Chambers
Crossword Dictionary

Chambers

CHAMBERS
An imprint of Chambers Harrap Publishers Ltd
7 Hopetoun Crescent
Edinburgh
EH7 4AY

www.chambers.co.uk

This edition first published by Chambers Harrap Publishers Ltd 2006
Reprinted 2007 (twice), 2008
Previous edition published 2000

A CIP catalogue record for this book is available from the British Library.

ISBN 978 0550 10081 8

Designed and typeset by Chambers Harrap Publishers Ltd, Edinburgh
Printed by Clays Ltd, St Ives plc

Contents

Contributors

Chambers Editor
Hazel Norris

Editors
Derek Arthur
Ross Beresford

Consultants
Derek Arthur
Ross Beresford
Jonathan Crowther
Don Manley
Tim Moorey

Contributors
Vicky Aldus
Katie Brooks

Crossword Essays
Jonathan Crowther
Don Manley
Tim Moorey

Data Management
Patrick Gaherty

Prepress Controllers
Nicolas Echallier
Susan Lawrie
Isla MacLean

Prepress Manager
Clair Simpson

Publishing Manager
Patrick White

The editors would like to thank the contributors to The Chambers Thesaurus, Chambers Crossword Lists and Chambers Concise Crossword Dictionary, extracts from which have been used in this text.

Preface

Solving crosswords is, by all accounts, an enjoyable way of spending one's leisure hours. More than 80 years after crosswords first appeared in the newspapers, and despite the temptations of sudoku and other puzzles, the crossword is still our favourite pastime. Yet so often crossword-solving can become a frustrating experience, accompanied by the gritting of teeth, the tearing-out of hair and the grumpy tossing aside of pens, as the clues prove baffling and the squares remain mockingly empty. *Chambers Crossword Dictionary* is a balm and a help for exactly those moments, providing as it does a wealth of potential solutions to even the thorniest and most apparently impenetrable clues.

That this new edition has undergone something of a quiet revolution will swiftly become apparent to those familiar with its previous incarnation. It has been thoroughly revised and massively expanded, and now includes more than 500,000 possible solutions to quick and cryptic clues, arranged in more than 19,600 entries. The entries comprise not only thesaurus-style synonyms, but also more than 1,200 reference lists of encyclopedic information, from famous pirates to ancient cities, baseball terms to types of grass. A list of the headwords at which these may be found is given on p.xlv.

Chambers Crossword Dictionary draws on material from across the authoritative Chambers reference range, and notably contains many thousands of terms from *The Chambers Dictionary*, including many of the archaic, literary and obscure words so beloved of cryptic crossword compilers. This new edition also makes use of the Chambers clue database, a huge and ever-growing record of the way words are actually used in crosswords. You will now find included abbreviations, symbols, codes and typical crossword jargon, such as 'AB' for 'sailor', or 'flower' to mean 'river'.

A new feature is the inclusion of 'indicators' denoting terms that may be used in a cryptic clue to show that a word or words should be reversed, anagrammatized or otherwise manipulated. For those new to cryptic crosswords, or wishing to brush up on their understanding, a new article that explains how indicators are used in cryptic clues may be found on p.xxvi, while lists of words that may be used as indicators are given on p.xxxiii.

Additional insights into the world of cruciverbalism are given in our highly-regarded introductory essays. 'The art of the crossword setter' by Jonathan Crowther offers an insight into the creation of these puzzles, while 'Crossword English' by Don Manley explains the types of clues that might be encountered and offers advice on how to approach the solving of cryptic crosswords. Tim Moorey writes on 'The art of the crossword clue', discussing the qualities that make for a memorable clue and offering examples of the finest clues so far devised.

This new edition of *Chambers Crossword Dictionary* has benefited immeasurably from the thoughtful advice and skilful editing of Ross Beresford and Derek Arthur, respectively a former and current co-editor of *The Listener* crossword in *The Times*. Their expertise is unsurpassed and their contribution throughout the project has been invaluable. We are also grateful to the previous edition's crossword consultants, Jonathan Crowther and Don Manley, and to Tim Moorey who joined the team for this second edition; their authoritative comments have shaped and immensely improved the dictionary. Finally, we would like to thank the many other people who have been involved in the preparation of this book, and also those who contributed to the first edition, notably Una McGovern and the late Catherine Schwarz. However, any errors, infelicities or omissions remain the sole responsibility of the publishers.

We warmly welcome all comments and suggestions from members of the public, which will be considered for incorporation in future editions. These should be sent to The Editor, *Chambers Crossword Dictionary*, Chambers Harrap Publishers Ltd, 7 Hopetoun Crescent, Edinburgh EH7 4AY.

The Publisher
Edinburgh, 2006

Introduction

Chambers Crossword Dictionary contains more than 500,000 possible solutions to quick and cryptic crossword clues. It draws on *The Chambers Dictionary, The Chambers Thesaurus* and other books in the Chambers reference range; it also uses the Chambers crossword clue database.

It does not contain definitions, parts of speech, usage labels or similar material. To check the exact meaning of a word or phrase, a dictionary such as *The Chambers Dictionary* is recommended.

This Introduction contains the following information:

Content
Word forms
Word length
Organization of entries
Expressions of ...
Indicators
Reference lists
Cross-references

Content

Entries in the *Crossword Dictionary* include both single words and phrases. Also included are abbreviations, short forms, acronyms, symbols, codes and the like, for the answers to crossword clues are often built up from these small pieces. Solvers will also find crossword jargon, such as 'tar' under 'sailor' and 'goat' under 'butter'. Anagrams, however, have not been included; so, for example, an entry for 'rotten time' would not list 'emit'.

Consideration has been given to the differing needs of various kinds of crosswords, from concise to advanced cryptics, and nothing has been excluded simply on the grounds of obscurity. Archaic, dialect, literary and uncommon words have been included, as these are often found in a variety of crosswords, not just (although undoubtedly most frequently) in advanced cryptics such as Azed in *The Observer* and *The Listener* in *The Times*. An emphasis has been placed on unusual short words with helpful letter sequences – for example 'tana' under 'police station' – as these often form the 'building blocks' which make up a cryptic solution. Variant spellings listed in *The Chambers Dictionary* have often been included. Where a usage is dubious but technically possible, as with an archaic variant of a synonym where it is unclear whether the variant is also synonymous with the headword, a degree of leniency has been employed.

The content of the *Crossword Dictionary* is broadly international in scope, with words from Australian, New Zealand, American, Anglo-Indian and other varieties of English included. Some common short foreign words sometimes found in crosswords are included too, such as 'mer' under 'sea' or 'ici' under 'here'.

Synonyms which are only loosely associated with the headword have not been included (for example 'twelfth' will not be found at 'grouse'). However, some names are included, as crossword convention allows references to people by first name or surname; for example 'Berlin' with the synonym 'Irving', 'Lincoln' for 'Abe' or 'Milne' for 'AA'. While a smattering of those most commonly found have been included, the list is not exhaustive and there will be others.

There is debate in crossword circles over what constitutes a 'sound' clue, and some crossword setters and editors do not employ particular uses of words or senses which others consider to be permissible. So as to be of maximum use to solvers of crosswords from a variety of sources, terms have been included in this book even if frowned upon by some. However, some usages considered to be especially contentious (usually as a result of word spacing and grammatical links having been ignored) have not been included, such as 'G' for 'Gateshead', 'm' for 'topmast' or 'fats' for 'breakfast'.

No attempt has been made to ensure that entries are 'symmetrical', ie that a synonym found under one headword (for example 'lucky') will also be found under another broadly synonymous entry (for example 'fortunate'). Since it is impossible to anticipate every reference a clue-writer will come up with, there are bound to be gaps. This deficiency can be mitigated by searching under different headwords, and there may be hints to be picked up from what is given. For example, the entry for 'swimmer' lists 'fish' as a synonym, which suggests that looking at the main entry for 'fish' may be helpful; here the intended solution, say 'eel', may be found.

Plural and inflected forms of words have generally not been given. Solvers should remember that if the wording of a cryptic clue suggests that a plural or verb form is required, they may need to pluralize or otherwise inflect a possible solution found in this *Dictionary*. Some abbreviations listed in the *Dictionary* stand for both singular and plural forms of a word (for example 'kg' can be kilogram or kilograms). For parts of cryptic solutions, plural and other forms may not be straightforward; for example, where 'duck' can conventionally be 'O', then 'ducks' in a clue may indicate 'Os' or 'OO'. This may also be encountered with the reference list of collective nouns, as setters may use 'crows', for example, for 'murder'.

This is also true for comparatives and superlatives; if a clue says 'more' or 'most', for example, it may be that an -er or -est ending needs to be added (for example 'more sensible' for 'saner' or 'most stupid' for 'dopiest'). Similarly, solvers should bear in mind that 'not' may be used in a clue to indicate the prefix 'un-' (for example 'not hidden' for 'unconcealed'), that 'again' may be used for the prefix 're-' (for example 'publish again' for 'reissue'), and so on.

Numbers, and terms which include both numbers and letters, have been included in many instances as some – although not all – setters and editors allow the number 1 to be converted to the letter I (as in the Roman numeral). Thus, 'M1' may be rendered as part of a solution as 'MI', and '1st' as 'IST'.

Word forms

The forms -*ize* and -*ization* are used throughout, but the alternative -*ise* or -*isation* spellings may be needed for the solutions to some crossword clues.

Similarly, the form 'your' is used in place of 'one's' in phrases such as 'put your foot down'. Solvers should remember that 'one's' may be required instead for a crossword solution. In some instances this may be reflected in the indication of word-length given in a clue: for example, 'sure of yourself' would be denoted as (4,2,8), hence listed here under **14**, whereas 'sure of oneself' would be (4,2,7), which would have been **13**.

Italics have not been used, even where conventionally a word or letter is italicized. This may be noted especially in relation to physics terms, for example, under 'Boltzmann constant' the symbol 'k' is given in roman type, whereas in *The Chambers Dictionary* it is italicized as *k*. Similarly, titles of novels and films, names of ships and other similar instances will all be found in roman type.

Where words can be hyphenated (as a noun) or unhyphenated (as a phrasal verb) both forms are usually included in synonym lists (for example 'back-up' and 'back up' at 'second').

Word length

The words and phrases given in this dictionary contain 15 letters or fewer, reflecting the most commonly used crossword grids. However, where a list represents a closed set, that is, where a list is clearly defined and limited, then all relevant terms have been included regardless of length. For example, all of the US states and all of the plays of Shakespeare have been included, even though some of these are longer than 15 letters in length.

Organization of entries

Within the dictionary, words have been sorted into over 19,600 one-stop alphabetical entries by meaning or subject category. Entries provide a range of words that are relevant to the headword, in two types of list:

- synonym lists, which present words with similar meanings to the headword
- reference lists, which present encyclopedic information related to the headword, such as people's names, place names and types of item

Some entries include only one type of list, whereas others include a range of synonyms plus one or more reference lists. For example:

abbey
03 Abb **06** abbacy, friary, priory
07 convent, minster, nunnery
08 cloister, seminary **09** cathedral,
monastery

Abbeys include:

04 Bath, Iona
05 Cluny, Kelso, Meaux, Roche, Royal
06 Bolton, Byland, Hexham, Whitby,
 Woburn
07 Citeaux, Furness, Melrose, Tintern,
 Waltham
08 Buckfast, Crowland, Dryburgh,
 Fontenay, Fonthill, Holyrood,
 Jedburgh, Newstead, Rievaulx
09 Clairvaux, Fountains, Holy Cross,
 Kirkstall, Nightmare, Sherborne
10 Malmesbury, Northanger
11 Westminster

Reference lists always follow thesaurus-style lists.

Within entries, words are grouped firstly by length, that is by the total number of letters in each word or phrase, and then ordered alphabetically within these word-length sections:

aisle
04 lane, path **07** gangway, passage,
walkway **08** alleyway, corridor
10 passageway **12** deambulatory

Alphabetization is strictly by letter, and some stylistic conventions have been disregarded: for example, 'Mc' will be found at 'Mc' rather than mingled with 'Mac'.

No distinction is made between parts of speech, or between homonyms (words spelled the same but with different meanings), as crossword setters play on multiple meanings and possible ambiguity in clues. For example, the entry for 'rebel' lists synonyms for the adjective, verb and noun senses:

rebel
◇ *anagram indicator*
04 defy, riot **06** flinch, mutine, mutiny, oppose, recoil, resist, revolt, rise up, shrink **07** aginner, beatnik, defiant, disobey, dissent, heretic, run riot, shy away **08** agitator, apostate, mutineer, mutinous, pull back, recusant, revolter **09** dissenter, guerrilla, insurgent **10** malcontent, rebellious, schismatic **11** disobedient, turn against **12** malcontented, paramilitary **13** insubordinate, nonconformist, revolutionary **14** freedom fighter **15** insurrectionary

and the entry for 'dock' presents synonyms for what are, in fact, three separate words, one being a type of plant, another meaning a wharf or to land at a wharf and the third meaning to cut short:

dock
◇ *tail deletion indicator*
02 dk **03** bob, cut, pen **04** clip, crop, land, moor, pier, quay, rump **05** basin, berth, jetty, put in, Rumex, tie up, wharf **06** anchor, deduct, detail, lessen, marina, reduce, remove, sorrel **07** bistort, curtail, harbour, shorten **08** boat yard, canaigre, decrease, diminish, patience, quayside, subtract, truncate, withhold **09** grapetree, polygonum **10** drop anchor, tidal basin, waterfront **12** monk's rhubarb, submarine pen **15** fitting-out basin

Synonym lists for idioms and phrasal verbs derived from many of the headwords are also included and are marked by •:

vouch
• **vouch for**
04 back **06** affirm, assert, assure, avouch, uphold, verify **07** certify, confirm, endorse, support, swear to, warrant **08** attest to, speak for **09** answer for, guarantee **10** asseverate

There may be more than one entry in the *Crossword Dictionary* for a word or phrasal verb. For example, 'shake up' appears as a phrasal verb at the entry for 'shake', but there is also an entry for the noun 'shake-up' as a headword in its own right.

Phrases, idioms and phrasal verbs have been located under the key headword contained and so should be found in an appropriate and intuitive place; *The Chambers Dictionary* has been followed in most instances. However, if a term cannot be found in the first place sought, solvers should try under other likely headwords.

Expressions of ...

Interjections and similar terms related to emotions are often found in cryptic crossword clues and introduced by 'expression of...' or a similar phrase. In this *Dictionary* these are listed under the relevant headword; for example 'expression of hesitation' may require 'um' or 'er', and these can be found under the headword 'hesitation'.

If expressions relating to a particular emotion cannot be found in the first place sought, solvers should look under a likely alternative; for example, if seeking an 'expression of disapprobation' but finding nothing under 'disapprobation', solvers should then try 'disapproval'.

Lists of interjections, cries, shouts and expressions may be found at the following headwords:

admiration	disgust	greeting	reproof
agreement	dismay	grief	resignation
annoyance	dismissal	hesitation	sarcasm
appreciation	dissatisfaction	hunting	scepticism
approval	distaste	impatience	silence
attention	doubt	invocation	stop
concession	drinking	joy	stupidity
contempt	emotion	misfortune	success
defiance	emphasis	pain	support
derision	encouragement	pleasure	surprise
disagreement	enthusiasm	praise	sympathy
disappointment	excitement	protest	triumph
disapproval	farewell	puzzlement	warning
disbelief	frenzy	realization	weariness
discovery	fright	regret	wonder
disdain	gratitude	relief	worry

Indicators

Terms which are often used as wordplay indicators in cryptic crossword clues are denoted with a diamond icon and the type of indicator – anagram, hidden, reversal, etc – is given:

adrift
◇ *anagram indicator*
04 lost **05** at sea **07** aimless
08 drifting, goalless, insecure, rootless
09 off course, unsettled **10** anchorless,
unanchored **11** disoriented
13 directionless, disorientated

Some words can be used as indicators of more than one kind of word play:

oddly
◇ *anagram indicator*
◇ *hidden alternately indicator*
07 weirdly **09** curiously, strangely,
unusually **10** abnormally, remarkably
11 irregularly

Indicators always follow the headword, idiom or phrasal verb. There may be instances in which an idiom or phrasal verb is followed only by an indicator, and not by synonym entries; this is because it was felt helpful to include the term for its usefulness as an indicator, but where it does not have synonyms in the usual way.

Indicators may not always appear in a cryptic clue in the way in which they appear in the *Dictionary*, but rather may be encountered in an inflected form: for example, 'digest' is marked as an anagram indicator, but solvers may be more likely to encounter it in a cryptic clue as 'digested'. While efforts have been made to denote all common indicators, the lists can never be exhaustive.

More information on the use of indicators in cryptic clues can be found on p.xxvi, and lists of words that may be used as indicators are given on p.xxxiii.

Reference lists

The reference lists have been derived from *Chambers Crossword Lists* and from other authoritative Chambers reference databases. Lists are entered in the *Dictionary* at the appropriate headword; a list of the headwords at which they may be found is given on p.xlv.

The reference lists are not intended to be all-inclusive, but to strike a balance between comprehensiveness and the likelihood of the words and phrases actually occurring as the solutions to crossword clues. For more comprehensive reference lists, *Chambers Crossword Lists* is recommended.

The reference lists include both historical and current information; for example, in the list of actors are not only contemporary figures like Sir Ian McKellen and Robin Williams, but also notable actors from the past like Richard Burbage and Edward Alleyn. Similarly, the lists may contain both real and fictional or legendary items. For example, the list of heroes includes the legendary Robin Hood, the literary D'Artagnan, the historical William Wallace, the cinematic Indiana Jones and the comic strip Superman.

Reference lists have been subdivided to make finding information easier. For example, there is not one list of singers, but separate lists of classical, folk, jazz, opera, pop and other singers.

Some of the reference lists contain additional information in brackets following core information. For example, first names or nicknames are given in brackets following a surname. In such lists, the core term (the unbracketed term) is presented in bold type to make browsing easier:

Pirates include:

03 **Tew** (Thomas)
04 **Bart** (Jean), **Gunn** (Ben), **Hook** (Captain), **Kidd** (William), **Otto**, **Read** (Mary), **Smee**
05 **Barth** (Jean), **Bones** (Billy), **Bonny** (Anne), **Bunce** (Jack), **Drake** (Sir Francis), **Every** (Henry), **Ewart** (Nanty), **Flint** (Captain), **Tache** (Edward), **Teach** (Edward)
06 **Aubery** (Jean-Benoit), **Conrad**, **Jonsen** (Captain), **Morgan** (Sir Henry), **Silver** (Long John), **Thatch** (Edward), **Walker** (William)
07 **Dampier** (William), **Lafitte** (Jean), **O'Malley** (Grace), **Rackham** (John), **Roberts** (Bartholomew), **Sparrow** (Captain Jack), **Trumpet** (Solomon)
08 **Altamont** (Frederick), **Black Dog**, **Blackett** (Nancy), **Blackett** (Peggy), **Blind Pew**, **Redbeard**, **Ringrose** (Basil)
09 **Black Bart**, **Cleveland** (Clement)
10 **Barbarossa** (Khair-ed-din), **Blackbeard**, **Calico Jack**
14 **Long John Silver**

Additional bracketed information is not included in the word-length count although it may form part of the solution to some crossword clues. The regnal numbers of individual popes, queens and kings have generally been omitted.

Common generic terms have often been omitted from the names and terms presented in reference lists, to avoid unwieldy and unnecessary repetition. For example, the word 'abbey' has not been included in names in the list of abbeys, and the word 'saw' has been omitted from the list of saws. Users should be aware that these terms may form part of the solution to some crossword clues.

The reference material has been selected to be as wide-ranging in scope as possible. Solvers should note that:

- numbers may be found in solutions in some instances, as numbers may be encountered or referenced in some form in cryptic puzzles. For example, the list of films includes *2001: A Space Odyssey* and *Apollo 13*.

- some items are included under a certain headword on the grounds of usefulness, even if they are not strictly types of the headword. For example, 'Washington DC' is included in the list of US states and 'tomato' is included in the list of vegetables. Similarly, items which are related to the headword may be included; succulents in the list of cacti, for example.

- variant spellings have been included, for example 'topi' and 'topee' in the list of hats.

some entries without a distinct reference list, both synonyms and reference-list type formation may be found intermingled.

Cross-references

Chambers Crossword Dictionary is extensively cross-referenced to make finding solutions easy. here are two forms of cross-reference; those at main headwords directing users elsewhere:

lough *see* **lake**

nd those which suggest that additional information may be found at other entries:

petrol
03 gas, LRP **05** ethyl, juice, super
08 gasolene, gasoline
See also **fuel**

many of the latter instances, the cross-reference directs solvers to a relevant reference list. may also direct solvers to a similar but longer entry with additional synonyms, or may make xplicit some crossword jargon or other slang; for example, a cross-reference at 'bloomer' to lower', or a cross-reference at 'stir' to 'prison'.

The art of the crossword setter

Jonathan Crowther (Azed of *The Observer*)

I am regularly asked – as often by people who habitually solve crosswords as by those wh
never do – how I set about compiling a puzzle, and especially what order I do things in. (Th
other commonly-asked question is how long each puzzle takes me, but I usually hedge whe
answering this one. A puzzle is best constructed over several sittings, and I have neve
bothered to calculate accurately the total time involved.) For most normal crosswords ther
are three distinct stages, each more time-consuming than the last: (i) constructing the gri
pattern, (ii) filling this with words and (iii) writing the clues. The three stages demand differer
skills, and for this reason I often compartmentalize the first two, constructing several gri
patterns at a sitting and then filling all of these with words before returning to the first grid t
start the lengthier and more creative process of writing the clues. Let us now look at eac
stage in turn.

Crossword grids

There is no absolute rule that crosswords should be symmetrical in design, ie with their blocke
squares or bars arranged so that they look the same if the grid is turned upside down or if it i
given a quarter-turn. The fact is that most are, and this is the widely-accepted norm. It is als
aesthetically pleasing, by no means a negligible consideration. Most importantly, the grid desig
should ensure a range of entries of varying lengths and a fair distribution of unchecked letter
(those which belong to only one word, across or down, and are not 'checked' by a word entere
in the other direction). In general the number of unchecked letters is greater in a blocked gri
than in a barred one. As a rule of thumb (though one that is regularly infringed by puzzles in
number of our national dailies), no more than half the letters of a solution should be unchecked i
a blocked grid. In barred grids, like mine in *The Observer*, the solver can expect a more generou
quota of cross-checked letters because such puzzles tend to use more rare and unusual words. I
both types of puzzle the inclusion of consecutive unchecked letters in answers is considered ba
practice and generally frowned on. It is all a question of fairness to the solver.

There is a fundamental difference in standard grid design between British-style and Americar
style crosswords. British crosswords, with their tradition of cryptic clues and unchecke
letters, normally require the solver to solve every clue in order to complete the puzzle. I
most American crosswords, whose clues are not cryptic in the British sense, there ar
proportionally far fewer blocked squares and they are arranged in such a way that *every* lette
is cross-checked, so that, in theory at least, it is possible to complete a puzzle by solving onl
about half its clues.

In practice, setters of most normal blocked grids in daily or Sunday newspapers in both Britai
and the US do not have to concern themselves with grid construction. Each paper uses
limited number of basic patterned grids to which the setter is restricted. In an age of eve
greater standardization this is perhaps inevitable, and it reduces the risk of error, but I sti
regard it as regrettable and am pleased that no such restriction is placed on me. I derive muc
satisfaction from exploring the many different grid designs possible within the establishe
parameters: grid size (normally 12 × 12 in my case), number of entries (usually 36), a goo
spread of entry lengths, and a fair number of unchecked letters. My predecessor Derric
Macnutt (the legendary Ximenes) preferred to let his patterns grow, organically as it wer
around the words he wanted to include in his puzzles, effectively merging my first two stage
of crossword construction into a single process. My own routine is as I have described, since

start with no preconceptions as to the words I want to use, and this only goes to show that there is no universally prescribed method. There are also no Mosaic laws governing the *size* of crosswords. Blocked grids in daily papers are usually 15 × 15, with about 32 answers (16 across and 16 down), but recent years have seen a growth in the number of 'jumbo' puzzles (typically 27 × 27, with 76 answers), presenting new challenges to solvers and setters alike by the inclusion of longer words and multi-word phrases. In a more modest way, the Azed crossword is now sometimes 13 × 11, enabling me to include 13-letter words on a regular basis. More specialized crosswords explore other designs, including circular diagrams with entries arranged circularly and radially, but these will probably remain the exception and the domain of the seriously dedicated solver.

Word choice

Having completed the grid, or having chosen it from the available range, the setter moves on to fill it with words. There are computer programs which can do this in the twinkling of an eye, though they are limited to the word-lists in the program's memory. The human brain takes much longer but it can select or reject words according to their suitability for cluing and its own real-world knowledge, a crucial factor in the writing of clues. Which words does one choose, and where does one start? I personally start from what seems the natural place, the top left-hand corner of the grid, extending down and across more or less at the same time while keeping a weather eye open for potential problem areas. Anything in the dictionary is fair game, and for me this means *The Chambers Dictionary*. My task is made easier by *Chambers Words* and *Chambers Back-Words for Crosswords*, books which present words alphabetically (or reverse-alphabetically) by length, so that I can see at a glance, say, all the 7-letter words beginning or ending with L. These aids are available to the solver as well as the setter, of course, but I like to think that whereas they are an invaluable tool for the hard-pressed setter, the solver will turn to them only as a last resort. Solving clues should be a contest of minds between setter and solver, not a series of conundrums to be resolved by reference to a published word-list. I also think the setter should be free to include non-dictionary words and phrases, especially topical ones, if these are sufficiently well known. Assessing what is and is not familiar enough to include here is of course a matter of fine judgement. Some newspapers have a policy of not allowing certain taboo words to be used as answers in their crosswords. In these liberated days such bowdlerization strikes me as rather old-fashioned. Crossword setters, like journalists and other writers, should be trusted to know where to draw the line.

The task of filling a grid with words is naturally easier in blocked diagrams than in barred ones, since the number of unchecked letters is significantly greater in blocked diagrams. In both types the setter develops with experience a feel for the 'shape' of words: common letter-clusters, the distribution of consonants and vowels, 'danger' letters (especially at the ends of words), helpful affixes and inflections, and so on. He or she must think ahead to avoid getting boxed into an awkward corner which will involve undoing part of the grid construction, an agonizing waste of time when deadlines are tight. The *Chambers Crossword Completer* is another valuable tool in this context, especially when setting blocked puzzles. This time words are arranged alphabetically by word length according to the alternate letters of each word, first the odd letters (first, third, fifth, etc) and then the even ones (second, fourth, sixth, etc). Special care needs to be taken with shorter words, especially those of four or five letters. There are comparatively few of these in the language (and of these far fewer begin with vowels than with consonants), so most will have been clued many times already. Good setters try to avoid reusing old clues, however proud of them they may be, and they should also not reuse *words* too often. Guarding against this is not easy, and inevitably, there being no copyright in good ideas, similar or identical clues to the same word will recur, but I do make a conscious effort not to repeat myself and think other setters should do likewise. (As a matter of passing interest, there are more different words in the language of eight letters than of any other word length.)

I have already mentioned fair play between setter and solver. This is an important principle in grid construction, just as much as in the writing of clues. Consonants, especially the less common ones, are generally more helpful to the solver as cross-checking letters than vowels are (with obvious exceptions like I or U in final position), and the setter should recognize this. I know that as a solver I feel hard done by if faced by −A−E, one of the most frequent four-letter-word patterns, especially if the setter has made matters worse by giving the word an extra-difficult clue!

Clues

The writing of the clues for a crossword is the last and much the most important task for the setter, for it is here that one stamps one's character and personal style on the puzzle. Seasoned solvers develop clear preferences for the style of this or that setter, and satisfied solvers usually remain loyal to a particular puzzle (even, sometimes, if they are less than happy with other aspects of the paper in which it appears). I firmly believe that an impersonal style of cluing can be boring, and there is no harm at all in letting one's own interests, sense of humour, even prejudices, emerge through one's clues, provided always that these are fair and accurate. Don Manley in his essay on 'Crossword English' describes in detail the range of different clue types regularly used by setters. As a setter myself, I follow a method which has not changed greatly over the years. I always write clues in the order in which they appear in the puzzle. Taking the more colourful words first means leaving a 'sump' of less interesting ones till last, an encouragement to treat the latter as second-class citizens and produce second-class clues as a result. I write no more than nine or ten clues at a sitting, having found that if I try to do more staleness sets in and pedestrian clues result. The restorative effects of even quite a short break doing other things can be truly remarkable! At the same time it is important to see the puzzle as a whole and to present a reasonable variety of clue types (not too many anagrams, for example) to ensure a balanced fare for the solver. This can be tricky when a word cries out for one particular treatment but that treatment has already been used for other words in the puzzle (or for the same word in an earlier puzzle), but the principle is sound. The aim must be to divert the solver, not to massage the setter's ego, so variety is important.

Some words are much more difficult to clue interestingly than others. Scientific terms come high on my list of unfavourite words, mainly because their meaning is very specific and does not lend itself to the sort of wordplay that is at the heart of cryptic clue-writing. A word with many meanings offers far greater scope for punning and similar red herrings to strew in the solver's path. But whichever word I am cluing I always strive (with varying success, I'm sure) for three key ingredients in a clue: accuracy, economy and wit. Every clue should lead accurately and unmistakably to its solution, saying precisely and grammatically what it means (though it may not always mean what it appears to say − taking advantage of the manifold ambiguities of our language is an essential part of cryptic clue-writing). It should do this in as few words as are consistent with fair play, avoiding all superfluous verbiage or mere padding. And it should if at all possible be enjoyable to solve, leaving successful solvers feeling both satisfied at their success and pleasurably diverted by the experience.

About the author

Jonathan Crowther is better known to many cryptic crossword solvers as Azed of *The Observer*. He has also set puzzles under the pseudonyms Gong and Ozymandias. His *Book of Azed Crosswords* is published by Chambers.

Crossword English

Don Manley (crossword setter and
author of *Chambers Crossword Manual*)

I am a monoglot, more or less. Although I studied French at school, I can't say I use it much – except when I have to on holiday, and even then it's a sort of pidgin French. But at least I feel I know English, and since (as Bernard Shaw put it) England and America are two countries divided by a common language, maybe one can be a polyglot just by watching television. Or maybe I can be a polyglot just by coming from Devon, where 'thistles' used to be called 'dashels'.

So what has this to do with crosswords? Well, in a sense Crossword English is rather like a foreign language – and it is a language that must be learnt. What may seem odd (if the cross-section of crossword setters I know is anything to go by) is that the polyglots who can speak French and English are not necessarily polyglots in the sense of knowing English and Crossword English. You're more likely to find that a crossword setter is a computer scientist, a physicist or a mathematician than a French teacher these days.

The irritating thing – to anyone who has not yet learnt Crossword English – is that it looks so like Everyday English. For the crossword which offers definitions only, this is perfectly obvious. So if the clue reads 'Cry of an ass (4)' you can write in BRAY straight away. You might have a few alternative answers for 'River (5)', and if you are living in Nottinghamshire you may be disposed to write in TRENT, but when faced with 'River in Paris (5)' you'll know that anything other than SEINE just isn't sane. So for the definition puzzle we're looking at a test of our ability to recognize synonyms or at a quiz with questions that would crop up early on in 'Who Wants To Be A Millionaire?'. This is as far as most people get with solving crosswords – the verbal quiz solved with a little help from reference books: a dictionary, an atlas and possibly an encyclopedia. They know English but not Crossword English.

So what is Crossword English? It is the language of the cryptic crossword, a language which looks like ordinary English but which has its own strange rules of grammar and construction and which has its own vocabulary. Crossword English is a series of mini-statements, mini-pictures, and mini-stories even, but the statements, the pictures, and the stories are each designed to hide a sort of riddle. So a riddle isn't a bad place to start with as an example of a cryptic clue:

> My first is in Cornwall but isn't in Devon
> For my second shun Hell and start looking in Heaven
> My third you may find in this or in that
> My whole is a creature that sits on the mat

Thus in a woeful verse of 39 words we have written a cryptic clue for CAT, and at each stage along the way we are spoon-fed with a letter at a time. It's obviously a puzzle, even if it's a pretty heavy-handed one.

Now look at these little riddles and see what you make of them:

1. Lady I rather fancy (7)
2. There's nothing in Basildon I like (3)
3. Delightful tea with the best china (8)
4. It's best to have cold sheets (5)
5. Delicate proposal (6)

6. The clock's put back? Relax! (5)
7. Company car? (3-6)
8. It could deflect battle spear (11)
9. Writer gathers wood as something that'll burn quickly (8)
10. Marsh plant enthrals artist (6)
11. Defeat brought by bowling gaining wicket – something captain controls? (9)
12. Amuse the French after a short time (6)
13. Did he have spelling lessons? (3,9,10)
14. Who you'd expect to find at gay weddings in the Isles?! (8)
15. Female beheaded in the sultanate (4)
16. Lab in, Tory out would suit him (4,5)
17. Boyfriend tied ribbon from what we hear (4)
18. Rejected young troublemaker longed to be free (8)
19. Fool about fifty, one not altogether bright (6)
20. 014? (6,5)

Here are twenty 'portrayals' – perfectly sensible 'portrayals' in generally understandable English – though 20 looks a bit odd. All of these were written by myself at some stage over the past fifteen years or so, and as I look at them I see not only Crossword English but a certain kind of Englishness. There is romance in 1 and 17 (and perhaps 5); there is an austere and rather snooty middle-Englishness about 2, 3 and 4; a concern with cricket in 11; hints of a threatening world outside modern England in 8 and 15; and so on. There may even be a touch of humour here and there. This is English language and English culture.

There are twenty puzzles to solve, so how are these clues different from those for BRAY and SEINE? The answer is (fairly) simple, though the implications of the answer may be complicated. It is this. In each cryptic clue there will still be a definition but the clue writer will have done one of two things. He (sometimes she – and, to be honest, we could do with more 'shes') will have either wrapped up the definition in 'cryptic language' or will have provided a definition plus some indication of the letters in the answer. Sometimes the crossword setter will have done both. In most cryptic clues there will be what we call a 'definition' followed by what we call a 'subsidiary indication' (sometimes also called 'wordplay'), or a subsidiary indication followed by a definition, or even an indication and a definition rolled into one. The secret in decoding a clue lies in trying to solve the answer from either or both of these components while using any letters that are already filled in.

If that all sounds horrible, it's because I've tried to give you a grammar lesson, and (as we all know) it's really much better to start learning a language by speaking it or writing it. No one ever really taught me 'all that grammar stuff' when I was a fledgling cruciverbalist (someone who 'does' crosswords). I was lucky enough to have a father who taught me how to solve clues when I was barely out of short trousers, and the best way I can explain Crossword English is to take you through the clues one by one. ·

1. *Lady I rather fancy (7)*
   The word 'fancy' is one of a huge set of **anagram indicators**. It tells us that the letters next to it are to be made 'fancy' or jumbled up. If you jumble up 'I rather' you get HARRIET, a lady. This clue, then is an **anagram**, perhaps the one form of cryptic clue everyone knows.

2. *There's nothing in Basildon I like (3)*
   If you look carefully, you'll see that there is indeed a word meaning nothing in the sequence of letters 'Basildon I like' and it's NIL. This is a **hidden word**.

3. *Delightful tea with the best china (8)*
   If you put a word for 'tea' and add it to a word for 'the best china', you will add 'char' to 'Ming' to form CHARMING, meaning 'delightful'. This is a **charade clue**.

4. *It's best to have cold sheets (5)*
As it happens, this is another charade, but this time we join an **abbreviation** 'c' to the sheets (= ream) to form CREAM (the best). Abbreviations are common in subsidiary indications.

5. *Delicate proposal (6)*
This is a **double-definition** clue, so you can look upon one definition as the official 'definition' and the other one as the 'subsidiary indication' – or vice versa. What word means both 'delicate' and 'proposal'? Answer: TENDER.

6. *The clock's put back? Relax! (5)*
This suggests (quite rightly) that you'll get an extra hour in bed when the clocks go back. But if you put back a 'timer' you will get REMIT, which means 'relax'. This is a **reversal** clue. In down clues you may see the word 'up' suggesting a reversal. And here the definition is at the end.

7. *Company car? (3-6)*
You may be tempted to think of this as another double-definition clue and look for a word that means both 'company' and 'car'. In fact the setter is inviting you to think of 'two's company, three's none', and so the answer is TWO-SEATER. There is no indication of letters in this clue, but we have noticed that it has a **cryptic definition**.

8. *It could deflect battle spear (11)*
We're looking for an anagram of 'battle spear' and find it in BREASTPLATE, but we notice that the clue as a whole is a definition. Every word in the clue is serving as a definition and as part of the subsidiary indication. We call this an **&lit.** clue. This particular type is **anag. &lit.**

9. *Writer gathers wood as something that'll burn quickly (8)*
The word 'gathers' suggests that a word for 'wood' might be inside a writer. Put 'fir' inside 'Wilde' and you'll find WILDFIRE. This is known as a **container-and-contents** clue.

10. *Marsh plant enthrals artist (6)*
This is another container-and contents clue. This time we have an abbreviation for artist (RA) inside a plant (moss) to give MORASS.

11. *Defeat brought by bowling gaining wicket – something captain controls? (9)*
If you solve crosswords you'll need to get used to **cricket vocabulary**. In this charade bowling is 'over', wicket is 'w', and something the captain controls is 'helm'. Put the three together to get OVERWHELM (defeat).

12. *Amuse the French after a short time (6)*
Although we're talking about Crossword English, we do allow a few **foreign words** to creep in, especially definite and indefinite articles of common European languages. In this charade a short time is 'tick' added to 'the French', which in this case is 'le', giving the answer TICKLE (amuse).

13. *Did he have spelling lessons? (3,9,10)*
The setter is tempting you to think about spelling in the sense of getting the right letters in sequence. In fact you should think about spelling in the sense of magic. The answer is THE SORCERER'S APPRENTICE, another cryptic definition, this one being set in what we call a **misleading context** occasioned by the **double-meaning** of 'spelling'. You'll find many other double meanings including 'flower' which can mean river. One of the delights of learning Crossword English is to work these out for yourself!

14. *Who you'd expect to find at gay weddings in the Isles?! (8)*
This is an outrageous charade, the answer being 'he brides' (ie HEBRIDES). No one ever seems to have taken offence. Every crossword should have at least one clue with an element of **humour.**

15. *Female beheaded in the sultanate (4)*
    This is a particular type of **subtractive** clue. Take the head letter off 'woman' to give the sultanate OMAN. If you take up cryptic crosswords you will also learn about 'endless' and 'heartless'.

16. *Lab in, Tory out would suit him (4,5)*
    This is another **anag. &lit.** Note that 'out' is a very common anagram indicator. You should be able to see TONY BLAIR quite easily.

17. *Boyfriend tied ribbon from what we hear (4)*
    When you see words like 'we hear' or 'they say' you almost certainly have a **homophone** clue. Here 'tied ribbon' is 'bow' and BEAU is bow 'from what we hear', ie 'beau' and 'bow' are homophones.

18. *Rejected young troublemaker longed to be free (8)*
    This is a **complex** clue in that it consists of the reverse of one word in a charade with another. A rejected troublemaker is 'Ted' backwards ('det') and longed is 'ached', which when attached makes DETACHED. Who ever calls unruly troublemakers 'teddy-boys' or 'teds' these days? Well, we do in crosswords. This is one example of **preserved obsolescence** in an area of language where we still have an extended-play record (EP) and sex appeal is still 'it'.

19. *Fool about fifty, one not altogether bright (6)*
    In this container-and-contents clue we make use of our knowledge of **Roman numerals**. Fifty is 'L' and 'twit' about 'L, I' is TWILIT. And there's a slightly misleading context here, isn't there?

20. *014? (6,5)*
    This last clue is what one might call a **zany** or **improvised** clue – a sort of one-off cryptic definition. It depends on the solver seeing that 014 = 2 x 007. Since 007 is the agent James Bond, the answer must be DOUBLE AGENT.

With these twenty clues we have touched on all of the most important aspects of Crossword English, and maybe I have already been rather too 'English English' for some. What about other Englishes? Well, I'm writing this introduction for a Scottish publisher with a very special dictionary, *The Chambers Dictionary*. This is of course an excellent 'English English' dictionary but it also contains some excellent English words from the past and some highly unusual Scottish words. *Chambers* should be in every self-respecting crossworder's library, but its greatest treasures tend to come into play in the more difficult puzzles where Edmund (Spenser) and Jock (the archetypal Scot) make frequent appearances.

Across the Atlantic, in the USA and Canada, 'American Crossword English' is developing as cryptic puzzles, based on British puzzles, become more popular. British solvers will find one or two unfamiliar abbreviations, maybe, and the contexts will be more American – but the similarities tend to contradict Shaw's assertion mentioned earlier.

It has often been pointed out that English is ideal for the crossword because words split up so agreeably. How convenient that 'astronomer' is an anagram of 'moon-starer' and how nicely 'bestride' splits into 'best ride'. Clearly it would be difficult to imagine Crossword Urdu, and yet cryptic crosswords do exist in Hebrew, Bengali, Welsh and Dutch – and other languages too, I dare say.

It's time for a final word about the 'custodians' of Crossword English and what they are trying to do. The word 'custodian' may suggest conservatism and a grammar rule-book. There's more to it than that, of course, but there is a necessary element of grammar in crosswords which needs to be preserved. There are, after all, limits to what is acceptable in Everyday English, and it is the same in Crossword English.

In our language the strict grammarians call themselves **Ximeneans** after Ximenes, *The Observer* crossword setter who died in 1971. There is no space here for a digression into the grammar over which crossword setters and their editors argue, but there is an ongoing debate about what is acceptable and what is not. Today the tradition of Ximenes is upheld by his successor Azed, who tells us about his approach to crossword setting elsewhere in this book. Many of today's crossword setters have been competitors in Azed's clue-writing competitions, and so it is no surprise that many of the crossword setters in our national dailies are Ximenean – as are their crossword editors. Puzzles will inevitably vary in style and in level of difficulty. Crossword setters are turning Crossword English Language into Crossword English Literature and different readers' (solvers) will inevitably have their own favourite 'authors' (setters). But there are rules within which the custodians make sure that Crossword English operates – rules not just of grammar, but rules of taste. Practitioners of this language don't have to be absolutely politically correct, but their language is still that of the polite drawing-room, not that of the gutter. We can gently poke fun at pompous bishops and politicians (though not by name specifically!), and we can make wry comments about modern society, but we aim to entertain and not to give offence.

We want to give pleasure and intellectual challenge. Crossword English began as a sort of 20th-century poetry for all to enjoy. Long may it continue into the 21st century and beyond.

About the author

Don Manley sets crosswords under a variety of pseudonyms (Bradman, Duck, Quixote, Pasquale and Giovanni) for many national newspapers (including *The Times, The Guardian, The Independent on Sunday, the Financial Times* and *The Sunday Telegraph*). He is the author of the authoritative *Chambers Crossword Manual*.

The art of the crossword clue

Tim Moorey (Mephisto of *The Sunday Times*)

What is it that makes certain clues stay in the memory when the vast majority are forgotten as soon as their solutions are discovered? I will try to answer the question by identifying characteristics and qualities that setters strive to find and solvers tend to appreciate. Each is illustrated with my choice of clue examples based on over 50 years of crossword solving, and also with choices made by fellow setters from their own past clues and those of other setters. In addition, having had the task of selecting a 'Clue of the Week' for *The Week* magazine since its inception, I regularly have to consider what constitutes a good clue, and my focus there – and here – is on what solvers are likely to have found satisfying. To an increasing extent, it is also based on actual feedback from *The Sunday Times* and *The Week* solvers, following the introduction several years ago of invitations to respond by email.

It is fairly clear which qualities are enjoyed in favoured clues: in a nutshell, short, simple, well-crafted sentences that paint a coherent and believable but misleading picture are well regarded. If these can be supplemented with topicality and wit, so much the better. Technical soundness is taken for granted, albeit that crossword professionals sometimes heatedly debate exactly what is technically sound. Solvers, I think, are unconcerned with this aspect; if a warm glow of recognition on uncovering the answer is obtained, they will value a clue that some professionals (including this one) rate as 'unsound'.

So here are four things I look for in clue selection:

1. Definition
My test is whether the word or words used in the clue could be substituted for the solution in a normal English sentence.

2. Ease of solving
The clue answer should not be immediately apparent; and the penny should drop after not too long an interval of puzzlement.

3. Clue length
Anything over ten words can make for indigestibility, but I wouldn't rule out clues that are slightly longer.

4. Artificiality in wording
There should be no strain evident, and especially no sign that the clue-writer would ideally have preferred to use a different word or words, but was unable to do so in the interest of clueing integrity.

The clues chosen as examples for this essay include what may be regarded as 'classics', that is to say that they are spoken of and quoted still, in most cases despite having appeared some years ago. I also include more recent clues that have featured as 'Clue of the Week'. In most cases, to give readers a better chance of solving, the solutions are fairly common words.

Now for the qualities and characteristics of memorable clues, with illustrations. Hints are given in italics alongside clues, with solutions provided at the end of the essay.

1. Short and succinct

Cryptic definition clues fit this category best, albeit that they may have the disadvantage of not conveying a picture. However, their neatness and deviousness appeal. Ideally, there can only be a unique solution to each of these; note that the bracketed number of letters can sometimes rule out possible alternatives, as in the last of the examples.

Art master (8) *Think old English*
Stiff examination (4,6) *Think Latin*
This cylinder is jammed (5,4) *Think food*
A pound of sultanas (8) *Nothing to do with food*
Bar of soap (6,6) *Two of the three words mislead*

Double definitions – where either word could define the answer – can also be mentioned here. Perhaps the two best known are:

Let rip (4) *Ideas associated with a tear mustn't be shed here*
Driving licence (2-5) *Think of driving in the 'pushy' sense*

2. Well-crafted, painting a believable picture

If these qualities can be included in a totally misleading sentence, then you may have a fine clue.

Neglectful having left off dicky bow (9) *Dicky and bow mislead*
Seems a hip replacement brings about stress (9) *Anagram*
Licking for Persians is a prolonged exercise (8) *Two definitions; think ancient battles*
Amazon order mailed with shrink wrapping (6-3) *A very tough but wonderful clue for a rare word; shrink = shy*
In autumn, we're piling up the last of the leaves (8) *Partial anagram*
Tumbler, nuts, smoke, rapture! (7-5) *Anagram*

3. Topicality

The references in these clues, in order, are: an infamous fatwa issued against an English novelist; a disastrous attempt in 1980 to rescue US hostages from Iran; fears before the 1990 World Cup relating to unruly English soccer fans; and finally the Iraq war.

He's rued his novel (7) *Anagram*
Carter coup tails off in disarray – prepare for war? (8) *Adjusted anagram*
Trouble Italy has looming? (11) *Anagram*
War's started by Bush? Completely! (6) *W is the answer's first letter*

Also topical was this prize-winning effort to celebrate puzzle number 1000 by Ximenes (or X as he was often known) in 1968; C refers to Chambers.

Up to date product of X and C (8) *Think multiplication*

4. Wit and humour

Undoubtedly appreciated by the solver, this is probably the category hardest for setters to achieve, and thus most rarely found. The fine first example won a prize in a Ximenes competition in *The Observer* in 1967, when the recently-coined solution word had not yet made it into the dictionary.

Abbreviations not in Chambers but should not be looked up anyway (4-6) *Think feminine clothes*

Silicone valley! (8) *Think feminine*

Roman marbles lost (3,6,6) *Think Latin*

In which three couples get together for sex (5) *Last word is the key*

Odd if no males could be found here (4,2,3) *Anagram*

Variety of *English* pastry – Dane would look down on it! (7) *Anagram*

Stiff collaring's my trade – it shows what can be done by starch (4,8) *Anagram*

5. Definition and secondary indications being the same ('& lit.' type clues)

Often considered as the pinnacle of the clue-writer's art, the best of this type have a conciseness of wording and do not reveal their charms too easily.

We'll get excited with Ring seat (10) *Anagram*

No fellow for mixing (4,4) *Anagram*

I rifle tubs at sea (10) *Anagram*

What you might find in Lechtal overlooking lake? (6) *Overlook here means 'ignore'*

What's tea passed round in? (5) *Tea is 'cha'*

Waitress with large bust could model as this (7-4) *Bust here means 'broken'*

Names I must jot endlessly (8) *Must here means 'in a frenzy'*

What grass is (even for a fool) (5) *Substitute one word for another*

By it 'truth' and 'lie' looked alternately interchangeable (6-5) *Anagram*

6. Subtlety of language

This type often requires a second, careful reading of a word or words, not necessarily prominent ones.

Lass I love moving upwards you may find well beneath this (3,3) *Down clue*

A chap could attend this celebration but never does (4,5) *Read it again*

Drink causing a problem? What if it is! (9) *An additive clue*

Item Gran arranged family slides in (5,7) *Family is 'clan'*

Shot with craft on course (9) *Golf and poetry cleverly in play*

A murder suspect, one hears (7) *Last two words especially mislead*

Dive made from upturned punts? (7) *A down clue; think Ireland*

7. Technical virtuosity

Long anagrams, as in the first two examples, are often quoted by solvers. This shows that work by setters (whether by computer or not) is appreciated. The third example of virtuosity is also one of the most deceptive clues ever published.

Ground with the Arsenal not getting the least bit of sympathy (5,4,4) *Ground, the past tense of grind*

Poetical scene with surprisingly chaste Lord Archer vegetating (3,3,8,12) *Brooke*

Some job at hand? We'll soon see (4,3,5) *Last word misleads*

8. Highly original clues not obviously fitting into any category

These typically require a leap of imagination on the part of the solver and maybe raise an especially wide smile when the penny drops. Even though the first two of the following clues are often considered 'unsound', they do get plaudits from solvers.

HIJKLMNO (5) *Chemistry; no direct definition included*

ONMLKJIH (9) *No direct definition included*
I can identify vehicles here (5) *IVR code knowledge needed*
014? (6,5) *Think spooks*
His, for example (9) *Plural answer*

Finally, the clue most suggested by fellow setters, and my own favourite, goes back over 25 years. It was originated by Les May, who won first prize in *The Observer*'s Azed competition, and could have been included in several of the other categories. A tough one to crack but solving it for real would be highly satisfying nonetheless.

Bust down reason (9) *Solution splits into three separate words for the purposes of the secondary reading*

Solutions and (where known) authors

Where the clue originally appeared under a pseudonym, the pseudonym is shown in brackets after the author's real name. Where there is no pseudonym or no name at all, the clue's author is unknown to me, or it may have featured either in clue-writing competitions or in publications such as *The Times* or *The Daily Telegraph* where setters are unnamed (though in three instances where names are known to me, due credit is given below).

1. TEACHEST; POST MORTEM; SWISS ROLL Adrian Bell *The Times*; SERAGLIO Valerie Coleman; ROVER'S RETURN; RENT; GO-AHEAD Norman Goddard;

2. GENUFLECT; EMPHASISE John Halpern (Mudd); MARATHON and SHIELD-MAY Ross Beresford; FAREWELL *anag we're in fall* H S Tribe; POSTURE-MAKER I M Raab;

3. RUSHDIE John Grimshaw; ACCOUTRE Tim Moorey; HOOLIGANISM Malcolm Barley; WHOLLY Michael Curl (Orlando); THOUSAND Sir Jeremy Morse;

4. MINI-SKIRTS M C Raphael; CLEAVAGE Roy Dean *The Times*; NON COMPOS MENTIS; LATIN *three times two is six* Brian Greer; ISLE OF MAN; YAPSTER Paul Henderson; BODY SNATCHER Sir Jeremy Morse;

5. WAGNERITES Derrick Macnutt (Ximenes); LONE WOLF Don Manley (Quixote); FILIBUSTER A N Clark; CHALET John Tozer; CHINA; SWEATER-GIRL Tim Moorey (Mephisto); AMNESIAC Kathleen Bissett; GREEN *een for ass* Richard Morse; DOUBLE-THINK Colin Dexter;

6. OIL RIG Jonathan Crowther (Azed); STAG PARTY; SUPPOSING; MAGIC LANTERN Colin Dexter; ALBATROSS; EARDRUM; NITERIE *Eire tin reversed* Roger Hooper;

7. WHITE HART LANE Richard Palmer (Merlin); THE OLD VICARAGE GRANTCHESTER John Graham (Araucaria); BATH AND WELLS *hidden clue* Brian Greer;

8. WATER; BACKWATER John Grimshaw *The Times*; ITALY; DOUBLE AGENT 007 Don Manley (Quixote); GREETINGS; BRAINWASH *bra in wash* Les May.

About the author

Tim Moorey sets crosswords as one of the three-strong Mephisto team for *The Sunday Times*, for which he also regularly contributes *The Sunday Times* crossword. He has additionally appeared as Owzat in newspapers such as *The Independent*, *The Sunday Telegraph* and *The Listener* crossword in *The Times*. He is the crossword editor of *The Week* magazine, gives talks on crosswords and runs regular crossword workshops.

Indicators in cryptic crossword clues

Tim Moorey (Mephisto of *The Sunday Times*)

Why do crosswords have 'indicators'?

As compared to definition-only crosswords (general knowledge, quick, easy and the like) which have clues offering only one means of arriving at each solution, cryptic crossword clues usually have two. These are a definition and a secondary way, often termed 'wordplay'. This in effect, acts as a check on the definition, or vice versa if the solver finds the definition elusive. Wordplay relies on 'indicators', of which there are many types. In effect, an indicator shows how the setter has manipulated the solution, in that a whole word (or part) may have been subject to one or more tricks, such as the following:

	Type of indicator
Changed into another word by a letter mix	Anagram
Split into parts with one part inside another	Containment/Insertion
Letter(s) chosen for subtraction	Deletion
Concealed inside the rest of the clue	Hidden
Considered as spoken, giving a different word	Homophone
Linked to other part(s)	Juxtaposition
Written backwards (or upwards for a Down clue)	Reversal
Letter(s) chosen for manipulation	Selection

How are indicators used?

Indicators are designed to signal to solvers:

- which type of wordplay is to be unravelled
- how to adjust a letter or letters within the clue
- how the whole clue sentence fits together

What are the main types of indicator?

In the clue examples that follow, the indicator is denoted in bold type.

1   Anagram

In nearly all cryptic crosswords solvers are expected to unravel some solutions from a mix of letters, and there is a need for this wordplay to be flagged up. Hence the anagram indicator of which there are a huge number. Most – but not all – imply some form of movement, lack of order, change, uncertainty or instability (especially in assumed mental or physical state) in their meanings, albeit often in a concealed surface reading. Anagram indicators such as 'ground' being the past tense of 'grind', and 'bananas' and 'potty' with their double meanings show such concealment.

There are also some indicators that can only be fully justified by well-established convention. For example, the many synonyms of 'drunk' such as 'pickled', 'stoned' and the like are commonly used, it being assumed that cruciverbal tipplers are wobbly rather than flat out! Nor are setters static in their usages: a modern synonym for 'crazy' such as 'out to lunch' makes a highly misleading anagram indicator, as does 'supply' in the second example.

People seen **working** in Basra (5)

The indicator 'working' for this purpose is in the sense of 'being in action' and it signals a letter mix for the solution ARABS.

Monn (Caterers) **supply** beef and grouse (12)

Here the adverb of 'supple' meaning 'pliant' shows that the first two words must be anagrammatized into REMONSTRANCE meaning complaint, or 'beef' and 'grouse'. Note that as well as wordplay there are two definitions here, a practice often found in advanced puzzles such as Azed or Mephisto.

2 Containment

A solution may be split such that one part of it can be seen as being 'outside' another, duly shown by the many indicators of this type. Containment and insertion indicators have the same effect.

Opportunity to **go round** one Italian city (5)

'Opportunity' is 'turn', and when that is put outside 'I' for 'one' you get the Italian city TURIN. Here 'to go round' is the indicator and 'one' for '1' for 'I' is a common crossword convention.

Saw dog **wearing** lead (7)

This requires 'Rover' for 'dog' to be placed inside 'lead' – or rather the metal's abbreviation 'Pb' – to give PROVERB, or 'saw'.

Is **trapped in** burning lift (5)

The indicator 'trapped in' signals that 'is' has to be contained by, ie put inside, 'burning' meaning 'hot' for the solution HOIST, which defines 'lift'.

3 Insertion

These have the same effect as containment indicators. A solution may be split such that one part is viewed as being 'inside' another.

Disreputable type in favour of **cutting** discount (9)

If you put 'pro', meaning 'in favour of', inside (ie 'cutting') the term 'rebate' meaning 'discount', the solution REPROBATE, a 'disreputable type', appears.

Crumpet may be so to speak **in** bed (8)

Here the well-concealed definition ends at the word 'so'. The wordplay is then 'utter' meaning 'to speak' in 'bed' leading us nicely to BUTTERED. (Note that the 'to' is to be ignored, as is commonly the practice with verbs in wordplay).

4 Deletion

These indicators signal the deletion of a letter or letters (as in the first example), or a whole word within a clue (as in the second example).

Applause left **out** in graduation ceremony (7)

'Applause' is 'clapping' and the indicator demands that its L for 'left' be taken out to leave CAPPING, a 'graduation ceremony'.

Surgeon **fails to get** on in this swell (5)

Take 'on' from 'surgeon' to get to SURGE which is the definition for 'swell'.

Note that the word 'in' here in both deletion examples is being used not as an indicator but as common crossword shorthand, in effect for 'leading to ...' or 'coming from ...'.

Other specific deletion indicators are discussed in Ends deletion indicators, Head deletion indicators, Middle deletion indicators and Tail deletion indicators.

5 Ends indicators

5a Ends selection

The first and last letters of a word within a clue are indicated for addition to some other letters, or to a whole word, in order to form the solution.

Urges for example, **both sides** in games (4)

The indicator 'both sides' when applied to 'games' gives two letters G and S. Put these together with 'eg', meaning 'for example', and you have EGGS as in to egg or urge someone on.

5b Ends deletion

The first and last letters of a word within a clue are indicated for deletion in order to form the solution.

Shell prawn uncooked (3)

'Shell' in the sense of 'separate from the shell or covering' implies removing the first and last letters of 'prawn' to give RAW meaning 'uncooked'.

6 Head indicators

There is a common (but not universally applied) convention that Down solutions should be indicated as the word appears in the completed grid. This means that a distinction is sometimes made between Across and Down clues as regards what constitutes 'heads'. For example, head selection indicators such as 'summit' or 'top' are sometimes said to be applicable to Down clues only.

6a Head selection

The first letter of a word within a clue is indicated for addition to some other letters or, as below, to a whole word to form the solution.

Starter with pork and mild pickle (6)

Here the indicator 'starter' is applied to 'pork' to give 'P'. Added to 'light' meaning 'mild' this provides the solution PLIGHT, or a 'pickle' – a predicament if you are in one.

6b Head deletion

The first letter of a word is indicated for deletion in order to form the solution.

Colleague in Monte Carlo event **failing to start** (4)

A 'Monte Carlo event' is a 'rally' which 'fails to start', ie it loses its initial letter. This leaves the answer ALLY, meaning 'colleague'.

7 Middle indicators

7a Middle selection

The middle letter (or letters) of a word within a clue is indicated for addition to some other letters, or to a whole word, in order to form the solution.

Plastic building toy on **centre** of floor (4)

'On' for 'leg' (as in cricket) plus the middle letter of floor, 'O', makes LEGO, the required toy.

b Middle deletion

The middle letter (or letters) of a word within a clue is indicated for deletion in order to form the solution.

Royal Artillery really **disheartened**? Seldom (6)

The central two letters 'AL' are eliminated from 'really' to give 'RELY', which put after 'RA' (an abbreviation of 'Royal Artillery') gives RARELY, 'seldom'

Tail indicators

a Tail selection

The last letter (or letters) of a word within a clue is indicated for addition to some other letters, or to a whole word, in order to form the solution.

Dull **back** of road could be a cul-de-sac (4,3)

'Dull' is 'deaden', to which an added 'D' from 'back of road' provides DEAD END, a 'cul-de-sac'.

b Tail selection down

This is similar to that above, but this indicator is for a Down clue only (see Head indicators above for an explanation of this convention). The above Across clue could be adapted as follows, with 'bottom' as the Tail Selection Down indicator.

Dull **bottom** of road could be a cul-de-sac (4,3)

This gives a Down clue with the same solution DEAD END, a 'cul-de-sac'.

c Tail deletion

The last letter (or letters) of a word is indicated for deletion in order to form the solution.

English poet messing around **endlessly** (6)

'Messing around' is 'larking' which becomes (Philip) LARKIN, the poet, when its last letter is taken off.

d Tail deletion down

This is similar to that above, but this indicator is for a Down clue only.

Baseless worry for vehicle (3)

If the final letter of 'care' for 'worry' is ignored, CAR, a 'vehicle', comes out as the Down clue answer.

Hidden

a Hidden

The indicator instructs solvers to look for the solution within the clue sentence, or wholly within one of the clue's words.

In Amritsar it's a common habit (4)

Indicated by 'in', the challenge is to uncover a hidden but defined four-letter word. This is SARI – formed from the last three letters of 'Amritsar' and the first letter of 'it's' – a common habit with the final word in its 'dress' sense.

Sensation **concealed by** Chopin, Sand – needlessly (4,3,7)

Not quite so easy to spot, as a result of its misleading punctuation, is the hidden phrase PINS AND NEEDLES, a sensation.

9b Hidden alternately

A second form of this indicator applies where every other letter has to be taken to form the solution word. The indicator will not necessarily always signal whether it's the even or odd letters to be used. For example, the indicator 'regularly' may refer to either even or odd letters.

Select **even parts** of strongest gear (4)

The instruction 'select' indicates taking the even letters in 'strongest' to form a word meaning 'gear'. Hence the solution is TOGS.

10 Homophone

In this type, the definition when spoken becomes another word which forms the wordplay. Sometimes with careless word placement, setters do not make clear which is the solution and which the homophone, though this may be established from the word-length. It can also be a problem for solvers as to which part of the English-speaking world, with its many differing pronunciations, is deemed to be speaking the homophone.

It's cold in a S American country **reportedly** (6)

'Reportedly' is an indicator that the solver is looking for a word that sounds like another meaning of 'cold'. 'Chile' clearly fits the bill as a homonym of CHILLY, the answer.

Check **on radio** for weather forecast? (4)

If listening to the radio, 'rein' (meaning 'check') would sound like RAIN, the solution.

11 Juxtaposition

11a Juxtaposition

The indicator shows that the two words or parts of words need to be placed together for the solution.

Endeavour perhaps to be **alongside** learner in a scrap (6)

Morse ('Endeavour', the first name of Inspector Morse in the novels by Colin Dexter) is juxtaposed with 'L' for 'learner' to make 'scrap', a MORSEL.

11b Juxtaposition down

This is similar to that above, but this indicator is for a Down clue only (see Head indicators above for an explanation of this convention).

One **above** Bishop given the answer: forgiveness (10)

'A' for 'one' put on top of 'B' for 'bishop' and 'solution' for 'answer' makes ABSOLUTION, meaning 'forgiveness'. Actually there are two juxtaposition indicators here, in that as well as 'above' the word 'given' also shows that some words are to be placed together.

12 Reversal

12a Reversal

The whole of a solution word can sometimes be reversed to form another different word (or the same word in the case of a palindrome – see below). It's the job of reversal indicators to show this, and sometimes also reversals of only part of a word which is then subject to more wordplay, as in the second example.

Huge flans **all round** – that's the plan (9)

'Huge flans' are 'mega tarts', which when reversed gives STRATAGEM or 'plan'.

Optimistic US president admitting bad **back** (7)

Reversing 'ill' for 'bad' and putting this inside (further wordplay signalled by 'admitting') Bush gives BULLISH, or 'optimistic'.

12b Reversal down

Reversal indicators used in Down clues will often be, for example, 'rising' or 'brought up' rather than those used in Across clues implying reversal horizontally such as 'all round' (as above) or as 'backwards' (see Head indicators above for further explanation of this convention). Using this in the preceding example, a Down clue could have been:

Huge flans **served up** – that's the plan (9)

It's 'served up' showing the necessary upwards movement in 'mega tarts' to lead to the same STRATEGEM solution.

12c Reversal palindrome

The third type of reversal indicator applies to palindromic solutions, for which there are a small number of indicators.

This note is small **whichever way you look at it** (5)

The indicator signals that the solution is the same as its reversal, in this case MINIM, the 'small note' of the clue.

Other indicators

In addition to the most important indicators already covered above, there are some others met in cryptic puzzles that can be mentioned briefly. They tend to be self-explanatory.

Foreign

Many European languages, especially French, can be indicated, usually obviously but occasionally not so, as in this example:

Nice girl has time for a piece of beef (6)

The indicator refers to the French city of Nice, where the word for 'girl' would be 'fille'. Put next to 'T' for 'time', you have FILLET, a piece of beef.

Archaic

Rather than use the mundane 'archaic' or 'obsolete' as indicators, setters find more interesting and misleading ways of expressing words that are no longer in general usage.

Mark **antique** articles rubbish! (2,3)

'M' for 'mark' (as in Germany before the euro), plus 'ye ye' or two archaic definite 'articles' will show as MY EYE, meaning 'rubbish!'

Dialect

Different regional words and accents may be referred to, especially British ones such as Scottish and Cockney.

The **Yorkshire** beer in fiction (4)

The solution TALE, meaning 'fiction' in the sense of a lie, comes from 'T' for 'the' as supposedly used in 'Yorkshire' plus 'ALE' for 'beer'.

Repetition

A small number of indicators show, nearly always self-evidently, when letters or words need to be included more than once in a solution.

The Queen **repeatedly** behind grown-up man of affairs (9)

Thus 'grown-up' is 'adult' which when preceding 'ER' (the Queen) twice gives 'ADULTERER', the 'man of affairs' being sought.

Conclusion

In the foregoing examples there is mostly only one type of indicator used in any one example. However, it is not uncommon in advanced puzzles to find one or more indicators of the same or different type being used in one clue. For example:

Clever wordplay recalled Thomas Mann's last book about love (3,3)

Here the solver is asked to do all the following:

	Indicator (and type)
Abbreviate *Thomas* to TOM	none given
Take *Mann's last* as N	*last* (tail selection)
Abbreviate *book* to B	none given
Abbreviate *love* to O	none given
Put TOM N B outside O	*about* (containment)

Amongst other possibilities, this gives TOMNOB.

Reverse this to get BONMOT   *recalled* (reversal)

And finally split it (3,3) to get BONMOT, meaning 'clever wordplay'.

Note that, as is almost always the case, abbreviations have to be identified without the aid of indicators. The clue is perhaps over-complex and you may or not agree that it offers clever wordplay!

About the author

Tim Moorey sets crosswords as one of the three-strong Mephisto team for *The Sunday Times*, for which he also regularly contributes *The Sunday Times* crossword. He has additionally appeared as Owzat in newspapers such as *The Independent*, *The Sunday Telegraph* and *The Listener* crossword in *The Times*. He is the crossword editor of *The Week* magazine, gives talks on crosswords and runs regular crossword workshops.

Indicator lists

The following lists show those headwords, phrasal verbs and idioms that are denoted in the *Crossword Dictionary* as being indicators of cryptic crossword clue wordplay.

The lists have been compiled on the basis of those indicators most commonly seen in crosswords. They are not, and never could be, definitive. The lists reflect the way that these words have been used in actual cryptic clues. Appearance in a list does not mean that such a usage is considered acceptable by all crossword setters and editors.

As explained in the Introduction, indicators may not appear in a cryptic clue in the way in which they appear here, but rather may be encountered in an inflected form – for example the anagram indicator 'digest' is more frequently encountered as 'digested' – or as part of a phrase, for example 'not reaching a conclusion' to indicate a tail deletion. As the lists reflect the headwords of the *Crossword Dictionary*, not every form of every indicator is included.

Additionally, there are some indicators which may be encountered in cryptic clues, but which are not denoted in the text or in the following lists. Examples of these include:

Type	Indicator example
Abbreviation to be used	short
Colloquial usage	commonly
First half, second half of word selected	left half, right half
Insertion between letters SS	aboard ship, on board
Move first letter to end	brings first to last, runs down
Move internal letter to front	puts foremost
Not all letters used	not entirely
One of two central letters deleted	half-heartedly
Only limited wordplay	slightly
Only two, three, etc letters selected	two of, three of, etc
Plural word loses final S	singular
Proportion of letters in a word selected	half, two-thirds
Selection of second, third, fourth, etc letter	second, third, fourth, etc
Selection of two letters	couple of
Single letter instead of double	just one
Substitute letters	replace, take instead, change, changing
Unusual homophone	drunkard says (*for a homophone that sounds slurred, eg 'mesh' for 'mess'*)

It should also be noted that as the number of foreign word indicators is potentially unlimited – any person or place might be used – only the most general have been included here. For example, 'article from Paris', 'day in Calais', 'Renoir's here', 'lake in Savoie' or 'of Chirac's' could all indicate that a French word is required (in these instances, 'la' or 'le', 'jour', 'ici', 'lac' and 'de' respectively).

Anagram indicators

Anagram indicators include:

abandon	another	beaten	buckle
abandoned	anxious	beat up	buffeted
aberrant	anyhow	become	building
abnormal	anyway	bedevil	built
abominable	apart	bedlam	bully
about	appalling	befuddle	bum
abroad	appallingly	belabour	bumble
absurd	appliance	belt	bumbling
abuse	applied	bemuse	bundle
abysmal	appointed	bemused	bungle
abysmally	appraisal	bend	burst
accident	arch	bendy	bust
accidentally	around	bent	bustle
acrobatics	arousal	berserk	bustling
acting	arouse	bespoke	busy
action	arrange	bewildered	butcher
activate	arrangement	biased	Byzantine
active	array	bizarre	calamitous
activity	artefact	bizarrely	camouflage
adapt	artful	blast	capricious
adaptable	artfully	blasted	career
adaptation	articulate	blazing	careless
adjust	articulated	blend	carelessly
adjustment	askew	blessed	carve
administer	assassinate	blight	carve up
adrift	assassination	blotchy	cast
affected	assemble	blow up	cavort
afflicted	assorted	blue	change
afresh	astonishing	blunder	changeable
after injury	astray	blur	chaotic
aggrieved	at fault	blurred	chew
agile	at random	body	choppy
agitate	atrocious	bogus	chop up
agitated	at sea	boil	churn
ague	away	boiled	circulate
alarm	awful	boiling	clobber
allocate	awfully	boisterous	clumsy
allocation	awkward	bomb	cocktail
all over the place	awkwardly	boozy	cock up
alloy	awry	boss	cock-up
alter	bad	botch	code
alteration	badly	bother	collapse
alternative	baffle	bottle	collected
alternatively	baffling	bouncing	collection
amazing	bake	bouncy	combustible
amend	bamboozle	brain	compilation
amendment	bananas	break	compile
amiss	bandy	break up	complex
amok	barbaric	breeze	complicate
analyse	barbarous	brew	complicated
analysis	barge	brittle	complication
anarchic	barking	broach	component
anew	baroque	broadcast	compose
angrily	bastard	broke	composed
angry	bats	broken	composition
animated	batter	broth	compound
animatedly	battered	bruise	compromise
anomalous	batting	bubbly	concerned
anomaly	batty	buck	concoct

condemn
condemnation
condition
confection
confound
confuse
confused
confusing
confusion
constituent
construct
construe
contaminate
contamination
contort
contrive
contrived
conversion
convert
convertible
convoluted
convulse
cook
cooked
cook up
correct
correction
corrupt
could be
could become
crack
cracked
crackers
crackpot
crack up
craft
craftily
crafty
cranky
crash
crazed
crazily
crazy
creation
criminal
crocked
crook
crooked
cross
crude
crudely
cruel
crumble
crumbly
crush
cuckoo
cultivate
cure
curious
curiously
cut
daft

damage
damaged
dance
dash
dashing
dazed
debris
decompose
defective
deficient
defile
deform
deformed
delirious
deliriously
demented
demolish
deplorable
deploy
deranged
desecrate
design
desperate
desperately
destabilize
destroy
destruction
desultory
deterioration
detour
devastate
devastated
develop
deviant
deviate
deviation
devilish
devious
diabolical
dicky
different
differently
digest
dilapidated
dire
direct
disarrange
disarray
disastrous
disband
discomfit
discompose
disconcert
disconcerting
discord
discordant
discover
diseased
disfigure
disgruntled
disguise
disguised

dish
dishevelled
dish out
disintegrate
disintegration
disjointed
dislocate
dislocation
dismantle
disorder
disordered
disorderly
disorganization
disorganize
disorganized
disorientate
disorientated
disorientation
dispel
disperse
dispersion
disport
dispose
disposed
disposition
disrupt
disruption
dissipate
dissipated
dissolute
dissonant
distillation
distort
distorted
distract
distracted
distraught
distribute
distribution
disturb
disturbance
disturbed
disturbing
dither
diverse
divert
diverting
dizzy
do
doctor
doddering
doddery
dodgy
done
dotty
doubtfully
drastic
drawn
dreadful
dreadfully
dress
dressing

dress up
drift
drunk
drunken
dubious
duff
dynamic
easily
easy
eccentric
edit
effervescent
elaborate
elastic
elevated
embarrass
embarrassed
embroil
emend
emendation
emerge
employ
engineer
enigmatic
enliven
entangle
entanglement
entwine
err
errant
erratic
erratically
erring
erroneous
error
erupt
eruption
evolution
evolve
exchange
excite
excited
excruciate
exercise
exotic
explode
explosive
extract
extraordinarily
extraordinary
extravagant
fabricate
fake
fall
false
faltering
fan
fanciful
fancy
fantastic
fashion
fault

faulty
fearful
ferment
fettle
feverish
fickle
find in
finesse
finicky
fishy
fit
fix
fixed
flabbergasted
flail
flake
flaky
flap
flash
flawed
flexible
flighty
flit
floating
flog
flop
floppy
flounder
flourish
flourished
flourishing
flow
fluctuate
fluff
fluid
flurried
flurry
fluster
flutter
fly
fly open
fog
foolish
foolishly
force
forced
foreign
forge
forged
forlorn
form
foul
founder
found in
fracture
frantic
frantically
freak
freak out
free
freely
frenetic

frenetically
frenzy
fresh
freshen
freshly
frightful
frightfully
frilly
frisky
frolic
frolicsome
fuddled
fudge
full
fumble
funnily
funny
furious
fussy
fuzzy
gaffe
gambol
garble
garbled
generate
giddily
giddy
ginger
gnarled
go crazy
gone
go off
grim
groggy
groom
gross
grotesque
ground
hairy
ham
hammer
hammered
hammer out
hamper
haphazard
haphazardly
happy
harass
harassed
harm
hash
hatch
havoc
haywire
hazy
head over heels
heat
hectic
hellish
helter-skelter
hideous
higgledy-piggledy

high
hit
hopeless
hopelessly
horrible
horribly
horrid
horrific
hotchpotch
hurl
hurt
hybrid
idiotic
ill
ill-assorted
ill at ease
ill-bred
ill-treat
imbecile
impair
impaired
imperfect
implicate
implicated
improper
improperly
inaccurate
incapable
in circulation
incorrect
indecent
indiscriminate
inebriated
inept
ingredient
injure
injured
inky
in motion
inordinate
in pieces
insane
insanely
insanity
insecure
intoxicate
intoxicated
intricate
invalid
invention
involve
involved
irregular
irritated
itinerant
jagged
jangle
jar
jaunty
jazz
jerk
jerky

jig
jiggle
jitters
jittery
jockey
jog
jolt
jostle
judder
juggle
jumble
jumbled
jump
junk
kick
kind of
kink
kinky
knead
knock
knock over
knot
knotty
labour
laboured
labyrinthine
lace
lamentable
lark
launder
lawless
lax
layout
lazily
leap
liberal
light
lit
lively
loaded
loony
loose
loosely
lost
lousy
ludicrous
lunatic
mad
madden
maddening
made-up
madly
madness
make
make up
make-up
maladjusted
malformed
malfunction
malleable
maltreat
mangle

manic
manically
manifest
manifestation
manipulate
manipulation
manoeuvre
manufacture
mar
marshal
mash
masquerade
massage
maul
maybe
mayhem
maze
meandering
meddle
medley
melange
mêlée
melt
mental
merry
mess
messy
metamorphose
metamorphosis
mill
mince
mint
misbehave
misbehaviour
mischievous
mischievously
misconduct
misconstrue
misdirect
miserable
miserably
misfit
misguided
mishandle
mishap
misinterpret
mislead
misleading
mismanage
mismanagement
misplace
misprint
misread
misrepresent
misrepresentation
misshapen
misspell
mistake
mistaken
mistakenly
mistreat
misuse

mix
mixed
mixed up
mix in
mixture
mix up
mix-up
mobile
mobilize
model
modification
modify
mongrel
mortal
mould
mouldy
move
movement
moving
muddle
muddled
muddy
muff
mushy
muss
must
musty
mutate
mutation
mutilate
mutilation
mutinous
mysterious
mysteriously
nastily
nasty
naughty
neaten
neglect
neglected
negligence
negligent
negotiate
negotiation
nervous
nervously
new
newly
nobble
nonsensical
not
novel
nuts
obfuscate
oblique
obscure
obstreperous
odd
oddball
oddly
off
off-colour

on
on the rampage
operate
order
orderly
organization
organize
organized
original
ornate
other
otherwise
out
outlandish
out of hand
out of order
out of place
out of sorts
output
outrageous
outré
outside
overthrow
overturn
painfully
panic
paranormal
pastiche
patchy
pathetic
peculiar
peculiarly
peddle
pell-mell
perform
perhaps
perplex
perturb
perturbed
perverse
perversely
perversion
perversity
pervert
perverted
phoney
pickle
pie
piece
plan
plastered
plastic
play
play around with
play with
ply
police
pollute
pollution
poor
poorly
pop

possible
possibly
potential
potentially
potty
prance
precarious
precariously
preparation
prepare
prepared
preposterous
problem
problematic
process
produce
production
promiscuous
protean
provide
pulverize
pummel
punish
puzzle
quaint
quake
queer
questionable
quirky
quiver
raddled
rag
rage
ragged
ramble
rambling
rampage
rampant
ramshackle
random
randomly
rare
rash
rattle
ravage
ravaged
rave
raving
react
reactionary
realign
rearrange
reassemble
rebel
rebellious
rebuild
recast
reckless
recklessly
recollect
recollection
recondition

reconfigure	revamp	scratch	special
reconstitute	reveal	screw	specially
reconstruct	revel	screwy	speech
recover	review	scruffy	spin
recreate	revise	scuffle	splash
recycle	revolt	sculpt	splice
red	revolting	sculpture	spoil
redeploy	revolution	scuttle	spongy
redevelop	revolutionary	seedy	sport
redevelopment	rework	seethe	sporting
redistribute	rewrite	serve	spray
redistribution	rickety	set	spread
redraft	ridiculous	set out	spring
re-edit	ridiculously	settlement	sprinkle
reel	rifle	shake	spurious
refashion	rig	shaky	squiffy
refine	rile	sham	squirm
refit	riot	shape	stagger
reform	riotous	shapeless	staggered
reformat	riotously	shatter	staggering
reformation	rip	shattered	steaming
refurbish	ripple	shell	stew
refurbishment	rock	shift	stir
refuse	rocky	shifty	stirring
regenerate	rogue	shimmer	storm
regenerated	roll	shimmering	stormy
regulate	rollicking	shiver	straighten
rehash	rolling	shock	strange
rejig	rot	shoddy	strangely
relax	rotten	shot	stray
relaxed	rough	shower	stress
relay	roughen	show off	structure
remake	roughly	shuffle	struggle
remarkable	round	sick	stumble
remedy	rouse	signal	stupid
remodel	rove	silliness	stupidly
render	rub	silly	style
renegade	rubbish	sink	subtle
renegotiate	rude	sketchy	subtly
renew	ruffle	skip	suffer
renovate	ruin	slack	suffering
rent	ruined	slapdash	sunk
reorder	rum	slaughtered	supply
reorganize	run	slide	surprising
repackage	running	slip	suspect
repair	runny	slippery	suspicious
replace	run riot	slipshod	swap
reposition	run wild	sloppy	swill
represent	rupture	slosh	swim
representation	rustic	slovenly	swimming
reprocess	sabotage	slyly	swing
reproduce	sack	smash	swinging
resettle	sad	snarl	swirl
reshape	sadly	solution	switch
reshuffle	salad	solve	swop
resolution	scatter	somehow	synthetic
resolve	scatty	sorry	tailor
resort	scheme	sort	taint
restless	scour	soup	tangle
restoration	scraggy	sozzled	tangled
restore	scramble	spasmodic	tattered
re-use	scrappy	spatter	tease

teeter	turn	unrestrained	wacky
terrible	turning	unrestricted	wag
terribly	tweak	unruly	waggle
throb	twiddle	unscramble	wander
throw	twinkle	unseemly	wanton
tidy	twinkling	unsettle	warp
tight	twirl	unsettled	warring
tipsy	twirling	unsound	waste
topple	twist	unstable	wasted
topsy-turvy	twisted	unsteady	wave
torment	twitch	untidy	waver
torn	type	untrue	wavering
tortuous	ugly	unusual	way
torture	unbalanced	unusually	weave
toss	uncertain	unwind	weird
totter	uncommon	unwise	whip
tour	uncommonly	upset	whip up
tragic	uncomplicated	upsetting	whirl
train	uncontrolled	upturn	whisk
trammel	unconventional	use	wicked
transfer	unco-ordinated	used	wild
transfigure	uncouth	useless	wildly
transform	undisciplined	vacillate	wind
transformation	undo	vacillating	winding
translate	undoing	vacillation	wobble
translation	undone	vagrant	wobbly
transmute	unduly	vague	woeful
transport	uneasy	vaguely	work
transported	uneven	vandalize	working
transpose	unexpected	variant	worried
trash	unexpectedly	variation	worry
travelling	unfair	varied	wound
treat	unfairly	variegated	wrack
treatment	unfamiliar	variety	wreck
tremble	unfit	various	wreckage
trembling	unfortunate	vary	wrestling
tremulous	unfortunately	vault	wretched
trick	ungainly	versatile	writhe
tricky	unhappily	version	wrong
trip	unhappy	vibrate	wrongly
trouble	unholy	vigorous	wrought
troubled	unkempt	vigorously	yank
troublesome	unnatural	vile	yearning
tumble	unnaturally	violate	yield
tumbledown	unorthodox	violation	yielding
tumult	unpredictable	violent	zany
turbulence	unravel	violently	
turbulent	unreliable	volatile	
turmoil	unrest	vulnerable	

Containment indicators

Containment indicators include:

about	admit	bag	box
absorb	adopt	bear	bracket
absorbed	around	bearing	break up
accept	arrest	beset	bring in
accommodate	assimilate	besiege	bring round
accommodating	assume	bewilder	bury
accommodation	astride	bite	capture
acquire	ate	biting	carry

casing	enfold	harbour	protect
catch	engulf	hedge	purse
catching	ensnare	herein	receive
caught	entertain	hide	repress
circle	entertaining	hiding	restrain
clasp	enthral	hold	restrict
cleft	enthralling	host	retain
clutch	envelop	house	round
collect	fence	housing	sandwich
come to grips with	flank	hug	secure
comprehend	found in	imbibe	see around
comprise	frame	imprison	seize
conceal	framework	include	shelter
concealed	gather	including	snare
consume	gathering	incorporate	squeeze
consuming	get around	in possession	stow
contain	get hold of	introduce	stuffing
cover	get round	keep	superficial
crossing	get to grips with	limit	surround
custody	go about	lock up	surrounding
describe	go around	net	swallow
detectable	gobble	nurse	tackle
drape	go round	obstruct	take in
draw in	grab	occlude	trap
eat	grasp	outside	trapped
embody	grasping	over	wearing
embrace	grip	overshadow	welcome
encapsulate	gripping	pen	without
encircle	guard	pinch	wrap
enclose	gulp	pocket	
encompass	hamper	possess	

Insertion indicators

Insertion indicators include:

aboard	divide	held in	penetrate
amid	don	imprisoned	penetrating
amidst	during	in	pierce
among	engage in	infuse	piercing
at heart	enter	inside	puncture
between	feed	intercept	seduce
bisect	fill	interception	set in
block	filling	interrupt	split
break	find in	interruption	tuck in
cleave	get into	invest	tuck into
collected	go into	involve	wear
cut	half	occupy	within
cutting	halve	part	
devour	held by	parting	

Deletion indicators

Deletion indicators include:

abandon	disregard	heave	lose
absent	drop	ignore	missing
cut	edit	junk	nearly
disappear	elude	lack	no
disappearance	excision	lacking	not
dismiss	excluding	leave	out
dismissal	fail to get	left	regardless

sack	scrub	skip	withdraw
sacrifice	shed	small	withhold
scratch	shun	take off	

Ends indicators

Ends selection indicators include:

banks	bounds	edge	limit
borders of	casing	extreme	side
both sides	determination	fringe	

Ends deletion indicators include:

limited	peel	top and tail	wingless
limitless	shell	unlimited	

Head indicators

Head selection indicators include:

at first	front	leader	start
beginner	head	leadership	starter
beginning	heading	leading	summit
capital	initial	minimum	tip
extreme	initially	opener	top
first	introduction	opening	
foremost	lead	primarily	

Head deletion indicators include:

behead	fail to start	leaderless	topless
decapitate	headless	limitless	trim
deface	head off	tip-off	

Middle indicators

Middle selection indicators include:

at heart	centre	heartily	middle
central	heart	innards	nucleus

Middle deletion indicators include:

disembowel	empty	heartless
disheartened	gutless	heartlessly

Tail indicators

Tail selection indicators include:

at last	endmost	finally	tail
at the end of	extreme	finish	terminal
back	far end	foundation	ultimate
behind	far side	last	ultimately
end	final	lastly	
ending	finale	rear	

Tail selection down indicators include:

base of
bottom
south

Tail deletion indicators include:

abbreviate	curtail	immature	reduction
abridged	curtailment	incomplete	short
abrupt	cut short	limit	shorten
almost	detail	limitless	shortened
brief	detailed	Manx	shortly
briefly	dock	most	trim
clip	endless	nearly	unfinished
contract	endlessly	reduce	

Tail deletion down indicators include:
baseless
bottom

Hidden indicators

Hidden indicators include:

amid	continuous	from	lock up
amidst	continuously	held by	part
among	cover	held in	part of
apparent	cover up	hidden	piece
belonging to	deposit	hide	sample
bit	discover	immerse	show
bottle	embrace	immersed	slice
central	emerge	in	some
characters in	extract	include	stuffing
concealed	find in	in part	within
contain	found in	inside	
content	fragment	keep	

Hidden alternately indicators include:

alternate	evenly	ignore the odds	oddly
even	even parts	odd	odd parts

Homophone indicators

Homophone indicators include:

aloud	hear	on telephone	sound
announce	hearing	oral	speak
articulate	hearsay	orally	speech
articulated	inform	pronounce	spoken
audible	list	pronounced	state
aural	listen	read aloud	told
broadcast	listen in	report	utter
conversation	murmur	reportedly	verbal
conversational	mutter	said	vocal
converse	narrate	say	
ear	on radio	saying	

Juxtaposition indicators

Juxtaposition indicators include:

abut	after	altogether	associate
add	against	and	associated
adjacent	ahead	append	at the end of
adjoin	also	approach	before
adjoining	alongside	arrive	behind

beside	continuously	go together	take on
by	first	in front	trail
chase	follow	in front of	with
come first	following	join	
continuous	given	meet	

Juxtaposition down indicators include:

above	go under	subordinate	topping
below	on	support	under
beneath	over	supporter	

Reversal indicators

Reversal indicators include:

about	go around	rebellious	reversal
all round	go back	recall	reverse
around	go back on	recede	reversion
back	go round	recess	revert
backfire	go west	recoil	review
backing	head over heels	recollect	revolution
backslide	hinge	recurrent	revolutionary
backsliding	in retrospect	reflect	rotate
backtrack	in return	reflection	round
backward	inversion	regress	set back
backwards	invert	reject	setback
boomerang	keep back	repel	switch
bring back	knock back	retire	turn
capsize	make a comeback	retired	turn back
come back	on the contrary	retiring	turned
contrary	preposterous	retreat	turning
cutback	raise	retrograde	turnover
east	rampant	retrogress	volte-face
fall	reactionary	retrospective	wheel
flip	rear	return	

Reversal down indicators include:

arise	hold up	send up	uprising
ascend	keel over	serve up	upset
ascendant	mount	set up	upside down
bring up	over	set-up	upturn
climb	overturn	take up	upward
come up	put up	turn over	use up
elevate	raised	turn up	
elevated	rise	up	
give rise to	rising	uplift	

Palindrome indicators include:

back and forth	to and fro	whichever way you
either way	up and down	look at it

Foreign indicators

Foreign word indicators include:

European	French	local
foreign	in France	translate

Archaic indicators

Archaic indicators include:

> antique
> old
> old-fashioned
> once

Dialect indicators

Dialect indicators include:

American	East End	Sandy	US
Cockney	local	Scot	Yorkshire
Cumbrian	New York	Scottish	

Repetition indicators

Repetition indicators include:

couple	repeat	repeatedly	twice
double	repeated	repetition	

Reference lists

Headwords followed by one or more reference list:

abbey
aboriginal
accommodation
acid
activist
actor, actress
administrative
admiral
Africa
African
agriculture
aircraft
airline
airport
alga, algae
alphabet
America
American
American football
amino acid
amphibian
anaesthetic
analgesic
anatomy
anchor
angel
animal
anniversary
ant
antelope
anthropology
antibiotic
antique
antiseptic
ape
apocryphal
apostle
apple
Arab
arch
archaeology
archbishop
archipelago
architect
architecture
armour
army
art
arthropod
artist

Asia
Asian
asteroid
astronaut
astronomer
athlete
athletics
atmosphere
Australia
Australian football
author
aviation
aviator
award

bacteriology
bacterium
badminton
bag
ballet
baseball
basketball
bat
battle
bay
beach
bean
bear
bed
bedclothes
beer
beetle
belief
believer
berry
bet
Bible
bicycle
biochemistry
biography
biology
bird
birth
biscuit
bishop
black
blemish
blue
bomb
bomber

bone
book
bookbinding
boot
border
botany
bottle
boxer
boxing
boy
brain
bread
bridge
bridle
brown
building
bulb
bushranger
business
businessman,
   businesswoman
butterfly

cactus
cake
calendar
camera
Canada
canal
canonical
cape
captain
car
cardinal
carpet
carriage
cartoon
castle
cat
cathedral
cattle
cave
celebration
cell
cemetery
cereal
ceremony
chair
channel
charity

cheese
chef
chemical
chemist
chemistry
chess
chicken
choreography
Christmas
church
cicada
cigarette
cinema
circle
circus
city
classification
clean
cloak
clock
clothes, clothing
cloud
clown
club
coat
cocktail
coffee
coin
collar
collective
collector
college
colour
comedian
comedy
comet
comic
command
commander
commonwealth
communication
compass
competition
composer
computer
conductor
constellation
container
continent
contraceptive

cook
cookery
cosmetic
cotton
council
country
county
court
cricket
crime
criminal
crop
cross
crossword
crust
crustacean
currency
cutlery
cutter
cyclist

dagger
dairy
dam
dance
dancer
dandy
daughter
day
death
deer
deficiency
delivery
department
desert
despot
dessert
detective
device
diamond
diary
dinosaur
diocese
director
disease
district
divination
doctor
dog
doll
domestic
dress
drink
drug
duck
dwarf
dye
dynasty

ear
eat
economics

economist
educational
eel
Egyptian
electorate
electrical
element
emblem
embroidery
emperor
empire
empress
engine
engineer
entertainer
entertainment
environment
enzyme
equestrian
essayist
Europe
European
execution
exercise
explorer
explosive
eye

fable
fabric
face
fairground
fairy tale
falcon
farm
fashion
fast
fastener, fastening
fate
feminism
fencing
fern
festival
fever
fictional
fictitious
Field Marshal
fighter
figure
film
fireplace
fireworks
firth
fish
fishing
flag
flower
fly
food
fool
football
footballer

footwear
forest
fortification
fossil
Frenchman
fruit
fuel
fungus
fur
furniture
fury

galaxy
gambling
game
garden
gardener
gardening
gas
gauge
gem
genealogy
general
genetics
geography
geology
German
giant
girl
gland
glass
god, goddess
golf
golf club
golfer
government
governor
grace
grass
Greek
green
grey
grouse
gulf
gun
gymnastics

hair
hairdresser
hairstyle
hat
headdress
heart
heraldry
herb
hero
heroine
highwayman
hill
historian
historical
hobby

hockey
holiday
honour
hormone
horse
horseman,
  horsewoman
hour
house
household
humour
hybrid
hydrocarbon

ice
ice hockey
ice skating
incarnation
inflammation
insect
insecticide
institute
instrument
insulator
inventor
invertebrate
Ireland
Irish
island

Japanese
jazz
jewellery
journalism
journalist
judge

karate
key
king
knife
knight
knit
knot

laboratory
lace
lake
language
Latin
law
lawyer
leaf
leather
legal
legend
letter
lettuce
lexicographer
libretto
lie
lily

liqueur
literary
literature
lizard
lock
London
lover
luggage

machinery
mammal
mania
Maori
marriage
marshal
marsupial
martial art
massacre
mathematics
meal
measurement
measuring instrument
meat
medical
medicine
metal
meteor
meteorology
Middle East
military
mineral
miser
missile
missionary
mollusc
monarch
monastery
monk
monkey
monster
month
monument
moon
moss
moth
mountain
mountaineering
mouth
murderer
muscle
muse
museum
mushroom
music
musical
musician
musketeer
Muslim
mythical
mythology

name

narcotic
nationality
NATO
navigation
nerve
news
newspaper
New York
New Zealand
Nobel Prize
nobility
non-fiction
note
novel
number
numeral
nurse
nut

observatory
occult
occupation
ocean
office
official
oil
Olympics
OPEC
opera
optical
orange
oratorio
orchestra
orchid
ore
organ
overture

paint
painter
painting
palace
palaeontologist
palm
pantomime
paper
parasite
Paris
park
parliament
parrot
particle
party
passage
pasta
pastry
patriarch
peninsula
people
pepper
pet
pharaoh

philosopher
philosophy
phobia
photographer
photographic
physics
physiology
pianist
picture
pig
pigment
pike
pine
pink
pirate
plague
plain
planet
plant
plastic
play
playwright
plumbing
poem
poet
poetry
poison
poisoning
poker
police
police officer
political
politician
pope
porcelain
port
potato
pottery
poultry
power
prayer
precipitation
premier
president
priest
primate
prime minister
prince
princess
printing
prison
probe
prophet, prophetess
prosody
protein
province
pseudonym
psychiatrist
psychology
public house
publish
punctuation

punishment
purple
puzzle

qualification
queen
quiz

rabbi
rabbit
race
racecourse
racing
radiation
radio
railway
rainbow
rank
rebel
rebellion
recording
red
refine
reformer
regiment
region
reindeer
relative
religion
religious
reptile
republic
resort
restaurant
revolution
revolutionary
rhetorical
rhyme
river
road
rock
rodent
Roman
roof
room
rope
rowing
rubber
rugby
ruler
ruminant
Russia
Russian

sage
sail
sailing
sailor
saint
salad
sale
salt

satellite
satirist
sauce
sausage
saw
Scandinavian
scanner
scarf
school
science
scientific
Scottish
scripture
sculptor
sculpture
sea
seafood
seal
season
seaweed
sect
sedative
sedge
servant
service
Seven against
  Thebes
Shakespeare
shark
sheep
ship
shipping
shop
shout
shrub
SI
siege
sight
signal
sin
singer
skier
skiing
skin
smell
snake

snow
soap
society
sofa
soldier
son
song
songwriter
sound
soup
spa
space
spaniel
specialist
speech
spider
spirits
sport
sportsperson
spread
spy
square
stadium
stamp
star
state
stationery
stick
storm
strait
study
sugar
suit
surgeon
surgery
swan
sweet
swimming
sword
symbol

table
taste
tax
tea
teacher

team
teeth
television
tennis
tense
tent
term
terrier
theatre
theatrical
theologian
theory
therapy
thief
tie
time
title
tobacco
tool
torture
tower
town
toy
train
transport
travel
treaty
tree
triangle
tribe
trophy
tumour
tunnel
twin
typeface

umbrella
uncle
underground
underwear
union
United Kingdom
United Nations
United States of
  America
university

utensil
valve
vegetable
vehicle
vein
vermin
vestment
villain
virtue
virus
vitamin
volcano

wall
war
water
waterfall
weapon
weather
weed
welsh
whale
wheel
whisky
white
wind
window
wine
wise
witch
womanizer
wonder
wood
world
worm
worship
wrestling
writer
writing

year
yellow

zodiac
zoology

A

a
02 an **03** ane, one, per **05** alpha
● **a French**
02 un **03** une
● **a German**
03 ein **04** eine

aardvark
07 antbear **08** anteater, earth-hog
09 groundhog

aback
● **take aback**
04 stun **05** shock, upset **06** dismay
07 astound, set back, stagger, startle
08 astonish, bewilder, knock out,
surprise **09** dumbfound **10** disconcert
11 flabbergast

abalone
04 paua, pawa

abandon
◇ *anagram indicator*
◇ *deletion indicator*
04 cede, drop, dump, jilt, quit, sink,
stop **05** abort, cease, chuck, ditch,
forgo, leave, let go, scrap, waive, yield
06 banish, desert, desist, escape,
forego, forhow, get out, give up, jack in,
maroon, pack in, resign, strand, vacate
07 bail out, forsake, yield to
08 abdicate, evacuate, forswear,
jettison, jump ship, part with,
renounce, run out on, wildness
09 break away, give way to, sacrifice,
stop doing, surrender, walk out on
10 break loose, depart from, go away
from, relinquish, resign from
11 discontinue, impetuosity, leave
behind, unrestraint **12** be overcome by,
break off with, carelessness, dispense
with, kick the habit, leave for dead,
recklessness, withdraw from **13** break
free from, impulsiveness, leave it at that
14 break it off with, give the elbow to,
lose yourself in **15** leave high and dry,
leave in the lurch, thoughtlessness,
uninhibitedness

abandoned
◇ *anagram indicator*
03 mad, old **04** left, wild **05** crazy,
empty **06** unused, vacant, wanton,
wicked **07** corrupt, disused, forlorn,
immoral **08** derelict, deserted,
desolate, forsaken, reckless
09 debauched, dissolute, neglected,
reprobate **10** profligate, unoccupied
11 uninhibited **12** unrestrained

abandonment
05 drift, loose **07** cession, discard,
Dunkirk, jilting, leaving, neglect,
waiving **08** ditching, dropping, giving-
up, stopping **09** cessation, desertion,
forsaking, marooning, sacrifice,
scrapping, stranding, surrender
10 abdication, decampment,
exposition **11** dereliction, reprobation,
resignation **12** renunciation, running
out on **13** leaving behind
14 discontinuance, relinquishment
15 discontinuation, resignation from

abase
05 crawl, lower **06** debase, demean,
humble, kowtow, malign **07** degrade,
mortify, put down **08** belittle, cast
down, suck up to **09** disparage,
humiliate

abasement
08 crawling, humility **09** demeaning
10 debasement, humbleness
11 humiliation, sucking up to
13 disparagement, mortification

abash
03 cow **05** quell, shame **06** humble
07 astound **08** confound, face down
09 embarrass, humiliate **10** disconcert
14 discountenance

abashed
07 ashamed, floored, humbled
08 confused **09** affronted, mortified,
perturbed, shamefast **10** bewildered,
confounded, humiliated, nonplussed,
remorseful, shamefaced, taken aback
11 discomfited, discomposed,
dumbfounded, embarrassed
12 disconcerted **15** discountenanced

abate
04 alay, ease, fade, faik, fall, sink, slow,
vail, wane **05** aleye, allay, allow, appal,
let up, quell, remit, slake **06** lessen,
pacify, rebate, reduce, relent, soothe,
weaken **07** assuage, decline, detract,
die down, drop off, dwindle, fall off,
qualify, relieve, slacken, subside
08 decrease, diminish, mitigate,
moderate, peter out, pluck off, taper off
09 alleviate, attenuate

abatement
04 wane **05** let-up, lysis **06** easing,
relief **07** decline **08** decrease, lowering
09 allowance, deduction, dwindling,
dying-down, lessening, reduction,
remission, weakening **10** diminution,
mitigation, moderation, palliation,
slackening, subsidence **11** alleviation,
assuagement, attenuation, dropping-off

abattoir
08 butchery, shambles
14 slaughterhouse

abbess
03 Abb **09** prelatess

abbey
03 Abb **06** abbacy, friary, priory
07 convent, minster, nunnery
08 cloister, seminary **09** cathedral,
monastery

Abbeys include:

04 Bath, Iona
05 Cluny, Kelso, Meaux, Roche, Royal
06 Bolton, Byland, Hexham, Whitby,
Woburn
07 Citeaux, Furness, Melrose, Tintern,
Waltham
08 Buckfast, Crowland, Dryburgh,
Fontenay, Fonthill, Holyrood,
Jedburgh, Newstead, Rievaulx
09 Clairvaux, Fountains, Holy Cross,
Kirkstall, Nightmare, Sherborne
10 Malmesbury, Northanger
11 Westminster

abbot
03 Abb **07** prelate **11** commendator
13 archimandrite

abbreviate
◇ *tail deletion indicator*
03 cut **04** clip, trim **06** digest, lessen,
précis, reduce, shrink **07** abridge,
curtail, cut down, shorten **08** abstract,
compress, condense, contract,
truncate **09** constrict, summarize

abbreviated
03 cut **05** short **07** clipped, compact,
reduced, summary **08** abridged
09 condensed, shortened, truncated
10 contracted

abbreviation
05 short **06** digest, précis, résumé
07 acronym, summary **08** abstract,
clipping, mnemonic, synopsis
09 reduction, short form **10** initialism,
shortening, truncation
11 abridgement, compression,
contraction, curtailment **13** shortened
form, summarization, truncated form

See also **county**; **United States of
America**

abdicate
04 cede, quit **05** forgo, shirk, yield
06 abjure, disown, forego, give up,
reject, resign, retire **07** abandon,
forsake **08** abnegate, renounce, step
down **09** repudiate, stand down,
surrender **10** relinquish **14** turn your
back on **15** give up the throne, wash
your hands of

abdication
07 refusal **08** giving-up **09** disowning, rejection, surrender **10** abjuration, abnegation, retirement **11** abandonment, repudiation, resignation **12** renunciation, standing-down, stepping-down **14** relinquishment

abdomen
03 maw, tum **04** guts, puku, womb **05** belly, bingy, heart, pleon, tummy **06** gaster, middle, paunch, venter **07** beer gut, insides, midriff, stomach **08** pot belly **09** beer belly, ventricle **10** little Mary **11** bread-basket, corporation, opisthosoma

abdominal
02 ab **05** belly **07** coeliac, gastric, ventral **08** visceral **10** intestinal **11** ventricular

abduct
05 seize **06** kidnap, ravish, snatch **07** capture **08** carry off, shanghai **09** lay hold of **10** run off with, spirit away **11** appropriate, make off with, run away with, take by force **12** hold to ransom **13** take as hostage **15** take away by force

abduction
04 rape **06** kidnap **07** capture, seizure **09** ravishing, seduction, snatching **10** enlevement, kidnapping **11** carrying off **15** taking as hostage

aberrant
◇ *anagram indicator*
03 odd **05** rogue **06** quirky **07** corrupt, deviant **08** abnormal, atypical, freakish, peculiar, straying **09** anomalous, defective, deviating, different, divergent, eccentric, irregular, wandering **11** incongruous

aberration
05 lapse **06** oddity **07** anomaly, mistake **08** delusion, straying **09** deviation, oversight, variation, wandering **10** deliration, divergence **11** abnormality, instability, peculiarity **12** eccentricity, irregularity **13** nonconformity

abet
03 aid **04** back, help, spur **05** egg on **06** assist, back up, incite, second **07** condone, endorse, promote, succour, support **08** sanction **09** encourage, lend a hand **11** collude with

abeyance
• **in abeyance**
05 on ice **06** on hold **07** disused, dormant, pending, shelved **09** postponed, suspended **11** hanging fire **12** in suspension **13** no longer in use **14** not in operation

abhor
04 hate, shun **05** spurn **06** detest, loathe, reject **07** despise **08** execrate **09** abominate, shudder at **10** cannot bear, recoil from, shrink from **11** cannot abide, cannot stand

abhorrence
04 hate **05** odium **06** enmity, hatred, horror, malice **07** disgust **08** aversion, contempt, distaste, loathing **09** animosity, revulsion **10** execration, repugnance **11** abomination, detestation

abhorrent
05 hated, yucky **06** horrid, odious **07** hateful, heinous **08** absonant, detested, horrible **09** detesting, execrable, loathsome, obnoxious, offensive, repellent, repugnant, repulsive, revolting **10** abominable, detestable, disgusting, nauseating **11** distasteful

abide
03 lie, won **04** bear, hack, last, stay, take **05** brook, dwell, stand, thole **06** accept, endure, live on, remain, reside **07** persist, stomach, survive **08** continue, tolerate **09** put up with
• **abide by**
04 obey **05** stand **06** accept, follow, fulfil, hold to, keep to, uphold **07** agree to, observe, respect, stand by **08** adhere to, carry out, submit to **09** conform to, discharge **10** comply with, toe the line **11** go along with, go by the book **15** stick to the rules

abiding
04 firm **05** fixed **06** stable **07** chronic, durable, eternal, lasting **08** constant, enduring, immortal, lifelong, long-term, standing, unending **09** continual, immutable, permanent **10** continuous, persistent, persisting, unchanging **11** continuance, everlasting, long-lasting, long-running **12** unchangeable

ability
04 gift **05** flair, forte, knack, means, power, savvy, skill, touch **06** genius, powers, talent **07** calibre, faculty, knowhow, prowess, the hang **08** aptitude, capacity, deftness, facility, strength, the knack **09** adeptness, dexterity, endowment, expertise, potential, resources **10** adroitness, capability, competence, competency, motivation, propensity **11** proficiency, savoir-faire, what it takes, wherewithal **12** potentiality **13** qualification

ab initio
07 at first, firstly **09** initially, primarily **10** at the start, originally **11** to begin with, to start with **12** from the start **14** at the beginning

abject
03 low **04** base, mean, vile **05** awful **06** sordid, woeful **07** debased, forlorn, ignoble, outcast, pitiful, servile, slavish **08** degraded, hopeless, pathetic, pitiable, shameful, wretched **09** execrable, miserable, worthless **10** degenerate, deplorable, despicable, grovelling, submissive **11** humiliating, ignominious **12** contemptible, ingratiating **13** dishonourable

abjure
04 deny, reny **05** renay, reney **06** disown, eschew, recant, reject **07** abandon, disavow, forsake, retract **08** abdicate, abnegate, disclaim, forswear, renege on, renounce **09** repudiate **10** relinquish **12** dispense with

ablaze
03 lit **04** alow **05** afire, aglow, alowe, angry, fiery, lit up **06** aflame, alight, ardent, fuming, on fire, raging **07** aroused, blazing, burning, excited, fervent, flaming, furious, glowing, ignited, intense, lighted, radiant **08** flashing, frenzied, gleaming, incensed, in flames, luminous **09** brilliant, sparkling **10** passionate, shimmering, stimulated **11** exhilarated, illuminated, impassioned **12** enthusiastic, incandescent

able
03 fit **04** deft, fere **05** adept **06** adroit, clever, expert, fitted, gifted, strong, up to it **07** capable, clued up, skilful, skilled **08** all there, masterly, powerful, talented **09** competent, cut out for, dexterous, effective, efficient, ingenious, on the ball, practised, qualified **10** proficient **11** experienced, intelligent **12** accomplished
• **able to**
05 fit to **06** free to **09** allowed to, capable of **10** prepared to **11** competent to, qualified to

able-bodied
02 AB **03** fit **04** fine, hale **05** burly, hardy, lusty, sound, stout, tough **06** hearty, robust, rugged, strong, sturdy **07** healthy, staunch **08** powerful, stalwart, vigorous **09** strapping **12** in good health **13** hale and hearty **14** as fit as a fiddle

ablution
05 laver **07** bathing, rinsing, soaking, washing **08** cleaning **09** cleansing, scrubbing, showering

abnegate
04 deny **06** abjure, eschew, give up, refuse, reject **07** abandon, abstain, disavow, forbear **08** forswear, renounce **09** repudiate, surrender **10** relinquish

abnegation
08 eschewal, giving-up **09** surrender **10** abjuration, abstinence, self-denial, temperance **11** forbearance, repudiation **12** renunciation **13** self-sacrifice **14** relinquishment

abnormal
◇ *anagram indicator*
03 odd **04** para- **05** outré, queer, weird **07** curious, deviant, erratic, oddball, strange, uncanny, unusual, wayward **08** aberrant, atypical, peculiar, singular, uncommon **09** anomalous, different, divergent, eccentric, irregular, unnatural **10** paranormal, unexpected

11 exceptional **13** extraordinary, funny peculiar, idiosyncratic, preternatural

abnormality
04 flaw **06** oddity **07** anomaly
08 enormity, vitiligo **09** deformity, deviation, exception, palilalia, water-core **10** aberration, difference, divergence **11** atypicality, bizarreness, dysfunction, monstrosity, pathography, peculiarity, singularity, strangeness, unusualness **12** eccentricity, irregularity, malformation, monstruosity, uncommonness **13** unnaturalness

abnormally
09 extremely, unusually **10** especially, remarkably, uncommonly
12 particularly **13** exceptionally
15 extraordinarily, preternaturally

aboard
◇ *insertion indicator*
02 in, on **04** into, onto **07** on board **09** alongside **11** on board ship

abode
02 in **03** inn, pad, won **04** home, seat, stay **05** lodge, whare **06** libken, remain **07** domicil, habitat, mansion, presage **08** domicile, dwelling, lodgings **09** residence, residency
10 habitation **11** inhabitance, inhabitancy **13** dwelling-place

abolish
03 axe, ban, end **04** chop, dump, sink, stop **05** annul, quash, scrap **06** cancel, repeal, revoke **07** blot out, destroy, expunge, nullify, rescind, subvert, vitiate, wipe out **08** abrogate, down with, get rid of, overturn, stamp out, suppress **09** eliminate, eradicate, overthrow, terminate **10** annihilate, do away with, invalidate, obliterate, put an end to **11** discontinue, exterminate

abolition
03 axe **04** chop **06** ending, repeal **07** dumping, voiding **08** chopping, quashing, stopping **09** annulment, overthrow, scrapping, vitiation
10 abrogation, extinction, rescission, revocation, subversion, withdrawal
11 blotting-out, destruction, dissolution, elimination, eradication, extirpation, rescindment, suppression, termination **12** annihilation, cancellation, invalidation, obliteration **13** doing-away with, extermination, nullification

abomasum
04 read

abominable
◇ *anagram indicator*
04 base, foul, vile **06** cursed, horrid, nefast, odious **07** hateful, heinous
08 damnable, dreadful, god-awful, horrible, terrible, wretched
09 abhorrent, appalling, atrocious, execrable, loathsome, nefandous, obnoxious, offensive, repellent, repugnant, repulsive, revolting

10 despicable, detestable, disgusting, nauseating **12** contemptible
13 reprehensible

abominably
07 beastly **08** horribly, odiously, terribly **09** execrably **10** dreadfully
11 appallingly, obnoxiously
12 disgustingly **13** reprehensibly

abominate
04 hate **05** abhor **06** detest, loathe **07** condemn, despise **08** execrate

abomination
04 evil, hate **05** curse, odium
06 hatred, horror, plague **07** disgust, offence, outrage, torment
08 anathema, atrocity, aversion, disgrace, distaste, loathing **09** hostility, revulsion **10** abhorrence, execration, repugnance **11** detestation

aboriginal
05 first, Koori, local, Murri, Nunga
06 Anangu, native, primal **07** ancient, initial **08** earliest, original, primeval
09 primaeval, primitive **10** indigenous
13 autochthonous, tangata whenua

Aboriginal activists include:
04 Mabo (Eddie)
05 Scott (Evelyn)
06 Dodson (Mick), Dodson (Patrick), O'Shane (Pat)
07 Bandler (Faith), Gilbert (Kevin), Pearson (Noel), Perkins (Charles)
09 Yunupingu (Galarrwuy)
12 Burnum Burnum

Aboriginal tribes include:
03 Wik
04 Tiwi
05 Bardi, Yanda
06 Aranda, Dharug
07 Noongar, Nyungar
08 Gurindji, Warlpiri
09 Kuring-gai, Wiradjuri
10 Bundjalung, Pitta Pitta, Wemba Wemba
14 Pitjantjatjara

aborigine
03 gin **05** koori, Maori, myall **06** native **08** indigene **11** black-fellow **15** first inhabitant

abort
03 axe, end **04** fail, halt, stop **05** check **06** thwart **07** call off, nullify, suspend
08 cut short, miscarry **09** frustrate, terminate **11** come to an end, discontinue **12** bring to an end **13** pull the plug on

abortion
08 misbirth **09** foeticide **10** aborticide
11 miscarriage, termination

abortive
04 idle, vain **06** barren, failed, futile
07 misborn, sterile, useless
08 bootless, thwarted **09** fruitless
10 unavailing **11** ineffective, ineffectual
12 unproductive, unsuccessful
13 inefficacious

abound
04 flow, teem **05** crowd, swarm, swell
06 be full, thrive **07** bristle **08** brim over, flourish, increase, overflow
09 exuberate, luxuriate **10** be abundant **11** be plentiful, proliferate, superabound

about
◇ *anagram indicator*
◇ *containment indicator*
◇ *reversal indicator*
01 a, c **02** ca, on, re **03** cir **04** circ, near, over **05** anent, circa, close, round **06** almost, approx, around, beside, nearby, nearly **07** all over, close by, close to, nearing, roughly **08** to and fro **09** apropos of, as regards, regarding
10 adjacent to, concerning, encircling, more or less, relating to, throughout
11 approaching, dealing with, referring to, surrounding, within reach
12 encompassing, here and there, with regard to **13** approximately, concerned with, connected with, in the matter of, in the region of, with respect to **14** on the subject of **15** in the vicinity of, with reference to
• **about to**
06 all but, soon to **07** going to, ready to **08** all set to **11** intending to, preparing to **12** on the point of, on the verge of

about-turn
03 uey **05** U-turn **08** reversal
09 about-face, turnabout, volte-face
10 turnaround **13** enantiodromia

above
◇ *juxtaposition down indicator*
03 sup, sur **04** atop, over, owre, upon
05 aloft, prior, sopra, super-, supra-
06 before, beyond, higher, high up, on high **07** earlier, on top of **08** immune to, overhead, previous, senior to
09 aforesaid, exceeding, foregoing, not open to, preceding **10** exempt from, higher than, in excess of, prevenient, previously, superior to, surpassing **11** above-stated, greater than, not liable to **12** not exposed to **14** above-mentioned, aforementioned
• **above all**
07 chiefly, firstly, notably **09** most of all, primarily **10** first of all **15** most importantly
• **above yourself**
04 smug, vain **05** cocky, proud
07 haughty, stuck-up **08** arrogant, boastful, immodest, puffed-up
09 bigheaded, conceited
10 complacent **11** egotistical, toffee-nosed **12** narcissistic, supercilious, vainglorious **13** self-important, self-satisfied, swollen-headed **14** full of yourself
• **as above**
02 us **03** ut supra

above-board
04 open, true **05** frank, legit
06 candid, dinkum, honest, kosher, square **07** upright **08** straight, truthful
09 guileless, reputable, veracious

10 forthright, honourable, legitimate, on the level **11** trustworthy **13** fair and square **15** straightforward

abracadabra
05 spell **09** gibberish, magic word **10** hocus pocus, mumbo-jumbo, open sesame

abrade
03 rub **04** stun **05** awake, chafe, erode, grate, graze, grind, rouse, scour, start **06** scrape **07** scratch, wear off **08** wear away, wear down **10** scrape away

abrasion
03 cut **05** chafe, graze **06** scrape **07** chafing, erosion, grating, rubbing, scratch **08** abrading, friction, grinding, scouring, scraping **10** scratching **11** excoriation, wearing-away, wearing-down

abrasive
04 bort **05** boart, emery, harsh, nasty, rough, sharp **06** biting **07** brusque, caustic, chafing, erodent, erosive, grating, hurtful **08** annoying, grinding, scraping **09** corrosive, sandpaper **10** frictional, glasspaper, irritating, scratching, unpleasant **11** attritional, garnet-paper, ground glass **14** silicon carbide

abreast
02 up **03** hep **05** level **06** afront, au fait, well up **07** in touch **08** familiar, informed, up to date **09** au courant, on the ball **10** acquainted, conversant, side by side **11** cheek by jowl **12** in the picture **13** knowledgeable **15** beside each other, next to each other

abridge
03 cut, lop **04** clip **05** elide, prune **06** digest, lessen, précis, reduce **07** curtail, cut down, shorten **08** abstract, compress, condense, contract, cut short, decrease, truncate **09** epitomize, summarize, synopsize **10** abbreviate **11** concentrate **12** circumscribe

abridged
◇ *tail deletion indicator*
03 abd, abr **05** short **06** potted **07** clipped, cut down, reduced, shorter **08** cut short, digested **10** contracted, summarized **11** abbreviated

abridgement
03 abr **06** abrégé, digest, précis, résumé **07** compend, cutting, epitome, outline, pastime, summary **08** abstract, decrease, synopsis **09** reduction **10** compendium, conspectus, diminution, shortening, truncation **11** contraction, curtailment, diminishing, restriction **12** abbreviation, abbreviature, short version **13** concentration

abroad
◇ *anagram indicator*
◇ *foreign word indicator*
03 out **04** away **05** about, forth

06 around, astray, widely **07** at large, current **08** offshore, overseas, publicly **10** far and wide **11** circulating, extensively **14** doing your OE, in foreign parts, to foreign parts **15** out of the country

• **go abroad**
08 emigrate

abrogate
03 axe, end **04** chop, dump, stop **05** annul, scrap **06** cancel, repeal, revoke **07** abolish, rescind, retract, reverse, vitiate **08** disenact, dissolve **09** disaffirm, repudiate **10** do away with, invalidate **11** countermand

abrogation
03 axe **04** chop **06** repeal **07** dumping **08** recision, reversal **09** abolition, annulment, repealing, scrapping, vitiation **10** overruling, rescinding, rescission, revocation **11** dissolution, repudiation, rescindment **12** cancellation, invalidation **14** countermanding, disaffirmation

abrupt
◇ *tail deletion indicator*
03 off **04** bold, curt, rude, snap **05** blunt, brisk, gruff, hasty, quick, rapid, rough, sharp, sheer, short, squab, steep, swift, terse **06** direct, snappy, sudden **07** brusque, hurried, instant, offhand, prerupt, uncivil **08** dramatic, impolite, snappish, vertical **09** immediate, startling **10** dismissive, surprising, unexpected, unforeseen, unfriendly **11** declivitous, precipitate, precipitous, unannounced **12** discourteous **13** instantaneous, unceremonious

abruptly
04 bang **05** short **06** curtly, rudely **07** bluntly, briskly, gruffly, hastily, offhand, quickly, rapidly, roughly, shortly, swiftly, tersely **08** directly, snappily, suddenly **09** brusquely, hurriedly, instantly **10** impolitely, snappishly **11** immediately **12** dismissively, unexpectedly **13** precipitately **14** discourteously **15** instantaneously, unceremoniously

abscess
04 boil, noma, sore **05** ulcer **06** canker **07** gumboil **08** swelling **09** gathering, impostume, infection **10** imposthume, ulceration **12** inflammation

abscond
03 fly **04** bolt, flee, quit **05** scram **06** beat it, decamp, escape, run off, vanish **07** do a bunk, make off, run away, scarper, vamoose **08** clear off, clear out, jump bail, run for it **09** disappear, do a runner, skedaddle **12** absquatulate **15** take French leave

absence
03 abs **04** lack, need, want **06** dearth **07** default, paucity, skiving, truancy, vacancy, vacuity **08** omission, scarcity

09 privation **10** bunking off, deficiency **11** absenteeism, abstraction, inattention **12** non-existence **13** non-appearance, non-attendance, playing hookey **14** unavailability

• **feel absence**
04 miss

absent
◇ *deletion indicator*
01 a **03** abs, MIA, off, out **04** away, AWOL, gone **05** blank **06** dreamy, truant, vacant **07** faraway, lacking, missing, not here, unaware **08** not there **09** elsewhere, miles away, not around, oblivious, unheeding **10** distracted, in absentia, not present **11** daydreaming, inattentive, preoccupied, unavailable **12** absent-minded

• **absent yourself**
04 exit **06** depart, retire **07** back out, retreat **08** slip away, withdraw **13** take your leave

absentee
06 no-show, truant **11** non-attender

absently
07 blankly **08** dreamily **12** abstractedly **13** inattentively **14** absent-mindedly

absent-minded
06 absent, dreamy, musing, scatty **07** faraway, pensive, unaware **08** absorbed, distrait, dreaming, heedless, yonderly **09** distraite, engrossed, forgetful, miles away, oblivious, unheeding, withdrawn **10** abstracted, distracted, unthinking **11** impractical, inattentive, not all there, preoccupied, unconscious **13** somewhere else, wool-gathering **14** dead to the world, scatterbrained

absent-mindedly
07 blankly **08** absently **12** abstractedly **13** inattentively

absolute
01 A **03** abs, set **04** dead, firm, full, meer, mere, pure, rank, sure, true **05** final, fixed, rigid, sheer, total, utter **06** entire **07** certain, decided, genuine, perfect, settled, supreme, unmixed **08** almighty, complete, decisive, definite, despotic, outright, positive, thorough **09** autarchic, boundless, downright, out-and-out, sovereign, undivided, universal, unlimited **10** autocratic, conclusive, consummate, definitive, exhaustive, high-handed, omnipotent, peremptory, tyrannical **11** autarchical, categorical, dictatorial, established, indubitable, non-variable, unalterable, unambiguous, unequivocal, unmitigated, unqualified **12** totalitarian, unrestrained, unrestricted **13** authoritarian, non-negotiable, unadulterated, unconditional **14** unquestionable

absolutely
03 abs, yes **04** bang, dead, just, mere, very **05** fully, quite, truly **06** fairly,

rely, surely, wholly **07** clearly,
actly, finally, for sure, no doubt,
ainly, quite so, totally, utterly
 entirely, of course **09** assuredly,
rtainly, decidedly, doubtless,
nuinely, naturally, obviously,
rfectly, precisely, supremely **10** by all
eans, completely, decisively,
finitely, in every way, infallibly,
sitively, separately, thoroughly,
deniably **11** à toute force,
ubtlessly, undoubtedly
 conclusively, despotically,
haustively, high-handedly,
rannically **13** categorically,
ctatorially, unambiguously,
equivocally, without a doubt
 autocratically, in every respect,
questionably, wholeheartedly
 unconditionally

bsolution
 mercy **06** pardon, shrift
 amnesty, freedom, release
 acquittal, discharge, pardoning,
rgation, remission **10** assoilment,
ting off, liberation, redemption
 deliverance, exculpation,
oneration, forgiveness, vindication
 emancipation **13** justification

bsolve
 free, quit **05** clear, loose, quite,
yte, remit **06** acquit, assoil, excuse,
 off, pardon, quight **07** deliver,
rgive, justify, release, set free
 liberate **09** assoilzie, discharge,
culpate, exonerate, vindicate
 accomplish, emancipate **11** have
ercy on

bsorb
containment indicator
 fill, hold, soak, sorb, suck, wrap
 eat up, mop up, use up **06** blot up,
vour, digest, draw in, engage, engulf,
 up, imbibe, ingest, occupy, retain,
ak up, suck up, take in, take up
 consume, drink in, engross, enthral,
volve, receive **08** sponge up
 captivate, fascinate, integrate,
eoccupy, swallow up **10** assimilate,
onopolize, understand
 incorporate

bsorbed
containment indicator
 rapt **07** riveted **08** involved,
ccupied **09** engrossed **10** captivated,
thralled, fascinated, interested,
ellbound **11** preoccupied, taken up
ith

bsorbent
 abs **04** dope **06** porous, spongy
 soaking **08** bibulous, blotting,
rvious **09** permeable, receptive,
sorbent, retentive **10** absorptive,
ongiform **12** assimilative,
rbefacient

bsorbing
 amusing **08** gripping, riveting
 diverting, enjoyable
 compelling, compulsive,
grossing, intriguing **11** captivating,

enthralling, fascinating, interesting
12 entertaining, preoccupying,
spellbinding **13** unputdownable

absorption
07 holding, osmosis **08** monopoly,
raptness, riveting, taking-in
09 devouring, drawing-in, immersion,
ingestion, soaking-up **10** engagement,
engrossing, intentness, occupation
11 captivating, consumption,
involvement **12** assimilation
13 attentiveness, concentration,
preoccupation

abstain
04 fast, pass, quit, shun, stop **05** avoid,
forgo, spare **06** cut out, desist, eschew,
forego, give up, jack in, refuse, reject,
resist **07** decline, forbear, not vote,
refrain **08** hold back, renounce,
restrain **09** be neutral, do without, go
without **11** stop short of **12** deny
yourself, refuse to vote **13** sit on the
fence

abstainer
02 TT **06** tee-tee, wowser **08** teetotal
09 Rechabite **11** teetotaller **12** water-
drinker
• **abstainers**
02 AA, TT

abstemious
02 TT **05** sober **06** frugal **07** ascetic,
austere, sparing **08** moderate, teetotal
09 abstinent, temperate **10** restrained
11 disciplined, self-denying **14** self-
abnegating **15** self-disciplined

abstention
08 celibacy **09** not voting
10 neutrality **13** refusal to vote
15 declining to vote

abstinence
04 fast **07** fasting, refusal
08 eschewal, giving-up, sobriety
09 avoidance, frugality, nephalism,
restraint **10** abjuration, abstaining,
asceticism, continence, continency,
declension, desistance, moderation,
refraining, self-denial, temperance,
water wagon **11** forbearance, self-
control, teetotalism **12** going-without,
renunciation **13** non-indulgence, self-
restraint **14** abstemiousness, self-
discipline
See also **fast**

abstinent
05 sober **06** frugal **07** ascetic
08 moderate, teetotal **09** continent,
temperate **10** abstaining, abstemious,
forbearing, restrained **11** self-denying
12 non-indulgent **14** self-controlled,
self-restrained **15** self-disciplined

abstract
03 abs, cut, tap **04** deep **06** arcane,
detach, digest, précis, remove, résumé,
subtle **07** abridge, complex, cut down,
draw off, epitome, extract, general,
isolate, outline, shorten, subduce,
subduct, summary, take out
08 abstruse, academic, compress,
condense, discrete, ideative, notional,

prescind, profound, separate, syllabus,
symbolic, synopsis, take away,
withdraw **09** contrived, recondite,
summarize **10** abbreviate,
compendium, conceptual,
conspectus, dissociate, ideational,
indefinite **11** abridgement,
compression, generalized, non-
concrete, suppositive, theoretical,
unpractical, unrealistic
12 hypothetical, intellectual,
metaphysical, non-realistic
13 philosophical, suppositional
14 recapitulation
• **in the abstract**
07 on paper **08** in theory **09** generally
10 notionally **11** in abstracto
12 conceptually **13** theoretically
14 hypothetically **15** philosophically

abstracted
06 absent, dreamy, musing, scatty
07 bemused, faraway, pensive,
unaware **08** absorbed, dreaming,
heedless **09** engrossed, forgetful,
miles away, oblivious, unheeding,
withdrawn **10** distracted, unthinking
11 impractical, inattentive, inconscient,
preoccupied, unconscious **12** absent-
minded **13** wool-gathering
14 scatterbrained

abstractedly
07 blankly **08** absently **13** inattentively
14 absent-mindedly

abstraction
04 idea **05** dream **06** entity, notion,
revery, theory **07** absence, concept,
formula, removal, reverie, theorem,
thought **09** isolation **10** absorption,
conception, conjecture, dreaminess,
extraction, generality, hypothesis,
remoteness, separation, withdrawal
11 bemusedness, distraction,
inattention, pensiveness
13 preoccupation **14** generalization

abstruse
04 deep, high, long **06** arcane, hidden,
subtle **07** complex, cryptic, Delphic,
obscure **08** esoteric, hermetic,
profound, puzzling **09** enigmatic,
exquisite, recherché, recondite
10 hermetical, mysterious, perplexing
11 inscrutable **12** unfathomable

absurd
◇ *anagram indicator*
04 daft **05** crazy, funny, gonzo, inane,
silly **06** stupid **07** asinine, comical,
foolish, idiotic, Laputan, risible
08 cockeyed, derisory, farcical,
humorous, Laputian **09** fantastic,
grotesque, illogical, laughable,
ludicrous, priceless, senseless,
unearthly, untenable **10** irrational,
ridiculous **11** harebrained, implausible,
incongruous, meaningless,
nonsensical, paradoxical
12 preposterous, unreasonable

absurdity
04 joke **05** farce, folly **06** drivel,
humour, idiocy **07** charade, inanity,
paradox, rubbish, twaddle

08 claptrap, daftness, malarkey, nonsense, ridicule, solecism, travesty **09** craziness, gibberish, silliness, stupidity **10** balderdash, caricature **11** fatuousness, foolishness, incongruity **12** illogicality **13** irrationality, ludicrousness, senselessness **14** implausibility, ridiculousness **15** meaninglessness

absurdly
07 crazily, funnily, inanely **08** stupidly **09** comically, foolishly, laughably, untenably **10** farcically, humorously **11** idiotically, implausibly, ludicrously, senselessly **12** irrationally, ridiculously, unreasonably **13** fantastically, incongruously, meaninglessly, nonsensically, paradoxically **14** preposterously

abundance
04 bags, glut, load, lots **05** feast, flush, fouth, fowth, heaps, loads, piles, routh, rowth, scads, sonce, sonse, store **06** bounty, excess, masses, oodles, plenty, riches, stacks, wealth **07** bonanza, fortune, lashing, oodlins, pleroma, tallent **08** fullness, lashings, opulence, overflow, plethora, richness **09** affluence, amplitude, fertility, plenitude, profusion **10** exuberance, generosity, lavishness, luxuriance, profligacy **11** copiousness, corn in Egypt, great supply, munificence, prodigality **12** extravagance, milk and honey **13** plentifulness, rack and manger **14** stouth and routh

abundant
04 full, rank, rich **05** ample, hefty, large, thick **06** filled, galore, lavish, strong **07** copious, opulent, profuse, teeming **08** affluent, generous, in plenty, prolific **09** bounteous, bountiful, exuberant, luxuriant, plenteous, plentiful **11** overflowing **12** well-supplied **14** more than enough

abundantly
04 very, well **05** amply, jolly **06** highly, plenty, really **07** acutely, awfully, greatly, utterly **08** severely, terribly **09** copiously, decidedly, extremely, intensely, profusely, unusually **10** completely, dreadfully, remarkably, thoroughly, uncommonly **11** exceedingly, excessively, extensively, exuberantly, frightfully, in abundance, in profusion, plentifully **12** immoderately, inordinately, prolifically, terrifically, unreasonably **13** exceptionally **15** extraordinarily

abuse
◇ *anagram indicator*
03 hit, mud **04** beat, harm, hurt, rail, rape **05** bully, curse, libel, scold, serve, slate, smear, snash, wrong **06** batter, damage, defame, impugn, injure, injury, insult, jawing, malign, misuse, molest, oppugn, pick on, revile, tirade, verbal **07** affront, beating, calumny, censure, cruelty, cursing, exploit,

insults, jobbery, miscall, offence, oppress, slag off, slander, swear at, torture, upbraid, violate, vitriol **08** be rude to, bullyrag, chuck off, derision, diatribe, ill-treat, maltreat, misapply, mistreat, reproach, scolding, swearing **09** call names, castigate, contumely, denigrate, disparage, invective, misemploy, swear-word, victimize **10** calumniate, chuck off at, defamation, imposition, oppression, upbraiding, vituperate **11** castigation, clapperclaw, denigration, hurl abuse at, malediction, molestation, mud-slinging, name-calling **12** billingsgate, calumniation, exploitation, ill-treatment, interference, maltreatment, mistreatment, vilification, vituperation **13** disparagement, interfere with, misemployment, sexual assault, treat like dirt **14** harass sexually, misapplication **15** assault sexually, take advantage of

abusive
04 rude **05** cruel **06** bitchy, brutal **07** harmful, hurtful, railing, satiric **08** reviling, scathing, scolding, scornful **09** injurious, insulting, invective, libellous, maligning, offensive, satirical, vilifying **10** censorious, defamatory, derogatory, pejorative, scurrilous, slanderous, upbraiding **11** blasphemous, castigating, denigrating, destructive, disparaging, opprobrious, reproachful **12** calumniating, contumelious, vituperative

abusively
06 rudely **07** cruelly **08** bitchily, brutally **10** revilingly, scathingly, scoldingly, scornfully **11** injuriously, insultingly, offensively **12** calumniously, censoriously, pejoratively, scurrilously, upbraidingly **13** blasphemously, denigratingly, disparagingly, opprobriously, reproachfully **14** contumeliously, vituperatively

abut
◇ *juxtaposition indicator*
04 join, lean **05** touch **06** adjoin, border **07** conjoin, impinge, verge on **08** be next to

abysmal
◇ *anagram indicator*
05 awful, utter **06** dismal **08** complete, dreadful, shocking, terrible **09** appalling, frightful **10** bottomless **11** disgraceful **12** unfathomable

abysmally
◇ *anagram indicator*
07 awfully **08** terribly **10** dreadfully **11** appallingly, frightfully **13** disgracefully

abyss
03 pit **04** gulf, hell, void **05** abysm, chasm, depth, gorge, gulph **06** abrupt, canyon, crater, depths, ravine **07** Avernus, fissure, swallow

08 crevasse, profound, Tartarus **09** barathrum **13** bottomless pit

acacia
03 koa **05** babul, boree, mulga, myall, sally **06** bablah, gidgee, gidjee, mimosa, sallee **07** robinia, shittah **08** brigalow **09** blackwood, doornboom, fever tree, flame-tree **10** locust tree **11** shittah tree **12** golden wattle **13** kangaroo-thorn

academic
03 don **04** acca **05** smart, tutor **06** brainy, fellow, master, pedant **07** bookish, donnish, erudite, learned, scholar, serious, student, teacher, trainer **08** abstract, bookworm, educated, educator, highbrow, lecturer, literary, notional, studious, well-read **09** pedagogue, professor, scholarly **10** conceptual, instructor, irrelevant, ivory-tower, scholastic **11** conjectural, educational, impractical, pedagogical, speculative, theoretical **12** hypothetical, intellectual, man of letters, well-educated **13** instructional, suppositional **14** woman of letters

academician
01 A **02** RA **03** ARA, RSA

academy
01 A **02** RA **03** RAM **04** RADA **05** forty **06** school **07** academe, college **08** immortal, seminary **09** institute **10** university **11** charm school

acanthus
07 ruellia **08** many-root **10** thunbergi **11** bear's-breech, brankursine, shrimp plant

accede
05 admit, agree, bow to **06** accept, assume, attain, come to, concur, give i **07** agree to, consent, inherit, succeed **08** assent to, back down, take over **09** acquiesce, consent to, succeed to **10** comply with

accelerate
05 hurry, speed **06** hasten, open up, spur on, step up **07** advance, forward, further, promote, quicken, speed up **08** antedate, expedite, go faster, step on it **09** festinate, stimulate **10** facilitate **11** drive faster, gather speed, pick up speed, precipitate, put on a spurt **12** gain momentum, step o the gas **14** step on the juice **15** put your foot down

acceleration
01 a, g **07** speed-up **08** momentum **09** hastening, promotion **10** expedition, forwarding, speeding-up, stepping-up **11** advancement, furtherance, stimulation **14** gathering speed, rate of increase

accent
04 beat, dash, tone **05** acute, force, grave, ictus, pitch, pulse, twang **06** brogue, rhythm, stress, timbre, tittl

7 cadence, diction **08** emphasis, priority **09** diacritic, intensity, pulsation **10** circumflex, importance, inflection, intonation, modulation, prominence **11** enunciation, underlining **12** accentuation, articulation, highlighting **13** pronunciation **15** diacritical mark

accentuate
6 accent, deepen, show up, stress **7** point up **08** heighten **9** emphasize, highlight, intensify, spotlight, underline **10** strengthen, underscore **15** make great play of

accept
◊ containment indicator
3 buy, get **04** bear, gain, have, take, wear **05** abide, admit, adopt, allow, bow to, grasp, stand, trust **06** come by, credit, endure, give in, honour, jump at, obtain, pocket, secure, suffer, take on, take up **07** abide by, acquire, agree to, approve, believe, embrace, fall for, let go of, receive, stomach, swallow, welcome, yield to **08** accede to, back down, face up to, say yes to, tolerate **9** approbate, believe in, consent to, integrate, put up with, recognize, undertake **10** comply with, concur with, not say no to **11** acknowledge, acquiesce in, be certain of, go along with, take on board **12** be resigned to **3** make the best of, receive warmly **5** come to terms with

acceptable
1 U **02** OK, on **04** so-so **06** not bad **7** welcome **08** adequate, all right, moderate, passable, pleasant, pleasing **9** agreeable, allowable, desirable, tolerable **10** admissible, delightful, gratifying, reasonable **11** appreciated, appropriate, permissible **12** satisfactory, the done thing **15** unexceptionable
▸ **make acceptable**
4 sell

acceptably
8 passably, suitably **09** agreeably, desirably, tolerably **10** adequately, moderately, reasonably **3** appropriately **14** satisfactorily

acceptance
2 OK **03** acc, nod **04** acpt **05** faith, trust **06** assent, belief, buying, taking **7** bearing, consent, gaining, getting, receipt, welcome **08** adoption, approval, credence, currency, giving-in, securing, taking on, taking-up **9** accepting, accession, acquiring, admission, agreement, embracing, endurance, obtaining, receiving, tolerance, welcoming **10** admittance, assumption, compliance, facing up to, falling for **11** affirmation, backing-down, concurrence, endorsement, integration, recognition, resignation, undertaking **12** acquiescence, ratification **13** putting up with, taking on board **14** going along with, seal of approval **15** acknowledgement, making the best of, stamp of approval

accepted
01 a **04** taen **05** taken, usual **06** agreed, common, normal **07** correct, regular **08** admitted, approved, orthodox, ratified, received, standard **09** confirmed, customary, universal **10** acceptable, authorized, recognized, sanctioned **11** appropriate, established, traditional **12** acknowledged, conventional, time-honoured

access
03 key, use **04** door, path, read, road **05** drive, entry, log on, way in **06** course, entrée, locate **07** gateway, ingress, passage **08** approach, driveway, entering, entrance, retrieve **09** admission **10** admittance **12** gain access to, means of entry, right of entry **13** accessibility **15** means of approach, permission to see

accessibility
11 convenience **12** availability, ease of access **13** attainability, obtainability **15** approachability, intelligibility

accessible
04 near, open **05** handy, ready **06** nearby, on hand, patent **07** general **09** available, get-at-able, reachable **10** achievable, attainable, come-at-able, convenient, easy to read, obtainable, procurable **11** close at hand, close to hand, within cooee **12** approachable, easy to follow, intelligible, user-friendly **14** comprehensible, understandable

accession
04 gain, gift **06** afflux, influx **08** addition, increase, purchase **09** affluxion, attaining **10** assumption, possession, succession, taking over **11** acquisition, inheritance

accessorize
04 trim **05** add to, adorn **06** bedaub, set off **07** augment, bedizen, enhance **08** contrast, decorate, round off **10** complement, supplement

accessory
03 aid, hat **04** belt, help **05** add-in, add-on, extra, frill, shoes **06** gloves, helper **07** abettor, adjunct, cathead, fitting, handbag, partner **08** addition, conniver, ornament, trimming **09** adornment, ancillary, appendage, assistant, associate, attribute, auxiliary, colleague, component, extension, jewellery, secondary **10** accomplice, additional, attachment, complement, decoration, incidental, peripheral, subsidiary, supplement **11** confederate, subordinate **12** appurtenance, contributory, supplemental **13** embellishment, supplementary

accident
◊ anagram indicator
03 cva, hap, RTA **04** blow, fate, luck **05** crash, fluke, freak, prang, shunt, smash, wreck **06** bingle, chance, hazard, mishap, pile-up, upcast

07 fortune, smash-up, tragedy **08** blowdown, calamity, casualty, disaster, fatality, fortuity, good luck **09** collision, mischance **10** misfortune **11** coincidence, contingency, contretemps, good fortune, serendipity **12** circumstance, happenstance, misadventure

accidental
04 flat **05** fluky, sharp **06** casual, chance, flukey, random **07** natural, outward **08** aleatory, external **09** adventive, dividuous, haphazard, uncertain, unplanned, unwitting **10** contingent, fortuitous, incidental, unexpected, unforeseen, unintended **11** inadvertent, promiscuous, unlooked-for **12** adventitious, uncalculated **13** serendipitous, unanticipated, unintentional **14** unpremeditated

accidentally
◊ anagram indicator
08 bechance, by chance, randomly **09** by mistake **10** by accident **11** ex accidenti, haphazardly, unwittingly **12** fortuitously, incidentally, unexpectedly **13** inadvertently **14** adventitiously **15** serendipitously, unintentionally

acclaim
04 clap, hail, laud **05** cheer, exalt, extol, toast, voice **06** cheers, eulogy, homage, honour, praise, salute **07** applaud, commend, fanfare, ovation, tribute, welcome **08** applause, approval, bouquets, cheering, clapping, eulogium, eulogize, plaudits, shouting **09** celebrate, extolment, laudation, publicity, rave about **10** exaltation **11** acclamation, approbation, celebration **12** commendation

acclaimed
05 famed, great, noted **06** famous **07** admired, eminent, exalted, notable, revered **08** honoured, renowned **09** legendary, prominent **10** celebrated **11** illustrious, outstanding **13** distinguished

acclamation
03 rap **04** wrap **05** paean **06** bravos, eulogy, homage, honour, praise **07** fanfare, ovation, tribute, welcome **08** applause, approval, cheering, clapping, shouting **09** panegyric **10** enthusiasm, exaltation, laudations **11** approbation, celebration **12** commendation **13** felicitations **15** congratulations

acclimatization
10 adaptation, adjustment **11** acclimation, habituation, orientation **13** accommodation, acculturation **14** naturalization **15** familiarization

acclimatize
04 salt **05** adapt, inure **06** adjust, attune **07** conform **08** accustom

09 acclimate, get used to, habituate
10 naturalize **11** accommodate,
acculturate, familiarize **12** find your
feet **15** get your bearings

accolade
05 award **06** homage, honour, praise
07 dubbing, embrace, tribute
11 recognition, testimonial **12** pat on
the back

accommodate
◇ *containment indicator*
03 aid, fit **04** help, hold, seat, take
05 adapt, board, house, lodge, put up,
serve **06** adjust, assist, attune, bestow,
billet, comply, modify, oblige, settle,
supply, take in **07** compose, conform,
provide, quarter, shelter **08** accustom,
cater for, domicile **09** fit in with,
habituate, harmonize, reconcile
11 acclimatize, be helpful to, give a
hand to, have room for, lend a hand to
12 have space for

accommodating
◇ *containment indicator*
04 kind **07** helpful, pliable, willing
08 friendly, obliging **09** agreeable,
compliant, indulgent, unselfish
10 hospitable **11** complaisant,
considerate, co-operative,
sympathetic

accommodation
◇ *containment indicator*
04 home **05** abode, board, place,
rooms **07** harmony, housing, lodging,
quarter, storage **08** dwelling, lodgings,
quarters **09** agreement, residence
10 compromise, conformity,
settlement **11** negotiation
12 negotiations **13** understanding
14 reconciliation

Accommodation types include:

03 inn, pad, pod
04 camp, digs, flat, gaff, gite, tent, yurt
05 b and b, cabin, hotel, house, igloo,
lodge, motel, squat, villa
06 bedsit, billet, camper, duplex,
flotel, hostel, jack-up, refuge, studio,
succah, sukkah
07 caravan, cottage, dockage, floatel,
lairage, parador, pension, shelter,
taverna
08 barracks, berthage, crashpad, pod
hotel, roomette, shipping, stabling,
tenement, wharfage
09 apartment, bedsitter, bunkhouse,
camper van, dormitory, full board,
half board, penthouse, residence,
rooming-in, timeshare
10 guardhouse, guest house, labour
camp, mobile home
11 bachelor pad, bed and board, youth
hostel
12 halfway house, hunting-lodge,
room and board, self-catering
13 boarding-house, habitat module
14 loft conversion
15 bed and breakfast, hall of
residence, married quarters

See also **building**; **house**; **tent**

accompaniment
04 vamp **06** backup, patter
07 adjunct, backing, bourdon,
descant, support **08** addition, obligato
09 accessory, obbligato, orchestra,
side order **10** background,
complement, supplement
11 coexistence, concomitant,
tracklement
• **provide accompaniment**
04 la-la

accompanist
04 comp **11** accompanier **12** backing
group **15** instrumentalist

accompany
04 back, chum **05** usher **06** assist,
attend, convoy, escort, follow, go with,
squire, wait on **07** coexist, conduct,
consort, partner, support **08** belong
to, chaperon, coincide, come with,
play with, tag along, wait upon, walk
with **09** associate, chaperone,
companion, occur with
10 complement, supplement, travel
with **11** go along with **12** tag along
with **13** associate with, come along
with **14** go together with, hang around
with

accomplice
04 aide, ally, mate **05** shill, stale
06 bonnet, button, helper **07** abettor,
fedarie, nobbler, partner **08** approver,
complice, copemate, federary,
foedarie, henchman, sidekick,
swagsman **09** accessory, assistant,
associate, colleague, copesmate,
federarie **11** confederate, conspirator
12 collaborator, participator, right-
hand man **14** right-hand woman

accomplish
02 do **06** attain, effect, finish, fulfil,
hack it, manage, obtain, wangle
07 achieve, compass, execute,
perform, produce, realize **08** bring off,
carry out, complete, complish,
conclude, engineer **09** discharge, pull
it off **10** bring about, consummate,
effectuate **15** carry into effect, deliver
the goods

accomplished
03 ace **04** arch, done, over **05** adept
06 adroit, expert, gifted, savant,
wicked **07** learned, savante, skilful,
skilled **08** compleat, masterly,
polished, talented **09** practised
10 consummate, cultivated, proficient
11 experienced **12** professional

accomplishment
03 act, art **04** deed, feat, gift **05** doing,
forte, knack, skill **06** stroke, talent,
virtue **07** ability, exploit, faculty,
finesse, prowess, quality, triumph
08 aptitude, exercise, fruition
09 discharge, effecting, execution,
finishing, operation **10** attainment,
capability, completion, conclusion,
fulfilling, fulfilment, futurition,
management, perfection, production
11 achievement, carrying-out,
performance, proficiency, realization

12 consummation **13** qualification
14 stroke of genius

accord
04 deal, give, jibe, pact, sort, suit
05 agree, allow, chime, endow, grant,
match, unity, yield **06** assent, bestow,
concur, confer, extend, square, tender,
treaty **07** compact, concert, conform,
congree, consort, harmony, present
08 contract, sympathy **09** agreement,
concordat, congruity, consensus,
harmonize, unanimity, vouchsafe
10 accordance, conformity,
congruence, convention, correspond,
settlement **11** be in harmony,
concurrence **13** be in agreement
14 correspondence
• **of your own accord**
06 freely **09** willingly **11** voluntarily
• **with one accord**
09 of one mind **11** unanimously

accordance
• **in accordance with**
02 by **05** after, under **10** in line with,
obedient to **12** in relation to, in the light
of **13** in concert with, in keeping with,
in the manner of **14** consistent with, in
proportion to **15** in agreement with

according
03 acc
• **according to**
03 per **05** after, as per **08** as said by,
secundum **10** as stated by, in line with,
obedient to **11** as claimed by,
depending on **12** in relation to, in the
light of **13** in keeping with, in the
manner of, on the report of
14 consistent with, in proportion to

accordingly
02 so **04** duly, ergo, thus **05** fitly, hence
08 properly, suitably **09** agreeably, as
result, therefore **10** sure enough,
thereafter **12** consequently,
consistently **13** appropriately, for that
reason, in consequence
15 correspondingly

accost
04 bord, hail, halt, stop **05** abord,
assay, board, boord, borde **06** attack,
boorde, detain, molest, nobble, waylay
07 address, solicit **08** approach,
confront **09** importune **10** buttonhole

account
02 a/c **03** acc, tab **04** acct, bill, deem,
hold, sake, tale **05** books, count, story,
value **06** assess, behalf, detail, esteem,
import, ledger, memoir, moment,
reckon, record, regard, report, sketch,
view as **07** adjudge, believe, charges,
details, history, invoice, journal,
version, write up **08** appraise,
consider, look upon, regard as, register
09 chronicle, inventory, narration,
narrative, portrayal, statement
10 commentary, importance
11 consequence, description,
distinction, explanation
12 presentation, significance
• **account for**
04 give, kill **06** defeat, make up, say

accountability

why, supply **07** clear up, destroy, explain, justify, provide **08** comprise **09** answer for, eliminate, elucidate, represent, vindicate **10** constitute, illuminate **11** rationalize **14** give reasons for
• **falsify accounts**
04 cook, rort **12** cook the books
• **give an account of**
04 tell **06** relate
• **on account of**
02 o/a **03** for **04** over **05** along **07** because, owing to, through **08** in view of **09** because of **10** by virtue of, in virtue of **11** the reason is **12** for the sake of
• **on no account**
05 never, no way **12** certainly not **13** not on your life

accountability
09 liability, reporting **10** obligation **11** amenability **13** answerability **14** responsibility

accountable
05 bound **06** liable **07** obliged **08** amenable **09** comptable, comptible, obligated **10** answerable, chargeable, explicable **11** charged with, responsible

accountant
02 CA **03** ACA, acc, CPA **06** bookie **09** bookmaker **11** bean counter

accoutrements
03 kit **04** gear **05** stuff **06** outfit, things **07** clobber **08** fittings, fixtures **09** caparison, equipment, trimmings **10** adornments **11** decorations, furnishings, odds and ends **12** appointments **13** appurtenances, bits and pieces, paraphernalia

accredit
06 depute **07** approve, certify, endorse, license, warrant **09** attribute, authorize, recognize **10** commission **11** certificate

accredited
07 deputed **08** approved, endorsed, licensed, official **09** appointed, certified, qualified **10** authorized, recognized **12** certificated, commissioned

accretion
05 add-on **06** growth **07** build-up **08** addition, increase **09** gathering, increment **10** collecting, cumulation, supplement **12** accumulation, augmentation

accrue
05 amass, mount **07** augment, be added, build up, collect, mount up **08** increase **10** accumulate

accumulate
04 gain, grow, pile, pool **05** amass, hoard, stash, store, tot up **06** accrue, distil, garner, gather, pile up **07** acquire, augment, build up, collect, congest, distill **08** assemble, cumulate, increase, multiply, snowball **09** aggregate, stockpile

accumulation
04 gain, heap, mass, pile **05** hoard, stack, stock, store **06** growth **07** accrual, build-up, reserve **08** assembly, increase **09** accretion, aggregate, gathering, stockpile **10** building-up, collection, cumulation **11** acquisition **12** augmentation **14** conglomeration, multiplication

accumulative
07 growing **08** mounting **09** enlarging **10** increasing **11** multiplying, snowballing

accuracy
05 truth **06** verity **08** fidelity, veracity **09** closeness, exactness, precision **10** exactitude **11** carefulness, correctness **12** authenticity, faithfulness, scrupulosity, truthfulness, veridicality **14** meticulousness

accurate
04 fair, nice, true **05** close, exact, right, sound, valid **06** bang on, dead-on, spot-on, strict **07** correct, factual, literal, perfect, precise **08** faithful, on target, rigorous, truthful, unerring **09** authentic, faultless, on the mark, veracious, veridical, well-aimed **10** meticulous **11** word-for-word, word-perfect **12** well-directed **13** letter-perfect

accurately
05 truly **07** closely, exactly **08** strictly **09** correctly, literally, perfectly, precisely **10** faithfully, rigorously, truthfully, unerringly **11** faultlessly, veraciously, veridically **12** meticulously

accursed
05 blest, hated **06** damned, doomed, goddam, sacred **07** blessed, goddamn, hateful **08** maledict, wretched **09** bewitched, condemned, execrable, goddamned, loathsome **10** abominable, bedevilled, despicable, detestable **13** anathematized

accusation
03 tax **04** bill **05** blame, cause, libel, smear **06** charge, threap, threep **08** citation, delation, gravamen **09** challenge, complaint, invective **10** allegation, imputation, indictment **11** arraignment, crimination, impeachment, inculpation, information, prosecution **12** denunciation **13** incrimination, recrimination

accuse
03 tax **04** book, cite **05** blame, frame, peach **06** allege, appeal, charge, detect, impugn, impute, indict **07** appeach, arraign, asperse, attaint, censure, impeach, reprove **08** confront, denounce **09** attribute, challenge, criminate, implicate, prosecute **10** put on trial **11** incriminate, recriminate **12** bring charges, press charges **13** inform against **14** throw the book at **15** hold

responsible, make accusations, make allegations

accustom
03 use **05** adapt, enure, inure, teach **06** adjust, attune **07** conform **08** occasion **09** acclimate, climatize, get used to, habituate **11** acclimatize, accommodate, familiarize **15** get familiar with

accustomed
03 old **04** tame, used, wont **05** fixed, given, usual **06** at home, inured, normal, wonted **07** general, regular, routine **08** everyday, familiar, frequent, habitual, ordinary **09** customary **10** acquainted, habituated, prevailing **11** established, traditional **12** acclimatized, conventional, in the habit of **14** consuetudinary

ace
01 A **03** jot, one, Tib **04** cool, neat, unit **05** basto, brill, great, whizz **06** expert, genius, grouse, master, superb, wicked, winner **07** dab hand, hotshot, maestro, perfect **08** champion, spadille, terrific, top-notch, very good, virtuoso **09** brilliant, excellent **10** first-class **11** outstanding

acerbic
05 harsh, sharp, spiky **06** biting **07** caustic, mordant **08** abrasive, stinging **09** rancorous, sarcastic, trenchant, vitriolic **10** astringent **11** acrimonious

ache
01 H **03** die, yen **04** hurt, itch, kill, long, pain, pang, pine, work **05** agony, aitch, crave, pound, smart, sting, throb, yearn **06** be sore, desire, hanker, hunger, play up, stound, stownd, suffer, thirst, twinge **07** agonize, anguish, craving, longing **08** pounding, smarting, soreness, stinging, yearning **09** be in agony, be painful, hankering, suffering, throbbing

achieve
02 do **03** get, win **04** earn, gain **05** reach **06** attain, effect, finish, fulfil, manage, obtain, wrap up **07** acquire, execute, perform, procure, produce, realize, succeed **08** carry out, complete **09** polish off **10** accomplish, bring about, consummate, effectuate

achievement
03 act **04** deed, feat **06** action, effort, stroke **07** exploit, success, triumph **08** activity, fruition **09** execution **10** attainment, chevisance, completion, fulfilment **11** acquirement, performance, procurement, realization **12** consummation, effectuation **14** accomplishment, stroke of genius

achiever
04 doer **08** go-getter, live wire, whizz kid **09** high-flyer, performer, succeeder **12** success story

Achilles' heel
05 fault **07** failing **08** weakness, weak spot **09** weak point **12** imperfection **15** vulnerable point

acid
04 keen, sour, tart **05** catty, harsh, sharp, sugar **06** acidic, biting, bitter, morose, unkind **07** acerbic, acetous, caustic, cutting, hurtful, mordant, pungent **08** critical, incisive, stinging, vinegary **09** acidulous, corrosive, sarcastic, trenchant, vitriolic **10** astringent, ill-natured **11** unsweetened

Acids include:

03 DNA, LSD, RNA
04 acyl, EDTA, uric
05 amino, boric, fatty, folic
06 acetic, citric, formic, lactic, nitric, oxalic, phenol, tannic
07 acrylic, benzoic, boracic, chloric, nitrous, nucleic, prussic, pyruvic, silicic, stearic
08 abscisic, ascorbic, carbolic, carbonic, ethanoic, lysergic, palmitic, periodic, retinoic, tartaric
09 methanoic, nicotinic, propionic, salicylic, sulphonic, sulphuric
10 aqua fortis, barbituric, carboxylic, phosphoric, sulphurous
11 hydrocyanic, ribonucleic
12 hydrochloric, hydrofluoric
13 thiosulphuric, tricarboxylic

See also **amino acid**

• **acid test**
02 pH
• **work with acid**
04 etch

acknowledge
03 con, own **04** avow, hail, mark **05** admit, allow, grant, greet, thank **06** accede, accept, affirm, agnize, answer, avouch, honour, notice, salute, wave to **07** address, agree to, concede, confess, confirm, declare, own up to, react to, reply to **08** signal to **09** acquiesce, celebrate, recognize, respond to **10** be grateful **11** say thank you, write back to **13** give thanks for

acknowledged
06 avowed **08** accepted, admitted, approved, attested, declared **09** confirmed, professed **10** accredited, recognized

acknowledgement
03 nod **04** wave **05** reply, smile **06** answer, avowal, credit, homage, notice, praise, thanks **07** tribute, welcome **08** bouquets, cognovit, comeback, granting, greeting, reaction, response **09** admission, allowance, deference, gratitude **10** acceptance, confession, profession, salutation **11** declaration, recognition **12** appreciation, gratefulness, recognizance

acme
04 apex, peak **05** crown, prick **06** apogee, climax, comble, height,

summit, zenith **07** optimum **08** pinnacle **09** high point **11** culmination, sublimation **12** highest point

acolyte
06 helper **08** adherent, altar boy, follower, hanger-on, sidekick, thurifer **09** assistant, attendant **11** acolouthite

acorn
04 mast **05** glans **07** oak mast, valonea, valonia **08** racahout, vallonia **09** raccahout

acoustic
05 aural, sound **06** audile **07** hearing **08** auditory

acquaint
04 tell **05** brief **06** advise, inform, notify, reveal **07** apprise, divulge, let know, possess **08** accustom, announce, disclose **09** enlighten **11** familiarize, make aware of **14** make conversant **15** put in the picture

acquaintance
04 mate **06** friend, pick-up **07** contact, homeboy **08** confrère, habitude, hanger-on, intimacy **09** associate, awareness, colleague, companion, knowledge **10** cognizance, connection, experience, fellowship **11** association, conversance, familiarity **12** relationship **13** companionship, social contact, understanding

acquainted
05 aware **06** au fait, versed **07** abreast **08** apprised, familiar, friendly, intimate **09** au courant, cognizant, in the know, up to speed **10** conversant, well-versed **11** on good terms **13** knowledgeable **15** on friendly terms
• **be acquainted with**
03 ken **04** know

acquiesce
05 agree, allow, defer **06** accede, accept, assent, concur, give in, permit, submit **07** approve, consent **12** give the nod to

acquiescence
03 nod **05** say-so **06** assent **07** consent, go-ahead **08** approval, thumbs-up, yielding **09** agreement, deference **10** acceptance, compliance, green-light, submission **11** concurrence, countenance

acquiescent
07 servile **08** acceding, agreeing, amenable, obedient, yielding **09** accepting, agreeable, approving, compliant **10** concurring, consenting, submissive **11** complaisant, deferential

acquire
◇ *containment indicator*
03 bag, buy, cop, ern, get, net, win **04** earn, gain, grab **05** amass **06** attain, collar, come by, gather, obtain, pick up, secure, snap up, take on **07** achieve, collect, procure, realize, receive,

snaffle, usucapt **08** purchase **10** accumulate **11** appropriate, splash out on

acquisition
03 buy **04** gain **05** prize **07** acquest, gaining **08** property, purchase, securing, takeover **09** accession, obtaining, usucapion **10** attainment, investment, possession, usucaption **11** achievement, procurement **13** appropriation

acquisitive
04 avid **06** greedy **08** covetous, grasping, hoarding **09** predatory, rapacious, voracious **10** avaricious **12** accumulative

acquisitiveness
05 greed **07** avarice, avidity **08** cupidity, rapacity, voracity **12** covetousness, graspingness **13** predatoriness

acquit
02 do **03** act **04** bear, free **05** clear, prove, repay **06** assoil, behave, bestow, excuse, let off, settle **07** absolve, comport, conduct, deliver, dismiss, perform, release, relieve, satisfy, set free **08** liberate, reprieve, uncharge **09** discharge, exculpate, exonerate, vindicate **11** make a bad job **12** make a good job **13** let off the hook

acquittal
06 relief **07** freeing, release **08** clearing, excusing, reprieve **09** clearance, discharge, dismissal **10** absolution, liberation **11** deliverance, exculpation, exoneration, vindication **12** compurgation

acre
01 a **02** ac

acrid
04 acid, sour, tart **05** harsh, nasty, sharp **06** biting, bitter **07** acerbic, burning, caustic, cutting, mordant, pungent **08** incisive, sardonic, stinging, venomous, virulent **09** malicious, sarcastic, trenchant, vitriolic **10** astringent **11** acrimonious

acrimonious
05 sharp **06** bitchy, biting, bitter, severe **07** abusive, acerbic, caustic, crabbed, cutting, waspish **08** petulant, spiteful, venomous, virulent **09** irascible, rancorous, splenetic, trenchant, vitriolic **10** astringent, censorious **11** atrabilious, ill-tempered

acrimony
04 gall **05** spite, venom **06** spleen **07** ill will, rancour, sarcasm, vitriol **08** acerbity, acridity, asperity, mordancy **09** harshness, ill temper, petulance, virulence **10** bitterness, causticity, ill feeling, resentment, trenchancy **11** astringency **12** irascibility

acrobat
05 speel **07** gymnast, speeler, tumbler **08** balancer, posturer, stuntman

9 aerialist, posturist **10** rope-dancer, rope-walker, stuntwoman, wing-walker **11** equilibrist, funambulist **12** somersaulter, trick cyclist **13** contortionist, trapeze artist **15** tightrope-walker

acrobatics
◇ anagram indicator
06 stunts **09** balancing **10** gymnastics **11** equilibrity, funambulism, rope-walking, wire-walking **13** somersaulting

across
01 a **02** ac **03** dia-, tra- **04** over, tran- **05** trans- **06** thwart **07** athwart **08** à travers

act
02 be, do **03** bit, gig, kid, law **04** bill, deal, deed, fake, feat, item, mime, move, part, play, sham, show, skit, step, turn, work **05** canon, doing, edict, enact, feign, front, mimic, put on, react, serve **06** action, affect, assume, be busy, behave, decree, number, ruling, sketch, stroke **07** episode, exploit, go about, imitate, measure, operate, perform, portray, pretend, respond, routine, section, statute **08** be active, division, feigning, function, pretence, put-up job, simulate **09** dissemble, execution, manoeuvre, operation, ordinance, represent, take steps **10** do the job of, enterprise, resolution, subsection, take action, take effect **11** achievement, affectation, counterfeit, dissimulate, impersonate, make-believe, performance, undertaking **12** characterize, dissemblance, go on the stage, have an effect, take measures **13** be efficacious, dissimulation, exert yourself **14** accomplishment, acquit yourself **15** comport yourself, conduct yourself

See also **law**
• **act badly**
03 ham
• **act on**
04 heed, obey, take **05** alter **06** affect, change, follow, fulfil, modify, work on **08** carry out **09** conform to, influence, transform **10** comply with
• **act the part of**
04 come
• **act up**
04 fail **06** pack up, play up **07** carry on, conk out, go kaput, go wrong, not work **09** break down, mess about, misbehave **10** give bother, muck around **11** behave badly, malfunction, stop working **12** cause trouble

acting
◇ anagram indicator
01 a **03** act **04** actg **05** drama **06** action, deputy, fill-in, pro tem, relief, supply **07** interim, reserve, showbiz, stand-by, stand-in, stopgap, theatre **08** artistry, covering **09** dramatics, imitating, in place of, luvviedom, melodrama, portrayal, short-term, surrogate, temporary **10** footlights,

performing, play-acting, stagecraft, substitute **11** histrionics, performance, provisional, theatricals, Thespianism **12** show business **13** impersonation, standing in for **14** performing arts

actinium
02 Ac

actinon
02 an

action
◇ anagram indicator
03 act, pas **04** case, deed, feat, fray, move, step, suit, work **05** clash, doing, fight, force, power **06** affray, battle, combat, effect, effort, energy, events, motion, result, spirit, vigour **07** exploit, lawsuit, measure, pizzazz, process, warfare **08** activity, conflict, exercise, exertion, fighting, goings-on, movement, practice, skirmish, vitality **09** encounter, endeavour, influence, mechanism, operation **10** activities, engagement, enterprise, excitement, get-up-and-go, happenings, litigation, liveliness, proceeding **11** achievement, functioning, hostilities, performance, proceedings, prosecution, stimulation, undertaking **12** exhilaration, forcefulness **14** accomplishment, course of action
• **check action**
04 stay
• **course of action**
04 path
• **critical time of action**
04 D-day

activate
◇ anagram indicator
04 fire, move, stir, trip **05** impel, put on, rouse, start **06** arouse, bestir, excite, prompt, propel, set off, turn on **07** actuate, animate, trigger **08** energize, get going, initiate, mobilize, motivate, set going, switch on **09** derepress, galvanize, kick-start, stimulate **10** trigger off **11** set in motion **12** start working **13** push the button **14** press the button, throw the switch

active
◇ anagram indicator
01 a **03** act **04** at it, busy, go-go, spry **05** agile, alert, astir, manic, quick, vital, yauld, zippy **06** birkie, lively, mobile, nimble, quiver, wimble **07** devoted, engaged, forward, in force, on the go, running, springe, vibrant, working **08** activist, animated, diligent, forceful, frenetic, involved, militant, occupied, practive, spirited, vigorous **09** committed, effectual, energetic, operative, sprightly, stirabout **11** functioning, hard-working, hyperactive, industrious, in operation, light-footed, operational **12** contributing, enterprising, enthusiastic **13** indefatigable
• **be active**
02 do **03** hum

activist
07 inciter, stirrer **08** agitator, fomenter,

henchman, militant **09** firebrand **10** incendiary, subversive **12** troublemaker **13** revolutionary

See also **aboriginal**

activity
◇ anagram indicator
02 do, go **03** act, job **04** deed, life, play, stir, task, work **05** hobby **06** action, bustle, labour, motion, scheme **07** pastime, project, pursuit, venture **08** business, exercise, exertion, industry, interest, movement **09** avocation, commotion, diversion, endeavour **10** activeness, enterprise, hurly-burly, liveliness, occupation **11** distraction, undertaking **13** something to do **14** toing and froing **15** a hive of activity, a hive of industry, hustle and bustle
• **bustling activity**
04 rush **06** bustle **07** beehive
• **focus of activity**
03 hub
• **furious activity**
04 rage
• **increase in activity**
04 boom

actor, actress
03 ham **04** feed, mime, mute, supe **05** buffa, buffo, comic, extra, luvvy, super, thesp **06** artist, luvvie, mummer, player, stager, stooge, walk-on **07** artiste, comique, histrio, ingénue, Roscius, starlet, support, trouper **08** comedian, epilogue, film star, histrion, juvenile, thespian **09** bit player, film actor, hamfatter, movie star, performer, play actor, principal, tragedian **10** leading man, mime artist, movie actor, understudy, utility man **11** leading lady, matinée idol, pantomimist, protagonist, straight man, tragedienne, tritagonist **12** impersonator, spear carrier **13** deuteragonist, supernumerary **14** character actor, dramatic artist, stage performer **15** strolling player

Kean (Edmund), **Lowe** (Rob), **Peck**
(Gregory), **Penn** (Sean), **Pitt** (Brad),
Reed (Oliver), **Sher** (Sir Antony),**Tati**
(Jacques),**Thaw** (John),**Tree** (Sir
Herbert Beerbohm),**Wood** (Elijah)

05 Allen (Woody), **Bacon** (Kevin),
Bates (Alan), **Brody** (Adrien), **Caine**
(Sir Michael), **Clift** (Montgomery),
Craig (Daniel), **Crowe** (Russell),
Dafoe (Willem), **Damon** (Matt),
Dance (Charles), **Firth** (Colin), **Flynn**
(Errol), **Fonda** (Henry), **Gable**
(Clark), **Grant** (Cary), **Grant** (Hugh),
Grant (Richard E), **Hanks** (Tom),
Hardy (Oliver), **Irons** (Jeremy), **Kelly**
(Gene), **Kempe** (Will), **Kline**
(Kevin), **Leung** (Tony), **Lewis** (Jerry),
Lloyd (Harold), **Lorre** (Peter),
Mason (James), **Mills** (Sir John),
Moore (Roger), **Neill** (Sam), **Nimoy**
(Leonard), **Niven** (David), **Nolte**
(Nick), **Price** (Vincent), **Quinn**
(Anthony), **Reeve** (Christopher),
Robey (Sir George), **Scott** (George
C), **Sheen** (Charlie), **Sheen** (Martin),
Smith (Will), **Spall** (Timothy),
Stamp (Terence), **Sydow** (Max von),
Tracy (Spencer),**Wayne** (John)

06 Alleyn (Edward), **Beatty** (Warren),
Bogart (Humphrey), **Brando**
(Marlon), **Brooks** (Mel), **Burton**
(Richard), **Cagney** (James), **Carrey**
(Jim), **Chaney** (Lon), **Coburn**
(James), **Cooper** (Gary), **Cruise**
(Tom), **Curtis** (Tony), **De Niro**
(Robert), **DeVito** (Danny), **Dillon**
(Matt), **Finney** (Albert), **Gambon**
(Sir Michael), **Gibson** (Mel), **Glover**
(Danny), **Harris** (Richard), **Heston**
(Charlton), **Hopper** (Dennis),
Howard (Trevor), **Hudson** (Rock),
Irving (Sir Henry), **Jacobi** (Sir
Derek), **Jolson** (Al), **Jouvet** (Louis),
Keaton (Buster), **Keitel** (Harvey),
Kemble (John Philip), **Laurel** (Stan),
Laurie (Hugh), **Lemmon** (Jack),
Lugosi (Bela), **Martin** (Steve),
Murphy (Eddie), **Murray** (Bill),
Neeson (Liam), **Newman** (Paul),
Oldman (Gary), **O'Toole** (Peter),
Pacino (Al), **Phelps** (Samuel),
Quayle (Sir Anthony), **Reagan**
(Ronald), **Reeves** (Keanu), **Rooney**
(Mickey), **Rourke** (Mickey), **Sharif**
(Omar), **Sinden** (Sir Donald), **Slater**
(Christian), **Spacey** (Kevin), **Swayze**
(Patrick),**Walken** (Christopher),
Welles (Orson),**Wilder** (Gene),
Willis (Bruce),**Wolfit** (Sir Donald)

07 Astaire (Fred), **Auteuil** (Daniel),
Aykroyd (Dan), **Benigni** (Roberto),
Berkoff (Steven), **Bogarde** (Sir
Dirk), **Branagh** (Kenneth), **Bridges**
(Jeff), **Bridges** (Lloyd), **Bronson**
(Charles), **Brosnan** (Pierce),
Brynner (Yul), **Burbage** (Richard),
Carlyle (Robert), **Chaplin** (Charlie),
Clooney (George), **Connery** (Sir
Sean), **Costner** (Kevin), **Crystal**
(Billy), **Cushing** (Peter), **Douglas**
(Kirk), **Douglas** (Michael), **Everett**
(Rupert), **Fiennes** (Joseph), **Fiennes**

(Ralph), **Forrest** (Edwin), **Freeman**
(Morgan), **Garrick** (David), **Gielgud**
(Sir John), **Hoffman** (Dustin),
Hopkins (Sir Anthony), **Hordern** (Sir
Michael), **Jackson** (Samuel L),
Karloff (Boris), **Marceau** (Marcel),
Matthau (Walter), **McQueen**
(Steve), **Mitchum** (Robert),
Montand (Yves), **Nielsen** (Leslie),
Olivier (Laurence, Lord), **Poitier**
(Sidney), **Redford** (Robert),
Rickman (Alan), **Robbins** (Tim),
Robeson (Paul), **Roscius**, **Russell**
(Kurt), **Savalas** (Telly), **Selleck** (Tom),
Sellers (Peter), **Shatner** (William),
Steiger (Rod), **Stewart** (James),
Ustinov (Sir Peter)

08 Atkinson (Rowan), **Barrault** (Jean-
Louis), **Day-Lewis** (Daniel),
DiCaprio (Leonardo), **Dreyfuss**
(Richard), **Eastwood** (Clint),
Goldblum (Jeff), **Guinness** (Sir
Alec), **Harrison** (Sir Rex), **Kingsley**
(Ben), **Laughton** (Charles),
Macready (William Charles),
McGregor (Ewan), **McKellen** (Sir
Ian), **Redgrave** (Sir Michael),
Reynolds (Burt), **Robinson** (Edward
G), **Scofield** (Paul), **Stallone**
(Sylvester),**Travolta** (John),**Van
Cleef** (Lee),**Van Damme** (Jean-
Claude), **von Sydow** (Max),
Williams (Robin),**Woodward**
(Edward)

09 Barrymore (Lionel), **Broadbent**
(Jim), **Broderick** (Matthew),
Chevalier (Maurice), **Courtenay** (Sir
Tom), **Depardieu** (Gérard),
Fairbanks (Douglas), **Fernandel**,
Hawthorne (Sir Nigel), **Lancaster**
(Burt), **Malkovich** (John), **Nicholson**
(Jack), **Pleasence** (Donald),
Strasberg (Lee),**Valentino**
(Rudolph)

10 Richardson (Sir Ralph), **Sutherland**
(Donald), **Sutherland** (Kiefer),
Washington (Denzel)

11 Mastroianni (Marcello),
Weissmuller (Johnny)

12 Attenborough (Richard, Lord),
Garcia Bernal (Gael), **Stanislavsky**
(Konstantin)

14 Schwarzenegger (Arnold)

See also **comedian**

Actresses include:

03 Bow (Clara), **Cox** (Courteney), **Day**
(Doris), **Loy** (Myrna)

04 Ball (Lucille), **Dern** (Laura), **Diaz**
(Cameron), **Dors** (Diana), **Duse**
(Eleonora), **Gish** (Lillian), **Gwyn**
(Nell), **Hawn** (Goldie), **Hird** (Dame
Thora), **Rigg** (Dame Diana), **Ryan**
(Meg),**West** (Mae),**Wood** (Natalie),
York (Susannah)

05 Allen (Gracie), **Berry** (Halle), **Bloom**
(Claire), **Close** (Glenn), **Davis**
(Bette), **Davis** (Geena), **Dench**
(Dame Judi), **Derek** (Bo), **Evans**
(Dame Edith), **Fonda** (Jane), **Gabor**
(Zsa Zsa), **Garbo** (Greta), **Jolie**
(Angelina), **Kelly** (Grace), **Lange**

(Jessica), **Leigh** (Janet), **Leigh**
(Vivien), **Lopez** (Jennifer), **Loren**
(Sophia), **Mills** (Hayley), **Moore**
(Demi), **Ryder** (Winona), **Smith**
(Dame Maggie), **Stone** (Sharon),
Swank (Hilary),**Terry** (Dame Ellen),
Welch (Raquel)

06 Adjani (Isabelle), **Bacall** (Lauren),
Bardot (Brigitte), **Bisset**
(Jacqueline), **Cheung** (Maggie),
Curtis (Jamie Lee), **Farrow** (Mia),
Fisher (Carrie), **Foster** (Jodie),
Grable (Betty), **Hannah** (Daryl),
Harlow (Jean), **Hedren** (Tippi),
Hunter (Holly), **Huston** (Anjelica),
Keaton (Diane), **Kemble** (Fanny),
Kidman (Nicole), **Kinski**
(Nastassja), **Lamarr** (Hedy), **Lumley**
(Joanna), **Midler** (Bette), **Mirren**
(Helen), **Monroe** (Marilyn),
Moreau (Jeanne), **Robson** (Dame
Flora), **Rogers** (Ginger), **Spacek**
(Sissy), **Streep** (Meryl), **Suzman**
(Janet),**Tautou** (Audrey),**Taylor**
(Dame Elizabeth),**Temple** (Shirley),
Turner (Kathleen),**Turner** (Lana),
Ullman (Tracey),**Weaver**
(Sigourney),**Winger** (Debra)

07 Andress (Ursula), **Andrews** (Dame
Julie), **Aniston** (Jennifer), **Bergman**
(Ingrid), **Binoche** (Juliette), **Colbert**
(Claudette), **Deneuve** (Catherine),
Gardner (Ava), **Garland** (Judy),
Hepburn (Audrey), **Hepburn**
(Katharine), **Jackson** (Glenda),
Johnson (Dame Celia), **Langtry**
(Lillie), **Lombard** (Carole), **Paltrow**
(Gwyneth), **Roberts** (Julia), **Russell**
(Jane), **Seymour** (Jane), **Siddons**
(Sarah), **Swanson** (Gloria),**Walters**
(Julie),**Winslet** (Kate)

08 Ashcroft (Dame Peggy), **Bancroft**
(Anne), **Bankhead** (Tallulah),
Basinger (Kim), **Campbell** (Mrs
Patrick), **Charisse** (Cyd), **Christie**
(Julie), **Crawford** (Joan), **Dietrich**
(Marlene), **Fontaine** (Joan),
Goldberg (Whoopi), **Griffith**
(Melanie), **Hayworth** (Rita),
MacLaine (Shirley), **Minnelli** (Liza),
Pfeiffer (Michelle), **Pickford**
(Mary), **Rampling** (Charlotte),
Redgrave (Vanessa), **Sarandon**
(Susan), **Shepherd** (Cybill), **Signoret**
(Simone), **Stanwyck** (Barbara),
Thompson (Emma)

09 Barrymore (Drew), **Bernhardt**
(Sarah), **Blanchett** (Cate),
Johansson (Scarlett), **MacDowell**
(Andie), **Mansfield** (Jayne),
Plowright (Joan Ann), **Streisand**
(Barbra),**Thorndike** (Dame Sybil),
Zellweger (Renée), **Zeta Jones**
(Catherine)

10 Rossellini (Isabella), **Rutherford**
(Dame Margaret)

11 Bracegirdle (Anne), **de Havilland**
(Olivia), **Mistinguett**, **Scott-
Thomas** (Kristin)

12 Bonham Carter (Helena),
Lollobrigida (Gina)

See also **comedian**

• actor's portrayal
04 part, role
• bad actor
03 ham

actors
04 cast 07 company

actress *see* actor, actress

actual
04 real, true, very 07 certain, de facto, actual, genuine 08 absolute, bona fide, concrete, definite, existent, material, physical, positive, real life, tangible, truthful, verified 09 authentic, confirmed, realistic 10 legitimate 11 substantial 12 indisputable 14 unquestionable

actuality
03 ens 04 fact 05 truth 07 realism, reality 08 solidity 09 entelechy, existence, substance 10 factuality 11 historicity, materiality 12 corporeality 14 substantiality

actually
04 even 05 truly 06 indeed, in fact, really 07 de facto, insooth, in truth, soothly 09 in reality 10 absolutely 11 as it happens 12 surprisingly 14 believe it or not 15 as a matter of fact

actuate
04 move, stir 05 rouse, start 06 arouse, kindle, prompt, set off, turn on 07 animate, trigger 08 activate, motivate, set going, switch on 09 instigate, stimulate 10 trigger off 11 set in motion 12 start working

acumen
03 wit 05 sense 06 wisdom 07 insight 08 gumption, keenness, sagacity, sapience 09 ingenuity, intuition, judgement, quickness, sharpness, smartness 10 astuteness, cleverness, perception, shrewdness 11 discernment, penetration, percipience, perspicuity 12 intelligence, perspicacity 13 judiciousness 14 discrimination

acupressure
04 do-in 07 shiatsu, shiatzu 09 Jin Shin Do®

acute
04 dire, keen 05 canny, grave, sharp, smart, vital 06 astute, clever, severe, shrewd, urgent 07 crucial, cutting, drastic, extreme, intense, sapient, serious, violent 08 critical, decisive, incisive, peracute, piercing, poignant 09 dangerous, judicious, observant, sensitive 10 discerning, insightful, perceptive, percipient, unbearable 11 distressing, penetrating, sharp-witted 13 perspicacious

acutely
04 very 06 keenly 07 gravely, sharply 08 markedly, severely, strongly 09 extremely, intensely, seriously

adage
03 saw 05 axiom, gnome, maxim 06 byword, saying 07 precept, proverb 08 aphorism, paroemia 10 apophthegm, whakatauki

adamant
03 set 04 firm, hard 05 fixed, rigid, stiff, tough 07 diamond 08 obdurate, resolute, stubborn 09 immovable, insistent, lodestone, unbending 10 determined, inflexible, unshakable, unwavering, unyielding 11 unrelenting, unshakeable 12 intransigent 14 uncompromising

Adamson
04 Abel, Cain, Seth

adapt
◇ *anagram indicator*
03 apt, fit 04 suit 05 alter, apply, frame, match, shape, tally 06 adjust, change, comply, modify, reduce, tailor 07 arrange, conform, convert, exploit, fashion, get used, prepare, qualify, remodel 08 attemper, settle in 09 contemper, customize, harmonize 10 specialize 11 accommodate 13 get accustomed

adaptable
◇ *anagram indicator*
07 open-end, plastic, pliable 08 amenable, flexible, variable 09 alterable, compliant, easy-going, malleable, open-ended, versatile 10 adjustable, changeable, modifiable 11 conformable, convertible

adaptation
◇ *anagram indicator*
05 shift 06 change 07 fitting, shaping 08 matching, revision 09 refitting, reshaping, reworking, variation 10 adjustment, alteration, conformity, conversion, fashioning 11 getting used, habituation, preparation, remodelling 12 conformation, modification, refashioning 13 accommodation, customization, harmonization 14 transformation 15 acclimatization, familiarization

add
◇ *juxtaposition indicator*
03 eik, eke, put, sum, tot 04 go on, join, tote 05 affix, annex, boost, count, put in, put on, raise, top up, total, tot up 06 adjoin, append, attach, deepen, extend, hike up, prefix, suffix, tack on 07 augment, build on, carry on, combine, count up, enhance, improve, include, postfix, summate, throw in 08 complete, continue, heighten, increase 09 aggravate, go on to say, increment, intensify, introduce 10 supplement 15 work out the total
• add up
03 fit 04 cast, make, mean 05 count, run to, spell, sum up, tally, total, tot up 06 amount, come to, reckon 07 compute, count up, include, signify, stack up 08 figure up, indicate, ring true 09 calculate, make sense 10 constitute 11 add together, be plausible 12 be

consistent, be reasonable, hang together 13 stand to reason

added
03 new 04 more 05 extra, fresh, spare 07 adjunct, another, further 10 additional 13 supplementary

addendum
02 PS 03 add 05 annex 07 adjunct, allonge, codicil 08 addition, appendix 09 appendage 10 attachment, postscript, supplement 11 endorsement 12 augmentation

addict
03 fan 04 buff, head, hype, user 05 fiend, freak, hound, junky 06 junkie, stoner 07 devotee, druggie, fanatic, hop-head, tripper 08 adherent, coke-head, drug user, follower, snowbird 09 clay eater, crackhead, dope-fiend, drug fiend, drug taker, mainliner, smackhead 10 enthusiast 14 cruciverbalist

addicted
04 daft, fond, nuts, wild 05 crazy, given, potty 06 hooked 07 devoted 08 absorbed, bibulous, frequent, inclined, obsessed 09 confirmed, dedicated, dependent, fanatical, strung out 10 dissipated 13 drug-dependent

addiction
04 need 05 habit, mania, thing 06 monkey 07 craving 08 caffeism, opiumism, vinosity 09 cocainism, ergomania, obsession 10 caffeinism, compulsion, dependence, dependency, femininism 11 a colt's tooth, etheromania

addictive
09 obsessive 10 compulsive 12 habit-forming, irresistible 14 uncontrollable

addition
02 PS 03 eik, eke, PPS 04 also, gain, plus 05 extra, rider 06 adding, annexe 07 adjunct, codicil 08 addendum, additive, appendix, counting, increase 09 accession, accessory, accretion, appendage, extension, inclusion, increment, reckoning, summing-up, totalling, totting-up 10 annexation, attachment, increasing, postscript, supplement 11 computation, enlargement 12 afterthought, appurtenance, augmentation
• in addition
03 too 04 also 05 forby 06 as well, to boot, withal 07 besides, further, thereto 08 as well as, moreover 09 thereunto 11 furthermore 12 additionally, not to mention, over and above 14 for good measure, into the bargain

additional
03 new, odd 04 more, plus 05 added, extra, fresh, other, spare 07 another, further 09 increased 10 excrescent 12 adscititious, adventitious, supervenient, supplemental 13 supplementary

additionally
03 too **04** also **05** forby **06** as well, to boot, withal **07** besides, further **08** moreover **10** in addition **11** furthermore **12** over and above **14** for good measure, into the bargain

additive
04 MTBE **05** extra **07** E-number **08** addition **09** oxygenate, summative **10** emulsifier, stabilizer, supplement **12** preservative **13** canthaxanthin **14** canthaxanthine

addle
03 bad **04** daze, faze **05** empty **06** barren, muddle, putrid **07** confuse, fluster, muddled, perplex **08** befuddle, bewilder

addled
04 lost **05** fazed **07** mixed-up, muddled **08** confused **09** befuddled, flustered, perplexed **10** bewildered

address
03 add **04** call, flat, hail, home, lord, mail, post, send, talk **05** abode, greet, house, label, orate, place, remit, spiel, uncle **06** accost, convey, direct, invoke, mister, prayer, sermon, speech, talk to **07** accoast, bespeak, lecture, lodging, oration, speak to, welcome, write to **08** diatribe, dwelling, greeting, harangue, location, mistress, petition, preach to **09** apartment, designate, discourse, epirrhema, inaugural, intend for, monologue, philippic, residence, rhetorize, sermonize, situation, soliloquy **10** allocution, apostrophe, directions, invocation, salutation **11** communicate, give a talk to, inscription, make a speech, superscribe, superscript, valedictory, whereabouts **12** disquisition, dissertation **13** give a speech to, poste restante **14** deliver a speech
• **address yourself to**
06 tackle **07** focus on **08** attend to, deal with, engage in **09** undertake **10** take care of **12** buckle down to **13** concentrate on **15** apply yourself to

adduce
04 cite, lead, name **05** quote **06** assign, object **07** mention, present, proffer, refer to, trot out, upbraid **08** allude to, evidence, point out **10** put forward

adept
03 ace, don **04** able, deft, good **05** handy, sharp, swell **06** adroit, clever, deacon, expert, genius, master, nimble, versed, wicked, wizard **07** capable, dab hand, maestro, mahatma, skilled, veteran **08** hot stuff, masterly, polished **09** competent, practised **10** proficient **11** experienced, nobody's fool **12** accomplished

adequacy
07 ability, fitness, measure **08** fairness **10** capability, competence, mediocrity **11** passability, sufficiency, suitability **12** indifference, tolerability **13** acceptability, requisiteness, tolerableness **14** reasonableness, serviceability

adequate
02 OK **03** fit **04** able, enow, good **05** equal, ho-hum, valid **06** enough, patchy, will do, worthy **07** average, capable, working **08** all right, passable, suitable **09** competent, requisite, tolerable **10** acceptable, reasonable, sufficient **11** appropriate, indifferent, serviceable **12** commensurate, could be worse, run of the mill, satisfactory **13** could be better, no great shakes, unexceptional **14** fair to middling **15** undistinguished

adequately
08 passably, suitably **09** tolerably **10** acceptably, reasonably **12** sufficiently **13** appropriately **14** satisfactorily

adhere
03 fix **04** bond, glue, grip, heed, hold, join, keep, link, obey **05** cling, paste, stick **06** attach, cement, cleave, cohere, defend, fasten, follow, fulfil, solder **07** abide by, accrete, combine, espouse, observe, respect, stand by, support **08** cleave to, coalesce, hold fast **10** comply with, stick up for **11** go along with **13** stick together

adherence
05 cling **07** defence, respect, support **08** advocacy, fidelity **10** compliance, fulfilment, observance

adherent
03 bur, fan, nut **04** buff, burr, Jain, Sikh, Sofi, Sufi **05** Bahai, child, freak, Hindu, Jaina **06** Hindoo, Maoist, Sabean, votary **07** admirer, devotee, engager, Genevan, gnostic, Patarin, Sabaean, sceptic, sectary, skeptic **08** advocate, believer, catholic, disciple, follower, groupist, hanger-on, henchman, Jacobite, loyalist, partisan, partizan, Patarine, rightist, royalist, sectator, servitor, sticking, upholder, Vichyite, Wesleyan **09** Caesarean, Caesarian, Communard, Gothicist, ideologue, Oliverian, Samaritan, satellite, socialist, Spinozist, supporter, Wagnerist, Wagnerite **10** aficionado, Bourbonist, enthusiast, Protestant **12** episcopalian, hereditarian **13** sun worshipper **14** restorationist **15** hereditarianist, parliamentarian

adhesion
04 bond, grip **08** cohesion, purchase, sticking, synechia **09** adherence **10** attachment **12** adhesiveness **15** holding together

adhesive
03 gum **04** bond, glue, tape **05** glair, gluey, gummy, paste, tacky **06** Blu-tak®, cement, clammy, Cow Gum®, gummed, sticky **07** Band-aid®, Blu-tack®, holding, hot melt, stick-on **08** adherent, adhering, clinging, cohesive, fixative, goldsize, mountant mucilage, sticking **09** attaching, emplastic, glutinous, Sellotape®, Superglue® **10** sticky tape **11** Elastoplast®, hot-melt glue **12** mucilaginous, passe-partout, rubber cement, self-adhesive

ad hoc
05 ad-lib **09** extempore, makeshift **10** improvised, off the cuff, unprepared, unscripted **11** spontaneous, unrehearsed **13** spontaneously

adieu
03 bye **04** ciao, ta-ta **05** adios **06** bye bye, cheers, kia ora, see you, so long **07** cheerio, goodbye, haere ra **08** au revoir, farewell, take care **10** all the best **11** arrivederci, be seeing you, leave-taking, see you later, valediction valedictory **12** have a nice day, mind how you go, see you around **14** auf Wiedersehen

ad infinitum
03 aye **07** for ever **08** evermore **09** endlessly, eternally **10** at all times, constantly **11** continually, incessantly, permanently, perpetually **12** till doomsday

adjacent
◊ *juxtaposition indicator*
04 near, next, nigh **05** close **06** beside **07** closest, nearest, vicinal **08** abutting, next-door, touching **09** adjoining, alongside, bordering, proximate **10** contiguous, coterminal, juxtaposed **11** conterminal, coterminant, coterminate, coterminous **12** conterminant, conterminate, conterminous, neighbouring

adjective
01 a **03** adj

adjoin
◊ *juxtaposition indicator*
03 add **04** abut, join, link, meet **05** annex, touch, unite, verge **06** append, attach, be next, border, couple **07** combine, connect **09** juxtapose, neighbour **12** interconnect

adjoining
◊ *juxtaposition indicator*
04 near, next **07** joining, linking, uniting, verging, vicinal **08** abutting, adjacent, next door, touching **09** bordering, combining, impinging, proximate **10** conjoining, connecting, contiguous, juxtaposed **12** neighbouring **15** interconnecting

adjourn
04 stay **05** defer, delay, pause **06** put off, recess, repair, retire **07** retreat, suspend **08** break off, continue, postpone, prorogue, withdraw **09** interrupt **11** discontinue **14** betake yourself **15** stop temporarily

adjournment
04 stay **05** break, delay, let-up, pause **06** recess **08** deferral, interval **09** deferment **10** moratorium, putting-off, suspension **11** continuance, dissolution, prorogation **12** intermission, interruption, postponement **15** discontinuation

adjudge
04 aret, cide, deem, side **05** aread, arede, arett, award, judge **06** addeem, addoom, assign, decide, decree, reckon, regard **07** arreede **08** consider **09** determine

adjudicate
04 pass **05** award, judge **06** decide, settle, umpire **07** adjudge, referee **09** arbitrate, determine, pronounce

adjudication
06 decree, ruling **07** verdict **08** decision **09** judgement **10** conclusion, settlement **11** arbitration **13** determination, pronouncement

adjudicator
03 ref, ump **05** judge **06** umpire **07** arbiter, referee **08** mediator **10** arbitrator

adjunct
05 added **06** joined **07** apanage **08** addition, appanage **09** accessory, appendage, appendant **10** complement, supplement **11** concomitant **13** accompaniment

adjust
◇ anagram indicator
03 fit, fix, set **04** gang, sort, suit, tram, true, tune **05** adapt, align, alter, amend, coapt, frame, shape, tweak **06** change, modify, reduce, repair, revise, settle, square, temper **07** arrange, balance, compose, concert, conform, convert, dispose, measure, rectify, remodel, reshape **08** fine-tune, modulate, register, regulate **09** get used to, harmonize, reconcile, refashion **11** accommodate **14** grow accustomed **15** make adjustments

adjustable
07 movable **08** flexible **09** adaptable, alterable, versatile **10** modifiable **11** convertible

adjustment
◇ anagram indicator
03 adj **04** COLA **06** change, fixing, tuning **07** fitting, setting, shaping **08** ordering, revision, tweaking **09** amendment, arranging **10** adaptation, alteration, coaptation, conforming, conversion, fine-tuning, regulation, settlement, settling in **11** arrangement, habituation, orientation, rearranging, remodelling **12** modification, settling down **13** accommodation, getting used to, harmonization, rearrangement, rectification **14** naturalization, reconciliation **15** acclimatization

adjutant
03 adj **04** adjt **06** argala **07** marabou **08** marabout

ad-lib
06 freely, invent, made-up, make up, wing it **09** extempore, impromptu, improvise **10** improvised, off the cuff, unprepared **11** extemporize, impulsively, play it by ear, spontaneous, unrehearsed **12** extemporized **13** spontaneously **14** extemporaneous, unpremeditated **15** speak off the cuff

administer
◇ anagram indicator
03 run **04** drug, give, head, lead, rule **05** anele, apply, fetch, guide **06** direct, govern, impose, manage, supply **07** adhibit, conduct, control, deliver, dole out, execute, exhibit, give out, mete out, oversee, provide **08** disburse, dispense, organize, regulate **09** discharge, officiate, supervise **10** distribute, measure out **11** preside over, superintend

administration
05 admin **06** regime, ruling, senate **07** cabinet, command, control, council, red tape, running **08** congress, ministry **09** direction, discharge, execution, executive, governing, paperwork, provision, supplying **10** government, imposition, leadership, management, overseeing, parliament **11** application, supervision **12** directorship, dispensation, organization, powers that be, term of office **13** administering, governing body **15** superintendence

administrative
09 executive **10** management, managerial, regulatory **11** directorial, legislative, supervisory **12** governmental **13** authoritative, gubernatorial **14** organizational

Administrative areas include:
04 area, city, town, ward, zila, zone **05** shire, state, theme **06** county, oblast, parish, region, sector, zillah **07** borough, commune, enclave, pargana, village **08** district, division, precinct, province, township **09** pergunnah, territory **11** conurbation **12** constituency, municipality

See also **borough**; **council**; **county**; **department**; **district**; **province**; **state**

administrator
04 boss, head **05** chief, elder, ruler **06** bigwig, leader, top dog **07** manager, trustee **08** big noise, chairman, director, governor, guardian, overseer **09** big cheese, commander, custodian, executive, organizer, patrician, president **10** controller, supervisor **11** dispensator **14** chief executive, judicial factor,

superintendent **15** director-general, judicial trustee

admirable
04 cool, fine, rare **05** brill **06** choice, wicked, worthy **07** slammin' **08** laudable, masterly, slamming, superior, terrific, valuable **09** deserving, estimable, excellent, exquisite, respected, wonderful **10** creditable **11** commendable, exceptional, magnificent, meritorious **12** praiseworthy, second to none **14** out of this world

admirably
09 eminently, supremely **11** commendably, deservingly, excellently, wonderfully **13** exceptionally, magnificently

admiral
02 AF, RA, VA **03** Adm **07** capitan, navarch, vanessa

Admirals include:
04 Byng (George, Viscount Torrington), Hood (Samuel, Viscount), Howe (Richard, Earl), Togo (Heihachiro, Count) **05** Blake (Robert), Croft, Doria (Andrea), Hawke (Edward, Lord), Rooke (Sir George) **06** Beatty (David, Earl), Benbow (John), Dönitz (Karl), Fisher (John, Lord), Grasse (François, Comte de), Halsey (William F, Jnr), Nelson (Horatio, Lord), Nimitz (Chester), Raeder (Erich), Vernon (Edward) **07** Old Grog, Tirpitz (Alfred von), Wrangel (Ferdinand, Baron von) **08** Cochrane (Thomas), Jellicoe (John, Earl) **09** Artemisia **10** Villeneuve (Pierre Charles) **11** Collingwood (Cuthbert, Lord), Mountbatten (Louis, Earl)

admiration
03 yen **04** mana **05** kudos **06** esteem, fureur, praise, regard, wonder **07** acclaim, delight, idolism, respect, worship **08** approval, pleasure, surprise **09** adoration, adulation, affection, amazement, reverence **10** high esteem, high regard, veneration **11** approbation, hero-worship **12** appreciation, astonishment, commendation
• **expression of admiration**
01 O **02** oh **03** man, wow **05** golly, wowee **06** by Jove **07** caramba, gee whiz, respect

admire
04 laud, like **05** adore, prize, value **06** esteem, praise, revere, wonder **07** applaud, approve, iconize, idolize, respect, worship **08** look up to, venerate **09** approve of **10** appreciate **11** hero-worship **12** esteem highly, like very much **13** think highly of **14** put on a pedestal **15** think the world of

admirer
03 fan **04** beau, buff **05** fiend, freak, lover, wooer **06** suitor **07** amateur,

beloved, devotee, gallant
08 adherent, disciple, follower, idolater, idolator, idolizer
09 boyfriend, supporter
10 aficionado, enthusiast, girlfriend, sweetheart, worshipper

admissible
02 OK **05** legit, licit **06** lawful
07 allowed **08** passable **09** allowable, permitted, tolerable, tolerated
10 acceptable, legitimate **11** justifiable, permissible

admission
06 access, avowal, entrée, exposé
07 ingress, peccavi **08** entrance, granting, mea culpa **09** allowance
10 acceptance, admittance, concession, confession, confidence, disclosure, divulgence, ordination, permission, profession, revelation
11 affirmation, declaration, entrance fee, entry charge, recognition
12 admission fee, asseveration, grande entrée, right of entry **13** right of access
14 acknowledgment
15 acknowledgement, enfranchisement

admit
◊ *containment indicator*
03 gie, own **04** give, take **05** adopt, agree, allow, enter, grant, let in, own up, yield **06** accept, affirm, fess up, ordain, reveal, take in **07** adhibit, concede, confess, declare, divulge, embrace, profess, receive, swear in, welcome
08 blurt out, disclose, initiate, intromit
09 come clean, introduce, recognize
10 allow entry, give access
11 acknowledge, matriculate **12** allow to enter, eat your words **13** give admission

admittance
05 entry **06** access, entrée **07** ingress
08 audience, entrance **09** admission, admitting, letting in, reception
10 acceptance, initiation
12 introduction, right of entry **13** right of access

admitted
05 given **07** confest, granted
08 accepted, affirmed, declared
09 confessed, confirmed, professed
10 recognized **12** acknowledged

admittedly
07 granted **08** avowedly **09** allowedly, certainly **11** confessedly

admitting
03 tho' **06** though

admixture
03 mix **05** alloy, blend **06** fusion
07 amalgam, mixture **08** compound, tincture **10** commixture
11 combination **12** amalgamation, intermixture

admonish
04 warn **05** chide, scold **06** berate, exhort, rebuke, school **07** censure, correct, counsel, reprove, tell off,

upbraid **09** reprimand **10** discipline
13 tear a strip off

admonition
05 pi-jaw **06** advice, earful, rebuke
07 censure, counsel, reproof, warning, wigging **08** berating, moniment, monument, scolding **09** reprimand
10 correction, telling-off, ticking-off
11 exhortation **12** dressing-down, reprehension

ad nauseam
08 boringly **09** endlessly
10 constantly **11** continually, perpetually **12** continuously, interminably, monotonously

ado
04 flap, fuss, stir, to-do **05** hoo-ha, tizzy **06** bother, bustle, hassle
07 stashie, stishie, stushie, trouble
08 stooshie **09** commotion
10 difficulty, hurly-burly **11** piece of work **12** song and dance

adolescence
05 teens, youth **07** boyhood, puberty
08 girlhood, minority **10** boyishness, immaturity, juvenility, pubescence
11 development, girlishness
12 juvenescence, teenage years, youthfulness **14** young adulthood

adolescent
03 ned, Ted **04** teen **05** minor, young, youth **06** boyish, neanic **07** girlish, growing, puerile, teenage **08** childish, immature, juvenile, subadult, Teddy boy, teenager, youthful **09** infantile, pubescent, Teddy girl **10** bobbysoxer, developing, young adult
11 juvenescent, young person

adopt
◊ *containment indicator*
04 back, take, vote **05** elect **06** accept, assume, borrow, choose, father, follow, foster, mother, ratify, select, take in, take on, take up **07** appoint, approve, embrace, endorse, espouse, support
08 arrogate, decide on, maintain, nominate, settle on **10** naturalize
11 appropriate **13** take as your own

adoption
04 vote **06** choice **07** backing, support
08 approval, election, espousal, taking-in, taking-on, taking-up **09** embracing, fostering, selection **10** acceptance, nomination **11** appointment, approbation, embracement, endorsement **12** ratification
13 appropriation **15** taking as your own

adorable
04 dear **05** sweet **07** darling, lovable, winning, winsome **08** charming, fetching, pleasing, precious
09 appealing, wonderful **10** attractive, bewitching, delightful, enchanting
11 captivating

adoration
04 love **06** esteem, homage, praise, regard **07** worship **08** devotion, doting on, idolatry **09** laudation,

reverence **10** admiration, cherishing, exaltation, high regard, veneration
11 idolization **12** thanksgiving
13 glorification, magnification

adore
04 love **05** enjoy **06** admire, dote on, esteem, honour, relish, revere, savour
07 cherish, worship **08** be fond of, hold dear, venerate **10** idolatrize **11** be devoted to, be partial to **12** enjoy greatly, esteem highly, like very much
15 think the world of

adorn
04 deck, dink, do up, gild, trim
05 array, begem, besee, crown, dight, dress, grace, paint **06** aguise, attire, attrap, bedeck, doll up, enrich, honour, invest, ornate, set out, tart up
07 adonize, apparel, bedight, bedizen, bejewel, bestick, commend, emblaze, enhance, festoon, furbish, garnish, impearl, miniate **08** beautify, decorate, emblazon, ornament **09** bespangle, embellish **10** illustrate

adornment
05 frill **06** fallal **07** decking, falbala, figgery, flounce, garnish, gilding
08 frippery, furbelow, ornament
09 accessory, fallalery, fandangle, garnishry, garniture, jewellery, trappings, trimmings **10** decorating, decoration, enrichment, ornateness, tawdry lace **11** bedizenment
13 embellishment, ornamentation
14 beautification

adrift
◊ *anagram indicator*
04 lost **05** at sea **07** aimless
08 drifting, goalless, insecure, rootless
09 off course, unsettled **10** anchorless, unanchored **11** disoriented
13 directionless, disorientated

adroit
04 able, deft, neat, pert **05** adept, slick, trick **06** clever, expert, habile
07 skilful **08** dextrous, tactical
09 dexterous, ingenious, masterful
10 proficient **11** resourceful

adroitly
04 ably **06** deftly **08** cleverly, expertly
09 skilfully **11** dexterously, masterfully
12 proficiently **13** resourcefully

adroitness
05 skill **07** ability, address, finesse, mastery **08** deftness, facility
09 adeptness, dexterity, expertise
10 cleverness, competence
11 proficiency, skilfulness
15 resourcefulness

adulation
06 praise **07** fawning, incense
08 flattery **10** admiration, sycophancy
11 assentation, bootlicking, hero worship, idolization **12** blandishment
13 pats on the back **15** personality cult

adulatory
07 fawning, fulsome, servile
08 praising, unctuous **10** flattering,

obsequious **11** blandishing, bootlicking, sycophantic **13** complimentary

adult
01 A, X **03** man **04** blue, ripe **05** of age, woman **06** fruity, mature, sleazy, X-rated **07** grown-up, obscene, raunchy, ripened **08** hard-core, indecent **09** developed, full-grown **10** fully-grown **11** grown person, near the bone **12** fully-fledged, pornographic **14** near the knuckle

adulterate
04 card, lime, load **05** taint, water **06** debase, defile, dilute, weaken **07** corrupt, degrade, devalue, falsify, pollute, vitiate **09** attenuate, water down **10** bastardize, make impure **11** contaminate, deteriorate **12** sophisticate

adulteration
08 dilution **09** pollution, vitiation, weakening **10** corruption, debasement, defilement **13** contamination, deterioration

adulterer
03 cad **04** rake, roué, stud, wolf **05** flirt **06** lecher **07** Don Juan, playboy **08** Casanova, deceiver **09** avouterer, ladies' man, libertine, womanizer **10** lady-killer, profligate **11** philanderer

adulterous
05 false **08** cheating, disloyal **09** deceitful, faithless, two-timing **10** inconstant, unfaithful

adultery
06 affair **07** avoutry, liaison **08** cheating **09** two-timing **10** flirtation, infidelity, misconduct, unchastity **11** fornication **12** entanglement **13** a bit on the side, playing around **14** unfaithfulness **15** extramarital sex, playing the field

advance
01 a **03** pay, sub **04** ante, cite, give, grow, help, lend, loan, pass, push, rise, seek, step **05** early, march, offer, prior, raise **06** adduce, allege, assist, avaunt, better, come on, credit, foster, growth, incede, move on, submit, supply, thrive **07** benefit, deposit, develop, forward, furnish, further, go ahead, headway, imprest, improve, leading, present, proceed, proffer, promote, prosper, provide, suggest, support, upgrade **08** flourish, get ahead, increase, move in on, progress, retainer, vanguard **09** go forward **10** betterment, facilitate, forge ahead, gain ground, prepayment, put forward **11** advancement, come forward, development, down payment, furtherance, improvement, make earlier, make headway, move forward, preliminary, progression, step forward **12** amelioration, breakthrough, bring forward, going forward, make progress, pay in advance, surge forward **13** expeditionary, moving

forward, pay beforehand **14** onward movement **15** forward movement, marching forward

• in advance
02 on **05** ahead, early **06** sooner **07** earlier, forward, in front, up front **09** aforehand, in the lead **10** beforehand, previously **11** ahead of time **14** in the forefront

advanced
01 a **03** far **04** high, lent, shot **05** ahead, early **06** higher, hi-tech, onward **07** complex, forward, leading **08** foremost, high-tech, up-to-date **09** high-level **10** avant-garde, precocious **11** progressive, ultra-modern **13** sophisticated, state-of-the art **14** forward-looking **15** ahead of the times

advancement
04 gain, rise **06** ascent, growth **07** advance, headway **08** progress **09** evolution, promotion, upgrading **10** betterment, furthering, preferment, proceeding, upward step **11** development, furtherance, improvement **12** kick upstairs

advances
05 moves, offer **08** approach **09** addresses, overtures **10** approaches, attentions, suggestion **11** proposition

advantage
02 ad **03** aid, pro, use, van **04** boon, boot, edge, gain, good, head, help, lead, odds, plus, pull, sake, sted, sway **05** asset, avail, cause, favor, fruit, prise, prize, stead, value **06** beauty, favour, ground, pay-off, profit, reward, virtue **07** account, benefit, box-seat, service, utility, vantage, welfare **08** blessing, eminence, interest, leverage, whip hand **09** dominance, emolument, good point, head start, obvention, plus point, privilege, upper hand **10** assistance, percentage, perquisite, precedence, proceeding, usefulness, whip handle **11** convenience, helpfulness, pre-eminence, superiority, weather gage **12** weather gauge **14** on the windy side

advantageous
04 plus **06** useful **07** gainful, helpful **08** valuable **09** favorable, of service, opportune, rewarding **10** beneficial, convenient, favourable, profitable, propitious, worthwhile **11** furthersome, serviceable **12** of assistance, remunerative

advent
03 adv **04** dawn **05** birth, onset **06** coming **07** arrival, looming **08** approach, entrance **09** accession, beginning, emergence, inception **10** appearance, occurrence **12** introduction

adventitious
07 foreign **09** unplanned **10** accidental, additional, fortuitous,

unexpected, unforeseen, unintended **12** uncalculated

adventure
04 gest, kick, risk **05** kicks, peril, quest **06** aunter, chance, danger, hazard, thrill **07** exploit, romance, venture **08** escapade, incident **09** happening **10** enterprise, excitement, experience, occurrence **11** speculation, undertaking

adventurer
04 hero **06** pirate **07** heroine, Ulysses, voyager **08** Argonaut, Odysseus, venturer, wanderer **09** daredevil, traveller **10** filibuster, speculator **11** bandeirante, enterpriser, opportunist **12** carpetbagger, swashbuckler

adventurous
04 bold, rash **05** gutsy, risky **06** daring, spunky **07** dareful **08** exciting, intrepid, perilous, reckless, romantic **09** audacious, dangerous, daredevil, hazardous, impetuous **10** headstrong, precarious **11** venturesome **12** enterprising **13** swashbuckling

adversary
03 foe **05** enemy, rival, Satan **07** opposer **08** attacker, copemate, opponent **09** assailant, copes-mate **10** antagonist, competitor, contestant

adverse
05 cross **06** thwart **07** awkward, counter, harmful, hostile, hurtful, opposed, unlucky **08** contrary, negative, opposing, opposite, perverse, untoward **09** injurious **10** unfriendly **11** conflicting, detrimental, inexpedient, inopportune, uncongenial, unfortunate **12** antagonistic, inauspicious, unfavourable, unpropitious **15** disadvantageous

adversely
09 harmfully, unluckily **10** negatively **12** unfavourably **13** detrimentally, unfortunately **14** inauspiciously, unpropitiously

adversity
03 woe **04** hell **05** cross, trial **06** misery, sorrow **07** bad luck, ill luck, reverse, the pits, trouble **08** calamity, disaster, distress, hardship, traverse **09** hard times, suffering **10** affliction, ill fortune, living hell, misfortune, perversity **11** catastrophe, tribulation **12** wretchedness

advertise
04 bark, bill, hype, plug, post, puff, push, sell, tout **05** boost, quack, trail **06** inform, market, notify, poster, praise, talk up **07** declare, display, promote, publish **08** announce, proclaim **09** broadcast, make known, publicize **10** make public, promulgate **11** merchandize

advertisement
02 ad, PR **04** bill, hype, plug, puff
05 blurb, promo **06** advert, jingle,
notice, poster, teaser, tele-ad, want ad
07 display, handout, leaflet, placard,
trailer **08** banner ad, bulletin,
circular, handbill **09** marketing,
promotion, publicity, throwaway
10 commercial, propaganda
12 announcement

advice
03 tip **04** help, rede, reed, view, word
05 reede **06** notice, wisdom
07 caution, conseil, counsel, opinion,
warning **08** guidance **09** direction
10 admonition, injunction,
memorandum, suggestion
11 counselling, dos and don'ts,
information, instruction **12** notification
13 communication, encouragement
14 recommendation
• **source of advice**
03 CAB **10** counsellor

advisability
06 wisdom **07** aptness **08** prudence
09 soundness **10** expediency
11 suitability **12** desirability
13 judiciousness, preferability
15 appropriateness

advisable
03 apt, fit **04** best, well, wise **05** sound
06 proper, wisest **07** correct, fitting,
politic, prudent **08** sensible, suitable
09 desirable, expedient, judicious,
suggested **10** beneficial, preferable,
profitable **11** appropriate,
recommended

advise
04 read, rede, tell, urge, vise, warn
05 guide, reede, teach, tutor
06 enjoin, inform, notify, preach,
report **07** apprise, caution, commend,
counsel, suggest **08** acquaint, fill in on,
forewarn, instruct **09** make known,
recommend **10** give notice **11** give
counsel **12** give guidance **14** give the
low-down **15** give suggestions, make
suggestions

advisedly
06 wisely **09** carefully, prudently
10 cautiously **11** judiciously
13 intentionally

adviser
03 IFA **04** aide, guru **05** angel, coach,
guide, tutor **06** Egeria, helper, lawyer,
mentor, minder **07** counsel, monitor,
starets, staretz, teacher **08** assessor
09 agony aunt, authority, confidant,
therapist, town clerk **10** confidante,
consultant, counsellor, instructor, law-
officer, pensionary **12** amicus curiae,
right-hand man **13** company doctor
14 right-hand woman **15** Attorney-
General

advisory
03 adv **07** helping **08** advising
10 consulting **11** counselling
12 consultative, consultatory,
recommending

advocacy
06 avowry **07** backing, defence,
pushing, support **08** adoption,
espousal, proposal **09** patronage,
promotion, upholding
11 advancement, campaigning,
championing, propagation
12 promulgation **13** encouragement,
justification **14** recommendation

advocate
02 KC, QC **03** adv **04** back, peat, plug,
urge **05** adopt, be pro, lobby
06 advise, back up, defend, favour,
lawyer, preach, syndic, uphold
07 counsel, endorse, espouse, justify,
pleader, promote, propose, push for,
speaker, support **08** argue for,
attorney, be behind, champion,
defender, exponent, plead for,
preacher, press for, promoter, upholder
09 barrister, believe in, encourage,
paraclete, patronize, prescribe,
proponent, recommend, solicitor,
spokesman, supporter **10** campaigner,
evangelist, vindicator **11** campaign for,
countenance, protagonist,
spokeswoman, subscribe to **12** King's
Counsel, spokesperson **13** Queen's
Counsel **14** sympathize with

aegis
04 wing **06** favour **07** backing,
support **08** advocacy, auspices
09 patronage **10** protection
11 sponsorship **12** championship,
guardianship

aeon
03 age, eon, era **04** span, time, year
05 epoch, years **08** duration, eternity
10 generation

aerate
06 excite, gasify **07** lighten, perturb,
refresh **09** oxygenate, ventilate **10** put
air into **13** charge with air, charge with
gas

aerial
04 aery, dish, yagi **05** aerie **06** dipole,
duplex, midair **07** aeolian, antenna,
booster, scanner **08** air-to-air, in the
air, radiator, receiver, squarial
13 satellite dish **14** above the ground

aeroplane
03 bus **04** kite **05** crate
See also **aircraft**

aesthetic
04 arty, fine **07** elegant, stylish
08 adorning, artistic, tasteful
10 decorative, ornamental
11 beautifying **12** embellishing
15 greenery-yallery

afar
06 far off **07** far away **08** a long way
09 distantly **13** a long distance

affability
06 warmth **08** courtesy, facility,
matiness, mildness, openness
09 benignity, geniality, palliness
10 amiability, chumminess, cordiality,
good humour, good nature, kindliness

11 amicability, benevolence,
sociability **12** congeniality,
friendliness, graciousness,
obligingness, pleasantness
15 approachability, conversableness

affable
04 maty, mild, open, warm **05** matey,
pally, suave **06** chummy, facile, genial,
kindly **07** amiable, cordial **08** amicable,
friendly, gracious, obliging, pleasant,
sociable **09** agreeable, congenial,
courteous, expansive **10** benevolent,
soft-spoken **11** good-natured
12 approachable, good-humoured

affair
02 go **03** biz **04** gear, love, ploy, shew,
show **05** amour, cause, event, fling,
issue, thing, topic **06** effeir, effere,
matter, pidgin, pigeon **07** affaire, carry-
on, concern, episode, funeral, liaison,
pidgeon, project, romance, shebang,
subject **08** activity, amour fou,
business, hypothec, incident, interest,
intrigue, question **09** happening,
operation **10** love affair, occurrence,
proceeding **11** transaction,
undertaking **12** circumstance,
relationship **13** affaire d'amour, grande
passion **14** affaire de coeur,
responsibility

affect
03 hit **04** do to, fake, faze, move, sham,
stir, sway, take **05** act on, adopt, alter,
amove, assay, feign, pinch, put on, taint,
throw, touch, up-end, upset
06 assume, attack, change, impact,
modify, regard, salute, strike **07** apply
to, concern, disturb, imitate, impress,
involve, perturb, pretend, profess,
trouble **08** bear upon, come home,
interest, overcome, relate to, simulate
09 influence, transform **10** do things
to, take hold of **11** counterfeit, impinge
upon, prevail over **14** have an effect on

affectation
03 act **04** airs, pose, sham, show
06 façade **07** charade, foppery,
ladyism **08** pretence, pretense
09 affection, imitation, mannerism
10 appearance, minauderie,
simulation **11** insincerity, theatricism
12 false display **13** airs and graces,
artificiality **15** pretentiousness

affected
◇ *anagram indicator*
04 camp, fake, posy, sham, twee
05 ditsy, ditzy, posey, put-on, stiff
06 chichi, la-di-da, phoney
07 assumed, feigned, foppish,
mincing, minikin, pompous, stuck up,
studied **08** literose, mannered,
precious **09** contrived, insincere,
simpering, simulated, unnatural
10 artificial, euphuistic, histrionic,
hoity-toity **11** counterfeit, highfalutin,
pretentious **12** highfaluting,
histrionical, niminy-piminy

affecting
03 sad **06** moving **07** piteous, pitiful
08 pathetic, pitiable, poignant,

powerful, stirring, touching
09 troubling **10** impressive **12** heart-rending **13** heartbreaking

affection
03 luv **04** care, love **05** amity
06 caring, desire, favour, liking, storge, warmth **07** feeling, passion, worship
08 calf-love, devotion, fondness, goodwill, kindness, localism, penchant
10 attachment, endearment, partiality, proclivity, propensity, tenderness, topophilia **11** inclination
12 friendliness, predilection
14 predisposition

affectionate
04 fond, kind, warm **05** eager
06 caring, doting, loving, tender
07 adoring, amiable, cordial, devoted, fervent, fulsome **08** attached, friendly, Platonic, sisterly **09** brotherly
10 passionate **11** warm-hearted

affectionately
06 dearly, fondly, kindly, warmly
07 amiably **08** lovingly, tenderly
09 adoringly, cordially, devotedly

affiliate
04 ally, join **05** annex, merge, unite
06 team up **07** combine, conjoin, connect, filiate **09** associate, syndicate
10 amalgamate, fraternize
11 confederate, incorporate **12** band together

affiliated
06 allied **07** related **08** in league
09 connected **10** associated, integrated **11** amalgamated
12 incorporated **13** in partnership

affiliation
03 tie **04** bond, link **05** union
06 league, merger **07** joining
08 alliance **09** coalition, filiation
10 connection, federation, membership **11** association, combination **12** amalgamation, relationship **13** confederation, incorporation

affinity
03 kin **04** bond **06** kinred, liking
07 analogy, empathy, kindred, kinship, rapport **08** affiance, fondness, homology, likeness, sympathy
09 chemistry, good terms
10 attraction, partiality, propensity, similarity, similitude **11** resemblance
12 relationship **13** comparability, compatibility **14** correspondence, predisposition

affirm
03 say **04** aver, avow **05** state, swear
06 adhere, assert, attest, avouch, ratify, uphold **07** certify, confirm, declare, endorse, support, testify, witness
08 maintain **09** predicate, pronounce
10 asseverate **11** corroborate

affirmation
02 ay **03** aye, yes **04** oath **06** avowal
07 protest, witness **08** averment
09 assertion, statement, testimony

10 affirmance, avouchment, deposition **11** attestation, declaration, endorsement **12** asseveration, confirmation, ratification
13 certification, corroboration, pronouncement

affirmative
02 ay, OK **03** aye, yea, yes
08 agreeing, dogmatic, emphatic, positive **09** agreement, approving, assenting, asserting, assertory
10 acceptance, concurring, confirming, consenting
11 concurrence, predicatory
12 acquiescence, confirmation, ratification **13** corroborative

affix
03 add, put, tag **04** bind, glue, join, tack **05** annex, paste, pin on, set to, stick **06** adhere, adjoin, append, attach, fasten, prefix, suffix
07 connect, subjoin **09** privative
13 frequentative

afflict
03 ail, try **04** harm, hurt, pain, prey
05 assay, beset, curse, gripe, smite, visit, wound **06** bother, burden, grieve, harass, plague, strain, stress, strike
07 anguish, inflict, oppress, scourge, torment, torture, trouble **08** distress, lacerate **09** persecute **12** bear hard upon

afflicted
◇ *anagram indicator*
03 ill, sad **04** hurt, sick, sore **05** beset, woful **06** cursed, humble, pained, struck, woeful **07** injured, laid low, plagued, wounded, wracked
08 affected, bothered, burdened, harassed, strained, stricken, tortured, troubled **09** aggrieved, anguished, depressed, disturbed, miserable, oppressed, sorrowful, suffering, tormented **10** distressed, overthrown
11 traumatized **13** grief-stricken

affliction
03 woe **04** care, pain, sore, teen, tene, tine, tyne **05** anger, cross, curse, grief, night, teene, trial **06** misery, ordeal, plague, sorrow, unweal **07** disease, furnace, illness, languor, scourge, torment, trouble **08** calamity, disaster, distress, hardship, sickness
09 adversity, suffering **10** depression, heart-grief, misfortune, visitation
11 tribulation **12** wretchedness

affluence
06 inflow, plenty, riches, wealth
07 fortune, tidy sum **08** opulence, property **09** abundance, megabucks, profusion, substance **10** easy street, prosperity **11** wealthiness

affluent
04 rich **05** flush **06** loaded
07 moneyed, opulent, wealthy, well-off **08** well-to-do **09** abounding, inflowing **10** in the money, prosperous, well-heeled **11** comfortable, rolling in it **12** on easy street

afford
04 bear, give **05** allow, grant, offer, spare, yield **06** answer, impart, manage, pay for, supply **07** furnish, present, produce, provide, sustain
08 generate **09** stretch to **11** be able to pay **13** have enough for **15** have the money for

affordable
05 cheap **06** budget **07** low-cost
08 moderate **09** dirt cheap, low-priced **10** economical, manageable, reasonable **11** inexpensive, sustainable

affray
03 row **04** fear, feud, fray, riot
05 brawl, brush, fight, mêlée, scrap, set-to **06** fracas, tussle **07** contest, disturb, punch-up, quarrel, scuffle, startle, wrangle **08** frighten, skirmish, squabble **10** fisticuffs, free-for-all
11 disturbance

affront
03 vex **04** face, slur, snub **05** abuse, anger, annoy, facer, pique, wrong
06 injury, insult, offend, slight
07 incense, offence, outrage, provoke
08 confront, dishonor, irritate, rudeness, vexation **09** aspersion, dishonour, displease, indignity
10 disrespect **11** discourtesy, provocation **13** slap in the face **14** kick in the teeth

affronted
05 angry, vexed **06** piqued
07 annoyed, injured **08** incensed, insulted, offended, outraged, slighted
09 irritated **10** displeased

Afghanistan
03 AFG

aficionado
03 fan, nut **04** buff **05** fiend, freak
06 expert **07** admirer, devotee
09 authority **10** enthusiast, specialist
11 connoisseur

aflame
02 in **03** lit **05** aglow, lit up **06** ablaze, alight, bright, on fire **07** burning, ignited, lighted, radiant, shining
11 illuminated

afloat
05 aswim, at sea, awash, sound
06 viable **07** buoyant, solvent, unfixed
08 drifting, floating, swimming, watching **09** out of debt **10** in the black, unsinkable

afoot
02 up **05** about, agate, astir
06 abroad, around **07** brewing, current, going on **08** in the air **09** in the wind **10** going about **11** circulating
13 in the pipeline

aforementioned
04 this **07** the same **09** aforesaid
10 aforenamed

afraid
03 rad **04** nesh **05** adrad, adred, afear, sorry, timid **06** afeard, aghast, craven,

feared, scared **07** affeard, alarmed, anxious, daunted, fearful, nervous **08** affrayed, cowardly, effraide, timorous **09** concerned, petrified, regretful, reluctant, terrified, tremulous **10** apologetic, frightened, suspicious **11** distrustful, in a blue funk, intimidated **12** apprehensive, faint-hearted, in a cold sweat **13** having kittens, panic-stricken, scared to death
• **be afraid**
05 quake

afresh
◊ *anagram indicator*
04 anew **05** again, newly **08** once more **09** once again, over again

Africa

African countries include:

04 Chad, Mali, Togo
05 Benin, Congo, Egypt, Gabon, Ghana, Kenya, Libya, Niger, Sudan
06 Angola, Guinea, Malawi, Rwanda, Uganda, Zambia
07 Algeria, Burundi, Comoros, Eritrea, Lesotho, Liberia, Morocco, Namibia, Nigeria, Senegal, Somalia, Tunisia
08 Botswana, Cameroon, Djibouti, Ethiopia, Tanzania, Zimbabwe
09 Cape Verde, Mauritius, Swaziland, The Gambia
10 Madagascar, Mauritania, Mozambique, Seychelles
11 Burkina Faso, Côte d'Ivoire, Sierra Leone, South Africa
12 Guinea-Bissau
13 Western Sahara
16 Equatorial Guinea
18 São Tomé and Príncipe
22 Central African Republic
28 Democratic Republic of the Congo

African landmarks include:

04 Giza, Nile
05 Congo, Luxor
06 Karnak, Sphinx
07 Zambezi
08 Aswan Dam, Kalahari, Lake Chad, Okavango, Pyramids
09 Lake Nyasa, Masai Mara, River Nile, Serengeti, Suez Canal
10 Lake Malawi, Lake Nasser, River Congo, River Niger
11 Drakensberg, Great Sphinx, Kilimanjaro, Luxor Temple
12 Aswan High Dam, Great Pyramid, Lake Victoria, Sahara Desert, Zambezi River
13 Mt Kilimanjaro, Okavango Delta, Table Mountain, Victoria Falls
14 Atlas Mountains, Cape of Good Hope, Kalahari Desert, Lake Tanganyika
15 Great Rift Valley

African

Africans include:

03 Ibo, Kru, Twi
04 Boer, Efik, Igbo, Kroo, Moor, Susu, Tshi, Zulu
05 Masai, Swazi, Temne, Tonga

06 Griqua, Herero, Kenyan, Kikuyu, Libyan, Malian, Somali, Tuareg, Yoruba
07 Angolan, Basotho, Chadian, Gambian, Guinean, Ivorian, Mosotho, Rwandan, Sahrawi, Swahili, Ugandan, Zambian
08 Algerian, Batswana, Beninese, Egyptian, Eritrean, Gabonese, Ghanaian, Liberian, Malagasy, Malawian, Moroccan, Motswana, Namibian, Nigerian, Nigerien, Sahraoui, Sudanese, Togolese, Tunisian
09 Burkinabé, Burundian, Congolese, Ethiopian, Sahrawian, Santoméan, São Toméan, Tanzanian
10 Djiboutian, Mozambican, Sahraouian, Senegalese, Zimbabwean
11 Cameroonian, Cape Verdean, Mauritanian
12 South African
13 Equatoguinean, Sierra Leonean
14 Central African, Guinea-Bissauan

after
◊ *juxtaposition indicator*
02 on **03** epi-, for **04** past **05** about, since **06** behind **07** chasing, owing to, wanting **09** because of, following, posterior, regarding **10** concerning, in honour of **11** as a result of, in pursuit of, on account of, trying to get **12** subsequent to, with regard to **15** in consequence of
• **after all**
08 in the end **09** most of all, primarily **10** first of all **12** nevertheless **15** most importantly
• **after that**
04 then **05** later
• **after which**
04 when
• **immediately after**
04 next
• **not after**
02 by
• **until after**
04 over

after-effect
06 result, upshot **07** spin-off **09** aftermath **11** consequence **12** repercussion

aftermath
03 end **04** rawn, wake **05** rowan **06** rawing, rowing, upshot **07** effects, fallout, outcome, results **08** backwash **10** lattermath **11** aftergrowth **12** after-effects, consequences **13** repercussions

afternoon
01 a **02** pm **04** arvo **06** undern **07** evening **12** postmeridian
• **pleasant Sunday afternoon**
03 PSA

afterpiece
03 jig **05** exode

afterthought
02 PS **03** PPS **05** rider **07** codicil **10** postscript

afterwards
03 eft **04** next, syne, then **05** later **07** later on **09** after that, thereupon **12** subsequently

again
02 do, re **03** eft **04** anew, back, more, over, then **05** ditto **06** afresh, encore, iterum **07** further **08** once more, yet again **09** once again, over again **11** another time, one more time
• **again and again**
05 often **10** constantly, frequently, repeatedly **11** continually **12** time and again

against
◊ *juxtaposition indicator*
01 v **02** on, to, vs **03** con **04** anti **06** facing, versus **07** harmful **08** abutting, fronting, in case of, opposing, touching **09** close up to, hostile to, opposed to, resisting **10** adjacent to, opposite to **11** confronting, detrimental, in the face of, prejudicial **12** in contrast to, in defiance of, unfavourable **13** in contact with **14** antagonistic to, in opposition to **15** disadvantageous

agate
04 onyx **05** afoot, astir, murra **06** astray, murrha, pebble **10** Mocha stone **11** chalcedonyx, dendrachate **12** Scotch pebble

agave
05 sisal **06** maguey **08** henequen, henequin, heniquin **12** American aloe, century plant

age
03 day, eon, era, yug **04** aeon, date, days, span, time, yuga **05** epoch, ripen, years **06** dotage, grow up, mature, mellow, old age, period, season, wither **07** century, decline, grow old **08** duration, maturity, senility **09** become old, come of age, seniority **10** degenerate, generation, senescence **11** decrepitude, deteriorate, elderliness **14** advancing years, declining years

See also **old age**

aged
02 ae, of **03** aet, old **04** grey **05** aging, hoary **06** ageing, mature, past it, senior **07** ancient, doddery, elderly **08** advanced, wintered **09** geriatric, getting on, senescent **11** over the hill, patriarchal **13** superannuated **15** advanced in years, no spring chicken

agency
04 firm, work **05** force, means, power **06** action, bureau, effect, medium, office **07** company, vehicle **08** activity, business, workings **09** influence, mechanism, operation **10** department **11** involvement **12** intervention, organization **15** instrumentality

See also **news**; **spy**

agenda
04 list, menu, plan **05** diary
06 scheme **08** calendar, schedule, to-do list **09** programme, timetable
12 scheme of work

agent
03 agt, Fed, rep, spy, way **04** Bond, doer, G-man, mole, narc, nark, root, spie, wait **05** cause, envoy, force, means, mover, narco, plant, proxy, route, spial, spook **06** agency, beagle, broker, deputy, engine, factor, medium, setter, shadow, source, worker **07** channel, liaison, sleeper, trustee, vehicle **08** assignee, delegate, emissary, Mata Hari, minister, mouchard, operator **09** go-between, middleman, operative, performer
10 instrument, negotiator, substitute
11 double agent, functionary
12 intermediary **14** representative
See also **publicity**

age-old
03 old **04** aged **07** ancient, antique, very old **08** primeval, time-worn
09 long-lived, primaeval

agglomeration
04 mass **05** stash, store **07** build-up
08 increase **09** aggregate, gathering, stockpile **10** collection **11** aggregation
12 accumulation, augmentation

aggrandize
05 exalt, widen **06** enrich **07** advance, amplify, dignify, elevate, enhance, enlarge, ennoble, glorify, inflate, magnify, promote, upgrade
09 glamorize **10** exaggerate, make richer

aggrandizement
09 elevation, promotion **10** exaltation
11 advancement, enhancement, enlargement **12** exaggeration
13 magnification

aggravate
03 irk, try, vex **05** annoy, get at, tease
06 harass, needle, pester, wind up, worsen **07** incense, inflame, magnify, provoke **08** compound, heighten, increase, irritate **09** intensify, make worse **10** exacerbate, exaggerate, exasperate

aggravation
05 aggro **06** hassle **07** teasing
08 vexation **09** annoyance
10 irritation **11** irksomeness, provocation **12** exasperation **15** thorn in the flesh

aggregate
03 ore, ped, sum **04** full, mass **05** gross, total, whole **06** amount, domain, entire
08 assemble, combined, complete, dendrite, detritus, entirety, manifold, point set, potstone, sum total, totality
09 complexus, inclusive, summation
10 collection, generality, grand total
11 accumulated, combination, total amount, whole amount
12 accumulation **13** comprehensive, hypersthenite

aggression
04 rage, raid **06** attack, injury, strike
07 air rage, assault, offence
08 invasion, road rage **09** hostility, incursion, intrusion, militancy, offensive, onslaught, pugnacity
10 antagonism **11** bellicosity, provocation **12** belligerence, encroachment, forcefulness, infringement **13** combativeness
14 aggressiveness

aggressive
04 bold **05** lairy, pushy **06** bad-ass, brutal, chippy, feisty, full-on, savage
07 bullish, go-ahead, hostile, kick-ass, zealous **08** forceful, invasive, ruthless, vigorous **09** assertive, bellicose, combative, cut-throat, ferocious, incursive, intrusive, in-yer-face, offensive, truculent **10** in-your-face, pugnacious **11** bareknuckle, belligerent, competitive, contentious, destructive, provocative, quarrelsome
12 bareknuckled **13** argumentative

aggressor
07 invader **08** attacker, intruder, offender, provoker **09** assailant, assaulter **10** instigator

aggrieved
◇ *anagram indicator*
04 hurt, sore **05** angry, upset **06** bitter, miffed, pained, peeved **07** annoyed, ill-used, injured, unhappy, wronged
08 insulted, offended, saddened
09 pissed off, resentful **10** distressed, maltreated **11** disgruntled

aghast
06 amazed **07** shocked, stunned
08 appalled, dismayed, startled
09 astounded, horrified, stupefied
10 astonished, confounded **12** horror-struck **13** thunderstruck

agile
◇ *anagram indicator*
04 deft, spry **05** acute, alert, brisk, fleet, lithe, nifty, quick, sharp, swank, swift, withy **06** active, astute, clever, limber, lissom, lively, mobile, nimble, supple **07** lissome **08** athletic, flexible **09** dexterous, sprightly
11 quick-witted

agility
08 deftness, mobility **09** alertness, briskness, quickness, sharpness, swiftness **10** activeness, astuteness, liveliness, nimbleness, suppleness
11 flexibility **15** quick-wittedness

agitate
◇ *anagram indicator*
03 vex **04** beat, faze, fuss, heat, poss, rile, rock, stir, toss **05** alarm, argue, blend, churn, fight, rouse, shake, upset, whisk, worry **06** arouse, battle, betoss, dither, excite, flurry, incite, rattle, ruffle, rumble, stir up, wind up, work up
07 commove, confuse, disturb, ferment, fluster, inflame, perturb, torment, trouble, unnerve
08 campaign, convulse, disquiet,

distract, kefuffle, unsettle **09** carfuffle, curfuffle, kerfuffle, stimulate
10 discompose, disconcert, perturbate

agitated
◇ *anagram indicator*
04 wild **05** het up, upset **06** heated, hectic, mobled, stormy **07** agitato, anxious, excited, nervous, ruffled, worried **08** hopped-up, in a tizzy, troubled, unnerved **09** disturbed, ebullient, flustered, in a lather, steamed up, troublous, unsettled, wrought up
10 distraught, tumultuous
11 highwrought **12** all of a dither, all of a doodah, disconcerted **14** hot and bothered

agitation
04 fret **05** alarm, tweak, worry
06 battle, flurry, frenzy, jabble, lather, motion, moving, pucker, ruffle, taking
07 anxiety, beating, concern, crusade, emotion, fanteeg, ferment, fluster, flutter, shaking, tempest, tension, tossing, trouble, turning **08** blending, disquiet, distress, fantigue, fighting, kefuffle, movement, stirring, striving, struggle, whisking **09** carfuffle, commotion, curfuffle, kerfuffle
10 ebullition, excitement
11 campaigning, distraction, disturbance, jactitation, trepidation
12 perturbation, restlessness

agitator
07 inciter, stirrer **08** activist, fomenter
09 Bolshevik, firebrand **10** instigator, subversive **12** rabble-rouser, troublemaker **13** revolutionary

agnostic
07 doubter, sceptic **08** doubting
09 sceptical **10** questioner, unbeliever
11 questioning, unbelieving
12 disbelieving **14** doubting Thomas

ago
04 back, gone, past, syne **05** since
06 before **07** earlier **09** in the past
10 previously **12** from that time

agog
04 avid, keen **05** eager **07** anxious, curious, excited, pop-eyed
09 impatient **10** enthralled, in suspense **12** enthusiastic **13** on tenterhooks

agonize
04 fret **05** worry **06** labour, strain, strive **07** contend, trouble, wrestle
08 struggle

agonizing
07 painful, racking **08** piercing, worrying **09** harrowing, torturous
10 tormenting **11** distressing
12 excruciating, heart-rending

agony
03 woe **04** hurt, pain **05** spasm
06 misery, throes **07** anguish, torment, torture **08** distress **09** suffering
10 affliction **11** tribulation
12 wretchedness

agrarian
07 bucolic, farming, georgic, predial
08 geoponic, praedial 09 agronomic
10 cultivated 12 agricultural

agree
02 OK 03 fit, yes 04 gree, jibe, jump,
okay, sort, suit 05 admit, align, aline,
allow, apply, atone, chime, close, fadge,
get on, grant, match, tally, yield
06 accede, accept, accord, adhere,
assent, assort, attone, clinch, comply,
concur, cotton, decide, go with,
permit, settle, square 07 be at one,
comport, concede, concord, conform,
congree, congrue, consent, consort,
paction 08 coincide, compound, hit it
off, say yes to, strike in 09 determine,
harmonize, subscribe, symbolize
10 compromise, condescend,
correspond, fall in with, homologate,
underwrite 11 acquiesce in, be of one
mind, go along with, meet halfway,
rubber-stamp, see eye to eye 12 be
consistent, share the view 14 give the
go-ahead, strike a bargain 15 give the
thumbs-up, make concessions

agreeable
04 fine, kind, nice 05 jolly, sapid
07 likable, willing 08 amenable,
amicable, charming, euphonic,
friendly, likeable, pleasant
09 compliant, congenial, desirable,
enjoyable, toothsome 10 acceptable,
attractive, delightful, euphonical,
euphonious 11 complaisant,
conformable, good-natured,
sympathetic 12 approachable
13 companionable, consentaneous

agreeably
09 enjoyably 10 acceptably,
pleasantly, pleasingly 11 accordingly
12 attractively, delightfully

agreement
03 agt, FTA 04 amen, band, deal,
deed, GATT, pact, repo, whiz
05 chime, covin, NAFTA, tally, union,
whizz 06 accord, assent, comart,
covyne, pre-nup, treaty, unison
07 analogy, bargain, closing, compact,
concert, concord, consent, consort,
contrat, entente, fitting, harmony,
syntony 08 affinity, contract,
covenant, matching, Mercosur,
sortance, sponsion, sympathy
09 Ausgleich, collusion, community,
concordat, consensus, indenture,
unanimity 10 compliance, conformity,
congruence, congruency, consonance,
convention, settlement, similarity,
uniformity 11 arrangement,
concordance, concurrence,
consistence, consistency,
respondence, supersedere,
transaction 12 complaisance
13 compatibility, embellishment,
understanding 14 correspondence,
correspondency
See also **treaty**

• **expression of agreement**
01 I 02 ay, OK 03 aye, oke, olé

04 amen, done, good, okay, sure
05 right, uh-huh, wilco 06 quotha,
rather, righto 07 d'accord, right-ho

agricultural
05 rural 06 farmed 07 bucolic,
farming, georgic 08 agrarian,
geoponic, pastoral, praedial
09 agronomic 10 cultivated,
geoponical 11 countryside
See also **farm**

agriculture
03 agr 04 plow 06 plough
07 farming, tillage, tilling
08 agronomy 09 geoponics,
husbandry 10 agronomics
11 agroscience, cultivation
12 agribusiness

Agriculturists include:
04 Coke (Thomas William), Tull
(Jethro)
05 Lawes (Sir John Bennet), Young
(Arthur)
06 Carver (George Washington)
07 Borlaug (Norman), Burbank
(Luther)
08 Bakewell (Robert)
09 McCormick (Cyrus)
12 Boussingault (Jean-Baptiste)

aground
05 stuck 06 ashore, neaped
07 beached, wrecked 08 grounded,
marooned, stranded 09 foundered
10 high and dry, on the rocks

ague
◇ *anagram indicator*
05 exies, fever 07 malaria 10 the
shivers

ah
02 ay, la 10 alas the day 12 alas the
while

ahead
◇ *juxtaposition indicator*
02 up 05 forth 06 before, onward
07 forward, in front, leading, onwards,
winning 08 advanced, forwards,
headlong, superior 09 at the head,
earlier on, in advance, in the lead, to the
fore 13 at an advantage, in the
vanguard 14 in the forefront

aid
04 ease, gift, hand, help, prop
05 boost, grant, serve 06 a leg up,
assist, backup, favour, hasten, oblige,
relief, second 07 backing, benefit,
charity, funding, promote, relieve,
service, speed up, subsidy, succour,
support, sustain 08 donation,
expedite 09 encourage, patronage,
subsidize 10 assistance, facilitate, rally
round, subvention 11 accommodate,
helping hand, sponsorship
12 contribution 13 a shot in the arm,
co-operate with, encouragement

aide
02 PA 06 minder, Sherpa 07 adviser,
attaché 08 adjutant, advocate,
disciple, follower 09 assistant,
confidant, supporter 10 aide-de-camp,

confidante 12 right-hand man 14 right-
hand woman

ail
04 fail, pain 05 upset, worry
06 bother, sicken, weaken 07 afflict,
trouble 08 distress, irritate
13 indisposition

ailing
03 ill 04 poor, sick, weak 05 frail, unfit
06 feeble, infirm, poorly, sickly, unwell
07 failing, invalid, unsound
08 diseased 09 deficient, insolvent,
off-colour, suffering 10 foundering,
inadequate, indisposed, out of sorts
11 debilitated, languishing 12 in poor
health 15 under the weather

ailment
03 ill, pip 04 waff, worm 05 cough
06 malady 07 disease, illness, passion
08 disorder, sickness, weakness
09 complaint, infection, infirmity
10 affliction, disability 11 dog's disease
13 indisposition

aim
03 end, eye, try 04 bend, goal, gole,
hope, mark, mean, plan, sake, seek,
vizy, want, wish 05 dream, ettle, level,
point, sight, telos, train, visie 06 aspire,
course, design, desire, direct, intend,
intent, line up, motive, object, scheme,
strive, target, vizzie 07 attempt,
mission, propose, purpose, resolve,
shoot at, take aim 08 ambition, zero in
on 09 direction, endeavour, intention,
objective 10 aspiration 11 work
towards 15 set your sights on

aimless
05 stray 06 chance, futile, random
07 erratic, wayward 08 drifting,
goalless, rambling, unguided
09 haphazard, pointless, shiftless,
unsettled, wandering 10 irresolute,
undirected 11 purposeless,
unmotivated 13 directionless,
unpredictable

air
03 sky 04 aero-, aria, aura, ayre, lift,
lilt, look, mien, puff, song, tell, tune,
waft, wind 05 blast, dirge, ditty, ether,
ozone, state, utter, voice, whiff
06 aerate, allure, aspect, breath,
breeze, demean, effect, expose,
manner, oxygen, reveal, screen, zephyr
07 arietta, bearing, canzona, canzone,
declare, demaine, demayne, demeane,
divulge, draught, express, feeling,
freshen, heavens, publish
08 ambience, carriage, cavatina,
disclose, fresh air, serenade
09 broadcast, character, circulate,
demeanour, make known, publicize,
ventilate 10 appearance, atmosphere,
expression, give vent to, impression,
make public 11 chansonette,
communicate, disseminate, have your
say 13 speak your mind
• **air defence**
02 AD
• **Air Transport Association**
03 ATA

airbed
04 Lilo®

airborne
02 a/b 06 flying 07 winging
08 hovering, in flight, in the air

aircraft

Aircraft include:

01 B, F
03 jet, MiG
04 Hawk, kite, Moth, STOL, VTOL
05 blimp, Comet, jumbo, Piper, plane, Stuka
06 Airbus®, Boeing, bomber, Cessna, copter, Fokker, glider, Mirage, Nimrod
07 airship, air taxi, balloon, biplane, Chinook, chopper, fighter, Halifax, Harrier, jump-jet, prop-jet, Tornado, Tristar, Typhoon
08 airliner, Blenheim, Concorde, Hercules, jumbo jet, Mosquito, seaplane, Spitfire, spy plane, superjet, triplane, turbojet, warplane, Zeppelin
09 aeroplane, amphibian, aquaplane, Boeing 747, delta-wing, dirigible, freighter, Gipsy Moth, Hurricane, Lancaster, monoplane, swing-wing, Tiger Moth, turboprop, two-seater
10 dive-bomber, hang-glider, helicopter, microlight, Sunderland, Wellington, whirlybird
11 battleplane, de Havilland, Flying Tiger, intercepter, rocket plane, Thunderbolt
12 air ambulance, single-seater, Sopwith Camel, troop-carrier
13 hot-air balloon, Messerschmitt, Stealth Bomber

Aircraft include:

04 R101
06 Bell X-1
07 Voyager
08 Enola Gay
09 Winnie Mae
10 Hindenburg
11 Air Force One, Lucky Lady II, Spruce Goose, Wright Flyer
12 Graf Zeppelin, Memphis Belle
15 Spirit of St Louis

Aircraft parts include:

03 fin, rib
04 cowl, flap, hood, skid, wing
05 cabin, radar, radio, stick
06 canopy, engine, rudder
07 aileron, ammeter, cockpit, cowling, fairing, tail fin, winglet
08 elevator, fuselage, intercom, joystick, tail boom, turbojet, wing flap
09 altimeter, nose wheel, propeller, tailplane, tail wheel
10 flight deck
11 chronometer, landing flap, landing gear, vertical fin
12 control stick, equilibrator, radio compass, rudder pedals
13 accelerometer, control column, undercarriage
14 radar altimeter
15 landing-carriage, magnetic compass

aircraftsman, aircraftswoman
02 AC 03 ACW, erk, LAC 04 LACW

air force
03 RAF 04 RAAF, RCAF, USAF, WAAF, WRAF 05 RNZAF, WRAAF
06 RAuxAF 09 Luftwaffe 11 Flying Corps

See also **rank**

airily
07 lightly, readily 08 breezily, casually, jauntily 10 flippantly 12 nonchalantly
14 light-heartedly

airing
07 venting, voicing 08 aeration, exposure, uttering 09 broadcast, statement 10 disclosure, divulgence, expression, freshening, refreshing, revelation 11 circulation, declaration, making known, publication, ventilation 13 communication, dissemination

airless
05 close, heavy, muggy, musty, stale
06 stuffy, sultry 08 stifling
10 breathless, oppressive
11 suffocating 12 unventilated
15 badly ventilated

airline

Airlines include:

02 BA, UA
03 BEA, BMI, JAL, KLM, PIA, SAS, TWA
04 BOAC, El Al
05 Pan Am
06 Qantas
07 EasyJet, Ryanair
08 Aeroflot, Alitalia
09 Aer Lingus, Air Canada, Air France, Lufthansa
13 Air New Zealand, Cathay Pacific
14 British Airways, British Midland, United Airlines, Virgin Atlantic

airman
02 AC, AR 03 ace, erk, LAC

airport
08 STOLport 09 aerodrome, vertiport

Airports include:

03 JFK, Zia
04 Orly
05 Luton, McCoy, O'Hare
06 Cannon, Changi, Dulles, Midway, V C Bird
07 Ataturk, Bradley, D F Malan, Entebbe, Gatwick, Hopkins, Lincoln, Lubbock, Roberts
08 Ciampino, El Dorado, G Marconi, Heathrow, Jan Smuts, La Aurora, McCarran, Mohamed V, Sangster, Schiphol, Stansted
09 Ben Gurion, Charleroi, Fiumicino, James M Cox, J F Kennedy, Jose Marti, Lindbergh, Marco Polo, Queen Alia
10 George Bush, Golden Rock, Hellenikon, John Lennon, King Khaled, Louis Botha, Sky Harbour, Will Rogers
11 Capodichino, Jorge Chavez, Las Americas, Ninoy Aquino, Owen Roberts, Pointe Noire, Tito Menniti
12 Benito Juarez, Berline-Tegel, Eduardo Gomes, Hancock Field, Indira Gandhi, Jomo Kenyatta, Norman Manley, Queen Beatrix, Simon Bolivar
13 Château Bougon, Chiang Kai Shek, Grantley Adams, King Abdul Aziz, Mariscal Sucre, Robert Mueller
14 Galileo Galilei, Juan Santa Maria, Kingsford Smith, Lester B Pearson, Murtala Mohamed
15 Augusto C Sandino, Charles de Gaulle, General Mitchell, Hamilton Kindley, Leonardo da Vinci, Theodore Francis

airs
05 swank 06 frills, posing 07 hauteur
09 arrogance, pomposity
10 snootiness 11 affectation, haughtiness, pretensions
12 affectedness 13 artificiality
15 pretentiousness

airtight
06 closed, sealed 08 flawless
09 windtight 10 conclusive
11 impermeable, indubitable, irrefutable 12 impenetrable, indisputable, tight-fitting 13 beyond dispute, incontestable 14 beyond question, unquestionable

airy
04 open 05 blowy, fresh, gusty, happy, roomy, windy 06 aerial, breezy, casual, jaunty, lively 07 offhand 08 cheerful, draughty, ethereal, etherial, flippant, spacious 09 spiritual, sprightly
10 immaterial, intangible, nonchalant, spirit-like 11 incorporeal 12 high-spirited, light-hearted 13 unsubstantial
14 well-ventilated

aisle
04 lane, path 07 gangway, passage, walkway 08 alleyway, corridor
10 passageway 12 deambulatory

ajar
04 agee, ajee, open 08 half open, unbolted, unclosed, unlocked
09 unlatched 10 unfastened
12 slightly open

akin
03 sib 04 like, near, sibb 05 close, sybbe 07 related, similar 08 congener
10 comparable, equivalent
13 corresponding

Alabama
02 AL 03 Ala

alacrity
06 ardour 07 fervour 08 keenness
09 briskness, eagerness, readiness
10 enthusiasm, impatience, promptness 11 willingness

alarm
◇ *anagram indicator*
03 din **04** bell, fear, horn **05** alert, daunt, larum, panic, scare, shock, siren **06** arouse, beat up, dismay, fright, horror, rattle, terror, tirrit, tocsin **07** agitate, anxiety, perturb, startle, terrify, unnerve, warning, whistle **08** affright, distress, frighten, Teasmade® **09** alarm-bell **10** make afraid, uneasiness **11** nervousness, trepidation **12** apprehension, danger signal, perturbation, put the wind up **13** consternation, smoke detector **14** distress signal

alarming
05 scary **07** ominous **08** daunting, dreadful, shocking, worrying **09** dismaying, startling, unnerving **10** disturbing, perturbing, terrifying **11** distressing, frightening, threatening

alarmist
09 doomsayer, jitterbug, pessimist **11** doomwatcher, scaremonger **12** doom-merchant **13** prophet of doom

alas
02 ay **03** out **04** haro, waly **06** harrow **07** welaway **08** waesucks, welladay, wellaway **09** alack-a-day, wellanear

Alaska
02 AK

Albania
02 AL **03** ALB

albatross
10 gooneybird, Quaker-bird

Alberta
02 AB

album
04 disc

albumin
05 ricin **06** myogen **08** leucosin

alchemist
05 adept **06** chemic **08** spagyric **09** spagyrist

alcohol
03 jar **04** bowl, diol, grog, lush, slug **05** booze, drink, juice, mahua, mahwa, sauce, skink, tinct **06** fuddle, gutrot, liquor, sterol, strunt, tiddly, tipple **07** butanol, ethanol, liqueur, mannite, shebeen, spirits, xylitol **08** catechol, farnesol, geraniol, glycerin, glycerol, linalool, mannitol, methanol, propanol, stimulus **09** aqua vitae, firewater, glycerine, hard stuff, the bottle **10** intoxicant **11** jungle juice, sphingosine, strong drink, the creature, tickle-brain **12** Dutch courage, spirit of wine

See also **drink**

• **low in alcohol**
04 lite

alcoholic
03 sot **04** alky, hard, lush, soak, wino **05** alkie, bloat, dipso, drunk, souse, toper **06** ardent, boozer, brewed, sponge, strong **07** Bacchus, drinker, tippler, tosspot **08** drunkard, habitual **09** distilled, fermented, inebriate **10** spirituous, wine-bibber **11** dipsomaniac, hard drinker, inebriating **12** heavy drinker, intoxicating

See also **drink**

• **very alcoholic**
04 hard

alcove
03 bay **04** nook **05** booth, niche **06** carrel, corner, recess, shrine **07** carrell, cubicle, dinette, opening **09** cubbyhole, ingleneuk, inglenook **11** compartment

alderman
02 CA **03** Ald **09** ealdorman

Alderney
03 GBA

ale
03 nog **04** beer, mild, nogg, purl **05** nappy, swats **06** alegar, tipper **07** morocco, October **08** heavy wet, twopenny **10** barley-bree, barley-broo **11** barley-broth

alehouse *see* **pub**

alert
04 gleg, warn, wary **05** agile, alarm, awake, brisk, quick, ready, shake, sharp **06** active, inform, lively, nimble, notice, notify, signal, sprack, tip off, tip-off **07** apprise, careful, caution, heedful, warning **08** all there, forewarn, prepared, spirited, vigilant, watchful **09** attentive, observant, on the ball, on the spot, sharp-eyed, up to snuff, wide-awake **10** on your toes, perceptive, presential, wake-up call **11** circumspect, sharp-witted **12** notification, on the lookout, on the qui vive

alertness
08 wariness **09** vigilance **10** observance **12** watchfulness **14** attentivenenss, perceptiveness **15** sharp-wittedness

alga, algae

Algae and lichens include:

05 chara, manna, usnea **06** archil, corkir, crotal, desmid, diatom, korkir, nostoc, volvox **07** crottle, cup moss, euglena, oak lump, parella, seaweed, Valonia **08** anabaena, conferva, frustule, lecanora, lungwort, pond scum, red algae, sea ivory, stonerag, stoneraw, tree moss, Ulothrix, wall moss, wartwort **09** chlorella, cup lichen, Isokontae, rock tripe, spirogyra, stonewort **10** brown algae, Conjugatae, cyanophyte, fallen star, green algae, heterocont, heterokont, rock violet, water bloom **11** blanketweed, Iceland moss, manna-lichen, Protococcus **12** Cyanophyceae, Phaeophyceae, reindeer moss, Rhodophyceae, stromatolite, water flowers **13** chlamydomonas, Protococcales, Schizophyceae, witches' butter **14** blue-green algae, cyanobacterium, dinoflagellate

See also **seaweed**

Algeria
02 DZ **03** Alg, DZA

alias
03 aka, née **06** anonym **07** allonym, moniker, pen name **08** formerly, monicker, nickname **09** false name, otherwise, pseudonym, sobriquet, stage name **10** also called, nom de plume, soubriquet **11** also known as, assumed name, nom de guerre **14** under the name of

alibi
05 story **06** excuse, reason **07** cover-up, defence, pretext **11** explanation, vindication **13** justification

alien
02 ET **03** LGM, odd **05** metic **06** exotic, remote **07** foreign, incomer, Martian, opposed, strange, unusual **08** contrary, forinsec, inimical, newcomer, outsider, peculiar, stranger **09** estranged, foreigner, immigrant, non-native, offensive, repugnant **10** extraneous, forinsecal, outlandish, unfamiliar **11** conflicting, incongruous **12** antagonistic, incompatible **14** little green man

alienate
05 sever **06** cut off, devest **07** divorce, turn off **08** amortize, estrange, separate, turn away **09** disaffect **10** antagonize, set against **11** make hostile

alienation
07 divorce, rupture **08** disunion **09** diversion, isolation, severance **10** detachment, remoteness, separation **11** turning away **12** disaffection, estrangement, indifference **14** antagonization

alight
02 in **03** lit, pop **04** fall, land, rest **05** alive, avail, avale, fiery, light, lit up, perch, pitch **06** ablaze, aflame, availe, bright, debark, get off, lively, on fire, settle, strike **07** blazing, burning, descend, detrain, flaming, get down, ignited, lighted, radiant, shining **08** come down, dismount, gleaming **09** brilliant, disembark, touch down **10** come to rest, disentrain **11** illuminated

align
04 ally, even, join, side, tram **05** agree, order, range, unite **06** adjust, even up, line up **07** arrange, combine **08** regulate **09** affiliate, associate, co-operate, orientate **10** co-ordinate, join forces, regularize, straighten, sympathize **12** make parallel

alignment
04 line 05 order 06 lining, siding
07 ranging 08 alliance, lining up,
sympathy 09 agreement 10 alineation
11 affiliation, allineation, arrangement,
association, co-operation
13 straightening

alike
04 akin, even 05 equal, samey 06 at
once 07 cognate, equally, similar, the
same, uniform 08 in common,
matching, parallel 09 analogous,
duplicate, identical, similarly
10 comparable, equivalent,
resembling 11 analogously, much the
same 12 in the same way
13 corresponding 15 correspondingly

alimony
06 upkeep 07 aliment, support
08 palimony 09 allowance
11 maintenance 12 child support

alive
04 live, vive 05 alert, awake, brisk,
quick, vital 06 active, chirpy, extant,
full of, lively, living 07 alert to, animate,
awake to, aware of, in force, running,
vibrant, working, zestful 08 animated,
existent, spirited, vigorous
09 breathing, energetic, heedful of, on
the hoof, surviving, to the fore,
vivacious 10 carrying on, full of life,
having life, in the flesh 11 abounding in,
above-ground, cognizant of,
conscious of, functioning, going
strong, in existence, in operation,
sensitive to, teeming with 12 crawling
with, swarming with, thronged with
15 overflowing with

alkaloid
06 emetin, harmin, theine 07 atropin,
betaine, brucine, caffein, cocaine,
codeine, coniine, emetine, harmine,
morphia, narceen 08 atropine,
caffeine, curarine, cytisine, daturine,
harmalin, hyoscine, ibogaine, lobeline,
mescalin, morphine, narceine,
nicotine, piperine, thebaine, veratrin
09 aconitine, bebeerine, berberine,
chaconine, ephedrine, gelsemine,
harmaline, mescaline, muscarine,
narcotine, quinidine, rhoeadine,
sparteine, veratrine, yohimbine
10 apomorphia, cinchonine,
colchicine, corydaline, ergotamine,
papaverine, pilocarpin, strychnine
11 apomorphine, gelseminine,
hyoscyamine, pilocarpine,
scopolamine, theobromine, vincristine
15 castanospermine

all
01 a' 03 sum 04 each, even, full, just
05 every, fully, quite, total, tutti, utter,
whole 06 apiece, entire, the lot,
utmost, wholly 07 perfect, totally,
utterly 08 complete, entirely, entirety,
everyone, greatest, outright
09 aggregate, everybody, wholesale
10 altogether, completely, every bit of,
every one of, everything, infinitely, the
whole of 11 every single, total amount,

whole amount 12 each and every,
universality 13 in its entirety
• **at all**
03 any, ava, eer 04 ever 10 oughtlings
14 in the slightest

allay
04 calm, cool, ease, stay 05 blunt,
check, quell, quiet, slake 06 alegge,
allege, lessen, pacify, reduce, smooth,
soften, solace, soothe, stanch
subdew, subdue 07 allegge, appease,
assuage, compose, mollify, relieve,
smoothe, staunch 08 decrease,
diminish, moderate 09 alleviate
12 tranquillize

allegation
04 plea 05 claim, story 06 avowal,
charge 07 surmise 08 averment,
citation 09 assertion, statement,
testimony 10 accusation, deposition,
profession 11 affirmation, declaration
12 asseveration

allege
04 aver, hold, urge 05 allay, claim,
plead, state, trump 06 affirm, assert,
attest, insist, obtend 07 contend,
declare, profess 08 maintain
09 alleviate, represent 10 asseverate,
put forward

alleged
06 stated 07 claimed, dubious,
reputed, suspect 08 declared,
doubtful, inferred, putative, so-called,
supposed 09 described, professed,
purported 10 designated, ostensible

allegedly
09 dubiously 10 apparently, doubtfully,
ostensibly, putatively, reportedly,
supposedly 11 purportedly 13 by all
accounts

allegiance
03 foy 04 duty 06 fealty 07 loyalty,
support 08 devotion, fidelity,
liegedom 09 adherence, constancy,
obedience 10 friendship, obligation,
solidarity 12 faithfulness

allegorical
06 mystic 07 typical 08 symbolic
09 parabolic 10 emblematic,
figurative 11 symbolizing
12 metaphorical 13 significative
14 representative

allegory
04 myth, tale 05 fable, story
06 emblem, legend, symbol
07 analogy, parable 08 apologue,
metaphor 09 symbolism
10 comparison

allergic
06 averse 07 hostile, opposed
08 affected 09 sensitive
11 disinclined, dyspathetic, susceptible
12 antagonistic 14 hypersensitive

allergy
08 aversion, dyspathy 09 antipathy,
hostility 10 antagonism, opposition
11 sensitivity 14 disinclination,
susceptibility

alleviate
04 alay, dull, ease, kill 05 abate, aleye,
allay, check 06 alegge, allege, deaden,
lessen, reduce, soften, soothe, subdue,
temper 07 allegge, assuage, cushion,
mollify, relieve 08 diminish, mitigate,
moderate, palliate 14 take the edge off

alleviation
06 easing, relief 07 dulling
08 soothing 09 abatement,
deadening, lessening, reduction
10 allegeance, diminution, mitigation,
moderation, palliation 11 aleggeaunce,
assuagement, consolation
13 mollification

alley
03 taw 04 gate, lane, mall, road, walk,
wynd 05 close 06 ginnel, marble,
street, vennel 07 dead end, passage,
pathway 08 alleyway, cul-de-sac, pall-
mall, rope-walk 10 back street,
passageway

alliance
04 axis, bloc, bond, NATO, pact
05 Anzus, guild, union 06 cartel,
league, treaty 07 compact, kinship
08 marriage 09 agreement, coalition,
concordat, syndicate 10 connection,
consortium, federation, Warsaw Pact
11 affiliation, association, combination,
confederacy, partnership
12 conglomerate, consociation,
popular front 13 confederation

allied
03 wed 05 bound, joint 06 agnate,
joined, linked, united 07 cognate,
connate, coupled, kindred, married,
related, unified 08 combined, in
league 09 connected, federated, in
cahoots 10 affiliated, associated
11 amalgamated, confederate, hand in
glove 12 confederated

allocate
04 mete, task 05 allot, allow, issue
06 assign, budget, divide, ration
07 deal out, dole out, earmark, mete
out 08 dispense, set aside, share out
09 admeasure, apportion, designate,
parcel out 10 distribute

allocation
03 cut, lot 05 grant, quota, share, stint,
whack 06 budget, ration 07 measure,
portion 09 allotment, allowance,
giving-out 10 sharing-out
12 distribution 13 apportionment
14 slice of the cake

allot
03 lot 04 aret, mete, rate, sort
05 allow, arett, grant, stint, teene
06 affect, assign, budget, divide, ration
07 dole out, earmark, mete out,
portion 08 allocate, dispense, set
aside, share out 09 admeasure,
apportion, designate 10 distribute

allotment
03 cut, lot 04 land, plot 05 grant,
quota, share, stint, whack 06 ration
07 measure, portion 08 division
09 allowance, partition 10 allocation,

percentage, plot of land **12** distribution
13 apportionment **14** slice of the cake

all-out
04 full **05** total **06** utmost
07 maximum **08** complete, forceful,
powerful, resolute, thorough, vigorous
09 energetic, full-scale, intensive,
undivided, unlimited, unstinted,
wholesale **10** determined, exhaustive,
forcefully, powerfully, resolutely,
thoroughly, vigorously **11** intensively,
unremitting **12** determinedly,
exhaustively, unrestrained
13 comprehensive, energetically, no-
holds-barred, thoroughgoing,
unremittingly

allow
02 OK **03** let, own **04** give, okay
05 admit, agree, allot, grant, spare
06 afford, assign, beteem, enable,
endure, permit, suffer **07** agree to,
approve, beteeme, concede, confess,
consent, earmark, provide, warrant
08 allocate, sanction, say yes to, set
aside, tolerate **09** apportion,
authorize, consent to, give leave, put
up with **11** acknowledge **15** give your
consent
• **allow for**
07 foresee, include, plan for
08 consider **09** budget for **10** arrange
for, bear in mind, keep in mind, provide
for **15** take into account

allowable
02 OK **04** okay **05** legal, legit, licit
06 lawful **07** rulable **08** all right,
approved **09** excusable
10 acceptable, admissible, legitimate
11 appropriate, justifiable, permissible
12 sanctionable

allowance
03 DLA, fya, ICA, JSA, law, lot, RDA
04 diet, feed, mags, size, tare, tret
05 batta, cloff, grant, maggs, quota,
ratio, share, stint **06** amount, budget,
corody, income, livery, milage, ration,
rebate, sequel **07** aliment, alimony,
annuity, benefit, bursary, charter,
corrody, dietary, leakage, mileage,
payment, pension, portion, provand,
provend, stipend, subsidy, windage
08 discount, expenses, latitude,
pittance, proviant **09** baby bonus,
deduction, reduction, risk money, salt-
money, strike pay, weighting
10 allocation, assistance, concession,
exhibition, husbandage, percentage,
privy purse, remittance, table money,
toleration **11** appointment, deferred
pay, maintenance, pocket money
12 child benefit, contribution,
severance pay **15** capitation grant
• **make allowances**
06 excuse, pardon **07** condone,
forgive **08** bear with, consider,
overlook **10** bear in mind, keep in mind
15 take into account

allowed
02 OK **03** let **04** luit, okay **05** legal,
legit, licit **06** lawful **08** accepted, all

right, approved **09** of warrant,
permitted, tolerated **10** authorized

alloy
◇ *anagram indicator*
04 bras **05** blend, brass, Invar®, metal,
potin, terne **06** Alnico®, Babbitt, billon,
bronze, eureka, fusion, latten,
Magnox®, occamy, ormolu, oroide,
pewter, solder, tambac, tombac,
tombak **07** amalgam, Babbitt,
chromel, mixture, Nitinol, shakudo,
similor, tinfoil, tutenag **08** cast iron,
compound, electron, gunmetal,
Manganin®, Nichrome®, orichalc, pot
metal, zircaloy, Zircoloy®
09 admixture, bell-metal, composite,
Duralumin®, Dutch gold, Dutch leaf,
eutectoid, magnalium, oricalche,
pinchbeck, platinoid, shibuichi, type
metal **10** constantan, Dutch metal,
iridosmine, iridosmium, mischmetal,
Monel metal®, mosaic gold, nicrosilal
11 coalescence, combination,
cupronickel, white copper **12** fusible
metal, German silver, prince's metal
13 Babbitt's metal, speculum metal
14 Britannia metal, high-speed steel,
phosphor bronze **15** aluminium
bronze, Corinthian brass
See also **metal**

all-powerful
05 great **07** supreme **08** absolute,
almighty **10** omnipotent, pre-eminent
12 totalitarian

all-purpose
08 all-round, flexible **09** adaptable,
versatile **12** multi-purpose **14** general-
purpose

all right
02 OK **03** A-OK, yes **04** fair, fine, okay,
safe, well **05** hunky, right, sound,
sweet, whole **06** agreed, indeed,
secure, unhurt **07** average, healthy, no
doubt **08** adequate, passable,
passably, suitable, suitably, unharmed,
very well **09** allowable, all serene,
certainly, hunky-dory, uninjured
10 absolutely, acceptable, acceptably,
adequately, definitely, good enough,
reasonable, reasonably, unimpaired,
well enough **11** right as rain
12 satisfactory **13** appropriately
14 satisfactorily **15** unobjectionable,
unobjectionably, without question

allspice
07 pimento **11** calycanthus **13** Jamaica
pepper

allude
04 hint **05** imply, infer, refer **06** remark
07 mention, speak of, suggest, touch
on **08** intimate **09** adumbrate,
insinuate, touch upon

allure
02 it, SA **03** air, win **04** coax, draw,
gait, lure, mien, pull **05** charm, decoy,
tempt, train, troll **06** appeal, cajole,
disarm, entice, lead on, seduce, work
on **07** attract, beguile, enchant,
glamour, win over **08** entrance,

interest, persuade, sirenize
09 captivate, fascinate, magnetism,
seduction **10** attraction, come-hither,
enticement, temptation **11** captivation,
enchantment, fascination **13** give the
come-on

alluring
04 sexy **05** siren **06** taking
07 agaçant, winning **08** agaçante,
arousing, engaging, enticing, fetching,
inviting, sensuous, tempting, to die for
09 beguiling, desirable, glamorous,
seductive **10** attractive, bewitching,
come-hither, enchanting, intriguing
11 captivating, fascinating, interesting

allusion
04 hint **06** glance, remark
07 comment, mention **08** citation
09 quotation, reference **10** intimation,
side glance, suggestion **11** implication,
insinuation, observation

ally
03 taw **04** join, link, side **05** marry,
unify, unite **06** friend, helper, league,
marble, team up **07** combine,
connect, consort, partner **08** co-
worker, sidekick **09** accessory, affiliate,
associate, colleague, supporter
10 accomplice, amalgamate,
foederatus, fraternize, join forces
11 collaborate, confederate **12** band
together, collaborator

almanac
06 annual, Wisden **08** calendar, register,
yearbook **09** ephemeris, Whitaker's

almighty
04 huge **05** awful, great **06** severe
07 immense, intense, supreme
08 absolute, enormous, terrible
09 desperate, very great **10** invincible,
omnipotent **11** all-powerful,
exceedingly, plenipotent **12** irresistible,
overpowering, overwhelming

almond
06 comfit **07** amygdal, praline

almost
◇ *tail deletion indicator*
03 nie, sub- **04** near, nigh **05** about,
quasi- **06** all but, nearly, next to, nighly,
nigh on, uneath **07** close on, close to,
nearing **08** as good as, nigh-hand, not
quite, well-nigh **09** just about, virtually
10 more or less, not far from, pretty
much, pretty well **11** approaching,
practically **12** pretty nearly
13 approximately

alms
05 gifts **06** awmous **07** charity
08 devotion, handouts, largesse
09 donations, endowment
13 contributions

aloft
02 up **04** high **05** above **06** high up
07 aheight **08** in the air, in the sky,
overhead **12** off the ground

alone
03 sad **04** just, only, sola, sole, solo
05 apart, solus **06** lonely, simply,

single, singly, solely, unique **07** forlorn, herself, himself, insular, private, unaided, unhappy **08** by itself, deserted, desolate, detached, forsaken, high-lone, isolated, lonesome, rejected, separate, solitary, uniquely **09** destitute, miserable, on your own, on your tod **10** by yourself, cloistered, unassisted, unattended, unescorted **11** exclusively, sequestered, without help **12** single-handed **13** companionless, independently, off your own bat, unaccompanied

along
02 on, up **04** down, near **05** ahead **06** beside, next to **07** close to, further, onwards, with you **09** alongside, as company **10** adjacent to, as a partner **11** at the side of
• **all along**
06 always **07** for ever **10** all the time, constantly **11** continually
• **along with**
09 including **12** in addition to, not to mention, over and above, together with **14** to say nothing of

alongside
◊ *juxtaposition indicator*
02 by **04** near **05** aside **06** beside **08** adjacent

aloof
03 off **04** cold, cool **05** chill **06** abeigh, chilly, formal, offish, remote, skeigh **07** distant, haughty, insular, stuck-up **08** detached, reserved **09** exclusive **10** antisocial, forbidding, unfriendly, unsociable **11** indifferent, standoffish **12** inaccessible, supercilious, uninterested, unresponsive **13** unforthcoming, unsympathetic **14** unapproachable

aloud
◊ *homophone indicator*
06 loudly **07** audibly, clearly, noisily, out loud, plainly **10** à haute voix, distinctly, sonorously **12** for all to hear, intelligibly, resoundingly, vociferously

alpha
01 A

alphabet
05 abcee, absey **06** script **13** criss-cross-row **14** Christ-cross-row

Alphabets and writing systems include:
03 ABC, IPA, ITA
04 Cree, kana, ogam
05 Greek, kanji, Kufic, Latin, oghram, Roman, runic
06 Arabic, Brahmi, finger, Glagol, Hebrew, nagari, naskhi, Pinyin, romaji
07 Braille, futhark, futhorc, futhork, Glossic, linear A, linear B
08 Cyrillic, Georgian, Gurmukhi, hiragana, katakana, phonetic
09 Byzantine, cuneiform, ideograph, logograph, syllabary

10 Chalcidian, devanagari, estrangelo, pictograph
11 estranghelo, hieroglyphs
14 Augmented Roman
15 Initial Teaching

Letters of the Arabic alphabet:
02 ba, fa, ha, ra, ta, ya, za
03 ayn, dad, dai, jim, kaf, kha, lam, mim, nun, qaf, sad, sin, tha, waw, zay
04 alif, dhai, shin
05 ghayn

Letters of the English alphabet:
01 A, B, C, D, E, F, G, H, I, J, K, L, M, N, O, P, Q, R, S, T, U, V, W, X, Y, Z
02 ar, ay, ee, ef, el, em, en, es, ex, oh, wy
03 bee, cee, cue, dee, eff, eks, ell, enn, ess, eye, gee, jay, kay, kew, pee, see, tee, vee, you, zed, zee
05 aitch
06 haitch
07 double-u
09 double-you

Letters of the Greek alphabet:
02 mu, nu, pi, xi
03 chi, eta, phi, psi, rho, san, tau, vau
04 beta, iota, zeta
05 alpha, delta, gamma, kappa, koppa, omega, sampi, sigma, theta
06 lambda
07 digamma, epsilon, omicron, upsilon, ypsilon
08 episemon

Letters of the Hebrew alphabet:
02 fe, he, pe
03 bet, heh, het, kaf, mem, nun, peh, qof, sin, tav, taw, tet, vav, waw, yod
04 alef, ayin, beth, chaf, heth, kaph, khaf, koph, qoph, resh, sade, shin, teth, yodh
05 aleph, cheth, dalet, gimel, lamed, sadhe, tsadi, tzade, zayin
06 daleth, lamedh, saddhe, samech, samekh

Letters of the NATO phonetic alphabet:
04 echo, golf, kilo, lima, mike, papa, xray, zulu
05 alpha, bravo, delta, hotel, india, oscar, romeo, tango
06 juliet, quebec, sierra, victor, yankee
07 charlie, foxtrot, uniform, whiskey
08 november

already
05 by now **06** by then, so soon **07** even now, just now, so early, thus far **08** even then, hitherto **09** before now **10** beforehand, by that time, by this time, heretofore, previously **12** so soon as this

alright *see* **all right**

also
◊ *juxtaposition indicator*
03 and, eke, too **04** item, plus **06** as well **07** besides, further **08** as well as, likewise, moreover **09** along with,

including **10** in addition **11** furthermore **12** additionally

alter
◊ *anagram indicator*
04 turn, vary **05** adapt, amend, emend, shift, tweak **06** adjust, bushel, change, deform, modify, recast, reform, revise, rework **07** antique, convert, disform, distort, improve, qualify, remodel, reshape **08** airbrush, innovate **09** diversify, transform, transmute, transpose **10** manipulate, metaphrase **12** metamorphose **13** make different
• **alter ego**
04 Hyde (Mr)

alteration
◊ *anagram indicator*
05 shift, tweak **06** change **07** massage **08** revision, variance **09** amendment, reshaping, reworking, variation **10** adaptation, adjustment, conversion, difference, emendation **11** reformation, remodelling, vicissitude **12** modification **13** metamorphosis, transmutation, transposition **14** transformation **15** diversification, transfiguration

altercation
03 row, wap **04** beef, miff, whid, yike **05** broil, clash, scrap, set-to **06** barney, bicker, breach, breeze, bust-up, dust-up, fracas, fratch, ruffle, square **07** brattle, discord, dispute, punch-up, quarrel, wrangle **08** argument, squabble **09** high words, logomachy **10** dependence, difference, difficulty, dissension **12** disagreement **13** slanging match

alternate
◊ *hidden alternately indicator*
03 alt **04** vary **05** alter, other **06** change, rotate, second **07** in turns **08** rotating **09** fluctuate, oscillate, take turns **10** every other, reciprocal, substitute **11** alternating, consecutive, every second, interchange, intersperse, reciprocate **13** chop and change, interchanging, take it in turns

alternative
◊ *anagram indicator*
02 or **05** other, wacky **06** back-up, choice, fringe, option, second **07** another, oddball, unusual **08** alterant, fall-back, recourse, uncommon **09** different, duplicate, selection, surrogate **10** preference, substitute, unorthodox **12** second string **14** nontraditional, unconventional

alternatively
◊ *anagram indicator*
02 or **06** or else **07** instead **09** otherwise **13** as a substitute **14** on the other hand **15** as another option

although
03 and **04** albe, as if, when **05** while **06** albeit, even if, much as, though, whilst **07** howbeit **08** as much as

altitude

09 howsoever 10 even though
11 granted that 13 even supposing
15 notwithstanding

altitude

03 alt 05 depth 06 height 07 stature
08 tallness 09 elevation, loftiness

alto

01 a 03 alt

altogether

◊ *juxtaposition indicator*
04 alto 05 all-to, fully, in all, joint, quite,
slick, whole 06 algate, in toto, wholly
07 algates, all told, in total, overall,
totally, utterly 08 all in all, all to one,
entirely 09 perfectly 10 absolutely,
completely, holus-bolus, thoroughly
12 first and last

altruism

06 unself 10 generosity
11 benevolence, disinterest,
magnanimity 12 selflessness 13 self-
sacrifice, unselfishness
15 considerateness

altruistic

06 humane 08 generous, selfless
09 unselfish 10 benevolent, charitable
11 considerate, magnanimous
12 humanitarian 13 disinterested,
philanthropic 14 public-spirited
15 self-sacrificing

aluminium

02 Al

alumnus

02 OB 06 old boy 07 old girl

always

02 ay 03 aye, e'er 04 ever 05 still
06 algate, semper, sempre 07 algates,
forever 08 evermore 09 endlessly,
eternally, every time, regularly 10 all
the time, constantly, habitually,
invariably, repeatedly 11 continually, in
perpetuum, perpetually, unceasingly,
unfailingly 12 consistently 13 again
and again 14 on each occasion 15 on
every occasion

amalgam

05 alloy, blend, union 06 fusion,
merger 07 mixture 08 compound
09 admixture, aggregate, synthesis
10 commixture 11 coalescence,
combination

amalgamate

04 ally, fuse 05 alloy, blend, merge,
unify, unite 06 mingle 07 combine
08 coalesce, compound, intermix
09 commingle, integrate
10 homogenize, synthesize
11 incorporate

amalgamation

05 blend, union, unity 06 fusion,
merger 07 joining, merging
08 alliance, blending, compound
09 admixture, synthesis
11 coalescence, combination,
commingling, integration,
unification 13 incorporation
14 homogenization

amass

04 gain, heap, pile 05 hoard, store
06 accrue, garner, gather, heap up, pile
up 07 acquire, collect, store up
08 assemble 09 aggregate
10 accumulate, foregather
11 agglomerate, agglutinate

amateur

01 A 02 Am 03 DIY, ham 04 buff
06 layman 07 admirer, dabbler,
fancier, varment, varmint 08 armchair
09 lay person 10 aficionado,
Corinthian, dilettante, enthusiast
11 afficionado 12 do-it-yourself
15 non-professional

amateurish

03 lay 05 crude, hammy, inept
06 clumsy, unpaid 08 bungling,
inexpert 09 unskilful, untrained
10 blundering 11 incompetent,
unqualified 14 unprofessional 15 non-
professional

amatory

04 fond 05 randy 06 erotic, loving,
sexual, tender 07 amorous, lesbian
10 passionate 11 impassioned
12 affectionate

amaze

03 wow 04 daze, kill, stun 05 floor,
panic, shock 06 awhape, dazzle,
dismay 07 astound, flatten, stagger,
startle, stupefy 08 astonish, bewilder,
bowl over, confound, gobsmack,
surprise 09 dumbfound 10 disconcert,
strike dumb 11 flabbergast, knock for
six 12 blow your mind

amazed

05 dazed 06 agazed 07 floored,
stunned 08 startled 09 astounded,
surprised 10 astonished, bewildered,
gobsmacked, speechless
11 dumbfounded, open-mouthed
13 flabbergasted, thunderstruck

amazement

04 maze 05 shock 06 dismay, marvel,
wonder 08 surprise 09 confusion
10 admiration, perplexity,
wonderment 11 incredulity
12 astonishment, bewilderment,
stupefaction 13 consternation

amazing

◊ *anagram indicator*
06 awsome, far-out, unreal
07 awesome 08 dazzling, exciting,
fabulous, stunning 09 thrilling,
wonderful 10 astounding, formidable,
impressive, incredible, marvellous,
monumental, staggering, surprising
11 astonishing, bewildering, jaw-
dropping, magnificent, spectacular
12 awe-inspiring, overwhelming
13 disconcerting

amazon

06 virago 09 shield-may 10 shield-
maid 12 shield-maiden

ambassador

05 agent, elchi, envoy 06 backer,
consul, deputy, elchee, eltchi, ledger,

legate, leiger, lieger, nuncio 07 leaguer,
leidger 08 advocate, delegate,
diplomat, emissary, minister
09 pronuncio, supporter
10 campaigner 14 representative
15 plenipotentiary

ambience

03 air 04 aura, feel, mood, tone
05 tenor, vibes 06 milieu, spirit
07 climate, feeling, flavour
09 character 10 atmosphere,
impression, vibrations 11 environment
12 surroundings

ambiguity

05 doubt 06 enigma, puzzle
07 dubiety, paradox 08 polysemy
09 confusion, obscurity, vagueness
10 double-talk, woolliness
11 ambivalence, double-speak,
dubiousness, imprecision, uncertainty,
unclearness 12 doubtfulness,
equivocality, equivocation 13 double
meaning 14 double entendre

ambiguous

05 vague 06 double, louche, woolly
07 cryptic, dubious, obscure, unclear
08 confused, doubtful, oracular,
puzzling, two-edged 09 confusing,
enigmatic, equivocal, imprecise,
oraculous, uncertain 10 back-handed,
homonymous, indefinite, multivocal
11 double-edged, paradoxical
12 inconclusive 13 double-meaning,
indeterminate

ambit

04 area 05 range, realm, scope, sweep
06 bounds, extent, sphere 07 breadth,
compass 08 confines

ambition

03 aim 04 goal, hope, push, wish, zeal
05 dream, drive, graal, grail, ideal
06 design, desire, grayle, hunger,
intent, object, target, thrust 07 craving,
longing, purpose 08 striving, yearning
09 eagerness, hankering, holy grail,
objective 10 aspiration, commitment,
enterprise, get-up-and-go, initiative
11 what it takes 13 determination
15 fire in your belly

ambitious

04 bold, hard, keen 05 eager, pushy
06 driven, intent 07 arduous, driving,
emulate, go-ahead, hopeful, zealous
08 aspirant, aspiring, desirous,
exacting, full of go, striving
09 assertive, demanding, difficult,
elaborate, energetic, go-getting,
grandiose, strenuous 10 determined,
formidable, impressive, purposeful
11 challenging, industrious, power-
hungry, pretentious 12 enterprising,
enthusiastic

ambivalence

05 clash, doubt 08 conflict, wavering
09 confusion 10 hesitation,
opposition, unsureness 11 fluctuation,
uncertainty, vacillation
12 equivocation 13 contradiction,
inconsistency 14 irresoluteness

mbivalent

5 mixed **06** unsure **07** opposed,
arring **08** clashing, confused,
oubtful, hesitant, wavering
9 debatable, equivocal, uncertain,
ndecided, unsettled **10** irresolute,
nresolved **11** conflicting, fluctuating,
icillating **12** inconclusive,
consistent **13** contradictory

mble

4 pace, walk **05** drift **06** dawdle,
mble, stroll, toddle, wander
7 meander, saunter **09** promenade
0 mosey along, single-foot
perambulate

mbulance

7 pannier **09** meat wagon **10** blood-
agon

mbush

4 jump, trap, wait **05** await, lurch,
are **06** attack, entrap, turn on, waylay
7 ensnare, forelay, lay wait
8 embusqué, lie perdu, pounce on,
irprise **09** ambuscade, bushwhack,
mboscata, lie in wait, lie perdue,
aylaying **11** lay a trap for **14** surprise
tack

meliorate

4 ease, mend **05** amend **06** better,
emedy **07** benefit, elevate, enhance,
nprove, promote, rectify, relieve
8 mitigate **09** alleviate **10** make
etter

melioration

4 help **07** benefit **09** amendment,
ettering **10** mitigation, refinement
1 alleviation, enhancement,
nprovement **13** rectification

menable

4 open **06** docile **07** pliable, subject,
illing **08** biddable, flexible
9 agreeable, compliant, tractable
0 responsive, submissive
1 acquiescent, complaisant,
ersuadable, responsible, susceptible
3 accommodating

mend

anagram indicator
3 fix **04** cure, heal, mend **05** alter,
mend **06** adjust, better, change,
iodify, reform, remedy, repair, revise
7 correct, enhance, improve, qualify,
ecover, rectify, redress **08** emendate
0 ameliorate

mendment

anagram indicator
3 ERA **05** Fifth **06** change, reform,
emedy **07** adjunct **08** addendum,
ddition, revision **10** adjustment,
teration, attachment, correction,
mendation **11** corrigendum,
nhancement, improvement,
eformation **12** modification
3 clarification, qualification,
ectification

mends

7 redress **08** requital **09** atonement,
xpiation, indemnity **10** recompense,

reparation **11** restitution, restoration
12 compensation, satisfaction
15 indemnification

• make amends

05 atone

amenity

07 service, utility **08** civility, facility,
resource **09** advantage
11 arrangement, convenience,
opportunity

America

01 A **02** Am, US **03** USA **04** Amer
See also **United States of America**

04 Cuba, Peru
05 Chile, Haiti
06 Belize, Brazil, Canada, Guyana,
Mexico, Panama
07 Bolivia, Ecuador, Grenada, Jamaica,
St Lucia, Uruguay
08 Colombia, Dominica, Honduras,
Paraguay, Suriname
09 Argentina, Costa Rica, Guatemala,
Nicaragua, Venezuela
10 El Salvador, The Bahamas
15 St Kitts and Nevis
17 Antigua and Barbuda, Dominican
Republic, Trinidad and Tobago
21 United States of America
25 St Vincent and the Grenadines

South American landmarks
include:

04 moai
05 Andes, Colca, llano, Plata, Plate,
selva
06 Amazon, Iguaçu, Itaipu, Osorno,
pampas, Paraná
07 Atacama, Ipanema, Orinoco
08 Cape Horn, Cotopaxi, Titicaca
09 Aconcagua, Cartagena, Galápagos,
Gran Chaco, Itaipu Dam, Patagonia
10 Angel Falls, Copacabana, Mato
Grosso, River Plate, Salto ángel
11 Colca Canyon, Iguaçu Falls, Machu
Picchu, Mt Aconcagua, Pico Bolívar
12 Easter Island, Lake Titicaca, Perito
Moreno, Río de la Plata
13 Atacama Desert, Kaieteur Falls
14 Cristo Redentor, Tierra del Fuego
15 Guiana Highlands

• Central America

02 CA

• South America

02 SA

American

◇ *dialect word indicator*
01 A **02** Am, US **04** Amer, Yank
06 Yankee, yanqui **08** Jonathan
09 stateside
See also **president**; **United States of**
America

Native American peoples include:

02 Ge
03 Fox, Han, Mam, Ofo, Ute, Zia
04 Adai, Coos, Cree, Crow, Erie, Hopi,
Hupa, Inca, Innu, Iowa, Maya,
Pomo, Suma, Tewa, Yana, Yuit, Yuma,
Zuñi

05 Aztec, Carib, Creek, Haida, Huron,
Inuit, Kaska, Mayan, Olmec,
Omaha, Opata, Osage, Sioux,
Tache, Wappo, Wiyot, Yupik
06 Apache, Arawak, Beaver, Bororo,
Cayuga, Chiaha, Dakota, Haihai,
Haisla, Iquito, Jumano, Kitsai,
Konkow, Lakota, Micmac, Mixtec,
Mohawk, Mojave, Nakipa, Navaho,
Navajo, Nootka, Ojibwa, Oneida,
Ottawa, Paipai, Paiute, Pawnee,
Pueblo, Quapaw, Santee, Seneca,
Toltec, Yakama, Yamana
07 Arapaho, Atakapa, Bannock,
Chibcha, Chinook, Choctaw,
Hohokam, Huastec, Ingalik,
Koskimo, Koyukon, Kwatami,
Mahican, Miskito, Mohegan,
Mohican, Nahuatl, Natchez,
Secotan, Shawnee, Tlingit, Walapai,
Wanapum, Zapotec
08 Algonkin, Cherokee, Cheyenne,
Comanche, Delaware, Iroquois,
Kwakiutl, Menomini, Onondaga,
Seminole, Shoshone, Shoshoni,
Squamish, Tarascan, Yanomamo
09 Algonquin, Blackfoot, Chickasaw,
Menominee, Tuscarora, Winnebago
10 Athabascan, Athabaskan,
Potawatomi, Wallawalla

• North American

04 Yank **06** Yankee **08** Canadian

American football

American football teams:

11 New York Jets, St Louis Rams
12 Buffalo Bills, Chicago Bears, Detroit
Lions
13 Dallas Cowboys, Denver Broncos,
Houston Texans, Miami Dolphins,
New York Giants
14 Atlanta Falcons, Oakland Raiders
15 Baltimore Ravens, Cleveland
Browns, Green Bay Packers, Seattle
Seahawks, Tennessee Titans
16 Arizona Cardinals, Carolina
Panthers, Kansas City Chiefs,
Minnesota Vikings, New Orleans
Saints, San Diego Chargers
17 Cincinnati Bengals, Indianapolis
Colts, San Francisco 49ers
18 New England Patriots, Philadelphia
Eagles, Pittsburgh Steelers, Tampa
Bay Buccaneers, Washington
Redskins
19 Jacksonville Jaguars

American football-related terms
include:

03 AFC, NFC, NFL
04 down, flag, pass, play, punt, sack,
snap
05 blitz, block, drive, field, guard,
sneak
06 center, fumble, huddle, pocket,
punter, safety, tackle
07 defense, end zone, lateral, lineman,
offense, quarter, rushing, shotgun,
time out
08 fullback, gridiron, halfback,
linesman, overtime, receiver,
scramble, tailback, tight end

09 field goal, reception, secondary, Super Bowl, touchdown
10 completion, cornerback, extra point, linebacker, nose tackle
11 quarterback, running back
12 defensive end, interception, interference, special teams, wide receiver
13 defensive back
15 run interference

American footballers include:

04 Camp (Walter Chauncy), Monk (Art), Rice (Jerry)
05 Allen (Marcus), Baugh (Sammy), Brown (Jim), Brown (Paul), Craig (Roger), Elway (John), Favre (Brett), Fouts (Dan), Halas (George), Perry (Joe), Perry (William), Shula (Don), Smith (Emmitt), White (Reggie)
06 Blanda (Frederick), Butkus (Dick), Graham (Otto), Grange (Red), Greene (Joe), Hutson (Don), Landry (Tom), Madden (John), Marino (Dan), Namath (Joe Willie), Payton (Walter), Rockne (Knute), Sayers (Gale), Taylor (Lawrence), Thorpe (Jim), Unitas (Johnny Constantine)
07 Lambeau (Curly), Montana (Joe), Sanders (Barry), Sanders (Deion), Simpson (OJ)
08 Campbell (Earl), Lombardi (Vince), Staubach (Roger)
09 Tarkenton (Frank)

American Samoa
03 ASM

americium
02 Am

amiability
06 warmth 08 kindness 10 cordiality, likability 11 likeability 12 cheerfulness, friendliness, pleasantness 15 warm-heartedness

amiable
04 kind, maty, warm 05 matey, pally, sweet 06 chummy, genial, gentle 07 affable, cordial, likable, lovable 08 charming, cheerful, engaging, friendly, likeable, loveable, obliging, pleasant, sociable 09 agreeable, clubbable, congenial, gemütlich 11 good-natured, warm-hearted 12 approachable, good-tempered 13 companionable 15 easy to get on with

amicable
05 civil 07 cordial 08 friendly, peaceful 09 civilized 10 harmonious 11 good-natured

amicably
07 civilly 09 cordially, peaceably 12 harmoniously 13 good-naturedly

amid, amidst
◇ *hidden indicator*
◇ *insertion indicator*
05 among, midst 06 amidst 07 amongst 12 in the midst of, in the thick of, surrounded by 13 in the middle of

Amin
03 Idi

amino acid

Amino acids include:

04 dopa
06 glycin, leucin, lysine, serine, valine
07 alanine, glycine, leucine, proline
08 arginine, cysteine, tyrosine
09 glutamine, histidine, ornithine, threonine
10 asparagine, citrulline, domoic acid, isoleucine, methionine, tryptophan
11 tryptophane
12 aspartic acid, glutamic acid, phenylalanin
13 phenylalanine
14 glutaminic acid

amiss
◇ *anagram indicator*
02 up 03 ill 04 awry, evil 05 false, wonky, wrong 06 astray, faulty 07 misdeed, wrongly 08 faultily, improper, untoward 09 defective, imperfect, incorrect 10 improperly, inaccurate, out of order, unsuitable 11 out of kilter 13 inappropriate

amity
05 peace 06 accord, comity 07 concord, harmony 08 goodwill, kindness, sympathy 10 cordiality, fellowship, fraternity, friendship 12 friendliness, peacefulness 13 brotherliness, understanding

ammo *see* **ammunition**

ammonia
• **derivative of ammonia**
05 amide, amine

ammunition
04 ammo, mine, shot 05 bombs, round, slugs 06 rounds, shells 07 bullets, rockets 08 grenades, missiles 09 gunpowder 10 cartridges, explosives 11 projectiles

amnesty
05 mercy 06 pardon 07 freedom, liberty, release 08 immunity, lenience, oblivion, reprieve 09 discharge, remission 10 absolution, indulgence 11 forgiveness 12 dispensation

amok
◇ *anagram indicator*
05 crazy, madly 06 wildly 07 berserk 08 frenzied, insanely 09 in a frenzy, violently 12 like a lunatic, on the rampage, out of control 14 uncontrollably

among
◇ *hidden indicator*
◇ *insertion indicator*
02 in, of 04 amid, with 05 midst 06 amidst 07 amongst, between 12 in the midst of, in the thick of, surrounded by, together with 13 in the middle of 14 in the company of

amorous
04 fond, warm 05 kissy, nutty, randy 06 erotic, in love, lovely, loving, sexual,

tender, wanton 07 amatory, gallant, lustful 08 lovesick 10 cupidinous, passionate 11 flirtatious, impassioned 12 affectionate

amorphous
05 vague 08 formless, inchoate, nebulous, unformed, unshapen 09 irregular, shapeless, undefined 10 indistinct 11 featureless 12 unstructured 13 indeterminate

amount
03 lot, sum 04 bulk, come, mass 05 quota, total, whole 06 degree, extent, figure, number, supply, volume 07 expanse, measure, quantum 08 entirety, quantity, sum total 09 aggregate, magnitude
• **amount to**
04 come, make, mean 05 equal, run to, spell, total, tot up 06 come to, number 07 add up to, run into, tot up to 09 aggregate, inventory 10 boil down to, come down to 12 correspond to 14 be equivalent to, be tantamount to
• **large amount**
03 lot 04 peck, slew, slue, tons
• **small amount**
03 tad 04 haet, ha'it, hate, iota, whit

amphetamine
04 whiz 05 benny, crank, speed, whizz 06 bomber 07 crystal 10 Benzedrine®, Methedrine®

amphibian
04 duck 06 weasel 07 amtrack
See also **animal**

Amphibians include:

03 ask, eft, olm
04 frog, hyla, newt, pipa, Rana, toad
05 Anura
06 Anoura, peeper
07 axolotl, paddock, proteus, puddock, tadpole
08 bullfrog, cane-toad, mudpuppy, platanna, tree frog, tree toad
09 Ambystoma, caecilian, green toad, marsh frog, Nototrema, warty newt
10 Amblystoma, common frog, common toad, edible frog, flying frog, hellbender, horned toad, natterjack, salamander, smooth newt
11 midwife toad, painted frog, Surinam toad
12 springkeeper, spring peeper
14 common treefrog, fire salamander, natterjack toad
15 arrow-poison frog, common spadefoot

amphitheatre
04 bowl, ring 05 arena 06 circus

ample
03 big 04 full, good, rich, wide 05 broad, great, large, roomy, wally 06 enough, plenty 07 copious, liberal, profuse 08 abundant, adequate, generous, handsome, spacious 09 expansive, extensive, plenteous, plentiful 10 commodious, sufficient,

oluminous **11** substantial
2 considerable, unrestricted **14** more
han enough

amplification
07 raising **08** addition, boosting,
ncrease **09** expansion, loudening
0 supplement **11** development,
elaboration, enlargement
2 augmentation, making louder
3 strengthening **15** intensification

amplify
5 add to, boost, raise, widen
6 deepen, expand, extend, louden
7 augment, broaden, bulk out,
develop, enhance, enlarge, fill out
8 enlargen, flesh out, heighten,
ncrease, lengthen **09** enlarge on,
ntensify **10** make louder, strengthen,
supplement **11** elaborate on, expatiate
on **13** go into details

amplitude
4 bulk, mass, size **05** throw, width
6 extent, volume **07** expanse
8 capacity, fullness, vastness
9 greatness, largeness, magnitude,
plenitude, profusion **11** copiousness
2 spaciousness **13** capaciousness

ampoule
4 vial

amputate
3 lop **04** dock **05** sever **06** cut off,
op off, remove **07** chop off, curtail,
hack off **08** dissever, separate,
truncate

amulet
4 juju, tiki **05** charm **06** fetish, grigri,
mascot, scarab **07** abraxas, periapt,
ea bean **08** churinga, greegree,
grisgris, pentacle, talisman
9 toadstone **10** lucky charm,
phylactery

amuse
4 play, slay **05** charm, cheer, crack,
olly, relax, sport, swing **06** absorb,
crease, divert, engage, occupy, please,
popjoy, regale, tickle, trifle **07** cheer
up, delight, disport, engross, enthral,
gladden **08** distract, interest, recreate
9 entertain, make laugh

amusement
3 fun, toy **04** game, play **05** flume,
hobby, mirth, R and R, sport, swing
6 solace **07** cockshy, delight,
Dodgems®, pastime **08** cottabus, flip-
flop, hilarity, interest, laughter, pleasure
9 big dipper, diversion, enjoyment,
merriment, parish top **10** recreation
11 distraction **12** fruit machine
3 entertainment, scenic railway
5 shooting gallery

amusing
3 fun **04** zany **05** a hoot, drôle, droll,
funny, jolly, light, witty **07** a scream,
comical, jocular, killing, waggish
8 charming, humorous, pleasant
9 diverting, enjoyable, facetious,
funny ha-ha, hilarious, laughable,
ludicrous, quizzical **10** delightful,

recreative **11** interesting
12 entertaining

amusingly
07 wittily **09** comically, enjoyably
10 humorously, pleasantly
11 hilariously **12** delightfully
13 interestingly **14** entertainingly

anaconda
04 boma **08** sucurujú, water boa

anaemic
03 wan **04** lame, pale, poor, tame,
weak **05** ashen, bland, frail, livid, pasty,
stale **06** chalky, feeble, infirm, pallid,
sallow, sickly **07** insipid **09** bloodless,
enervated, hackneyed, whey-faced
10 colourless, exsanguine, uninspired,
unoriginal **11** ineffective, ineffectual
12 exsanguinous **13** unimaginative

anaesthetic
05 local **06** number, opiate, premed
07 anodyne, general **08** epidural,
narcotic, sedative **09** analgesic,
soporific **10** nerve block, painkiller,
palliative **12** stupefacient, stupefactive
13 premedication

Anaesthetics include:

03 gas, PCP
05 ether, trike
06 eucain, Evipan®, spinal
07 Avertin®, cocaine, eucaine,
urethan
08 ketamine, metopryl, procaine,
stovaine, urethane
09 Fluothane®, halothane, lidocaine,
Pentothal®
10 benzocaine, chloroform,
lignocaine, nerve block,
orthocaine, thiopental
11 Dutch liquid, laughing gas,
thiopentone
12 cyclopropane, hexobarbital,
nitrous oxide
13 hexobarbitone, phencyclidine
14 methyl chloride
15 tribromoethanol

anaesthetize
04 dope, drug, dull, numb **06** deaden,
freeze **07** stupefy **09** cocainize **10** put
to sleep **11** desensitize

analgesic
10 painkiller

Analgesics include:

06 Calpol®
07 aspirin, codeine, Disprin®,
Disprol®, menthol, metopon,
morphia, Nurofen®, Panadol®,
quinine, salicin
08 Cuprofen®, fentanyl, ketamine,
morphine, salicine, stovaine
09 Calprofen®, co-codamol,
ibuprofen, pethidine
10 diclofenac
11 aminobutene, Distalgesic®,
indometacin, paracetamol,
pentazocine
12 indomethacin, salicylamide
13 carbamazepine, phencyclidine
14 phenylbutazone

analogous
04 like **07** kindred, similar **08** agreeing,
matching, parallel, relative
10 comparable, equivalent, resembling
11 correlative **13** corresponding

analogy
06 simile **08** likeness, metaphor,
parallel, relation **09** agreement,
semblance **10** comparison, similarity,
similitude **11** correlation, equivalence,
resemblance **14** correspondence

analyse
◇ *anagram indicator*
04 scan, sift, test **05** assay, judge,
parse, study **06** divide, reduce, review
07 dissect, examine, inquire, process,
resolve **08** calendar, consider,
construe, critique, estimate, evaluate,
separate **09** anatomize, break down,
criticize, interpret, metricize, take apart
10 scrutinize **11** investigate,
phonemicize

analysis
◇ *anagram indicator*
04 test **05** assay, check, study
06 review **07** anatomy, check-up,
inquiry, opinion, sifting **08** division,
scrutiny **09** blood test, breakdown,
judgement, reasoning, reduction
10 dissection, estimation, evaluation,
exposition, inspection, resolution,
separation **11** examination,
explanation, explication, navel-gazing
13 anatomization, introspection,
investigation **14** interpretation

analyst
06 prober, tester **07** assayer, chemist
08 analyser, inquirer **09** dissector
10 researcher **12** experimenter
15 experimentalist

analytical
07 in-depth, logical **08** analytic,
clinical, critical, detailed, rational,
studious **09** inquiring, searching
10 diagnostic, dissecting, expository,
methodical, systematic **11** explanatory,
inquisitive, questioning
13 investigative **14** interpretative

anarchic
◇ *anagram indicator*
07 chaotic, lawless, riotous
08 confused, mutinous, nihilist
10 disordered, rebellious, ungoverned
11 anarchistic, libertarian
12 disorganized **13** revolutionary

anarchism
05 chaos **07** mob-rule **08** disorder,
rent-a-mob, sedition **09** mobocracy,
rebellion **10** insurgency, ochlocracy,
revolution **11** lawlessness
12 insurrection, racketeering

anarchist
05 rebel **08** nihilist **09** Bolshevik,
insurgent, terrorist **11** libertarian
13 revolutionary

anarchy
04 riot **05** chaos **06** mutiny, unrule
07 misrule **08** disorder, nihilism

09 anarchism, confusion, rebellion **10** revolution **11** lawlessness, pandemonium **12** insurrection

anathema
04 bane **05** curse, taboo **07** bugbear **08** aversion **09** bête noire **10** abhorrence **11** abomination **12** proscription

anatomy
05 build, frame **06** make-up **07** zootomy **08** analysis, topology **09** framework, phytotomy, sarcology, structure **10** dissection **11** composition, vivisection **12** anthropotomy, constitution, construction

Anatomical terms include:

04 bone, hock, limb, oral, vein, womb **05** aorta, aural, bowel, digit, elbow, gland, groin, helix, ileum, nasal, pedal, renal, spine, uvula, volar, vulva **06** artery, axilla, biceps, buccal, carpal, carpus, dental, dermal, dorsal, gullet, lumbar, muscle, neural, ocular, septum, tendon, thymus, uterus **07** abdomen, alveoli, auricle, cardiac, cochlea, gastric, glottis, gristle, hepatic, jugular, mammary, membral, optical, patella, sternum, thyroid, triceps **08** cerebral, duodenal, foreskin, gingival, ligament, mandible, pectoral, thoracic, vena cava, vertebra, voice-box, windpipe **09** capillary, cartilage, diaphragm, epidermis, funny bone, genitalia, hamstring, lachrymal, lymph node, pulmonary, sphincter, umbilicus, ventricle **10** cerebellum, epiglottis, oesophagus **11** intercostal, solar plexus **14** Fallopian tubes

See also **bone**; **brain**; **ear**; **eye**; **gland**; **heart**; **hormone**; **mouth**; **muscle**; **teeth**; **vein**

Anatomists include:

04 Baer (Karl), Bell (Sir Charles), Dart (Raymond), Knox (Robert) **05** Clark (Sir Wifred le Gros), Graaf (Regnier de), Monro (Alexander) **06** Adrian (Edgar, Lord), Cowper (William), Cuvier (Georges, Lord), Haller (Albrecht von), Stubbs (George), Tobias (Phillip) **07** Colombo (Matteo Realdo), Galvani (Luigi) **08** Alcmaeon, Malpighi (Marcello), Vesalius (Andreas) **09** Bartholin (Caspar), Eustachio (Bartolomeo), Fallopius (Gabriel), Zuckerman (Solly, Lord) **10** Herophilus **13** Waldeyer-Hartz (Wilhelm)

ancestor
04 sire **05** elder **06** father, mother, tipuna, tupuna **07** forbear **08** forebear **09** ascendant, ascendent, grandsire,

precursor **10** antecedent, antecessor, forefather, forerunner, progenitor **11** predecessor **12** primogenitor **13** primogenitrix

ancestral
06 avital, lineal **07** genetic **08** familial, parental **09** inherited **10** hereditary **12** genealogical

• **ancestral image**
04 tiki

ancestry
04 line, race **05** blood, roots, stock **06** family, linage, lynage, origin, stirps **07** descent, lignage, lineage **08** breeding, heredity, heritage, pedigree **09** ancestors, ancientry, forebears, genealogy, offspring, parentage, whakapapa **10** derivation, extraction, family tree **11** forefathers, progenitors

anchor
03 fix **04** hook, host, moor **05** affix, berth, tie up **06** attach, fasten **07** bulwark, compère, mooring, mudhook, recluse, support **08** backbone, linchpin, mainstay, make fast **09** anchorman, announcer, presenter **10** foundation, newsreader **11** anchorwoman **15** tower of strength

Anchors include:

03 car, CQR, ice, sea **04** navy, rond **05** bower, drift, kedge, sheet, waist **06** drogue, plough, stream **07** grapnel, killick, killock, stocked, weather **08** mushroom **09** admiralty, stockless, yachtsman **12** double fluked

• **lie at anchor**
04 ride

anchorage
04 cell, road, rode **06** riding

anchorite
04 monk **05** loner **06** anchor, hermit **07** ascetic, eremite, recluse, stylite **08** solitary **09** anchoress **10** solitarian

ancient
03 old **04** aged **05** early, first, hoary, passé **06** age-old, antick, bygone, démodé **07** antique, archaic **08** earliest, obsolete, original, outmoded, primeval, pristine, time-worn, world-old **09** antiquary, atavistic, auld-warld, out-of-date, primaeval, primitive **10** antiquated, fossilized, immemorial, primordial **11** prehistoric **12** antediluvian, old-fashioned **13** superannuated **15** as old as the hills

See also **city**; **Egyptian**; **festival**

ancillary
05 extra **07** helping **08** adjuvant **09** accessory, auxiliary, secondary **10** additional, subserving, subsidiary, supporting **11** adminicular, ministering, subordinate **12** contributory **13** supplementary

and
◇ *juxtaposition indicator*
01 'n' **02** an' **03** too **04** also, plus, then, with **06** as well **07** ampassy, besides **08** as well as, by the way, moreover, together **09** along with, ampersand, amperzand, including, what's more **10** ampussy-and, in addition **11** furthermore **12** in addition to, together with

andiron
03 dog **06** chenet **07** firedog

Andorra
03 AND

androgynous
08 bisexual **09** polygamic **10** monoecious **11** monoclinous, protogynous **12** heterogamous **13** gynodioecious, hermaphrodite, male and female **14** androdioecious

anecdotal
08 everyday, informal **09** narrative **10** unofficial **11** reminiscing **12** storytelling, unscientific

anecdote
04 tale, yarn **05** story **06** sketch **08** exemplum **09** narrative, urban myth **11** urban legend **12** reminiscence

anecdotes
03 ana

anew
◇ *anagram indicator*
05 again **06** afresh, de novo, iterum **07** freshly **08** once more **09** de integro, once again **12** all over again

angel
03 gem **05** ideal, saint **07** darling, paragon, watcher **08** guardian, treasure **09** nonpareil **13** heavenly being **14** messenger of God **15** divine messenger

Angels include:

05 Ariel, Eblis, Iblis, Satan, Uriel **06** Abdiel, Arioch, Azrael, Belial, Mammon, Moloch, Zephon **07** Gabriel, Israfel, Lucifer, Michael, Raphael, Zadkiel **08** Ithuriel **09** Beelzebub

Orders of angel include:

05 angel, power **06** cherub, seraph, throne, virtue **08** dominion **09** archangel **10** domination **12** principality

angelic
04 holy, pure **05** pious **06** divine, lovely **07** saintly **08** adorable, beatific, cherubic, empyrean, ethereal, heavenly, innocent, seraphic, virtuous **09** beautiful, celestial, unworldly **10** cherubical, cherubimic

anger
03 bug, ire, irk, vex, wax **04** face, fuff, fury, gall, gram, huff, miff, mood, move

nark, pelt, rage, rile, roil, teen, tene **05** annoy, blood, flake, get at, pique, teene, wrath **06** bother, choler, dander, emboil, enrage, madden, monkey, needle, nettle, offend, ruffle, temper, wind up **07** affront, air rage, bluster, chagrin, dudgeon, incense, inflame, kippage, offence, offense, outrage, provoke, rancour **08** bad blood, drive mad, irritate, paroxysm, road rage, vexation **09** aggravate, annoyance, infuriate, make angry **10** antagonism, antagonize, bitterness, conniption, drive crazy, exasperate, fit of anger, irritation, resentment **11** displeasure, indignation **12** boiling-point, drive bananas, exasperation, irritability **13** make sparks fly **14** drive up the wall
• **show anger**
06 bridle

angle
03 aim **04** bend, edge, face, fish, fork, hook, knee, nook, side, spin, take, tilt, turn **05** crook, elbow, facet, point, slant **06** aspect, corner, crotch, direct **07** flexure, outlook **08** approach, gradient, position **09** direction, viewpoint **10** projection, standpoint **11** inclination, perspective, point of view **12** intersection
• **angle for**
03 aim **04** seek **05** go for **07** fish for **08** shoot for, try to get **11** make a bid for **12** seek to obtain
• **angle in botany**
04 axil
• **angle in mining**
04 hade
• **angle of 45°**
05 mitre
• **reflex angle**
02 in

angler
03 rod **06** fisher, Walton **07** rodster, wide-gab **08** frogfish, monkfish, piscator **09** devilfish, fisherman, goose-fish, piscatrix, Waltonian

Anglican
02 CE

angling *see* **fishing**

Anglo-French
02 AF

Angola
02 AN **03** AGO

angrily
◇ *anagram indicator*
05 hotly **06** warmly **07** crossly, irately **08** bitterly **09** furiously, stroppily **10** wrathfully **11** indignantly, rancorously, resentfully **12** passionately

angry
◇ *anagram indicator*
03 hot, mad **04** evil, high, warm, wild, yond **05** black, cross, het up, irate, livid, moody, radge, ratty, spewy, wrath **06** bitter, choked, heated, raging, sullen, sultry **07** annoyed, berserk,

blazing, crooked, enraged, furious, ropable, stroppy, uptight **08** burned up, choleric, foribund, hairless, in a paddy, incensed, moody-mad, outraged, ropeable, seething, steaming, up in arms, wrathful **09** in a lather, in a temper, indignant, infuriate, irritated, pissed off, rancorous, raving mad, resentful, seeing red, splenetic, ticked off **10** aggravated, displeased, hopping mad, infuriated, passionate, stomachful, up in the air **11** disgruntled, exasperated, fit to be tied **12** on the rampage, on the warpath **14** beside yourself
• **make angry**
07 incense

angst
05 dread, worry **06** stress **07** anguish, anxiety, tension **08** distress **09** worriment **10** foreboding, uneasiness **11** disquietude **12** apprehension

angstrom
01 A

Anguilla
03 AIA

anguish
03 woe **04** dole, pain, pang, rack **05** agony, dolor, grief **06** dolour, misery, sorrow **07** anxiety, torment, torture **08** distress **09** heartache, suffering **10** affliction, desolation, heartbreak **11** tribulation **12** wretchedness

anguished
08 dolorous, harrowed, stressed, stricken, tortured, wretched **09** afflicted, miserable, suffering, tormented **10** distressed

angular
04 bony, lank, lean, thin **05** gaunt, gawky, lanky, spare **06** skinny **07** scrawny **08** rawboned **12** sharp-pointed

animal
03 pig **04** wild, zoic **05** beast, brute, swine **06** bodily, carnal, mammal, savage **07** bestial, brutish, critter, fleshly, inhuman, monster, sensual **08** animalic, creature, physical **09** barbarian **11** furry friend, instinctive **13** theriomorphic

stag, tahr, tegu, tehr, thar, titi, toad, unau, ursa, urus, urva, wolf
05 adder, bison, camel, civet, coney, eland, horse, hyena, koala, lemur, llama, loris, moose, mouse, otter, panda, ratel, sheep, skunk, tiger, whale, zebra
06 baboon, badger, beaver, cougar, ermine, ferret, gerbil, gibbon, impala, jaguar, monkey, ocelot, rabbit, racoon, walrus, weasel, wombat
07 buffalo, caribou, cheetah, dolphin, gazelle, giraffe, gorilla, hamster, leopard, panther, polecat, sealion, wallaby
08 aardvark, antelope, elephant, hedgehog, kangaroo, kinkajou, mongoose, platypus, reindeer, sea otter, squirrel
09 armadillo, orang-utan, polar bear, wolverine
10 camelopard, chimpanzee, giant panda, rhinoceros
11 grizzly bear
12 hippopotamus

See also **amphibian; ape; beetle; bird; butterfly; cat; cattle; chicken; collective; crustacean; deer; dinosaur; disease; dog; duck; farm; fish; game; horse; insect; invertebrate; lair; lizard; mammal; marsupial; mollusc; monkey; moth; pig; poultry; reptile; rodent; shark; sheep; snake; sound; spider; whale; worm**

Animal lairs, nests and homes include:

03 den, nid, pen, sty
04 bike, bink, byre, cage, coop, drey, fold, form, hive, hole, holt, nest, sett
05 earth, eyrie, lodge, shell
06 burrow, warren, wurley
08 dovecote, fortress, vespiary
09 formicary
11 formicarium, termitarium

Adjectives relating to animals include:

05 apian, avian, avine, ovine
06 bovine, canine, equine, feline, hippic, larine, lupine, murine, simian, ursine
07 acarine, anguine, asinine, caprine, cervine, corvine, hircine, leonine, milvine, otarine, pardine, phocine, piscine, porcine, saurian, sebrine, taurine, tigrine, turdine, vespine, vulpine
08 anserine, aquiline, bubaline, cameline, chthyoid, elaphine, ichthyic, lemurine, leporine, limacine, ophidian, pavonine, sciurine, soricine, suilline, viperine, vituline
09 caballine, chelonian, colubrine, columbine, crotaline, falconine, hirundine, musteline, ornithoid, viverrine, volucrine, vulturine
10 psittacine, serpentine
11 accipitrine, elephantine, fringilline, lacertilian

12 gallinaceous, oryctolagine
13 rhopalocerous
14 papilionaceous

Animal-related terms include:

03 ear, egg, eye, fin, fur, leg, paw, pet
04 beak, bill, bite, claw, coat, crop, dock, gill, gula, hoof, horn, hump, jowl, loin, mane, mate, prey, rump, tail, teat, tusk, wild, wing, wool
05 chine, crest, fangs, feral, moult, pouch, scale, shell, snout, spine, sting, trunk, udder, venom
06 antler, barrel, dewlap, jubate, mantle, muzzle, thorax, ungula
07 abdomen, antenna, feather, flehmen, flipper, gizzard, habitat, migrate, mimicry, pallium, segment, withers
08 coupling, domestic, forefoot, forewing, halteres, hindfoot, hindwing, predator, torquate, ungulate, whiskers
09 marsupium, oviparous, prehallux, proboscis, pygostyle, syndactyl, taligrade
10 camouflage, gressorial, ovipositor, viviparous, webbed feet
11 compound eye, lateral line, search image, swim bladder, waggle dance
12 forked tongue
13 electric organ, metamorphosis
14 startle colours
15 prehensile thumb

Female animals include:

03 cow, doe, ewe, hen, pen, ree, sow
04 gill, hind, jill, jomo, mare
05 bitch, dsomo, jenny, nanny, queen, reeve, vixen, zhomo
06 peahen
07 greyhen, lioness, tigress
08 water cow
09 dolphinet, guinea hen, turkey hen
10 leopardess, weasel coot

Male animals include:

03 cob, dog, hob, nun, ram, tom, tup
04 boar, buck, bull, cock, hart, jack, stag, zobo, zobu
05 billy, drake, drone, dsobo
06 gander, musket, old man, ramcat
08 seecatch, stallion
09 blackcock
10 turkey cock
12 throstle-cock

Young animals include:

03 cub, elt, fry, kid, kit, nit
04 brit, calf, colt, eyas, fawn, foal, gilt, grig, joey, lamb, maid, parr, peal, sild, slip, yelt
05 chick, elver, owlet, piper, puppy, scrod, shote, smolt, squab, steer, whelp
06 alevin, cygnet, eaglet, gimmer, grilse, heifer, hidder, kitten, lionet, piglet, pullet, samlet, weaner
07 codling, eelfare, gosling, leveret, pigling, sardine, skegger, sounder, tadpole, wolfkin

08 brancher, duckling, goatling, nestling, pea-chick
09 fledgling

Animals representing years in the Chinese calendar:

02 ox
03 dog, pig, rat
04 boar, cock, goat, hare
05 horse, sheep, snake, tiger
06 dragon, monkey, rabbit
07 buffalo, rooster, serpent

• **animal display**
03 zoo **09** menagerie
• **animal's body**
04 soma
• **stock of animals**
04 team, teme
• **tame animal**
03 pet
• **unsuitable animal**
04 cull

animate
04 fire, goad, live, move, spur, stir, urge, wake **05** alive, impel, quick, rouse, spark, vital **06** arouse, buck up, ensoul, excite, incite, inform, insoul, kindle, living, revive, vivify **07** enliven, inspire, quicken **08** activate, embolden, energize, inspirit, vitalize
09 breathing, conscious, encourage, galvanize, instigate, stimulate
10 invigorate, reactivate **11** bring to life

animated
◇ *anagram indicator*
03 hot **05** alive, brisk, eager, peppy, quick, vital, zappy **06** active, ardent, chirpy, lively **07** buoyant, chipper, excited, fervent, glowing, radiant, vibrant **08** instinct, spirited, vehement, vigorous **09** ebullient, energetic, sparkling, sprightly, vivacious
10 passionate **11** full of beans, impassioned **12** enthusiastic **15** bright and breezy

animatedly
◇ *anagram indicator*
05 mosso **07** briskly, eagerly
08 actively, ardently **09** excitedly, fervently, radiantly, vibrantly
10 vehemently, vigorously
11 vivaciously **12** passionately
13 energetically

animation
02 go **03** pep **04** fire, heat, life, zeal, zest, zing **05** verve **06** action, energy, spirit, vigour **07** elation, fervour, passion, sparkle **08** activity, radiance, vibrancy, vitality, vivacity **10** claymation, ebullience, enthusiasm, excitement, liveliness **11** high spirits **12** exhilaration **13** sprightliness, vivaciousness

animosity
04 feud, hate **05** odium, pique, spite
06 animus, enmity, hatred, malice **07** ill will, rancour **08** acrimony, friction, loathing **09** antipathy, hostility, malignity **10** abhorrence, antagonism, bitterness, ill feeling, race hatred, resentment **11** malevolence

ankle
04 coot, cuit, cute, hock **05** hough, talus **06** tarsus

annals
04 acta **05** fasti **07** history, memoirs, records, reports **08** accounts, archives, journals **09** registers
10 chronicles

annex
03 add **04** join **05** affix, seize, unite, usurp **06** adjoin, append, attach, fasten, occupy, take in **07** acquire, connect, conquer, purloin
08 arrogate, take over **09** extension, mediatize **11** appropriate, incorporate

annexation
07 seizure **08** conquest, takeover, usurping **10** arrogation, occupation
11 acquisition **13** appropriation

annexe
04 wing **08** addition **09** expansion, extension **10** attachment, supplement

annihilate
04 raze, rout **05** erase **06** defeat, murder, rub out, thrash **07** abolish, conquer, destroy, take out, trounce, wipe out **09** eliminate, eradicate, extirpate, liquidate **10** extinguish, obliterate **11** assassinate, exterminate

annihilation
03 end **06** defeat, murder **07** erasure
09 abolition **10** extinction
11 destruction, elimination, eradication, extirpation, liquidation
12 obliteration **13** assassination, extermination

anniversary
04 obit **07** jubilee **08** birthday, yahrzeit **09** centenary, millenary
10 birthnight, centennial, millennium, wedding day **11** bicentenary, bimillenary, octingenary, semi-jubilee
12 bicentennial, quinquennial, sexcentenary, tercentenary
13 novocentenary, octocentenary, quincentenary, tercentennial
14 octingentenary
15 quatercentenary, sesquicentenary

Anniversaries include:

04 D-Day
05 VE Day, VJ Day
07 Flag Day
08 Anzac Day
09 Canada Day, Empire Day
10 Burns Night, Victory Day
11 Bastille Day, Columbus Day, Dominion Day, Oak-apple Day, Republic Day, Waitangi Day
12 Armistice Day, Australia Day, Discovery Day, Fourth of July, Thanksgiving
13 King's Birthday, Liberation Day, Revolution Day
14 Guy Fawkes Night, Queen's Birthday, Remembrance Day, Unification Day
15 Constitution Day, Emancipation Day, Independence Day

Wedding anniversaries include:

03 fur, tin
04 gold, iron, jade, lace, ruby, silk, wood, wool
05 china, coral, fruit, glass, ivory, linen, paper, pearl, steel, sugar
06 bronze, clocks, copper, cotton, silver, willow
07 crystal, diamond, emerald, flowers, leather, pottery, watches
08 desk sets, platinum, sapphire, textiles
09 aluminium
10 appliances, silverware
13 gold jewellery

annotate
04 note **05** gloss **07** comment, explain **09** elucidate, explicate, interpret **10** add notes to
11 marginalize

annotation
04 note **05** gloss **07** comment
08 exegesis, footnote, scholion, scholium **10** commentary
11 elucidation, explanation, explication
12 commentation

announce
◇ *homophone indicator*
04 bill, post **05** sound, state **06** advise, blazon, notify, report, reveal
07 betoken, declare, divulge, gazette, give out, publish **08** denounce, disclose, intimate, proclaim, propound
09 advertise, broadcast, make known, preconize, publicize **10** make public, promulgate **12** blazon abroad **14** make a statement **15** issue a statement

announcement
04 card **06** notice, report **07** message, release **08** bulletin, dispatch, handbill, obituary **09** broadcast, giving-out, ipse dixit, publicity, reporting, statement **10** communiqué, disclosure, divulgence, intimation, revelation **11** declaration, information, making known, publication, publicizing **12** making public, notification, proclamation, promulgation **13** advertisement
14 pronunciamento

announcer
02 MC **04** host **06** anchor, herald
07 compère **09** anchorman, messenger, presenter, town crier
10 newscaster, newsreader, speakerine **11** anchorwoman, annunciator, broadcaster, commentator

annoy
03 bug, din, hip, hyp, irk, nag, noy, try, vex **04** fash, gall, hump, miff, nark, ride, rile, roil **05** anger, cross, sturt, tease
06 bother, harass, hassle, hatter, hector, madden, molest, nettle, pester, plague, ruffle, tee off, wind up
07 chagrin, disturb, hack off, provoke, tick off, trouble **08** brass off, contrary, irritate **09** aggravate, cheese off, displease, drive nuts, importune
10 drive crazy, exasperate **11** get your

goat **12** drive bananas **13** get on your wick, get up your nose, get your back up, make sparks fly **14** drive up the wall, get your blood up, give you the hump, piss someone off, take the michael **15** get on your nerves, get your dander up

annoyance
04 bind, bore, drag, fash, hump, pain, pest **05** anger, sturt, tease **06** bother, injury, molest, pester, ruffle
07 bugbear, chagrin, noyance, trouble
08 headache, irritant, mischief, nuisance, vexation **09** bête noire
10 harassment, irritation
11 aggravation, displeasure, disturbance, provocation
12 exasperation, excruciation **13** pain in the butt, pain in the neck **14** thorn in the side

• **expression of annoyance**
03 dam, dee, god, hey, sod, tut
04 damn, drat, heck, hell, hoot, phew, rats **05** blast, blimy, damme, devil, Jesus, my God!, shoot, waugh
06 blimey, bother, Christ, dammit, shucks, zounds **07** caramba, doggone **08** honestly, hoot-toot
09 cor blimey, do you mind?, good grief, gorblimey **10** hell's bells, hell's teeth, hoots-toots **11** botheration, for God's sake, for pete's sake, that's torn it **12** Donnerwetter
13 Gordon Bennett **14** for Christ's sake, for heaven's sake **15** for goodness sake

annoyed
04 sore **05** angry, cross, fed up, upset, vexed **06** bugged, hipped, miffed, narked, peeved, piqued, shirty
07 chocker, hassled, in a huff, pig sick, stroppy **08** harassed, in a paddy, provoked **09** indignant, irritated, pissed off, ticked off **10** brassed off, cheesed off, displeased, driven nuts, got the hump **11** driven crazy, exasperated

annoying
05 pesky **06** trying **07** galling, irksome, teasing **08** infernal, niggling, tiresome **09** harassing, intrusive, maddening, offensive, provoking, unwelcome, vexatious
10 bothersome, disturbing, irritating, plaguesome **11** aggravating, importunate, infuriating, pestiferous, troublesome **12** exasperating

annual
06 yearly **07** almanac **08** calendar, register, yearbook
• **annual return**
02 AR

annul
04 undo, void **05** quash **06** cancel, defeat, negate, recall, reduce, repeal, revoke, vacate **07** abolish, cashier, nullify, rescind, retract, reverse, suspend, vacuate **08** abrogate, disannul, dissolve, overrule, set aside
10 invalidate **11** countermand

annulment
06 defeat, recall, repeal **07** reverse, voiding **08** negation, quashing
09 abolition, cassation **10** abrogation, rescission, revocation, suspension
11 countermand, dissolution, rescindment **12** cancellation, invalidation **13** nullification

anodyne
04 dull **05** bland **07** neutral
08 harmless, innocent **09** analgesic, deadening, innocuous **11** inoffensive

anoint
03 oil, rub **04** balm, daub, nard, oint
05 anele, bless, salve, smear
06 grease, hallow, ordain, pomade
08 dedicate, sanctify, set apart
09 embrocate, lubricate **10** apply oil to, consecrate

anomalous
◇ *anagram indicator*
03 odd **04** rare **05** freak **07** deviant, unusual **08** abnormal, atypical, freakish, peculiar, singular
09 eccentric, irregular **11** exceptional, incongruous **12** inconsistent

anomaly
◇ *anagram indicator*
05 freak **06** misfit, oddity, rarity
09 departure, deviation, exception
10 aberration, divergence
11 abnormality, incongruity, peculiarity
12 eccentricity, irregularity
13 inconsistency

anon
04 soon **06** coming **07** by and by, shortly **09** quite soon **10** before long
11 immediately **14** in a little while **15** in the near future

anonymous
01 a **02** an **04** anon, gray, grey
07 unknown, unnamed **08** faceless, nameless, unsigned **09** incognito
10 authorless, impersonal, innominate, unattested
11 nondescript, unspecified
12 unattributed, unidentified, unremarkable **13** unexceptional
14 unacknowledged

anorak
04 nerd, nurd, spod, wonk **06** cagoul, kagool, kagoul **07** cagoule, kagoule
11 windcheater **12** trainspotter

another
◇ *anagram indicator*
04 more **05** added, extra, other, spare
06 second **07** further, variant
09 different, some other **10** additional, not the same **11** alternative

answer
01 a **03** ans, fit, get, key **04** fill, meet, pass, rein, suit **05** agree, match, react, reply, serve **06** fulfil, pick up, refute, result, retort, return **07** conform, resolve, respond, riposte, satisfy
08 comeback, quick fix, reaction, rebuttal, rescript, response, solution
09 correlate, get back to, match up to,

rejoinder, retaliate, write back **10** come back to, resolution **11** acknowledge, explanation, replication, retaliation, unravelling **12** correspond to **15** acknowledgement

• **answer back**
04 sass **05** argue, rebut **06** retort **07** dispute, riposte **08** backchat, disagree, talk back **09** retaliate **10** be cheeky to, contradict

• **answer for**
06 pay for **08** speak for, vouch for **09** engage for, suffer for **11** be liable for **13** be punished for

• **answer to**
08 report to **09** work under **15** be accountable to, be responsible to

answerable
06 liable **07** to blame **08** suitable **10** chargeable, equivalent **11** accountable, blameworthy, responsible

ant
05 emmet, nurse **06** ergate, nasute, neuter **07** ergates, pismire, termite

Ants include:

03 red
04 army, fire, leaf, wood
05 black, crazy
06 Amazon, driver, weaver
07 bulldog, forager, pharaoh, soldier
08 honeydew
09 black lawn, carpenter, harvester
10 leaf-cutter
12 red harvester

antagonism
06 enmity **07** discord, ill will, rivalry **08** conflict, friction **09** animosity, antipathy, hostility **10** antibiosis, contention, dissension, ill feeling, opposition, oppugnancy

antagonist
03 foe **04** peer **05** enemy, rival **08** opponent **09** adversary, contender **10** competitor, contestant

antagonistic
06 averse **07** adverse, hostile, opposed **08** opponent **10** at variance, unfriendly **11** adversarial, belligerent, conflicting, contentious, ill-disposed **12** incompatible

antagonize
03 bug **04** miff, rile **05** anger, annoy, get at, repel **06** insult, needle, nettle, offend, wind up **07** incense, provoke **08** alienate, drive mad, embitter, estrange, irritate **09** aggravate, disaffect **10** drive crazy **12** drive bananas **13** make sparks fly **14** drive up the wall

Antarctica
03 ATA

Antarctic animal
07 Penguin

antbear
08 aardvark, tamanoir
12 Myrmecophaga

anteater
05 Manis **07** echidna, tamandu **08** aardvark, pangolin, tamandua

antecedent
04 race **05** blood, roots, stock **06** stirps, tipuna, tupuna **09** ancestors, forebears, genealogy, precedent, preceding, precursor **10** extraction, forerunner, prevenient **11** forefathers, preparatory, progenitors

antedate
07 precede, predate, prevene **08** antecede, go before **10** come before

antediluvian
03 old **05** early, passé **06** bygone, old hat **07** archaic **08** outmoded **10** antiquated **11** out of the Ark **15** as old as the hills

antelope

Antelopes include:

03 bok, doe, gnu, kid, kob
04 kudu, oryx, puku, suni, thar, topi
05 addax, bubal, chiru, eland, goral, nagor, nyala, oribi, sable, saiga, sasin, serow
06 bosbok, dik-dik, duiker, duyker, dzeren, impala, inyala, koodoo, lechwe, nilgai, nilgau, pygarg, reebok
07 blaubok, blesbok, bloubok, bubalis, chamois, chikara, gazelle, gemsbok, gerenuk, grysbok, madoqua, nylghau, sassaby
08 Antilope, bontebok, boschbok, bushbuck, palebuck, reedbuck, steenbok, tsessebe
09 blackbuck, sitatunga, situtunga, springbok, steinbock, tragelaph, waterbuck
10 Alcelaphus, hartebeest, ox-antelope, wildebeest
11 zebra duiker
12 goat-antelope, klipspringer
13 sable antelope

antenna
04 horn **06** aerial, feeler

anteroom
04 hall **05** foyer, lobby, porch **09** vestibule **11** antechamber, waiting-room **12** entrance hall, voiding-lobby

anthem
04 hymn, song **05** chant, motet, paean, psalm **06** motett, waiata **07** chorale, introit **08** antiphon, canticle, isodicon **10** responsory **12** Marseillaise, song of praise

anthology
06 digest **07** omnibus **08** treasury **09** selection, spicilege **10** collection, compendium, miscellany **11** compilation, florilegium **12** chrestomathy

Anthony
04 Tony

anthrax
04 sang

anthropology
09 ethnology

Anthropologists include:

04 Boas (Franz), Buck (Sir Peter), Mead (Margaret)
05 Hiroa (Te Rangi), Tylor (Sir Edward)
06 Frazer (Sir J G), Leakey (Louis), Marett (R R)
07 Métraux (Albert)
09 Heyerdahl (Thor)
10 Malinowski (Bronislaw)
11 Lévi-Strauss (Claude)
14 Radcliffe-Brown (Alfred)

antibiotic

Antibiotics include:

05 Cipro®
08 neomycin, nystatin
09 avoparcin, kanamycin, Neosporin®, polymyxin, quinolone
10 ampicillin, Aureomycin®, bacitracin, gramicidin, lincomycin, meticillin, penicillin, polymyxin B, rifampicin, Terramycin®, vancomycin
11 amoxicillin, amoxycillin, clindamycin, cloxacillin, cycloserine, doxorubicin, doxycycline, fusidic acid, methicillin
12 erythromycin, griseofulvin, streptomycin, tetracycline, trimethoprim
13 cephalosporin, ciprofloxacin, co-trimoxazole, metronidazole, spectinomycin, virginiamycin
15 chloramphenicol, oxytetracycline

antibody
03 MAB **06** reagin **10** agglutinin, amboceptor, immune body, precipitin **13** isoagglutinin

antic
04 dido **05** caper, clown **07** buffoon **09** fantastic, grotesque **10** mountebank

Antichrist
08 man of sin, the Beast **10** lawless one

anticipate
05 await, guess **06** bank on, expect **07** count on, foresee, hope for, look for, obviate, precede, predict, pre-empt, prepare, prevene, prevent **08** antedate, beat to it, figure on, forecast, preclude, reckon on **09** apprehend, count upon, forestall, intercept **10** prepare for **11** preoccupate, second-guess, think likely **13** look forward to

anticipation
04 hope, type **08** forecast **09** foretaste, intuition, prejudice, prolepsis **10** excitement, expectancy, prediction, prevention **11** bated breath, expectation, preparation **12** apprehension, presentiment

anticlimax
06 bathos, fiasco **07** let-down

8 comedown, non-event 09 damp
quib 14 disappointment

antics
6 capers, doings, pranks, stunts, tricks
7 foolery, frolics 08 clowning,
mischief 09 horseplay, silliness
10 buffoonery, shenanigan, skylarking,
tomfoolery 11 playfulness,
shenanigans 12 monkey-tricks

antidote
4 cure 05 serum 06 bezoar, remedy,
senega 07 theriac, treacle 08 naloxone,
Orvietan, theriaca 09 antitoxin,
antivenin 10 corrective, mithridate
11 contrayerva, dimercaprol, neutralizer
12 alexipharmic, counter-agent
13 counter-poison, Venice treacle
14 alexipharmakon, countermeasure

Antigua and Barbuda
03 ATG

antimony
2 Sb

antipathy
4 hate 05 odium 06 animus, enmity,
hatred 07 allergy, disgust, dislike, ill will
08 aversion, bad blood, distaste,
dyspathy, loathing 09 animosity,
hostility, repulsion 10 abhorrence,
antagonism, opposition, repugnance
15 incompatibility

antiquated
5 dated, passé 06 bygone, démodé,
ogram, fossil, old hat 07 ancient,
archaic, outworn 08 obsolete,
outdated, outmoded 09 out-of-date,
primitive 10 fossilized 11 on the way
out, prehistoric 12 antediluvian, old-
fashioned 13 anachronistic,
prehistorical

antique
◇ archaic word indicator
03 old 05 curio, relic 06 bygone,
quaint, rarity 07 ancient, archaic,
veteran, vintage 08 Egyptian,
heirloom, obsolete, outdated
09 antiquity, curiosity 10 antiquated
11 antiquarian, museum piece, period
piece 12 old-fashioned 13 object of
virtu 14 collector's item

Antiques-related terms include:
04 Goss, Ming, ring, T'ang
05 glaze, ivory
06 barock, dealer, empire, Gothic,
lustre, patina, period, rococo
07 art deco, auction, barocco,
baroque, ceramic, federal, impasto,
opaline, pilgrim, pottery, Tiffany
08 filigree, Georgian, Jacobean,
majolica, Sheraton, trecento
09 bone china, collector, Delftware,
Edwardian, porcelain, Queen Anne,
soft paste, stoneware, valuation,
Victorian
10 art nouveau, millefiori
11 chinoiserie, Chippendale,
cinquecento, haute époque,
Hepplewhite, period piece,
restoration

12 antiques fair, arts and craft, blanc de
Chine, blue and white,
reproduction, transitional
13 willow pattern
15 churrigueresque

antiquity
03 age, eld 06 old age 07 oldness
08 agedness 09 ancientry, olden days
10 days of yore 11 ancientness, distant
past 12 ancient times 14 time
immemorial

antiseptic
04 pure 05 clean 07 aseptic, sterile
08 cleanser, germ-free, hygienic,
purifier, sanitary 09 germicide,
medicated, mouthwash, sanitized
10 sterilized, unpolluted 11 bactericide
12 disinfectant 14 uncontaminated

Antiseptics include:
03 TCP®
05 eupad, eusol
06 cresol, Dettol®, flavin, formol,
phenol, Savlon®, thymol
07 benzoin, flavine
08 creasote, creosote, formalin,
iodoform
09 cassareep, cassaripe, cetrimide,
Germolene®, Listerine®,
merbromin, zinc oxide
10 acriflavin
11 acriflavine
12 carbolic acid, methyl violet
13 chlorhexidine, crystal violet, flowers
of zinc, gentian violet, silver nitrate
14 Dakin's solution, rubbing alcohol,
sodium benzoate, sodium chlorate
15 hexachlorophane, hexachlorophene

antisocial
07 asocial, hostile, lawless
08 anarchic, reserved, retiring
09 alienated, withdrawn 10 disorderly,
disruptive, rebellious, unfriendly,
unsociable 11 belligerent
12 antagonistic, misanthropic,
unacceptable 13 unforthcoming
14 unapproachable
15 uncommunicative

antisubmarine
02 AS

antithesis
07 reverse 08 contrast, converse,
opposite, reversal 10 opposition
13 contradiction 15 opposite extreme

antithetical
07 opposed 08 clashing, contrary,
opposing 11 conflicting
12 incompatible, in opposition
13 contradictory 14 irreconcilable

antler
04 horn 08 staghorn 09 hartshorn

antler
04 horn 08 staghorn 09 hartshorn

Antony
04 Tony

anxiety
03 tiz 04 care, cark, fear, rack, stew
05 angst, dread, sweat, tizzy, worry

06 fantad, fantod, hang-up, nerves,
strain, stress 07 anguish, concern,
fantads, fanteeg, fantods, jitters,
tension, thought, willies 08 disquiet,
distress, fantigue, suspense
09 dysthymia, misgiving, worriment
10 foreboding, impatience, solicitude,
uneasiness 11 butterflies, disquietude,
fretfulness, nervousness
12 apprehension, collywobbles,
hypochondria, restlessness
13 consternation, heebie-jeebies
14 solicitousness
See also **phobia**
• **free from anxiety**
04 ease

anxious
◇ anagram indicator
04 keen, taut, toey 05 eager, het up,
tense, upset 06 afraid, uneasy
07 careful, fearful, fretful, in a stew,
jittery, longing, nervous, uptight,
worried 08 desirous, dismayed, in a
tizzy, insecure, restless, tortured,
troubled, yearning 09 concerned,
desperate, disturbed, expectant, ill at
ease, impatient, on the rack,
tormented 10 distressed, in suspense,
solicitous 11 overwrought
12 apprehensive, enthusiastic
13 grandmotherly, on tenterhooks
14 hot and bothered, valetudinarian
15 a bundle of nerves

anxiously
07 tensely 08 uneasily 09 fearfully,
fretfully, nervously 10 restlessly
11 impatiently, tormentedly
12 solicitously 14 apprehensively

any
03 ary, one 04 a few, some 05 arrow,
at all 06 a bit of 09 whichever 10 a
single one, in the least 11 the least bit,
to any extent 12 to some extent

anybody
03 one

anyhow
◇ anagram indicator
06 anyway 07 anyways 08 at random,
untidily 09 at any rate, in any case
10 carelessly, in any event, not in order,
regardless 11 at all events, haphazardly
12 nevertheless, no matter what
13 indifferently

anyone
03 you

anything
03 owt 05 ought

anyway
◇ anagram indicator
06 anyhow 07 anyroad 09 in any case
10 in any event, regardless 11 at all
events 12 nevertheless, no matter
what

apace
04 fast 07 hastily, quickly, rapidly,
swiftly 08 speedily 10 at top speed
11 at full speed, double-quick
12 without delay

apart

◇ *anagram indicator*
04 afar, away **05** alone, aloof, aside
06 beside, cut off, in bits, singly, to bits
07 asunder, distant **08** by itself,
distinct, divorced, excluded, in pieces,
isolated, separate, to pieces **09** into
parts, on your own, piecemeal,
privately, separated, to one side **10** by
yourself, separately **11** not together
12 individually **13** independently
• **apart from**
04 save **06** beyond, but for, except
07 besides, outside **08** excepted
09 aside from, except for, excluding
11 not counting

apartment

03 apt, pad **04** flat, gaff, room, unit
05 bower, condo, split **06** duplex,
walk-up **07** chamber, mansion
08 home unit, paradise, tenement
11 condominium **12** privy chamber
13 accommodation **15** duplex
apartment
See also **room**

apathetic

04 cold, cool, numb **05** blasé, ho-hum
07 passive, unmoved **08** listless,
lukewarm **09** impassive, lethargic,
unfeeling **10** insouciant, uninvolved
11 emotionless, half-hearted,
indifferent, unambitious,
unconcerned, unemotional
12 uninterested, unresponsive

apathy

06 acedia, torpor **07** accidie, inertia,
languor **08** coldness, coolness,
lethargy **09** passivity, unconcern
11 impassivity **12** indifference,
listlessness, sluggishness
13 insensibility, lack of concern **14** lack
of interest

ape

04 copy, echo, mock **05** magot, mimic
06 affect, mirror, parody, parrot, send
up, simian **07** imitate, take off
09 proconsul **10** anthropoid,
caricature, jackanapes, troglodyte
11 counterfeit
See also **animal; monkey; primate**

Apes include:

05 chimp, drill, jocko, orang, pigmy,
pongo, pygmy, satyr
06 baboon, bonobo, chacma, dog-
ape, gelada, gibbon, monkey, wou-
wou, wow-wow
07 gorilla, hoolock, macaque,
siamang
08 hylobate, mandrill
09 hamadryad, orang-utan
10 chimpanzee, silverback
11 orang-outang
12 Cynocephalus, ourang-outang,
paranthropus
13 Kenyapithecus
15 pygmy chimpanzee

aperture

03 eye, gap **04** hole, rent, slit, slot, vent
05 chink, cleft, crack, light, mouth,
space **06** breach, choana, oscule,
rictus, throat, window **07** fissure,
foramen, opening, orifice, osculum,
passage, punctum, swallow
08 fenestra, overture, punctule
09 sight-hole **10** interstice
11 perforation **14** counter-opening

apex

03 tip, top **04** acme, peak **05** crest,
crown, point **06** apogee, climax,
height, summit, vertex, zenith
08 pinnacle **09** fastigium, high point
10 apotheosis, pyramidion
11 culmination **12** consummation
13 crowning point

aphid, aphis

06 ant cow **08** blackfly, greenfly
09 bark-louse **10** dolphin-fly, plant
louse, smother-fly

aphorism

03 saw **05** adage, axiom, gnome,
maxim **06** dictum, saying **07** epigram,
precept, proverb **08** sentence
09 witticism **10** apophthegm,
whakatauki

aphrodisiac

06 erotic **07** amative, amatory, philter,
philtre **08** venerous **09** cantharis,
erogenous, stimulant, venereous
10 love potion, Spanish fly
11 erotogenous, stimulative

Aphrodite

05 Venus

apiece

03 all **04** each **06** singly **07** per head
09 per capita, per person
10 separately **12** individually,
respectively

aplomb

05 poise **08** calmness, coolness
09 assurance, composure, sangfroid
10 confidence, equanimity **11** savoir-
faire **13** self-assurance **14** self-
confidence, self-possession,
unflappability

apocryphal

06 made-up **07** dubious **08** doubtful,
fabulous, mythical, spurious
09 concocted, equivocal, imaginary,
legendary **10** fabricated, fictitious,
unverified **11** unsupported
12 questionable **15** unauthenticated,
unsubstantiated

Apocryphal books of the Bible include:

03 Bar, Esd, Jud, Sir, Sus, Tob
04 Macc, Wisd
05 Bel&Dr, Tobit (Book of)
06 Baruch (Book of), Ecclus, Esdras
(Books of), Judith (Book of)
07 Pr of Man, Susanna (History of)
08 Manasseh (Prayer of)
09 Maccabees
14 Ecclesiasticus (Book of)
15 Bel and the Dragon, Wisdom of
Solomon (Book of)

See also **Bible**

apologetic

05 sorry **06** rueful **08** contrite,
penitent **09** regretful, repentant
10 excusatory, remorseful

apologetically

08 ruefully **10** contritely, penitently
11 regretfully, repentantly
12 remorsefully

apologia

07 defence **08** argument
11 explanation, explication, vindication

apologist

06 backer **08** advocate, defender,
endorser, upholder **09** supporter
10 vindicator

apologize

05 plead **06** grovel, regret **07** confess,
explain, justify **08** say sorry **09** ask
pardon **11** acknowledge **12** be
apologetic, eat humble pie, eat your
words **14** ask forgiveness, say you are
sorry

apology

04 oops, plea **05** sorry **06** excuse
07 defence, mockery, regrets
08 excuse me, pardon me, travesty
10 caricature, confession, corruption,
distortion, palliation **11** explanation,
saying sorry, vindication **12** poor
specimen **13** justification **14** poor
substitute **15** acknowledgement

apoplectic

03 mad **04** high **05** cross, irate, livid,
moody, radge, ratty, spewy, wrath,
wroth **06** bitter, choked, raging, sullen,
sultry **07** annoyed, crooked, enraged,
furious, ropable, stroppy, uptight
08 burned up, choleric, foribund,
hairless, in a paddy, incensed,
outraged, seething, up in arms,
wrathful **09** in a lather, in a temper,
indignant, irritated, pissed off,
rancorous, raving mad, resentful,
seeing red, splenetic, ticked off, very
angry **10** hopping mad, infuriated,
passionate, up in the air **11** disgruntled,
exasperated, fit to be tied **12** on the
rampage, on the warpath **14** beside
yourself

apostasy

06 heresy **07** perfidy, rattery, ratting
09 defection, desertion, falseness,
recreance, recreancy, treachery
10 disloyalty, renegation
12 renunciation **13** faithlessness
14 unfaithfulness

apostate

03 rat **07** heretic, traitor **08** defector,
deserter, recreant, renegade,
runagate, turncoat **10** recidivist
13 tergiversator

apostle

07 pioneer, teacher **08** advocate,
champion, crusader, disciple,
preacher, reformer **09** apologist,
messenger, proponent, supporter
10 evangelist, missionary
12 proselytizer

Apostles of Jesus Christ:

04 John
05 James, Judas, Peter, Simon
06 Andrew, Philip, Thomas
07 Matthew
08 Matthias, Thaddeus
11 Bartholomew
13 Judas Iscariot
14 Simon the Zealot
15 James of Alphaeus
17 Simon the Canaanite

apotheosis

03 tip **04** acme, apex, peak **05** crest, crown, point **06** apogee, climax, height, summit, vertex, zenith **08** pinnacle **09** fastigium, high point **11** culmination, deification **12** consummation **13** crowning point, glorification

appal

05 alarm, daunt, scare, shock **06** dismay **07** disgust, horrify, outrage, terrify, unnerve **08** frighten **10** disconcert, intimidate

appalling

◇ *anagram indicator*
04 dire, grim, naff, poor, ropy **05** awful, lousy, pants, ropey **06** horrid **07** ghastly, hideous, the pits, very bad **08** alarming, daunting, dreadful, hopeless, horrible, horrific, inferior, pathetic, shocking, terrible **09** atrocious, frightful, harrowing, loathsome, unnerving **10** disgusting, horrifying, inadequate, outrageous, terrifying **11** frightening, nightmarish **12** intimidating, unacceptable **14** unsatisfactory

appallingly

◇ *anagram indicator*
07 awfully **08** horribly, terribly **09** hideously **10** dreadfully, hopelessly, shockingly **11** frightfully **12** horrifically, pathetically, unacceptably

apparatus

03 rig **04** bank, gear, tool **05** means, set-up, tools **06** device, gadget, outfit, system, tackle **07** machine, network **08** utensils **09** appliance, equipment, framework, implement, machinery, materials, mechanism, structure **10** implements, instrument **11** contraption

See also **laboratory**

apparel

03 kit **04** garb, gear, tire, togs **05** besee, dress, get-up, weeds **06** attire, outfit, robing, vestry **07** clobber, clothes, costume, raiment, vesture **08** clothing, garments, wardrobe **09** garniture **11** habiliments

apparent

◇ *hidden indicator*
02 ap **03** app **04** open **05** clear, overt, plain **06** marked, patent **07** evident, obvious, outward, seeming, visible **08** declared, distinct, manifest **10** detectable, noticeable, ostensible **11** conspicuous, perceptible, superficial **12** unmistakable **13** be standing out

apparently

02 ap **03** app **07** clearly, plainly **08** patently **09** evidently, obviously, outwardly, reputedly, seemingly **10** manifestly, ostensibly **12** on the surface **13** on the face of it, superficially

apparition

05 fetch, ghost, shape, spook, taish **06** double, spirit, taisch, vision, wraith **07** chimera, eidolon, gytrash, phantom, specter, spectre **08** illusion, manifest, phantasm, presence, visitant **09** hobgoblin, semblance **10** appearance **12** doppelgänger **13** manifestation **15** materialization

appeal

02 it, SA **03** ask, beg, cry, SOS, sue **04** call, draw, lure, peal, pele, plea, pray, suit **05** apply, charm, claim, oomph, plead, tempt **06** allure, ask for, avouch, beauty, call on, engage, entice, invite, invoke, orison, please, prayer, review **07** address, attract, beseech, entreat, implore, provoke, reclaim, request, retrial, solicit **08** approach, call upon, charisma, entreaty, interest, petition **09** fascinate, magnetism **10** adjuration, attraction, invocation, recusation, supplicate **11** application, conjuration, enchantment, fascination, imploration, winsomeness **12** re-evaluation, solicitation, supplication **13** re-examination **14** attractiveness **15** reconsideration

• **solemn appeal**
04 oath

appealing

07 winning, winsome **08** alluring, charming, engaging, enticing, inviting, magnetic, pleasing, tempting **10** attractive, enchanting **11** charismatic, fascinating, interesting

appear

◇ *homophone indicator*
03 act, eye **04** go on, look, loom, peer, play, rise, seem, shew, show, star **05** arise, bob up, break, enter, issue, kithe, kythe, occur, pop up **06** arrive, attend, cast up, co-star, crop up, emerge, figure, show up, spring, turn up **07** come out, compear, develop, perform, surface, topline, turn out **08** platform, take part **09** be on stage, be present, come along **10** be a guest in **11** be published, come to light, materialize, show signs of **12** come across as, come into view, show your face **13** become visible, come into sight **14** take the guise of **15** become available

• **begin to appear**
03 ope **04** open

appearance

03 air, hew, hue **04** broo, brow, face, form, garb, look, mien, rise, show, view **05** debut, front, ghost, guise, image, looks **06** advent, aspect, coming, effeir, effere, façade, figure, manner, ostent, visage **07** arrival, bearing, outward **08** exterior, illusion, presence, pretence **09** appearing, demeanour, emergence, semblance **10** apparition, attendance, complexion, expression, impression **11** outward form **12** introduction **14** coming into view

• **final appearance**
08 swansong

• **personal appearance**
02 PA

appease

04 stay **05** allay, atone, quiet, still **06** aslake, attone, defray, pacify, soothe **07** mollify, placate, qualify, satisfy **08** mitigate **09** reconcile **10** conciliate, propitiate **13** make peace with

appeasement

09 placation **11** peacemaking **12** conciliation, pacification, satisfaction **14** reconciliation

appellation

04 name **05** title **07** epithet **08** monicker, nickname **09** most noble, sobriquet **10** soubriquet **11** description, designation **12** compellation, denomination

append

◇ *juxtaposition indicator*
03 add, put, tag **04** join **05** affix, annex **06** adjoin, attach, fasten, tack on **07** conjoin, subjoin **08** pickback **09** pickaback, pickapack, piggyback

appendage

03 lug **04** aril **05** affix, aglet, whisk **06** aiglet, arista, barbel, cercus, stipel, uropod **07** adjunct, arillus, auricle, foretop, maxilla, stipule **08** addendum, addition, appendix, gnathite, nose-leaf, pedipalp, pendicle **09** allantois, chelicera, swimmeret, tailpiece **10** paraglossa, parapodium, supplement **11** aiguillette **12** appurtenance

appendix

03 app **05** annex, rider **07** adjunct, codicil, pendant, pendent **08** addendum, addition, epilogue, schedule **09** appendage **10** postscript, supplement

appertain

05 apply, refer **06** bear on, effeir, effere, regard, relate **07** concern, pertain **10** be relevant **14** have a bearing on

appetite

03 maw, yen **04** lust, urge, zeal, zest **05** taste, tooth, twist **06** desire, hunger, liking, orexis, relish, thirst **07** craving, longing, malacia, passion, stomach **08** inner man, yearning **09** eagerness **10** inner woman, propensity **11** inclination **13** concupiscence

• **sharpness of appetite**
04 edge

appetizer
04 meze, tapa, whet **05** bhaji, mezze, tapas **06** bhagee, bhajee, canapé, dim sum, relish **07** starter **08** antepast, apéritif, cocktail **09** antipasto **11** amuse-bouche, amuse-gueule, first course, hors d'oeuvre **13** prawn cocktail

appetizing
05 tasty, yummy **06** morish **07** moreish, piquant, savoury, scrummy **08** inviting, tempting **09** appealing, delicious, palatable, succulent, toothsome **11** lip-smacking, scrumptious **13** mouthwatering

applaud
03 hum **04** clap, laud, root, ruff **05** cheer, extol **06** cry aim, praise **07** acclaim, approve, commend **08** eulogize **10** compliment **12** congratulate **14** cheer to the echo, give a big hand to **15** give an ovation to

applause
04 hand, ruff **05** éclat, salvo, vivat **06** bravos, cheers, praise **07** acclaim, ovation, plaudit **08** a big hand, accolade, approval, cheering, clapping, encomium, plaudits **11** acclamation, Kentish fire **12** commendation **14** congratulation **15** standing ovation

apple
04 pome

Apples include:

03 Cox
04 Cox's, crab, snow
05 Coxes, eater
06 biffin, codlin, cooker, eating, idared, pippin, russet
07 Baldwin, Bramley, codling, cooking, costard, crispin, ribston, Sturmer, wine-sap
08 Braeburn, Jonathan, McIntosh, pearmain, Pink Lady, queening, ribstone, sweeting
09 delicious, jenneting, king-apple, nonpareil, Royal gala
11 Granny Smith, McIntosh red, russet apple
12 Red Delicious
13 Ribston pippin, Sturmer Pippin
15 Golden Delicious

- **apple core**
04 runt
- **big apple**
02 NY **03** NYC

appliance
03 use **04** iron, tool **05** gizmo, truss, value, waldo **06** device, gadget, praxis **07** machine **08** function **09** apparatus, implement, mechanism, relevance **10** fire engine, instrument **11** application, carrying-out, contraption, contrivance
See also **domestic**; **utensil**

applicable
03 apt, fit **04** live **05** valid **06** proper, suited, useful **07** fitting **08** apposite, relevant, suitable **09** pertinent **10** legitimate **11** appropriate
- **not applicable**
02 n/a

applicant
06 suitor **08** aspirant, claimant, inquirer **09** candidate, postulant **10** competitor, contestant, petitioner **11** interviewee

application
03 use **04** suit **05** claim, study, value **06** appeal, demand, effort, praxis **07** aptness, bearing, inquiry, program, purpose, request, rubbing **08** function, hard work, industry, keenness, petition, smearing, software **09** anointing, assiduity, diligence, putting on, relevance, spreading, treatment **10** commitment, dedication, pertinence **11** germaneness **12** perseverance, sedulousness, significance **13** attentiveness **15** industriousness
- **make application**
03 sue

applied
◇ *anagram indicator*
04 real **06** actual, useful **07** hands-on **08** relevant **09** practical **10** functional
- **applied to**
02 on

apply
03 fit, lay, ply, put, rub, set, sue, use **04** give, suit, turn **05** brush, claim, exert, lay on, order, paint, put on, refer, smear, study, wield **06** affect, anoint, appeal, appose, ask for, assign, bestow, betake, commit, devote, direct, draw on, employ, engage, relate, resort **07** address, adhibit, execute, harness, inquire, involve, pertain, present, request, solicit, utilize **08** dedicate, exercise, petition, practise, put in for, resort to, spread on, work hard **09** appertain, cover with, implement, persevere, treat with **10** administer, be diligent, be relevant, buckle down, settle down **11** bring to bear, concentrate, knuckle down, requisition, write off for **12** make an effort, write away for **13** be industrious, be significant, bring into play **14** commit yourself, devote yourself, fill in a form for **15** put into practice
- **apply carelessly**
04 slap

appoint
03 fix, set **04** cast, hire, make, name, pick, post **05** allot, co-opt, elect, limit, place, put in, voice **06** assign, charge, choose, decide, decree, depute, detail, direct, employ, engage, ordain, select, settle, take on **07** arrange, command, specify, station **08** delegate, nominate **09** designate, determine, establish **10** commission, constitute **13** be shortlisted

appointed
◇ *anagram indicator*
03 due, set **05** fixed **06** chosen **07** decided, decreed, settled **08** allotted, arranged, assigned, destined, ordained **09** scheduled **10** designated, determined **11** established, pre-arranged, preordained

appointment
03 job **04** date, post, room **05** place, tryst **06** choice, naming, office **07** meeting **08** choosing, election, position **09** interview, selection, situation **10** delegation, engagement, nomination, rendezvous **11** arrangement, assignation **12** consultation **13** commissioning
- **keep an appointment**
04 meet

apportion
04 deal, mete **05** allot, carve, grant, share, stint, weigh **06** assign, divide, morsel, number, ration **07** deal out, dole out, hand out, mete out **08** allocate, dispense, share out **09** admeasure, ration out **10** distribute, measure out

apportionment
05 grant, share **06** ration **07** dealing, handout, sharing **08** division **09** allotment, rationing **10** allocation, assignment **12** dispensation, distribution

apposite
03 apt **06** suited **07** apropos, germane, in point **08** relevant, suitable **09** befitting, pertinent **10** applicable, to the point **11** appropriate **12** to the purpose

appraisal
◇ *anagram indicator*
05 assay, prise, prize **06** rating, review, survey **07** opinion **08** estimate, once-over **09** judgement, reckoning, valuation **10** assessment, estimation, evaluation, inspection **11** examination **12** appreciation

appraise
04 rate **05** assay, judge, sum up, value **06** assess, review, size up, survey **07** examine, inspect, valuate **08** estimate, evaluate, once-over

appreciable
04 vast **08** definite, sensible **10** noticeable, ponderable **11** discernible, perceptible, significant, substantial **12** considerable, recognizable

appreciably
08 markedly **10** definitely, noticeably **11** perceptibly **12** considerably **13** significantly, substantially

appreciate
03 see **04** gain, go up, grow, know, like, rise **05** enjoy, grasp, mount, prize, sense, thank, value **06** admire, esteem, regard, relish, savour **07** apprise,

 prize, cherish, enhance, improve,
late, realize, respect, welcome
 increase, perceive, treasure **09** be
vare of, recognize **10** comprehend,
rengthen, understand
 acknowledge **12** be indebted to,
ke kindly to **13** be conscious of, be
ateful for, be sensitive to, give thanks
r, think highly of **14** be appreciative,
mpathize with

ppreciation
 gain, rise **05** grasp, sense
 esteem, growth, liking, notice,
aise, regard, relish, review, thanks
 feeling, respect, valuing
 analysis, critique, increase,
mpathy **09** awareness, enjoyment,
atitude, inflation, judgement,
nowledge, valuation **10** admiration,
sessment, cognizance, commentary,
calation, estimation, evaluation,
ligation, perception, respecting
 enhancement, high opinion,
provement, realization, recognition,
nsitivity **12** gratefulness,
debtedness, thankfulness
 comprehension, understanding
 responsiveness
 acknowledgement
expression of appreciation
 ta **05** merci, mercy, super
 cheers!, phwoah, phwoar, thanks
 thank you **10** danke schon

ppreciative
 mindful, obliged, pleased
 admiring, beholden, grateful,
debted, thankful **09** conscious,
nsitive **10** perceptive, respectful,
sponsive, supportive **11** encouraging
 enthusiastic **13** knowledgeable

pprehend
 nab, see **04** bust, grab, nick, take,
vig **05** catch, grasp, run in, seize
 arrest, collar, detain, pick up, pull in
 believe, capture, realize
 conceive, consider, perceive
 deprehend, recognize
 comprehend, understand

pprehension
 fear **05** alarm, doubt, dread, grasp,
alm, worry **06** arrest, belief, noesis,
king, unease, uptake **07** anxiety,
pture, concern, jitters, seizure,
llies **08** disquiet, mistrust
 detention, misgiving, suspicion
 cognizance, conception,
reboding, perception, the willies,
easiness **11** butterflies, discernment,
rvousness, realization, recognition,
pidation **12** collywobbles,
ellection, perturbation
 comprehension, heebie-jeebies,
derstanding

pprehensive
 toey **06** afraid, uneasy **07** alarmed,
xious, fearful, nervous, worried
 bothered, doubtful, insecure
 concerned **10** suspicious
 distrustful, mistrustful **13** on
nterhooks

apprehensively
08 uneasily **09** anxiously, fearfully,
nervously **10** doubtfully
12 suspiciously **13** distrustfully,
mistrustfully

apprentice
01 L **03** app, cub **04** snob, tiro, tyro
05 cadet, maiko, pupil **06** commis,
indent, intern, novice, rookie **07** flat
cap, learner, recruit, starter, student,
trainee **08** beginner, improver,
newcomer, prentice, servitor, turnover
11 probationer **13** printer's devil

apprenticeship
09 Lehrjahre, novitiate **11** studentship,
traineeship, trial period **14** training
period

apprise
04 tell, warn **05** brief **06** advise,
inform, notify, tip off **08** acquaint,
intimate **09** ascertain, enlighten
11 communicate

approach
◇ *juxtaposition indicator*
03 nie, way **04** cost, draw, meet, near,
nigh, plea, road **05** abord, anear, angle,
begin, close, coast, coste, drive, greet,
knock, means, reach, run-in, slant,
style, treat **06** access, accost, advent,
appeal, arrive, avenue, broach,
coming, gain on, go near, invite,
manner, method, stance, system,
tackle, talk to **07** accoast, address,
advance, apply to, arrival, catch up,
contact, doorway, get onto, mention,
opinion, passage, request, speak to,
succeed, tactics **08** advances, appeal
to, attitude, bear down, border on,
commence, deal with, draw near,
driveway, embark on, entrance, go
nearer, landfall, oncoming, overture,
position, proposal, set about, sound
out, strategy **09** introduce, overtures,
procedure, technique, threshold,
undertake, viewpoint **10** buttonhole,
come closer, come nearer, come near
to, coming near, invitation, launch into,
standpoint, suggestion **11** application,
appropinque, approximate, come
close to, coming close, compare with,
get closer to, move towards,
perspective, point of view, proposition,
suggestions **12** make advances
13 appropinquate, make overtures,
modus operandi **14** advance towards,
course of action, get in touch with,
proceed towards

approachable
04 open, warm **07** affable **08** friendly,
informal, pleasant, sociable
09 agreeable, congenial, get-at-able,
reachable, welcoming **10** accessible,
attainable **15** easy to get on with

approbation
06 esteem, favour, praise **07** respect
08 applause, approval **09** allowance,
laudation **10** acceptance, well-liking
11 countenance, endorsement, good
opinion, recognition
12 commendation **13** encouragement

appropriate
03 apt, fit, nab **04** jump, lift, meet,
nick, sink, take **05** annex, filch, pinch,
right, seize, steal, swipe, usurp
06 assume, choice, pilfer, pocket,
proper, seemly, spot-on, suited, thieve,
timely **07** apropos, correct, fitting,
germane, impound, in order, pre-
empt, purloin, trouser **08** accepted,
arrogate, becoming, embezzle, glom
on to, knock off, liberate, peculate,
property, relevant, suitable
09 befitting, congruous, expedient,
opportune, pertinent, well-timed
10 applicable, commandeer,
confiscate, felicitous, seasonable, to
the point, well-chosen
11 appurtenant, expropriate, in
character, make off with, requisition
12 appertaining **14** misappropriate

appropriately
07 apropos **08** properly, suitably
09 correctly, fittingly **10** relevantly
12 felicitously

approval
02 OK **03** nod **04** okay, wink **05** favor,
leave, voice **06** assent, esteem, favour,
honour, liking, praise, regard
07 acclaim, approof, consent, go-
ahead, licence, mandate, plaudit,
respect, support **08** agrément,
applause, blessing, sanction, thumbs-
up **09** agreement **10** acceptance,
admiration, green light, imprimatur,
permission, validation **11** acclamation,
approbation, concurrence,
endorsement, good opinion, rubber
stamp **12** appreciation,
commendation, confirmation,
ratification **13** authorization,
certification **14** recommendation
• **expression of approval**
02 ay, OK **03** aye, oke, olé, rah, yay
04 good, hear, okay, viva, vive
05 bravo, hurra, huzza, there, vivat
06 beauty, hooray, hurrah, hurray
07 attaboy, too much, top-hole, way to
go! **08** attagirl, long live, zindabad
09 full marks, good on you **10** good for
you, hubba hubba

approve
02 OK **03** buy, dig **04** amen, back, like,
pass **05** adopt, allow, bless, carry
06 accept, admire, concur, esteem,
favour, permit, praise, ratify, regard,
second, uphold **07** acclaim, agree to,
applaud, commend, confirm, endorse,
mandate, support **08** accede to, assent
to, hold with, sanction, validate
09 authorize, consent to, recommend
10 appreciate, homologate
11 countenance, rubber-stamp, think
well of **12** give the nod to **13** be
pleased with, think highly of

approved
03 app **06** proper **07** correct
08 accepted, favoured, official,
orthodox **09** permitted, preferred
10 authorized, recognized, sanctioned
11 comme il faut, permissible,
recommended **13** authoritative

approving
08 admiring, praising **09** laudatory
10 favourable, respectful, supportive
12 appreciative, commendatory

approvingly
10 admiringly, favourably **12** with
pleasure **14** appreciatively

approximate
03 app **04** like, near, wild **05** close,
loose, rough, round **06** coarse
07 guessed, inexact, similar, verge on
08 approach, ballpark, border on,
relative, resemble **09** estimated,
imprecise **10** come near to **11** be
similar to, come close to **14** be
tantamount to

approximately
01 c **02** ca **03** odd, say **04** or so, some
05 about, circa **06** around, nearly
07 close to, loosely, roughly **09** just
about, not far off, rounded up **10** give
or take, more or less, round about
11 approaching, rounded down **13** in
the region of, or thereabouts,
something like **14** in round figures, in
round numbers **15** in the vicinity of

approximation
05 guess **08** approach, estimate,
likeness **09** rough idea, semblance
10 conjecture, estimation, similarity
11 guesstimate, resemblance
14 ballpark figure, correspondence

appurtenance
09 equipment, trappings
10 belongings **11** accessories,
impedimenta **13** paraphernalia

April
03 Apr

a priori
07 deduced **08** inferred
11 conjectural, theoretical
12 hypothetical **13** suppositional

apron
03 bay, bib, rim **04** brat, edge, tier
05 dicky, skirt **06** border, dickey,
dickie, fringe, napron, pinnie, tabard
07 placket, tablier **08** pinafore,
standing **09** barm-cloth, forecourt,
periphery **10** loading bay **12** hard-
standing

apropos
02 re **03** apt **05** right **06** proper,
seemly, timely **07** correct, fitting
08 accepted, becoming, relevant,
suitable **09** befitting, opportune,
pertinent, regarding **10** applicable,
felicitous, respecting, seasonable, to
the point, well-chosen **11** in respect of
12 in relation to, with regard to **13** with
respect to **14** on the subject of **15** with
reference to

apse
04 bema **06** concha, exedra
07 exhedra **09** apsidiole, prothesis

apt
03 fit **04** gleg **05** given, happy, prone,
ready **06** liable, likely, proper, seemly,
spot-on, timely, toward **07** correct,
fitting, germane, subject, tending
08 accurate, apposite, disposed,
inclined, relevant, suitable
10 acceptable, applicable, seasonable
11 appropriate

aptitude
04 bent, gift, turn **05** flair, skill
06 talent **07** ability, faculty, fitness,
leaning **08** capacity, facility, tendency
09 endowment, quickness
10 capability, cleverness
11 disposition, inclination, proficiency
12 intelligence **14** natural ability

aptly
05 fitly **08** suitably **09** fittingly
10 appositely, relevantly, to the point
13 appropriately

aquatic
03 sea **05** fluid, river, water **06** liquid,
marine, watery **07** fluvial **08** maritime,
nautical

aquiline
06 hooked **10** hooknosed

Arab
02 Ar

Arabic
02 Ar **04** Arab
See also **alphabet**

arable
03 lay, lea, lee, ley **06** fecund **07** fertile
08 farmable, fruitful, tillable
10 cultivable, ploughable, productive
See also **crop**

arachnid *see* **spider**

arbiter
05 judge **06** expert, master, pundit,
umpire **07** oddsman, referee
08 governor **09** authority, birlieman,
byrlaw-man **10** controller
11 adjudicator

arbitrarily
08 by chance, randomly **11** illogically
12 irrationally, subjectively,
unreasonably **14** inconsistently

arbitrary
06 chance, random **08** absolute,
despotic, dogmatic, personal
09 illogical, imperious, whimsical
10 autocratic, capricious, dominative,
high-handed, irrational, subjective,
tyrannical, unreasoned **11** dictatorial,
domineering, instinctive, magisterial,
overbearing **12** conventional,
inconsistent, unreasonable
13 discretionary

arbitrate
05 judge **06** decide, settle, umpire
07 mediate, referee **09** determine
10 adjudicate **13** pass judgement **14**
in judgement

arbitration
08 decision **09** arbitrage, judgement
mediation **10** compromise, settleme
11 arbitrament, negotiation
12 adjudication, intervention
13 determination

arbitrator
03 ref, ump **05** judge **06** umpire
07 arbiter, referee **08** mediator
09 go-between, moderator
10 negotiator **11** adjudicator
12 intermediary

arbour
03 bay **05** bower **06** alcove, grotto,
herbar, recess **07** pergola, retreat,
shelter **09** sanctuary

arc
03 bow **04** arch, bend, spin, turn
05 curve, round **06** swerve
09 curvature **10** curved line,
semicircle

arcade
04 mall, stoa **05** plaza **06** loggia,
piazza **07** gallery, portico **08** cloiste
galleria, precinct **09** colonnade,
peristyle, triforium **10** covered way
12 shopping mall

arcane
06 hidden, occult, secret
07 cryptic, obscure **08** abstruse,
esoteric, mystical, profound
09 concealed, enigmatic, recondite
10 mysterious

arch
◇ *anagram indicator*
03 arc, bow, hog, sly **04** bend, dome
hoop, span **05** chief, curve, embow,
ogive, roach, vault **06** bridge, cambe
diadem, girdle, invert, portal, shrewd
zygoma **07** archway, concave,
cunning, playful, roguish, squinch,
waggish **08** cross-rib, espiègle,
platband **09** curvature, principal
10 manteltree, mysterious, semicircl
11 counterfort, mischievous **13** arc d
triomphe

rchaeology

Archaeological terms include:

3 cup, dig, jar, jug, tor, urn
4 adze, bowl, celt, cist, core, kist, site, tell
5 blade, burin, cairn, ditch, flake, flask, flint, henge, hoard, mound, mummy, shard, sherd, stele, whorl
6 barrow, beaker, bogman, dolmen, dromos, eolith, menhir, midden, mosaic, patina, strata, trench
7 amphora, anomaly, cave art, crannog, handaxe, Iron Age, neolith, obelisk, papyrus, rock art, sondage, stratum, tumulus
8 artefact, artifact, cromlech, excavate, hill fort, knapping, ley lines, megalith, post hole, Stone Age
9 arrowhead, Bronze Age, cartouche, crop-marks, earthwork, enclosure, hypocaust, longhouse, Neolithic
10 Anglo-Saxon, assemblage, excavation, geophysics, grave goods, inhumation, roundhouse, tear bottle
1 burial mound, rock shelter, stone circle
2 amphitheatre, archaeometry, carbon dating, field walking, Interglacial, Palaeolithic, stratigraphy
3 kitchen-midden, standing stone, treasure trove, wattle and daub
4 hunter-gatherer

Archaeologists include:

4 Uhle (Max)
5 Clark (Grahame), Evans (Sir Arthur)
6 Anning (Mary), Breuil (Henri), Carter (Howard), Childe (Gordon), Clarke (David L), Daniel (Glyn), Hawkes (Jacquetta), Kidder (A V), Layard (Sir Austen), Leakey (Louis), Leakey (Mary), Petrie (Sir Flinders), Putnam (Frederic Ward)
7 Binford (Lewis), Renfrew (Colin, Lord), Thomsen (Christian), Wheeler (Sir Mortimer), Woolley (Sir Leonard), Worsaae (Jens Jacob)
8 Breasted (J H), Cunliffe (Barry), Fiorelli (Giuseppe), Koldewey (Robert), Mallowan (Sir Max), Mariette (Auguste), Marshall (Sir John)
9 Andersson (Johan Gunnar)
10 Pitt-Rivers (Augustus), Schliemann (Heinrich)
1 Champollion (Jean François)

rchaic

3 old **5** passé **6** bygone, old hat, quaint **7** ancient, antique
8 medieval, obsolete, outdated, utmoded **09** mediaeval, out-of-date, rimitive **10** antiquated
1 obsolescent, out of the ark
2 antediluvian, old-fashioned

rchangel

8 hierarch **10** dead-nettle **14** garden ngelica

ee also **angel**

archbishop

03 abp **07** primate **12** metropolitan
See also **cardinal**

Archbishops include:

04 Gray (Gordon), Hope (David), Hume (Basil), Kemp (John), Lang (Cosmo), Laud (William), Tutu (Desmond)
05 Beran (Josef), Carey (George), Glemp (Jozef)
06 Anselm, Beaton (David), Becket (Thomas à), Benson (Edward White), Blanch (Stuart), Coggan (Donald), Edmund (St), Fisher (Geoffrey), Heenan (John Carmel), Hilary (of Poitiers, St), Mannix (Daniel), Morton (John), Parker (Matthew), Potter (John), Ramsay (Michael), Runcie (Robert), Temple (Frederick), Temple (William), Trench (Richard Chenevix), Ussher (James), Walter (Hubert), Warham (William), Wolsey (Thomas)
07 Arundel (Thomas), Cranmer (Thomas), Dunstan (St), Habgood (John), Langton (Stephen), Mendoza (Pedro Gonzalez de), Sentamu (John), Sheldon (Gilbert), Wiseman (Nicholas)
08 Adalbert, Cuthbert, Davidson (Randall), Ethelred, Makarios, Whitgift (John), Williams (Rowan)
09 Augustine (St), Wyszynski (Stefan)
10 Damaskinos, Huddleston (Trevor)

archdiocese *see* diocese

archer

04 Eros, Tell **05** Cupid **06** bow-boy, bowman **09** sagittary **11** Sagittarius, toxophilite

archetypal

05 ideal, model, stock **07** classic, typical **08** original, standard
09 exemplary **12** paradigmatic
14 characteristic, quintessential, representative

archetype

04 form, idea, type **05** ideal, model
06 entity **07** classic, epitome, pattern
08 exemplar, original, paradigm, standard **09** precursor, prototype
10 stereotype **12** quintessence, typification

archipelago

Archipelagoes include:

04 Cuba, Fiji, Sulu
05 Åland, Gulag, Japan, Malay, Malta, Tonga
06 Arctic, Azores, Chagos, Kosrae, Tuvalu
07 Bahamas, Mayotte, Tuamotu
08 Bismarck, Cyclades, Kiribati, Maldives, Moluccas, Svalbard
09 Alexander, Antarctic, Cape Verde, Catherine, Galápagos, Indonesia, Louisiade, Marquesas, North Land
10 Ahvenanmaa, Les Iles d'Or, Seychelles, Vesterålen, West Indies
11 Iles d'Hyères, Line Islands, Philippines, Spitsbergen, Vesteraalen
12 Kuril Islands, Novaya Zemlya, Pearl Islands, Spice Islands, Sunda Islands
13 Aegean Islands, Caicos Islands, Canary Islands, Ellice Islands, Ionian Islands, Tubuai Islands
14 Austral Islands, Bijagos Islands, Channel Islands, Franz Josef Land, Gilbert Islands, Leeward Islands, Lofoten Islands, Nicholas II Land, Oki Archipelago, Papua New Guinea, Phoenix Islands, Solomon Islands, Tierra del Fuego, Visayan Islands
15 Balearic Islands, Friendly Islands, Marshall Islands, Pitcairn Islands, Severnaya Zemlya, Wallis and Futuna, Windward Islands

architect

05 maker **06** author, shaper
07 creator, founder, planner
08 designer, engineer, inventor
10 instigator, mastermind, originator, prime mover **11** constructor, draughtsman **13** master builder

Architects include:

04 Adam (Robert), Drew (Dame Jane), Loos (Adolf), Nash (John), Shaw (Norman), Wren (Sir Christopher)
05 Aalto (Alvar), Barry (Sir Charles), Costa (Lucio), Dudok (Willem), Gaudí (Antonio), Jones (Inigo), Meier (Richard), Nervi (Pier Luigi), Piano (Renzo), Pugin (Augustus), Scott (Sir George Gilbert), Scott (Sir Giles Gilbert), Soane (Sir John), Speer (Albert), Velde (Henri van de)
06 Casson (Sir Hugh), Cubitt (Thomas), Foster (Sir Norman), Giotto, Howard (Sir Ebenezer), Lescot (Pierre), Morris (William), Paxton (Sir Joseph), Pisano (Giovanni), Rogers (Sir Richard), Semper (Gottfried), Serlio (Sebastiano), Spence (Sir Basil), Wright (Frank Lloyd)
07 Alberti (Leon Battista), Asplund (Erik Gunnar), Behrens (Peter), Bernini (Gian Lorenzo), Gropius (Walter), Ictinus, Imhotep, Lutyens (Sir Edwin), Olmsted (Frederick Law), Vignola (Giacomo da)
08 Bramante (Donato), Jacobsen (Arne), Miralles (Enric), Niemeyer (Oscar), Palladio (Andrea), Piranesi (Giambattista), Saarinen (Eero), Sottsass (Ettore), Stirling (James), Sullivan (Louis), Vanbrugh (Sir John)
09 Borromini (Francesco), Haussmann (Georges, Baron), Hawksmoor (Nicholas), Libeskind (Daniel), Mackmurdo (Arthur), Vitruvius
10 Mackintosh (Charles Rennie)
11 Le Corbusier
12 Brunelleschi (Filippo), Viollet-Le-Duc (Eugène)
14 Mies van der Rohe (Ludwig)
15 Leonardo da Vinci

architecture

04 form **05** frame, set-up, style
06 design, make-up, system
08 building, planning **09** designing,
framework, structure **11** arrangement,
composition **12** conformation,
constitution, construction,
organization **13** configuration
14 architectonics

Architecture styles include:

04 Adam
05 Greek, Saxon
06 Gothic, modern, Norman, rococo
07 barocco, baroque, Italian, Lombard,
mission, mudéjar
08 baronial, high tech
09 beaux arts, brutalism, Byzantine,
Cape Dutch, decorated, Palladian,
Queen Anne
10 art nouveau, Corinthian,
Romanesque
11 Elizabethan, Renaissance
13 Gothic revival, international,
neoclassicism, Perpendicular, post-
modernism
15 churrigueresque

Architectural features include:

03 orb, web
04 anta, apse, arch, base, bell, boss,
cove, crop, cusp, cyma, dado, drum,
list, neck, ribs, vase, void
05 antae, attic, congé, crown, flute,
gable, gavel, glyph, groin, gutta,
hance, helix, mould, nerve, ogive,
print, pylon, quirk, scape, socle,
spire, stria, talon, tenia, tondo,
torus, tower, truss, vault
06 abacus, atrium, canton, caulis,
chevet, cinque, cippus, column,
concha, congee, coping, corona,
coving, crenel, dentil, facade,
fascia, fillet, finial, flèche, fornix,
frieze, haunch, impost, lierne,
metope, patera, patten, pillar,
podium, portal, reglet, regula,
rosace, scotia, severy, striae, taenia,
turret, wreath
07 aileron, annulet, balloon, bandrol,
capital, cavetti, cavetto, conchae,
corbeil, cornice, crocket, diglyph,
doucine, echinus, fantail, festoon,
fronton, fusarol, grecque, larmier,
mullion, necking, nervure, pannier,
parapet, Persian, pilotis, portico,
rosette, solidum, squinch, surbase,
tambour, telamon, tondino
08 abutment, accolade, apophyge,
astragal, baguette, bandelet,
banderol, bannerol, bellcote,
buttress, canephor, cartouch,
chapiter, chaptrel, ciborium,
cincture, crenelle, diastyle, dipteral,
dipteros, entresol, epistyle,
frontoon, fusarole, gorgerin,
imperial, intrados, mascaron,
moulding, pediment, pilaster,
prostyle, pulpitum, rockwork, sept-
foil, skewback, spandrel, spandril,
terminus, triglyph, tympanum,
voussoir
09 apsidiole, archivolt, balection,

banderole, bolection, cartouche,
crossette, cul-de-four, decastyle,
embrasure, embrazure, foliation,
guilloche, hypostyle, mezzanine,
modillion, octastyle, octostyle,
peristyle, strap work, stylobate,
tierceron, triforium, water leaf
10 acroterion, architrave, ball-flower,
bratticing, cauliculus, chambranle,
clearstory, clerestory, demicupola,
ditriglyph, egg-and-dart, eye-
catcher, feathering, jerkinhead,
pendentive, quatrefoil, subarcuate,
water table, weathering
11 brattishing, entablature, paternoster
12 egg-and-anchor, egg-and-tongue,
frontispiece
13 chain moulding, interpilaster,
quatrefeuille, vermiculation
14 Catherine-wheel, flying buttress

See also **arch**

Architectural and building terms include:

04 dado, dome, jamb, roof
05 Doric, eaves, groin, Ionic, ridge,
Tudor
06 alcove, annexe, coving, duplex,
façade, fascia, fillet, finial, frieze,
Gothic, lintel, Norman, pagoda,
plinth, reveal, rococo, scroll, soffit,
stucco, Tuscan
07 baroque, cornice, festoon, fletton,
fluting, mullion, pantile, parapet,
rafters, Regency, rotunda
08 baluster, capstone, dogtooth, dry-
stone, gargoyle, Georgian,
pinnacle, sacristy, terrazzo,
wainscot
09 bas relief, classical, Edwardian,
elevation, gatehouse, Queen Anne,
roughcast
10 architrave, barge-board,
Corinthian, drawbridge,
flamboyant, groundplan,
Romanesque, weathering
11 coping stone, corner-stone,
Elizabethan, Flemish bond
12 Early English, frontispiece, half-
timbered

archives

04 roll **05** deeds **06** annals, papers
07 ledgers, records **09** documents,
memorials, registers **10** chronicles
11 memorabilia

arctic

05 polar **06** boreal, frosty, frozen
07 glacial, subzero **08** Far North,
freezing, Siberian **11** far northern,
hyperborean **12** bitterly cold, freezing
cold
• **arctic animal**
09 polar bear

ardent

03 hot **04** avid, keen, warm **05** eager,
fiery **06** fervid, fierce, strong
07 burning, devoted, fervent, intense,
mettled, zealous **08** sanguine, spirited,
vehement **09** dedicated, perfervid,
spiritous **10** mettlesome, passionate
11 empassioned, evangelical,

impassioned, warm-blooded
12 enthusiastic **14** enthusiastical
• **be ardent**
04 glow

ardently

05 hotly **06** avidly, warmly **07** eagerly
08 strongly **09** devotedly, fervently,
intensely, zealously **10** vehemently
12 passionately

ardour

04 fire, heat, lust, rage, zeal, zest
05 flame, wrath **06** duende, fervor,
spirit, warmth **07** avidity, fervour,
passion **08** covetise, devotion,
keenness **09** animation, eagerness,
intensity, vehemence **10** dedication,
enthusiasm **12** empressement

arduous

04 hard **05** chore, harsh, heavy, steep,
stiff, tough **06** severe, taxing, tiring,
uphill **07** be a slog, onerous **08** be
murder, daunting, rigorous, wearying
09 difficult, fatiguing, gruelling,
laborious, punishing, strenuous
10 burdensome, exhausting,
formidable **12** backbreaking

are

01 A **04** live **05** exist

area

01 A **04** beat, part, size, zone **05** field,
manor, patch, place, range, realm,
scope, tract, width, world **06** branch,
domain, extent, parish, region, sector,
sphere **07** breadth, compass, enclave,
expanse, portion, quarter, section,
stretch, terrain **08** district, environs,
locality, precinct, province **09** territory
10 department **11** environment,
reserve area **13** catchment area,
neighbourhood

See also **administrative**; **council**;
county; **district**

arena

04 area, bowl, ring **05** field, realm,
scene, world **06** domain, ground, sphere
07 stadium, theatre **08** coliseum,
province **10** department, hippodrome
11 battlefield **12** amphitheatre,
battleground **14** area of conflict

Ares

04 Mars

Argentina

02 RA **03** ARG

argon

02 Ar

argot

04 cant **05** idiom, slang **06** jargon
08 parlance

arguable

04 moot **09** debatable, uncertain,
undecided **10** disputable
11 contentious, open to doubt
12 questionable **14** controvertible,
open to question

arguably

05 maybe **08** possibly, probably
10 most likely **15** in all likelihood

gue

rag, row **04** feud, hold, moot, show,
ar **05** claim, fight, imply, nyaff, plead,
ove **06** assert, bicker, cangle,
bate, denote, haggle, hassle, reason
accurse, contend, declare, discuss,
play, dispute, exhibit, fall out,
arrel, quibble, suggest, wrangle,
estle **08** convince, disagree,
suade, have a row, indicate, logicize,
aintain, manifest, persuade,
estion, squabble **09** altercate, chop
gic, have it out, have words, join
ue, take issue, talk out of **10** chew
e fat, chew the rag, contradict, hold a
ef **11** cross swords, demonstrate,
ostulate, remonstrate **13** be
idence for, have it out with
be at loggerheads, have a bone to
ck

gument

pro, row **04** beef, blue, case, feud,
ot, spat, tiff, yike **05** claim, clash,
ht, lemma, logic, run-in, set-to,
eme, topic, yikes **06** barney, bust-up,
ntra, debate, dust-up, hassle, reason,
ckus, rumpus, tangle, thesis
contest, defence, dispute, fallacy,
tline, polemic, quarrel, summary,
angle **08** conflict, ding-dong,
idence, exchange, squabble,
nopsis, trilemma **09** argy-bargy,
ertion, enthymeme, objection,
odlibet, rationale, reasoning,
ogism **10** contention, discussion
altercation, controverse,
ntroversy, declaration
antistrophon, disagreement
argumentation, demonstration,
postulation, justification, running
ttle, shouting-match, slanging-
tch **14** heated exchange

gumentation

case **05** claim, logic **06** debate
defence **08** argument, disproof,
idence **09** rationale, reasoning
contention **13** expostulation,
tification

gumentative

chippy **07** stroppy **08** captious,
ntrary, perverse **09** litigious,
lemical, truculent **11** belligerent,
ntentious, dissentious, opinionated,
arrelsome **12** cantankerous,
putatious

id

dry **04** drab, dull, flat **05** baked,
id, waste **06** barren, boring, desert,
eary, jejune, meagre, torrid
parched, sterile, tedious **08** lifeless
infertile, torrefied, waterless
colourless, dehydrated,
siccated, monotonous, spiritless,
nspired **12** moistureless,
ivelled up, unproductive
uninteresting

ight

OK **05** aptly, fitly, truly **07** exactly,
htly **08** properly, suitably
correctly **10** accurately

arise

◇ *reversal down indicator*
04 come, flow, go up, lift, rise, soar,
stem **05** begin, climb, ensue, get up,
issue, mount, occur, start, tower
06 appear, ascend, come up, crop up,
derive, emerge, follow, happen, result,
rise up, spring **07** emanate, proceed,
stand up **08** commence **10** be caused
by **11** be a result of, come to light
12 straighten up **13** come into being,
get to your feet, present itself

aristocracy

04 nobs, rank **05** élite, lords, peers,
toffs **06** gentry, ladies **07** peerage
08 nobility, noblemen **09** gentility,
optimates, top drawer **10** haute
monde, noblewomen, patricians,
patriciate, upper class, upper crust
11 aristocrats, high society, ruling class
15 privileged class

aristocrat

03 nob **04** lady, lord, peer, toff
05 noble **06** Junker **07** grandee,
high-hat, peeress **08** eupatrid,
nobleman, optimate **09** patrician
10 grande dame, noblewoman
13 grand seigneur

See also **nobility**

aristocratic

01 U **05** élite, noble **06** lordly, titled
07 courtly, elegant, refined
08 highborn, well-born **09** dignified,
patrician **10** upper-class, upper-crust
11 blue-blooded **12** thoroughbred

arithmetic

07 algebra **08** algorism, logistic
11 computation

Arizona

02 AZ **04** Ariz

Arkansas

02 AR **03** Ark

Arkwright

04 Noah

arm

03 bay, fin, rig **04** barb, cove, gird, heel,
iron, limb, loch, prop, whip, wing
05 array, brace, crank, creek, equip,
firth, force, index, inlet, issue, might,
power, prime, rearm, steel, wiper
06 branch, outfit, sleeve, supply,
weapon **07** channel, estuary, euripus,
forearm, fortify, furnish, passage,
prepare, protect, provide, quillon, sea
loch, section **08** accoutre, brachium,
division, embattle, offshoot, strength
09 appendage, authority, extension,
reinforce, upper limb **10** department,
detachment, projection, strengthen
12 embranchment **15** windscreen-
wiper

armada

04 navy **05** fleet **08** flotilla, squadron
10 naval force

armadillo

04 peba **05** tatou **07** Dasypus, tatouay
10 pichiciego

armaments

04 arms, guns **06** cannon **07** weapons
08 ordnance, weaponry **09** artillery,
munitions **10** ammunition

armed

06 fitted **07** packing **08** tooled up
• **armed man**
03 gun

armed services *see* **army**; **air force**;
military; **navy**; **rank**

Armenia

02 AM **03** ARM

armistice

04 pact **05** peace, truce **09** ceasefire
10 still-stand **11** peace treaty

armour

04 gear, gere, mail, weed **05** plate,
proof, stand **06** corium, shield
07 panoply **08** armature **12** iron-
cladding

Armour includes:

04 cush, jack, jamb, lame, mail, suit,
tace
05 armet, brace, cuish, culet, curat,
jambe, salet, tasse, visor
06 beaver, byrnie, casque, couter,
crinet, cuisse, curiet, faulds, gorget,
greave, grille, gusset, helmet,
jamber, morion, poleyn, rondel,
salade, sallet, taslet, tasset, tonlet,
tuille, voider
07 ailette, barding, basinet, besagew,
brasset, buckler, cap-à-pie, corslet,
cuirass, harness, hauberk, jambeau,
jambeux, jambier, lamboys,
morrion, palette, placcat, placket,
poitrel, puldron, sabaton, surcoat,
ventail
08 aventail, bascinet, brassard,
brassart, chaffron, chamfron,
chausses, corselet, gauntlet,
giambeux, jambeaux, jazerant,
pauldron, pectoral, placcate,
pouldron, shynbald, solleret,
spaulder, vambrace, ventaile,
ventayle
09 aventaile, backpiece, backplate,
chain mail, chamfrain, garniture,
habergeon, jesserant, mandilion,
mandylion, nosepiece, rerebrace,
vantbrace, vantbrass
10 body armour, cataphract, coat-
armour, coat of mail
11 breastplate, genouillère,
mentonnière, plate armour, scale
armour
12 splint armour

---

armoured

06 plated **08** iron-clad, loricate
09 bomb-proof, protected, toughened
10 reinforced **11** bullet-proof, steel-
plated **12** armour-plated

armoury

05 depot, stock **07** arsenal
08 magazine **09** arms depot,
garderobe, stockpile **10** repository
13 ordnance depot **14** ammunition
dump

armpit
05 oxter **06** axilla

arms
04 guns **05** crest **06** cannon, emblem, shield **07** weapons **08** blazonry, firearms, heraldry, insignia, missiles, ordnance, weaponry **09** armaments, artillery, munitions **10** ammunition, coat-of-arms, escutcheon **11** projectiles **14** heraldic device

army
03 mob **04** host, pack, sena **05** crowd, horde, swarm **06** throng, troops **07** cohorts, legions, militia **08** brachial, infantry, military, soldiers, soldiery **09** multitude **10** armed force, arrière-ban, land forces **11** thin red line

Armies include:

02 AA, SA, TA
03 AVR, GAR, IRA, USA, WLA
04 BAOR, INLA
05 Sally
06 Church, Tartan
08 New Model
09 Eurocorps, Salvation
10 Blue Ribbon, Women's Land
11 Grande Armée, Territorial

See also rank; regiment
• **army corps** *see* regiment
• **army regulation**
02 AR

aroma
04 nose **05** fumet, odour, scent, smell **06** savour **07** bouquet, fumette, perfume **09** fragrance, redolence

aromatic
05 balmy, fresh, spicy **07** pungent, savoury, scented **08** fragrant, perfumed, redolent **11** odoriferous **12** sweet-scented **13** sweet-smelling

around
◇ *anagram indicator*
◇ *containment indicator*
◇ *reversal indicator*
01 c **02** ca **04** near **05** about, circa, close, round **06** at hand, nearby, nearly **07** all over, close by, close to, roughly **08** framed by, to and fro **09** enclosing **10** encircling, everywhere, more or less, on all sides, throughout **11** surrounding, within reach **12** circumjacent, encompassing, everywhere in, here and there, on all sides of, to all parts of **13** approximately, circumambient, on every side of **15** in all directions

arousal
◇ *anagram indicator*
06 firing **08** stirring **09** agitation, evocation **10** excitement **11** provocation, titillation **12** getting going, inflammation

arouse
◇ *anagram indicator*
04 fire, goad, move, spur, whet **05** alarm, cause, evoke, incur, pique, rouse, spark, tease, waken **06** awaken, beat up, bestir, excite, incite, induce,

kindle, prompt, stir up, turn on, wake up, whip up **07** agitate, animate, inflame, knock up, provoke, quicken, sharpen, startle, trigger, upraise **08** get going, summon up **09** call forth, eroticize, galvanize, impassion, instigate, stimulate, suscitate, titillate **11** disentrance

arraign
06 accuse, charge, impugn, indict **07** appoint, empeach, impeach **09** prosecute **11** incriminate **13** call to account

arraignment
04 case **05** trial **06** charge **07** summons **10** accusation, indictment **11** impeachment, legal action **13** incrimination

arrange
◇ *anagram indicator*
02 do **03** fix, set **04** cast, comb, file, gang, list, make, plan, sift, size, sort, stow, tidy, tile, trim **05** adapt, agree, align, aline, array, braid, class, dress, fix up, grade, group, ink in, order, place, preen, range, score, set up, swing **06** adjust, blouse, codify, decide, design, devise, digest, fettle, format, gather, lay out, line up, make up, ordain, set out, settle **07** address, article, blow-dry, concert, dispose, echelon, enrange, marshal, prepare, process, project, rummage, seriate, set out, windrow **08** alphabet, classify, conclude, contrive, embattle, engineer, enraunge, organize, pencil in, position, regulate, rustle up, settle on, stratify **09** catalogue, collocate, determine, harmonize, methodize, negotiate, serialize **10** categorize, co-ordinate, distribute, foreordain, instrument, put in order, transcribe **11** choreograph, configurate, orchestrate, systematize **12** chronologize

arranged
03 arr

arrangement
◇ *anagram indicator*
03 lay **04** form, pack, plan **05** array, order, plans, score, set-up, taxis, terms **06** design, detail, fixing, format, layout, line-up, method, scheme, system **07** details, display, setting, version **08** contract, disposal, grouping, ordnance, planning, position, schedule **09** agreement, Ausgleich, bandobast, bundobust, digestion, formation, preparing, structure **10** adaptation, compromise, groundwork, schematism, settlement **11** disposition, positioning, preparation **12** modus vivendi, organization, preparations **13** configuration, harmonization, orchestration **14** classification, interpretation **15** instrumentation

arranger
03 arr

arrant
04 rank, vile **05** gross, utter **06** braze, **07** blatant, extreme **08** absolute, complete, flagrant, infamous, outrigh, rascally, thorough **09** barefaced, downright, egregious, notorious, out and-out **11** unmitigated **12** incorrigib **13** thoroughgoing

array
◇ *anagram indicator*
03 set **04** deck, garb, robe, show, tri **05** adorn, align, dress, group, herse, order, range **06** attire, attrap, clothe, draw up, effeir, effere, lay out, line up line-up, matrix, muster, parade, pligh spread **07** apparel, arrange, bedight, bedizen, display, dispose, exhibit, marshal, panoply **08** accoutre, assemble, decorate, position **09** formation **10** assemblage, assortment, collection, exhibition, exposition, habilitate **11** arrangemer disposition, marshalling

arrears
04 debt **05** debts **07** balance, defici **10** amount owed, money owing **11** liabilities **14** sum of money owed
• **in arrears**
04 late **05** owing **06** behind, in debt **07** overdue **10** behindhand **11** back-ganging, outstanding

arrest
◇ *containment indicator*
02 do **03** cop, lag, nab, nip, sus **04** book, bust, grab, grip, halt, hold, l nail, nick, slow, stem, stop, suss **05** block, catch, check, delay, pinch, rivet, run in, seize, stall **06** absorb, attach, collar, detain, engage, fixate, hinder, impede, nobble, pick up, pull retard, stasis, take up **07** attract, captiv capture, engross, inhibit, seizure, snabble, snaffle **08** intrigue, obstruct, restrain, slow down **09** apprehend, detention, epistasis, fascinate, interrup **11** nip in the bud **12** apprehension **15** take into custody
• **under arrest**
06 copped **09** in custody **11** in captiv

arresting
07 amazing, notable **08** engaging, riveting, striking, stunning **10** impressive, noteworthy, noticeab remarkable, surprising **11** conspicuo eye-catching, outstanding **13** extraordinary

arrival
03 arr **04** dawn **05** birth, comer, ent guest, start **06** advent, blow-in, coming, income, origin **07** entrant, fresher, incomer, visitor **08** approac debutant, entrance, freshman, newcomer, visitant **09** debutante, emergence, invention **10** appearanc homecoming, occurrence **11** development

arrive
◇ *juxtaposition indicator*
03 arr, get, hit **04** come, dock, gain, land, make, show **05** enter, fetch, ge

), occur, reach **06** accede, appear,
ttain, become, blow in, come in, come
), drop in, happen, make it, obtain, pull
, roll in, roll up, show up, swan in,
wan up, turn up **07** achieve, check in,
lock in, get here, pitch up, succeed,
urface **08** get there **09** be present,
ammer out, thrash out, touch down
0 accomplish, be a success, be
roduced, come to hand **11** get to the
op, materialize **12** become famous
4 come on the scene **15** become
vailable, come on the market

rrogance
4 side **05** nerve, pride, scorn
6 hubris, hybris, morgue, vanity
7 conceit, disdain, egotism, hauteur,
pinion **08** assuming, boasting,
ontempt, high hand, surquedy
9 contumely, insolence, lordiness,
omposity, surquedry **11** haughtiness,
resumption, superiority
2 snobbishness **13** condescension,
nperiousness **14** high-handedness,
elf-importance

rrogant
4 high **05** cobby, proud, stout
6 lordly, uppity, wanton **07** haughty,
:uck-up, topping **08** assuming,
oastful, insolent, jumped-up,
cornful, snobbish, superior
9 bigheaded, conceited, dangerous,
gotistic, hubristic, imperious
0 disdainful, high-handed, hoity-toity
1 overbearing, overweening,
atronizing, toffee-nosed
2 contemptuous, presumptuous,
upercilious **13** condescending, high
nd mighty, self-important **14** full of
ourself, on the high ropes

rrogantly
4 high **07** proudly **09** haughtily
0 boastfully, insolently, scornfully,
nobbishly **11** conceitedly, imperiously
2 disdainfully, high-handedly
3 hubristically, overbearingly,
verweeningly, patronizingly
4 contemptuously, presumptuously,
uperciliously **15** condescendingly,
elf-importantly

rrogate
5 seize, usurp **06** assume
7 presume **08** take over
0 commandeer **11** appropriate
4 misappropriate

rrogation
7 seizure **10** assumption, possession,
aking over **13** appropriation,
ommandeering

rrow
3 any, ary **04** bolt, dart **05** shaft
6 flight, marker, quar'le **07** dogbolt,
ointer, quarrel, sagitta **08** bird-bolt
9 butt-shaft, indicator **11** swallowtail
3 grey-goose wing **14** cloth-yard
aft, grey-goose quill, grey-goose
haft

rrowhead
4 fork

---

arrowroot
03 pia **07** Maranta

arsenal
05 depot, stock **06** armory
07 armoury, weapons **08** magazine,
weaponry **09** arms depot, garderobe,
stockpile **10** repository **13** ordnance
depot **14** ammunition dump

arsenic
02 As

arson
09 pyromania, saddlebow
11 firebombing, fire-raising
12 incendiarism

arsonist
05 torch **07** firebug **10** firebomber,
fire-raiser, incendiary, pyromaniac

art
04 feat, gift **05** craft, flair, guile, knack,
skill, trade **06** Arthur, deceit, design,
method, talent **07** artwork, cunning,
daubery, finesse, knowhow, mastery,
sleight, slyness **08** aptitude, artistry,
facility, strategy, trickery, wiliness
09 dexterity, expertise, ingenuity,
technique **10** adroitness, artfulness,
astuteness, craftiness, profession,
shrewdness, virtuosity **12** creative
work **13** craftsmanship
15 draughtsmanship

See also **Japanese**; **painting**; **sculpture**

Arts and crafts include:

04 film
05 batik, video
06 fresco, mosaic, saikei
07 carving, collage, crochet, drawing,
etching, ikebana, origami, pottery,
weaving
08 ceramics, graphics, knitting,
painting, pencraft, spinning,
tapestry, tsutsumu
09 animation, cloisonné, engraving,
jewellery, marquetry, metalwork,
modelling, patchwork, sculpture,
sketching, woodcraft
10 basketwork, caricature,
embroidery, enamelling,
needlework, xylography
11 calligraphy, lithography,
needlecraft, oil painting,
photography, portraiture,
psaligraphy, stitchcraft, watercolour,
woodcarving, wood cutting
12 animatronics, architecture,
chalcography, illustration, stained
glass
13 digital design, graphic design, wood
engraving
14 relief printing, screenprinting

See also **picture**

*Schools, movements and styles of
art include:*

05 Nabis, Op Art, video
06 Cubism, Gothic, Pop Art, Purism,
Rococo
07 Art Brut, Art Deco, Baroque,
Bauhaus, Brit art, Dadaism, digital,
Fauvism, folk art, Realism

---

08 abstract, Barbizon, Bohemian,
Futurism, Japonism, Venetian
09 Byzantine, formalism, Mannerism,
Modernism, Symbolism, Vorticism
10 arte povera, Art Nouveau,
automatism, classicism, Florentine,
literalism, Minimal Art, Naturalism,
New Realism, Romanesque,
Surrealism
11 Hellenistic, Pointillism, Primitivism,
renaissance, Romanticism,
Suprematism
12 Aestheticism, magic realism,
Quattrocento, Superrealism
13 Arts and Crafts, Conceptual Art,
Expressionism, Impressionism,
Neoclassicism, Neo-Plasticism,
Post-Modernism, Preraphaelite
14 action painting, Constructivism

*Art materials and art-related
terms include:*

03 ink
04 term, wash
05 cameo, easel, fitch, liner, sable,
smock, turps, video
06 badger, crayon, fusain, pastel,
pencil, relief, sketch, tusche
07 atelier, cartoon, digital, modello,
organic, palette, scumble,
torchon
08 abstract, alfresco, charcoal,
gumption, intaglio, Luminism,
monotint, paintbox, pastille
09 lay-figure, pen and ink, stretcher
10 delineavit, from nature, paint brush,
sketchbook
11 perspective, trompe l'oeil, wash
drawing
12 installation, underdrawing
13 social realism
15 oil of turpentine

• **work of art**
06 doodle **09** Old Master

artefact
◇ *anagram indicator*
04 item, tool **05** thing **06** object
07 neolith **09** something
10 palaeolith

Artemis
05 Diana

artery
02 M1 **04** duct, road, tube **06** vessel
07 channel, conduit **11** blood vessel

See also **vein**

artful
◇ *anagram indicator*
03 sly **04** foxy, rusé, wily **05** dodgy,
sharp, smart **06** cautel, clever, crafty,
shrewd, subtle, tricky **07** cunning,
devious, skilful, vulpine **08** masterly,
scheming **09** cautelous, deceitful,
designing, dexterous, ingenious
11 resourceful

artfully
◇ *anagram indicator*
05 slyly **08** cleverly, craftily, shrewdly
09 cunningly, deviously, skilfully
11 deceitfully, ingeniously

arthropod

Arthropods include:

09 trilobite, water bear
10 tardigrade
14 bear-animalcule

See also **crustacean**; **insect**;
invertebrate; **spider**

Arthurian legend *see* **knight**;
legend

article

01 a **02** an, el, il, la, le, un **03** art, ein,
les, the, une **04** eine, item, part, term,
unit **05** curio, essay, paper, piece,
point, story, thing **06** clause, exposé,
object, report, review **07** account,
exhibit, feature, portion, section,
whatsit, write-up **08** artefact,
offprint **09** commodity, editorial,
monograph, paragraph, something,
thingummy **10** boondoggle,
commentary, subsection
11 composition, constituent
12 thingummybob, thingummyjig
14 what-d'you-call-it

articulate

◇ *homophone indicator*
◇ *anagram indicator*

03 say **04** talk **05** clear, frame, lucid,
speak, state, utter, vocal, voice
06 fluent, tongue, verbal **07** breathe,
enounce, express, jointed, realize
08 coherent, distinct, eloquent,
vocalize **09** enunciate, pronounce,
verbalize **10** expressive, meaningful,
well-spoken **12** intelligible
13 communicative
14 comprehensible, understandable

articulated

◇ *homophone indicator*
◇ *anagram indicator*

05 joint **06** hinged, joined, linked
07 coupled, jointed **08** attached,
fastened **09** connected, segmented
10 vertebrate **11** interlocked **14** fitted
together

articulately

07 clearly, lucidly **08** fluently
10 coherently, distinctly, eloquently
12 expressively, intelligibly
14 comprehensibly

articulation

05 joint **06** saying **07** diction,
segment, talking, voicing **08** coupling,
delivery, jointing, junction, speaking,
tonguing **09** arthrosis, clavation,
consonant, gomphosis, utterance
10 connection, expression
11 diarthrosis, enunciation
12 schindylesis, synarthrosis,
vocalization **13** pronunciation,
verbalization

artifice

03 art, con, gin **04** ruse, scam, wile
05 craft, dodge, fraud, guile, reach, set-
up, shift, trick **06** deceit, device,
scheme, tactic **07** cunning, shuffle,
slyness **08** strategy, subtlety, trickery
09 chicanery, deception, stratagem

10 artfulness, cleverness, craftiness,
subterfuge **11** contrivance,
deviousness **12** contrivement
14 davenport-trick

artificial

03 art **04** fake, faux, mock, sham
05 bogus, false, paste, pseud
06 ersatz, forced, made-up, phoney,
pseudo **07** assumed, feigned, man-
made, plastic, studied **08** affected,
mannered, specious, spurious
09 contrived, imitation, insincere,
pretended, processed, simulated,
synthetic, unnatural **10** non-natural
11 counterfeit **12** manufactured

artificiality

04 sham **07** falsity **08** pretence
10 simulation **11** insincerity
12 speciousness, spuriousness
13 theatricalism, theatricality,
unnaturalness

artificially

07 falsely **10** speciously, spuriously
11 insincerely, unnaturally
13 synthetically

artillery

02 RA **03** AAA, art, RHA **04** arty, guns
05 train **07** cannons, gunnery,
weapons **08** cannonry, missiles,
ordnance **09** heavy guns, munitions
12 heavy weapons

artisan

06 expert **07** pioneer **08** mechanic
09 artificer, craftsman, operative
10 journeyman, technician
11 craftswoman **12** craftsperson
13 skilled worker **14** handicraftsman

artist

02 RA **03** ace, ARA, pro **04** poet
05 actor, maker, maven, mavin
06 author, dancer, expert, writer
07 creator, dab hand, founder, maestro
08 Bohemian, composer, inventor,
musician **09** authority, mannerist,
performer **10** originator, specialist,
trecentist **12** professional
13 perspectivist

Artists, craftsmen and
craftswomen include:

06 etcher, master, potter, weaver
07 painter, printer
08 animator, designer, engraver,
  sculptor
09 architect, carpenter, goldsmith
10 blacksmith, cartoonist, oil painter
11 coppersmith, draughtsman,
  illustrator, miniaturist, portraitist,
  silversmith, web designer
12 caricaturist, lithographer,
  photographer
13 draughtswoman, graphic artist,
  screenprinter
14 graffiti artist, pavement artist,
  watercolourist
15 graphic designer

See also **painter**; **photograph**; **sculpture**

• **great artist**
09 Old Master

artiste

05 actor, comic **06** dancer, player,
singer **07** actress, trouper
08 comedian, musician **09** performer
10 comedienne **11** entertainer
12 vaudevillian **13** variety artist

artistic

04 fine **06** gifted **07** elegant, refined,
skilled, stylish **08** creative, cultured,
graceful, original, talented, tasteful
09 aesthetic, beautiful, exquisite,
sensitive **10** attractive, cultivated,
decorative, expressive, harmonious,
ornamental **11** imaginative

artistry

05 craft, flair, skill, style, touch
06 genius, talent **07** ability, finesse,
mastery **08** deftness **09** expertise
10 brilliance, creativity **11** proficiency,
sensitivity, workmanship
13 craftsmanship **14** accomplishment

artless

04 open, pure, true **05** frank, naive,
naked, plain **06** candid, direct,
honest, simple, unwary **07** genuine,
natural, sincere **08** homespun,
innocent, trusting **09** childlike,
guileless, ingenuous, unworldly
10 unaffected **11** undesigning
13 unpretentious **15** straightforward,
unsophisticated

artlessly

05 truly **06** openly, purely, simply
07 frankly, naively, plainly **08** candidly,
directly **09** naturally, sincerely
10 innocently **11** ingenuously
15 unpretentiously

Aruba

03 ABW

as

02 eg, so, ut **03** als, qua **04** kame, like,
when **05** being, esker, since, while
06 just as, such as, whilst **07** arsenic,
because, owing to, through
09 forasmuch, similar to **10** for
example, inasmuch as, seeing that
11 as a result of, for instance, in the role
of, on account of **12** in the guise of
13 at the same time, functioning as,
with the part of **14** simultaneously
15 at the same time as, considering tha

• **as for**
07 apropos **09** as regards
10 concerning, respecting **12** in
relation to, with regard to **13** with
respect to **14** on the subject of, with
relation to **15** with reference to

• **as it were**
05 quasi **06** in a way, kind of, second,
sort of **07** so to say **09** in some way, so
to speak **10** in some sort **11** as it might
be

asafoetida

04 hing

asbestos

07 amosite **08** amiantus, rock wood
09 amianthus, earthflax **10** chrysotile
11 crocidolite **12** mountain wood

ascend
◇ *reversal down indicator*
03 sty **04** go up, rise, soar, upgo
05 arise, climb, fly up, get up, mount, scale, tower **06** climax, come up, move up **07** float up, lift off, take off
10 gain height **12** slope upwards

ascendancy
04 edge, sway **05** power
07 command, control, mastery
08 dominion, hegemony, lordship, prestige **09** authority, dominance, dominancy, influence, mobocracy, supremacy, upper hand
10 domination, prevalence **11** pre-eminence, superiority
12 predominance

ascendant
◇ *reversal down indicator*
07 growing **08** dominant, powerful, superior **09** prevalent **10** developing
11 predominant **12** on the up and up
13 rising in power

ascending
02 up

ascent
04 hill, pull, ramp, rise **05** climb, slope
06 rising, uphill **07** advance, incline, scaling **08** anabasis, climbing, gradient, mounting, progress **09** acclivity, ascending, ascension, elevation
10 escalation **11** advancement

ascertain
03 fix, see **04** twig **05** learn, prove
06 detect, locate, settle, verify
07 confirm, find out, pin down, suss out **08** discover, identify, make sure
09 determine, establish, get to know
10 come to know, make sure of
11 make certain

ascetic
03 nun **04** Jain, monk, yogi **05** fakir, harsh, Jaina, plain, sadhu, stern
06 Essene, hermit, saddhu, severe, strict **07** austere, dervish, Jainist, puritan, recluse, spartan, stylite
08 celibate, Nazarite, rigorous, sannyasi, solitary **09** abstainer, abstinent, anchorite, Montanist, pillarist **10** abstemious **11** pillar-saint, puritanical, self-denying **14** self-controlled **15** self-disciplined

asceticism
07 ascesis **08** severity **09** austerity, harshness **10** abstinence, self-denial
11 monasticism, self-control **14** self-discipline

ascidian
08 tunicate **09** sea squirt
15 appendicularian

ascribe
05 apply **06** assign, charge, credit, impute **07** put down, set down
08 accredit, arrogate **09** attribute
12 give credit to

ash
04 kali, kelp, kilp **05** aizle, easle, rowan
06 embers, tephra **07** cinders, clinker,

residue, witchen **08** charcoal, Ygdrasil
09 xanthoxyl, Yggdrasil **10** Yggdrasill
11 nuée ardente **13** toothache tree
15 Pharaoh's serpent

ashamed
05 loath, sorry **06** guilty, modest
07 abashed, bashful, humbled
08 blushing, contrite, hesitant, penitent, red-faced, sheepish **09** mortified, reluctant, unwilling **10** apologetic, distressed, humiliated, remorseful, shamefaced **11** crestfallen, discomfited, discomposed, embarrassed **12** on a guilt trip **13** self-conscious

ashen
03 wan **04** grey, pale **05** livid, pasty, white **06** leaden, pallid **07** anaemic, ghastly **08** blanched, bleached
09 pale-faced **10** colourless

ashore
05 aland **11** onto the land **12** onto the beach, onto the shore **15** towards the shore

Asia

04 Laos
05 Burma, China, India, Japan, Nepal
06 Bhutan, Taiwan
07 Myanmar, Vietnam
08 Cambodia, Malaysia, Maldives, Mongolia, Pakistan, Sri Lanka, Thailand
09 East Timor, Indonesia, Singapore
10 Bangladesh, Kazakhstan, Kyrgyzstan, North Korea, South Korea, Tajikistan, Uzbekistan
11 Afghanistan, Philippines
12 Turkmenistan
16 Brunei Darussalam

05 Indus
06 Ganges, Mekong, Mt Fuji
07 Everest, Yangtze
08 Krakatoa, Lake Sebu, Red River, Taj Mahal
09 Angkor Wat, Annapurna, Great Wall, Himalayas, Hiroshima, Ming Tombs, Mt Everest
10 Gobi Desert, River Indus, Sagarmatha, Sea of Japan, Thar Desert
11 Brahmaputra, Mekong River, Three Gorges, Yellow River
12 Golden Temple, Potala Palace, Raffles Hotel
13 Forbidden City, Kangchenjunga
14 Jaganath Temple
15 Tiananmen Square

Asian

03 Han, Lao
04 Ainu, Cham, Nair, Shan, Sulu, Thai
05 Bajau, Karen, Kazak, Nayar, Tajik, Tamil, Uzbeg, Uzbek, Vedda
06 Afghan, Baluch, Gurkha, Indian, Kazakh, Kyrgyz, Manchu, Mongol, Pathan, Tadjik, Telugu

07 Baluchi, Burmese, Chinese, Goanese, Goorkha, Karenni, Kirghiz, Laotian, Manchoo, Maratha, Russian, Tadzhik, Tagálog, Turkish, Turkmen
08 Bruneian, Canarese, Filipina, Filipino, Japanese, Kanarese, Mahratta, Nepalese
09 Bhutanese, Cambodian, Malaysian, Mongolian, Pakistani, Sri Lankan, Taiwanese
10 Indonesian, Myanmarese, Vietnamese
11 Azerbaijani, Bangladeshi, Kazakhstani, North Korean, Singaporean, South Korean, Tajikistani

aside
02 by **04** away **05** alone, apart
07 whisper **08** secretly **09** alongside, departure, monologue, on one side, privately, soliloquy, to one side
10 apostrophe, digression, separately
11 in isolation, out of the way, parenthesis **12** obiter dictum, stage whisper **13** cursory remark
15 notwithstanding

asinine
04 daft **05** crazy, inane, potty, silly
06 absurd, stupid **07** fatuous, foolish, idiotic, moronic **08** gormless
09 imbecilic, ludicrous, senseless
10 half-witted **11** nonsensical

ask
03 beg, bid, eft, sue **04** evet, newt, poll, pose, pray, pump, quiz, seek
05 crave, grill, order, plead, posit, press, query, speer, speir, yearn
06 appeal, demand, desire, invite, summon **07** beseech, bespeak, canvass, clamour, enquire, entreat, fire off, implore, inquire, propose, request, require, solicit, suggest **08** approach, have over, petition, propound, question **09** entertain, have round, interview, postulate **10** put forward, supplicate **11** interrogate, requisition
12 cross-examine, put on the spot
13 cross-question **14** put a question to
15 give a grilling to

askance
04 awry **07** asconce **08** sideways
09 dubiously, obliquely **10** doubtfully, indirectly, scornfully **11** sceptically
12 disdainfully, suspiciously
13 distrustfully, mistrustfully
14 contemptuously, disapprovingly

askew
◇ *anagram indicator*
04 awry, skew **05** aglee, agley, tipsy
06 skivie, squint **07** crooked, oblique
08 lopsided, sideways **09** crookedly, obliquely, off-centre, out of line, skew-whiff **10** lopsidedly **12** asymmetrical
14 asymmetrically

asleep
04 numb **05** inert **06** dozing
07 dormant, napping, resting
08 comatose, inactive, reposing,

sleeping, snoozing **09** conked out, flaked out, nodded off, popped off **10** crashed out, fast asleep, sparked out **11** sound asleep, unconscious **13** out like a light **14** dead to the world, in the land of Nod, out for the count

asparagus
05 sprew, sprue **06** smilax

aspect
03 air **04** brow, face, look, side, view **05** angle, facet, light, phase, point, trine, visor, vizor **06** facies, factor, manner, phasis **07** bearing, contour, feature, outlook, respect, sextile **08** position, quartile, quincunx, quintile **09** dimension, direction, landscape **10** apparition, appearance, biquintile, complexion, expression, standpoint **11** conjunction, countenance, physiognomy, point of view **13** configuration

asperity
08 acerbity, acrimony, severity, sourness **09** crossness, harshness, roughness, sharpness **10** bitterness, causticity **11** astringency, crabbedness, peevishness **12** abrasiveness, churlishness, irascibility, irritability

aspersion
04 slur **07** calumny, slander
• **cast aspersions on**
04 slur **05** knock, slate, smear **06** defame, vilify **07** censure, run down, slander **08** reproach **09** criticize, denigrate, deprecate, disparage **10** calumniate, sling mud at, throw mud at

asphalt
08 uintaite **09** gilsonite, Jew's-pitch, uintahite **12** mineral pitch

asphyxiate
03 gas **05** choke **06** stifle **07** smother **08** strangle, throttle **09** suffocate **11** strangulate

asphyxiation
07 choking **08** stifling **10** smothering **11** suffocation **13** strangulation

aspirant
06 donzel, squire **09** candidate

aspirate
05 rough

aspiration
03 aim, yen **04** goal, hope, wish **05** dream, ideal **06** desire, intent, object **07** craving, longing, purpose **08** ambition, yearning **09** breathing, endeavour, hankering, objective **10** pretension

aspire
03 aim, yen **04** hope, long, mint, seek, wish **05** crave, dream, ettle, yearn **06** desire, hanker, intend, pursue **07** pretend, purpose **11** have as a goal, have as an aim

aspiring
04 keen **05** eager **07** budding, hopeful, longing, wishful, would-be

08 aspirant, striving **09** ambitious, intending **10** optimistic **12** endeavouring, enterprising

ass
03 fon, git, mug, nit, oaf, sot, yap **04** berk, cake, clot, cony, coof, dill, dope, dork, fool, geek, goop, gowk, gull, joss, moke, mule, nana, nerd, nerk, nong, pony, prat, soft, twit, yo-yo **05** burro, cluck, cuddy, dicky, dweeb, galah, hinny, idiot, Jenny, kiang, klutz, kulan, kyang, neddy, ninny, patch, schmo, snipe, sumph, twerp, wally **06** bampot, cretin, dickey, dimwit, donkey, dottle, drongo, koulan, nidget, nitwit, numpty, onager, quagga, sawney, turkey, wigeon **07** airhead, asinico, buffoon, gubbins, halfwit, jackass, jughead, lemming, muggins, natural, plonker, saphead, want-wit **08** dipstick, flathead, fondling, imbecile, innocent, lunkhead, mooncalf, numskull, omadhaun, Tom-noddy **09** blockhead, capocchia, dumb-cluck, dziggetai, lack-brain, lame brain, mumchance, schlemiel **10** nincompoop **11** jenny donkey, knuckle-head **13** Jerusalem pony, proper Charlie
See also **fool**

assail
03 din, rag, row **04** peal, pelt, slam **05** assay, beset, go for, slate, worry **06** attack, invade, malign, plague, rattle, revile, strafe, straff, strike **07** barrage, bedevil, belabor, bestorm, bombard, disturb, lay into, perplex, rubbish, run down, set upon, slag off, torment, trouble **08** badmouth, ballyrag, belabour, bludgeon, bullyrag, maltreat, overfall, set about, tear into **09** criticize, pitch into **10** fall foul of, set against

assailant
05 enemy **06** abuser, mugger **07** invader, reviler **08** assailer, attacker, onsetter, opponent **09** adversary, aggressor, assaulter

assassin
04 thug **05** bravo, ninja **06** gunman, hit-man, killer, slayer **07** sworder **08** murderer **09** cut-throat **10** hatchet man, liquidator **11** contract man, executioner
See also **murderer**

assassinate
◇ *anagram indicator*
03 hit **04** do in, kill, slay **06** murder **07** bump off, execute **08** dispatch **09** eliminate, liquidate, slaughter

assassination
◇ *anagram indicator*
06 murder **07** killing **09** execution, slaughter, taking-off **11** termination

assault
02 do **03** GBH, hit, mug **04** raid, rape **05** abuse, assay, blitz, feint, go for, onset, smite, stoor, storm, stour **06** affray, attack, beat up, charge, do

over, fall on, insult, invade, molest, stound, stownd, stowre, strike **07** attempt, battery, bombard, lay into, mugging, offence, offense, set upon **08** invasion, storming **09** fusillade, incursion, offensive, onslaught **10** hamesucken, violent act **11** molestation **13** interfere with **15** act of aggression, throw yourself on

assay
04 test **05** check, cupel, ELISA **08** analysis **09** appraisal, judgement **10** assessment, evaluation, inspection **11** examination

assemblage
04 mass **05** crowd, flock, group, rally, shoal, strew **06** galaxy, school, throng **07** montage **09** aggregate, gathering, multitude **10** collection, collective, parliament **12** accumulation

assemble
◇ *anagram indicator*
04 band, join, make, mass, meet **05** amass, build, flock, group, rally, relie, set up, troop **06** accoil, cobble, gather, join up, muster, relide, roll up, summon **07** collate, collect, compose, connect, convene, convoke, marshal, round up, summons **08** mobilize **09** aggregate, construct, fabricate **10** accumulate, congregate, rendezvous **11** fit together, get together, manufacture, put together **12** come together **13** bring together, piece together

assembly
03 hui, mob **04** body, Dáil, diet, feis, meet, moot, Sejm **05** agora, bench, court, crowd, divan, flock, gemot, group, jirga, rally, synod, thing **06** indaba, kgotla, Majlis, Mejlis, muster, plenum, throng **07** chamber, chapter, company, council, gorsedd, Knesset, Landtag, meeting, squeeze, turnout, zemstvo **08** audience, building, bun fight, conclave, congress, ecclesia, folkmoot, panegyry, presence, Sobranje, Sobranye, Storting **09** Aula Regis, concourse, frequence, gathering, multitude, Skupstina, Storthing, synagogue, synedrion, synedrium, volksraad **10** assemblage, bear garden, collection, conference, consistory, convention, Curia Regis, Donnybrook, masquerade, Oireachtas, Skupshtina **11** church court, convocation, Dáil Eireann, fabrication, manufacture, Pandemonium **12** body of people, common vestry, congregation, construction, Pandaemonium **15** piecing together, putting together
See also **parliament**
• **General Assembly**
02 GA

assent
03 buy **05** agree, allow, grant, yield **06** accede, accept, accord, comply, concur, permit, submit **07** approve, concede, consent, go-ahead

08 approval, sanction, thumbs-up
09 accession, acquiesce, agreement, subscribe **10** acceptance, compliance, concession, green light, permission, submission **11** approbation, concurrence **12** acquiescence, capitulation **14** give the go-ahead **15** give the thumbs-up
• **expression of assent**
01 I **02** ay, OK **03** aye, oke, olé
04 done, good, okay **07** d'accord **09** I am agreed **10** I am content

assert
03 put, say **04** have, hold, pose
05 argue, claim, state, swear, vouch
06 affirm, attest, avouch, defend, stress, uphold **07** confirm, contend, declare, lay down, profess, protest
08 constate, insist on, maintain
09 establish, predicate, pronounce, testify to, vindicate **10** stand up for **12** crack the whip

assertion
03 vow **04** word **05** claim, vouch
06 avowal, threap, threep
08 averment, pretence, pretense, sentence **09** statement **10** affirmance, allegation, contention, insistence, profession **11** affirmation, attestation, declaration, jactitation, predication, testificate, vindication **12** constatation, gratis dictum **13** pronouncement

assertive
04 bold, firm **05** perky, pushy
07 decided, forward **08** assuming, dogmatic, dominant, emphatic, forceful, immodest, positive
09 confident, insistent **10** aggressive, determined **11** domineering, opinionated, overbearing, self-assured
12 presumptuous, strong-willed
13 self-confident **14** sure of yourself **15** feeling your oats

assertively
06 boldly, firmly **10** dominantly, forcefully, positively **11** confidently, insistently **12** aggressively
14 presumptuously **15** self-confidently

assess
03 fix, tax **04** levy, rate **05** cense, gauge, Jenny, judge, stent, sum up, teind, value, weigh **06** affeer, assize, demand, extend, impose, modify, review, size up **07** compute
08 appraise, check out, consider, estimate, evaluate **09** calculate, determine **11** jenny donkey

assessment
04 levy, rate, toll **05** recce, stent
06 demand, review, tariff **07** opinion, testing **09** appraisal, judgement, valuation **10** estimation, evaluation, imposition **11** computation
12 appraisement **13** consideration

assessor
05 judge **06** expert, gauger, umpire, valuer **07** adviser, arbiter, referee
08 examiner, measurer, recorder, reviewer, valuator **09** appraiser,

estimator, inspector **10** arbitrator, consultant, counsellor **11** adjudicator
12 loss adjuster **15** average adjuster

asset
03 aid **04** boon, help, plus **05** funds, goods, means, money **06** estate, virtue, wealth **07** benefit, capital, savings **08** blessing, holdings, property, reserves, resource, seed corn, strength, tangible **09** advantage, liability, plus point, resources, valuables **10** securities **11** hot property, possessions, receivables, strong point

asseverate
04 aver, avow **05** claim, state
06 affirm, assert, attest **07** confirm, declare, profess **08** maintain

assiduity
08 devotion, hard work, industry, sedulity **09** constancy, diligence
10 dedication **11** persistence
12 perseverance **14** meticulousness **15** industriousness

assiduous
06 steady **07** careful, devoted
08 constant, diligent, sedulous, studious, thorough, untiring
09 attentive, dedicated **10** meticulous, persistent, unflagging **11** hard-working, industrious, persevering
13 conscientious, indefatigable

assign
03 fix, put, set **04** aret, cast, give, name, rank, sort **05** allot, allow, apply, arett, grant, range **06** affect, choose, convey, detail, impute, ordain, select
07 adjudge, appoint, ascribe, consign, endorse, hive off, indorse, install, put down, specify, station **08** accredit, allocate, arrogate, delegate, dispense, hand over, make over, nominate, relegate, transfer, transmit
09 apportion, attribute, chalk up to, designate, determine, stipulate
10 commission, distribute
11 appropriate

assignation
04 date **05** tryst **10** engagement, rendezvous **11** appointment, arrangement **13** secret meeting

assignment
03 job **04** duty, post, task **05** grant
06 charge, errand **07** project
08 position, transfer **09** selection
10 allocation, commission, conveyance, delegation, nomination, obligation **11** appointment, consignment, designation, disposition **12** distribution **14** responsibility

assimilate
◇ *containment indicator*
03 mix **05** adapt, blend, grasp, learn, unite **06** absorb, adjust, imbibe, mingle, pick up, take in **08** accustom
09 integrate **11** acclimatize, accommodate, incorporate, internalize

assimilation
07 osmosis **08** blending, grasping, learning, mixing in, taking in
09 digestion **10** absorption, adaptation, adjustment, resorption
11 integration **13** accommodation, incorporation **15** acclimatization, internalization

assist
03 aid **04** abet, back, help **05** serve
06 back up, enable, second
07 advance, benefit, further, pitch in, relieve, succour, support, sustain
08 expedite **09** co-operate, do your bit, encourage, give a hand, lend a hand, reinforce **10** facilitate, make easier, rally round **11** collaborate
12 give a leg up to

assistance
03 aid **04** hand, help **05** boost **06** a leg up, relief **07** backing, benefit, service, subsidy, succour, support
08 easement **09** adjutancy
10 friendship **11** co-operation, furtherance **12** a helping hand
13 collaboration, reinforcement

assistant
02 PA **03** cad, PDA **04** aide, ally, mate
05 clerk, usher **06** backer, curate, deputy, helper, intern, leg-man, nipper, second, yeoman **07** abettor, acolyte, acolyth, best boy, fireman, matross, nobbler, omnibus, partner
08 chainman, leg-woman, mud-clerk, right arm, salesman, servitor
09 accessory, ancillary, associate, auxiliary, coadjutor, colleague, land-reeve, midinette, prorector, secretary, suffragan, supporter, toad-eater, whipper-in **10** accomplice, aide-de-camp, amanuensis, copyholder, evangelist, proproctor, reading-boy, roughrider, sales clerk, saleswoman, subsidiary **11** confederate, merry-andrew, salesperson, subordinate
12 brigade major, collaborator, demonstrator, driving force, right-hand man **13** counter-jumper
14 boatswain's mate, checkout person, Common Serjeant, counter-skipper **15** second-in-command, vice-chamberlain

associate
◇ *juxtaposition indicator*
01 A **03** Ass, mix, pal **04** ally, band, chum, gang, herd, join, link, mate, mell, pair, peer, yoke **05** crony, haunt, unite
06 attach, couple, fellow, friend, helper, hobnob, league, mingle, relate
07 combine, company, compeer, comrade, connect, consort, goombah, hang out, partner, sociate
08 complice, confrère, co-worker, follower, identify, sidekick, sororize, yoke-mate **09** accompany, affiliate, assistant, coadjutor, colleague, companion, correlate, hang about, neighbour, socialize, syndicate
10 accomplice, amalgamate, be involved, coadjutrix, consociate, fraternize, hang around, yokefellow

11 coadjutress, confederate, keep company **12** band together, collaborator, go hand in hand, rub shoulders **15** think of together

associated
◇ *juxtaposition indicator*
03 Ass **05** alike **06** allied, linked **07** coupled, related, similar **08** combined, in league **09** connected, consorted **10** affiliated, correlated, syndicated **11** amalgamated **12** confederated **13** corresponding, in partnership

association
03 Ass, tie **04** band, bond, club, gild, hunt, link **05** group, guild, tie-up, union **06** cartel, chapel, clique, league, Probus, thrift, Verein **07** combine, company, contact, job club, society **08** alliance, clanship, intimacy, relation, sodality **09** coalition, goose-club, syndicate **10** connection, consortium, craft guild, federation, fellowship, fraternity, friendship, Jockey Club, Land League, propaganda, Young Italy **11** affiliation, confederacy, corporation, correlation, familiarity, involvement, partnership, triumvirate **12** consociation, Gesellschaft, organization, relationship **13** companionship, confederation, incorporation, interrelation **14** Burschenschaft, identification, Primrose League **15** friendly society

assorted
◇ *anagram indicator*
05 mixed **06** divers, motley, sundry, varied **07** diverse, several, various **08** manifold, sortable **09** different, differing **10** variegated **11** farraginous **12** multifarious **13** heterogeneous, miscellaneous

assortment
03 lot, mix **05** array, bunch, group **06** choice, jumble, medley **07** farrago, mixture, variety **08** grouping, mixed bag **09** diversity, menagerie, potpourri, selection **10** collection, miscellany, salmagundi **11** arrangement, olla-podrida, smörgåsbord **13** bits and pieces

assuage
04 beet, bete, calm, ease, lull **05** allay, lower, mease, slake, swage **06** lenify, lessen, pacify, quench, reduce, soften, soothe **07** appease, lighten, mollify, relieve, satisfy **08** mitigate, moderate, palliate **09** alleviate

assume
◇ *containment indicator*
03 don **04** bear, take **05** adopt, fancy, feign, guess, infer, posit, put on, seize, think, usurp **06** accept, affect, deduce, expect, strike, take it, take on **07** acquire, believe, embrace, imagine, pre-empt, presume, pretend, suppose, surmise **08** arrogate, shoulder, simulate, take over **09** enter upon, postulate, undertake **10** come to have, commandeer, presuppose, take as

read, understand **11** appropriate, counterfeit **14** take for granted

assumed
04 fake, sham **05** bogus, false **06** made-up, phoney **07** feigned **08** affected, borrowed, putative, supposed **09** pretended, simulated **10** fictitious **11** counterfeit **12** adscititious, hypothetical, pseudonymous **14** supposititious

assumption
04 idea **05** axiom, donné, fancy, guess **06** belief, donnée, notion, theory **07** embrace, premise, seizure, surmise **08** adoption, takeover **09** inference, postulate **10** acceptance, arrogation, conclusion, conjecture, hypothesis, pre-emption, usurpation **11** embarkation, expectation, postulation, presumption, shouldering, supposition, undertaking **13** appropriation, commandeering **14** presupposition

assurance
03 vow **04** gall, oath, word **05** nerve, poise **06** aplomb, pledge **07** courage, promise, surance, warrant **08** audacity, boldness, security, sureness **09** assertion, certainty, guarantee **10** confidence, conviction, positivism **11** affirmation, assuredness, declaration, undertaking **12** self-reliance **13** self-assurance **14** self-confidence, unflappability

assure
03 vow **04** affy, hete, seal, tell **05** hecht, hight, swear **06** affirm, attest, avouch, ensure, pledge, secure, soothe **07** certify, comfort, confirm, hearten, promise, resolve, warrant **08** convince, persuade, reassure **09** ascertain, encourage, guarantee

assured
04 bold, calm, sure **05** fixed **06** secure **07** certain, ensured, settled **08** definite, positive, promised **09** assertive, audacious, confident, confirmed, thoughten **10** guaranteed **11** cut and dried, irrefutable, self-assured **12** indisputable **13** self-confident, self-possessed **14** sure of yourself
● **be assured of**
04 know

assuredly
05 pardi, pardy, perdy **06** pardie, perdie, surely **07** my certy **08** my certie **09** by my certy, certainly, of a verity **10** by my certie, definitely, for certain **12** and no mistake, indisputably, without doubt **14** unquestionably **15** without question

astatine
02 At

astern
03 aft **04** baft **05** abaft, apoop

asteroid
09 planetoid **11** minor planet

04 Eros, Hebe, Iris, Juno
05 Ceres, Flora, Metis, Vesta
06 Apollo, Cybele, Davida, Europa, Hygiea, Icarus, Pallas, Psyche, Trojan
07 Eunomia
10 Interamnia

astir
05 afoot, agate **07** abroach, humming **09** in the wind

astonish
03 wow **04** daze, stun **05** amaze, floor, shock, stony **07** astound, flummox, stagger, startle, stupefy **08** bewilder, bowl over, confound, dumfound, gobsmack, surprise **09** dumbfound, electrify, take aback **11** flabbergast, knock for six **12** blow your mind

astonished
05 dazed **06** amazed **07** shocked, stunned **08** open-eyed, startled, wide-eyed **09** astounded, staggered, surprised **10** bewildered, bowled over, confounded, gobsmacked, taken aback **11** dumbfounded **12** lost for words **13** flabbergasted, knocked for six, thunderstruck

astonishing
◇ *anagram indicator*
07 amazing **08** shocking, striking, stunning **09** startling **10** astounding, impressive, marvellous, prodigious, staggering, surprising **11** bewildering, mind-blowing **12** awe-inspiring, breathtaking, mind-boggling, unbelievable

astonishment
05 shock **06** dismay, marvel, wonder **08** surprise **09** amazement, confusion, disbelief **10** admiration, wonderment **12** bewilderment, stupefaction **13** consternation

astound
04 stun **05** abash, amaze, floor, shock **06** stound **07** flummox, startle, stupefy **08** astonish, bewilder, bowl over, surprise **09** overwhelm **11** knock for six

astounding
07 amazing **08** shocking, stunning **09** startling **10** staggering, stupefying, stupendous, surprising **11** astonishing, bewildering **12** breathtaking, overwhelming

astray
◇ *anagram indicator*
04 awry, lost, miss, will, wull **05** abord, agate, amiss, wrong **06** abroad, adrift, errant, erring **07** missing **09** off course **10** miswandred, off the mark **11** off the rails

astride
◇ *containment indicator*
08 straddle **10** en cavalier **12** colossus-wise

astringent

04 acid, hard, kino **05** harsh, rough,
stern **06** biting, gambir, severe
07 acerbic, austere, caustic, gambier,
guaraná, mordant, puckery, rhatany,
styptic **08** alum-root, critical,
krameria, scathing **09** obstruent,
tormentil, trenchant, zinc oxide
10 astrictive, witch-hazel
11 restringent

astrologer

09 stargazer **10** genethliac
11 horoscopist, Nostradamus
12 figure-caster **14** archgenethliac

astronaut

08 lunanaut, spaceman
09 cosmonaut, lunarnaut, taikonaut
10 spacewoman **14** space traveller

Astronauts and space travellers include:

03 Ham
04 Bean (Alan), Ride (Sally), Tito
(Dennis)
05 Foale (Michael), Glenn (John), Irwin
(James), Laika, Scott (David), Titov
(Gherman), White (Edward)
06 Aldrin (Buzz), Conrad (Pete),
Leonov (Aleksei), Lovell (Jim)
07 Chaffee (Roger), Collins (Michael),
Gagarin (Yuri), Grissom (Gus),
Schirra (Wally), Sharman (Helen),
Shepard (Alan)
08 Mitchell (Edgar)
09 Armstrong (Neil)
10 Tereshkova (Valentina)

• **would-be astronaut**
10 space cadet

astronomer

04 astr **06** astron **09** stargazer

Astronomers and astrophysicists include:

04 Airy (Sir George), Biot (Jean-
Baptiste), Gold (Thomas), Hale
(George), Lyot (Bernard), Oort
(Jan), Pond (John), Rees (Sir
Martin), Ryle (Sir Martin), Saha
(Meghnad), Webb (James E)
05 Adams (John Couch), Adams
(Walter S), Baade (Walter), Baily
(Francis), Bliss (Nathaniel), Brahe
(Tycho), Dyson (Sir Frank), Gauss
(Carl Friedrich), Hoyle (Sir Fred),
Jeans (Sir James), Jones (Sir Harold
Spencer), Moore (Sir Patrick),
Sagan (Carl), Smith (Sir Francis),
Vogel (Hermann Carl)
06 Bessel (Friedrich), Halley (Edmond),
Hewish (Antony), Hubble (Edwin),
Jansky (Karl), Kepler (Johannes),
Kuiper (Gerard), Lovell (Sir
Bernard), Olbers (Heinrich), Piazzi
(Giuseppe), Roemer (Olaus)
07 Babcock (Harold D), Barnard
(Edward Emerson), Bradley (James),
Cassini (Giovanni), Celsius (Anders),
Galilei (Galileo), Galileo, Hawking
(Stephen), Huggins (Sir William),
Langley (Samuel), Laplace (Pierre),
Lockyer (Sir Norman), Maunder

(E W), Penrose (Roger), Penzias
(Arno), Ptolemy, Russell (Henry
Norris), Sandage (Allan), Schmidt
(Maarten), Seyfert (Carl), Shapley
(Harlow), Whipple (Fred), Woolley
(Sir Richard)
08 Burbidge (Geoffrey), Burbidge
(Margaret), Chandler (Seth Carlo),
Christie (Sir William), Friedman
(Herbert), Herschel (Caroline),
Herschel (Sir John), Herschel (Sir
William), Lemaître (Georges),
Tombaugh (Clyde W)
09 Eddington (Sir Arthur), Fabricius
(David), Flamsteed (John),
Maskelyne (Nevil), Sosigenes
10 Carrington (Richard), Copernicus
(Nicolas), Hipparchos, Wolfendale
(Sir Arnold)
11 Bell Burnell (Jocelyn), Graham-
Smith (Sir Francis), Hertzsprung
(Ejnar), Tsiolkovsky (Konstantin)
12 Schiaparelli (Giovanni)
13 Chandrasekhar (Subrahmanyan),
Schwarzschild (Karl)
14 Galileo Galilei

astronomical

04 astr, huge, vast **06** astron, cosmic
07 immense, mammoth, massive,
stellar **08** colossal, enormous,
gigantic, heavenly, infinite, thumping,
whopping **09** celestial, planetary
10 tremendous **11** substantial
12 considerable, cosmological,
immeasurable, interstellar
• **astronomical model**
06 orrery

astronomy

04 astr **06** astron **08** star-read
09 uranology

astrophysicist *see* **astronomer**

astute

03 sly **04** cute, keen, sage, wide,
wily, wise **05** canny, sharp **06** clever,
crafty, shrewd, subtle **07** cunning,
knowing, prudent **09** sagacious
10 discerning, perceptive
11 intelligent, penetrating, sharp-
witted **13** perspicacious

astutely

06 keenly, wisely **08** craftily, shrewdly
12 perceptively **13** intelligently, sharp-
wittedly

asunder

02 up **05** apart, in two **06** atwain **07** in
twain **08** in pieces, to pieces

asylum

03 bin **05** girth, grith, haven
06 bedlam, refuge **07** retreat, shelter
08 madhouse, Magdalen, nuthouse
09 dark-house, funny farm, sanctuary
10 frithsoken **11** institution
12 penitentiary, port in a storm
13 place of safety **14** mental hospital

asymmetrical

04 awry, skew **06** uneven **07** anaxial,
crooked, oblique, unequal
08 lopsided **09** distorted, irregular,

malformed **10** unbalanced
13 unsymmetrical

asymmetry

09 imbalance **10** distortion,
handedness, inequality, unevenness,
unsymmetry **11** crookedness
12 irregularity, lopsidedness,
malformation

at

02 in, to **08** astatine

ate

◇ *containment indicator*

atheism

07 impiety **08** nihilism, paganism,
unbelief **09** disbelief, non-belief
10 heathenism, infidelity, irreligion,
scepticism **11** godlessness, rationalism,
ungodliness **12** freethinking

atheist

05 pagan **07** heathen, heretic, infidel,
sceptic **08** humanist, nihilist
10 unbeliever **11** disbeliever,
freethinker, non-believer, nullifidian,
rationalist

Athene

07 Minerva

athlete

04 jock **05** miler **06** player, runner
07 gymnast, hurdler **09** contender,
sportsman **10** competitor, contestant
11 sportswoman **12** quarter-miler

Athletes include:

03 Coe (Sebastian, Lord)
04 Budd (Zola), Cram (Steve), Koch
(Marita), Mota (Rosa)
05 Bubka (Sergey), Jones (Marion),
Keino (Kip), Lewis (Carl), Lewis
(Denise), Moses (Ed), Nurmi
(Paavo), Ottey (Merlene), Ovett
(Steve), Owens (Jesse), Waitz
(Grete), Wells (Allan)
06 Aouita (Said), Barber (Eunice),
Beamon (Bob), Devers (Gail),
Foster (Brendan), Greene
(Maurice), Holmes (Kelly), Mutola
(Maria), Oerter (Al), Peters (Mary)
07 Backley (Steve), Edwards
(Jonathan), Fosbury (Dick),
Freeman (Cathy), Gunnell (Sally),
Jackson (Colin), Johnson (Ben),
Johnson (Michael), Liddell (Eric),
Zatopek (Emil), Zelezny (Jan)
08 Christie (Linford), Guerrouj
(Hicham el-), Kipketer (Wilson),
McColgan (Liz), Pieterse (Zola),
Thompson (Daley)
09 Bannister (Sir Roger), O'Sullivan
(Sonia), Radcliffe (Paula),
Sanderson (Tessa), Whitbread
(Fatima)
12 Blankers-Koen (Fanny),
Gebrselassie (Haile), Grey-
Thompson (Dame Tanni)
14 Griffith Joyner (Florence 'Flo-Jo')

athletic

01 A **03** fit **04** wiry **05** games, leish
06 active, brawny, muscly, robust,
sinewy, sports, sporty, strong, sturdy

08 muscular, powerful, sporting, vigorous, well-knit **09** energetic, gymnastic, strapping

athletics
05 games, races **06** sports **07** matches **08** aerobics **09** exercises **10** gymnastics **11** field events, track events **13** callisthenics
See also **sport**

Athletics events include:
04 ball, shot, walk
05 relay
06 discus, hammer, sprint
07 hurdles, javelin, shot put
08 biathlon, high jump, long jump, marathon, tug-of-war
09 broad jump, caber toss, decathlon, pole vault, sheaf toss, triathlon
10 heptathlon, pentathlon, tetrathlon, triple jump
11 discus throw, fell running, fifty metres, hammer throw, race walking
12 cross-country, half marathon, javelin throw, steeplechase
14 hop, step and jump
15 tossing the caber

athwart
04 awry **06** across, aslant **07** asklent

atmosphere
03 air, atm, fug, sky **04** aura, feel, mood, tone **05** ether, miasm, tenor, vibes **06** miasma, milieu, spirit, welkin **07** climate, feeling, flavour, heavens, quality, setting **08** ambience, empyrean **09** aerospace, character, firmament **10** background **11** environment **12** surroundings **13** vault of heaven

Atmosphere layers include:
09 exosphere, ionopause, mesopause
10 ionosphere, mesosphere, ozone layer, tropopause
11 stratopause, troposphere
12 stratosphere, thermosphere

atom
03 bit, jot **04** hint, iota, mite, spot, whit **05** crumb, grain, scrap, shred, speck, trace **06** morsel **08** fragment, molecule, particle **09** scintilla
See also **particle**

atomic
01 A
• **atomic mass unit**
03 amu
• **atomic number**
04 at no **06** at numb
• **atomic weight**
01 A **03** AWU **04** at wt

atone
03 aby **04** abye **06** offset, pay for, ransom, redeem, remedy, repent **07** appease, expiate, redress, satisfy **08** make good **09** indemnify, make right, make up for, reconcile **10** compensate, make amends, propitiate, recompense **14** make reparation

atonement
06 amends, ransom **07** payment, penance, redress **08** requital **09** expiation, indemnity, repayment **10** recompense, redemption, reparation **11** appeasement, eye for an eye, restitution, restoration **12** compensation, propitiation, satisfaction **13** acceptilation, reimbursement

atrocious
◇ *anagram indicator*
05 awful, cruel, enorm **06** brutal, savage, wicked **07** ghastly, heinous, hideous, vicious **08** dreadful, enormous, fiendish, grievous, horrible, ruthless, shocking, terrible **09** appalling, frightful, merciless, monstrous, nefarious **10** abominable, diabolical, disgusting, flagitious, horrendous

atrociously
07 cruelly **08** brutally, horribly, terribly, wickedly **09** heinously **10** abominably, dreadfully, fiendishly, ruthlessly, shockingly **11** appallingly, monstrously

atrocity
04 evil **06** horror **07** cruelty, outrage **08** enormity, savagery, vileness, villainy **09** barbarity, brutality, violation **10** wickedness **11** abomination, heinousness, hideousness, monstrosity, viciousness **13** atrociousness **14** flagitiousness

atrophy
04 fade **05** decay, waste **06** shrink, sweeny, tabefy, wither **07** decline, dwindle, shrivel, wasting **08** diminish, emaciate, marasmus **09** waste away, withering **10** amyotrophy, degenerate, diminution, emaciation, involution **11** deteriorate, shrivelling, tabefaction, wasting away **12** degeneration **13** deterioration

attach
03 add, fix, lay, pin, put, sew, tag, tie **04** ally, bind, join, link, nail, send, tack, weld **05** add on, affix, annex, cling, place, put on, snell, stick, unite **06** adhere, append, assign, belong, couple, detail, fasten, impute, limber, second, secure, solder **07** adhibit, ascribe, Blu-Tack®, connect, harness, plaster **08** allocate, relate to **09** affiliate, align with, associate, attribute, factorize, latch onto, piggyback **10** articulate, make secure **11** combine with **13** affiliate with, associate with

attached
04 fond **06** liking, loving, tender **07** devoted, engaged, married **08** friendly **09** affianced, appendant, spoken for **11** going steady **12** affectionate **15** in a relationship

attachment
03 tie **04** bond, frog, link, love **05** extra **06** fetich, fetish, liking **07** adapter, adaptor, adjunct, codicil,

fetiche, fitment, fitting, fixture, loyalty **08** addition, adhesion, affinity, calf-love, devotion, fixation, fondness **09** accessory, affection, appendage, closeness, extension **10** attraction, commitment, friendship, partiality, supplement, tenderness **12** accoutrement, appurtenance **13** grande passion

attack
03 fit, gas, get, lam, mob, mug, pan, pin, TIA **04** bash, bomb, bout, chin, fake, flak, fork, gang, go at, jump, Mace®, nuke, prey, push, raid, rear, roll, rush, Scud, slam, tilt **05** abuse, alert, begin, blame, blast, blitz, board, brash, decry, fling, fly at, foray, glass, go for, ictus, knock, prang, sally, scrag, siege, slate, snipe, spasm, start, storm, touch **06** access, affect, ambush, assail, batter, beat up, berate, bodrag, bottle, charge, come at, do over, duff up, extent, fall on, hold-up, impugn, infect, insult, invade, jump on, malign, molest, napalm, oppugn, pounce, rebuke, revile, rocket, savage, send in, shower, sortie, strafe, strike, stroke, tackle, tongue, vilify, wade in, waylay **07** address, aggress, air-raid, assault, attempt, battery, besiege, blister, bombard, bulldog, censure, clobber, destroy, fly upon, focus on, handbag, hiccups, inveigh, kicking, lampoon, lay into, reprove, round on, rubbish, run down, sandbag, seizure, set upon, slag off, slating, torpedo **08** attend to, camisade, camisado, commence, deal with, denounce, dive-bomb, embark on, firebomb, invasion, knocking, paroxysm, pounce on, roasting, set about, slamming, storming, strike at, tear into, tomahawk **09** broadside, cannonade, criticism, criticize, go wilding, have a go at, hiccoughs, incursion, invective, irruption, light into, obsession, offensive, onslaught, pull apart, stand upon, submarine, undertake, weigh into **10** bitch about, calumniate, chuck off at, convulsion, coup de main, crise de foi, get stuck in, hatchet job, have a pop at, impugnment, revilement, take a pop at, vituperate, weight into **11** bombardment, infestation, pick holes in **12** crise de nerfs, get started on, get stuck into, go over the top, leave for dead, Pearl Harbour, pull to pieces, put in the boot, put the boot in, tear to pieces, tear to shreds, vilification **13** feeding frenzy, find fault with **14** a warm reception, make a dead set at **15** act of aggression, apply yourself to, go for the jugular, throw yourself on

attacker
06 abuser, critic, mugger, raider **07** invader, reviler, striker **09** aggressor, assailant, assaulter, detractor **10** persecutor

attain
03 get, hit, net, win **04** earn, find, gain **05** fetch, grasp, reach, seize, touch

06 effect, fulfil, obtain, secure
07 achieve, acquire, possess, procure, realize, recover **08** arrive at, complete **10** accomplish

attainable
06 at hand, doable, viable **08** feasible, possible, probable **09** potential, reachable, realistic **10** accessible, achievable, imaginable, manageable, obtainable **11** conceivable, practicable, within reach

attainment
03 art **04** feat, gift **05** skill **06** talent **07** ability, mastery, success **08** aptitude, facility **10** capability, competence, completion, fulfilment **11** achievement, acquirement, procurement, proficiency, realization **12** consummation **14** accomplishment

attempt
02 go **03** aim, bid, shy, try **04** bash, burl, fand, fond, make, mint, push, seek, shot, stab, trie **05** assay, crack, essay, foray, offer, trial, whack **06** aspire, effort, set out, strive, tackle **07** have a go, pretend, venture **08** attentat, endeavor, have a try, struggle **09** endeavour, give it a go, have a bash, have a shot, have a stab, tentative, undertake **10** coup d'essai, experiment, give it a try, have a crack **11** have a stab at, try your hand, undertaking **12** give it a whirl **13** see if you can do, try your hand at **15** do your level best

attend
04 go to, hear, heed, help, mark, mind, note, page, show, stay, tend, wait **05** audit, await, guard, holla, nurse, serve, usher, visit, watch **06** appear, assist, be here, escort, follow, listen, notice, show up, squire, turn up **07** be there, care for, give ear, go along, observe **08** chaperon, frequent, take note, wait upon **09** accompany, chaperone, come along, look after **10** minister to, take care of, take notice, take part in **11** be present at, concentrate **12** pay attention
• **attend to**
03 fix **04** heed, mind, sort, tent **05** see to, valet **06** direct, handle, manage, notice **07** control, oversee, process **08** consider, cope with, deal with, follow up, see about **09** look after, supervise **10** follow up on, take care of **11** give an eye to

attendance
04 duty, gate **05** crowd, house **06** escort, roll-up **07** showing, turnout **08** audience, courting, presence **09** appearing, showing up **10** appearance

attendant
03 man **04** aide, jack, mute, page, sice, syce **05** angel, gilly, guard, guide, jäger, saice, sowar, usher, woman **06** batman, bedral, escort, gillie, helper, jaeger, keeper, porter, varlet, verger, waiter **07** acolyte, acolyth,

bederal, best man, bulldog, checker, custrel, equerry, esquire, famulus, footboy, footman, ghillie, janitor, linkboy, linkman, marshal, orderly, related, servant, snuffer, steward **08** attached, batwoman, beach boy, chaperon, chasseur, follower, footpage, handmaid, janitrix, retainer, waitress **09** assistant, auxiliary, boxkeeper, chaperone, chaprassi, chaprassy, chuprassy, companion, custodian, groomsman, janitress, kennelman, lady's-maid, observant, pew-opener, resultant, satellite **10** associated, conclavist, consequent, handmaiden, incidental, kennelmaid, led captain, lock-keeper, ministrant, pursuivant, subsequent, vivandière **11** apple-squire, body servant, concomitant, gentlewoman, loblolly-boy **12** accompanying, bottle-holder, shield-bearer **13** church officer, gillie-wetfoot **14** gentleman usher, valet de chambre **15** gillie-white-foot

attention
03 ear, eye **04** care, gaum, gorm, heed, help, mind, 'shun **06** notice, regard **07** concern, respect, service, therapy, thought **08** civility, courtesy, scrutiny **09** alertness, awareness, gallantry, limelight, treatment, vigilance **10** advertence, advertency, attendance, politeness **11** compliments, high profile, mindfulness, observation, recognition **13** concentration, consideration, contemplation, preoccupation
• **expressions relating to attracting or directing attention**
02 hi, ho, la, lo, oi, 'st, yo **03** hem, hey, hoa, hoh, hoi, hoy, pst, say, see, why **04** ahem, ecce, ecco, here, hist, look, oyes, oyez, psst, 'shun, soho, what, yo-ho **05** cooee, cooey, hallo, hello, holla, hollo, hullo, voilà **06** behold, halloa, halloo, yo-ho-ho, yoo-hoo **07** whoa-hoa **08** whoa-ho-ho **10** view-halloo
• **pay attention**
04 gaum, gorm, heed **06** listen **07** focus on, hearken, observe **10** get a load of, take notice **13** concentrate on **14** watch carefully **15** focus your mind on, listen carefully

attentive
04 kind **05** alert, awake, aware, civil, tenty, whist **06** polite, tentie **07** all ears, careful, devoted, dutiful, gallant, heedful, listful, mindful **08** gracious, noticing, obliging, vigilant, watchful, watching **09** advertent, adviceful, avizefull, courteous, listening, observant, on the ball, regardant **10** chivalrous, particular, thoughtful **11** advertising, considerate, punctilious **12** on the qui vive **13** accommodating, concentrating, conscientious

attentively
09 carefully, mindfully **10** watchfully **11** observantly **15** conscientiously

attenuated
04 bony, fine, slim, thin **06** narrow, skinny, slight **07** scraggy, scrawny, slender

attest
04 aver, show **05** prove **06** adjure, affirm, assert, depose, evince, verify **07** certify, confirm, declare, display, endorse, witness **08** evidence, manifest, proclaim, vouch for **10** asseverate **11** corroborate, demonstrate **13** bear witness to

attic
04 loft **06** garret **07** mansard **10** sky parlour

attire
04 garb, gear, suit, tire, togs, wear **05** dress, habit **06** finery, outfit, rig-out **07** apparel, clobber, clothes, costume **08** clothing, garments **10** habiliment, habilitate **11** habiliments **13** accoutrements

attired
05 ready **07** adorned, arrayed, clothed, dressed **09** decked out, rigged out, turned out **11** habilitated

attitude
04 mood, pose, song, view **05** piety, sense, stand **06** aspect, manner, stance **07** bearing, feeling, mindset, opinion, outlook, posture **08** approach, carriage, position **09** mentality, sentiment, viewpoint, world-view **10** Anschauung, deportment **11** disposition, perspective, point of view **13** way of thinking **14** Weltanschauung

attorney
02 AG, DA, QC **03** Att **04** Atty **05** brief **06** lawyer **07** counsel, proctor **08** advocate **09** barrister, solicitor **12** legal adviser

attract
04 draw, hook, lure, pull **05** charm, rivet, swing, tempt **06** allure, engage, entice, excite, induce, invite, pull in, seduce **07** bewitch, bring in, enchant, incline **08** appeal to, interest **09** captivate, fascinate, magnetize

attraction
02 it, SA **04** bait, bond, draw, hook, lure, pull **05** charm, sight **06** allure, appeal, favour **07** draught, feature, glamour **08** activity, affinity, building, cohesion, interest **09** box office, diversion, magnetism, seduction **10** enticement, inducement, invitation, temptation **11** captivation, enchantment, fascination, Ferris wheel **13** entertainment
• **centre of attraction**
04 clou

attractive
03 bad, fit, hot **04** cute, fair, foxy, sexy, taky **05** bonny, dishy, hunky, tasty, triff **06** catchy, comely, glossy, lovely, nubile, pretty, snazzy **07** dashing, elegant, nymphic, shapely, triffic,

winning, winsome **08** all right, beddable, catching, charming, engaging, enticing, epigamic, fetching, gorgeous, handsome, hot stuff, inviting, knockout, luscious, magnetic, pleasant, pleasing, striking, stunning, tempting, terrific **09** agreeable, appealing, appetible, beautiful, desirable, fanciable, glamorous, insidious, seductive, toothsome **10** adamantine, personable, photogenic, voluptuous **11** captivating, charismatic, fascinating, good-looking, interesting, picturesque **12** irresistible **13** prepossessing **14** a bit of all right

attribute
03 lay **04** mark, note, side, sign **05** apply, blame, facet, point, quirk, refer, trait **06** aspect, assign, charge, credit, impute, reckon, streak, symbol, virtue **07** adjunct, apanage, ascribe, feature, put down, quality, set down **08** accredit, appanage, arrogate, property **09** affection, indicator **11** peculiarity **12** idiosyncrasy **14** characteristic

attrition
07 chafing, erosion, rubbing **08** abrasion, friction, grinding, scraping **09** detrition, weakening **10** harassment **11** attenuation, wearing away, wearing down

attuned
03 set **05** tuned **07** adapted **08** adjusted **09** regulated **10** accustomed, harmonized **11** assimilated, co-ordinated **12** acclimatized, familiarized

atypical
07 deviant, unusual **08** aberrant, abnormal, freakish, uncommon **09** anomalous, divergent, eccentric, untypical **11** exceptional **13** extraordinary **14** unconventional

aubergine
07 brinjal **08** eggplant, mad-apple

auburn
04 rust **05** henna, tawny **06** copper, russet, Titian **07** dark-red **08** chestnut **12** reddish-brown

auction
04 cant, roup, sale **06** outcry, vendue **07** outroop **09** trade sale **11** warrant sale **12** subhastation

auctioneer
09 outrooper **11** rouping-wife

audacious
04 bold, pert, rash, rude **05** brave, fresh, lippy, nervy, risky, saucy **06** brazen, cheeky, daring, plucky **07** assured, forward, valiant **08** assuming, fearless, impudent, insolent, intrepid, reckless **09** dauntless, shameless, unabashed **10** courageous **11** adventurous, impertinent, venturesome **12** devil-may-care, enterprising, presumptuous **13** disrespectful

audacity
04 grit, guts, neck, risk **05** cheek, nerve, pluck **06** bottle, daring, valour **07** bravery, courage **08** boldness, defiance, forehead, pertness, rashness, rudeness **09** assurance, hardihead, hardihood, impudence, insolence **10** brazenness, effrontery, enterprise **11** forwardness, intrepidity, presumption **12** fearlessness, impertinence, recklessness **13** dauntlessness, shamelessness **15** adventurousness

audible
◇ *homophone indicator*
05 clear, heard **08** distinct, hearable **10** detectable **11** appreciable, discernible, perceptible **12** recognizable

audience
04 fans **05** audit, crowd, house **06** public **07** hearing, meeting, patrons, ratings, theater, theatre, turnout, viewers **08** assembly, auditory, devotees, regulars **09** followers, following, gathering, interview, listeners, onlookers, reception **10** auditorium, conference, discussion, spectators **11** bums on seats **12** congregation, consultation

audit
05 check **06** go over, review, survey, verify **07** analyse, balance, examine, inspect **08** analysis, scrutiny **09** balancing, go through, statement **10** inspection, scrutinize **11** examination, investigate, work through **12** verification **13** investigation

audition
05 trial **07** hearing

auditorium
04 hall **05** front, house **07** chamber, theatre **09** playhouse, sphendone **10** opera house **11** concert hall **12** assembly room **14** conference hall

au fait
05 aware **06** versed **07** abreast, in touch **08** familiar, up to date **09** au courant **10** conversant **13** knowledgeable

augment
03 ech, ich **04** eche, eech, grow **05** add to, boost, put on, raise, swell **06** expand, extend **07** amplify, build up, enhance, enlarge, inflate, magnify **08** heighten, increase, multiply **09** intensify, reinforce **10** strengthen **11** make greater

augmentation
05 boost **06** growth **07** build-up **08** increase **09** expansion, extension **11** enlargement **13** amplification, magnification, strengthening **15** intensification

augur
04 bode, spae **06** herald **07** betoken, portend, predict, presage, promise,

signify **08** forebode, foretell, prophesy **09** auspicate, be a sign of, harbinger

augury
04 omen, sign **05** sooth, token **06** herald **07** portent, promise, warning **08** prodrome, prophecy **09** harbinger **10** foreboding, forerunner, prediction **11** forewarning **12** ornithoscopy **13** haruspication **15** prognostication

august
03 Aug **05** grand, lofty, noble **06** solemn **07** exalted, stately, sublime **08** glorious, imperial, imposing, majestic **09** dignified, respected, venerable **10** impressive **11** magnificent **12** awe-inspiring **13** distinguished

Augustines
03 OSA

auk
04 roch **05** rotch **06** rotche **07** Alcidae, dovekie, penguin, rotchie, sea dove **08** garefowl **09** razorbill

Auntie
03 BBC **04** Beeb

aura
03 air **04** feel, hint, mood **05** vibes **06** nimbus **07** feeling, quality **08** ambience, mystique **09** emanation **10** atmosphere, genius loci, suggestion, vibrations

aural
◇ *homophone indicator*

aurora
03 Eos **11** polar lights **12** merry dancers **14** northern lights, southern lights

auspices
• **under the auspices of**
11 in the care of **13** in the charge of **15** under the aegis of

auspicious
04 rosy **05** happy, lucky, white **06** bright, timely **07** hopeful **08** cheerful **09** fortunate, opportune, promising **10** fair-boding, favourable, felicitous, optimistic, propitious, prosperous **11** encouraging

austere
04 cold, grim, hard **05** basic, bleak, grave, harsh, plain, rigid, sober, stark, stern, stoic, stoor, stour, sture **06** chaste, formal, frugal, severe, simple, solemn, sombre, stowre, strict **07** ascetic, Dantean, distant, killjoy, serious, spartan **08** exacting, rigorous **09** stringent, unadorned, unbending, unfeeling **10** abstemious, astringent, economical, forbidding, functional, inflexible, restrained, Waldensian **11** puritanical, self-denying **12** unornamented **14** self-abnegating **15** self-disciplined

austerity
06 rigour **07** economy **08** coldness, hardness, severity **09** formality, harshness, plainness, solemnity

10 abstinence, asceticism, puritanism, self-denial, simplicity **13** inflexibility **14** abstemiousness, self-discipline

Australia

01 A **02** Oz **03** AUS **04** Aust **05** Austr **09** down under

See also **electorate; governor; Prime Minister; state; team**

Australian cities and notable towns include:

05 Perth
06 Cairns, Darwin, Hobart, Sydney
08 Adelaide, Brisbane, Canberra
09 Fremantle, Melbourne
12 Alice Springs

Australian landmarks include:

05 Uluru
08 Lake Eyre, Shark Bay
09 Ayers Rock, Botany Bay, Pinnacles, Purnululu
10 Bondi Beach, Yarra River
11 Barrier Reef, Mt Kosciusko, Murray River
12 Darling River, Fraser Island, Gibson Desert, Hunter Valley, Rialto Towers
13 Barossa Valley, Blue Mountains, Bungle Bungles, Devil's Marbles, Dividing Range, Flinders Range, Harbour Bridge, Simpson Desert
14 Australian Alps, Nullarbor Plain, Pinnacle Desert, Snowy Mountains, Twelve Apostles, Uluru–Kata Tjuta, Victoria Desert

Australian

01 A **02** Oz **03** gin **05** koori, myall, ocker **06** Aussie, Strine

See also **Aboriginal; state**

Australian football

Australian football-related terms include:

03 AFL
04 goal, mark, ruck, wing
05 rover
06 ball up, behind, centre, tackle, time on, umpire
07 dispose, kick out, quarter, ruckman
08 follower, free kick, full back, half back, handball, handpass, left wing, screamer, stab pass
09 playfield, right wing, ruck rover
10 back pocket, banana kick, behind post, centre line, goal square, goal umpire, off the boot
11 Aussie Rules, daisy cutter, full forward, half forward
12 boundary line, centre bounce, centre square, Magarey Medal
13 Brownlow Medal, checkside punt, fifty-metre arc, forward pocket, half-back flank, Sandover Medal
14 aerial pingpong, boundary umpire, centre half back
15 chewy on your boot

Australian football players include:

04 Dyer (Jack)
05 Carey (Wayne)

06 Ablett (Gary), Blight (Malcolm), Bunton (Haydn), Capper (Warwick), Cazaly (Roy), Farmer (Graham 'Polly')
07 Barassi (Ron), Jackson (Mark), Lockett (Tony), Whitten (Ted)
08 Bartlett (Kevin), Brereton (Dermot), Brownlow (Charles), Matthews (Leigh), Richards (Lou)
10 Jesaulenko (Alex)

Australian Football League team nicknames include:

04 Cats
05 Blues, Crows, Hawks, Lions, Power, Swans
06 Demons, Eagles, Saints, Tigers
07 Bombers, Dockers, Magpies
08 Bulldogs
09 Kangaroos

Austria

01 A **03** AUT

authentic

04 echt, real, true **05** legal, valid **06** actual, dinkum, honest, kosher, lawful **07** certain, correct, factual, genuine **08** accurate, attested, bona fide, credible, faithful, reliable, sterling **10** dependable, historical, legitimate, true-to-life, undisputed **11** trustworthy **12** the real McCoy, the real thing

authentically

04 echt **06** really **08** actually, credibly, lawfully, reliably **09** genuinely **10** accurately, faithfully **12** historically, legitimately

authenticate

04 test **05** prove **06** attest, ratify, signet, verify **07** certify, confirm, endorse, warrant **08** accredit, notarize, validate, vouch for **09** authorize, guarantee **11** corroborate **12** substantiate

authentication

10 validation **11** attestation, endorsement **12** confirmation, ratification, verification **13** accreditation, authorization, corroboration **14** substantiation

authenticity

05 truth **07** honesty **08** accuracy, fidelity, legality, validity, veracity **09** certainty **10** legitimacy **11** correctness, credibility, genuineness, reliability **12** faithfulness, truthfulness **13** dependability **15** trustworthiness

author

03 pen **04** hand, poet **05** maker, mover **06** parent, penman, writer **07** creator, founder, planner **08** composer, designer, essayist, inventor, lyricist, novelist, penwoman, producer, reporter, volumist **09** architect, dramatist, garreteer, initiator, ink-jerker, scribbler **10** biographer, ink-slinger, journalist, librettist, originator, playwright, prime mover, songwriter, trecentist

11 contributor, hedge-writer **12** man of letters, paper-stainer, screenwriter **13** Deuteronomist, revelationist **14** woman of letters

See also **writer**

Authors include:

03 Eco (Umberto), Kee (Robert), Lee (Harper), Lee (Laurie), Poe (Edgar Allan), Pym (Barbara), RLS, Roy (Arundhati)
04 Amis (Kingsley), Amis (Martin), Behn (Aphra), Böll (Heinrich), Boyd (William), Buck (Pearl S), Cary (Joyce), Dahl (Roald), Dane (Clemence), Fine (Anne), Ford (Ford Madox), Gide (André), Grey (Zane), Hogg (James), Hope (Anthony), Hugo (Victor), Jane (Fred T), King (Stephen), Levi (Primo), Loos (Anita), Mann (Thomas), Okri (Ben), Puzo (Mario), Rhys (Jean), Roth (Philip), Sade (Marquis de), Saki, Sand (George), Seth (Vikram), Shah (Eddy), Snow (C P), Wain (John), West (Dame Rebecca), Wood (Mrs Henry), Zola (Emile)
05 Adams (Douglas), Adams (Richard), Agnon (Shmuel Yosef), Banks (Iain), Banks (Lynne Reid), Bates (H E), Behan (Brendan), Benét (Stephen), Bowen (Elizabeth), Bragg (Melvyn), Brink (André), Brown (George Mackay), Bunin (Ivan), Byatt (A S), Camus (Albert), Chase (James Hadley), Craik (Dinah), Crane (Stephen), Dante, Defoe (Daniel), Desai (Anita), Doyle (Roddy), Doyle (Sir Arthur Conan), Dumas (Alexandre, fils), Dumas (Alexandre, père), Eliot (George), Ellis (Alice Thomas), Elton (Ben), Faure (Edgar), Frayn (Michael), Genet (Jean), Gogol (Nikolai), Gorky (Maxim), Grass (Günter), Hardy (Thomas), Hasek (Jaroslav), Hesse (Hermann), Heyer (Georgette), Innes (Hammond), James (Henry), James (P D), Joyce (James), Kafka (Franz), Keane (Molly), Kesey (Ken), Laski (Marghanita), Lewis (C S), Lewis (M G 'Monk'), Lewis (Sinclair), Lewis (Wyndham), Lodge (David), Lowry (Malcolm), Marsh (Dame Ngaio), Milne (A A), Moore (Brian), Moore (Thomas), Munro (H H), O'Hara (John), Paton (Alan), Peake (Mervyn), Plath (Sylvia), Powys (John), Queen (Ellery), Reade (Charles), Sagan (Françoise), Scott (Paul), Scott (Sir Walter), Shute (Nevil), Simon (Claude), Smith (Dodie), Smith (Stevie), Smith (Wilbur), Spark (Dame Muriel), Staël (Madame de), Stowe (Harriet Beecher), Swift (Graham), Swift (Jonathan), Twain (Mark), Tyler (Anne), Verne (Jules), Vidal (Gore), Waugh (Auberon), Waugh (Evelyn), Wells (H G), White (Patrick), White

(T H), Wilde (Oscar), Wolfe (Thomas Clayton), Wolfe (Tom), Woolf (Virginia), Yates (Dornford), Yonge (Charlotte)

06 Achebe (Chinua), Alcott (Louisa May), Aldiss (Brian), Ambler (Eric), Aragon (Louis), Archer (Jeffrey), Asimov (Isaac), Atwood (Margaret), Austen (Jane), Auster (Paul), Balzac (Honoré de), Barker (Pat), Barnes (Julian), Barrie (Sir J M), Bellow (Saul), Binchy (Maeve), Blixen (Karen, Lady), Blyton (Enid), Borges (Jorge Luis), Braine (John), Bratby (John), Brazil (Angela), Brontë (Anne), Brontë (Charlotte), Brontë (Emily), Bryson (Bill), Buchan (John), Bunyan (John), Burney (Fanny), Butler (Samuel), Capote (Truman), Carter (Angela), Cather (Willa), Chopin (Kate), Clancy (Tom), Clarke (Arthur C), Conrad (Joseph), Cooper (James Fenimore), Cooper (Jilly), Cronin (A J), Faulks (Sebastian), Fowles (John), France (Anatole), Fuller (Margaret), Gibbon (Lewis Grassic), Godden (Rumer), Godwin (William), Goethe (Johann Wolfgang von), Graham (Winston), Graves (Robert), Greene (Graham), Haddon (Mark), Hamsun (Knut), Heller (Joseph), Hilton (James), Holtby (Winifred), Hornby (Nick), Hughes (Thomas), Huxley (Aldous), Ibáñez (Vicente Blasco), Jensen (Johannes V), Jerome (Jerome K), Keller (Gottfried), Kelman (James), Laclos (Pierre Choderlos de), Larkin (Philip), Le Fanu (Sheridan), Lively (Penelope), London (Jack), Mailer (Norman), Malouf (David), McEwan (Ian), Miller (Henry), Morgan (Charles), Nesbit (E), O'Brien (Edna), O'Brien (Flann), Orwell (George), Porter (Katherine Anne), Powell (Anthony), Proulx (E Annie), Proust (Marcel), Rankin (Ian), Sapper, Sartre (Jean-Paul), Sayers (Dorothy L), Sewell (Anna), Sharpe (Tom), Singer (Isaac Bashevis), Steele (Danielle), Sterne (Laurence), Stoker (Bram), Storey (David), Tagore (Rabindranath), Thomas (Dylan), Traven (B), Undset (Sigrid), Updike (John), Walker (Alice), Warner (Marina), Warren (Robert Penn), Weldon (Fay), Wesley (Mary), Wilder (Thornton), Wilson (Sir Angus), Wright (Richard)

07 Ackroyd (Peter), Aksakov (Sergei), Angelou (Maya), Arrabal (Fernando), Baldwin (James), Ballard (J G), Beckett (Samuel), Bennett (Arnold), Bentine (Michael), Burgess (Anthony), Burnett (Frances Hodgson), Calvino (Italo), Canetti (Elias), Carroll (Lewis), Chatwin (Bruce), Chekhov (Anton), Clavell (James), Cleland (John), Cocteau (Jean),

Coetzee (J M), Colette, Collins (Wilkie), Cookson (Catherine), Deledda (Grazia), Dickens (Charles), Diderot (Denis), Dineson (Isaac), Douglas (Norman), Drabble (Margaret), Durrell (Gerald), Durrell (Lawrence), Fleming (Ian), Forster (E M), Forster (Margaret), Forsyth (Frederick), Francis (Dick), Gaskell (Mrs Elizabeth), Gautier (Théophile), Gibbons (Stella), Gissing (George), Golding (William), Grahame (Kenneth), Grisham (John), Haggard (Sir H Rider), Hammett (Dashiell), Hartley (L P), Kerouac (Jack), Kipling (Rudyard), Kundera (Milan), Lardner (Ring), Laxness (Halldór), Le Carré (John), Lehmann (Rosamond), Lessing (Doris), Maclean (Alistair), Mahfouz (Naguib), Malamud (Bernard), Malraux (André), Manning (Olivia), Manzoni (Alessandro), Marryat (Captain Frederick), Maugham (W Somerset), Mauriac (François), Mérimée (Prosper), Mishima (Yukio), Mitford (Nancy), Moravia (Alberto), Murdoch (Dame Iris), Nabokov (Vladimir), Naipaul (V S), Peacock (Thomas Love), Prévost (l'Abbé), Pullman (Philip), Pushkin (Alexander), Pynchon (Thomas), Ransome (Arthur), Raphael (Frederic), Renault (Mary), Rendell (Ruth), Richler (Mordecai), Robbins (Harold), Rolland (Romain), Rowling (J K), Rushdie (Salman), Sassoon (Siegfried), Shelley (Mary), Shields (Carol), Simenon (Georges), Sitwell (Sir Osbert), Soyinka (Wole), Spender (Sir Stephen), Surtees (Robert Smith), Theroux (Paul), Tolkien (J R R), Tolstoy (Leo, Count), Tremain (Rose), Wallace (Lewis), Walpole (Sir Hugh), Wharton (Edith), Wyndham (John)

08 Andersen (Hans Christian), Apuleius (Lucius), Asturias (Miguel), Barbusse (Henri), Beckford (William Thomas), Beerbohm (Sir Max), Björnson (Björnstjerne), Bradbury (Malcolm), Bradbury (Ray), Bradford (Barbara Taylor), Brittain (Vera), Brookner (Anita), Bulgakov (Mikhail), Caldwell (Erskine), Cartland (Barbara), Chandler (Raymond), Christie (Dame Agatha), Constant (Benjamin), Cornwell (Patricia), Crompton (Richmal), Day-Lewis (Cecil), Deighton (Len), De La Mare (Walter), Disraeli (Benjamin), Donleavy (J P), Faulkner (William), Fielding (Henry), Flaubert (Gustave), Forester (C S), Francome (John), Goncourt (Edmond de), Gordimer (Nadine), Hochhuth (Rolf), Huysmans (J K), Ishiguro (Kazuo), Jhabvala (Ruth Prawer),

Kawabata (Yasunari), Keneally (Thomas), Kingsley (Charles), Koestler (Arthur), Lagerlöf (Selma), Lawrence (D H), Lockhart (John Gibson), Macaulay (Dame Rose), McCarthy (Mary), Melville (Herman), Meredith (George), Michener (James A), Milligan (Spike), Mitchell (Margaret), Morrison (Toni), Mortimer (John), Murasaki (Shikibu), Oliphant (Margaret), Ondaatje (Michael), Remarque (Erich Maria), Rousseau (Jean Jacques), Salinger (J D), Sillitoe (Alan), Sinclair (Upton), Smollett (Tobias), Spillane (Mickey), Stendhal, Tanizaki (Junichiro), Trollope (Anthony), Trollope (Joanna), Turgenev (Ivan), Voltaire, Vonnegut (Kurt, Junior)

09 Allingham (Margery), Bernières (Louis de), Bleasdale (Alan), Burroughs (Edgar Rice), Burroughs (William S), Cervantes (Miguel de), Charteris (Leslie), Chatterji (Bankim), D'Annunzio (Gabriele), Delafield (E M), De La Roche (Mazo), De Quincey (Thomas), Dos Passos (John), Du Maurier (Dame Daphne), Du Maurier (George), Edgeworth (Maria), Gerhardie (William), Goldsmith (Oliver), Greenwood (Walter), Grossmith (George), Grossmith (Weedon), Guareschi (Giovanni), Hauptmann (Gerhart), Hawthorne (Nathaniel), Hemingway (Ernest), Highsmith (Patricia), Hölderlin (Friedrich), Hopkinson (Sir Tom), Isherwood (Christopher), Lampedusa (Giuseppe Tomasi de), Lermontov (Mikhail), Linklater (Eric), Llewellyn (Richard), Mackenzie (Sir Compton), Mankowitz (Wolf), Mansfield (Katherine), Marinetti (Filippo Tommaso), Masefield (John), McCullers (Carson), Mitchison (Naomi), Monsarrat (Nicholas), Pasternak (Boris), Pratchett (Terry), Priestley (J B), Radcliffe (Ann), Santayana (George), Sholokhov (Mikhail), Steinbeck (John), Stevenson (Robert Louis), Thackeray (William Makepeace), Wodehouse (Sir P G)

10 Bainbridge (Beryl), Ballantyne (R M), Chesterton (G K), De Beauvoir (Simone), Dostoevsky (Fyodor), Fairbairns (Zoë), Fitzgerald (F Scott), Galsworthy (John), Lagerkvist (Pär), Maupassant (Guy de), Pirandello (Luigi), Richardson (Dorothy M), Richardson (Samuel), Strindberg (August), Van der Post (Sir Laurens), Waterhouse (Keith)

11 Kazantzakis (Nikos), Sienkiewicz (Henryk), Vargas Llosa (Mario)

12 Quiller-Couch (Sir Arthur), Robbe-Grillet (Alain), Saint-Exupéry (Antoine de), Solzhenitsyn (Aleksandr)

13 Alain-Fournier (Henri), García Márquez (Gabriel), Sackville-West (Vita)
14 Compton-Burnett (Dame Ivy)
15 Somerset Maugham (William)

See also **playwright; poet**

authoritarian
05 harsh, rigid, tough **06** despot, severe, strict, tyrant **08** absolute, autocrat, despotic, dictator, dogmatic **09** imperious, Orwellian **10** absolutist, autocratic, inflexible, oppressive, tyrannical, unyielding **11** dictatorial, doctrinaire, domineering, magisterial **12** totalitarian **14** disciplinarian

authoritarianism
06 Nazism **07** Fascism **09** autocracy, despotism **10** absolutism, oppression, repression **12** dictatorship **15** totalitarianism

authoritative
04 bold, true **05** crisp, sound, valid **07** factual, learned **08** accepted, accurate, approved, decisive, faithful, imposing, official, reliable, truthful **09** assertive, audacious, authentic, confident, masterful, scholarly **10** authorized, commanding, convincing, definitive, dependable, imperative, legitimate, sanctioned **11** cathedratic, magisterial, self-assured, trustworthy **13** self-confident, self-possessed **14** sure of yourself

authoritatively
06 boldly **08** reliably **09** factually **10** accurately, decisively, dependably, ex cathedra, faithfully **11** assertively, audaciously, confidently **12** convincingly, definitively **13** authentically **15** self-confidently

authority
03 bar **04** buff, mana, name, rule, sage, sway, them, they **05** adept, bible, clout, force, leave, power, right, say-so, state **06** expert, master, muscle, permit, pundit **07** command, consent, control, council, faculty, go-ahead, licence, prelacy, royalty, scepter, sceptre, scholar, Vatican, warrant **08** dominion, lordship, sanction, thumbs-up **09** influence, provostry, supremacy, vicariate **10** domination, fatherhood, government, green light, inquirendo, management, permission, specialist **11** bureaucracy, connoisseur, credentials, imperialism, landlordism, officialdom, prerogative, sovereignty **12** carte blanche, jurisdiction, professional, protectorate **13** authorization, establishment **14** administration, patria potestas **15** the powers that be
• **emblem of authority**
03 rod **04** vare, wand **05** sword **07** scepter, sceptre
• **post of authority**
04 seat

authorization
02 OK **04** okay, pass **05** leave, stamp **06** permit **07** consent, go-ahead, licence, mandate, warrant **08** approval, passport, retainer, sanction, thumbs-up, warranty **09** authority **10** commission, empowering, green light, permission, validation, warrantise **11** credentials, entitlement, procuratory **12** confirmation, ratification **13** accreditation

authorize
02 OK **03** let **04** okay **05** allow **06** enable, permit, ratify **07** approve, confirm, empower, entitle, licence, license, mandate, warrant **08** accredit, legalize, sanction, validate **09** consent to, make legal, privilege **10** commission **15** give authority to

authorized
05 legal, legit **06** lawful **08** approved, licensed, official **09** permitted, warranted **10** accredited, recognized **12** commissioned, under licence

autobahn
02 AB

autobiography
02 CV **05** diary **06** memoir **07** journal, memoirs **09** life story **15** story of your life

autocracy
07 fascism, tyranny **08** autarchy **09** despotism **10** absolutism **12** dictatorship **15** totalitarianism

autocrat
04 cham **06** Caesar, despot, Hitler, tyrant **08** dictator **10** absolutist, panjandrum **12** little Hitler, totalitarian **13** authoritarian

autocratic
08 absolute, despotic **09** autarchic, imperious **10** tyrannical **11** all-powerful, dictatorial, domineering, overbearing **12** totalitarian **13** authoritarian

autograph
04 mark, name, sign **07** endorse, initial **08** initials, monicker **09** signature **11** countersign, endorsement, inscription, put your mark **13** write your name

automatic
06 reflex **07** certain, natural, robotic, routine **08** knee-jerk, unmanned, unwilled **09** automated, necessary, Pavlovian **10** inevitable, mechanical, mechanized, programmed, push-button, self-acting, unthinking **11** inescapable, instinctive, involuntary, spontaneous, unavoidable **12** computerized **14** self-activating, self-propelling, self-regulating, uncontrollable

See also **gun**

automatically
09 certainly, naturally, routinely **10** inevitably **11** inescapably,

necessarily, robotically, unavoidably **12** mechanically, unthinkingly **13** instinctively, involuntarily, spontaneously, unconsciously **14** uncontrollably

automobile
03 car **05** motor **07** vehicle **08** motor car **12** motor vehicle

See also **car**

autonomous
04 free **09** sovereign **11** independent **13** self-directing, self-governing **15** self-determining

autonomy
07 autarky, freedom **08** free will, home rule, self-rule **11** sovereignty **12** independence **14** rangatiratanga, self-government **15** self-sufficiency

autopsy
08 necropsy **10** dissection, post-mortem

autumn
04 fall **07** back-end, harvest **08** leaf-fall

auxiliary
03 aid **05** extra, spare **06** aiding, backer, back-up, helper, second **07** helping, partner, reserve **09** accessory, adminicle, ancillary, assistant, assisting, emergency, secondary, supporter **10** additional, peripheral, subsidiary, substitute, supporting, supportive **11** subordinate **12** right-hand man **13** supplementary **14** right-hand woman **15** second-in-command

avail
03 dow, use **04** doff, vail **05** lower, serve, stead **06** accept, alight, draw on **07** bestead, prevail, succeed, utilize **08** exercise, resort to **09** make use of **15** take advantage of
• **to no avail**
06 in vain, vainly **11** fruitlessly **13** ineffectually **14** unsuccessfully, without success

available
02 on **04** free, open **05** handy, on tap, ready, to let **06** at hand, on hand, single, to hand, usable, vacant **07** not busy, untaken **09** at liberty **10** accessible, convenient, disposable, obtainable, procurable, unoccupied, up for grabs **11** contactable, forthcoming, off the shelf, within reach **12** up your sleeve **13** at your command **14** at your disposal

avalanche
04 wave **05** flood **06** deluge **07** barrage, cascade, lauwine, torrent **08** landslip, snowslip **09** landslide **10** inundation

avant-garde
06 far-out, modern, way-out **07** go-ahead **08** advanced, original **09** inventive **10** futuristic, innovative, innovatory, pioneering **11** progressive **12** contemporary, enterprising,

experimental **14** forward-looking, ground-breaking, unconventional

avarice
05 greed **06** misery **07** avidity
08 meanness **09** pleonexia, the gimmes **10** greediness
11 gourmandise, materialism, miserliness, selfishness
12 covetousness **15** acquisitiveness

avaricious
04 avid, gare, mean **06** greedy, grippy, sordid **07** griping, gripple, miserly
08 covetous, grasping **09** mercenary, rapacious **10** pleonectic **11** acquisitive
12 curmudgeonly

avatar *see* **incarnation**

avenge
05 repay, right, venge, wreak
06 punish **07** pay back, requite **09** get back at, retaliate, vindicate **11** get even with **14** get your own back, take revenge for

avenger
04 goel

avenue
02 Av **03** ave, way **04** line, road, walk
05 allée, corso, drive, grove, vista
06 dromos, method, midway, scheme, street **07** Madison, passage
08 approach, broadway **09** boulevard
10 cradlewalk **12** thoroughfare
13 modus operandi **14** course of action

aver
04 avow **05** state **06** affirm, attest, cattle **07** confirm, declare **08** maintain
09 make known **11** possessions

average
02 av **03** ave, par, run **04** fair, mean, mode, norm, rule, so-so **05** usual
06 centre, common, medial, median, medium, middle, Nikkei, normal
07 regular, routine, typical **08** Dow-Jones, everyday, mediocre, middling, mid-point, moderate, ordinary, passable, standard **09** tolerable **10** not much cop **11** indifferent, not up to much **12** intermediate, run-of-the-mill, satisfactory **13** no great shakes, unexceptional **14** common-or-garden, fair to middling, nothing special **15** undistinguished
• **on average**
06 mainly, mostly **07** as a rule, chiefly, usually **08** normally **09** generally, in the main, routinely, typically **10** by and large, on the whole, ordinarily

averse
05 loath **07** hostile, opposed
09 reluctant, unwilling **10** indisposed
11 disinclined, ill-disposed
12 antagonistic, antipathetic, unfavourable

aversion
04 hate **06** hatred, horror, phobia
07 disgust, dislike **08** distaste, loathing
09 antipathy, hostility, repulsion, revulsion **10** abhorrence, antagonism,

opposition, reluctance, repugnance
11 abomination, detestation
13 unwillingness **14** disinclination
See also **phobia**

avert
03 wry **04** stop **05** avoid, evade, parry
07 deflect, fend off, forfend, head off, obviate, prevent, ward off **08** preclude, stave off, turn away **09** forestall, frustrate, turn aside

aviary
06 volary

aviation
06 flight, flying **11** aeronautics

Aviation-related terms include:
04 dive, drag, flap, taxi
05 fly-by, pilot, plane, prang
06 airway, hangar, runway, thrust
07 airline, air miss, airport, airship, captain, console, fly-past, landing, lift-off, spoiler, take-off
08 aircraft, airfield, airplane, airspace, airstrip, altitude, black box, nose dive, subsonic, windsock, wingspan
09 aeroplane, aerospace, crash dive, fixed-wing, fly-by-wire, jetstream, overshoot, parachute, sonic boom, test pilot, touchdown
10 chocks away, flight crew, Mach number, solo flight, supersonic, test flight, undershoot
11 ground speed, loop-the-loop, night-flying, vapour trail
12 control tower, crash-landing, landing strip, maiden flight, sound barrier
13 ground control, jet propulsion
14 automatic pilot, flight recorder, holding pattern

aviator
05 flyer, pilot **06** airman **08** airwoman
12 aircraftsman **14** aircraftswoman

Aviators include:
04 Byrd (Richard Evelyn), Rust (Mathias), Udet (Ernst)
05 Bader (Sir Douglas), Balbo (Italo, Count), Brown (Sir Arthur Whitten), Johns (Captain W E), Smith (Sir Ross)
06 Alcock (Sir John), Cessna (Clyde), Gibson (Guy), Harris (Sir Arthur 'Bomber'), Hughes (Howard), Nobile (Umberto), Wright (Orville), Wright (Wilbur), Yeager (Chuck)
07 Bennett (Floyd), Blériot (Louis), Branson (Richard), Cochran (Jacqueline), Dornier (Claudius), Douglas (Donald Wills), Earhart (Amelia), Fossett (Steve), Giffard (Henri), Goering (Hermann), Hinkler (Bert), Johnson (Amy), Korolev (Sergei), Piccard (Auguste), Sopwith (Sir Thomas)
08 Brabazon (John, Lord), Cheshire (Leonard, Lord), Zeppelin (Count Ferdinand von)
09 Blanchard (Jean Pierre), Lindbergh (Charles), McDonnell (James Smith)

10 Lindstrand (Per), Richthofen (Manfred, Baron von)
11 Montgolfier (Jacques), Montgolfier (Joseph)
12 Saint-Exupéry (Antoine de)
13 Messerschmitt (Willy)

avid
03 mad **04** keen **05** crazy, eager, great
06 ardent, greedy, hungry **07** athirst, devoted, earnest, fervent, intense, thirsty, zealous **08** covetous, grasping, ravenous **09** dedicated, fanatical
10 insatiable, passionate
12 enthusiastic

avidly
05 madly **06** keenly **07** eagerly
08 ardently, greedily, hungrily
09 devotedly, earnestly, fervently, intensely, thirstily, zealously
10 covetously, insatiably, ravenously
11 fanatically **12** passionately

avocado
08 aguacate **09** guacamole
13 alligator pear

avocet
07 awlbird, scooper

avoid
03 fly **04** balk, duck, miss, shun
05 avert, dodge, elude, evade, evite, hedge, shirk **06** bypass, escape, eschew **07** decline, evitate, forbear, prevent **08** get out of, get round, sidestep **09** give a miss **10** circumvent
11 abstain from, make a detour, refrain from, run away from, shy away from
12 hold back from, keep away from, stay away from, steer clear of

avoidable
08 eludible, evitable **09** avertible, escapable, stoppable **11** preventable

avow
03 vow **04** aver **05** admit, state, swear
06 assert, attest, avouch **07** confess, declare, profess **08** maintain
11 acknowledge

avowed
04 open **05** overt, sworn **07** confest
08 admitted, declared **09** barefaced, confessed, professed **10** professing
12 acknowledged **13** self-confessed
14 self-proclaimed

await
04 bide, stay **05** tarry **06** expect, remain **07** hope for, look for, wait for
10 anticipate **12** be in store for, lie in wait for **13** look forward to

awake
04 stir, wake **05** abray, alert, alive, aware, rouse, waken **06** abrade, abraid, arouse, awaken, wake up
07 aroused, mindful, wakeful
08 stirring, vigilant, watchful
09 attentive, conscious, observant, sensitive, wide awake **12** appreciative

awaken
04 stir, wake **05** awake, rouse, waken
06 abraid, excite, wake up **07** inspire

8 engender, generate **09** stimulate
1 disentrance **14** cause to realize

awakening
5 birth **06** waking **07** arousal,
waking, revival, rousing **08** wakening
9 animating **10** activation, enlivening
1 reanimating, revivifying, stimulation
2 vivification

award
3 cup **04** aret, gift, give, gong
5 allot, allow, arett, endow, grant,
medal, order, prize **06** accord,
addeem, addoom, adward, assign,
bestow, confer, modify, reward, trophy
7 adjudge, bursary, honours,
payment, present, rosette
8 accolade, allocate, bestowal,
citation, decision, decorate, dispense
9 allotment, allowance, apportion,
conferral, determine, endowment,
judgement **10** adjudicate, decoration,
distribute, palatinate, settlement,
subvention **11** certificate, scholarship
2 adjudication, commendation,
dispensation, presentation

Awards and prizes include:
2 CH, MM, OM
3 CBE, OBE
4 Brit, Emmy, Tony
5 Bafta, César, Nobel, Oscar
6 Booker, Grammy, Orange, Turner
7 Academy, Olivier
8 Palme d'Or, Pulitzer, Stirling
9 Grand Jury, Grand Prix, Man
    Booker, Templeton
0 Golden Bear, Golden Palm
1 Fields Medal, Golden Globe
2 Prix Goncourt
3 Whitbread Book

ee also **honour; military**

aware
3 hip **05** alert, awake, sharp
6 shrewd, sussed **07** alive to, clued
up, heedful, knowing, mindful
8 apprised, familiar, informed,
sensible, sentient, vigilant **09** attentive,
au courant, cognizant, conscient,
conscious, in the know, observant, on
the ball, sensitive **10** acquainted,
conversant **11** enlightened, recognizant
2 appreciative **13** knowledgeable
• **aware of**
4 on to
• **be aware of**
3 ken **04** feel, know

awareness
3 sus **04** suss **05** grasp **06** vision
7 insight, samadhi **09** knowledge
0 cognizance, perception
1 familiarity, panesthesia, recognition,
sensitivity **12** acquaintance,
appreciation, panaesthesia
3 consciousness, sensitiveness,
understanding

awash
4 full **05** alive **06** packed, soaked
7 flooded, replete, teeming
8 crawling, drenched, swarming
9 inundated, saturated, submerged

away
◇ *anagram indicator*
02 by **03** far, fro, off, out **04** from
05 apart, aside, hence **06** abroad,
absent **08** from here **09** elsewhere,
from there, not at home, not at work,
on holiday **10** on vacation **11** at a
distance

awe
04 fear **05** dread **06** honour, terror,
wonder **07** respect **09** amazement,
reverence **10** admiration, veneration,
wonderment **12** apprehension,
astonishment, stupefaction

awed
06 amazed, solemn **07** fearful,
stunned **09** awe-struck **10** astonished
11 reverential **12** lost for words

awe-inspiring
06 moving, solemn **07** amazing,
awesome, exalted, sublime
08 daunting, dazzling, fearsome,
imposing, majestic, numinous, striking,
stunning **09** wonderful **10** formidable,
impressive, stupefying, stupendous
11 astonishing, magnificent,
spectacular **12** breathtaking,
intimidating, mind-boggling,
overwhelming

awesome
07 amazing **08** daunting, stunning
10 formidable, impressive
11 astonishing, jaw-dropping,
spectacular **12** breathtaking,
intimidating, mind-boggling,
overwhelming **13** extraordinary

awestruck
04 awed **06** amazed **09** awe-struck,
impressed **10** astonished **12** lost for
words

awful
◇ *anagram indicator*
03 ill **04** crap, dire, naff, sick **05** lousy,
nasty, pants, rough, seedy, spewy
06 crummy, horrid, in pain, poorly,
unwell **07** abysmal, fearful, ghastly,
heinous, the pits **08** alarming,
dreadful, gruesome, horrible, horrific,
inferior, pathetic, shocking, terrible,
very poor **09** appalling, atrocious,
frightful, third-rate, washed out
10 disgusting, horrifying, inadequate,
second-rate, unpleasant **11** distressing
14 a load of rubbish, unsatisfactory
15 under the weather

awfully
◇ *anagram indicator*
04 very **06** deeply, really **07** greatly
08 terribly **09** extremely, immensely
10 absolutely, dreadfully, remarkably
12 particularly, tremendously,
unbelievably

awhile
10 for a moment **11** for some time
13 for a short time

awkward
◇ *anagram indicator*
03 shy **04** rude **05** blate, gawky, inept,

nasty **06** clumsy, clunky, fiddly,
gauche, rustic, thumby, touchy, tricky,
ungain **07** bashful, boorish, cubbish,
loutish, prickly, spastic, stroppy,
uncouth **08** annoying, bungling,
clownish, delicate, handless, inexpert,
lubberly, stubborn, ungainly, untoward,
unwieldy **09** all thumbs, difficult,
graceless, ham-fisted, ill at ease,
inelegant, irritable, maladroit,
obstinate, unskilful **10** cumbersome,
left-handed, perplexing, ungraceful,
unpleasant **11** disobliging,
embarrassed, heavy-handed,
obstructive, problematic, troublesome
12 bloody-minded, embarrassing,
inconvenient **13** chuckle-headed,
oversensitive, uncomfortable, unco-
operative, unco-ordinated
15 unaccommodating

awkwardly
◇ *anagram indicator*
05 shyly **07** ineptly **08** clumsily,
uneasily, ungainly **09** bashfully
10 inexpertly **11** gracelessly, ham-
fistedly, inelegantly, maladroitly,
unskilfully **12** ungracefully **13** heavy-
handedly, uncomfortably

awkwardness
09 confusion, gawkiness, inaptness
10 clumsiness, inaptitude, inelegance,
maladdress, uneasiness **11** bashfulness
12 discomfiture, ungainliness
13 embarrassment, gracelessness, left-
handiness **15** heavy-handedness

awl
04 brog, prod, stob **05** elsin **06** elshin

awn
05 beard

awning
04 tilt **05** blind, cover, shade
06 canopy **07** shelter **08** covering,
shamiana, sunblind, sunshade,
velarium **09** shamianah

awry
◇ *anagram indicator*
03 cam, kam **04** skew **05** aglee, agley,
amiss, askew, kamme, tipsy, wonky,
wrong **06** skivie, uneven **07** askance,
athwart, crooked, haywire, oblique,
tortive, twisted **08** cockeyed
09 off-centre, skew-whiff
10 misaligned, out of joint
12 asymmetrical, by transverse

axe
03 cut, hew **04** bill, celt, chop, fell, fire,
sack **05** split **06** cancel, cleave, guitar,
labrys, piolet, remove, sparth
07 chopper, cleaver, cut down, dismiss,
gisarme, halberd, hatchet, sparthe,
twibill **08** get rid of, palstaff, palstave,
partisan, throw out, tomahawk,
withdraw **09** battle-axe, discharge,
eliminate, saxophone, terminate
11 coup de poing, discontinue,
thunderbolt **12** Jeddart staff
• **get the axe**
10 get the boot, get the chop, get the
sack **11** be cancelled

axiom
02 ax 05 adage, maxim, truth
06 byword, dictum, truism
07 precept 08 aphorism, petition
09 postulate, principle
11 fundamental

axiomatic
05 given 06 gnomic 07 assumed,
certain, granted 08 accepted, manifest
10 aphoristic, proverbial, understood
11 fundamental, indubitable,
presupposed, self-evident
12 unquestioned 14 apophthegmatic,
unquestionable

axis
01 X, Y, Z 03 cob 04 axle 05 henge,
hinge, pivot 06 chital, rachis
07 rhachis 08 backbone, modiolus,
vertical 10 centre-line, horizontal
13 macrodiagonal 14 brachydiagonal
• **end of axis**
04 pole

axle
03 pin, rod 04 axis 05 pivot, shaft,
truck 07 mandrel, mandril, spindle
11 paddle-shaft

Azerbaijan
02 AZ 03 AZE

azure
04 Saxe 07 sky-blue 08 cerulean, pale
blue 09 light blue 11 nattier blue
13 Cambridge blue

B

B
04 beta **05** bravo

babble
03 gab, jaw **05** babel, prate **06** burble, cackle, gabble, gibber, gurgle, hubbub, jabber, jawing, mumble, murmur, mutter, waffle, witter **07** blabber, brabble, chatter, clamour, prattle, twaddle, twattle **08** rabbit on **09** gibberish, wittering **10** tongue-work **12** bibble-babble

babe
03 sis, tot **04** baby **05** child **06** infant **07** newborn, tiny tot **08** suckling **10** babe in arms **11** newborn baby

babel
03 din **05** chaos **06** babble, bedlam, hubbub, tumult, uproar **07** clamour, turmoil **08** disorder **09** commotion, confusion **10** hullabaloo **11** pandemonium

baboon
05 drill **06** chacma, dog-ape, gelada **08** mandrill **09** hamadryad **12** Cynocephalus

baby
03 bub, sis, tot, wee **04** babe, dear, love, mini, mite, tiny **05** bairn, bubby, child, dwarf, honey, small, sprog, teeny **06** infant, little, midget, minute **07** darling, dearest, neonate, newborn, papoose, sweetie, tiny tot, toddler **08** killcrop, pint-size, suckling **09** miniature, pint-sized **10** diminutive, small-scale, sweetheart **11** newborn baby

babyish
04 baby, soft **05** naive, silly, sissy, young **07** foolish, puerile **08** childish, immature, juvenile **09** infantile

Babylonian *see* **god, goddess**

bacchanalian
• **bacchanalian expression**
04 euoi, evoe, upsy **05** evhoe, evohe, upsee, upsey

Bacchus
08 Dionysus

bachelor
01 B **02** BA **04** Bach **05** batch

bacillus
02 TB **03** bcg **07** anthrax **08** coliform **11** micrococcus

back
◊ *reversal indicator*
◊ *tail selection indicator*
03 aft, ago, aid, bet, bid, end, off

04 abet, ante, away, help, hind, past, rear, risk, tail **05** boost, other, spine, stake, stern, wager **06** assist, before, behind, bygone, chance, dorsum, far end, favour, former, gamble, rachis, recede, recoil, retire, second, tergum **07** bolster, confirm, earlier, elapsed, endorse, finance, promote, rear end, regress, retreat, reverse, sponsor, support, sustain, tail end, venture **08** advocate, back away, backbone, backside, be behind, champion, hindmost, hind part, obsolete, outdated, previous, sanction, side with, withdraw **09** backtrack, backwards, encourage, get behind, other side, out of date, posterior, speculate, subsidize, to the rear **10** previously, underwrite **11** countenance, countersign, go backwards, reverse side **12** hindquarters **13** move backwards
• **back and forth**
◊ *palindrome indicator*
• **back away**
06 recede, recoil **07** retreat **08** draw back, fall back, move back, step back, withdraw **10** give ground
• **back down**
05 yield **06** give in, submit **07** abandon, concede, retreat **08** withdraw **09** back-pedal, backtrack, climb down, surrender
• **back out**
◊ *reversal indicator*
06 cancel, cry off, give up, recant, resign, resile **07** abandon, call off, pull out, retreat **08** crawfish, go back on, withdraw **10** chicken out **11** get cold feet
• **back up**
03 aid **04** abet **06** assist, second, soothe, verify **07** bear out, bolster, confirm, endorse, reserve, stand by, stand to, support **08** champion, validate **09** reinforce **11** corroborate **12** substantiate
• **behind your back**
05 slyly **08** covertly, secretly, sneakily **09** furtively **11** deceitfully **15** surreptitiously
• **turn your back on**
04 quit **05** leave **06** ignore, reject **07** abandon, exclude **08** throw out **09** repudiate **15** wash your hands of

backbiting
05 abuse, catty, libel, slurs, spite **06** bitchy, gossip, malice **07** abusive, calumny, cattish, insults, slander **08** spiteful **09** aspersion, cattiness, criticism, libellous, malicious, vilifying **10** bitchiness, defamation, detraction, revilement, rubbishing, slanderous

11 denigration, disparaging, mud-slinging, slagging off **12** back-wounding, spitefulness, vilification, vituperation **13** disparagement

backbone
04 core, grit, guts **05** basis, chine, nerve, pluck, power, spine **06** bottle, mettle **07** courage, nucleus, resolve, stamina, support **08** firmness, mainstay, strength, tenacity **09** character, toughness, vertebrae, willpower **10** foundation, resolution **11** cornerstone **12** spinal column, vertebration **13** determination, steadfastness **15** vertebral column

backbreaking
04 hard **05** heavy **07** arduous, killing, onerous **08** crushing, grueling **09** gruelling, laborious, punishing, strenuous **10** exhausting

backchat
03 lip **04** face **05** cheek, mouth, nerve, snash **08** back talk, repartee, rudeness **09** brass neck, cross-talk, impudence, insolence, sauciness **12** impertinence

backer
05 angel **06** friend, funder, patron, second **07** sponsor **08** advocate, champion, investor, promoter, seconder, stickler **09** supporter **10** benefactor, subscriber, subsidizer, well-wisher **11** underwriter **12** bottle-holder

backfire
◊ *reversal indicator*
04 fail, flop **06** blow up, recoil **07** explode, misfire, rebound **08** detonate, miscarry, ricochet **09** boomerang, discharge **10** strike back **12** defeat itself **14** score an own goal **15** be self-defeating, come home to roost

backgammon
08 tick-tack, tric-trac, verquere **10** trick-track

background
04 fond **05** field, scene **06** canvas, family, milieu, record, status **07** context, culture, factors, history, origins, setting **08** backdrop, breeding, surround **09** backcloth, cyclorama, education, framework, grounding, tradition **10** experience, influences, upbringing **11** credentials, environment, preparation **12** surroundings **13** circumstances **14** qualifications, social standing

backhanded
06 ironic 07 awkward, dubious, oblique, reverse 08 indirect, sardonic, two-edged 09 ambiguous, equivocal, insincere, sarcastic 11 double-edged

backing
◊ *reversal indicator*
03 aid 04 help, vamp 05 funds, grant 06 backup, facing, favour, lining 07 finance, funding, helpers, padding, subsidy, support 08 advocacy, approval, sanction 09 obbligato, patronage, promotion, seconding 10 assistance, stiffening 11 championing, co-operation, endorsement, interlining, sponsorship 12 commendation, moral support 13 accompaniment, encouragement, reinforcement

backlash
06 recoil 08 backfire, kickback, reaction, reprisal, response 09 boomerang 11 retaliation 12 repercussion 13 counteraction

backlog
04 heap, pile 05 hoard, stock 06 excess, supply 07 reserve 08 mountain, reserves 09 resources 12 accumulation

back-pedal
05 yield 06 give in, renege, submit 07 abandon, concede, retract, retreat 08 do a U-turn, go back on, take back, withdraw 09 about-face, about-turn, backtrack, climb down, surrender 12 tergiversate 14 change your mind

backslide
◊ *reversal indicator*
03 sin 04 slip 05 lapse, stray 06 defect, desert, go back, renege, revert 07 default, regress, relapse 08 go astray, turn away 10 apostatize 12 tergiversate, turn your back 13 fall from grace

backslider
07 reneger 08 apostate, defector, deserter, recreant, renegade, turncoat 09 defaulter 10 recidivist 13 tergiversator

backsliding
◊ *reversal indicator*
05 lapse 07 relapse 08 apostasy 09 defection, desertion 10 defaulting, regression 14 tergiversation

backtrack
◊ *reversal indicator*
06 renege 08 do a U-turn, go back on, withdraw 09 back-pedal, climb down 12 tergiversate 14 change your mind

backup
03 aid 04 help 07 support 10 assistance 11 endorsement 12 confirmation 13 encouragement, reinforcement

backward
◊ *reversal indicator*
03 shy 04 hind, slow 05 timid

06 arrear, averse, behind 07 arriéré, bashful, reverse 08 hesitant, immature, rearward, retarded, reticent, retiring, wavering 09 reluctant, shrinking, subnormal, to the back, unwilling 10 hesitating, regressive, retrograde 11 undeveloped 13 retrogressive 14 underdeveloped 15 unsophisticated

backwards
◊ *reversal indicator*
05 aback, retro- 09 rearwards, to the back 12 regressively 15 retrogressively

backwash
04 flow, path, wake, wash 05 swell, waves 06 result 07 results 08 reaction 09 aftermath 11 after effect, consequence 12 after effects, consequences, repercussion 13 repercussions 14 reverberations

backwater
05 bogan, scrub 06 slough 08 Woop Woop 11 remote place 13 isolated place

backwoods
04 bush 05 brush 07 outback 08 backveld 09 backwater, the sticks 10 back-blocks, the boonies 11 remote place 12 back of beyond, the boondocks 13 isolated place 15 middle of nowhere

bacon
04 bard, spek 05 Roger, speck 06 collar, gammon, lardon, rasher 07 Francis, lardoon 08 forehock, pancetta

bacteria *see* **bacterium**

bacteriology

Bacteriologists include:

04 Cohn (Ferdinand), Gram (Hans), Koch (Robert), Roux (Émile) 05 Avery (Oswald), Smith (Theobald), Twort (Frederick) 06 Enders (John) 07 Behring (Emil von), Buchner (Hans), Ehrlich (Paul), Fleming (Sir Alexander), Löffler (Friedrich) 08 Calmette (Albert), Kitasato (Shibasaburo) 10 Wassermann (August von)

See also **biology**

bacterium
03 bug, rod 04 cell, germ 06 mother, packet, strain 07 microbe 08 parasite, serotype, superbug 13 micro-organism

Bacteria include:

04 MRSA 06 coccus, vibrio 07 Proteus 08 bacillus, listeria, Shigella, yersinia, zoogloea 09 Azobacter, peritrich, ray fungus, Rhizobium, spirillum, treponema, treponeme 10 gonococcus, Klebsiella, Leptospira, salmonella, saprophyte

11 acidophilus, Actinomyces, Azotobacter, Bacillaceae, clostridium, Escherichia, Pasteurella, Penicillium, pseudomonad, pseudomonas, spirochaete 12 enterococcus, helicobacter, pneumococcus, vinegar plant 13 campylobacter, Eubacteriales, fission fungus, lactobacillus, Mycobacterium, streptococcus 14 actinobacillus, Corynebacteria, staphylococcus, trichobacteria, Vibrio cholerae, Yersinia pestis 15 Escherichia coli, intestinal flora, sulphur bacteria

bad
◊ *anagram indicator*
03 hot, ill, mal-, off 04 blue, eale, edgy, evil, foul, high, hurt, lewd, mean, naff, nice, poor, poxy, ropy, rude, sick, sour, vile, wack, weak 05 acute, angry, awful, black, cross, crude, dirty, gammy, grave, gross, harsh, humpy, juicy, lousy, narky, nasty, onkus, pants, ratty, sorry, testy 06 aching, coarse, crabby, crummy, faulty, feisty, filthy, gallus, gloomy, grumpy, guilty, in pain, mouldy, poorly, putrid, rancid, rotten, severe, shirty, shoddy, sinful, smutty, snappy, spoilt, stingy, tetchy, unruly, unwell, vulgar, wicked 07 abusive, adverse, ashamed, bilious, bolshie, botched, corrupt, crabbed, decayed, gnarled, grouchy, harmful, hurtful, immoral, in a huff, in a sulk, injured, intense, naughty, obscene, painful, peppery, prickly, profane, raunchy, ruinous, serious, stroppy, tainted, the pits, unhappy, useless, wayward, wounded 08 choleric, contrite, criminal, critical, damaging, diseased, dreadful, hopeless, impaired, impolite, indecent, inferior, mediocre, pathetic, petulant, shameful, terrible 09 appalling, atrocious, crotchety, dangerous, defective, deficient, difficult, dishonest, dyspeptic, fractious, impatient, imperfect, injurious, insulting, irascible, irritable, offensive, querulous, reprobate, splenetic, third-rate, unhealthy 10 apologetic, capernoity, degenerate, deplorable, despondent, ill-behaved, inadequate, mismanaged, outrageous, putrescent, refractory, remorseful, second-rate, shamefaced, unpleasant, unsuitable 11 a load of crap, bad-tempered, blasphemous, carnaptious, deleterious, destructive, detrimental, disobedient, distressing, incompetent, ineffective, ineffectual, mischievous, substandard, thin-skinned, undesirable, unfortunate, unwholesome 12 badly-behaved, cantankerous, contaminated, disagreeable, discourteous, inauspicious, inconvenient, putrefactive, unacceptable, unfavourable 13 inappropriate, quick-tempered, reprehensible 14 a load of garbage, a load of rubbish,

uncontrollable, unsatisfactory
15 under the weather
• **not bad**
02 OK **04** fair, so-so **07** average
08 adequate, all right, passable
09 quite good, tolerable
10 acceptable, reasonable
12 satisfactory

badge
03 mon **04** blue, logo, mark, sign, star
05 brand, crest, eagle, patch, stamp,
token, wings **06** button, device,
emblem, ensign, rondel, shield, symbol
07 cockade, insigne, kikumon, rosette
08 episemon, insignia, numerals,
vernicle **09** indicator, trademark
10 cognizance, escutcheon, indication
14 identification

badger
03 nag **04** bait, goad, ride **05** brock,
bully, harry, hound, ratel **06** chivvy, go
on at, harass, hassle, keep at, pester,
plague, teledu **07** torment **08** ballyrag,
bullyrag, keep on at **09** importune
• **badger-like animal**
05 ratel
• **badgers**
04 cete

badinage
05 borak, chaff **06** banter, humour
07 mockery, ribbing, teasing, waggery
08 dicacity, drollery, raillery, repartee,
wordplay **10** jocularity, persiflage
11 give and take

badly
◊ *anagram indicator*
03 ill, mis- **06** deeply, evilly, poorly
07 acutely, awfully, cruelly, gravely,
greatly, ineptly, wrongly **08** bitterly,
faultily, severely, sinfully, terribly,
unfairly, very much, wickedly
09 adversely, crucially, extremely,
immorally, intensely, painfully, seriously,
unhappily, uselessly **10** carelessly,
criminally, critically, enormously,
improperly, shamefully **11** appallingly,
dangerously, defectively, desperately,
dishonestly, exceedingly, imperfectly,
incorrectly, negligently, offensively
12 inadequately, pathetically,
tremendously, unacceptably,
unfavourably **13** incompetently,
ineffectually, unfortunately
14 unsuccessfully
• **badly off**
04 poor **05** needy **06** in need

bad-mannered
04 rude **05** crude **06** coarse
07 boorish, cubbish, ill-bred, loutish,
uncivil, uncouth **08** churlish, impolite,
insolent **10** ill-behaved, unmannerly
11 ill-mannered, insensitive **12** badly-
behaved, discourteous

badminton

Badminton-related terms include:
03 net, set
04 bird, kill
05 clear, court, drive, flick, rally, serve,
smash

06 racket
07 doubles, racquet, singles
08 drop shot, wood shot
11 shuttlecock
12 service court
13 underarm clear

badness
03 sin **04** evil **07** cruelty **08** foulness,
vileness **09** depravity, nastiness
10 corruption, dishonesty, immorality,
wickedness **12** shamefulness
14 unpleasantness

bad-tempered
04 edgy, mean **05** black, cross, humpy,
narky, ratty, sulky, testy, vixen **06** crabby,
feisty, gnarly, grumpy, shirty, snappy,
stingy, tetchy **07** bilious, crabbed,
crabbit, gnarled, grouchy, in a huff, in a
mood, in a sulk, peppery, prickly,
stroppy, vicious, vixenly **08** choleric,
petulant, scratchy, vixenish
09 crotchety, dyspeptic, fractious,
impatient, irascible, irritable, querulous,
splenetic **10** capernoity, ill-natured, in a
bad mood **11** carnaptious, curnaptious,
dyspeptical, ill-humoured, thin-skinned
12 cantankerous **13** quick-tempered

baffle
◊ *anagram indicator*
03 bar, fox, get **04** daze, faze, foil, mate
05 block, check, elude, evade, stump,
throw, upset **06** bemuse, defeat, fickle,
hinder, puzzle, thwart **07** bumbaze,
confuse, flummox, mystify, nonplus,
perplex **08** bewilder, confound
09 bamboozle, dumbfound, frustrate
10 disconcert **13** bring to naught

baffling
◊ *anagram indicator*
07 amazing, cryptic **08** bemusing,
puzzling **09** confusing, enigmatic
10 astounding, mysterious, perplexing,
stupefying, surprising **11** bewildering
12 unfathomable **13** disconcerting,
extraordinary

bag
◊ *containment indicator*
03 cod, get, net, pot, sac **04** gain, grab,
kill, land, pock, poke, port, take, trap
05 catch, pouch, shoot **06** come by,
corner, obtain, pocket, secure
07 acquire, capture, reserve
09 container **10** commandeer,
receptacle **11** appropriate

Bags include:
03 bum, jag, kit, pod
04 caba, case, grip, hand, mail, pack,
sack, tote, wash
05 bulse, cabas, dilli, dilly, ditty, money,
purse, scrip
06 carpet, clutch, duffel, flight, sachel,
saddle, tucker, valise, vanity, wallet
07 carrier, evening, holdall, satchel,
shopper, utricle
08 backpack, carry-all, gripsack,
knapsack, mailsack, meal-poke,
pochette, reticule, rucksack,
shopping, shoulder, suitcase,
wineskin, woolpack

09 briefcase, fanny pack, Gladstone,
haversack, moneybelt, overnight
10 sabretache
11 attaché-case, portmanteau

baggage
04 bags, gear, swag **05** cases
06 things **07** clobber, dunnage,
effects, luggage **08** carriage, materiel
09 equipment, suitcases, viaticals
10 belongings **11** impedimenta
13 accoutrements, paraphernalia
See also **prostitute**

baggy
05 kneed, loose, roomy, slack
06 bulged, droopy, floppy, pouchy,
sloppy **07** bulging, sagging
08 oversize **09** billowing, shapeless
10 ballooning, extra large, ill-fitting
12 loose-fitting

bagpipe
05 gaita, pipes **07** musette, piffero
08 dulcimer, zampogna
09 cornemuse **10** small-pipes,
sourdeline **12** uillean pipes **13** uileann
pipes
• **bagpipe composition**
04 port **07** pibroch

Bahamas
02 BS **03** BHS

Bahrain
03 BHR, BRN

bail
04 bond, hoop **05** ladle **06** pledge,
surety **07** caution, custody, replevy
08 security, warranty **09** guarantee
10 collateral **12** jurisdiction
• **bail out**
03 aid **04** help, quit, save **05** eject,
ladle, scoop **06** assist, escape, get out,
rescue **07** back out, finance, relieve,
retreat **08** get clear, withdraw

bailiff
04 foud **05** agent, reeve **06** beagle
07 nut-hook **08** huissier **09** bum-
baylie, hundreder, hundredor
10 philistine **11** land-steward
12 shoulder knot **15** shoulder-clapper

bait
03 dap, irk, lug **04** goad, lure, rage
05 annoy, bribe, decoy, harry, hound,
leger, slate, snare, squid, taunt, tease,
tie-up, yabby **06** badger, berley, burley,
caplin, gentle, harass, hassle, ledger,
lidger, needle, plague, yabbie
07 capelin, catworm, lugworm,
provoke, ragworm, torment **08** irritate
09 anchoveta, angleworm, brandling,
incentive, killifish, persecute, propeller,
white worm **10** allurement, attraction,
enticement, incitement, inducement,
temptation **11** hellgramite, refreshment
12 hellgrammite, night crawler **15** give
a hard time to

bake
◊ *anagram indicator*
03 dry **04** burn, cake, cook, fire, heat,
shir **05** brown, parch, roast, shirr
06 harden, scorch, wither **07** shrivel

08 pot-roast **09** oven-roast, spit-roast **12** porcellanize

balance
03 bal, set **04** meet, rest, trim, tron **05** agree, level, Libra, match, pease, peaze, peise, peize, peyse, poise, pound, tally, weigh **06** adjust, aplomb, equate, equity, even up, excess, juggle, launce, make up, offset, parity, review, square, stasis, steady **07** compare, even out, librate, residue, surplus, weigh up **08** appraise, calmness, consider, equality, equalize, estimate, evaluate, evenness, symmetry **09** assurance, composure, equipoise, remainder, sangfroid, stability, stabilize **10** correspond, counteract, difference, equanimity, neutralize, set against, steadiness, uniformity **11** equilibrate, equilibrium, equivalence, self-control **12** counterweigh **13** compensate for, equiponderate **14** cool-headedness, correspondence, counterbalance, self-possession, unflappability **15** level-headedness
• **balance sheet**
02 bs
• **in the balance**
04 iffy **06** unsure **07** unknown **08** in the air **09** knife-edge, uncertain, undecided, unsettled **10** indefinite, touch and go **12** undetermined **13** unpredictable
• **on balance**
07 overall **08** all in all **09** generally **12** in conclusion

balanced
04 calm, even, fair **05** equal, level, sound **06** poised **07** assured, healthy, weighed **08** complete, sensible, straight, unbiased **09** equitable, impartial, objective **10** cool-headed, even-handed **11** level-headed, well-rounded **12** unprejudiced **13** dispassionate, self-possessed

balcony
04 gods **06** loggia **07** gallery, portico, sundeck, terrace, veranda **09** mezzanine **10** moucharaby **11** upper circle **14** quarter-gallery

bald
04 bare **05** bleak, blunt, naked, plain, stark **06** barren, direct, paltry, peeled, severe, simple, smooth **07** exposed, obvious, pollard, trivial **08** glabrate, glabrous, hairless, outright, straight, tonsured, treeless **09** depilated, downright, outspoken, unadorned, uncovered **10** bald-headed, forthright **11** bald as a coot, unambiguous, undisguised, unsheltered **15** straightforward

balderdash
03 rot **04** blah, bosh, bull, bunk, crap, guff, jazz **05** bilge, borak, hooey, trash, tripe **06** blague, bunkum, drivel, faddle, havers, hot air, piffle **07** baloney, eyewash, hogwash, rhubarb, rubbish, twaddle **08** blethers, bulldust, claptrap, cobblers, doggerel,

malarkey, nonsense, tommyrot **09** bull's wool, gibberish, moonshine, poppycock **10** codswallop, galimatias **12** clamjamphrie

balding
04 bald **08** receding **09** thin on top **14** losing your hair

baldmoney
03 meu **07** spignel

baldness
07 fox-evil **08** alopecia, bareness, hair loss, psilosis **09** calvities, madarosis, starkness **12** glabrousness, hairlessness **14** alopecia areata, bald-headedness

bale
02 bl **04** lave, pack **05** ladle, seron, truss **06** bundle, parcel, seroon **07** confine, package **08** woolpack
• **bale out**
04 quit **06** escape, get out **07** back out, retreat **08** get clear, withdraw

baleful
04 evil **05** swart **06** deadly, malign, sullen, swarth **07** harmful, hurtful, malefic, noxious, ominous, painful, ruinous **08** menacing, mournful, sinister, venomous **09** injurious, malignant, sorrowful **10** lugubrious, malevolent, pernicious **11** destructive, threatening

balefully
09 harmfully, hurtfully **10** menacingly **11** dangerously **13** destructively, detrimentally, threateningly

balk, baulk
03 bar, hen, jib **04** chop, foil **05** avoid, check, demur, dodge, evade, reest, reist, shirk, stall **06** baffle, boggle, defeat, eschew, flinch, hinder, ignore, impede, pull up, recoil, refuse, resist, shrink, thwart **07** decline, prevent **08** hesitate, obstruct **09** discomfit, forestall, frustrate **10** counteract, disconcert **11** frustration **14** disappointment

ball
01 O **02** ba **03** cop, nur, orb **04** clew, clue, drop, knur, nurr, pill, shot, slug, tice **05** dance, fungo, globe, Jaffa, knurr, party **06** beamer, bullet, googly, pellet, soirée, sphere, strike, yorker **07** bouncer, globule, long hop, shooter, swinger **08** assembly, carnival, Chinaman, delivery, full toss, gazunder, leg break, off break **09** inswinger **10** masquerade, outswinger, projectile **11** daisy-cutter, dinner-dance **14** conglomeration
• **high ball**
03 lob
• **play ball**
07 go along, respond **09** co-operate, play along **11** collaborate, reciprocate, show willing
• **position of ball**
03 lie

ballad
03 jig **04** poem, song **05** carol, ditty,

mento **06** shanty **07** ballant, calypso, romance **08** folk-song, singsong **09** cantilena **10** forebitter **12** Lillibullero

ballet
07 dancing **11** leg-business **13** ballet-dancing
See also **choreography; dance; dancer**

Ballets include:
05 Manon, Rodeo, Rooms
06 Apollo, Boléro, Carmen, Façade, Ondine, Onegin, Parade
07 Giselle, La Valse, Orpheus, Requiem
08 Coppélia, Les Noces, Nocturne, Swan Lake
09 Anastasia, Les Biches, Mayerling
10 Cinderella, Don Quixote, La Sylphide, Petroushka, Prince Igor, Pulcinella
11 Billy the Kid, Las Hermanas, The Firebird
12 Les Sylphides, Schéhérazade
13 Pineapple Poll, The Nutcracker
14 Daphnis et Chloé, Romeo and Juliet, The Prodigal Son
15 The Rite of Spring

Ballet-related terms include:
03 bar, pas
04 jeté, plié, posé, tutu
05 barre, battu
06 à terre, attack, ballon, chassé, écarté, en face, en l'air, pointe, school, splits
07 à pointe, bourrée, bras bas, ciseaux, company, danseur, en avant, fouetté, leotard, maillot, pointes, premier
08 attitude, batterie, cabriole, capriole, coryphée, couronne, danseuse, en pointe, ensemble, fish dive, glissade, première, stulchak
09 arabesque, ballerina, battement, cou de pied, elevation, entrechat, pas de chat, pas de deux, pas de seul, pirouette, point shoe, promenade, régisseur
10 ballet shoe, répétiteur
11 Laban system, ports de bras
12 ballet-dancer, ballet-master, choreography, labanotation
13 corps de ballet, five positions, sur les pointes
14 divertissement, maître de ballet, petit battement, premier danseur, prima ballerina
15 grande battement, principal dancer

balloon
03 bag **04** soar **05** belly, bulge, swell **06** billow, blow up, dilate, expand, rocket **07** distend, enlarge, fumetto, inflate, puff out **08** aerostat, escalate, snowball **09** dirigible, skyrocket **11** grow rapidly, montgolfier **12** ballon d'essai **15** increase rapidly

ballot
04 poll, vote **06** voting **07** polling **08** election **10** plebiscite, referendum
• **ballot-box**
03 urn

ballyhoo
04 fuss, hype, to-do **05** noise
06 hubbub, racket, tumult **07** build-up, clamour **09** agitation, commotion, hue and cry, kerfuffle, promotion, publicity **10** excitement, hullabaloo, propaganda **11** advertising, disturbance

balm
04 nard, tolu **05** cream, salve
06 balsam, lotion, relief **07** anodyne, bromide, comfort, unguent
08 curative, lenitive, ointment, sedative **09** calmative, emollient, opobalsam **10** palliative
11 consolation, embrocation, restorative

balmy
04 mild, soft, warm **06** gentle
07 clement, summery **08** pleasant, soothing **09** temperate

balsam
04 heal, Tolu **06** embalm **07** wood oil
09 impatiens, spikenard **13** noli-me-tangere

Balt
04 Esth, Lett

bamboozle
◇ *anagram indicator*
03 con **04** daze, dupe, fool, gull, rook
05 cheat, trick, upset **06** bemuse, diddle, puzzle **07** bumbaze, confuse, deceive, mystify, nonplus, perplex, swindle **08** bewilder, confound, hoodwink **09** dumbfound
10 disconcert **14** pull a fast one on

ban
03 bar **04** band, tabu, tapu, veto
05 black, curse, taboo **06** banish, censor, forbid, outlaw **07** abolish, boycott, embargo, exclude
08 disallow, outlawry, prohibit, restrict, stoppage, suppress **09** ostracize, proscribe, sanctions **10** banishment, censorship, disqualify, injunction, moratorium **11** prohibition, restriction, suppression **12** anathematize, condemnation, denunciation, interdiction, proclamation, proscription

banal
04 dull, flat **05** bland, corny, empty, inane, stale, stock, tired, trite, vapid
06 boring, old hat **07** cliché'd, humdrum, mundane, trivial
08 clichéed, cornball, everyday, ordinary, overused **09** hackneyed
10 threadbare, unoriginal
11 commonplace, nondescript, stereotyped, wearing thin
13 unimaginative

banality
06 cliché, truism **07** bromide, fatuity
08 cornball, dullness, vapidity
09 emptiness, inaneness, platitude, staleness, tiredness, triteness
10 prosaicism, triviality
11 commonplace, old chestnut
12 ordinariness **13** unoriginality

banana
08 plantain

bananas
◇ *anagram indicator*
03 mad **04** hand, Musa **05** bunch, crazy
• **go bananas**
04 flip **05** freak **08** freak out

band
02 CB **03** bar, rib, rim, tie **04** ally, belt, body, bond, club, cord, core, crew, fess, frog, gang, ging, herd, hoop, join, line, link, ring, sash, tape, team, teme, tire, tyre, welt, with, zona, zone **05** chain, crowd, fesse, flock, group, horde, merge, music, party, strap, strip, thong, troop, unite, withe **06** clique, fetter, gather, girdle, ribbon, streak, stripe, swathe, team up, throng **07** bandage, binding, company, manacle, shackle, society **08** ensemble, federate, ligature, pop group **09** affiliate, gathering, orchestra **10** amalgamate, close ranks, connection, contingent, join forces, music group **11** association, collaborate, consolidate **12** club together, musical group, pull together
13 stand together, stick together
See also **singer**
• **raised band**
03 rib
• **twisted band**
04 torc, with **05** withe **06** torque

bandage
01 T **04** bind, lint, wrap **05** cover, dress, gauze, spica **06** binder, bind up, swathe **07** Band-aid®, bandeau, plaster, scapula, swaddle **08** capeline, compress, dressing, ligature, Tubigrip®
09 capelline, suspensor **10** tourniquet
11 Elastoplast®

bandicoot
05 bilby **06** pig-rat **10** Malabar-rat

bandit
05 crook, thief **06** cowboy, gunman, mugger, outlaw, pirate, raider, robber
07 brigand **08** criminal, gangster, hijacker, marauder **09** buccaneer, desperado, plunderer, racketeer
10 highwayman

bandsman
04 wait

bandy
◇ *anagram indicator*
04 bent, pass, swap, toss **05** bowed, fight, fling, throw, trade **06** barter, curved, spread, strive **07** chaffer, crooked **08** exchange **09** bow-legged, misshapen **11** interchange, reciprocate

bane
03 woe **04** evil, harm, pest, ruin
05 curse, death, trial **06** blight, burden, misery, ordeal, plague, poison
07 scourge, torment, trouble
08 calamity, disaster, distress, downfall, mischief, nuisance, vexation
09 adversity, annoyance, bête noire

10 affliction, irritation, misfortune, pestilence **11** destruction **14** thorn in the side **15** thorn in the flesh

baneful
07 harmful, noxious, painful, ruinous
08 annoying **09** poisonous
10 disastrous, pernicious
11 destructive, distressing, troublesome **12** pestilential

bang
03 hit, pop, rap **04** bash, benj, blow, boom, bump, clap, dead, drum, echo, hard, peal, shot, slam, slap, sock, thud, wham **05** burst, clang, clash, crack, crash, knock, noise, pound, punch, right, smack, spang, stamp, thump, whack **06** blow up, hammer, report, strike, stroke, thwack, wallop
07 clatter, exactly, explode, noisily, resound, thunder **08** abruptly, bump into, cannabis, detonate, directly, headlong, slap-bang, straight, suddenly **09** collision, crash into, explosion, precisely **10** absolutely, detonation

banger
04 bomb, heap **05** crate **06** jalopy
07 clunker, jaloppy, sausage **09** tin lizzie

Bangladesh
02 BD **03** BGD

bangle
04 band, kara **06** anklet **07** circlet
08 bracelet, wristlet

banish
03 ban, bar **04** band, oust **05** debar, eject, evict, exile, expel **06** deport, dispel, forsay, outlaw, remove
07 abandon, cast out, discard, dismiss, exclude, foresay, shut out **08** dislodge, get rid of, relegate, send away, throw out **09** drive away, eliminate, eradicate, extradite, ostracize, rusticate, transport
10 disimagine, expatriate, repatriate
13 excommunicate

banishment
03 ban **05** exile **08** eviction, outlawry
09 exclusion, exilement, expulsion, ostracism **11** deportation, extradition
12 expatriation **14** transportation
15 excommunication

banisters
04 rail **07** railing **08** handrail
10 balustrade

bank
02 as, bk **03** bar, dam, row, tip **04** bink, brae, edge, fund, heap, keep, line, link, mass, pile, pool, rank, reef, rise, rive, save, side, sunk, tier, tilt **05** amass, array, bench, bluff, cache, drift, group, hoard, hurst, knoll, lay by, levee, mound, panel, pitch, ridge, shore, slant, slope, stack, stock, store, train **06** heap up, margin, pile up, rivage, save up, series, supply **07** deposit, hillock, incline, parados, pottery, rampart, reserve, savings, stack up **08** put aside, sequence, treasury **09** earthwork,

reservoir, stash away, stockpile
10 accumulate, depository,
embankment, repository, succession
11 put together, savings bank
12 accumulation, clearing bank,
finance house, merchant bank
14 finance company, high-street bank
15 building society
• **banking system**
04 giro
• **bank on**
05 bet on, trust **06** rely on **07** count on
08 depend on **09** bargain on, believe
in **14** pin your hopes on
• **bank rate**
02 br
• **banks**
◊ *ends selection indicator*
• **bank up**
04 hele, hill

banker
05 gnome **06** shroff **07** Lombard
09 exchanger
See also **river**

banknote
03 fin **04** bill, note **05** fiver, scrip
06 flimsy, greeny, single, tenner, twenty
07 greenie, iron man, sawbuck
09 greenback **10** paper money
12 treasury note

bankrupt
04 bung, bust, duck, ruin **05** break,
broke, spent **06** beggar, bereft,
broken, debtor, dyvour, failed, folded,
hard up, pauper, ruined **07** cripple,
lacking, wanting, without
08 beggared, depleted, deprived, in
the red, lame duck **09** deficient,
destitute, exhausted, gone under,
insolvent, penurious, sequester
10 impoverish, on the rocks, stony
broke, trade-falne **11** impecunious,
trade-fallen **12** impoverished, on your
uppers **13** gone to the wall, in
liquidation

bankruptcy
04 lack, ruin **05** smash **06** penury,
stumer **07** beggary, dyvoury, failure
08 disaster **09** ruination
10 exhaustion, insolvency **11** Carey
Street, liquidation **12** indebtedness
13 financial ruin, sequestration
• **to bankruptcy**
04 scat **05** skatt

banner
04 flag, sign **06** burgee, ensign,
fanion, pennon **07** bandrol, colours,
labarum, pennant, placard
08 banderol, bannerol, gonfalon,
gumphion, standard, streamer,
vexillum **09** banderole, bannerall,
oriflamme

banquet
04 dine, meal **05** feast, party, treat
06 dinner, junket, spread **11** dinner
party **13** entertainment

banter
03 kid, pun, rag, rib **04** jest, joke, josh,
mock, quiz, rail **05** borak, borax, chaff,

rally, roast, tease **06** deride, joking
07 jesting, kidding, mockery, ribbing
08 badinage, chaffing, derision,
dicacity, raillery, repartee, ridicule,
word play **09** make fun of
10 persiflage, pleasantry

Bantu
04 Hutu, Xosa, Zulu **05** Nguni, Sotho,
Swazi, Tonga, Tutsi, Xhosa **06** Herero,
Nyanja, Tswana **07** Basotho, Lingala,
Sesotho, Swahili **08** Congoese
09 Congolese

baptism
05 debut **06** launch, naming
07 mersion **08** affusion **09** aspersion,
beginning, immersion, launching
10 dedication, initiation, sprinkling
11 christening, parabaptism
12 inauguration, introduction,
paedobaptism, purification

baptize
03 dip **04** call, name, term **05** admit,
enrol, style, title **06** purify **07** cleanse,
immerse, recruit **08** christen, initiate,
sprinkle **09** introduce

bar
01 T, Z **03** ban, fen, fid, gad, inn, pub,
rib, rod, zed, zee **04** bolt, cake, dive,
howf, hunk, lock, lump, pole, rail, risp,
rung, save, shet, shut, slab, slot, snug,
spar, stop, swee, toll **05** block, check,
chunk, court, debar, estop, grill, ingot,
latch, lever, shaft, stake, stick, table,
wedge **06** batten, bistro, boozer, but
for, except, fasten, forbid, hinder,
lounge, nugget, paling, saloon, secure,
tavern **07** barrier, counsel, counter,
exclude, lawyers, padlock, prevent,
railing, suspend, taproom
08 blockade, drawback, hostelry,
obstacle, obstruct, omitting, preclude,
prohibit, restrain, snuggery, tribunal
09 advocates, apart from, aside from,
barricade, brasserie, deterrent, except
for, excepting, excluding, hindrance,
lounge bar, stanchion **10** barristers,
beer-parlor, crosspiece, disqualify,
impediment **11** obstruction, public
house **12** beverage room, watering-
hole

barb
03 dig, mow **04** gibe, harl, herl, tang,
trim **05** arrow, beard, fluke, point,
prong, ramus, scorn, shave, sneer,
spike, sting, thorn **06** insult, needle,
rebuff **07** affront, bristle, killick,
killock, prickle

Barbados
03 BDS, BRB

barbarian
03 Hun, oaf **04** boor, Goth, lout, wild
05 brute, crude, rough **06** coarse,
savage, vandal, vulgar **07** brutish,
loutish, ruffian, uncouth **08** hooligan
09 Hottentot, ignoramus **10** illiterate,
philistine, tramontane, uncultured,
wild person **11** Neanderthal,
uncivilized **12** uncultivated
15 unsophisticated

barbaric
◊ *anagram indicator*
04 rude, wild **05** crude, cruel
06 brutal, coarse, fierce, savage, vulgar
07 bestial, brutish, foreign, inhuman,
uncouth, vicious **08** ruthless
09 barbarous, ferocious, murderous,
primitive **11** uncivilized

barbarism
07 cruelty **08** enormity, ferocity,
rudeness, savagery, wildness
09 brutality, crudeness, vulgarity
10 bestiality, coarseness, corruption,
fierceness, heathenism **11** brutishness,
inhumanness, uncouthness,
viciousness **12** ruthlessness
13 murderousness **15** uncivilizedness

barbarity
07 cruelty, outrage **08** atrocity,
enormity, ferocity, savagery, wildness
09 brutality **10** inhumanity, savageness
11 brutishness, viciousness
12 ruthlessness **13** barbarousness

barbarous
◊ *anagram indicator*
04 rude, wild **05** crude, cruel, harsh,
rough **06** brutal, fierce, Gothic, savage,
vulgar **07** bestial, brutish, corrupt,
inhuman, vicious **08** barbaric,
ignorant, ruthless **09** barbarian,
ferocious, heartless, murderous,
primitive, unrefined **10** uncultured,
unlettered **11** uncivilized, unscholarly
15 unsophisticated

barbecue
03 BBQ **04** bake, cook **05** braai, broil,
brown, grill, roast **06** barbie
07 cookout, griddle, hibachi, stir-fry
09 spit-roast **10** braaivleis

barbed
04 acid **05** armed, catty, jaggy, nasty,
snide, spiky, spiny **06** bitchy, hooked,
jagged, spiked, tanged, thorny, unkind
07 bearded, caustic, cutting, hostile,
hurtful, pointed, prickly, pronged,
toothed **08** barbated, critical, spiteful,
wounding **09** sarcastic

barber
04 Todd **05** shave, strap **06** Figaro,
shaver, tonsor **07** scraper
11 hairdresser, Sweeney Todd

bard *see* **poet**

bare
04 bald, cold, hard, lewd, mere, nude,
peel, pure, very **05** basic, bleak, clear,
empty, naked, plain, sheer, stark, strip,
utter **06** barren, expose, reveal, simple,
unmask, unveil, vacant **07** denuded,
display, exposed, lay bare, uncover,
undress **08** absolute, complete,
desolate, in the nip, in the raw, stripped,
treeless, unclothe, unwooded,
woodless **09** essential, in the buff, in
the nude, in the scud, unadorned,
unclothed, uncovered, undressed,
very least **10** defoliated, no more than,
stark-naked, unforested
11 unfurnished, unsheltered **13** with
nothing on **15** straightforward

barefaced

04 bald, bold, open 05 brash, naked
06 arrant, avowed, brazen, patent
07 blatant, glaring, obvious
08 flagrant, impudent, insolent,
manifest, palpable 09 audacious, bald-
faced, beardless, shameless,
unabashed 11 transparent,
unconcealed, undisguised

barefooted

06 unshod 08 barefoot, shoeless
09 discalced

barely

04 just, only 05 scant 06 almost,
hardly, openly, scrimp 07 halfway,
nakedly, none too, plainly
08 narrowly, no sooner, only just,
scarcely 10 by a whisker, explicitly
12 be a near thing, by a short head
13 be a close thing

bargain

02 go 03 buy 04 deal, pact, sell, snip,
whiz 05 broke, cheap, steal, trade,
truck, whizz 06 barter, broker, clinch,
haggle, indent, market, pledge, settle,
treaty 07 chaffer, cheapen, good buy,
promise, traffic 08 beat down, cheap
buy, contract, covenant, discount,
giveaway, purchase, transact,
Tamworth 09 agreement, bon
marché, concordat, negotiate,
reduction 11 arrangement,
negotiation, transaction 12 special
offer 13 understanding, value for
money

bargain for

06 expect 07 foresee, imagine,
include, look for, plan for 08 consider,
contract, figure on, reckon on
10 anticipate 11 contemplate
13 be prepared for 15 take into
account

into the bargain

04 also 06 as well 07 besides 10 in
addition 11 furthermore
12 additionally

bargaining

05 trade 06 barter, buying, dicker,
outcry 07 chaffer, dealing, selling
08 dealings, haggling 09 bartering
11 negotiation, trafficking,
transaction 12 horsetrading
14 wheeler-dealing

barge

anagram indicator
03 hit 04 bump, keel, pram, push, rush,
scow 05 barca, butty, casco, elbow,
praam, press, shove, smash 06 galley,
hopper, jostle, plough, push in, wherry
07 birlinn, budgeon, collide, gabbard,
gabbart, lighter, piragua, pirogue,
pontoon 08 budgerow, flatboat,
keelboat, periagua 09 Bucentaur,
canal-boat, houseboat 10 narrowboat
11 galley-foist, push your way 12 force
your way

barge in

05 cut in 06 butt in 07 break in, burst
in, intrude 09 gatecrash, interfere,
interrupt

baritone

03 bar

barium

02 Ba

bark

03 bay, cry, tan, wow, yap 04 bass,
bast, bawl, cork, hide, howl, husk, kina,
peel, rind, skin, snap, tapa, waff, woof,
yaff, yawp, yell, yelp 05 china, cough,
crust, growl, quest, quill, quina, shell,
shout, snarl, suber, tappa 06 bellow,
bowwow, casing, cortex 07 cascara,
encrust, pereira, thunder 08 calisaya,
cinchona, cinnamon, covering,
simaruba, tan balls 09 bull's wool,
quebracho, sassafras, simarouba,
xanthoxyl 10 cascarilla, integument,
quercitron 11 slippery elm 13 cascara
amarga 14 cascara sagrada

barking

◇ *anagram indicator*
03 bay, mad, odd 04 daft, nuts
05 barmy, batty, crazy, dippy, dotty,
loony, loopy, nutty, potty 06 cuckoo,
insane 07 bananas, bonkers 08 crackers
09 latration 10 off your nut, unbalanced
11 off your head 12 mad as a hatter,
round the bend 13 off your rocker,
round the twist 14 off your trolley

barley

04 bear, bere, bigg, malt 07 Hordeum

barmy

03 mad, odd 04 daft, nuts 05 batty,
crazy, dippy, dotty, loony, loopy, nutty,
silly 06 cuckoo, frothy, insane, stupid
07 foolish, idiotic 08 crackers
10 fermenting, off your nut, out to
lunch, unbalanced 11 off your head
12 round the bend 13 off your rocker,
round the twist 14 off your trolley

barn

06 grange 07 skipper

barometer

07 aneroid 09 barograph
10 statoscope 12 weather glass
13 sympiesometer

baron

01 B 02 Bn 04 lord, peer 05 mogul
06 bigwig, fat cat, tycoon 07 big shot,
magnate 08 nobleman 09 big cheese,
executive 10 aristocrat, Münchausen
12 entrepreneur 13 industrialist

baroness

04 lady, peer 07 baronne
10 aristocrat, noblewoman

baronet

02 Bt 04 Bart

baroque

◇ *anagram indicator*
04 bold 05 showy 06 florid, ornate,
rococo 07 flowery 08 fanciful,
vigorous 09 decorated, elaborate,
exuberant, fantastic, grotesque,
whimsical 10 convoluted, flamboyant
11 embellished, extravagant,
overwrought 13 overdecorated,
overelaborate 15 churrigueresque

barrack

03 boo 04 hiss, jeer 05 taunt
06 casern, heckle 07 caserne
09 interrupt, shout down

barracking

04 boos 07 hissing, jeering
08 heckling 12 interruption
13 interruptions

barracks

03 bks 04 camp, fort 06 billet, casern
07 lodging 08 garrison, quarters
10 encampment, glasshouse,
guardhouse 11 gendarmerie
13 accommodation

barrage

03 dam 04 dyke, hail, mass, rain, wall
05 burst, flood, onset, salvo, storm
06 attack, deluge, shower, stream,
volley 07 assault, barrier, battery,
gunfire, torrent 08 shelling
09 abundance, barricade, broadside,
cannonade, fusillade, onslaught,
profusion 10 embankment
11 bombardment, obstruction

barrel

01 b 02 bl 03 bbl, but, keg, tub, tun
04 butt, cade, cask, drum, pipe, wood
05 pièce 06 clavie, firkin, runlet, tierce,
tumble 07 oil drum, rundlet
08 hogshead 09 water-butt
10 Morris-tube

barren

03 dry 04 arid, dull, eild, flat, yeld, yell
05 addle, bleak, blunt, empty, gaunt,
vapid, waste 06 desert, effete, meagre
07 hirstie, sterile, useless 08 desolate,
infecund, teemless 09 childless,
fruitless, infertile, pointless, unbearing,
valueless 10 profitless, unfruitful,
unprolific 11 purposeless, uninspiring,
unrewarding 12 inhospitable,
uncultivable, unproductive
13 uninformative, uninstructive,
uninteresting

barrenness

06 dearth 07 aridity, dryness
08 dullness 09 emptiness, sterility
11 infecundity, infertility, uselessness
13 pointlessness 14 unfruitfulness

barricade

03 bar 04 shut 05 block, close, fence
06 defend 07 barrier, bulwark, close
up, defence, fortify, protect, rampart,
shut off 08 blockade, obstacle,
obstruct, palisade, stockade
10 protection, strengthen
11 obstruction

Barrie

02 JM

barrier

03 bar, dam 04 bail, boom, doll, gate,
ha-ha, wall 05 block, check, ditch,
fence, hedge, rails, spina 06 haw-haw,
hurdle 07 barrage, curtain, railing,
rampart 08 blockade, boundary,
bulkhead, division, drawback, frontier,
handicap, obstacle, railings, stockade,
tick gate, traverse, turnpike

09 barricade, enclosure, hindrance, inclosure, partition, restraint, ring-fence, roadblock **10** breakwater, difficulty, dingo fence, impediment, limitation, tariff wall **11** iron curtain, mental block, obstruction, restriction **12** glass ceiling **13** bamboo curtain, fortification, kangaroo fence **14** stumbling-block **15** cordon sanitaire, dingo-proof fence

barring
02 if **03** bar **06** except, unless **09** except for

barrister
02 KC, QC **03** Bar **04** silk **05** brief **06** lawyer **07** counsel, Rumpole **08** advocate, attorney, recorder, serjeant **09** counselor, solicitor **10** counsellor **12** King's Counsel **13** Queen's Counsel, serjeant-at-law
See also **lawyer**

barrow
03 how **04** cart, howe, tump **05** hurly, truck **07** tumulus **08** push-cart **11** horned cairn

bartender
06 barman **07** barkeep, barmaid **08** publican **09** barkeeper **10** mixologist

barter
04 chop, cope, coup, deal, sell, swap, swop **05** trade, truck **06** dicker, haggle, niffer **07** bargain, dealing, trading, traffic **08** exchange, haggling, swapping, truckage **09** negotiate **10** bargaining **11** negotiation, permutation, trafficking

basalt
04 trap, whin **05** wacke **07** diabase **08** basanite, traprock **09** toadstone, whinstone

base
01 e **02** HQ **03** bed, dog, key, low, ten **04** camp, core, evil, foot, home, mean, poor, post, prop, rest, root, seat, site, stay, vile **05** basis, build, depot, found, heart, hinge, layer, lowly, stand **06** abject, bottom, centre, depend, derive, fundus, ground, locate, origin, plinth, sordid, source, vulgar, wicked **07** bedrock, coating, corrupt, essence, immoral, install, pitiful, situate, station, support **08** backbone, covering, depraved, infamous, keystone, pedestal, position, shameful, wretched **09** component, construct, essential, establish, low-minded, miserable, principal, reprobate, thickness, valueless, worthless **10** despicable, foundation, groundwork, scandalous, settlement, substratum, underneath **11** disgraceful, fundamental, ignominious **12** contemptible, disreputable, have as a basis, headquarters, substructure, unprincipled **13** starting-point **14** understructure **15** foundation stone
• **base of**
◇ *tail selection down indicator*

baseball

Baseball players include:

03 Ott (Mel)
04 Cobb (Ty), Mack (Connie), Mays (Willie), Ruth (Babe), Ryan (Nolan)
05 Aaron (Hank), Bench (Johnny), Berra (Yogi), Paige (Satchel), Spahn (Warren), Young (Cy)
06 Gehrig (Lou), Gibson (Bob), Gibson (Josh), Koufax (Sandy), Mantle (Mickey), Musial (Stan), Ripken (Cal)
07 Clemens (Roger), Jackson (Reggie), McGwire (Mark), Stengel (Casey)
08 Clemente (Roberto), DiMaggio (Joe), Robinson (Brooks), Robinson (Jackie), Williams (Ted)
09 Alexander (Grover Cleveland), Mathewson (Christy)

Major league baseball teams:

11 Chicago Cubs, New York Mets
12 Boston Red Sox, Texas Rangers
13 Atlanta Braves, Detroit Tigers, Houston Astros
14 Cincinnati Reds, Florida Marlins, Minnesota Twins, New York Yankees, San Diego Padres
15 Chicago White Sox, Colorado Rockies, Seattle Mariners, Toronto Blue Jays
16 Baltimore Orioles, Cleveland Indians, Kansas City Royals, Milwaukee Brewers, Oakland Athletics, St Louis Cardinals
17 Los Angeles Dodgers, Pittsburgh Pirates, Tampa Bay Devil Rays
18 San Francisco Giants
19 Arizona Diamondbacks, Washington Nationals
20 Philadelphia Phillies
25 Los Angeles Angels of Anaheim

Baseball terms include:

03 ace, ERA, hit, out, RBI, run, tag
04 balk, ball, base, bunt, cage, mitt, safe, walk
05 alley, bench, error, mound, pitch, plate
06 assist, batter, bottom, closer, double, dugout, fly out, inning, on deck, single, sinker, slider, strike, triple, wind-up
07 all-star, base hit, battery, bull pen, catcher, chopper, diamond, fly ball, home run, infield, pennant, pitcher, rundown, shutout
08 ballpark, baseline, fair ball, fastball, foul ball, foul pole, nightcap, no-hitter, outfield, set-up man
09 cut-off man, earned run, first base, gold glove, grand slam, ground out, hit-and-run, home plate, infielder, in the hole, left field, line drive, sacrifice, screwball, strike out, third base, wild pitch
10 baserunner, batter's box, double play, ground ball, outfielder, passed ball, right field, second base, strike zone

11 base on balls, basket catch, centre field, knuckleball, left fielder, perfect game, pinch hitter, pinch runner, run batted in, unearned run
12 breaking ball, double-header, extra innings, load the bases, right fielder, warning track
13 centre fielder, foul territory, relief pitcher, safety squeeze
14 American League, backdoor slider, batting average, fielder's choice, National League, suicide squeeze
15 starting pitcher

• **baseball statistic**
03 ERA, RBI

baseless
◇ *tail deletion down indicator*
04 idle **06** untrue **09** unfounded **10** fabricated, gratuitous, groundless, ill-founded, unattested **11** uncalled-for, unconfirmed, unjustified, unsupported **15** unauthenticated, unsubstantiated

basement
05 crypt, dunny, vault **06** cellar

bash
02 go **03** box, hit, ram, try **04** bang, beat, belt, biff, blow, bump, clip, dent, rave, shot, slug, sock, stab **05** blast, break, crack, crash, knock, party, punch, smack, smash, thump, whack, whirl **06** batter, rave-up, strike, thrash, wallop **07** attempt, clobber **11** celebration

bashful
03 coy, shy **05** blate, timid **06** modest **07** abashed, laithfu', nervous **08** backward, blushing, hesitant, reserved, reticent, retiring, sheepish, timorous **09** diffident, inhibited, shamefast, shrinking **10** shamefaced, sheep-faced **11** embarrassed **12** self-effacing **13** self-conscious, unforthcoming

bashfully
05 shyly **07** timidly **08** modestly **09** nervously **10** hesitantly, reticently, sheepishly **11** diffidently **14** self-effacingly **15** self-consciously

bashfulness
05 shame **07** blushes, coyness, modesty, reserve, shyness **08** timidity **09** hesitancy, reticence **10** diffidence, inhibition **11** nervousness **12** sheepishness **13** embarrassment, mauvaise honte **14** self-effacement, shamefacedness

basic
03 gut, key **04** bare, root **05** crude, first, plain, stark, vital **06** simple, staple **07** austere, bedrock, central, minimum, primary, radical, spartan **08** inherent, no-frills, standard, starting **09** essential, important, intrinsic, necessary, primitive, unadorned **10** elementary, underlying **11** bog standard, fundamental, lowest level, preparatory, rudimentary **12** down-and-dirty **13** indispensable **14** unsophisticate **15** unsophisticated

basically

6 mainly **07** at heart **08** at bottom
9 in essence, in the main, primarily,
radically **10** inherently **11** essentially, in
principle, principally
13 fundamentally, intrinsically,
substantially

basics

3 ABC **04** core **05** abcee, absey, facts
7 bedrock **08** alphabet, elements
9 realities, rudiments **10** brass tacks,
essentials, principles, rock bottom
11 necessaries, nitty-gritty
12 fundamentals, introduction, nuts
and bolts **14** practicalities **15** first
principles

basin

3 bed, dip, pan, pot **04** bowl, dish,
dock, park, sink, tank **05** bidet, docks,
gully, laver, playa **06** cavity, crater,
hollow, lavabo, valley **07** channel,
piscina **08** birdbath, washbowl
9 impluvium, reservoir
10 aquamanile, aquamanile,
depression

basis

3 key, way **04** base, core, fond, root
5 heart, radix, terms **06** bottom,
ground, method, reason, status,
system, thrust **07** bedrock, essence,
footing, grounds, keynote, premise,
reasons, support **08** approach,
pedestal, platform **09** condition,
essential, principle, procedure,
rationale **10** conditions, essentials,
foundation, grass-roots, groundwork,
hypostasis, substratum
11 arrangement, cornerstone,
fundamental **12** fundamentals,
quintessence **13** alpha and omega,
starting-point **14** main ingredient
15 first principles

ask

3 lie, sun **04** laze, loll **05** bathe, enjoy,
lap up, relax, revel **06** lounge, relish,
savour, sprawl, wallow **08** apricate,
sunbathe **09** delight in, luxuriate
14 take pleasure in

asket

3 bin, box, cob, fan, rip, van, wpb
4 case, cauf, chip, coop, corf, crib,
coal, hask, kipe, leap, skep, trug
5 cabas, creel, frail, maund, scull,
skull, willy **06** gabion, hamper, holder,
junket, mocock, mocuck, murlan,
hurlin, petara, pottle, punnet, willey,
visket **07** corbeil, cresset, flasket,
purlain, pannier, scuttle, seedlip,
whopper, trolley **08** bassinet, calathus
9 container, corbeille, fish-creel,
meat-creel **10** receptacle **12** wagger-
dagger

asketball

bass

01 B **03** low **04** base, bast, deep, full,
rich **05** fibre, grave **06** burden,
phloem **07** bourdon, burthen, matting,
sea dace, sea wolf **08** continuo,
diapason, low-toned, resonant, sea
perch, sonorous **09** deep-toned, full-
toned, loup de mer, succentor **10** low-
pitched **11** deep-pitched

bast

04 bass **05** fibre, liber **06** phloem,
raffia **07** leptome, matting

bastard

◇ anagram indicator
03 git **05** slink **06** basket, by-blow,
mamzer **07** buzzard **08** sideslip,
spurious **09** come-o'-will, love child
10 lucky-piece, misfortune **12** come-
by-chance, illegitimate, natural child
13 filius nullius

bastardize

06 debase, defile, demean
07 cheapen, corrupt, degrade,
devalue, distort, pervert, vitiate
10 adulterate, degenerate, depreciate
11 contaminate

bastion

04 prop, rock **06** pillar **07** bulwark,
citadel, defence, lunette, moineau,
redoubt, support **08** defender,
fortress, mainstay **10** protection,
stronghold

bat

04 blow, club, lath, rate **05** fungo, lingo,
speed, spree, stick **06** paddle, racket,
willow **07** batsman, battery, flutter
09 battalion, rearmouse, reremouse,
trap stick **10** battledoor, battledore,
Scotch hand **12** flitter-mouse

batch

03 lot, set **04** mass, pack **05** bunch,
crowd, group **06** amount, parcel
07 cluster **08** quantity **09** aggregate
10 assemblage, assortment,
collection, contingent **11** consignment
12 accumulation **14** conglomeration

bath

03 dip, spa, tub **04** soak, stew, wash
05 banya, bathe, clean, sauna, scrub,
stove, therm **06** douche, hammam,
hot tub, hummum, mikvah, mikveh,
shower, therms **07** bathtub,
hummaum, Jacuzzi®, spa pool,
thermae **08** aerotone, balneary
09 bain-marie, freshen up, have a bath,
steam bath, steam room, take a bath,
whirlpool **10** Aquae Sulis **11** slipper
bath, Turkish bath

bathe

03 bay, dip, tub, wet **04** bath, baye,
dook, lave, soak, stew, surf, swim, wash

05 beath, clean, cover, embay, flood, rinse, steep **06** paddle **07** cleanse, embathe, imbathe, immerse, Jacuzzi®, moisten, suffuse **08** permeate, saturate, take a dip **09** encompass, skinny-dip

bathos
07 let-down **08** comedown **10** anticlimax **14** disappointment

baton
03 rod **05** staff, stick **06** cudgel, warder **07** scepter, sceptre **09** truncheon

bats
◇ anagram indicator
03 mad **04** nuts **05** crazy
07 Mormops **15** Megacheiroptera, Microchiroptera

batsman
• **first batsman**
06 opener
• **weaker batsmen**
04 tail

battalion
02 bn **03** bat, mob **04** army, herd, host, mass, unit **05** crowd, force, horde **06** battle, legion, throng, troops **07** brigade, company, platoon, section **08** division, garrison, regiment, squadron **09** multitude **10** contingent, detachment

batten
03 bar, fix **04** bolt **05** board, strip **06** fasten, secure **07** board up, tighten **08** nail down **09** barricade, clamp down

batter
◇ anagram indicator
03 hit, lam, ram **04** bash, beat, club, dash, hurt, lash, maul, pelt **05** abuse, erode, pound, smash, whack **06** beat up, bruise, buffet, damage, hatter, injure, mangle, pummel, strike, thrash, wallop **07** assault, bombard, destroy, lay into, rough up, wear out **08** demolish, ill-treat, maltreat, wear down **09** cannonade, disfigure **10** knock about **11** overweather
• **batter down**
04 ruin **05** smash, wreck **07** destroy **08** demolish **09** break down

battered
◇ anagram indicator
03 hit **06** abused, beaten, shabby **07** bruised, crushed, damaged, injured, run-down **09** crumbling **10** ill-treated, maltreated, ramshackle, tumbledown **11** dilapidated **13** weather-beaten

battery
03 bat, row, set **04** bank, cell, guns, pram **05** array, cycle, force, group, nicad, praam **06** attack, cannon, series **07** assault, beating, mugging **08** cannonry, ordnance, sequence, striking, violence **09** artillery, thrashing **10** button cell, succession **12** emplacements

batting
◇ anagram indicator
02 in

battle
02 by **03** bye, row, war **04** feud, fray, race, wage **05** argue, brawl, clash, drive, field, fight, scrap, set-to, stoor, stour **06** action, affair, attack, buffet, combat, debate, engage, stoush, stowre, strife, strive **07** agitate, clamour, contend, contest, crusade, dispute, fertile, hosting, quarrel, warfare **08** campaign, conflict, darraign, disagree, naumachy, sea-fight, skirmish, struggle **09** battalion, encounter, naumachia **10** Armageddon, engagement, free-for-all, nourishing, tournament **11** altercation, competition, controversy, final battle, hostilities, turkey-shoot **12** disagreement **13** armed conflict, confrontation

See also **siege**; **war**

Battles include:

04 Jena, Loos, Neva, Nile, Zama
05 Alamo, Anzio, Boyne, Bulge, Crécy, Issus, Liège, Maipó, Maipú, Marne, Mylae, Pavia, Rhine, Sedan, Sluys, Somme, Spurs, Valmy, Varna, Ypres
06 Actium, Amiens, Arnhem, Cannae, Crimea, Harlaw, Kosovo, Lützen, Midway, Mohács, Mycale, Naseby, Pinkie, Quebec, Shiloh, Tobruk, Towton, Verdun, Wagram
07 Antwerp, Britain, Bull Run, Cambrai, Cassino, Colenso, Corunna, Cowpens, Dresden, Dunkirk, Flodden, Iwo Jima, Jutland, Leipzig, Lepanto, Leuctra, Marengo, Okinawa, Plassey, Salamis, Salerno, Thapsus
08 Atlantic, Ayacucho, Blenheim, Carabobo, Culloden, Fontenoy, Formigny, Granicus, Hastings, Mafeking, Marathon, Monmouth, Omdurman, Philippi, Poitiers, Pyramids, Saratoga, Spion Kop, St Albans, Waterloo, Yorktown
09 Agincourt, Balaclava, Bay of Pigs, Chaeronea, El Alamein, Pharsalus, Ramillies, Sedgemoor, Seven Days, Solferino, Trafalgar, Vicksburg
10 Aboukir Bay, Adrianople, Austerlitz, Brandywine, Bunker Hill, Charleston, Cold Harbor, Copenhagen, Gettysburg, Malplaquet, Oudenaarde, River Plate, Stalingrad, Tannenberg, Tel-El-Kebir, Wilderness
11 Bannockburn, Guadalcanal, Hohenlinden, Marston Moor, Navarino Bay, Pearl Harbor, Prestonpans, Wounded Knee
12 Mons Graupius, Monte Cassino, Tet offensive
13 Bosworth Field, Cape St Vincent, Killiecrankie, Little Bighorn, Magersfontein, Passchendaele
14 Fredericksburg

battle-axe
03 axe, hag **04** bill, fury, wife **05** shrew, witch **06** dragon, poleax, sparth, Tartar, virago **07** gisarme, poleaxe, sparthe **08** harridan, martinet **09** termagant **12** Jeddart staff **14** disciplinarian

battle-cry
05 motto **06** banzai, slogan, war cry **07** war song **09** catchword, watchword **11** catchphrase, rallying cr **12** rallying call

battlefield
05 arena, field, front, place **07** war zone **09** front line **10** Armageddon, combat zone **12** battleground **13** field of battle

battlement
07 barmkin **08** bartisan, bartizan

batty
◇ anagram indicator
03 mad, odd **04** bats, daft, nuts **05** barmy, buggy, crazy, dippy, dotty, loony, loopy, nutty, silly **06** insane, stupid **07** bonkers, foolish, idiotic **08** crackers, demented, peculiar **09** eccentric **10** off your nut, out to lunch **11** off your head **12** round the bend **13** off your rocker, round the twist

bauble
03 toy **06** gewgaw, tinsel, trifle **07** bibelot, flamfew, trinket **08** gimcrack, kickshaw, ornament **09** bagatelle, plaything **10** knick-knack

baulk *see* **balk, baulk**

bawd
04 pimp **05** madam **08** procurer **09** panderess, procuress **13** brothel-keeper

bawdy
04 blue, lewd, rude **05** adult, dirty, gross **06** coarse, erotic, ribald, risqué smutty, vulgar, X-rated **07** lustful, obscene, raunchy **08** improper, indecent, prurient **09** lecherous, salacious **10** indecorous, indelicate, lascivious, libidinous, licentious, sculduddry, suggestive **11** sculduddr, skulduddery **12** pornographic **14** nea the knuckle

bawl
03 cry, sob **04** call, gape, howl, roar, wail, weep, yell, yowl **05** shout **06** bellow, cry out, gollar, goller, holle scream, snivel, squall **07** blubber, call out, screech **10** vociferate
• **bawl out**
05 scold **06** rebuke, yell at **07** rouse on, tell off **09** dress down, reprimand

bay
03 arm, cry, vae, voe **04** bark, bawl, bell, cove, gulf, howl, loch, nook, roar, yelp, yowl **05** bathe, bight, booth, creek, firth, fleet, inlet, niche, reach, sound, stall **06** alcove, bellow, carrel, holler, lagoon, laurel, recess **07** clamour, classis, cubicle, estuary,

pening **09** cubbyhole, embayment
1 compartment, indentation

4 Acre, Clew, Daya, Kiel, Luce, Lyme,
Pigs, Tees
5 Algoa, Blind, Cloud, Enard,
Evans, False, Fundy, Hawke, Shark,
Table
6 Baffin, Bantry, Bengal, Biscay,
Botany, Broken, Colwyn, Dingle,
Dublin, Galway, Hervey, Hudson,
Lubeck, Mounts, Naples, Plenty,
Tasman, Torbay, Walvis
7 Bustard, Chaleur, Donegal,
Dundalk, Fortune, Halifax,
Hudson's, Montego, Moreton,
Pegasus, Prudhoe, Thunder, Trinity,
Volcano
8 Campeche, Cardigan, Delaware,
Georgian, Hang-Chow, Portland,
Quiberon, San Pablo, Tremadog,
Weymouth
9 Admiralty, Discovery, Encounter,
Frobisher, Galveston, Geographe,
Hermitage, Mackenzie,
Morecambe, Notre Dame,
Placentia
0 Barnstaple, Bridgwater,
Carmarthen, Chesapeake,
Conception, Heligoland,
Providence, Robin Hood's
1 Port Jackson, Port Phillip, Saint
Bride's, Saint Magnus
2 Saint George's, San Francisco

• **bay with spots**
4 roan

ayonet
4 pike, stab **05** blade, knife, spear,
pike, stick, sword **06** dagger,
mpale, pierce **07** poniard **08** white
rm

azaar
4 fair, fête, mart, sale, souk **06** market
7 alcázar **08** exchange **10** alcaicería,
umble sale **11** bring-and-buy,
narketplace **13** nearly-new sale

BC
4 Beeb **06** Auntie

e
3 lie **04** form, last, live, make, stay
5 abide, arise, dwell, exist, occur,
tand **06** befall, endure, happen, make
p, obtain, remain, reside **07** add up to,
e alive, breathe, develop, inhabit,
ersist, prevail, survive **08** amount to,
ontinue **09** be located, be present,
eryllium, come about, represent,
ake place, transpire **10** account
or, be situated, come to pass,
onstitute

each
4 hard, land, lido, sand **05** coast,
lage, sands, shore **06** ground, strand
7 machair, seaside, shingle **08** go
shore, littoral, seaboard, seashore
9 coastline, run ashore **10** be
rounded, be stranded, run aground,
vater's edge

04 Gold, Juno, Long, Palm, Utah
05 Bells, Bondi, Cable, Manly, Miami,
Omaha, Sword
06 Chesil, Malibu, Sunset, Tahiti,
Venice
07 Daytona, Glenelg, Ipanema,
Pattaya, Waikiki
08 Hotwater, St Tropez, Virginia
09 Blackpool
10 Copacabana, Ninety Mile
11 Coney Island
13 Skeleton Coast
15 Surfers Paradise

beachcomber
06 loafer **07** forager **08** loiterer,
wayfarer **09** scavenger

beacon
04 beam, fire, sign **05** fanal, flare, light,
racon **06** pharos, rocket, signal
07 bonfire **08** bale-fire, needfire
09 watch fire **10** lighthouse,
watchtower **12** danger signal, warning
light

bead
03 dot **04** ball, bede, blob, drip, drop,
gaud, glob, nurl, tear **05** bugle, jewel,
knurl, ojime, pearl **06** bubble, pellet,
prayer **07** cabling, droplet, globule
08 moulding, spheroid **10** adderstone
11 paternoster, spacer plate **13** cable-
moulding

beadle
06 bedral, Bumble **07** bederal
09 apparitor **10** bluebottle **13** church
officer

beak
02 JP **03** neb, nib, ram **04** bill, nose
05 becke, snout **07** rostrum
09 mandibles, proboscis, rostellum
10 magistrate **12** schoolmaster
14 schoolmistress

beaker
03 cup, jar, mug **05** glass **07** tankard,
tumbler

beam
03 aim, bar, ray, RSJ, tie **04** balk, boom,
emit, glow, grin, lath, send, spar, yard
05 baulk, board, chink, flare, flash,
glare, gleam, glint, joist, laugh, plank,
relay, shaft, shine, smile, smirk, stock,
strut, trave **06** binder, bumkin, direct,
gibbet, girder, hurter, lintel, needle,
pencil, purlin, rafter, solive, streak,
stream, summer, timber **07** bumpkin,
carling, effulge, glimmer, glitter,
radiate, sleeper, sparkle, support,
transom, trimmer **08** herisson,
kingpost, stanchel, stancher, streamer,
stringer, transmit **09** broadcast,
crosshead, outrigger, principal, queen
post, scantling, stanchion, weigh-bauk
10 bressummer, cantilever
12 breastsummer

• **off beam**
05 wrong **08** mistaken **09** incorrect,
misguided, off target **10** inaccurate
11 wrong-headed **13** wide of the mark

bean

03 dal, Goa, pea, soy, urd, wax
04 dahl, dhal, fava, gram, guar, jack,
Lens, lima, loco, mung, navy, okra,
snap, soja, soya
05 aduki, berry, black, broad, carob,
dholl, green, horse, moong, pinto,
sugar, tonga, tonka
06 adsuki, adzuki, butter, cherry,
chilli, coffee, cowpea, French,
frijol, kidney, lablab, legume,
lentil, locust, runner, string,
winged
07 alfalfa, Calabar, fasolia, frijole,
haricot, jumping, Molucca, scarlet,
snow pea, tonquin
08 black-eye, borlotti, chickpea,
garbanzo, pichurim, snuffbox, split
pea, sugar pea, yard-long
09 black-eyed, black gram, flageolet,
green gram, jequirity, mangetout,
pigeon pea, puy lentil, red kidney,
red lentil
10 cannellini, golden gram, prayer
bead
11 black-eye pea, garbanzo pea, green
lentil
12 asparagus pea, black-eyed pea,
marrowfat pea, sassafras nut, St
John's bread
13 scarlet runner

bear
◇ containment indicator
02 go **03** act, hae, owe, pay, sit
04 bend, dree, hack, have, hold,
hump, keep, like, move, show, take,
teem, tote, turn, veer **05** abear, abide,
admit, allow, beget, breed, bring,
brook, carry, curve, drive, fetch,
stand, thole, yield **06** accept, acquit,
behave, convey, endure, foster,
give up, hold up, keep up, permit,
suffer, swerve, uphold **07** abrooke,
cherish, comport, conduct, deliver,
develop, deviate, display, diverge,
endorse, exhibit, harbour, produce,
stomach, support, sustain
08 engender, fructify, generate, live
with, maintain, shoulder, tolerate
09 entertain, propagate, put up with,
transport **10** bring forth **11** give birth to
13 grin and bear it

03 sea, sun
04 balu, cave, Pooh, Yogi
05 baloo, black, brown, Bruin,
Great, honey, koala, Nandi,
polar, sloth, teddy, water,
white
06 Little, native, Rupert, woolly
07 grizzly, Malayan
08 cinnamon
09 Ursa Major, Ursa Minor
10 giant panda, Paddington
13 Teddy Robinson, Winnie the
Pooh

• **bear down on**
08 approach, browbeat, move in on
09 advance on, close in on

- **bear in mind**
04 mind, note **06** keep in **08** consider, remember **10** keep in mind **11** be mindful of **15** make a mental note, take into account
- **bear out**
05 prove **06** back up, ratify, uphold, verify **07** confirm, endorse, justify, support, warrant **08** validate **09** vindicate **11** corroborate, demonstrate **12** substantiate
- **bear up**
04 buoy, cope **06** endure, suffer **07** carry on, survive **09** persevere, soldier on, withstand **13** grin and bear it
- **bear with**
06 endure, suffer **07** forbear **08** tolerate **09** put up with **13** be patient with

bearable
07 livable **08** liveable, passable, portable **09** endurable, tolerable **10** acceptable, admissible, manageable, sufferable **11** supportable, sustainable

beard
03 awn **04** dare, defy, face, kesh, peak, tuft, ziff **05** brave **06** beaver, goatee, oppose, pappus **07** bristle, Charley, Charlie, stubble, vandyke **08** confront, imperial, whiskers **09** challenge, moustache, sideburns **10** face-fungus, facial hair, sideboards **11** mutton chops **12** Newgate frill **13** Newgate fringe **14** stand up against

bearded
05 awned, bushy, hairy **06** barbed, shaggy, tufted **07** bristly, hirsute, prickly, stubbly **08** barbated, unshaven **09** pogoniate, whiskered **11** bewhiskered

bearer
05 agent, owner, payee **06** holder, porter, runner **07** carrier, courier, jampani **08** chairman, conveyor, jampanee **09** consignee, messenger, possessor **11** beneficiary, transporter

bearing
◇ *containment indicator*
01 E, N, S, W **03** aim, air, way **04** east, gait, gest, mien, port, west **05** geste, north, poise, south, track **06** aspect, course, manner **07** concern, posture, stature **08** attitude, carriage, location, portance, position, relation **09** behaviour, demeanour, direction, influence, reference, relevance, situation **10** connection, deportment, pertinence **11** comportment, orientation, whereabouts **12** significance
- **strewn with bearings**
04 semé **05** semée

beast
03 pig **04** bête, ogre **05** brute, devil, fiend, swine **06** animal, savage, tarand **07** monster, salvage **08** behemoth, creature, opinicus **09** barbarian
See also **animal**

- **mark of the Beast**
02 mb

beastly
04 foul, mean, vile **05** awful, cruel, nasty **06** brutal, horrid, rotten **07** swinish **08** horrible, terrible **09** brutishly, repulsive **10** abominably, unpleasant **11** frightfully **12** disagreeable

beat
02 do **03** box, gub, hit, lam, mix, pug, ram, tan, tap, way, wop **04** bang, bash, belt, best, biff, blow, cane, club, cuff, dash, ding, drub, dust, firk, flap, flay, flog, form, lash, lick, mall, maul, path, pelt, race, rout, ruin, slap, slat, stir, thud, tick, time, tund, walk, welt, wham, whip, whop, work, yerk, yirk **05** all in, birch, blend, clout, crush, excel, forge, knock, knout, metre, mould, outdo, paste, pound, pulse, punch, quake, quell, repel, rhyme, round, route, shake, shape, smack, smash, stamp, strap, swing, swipe, tempo, throb, thump, tired, whack, whisk, worst **06** accent, batter, bruise, buffet, bushed, course, cudgel, done in, exceed, fill in, granny, hammer, outrun, outwit, pooped, pummel, quiver, reject, rhythm, rounds, stress, strike, stroke, subdue, thrash, thresh, thwack, wallop, zonked **07** banging, cadence, circuit, clobber, combine, conquer, contuse, eclipse, fashion, flutter, journey, knubble, lambast, lay into, measure, outplay, pulsate, surpass, tremble, trounce, vibrate, wearied, whacked, worn out **08** dead-beat, dog-tired, fatigued, jiggered, knocking, malleate, outmatch, outscore, outsmart, outstrip, overcome, pounding, rib-roast, striking, throw out, tired out, vanquish, vapulate **09** devastate, discomfit, exhausted, knackered, marmelize, overpower, overthrow, overwhelm, palpitate, pooped out, pulsation, pulverize, slaughter, subjugate, territory, transcend, vibration, zonked out **10** annihilate, clapped-out, knock about **11** palpitation, tuckered out **13** have the edge on, put to the worse, run rings round **14** get the better of **15** make mincemeat of
- **beat against the wind**
03 ply
- **beat off**
05 repel **07** hold off, repulse, ward off **08** beat back, fight off, overcome, push back **09** drive back, force back, keep at bay
- **beats per minute**
03 BPM **05** pulse **09** pulse rate
- **beat up**
◇ *anagram indicator*
02 do **03** mug **05** scrag **06** arouse, attack, bang up, batter, donder, do over, duff up, switch **07** assault, clobber, disturb, rough up, scare up **08** duff over, work over **10** knock about **11** knock around

beaten
◇ *anagram indicator*
04 flat, ybet **05** foamy, mixed, trite **06** forged, formed, frothy, shaped, worked **07** blended, moulded, stamped, stirred, trodden, whipped, whisked, wrought **08** foliated, hammered, trampled, well-used, well-worn **09** exhausted, fashioned, stonkered **11** well-trodden

beatific
06 divine, joyful **07** angelic, blessed, exalted, sublime **08** blissful, ecstatic, glorious, heavenly, seraphic **09** rapturous

beatification
10 exaltation **12** canonization **13** glorification **14** sanctification

beatify
05 bless, exalt **07** glorify **08** canonize, macarize, sanctify

beating
04 loss, rout, ruin, warm **05** laldy, pandy, pulse, socks **06** caning, defeat hiding, lacing, laldie **07** battery, belting, duffing, hitting, lashing, pasting, pugging, tanning, the cane, warming **08** bruising, clubbing, conquest, downfall, drubbing, flogging, knocking, once-over, punching, slapping, smacking, the birch, the strap, thumping, whacking, whipping, whupping **09** bastinade, bastinado, battering, doing-over, duffing-up, going-over, hammering, overthrow, pulsation, pulsatory, slaughter, thrashing, trouncing, walloping **10** clobbering, loundering, outwitting, paddy-whack **11** duffing-over, outsmarting, vanquishing **12** annihilation, chastisement, overpowering, overwhelming

beatitude
07 delight, ecstasy, elation, rapture **08** macarism **09** happiness **11** blessedness **13** contentedness

beau
03 fop, guy **04** buck **05** dandy, lover, spark **06** Adonis, escort, fiancé, suitor **07** admirer, coxcomb **08** muscadin, popinjay **09** boyfriend **10** sweethear

beautician
07 friseur **09** visagiste **11** cosmetician hairdresser **12** aesthetician

beautiful
04 fair, fine **05** bonny, sheen **06** brigh comely, lovely, pretty, seemly **07** auroral, radiant, smicker **08** alluring, aurorean, becoming, charming, gorgeous, graceful, handsome, pleasing, smashing, specious, striking, stunning **09** appealing, exquisite, fair-faced, fairytale, ravishing **10** attractive, delightful, voluptuous **11** good-looking, hyacinthine, magnificent **14** out of this world, poetry in motion **15** pulchritudinous

beautifully
6 fairly, lovely **09** radiantly
0 charmingly, gracefully, pleasantly, pleasingly, strikingly, stunningly
2 attractively, delightfully

beautify
4 deck, gild **05** adorn, array, grace
6 bedeck, doll up, tart up
7 enhance, garnish, improve, smarten
8 decorate, flourish, ornament, spruce up, titivate **09** embellish, glamorize, smarten up

beauty
4 boon, dish, fair, form **05** asset, belle, bonus, charm, doozy, glory, grace, looks, merit, peach, pride, siren, Venus **06** allure, appeal, corker, doozer, glamor, virtue **07** benefit, charmer, cracker, delight, feature, glamour, harmony, smasher, stunner
8 blessing, dividend, Greek god, knockout, radiance, strength, symmetry **09** advantage, beau ideal, good looks, good point, good thing, plus point **10** attraction, excellence, good-looker, loveliness, prettiness, seemliness **11** femme fatale, pulchritude **12** gorgeousness, gracefulness, handsomeness
3 exquisiteness **14** attractiveness, beauté du diable

beaver
4 flix **05** beard **06** castor **08** sewellel
• beaver away
4 slog **06** work at **07** persist **08** plug away, work hard **09** persevere, slave away

becalmed
4 idle **05** still, stuck **07** at a halt
8 marooned, stranded **10** motionless
3 at a standstill

because
2 as **03** 'cos, for **05** due to, since
6 for why **07** owing to, through
8 seeing as, thanks to **09** forasmuch
0 by reason of, by virtue of **11** as a result of, on account of
• because of
2 in **07** owing to **08** what with **10** by virtue of, in virtue of **11** on account of

beckon
3 nod **04** call, coax, draw, lure, pull, waft, wave **05** tempt **06** allure, entice, induce, invite, motion, signal, summon
7 attract, gesture **08** persuade
1 gesticulate

become
◇ anagram indicator
2 go **03** get, run, set, wax, won
4 come, fall, grow, suit, take, turn
5 befit, grace, worth **06** beseem, resort, set off **07** enhance, flatter
8 come to be, grow into, ornament, pass into **09** embellish, harmonize
0 change into, look good on, mature into **11** develop into, turn out to be
3 be changed into
• become of
6 befall **08** happen to **11** be the fate of

becoming
03 fit **06** comely, decent, pretty, seemly **07** elegant, fitting
08 charming, decorous, fetching, graceful, gracious, handsome, suitable, tasteful **09** befitting, besitting, congruous **10** attractive, compatible, consistent, flattering **11** appropriate

becomingly
09 elegantly **10** charmingly, fetchingly, gracefully, tastefully **12** attractively

bed
03 fix, hay, kip, mat, pad, pit, row, set
04 area, base, bury, doss, plot, sack
05 basis, embed, floor, found, inlay, layer, patch, plant, space, strip
06 border, bottom, garden, ground, insert, matrix, settle **07** channel, implant, stratum **09** establish
10 foundation, groundwork, substratum **11** watercourse

Beds include:
01 Z
03 box, cot, day
04 bunk, camp, cott, crib, sofa, twin
05 berth, couch, divan, futon, water
06 cradle, double, litter, pallet, Put-u-up®, single
07 folding, hammock, trestle, truckle, trundle
08 bassinet, foldaway, king-size, mattress, platform, put-you-up
09 couchette, king-sized, lit bateau, palliasse, queen-size, shakedown
10 adjustable, four-poster, mid sleeper, queen-sized
11 high sleeper
12 chaise longue

• bed down
03 kip **05** sleep **06** turn in **07** go to bed, kip down **08** doss down **09** hit the hay **10** call it a day, get some kip, hit the sack, settle down
• dry bed
04 wadi, wady
• get out of bed
04 rise **07** surface, turn out **08** show a leg, tumble up **10** hit the deck **12** rise and shine
• out of bed
02 up **05** astir, risen

bedaub
04 clag, moil **05** smear **06** parget
07 besmear, plaster **08** slaister
09 beslubber

bedbug
01 B **05** B flat **06** chinch

bedclothes
06 covers **07** bedding **08** bed-linen

Bedclothes include:
05 doona, duvet, quilt, sheet
06 downie, pillow
07 bedroll, blanket, bolster, valance
08 coverlet
09 bed canopy, bedspread, comforter, eiderdown, throwover
10 duvet cover, pillowcase, pillow sham, pillowslip, quilt cover
11 counterpane, fitted sheet, sleeping bag
13 mattress cover, valanced sheet, Witney blanket
14 patchwork quilt
15 cellular blanket, electric blanket

bedeck
04 deck, trim **05** adorn, array
07 festoon, garnish, trick up
08 beautify, decorate, ornament, trick out **09** embellish

bedevil
◇ anagram indicator
03 irk, vex **04** fret **05** annoy, beset, tease, worry **06** harass, pester, plague
07 afflict, besiege, torment, torture, trouble **08** confound, distress, irritate
09 frustrate

bedfellow
04 ally **06** fellow, friend **07** partner
09 associate, colleague, companion

bedlam
◇ anagram indicator
05 babel, chaos, noise **06** furore, hubbub, madman, tumult, uproar
07 anarchy, clamour, turmoil
08 madhouse **09** commotion, confusion **10** hullabaloo
11 pandemonium

bedraggled
03 wet **05** dirty, messy, muddy
06 soaked, sodden, soiled, untidy
07 muddied, scruffy, soaking, unkempt
08 drenched, dripping, slovenly
10 disordered, soaking wet
11 dishevelled

bedridden
06 bedrid, laid up **07** worn-out
10 housebound **13** confined to bed, incapacitated **14** flat on your back

bedrock
04 base, core **05** basis, heart
06 basics, bottom, reason **07** essence, footing, premise, reasons, support
09 rationale **10** essentials, foundation, rock bottom **12** fundamentals
13 starting-point **15** first principles

bedroom
02 br **06** dormer **07** cubicle
08 roomette **09** bed-closet
10 bedchamber

bee
01 B **04** king **05** drone, nurse, queen
06 hummer, neuter, worker **07** royalty
10 drumbledor, dumbledore, leaf-cutter

beech
05 Fagus **06** myrtle **15** Tasmanian myrtle

beef
03 gag, sey **04** moan, rump, shin
05 bully, chuck, filet, flank, gripe, keema, mouse, round, skink, steak, T-bone **06** grouse, object, runner
07 charqui, dispute, grumble, sirloin, surloin, topside **08** bresaola, complain, disagree, pastrami, salt-junk

09 aitchbone, criticize, rump steak, salt horse, tournedos **10** mousepiece, silverside **11** filet mignon, sauerbraten **12** mouse-buttock **13** Chateaubriand, Scotch collops **15** scotched collops

• **beef up**
07 build up, toughen **08** flesh out **09** establish, reinforce, toughen up **10** invigorate, strengthen **11** consolidate **12** substantiate **15** give new energy to

beefeater
04 exon **06** ox-bird, yeoman **07** Buphaga **08** oxpecker

beefy
03 fat **05** bulky, burly, heavy, hefty, tubby **06** brawny, fleshy, robust, stocky, stolid, sturdy **07** hulking **08** muscular, stalwart **09** corpulent

beehive
03 gum **04** skep

beer
04 brew, grog, half, pint **06** liquor **07** brewski **11** amber liquid

Beers include:

03 ale, dry, ice, IPA, keg
04 bock, mild, Pils, rice
05 black, fruit, guest, heavy, honey, kvass, lager, plain, sixty, stout, wheat, white
06 bitter, eighty, export, old ale, porter, shandy, Stella®
07 bottled, draught, pale ale, Pilsner, real ale, seventy
08 amber ale, brown ale, Guinness®, home brew, light ale, Pilsener, trappist
09 microbrew, milk stout, snakebite, wheat beer
10 barley wine, low-alcohol, malt liquor, sweet stout, Weisse Bier
11 black-and-tan
12 Christmas ale, India Pale Ale
13 sixty shilling
14 eighty shilling
15 cask-conditioned, seventy shilling

See also **glass**

beetle
03 nip, run, zip **04** dash, maul, rush, tear **05** hurry, scoot **06** batler, batlet, bustle, mallet, scurry **07** scamper

See also **animal**; **insect**

Beetles include:

03 dor, may, oil
04 bark, dorr, dung, leaf, musk, pine, rove, stag
05 black, click, clock, shard, tiger, water
06 carpet, chafer, dor-fly, ground, may bug, sacred, scarab, sexton, weevil
07 burying, cadelle, carabid, carrion, goliath, hop-flea, hornbug, rose bug
08 bum-clock, cardinal, Colorado, glow-worm, Hercules, Japanese, ladybird, longhorn, wireworm, woodworm
09 furniture, goldsmith, longicorn, tumblebug, whirligig

10 bombardier, cockchafer, deathwatch, rhinoceros, rose chafer, scarabaean, scarabaeid, tumbledung, turnip flea
11 coprophagan, typographer

• **beetle-crusher**
03 cop **09** policeman **11** infantryman

beetling
07 jutting, pendent **09** poking out, prominent **10** projecting, protruding **11** leaning over, overhanging, sticking out

befall
04 fall **05** ensue, occur **06** arrive, astart, betide, chance, follow, happen, result, strike **07** fortune **08** bechance, come over, come upon, fall upon, happen to **09** befortune, overwhelm, supervene, take place **11** materialize

befit
03 set, sit **04** seem, sort, suit **05** match **06** become, befall, behove, beseem, besort **10** complement **13** harmonize with

befitting
03 apt, fit **04** like, meet **05** right **06** decent, proper, seemly **07** correct, fitting **08** becoming, sortable, suitable **11** appropriate **12** well-becoming **13** well-beseeming

before
◇ *juxtaposition indicator*
01 a **02** an, or, to **03** bef, ere, pre, pro- **04** ante, once, onst, prae- **05** ahead **07** ahead of, already, earlier, in front, prior to **08** formerly **09** in advance, in front of **10** on the eve of, previously, previous to, sooner than **11** earlier than **12** in the sight of, not later than **15** in the presence of

• **as before**
02 do **05** ditto

beforehand
03 pre- **04** fore-, prae- **05** afore, early **06** before, former, sooner **07** already, earlier **08** paravant **09** aforehand, in advance, paravaunt **10** previously **11** ahead of time **13** preliminarily

befriend
03 aid **04** back, help **06** assist, defend, favour, uphold **07** benefit, comfort, protect, stand by, succour, support, sustain, welcome **09** encourage, get to know, look after **10** fall in with, stick up for **11** keep an eye on **13** make a friend of **15** make friends with

befuddle
◇ *anagram indicator*
04 daze, faze **06** baffle, muddle, puzzle **07** confuse, nonplus, perplex, stupefy **08** bewilder **09** disorient

beg
03 ask, bum **04** pray, prog, thig **05** cadge, crave, maund, mooch, mouch, plead **06** appeal, ask for, desire, fleech, sponge, turn to **07** beseech, beseeke, entreat, implore, intreat, maunder, request, require,

schnorr, skelder, solicit **08** governor, mooch off, petition, scrounge, stand pad **09** importune, panhandle **10** supplicate **11** ask for money **13** touch for money

beget
03 get **04** kind, sire **05** breed, cause, spawn **06** create, effect, father, gender, lead to **07** produce, propage **08** engender, generate, occasion, result in **09** procreate, propagate **10** bring about, give rise to

beggar
03 bum **04** defy **05** randy, tramp **06** baffle, blowse, blowze, cadger, canter, craver, exceed, mumper, pauper, randie, toerag **07** bludger, jarkman, maunder, moocher, ruffler, sponger, surpass, vagrant **08** Abram-man, beadsman, bedesman, besognio, besonian, bezonian, blighter, glassman, palliard, vagabond, whipjack **09** challenge, lazzarone, mendicant, schnorrer, scrounger, sundowner, transcend **10** Abraham-man, beadswoman, down-and-out, freeloader, panhandler, supplicant, upright-man **11** gaberlunzie **12** down-and-outer, hallan-shaker

beggarly
03 low **04** mean, poor **05** needy **06** abject, meagre, modest, paltry, slight, stingy **07** miserly, pitiful **08** pathetic, wretched **09** niggardly, worthless **10** despicable, inadequate **12** contemptible **13** insubstantial

begin
02 go **03** gin, ope **04** open, take **05** arise, enter, found, get at, set in, set up, shoot, spark, start **06** appear, broach, come on, crop up, embark, emerge, incept, set off, set out, spring **07** actuate, do first, enter on, kick off, take off **08** activate, commence, embark on, fire away, get going, inchoate, initiate, set about, shoot off, strike up **09** enter upon, instigate, institute, introduce, originate **10** launch into **11** get cracking, give birth to, open the ball, set in motion **13** take the plunge

beginner
◇ *head selection indicator*
01 L **03** cub, deb **04** tiro, tyro **05** pupil, rooky **06** author, newbie, novice, rookie **07** fresher, learner, new chum, recruit, starter, student, trainee **08** freshman, initiate, neophyte, newcomer **09** fledgling, greenhorn, Johnny-raw **10** apprentice, raw recruit, tenderfoot **11** abecedarian, probationer **13** alphabetarian

beginning
◇ *head selection indicator*
03 ord **04** dawn, germ, rise, root, seed **05** birth, debut, get-go, intro, onset, start **06** day one, launch, origin, outset, source **07** genesis, kick-off, new leaf, opening, preface, prelude **09** emergence, first base, first part,

**...ception, square one, the word go
...conception, fresh start, inchoation,
...cipience, initiation 11 institution,
...pening part, pastures new
...2 commencement, fountainhead,
...auguration, introduction
...3 establishment, new beginnings,
...arting-point
  from beginning to end**
...4 over 07 through 08 from A to Z

egone
...4 away 05 hence 06 avaunt 10 aroint
...ee 11 allez-vous-en

egrudge
...4 envy, mind 05 covet, stint
...6 grudge, resent 08 object to 11 be
...alous of 13 be resentful of

eguile
...4 dupe, fool, gull, wile 05 amuse,
...end, charm, cheat, cozen, guile,
...uyle, trick 06 delude, divert, occupy,
...educe 07 attract, bewitch, deceive,
...elight, enchant, engross, mislead
...8 distract, hoodwink 09 captivate,
...ntertain

eguiling
...8 alluring, charming, enticing
...9 appealing, diverting, seductive
...0 attractive, bewitching, delightful,
...nchanting, intriguing 11 captivating,
...teresting 12 entertaining

ehalf
...4 name, part, sake 07 account,
...enefit 08 interest
  on behalf of
...2 pp 03 for 06 per pro 09 acting for
...l in support of, in the name of 12 for
...ccount of, for the good of, for the sake
...f, representing 13 to the profit of
...5 for the benefit of

ehave
...2 be, do 03 act, use 04 bear, go on,
...uit, walk, work 05 abear, carry, quite,
...uyte, react 06 acquit, be good,
...emean, deport, quight 07 comport,
...onduct, operate, perform, respond
...8 function 10 act your age 11 act
...olitely, act properly 12 not mess
...bout, not muck about 13 be well-
...ehaved 14 acquit yourself
...5 comport yourself, conduct yourself,
...ind your manners, mind your p's and
...'s

ehaviour
...4 form, ways 06 action, doings,
...abits, manner 07 conduct, manners
...8 dealings, reaction, response
...9 attitudes, demeanour, operation
...0 deportment 11 comportment,
...nctioning, performance, way of
...cting

ehead
  head deletion indicator
...4 head, kill 07 execute 09 decollate
...0 decapitate, guillotine, put to death

ehest
  at the behest of
...l at the hest of 12 at the order of 13 on

---

the wishes of 14 at the bidding of, at
the command of, at the request of

behind
  ◇ *juxtaposition indicator*
  ◇ *tail selection indicator*
03 aft, ass, bum, for 04 back, baft, butt,
late, next, post, rear, rump, slow
05 abaft, after, ahind, ahint, retro-,
stern 06 arrear, astern, back of, bottom,
heinie, in debt 07 backing, causing,
close on, delayed, overdue
08 backside, buttocks, derrière, in
back of 09 at the back, at the rear,
endorsing, following, in arrears, in the
rear, later than, posterior
10 behindhand, explaining, initiating,
supporting 11 at the back of, at the rear
of, instigating, on the side of, running
late 12 giving rise to, subsequently
13 accounting for, at the bottom of
14 responsible for 15 slower than
usual

behindhand
03 lag 04 down, late, slow 05 tardy
06 behind, remiss 07 delayed
08 backward, dilatory 09 in arrears,
out of date 14 behind schedule

behold
02 la, lo 03 see 04 ecce, ecco, espy,
look, mark, note, scan, view 05 voici,
voilà, watch 06 descry, gaze at, look at,
regard, survey 07 discern, observe,
witness 08 consider, perceive
11 contemplate

beholden
05 bound, owing 07 obliged
08 addebted, grateful, indebted,
thankful 09 obligated 12 appreciative
15 under obligation

behove
05 befit 06 import, profit 07 benefit,
stand on 08 be proper, be seemly
11 be essential, be necessary 13 be
suitable for 14 be advantageous

beige
03 tan 04 buff, ecru, fawn 05 camel,
khaki, sandy, suede, taupe 06 coffee,
greige, oyster 07 neutral, oatmeal
08 mushroom

being
03 ens, man 04 esse, life, soul, will
05 beast, heart, human, thing, woman
06 animal, entity, living, mortal, nature,
person, psyche, spirit 07 essence,
reality 08 creature, emotions
09 actuality, animation, existence,
haecceity, inner self, substance
10 human being, individual, inner
being 11 personality 13 heart of hearts

belabour
  ◇ *anagram indicator*
03 hit 04 beat, belt, flay, flog, whip
05 sauce 06 attack, pummel, strike,
thrash 07 dwell on 09 lay on load,
reiterate 11 flog to death, harp on
about 14 go on and on about

Belarus
02 BY, SU 03 BLR

---

belated
04 late 05 lated, tardy 07 delayed,
overdue 09 benighted, out of date
10 behindhand, unpunctual 14 behind
schedule

belatedly
07 tardily 12 unpunctually 14 behind
schedule

belch
03 yex 04 boak, bock, boke, burp,
emit, gush, rift, spew, vent, yesk
05 eject, eruct, issue 06 hiccup
07 give off, give out 08 disgorge,
eructate 09 discharge 10 eructation
11 bring up wind

beleaguered
05 beset, vexed 07 plagued, worried
08 badgered, besieged, bothered,
harassed, pestered, troubled
09 blockaded, tormented
10 persecuted, surrounded, under siege

Belgium
01 B 03 BEL 04 Belg

belie
04 deny 06 negate, refute 07 conceal,
confute, cover up, deceive, falsify,
gainsay, mislead 08 disguise, disprove
10 contradict 12 misrepresent, run
counter to

belief
03 ism 04 idea, view 05 creed,
dogma, ethic, faith, ideal, tenet, trust
06 credit, notion, theory, threap,
threep 07 feeling, opinion
08 credence, doctrine, ideology,
reliance, sureness, teaching
09 assurance, certainty, intuition,
judgement, knowledge, principle,
tradition, viewpoint 10 confidence,
conviction, impression, persuasion
11 expectation, point of view,
presumption

Beliefs include:
06 holism, malism, racism
07 animism, atheism, elitism
08 demonism, feminism, hedonism,
humanism, nihilism, Satanism
09 pantheism, physicism, tritheism
10 liberalism, Manicheism,
monotheism, polytheism
11 agnosticism, parallelism,
supremacism, tetratheism
12 Manicheanism
13 ethnocentrism, individualism,
structuralism
14 fundamentalism, traditionalism,
tripersonalism
15 supernaturalism

See also **religion**

believable
06 likely 07 credent 08 credible,
possible, probable, reliable
09 plausible 10 acceptable,
imaginable 11 conceivable,
trustworthy 13 authoritative

believe
03 buy, wis 04 deem, feel, hold, trow,
wear, ween, wish, wist 05 faith, guess,

judge, opine, think, trust **06** accept,
assume, credit, figure, gather, reckon
07 fall for, imagine, suppose, swallow
08 consider, maintain, perceive
09 postulate, speculate **10** Adam and
Eve, conjecture, understand **11** be
certain of, take on board **13** be
convinced by, be persuaded by
• **believe in**
04 rate **05** trust **06** favour, follow, hold
by, rely on **07** swear by **08** depend on
09 approve of, encourage,
recommend **11** value highly **12** be in
favour of **13** be convinced of, be
persuaded by **15** set great store by
• **hard to believe**
04 tall

believer
06 zealot **07** convert, devotee
08 adherent, disciple, follower,
upholder **09** proselyte, supporter

Believers include:

03 Jew
04 Babi, Jain, Sikh, Sofi, Sufi
05 Babee, Hindu, Jaina
06 holist, Muslim
07 Alawite, animist, Bahaist, Genevan,
Lollard, Scotist
08 Arminian, Buddhist, Calixtin,
Catholic, demonist, Erastian,
Glassite, humanist, Lutheran,
Nazarean, Nazarene, Pelagian,
Salesian, Satanist, Wesleyan
09 animalist, Calixtine, Christian,
Confucian, Eutychian, Gregorian,
Methodist, Nestorian, Origenist,
pantheist, Sabellian, Simeonite,
Wyclifite
10 Bergsonian, Berkeleian,
Cameronian, Capernaite, Holy
Roller, Marcionite, polytheist,
Wycliffite
11 Sandemanian, Valentinian
12 Apollinarian, Southcottian
13 Hutchinsonian, Roman Catholic,
Swedenborgian
14 fundamentalist, the Oxford group
15 supernaturalist

belittle
04 slag, slam **05** abase, decry, knock,
scorn, slate **06** demean, deride, do
down, dump on, lessen **07** dismiss,
rubbish, run down, slag off
08 diminish, minimize, play down,
ridicule **09** deprecate, disparage,
downgrade, sell short, underrate
10 trivialize, understate, undervalue
11 detract from, pick holes in **12** pull to
pieces, tear to shreds
13 underestimate **15** do a hatchet job
on

Belize
02 BH, BZ **03** BLZ

bell
03 tom **04** gong, horn, peal, ring
05 bleep, chime, knell, larum, siren
06 alarum, curfew, hooter, signal,
tocsin, vesper **07** angelus, bleeper,
tinkler, warning **08** pavilion
13 tintinnabulum

• **sound of bell, sound of bells**
04 clam, dong, peal, ring, ting, tink, toll
05 chime, knell **06** firing, tinkle
08 ding-dong **09** ding-a-ling

bellbird
08 araponga, arapunga
09 campanero

belle
05 peach, siren, Venus **06** beauty,
corker **07** charmer, cracker, smasher,
stunner **08** knockout **10** good-looker
11 femme fatale

bellicose
07 violent, warlike, warring
08 bullying, militant **09** combative
10 aggressive, pugnacious
11 belligerent, contentious,
quarrelsome **12** antagonistic
13 argumentative

belligerence
03 war **08** bullying, violence
09 militancy, pugnacity **10** aggression,
antagonism **11** provocation
12 warmongering **13** combativeness,
sabre-rattling **14** unfriendliness
15 contentiousness, quarrelsomeness

belligerent
06 chippy **07** hostile, scrappy, violent,
warlike, warring **08** bullying, militant
09 combative, truculent **10** aggressive,
pugnacious **11** contentious,
provocative, quarrelsome
12 antagonistic, disputatious,
warmongering **13** argumentative,
sabre-rattling

bellow
03 cry **04** bawl, howl, roar, rout, yell
05 shout, troat **06** buller, holler,
scream, shriek **07** clamour, thunder
14 raise your voice

belly
03 gut, pot, tum, wem **04** bulk, bunt,
guts, kite, kyte, puku, wame, webm
05 gastr-, tummy, weamb **06** gastro-,
paunch, venter **07** abdomen, gastero-,
insides, stomach **08** pot-belly **09** beer
belly **10** intestines **11** bread basket,
corporation

belong
02 go **03** fit **04** be in, long **05** fit in
06 go with **07** be found, be yours,
pertain **08** attach to, be part of, be
sorted, relate to **09** appertain, be
owned by, tie up with **10** be included,
be situated, link up with **11** be a
member of **12** be classified **13** be
categorized, have as its home **14** be
affiliated to, be an adherent of, have as
its place **15** be connected with, be the
property of

belonging
04 link **05** links **07** kinship, loyalty,
rapport **08** affinity **09** closeness
10 acceptance, attachment, fellowship
11 affiliation, association **12** relationship
13 compatibility, fellow-feeling
• **belonging to**
◊ *hidden indicator*

belongings
03 kit **04** gear **05** goods, stuff, traps
06 tackle, things **07** clobber, effects
08 chattels, property **11** possessions
13 accoutrements, appurtenances,
paraphernalia

beloved
02 jo **03** joe, joy, pet **04** baby, bird,
dear, duck, leve, lief, love, wife
05 angel, fella, honey, lieve, loved,
lover, sweet **06** adored, fiancé, liking
prized, spouse, tender **07** admired,
darling, dearest, fiancée, husband,
partner, revered, sweetie
08 endeared, lady-love, loved one,
precious, true-love **09** belamoure,
betrothed, boyfriend, cherished,
favourite, heart-dear, inamorata,
inamorato, much loved, treasured
10 bellamoure, girlfriend, sweetheart
worshipped **12** alder-liefest **13** speci
friend

below
◊ *juxtaposition down indicator*
03 inf, sub- **04** down **05** infra, later,
lower, under **07** beneath **09** further
on, hereunder, lower down, lower
than, subject to **10** inferior to, lesser
than, underneath **13** at a later place,
subordinate to **15** lower in rank than

belt
◊ *anagram indicator*
03 box, fly, hit, tan, zip **04** area, band
bang, bash, biff, blow, cane, cord, das
flay, flog, lash, loop, pelt, rush, sash,
slap, tear, whip, zona, zone **05** apron
birch, chain, clout, girth, knock, layer,
mitre, punch, slosh, smack, speed,
strap, strip, swipe, thump, tract, want
whack **06** bruise, career, cestus,
charge, corset, extent, girdle, region,
sector, strike, swathe, thwack, wallop
waspie **07** baldric, bashing, clobber,
harness, stretch, zonulet **08** baldrick,
ceinture, cincture, cingulum, district
09 bandoleer, bandolier, hip-girdle,
Sam Browne, waistband
10 cummerbund

See also **karate**

• **below the belt**
05 dirty **06** unfair, unjust
09 dishonest, underhand, unethical
10 out of order **11** uncalled-for,
unjustified **12** unscrupulous
• **belt up**
02 sh, st **03** shh **04** hist **05** shush,
whish, whist **06** shut up, whisht, wrar
up **07** be quiet, wheesht **08** button u
cut it out, pipe down **10** keep shtoon
stay shtoom **12** put a sock in it, shut
your face **13** button your lip, shut you
mouth

belvedere
06 gazebo **07** mirador

bemoan
03 rue **04** moan, pity, wail **05** mourn
06 bewail, lament, regret **07** deplore
sigh for, weep for **09** grieve for
10 sorrow over

emuse
anagram indicator
4 daze, faze 05 floor, throw
6 baffle, muddle, puzzle 07 confuse,
erplex, stupefy 08 befuddle,
ewilder 09 bamboozle

emused
anagram indicator
5 dazed, fazed, mused 07 baffled,
oored, muddled, puzzled
8 confused 09 astounded,
efuddled, perplexed, pixilated,
tupefied 10 astonished, bamboozled,
ewildered, pixillated
1 overwhelmed 12 disconcerted

emusement
4 daze 09 confusion 10 bafflement,
erplexity, puzzlement
2 bewilderment, stupefaction
4 disorientation

en
3 Hur

ench
3 pew 04 banc, bank, bink, form,
eat 05 board, court, judge, ledge,
all, table, thoft 06 banker, exedra,
ettle, thwart 07 counter, exhedra,
ibune 08 rout-seat, tribunal
9 courtroom, judiciary, shopboard,
orkbench, worktable 10 judicature,
nife-board, magistrate 13 judgement-
eat

enchmark
4 norm 05 basis, gauge, level, model,
cale 07 example, pattern 08 standard
9 criterion, guideline, reference,
ardstick 10 guidelines, touchstone
1 reference-point

end
anagram indicator
1 S, U, Z 02 es 03 arc, bow, ess, out,
ly, sag 04 arch, curb, flex, genu, hook,
ump, kink, knot, lean, loop, ramp,
way, trap, turn, veer, warp, wind
5 angle, bight, courb, crimp, crook,
urve, elbow, embow, hinge, hunch,
neel, mould, ox-bow, plash, round,
hape, squat, stoop, trend, twist, wring
6 affect, bought, buckle, compel,
orner, crouch, cut-off, deflex, direct,
og-leg, recede, reflex, spring, swerve,
rimple, zigzag 07 compass, contort,
rankle, decline, deflect, deviate, dip-
ap, diverge, flexion, flexure, incline,
ncurve, inflect, meander, recline,
ecurve, reflect, turning, whimple,
riggle 08 persuade, swan neck
9 curvature, genuflect, incurvate,
nflexure, influence, prostrate, retroflex
0 circumflex, deflection, divergence,
nake curved, manipulate
1 circumflect, hairpin bend,
nclination, incurvation
  bend over
4 lean 08 double up
  bend over backwards
8 go all out 10 do your best 11 try
ery hard 13 exert yourself 14 put
ourself out 15 trouble yourself

bendy
◇ *anagram indicator*
08 flexible

beneath
◇ *juxtaposition down indicator*
03 sub 05 below, lower, neath, under
06 aneath 09 lower down, lower than
10 unbecoming, underneath,
unworthy of 11 unbefitting

Benedictines
03 OSB

benediction
05 grace 06 favour, prayer 07 benison
08 blessing 10 invocation
11 blessedness 12 consecration,
thanksgiving

benefactor
05 angel, donor, giver 06 backer,
friend, helper, patron 07 sponsor
08 promoter, provider 09 supporter
10 subscriber, subsidizer, well-wisher
11 contributor 14 fairy godmother,
philanthropist

beneficent
04 kind 06 benign 07 benefic, helpful,
liberal 08 generous 09 bountiful,
unselfish 10 altruistic, benevolent,
charitable, munificent
12 Grandisonian 13 compassionate

beneficial
04 good 06 useful 07 helpful
08 edifying, salutary, valuable
09 benignant, improving, promising,
rewarding, wholesome 10 favourable,
profitable, propitious, worthwhile
11 serviceable 12 advantageous
  • **beneficial to**
03 for

beneficiary
04 heir 05 payee 07 heiress, legatee
08 receiver 09 inheritor, recipient,
successor 10 the assured

benefit
03 ACC, aid, DPB, pay, use 04 boon,
broo, dole, gain, good, help, perk, sake
05 asset, avail, bonus, buroo, compo,
merit, serve 06 assist, behalf, behoof,
better, credit, favour, income, milage,
pay-off, profit, reward 07 advance,
bespeak, enhance, further, improve,
mileage, payment, pension, promote,
service, sick pay, spin-off, support,
vantage, welfare 08 blessing, dividend,
do good to, interest, kindness
09 advantage, allowance, good point
10 assistance, perquisite
11 benefaction 13 be of service to,
fringe benefit, income support
14 social security 15 be of advantage to

benevolence
04 care, pity 05 grace, mercy
08 altruism, goodness, goodwill,
kindness 09 tolerance 10 compassion,
generosity, humaneness, liberality
11 magnanimity, munificence
12 friendliness, philanthropy
14 charitableness 15 considerateness,
humanitarianism, kind-heartedness

benevolent
04 good, guid, kind 06 benign, caring,
humane, kindly 07 liberal 08 friendly,
generous, gracious, merciful, tolerant
10 altruistic, charitable, munificent
11 considerate, kind-hearted,
magnanimous, soft-hearted
12 humanitarian, well-disposed
13 compassionate, philanthropic
15 philanthropical

benevolently
06 kindly 08 benignly, humanely
09 liberally 10 charitably, generously,
graciously, mercifully, tolerantly
13 considerately, kind-heartedly,
magnanimously, soft-heartedly
14 altruistically 15 compassionately

benighted
07 belated, nighted 08 backward,
ignorant 09 unknowing 10 illiterate,
uncultured, uneducated, unlettered,
unschooled 11 unfortunate
13 inexperienced, unenlightened

benign
04 good, kind, mild, warm 05 sweet,
trine 06 genial, gentle, kindly
07 affable, amiable, benefic, cordial,
curable, healthy, liberal 08 benedict,
friendly, generous, gracious, harmless,
innocent, obliging 09 agreeable,
avuncular, opportune, temperate,
treatable, wholesome 10 auspicious,
beneficial, benevolent, charitable,
favourable, propitious, refreshing,
salubrious 11 restorative,
sympathetic, warm-hearted
12 advantageous, non-malignant,
providential

benignly
06 kindly 07 affably, amiably
08 genially 10 charitably, generously,
graciously, obligingly 12 benevolently
15 sympathetically

Benin
02 DY, RB 03 BEN

bent
◇ *anagram indicator*
04 curb, gift, turn 05 bowed, corbe,
courb, dodgy, flair, forte, knack, wrong
06 angled, arched, curved, fiorin,
folded, redtop, reflex, talent, warped
07 ability, corrupt, crooked, curvate,
doubled, embowed, faculty, falcate,
hunched, illegal, leaning, stooped,
strepto-, twafald, twisted 08 aptitude,
capacity, criminal, cup of tea, curvated,
facility, falcated, fondness, inclined,
inflexed, penchant, reflexed, retorted,
tendency 09 contorted, dishonest,
infracted, refracted, retroflex,
swindling 10 fraudulent, geniculate,
preference, proclivity, propensity
11 disposition, geniculated, inclination
12 predilection 13 untrustworthy
14 predisposition
  • **bent on**
05 set on 07 fixed on 08 intent on
10 disposed to, inclined to, resolved to
11 insistent on 12 determined to

bequeath
04 give, will **05** endow, grant, leave
06 assign, bestow, commit, demise,
devise, impart, pass on **07** consign,
entrust **08** hand down, make over,
transfer, transmit

bequest
04 gift **05** trust **06** estate, legacy
07 devisal **08** bestowal, donation,
heritage, pittance **09** endowment
10 bequeathal, settlement
11 inheritance **13** mortification

berate
05 blast, chide, scold, slate **06** rail at,
rebuke, revile **07** censure, chew out,
reprove, start on, tell off, upbraid
08 chastise, give hell, reproach
09 castigate, criticize, dress down,
fulminate, reprimand, start in on
10 vituperate **13** give a rocket to, tear a
strip off

bereaved
03 orb **04** lost **06** robbed
07 widowed **08** deprived, divested,
grieving, orphaned **12** dispossessed

bereavement
04 loss **05** death, grief **06** orbity,
sorrow **07** passing, sadness
08 deprival **11** deprivation, passing-
away **13** dispossession

bereft
• **bereft of**
05 minus **07** lacking, wanting
08 devoid of, robbed of **10** cut off
from, deprived of, parted from,
stripped of **11** destitute of

berkelium
02 Bk

Berlin
06 Irving

Bermuda
03 BMU

berry
05 bacca **06** acinus

Berries include:
05 lichi
06 lichee, litchi, lychee
07 bramble, leechee
08 bilberry, dewberry, goosegog,
  mulberry, tayberry
09 blaeberry, blueberry, cranberry,
  raspberry, whimberry
10 blackberry, cloudberry, elderberry,
  gooseberry, loganberry, redcurrant,
  strawberry
11 boysenberry, huckleberry
12 blackcurrant, serviceberry,
  whitecurrant, whortleberry

berserk
◇ *anagram indicator*
03 mad **04** nuts, wild **05** angry, barmy,
batty, berko, crazy, manic, rabid
06 crazed, insane, raging, raving
07 frantic, furious, violent **08** baresark,
demented, deranged, frenzied,
maniacal **10** hysterical **11** off your
head **13** off the deep end, out of

your mind **14** beside yourself,
uncontrollable

berth
03 bed **04** bunk, dock, land, moor,
port, quay **05** tie up, wharf **06** anchor,
billet **07** hammock, harbour, mooring,
sleeper **09** anchorage, couchette
10 cast anchor, drop anchor
• **give a wide berth to**
04 shun **05** avoid, dodge, evade
06 eschew **09** give a miss **12** steer
clear of

beryl
07 emerald **08** emeraude, heliodor
09 morganite **10** aquamarine

beryllium
02 Be

beseech
03 ask, beg, sue **04** pray **05** crave,
plead **06** adjure, call on, desire, exhort
07 entreat, implore, intreat, solicit
08 appeal to, petition **09** deprecate,
importune, obsecrate **10** supplicate

beset
◇ *containment indicator*
03 lay, rag **04** bego **05** belay, hem in,
press, worry **06** assail, attack, bestad,
bested, harass, hassle, obsess, pester,
plague, preace, prease **07** bedevil,
besiege, bestead, preasse, torment
08 bestadde, entangle, scabrous,
surround

besetting
08 constant, dominant, habitual
09 harassing, obsessive, prevalent,
recurring **10** compulsive, inveterate,
persistent **11** troublesome
12 irresistible **14** uncontrollable

beside
◇ *juxtaposition indicator*
02 by, on, to **04** near **06** next to
07 close to, upsides **08** abutting,
adjacent **09** abreast of, alongside,
bordering **10** next door to **11** by the
side of, overlooking **12** neighbouring
• **beside yourself**
03 mad **05** crazy **06** crazed, insane
07 berserk, frantic **08** demented,
deranged, frenetic, frenzied,
overcome, unhinged **09** delirious
10 distraught, unbalanced **13** out of
your mind

besides
02 by **03** too, yet **04** also, else
05 forby **06** as well, either, forbye,
foreby, withal **07** au reste, further
08 as well as, moreover **09** apart from,
aside from, excluding, other than,
otherwise, what's more **10** in addition
11 furthermore **12** additionally, in
addition to, over and above

besiege
◇ *containment indicator*
03 nag **05** belay, beset, besit, hem in,
hound, worry **06** assail, badger,
bother, harass, invest, obsess, pester,
plague, shut in **07** assiege, confine,
oppress, torment, trouble

08 blockade, encircle, surround
09 beleaguer, encompass, importune
overwhelm **10** lay siege to

besmirch
04 slur, soil **05** dirty, smear, stain, sully
06 damage, defame, defile
07 besmear, blacken, slander, tarnish
08 besmutch **09** dishonour

besom
03 cow, kow **05** broom

besotted
03 mad **04** wild **05** crazy, potty
06 doting, sotted, stupid **07** bedazed
drunken, smitten **08** obsessed
09 bedazzled, bewitched, stupefied
10 bowled over, hypnotized,
infatuated, spellbound **11** intoxicated

bespatter
04 dash, drop, soil **05** bemud, dirty,
smear, spray, stain **06** bedash, befoam
defame, shower, splash **07** asperse,
scatter, spatter, splodge **08** splatter,
sprinkle

bespeak
04 show **05** imply **06** attest, denote,
engage, evince, reveal **07** betoken,
display, exhibit, signify, suggest
08 evidence, indicate, proclaim, spea
for **11** demonstrate

bespoke
◇ *anagram indicator*
09 dedicated **10** tailor-made

best
02 A1 **03** ace, cap, top **04** beat, lick,
most, pick, plum, rout, star, tops
05 cream, élite, first, ideal, jewel,
prime, worst **06** choice, defeat, finest
flower, hammer, outwit, subdue,
thrash, utmost **07** clobber, conquer,
greatly, hardest, highest, largest,
leading, optimal, optimum, outplay,
perfect, premium, supreme, the tops,
trounce **08** foremost, greatest,
outsmart, overcome, peerless,
ultimate, vanquish **09** damnedest,
excellent, extremely, favourite, first-
rate, highlight, matchless, nonpareil,
number one, overpower, overwhelm,
slaughter, supremely, top-drawer,
worthiest **10** annihilate, first-class, pre
eminent, unbeatable, unequalled,
unrivalled **11** excellently, matchlessly,
outstanding, superlative, unsurpassed
12 incomparable, incomparably,
second to none **13** exceptionally, have
the edge on, one in a million,
outstandingly, superlatively,
unsurpassedly **14** crème de la crème,
get the better of, greatest effort, record
breaking

bestial
04 rude, vile **05** cruel, feral, gross
06 animal, brutal, carnal, savage,
sordid **07** beastly, brutish, inhuman,
sensual **08** barbaric, degraded,
depraved **09** barbarous, unrefined

bestiality
07 cruelty **08** savagery **09** barbarism

10 inhumanity, sordidness **15** animal behaviour

bestir
05 exert **06** arouse, awaken, incite **07** actuate, animate **08** activate, energize, motivate **09** galvanize, stimulate

bestow
02 do **04** give **05** allot, award, endow, grant, spend, wreak **06** accord, commit, confer, donate, estate, impart, lavish **07** dispose, entrust, present **08** bequeath, transmit **09** apportion **11** communicate

bestride
05 cross **06** defend **07** command, protect **08** dominate, straddle **10** bestraddle, overshadow, sit astride **12** stand astride

bestseller
03 hit **07** success, triumph **08** smash hit **11** blockbuster, brand leader

bestselling
03 top **06** famous **07** leading, popular **08** unbeaten

bet
02 go **03** bid, lay, pot, put **04** ante, back, hold, punt, risk, view **05** place, pound, stake, wager **06** be sure, chance, choice, expect, gamble, hazard, notion, option, pledge, theory **07** feeling, flutter, lottery, opinion, venture **09** be certain, intuition, judgement, speculate, viewpoint **10** conviction, impression, prediction **11** alternative, be convinced, point of view, speculation **12** have a flutter, play for money **14** course of action, not be surprised

See also **gambling**

Bets and betting systems include:
03 TAB
04 tote
06 double, parlay, roll-up, tierce, treble, triple, Yankee
07 à cheval, each way
08 ante-post, forecast, perfecta, quinella, trifecta
09 on the nose, quadrella
10 martingale, pari-mutuel, superfecta, sweepstake
11 accumulator, daily double
13 double or quits

• **accept bet**
03 see

betel
03 pan **04** paan, pawn, siri **05** sirih

bête noire
04 bane **05** curse **07** bugbear, pet hate **08** anathema, aversion **11** abomination, pet aversion **14** thorn in the side **15** thorn in the flesh

betide
05 ensue, occur **06** befall, betime, chance, happen **07** develop **08** overtake **09** supervene, take place

betoken
04 bode, mark, mean, sign **05** augur, token **06** betide, denote, signal **07** bespeak, declare, portend, presage, promise, signify, suggest **08** evidence, forebode, indicate, manifest **09** represent, symbolize **13** prognosticate

betray
03 dob **04** dupe, sell, shop, show, tell **05** abuse, cross, dob in, grass, peach, rat on **06** bewray, delude, desert, expose, reveal, rumble, tell on, unmask **07** abandon, confess, deceive, divulge, forsake, let down, let slip, mislead, sell out, split on, stool on **08** disclose, give away, go back on, inform on, manifest, renege on, squeal on **09** play false, walk out on **11** double-cross, turn traitor **12** be disloyal to, bring to light **13** stab in the back **14** be unfaithful to, break faith with

betrayal
05 abuse **06** duping **07** perfidy, sell-out, treason **08** giveaway, trickery **09** deception, duplicity, falseness, treachery **10** disloyalty **11** double-cross **13** breaking faith, double-dealing, stab in the back **14** double-crossing, traitorousness, unfaithfulness

betrayer
05 grass, Judas **07** stoolie, traitor **08** apostate, deceiver, informer, renegade, traditor, treacher **09** treachour **10** supergrass **11** backstabber, conspirator, stool pigeon **13** double-crosser, whistle-blower

betrothal
03 vow **04** vows **05** troth **07** promise **08** affiance, contract, espousal, handfast **09** assurance **10** engagement **11** fiançailles, handfasting, hand-promise, subarration, trothplight **12** subarrhation

betrothed
05 troth **07** assured, engaged, pledged **08** espoused, promised **09** affianced, combinate **10** contracted **11** trothplight **13** trothplighted

better
03 cap, top **04** beat, best, mend, well **05** cured, finer, outdo, raise **06** bigger, enrich, exceed, fitter, healed, larger, longer, punter, reform **07** correct, enhance, forward, further, gambler, greater, improve, promote, rectify, surpass **08** improved, outstrip, overtake, restored, stronger, superior, worthier **09** a cut above, healthier, improve on, improving, on the mend, recovered **10** ameliorate, make better, preferable, recovering, speculator, surpassing **11** more fitting, progressing **12** more valuable **14** fully recovered, more acceptable **15** go one better than, of higher quality

betterment
10 enrichment **11** advancement, edification, enhancement, furtherance, improvement, melioration **12** amelioration

betting *see* **bet**

between
◇ *insertion indicator*
03 bet, mid **04** amid **05** among, inter- **06** amidst **07** amongst, halfway **11** in the middle **13** in the middle of

bevel
04 bias, cant, tilt **05** angle, basil, bezel, mitre, slant, slope, splay **07** chamfer, oblique **08** diagonal

beverage
04 brew **05** drink **06** liquid, liquor **07** draught, potable **08** ambrosia, potation **11** refreshment
See also **drink**

bevy
04 band, gang, pack **05** bunch, crowd, flock, group, troop **06** gaggle, throng, troupe **07** company **08** assembly **09** gathering **10** collection

bewail
03 rue **04** keen, moan **05** mourn **06** bemoan, lament, regret, repent **07** cry over, deplore **08** sigh over **10** grieve over, sorrow over **14** beat your breast

beware
04 cave, mind, shun, ware **05** avoid, watch **06** be wary, caveat **07** look out, mind out **08** take heed, watch out **09** be careful **10** be cautious **12** guard against, steer clear of **13** be on your guard

bewilder
◇ *containment indicator*
04 daze, faze, lose, maze **05** amaze, floor, mix up, stump **06** baffle, bemuse, fickle, muddle, puzzle, wander, wilder **07** buffalo, bumbaze, confuse, flummox, mystify, nonplus, perplex, stupefy **08** confound **09** bamboozle, disorient, obfuscate **10** disconcert, take to town **12** tie up in knots

bewildered
◇ *anagram indicator*
04 lost, will, wull **05** at sea, dizzy, fazed, muzzy **06** fogged, tavert **07** baffled, bemazed, bemused, floored, mixed up, muddled, pixy-led, puzzled, stunned, taivert **08** all at sea, confused, jiggered, pathless, wandered **09** flummoxed, mystified, perplexed, pixilated, surprised, trackless, uncertain **10** bamboozled, distracted, nonplussed, pixillated, speechless, taken aback **11** disoriented

bewildering
05 dizzy **07** amazing, cryptic **08** baffling, puzzling **09** confusing, enigmatic **10** astounding, mysterious, mystifying, perplexing, surprising **12** unfathomable

bewilderment

03 awe, fog **04** daze, maze **05** amaze
06 muddle, puzzle **07** mizmaze
08 surprise **09** amazement, confusion, égarement, puzzledom
10 amazedness, perplexity, puzzlement **11** uncertainty
12 stupefaction **13** disconcertion, mystification **14** disorientation

bewitch

03 hex, obi **04** obia, take, wish
05 charm, obeah, witch **06** allure, hoodoo, obsess, seduce, strike, voodoo, voudou **07** beguile, delight, enchant, enthral, glamour, possess **08** elf-shoot, entrance, forspeak, intrigue, overlook, sirenize, transfix **09** captivate, enrapture, ensorcell, fascinate, forespeak, hypnotize, mesmerize, spellbind, tantalize

beyond

04 over, past **05** above, after, ayont, trans- **08** away from **09** apart from, later than, upwards of **10** remote from
11 further than, greater than **12** out of range of, out of reach of **14** on the far side of

Bhutan

03 BTN

bias

04 bent, load, sway, warp **05** angle, cross, poise, slant, twist **06** colour, earwig, weight **07** bigotry, distort, leaning, oblique **08** diagonal, jaundice, penchant, tendency
09 influence, parti pris, prejudice, preoccupy, slantwise **10** distortion, partiality, partialize, predispose, prepossess, proclivity, propensity, unfairness **11** favouritism, inclination, intolerance, load the dice, prejudicate
12 one-sidedness, predilection, stereotyping **13** prepossession

biased

◊ *anagram indicator*
04 skew **06** angled, loaded, skewed, swayed, unfair, warped **07** bigoted, partial, slanted, twisted **08** one-sided, partisan, partizan, weighted
09 blinkered, distorted, jaundiced
10 influenced, interested, prejudiced, subjective, tendential **11** predisposed, prejudicate, tendencious, tendentious
12 prepossessed **14** discriminatory

bib

04 pout **05** Bible, blain **06** brassy, feeder

Bible

02 NT, OT **03** ABC, Bib, law **05** canon
06 fardel, manual, omasum, primer
07 Gospels, letters, lexicon
08 epistles, good book, handbook, holy writ, prophets, textbook, writings **09** Apocrypha, authority, companion, directory, guidebook, Holy Bible, manyplies **10** dictionary, Pentateuch, psalterium, revelation, Scriptures **12** encyclopedia,
New Testament, Old Testament
13 reference book **14** holy Scriptures

See also **plague**; **scripture**

08 Bethesda, Dalmatia, Damascus, Golgotha, Gomorrah, Mt Ararat, Nazareth
09 Bethlehem, Jerusalem, Palestine
10 Alexandria, Gethsemane
11 River Jordan
12 Garden of Eden, Sea of Galilee

See also **apocryphal**

bibliography
06 record **08** book list **09** catalogue
10 bibliology **11** bibliotheca, list of books

bicker
03 row **04** spar, spat **05** argue, clash, fight, scrap **06** patter, quiver
07 dispute, fall out, glitter, quarrel, wrangle **08** disagree, squabble
09 altercate

bickering
06 at odds **07** arguing **08** clashing
09 scrapping **10** squabbling
11 disagreeing, quarrelling **13** at loggerheads **15** like cats and dogs

bicycle
04 bike **05** cycle, wheel **10** pedal cycle

Bicycles include:
03 BMX
04 push, quad, solo
05 hobby, racer
06 safety, tandem
07 chopper, Raleigh®, touring
08 draisene, draisine, exercise, kangaroo, mountain, ordinary, push-bike, tricycle, unicycle
09 recumbent
10 all-terrain, boneshaker, dandy-horse, fairy-cycle, fixed-wheel, stationary, two-wheeler, velocipede
12 mountain bike
13 penny farthing
14 all-terrain bike

Bicycle parts include:
03 hub
04 bell, fork, gear, lamp, pump, tire, tyre
05 brake, chain, crank, frame, pedal, spoke, wheel
06 dynamo, fender, hanger, pulley, saddle, spokes
07 bar ends, carrier, headset, hub gear, pannier, rim tape, toe clip, tool bag, top tube
08 aero bars, cassette, chainset, crankset, crossbar, down tube, head tube, mudguard, rim brake, rod brake, seat post, seat tube, sprocket, wheel nut, wheel rim
09 brake shoe, chain link, chain ring, disc brake, drum brake, gear cable, gear lever, gearwheel, inner tube, kickstand, prop stand, reflector, seat stays, tyre valve, wheel lock
10 brake block, brake cable, brake lever, chain guard, chain guide, chain stays, chain wheel, crank lever, derailleur, drive train,

handlebars, seat pillar, stabilizer, Woods® valve
11 gear shifter, lamp bracket, Presta® valve, roller chain, speedometer
12 brake caliper, coaster brake, diamond frame, spoke nipples, steering head, steering tube, stirrup guide, wheel bearing, wheel spindle
13 bottom bracket, clipless pedal, freewheel unit, handlebar stem, Schrader® valve, shock absorber, sprocket wheel
14 drop handlebars, side-pull brakes

bid
02 go **03** ask, say, sum, try, vie
04 bode, call, pray, tell, wave, wish
05 greet, offer, order, price, put up
06 amount, charge, demand, desire, direct, effort, enjoin, invite, submit, summon, tender **07** advance, attempt, call for, command, proffer, propose, request, require, solicit, venture
08 instruct, proposal **09** endeavour
10 put forward, submission

• **no bid**
04 pass

biddable
04 meek **08** amenable, obedient
09 compliant, easy-going, malleable, tractable **10** submitting **11** subservient

bidding
04 call **05** order **06** behest, charge, demand, desire **07** command, request, summons **09** direction **10** injunction, invitation **11** instruction, requirement

• **bidding system**
04 Acol **06** canapé **09** blackwood

big
02 OS **03** fat **04** huge, loud, main, mega, tall, vast **05** adult, beefy, build, bulky, burly, elder, giant, great, hefty, jumbo, large, major, obese, older, stout
06 brawny, bumper, famous, mature, pile up, valued **07** eminent, grown-up, hulking, immense, leading, mammoth, massive, pompous, radical, salient, serious, sizable, weighty **08** boastful, colossal, critical, enormous, generous, gigantic, gracious, muscular, powerful, sizeable, spacious, whopping
09 cavernous, corpulent, extensive, ginormous, humungous, important, momentous, principal, prominent, unselfish, well-built, well-known
10 benevolent, extra large, munificent, noteworthy, voluminous
11 fundamental, influential, kind-hearted, magnanimous, outstanding, pretentious, significant, substantial
12 considerable **13** distinguished

bigheaded
04 vain **05** cocky **07** haughty, stuck-up **08** arrogant **09** conceited **11** swell-headed **12** vainglorious **13** self-important, self-satisfied, swollen-headed **14** full of yourself

bigot
03 MCP **06** racist, sexist, zealot

07 fanatic **08** partisan **09** dogmatist, homophobe, sectarian **10** chauvinist
11 religionist

bigoted
06 biased, closed, narrow, swayed, warped **07** partial, twisted
08 dogmatic, one-sided **09** blinkered, fanatical, hidebound, illiberal, jaundiced, obstinate **10** influenced, intolerant, prejudiced **11** opinionated
12 narrow-minded

bigotry
04 bias **06** racism, sexism **08** jingoism
09 dogmatism, injustice, prejudice, racialism **10** chauvinism, fanaticism, partiality, unfairness **11** intolerance, religionism **12** sectarianism
14 discrimination

bigwig
03 nob, VIP **04** tuan **05** mogul, swell
06 big gun, honcho, worthy **07** big shot, notable **08** big noise, somebody
09 big cheese, celebrity, dignitary, personage **10** panjandrum
11 heavyweight

bijou
03 wee **04** tiny **05** jewel, small
06 little, minute, petite, pocket
07 compact, trinket **10** diminutive

bile
04 gall **05** anger **06** choler, spleen
07 rancour **09** bad temper, ill-humour, testiness **10** bitterness, melancholy
11 peevishness, short temper
12 irascibility, irritability

bilge
03 rot **04** crap **05** balls, trash, tripe
06 drivel, faddle, hot air, piffle
07 rubbish, twaddle **08** blethers, claptrap, cobblers, nonsense, tommyrot **09** gibberish, poppycock
10 codswallop **12** clamjamphrie

bilious
04 edgy, sick **05** cross, lurid, testy
06 crabby, garish, grumpy, queasy, sickly **07** grouchy, peevish
08 choleric **09** crotchety, irritable, nauseated **10** disgusting, nauseating, out of sorts **11** bad-tempered, ill-humoured, ill-tempered **13** short-tempered

bilk
02 do **03** con **05** cheat, elude, sting, trick **06** diddle, fleece **07** deceive, defraud, do out of, swindle
09 bamboozle **14** pull a fast one on

bill
02 a/c, ad, ax **03** acc, act, axe, fin, IOU, neb, nib, tab **04** acct, beak, chit, note, post **05** check, debit, flyer, score, tally
06 advert, charge, notice, poster
07 account, charges, handout, invoice, leaflet, measure, placard, promote, rostrum, statute, William **08** announce, banknote, bulletin, circular, handbill, mandible, playbill, proposal
09 advertise, list costs, programme, reckoning, statement **10** broadsheet,

give notice **11** legislation
12 announcement **13** advertisement,
send an account, send an invoice
14 send a statement
• **bill of sale**
02 bs

billet
03 job **04** post **05** berth, lodge, put up,
rooms **06** casern, coupon, office
07 caserne, housing, lodging, quarter,
station **08** barracks, position, quarters
09 situation **10** employment,
occupation **11** accommodate
13 accommodation **14** living quarters

billow
04 mass, rise, roil, roll, rush, wave
05 bulge, cloud, flood, heave, surge,
swell **06** expand **07** balloon, breaker,
fill out, puff out **08** undulate

billowy
06 waving **07** heaving, rolling, surging,
tossing **08** rippling, swelling, swirling
09 billowing **10** undulating

Billy
06 Bunter

bin
03 box **04** bing, bunk **05** chest
06 basket, bucket, holder **07** wheelie
09 container **10** garbage can,
receptacle **11** waste basket

bind
03 oop, oup, tie, wap **04** bond, bore,
gage, gird, hold, hole, join, lash, pain,
rope, spot, tape, whip, wrap, yoke
05 chain, clamp, cover, dress, force,
impel, leash, stick, strap, thirl, tie up,
truss, unify, unite **06** attach, compel,
embale, fasten, fetter, hamper, objure,
oblige, secure, swathe, tether
07 astrict, bandage, combine, confine,
dilemma, embrace, impasse, require,
shackle **08** astringe, enfetter, nuisance,
quandary, restrain, restrict **09** colligate,
constrain, tight spot **10** close ranks,
difficulty, irritation **11** necessitate,
predicament **12** knit together, pull
together **13** embarrassment,
inconvenience, pain in the neck, stand
together

binding
04 tape, yapp **05** cover, tight, valid
06 border, edging, strict **07** bandage
08 covering, ligation, rigorous,
trimming, wrapping **09** mandatory,
necessary, permanent, requisite,
stringent **10** compulsory, conclusive,
obligatory **11** irrevocable,
unalterable, unbreakable
12 indissoluble

bindweed
08 bearbine, bellbind, withwind,
woodbind, woodbine **09** withywind
11 convolvulus

binge
02 do **03** jag **04** bout, orgy, sesh, toot,
tout **05** beano, blind, fling, spree
06 bender, guzzle **07** blow-out,
session

biochemistry

Biochemists include:

04 Abel (John Jacob), Cori (Carl), Duve
(Christian de)
05 Boyer (Herbert), Brown (Rachel
Fuller), Chain (Sir Ernst B), Doisy
(Edward A), Krebs (Sir Edwin G),
Krebs (Sir Hans), Monod (Jacques),
Moore (Stanford)
06 Asimov (Isaac), Beadle (George),
Domagk (Gerhard), Martin
(Archer), Mullis (Kary B), Oparin
(Alexandr), Perutz (Max), Porter
(Rodney R), Sanger (Frederick)
07 Edelman (Gerald M), Fischer
(Edmond H), Hopkins (Sir
Frederick), Khorana (Har Gobind),
Stanley (Wendell M), Waksman
(Selman), Warburg (Otto)
08 Anfinsen (Christian B), Chargaff
(Erwin), Kornberg (Arthur),
Meyerhof (Otto), Northrop (John
H), Weinberg (Robert)
09 Bergström (Sune), Butenandt
(Adolf), Michaelis (Leonor)
11 Hoppe-Seyler (Felix)
12 Szent-Györgyi (Albert von)

See also **biology**

biography
02 CV **03** bio **04** biog, life **05** diary
06 biopic, letter, memoir, record,
résumé **07** account, diaries, history,
journal, letters, memoirs, profile
08 journals **09** life story
11 hagiography **12** recollection
13 autobiography, prosopography,
recollections **15** curriculum vitae

Biographers include:

05 Spark (Dame Muriel), Weems
(Mason Locke)
06 Aubrey (John), Morley (John,
Viscount), Motion (Andrew),
Napier (Mark), Wilson (Andrew
Norman)
07 Ackroyd (Peter), Bedford (Sybille),
Bolitho (Hector), Boswell (James),
Debrett (John), Ellmann (Richard),
Holroyd (Michael), Lubbock
(Percy), Pearson (Hesketh), Sitwell
(Sacheverell)
08 Lockhart (John Gibson), Plutarch,
Strachey (Lytton)
09 Aldington (Richard), Kingsmill
(Hugh), Suetonius

biology

Biological terms include:

02 GM
03 DNA, RNA
04 cell, gene
05 class, genus, virus
06 coccus, enzyme, family, fossil,
tissue
07 meiosis, microbe, mitosis, nucleus,
osmosis, protein, species
08 bacillus, bacteria, cultivar, genetics,
membrane, molecule, mutation,
organism, parasite, ribosome, stem
cell

09 amino acid, cell cycle, corpuscle,
cytoplasm, diffusion, ecosystem,
ectoplasm, evolution, food chain,
Mendelism, pollution, reticulum,
symbiosis
10 alpha helix, chromosome,
extinction, Lamarckism,
metabolism, parasitism,
protoplasm
11 Haeckel's law, homeostasis,
respiration
12 conservation, mitochondria,
reproduction
13 flora and fauna, micro-organism,
mitochondrion
14 Golgi apparatus, photosynthesis
15 nuclear membrane, ribonucleic
acid

Biologists and naturalists include:

03 His (Wilhelm)
04 Axel (Richard), Baer (Karl Ernst
von), Berg (Paul), Hess (Walter),
Hunt (Tim), Katz (Sir Bernard), Koch
(Ludwig), Lyon (Mary)
05 Arber (Werner), Bacon (Francis,
Viscount), Bates (Henry Walter),
Beebe (William), Bruce (Sir David),
Crick (Francis), Golgi (Camillo),
Lewis (Edward B), Luria (Salvador),
Lwoff (André), Nurse (Sir Paul M),
Sabin (Albert), Scott (Sir Peter),
Sharp (Phillip), Smith (Hamilton),
White (Gilbert)
06 Altman (Sidney), Anning (Mary),
Bishop (Michael), Blobel (Günter),
Boveri (Theodor), Buffon (George-
Louis, Comte de), Cairns (Hugh),
Cannon (Walter), Carson (Rachel),
Claude (Albert), Darwin (Charles),
Friend (Charlotte), Huxley (Sir
Julian), Huxley (T H), Isaacs (Alick),
Kandel (Eric), Lartet (Edouard),
Morgan (Thomas Hunt), Palade
(George), Sloane (Sir Hans), Varmus
(Harold), Watson (James), Wilson
(Edward)
07 Adamson (Joy), Agassiz (Louis),
Andrews (Roy), Beneden
(Edouard), Brenner (Sydney),
Dawkins (Richard), Driesch (Hans),
Durrell (Gerald), Epstein (Sir
Anthony), Flavell (Richard), Gilbert
(Walter), Haeckel (Ernst), Haldane
(J B S), Hershey (A D), Jackson
(Barbara, Lady), Kendrew (Sir John),
Lamarck (Jean), Lubbock (Sir John),
Nathans (Daniel), Pasteur (Louis),
Roberts (Richard), Steptoe
(Patrick), Wallace (Alfred)
08 Cousteau (Jacques), Delbrück
(Max), Flemming (Walther),
Franklin (Rosalind), Hartwell (Lee),
Humboldt (Alexander, Baron von),
Jeffreys (Sir Alec), Linnaeus (Carl),
Li Shizen, Margulis (Lynn),
Meselson (Matthew), Milstein
(Cesar), Purkinje (Jan), Sielmann
(Heinz), Starling (Ernest), Tonegawa
(Susumu), Weismann (August)
09 Lederberg (Joshua), Schaudinn
(Fritz), Wieschaus (Eric)

10 Ingen-Housz (Jan)
11 Deisenhofer (Johan),
Leeuwenhoek (Antoni van),
Metchnikoff (Elie), **Ramón y Cajal**
(Santiago), **Spallanzani** (Lazaro)
12 Attenborough (Sir David),
Maynard Smith (John)
13 Du Bois-Reymond (Emil Heinrich)
14 Levi-Montalcini (Rita)
15 Nusslein-Volhard (Christiane)

See also **bacteriology; biochemistry;
palaeontologist; physiology**

birch
03 rod **04** birk, flog, twig **05** swish
06 Betula

bird
03 jug **04** avis, babe, gaol, girl, jail,
nick, quod, shop, stir, time **05** choky,
clink **06** chokey, lumber, prison
07 college, slammer **10** girlfriend
See also **animal; chicken; duck; game;
hen; poultry**

Birds include:

02 ka
03 ani, auk, bat, cob, daw, doo, emu,
hae, hen, jay, kea, kia, mag, maw,
mew, moa, owl, pie, roc, tit, tui
04 barb, chat, cirl, cobb, cock, coot,
crow, dodo, dove, duck, emeu,
erne, eyas, fowl, gled, guan, gull,
hawk, hern, huia, ibis, jynx, kagu,
kaka, kite, kiwi, knot, kora, kuku,
lark, loom, loon, lory, mina, myna,
nene, nyas, pavo, pern, pica, piet,
pyat, pyet, pyot, rail, rhea, rook, ruff,
runt, ruru, rype, shag, skua, smee,
sora, swan, taha, teal, tern, tody,
weka, wren, xema, yite
05 agami, ariel, booby, capon, chick,
crane, diver, eagle, egret, eider,
finch, fleet, flier, galah, glede,
goose, grebe, heron, hobby,
macaw, mynah, ousel, piper, pipit,
pitta, potoo, quail, raven, robin,
scops, snipe, solan, squab, stilt,
stork, swift, tewit, twite, vireo,
wader
06 avocet, bantam, barbet, budgie,
bulbul, canary, chough, condor,
cuckoo, curlew, cushat, darter,
dipper, drongo, dunlin, falcon,
fulmar, gannet, godwit, grouse,
hoopoe, houdan, jabiru, jacana,
kakapo, linnet, magpie, martin,
merlin, mesite, motmot, oriole,
osprey, parrot, peahen, peewit,
petrel, pigeon, plover, puffin, pullet,
raptor, redcap, roller, sea-mew,
shrike, siskin, takahe, thrush, tom-
tit, toucan, trogon, turaco, turkey,
yaffle, zoozoo
07 antbird, apteryx, babbler, barn owl,
bittern, bluecap, blue jay, bluetit,
bullbat, bunting, bustard, buzzard,
chicken, coal-tit, cotinga, courser,
cowbird, creeper, dottrel, dunnock,
fantail, finfoot, goshawk, grackle,
halcyon, harrier, hoatzin, jacamar,
jackdaw, kestrel, lapwing, leghorn,
limpkin, mallard, manakin,

moorhen, mudlark, oilbird, ostrich,
peacock, pelican, penguin,
phoenix, pintail, poultry, quetzal,
redpoll, redwing, rooster,
ruddock, seagull, seriema,
skimmer, skylark, spadger, sparrow,
sunbird, swallow, tanager, tiercel,
tinamou, titlark, touraco, vulture,
wagtail, warbler, waxbill, wrybill,
wryneck
08 aasvogel, accentor, adjutant,
aigrette, bee-eater, bellbird,
blackcap, bobolink, cockatoo,
currasow, dabchick, dotterel, fish-
hawk, flamingo, great tit, grosbeak,
hernshaw, hornbill, landrail,
laverock, leafbird, lorikeet,
lovebird, lyrebird, megapode, myna
bird, nightjar, nuthatch, ovenbird,
ox-pecker, palmchat, parakeet,
pheasant, puffbird, rainbird,
redshank, redstart, ringtail,
screamer, sea eagle, shoebill,
starling, tapaculo, water-hen,
whimbrel, white-eye, woodcock
09 aepyornis, albatross, bald eagle,
bergander, blackbird, blackhead,
bowerbird, broadbill, bullfinch,
cassowary, chaffinch, chickadee,
cockatiel, cormorant, corncrake,
eider duck, fairy tern, fieldfare,
frogmouth, gerfalcon, gnateater,
goldfinch, goosander, guillemot,
jack-snipe, kittiwake, little owl,
merganser, mollymawk,
mousebird, mynah bird, nighthawk,
ossifrage, partridge, peregrine,
phalarope, ptarmigan, razorbill,
sandpiper, scrub-bird, sheldrake,
thornbill, trumpeter, turnstone,
wind-hover
10 budgerigar, chiff-chaff, fledgeling,
flycatcher, goatsucker,
gobemouche, greenfinch,
greenshank, guinea fowl,
hammerhead, harpy eagle,
honeyeater, honeyguide,
kingfisher, kookaburra, nutcracker,
sanderling, sandgrouse,
shearwater, sheathbill, song thrush,
sunbittern, tropicbird, turtledove,
wattlebird, woodpecker, wood
pigeon
11 butcherbird, frigatebird, golden
eagle, hummingbird, mockingbird,
nightingale, plantcutter, reed-
warbler, snow bunting, song
sparrow, sparrowhawk, stone-
curlew, storm petrel, thunderbird,
tree-creeper, woodcreeper, wood-
swallow
12 adjutant bird, cuckoo-roller, diving
petrel, flowerpecker, golden plover,
honeycreeper, missel-thrush,
mistle-thrush, sedge warbler,
yellowhammer
13 archaeopteryx, barnacle goose,
oystercatcher, secretary bird,
willow warbler
14 bird of paradise, plains wanderer
15 blue-footed booby, passenger
pigeon, peregrine falcon

Birds of prey include:

03 owl
04 erne, hawk, kite, pern
05 eagle, hobby
06 falcon, lanner, merlin, osprey, raptor
07 barn owl, buzzard, goshawk,
harrier, hawk owl, kestrel, red kite
08 bateleur, berghaan, duck-hawk,
eagle owl, fish-hawk, Scops owl,
sea eagle, spar-hawk, tawny owl
09 bald eagle, black kite, eagle-hawk,
fish eagle, gyrfalcon, little owl,
marsh hawk, peregrine, stone hawk
10 harpy eagle, hen harrier, tawny
eagle
11 booted eagle, chicken hawk,
Cooper's hawk, golden eagle,
sparrowhawk, stone falcon
12 great grey owl, honey buzzard,
long-eared owl, marsh harrier
13 American eagle, Iceland falcon,
imperial eagle, lesser kestrel, pallid
harrier, secretary bird, short-eared
owl
14 short-toed eagle
15 Montagu's harrier, peregrine falcon,
red-footed falcon

Flightless birds include:

03 emu
04 dodo, emeu, kiwi, rhea, weka
06 kakapo, ratite, takahe
07 ostrich, penguin
08 great auk, notornis
09 cassowary, owl-parrot, solitaire

Mythical birds include:

03 fum, roc, rok, ruc
04 fung, huma, rukh
07 phoenix
08 whistler
09 impundulu
11 thunderbird
12 bird of wonder

Seabirds include:

03 auk, cob, maw, mew
04 cobb, guga, gull, shag, skua, tern,
Xema
05 solan
06 fulmar, gannet, petrel, puffin
07 pickmaw, seagull
08 comorant
09 black tern, great skua, guillemot,
kittiwake, little auk, mallemuck,
razorbill, swart-back
10 Arctic skua, Arctic tern, common
gull, common tern, little gull, little
tern, saddleback, solan goose
11 herring gull, Iceland gull, roseate
tern, Sabine's gull, storm petrel
12 glaucous gull, Leach's petrel,
pomarine skua, sandwich tern
14 black guillemot, long-tailed skua,
Manx shearwater
15 black-backed gull, black-headed gull

Wading birds include:

03 ree
04 hern, ibis, knot, ruff
05 crake, crane, heron, reeve, snipe,
stilt, stint, stork

06 avocet, curlew, dunlin, godwit, plover
07 bittern, bustard, lapwing
08 dotterel, flamingo, redshank, whimbrel, woodcock
09 dowitcher, grey heron, phalarope, sandpiper, turnstone
10 greenshank, sanderling
11 little stint, stone curlew
12 golden plover, great bustard, ringed plover
13 little bustard, oystercatcher

• **birds**
04 Aves **05** ornis

birth
04 dawn, line, race, rise, root, seed
05 blood, house, start, stock
06 advent, family, labour, origin, source, strain **07** arrival, descent, genesis, lineage, origins **08** ancestry, breeding, delivery, nativity, pedigree
09 beginning, emergence, genealogy, parentage **10** appearance, background, childbirth, derivation, extraction **11** confinement, parturition
12 commencement, fountainhead
13 starting-point

Birth flowers:

04 rose
05 aster, daisy, holly, poppy
06 cosmos, violet
07 jonquil
08 hawthorn, larkspur, primrose, snowdrop, sweet pea
09 calendula, carnation, gladiolus, narcissus, water lily
10 poinsettia
11 honeysuckle
12 morning glory
13 chrysanthemum
15 lily of the valley

Birth stones:

04 opal, ruby
05 pearl, topaz
06 garnet, zircon
07 diamond, emerald, peridot
08 amethyst, sapphire, sardonyx
09 moonstone, turquoise
10 aquamarine, bloodstone, tourmaline
11 alexandrite

• **give birth to**
03 cub, ean, kid, lay, pig, pup **04** bear, drop, fawn, foal, have, lamb, yean
05 calve, found, throw **06** create, farrow, kitten, litter, mother **08** initiate
09 establish **10** bring forth, give rise to, inaugurate **12** cause to exist

birthday
03 dob **10** day of birth **11** anniversary

birthmark
04 mole **05** naeve, nevus, patch
06 naevus **07** blemish **10** beauty spot, mother spot **13** discoloration, port-wine stain **14** strawberry mark

birthplace
02 bp **03** b pl **04** home, root **05** fount, roots **06** cradle, source **08** home town

10 fatherland, incunables, incunabula, native town, provenance **12** place of birth **13** mother country, native country, place of origin

birthright
03 due **06** legacy **08** birthdom
09 privilege **11** inheritance, prerogative

biscuit
04 bake, cake **05** biccy **06** bickie

Biscuits include:

03 dog, nut, sea, tea
04 kiss, Nice, puff, rice, rusk, ship, snap, tack, thin, Twix®, wine
05 Marie, ship's, wafer, water
06 cookie, hob-nob, Kit-Kat®, parkin, perkin
07 Bourbon, cracker, fig roll, Gold Bar®, iced gem, Lincoln, oatcake, Penguin®, pretzel, ratafia, rich tea, saltine
08 biscotto, captain's, cracknel, flapjack, hardtack, macaroon, Zwieback
09 Abernethy, Breakaway®, chocolate, digestive, four-by-two, garibaldi, ginger nut, jaffa cake, party ring, petit four, pink wafer, shortcake
10 Bath Oliver, Blue Riband®, brandy snap, butter-bake, crispbread, dunderfunk, florentine, gingersnap, malted milk, shortbread, Wagon Wheel®
11 brown George, fly cemetery, soda cracker, squashed fly
12 cream cracker, custard cream, jammie dodger, langue de chat
14 gingerbread man

• **soften biscuit**
04 dunk

bisect
◇ *insertion indicator*
04 fork **05** cross, halve, split **06** divide
08 cut in two, separate **09** bifurcate, cut in half, intersect **13** divide into two

bisexual
02 bi **04** AC/DC **07** epicene
11 androgynous, monoclinous
12 ambidextrous, switch hitter
13 hermaphrodite
15 gynandromorphic

bishop
01 B **02** Bp, DD, RR **04** abba, lord
06 exarch, magpie, primus **07** pontiff, prelate, primate **08** diocesan
09 coadjutor, patriarch, suffragan
10 archbishop, episcopant, metropolis
11 intercessor **12** metropolitan
13 spiritual peer **14** vicar-apostolic

Bishops include:

05 Aidan (St), Peter (St)
06 Blaise, Ninian (St), Osmund (St)
07 Ambrose (St), Carroll (John), Hadrian, Patrick (St)
08 Geoffrey (of Monmouth), Holloway (Richard), Nicholas (St), Sheppard (David)

11 Elphinstone (William), Odo of Bayeux

See also **archbishop**

bishopric
03 see **07** diocese, Holy See
10 episcopacy, episcopate
See also **diocese**

bismuth
02 Bi

bison
04 gaur **06** wisent **07** aurochs, bonasus, buffalo **08** bonassus

bit
◇ *hidden indicator*
03 ate, dot, jot, ort, tad **04** atom, chip, curb, dash, doit, drap, drop, haet, hint, iota, lump, mite, part, what, whit
05 chunk, crumb, drill, flake, fleck, grain, piece, scrap, shred, slice, speck, touch, trace **06** cannon, morsel, nibble, pelham, sliver, tittle
07 kenning, portion, segment, snaffle, soupçon, vestige **08** fragment, mouthful, particle **09** scintilla **10** small piece **12** small portion
• **a bit**
04 tick **05** jiffy **06** a while, fairly, minute, moment, rather **07** a little, a moment, not much, not very
08 slightly **10** a short time, few minutes, few moments **12** a little while
• **bit by bit**
06 slowly **08** in stages **09** gradually, piecemeal **10** step by step **14** little by little
• **bit of**
◇ *head selection indicator*
• **last bit of**
◇ *tail selection indicator*

bitch
03 cat, cow, pig **04** moan, slut
05 brach, gripe, harpy, shrew, swine, trial, vixen, whine **06** ordeal, virago, whinge **07** doggess, grumble, torment
08 badmouth, complain **09** criticize, female dog, nightmare **13** find fault with **15** be spiteful about

bitchiness
05 spite, venom **06** malice **07** cruelty
08 meanness **09** cattiness, nastiness
13 maliciousness

bitchy
04 mean **05** catty, cruel, nasty, snide
07 cutting, vicious **08** shrewish, spiteful, venomous, vixenish
09 malicious, rancorous
10 backbiting, vindictive

bite
◇ *containment indicator*
03 bit, eat, nip **04** chew, crop, gnaw, grip, hold, kick, peck, pick, rend, snap, take, tang, tear, work **05** champ, chomp, crush, force, gnash, munch, piece, pinch, power, prick, punch, seize, smart, snack, spice, sting, taste, wound **06** begnaw, crunch, effect, impact, lesion, morsel, nibble, pierce, tingle **07** morsure, remorse

08 mouthful, piquancy, puncture, pungency, smarting, strength
09 influence, light meal, masticate, sharpness, spiciness **10** impression, take effect **11** refreshment

biting
◇ *containment indicator*
03 raw **04** acid, cold, keen, tart
05 acrid, harsh, nippy, sharp **06** bitter, severe, shrewd, toothy **07** caustic, cutting, cynical, hurtful, mordant, nipping, pointed, pungent, vicious
08 freezing, incisive, piercing, scathing, stinging **09** sarcastic, trenchant, vitriolic **10** astringent, mordacious **11** penetrating

bitter
03 ale, raw, sad, wry **04** acid, keen, sore, sour, tart **05** acerb, acidy, acrid, angry, aygre, cruel, eager, harsh, nippy, parky, sharp, tangy, wersh **06** arctic, biting, fierce, morose, porter, savage, severe, sullen, tragic **07** acerbic, caustic, cynical, hostile, intense, painful, pungent, unhappy
08 freezing, piercing, sardonic, scathing, spiteful, stinging, venomous, vinegary, virulent **09** aggrieved, harrowing, indignant, jaundiced, merciless, rancorous, resentful, vitriolic
10 astringent, begrudging, embittered, malevolent, vindictive, wry-mouthed
11 acrimonious, disgruntled, distressing, penetrating, unsweetened
12 freezing cold, gut-wrenching, heart-rending, vituperative
13 disappointing, heartbreaking

bitterly
05 wryly **06** sourly **07** angrily, cruelly
08 bitingly, morosely, savagely, severely, sullenly **09** cynically, hostilely, intensely, painfully **10** grievously, grudgingly, piercingly, scathingly, spitefully, venomously **11** acerbically, caustically, indignantly, rancorously, resentfully, with vitriol **12** begrudgingly, embitteredly, malevolently, sardonically, vindictively **13** acrimoniously, penetratingly **14** vituperatively

bittern
05 Ardea **06** bittor, bittur **07** bittour
08 mire-drum **10** butter-bump
11 mossbluiter **12** bull-of-the-bog

bitterness
04 bite, edge, fell, gall, pain **05** anger, marah, spite, venom **06** enmity, grudge, rancor, spleen **07** acidity, cruelty, iciness, rancour, rawness, sadness, tragedy, vinegar **08** acrimony, coldness, cynicism, distress, ferocity, jaundice, pungency, severity, sourness, tartness, wormwood **09** harshness, hostility, intensity, sharpness, tanginess, virulence **10** acerbity, antagonism, chilliness, frostiness, moroseness, resentment, sullenness **11** indignation, malevolence, painfulness, penetration, unhappiness **12** embitterment, heart-rending **13** heartbreaking
14 disappointment, vindictiveness

bitty
06 broken, fitful **07** scrappy
09 piecemeal **10** disjointed, fragmented, incoherent
12 disconnected

bitumen
03 tar **05** slime **09** albertite, elaterite
11 pissasphalt

bivalve
06 cockle, oyster, tellen, tellin
07 geoduck, scallop, scollop **08** ark-shell **10** otter shell

bizarre
◇ *anagram indicator*
03 odd **05** funny, gonzo, outré, queer, wacky, weird **06** way-out **07** comical, curious, deviant, oddball, offbeat, strange, surreal, unusual **08** abnormal, freakish, peculiar, uncommon
09 eccentric, fantastic, grotesque, left-field, ludicrous **10** off the wall, outlandish, ridiculous **11** extravagant, Pythonesque **13** extraordinary
14 unconventional

bizarrely
◇ *anagram indicator*
05 oddly **07** weirdly **09** comically, curiously, strangely, unusually
10 abnormally, freakishly, peculiarly
11 ludicrously **12** outlandishly, ridiculously **13** extravagantly

blab
04 blat, leak, tell **05** prate **06** gossip, reveal, squeal, tattle **07** blister, divulge, let slip, tattler **08** blurt out, disclose, tattling **11** blow the gaff **15** give the game away

blabber
04 chat **06** babble, gabble, gossip, jabber, witter **07** blather, blether, chatter, prattle, swollen, twattle, twitter

black
01 B **03** bad, dim, sad **04** dark, evil, inky, sick, slae, sloe, vile **05** angry, awful, bleak, cruel, dingy, dirty, dusky, grimy, gross, gungy, muddy, raven, sooty, unlit, wrong **06** bitter, dismal, filthy, gloomy, grotty, grubby, odious, soiled, sombre, sullen, tragic, vulgar, wicked **07** cynical, demonic, heinous, immoral, satanic, stained, Stygian, subfusc, swarthy, unclean, unhappy
08 coloured, devilish, funereal, hopeless, menacing, moonless, mournful, overcast, starless
09 Cimmerian, depressed, malicious, miserable, nefarious, resentful, tasteless, tenebrous **10** depressing, diabolical, fuliginous, in bad taste, lugubrious, malevolent, melancholy, melanistic, nigrescent, pitch-black
11 black as coal, crepuscular, dark-skinned, distressing, threatening
13 unilluminated

Blacks include:
03 jet
04 blae, ebon, jeat
05 dwale, ebony, sable

08 jet-black
09 coal-black

• **black and white**
02 b/w **04** gray, grey **05** plain
07 brocked, brockit, on paper, piebald, printed, pyebald, written **08** clear-cut, definite, distinct, on record
11 categorical, unambiguous, unequivocal, well-defined, written down **12** monochromist **13** pepper-and-salt

• **black eye** *see* eye
• **black out**
03 gag **05** faint **06** censor, darken
07 conceal, cover up, eclipse, pass out
08 collapse, flake out, keel over, suppress, withhold

• **in the black**
03 ban, bar, fly **05** punch, taboo
06 bruise, injure **07** blacken, boycott, embargo, solvent **08** in credit
09 blacklist, out of debt **11** without debt

• **very black**
02 BB **04** inky

blackball
03 ban, bar, pip **04** oust, pill, snub, veto
05 debar, expel **06** reject **07** drum out, exclude, shut out **08** throw out
09 blacklist, ostracize, repudiate
11 vote against

blacken
03 ink, tar **04** cork, soil **05** black, cloud, decry, dirty, libel, smear, smoke, stain, sully, taint **06** besmut, darken, defame, defile, impugn, malign, revile, smudge, vilify **07** detract, nigrify, run down, slander, tarnish **08** besmirch
09 denigrate, discredit, dishonour, make dirty **10** calumniate

blackguard
05 crook, devil, knave, rogue, sweep, swine **06** rascal, rotter, wretch
07 bleeder, bounder, scumbag, stinker, villain **08** blighter **09** miscreant, reprobate, scoundrel **10** vituperate

blackleg
03 leg **04** fink, scab, snob
09 knobstick

blacklist
03 ban, bar **04** snub, veto **05** debar, expel, taboo **06** outlaw, reject
07 boycott, exclude, shut out
08 disallow, preclude **09** ostracize, proscribe, repudiate

blackmail
04 milk **05** black, bleed, chout, exact, force **06** coerce, compel, demand, extort, lean on, ransom, strike
07 bribery, squeeze **08** chantage, exaction, threaten **09** extortion, greenmail, hush money, shakedown
10 pressurize **12** hold to ransom, intimidation **14** put the screws on

blackmailer
07 vampire **08** hijacker **10** highbinder, highjacker **11** bloodsucker, extortioner
12 extortionist

blackout
04 coma **05** faint, swoon **07** cover-up, embargo, secrecy, silence, syncope **08** brownout, oblivion, power cut **10** censorship, flaking-out, passing out **11** concealment, suppression, withholding **12** power failure **15** unconsciousness

blacksmith
06 vulcan **09** hammerman, ironsmith **11** burn-the-wind

bladder
04 swim **05** sound **06** vesica **07** blister, utricle, vesicle **09** cholecyst

blade
03 fan, oar **04** edge, peel, vane, wash **05** float, knife, lance, razor, skate, spear, sword **06** dagger, lamina, paddle, scythe, Toledo **07** bayonet, scalpel, spatula **10** cream-slice, paperknife **11** cutting edge
See also **dagger**; **sword**

blame
03 rap, tax **04** onus, wite, wyte **05** chide, decry, fault, guilt, odium, stick, thank, wight **06** accuse, berate, charge, dirdam, dirdum, injury, rebuke **07** appoint, censure, condemn, pin it on, reproof, reprove, upbraid **08** admonish, berating, reproach, tear into **09** criticism, criticize, dispraise, inculpate, liability, name names, reprehend, reprimand, scapegoat **10** accusation, confounded, disapprove, discommend, find guilty, hold liable **11** culpability **12** condemnation, name and shame **13** find fault with, incrimination, recrimination **14** accountability, responsibility **15** hold accountable, hold responsible

blameless
05 clear **07** perfect, sinless, upright **08** innocent, virtuous, witeless **09** faultless, guiltless, lily-white, stainless **10** inculpable, unblamable, unreproved **11** unblemished **12** irreprovable, without fault **13** above reproach, unimpeachable **14** irreproachable **15** irreprehensible

blameworthy
06 guilty **07** at fault **08** culpable, shameful, unworthy **10** flagitious **11** inexcusable, responsible **12** disreputable, indefensible, reproachable **13** discreditable, reprehensible

blanch
04 boil **05** scald **06** blench, whiten **07** go white, lighten **08** etiolate, grow pale, turn pale **09** turn white **10** become pale, grow pallid **11** become white **12** become pallid

blancmange
04 mold **05** mould **08** flummery

bland
04 dull, flat, mild, weak **05** suave **06** boring, smooth, spammy

07 anodyne, humdrum, insipid, mundane, tedious, vanilla **08** ordinary **09** tasteless **10** antiseptic, monotonous, unexciting **11** flavourless, inoffensive, nondescript, uninspiring **13** characterless, uninteresting

blandishments
05 sooth, spiel **07** blarney, coaxing, fawning, flannel, treacle **08** cajolery, flattery, lipsalve, soft soap **09** agréments, sweet talk, wheedling **10** sycophancy **11** compliments, enticements, inducements **12** ingratiation, inveiglement **14** persuasiveness

blank
03 gap **04** bare, void **05** break, clean, clear, empty, plain, space, white **06** glazed, vacant, vacuum **07** deadpan, vacancy, vacuity, vacuous **08** lifeless, unfilled, unmarked **09** apathetic, emptiness, impassive, unwritten **10** empty space, poker-faced **11** emotionless, indifferent, inscrutable, nothingness **12** uninterested **14** expressionless, without feeling **15** uncomprehending

blanket
04 coat, film, hide, mask **05** bluey, cloak, cloud, cover, layer, manta, quilt, sheet, total **06** afghan, carpet, deaden, global, mantle, muffle, poncho, sarape, serape, stroud **07** coating, conceal, eclipse, obscure, overall, overlay, whittle, wrapper **08** bedcover, coverage, covering, coverlet, envelope, mackinaw, suppress, surround, sweeping, wrapping **09** bedspread, eiderdown, inclusive, wholesale **11** wide-ranging **12** all-embracing, all-inclusive, underblanket **13** comprehensive **14** across-the-board, indiscriminate

blankly
08 vacantly **09** vacuously **10** lifelessly **11** impassively **13** apathetically, emotionlessly, indifferently **14** uninterestedly, without feeling

blare
04 boom, honk, hoot, peal, ring, roar, toot **05** blast, clang **07** boom out, clamour, resound, thunder, trumpet **08** blast out **11** sound loudly

blarney
05 spiel, taffy **06** cajole, sawder **07** coaxing, flannel **08** cajolery, flattery, soft soap **09** sweet talk, wheedling **10** soft sawder, soft sowder **13** blandishments **14** persuasiveness

blasé
04 cool **05** bored, jaded, weary **07** offhand, unmoved **08** lukewarm **09** apathetic, impassive, unexcited **10** nonchalant, phlegmatic, uninspired **11** indifferent, unconcerned, unimpressed **12** uninterested

blaspheme
04 cuss, damn **05** abuse, curse, swear **06** revile **07** profane **08** execrate

09 desecrate, imprecate **10** utter oaths **12** anathematize

blasphemous
07 godless, impious, profane, ungodly **10** irreverent, sulphurous **11** imprecatory, irreligious **12** sacrilegious

blasphemously
09 profanely **12** irreverently **14** sacrilegiously **15** disrespectfully

blasphemy
05 curse, oaths **07** cursing, impiety, outrage **08** swearing **09** expletive, profanity, sacrilege, violation **10** execration, unholiness **11** desecration, impiousness, imprecation, irreverence, profaneness, ungodliness

blast
◇ *anagram indicator*
03 dee, wap **04** bang, blow, bomb, boom, clap, dang, drat, gale, gust, honk, hoot, parp, peal, puff, roar, ruin, rush, shot, slam, toot, tout, waff, wail, zonk **05** blare, burst, clang, crack, crash, pryse, scath, slate, sound, storm, trump, whiff, whift **06** assail, attack, bellow, berate, blow up, blow-up, flatus, flurry, jigger, rebuke, scaith, scathe, scream, shriek, skaith, squall, strike, volley, wuther **07** blaring, blatter, bluster, booming, boom out, clamour, destroy, draught, explode, gun down, reprove, roaring, shatter, tantara, tell off, tempest, thunder, upbraid, whither **08** blare out, demolish, outburst, siderate **09** criticize, discharge, explosion, reprimand, shoot down, tantarara **10** detonation, sideration **12** blow to pieces **13** thunder-stroke

• **blast off**
07 lift off, take off **10** be launched

blasted
◇ *anagram indicator*
05 ruddy **06** cursed, damned, darned **07** flaming **08** annoying, blighted, blooming, dratting, flipping, infernal **10** confounded, unpleasant **12** planet-struck **14** planet-stricken

blatant
04 bald, open **05** naked, overt, sheer **06** arrant, brazen, coarse, full-on, patent **07** glaring, obvious **08** flagrant, hard-core, manifest, outright **09** bald-faced, barefaced, clamorous, obtrusive, out-and-out, prominent, shameless, unashamed **10** pronounced **11** conspicuous, undisguised, unmitigated **12** ostentatious

blatantly
06 openly **08** brazenly, patently **09** glaringly, obviously, out-and-out **10** flagrantly, manifestly **11** shamelessly, unashamedly **13** conspicuously

blaze
03 low **04** beam, boil, burn, fire, glow, lowe, lunt, rage **05** blast, burst, erupt,

flame, flare, flash, glare, gleam, light, shine, shoot **06** blow up, flames, ignite, let fly, let off, see red, seethe, set off **07** bonfire, explode, flare up, flare-up, glitter, inferno **08** be alight, be on fire, outburst, radiance **09** be radiant, catch fire, discharge, explosion, firestorm **10** brilliance **11** be brilliant **13** conflagration **15** burst into flames

blazing
◊ *anagram indicator*
05 angry **06** on fire **07** burning

blazon
05 vaunt **06** flaunt, herald **07** trumpet **08** announce, flourish, proclaim **09** broadcast, celebrate, make known, publicize

bleach
04 fade, pale **06** blanch, whiten **07** lighten **08** decolour, etiolate, make pale, peroxide, turn pale **09** make white, turn white **10** decolorize

bleak
03 raw **04** arid, bare, blae, blay, bley, cold, dark, drab, dull, grim, open **05** ablet, empty, harsh, windy **06** barren, chilly, dismal, dreary, gloomy, leaden, sombre **07** exposed, joyless, spartan **08** desolate, hopeless, soulless, wretched **09** cheerless, desperate, miserable, windswept **10** depressing **11** comfortless, unpromising, unsheltered **12** discouraging, unfavourable **13** disheartening, weather-beaten

bleakly
06 grimly **08** dismally, drearily, gloomily, sombrely **09** joylessly, miserably **10** wretchedly **11** cheerlessly **12** unfavourably **13** unpromisingly

bleary
03 dim **05** tired **06** blurry, cloudy, drowsy, rheumy, watery **07** blurred **09** unfocused **10** bleary-eyed

bleat
03 baa, cry, maa **04** beef, blat, bray, call, moan **05** gripe, whine **06** grouse, kvetch, whinge **07** grumble, whicker **08** complain **09** complaint

bleed
03 run, sap **04** flow, gush, melt, milk, ooze, seep, weep **05** blood, drain, exude, flood, glide, merge, spurt **06** extort, reduce **07** deplete, exhaust, extract, squeeze, suck dry, trickle **08** let blood **09** lose blood, shed blood **10** bleed white **11** extravasate, haemorrhage **12** exsanguinate, phlebotomize

blemish
03 mar **04** blot, blur, flaw, mark, mote, tash, vice, want **05** botch, fault, speck, spoil, stain, sully, taint, touch **06** blotch, damage, deface, defame, defect, impair, smudge **07** tarnish **08** disgrace **09** deformity, disfigure, dishonour **10** compromise **12** imperfection **13** discoloration, disfigurement

03 zit
04 acne, boil, bump, corn, mole, scab, scar, spot, wart
06 bunion, callus, naevus, pimple
07 blister, freckle, pustule, verruca
08 pockmark
09 birthmark, blackhead, carbuncle, chilblain, whitehead
14 strawberry mark

blench
03 shy **05** cower, quail, quake, start, wince **06** falter, flinch, quiver, recoil, shrink **07** shudder **08** draw back, hesitate, pull back

blend
◊ *anagram indicator*
03 fit, mix **04** beat, fuse, meld, melt, stir, suit **05** admix, alloy, match, merge, union, unite, whisk **06** commix, fusion, go with, mingle, set off **07** amalgam, combine, merging, mixture, uniting **08** coalesce, compound, intermix **09** admixture, commingle, composite, contemper, harmonize, synthesis **10** amalgamate, commixture, complement, concoction, go together, go well with, homogenize, intertwine, interweave, synthesize **11** combination, portmanteau, run together **12** amalgamation

bless
04 laud **05** exalt, extol, thank, wound **06** anoint, favour, hallow, honour, ordain, praise, thrash **07** glorify, magnify, worship **08** brandish, dedicate, sanctify **10** consecrate, lay hands on **13** be grateful for, be thankful for, give thanks for
• **bless you**
10 benedicite, Gesundheit

blessed
◊ *anagram indicator*
04 glad, holy **05** happy, lucky **06** adored, divine, graced, joyful, joyous, sacred **07** endowed, revered **08** benedict, favoured, hallowed, heavenly, provided **09** benedight, contented, fortunate **10** prosperous, sanctified **11** consecrated

blessing
02 OK **04** boon, gain, gift, help **05** grace, leave **06** bounty, favour, profit **07** backing, benefit, benison, consent, darshan, go-ahead, godsend, kiddush, service, support **08** approval, felicity, sanction, thumbs-up, windfall **09** advantage, agreement, authority, good thing **10** benedicite, dedication, green light, invocation, permission **11** approbation, benediction, concurrence, good fortune **12** commendation, consecration, thanksgiving

blight
◊ *anagram indicator*
03 mar, rot, woe **04** bane, dash, evil, kill, ruin, take **05** blast, check, crush, curse, decay, spoil, wreck **06** cancer,

canker, damage, fungus, injure, mildew, strike, wither **07** destroy, disease, scourge, scowder, setback, shatter, shrivel, trouble **08** calamity, scouther, scowther **09** blastment, fire-blast, frustrate, pollution, undermine **10** affliction, annihilate, corruption, disappoint, misfortune, sideration **11** infestation **13** contamination

blimey
03 coo, lor

blind
03 mad **04** hood, mask, rash, seal, seel, slow, trap, wild **05** blend, chick, cloak, cover, front, hasty, shade, trick **06** bisson, closed, dazzle, façade, hidden, screen **07** confuse, cover-up, curtain, deceive, eyeless, mislead, shutter, unaware, winking **08** careless, heedless, ignorant, mindless, obscured, reckless, unseeing, Venetian **09** concealed, impetuous, impulsive, make blind, oblivious, sightless, unmindful, unsighted **10** beetle-eyed, camouflage, intimidate, irrational, masquerade, neglectful, obstructed, out of sight, uncritical, unthinking, visionless **11** distraction, inattentive, indifferent, injudicious, insensitive, roller blind, smokescreen, thoughtless, unconscious, unobservant, unreasoning, window shade **12** festoon blind, imperceptive **13** Austrian blind, inconsiderate, Venetian blind **14** deprive of sight, indiscriminate **15** block your vision, deprive of vision, put the eyes out of
See also **sight**

blindly
05 madly **06** rashly, wildly **10** carelessly, mindlessly, recklessly, unseeingly **11** impetuously, impulsively, senselessly, sightlessly **12** incautiously, irrationally, uncritically, unthinkingly, without sight **13** thoughtlessly, without vision

blink
04 peep, pink, wink **05** flash, gleam, shine, twink **06** glance, wapper **07** flicker, flutter, glimmer, glimpse, glitter, nictate, sparkle, twinkle **09** nictitate **11** scintillate

blip
03 pip **04** buzz **05** bleep **06** glitch, hiccup, squeal **07** screech

bliss
03 joy **06** heaven, utopia **07** ecstasy, elation, nirvana, rapture **08** euphoria, gladness, paradise **09** happiness **11** blessedness **12** blissfulness **13** seventh heaven

blissful
05 happy **06** elated, joyful, joyous **07** idyllic **08** ecstatic, euphoric, seraphic **09** delighted, enchanted, rapturous **10** enraptured, seraphical

blister
03 wen **04** blab, bleb, boil, cyst, sore **05** blain, bulla, ulcer **06** canker,

blistering

papula, pimple **07** abscess, measles, papilla, pustule, vesicle **08** cold sore, furuncle, overgall, swelling, vesicate, vesicula **09** carbuncle, phlyctena, pompholyx **10** phlyctaena

blistering
03 hot **05** cruel **06** fierce, savage **07** caustic, extreme, intense, vicious **08** scathing, vesicant, virulent **09** ferocious, sarcastic, scorching, withering **10** epispastic

blithe
05 happy, merry **06** casual, cheery **08** carefree, careless, cheerful, heedless, uncaring **10** unthinking, untroubled **11** thoughtless, unconcerned **12** light-hearted

blithely
08 casually **10** carelessly **12** unthinkingly **13** thoughtlessly

blitz
04 raid **06** attack, effort, strike **07** attempt **08** campaign, exertion **09** endeavour, offensive, onslaught **10** blitzkrieg **11** bombardment **12** all-out effort

blizzard
05 buran, storm **06** squall **07** tempest **08** white-out **09** snowstorm

bloated
04 full **05** puffy **06** sodden **07** blown up, dilated, stuffed, swollen **08** enlarged, expanded, inflated, puffed up **09** distended, puffed out

blob
01 O **03** dab, gob **04** ball, bead, drop, duck, glob, lump, mass, pill, spot, tear **05** pearl **06** bubble, pellet, splash **07** droplet, globule

bloc
04 axis, ring **05** block, cabal, group, union **06** cartel, clique, league **07** entente, faction **08** alliance **09** coalition, syndicate **10** federation **11** association

block
◇ *insertion indicator*
03 bar, dam, dit, jam, let, ped **04** cake, clog, cube, halt, hunk, lump, mass, plug, seal, slab, stop **05** batch, brick, check, choke, chunk, close, dam up, delay, deter, group, piece, wedge **06** arrest, bung up, clog up, hamper, hinder, impede, scotch, series, square, stop up, thwart **07** barrier, cluster, complex, occlude, section **08** blockage, building, drawback, obstacle, obstruct, quantity, stoppage **09** deterrent, frustrate, hindrance, stonewall, structure **10** be in the way, impediment, resistance **11** development, obstruction **14** stumbling-block
• **block off**
04 seal, stop **05** close **06** stop up **07** close up, shut off
• **block out**
04 hide, mask, veil **06** screen **07** blot

out, conceal, eclipse, obscure, repress, shut out **08** blank out, suppress **10** obliterate
• **block up**
03 ram **04** cloy

blockade
03 ram **04** cloy, stop **05** block, check, siege **06** hinder **07** barrier, besiege, choke up, closure, prevent **08** encircle, keep from, obstacle, obstruct, oppilate, stoppage, surround **09** barricade **10** investment **11** obstruction, restriction **12** encirclement, prevent using **15** prevent entering, prevent reaching

blockage
03 jam **04** clot **05** block **06** log jam **08** blocking, snifters, stoppage **09** hindrance, occlusion **10** bottleneck, congestion, impediment **11** obstruction

blockhead
03 git **04** dope, dork, fool, geek, jerk, mome, mutt, nerd, prat, twit **05** chump, dunce, goosy, idiot, ninny, twerp, wally **06** dimwit, goosey, nitwit, noodle, oxhead, tumphy **07** dizzard, jackass, log-head, plonker **08** bonehead, clotpoll, dipstick, imbecile, jolthead, lunkhead, numskull **09** besom-head, doddipoll, doddypoll, dottipoll, numbskull, pigsconce, thickhead, thickskin **10** bufflehead, jolterhead, loggerhead, muddle-head, nincompoop, thick-skull, woodenhead **11** chuckle-head, leather-head

bloke
03 boy, guy, man, oik **04** chap, male **05** fella **06** fellow **09** character **10** individual
See also **boy**

blond, blonde
04 fair **05** light **06** cendré, flaxen, golden **08** bleached **10** fair-haired **11** tow-coloured **12** golden-haired **13** light-coloured

blood
03 nut **04** Blut, gore, knut, ruby, sang **05** birth **06** claret, family **07** descent, kindred, kinship, lineage **08** ancestry **09** lifeblood, relations **10** extraction, vital fluid **11** descendants **12** relationship
• **draw blood**
03 cup **05** bleed
• **mass of blood**
04 clot

bloodcurdling
05 scary **06** horrid **07** fearful **08** chilling, dreadful, horrible, horrific **09** appalling **10** horrendous, horrifying, terrifying **11** frightening, hair-raising **13** spine-chilling

bloodgroup
01 A, B, O **02** AB

bloodhound
04 lime, lyam, lyme **06** sleuth

07 coondog **09** coonhound, detective, lime-hound, lyam-hound, lyme-hound **11** sleuth-hound

bloodless
03 wan **04** cold, dead, pale **05** ashen, pasty, white **06** chalky, feeble, pallid, sallow, sickly, torpid **07** anaemic, drained, insipid, languid **08** lifeless, listless, peaceful **09** unfeeling, unwarlike **10** colourless, non-violent, spiritless, strife-free **11** passionless, unemotional

bloodshed
04 gore **06** murder, pogrom **07** carnage, killing, slaying **08** butchery, massacre **09** bloodbath, slaughter **10** decimation **12** bloodletting

bloodsucker
04 flea, gnat, tick **05** lamia, leech **06** gadfly **07** deer fly, sponger, tabanid, vampire **08** birch fly, black fly, mosquito, parasite, simulium **09** stable fly **10** horseleech, vampire bat **11** blackmailer, buffalo gnat, extortioner **12** extortionist, sucking louse

bloodthirsty
05 cruel **06** brutal, savage **07** inhuman, vicious, warlike **08** barbaric, ruthless **09** barbarous, ferocious, homicidal, murderous **10** sanguinary

bloody
03 red **04** gory, rare **05** bally, cruel, ruddy **06** bluggy, brutal, fierce, purple, savage **08** bleeding, blinking, blooming, sanguine **09** ferocious, homicidal, murderous **10** sanguinary **11** ensanguined, sanguineous **12** bloodstained, bloodthirsty, sanguinolent **13** ensanguinated

bloody-minded
05 cruel **06** touchy **07** awkward, stroppy **08** stubborn **09** difficult, irritable, obstinate, unhelpful **11** obstructive **13** unco-operative

bloom
03 bud **04** blow, glow, grow, open **05** blush, chill, flush, prime **06** beauty, flower, health, heyday, lustre, mature, pruina, sprout, thrive, vigour **07** blossom, develop, prosper, red tide **08** flourish, radiance, rosiness, strength **09** freshness **10** perfection **11** florescence **13** efflorescence
• **in bloom**
03 out

bloomer *see* **flower; mistake**

blooming
04 rosy **05** bonny, primy, ruddy **07** healthy **09** flowering **10** blossoming, florescent

blossom
03 bud, may, pip **04** blow, grow **05** bloom **06** flower, mature, pruina, thrive **07** bloosme, burgeon, develop,

prosper, succeed **08** flourish, progress **10** effloresce **11** florescence **13** efflorescence

blot
03 dot, dry, mar **04** blur, flaw, mark, soak, spot **05** dry up, fault, smear, spawn, speck, spoil, stain, sully, taint **06** absorb, blotch, defect, smudge, soak up **07** blacken, blemish, splodge, tarnish **08** disgrace **09** black mark, disfigure **10** tarnishing **12** imperfection, obliteration
• **blot out**
04 bury, hide **05** blank, erase **06** cancel, darken, delete, efface, screen, shadow **07** conceal, eclipse, expunge, obscure **08** black out **10** obliterate

blotch
04 blot, dash, mark, monk, spot **05** patch, stain **06** smudge, splash **07** blemish, pustule, splodge, splotch **08** heatspot

blotched
06 marked, pimply, spotty **07** blotchy, freckly, scarred, spotted, stained **09** blemished, centonate, scratched

blotchy
◊ *anagram indicator*
06 patchy, smeary, spotty, uneven **07** spotted **08** inflamed, reddened **09** blemished

blouse
05 middy, shirt, smock, tunic, waist **09** garibaldi **10** shirtwaist

blow
03 bat, bob, bop, box, cut, dad, fan, hit, rap, tip, wap **04** bang, bash, belt, biff, buff, butt, chop, clap, clip, conk, cuff, daud, dint, flow, flub, fuse, gale, gust, hook, jolt, lick, melt, oner, paik, pant, pash, pelt, pipe, play, plug, puff, ruin, rush, scat, slap, snot, sock, stot, swat, tear, toot, waff, waft, welt, whop, wind, wipe, yank **05** appel, blare, blast, botch, break, burst, carry, clout, drift, drive, fling, float, fluff, knock, one-er, peise, punch, shock, skiff, smack, sound, souse, spang, split, spoil, sweep, swipe, thump, upset, waste, whack, whang, whirl, whisk, wreck **06** buffet, bungle, cock up, devvel, exhale, flurry, inhale, stream, stroke, thwack, wallop, whammy, wunner, wuther **07** blow out, breathe, flutter, lounder, puff out, reverse, rupture, screw up, setback, shocker, trumpet, whample, whirret **08** calamity, comedown, disaster, misspend, puncture, squander, surprise **09** bombshell, dissipate, miss out on **10** affliction, breathe out, concussion, exsufflate, insufflate, misfortune **11** catastrophe, fritter away, make a mess of, miss the boat, spend freely **12** short-circuit **13** rude awakening **14** disappointment, spend like water **15** bolt from the blue
• **blow out**
04 tear **05** burst, snift, split **06** put out

07 rupture, smother **08** puncture, snuff out **10** extinguish
• **blow over**
03 end **04** pass **05** abate, cease **06** finish, vanish **07** die down, subside **08** peter out **09** disappear, dissipate, fizzle out **10** settle down **11** be forgotten
• **blow up**
◊ *anagram indicator*
04 bomb, fill, flip, gale, go up, gust, puff, wind **05** blast, bloat, blore, burst, go ape, go mad, go off, scold, storm, swell **06** dilate, expand, flurry, puff up, pump up, squall **07** balloon, distend, draught, enlarge, explode, fill out, inflate, magnify, tempest **08** detonate **09** overstate **10** exaggerate, hit the roof **11** become angry, blow your top, flip your lid, go ballistic **12** get into a rage **14** lose your temper **15** fly off the handle
• **gentle blow**
03 tip **04** peck
• **heavy blow**
02 KO **04** bang, bash, bump, oner, slog, slug, swat **05** douse, dowse, one-er, slosh, souse, swash, thump **06** lander, wallop, wunner **07** lounder **08** knockout **11** neck-herring

blow-out
04 bash, flat, rave **05** binge, feast, party **06** rave-up **07** knees-up **08** flat tyre, puncture **09** beanfeast, burst tyre **11** celebration

blowpipe
03 hod **06** sumpit **07** blowgun **08** sumpitan **09** sarbacane

blowy
05 fresh, gusty, windy **06** breezy, stormy **07** squally **08** blustery

blowzy
05 messy **06** sloppy, untidy **07** tousled, unkempt **08** slipshod, slovenly **09** ungroomed **10** bedraggled **11** dishevelled

blubber
03 cry, sob **04** blub, spek, weep **05** speck **06** bubble, snivel **07** sniffle, snotter, whimper **09** jellyfish

bludgeon
03 hit, sap **04** beat, club, cosh **05** baton, bully, force **06** badger, batter, coerce, compel, cudgel, harass, hector, strike **07** clobber, dragoon **08** browbeat, bulldoze **09** terrorize, truncheon **10** intimidate, pressurize

blue
◊ *anagram indicator*
03 low, sad **04** down, glum, lewd, rude, Tory **05** adult, bawdy, dirty, fed up, saucy **06** coarse, dismal, erotic, fruity, gloomy, morose, risqué, smutty, steamy, vulgar, X-rated **07** obscene, raunchy, unhappy **08** dejected, downcast, improper, indecent **09** depressed, miserable, off-colour, offensive **10** despondent, dispirited, melancholy **11** downhearted, near the

bone **12** Conservative, pornographic **14** down in the dumps, near the knuckle

03 sky **04** anil, aqua, bice, blae, cyan, navy, Saxe, teal **05** azure, perse, smalt **06** cerule, cobalt, haüyne, indigo **07** caerule, gentian, ice-blue, jacinth, sea-blue, sky-blue, watchet **08** baby blue, cerulean, dark blue, mazarine, navy blue, Nile blue, sapphire, Saxe blue **09** caerulean, royal blue, steel-blue, turquoise **10** aquamarine, Berlin blue, cornflower, kingfisher, Oxford blue, periwinkle, petrol blue, powder blue **11** duck-egg blue, lapis lazuli, nattier blue, peacock-blue, ultramarine **12** air-force blue, dumortierite, electric blue, midnight blue, Prussian blue, Wedgwood blue **13** Cambridge blue, robin's-egg blue **15** lapis lazuli blue

bluebottle
06 beadle **07** blawort, blewart, blowfly, brommer **09** policeman

blueprint
04 plan **05** draft, guide, model, pilot **06** design, scheme, sketch **07** outline, pattern, project **08** strategy **09** archetype, cyanotype, programme, prototype **14** representation

blues
05 dumps, gloom **06** cafard **07** sadness **08** doldrums, glumness, miseries **09** dejection, moodiness **10** depression, gloominess, melancholy **11** despondency, unhappiness

bluff
03 lie **04** bank, brow, crag, fake, fool, open, peak, sham, show **05** blind, blunt, cliff, feign, feint, frank, fraud, ridge, scarp, surly, trick **06** candid, deceit, delude, direct, escarp, genial, hearty, height, humbug **07** affable, bravado, deceive, leg-pull, mislead, pretend **08** foreland, headland, hoodwink, pretence **09** bamboozle, deception, downright, four-flush, idle boast, outspoken, precipice **10** blustering, escarpment, promontory, subterfuge **11** braggadocio, good-natured, plain-spoken **15** straightforward

blunder
◊ *anagram indicator*
03 err **04** bish, boob, flub, gaff, goof, slip **05** bevue, boner, botch, break, error, fault, fluff, gaffe **06** bêtise, booboo, bumble, bungle, cock up, cock-up, goof up, howler, mess up, muck up, muddle, ricket, slip up, slip-up **07** bloomer, clanger, faux pas, floater, go wrong, mistake, screw up,

stumble 08 flounder, get wrong, misjudge, pratfall, solecism **09** mismanage, oversight **10** inaccuracy **12** drop a clanger, indiscretion, make a mistake, miscalculate, misjudgement

blunt
04 bald, bate, curt, dull, numb, rude, worn **05** abate, allay, frank, stark **06** abrupt, candid, dampen, deaden, direct, honest, obtund, obtuse, rebate, retund, soften, unedge, weaken **07** brusque, disedge, rounded, stubbed, uncivil **08** edgeless, explicit, hebetate, impolite, not sharp, tactless **09** alleviate, downright, outspoken, pointless **10** forthright, point-blank **11** insensitive, plain-spoken, unsharpened **12** anaesthetize **13** unceremonious **14** take the edge off **15** straightforward

bluntly
06 rudely **07** frankly, roundly **08** candidly, directly **09** brusquely **10** explicitly, impolitely, point-blank, tactlessly **12** forthrightly **13** insensitively **15** unceremoniously

blur
◇ *anagram indicator*
03 dim, fog **04** dull, fuzz, haze, mask, mist, muzz, slur, spot, veil **05** befog, blear, cloud, mudge, smear, stain **06** blotch, darken, mackle, muddle, smudge, soften **07** becloud, blemish, conceal, confuse, dimness, obscure **09** confusion, disfigure, fuzziness, make vague, obscurity **10** cloudiness **14** indistinctness, make indistinct

blurb
04 copy, hype, puff **05** spiel **12** commendation **13** advertisement

blurred
◇ *anagram indicator*
03 dim **04** hazy, soft **05** blear, faint, foggy, fuzzy, misty, muzzy, vague, woozy **06** bleary, cloudy **07** clouded, obscure, unclear **08** confused **10** ill-defined, indistinct, out of focus

blurt
• **blurt out**
03 cry **04** blab, blat, gush, leak, tell **05** plump, spout, utter **06** cry out, let out, reveal **07** call out, divulge, exclaim, let slip **08** disclose **09** ejaculate **11** come out with **13** spill the beans **15** give the game away

blush
03 red **04** glow **05** flush, go red, rouge **06** colour, mantle, redden **07** crimson, scarlet, turn red **08** colour up, rosiness **09** reddening, ruddiness

blushing
03 red **04** rosy **06** modest **07** ashamed, flushed, glowing, red face **08** confused **09** rubescent **10** erubescent **11** embarrassed **12** apple-cheeked

bluster
04 brag, crow, huff, rage, rant, roar **05** bluff, boast, bully, storm, strut, vaunt **06** hector, ruffle **07** bravado, crowing, roister, royster, show off, swagger, talk big **08** boasting, harangue **11** braggadocio, domineering, fanfaronade, rodomontade

blustery
04 wild **05** gusty, windy **06** stormy **07** squally, violent **10** boisterous, swaggering **11** tempestuous

boar
03 hog **05** brawn **06** barrow, tusker **07** sounder **08** sanglier

board
02 bd **04** beam, deal, food, grub, jury, nosh, slab, slat, tray **05** catch, embus, enter, get in, get on, meals, mount, Ouija®, panel, plank, sheet **06** embark, timber **07** council, emplane, entrain, get into, rations **08** advisers, trustees, victuals **09** committee, directors, governors **10** commission, head office, management, provisions, step aboard, sustenance **11** directorate **12** working party **13** advisory group
• **board up**
04 seal, shut **05** close, cover **06** shut up **07** close up, cover up
• **on board**
02 SS
• **put on board**
04 lade **06** embark
• **remove from board**
04 bear

boarder
02 PG **09** pensioner

board game *see* **game**

boast
03 gab, gem, joy **04** blow, brag, crow, have, yelp **05** claim, crack, crake, enjoy, glory, prate, pride, skite, strut, swank, vapor, vaunt **06** avaunt, bounce, hot air, vapour **07** big-note, bluster, crowing, exhibit, possess, show off, swagger, talk big, trumpet **08** mouth off, sound off, talk tall, treasure **09** gasconade, gasconism, jactation, loudmouth, overstate, vainglory **10** blustering, exaggerate, self-praise **11** fanfaronade, rodomontade **12** cry roast-meat **13** overstatement **15** blow your own horn, pride yourself on

boastful
03 big **04** vain **05** cocky, proud, windy **06** hot-air, swanky **07** crowing **08** arrogant, braggart, bragging, glorious, immodest, puffed up **09** bigheaded, blustrous, cock-a-hoop, conceited, thrasonic **10** blusterous, swaggering **11** egotistical, spread-eagle, swell-headed, thrasonical **12** self-glorious, vainglorious **13** swollen-headed **14** self-flattering
• **boastful talk**
03 gas **05** mouth

boastfully
03 big **07** cockily, proudly **09** crowingly **10** arrogantly **11** conceitedly **13** egotistically **14** vaingloriously

boat
03 tub
See also **sail**; **ship**

boatman
05 rower **06** bargee, sailor **07** oarsman **08** ferryman, hoveller, voyageur, waterman, water rat **09** gondolier, oarswoman, yachtsman **11** yachtswoman

bob
01 s **03** bow, dop, hod, hop, nod, tap **04** dock, jerk, jolt, jump, leap, skip **05** float **06** bobble, bounce, curtsy, popple, quiver, Robert, spring, twitch, wobble **08** shilling **09** oscillate
• **bob up**
04 rise **05** arise, pop up **06** appear, arrive, crop up, emerge, show up **07** surface **08** spring up **11** materialize

bobbin
04 bone, pirn, reel **05** quill, spool

bobby *see* **police officer**

bobsleigh run
04 lauf

bode
03 bid **04** sign, warn **05** augur, dwelt, offer **06** herald, waited **07** betoken, endured, portend, predict, presage, purport, signify **08** forebode, foreshow, foretell, forewarn, indicate, intimate, prophesy, remained, threaten **09** adumbrate, foretoken **10** foreshadow **13** prognosticate

bodge
04 flub, goof, mess, ruin **05** botch, fluff, spoil **06** bungle, foul up, goof up, mess up, muck up **07** blunder, louse up, screw up **11** make a hash of

bodice
04 body **05** choli, gilet, jumps, waist **06** Basque, corset, halter **07** bustier, corsage **08** camisole, jirkinet, overslip **10** chemisette

bodily
04 real **05** as one, fully **06** actual, carnal, in toto, wholly **07** en masse, fleshly, totally **08** as a whole, concrete, entirely, material, physical, tangible **09** corporeal **10** altogether, completely **11** substantial **12** collectively
See also **humour**

body
◇ *anagram indicator*
03 bod, lot, mob, nub **04** area, band, bloc, bouk, buik, buke, bulk, clay, core, form, lich, mass, soma **05** build, crowd, frame, group, heart, range, shell, stiff, torso, trunk **06** amount, cartel, casing, corpse, extent, figure, kernel, throng, volume, weight **07** anatomy, cadaver, carcase, chassis, company, council,

body

density, essence, expanse, phalanx, society, stretch **08** congress, dead body, firmness, fullness, main part, physique, quantity, richness, skeleton, solidity **09** authority, framework, multitude, structure, substance, syndicate **10** collection **11** association, central part, consistency, corporation, largest part **12** organization **13** confederation
• **body odour**
02 BO

bodyguard
02 SS **05** guard **06** minder **08** defender, guardian **09** lifeguard, protector **10** triggerman **11** Swiss Guards **13** Schutzstaffel **15** praetorian guard

boffin
05 brain **06** expert, genius, wizard **07** egghead, planner, thinker **08** designer, engineer, inventor **09** intellect, scientist **10** mastermind **11** backroom-boy **12** intellectual

bog
02 WC **03** can, fen, lav, loo **04** dike, dyke, john, kazi, mire, moss, quag, sink, pew, spue, sump **05** dunny, gents, carsy, karzy, khazi, lavvy, marsh, privy, swamp, yarfa **06** carsey, karsey, ladies', lavabo, morass, muskeg, office, petary, lough, stodge, throne, toilet, yarpha **07** cludgie, latrine **08** bathroom, dunnakin, quagmire, washroom, wetlands **09** cloakroom, marshland, swampland **10** facilities, quicksands **11** convenience, water closet **12** smallest room
• **bog down**
04 halt, mire, sink, trap **05** delay, stall, stick **06** deluge, hinder, hold up, impede, retard, slow up **07** set back **08** encumber, slow down **09** overwhelm
• **bog myrtle**
04 gale **06** Myrica **09** sweet-gale
• **hole in bog**
03 hag **04** hagg

boggle
03 jib **05** alarm, amaze, demur **06** bungle, marvel, wonder **07** astound, confuse, scruple, stagger, startle **08** bowl over, hesitate, surprise **09** objection, overwhelm **11** flabbergast

boggy
04 miry, oozy, soft **05** fenny, moory, mossy, muddy, soggy, spewy **06** marshy, quaggy, sodden, spongy, swampy **07** moorish, morassy, paludal, queachy, queechy **11** waterlogged

bogus
◇ anagram indicator
03 bad **04** fake, sham **05** dummy, false, pseud, spoof **06** forged, phoney, pseudo **08** spurious **09** imitation **10** artificial, fraudulent **11** counterfeit, make-believe **13** disappointing

bohemian
04 arty, boho **06** exotic, hippie, wayout **07** beatnik, bizarre, drop-out, oddball, offbeat **08** artistic, original **09** eccentric **10** avant-garde, off-thewall, unorthodox **11** alternative **12** trustafarian **13** nonconformist **14** unconventional

bohrium
02 Bh

boil
◇ anagram indicator
03 jug **04** brew, cook, fizz, foam, fume, heat, leep, rage, rave, sore, stew **05** blain, botch, erupt, froth, steam, storm, ulcer **06** bubble, bunion, decoct, growth, gurgle, pimple, see red, seethe, simmer, tumour, wallop **07** abscess, anthrax, blister, explode, gumboil, parboil, pustule **08** furuncle, ganglion, swelling **09** blow a fuse, carbuncle, fulminate, gathering **10** effervesce, hit the roof **11** blow your top **12** fly into a rage, inflammation **13** come to the boil **14** bring to the boil **15** fly off the handle, go off the deep end
• **boil down**
06 amount, digest, distil, reduce **07** abridge **08** abstract, condense **09** summarize **11** concentrate

boiled
◇ anagram indicator
03 sod **06** sodden

boiler
06 kettle

boiling
◇ anagram indicator
03 hot **05** angry, surge **06** baking, fuming, torrid **07** coction, enraged, flaming, furious **08** broiling, bubbling, gurgling, incensed, roasting, scalding, steaming **09** indignant, scorching, turbulent **10** blistering, ebullition, infuriated, sweltering **12** effervescent

boisterous
◇ anagram indicator
04 loud, wild **05** noisy, randy, rough, rowdy **06** active, bouncy, lively, randie, stormy, unruly **07** laddish, riotous, romping **08** animated, roisting, roysting, spirited **09** clamorous, energetic, exuberant, goustrous, turbulent **10** disorderly, knockabout, rollicking, strepitoso, tumultuous **11** dithyrambic, hyperactive, rumbustious **12** obstreperous, rambunctious, unrestrained

boisterously
06 loudly, wildly **07** noisily, roughly, rowdily **08** actively **09** riotously **10** animatedly, spiritedly **11** clamorously, exuberantly, turbulently **12** tumultuously **13** energetically, hyperactively **14** obstreperously, unrestrainedly

bold
02 bf **04** free, loud, pert **05** brash, brave, heavy, saucy, showy, steep, thick, vivid **06** abrupt, brassy, brazen, bright, cheeky, daring, flashy, heroic, manful, plucky, strong **07** assured, defiant, forward, gallant, haughty, naughty, valiant **08** definite, distinct, fearless, impudent, insolent, intrepid, malapert, outgoing, spirited, striking, valorous **09** audacious, bald-faced, barefaced, chivalric, colourful, confident, dauntless, foolhardy, prominent, shameless, unabashed, undaunted **10** chivalrous, courageous, diastaltic, flamboyant, in-your-face, noticeable, pronounced **11** adventurous, bold as a lion, bold as brass, conspicuous, eye-catching, venturesome **12** enterprising, highspirited, presumptuous
• **be bold**
04 dare

boldly
06 crouse **07** bravely, vividly **08** brightly, daringly, pluckily, risoluto, strongly **09** valiantly **10** definitely, distinctly, fearlessly, heroically, intrepidly, strikingly **11** audaciously, confidently, prominently **12** courageously **13** adventurously

Bolivia
03 BOL

bolshie
04 rude **06** touchy **07** awkward, prickly, problem, stroppy **08** stubborn **09** difficult, irritable, obstinate, unhelpful **10** unpleasant **12** bloody-minded **13** oversensitive, unco-operative

bolster
03 aid, pad **04** help, prop, stay **05** boost, brace **06** assist, buoy up, firm up, pillow **07** augment, cushion, shore up, stiffen, support **08** buttress, maintain **09** Dutch wife, reinforce **10** invigorate, revitalize, strengthen, supplement

bolt
01 U **03** bar, fly, peg, pin, rat, ray, rod, run **04** cram, dart, dash, flee, gulp, lock, rush, slot, sneb, snib, stud, wolf **05** arrow, blaze, burst, catch, elope, flare, flash, gorge, latch, rivet, scoff, screw, shaft, shoot, spark, stuff **06** devour, escape, fasten, gobble, guzzle, hurtle, pintle, run off, secure, sperre, sprint, streak **07** abscond, run away, scarper **08** fastener, wolf down

Boltzmann constant
01 k

bomb
◇ anagram indicator
03 egg **05** prang, speed **06** attack, blow up, device, mortar **07** bombard, destroy **09** bombshell, explosive **10** projectile

01 A, H
02 V-1, V-2
03 car

bombard

04 aero, atom, buzz, dumb, fire, mine, MOAB, nail, pipe, time
05 dirty, E-bomb, Mills, shell, smart, smoke, stink
06 binary, candle, cobalt, drogue, flying, fusion, letter, parcel, petrol, radium, rocket
07 bomblet, cluster, fission, grenade, missile, neutron, nuclear, plastic, tallboy, torpedo
08 bouncing, firebomb, hydrogen, landmine
09 doodlebug, Grand Slam, pineapple
10 incendiary
11 blockbuster, daisy-cutter, depth charge, penetration, sensor fuzed, stun grenade, thermobaric
12 bunker buster, rifle grenade
13 fragmentation, thermonuclear
15 Molotov cocktail

bombard
04 bomb, pelt, raid **05** blast, blitz, flood, hound, pound, shell, stone, swamp **06** assail, attack, batter, bother, deluge, harass, mortar, pellet, pester, strafe, straff **07** besiege, torpedo **08** inundate **09** blackjack

bombardment
04 fire, flak, hail **05** blitz, salvo, stonk **06** attack **07** air raid, assault, barrage, bombing, stonker **08** hounding, pounding, shelling **09** besieging, bothering, cannonade, fusillade, harassing, onslaught, pestering, shellfire

bombast
03 pad **04** rant **05** stuff **06** hot air **07** bluster, fustian, heroics, inflate, padding **08** euphuism, inflated, stuffing **09** dithyramb, pomposity, verbosity, wordiness **10** sophomoric, turgidness **11** ampullosity **13** magniloquence **14** grandiloquence **15** pretentiousness

bombastic
04 tall **05** puffy, tumid, windy, wordy **06** turgid **07** bloated, fustian, pompous, verbose **08** affected, inflated **09** grandiose, high-flown **10** euphuistic, portentous, sophomoric **11** pretentious, spread-eagle **12** magniloquent, ostentatious, sophomorical **13** grandiloquent

bomber
01 B

Bombers include:

03 B-10, B-17, B-19, B-52, MB-1
04 dive
05 Stuka
06 Gotha G, Harris, Sukhoi
07 Avenger, Heinkel, Junkers, stealth, suicide, Tupolev, Warthog
08 Mitchell
09 Lancaster, Liberator
13 Superfortress
14 Flying Fortress

bona fide
04 real, true **05** legal, valid **06** actual, dinkum, honest, kosher, lawful **07** genuine **09** authentic **10** legitimate **12** the real McCoy

bonanza
04 boon **07** godsend **08** blessing, windfall **12** stroke of luck, sudden wealth

bond
02 bd **03** gum, tie, vow **04** band, bind, cord, deal, fuse, glue, join, knot, link, pact, seal, ties, weld, word, yoke **05** chain, nexus, noose, paste, starr, stick, union, unite **06** attach, cement, copula, fasten, fetter, league, pledge, treaty **07** binding, connect, liaison, linkage, manacle, promise, rapport, shackle, statute, valence **08** affinity, contract, covenant, ligament, mateship, relation, vinculum, yearling **09** agreement, chemistry **10** attachment, connection, friendship, obligation **11** affiliation, transaction **12** relationship

bondage
04 yoke **06** thrall **07** serfdom, slavery **08** nativity, thraldom **09** captivity, restraint, servitude, thralldom, vassalage **10** subjection, villeinage **11** confinement, enslavement, subjugation **12** imprisonment, subservience **13** incarceration

bone
03 nab, tot **05** seize **06** bobbin

Bones include:

01 T
02 os
03 hip, jaw, luz, rib
04 back, coxa, knee, shin, ulna
05 ankle, anvil, cheek, costa, femur, funny, hyoid, ilium, incus, jugal, pubis, skull, spine, talus, thigh, thumb, tibia, vomer, wrist
06 breast, carpal, coccyx, collar, fibula, hammer, pecten, pelvis, radius, sacrum, saddle, stapes, tarsus
07 cranium, ethmoid, humerus, ischium, kneecap, knuckle, malleus, ossicle, patella, phalanx, scapula, sternum, stirrup
08 clavicle, lower jaw, mandible, parietal, scaphoid, shoulder, upper jaw, vertebra
09 calcaneum, calcaneus, occipital, trapezium, zygomatic
10 metacarpal, metatarsal
12 pelvic girdle
13 shoulder-blade

bones
02 Dr, GP, MO **03** doc **04** dice, ossa **06** doctor **08** skeleton

bonfire
04 pyre **08** bale-fire **09** feu de joie

bonhomie
08 sympathy **09** geniality **10** affability, amiability, good nature, tenderness **12** conviviality, friendliness **15** kind-heartedness, warm-heartedness

bon mot
04 quip **07** riposte **08** one-liner, repartee **09** wisecrack, witticism **10** pleasantry

bonnet
03 cap **04** hood, poke **06** kiss-me, toorie, tourie **08** balmoral, bongrace **11** kiss-me-quick
• **bonnet monkey**
04 zati

bonny
04 fair, fine **05** bonie, merry, plump **06** cheery, comely, joyful, lovely, pretty **07** smiling **08** blooming, bouncing, cheerful, handsome **09** beautiful **10** attractive, sweetheart

bonus
03 tip **04** gain, gift, perk, plus **05** bribe, extra, prize **06** reward **07** benefit, handout, premium **08** dividend, gratuity **09** advantage, lagniappe **10** commission, honorarium, perquisite **14** fringe benefits

bony
04 lean, thin **05** drawn, gaunt, gawky, lanky **06** skinny **07** angular, osseous, scraggy, scrawny **08** gangling, rawboned, sclerous, skeletal **09** emaciated

book
01 b **02** bk **03** bag, lib, log, vol **04** text, tome, work **05** Bible, blame, enter, folio, order, tract **06** accuse, arrest, charge, engage, script, volume **07** arrange, booklet, charter, procure, reserve **08** accuse of, libretto, organize, schedule **09** programme **10** prearrange **11** publication

Books include:

03 pad
04 A to Z, bath, chap, cook, copy, days, hand, hymn, note, text, work, year
05 album, atlas, audio, board, cloth, comic, diary, e-book, guide, novel, pop-up, scrap, story
06 annual, gradus, hymnal, jotter, ledger, manual, missal, phrase, prayer, primer, sketch
07 almanac, fiction, Filofax®, journal, lexicon, omnibus, picture, psalter
08 exercise, grimoire, hardback, libretto, self-help, softback, thriller
09 anthology, biography, catalogue, children's, detective, directory, gazetteer, paperback, reference, thesaurus
10 bestseller, compendium, dictionary, large print, lectionary, manuscript
11 coffee-table, concordance, instruction, travel guide
12 encyclopedia
13 penny dreadful, travel journal
15 pocket companion

See also **apocryphal; Bible**

• **book in**
05 enrol **07** check in **08** register
• **book of rules**
03 pie, pye **07** ordinal **11** penitential

bookbinding

10 bibliopegy

Bookbinding terms include:

03 aeg

04 case, head, limp, tail, yapp

05 bolts, hinge, spine

06 boards, gather, jacket, lining, Linson®, sewing

07 binding, buckram, drawn-on, flyleaf, headcap, morocco

08 backbone, blocking, casing-in, doublure, drilling, endpaper, fore edge, hardback, headband, open-flat, shoulder, smashing, stamping, tailband

09 backboard, book block, casebound, debossing, dust cover, embossing, full bound, half bound, loose-leaf, millboard, paperback, signature, soft-cover

10 back lining, binder's die, front board, laminating, pasteboard, raised band, side-stitch, square back, stab-stitch, strawboard, varnishing, whole bound

11 comb binding, ring binding, velo binding, wire binding, wiro binding

12 all edges gilt, binder's board, binder's brass, cloth binding, flexi binding, notch binding, quarter bound, saddle-stitch, thread sewing

13 back cornering, blind blocking, spiral binding, unsewn binding, wire stitching

14 library binding, perfect binding

15 adhesive binding, cloth-lined board, hot foil stamping

booking

11 appointment, arrangement, reservation

bookish

07 donnish, erudite, inkhorn, learned

08 academic, cultured, highbrow, lettered, literary, pedantic, studious, well-read **09** scholarly **10** scholastic

12 bluestocking, intellectual

booklet

06 folder, notice **07** handout, leaflet

08 brochure, circular, pamphlet

09 programme

books

02 bb, NT, OT **03** bks **07** ledgers, records **08** accounts **12** balance sheet

boom

03 jib **04** bang, clap, gain, grow, jump, leap, roar, roll, spar **05** blare, blast, boost, burst, crash, spurt, surge, swell **06** bellow, do well, expand, growth, rumble, thrive, upturn **07** advance, burgeon, develop, explode, prosper, resound, succeed, success, thunder, upsurge, upswing **08** escalate, flourish, increase, mushroom, progress, snowball **09** bombilate, bombinate, expansion, explosion, intensify, loud noise, resonance, skyrocket **10** escalation, strengthen

11 development, improvement, reverberate **13** reverberation

boomerang

◇ *reversal indicator*

05 kiley, kylie **06** recoil **07** rebound, reverse **08** backfire, ricochet

10 bounce back, spring back, throw stick

boon

04 bene, gift, help, plus **05** bonus, grant **06** favour, jovial **07** benefit, godsend, present, request **08** blessing, gratuity, intimate, kindness, petition, windfall **09** advantage, convivial

• **boon companion**

06 cupman, Trojan **07** franion

09 confidant **10** best friend, confidante, dear friend **11** bosom friend, close friend **13** special friend

boor

03 hog, lob, oaf, oik, yob **04** clod, Jack, kern, lout, pleb, slob **05** chuff, clown, kerne, ocker, yahoo, yobbo, yokel

06 chough, keelie, rustic **07** Grobian, peasant **08** plebeian **09** barbarian, lager lout, vulgarian **10** clodhopper, philistine **14** country bumpkin

boorish

04 rude **05** borel, crass, crude, gross, gruff, ocker, rough, swain **06** borrel, coarse, jungli, lumpen, oafish, rustic, vulgar **07** borrell, ill-bred, loutish, uncouth **08** ignorant, impolite, swainish **09** unrefined **10** uneducated

11 clodhopping, ill-mannered, uncivilized

boost

03 aid, rap **04** boom, help, hype, lift, plug, rise, spur, wrap **05** put up, raise, steal **06** assist, expand, fillip, foster, play up, praise, talk up, uplift

07 advance, amplify, augment, bolster, develop, ego-trip, enhance, enlarge, further, improve, inspire, promote, support **08** addition, heighten, increase, maximize, shoplift, stimulus **09** advertise, encourage, expansion, increment, promotion, publicity, publicize, stimulate **10** assistance, potentiate, supplement **11** development, enhancement, enlargement, furtherance, improvement, inspiration

12 augmentation, shot in the arm

13 advertisement, amplification, encouragement

boot

04 kick **05** shove, trunk **06** profit

09 advantage

Boots include:

03 gum, top, ugg

04 crow, half, jack, lace, moon, snow

05 ankle, kamik, rugby, thigh, wader, welly

06 bootee, buskin, chukka, combat, finsko, galosh, golosh, hiking, jemima, mucluc, mukluk, riding

07 blucher, bottine, Chelsea, cracowe, finnsko, galoche, Hessian, walking

08 balmoral, bootikin, climbing, finnesko, football, high shoe, larrigan, muckluck, overshoe

09 scarpetto

10 Doc Martens®, wellington

13 beetle-crusher

• **boot out**

04 fire, sack, shed **05** eject, expel

06 lay off **07** dismiss, kick out, suspend

10 give notice **12** give the heave

13 make redundant

• **to boot**

03 too **06** as well **07** besides **10** in addition **14** into the bargain

booth

03 box, hut **05** crame, kiosk, stall, stand **06** bothan, carrel **07** cubicle

11 compartment, luckenbooth

bootleg

05 wrong **06** banned, barred, pirate

07 illegal, illicit, pirated, smuggle

08 criminal, outlawed, smuggled, unlawful **09** forbidden **10** prohibited, proscribed **11** black-market, interdicted **12** unauthorized **15** under-the-counter

bootless

04 vain **06** barren, futile **07** sterile, useless **09** fruitless, pointless

10 profitless, unavailing **11** ineffective

12 unprofitable, unsuccessful

booty

04 haul, loot, prey, swag **05** bribe, gains, prize, spoil **06** bottom, creach, creagh, shikar, spoils **07** pillage, plunder, profits, takings **08** pickings, purchase, winnings

booze

03 jar **04** grog, slug, tank **05** drink, juice, skink, tinct **06** fuddle, liquor, strunt, tiddly, tipple **07** alcohol, indulge, liqueur, spirits **08** stimulus

09 firewater, get pissed, hard stuff, the bottle, the cratur **10** have a drink, intoxicant **11** jungle juice, strong drink, the creature **12** Dutch courage, hit the bottle **14** drink like a fish

See also **beer; cocktail; drink; liqueur; liquor; spirits; wine**

boozer

03 bar, inn, pub, sot **04** howf, lush, soak, wino **05** alkie, bloat, dipso, drunk, local, souse, toper **06** lounge, saloon, sponge, tavern **07** Bacchus, drinker, tippler, tosspot **08** drunkard, habitual, hostelry **09** alcoholic, inebriate, lounge bar **10** wine-bibber

11 dipsomaniac, hard drinker, public house **12** heavy drinker, watering-hole

boozy

◇ *anagram indicator*

See **drunken**

bop

03 hop, jig **04** blow, jive, jump, leap, rock, spin, sway **05** dance, stomp, twirl, twist, whirl **06** boogie, gyrate, hoof it, strike **09** pirouette, shake a leg

11 move to music

borage
07 alkanet, anchusa, bugloss, comfrey, manjack, myosote **08** gromwell, lungwort, myosotis, sebesten **09** stickseed, Symphytum **10** dog's-tongue, heliotrope, Pulmonaria **11** cool-tankard, oyster plant **12** hound's-tongue, lithospermum **13** viper's bugloss

border
03 bed, hem, mat, rim **04** abut, bank, bord, brim, cost, curb, dado, edge, join, kerb, limb, line, list, mark, mete, orle, rand, roon, rund, side, trim, welt **05** apron, board, boord, borde, bound, brink, coast, coste, flank, frill, limit, march, skirt, swage, touch, verge **06** accost, adjoin, boorde, bounds, cotise, frieze, fringe, margin, purfle, screed, trench, weeper **07** accoast, bordure, confine, connect, cottise, enclose, engrail, impinge, marches, margent, selvage, valance, valence, wayside **08** be next to, boundary, confines, dentelle, emborder, frontier, furbelow, headland, roadside, selvedge, surround, trimming **09** cartouche, guilloche, lie next to, perimeter, periphery, state line **10** borderline, limitrophe, marchlands **11** demarcation **12** be adjacent to, circumscribe **13** circumference

Borders and boundaries include:
07 Rubicon
09 Green Line
10 Berlin Wall, no-man's-land
11 Iron Curtain, Maginot Line
13 Bamboo Curtain
14 Mason–Dixon line
15 cordon sanitaire

• border on
07 verge on **08** approach, be almost, be nearly, resemble **13** approximate to **14** be tantamount to

• borders of
◇ *ends selection indicator*
08 purlieus

borderline
04 iffy, line **05** limit **06** divide **08** boundary, division, doubtful, marginal **09** uncertain **10** ambivalent, indecisive, indefinite **11** problematic **12** dividing-line **13** indeterminate **15** demarcation line, differentiation
See also **border**

bore
03 awl, dig, irk, sap, sat, tap, vex **04** bare, bind, drag, eger, jade, mine, pain, sink, tire **05** annoy, drill, eager, eagre, ennui, grind, weary, worry **06** bother, burrow, dig out, hollow, jostle, pall on, pierce, tunnel **07** exhaust, fatigue, sondage, trouble, turn off, turn-off, wear out **08** headache, irritate, nuisance, puncture **09** hollow out, make tired, penetrate, perforate, terebrant, terebrate, undermine **11** be tedious to, send to sleep **13** pain in the neck **15** bore the pants off

• enlarge bore
04 ream, rime

bored
05 fed up, tired **06** ennuyé, in a rut **07** ennuied, wearied **09** exhausted, turned off, unexcited **10** bored stiff, brassed off, browned off, cheesed off **12** bored to tears, sick and tired, uninterested

boredom
05 ennui **06** acedia, apathy, tedium **07** humdrum, malaise, taedium, vapours **08** dullness, flatness, monotony, sameness **09** weariness **11** frustration, tediousness **12** listlessness **14** world-weariness

boring
03 dry **04** dull, flat, slow, tedy **05** dully, ho-hum, samey, stale, trite **06** draggy, dreary, flatly, jejune, stupid, tiring **07** humdrum, insipid, mundane, prosaic, routine, tedious, tritely **08** drearily, tiresome, unvaried **09** insipidly, tediously **10** long-winded, monotonous, tiresomely, uneventful, unexciting, uninspired **11** commonplace, prosaically, repetitious, stultifying, uninspiring **12** long-windedly, monotonously, uneventfully, unexcitingly **13** repetitiously, stultifyingly, unimaginative, uninteresting **14** soul-destroying **15** unimaginatively, uninterestingly

• boring piece
05 drill

born
01 b, n **02** né **03** nat, née **05** natus

boron
01 B

borough
03 bor **04** area, port, town **05** borgo, burgh **06** parish **08** district **09** community **12** constituency
See also **London; New York**

borrow
03 use **04** draw, hire, rent, take **05** adopt, cadge, lease, lever, usurp **06** derive, obtain, pledge, scunge, sponge, surety, take up **07** acquire, charter **08** scrounge, take over **10** have on loan, take on loan **11** appropriate **12** have the use of, take out a loan **14** use temporarily

borrowing
03 IOU, use **04** debt, hire, loan **06** calque, rental **07** charter, leasing **08** adoption, loan-word, takeover **10** derivation **11** acquisition **12** temporary use **15** loan-translation

Bosnia and Herzegovina
03 BIH

bosom
03 pap, tit **04** boob, boon, bust, core, dear **05** booby, chest, close, diddy, heart, midst **06** breast, centre, desire, loving **07** breasts, devoted, shelter

08 faithful, intimate **09** sanctuary **10** protection **12** confidential

boss
◇ *anagram indicator*
03 cow, don, gov, guv **04** calf, head, knob, knot, stud, umbo **05** bully, chief, empty, jewel, owner, stock **06** bigwig, gaffer, hollow, honcho, leader, manage, master, oubaas, pellet, top dog, top man **07** cacique, captain, cazique, control, foreman, manager, mistake, supremo **08** browbeat, bulldoze, bull's-eye, chairman, director, dominate, domineer, employer, governor, omphalos, overseer, superior, top woman **09** big cheese, excellent, executive, top banana, tyrannize **10** chairwoman, order about, push around, supervisor **11** chairperson, order around **12** give orders to **13** administrator, lay down the law **14** superintendent

bossiness
07 tyranny **09** autocracy, despotism **13** assertiveness, imperiousness **14** high-handedness

bossy
03 cow **04** calf **06** lordly **08** despotic, exacting **09** assertive, demanding, imperious, insistent **10** autocratic, dominating, high-handed, oppressive, tyrannical **11** dictatorial, domineering, overbearing **13** authoritarian

botany
03 bot **09** phytology **11** phytography

Botanists include:
03 Mee (Margaret Ursula), Ray (John)
04 Bary (Heinrich Anton de), Bose (Sir Jagadis Chandra), Cohn (Ferdinand Julius), Gray (Asa)
05 Banks (Sir Joseph), Brown (Robert), Hales (Stephen), Sachs (Julius von), Vries (Hugo de)
06 Biffen (Sir Rowland Harry), Carver (George Washington), Haller (Albrecht von), Hooker (Sir Joseph Dalton), Hudson (William), Mendel (Gregor Johann), Nägeli (Karl Wilhelm von), Torrey (John)
07 Bartram (John), Bellamy (David), Bentham (George), De Vries (Hugo Marie), Pfeffer (Wilhelm), Tansley (Sir Arthur George), Vavilov (Nikolai)
08 Blackman (Frederick Frost), Candolle (Augustin Pyrame de), Linnaeus (Carolus)
09 Boerhaave (Hermann), Schleiden (Matthias Jakob)
10 Camerarius (Rudolph Jacob), Hofmeister (Wilhelm Friedrich Benedikt), Pringsheim (Nathaniel)

botch
◇ *anagram indicator*
03 mar, mux **04** boil, flop, flub, goof, hash, mess, muff, ruin, sore **05** bodge, farce, fluff, patch, spoil **06** bungle, clatch, cock up, cock-up, foul up, goof up, mess up, muck up, muddle, pimple

7 blemish, blunder, butcher, clamper, ailure, louse up, screw up **8** shambles **09** mismanage **11** make a ash of, make a mess of, miscarriage **3** make a bad job of

ooth
4 each **06** as well, the two **07** the air

other
▷ *anagram indicator*
3 ado, bug, irk, nag, vex **04** drat, fash, uss, pest **05** aggro, alarm, annoy, eave, deeve, grief, grind, pains, tease, pset, worry **06** bovver, bustle, ismay, effort, flurry, harass, hassle, nolest, pester, plague, put out, umpus, shtook, shtuck, strain, unrest **7** concern, disturb, fluster, perplex, roblem, schtook, schtuck, trouble **8** disorder, distress, exertion, fighting, rritate, nuisance, vexation **9** annoyance, incommode **0** aggravate, difficulty, irritation **1** disturbance **12** make an effort **3** inconvenience, make the effort, ain in the neck **14** think necessary **5** concern yourself

othersome
5 pesky **06** boring, vexing **07** brickle, rksome, tedious **08** annoying, ashious, tiresome **09** laborious, exatious, wearisome **10** irritating **1** aggravating, distressing, infuriating, roublesome **12** exasperating, nconvenient

Botswana
2 BW, RB **03** BWA

ottle
▷ *anagram indicator*
▷ *hidden indicator*
3 bot **04** grit, guts **05** nerve, spunk **6** daring, valour **07** bravery, courage **8** boldness **09** container **1** intrepidity **12** Dutch courage

Bottles include:
3 bed, gas, ink, pig
4 beer, case, codd, jack, junk, mick, milk, tear, vial, wash, wine
5 bidon, cruet, cruse, dumpy, flask, gourd, Klein, phial, scent, snuff, water
6 carafe, carboy, cutter, feeder, fiasco, flacon, flagon, hottie, inkpot, lagena, magnum, poison, pooter, siphon, stubby, syphon, Woulfe
7 amphora, ampulla, costrel, feeding, flacket, pilgrim, pitcher, squeezy, sucking, torpedo, vinegar, washing
8 calabash, decanter, demijohn, hip flask, hot-water, magnetic, medicine, screwtop, smelling, weighing
9 Aristotle
0 apothecary, lachrymary, winchester
1 vinaigrette, water bouget
2 Bologna phial, lachrymatory, Thermos® flask

See also **wine**

• bottle up
04 curb, hide **06** cork up, shut in **07** conceal, confine, contain, enclose, inhibit, repress **08** disguise, hold back, keep back, restrain, restrict, suppress **11** keep in check

bottleneck
05 block **06** hold-up **07** snarl-up **08** blockage, clogging, gridlock, obstacle **09** narrowing **10** congestion, traffic jam **11** obstruction, restriction **12** constriction

bottom
◇ *tail selection down indicator*
03 ass, bed, bum, end **04** base, butt, coit, foot, prat, rear, rump, seat, sill, sole, tail, tush **05** basis, batty, booty, botty, floor, lower, nadir, quoit, tushy **06** behind, depths, far end, fundus, ground, heinie, lowest, plinth, seabed, tushie **07** bedrock, staddle, support **08** backside, buttocks, pedestal, sea floor **09** posterior, undermost, underside **10** foundation, underneath **11** farthest end, furthest end, lowest level **12** substructure, underpinning

See also **buttocks**

bottomless
◇ *tail deletion down indicator*
04 deep **07** abysmal, abyssal **08** infinite, profound **09** boundless, depthless, limitless, subjacent, unfounded, unlimited, unplumbed **10** fathomless, unbottomed, unfathomed **11** measureless **12** immeasurable, unfathomable **13** inexhaustible

bough
04 limb **06** branch **07** gallows, roughie

bought
04 coft

boulder
04 rock **05** stone **06** gibber **07** bowlder **10** niggerhead

boulevard
04 Blvd, Boul, mall, road **05** drive **06** avenue, parade, street **08** corniche, prospect **09** promenade **12** thoroughfare

bounce
02 go **03** bob, dap, lie, zip **04** bang, beat, give, jump, leap, stot, thud **05** boast, boing, boink, bound, pitch, stoit, styte, throw **06** energy, morgay, recoil, spring, vigour **07** dogfish, rebound **08** boasting, dynamism, ricochet, vitality, vivacity **09** animation, dismissal **10** ebullience, elasticity, exaggerate, exuberance, get-up-and-go, liveliness, resilience, spring back **11** springiness **12** spiritedness

• bounce back
07 improve, recover **09** get better **13** make a comeback **15** get back to normal

bouncer
03 dud **04** liar **05** bully **06** bumper **10** chucker-out

bouncing
◇ *anagram indicator*
05 bonny **06** hearty, lively, robust, strong **07** healthy **08** blooming, thriving, vigorous **09** energetic, walloping

bouncy
◇ *anagram indicator*
04 spry **05** alive **06** active, lively, spongy **07** dynamic, elastic, rubbery, springy **08** flexible, spirited, stretchy, vigorous **09** energetic, resilient, sprightly, vivacious **11** full of beans

bound
◇ *containment indicator*
02 bd **03** bob, hop, lep, off **04** curb, edge, held, jump, leap, line, mere, skip, sten, stot, sure, tied, tyde **05** brink, caper, check, dance, fated, fixed, flank, frisk, going, limit, off to, roped, scoup, scowp, skelp, skirt, sling, spang, stend, sworn, vault, verge **06** border, bounce, cavort, coming, doomed, forced, fringe, frolic, gambol, headed, hurdle, lashed, liable, limits, lollop, margin, prance, spring, tied up **07** affined, certain, chained, clamped, confine, contain, control, enclose, galumph, gambado, heading, obliged, outline, pledged, secured, trussed **08** articled, attached, bandaged, beholden, confines, definite, destined, fastened, fettered, gallumph, handfast, moderate, regulate, required, restrain, restrict, shackled, strapped, surround, tethered **09** committed, compelled, duty-bound, extremity, perimeter, restraint **10** borderline, covenanted, limitation, proceeding, restricted, travelling **11** constrained, demarcation, on your way to, restriction, termination **12** circumscribe **13** circumference

• bound up with
07 involve **09** related to **10** linked with, tied up with **11** dependent on **13** connected with **14** associated with, hand in hand with

boundary
02 IV, VI **03** six **04** edge, four, goal, gole, limb, line, list, mark, mere, mete, pale, term **05** bourn, brink, limes, limit, march, meith, score, verge **06** border, bounds, bourne, fringe, limits, margin **07** barrier, confine, marches, Rubicon, surface **08** confines, frontier **09** extremity, parameter, perimeter, periphery **10** borderline **11** demarcation, termination **15** point of no return

See also **border**

bounded
05 edged **07** cramped, defined, limited **08** bordered, confined, enclosed, hemmed in, walled in **09** delimited, encircled **10** controlled, demarcated, restrained, restricted, surrounded **11** encompassed **13** circumscribed

bounder
03 cad, cur, pig, rat, roo **04** euro **05** cheat, knave, rogue, swine

06 hopper, jumper, rotter **07** dastard, wallaby **08** blighter, dirty dog **09** miscreant **10** blackguard

boundless
04 vast **06** untold **07** endless, immense **08** infinite, unending **09** countless, limitless, shoreless, unbounded, unlimited **10** numberless, unconfined, unflagging **11** everlasting, illimitable, innumerable, measureless, never-ending **12** immeasurable, incalculable, interminable **13** indefatigable, inexhaustible

bounds
◊ *ends selection indicator*
05 edges, scope **06** limits **07** borders, fringes, marches, margins **08** confines **09** perimeter, periphery **10** boundaries, parameters **11** extremities **12** demarcations, restrictions **13** circumference
• **out of bounds**
02 OB **04** tapu **05** taboo **06** banned, barred **09** forbidden, off limits **10** disallowed, not allowed, prohibited

bountiful
05 ample **06** lavish **07** copious, liberal, profuse **08** abundant, generous, princely, prolific **09** boundless, bounteous, exuberant, luxuriant, plenteous, plentiful **10** munificent, open-handed, ungrudging, unstinting **11** magnanimous, overflowing

bounty
03 tip **04** gift **05** bonus, grant **06** reward **07** charity, premium, present **08** donation, gratuity, kindness, largesse **09** allowance **10** almsgiving, generosity, liberality, recompense **11** beneficence, magnanimity, munificence **12** philanthropy

bouquet
04 nose, posy **05** aroma, bunch, odour, scent, smell, spray **06** eulogy, favour, honour, praise, wreath **07** corsage, garland, nosegay, perfume, tribute **08** accolade, approval **09** fragrance, redolence **10** buttonhole, compliment **11** boutonnière **12** commendation, felicitation, pat on the back **15** congratulations, odoriferousness

bourgeois
04 dull **05** banal, trite **06** square **07** humdrum **08** ordinary **09** hidebound, Pooterish **10** capitalist, conformist, pedestrian, uncreative, uncultured, uninspired, unoriginal **11** Biedermeier, commonplace, middle-class, traditional **12** conservative, conventional **13** materialistic, unadventurous, unimaginative **15** money-orientated

bout
02 go **03** fit, jag, run **04** bend, bust, dose, fall, game, heat, lush, sesh, term, time, turn **05** binge, boose, booze, bouse, brash, burst, drunk, fight,

match, round, set-to, spasm, spell, spree, stint, touch, veney, venue **06** attack, battle, beer-up, bottle, course, fuddle, period, screed, venewe **07** booze-up, carouse, contest, session, splurge, stretch, wassail, wrestle **08** struggle **09** encounter **10** engagement, makunouchi **11** competition

bovine
04 dull, dumb, slow **05** dense, thick **06** stupid **07** cowlike, doltish **09** dim-witted **10** cattlelike, slow-witted
• **bovine animals**
04 cows, neat **06** cattle

bow
03 arc, bob, nod, tie, yew **04** arch, arco, beak, beck, bend, duck, eugh, head, jook, jouk, knot, loop, lout, lowt, move, prow, ring, stem **05** crook, crush, curve, defer, dicky, drail, front, slope, stick, stoop, yield **06** accede, accept, circle, comply, crouch, curtsy, dickey, dickie, give in, humble, kowtow, salaam, subdue, submit **07** bending, concede, conquer, consent, incline, namaste, rostrum, succumb **08** forepart, namaskar, vanquish **09** acquiesce, genuflect, give way to, humiliate, lavaliere, obeisance, overpower, subjugate, surrender **10** capitulate, lavallière, salutation **11** fiddlestick, genuflexion, inclination, prostration **12** dorsiflexion **13** make obeisance **15** acknowledgement
• **bow out**
04 quit **05** leave **06** defect, desert, give up, resign, retire **07** abandon, back out, pull out **08** step down, withdraw **09** stand down **10** chicken out
• **part of bow**
03 nut **04** frog, heel, luff
• **with bow**
04 arco

bowdlerize
03 cut **04** edit **05** purge **06** censor, excise, modify, purify **07** clean up, expunge **09** expurgate **10** blue-pencil

bowels
04 core, guts **05** belly, colon, heart **06** cavity, centre, depths, inside, middle **07** innards, insides, viscera **08** entrails, interior **09** entralles **10** intestines

bower
03 bay **05** arbor **06** alcove, arbour, grotto, recess **07** retreat, shelter **09** sanctuary

bowl
03 cap, cog, pan **04** caup, dish, hurl, race, roll, rush, sink, spin, wood **05** basin, cogie, fling, hurry, joram, jorum, mazer, motor, pitch, speed, tazza, throw, whirl **06** beaker, bicker, career, coggie, crater, goblet, krater, piggin, propel, rotate, vessel **07** brimmer, cage-cup, chalice, écuelle, revolve **08** jeroboam, monteith **09** container, porringer,

posset cup, pottinger **10** receptacle **11** fingerglass **12** move steadily
• **bowled**
01 b
• **bowl over**
03 wow **04** fell, stun **05** amaze, floor, shock **06** topple **07** astound, stagger, startle **08** astonish, push into, surprise **09** dumbfound, knock down, overwhelm, unbalance **11** flabbergast **12** affect deeply **14** impress greatly

bowler
03 hat **04** skip **05** Derby **06** pot hat, seamer **07** Christy, hard hat, spinner **08** Christie

box
◊ *containment indicator*
02 tv **03** ark, dan, hit, pew, pix, pyx, urn **04** butt, case, cuff, etui, fist, fund, inro, loge, mill, pack, slap, slug, sock, spar, tele, wrap **05** bijou, chest, clout, fight, lodge, punch, pyxis, telly, thump, whack **06** batter, buffet, carton, casket, coffin, encase, packet, parcel, strike, wallop **07** coffret, package, present **09** baignoire, container **10** receptacle, television
• **box in**
04 cage, trap **05** hem in **06** bail up, coop up, corner, shut in **07** block in, confine, contain, enclose, fence in **08** imprison, restrain, restrict, surround **09** cordon off **12** circumscribe

boxer
03 ham, pug **07** cruiser, fighter **08** pugilist, southpaw **12** prizefighter **15** sparring partner

Boxers, managers and promoters include:

03 Ali (Muhammad)
04 Benn (Nigel), Clay (Cassius), Khan (Amir), King (Don)
05 Bruno (Frank), Duran (Roberto), Hamed ('Prince' Naseem), Lewis (Lennox), Louis (Joe), Moore (Archie), Tyson (Mike)
06 Cooper (Henry), Dundee (Angelo), Eubank (Chris), Holmes (Larry), Liston (Sonny), Spinks (Leon)
07 Dempsey (Jack), Foreman (George), Frazier (Joe), Leonard (Sugar Ray)
08 Marciano (Rocky), McGuigan (Barry), Robinson (Sugar Ray)
09 Armstrong (Henry), Holyfield (Evander), Honeyghan (Lloyd)
11 Fitzsimmons (Bob), Queensberry (Sir John Sholto Douglas, Marquis of)

boxing
04 ring **06** savate **08** fighting, pugilism, sparring **10** fisticuffs, infighting, the science **11** the noble art **13** prizefighting **15** the noble science
See also **sport**

Professional boxing weight divisions include:

09 flyweight
11 heavyweight, lightweight, strawweight

12 bantamweight, middleweight, welterweight
13 cruiserweight, featherweight, mini flyweight, minimum weight
14 light flyweight, super flyweight
15 junior flyweight

• **boxing match**
04 bout, mill, spar **10** glove-fight, prizefight

boy
03 bub, cub, kid, lad, son, tad **04** boyo, loon, lown, male, tama **05** bubby, bucko, child, gilpy, groom, knave, lowne, sprog, youth **06** chield, chokra, chummy, fellow, garçon, junior, loonie, nickum, nipper, shaver **07** galopin, gorsoon, gossoon **08** man-child, spalpeen, teenager, young man **09** dandiprat, dandyprat, Jack-a-Lent, schoolboy, stripling, youngster **10** adolescent, knave-bairn **11** guttersnipe, kinchin-cove **14** whippersnapper

Boys' names include:
02 Al, Cy, Ed, Ik, Jo
03 Abe, Alf, Ali, Asa, Bat, Baz, Ben, Bob, Dai, Dan, Deb, Dee, Del, Den, Dev, Dob, Don, Gay, Gaz, Gil, Gus, Guy, Hew, Huw, Ian, Ike, Iky, Ira, Ivo, Jay, Jem, Jim, Joe, Jon, Jos, Ken, Kim, Kit, Lal, Lee, Len, Leo, Lew, Mat, Max, Nat, Ned, Nye, Pat, Pip, Rab, Rae, Ray, Reg, Rex, Rob, Rod, Ron, Roy, Sam, Sim, Sol, Tam, Ted, Tim, Tom, Val, Vic, Viv, Wat, Wyn, Zia
04 Adam, Adil, Alan, Alec, Aled, Alex, Algy, Alun, Amin, Andy, Anil, Arch, Arun, Bart, Bert, Bill, Bram, Bryn, Carl, Ceri, Chad, Chae, Chay, Clem, Colm, Dave, Davy, Dean, Dewi, Dick, Dirk, Doug, Drew, Eddy, Egon, Eoin, Eric, Eryl, Euan, Evan, Ewan, Ewen, Ezra, Finn, Fred, Gabi, Gary, Gaye, Gene, Glen, Glyn, Gwyn, Hani, Hank, Hari, Hope, Huey, Hugh, Hugo, Iain, Ifor, Ivan, Ivon, Ivor, Jack, Jake, Jeff, Jock, Joel, Joey, John, Josh, Joss, Jude, Jule, Karl, Kirk, Kurt, Liam, Luke, Mark, Matt, Mick, Mike, Neal, Neil, Nick, Noam, Noel, Omar, Owen, Ozzy, Paul, Pete, Phil, Rana, Ravi, Raza, René, Rhys, Rick, Rolf, Rory, Ross, Ryan, Saul, Sean, Seth, Siôn, Theo, Thos, Toby, Tony, Trev, Umar, Walt, Will, Yves, Zach, Zack
05 Aaron, Abd-al, Abdul, Abram, Adeel, Adnan, Ahmad, Ahmed, Aidan, Aiden, Alfie, Allan, Allen, Alwin, Alwyn, Amrit, Andie, Angel, Angus, Anwar, Archy, Arran, Barry, Basil, Bazza, Benny, Billy, Bobby, Boris, Brent, Brett, Brian, Bruce, Bruno, Bryan, Bunny, Cahal, Calum, Cecil, Chaim, Chris, Chuck, Claud, Clint, Clive, Clyde, Colin, Colum, Conor, Corin, Cosmo, Craig, Cyril, Cyrus, Damon, Danny, David, Davie, Denis, Denny, Denys, Derek, Dicky, Dilip, Dipak, Donal, Duane, Dwane, Dylan, Eddie, Edgar, Edwin, Elroy,

Elton, Elvis, Elwyn, Emlyn, Emrys, Enoch, Ernie, Errol, Farid, Faruq, Felix, Fionn, Floyd, Frank, Gabby, Gamal, Garry, Gavin, Geoff, Gerry, Giles, Glenn, Gopal, Hamza, Harry, Harun, Hasan, Haydn, Henry, Homer, Howel, Humph, Husni, Hywel, Idris, Ieuan, Inigo, Isaac, Jacob, Jamal, James, Jamie, Jamil, Jared, Jason, Jerry, Jesse, Jimmy, Jools, Kamal, Kasim, Keith, Kelly, Kenny, Kerry, Kevan, Kevin, Kiran, Kumar, Lance, Larry, Leigh, Lenny, Leroy, Lewie, Lewis, Linus, Lloyd, Logan, Lorne, Louie, Louis, Lucas, Madoc, Manny, Micky, Miles, Moray, Moses, Moshe, Mungo, Murdo, Myles, Neale, Neddy, Niall, Nicky, Nicol, Nigel, Ollie, Orson, Oscar, Ozzie, Paddy, Patsy, Percy, Perry, Peter, Piers, Qasim, Rajiv, Ralph, Randy, Ricky, Roald, Robin, Roddy, Roger, Rowan, Rufus, Sacha, Salim, Sammy, Sandy, Sasha, Scott, Shane, Shaun, Shawn, Silas, Simon, Solly, Steve, Sunil, Taffy, Tariq, Teddy, Terry, Tommy, Tudor, Ulric, Ultan, Vijay, Vinay, Waldo, Walid, Wally, Wasim, Wayne, Willy, Wynne
06 Adrian, Albert, Alexei, Alexej, Alexis, Alfred, Andrew, Antony, Archie, Arnold, Arthur, Ashley, Ashraf, Aubrey, Austin, Barney, Benjie, Bernie, Bertie, Bharat, Billie, Blaise, Bobbie, Callum, Calvin, Caspar, Cathal, Cedric, Ciaran, Clancy, Claude, Clovis, Colley, Connor, Conrad, Dafydd, Damian, Damien, Daniel, Darren, Declan, Deepak, Delroy, Dennis, Denzil, Dermot, Deryck, Devdan, Dicken, Dickie, Dickon, Dilwyn, Dobbin, Donald, Donnie, Dougal, Dudley, Dugald, Duggie, Duncan, Dustin, Eamonn, Eamunn, Edmund, Edward, Ernest, Esmond, Eugene, Faisal, Fareed, Faysal, Fergus, Finbar, Fingal, Finlay, Finley, Fintan, Freddy, Gareth, Garret, George, Georgy, Gerald, Gerard, Gerrie, Gideon, Gobind, Gordon, Govind, Graeme, Graham, Gussie, Hamish, Harold, Haroun, Harvey, Hassan, Hayden, Haydon, Hector, Herbie, Hervey, Hilary, Horace, Howard, Howell, Hubert, Hughie, Husain, Isaiah, Iseult, Ismail, Israel, Jarvis, Jasper, Jeremy, Jerome, Jervis, Jethro, Jimmie, Jolyon, Jordan, Joseph, Joshua, Julian, Julius, Justin, Kelvin, Kennie, Kieran, Kieron, Laurie, Lawrie, Lennie, Leslie, Lester, Lionel, Lorcan, Lucius, Luther, Lynsey, Magnus, Mahmud, Marcel, Marcus, Marlon, Martin, Martyn, Marvin, Melvin, Melvyn, Mervyn, Milton, Morgan, Morris, Murray, Nathan, Neddie, Nichol, Ninian, Norman, Oliver, Osbert, Oswald, Pascal, Pearce, Philip, Pierce, Rajesh, Randal, Ranulf, Reggie, Reuben, Richie, Robbie, Robert, Rodney,

Roland, Ronald, Rudolf, Rupert, Saleem, Samuel, Sanjay, Seamas, Seamus, Seumas, Shamus, Sharif, Sidney, Sorley, Steven, Stevie, St John, Stuart, Sydney, Teddie, Thomas, Timmie, Tobias, Trevor, Tyrone, Vernon, Victor, Vikram, Virgil, Vivian, Vyvian, Vyvyan, Walter, Willie, Xavier
07 Abraham, Alister, Ambrose, Aneurin, Anthony, Auberon, Barnaby, Bernard, Bertram, Brendan, Chandra, Charles, Charley, Charlie, Christy, Clement, Crispin, Derrick, Desmond, Dominic, Douglas, Eustace, Feargal, Finbarr, Francie, Francis, Frankie, Freddie, Gabriel, Geordie, Georgie, Geraint, Gervase, Gilbert, Godfrey, Grahame, Gwillym, Herbert, Humphry, Hussain, Hussein, Ibrahim, Isadore, Isidore, Isodore, Jeffrey, Johnnie, Kenneth, Killian, Krishna, Lachlan, Leonard, Leopold, Lindsay, Lindsey, Ludovic, Malcolm, Matthew, Maurice, Michael, Murdoch, Mustafa, Neville, Nicolas, Orlando, Patrick, Peredur, Phillip, Quentin, Quintin, Quinton, Randall, Randolf, Ranulph, Raymond, Reynold, Richard, Rowland, Rudolph, Russell, Shankar, Shelley, Solomon, Stanley, Stephen, Stewart, Terence, Timothy, Torquil, Tristan, Vaughan, Vincent, Wilfred, Wilfrid, William, Winston, Zachary
08 Alasdair, Alastair, Algernon, Alistair, Augustus, Barnabas, Benedick, Benedict, Benjamin, Beverley, Christie, Clarence, Clifford, Crispian, Cuthbert, Dominick, Emmanuel, Frederic, Geoffrey, Humphrey, Jonathan, Jonathon, Kimberly, Kingsley, Lancelot, Laurence, Lawrence, Llewelyn, Matthias, Meredith, Mordecai, Muhammad, Nicholas, Perceval, Percival, Randolph, Reginald, Roderick, Ruaidhri, Ruairidh, Ruaraidh, Rupinder, Terrance, Theodore, Tristram
09 Alexander, Archibald, Augustine, Christian, Ferdinand, Frederick, Kimberley, Launcelot, Nathaniel, Peregrine, Sebastian, Siegfried, Somhairle, Sylvester, Valentine
10 Maximilian
11 Bartholomew, Christopher

boycott
03 ban, bar **04** snub **05** avoid, black, spurn **06** eschew, ignore, outlaw, refuse, reject **07** embargo, exclude, refusal **08** disallow, prohibit, spurning **09** blacklist, exclusion, ostracism, ostracize, proscribe, rejection **11** prohibition **12** cold-shoulder, proscription **14** send to Coventry

boyfriend
03 ami, guy, man **04** beau, date **05** bloke, fella, lover **06** fellow, fiancé, steady, suitor, toyboy **07** admirer, best

boy, partner, squeeze **08** young man **09** cohabitee **10** sweetheart **11** live-in lover **15** common-law spouse

boyish
05 gamin, green, young **06** gamine, tomboy **07** puerile **08** childish, immature, innocent, juvenile, youthful **09** childlike **10** adolescent, unfeminine, unmaidenly

brace
02 II, PR **03** duo, tie, two **04** beam, bend, bind, pair, prop, stay, vice **05** clamp, nerve, shore, steel, strap, strut, truss **06** couple, fasten, gear up, hold up, prop up, secure, steady, wimble **07** bandage, bolster, compose, fortify, prepare, psych up, shore up, shoring, support, tighten, twosome **08** accolade, bridging, buttress, fastener, get ready **09** reinforce, stanchion, undergird **10** strengthen **13** reinforcement

bracelet
04 band **05** armil **06** bangle **07** armilla, circlet **08** handcuff, wristlet

bracing
05 brisk, crisp, fresh, tonic **07** rousing **08** reviving, vigorous **09** energetic **10** energizing, enlivening, fortifying, refreshing **11** stimulating **12** exhilarating, invigorating **13** strengthening

bracken
04 tara **05** brake

bracket
◇ containment indicator
03 lot **04** prop, rest, stay **05** batch, brace, class, frame, group **06** becket, cohort, corbel, gusset, holder, mutule, trivet **07** cripple, potence, support **08** category, grouping **09** goose-neck, modillion **10** cantilever, misericord **11** misericorde, parenthesis **14** classification

brackish
04 brak, salt **05** briny, salty **06** bitter, saline **07** saltish **11** salsuginous

bract
05 glume, palea **06** spathe **08** phyllary **10** hypsophyll

brad
04 nail

brag
03 gab **04** bull, crow **05** boast, proud, vapor, vaunt **06** vapour **07** big-note, bluster, proudly, show off, swagger, talk big **08** mouth off **10** shoot a line **11** hyperbolize, rodomontade **12** cry roast-meat, lay it on thick **15** blow your own horn

braggart
06 gascon **07** bluffer, boaster, show-off, swasher, windbag **08** bangster, big mouth, boastful, fanfaron, puckfist **09** blusterer, loud-mouth, swaggerer **11** braggadocio **12** rodomontader, swashbuckler

bragging
06 hot air **07** bluster, bravado **08** boasting, vauntery **09** thrasonic **10** showing-off **11** jactitation, thrasonical **12** boastfulness, exaggeration **13** tongue-doubtie

braid
04 cord, lace, tail, wind, yarn **05** plait, pleat, queue, ravel, tress, twine, twist, weave **06** caddis, ric-rac, sennit, sinnet, thread **07** caddice, embraid, entwine **08** reproach, rick-rack, soutache **09** interlace, passement **10** intertwine, interweave **13** scrambled eggs

brain
◇ anagram indicator
03 wit **04** head, mind, nous **05** savvy, sense **06** acumen, boffin, brains, expert, genius, pundit, reason **07** egghead, prodigy, scholar **08** brainbox, highbrow, pia mater, sagacity **09** intellect, sensorium **10** encephalon, grey matter, mastermind, shrewdness **11** cleverclogs, common sense, upper storey **12** intellectual, intelligence **13** understanding

> Brain parts include:

04 falx, lobe, lobi, pons
06 cortex
07 cinerea
08 amygdala, cerebrum, meninges, midbrain, thalamus
09 brainstem, forebrain, hindbrain, ventricle
10 Broca's area, cerebellum, grey matter, pineal body, spinal cord
11 frontal lobe, hippocampus, white matter
12 hypothalamus, limbic system, parietal lobe, Purkinje cell, temporal lobe, visual cortex
13 choroid plexus, mesencephalon, occipital lobe, olfactory bulb, optic thalamus, Wernicke's area
14 cerebral cortex, corpus callosum, left hemisphere, pituitary gland
15 right hemisphere, substantia nigra

brainless
04 daft **05** crazy, inept, silly **06** stupid **07** foolish, idiotic **08** mindless **09** hen-witted, senseless **10** half-witted **11** incompetent, thoughtless **12** simple-minded

brains
02 IQ **03** wit **04** loaf, nous **05** harns, savey, savvy **06** common, savvey, sconce, wisdom **08** gumption **10** grey matter

brainteaser
05 poser **06** puzzle, riddle **07** problem **09** conundrum **10** mind-bender **12** brain-twister

brainwashing
08 grilling **09** menticide **10** persuasion **11** mind-bending, re-education **12** conditioning, pressurizing **14** indoctrination

brainy
04 wise **05** smart **06** bright, clever, gifted **07** sapient **09** brilliant **11** intelligent **12** intellectual

brake
04 curb, drag, fern, halt, rein, slow, stop **05** check **06** harrow, pull up, retard **07** bracken, control, slacken, thicket **08** moderate, slow down **09** restraint **10** constraint, decelerate, retardment **11** reduce speed, restriction
• **braking system**
03 ABS

bramble
05 Rubus **06** lawyer **08** dewberry **10** blackberry, cloudberry **12** Penang-lawyer

bran
06 chesil, chisel, shorts **07** pollard **08** roughage

branch
02 br **03** arm, cow, leg, lye **04** axis, fork, limb, lobe, loop, part, reis, rice, stem, whip, wing **05** bough, corps, prong, ramus, scrog, shoot, sprig, withy **06** agency, bureau, office **07** braunch, cladode, section **08** division, offshoot **09** affiliate, succursal, tributary **10** department, discipline, subsection, subsidiary **11** local office, phylloclade, subdivision **12** ramification **14** regional office
• **branch off**
04 fork **06** divide, offset, spring **07** deviate, diverge, furcate **08** separate **09** bifurcate
• **branch out**
04 vary **05** add to **06** expand, extend, ramify **07** develop, enlarge **08** increase, multiply **09** diversify, spread out, subdivide **10** broaden out **11** proliferate

brand
03 tag **04** burn, chop, kind, line, logo, make, mark, sear, sere, sign, sort, type, wipe **05** class, grill, label, stain, stamp, taint **06** burn in, emblem, marque, symbol **07** censure, quality, species, variety **08** besmirch, denounce, disgrace, hallmark, typecast **09** brand-name, discredit, trademark, tradename **10** stigmatize **14** identification **15** identifying mark

brandish
03 wag **04** wave **05** bless, flash, raise, shake, swing, wield **06** flaunt, hurtle, parade, waving **07** display, exhibit, vibrate, wampish **08** flourish

brandy
03 dop **04** fine, marc **05** bingo, mobby, Nantz, peach, smoke **06** Cognac, grappa, mobbie **07** quetsch **08** Armagnac, Calvados, eau de vie, mahogany, slivovic **09** apple-jack, aqua vitae, Cape smoke, mirabelle, slivovica, slivovitz **10** ball of fire **11** aguardiente, cold-without, water of life **12** cherry bounce **13** fine Champagne

rash

bold, rash, rude **05** cocky, crude,
sty, pushy **06** brazen, flashy
assured, brittle, forward
impudent, insolent, reckless
assertive, audacious, bumptious,
olhardy, heartburn, impetuous,
pulsive **10** incautious, indiscreet
impertinent, precipitate **13** self-
nfident

rashly

boldly, rashly, rudely **07** cockily,
stily, pushily **08** brazenly
assuredly, forwardly **10** impudently,
solently, recklessly **11** assertively,
daciously, foolhardily, impetuously,
pulsively **12** incautiously,
discreetly **13** impertinently,
ecipitately **15** self-confidently

rashness

audacity, boldness, rashness,
deness **09** hastiness, impudence,
caution, insolence, pushiness
brazenness **12** impertinence,
cklessness **13** assertiveness,
olhardiness **14** self-confidence

rass

gall, loot, sass **05** cheek, money,
rve **06** latten **08** audacity,
utzpah, orichalc, rudeness, temerity
brass neck, impudence, insolence,
cessary, oricalche **10** brass nerve,
azenness, effrontery **11** presumption
impertinence

top brass

VIPs

rassy

bold, hard, loud **05** brash, cocky,
rsh, noisy, pushy, sassy, saucy
brazen **07** blaring, forward, grating,
rring, raucous **08** insolent, jangling,
ercing, strident **09** dissonant,
ameless **11** loud-mouthed

rat

get, imp, kid **04** gait, geit, gyte
brach, puppy **06** nipper, rascal
brachet **08** bantling, bratchet
youngster **10** jackanapes
guttersnipe **14** whippersnapper

ravado

show, talk **05** boast, brave
parade **07** bluster, bombast,
avery, swagger **08** boasting,
agging, pretence, vaunting
swaggerer **10** showing-off
braggadocio, fanfaronade,
domontade

rave

bear, bold, dare, defy, face
bravo, bully, gutsy, hardy, manly,
ble, showy **06** daring, endure, feisty,
tty, heroic, plucky, spunky, suffer
doughty, gallant, stoical, valiant
confront, face up to, fearless,
ndsome, intrepid, resolute, stalwart,
afraid, valorous, yeomanly
audacious, challenge, dauntless,
cellent, put up with, stand up to,
daunted, withstand **10** courageous

11 indomitable, lion-hearted,
unflinching **12** face the music, not turn
a hair, stout-hearted **14** game as Ned
Kelly, keep your chin up

bravely

06 boldly **07** hardily **08** daringly,
pluckily, yeomanly **09** doughtily,
gallantly, stoically, valiantly
10 fearlessly, heroically, intrepidly,
resolutely, stalwartly, valorously
11 audaciously, dauntlessly,
indomitably, undauntedly
12 courageously **13** unflinchingly
14 stout-heartedly

bravery

04 grit, guts **05** pluck, spunk, valor
06 daring, finery, mettle, spirit, valour
07 bravado, courage, heroism,
prowess **08** audacity, boldness,
chivalry, tenacity, valiance
09 fortitude, gallantry, hardiness
10 resolution **11** intrepidity
12 fearlessness, stalwartness
13 dauntlessness **14** courageousness,
indomitability

bravo

01 B **03** olé **04** euge **08** well done
09 excellent, spadassin

bravura

04 dash, élan **06** spirit **07** sparkle
10 brilliance **12** magnificence

brawl

03 row **04** dust, fray, rout **05** argue,
broil, clash, fight, flite, flyte, mêlée,
scold, scrap **06** affray, bundle, bust-up,
dust-up, fracas, fratch, ruckus, rumpus,
stoush, tussle **07** bagarre, brabble,
brangle, dispute, punch-up, quarrel,
scuffle, tuilyie, tuilzie, wrangle, wrestle
08 argument, disorder, skirmish,
squabble **09** altercate
10 Donnybrook, fisticuffs, free-for-all,
rough-house **11** altercation

brawn

04 beef, boar, bulk **05** might, power
06 muscle, sinews **07** muscles
08 beefcake, strength **09** beefiness,
bulkiness **10** headcheese, robustness
11 muscularity

brawny

05 beefy, bulky, burly, hardy, hefty,
hunky, husky, meaty, solid **06** fleshy,
robust, sinewy, strong, sturdy
07 hulking, massive **08** athletic,
muscular, powerful, stalwart, vigorous
09 strapping, well-built

bray

04 bell, hoot, roar **05** blare, neigh
06 bellow, heehaw, whinny
07 screech, trumpet

brazen

04 bold, pert **05** brash, pushy, saucy
06 brassy **07** blatant, defiant, forward
08 flagrant, immodest, impudent,
insolent **09** audacious, bald-faced,
barefaced, shameless, unabashed,
unashamed **10** hard-boiled, in-your-
face

• brazen it out

04 defy **09** be defiant **11** be
unashamed **12** be impenitent

brazenly

06 boldly **09** blatantly, defiantly
10 flagrantly, immodestly, impudently,
insolently **11** audaciously, shamelessly,
unashamedly

brazier

06 hearth, mangal **07** brasero
08 scaldino **10** fire-basket

Brazil

02 BR **03** BRA **04** Braz

breach

03 gap **04** gulf, hole, rift, slap
05 break, chasm, cleft, crack, lapse,
space, split, unlaw **06** open up, saltus,
schism **07** crevice, fissure, offence,
offense, opening, parting, quarrel,
rupture, violate **08** aperture, breakers,
breaking, division, fraction, infringe,
solution, trespass, variance **09** break
open, severance, violation
10 alienation, contravene, difference,
disruption, dissension, infraction,
separation **12** break through, burst
through, disaffection, disagreement,
disobedience, dissociation,
estrangement, infringement
13 contravention, transgression

bread

03 fat, tin **04** cash, diet, dosh, fare,
food, pane **05** dough, dumps, funds,
lolly, money, sugar **06** crusts
07 shekels **08** sandwich, victuals
09 nutriment **10** livelihood, provisions,
sustenance **11** necessities,
nourishment, spondulicks, subsistence
12 the necessary

Bread and rolls include:

03 bap, cob, nan, rye, tea
04 azym, cake, corn, diet, farl, flat, loaf,
milk, naan, pita, pone, roti, soda
05 arepa, azyme, bagel, black, brown,
cheat, fancy, horse, matza, matzo,
pitta, plait, poori, ravel, white
06 burger, damper, French, garlic,
graham, hoagie, hot dog, Indian,
injera, lavash, matzah, matzoh,
panini, panino, simnel, stotty, wastel
07 bannock, bloomer, brioche,
brownie, buttery, challah, chapati,
currant, ficelle, granary, jannock,
manchet, paratha, pretzel, stollen,
stottie, wheaten
08 baguette, barm cake, chapatti,
ciabatta, corn pone, focaccia,
grissini, leavened, milk loaf,
ravelled, ryebread, schnecke,
standard, tortilla
09 bara brith, barmbrack, batch loaf,
burger bun, cornbread, croissant,
flatbread, hamburger, petit pain,
schnecken, shewbread,
showbread, sourdough, wholemeal
10 breadstick, bridge roll, finger roll,
French loaf, stotty cake,
unleavened, vienna loaf,
wholewheat

11 cottage loaf, French stick, morning roll, potato bread, potato scone
12 pumpernickel
13 farmhouse loaf
14 pain au chocolat

- **bread and butter**
11 maintenance
- **bread in milk**
03 sop

breadbasket
03 tum **05** tummy **07** stomach

breadth
01 b **04** beam, size, span **05** range, reach, scale, scope, sweep, width **06** extent, spread **07** compass, expanse, measure **08** latitude, vastness, wideness **09** amplitude, beaminess, broadness, dimension, magnitude, thickness **10** distension **13** extensiveness

break
◇ anagram indicator
◇ insertion indicator
03 gap, vac **04** beat, bust, dash, dawn, fail, gash, halt, hole, kick, lash, luck, lull, open, part, quit, rend, rest, rift, rise, ruin, snap, stop, tame, tear, tell, vary **05** begin, cleft, crack, crash, crush, excel, flout, let-up, outdo, pause, pound, sever, smash, solve, split **06** appear, be born, better, breach, chance, change, cut off, cut out, decode, divide, emerge, exceed, falter, give up, go phut, impair, impart, inform, lessen, open up, pack up, pierce, reduce, reveal, schism, shiver, soften, strike, subdue, weaken, worsen **07** abandon, conk out, crevice, cushion, decrypt, destroy, disobey, disturb, divulge, fissure, fortune, go kaput, holiday, improve, lighten, opening, respite, rupture, shatter, smoke-ho, stammer, stumble, stutter, surpass, suspend, time off, time-out, unravel, violate, work out **08** announce, breather, decipher, demolish, diminish, disclose, enfeeble, fracture, infringe, interval, outstrip, overcome, puncture, separate, shake off, splinter, vacation **09** advantage, dishonour, figure out, interlude, interrupt, perforate, undermine **10** contravene, demoralize, relinquish, separation **11** discontinue, malfunction, opportunity, stop working **12** bring to an end, disintegrate, estrangement, go on the blink, intermission, interruption, stroke of luck **13** interfere with
- **break away**
03 fly **04** flee, quit **05** leave, split, start **06** depart, detach, escape, secede **07** run away **08** separate, split off **11** part company **13** make a run for it
- **break down**
02 go **04** cark, conk, fail, kark, stop **05** crash, crock, crush, plash, smash **06** detail, go down, go phut, pack up **07** analyse, burn out, conk out, crack

up, crock up, destroy, dissect, founder, give way, itemize, seize up **08** collapse, demolish, separate **09** attenuate, decompose, knock down **10** be overcome, categorize, go to pieces **11** fall through, lose control, stop working **13** come to nothing
- **break in**
03 rob **04** raid, tame, wear **05** cut in, prime, start, train **06** burgle, butt in, irrupt **07** impinge, intrude **08** accustom, encroach **09** condition, cultivate, get used to, interject, interpose, interrupt, intervene **14** enter illegally
- **break off**
03 end **04** halt, part, stop **05** cease, pause, sever **06** detach, divide, finish **07** snap off, suspend **08** dissever, separate **09** interrupt, terminate **10** disconnect **11** discontinue **12** bring to an end
- **break out**
03 rip **04** bolt, flee **05** arise, begin, erupt, occur, shout, start **06** blow up, emerge, escape, happen **07** abscond, exclaim, flare up **08** burst out, commence **09** come out in, interject **13** begin suddenly
- **break through**
04 pass **06** emerge **07** succeed **08** fracture, overcome, progress **09** penetrate **10** gain ground **11** leap forward, make headway
- **break up**
◇ anagram indicator
◇ containment indicator
04 part, stop **05** sever, split, stave **06** divide, finish, reduce, reform **07** adjourn, destroy, disband, divorce, resolve, split up, suspend **08** demolish, diffract, disperse, dissolve, separate, splinter, to-bruise **09** dismantle, dismember, take apart, terminate **11** come to an end, discontinue, part company **12** bring to an end, disintegrate
- **break with**
04 drop, jilt **05** ditch **06** reject **08** part with, renounce **09** repudiate **10** finish with **12** separate from

breakable
05 frail **06** flimsy **07** brittle, fragile, friable **08** delicate **09** frangible **10** jerry-built **12** easily broken **13** insubstantial

breakaway
05 rebel **06** escape, revolt **08** apostate, renegade, seceding **09** defection, heretical, secession **10** dissenting, schismatic, separatist, withdrawal **12** secessionist

breakdown
07 failure **08** analysis, collapse, stoppage **10** cracking-up, dissection **11** itemization, malfunction **12** interruption **13** going to pieces **14** categorization, classification, disintegration
- **breakdown service**
02 AA **03** RAC

breaker
04 wave **06** billow, buster, roller **10** roughrider **11** white horses

breakfast
07 dejeune, disjune **08** déjeuner **10** chota hazri **13** petit déjeuner
See also **cereal**

break-in
04 raid **07** larceny, robbery **08** burglary, invasion, trespass **09** intrusion **13** house-breaking

breakneck
05 rapid, swift **06** speedy **07** express **08** headlong, very fast **09** very quick **11** precipitate **13** like lightning

breakthrough
04 find, gain, leap, step **07** advance, finding, headway **08** progress **09** discovery, invention, milestone **10** innovation **11** development, improvement, leap forward, quantum leap, step forward

break-up
03 end **04** rift **05** split **06** finish **07** debacle, divorce, parting, upbreak **09** crumbling, dispersal **10** separation **11** dissolution, splitting-up, termination **14** disintegration

breakwater
04 dock, mole, pier, quay, spur **05** jetty, wharf **06** groyne **07** bulwark, sea wall

bream
03 tai **05** porgy **06** braise, braize, porgie, sargos, sargus **08** tarwhine

breast
03 dug, pap, tit **04** boob, bust, stem, teat **05** booby, bosom, chest, diddy, front, heart, mamma, titty **06** nipple, thorax **07** brisket, bristol, knocker **08** breaskit

breastplate
06 byrnie, thorax **07** cuirass, placket **08** pectoral, plastron, rational

breath
03 air **04** gasp, gulp, gust, hint, pant, puff, sigh, waft, wind **05** aroma, odour, prana, smell, whiff **06** breeze, flatus, murmur, pneuma, spirit **07** whisper **09** breathing, suspicion, undertone **10** exhalation, inhalation, suggestion **11** inspiration, respiration

breathe
04 gasp, pant, puff, sigh, tell **05** imbue, snore, utter, voice **06** exhale, expire, impart, infuse, inhale, inject, instil, murmur **07** express, inspire, respire, suspire, whisper **09** embreathe, inbreathe, transfuse **10** articulate, insufflate

breather
04 gill, halt, lung, nare, rest, walk **05** break, pause **06** recess **07** respite **10** relaxation **14** breathing space, constitutional

breathless
04 agog, dead **05** eager **06** pooped,

puffed, winded **07** airless, anxious, choking, excited, gasping, panting, puffing **08** feverish, wheezing **09** exhausted, expectant, impatient, pooped out, puffed out **10** in suspense **11** open-mouthed, out of breath, short-winded, tuckered out

breathtaking
06 moving **07** amazing **08** drop-dead, exciting, stirring, stunning **09** thrilling **10** astounding, impressive, stupendous **11** astonishing, magnificent, spectacular **12** awe-inspiring, overwhelming

breathtakingly
09 amazingly **10** excitingly, stirringly, stunningly **11** thrillingly **12** impressively, stupendously **13** astonishingly, spectacularly **14** awe-inspiringly, overwhelmingly

breeches
04 hose **05** slops **06** breeks, tights, trouse, trunks **07** plushes, trusses **08** chausses, jodhpurs, leathers, trossers, trousers **09** buckskins, knee-cords, strossers, trunk hose **12** galligaskins, pedal pushers, small-clothes **14** knickerbockers

breed
04 bear, kind, line, make, race, rear, sort, type **05** cause, class, hatch, raise, stamp, stock **06** arouse, create, family, foster, hybrid, strain **07** bring up, calibre, develop, lineage, nourish, nurture, produce, progeny, species, variety **08** engender, generate, multiply, occasion, pedigree **09** cultivate, originate, procreate, propagate, pullulate, reproduce **10** bring about, bring forth, give rise to **11** give birth to

breeding
05 stock **06** polish **07** culture, lineage, manners, nurture, raising, rearing **08** ancestry, civility, gentrice, training, urbanity **09** education, gentility **10** politeness, refinement, upbringing **11** cultivation, development, good manners, procreation, savoir-vivre **12** reproduction
• **breeding establishment**
04 stud

breeding-ground
04 nest **06** cradle, hotbed, school **07** nursery **08** hothouse **14** training ground

breeze
◇ *anagram indicator*
03 air **04** flit, gust, puff, sail, trip, waft, wind **05** glide, hurry, sally, slant, snift, sweep **06** breath, doctor, flurry, wander, zephyr **07** cat's paw, draught, saunter, snifter **08** sniffler **12** periodic wind

breezy
04 airy **05** blowy, brisk, fresh, gusty, light, windy **06** blithe, bright, casual, jaunty, lively **07** blowing, buoyant, relaxed, squally **08** animated,

blustery, carefree, cheerful, debonair, informal **09** confident, easy-going, vivacious **12** exhilarating, light-hearted

Brenda
02 ER

brevity
07 economy, fewness **08** curtness, laconism **09** briefness, concision, crispness, pithiness, shortness, terseness **10** abruptness, transience **11** compactness, conciseness **12** ephemerality, impermanence, incisiveness, succinctness **14** transitoriness

brew
◇ *anagram indicator*
04 boil, cook, loom, make, mash, plan, plot, soak, stew **05** blend, drink, hatch, steep **06** devise, excite, foment, gather, infuse, liquor, potion, scheme, seethe **07** build up, concoct, develop, ferment, mixture, prepare, project **08** beverage, compound, contrive, infusion **10** be on its way, concoction **11** combination, preparation **12** distillation, fermentation **13** be in the offing **15** be in preparation

bribe
03 buy, fix, sop **04** bung, dash, gift, palm, vail, wage **05** bonus, booty, drink, sling, spoil, touch, vails, vales **06** boodle, buy off, carrot, grease, hamper, nobble, pay off, pay-off, payola, reward, square, suborn **07** buy over, corrupt, douceur, palm-oil, pension **08** kickback, the drink **09** hush money, incentive, keep sweet, lubricate, refresher, slush fund, sweetener **10** allurement, back-hander, enticement, inducement, palm-grease, take care of **12** straightener **13** gratification **15** protection money

bribery
05 graft **09** embracery **10** corruption, inducement, protection **11** subornation **12** malversation, palm-greasing

bric-à-brac
06 curios **07** baubles, gewgaws **08** antiques, bibelots, trinkets, trumpery **09** gimcracks, ornaments **10** Japanesery, rattletrap, Victoriana **11** knick-knacks, odds and ends **13** bits and pieces

brick
03 bar, bur, pal **04** burr, chum, lump, mass, mate, rock, slab **05** adobe, block, buddy, gault, piece, stone, wedge **06** header, rubber, rustic **07** clinker, fletton, klinker, nogging, soldier **09** briquette, firebrick, stretcher **10** real friend **11** breeze block **12** Dutch clinker
• **brick waste**
04 grog
• **piece of brick**
03 bat

bridal
07 marital, nuptial, wedding **08** conjugal, marriage **09** connubial **11** matrimonial

bride
04 wife **06** spouse **07** GI bride **08** newly-wed, war bride, wife-to-be **09** bride-to-be **11** honeymooner **15** marriage partner

bridegroom
05 groom **06** spouse **07** husband **08** newly-wed **11** honeymooner, husband-to-be **15** marriage partner

bridge
02 br **03** tie **04** bind, bond, fill, join, link, pons, rest, span **05** cross, unite **06** couple, go over **07** connect, spanner **08** traverse **10** connection **11** reach across

Bridge types include:
03 air, fly
04 arch, beam, deck, draw, foot, leaf, over, raft, road, rope, skew, toll, wire
05 chain, pivot, swing
06 Bailey, flying, girder
07 bascule, flyover, lattice, lifting, pontoon, railway, through, viaduct
08 aqueduct, causeway, floating, humpback, overpass
09 box girder
10 cantilever, suspension, traversing
11 cable-stayed

Bridges include:
03 Tay
04 Skye, Tyne
05 Forth, Sighs, Tower
06 Bailey, Humber, Kintai, London, Rialto, Severn
07 Bifrost, Clifton, Rainbow, Tsing Ma, Yichang
08 Bosporus, Brooklyn, Jiangyin, Mackinac, Waterloo
09 Evergreen, Forth Road, Kurushima, River Kwai
10 Bosporus II, Golden Gate, Höga Kusten, Ironbridge, Millennium, Pont du Gard, Storebaelt
11 Brocade Sash
12 Akashi-Kaikyo, Pont d'Avignon, Ponte Vecchio
13 Great Belt East, Kita Bisan-seto, Millau Viaduct, Sydney Harbour
14 Ponte 25 de Abril, Quebec Railroad
15 Minami Bisan-Seto

• **bridge player**
01 e, n, s, w **04** east, west **05** north, south
• **bridge support**
04 pier
• **bridge system**
04 Acol **06** canapé **09** blackwood

bridle
05 check **06** branks, govern, halter, master, subdue **07** bristle, contain, control, repress **08** hold back, moderate, restrain **09** hackamore, restraint **12** be offended by **15** become indignant

Bridle parts include:
03 bit
04 curb
05 cheek
06 musrol, pelham
07 bridoon, eye-flap, snaffle
08 browband, noseband
09 headstall
10 cheekpiece

See also **horse**

brief
◊ *tail deletion indicator*
02 KC, QC **04** case, curt, data, tell
05 blunt, breve, crisp, gen up, guide,
hasty, pithy, prime, quick, remit, sharp,
short, surly, swift, terse **06** abrupt,
advice, advise, digest, direct, fill in,
flying, inform, lawyer, orders, précis
07 brusque, compact, concise,
cursory, defence, dossier, explain,
laconic, limited, mandate, outline,
passing, prepare, summary
08 abridged, abstract, argument,
breviate, briefing, capsular, evidence,
fleeting, instruct, succinct **09** barrister,
condensed, directive, ephemeral,
fugacious, laconical, momentary,
temporary, thumbnail, tout court,
transient **10** aphoristic, compressed,
directions, evanescent, short-lived,
transitory **11** abridgement, information
12 instructions **13** bring up to date,
short and sweet **14** responsibility

briefing
03 gen **06** advice, orders **07** low-
down, meeting, priming, run-down
08 guidance **09** filling-in
10 conference, directions, intimation
11 information, preparation
12 instructions

briefly
◊ *tail deletion indicator*
05 in few, short **07** in a word, in brief, in
short, quickly, shortly, tersely
09 concisely, cursorily, precisely,
summarily **10** succinctly, to the point
11 in a few words, in a nutshell

brigade
03 Bde **04** band, body, crew, team, unit
05 corps, force, group, party, squad,
troop **07** company **10** contingent
• **Boys' Brigade**
02 BB

brigand
06 bandit, haiduk, outlaw, robber
07 cateran, heyduck, ruffian
08 gangster, marauder **09** desperado,
plunderer **10** bushranger, freebooter,
highwayman **11** trailbaston

bright
03 gay, lit, net **04** fine, glad, keen, nett,
rosy **05** acute, clear, happy, jolly, light,
merry, quick, sharp, smart, sunny, vivid
06 astute, brainy, clever, genial, joyful,
lively **07** beaming, blazing, glaring,
glowing, hopeful, intense, radiant,
shining **08** blinding, cheerful,
dazzling, flashing, gleaming, glorious,
luminous, lustrous, pleasant, splendid

09 beautiful, brilliant, cloudless,
effulgent, promising, refulgent,
sparkling, twinkling, unclouded,
vivacious **10** auspicious, favourable,
glistening, glittering, optimistic,
perceptive, propitious, shimmering
11 encouraging, illuminated, illustrious,
intelligent, quick-witted, resplendent
12 incandescent **15** bright as a button

brighten
03 rub **04** glow, jazz **05** gleam, pep
up, rub up, shine **06** buck up, buoy up,
jazz up, perk up, polish **07** burnish,
cheer up, clear up, enhance, enliven,
gladden, hearten, lighten, light up, liven
up **09** encourage, irradiate, refurbish,
smarten up **10** illuminate, make bright

brightly
06 ablaze, gladly **07** happily
08 joyfully **09** glaringly, glowingly,
intensely, radiantly **10** blindingly,
cheerfully, dazzlingly, splendidly
11 brilliantly, vivaciously

brilliance
04 tone **05** glare, glory, gloss, sheen
06 dazzle, genius, lustre, talent
07 bravura, glamour, prowess, sparkle
08 aptitude, fulgency, radiance,
splendor **09** greatness, intensity,
splendour, vividness **10** brightness,
cleverness, effulgence, excellence,
refulgence, virtuosity **11** coruscation,
distinction **12** magnificence,
resplendence

brilliant
03 ace, def **04** cool, hard, mega, neat,
pear, star **05** brill, gemmy, great, quick,
showy, vivid **06** astute, brainy, bright,
clever, expert, famous, gifted, glossy,
superb, wicked **07** blazing, crucial,
erudite, fulgent, glaring, intense,
lambent, radical, shining, skilful
08 dazzling, glorious, masterly,
smashing, splendid, talented, terrific,
top-notch **09** effulgent, excellent,
fantastic, refulgent, sparkling,
splendent, sunbright, wonderful
10 brightsome, celebrated, glittering,
remarkable **11** exceptional, illustrious,
intelligent, magnificent, outstanding,
resourceful, resplendent
12 accomplished, enterprising, second
to none **13** scintillating **14** out of this
world

brilliantly
07 vividly **08** brightly, cleverly,
superbly **09** intensely, skilfully
10 dazzlingly, gloriously, splendidly
11 masterfully, wonderfully
13 magnificently, resplendently

brim
03 lip, rim, top **04** edge, poke
05 brink, limit, verge **06** border,
margin **09** perimeter **10** be full with
12 be filled with, overflow with
13 circumference

brimful
04 full **05** abrim **06** filled, jammed
07 bulging, crammed, stuffed

09 packed out **11** chock-a-block,
overflowing

brindled
04 pied **05** tabby **06** dotted **07** dappled,
flecked, mottled, piebald **08** speckled,
stippled, streaked **10** variegated

bring
03 fet, get, lay **04** bear, lead, take
05 carry, cause, fetch, force, guide,
usher **06** convey, create, escort,
prompt, submit **07** conduct, deliver,
present, produce, provoke
08 engender, initiate, result in
09 accompany, transport **10** make
happen, put forward
• **bring about**
04 make **05** cause, frame, wreak
06 create, effect, fulfil, manage
07 achieve, compass, inspire, operate,
perform, procure, produce, provoke,
realize **08** contrive, generate,
occasion, purchase **09** encompass,
instigate **10** accomplish
• **bring back**
◊ *reversal indicator*
05 evoke, recal **06** call up, recall,
reduce, relate, remind **07** recover,
reverse, suggest **13** take you back to
14 make you think of
• **bring down**
04 drop, oust, pull, stop **05** abate,
lower, shoot **06** defeat, depose,
derive, embace, embase, humble,
imbase, reduce, sadden, topple, unseat
07 destroy **08** decrease, dismount,
vanquish **09** knock down, overthrow,
shoot down **11** cause to drop, cause to
fall
• **bring forward**
05 raise **06** adduce, allege, object
07 advance, prepone, present,
produce, propose, suggest, trot out
10 put forward **11** make earlier
• **bring in**
◊ *containment indicator*
03 net **04** earn, make, wind **05** fetch,
gross, set up, yield **06** accrue, import,
induce, launch, return **07** pioneer,
produce, realize, usher in **08** initiate
09 introduce, originate, pronounce
10 inaugurate
• **bring off**
03 win **06** fulfil, rescue **07** achieve,
execute, perform, pull off
09 discharge, put across, succeed in
10 accomplish, consummate
• **bring on**
05 cause, infer **06** foster, induce, lead
to, prompt **07** advance, improve,
inspire, nurture, provoke **08** expedite,
generate, occasion **10** accelerate, give
rise to, make happen **11** precipitate
• **bring out**
05 issue, print **06** launch, stress
07 draw out, enhance, produce,
publish **09** emphasize, highlight,
introduce **10** accentuate
• **bring round**
◊ *containment indicator*
04 coax **05** rouse **06** awaken, cajole,
revive, wake up **07** bring to, convert,

in over **08** convince, persuade
11 resuscitate

bring up
reversal down indicator
03 cat **04** barf, form, puke, rear
05 breed, nurse, raise, teach, train,
vomit **06** broach, foster, nousle,
nuzzle, submit **07** care for, educate,
mention, nourish, noursle, nousell,
nurture, propose, throw up, touch on
09 introduce **11** regurgitate

brink
03 lip, rim **04** bank, brim, edge
05 limit, marge, verge **06** border,
hinge, margin **08** boundary
09 extremity, threshold

brio
03 pep, zip **04** dash **05** force, gusto,
oomph, verve **06** energy, spirit, vigour
08 dynamism, vivacity **09** animation
10 liveliness

brisk
04 busy, cant, cold, fast, good, perk,
pert, yare **05** agile, alert, cobby, crisp,
fresh, kedge, kedgy, kidge, quick, rapid,
sharp, smart **06** active, crouse, lively,
nimble, snappy **07** allegro, bracing
08 brushing, bustling, friskful, galliard,
spirited, vigorous **09** energetic,
brightly **10** no-nonsense, refreshing
11 stimulating **12** businesslike,
exhilarating, invigorating

briskly
04 well **06** busily, nimbly **07** allegro,
on moto, quickly, rapidly, sharply
08 abruptly **09** brusquely
10 decisively, vigorously
13 energetically

bristle
03 awn **04** barb, hair, rise, seta
05 birse, quill, spine, thorn **06** arista,
bridle, chaeta, seethe, setule, stilet,
striga, stylet **07** hum with, prickle,
stubble, whisker **08** abound in, bridle
at, teem with, vibrissa **09** swarm with
10 seethe with, stand on end,
chbraculum **11** be thick with, horripilate
12 be incensed at **14** draw yourself up

bristly
05 hairy, rough, spiky, spiny **06** hispid,
thorny **07** bearded, hirsute, prickly,
stubbly **08** echinate, unshaven
09 echinated, whiskered **10** barbellate

British
1 B **02** Br, GB, UK **03** pom **04** Brit
05 pommy
see also **monarch**

British Columbia
2 BC

brittle
anagram indicator
04 curt, edgy, hard **05** birsy, brash,
crisp, frail, frowy, frush, harsh, nervy,
sharp, short, spall, spalt, tense
06 frowie **07** bruckle, crackly, crumbly,
fragile, friable, froughy, grating,
nervous, redsear, shivery **08** delicate,
spot-short, redshare, redshire, redshort,

---

shattery, unstable **09** breakable, cold-
short, crumbling, frangible, irritable,
sensitive **12** easily broken

broach
◇ *anagram indicator*
03 tap **04** open, spit **05** begin, raise
06 hint at, open up, pierce, strike
07 bring up, mention, propose, refer to,
suggest **08** allude to **09** introduce

broad
04 free, open, vast, wide **05** ample,
clear, large, plain, roomy, vague
06 coarse, direct, marked, strong,
vulgar **07** evident, general, obvious
08 catholic, eclectic, spacious,
sweeping, unsubtle **09** capacious,
extensive, inclusive, outspoken,
universal, unlimited **10** noticeable,
widespread **11** compendious, far-
reaching, not detailed, unconcealed,
undisguised, wide-ranging **12** all-
embracing, encyclopedic, latitudinous
13 comprehensive

broadcast
◇ *anagram indicator*
◇ *homophone indicator*
03 air, sow **04** beam, show **05** aired,
cable, relay **06** repeat, report, spread
07 network, publish, radiate, scatter,
trailer, webcast **08** announce,
newscast, teletext, televise, transmit
09 advertise, cablecast, circulate,
make known, programme, publicize,
simulcast, soap opera **10** promulgate,
sportscast, telebridge **11** disseminate
12 transmission **15** access broadcast

• **outside broadcast**
02 OB **06** remote

broaden
05 widen **06** expand, extend, open up,
spread **07** augment, develop, enlarge,
stretch **08** increase **09** branch out,
diversify

broadly
05 fully **06** mainly, mostly, widely
07 as a rule, largely, usually
08 commonly, normally **09** generally
10 by and large, more or less, on the
whole, thoroughly **11** extensively, in
most cases, in principle **14** for the most
part **15** comprehensively

broad-minded
07 liberal **08** tolerant, unbiased
09 impartial, indulgent, receptive
10 forbearing, open-minded,
permissive **11** enlightened, progressive
12 free-thinking, unprejudiced
13 dispassionate

broadside
04 tire **05** blast, salvo, stick **06** attack,
volley **07** assault, censure **08** brickbat,
diatribe, harangue **09** battering,
cannonade, criticism, invective,
philippic **11** bombardment,
fulmination **12** counterblast,
denunciation

brochure
05 flyer **06** folder **07** booklet,
handout, leaflet **08** circular, handbill,

---

pamphlet **09** throwaway
10 broadsheet, prospectus

broil
03 fry **04** cook **05** grill, roast, toast
08 barbecue, stramash

broiling
03 hot **06** baking **07** boiling
08 roasting **09** scorching **10** blistering,
sweltering

broke
◇ *anagram indicator*
04 bust, poor **05** skint, stony **06** hard
up, ruined **07** bargain **08** bankrupt,
indigent, strapped **09** destitute,
insolvent, negotiate, penniless,
penurious **10** cleaned out, stony-
broke **11** impecunious
12 impoverished, on your uppers
14 on your beam ends **15** poverty-
stricken, strapped for cash

broken
◇ *anagram indicator*
04 bust, down, duff, rent, weak
05 burst, ended, kaput, tamed, wonky
06 beaten, failed, faulty, feeble, fitful,
pakaru **07** crushed, damaged, erratic,
halting, severed, smashed, subdued
08 defeated, divorced, ruptured
09 defective, destroyed, disturbed,
exhausted, faltering, fractured, gone
wrong, imperfect, knackered,
oppressed, separated, shattered,
spasmodic **10** demolished, disjointed,
dispirited, hesitating, not working, on
the blink, on the fritz, out of order,
stammering, vanquished
11 demoralized, fragmentary,
inoperative, interrupted, out of action
12 disconnected, intermittent
13 discontinuous **14** malfunctioning

• **not to be broken**
04 iron

broken-down
03 ill **04** bust, duff **05** kaput
06 broken, faulty, ruined **07** damaged,
decayed, rickety, worn-out
08 decrepit **09** collapsed, defective
10 on the blink, on the fritz, out of
order, ramshackle **11** dilapidated, in
disrepair, inoperative

broken-hearted
03 sad **04** down **07** forlorn, unhappy
08 dejected, desolate, dolorous,
mournful, wretched **09** miserable,
sorrowful **10** despairing, despondent,
devastated, prostrated **11** crestfallen,
heartbroken **12** disappointed,
disconsolate, inconsolable **13** grief-
stricken **14** down in the dumps

broker
03 job **04** deal **05** agent, agree, bania
06 banian, banyan, clinch, dealer,
factor, jobber, settle **07** arrange,
bargain, execute, handler, mediate
08 complete, conclude, organize
09 arbitrate, go-between, land agent,
middleman, negotiate **10** negotiator
11 arbitrageur, stockbroker,
stockjobber **12** intermediary

bromide
06 cliché, downer, opiate, truism
07 anodyne 08 banality, narcotic,
sedative 09 calmative, platitude
10 stereotype 11 barbiturate,
commonplace 12 sleeping pill
13 tranquillizer

bromine
02 Br

bronze
02 br 03 tan 04 rust 05 brass
06 auburn, copper, Titian 07 aeneous,
vermeil 08 chestnut 09 impudence
10 horseflesh 12 reddish-brown
14 copper-coloured

bronzed
05 brown 06 bronze, tanned
07 browned 08 hardened, sunburnt
09 sunburned, suntanned

brooch
03 pin 04 clip, ouch, prop 05 badge,
broch, clasp 06 fibula, tiepin 08 lapel
pin 09 breastpin

brood
03 eye, nid, nye, sit 04 aery, clan, eyry,
fret, kind, mope, muse, nest, nide, race,
sulk, team 05 aerie, ayrie, breed,
cleck, clock, cover, covey, eyrie, hatch,
issue, spawn, sperm, tribe, young
06 chicks, clutch, family, go over,
kindle, litter, ponder 07 agonize, dwell
on, eelfare, progeny 08 children,
clecking, incubate, meditate, mull over,
rehearse, ruminate 09 bairn-team,
bairn-time, fret about, household,
offspring, parentage 10 extraction,
worry about

brook
04 bear, beck, burn, gill, kill, purl, rill
05 allow, creek, fleet, ghyll, inlet, stand
06 accept, branch, endure, permit,
runnel, stream 07 abrooke, channel,
rivulet, stomach, support 08 tolerate
09 put up with, withstand
11 countenance, watercourse

broom
04 wisp 05 besom, scrub, spart
06 retama 07 cytisus, hag-weed
09 knee-holly, Turk's head 10 Jew's-
myrtle 15 shepherd's myrtle

broth
◇ anagram indicator
04 kail, kale, soup 05 ramen
06 brewis, cullis 08 bouillon, hotchpot
09 pot liquor 10 beef-brewis,
hodgepodge, hotchpotch, muslin-kale

brothel
03 kip 04 crib, stew 05 stews
06 bagnio, bordel 07 Corinth
08 bordello, cathouse, hothouse, red
light 10 bawdy-house, flash-house,
whorehouse 12 knocking-shop,
leaping-house 13 sporting house,
vaulting-house 14 house of ill fame,
massage parlour 15 disorderly house

brother
02 br 03 bro, fra, pal, sib 04 bhai, brer,
chum, mate, monk, sibb 05 billy,

buddy, frère, friar 06 billie, fellow,
friend, german 07 comrade, partner,
sibling 08 relation, relative
09 associate, colleague, companion
11 full brother, half-brother, twin-
brother 12 blood-brother 13 brother-
german
• **big brother**
05 prior 08 dictator

brotherhood
03 PRB 05 guild, union 06 clique,
league 07 society 08 alliance,
confrère 09 community, confrérie,
Félibrige 10 fellowship, fraternity,
friendship 11 association,
cameraderie, comradeship,
confederacy 12 fraternalism,
friendliness 13 confederation,
confraternity

brotherly
04 kind 05 loyal 06 caring, loving
08 amicable, friendly 09 fraternal
10 benevolent 11 sympathetic
12 affectionate 13 philanthropic

brow
03 tip, top 04 peak 05 brink, cliff,
ridge, verge 06 summit 07 pit-head,
temples 08 forehead

browbeat
05 bully, force, hound 06 coerce,
hector 07 dragoon, oppress
08 bulldoze, domineer, overbear,
threaten 09 tyrannize 10 intimidate

brown
02 br 03 fry 04 cook, fusc, seal
05 grill, singe, toast 06 tanned
07 bronzed, browned, embrown,
fuscous 08 sunburnt 09 infuscate

Browns include:

03 bay, dun, tan
04 buff, drab, ecru, fawn, pine, rust,
   sand, teak
05 beige, camel, cocoa, dusky, hazel,
   honey, khaki, mocha, ochre, rusty,
   sepia, taupe, tawny, tenné,
   umber
06 auburn, bister, bistre, bronze,
   burnet, coffee, copper, ginger,
   russet, sorrel, walnut
07 biscuit, caramel, chamois, filemot,
   oatmeal, oxblood
08 brunette, chestnut, cinnamon,
   mahogany, mushroom, nut-brown,
   philamot, raw umber
09 chocolate, earth-tone
10 burnt umber, café au lait, terracotta
11 burnt sienna, orange-tawny
12 vandyke brown

browned off
05 bored, fed up, weary 07 annoyed
09 hacked off, irritated, pissed off
10 bored stiff, brassed off, cheesed
off, dispirited 11 discouraged,
disgruntled, downhearted,
exasperated 12 discontented,
disheartened

brownie
03 hob, nis 05 nisse

browse
03 eat 04 feed, look, scan, skim, surf
05 graze 06 nibble, peruse, survey
07 dip into, pasture 09 quick read
11 leaf through 12 flick through, flick-
through

bruise
◇ anagram indicator
04 beat, hurt, mark, stun 05 break,
clour, crush, frush, pound, spoil, upse
wound 06 damage, grieve, injure,
injury, insult, intuse, lesion, offend,
shiner 07 blacken, blemish, contuse,
rainbow, surbate 08 black eye, to-
bruise 09 contusion, discolour
10 ecchymosis 13 discoloration

bruiser
04 thug 05 bully, rough, tough
07 hoodlum, ruffian 08 bully boy
09 bovver boy, roughneck 12 prize-
fighter

Brunei
03 BRN, BRU

brunt
05 force, shock 06 burden, impact,
strain, thrust, weight 07 impetus
08 pressure 09 main force 10 full
weight

brush
03 hog, rub 04 bush, dust, kiss, swak
wipe 05 besom, broom, clash, clean
clear, fight, fitch, flick, frith, graze,
scrap, scrub, scuff, set-to, shine, swee
touch, whisk 06 badger, bushes,
caress, duster, dust-up, fracas, pallet,
polish, putois, scrape, shrubs, stroke,
tussle 07 burnish, contact, fox-tail,
stipple, sweeper, thicket, tickler
08 argument, conflict, skirmish
09 brushwood, currycomb, encount
pope's head, underwood 10 hair-
pencil 11 ground cover, overgrainer,
undergrowth 12 disagreement
13 confrontation
• **brush aside**
05 flout 06 ignore 07 dismiss
08 belittle, override, pooh-pooh
09 disregard
• **brush off**
04 snub 05 spurn 06 disown, ignore
rebuff, reject, slight 07 dismiss, repul
09 disregard, repudiate 12 cold-
shoulder
• **brush up**
04 cram, swot, tidy 05 clean, study
06 go over, read up, revise, tidy up
07 improve, refresh, relearn 08 bone
up on, polish up 09 freshen up
15 clean yourself up, refresh yourself

brush-off
04 snub 06 rebuff, slight 07 kiss-off,
refusal, repulse 09 dismissal, rejectio
11 repudiation 12 cold shoulder
14 discouragement

brushwood
03 hag 04 hagg, reis, rice 05 bavin,
firth, frith, scrub 06 jungle 07 fascin
08 mattress, ovenwood 09 chaparra
10 underscrub

brusque

04 curt 05 blunt, brief, gruff, sharp, short, surly, terse 06 abrupt 07 uncivil 08 impolite, tactless 09 downright 12 discourteous, undiplomatic

brutal

05 cruel, frank, harsh, plain, tough 06 animal, coarse, savage, severe 07 beastly, bestial, boarish, brutish, callous, doggish, inhuman, ruffian, vicious, violent 08 inhumane, pitiless, ruthless 09 barbarous, ferocious, heartless, merciless, unfeeling, unsparing 10 Rottweiler 11 insensitive, iron-hearted, remorseless 12 bloodthirsty, down-and-dirty 15 straightforward

brutality

07 cruelty 08 atrocity, ferocity, savagery, violence 09 barbarism, barbarity, callosity, roughness 10 coarseness, inhumanity 11 brutishness, callousness, viciousness 12 ruthlessness

brutalize

03 hit 04 beat, flog 05 inure, pound 06 attack, batter, deaden, harden, thrash 07 assault, degrade 09 animalize 10 dehumanize 11 desensitize

brutally

07 cruelly, frankly, harshly 08 savagely, severely 09 brutishly, callously, viciously 10 inhumanely, pitilessly, ruthlessly 11 barbarously, ferociously, heartlessly, mercilessly, unfeelingly 13 insensitively

brute

04 bête, lout, ogre 05 beast, bully, rude, devil, fiend, gross, swine, yahoo 06 animal, bodily, carnal, coarse, sadist, savage, stupid 07 Caliban, fleshly, monster, ruffian, sensual 08 creature, depraved, mindless, physical 09 senseless 10 irrational, Rottweiler, unthinking 11 instinctive

brutish

05 crass, crude, cruel, feral, gross 06 animal, brutal, coarse, ferine, savage, stupid, vulgar 07 bestial, loutish, uncouth 08 barbaric 09 barbarian, barbarous 11 uncivilized

bubble

04 ball, bead, bell, bleb, boil, drop, fizz, foam, head, lock, seed, suds 05 fraud, froth, gloop, spume 06 bounce, burble, dimple, gurgle, lather, mantle, seethe, trifle, vanity, wallop 07 air-bell, air-lock, blister, blubber, droplet, fantasy, globule, sparkle, vesicle 08 belated, be filled, blowhole, delusion, fleeting, illusion, rowndell 09 ball of air, be excited, deceptive, transient 10 depression, effervesce 13 effervescence, insubstantial

bubbly

◇ anagram indicator
04 fizz 05 fizzy, happy, merry, sudsy 06 bouncy, elated, frothy, lively

07 excited, foaming 08 animated, champers 09 champagne, ebullient, exuberant, sparkling, vivacious 10 carbonated 12 effervescent

buccaneer

06 pirate 07 corsair, sea wolf 08 sea rover 09 privateer, sea robber 10 filibuster, freebooter

buck

◇ anagram indicator
03 bok 04 soar, sore 05 cheer, dandy, soare, sorel 06 buoy up, dollar, ignore, marker, oppose, resist, sorell, sorrel 07 counter, hearten, pricket 08 reassure 09 encourage 10 contradict 13 break the rules
• **buck up**
05 cheer, gee up, hurry, rally 06 hasten, perk up 07 cheer up, enliven, hearten, hurry up, improve 08 inspirit, step on it 09 encourage, stimulate, take heart 10 get a move on 14 rattle your dags 15 get your skates on

bucket

03 can, dip, tub 04 bail, bale, pail 05 ladle, stoop, stope, stoup 06 dipper, kibble, situla, stoope, vessel 07 pitcher, scuttle 09 clamshell
• **bucket down**
04 pour 08 pelt down, pour down 11 rain heavily 15 rain cats and dogs
• **bucket chain**
05 noria 12 Jacob's ladder

buckle

◇ anagram indicator
04 bend, clip, fold, hasp, hook, kink, warp 05 bulge, catch, clasp, close, hitch, twist 06 cave in, fasten, secure 07 connect, crumple, distort, wrinkle 08 collapse, fastener 10 contortion, distortion
• **buckle down**
08 go all out 11 get down to it, knuckle down 15 start to work hard

buckler

05 pelta 06 target 08 rondache 09 protector 10 protection

bucolic

05 rural 06 rustic 07 country 08 agrarian, pastoral 11 countrified 12 agricultural

bud

03 eye, gem 04 bulb, germ, grow, knop, knot 05 caper, clove, gemma, knosp, shoot, sprig 06 bulbel, bulbil, button, embryo, friend, sprout, turion 07 brother, burgeon, cabbage, develop, plumule 09 débutante, pullulate 11 heart of palm, palm-cabbage 12 hibernaculum

Buddhist

03 Zen 04 lama 05 bonze 08 talapoin 09 Dalai Lama
• **Buddhist dome**
04 tope 05 stupa 06 dagaba, dagoba

budding

07 growing, nascent 09 embryonic, fledgling, flowering, gemmation,

germinant, incipient, potential, promising 10 burgeoning, developing 11 up-and-coming

buddy

03 pal 04 chum, mate 05 crony 06 cobber, friend 07 brother, comrade 09 companion 10 buddy-buddy, good friend

budge

03 jee 04 bend, give, move, push, roll, stir, sway 05 bodge, bouge, shift, slide, stiff, yield 06 change, give in, remove 07 give way, pompous 08 convince, dislodge, persuade 09 influence 13 not compromise 14 change your mind

budget

04 plan 05 allot, allow, funds, means, quota 06 afford, bouget, bowget, ration 08 allocate, estimate, finances, schedule, set aside 09 allotment, allowance, apportion, economics, resources 10 allocation 13 financial plan

buff

03 fan, rub, tan 04 blow, fawn 05 beige, brush, fiend, freak, khaki, maven, rub up, sandy, shine, straw 06 addict, expert, nankin, polish, smooth, stroke 07 admirer, burnish, devotee, fanatic, nankeen, natural 09 yellowish 10 aficionado, enthusiast 11 connoisseur 14 yellowish-brown
• **in the buff**
04 bare, nude 05 naked 08 in the raw, starkers, stripped 09 unclothed, uncovered, undressed 10 stark-naked 12 not a stitch on 13 with nothing on 15 in the altogether

buffalo

04 anoa, arna 05 bison, bugle 07 Bubalus, carabao, overawe, tamarao, tamarau, timarau, zamouse 08 bewilder, water cow

buffer

03 pad 06 absorb, bumper, deaden, fender, lessen, pillow, reduce, screen, shield, soften 07 bulwark, cushion, protect 08 diminish, mitigate, polisher, suppress 12 intermediary 13 shock absorber

buffet

03 box, hit, jar, tax 04 bang, beat, blow, buff, bump, café, cuff, harm, jolt, push, slap 05 clout, knock, pound, shove, smack, thump, weigh 06 batter, battle, blight, burden, pummel, strike 07 afflict, counter, disturb, oppress, trouble 08 cold meal, distress, snackbar 09 cafeteria, cold table, weigh down 11 self-service, smorgasbord 12 help yourself

buffeted

◇ anagram indicator

buffoon

03 wag 04 fool, mime, mome, Vice, zany 05 antic, clown, comic, droll, joker 06 antick, jester, Scogan

07 anticke, antique, farceur, Scoggin, tomfool **08** comedian, farceuse, Iniquity **09** harlequin **10** mountebank, Scaramouch **11** Jack-pudding, merry-andrew, Punchinello, Scaramouche

buffoonery
05 farce **07** jesting, zanyism **08** clowning, drollery, nonsense **09** pantomime, silliness **10** tomfoolery **11** waggishness **12** harlequinade, pantalooneery **13** Pantagruelism

bug
03 fad, irk, tap, vex, wog **04** flaw, flea, germ, mite, snag **05** annoy, craze, error, fault, mania, thing, virus **06** bother, cootie, defect, harass, insect, needle, pester, wind up **07** blemish, disease, disturb, failing, gremlin, illness, microbe, monitor, wiretap **08** irritate, listen in, phone-tap **09** aggravate, bacterium, eavesdrop, infection, obsession **10** listen in on, listen in to **11** eavesdrop on **12** creepy-crawly, imperfection **13** micro-organism **15** listening device

bugbear
03 bug **04** bane, bogy **05** bogey, bogle, dread, fiend, poker **06** horror **07** pet hate, rawhead **08** anathema **09** bête noire, nightmare **10** Mumbo-jumbo

bugle
10 flügelhorn **11** hunting-horn

bugle-call
04 post, taps **07** hallali, retreat **08** last post, reveille **09** first post, lights out **15** boots and saddles

build
03 big, set **04** body, form, make, rear, size **05** begin, edify, erect, frame, mason, put up, raise, shape, start **06** extend, figure, timber **07** augment, develop, enlarge, fashion, upbuild **08** assemble, escalate, increase, initiate, physique, throw out **09** construct, fabricate, institute, intensify, overbuild, structure, substruct **10** constitute, inaugurate **11** put together **13** knock together
• **build up**
03 add **04** grow, hype, plug, rear **05** amass, boost, mount, set up **06** expand, extend, gather **07** aggrade, amplify, augment, collect, develop, enhance, enlarge, fortify, improve, mount up, promote **08** assemble, escalate, heighten, increase, snowball **09** advertise, construct, elaborate, establish, intensify, publicize, reinforce, structure **10** accumulate, strengthen **11** put together **13** piece together

builder
05 jerry, mason **06** waller **08** labourer **09** craftsman **11** craftswoman **12** craftsperson, manual worker **13** skilled worker

building
◊ *anagram indicator*
04 pile **07** edifice **08** dwelling,

erection **09** structure **11** development, fabrication **12** architecture, construction

See also **architecture**

03 inn, pub
04 barn, café, fort, mews, mill, pier, shed, shop, silo
05 abbey, arena, cabin, hotel, house, store, villa
06 castle, chapel, church, cinema, garage, gazebo, mandir, mosque, museum, pagoda, palace, prison, school, stable, temple
07 chateau, college, cottage, factory, library, low-rise, mansion, theatre
08 barracks, beach hut, bungalow, dovecote, fortress, gurdwara, high-rise, hospital, monument, outhouse, pavilion, showroom, skilling, skillion, windmill
09 apartment, boathouse, cathedral, farmhouse, gymnasium, mausoleum, monastery, multiplex, synagogue, warehouse
10 lighthouse, maisonette, restaurant, skyscraper, sports hall, tower block, university
11 condominium, observatory, office block, public house, summerhouse
12 block of flats, power station
14 apartment house, sliver building

See also **accommodation; house; tent**

05 Duomo
07 BT Tower, CN Tower, Kremlin, La Scala, St Paul's, UN Plaza
08 Casa Milà, Cenotaph, Chrysler, Flatiron, Pantheon, St Peter's, Taj Mahal
09 Acropolis, Coit Tower, Colosseum, Notre Dame, Old Bailey, Parthenon, Reichstag, St Pancras, Taipei 101, The Louvre, US Capitol
10 Guggenheim, Sears Tower, Tate Modern, The Gherkin, Trump Tower, Versailles, White House
11 Canary Wharf, Eden Project, Eiffel Tower, Empire State, Musée d'Orsay, Space Needle, The Alhambra, The Panthéon, The Pentagon, Tower Bridge, Tower of Pisa
12 Globe Theatre, Great Pyramid, Mont St Michel, Telecom Tower, The Parthenon, Winter Palace
13 Crystal Palace, Dome of the Rock, Musée du Louvre, Royal Crescent, Somerset House, Tower of London
14 Balmoral Castle, Barbican Centre, Blenheim Palace, Centre Pompidou, Hoover Building, Millennium Dome, Petronas Towers, Pompidou Centre, Sagrada Familia, UN Headquarters, Wells Cathedral
15 Ashmolean Museum, Banqueting House, Brandenburg Gate, Capitol Building, Edinburgh Castle, Lincoln

Memorial, Post Office Tower, Royal Opera House, Statue of Liberty, Westminster Hall

See also **religious; tower**

03 MDF
04 clay, sand, tile, wood
05 brick, glass, grout, slate, steel, stone
06 ashlar, cement, girder, gravel, gypsum, lintel, lumber, marble, mastic, mortar, pavior, siding, tarmac, thatch, timber
07 asphalt, bitumen, decking, drywall, fixings, granite, lagging, plaster, plastic, plywood, sarking, shingle
08 asbestos, cast iron, cladding, concrete, hard core, roof tile, wall tile
09 aggregate, aluminium, chipboard, clapboard, flagstone, floor tile, hardboard, sandstone, steel beam
10 glass fibre, insulation, matchboard
11 breeze block, paving stone, roofing felt
12 plasterboard
13 building block, wattle and daub
14 foam insulation, stainless steel

• **building area**
04 site

build-up
04 gain, heap, hype, load, mass, plug, puff **05** drift, stack, store **06** growth **08** increase **09** accretion, expansion, marketing, promotion, publicity, stockpile **10** escalation **11** advertising, development, enlargement **12** accumulation

built
◊ *anagram indicator*

built-in
05 fixed **06** fitted **07** in-built **08** implicit, included, inherent, integra **09** essential, intrinsic, necessary **11** fundamental, inseparable **12** incorporated

bulb
03 set **05** globe **11** Rupert's drop

04 cive, eddo, iris, ixia, lily, taro
05 camas, chive, onion, tulip
06 allium, camash, camass, chives, crinum, crocus, garlic, nerine, scilla, squill
07 anenome, jonquil, muscari, peacock, quamash
08 amarylis, bluebell, camassia, curtonis, cyclamen, daffodil, endymion, galtonia, gladioli, harebell, hyacinth, scallion, snowdrop, sparaxis
09 amaryllis, colchicum, crocosmia, galanthus, gladiolus, narcissus, snowflake, tiger lily
10 agapanthus, chionodoxa, fritillary, giant rouge, montbretia, ranunculus, snake's head, solfaterre wand flower

acidanthera, African lily, erythronium, fritillaria, hippeastrum, lapeirousia, naked ladies, spring onion, sternbergia, tiger flower
autumn crocus, ornithogalum, Solomon's seal, wild hyacinth
crown imperial, grape hyacinth, lily-of-the-Nile, striped squill, winter aconite
belladonna lily, chincherinchee, glory of the snow, Ithuriel's spear
dog's tooth violet, lily-of-the-valley

ulbous
convex, puffed **07** bloated, ulging, rounded, swollen
swelling, tuberous **09** distended, uffed out, pulvinate **10** pulvinated

ulgaria
BG **03** BGR **04** Bulg

ulge
bag, bug, sag **04** bias, bulb, bump, ump, lump, rise **05** belly, pouch, strut, arge, swell **06** billow, dilate, expand, rout **07** blister, distend, enlarge, roject, puff out, upsurge **08** increase, otrude, shoulder, swelling
distension, projection
protuberance **15** intensification

ulk
body, bouk, feck, hold, hull, mass, ost, size **05** cargo, great, gross
extent, volume, weight **07** bigness
majority, quantity, roughage
amplitude, immensity, largeness, agnitude, nearly all, substance
dimensions, lion's share
preponderance

bulk out, bulk up
fill **06** expand, extend, fill up, pad at **07** fill out **08** increase **10** make gger

ulky
big **04** huge **05** ample, gross, eavy, hefty, large, lofty, lusty
awkward, hulking, immense, mping, mammoth, massive, lumed, weighty **08** colossal, normous, unwieldy **10** cumbersome, luminous **11** substantial
unmanageable

ull
ox **03** rot **04** brag, male, mick, neat
micky **06** mickey, strong, Taurus
massive **08** nonsense
policeman **10** Unigenitus Hibernicism **12** Hibernianism

ulldoze
push, raze **05** bully, clear, force, vel **06** coerce **07** flatten
browbeat, demolish **09** knock own **10** intimidate **11** push through, eamroller

ullet
ball, shot, slug **06** dumdum, pellet
missile **08** Biscayan **09** cartouche, rtridge, lead towel, Minié ball
projectile, propellant

bulletin
06 report, update **07** leaflet, message, release **08** dispatch **09** newsflash, newspaper, news sheet, statement **10** communiqué, newsletter **12** announcement, notification **13** communication

bullfight
07 corrida **10** tauromachy **14** corrida de toros

bullfighter
07 matador, picador **08** matadore, toreador **10** rejoneador **12** banderillero

bullish
06 upbeat **07** buoyant, hopeful **08** cheerful, positive, sanguine **09** confident, obstinate **10** aggressive, optimistic

bully
◊ *anagram indicator*
03 cow **04** good, haze, huff, prey, thug **05** brave, bucko, great, heavy, tough, tyran **06** coerce, cuttle, hector, pick on, tyrant **07** bluster, bouncer, hoodlum, killcow, oppress, ruffian, torment **08** browbeat, bulldoze, bully-boy, bullyrag, domineer, overbear **09** excellent, persecute, souteneur, terrorize, tormentor, tyrannize, victimize **10** blustering, browbeater, Drawcansir, intimidate, persecutor, push around **11** intimidator **12** swashbuckler

bulrush
04 tule **08** cat's-tail

bulwark
04 wall **05** guard **06** buffer **07** bastion, defence, outwork, rampart, redoubt, sea-wall, support **08** buttress, mainstay, security **09** partition, safeguard **10** breakwater, embankment, protection **13** fortification

bum
◊ *anagram indicator*
03 ass, bad, beg, dud, low **04** butt, coit, duff, hobo, hurl, loaf, naff, poor, rear, rump, seat, tail, toss **05** awful, booty, cadge, false, quoit, spree, tramp, wrong **06** behind, borrow, bottom, crummy, dosser, sponge **07** adverse, gangrel, rubbish, sponger, useless, vagrant **08** backside, beach boy, buttocks, scrounge, terrible, vagabond **09** imperfect, worthless **10** despicable, inadequate, unpleasant **12** disagreeable, unacceptable **14** unsatisfactory

bumble
◊ *anagram indicator*
05 drone, idler, lurch **06** beadle, bungle, falter, teeter, totter **07** blunder, bungler, stagger, stumble

bumbling
◊ *anagram indicator*
05 inept **06** clumsy **07** awkward, muddled **08** botching, bungling

09 lumbering, maladroit, stumbling **10** blundering **11** incompetent, inefficient

bump
03 hit, jar **04** bang, blow, hump, jerk, jole, joll, jolt, jowl, knur, lump, slam, thud, whap, whop **05** barge, bulge, crash, dunch, dunsh, joule, knock, prang, shake, shock, shove, smash, thump **06** bounce, impact, injury, jostle, jounce, nodule, rattle, strike **07** collide, papilla **08** dislodge, swelling **09** collision, speed bump **10** protrusion, tumescence **11** collide with **12** irregularity, protuberance
• **bump into**
04 meet **07** run into **09** encounter, light upon **10** chance upon, come across, happen upon **12** meet by chance
• **bump off**
03 top **04** do in, kill **06** murder, remove, rub out **08** blow away **09** eliminate, liquidate **11** assassinate

bumper
03 big **04** rich **05** great, jumbo, kelty, large, rouse **06** keltie **07** bouncer, massive **08** abundant, enormous, whopping **09** excellent, ginormous, plentiful **11** exceptional **12** supernaculum

bumpkin
03 oaf, put, yap **04** boor, hick, lout, lowt, putt, rube **05** clown, yokel **06** rustic **07** hawbuck, hayseed, peasant **08** clodpate, clodpole, clodpoll **09** hillbilly **10** clodhopper, provincial **11** bushwhacker **12** country yokel **14** country bumpkin

bumptious
04 coxy **05** brash, cocky, pushy **06** cocksy, uppish **07** forward, pompous **08** arrogant, boastful, impudent **09** assertive, conceited, egotistic, officious **10** swaggering **11** overbearing **12** presumptuous **13** over-confident, self-important **14** full of yourself

bumpy
05 jerky, lumpy, rough **06** bouncy, choppy, knobby, uneven **07** jolting, knobbly **08** pot-holed **09** irregular

bun
03 wad **04** chou **05** brick **06** cookie **07** Bath bun, huffkin, teacake **08** black bun, cream bun, crescent, cross bun, rock cake **09** burger bun **10** Chelsea bun, currant bun, Eccles cake **11** hot cross bun **12** mosbolletjie

bunch
03 bob, lot, mob, wad **04** band, club, crew, gang, heap, herd, hump, lump, mass, pack, pile, posy, team, tuft, wisp **05** batch, clump, crowd, flock, group, party, sheaf, spray, stack, swarm, troop **06** bundle, gather, huddle, number, string **07** bouquet, cluster, collect, corsage, nosegay **08** assemble, boughpot, fascicle, quantity, swelling

09 fascicule, gathering, multitude
10 assortment, châtelaine, collection, congregate, fasciculus, racemation **11** concentrate **12** tussie mussie **13** agglomeration

bundle
◇ *anagram indicator*
03 bag, box, jag, kit, set, tie, wad, wap **04** bale, bind, drum, heap, mass, pack, pile, roll, rush, swag, wisp, wrap, yelm **05** batch, bavin, bluey, brawl, bunch, group, hurry, sheaf, shook, shove, skein, stack, truss, whisk **06** bottle, carton, faggot, fasces, fasten, gather, huddle, hustle, knitch, packet, parcel, tumble **07** cluster, dorlach, fascine, package **08** fascicle, quantity, shiralee, woolpack **09** fascicule, shirralee, trousseau **10** assortment, collection, fasciculus **11** consignment, push roughly **12** accumulation

bung
03 pay, tip **04** cork, dead, dook, plug, seal **05** bribe, purse, shive **06** spigot **07** stopper, useless **08** bankrupt, cutpurse **10** pickpocket

bungle
◇ *anagram indicator*
03 mar **04** boob, duff, flub, goof, mash, mess, muff, mull, ruin **05** blunk, bodge, botch, fluff, fudge, spoil **06** bobble, boggle, bumble, bummle, cock up, foozle, foul up, goof up, mangle, mess up, muck up, muddle **07** bauchle, blunder, louse up, screw up **09** misguggle, mishandle, mismanage **10** mishguggle **11** make a mess of

bungler
04 muff **05** blunk **06** bumble, bummle, duffer, tinker **07** blunker, botcher, bumbler **08** shlemiel **09** blunderer, schlemiel, schlemihl **11** incompetent **13** butterfingers

bungling
05 inept, messy **06** clumsy **07** awkward **08** botching **09** ham-fisted, ham-handed, maladroit, unskilful **10** amateurish, blundering, cack-handed **11** incompetent

bunk
04 flee **05** berth, sleep **06** humbug **08** claptrap

bunker
03 bin **04** fuel, trap **06** hazard **07** shelter **08** sand trap

bunkum
02 BS **03** rot **04** blah, bosh, bull, bunk **05** balls, bilge, hooey, trash, tripe **06** humbug, piffle **07** baloney, garbage, hogwash, rubbish, twaddle **08** blah-blah, bulldust, claptrap, cobblers, malarkey, nonsense, tommyrot **09** poppycock **10** balderdash, codswallop **12** blah-blah-blah **13** horsefeathers

bunting
04 cirl **05** flags, junco **07** ortolan **08** longspur **09** snowflake, snowfleck,

snowflick **10** dickcissel **11** decorations, reed-sparrow, yellow-ammer **12** yellowhammer **13** writing-master

buoy
03 dan **04** rise **05** float **06** beacon, marker, signal **07** dolphin, mooring
● **buoy up**
04 lift **05** boost, cheer, raise **06** bear up **07** cheer up, hearten, support, sustain **09** encourage

buoyancy
03 joy, pep **06** bounce, growth, vigour **07** flotage **08** floatage, gladness, optimism, strength **09** geniality, happiness, jolliness, lightness, toughness **10** brightness, confidence, enthusiasm, resilience
11 development, good spirits **12** cheerfulness, floatability

buoyant
05 happy, hardy, light, peppy, tough **06** afloat, blithe, bouncy, bright, joyful, lively, strong **07** bullish, growing **08** animated, carefree, cheerful, debonair, floating, thriving, youthful **09** adaptable, floatable, resilient, vivacious **10** developing, optimistic, weightless **12** light-hearted

burble
03 lap **04** purl **06** babble, gurgle, murmur, tangle **07** confuse

burden
03 bob, tax **04** bear, care, cark, duty, lade, load, onus, task, tote, yoke **05** beare, cargo, cross, crush, drone, trial, worry **06** bother, charge, fading, impose, lumber, monkey, saddle, sorrow, strain, stress, weight **07** anxiety, burthen, holding, oppress, present, refrain, trouble **08** carriage, encumber, handicap, incumber, land with, overbulk, overload, pressure **09** agistment, cumbrance, grievance, lie hard on, millstone, overpress, overwhelm, undersong, weigh down **10** affliction, dead-weight, imposition, lie heavy on, obligation, overburden, overextend, overstress **11** encumbrance **14** responsibility

burdensome
05 heavy **06** taxing, trying **07** irksome, onerous, weighty **08** crushing, exacting, grievous **09** chargeful, difficult, importune, wearisome **10** chargeable, oppressive **11** importunate, troublesome

burdock
04 gobo **05** clote **07** clotbur, hardoke **08** clotebur **09** cocklebur

bureau
04 desk **06** agency, branch, office **07** counter, service **08** division **10** department **11** writing-desk

bureaucracy
07 red tape **08** city hall, ministry **09** beadledom, paperwork, the system **10** government **11** officialdom

12 civil service **13** officiousness **14** administration, the authorities

bureaucrat
04 suit **07** officer **08** Eurocrat, mandarin, minister, official **09** chinovnik **11** apparatchik, functionary **12** civil servant, office-holder **13** administrator **15** committe member

bureaucratic
05 rigid **08** official **10** inflexible, procedural **11** complicated, ministeri **12** governmental **14** administrative

burgeon
04 grow **05** swell **06** expand, extend **07** develop, enlarge **08** escalate, increase, snowball **11** proliferate

burglar
04 yegg **05** thief **06** robber **07** yeggman **08** pilferer **09** cracksma **10** cat-burglar, trespasser **12** housebreaker

burglary
05 heist, theft **07** break-in, larceny, robbery **08** stealing, trespass **09** pilferage **13** housebreaking

burgle
03 rob **05** screw **09** break into, burst into, steal from **10** burglarize

burial
07 burying, funeral **08** exequies **09** committal, interment, obsequies, sepulchre **10** entombment, inhumation

burial place
05 crypt, grave, vault **06** kurgan **07** charnel, tumulus **08** catacomb, cemetery, God's acre, Golgotha, Pantheon **09** graveyard, mausoleum sepulcher, sepulchre **10** churchyard, necropolis **12** potter's field
See also **cemetery**

Burkina Faso
02 BF **03** BFA

burlesque
04 mock **05** comic, spoof **06** parod satire, send-up **07** mockery, mockin take-off **08** derisive, farcical, ridicule travesty **09** parodying, satirical **10** caricature, heroi-comic **11** caricatural, hudibrastic **12** heroi-comical, mickey-taking **13** Pantagruelism

burly
03 big **05** beefy, heavy, hefty **06** brawny, knotty, stocky, strong, sturdy **07** buirdly, hulking **08** athleti muscular, powerful, thickset **09** strapping, well-built

burn
03 fry, gut **04** bite, bren, char, fume, glow, hurt, itch, long, plot, sear, sere **05** blaze, brand, brook, cense, chark flame, flare, flash, grill, inure, light, parch, ploat, scald, singe, smart, smoke, sting, swale, swayl, sweal, sweel, toast, yearn **06** brenne, desire

mboil, ignite, kindle, scorch, seethe, immer, stream, tingle **07** be eager, combust, consume, corrode, cremate, destroy, flare up, flicker, glimmer, nflame, scowder, shrivel **08** be ablaze, be on fire, burn down, scouther, scowther, smoulder **09** catch fire, cauterize, incremate, set alight, set fire o **10** be in flames, deflagrate, ncinerate **11** catch ablaze, conflagrate, o up in smoke, put a match to **12** be onsumed by, go up in flames **13** put to he torch **15** burst into flames

burning
2 in **03** hot, lit **04** live, sear **05** acrid, cute, afire, eager, fiery, quick, seare, rrent, vital **06** ablaze, aflame, alight, rdent, biting, cauter, fervid, urgent, stion **07** blazing, caustic, cautery, rucial, earnest, fervent, flaming, antic, glowing, intense, pungent, earing **08** flagrant, flashing, frenzied, leaming, piercing, pressing, scalding, marting, stinging, swealing, tingling, ehement **09** consuming, essential, nportant, inburning, prickling, corching **10** passionate 1 conflagrant, illuminated, npassioned, significant, smouldering **2** incendiarism **13** conflagration

burnish
4 buff **05** glaze, shine **06** lustre, olish **08** brighten, polish up

burp
4 wind **05** belch **08** eructate 0 eructation **11** bring up wind

burrow
3 den, dig, set **04** bury, hole, howk, air, mine, root, sett **05** delve, earth, vroot **06** gopher, nuzzle, search, unnel, warren **07** retreat, rummage, helter **08** excavate, fox-earth **9** undermine **10** rabbit hole

bursar
6 purser **07** cashier **09** treasurer

bursary
5 award, grant **09** endowment 0 exhibition, fellowship **11** scholarship

burst
anagram indicator
3 fit, fly, pop, run **04** bang, blow, clap, art, gush, gust, loup, part, race, rush, ear **05** barge, blaze, blitz, brash, reak, crack, erupt, flash, go off, go op, hurry, plump, salvo, spate, split, pout, spurt, start, surge **06** blow up, ounce, go bang, shiver, spring, volley **7** blow-out, dehisce, disrupt, xplode, rupture, shatter, torrent **8** distrain, fragment, outbreak, utburst, puncture **09** break in on, reak open, discharge, fusillade, pull part, split open **10** outpouring 1 push your way **12** disintegrate
• **burst out**
3 cry **04** buff **05** begin, flash, start, tter **06** cry out, irrupt **07** call out, xclaim, explode **08** blurt out, ommence **10** break forth

Burundi
02 RU **03** BDI

bury
◇ *containment indicator*
04 eard, hide, sink, tomb, yerd, yird **05** cover, earth, embed, grave, inter, plant, yeard **06** absorb, burrow, engage, engulf, entomb, inhume, occupy, shroud **07** conceal, enclose, engross, immerse, implant, inearth, inherce **08** enshroud, inhearse, submerge **09** lay to rest, sepulchre **15** put six feet under

bus
03 ISA, PCI, USB **05** coach, trunk **06** jitney, pirate **09** two-decker, vaporetto **10** mammy-wagon, service car **11** park-and-ride **12** double-decker, single-decker

bush
03 tod **05** brush, crude, hedge, plant, scrog, scrub, shrub, todde, wilds **06** busket, tavern **07** bramble, outback, thicket **09** backwoods, makeshift, primitive, scrubland **11** uncivilized **13** rough and ready
• **not beat about the bush**
11 speak openly **12** speak plainly **14** come to the point, commit yourself

bushbaby
06 galago **07** nagapie **08** night-ape

bushel
02 bu **03** fou

bushranger
06 outlaw **07** brigand **10** highwayman **12** backwoodsman

bushy
04 wiry **05** bosky, fuzzy, rough, stiff, thick, woody **06** dumose, dumous, fluffy, shaggy, unruly **07** bristly **09** bristling, luxuriant, spreading **12** dasyphyllous

busily
04 hard **07** briskly **08** actively, speedily **09** earnestly **10** diligently **11** assiduously, strenuously **12** purposefully **13** energetically, industriously

business
02 co **03** biz, bus, job **04** baby, deal, duty, firm, gear, line, task, work **05** issue, point, topic, trade **06** affair, buying, career, matter, métier, outfit, pigeon **07** calling, company, concern, problem, selling, subject, trading, venture **08** commerce, dealings, flagship, industry, question, vocation **09** franchise, operation, syndicate **10** bargaining, consortium, employment, enterprise, occupation, profession **11** corporation, partnership **12** conglomerate, organization, transactions **13** establishment, manufacturing, merchandizing, multinational, parent company **14** holding company, responsibility

15 American Express, DaimlerChrysler, Deutsche Telekom, Electrolux Group, General Electric, GlaxoSmithKline, Legal and General, Marks and Spencer, National Express, News Corporation

- **business centre**
04 city
- **do business**
04 deal, sell
- **go out of business**
04 fold

businesslike
05 slick **06** formal **07** correct, orderly, precise **08** thorough **09** efficient, organized, practical, pragmatic **10** impersonal, methodical, systematic **11** painstaking, well-ordered **12** matter-of-fact, professional

businessman, businesswoman
06 trader, tycoon, wallah **07** Babbitt, magnate **08** city gent, employer, merchant **09** boxwallah, executive, financier **10** capitalist **12** entrepreneur, manufacturer **13** industrialist

Businesspeople include:

04 Benz (Karl Friedrich), Bond (Alan), Boot (Sir Jesse), Cook (Thomas), Ford (Henry), Jobs (Steven), Mond (Ludwig), Shah (Eddy), Tate (Sir Henry), Wang (An)
05 Arden (Elizabeth), Astor (John, Lord), Bosch (Carl), Fayed (Mohamed al-), Forte (Charles, Lord), Gates (Bill), Getty (Jean Paul), Grade (Michael), Heinz (Henry John), Honda (Soichiro), Krupp (Friedrich), Laker (Sir Freddie), Leahy (Sir Terry), Lyons (Sir Joseph), Marks (Simon, Lord), Nobel (Alfred), Rolls (Charles), Royce (Sir Henry), Sugar (Sir Alan), Trump (Donald), Zeiss (Carl)
06 Ansett (Sir Reg), Boeing (William Edward), Browne (John, Lord), Butlin (Billy), Conran (Sir Terence), Cunard (Sir Samuel), Dunlop (John Boyd), du Pont (Pierre Samuel), Fugger (Johannes), Gamble (Josias), Hammer (Armand), Hilton (Conrad Nicholson), Hoover (William Henry), Hughes (Howard), Mellon (Andrew William), Morgan (J Pierpont), Packer (Kerry), Turner (Ted)
07 Agnelli (Giovanni), Barclay (Robert), Branson (Sir Richard), Bugatti (Ettore), Cadbury (George), Cadbury (John), Citroën (André Gustave), Iacocca (Lee), Kennedy (Joseph P), Maxwell (Robert), Murdoch (Rupert), Onassis (Aristotle), Roddick (Anita), Sotheby (John), Tiffany (Charles Lewis)
08 Birdseye (Clarence), Carnegie (Andrew), Christie (James), Gillette (King Camp), Guinness (Sir Benjamin Lee), Michelin (André),

Nuffield (William Richard Morris, Viscount), Olivetti (Adriano), Pulitzer (Joseph), Rathenau (Walther), Rowntree (Joseph), Sinclair (Sir Clive)
09 Arkwright (Sir Richard), Carothers (Wallace), Firestone (Harvey Samuel), Sainsbury (Alan John, Lord), Selfridge (Harry Gordon), Woolworth (Frank Winfield)
10 Berlusconi (Silvio), Guggenheim (Meyer), Leverhulme (William Hesketh Lever, Viscount), Pilkington (Sir Alastair), Rothschild (Meyer Amschel), Vanderbilt (Cornelius)
11 Beaverbrook (Max, Lord), Harvey-Jones (Sir John), Rockefeller (John D)

busker
14 street-musician

bust
◇ *anagram indicator*
04 duff, head, herm, phut, raid, term **05** boobs, bosom, break, chest, crack, herma, kaput, punch, smash, spree, torso, wonky **06** arrest, breast, broken, damage, demote, faulty, ruined, statue **07** breasts, destroy, shatter **08** terminus **09** defective, penniless, sculpture **10** on the blink, on the fritz, out of order **11** out of action
- **go bust**
04 fail, flop, fold **05** crash **06** go bung **07** founder **08** collapse **09** close down **11** go to the wall **14** become bankrupt **15** become insolvent

bustle
◇ *anagram indicator*
03 ado **04** belt, buzz, dash, fuss, rush, stir, tear, to-do, trot, whew **05** haste, hurry **06** bestir, bumble, bummle, flurry, hasten, pother, ruffle, rustle, scurry, tumult **07** fluster, scamper, the rush **08** activity, rush hour, scramble, to and fro, tournure **09** agitation, commotion, stirabout **10** excitement, hurly-burly **11** hurry-scurry, hurry-skurry **12** rush to and fro **13** dress-improver **15** a hive of activity, hustle and bustle

bustling
◇ *anagram indicator*
04 busy, full **05** astir **06** active, hectic, lively **07** abustle, buzzing, crowded, humming, rushing, teeming **08** eventful, restless, stirring, swarming, thronged **09** energetic, on the trot

busy
◇ *anagram indicator*
04 at it, full **05** manic **06** absorb, active, bustle, eident, embusy, employ, engage, hectic, lively, occupy, red-hot, throng, tied up, tiring **07** concern, crowded, engaged, engross, frantic, go about, immerse, involve, on the go, teeming, vibrant, working **08** bustling, diligent, employed, eventful, hard at it, interest, involved, meddling, occupied,

on the job, restless, sedulous, swarming, tireless **09** assiduous, detective, energetic, engrossed, on the trot, stirabout, strenuous **10** busy as a bee **11** industrious, snowed under, unavailable **12** having a lot on, in conference **13** under pressure **14** fully stretched, having a lot to do, in the thick of it
- **be busy**
03 hum

busybody
03 pry **05** snoop **06** gossip **07** meddler, snooper **08** intruder, quidnunc **09** pragmatic **10** interferer **11** Nosey Parker **12** eavesdropper, troublemaker **13** mischief-maker, scandalmonger **14** pantopragmatic

but
03 bar, nay, sed **04** just, only, save **06** anyway, at most, even so, except, merely, purely, simply **07** barring, besides, however **08** omitting **09** apart from, aside from, excepting, excluding, objection, other than **10** all the same, for all that, leaving out, no more than **11** just the same, nonetheless **12** nevertheless **15** notwithstanding
- **all but**
04 near **06** almost

butch
04 male **05** macho, tough **06** virile **07** manlike, mannish **09** masculine

butcher
◇ *anagram indicator*
04 kill, slay **05** botch, spoil **06** killer, slayer **07** destroy, flesher **08** massacre, murderer, mutilate **09** destroyer, liquidate, slaughter **10** meat trader **11** assassinate, exterminate, meat counter, slaughterer, supermarket **12** mass murderer, meat retailer

butchery
06 murder **07** carnage, killing **08** abattoir, butcher's, massacre, shambles **09** bloodshed, meat trade, slaughter **10** mass murder **11** meat-selling **12** blood-letting **13** meat retailing **14** slaughterhouse **15** mass destruction

butler
03 RAB **08** khansama **09** khansamah, sommelier **12** bread-chipper

butt
03 box, bum, but, end, hit, jab, keg, nip, nut, ram, tip, tun **04** base, bump, bunt, cask, dout, dupe, foot, haft, horn, mark, pipe, poke, prod, push, stub **05** dunch, dunsh, knock, punch, roach, shaft, shove, snipe, stock, stump **06** barrel, bottom, buffet, bumper, dog-end, fag end, firkin, handle, object, stooge, target, thrust, tierce, victim **07** butt end, remnant, rundlet, subject, tail end **08** buttocks, hogshead **09** posterior, scapegoat **10** table-sport **12** jesting-stock **13** laughing-stock

- **butt in**
05 cut in 06 horn in, meddle 07 break in, intrude 09 interfere, interject, interpose, interrupt 12 put your oar in 15 stick your nose in

butter
03 ghi, ram 04 drop, ghee, goat 06 beurre 08 flattery

- **butter producer**
04 mowa, shea 05 mahua, mahwa, mowra

- **butter up**
04 coax 06 cajole, kowtow, praise 07 blarney, flatter, wheedle 08 kowtow to, pander to, soft-soap, suck up to 14 be obsequious to

buttercup
06 gilcup 07 giltcup, kingcup 08 crowfoot 10 goldilocks, ranunculus

butterfingers
04 muff

butterfly
05 light 07 flighty 10 dilettante
See also **animal**; **insect**; **moth**

Butterflies include:

03 map
04 blue, wall
05 argus, comma, elfin, heath, satyr, white
06 apollo, copper, hermit, morpho, pierid, psyche
07 admiral, cabbage, monarch, Papilio, peacock, ringlet, satyrid, skipper, thistle, Ulysses, vanessa
08 birdwing, cardinal, grayling, hesperid, milk-weed
09 brimstone, cleopatra, Hesperian, holly-blue, nymphalid, orange-tip, wall brown, wood white
10 brown argus, common blue, fritillary, gatekeeper, hairstreak, red admiral
11 large copper, meadow-brown, painted lady, Scotch argus, swallowtail
12 cabbage-white, dingy skipper, Essex skipper, marbled-white, white admiral
13 chalkhill blue, clouded yellow, mourning cloak, purple emperor, tortoiseshell
15 black hairstreak, brown hairstreak, green hairstreak, grizzled skipper, heath fritillary, Lulworth skipper, marsh fritillary, mountain ringlet

buttocks
03 ass, bum, can, fud 04 buns, butt, coit, doup, duff, prat, rear, rump, seat, tail, tush 05 booty, fanny, nates, pratt, quoit, tushy 06 behind, bottom, breech, cheeks, heinie, tushie 07 crouper, croupon, gluteus, hurdies, keister, sit-upon 08 backside, derrière, haunches 09 fundament, hinder-end, posterior 10 hinderlans, hinderlins 11 hinderlands, hinderlings 12 hindquarters
See also **bottom**

button
04 disc, frog, knob, link, stud 05 catch, clasp, lever 06 barrel, olivet, switch, toggle 08 bell push, fastener 09 fastening

buttonhole
03 nab 04 grab 05 catch 06 accost, collar, corner, detain, waylay 09 importune, take aside 11 boutonnière

buttress
04 pier, prop, stay 05 brace, shore, strut 06 back up, hold up, prop up 07 shore up, support, sustain, tambour 08 abutment, mainstay, underpin 09 bolster up, reinforce, stanchion 10 strengthen 11 counterfort 13 reinforcement

buxom
05 ample, busty, jolly, plump, sonsy 06 bosomy, chesty, comely, lively, sonsie, zaftig 07 bucksom, elastic 08 yielding 09 Junoesque, pneumatic 10 Rubenesque, voluptuous 11 full-figured, well-endowed, well-rounded, well-stacked 12 full-breasted 13 large-breasted

buy
03 fix, get, job 04 chop, coff, deal, take 05 bribe, hedge, scalp, trade 06 buy off, market, nobble, obtain, pay for, pick up, redeem, snap up, suborn 07 acquire, bargain, emption, engross, overbuy, procure, shop for 08 invest in, panic-buy, purchase, underbuy 09 speculate, stock up on, subsidize 10 go shopping, shop around 11 acquisition, merchandize, splash out on 13 do the shopping

buyer
06 broker, client, dealer, emptor, patron, vendee 07 shopper 08 consumer, customer 09 purchaser

buzz
03 fad, hum 04 call, high, kick, purr, race, ring, zing 05 craze, drone, kicks, pulse, throb, throw, whirr 06 bustle, gossip, latest, murmur, rumour, thrill 07 buzzing, hearsay, resound, scandal 08 resonate, susurrus, tinnitus 09 bombilate, bombinate, phone call, susurrate 10 enthusiasm, excitement 11 bombilation, bombination, reverberate, stimulation, susurration 15 word on the street

buzzard
04 pern 05 buteo 07 bee-kite, puttock 08 zopilote 09 gallinazo

buzzer
03 bee 08 telltale 09 whisperer

by
◇ juxtaposition indicator
01 X 02 at, in, of, on 03 gin, per, via 04 away, near, over, past, with 05 along, aside, close, forby, handy, times, using 06 at hand, before, beside, beyond, next to 07 close by, close to, through 09 alongside, by means of 11 according to, no later than 12 in relation to 15 under the aegis of

bygone
04 lost, past 05 olden 06 former 07 ancient, antique, one-time 08 departed, forepast, previous 09 erstwhile, forgotten 10 antiquated, dinosauric

bypass
04 CABG, omit 05 avoid, dodge, evade, shunt, skirt 06 detour, ignore 07 neglect 08 ring road, sidestep, slip road 09 diversion, sidetrack 10 circumvent 12 steer clear of 13 find a way round

by-product
06 result 07 fallout, spin-off 10 derivative, entailment, side effect 11 after-effect, concomitant, consequence 12 repercussion 13 epiphenomenon, knock-on effect

bystander
07 watcher, witness 08 looker-on, observer, onlooker, passer-by, talesman 09 spectator 10 eyewitness, rubberneck

byword
03 saw 05 adage, ideal, maxim, model, motto 06 ayword, dictum, saying, slogan 07 epitome, example, nayword, paragon, precept, proverb 08 aphorism, exemplar, overcome, standard 09 catchword, watchword 10 apophthegm, embodiment 14 perfect example

Byzantine
◇ anagram indicator
06 knotty 07 complex 08 tortuous 09 intricate 11 complicated 12 labyrinthine

C

C
03 cee, san, see **07** Charlie

cab
04 taxi **05** cabin, noddy **06** drosky, fiacre, hansom **07** droshky, growler, minicab, taxicab, vettura **08** quarters **10** two-wheeler **11** compartment, four-wheeler **15** hackney carriage

cabal
03 set **04** plot **05** junta, junto, party **06** clique, league **07** coterie, faction **08** conclave, intrigue, plotters **09** camarilla, coalition

cabaret
04 acts, club, show **05** turns **06** comedy **07** dancing, singing, variety **09** night club **10** restaurant **11** performance **13** entertainment

cabbage
04 chou, cole, gobi, kail, kale, wort **05** savoy, steal **06** greens **07** bok choy, castock, custock, pak choi, purloin **08** colewort, drumhead, kohlrabi **09** banknotes **10** choucroute, greenstuff, paper money, sauerkraut **11** cauliflower, sea colewort **13** Chinese leaves **14** Brussels sprout

cabbage-head
04 loaf

cabin
03 hut **04** room, shed **05** berth, bothy, coach, cuddy, lodge, shack **06** cabana, chalet, refuge, saloon, shanty **07** cottage, gondola, shelter **08** loghouse, quarters **09** signal box, stateroom **10** roundhouse **11** compartment

cabinet
04 case **05** bahut, chest, filer, store **06** closet, locker, senate, shrine **07** almirah, console, dresser **08** cupboard, vargueño **09** executive, ministers **10** encoignure, government, leadership, secretaire **11** chiffonnier **12** Privy Council **14** administration, official family

cable
03 fax, guy **04** co-ax, cord, flex, lead, line, rope, stay, wire **05** chain, e-mail, radio **06** feeder, halser, hawser **07** coaxial **08** telegram, transmit **09** facsimile, send a wire, telegraph **11** Telemessage® **13** send a telegram **15** send by telegraph

cache
04 fund, hide **05** hoard, stash, stock, store **06** garner, supply **07** reserve **09** stockpile **10** collection, repository, storehouse **12** accumulation **13** treasure-store **14** hidden treasure

cachet
06 esteem, favour, status **08** approval, eminence, prestige **10** estimation, reputation, street cred **11** distinction

cack-handed
05 gawky, inept **06** clumsy **07** awkward **08** bungling **09** all thumbs, ham-fisted, unskilful **10** blundering, left-handed, ungraceful **11** heavy-handed **13** unco-ordinated

cackle
04 crow **05** clack **06** gabble, gaggle, giggle, keckle, titter **07** chortle, chuckle, snigger **09** loud laugh **11** laugh loudly **15** unpleasant laugh

cacophonous
04 loud **05** harsh **07** grating, jarring, raucous **08** strident **09** dissonant **10** discordant **11** horrisonant **12** inharmonious

cacophony
03 din **06** racket **07** discord, jarring **09** charivari, harshness, stridency **10** disharmony, dissonance **11** raucousness **12** caterwauling

cactus

Cacti include:

04 crab, toad, tuna
05 dildo, nopal
06 barrel, cereus, cholla, Easter, mescal, old man, orchid, peanut, peyote
07 jointed, old lady, opuntia, rainbow, saguaro
08 dumpling, gold lace, hedgehog, rat's tail, snowball, starfish, Turk's cap
09 bunny ears, Christmas, goat's horn, gold charm, Indian fig, mistletoe, sea-urchin
10 cotton-pole, sand dollar, silver ball, strawberry, zygocactus
11 grizzly bear, mammillaria, prickly pear, scarlet ball, silver torch
12 golden barrel
13 Bristol beauty, schlumbergera
14 drunkard's dream
15 queen of the night, snowball cushion

cad
03 oik, rat **04** heel **05** devil, knave, rogue, swine **06** rascal, rotter, wretch **07** bleeder, bounder, scumbag, stinker, villain **08** blighter, deceiver **09** miscreant, reprobate, scoundrel **10** blackguard

cadaver
04 body **05** stiff **06** corpse **07** carcase, remains **08** dead body

cadaverous
03 wan **04** pale, thin **05** ashen, gaunt **07** ghostly, haggard **08** skeletal **09** death-like, emaciated **10** corpse-like

caddy
05 chest

cadence
04 beat, fall, lilt, rate **05** close, metre, pulse, swing, tempo, throb, trope **06** accent, euouae, evovae, rhythm, stress **07** falling, measure, pattern, sinking **09** half-close **10** inflection, intonation, modulation

cadge
03 beg, bot, bum **05** mooch, mouch, ponce **06** sponge **08** scrounge

cadmium
02 Cd

cadre
03 set **04** band, crew, gang, team **05** corps, squad **10** small group

caesium
02 Cs

café
04 caff **06** bistro, buffet, pull-in **07** noshery, tea room, tea shop, wine bar **08** snackbar **09** brasserie, cafeteria, coffee bar, cybercafé, estaminet, truck stop **10** coffee shop, restaurant **11** greasy spoon

cafeteria
04 café, caff **06** buffet **07** canteen **10** restaurant **15** self-service café

cage
03 mew, pen **04** coop, corf, dray, drey **05** cavie, grate, hutch, pound **06** aviary, corral, keavie, lock-up **07** tumbler **09** enclosure

caged
05 mewed **06** shut up **07** encaged **08** confined, cooped up, fenced in, locked up **09** impounded **10** imprisoned, restrained **12** incarcerated

cagey
04 wary, wily **05** chary **06** shrewd **07** careful, guarded **08** cautious, discreet **09** secretive **11** circumspect **12** non-committal

cahoots
• in cahoots
08 in league **09** colluding
10 conspiring, in alliance **11** hand in
glove, in collusion **13** collaborating

cairn
03 man **04** barp **05** raise

cajole
04 coax, dupe, lure, wile, work
05 moody, tempt **06** beflum, chat up,
diddle, entice, humbug, seduce,
soothe, whilly **07** beguile, blarney,
cuittle, flatter, mislead, wheedle
08 blandish, butter up, get round,
inveigle, persuade, soft-soap
09 sweet-talk, whillywha
10 whillywhaw **12** work yourself

cajolery
05 wiles **06** duping **07** blarney,
coaxing **08** flattery, soft soap **09** sweet
talk, wheedling, whillywha
10 cajolement, enticement,
inducement, inveigling, misleading,
persuasion, whillywhaw
11 beguilement, inducements
12 blandishment, inveiglement
13 blandishments

cake
03 bar, dry, pan **04** coat, cube, farl,
loaf, lump, mass, pone, slab **05** block,
chunk, cover, fancy, farle **06** harden,
pastry, tablet **07** congeal, encrust,
plaster, thicken **08** solidify
09 coagulate **11** consolidate

*Cakes, pastries and puddings
include:*

03 bun, pie
04 baba, flan, fool, puri, roti, tart
05 bombe, crêpe, jelly, poori, scone,
sweet, torte
06 éclair, gateau, junket, mousse,
muffin, parkin, sponge, trifle, waffle,
yum-yum
07 baklava, Banbury, bannock, Bath
bun, brioche, brownie, crumble,
crumpet, cupcake, fig roll, fritter,
iced bun, jam roll, jam tart, oatcake,
pancake, Pavlova, plum pie, ratafia,
rum baba, saffron, savarin, soufflé,
stollen, strudel, tartlet, teacake,
wedding, Yule log
08 apple pie, black bun, doughnut,
flummery, macaroon, malt loaf,
meringue, mince pie, pecan pie,
plum-cake, rock cake, sandwich,
seedcake, syllabub, tiramisu,
turnover, whim-wham
09 angel cake, cherry-pie, clafoutis,
cranachan, cream cake, cream
horn, cream puff, drop scone, fairy
cake, fruitcake, fruit tart, fudge
cake, Genoa cake, lamington, lardy
cake, lemon tart, madeleine,
panettone, pound cake, queen
cake, Sally Lunn, shortcake, Swiss
roll
10 banana cake, Battenburg, carrot
cake, cheesecake, Chelsea bun,
coffee cake, Dundee cake, Eccles
cake, ginger cake, girdle cake, key

lime pie, marble cake, panna cotta,
pumpkin pie, simnel cake, sponge
cake, tarte tatin
11 baked Alaska, banana bread,
banoffee pie, crème brulée, currant
cake, custard tart, gingerbread, hot
cross bun, jam roly-poly, lady's
finger, Linzertorte, Madeira cake,
plum pudding, profiterole, rice
pudding, Sachertorte, sago
pudding, spotted dick, treacle tart,
wedding cake
12 apfel strudel, Bakewell tart,
birthday cake, chocolate log,
custard slice, Danish pastry, figgy
pudding, hasty pudding, pease
pudding, sandwich cake
13 apple dumpling, apple turnover,
chocolate cake, Christmas cake,
Scotch pancake, sponge pudding,
summer pudding
14 apple charlotte, charlotte russe,
Pontefract cake, steamed pudding,
toasted teacake, upside-down
cake, Victoria sponge
15 chocolate éclair, queen of puddings

See also **bun**

calamitous
◇ *anagram indicator*
04 dire **05** fatal **06** deadly, tragic,
woeful **07** ghastly, ruinous
08 dreadful, grievous, wretched
10 disastrous **11** cataclysmic,
devastating **12** catastrophic

calamity
02 wo **03** wae, woe **04** blow, Jane,
ruin, ruth, woes **05** trial **06** mishap
07 reverse, scourge, tragedy, trouble
08 disaster, distress, downfall
09 adversity, mischance **10** affliction,
misfortune **11** catastrophe, tribulation
12 misadventure **15** sword of
Damocles

calcium
02 Ca

calculate
03 aim **04** cast, make, plan, rate, work
05 add up, count, gauge, judge, tally,
think, value, weigh **06** assess, cipher,
cypher, derive, design, figure, intend,
reckon **07** compute, measure,
purpose, suppose, work out
08 consider, estimate, reckon up
09 determine, enumerate

calculated
06 wilful **07** planned **08** computed,
intended, measured, purposed,
reckoned, tactical **10** considered,
deliberate, purposeful, well-judged
11 intentional **12** premeditated

calculating
03 sly **04** wily **05** sharp **06** crafty,
shrewd **07** cunning, devious
08 scheming **09** designing
10 contriving **11** circumspect
12 manipulative **13** Machiavellian
• calculating aid
03 log **04** abac **06** abacus **07** soroban
08 computer, isopleth, nomogram

09 nomograph, slide rule **10** calculator
12 arithmometer **14** alignment chart
15 digital computer

calculation
03 sum **06** answer, result **08** estimate,
figuring, forecast, logistic, planning
09 evolution, judgement, reckoning
10 alligation, arithmetic, assessment,
estimation, figurework, working-out
11 computation, mensuration
12 deliberation

calculus
04 lith- **06** tartar **07** urolith
08 fluxions **09** sialolith
11 quaternions

calendar

Calendars include:

05 Bahà'í, Hindu, lunar, Roman, solar
06 Coptic, Hebrew, Jewish, Julian
07 Chinese, Islamic, Persian
09 arbitrary, Gregorian, lunisolar
10 republican
13 revolutionary

See also **animal**; **month**

calf
04 boss, dogy, veal **05** bossy, dogie,
poddy, slink **06** vealer **08** maverick

calibre
03 cal **04** bore, gage, size **05** gauge,
gifts, merit, worth **06** league, talent
07 ability, faculty, measure, quality,
stature **08** capacity, diameter, strength
09 character **10** competence,
endowments, excellence
11 distinction

California
02 CA **05** Calif

californium
02 Cf

call
02 ca', go **03** bid, caa', cap, cry, dub,
mot, run **04** bawl, bell, buzz, caul, cite,
hail, name, need, nemn, pink, plea,
ring, roar, term, toll, yell **05** brand,
cause, claim, cleep, clepe, cooee,
cooey, hight, label, order, phone, pop
in, right, shout, style, title, visit
06 appeal, ask for, bellow, call in, come
by, cry out, demand, drop in, excuse,
invite, market, reason, reckon, rename,
ring up, scream, shriek, signal, stop by,
summon, tinkle **07** baptize, command,
contact, convene, enstyle, entitle,
exclaim, grounds, hallali, phone up,
request, send for, summons, warning
08 assemble, christen, occasion
09 call round, designate, pay a visit,
telephone **10** denominate, describe
as, invitation **11** ask to come in,
exclamation **12** announcement
13 justification **14** ask to come round
• call for
04 levy, need, take **05** claim, fetch, go
for **06** demand, entail, pick up
07 collect, involve, justify, push for,
require, solicit, suggest, warrant
08 occasion, press for **11** necessitate
13 make necessary

- **call off**
04 drop 05 scrub 06 cancel, revoke,
shelve 07 abandon, rescind 08 break
off, withdraw 11 discontinue
- **call on**
03 ask, bid, gam, put, see 04 urge
05 plead, visit 06 appeal, demand,
invoke, summon, wait on 07 entreat,
request 08 appeal to, go and see, look
in on, press for, wait upon 10 supplicate
- **call up**
04 buzz, pick, ring 05 phone, raise
06 choose, enlist, invite, ring up,
select, sign up, summon, take on
07 contact, display, phone up, recruit
08 settle on 09 conscript, telephone
- **on call**
05 ready 06 on duty 09 on standby
10 standing by

called
03 hot 04 hote 05 nempt

call girl
04 tart 05 whore 06 harlot, hooker
07 hustler 10 loose woman, prostitute
12 street-walker 14 lady of the night

calling
03 job 04 line, work 05 field, trade
06 career, métier 07 mission, pursuit
08 business, province, vocation
10 employment, line of work,
occupation, profession 14 line of
business

callous
04 cold 05 cruel, harsh, horny, stony,
tough 06 seared 08 hardened,
indurate, obdurate, uncaring
09 heartless, insensate, unfeeling
10 hard-bitten, hard-boiled, insensible,
iron-headed 11 cold-blooded, cold-
hearted, hard as nails, hard-hearted,
indifferent, insensitive 12 case-
hardened, stony-hearted, thick-
skinned 13 unsympathetic

callously
06 coldly 07 harshly 11 heartlessly,
unfeelingly 13 cold-bloodedly, hard-
heartedly, insensitively

callow
03 raw 05 green, naive 06 jejune,
rookie 07 puerile, untried
08 immature, innocent, juvenile
09 fledgling, guileless, unbearded,
unfledged 11 uninitiated
13 inexperienced 15 unsophisticated

calm
03 cam 04 alay, came, caum, cool,
ease, even, hush, loun, lown, lull, mild
05 aleye, allay, lound, lownd, peace,
quiet, relax, sleek, still 06 becalm,
pacify, placid, poised, repose, sedate,
serene, settle, smooth, soothe, steady,
stilly 07 appease, assuage, compose,
halcyon, mollify, placate, quieten,
relaxed, reposed, restful, unmoved
08 ataraxia, calmness, composed,
cool down, dead-wind, laid-back,
peaceful, pipeclay, quietude, serenity,
tranquil, waveless, windless
09 collected, composure, impassive,

lighten up, limestone, nerveless,
placidity, sangfroid, stillness,
supercool, unclouded, unexcited,
unruffled 10 cool-headed, equanimity,
phlegmatic, settle down, simmer
down, untroubled 11 contentment,
impassivity, restfulness, undisturbed,
unemotional, unexcitable,
unflappable, unflustered, unpassioned,
unperturbed 12 even-tempered, keep
your head, on an even keel,
peacefulness, tranquillity, tranquillize,
unpassionate 13 dispassionate,
impassiveness, imperturbable, self-
possessed, unimpassioned
14 presence of mind, self-controlled,
unapprehensive, unflappability
15 cool as a cucumber

calmly
08 steadily 11 impassively 12 on an
even keel 13 unemotionally
14 phlegmatically 15 dispassionately

calorie
03 cal

calumny
05 abuse, libel, lying, smear 06 attack,
insult, mud pie 07 obloquy, slander
09 aspersion 10 backbiting,
defamation, derogation, detraction,
revilement 11 denigration, slagging-off
12 vilification, vituperation
13 disparagement

camaraderie
08 affinity, intimacy 09 closeness
10 fellowship, friendship
11 brotherhood, comradeship,
sociability 12 togetherness
13 brotherliness, companionship,
esprit de corps 14 fraternization, good
fellowship

Cambodia
01 K 03 KHM

Cambridge University *see* **college**

camel
04 oont 08 Bactrian 09 dromedare,
dromedary 15 ship of the desert

camera

Cameras include:

02 TV
03 APS, SLR, TLR
04 CCTV, cine, disc, film, Fuji®, view
05 Canon®, Kodak®, Leica®, Nikon®,
plate, press, sound, still, video
06 Konica®, Pentax®, reflex, Rollei®,
stereo, Super 8®, Webcam
07 bellows, compact, digital,
Minolta®, obscura, Olympus®,
pinhole, Yashica®
08 dry-plate, Polaroid®, Praktica®,
security, wet-plate
09 automatic, binocular, camcorder,
half-plate, miniature, panoramic,
Rolliflex®, single use, Steadicam®
10 box Brownie®, disposable,
Instamatic®, sliding box
11 large-format
12 quarter-plate, subminiature,
surveillance

13 daguerreotype, folding reflex,
point-and-press
14 twin-lens reflex
15 cinematographic

- **move camera**
03 pan 05 track

Cameroon
03 CAM, CMR

camouflage
◇ *anagram indicator*
04 hide, mask, veil 05 blind, cloak,
cover, front, guise 06 façade, screen
07 conceal, cover up, cover-up,
deceive, obscure 08 disguise
09 deception 10 maskirovka,
masquerade 11 concealment,
counterfeit

camp
03 set 04 duar, laer, side, tent
05 campy, crowd, douar, dowar, group,
gypsy, party, tents 06 caucus, clique,
encamp, laager, outlie 07 bivouac,
faction, leaguer, rough it, section
08 affected, campsite, mannered
09 pitch camp, posturing, set up camp
10 artificial, effeminate, encampment,
over the top, pitch tents, theatrical
11 camping-site, exaggerated
12 ostentatious 13 camping-ground,
sleep outdoors
- **confined to camp**
02 CC

campaign
03 war 04 push, work 05 blitz,
drive, fight, jehad, jihad, lobby
06 attack, battle, strive 07 canvass,
crusade, journey, promote
08 advocate, movement, strategy,
struggle 09 offensive, operation,
promotion 10 expedition 14 course
of action

campaigner
06 zealot 07 fighter 08 activist,
advocate, champion, crusader,
promoter, reformer 10 enthusiast

camp-follower
03 boy 05 toady 06 bummer, lackey,
lascar 08 hanger-on, henchman
11 leaguer-lady, leaguer-lass

can
03 dow, jar, jug, lav, loo, mug, tin
04 dows, jail, pail, stir 06 prison, toilet
08 canister, jerrycan, lavatory, preserve
09 container 10 chimney pot,
receptacle 11 depth charge
See also **prison**; **toilet**
- **can it** *see* **quiet**; **shut up** *under* **shut**

Canada
03 CAN, CDN
See also **Prime Minister**; **province**

Canadian cities and notable
towns include:

06 Ottawa, Quebec, Regina
07 Calgary, Halifax, Toronto
08 Edmonton, Montreal, Victoria,
Winnipeg
09 Saskatoon, Vancouver

Canadian landmarks include:

06 Mt Thor
07 CN Tower, Mt Logan, Niagara, Rockies, Sky Dome
08 Lake Erie
09 Hudson Bay, Lake Huron, Mt Seymour
10 Great Lakes, St Lawrence
11 Lake Ontario
12 Lake Superior, Niagara Falls
13 Algonquin Park, Parc Olympique
14 Horseshoe Falls, Rocky Mountains

Canadian
03 Can, Cdn **06** Canuck

canal
03 Can, gut **04** duct, foss, moat, tube **05** ditch, fosse, zanja **06** groove, trench **07** channel, enteron, passage, shipway **08** waterway **10** navigation **11** watercourse **14** digestive tract

Canals include:

04 Erie, Kiel, Suez
05 Grand
06 Panama, Rideau
07 Corinth, Midland, Welland
10 Caledonian, Mittelland
11 Welland Ship
14 Manchester Ship

cancel
03 axe, nix **04** drop, kill, stop, undo, wipe **05** abort, adeem, annul, erase, quash, scrap, scrub **06** delete, offset, repeal, revoke, shelve, strike **07** abandon, abolish, call off, nullify, red-line, rescind, retract, vitiate, wash out **08** abrogate, break off, cross out, dissolve, override, postpone, suppress, withdraw, write off **09** eliminate, strike out **10** declare off, invalidate, obliterate, scrub round **11** countermand, discontinue **14** counterbalance
• **cancel out**
06 offset, redeem **07** balance, nullify **09** make up for **10** compensate, counteract, neutralize **14** counterbalance

cancellation
06 repeal **08** deletion, dropping, quashing, shelving, stopping **09** abolition, annulment, scrubbing **10** abandoning, calling-off, nullifying, revocation **11** abandonment, elimination **12** invalidation **14** neutralization

cancer
03 rot **04** Big C, Crab, evil **06** blight, canker, growth, plague, tumour **07** disease, scourge, the Big C, the Crab **08** cancroid, sickness **09** carcinoma **10** corruption, malignancy, pestilence **15** malignant growth

candelabrum
07 menorah **09** lampadary **11** candlestick

candid
04 fair, open **05** blunt, clear, frank,

plain, round, white **06** honest, simple **07** liberal, shining, sincere, unposed **08** informal, truthful, unbiased **09** guileless, impartial, ingenuous, outspoken **10** forthright **11** plain-spoken, unequivocal, unrehearsed **12** heart-to-heart **15** straightforward

candidate
03 PPC **06** runner, seeker **07** entrant, nominee **08** aspirant, examinee **09** applicant, contender, postulant, pretender **10** competitor, contestant **11** possibility
• **candidate list**
04 leet **06** ticket

candidly
06 openly, simply **07** bluntly, clearly, frankly, plainly, roundly, up-front **08** honestly **09** liberally, sincerely **10** truthfully **11** guilelessly, ingenuously, outspokenly **12** forthrightly **13** unequivocally

candle
03 dip **04** slut **05** cerge, sperm, taper, torch **06** bougie, ulicon, ulikon **07** oolakan, oulakan, shammes, ulichon **08** amandine, eulachan, eulachon, luminary, oulachon, shammash, wax light **09** tallow dip **10** night-light **12** tallow candle

candour
06 purity **07** honesty, naivety **08** kindness, openness **09** bluntness, franchise, frankness, plainness, sincerity, whiteness **10** directness, liberality, simplicity **11** artlessness, brusqueness **12** impartiality, plain-dealing, truthfulness **13** guilelessness, ingenuousness, outspokenness **14** forthrightness **15** unequivocalness

candy
05 glacé, kandy **06** candie, sweets **07** cocaine, encrust, toffees **10** chocolates **11** crystallize **13** confectionery

cane
03 rod **05** crook, ratan, staff, stick, swish, swits **06** ferule, jambee, rattan, switch **07** tickler, whangee **09** riding rod **10** alpenstock, supplejack **12** swagger-stick, walking-stick

canine
01 c **04** tush **06** cuspid **08** dogtooth, eye tooth
See also **dog**

canker
03 rot **04** bane, boil, evil, sore **05** decay, ulcer **06** blight, cancer, infect, lesion, plague **07** corrupt, destroy, disease, pollute, scourge **08** sickness **09** corrosion, infection **10** cankerworm, corruption, pestilence, ulceration

cannabis
03 kef, kif, pot, tea **04** benj, blow, dope, gage, hash, hemp, kaif, leaf, puff, punk, toke, weed **05** bhang, blunt, ganja, gauge, grass, joint, roach, skunk,

splay **06** bomber, greens, reefer, spliff **07** hashish **08** locoweed, Mary Jane **09** marihuana, marijuana, substance **10** sinsemilla, wacky baccy **12** electric puha

cannibal
08 man-eater **09** Thyestean, Thyestian **11** people-eater **15** anthropophagite

cannibalism
08 exophagy **09** endophagy, man-eating **12** people-eating **13** anthropophagy

cannibalistic
09 man-eating, Thyestean **10** exophagous **11** endophagous **12** people-eating **15** anthropophagous

cannily
06 subtly **07** acutely, sharply **08** astutely, cleverly, shrewdly **09** knowingly, skilfully

cannon
03 gun **05** carom, saker **06** barker, big gun, curtal, falcon, monkey, mortar, Quaker **07** battery, bombard, chamber, nursery **08** basilisk, culverin, field gun, great gun, howitzer, murderer, oerlikon, ordnance, spitfire **09** artillery, carambole, carronade, Quaker gun, zumbooruk **10** fieldpiece, serpentine **11** stern-chaser **12** demi-culverin **14** murdering-piece

cannonade
05 salvo **06** volley **07** barrage **08** pounding, shelling **09** broadside **11** bombardment

canny
03 sly **04** good, nice, wice, wise **05** acute, lucky, pawky, sharp **06** artful, astute, clever, gentle, shrewd, subtle **07** careful, knowing, prudent, skilful **08** cautious, innocent **09** fortunate, judicious, sagacious **11** circumspect, worldly-wise **13** perspicacious

canoe
04 waka **05** kaiak, kayak **06** dugout **07** piragua **08** montaria, woodskin **09** monoxylon

canon
03 can, law **04** line, rota, rule **05** round, vicar **06** priest, square, squier, squire **07** brocard, dictate, precept, statute **08** Mathurin, minister, reverend, standard, vice-dean **09** clergyman, criterion, Mathurine, principle, yardstick **10** prebendary, regulation **12** residentiary

canonical
07 regular **08** accepted, approved, orthodox **10** authorized, recognized, sanctioned **13** authoritative
• **canonical hours**

Canonical hours include:

04 none, sext
05 lauds, nones, prime, terce
06 matins, tierce

07 complin, orthros, vespers
08 compline, evensong

canonize
05 bless, saint **07** beatify, besaint
08 sanctify

canopy
03 sky **04** dais, tilt **05** cover, herse, shade, state **06** awning, estate, hearse, huppah, tester **07** chuppah, majesty, marquee, shelter, veranda
08 ciborium, covering, marquise, pavilion, shamiana, sunshade, umbrella, verandah **09** baldachin, baldaquin, clamshell, parachute, shamianah **10** cooker hood, tabernacle **11** baldacchino **12** cloth of state

cant
04 kant, tilt **05** argot, brisk, lingo, merry, slang, slope **06** jargon, lively, snivel **07** snuffle **09** hypocrisy
10 vernacular **11** insincerity, rogues' Latin **12** thieves' Latin
15 pretentiousness

cantankerous
05 cross, testy **06** crabby, crusty, grumpy, ornery **07** crabbed, grouchy, peevish, piggish **08** contrary, perverse, stubborn **09** crotchety, difficult, irascible, irritable **11** bad-tempered, carnaptious, curnaptious, ill-humoured, quarrelsome **13** quick-tempered

canteen
04 café **05** flask, Naafi **06** buffet
08 snackbar **09** cafeteria, refectory
10 commissary, restaurant

canter
03 jog, ren, rin, run **04** lope, trot
05 amble, titup **06** gallop, tittup
07 jogtrot, tripple **11** false gallop

canton
03 can **04** Vaud **05** space **06** corner
08 division, ordinary

canvas
04 tent **05** Binca®, sails, tents
06 burlap, muslin **08** oilcloth

canvass
04 poll, scan, sift **05** study **06** debate, survey **07** agitate, analyse, discuss, examine, explore, find out, inspect
08 campaign, evaluate **09** seek votes
10 scrutinize **11** ask for votes, electioneer, inquire into, investigate
12 solicit votes **13** drum up support

canyon
05 abyss, cañon, chasm, gorge, gully
06 cañada, ravine, valley

cap
03 hat, lid, mob, taj, tam, top **04** beat, bung, call, caul, coat, coif, curb, kepi, plug **05** beret, chaco, cover, crown, excel, kippa, limit, mutch, outdo, quoif, shako, tammy, toque, tuque
06 amorce, barret, berret, better, biggin, bonnet, bunnet, calpac, chapka, czapka, exceed, granny,

kalpak, pileus, shacko **07** biretta, bycoket, calotte, calpack, control, eclipse, ferrule, grannie, montero, stopper, surpass **08** capeline, chaperon, gorblimy, outshine, outstrip, restrain, restrict, schapska, trencher, yarmulka, yarmulke, zuchetta, zuchetto **09** capelline, chaperone, cock's-comb, crown cork, glengarry, gorblimey, transcend, trenchard, zucchetto **10** cockernony, Kilmarnock
11 bonnet-rouge, mortarboard, Tam o' Shanter **12** cheesecutter
13 international **15** go one better than
See also **hat**

capability
05 means, power, skill **06** talent
07 ability, faculty **08** aptitude, capacity, facility **09** potential
10 competence, efficiency
11 proficiency, skilfulness
13 qualification **14** accomplishment

capable
04 able **05** adept, apt to, smart
06 clever, fitted, gifted, suited
07 needing, notable, skilful
08 allowing, liable to, masterly, talented **09** competent, efficient, qualified, tending to **10** disposed to, inclined to, proficient **11** experienced, intelligent **12** accomplished, businesslike **13** comprehensive

capably
04 ably **07** adeptly **08** cleverly
09 skilfully **11** competently, efficiently
12 proficiently **13** intelligently

capacious
03 big **04** huge, vast, wide **05** ample, broad, large, roomy, womby **07** liberal, sizable **08** generous, spacious
09 expansive, extensive
10 commodious, voluminous
11 comfortable, elephantine, substantial **13** comprehensive

capacity
03 cap, job **04** bind, gift, post, role, room, size **05** power, range, scope, skill, space **06** extent, genius, office, talent, volume **07** ability, compass, content, faculty **08** aptitude, function, position **09** largeness, magnitude, potential, readiness, resources
10 capability, cleverness, competence, competency, dimensions, efficiency
11 appointment, proficiency, proportions, sufficiency
12 intelligence
• **in the capacity of**
03 qua

cape
01 C **03** ras **04** coat, head, naze, neck, ness, robe, scaw, skaw, wrap **05** amice, cloak, fanon, fichu, point, shawl, talma
06 almuce, domino, mantle, muleta, poncho, sontag, tippet, tongue
07 burnous, manteel, mozetta, pelisse
08 burnouse, headland, pelerine
09 peninsula **10** promontory
See also **cloak**; **peninsula**

Capes include:
03 Cod
04 Fear, Horn, York
05 Wrath
06 Cretin, Orange
07 Kennedy, Leeuwin, Lookout
08 Farewell, Foulwind, Good Hope, Suckling
09 Canaveral, Carbonara, St Vincent, Trafalgar, Van Diemen
10 Finisterre, Kidnappers, Providence
11 Three Points, Tribulation
12 Hopes Advance
13 Prince of Wales

caper
03 hop **04** dido, jape, jest, jump, lark, leap, romp, skip **05** antic, bound, crime, dance, flisk, frisk, prank, scoup, scowp, stunt **06** affair, antics, bounce, cavort, frolic, gambol, prance, spring
07 gambado **08** business, capriole, escapade, mischief **09** high jinks
10 pigeon-wing

Cape Verde
03 CPV

capital
◊ *head selection indicator*
02 A1, uc **03** cap **04** cash, head, main, seat **05** chief, first, fonds, funds, major, means, money, prime, stock **06** assets, uncial, wealth **07** central, finance, leading, primary, savings, serious
08 cardinal, foremost, main city, property, reserves **09** excellent, important, majuscule, principal, resources **10** investment **11** block letter, investments, wherewithal
12 block capital, liquid assets
13 capital letter **15** upper-case letter
See also **city**; **currency**
• **small capitals**
02 sc

capitalism
12 laissez-faire **14** free enterprise

capitalist
05 mogul **06** banker, fat cat, tycoon
07 magnate, moneyer **08** investor, moneyman **09** bourgeois, financier, moneybags, plutocrat **12** money-spinner **13** person of means

capitalize
• **capitalize on**
07 exploit **08** cash in on **10** profit from
13 make the most of **15** take advantage of

capitulate
05 yield **06** give in, give up, relent, submit **07** succumb **08** back down
09 surrender **15** throw in the towel

capitulation
08 giving-in, giving-up, yielding
09 relenting, surrender **10** submission, succumbing **11** backing-down

caprice
03 fad **04** whim **05** fancy, freak, humor, quirk **06** humour, megrim,

notion, spleen, vagary, vapour, whimsy
07 fantasy, impulse **08** humoresk,
migraine, phantasy **09** capriccio
10 fickleness, fitfulness, humoresque
11 inconstancy **14** changeableness

capricious
◇ *anagram indicator*
03 odd **05** freak, queer **06** fickle, fitful,
kittle, quirky, wanton **07** erratic,
wayward **08** fanciful, freakish,
humorous, perverse, petulant, variable
09 arbitrary, fantastic, impulsive,
mercurial, uncertain, whimsical
10 capernoity, changeable,
humoursome, inconstant
11 capernoitie, cappernoity, fantastical
13 unpredictable

capsize
◇ *reversal indicator*
04 purl **05** upset **06** invert **07** tip over,
whemmle, whomble, whommle,
whummle **08** keel over, overturn, roll
over, turn over **10** turn turtle
11 overturning

capsule
03 pod, urn **04** boll, pill **05** craft, jelly,
probe, shell **06** bomber, caplet,
cocoon, module, ovisac, sheath, tablet
07 habitat, lozenge, sandbox
08 pyxidium, spansule **09** container,
poppy-head, radio pill
10 nidamentum, receptacle
11 sporogonium

captain
03 cid **04** boss, head, lead, skip
05 chief, owner, pilot **06** direct, guider,
leader, manage, master, old man,
patron **07** command, control, officer,
patroon, skipper **08** capitayn
09 commander, commodore,
supervise **10** ritt-master, shipmaster
12 be in charge of **13** master-mariner,
protospataire, whaling-master
14 protospathaire **15** protospatharius

caption
04 note **05** title **06** arrest, legend,
titles **07** cutline, heading, wording
08 headline **09** underline
11 inscription

captious
07 carping, peevish **08** critical,
niggling **09** quibbling **10** nit-picking,
scrupulous **13** hair-splitting,
hypercritical

captivate
03 get, win **04** lure, take **05** charm

06 allure, dazzle, seduce **07** attract,
beguile, bewitch, delight, enamour,
enchant, enthral **09** enrapture,
fascinate, hypnotize, infatuate,
mesmerize **11** take by storm

captivating
06 taking **07** winsome **08** alluring,
catching, charming, dazzling
09 beautiful, beguiling, seductive
10 attractive, bewitching,
delightful, enchanting **11** enthralling,
fascinating

captive
03 POW **05** caged, slave **06** secure,
shut up **07** caitive, convict, hostage,
subject, triumph **08** confined,
detained, detainee, enslaved,
ensnared, interned, internee, jailbird,
locked up, prisoner **09** enchained, in
bondage **10** imprisoned, locked away,
restrained, restricted **12** incarcerated
13 held in custody

captivity
05 bonds, exile **06** duress
07 bondage, custody, slavery
09 detention, endurance, restraint,
servitude **10** constraint, internment
11 confinement, enslavement
12 imprisonment **13** incarceration

captor
05 guard **06** jailor, keeper, warder
09 custodian **12** incarcerator

capture
◇ *containment indicator*
03 cop, nab, net, win **04** land, nick,
rush, take, trap, with **05** carry, catch,
mop up, seize, snare, withe **06** arrest,
collar, cut out, entrap, occupy, pick up,
record, secure, taking **07** embrace,
ensnare, express, nabbing, nicking, run
down, seizure, snabble, snaffle
08 catching, hit a blot, hunt down,
imprison, surprise, trapping
09 apprehend, collaring, recapture,
represent, reproduce **11** encapsulate
12 imprisonment, take prisoner
13 taking captive **14** taking prisoner
• **be captured**
04 fall

capuchin
03 sai **05** Cebus, sajou **07** sapajou

car
04 auto, cart, heap **05** motor
07 chariot, clunker, vehicle, vettura
08 motor car **09** speedster
10 automobile, rust bucket **12** motor
vehicle **13** shooting brake

11 accelerator, anti-roll bar, exhaust pipe, ignition key, number plate, parcel shelf, speedometer
12 licence plate, parking-light, quarterlight, transmission
13 centre console, courtesy light, cruise control, flasher switch, pneumatic tyre, rack and pinion, radial-ply tyre, reclining seat, shock absorber, side-impact bar, steering-wheel
14 air-conditioner, central locking, electric window, emergency light, four-wheel drive, hydraulic brake, rear-view mirror, reversing light, steering-column
15 windscreen-wiper

Car and motoring-related terms include:

02 AA
03 dip, GPS, LRP, map, MOT, RAC, tow
04 exit, park, skid, SORN, stop
05 amber, brake, crash, cut up, flash, layby, on tow, prang, shunt
06 diesel, fill up, filter, garage, hold-up, L-plate, octane, petrol, pile-up, pull in
07 blowout, bollard, bus lane, car park, car wash, cat's-eye, give way, logbook, MOT test, neutral, pull out, reverse, road map, snarl-up, tax disc, traffic
08 accident, change up, coasting, declutch, fast lane, flat tyre, gridlock, indicate, junction, main beam, overtake, puncture, red light, road rage, services, slip road, slow lane, speeding, tailback, taxi rank, turn left, unleaded
09 blind spot, breakdown, collision, cycle lane, fifth gear, first gear, green card, hit-and-run, radar trap, road atlas, road studs, roadworks, sixth gear, third gear, T junction, turn right, wheelspin, white line
10 accelerate, amber light, arm signals, bottleneck, change down, change gear, change lane, contraflow, crossroads, fourth gear, green light, inside lane, middle lane, pedestrian, petrol pump, roundabout, second gear, speed limit, stay in lane, straight on, tailgating, traffic jam, yellow line
11 box junction, crawler lane, drink-driver, driving test, hand signals, highway code, outside lane, speed camera, traffic cone, traffic cops, traffic news, zigzag lines
12 drink-driving, hard shoulder, left-hand lane, motorway toll, one-way system, parking meter, passing place, road junction, speeding fine, tyre pressure
13 Belisha beacon, drink and drive, driving lesson, driving school, flashing amber, handbrake turn, jump the lights, left-hand drive, level crossing, no-claims bonus, parking ticket, pay and display, penalty points, petrol station,

power steering, right-hand lane, super unleaded, traffic lights, traffic police, zebra crossing
14 cadence braking, double declutch, driving licence, four-wheel drive, mini-roundabout, MOT certificate, motorway pile-up, overtaking lane, poor visibility, puffin crossing, right-hand drive, service station, speeding ticket, unleaded petrol
15 pelican crossing, put your foot down, road fund licence, test certificate, traction control, warning triangle

See also **motor vehicle**

carafe
03 jug **05** flask **06** bottle, flagon **07** pitcher **08** decanter

caravan
02 RV **03** van **04** line **05** group, train **06** cafila, convoy, kafila **07** caffila, trailer **09** camper van, Dormobile®, motor home, Winnebago® **10** mobile home

carbon
01 C **04** copy **07** diamond **08** graphite **09** buckyball
• **carbon copy**
02 cc **03** bcc **06** flimsy **08** manifold

carbuncle
04 boil, bump, lump, sore **06** bunion, pimple **07** anthrax, blister **12** inflammation

carcase, carcass
04 body, hulk **05** shell **06** corpse, cutter **07** cadaver, remains **08** dead body, skeleton **09** framework, structure
See also **meat**

card
03 ace, map, mix **04** Amex, club, comb, jack, king, tose, toze **05** deuce, heart, joker, knave, queen, spade, toaze **06** domino, master, meishi **07** diamond **10** adulterate **13** carte-de-visite
See also **eccentric; game**
• **cards suits**
01 c, d, h, s **05** clubs **06** hearts, spades **08** diamonds
• **on the cards**
06 likely **08** possible, probable **11** looking as if, looking like **13** the chances are
• **playing cards**
04 deck, hand **11** devil's books

cardinal
02 HE **03** key **04** main **05** basic, chief, first, pivot, prime **06** number, red hat **07** capital, central, highest, leading, primary **08** foremost, greatest, grosbeak **09** essential, important, paramount, principal **10** pre-eminent **11** fundamental **14** apostolic vicar
See also **archbishop; number**

Cardinals include:

03 Sin (Jaime)
04 Gray (Gordon), Hume (Basil), Pole

(Reginald), **Retz** (Jean Françoise de)
05 **Chigi** (Fabio)
06 **Beaton** (David), **Borgia** (Rodrigo), **Fisher** (John), **Heenan** (John Carmel), **Medici** (Giovanni de'), **Newman** (John Henry), **Rovere** (Francesco della), **Stuart** (Henry, Duke of York), **Wolsey** (Thomas)
07 **Bethune** (David), **Langham** (Simon), **Langton** (Stephen), **Mazarin** (Jules), **Mendoza** (Pedro Gonzalez de), **Pandulf, Vaughan** (Herbert), **Wiseman** (Nicholas), **Ximenes** (Francisco)
08 **Alberoni** (Giulio), **Aubusson** (Pierre d'), **Beaufort** (Henry), **Stepinac**
09 **Richelieu** (Armand Jean Duplessis, Duc de), **Wyszynski** (Stefan)
10 **Bellarmine** (Robert), **Breakspear** (Nicolas), **Mindszenty** (József)
13 **Murphy-O'Connor** (Cormac)

• **cardinal's office**
03 hat

care
04 cark, fear, heed, mind, reck, reke, ward **05** kaugh, pains, worry **06** bother, burden, charge, hang-up, kiaugh, regard, strain, stress, tender **07** anxiety, caution, concern, control, custody, keeping, minding, tending, thought, trouble **08** accuracy, disquiet, distress, interest, pressure, prudence, tutelage, vexation **09** attention, give a damn, oversight, vigilance **10** affliction, attendance, protection **11** be concerned, carefulness, forethought, heedfulness, safekeeping, supervision, tribulation **12** be interested, guardianship, looking-after, watchfulness, watching-over **13** consideration **14** circumspection, meticulousness, responsibility
• **care for**
04 like, love, mind, tend, want **05** enjoy, nurse **06** attend, desire **07** cherish, protect **08** be fond of, be keen on, maintain **09** be close to, delight in, look after, watch over **10** minister to, provide for, take care of **12** be in love with
• **care of**
01 c/- **02** c/o

career
◇ *anagram indicator*
03 job, ren, rin, run **04** bolt, dash, life, past, race, rush, tear **05** shoot, speed, trade, whang **06** gallop, hurtle, métier **07** calling, cariere, pursuit **08** life-work, vocation **10** employment, livelihood, occupation, profession

carefree
05 happy **06** blithe, breezy, cheery **07** halcyon **08** cheerful, debonair, laid-back **09** easy-going, fancy-free, unworried **10** debonnaire, insouciant, nonchalant, rollicking, untroubled **11** thoughtless, unconcerned **12** happy-go-lucky, light-hearted **13** irresponsible

careful
04 mean, wary, wise **05** alert, aware, chary, close, heedy, tight **06** eyeful, frugal, stingy **07** anxious, guarded, heedful, mindful, miserly, precise, prudent, sparing, tactful, thrifty **08** accurate, cautious, detailed, diligent, discreet, rigorous, sensible, thorough, vigilant, watchful **09** assiduous, attentive, judicious, niggardly, penny-wise **10** deliberate, economical, fast-handed, fastidious, hard-fisted, methodical, meticulous, particular, scrupulous, solicitous, systematic, thoughtful **11** circumspect, close-fisted, close-handed, painstaking, punctilious, tight-fisted **12** parsimonious, softly-softly **13** conscientious, penny-pinching

carefully
05 hooly **06** warily **07** charily, closely **09** guardedly, heedfully, mindfully, precisely, prudently, tactfully **10** accurately, cautiously, diligently, discreetly, handsomely, rigorously, solicitous, thoroughly, vigilantly, watchfully **11** assiduously, attentively, judiciously, punctilious **12** deliberately, fastidiously, methodically, meticulously, scrupulously, thoughtfully **13** circumspectly, painstakingly **14** systematically **15** conscientiously

careless
◊ anagram indicator
03 lax **04** nice **05** hasty, messy, slack **06** breezy, casual, remiss, secure, shoddy, simple, sloppy, untidy **07** artless, cursory, négligé, offhand, untenty **08** carefree, cheerful, heedless, laid-back, reckless, slapdash, slipshod, tactless, uncaring **09** easy-going, forgetful, negligent, unguarded, unmindful, unworried **10** disorderly, inaccurate, incautious, indiscreet, insouciant, neglectful, nonchalant, regardless, unthinking, untroubled **11** inattentive, perfunctory, superficial, thoughtless, unconcerned **12** absent-minded, disorganized, happy as a clam, happy-go-lucky, light-hearted **13** inconsiderate, irresponsible **15** happy as a sandboy

carelessly
◊ anagram indicator
06 anyhow **07** hastily **08** casually, remissly, shoddily, slam-bang, slapdash, sloppily **09** cursorily **10** heedlessly, recklessly, tactlessly, uncaringly **11** forgetfully, negligently, offhandedly, unguardedly, unmindfully **12** incautiously, indiscreetly, neglectingly, unthinkingly **13** inattentively, irresponsibly, perfunctorily, superficially, thoughtlessly, unconcernedly **14** absent-mindedly **15** inconsiderately

caress
03 coy, hug, pat, pet, rub **04** bill, kiss **05** grope, touch **06** cuddle, feel up,

fondle, nuzzle, stroke **07** embrace, petting, touch up **08** canoodle, lallygag, lollygag **10** endearment **13** butterfly kiss, slap and tickle

caretaker
06 acting, fill-in, keeper, porter, pro tem, sexton, verger, warden **07** curator, dvornik, janitor, ostiary, shammes, stand-in, steward **08** janitrix, shammash, watchman **09** concierge, custodian, janitress, short-term, temporary **10** doorkeeper, substitute **11** provisional **14** superintendent

careworn
04 worn **05** gaunt, tired, weary **07** anxious, haggard, worn-out, worried **08** fatigued **09** exhausted

cargo
04 bulk, haul, last, load **05** goods **06** lading **07** baggage, fraught, freight, payload, tonnage **08** contents, deck-load, frautage, shipment **10** fraughtage **11** consignment, merchandise

Caribbean
02 WI **10** West Indies

caricature
04 mock **05** mimic **06** parody, satire, send up, send-up **07** cartoon, distort, lampoon, mimicry, take off, take-off **08** ridicule, satirize, travesty **09** burlesque, imitation **10** distortion, exaggerate **14** representation

caring
04 fond, kind, warm **06** loving, tender **07** devoted, helpful **08** friendly **10** altruistic, benevolent, thoughtful **11** good-natured, kind-hearted, sympathetic **12** affectionate **13** compassionate, philanthropic, tender-hearted

carnage
06 murder **07** killing **08** butchery, genocide, massacre **09** bloodbath, bloodshed, holocaust, slaughter **10** mass murder **15** ethnic cleansing

carnal
04 lewd **05** belly, human **06** animal, bodily, erotic, impure, sexual **07** fleshly, lustful, natural, outward, sensual **08** physical **09** corporeal, lecherous, murderous **10** lascivious, libidinous, licentious **11** flesh-eating, unspiritual

carnival
04 fair, fête, gala **05** carny **06** carney, fiesta **07** holiday, jubilee, revelry **08** Fasching, festival, jamboree **09** amusement, Mardi Gras, merriment **11** celebration, merrymaking

carnivorous
10 meat-eating, zoophagous **11** creophagous, flesh-eating

carol
04 hymn, noel, sing, song **06** carrel, chorus, strain **07** carrell, wassail **13** Christmas song

carousal
04 upsy **05** feast, rouse, upsee, upsey

carouse
04 birl **05** birle, booze, drink, party, quaff, revel, spree **06** imbibe **07** roister, wassail **09** celebrate, make merry **11** drink freely, wassail bout

carousing
08 drinking, partying **11** celebrating, compotation, merrymaking **13** mallemaroking

carp
02 id **03** ide, koi, nag **04** yerk **05** gibel, knock, pinch **06** go on at, twitch **07** censure, crucian, crusian, nit-pick, quibble **08** complain, cyprinid, goldfish, reproach **09** criticize, find fault, round fish **10** find faults, silverfish **11** have a shot at **14** ultracrepidate

carpenter
05 chips **06** chippy, joiner, Joseph, Quince, wright **10** cartwright, shipwright, woodworker **12** cabinet-maker

carpet
03 bed, mat, rug **04** cake, coat, wrap **05** cover, dress, layer **06** clothe, encase, spread **07** blanket, matting, overlay **08** covering **10** tablecloth **13** floor-covering

Carpets and rugs include:
03 rag, red, rya
04 kali
05 Dutch, kelim, kilim, magic, pilch, stair, throw
06 hearth, hooked, khilim, Kirman, numdah, runner, prayer, Turkey, Wilton
07 bergama, flokati, Persian, Turkish
08 Aubusson, bergamot, Brussels, moquette
09 Axminster, prayer rug, sheepskin
10 travelling
11 Bessarabian, buffalo robe
13 Kidderminster

carping
07 nagging, Zoilism **08** captious **09** cavilling, quibbling **10** nit-picking **11** complaining, criticizing **12** fault-finding

carriage
03 air, car, cge, job, set **04** gait, mien, port **05** guise, poise, tenue **06** burden, clatch, manner, stance **07** baggage, bearing, conduct, freight, portage, postage, posture, turnout, vehicle, voiture **08** attitude, carrying, delivery, equipage, portance, presence, truckage **09** behaviour, demeanour, porterage, transport **10** conveyance, deportment **14** transportation

Carriages include:
03 cab, fly, gig
04 arba, baby, chay, drag, dray, ekka, mail, pony, pram, rath, shay, trap

05 araba, aroba, bandy, buggy, coach, coupé, dilly, ratha, stage, sulky, T-cart, wagon
06 berlin, calash, chaise, drosky, go-cart, hansom, herdic, landau, pochay, purdah, spider, spring, surrey
07 britska, britzka, cariole, caroche, chariot, dogcart, droshky, hackney, phaeton, pillbox, ricksha, tilbury, vettura, vis-à-vis
08 barouche, britzska, brougham, carriole, carryall, clarence, diligent, jump-seat, po'chaise, rickshaw, rockaway, sociable, stanhope, victoria
09 britschka, cabriolet, landaulet, wagonette
10 four-in hand, post chaise, stagecoach
11 family coach, hurly-hacket, village cart
13 désobligeante, mourning coach, spider phaeton, thoroughbrace

carried away
04 rapt **06** enlevé, way-out
• **get carried away**
06 lose it **13** become excited
See also **carry**

carrier
06 bearer, porter, runner, telfer, vector
07 airline, telpher, tranter, vehicle
08 conveyor, horseman, kurveyor
09 messenger **10** plastic bag
11 transmitter, transporter
12 roundsperson **13** dispatch rider
14 delivery-person, transport rider

carrion
03 ket
• **carrion feeder**
04 hyen **05** hyena **06** hyaena
07 vulture **08** aardwolf **09** scavenger

carry
◇ *containment indicator*
03 act, lug **04** bear, cart, gain, haul, have, hold, hump, lead, mean, move, pass, pipe, sell, show, take, tote, wain
05 adopt, bring, cover, drive, fetch, mount, print, reach, relay, shift, stand, stock **06** accept, acquit, behave, convey, effect, entail, hold up, lead to, pass on, ratify, retail, suffer, travel, uphold, wheech **07** approve, be heard, comport, conduct, contain, deliver, display, involve, present, publish, release, support, sustain, vote for **08** hand over, maintain, result in, sanction, shoulder, transfer, transmit, underpin **09** authorize, be audible, broadcast, transport **11** communicate, disseminate, have for sale, keep in stock **12** vote in favour **14** be infected with
• **carry away**
03 rap **04** lift **06** asport, ravish
08 bear away **09** transport
• **carry off**
03 lag, net, rob, win **04** gain, hent, land, rape **05** crack **06** abduct, kidnap, pick up, secure **07** achieve

08 complete **09** succeed in, transport
12 come away with
• **carry on**
03 ren, rin, run **04** go on, hold, keep, last, wage **06** bash on, endure, keep on, keep up, manage, play up, pursue, resume **07** conduct, operate, persist, proceed, restart **08** continue, engage in, maintain, progress, return to
09 misbehave, persevere
10 administer, be involved, mess around, play around **12** have an affair
15 behave foolishly
• **carry out**
02 do **04** fill **05** mount **06** effect, fulfil
07 achieve, conduct, deliver, execute, perform, realize **08** bring off
09 discharge, implement, undertake
10 accomplish **12** give effect to **13** put into effect **15** deliver the goods, put into practice

carry-on
04 flap, fuss, stir, to-do **05** hoo-ha
06 bother, hassle **07** trouble
09 commotion, kerfuffle

cart
03 car, jag, lug **04** bear, dray, gill, haul, hump, jill, lead, move, pram, tote
05 bandy, carry, float, furby, gambo, shift, truck, wagon **06** barrow, convey, furphy, gurney **07** cariole, hackery, shandry, trailer, tumbrel, tumbril
08 carriole, democrat, handcart, transfer **09** transport **11** wheelbarrow

cartilage
07 cricoid, gristle **08** chondrus, meniscus

carton
03 box, tub **04** case, pack **06** packet, parcel **07** package **09** container

cartoon
04 toon **05** anime, manga **06** bubble, parody, send-up, sketch **07** balloon, drawing, fumetto, lampoon, picture, take-off **09** animation, burlesque
10 caricature, comic strip **12** animated film, strip cartoon

Cartoon characters include:
03 PHB, Ren, Tom
04 Bart, Fred, Huey, Kyle, Lisa, Stan
05 Alice, Bluto, Dewey, Dumbo, Goofy, Homer, Jerry, Kenny, Louey, Marge, Mr Men, Robin, Rocky, Snowy, Wally
06 Batman, Beavis, Boo Boo, Calvin, Daphne, Droopy, Hobbes, Maggie, Obelix, Popeye, Shaggy, Snoopy, Stimpy, Thelma, Tintin, Top Cat
07 Asterix, Cartman, Custard, Dilbert, Gnasher, Muttley, Penfold, Roobarb
08 Andy Capp, Butthead, Clouseau, Garfield, Krazy Kat, Olive Oyl, Super Man, Superted, Tank Girl, The Joker, Yogi Bear
09 Betty Boop, Bugs Bunny, Chip 'n' Dale, Daffy Duck, Daisy Duck, Dastardly, Dick Tracy, Elmer Fudd, Marmaduke, Oor Wullie, Pepe le Pew, Scooby Doo, Spider Man, Sylvester, The Broons, Tweety Pie

10 Bullwinkle, Donald Duck, Judge Dredd, Road Runner, Scrappy Doo, The Riddler
11 Bart Simpson, Betty Rubble, Danger Mouse, Felix the Cat, Flash Gordon, Fred Bassett, Korky the Cat, Lisa Simpson, Mickey Mouse, Minnie Mouse, The Simpsons, Wile E Coyote
12 Barney Rubble, Charlie Brown, Desperate Dan, Homer Simpson, Little Misses, Marge Simpson, Ren and Stimpy
13 Dick Dastardly, Maggie Simpson, Modesty Blaise, Rupert the Bear, Scrooge McDuck
14 Bash Street Kids, Foghorn Leghorn, Fred Flintstone, Incredible Hulk, The Pink Panther
15 Calvin and Hobbes, Dennis the Menace, Penelope Pitstop, Steamboat Willie, Wilma Flintstone

Cartoonists include:
02 HB
03 Low (Sir David)
04 Capp (Al), Kane (Bob), Rémi (Georges)
05 Adams (Scott), Avery (Tex), Block (Herbert L), Davis (Jim), Doyle (John), Giles, Hanna (William), Hergé, Jones (Chuck), Lantz (Walter), McCay (Winsor), Segar (Elzie), Silas
06 Addams (Charles), Disney (Walt), Fisher (Bud), Iwerks (Ub), Larson (Gary), Scarfe (Gerald), Schulz (Charles M), Searle (Ronald), Siegel (Jerry), Smythe (Reg)
07 Barbera (Joseph), Shuster (Joseph), Tenniel (Sir John), Trudeau (Garry), Watkins (Dudley D), Webster (Tom)
08 Goldberg (Rube), Groening (Matt), Herblock, Herriman (George), Robinson (Heath)
09 Baxendale (Leo), Fleischer (Max), Watterson (Bill)
12 Bairnsfather (Bruce), Hanna-Barbera

cartridge
04 case, tube **05** blank, round, shell
06 charge **07** capsule, torpedo
08 canister, cassette, cylinder, magazine, streamer **09** container
11 central fire

caruncle
04 aril **08** arillode **10** strophiole

carve
◇ *anagram indicator*
03 cut, hew **04** chip, chop, etch, form, hack **05** cut up, kerve, mould, notch, sculp, shape, slice, write **06** chisel, entail, incise, indent, sculpt, unlace
07 engrave, entayle, fashion, insculp, whittle **09** apportion, dismember, sculpture, truncheon **10** distribute
11 insculpture
• **carve up**
◇ *anagram indicator*
05 share, split **06** divide **07** split up
08 separate, share out **09** parcel out, partition **10** distribute

carving

03 cut **04** bust **05** model, round, tondo
06 statue **08** incision, knotwork,
tympanum **09** scrimshaw, sculpture,
statuette **10** lithoglyph, petroglyph,
rosemaling **11** dendroglyph,
scrimshandy **12** mezzo-relievo,
mezzo-rilievo, scrimshander

cascade

03 lin **04** fall, gush, linn, pour, rush
05 chute, falls, flood, pitch, spill, surge
06 deluge, plunge, shower, tumble
07 descend, torrent, trickle
08 cataract, fountain, overflow
09 avalanche, waterfall **10** outpouring,
water chute, waterworks

case

◇ ends selection indicator
03 bag, box **04** étui, sted, suit
05 cause, chest, cover, crate, crime,
event, point, shell, state, stead, stede,
trial, trunk **06** action, affair, carton,
casing, casket, client, dative, essive,
holder, jacket, sheath, valise, victim
07 attaché, cabinet, capsule, context,
defence, dispute, elative, examine,
example, grounds, holdall, inquiry,
invalid, keister, lawsuit, patient,
process, wrapper **08** abessive,
ablative, adessive, allative, argument,
canister, evidence, genitive, illative,
incident, inessive, instance, kalamdan,
locative, occasion, position, showcase,
specimen, suitcase, vasculum,
vocative **09** briefcase, cartridge,
chrysalid, chrysalis, condition,
container, flight bag, papeterie,
portfolio, reasoning, situation, travel
bag **10** accusative, comitative,
nominative, occurrence, receptacle,
subjective, vanity-case **11** attaché
case, contingency, hand luggage,
portmanteau, proceedings, reconnoitre,
translative, writing desk **12** illustration,
overnight bag **13** circumstances,
investigation, particularity

cases

02 ca

cash

03 tin **04** cent, dime, dosh, loot
05 blunt, brass, bread, coins, dough,
funds, gravy, lolly, money, notes, Oscar,
ready, rhino, smash **06** change,
encash, greens, moolah, stumpy
07 bullion, capital, finance, readies,
realize, scratch, shekels **08** currency,
exchange, greenies **09** banknotes,
hard money, liquidate, megabucks,
resources **10** ready money **11** legal
tender, spondulicks, wherewithal
12 hard currency, turn into cash

• **cash return**
07 jackpot

cashier

04 fire, sack **05** annul, break, clerk,
expel **06** banker, bursar, purser, teller
07 checker, discard, dismiss, drum out,
unfrock **08** get rid of, throw out
09 bank clerk, discharge, treasurer
10 accountant

casing

◇ containment indicator
◇ ends selection indicator
03 cup, tub **04** cast, core **05** cover,
shell **06** jacket, sheath **07** cowling,
housing **08** binnacle, covering,
envelope, pair case, trunking,
wrapping **09** air-jacket, crankcase, oil
string, sheathing **10** protection **11** bell-
housing, junction box, steam jacket,
water jacket **13** cylinder block

cask

03 but, keg, pin, tub, tun, vat **04** butt,
cade, pipe, wood **05** flask **06** barrel,
casket, casque, firkin, octave, tierce
07 barrico, breaker, leaguer
08 hogshead, puncheon **09** kilderkin
11 scuttlebutt

casket

03 box **04** case, kist **05** chest, pyxis,
shell **06** coffer, coffin, larnax
08 cassette, jewel-box **11** sarcophagus
12 pine overcoat, wooden kimono
14 wooden overcoat

cassava

04 yuca **05** yucca **06** manioc
07 mandioc, manihoc, tapioca
08 mandioca **09** mandiocca

casserole

04 stew **06** diable **07** cocotte, stew-
pan, terrine, tzimmes **08** pot-au-feu
09 Dutch oven **10** slow cooker

cast

◇ anagram indicator
03 die, lob, mew, put, see, shy **04** drop,
emit, form, hurl, look, putt, seek, shed,
slip, toss, turn, veer, view, vote, warp
05 add up, drive, fling, found, fusil,
heave, impel, model, mould, moult,
pitch, place, shape, shoot, sling, stamp,
throw **06** actors, assign, chance,
create, direct, fusile, glance, launch,
look at, manner, record, reject, spread,
thrown, troupe **07** appoint, casting,
company, condemn, diffuse, discard,
dismiss, fashion, give off, give out,
glimpse, moulded, players, predict,
project, quality, radiate, redound,
reflect, scatter **08** covering, register,
rejected **09** calculate, formulate
10 catch sight, characters, performers
12 entertainers **13** put in jeopardy
14 mark with a cross

• **cast aside**
06 reject **07** discard, say no to
08 get rid of, turn down **12** dispense
with

• **cast down**
05 abase, crush **06** abattu, deject,
sadden **07** depress **08** dejected,
desolate **10** discourage, dishearten

• **cast out**
09 ostracize

caste

04 race, rank **05** class, grade, group,
order **06** degree, estate, status
07 lineage, station, stratum
08 position **10** background **11** social
class **14** social standing

castigate

03 rap **04** slam **05** chide, emend,
scold **06** berate, punish, rebuke
07 censure, chasten, correct, reprove,
upbraid **08** admonish, chastise
09 criticize, dress down, reprimand
10 discipline **13** tear a strip off **15** give
someone hell

castle

01 R **04** fort, keep, rook **05** tower, villa
06 kasbah, palace **07** château, citadel,
mansion, schloss **08** fastness, fortress
10 stronghold **11** stately home
12 country house

Castles include:

03 Doe, Eye, Lea, Mey
04 Clun, Drum, Leap, Peel, Trim, Ward,
York
05 Black, Burgh, Corfe, Croft, Doune,
Flint, Knock, Leeds, Skibo, White
06 Cawdor, Durham, Fraser, Glamis,
Howard, Ludlow, Maiden, Sandal,
Swords
07 Alnwick, Arundel, Braemar, Caister,
Culzean, Dunster, Harlech, Lismore,
Old Wick, Peveril, Scotney,
Warwick, Windsor
08 Balmoral, Bamburgh, Bastille,
Broughty, Corgarff, Dunottar,
Dunvegan, Egremont, Elsinore,
Goodrich, Jedburgh, Kilkenny,
Monmouth, Pembroke, Stirling,
Stokesay, Tintagel, Urquhart
09 Beaumaris, Blackrock, Chipchase,
Dunsinane, Edinburgh, Hermitage,
Inverness, Lancaster, Lochleven, St
Andrews, Tantallon
10 Bridgnorth, Caernarvon, Caerphilly,
Carmarthen, Jewel Tower,
Kenilworth, Montgomery,
Okehampton, Pontefract,
Rockingham
11 Castell Coch, Chillingham,
Craigmillar, Eilean Donan,
Fotheringay, Lindisfarne, Narrow
Water, Ravenscraig, Scarborough,
Tattershall, Thirlestane
12 Conisborough
13 Carrickfergus
15 St Michael's Mount

Castle parts include:

04 berm, keep, moat, ward
05 ditch, fosse, motte, mound, scarp,
tower
06 bailey, chapel, corbel, crenel,
donjon, merlon, turret
07 bastion, dungeon, parados,
parapet, postern, rampart
08 approach, barbican, bartizan,
brattice, buttress, crosslet,
loophole, stockade, wall walk
09 arrow-slit, courtyard, embrasure,
gatehouse, inner wall
10 drawbridge, murder hole,
portcullis, watchtower
11 battlements, curtain wall, outer bailey
12 crenellation, lookout tower
13 enclosure wall

• **castles**
02 O-O **03** O-O-O

castrate
03 cut, fix **04** geld, glib, swig **05** alter, unman, unsex **06** doctor, neuter **07** evirate, knacker **10** emasculate

casual
03 odd **04** orra **05** blasé, stray **06** chance, random **07** cursory, leisure, offhand, passing, relaxed, scratch **08** careless, informal, laid-back, lukewarm, part-time **09** apathetic, easy-going, irregular, negligent, short-term, temporary, throwaway **10** accidental, fortuitous, incidental, insouciant, nonchalant, occasional, unexpected, unforeseen **11** comfortable, free-and-easy, indifferent, promiscuous, provisional, spontaneous, superficial, unconcerned **12** happy-go-lucky, intermittent **13** lackadaisical, serendipitous, unceremonious, unintentional **14** unpremeditated

casually
06 overly **08** sportily **10** informally, off the cuff **11** comfortably **12** occasionally **13** spontaneously **15** parenthetically

casualty
04 loss **05** death **06** caduac, injury, victim **07** injured, missing, wounded **08** accident, fatality, sufferer **10** dead person, misfortune **13** injured person

casuistry
07 sophism **09** chicanery, sophistry **12** equivocation, speciousness

cat
03 man, mog, tom **04** chap, puss **05** moggy, pussy, queen, rumpy **06** feline, kitten, mouser, neuter, tomcat **08** baudrons, pussy cat **09** catamaran, grimalkin

See also **animal**; **vomit**

03 rex
04 Manx
05 Korat, tabby
06 Angora, Bengal, Birman, Bombay, Cymric, Havana, LaPerm, Ocicat, Somali
07 Burmese, Persian, rag-doll, Siamese, Tiffany
08 Balinese, Burmilla, Devon rex, Snowshoe, Tiffanie
09 Himalayan, Maine Coon, Singapura, Tonkinese
10 Abyssinian, Carthusian, chinchilla, Cornish rex, Selkirk Rex, Turkish Van
11 Egyptian Mau, Foreign Blue, Russian Blue, silver tabby
12 Foreign White, Scottish Fold
13 domestic tabby, Tortoiseshell, Turkish Angora
15 British longhair, Exotic shorthair, Japanese Bobtail, Norwegian Forest

Wild and big cats include:

03 bob
04 eyra, lion, lynx, pard, puma
05 feral, tiger

06 cougar, jaguar, kodkod, margay, ocelot, pampas
07 cheetah, leopard
08 mountain
09 Geoffroy's
10 jaguarundi
11 snow leopard
12 mountain lion, Scottish wild
13 little spotted
14 clouded leopard

Famous cats include:

03 Tom
04 Bast, Jess
05 Dinah, Felix, Korky
06 Arthur, Bastet, Ginger, Kaspar, Top Cat, Ubasti
07 Bagpuss, Custard, Simpkin
08 Beerbohm, Garfield, Humphrey, Krazy Kat, Macavity
09 Mehitabel, Mrs Norris, Sylvester, Thomasina, Tom Kitten
10 El Brooshna, Heathcliff
11 Cat in the Hat, Cheshire Cat, Crookshanks, Korky the Cat, Pink Panther, Puss in Boots
14 Bustopher Jones, Mr Mistoffelees, Old Deuteronomy, The Cat in the Hat

cataclysm
04 blow **07** debacle **08** calamity, collapse, disaster, upheaval **10** convulsion **11** catastrophe, devastation

cataclysmic
05 awful, fatal **06** tragic **08** dreadful, terrible **10** calamitous, disastrous **11** catastrophe, devastating

catacomb
04 tomb **05** crypt, vault **07** ossuary **09** mausoleum **11** burial-vault

catalogue
03 cat **04** file, list, roll **05** guide, index, table **06** litany, ragman, record, roster **07** catelog, magalog, notitia, ragment **08** brochure, bulletin, calendar, classify, manifest, register, schedule, tabulate **09** checklist, directory, gazetteer, inventory, make a list **10** categorize, prospectus **11** alphabetize, iconography, specialogue **12** compile a list **14** classification, Durchmusterung

catapult
01 Y **04** fire, hurl, toss **05** fling, pitch, shoot, sling, throw **06** hurtle, launch, propel **07** balista, bricole **08** ballista, scorpion, shanghai **09** slingshot

cataract
03 lin **04** linn **05** falls, force, pearl **06** deluge, rapids **07** cascade, torrent **08** downpour, overfall, pearl-eye **09** floodgate, pin and web, waterfall **10** portcullis, waterspout

catastrophe
04 blow, doom, rear, ruin **06** fiasco **07** debacle, failure, reverse, tragedy, trouble **08** calamity, disaster, upheaval **09** adversity, cataclysm,

mischance **10** affliction, misfortune **11** devastation

catastrophic
05 awful, fatal **06** tragic **08** dreadful, terrible **10** calamitous, disastrous **11** cataclysmic, devastating

catcall
03 boo **04** gibe, hiss, jeer, jibe **07** whistle **09** raspberry **10** barracking, Bronx cheer

catch
◇ *containment indicator*
03 bag, cop, get, kep, nab, net **04** bolt, clip, draw, fang, find, fish, grab, grip, hank, hasp, haul, hear, hold, hook, lock, make, nail, nick, pawl, rope, sear, snag, sneb, snib, tack, take, trap, twig **05** board, clasp, get it, get on, grasp, hitch, latch, phang, seize, snare, sneck, watch **06** arrest, clutch, collar, corner, detect, detent, engage, entrap, expose, fathom, follow, pick up, snatch, take in, unmask **07** attract, capture, develop, discern, ensnare, find out, make out, problem, round up, seizure, startle **08** contract, discover, drawback, fastener, holdfast, hunt down, obstacle, overtake, perceive, surprise **09** apprehend, deprehend, lay hold of, recapture, recognize, succumb to **10** comprehend, difficulty, go down with, understand **11** be in time for **12** disadvantage, get the hang of **13** become ill with, catch in the act **14** catch red-handed

See also **haul**; **song**

• catch on
05 grasp **06** fathom, follow, take in **10** comprehend, understand **13** become popular

• catch up
06 gain on **08** overtake **09** draw level

catching
◇ *containment indicator*
06 taking **10** attractive, contagious, infectious **11** captivating **12** communicable **13** transmissible, transmittable

catchphrase
05 motto **06** byword, jingle, saying, slogan, wheeze **07** formula **08** password **09** catchword, parrot-cry, watchword **10** shibboleth

catchy
07 melodic, popular, tuneful **08** haunting **09** appealing, deceptive, memorable **10** attractive **11** captivating **13** unforgettable

catechize
04 test **05** drill, grill **07** examine **08** instruct, question **11** interrogate **12** cross-examine

categorical
05 clear, total, utter **06** direct **07** express **08** absolute, definite, emphatic, explicit, positive **09** downright **10** conclusive,

unreserved 11 unequivocal, unqualified **13** unconditional

categorically
7 clearly, utterly **08** directly
09 expressly **10** absolutely, definitely, explicitly, positively **12** emphatically, unreservedly **13** unequivocally
5 unconditionally

categorization
7 listing, ranking, sorting
8 grouping, ordering **11** arrangement
4 classification

categorize
3 peg **04** list, rank, sort **05** class, grade, group, order **06** docket
7 arrange, docquet **08** classify, tabulate **09** phenotype
0 pigeonhole, stereotype

category
4 head, kind, list, rank, sort, type
5 class, genre, grade, group, order, tirp, stuff, taxon, title **06** rubric, stirps
7 bracket, chapter, heading, listing, section, variety **08** division, grouping
0 department, superclass, superorder **11** superphylum
4 classification

cater
5 serve **06** pander, supply **07** furnish, indulge, provide, satisfy, victual
9 provision

caterwaul
3 cry **04** bawl, howl, wail, yowl
5 miaow, wrawl **06** scream, shriek, squall **07** screech

catharsis
7 purging, release **09** cleansing, depuration, purifying **10** abreaction, abstersion, lustration **12** purification

cathartic
7 lustral, purging, release, scourer
9 cleansing, purgative, purifying
0 abreactive, abstersive, eccoprotic

cathedral
4 dome **05** duomo **07** minster
2 procathedral
See also **church**

• **cathedral city**
03 see

catholic
01 C **02** RC **04** Tory, wide **05** broad, Latin, Roman **06** global, varied
07 diverse, general, liberal **08** eclectic, Jebusite, Romanish, Romanist, tolerant
09 inclusive, universal **10** broad-based, left-footer, open-minded, Tridentine, widespread **11** broad-minded, wide-ranging **12** all-embracing, all-inclusive
13 comprehensive **15** all-encompassing

catholicism
04 Rome **06** popery **08** Romanism

catmint
03 nep, nip **06** catnep, catnip, nepeta

cats and dogs
04 rain

cattle
02 ky **03** fee, kye **04** aver, cows, kine, kyne, neat, nout, nowt, oxen **05** bulls, stock **06** beasts, beeves **09** livestock
See also **animal**

catty
03 kin **04** kati, mean **05** katti
06 bitchy **07** vicious **08** spiteful, venomous **09** malicious, rancorous
10 backbiting, ill-natured, malevolent

caucus
03 set **06** clique, parley **07** meeting, session **08** assembly, conclave
09 gathering **10** convention **11** get-together

caught
◇ *containment indicator*
01 c **02** ct **03** had **04** held **06** keight, netted **11** in by the week

cauliflower
04 gobi
• **head of cauliflower**
04 curd

causative
04 root **07** causing, factive
09 factitive

cause
03 aim, end, gar **04** call, make, root, sake **05** agent, basis, beget, begin, breed, causa, force, garre, ideal, maker, mover **06** agency, author, belief, compel, create, effect, factor, incite, induce, lead to, motive, object, origin, parent, prompt, reason, render, source, spring **07** because, creator, grounds, impulse, produce, provoke, purpose, trigger **08** generate, motivate, movement, occasion, producer, result in, stimulus **09** beginning, incentive, originate, principle, stimulate, wherefore **10** accusation, bring about, conviction, enterprise, give rise to, inducement, mainspring, make happen, motivation, originator, prime mover, trigger off **11** explanation, precipitate, undertaking **12** be the cause of **13** be at the root of, justification

caustic
04 acid, keen, tart **05** snide **06** biting, bitter, severe **07** burning, cutting, erodent, mordant, pungent
08 scathing, stinging, virulent
09 acidulent, acidulous, corroding, corrosive, sarcastic, trenchant, vitriolic
10 astringent, escharotic
11 acrimonious, destructive

caustically
08 bitterly, severely **10** scathingly, virulently **11** trenchantly
13 acrimoniously, sarcastically, vitriolically

cauterize
04 burn, fire, sear **05** singe **06** scorch
09 carbonize, disinfect, sterilize

caution
04 bail, care, heed, urge, warn 05 alert,
deter, guard 06 advice, advise, cautel,
caveat, surety, tip off, tip-off 07 counsel,
warning 08 admonish, prudence,
security, wariness 09 alertness,
reprimand, vigilance 10 admonition,
discretion, injunction 11 carefulness,
forethought, heedfulness, mindfulness
12 deliberation, watchfulness
14 circumspection
• lacking caution
04 rash

cautious
04 safe, ware, wary 05 alert, cagey,
chary 06 Fabian, shrewd 07 careful,
guarded, heedful, prudent, tactful
08 discreet, gingerly, vigilant, watchful
09 cautelous, defensive, judicious,
tentative 10 deliberate 11 circumspect
12 conservative, softly-softly
13 unadventurous

cautiously
08 gingerly 09 carefully, prudently,
tactfully 10 discreetly 11 defensively,
judiciously, tentatively 12 deliberately
13 circumspectly 14 conservatively

cavalcade
05 array, train, troop 06 parade
07 cortège, retinue, sowarry
08 sowarree 09 march-past,
motorcade 10 procession

cavalier
04 curt 05 lofty, spahi 06 casual,
escort, knight, lordly 07 gallant,
haughty, offhand, partner, warlike
08 arrogant, chasseur, horseman,
insolent, Ironside, royalist, scornful
09 chevalier, gentleman, Malignant
10 cavalryman, disdainful, equestrian,
incautious, swaggering 11 Bashi-
Bazouk, free-and-easy, patronizing
12 devil-may-care, horse soldier,
supercilious 13 condescending

cavalry
05 horse 07 hussars, lancers, reiters
08 dragoons, horsemen, sabreurs,
troopers 09 chasseurs, Ironsides,
risaldars 10 cavalrymen, light-horse,
the heavies 11 equestrians, ritt-masters
13 horse soldiers, mounted troops

cave
03 den 04 grot, hole 05 antar, antre,
delve 06 beware, cavern, cavity,
dugout, grotto, hollow, tunnel
07 pothole 09 Domdaniel

Caves include:
04 Zitu
06 Berger, Vqerdi
08 Badalona
09 G E S Malaga, Snezhnaya
10 Schneeloch
11 Batmanhöhle, Jean Bernard
14 Lamprechtsofen, Pierre-St-Martin,
Sistema Huautla

• cave in
04 fall, slip 05 yield 06 fall in 07 give
way, subside 08 collapse

caveat
05 alarm 06 notice 07 caution,
proviso, warning 10 admonition

cavern
03 den 04 cave, cove 05 vault
06 cavity, dugout, Erebus, grotto,
hollow, tunnel 07 pothole
08 catacomb, vaultage

cavernous
04 dark, deep, huge, vast 05 large
06 gaping, gloomy, hollow, sunken
07 concave, echoing, immense,
yawning 08 resonant, spacious
09 depressed 10 bottomless
12 unfathomable

cavil
03 nag 04 carp 06 haggle 07 censure,
nit-pick, quarrel, quibble 08 complain,
reproach 09 criticize 10 find faults

cavity
03 gap, pit, sac, vug 04 bore, cell,
dent, hole, mine, tear, vein, well, womb
05 celom, crypt, druse, geode, lumen,
purse, sinus, vitta 06 antrum, atrium,
camera, coelom, concha, cotyle,
crater, hollow, lacuna, pelvis, pocket
07 chamber, cochlea, coelome,
eardrum, glenoid, orifice, vacuole,
vesicle 08 aperture, brood-sac
09 ventricle, vestibule 10 acetabulum,
blastocoel, brood-pouch, cavitation,
excavation, hollowness, thunder-egg
11 conceptacle, haematocele,
mediastinum, rhynchocoel
13 neuroblastoma, splanchnocele

cavort
◇ *anagram indicator*
04 romp, skip 05 caper, dance, frisk,
sport 06 frolic, gambol, prance

cavy *see* guinea pig

Cayman Islands
03 CYM

cease
03 die, end, lin 04 blin, fail, halt, poop,
quit, stay, stop, unbe 05 abate, cesse,
leave, let up, stint 06 desist, devall,
finish, lay off, pack in 07 poop out,
refrain, suspend 08 break off,
conclude, give over, leave off, peter
out, surcease 09 call a halt, cessation,
fizzle out, terminate 11 come to a halt,
come to an end, discontinue 12 bring
to a halt, bring to an end

ceaseless
07 endless, eternal, non-stop
08 constant, unending, untiring
09 continual, incessant, perpetual,
unceasing 10 continuous, persistent
11 everlasting, never-ending,
unremitting 12 interminable
13 uninterrupted

ceaselessly
07 for ever 09 endlessly, eternally
10 constantly, unendingly 11 day in day
out, incessantly, unceasingly
12 continuously, interminably
13 everlastingly, unremittingly 14 for
ever and ever 15 uninterruptedly

cedar
06 arolla, deodar 11 cryptomeria

cede
05 allow, grant, yield 06 convey, give
up, resign 07 abandon, concede,
deliver 08 abdicate, hand over,
renounce, transfer, turn over
09 surrender 10 relinquish

ceiling
04 loft, most, roof 05 beams, limit,
vault 06 awning, canopy, cupola, soft
07 lacunar, maximum, plafond, rafters
seeling 08 overhead 09 laquearia
10 upper limit 11 cut-off point

celebrate
03 wet 04 hold, hymn, keep, laud,
mark, rave, sing, tune 05 binge, bless
carol, chant, extol, go out, revel, soun
toast 06 besing, chaunt, honour,
record, renown, repeat, shrove, sonn
07 drink to, emblaze, have fun, maffic
observe, perform, poetize, rejoice,
triumph, trumpet 08 emblazon, live i
up, memorize, remember 09 have a
ball, solemnize, whoop it up 10 have
party, procession 11 commemorate,
throw a party 12 concelebrate
13 enjoy yourself, go on the razzle
14 go out on the town, push the boat
out, put the flags out 15 paint the tow
red

celebrated
03 cel 05 famed, great, noted
06 famous 07 admired, eminent,
exalted, notable, popular, revered
08 fabulous, glorious, renowned
09 acclaimed, legendary, prominent,
well-known 11 illustrious, outstanding
13 distinguished

celebration
02 do 03 ale, jol 04 fete, gala, orgy,
rave 05 beano, binge, feast, jolly, spre
06 hooley, junket, rave-up 07 jubilee,
revelry, shindig 08 festival, jamboree,
occasion, Olympiad 09 festivity,
gaudeamus 10 observance
11 merrymaking 13 jollification
See also **festival**

Celebrations include:
04 fête, gala
05 feast, party
06 May Day
07 banquet, baptism, jubilee, name-
day, reunion, tribute, wedding
08 birthday, festival, hen night,
marriage
09 centenary, Labour Day, reception,
saint's day, stag night
10 bar mitzvah, bat mitzvah,
dedication, graduation,
homecoming, retirement
11 anniversary, christening, coming-
of-age, harvest-home
12 thanksgiving
13 commemoration
15 harvest festival, Independence Day

celebratory
06 festal

elebrity
3 VIP **04** fame, lion, name, note, star **5** celeb **06** bigwig, esteem, legend, *nown, worthy **07** big name, big shot, *otable, stardom **08** eminence, *minary **09** dignitary, greatness, *otoriety, personage, superstar **)** notability, prominence, reputation **4** distinction, personality **12** famous *erson, living legend **13** household *ame **15** illustriousness

elerity
5 haste, speed **08** dispatch, fastness, *pidity, velocity **09** fleetness, *uickness, swiftness **10** expedition, *romptness

elestial
6 astral, divine, starry, uranic **7** angelic, Chinese, elysian, eternal, *odlike, sublime **08** empyrean, ethereal, *eavenly, immortal, seraphic, supernal **9** spiritual, unearthly **10** paradisaic, *perlunar **11** superlunary, translunary **2** supernatural **14** transcendental

elestially
8 divinely **09** eternally, sublimely **0** immortally **11** angelically, spiritually **4** supernaturally

elibacy
6 purity **08** chastity **09** virginity **0** abnegation, abstinence, *ontinence, maidenhood, self-denial, *ngleness **12** bachelorhood, *pinsterhood **13** self-restraint

elibate
4 pure **05** unwed **06** chaste, single, *irgin **08** bachelor, spinster **9** abstinent, unmarried

ell
3 set **04** coop, cyte, jail, room, unit **5** ascus, crowd, crypt, group, party, *eter, spore **06** caucus, clique, lock-*p, matrix, prison, zygote **07** battery, *hamber, cubicle, dungeon, faction, *ucleus, section **08** organism **9** anchorage, black hole, cytoplasm, *nclosure, hermitage, reclusory **0** protoplasm, protoplast **1** compartment, electric eye

Cells include:
1 B, T
3 egg, PEC, red, rod, sex, wet **4** cone, fuel, germ, HeLa, mast, ovum, stem
5 blood, guard, nerve, plant, solar, sperm, water, white
6 animal, cancer, collar, diaxon, gamete, goblet, Hadley, killer, memory, mother, neuron, oocyte, plasma, target, tumour
7 cadmium, Daniell, gravity, helper T, initial, neurone, primary, Schwann, Sertoli, somatic, voltaic
8 akaryote, basophil, daughter, galvanic, gonidium, gonocyte, monocyte, myoblast, neoblast, parietal, platelet, Purkinje, red blood, retinula, sclereid, selenium, tracheid, zooblast

09 acidophil, antipodal, astrocyte, coenocyte, corpuscle, fibrocyte, haemocyte, hybridoma, idioblast, Leclanché, leucocyte, leukocyte, macrocyte, microcyte, myofibril, phagocyte, photocell, prokaryon, sclereide, secondary, spermatid, syncytium, thymocyte, tracheide
10 choanocyte, cnidoblast, enterocyte, eosinophil, fibroblast, gametocyte, hepatocyte, histiocyte, histoblast, leucoblast, leukoblast, lymphocyte, macrophage, melanocyte, myeloblast, neuroblast, neutrophil, osteoblast, osteoclast, spherocyte, suppressor, thread-cell, white blood
11 B lymphocyte, erythrocyte, granulocyte, lymphoblast, megaloblast, odontoblast, poikilocyte, thrombocyte, T lymphocyte
12 chondroblast, erythroblast, haematoblast, red corpuscle, reticulocyte, spermatocyte, spermatozoid, spermatozoon
13 chromatophore, natural killer, photoelectric, spermatoblast
14 blood corpuscle, spermatogonium, white corpuscle

• **mass of cells**
05 nodus **06** morula

cellar
04 vaut **05** crypt, dunny, vault, vaute **08** basement, coal hole, vaultage **09** storeroom, wine vault **10** wine cellar, wine vaults

Celtic *see* **mythology**

cement
03 fix, gum **04** bind, bond, glue, join, lime, lute, weld **05** affix, compo, grout, paste, putty, stick, trass, union, unite **06** attach, cohere, fasten, gunite, maltha, mastic, matrix, mortar, screed, slurry, solder, stucco **07** bonding, combine, mastich, plaster **08** adhesive, concrete, fixative, grouting, pointing, rice glue, solution **11** ciment fondu

cemetery
05 tombs **06** graves **08** boneyard, God's acre, urnfield **09** graveyard **10** burial site, campo santo, churchyard, necropolis **11** burial place **12** burial ground, charnel house

Cemeteries and burial places include:
07 Nunhead
08 Brompton, Highgate, Panthéon
09 Abney Park, Arlington
10 El Escorial, La Almudena, Montmartre, Mount Holly, San Michele, Weissensee
11 Kensal Green, Mount Olivet, West Norwood
12 Golders Green, Les Invalides, Montparnasse, Père Lachaise, Tower Hamlets

13 Mount of Olives
15 Island of the Dead

censor
03 ban, cut **04** Cato, edit **06** delete, editor **08** examiner, make cuts **09** expurgate, inspector **10** blue-pencil, bowdlerize, expurgater **11** bowdlerizer

censorious
06 severe **07** carping **08** captious, critical, negative **09** cavilling **10** fuddy-duddy **11** disparaging **12** condemnatory, disapproving, fault-finding, overcritical **13** hypercritical

censoriously
08 severely **10** captiously, critically **13** disparagingly **14** disapprovingly, overcritically **15** hypercritically

censure
03 rap **04** damn, Hell, slam **05** blame, chide, fault, judge, scold, strop, taunt **06** jump on, rebuke, taxing **07** appeach, condemn, obloquy, reproof, reprove, scandal, tell off, trounce, upbraid **08** admonish, denounce, reproach, scolding, sentence **09** castigate, criticism, criticize, dispraise, reprehend, reprimand, reprobate, syndicate **10** admonition, imputation, perstringe, reflection, telling-off, upbraiding **11** castigation, disapproval, remonstrate, reprobation **12** admonishment, condemnation, denunciation, disapprove of, pull to pieces, remonstrance, reprehension, vituperation **15** come down heavy on

cent
01 c **02** ct **03** red **05** penny

centimes
01 c

centipede
08 scutiger **11** scolopendra **12** scolopendrid, thousand-legs

central
◇ *hidden indicator*
◇ *middle selection indicator*
03 cen, key, mid **04** cent, core, main **05** basic, chief, focal, inner, major, prime, vital **06** centre, medial, median, middle **07** crucial, pivotal, primary **08** dominant, foremost, interior **09** essential, principal **11** fundamental, significant **13** most important
• **central heating**
02 ch

Central African Republic
03 CAF, RCA

Central America *see* **America; god, goddess**

centralization
08 focusing **11** convergence, unification **12** amalgamation, streamlining **13** concentration, consolidation, incorporation **15** rationalization

centralize
05 focus, unify **07** compact
08 condense, converge
10 amalgamate, streamline
11 concentrate, consolidate, incorporate, rationalize **13** bring together **14** gather together

centre
◇ *middle selection indicator*
03 hub, mid **04** core, crux **05** arena, focus, heart, hinge, pivot **06** kernel, middle, resort **07** nucleus, revolve
08 bull's-eye, converge, linchpin, midpoint, omphalos **09** gravitate
10 focal point, metropolis, stronghold
11 concentrate
• **in centre**
◇ *hidden indicator*

centre-forward
02 cf

centre-half
02 ch

centrepiece
04 best, peak **05** cream **06** climax
07 epergne **08** duchesse, high spot
09 highlight, high point **13** duchesse cover

century
01 c **03** age, cen, ton **04** cent
09 centenary
• **half century**
01 l

cephalopod
05 Sepia, squid **06** cuttle, loligo
07 octopus **08** ammonite, nautilus
09 goniatite, nautiloid **10** cuttlefish
13 paper nautilus **14** pearly nautilus

ceramics
04 raku, ware **06** bisque **07** faience, pottery **09** ironstone, porcelain
11 earthenware

cereal
05 grain

Cereals include:
03 oat, rye, tef, zea
04 bear, bere, corn, oats, rice, sago, teff, yuca
05 bajra, emmer, maize, spelt, wheat
06 barley, bulgur, manioc, millet
07 bulghur, cassava, mandioc, manihoc, oatmeal, sorghum, tapioca
08 amaranth, amelcorn, couscous, mandioca, semolina
09 buckwheat, mandiocca, sweetcorn, triticale
10 guinea corn, Indian corn, Kaffir corn
11 pearl millet
12 common millet
13 bulrush millet, foxtail millet, grain amaranth, Italian millet

Breakfast cereals include:
04 bran
05 Alpen®
06 muesli
07 All Bran®, granola
08 Cheerios®, Coco Pops®, Frosties®, porridge, Ricicles®, Special K®, Weetabix®
09 Ready Brek®, Shreddies®
10 Bran Flakes®, cornflakes, Quaker Oats®, Sugar Puffs®
11 Fruit'n'Fibre®, Puffed Wheat®, Sultana Bran®
12 Country Crisp®, Rice Krispies®
13 Fruit and Fibre®, Golden Grahams®, Honey Nut Loops®, Shredded Wheat®

ceremonial
04 rite **05** state **06** custom, formal, ritual, solemn **07** mummery, stately
08 ceremony, official, protocol
09 dignified, formality, solemnity
11 ritualistic

ceremonially
08 formally, ritually, solemnly
10 officially

ceremonious
05 civil, exact, grand, stiff **06** formal, polite, ritual, solemn **07** courtly, precise, starchy, stately **08** imposing, majestic, official **09** courteous, dignified **10** scrupulous **11** deferential, punctilious

ceremoniously
07 civilly, exactly, grandly, stiffly
08 formally, politely, solemnly
09 precisely, starchily **10** officially
11 courteously **12** scrupulously
13 deferentially, punctiliously
15 ritualistically

ceremony
04 form, gaud, pomp, rite, show
05 order **06** custom, parade, ritual
07 decorum, liturgy, service
08 exercise, festival, function, niceties, occasion, protocol **09** etiquette, formality, induction, ordinance, pageantry, propriety, punctilio, sacrament, solemnity, tradition, unveiling **10** ceremonial, coronation, dedication, graduation, initiation, observance **11** anniversary, celebration, investiture
12 circumstance, commencement, inauguration **13** commemoration, spit and polish

Ceremonies include:
05 amrit, doseh, tangi
06 maundy, nipter
07 baptism, capping, chanoyu, chuppah, matsuri, wedding
08 marriage, nuptials
09 committal, matrimony
10 bar mitzvah, bat mitzvah, corroboree, graduation, initiation
11 christening, fire-walking
12 confirmation
• **funeral ceremonies**
04 obit

Ceres
07 Demeter

cerium
02 Ce

certain
04 safe, some, sure, true **05** bound, clear, fated, fixed, plain, small
06 doomed, siccar, sicker **07** assured, dead set, decided, evident, express, limited, obvious, partial, perfect, precise, regular, settled, special
08 absolute, definite, destined, in the bag, positive, reliable, resolved, specific **09** confident, convinced, indubious, persuaded, undoubted, unfailing **10** conclusive, convincing, dependable, determined, home and dry, individual, inevitable, inexorable, particular, undeniable **11** cut and dried, established, indubitable, ineluctable, inescapable, irrefutable, open-and-shut, unavoidable
12 indisputable, no ifs and buts
13 bound to happen, meant to happen
14 unquestionable
• **a certain**
03 one **04** some
• **make certain**
06 ensure

certainly
02 OK **03** oke, yes **04** iwis, okay, sure, ywis **06** and how!, certes, siccar, sicker, surely, you bet **07** clearly, for sure, no doubt, plainly **08** forsooth, of course, to be sure **09** assuredly, doubtless, naturally, obviously, sure thing **10** absolutely, by all means, definitely, in very deed, positively, undeniably **11** beyond doubt, doubtlessly, if you please, indubitably, past dispute, undoubtedly **12** as sure as a gun, bang to rights, questionless, without doubt **13** beyond dispute, without a doubt **14** beyond question, unquestionably, without dispute **15** in all conscience

certainty
03 nap **04** cert, fact, lock, snip
05 cinch, faith, moral, trust, truth
06 banker, surety **07** natural, reality, safe bet **08** dead cert, security, sureness, validity **09** assurance, constancy, sure thing **10** confidence, conviction, positivism **11** assuredness
12 positiveness **13** inevitability
14 matter of course

certificate
04 pass **05** award, lines, proof, scrip, title **06** cocket, docket, patent, ticket
07 diploma, licence, voucher, warrant
08 aegrotat, document, navicert, register, testamur **09** clearance, debenture, guarantee, land-scrip
10 securities **11** credentials, endorsement, smart-ticket, testimonial
12 bill of health, Tyburn-ticket
13 authorization, certificatory, marriage-lines, qualification

certify
04 aver **05** vouch **06** assure, attest, inform, ratify, verify **07** confirm, declare, endorse, license, testify, warrant, witness **08** accredit, validate
09 authorize, guarantee, pronounce, recognize **11** corroborate

12 authenticate, substantiate **13** bear witness to

certitude
08 sureness **09** assurance, certainty **10** confidence, conviction, plerophory **11** assuredness, plerophoria **12** positiveness **13** full assurance

cessation
02 ho **03** end, hoa, hoh **04** blin, halt, rest, stay, stop **05** break, cease, let-up, pause, stint **06** ending, hiatus, recess **07** ceasing, failure, halting, respite **08** abeyance, breakoff, interval, stoppage, stopping, surcease, suspense **09** remission **10** conclusion, desistance, standstill, suspension **11** termination **12** intermission, interruption **13** discontinuing **14** discontinuance **15** discontinuation

Chad
03 TCD, TCH

chafe
03 rub, vex **04** bind, fret, rasp, wear **05** anger, annoy, grate, peeve **06** abrade, chauffe, chauff, enrage, scrape **07** be angry, incense, inflame, provoke, scratch **08** irritate, wear away, wear down **09** excoriate **10** exasperate

chaff
03 kid, rag, rib, rot **04** chip, jest, joke, josh, mock, pods **05** cases, husks, tease **06** banter, have-on, joking, shells **07** jesting, kidding, ribbing, rubbish, teasing **08** badinage, repartee **09** make fun of

chagrin
03 irk, vex **05** annoy, peeve, shame **07** mortify **08** disquiet, irritate, shagreen, vexation, wormwood **09** annoyance, displease, embarrass, humiliate **10** disappoint, dissatisfy, exasperate, irritation **11** displeasure, fretfulness, humiliation, indignation **12** discomfiture, discomposure, exasperation **13** embarrassment, mortification **14** disappointment **15** dissatisfaction

chain
02 ch **03** row, set, tie **04** bind, bond, boom, curb, firm, line, link, rode, seal, team **05** group, guard, hitch, range, slang, train, union **06** albert, catena, fasten, fetter, secure, series, string, tether, traces **07** company, confine, creeper, enslave, manacle, measure, shackle, trammel **08** coupling, handcuff, restrain, sequence **09** fanfarona, restraint **10** succession, watchguard **11** progression **13** concatenation

chair
02 MC **04** lead, seat **05** emcee **06** direct **07** convene, speaker **08** chairman, convenor, director, moderate **09** organizer, president, supervise **10** chairwoman **11** chairperson, preside over, toastmaster **13** act as chairman, professorship **15** act as chairwoman

03 arm, lug, pew **04** Bath, camp, cane, deck, easy, form, high, push, wing **05** bench, elbow, king's, night, potty, sedan, stool, wheel **06** basket, carver, curule, dining, estate, jampan, Morris, pouffe, rocker, sag bag, sledge, swivel, throne, wicker **07** beanbag, Berbice, bergère, commode, guérite, kitchen, lounger, nursing, rocking, Windsor **08** captain's, electric, fauteuil, prie-dieu, recliner, wainscot **09** director's **10** boatswain's, fiddle-back, frithstool, ladder-back **11** Cromwellian, gestatorial **12** ducking-stool

See also **seat**

chairman, chairwoman
02 MC **03** Chm **04** chmn, prof **05** emcee **06** preses **07** praeses **08** convenor, director **09** organizer, president, professor, spokesman **10** prolocutor **11** chairperson, spokeswoman **12** spokesperson

chalcedony
04 sard **05** agate **06** plasma **07** sardius **09** hornstone, moss agate **10** bloodstone **11** chrysoprase

chalk
• **chalk up**
03 log **04** gain **05** score, tally **06** attain, charge, credit, record **07** achieve, ascribe, put down **08** register **09** attribute **10** accumulate

chalky
03 wan **04** pale **05** ashen, dusty, white **06** ground, pallid **07** crushed, powdery **10** calcareous, colourless, cretaceous, granulated

challenge
03 hen, tax, try, vie **04** call, dare, defy, gage, risk, test **05** assay, brave, claim, demur, query, stand, stump, trial **06** accost, accuse, appeal, cartel, charge, hazard, henner, hurdle, invite, strain, summon, tackle, why-not **07** bidding, darrain, darrayn, deraign, dispute, problem, protest, provoke, stretch, summons **08** champion, confront, darraign, darraine, defiance, object to, obstacle, question **09** darraigne, objection, stimulate, ultimatum **10** accusation, opposition **11** opportunity, provocation, questioning **12** disagreement, disagree with **13** confrontation, interrogation **14** call in question **15** take exception to

challenging
06 gnarly, taxing **07** testing **08** exacting, exciting **09** demanding **10** stretching

chamber
02 po **03** pot **04** hall, room, silo **05** divan, fogou, house, jerry, potty,

vault **06** camera, cavern, cavity, chanty, durbar, hollow, jordan, serdab, urinal **07** bedroom, boudoir, confine, council **08** assembly, casemate, gazunder, hypogeum, moot-hall, thalamus **09** apartment, combustor, hypogaeum, mattamore, stokehold, ventricle **10** auditorium, close-stool, parliament, souterrain, subterrain, subterrane, thunderbox **11** compartment, legislature **12** assembly room, meeting-place

See also **room**

champagne
03 fiz, pop **04** fizz **06** bubbly, simkin **07** Sillery, simpkin **08** champers, the Widow **10** gooseberry

See also **wine**

champion
02 Ch **03** ace, Cid, gun **04** back, hero, kemp **05** angel, champ, ozeki **06** backer, defend, expert, kemper, knight, patron, uphold, victor, winner **07** apostle, espouse, messiah, promote, protect, saviour, support, tribune **08** advocate, asserter, assertor, defender, douzeper, guardian, maintain, Palmerin, stand for, upholder, yokozuna **09** campeador, challenge, conqueror, deliverer, doucepere, excellent, promachos, proponent, protector, supporter **10** kempery-man, stand up for, vindicator **11** excellently, protagonist, title-holder **13** hold a brief for

See also **seven**

chance
03 hap, run, try **04** cast, fate, luck, odds, risk, show, time **05** arise, break, essay, fluke, occur, stake, wager **06** crop up, fair go, flukey, follow, gamble, happen, hazard, random, result, strike, upcast **07** destiny, develop, fortune, opening, venture **08** accident, Buckley's, fortuity, occasion, prospect **09** arbitrary, come about, haphazard, speculate, take place **10** likelihood, play a hunch, providence **11** bet your life, coincidence, contingency, opportunity, possibility, probability, serendipity, speculation, take a chance **12** bet your boots, happenstance, push your luck, your best shot **14** Buckley's chance, chance your luck

• **by chance**
07 happily **08** bechance, randomly **09** by mistake **10** by accident **11** haphazardly, unwittingly **12** accidentally, fortuitously, incidentally, peradventure, unexpectedly **13** inadvertently **14** adventitiously **15** serendipitously, unintentionally

• **chance on, chance upon**
04 meet **06** casual, flukey, random **07** run into **08** bump into, discover **09** arbitrary, haphazard, run across, stumble on **10** accidental, come across, fortuitous, incidental,

unexpected, unforeseen, unintended **11** inadvertent, unlooked-for **12** find by chance **13** serendipitous, unanticipated, unintentional
• **decision by chance**
03 lot **04** draw **07** lottery

Chancellor of the Exchequer
02 CE

chancy
04 safe **05** dicey, dodgy, lucky, risky **06** tricky **07** fraught **09** dangerous, hazardous, uncertain **11** speculative **13** problematical, unpredictable

chandelier
06 corona, lustre **09** girandola, girandole **11** corona lucis, electrolier

change
◇ *anagram indicator*
02 go **03** mew **04** cash, chop, move, pass, peal, swap, turn, vary **05** adapt, alter, amend, coins, renew, shift, trade, trend, U-turn, waver **06** adjust, barter, become, evolve, modify, mutate, reform, revise, rotate, silver, switch **07** commute, connect, convert, coppers, develop, novelty, remodel, renewal, replace, shake-up, variate, variety **08** do a U-turn, exchange, movement, mutation, reversal, revision, rotation, transfer, upheaval **09** about-face, about-turn, alternate, amendment, customize, diversion, evolution, fluctuate, transform, transpose, turnabout, vacillate, variation, volte-face **10** adaptation, adjustment, alteration, conversion, difference, ebb and flow, innovation, reorganize, revolution, substitute, transition **11** alternation, development, fluctuation, interchange, remodelling, replacement, restructure, state of flux, transfigure, transmutate, vacillation, vicissitude **12** metamorphose, modification, substitution **13** chop and change, customization, make different, metamorphosis, restructuring, transmutation, transposition **14** reconstruction, reorganization, transformation **15** become different, make a connection, transfiguration

changeable
◇ *anagram indicator*
05 fluid, windy **06** fickle, labile, mobile, wankle, whimsy **07** erratic, flighty, movable, mutable, Protean, various, varying, voluble, whimsey **08** moveable, shifting, skittish, unstable, unsteady, variable, volatile, wavering **09** changeful, irregular, mercurial, uncertain, unsettled, versatile **10** capricious, inconstant, unreliable **11** chameleonic, fluctuating, vacillating **12** inconsistent **13** chameleon-like, kaleidoscopic, unpredictable **15** vicissitudinous

changeless
05 final, fixed **06** static **07** eternal **08** constant, timeless **09** immutable, permanent **10** invariable, unchanging **11** unalterable **12** unchangeable

changeling
03 auf, oaf **08** elf-child, killcrop

channel
02 ea **03** bed, eau, gut, sny, sow, use, way **04** duct, feed, gate, kill, lake, lane, lead, main, neck, path, race, send, snye, sure, tube **05** agent, canal, chime, ditch, drain, falaj, flume, focus, force, glyph, guide, gully, latch, letch, level, major, means, radio, rigol, route, sewer, sloot, sluit, sound, stank, trunk **06** agency, airway, artery, avenue, convey, course, cut-off, direct, furrow, gravel, groove, grough, gullet, gulley, gutter, hollow, limber, medium, narrow, rigoll, sheuch, siphon, sluice, strait, trench, trough **07** chamfer, conduct, conduit, culvert, fairway, limbers, narrows, offtake, passage, raceway, shingle, station, wireway **08** approach, aqueduct, headrace, millrace, overflow, tailrace, transmit, wash-away, waterway **11** canaliculus, concentrate, katabothron, katavothron, spill-stream, watercourse

> **Channels include:**

03 Kii
04 Foxe
05 Bashi, Bungo, Kaiwi, Kauai, Lamma, Minas, Minch, North
06 Akashi, Kalohi, Manche, Queens
07 Babuyan, Bristol, English, Jamaica, Massawa, Pailolo, Sandwip, St Lucia, Yucatán
08 Dominica, La Manche, Nicholas, Santaren, Sicilian, St Andrew, The Minch
09 Balintang, Capricorn, East Lamma, Geographe, Kaulakahi, Northwest, Old Bahama, Skagerrak, St George's, West Lamma
10 Alalakeiki, Alenuihaha, McClintock, Mozambique, North Minch
11 Little Minch
12 Kealaikahiki, Santa Barbara

See also **television**

• **Channel Islands**
02 CI

> **The Channel Islands:**

04 Herm, Sark
06 Jersey, Jethou
07 Brechou
08 Alderney, Guernsey
10 the Caskets
11 the Chauseys
12 the Minquiers

chant
03 cry **04** haka, sing, song, yo-ho **05** ditty, psalm, shout **06** cantus, chorus, incant, intone, mantra, melody, recite, slogan, warcry, yo-ho-ho **07** refrain **09** decantate, plainsong, yo-heave-ho **10** cantillate, intonation, recitation **11** Hare Krishna, incantation

chaos
◇ *anagram indicator*
04 mess, muss, riot **05** abyss, havoc, musse, snafu **06** bedlam, mayhem,

tumult, uproar **07** anarchy **08** disarray, disorder, madhouse, shambles, tohu bohu, upheaval **09** confusion **10** disruption, dog's dinner **11** lawlessness, pandemonium **13** pig's breakfast **14** Rafferty's rules **15** disorganization

chaotic
◇ *anagram indicator*
05 snafu **06** unruly **07** lawless, riotous **08** anarchic, confused, deranged **09** disrupted, orderless, shambolic **10** disordered, disorderly, topsy-turvy, tumultuary, tumultuous **12** disorganized, uncontrolled **14** all over the shop **15** all over the place

chap
03 boy, cat, cod, guy, jaw, man, mun, oik, sod **04** boyo, chop, cove, hack, sort, type **05** bloke, bucko, cheek, crack, knock, spray **06** codger, fellow, Johnny, shaver, strike **07** bastard, Johnnie, spreaze, spreeze **08** spreathe, spreethe **09** character **10** individual, male person

chapel
05 crypt **06** Beulah **07** chantry, galilee, martyry, oratory **08** chauntry, feretory, parabema, sacellum **09** beadhouse, prothesis **13** Nonconformist **15** chapelle ardente

chaperon, chaperone
04 mind **05** guard **06** attend, duenna, escort **07** protect **08** sheepdog, shepherd **09** accompany, companion, look after, matronize, safeguard, watch over **10** take care of

chapped
03 raw **04** sore **06** chafed **07** cracked, sprayed

chapter
01 c **02** ch **03** cap **04** chap, part, sura, time **05** caput, phase, stage, surah, topic **06** branch, clause, period **07** capital, episode, portion, section **08** division **10** department

char
02 do **03** tea **04** burn, coal, sear **05** brown, singe, togue, woman **06** Mrs Mop, scorch **07** blacken, Mrs Mopp, torgoch **08** redbelly, saibling **09** carbonize, cauterize **10** accomplish, brook trout **11** Dolly Varden

character
04 aura, card, case, hair, logo, mark, part, role, rune, sign, sort, tone, type **05** charm, ethos, image, stamp, style, trait, write **06** appeal, cipher, device, emblem, figure, honour, letter, make-up, nature, oddity, person, psyche, status, symbol, temper **07** calibre, courage, engrave, essence, feature, honesty, imprint, oddball, persona, quality **08** backbone, describe, identity, interest, original, position, property, strength **09** delineate, eccentric, ideograph, integrity, reference, represent **10** attributes,

hieroglyph, human being, individual, moral fibre, reputation **11** disposition, peculiarity, personality, specialness, temperament, uprightness **12** constitution **13** determination, individuality **14** attractiveness **15** characteristics, eccentric person

See also **alphabet; Bible; cartoon; fairy tale; legend; letter; literary; mythology; opera; pantomine; Shakespeare**

• **character part**
04 role

• **characters in**
◇ *hidden indicator*

• **proper character**
03 him

characteristic
04 mark, note **05** point, right, trait **06** factor **07** feature, quality, special, symptom, typical **08** hallmark, peculiar, property, specific, symbolic **09** attribute, mannerism, trademark **10** individual **11** distinctive, peculiarity, symptomatic **12** idiosyncrasy **13** idiosyncratic **14** discriminative, distinguishing, representative

characteristically
09 typically **10** peculiarly **12** individually **13** distinctively

characterization
09 depiction, portrayal **11** description **12** presentation **14** representation

characterize
04 mark **05** brand, stamp **06** depict, typify **07** portray, present, qualify, specify **08** describe, identify, indicate **09** designate, represent **10** stereotype **11** distinguish

• **be characterized by**
04 have

characterless
05 inane **12** invertebrate

charade
04 fake, sham **05** farce **06** parody, riddle **07** mockery **08** pretence, travesty **09** pantomime

charge
01 Q **03** ask, chg, due, fee, ion, rap, tax **04** bill, care, cost, debt, dues, duty, fill, levy, load, mine, rate, rent, rush, shot, tear, tilt, toll, ward **05** blame, debit, exact, imbue, onset, order, price, prime, storm, terms, trust **06** accuse, affect, amount, ask for, assail, attack, burden, demand, dittay, impose, impute, indict, infuse, onrush, outlay, rental, sortie, tariff, thrill **07** arraign, assault, command, custody, expense, impeach, keeping, mandate, payment, pervade, suffuse **08** godchild, saturate, storming **09** challenge, fix a price, inculpate, incursion, offensive, onslaught, overwhelm, put down to, set a price **10** accusation, accusement, allegation, imputation, indictment, objuration, obligation, protection **11** arraignment, expenditure, impeachment, incriminate, rush

forward, safekeeping **12** guardianship **13** incrimination **14** responsibility **15** ask someone to pay, demand in payment

See also **heraldry**

• **clear of charges**
03 net **04** nett

• **in charge of**
02 i/c **07** leading **08** managing **09** directing, heading up **10** overseeing **11** controlling, supervising **12** looking after, taking care of **14** responsible for

charged
04 live **08** instinct

chariot
03 car **04** biga, rath, wain **05** ratha, wagon **06** charet, vimana, waggon **08** quadriga

charioteer
03 Hur **04** Jehu **06** Ben-Hur **07** wagoner **08** waggoner

charisma
04 draw, lure, pull **05** charm **06** allure, appeal **09** magnetism **10** attraction **12** drawing-power

charismatic
08 charming, magnetic **09** appealing, glamorous **10** attractive **11** captivating, fascinating **12** irresistible

charitable
04 kind **06** benign, kindly **07** lenient, liberal **08** generous, gracious, tolerant **09** bounteous, forgiving, indulgent **10** beneficent, benevolent, open-handed **11** broad-minded, considerate, magnanimous, sympathetic **12** eleemosynary, humanitarian **13** compassionate, philanthropic, understanding

• **charitable person**
04 Lion

charitably
06 kindly **09** liberally **10** generously, graciously, tolerantly **11** bounteously **12** open-mindedly **13** considerately **15** compassionately, sympathetically

charity
03 aid **04** alms, fund, gift, love **05** trust **06** relief **07** caritas, concern, funding, handout, mission **08** altruism, clemency, donation, goodness, goodwill, hospital, humanity, kindness, leniency, sympathy **09** affection, tolerance **10** almsgiving, assistance, benignness, compassion, foundation, generosity, indulgence **11** beneficence, benevolence, institution, munificence **12** contribution, graciousness, philanthropy **13** bountifulness, confraternity, consideration, unselfishness **14** thoughtfulness **15** considerateness, kind-heartedness

03 DEC, NCH
04 PDSA, RNIB, RNLI, RSPB, WRVS
05 CAFOD, NSPCC, Oxfam, RSPCA, Scope

09 ActionAid, Barnardo's
10 Greenpeace
11 Comic Relief, Help the Aged
12 Christian Aid
13 National Trust, Wellcome Trust, Woodland Trust
15 Leonard Cheshire, Save the Children, St John Ambulance

06 fun run, raffle
08 telethon
09 radiothon, swimathon
10 jumble sale
12 slave auction
13 coffee morning, sponsored swim, sponsored walk
14 charity auction
15 bring-and-buy sale

charlatan
04 fake, sham **05** cheat, fraud, quack **06** con man, phoney **08** impostor, swindler **09** pretender, trickster **10** confidence, mountebank **11** bogus caller, illywhacker **13** bogus official

charlie
01 C

See also **fool**

charm
02 it **03** obi, win **04** draw, idol, ju-ju, mojo, obia, take, tiki **05** aroma, magic, obeah, spell, weird **06** allure, amulet, appeal, cajole, enamor, fetish, glamor, grigri, mascot, please, seduce **07** abraxas, attract, becharm, beguile, bewitch, delight, enamour, enchant, encharm, glamour, hei tiki, periapt, sorcery, trinket, windbag **08** comether, greegree, grisgris, intrigue, medicine, nephrite, ornament, prestige, talisman **09** captivate, cramp-bone, enrapture, fascinate, magnetism, mesmerize **10** allurement, attraction, night-spell, phylactery **11** abracadabra, captivation, enchantment, fascination, hand of glory, what it takes **12** desirability, porte-bonheur **14** attractiveness, delightfulness

charming
04 cute, nice **05** elfin, sweet **06** lovely, pretty, quaint, smooth **07** winning, winsome **08** adorable, alluring, engaging, fetching, pleasant, pleasing, tasteful, tempting **09** appealing, disarming, glamorous, seductive **10** attractive, bewitching, delectable, delightful, enchanting, entrancing **11** captivating, fascinating **12** chocolate-box, irresistible

charmingly
07 sweetly **09** winsomely **10** alluringly, delectably, pleasantly, pleasingly **11** glamorously **12** attractively, delightfully, enchantingly, irresistibly

chart
02 ch **03** map **04** abac, draw, list, mark, note, plan, plot **05** draft, graph,

place, table **06** follow, league, map out, record, sketch **07** diagram, monitor, observe, outline, sea card **08** bar chart, document, isopleth, nomogram, pie chart, register **09** blueprint, delineate, flow chart, flow sheet, hit parade, modulator, nomograph, sociogram, top twenty **10** hyetograph, organogram **11** put on record **13** keep a record of

charter
04 bond, deed, hire, rent **05** carta, grant, lease, right **06** charta, employ, engage, patent, permit **07** licence, license, warrant **08** contract, covenant, document, sanction **09** allowance, authority, authorize, franchise, indenture, novodamus, privilege **10** commission, concession **11** prerogative **13** accreditation, authorization

chary
03 shy **04** cagy, slow, wary **05** cagey, leery **06** tender, uneasy **07** careful, guarded, heedful, prudent **08** cautious, precious **09** reluctant, unwilling **10** fastidious, suspicious **11** circumspect

chase
◇ *juxtaposition indicator*
03 sic **04** fall, hunt, rush, seek, sick, tail **05** chevy, chivy, drive, expel, hound, hurry, track, trail **06** chivvy, course, follow, groove, pursue, quarry, scorse, shadow **07** engrave, hot-trod, hunting, pursuit **08** coursing, run after, send away **09** give chase, prosecute **12** running after **13** hare and hounds

chasm
03 gap **04** gape, gulf, rift, void, yawn **05** abyss, cleft, crack, gorge, split **06** breach, canyon, cavity, crater, hollow, ravine **07** divorce, fissure, opening, quarrel **08** crevasse **10** alienation, separation **12** disagreement, estrangement

chassis
05 frame **08** bodywork, fuselage, skeleton **09** framework, structure **12** substructure **13** undercarriage

chaste
03 ren, rin, run **04** bare, pure, sick **05** moral, plain, worry **06** decent, demure, graced, honest, modest, scorse, simple, single, vestal **07** austere, classic **08** celibate, innocent, virginal, virtuous **09** abstinent, continent, unadorned, undefiled, unmarried, unsullied **10** immaculate, restrained **13** unembellished

chasten
04 curb, tame **06** humble, punish, purify, refine, soften, subdue, temper **07** correct, repress, reprove **08** chastise, moderate, restrain **09** castigate, humiliate **10** discipline

chastise
03 fix **04** beat, cane, flog, lash, whip **05** scold, smack, spank, strap **06** berate, disple, punish, purify, refine, reform, swinge, wallop **07** censure, correct, reprove, scourge, upbraid **08** admonish, moderate, restrain **09** castigate, dress down, reprimand **10** discipline, take to task

chastisement
07 beating, censure, what for **08** flogging, scolding, smacking, spanking, whipping **09** walloping **10** admonition, correction, discipline, punishment **11** castigation **12** dressing-down

chastity
05 honor **06** honour, purity, virtue **07** honesty, modesty **08** celibacy **09** innocence, virginity **10** abstinence, continence, continency, maidenhood, moderation, singleness **13** temperateness **14** immaculateness, unmarried state

chat
03 gas, jaw, rap **04** coze, talk **05** crack, louse, visit, wongi **06** babble, confab, cosher, gossip, jabber, natter, rabbit, waffle, yabber **07** blather, blether, chatter, chinwag, prattle, schmooz, shmoose, shmooze **08** causerie, chitchat, converse, cosy chat, rabbit on, schmooze **09** small talk, tête-à-tête **10** chew the fat, chew the rag **11** confabulate **12** conversation, heart-to-heart, tittle-tattle **13** confabulation **14** clash-ma-clavers, shoot the breeze

• chat up
03 eye **04** ogle **06** leer at **08** come on to **09** flirt with **11** make a pass at **14** make advances to **15** try to get off with

chatter
03 gab, gas, jaw, mag, yap **04** chat, talk **05** clack, clash, froth, skite **06** babble, cackle, confab, gabble, gammon, gossip, jabber, jargon, natter, patter, rabbit, rattle, tattle, waffle, witter, yatter **07** blether, chinwag, chitter, chunder, chunner, chunter, clatter, earbash, gabnash, nashgab, palaver, prattle, twattle **08** chitchat, chounter, rabbit on, rattle on **09** tête-à-tête **10** talky-talky, tongue-work **12** conversation, gibble-gabble, talkee-talkee, tittle-tattle, yada yada yada **14** clitter-clatter **15** yadda yadda yadda

chatterbox
06 gabber, gasbag, gasser, gossip, talker **07** babbler, gabnash, tattler, windbag **08** big mouth, jabberer, natterer **09** chatterer, gossipper, loudmouth **12** blabbermouth **13** tittle-tattler **14** telephone kiosk

chatterer
03 pie **06** chewet, gabber, tatler **07** gabnash, nashgab, tattler

chatty
04 glib **05** dirty, gabby, lousy, newsy **06** casual, mouthy **07** gossipy, gushing, verbose **08** effusive, familiar, friendly, informal **09** garrulous, talkative **10** colloquial, long-winded, loquacious **13** communicative **14** conversational

chauvinism
04 bias **06** sexism **08** jingoism **09** prejudice **10** flag-waving **11** nationalism **12** partisanship **14** male chauvinism

chauvinist
03 MCP **05** jingo **06** biased, sexist **08** jingoist **10** flag-waving, prejudiced **11** nationalist **14** male chauvinist

chauvinistic
06 biased, sexist **10** jingoistic, prejudiced **13** nationalistic

cheap
03 low **04** mean, poor, sale **05** a snip, tacky, tatty **06** a steal, budget, cheapo, chintz, common, jitney, paltry, shoddy, sordid, tawdry, two-bit, vulgar **07** bargain, chintzy, economy, low-cost, reduced, slashed **08** a good buy, cut-price, dog-cheap, giveaway, inferior, low-price, no-frills, sixpenny, twopenny **09** bon marché, cheapjack, cheap-rate, dirt-cheap, good-cheap, knock-down, rinky-dink, tasteless, ten a penny, throwaway, worthless **10** à bon marché, affordable, despicable, discounted, economical, improvised, marked-down, ramshackle, reasonable, rock-bottom, second-rate **11** a dime a dozen, gingerbread, inexpensive, reduced-rate **12** contemptible **13** cheap and nasty, going for a song, on a shoestring, value-for-money **14** on special offer **15** bargain-basement

cheapen
05 lower **06** demean **07** degrade, devalue **08** belittle, derogate **09** denigrate, discredit, disparage, downgrade **10** depreciate

cheaply
09 at low cost, bon marché **10** à bon marché, affordably, reasonably **12** at a cheap rate, economically, with no frills **13** inexpensively **14** at a reduced rate, on special offer

cheat
02 do **03** bam, bob, cog, con, fix, fob, fox, gum, gyp, jew, rig **04** bilk, chiz, clip, colt, deny, dupe, fake, fool, gull, have, jink, mump, slur, snap, swiz, take, trim **05** biter, bluff, check, chess, chizz, cozen, crook, cully, dingo, fraud, fudge, hocus, queer, rogue, screw, shark, stiff, sting, touch, trick, welsh **06** baffle, begunk, cajole, chisel, chouse, con man, diddle, dodger, do down, fiddle, fleece, intake, rip off, smouch, take in, thwart **07** beguile, cheater, cozener, deceive, defraud, deprive, escheat, forfeit, gudgeon, mislead, prevent, sharper, skelder, swindle, swizzle, twister, two-time **08** deceiver, hoodwink, impostor, picaroon, swindler **09** bamboozle, charlatan,

hiseller, cony-catch, deception,
luckshove, frustrate, trickster,
victimize **10** do a flanker **11** cony-
catcher, do one over on, double-cross,
extortioner, gull-catcher,
hornswoggle, short-change **12** do the
dirty on, take for a ride **13** double-
crosser

heck
02 ch **03** bar, nip, tab **04** balk, bill,
curb, damp, foil, halt, rein, scan, slow,
neb, snub, stem, stop, test, tick
05 audit, baulk, crush, delay, limit,
pinch, probe, punch, sneap, study,
stunt, tally, token **06** arrest, blight,
bridle, coupon, hinder, impede, look
at, police, rebuff, rebuke, rein in, retard,
screen, tartan, thwart, ticket, verify
07 account, analyse, charges, check-
up, compare, confirm, contain, control,
examine, inhibit, inquiry, inspect,
invoice, monitor, repress, repulse,
setback, shorten, staunch **08** analysis,
holdback, make sure, obstruct, once-
over, research, restrain, scrutiny, slow
down, suppress, validate **09** going-
over, go through, reckoning,
reprimand, restraint, statement, take
stock **10** cross-check, inspection,
monitoring, scrutinize **11** corroborate,
counterfoil, examination, inquire into,
investigate **12** confirmation,
substantiate, verification
3 investigation, look at closely **15** give
the once-over
• **check in**
05 enrol **06** book in **08** register
• **check out**
04 case, test **05** leave, recce, study
06 depart **07** examine, inspect
08 look into, settle up **10** pay the bill
1 investigate
• **check up**
04 test **05** probe **06** assess, verify
07 analyse, confirm, examine, inspect
08 evaluate, make sure **09** ascertain
1 inquire into, investigate
• **hold in check, keep in check**
04 curb, stop **06** arrest, bridle, hinder,
impede, rein in **07** control, prevent,
repress **08** hold back, keep back,
obstruct, restrain, suppress

heck-up
04 test **05** audit, probe **07** inquiry
08 analysis, research, scrutiny
09 appraisal **10** evaluation, inspection,
monitoring **11** examination
2 confirmation, verification
3 investigation

heek
03 jaw, lip **04** chap, chop, gall, gena,
ole, joll, jowl, neck, sass, wang
05 chaft, mouth, nerve, sauce
06 chafts, dimple **08** attitude,
audacity, chutzpah, temerity **09** brass
neck, impudence, insolence
10 brazenness, disrespect, effrontery
2 impertinence

heekily
6 pertly **10** impudently, insolently
3 impertinently **15** disrespectfully

cheeky
04 pert, rude **05** fresh, lippy, sassy,
saucy **06** brazen, mouthy **07** forward
08 impudent, insolent **09** audacious
11 impertinent **12** overfamiliar
13 disrespectful

cheep
04 peep, pipe, sing **05** chirp, trill,
tweet **06** warble **07** chirrup, twitter,
whistle

cheer
03 hip, joy, olé, rah **04** buck, buoy, clap,
face, fare, food, glad, hail, hoop, warm,
yell **05** bravo, elate, shout, whoop
06 buck up, buoy up, cherry, hurrah,
perk up, salute, solace, spirit, uplift
07 acclaim, applaud, comfort, console,
enliven, fanfare, gladden, hearten,
ovation, revelry, root for, support,
welcome **08** applause, brighten,
clapping, gladness, inspirit, plaudits,
semblant **09** celebrate, encourage,
enhearten, happiness, merriment
10 barrack for, exhilarate, joyfulness
11 acclamation, high spirits,
hopefulness, merrymaking
12 cheerfulness **13** entertainment
• **cheer up**
05 liven, rally **06** buck up, perk up
07 chirrup, comfort, console, hearten,
liven up **08** brighten **09** encourage,
take heart **10** brighten up
• **be cheered**
04 rise

cheerful
03 gay **04** glad, joco, warm **05** bonny,
cadgy, canty, happy, jolly, light, merry,
riant, sunny **06** blithe, bubbly, breezy,
bright, bubbly, cheery, chirpy, genial,
hearty, jaunty, jocund, jovial, joyful,
joyous, kidgie, lively, smiley, upbeat
07 buoyant, chipper, holiday, smiling,
winsome **08** animated, carefree,
chirrupy, eupeptic, laughing, pleasant,
pleasing, spirited, stirring
09 agreeable, contented, exuberant,
inspiring, lightsome, sparkling
10 attractive, comforting, delightful,
heartening, optimistic **11** encouraging
12 enthusiastic, good-humoured,
high-spirited, light-hearted **13** in good
spirits

cheerily
06 gladly **07** happily **08** brightly,
jovially **10** cheerfully **14** light-
heartedly

cheerio
03 bye **04** ta-ta **05** adieu **06** bye-bye,
cheers, hooray, hooroo, see you, so
long **07** goodbye, haere ra **08** au
revoir, farewell **11** see you later
See also **farewell**

cheerless
03 sad **04** cold, dank, dark, dead, drab,
dull, grim **05** bleak, dingy, drab, barren,
dismal, dreary, gloomy, lonely, sombre,
sullen, wintry **07** austere, forlorn,
joyless, sunless, unhappy, wintery
08 dejected, desolate, dolorous,

mournful, winterly **09** miserable,
sorrowful **10** depressing, despondent,
melancholy, uninviting **11** comfortless
12 disconsolate

cheers
02 ta **03** bye **04** rivo, skol, ta-ta, tope
05 adieu, skoal **06** bye-bye, health,
prosit, see you, so long **07** cheerio,
goodbye, haere ra, slàinte, wassail
08 au revoir, bless you, chin-chin,
farewell, thank you, waes hail
09 bottoms up, drink hail **10** all the
best, here's to you, many thanks,
thanks a lot **11** much obliged, see you
later **12** down the hatch, mud in your
eye **13** happy landings **14** your good
health **15** to absent friends

cheery
03 gay **04** glad **05** happy, jolly, merry
06 breezy, bright, chirpy, genial, hearty,
jaunty, jovial, joyful, lively **07** buoyant,
smiling **08** animated, carefree,
cheerful, laughing, spirited
09 contented, exuberant, sparkling
10 optimistic **12** back-slapping,
enthusiastic, light-hearted **13** in good
spirits

cheese

Cheeses include:

03 ewe, Oka
04 Brie, curd, Edam, feta, goat, hard,
skyr, soft
05 Caboc, Carré, Derby, Gouda, quark
06 Cantal, chèvre, Dunlop, junket,
Orkney, paneer, Romano, Tilsit
07 Boursin, Cheddar, crottin, crowdie,
Fontina, Gruyère, kebbock,
kebbuck, Limburg, Münster, ricotta,
sapsago, Stilton®
08 bel paese, Cheshire, Churnton,
Emmental, halloumi, Huntsman,
manchego, Parmesan, pecorino,
raclette, Taleggio, vacherin
09 Amsterdam, Blue Vinny,
Cambozola®, Camembert,
chevreton, Emmenthal, ewe-
cheese, Ilchester, Jarlsberg®,
Killarney, Leicester, Limburger,
Lymeswold®, mouse-trap, Port
Salut, processed, provolone,
reblochon, Roquefort, sage Derby
10 blue cheese, Caerphilly, curd
cheese, Danish blue, dolcelatte,
Emmentaler, Gloucester,
Gorgonzola, hard cheese,
Lancashire, mascarpone,
mozzarella, Neufchâtel, Red
Windsor, soft cheese, stracchino,
vegetarian
11 Coulommiers, cream cheese, Petit
Suisse, Pont l'Évêque, Saint-Paulin,
Wensleydale
12 Blue Cheshire, fromage frais,
Monterey Jack, Philadelphia®, Red
Leicester
13 Bleu d'Auvergne, cottage cheese

• **big cheese**
03 nob, VIP **04** tuan **05** mogul, swell
06 big gun, bigwig, honcho, worthy
07 big shot, notable **08** big noise,

somebody **09** celebrity, dignitary, personage **10** panjandrum **11** heavyweight

cheesed off
05 bored, fed up **07** annoyed **09** depressed, disgusted, hacked off, pissed off **10** brassed off, browned off **11** disgruntled **12** disappointed, discontented, dissatisfied, sick and tired

chef
Chefs, restaurateurs and cookery writers include:

03 Hom (Ken)
04 Gray (Rose), Roux (Albert), Roux (Michel), Spry (Constance)
05 Allen (Betty), Blanc (Raymond René), David (Elizabeth), Delia, Floyd (Keith), Leith (Prue), Roden (Claudia), Smith (Delia), Soyer (Alexis), Stein (Rick), White (Marco Pierre)
06 Appert (Nicolas François), Beeton (Mrs Isabella Mary), Carême (Marie Antoine), Farmer (Fannie), Lawson (Nigella), Oliver (Jamie), Ramsay (Gordon), Rhodes (Gary), Rogers (Ruth), Slater (Nigel), Wilson (David)
07 Cradock (Fanny), Erikson (Gunn), Grigson (Jane), Grigson (Sophie), Jaffrey (Madhur), Ladenis (Nico)
08 Dimbleby (Josceline), Grossman (Loyd), Harriott (Ainsley), Mosimann (Anton), Paterson (Jennifer)
09 Carluccio (Antonio), Escoffier (Auguste), McCartney (Linda)
12 Two Fat Ladies
13 Dickson Wright (Clarissa)
14 Brillat-Savarin (Anthelme)
15 Worrall Thompson (Antony)

chemical
Chemical compounds include:

03 PVC
04 alum, DEET, urea
05 epoxy
06 phenol
07 ammonia, borazon, chloral, ethanol, styrene, toluene
08 kerosene, methanol, paraffin
10 chloramine, chloroform
12 benzaldehyde, borosilicate
13 carbon dioxide, chlorhexidine, chlorobromide
14 carbon monoxide, chloral hydrate
15 organophosphate, sodium hydroxide

See also **element**

chemist
Chemists include:

03 Lee (Yuan T)
04 Abel (Sir Frederick), Davy (Sir Humphry), Hess (Germain Henri), Kuhn (Richard), Mond (Ludwig), Urey (Harold Clayton)
05 Abegg (Richard), Black (Joseph), Boyle (Robert), Curie (Marie),

Darby (Abraham), Dewar (Sir James), Haber (Fritz), Hooke (Robert), Kroto (Sir Harold), Libby (Willard Frank), Meyer (Lothar), Nobel (Alfred), Soddy (Frederick)
06 Baeyer (Adolf von), Barton (Sir Derek), Bunsen (Robert Wilhelm), Dalton (John), Eyring (Henry), Hevesy (George Charles von), Liebig (Justus von), Miller (Stanley Lloyd), Nernst (Walther), Porter (George, Lord), Ramsay (Sir William)
07 Abelson (Philip H), Bergius (Friedrich), Buchner (Eduard), Faraday (Michael), Fischer (Emil Hermann), Fischer (Hans), Hodgkin (Dorothy), Pasteur (Louis), Pauling (Linus Carl), Scheele (Carl Wilhelm), Seaborg (Glenn Theodore)
08 Avogadro (Amedeo), Chevreul (Michel Eugène), Hadfield (Sir Robert Abbott), Klaproth (Martin Heinrich), Langmuir (Irving), Lonsdale (Dame Kathleen), Lovelock (James), Mulliken (Robert Sanderson), Regnault (Henri Victor), Robinson (Sir Robert), Sidgwick (Nevil Vincent), Svedberg (Theodor), Tiselius (Arne Wilhelm Kaurin)
09 Arrhenius (Svante August), Baekeland (Leo Hendrik), Berzelius (Jöns Jacob), Cavendish (Henry), Gay-Lussac (Joseph Louis), Lavoisier (Antoine Laurent), Priestley (Joseph), Prigogine (Ilya, Vicomte)
10 Cannizzaro (Stanislao), Mendeleyev (Dmitri)
12 Boussingault (Jean Baptiste Joseph)

• chemists
03 ICI, RSC **04** BASF **06** IChemE

chemistry
Chemistry terms include:

02 IR, pH
03 cis, gas, ion
04 acid, atom, base, bond, mass, mole, rate, salt, weak
05 assay, block, cycle, ester, group, IUPAC, lipid, order, phase, polar, redox, shell, solid, trans, yield
06 alkali, alkane, alkene, buffer, chiral, dalton, dilute, dipole, fusion, halide, isomer, ketone, ligand, liquid, matter, period, phenyl, pi bond, proton, strong, symbol
07 chelate, chemist, colloid, crystal, element, entropy, fission, formula, halogen, isotope, lattice, mixture, neutral, neutron, nucleus, orbital, organic, polymer, product, racemic, reagent, soluble, solvent, valency
08 analysis, aromatic, catalyst, compound, cracking, dialysis, electron, emulsion, end point, enthalpy, fixation, half life, inert gas, miscible, molecule, noble gas, reactant, reaction, solution

09 aliphatic, allotrope, anhydrous, catalysis, corrosion, diffusion, electrode, empirical, hydroxide, indicator, inorganic, insoluble, ionic bond, oxidation, reduction, saturated, side chain, sigma bond, substance, synthesis, titration
10 amphoteric, atomic mass, combustion, curly arrow, double bond, exothermic, free energy, hydrolysis, immiscible, litmus test, reversible, single bond, suspension, triple bond, zwitterion
11 crystallize, diffraction, electrolyte, endothermic, equilibrium, evaporation, free radical, ground state, hydrocarbon, litmus paper, precipitate, respiration, sublimation
12 atomic number, atomic radius, atomic weight, biochemistry, chemical bond, chlorination, concentrated, condensation, covalent bond, dissociation, distillation, electrolysis, fermentation, hydrogen bond, melting point, metallic bond, spectroscopy
13 chain reaction, decomposition, fractionation, periodic table, radioactivity, stoichiometry
14 Avogadro number, Brownian motion, buffer solution, chromatography, saponification
15 atomic structure, aufbau principle, chemical element, collision theory, transition metal, transition state

cheque
03 dud **04** giro **06** stumer **07** bouncer **11** counterfoil

chequer
04 dice **09** interrupt, variegate **10** chessboard **13** counterchange

chequered
05 diced, mixed **06** checky, chequy, varied **07** checked, diverse, striped **08** eventful **10** variegated **13** multicoloured, particoloured **15** with ups and downs

cherish
03 hug **04** love **05** adore, brood, nurse, prize, value **06** foster, nestle, tender **07** brood on, care for, harbour, nourish, nurture, shelter, support, sustain **08** enshrine, hold dear, treasure **09** encourage, entertain, look after **10** make much of, take care of **11** have at heart, refocillate **14** take good care of

cherished
03 pet **08** precious

cherry
04 gean **05** cheer, morel, ruddy **06** cornel, mazard **07** may-duke, mazzard, morello **08** hagberry **09** Malpighia **10** blackheart

cherub
05 angel **06** seraph

cherubic
04 cute **05** sweet **06** lovely
07 angelic, lovable **08** adorable,
heavenly, innocent, loveable, seraphic
09 appealing

chess

chest
03 ark, box, cub **04** case, kist
05 bahut, caddy, crate, hutch, trunk
06 breast, bunker, bureau, casket,
coffer, girnel, larnax, scrine, shrine,
thorax **07** cap-case, cassone,
commode, dresser, meal-ark, sternum,
tallboy **08** corn-kist, treasury,
wakahuia **09** slop-chest, strongbox
10 chiffonier

chestnut
02 ch **05** favel **06** cliché, conker, favell,
sorrel **07** badious, buckeye, caltrop,

horn-nut, saligot **08** bean tree,
Castanea **09** chincapin, chinkapin
10 chinquapin **14** Castanospermum

chevron
01 V **06** stripe **08** dancette

chew
◊ *anagram indicator*
03 eat **04** bite, chaw, gnaw, quid
05 champ, chomp, grind, munch
06 crunch **07** reflect **08** meditate,
ruminate **09** manducate, masticate
• **chew over**
06 muse on, ponder **07** weigh up
08 consider, mull over **10** meditate on,
ruminate on **14** deliberate upon

chic
05 smart, style **06** chichi, dapper,
modish, snazzy, trendy, with it **07** à la
mode, elegant, stylish **08** elegance
11 fashionable **13** sophisticated

chicanery
05 dodge, fraud, guile, wiles
08 artifice, cheating, intrigue, trickery
09 deception, duplicity, quibbling,
sophistry **10** dishonesty, subterfuge
11 deviousness, hoodwinking
13 deceitfulness, double-dealing,
jiggery-pokery, sharp practice
15 underhandedness

chick
04 bird

chicken
03 hen **04** poot, pout **05** biddy,
chook, chuck, poule, poult, rumpy,
squab **06** scared **07** broiler, chookie,
chuckie, poussin **08** coq au vin,
cowardly, springer, yakitori
09 howtowdie **10** frightened
See also **animal**; **cowardly**; **hen**

chickpea
04 gram **05** chana, chich **08** garbanzo

chide
03 row **04** rate, twit **05** blame, dress,
scold, shend **06** berate, rebuke
07 censure, lecture, quarrel, reprove,
tell off, upbraid **08** admonish, chastise,
reproach **09** criticize, objurgate,
reprehend, reprimand

chief
02 Ch **03** cid, key, oba **04** arch, boss,
cock, head, jarl, kaid, khan, lead, lord,
main, raja, ratu **05** ariki, chair, first,
grand, great, major, prime, rajah, ratoo,
ruler, sheik, vital **06** big gun, gaffer,
honcho, leader, master, primal,

sachem, sheikh, sudder, top dog
07 cacique, captain, cazique, central,
headman, highest, leading, manager,
mugwump, premier, primary, supreme,
supremo **08** big noise, cardinal,
chairman, director, dominant,
foremost, governor, intimate, overlord,
sagamore, superior, suzerain **09** big
cheese, chieftain, commander,
directing, essential, head-woman,
important, number one, paramount,
pendragon, president, principal,
rangatira, top banana, uppermost
10 chairwoman, coryphaeus, head
bummer, pre-eminent, prevailing,
ringleader **11** chairperson, controlling,
outstanding, predominant, supervising
13 most important, prime minister
14 chief executive, superintendent

See also **emperor**; **empress**; **governor**;
king; **president**; **queen**; **ruler**

chiefly
06 mainly, mostly **07** usually
09 capitally, generally, in the main,
primarily **10** especially, on the whole
11 essentially, principally
13 predominantly **14** for the most
part

child
02 ch, it **03** boy, elf, get, imp, kid, son,
tot **04** babe, baby, brat, chit, dalt, gait,
geit, girl, gyte, mite, puss, tama, tike,
tiny, trot, tyke, waif, wean **05** bairn,
chick, dault, elfin, issue, mardy, minor,
scamp, slink, smout, smowt, sprog,
totty, wench, youth **06** cherub, enfant,
infant, kidlet, moppet, nipper, pledge,
rug rat, toddle, tottie, urchin, wanton
07 bambino, dilling, gangrel, hellion,
kinchin, littlin, name-son, neonate,
papoose, preteen, prodigy, progeny,
subteen, tiny tot, toddler, young 'un
08 adherent, bantling, Benjamin,
daughter, disciple, godchild, innocent,
juvenile, little 'un, littling, munchkin,
suckling, tamariki, teenager, weanling,
young one **09** kiddywink, littleane,
little boy, little one, monthling,
offspring, stepchild, underfive,
youngster **10** adolescent, ankle-biter,
changeling, descendant, eyas-musket,
fosterling, grandchild, inhabitant,
jackanapes, kiddiewink, knave-bairn,
little girl, orphanmite, ragamuffin,
wunderkind, young adult **11** ankle-
nipper, butter-print, encumbrance,
guttersnipe, olive branch, preschooler,
schoolchild, weeny-bopper, young
person **12** kiddiewinkie
• **only child**
02 oc

childbirth
05 pains **06** labour **07** lying-in, travail
08 delivery **09** maternity, pregnancy,
puerperal **11** confinement, parturition
12 accouchement, child-bearing

childhood
05 youth **07** boyhood, infancy
08 babyhood, girlhood, minority
09 early days **10** early years,

immaturity, schooldays
11 adolescence

childish
05 silly **06** boyish **07** babyish, foolish, girlish, puerile **08** immature, juvenile, trifling **09** frivolous, infantile **10** namby-pamby **13** irresponsible

childishly
09 foolishly **10** immaturely **13** irresponsibly

childless *see* **without issue** *under* **issue**

childlike
05 naive **06** docile, simple **07** artless, natural **08** innocent, trustful, trusting **09** credulous, guileless, ingenuous **10** unaffected

children
05 issue

Chile
03 CHL, RCH

chill
03 flu, ice, icy, nip, raw **04** bite, cold, cool, fear **05** algid, aloof, bleak, dread, fever, nippy, oorie, ourie, owrie, parky, relax, scare, sharp, virus **06** biting, chilly, dampen, dismay, freeze, frigid, frosty, shiver, wintry **07** anxiety, depress, iciness, petrify, rawness, terrify **08** coldness, cool down, coolness, freezing, frighten, make cold **09** crispness, influenza **10** become cold, depressing, discourage, dishearten, make colder, unfriendly **11** refrigerate **12** apprehension, become colder
● **chilled**
05 on ice **07** relaxed
● **chill out**
05 relax **06** unwind **08** calm down **09** have a rest **10** take it easy

chilly
03 icy, raw **04** cold, cool **05** aloof, bleak, brisk, crisp, fresh, gelid, nippy, parky, sharp, stony **06** biting, frigid, wintry **07** distant, hostile **08** freezing **10** unfriendly **11** unwelcoming **12** unresponsive **13** unsympathetic **14** unenthusiastic

chime
04 boom, ding, dong, peal, ring, tink, toll **05** agree, clang, rhyme, sound **06** accord, jingle, strike, tinkle **07** harmony, resound **11** reverberate **13** reverberation **14** tintinnabulate
● **chime in**
05 agree, blend, cut in, fit in **06** butt in, chip in **09** be similar, harmonize, interject, interpose, interrupt **10** correspond **12** be consistent

chimera
05 dream, fancy **07** fantasy, ratfish, spectre **08** delusion, illusion **09** idle fancy **12** will-o'-the-wisp **13** hallucination

chimney
03 lum **04** flue, vent **05** cleft, shaft, stack, stalk **06** funnel, tunnel **07** chimley, chumley, crevice **08** femerall **10** flare stack, smokestack **12** chimney stalk
● **chimney pot**
03 can **06** top-hat

china
02 Ch, RC **03** CHN, TWN **04** Chin, kina, mate **05** quina **06** dishes, plates **07** ceramic, pottery, quinine **08** crockery **09** porcelain, tableware **10** terracotta **11** earthenware **13** dinner service **14** cups and saucers, the flowery land **15** Celestial Empire, People's Republic
See also **friend; porcelain**

Chinese
02 Ch **03** Han **04** Chin, Sino- **05** Seric, Sinic **07** Cataian, Catayan, Sinaean **08** Cathaian, Cathayan
See also **animal; dynasty**
● **Chinese society**
04 tong

chink
03 cut, gap **04** gasp, rift, rima, rime, slit, slot **05** cleft, crack, money, space, split **06** cavity, cranny, rictus **07** crevice, fissure, opening **08** aperture

chip
03 bit, fry **04** dent, disc, EROM, flaw, gash, nick, pare **05** break, chaff, crack, crisp, EPROM, flake, nacho, notch, piece, scrap, shard, shred, slice, snick, spale, spall, tease, token, wafer **06** chisel, damage, gallet, paring, sliver **07** blitter, counter, crumble, Pentium®, pinning, scratch, shaving, whittle **08** break off, fragment, splinter **09** French fry **10** transputer **11** fried potato **14** microprocessor
See also **computer**
● **chip in**
03 pay **05** cut in **06** butt in, donate **07** chime in **09** interject, interpose, interrupt, subscribe **10** contribute **12** club together **13** make a donation **14** have a whip-round **15** have a collection

chirp
03 pip **04** peep, pipe, sing **05** cheep, chirk, chirm, chirr, trill, tweet **06** chirre, warble **07** chirrup, chitter, twitter, whistle **10** tweet-tweet

chirpy
03 gay **04** glad **05** happy, jolly, merry, perky **06** blithe, bright, cheery, jaunty, lively **08** cheerful

chisel
03 gad **04** bran, burr **05** burin, cheat, drove, gouge **06** firmer, gravel **07** boaster, bolster, scauper, scorper, shingle **12** pitching tool
See also **carve; cheat; sculpt**

chit-chat
04 chat, talk **06** confab, gossip, natter **07** chatter, chinwag, prattle **08** cosy chat **09** small talk, tête-à-tête **10** idle

gossip **12** conversation, heart-to-heart, tittle-tattle

chivalrous
04 bold **05** brave, noble **06** heroic, polite **07** gallant, valiant **08** gracious, knightly **09** courteous **10** courageous, honourable **11** gentlemanly **12** well-mannered

chivalry
06 honour **07** bravery, bushido, courage **08** boldness, courtesy, noblemen **09** gallantry, integrity **10** politeness **11** courtliness, good manners **12** graciousness, truthfulness **15** gentlemanliness

chivvy
03 bug, nag **04** goad, hunt, prod, urge **05** annoy, chase, hound, hurry **06** badger, harass, hassle, pester, plague **07** hurry up, pursuit, torment **08** pressure **09** importune

chlorine
02 Cl

chock-a-block
04 full **06** jammed, packed **07** brimful, chocker, crammed, crowded **08** overfull **09** congested, jam-packed **14** full to bursting

choice
03 try **04** best, fine, list, plum, rare, trye, wale, will **05** prime, prize, range, taste **06** answer, dainty, finest, opting, option, select **07** Auslese, picking, special, variety **08** choosing, decision, druthers, election, precious, solution, superior, valuable **09** excellent, exclusive, exquisite, first-rate, selection **10** first-class, hand-picked, preference **11** alternative, appropriate **14** discrimination

choke
03 bar, dam, gag **04** clog, glut, plug, silt, stap, stop **05** block, close, cough, dam up, retch, worry **06** accloy, silt up, stifle **07** congest, occlude, smother **08** obstruct, strangle, suppress, throttle **09** constrict, overpower, overwhelm, suffocate **10** asphyxiate
● **choke back**
04 curb **05** check **07** contain, control, inhibit, repress **08** restrain, strangle, suppress **09** fight back

chokey, choky *see* **prison**

choleric
05 angry, fiery, testy **06** crabby, touchy **07** crabbed, peppery **08** petulant **09** crotchety, irascible, irritable **10** passionate **11** bad-tempered, hot-tempered, ill-tempered **13** quick-tempered

choose
03 opt **04** list, pick, take, wale, want, will, wish **05** adopt, chuse, elect, fix on, go for **06** decide, desire, favour, opt for, prefer, see fit, select, take up **07** appoint, espouse, extract, pick out, vote for **08** decide on, plump for, settle on **09** designate, determine,

ingle out **10** predestine **14** make up
our mind

hoosy
5 faddy, fussy, picky **07** finicky
8 exacting **09** selective **10** fastidious,
particular, pernickety **11** persnickety
4 discriminating

hop
2 ax **03** axe, cut, eat, hew, jaw, lop,
aw **04** chap, clap, dice, fell, food,
ack, hash, seal, snap **05** brand, carve,
rack, cut up, mince, sever, share, slash,
lice, split **06** barter, change, cleave,
livide, thrust **07** dissect, fissure
8 exchange, truncate **09** côtelette
• **chop up**
› *anagram indicator*
3 cut **04** cube, dice **05** cut up, grate,
rind, mince, shred, slice **06** divide
7 slice up **13** cut into pieces

hoppy
› *anagram indicator*
4 wavy **05** rough **06** broken, stormy,
uneven **07** ruffled, squally **08** blustery
9 turbulent **11** tempestuous

hore
3 job **04** duty, task **05** truck
6 burden, errand **07** routine **11** piece
of work

horeography

horisters
5 choir

hortle
4 crow **05** laugh, snort **06** cackle,
uffaw **07** chuckle, snigger

horus
4 call **05** choir, shout **06** burden,
train **07** refrain, singers **08** ensemble,
esponse **09** vocalists **10** choristers
1 choral group

Christ
01 X **02** Ch, JC, XP, Xt **03** Chr, I am
04 Lord **06** the Son **07** Holy One,
Messiah, Saviour **08** Immanuel,
Redeemer, Son of God, Son of Man
09 deliverer, Lamb of God,Word of
God **11** King of kings, Lord of lords, the
Redeemer **12** Good Shepherd
13 Prince of Peace

christen
03 dub **04** call, name, term **05** style,
title **07** baptize, immerse **08** sprinkle
09 designate **10** begin using,
inaugurate **11** give a name to

Christian
02 Xn **03** Chr **04** Copt, Xian **05** Xtian

Christmas
02 Xm **04** Noel, Xmas,Yule **05** Nowel
06 Crimbo, Nowell **08** Chrissie,
Nativity,Yuletide

See also **wise man** *under* **wise**

Christmas Island
03 CXR

Christ's-thorn
04 nabk

chromium
02 Cr

chromosome
• **part of chromosome**
02 id **07** cistron

chronic
04 naff, ropy **05** awful, pants
07 abysmal, the pits **08** constant,
dreadful, habitual, hardened, long-
term, terrible **09** appalling, atrocious,
confirmed, continual, frightful,
incessant, ingrained, recurring
10 deep-rooted, deep-seated,
deplorable, inveterate, persistent
11 long-lasting **12** incorrigible, long-
standing **14** a load of rubbish

chronically
08 long-term **10** constantly, habitually
11 continually, incessantly, recurrently
12 deep-rootedly, incorrigibly,
inveterately, persistently

chronicle
04 epic, list, saga, tell **05** chron, diary,
enter, story **06** annals, record, relate,
report **07** account, history, journal,

narrate, recount, set down
08 archives, calendar, register
09 narrative, write down **11** put on
record
• **entry in chronicle**
05 annal

chronicler
06 scribe **07** diarist **08** annalist,
narrator, recorder, reporter
09 archivist, historian
11 chronologer **13** chronographer
15 historiographer

chronological
06 serial **07** in order, ordered
10 historical, in sequence, sequential
11 consecutive, progressive

chubby
03 fat **04** full **05** fubby, fubsy, plump,
podgy, round, stout, tubby **06** flabby,
fleshy, portly, rotund **07** paunchy
08 roly-poly

chuck
03 put, shy **04** cast, dump, food, hurl,
jilt, lump, quit, toss **05** chunk, fling,
heave, pitch, sling, throw **06** give up,
pack in, pebble, reject **07** abandon,
chicken, discard, dismiss, forsake
08 get rid of, jettison **12** give the elbow
15 give the brush-off

chuckle
04 crow **05** laugh, snort **06** cackle,
clumsy, giggle, titter **07** chortle,
snigger **12** laugh quietly

chum
03 pal **04** mate, tosh **05** buddy, butty,
crony **06** cobber, friend **07** comrade
09 accompany, associate, companion
See also **friend**

chummy
04 maty **05** close, matey, pally, thick
08 criminal, friendly, intimate, sociable
12 affectionate

chunk
03 nub **04** hunk, junk, lump, mass, slab
05 block, chuck, piece, wedge, wodge
06 dollop **07** portion

chunky
05 broad, bulky, dumpy, heavy, large,
solid, thick **06** blocky, stocky
07 awkward, weighty **08** thickset,
unwieldy **09** well-built
10 cumbersome **11** substantial

church
02 CE, Ch **04** cult, fold, kirk, sect
05 abbey, flock **06** bethel, chapel,
shrine, temple **07** chantry, minster
08 assembly, basilica, Bethesda,
ecclesia, grouping **09** cathedral,
community, tradition **10** fellowship,
house of God, Lord's house,
tabernacle **11** people of God **12** body
of Christ, congregation, denomination,
meeting-house, procathedral **13** bride
of Christ, house of prayer **14** house of
worship, place of worship, preaching-
house
See also **cathedral**

Church and cathedral parts include:

03 pew
04 apse, arch, font, nave, rood, tomb
05 aisle, altar, choir, crypt, porch, slype, spire, stall, stoup, tower, vault
06 adytum, arcade, atrium, belfry, chapel, chevet, corona, parvis, portal, pulpit, sedile, shrine, squint, vestry
07 almonry, chancel, frontal, gallery, lectern, lucarne, narthex, piscina, reredos, steeple, tambour
08 cloister, credence, crossing, keystone, parclose, pinnacle, predella, sacellum, sacristy, transept
09 antechoir, bell tower, sacrarium, sanctuary, sepulchre, stasidion, triforium
10 ambulatory, baptistery, bell screen, clerestory, diaconicon, fenestella, frithstool, misericord, presbytery, retrochoir, rood screen
12 chapterhouse, confessional, deambulatory
14 ringing chamber, schola cantorum

churchman *see* **clergyman, clergywoman**

churchyard
05 house **07** charnel **08** boneyard, cemetery, God's acre, kirkyard **09** graveyard, kirkyaird **10** burial site, necropolis **11** burial place **12** burial ground

churlish
04 rude **05** harsh, rough, surly **06** morose, oafish, sullen **07** boorish, brusque, carlish, crabbed, doggish, ill-bred, loutish, uncivil **08** impolite **10** ungracious, unmannerly, unsociable **11** bad-tempered, ill-mannered, ill-tempered **12** discourteous **13** unneighbourly **14** ill-conditioned

churn
◇ *anagram indicator*
04 beat, boil, foam, kirn, puke, stir, toss, turn **05** froth, heave, retch, swirl, vomit **06** be sick, seethe, writhe **07** agitate, disturb, throw up **08** convulse
• **churn out**
07 knock up, pump out, turn out **13** throw together

chute
03 lin **04** linn, ramp **05** flume, rapid, shaft, shoot, shute, slide, slope, spout, trunk **06** funnel, gutter, runway, trough **07** channel, incline **09** parachute, waterfall **10** water shoot

chutzpah
03 lip **04** gall **05** cheek, mouth, nerve, sauce **08** audacity **09** brass neck, impudence, insolence **10** brazenness, disrespect, effrontery **12** impertinence

cicada
06 tettix **10** harvest-fly **11** balm-cricket

Cicadas include:

05 Myer's
06 red-eye
09 Union Jack
10 blue prince
11 black prince, floury baker, greengrocer, green Monday, masked devil
12 floury miller, yellow Monday
13 double drummer

cigarette
03 cig, fag, tab **04** weed **05** cigar **06** dog end, fag end **10** coffin-nail, paper-cigar **11** cancer-stick

Cigarettes and cigars include:

04 bidi, burn
05 beedi, blunt, ciggy, claro, joint, paper, roach, segar, smoke, snout, stogy, whiff
06 beedie, bomber, ciggie, concha, gasper, Havana, low-tar, manila, reefer, roll-up, spliff, stogey, stogie
07 cheroot, high-tar, manilla, menthol, regalia
08 king-size, long-nine, perfecto
09 cigarillo, filter tip, panatella
10 tailor-made
11 corona lucis, roll-your-own

cinch
04 snip **06** doddle, scoosh, stroll **08** cakewalk, duck soup, pushover, walkover **09** certainty **10** child's play **11** piece of cake

cinders
04 coal, coke, slag **05** ashes **06** dander, embers **07** clinker **08** charcoal

cinema
05 films, scope **06** flicks, movies **07** drive-in, fleapit, theatre **08** bioscope, bughouse, pictures **09** big screen, multiplex **10** movie house **11** film theatre, nickelodeon **12** movie theatre, picture-house, silver screen **13** picture-palace **14** motion pictures, moving pictures

Cinema and theatre names include:

03 ABC, MGM, Rex, Rio, UCI, UGC
04 Gala, IMAX, Ritz, Roxy
05 Byron, Cameo, Forum, Grand, Kings, Lyric, Metro, Odeon, Orion, Plaza, Regal, Royal, Savoy, Scala, Tower
06 Albany, Apollo, Cannon, Casino, Curzon, Empire, Gaiety, Lyceum, Marina, New Vic, Old Vic, Palace, Queens, Regent, Rialto, Robins, Tivoli, Virgin
07 Adelphi, Almeida, Arcadia, Astoria, Capitol, Carlton, Central, Century, Circuit, Classic, Coronet, Embassy, Essoldo, Gaumont, Granada, La Scala, Locarno, Mayfair, Orpheum, Paragon, Phoenix, Picardy
08 Alhambra, Broadway, Charlton, Cineplex, Citizens, Coliseum, Colonial, Dominion, Electric, Everyman, Festival, Imperial, Landmark, Majestic, Memorial, Pavilion, Windmill
09 Alexandra, Cineworld, Filmhouse, Hollywood, Palladium, Paramount, Playhouse
10 Ambassador, Hippodrome, Lighthouse
11 Her Majesty's, His Majesty's, New Victoria, Ster Century
12 Metropolitan, Picturedrome, Picturehouse, Thefilmworks
13 LyceumTheatre, Picture Palace, Warner Village
14 Electric Palace
15 Screen on the Hill

cipher
01 O **03** nil **04** code, null, zero **05** zilch **06** Enigma, naught, nobody, nought, yes-man **07** nothing **09** calculate, character, nonentity **10** cryptogram **11** cryptograph **12** coded message, secret system **13** secret writing

circa
01 c **02** ca **03** cir, odd **04** circ, some **05** about **06** around, nearly **07** close to, loosely, roughly **09** just about, not far off **10** more or less, round about **11** approaching **13** approximately, in the region of, or thereabouts, something like **15** in the vicinity of

circle
◇ *containment indicator*
01 O **03** set **04** club, gang, gird, wind **05** crowd, group, hem in, pivot, whirl **06** clique, gyrate, rotate, swivel **07** circlet, company, coterie, cycloid, enclose, envelop, hedge in, revolve, rondure, rounder, society **08** assembly, encircle, surround **09** circulate, encompass, move round **10** fellowship, fraternity **12** circumscribe **14** circumnavigate

Circles include:

03 lap, orb
04 ball, band, belt, coil, corn, crop, curl, disc, eddy, gyre, halo, hoop, hour, loop, oval, ring, turn, tyre
05 crown, cycle, dress, globe, grand, great, magic, mural, orbit, pitch, plate, polar, round, stone, upper, wheel
06 Arctic, circus, cordon, discus, girdle, rundle, saucer, sphere, spiral, tropic, vortex, wreath
07 annulet, annulus, circuit, compass, coronet, ellipse, equator, roundel, traffic, transit, turning, vicious
08 epicycle, gyration, meridian, rotation, roundure, striking, virtuous
09 Antarctic, perimeter, whirlpool, whirlwind
10 almacantar, almucantar, Circassian revolution
13 circumference

• **stone circle**
08 cromlech **09** cyclolith
10 Stonehenge **11** peristalith

circuit

2 IC **03** lap **04** area, beat, eyre, tour
5 ambit, limit, orbit, range, round,
route, track **06** bounds, course,
diadem, region **07** compass, rondure,
rounder **08** boundary, district,
progress, roundure **09** perimeter, race
track **10** revolution **12** running-track
3 circumference, perambulation

• closed circuit
2 CC

• logic circuit
2 OR **03** AND, NOR, NOT, XOR
4 NAND

circuitous

7 devious, oblique, winding
8 indirect, rambling, tortuous
9 meandrian, meandrous
0 meandering, roundabout
1 anfractuous **12** labyrinthine,
periphrastic

circular

5 flyer, orbed, round **06** folder, letter,
notice **07** annular, leaflet **08** handbill,
pamphlet **09** spherical **10** disc-
shaped, hoop-shaped, ring-shaped,
round robin **12** announcement
3 advertisement

circulate

> *anagram indicator*
4 flow, pass, walk **05** float, issue,
rumor, swirl, troll, utter, whirl
6 gyrate, report, rotate, rumour,
spread **07** diffuse, give out, go about,
go round, publish, revolve **08** go
abroad, go around, put about, transmit
9 broadcast, get around, pass round,
propagate, publicize, send round
0 distribute, promulgate
1 disseminate, go the rounds, spread
about **12** spread around **13** make the
rounds

circulation

4 flow **05** cycle **06** motion, spread
7 issuing **08** circling, currency,
cyclosis, movement, rotation
9 blood-flow, publicity **10** readership
1 propagation, publication
2 distribution, transmission
3 dissemination

• in circulation
> *anagram indicator*
5 in use **06** afloat, around, issued
7 current, printed **09** available,
published **11** distributed, spread about
2 spread around

circumference

3 arc, rim **04** edge **05** girth, round,
verge **06** border, bounds, circle, fringe,
limits, margin **07** circuit, compass,
outline **08** boundary, confines
9 extremity, perimeter, periphery

circumlocution

6 ambage **08** pleonasm
9 euphemism, prolixity, tautology,
verbosity, wordiness **10** periphrase,
redundancy **11** convolution,
diffuseness, periphrasis
2 indirectness **14** discursiveness,
roundaboutness

circumlocutory

05 wordy **06** prolix **07** diffuse,
verbose **08** elliptic, indirect
09 ambagious, redundant
10 convoluted, discursive, elliptical,
long-winded, pleonastic, roundabout
11 euphemistic **12** periphrastic,
tautological

circumscribe

04 trim **05** bound, hem in, limit, pen in
06 define **07** abridge, confine, curtail,
delimit, enclose **08** encircle, restrain,
restrict, surround **09** delineate,
demarcate, encompass

circumspect

04 wary, wise **05** canny **07** careful,
guarded, politic, prudent **08** cautious,
discreet, vigilant, watchful
09 attentive, judicious, observant,
sagacious **10** deliberate **11** calculating
14 discriminating

circumspection

04 care **07** caution **08** prudence,
wariness **09** canniness, chariness,
examining, vigilance **10** discretion
11 carefulness, guardedness
12 deliberation, watchfulness

circumstance

03 lot **04** case, fact, fate, item, nark,
this **05** event, means, state, thing
06 detail, factor, plight, status
07 element, fortune, respect, situate
08 accident, ceremony, position
09 condition, happening, lifestyle,
resources, situation **10** background,
occurrence, particular
11 arrangement, environment **12** lie of
the land **14** how the land lies, state of
affairs

circumstantial

04 tiny **06** minute **07** deduced,
hearsay **08** indirect, inferred,
presumed **10** contingent, evidential,
incidental **11** conjectural, inferential,
presumptive, provisional

circumvent

04 dish **05** avoid, dodge, evade
06 bypass, outwit, thwart **07** get past
08 get out of, get round, go beyond,
outflank, sidestep **09** encompass
12 steer clear of

circumvention

07 dodging, evasion **09** avoidance,
bypassing, thwarting **12** sidestepping
13 steering clear

circus

06 cirque **10** hippodrome

Circus-related terms include:

03 top
04 geek, ring, tent
05 clown
06 big top, pie car
07 acrobat, balloon, juggler, sawdust,
trapeze, tumbler
08 carnival, conjurer, conjuror, drum
roll, high wire, magician, sideshow,
unicycle
09 aerialist, fire-eater, lion tamer,

menagerie, safety net, strongman,
tightrope
10 acrobatics, acrobatism, candy floss,
custard pie, ringmaster, roustabout,
somersault, trick-rider, unicyclist
11 funambulist, greasepaint
12 escape artist, roll up! roll up!,
stiltwalking, trick cyclist
13 bareback rider, contortionist,
trapeze artist

cissy

03 wet **04** baby, soft, tonk, weak,
wimp, wuss **05** pansy, softy
06 coward, feeble **07** crybaby,
milksop, unmanly, wimpish
08 cowardly, weakling **09** mummy's
boy **10** effeminate, namby-pamby

cistern

03 vat **04** sink, tank **05** basin **08** feed-
head, flush-box **09** reservoir

citadel

04 fort, keep **05** tower **06** castle
07 bastion, kremlin **08** fortress
09 acropolis **10** stronghold
13 fortification

citation

03 cit **05** award, quote **06** honour,
source **07** cutting, excerpt, mention,
passage **08** allusion, epigraph
09 quotation, reference **10** allegation
12 commendation, illustration

cite

04 call, name **05** bring, quote, state,
vouch **06** adduce, allege, summon
07 advance, bring up, convent,
mention, refer to, specify **08** allude to,
evidence **09** enumerate, exemplify
13 give an example

citizen

03 cit **05** local, voter **07** burgher,
denizen, freeman, oppidan, subject
08 civilian, national, resident, taxpayer,
townsman, urbanite **10** inhabitant,
townswoman **11** city-dweller,
householder

city

02 EC **04** seat, town **08** big smoke,
downtown, precinct **09** inner city,
metroplex, Weltstadt **10** city centre,
cosmopolis, metropolis, micropolis,
pentapolis **11** conurbation,
megalopolis, urban sprawl
12 municipality **13** urban district
14 concrete jungle

Ancient cities include:

02 Ur
04 Acre, Axum, Ebla, Nuzi, Rome,
Susa, Troy, Tula, Tyre, Uruk
05 Aksum, Argos, Bosra, Bursa, Copán,
Cuzco, Eridu, Hatra, Huari, Mitla,
Moche, Petra, Saida, Sidon, Tikal,
Uxmal
06 Athens, Byblos, Cyrene, Jabneh,
Jamnia, Napata, Nippur, Sardis,
Shiloh, Sparta, Thebes, Ugarit
07 Antioch, Babylon, Bukhara, Corinth,
El Tajin, Ephesus, Megiddo, Miletus,
Mycenae, Nineveh, Paestum,

Plataea, Pompeii, Samaria, Sybaris, Vergina
08 Carthage, Damascus, Hattusas, Hattusha, Kerkuane, Palenque, Pergamon, Pergamum, Sigiriya, Tashkent, Thysdrus
09 Byzantium, Cartagena, Epidaurus, Sukhothai
10 Alexandria, Angkor Thom, Carchemish, Heliopolis, Hierapolis, Monte Albán, Persepolis
11 Chichén Itzá, Herculaneum, Machu Picchu, Polonnaruwa, Teotihuacán
12 Anuradhapura
13 Halicarnassus
14 Constantinople

Capital cities include:

04 Apia, Baku, Bern, Dili, Doha, Kiev, Lima, Lomé, Malé, Oslo, Riga, Rome, San'a, Suva
05 Abuja, Accra, Amman, Berne, Cairo, Dacca, Dakar, Dhaka, Hanoi, Kabul, Koror, La Paz, Minsk, Paris, Praia, Quito, Rabat, Sana'a, Seoul, Sofia, Sucre, Tokyo, Tunis, Vaduz
06 Akmola, Ankara, Asmara, Astana, Athens, Bamako, Bangui, Banjul, Beirut, Berlin, Bissau, Bogotá, Dodoma, Dublin, Harare, Havana, Kigali, Lisbon, London, Luanda, Lusaka, Madrid, Majuro, Malabo, Manama, Manila, Maputo, Maseru, Monaco, Moroni, Moscow, Muscat, Nassau, Niamey, Ottawa, Peking, Prague, Riyadh, Roseau, Skopje, T'aipei, Tarawa, Tehran, Tirana, Vienna, Warsaw, Yangon, Zagreb
07 Abidjan, Algiers, Alma-Ata, Baghdad, Bangkok, Beijing, Belfast, Bishkek, Caracas, Cardiff, Cayenne, Colombo, Conakry, Cotonou, El Aaiún, Godthab, Honiara, Jakarta, Kampala, Lobamba, Managua, Mbabane, Nairobi, Nicosia, Palikir, Papeete, Rangoon, San José, San Juan, São Tomé, St John's, Tallinn, Tbilisi, Teheran, Thimphu, Tripoli, Valetta, Vilnius, Yaoundé, Yerevan
08 Abu Dhabi, Ashgabat, Asunción, Belgrade, Belmopan, Brasília, Brussels, Budapest, Canberra, Cape Town, Castries, Chisinau, Damascus, Djibouti, Dushanbe, Freetown, Gaborone, Helsinki, Khartoum, Kingston, Kinshasa, Kishinev, Lilongwe, Monrovia, N'Djamena, New Delhi, Port-Vila, Pretoria, Santiago, Sarajevo, Tashkent, The Hague, Tórshavn, Valletta, Victoria, Windhoek
09 Amsterdam, Ashkhabad, Bucharest, Bujumbura, Edinburgh, Fongafale, Islamabad, Jerusalem, Kathmandu, Kingstown, Ljubljana, Mogadishu, Nuku'alofa, Phnom Penh, Port Louis, Porto Novo, Pyongyang, Reykjavík, San Marino, Singapore, St George's, Stockholm, Ulan Bator, Vientiane
10 Addis Ababa, Basseterre, Bratislava, Bridgetown, Copenhagen,

Georgetown, Kuwait City, Libreville, Luxembourg, Mexico City, Montevideo, Nouakchott, Panama City, Paramaribo, Wellington, Willemstad
11 Brazzaville, Buenos Aires, Kuala Lumpur, Monaco-Ville, Ouagadougou, Port Moresby, Port of Spain, San Salvador, Tegucigalpa, Vatican City
12 Antananarivo, Bloemfontein, Fort-de-France, Port-au-Prince, Santo Domingo, Tel Aviv-Jaffa, Washington DC, Yamoussoukro
13 Guatemala City, Yaren District
14 Andorra la Vella
17 Bandar Seri Begawan
23 Sri Jayawardenepura Kotte

Cities and towns include:

02 Bo, LA, NY
03 Åbo, Ayr, Ely, Fès, Fez, Gao, Hué, Lae, Nis, NYC, Pau, Qom, Ufa, Ulm, Vac, Zug
04 Acre, Aden, Agra, Ajme, Amoy, Bari, Bath, Bonn, Brno, Bury, Caen, Cali, Cebu, Como, Cork, Dazu, Deal, Edam, Elat, Eton, Faro, Gand, Gent, Gifu, Graz, Györ, Homs, Hove, Hull, Iasi, Icel, Ipoh, Jima, Jixi, Kano, Kiel, Kobe, Köln, Kota, La-sa, León, Linz, Lódz, Lugo, Luik, Lund, Lvov, Metz, Mold, Mons, Naas, Naha, Nara, Nice, Nuuk, Oban, Oita, Omsk, Oran, Oulu, Pécs, Pegu, Perm, Pisa, Pula, Pune, Rand, Reno, Rhyl, Ruse, Ryde, Safi, Sale, Salt, Sfax, Sian, Sion, Soul, St-Lô, Suez, Sumy, Tema, Thun, Tula, Tyre, Umeå, Vasa, Vigo, Waco, Wick, Wien, Wuhu, Wuxi, Xi'an, York, Zibo, Zörs
05 Adana, Ahvaz, Åland, Al Ayn, Aosta, Aqaba, Argos, Århus, Arica, Arles, Arras, Aspen, Aswan, Ávila, Baden, Banff, Baoji, Basle, Basra, Beira, Belém, Benxi, Blida, Blyth, Boise, Bondi, Borga, Bouar, Breda, Brest, Braga, Bursa, Busan, Cádiz, Canea, Cavan, Ceuta, Chiba, Chita, Colón, Conwy, Cowes, Crewe, Cuzco, Davao, Davos, Delft, Delhi, Derby, Dijon, Dover, Duala, Dubai, Dukou, Eilat, Elche, Epsom, Essen, Eupen, Évora, Fiume, Frome, Fuxin, Genoa, Ghent, Gijón, Gomel, Gorky, Gouda, Gweru, Hagen, Haifa, Halle, Hefei, Hohot, Honan, Ichun, Ieper, Iwaki, Izmir, Jaffa, Jedda, Jilin, Jinan, Jinja, Kaédi, Kandy, Karaj, Kazan, Kelso, Kirov, Kitwe, Kochi, Konya, Köseg, Kursk, Kyoto, Lagos, Leeds, Lewes, Lhasa, Liège, Lille, Limbe, Luton, Luxor, Lyons, Mâcon, Mainz, Malmö, Masan, Mecca, Medan, Miami, Milan, Mitla, Mopti, Mosul, Namen, Namur, Nancy, Nasik, Natal, Ndola, Nîmes, Ohrid, Omagh, Omaha, Omiya, Oryol, Osaka, Otley, Oujda, Padua, Parma, Patan, Patna, Pavia, Penza, Perth, Plzen, Ponce, Poole, Poona, Pusan, Reims, Resit, Ripon, Ronda, Rouen,

Rovno, Rugby, Sakai, Salem, Salta, Sebha, Ségou, Sidon, Siena, Skien, Sochi, Sopot, Split, Suita, Surat, Suwon, Taegu, Talca, Tampa, Tanga, Tanta, Tempe, Thane, Thiès, Tomar, Tomsk, Torun, Tours, Trier, Troon, Truro, Tulsa, Tunja, Turin, Turku, Tzu-po, Udine, Ulsan, Urawa, Utica, Vaasa, Varna, Vejle, Vlorë, Wells, Wigan, Worms, Wuhan, Ypres, Zadar, Zaria, Zarqa
06 Aachen, Aarhus, Agadez, Agadir, Albany, Aleppo, Amiens, Annaba, Annecy, Anshan, Anvers, Anyang, Arezzo, Armagh, Arnhem, Arusha, Ashdod, Atbara, At Taif, Austin, Avarua, Baguio, Bangor, Baotou, Bastia, Bengpu, Bergen, Bhopal, Bilbao, Biloxi, Bitola, Bochum, Bolton, Bombay, Bootle, Boston, Brasov, Bremen, Bruges, Brugge, Burgos, Buxton, Cairns, Calais, Callao, Calmar, Camden, Campos, Cancún, Cannes, Canton, Carlow, Casper, Chania, Chi-nan, Chonju, Cochin, Cracow, Crosby, Cuenca, Dalian, Dallas, Da Nang, Danzig, Daqing, Darhan, Darwin, Datong, Dayton, Denver, Dieppe, Douala, Dudley, Duluth, Dundee, Durban, Durham, Durrës, El Gîza, El Paso, Eugene, Evreux, Exeter, Fatima, Fresno, Frunze, Fu-chou, Fushun, Fuzhou, Galway, Gdansk, Gdynia, Geneva, Gitega, Grodno, Grozny, Guelph, Guilin, Guimar, Gujrat, Guntur, Ha'apai, Hamina, Handan, Han-kou, Harbin, Harlem, Harlow, Harrow, Hebron, Hegang, Himeji, Hobart, Howrah, Ibadan, Inchon, Indore, Jaffna, Jaipur, Jarash, Jarrow, Jeddah, Jiddah, Jilong, Juneau, Kalmar, Kaluga, Kankan, Kanpur, Kaolan, Kassel, Kaunas, Kendal, Khulna, Kirkby, Kirkuk, Kosice, Kraków, Kumasi, Kurgan, Lahore, Lanark, Leiden, Le Mans, Leshan, Leuven, Leyden, Lübeck, Lublin, Ludlow, Lugano, Maceio, Madras, Makale, Málaga, Malang, Manaus, Mantua, Matrah, Medina, Meerut, Mekele, Meknès, Meshed, Mobile, Mukden, Multan, Muncie, Munich, Murcia, Mysore, Nablus, Nagano, Nagoya, Nagpur, Nantes, Napier, Naples, Narvik, Newark, Ningbo, Nouméa, Odense, Odessa, Oldham, Olinda, Oporto, Örebro, Osasco, Osijek, Ostend, Oviedo, Oxford, Padang, Paphos, Phuket, Piatra, Pierre, Pilsen, Porvoo, Potosí, Poznan, Presov, Puebla, Quebec, Queluz, Quetta, Raipur, Rajkat, Ranchi, Recife, Redcar, Reggio, Regina, Rennes, Rheims, Rijeka, Ryazan, Saigon, Salala, Samara, Santos, Schwyz, Sefadu, Sendai, Shiraz, Silves, Sining, Sintra, Skikda, Sliema, Slough, Smyrna, Sokodé, Sousse, Soweto, Sparta, St Ives, St John, St Malo, St Paul, Stroud, Stuart, Suchow, Sukkur, Suzhou,

Sydney, Szeged, Tabriz, Tacoma, Tadmur, Taejon, Tahoua, Tainan, Tamale, Tambov, Tarbes, Tarsus, Tat'ung, Teruel, Thurso, Tipasa, Tobruk, Toledo, Toluca, Topeka, Torbay, Toulon, Toyama, Toyota, Tralee, Trento, Treves, Tromsø, Troyes, Tsinan, Tubruq, Tucson, Tyumen, Urumqi, Vannes, Vargas, Venice, Verona, Viborg, Weimar, Whitby, Widnes, Woking, Xiamen, Xining, Xuzhou, Yangku, Yantai, Yeovil, Yichun, Yunnan, Zabrze, Zigong, Zinder, Zurich, Zwolle

7 Aberfan, Airdrie, Aligarh, Alnwick, Antibes, Antioch, Antwerp, Aracaju, Atlanta, Augusta, Auxerre, Avignon, Baalbek, Badajoz, Bairiki, Banares, Banbury, Bandung, Baoding, Barnaul, Barossa, Bayamón, Bedford, Beeston, Benares, Bendigo, Berbera, Bergama, Bergamo, Bexhill, Bizerta, Blarney, Bologna, Bolzano, Boulder, Bourges, Braemar, Brescia, Bristol, Bryansk, Buffalo, Burnley, Cáceres, Calgary, Calicut, Cardiff, Catania, Chalcis, Changan, Cheadle, Cheddar, Chelsea, Chengde, Chengdu, Cheng-tu, Chester, Chicago, Chifeng, Chi-lung, Chongju, Chungho, Clonmel, Coblenz, Coimbra, Cologne, Concord, Córdoba, Corinth, Corinto, Corunna, Crawley, Dandong, Detroit, Devizes, Donetsk, Douglas, Dresden, Dundalk, Dunedin, Dunkirk, Durango, Entebbe, Erdenet, Esbjerg, Evesham, Exmouth, Falkirk, Fareham, Ferrara, Foochow, Fukuoka, Funchal, Ganzhou, Geelong, Glasgow, Goiânia, Gosport, Granada, Grimsby, Guiyang, Gwalior, Gwangju, Haerbin, Halifax, Hamburg, Hamhung, Hanover, Harwich, Henzada, Heredia, Houston, Huaibai, Huainan, Ipswich, Iquique, Iquitos, Irkutsk, Isfahan, Ivanovo, Izhevsk, Jackson, Jericho, Jiamusi, Jinzhou, Jodhpur, Kaesong, Kaifeng, Kalinin, Kananga, Karachi, Kassala, Kayseri, Keelung, Kenitra, Keswick, Kharkov, Kherson, Koblenz, Kolding, Kuching, Kunming, Kutaisi, Lansing, Lanzhou, La Plata, Larnaca, Latakia, Leghorn, Le Havre, Leipzig, Lerwick, Liberia, Limoges, Lincoln, Lipetsk, Liuzhou, Livorno, Logroño, Louvain, Lucerne, Lucknow, Lugansk, Lumbini, Luoyang, Machida, Madison, Madurai, Malvern, Manzini, Maracay, Marburg, Margate, Mashhad, Massawa, Matlock, Matsudo, Melilla, Memphis, Mendoza, Mildura, Mindelo, Miskolc, Mitsiwa, Mogilev, Mombasa, Morpeth, Münster, Nanjing, Nanking, Nanning, Nantong, Newbury, Newport, Newquay, New Ross,

New York, Niigata, Niterói, Norfolk, Norwich, Novi Sad, Oakland, Okayama, Okinawa, Olympia, Orlando, Orleans, Ostrava, Pahsien, Paisley, Palermo, Panshan, Pattaya, Peebles, Penrith, Perugia, Phoenix, Piraeus, Pistoia, Pitesti, Plovdiv, Poltava, Popayán, Portree, Potsdam, Preston, Prizren, Qingdao, Qiqihar, Quimper, Raleigh, Randers, Ravenna, Reading, Redwood, Reigate, Roanoke, Rosario, Rostock, Rotorua, Runcorn, Sagunto, Salamis, Salerno, Salford, Sandown, Santa Fe, São Luis, Sapporo, Saransk, Saratov, Sassari, Seattle, Segovia, Setúbal, Seville, Shannon, Shantou, Shihezi, Shikoku, Shkodër, Sialkot, Sinuiju, Songnam, Spokane, Spoleto, Staines, Stanley, St Denis, St Louis, Sudbury, Swansea, Swindon, Taiyuan, Tampere, Tampico, Tangier, Taunton, Tel Aviv, Telford, Tétouan, Tianjin, Tijuana, Tilburg, Tilbury, Toronto, Torquay, Tournai, Trenton, Trieste, Tucumán, Ulan-Ude, Uppsala, Utrecht, Ventnor, Vicenza, Vitebsk, Vitosha, Walsall, Warwick, Watford, Weifang, Wenzhou, Wexford, Wichita, Windsor, Wrexham, Wroclaw, Wuhsien, Yakeshi, Yichang, Yingkou, Yonkers, Zermatt, Zhuzhou, Zwickau

08 Aberdeen, Acapulco, Adelaide, Akureyri, Alajuela, Albacete, Alicante, Amarillo, Amritsar, Arbroath, Arequipa, Auckland, Augsburg, Aviemore, Ayia Napa, Ballarat, Banghazi, Bareilly, Barnsley, Bathurst, Bayreuth, Beauvais, Belgorod, Benghazi, Benguela, Benidorm, Besançon, Bhadgaon, Biarritz, Bismarck, Blantyre, Bobruysk, Bordeaux, Boulogne, Bradford, Braganza, Brighton, Brindisi, Brisbane, Bulawayo, Burgundy, Cagliari, Calcutta, Campinas, Carlisle, Changsha, Chartres, Chemnitz, Chepstow, Cheyenne, Chiclayo, Chimbote, Chimkent, Ching-tao, Chongjin, Clevedon, Columbia, Columbus, Contagem, Coventry, Culiacán, Curitiba, Dartford, Dearborn, Debrecen, Djakarta, Dortmund, Drogheda, Duisburg, Dumfries, Dunhuang, Dunleary, Durgapur, Dzhambul, Ebbw Vale, Edmonton, El Kharga, Elsinore, Europort, Falmouth, Florence, Flushing, Freeport, Fribourg, Fujisawa, Fukuyama, Gaoxiong, Gisborne, Gorlovka, Grantham, Grasmere, Greenock, Grenoble, Guernica, Hachioji, Haiphong, Hakodate, Hamilton, Hangchow, Hangzhou, Hannover, Hartford, Hastings, Hengyang, Hereford, Hertford, Hirakata, Holyhead, Holywell, Hong Kong, Honolulu, Huangshi, Hunjiang, Ichikawa, Iowa City, Istanbul, Jabalpur, Jaboatoa,

Kairouan, Kanazawa, Kandahar, Karlsbad, Katowice, Kawasaki, Keflavik, Kemerovo, Kilkenny, Kirkwall, Kismaayo, Klosters, Kolhapur, Konstanz, Koriyama, Kuei-yang, Kumamoto, Laâyoune, La Laguna, Las Vegas, Lausanne, Legoland, Leskovac, Liaoyang, Liaoyuan, Limassol, Limerick, Londrina, Longford, Lüderitz, Ludhiana, Lyallpur, Makassar, Mandalay, Mannheim, Marbella, Mariupol, Mariupol, Mayaguez, Mazatlán, Medellín, Mercedes, Mexicali, Montreal, Montreux, Montrose, Mufulira, Mulhouse, Murmansk, Myingyan, Nagasaki, Namangan, Nanchang, Nazareth, New Haven, Newhaven, Nijmegen, Novgorod, Nuneaton, Nürnberg, Oak Ridge, Omdurman, Oostende, Orenburg, Oswestry, Pago Pago, Pamplona, Panchiao, Pasadena, Pavlodar, Penzance, Peshawar, Piacenza, Ploiesti, Plymouth, Poitiers, Portland, Portrush, Port Said, Pristina, Ramsgate, Rancagua, Randstad, Redditch, Richmond, Road Town, Rochdale, Rockford, Roskilde, Rosslare, Sabadell, Salonica, Salzburg, Saltillo, Salvador, Salzburg, San Diego, Santa Ana, Santarém, São Paulo, Satu Mare, Savannah, Schwerin, Semarang, Shanghai, Shanklin, Shaoguan, Shenyang, Shizuoka, Sholapur, Silk Road, Simbirsk, Skegness, Smolensk, Solihull, Solingen, Sorocaba, Southend, Srinagar, Stafford, St Albans, Stamford, St David's, St Gallen, St Helens, St Helier, Stirling, St Moritz, Stockton, Strabane, St-Tropez, Subotica, Suicheng, Surabaya, Swan Hill, Syracuse, Szczecin, Taganrog, Taichung, Tamworth, Tangshan, Teresina, Thetford, Thonburi, Tiberias, Tientsin, Timbuktu, Titograd, Tolyatti, Tongeren, Toulouse, Toyohasi, Toyonaka, Trujillo, Tsingtao, Tübingen, Uleaborg, Ullapool, Vadodara, Valencia, Valletta, Varanasi, Veracruz, Vila Real, Vinnitsa, Vittoria, Vladimir, Voronezh, Wakayama, Wallasey, Wallsend, Warangal, Weymouth, Winnipeg, Worthing, Würzburg, Xiangfan, Xiangtan, Xinxiang, Yangchow, Yangquan, Yangzhou, Yinchuan, Yin-hsien, Yokohama, Yokosuko, Yorktown, Zakopane, Zanzibar, Zhitomir

09 Adis Abeba, Ahmadabad, Alba Iulia, Albufeira, Aldershot, Algeciras, Allahabad, Amagasaki, Ambleside, Anchorage, Annapolis, Archangel, Asahikawa, Astrakhan, Audenarde, Aylesbury, Bakhtaran, Baltimore, Bangalore, Barcelona, Beersheba, Berbérati, Bethlehem, Bhavnagar, Bialystok, Blackburn,

Blackpool, Bossangoa, Botany Bay, Brunswick, Bydgoszcz, Cambridge, Cartagena, Castlebar, Changchun, Changzhou, Charleroi, Charlotte, Chengchow, Cherbourg, Chernobyl, Chiang Mai, Chihuahua, Choluteca, Chongqing, Chungking, Cleveland, Colwyn Bay, Constance, Constanta, Des Moines, Doncaster, Dordrecht, Dubrovnik, Dudelange, Dumbarton, Dungannon, Dunstable, Eastleigh, Eindhoven, Eskisehir, Esztergom, Fairbanks, Famagusta, Faridabad, Fishguard, Fleetwood, Fortaleza, Fort Worth, Frankfort, Frankfurt, Fremantle, Funabashi, Galveston, Gateshead, Gaziantep, Gippsland, Gold Coast, Gorakhpur, Gravesend, Greenwich, Groningen, Guangzhou, Guarulhos, Guayaquil, Guildford, Hallstatt, Hamamatsu, Harrogate, Haslemere, Helsingør, Heraklion, Hilversum, Hiroshima, Humpty Doo, Hyderabad, Immingham, Innsbruck, Inverness, Ismailiya, Jalandhar, Jamestown, Johnstone, Jönköping, Kagoshima, Kamchatka, Kaohsiung, Karaganda, Karlsruhe, Kawaguchi, Killarney, Kimberley, King's Lynn, Kirkcaldy, Kisangani, Kishinyov, Kitzbühel, Kórinthos, Kozhikode, Krasnodar, Krivoy Rog, Kurashiki, Kuybyshev, Kwang-chow, Lancaster, Las Cruces, Leicester, Lexington, Lichfield, Liverpool, Llangefni, Long Beach, Lowestoft, Lymington, Magdeburg, Mahajanga, Maidstone, Makeyevka, Mamoudzan, Manizales, Mansfield, Maracaibo, Maralinga, Marrakesh, Matsuyama, Melbourne, Middleton, Milwaukee, Monterrey, Moradabad, Morecambe, Mullingar, Nashville, Neuchâtel, Newcastle, Newmarket, Nikolayev, Nuremberg, Ogbomosho, Osnabrück, Palembang, Pamporovo, Perpignan, Peterhead, Pingxiang, Pontianak, Port Natal, Port Sudan, Pressburg, Prestwick, Princeton, Qinghai Hu, Querétaro, Riverside, Rochester, Rotherham, Rotterdam, Rovaniemi, Salisbury, Samarkand, San Miguel, Santa Cruz, Santander, Saragossa, Saskatoon, Shanchung, Sheerness, Sheffield, Sioux City, South Bend, Southport, Southwark, St Andrews, Stavanger, Stavropol, St-Étienne, Stevenage, St-Nazaire, Stockport, Stornoway, St-Quentin, Stranraer, Stuttgart, Sukhothai, Sundsvall, Surakarta, Takamatsu, Takatsuki, Tarragona, Tenkodogo, T'ien-ching, Timisoara, Toamasina, Togliatti, Toowoomba, Trondheim, Tullamore, Ulyanovsk, Vancouver, Velingrad, Vicksburg, Volgograd, Wakefield, Walvis Bay, Waterford, Wiesbaden, Wimbledon, Wolfsburg, Worcester, Wuppertal, Xiangyang, Yaroslavl, Zamboanga, Zaozhuang, Zhengzhou, Zhenjiang, Zrenjanin

10 Alexandria, Baton Rouge, Belize City, Birkenhead, Birmingham, Bridgeport, Bridgwater, Broken Hill, Caernarvon, Caerphilly, Canterbury, Carmarthen, Carnoustie, Carson City, Casablanca, Chandigarh, Charleston, Cheboksary, Chelmsford, Cheltenham, Chenghsien, Chichester, Chittagong, Cienfuegos, Cincinnati, Cluj-Napoca, Coatbridge, Cochabamba, Coimbatore, Colchester, Concepción, Darjeeling, Darlington, Diyarbakir, Dorchester, Düsseldorf, Dzerzhinsk, Eastbourne, El Mansoura, Faisalabad, Felixstowe, Folkestone, Fray Bentos, Galashiels, George Town, Gillingham, Glenrothes, Gloucester, Goose Green, Gothenburg, Gujranwala, Haddington, Harrisburg, Hartlepool, Heidelberg, Hermosillo, Hildesheim, Huntingdon, Huntsville, Jamshedpur, Jingdezhen, Joao Pessoa, Juiz de Fora, Kakopetria, Kalgoorlie, Kansas City, Kenilworth, Khabarovsk, Kilmarnock, Kita-Kyushu, Kompong Som, Lake Placid, Las Piedras, Launceston, Leeuwarden, Letchworth, Linlithgow, Little Rock, Liupanshui, Livingston, Llangollen, Los Angeles, Louisville, Lubumbashi, Luluabourg, Maastricht, Maidenhead, Manchester, Marseilles, Medjugorje, Miami Beach, Monte Carlo, Montego Bay, Montgomery, Montpelier, Mostaganem, Motherwell, Mudanjiang, New Orleans, Nottingham, Nouadhibou, Nova Iguacu, Oranjestad, Oudenaarde, Palmerston, Petersburg, Pittsburgh, Pontefract, Portishead, Portsmouth, Providence, Quezon City, Quinnipiac, Rawalpindi, Regensburg, Sacramento, Sagamihara, San Antonio, San Ignacio, Santa Marta, Santo André, São Gonçalo, Scunthorpe, Sebastopol, Shepparton, Shreveport, Shrewsbury, Simferapol, Sioux Falls, Södertälje, Strasbourg, Sunderland, Sverdlovsk, Talcahuano, Tammerfors, Tananarive, Thunder Bay, Townsville, Trivandrum, Trowbridge, Tsaochuang, Utsunomiya, Valladolid, Valparaíso, Vijayawada, Viña del Mar, Vlissingen, Wadi Medani, Wagga Wagga, Warrington, Washington, Whitehorse, Wilmington, Winchester, Windermere, Winterthur, Wittenberg, Wollongong, Workington, Yogyakarta, Yoshkar Ola, Zaporozhye

11 Aberystwyth, Albuquerque, Antofagasta, Bahía Blanca, Banjarmasin, Basingstoke, Bhilai Nagar, Bognor Regis, Bournemouth, Brandenburg, Bremerhaven, Bridlington, Broadstairs, Brownsville, Bucaramanga, Campo Grande, Carcassonne, Charlestown, Chattanooga, Chelyabinsk, Cherepovets, Cirencester, Cleethorpes, Cockermouth, Cone Island, Conisbrough, Constantine, Cumbernauld, Dar es Salaam, Differdange, Downpatrick, Dunfermline, Enniskillen, Farnborough, Fort William, Francistown, Fraserburgh, Fredericton, Glastonbury, Grangemouth, Guadalajara, Guisborough, Hälsingborg, Helsingborg, Helsingfors, High Wycombe, Johor Baharu, Juan-les Pins, Kaliningrad, Kampong Saom, Karlovy Vary, Kompong Saom, Komsomolosk, Krasnoyarsk, Lianyungang, Londonderry, Lossiemouth, Makhachkala, Mar del Plata, Medicine Hat, Medway Towns, Minneapolis, Montpellier, Narayanganj, Newport News, New York City, Nishinomiya, Northampton, Novosibirsk, Palm Springs, Pointe-Noire, Polonnaruwa, Port Augusta, Porto Alegre, Prestonpans, Punta Arenas, Qinhuangdao, Resistencia, Rockhampton, Rostov-on-Don, Saarbrücken, Scarborough, Southampton, Spanish Town, Springfield, Stourbridge, Szombathely, Tallahassee, Trincomalee, Tselinograd, Vladivostok, Westminster, White Plains, Wu-lu-k'o-mu-shi, Yellowknife, Zhangjiakou

12 Alice Springs, Anuradhapura, Atlantic City, Barquisimeto, Barranquilla, Beverly Hills, Bloemfontein, Buenaventura, Caloocan City, Chesterfield, Christchurch, Ciudad Juárez, East Kilbride, Great Malvern, Higashiosaka, Hubli-Dharwar, Huddersfield, Indianapolis, Jacksonville, Johannesburg, Keetmanshoop, Kota Kinabalu, Kristianstad, Léopoldville, Lisdoonvarna, Loughborough, Luang Prabang, Ludwigshafen, Macclesfield, Magnitogorsk, Mazar-e-Sharif, Milton Keynes, New Amsterdam, Nizhniy Tagil, Novokuznetsk, Oklahoma City, Petaling Jaya, Peterborough, Philadelphia, Pingdingshan, Pointe-à-Pitre, Ponta Delgada, Port Harcourt, Puerto Cortes, Rio de Janeiro, Salt Lake City, San Cristobal, San Francisco, San Pedr Sula, San Sebastian, Santa Barbara Schaffhausen, Shijiazhuang,

Shuangyashan, Sidi bel Abbès, Skelmersdale, South Shields, Speightstown, Stanleyville, St Catherines, Stoke-on-Trent, St Petersburg, Tel Aviv-Jaffa, Tennant Creek, Thessaloníki, Trichinopoly, Ujung Pandang, Villahermosa, West Bromwich, Williamsburg, Winston-Salem

3 Aix-en-Provence, Belo Horizonte, Bobo-Dioulasso, Charlottetown, Ciudad Guayana, Duque de Caxias, Ellesmere Port, Epsom and Ewell, Great Yarmouth, Ho Chi Minh City, Jefferson City, Kidderminster, Kirkcudbright, Kirkintilloch, Leamington Spa, Lytham St Anne's, Middlesbrough, Ordzhonikidze, Port Elizabeth, Portlaoighise, Quezaltenango, Ribeirao Preto, San Bernardino, San Luis Potosí, Semipalatinsk, Sihanoukville, Veliko Turnovo, Virginia Beach, Visakhapatnam, Wolverhampton, Yekaterinburg, Zlatni Pyasaci

4 Andorra-la-Vella, Dnepropetrovsk, Elisabethville, Feira de Santana, Hemel Hempstead, Henley-on-Thames, Louangphrabang, Santiago de Cuba, Shihchiachuang, Stockton-on-Tees, Székesfehérvár, Tunbridge Wells, Ust-Kamenogorsk, Voroshilovgrad

5 Alcalá de Henares, Angra do Heroísmo, Barrow-in-Furness, Burton-upon-Trent, Charlotte Amalie, Charlottesville, Chester-le-Street, Clermont-Ferrand, Colorado Springs, Frankfurt am Main, Netzahaulcoyotl, Nizhniy Novgorod, Palma de Mallorca, Palmerston North, Sáo Joáo de Meriti, Sekondi-Takoradi, Shoubra el-Kheima, Sutton Coldfield, Weston-super-Mare

ee also **Australia; Canada; Ireland; ew Zealand; Russia; United ingdom; United States of America**

city area
2 EC

ivet
5 genet, rasse, zibet **07** genette, nsang, nandine, Viverra **8** mongoose, suricate, toddy cat **9** binturong, delundung, ichneumon, weasel cat **10** paradoxure

ivic
4 city, town **05** local, urban **06** public **7** borough **08** communal **9** community, municipal **2** metropolitan

ivil
3 civ, lay **04** fair, home **05** civic, local, ate **06** polite, public, urbane **7** affable, courtly, refined, secular **8** civilian, communal, domestic, nterior, internal, mannerly, national, obliging, polished, temporal, well-red **09** civilized, community, ompliant, courteous, municipal

---

10 cultivated, respectful **11** complaisant **12** well-mannered **13** accommodating, parliamentary

civilian
03 civ **05** civvy, mufti **07** citizen, gownman **08** gownsman **12** non-combatant

civility
04 tact **06** comity, notice **07** amenity, manners, respect **08** breeding, courtesy, urbanity **09** attention **10** affability, politeness, refinement **11** good manners **12** graciousness, pleasantness **13** courteousness

civilization
06 Kultur, people **07** culture, customs, society **08** progress, urbanity **09** community, education **10** refinement **11** advancement, cultivation, development **12** human society **13** enlightenment **14** sophistication

civilize
04 tame **05** edify **06** polish, refine **07** educate, improve, perfect **08** humanize, instruct **09** cultivate, enlighten, socialize **12** sophisticate

civilized
06 polite, urbane **07** refined **08** advanced, cultured, educated, sensible, sociable **09** courteous, developed **10** cultivated, reasonable **11** enlightened **12** well-mannered **13** sophisticated

civilly
07 courtly **08** mannerly, politely, urbanely **10** obligingly **11** courteously **12** respectfully

clad
06 vested **07** attired, clothed, covered, dressed, wearing

claim
03 ask, bag, own, sue **04** aver, avow, call, hold, kill, need, plea, pose, take **05** cause, clame, exact, right, shout, state **06** affirm, allege, assert, assume, avowal, demand, insist **07** collect, contend, darrain, darrayn, declare, deraign, deserve, pretend, profess, purport, request, require **08** averment, darraign, darraine, maintain, petition, put in for **09** assertion, challenge, darraigne, postulate, privilege **10** allegation, contention, insistence, lay claim to, pretension, profession **11** affirmation, application, declaration, entitlement, requirement, requisition **12** asseveration, be entitled to, have a right to

claimant
06 titler **08** litigant **09** applicant, candidate, pretender, suppliant **10** challenger, petitioner, pretendant, pretendent, suppliant

clairvoyance
03 ESP **09** telepathy **11** second sight **13** psychic powers **14** cryptaesthesia, fortune-telling, hyperaesthesia

---

clairvoyant
04 seer **05** augur **06** oracle **07** diviner, prophet, psychic **08** telepath **09** prophetic, visionary **10** prophetess, soothsayer, telepathic **12** extrasensory **13** fortune-teller

clam
03 Mya **05** cohog **06** quahog **07** quahaug, scallop **08** tridacna **11** black quahog

clamber
04 claw, shin **05** climb, mount, scale **06** ascend, shinny **08** scrabble, scramble, sprackle **09** spraickle

clammy
04 damp, dank **05** close, heavy, moist, muggy, slimy **06** sticky, sweaty, viscid **08** sweating

clamorous
04 loud **05** lusty, noisy, vocal **07** blaring, blatant, riotous **08** blattant, vehement **09** deafening, insistent **10** boisterous, strepitant, tumultuous, uproarious, vociferant, vociferous **11** open-mouthed **12** obstreperous

clamour
03 cry, din, hue **04** bark, rout, urge, utis **05** blare, claim, noise, raird, reird, rumor **06** demand, hubbub, insist, outcry, racket, rumour, uproar **07** brabble, call for, outrage **08** brouhaha, press for, shouting, stramash **09** agitation, commotion, hue and cry **10** complaints **11** vociferance **12** katzenjammer, vociferation **13** ask for noisily

clamp
03 fix **04** grip, heap, hold, vice **05** brace, clasp, press, stack, tread **06** clench, clinch, fasten, secure **07** bracket, squeeze **08** fastener **09** hand-screw, pinchcock, potato pit **10** Denver boot, immobilize **11** immobilizer
• **clamp down on**
04 stop **05** limit **07** confine, control, prevent **08** restrain, restrict, suppress **10** put a stop to **11** crack down on **14** come down hard on

clampdown
04 stop **05** limit **07** control **09** crackdown, restraint **10** prevention **11** restriction, suppression

clan
03 set **04** band, gens, hapu, line, name, race, sect, sept **05** group, horde, house, tribe **06** circle, clique, family, kinred **07** coterie, faction, kindred, society **10** fraternity **11** brotherhood **13** confraternity

See also **Scottish**

clandestine
03 sly **06** closet, covert, hidden, secret, sneaky **07** furtive, private **08** backdoor, backroom, stealthy **09** concealed, underhand **10** behind-door, fraudulent, undercover **11** underground **13** surreptitious

14 cloak-and-dagger **15** under-the-counter

clandestinely
05 slyly **07** on the QT **08** covertly, secretly, sneakily **09** furtively, privately **10** on the quiet, stealthily **12** fraudulently **15** surreptitiously, under the counter

clang
04 bong, peal, ring, toll **05** chime, clank, clash, clink, clunk, klang **06** jangle, timbre **07** clatter, resound **11** reverberate **13** reverberation

clanger
04 boob, flub, goof, slip **05** boner, error, fault, gaffe **06** booboo, cock-up, howler, slip-up, stumer **07** bloomer, blunder, faux pas, mistake **08** solecism **09** oversight **10** inaccuracy **12** indiscretion, misjudgement

clank
04 ring, toll **05** clang, clash, clink, clunk **06** jangle **07** clatter, resound **10** resounding **11** reverberate **13** reverberation

clannish
06 narrow, select **07** cliquey, insular **08** cliquish **09** exclusive, parochial, sectarian **10** unfriendly

clap
03 hit, pat, ray **04** bang, bolt, chop, slap **05** blaze, burst, cheer, crack, flare, flash, shaft, smack, spark, whack **06** streak, strike, wallop **07** acclaim, applaud, ovation **08** applause, handclap, plaudite **11** thunderbolt **15** round of applause, standing ovation

claptrap
03 rot **04** blah, bosh, bull, bunk, guff **05** balls, bilge, hokum, trash, tripe **06** bunkum, drivel, faddle, hot air, piffle **07** baloney, blarney, eyewash, hogwash, rhubarb, rubbish, twaddle **08** blethers, buncombe, cobblers, nonsense, tommyrot **09** gibberish, poppycock **10** codswallop

clarification
05 gloss **10** definition, exposition **11** elucidation, explanation **12** illumination **14** interpretation, simplification

clarify
05 clear, gloss, purge **06** define, filter, purify, refine **07** clear up, explain, resolve **08** simplify, spell out **09** elucidate, make clear, make plain **10** illuminate **11** shed light on **12** throw light on

clarity
08 lucidity **09** chiarezza, clearness, plainness, precision, sharpness **10** definition, simplicity, visibility **11** obviousness **12** explicitness, transparency **15** intelligibility, unambiguousness

clash
03 jar, war **04** bang, feud, slam, snap **05** brush, clang, clank, crash, fight, noise, swash **06** gossip, hurtle, jangle, rattle, scream, strike **07** chatter, clatter, collide, contend, co-occur, grapple, jarring, quarrel, warring, wrangle **08** argument, coincide, conflict, disagree, fall foul, fighting, mismatch, not match, showdown, striking **09** collision, not go with **10** fall foul of **11** altercation, discordance, misalliance **12** be discordant, disagreement, irregularity **13** confrontation, not go together **14** be incompatible, look unpleasant **15** incompatibility

clasp
◇ *containment indicator*
03 hug, pin **04** clip, grip, hasp, hold, hook, tach **05** bosom, catch, grasp, press, slide, spang, tache, unite **06** attach, brooch, buckle, clutch, cuddle, enfold, fasten, preace, prease, tassel **07** agraffe, cling to, connect, embosom, embrace, enclasp, grapple, preasse, squeeze **08** fastener **09** fastening, hair slide, interlock, safety pin **10** infibulate

class
03 set **04** chic, form, kind, race, rank, rate, sort, type, year **05** brand, caste, genre, genus, grade, group, level, order, style, taste **06** course, league, lesson, period, phylum, reckon, sphere, status, stream **07** arrange, lecture, quality, section, seminar, species, teach-in **08** category, classify, division, elegance, grouping, standing, tutorial, workshop **09** designate **10** background, categorize, department, pigeonhole, study group **11** distinction, social order, stylishness **12** denomination, pecking order, social status **14** classification, social division, social standing, sophistication

See also **classification**

classic
04 best, Oaks, true **05** Derby, great, ideal, model, prime, usual **06** finest, simple **07** abiding, ageless, elegant, lasting, regular, St Leger, The Oaks, typical, undying **08** Augustan, enduring, exemplar, immortal, masterly, standard, timeless **09** brilliant, excellent, exemplary, first-rate, prototype **10** archetypal, consummate, definitive, first-class, masterwork **11** established, masterpiece, outstanding, traditional, undecorated, understated **12** paradigmatic, time-honoured **13** authoritative **14** characteristic, quintessential, representative **15** established work, unsophisticated

classical
04 pure **05** Attic, Latin, plain **06** humane, simple **07** concert, elegant, Grecian, refined, serious **08** Hellenic **09** excellent, symphonic **10** harmonious, restrained **11** symmetrical, traditional **12** ancient Greek, ancient Roman

See also **musician**; **singer**

classically
06 purely, simply **07** as a rule, plainly, usually **08** normally **09** elegantly, typically **10** ordinarily, originally **11** customarily **12** harmoniously, historically **13** symmetrically, traditionally

classification
05 group **06** method **07** grading, sorting **08** classing, grouping, taxonomy **10** tabulation **11** arrangement, cataloguing **12** codification, distribution **14** categorization **15** systematization

Classifications of living organisms include:

05 class, genus, order
06 domain, empire, family, phylum
07 kingdom, species
08 division

Kingdoms, domains and empires include:

05 fungi
06 monera, plants
07 animals, archaea
08 bacteria, protista
10 eubacteria, eukaryotes
11 prokaryotes
14 archaebacteria

Classes include:

04 Aves
07 Insecta
08 Amphibia, Bivalvia, Mammalia
09 Arachnida, Bryopsida, Pinopsida
10 Gastropoda, Liliopsida
11 Cephalopoda
12 Malacostraca
13 Magnoliopsida

classify
03 peg **04** file, rank, sort, type **05** class, grade, group, order, range **06** assort, codify, divide **07** arrange, dispose, include, sort out **08** regiment, serotype, stratify, tabulate **09** catalogue **10** categorize, distribute, pigeonhole **11** systematize

classy
04 fine, posh **05** grand, ritzy **06** select, smooth, swanky **07** elegant, stylish **08** gorgeous, superior, up-market **09** exclusive, expensive, exquisite, high-class **13** sophisticated

clatter
03 jar **04** bang **05** clang, clank, clunk, crash **06** gossip, hotter, jangle, rattle, strike **07** blatter, chatter

clause
04 item, part **05** point, rider, salvo **06** phrase **07** adjunct, article, chapter, heading, passage, proviso, section **08** clausula, loophole, particle, tenendum **09** condition, novodamus, paragraph, provision, reddendum **10** subsection **13** specification

claw
3 rip 04 clat, crab, fang, maul, nail, ...ere, tear 05 chela, claut, cloye, graze, ...riff, seize, talon 06 clutch, griffe, ...angle, nipper, pincer, pounce, ...crape, unguis 07 falcula, flatter, ...ripper, scratch 08 lacerate, scrabble ...clapperclaw

clay
3 cam, pug, wax 04 bole, calm, ...aum, glei, gley, loam, lute, marl, pisé, ...lip, soil, tile, till 05 argil, blaes, brick, ...loam, earth, fango 06 blaise, blaize, ...lunch, ground, kaolin 07 kaoline, ...ottery 08 ceramics, cimolite, ...luvium, laterite 09 bentonite
0 lithomarge, meerschaum, plastilina
clay-chalk mixture
4 malm

clean
3 net, new, rub 04 char, even, fair, ...ood, just, neat, nett, pure, tidy, wash, ...ipe 05 blank, crisp, empty, final, ...esh, fully, moral, quite, rinse, scour, ...weep, total, utter, whole 06 chaste, ...ecent, emunge, hollow, honest, ...odest, proper, scrape, simple, ...mooth, soogee, soogie, unused, ...ashed 07 aseptic, elegant, ethical, ...under, perfect, regular, sterile, totally, ...pright 08 clean-cut, cleansed, clear-...ut, complete, decisive, directly, ...ntirely, flawless, graceful, hygienic, ...nnocent, pristine, purified, sanitary, ...moothly, spotless, straight, unerring, ...nmarked, unsoiled, virtuous
9 faultless, guiltless, laundered, ...eputable, righteous, speckless, ...nspotted, unstained, unsullied, ...wholesome 10 above board, ...ntiseptic, completely, conclusive, ...ven-handed, honourable, ...mmaculate, sterilized, unpolluted, ...pstanding 11 appropriate, ...espectable, unblemished, ...ncorrupted, well-defined 12 spick ...nd span, squeaky-clean
3 unadulterated 14 clean as a new ...in, decontaminated, uncontaminated

• **clean out**
3 fay, fey
• **come clean**
5 admit, own up 06 fess up, reveal
7 confess, tell all 11 acknowledge
3 spill the beans

clean-cut
4 neat, tidy, trim 05 fresh, natty, ...mart, terse 06 spruce 07 orderly
1 uncluttered

cleaner
03 vac 04 char 05 daily, wiper
06 Hoover®, Mrs Mop, vacuum
07 Mrs Mopp, orderly 08 charlady
09 charwoman

cleanliness
06 purity 09 cleanness, freshness
10 perfection 12 spotlessness

cleanse
04 pure, wash 05 bathe, clean, clear,
flush, porge, purge, rinse, scour
06 garble, purify 07 absolve, deterge,
launder, mundify 08 absterge, lustrate,
scavenge 09 disinfect, sterilize
12 make free from

cleanser
04 soap 07 cleaner, scourer, solvent
08 purifier 09 detergent 10 soap
powder 12 disinfectant 14 scouring
powder

clear
02 go 03 net, rid 04 earn, fair, fine,
free, full, gain, jump, keen, land, make,
move, neat, nett, open, pass, pure, quit,
sure, tidy, void, wipe 05 allow, bring,
clean, empty, erase, let go, light, lucid,
overt, plain, quick, quite, sharp, sheer,
shift, sunny, vault 06 acquit, bright,
decode, excuse, filter, glassy, go over,
limpid, liquid, loosen, pardon, patent,
permit, pocket, refine, remble,
remove, serene, settle, unclog, unload,
unstop, vacate, vanish, wholly
07 absolve, approve, audible, bring in,
certain, cleanse, evident, express,
fogless, hyaline, justify, logical,
obvious, plainly, precise, release,
through, unblock 08 apparent,
coherent, definite, distinct, evacuate,
evanesce, explicit, get rid of, innocent,
jump over, leap over, liberate, luculent,
luminous, manifest, melt away,
pellucid, positive, pregnant, sanction,
sensible, take away, take home,
undimmed, undulled 09 authorize,
blameless, cloudless, convinced,
decongest, disappear, discharge,
evaporate, exculpate, exonerate,
extricate, guiltless, unblocked,
unclouded, unimpeded, vindicate
10 articulate, colourless, diaphonous,
disengaged, in the clear, perceptive,
pronounced, reasonable, see-through,
unhindered, unscramble, untroubled
11 acquittance, beyond doubt,
conspicuous, crystalline, disentangle,
make a profit, penetrating, perceptible,
translucent, transparent,
unambiguous, unequivocal, well-
defined 12 clear as a bell, crystal-clear,
intelligible, recognizable, twenty-
twenty, unmistakable, unobstructed
13 find not guilty 14 beyond
question, comprehensible, give
permission, give the go-ahead, having
no qualms, understandable,
unquestionable
• **all clear**
09 copacetic, copasetic, kopacetic
• **clear away**
03 mop

• **clear off**
04 quit 06 get out, go away 07 buzz
off, gertcha, push off 08 cheese it, run
along, shove off
• **clear out**
03 get 04 sort, tidy 05 empty, hop it,
leave, scour 06 beat it, depart, get out,
go away, tidy up, vacate 07 get lost,
push off, sort out 08 clear off, shove off,
throw out, withdraw
• **clear up**
03 red 04 fair, redd, sort, tidy
05 crack, order, salve, solve
06 answer, remove 07 clarify, explain,
improve, iron out, resolve, sort out,
unravel 08 brighten 09 elucidate,
liquidate, rearrange 10 become fine,
brighten up, put in order, straighten
11 become sunny, stop raining
12 straighten up 13 straighten out
• **not clear**
02 nl 09 non liquet

clearance
02 OK 03 gap 04 room 05 leave, say-
so, space, sweep 06 margin, moving
07 consent, freeing, go-ahead,
removal 08 clearing, emptying,
headroom, riddance, sanction,
shifting, vacating 09 allowance,
cleansing, unloading 10 demolition,
evacuation, green light, permission,
taking-away 11 endorsement
13 authorization

clear-cut
05 clean, clear, plain, sharp 07 precise
08 definite, distinct, explicit, sharp-
cut, specific 09 trenchant 11 cut and
dried, unambiguous, unequivocal,
well-defined 13 black and white
15 straightforward

clear-headed
04 wise 05 sober 08 rational, sensible
09 practical, realistic 11 intelligent

clearing
03 gap 04 dell 05 glade, slash, space
06 assart 07 opening 08 scouring,
slashing

clearly
04 well 05 plain 06 bright, openly
07 lucidly, plainly 08 markedly,
patently 09 evidently, obviously
10 coherently, distinctly, explicitly,
manifestly, undeniably 11 undoubtedly
12 indisputably, intelligibly,
unmistakably, without doubt
13 conspicuously, incontestably
14 comprehensibly

cleave
◇ *insertion indicator*
03 cut, hew 04 chop, hold, open, part,
rend, rift 05 cling, crack, halve, sever,
share, slice, split, stick, unite 06 adhere,
attach, cohere, divide, pierce, remain,
sunder 07 fissure 08 dissever, disunite,
separate 09 crack open, split open

cleft
◇ *containment indicator*
03 gap, jag 04 rent, rift, riva 05 break,
chasm, chink, cloff, crack, slack, split

06 breach, cranny, parted, sexfid
07 chimney, crevice, divided, fissure, octofid, opening, pharynx
08 cleaving, crevasse, fissured, fracture, scissure **09** bisulcate, quadrifid, septemfid **13** quadripartite

clemency
04 pity **05** mercy **06** lenity
08 humanity, kindness, leniency, mildness, sympathy **10** compassion, generosity, indulgence, moderation, tenderness **11** forbearance, forgiveness, magnanimity
12 mercifulness **15** soft-heartedness

clench
04 grip, grit, hold, seal, shut **05** clasp, close, grasp, press **06** clinch, clutch, double, fasten **07** squeeze **08** double up **12** close tightly **13** press together

clergy
06 church **07** clerics **08** learning, ministry, the cloth **09** churchmen, clergymen, education, the church
10 holy orders, priesthood
11 churchwomen, clergywomen, spiritualty **12** spirituality

clergyman, clergywoman
02 DD, RR **03** Rev **04** dean, imam, papa **05** canon, clerk, padre, rabbi, vicar **06** bishop, cleric, curate, deacon, divine, father, josser, Levite, mother, mullah, parson, pastor, priest, rector
07 diocese, dominie, muezzin, prelate, secular **08** cardinal, chaplain, man of God, minister, Nonjuror, preacher, reverend, sky pilot, spintext, squarson, vartabed **09** churchman, deaconess, presbyter, rural dean **10** arch-priest, prebendary, woman of God
11 churchwoman **12** ecclesiastic
13 man of the cloth **14** superintendent
15 woman of the cloth

clerical
06 filing, office, typing **08** official, pastoral, priestly, reverend
09 canonical, episcopal **10** pen-pushing, sacerdotal **11** keyboarding, ministerial, secretarial, white-collar
14 administrative, ecclesiastical
See also **vestment**

clerk
04 babu **05** baboo **06** circar, notary, priest, scribe, sircar, sirkar, teller, typist, writer **07** actuary, copyist, scholar
08 cursitor, official, Petty Bag, quillman, servitor **09** assistant, clergyman, pen-driver, pen-pusher, secretary **10** book-keeper **11** paper-pusher, protocolist, protonotary, quill-driver **12** prothonotary, receptionist, record-keeper, stenographer
13 account-keeper, administrator, shop-assistant

clever
03 apt **04** able, cute, deft, gleg, keen
05 natty, quick, sharp, smart, witty
06 adroit, artful, brainy, bright, expert, gifted, pretty, shrewd, souple
07 capable, cunning, knowing,

notable, sapient, skilful **08** rational, sensible, talented **09** brilliant, conceited, dexterous, ingenious, inventive, sagacious, spiritual
10 discerning, perceptive
11 intelligent, quick-witted, resourceful, sharp-witted
12 apprehensive **13** knowledgeable

cleverly
04 ably **07** capably **08** artfully, astutely, craftily, expertly, shrewdly
09 skilfully **11** ingeniously
12 discerningly **13** intelligently, knowledgeably, quick-wittedly

cliché
06 truism **07** bromide **08** banality, chestnut **09** platitude **10** stereotype
11 commonplace, old chestnut
15 hackneyed phrase

cliché'd, clichéed
04 dull, worn **05** banal, corny, stale, stock, tired, trite **06** common
07 routine, worn-out **08** overused, time-worn **09** hackneyed
10 overworked, pedestrian, threadbare **11** commonplace, stereotyped, wearing thin **12** run-of-the-mill **13** platitudinous, unimaginative

click
04 beat, snap, snip, tick, twig **05** clack, clink, forge, get on, snick **08** cotton on, get along, hit it off **09** get on well, implosive, make sense **10** understand
11 become clear, suction stop **13** fall into place, suctional stop

client
04 user **05** buyer **06** patron, punter, vassal **07** patient, regular, shopper
08 consumer, customer, hanger-on
09 applicant, dependant, purchaser

clientèle
05 trade, users **06** buyers, market
07 clients, patrons **08** business, regulars, shoppers **09** consumers, customers, following, patronage
10 purchasers

cliff
03 tor **04** clef, crag, face, scar **05** bluff, cleve, scarp, scaur **06** cleeve
08 overhang, rock-face **09** precipice
10 escarpment, promontory

climactic
05 final **07** crucial **08** critical, decisive, exciting **09** paramount

climate
04 mood **05** trend **06** milieu, region, spirit, temper **07** feeling, setting, weather **08** ambience, tendency
10 atmosphere **11** disposition, environment, temperament, temperature

climax
03 top **04** acme, apex, head, peak
06 apogee, finale, height, summit, zenith **08** pinnacle **09** crescendo, highlight, high point **11** catastrophe, culmination

climb
◇ *reversal down indicator*
03 sty, top **04** go up, move, ramp, rise, scan, shin, soar, stie, stir, stye **05** juma, mount, scale, sclim, shift, sklim, speel, swarm **06** ascend, ascent, prusik, shin up **07** clamber, going up, shoot up
08 increase, scramble, surmount
11 herringbone, mountaineer, upward slope **14** uphill struggle
• **climb down**
05 yield **07** concede, descend, retract retreat **08** back down **09** surrender
12 eat your words
• **climbing party**
04 rope

climb-down
07 retreat **08** yielding **09** surrender
10 concession, retraction, withdrawal

climber
03 ivy **04** Jack, Jill, vine **07** speeler
10 nasturtium **11** balloon-vine, honeysuckle, Jack and Jill, mountainee
12 kangaroo vine, morning glory
13 scarlet runner **14** Scotch attorney

clinch
03 pun **04** land, seal **05** clink, close, rivet **06** clench, decide, secure, settle, verify **07** confirm, embrace, grapple
08 conclude **09** determine

cling
03 hug **04** grip, hold **05** clasp, grasp, stick **06** adhere, attach, cleave, clutch, defend, fasten, hold on, shrink
07 embrace, shrivel, stand by, support
08 hold on to, stay true **09** adherence
10 be faithful

clinic
07 doctor's **08** hospital **09** infirmary
10 sanatorium **12** health centre
13 medical centre

clinical
04 cold **05** basic, plain, stark
06 simple **07** austere, medical, patient
08 analytic, detached, hospital
09 impassive, objective, unadorned, unfeeling **10** analytical, antiseptic, impersonal, scientific, uninvolved
11 emotionless, unemotional
12 businesslike **13** disinterested, dispassionate

clinically
09 medically **14** scientifically

clink *see* **prison**

clip
◇ *tail deletion indicator*
03 box, cut, dod, fix, hit, pin **04** crop, cuff, dock, hold, mute, pare, poll, slap, snip, trim **05** cheat, clout, D-ring, graze, jumar, prune, punch, shear, smack, thump, tough, whack
06 attach, crutch, cut off, cut out, fasten, reduce, staple, strike, tingle, wallop **07** Bulldog®, curtail, cutting, embrace, excerpt, extract, passage, pollard, run into, section, shorten, snippet **08** citation, cut short, encircle, fastener, truncate **09** crash into,

quotation **10** abbreviate, clothes-peg, clothes-pin, jumar clamp, overcharge **11** collide with, music holder

See also **cut**

clipping
04 clip **05** scrow, shear, shred **06** paring **07** cutting, excerpt, extract, passage, section, snippet, topiary **08** citation, snipping, trimming **09** quotation

clique
03 set **04** band, clan, club, gang, pack, ring **05** bunch, crowd, group **06** circle, set-out **07** coterie, faction, in-crowd, society **08** grouplet **10** fraternity

cloak
04 cape, coat, hide, mask, pall, rail, robe, veil, wrap **05** blind, cloke, cover, front **06** mantle, screen, shield, shroud **07** conceal, obscure, pretext **08** covering, disguise **10** camouflage

Cloaks include:
04 capa **05** amice, grego, jelab, manta, pilch, sagum, shawl, talma **06** abolla, capote, dolman, domino, poncho, visite **07** chlamys, galabea, galabia, jellaba, korowai, manteel, mantlet, paenula, pelisse, pluvial, rocklay, rokelay, sarafan **08** capuchin, cardinal, djellaba, galabeah, galabiah, gallabea, gallabia, himation, mantelet, mantilla, palliate **09** djellabah, gabardine, gaberdine, gallabeah, gallabiah, gallabieh, gallabiya **10** gallabiyah, gallabiyeh, paludament, roquelaure **11** buffalo robe **12** mousquetaire, paludamentum

clobber
◊ *anagram indicator*
03 hit, kit, zap **04** bash, beat, belt, capa, garb, gear, lick, rout, ruin, slap, sock, togs **05** clout, crush, knock, punch, stuff, thump, whack **06** attack, defeat, hammer, strike, tackle, things, thrash, wallop **07** baggage, conquer, trounce **08** clothing, garments **09** equipment, overpaint, overwhelm **10** belongings **11** bits and bobs, possessions **13** bits and pieces, paraphernalia

clock
03 hit, sit **04** face **05** brood, cluck **06** beetle, notice **07** observe **08** ornament **10** mileometer, timekeeper **11** speedometer

Clocks and watches include:
03 fob, Tim **04** ring, stop **05** alarm, wrist **06** atomic, cuckoo, mantel, quartz **07** bracket, digital, pendant, sundial **08** analogue, carriage, longcase, speaking **09** repeating **10** travelling **11** chronograph, chronometer, grandfather, grandmother

• clock up
03 log **05** reach **06** attain, record **07** achieve, archive, chalk up, notch up **08** register

• round the clock
10 constantly **11** ceaselessly, day and night **12** continuously **15** twenty-four seven, without stopping

clod
04 hunk, lump, mass, mool, pelt, slab **05** block, chunk, clump, glebe, throw, wedge **06** ground

clog
03 dam, jam, log, mud **04** ball, gaum, gorm **05** block, choke, dam up, sabot **06** accloy, ball up, bung up, burden, chopin, galosh, golosh, hamper, hinder, hobble, impede, patten, pester, stop up **07** chopine, clutter, congest, galoche, occlude **08** encumber, obstruct

cloister
05 aisle **06** arcade **07** portico, walkway **08** corridor, pavement **10** ambulatory

cloistered
08 confined, enclosed, hermitic, isolated, secluded, shielded **09** cloistral, insulated, protected, reclusive, sheltered, withdrawn **10** restricted **11** sequestered

close
03 bar, Clo, end, row **04** best, bolt, clog, cork, dear, fail, fill, flop, fold, fuse, good, hard, join, keen, lane, like, lock, mean, mews, mure, near, plug, road, seal, shet, shut, slam, stop, true **05** block, bosom, cease, court, dense, exact, fixed, fuggy, heavy, humid, muggy, pause, place, quiet, solid, tight, union, unite **06** at hand, clinch, decide, direct, ending, fasten, finale, finish, gain on, go bust, hidden, lessen, lock up, loving, marked, narrow, nearby, nearly, not far, packed, secret, secure, settle, shut up, square, sticky, stingy, stop up, strait, street, strict, strong, stuffy, sultry, verify, wind up **07** adjourn, airless, block up, cadence, careful, close by, compact, confirm, cramped, crowded, densely, devoted, grapple, intense, literal, miserly, occlude, padlock, precise, private, similar, terrace, tightly **08** accurate, adjacent, approach, attached, block off, collapse, complete, conclude, conflict, cul-de-sac, detailed, distinct, faithful, familiar, imminent, intimate, junction, obstruct, reserved, reticent, rigorous, round off, secluded, secretly, shut down, stifling, straight, streight, taciturn, thorough **09** adjoining, cessation, close down, close-knit, condensed, courtyard, determine, enclosure, encounter, establish, immediate, impending, niggardly, searching, secretive, terminate, winding-up **10** come closer, comparable, completion, conclusion, dénouement, go bankrupt, hard-fought, methodical, oppressive, quadrangle, sweltering **11** adjournment, approaching, catch up with, culmination, discontinue, draw to an end, get closer to, go to the wall, inseparable, neck and neck, painstaking, suffocating, well-matched **12** a stone's throw, bring to an end, concentrated, confidential, neighbouring, on the brink of, on the verge of, parsimonious, unventilated **13** corresponding, evenly matched, in the vicinity, penny-pinching, unforthcoming **14** cease operating, on your doorstep **15** cease operations, uncommunicative

• close in
04 shut **08** approach, draw near, encircle, surround **10** come nearer

• close to
02 on **04** near, nigh **06** fast by, nearby

• keep close to
03 hug

closed
02 to **04** dark, shut **05** drawn **06** lucken

• not closed
04 agee, ajar, ajee, open

closet
04 zeta **05** press, privy **06** covert, hidden, recess, secret **07** cabinet, confine, furtive, isolate, private, seclude **08** cloister, cupboard, shut away, wardrobe **10** undercover, unrevealed **11** storage room, underground **13** surreptitious

closure
03 gag **05** block **07** cloture, failure, folding **08** blocking, shutdown, shutting **09** stricture, winding-up **10** bankruptcy, guillotine, stopping-up **11** closing-down, obstruction **12** laryngospasm

clot
03 gel, git, mug, nit, set **04** clag, dope, dork, fool, glob, lump, mass, nerd, prat, twit **05** clump, cruor, grume, idiot, twerp, wally **06** curdle, gobbet, lapper, lopper **07** congeal, embolus, plonker, splatch, thicken **08** clotting, coalesce, imbecile, solidify, thrombus **09** blockhead, coagulate **10** bufflehead, nincompoop, thrombosis **11** coagulation, obstruction **12** crassamentum

cloth
03 lap, rag **05** sails, stuff, towel **06** duster, fabric, lappie **07** flannel, textile **08** material **09** churchmen, clergymen, dishcloth, facecloth, the church, the clergy **10** floorcloth, holy orders, upholstery **11** churchwomen, clergywomen, the ministry

See also **fabric**

• measure of cloth
03 ell, end

- **piece of cloth**
03 lap, rag **04** fent, gair, pane, sash
05 clout, godet, lapje **06** lappie
07 remnant

clothe
03 rig **04** coat, cour, deck, gird, robe,
vest, wrap **05** cover, drape, dress,
endew, endue, equip, habit, indew,
indue, put on **06** attire, carpet,
emboss, enrobe, fit out, invest, outfit
07 apparel, bedizen, blanket, envelop,
garment, overlay, vesture **08** accoutre
09 caparison

clothes, clothing
03 kit **04** drag, duds, garb, gear, togs,
wear, weed **05** braws, claes, dress, get-
up **06** attire, outfit **07** apparel, clobber,
costume, raiment, threads, toggery,
uniform, vesture **08** cast-offs, clothing,
dressing, garments, glad rags, wardrobe
09 trousseau, vestiture, vestments
11 habiliments, hand-me-downs

See also **boot**; **cloak**; **coat**; **dress**;
footwear; **hat**; **headdress**; **jacket**;
scarf; **vestment**

Clothes include:

02 gi
03 aba, boa, bra, fur, gie, obi, PJs, tie,
top
04 501s®, abba, belt, body, buff, capa,
cape, coat, furs, gown, kilt, maud,
midi, mink, mitt, muff, rami, ruff,
sack, sari, sash, slip, slop, sock, spat,
suit, sulu, toga, toge, veil, vest, wrap
05 abaya, burka, cloak, cords, dhoti,
dress, frock, glove, ihram, jeans,
kanzu, Levis®, lungi, pants, parka,
ruana, scarf, shawl, shift, shirt,
shrug, skirt, smock, stole, teddy,
thong, tunic
06 basque, bikini, blouse, bodice,
boorka, bow-tie, boxers, braces,
briefs, caftan, corset, cravat,
denims, dirndl, fleece, garter,
girdle, jersey, jubbah, jumper,
kaross, kimono, mitten, poncho,
sacque, samfoo, sarong, shorts,
slacks, tabard, tights, T-shirt
07 catsuit, crop top, doublet, g-string,
hosiery, jimjams, leotard, muffler,
necktie, nightie, overall, panties,
pyjamas, singlet, spattee, sweater,
tank top, twin-set, uniform, vest
top, wet suit, yashmak, Y-fronts
08 bathrobe, bedsocks, breeches,
camisole, cardigan, culottes,
earmuffs, flannels, guernsey,
hipsters, hot pants, jodhpurs,
jumpsuit, leggings, lingerie,
negligee, pashmina, pinafore, polo-
neck, pullover, raincoat, swimsuit,
tee-shirt, trousers
09 balaclava, bed-jacket, brassière,
coveralls, dress suit, dungarees, hair
shirt, housecoat, jockstrap, mini
skirt, outerwear, pantihose,
petticoat, plus-fours, polo shirt,
salopette, separates, shahtoosh,
shell suit, Sloppy Joe, stockings,
tracksuit, underwear, waistcoat
10 boiler suit, Capri pants,
cummerbund, dinner-gown,
drainpipes, dress-shirt, flying suit,
leg-warmers, lounge suit,
nightdress, nightshirt, romper suit,
rugby shirt, string vest, suspenders,
sweat-shirt, turtle-neck,
underpants
11 bell-bottoms, boiled shirt, boxer-
shorts, leisure suit, morning suit,
pencil-skirt, thermal vest, trouser
suit
12 body stocking, camiknickers,
divided-skirt, dressing-gown,
evening-dress, palazzo pants,
pedal-pushers, shirtwaister
13 Bermuda shorts, cycling shorts,
liberty bodice, pinafore skirt,
shalwar-kameez, suspender belt
14 bathing-costume, combat trousers,
double-breasted, French knickers,
jogging bottoms, single-breasted,
swimming trunks, three-piece suit
15 swimming costume

- **plain clothes**
05 mufti
- **shabby clothes**
03 tat

cloud
03 dim, fog **04** blur, dull, mist, puff,
rack, veil, weft **05** chill, cover, shade
06 billow, darken, defame, mantle,
muddle, shadow, shroud **07** confuse,
eclipse, obscure **08** dullness,
woolpack **09** obfuscate
10 overshadow

Clouds include:

06 cirrus, nimbus
07 cumulus, stratus
10 mare's-tails
11 altocumulus, altostratus
12 cirrocumulus, cirrostratus,
cumulonimbus, nimbostratus
13 fractocumulus, fractostratus,
stratocumulus

cloudless
03 dry **04** fair, fine **05** clear, sunny
06 bright **08** pleasant **09** unclouded

cloudy
01 c **03** dim **04** dark, dull, grey, hazy
05 foggy, heavy, milky, misty, muddy,
murky, vague **06** blurry, gloomy,
leaden, opaque, sombre **07** blurred,
muddled, obscure, sunless
08 confused, lowering, nebulous,
nubilous, overcast **10** indistinct

clout
03 box, hit **04** blow, cuff, pull, slap,
slug, sock **05** patch, power, punch,
smack, thump, whack **06** muscle,
strike, wallop, weight **07** garment
08 prestige, standing **09** authority,
influence

cloven
05 cleft, split **07** divided **08** bisected

clown
04 dork, fool, geek, jerk, jest, joke,
nerd, twit, zany **05** antic, chuff, comic,
idiot, joker, ninny, twerp, wally
06 antick, august, chough, dimwit,
jester, joskin, nitwit, Pompey, rustic
07 anticke, antique, auguste, buffoon,
bumpkin, Costard **08** comedian,
dipstick, gracioso, imbecile, numskull
09 blockhead, grotesque, harlequin,
muck about, patchocke, Whiteface
10 act the fool, fool around, goof
around, mess around, nincompoop,
patchcocke, Touchstone **11** carpet
clown, merry-andrew, play the fool
12 act foolishly **13** pickle-herring

Clowns include:

04 Bozo, Coco, Hobo, Joey
05 Tramp
07 Pierrot
08 Grimaldi, Owl-glass, Trinculo
09 Owle-glass
10 Howleglass, Owlspiegle
14 Joseph Grimaldi

cloying
04 icky **06** sickly **07** choking, fulsome
08 luscious **09** excessive, oversweet,
sickening **10** disgusting, nauseating

club
03 hit, set **04** bash, beat **05** bunch,
clout, group, guild, order, union
06 batter, beat up, circle, clique,
fascio, league, priest, pummel, strike
07 chapter, clobber, combine,
company, society, sorosis **08** hetairia
09 auxiliary **10** federation, fraternity,
sisterhood **11** association,
brotherhood, combination, free-and-
easy **12** organization **13** life-preserver

See also **football**; **golf club**

Clubs include:

03 bar, bat
04 cosh, mace, patu, polt
05 bandy, billy, caman, nulla, staff,
stick, waddy
06 cudgel, hurley
07 bourdon
08 bludgeon, trunnion
09 blackjack, truncheon
10 knobkerrie, nulla-nulla
12 shinty-stick

Club types include:

03 fan, job
04 boat, book, glee, golf
05 disco, field, goose, night, slate, strip,
yacht, youth
06 bridge, health, social, tennis
07 cabaret, country, singles
09 warehouse
10 investment
11 discotheque
12 Darby and Joan

Club names include:

03 MCC, RAC, Ski
04 Arts, Turf
05 Buck's, Naval
06 Alpine, Cotton, Drones, Jockey,
Kennel, Kitcat, Pratt's, Queen's,
Reform, Rotary, Savage, Savile,
United, White's

7 Almack's, Authors', Boodle's, Brooks's, Canning, Carlton, Country, Farmers, Garrick, Groucho, Kiwanis, Leander, Railway, Variety
8 Hell-fire, National, Oriental, Portland
9 Athenaeum, Beefsteak, East India, Green Room, Lansdowne, Wig and Pen
0 Caledonian, City Livery, Crockford's, Flyfishers', Hurlingham, Oddfellows, Roehampton, Travellers
1 Army and Navy, Arts Theatre, Chelsea Arts
2 Anglo-Belgian, City of London, London Rowing, New Cavendish, Thames Rowing
3 Royal Air Force
4 American Women's, City University
5 National Liberal, Royal Automobile, Victory Services

club together
6 chip in **09** give money
0 contribute, join forces **12** share the cost **14** have a whip-round
in the club *see* **pregnant**

lubhouse
2 ch **14** nineteenth hole

lubs
1 C
jack of clubs
3 pam

lue
3 tip **04** hint, idea, lead, sign **05** fix, tip, light, trace **06** clavis, notion, thread, tip-off **07** inkling, pointer **8** evidence, signpost **09** master-key, suspicion **10** indication, intimation, suggestion

lueless
4 dumb **05** dense, thick **06** stupid **8** helpless, ignorant **09** unlearned **0** uninformed, unschooled **11** not all there, uninitiated **13** inexperienced

lump
3 lot, mot **04** beat, blow, clot, knot, mass, mott, plod, thud, tuft, tump **5** amass, bluff, bunch, clomp, group, motte, plump, stamp, stomp, thump, ramp **06** bundle, lumber, spinny, rudge **07** cluster, spinney, stumble, thicket, tussock **10** accumulate, collection **11** agglutinate **2** accumulation **13** agglomeration, agglutination

lumsy
◊ anagram indicator
3 ham **04** rude **05** bulky, crude, Dutch, gawky, heavy, hulky, inept, booby, rough, squab **06** clunky, gauche, oafish, thumby, wooden **7** awkward, chuckle, hulking, ill-made, spastic, uncouth, unhandy **8** bungling, clumping, tactless, ungainly, unheppen, unwieldy **09** all thumbs, ham-fisted, ham-handed, lumbering, maladroit, shapeless, two-fisted, unskilful **10** blundering,

cack-handed, cumbersome, Dutch-built, kack-handed, ungraceful, unhandsome **11** heavy-handed, insensitive **12** hippopotamic, unmanageable **13** accident-prone, chuckle-headed, hippopotamian, unco-ordinated **14** banana-fingered

cluster
03 bob **04** band, knot, mass, tuft **05** batch, bunch, clump, crowd, flock, group, plump, strap, truss **06** gather, huddle, raceme **07** collect, panicle **08** assemble, assembly **09** gathering **10** assemblage, assortment, collection, congregate, racemation **11** constellate **12** come together **13** agglomeration, group together, inflorescence

clustered
06 massed **07** bunched, grouped **08** gathered **09** assembled, glomerate **11** agglomerate

clutch
◊ *containment indicator*
03 set **04** claw, grab, grip, hold, jaws, sway **05** brood, catch, clasp, claws, grasp, gripe, group, hands, hatch, mercy, power, seize **06** clench, graple, number, snatch **07** claucht, claught, cling to, control, custody, embrace, grapple, gripper, keeping, setting, sitting **08** dominion, hang on to, hatching **09** get hold of **10** incubation, possession, take hold of

clutter
04 fill, mess, stir **05** chaos, cover, noise, strew **06** jumble, litter, mess up, midden, muddle **07** scatter **08** disarray, disorder, encumber **09** confusion, make a mess **10** make untidy, untidiness **12** fill untidily

coach
03 bus, cab, car, gig **04** coch, cram, drag, post, trap **05** drill, prime, teach, train, tutor, wagon **06** fiacre, hansom, landau, mentor, school **07** droshky, grinder, hackney, minibus, prepare, railbus, rattler, tally-ho, teacher, trainer **08** barouche, brougham, carriage, educator, instruct, motor-bus **09** battlebus, buffet car, cabriolet, charabanc, Greyhound **10** four-in-hand, griddle car, instructor, motor-coach, répétiteur **12** express coach
See also **carriage**

coagulate
03 gel, ren, rin, run, set **04** cake, clot, melt **06** curdle **07** clotted, clotter, congeal, curdled, thicken **08** solidify

coagulation
08 clotting **10** congealing, thickening **11** solidifying

coal
03 jet, jud, nut **04** char, jeat, smut **05** dross, ember, small **06** cinder, splint **07** lignite **10** anthracite **13** black diamonds
• **coal dust**
04 coom, culm, duff

• **coal scuttle**
03 hod **09** purdonium
• **coal yard**
03 ree **04** reed

coalesce
03 mix **04** fuse, join **05** blend, merge, unite **06** cohere, commix **07** combine **09** affiliate, commingle, integrate **10** amalgamate **11** consolidate, incorporate **12** join together

coalescence
06 fusion, merger **07** mixture **08** blending **09** immixture **11** affiliation, combination, integration **12** amalgamation, concrescence **13** consolidation, incorporation

coalition
04 bloc **05** union **06** fusion, league, merger **07** compact, joining **08** alliance **10** federation **11** affiliation, association, combination, confederacy, conjunction, integration, partnership **12** amalgamation **13** confederation

coarse
03 ham **04** base, blue, rank, rude **05** bawdy, broad, brute, crass, crude, gross, hairy, harsh, lumpy, rough, rudas, scaly **06** blowsy, blowzy, brutal, common, earthy, incult, ribald, ribaud, rugged, shaggy, smutty, uneven, vulgar **07** abusive, boorish, bristly, loutish, obscene, prickly, raunchy, rybauld, uncivil **08** gorblimy, immodest, impolite, improper, indecent, inferior, porterly, unbolted **09** gorblimey, off-colour, offensive, unrefined **10** indelicate, unfinished, unpolished, unpurified **11** foul-mouthed, ill-mannered, unprocessed

coarsely
06 rudely **07** bawdily, crudely, roughly **08** ruggedly, unevenly, vulgarly **09** boorishly, loutishly, obscenely **10** immodestly, impolitely, improperly, indecently **11** irregularly, offensively

coarsen
04 dull **05** blunt **06** deaden, harden **07** roughen, thicken **08** indurate **11** desensitize

coarseness
04 smut **06** raunch **07** crudity, hoggery **08** ribaldry **09** bawdiness, hairiness, immodesty, indecency, obscenity, roughness, vulgarism, vulgarity **10** crassitude, earthiness, indelicacy, ruggedness, smuttiness, unevenness **11** grossièreté, prickliness **12** irregularity **13** offensiveness

coast
04 cost, sail, side, taxi **05** beach, coste, drift, glide, limit, shore, slide, terms **06** border, cruise, region, strand **07** footing, seaside **08** littoral, seaboard, seashore **09** coastline, direction, foreshore, freewheel
• **coast road**
04 prom

coaster
04 grab **05** doily, doyly, smack
07 beermat

coat
04 cake, daub, film, hair, hide, mack, pave, pelt, skin, wool **05** apply, cover, glaze, layer, paint, put on, quote, sheet, skirt, smear **06** clothe, enamel, finish, mantle, spread, veneer **07** coating, encrust, overlay, plaster, put over, varnish **08** cladding, covering, laminate, pellicle **10** integument, lamination

Coats include:

03 box, car, fur, mac
04 baju, buff, cape, jack, jump, maxi, midi, over, pink, rain, sack, tail, warm
05 acton, cimar, cloak, cymar, drape, dress, frock, gilet, great, grego, jupon, lammy, loden, parka, sayon, wamus
06 achkan, Afghan, anorak, Basque, blazer, bolero, cagoul, covert, dolman, duffel, fleece, jacket, jerkin, kagool, kagoul, kirtle, lammie, poncho, reefer, riding, sacque, sports, tabard, taberd, trench, tuxedo, Zouave
07 Barbour®, blanket, blouson, cagoule, cutaway, kagoule, Mae West, matinée, morning, overall, snorkel, surtout, swagger, vareuse, zamarra, zamarro
08 Burberry®, camisole, gambeson, haqueton, mackinaw, sherwani
09 bed jacket, gabardine, gaberdine, hacqueton, macintosh, Mao-jacket, newmarket, pea-jacket, petticoat, redingote, shortgown
10 body-warmer, bumfreezer, bush jacket, carmagnole, claw-hammer, Eton jacket, flak jacket, half-kirtle, life jacket, mackintosh, mess jacket, roundabout, windjammer
11 biker jacket, puffa jacket, shell jacket, swallowtail, Windbreaker®, windcheater
12 bomber jacket, combat jacket, dinner jacket, donkey jacket, lumberjacket, monkey jacket, Prince Albert, pyjama jacket, safari jacket, sports jacket, straitjacket
13 hacking jacket, matinee jacket, Norfolk jacket, reefing-jacket
14 shooting jacket

coating
03 fur **04** coat, film, skin, wash **05** crust, glaze, layer, sheet **06** crusta, enamel, finish, patina, resist, slough, veneer **07** blanket, dusting, overlay, varnish, washing **08** covering, membrane **10** colourwash, lamination, pebbledash

coax
03 pet **04** draw, wile **05** carny, tempt **06** allure, cajole, carney, entice, fleech, humour, induce, soothe **07** beguile, cuittle, flatter, wheedle, win over **08** blandish, collogue, get round, inveigle, persuade, soft-soap, talk into,

win round **09** sweet-talk, whillywha **10** whillywhaw **11** prevail upon

cobalt
02 Co

cobber *see* friend

cobble
04 pave
• **cobble together**
07 knock up **09** improvise **11** make quickly, make roughly, put together **13** throw together **14** prepare quickly, prepare roughly, produce quickly, produce roughly

cobbler
04 snab, snob **05** sutor **06** cosier, cozier, soutar, souter, sowter

cobblers *see* rubbish

cobra
03 asp **04** naga, Naia, Naja **05** aspic **09** hamadryad

cocaine
01 C **04** blow, coke, snow **05** candy, crack **07** charlie, crystal **08** freebase **09** nose candy, ready-wash **10** white stuff

cock
03 dog, tap, tip **04** bend, lift, tilt **05** capon, henny, point, raise, slant, strut **07** chicken, gobbler, incline, rooster, swagger **08** cockerel, nonsense, shake-bag **10** bubbly-jock, roadrunner **11** chanticleer, game-chicken
• **cock up**
◇ *anagram indicator*
04 hash, muff, ruin **05** bodge, farce, fluff **06** bungle, foul up, mess up, muck up **07** blunder, screw up **08** shambles **11** make a hash of, make a mess of

cockeyed
04 awry, daft **05** askew, barmy, crazy, tipsy **06** absurd **07** crooked **08** lopsided **09** half-baked, ludicrous, senseless, skew-whiff **11** nonsensical **12** asymmetrical, preposterous

cockily
08 cheekily **10** impudently, insolently **13** impertinently **15** disrespectfully

Cockney
◇ *dialect indicator*
04 'Arry **06** 'Arriet **09** Londonese **10** pearly king **11** pearly queen

cocksure
04 vain **05** brash, cocky **08** arrogant **09** conceited **10** swaggering **11** egotistical, self-assured, swell-headed **13** overconfident, self-confident, self-important, swollen-headed

cocktail
◇ *anagram indicator*

Cocktails include:

04 Sour
05 Bronx
06 eggnog, Gimlet, Mai tai, mojito, Rickey, Rob Roy

07 Bellini, Collins, Martini®, negroni, pink gin, Sazerac®, Sidecar, Slammer, Stinger
08 Acapulco, Brown Cow, Bullshot, Daiquiri, Pink Lady, salty dog, snowball
09 buck's fizz, Kir Royale, long vodka, Manhattan, Margarita, Rusty Nail, Sea Breeze, whisky mac, White Lady
10 Bloody Mary, blue lagoon, Caipirinha, Horse's Neck, margharita, Moscow Mule, piña colada, Tom Collins, whisky sour
11 black velvet, gin-and-tonic, gloom raiser, Screwdriver
12 Black Russian, Cosmopolitan, Old Fashioned, White Russian
13 Planter's Punch
14 American Beauty, Singapore Sling, tequila slammer, Tequila Sunrise
15 Brandy Alexander

See also **liqueur**; **spirits**

cocky
04 pert, vain **05** brash, perky **06** bouncy **08** arrogant, cocksure, jumped-up **09** bumptious, conceited, hubristic **10** swaggering **11** egotistical, self-assured **13** overconfident, self-confident, self-important, swollen-headed

cocoon
03 pod **04** wrap **05** cover **06** defend, dupion, swathe **07** cushion, envelop, isolate, protect **08** cloister, insulate, preserve **11** overprotect

coddle
03 pet **04** baby **05** spoil **06** cosher, cosset, humour, pamper **07** indulge, protect **11** mollycoddle, overprotect

code
◇ *anagram indicator*
03 law **04** laws **05** codex, fuero, Morse, rules, signs **06** cipher, codify, custom, cypher, ethics, morals, system, volume **07** bar code, conduct, letters, manners, numbers, symbols, zip code **08** morality, postcode, practice **09** etiquette, iddy-umpty, local code, Morse code **10** convention, cryptogram, postal code, principles **11** cryptograph, machine code, regulations **12** dialling code, national code **13** secret message, secret writing **14** secret language

codify
05 group, order **06** digest **07** marshal, sort out **08** classify, organize **09** catalogue **11** systematize

coerce
05 bully, drive, force **06** compel, lean on **07** dragoon **08** bludgeon, browbeat, bulldoze, pressure, railroad, threaten, use force **09** constrain, pressgang, strongarm **10** intimidate, pressurize **14** put the screws on

coercion
04 heat **05** force **06** duress **07** duresse, threats **08** big stick,

bullying, pressure **09** restraint
10 compulsion, constraint **11** arm-
twisting, browbeating **12** direct action,
intimidation

coffee
03 joe

Coffee roasts and blends include:

04 Java
05 decaf
06 filter, ground, Kenyan
07 Arabica, instant
09 Colombian, dark roast
10 Costa Rican, light roast, percolated
11 French roast
12 Blue Mountain
13 decaffeinated

Coffees include:

05 black, Irish, latte, milky, Mocha,
white
06 filter, Gaelic
07 Turkish
08 café noir, espresso
09 Americano, cafetière, demitasse
10 café au lait, café filtre, cappuccino
11 skinny latte

• coffee house
04 cafe, caff

coffer
03 ark, box **04** case, cash, safe
05 chest, funds, hoard, means,
money, store, trunk **06** assets, casket,
wealth **07** backing, capital, coffret,
finance, lacunar **08** moneybox,
treasury **09** resources, strongbox
10 repository

coffin
03 box **04** kist **05** flask, shell
06 casket, larnax **11** sarcophagus
12 pine overcoat, wooden kimono
14 wooden overcoat

cogency
05 force, power **06** weight
07 potency, urgency **08** strength
09 influence **12** forcefulness,
plausibility **13** effectiveness

cogent
06 potent, strong, urgent **07** weighty
08 forceful, forcible, powerful,
pregnant **09** effective **10** compelling,
conclusive, convincing, persuasive
11 influential **12** irresistible,
unanswerable

cogently
08 forcibly, potently, strongly, urgently
10 forcefully, powerfully **11** effectively
12 compellingly, conclusively,
convincingly, persuasively

cogitate
04 mull, muse **06** ponder **07** reflect
08 consider, meditate, mull over,
ruminate **09** cerebrate **10** deliberate
11 contemplate, think deeply

cognate
03 cog **04** akin **05** alike **06** agnate,
allied, kinred **07** kindred, related,
similar **09** analogous, conjugate,

connected **10** affiliated, associated,
congeneric **11** consanguine
13 corresponding

cognition
06 reason **07** insight **08** learning,
thinking **09** awareness, knowledge,
reasoning **10** perception
11 discernment, rationality
12 apprehension, intelligence
13 comprehension, consciousness,
enlightenment, understanding

cognizance
• take cognizance of
06 accept, regard **09** recognize
11 acknowledge **12** take notice of
13 become aware of

cognizant
05 aware **06** versed **07** witting
08 acknowne, apprised, familiar,
informed **09** conscious
10 acquainted, conversant
13 knowledgeable

cohabit
03 bed **06** occupy **07** company, shack
up **08** live with **09** live in sin, live tally
12 live together **13** sleep together

cohere
04 bind, fuse, hold **05** add up, agree,
cling, stick, unite **06** adhere, square
07 combine **08** coalesce
09 harmonize, make sense
10 correspond **11** consolidate **12** be
consistent, hang together, hold
together

coherence
05 sense, union, unity **07** harmony
09 agreement, congruity, connexion
10 connection, consonance, logicality
11 concordance, consistency
14 correspondence

coherent
05 clear, lucid **07** logical, orderly
08 joined-up, rational, reasoned,
sensible **09** connected, organized
10 articulate, consistent, meaningful,
systematic **11** well-planned
12 intelligible **14** comprehensible,
well-structured

cohesion
05 sense, union, unity, whole
07 harmony **09** agreement
10 connection, solidarity
11 consistency **12** togetherness
14 correspondence

cohesive
05 close **06** joined, united
08 coherent, together **09** connected,
tenacious **10** continuous
12 interrelated

cohort
03 lot, set **04** band, body, mate, unit
05 batch, buddy, class, group, squad,
troop **06** column, legion **07** bracket,
brigade, company, partner
08 category, division, follower,
myrmidon, regiment, sidekick,
squadron **09** assistant, associate,
companion, supporter **10** accomplice,

contingent **11** combination
14 categorization, classification

coil
04 clew, clue, curl, fake, fank, fuss,
hank, loop, ring, roll, turn, wind
05 bight, choke, helix, noise, round,
skein, snake, spire, twine, twirl, twist,
whorl, wring **06** bought, hubbub,
spiral, toroid, tumult, wreath, writhe
07 entwine, primary, rouleau, wreathe
08 solenoid, volution **09** convolute,
corkscrew **11** convolution

coin
04 bean, cash, cast, dump, mint
05 forge, money, piece, quoin, stamp
06 change, create, devise, invent,
make up, silver, specie, strike **07** dream
up, produce, think up **08** brockage,
conceive, hard cash **09** fabricate,
formulate, hard money, neologize,
originate **10** lucky-piece
11 cornerstone, loose change, small
change
See also **currency**

Coins include:

02 as, at, xu
03 bit, bob, cob, dam, écu, esc, fen,
hao, joe, mag, mil, mna, moy, ore,
pul, pya, rap, sen, sol, sou, ure, zuz
04 anna, buck, cent, chon, dime, doit,
duro, fals, fils, jane, jiao, joey, kuru,
lion, lwei, maik, make, merk, mina,
mite, mule, obol, para, paul, peni,
quid, real, rial, ryal, sent, tael, zack
05 angel, baisa, bodle, brock, brown,
butut, conto, copec, crown, ducat,
eagle, gerah, gopik, groat, khoum,
kopek, laari, lepta, livre, louis,
mopus, noble, obang, paolo,
pence, penny, piece, pound, royal,
scudo, scute, stamp, taler, thebe,
unite
06 aureus, bezant, boddle, copeck,
copper, denier, dirham, dollar,
double, escudo, florin, guinea,
hansel, kopeck, nickel, obolus,
pagoda, pesewa, satang, sequin,
stater, talent, tanner, thaler
07 austral, carolus, centavo, centime,
centimo, chetrum, crusado,
drachma, guilder, ha'penny,
jacobus, moidore, Pfennig, piastre,
pistole, pollard, quarter, sextant,
solidus, spanker
08 denarius, doubloon, ducatoon,
farthing, Groschen, half anna, half
mark, imperial, louis d'or, millième,
napoleon, new penny, picayune,
qindarka, sesterce, shilling,
sixpence, solidare, stotinka, ten
pence, two pence, two pound
09 centesimo, dandiprat, five pence,
gold crown, gold penny, half-
crown, half groat, halfpenny, pound
coin, sovereign, yellow-boy
10 broadpiece, fifty pence, half florin,
half guinea, krugerrand, sestertius
11 bonnet-piece, double eagle,
sixpenny bit, spade guinea, twenty
pence, twopenny bit

12 antoninianus, silver dollar, two pound coin
13 brass farthing, half sovereign, quarter dollar, sixpenny piece, ten pence piece, tenpenny piece, threepenny bit, two pence piece, twopenny piece
14 five pence piece
15 fifty pence piece, threepenny piece

• **counterfeit coin**
03 rag **04** shan, slip **05** shand
06 doctor, duffer, stumer
• **material for coin**
04 flan
• **supposed coin**
03 moy

coincide
05 agree, clash, match, tally **06** accord, concur, square **07** coexist **09** be the same, harmonize **10** correspond
11 synchronize **14** happen together

coincidence
04 luck, step **05** clash, fluke
06 chance **08** accident, clashing, conflict, fortuity, synastry
11 coexistence, concurrence, conjunction, consilience, correlation, eventuality, serendipity, synchronism
12 simultaneity **13** synchronicity
14 correspondence
15 synchronization

coincident
04 like **05** alike, close **07** related, similar, the same **09** in harmony
10 coexisting, coinciding, comparable, concurrent, consistent, equivalent
11 coterminous, in agreement
12 conterminous, simultaneous
13 corresponding
15 contemporaneous

coincidental
05 lucky **06** casual, chance, flukey
09 unplanned **10** accidental, fortuitous **13** serendipitous, unintentional

coincidentally
07 luckily **08** by chance
12 accidentally **15** unintentionally

coke *see* **cocaine**

cold
01 c **03** ice, icy, raw **04** brrr, cool, dead, jeel, keen, numb, rimy, rume, snow
05 agued, aloof, bleak, cauld, chill, fremd, fresh, frore, frost, gelid, nippy, parky, polar, rheum, stony **06** arctic, biting, bitter, brumal, chilly, frigid, frosty, frozen, numbed, remote, winter, wintry **07** brumous, callous, catarrh, chilled, cutting, distant, glacial, hostile, ice-cold, iciness, rawness, shivery, unmoved **08** clinical, coldness, coolness, freezing, lukewarm, reserved, Siberian, uncaring, unheated
09 chillness, frigidity, heartless, repulsive, unfeeling **10** chilliness, Decemberly, impersonal, phlegmatic, spiritless, unfriendly **11** Decemberish, indifferent, insensitive, passionless, standoffish, unemotional, unexcitable

12 antagonistic, unresponsive
13 unsympathetic **15** undemonstrative
• **cold and wet**
04 sour

cold-blooded
05 cruel **06** brutal, savage **07** callous, inhuman **08** barbaric, pitiless, ruthless
09 barbarous, heartless, merciless, unfeeling **10** iron-headed
14 poikilothermal, poikilothermic

cold-hearted
04 cold **06** flinty, unkind **07** callous, inhuman **08** detached, uncaring
09 heartless, unfeeling **10** iron-headed **11** indifferent, insensitive
12 stony-hearted **13** unsympathetic
15 uncompassionate

coldly
09 callously **11** heartlessly, unfeelingly
13 insensitively, unemotionally

colic
03 bot **04** bott **05** batts **10** mulligrubs

collaborate
04 join **05** unite **06** assist, betray, team up **07** collude **08** conspire **09** co-operate **10** fraternize, join forces
11 participate, turn traitor, work jointly
12 work together **13** associate with, combine forces **14** work as partners

collaboration
05 union **08** alliance, teamwork
09 collusion **10** conspiring
11 association, co-operation, joint effort, partnership **12** fraternizing
13 participation **14** combined effort

collaborator
07 partner, traitor **08** betrayer, colluder, co-worker, quisling, renegade, teammate, turncoat
09 assistant, associate, colleague
10 accomplice **11** conspirator, fraternizer **12** fellow worker

collapse
◊ *anagram indicator*
03 rot **04** blow, bust, fail, fall, flop, fold, ruin, sink **05** break, close, faint, slump, swoon **06** attack, cave in, cave-in, fall in, finish, fold up, go bung, tumble
07 burst-up, crack up, crumble, crumple, debacle, deflate, failure, founder, give way, pancake, pass out, sinking, subside **08** black out, blackout, downfall, fainting, fall down, flake out, keel over **09** break down, breakdown, come apart, fall about, fall apart, falling-in, giving way
10 concertina, foundering, go to pieces, passing-out, subsidence
11 come to an end, coming apart, falling-down, fall through, go to the wall, keeling-over, lose control
12 disintegrate, fall to pieces **13** come to nothing, loss of control
14 disintegration, falling-through, have a breakdown **15** falling to pieces

collar
03 bag, nab **04** band, bust, grab, nick, ring, stop **05** catch, seize **06** arrest,

haul in **07** capture **08** neckband
09 apprehend

03 dog
04 Eton, flea, roll, ruff, wing
05 horse, ox-bow, shawl, steel, storm, whisk
06 bertha, choker, collet, gorget, jampot, rabato, rebato
07 brecham, partlet, rebater, stick-up, tie-neck, vandyke
08 carcanet, clerical, granddad, mandarin, Peter Pan, polo neck, rabatine, turn-down
09 holderbat, piccadell, piccadill
10 chevesaile, piccadillo, piccadilly
11 falling band
12 mousquetaire

collate
04 edit, sort **05** order **06** gather
07 arrange, collect, compare, compile, compose **08** organize **10** put in order
11 put together

collateral
05 funds, rival **06** pledge, surety
07 deposit **08** security **09** assurance, guarantee **10** additional, subsidiary
12 contemporary **13** corresponding

collation
07 editing **08** ordering **09** gathering
11 arrangement, compilation, composition **12** organization
15 putting together

colleague
04 aide, ally **06** helper, winger
07 comrade, partner **08** confrère, conspire, co-worker, teammate, workmate **09** assistant, associate, auxiliary, bedfellow, companion
11 confederate **12** collaborator, fellow worker

collect
◊ *containment indicator*
03 get **04** form, heap, mass, meet, save
05 amass, fetch, hoard, rally **06** gather, make up, muster, pick up, pile up, semble, take up, uplift **07** acquire, call for, come for, compose, convene, prepare, recover, solicit **08** assemble, converge, go and get **09** aggregate, go and take, stockpile **10** accumulate, congregate, go and bring, raise money
11 come to money **12** come together, have as a hobby **14** be interested in, gather together **15** ask people to give

collected
◊ *anagram indicator*
◊ *insertion indicator*
04 calm, cool **06** placid, poised, serene **07** unfazed **08** composed, unshaken **09** unruffled **10** controlled
11 unflappable, unperturbed
13 imperturbable, self-possessed
14 self-controlled

collection
◊ *anagram indicator*
03 set **04** gift, heap, mass, pack, pile, sort **05** gifts, group, hoard, plate, store

06 basket, job-lot, rickle, series
07 boiling, cluster, variety
08 assembly, caboodle, donation, jingbang, offering **09** anthology, composure, congeries, donations, gathering, offertory, selection, stockpile, whip-round **10** assemblage, assortment **11** compilation, ingathering, olla-podrida
12 accumulation, conglomerate, contribution, subscription
13 contributions **14** collected works, conglomeration, omnium-gatherum

collective
05 joint **06** common, moshav, shared, united **07** commune, kibbutz, kolkhoz
08 combined **09** aggregate, community, composite, concerted, corporate, gathering, unanimous
10 assemblage, cumulative, democratic **11** congregated, co-operative **13** collaborative

Collective nouns for animals include:

03 bed (clams, oysters), cry (hounds), gam (whales), mob (kangaroos), nid (pheasants), nye (pheasants), pod (seals, whales)
04 army (caterpillars, frogs), bale (turtles), band (gorillas), bask (crocodiles), bevy (larks, pheasants, quail, swans), cete (badgers), dole (doves, turtles), erst (bees), herd (buffalo, cattle, deer, elephants, goats, horses, kangaroos, oxen, seals, whales), hive (bees), pace (asses), pack (dogs, grouse, hounds, wolves), romp (otters), rout (wolves), safe (ducks), span (mules), team (ducks), trip (goats, sheep), zeal (zebras)
05 bloat (hippopotami), brace (ducks), brood (chickens, hens), charm (finches, goldfinches), covey (partridges, quail), crash (rhinoceros), drift (hogs, swine), drove (cattle, horses, oxen, sheep), flock (birds, ducks, geese, sheep), grist (bees), shoal (fish), siege (cranes, herons), skein (geese), swarm (ants, bees, flies, locusts), tower (giraffes), tribe (goats), troop (baboons, kangaroos, monkeys), watch (nightingales), wedge (swans)
06 ambush (tigers), cackle (hyenas), colony (ants, bees, penguins, rats), gaggle (geese), kindle (kittens), labour (moles), litter (kittens, pigs), murder (crows), muster (peacocks, penguins), parade (elephants), parcel (penguins), rafter (turkeys), school (dolphins, fish, porpoises, whales), string (horses, ponies), tiding (magpies)
07 bouquet (pheasants), clowder (cats), company (parrots), prickle (porcupines), turmoil (porpoises)
08 building (rooks), paddling (ducks)
09 intrusion (cockroaches), mustering (storks), obstinacy (buffalo)

10 exaltation (larks), parliament (owls, rooks), shrewdness (apes), unkindness (ravens)
11 convocation (eagles), murmuration (starlings), ostentation (peacocks), pandemonium (parrots)
12 congregation (plovers)

collector

Collectors and enthusiasts include:

05 gamer
07 gourmet
08 neophile, zoophile
09 antiquary, cinephile, ex-librist, logophile, oenophile, philomath, xenophile
10 arctophile, audiophile, cartophile, discophile, ephemerist, gastronome, hippophile, monarchist
11 ailurophile, balletomane, bibliophile, canophilist, etymologist, notaphilist, numismatist, oenophilist, philatelist, scripophile, technophile, toxophilite
12 ailourophile, cartophilist, coleopterist, Dantophilist, deltiologist, entomologist, incunabulist, ophiophilist, phillumenist, stegophilist
13 arachnologist, campanologist, chirographist, lepidopterist, ornithologist, tegestologist, timbrophilist
14 cruciverbalist
15 conservationist, stigmatophilist

college
01 c **04** coll, Eton, hall, poly, tech
06 lyceum, prison, school
07 academy, madrasa **08** madrasah, madrassa, seminary **09** institute, madrassah, medresseh **10** university
11 polytechnic

See also **educational**; **university**

Colleges and halls of Cambridge University:

05 Clare, Jesus, King's
06 Darwin, Girton, Queens', Selwyn
07 Christ's, Downing, New Hall, Newnham, St John's, Trinity, Wolfson
08 Emmanuel, Homerton, Pembroke, Robinson
09 Churchill, Clare Hall, Magdalene, St Edmund's
10 Hughes Hall, Peterhouse
11 Fitzwilliam, Trinity Hall
12 Sidney Sussex, St Catharine's
13 Corpus Christi, Lucy Cavendish
16 Gonville and Caius

Colleges and halls of Oxford University:

03 New
05 Green, Jesus, Keble, Oriel
06 Exeter, Merton, Queen's, Wadham
07 Balliol, Kellogg, Linacre, Lincoln, St Anne's, St Cross, St Hugh's, St John's, Trinity, Wolfson

08 All Souls, Hertford, Magdalen, Nuffield, Pembroke, St Hilda's, St Peter's
09 Brasenose, Mansfield, St Antony's, Templeton, The Queen's, Worcester
10 Somerville, University
11 Campion Hall, Regent's Park
12 Christ Church, St Benet's Hall, St Catherine's, St Edmund Hall, Wycliffe Hall
13 Corpus Christi
14 Greyfriars Hall
15 Blackfriars Hall, St Stephen's House
16 Harris Manchester, Lady Margaret Hall

• **at college**
02 up
• **college head**
04 dean
• **college square**
04 quad

collide
03 hit, war **04** bump, feud, foul
05 clash, crash, fight, prang, smash
06 cannon, go into **07** contend, grapple, quarrel, run into, wrangle
08 bump into, conflict, disagree
09 crash into, smash into **10** meet head on, plough into **12** be in conflict

collision
04 bump, feud **05** brush, clash, crash, fight, prang, shunt, smash, wreck
06 impact, pile-up **07** quarrel, warring, wrangle **08** accident, clashing, conflict, disaster, fighting, showdown **09** rencontre
10 opposition, rencounter
12 disagreement, fender bender
13 confrontation

colloid
03 gel, sol **08** emulsoid **10** suspensoid
11 carrageenan, carrageenin
12 carragheenin

colloquial
06 casual, chatty **07** demotic, popular
08 everyday, familiar, informal
09 idiomatic **10** vernacular
14 conversational

colloquially
09 popularly **10** familiarly, informally

collude
04 plot **06** scheme **07** connive
08 conspire, intrigue **09** machinate
11 be in cahoots, collaborate

collusion
04 plot **06** deceit, league, scheme
07 cahoots **08** artifice, intrigue, scheming **10** complicity, connivance, conspiracy **11** machination
13 collaboration

Colombia
02 CO **03** COL

colonist
04 boor **05** colon **07** pioneer, planter, settler **08** colonial, emigrant, Siceliot, Sikeliot **09** colonizer, immigrant, inhabiter **12** Australasian
See also **governor**

colonize
05 found, plant **06** occupy, people, settle **07** pioneer **08** populate

colonnade
04 stoa **05** porch **06** arcade, xystus **07** eustyle, portico **08** diastyle **09** areostyle, cloisters, peristyle **10** araeostyle **11** covered walk **12** columniation

colony
04 hive **05** apery, group, swarm **07** outpost **08** dominion, province **09** coenobium, community, formicary, hydrosoma, hydrosome, polyzoary, satellite, territory **10** dependency, plantation, possession, settlement **11** association, formicarium, polyzoarium **12** protectorate **14** satellite state

Colorado
02 CO **04** Colo

colossal
04 huge, vast **05** great, jumbo **07** immense, mammoth, massive **08** enormous, gigantic, whopping **09** herculean, monstrous **10** gargantuan, monumental **14** Brobdingnagian

colossus
04 ogre **05** giant, titan **07** Cyclops, Goliath, monster **08** Hercules

colour
03 dye, hew, hue, ink, kit **04** bias, flag, glow, kick, leer, life, race, sway, tint, tone, wash **05** badge, blush, flush, get-up, go red, oomph, paint, shade, slant, stain, strip, taint, tinge **06** affect, banner, crayon, emblem, ensign, reason, redden, tackle, timbre **07** distort, falsify, pervert, pigment, pizzazz, pretext, redness, turn red, variety **08** clothing, colorant, disguise, insignia, pinkness, richness, rosiness, standard, tincture **09** animation, highlight, influence, overstate, prejudice, ruddiness, vividness **10** appearance, brilliance, coloration, complexion, exaggerate, liveliness, skin colour **11** ethnic group, nationality, racial group **12** misrepresent, pigmentation, plausibility

Colours include:
03 dun, jet, red, sky, tan
04 anil, blae, blue, buff, cyan, dove, drab, ecru, fawn, gold, gray, grey, guly, hoar, jade, navy, opal, pink, plum, puce, roan, rose, rosy, ruby, rust, sage, sand, wine
05 amber, beige, black, brown, coral, cream, ebony, green, khaki, lemon, lilac, mauve, milky, ochre, peach, sepia, taupe, topaz, umber, white
06 auburn, bottle, bronze, canary, cerise, cherry, cobalt, copper, indigo, maroon, orange, purple, salmon, silver, violet, yellow
07 apricot, avocado, crimson, emerald, gentian, magenta, saffron, scarlet
08 burgundy, charcoal, chestnut, cinnamon, eau de nil, lavender, magnolia, mahogany, sapphire
09 aubergine, chocolate, nile green, tangerine, turquoise, vermilion
10 aquamarine, chartreuse, cobalt blue, grass-green
11 burnt sienna, lemon yellow

See also **black; blue; dye; green; grey; orange; pigment; pink; purple; rainbow; red; white; yellow**

• lose colour
04 fade, pale

coloured
01 C **09** chromatic

colourful
03 gay **04** deep, rich **05** gaudy, vivid **06** bright, garish, lively **07** graphic, intense, vibrant **08** animated, exciting **09** brilliant **10** flamboyant, polychrome, variegated **11** interesting, picturesque, stimulating **12** many-coloured **13** kaleidoscopic, multicoloured, parti-coloured

colourfully
08 brightly **09** intensely, vibrantly **11** brilliantly

colourless
03 wan **04** drab, dull, fade, grey, pale, tame **05** ashen, bleak, faded, plain, white **06** boring, dreary, sickly **07** anaemic, insipid, neutral **08** bleached **09** washed out **10** lacklustre, monochrome, uncoloured **11** transparent, unmemorable **13** characterless, uninteresting **14** complexionless **15** in black and white

colt
01 c **04** beat, cade, stag **05** staig **06** hogget

Columbia *see* **British; District of Columbia** *under* **district**

column
03 col, row **04** anta, file, item, line, list, pier, pole, post, rank **05** Atlas, piece, queue, shaft, story **06** parade, pillar, string **07** article, columel, feature, obelisk, support, telamon, upright **08** caryatid, pilaster **10** procession

• shaft of column
04 fust, tige **05** scape, trunk **06** scapus

columnist
06 critic, editor, writer **08** reporter, reviewer **10** journalist **11** contributor **13** correspondent

coma
03 PVS **05** sopor **06** stupor, torpor, trance **08** hypnosis, lethargy, oblivion **09** catalepsy **10** drowsiness, somnolence **13** insensibility **15** unconsciousness

comatose
03 out **05** dazed **06** drowsy, sleepy, torpid **07** in a coma, out cold, stunned **08** sluggish, soporose **09** lethargic, somnolent, stupefied **10** cataleptic, insensible **11** unconscious

comb
03 red **04** card, hunt, kaim, kame, kemb, rake, redd, sift, tidy, tose, toze **05** combe, coomb, crest, dress, groom, scour, sweep, tease, toaze, trawl **06** coombe, hackle, kangha, neaten, screen, search **07** arrange, explore, ransack, rummage **08** scribble, untangle **09** go through **11** disentangle **14** turn upside down

combat
03 war **04** agon, bout, defy, duel **05** clash, fight, lists **06** action, battle, debate, oppose, resist, strive **07** contend, contest, wage war, warfare **08** conflict, do battle, fighting, skirmish, struggle **09** encounter, monomachy, rencontre, withstand **10** engagement, rencounter, take up arms **11** hostilities

• unarmed combat
04 judo **06** karate **07** ju-jitsu **08** jiu-jitsu

combatant
05 enemy **07** fighter, soldier, warrior **08** opponent **09** adversary, contender, gladiator **10** antagonist, batteilant, serviceman **11** belligerent, protagonist **12** servicewoman

combative
06 bantam **07** hawkish, warlike, warring **08** militant **09** agonistic, bellicose, truculent **10** aggressive, pugnacious **11** adversarial, belligerent, contentious, quarrelsome **12** antagonistic **13** argumentative

combination
03 mix **04** club **05** blend, cross, group, union **06** fusion, merger **07** amalgam, combine, mixture, synergy **08** alliance, clubbing, compound, junction, solution **09** coalition, composite, syndicate, synthesis **10** collection, conflation, connection, consortium, federation **11** association, coalescence, composition, confederacy, conjunction, co-operation, integration, unification **12** amalgamation, co-ordination **13** confederation

combine
03 mix **04** ally, bind, bond, club, fuse, join, link, meld, pool, stir, weld **05** admix, alloy, blend, marry, merge, piece, trust, unify, unite **06** mingle, team up **07** conjoin, connect **08** compound, conflate, cumulate, restrict **09** associate, coadunate, co-operate, integrate, syndicate **10** amalgamate, homogenize, join forces, synthesize **11** incorporate, put together **12** club together **13** bring together

• combined
08 together

• combined with
03 cum

combustible
◇ *anagram indicator*
05 tense **06** ardent, stormy
07 charged **08** volatile **09** excitable,
explosive, flammable, ignitable,
sensitive **10** incendiary, phlogistic
11 inflammable

combustion
06 firing **07** burning **08** igniting,
ignition
• **internal combustion**
02 IC

come
02 be **04** gain, hail, near, stem, turn
05 arise, enter, issue, occur, reach,
yield **06** allons, appear, arrive, attain,
attend, become, climax, dawn on,
evolve, follow, happen, secure, show
up, strike, turn up **07** achieve, advance,
barge in, burst in, develop, get here,
occur to, surface, think of
08 approach, draw near, get there, pass
into, remember **09** be on offer, come
about, go as far as, originate, take
place, transpire **10** be caused by, be
produced, come to pass, evolve into,
move nearer, result from **11** be a native
of, be available, develop into,
materialize, move forward, move
towards **13** be on the market, present
itself, reach an orgasm, travel towards
14 have as your home **15** come to the
mind of, have its origin, have as its
source
• **come about**
04 fall, sort **05** arise, occur **06** arrive,
befall, happen, result **09** take place,
transpire **10** come to pass
• **come across**
04 find, meet, seem **06** appear, notice
07 run into **08** bump into, come over,
discover, meet in wi' **09** encounter
10 chance upon, happen upon, meet
in with **11** communicate **12** find by
chance, meet by chance **13** stumble
across
• **come along**
04 mend **05** rally **06** arrive
07 advance, develop, hurry up,
improve, recover **08** progress **09** get
better, shake a leg **10** get a move on,
recuperate **11** get cracking, make
headway **12** make progress **15** get
your skates on
• **come apart**
04 tear **05** break, split **07** break up,
crumble **08** collapse, separate **10** fall
to bits **12** disintegrate, fall to pieces
• **come back**
◇ *reversal indicator*
06 go back, remind, return **07** get back
08 come home, reappear **10** be
recalled **11** be suggested **12** be
remembered **13** be recollected
• **come between**
04 part **06** divide **07** split up
08 alienate, disunite, estrange,
separate **09** interpose
• **come by**
03 get **05** visit **06** obtain, secure
07 acquire, procure **09** get hold of

• **come down**
04 drop, fall **05** avail, avale, light
06 availe, reduce, worsen **07** decline,
descend **08** decrease, dismount
10 degenerate **11** deteriorate
• **come down on**
05 blame, chide, knock, slate
06 berate, rebuke **07** reprove, upbraid
08 admonish, tear into **09** criticize,
reprehend, reprimand **13** find fault
with
• **come down to**
04 mean **07** add up to **08** amount to
10 boil down to **12** correspond to
14 be equivalent to, be tantamount to
• **come down with**
03 get **05** catch **06** pick up
07 develop **08** contract **09** succumb
to **10** go down with **11** fall ill with
13 become ill with
• **come forward**
05 offer **06** accede, step up
09 volunteer **11** step forward **13** offer
yourself
• **come in**
05 enter **06** appear, arrive, entrez,
finish, show up **07** receive
• **come in for**
03 get **04** bear **06** endure, suffer
07 receive, sustain, undergo
10 experience **13** be subjected to
• **come into**
04 heir **06** be left **07** acquire, inherit,
receive **08** be heir to, contract
• **come off**
04 mend, work **05** end up, occur, rally,
strip **06** appear, go well, happen, pay
off, thrive **07** advance, develop,
improve, proceed, recover, succeed,
work out **08** progress **09** get better,
take place **10** recuperate, take effect
11 be effective **12** be successful, make
progress
• **come on**
03 via **04** mend **05** begin, rally
06 allons, appear, thrive **07** advance,
develop, improve, proceed, recover,
succeed **08** progress **09** get better
10 recuperate **12** make progress
• **come out**
03 end **05** admit, end up, erupt, issue
06 appear, emerge, finish, result, strike
07 leak out **08** conclude **09** terminate
10 be produced, be released, be
revealed **11** become known, be
published, come to light **12** be made
public **13** declare openly **15** become
available
• **come out with**
03 say **05** state, utter **06** affirm
07 declare, divulge, exclaim **08** blurt
out, disclose
• **come round**
04 veer, wake **05** agree, allow, awake,
grant, occur, recur, visit, yield
06 accede, come to, happen, relent
07 concede, recover **08** reappear
09 be won over, take place **11** be
persuaded **13** be converted to
14 change your mind
• **come through**
04 pass, ride **06** endure **07** achieve,

prevail, ride out, succeed, survive,
triumph **09** withstand **10** accomplish
11 pull through
• **come to**
04 make, stop, wake **05** awake, equal,
run to, total **06** obtain **07** add up to,
recover **08** amount to **09** aggregate,
come round
• **come together**
03 gel **04** jell, meet **05** close, rally
07 collect, convene
• **come up**
◇ *reversal down indicator*
04 rise **05** arise, occur **06** appear,
crop up, happen, turn up **13** present
itself
• **come up to**
04 meet **05** equal, reach
08 approach, live up to **09** match up to
11 compare with, measure up to
12 make the grade
• **come up with**
05 offer **06** devise, submit
07 advance, dream up, present,
produce, propose, suggest, think of
08 conceive **10** put forward

comeback
05 rally **06** retort, return **07** revival
08 recovery **09** rejoinder
10 resurgence **12** reappearance
13 recrimination
• **make a comeback**
◇ *reversal indicator*

comedian
03 wag, wit **05** clown, comic, joker
06 gagman **07** gagster **08** funny man,
humorist **10** comedienne, funny
woman **11** entertainer

Comedians include:

03 Dee (Jack), Fry (Stephen), Lom
(Herbert), Sim (Alastair), Wax
(Ruby)
04 Cook (Peter), Dodd (Ken), Hill
(Benny), Hill (Harry), Hope (Bob),
Idle (Eric), Kaye (Danny), Marx
(Chico), Marx (Groucho), Marx
(Harpo), Marx (Zeppo), Sims
(Joan), Tati (Jacques), Wise (Ernie),
Wood (Victoria)
05 Abbot (Russ), Allen (Dave), Allen
(Woody), Brand (Jo), Bruce (Lenny),
Burns (George), Cosby (Bill), Davro
(Bobby), Elton (Ben), Emery (Dick),
Hardy (Oliver), Henry (Lenny),
Inman (John), James (Sid), Jones
(Griff Rhys), Jones (Terry), Kempe
(Will), Lewis (Jerry), Lloyd (Harold),
Lucas (Matt), Moore (Dudley),
Oddie (Bill), Palin (Michael), Pryor
(Richard), Robey (Sir George),
Sayle (Alexei), Smith (Mel), Starr
(Freddie), Sykes (Eric)
06 Abbott (Bud), Bailey (Bill), Barker
(Ronnie), Brooks (Mel), Cleese
(John), Coogan (Steve), Cooper
(Tommy), Dawson (Les), Fields
(W C), French (Dawn), Garden
(Graeme), Howerd (Frankie),
Jordan (Dorothy), Keaton (Buster),
Lauder (Sir Harry), Laurel (Stan),
Laurie (Hugh), Martin (Steve),

Mayall (Rik), **Merton** (Paul), **Murphy** (Eddie), **Murray** (Bill), **Reeves** (Vic), **Ullman** (Tracey), **Wilder** (Gene), **Wisdom** (Norman)

07 Aykroyd (Dan), **Baddiel** (David), **Bentine** (Michael), **Bremner** (Rory), **Carrott** (Jasper), **Chaplin** (Charlie), **Chapman** (Graham), **Corbett** (Ronnie), **Deayton** (Angus), **Enfield** (Harry), **Everett** (Kenny), **Feldman** (Marty), **Gervais** (Ricky), **Hancock** (Tony), **Handley** (Tommy), **Jacques** (Hattie), **Manning** (Bernard), **Matthau** (Walter), **Newhart** (Bob), **Roscius**, **Secombe** (Harry), **Sellers** (Peter), **Tarbuck** (Jimmy), **Ustinov** (Sir Peter)

08 Atkinson (Rowan), **Coltrane** (Robbie), **Connolly** (Billy), **Coquelin** (Benoît Constant), **Costello** (Lou), **Grimaldi** (Joseph), **Milligan** (Spike), **Mitchell** (Warren), **Mortimer** (Bob), **Roseanne**, **Saunders** (Jennifer), **Seinfeld** (Jerry), **Sessions** (John), **The Goons**, **Walliams** (David), **Williams** (Kenneth), **Williams** (Robin)

09 Edmondson (Adrian), **Fernandel**, **Grossmith** (George), **Morecambe** (Eric), **Rhys Jones** (Griff), **Whitfield** (June)

10 The Goodies, **Whitehouse** (Paul)

11 Monty Python, **Terry-Thomas**

12 Brooke-Taylor (Tim)

14 Laurel and Hardy, **Little and Large**

15 The Marx Brothers

See also **actor, actress**

comedown

04 blow **06** bathos **07** decline, descent, let-down, reverse **08** demotion, reversal **09** deflation **10** anticlimax **11** degradation, humiliation **14** disappointment

comedy

03 com, fun **06** humour, joking **07** jesting **08** clowning, drollery, hilarity **09** funniness, pantomime **13** entertainment, facetiousness

Comedy types include:

03 gag, low, pun, wit

05 high, joke, sick

05 black, farce, Greek

06 modern, satire, sitcom, visual

07 musical, stand-up

08 romantic

09 burlesque, satirical, screwball, situation, slapstick

10 comic opera, sketch show, television, theatrical, vaudeville

11 alternative, Pythonesque, restoration, tragicomedy

12 Chaplinesque, neoclassical

13 Shakespearian

15 comedy of humours, comedy of manners, improvisational, situation comedy

comely

04 fair, fine, tidy **05** ample, bonny, buxom, sonsy **06** bonnie, gainly, goodly, likely, lovely, pretty, proper,

sonsie **07** sightly, winsome **08** blooming, graceful, handsome, pleasing **09** beautiful, excellent **10** attractive **11** good-looking **15** pulchritudinous

come-on

04 lure **10** allurement, attraction, enticement, inducement, persuasion, temptation **13** encouragement

comet

Comets include:

04 West, Wolf

05 Cruls, Encke, Kirch, Mrkos, Tycho

06 Donati, Halley, Lexell, Newton

07 Bennett, Humason, Tebbutt

08 Daylight, Hale-Bopp, Kohoutek

09 Hyakutake, Ikeya-Seki, Morehouse, Seki-Lines

10 De Chéseaux, Flauergues, Great Comet

11 Arend-Roland, Swift-Tuttle

12 Pons-Winnecke

13 Shoemaker-Levy

14 Tago-Sato-Kosaka

comeuppance

04 dues **05** merit **06** rebuke **07** deserts **08** requital **10** chastening, punishment, recompense **11** just deserts, retribution **14** what you deserve

comfort

03 aid **04** cosy, cozy, ease, help, stay **05** cheer **06** luxury, plenty, relief, repose, solace, soothe **07** assuage, console, encheer, enliven, gladden, hearten, refresh, relieve, succour, support **08** cosiness, opulence, reassure, snugness **09** alleviate, empathize, encourage, enjoyment, recomfort, wellbeing **10** condolence, easy street, invigorate, relaxation, strengthen, sympathize **11** alleviation, consolation, contentment, reassurance **12** compensation, satisfaction **13** bring solace to, encouragement, Gemütlichkeit **15** freedom from pain, speak to the heart

comfortable

04 bein, bien, cosy, cozy, easy, lazy, safe, slow, snug, tosh, warm, well **05** comfy, cushy, happy, loose, roomy **06** at ease, couthy, gentle, homely, kindly, secure **07** couthie, opulent, relaxed, restful, well-off **08** affluent, armchair, carefree, homelike, laid-back, pleasant, relaxing, well-to-do **09** agreeable, confident, contented, enjoyable, gemütlich, leisurely, luxurious, rosewater, unhurried **10** commodious, convenient, delightful, prosperous **11** well-fitting **12** loose-fitting **13** unembarrassed

• **make yourself comfortable**

04 cose

comforting

07 helpful **08** cheering, soothing **09** analeptic, consoling **10** heartening, reassuring **11** consolatory,

encouraging, inspiriting **12** heartwarming

comic

03 wag, wit **04** card, rich, zany **05** buffo, clown, droll, funny, joker, light, witty **06** absurd, gagman, joking **07** amusing, buffoon, comical, gagster, jocular **08** comedian, farcical, funny man, humorist, humorous **09** diverting, facetious, hilarious, laughable, ludicrous, priceless **10** funny woman, ridiculous **11** entertainer **12** entertaining, knee-slapping **13** side-splitting

Comics include:

03 Viz

05 Beano, Bunty, Dandy

08 The Beano, The Dandy, The Eagle

comical

05 droll, funny, witty **06** absurd **07** amusing **08** farcical, humorous **09** diverting, hilarious, laughable, ludicrous, quizzical **10** ridiculous **12** entertaining

comically

07 funnily, wittily **08** absurdly **09** amusingly **10** farcically, humorously **11** hilariously, ludicrously **12** ridiculously

coming

03 due **04** anon, dawn, near, next **05** birth **06** advent, future, rising **07** arrival, nearing **08** approach, aspiring, imminent, upcoming **09** accession, advancing, impending, promising **11** approaching, forthcoming, up-and-coming

• **coming out**

09 emergence

command

03 bid, get **04** fiat, gain, head, hest, lead, rule, sway, warn, will **05** edict, heast, order, power, reign **06** adjure, behest, behote, charge, compel, decree, demand, direct, enjoin, govern, heaste, impose, manage, obtain, secure **07** be given, behight, bidding, control, dictate, mandate, mastery, precept, receive, require **08** dominate, dominion, instruct, pleasure **09** authority, direction, directive, supervise **10** ascendancy, domination, government, injunction, leadership, management **11** commandment, instruction, preside over, requirement, superintend, supervision **12** be in charge of, give orders to **13** be in control of **15** superintendence

Commands include:

03 hie, hup, hye

04 easy, halt, high, mush

05 be off, enter, gee up

06 come by, entrez, gee hup, huddup

07 give way

09 stand easy

10 quick march

12 be off with you

15 stand and deliver

commandeer
04 take 05 press, seize, usurp
06 hijack 07 impound 08 arrogate
09 sequester 10 confiscate
11 appropriate, expropriate, requisition, sequestrate

commander
03 Cdr, Com 04 boss, Cmdr, comm, head 05 bloke, chief, Comdr
06 leader, master

Commanders include:
03 aga, mir
04 agha, meer
06 sardar, sirdar
07 admiral, captain, general, officer, prefect, warlord
08 director, governor, hipparch, phylarch, risaldar, taxiarch, tetrarch
09 chieftain, chiliarch, imperator, polemarch, privateer, seraskier, trierarch
11 encomendero, turcopolier
13 generalissimo
14 superintendent
See also **admiral**; **field marshal**; **general**

commanding
05 lofty 06 strong 08 dominant, forceful, imperial, imposing, powerful, superior 09 assertive, confident, directing, strategic 10 autocratic, dominating, impressive, peremptory
11 controlling 12 advantageous
13 authoritative

commemorate
04 keep, mark 06 honour, salute
07 observe 08 remember
09 celebrate, recognize, solemnize
11 immortalize, memorialize 12 pay tribute to

commemoration
04 mind, obit 06 honour, memory, salute 07 tribute 08 ceremony
09 honouring 10 dedication, observance 11 celebration, recognition, recordation, remembrance

commemorative
07 marking 08 memorial, saluting
09 honouring 10 dedicatory, in honour of, in memoriam, in memory of
11 celebratory, remembering 12 as a tribute to 15 in recognition of, in remembrance of

commence
04 open 05 begin, start 06 launch
07 go ahead 08 embark on, initiate
09 originate 10 inaugurate, make a start 14 make a beginning

commencement
05 onset, start 06 launch, origin, outset 07 kick-off, opening
09 beginning 10 initiation

commend
03 rap 04 give, laud, wrap 05 adorn, extol, trust, yield 06 commit, praise, set off 07 acclaim, applaud, approve, confide, consign, deliver, entrust,

propose, suggest 08 advocate, eulogize, hand over 09 recommend
10 compliment 13 speak highly of

commendable
04 good 05 noble 06 pretty, worthy
08 laudable 09 admirable, deserving, estimable, excellent, exemplary, well-found 10 creditable 11 meritorious
12 praiseworthy

commendation
06 credit, praise 07 acclaim
08 accolade, applause, approval, encomion, encomium, good word
09 panegyric 10 approvance
11 acclamation, approbation, good opinion, high opinion, recognition
13 brownie points, encouragement
14 congratulation, recommendation, seal of approval, special mention
15 stamp of approval

commensurate
03 due 05 equal 07 fitting
08 adequate 10 acceptable, comparable, equivalent, sufficient
11 according to 13 appropriate to, corresponding, proportionate
14 compatible with, consistent with, in proportion to 15 corresponding to

comment
03 say 04 note, view 05 gloss, gloze, opine 06 remark 07 descant, explain, mention, observe, opinion, speak to
08 annotate, footnote, point out, scholion, scholium, sidenote
09 criticism, elucidate, interject, interpose, interpret, statement
10 annotation, commentary, exposition 11 elucidation, explanation, observation 12 illustration, marginal note, obiter dictum 13 give an opinion

commentary
04 comm 05 notes 06 Gemara, postil, remark, report, review 07 account
08 analysis, Brahmana, critique, exegesis, treatise 09 narration, voice-over 10 annotation, exposition, play-by-play 11 description, elucidation, explanation 14 interpretation

commentator
05 hakam 06 critic 07 exegete, glosser 08 narrator, reporter
09 annotator, commenter, expositor, glossator, scholiast 10 newscaster
11 broadcaster, interpreter
12 sportscaster 13 correspondent
See also **cricket**

commerce
03 com 05 trade 07 dealing, traffic
08 business, dealings, exchange, industry 09 marketing, relations
11 intercourse, trafficking
13 merchandizing

commercial
02 ad 04 bill, hype, plug 05 blurb, trade, venal 06 advert, jingle, notice, poster, shoppy 07 display, handout, leaflet, placard, popular, trading
08 business, circular, handbill, merchant, monetary, saleable, sellable

09 financial, lucrative, marketing, mercenary, promotion, publicity
10 industrial, mercantile, profitable, propaganda 11 moneymaking
12 announcement, profit-making
13 advertisement, materialistic, money-spinning 15 entrepreneurial

commiserate
07 comfort, console, feel for
10 sympathize, understand 12 feel sorry for 13 offer sympathy 15 express sympathy, send condolences

commiseration
04 pity 06 solace 07 comfort
08 sympathy 10 compassion, condolence 11 condolences, consolation 13 consideration, understanding

commission
03 cut, fee, job 04 duty, send, task, work 05 board, order, share, trust
06 ask for, assign, charge, depute, employ, engage, errand, select
07 appoint, arrange, council, empower, mandate, mission, rake-off, request, royalty, warrant 08 contract, delegate, function, nominate, poundage 09 allowance, authority, authorize, brokerage, committee
10 assignment, delegation, deputation, employment, percentage
11 appointment, piece of work
12 advisory body, compensation
13 advisory group 14 representative, responsibility 15 put in an order for

commit
02 do 03 put, sin 04 aret, bind, give, hete, send 05 admit, arett, enact, enure, hecht, hight, inure, trust
06 assign, decide, effect, engage, pledge 07 commend, confide, confine, consign, deliver, deposit, entrust, execute, get up to, intrust, perform, promise, put away
08 bequeath, carry out, covenant, dedicate, delegate, hand over, obligate
09 indulge in, recommend
10 perpetrate 15 cross the Rubicon

commitment
03 tie, vow 04 duty, word 06 effort, pledge 07 loyalty, promise
08 covenant, devotion, hard work
09 adherence, assurance, guarantee, liability 10 allegiance, dedication, engagement, obligation
11 involvement, undertaking
12 imprisonment 14 responsibility

committal
06 pledge 07 sending 09 admission
11 confinement, consignment
12 imprisonment

committed
05 loyal 06 active, engagé, paid up, red-hot 07 devoted, engaged, fervent, sold out, zealous 08 diligent, involved, studious 09 dedicated, sold out on
11 evangelical, hardworking, industrious 12 card-carrying, enthusiastic

committee
03 com 05 board, table 08 delegacy
09 Politburo 10 Propaganda
11 Politbureau

commodious
05 ample, large, roomy 08 spacious,
suitable 09 capacious, expansive,
extensive 10 convenient
11 comfortable, serviceable

commodity
04 item 05 goods, stock, thing, wares
06 output, profit 07 article, produce,
product 08 material 09 advantage,
privilege 10 expediency
11 convenience, merchandise

common
03 com, low 05 crude, daily, joint,
plain, sense, share, stray, usual
06 coarse, mutual, normal, public,
shared, simple, vulgar 07 average,
general, ill-bred, loutish, popular,
regular, routine, uncouth 08 accepted,
communal, everyday, familiar,
frequent, habitual, inferior, ordinary,
plebeian, standard, tritical, workaday
09 community, customary, prevalent,
ten a penny, two a penny, universal,
unrefined 10 collective, customable,
dime a dozen, prevailing, widespread
11 bog standard, commonplace
12 common as muck, conventional,
run-of-the-mill 13 unexceptional
15 undistinguished

commoner
02 MP 04 pleb 07 plebean
08 plebeian

common land
03 tie, tye 04 mark

commonly
05 often, vulgo 07 as a rule, usually
08 normally 09 generally, regularly,
routinely, typically 10 frequently 14 for
the most part

commonplace
05 banal, stale, stock, trite, usual
06 boring, common, modern, ornery,
vulgar 07 humdrum, mundane,
obvious, ordinar, prosaic, routine,
worn out 08 bromidic, copybook,
everyday, exoteric, frequent, ordinary,
overused 09 hackneyed, prosaical,
quotidian 10 pedestrian, threadbare,
widespread 11 a dime a dozen
13 unexceptional, uninteresting

common sense
04 nous 05 savey, savvy, sense
06 brains, reason, sanity, savvey,
wisdom 07 realism 08 gumption,
prudence 09 good sense, judgement,
mother wit, soundness 10 astuteness,
experience, pragmatism, shrewdness
11 discernment, rumgumption
12 practicality, sensibleness
13 judiciousness, rumelgumption,
rumgumption 14 hard-headedness,
rumblegumption, rummelgumption,
rummlegumption 15 level-
headedness

commonsense
04 sane, wise 05 sound 06 astute,
shrewd 07 prudent 08 sensible
09 judicious, practical, pragmatic,
realistic 10 discerning, hard-headed,
reasonable 11 down-to-earth,
experienced, level-headed 12 matter-
of-fact 14 commonsensical

commonwealth
03 Com 04 weal 12 Protectorate

Commonwealth member countries:
04 Fiji
05 Ghana, India, Kenya, Malta, Nauru,
Samoa, Tonga
06 Belize, Brunei, Canada, Cyprus,
Guyana, Malawi, Tuvalu, Uganda,
Zambia
07 Grenada, Jamaica, Lesotho,
Namibia, Nigeria, St Lucia, Vanuatu
08 Barbados, Botswana, Cameroon,
Dominica, Kiribati, Malaysia,
Maldives, Pakistan, Sri Lanka,
Tanzania, Zimbabwe
09 Australia, Mauritius, Singapore,
Swaziland, The Gambia
10 Bangladesh, Mozambique, New
Zealand, Seychelles, The Bahamas
11 Sierra Leone, South Africa
13 United Kingdom
14 Papua New Guinea, Solomon
Islands
15 St Kitts and Nevis
16 Brunei Darussalam
17 Antigua and Barbuda, Trinidad and
Tobago
21 St Christopher and Nevis
24 United Republic of Tanzania
25 St Vincent and the Grenadines

Commonwealth of Independent States members:
06 Russia
07 Armenia, Belarus, Georgia,
Moldova, Ukraine
10 Azerbaijan, Kazakhstan,
Kyrgyzstan, Tajikistan, Uzbekistan
12 Turkmenistan

commotion
03 ado, row 04 fuss, Hell, riot, stir, to-
do, toss 05 hurly, hurry, noise, steer,
stire, storm, styre, whirl 06 bustle,
bust-up, flurry, fracas, fraise, furore,
hotter, hubbub, pother, pudder, racket,
romage, rumpus, steery, tiswas, tizwas,
tumult, uproar 07 burst-up, clamour,
ferment, rummage, tempest, turmoil
08 ballyhoo, brouhaha, disorder,
disquiet, kefuffle, tirrivee, tirrivie,
upheaval 09 agitation, carfuffle,
confusion, curfuffle, hurricane,
kerfuffle, stirabout 10 excitement,
hullabaloo, hurly-burly 11 disturbance

communal
05 joint 06 common, public, shared
07 general 09 community 10 collective

communally
07 jointly 08 commonly
09 community, generally
12 collectively

commune
03 com, mir 06 colony 07 kibbutz
08 converse 09 community, discourse
10 collective, fellowship, get close to,
get in touch, settlement
11 communicate, co-operative, feel
close to, feel in touch, make contact
12 municipality

communicable
08 catching 09 infective
10 contagious, conveyable, infectious,
spreadable 12 transferable
13 transmissible, transmittable

communicate
04 talk 05 phone, reach, relay, speak,
write 06 bestow, convey, empart,
impart, inform, liaise, notify, pass on,
report, reveal, spread, unfold
07 commune, contact, declare,
deliver, diffuse, divulge, express, get
over, mediate, publish, put over
08 acquaint, announce, converse,
disclose, intimate, proclaim, transmit
09 be in touch, broadcast, get across,
make known, put across, telephone
10 correspond, get in touch
11 demonstrate, disseminate

communication
05 touch 07 contact, message
09 telephony 10 connection,
disclosure, intimation 11 information,
intercourse 12 intelligence,
transmission 13 dissemination
14 correspondence

Communication forms include:
02 IT, TV
03 fax, MMS, Net, PDA, SMS
04 memo, Moon, news, note, post,
wire, word
05 cable, e-mail, media, pager, pay TV,
press, radar, radio, telex, video
06 gossip, letter, notice, poster, report,
speech, tannoy, the net
07 bleeper, Braille, cable TV, journal,
leaflet, message, Prestel®,
webcast, website
08 access TV, aerogram, brochure,
bulletin, circular, computer,
dialogue, dispatch, Intelsat,
intercom, Internet, junk mail,
magazine, mailshot, pamphlet,
postcard, telegram, teletext, wireless
09 broadband, catalogue, digital TV,
facsimile, grapevine, mass media,
megaphone, Morse code,
newsflash, newspaper, publicity,
satellite, semaphore, statement,
telephone, voice mail
10 communiqué, dictaphone, loud-
hailer, pay-per-view, television,
typewriter
11 advertising, chain letter, satellite TV,
Telemessage®, teleprinter, text
message, the Internet
12 announcement, broadcasting,
conversation, press release, sign
language, walkie-talkie, World
Wide Web
13 video-on-demand, word processor
14 correspondence, subscription TV

communicative
04 free, open **05** frank **06** candid, chatty **07** voluble **08** friendly, outgoing, sociable **09** expansive, extrovert, talkative **10** unreserved **11** forthcoming, informative, intelligent

communion
02 HC **04** Mass **05** agape, unity **06** accord **07** concord, empathy, harmony, rapport **08** affinity, occasion, sympathy **09** closeness, communing, community, Eucharist, Sacrament **10** fellowship **11** intercourse, Lord's Supper **12** togetherness **13** participation **15** sharing feelings, sharing thoughts

communiqué
06 report **07** message **08** bulletin, dispatch **09** newsflash, statement **12** announcement, press release **13** communication

communism
06 Maoism **07** Marxism, Titoism **08** Leninism **09** socialism, sovietism, Stalinism **10** Bolshevism, Trotskyism **11** revisionism **12** collectivism **15** totalitarianism

communist
03 com, red **04** Trot **05** commo, commy, tanky **06** commie, Maoist, soviet **07** comrade, leftist, Marxist **08** Leninist, Viet Cong **09** communard, socialist, Stalinist **10** Bolshevist, Spartacist, Spartakist, Trotskyist, Trotskyite **11** revisionist **12** collectivist

community
04 body, town, umma **05** biome, group, order, state, tribe, ummah **06** ashram, colony, locale, nation, people, public, region, sangha **07** commune, dogtown, kibbutz, phalanx, section, society **08** district, Greekdom, locality, populace **09** Agapemone, agreement, coenobium, residents, sociation **10** commonness, fellowship, fraternity, population, settlement, sisterhood **11** association, brotherhood **13** neighbourhood

commute
05 remit **06** adjust, lessen, modify, reduce, soften **07** curtail, journey, lighten, shorten, shuttle **08** decrease, exchange, mitigate **10** substitute **12** travel to work

commuter
09 passenger, traveller **11** straphanger, suburbanite

Comoros
03 COM

compact
03 ram **04** bond, cram, deal, firm, neat, pact, snug, tamp **05** brief, close, dense, pithy, short, small, solid, terse, tight, union **06** accord, league, little, pocket, settle, treaty **07** bargain, concise, entente, flatten, squeeze

08 alliance, compress, condense, contract, covenant, flapjack, pack down, smallish, succinct, well-knit **09** agreement, concordat, condensed, indenture, press down, telescope **10** compressed, settlement **11** arrangement, close-packed, consolidate, transaction **12** close-grained, close-pressed, impenetrable **13** press together, understanding **15** pressed together

companion
03 lad, pal **04** aide, ally, feer, fere, mate **05** buddy, crony, feare, fiere **06** cohort, co-mate, cupman, escort, fellow, friend, marrow, pheere, potman, shadow, Trojan **07** compeer, comrade, consort, convive, franion, partner **08** barnacle, beau-pere, book-mate, chaperon, compadre, copemate, Ephesian, follower, intimate, playmate, sidekick, workmate **09** assistant, associate, attendant, bon vivant, chaperone, colleague, confidant, copes-mate, pew-fellow **10** accomplice, bon vivante, compotator, confidante, goodfellow **11** compotation, confederate, inseparable, skaines mate
See also **boon**

companionable
06 genial **07** affable, amiable, cordial **08** familiar, fellowly, friendly, informal, outgoing, sociable **09** agreeable, congenial, convivial, extrovert **10** gregarious **11** neighbourly, sympathetic **12** approachable

companionship
07 company, rapport, society, support **08** intimacy, sympathy **09** closeness **10** fellowship, friendship **11** association, camaraderie, comradeship **12** consociation, conviviality, togetherness **13** esprit de corps

company
02 AG, BV, Co, SA **03** Cia, Cie, Coy, PLC, set **04** band, body, cast, core, crew, firm, gang, ging, GmbH, heap, push, sort, team **05** crowd, group, house, party, troop, trust **06** cartel, circle, guests, throng, troupe **07** callers, concern, contact, society, support **08** assembly, business, ensemble, jingbang, presence, visitors **09** closeness, community, gathering, syndicate **10** attendance, consortium, fellowship, friendship, subsidiary **11** association, comradeship, corporation, partnership **12** conglomerate, conviviality, togetherness **13** companionship, establishment, multinational **14** holding company, limited company
See also **business; dance company** *under* **dance**

comparable
04 akin, like, near **05** alike, close, equal **07** cognate, related, similar **08** parallel **09** analogous **10** equivalent,

tantamount **12** commensurate, proportional **13** corresponding, proportionate

comparably
07 equally **09** similarly **11** analogously **14** proportionally **15** correspondingly, proportionately

comparative
02 -er **03** -est **08** relative **12** by comparison, in comparison

comparatively
10 relatively **12** by comparison, in comparison

compare
02 cf, cp **03** get, vie **04** even, like, link **05** equal, liken, match, touch, weigh **06** confer, equate **07** balance, compeer, compete, measure, paragon, provide, stack up **08** confront, contrast, parallel, resemble **09** analogize, correlate, juxtapose **10** be as good as, comparison, set against **13** hold a candle to, set side by side **14** bear comparison, be comparable to **15** regard as the same
• **beyond compare**
06 superb **07** supreme **08** peerless **09** brilliant, matchless, nonpareil, unmatched **10** unequalled, unrivalled **11** superlative, unsurpassed **12** incomparable, without equal **15** without parallel

comparison
07 analogy, parable **08** contrast, likeness, parallel **10** similarity, similitude **11** correlation, differences, distinction, parallelism, resemblance **12** relationship **13** comparability, juxtaposition **15** differentiation

compartment
03 bay, box, pew, pod **04** area, cage, cell, pane, part, room, till **05** berth, booth, niche, panel, stall **06** alcove, carrel, locker, locule **07** chamber, cubicle, loculus, section, sleeper **08** carriage, casemate, category, division, traverse **09** cubbyhole, partition **10** pigeonhole **11** subdivision

compartmentalize
03 tag **04** file, slot, sort **05** group **08** classify **09** catalogue **10** categorize, pigeonhole **11** alphabetize **12** sectionalize

compass
04 area, bend, dial, plot, zone **05** ambit, curve, field, gamut, grasp, limit, range, reach, realm, round, scale, scope, space, sweep, swing **06** bounds, circle, extent, limits, obtain, realms, sphere, spread **07** achieve, circuit, enclose, pelorus, stretch, trammel **08** boundary, contrive, diapason, register, surround **09** enclosure **10** accomplish, comprehend **13** circumference

03 ENE, ESE, NNE, NNW, SSE, SSW, WNW, WSW
04 east, E by N, E by S, N by E, N by W, S by E, S by W, W by N, W by S, west
05 NE by E, NE by N, north, NW by N, NW by W, SE by E, SE by S, south, SW by S, SW by W
09 north-east, north-west, south-east, south-west
11 east by north, east by south, north by east, north by west, south by east, south by west, west by north, west by south
13 east-north-east, east-south-east, west-north-west, west-south-west
14 north-north-east, north-north-west, south-south-east, south-south-west
15 north-east by east, north-west by west, south-east by east, south-west by west
16 north-east by north, north-west by north, south-east by south, south-west by south

compassion
04 care, pity **05** heart, mercy **06** bowels, sorrow, ubuntu **07** concern, remorse **08** humanity, kindness, leniency, sympathy **10** condolence, gentleness, tenderness **11** benevolence **13** commiseration, consideration, fellow-feeling, understanding

compassionate
06 benign, caring, gentle, humane, kindly, tender **07** clement, feeling, lenient, piteous, pitiful, pitying **08** bleeding, merciful **09** forgiving **10** benevolent, charitable, forbearing, passionate, remorseful, supportive **11** kind-hearted, sympathetic, warm-hearted **12** humanitarian **13** tender-hearted, understanding

compatibility
05 match **07** harmony, rapport **08** sympathy **11** consistence, consistency, suitability **12** adaptability **14** like-mindedness

compatible
06 suited **07** similar **08** matching, suitable **09** accordant, adaptable, congruent, congruous, consonant, in harmony **10** consistent, harmonious, like-minded, well-suited **11** conformable, sympathetic, well-matched **12** reconcilable **13** having rapport

compatriot
10 countryman **12** countrywoman **13** fellow citizen **14** fellow national

compel
03 gar **04** make, urge **05** bully, coact, drive, force, garre, impel **06** coerce, hustle, lean on, oblige **07** dragoon, efforce, enforce **08** browbeat, bulldoze, compulse, insist on, pressure **09** constrain, press-gang, strongarm **10** intimidate, pressurize **11** necessitate **14** put the screws on

compelling
06 cogent, urgent **07** weighty **08** coercive, forceful, gripping, mesmeric, powerful, pressing, riveting **09** absorbing **10** compulsive, compulsory, conclusive, convincing, imperative, overriding, persuasive **11** enthralling, fascinating, irrefutable **12** irresistible, spellbinding **13** unputdownable

compendious
05 brief, crisp, short, terse **07** compact, concise, summary **08** complete, succinct **09** condensed **10** to the point **12** all-embracing **13** comprehensive

compendium
06 digest, manual, symbol **07** summary **08** abstract, breviate, handbook, synopsis **09** anthology, companion, vade-mecum **10** abridgment, collection, shortening **11** abridgement, compilation

compensate
05 atone, repay **06** cancel, make up, offset, recoup, redeem, refund, reward **07** balance, nullify, redress, requite, restore, satisfy **08** make good, make up to **09** indemnify, make up for, reimburse **10** balance out, counteract, make amends, neutralize, recompense, remunerate **11** countervail **12** counterpoise **14** counterbalance, make reparation

compensation
04 boot, bote **05** compo **06** amends, refund, return, reward **07** comfort, damages, payment, redress **08** reprisal, requital, solatium **09** atonement, demurrage, indemnity, repayment **10** blood money, correction, recompense, reparation **11** consolation, restitution, restoration **12** remuneration, satisfaction **13** reimbursement **15** conscience money, indemnification

compère
02 MC **04** host **05** emcee, front **06** anchor **07** present **09** anchorman, announcer, presenter **10** link person **11** anchorwoman

compete
03 ren, rin, run, vie **04** play, race **05** enter, fight, match, rival **06** battle, jostle, oppose, strive **07** compare, contend, contest, go in for **08** struggle, take part **09** challenge **11** participate, pit yourself

competence
05 power, skill **07** ability, fitness, purview **08** aptitude, capacity, facility **09** authority, expertise, technique **10** capability, efficiency, experience **11** proficiency, sufficience, sufficiency, suitability **12** jurisdiction **13** legal capacity

competent
03 fit **04** able, good **05** adept, equal, tight **06** expert, habile, strong, useful

07 capable, skilful, skilled, trained **08** adequate, masterly, passable, suitable **09** efficient, qualified **10** acceptable, consummate, legitimate, proficient, reasonable, sufficient **11** appropriate, experienced, respectable **12** accomplished, satisfactory **13** well-qualified

competition
03 bee, cup **04** bout, game, goal, gole, meet, open, quiz, race **05** event, field, match, vying **06** rivals, strife, trials **07** contest, cook off, rivalry **08** concours, conflict, knockout, struggle **09** challenge, emulation, encounter, opponents, spelldown **10** contention, opposition, tournament **11** challengers, competitors, spelling bee **12** championship, cross-country **13** combativeness **15** competitiveness

02 TT
05 Ashes, Derby, FA Cup
06 Le Mans
07 Grey Cup, Masters, Uber Cup, UEFA Cup
08 Rose Bowl, Ryder Cup, Speedway, World Cup
09 Motocross, Super Bowl, Thomas Cup, World Bowl
10 Asian Games, Formula One, Solheim Cup, Stanley Cup
11 Admiral's Cup, America's Cup, Kinnaird Cup, World Series
12 Iditarod Race, Olympic Games, Tour de France
13 Grand National, Kentucky Derby, Leonard Trophy
15 Paralympic Games
17 Commonwealth Games

competitive
03 low **04** fair, just, keen **05** pushy **06** modest **07** average, cut-rate **08** moderate **09** ambitious, combative, cut-throat, dog-eat-dog **10** aggressive, reasonable **11** contentious, inexpensive **12** antagonistic **15** bargain-basement

competitively
03 low **06** fairly **08** modestly **10** moderately, reasonably **13** inexpensively

competitiveness
07 rat race, rivalry **08** ambition, keenness **09** challenge, pugnacity, pushiness **10** aggression, antagonism **13** ambitiousness, assertiveness, combativeness **14** aggressiveness **15** contentiousness

competitor
05 rival **06** player **07** agonist, entrant, roadman **08** corrival, emulator, Olympian, opponent, trialist **09** adversary, candidate, contender, triallist **10** antagonist, challenger, contestant, opposition **11** competition, pancratiast, participant, pentathlete

ompilation
anagram indicator
4 opus, work 05 album, segue
6 corpus 07 omnibus 08 treasury
9 amassment, anthology, collation,
otpourri, selection, thesaurus
0 assemblage, collection,
ompendium, miscellany
4 arrangement, collectanea,
omposition, florilegium
2 accumulation, chrestomathy,
rganization

ompile
anagram indicator
4 cull, edit 05 amass 06 garner,
ather 07 arrange, collate, collect,
ompose, marshal 08 assemble,
rganize 09 construct 10 accumulate
4 put together
compiler
1 l 02 me
compiler's
4 mine

omplacency
5 pride 07 triumph 08 gloating,
leasure, serenity, smugness
4 contentment, self-content
2 complaisance, satisfaction
3 gratification, self-assurance

omplacent
4 smug, vain 05 proud 06 serene
7 pleased 08 gloating, serenity
9 contented, gratified, satisfied
0 triumphant 11 complaisant, self-
ssured, unconcerned 13 self-
ontented, self-righteous, self-satisfied

omplain
3 nag 04 ache, beef, bind, carp, fuss,
rn, hurt, mean, mein, mene, moan,
ump 05 bitch, bleat, gripe, groan,
rowl, grump, meane, plain, whine
6 bemoan, bewail, endure, grouse,
rutch, kvetch, lament, object, repine,
nivel, squawk, squeal, whinge
7 carry on, grumble, protest,
vheenge 08 be in pain, feel pain
9 bellyache, criticize, find fault, make
fuss 10 make a noise, suffer from
4 expostulate, kick up a fuss, raise a
tink, remonstrate 12 moan and groan
4 file a complaint 15 have a bone to
ick, lodge a complaint

omplainer
4 nark 06 kvetch, moaner, whiner
7 bleater, fusspot, grouser, niggler,
vhinger 08 grumbler, kvetcher 09 nit-
icker 10 bellyacher, fussbudget
4 fault-finder

omplaint
4 beef, moan 05 bleat, gripe, groan,
lain, upset 06 charge, grouch, grouse,
rutch, malady, plaint, squawk, whinge
7 ailment, beefing, carping, censure,
isease, grumble, illness, malaise,
rotest, quarrel, quibble, trouble,
vheenge 08 bleating, disorder,
laining, sickness 09 annoyance,
ellyache, condition, criticism,
rievance, infection, objection,
uerimony, whingeing 10 accusation,

affliction 11 bellyaching 12 fault-
finding, inflammation 13 indisposition
14 representation 15 dissatisfaction
See also **disease**; **inflammation**

• **expression of complaint**
02 ah

complaisant
06 docile 07 amiable, willing
08 amenable, biddable, obedient,
obliging 09 agreeable, compliant,
tractable 10 complacent, solicitous
11 conformable, deferential
12 conciliatory 13 accommodating

complement
03 set, sum 05 crown, match, quota,
total 06 alexin, amount, number, set
off 08 addition, capacity, complete,
contrast, entirety, fullness, round off,
strength, totality 09 accessory,
accompany, aggregate, allowance,
companion 10 completion, go well
with 11 counterpart 12 consummation
13 accompaniment 14 go well
together 15 combine well with

complementary
04 twin 06 fellow 08 matching
09 companion, finishing
10 compatible, completing,
harmonious, perfecting, reciprocal,
supporting 11 correlative
12 interrelated 13 corresponding
14 interdependent
See also **medicine**

complete
02 do 03 all, cap, end 04 done, full,
over, real 05 clean, close, crown,
ended, pakka, pucka, pukka, total,
utter, whole 06 answer, clinch,
damned, entire, fill in, finish, fulfil,
intact, make up, settle, wind up
07 achieve, execute, fill out, fulfill,
perfect, perform, plenary, realize,
settled 08 absolute, achieved,
conclude, detailed, finalize, finished,
integral, outright, round off, thorough,
unbroken, unedited 09 completed,
concluded, discharge, downright,
finalized, integrate, out-and-out, polish
off, terminate, undivided
10 accomplish, consummate,
exhaustive, terminated, unabridged
11 unmitigated, unqualified,
unshortened 12 accomplished,
unexpurgated 13 comprehensive,
thoroughgoing, unabbreviated,
unconditional

completely
02 up 03 all, out 05 fully, quite, right,
whole 06 hollow, in full, wholly
07 good and, sheerly, solidly, totally,
utterly 08 entirely, outright 09 all ends
up, all the way, every inch, perfectly, to
the hilt, to the wide 10 absolutely,
abundantly, altogether, thoroughly
11 back to front, neck and crop, up to
the hilt 12 from top to toe, heart and
soul, stoop and roop, stoup and roup,
well and truly 13 bag and baggage,
head over heels, root and branch 14 in

every respect 15 down to the ground,
from first to last

completion
03 end, sum 05 close, crown 06 finish
08 fruition 09 discharge, execution
10 attainment, conclusion, fulfilling,
fulfilment, perfection, settlement
11 achievement, culmination,
realization, termination
12 consummation, finalization
14 accomplishment

complex
◇ *anagram indicator*
05 mixed, thing 06 hang-up, phobia,
scheme, system, varied 07 devious,
diverse, network 08 compound,
disorder, fixation, involved, multiple,
neurosis, ramified, tortuous
09 Byzantine, composite, difficult,
elaborate, institute, intricate, obsession,
plexiform, structure 10 circuitous,
complicate, convoluted 11 aggregation,
complicated, development
12 organization 13 establishment,
preoccupation, sophisticated

complexion
03 rud 04 blee, cast, kind, leer, look,
skin, sort, tone, type 05 guise, light,
stamp 06 aspect, colour, nature
07 texture 08 attitude 09 character,
colouring 10 appearance
11 perspective 12 pigmentation

complexity
07 variety 09 intricacy 10 complicacy,
complicity 11 convolution,
deviousness, diverseness, elaboration,
involvement 12 complication,
entanglement, multiplicity,
ramification, repercussion,
tortuousness 13 compositeness
14 circuitousness 15 complicatedness

compliance
01 C 06 assent 07 keeping 08 yielding
09 agreement, appliance, deference,
obedience, passivity 10 accordance,
conformity, submission 11 application,
concurrence 12 acquiescence,
complaisance 14 conformability,
submissiveness

compliant
05 civil 06 docile 07 passive, pliable
08 amenable, biddable, flexible,
obedient, yielding 09 agreeable,
appliable, indulgent, tractable
10 obsequious, sequacious,
submissive 11 acquiescent,
complaisant, conformable, deferential,
subservient 13 accommodating

complicate
◇ *anagram indicator*
05 mix up 06 jumble, muddle, puzzle,
tangle 07 complex, confuse, involve,
inweave, perplex 08 compound,
entangle 09 elaborate 12 make
involved 13 make difficult

complicated
◇ *anagram indicator*
06 fiddly, implex, tricky 07 complex,
cryptic 08 confused, involved,

complication

puzzling, tortuous **09** Byzantine, difficult, elaborate, intricate **10** convoluted, perplexing **11** problematic **12** labyrinthine

complication

◇ *anagram indicator*
03 web **04** node, snag **05** nodus **06** tangle **07** mixture, problem **08** drawback, obstacle **09** confusion, intricacy **10** complexity, difficulty **11** complexness, convolution, elaboration **12** ramification, repercussion **13** complexedness

complicity

08 abetment, approval **09** agreement, collusion, knowledge **10** complexity, connivance **11** concurrence, involvement **13** collaboration **14** being in cahoots

compliment

04 laud **05** extol **06** admire, eulogy, favour, homage, honour, praise, salute **07** applaud, bouquet, commend, devoirs, douceur, flatter, regards, tribute **08** accolade, approval, encomium, eulogize, flattery, respects **09** baisemain, greetings, laudation, sugarplum, trade-last **10** admiration, best wishes, felicitate, good wishes, salutation **11** speak well of **12** commendation, congratulate, felicitation, pat on the back, remembrances **13** speak highly of **15** congratulations
• **looking for compliments**
07 angling, fishing

complimentary

04 free **06** gratis **07** glowing **08** admiring, courtesy, honorary **09** approving **10** eulogistic, favourable, flattering, for nothing, on the house **11** meliorative, panegyrical **12** appreciative, commendatory **14** congratulatory

comply

04 meet, obey **05** agree, all in, defer, yield **06** accede, accord, assent, follow, fulfil, oblige, submit **07** abide by, conform, consent, observe, perform, respect, satisfy **09** acquiesce, discharge **10** condescend **11** accommodate

component

◇ *anagram indicator*
03 bit **04** item, part, unit **05** basic, piece **06** factor, module, widget **07** element, partial, section **08** inherent, integral **09** essential, intrinsic, spare part **10** ingredient **11** constituent **12** constitutive, integral part **15** constituent part
See also **electrical**

comport

03 act, use **04** bear **05** abear, carry **06** acquit, behave, demean, deport **07** conduct, perform

compose

◇ *anagram indicator*
03 pen, set **04** calm, dite, form, lull,

make **05** build, frame, quell, quiet, still, write **06** create, devise, draw up, indite, invent, make up, pacify, settle, soothe, steady **07** arrange, assuage, collect, compile, concoct, control, fashion, produce, stickle, think of, think up **08** assemble, calm down, comprise **09** construct, reconcile **10** constitute **11** choreograph, orchestrate, put together **12** tranquillize

composed

◇ *anagram indicator*
04 calm, cool **05** quite **06** at ease, placid, sedate, serene **07** relaxed **08** together, tranquil **09** collected, confident, unruffled, unworried **10** calmed down, controlled **11** level-headed, unflappable **13** imperturbable, quietened down, self-possessed **14** self-controlled **15** cool as a cucumber

composer

04 bard, poet **05** lyric, maker **06** author, master, writer **07** creator, maestro **08** arranger, melodist, musician, producer, psalmist, triadist **09** epitapher, songsmith, tunesmith **10** epitaphist, operettist, originator, songwriter, symphonist **12** balladmonger, variationist, vaudevillist **13** contrapuntist, dodecaphonist, orchestralist

Composers include:

03 Bax (Sir Arnold), Sor (Fernando)
04 Adam (Adolphe), Arne (Thomas), Bach (Carl Philipp Emanuel), Bach (Johann Christian), Bach (Johann Sebastian), Berg (Alban), Bull (John), Byrd (William), Cage (John), Ives (Charles), Orff (Carl), Pärt (Arvo), Weir (Judith)
05 Adams (John), Auric (Georges), Berio (Luciano), Bizet (Georges), Bliss (Sir Arthur), Boito (Arrigo), Boyce (William), Bruch (Max), D'Indy (Vincent), Dufay (Guillaume), Dukas (Paul), Durey (Louis), Elgar (Sir Edward), Falla (Manuel de), Fauré (Gabriel), Glass (Philip), Gluck (Christoph), Grieg (Edvard), Haydn (Joseph), Holst (Gustav), Lehár (Franz), Liszt (Franz), Lully (Jean Baptiste), Ogdon (John), Parry (Sir Hubert), Ravel (Maurice), Satie (Erik), Verdi (Giuseppe), Weber (Carl Maria von)
06 Barber (Samuel), Bartók (Béla), Bishop (Sir Henry Rowley), Boulez (Pierre), Brahms (Johannes), Busoni (Ferruccio), Casals (Pablo), Chopin (Frédéric), Clarke (Jeremiah), Coates (Eric), Delius (Frederick), Dvořák (Antonín), Franck (César), German (Sir Edward), Glinka (Mikhail), Gounod (Charles), Gurney (Ivor), Handel (George Frideric), Kodály (Zoltán), Ligeti (György), Mahler (Gustav), Morley (Thomas), Mozart (Wolfgang

Amadeus), **Previn** (André), **Rameau** (Jean Philippe), **Rubbra** (Edmund), **Tallis** (Thomas), **Varèse** (Edgard), **Wagner** (Richard), **Walton** (Sir William), **Webern** (Anton von), **Wilbye** (John)
07 Albéniz (Isaac), Allegri (Gregorio), Bellini (Vincenzo), Bennett (Sir Richard Rodney), Berlioz (Hector), Borodin (Alexander), Britten (Benjamin), Campion (Thomas), Copland (Aaron), Corelli (Arcangelo), Debussy (Claude), Delibes (Léo), Dowland (John), Duruflé (Maurice), Fricker (Peter), Gibbons (Orlando), Górecki (Henryk), Janáček (Leos), Menotti (Gian-Carlo), Milhaud (Darius), Nicolai (Otto), Nielsen (Carl), Poulenc (Francis), Puccini (Giacomo), Purcell (Henry), Rossini (Gioacchino), Salieri (Antonio), Shankar (Ravi), Smetana (Bedrich), Strauss (Johann), Strauss (Richard), Tavener (John), Tippett (Sir Michael), Vivaldi (Antonio), Xenakis (Iannis)
08 Berkeley (Sir Lennox), Bruckner (Anton), Couperin (François), Goossens (Sir Eugene), Grainger (Percy), Hoffmann (Ernst Theodor Wilhelm), Holliger (Heinz), Honegger (Arthur), Maconchy (Dame Elizabeth), Mascagni (Pietro), Massenet (Jules), Messiaen (Olivier), Respighi (Ottorino), Schubert (Franz), Schumann (Robert), Scriabin (Aleksandr), Sibelius (Jean), Sondheim (Steven), Stanford (Sir Charles Villiers), Sullivan (Sir Arthur), Telemann (Georg Philipp), Victoria (Tomás Luis de), Williams (John)
09 Beethoven (Ludwig van), Boulanger (Nadia), Buxtehude (Diderik), Donizetti (Gaetano), Hindemith (Paul), Meyerbeer (Giacomo), Offenbach (Jacques), Pachelbel (Johann), Prokofiev (Sergei), Scarlatti (Alessandro), Scarlatti (Domenico), Tortelier (Paul)
10 Birtwistle (Sir Harrison), Boccherini (Luigi), Kabalevsky (Dmitri), Monteverdi (Claudio), Mussorgsky (Modeste), Praetorius (Michael), Rubinstein (Anton), Saint-Saëns (Camille), Schoenberg (Arnold), Stravinsky (Igor), Villa-Lobos (Hector)
11 Humperdinck (Engelbert), Leoncavallo (Ruggiero), Mendelssohn (Felix), Rachmaninov (Sergei), Stockhausen (Karlheinz), Tchaikovsky (Piotr), Theodorakis (Mikis)
12 Shostakovich (Dmitri)
13 Khatchaturian (Aram), Maxwell Davies (Sir Peter)
14 Rimsky-Korsakov (Nikolai)
15 Vaughan Williams (Ralph)

See also **libretto**

composite

05 alloy, blend, fused, mixed **06** fusion
07 amalgam, blended, complex, mixture **08** combined, compound, pastiche **09** patchwork, synthesis
10 conflation **11** agglutinate, combination, synthesized
12 amalgamation, conglomerate
13 agglutination, heterogeneous

composition

◇ *anagram indicator*
02 op **04** book, dite, fine, form, opus, poem, port, task, text, work
05 compo, essay, motet, novel, opera, paper, piece, story, study, thing, verse
06 design, erotic, layout, make-up, making, motett, review, satire, sonata, thesis **07** article, balance, drawing, harmony, mixture, morceau, picture, writing **08** creation, devising, exercise, oratorio, painting, pencraft, rhapsody, symmetry, symphony, treatise
09 album-leaf, arranging, capriccio, character, exaration, formation, impromptu, invention, structure, work of art **10** adaptation, assignment, compromise, concoction, confection, consonance, mock-heroic, production, proportion, whipstitch
11 arrangement, combination, compilation, formulation
12 conformation, constitution, dissertation, organization
13 accompaniment, choral prelude, configuration **15** putting together

See also **musical**

compost

04 peat **05** humus, mulch **06** manure
07 grow-bag, mixture **08** dressing, leaf-soil **09** leaf-mould **10** fertilizer, growing-bag

composure

04 calm, ease **05** poise **06** aplomb, temper **07** dignity **08** calmness, coolness, serenity **09** assurance, character, placidity, sangfroid
10 collection, confidence, dispassion, equanimity **11** composition, impassivity, self-control, temperament
12 tranquillity **13** self-assurance
14 self-possession **15** level-headedness

compound

◇ *anagram indicator*
03 Cpd, mix, pen **04** fold, fuse, yard
05 add to, alloy, blend, court, fused, mixed, pound, put up, unite **06** corral, fusion, hybrid, make up, medley, mingle, worsen **07** amalgam, augment, blended, combine, complex, magnify, mixture, paddock
08 coalesce, combined, dispense, heighten, increase, multiple, stockade
09 admixture, aggravate, composite, enclosure, intensify, intricate, synthesis
10 amalgamate, complicate, exacerbate, synthesize **11** combination, complicated, composition, intermingle, put together, synthesized
12 amalgamation, conglomerate

See also **chemical**

comprehend

◇ *containment indicator*
03 see **04** know, twig **05** catch, cover, get it, grasp, sense **06** fathom, take in, tumble **07** catch on, compass, contain, discern, embrace, include, involve, make out, realize **08** comprise, conceive, perceive, tumble to
09 apprehend, encompass, penetrate
10 appreciate, assimilate, generalize, understand **11** make sense of **15** put your finger on

comprehensible

05 clear, lucid, plain **06** simple
08 coherent, explicit **09** graspable
10 accessible **11** conceivable, discernible **12** intelligible
14 understandable **15** straightforward

comprehension

03 ken **05** grasp, sense **07** insight
09 judgement, knowledge
10 conception, perception
11 discernment, realization
12 appreciation, apprehension, intelligence **13** understanding

comprehensive

04 full, wide **05** all-in, broad **06** global
07 blanket, capable, general, overall
08 complete, elliptic, sweeping, thorough **09** extensive, inclusive, universal **10** elliptical, exhaustive, widespread **11** compendious **12** all-embracing, all-inclusive, encyclopedic
14 across-the-board, encyclopedical

comprehensively

05 fully **06** widely **07** broadly
10 completely, thoroughly, widespread
11 extensively **12** exhaustively

compress

03 jam, ram, zip **04** cram, lace, pack, pump, tamp **05** crowd, crush, pinch, press, screw, stuff, wedge **06** impact, reduce, squash, strain **07** abridge, astrict, compact, embrace, flatten, shorten, squeeze **08** astringe, condense, contract, shoehorn
09 coarctate, constrict, summarize, synopsize, telescope **10** abbreviate, pressurize **11** concentrate, consolidate, strangulate

compression

07 packing, pumping **08** pinching, pressing, stuffing, thlipsis
09 squashing **10** condensing, flattening **12** constriction
13 concentration, consolidation

comprise

◇ *containment indicator*
04 form **05** cover **06** embody, make up, take in **07** compose, contain, embrace, include, involve **09** consist of, encompass **10** comprehend, constitute **11** incorporate **12** be composed of

compromise

◇ *anagram indicator*
04 deal, risk **05** adapt, agree, shame
06 adjust, damage, expose, settle, weaken **07** balance, bargain, concede,

imperil, involve **08** endanger, trade-off
09 agreement, arbitrate, discredit, dishonour, embarrass, implicate, mediation, middle way, negotiate, prejudice, settle for, undermine
10 adjustment, concession, jeopardize, settlement **11** arbitration, composition, co-operation, give and take, meet halfway, negotiation, temperament **12** bring shame to, modus vivendi **13** accommodation, understanding **15** make concessions

compulsion

04 need, urge **05** drive, force
06 demand, desire, duress **07** duresse, impulse, longing **08** coaction, coercion, distress, pressure
09 necessity, obsession **10** constraint, insistence, obligation, temptation
11 enforcement **13** preoccupation

compulsive

06 hooked, urgent **07** chronic, driving
08 addicted, gripping, habitual, hardened, hopeless, mesmeric, riveting **09** absorbing, besetting, dependent, incurable, obsessive
10 compelling, inveterate
11 enthralling, fascinating, unavoidable
12 incorrigible, irredeemable, irresistible, overpowering, overwhelming, pathological, spellbinding **14** uncontrollable

compulsively

09 incurably **10** habitually, inevitably
11 chronically, obsessively, unavoidably
12 incorrigibly, irresistibly
13 involuntarily **14** pathologically

compulsory

03 set **06** forced **07** binding
08 coactive, required **09** de rigueur, essential, mandatory, necessary, requisite **10** compelling, imperative, obligatory, stipulated **11** contractual

compunction

05 guilt, qualm, shame **06** qualms, regret, sorrow, unease **07** remorse
09 misgiving, penitence **10** contrition, hesitation, misgivings, reluctance, repentance, uneasiness

computation

03 sum **06** answer, result **08** estimate, figuring, forecast **09** reckoning
10 arithmetic, estimation, working-out
11 calculation, forecasting

compute

03 sum **04** rate **05** add up, count, tally, total **06** assess, figure, reckon
07 count up, measure, work out
08 estimate, evaluate **09** calculate, enumerate

computer

02 NC, PC **03** MPC **10** calculator
15 electronic brain

Computers include:

03 HAL, IBM, Mac, SAL
04 iMac, VIKI
05 Eddie, ENIAC, Holly, iBook
06 UNIVAC

08 Colossus, Deep Blue, Spectrum
09 The Matrix
11 DeepThought
12 Commodore Pet

Computer scientists include:

04 Bell (Gordon), Bush (Vannevar), Cray (Seymour), Hurd (Cuthbert Corwin), Jobs (Steven), Zuse (Konrad)
05 Aiken (Howard Hathaway), Burks (Arthur Walter), Gates (William Henry 'Bill'), Olsen (Kenneth Harry), Sugar (Alan)
06 Amdahl (Gene Myron), Backus (John), Comrie (Leslie John), Eckert (John Presper), Hopper (Grace Murray), Huskey (Harry Douglas), Michie (Donald), Milner (Robin Gorell), Porter (Arthur), Turing (Alan), Wilkes (Maurice Vincent)
07 Babbage (Charles), Kilburn (Tom), Mauchly (John William), Shannon (Claude Elwood), Stibitz (George Robert), Wheeler (David John)
08 Lovelace (Ada, Countess), Shockley (William Bradford), Sinclair (Sir Clive), Williams (Sir Frederic Calland)
09 Atanasoff (John Vincent), Forrester (Jay Wright), Goldstine (Herman Heine), Hollerith (Herman), Wilkinson (James Hardy)
10 Berners-Lee (Tim), Fairclough (John Whitaker), Michaelson (Sidney), Von Neumann (John)

Computing and Internet terms include:

02 CD, IT, PC, VR
03 bit, bot, bug, bus, CD-R, CPU, DOS, DTP, DVD, FAQ, FTP, GUI, hit, IDE, ISP, Mac®, net, P2P, PDF, RAM, ROM, RTF, URL, VDU, WAN, Web, WWW
04 BIOS, boot, byte, card, CD-RW, cell, chip, data, disk, dump, file, game, HTML, icon, iMac®, ISDN, menu, port, ring, SGML, Unix®, worm
05 ASCII, BASIC, cache, CD-ROM, e-mail, iBook®, JANET®, Linux, login, log on, Mac OS, macro, modem, mouse, MS-DOS®, pixel, shell, virus
06 access, backup, binary, bitmap, buffer, cursor, DVD-ROM, editor, format, Google®, laptop, log off, memory, plug-in, reboot, screen, script, server, the Net, the Web, toggle, window
07 browser, crawler, default, desktop, hacking, monitor, network, palmtop, Pentium®, pointer, printer, program, scanner, toolbar, Unicode, upgrade, Web page, Web site, Windows®, WYSIWYG, zip disk
08 Apple Mac®, autosave, bookmark, chat room, database, emoticon, firewall, freeware, gigabyte, graphics, handheld, hard disk, hardware, home page, Internet,

joystick, keyboard, kilobyte, megabyte, mouse mat, notebook, password, platform, protocol, software, template, terabyte, terminal, user name
09 character, debugging, directory, disk drive, e-commerce, hard drive, hyperlink, hypertext, interface, mainframe, newsgroup, shareware, sound card, utilities, video card
10 domain name, floppy disk, multimedia, netiquette, peer-to-peer, peripheral, rewritable, serial port
11 abandonware, application, compact disc, compression, cut and paste, floppy drive, motherboard, optical disk, screen saver, silicon chip, spreadsheet, Trojan horse, workstation
12 circuit board, graphics card, installation, laser printer, parallel port, search engine, spellchecker, subdirectory, World Wide Web
13 file extension, ink-jet printer, microcomputer, user interface
14 electronic mail, internal memory, microprocessor, read only memory, rich text format, virtual reality, word processing
15 operating system, wide area network

See also **key**; **language**

- **connected computers**
03 net, web **07** network

comrade
03 pal **04** aide, ally, mate **05** billy, buddy, butty, crony **06** billie, escort, fellow, frater, friend **07** Achates, consort, partner **08** chaperon, follower, intimate, sidekick, tovarich, tovarish **09** assistant, associate, attendant, bully-rook, chaperone, colleague, communist, companion, confidant, tovarisch **10** accomplice, confidante **11** bon camarade, confederate **12** pot companion

comradeship
08 affinity **09** closeness **10** fellowship, friendship, sisterhood **11** brotherhood, camaraderie, sociability **12** sisterliness, togetherness **13** brotherliness, companionship, esprit de corps

con
02 do **04** dupe, hoax, know, rook, scam, scan, show **05** bluff, cheat, fraud, knock, learn, teach, trick **06** fiddle, fleece, racket, rip off **07** against, deceive, defraud, mislead, swindle, tweedle **08** cheating, hoodwink, inveigle, prisoner **09** bamboozle, deception **11** acknowledge, double-cross **15** confidence trick

concatenation
05 chain, nexus, trail, train **06** course, series, string, thread **07** linking **08** progress, sequence **10** connection, procession, succession **11** progression **12** interlinking, interlocking

concave
04 arch **05** vault **06** cupped, hollow, sunken **07** invexed, scooped **08** curved in, hollowed, incurved, indented **09** depressed, excavated, incurvate **14** bending inwards

conceal
◇ *containment indicator*
◇ *hidden indicator*
04 bury, feal, heal, heel, hele, hide, mask, sink, veil **05** cloak, cloke, cover, stash **06** closet, hush up, keep in, pocket, screen, shroud, vizard **07** cover up, obscure, secrete, smother **08** disguise, keep dark, submerge, suppress, tuck away **09** dissemble, keep quiet, overgreen, whitewash **10** camouflage, keep hidden, keep secret, subterfuge **11** dissimulate, put the lid on **14** keep out of sight, keep under wraps

concealed
◇ *containment indicator*
◇ *hidden indicator*
05 perdu **06** covert, hidden, latent, masked, perdue, unseen **07** covered **08** screened **09** disguised, submerged **10** tucked away **11** clandestine **13** inconspicuous

concealment
◇ *containment indicator*
◇ *hidden indicator*
04 mask, veil **05** cloak, cover, wraps **06** hiding, screen, shroud **07** cover-up, hideout, mystery, privacy, secrecy, shelter **08** disguise, hideaway **09** secretion, whitewash **10** camouflage, protection **11** keeping dark, smokescreen, suppression **13** keeping secret

concede
03 owe, own **04** cede **05** admit, allow, grant, own up, yield **06** accede, accept, give up **07** confess, forfeit **08** hand over **09** recognize, sacrifice, surrender **10** condescend, relinquish **11** acknowledge

conceit
03 ego **04** fume, wind **05** image, pride, think **06** device, simile, vanity **07** bighead, egotism, imagine, swagger, thought **08** conceive, concetto, metaphor, puppyism, self-love **09** arrogance, cockiness, immodesty, vainglory **10** comparison, narcissism **11** complacency, haughtiness **12** boastfulness **13** bigheadedness, conceitedness, understanding **14** figure of speech, self-admiration, self-assumption, self-importance

conceited
04 smug, vain **05** cocky, flory, proud, windy, witty **06** clever, snotty **07** haughty, stuck-up **08** arrogant, boastful, immodest, puffed up **09** bigheaded, cat-witted, egotistic, upsetting **10** complacent, toffee-nose **11** egotistical, fantastical, overweening, swell-headed, toffee-nosed

narcissistic, supercilious, inglorious **13** above yourself, self-important, self-satisfied, swelled-headed, swollen-headed **14** full of ourself

onceivable
likely **07** tenable **08** credible, ossible, probable **09** cogitable, ausible, thinkable **10** believable, aginable

onceivably
possibly, probably **09** plausibly imaginably

onceive
see **04** form, take **05** brain, fancy, asp, guess, start, think **06** create, esign, devise, enwomb, invent believe, conceit, develop, express, ntasy, gestate, imagine, picture, oduce, realize, suppose, think of, ink up **08** contrive, envisage, erceive **09** apprehend, be fertile, rmulate, originate, reproduce, sualize **10** appreciate, come up with, mprehend, understand **11** get egnant, give birth to **14** become egnant **15** get into your head

oncentrate
mind **05** amass, bunch, crowd, cus, juice, rivet, think **06** apozem, tend, centre, direct, distil, elixir, ther, reduce **07** cluster, collect, ssence, extract, thicken **08** boil own, compress, condense, consider, nverge **09** decoction, decocture, aporate, intensify **10** accumulate, entralize, congregate **11** consolidate, ephlegmate, put your mind distillation, keep your mind, pay tention, quintessence **13** apply urself **15** devote attention

oncentrated
conc, deep, hard, rich **05** dense all-out, strong **07** intense, reduced vigorous **09** concerted, ondensed, distilled, intensive, renuous, thickened, undiluted, ndivided **10** compressed, aporated

oncentration
conc, heed, mass, mind **05** crowd cluster **08** devotion, focusing, ouping **09** attention, denseness, tensity, reduction, thickness absorption, collection application, boiling-down, mpression, convergence, deep ought, engrossment, evaporation accumulation, close thought, ngregation, distillation agglomeration, consolidation centralization, conglomeration

oncept
idea, idée, plan, view **05** image notion, theory, vision **07** picture, ought **09** dimension, intention, niversal **10** conception, hypothesis, pression **11** abstraction visualization

conception
04 clue, idea, plan, view **05** birth, image **06** design, notion, origin, outset, theory, vision **07** concept, genesis, inkling, picture, thought **09** beginning, formation, inception, intention, invention, knowledge, launching, pregnancy **10** conceiving, hypothesis, impression, initiation, perception **11** abstraction, fecundation, origination **12** appreciation, impregnation, inauguration, insemination, reproduction **13** comprehension, fertilization, understanding, visualization

conceptual
05 ideal **08** abstract, notional, thematic **11** speculative, theoretical **12** hypothetical **14** classificatory

concern
03 job **04** baby, busy, care, cern, duty, firm, heed, part, reck, reke, task **05** alarm, cover, field, issue, point, stake, topic, touch, upset, worry **06** affair, affect, bear on, bother, charge, debate, devote, indaba, matter, meddle, pidgin, pigeon, reckon, regard, sorrow, strain, tender, unease **07** anguish, anxiety, apply to, be about, company, disturb, involve, lookout, perturb, pidgeon, problem, refer to, subject, thought, trouble **08** argument, business, deal with, disquiet, distress, interest, pressure, question, relate to **09** attention, pertain to, syndicate **10** enterprise, solicitude **11** appertain to, association, concernment, corporation, disturbance, involvement, make anxious, make worried, partnership **12** apprehension, have to do with, organization, perturbation **13** attentiveness, consideration, establishment **14** prey on your mind, responsibility **15** be connected with

See also **company**; **business**

concerned
◇ *anagram indicator*
04 kind **05** upset **06** caring, uneasy **07** anxious, helpful, related, unhappy, versant, worried **08** affected, bothered, gracious, involved, troubled **09** attentive, connected, disturbed, perturbed, sensitive, unselfish **10** altruistic, charitable, distressed, implicated, interested, solicitous, thoughtful **11** considerate **12** apprehensive
• **be concerned**
04 care, mell
• **concerned with**
02 in, re **05** about

concerning
02 of, on, re **04** in re, over **05** about, after, anent **07** apropos **08** to do with, touching **09** as regards, regarding **10** relating to, relevant to, respecting **11** referring to **12** with regard to **13** in

the matter of, with respect to **14** on the subject of **15** with reference to

concert
03 gig **04** prom, show **05** quill, union **06** accord, smoker, soirée, unison **07** concord, harmony, recital **09** agreement, rendering, rendition, unanimity **10** appearance, consonance, engagement, hootenanny, jam session, production **11** concordance, co-operation, partnership, performance **12** presentation **13** collaboration, entertainment

concerted
05 joint **06** shared, united **07** planned **08** combined **09** organized **10** collective **11** co-operative, co-ordinated, interactive, prearranged **12** concentrated **13** collaborative

concession
03 cut, sop **05** grant, right **06** ceding, favour **07** forfeit **08** decrease, discount, giving-up, handover, yielding **09** admission, allowance, exception, franchise, privilege, reduction, sacrifice, surrender **10** acceptance, adjustment, compromise **11** recognition, synchoresis **12** special right **14** relinquishment **15** acknowledgement
• **expression of concession**
02 ou, ow

conciliate
06 disarm, pacify, soften, soothe **07** appease, mollify, placate, satisfy **09** reconcile **10** propitiate **11** disembitter

conciliation
09 placation **11** appeasement, peacemaking **12** pacification, propitiation **13** mollification **14** reconciliation

conciliator
04 dove **06** broker **08** mediator **09** go-between, middleman **10** negotiator, peacemaker, reconciler **11** intercessor **12** intermediary

conciliatory
06 irenic **07** pacific **09** appeasing, assuaging, disarming, peaceable, placatory **10** mollifying **11** peacemaking **12** pacificatory, propitiative, propitiatory, smooth-spoken **13** smooth-talking, smooth-tongued **14** reconciliatory

concise
04 curt **05** brief, crisp, pithy, short, terse, tight **07** compact, laconic, summary **08** abridged, elliptic, mutilate, succinct, synoptic **09** condensed, thumbnail **10** aphoristic, compressed, elliptical, to the point **11** abbreviated, compendious **12** epigrammatic **14** epigrammatical

concisely
06 curtly **07** briefly, crisply, in a word, in brief, in short, pithily, tersely

10 succinctly, to the point **11** in a nutshell, laconically

conclave
05 cabal **06** parley, powwow
07 cabinet, council, meeting, session
08 assembly **09** gathering
10 conference **13** confabulation, secret meeting

conclude
03 end **04** amen, make **05** agree, allow, cease, close, debar, infer, judge, uptie **06** assume, clinch, decide, deduce, effect, finish, gather, reason, reckon, settle, top off, wind up, wrap up **07** arrange, enclose, pull off, resolve, suppose, surmise, work out **08** bring off, complete, restrain **09** culminate, determine, establish, negotiate, polish off, terminate **10** accomplish, conjecture, consummate **11** come to an end, discontinue, draw to an end **12** bring to an end

conclusion
03 con, end **04** coda, fine **05** close, finis, issue, omega, point **06** answer, ending, finale, finish, result, riddle, upshot **07** come-off, finding, opinion, outcome, problem, verdict **08** decision, epilogue, explicit, illation, pirlicue, settling, solution **09** agreement, brokering, cessation, clinching, deduction, effecting, inference, judgement, punchline **10** assumption, completion, consectary, conviction, experiment, peroration, pulling-off, resolution, settlement, working-out **11** arrangement, consequence, culmination, negotiation, termination **12** consummation **13** determination, establishment **14** accomplishment, discontinuance
• in conclusion
04 ergo **06** in fine **07** finally, to sum up **09** in closing **10** to conclude

conclusive
03 net **04** nett **05** clear, final
08 decisive, definite, ultimate
10 convincing, definitive, unarguable, undeniable **11** irrefutable
12 indisputable, unanswerable, unappealable

conclusively
07 clearly, finally **10** decisively, definitely, ultimately, unarguably, undeniably **11** irrefutably
12 convincingly, definitively, indisputably

concoct
◇ *anagram indicator*
03 fix, mix **04** brew, cook, make, plan, plot **05** blend, frame, hatch **06** cook up, decoct, devise, invent, make up, mature **07** develop, dream up, prepare, think up **08** contrive, rustle up **09** fabricate, formulate
11 manufacture, put together

concoction
◇ *anagram indicator*
04 brew, myth **05** blend, fable, story

06 potion **07** fiction, mixture, untruth
08 compound, creation **09** hell-broth, love-juice **10** fairy story
11 combination, fabrication, preparation, witches' brew

concomitant
07 symptom **09** attendant, by-product, conjoined, secondary, syndromic **10** co-existent, concurrent, incidental, side effect **11** associative, synchronous **12** accompanying, coincidental, conterminous, contributing, simultaneous
13 accompaniment, complementary, epiphenomenon
15 contemporaneous

concord
04 pact **05** agree, amity, peace, union
06 accord, treaty, unison **07** compact, concent, entente, harmony, rapport
09 agreement, concentus, consensus, harmonize, unanimity **10** consonance, friendship **11** amicability

concourse
04 hall **05** crowd, crush, foyer, lobby, plaza, press, swarm **06** lounge, piazza, repair, resort, throng **07** meeting
08 assembly, entrance **09** gathering, multitude **10** collection, confluence

concrete
04 firm, real **05** béton, solid **06** actual
07 factual, genuine, Siporex®, visible
08 definite, explicit, material, physical, positive, specific, tangible
09 touchable **11** perceptible, substantial

concubine
05 leman, lover, madam **07** lorette, sultana **08** mistress, paramour
09 courtesan, guinea-hen, kept woman **11** apple-squire

concupiscence
04 lust **06** desire, libido **07** concupy, lechery **08** appetite, lewdness
09 horniness, lubricity, randiness
11 lustfulness **12** sexual desire
14 lasciviousness, libidinousness

concupiscent
04 lewd **05** horny, randy **07** lustful
09 lecherous **10** lascivious, libidinous, lubricious

concur
05 agree **06** accede, accord, assent, comply **07** approve, consent
08 coincide **09** acquiesce, co-operate, harmonize **11** be in harmony

concurrence
06 assent **07** consent **08** approval, syndrome **09** agreement, synchrony
10 acceptance, conspiracy
11 association, coexistence, coincidence, consilience, convergence
12 acquiescence, common ground, simultaneity **13** juxtaposition
15 contemporaneity

concurrent
10 coexistent, coexisting, coincident, coinciding **11** concomitant,

synchronous **12** accompanying, simultaneous **15** contemporaneous

concussion
10 head injury **11** brain injury, water hammer **15** unconsciousness

condemn
◇ *anagram indicator*
03 ban, bar **04** cast, damn, doom, his kest, slam **05** blame, decry, force, judge, knock, slate **06** berate, coerce compel, ordain, punish, revile
07 accurse, censure, consign, convict deplore, destine, destroy, reprove, run down, upbraid **08** demolish, denounce, reproach, sentence
09 castigate, criticize, deprecate, disparage, reprehend **10** disapprove, find guilty **12** declare unfit **13** declare unsafe, give a sentence, pass a sentence

condemnation
◇ *anagram indicator*
03 ban **04** doom **05** blame
07 censure, reproof **08** judgment, reproach, sentence **09** criticism, damnation, judgement **10** conviction thumbs-down **11** castigation, deprecation, disapproval, reprobation
12 denunciation **13** disparagement

condemnatory
08 accusing, critical **09** damnatory, reprobate **10** accusatory, censorious
11 deprecatory, judgemental, reprobative, reprobatory
12 denunciatory, disapproving, discouraging, proscriptive, unfavourable **13** incriminating

condensation
05 steam **06** digest, précis
07 summary **08** moisture, synopsis
09 reduction **11** abridgement, boiling down, compression, contraction, curtailment, evaporation
12 distillation, liquefaction
13 concentration, consolidation, deliquescence, precipitation

condense
03 cut **06** distil, précis, reduce
07 abridge, compact, curtail, cut down, shorten, thicken **08** boil down compress, contract, solidify
09 capsulize, coagulate, epitomize, evaporate, intensify, summarize
10 abbreviate, condensate, deliquesce, inspissate **11** concentrate encapsulate, precipitate

condensed
03 cut **04** rich **05** dense **06** potted, strong **07** capsule, clotted, compact, concise, cut down, reduced, summar
08 capsular **09** curtailed, shortened, thickened, undiluted **10** abstracted, coagulated, compressed, contracted, evaporated, summarized
12 concentrated

condescend
04 bend **05** agree, deign, grant, stoop
06 comply, see fit **07** concede, consent, decline, descend, specify

[c]ondescending

[0]9 patronize, vouchsafe 10 talk down [t]o 12 be snobbish to 13 lower yourself [1]4 demean yourself, humble yourself

condescending

[0]5 lofty 06 lordly, snooty 07 haughty, stuck-up 08 gracious, snobbish, superior 09 imperious 10 disdainful [1]1 patronizing, toffee-nosed [1]2 supercilious

condescendingly

[1]0 snobbishly 11 imperiously [1]2 disdainfully 13 patronizingly [1]4 superciliously

condescension

[0]4 airs 05 stoop 07 disdain [0]9 loftiness 10 lordliness [1]1 haughtiness, superiority [1]2 snobbishness

condiment

[0]4 salt 05 spice 06 ginger, pepper, relish, season 07 caraway, chutney, mustard, pickles, vinegar 08 carraway, chow-chow 09 seasoning [1]1 horseradish, tracklement 13 French mustard 14 English mustard

condition

◊ anagram indicator

[0]2 do, if 03 -dom, ply 04 case, form, nick, pass, rule, sted, tone, trim, tune [0]5 adapt, equip, groom, limit, mould, order, prime, set-up, shape, state, stead, stedd, stede, steed, teach, terms, train, treat 06 adjust, defect, demand, factor, fettle, health, kilter, malady, milieu, plight, revive, season, stedde, temper 07 ailment, climate, context, disease, educate, factors, fitness, illness, improve, nourish, prepare, problem, proviso, restore, setting [0]8 accustom, disorder, position, quandary, restrict, weakness [0]9 brainwash, complaint, essential, infirmity, influence, necessity, provision, situation, transform, way of life 10 atmosphere, background, imitation, obligation 11 environment, familiarize, make healthy, predicament, requirement, restriction, stipulation 12 indoctrinate, precondition, prerequisite, surroundings, working order [1]3 circumstances, qualification, state of health

See also **disease; psychological; skin**

• **in good condition**

[0]2 OK 03 fit 04 okay, taut, tidy, well [0]5 sound 07 in flesh, in shape, thrifty [1]3 well-preserved

• **in perfect condition**

[0]2 go 06 groovy 12 sound as a bell

• **in such condition**

[0]2 so

• **in what condition**

[0]3 how

[co]nditional

[0]4 tied 05 based 07 limited, subject [0]8 relative 09 dependent, provisory, qualified 10 contingent, restricted [1]1 provisional

conditionally

09 limitedly 10 relatively 11 qualifiedly 13 provisionally

conditioning

07 shaping 08 moulding 09 influence 10 adaptation, adjustment 11 preparation 12 transforming

condolence

04 pity 07 comfort, support 08 sympathy 10 compassion 11 consolation 13 commiseration

condom

04 safe 06 johnny, rubber, sheath 07 Femidom®, johnnie, scumbag 10 protective 12 female condom, French letter, prophylactic 13 contraceptive

condone

05 allow, brook 06 accept, excuse, ignore, pardon 07 forgive, let pass 08 overlook, tolerate 09 disregard 15 turn a blind eye to

conducive

06 useful 07 helpful, leading, tending 09 promoting 10 beneficial, favourable, productive 11 encouraging, ministerial 12 advantageous, contributing, contributory, instrumental

conduct

02 do 03 act, ren, rin, run 04 bear, hold, keep, lead, show, take, ways 05 bring, carry, chair, guide, pilot, steer, usher 06 acquit, behave, convey, direct, escort, handle, manage 07 actions, bearing, comport, control, manners, operate, perform, running, solicit 08 attitude, behavior, carry out, guidance, organize, practice, regulate, transmit 09 accompany, behaviour, demeanour, direction, operation 10 administer, deportment, leadership, management 11 comportment, orchestrate, supervision 12 be in charge of, organization 14 administration

conductance

01 G

conductor

06 leader 07 clippie, maestro, manager 11 non-electric

Conductors include:

04 Böhm (Karl), Wood (Sir Henry) 05 Boult (Sir Adrian), Bülow (Hans von), Davis (Sir Andrew), Davis (Sir Colin), Elgar (Sir Edward), Hallé (Sir Charles), Kempe (Rudolf), Solti (Sir Georg), Sousa (John Philip) 06 Abbado (Claudio), Boulez (Pierre), Casals (Pablo), Gibson (Sir Alexander), Maazel (Lorin), Mahler (Gustav), Previn (André), Rattle (Sir Simon), Walter (Bruno) 07 Beecham (Sir Thomas), Gergiev (Valery), Haitink (Bernard), Harding (Daniel), Jansons (Mariss), Karajan (Herbert von), Lambert (Constant), Nicolai (Otto), Richter (Hans),

Sargent (Sir Malcolm), Smetana (Bedrich), Strauss (Johann), Strauss (Richard) 08 Goossens (Sir Eugene) 09 Ashkenazy (Vladimir), Barenboim (Daniel), Bernstein (Leonard), Boulanger (Nadia), Klemperer (Otto), Mackerras (Sir Charles), Stokowski (Leopold), Tortelier (Paul), Toscanini (Arturo) 10 Barbirolli (Sir John), Villa-Lobos (Heitor) 11 Furtwängler (Wilhelm) 12 Rostropovich (Mstislav)

conduit

04 duct, main, pipe, tube 05 canal, chute, ditch, drain, flume, trunk 06 gutter, trough, tunnel 07 channel, culvert, passage, wireway 08 fountain, penstock, waterway 10 passageway 11 watercourse

cone

03 puy 05 spire 06 cornet, funnel 09 monticule, strobilus

confection

◊ anagram indicator

See **dessert**

confectionery

05 candy 06 sweets 07 bonbons, goodies, junkets, toffees 08 licorice, sweeties 09 liquorice 10 chocolates, confiserie, sweetmeats, sweet-stuff

See also **sweet**

confederacy

04 band, Bund 05 junta, junto, union 06 league 07 compact 08 alliance 09 coalition 10 conspiracy, federation 11 Five Nations, partnership 13 confederation

confederate

04 ally, band 05 cover 06 allied, friend, united 07 abettor, fedarie, federal, partner 08 combined, federary, federate, foedarie 09 accessory, assistant, associate, colleague, federarie, supporter 10 accomplice, associated 11 conspirator 12 collaborator

confederation

04 zupa 05 union 06 league 07 compact 08 alliance 09 coalition, hermandad 10 federation 11 association, confederacy, partnership 12 amalgamation

confer

02 cf, do 03 pay 04 give, lend, talk 05 award, grant, parle, pawaw 06 accord, bestow, debate, impart, parley, powwow 07 compare, consult, discuss, give out, present 08 converse 10 deliberate 13 exchange views

conference

03 hui 04 diet, pear 05 forum 06 debate, huddle, indaba, parley, powwow, summit 07 meeting, palaver, seminar 08 colloquy, congress, dialogue 09 symposium 10 colloquium, convention,

discussion, imparlance, pourparler
11 convocation, emparlaunce, get-together **12** consultation, council of war

confess
03 own **04** avow, sing **05** admit, cough, grant, own up **06** affirm, agnize, assert, expose, fess up, reveal, shrive, squeak **07** concede, confide, declare, divulge, profess, tell all, unbosom **08** disclose, unburden **09** come clean, make known, recognize **11** accept blame, acknowledge **13** come out with it, spill the beans, spill your guts **15** get off your chest

confession
06 avowal, shrift **08** exposure, owning-up **09** admission, assertion **10** disclosure, divulgence, profession, revelation, submission, unbosoming **11** affirmation, declaration, making known, short shrift, unburdening **14** acknowledgment **15** acknowledgement, amende honorable

confidant, confidante
03 pal **04** chum, mate **05** buddy, crony **06** friend **08** alter ego, intimate **09** companion **10** best friend, bosom buddy, repository **11** bosom friend, close friend

confide
04 affy, tell **05** admit **06** impart, reveal **07** breathe, confess, divulge, entrust, unbosom, whisper **08** disclose, intimate, unburden **11** tell a secret **15** get off your chest

confidence
03 con **04** hope **05** faith, poise, trust **06** aplomb, belief, secret **07** courage **08** boldness, calmness, credence, forehead, intimacy, reliance **09** assurance, certainty, composure **10** conviction, dependence, self-belief **11** assuredness **12** positiveness, self-reliance **13** private matter, self-assurance **14** self-confidence, self-possession
• **in confidence**
08 in secret, secretly **09** entre nous, in privacy, in private, privately **10** personally **11** just quietly **12** under the rose **14** confidentially **15** between you and me

confident
04 bold, calm, cool, sure **05** happy, hardy **06** crouse, secure, upbeat **07** assured, certain **08** composed, definite, fearless, positive, sanguine **09** convinced, dauntless, unabashed **10** courageous, optimistic, sure-footed **11** comfortable, self-assured, self-reliant **12** unhesitating **13** self-confident, self-possessed **14** sure of yourself **15** unselfconscious

confidential
04 pack **05** bosom, privy **06** inward, secret **07** a latere, private **08** hush-hush, intimate, man-to-man, personal

09 sensitive, tête-à-tête, top secret **10** classified, restricted **12** off-the-record, woman-to-woman

confidentially
07 privily, sub rosa **08** in camera, in secret **09** entre nous, in privacy, in private, privately **10** on the quiet, personally **12** in confidence **15** between you and me

confidently
06 boldly, calmly, coolly, surely **09** assuredly **10** composedly, fearlessly, positively **11** comfortably **12** courageously **14** optimistically, unhesitatingly

configuration
04 cast, face, form **05** shape **06** figure **07** contour, outline **11** arrangement, composition, disposition **12** conformation

confine
03 fix, mew, pen **04** bail, bale, bind, cage, coop, crib, edge, gate, hold, keep, mure, shut **05** bound, cramp, emmew, enmew, immew, limit, pound, scope, stick, thirl **06** border, coop up, immure, inhoop, intern, keep in, lock up, narrow, prison, shut in, shut up **07** chamber, control, delimit, enclose, impound, inclose, inhibit, repress, shackle, trammel **08** bottle up, boundary, frontier, imprison, lock away, regulate, restrain, restrict, shut away **09** constrain, immanacle, parameter, perimeter, prescribe **10** limitation **11** hold captive, incarcerate, restriction **12** circumscribe, hold prisoner **13** circumference, hold in custody

confined
04 pent, poky **05** caged, close, pokey, small **06** narrow, penned, poking **07** captive, cramped, limited, squeezy **08** enclosed **09** chambered **10** controlled, housebound, imprisoned, restricted **11** constrained, constricted **13** circumscribed

confinement
05 birth **06** burden, labour **07** custody, lying-in **08** delivery, solitary **09** captivity, detention, restraint **10** childbirth, constraint, internment, prisonment **11** house arrest, parturition **12** imprisonment **13** incarceration

confirm
03 fix, tie **04** aver, back **05** check, prove **06** affirm, assert, assure, bishop, clinch, harden, obsign, pledge, ratify, settle, soothe, uphold, verify **07** approve, certify, endorse, fortify, gazette, promise, qualify, support, warrant **08** evidence, reassure, sanction, validate **09** authorize, establish, guarantee, obsignate, reinforce **10** asseverate, homologate, strengthen **11** corroborate, demonstrate **12** authenticate, substantiate **14** give credence to

confirmation
05 proof **06** assent, chrism **07** backing, support **08** approval, evidence, sanction **09** agreement, testimony **10** acceptance, affirmance, validation **11** affirmation, approbation, endorsement **12** ratification, verification **13** accreditation, corroboration **14** authentication, substantiation

confirmed
03 set **04** firm **05** fixed, sworn, vowed **06** inured, rooted **07** affear'd, chronic, settled **08** addicted, affeered, habitual, hardened, seasoned **09** incurable **10** double-dyed, entrenched, inveterate **11** corroborate, established **12** incorrigible, long-standing **13** dyed-in-the-wool **15** long-established

confiscate
05 seize **06** remove **07** escheat, forfeit, impound **08** arrogate, take away **09** forfeited, sequester **10** commandeer **11** appropriate, expropriate

confiscation
07 escheat, removal, seizure **08** takeover **09** distraint **10** forfeiture, impounding **12** distrainment **13** appropriation, commandeering, expropriation, sequestration

conflagration
04 fire **05** blaze **06** flames **07** burning, inferno **09** holocaust **12** deflagration

conflate
04 fuse **05** blend, merge **07** combine **08** compound **09** integrate **10** amalgamate, synthesize **11** incorporate, put together **13** bring together

conflict
03 jar, row, war **04** agon, camp, feud, muss **05** agony, brawl, clash, close, fight, mêlée, musse, scrap, set-to **06** battle, bust-up, combat, differ, dust-up, fracas, oppose, scrape, strife, strive, tangle, thwart, unrest **07** collide, contend, contest, discord, dispute, ill-will, quarrel, warfare **08** antinomy, be at odds, clashing, disagree, friction, skirmish, struggle, variance **09** antipathy, collision, encounter, front line, go against, hostility **10** antagonism, contention, contradict, dissension, dissonance, engagement, opposition **12** be at variance, disagreement **13** be incongruous, confrontation **15** be in opposition, be at loggerheads, incompatibility
See also **battle; war**

conflicting
06 at odds, off-key **08** clashing, contrary, opposing **09**

conflicting
06 at odds, off-key **08** clashing, contrary, opposing **09** competing, dissonant **10** at variance

11 incongruous **12** antithetical, incompatible, inconsistent **13** contradictory

confluence
05 union **06** infall **07** conflux, meeting **08** junction **09** concourse **10** watersmeet **11** concurrence, convergence **12** meeting-point

conform
03 fit **04** obey, suit **05** adapt, agree, match, tally **06** accord, adjust, comply, follow, square **07** abide by, observe **08** parallel, quadrate **09** be uniform, harmonize **10** comply with, correspond, fall in with, toe the line **11** accommodate **12** fall into line **13** go with the flow **14** be conventional, do the same thing, follow the crowd **15** go with the stream

conformist
03 Con **06** yes-man **11** rubber-stamp **13** stick-in-the-mud **14** traditionalist **15** conventionalist

conformity
07 harmony **08** affinity, likeness **09** agreement, congruity, obedience, orthodoxy **10** accordance, accordancy, adjustment, compliance, consonance, observance, similarity, uniformity **11** resemblance **13** accommodation **14** correspondence, traditionalism **15** conventionality

confound
◇ anagram indicator
03 mix **04** beat, dash, faze, mate, ruin, stun **05** abash, amaze, floor, knock, stump, throw, upset **06** awhape, baffle, defeat, puzzle, rabbit, thwart **07** astound, confuse, destroy, flummox, mystify, nonplus, perplex, stagger, startle, stupefy, unshape **08** astonish, bewilder, demolish, surprise **09** bamboozle, discomfit, dumbfound, frustrate, overthrow, overwhelm **10** spiflicate **11** flabbergast, spifflicate

confront
04 defy, face, meet, show **05** brave, cross **06** accost, appose, attack, oppose, resist, tackle **07** address, affront, assault, compare, eyeball, present **08** cope with, deal with, face down, face up to **09** challenge, encounter, stand up to, withstand **10** meet head on, reckon with **11** contend with **12** face the music **15** come to grips with, come to terms with

confrontation
05 brush, clash, fight, set-to **06** battle **07** contest, face-off, quarrel **08** conflict, showdown **09** collision, encounter **10** engagement **12** disagreement

confuse
◇ anagram indicator
03 fog **04** faze, lose, maze **05** addle, bemud, dizzy, floor, mix up, mudge,

stump, throw, upset **06** baffle, bemuse, burble, didder, dither, fickle, flurry, fuddle, jumble, mess up, mingle, mither, mizzle, moider, muddle, puzzle, tangle **07** bumbaze, flummox, fluster, involve, mistake, moither, mortify, mystify, perplex **08** bemuddle, bewilder, compound, confound, disorder, distract, dumfound, entangle, surprise **09** bamboozle, disorient, dumbfound, elaborate, embarrass, embrangle, imbrangle, obfuscate **10** complicate, disarrange, discompose, disconcert, tie in knots **12** disorientate, make involved, mingle-mangle **13** make difficult

See also **baffle; tangle**

confused
◇ anagram indicator
04 hazy, lost, mazy, mixt, mixy **05** dazed, dizzy, messy, mixed, muddy **06** addled, untidy **07** baffled, bemused, chaotic, floored, in a flap, jumbled, maffled, mixed-up, muddled, puzzled **08** all at sea, flustery **09** delirious, disturbed, flummoxed, flustered, mystified, perplexed **10** bamboozled, bewildered, confounded, désorienté, disordered, disorderly, distracted, hurly-burly, indistinct, nonplussed, out of order, topsy-turvy, unbalanced, up a gumtree **11** complicated, disarranged, in a flat spin, muddy-headed **12** disconcerted, disorganized, inextricable **13** disorientated, helter-skelter, muddle-brained **15** all over the place

confusing
◇ anagram indicator
05 dizzy **07** cryptic, unclear **08** baffling, involved, muddling, puzzling, tortuous **09** ambiguous, difficult **10** misleading, perplexing **11** bewildering, complicated **12** inconclusive, inconsistent **13** contradictory

confusion
◇ anagram indicator
02 pi **03** fog, pie, pye **04** mess, muss, toss **05** chaos, lurry, mix-up, musse, shame **06** baffle, bumble, bummle, cock-up, dudder, fuddle, guddle, huddle, jumble, mess-up, muddle **07** clutter, flutter, turmoil, whemmle, whomble, whommle, whummle **08** disarray, disorder, mish-mash, shambles, upheaval **09** commotion, égarement, overthrow, perdition **10** bafflement, hurly-burly, perplexity, puzzlement, topsy-turvy, untidiness **12** bewilderment, entanglement, hubble-bubble, hugger-mugger **13** disconcertion, embarrassment, indistinction, mystification **14** disarrangement **15** disorganization

confute
05 rebut, refel **06** debunk, negate, refute **07** put down **08** disprove, redargue **09** discredit **10** contradict, controvert, prove false

congeal
03 gel, set **04** cake, clot, fuse, geal, jeel **05** jelly **06** curdle, freeze, harden **07** pectize, stiffen, thicken **08** coalesce, solidify **09** coagulate **11** concentrate

congenial
04 cosy **06** genial, homely, kinred **07** kindred **08** friendly, pleasant, pleasing, relaxing, suitable **09** agreeable, simpatico **10** compatible, delightful, favourable, like-minded, well-suited **11** complaisant, sympathetic, sympathique **13** companionable

congenital
05 utter **06** inborn, inbred, innate, inured **07** chronic, connate, natural **08** complete, habitual, hardened, inherent, seasoned, thorough **09** incurable, inherited **10** compulsive, connatural, entrenched, hereditary, inveterate **12** incorrigible **14** constitutional

congested
04 full **06** choked, jammed, packed **07** blocked, clogged, crammed, crowded, stuffed, teeming **08** engorged **11** overcharged, overcrowded, overflowing

congestion
03 jam **07** choking, snarl-up **08** blockage, blocking, clogging, crowding, gridlock **10** bottleneck, pinchpoint, traffic jam **12** overcrowding

conglomerate
04 firm **05** group, trust **06** cartel, merger **07** combine, company, concern **08** business, fullness **10** consortium, traffic jam **11** association, corporation, engorgement, partnership **13** establishment, multinational

conglomeration
04 mass **06** medley **09** composite **10** assemblage, assortment, collection, hotchpotch **11** aggregation **12** accumulation **13** agglomeration

Congo
03 COD, COG, RCB, ZRE

congratulate
05 greet **06** praise **08** wish well **09** gratulate **10** compliment, felicitate **12** pat on the back **13** say well done to **15** wish happiness to
• **congratulate yourself**
05 plume, preen, pride **09** delight in

congratulations
04 euge **07** bouquet **08** bouquets, congrats, mazeltov, well done **09** good on you, greetings **10** best wishes, good for you, good wishes **11** compliments **12** pat on the back **13** felicitations

congregate
04 form, mass, meet **05** clump, crowd, flock, rally **06** gather, muster, throng **07** cluster, collect, convene

08 assemble, converge
10 accumulate, rendezvous 12 come together

congregation
04 fold, host, mass 05 crowd, flock, group, laity 06 parish, people, throng 07 meeting 08 assembly 09 multitude 10 fellowship 12 parishioners

congress
03 hui 04 diet 05 forum, synod 07 council, meeting 08 assembly, conclave 09 gathering 10 conference, convention, parliament 11 convocation, legislature

congruence
05 match 07 harmony 08 identity 09 agreement 10 concinnity, conformity, consonance, similarity 11 coincidence, concurrence, consistency, parallelism, resemblance 13 compatibility 14 correspondence

congruent
07 similar 08 parallel, suitable 09 consonant 10 compatible, concurrent, consistent, harmonious 13 corresponding

conical
06 spired 07 pointed, tapered 08 tapering 09 pyramidal, turbinate 10 cone-shaped, fastigiate 12 funnel-shaped, infundibular 13 infundibulate, pyramid-shaped

conifer *see* **pine; tree**

conjectural
07 assumed, posited 08 academic, supposed, surmised 09 tentative 10 divinatory, postulated, stochastic 11 speculative, theoretical 12 divinatorial, hypothetical 13 suppositional

conjecture
03 aim 05 augur, fancy, guess, infer 06 assume, notion, reckon, theory 07 imagine, presume, suppose, surmise, suspect 08 estimate, theorize 09 guesswork, inference, speculate, suspicion 10 assumption, conclusion, divination, estimation, hypothesis, presuppose, projection 11 guesstimate, hypothesize, presumption, speculation, supposition 13 extrapolation 14 presupposition

conjoin
04 join, link 05 match, unify, unite 06 concur 07 combine, connect 08 alligate 10 amalgamate, synthesize 12 join together

conjugal
06 bridal, wedded 07 marital, married, nuptial, spousal 08 hymeneal 09 connubial 11 epithalamic, matrimonial
• **conjugal union**
03 bed

conjunction
05 synod, union 06 syzygy 07 unition 10 alligation, connection, copulative,

injunction 11 association, coexistence, coincidence, colligation, combination, concurrence, unification 12 amalgamation, co-occurrence 13 juxtaposition
• **in conjunction with**
04 with 09 alongside, along with 12 combined with, together with 13 in company with

conjure
05 charm, evoke, raise, rouse 06 call up, compel, invoke, juggle, summon 07 bewitch, do magic 08 do tricks 09 fascinate 10 make appear 11 materialize 12 perform magic 13 perform tricks
• **conjure up**
05 evoke 06 awaken, create, excite, invoke, recall 07 produce 08 summon up 09 recollect 10 call to mind 11 bring to mind

conjurer
06 wizard 08 magician, sorcerer 10 mystery-man 11 illusionist, thaumaturge 12 prestigiator 13 miracle-worker 15 prestidigitator
• **conjurer's skill**
11 legerdemain 13 sleight of hand
• **conjurer's words**
09 hey presto 10 hocus-pocus 11 abracadabra

conk
04 head, nose
• **conk out**
03 die 04 fail 06 go bust, go phut, pack up 07 go kaput 08 collapse 09 break down, go haywire 12 go on the blink

con man
04 liar 05 bunco, cheat, crook 06 rorter, usurer 07 blagger, grifter, hustler 08 deceiver, swindler, tweedler 09 con artist 11 bunco artist, illy whacker, overcharger 12 bunko-steerer, extortionist, rip-off artist

connect
03 put, tie 04 ally, bolt, bond, fuse, join, link 05 affix, clamp, unite 06 attach, bridge, couple, equate, fasten, relate, secure 07 bracket, combine 08 identify, relate to 09 associate, correlate 10 articulate 11 compaginate, concatenate 12 hang together

connected
04 akin, tied 06 allied, joined, linked, united 07 coupled, related, secured 08 coherent, combined, fastened 09 associate, conjugate 10 affiliated, associated

Connecticut
02 CT 04 Conn

connection
03 tie 04 bond, link, pons 05 clasp, joint, tie-in, tie-up 06 friend, hook-up, link-up 07 analogy, contact, context, liaison, linkage, rapport, sponsor 08 alliance, coupling, intimacy, junction, parallel, relation, relative

09 coherence, fastening, reference, relevance 10 attachment 11 association, colligation, conjunction, correlation, intercourse 12 acquaintance, relationship 13 communication, consanguinity, interrelation 14 correspondence
• **in connection with**
02 re 04 as to 05 about 07 apropos 09 as regards, regarding 10 concerning, in regard to 12 in relation to, with regard to 13 with respect to 14 on the subject of 15 with reference to

conning-tower
04 sail

connivance
07 consent 08 abetment, abetting 09 collusion, condoning 10 complicity, conspiracy, lenocinium

connive
04 plot, wink 05 allow, brook, cabal, coact, let go 06 ignore, scheme, wink at 07 collude, complot, condone, let pass 08 conspire, intrigue, overlook, pass over, tolerate 09 disregard, gloss over 11 collaborate 15 turn a blind eye to

conniving
05 nasty 07 corrupt, immoral 08 plotting, scheming 09 colluding 10 conspiring 12 manipulative, unscrupulous

connoisseur
04 buff 05 judge 06 expert, pundit 07 arbiter, devotee, epicure, gourmet 08 aesthete, oenophil, virtuoso 09 authority 10 aficionado, gastronome, specialist 11 cognoscente, gastronomer, oenophilist 12 iconophilist

connotation
04 hint 06 intent, nuance 08 allusion, overtone 09 colouring, undertone 10 intimation, suggestion 11 association, implication, insinuation 12 undercurrent 13 comprehension

connote
05 imply 06 hint at, import 07 betoken, purport, signify, suggest 08 allude to, indicate, intimate 09 associate, connotate, insinuate

conquer
03 win 04 beat, best, rout, take 05 annex, crush, debel, quell, seize, worst 06 defeat, humble, master, obtain, occupy, subdew, subdue 07 acquire, control, overrun, possess, succeed, trounce 08 overcome, suppress, surmount, vanquish 09 overpower, overthrow, rise above, subjugate 11 appropriate, prevail over, triumph over 14 get the better of

conqueror
04 hero, lord, Moor 05 champ, Mogul 06 master, victor, winner 08 champion 10 subjugator, vanquisher 12 conquistador

conquest
03 win **04** coup, rout **05** catch, lover
06 defeat **07** beating, captive, capture,
mastery, seizing, success, triumph,
victory **08** crushing, invasion
09 overthrow, trouncing
10 annexation, occupation,
possession, subjection **11** acquisition,
overrunning, subjugation
12 overpowering, vanquishment
13 appropriation

conscience
05 inwit **06** ethics, morals, qualms
08 scruples **09** diligence, moral code,
standards **10** moral sense, principles,
syneidesis, synteresis **11** voice within
12 sense of right **14** scrupulousness
15 still small voice

conscience-stricken
05 sorry **06** guilty **07** ashamed
08 contrite, penitent, troubled
09 disturbed, regretful, repentant
10 remorseful **11** guilt-ridden
12 compunctious, on a guilt trip

conscientious
06 honest **07** careful, dutiful, upright
08 diligent, faithful, thorough
09 assiduous, attentive, dedicated
10 methodical, meticulous, particular,
scrupulous **11** hard-working,
industrious, painstaking, punctilious,
responsible

conscious
05 alert, alive, awake, aware **06** wilful
07 heedful, knowing, mindful, studied,
witting **08** rational, sensible, sentient
09 cognizant, conscient, on purpose,
reasoning, voluntary **10** calculated,
deliberate, percipient, responsive,
volitional **11** intentional, recognizant
12 premeditated **13** self-conscious
• **be conscious of**
04 feel **06** savour

consciously
08 wilfully **09** knowingly, on purpose
11 voluntarily **12** deliberately
13 intentionally

consciousness
04 mind **06** psyche **07** thought
09 alertness, awareness, intuition,
knowledge, sentience **10** being awake,
cognizance, perception
11 cenesthesia, cenesthesis,
realization, recognition, sensibility,
wakefulness **12** apprehension
13 coenaesthesia, coenaesthesis

conscript
05 draft **06** call up, enlist, induct,
muster, take on **07** draftee, recruit,
round up **08** enlistee, enrolled,
inductee **10** registered

conscription
05 draft **08** drafting

consecrate
03 vow **05** bless, exalt **06** anoint,
devote, hallow, ordain, revere
07 devoted **08** dedicate, make holy,
sanctify, venerate **10** sanctified

consecutive
06 in a row, in turn, serial **07** running,
sequent, seriate **08** parallel, straight,
unbroken **09** following, on the trot
10 back to back, continuous,
sequential, succeeding, successive
13 uninterrupted

consecutively
06 in a row, in turn **09** on the trot
10 back to back **11** hand-running
12 continuously, sequentially,
successively **15** uninterruptedly

consensus
05 unity **07** concord, consent,
harmony **09** agreement, unanimity
10 consension **11** concurrence
12 consentience, majority view

consent
05 admit, agree, allow, grant, yield
06 accede, accept, afford, assent,
comply, concur, permit, submit
07 affoord, approve, concede, go-
ahead **08** approval, sanction
09 acquiesce, agreement, authorize,
clearance **10** acceptance, compliance,
concession, condescend, green light,
homologate, permission
11 concurrence, go along with
12 acquiescence **13** authorization
14 give the go-ahead **15** give the
thumbs-up

consequence
03 end **04** note **05** issue, value
06 effect, import, moment, result,
upshot, weight **07** concern, outcome
08 eminence, sequence **09** aftermath,
inference, substance **10** importance,
importancy, prominence, side effect
11 distinction, eventuality, implication
12 repercussion, significance
13 reverberation

consequent
07 ensuing, sequent **09** appendant,
corollary, following, resultant, resulting
10 consectary, sequential,
subsequent, successive

consequential
03 key **05** vital **07** crucial, ensuing,
serious, weighty **08** material, relevant,
valuable **09** following, important,
momentous, prominent, resultant,
resulting **10** noteworthy, sequential,
subsequent, successive **11** far-
reaching, significant, substantial

consequently
04 ergo, then, thus **05** hence **06** so
that **09** as a result, therefore
11 accordingly, necessarily
12 subsequently **13** inferentially
15 consequentially

conservation
03 con **04** care **06** saving, upkeep
07 custody, ecology, economy,
keeping **09** husbandry **10** protection
11 maintenance, safe-keeping
12 preservation, safeguarding

conservationist
05 green **06** econut **07** greenie

consider
08 ecofreak **09** ecologist **10** tree-
hugger **15** preservationist
• **conservationists**
02 NT **03** WWF

conservatism
09 orthodoxy **14** traditionalism
15 conventionalism

conservative
01 C **03** Con **04** blue, cons, Tory
05 right, sober **06** hunker **07** careful,
diehard, guarded, old-line
08 cautious, moderate, old-liner,
orthodox, Unionist, verkramp
09 bourgeois, hidebound, right-wing
10 inflexible **11** reactionary, right-
winger, traditional **12** buttoned-down,
conventional **13** set in your ways, stick-
in-the-mud, unprogressive
14 traditionalist **15** backward-looking,
middle-of-the-road

conservatory
06 school **07** academy, college
08 hothouse **09** institute
10 glasshouse, greenhouse,
storehouse **11** music school **12** drama
college, preservatory **13** conservatoire

conserve
03 jam **04** keep, save **05** guard,
gumbo, hoard, jelly **06** retain
07 husband, protect, store up **08** keep
back, maintain, preserve **09** comfiture,
marmalade, safeguard **10** take care of
13 keep in reserve

consider
03 see **04** deem, feel, hold, muse,
note, rate, view, vise **05** count, judge,
study, think, weigh **06** debate, devise,
esteem, ponder, regard, reward
07 believe, bethink, examine, reflect,
respect, toy with, weigh up **08** chew
over, cogitate, envisage, meditate, mull
over, prepense, regard as, remember,
ruminate, see about **09** apprehend,
kick about **10** animadvert, bear in
mind, deliberate, keep in mind, kick
around **11** contemplate **13** give
thought to **15** take into account

considerable
03 big, gay, gey **04** some, tidy, vast
05 ample, great, large, smart **06** lavish,
marked, pretty **07** healthy, notable,
serious, sizable **08** abundant,
generous, sizeable **09** important,
plentiful, tolerable **10** noteworthy,
noticeable, reasonable **11** appreciable,
influential, perceptible, respectable,
significant, substantial, substantive
13 distinguished

considerably
03 gay, gey **04** much **07** greatly
08 markedly **10** abundantly,
noticeably, remarkably **11** appreciably
13 significantly, substantially

considerate
04 kind **06** caring **07** helpful, tactful
08 discreet, generous, gracious,
obliging, selfless **09** attentive,
concerned, courteous, sensitive,
unselfish **10** altruistic, charitable,

deliberate, respective, solicitous, thoughtful **11** sympathetic **13** compassionate

consideration

04 care, fact, heed, tact **05** count, issue, point **06** factor, motive, notice, reason, regard, review **07** account, concern, payment, respect, thought **08** altruism, analysis, kindness, scrutiny, sympathy **09** attention, reckoning **10** cogitation, compassion, discretion, generosity, importance, inspection, meditation, recompense, reflection, rumination **11** examination, helpfulness, sensitivity **12** circumstance, deliberation, graciousness, selflessness **13** contemplation, unselfishness **14** thoughtfulness
- **lacking consideration**
04 nude
- **take into consideration**
05 study **07** plan for **08** allow for, consider **10** bear in mind, keep in mind **13** give thought to **15** take into account

considering

08 all in all, in view of **10** respecting **12** in the light of **13** bearing in mind

consign

04 seal, send, ship, sign **06** assign, banish, commit, convey, devote **07** commend, deliver, entrust **08** give over, hand over, relegate, transfer, transmit **09** recommend

consignment

04 load **05** batch, cargo, goods **08** delivery, shipment

consist

03 lie **05** exist **06** embody, inhere, reside **07** contain, embrace, include, involve, subsist **08** amount to, be formed, be made up, comprise **10** be composed **11** be contained, incorporate

consistency

07 density, harmony, keeping **08** cohesion, evenness, firmness, identity, sameness **09** agreement, coherence, coherency, congruity, constancy, stability, substance, thickness, viscosity **10** accordance, conformity, consonance, continuity, regularity, smoothness, steadiness, uniformity **11** persistence, reliability **12** lack of change **13** compatibility, dependability, steadfastness **14** correspondence

consistent

04 same **06** stable, steady **07** logical, regular, uniform **08** agreeing, coherent, constant, matching, straight **09** accordant, congruous, consonant, unfailing **10** coinciding, compatible, conforming, dependable, harmonious, persistent, unchanging **11** predictable, undeviating **13** consentaneous, corresponding **15** hanging together

consistently

09 regularly, uniformly **10** constantly,

dependably **11** predictably, unfailingly **12** persistently

consolation

03 aid **04** ease, help **05** cheer **06** relief, solace **07** comfort, succour, support **08** soothing, sympathy **11** alleviation, assuagement, reassurance **12** recomforture **13** commiseration, encouragement

console

04 calm, help, Xbox® **05** ancon, board, cheer, dials, knobs, panel **06** levers, solace, soothe **07** buttons, comfort, hearten, relieve, succour, support **08** controls, Gamecube®, keyboard, Nintendo®, reassure, switches **09** consolate, dashboard, encourage, recomfort **11** instruments, PlayStation® **12** control panel **14** sympathize with **15** commiserate with

consolidate

03 pun **04** fuse, join **05** merge, unify, unite **06** cement, secure, united **07** combine, compact, fortify **09** reinforce, stabilize **10** amalgamate, make secure, make stable, make strong, strengthen **12** make stronger **14** make more secure, make more stable

consolidation

06 fusion, merger **07** joining, uniting **08** alliance, securing **09** cementing **10** federation **11** affiliation, association, combination, unification **12** amalgamation **13** confederation, fortification, reinforcement, stabilization, strengthening

consonance

07 concord, harmony **09** agreement, congruity **10** accordance, conformity **11** consistency, suitability **13** compatibility **14** correspondence

consonant

05 lenis, velar **06** fortis, sonant, uvular **08** agreeing, alveolar, bilabial, ejective, emphatic, suitable **09** accordant, according, congruous, implosive, in harmony **10** compatible, conforming, consistent, harmonious **11** in agreement **12** articulation, in accordance **13** correspondent

consort

03 mix **04** lady, maik, make, mate, wife **05** agree, troop **06** accord, escort, mingle, spouse **07** husband, partner **09** accompany, agreement, associate, companion, spend time **10** fraternize **11** keep company

consortium

04 bloc, bond, pact **05** guild, union **06** cartel, league, treaty **07** compact, company **08** alliance, marriage **09** agreement, coalition, syndicate **10** federation, fellowship **11** affiliation, association, combination, corporation, partnership **12** conglomerate, organization **13** confederation

conspicuous

05 clear, showy **06** flashy, garish, marked, patent **07** blatant, eminent, evident, glaring, obvious, shining, visible **08** apparent, flagrant, kenspeck, manifest, remarked, striking **09** prominent **10** easily seen, kenspeckle, noticeable, observable, remarkable **11** discernible, perceptible **12** ostentatious, recognizable **13** easily noticed

conspicuously

07 clearly, showily, visibly **08** flashily, garishly, markedly, patently **09** blatantly, evidently, glaringly, obviously **10** flagrantly, manifestly, noticeably, observably, remarkably, strikingly **11** discernibly, perceptibly, prominently **12** recognizably **14** ostentatiously

conspiracy

03 fix **04** plot **05** cabal, covin, set-up **06** covyne, league, scheme **07** complot, consult, frame-up, treason **08** intrigue **09** collusion, stratagem **10** connivance **11** concurrence, confederacy, machination **13** collaboration

conspirator

05 Casca, Cinna **06** Brutus **07** Cassius, plotter, schemer, traitor **08** Catiline, colluder **09** conspirer, intriguer **10** highbinder, practisant **12** collaborator
- **group of conspirators**
04 band **05** cabal

conspire

04 ally, join, link, plan, plot **05** unite **06** devise, scheme **07** collude, combine, complot, conjure, connect, connive **08** intrigue **09** associate, colleague, co-operate, machinate, manoeuvre **10** hatch a plot, join forces **11** act together, collaborate **12** work together

constable

02 PC, SC **03** cop, WPC **04** Dull **05** jawan, wolly **06** cotwal, harman, kotwal **09** catchpole, catchpoll **10** harman-beck **11** headborough **12** thirdborough
See also **police officer**

constancy

05 truth **07** loyalty **08** devotion, fidelity, firmness, tenacity **09** certainty, fixedness, stability **10** permanence, regularity, resolution, steadiness, uniformity **11** consistency, persistence **12** faithfulness, perseverance **13** dependability, steadfastness **15** trustworthiness, unchangeability

constant

01 c, G, h, k **04** even, firm, trew, true **05** daily, fixed, loyal **06** stable, stanch, steady **07** chronic, devoted, endless, eternal, non-stop, regular, staunch, uniform **08** faithful, resolute, unbroken **09** ceaseless, continual, immutable, incessant, permanent, perpetual,

steadfast, unfailing, unvarying
10 changeless, consistent, continuous, dependable, invariable, persistent, relentless, unchanging, unflagging, unwavering **11** everlasting, never-ending, persevering, trustworthy, unalterable, unremitting
12 interminable, unchangeable
13 uninterrupted **14** without respite

constantly
03 aye **05** daily, still **06** always **07** for ever, non-stop, on and on **09** ad nauseam, endlessly **10** all the time, invariably **11** ceaselessly, continually, day in day out, incessantly, perennially, permanently, perpetually
12 continuously, interminably, relentlessly **13** everlastingly
15 twenty-four seven

constellation

Constellations include:

03 Ara, Cup, dog, Fly, Fox, Leo, Net, Ram
04 Apus, Argo, Bull, Crab, Crow, Crux, Dove, Grus, Hare, Harp, Keel, Lion, Lynx, Lyra, Pavo, Swan, Vela, Wolf
05 Altar, Aries, Arrow, Cetus, Clock, Crane, Draco, Eagle, Easel, Hydra, Indus, Lepus, Level, Libra, Lupus, Mensa, Musca, Norma, Orion, Pyxis, Sails, Table, Twins, Virgo, Whale
06 Antlia, Aquila, Archer, Auriga, Boötes, Caelum, Cancer, Carina, Chisel, Corvus, Crater, Cygnus, Dorado, Dragon, Fishes, Fornax, Gemini, Hydrus, Indian, Lizard, Octans, Octant, Pictor, Pisces, Puppis, Scales, Scutum, Shield, Taurus, Toucan, Tucana, Virgin, Volans
07 Air Pump, Centaur, Cepheus, Columba, Dolphin, Furnace, Giraffe, Lacerta, Peacock, Pegasus, Perseus, Phoenix, Sagitta, Sea Goat, Serpens, Serpent, Sextans, Sextant, Unicorn
08 Aquarius, Circinus, Equuleus, Eridanus, Great Dog, Hercules, Herdsman, Leo Minor, Scorpion, Scorpius, Sculptor, Triangle
09 Andromeda, Centaurus, Chameleon, Compasses, Delphinus, Great Bear, Little Dog, Monoceros, Ophiuchus, Reticulum, Swordfish, Telescope, Ursa Major, Ursa Minor, Vulpecula
10 Canis Major, Canis Minor, Cassiopeia, Chamaeleon, Charioteer, Flying Fish, Horologium, Little Bear, Little Lion, Microscope, Sea Serpent, Ship's Stern, Triangulum, Water Snake
11 Capricornus, Hunting Dogs, Little Horse, Sagittarius, Telescopium, Water Bearer, Winged Horse
12 Microscopium, Southern Fish
13 Berenice's Hair, Canes Venatici, Coma Berenices, Northern Crown, River Eridanus, Serpent Bearer, Southern Cross, Southern Crown

14 Bird of Paradise, Camelopardalis, Corona Borealis
15 Corona Australis, Mariner's Compass, Piscis Austrinus

consternation
03 awe **04** fear **05** alarm, dread, panic, shock **06** dismay, fright, horror, terror
07 anxiety **08** distress **11** disquietude, trepidation **12** bewilderment, perturbation

constipated
05 bound

constituency
04 area, seat, ward, zone **05** burgh, shire **06** parish, region, Riding
07 borough **08** district, division, Euroseat, marginal, precinct
09 community **10** electorate

constituent
◇ *anagram indicator*
03 bit **04** part, unit **05** basic, voter
06 factor **07** content, elector, element, section **08** electing, inherent, integral
09 component, essential, intrinsic, principle **10** ingredient **12** constitution
13 component part

constitute
02 be **04** form, make, mean **05** found, set up **06** create, make up, strike
07 add up to, appoint, charter, compose, empower **08** amount to, comprise, initiate **09** authorize, establish, institute, represent
10 commission, inaugurate **12** be regarded as **14** be equivalent to, be tantamount to

constitution
03 set **04** code, laws **05** fuero, habit, rules, state **06** health, make-up, nature, policy, polity, temper, upmake
07 charter **08** habitude, physique, statutes **09** character, condition, formation, structure **10** social code
11 codified law, composition, disposition, temperament
temperature 12 bill of rights, idiosyncrasy, organization
13 configuration **15** basic principles

constitutional
04 turn, walk **05** amble, by law, legal
06 airing, lawful, stroll, vested
07 politic, saunter **08** codified, ratified
09 promenade, statutory
10 authorized, legitimate **11** legislative
12 governmental

constrain
03 put **04** bind, curb, rein, urge
05 check, drive, force, impel, limit
06 coerce, compel, hinder, oblige, strain **07** confine **08** hold back, obligate, pressure, restrain, restrict
09 constrict **10** perstringe, pressurize
11 necessitate

constrained
04 hard **05** stiff **06** forced, uneasy
07 awkward, guarded **08** reserved, reticent **09** compelled, inhibited, unnatural **11** embarrassed

constraint
04 curb, rein **05** check, force
06 damper, demand, duress
07 duresse, shackle **08** coercion, pressure **09** hindrance, necessity, restraint, reticence, stiffness
10 compulsion, forcedness, impediment, inhibition, insistence, limitation, obligation **11** awkwardness, confinement, guardedness, restriction, self-control **13** embarrassment, unnaturalness

constrict
04 bind, curb **05** check, choke, close, cramp, limit, pinch **06** hamper, hinder, impede, narrow, shrink **07** confine, inhibit, squeeze, tighten **08** compress, contract, hold back, obstruct, restrict, strangle **09** constrain **10** make narrow
11 strangulate

constriction
04 curb **05** check, choke, cramp
07 isthmus **08** blockage, pressure, stenosis, thlipsis **09** hindrance, narrowing, reduction, squeezing, stegnosis, stricture, tightness
10 constraint, impediment, limitation, tightening **11** compression, contraction, restriction
13 constringency, incarceration

construct
◇ *anagram indicator*
04 form, make **05** build, craft, erect, found, model, patch, put up, raise, set up, shape, weave **06** create, design, devise, fabric **07** compile, compose, elevate, fashion, knock up, throw up
08 assemble, engineer **09** carpenter, establish, fabricate, formulate, structure **11** manufacture, put together
13 knock together, throw together

construction
04 form **05** model, order, shape
06 fabric, figure, make-up, making
07 edifice, meaning, reading
08 assembly, building, erection
09 deduction, elevation, formation, framework, inference, structure
11 arrangement, composition, disposition, fabrication, manufacture
12 organization **13** configuration, establishment **14** interpretation

constructive
06 useful **07** helpful **08** inferred, positive, valuable **09** practical
10 beneficial, productive
12 advantageous **13** architectonic

constructively
08 usefully **09** helpfully **10** positively
11 practically **12** beneficially, productively **14** advantageously

construe
◇ *anagram indicator*
04 read **05** infer, see as **06** deduce, render **07** analyse, explain, expound
08 regard as **09** interpret **10** take to mean, understand

consul
03 Con **05** agent, elchi, envoy

06 ledger, legate, nuncio 07 leaguer
08 delegate, diplomat, emissary,
minister 10 ambassador
14 representative 15 plenipotentiary

consult

03 see 04 talk, vide 06 confer, debate,
look up, turn to 07 discuss, refer to
08 question 09 ask advice
10 deliberate, seek advice
11 interrogate 14 ask information
15 seek information

consultant

06 expert 07 adviser 09 associate,
authority 10 specialist

consultation

04 talk 05 forum 07 counsel, hearing,
meeting, session 08 dialogue
09 interview 10 conference,
discussion 11 appointment,
examination 12 deliberation

consultative

07 helping 08 advising, advisory
10 consulting 11 counselling
12 consultatory, recommending

consume

◊ containment indicator
03 eat, gut, use 04 burn, grip, kill, pine,
take, wear 05 drain, drink, eat up, scoff,
shift, snarf, spend, touch, use up, waste
06 absorb, bezzle, burn up, damage,
devour, expend, gobble, guzzle, ingest,
murder, obsess, punish, ravage, tuck in
07 deplete, destroy, discuss, drink up,
engross, exhaust, swallow, torment,
utilize 08 demolish, dominate, lay
waste, mainline, squander, wear down
09 devastate, dispose of, dissipate, go
through, overwhelm, polish off,
preoccupy 10 annihilate, get through,
monopolize 11 fritter away 12 get
stuck into

consumer

04 user 05 buyer, mouth 06 client,
patron 07 end-user, shopper
08 customer 09 purchaser

consuming

◊ containment indicator
07 wasting, wearing 08 gripping
09 absorbing, devouring, obsessive
10 compelling, destroying,
dominating, engrossing, immoderate,
tormenting 12 monopolizing,
overwhelming, preoccupying

consummate

03 cap, end 05 crown, exact, total,
utter 06 finish, fulfil, gifted, made up,
superb 07 achieve, execute, perfect,
perform, realize, skilled, supreme
08 absolute, complete, conclude,
finished, polished, superior, ultimate
09 competent, exemplary, matchless,
practised, terminate 10 accomplish,
effectuate, proficient 11 replenished,
unqualified 12 accomplished,
transcendent 13 distinguished

consummation

03 end 04 pass 06 finish 07 capping
08 crowning 09 execution

10 completion, conclusion, fulfilment,
perfection 11 achievement,
culmination, performance, realization,
termination 12 effectuation
13 actualization 14 accomplishment

consumption

02 TB 05 waste 06 eating 07 decline,
using-up 08 draining, drinking,
guzzling, scoffing, spending
09 depletion, devouring, expending,
ingestion, tucking-in 10 absorption,
exhaustion, swallowing
11 expenditure, squandering,
utilization 12 going-through,
tuberculosis 14 getting-through

contact

03 fax 04 call, ring 05 e-mail, phone,
reach, touch, union 06 friend, impact,
notify 07 apply to, get onto, meeting,
speak to, sponsor, taction, write to
08 approach, junction, relation,
relative, tangency, touching 09 get
hold of, proximity, telephone
10 connection, contiguity
11 association, contingence
12 acquaintance, get through to
13 communication, juxtaposition
14 get in touch with 15 communicate
with

• **in contact with**

02 to 04 into

contagion

06 poison 08 tainting 09 infection,
pollution 10 corruption, defilement
13 contamination

contagious

07 noxious 08 catching, epidemic,
pandemic 09 spreading
10 compelling, infectious
12 communicable, irresistible
13 transmissible, transmittable

contain

◊ containment indicator
◊ hidden indicator
04 curb, hold, seat, stop, take 05 carry,
check, limit 06 embody, enseam,
enwomb, hold in, rein in, retain, stifle,
take in 07 control, embrace, enclose,
include, involve, repress 08 comprise,
keep back, restrain, suppress 09 keep
under 10 have inside
11 accommodate, incorporate, keep in
check

container

◊ hidden indicator
06 holder, vessel 10 receptacle,
repository

Containers include:

03 bag, bin, box, can, cup, jar, jug, keg,
mug, pan, pot, tin, tub, urn, vat
04 bowl, case, cask, dish, drum,
Esky®, pack, pail, sack, silo, tank,
tube, vase, vial, well
05 basin, chest, churn, crate, crock,
glass, purse, trunk
06 barrel, basket, beaker, bottle,
bucket, carton, casket, hamper,
kettle, locker, packet, punnet,
teapot, trough, tureen

07 cistern, dustbin, pannier, pitcher,
tumbler
08 canister, cauldron, cylinder,
suitcase, tea caddy, tea chest, waste
bin
09 water-butt

containment

04 curb 05 check 07 control
08 stifling 09 restraint 10 limitation,
repression 11 suppression

contaminate

◊ anagram indicator
04 foul, harm, soil 05 decay, spike,
spoil, stain, sully, taint 06 debase,
defile, infect 07 corrupt, deprave,
pollute, tarnish, vitiate 10 adulterate,
make impure

contamination

◊ anagram indicator
04 harm 05 decay, filth, stain, taint
07 soiling, tarnish 08 foulness,
impurity, spoiling, sullying
09 infection, pollution, vitiation
10 corruption, debasement,
defilement, rottenness 11 desecration
12 adulteration

contemplate

04 muse, plan, view 05 spell, study,
weigh 06 behold, design, expect,
intend, look at, ponder, regard, survey
07 dwell on, examine, foresee, inspect
observe, propose, weigh up
08 cogitate, consider, envisage,
meditate, mull over, ruminate
09 reflect on 10 deliberate, have in
mind, have in view, scrutinize, think
about 11 have an eye to 13 give
thought to

contemplation

04 muse, view 05 dwell, study
06 gazing, musing, regard, survey
07 purpose, thought, viewing
08 mind's eye, scrutiny, weighing
09 beholding, pondering, regarding
10 cogitation, inspection, meditation,
reflection, rumination, weighing up
11 cerebration, examination, mulling-
over, observation 12 deliberation,
recollection 13 consideration

contemplative

04 rapt 06 intent, musing 07 pensive
08 cerebral 10 meditative, reflective,
ruminative, thoughtful 13 deep in
thought, introspective

contemporaneous

06 coeval 10 coetaneous, coexistent,
concurrent 11 synchronous
12 simultaneous

contemporary

02 AD 03 now 04 peer 05 equal
06 coeval, fellow, latest, modern,
recent, today's, trendy, with it
07 current, partner, present, topical
08 confrère, co-worker, parallel, up-
to-date 09 associate, colleague
10 avant-garde, coetaneous,
coexistent, collateral, concurrent,
futuristic, new-fangled, present-day

11 counterpart, fashionable, present-time, synchronous, ultra-modern **12** simultaneous **13** up-to-the-minute **14** contemporanean **15** contemporaneous

contempt

05 scorn **06** hatred **07** disdain, dislike, mockery, neglect **08** derision, despisal, disgrace, loathing, ridicule **09** contumely, dishonour, disregard **10** disrespect **11** detestation **13** condescension

• **expression of contempt**
02 ho **03** ach, aha, bah, boo, foh, gup, hoa, hoh, mew, och, pho, poh, rot, sis, yah **04** booh, nuts, phew, phoh, pish, poof, pooh, push, quep, rats, tush, yech **05** pshaw, snoot, sucks! **06** phooey **10** sucks to you!

• **sign of contempt**
04 fico, figo **05** sneer **11** Harvey Smith

• **term of contempt**
03 cit, dog, nit **05** sprat **06** monkey **07** jive-ass **08** whipster

contemptible

03 low **04** base, mean, vile **05** petty **06** abject, cruddy, ornery, paltry, scurvy, shabby **07** hateful, pelting, pitiful **08** pitiable, shameful, unworthy, wretched **09** loathsome, miserable, worthless **10** degenerate, despicable, detestable, lamentable **11** ignominious

• **contemptible person**
04 crud, scut, snot, toad **05** crumb, diddy, droob, snipe, squit, twerp **06** fellow, louser **07** dogbolt, hangdog **08** dirty dog, scullion, whiffler

contemptuous

05 tossy **06** snorty **07** cynical, haughty, jeering, mocking **08** arrogant, derisive, derisory, insolent, scornful, sneering **09** insulting, withering **10** despiteful, disdainful, dispiteous **12** contumelious, supercilious **13** condescending, disrespectful, high and mighty

contend

03 vie, war **04** aver, cope, deal, face, hold, wage **05** argue, brave, claim, clash, fight, rival, state **06** affirm, allege, assert, battle, combat, debate, oppose, reckon, strive, tackle, tussle **07** address, agonize, compete, contest, declare, dispute, grapple, profess, wrestle **08** conflict, face up to, maintain, militate, struggle **09** challenge **10** asseverate, meet head on **11** come to grips, come to terms

content

◊ *hidden indicator*
04 ease, gist, glad, load, size, text **05** happy, ideas, items, parts, peace, theme, topic **06** amount, at ease, be glad, burden, humour, matter, pacify, please, soothe, volume **07** appease, be happy, chapter, comfort, delight, essence, gratify, indulge, meaning, measure, placate, pleased, satisfy,

section, subject, willing **08** capacity, cheerful, contents, division, elements, gladness, material, pleasure, serenity **09** be pleased, contented, fulfilled, happiness, satisfied, substance, unworried **10** components, equanimity, fulfilment, proportion, untroubled **11** comfortable, contentment, ingredients **12** cheerfulness, constituents, peacefulness, satisfaction, significance, things inside **13** gratification, subject matter **14** component parts **15** what is contained

• **remove contents**
03 gut **05** empty **10** disembowel

contented

04 glad **05** happy **07** content, perfect, pleased, relaxed **08** cheerful **09** fulfilled, satisfied, unworried **10** untroubled **11** comfortable

contention

04 bate, case, plea, toil, view **05** claim, stand, sturt, words **06** belief, debate, enmity, jangle, notion, strife, theory, thesis **07** discord, dispute, feeling, feuding, opinion, rivalry **08** argument, position, struggle **09** assertion, hostility, intuition, judgement, logomachy, viewpoint, wrangling **10** conviction, difference, differency, dissension, impression, persuasion **11** controversy, point of view **12** disagreement

contentious

07 hostile **08** captious, disputed, doubtful, perverse **09** bellicose, bickering, debatable, polemical, querulous **10** debateable, disputable, pugnacious **11** dissentious, quarrelsome, tendentious **12** antagonistic, questionable **13** argumentative, controversial

contentment

04 ease **05** peace **07** comfort, content **08** gladness, pleasure, serenity **09** happiness **10** equanimity, fulfilment **11** complacency **12** cheerfulness, peacefulness, satisfaction **13** contentedness, gratification

contest

03 vie, war **04** bout, deny, game, jump, race **05** doubt, event, fight, match, pairs, set-to, vying **06** battle, combat, debate, defend, oppose, pingle, refute, strife, strive, tussle **07** brabble, compete, contend, dispute, matchup **08** argument, concours, conflict, litigate, object to, question, skirmish, struggle **09** challenge, emulation, encounter, try to beat **10** tournament **11** competition, controversy **12** argue against, championship, contestation

• **in contest against**
04 with

• **part of contest**
03 leg

contestant

05 rival **06** player, prizer **07** entrant **08** aspirant, opponent **09** adversary, candidate, contender, disputant **10** competitor **11** participant

context

07 factors, setting **08** position **09** connexion, framework, situation **10** background, conditions, connection **12** surroundings **13** circumstances **14** state of affairs

contiguous

04 near, next **05** close **06** beside **07** vicinal **08** abutting, adjacent, touching **09** adjoining, bordering **10** coadjacent, conjoining, juxtaposed, tangential **12** conterminous, neighbouring **15** juxtapositional

continent

08 mainland, virtuous **09** temperate **10** terra firma

Continents:

04 Asia
06 Africa, Europe
07 Oceania
10 Antarctica
11 Australasia
12 North America, South America

contingency

05 event **06** chance **07** contact **08** accident, fortuity, incident, juncture **09** emergency, happening **10** incidental, randomness **11** chance event, eventuality, possibility, uncertainty **13** arbitrariness

contingent

03 set **04** band, body **05** based, batch, group, party, quota, share **07** company, mission, section, subject **08** division, relative **09** dependant, dependent **10** accidental, complement, delegation, deputation, detachment **11** conditional **15** representatives

continual

05 still **07** abiding, eternal, regular **08** constant, frequent, repeated **09** incessant, perpetual, recurrent, unceasing **10** persistent, repetitive **11** everlasting **12** interminable

continually

03 e'er **04** ever **06** always **07** forever, non-stop, on and on **09** endlessly, eternally, regularly **10** all the time, constantly, frequently, habitually, repeatedly **11** ceaselessly, incessantly, perpetually, recurrently **12** interminably, persistently **13** everlastingly

continuance

04 stay, term **06** period **07** abiding, durance **08** duration, dwelling, standing **09** endurance **10** permanence **11** adjournment, maintenance, persistence, protraction **12** continuation

continuation

06 return, sequel **07** renewal
08 addition, progress **09** extension
10 carrying-on, resumption,
supplement **11** development,
furtherance, lengthening,
maintenance, persistence, protraction
12 prolongation **13** starting again
14 recommencement
• in continuance
02 on

continue

02 on **04** dure, go on, hold, keep, last,
rest, stay **05** abide, renew **06** endure,
extend, hold on, keep on, keep up,
move on, pursue, remain, resume
07 adjourn, carry on, hold out, not
stop, persist, press on, proceed,
project, prolong, stick at, subsist,
survive, sustain **08** lengthen, maintain,
progress **09** keep going, persevere,
persist in, soldier on **10** begin again,
keep moving, keep on with, press
ahead, recommence, start again
11 keep walking, persevere in, take up
again **12** proceed again **14** keep
travelling

continuity

04 flow **07** linkage **08** cohesion,
sequence, synaphea **09** synapheia
10 connection, succession
11 progression **14** continuousness

continuous

◇ *hidden indicator*
◇ *juxtaposition indicator*
05 solid **07** endless, flowing, lasting,
non-stop, running **08** constant,
extended, seamless, unbroken,
unending **09** ceaseless, continued,
prolonged, unceasing **10** persistent,
relentless **11** consecutive, never-
ending, not stopping, unremitting,
with no let-up **12** interminable
13 uninterrupted, without a break

continuously

◇ *hidden indicator*
◇ *juxtaposition indicator*
04 away **08** together **09** endlessly
10 all the time, at a stretch, constantly
11 ceaselessly **12** interminably,
persistently, relentlessly
13 consecutively, unremittingly
15 twenty-four seven, uninterruptedly

contort

◇ *anagram indicator*
03 wry **04** knot, warp **05** gnarl, twist
06 deform, squirm, wrench, writhe
07 distort, screw up, wreathe, wriggle
08 misshape **09** convolute, disfigure
14 bend out of shape

contortionist

07 acrobat, gymnast, tumbler
08 balancer, stuntman **09** aerialist
10 rope-dancer, rope-walker,
stuntwoman **11** equilibrist, funambulist
12 posture-maker, somersaulter
13 posture-master, trapeze artist

contour

04 form **05** curve, lines, shape

06 aspect, figure, relief **07** isobase,
isobath, outline, profile, surface
08 contorno, tournure **09** character
10 silhouette

contraband

08 hot goods, smuggled **09** smuggling
10 prohibited **11** banned goods,
bootlegging **13** unlawful goods
14 illegal traffic **15** prohibited goods,
proscribed goods

contraceptive

Contraceptives include:

03 cap, IUD
04 coil, IUCD, loop, pill, safe
06 condom, johnny, rubber, sheath,
Vimule®
07 Femidom®, johnnie, the pill
08 Dutch cap, minipill
09 birth pill, diaphragm, prolactin
10 Lippes loop, protective
11 Depo-Provera®
12 female condom, French letter,
prophylactic

contract

◇ *tail deletion indicator*
03 get **04** bond, deal, knit, make, pact
05 agree, catch, purse, tense **06** draw
in, engage, lessen, narrow, pick up,
pledge, reduce, settle, shrink, take in,
treaty **07** abridge, appalto, arrange,
bargain, betroth, compact, curtail,
develop, promise, shorten, shrivel,
tighten, wrinkle **08** compress,
condense, covenant, decrease,
diminish, handfast **09** agreement,
betrothal, champerty, concordat,
constrict, indenture, negotiate,
stipulate, succumb to, undertake
10 abbreviate, agree terms,
commitment, constringe, convention,
engagement, go down with,
settlement **11** arrangement, make
shorter, make smaller, stipulation,
transaction **12** come down with
13 become ill with, become shorter,
become smaller, understanding **14** be
taken ill with
• contract out
06 get out **07** drop out, farm out
08 delegate, withdraw **09** outsource
11 subcontract **12** give to others, pass
to others

contraction

06 shrink **07** systole, tensing
09 drawing-in, lessening, narrowing,
reduction, shrinkage **10** abridgment,
shortening, tightening
11 abridgement, astringency,
compression, curtailment, shrivelling
12 abbreviation, constriction
13 shortened form

contradict

03 nay **04** deny **05** argue, belie, rebut
06 impugn, naysay, negate, oppose,
refute, threap, threep **07** confute,
counter, dispute, gainsay, outface,
sublate **08** contrary, traverse **09** argue
with, challenge, clash with, disaffirm,
go against **12** be at odds with, conflict

with, contrast with, disagree with
14 fly in the face of

contradiction

04 odds **05** clash **06** denial
07 démenti, dispute, paradox
08 antilogy, antinomy, conflict,
negation, rebuttal, traverse, variance
09 challenge **10** antithesis, opposition,
refutation **11** confutation, incongruity
12 disagreement **13** disaffirmance,
inconsistency **14** disaffirmation
15 counter-argument

contradictory

07 opposed **08** clashing, contrary,
opposing, opposite **09** dissonant,
repugnant **10** discordant, discrepant
11 conflicting, dissentient,
incongruous, paradoxical
12 antagonistic, antithetical,
incompatible, inconsistent
14 irreconcilable

contralto

01 c **04** alto

contraption

03 rig **05** gizmo, waldo **06** device,
doodad, doodah, doofer, gadget,
widget **07** machine **08** thingamy
09 apparatus, invention, mechanism
11 contrivance, thingamybob,
thingamyjig **12** what's-its-name

contrary

◇ *reversal indicator*
05 annoy **06** oppose **07** adverse,
awkward, counter, hostile, opposed,
reverse, stroppy, wayward **08** clashing,
converse, opposing, opposite,
perverse, stubborn **09** difficult,
obstinate **10** antipathic, antithesis,
discrepant, headstrong, overthwart,
refractory **11** conflicting, disobliging,
intractable **12** antagonistic,
cantankerous, cross-grained,
incompatible, inconsistent **13** unco-
operative **14** irreconcilable
• contrary to
10 at odds with **14** at variance with, in
conflict with, in opposition to
• on the contrary
◇ *reversal indicator*
08 not at all **09** far from it, per contra
10 conversely, e contrario **11** al
contrario, au contraire **14** just the
reverse **15** just the opposite, quite the
reverse, tout au contraire

contrast

04 foil **05** clash **06** differ, oppose,
relief, set-off **07** compare **08** be at
odds, chiasmus, conflict, disagree,
opposite **09** disparity, go against
10 antithesis, comparison, contradict,
difference, divergence, opposition
11 counter-view, distinction,
distinguish **12** be at variance, be in
conflict, discriminate
13 counterchange, differentiate,
dissimilarity, dissimilitude
14 contraposition **15** differentiation
• in contrast to
09 as against, opposed to **10** rather
than **14** in opposition to

contravene

04 defy **05** break, flout **06** breach, oppose **07** disobey, violate **08** infringe **10** transgress

contravention

06 breach **08** breaking **09** violation **11** dereliction **12** infringement **13** transgression

contretemps

04 tiff **05** brush, clash, hitch **06** mishap **08** accident, argument, squabble **10** difficulty, misfortune **11** predicament **12** disagreement, misadventure

contribute

04 edit, give, help, make **05** add to, cause, endow, grant, write **06** bestow, chip in, create, donate, kick in, lead to, submit, supply **07** chuck in, compile, compose, conduce, furnish, prepare, present, produce, promote, provide **08** generate, occasion, result in **09** originate, subscribe **10** bring about, give rise to, make happen **11** be a factor in, play a part in **13** give a donation

contribution

03 tax **04** gift, item, koha, levy, mite, shot **05** grant, input, paper, piece, story **06** column, report, review **07** article, feature, handout, present **08** addition, bestowal, donation, gratuity, offering **09** endowment **10** feuilleton, proportion, submission **11** Peter's pence **12** subscription **14** superannuation

contributor

05 donor, giver **06** author, backer, critic, patron, writer **07** sponsor **08** compiler, reporter, reviewer **09** columnist, freelance, supporter **10** benefactor, journalist, subscriber **13** correspondent

contrite

05 sorry **06** humble **07** ashamed **08** penitent, red-faced **09** chastened, regretful, repentant **10** remorseful **11** guilt-ridden, penitential

contrition

05 shame **06** regret, sorrow **07** remorse **09** penitence **10** repentance **11** compunction, humiliation **12** self-reproach

contrivance

03 art, gin **04** gear, plan, plot, ploy, ruse, tool **05** dodge, gizmo, shift, trick **06** design, device, doodad, doodah, doofer, engine, gadget, scheme, tactic, widget **07** machine, project **08** artifice, intrigue, thingamy **09** apparatus, appliance, equipment, expedient, implement, invention, mechanism, stratagem **10** compassing **11** contraption, imagination, machination, thingamybob, thingamyjig **12** excogitation, what's-its-name

contrive

◇ *anagram indicator*
04 brew, cook, form, plan, plot, work **05** frame, set up, spend, weave **06** create, cut out, design, devise, effect, engine, invent, manage, scheme, tamper, wangle **07** arrange, compass, concoct, imagine, succeed **08** conceive, engineer, find a way **09** construct, fabricate, manoeuvre **10** bring about, understand **11** orchestrate, stage-manage

contrived

◇ *anagram indicator*
05 false, hokey, set-up **06** forced **08** laboured, mannered, overdone, strained **09** elaborate, unnatural **10** artificial, factitious

control

03 ren, rin, run **04** curb, dial, head, keep, knob, lead, rein, ride, rule, sway, work **05** brake, check, lever, limit, power, reign **06** adjust, button, charge, direct, govern, make go, manage, reduce, subdue, switch, verify **07** command, contain, mastery, monitor, operate, oversee, repress **08** dominate, guidance, hold back, modulate, regulate, restrain, restrict **09** authority, be the boss, constrain, constrict, direction, dominance, hindrance, influence, oversight, reduction, restraint, supervise, supremacy **10** constraint, discipline, government, impediment, instrument, limitation, management, perstringe, regulation, repression, run the show **11** call the tune, keep in check, preside over, restriction, self-control, superintend, supervision **12** be in charge of, call the shots, jurisdiction, rule the roost **13** be in the saddle, self-restraint **14** pull the strings, put the brakes on, self-discipline **15** superintendence, wear the trousers

• **lose control**
04 slip, spaz **05** spazz **07** flip out

• **numerical control**
02 NC

controversial

04 moot **07** at issue, eristic, polemic **08** disputed, doubtful **09** debatable, polemical **10** disputable **11** contentious, tendentious **12** questionable **13** argumentative

controversy

06 debate, strife **07** discord, dispute, polemic, quarrel, wrangle **08** argument, friction, squabble **10** contention, debatement, discussion, dissension, war of words **11** altercation **12** cause célèbre, disagreement

contusion

04 bump, lump, mark **05** knock **06** bruise, injury **07** blemish **08** swelling **10** ecchymosis **13** discoloration

conundrum

05 guess, poser **06** enigma, puzzle, riddle, teaser **07** anagram, problem **08** quandary, word game **10** difficulty **11** brainteaser **12** brain-twister

conurbation

04 city, town **06** ghetto **08** big smoke, downtown, precinct, suburbia **09** inner city, metroplex, urban area **10** city centre, cosmopolis, metropolis, micropolis, pentapolis **11** megalopolis, urban sprawl **12** municipality **13** urban district **14** concrete jungle

convalesce

05 rally **06** pick up, revive **07** get well, improve, recover **09** get better **10** recuperate **11** get stronger, pull through

convalescence

08 recovery **09** anastasis **11** improvement, restoration **12** recuperation **13** getting better **14** rehabilitation

convene

04 call, meet **05** bring, rally **06** gather, muster, summon **07** collect, convoke **08** assemble **10** congregate **12** call together, come together **13** bring together

convenience

03 bog, lav, loo, use **04** help **06** behoof, device, gadget, toilet **07** amenity, benefit, fitness, service, utility **08** facility, lavatory, resource **09** advantage, appliance, commodity, ease of use, handiness, usability **10** expediency, usefulness **11** propinquity, suitability, water closet **12** availability **13** accessibility, accommodation, opportuneness **14** propitiousness, serviceability **15** appropriateness

See also **toilet**

convenient

03 fit **04** easy, gain, hend **05** handy **06** at hand, fitted, nearby, suited, timely, useful **07** adapted, favored, fitting, helpful **08** favoured, handsome, suitable **09** available, expedient, opportune, well-timed **10** accessible, beneficial, commodious, near at hand **11** appropriate, close at hand, within reach **12** labour-saving **13** advantageable **14** at your disposal

conveniently

04 well **05** patly **06** at hand, nearby **08** suitably, usefully **09** helpfully **10** accessibly, near at hand **11** close at hand, within reach **13** appropriately

convent

04 cite **05** abbey, house **06** fratry, friary, priory, summon **07** convene, fratery, nunnery **08** cloister **09** monastery

See also **monastery**

convention

03 use **04** bond, code, deal, pact **05** ethos, mores, synod, usage **06** accord, custom, treaty **07** bargain, compact, council, fashion, meeting **08** assembly, ceremony, conclave, congress, contract, covenant, practice, protocol **09** agreement, Blackwood, concordat, delegates, etiquette, formality, gathering, propriety, punctilio, tradition **10** commitment, conference, engagement, settlement **11** arrangement, convocation, transaction **12** matter of form **13** understanding **15** representatives

conventional
04 lame **05** nomic, trite, usual **06** common, formal, normal, proper, ritual **07** correct, pompier, regular, routine, uptight **08** accepted, copybook, expected, ordinary, orthodox, received, standard, straight **09** bourgeois, customary, hidebound, prevalent **10** conformist, mainstream, pedestrian, prevailing, unoriginal **11** commonplace, respectable, stereotyped, traditional **12** conservative, run-of-the-mill **14** common-or-garden

conventionally
07 usually **08** commonly, formally, normally **09** regularly, routinely **10** ordinarily **13** traditionally

converge
04 form, join, mass, meet **05** focus, merge, unite **06** gather **07** close in, combine **08** approach, coincide **09** intersect **11** concentrate, move towards **12** come together

convergence
05 union **07** meeting, merging **08** approach, blending, junction **10** confluence **11** coincidence, combination **12** intersection **13** concentration

conversant
• **conversant with**
08 versed in **09** skilled in **10** apprised of, au fait with **11** practised in **12** familiar with, proficient in **13** experienced in, informed about **14** acquainted with

conversation
◇ *homophone indicator*
03 rap **04** chat, talk **05** board, convo, crack, craic, wongi **06** confab, gossip, natter, yabber **07** chinwag, purpose **08** chitchat, colloquy, cosy chat, dialogue, exchange, parlance, question, speaking **09** discourse, small talk, table talk, tête-à-tête **10** discussion, pillow talk **12** heart-to-heart **13** communication, interlocution

conversational
◇ *homophone indicator*
06 casual, chatty **07** relaxed **08** informal **09** talkative **10** colloquial **13** communicative

converse
◇ *homophone indicator*
04 chat, talk **05** speak, wongi **06** confer, dialog, gossip, natter, reason, relate **07** chatter, commune, counter, discuss, obverse, propose, purpose, reverse **08** chitchat, collogue, colloquy, contrary, dialogue,

opposing, opposite, question, reversed **09** discourse **10** antithesis, chew the fat, chew the rag, colloquize, transposed **11** communicate **12** antithetical **13** other way round

conversely
09 e converso, obversely **10** contrarily **12** contrariwise **13** on the contrary **14** antithetically, on the other hand

conversion
◇ *anagram indicator*
06 change, switch **07** rebirth, turning **08** exchange, metanoia, mutation **09** preaching, reshaping **10** adaptation, adjustment, alteration, conviction, persuasion **11** proselytism, reformation, remodelling, translation **12** modification, regeneration, substitution **13** customization, metamorphosis, transmutation **14** evangelization, reconstruction, reorganization, transformation **15** proselytization, transfiguration

convert
◇ *anagram indicator*
03 put **04** goal, make, turn **05** adapt, alter **06** adjust, change, modify, mutate, reform, revise, switch **07** rebuild, remodel, reshape, restyle, win over **08** adherent, believer, convince, disciple, exchange, go over to, move over, neophyte, persuade, transfer, turn into **09** bring over, customize, new person, proselyte, refashion, transform, transmute **10** evangelize, reorganize, substitute, switch from **11** jump the dyke, loup the dyke, proselytize, reconstruct, restructure, transfigure **12** metamorphose **13** change beliefs, changed person **14** change religion

convertible
◇ *anagram indicator*
06 ragtop **07** soft top **09** adaptable, landaulet **10** adjustable, changeable, modifiable, permutable **11** landaulette **12** exchangeable **15** interchangeable

convex
04 nowy **05** bombé **07** bulging, gibbous, rounded **08** swelling **09** curved out **10** bow-fronted **11** protuberant **15** bending outwards

convey
03 put, tip **04** bear, have, lead, move, pipe, send, take, tell, wain **05** bring, carry, drive, fetch, guide, shift, steal **06** hand on, impart, import, pass on, relate, reveal **07** channel, conduct, deliver, express, forward, mediate, present **08** announce, disclose, transfer, transmit **09** make known, transport **11** communicate

conveyance
03 bus, cab, car, sac, van **04** cart, taxi **05** coach, grant, lorry, truck, wagon **06** ceding **07** bicycle, express, transit, vehicle **08** carriage, delivery, granting, mortgage, movement, transfer **09** transport **10** bequeathal,

motorcycle **11** consignment **12** transference, transmission **13** transportance **14** transportation
See also **aircraft**; **bicycle**; **car**; **carriage**; **ship**

convict
03 con, lag **05** crime, crook, felon, judge **06** canary, forçat, inmate **07** approve, attaint, condemn, culprit, old hand, reprove, villain **08** criminal, imprison, jailbird, offender, prisoner, sentence, yardbird **09** wrongdoer **10** canary-bird, emancipist, find guilty, lawbreaker

conviction
04 view **05** creed, faith, prior, tenet **06** belief **07** fervour, opinion **08** firmness, sentence **09** assurance, certainty, certitude, judgement, principle **10** confidence, persuasion, plerophory **11** earnestness, plerophoria **12** condemnation, imprisonment, satisfaction

convince
04 sell, sway **06** assure, induce, prompt **07** prove to, resolve, satisfy, win over **08** persuade, perswade, talk into, talk over **09** bring home, influence **10** bring round **11** prevail upon

convincing
06 cogent, likely **07** certain, telling **08** credible, forceful, luculent, positive, powerful, pregnant, probable **09** plausible **10** compelling, conclusive, conclusory, impressive, persuasive **12** satisfactory

convincingly
08 cogently, credibly **09** all ends up, plausibly, tellingly **10** forcefully, powerfully **12** compellingly, conclusively, impressively, persuasively

convivial
04 boon **05** jolly, merry **06** genial, hearty, jovial, lively, social **07** affable, cordial, festive **08** cheerful, friendly, sociable **09** fun-loving **11** Anacreontic

conviviality
03 fun **05** cheer, mirth **06** gaiety **07** jollity **08** bonhomie **09** festivity, geniality, joviality **10** cordiality, liveliness **11** good feeling, merrymaking, sociability **12** friendliness **14** goodfellowship

convocation
04 diet **05** forum, synod **07** council, meeting **08** assembly, conclave, congress **10** assemblage, conference, convention **12** congregation, forgathering

convoluted
◇ *anagram indicator*
04 mazy **07** complex, unclear, winding, writhen, wrythen **08** involved, tortuous, twisting **09** convolute, intricate, Vitruvian **10** meandering **11** complicated

convolution
04 coil, fold, loop, turn **05** gyrus, helix, twist, whorl **06** spiral **07** coiling, winding **08** curlicue **09** intricacy, sinuosity **10** complexity **11** involvement, sinuousness **12** complication, entanglement, tortuousness

convoy
04 line **05** fleet, group, guard, train **06** escort **07** company **10** attendance, protection

convulse
◇ *anagram indicator*
04 jerk **05** seize **07** disturb, shudder **08** unsettle **10** suffer a fit **14** shake violently, suffer a seizure

convulsion
03 fit, tic **05** cramp, ictus, spasm **06** attack, furore, tremor, tumult, unrest **07** seizure, turmoil **08** disorder, eruption, laughter, outburst, paroxysm, upheaval **09** agitation, commotion **10** turbulence **11** contraction, disturbance **13** electric shock

convulsive
05 jerky **06** fitful **07** violent **08** sporadic **09** spasmodic **11** spasmodical **12** uncontrolled
• **convulsive disorder**
03 DTs **15** delirium tremens

cook
◇ *anagram indicator*
02 do **03** pan **04** burn, chef, fake, heat, make, peep, ruin, warm **05** fryer, put on, spoil **06** doctor, greasy, overdo **07** babbler, concoct, falsify, prepare, scare up, underdo **08** overcook, rustle up **09** cuisinier, improvise, undercook **11** put together **13** throw together
See also **chef**

Cooking methods include:
03 fry
04 bake, boil, sear, stew
05 broil, brown, curry, grill, poach, roast, sauté, steam, toast
06 braise, coddle, flambé, pan-fry, simmer
07 deep-fry, parboil, stir-fry
08 barbecue, pot-roast, scramble
09 casserole, char-grill, fricassee, microwave, oven-roast, spit-roast
10 flame-grill

• **cook up**
◇ *anagram indicator*
04 brew, edit, plan, plot **06** devise, invent, make up, scheme **07** concoct, falsify, prepare **08** contrive **09** fabricate

cooked
◇ *anagram indicator*
• **lightly cooked**
04 rare, rear

cookery
Cookery styles include:
04 Thai
05 Greek, halal, Irish, mezze, rural, tapas, vegan, Welsh

06 French, fusion, German, Indian, kosher, Tex-Mex
07 African, British, Chinese, Eastern, English, Italian, Mexican, seafood, Spanish, Turkish
08 American, fast food, Japanese, Scottish
09 Cantonese, Caribbean, Malaysian, Provençal
10 cordon bleu, Far Eastern, gluten-free, Indonesian, Pacific Rim, vegetarian
11 home cooking, lean cuisine
12 haute cuisine
13 Mediterranean, Middle Eastern
14 cuisine minceur
15 nouvelle cuisine

Cookery-related terms include:
03 Aga, dip, gut, hob, ice
04 chef, chop, cook, cure, dice, mash, oven, rise, whip
05 baste, brown, carve, chill, chump, curry, daube, devil, dress, glaze, grate, knead, mince, mould, press, purée, score, shave, smoke, steep, stuff, whisk
06 batter, blanch, de-bone, entrée, fillet, fondue, infuse, kosher, leaven, recipe, reduce, season, spread
07 garnish, nibbles, proving, starter, tandoor, topping
08 cookbook, devilled, marinade, marinate, preserve
09 antipasto, percolate, reduction, tenderize
10 caramelize
11 hors d'oeuvre

Cook Islands
03 COK

cool
03 ace, fan, ice **04** calm, chic, cold, iced, keel, mega, neat **05** abate, allay, aloof, brill, chill, crisp, fresh, great, nervy, nippy, parky, poise, quiet, smart, tepid **06** breeze, breezy, caller, chilly, dampen, freeze, frigid, frosty, lessen, placid, poised, quench, reduce, sedate, temper, trendy, wicked **07** assuage, bracing, chilled, control, distant, draught, elegant, get cold, ice-cold, relaxed, stylish, subside, unmoved **08** calmness, coldness, composed, coolness, diminish, draughty, impudent, laid-back, lukewarm, make cold, moderate, reserved, smashing, terrific, turn cold **09** admirable, apathetic, collected, composure, crispness, excellent, fantastic, freshness, get colder, impassive, nippiness, sangfroid, unexcited, unruffled, wonderful **10** acceptable, become cold, chilliness, make colder, marvellous, refreshing, streetwise, turn colder, unfriendly, untroubled **11** fashionable, half-hearted, indifferent, level-headed, refrigerate, self-control, standoffish, undisturbed, unemotional, unexcitable, unflappable, unflustered, unperturbed, unwelcoming **12** air-condition,

become colder, second to none, uninterested, unresponsive **13** collectedness, defervescence, defervescency, disinterested, dispassionate, imperturbable, self-possessed, sophisticated **14** out of this world, self-discipline, self-possession, unapprehensive, unenthusiastic **15** cool as a cucumber, uncommunicative, undemonstrative

cooler *see* jail, gaol

cooling
08 chilling, freezing **10** refreshing **11** refrigerant, ventilation **13** defervescence, defervescency, refrigeration, refrigerative, refrigeratory **15** air-conditioning

coolly
06 calmly, coldly **07** quietly **08** frostily, placidly, sedately **09** distantly **10** composedly, impudently, reservedly **11** collectedly, impassively, unexcitably, unexcitedly **13** apathetically, half-heartedly, imperturbably, indifferently, level-headedly, standoffishly, unemotionally **14** uninterestedly, unresponsively **15** dispassionately

coop
03 box, mew, pen, ren, rin, rip, run **04** cage **05** cavie, hutch, pound **06** keavie **09** enclosure
• **coop up**
03 pen **04** cage, shut **06** bail up, immure, keep in, lock up, shut in, shut up **07** close in, confine, enclose, impound **08** imprison, lock away **11** incarcerate

Cooper
04 Gary

co-operate
03 aid **04** ally, help, play, pool **05** share, unite **06** assist, team up **07** combine, pitch in **08** conspire, play ball **09** play along **10** contribute, join forces **11** collaborate, participate, string along **12** band together, pull together, work together **14** pull your weight, work side by side

co-operation
03 aid **04** help **05** unity **08** teamwork **10** assistance, team spirit **11** give-and-take, helpfulness, helping hand, joint action **12** contribution, co-ordination **13** collaboration, esprit de corps, participation **15** concerted action, concerted effort, working together

co-operative
05 joint **06** shared, united **07** helpful, helping, willing **08** coactive, combined, obliging **09** assisting, compliant, concerted **10** collective, responsive, supportive **11** co-ordinated **13** accommodating, collaborative **15** working together

co-ordinate
01 x, y, z **02** go **04** mesh **05** adapt, blend, match, order **06** go well, join up

07 absciss, arrange, blend in
08 abscissa, abscisse, ordinate, organize, regulate, tabulate **09** co-operate, correlate, harmonize, integrate, mix 'n' match
10 complement, go together
11 collaborate, synchronize, systematize **12** be compatible, work together **14** make compatible

co-ordination
07 harmony **08** blending, matching, ordering **10** ordonnance
11 arrangement, co-operation, integration **12** organization
13 collaboration, compatibility
15 complementation

cop
02 PC **03** get, pig, top **04** bull, head, nark **05** bizzy, bobby, catch **06** arrest, copper, obtain, rozzer **07** acquire, capture, officer **08** flatfoot
09 constable, policeman **10** bluebottle
11 policewoman **13** police officer
See also **police officer**
• **cop out**
04 balk, duck, shun **05** avert, avoid, dodge, elude, evade, hedge, shirk
06 bypass, escape **07** prevent **08** get out of, get round, sidestep **09** give a miss **11** abstain from, make a detour, run away from, shy away from **12** hold back from, keep away from, stay away from, steer clear of

cope
04 meet **05** get by, match **06** barter, make do, manage **07** carry on, chlamys, contend, pluvial, subsist, succeed, survive **08** exchange
09 encounter **10** get through
• **cope with**
04 hack **05** touch, treat **06** endure, handle, manage, take up **07** weather
08 deal with **09** encounter **11** contend with, grapple with, wrestle with
12 struggle with

coping
04 skew

copious
04 full, huge, rich **05** ample, great, large **06** bags of, lavish **07** fulsome, liberal, profuse, teeming **08** abundant, generous, numerous **09** abounding, bounteous, bountiful, extensive, luxuriant, plenteous, plentiful, redundant **11** overflowing
13 inexhaustible

cop-out
05 alibi, dodge, fraud **06** excuse, get-out **07** evasion, pretext **08** pretence, shirking **14** passing the buck

copper
01 p **02** Cu
See also **coin**; **police officer**

cops *see* **police**

copse
04 bush, carr, wood **05** brush, grove
06 spinny, spring **07** coppice, spinney, thicket

copulate
03 tup **04** mate **07** have sex **08** make love **10** fool around, get off with, make it with **11** go all the way, go to bed with

copulation
03 sex **06** coitus, mating **07** coition
08 congress, coupling, embraces, intimacy **09** relations **10** commixtion, love-making **15** carnal knowledge

copy
02 cc **03** ape, bcc, CRC, fax **04** crib, echo, fake, scan **05** clone, forge, image, issue, mimic, model, print, stuff, trace, Xerox® **06** borrow, carbon, ectype, follow, mirror, parrot, pirate, repeat, sample **07** emulate, estreat, example, forgery, imitate, pattern, replica, tracing, vidimus **08** apograph, knock-off, likeness, manifold, simulate, specimen **09** archetype, borrowing, duplicate, facsimile, imitation, photocopy, Photostat®, polygraph, replicate, reproduce, semblance
10 carbon copy, mimeograph, plagiarism, plagiarize, transcribe, transcript, triplicate **11** counterfeit, counterpart, engrossment, impersonate, replication
12 reproduction **13** transcription
14 representation **15** exemplification

coquettish
06 flirty **07** amorous, flighty, teasing, vampish **08** dallying, inviting
09 seductive **10** come-hither
11 flirtatious, provocative

cord
03 guy, tie **04** bond, flex, lace, line, link, rope **05** cable, match, twine, twist
06 bobbin, myelon, ribbon, strand, string, tendon, thread **07** funicle, service **08** bell pull, chenille
09 funiculus **10** connection, draw-string **11** navel-string **12** spinal marrow

cordial
04 warm **05** shrub **06** genial, hearty
07 affable, cardiac, earnest, persico, ratafia, rosolio, sincere **08** amicable, anisette, cheerful, friendly, persicot, pleasant, rosoglio, sociable
09 agreeable, heartfelt, hippocras, rosa-solis, welcoming **10** pousse-café
11 Benedictine, stimulating, warm-hearted **12** affectionate, invigorating, wholehearted **13** aqua caelestis, aurum potabile

cordiality
05 heart **06** warmth **07** earnest, welcome **09** affection, geniality, sincerity **10** affability, heartiness
11 sociability **12** cheerfulness, friendliness **13** agreeableness

cordially
06 warmly **07** affably **08** amicably, genially, sociably **10** cheerfully, pleasantly **13** warm-heartedly
14 wholeheartedly

cordon
04 line, ring **05** chain, fence, plant
06 column, ribbon **07** barrier

• **cordon off**
07 enclose, isolate, seal off **08** close off, encircle, fence off, separate, surround

core
03 key, nub **04** crux, gang, gist, lead, main, nife, runt **05** basic, heart, shift, vital **06** centre, innate, kernel, middle
07 campana, central, company, corncob, crucial, essence, nucleus, typical **08** inherent, interior
09 essential, intrinsic, principal, substance **10** barysphere, definitive, underlying **11** constituent, fundamental, nitty-gritty **12** axis cylinder, quintessence
14 characteristic

cork
03 lid **04** bung, plug, seal, stop
05 cover, shive, suber **07** phellem, stopper

corm *see* **bulb**

cormorant
04 shag **05** scart, skart **06** duiker, duyker, scarth, skarth **07** sea crow

corn
03 mow, rye, Zea **04** oats **05** grain, maize, wheat **06** barley, cereal, farina, kernel, pinole **10** arable crop, cereal crop, intoxicate

corner
03 cor, fix, hog, jam **04** bend, fork, hole, nook, trap, tree **05** angle, catch, crook, curve, joint, niche **06** bail up, cantle, cavity, cranny, cut off, dièdre, pickle, plight, recess, scrape
07 confine, control, crevice, hideout, retreat, straits, turning **08** block off, dominate, hardship, hideaway, hunt down, junction **09** ingleneuk, inglenook, situation, tight spot
10 monopolize, run to earth
11 predicament **12** intersection
13 nowhere to turn **15** force into a place
• **around the corner**
04 near **05** close, local **06** at hand, coming, nearby **07** close by, looming
08 imminent, in the air **09** impending
10 accessible, convenient
11 approaching, within range, within reach **12** a stone's throw, neighbouring
13 about to happen
• **cut corners**
05 skimp

cornerstone
03 key **04** base, coin, core **05** basis, heart, quoin **06** thrust **07** bedrock, essence, keyhole, skew-put, support
08 keystone, mainstay **09** essential, principle, skew-table **10** essentials, groundwork, skew-corbel
11 fundamental **12** fundamentals
13 alpha and omega, starting-point
14 basic principle, main ingredient
15 first principles

Cornwall
02 SW

corny

04 dull **05** banal, horny, stale, trite **06** feeble, spammy **07** buckeye, cliché'd, maudlin, mawkish **08** clichéed, overused **09** hackneyed **11** commonplace, Mickey Mouse, sentimental, stereotyped **12** old-fashioned **13** platitudinous

corollary

05 rider **06** porism, result, upshot **08** function, illation **09** deduction, induction, inference **10** conclusion, consectary, consequent **11** consequence **13** supplementary

coronation

08 crowning **12** enthronement

coronet

05 crown, tiara **06** cornet, diadem, wreath **07** circlet, crownet, garland

corporal

03 Cpl, NCO, Nym **04** corp, naik, pall **06** actual, bodily, carnal **07** fleshly, somatic **08** concrete, material, physical, tangible **09** brigadier, corporeal **10** anatomical **11** substantial **13** lance sergeant

corporate

05 joint **06** allied, common, merged, pooled, shared, united **08** combined, communal **09** concerted **10** collective, collegiate **11** amalgamated **13** collaborative

corporation

04 firm, gild **05** belly, guild, house, trust **06** cartel, paunch **07** commune, company, concern, council, guildry **08** business, industry, pot-belly, township **09** authority, beer belly, syndicate **10** consortium **11** association, authorities, City Company, partnership **12** conglomerate, organization **13** burgh of barony, establishment, governing body, multinational **14** holding company

See also **paunch; stomach**

corporeal

05 human, hylic **06** actual, bodily, carnal, mortal **07** fleshly **08** concrete, corporal, material, physical, tangible **11** substantial

corps

01 C **02** CD **03** RAC **04** band, body, crew, team, unit **05** squad **07** brigade, company **08** division, regiment, squadron **10** contingent, detachment

corpse

04 body, like, mort **05** corse, mummy, relic, stiff, zombi **06** deader, relics, zombie **07** cadaver, carcase, carcass, remains **08** dead body, skeleton **09** flatliner

corpulent

03 fat **05** beefy, bulky, burly, large, obese, plump, poddy, podgy, stout, tubby **06** fleshy, portly, rotund **07** adipose, fattish **08** roly-poly **10** overweight, pot-bellied, well-padded **11** Falstaffian

corpus

04 body **05** whole **08** entirety **10** collection **11** aggregation, compilation

corral

03 sty **04** coop, fold **05** kraal, pound, stall **09** enclosure

correct

◇ *anagram indicator*

02 OK **03** fix **04** cure, edit, jake, just, mend, okay, real, sort, true **05** amend, debug, emend, exact, right, scold, tweak **06** actual, adjust, bang on, proper, punish, rebuke, reform, remedy, revise, seemly, spot-on, strict **07** fitting, improve, precise, rectify, redress, regular, reprove, right-on, sort out **08** accepted, accurate, admonish, disabuse, faithful, flawless, put right, regulate, set right, standard, suitable, truthful, unerring **09** faultless, reprimand **10** acceptable, ameliorate, blue-pencil, discipline **11** appropriate, comme il faut, put straight, put to rights, set to rights, word-perfect **12** conventional, rehabilitate **14** counterbalance

correction

◇ *anagram indicator*

05 tweak **06** rebuke, reform **07** reproof **08** equation, grafting, scolding **09** amendment, reduction, remedying, reprimand **10** adjustment, admonition, alteration, diorthosis, discipline, emendation, punishment **11** improvement, reformation **12** amelioration, chastisement, compensation, modification **13** rectification **14** rehabilitation

corrective

05 penal **08** curative, punitive, remedial **09** corrigent, medicinal **10** amendatory, emendatory, palliative **11** reformatory, restorative, therapeutic **12** disciplinary **14** rehabilitative

correctly

◇ *anagram indicator*

02 OK **04** okay **05** right **07** exactly, rightly **08** actually, properly, suitably **09** about east, fittingly, precisely **10** acceptably, accurately, flawlessly, unerringly **11** faultlessly **13** appropriately **14** conventionally

correlate

04 link **05** agree, tally, tie in **06** equate, relate **07** compare, connect **08** analogue, interact, parallel **09** associate **10** co-ordinate, correspond **15** show a connection

correlation

03 fit **04** link **10** connection **11** association, equivalence, interaction, interchange, reciprocity **12** relationship **14** correspondence **15** interdependence

correspond

03 fit, pen **05** agree, match, rhyme, tally, write **06** accord, answer, concur,

square **07** balance, conform, match up **08** assonate, coincide, dovetail, register **09** be similar, correlate, harmonize, represent **10** complement, sympathize **11** be analogous, communicate, fit together, keep in touch **12** be consistent, be equivalent **13** be in agreement **15** exchange letters

correspondence

03 fit **04** mail, post **05** e-mail, match **07** analogy, harmony, letters, writing **08** relation **09** agreement, assonance, congruity **10** comparison, conformity, consonance, similarity **11** coincidence, concurrence, correlation, equivalence, resemblance, suitability **13** communication, comparability

See also **letter**

correspondent

06 keypal, pen pal, writer **08** agreeing, reporter, suitable **09** answering, columnist, pen friend **10** journalist, responsive **11** contributor, responsible **12** letter-writer

corresponding

04 like **07** similar, suiting **08** agreeing, matching, parallel, relative **09** accordant, analogous, answering, congruent, facsimile, identical **10** collateral, comparable, equivalent, reciprocal **12** commensurate, interrelated **13** complementary

corridor

04 hall **05** aisle, lobby **07** gallery, gangway, hallway, passage **08** alleyway **09** penthouse **10** passageway

corroborate

05 prove **06** attest, back up, ratify, uphold, verify **07** bear out, certify, confirm, endorse, support, sustain **08** document, evidence, underpin, validate **09** confirmed **12** authenticate, substantiate

corroboration

10 validation **11** attestation, endorsement **12** confirmation, ratification, verification **14** authentication, substantiation

corroborative

09 endorsing, verifying **10** confirming, evidential, supporting, supportive, validating **11** evidentiary **12** confirmative, confirmatory, verificatory **14** substantiating

corrode

03 eat, rot **04** burn, etch, fret, rust **05** eat in, erode, waste **06** abrade, impair **07** consume, crumble, destroy, eat away, eat into, oxidize, tarnish **08** wear away **11** deteriorate **12** disintegrate

corrosion

03 rot **04** rust **07** burning, erosion, rotting, rusting, wasting **08** abrasion **09** prerosion **10** tarnishing **13** deterioration **14** disintegration

corrosive
04 acid **07** caustic, cutting, erosive, wasting, wearing **08** abrasive **09** consuming, corroding **11** destructive

corrugated
06 fluted, folded, ridged **07** creased, grooved, rumpled, striate **08** crinkled, furrowed, wrinkled **10** channelled

corrupt
◇ *anagram indicator*
03 buy, mar, rot **04** bent, evil, lure, warp **05** bribe, decay, shady, spoil, taint, venal **06** blight, bribed, buy off, canker, debase, defile, doctor, impure, infect, poison, putrid, rotten, seduce, sleazy, suborn, wicked **07** abusive, crooked, debauch, defiled, deprave, falsify, immoral, obscene, pervert, pollute, putrefy, subvert, tainted, vitiate **08** bribable, depraved, empoison **09** barbarize, barbarous, debauched, dishonest, dissolute, inquinate, unethical **10** adulterate, bastardize, degenerate, demoralize, fraudulent, lead astray, tamper with **11** contaminate **12** contaminated, unprincipled, unscrupulous **13** untrustworthy **15** be a bad influence

corruption
03 rot **04** evil, vice **05** abuse, bobol, fraud, graft **06** sleaze **07** bribery, leprosy **08** impurity, iniquity, villainy **09** depravity, extortion, pollution, shadiness **10** adaptation, alteration, debauchery, dishonesty, distortion, immorality, perversion, rottenness, subversion, wickedness **11** criminality, crookedness, degradation, subornation **12** degeneration, modification **13** contamination, sharp practice

corset
04 belt, busk **05** stays **06** bodice, girdle, roll-on, shaper, waspie **08** corselet **11** panty girdle

cortège
05 suite, train **06** column, parade **07** retinue **09** cavalcade, entourage **10** procession

cosh *see* **weapon**

cosily
06 safely, snugly, warmly **08** securely **10** intimately **11** comfortably

cosmetic
04 fard **05** minor **06** beauty, make-up, slight **07** shallow, surface, trivial **08** external, skin-deep **10** maquillage, peripheral **11** beautifying, superficial

Cosmetics include:
05 rouge, toner
07 blusher, bronzer, mascara, perfume
08 cleanser, eyeliner, face mask, face pack, lip gloss, lip liner, lipstick, panstick
09 concealer, eye shadow, face cream
10 face powder, foundation, kohl pencil, nail polish
11 greasepaint, moisturizer, nail varnish
13 eyebrow pencil, pressed powder

cosmic
04 huge, mega, vast **05** large **07** immense, in space, massive, mundane, orderly, seismic **08** colossal, enormous, infinite **09** from space, grandiose, limitless, universal, worldwide **11** measureless, significant **12** immeasurable

cosmonaut
08 lunanaut, spaceman **09** astronaut, lunarnaut, taikonaut **10** spacewoman **14** space traveller

cosmopolitan
06 urbane **07** worldly **08** cultured **09** universal **11** broad-minded, multiracial, worldly-wise **12** unprejudiced **13** international, multicultural, sophisticated, well-travelled

cosmos
06 galaxy, nature, system, worlds **08** creation, universe

cosset
03 pet **04** baby **05** spoil **06** coddle, cuddle, fondle, pamper **07** cherish, indulge **11** mollycoddle, overindulge

cost
03 fee, pay, tab **04** exes, harm, hurt, levy, loss, rate, take, toll **05** coast, fetch, go for, price, quote, value, worth **06** amount, ask for, budget, buy for, charge, come to, damage, figure, injure, injury, outlay, tariff **07** be worth, cost out, deprive, destroy, expense, payment, penalty, sell for, set back, stand in, work out **08** amount to, estimate, expenses, retail at, spending **09** calculate, cause harm, detriment, knock back, outgoings, overheads, quotation, sacrifice, suffering, valuation **10** be priced at, be valued at **11** asking price, cause injury, deprivation, expenditure **12** disbursement, selling price **13** disbursements **14** cause the loss of

Costa Rica
02 CR **03** CRI

costly
04 dear, posh, rich, salt **05** steep **06** lavish, pricey **07** harmful, premium, ruinous, sky-high **08** damaging, high-cost, precious, splendid, valuable **09** big-ticket, chargeful, excessive, expensive, priceless, sumptuous **10** disastrous, exorbitant, high-priced, loss-making, overpriced **11** deleterious, destructive, detrimental **12** catastrophic, costing a bomb, extortionate **15** costing the earth, daylight robbery

costume
02 gi **03** gie, tog **04** garb, suit **05** dress, get-up, habit, robes **06** attire, bather, bikini, cossie, judogi, livery, outfit, rig-out, toilet **07** apparel, clobber, clothes, fashion, threads, uniform **08** clothing, ensemble, garments **09** gala-dress, vestments **10** diving suit, fancy dress **11** diving dress **12** style of dress
See also **clothes, clothing**

cosy
04 cosh, safe, snug, warm **05** comfy **06** homely, intime, secure **08** intimate **09** congenial, gemütlich, sheltered **11** comfortable

Côte d'Ivoire
02 CI **03** CIV

coterie
03 set **04** camp, club, gang **05** cabal, group **06** caucus, circle, clique **07** cenacle, faction **09** camarilla, community **11** association

cottage
03 cot, hut **04** crib, gite **05** bothy, cabin, dacha, lodge, shack, villa **06** bothie, chalet, shanty **08** bungalow **09** home-croft

cotton
04 lint **05** ceiba

Cotton fabrics include:
04 aida, duck, jean
05 chino, denim, dhoti, drill, jaspé, jeans, kanga, piqué, surat, toile
06 Bengal, calico, canvas, chintz, coutil, dhooti, diaper, dimity, humhum, jersey, khanga, madras, moreen, muslin, nankin, Oxford, pongee, sateen, T-cloth
07 batiste, buckram, challis, duvetyn, fustian, galatea, gingham, jaconet, kitenge, Mexican, nankeen, percale, printer, silesia
08 chambray, corduroy, coutille, cretonne, drilling, frocking, lambskin, marcella, nainsook, organdie, osnaburg, shantung, thickset
09 cottonade, huckaback, longcloth, percaline, sailcloth, satin jean, swans-down, velveteen
10 Balbriggan, candlewick, monk's cloth, seersucker, winceyette
11 cheesecloth, flannelette, mutton cloth, nettle-cloth, Oxford cloth, sponge cloth
13 casement cloth

● **foreign particle in cotton**
04 moit, mote

couch
03 bed, set **04** bear, sofa, word **05** divan, frame, quick, utter **06** cradle, day bed, litter, pallet, phrase, quitch, scutch, settee, twitch **07** express, lounger, ottoman, quicken, sofa bed, support, vis-à-vis **08** dog-grass, dog-wheat **10** quack grass, quick grass, triclinium **11** quitch grass, scutch grass, twitch grass **12** chaise-longue, chesterfield

cough
03 hem, ugh **04** ahem, bark, hack, hawk, kink, rasp **05** croak, hoast

06 tisick, tussis **07** hawking **08** kink-host **09** chincough, kink-cough, pertussis **15** clear your throat
• **cough up**
03 pay **04** give **05** pay up **06** ante up, pay out **07** fork out, stump up **08** hand over, shell out

could
• **could be, could become**
◊ *anagram indicator*

council
04 body, diet, duma, jury **05** board, boule, cabal, crowd, divan, douma, flock, forum, group, jirga, junta, panel, rally, shura, synod, witan **06** senate, soviet, throng **07** cabinet, chamber, company, conseil, consult, meeting **08** advisers, assembly, congress, ministry, trustees **09** committee, directors, executive, gathering, governors, Landsting, Loya Jirga, multitude, panchayat, Sanhedrim, Sanhedrin, syndicate **10** commission, conference, convention, focus group, government, Landsthing, management, parliament, presidency **11** city fathers, convocation, corporation, directorate, witenagemot **12** advisory body, ayuntamiento, body of people, congregation, working party **13** advisory group, governing body **14** administration, local authority

---

Council areas of Scotland:

04 Fife
05 Angus, Moray
07 Falkirk
08 Highland, Stirling
10 Dundee City, Eilean Siar, Inverclyde, Midlothian
11 East Lothian, Glasgow City, West Lothian
12 Aberdeen City, East Ayrshire, Renfrewshire
13 Aberdeenshire, Argyll and Bute, North Ayrshire, Orkney Islands, South Ayrshire
15 City of Edinburgh, Perth and Kinross, Scottish Borders, Shetland Islands
16 Clackmannanshire, East Renfrewshire, North Lanarkshire, South Lanarkshire
18 East Dunbartonshire, West Dunbartonshire
19 Dumfries and Galloway

Council areas of Wales:

05 Conwy, Powys
07 Cardiff, Gwynedd, Newport, Swansea, Torfaen, Wrexham
08 Bridgend
10 Caerphilly, Ceredigion, Flintshire
12 Blaenau Gwent, Denbighshire
13 Merthyr Tydfil, Monmouthshire, Pembrokeshire
14 Isle of Anglesey
15 Carmarthenshire, Neath Port Talbot, Vale of Glamorgan
16 Rhondda Cynon Taff

---

councillor
02 CC, Cr, PC **04** Cllr **05** vezir, vizir **06** induna, visier, vizier, wizier **07** burgess, provost **08** decurion

counsel
02 KC, QC **04** read, rede, silk, urge, warn **05** aread, arede, guide, teach **06** advice, advise, direct, exhort, lawyer **07** arreede, caution, opinion, suggest **08** admonish, advising, advocate, attorney, guidance, instruct, moralism **09** barrister, direction, recommend, solicitor, viewpoint **10** admonition, advisement, conference, conferring, suggestion **11** exhortation, forethought, information **12** amicus curiae, consultation, deliberation, give guidance **13** consideration **14** recommendation **15** give your opinion

counsellor
04 guru **05** coach, guide, tutor **06** mentor, Nestor **07** teacher **08** director **09** authority, barrister, confidant, directrix, therapist **10** Achitophel, Ahithophel, confidante, consultant, directress, instructor

count
03 add, Ory, sum **04** deem, feel, Graf, hold, list, poll, tell **05** add up, check, compt, Fosco, grave, judge, score, sum up, tally, think, total, tot up, whole **06** census, county, esteem, matter, number, reckon, regard **07** account, compute, Dracula, include, qualify, signify **08** allow for, consider, look upon **09** calculate, enumerate, landgrave, numbering, palsgrave, reckoning, totting-up **10** cut some ice, full amount, Rhinegrave **11** be important, calculation, carry weight, computation, enumeration **13** mean something, take account of **15** make a difference, take into account

See also **nobility**
• **count in**
05 put in **06** rope in **07** include, involve, let in on **08** allow for **09** introduce
• **count on**
05 trust **06** bank on, expect, lean on, rely on **07** bargain, believe, swear by **08** depend on, reckon on **10** bargain for
• **count out**
04 omit, tell **06** ignore **07** exclude **08** leave out, pass over **09** disregard, eliminate **10** include out

countenance
04 back, face, look, mien **05** agree, allow, brook **06** endure, favour, permit, uphold, visage **07** approve, condone, endorse **08** features, sanction, semblant, stand for, tolerate **09** patronage, put up with **10** appearance, expression **11** approbation, physiognomy **12** acquiescence

counter
03 bar **04** buck, chip, coin, desk, disc, dump, fish, meet **05** merel, meril, parry, piece, stand, table, token **06** answer, buffet, combat, marker, merell, offset, oppose, resist, retort, return **07** adverse, against, dispute, opposed, respond, surface, worktop **08** contrary, opposing, opposite **09** hit back at, retaliate, shopboard **10** contradict, conversely **11** conflicting, contrasting, work surface **12** in opposition **13** contradictory

counteract
04 foil, undo **05** annul, check **06** defeat, hinder, negate, offset, oppose, remedy, resist, thwart **07** prevent **09** frustrate **10** act against, invalidate, neutralize **11** countervail **14** counterbalance

counterbalance
04 undo **05** poise **06** cancel, offset, set-off **07** balance, correct, requite **08** equalize **09** make up for **10** compensate, neutralize **11** countervail **12** counterpoise **13** compensate for

counterfeit
03 dud **04** base, copy, fake, sham **05** bogus, dummy, faked, false, feign, forge, fraud, phony, pseud, queer, snide **06** copied, forged, phoney, pirate, pseudo **07** falsify, feigned, forgery, imitate, pretend, simular **08** borrowed, disguise, phantasm, postiche, simulate, spurious **09** brummagem, fabricate, imitation, pretended, reproduce, simulated **10** artificial, camouflage, fraudulent **11** impersonate **12** reproduction

See also **counterfeit coin** *under* **coin**

countermand
05 annul, quash **06** cancel, repeal, revoke **07** rescind, reverse, unorder **08** abrogate, override, overturn **10** revocation

counterpart
04 copy, mate, peer, twin **05** equal, match, moral, tally **06** double, fellow **07** obverse **08** parallel **09** duplicate **10** complement, equivalent, supplement **14** opposite number

counterpoint
04 foil **06** relief, set off, set-off **07** descant, enhance **08** contrast, faburden, heighten, opposite **09** intensify **10** complement **11** counterpane **13** differentiate **15** differentiation, throw into relief

countless
06 legion, myriad, untold **07** endless, umpteen **08** infinite **09** boundless, limitless **10** numberless, unnumbered, without end **11** innumerable, measureless **12** immeasurable, incalculable **13** inexhaustible

countrified
04 hick **05** rural **06** rustic **07** bucolic,

idyllic, outback **08** agrarian, pastoral **10** provincial **12** agricultural

country
04 area, bush, land, pays, soil **05** power, realm, rural, state, wilds **06** landed, nation, people, public, region, rustic, sticks, voters **07** bucolic, idyllic, kingdom, outback, terrain **08** agrarian, citizens, district, electors, farmland, locality, moorland, pastoral, populace, republic **09** backwater, backwoods, community, green belt, provinces, residents, rural area, territory **10** population, provincial **11** countryside, inhabitants **12** agricultural, back of beyond, principality **13** neighbourhood **15** middle of nowhere

Countries:

02 UK
03 PRC, UAE, USA
04 Chad, Cuba, Fiji, Iran, Iraq, Laos, Mali, Oman, Peru, Togo
05 Benin, Burma, Chile, China, Congo, Egypt, Gabon, Ghana, Haiti, India, Italy, Japan, Kenya, Libya, Malta, Nauru, Nepal, Niger, Palau, Qatar, Samoa, Spain, Sudan, Syria, Tonga, Yemen
06 Angola, Belize, Bhutan, Brazil, Canada, Cyprus, España, France, Greece, Guinea, Guyana, Israel, Italia, Jordan, Kuwait, Latvia, Malawi, Mexico, Monaco, Norway, Panama, Poland, Russia, Rwanda, Sweden, Taiwan, Turkey, Tuvalu, Uganda, Zambia
07 Albania, Algeria, Andorra, Armenia, Austria, Bahrain, Belarus, Belgium, Bolivia, Burundi, Comoros, Croatia, Denmark, Ecuador, Eritrea, Estonia, Finland, Georgia, Germany, Grenada, Holland, Hungary, Iceland, Ireland, Jamaica, Lebanon, Lesotho, Liberia, Moldova, Morocco, Myanmar, Namibia, Nigeria, Romania, Senegal, Somalia, St Lucia, Tunisia, Ukraine, Uruguay, Vanuatu, Vatican, Vietnam
08 Barbados, Botswana, Bulgaria, Cambodia, Cameroon, Colombia, Djibouti, Dominica, Ethiopia, Honduras, Kiribati, Malaysia, Maldives, Mongolia, Pakistan, Paraguay, Portugal, Slovakia, Slovenia, Sri Lanka, Suriname, Tanzania, Thailand, Zimbabwe
09 Argentina, Australia, Cape Verde, Costa Rica, East Timor, Guatemala, Indonesia, Lithuania, Macedonia, Mauritius, Nicaragua, San Marino, Singapore, Swaziland, The Gambia, Venezuela
10 Azerbaijan, Bangladesh, El Salvador, Kazakhstan, Kyrgyzstan, Luxembourg, Madagascar, Mauritania, Mozambique, New Zealand, North Korea, Seychelles, South Korea, Tajikistan, The Bahamas, Uzbekistan
11 Afghanistan, Burkina Faso, Côte

d'Ivoire, Deutschland, Philippines, Saudi Arabia, Sierra Leone, South Africa, Switzerland
12 Guinea-Bissau, Turkmenistan
13 Czech Republic, Liechtenstein, United Kingdom, Western Sahara
14 Papua New Guinea, Solomon Islands, The Netherlands
15 Marshall Islands, St Kitts and Nevis
16 Brunei Darussalam, Equatorial Guinea
17 Antigua and Barbuda, Dominican Republic, Trinidad and Tobago
18 São Tomé and Príncipe, United Arab Emirates
19 Serbia and Montenegro
20 Bosnia and Herzegovina
21 United States of America
22 Central African Republic
25 St Vincent and the Grenadines
27 Federated States of Micronesia
28 Democratic Republic of the Congo

Country codes include:

03 ABW, AFG, AGO, AIA, ALB, AND, ANT, ARE, ARG, ARM, ASM, ATA, ATF, ATG, AUS, AUT, AZE, BDI, BEL, BEN, BFA, BGD, BGR, BHR, BHS, BIH, BLR, BLZ, BMU, BOL, BRA, BRB, BRN, BTN, BVT, BWA, CAF, CAN, CCK, CHE, CHL, CHN, CIV, CMR, COD, COG, COK, COL, COM, CPV, CRI, CUB, CXR, CYM, CYP, CZE, DEU, DJI, DMA, DNK, DOM, DZA, ECU, EGY, ERI, ESH, ESP, EST, ETH, FIN, FJI, FLK, FRA, FRO, FSM, GAB, GBR, GEO, GHA, GIB, GIN, GLP, GMB, GNB, GNQ, GRC, GRD, GRL, GTM, GUF, GUM, GUY, HGK, HMD, HND, HRV, HTI, HUN, IDN, IMN, IND, IOT, IRL, IRN, IRQ, ISL, ISR, ITA, JAM, JOR, JPN, KAZ, KEN, KGZ, KHM, KIR, KNA, KOR, KWT, LAO, LBN, LBR, LBY, LCA, LIE, LKA, LSO, LTU, LUX, LVA, MAC, MAR, MCO, MDA, MDG, MDV, MEX, MHL, MKD, MLI, MLT, MMR, MNG, MNP, MOZ, MRT, MSR, MTQ, MUS, MWI, MYS, MYT, NAM, NCL, NER, NFK, NGA, NIC, NIU, NLD, NOR, NPL, NRU, NZL, OMN, PAK, PAN, PCN, PER, PHL, PLW, PNG, POL, PRI, PRK, PRT, PRY, PYF, QAT, REU, ROU, RUS, RWA, SAU, SDN, SEN, SGP, SHN, SJM, SLB, SLE, SLV, SMR, SOM, SPM, STP, SUR, SVK, SVN, SWE, SWZ, SYC, SYR, TCA, TCD, TGO, THA, TJK, TKL, TKM, TLS, TON, TTO, TUN, TUR, TUV, TWN, TZA, UGA, UKR, URY, USA, UZB, VAT, VCT, VEN, VGB, VIR, VNM, VUT, WLF, WSM, YEM, YUG, ZAF, ZMB, ZWE

Former country names include:

04 Siam, USSR
05 Burma, Zaire
06 Bengal, Ceylon, Persia, Urundi
07 Dahomey, Formosa
08 Rhodesia
09 Abyssinia, Indochina, Kampuchea, Nyasaland

10 Basutoland, Ivory Coast, Senegambia, Tanganyika, Upper Volta, Yugoslavia
11 Dutch Guiana, French Sudan, New Hebrides, Ubangi Shari
12 Bechuanaland, French Guinea, Ruanda-Urundi
13 British Guiana, Ellice Islands, Khmer Republic, Spanish Guinea, Spanish Sahara, Trucial States
14 Czechoslovakia, French Togoland, Gilbert Islands
15 British Honduras, British Togoland, Dutch East Indies, South West Africa

See also **Africa**; **America**; **Arab**; **Asia**; **commonwealth**; **Europe**; **Middle East**

• **open country**
03 lay, lea, lee, ley **04** moor, veld, wold **05** field, heath, plain, range, veldt, weald

countryman, countrywoman
03 hob **04** boor, hick, hind **05** Hodge, yokel **06** farmer, rustic, yeoman **07** bumpkin, hayseed, landman, peasant **09** hillbilly **10** clodhopper, compatriot, provincial **11** bushwhacker **12** backwoodsman **13** fellow citizen **14** fellow national

countryside
06 nature **07** country, scenery **08** farmland, moorland, outdoors **09** green belt, landscape, rural area

countrywoman *see* countryman, countrywoman

county
02 Co **04** area **05** count, shire, state **06** parish, region **08** district, province **09** comitatus, territory **10** department

Counties and administrative areas of England:

04 Kent, York
05 Derby, Devon, Essex, Luton, Poole
06 Dorset, Durham, Halton, London, Medway, Slough, Surrey, Torbay
07 Cumbria, Norfolk, Reading, Rutland, Suffolk, Swindon
08 Cheshire, Plymouth, Somerset, Thurrock
09 Blackpool, Hampshire, Leicester, Wiltshire, Wokingham
10 Darlington, Derbyshire, East Sussex, Hartlepool, Lancashire, Merseyside, Nottingham, Portsmouth, Shropshire, Warrington, West Sussex
11 Bournemouth, Isle of Wight, Oxfordshire, Southampton, Tyne and Wear
12 Bedfordshire, Lincolnshire, Milton Keynes, Peterborough, Stoke-on-Trent, Warwickshire, West Midlands
13 City of Bristol, Herefordshire, Hertfordshire, Middlesbrough, North Somerset, Southend-on-Sea, Staffordshire, West Berkshire, West Yorkshire
14 Cambridgeshire, Leicestershire, Northumberland, North Yorkshire,

South Yorkshire, Stockton-on-Tees, Worcestershire
15 Bracknell Forest, Brighton and Hove, Buckinghamshire, Gloucestershire, Nottinghamshire
16 Northamptonshire, Telford and Wrekin
17 Greater Manchester, North Lincolnshire
18 Redcar and Cleveland
19 Blackburn with Darwen
20 South Gloucestershire, Windsor and Maidenhead
21 East Riding of Yorkshire, North East Lincolnshire
22 City of Kingston upon Hull
24 Bath and North East Somerset, Cornwall and Isles of Scilly

County abbreviations include:

02 Mx
03 Dev, Dur, Ess, Mon, Som, Sur, War
04 Beds, Camb, Ches, Corn, Cumb, Dors, Glos, Mont, Oxon, Suff
05 Berks, Bucks, Cambs, Cards, Derby, E Suss, Hants, Herts, Lancs, Leics, Lincs, Middx, Notts, Wilts, Worcs, Yorks
06 Caerns, Shrops, Staffs
08 Northumb
09 Northants

Counties of Ireland:

04 Cork, Leix, Mayo
05 Cavan, Clare, Kerry, Laois, Louth, Meath, Sligo
06 Carlow, Dublin, Galway, Offaly
07 Donegal, Kildare, Leitrim, Wexford, Wicklow
08 Kilkenny, Laoighis, Limerick, Longford, Monaghan
09 Roscommon, Tipperary, Waterford, Westmeath

See also **district**

• **home counties**
02 SE
• **county town** *see* **town**

coup
04 blow, deed, feat **05** stunt, upset **06** action, barter, putsch, revolt, stroke **07** exploit, success, triumph **08** exchange, overturn, takeover, uprising **09** coup d'état, manoeuvre, overthrow, rebellion **10** revolution **11** tour de force **12** insurrection, masterstroke **14** accomplishment

coup de grâce
04 kill **06** kibosh **07** quietus **08** clincher **09** death blow **11** kiss of death **13** finishing blow

coup d'état
04 coup **06** putsch, revolt **08** takeover, uprising **09** overthrow, rebellion **10** revolution **12** insurrection

couple
◇ *repetition indicator*
03 duo, two, wed **04** ally, bind, join, link, mate, meng, ming, pair, tway,

yoke **05** brace, clasp, hitch, marry, match, menge, twain, unite **06** attach, buckle, fasten, lovers, marrow **07** combine, conjoin, connect, diarchy, shackle, twosome **08** double up, partners **09** accompany, associate, integrate, newlyweds **12** Darby and Joan **14** husband and wife

coupon
04 form, slip, stub **05** check, token **06** billet, docket, ticket **07** voucher **11** certificate, counterfoil

courage
04 grit, guts **05** balls, heart, metal, moxie, nerve, pluck, spunk, valor **06** bottle, daring, mettle, spirit, valour **07** bravery, cojones, heroism, stomach **08** audacity, backbone, boldness, coraggio, gumption **09** fortitude, gallantry **10** resolution **11** intrepidity **12** fearlessness **13** dauntlessness, determination

courageous
04 bold, game **05** brave, gutsy, hardy, wight **06** ballsy, daring, feisty, heroic, manful, plucky, spunky **07** gallant, valiant **08** fearless, generous, intrepid, resolute, valorous **09** audacious, dauntless **10** determined, stomachous **11** adventurous, full-hearted, high-hearted, indomitable, lion-hearted **12** stout-hearted

• **courageous person**
04 hero, lion

courageously
06 boldly **07** bravely **09** gallantly, valiantly **10** fearlessly, heroically, intrepidly, resolutely **11** audaciously, dauntlessly, indomitably **13** adventurously

courier
03 rep **05** envoy, guide **06** bearer, escort, herald, legate, nuncio, runner **07** carrier, postman **08** emissary **09** estafette, messenger, tour guide **10** pursuivant **11** travel guide **13** dispatch rider **14** representative

course
03 ren, rin, run, way **04** beat, dash, dish, flow, gush, hunt, lane, line, mess, mode, move, part, path, plan, pour, race, rise, road, rota, span, tack, term, time **05** ambit, chase, lapse, march, orbit, order, route, spell, stage, surge, sweet, track, trail **06** entrée, follow, ground, manner, method, period, policy, pursue, remove, series, stream, system, voyage **07** advance, channel, circuit, classes, current, dessert, lessons, passage, passing, process, pudding, regimen, starter, studies **08** approach, duration, lectures, movement, progress, run after, schedule, sequence, syllabus **09** appetizer, direction, entremets, procedure, programme, racetrack, unfolding **10** curriculum, flight path, golf course, main course, racecourse, succession, trajectory

11 development, furtherance, hors d'oeuvre, progression
See also **compass**; **golf**; **race**; **racecourse**

• **alter course**
04 gybe, jibe, tack, wear
• **deviate from course**
03 bag, yaw
• **direct course**
03 aim **04** head
• **fixed course**
03 rut **04** race
• **in due course**
02 so **06** in time **07** finally **09** in due time **10** eventually **13** all in good time, sooner or later
• **of course**
02 ay **03** aye **04** sure **05** natch **06** surely **07** no doubt **08** to be sure **09** certainly, naturally **10** by all means, definitely **11** bien entendu, doubtlessly, indubitably, undoubtedly **12** indisputably **13** needless to say, without a doubt **14** not unnaturally
• **part of course**
03 leg

court
02 ct **03** bar, Hof, see, sew, sue, woo, wow **04** date, quad, ring, risk, seek, yard **05** alley, arena, bench, chase, green, patio, plaza, suite, track, train **06** castle, go with, ground, incite, invite, palace, piazza, prompt, pursue, square **07** attract, cortège, flatter, provoke, retinue, solicit **08** cloister, game area, go steady, pander to, try to win **09** courtyard, cultivate, curtilage, enclosure, entourage, esplanade, forecourt, go out with, household, judiciary, peristyle **10** attendants, cozy up with, judicatory, judicature, praetorium, quadrangle **11** conservancy, go round with, playing area **12** go around with **13** spheristerion **14** royal residence **15** curry favour with

Courts include:

03 law
04 eyre, Fehm, high, Lyon, moot, open, Vehm
05 burgh, civil, crown, prize, trial, World, youth
06 appeal, Arches, church, claims, county, family, Honour, police, record
07 appeals, assizes, borough, circuit, Diplock, divorce, federal, justice, Probate, Session, sheriff, Supreme
08 chancery, coroner's, criminal, district, juvenile, kangaroo, Requests, superior, tribunal
09 children's, Exchequer, Faculties, municipal, Old Bailey, Piepowder, Sanhedrim, Sanhedrin, the Arches
10 Commercial, commissary, consistory, Divisional, Piepowders, Protection
11 Arbitration, Common Bench, Common Pleas, High Justice, magistrates', police-court, Prerogative, small claims
12 Aulic Council, court-martial, House of Lords, Privy Council
13 first instance

14 Criminal Appeal, High Commission, High Justiciary
15 Central Criminal, European Justice, Lord Chancellor's

- **bring to court**
04 file
- **court case**
04 suit **05** trial **06** action **07** lawsuit
- **court house**
02 ch
- **in court**
02 up **08** at the bar
- **right to hold court**
03 sac, soc
- **take to court**
03 law, sue

courteous
04 hend, kind **05** civil **06** polite, urbane **07** affable, courtly, gallant, refined, tactful **08** debonair, gracious, ladylike, mannerly, obliging, polished, well-bred **09** attentive **10** chivalrous, debonnaire, diplomatic, respectful, well-spoken **11** considerate, deferential, gentlemanly **12** well-mannered

courteously
06 kindly **07** civilly **08** politely, urbanely **09** gallantly, refinedly, tactfully **10** graciously, obligingly **11** attentively **12** chivalrously, respectfully **13** considerately, deferentially **14** diplomatically

courtesy
04 tact **06** comity, curtsy, devoir, favour, gentry **07** manners, respect **08** breeding, chivalry, civility, kindness, urbanity **09** attention, deference, etiquette, gallantry, gentility **10** generosity, gentilesse, politeness, refinement **11** good manners **12** good breeding, graciousness **13** consideration

courtier
04 lady, lord, page **05** noble, toady **07** steward, subject **08** follower, liegeman, nobleman **09** attendant, cup-bearer, flatterer, sycophant **11** train-bearer **13** lady-in-waiting

courtly
05 aulic, civil **06** formal, lordly, polite **07** elegant, gallant, refined, stately **08** decorous, gracious, high-bred, obliging, polished **09** dignified **10** chivalrous, flattering **11** ceremonious **12** aristocratic

courtship
04 suit **05** spoon **06** affair, dating, wooing **07** chasing, pursuit, romance **08** courting, going-out, love-suit **10** attentions, lovemaking **11** going steady

courtyard
04 area, quad, ward, yard **05** court, garth, marae, patio, plaza **06** atrium, square **07** cortile **08** cloister **09** enclosure, esplanade, forecourt **10** quadrangle

cove
03 bay, man **04** chap **05** bight, creek, fiord, firth, inlet **06** cavern **07** estuary

covenant
03 vow **04** bond, deed, pact **05** agree, trust **06** engage, pledge, treaty **07** compact, promise **08** contract, warranty **09** agreement, concordat, indenture, stipulate, testament, undertake **10** commitment, convention, engagement **11** arrangement, stipulation, undertaking **12** dispensation

cover
◇ *containment indicator*
◇ *hidden indicator*
02 do, go **03** cap, cup, hap, hat, lay, lep, lid, set, top **04** bury, cake, case, coat, cour, cowl, daub, deck, film, heal, heel, hele, hide, hood, leap, mask, pall, skin, tell, tilt, veil, vele, wrap **05** apron, brood, cloak, cloke, coure, cross, dress, duvet, front, guard, layer, paten, quoit, throw, treat **06** attire, be over, canopy, carpet, clothe, defend, embody, encase, extend, façade, incase, insure, jacket, mantle, pay for, refuge, report, review, screen, shield, shroud, sleeve, spread, survey, take in, toilet, travel **07** analyse, bedding, binding, blanket, coating, conceal, contain, cover-up, defence, embrace, envelop, examine, garment, include, involve, journey, measure, narrate, obscure, overlay, package, plaster, present, pretext, protect, put over, relieve, replace, shelter, stretch, swaddle, wrapper, wreathe **08** accoutre, bedcover, bespread, blankets, clothing, comprise, consider, continue, covering, deal with, deputize, describe, disguise, enshroud, envelope, go across, overveil, pretence, security, traverse **09** assurance, bedspread, encompass, fill in for, indemnify, indemnity, insurance, make up for, place over, safeguard, sanctuary, talk about, whitewash **10** balance out, bedclothes, camouflage, complicity, conspiracy, extend over, overspread, protection, provide for, recompense, stand in for, travel over, underwrite, write about **11** be enough for, concealment, confederate, hiding-place, incorporate, investigate, pinch-hit for, smokescreen **12** compensation, take over from **13** compensate for, give details of **14** counterbalance **15** give an account of, indemnification

- **cover up**
◇ *hidden indicator*
03 hap **04** hide **05** blank, fudge **06** hush up **07** conceal, repress **08** enshroud, hoodwink, keep dark, suppress **09** dissemble, gloss over, whitewash **10** keep secret
- **original cover**
02 OC

coverage
04 item **05** story **06** report

07 account, blanket, reports **08** analysis **09** reportage, reporting **11** description **13** investigation

covering
03 cap, lag, rug, top **04** aril, cape, case, coat, cope, film, hood, husk, mask, pall, roof, skin **05** armor, cloak, cloke, cover, crust, layer, shell **06** armour, awning, carpet, casing, sheath, tegmen, veneer **07** blanket, coating, housing, overlay, roofing, shelter **08** clothing, pavilion, sheeting, wrapping **09** tarpaulin **10** encasement, incasement, integument, overlaying, protection **11** descriptive, explanatory **12** accompanying, introductory

covert
06 hidden, secret, sneaky, veiled **07** furtive, private, shelter **08** sidelong, stealthy, ulterior **09** concealed, disguised, underhand **10** dissembled **11** clandestine, unsuspected **13** subreptitious, surreptitious, under the table

covertly
08 secretly **09** furtively, privately **15** surreptitiously

cover-up
05 front **06** façade, screen **08** pretence **09** deception, whitewash **10** complicity, conspiracy **11** concealment, smokescreen

covet
04 envy, want **05** crave, fancy **06** desire **07** long for **08** begrudge, yearn for **09** hanker for, hunger for, lust after, thirst for

covetous
06 greedy **07** craving, envious, jealous, longing, wanting **08** desirous, grasping, yearning **09** hankering, hungering, rapacious, thirsting **10** avaricious, insatiable **11** acquisitive, close-fisted, close-handed

covey
03 nid, set **04** band, bevy **05** brood, flock, group, hatch, party, skein **06** flight **07** cluster, company

cow
02 ox **03** mog **04** boss, mart, neat, quey, runt **05** besom, bossy, bully, daunt, doddy, moggy, mooly, muley, scare, stirk **06** crummy, dismay, hawkey, hawkie, heifer, humlie, Jersey, milker, moggie, mulley, rattle, rother, subdue **07** kouprey, overawe, unnerve **08** Alderney, browbeat, domineer, Friesian, frighten, springer **09** terrorize **10** discourage, dishearten, intimidate

coward
03 cat **04** Noel, sook, wimp, wuss **05** dingo, sissy **06** craven **07** chicken, cowherd, crybaby, dastard, hilding, nithing, viliaco, viliago **08** cowheard, deserter, poltroon, recreant, renegade, villagio, villiaco, villiago, weakling **10** faint-heart, poultroone,

Scaramouch, scaredy-cat
11 Scaramouche, yellow-belly

cowardice
08 timidity **11** fearfulness
12 cowardliness, timorousness
13 pusillanimity, spinelessness
14 spiritlessness

cowardly
04 nesh, soft, weak **05** faint, mangy,
timid **06** coward, cowish, craven,
mangey, maungy, scared, yellow
07 chicken, dastard, fearful, gutless,
hilding, jittery, meacock, nithing,
unmanly, wimpish **08** timorous,
unheroic **09** dastardly, spineless, weak-
kneed **10** spiritless **11** lily-livered, milk-
livered **12** faint-hearted, weak-spirited,
white-livered **13** pusillanimous,
yellow-bellied **14** chicken-hearted,
chicken-livered

cowboy
05 cheat, rogue, waddy **06** drover,
gaucho, herder, rascal, waddie
07 bungler, cowhand, cowpoke,
herdboy, rancher, vaquero
08 buckaroo, buckayro, buckeroo,
herdsman, ranchero, stockman,
swindler, wrangler **09** cattleman,
fraudster, scoundrel **10** cowpuncher
11 incompetent **12** bronco-buster,
cattleherder

cower
04 ruck **05** quail, quake, shake, skulk,
wince **06** cringe, crouch, flinch, grovel,
recoil, shiver, shrink **07** croodle,
tremble **08** draw back

cowhouse
04 byre **07** shippen, shippon

co-worker
04 aide, ally **06** helper **07** comrade,
partner **08** confrère, teammate,
workmate **09** assistant, associate,
auxiliary, colleague, companion
11 confederate **12** collaborator, fellow
worker

cows
02 ky **03** kye **04** kine, neat

coxcomb
03 fop **04** head, prig **07** princox
08 popinjay, princock

coy
03 shy **04** arch, nice, prim **05** squab,
timid **06** caress, demure, modest,
skeigh **07** bashful, disdain, evasive,
prudish **08** backward, reserved,
retiring, skittish **09** diffident, kittenish,
reticence, shrinking, squeamish,
withdrawn **10** coquettish **11** flirtatious
12 self-effacing

coyly
06 primly **07** timidly **08** demurely,
modestly **09** bashfully, evasively,
prudishly **11** diffidently **12** coquettishly
13 flirtatiously **14** self-effacingly

crab
04 claw, cock **05** decry, scrog, wreck
06 Cancer, hermit, partan, scrawl

07 fiddler, limulus, pagurid, souring,
wilding **08** horseman, obstruct,
ochidore, pagurian **09** criticize,
frustrate, scrog-bush, scrog-buss, soft-
shell **12** saucepan-fish

crabbed, crabby
04 sour, tart **05** acrid, cross, harsh,
surly, testy, tough **06** cranky, morose,
snappy **07** awkward, cankery, fretful,
grouchy, iracund, prickly **08** cankered,
captious, churlish, perverse, petulant,
snappish **09** crotchety, difficult,
fractious, irascible, irritable, splenetic
10 ill-natured **11** acrimonious, bad-
tempered, ill-tempered
12 cantankerous, iracundulous,
misanthropic

crack
◇ *anagram indicator*
02 go **03** ace, dig, gag, gap, hit, pop,
try **04** bang, bash, beat, blow, boom,
bump, chap, chat, chip, chop, clap,
dope, dunt, fent, flaw, gibe, jest, joke,
leak, line, quip, rent, rift, rima, rock,
shot, slap, snap, stab, star **05** boast,
break, burst, check, chink, cleft, clout,
craic, crash, craze, joint, shake, slash,
smack, solve, split, whack, whirl
06 breach, cave in, cavity, choice,
cleave, cranny, decode, effort, expert,
go bang, gossip, report, spring, strike,
wallop **07** attempt, crackle, crevice,
decrypt, dope out, explode, fissure,
resolve, rupture, shatter, skilful, skilled,
unravel, work out **08** collapse,
crevasse, decipher, detonate, fracture,
fragment, one-liner, repartee, splinter,
superior, top-notch **09** break down,
brilliant, excellent, explosion, figure
out, first-rate, really-wash, wisecrack,
witticism **10** detonation, first-class, go
to pieces, hand-picked **11** lose control,
outstanding **15** find the answer to
● **crack down on**
03 end **04** stop **05** check, crush, limit
07 confine, control, repress **09** restrict,
suppress **10** act against, get tough on,
put a stop to **11** clamp down on
● **crack up**
◇ *anagram indicator*
05 go mad, laugh **06** praise **07** go
crazy **08** collapse **09** break down,
fall about, fall apart **10** go to pieces
11 go ballistic, lose control **14** split
your sides

crackdown
03 end **04** stop **05** check **08** crushing
09 clampdown **10** repression
11 suppression

cracked
◇ *anagram indicator*
03 mad **04** bats, daft, nuts, torn
05 barmy, batty, crazy, harsh, loony,
nutty, split **06** broken, crazed, faulty,
flawed, insane **07** chapped, chipped,
damaged, foolish, idiotic, starred
08 crackpot, deranged, dingbats,
fissured **09** defective, imperfect
12 crackbrained, round the bend
13 off your rocker, out of your tree

crackers
◇ *anagram indicator*
03 mad **04** daft, nuts **05** batty, crazy,
loony, matza, matzo, nutty **06** matzah,
matzoh **07** cracked, foolish, idiotic
08 crackpot **10** unbalanced
12 crackbrained, round the bend

crackle
04 snap **05** crack, money **06** rustle,
sizzle **08** crepitus **09** banknotes,
crepitate **10** paper money
11 crepitation, decrepitate
13 decrepitation

crackpot
◇ *anagram indicator*
04 fool **05** freak, idiot, loony
06 nutter, weirdo **07** nutcase, oddball
10 basket case

cradle
03 bed, cot **04** base, crib, hold, lull,
prop, rest, rock, tend **05** fount, frame,
mount, nurse, stand **06** holder, nestle,
origin, rocker, source, spring
07 berceau, infancy, nurture, shelter,
support **08** bassinet, carry-cot,
cunabula, mounting **09** beginning,
framework, travel-cot **10** birthplace,
gold-washer, incunabula, wellspring
11 Moses basket **12** fountain-head
13 starting-point

craft
◇ *anagram indicator*
03 art, job **04** boat, line, ship, work
05 flair, guile, knack, skill, trade, wiles
06 deceit, talent, vessel **07** ability,
calling, cunning, finesse, foxship,
mastery, pursuit, sleight, slyness
08 activity, aircraft, aptitude, artistry,
business, deftness, subtlety, trickery,
vocation **09** dexterity, expertise,
handiwork, ingenuity, sharpness,
spaceship, technique **10** adroitness,
artfulness, astuteness, cleverness,
craftiness, employment, expertness,
handicraft, occupation, shrewdness,
spacecraft **11** cunningness,
deviousness, skilfulness, workmanship
12 fiendishness, landing craft
13 deceitfulness, inventiveness
15 imaginativeness, resourcefulness
See also **art**; **ship**

craftily
◇ *anagram indicator*
05 slyly **08** artfully, astutely, shrewdly
09 cunningly, deviously **10** guilefully
11 deceitfully **12** fraudulently

craftsman, craftswoman
05 maker, smith **06** artist, expert,
master, wright **07** artisan, artsman,
workman **08** mechanic **09** artificer,
tradesman **10** technician
11 tradeswoman **12** craftsperson,
tradesperson **13** skilled worker
See also **artist**

craftsmanship
05 skill **07** mastery **08** artistry
09 dexterity, expertise, technique
11 skilfulness, workmanship

craftswoman *see* **craftsman, craftswoman**

crafty

◇ *anagram indicator*

03 sly **04** foxy, slim, wily **05** canny, loopy, sharp **06** artful, astute, knacky, shrewd, subtle **07** crooked, cunning, devious, tricksy, versute **08** guileful, knackish, scheming **09** conniving, deceitful, designing, subdolous **10** fraudulent **11** calculating, duplicitous **12** disingenuous **13** Machiavellian

crag

03 tor **04** neck, noup, peak, rock **05** bluff, cliff, craig, heuch, heugh, ridge, scarp, stoss **06** throat **08** pinnacle **10** escarpment

craggy

05 rocky, rough, stony **06** cliffy, jagged, marked, rugged, uneven **07** cliffed, cragged **09** rough-hewn **11** precipitous **13** weather-beaten

cram

03 bag, jam, lie, ram **04** crap, fill, glut, pack, pang, stap, stop, swot, tuck **05** crowd, crush, farce, force, frank, gorge, grind, mug up, press, prime, stuff **06** fill up, revise, stodge **07** compact, squeeze **08** bone up on, compress, overfeed, overfill **09** overcrowd, study hard

cramp

03 tie **04** ache, pain, pang, rein **05** check, crick, limit, spasm **06** arrest, bridle, hamper, hinder, impede, narrow, stitch, stymie, thwart, twinge **07** confine, cramped, inhibit, shackle **08** handicap, obstruct, restrain, restrict **09** constrain, constrict, frustrate, hamstring, restraint, stiffness **10** convulsion **11** contraction **14** pins and needles **15** overuse syndrome, scrivener's palsy

cramped

04 full, poky **05** small, tight **06** narrow, packed **07** bounded, crabbed, crowded, squeezy **08** closed in, confined, hemmed in, niggling, overfull, squashed, squeezed **09** congested, jam-packed **10** compressed, restricted **11** constricted, overcrowded **12** incommodious **13** uncomfortable

crane

05 davit, hoist, Jenny, sarus, winch **06** brolga, hooper, jigger, tackle **07** cranium, derrick, whooper **08** adjutant **10** demoiselle **12** adjutant bird, cherry picker **14** block and tackle **15** native companion

crank

04 kook, whim **05** freak, idiot, loony, wince, winch **06** madman, nutter, weirdo **07** oddball **08** crackpot **09** character, eccentric **11** amphetamine

• **crank up**

05 add to **06** hike up, step up **07** build

up, further **08** increase **09** intensify **10** strengthen

cranky

◇ *anagram indicator*

03 fey, odd **04** tart **05** cross, dotty, harsh, queer, shaky, surly, testy, wacky **06** crabby, Fifish, screwy, snappy **07** awkward, bizarre, crabbed, grouchy, prickly, strange **08** freakish, peculiar, unsteady **09** crotchety, difficult, eccentric, irritable **11** bad-tempered, ill-tempered **12** cantankerous **13** idiosyncratic **14** unconventional

cranny

03 gap **04** hole, nook, rent, slit **05** chink, cleft, crack **07** crevice, fissure, opening **08** cleavage **10** interstice

crash

◇ *anagram indicator*

03 din, hit, ram **04** bang, bash, boom, bump, clap, dash, fail, fall, fold, rack, ruin, thud, wham **05** break, clang, clank, clash, ditch, frush, knock, pitch, pound, prang, rapid, shunt, smash, thump, wreck **06** batter, bingle, cut out, fold up, fragor, go bust, go into, go phut, pack up, pile-up, plunge, racket, shiver, topple, urgent **07** clatter, collide, failure, founder, go kaput, go under, run into, shatter, smash-up, thunder **08** accident, collapse, downfall, fracture, fragment, meltdown, splinter **09** break down, collision, drive into, emergency, explosion, immediate, intensive, smash into **10** bankruptcy, depression, plough into, telescoped **11** accelerated, black Monday, come a gutser, go to the wall, malfunction, stop working, thunderclap **12** concentrated, disintegrate, go on the blink **13** round-the-clock

crass

04 naff, rude **05** crude, dense, gross, ocker **06** clumsy, coarse, oafish, obtuse, stupid **07** boorish, witless **08** tactless, unsubtle **09** tasteless, unrefined **10** blundering, indelicate **11** insensitive **15** unsophisticated

crassly

06 rudely **07** crudely **08** clumsily, coarsely, stupidly **10** tactlessly **11** tastelessly **12** indelicately **13** insensitively

crate

03 box, car **04** case, kist **05** chest, plane, seron **06** seroon **08** tea chest **09** container **10** packing-box **11** packing-case

crater

03 dip, pit **04** bowl, hole, maar **05** abyss, basin, chasm **06** cavity, hollow **07** caldera **09** shell-hole **10** depression

cravat

05 scarf, stock **06** o'erlay **07** overlay, owrelay, soubise **09** neckcloth, steenkirk, stenkirk

crave

03 beg **04** need, want, wish **05** claim, covet, fancy **06** desire, hunger **07** dream of, long for, longing, pant for, pine for, require, sigh for **08** yearn for **09** hunger for, lust after, thirst for **10** be dying for **11** hanker after

craven

04 soft, weak **05** timid **06** afraid, coward, scared, yellow **07** chicken, fearful, gutless **08** cowardly, poltroon, recreant, timorous, unheroic **09** spineless, weak-kneed **10** spiritless **11** lily-livered **12** faint-hearted, mean-spirited, weak-spirited, white-livered **13** pusillanimous **14** chicken-hearted, chicken-livered

craving

04 lust, need, pica, urge, wish **06** desire, greedy, hunger, pining, thirst **07** longing, malacia, panting, sighing **08** appetent, appetite, yearning **09** hankering **10** dipsomania, hydromania, methomania **11** toxicomania **13** morphinomania

crawl

04 drag, edge, fawn, inch, knee, swim, teem **05** creep, snail, swarm, toady **06** cringe, grovel, kowtow, seethe, squirm, suck up, writhe **07** bristle, flatter, slither, wriggle **08** be full of **09** be all over, freestyle **10** move slowly **11** curry favour **12** bow and scrape, go on all fours **13** advance slowly **14** be obsequious to

• **crawler**

06 insect

crayfish

05 yabby **06** gilgie, jilgie, marron, yabbie

craze

03 bug, fad **04** buzz, flaw, mode, rage, ramp, whim **05** crack, mania, thing, trend, vogue **06** frenzy, furore, impair, weaken **07** fashion, novelty, passion **08** insanity **09** melomania, obsession, the latest, typomania **10** anglomania, anthomania, enthusiasm **11** acronymania, infatuation, tulipomania **12** orchidomania, potichomania, theatromania **13** preoccupation

crazed

◇ *anagram indicator*

03 mad **04** nuts, wild **05** berko, crazy, loony **06** insane **07** berserk, lunatic **08** demented, deranged, unhinged **09** up the pole **10** moonstruck, unbalanced **12** moon-stricken, round the bend **13** off your rocker, out of your mind, round the twist

crazily

◇ *anagram indicator*

05 madly **06** wildly **08** insanely **09** manically **11** frantically **12** frenetically

crazy

◇ *anagram indicator*

03 mad, odd, wet **04** avid, bats, daft,

ond, gaga, gyte, keen, loco, nuts, wild,
zany **05** barmy, batty, buggy, daffy,
dippy, dotty, flaky, gonzo, loony, loopy,
manic, nutty, potty, silly, wacko, wacky,
wiggy **06** absurd, ardent, crazed,
cuckoo, dottle, fruity, insane, maniac,
mental, raving, screwy, stupid, unwise
07 bananas, barking, berserk, bonkers,
cracked, devoted, dottled, foolish,
frantic, haywire, idiotic, lunatic,
meshuga, rickety, smitten, strange,
zealous **08** crackers, crackpot,
demented, deranged, dingbats,
doolally, frenetic, peculiar, unhinged
09 disturbed, enamoured, fanatical,
foolhardy, half-baked, imprudent,
infuriate, ludicrous, lymphatic,
pixilated, senseless, up the wall
10 bestraught, distracted, distraught,
frantic-mad, infatuated, off the wall, off
your nut, outrageous, out to lunch,
passionate, pixillated, ridiculous,
unbalanced **11** hare-brained,
impractical, nonsensical, not all there,
off the rails, off your head, unrealistic
12 crackbrained, enthusiastic, mad
as a hatter, off your chump,
preposterous, round the bend
13 impracticable, irresponsible, off
your rocker, out of your head, out of
your mind, out of your tree, round the
twist **14** off your trolley, wrong in the
head
• **go crazy**
◇ *anagram indicator*
04 flip **05** go ape, go mad **06** blow up,
wig out **09** go bananas **11** flip your lid,
go ballistic **15** lose your marbles

creak
04 rasp **05** grate, grind, groan
06 scrape, screak, squeak, squeal
07 scratch, screech

creaky
05 rusty **07** grating, rasping, squeaky,
unoiled **08** grinding, groaning,
scraping **09** squeaking, squealing
10 scratching, screeching

cream
03 oil **04** best, pale, pick, ream, skim
05 creme, élite, ivory, milky, paste,
pasty, prime, salve, sweet **06** finest,
flower, lotion, thrash **07** unguent
08 cleanser, cosmetic, emulsion,
liniment, off-white, ointment
09 emollient **10** choice part, select
part **11** application, preparation
13 whitish-yellow **14** crème de la
crème, pick of the bunch, yellowish-
white

creamy
04 oily, pale, rich **05** ivory, milky, pasty,
reamy, thick **06** smooth **07** buttery,
velvety **08** off-white **13** cream-
coloured, whitish-yellow
14 yellowish-white

crease
04 fold, kris, line, ruck, tuck **05** crimp,
pleat, ridge **06** creese, furrow, groove,
kreese, pucker, ruckle, rumple, runkle
07 crinkle, crumple, wreathe, wrinkle

09 corrugate **10** line of life
11 corrugation
• **crease up**
05 amuse **09** make laugh

create
04 coin, form, make **05** build, cause,
erect, found, frame, hatch, mould, set
up, shape **06** design, devise, invent,
invest, lead to, ordain **07** appoint,
compose, concoct, develop, install,
produce **08** engender, generate,
initiate, occasion, result in
09 construct, establish, fabricate,
formulate, institute, originate **10** bring
about, give rise to, inaugurate **13** cause
to happen **14** bring into being

creation
◇ *anagram indicator*
04 life, work **05** birth, world
06 cosmos, design, making, nature,
origin **07** concept, genesis, product
08 universe **09** formation, handiwork,
handywork, invention, work of art
10 biopoiesis, brainchild, conception,
concoction, everything, foundation,
generation, initiation, innovation,
production **11** achievement, chef
d'oeuvre, composition, development,
fabrication, institution, masterpiece,
origination, procreation
12 constitution, construction
13 establishment

creative
06 clever, gifted **07** fertile **08** artistic,
inspired, naturing, original, talented
09 forgetive, ingenious, intuitive,
inventive, visionary **10** innovative,
productive **11** full of ideas, imaginative,
resourceful

creativity
04 gift **06** talent, vision **08** artistry
09 fertility, ingenuity **10** cleverness
11 imagination, inspiration, originality
13 inventiveness **14** productiveness
15 imaginativeness, resourcefulness

creator
03 God **05** maker **06** author, Brahma,
father, mother, Ormazd, Ormuzd
07 builder, founder **08** composer,
demiurge, designer, inventor, producer
09 architect, Artificer, demiurgus,
initiator **10** Ahura Mazda, first cause,
originator, prime mover

creature
03 man **04** bird, body, fish, soul, zoon
05 beast, being, human, thing, wight,
woman **06** animal, cratur, insect,
mortal, person, wretch **07** crathur,
critter, crittur **08** organism **10** human
being, individual **11** living thing
See also **animal**; **mythical**; **poison**

credence
05 faith, trust **06** belief, credit
07 support **08** reliance **09** sideboard
10 acceptance, confidence,
dependence **11** credibility

credentials
04 deed **05** title **06** papers, permit
07 diploma, licence, warrant

08 passport **09** documents, reference
11 certificate, testimonial **12** identity
card **13** accreditation, authorization
14 recommendation **15** proof of
identity

credibility
04 cred **09** integrity **10** likelihood
11 probability, reliability **12** plausibility
14 reasonableness **15** trustworthiness

credible
06 honest, likely **07** credent, sincere,
tenable **08** possible, probable, reliable
09 plausible, thinkable **10** believable,
convincing, dependable, imaginable,
persuasive, reasonable **11** conceivable,
trustworthy

credibly
08 honestly, possibly, reliably
09 plausibly, sincerely, thinkably
10 believably, dependably, imaginably,
reasonably **11** conceivably
12 convincingly, persuasively
13 trustworthily

credit
02 cr, HP **03** buy **04** fame, tick
05 asset, boast, faith, glory, kudos,
mense, pride, strap, tally, trust
06 accept, assign, belief, charge,
esteem, honour, impute, praise, rely on,
thanks **07** acclaim, ascribe, believe,
put down, swallow, tribute
08 accredit, approval, credence,
plaudits, prestige **09** attribute, have
faith, laudation **10** confidence,
estimation, reputation **11** distinction,
pride and joy, recognition, subscribe to
12 commendation
15 acknowledgement
• **in credit**
07 solvent **10** beforehand, in the black
• **on credit**
06 on tick **07** on lay-by, on trust **08** on
the tab **09** on account **10** on the slate
12 on the knocker **13** by instalments
14 on hire purchase **15** on the never-
never

creditable
04 good **06** worthy **08** laudable
09 admirable, deserving, estimable,
excellent, exemplary, reputable
10 honourable **11** commendable,
meritorious, respectable, trustworthy
12 praiseworthy

creditably
04 well **09** admirably **10** honourably
11 commendably, excellently,
respectably

creditor
02 cr **06** debtee, lender **07** Shylock
08 apprizer **09** loan shark
11 moneylender

credulity
07 naivety **09** silliness, stupidity
10 dupability, simplicity **11** gullibility
13 credulousness **14** uncriticalness

credulous
04 fond **05** naive **06** simple
07 credent, dupable **08** gullable,

gullible, trusting, wide-eyed
10 uncritical **12** overtrusting, unsuspecting

creed
05 canon, credo, dogma, faith
06 belief, Ophism, symbol, tenets
08 articles, doctrine, ideology, standard, teaching **09** catechism, the belief **10** persuasion, principles

creek
03 bay, geo, gio, goe, pow, voe
04 cove, wick **05** bight, brook, crick, fiord, firth, fjord, fleet, inlet **06** slough, stream **07** estuary

creep
04 edge, fawn, fear, geek, grew, grue, inch, worm **05** alarm, crawl, slink, snake, sneak, steal, toady **06** cringe, fawner, grovel, horror, squirm, terror, tiptoe, unease, writhe, yes-man
07 shudder, slither, wriggle **08** disquiet **09** revulsion, sycophant **10** bootlicker
13 move unnoticed

creeper
04 vine **05** liana, plant **06** runner
07 climber, rambler, trailer **08** trailing, woodbind, woodbine **09** Boston ivy
10 ampelopsis, monkey rope, tropaeolum **13** climbing plant, trailing plant
See also **snake**

creepy
05 eerie, scary, weird **06** crawly, spooky **07** macabre, ominous
08 gruesome, horrible, horrific, menacing, sinister **10** disturbing, horrifying, mysterious, terrifying, unpleasant **11** frightening, hair-raising, nightmarish, threatening
13 bloodcurdling, spine-chilling

crescent
04 Cres **06** waxing **07** growing
09 croissant **10** increasing

crescent-shaped
05 moony **06** lunate **07** falcate, lunated, lunular **08** falcated **09** bow-shaped, falciform **12** sickle-shaped

crest
03 mon, top **04** apex, comb, edge, head, knap, mane, peak, tuft **05** badge, chine, crown, plume, ridge **06** cimier, copple, crista, device, emblem, summit, symbol, tassel **07** cornice, feather, panache, regalia, topknot
08 aigrette, caruncle, insignia, pinnacle, surmount **09** cockscomb
10 coat of arms

crestfallen
03 sad **08** dejected, downcast
09 depressed **10** cheesed off, despondent, dispirited
11 discouraged, downhearted
12 disappointed, disconsolate, disheartened **13** in the doldrums
14 down in the dumps

cretin
03 ass, mug, nit **04** clot, dolt, dope, dork, fool, geek, jerk, prat, twit

05 chump, dumbo, dunce, idiot, moron, ninny, schmo, twerp, wally
06 dimwit, nitwit, sucker **07** fathead, halfwit, jughead, pillock, plonker, schmuck **08** imbecile **09** birdbrain, blockhead, ignoramus, simpleton
10 bufflehead, nincompoop

crevasse
03 gap **05** abyss, chasm, cleft, crack, split **07** fissure **11** bergschrund

crevice
03 gap **04** hole, rift, slit **05** break, chink, cleft, crack, split **06** cranny
07 fissure, opening **10** interstice

crew
03 lot, man, mob, set **04** band, crue, gang, pack, ship, team, unit **05** bunch, corps, crowd, eight, force, group, party, squad, troop **06** torpid **07** company
09 lower deck **10** complement

crew member *see* **sailor; ship**

crib
03 bed, cot, key **04** copy, lift, pony, putz, trot **05** cheat, horse, pinch, stall, steal **06** cratch, pirate **07** brothel, purloin **08** bassinet, carry-cot, cribbage **09** reproduce, travel-cot
10 plagiarize **11** Moses basket

crick
04 kink, pain, rick **05** cramp, creek, spasm **06** twinge **09** stiffness
10 convulsion

cricket
04 grig **05** stool **09** churr-worm

Cricket teams include:
04 Kent
05 Essex
06 Durham, Surrey, Sussex
08 Somerset, Victoria
09 Glamorgan, Hampshire, Middlesex, Yorkshire
10 Derbyshire, Lancashire, Queensland
12 Warwickshire
13 New South Wales
14 Leicestershire, South Australia, Worcestershire
15 Gloucestershire, Nottinghamshire

Cricket terms include:
01 b, c, M, w
02 by, CC, in, lb, nb, no, on, ro
03 bat, box, bye, CCC, cut, ECB, ICC, lbw, leg, MCC, net, ODI, off, pad, peg, run, six, ton
04 bail, ball, blob, bowl, deep, draw, duck, edge, four, go in, grub, hook, Oval, over, pair, poke, pull, slip, tail, test, tice, walk, wide
05 Ashes, break, c and b, catch, cover, dolly, drive, extra, glide, gully, knock, Lords, mid-on, pitch, plumb, point, silly, skyer, snick, stump
06 appeal, beamer, bowled, bowler, caught, crease, doosra, eleven, glance, googly, ground, howzat, leg bye, long on, maiden, middle, mid-off, no-ball, not out, opener, play

on, run out, single, square, stumps, the leg, umpire, whites, wicket, yorker
07 batsman, batting, bouncer, century, declare, dismiss, fielder, grubber, infield, innings, last man, leg side, leg slip, leg spin, long hop, long leg, long off, off spin, on the up, spinner, striker, stumped, wrong'un
08 bodyline, boundary, chinaman, delivery, fielding, flannels, follow on, full toss, how's that, leg guard, long slip, long stop, misfield, off break, off drive, off guard, one-dayer, outfield, pavilion, short leg, sledging, the Ashes, third man
09 batswoman, deep field, fieldsman, hit wicket, inswinger, leg before, leg theory, long field, mid-wicket, overpitch, short slip, square leg, test match, tip and run
10 all-rounder, cover drive, draw stumps, fast bowler, golden duck, leg spinner, maiden over, pace bowler, right guard, scoreboard, seam bowler, silly mid-on, skittle out, spin bowler, twelfth man
11 clean bowled, daisy-cutter, diamond duck, fast bowling, fieldswoman, grass-cutter, ground staff, half-century, limited-over, net practice, one-day match, pace bowling, seam bowling, sight screen, silly mid-off, spin bowling
12 carry your bat, wicketkeeper
13 break your duck, county cricket, keep your end up, maiden century, night-watchman, popping crease
14 off the back foot
15 bowl a maiden over, caught and bowled, leather on willow, leg before wicket, square leg umpire

See also **delivery**

Cricketers, commentators and umpires include:
03 Fry (Charles Burgess)
04 Ames (Leslie), Bedi (Bishen), Bird (Dicky), Hall (Wesley), Hick (Graeme), Khan (Imran), Lara (Brian), Lock (Tony), Lord (Thomas)
05 Abbas (Zaheer), Akram (Wasim), Allen (Sir Gubby), Amiss (Dennis), Crowe (Martin), Evans (Godfrey), Gibbs (Lance), Gooch (Graham), Gough (Darren), Gower (David), Grace (W G), Greig (Tony), Healy (Ian), Hobbs (Sir Jack), Knott (Alan), Laker (Jim), Lawry (William), Lloyd (Clive), Marsh (Rodney), Pilch (Fuller), Walsh (Courtney), Warne (Shane), Waugh (Mark), Waugh (Steve)
06 Arlott (John), Bailey (Trevor), Benaud (Richie), Border (Allan), Botham (Ian), Cronje (Hansie), Dexter (Ted), Donald (Allan), Dravid (Rahul), Edrich (Bill), Edrich (John), Garner (Joel), Hadlee (Sir Richard), Haynes (Desmond), Hutton (Len), Jessop (Gilbert), Lillee (Dennis), Miller (Keith), Rhodes (Wilfred),

Sobers (Sir Garfield), Thorpe (Graham), Titmus (Fred), Turner (Glenn), Warner (Sir Pelham 'Plum')

07 Ambrose (Curtley), Boycott (Geoffrey), Bradman (Sir Donald), Compton (Denis), Cowdrey (Colin, Lord), Denness (Michael), De Silva (Aravinda), Gatting (Mike), Holding (Michael), Hussain (Nasser), Jardine (Douglas), Larwood (Harold), Miandad (Javed), Pollock (Graeme), Simpson (Robert), Stewart (Alec), Thomson (Jeff), Trueman (Fred)

08 Atherton (Michael), Chappell (Greg), Chappell (Ian), Chappell (Trevor), Flintoff (Andrew), Gavaskar (Sunil), Kapil Dev (Nikhanj), Richards (Barry), Richards (Vivian), Sheppard (David)

09 D'Oliveira (Basil), Greenidge (Gordon), Ranatunga (Arjuna)

10 Azharuddin (Mohammad), Barrington (Ken), Lillywhite (William)

11 Heyhoe Flint (Rachel), Illingworth (Raymond), Trescothick (Marcus)

crier

06 beadle, herald **07** bellman **09** announcer, messenger, outrooper, town crier **10** proclaimer **15** bearer of tidings

crime

03 rap, sin **04** evil, fact, vice **06** crimen, felony **07** misdeed, offence, offense, outrage, villany **08** atrocity, enormity, iniquity, thievery, villainy **09** violation **10** illegal act, misconduct, wickedness, wrongdoing **11** delinquency, lawbreaking, lawlessness, malefaction, malfeasance, unlawful act **12** misdemeanour **13** transgression

Crimes include:

03 ABH, GBH
04 rape
05 arson, fraud, theft
06 hijack, murder, piracy
07 assault, battery, bribery, forgery, larceny, mugging, perjury, robbery, treason
08 burglary, filicide, homicide, poaching, sabotage, stalking
09 blackmail, extortion, hate crime, joy-riding, matricide, parricide, patricide, pilfering, terrorism, uxoricide, vandalism
10 corruption, cybercrime, fratricide, kidnapping
11 drug dealing, hooliganism, infanticide, shoplifting, sororicide, trespassing
12 drink-driving, embezzlement, manslaughter
13 assassination, drug smuggling, housebreaking
14 counterfeiting, insider dealing, insider trading
15 computer hacking

criminal

◇ anagram indicator

03 con **04** bent, crim, evil **05** felon, tough, wrong **06** chummy, guilty, outlaw, wicked **07** convict, corrupt, crooked, culprit, illegal, illicit, lawless, obscene, villain **08** crimeful, culpable, infamous, offender, prisoner, shameful, unlawful **09** dishonest, felonious, miscreant, nefarious, wrongdoer **10** delinquent, deplorable, disgusting, indictable, iniquitous, lawbreaker, malefactor, outrageous, scandalous, villainous **11** disgraceful, lawbreaking **12** preposterous **13** reprehensible

Criminal types include:

03 dip, lag
04 hood, thug, yegg
05 crook, thief
06 bandit, forger, gunman, killer, mugger, pirate, rapist, robber, vandal
07 abactor, brigand, burglar, filcher, hoodlum, mobster, poacher, prigger, rustler, stalker, tea leaf, yeggman
08 arsonist, assassin, batterer, bigamist, car-thief, gangster, hijacker, jailbird, joyrider, murderer, pederast, perjurer, receiver, saboteur, smuggler, swindler
09 buccaneer, cracksman, embezzler, kidnapper, larcenist, racketeer, ram-raider, strangler, terrorist
10 bootlegger, cat burglar, dope pusher, drug dealer, fire-raiser, highwayman, paedophile, pickpocket, shoplifter, trespasser
11 armed robber, blackmailer, bogus caller, drink-driver, kerb-crawler, safecracker, war criminal
12 drug smuggler, extortionist, housebreaker, sexual abuser
13 counterfeiter

Criminals include:

03 Ray (James Earl)
04 Aram (Eugene), Hare (William), Hood (Robin), Kray (Reginald), Kray (Ronnie), Rais (Gilles de), Todd (Sweeney), West (Frederick), West (Rosemary)
05 Biggs (Ronald), Blood (Thomas), Booth (John Wilkes), Brady (Ian), Burke (William), Ellis (Ruth), James (Jesse), Kelly (Ned), Lucan (Richard John Bingham, Lord)
06 Barrow (Clyde), Bonney (William H), Borden (Lizzie), Capone (Al), Corday (Charlotte), Meehan (Patrick), Nilsen (Dennis), Oswald (Lee Harvey), Parker (Bonnie), Rob Roy, Sirhan (Sirhan), Turpin (Dick)
07 Bathori (Elizabeth), Chapman (Mark), Crippen (Hawley), Hindley (Myra), Huntley (Ian), Ireland (William), Luciano (Charles 'Lucky'), Shipman (Harold), Winters (Larry)
08 Barabbas, Christie (John), Hanratty (James), Sheppard (Jack), Son of Sam

09 Berkowitz (David), Dillinger (John), Sutcliffe (Peter)
11 Billy the Kid
13 Jack the Ripper
14 Moors Murderers
15 Yorkshire Ripper

See also **highwayman**; **pirate**

crimp

04 bend, curl, fold, pote, tuck, wave **05** flute, pleat, quill, ridge **06** crease, furrow, gather, goffer, groove, hinder, pucker, rumple, thwart **07** crinkle, crumple, gauffer, wrinkle **09** corrugate

cringe

03 bow, shy **04** bend, duck, fawn **05** cower, crawl, creep, quail, sneak, start, stoop, toady, wince **06** blench, crouch, flinch, grovel, kowtow, quiver, recoil, shrink, suck up **07** flatter, tremble **08** draw back **09** be all over **11** curry favour **12** bow and scrape **14** tug the forelock

crinkle

04 curl, fold, line, ruck, tuck, wave **05** crimp, money, pleat, ridge, twist **06** crease, furrow, groove, pucker, ruffle, rumple **07** crumple, wrinkle **09** corrugate **10** paper money **11** corrugation

crinkly

05 curly, kinky, money **06** fluted, folded, frizzy, ridged, tucked **07** creased, crimped, grooved, pleated, rumpled, wrinkly **08** crinkled, crumpled, furrowed, gathered, puckered, wrinkled **10** corrugated, paper money

cripple

04 lame, maim, ruin **05** spoil **06** damage, hamper, impair, impede, injure, weaken **07** destroy, disable, lameter, lamiger, lamiter, vitiate **08** handicap, lammiger, mutilate, paralyse, sabotage **09** hamstring, undermine **10** debilitate, immobilize **12** incapacitate

crippled

04 halt, lame, maim **08** deformed, disabled **09** paralysed **11** handicapped **13** incapacitated

crisis

03 fit, fix, jam **04** acme, hole, mess, stew, turn **05** brunt, crise **06** crunch, pickle, scrape **07** dilemma, problem, trouble **08** calamity, disaster, exigency, hot water, quandary, solution **09** emergency, extremity **10** crossroads, difficulty **11** catastrophe, predicament **12** turning-point

crisp

04 chip, cool, firm, hard, neat **05** brief, brisk, clear, crump, fresh, pithy, short, terse **06** chilly, crispy, crumpy, snappy **07** bracing, brittle, chippie, concise, crackly, crumbly, crunchy, friable **08** decisive, incisive, succinct **09** breakable **10** refreshing **12** invigorating **13** authoritative

criterion
03 law **04** norm, rule, test **05** basis, canon, gauge, model, scale **06** square **07** measure **08** exemplar, standard **09** benchmark, principle, yardstick **10** shibboleth, touchstone

critic
05 judge **06** carper, censor, expert, pundit **07** analyst, knocker, monitor, Zoilist **08** attacker, censurer, observer, overseer, reviewer **09** Aristarch, authority, backbiter, find-fault, nit-picker **11** commentator, fault-finder
See also **literary**

critical
04 crit, nice **05** fatal, grave, major, vital **06** severe, urgent **07** carping, crucial, exigent, fateful, gingery, pivotal, probing, serious **08** captious, deciding, decisive, historic, niggling, perilous, pressing, scathing, venomous **09** cavilling, dangerous, essential, important, momentous, quibbling, vitriolic **10** analytical, censorious, compelling, derogatory, diagnostic, discerning, evaluative, expository, nit-picking, perceptive, precarious **11** climacteric, disparaging, explanatory, judgemental, penetrating, significant **12** all-important, condemnatory, disapproving, fault-finding, hypercorrect, life-and-death, sharp-tongued, vituperative **13** hypercritical **14** disapprobative, interpretative **15** uncomplimentary
• **critical position**
04 pass

critically
07 acutely, gravely, vitally **08** urgently **09** crucially, seriously **10** captiously, decisively, perilously **11** dangerously **12** analytically **13** disparagingly, significantly **14** diagnostically, disapprovingly **15** hypercritically

criticism
04 flak **05** blame, snipe, stick, strop **06** attack, niggle, review **07** censure, comment, reproof, ripping, slating, write-up, Zoilism **08** analysis, bad press, brickbat, critique, knocking, niggling, slamming **09** appraisal, judgement, stricture **10** assessment, commentary, evaluation, exposition, nit-picking, textualism **11** disapproval, explanation, explication **12** appreciation, condemnation, fault-finding **13** animadversion, disparagement **14** interpretation

criticize
03 bag, nag, pan, rip **04** carp, crab, flay, slag, slam, zing **05** blame, cut up, decry, judge, knock, roast, score, slash, slate, snipe, trash **06** assess, attack, hammer, impugn, niggle, peck at, review, tilt at **07** analyse, canvass, censure, condemn, dissect, explain, nit-pick, rip into, rubbish, run down, scarify, slag off, snipe at **08** appraise, badmouth, denounce, evaluate, wade into **09** castigate, denigrate, disparage,

excoriate, have a go at, interpret, pull apart, slaughter, take apart, tear apart **10** animadvert, come down on, go to town on, have a pop at, speak ill of, take a pop at, vituperate **11** have a shot at, pick holes in **12** disapprove of, pick to pieces, pull to pieces, put the boot in, tear to shreds **13** find fault with, tear a strip off **14** cast aspersions, ultracrepidate **15** do a hatchet job on, pass judgement on

critique
05 essay **06** review **07** write-up **08** analysis **09** appraisal, criticism, judgement **10** assessment, commentary, evaluation, exposition **11** explanation, explication **12** appreciation **14** interpretation

croak
03 caw, die **04** crow, gasp, kill, rasp **05** crake, croup, grunt **06** squawk, wheeze **07** grumble **12** speak harshly

Croatia
02 HR **03** HRV

crock
03 jar, pig, pot, urn **04** dirt, smut **06** vessel **07** disable **08** potsherd **09** break down

crocked
◊ *anagram indicator*
See **drunk**

crockery
05 china **06** dishes **07** pottery **08** brockage **09** porcelain, stoneware, tableware **11** earthenware **12** breakfast-set

crocodile
04 croc **06** caiman, cayman, garial, gavial, mugger **07** gharial **09** leviathan, teleosaur **11** river-dragon, Teleosaurus

croft
04 farm, plot **07** pightle **08** farmland **12** smallholding

Cronus
06 Saturn

crony
03 pal **04** ally, chum, mate **05** buddy **06** friend **07** comrade **08** familiar, follower, intimate, sidekick **09** associate, colleague, companion, confidant **10** accomplice, confidante

crook
◊ *anagram indicator*
03 bow, ill **04** bend, flex, hook, kink, sick, tilt, warp **05** angle, angry, cheat, cromb, crome, cross, curve, fraud, nasty, rogue, shark, slant, thief, twist, wrong **06** con man, deform, gibbet, kebbie, robber, unfair, unwell **07** crosier, crozier, distort, dubious, villain **08** criminal, crummack, crummock, inferior, offender, operator, swindler **09** card sharp, dishonest, sheep-hook **10** distortion, lawbreaker, unpleasant **13** pastoral staff

crooked
◊ *anagram indicator*
04 awry, bent **05** askew, bowed, shady, wrong **06** angled, camsho, curved, hooked, shifty, thrawn, tilted, uneven, warped, zigzag **07** buckled, corrupt, illegal, illicit, sinuous, twisted, winding **08** camshoch, criminal, deformed, lopsided, slanting, thraward, thrawart, tortuous, unlawful **09** camsheugh, contorted, deceitful, dishonest, distorted, irregular, misshapen, nefarious, off-centre, skew-whiff, underhand, unethical **10** asymmetric, fraudulent **11** anfractuous, treacherous **12** unprincipled, unscrupulous

crookedly
04 agee, ajee, awry **05** askew **08** unevenly **09** off-centre **10** lopsidedly **14** asymmetrically

croon
03 hum **04** lilt, sing **06** warble **08** vocalize
• **crooner**
04 Bing
See also **singer**

crop
03 cut, lop, lot, mow, rod, set **04** clip, crap, craw, pare, poll, reap, snip, stow, trim **05** batch, gorge, group, prune, shear, stand, yield **06** finial, fruits, gather, growth, reduce **07** curtail, harvest, produce, reaping, shorten, vintage **08** gleaning, wool clip **09** gathering, ingluvies **10** collection

Arable crops include:
03 pea, rye, yam
04 bean, corn, flax, hemp, kale, milo, oats, rape, rice
05 colza, maize, swede, wheat
06 barley, kharif, millet, potato, turnip
07 alfalfa, cassava, linseed, lucerne, oilseed, popcorn, sorghum, soy bean
08 mung bean, soya bean, teosinte
09 milo maize, sugar beet, sugar cane, sunflower, sweetcorn, triticale
11 oilseed rape, sweet potato
12 mangel wurzel

• **crop up**
05 arise, occur **06** appear, arrive, come up, emerge, happen, turn up **09** take place **10** come to pass **13** present itself

cross
◊ *anagram indicator*
01 X **03** cut, ill, irk, mix, woe, wry **04** arch, crux, defy, edgy, foil, ford, join, lace, load, meet, pain, sign, sore, span, vext, wade **05** angry, annoy, blend, block, check, grief, harsh, irate, short, surly, thraw, trial, vexed, worry **06** bridge, burden, crabby, franzy, grumpy, hamper, hinder, hybrid, impede, misery, oppose, peeved, put out, resist, shirty, snappy, sullen, thwart **07** adverse, amalgam, annoyed, awkward, fretful, grouchy, mixture,

mongrel, oblique, peevish, prickly, trouble **08** bestride, confront, converge, diagonal, disaster, go across, obstruct, opposite, pass over, snappish, traverse, walk over **09** adversity, balancing, crosswise, crotchety, decussate, difficult, dishonest, fractious, frustrate, hybridize, impatient, intersect, irascible, irritable, splenetic, suffering **10** affliction, criss-cross, crossbreed, displeased, interbreed, intertwine, interweave, misfortune, mixed breed, mongrelize, overthwart, reciprocal, transverse **11** bad-tempered, catastrophe, combination, ill-tempered, tribulation **12** cantankerous, disagreeable, interchanged, intersecting, neutralizing, travel across **14** cross-fertilize, cross-pollinate

See also **hybrid**

01 T
03 Red, tau
04 ankh, high, Iron, ring, rood, rose, rosy
05 fiery, Greek, Latin, papal, Rouen
06 ansate, botoné, Celtic, fleury, fylfot, Geneva, George, market, moline, potent, Y-cross
07 Avelian, Calvary, capital, Cornish, Maltese, Russian, saltire, Weeping
08 Buddhist, capuchin, cardinal, crosslet, crucifix, holy-rood, Lorraine, military, pectoral, quadrate, rood-tree, Southern, St Peter's, swastika, Victoria
09 encolpion, encolpium, Jerusalem, preaching, St Andrew's, St George's
10 St Anthony's
11 patriarchal
13 Constantinian, crux decussata
14 archiepiscopal

• **cross out**
06 cancel, cut out, delete, remove, rub out **07** edit out **09** strike out **10** blue-pencil, obliterate
• **make cross**
04 vote
• **make sign of cross over**
04 sain

cross-examination
04 quiz **08** grilling, quizzing **11** examination, questioning **13** interrogation **14** the third degree

cross-examine
04 pump, quiz **05** grill, targe **07** examine **08** question **11** interrogate **13** cross-question

crossing
◇ *containment indicator*
04 ford, trip **06** voyage **07** journey, passage, traject **08** junction, traverse **09** crosswalk, overgoing **10** crossroads, trajection **12** intersection **13** zebra crossing **14** Toucan crossing **15** grade separation, pelican crossing

crossover value
03 COV

crosswise
04 awry, over **06** across, aslant, thwart **07** athwart **08** sideways **09** crossways, obliquely **10** crisscross, diagonally, overthwart, transverse **11** catercorner **12** transversely **13** catercornered

crossword

03 Phi
04 Apex, Azed, Duck, Mass, Monk, Paul, Shed
05 Afrit, Owzat, Rufus, Wynne (Arthur)
06 Aelred, Crispa, Custos, Gemini, Merlin, Portia
07 Columba, Cyclops, Fidelio, Quixote, Spurius, Ximenes
08 Everyman, Giovanni, Mephisto, Pasquale
09 Araucaria, Beelzebub, Bunthorne, Cinephile, Virgilius
10 Enigmatist, Torquemada

crotch
04 fork **05** groin **06** crutch **08** genitals **11** bifurcation

crotchet
03 toy **04** whim **11** quarter note

crotchety
05 cross, surly, testy **06** crabby, crusty, grumpy **07** awkward, crabbed, grouchy, iracund, maggoty, peevish, prickly **08** contrary, petulant **09** difficult, fractious, irascible, irritable, whimsical **11** bad-tempered, ill-tempered **12** cantankerous, disagreeable, iracundulous, obstreperous **13** short-tempered

crouch
03 bow **04** bend, dare, duck, fawn, ruck **05** cower, hunch, kneel, squat, stoop **06** cringe

crow
03 daw, jay **04** brag, rook **05** boast, crake, exult, gloat, raven, vaunt **06** chough, corbie, corvid, hoodie **07** bluster, jackdaw, rejoice, show off, talk big, triumph **08** flourish **09** flute-bird **10** nutcracker, saddleback **12** cry roast-meat **13** Cornish chough **14** cock-a-doodle-doo **15** blow your own horn

crowd
03 jam, lot, mob, set **04** army, band, cram, gate, herd, host, mass, mong, pack, pile, push, raft, rout **05** bunch, crush, crwth, drove, elbow, flock, group, horde, house, meiny, press, shove, stuff, surge, swarm, three **06** bundle, circle, clique, gather, huddle, hustle, jostle, masses, meiney, meinie, menyie, muster, people, public, rabble, roll-up, squash, stream, throng, thrust **07** cluster, company, congest, scrooge, scrouge, squeeze, the many, turnout, viewers **08** assembly, audience, caboodle,

compress, converge, frequent, overflow, populace, riff-raff, scrowdge, varletry, watchers **09** frequence, gathering, listeners, multitude, revel-rout **10** attendance, collection, congregate, fraternity, spectators **12** grex venalium

crowded
04 busy, full, pang **05** close, thick **06** filled, jammed, mobbed, packed, throng **07** chocker, crammed, cramped, crushed, teeming **08** frequent, overfull, swarming, thronged **09** congested, jam-packed **11** chock-a-block, overcrowded, overflowing **13** overpopulated **14** full to bursting

crown
02 cr **03** cap, taj, tip, top **04** acme, apex, bays, king, noll, pate, peak, tiar **05** adorn, award, crest, glory, kudos, prize, queen, ruler, tiara, title **06** anoint, cantle, climax, corona, diadem, empire, fulfil, height, honour, induct, invest, krantz, reward, sconce, summit, trophy, vertex, wreath **07** aureola, aureole, circlet, coronal, coronet, dignify, emperor, empress, festoon, foretop, garland, install, laurels, monarch, perfect, pschent, royalty, thick'un **08** complete, enthrone, finalize, kingship, laureate, monarchy, pinnacle, round off **09** sovereign **10** consummate **11** culmination, distinction, sovereignty **13** ultimus haeres

crowning
03 top **05** final **07** highest, perfect, supreme **08** greatest, ultimate **09** climactic, paramount, sovereign, unmatched **10** consummate, coronation **11** culminating, investiture, unsurpassed **12** enthronement, inauguration, incoronation, installation

crucial
03 key **05** major, vital **06** trying, urgent **07** central, pivotal, testing **08** critical, deciding, decisive, historic, pressing **09** essential, important, momentous, searching **10** compelling **12** all-important

crucially
07 vitally **09** centrally **10** critically, decisively **11** essentially, importantly, momentously

crucify
04 mock, rack, slam **05** knock, slate **06** punish **07** execute, rubbish, run down, torment, torture **08** ridicule **09** criticize, denigrate, excoriate, persecute **10** put to death **12** pull to pieces, tear to pieces, tear to shreds **14** kill on the cross

crude
◇ *anagram indicator*
03 hot, raw **04** blue, lewd, rude **05** basic, bawdy, brash, brute, dirty, gross, juicy, rough **06** coarse, earthy, risqué, simple, smutty, vulgar

07 natural, obscene, raunchy, uncouth **08** immature, indecent **09** half-baked, makeshift, offensive, primitive, unrefined, untreated **10** inartistic, undigested, unfinished, unpolished, unprepared **11** barrelhouse, rudimentary, unconcocted, undeveloped, unprocessed **12** down-and-dirty **13** rough and ready

crudely

◇ *anagram indicator*
06 rudely, simply **07** roughly **08** coarsely **09** basically, obscenely **10** indecently **11** offensively, primitively

cruel

◇ *anagram indicator*
03 raw **04** evil, fell, grim, mean **05** felon, nasty **06** bitter, bloody, brutal, fierce, flinty, immane, savage, severe, unkind, wanton, wicked **07** callous, cutting, hellish, inhuman, painful, vicious **08** barbaric, diabolic, felonous, fiendish, indurate, inhumane, Neronian, pitiless, ruthless, sadistic, spiteful, vengeful **09** atrocious, barbarous, butcherly, ferocious, heartless, malicious, merciless, murderous, truculent, unfeeling **10** blistering, heathenish, implacable, inexorable, iron-headed, malevolent **11** cold-blooded, hard-hearted, remorseless, unrelenting **12** bloodthirsty, bloody-minded, excruciating, stony-hearted **13** marble-hearted **14** marble-breasted

cruelly

08 brutally, fiercely, immanely, savagely, unkindly **09** callously, inhumanly, painfully, viciously **10** implacably, inhumanely, pitilessly, ruthlessly, spitefully **11** ferociously, heartlessly, maliciously, mercilessly, truculently **13** cold-bloodedly, hard-heartedly, remorselessly

cruelty

05 abuse, spite, venom **06** malice, sadism **07** tyranny **08** bullying, ferocity, immanity, meanness, savagery, severity, violence **09** barbarity, brutality, harshness **10** bestiality, inhumanity, unkindness **11** callousness, viciousness **12** ruthlessness **13** heartlessness, mercilessness, murderousness **15** hard-heartedness

cruise

04 busk, sail, taxi, trip **05** coast, drift, glide, slide **06** travel, voyage **07** holiday, journey **09** freewheel

crumb

03 bit, jot **04** atom, iota, mite, nirl **05** flake, grain, piece, scrap, shred, speck **06** morsel, sliver, titbit **07** granule, snippet, soupçon **08** fragment, particle

crumble

◇ *anagram indicator*
03 rot **04** fail, mull, murl **05** crush, decay, grind, pound **06** powder **07** break up, moulder **08** collapse,

come away, fragment **09** break down, decompose, fall apart, pulverize **10** degenerate **11** deteriorate **12** disintegrate, fall to pieces

crumbly

◇ *anagram indicator*
04 nesh **05** frush, short **07** brittle, friable, powdery **11** pulverulent

crummy

04 poor, weak **05** cheap **06** grotty, rotten, shoddy, trashy **07** useless **08** inferior, pathetic, rubbishy **09** half-baked, miserable, third-rate, worthless **10** second-rate, unpleasant **11** substandard **12** contemptible

crumpet

04 head **05** woman, women **06** muffin **07** pikelet

crumple

04 fall, fold **05** crush **06** crease, pucker, raffle, rumple **07** crinkle, wrinkle **08** collapse, scrumple

crunch

04 bite, chew, crux, test **05** champ, chomp, crush, grind, munch, pinch, sit-up, smash **06** crisis **07** graunch, scranch, scrunch **09** emergency, masticate **13** critical point, moment of truth

crusade

03 war **04** push, work **05** cause, drive, fight, jihad **06** attack, battle, strive **07** holy war, promote **08** advocate, campaign, movement, strategy, struggle **09** offensive **10** expedition **11** undertaking

crusader

06 zealot **07** battler, fighter **08** activist, advocate, champion, promoter, reformer **10** campaigner, enthusiast, missionary

crush

◇ *anagram indicator*
03 jam **04** cram, love, mash, mill, mush, pack, pash, pulp, ruin **05** abash, break, chack, champ, check, crowd, grind, horde, pinch, pound, press, quash, quell, shame, smash, stamp, tread, upset **06** bruise, crease, crunch, defeat, liking, mangle, rumple, squash, squish, step on, subdue, throng **07** break up, conquer, contuse, crinkle, crumble, crumple, mortify, oppress, passion, put down, screw up, scrunch, shatter, squeeze, squelch, thrutch, wrinkle **08** compress, demolish, overcome, scrumple, squabash, suppress, vanquish **09** break down, comminute, devastate, humiliate, obsession, overpower, overwhelm, pulverize, telescope, triturate **10** annihilate **11** infatuation, steam-roller

• **crush down**
03 bow

crust

03 fur, reh **04** coat, film, husk, rind, scab, skin **05** argol, layer, shell, skull

06 caking, casing, gratin, pastry **07** caliche, capping, clinker, coating, outside, salband, surface, topping **08** beeswing, covering, exterior **09** wine-stone **10** concretion, livelihood **11** lithosphere **12** encrustation, impertinence, incrustation **13** efflorescence

Parts of the earth's crust include:

03 sal
04 sial, sima
06 craton, mantle

crustacean

Crustaceans include:

04 crab
05 krill, prawn, yabby
06 gilgie, hermit, jilgie, marron, partan, scampi, scrawl, shrimp, squill, yabbie
07 camaron, copepod, daphnia, dog-crab, fiddler, limulus, lobster, pagurid, pea-crab, pill bug
08 barnacle, crawfish, crayfish, crevette, king crab, land crab, ochidore, pagurian
09 centipede, devil-crab, fish louse, king prawn, langouste, millipede, phyllopod, schizopod, sea slater, shore crab, soft-shell, water flea, woodlouse
10 acorn-shell, edible crab, hermit crab, mitten-crab, robber crab, sandhopper, seed shrimp, spider crab, stomatopod, tiger prawn, velvet-crab, velvet worm, whale louse
11 brine shrimp, calling-crab, coconut crab, common prawn, Dublin prawn, fairy shrimp, fiddler crab, langoustine, rock lobster, soldier crab, spectre crab, tiger shrimp
12 common shrimp, mantis shrimp, mussel shrimp, saucepan-fish, sentinel crab, spiny lobster, squat lobster
13 acorn-barnacle, common lobster, goose barnacle, horseshoe crab, noble crayfish, Norway lobster, opossum shrimp, spectre shrimp, tadpole shrimp, velvet-fiddler
14 Dublin Bay prawn, skeleton shrimp, woolly-hand crab

See also **animal**

crusty

04 firm, hard **05** baked, cross, gruff, surly, testy **06** crabby, crispy, grumpy, snappy, touchy **07** awkward, brittle, brusque, crabbed, crumbly, crunchy, friable, grouchy, peevish, prickly **08** contrary, petulant, well-done **09** breakable, difficult, fractious, irascible, irritable, splenetic, well-baked **11** bad-tempered **12** cantankerous, disagreeable, obstreperous **13** short-tempered

crux

03 nub **04** core **05** cross, heart **06** centre, kernel, puzzle **07** essence, nucleus **13** the bottom line

See also **cross**

cry
03 caw, mew, sab, sob **04** bawl, blub, call, gowl, hoop, hoot, howl, keen, mewl, pipe, plea, rivo, roar, wail, weep, word, yawp, yell, yelp, yowl **05** bleat, chevy, chivy, clock, greet, havoc, mouth, neigh, pewit, shout, skirl, tears, whine, whoop **06** bellow, bubble, chivvy, lament, peewee, peewit, prayer, report, rumour, scream, shriek, slogan, snivel, squawk, squeal, yoicks **07** bawling, blubber, call out, clamour, exclaim, screech, tantivy, vagitus, whimper **08** peesweep, proclaim **09** alalagmos, be in tears, peaseweep, shed tears, watchword **11** ejaculation, exclamation, lamentation **14** burst into tears, cry your eyes out

See also shout; war cry *under* war

• cry off
06 cancel **07** back out **08** withdraw **13** decide against **14** change your mind, excuse yourself

• cry out for
04 need, want **06** demand **07** call for, require **11** necessitate

• cry up
04 sell **06** praise

crypt
04 tomb **05** vault **08** catacomb **09** mausoleum **10** undercroft **13** burial chamber

cryptic
04 dark **06** hidden, occult, secret, unseen, veiled **07** bizarre, obscure, strange **08** abstruse, esoteric, puzzling **09** ambiguous, enigmatic, equivocal **10** mysterious, perplexing

cryptically
08 secretly **09** bizarrely, obscurely, strangely **11** ambiguously **12** mysteriously **13** enigmatically

crystal
04 spar **05** macle, table **06** needle, raphis **07** cocaine, raphide, rhaphis, spicule **08** cut glass, rhaphide **09** microlite **10** watchglass **11** amphetamine, seeing stone

crystallize
04 form **05** candy, shoot **06** appear, emerge, harden **07** clarify **08** solidify **09** make clear **11** become clear, materialize **12** make definite **13** become clearer **14** become definite

cub
03 pup **04** baby, tiro **05** chest, puppy, whelp, young, youth **06** newbie, novice, rookie **07** fresher, learner, recruit, starter, student, trainee **08** beginner, freshman, initiate, neophyte **09** fledgling, greenhorn, offspring, youngster **10** apprentice, raw recruit, tenderfoot **11** probationer

Cuba
01 C **02** CU **03** CUB

cubbyhole
03 den **04** hole, slot **05** booth, niche **06** recess **07** cubicle **08** hideaway, tiny room **10** pigeonhole **11** compartment

cube
03 die **04** dice **05** block, solid **06** cuboid **10** hexahedron, triplicate

cuckoo
◇ *anagram indicator*
03 ani, mad **04** daft, gouk, gowk, koel, loco, nuts **05** batty, crazy, loony, nutty, silly **07** cracked, foolish, idiotic **08** crackpot, rainbird **12** crackbrained, round the bend **13** chaparral cock **14** brain-fever bird

See also fool; foolish

cucumber
05 choko, wolly **07** gherkin **10** dill pickle **11** bitter-apple

cuddle
03 hug, pet **04** hold, neck, snog **05** clasp, nurse **06** caress, enfold, fondle, nestle, smooch **07** embrace, smuggle, snuggle **08** canoodle

cuddly
04 cosy, soft, warm **05** plump **07** lovable **08** huggable, loveable **10** cuddlesome

cudgel
03 bat, hit **04** bash, beat, club, cosh, mace, patu, rung **05** clout, plant, pound, shrub, stick, towel **06** alpeen, ballow, batter, souple, strike, thwack, waster **07** clobber **08** bludgeon **09** bastinado, crabstick, fustigate, truncheon **10** shillelagh **12** an oaken towel

cue
01 Q **03** nod, rod **04** hint, mace, sign **06** prompt, signal **08** feed-line, half-butt, reminder, stimulus **09** catchword, incentive **10** indication, intimation, suggestion

cuff
03 box, hit **04** beat, belt, biff, clip, gowf, slap **05** clout, knock, scuff, smack, thump, whack **06** buffet, scruff, strike **07** armband, clobber, manacle **08** bracelet, gauntlet, handcuff, snitcher, wristlet **09** muffettee

• off the cuff
05 ad lib **09** extempore, impromptu **10** improvised, off the wall, unprepared, unscripted **11** unrehearsed **13** spontaneously

cuisine
07 cookery, cooking **10** cordon bleu **12** haute cuisine **15** nouvelle cuisine

cul-de-sac
04 loke **05** close **07** dead end **10** blind alley **13** no through road

cull
04 dupe, kill, pick, sift, thin **05** amass, glean, pluck **06** choose, gather, select **07** collect, destroy, pick out, thin out **09** slaughter

culminate
03 end **04** peak **05** close, crest, end up **06** climax, finish, wind up **08** conclude **09** terminate **10** consummate **11** come to a head **13** come to a climax

culmination
03 sum, top **04** acme, apex, head, peak, roof, turn **05** crown, point **06** apogee, climax, finale, height, heyday, summit, zenith **08** meridian, pinnacle **09** high point **10** completion, conclusion, perfection, perihelion **12** consummation

culpability
05 blame, fault, guilt **09** liability **13** answerability **14** accountability, responsibility **15** blameworthiness

culpable
05 wrong **06** faulty, guilty, liable, sinful **07** at fault, peccant, to blame **08** blamable, criminal **09** blameable, offending **10** answerable, censurable, in the wrong **11** blameworthy, responsible **13** reprehensible

culprit
05 felon **07** convict, villain **08** criminal, offender **09** miscreant, wrongdoer **10** delinquent, lawbreaker **11** guilty party

cult
03 fad **04** sect **05** craze, faith, mania, party, trend, vogue, Wicca **06** belief, cultus, school, Shinto **07** faction, fashion, in-thing, macumba **08** fixation, movement, navalism, religion **09** obsession **11** affiliation **12** denomination, macrobiotics

cultivate
◇ *anagram indicator*
03 aid, dig, sow, woo **04** back, farm, grow, help, tend, till, work **05** court, fancy, groom, plant, raise, train **06** assist, enrich, foster, garden, labour, manure, plough, polish, pursue, refine, work on **07** advance, bring on, cherish, culture, develop, enhance, forward, further, harvest, husband, improve, nurture, prepare, produce, promote, support **08** civilize **09** encourage, enlighten, fertilize

cultivated
04 tame **06** polite, sative, urbane **07** genteel, refined **08** advanced, cultured, educated, highbrow, polished, well-read **09** civilized, scholarly **10** discerning **11** enlightened **12** well-informed **13** sophisticated **14** discriminating

cultivation
05 tilth **06** sowing **07** backing, culture, farming, growing, nurture, support, tilling, working **08** planting **09** advancing, fostering, manurance, nurturing **10** assistance, cherishing, forwarding, furthering, harvesting, refinement **11** agriculture, development, improvement, preparation **12** civilization **13** encouragement

cultural
04 folk **06** ethnic, tribal **07** liberal **08** artistic, communal, edifying, national, societal **09** aesthetic, educative, elevating, enriching,

improving **10** broadening, civilizing, humanizing **11** educational, traditional **12** enlightening **13** developmental **15** anthropological

culture
04 arts, crop **05** mores, music **06** growth, habits **07** customs, history, society, the arts **08** heritage, learning, painting **09** behaviour, cultivate, education, lifestyle, nurturing, tendering, way of life **10** humanities, literature, philosophy, production, refinement, traditions **11** cultivation **12** civilization

cultured
04 arty **06** polite, urbane **07** erudite, genteel, learned, refined **08** advanced, artistic, educated, highbrow, polished, tasteful, well-bred, well-read **09** arty-farty, civilized, scholarly **10** cultivated **11** enlightened **12** intellectual, well-educated, well-informed **13** sophisticated

culvert
04 duct **05** drain, sewer **06** gutter **07** channel, conduit, ponceau **11** watercourse

cumbersome
04 slow **05** bulky, heavy **07** awkward, complex, onerous, weighty **08** cumbrous, involved, unwieldy, wasteful **09** difficult **10** burdensome **11** complicated, inefficient **12** incommodious, inconvenient, unmanageable **14** badly organized

Cumbrian
◊ *dialect indicator*

cumulative
07 growing **08** mounting **09** enlarging **10** collective, increasing **11** multiplying, progressive, snowballing

cunning
03 art, fly, sly **04** arch, deep, deft, foxy, rusé, slee, wily **05** canny, carny, craft, guile, guyle, leery, sharp, skill, wiles **06** artful, astute, carney, cautel, clever, crafty, dainty, deceit, knacky, policy, quaint, shifty, shrewd, slight, sneaky, subtle, tricky **07** crabbit, devious, finesse, knowing, practic, skilful, sleekit, sleight, slyness, varment, varmint, vulpine **08** artifice, deftness, fiendish, guileful, knackish, slippery, subtlety, trickery **09** deceitful, dexterous, ingenious, ingenuity, insidious, inventive, knowledge, sharpness **10** adroitness, artfulness, astuteness, cleverness, craftiness, shrewdness **11** cunningness, deviousness, imaginative, resourceful **12** fiendishness, manipulative **13** cunning as a fox, deceitfulness, inventiveness **15** imaginativeness, resourcefulness

cup
03 mug, nut, pot, tig, tot **04** bowl, tass, wine **05** award, bidon, calix, cruse, medal, plate, prize, punch **06** beaker, bumper, cotyle, goblet, hollow, noggin, quaich, quaigh, reward, rhyton, tassie, trophy **07** chalice, cyathus, scyphus, tankard, tumbler **08** pannikin **09** cantharus, gripe's egg **11** doch-an-doris **12** deuch-an-doris, doch-an-dorach **13** deoch-an-doruis

See also **drinking**

cupbearer
04 Hebe **08** Ganymede

cupboard
05 ambry, awmry, chest, press, store **06** almery, aumbry, awmrie, closet, locker, pantry **07** almirah, armoire, cabinet, dresser, tallboy **08** cellaret, hot press, meat safe, wardrobe **09** sideboard **12** clothes-press, Welsh dresser **14** Coolgardie safe

Cupid
04 Eros

cupidity
05 greed **06** hunger **07** avarice, avidity, itching, longing **08** rapacity, voracity, yearning **09** eagerness, hankering **10** greediness **12** covetousness, graspingness **13** rapaciousness **14** avariciousness **15** acquisitiveness

curable
08 operable **09** medicable, reparable, treatable **10** reformable, remediable **11** rectifiable

curative
05 tonic **07** healing **08** medcinal, remedial, salutary **09** healthful, medicinal, vulnerary **10** corrective, febrifugal **11** alleviative, restorative, therapeutic **12** health-giving

curator
06 keeper, warden, warder **07** steward **08** guardian **09** attendant, caretaker, custodian **11** conservator

curb
03 bit **04** bend, bent, rein **05** brake, check, corbe, courb **06** bridle, damper, hamper, hinder, impede, muzzle, rebuff, reduce, retard, subdue **07** contain, control, inhibit, refrain, repress **08** hold back, keep back, moderate, restrain, restrict, suppress **09** constrain, deterrent, hindrance, kerbstone, restraint, retardant **10** constraint, impediment, limitation, repression, unofficial **11** holding-back, keep in check, restriction, suppression

curdle
03 run **04** clot, earn, grew, grue, sour, turn, whig **05** yearn **06** lapper, lopper, posset **07** congeal, cruddle, ferment, thicken **08** solidify, turn sour **09** coagulate

curd, curds
04 skyr **06** junket
• **bean curd**
04 tofu

cure
◊ *anagram indicator*
03 dry, dun, fix **04** ease, heal, help, mend, salt **05** amend, break, reast, reest, reist, smoke, treat **06** elixir, hobday, kipper, pickle, remedy, repair **07** correct, cure-all, dry-salt, healing, panacea, recover, rectify, relieve, restore, therapy **08** antidote, barbecue, make well, medicine, preserve, recovery, smoke-dry, solution, specific, unpoison **09** alleviate, treatment **10** corrective, make better **11** alleviation, restorative **12** fever therapy

cure-all
06 elixir **07** nostrum, panacea **10** catholicon **12** panpharmacon **13** diacatholicon **15** universal remedy

curfew
04 gate

curie
02 Ci

curio
06 bygone **07** antique, bibelot, trinket **09** curiosity, objet d'art **10** knick-knack **12** objet de vertu **13** object of virtu **14** article of virtu

curiosity
05 curio, freak **06** bygone, gabion, marvel, oddity, prying, rarity, search, wonder **07** antique, exotica, inquiry, novelty, trinket **08** interest, nosiness, querying, snooping **09** objet d'art, spectacle **10** knick-knack, phenomenon **11** peculiarity, questioning **12** interference **15** inquisitiveness

curious
◊ *anagram indicator*
03 odd **04** agog, nosy, rare **05** funny, nosey, novel, queer, weird **06** exotic, prying, quaint, unique **07** bizarre, strange, unusual **08** freakish, meddling, peculiar, puzzling, querying, singular, snooping **09** inquiring, intrigued, searching **10** fascinated, interested, keen to know, meddlesome, mysterious, remarkable, unorthodox **11** inquisitive, interfering, questioning **13** extraordinary **14** unconventional, wanting to learn
• **be curious**
03 pry

curiously
◊ *anagram indicator*
05 oddly **08** quaintly **09** bizarrely, strangely, unusually **10** peculiarly, remarkably **11** inquiringly **12** meddlesomely, mysteriously **13** inquisitively, interferingly, questioningly

curium
02 Cm

curl
04 bend, coil, eddy, friz, kink, loop, purl, ring, roll, tong, turn, wave, wind **05** crimp, curve, dildo, frizz, helix, pinch, snake, swirl, twine, twirl, twist, whorl **06** becurl, ripple, scroll, spiral,

wreath, writhe **07** crimple, crinkle, earlock, frizzle, frounce, meander, inglet, wreathe **08** curlicue, kiss-curl, ovelock **09** corkscrew, favourite **12** heartbreaker **13** permanent wave

curly
04 wavy **05** fuzzy, kinky **06** curled, frizzy, permed **07** coiling, crimped, curling, looping, turning, winding **08** twirling, twisting **09** corkscrew, spiralled, wreathing **10** spiralling

currant
05 Ribes **06** rizard, rizzar, rizzer **07** rizzart

currency
03 tin **04** cash **05** bills, brass, coins, money, notes, vogue **07** coinage **08** exposure **09** publicity **10** acceptance, popularity, prevalence **11** circulation, legal tender **13** dissemination

Currencies include:
02 nu
03 ecu, kip, lat, lei, lek, leu, lev, som, sum, won, yen
04 baht, birr, cedi, dong, dram, euro, kina, kuna, kyat, lari, lats, lira, loti, mark, peso, pula, punt, rand, real, rial, riel, taka, tala, vatu, yuan
05 colón, denar, dinar, dobra, franc, frank, krona, krone, kroon, kunar, leone, litas, manat, marka, naira, nakfa, pence, pound, riyal, rupee, sucre, tenge, tolar, zaïre, zloty
06 ariary, balboa, dalasi, dirham, dollar, escudo, forint, gourde, gulden, hryvna, koruna, kwacha, kwanza, maloti, markka, new sol, pa'anga, pataca, peseta, rouble, rupiah, shekel, somoni, tugrik, tugrug
07 afghani, bolivar, cordoba, drachma, guarani, guilder, hyrvnia, lempira, metical, new peso, ouguiya, quetzal, ringgit, rufiyaa
08 new dinar, ngultrum, nuevo sol, renminbi, shilling, sterling, US dollar
09 boliviano, lilangeni, new dollar, schilling
10 emalangeni, Swiss franc
11 Deutschmark, French franc, karbovanets, Turkish lira
12 Belgian franc, Deutsche mark, renminbi yuan
14 Canadian dollar

See also **coin**

Former currencies include:
01 m
02 DM
03 pie
04 inti, lira, mark, pice, punt, reis
05 belga, franc, krone, sucre, zaïre
06 décime, ekuele, escudo, gilder, lepton, markka, peseta
07 austral, cruzado, drachma, guilder, milreis
08 cruzeiro, groschen
09 schilling
11 Deutschmark

current
01 I **02** AC, DC, in **03** amp, cur, ebb, jet, now **04** curt, eddy, flow, live, mood, race, rife, rill, soom, swim, tide **05** drift, going, juice, swirl, tenor, trend, valid **06** abroad, common, course, extant, modern, outset, stream, trendy **07** backset, bombora, draught, exhaust, feeling, flowing, general, indraft, instant, in vogue, ongoing, outflow, popular, present, running, thermal, topical **08** accepted, backwash, existing, movement, progress, reigning, tendency, tide race, up-to-date **09** direction, indraught, in fashion, prevalent **10** mainstream, present-day, prevailing, widespread **11** back-draught, fashionable, going around, present-time **12** contemporary, undercurrent **13** in circulation, up-to-the-minute

currently
03 now **05** today **07** just now **08** right now **09** at present, presently, these days **10** at this time **11** at the moment **15** for the time being

curriculum
06 course, module **07** program **08** subjects, syllabus **09** programme, timetable **10** discipline **13** course of study **14** core curriculum **15** course of studies

curry
04 beat **06** madras, quarry **07** cuittle, scratch **08** vindaloo

curse
02 wo **03** ban, eff, hex, moz, pox, woe **04** bane, blow, cuss, damn, evil, harm, jinx, mozz, oath, ruin **05** beset, blast, blind, shrew, spell, swear, weary, winze **06** berate, blight, maugre, ordeal, plague **07** accurse, afflict, beshrew, condemn, malison, scourge, torment, trouble **08** anathema, calamity, cussword, denounce, disaster, execrate, maledict **09** blaspheme, blasphemy, curse-word, expletive, fulminate, imprecate, obscenity, profanity, swear-word, vengeance **10** affliction, execration, Indian sign, misfortune, put a jinx on **11** bad language, eff and blind, imprecation, malediction, tribulation **12** anathematize, damn and blast **13** excommunicate **14** four-letter word, use bad language

cursed
04 vile **05** curst **06** bloody, cussed, damned, darned, dashed, odious **07** blasted, flaming, hateful, unlucky **08** annoying, blinking, blooming, dratting, fiendish, flipping, infamous, infernal **09** execrable, loathsome **10** abominable, confounded, detestable, pernicious, unpleasant

cursory
05 brief, hasty, quick, rapid **06** casual, slight **07** hurried, offhand, passing, summary **08** careless, fleeting,

slapdash **09** desultory **10** dismissive **11** perfunctory, superficial

curt
04 rude, tart **05** blunt, brief, gruff, pithy, sharp, short, squab, terse **06** abrupt **07** brittle, brusque, concise, laconic, offhand, summary, uncivil **08** snappish, succinct **10** ungracious **11** short-spoken **13** short and sweet, unceremonious

curtail
◇ *tail deletion indicator*
03 cut **04** clip, dock, pare, slim, trim **05** abate, limit, prune **06** hamper, lessen, reduce, shrink **07** abridge, cut back, cut down, shorten **08** cut short, decrease, pare back, pare down, restrict, truncate **09** cut back on **10** abbreviate, guillotine **12** circumscribe

curtailment
◇ *tail deletion indicator*
03 cut **06** paring **07** cutback, docking, pruning **08** decrease, slimming, trimming **09** lessening, reduction, shrinkage **10** abridgment, guillotine, limitation, shortening, truncation **11** abridgement, contraction, restriction **12** abbreviation, retrenchment

curtain
04 pall, swag, vail, veil **05** blind, cover, drape, scene **06** purdah, screen **07** drapery, hanging, shutter, vitrage **08** backdrop, portière, tapestry, traverse **10** net curtain **13** window hanging
• **theatre curtain**
03 tab **04** drop, iron **05** cloth

curtly
05 short **06** rudely **07** bluntly, briefly, gruffly, pithily, sharply, shortly, tersely **08** abruptly **09** brusquely, concisely, uncivilly **10** succinctly **11** laconically **12** ungraciously **15** unceremoniously

curtsy
03 bob, bow, dop **06** kowtow, salaam **08** courtesy **09** genuflect

curvaceous
05 buxom, curvy **06** bosomy, comely **07** shapely **09** curvesome **10** voluptuous **11** well-rounded, well-stacked

curve
03 arc, bow **04** arch, bend, coil, hook, kink, loop, ogee, turn, wind **05** bulge, crook, graph, helix, rhumb, round, swell, twist **06** bought, camber, circle, record, spiral, spiric, swerve **07** caustic, cissoid, compass, flexure, incurve, quadric, quartic, winding **08** apophyge, catenary, conchoid, crescent, envelope, liquidus, parabola, sinusoid, trochoid **09** curvature, loxodrome **10** epicycloid, isoseismal, meandering, trajectory **11** catacaustic, harmonogram **12** hypotrochoid **15** brachistochrone, Lissajous figure

curved

04 bent **05** bowed, wrong **06** arched, convex, cupped, humped, warped **07** arcuate, bending, bulging, concave, crooked, rounded, scooped, sinuous, twisted **08** sweeping, swelling, tortuous **09** curviform, incurvate **10** incurvated, serpentine

cushion

03 cod, mat, pad **04** bank, tyre **05** squab **06** absorb, buffer, dampen, deaden, lessen, muffle, pillow, prop up, reduce, soften, stifle **07** beanbag, bolster, bum roll, hassock, kneeler, padding, pillion, protect, sandbag, support **08** buttress, diminish, headrest, mitigate, pulvinus, suppress **09** pulvillus, upholster **10** lace-pillow, protection **11** booster seat **13** shock absorber **14** vegetable sheep

cushy

04 easy, plum, soft **05** jammy **11** comfortable, undemanding

cusp

04 horn **05** point **07** spinode

custard

04 flam **05** flamm, flawn **06** flaune **07** sabayon **08** zabaione **10** zabaglione

custodian

05 guard **06** custos, keeper, warden, warder **07** curator **08** claviger, guardian, overseer, watchdog, watchman **09** caretaker, castellan, protector **11** conservator **12** conservatrix **14** superintendent

custody

◇ *containment indicator*
04 bail, care, hand, hold, ward **05** hands **06** arrest, charge, prison **07** keeping **08** guarding, guidance, handfast, security, wardship, watching **09** captivity, detention, retention **10** possession, protection **11** confinement, safekeeping, supervision, trusteeship **12** guardianship, imprisonment, preservation **13** custodianship, incarceration **14** responsibility

custom

03 use, way, won **04** form, rite, thew **05** ethos, habit, mores, style, trade, usage **06** manner, policy, ritual **07** fashion, routine **08** business, ceremony, practice **09** etiquette, formality, patronage, procedure, rusticism, sacred cow, tradition **10** consuetude, convention, observance **11** institution **13** way of behaving

customarily

07 as a rule, usually **08** commonly, normally **09** generally, popularly, regularly, routinely **10** habitually, ordinarily **11** fashionably **13** traditionally **14** conventionally

customary

03 set **04** used **05** nomic, usual **06** common, normal, vulgar, wonted **07** general, popular, regular, routine **08** accepted, everyday, familiar, habitual, ordinary **10** obligatory, prevailing **11** established, fashionable, traditional **12** conventional, prescriptive **14** consuetudinary

customer

05 buyer, trick **06** client, patron, punter **07** regular, shopper **08** consumer, prospect **09** purchaser, shillaber

customize

03 fit **04** suit **05** adapt, alter, tweak **06** adjust, modify, tailor **07** convert **08** fine-tune **09** transform **11** personalize

customs

04 dues **05** mores, taxes **06** duties, excise, impost, levies **07** tariffs **08** protocol

cut

◇ *anagram indicator*
◇ *deletion indicator*
◇ *insertion indicator*
◇ *tail deletion indicator*
02 ax **03** axe, bit, end, hew, lop, mow, rip, saw **04** blow, burn, chop, clip, crop, curb, dash, dice, dock, edit, form, gash, hack, halt, kerf, make, nick, omit, pare, part, race, rase, raze, reap, sawn, shun, skip, slit, sned, snee, snip, snub, stab, stop, tape, trim **05** avoid, blank, block, break, carve, cross, fault, grate, joint, knife, lance, lower, mince, notch, piece, prune, quota, scalp, score, scorn, sever, shape, share, shave, shear, shred, slash, slice, slish, sneck, snick, split, spurn, style, whack, wound **06** chisel, chop up, cleave, delete, design, dilute, divide, excise, ignore, incise, insult, lessen, pierce, précis, ration, rebuff, record, reduce, saving, slight, stroke, trench **07** abridge, curtail, cutback, cut dead, diluted, dissect, economy, engrave, failure, fashion, incised, portion, profile, rake-off, scratch, section, shorten, suspend **08** break off, castrate, cleaving, condense, decrease, diminish, dividing, excision, incision, lacerate, lowering, obstruct, renounce, stoppage **09** breakdown, expurgate, intercept, interrupt, intersect, lessening, reduction, summarize, videotape **10** abbreviate, adulterate, allocation, cutting-out, diminution, disconnect, laceration, proportion, tape-record **11** adulterated, discontinue, make shorter **12** breaking-down, bring to an end, cold-shoulder, retrenchment **14** malfunctioning, send to Coventry, slice of the cake **15** pretend not to see

See also **hairstyle**; **meat**

● **cut across**
08 go beyond, surmount **09** intersect, rise above, transcend **11** leave behind

● **cut and dried**
05 clear, fixed **06** sewn up **07** certain, decided, settled **08** definite **09** automatic, organized **11** prearranged **13** predetermined

● **cut back**
03 lop **04** crop, curb, trim **05** check, lower, prune, slash **06** lessen, reduce **07** coppice, curtail **08** decrease, downsize, retrench **09** economize, scale down

● **cut down**
02 ax **03** axe, hew, lop, mow, saw **04** curb, fell, kill, maim, raze, reap **05** level, lower, prune, slash **06** lessen, reduce **07** curtail **08** chop down, decrease, diminish

● **cut in**
05 nip in **06** butt in **07** barge in, break in, intrude **09** interject, interpose, interrupt, intervene

● **cut off**
03 end **04** clip, halt, nick, stop **05** block, sever, shred **06** detach, excide, remove, unhook **07** abscind, chop off, exscind, handsel, isolate, seclude, shelter, suspend, take off, tear off **08** amputate, break off, insulate, obstruct, prescind, retrench, separate, smite off **09** intercept, interrupt, keep apart **10** disconnect, interclude, stormbound **11** discontinue **12** bring to an end

● **cut out**
04 clip, drop, edit, fail, omit, quit, stop **05** block, cease, debar, shape, sneck, snick **06** delete, desist, excise, exsect, go phut, lay off, pack in, pack up, remove **07** conk out, eclipse, exclude, extract, go kaput, go wrong, refrain, ride out, take out, tear out **08** carve out, contrive, knock off, leave off, leave out, separate, supplant **09** break down **11** discontinue, malfunction, stop working **12** go on the blink

● **cut out for**
04 good, made **05** right **06** suited **08** suitable **09** qualified **11** appropriate

● **cut short**
◇ *tail deletion indicator*
04 crop, dock, snub **05** roach **07** abridge, bobtail, chapped, concise, curtail **08** prescind, truncate **10** detruncate

● **cut slantwise**
04 bias

● **cut square across**
03 bob **04** bang

● **cut up**
04 chop, dice, hurt **05** break, carve, het up, mince, slash, slice, upset **06** chop up, divide, put out **07** annoyed, dissect, slice up, unhappy **08** bothered, saddened, tomahawk, troubled, worked up **09** dismember **10** distressed

cutback

◇ *reversal indicator*
03 cut **06** saving **07** economy **08** decrease, lowering, slashing **09** lessening, reduction **11** curtailment **12** retrenchment

cute

04 twee **05** ankle, sweet **06** astute, clever, lovely, pretty **07** lovable

08 adorable, charming, loveable
09 appealing, endearing **10** attractive, delightful

cutlery
06 silver **07** canteen **08** flatware

Cutlery items include:

04 fork
05 knife, ladle, spoon
08 fish fork, teaspoon
09 fish knife, fish slice, salt spoon, soupspoon
10 bread knife, caddy spoon, cake server, chopsticks, pickle fork, steak knife, sugar tongs, tablespoon
11 butter knife, carving fork, cheese knife, corn holders
12 apostle spoon, carving knife, dessertspoon, salad servers
14 vegetable knife

cutlet
04 chop **09** côtelette, schnitzel
15 Wiener schnitzel

cut-price
04 sale **05** cheap **07** bargain, cut-rate, reduced **08** discount **09** low-priced
10 marked-down

cutpurse
03 nip **04** bung **06** nipper
10 pickpocket

cutter
04 pone **05** axman **06** axeman
08 lapidary

Cutters include:

03 axe, fox, saw, sax
04 adze, bill, celt
05 bilbo, blade, brand, knife, mower, plane, razor, saber, sabre, sword
06 chisel, colter, culter, dagger, ice axe, jigsaw, labrys, lopper, meat-ax, piolet, poleax, rapier, scythe, shears, sickle, sparth
07 chopper, cleaver, coulter, cutlass, fretsaw, gisarme, hacksaw, halberd, hatchet, meat-axe, poleaxe, pollaxe, sparthe, twibill
08 battle-ax, billhook, chainsaw, claymore, clippers, palstaff, palstave, partisan, scimitar, scissors, shredder, stone axe, Strimmer®, tomahawk
09 battle-axe, double-axe, Excalibur, holing-axe, lawnmower, secateurs
10 broadsword, coal-cutter, corkcutter, guillotine, putty-knife, spokeshave
11 chaff-cutter, coup de poing, glasscutter, grass-cutter, Lochaber axe, paper-cutter, straw-cutter

12 cookie-cutter, hedgetrimmer, Jeddart staff, marble-cutter
13 mowing machine, pinking shears

See also **dagger**; **knife**; **saw**; **weapon**

cut-throat
04 keen, thug **05** cruel, razor
06 brutal, cutter, fierce **07** ruffian, sworder **08** assassin, pitiless, ruthless
09 dog-eat-dog, merciless, murderous
10 relentless **15** keenly contested

cutting
◇ *insertion indicator*
03 raw **04** acid, clip, keen, sect, sien, slip, syen **05** chill, piece, plant, scion, scrap, sharp, snide **06** bitchy, biting, bitter, secant **07** caustic, coupure, excerpt, extract, gingery, hurtful, mordant, pointed **08** clipping, incision, incisive, piercing, quickset, scathing, scission, scissure, stinging, wounding **09** malicious, sarcastic, trenchand, trenchant **11** penetrating

cuttle-bone
03 pen **06** pounce, sepium

cycle
03 age, eon, era, orb **04** aeon, bike, rota **05** epoch, order, phase, round, trike **06** circle, period, rhythm, series
07 pattern **08** go-around, rotation, sequence **09** biorhythm, body clock
10 revolution, succession **11** oscillation

cyclical
06 cyclic **07** regular **08** repeated
09 recurrent, recurring **10** repetitive

cyclist

Cyclists include:

03 Hoy (Chris)
04 Gaul (Charly)
05 Binda (Alfredo), Bobet (Louison), Coppi (Fausto), Kelly (Sean), Moser (Francesco), Zabel (Erik)
06 Burton (Beryl), Fignon (Laurent), Harris (Reg), LeMond (Greg), Merckx (Eddy)
07 Bartali (Gino), Hinault (Bernard), Museeuw (Johan), Pantani (Marco), Queally (Jason), Simpson (Tom), Ullrich (Jan), Van Looy (Rik)
08 Anquetil (Jacques), Boardman (Chris), Indurain (Miguel), Maertens (Freddy), Opperman (Sir Hubert), Poulidor (Raymond), Virenque (Richard)
09 Armstrong (Lance), Zoetemelk (Joop)
10 Bahamontes (Federico), van Moorsel (Leontien Ziljaard-)

11 De Vlaeminck (Roger)
13 Longo-Ciprelli (Jeannie)

cyclone
05 storm **07** monsoon, tempest, tornado, typhoon **09** hurricane, whirlwind, windstorm **10** cockeye bob, depression, willy-willy
11 cockeyed bob **13** tropical storm

cylinder
04 drum, reel, roll **05** spool **06** barrel, bobbin, column, roller **07** spindle

cymbal
03 zel **07** symbole

cynic
05 surly **07** doubter, killjoy, knocker, sceptic, scoffer **08** Diogenes, snarling
09 pessimist **10** spoilsport
11 misanthrope

cynical
05 surly **06** bitter, ironic **07** mocking
08 critical, derisive, Diogenic, doubtful, doubting, negative, sardonic, scoffing, scornful, snarling, sneering
09 hardnosed, sarcastic, sceptical
10 embittered, hard-boiled, streetwise, suspicious **11** distrustful, pessimistic, worldly-wise
12 contemptuous, disenchanted
13 disillusioned, unsentimental
14 Mephistophelic
15 Mephistophelean, Mephistophelian

cynically
08 bitterly **09** mockingly **10** critically, derisively, negatively, scornfully
11 sceptically **12** suspiciously
13 distrustfully **14** contemptuously
15 pessimistically

cynicism
05 doubt, irony, scorn **07** mocking, sarcasm **08** contempt, distrust, scoffing, sneering **09** disbelief, pessimism, surliness, suspicion
10 scepticism **11** misanthropy
13 heartlessness **14** disenchantment
15 disillusionment

Cyprus
02 CY **03** CYP

cyst
03 sac, wen **04** bleb **06** growth, ranula
07 abscess, bladder, blister, capelet, dermoid, hydatid, utricle, vesicle
08 atheroma, capellet, steatoma
09 chalazion

Czech Republic
02 CZ **03** CZE

D

D
03 dee **05** delta

dab
03 bit, mop, pat, tad, tap **04** blot, dash, daub, drop, peck, spot, swab, wipe **05** fleck, press, smear, speck, tinge, touch, trace **06** dollop, smudge, splash, stroke **07** smidgen, trickle **08** sprinkle **09** lemon sole **10** sandsucker
• **dab hand**
03 ace, dip, toy, wet **04** play **05** adept, dally **06** dampen, expert, paddle, potter, splash, tinker, trifle, wizard **07** amateur, dallier, moisten, trifler **08** splatter, sprinkle, tinkerer **09** lay person **10** dilettante, past master

dabble
03 dip, toy, wet **04** play **05** dally, flirt, plash **06** clatch, dampen, fiddle, guddle, muddle, paddle, potter, putter, splash, tinker, trifle **07** immerse, moisten, plotter, plouter, plowter, smatter **08** splatter, sprinkle

dabbler
07 amateur, dallier, trifler **08** tinkerer **09** lay person, literator **10** dilettante

dad *see* **father**

daemon
04 deva **05** demon, devil, force, geist **06** animus, genius, spirit **09** cacodemon **10** evil spirit, genius loci, good spirit

daft
◇ *anagram indicator*
03 dim, mad, odd **04** avid, dull, dumb, fond, keen, nuts, slow, wild **05** barmy, batty, crazy, daffy, dense, dopey, dotty, inane, loony, loopy, nutty, potty, silly, sweet, thick, wacky **06** absurd, ardent, crazed, insane, mental, simple, stupid, unwise **07** berserk, bonkers, devoted, fatuous, foolish, glaiket, glaikit, idiotic, lunatic, smitten, touched, zealous **08** crackpot, demented, deranged, dingbats, farcical, gormless, obsessed, peculiar, unhinged **09** dim-witted, disturbed, enamoured, fanatical, foolhardy, half-baked, imprudent, laughable, ludicrous, senseless **10** infatuated, irrational, outrageous, passionate, ridiculous, slow-witted, unbalanced **11** hare-brained, nonsensical, unrealistic **12** addle-brained, crackbrained, enthusiastic, preposterous, round the bend, simple-minded **13** impracticable, irresponsible, off your rocker, out of your mind, round the twist, thick as a plank

dagger
05 blade, knife **06** obelus

See also **knife; sword**

Dáil member
02 TD

daily
04 char **05** adays **06** common **07** cleaner, diurnal, journal, per diem, regular, routine **08** constant, day by day, day-to-day, everyday, habitual, ordinary **09** circadian, customary, quotidian, regularly **10** constantly **11** commonplace, day after day

See also **newspaper**

dainty
04 cate, fine, neat, nice, trim **05** dinky, faddy, fancy, fussy, genty, juicy, small, tasty **06** bonbon, choice, choosy, friand, little, luxury, mignon, morsel, petite, pretty, sunket, titbit **07** cunning, elegant, finicky, friande, genteel, minikin, refined, savoury **08** charming, delicacy, delicate, graceful, luscious, mignonne, tasteful **09** delicious, enjoyable, exquisite, lickerish, liquorish, succulent, sweetmeat **10** appetizing, delectable, delightful, fastidious, particular, scrupulous **11** bonne-bouche **12** hard to please **14** discriminating

dairy

dairymaid
03 dey **08** dey-woman

dais
05 stage, stand **06** estate, podium **07** haut pas, rostrum, staging **08** footpace, platform

daisy
05 gowan, ox-eye **07** felicia, guayule **08** feverfew, ox-tongue **10** cupid's dart, horse-gowan, marguerite, moonflower **14** hen-and-chickens

dale
03 cwm, den, ria **04** dean, dell, dene, gill, glen, vale **05** coomb, griff, grike, gulch, heuch, slade **06** dingle, strath, valley

dalliance
04 play **05** delay, sport **06** toying **07** playing **08** dawdling, flirting, sporting, tarrying, trifling **09** loitering, pottering

dally
03 toy **04** play **05** delay, flirt, tarry **06** coquet, dawdle, frivol, linger, loiter, pingle, trifle **07** carry on **08** coquette **10** tick and toy **12** take your time **13** procrastinate

dam
03 pen **04** bund, stem, sudd, wall, wear, weir **05** block, cauld, check, stank **06** anicut, mother **07** annicut, barrage, barrier, confine, staunch **08** blockage, obstruct, restrict **09** barricade, decametre, hindrance, restraint **10** draughtman, embankment, millstream **11** obstruction

11 Afsluitdijk, Grand Coulee, La Esmeralda, Three Gorges
13 Alberto Lleras, Alvaro Obregon, Grande Dixence, Manuel M Torres
14 Afsluitdijk Sea
15 Sayano-Shushensk

damage
◇ *anagram indicator*
3 mar, rip **04** cost, dent, fine, harm, hurt, loss, ruin **05** abuse, havoc, price, spoil, wreck, wrong **06** charge, deface, impair, injure, injury, weaken **07** blemish, destroy, empeach, expense, impeach, vitiate **08** decimate, mischief, mutilate, sabotage **09** desecrate, detriment, disprofit, indemnity, suffering, vandalism, vandalize **10** defacement, defilement, impairment, mutilation, recompense, reparation, tamper with **11** depredation, desecration, destruction, devastation, restitution **12** compensation, disadvantage, incapacitate, satisfaction **13** play havoc with, reimbursement, vandalization **14** wreak havoc with **15** indemnification

damaged
◇ *anagram indicator*
04 mard **07** cracked, unsound **08** impaired

damaging
03 bad **07** harmful, hurtful, ruinous **09** injurious **10** pernicious **11** deleterious, destructive, detrimental, prejudicial **12** unfavourable **15** disadvantageous

dame
03 DBE, DCB **04** Edna, lady **05** broad, woman **06** female, matron, mother **07** dowager, peeress **08** baroness **10** aristocrat, noblewoman

damn
01 d **03** dee, jot, pan **04** dang, darn, dash, doom, hang, hoot, iota, sink, slag, slam, toss **05** blank, blast, curse, decry, knock, slate, swear **06** attack, berate, jigger, revile **07** accurse, censure, condemn, inveigh, monkey's, run down, slag off **08** denounce, execrate, maledict, two hoots **09** blaspheme, castigate, criticize, denigrate, excoriate, fulminate, imprecate **10** come down on, denunciate **11** pick holes in, tinker's cuss **12** anathematize, pull to pieces, tear to shreds **13** brass farthing **14** use bad language

damnable
06 cursed, damned, wicked **07** hateful, hellish **08** horrible, infernal **09** atrocious, execrable, offensive **10** abominable, despicable, detestable, diabolical, iniquitous, pernicious, unpleasant **12** disagreeable **13** objectionable

damnation
04 doom, hell **08** anathema, hell-fire **09** perdition **12** condemnation,

denunciation, proscription
15 excommunication

damned
04 lost, very, vile **05** pocky **06** blamed, bloody, cursed, darned, dashed, deuced, doomed, effing, odious **07** blasted, flaming, hateful **08** accursed, annoying, blinking, blooming, complete, dratting, fiendish, flipping, infernal, jiggered, thorough **09** condemned, execrable, execrated, loathsome, reprobate **10** abominable, confounded, despicable, detestable, pernicious, unpleasant **11** exceedingly **13** anathematized, blankety-blank **14** blankety-blanky

damning
09 damnatory **10** condemning **11** implicating, implicative, inculpatory **12** accusatorial, condemnatory **13** incriminating

damp
03 dew, fog, wet **04** dank, dewy, dull, mist, rain **05** check, foggy, gloom, humid, misty, mochy, moist, muggy, rainy, soggy **06** clammy, fousty, mochie, moisty, rheumy, vapour **07** drizzle, drizzly, wetness, wettish **08** dampness, dankness, humidity, moisture, vaporous **09** moistened **10** clamminess, discourage **14** discouragement, unenthusiastic
• **damp down**
04 calm, dull **05** check **06** deaden, lessen, quench, reduce **08** decrease, diminish, moderate, restrain

dampen
03 wet **04** damp, dash, dull **05** check, deter, spray **06** deaden, dismay, lessen, muffle, reduce, stifle **07** depress, inhibit, moisten, smother **08** damp down, decrease, diminish, moderate, restrain **10** discourage, dishearten **12** put a damper on

damper
04 mute **07** sordino **10** wet blanket **13** register-plate
• **put a damper on**
04 dash, dull **05** check, deter **06** deaden, dismay, lessen, muffle, reduce, stifle, subdue **07** depress, inhibit, smother **08** damp down, decrease, diminish, moderate, restrain **10** discourage, dishearten

dampness
03 dew, fog, wet **04** damp, mist, rain **06** vapour **07** drizzle, wetness **08** dankness, humidity, moisture **09** mugginess **10** clamminess

damsel
04 girl, lass **06** lassie, maiden **09** young lady **10** young woman

dance
◇ *anagram indicator*
04 juke, jump, leap, play, rock, skip, spin, sway **05** caper, flash, frisk, swing, twirl, waver, whirl **06** bounce, cavort, frolic, gambol, gyrate, hoof it, prance, ripple, spring **07** flicker, shimmer,

sparkle, twinkle **09** pirouette, shake a leg **11** move lightly, move to music **13** tread a measure
See also **ballet**

stomp, strut, Suzi-Q, three, twist, whisk
06 aerial, breaks, bronco, chassé, circle, jockey, paddle, riffle, shimmy, uprock
07 box step, fan kick, feather, jig step, locking, lollies, popping, pop turn, rocking, scuffle, shuffle, six-step, swivels, toprock, twinkle
08 back step, crab walk, flat step, four-step, hair comb, headspin, heel pull, heel turn, hook turn, neck wrap, pas-de-bas, push spin, rock step, shedding, spot turn, swingout, throwout, time step, windmill
09 allemagne, applejack, crazy legs, cross over, cross turn, dile que no, grapevine, lindy turn, pas de deux, poussette, promenade, quick stop, sugarfoot, sugarpush
10 ball-change, chainé turn, change step, charleston, chassé turn, come-around, Cuban walks, cucarachas, inside turn, jackhammer, rubber legs, spiral turn, texas tommy, triple step
11 alemana turn, impetus turn, natural turn, outside turn, pas de basque, quarter turn, reverse turn, setting step
12 last shedding, shake and turn, under-arm turn
13 double-shuffle, fall off the log, first shedding
14 change of places, kick-ball-change, transition step, travelling step

• **dance company**
03 set

Dance companies include:

10 Ballet West
11 Kirov Ballet, Royal Ballet
12 Sadler's Wells, Kirov Ballet, Royal Ballet
13 Ballet Rambert, Ballets Russes, Bolshoi Ballet, Joffrey Ballet
14 National Ballet

dancer
04 alma, alme **05** almah, almeh
06 bopper, exotic, hoofer **07** baladin, danseur, kachina, morisco, skipper, slammer, waltzer **08** coryphée, danseuse, figurant, joncanoe, junkanoo, matachin, première, showgirl **09** ballerina, figurante, John Canoe, John Kanoo, tap-dancer **10** pyrrhicist **11** belly-dancer, comprimario **12** ballet dancer **13** terpsichorean **14** Jack-in-the-green

Dancers include:

03 Lee (Gypsy Rose)
04 Bull (Deborah), Edur (Thomas), Oaks (Agnes)
05 Ailey (Alvin, Jnr), Baker (Josephine), Cohan (Robert), Dolin (Anton), Kelly (Gene), Laban (Rudolf von), Lifar (Serge), Perón (Isabelita), Sleep (Wayne), Tharp (Twyla)
06 Ashton (Sir Frederick), Béjart (Maurice), Blasis (Carlo), Childs (Lucinda), Clarke (Michael), Cooper

(Adam), Davies (Siobhan), Dowell (Anthony), Duncan (Isadora), Fokine (Michel), Graham (Martha), Paxton (Steve), Petipa (Marius), Rogers (Ginger), Sibley (Antoinette), Wigman (Mary)
07 Astaire (Fred), Bussell (Darcey), Durante (Viviana), Edwards (Leslie), Fonteyn (Dame Margot), Guillem (Sylvie), Markova (Dame Alicia), Massine (Léonide), Nureyev (Rudolf), Pavlova (Anna), Rambert (Dame Marie), Seymour (Lynn), Ulanova (Galina)
08 Danilova (Alexandra), De Valois (Dame Ninette), Hayworth (Rita), Helpmann (Sir Robert), Humphrey (Doris), Nijinska (Bronislava), Nijinsky (Vaslav)
09 Diaghilev (Sergei), Macmillan (Sir Kenneth)
10 Balanchine (George), Cunningham (Merce), Mukhamedov (Irek)
11 Baryshnikov (Mikhail), Mistinguett

See also **ballet**

dandelion
09 kok-saghyz, taraxacum

dandle
03 pet **04** toss **05** dance **06** bounce, cradle, cuddle, doodle, fondle, jiggle

dandy
03 fop **04** beau, buck, dude, fine, lair, posh, toff **05** blade, blood, great, smart, swell **06** Adonis, masher **07** capital, coxcomb, jessamy, musk-cat, peacock, princox **08** macaroni, muscadin, popinjay, splendid **09** excellent, exquisite, fantastic, first-rate **10** beau garçon, dapperling, fantastico **12** man about town **13** puss-gentleman

Dandies include:

04 Nash (Richard 'Beau')
05 Crisp (Quentin), Wilde (Oscar)
06 Coward (Noel)
08 Beerbohm (Max), Brummell (George 'Beau')
12 Yankee Doodle

danger
04 risk **05** nasty, peril, power **06** hazard, menace, risque, threat **07** pitfall **08** jeopardy **09** liability **10** insecurity **11** imperilment **12** endangerment, perilousness **13** vulnerability **14** precariousness **15** snake in the grass
• **danger signal**
03 red **08** red light
• **hidden danger**
04 trap **07** pitfall

dangerous
03 hot **05** dicey, dodgy, grave, hairy, nasty, risky, tight **06** chancy, daring, severe, unsafe **07** exposed, no'canny, ominous, serious **08** alarming, arrogant, critical, high-risk, insecure, menacing, perilous, reckless, unchancy **09** breakneck, hazardous, minacious, mischancy **10** jeopardous,

periculous, precarious, vulnerable
11 defenceless, stand-offish, susceptible, threatening, treacherous

dangerously
07 acutely, gravely **08** severely
09 seriously **10** alarmingly, critically, menacingly, perilously **12** precariously
13 threateningly

dangle
03 sag **04** fall, flap, hang, loll, lure, sway, wave **05** droop, offer, swing, tempt, trail **06** entice, flaunt, seduce
07 hold out **08** flourish **09** tantalize

dank
03 wet **04** damp, dewy **05** madid, moist, musty, slimy, soggy **06** chilly, clammy, sticky

Daphne
08 lacebark, mezereon, mezereum
09 eaglewood, widow wail **12** spurge laurel

dapper
04 chic, neat, spry, tidy, trim **05** brisk, natty, smart **06** active, dainty, nimble, spruce **07** stylish **08** debonair, sprauncy **11** well-dressed, well-groomed **13** well-turned-out

dappled
04 pied **06** dotted **07** blotchy, flecked, mottled, piebald, spotted **08** blotched, freckled, speckled, stippled, streaked
09 chequered **10** bespeckled, variegated

dare
04 dace, dart, daze, defy, doze, face, goad, lurk, risk **05** brave, flout, stake, stare, stump, taunt **06** crouch, gamble, hazard, invite, resist, shrink
07 daunton, presume, provoke, venture **08** boldness, confront, endanger, frighten, gauntlet **09** adventure, challenge, go so far as, stand up to, ultimatum **11** provocation
12 be bold enough, go out on a limb
13 be brave enough **14** have the courage

daredevil
04 bold, rash **05** brave, hasty
06 daring, madcap, plucky
07 hothead, valiant **08** fearless, intrepid, reckless, stuntman **09** audacious, dauntless, desperado, hotheaded, impetuous, impulsive
10 adventurer **11** adventurous
12 swashbuckler

daring
04 bold, gall, grit, guts, rash, wild
05 brave, hardy, moxie, nerve, pluck, spunk **06** bottle, plucky, spirit, valour
07 bravery, courage, gallows, prowess, valiant **08** audacity, boldness, defiance, fearless, intrepid, rashness, reckless, shocking, ventrous, wildness
09 audacious, dauntless, foolhardy, impulsive, undaunted, venturous
10 courageous, jeopardous
11 adventurous, intrepidity, venturesome **12** fearlessness,

high-spirited, recklessness
13 foolhardiness 15 adventurousness

daringly
06 boldly 07 bravely 10 fearlessly
11 audaciously 12 courageously
13 adventurously

dark
02 dk 03 bad, dim, fog, sad, wan
04 base, drab, dusk, evil, foul, grim,
mirk, mist, murk, vile 05 awful, black,
bleak, blind, brown, dingy, dirty, dusky,
foggy, gloom, misty, moody, murky,
night, olive, sable, shade, shady, tawny,
unlit, wrong 06 arcane, auburn,
cloudy, dismal, gloomy, hidden,
morose, opaque, secret, sombre,
tanned, tragic, veiled, wicked
07 bronzed, crooked, cryptic,
dimness, evening, immoral, joyless,
mystery, obscure, ominous, pit-mirk,
privacy, secrecy, shadows, shadowy,
sunless, swarthy 08 abstruse, badly lit,
brunette, chestnut, darkness, dejected,
dimly lit, esoteric, hopeless, horrible,
menacing, mournful, overcast,
puzzling, sinister, twilight, worrying
09 blackness, cheerless, concealed,
enigmatic, half-light, ignorance,
intricate, murkiness, nightfall, night-
time, obscurity, poorly lit, recondite,
shadiness, suntanned, tenebrity,
tenebrose, tenebrous 10 caliginous,
cloudiness, dark-haired, despicable,
disastrous, forbidding, gloominess,
iniquitous, mysterious, tenebrious,
unpleasant 11 concealment,
crepuscular, dark-skinned, distressing,
frightening, inscrutable, sunlessness,
tenebrosity 12 crepusculous
13 unenlightened, unilluminated
14 unintelligible

darken
03 dim, fog 04 fade 05 blind, cloud,
colly, frown, sable, shade, sully
06 deject, sadden, shadow
07 benight, blacken, depress, eclipse,
embrown, imbrown, obscure 08 cast
down 09 cloud over, grow angry, look
angry, obfuscate, overshade, weigh
down 10 grow darker, make gloomy,
obnubilate, overshadow, sclerotize
11 become angry 12 become darker
13 disilluminate

darkly
05 dimly 06 glumly 07 at night,
blackly, by night 08 dismally, gloomily,
sullenly 09 obscurely 11 cryptically,
inscrutably 12 in the shadows,
mysteriously 13 enigmatically

darkness *see* dark

darling
03 hon, luv, pet 04 dear, duck, hero,
idol, love, peat 05 angel, honey, loved,
sugar, sweet 06 adored, dautie,
dawtie, minion, poppet, prized
07 acushla, asthore, beloved, dearest,
dilling, minikin, sweetie 08 dearling,
precious, sweeting, treasure
09 celebrity, cherished, favourite,
treasured 10 delightful, mavourneen,

sweetheart 11 blue-eyed boy,
teacher's pet, white-haired 13 fair-
haired boy 14 apple of your eye

darmstadtium
02 Ds

darn
03 sew 04 drat, mend 05 patch, sew
up 06 cobble, repair, stitch

dart
03 fly, run 04 barb, bolt, cast, cook,
dace, dare, dash, flit, hurl, leap, plan,
race, rush, send, skit, tear, toss
05 arrow, bound, flash, fling, lance,
lanch, scoot, shaft, shoot, sling, start,
throw 06 endart, flight, glance, launch,
pounce, propel, scheme, scurry,
spring, sprint, strike, wheech
07 feather, harpoon, project
08 spiculum 09 fléchette, love-arrow,
love-shaft 10 banderilla

dash
◇ *anagram indicator*
03 bit, cut, dad, dah, fly, hie, jaw, nip,
pop, run, tad, zip 04 bang, beat, bolt,
brio, dart, daud, ding, dive, drop, élan,
hint, hurl, lash, life, pash, race, ramp,
rash, ruin, rule, rush, slam, spot, tear,
toss 05 blank, blash, bound, break,
bribe, crash, crush, fling, force, grain,
gusto, hurry, pinch, plash, pound, scart,
shine, smash, souse, spang, speck,
speed, spoil, spurt, swash, swill, throw,
tinge, touch, trace, verve, wreck
06 blight, dampen, energy, hurtle,
jabble, little, relish, sadden, sluice,
spirit, splash, sprint, streak, strike,
stroke, thwart, vigour, wheech
07 depress, destroy, fervour, flavour, let
down, passion, pizzazz, scuttle,
shatter, smidgen, soupçon, sparkle,
viretot 08 confound, gratuity,
scramble, vitality, vivacity
09 animation, devastate, frustrate
10 disappoint, discourage, dishearten,
enthusiasm, liveliness, suggestion
• **dash off**
06 scrawl 07 jot down 08 scribble

dashing
◇ *anagram indicator*
04 bold 05 doggy, showy, smart
06 dapper, daring, lively, plucky, rakish
07 elegant, gallant, go-ahead, raffish,
stylish, varment, varmint 08 animated,
debonair, slap-bang, slashing,
smashing, spirited, vigorous
09 energetic, exuberant 10 attractive,
flamboyant 11 fashionable

dastard
06 coward 07 hilding

dastardly
03 low 04 base, evil, mean, vile
06 craven, wicked 07 nithing
08 cowardly, fiendish 09 underhand
10 despicable, diabolical, iniquitous
11 lily-livered 12 contemptible, faint-
hearted

data
04 info 05 facts, input 07 details,
figures 08 features, material, research

09 documents 10 statistics
11 information, particulars
• **collection of data**
04 file

date
01 d 03 age, day, era 04 ides, time,
week, year 05 court, epoch, go out,
month, stage, tryst 06 belong, decade,
epocha, escort, friend, go back, go
with, period, steady 07 century,
meeting, partner, take out 08 come
from, young man 09 boyfriend, exist
from, go out with, man friend,
obsolesce, originate, young lady 10 be
together, engagement, girlfriend, go
out of use, lady friend, millennium,
rendezvous, show its age
11 appointment, assignation, woman
friend 12 go steady with 14 become
obsolete, be involved with
• **to date**
03 yet 05 as yet, so far 07 up to now
08 until now 14 up to the present
• **without date**
02 sa, sd

dated
05 passé 06 old hat, square 07 archaic
08 obsolete, outdated, outmoded
09 out-of-date, unstylish
10 antiquated, superseded
11 obsolescent 12 old-fashioned
13 unfashionable

daub
03 dab 04 blot, coat, gaum, gorm,
spot, teer 05 cover, paint, slake,
smalm, smarm, smear, stain, sully
06 bedaub, blotch, clatch, smirch,
smudge, splash 07 plaster, slubber,
spatter, splodge, splotch 08 splatter
09 beplaster, bespatter 10 blottesque

daughter
01 d 03 dau 04 girl, lass 05 child, fille
06 lassie 08 disciple 09 offspring
10 descendant, inhabitant

Daughters include:

04 Anne (Princess), Hero, Kate, Page
(Anne)
05 Freud (Anna), Lloyd (Emily), Mills
(Hayley), O'Neal (Tatum), Regan
06 Bhutto (Benazir), Bianca, Fatima,
Fisher (Carrie), Forbes (Emma),
Gandhi (Indira), Imogen, Juliet,
Marina
07 Electra, Forsyte (Fleur), Goneril,
Jessica, Lavinia, Miranda, Ophelia,
Perdita, Presley (Lisa Marie)
08 Cordelia, Lovelace (Ada), Minnelli
(Liza), Williams (Shirley)
09 Cassandra, du Maurier (Daphne),
Katharina, McCartney (Stella),
Pankhurst (Christabel)
10 Beckinsale (Kate), Richardson
(Joely), Richardson (Natasha),
Rossellini (Isabella)
13 Princess Royal

daunt
03 cow 04 adaw, faze, pall 05 abash,
alarm, amate, deter, quail, scare, shake
06 dismay, put off, rattle, ruffle, subdue

07 overawe, unnerve **08** dispirit, frighten **09** take aback **10** demoralize, disconcert, discourage, dishearten, intimidate **11** disillusion

daunted
04 mate **05** quayd

daunting
05 scary **08** alarming **09** unnerving **11** dispiriting, frightening **12** demoralizing, discouraging, intimidating **13** disconcerting, disheartening

dauntingly
07 scarily **10** alarmingly **11** unnervingly **13** dispiritingly, frighteningly **14** demoralizingly, discouragingly, intimidatingly **15** disconcertingly, dishearteningly

dauntless
04 bold **05** brave, stout **06** daring, plucky **07** doughty, valiant **08** fearless, intrepid, resolute **09** undaunted **10** courageous, determined **11** indomitable

dawdle
03 lag **05** dally, delay, drawl, tarry, trail **06** diddle, linger, loiter, potter, putter **07** saunter **08** go slowly **09** faff about, hang about **10** dilly-dally **11** take too long **12** drag your feet, take your time

dawn
04 open, rise **05** begin, birth, break, gleam, onset, start, sun-up **06** advent, appear, arrive, Aurora, be born, emerge, origin, spring **07** arrival, day-peep, develop, genesis, glimmer, lighten, morning, sunrise **08** brighten, cock-crow, commence, daybreak, daylight **09** beginning, dayspring, emergence, grow light, inception, originate **10** break of day, first light **11** become light, crack of dawn **12** commencement **13** come into being
* **dawn on**
03 hit **05** click **06** sink in, strike **07** occur to, realize **12** register with

day
01 d **03** age, era **04** date, dies, Ides, jour, peak, time **05** bloom, epoch, flush, Nones, prime **06** heyday, period **07** calends, daytime, kalends **08** daylight **09** golden age **10** generation **13** daylight hours

See also **Christmas**
* **day after day**
09 endlessly, regularly **10** repeatedly **11** continually, perpetually **12** monotonously, persistently, relentlessly, time and again **13** again and again
* **day by day**
08 steadily **09** gradually **13** progressively **15** slowly but surely
* **day in, day out**
08 every day **09** endlessly, regularly **10** repeatedly **11** continually **12** monotonously, persistently, time and again **13** again and again
* **day's end**
03 e'en, ene, eve **04** even **07** evening
* **have had its day**
08 be past it **11** be out of date
* **number of days**
04 week, year **05** month **07** weekend **09** fortnight
* **these days**
02 AD
* **three times a day**
03 tid
* **time of day**
04 seal, seel, seil, sele

daybreak
04 dawn, morn **05** sun-up **06** Aurora **07** morning, sunrise **08** cock-crow, daylight **10** break of day, first light **11** crack of dawn **12** skreigh of day

daydream
04 muse, wish **05** dream, fancy **06** musing, trance, vision **07** fantasy, figment, imagine, reverie **09** fantasize, imagining, pipe dream, switch off **11** inattention **13** be lost in space, woolgathering **14** stare into space **15** be in a brown study, castles in the air, not pay attention

daydreamer
06 rêveur **07** dreamer, rêveuse **08** idealist, romantic **09** fantasist, visionary **10** Don Quixote, fantasizer **11** Walter Mitty

daylight
03 day **04** dawn **05** light, sun-up **07** daytime, high day, morning, sunrise **08** broad day, cock-crow, daybreak, sunlight **10** break of day, first light **11** crack of dawn **12** natural light

daze
04 dare, numb, spin, stun **05** amaze, blind, gally, knock, shock, whirl **06** baffle, dazzle, stupor, trance **07** astound, confuse, perplex, stagger, startle, stupefy **08** astonish, bewilder, blow away, bowl over, knock out, numbness, paralyse, surprise **09** confusion, dumbfound, take aback **11** distraction, flabbergast, knock for six **12** bewilderment

dazed
◇ *anagram indicator*
03 out **05** muzzy, silly, totty, woozy **06** amazed, groggy, numbed, punchy **07** baffled, dazzled, shocked, stunned **08** confused, startled **09** astounded, blown away, paralysed, perplexed, staggered, stupefied, surprised **10** astonished, bewildered, bowled over, punch-drunk, speechless, taken aback **11** dumbfounded, unconscious **13** flabbergasted

dazzle
03 awe, wow **04** blur, daze **05** amaze, blaze, blend, blind, flare, flash, glare, gleam **06** bedaze, strike **07** bewitch, confuse, glitter, impress, overawe, sparkle, stupefy **08** astonish, bedazzle, bowl over, knock out **09** dumbfound, fascinate, hypnotize, overpower, overwhelm, splendour **10** brightness, brilliance, razzmatazz **11** scintillate **12** magnificence **13** scintillation

dazzling
05 glaik, grand **06** bright, superb **07** glaring, radiant, shining **08** blinding, glorious, splendid, stunning **09** brilliant, ravishing, sparkling **10** foudroyant, glittering, impressive **11** psychedelic, sensational, spectacular **12** awe-inspiring, breathtaking **13** scintillating

dazzlingly
8 brightly, superbly **09** glaringly,
radiantly **10** blindingly, gloriously
11 brilliantly **12** impressively
13 sensationally, spectacularly
14 breathtakingly

deactivate
4 stop **07** disable **08** paralyse
10 immobilize **14** put out of action

dead
1 d **03** dec **04** bang, bung, bust, cold,
dull, flat, gone, late, numb, very
5 dated, exact, inert, kaput, napoo,
passé, quiet, quite, smack, stiff, tired,
total, utter, waned **06** asleep, barren,
benumb, boring, broken, deaden,
entire, frigid, no more, old hat, really,
sleepy, torpid **07** awfully, defunct,
disused, exactly, expired, extinct,
humdrum, perfect, tedious, utterly,
worn out **08** absolute, ad patres,
benumbed, complete, dead beat,
deceased, departed, directly, inactive,
feless, lukewarm, obsolete, outright,
passed on, perished, straight, terribly,
thorough, tired out, unerring
09 apathetic, bloodless, conked out,
deathlike, downright, exanimate,
exhausted, extremely, inanimate,
inelastic, insensate, knackered, out of
date, paralysed, thanatoid, unfeeling
10 absolutely, breathless, broken-
down, brown bread, completely,
insentient, not working, on the blink,
on the fritz, out of order, passed away,
spiritless, unexciting **11** dead as a dodo,
emotionless, gone to sleep,
immediately, indifferent, ineffective,
insensitive, off the hooks, ready to
drop, unemotional, unqualified
12 discontinued, six feet under,
unresponsive **13** exceptionally,
uninteresting, unsympathetic **14** no
longer spoken **15** dead as a doornail

deaden
4 dull, hush, mute, numb **05** abate,
allay, blunt, check, slake **06** benumb,
dampen, harden, lessen, muffle,
obtund, reduce, soothe, stifle, subdue,
weaken **07** assuage, mortify, quieten,
smother **08** diminish, mitigate,
moderate, paralyse, suppress
09 alleviate **11** desensitize
12 anaesthetize **14** take the edge off
15 make insensitive

deadline
4 term, time **06** time up **08** timeline
09 time limit **10** target date

deadlock
4 halt **05** stale **06** log jam **07** dead
end, impasse **08** stand-off, stoppage
09 checkmate, stalemate **10** standstill

deadly
4 dull, fell, grim, sure, true **05** fatal,
feral, great, hated, quite, toxic **06** bitter,
boring, fierce, funest, lethal, marked,
mortal, savage **07** deathly, extreme,
humdrum, intense, killing, noxious,
perfect, precise, serious, tedious,
totally, utterly **08** accurate, deathful,

entirely, flawless, mortific, unerring,
venomous **09** dangerous, deathlike,
effective, extremely, malignant,
murderous, perfectly, pestilent,
thanatoid, unfailing **10** absolutely,
completely, dreadfully, implacable,
monotonous, pernicious, thoroughly,
unexciting **11** destructive, internecine,
internecive **12** death-dealing
13 uninteresting **14** irreconcilable
15 life-threatening

deadpan
05 blank, empty **09** impassive
10 poker-faced **11** emotionless,
inscrutable **12** inexpressive,
unexpressive **13** dispassionate,
straight-faced **14** expressionless

deaf
04 surd **05** dunny **07** unmoved
08 heedless **09** oblivious, stone-deaf,
unmindful, untouched **10** cloth-eared,
impervious, unaffected **11** deaf as a
post, inattentive, indifferent,
unconcerned **13** hard of hearing
15 hearing-impaired

deafening
07 booming, ringing, roaring
08 piercing, very loud **09** very noisy
10 resounding, thundering,
thunderous **11** ear-piercing **12** ear-
splitting, overwhelming
13 reverberating

deal
02 go **03** act, buy, lot **04** flog, hand,
load, mart, mete, pact, push, vend
05 allot, reach, round, serve, share,
stock, trade, treat **06** amount, assign,
bestow, degree, direct, divide, export,
extent, handle, market, strike
07 bargain, deliver, dish out, dole out,
give out, inflict, mete out, operate,
portion, traffic **08** contract, covenant,
dispense, quantity **09** agreement,
apportion, negotiate, treatment
10 administer, buy and sell, distribute,
do business **11** arrangement,
transaction **12** distribution
13 understanding
• **deal out**
04 dole, help **06** divide **08** dispense
10 distribute
• **deal with**
04 cope, sort **05** cover, see to, touch,
treat **06** handle, manage, tackle
07 be about, concern, process,
sort out **08** attend to, consider, cope
with **09** look after **10** take care of
12 have to do with **14** get to grips
with
• **good deal**
07 bargain
• **great deal**
03 lot **04** heap, mort, much, some
05 heaps, power, sight, world

dealer
03 dlr **04** tout **05** agent, coper
06 broker, couper, hawker, monger,
pedlar, pusher, seller, totter, trader,
vendor **07** chapman, fripper
08 marketer, merchant, retailer,

salesman, supplier **09** brinjarry,
fripperer **10** saleswoman, trafficker,
wholesaler **11** distributor, salesperson
12 merchandizer

dealing, dealings
05 trade, truck **07** trading, traffic
08 business, commerce **09** marketing,
operation, relations **10** chevisance,
operations **11** association,
connections, intercourse,
merchandise, trafficking, transaction
12 negotiations, transactions
13 communication

dean
03 den **04** dell, dene, head
05 doyen, slade, Swift **08** director
09 principal, rural dean **11** chapter
head, vicar-forane **12** Very Reverend
13 head of faculty **14** cardinal-
bishop
• **rural dean**
02 RD **10** arch-priest **11** vicar-forane

dear
03 joy, pet **04** cher, chou, high, lamb,
leve, lief, love, posh, salt **05** angel,
chère, close, honey, lieve, loved, steep,
sugar, sweet **06** adored, costly, pricey,
scarce, valued **07** beloved, darling,
earnest, machree, sky-high, sweetie
08 esteemed, familiar, favoured,
grievous, high-cost, intimate, loved
one, not cheap, precious, treasure
09 big-ticket, chargeful, cherished,
endearing, excessive, expensive,
favourite, respected, treasured
10 exorbitant, high-priced,
mavourneen, overpriced, sweetheart
11 well-beloved **12** au poids de l'or,
costing a bomb, extortionate
15 costing the earth, daylight
robbery

dearer
04 loor

dearly
06 deeply, fondly **07** greatly
08 lovingly, tenderly, very much
09 adoringly, devotedly, earnestly,
extremely **10** a great deal, intimately,
profoundly, with favour **11** with respect
12 at a great cost, at a high price
13 with affection, with great loss
14 affectionately

dearth
04 lack, need, want **06** famine
07 absence, paucity, poverty
08 dearness, scarcity, shortage,
sparsity **10** barrenness, deficiency,
inadequacy, meagreness, scantiness
12 exiguousness **13** insufficiency

death
03 end **04** loss, ruin **06** finish
07 decease, undoing **08** curtains,
downfall, the grave **09** cessation,
departure, mortality, perishing
10 defunction, expiration, extinction
11 destruction, dissolution,
eradication, extirpation, termination
12 annihilation, obliteration
13 extermination

Death-related terms include:

03 DOA, RIP, urn
04 bier, cist, mort, obit, pall, pyre, sati, soul, toll, tomb, wake, will
05 ashes, bardo, cairn, dirge, elegy, éloge, elogy, grave, mourn, shiva, tangi, vigil, widow
06 Azrael, bedral, burial, chadar, coffin, corpse, demise, entomb, eulogy, exequy, fossor, grieve, hearse, lament, lethal, martyr, monody, mortal, orphan, rosary, shibah, shivah, shroud, suttee, wreath
07 autopsy, bederal, bereave, coroner, cortège, cremate, crucify, elogium, epitaph, funeral, inquest, karoshi, keening, mastaba, mourner, passing, quietus, requiem, widower
08 casualty, cemetery, cenotaph, deathbed, death row, deceased, disinter, dispatch, eulogium, fatality, grieving, hara-kiri, interred, last post, long home, mortbell, mortuary, mourning, necropsy, necrosis, obituary, yahrzeit
09 committal, cremation, dead march, death mask, graveside, graveyard, headstone, interment, last rites, mass grave, mausoleum, mortician, obsequies, passing on, sacrifice, sepulchre, testament, tombstone, year's mind
10 death knell, euthanasia, grim reaper, necropolis, obituarist, pall-bearer, posthumous, predecease, strae death, undertaker
11 bereavement, crematorium, eternal rest, funeral home, grave-digger, last honours, passing away, passing bell, requiem mass, rest in peace, rigor mortis, sarcophagus, suicide pact
12 burial ground, debt of nature, disinterment, last farewell, mercy killing, resting place, the other side
13 burial society, natural causes
14 extreme unction, funeral parlour
15 funeral director, resurrectionist

• **after death**
02 PM **10** posthumous, post-mortem
• **approach of death**
03 fit
• **by reason of death**
02 cm
• **put to death**
03 gas **04** do in, hang, kill **05** lynch, press, shoot, waste **06** behead, martyr, rub out **07** bump off, crucify, execute, take out **08** blow away, despatch, dispatch, knock off **09** transport
10 decapitate, guillotine
11 electrocute, exterminate
• **repose of death**
04 rest

deathless
07 eternal, undying **08** immortal, timeless **09** memorable **10** ever-living
11 everlasting, never-ending
12 imperishable **13** incorruptible, unforgettable

deathly
03 wan **04** grim, pale **05** ashen, fatal, white **06** deadly, mortal, pallid, utmost
07 extreme, ghastly, ghostly, haggard, harmful, intense **08** terrible
09 deathlike, ghost-like, thanatoid
10 cadaverous, colourless

debacle
04 hash, rout, ruin **05** farce, havoc
06 cock-up, defeat, fiasco, foul-up
07 failure, screw-up, turmoil, washout
08 collapse, disaster, downfall, reversal, stampede **09** cataclysm, overthrow, ruination **11** catastrophe, devastation **14** disintegration

debar
03 ban, bar **04** deny, stop **05** eject, expel **06** cut out, forbid, hamper, hinder **07** exclude, keep out, prevent, shut out, suspend **08** conclude, obstruct, preclude, prohibit, restrain
09 blackball, proscribe, segregate
10 disqualify

debarred
03 out

debase
05 abase, allay, alloy, lower, shame, taint **06** bemean, defile, demean, dilute, embace, embase, humble, imbase, reduce **07** cheapen, corrupt, degrade, devalue, pollute, vitiate
08 disgrace **09** discredit, dishonour, humiliate **10** adulterate, bastardize, sensualize **11** contaminate

debased
03 low **04** base, vile **05** hedge
06 abased, fallen, impure, shamed, sinful, sordid, vulgar **07** corrupt, defiled, humbled, immoral, tainted
08 degraded, devalued, polluted, reversed **09** cheapened, debauched, disgraced, perverted **10** degenerate, humiliated, prostitute **11** adulterated, discredited, dishonoured
12 contaminated

debasement
05 shame **08** disgrace **09** abasement, dishonour, pollution **10** cheapening, corruption, defilement, perversion
11 degradation, depravation, devaluation, humiliation
12 adulteration, degeneration
13 contamination

debatable
04 moot **06** unsure **07** dubious, unclear **08** arguable, doubtful
09 uncertain, undecided, unsettled
10 disputable **11** contentious, contestable **12** questionable
13 controversial, problematical
14 open to question

debate
05 argue, fight, flyte, forum, weigh
06 combat, ponder, powwow, reason
07 contend, contest, discept, discuss, dispute, flyting, polemic, reflect, teach-in, wrangle, wrestle
08 argument, cogitate, consider, mull over, polemics, talk over **09** altercate,

forensics, kick about, talk about, talkathon, think over, thrash out
10 contention, deliberate, discussion, kick around, knock about, meditate on, reflection **11** altercation, controversy, disputation, knock around, talk through **12** cut and thrust, deliberatio
13 consideration **15** exchange of views

debauch
03 wet **04** ruin **05** whore **06** debosh, ravish, seduce **07** corrupt, deprave, pervert, pollute, subvert, violate, vitiate **10** lead astray **11** over-indulge

debauched
04 lewd **06** wanton **07** corrupt, debased, immoral, riotous
08 decadent, degraded, depraved, rakehell **09** abandoned, carousing, corrupted, dissolute, excessive, perverted **10** degenerate, dissipated, licentious, profligate **11** intemperate, promiscuous **13** overindulgent

debauchery
04 lust, orgy, riot **05** revel **06** excess
07 licence, license **08** carousal, lewdness **09** decadence, depravity
10 corruption, degeneracy, immorality, rakishness, wantonness
11 degradation, dissipation, libertinage, libertinism
12 intemperance **13** dissoluteness
14 licentiousness, overindulgence
• **place of debauchery**
03 sty

debenture
04 bond

debilitate
03 sap **04** tire **05** drain **06** impair, weaken **07** cripple, exhaust, fatigue, wear out **08** enervate, enfeeble
09 undermine **10** devitalize
12 incapacitate

debilitating
06 tiring **09** crippling, fatiguing, impairing, weakening **10** enervating, enervative, enfeebling, exhausting, wearing out **11** undermining
14 incapacitating

debility
05 atony **07** fatigue, frailty, languor, malaise **08** asthenia, weakness
09 atonicity, faintness, infirmity, tiredness, weariness **10** enervation, exhaustion, feebleness, incapacity, myasthenia **11** decrepitude
12 enfeeblement, lack of energy, neurasthenia **14** lack of vitality

debit
• **direct debit**
02 DD

debonair
05 suave **06** breezy, jaunty, smooth, urbane **07** affable, buoyant, dashing, elegant, refined, stylish **08** carefree, charming, cheerful, cultured, well-bred **09** courteous, dignified **12** light-hearted **13** sophisticated

debrief

05 grill 07 examine 08 question
09 interview 11 interrogate 12 cross-examine 13 cross-question

debris

▷ anagram indicator

04 bits, muck 05 drift, dross, ruins, crap, trash, waste, wreck 06 bahada, bajada, litter, pieces, refuse, rubble, tephra 07 eluvium, remains, rubbish 08 detritus, wreckage 09 fragments, sweepings 12 pyroclastics
• **pile of debris**
03 tel 04 tell

debt

03 dew, due, IOU, sin 04 bill, duty, hock 05 claim, debit, score 06 charge 07 account, arrears 08 money due 09 amount due, liability, overdraft 10 aes alienum, commitment, money owing, obligation 11 amount owing 12 indebtedness
• **in debt**
06 in hock 08 in the red 09 gone under, in arrears, insolvent 10 owing money 11 in overdraft 13 gone to the wall, in Queer Street
• **indication of debt**
03 red
• **in someone's debt**
07 obliged 08 beholden, indebted, thankful 11 honour-bound 12 appreciative

debtor

02 Dr 07 debitor 08 bankrupt, borrower, deadbeat 09 defaulter, insolvent, mortgagor 10 abbey-laird, fly-by-night

debunk

04 mock 05 quash 06 expose, show up 07 deflate, explode, lampoon 08 disprove, puncture, ridicule 13 cut down to size

debut, début

05 start 06 launch 08 entrance, première 09 beginning, coming-out, first time, launching 10 first night, initiation 12 inauguration, introduction, presentation 14 first recording 15 first appearance

debutante, débutante

03 bud, deb 05 debby

decadence

04 fall 05 decay 07 decline 09 depravity 10 corruption, debasement, debauchery, degeneracy, immorality, perversion 11 dissipation, dissolution 12 degeneration 13 deterioration, retrogression 14 degenerateness, licentiousness, self-indulgence

decadent

06 effete 07 corrupt, debased, immoral 08 decaying, degraded, depraved 09 debauched, declining, dissolute, symbolist 10 Babylonian, degenerate, dissipated, licentious 12 degenerating, unprincipled 13 deteriorating, self-indulgent

decamp

03 fly, guy 04 bolt, flee, flit 05 lam it, scrap, slide, slope, split 06 desert, escape, hook it, levant, mizzle, run off 07 abscond, do a bunk, make off, run away, scamper, scarper, take off, vamoose 08 light out, slope off, up sticks 09 do a runner, skedaddle 10 hightail it, make tracks 12 absquatulate 14 take in on the lam

decant

03 tap 05 drain 07 draw off, pour out 08 transfer 09 siphon off

decapitate

◇ head deletion indicator

06 behead, unhead 07 execute 10 guillotine

decay

03 rot 04 blet, doat, dote, fail, ruin, rust, sink 05 faint, go bad, go off, mould, spoil, waste 06 blight, canker, caries, dry rot, empare, fading, fester, fungus, impair, mildew, perish, weaken, wet rot, wither 07 atrophy, corrode, crumble, decline, dwindle, empaire, empayre, failing, failure, forfair, go to pot, putrefy, rotting, shrivel, wasting 08 collapse, downfall, foxiness, going bad, wear away 09 crumbling, decadence, decadency, decompose, perishing, putridity, waste away, weakening, withering 10 debasement, declension, decompound, degenerate, go downhill 11 deteriorate, go to the dogs, labefaction, putrescence 12 degeneration, disintegrate, putrefaction 13 consenescence, consenescency, decomposition, deterioration, labefactation 14 disintegration

decayed

03 bad, off 04 rank, sour 05 druxy, stale 06 addled, failed, mouldy, putrid, rotten, sleepy, wasted 07 carious, carrion, doddard, rotting, ruinous, spoiled 08 corroded, doddered, mildewed, perished, withered 09 putrefied 10 decomposed, dirt-rotten, putrescent 12 impoverished

decease

03 die, end 04 rest 05 death, dying 06 demise 07 passing 09 departure, passing on 10 expiration 11 dissolution, passing away

deceased

03 dec 04 dead, gone, late, lost 06 asleep, former, no more 07 defunct, expired, extinct 08 departed, finished 12 six feet under 15 dead as a doornail

deceit

03 con 04 fake, game, ruse, sham, wile 05 abuse, dodge, feint, fraud, guile, guyle 06 barrat 07 cunning, forgery, glozing, slenter, slinter, slyness, swindle 08 artifice, cheating, coquetry, cozenage, pretence, trickery, wiliness 09 chicanery, deception, duplicity, falseness, gold brick, hypocrisy,

invention, malengine, phenakism, stratagem, treachery 10 craftiness, imposition, subterfuge 11 fraudulence 13 double-dealing 14 monkey business 15 underhandedness

deceitful

03 sly 04 foxy, jive, rusé 05 false, lying, Punic, sharp 06 braide, crafty, double, forked, sneaky, tricky 07 crooked, cunning, devious, elusory, knavish 08 coloured, guileful, illusory, two-faced 09 deceiving, deceptive, designing, dishonest, insincere, underhand 10 deceptious, fraudulent, Janus-faced, mendacious, perfidious, untruthful 11 counterfeit, dissembling, duplicitous, prestigious, treacherous 12 false-hearted, hypocritical 13 double-dealing, double-tongued, untrustworthy

deceitfully

05 slyly 06 double 07 falsely 08 craftily, sneakily 09 cunningly 11 deceivingly, deceptively, dishonestly, insincerely 12 fraudulently, mendaciously, perfidiously, untruthfully 13 duplicitously, treacherously, underhandedly 14 hypocritically

deceive

02 do 03 cog, con, gag, kid, lie 04 bite, do in, dupe, flam, fool, gull, hoax, mock 05 abuse, blind, bluff, cheat, false, put on, trick, trump 06 befool, betray, delude, entrap, have on, humbug, lead on, misuse, outwit, seduce, slip up 07 beguile, cheat on, chicane, defraud, ensnare, mislead, swindle, two-time 08 hoodwink, misguide, outsmart 09 bamboozle, dissemble, mislippen 10 camouflage, disappoint, impose upon 11 double-cross, hornswoggle, set a trap for, string along 12 put one over on, take for a ride 13 put a cheat upon 14 pull a fast one on

deceiver

04 fake 05 cheat, crook, fraud 06 abuser, con man, falser, guiler, guyler, hoaxer 07 deluder, diddler, seducer 08 betrayer, impostor, swindler, treacher 09 charlatan, hypocrite, inveigler, treachour, tregetour, trickster 10 dissembler, mountebank 11 treachetour 12 double-dealer

decelerate

04 slow 05 brake 06 retard 08 slow down 11 reduce speed 12 go more slowly 14 put the brakes on

December

03 Dec

decency

07 decorum, fitness, modesty 08 civility, courtesy, fairness 09 etiquette, good taste, integrity, propriety 10 politeness, seemliness 11 correctness, helpfulness, uprightness 14 respectability

decent

02 OK **03** fit **04** fair, kind, nice, pure **05** civil **06** chaste, honest, modest, polite, proper, seemly, worthy **07** correct, ethical, fitting, gradely, helpful, upright **08** adequate, becoming, decorous, generous, gracious, graithly, moderate, obliging, passable, pleasant, suitable, tasteful, virtuous, wise-like **09** befitting, competent, courteous, dignified, tolerable **10** acceptable, dependable, reasonable, salubrious, sufficient, thoughtful **11** appropriate, presentable, respectable, trustworthy **12** satisfactory **13** accommodating

decently

06 fairly, nicely **08** honestly, politely, properly, suitably **09** correctly, ethically, helpfully, tolerably **10** acceptably, adequately, becomingly, decorously, generously, graciously, obligingly, reasonably **11** courteously, presentably, respectably **12** sufficiently, thoughtfully **13** appropriately **14** satisfactorily

decentralize

07 devolve **08** delegate, localize **11** regionalize **13** deconcentrate **14** spread outwards **15** spread downwards

deception

03 cog, con, fib, kid, lie **04** hoax, hype, ruse, scam, sell, sham, wile **05** bluff, cheat, fraud, glaik, guile, kiddy, moody, set-up, snare, sting, trick **06** deceit, have-on, humbug, take-in **07** abusion, cunning, eyewash, fallacy, fubbery, gullery, leg-pull, swindle **08** artifice, cheating, flim-flam, illusion, nonsense, pretence, put-up job, trickery **09** chicanery, chicaning, duplicity, hypocrisy, imposture, stratagem, treachery **10** craftiness, hocus-pocus, maskirovka, pious fraud, subterfuge **11** dissembling, fraudulence, insincerity, supercherie **13** deceptiveness, double-dealing, funny business, jiggery-pokery **14** false pretences **15** smoke and mirrors, underhandedness

deceptive

03 sly **04** fake, foxy, mock, sham **05** bogus, false, sharp **06** bubble, catchy, crafty, hollow **07** amusive, crooked, cunning, elusive **08** cheating, delusive, delusory, fraudful, illusive, illusory, imposing, specious, spurious **09** ambiguous, dishonest, faithless, underhand **10** fallacious, fraudulent, misleading, unreliable **11** dissembling, duplicitous

deceptively

07 falsely **10** illusively, speciously, spuriously **11** ambiguously, dishonestly **12** fraudulently, misleadingly

decibel

02 dB

decide

03 end, fix, opt **04** pick, rule, seal **05** aread, arede, go for, judge, opt in **06** choose, clinch, define, make up, opt for, select, settle, wrap up **07** adjudge, arreede, darrain, darrayn, deraign, discuss, resolve, work out **08** conclude, darraign, darraine, plump for **09** arbitrate, darraigne, determine, establish **10** adjudicate, dijudicate **11** give a ruling **12** turn the scale **13** make a decision **14** commit yourself, give a judgement, make up your mind, reach a decision **15** come to a decision

decided

04 ared, firm **05** clear **06** marked **07** certain, express, obvious **08** absolute, clear-cut, decisive, definite, distinct, emphatic, positive, resolute **10** deliberate, determined, forthright, pronounced, purposeful, undeniable, undisputed, unswerving, unwavering, well-marked **11** categorical, unambiguous, unequivocal **12** indisputable, unhesitating, unmistakable **14** unquestionable

decidedly

04 very **05** quite **07** clearly **08** markedly **09** certainly, downright, obviously **10** absolutely, decisively, definitely, distinctly, noticeably, positively **12** unmistakably **13** unequivocally **14** unquestionably

decider

08 clincher **10** determiner **11** coup de grâce

deciding

03 key **05** chief, final, prime **06** crunch **07** crucial, supreme **08** critical, decisive **09** principal **10** conclusive **11** determining, influential, significant

decimate

05 tithe, tythe **07** destroy, flatten **09** devastate, eliminate, eradicate **10** annihilate, obliterate

decipher

04 dope **05** break, crack, solve **06** decode, detect, reveal **07** dope out, make out, suss out, unravel, work out **08** construe **09** figure out, interpret, translate **10** descramble, understand, unscramble **11** make sense of **13** transliterate

decision

05 arrêt, award, parti **06** decree, firman, result, ruling **07** finding, opinion, outcome, purpose, resolve, verdict **08** firmness, last word, sentence **09** judgement **10** conclusion, resolution, settlement **11** arbitration **12** adjudication, decisiveness, forcefulness **13** determination, pronouncement **14** recommendation

decisive

03 key **04** firm **05** crisp, fatal, final, prime **06** strong **07** crucial, decided,

fateful **08** absolute, critical, deciding, definite, forceful, positive, resolute **09** effectual, momentous, principal **10** conclusive, definitive, determined, forthright, purposeful, unswerving, unwavering **11** determinate, determining, influential, significant **12** single-minded, strong-minded

decisively

06 firmly **08** strongly **09** crucially, fatefully **10** absolutely, critically, forcefully, positively, resolutely **11** momentously **12** conclusively, definitively, determinedly, forthrightly, purposefully, unswervingly, unwaveringly **13** influentially, significantly **14** single-mindedly

deck

02 dk **03** rig, tog **04** pack, prim, trap, trim **05** adorn, array, cover, grace **06** bedeck, betrim, clothe, enrich, ground, tart up **07** festoon, garland, garnish, trick up **08** beautify, covering, decorate, ornament, platform, prettify, trick out **09** embellish

• deck out

03 rig, tog **04** do up, garb, robe **05** adorn, array, dress, get up, prick **06** clothe, doll up, tart up **07** dress up **08** decorate

declaim

04 rant **05** mouth, orate, spiel, spout **06** recite **07** bespout, elocute, lecture **08** disclaim, harangue, perorate, proclaim, sound off **09** hold forth, pronounce, sermonize **11** expostulate, speak boldly

declamation

04 rant **06** sermon, speech, tirade **07** address, lecture, oration **08** harangue **10** recitation **12** speechifying

declamatory

04 bold **05** stagy **07** fustian, orotund, pompous, stilted **08** dramatic, inflated, parlando **09** bombastic, grandiose, high-flown, overblown **10** discursive, oratorical, rhetorical, theatrical **12** magniloquent **13** grandiloquent

declaration

03 dec **04** call, dick, word **05** edict **06** avowal, decree **08** averment **09** affidavit, assertion, assurance, broadcast, manifesto, outgiving, statement, testimony **10** confession, deposition, disclosure, profession, revelation **11** affirmation, attestation, certificate, enunciation **12** announcement, asseveration, confirmation, denunciation, notification, proclamation, promulgation, protestation **13** communication, pronouncement **15** acknowledgement

declare

02 go **03** say, vie **04** aver, avow, read, show **05** aread, arede, claim, speak, state, swear **06** affirm, assert, attest, decree, notify, reveal **07** arreede,

certify, confess, confirm, discuss,
express, profess, protest, publish,
signify, testify, witness **08** announce,
disclose, maintain, manifest, proclaim,
set forth, validate **09** broadcast, make
known, pronounce **10** asseverate,
promulgate **11** communicate

declared
04 ared **06** avowed, stated **07** confest
09 confessed, professed

decline
03 dip, ebb, rot, sag, set **04** balk, deny,
drop, fade, fail, fall, flag, hill, nill, sink,
slip, wane, welk **05** abate, avoid, baulk,
decay, droop, forgo, lapse, quail, slant,
slide, slope, slump, stoop, traik
06 devall, forego, go down, lessen,
plunge, recede, reduce, refuse, reject,
sunset, waning, weaken, wither,
worsen **07** descend, descent, deviate,
drop-off, dwindle, evening, failing,
failure, fall off, get less, go to pot,
incline, plummet, regress, say no to,
subside, tail off **08** come down,
decrease, diminish, downturn, fall
away, lowering, nosedive, peter out,
turn down **09** abatement, catabasis,
decadence, decadency, declivity,
deviation, downswing, dwindling,
lessening, recession, reduction,
repudiate, weakening, worsening
10 become less, condescend, de-
escalate, degenerate, diminution,
divergence, falling-off, go downhill, go
to pieces, sunsetting **11** declination,
dégringoler, deteriorate **12** de-
escalation, degeneration
13 deterioration, retrogression

decode
04 dope **05** clear, crack **07** decrypt,
dope out, make out, unravel, work out
08 construe, decipher, uncipher
09 figure out, interpret, translate
10 understand, unscramble
13 transliterate

decomposable
10 degradable **12** destructible
13 biodegradable
14 decompoundable

decompose
◇ *anagram indicator*
03 rot **05** decay, go bad, go off, spoil
06 fester **07** break up, crumble,
degrade, putrefy **08** dissolve,
fragment, pyrolyse, separate **09** break
down **10** decompound
12 depolymerize, disintegrate

decomposition
03 rot **05** decay **07** rotting **08** going
bad, going off **09** perishing, putridity,
pyrolysis **10** corruption, hydrolysis,
photolysis, radiolysis **11** degradation,
dissolution, putrescence
12 electrolysis, fermentation,
putrefaction **14** disintegration

decontaminate
05 clean, purge **06** purify **07** cleanse
08 fumigate, sanitize **09** disinfect,
sterilize

décor
07 scenery **10** decoration
11 furnishings **12** colour scheme
13 ornamentation

decorate
03 ice **04** cite, deck, do up, hang, pink,
trim **05** adorn, array, chase, crown,
grace, paint, paper **06** bedaub, colour,
daiker, enrich, fangle, honour, parget,
reward, tart up **07** bedizen, bemedal,
deck out, embrave, festoon, furbish,
garland, garnish, smarten, trick up
08 beautify, damaskin, ornament,
prettify, renovate, spruce up, trick out
09 damascene, damaskeen,
damasquin, embellish, guilloche,
refurbish, scrimshaw, wallpaper
10 damasceene **12** give a medal to
13 give an award to **14** give an honour
to

decoration
04 paua, star **05** award, badge, cross,
crown, décor, frill, honor, medal, mural,
order, title **06** bauble, doodad,
doodah, emblem, honour, laurel,
parget, ribbon, scroll, wreath
07 bunting, colours, garland, garnish,
trinket **08** diamanté, flourish, frou-
frou, insignia, ornament, parament,
trimming **09** adornment
10 enrichment, Japanesery, knick-
knack **11** elaboration, enhancement,
furnishings **12** colour scheme
13 embellishment, ornamentation
14 beautification

See also **honour**; **military**

decorative
05 fancy **06** flashy, ornate, pretty,
rococo **08** adorning **09** elaborate,
enhancing **10** ornamental
11 beautifying, prettifying
12 embellishing **13** non-functional

decorous
03 fit **05** staid **06** comely, decent,
modest, polite, proper, sedate, seemly
07 correct, courtly, refined
08 becoming, mannerly, menseful,
suitable **09** befitting, dignified
11 appropriate, comme il faut, well-
behaved **13** parliamentary

decorum
05 grace **07** decency, dignity, honesty,
modesty **08** breeding, courtesy, good
form, protocol **09** behaviour,
etiquette, propriety, restraint
10 conformity, deportment,
politeness, seemliness **11** good
manners **14** respectability

decoy
04 bait, draw, lead, lure, tice, tole, toll,
trap **05** dummy, piper, roper, shill,
snare, stale, stall, tempt **06** allure,
bonnet, button, entice, entrap, seduce,
trepan **07** attract, deceive, ensnare,
pitfall, roper-in **08** inveigle, pretence
09 diversion **10** allurement, attraction,
enticement, inducement, red herring,
temptation **11** ensnarement, stool
pigeon, tame cheater

decrease
03 ebb **04** drop, ease, fall, loss, slim,
trim, wane **05** abate, decay, let up,
lower, slide, taper, wanze **06** decrew,
go down, lessen, plunge, reduce, shrink
07 curtail, cut back, cutback, cut down,
decline, dwindle, fall off, plummet,
slacken, subside **08** come down,
contract, diminish, downturn, lowering,
make less, peter out, rollback, slim down,
step-down, taper off **09** abatement,
decrement, dwindling, lessening,
reduction, scale down, shrinkage
10 become less, de-escalate, degression,
diminution, falling-off, subsidence
11 contraction **12** de-escalation

decree
03 act, law, saw **04** fiat, rule, will
05 edict, enact, grace, irade, novel,
order, ukase, write **06** decern, decide,
direct, enjoin, firman, modify, ordain,
ruling **07** command, dictate, lay down,
mandate, novelle, precept, statute
08 proclaim, psephism, rescript
09 determine, directive, enactment,
indiction, interdict, judgement,
manifesto, ordinance, prescribe,
pronounce, testament **10** regulation
11 hatti-sherif **12** interlocutor,
proclamation, promulgation
13 interlocution **14** senatus consult

decrepit
03 old **04** aged, weak **05** frail, warby
06 feeble, infirm, past it **07** elderly,
rickety, run-down, worn-out
08 battered, spavined **09** crumbling,
doddering, enfeebled, getting on,
senescent, tottering **10** broken-down,
clapped-out, in bad shape,
ramshackle, tumbledown
11 dilapidated, over the hill **12** falling
apart **13** falling to bits **14** in bad
condition **15** falling to pieces

decrepitude
04 ruin **05** decay **06** dotage, old age
08 debility, senility, weakness
09 infirmity **10** disability, feebleness,
incapacity, senescence **11** ricketiness
12 degeneration, dilapidation
13 deterioration **14** incapacitation

decriminalize
05 allow **06** permit, ratify **07** approve,
license, warrant **08** legalize, sanction,
validate **09** authorize **10** legitimize

decry
03 pan **04** carp, crab, slam **05** blame,
knock, slate, snipe **06** attack
07 censure, condemn, devalue, nit-
pick, run down, traduce **08** belittle,
denounce, derogate **09** criticize,
denigrate, disparage, excoriate,
underrate **10** animadvert, come down
on, depreciate, preach down,
undervalue **12** disapprove of, pull to
pieces, tear to shreds **13** find fault with,
tear a strip off **14** declaim against,
inveigh against **15** do a hatchet job on

dedicate
04 bind, give, name, open **05** bless,
offer **06** assign, commit, devote,

hallow, pledge **07** address, devoted, present **08** inscribe, make holy, sanctify, set apart **09** sacrifice, surrender **10** consecrate, give over to, inaugurate

dedicated
06 oblate **07** bespoke, devoted, sold out, staunch, zealous **08** diligent **09** committed, sold out on **10** customized, purposeful **11** custom-built, given over to, hard working, industrious **12** card-carrying, enthusiastic, single-minded, wholehearted **13** dyed-in-the-wool, single-hearted

dedication
04 wake, zeal **07** address, loyalty **08** blessing, devotion **09** adherence, hallowing **10** allegiance, attachment, commitment, enthusiasm **11** benediction, inscription **12** consecration, faithfulness, presentation **13** self-sacrifice **14** sanctification

deduce
04 dope, draw, suss **05** glean, infer **06** derive, gather, reason **07** dope out, surmise, work out **08** conclude **09** figure out, syllogize **10** understand

deduct
04 dock **06** deduce, reduce, remove, weaken **07** take off **08** knock off, reduce by, separate, subtract, take away, take from, withdraw **09** strike off **10** decrease by

deduction
04 dock **06** result **07** finding, removal, reprise **08** decrease, discount **09** abatement, allowance, corollary, inference, reasoning, reduction, surmising, taking off **10** assumption, conclusion, consectary, diminution, hypothesis, taking away, withdrawal **11** consequence, presumption, subtraction **12** off-reckoning
• **clear of deductions**
03 net **04** nett

deed
03 act **04** fact, feat, work **05** issue, starr, title, truth **06** action, escrow, factum, record **07** charter, exploit, reality **08** activity, contract, document, mortgage, valiance, valiancy **09** actuality, agreement, endeavour, indenture, quitclaim, specialty **10** attainment, backletter, bill of sale **11** achievement, disposition, enfeoffment, infeudation, performance, transaction, undertaking **14** accomplishment

deem
03 see **04** hold **05** judge, think **06** esteem, reckon, regard **07** account, adjudge, believe, imagine, opinion, suppose **08** conceive, consider, estimate

deep
03 far, low, sea **04** bass, dark, full, lost, main, rapt, rich, warm, wise **05** briny,

grave, ocean, quiet, sound, thick, vivid **06** arcane, ardent, astute, clever, gaping, intent, severe, strong **07** abysmal, abyssal, booming, cunning, earnest, extreme, faraway, fervent, glowing, intense, learned, obscure, serious, yawning **08** absorbed, abstruse, a long way, esoteric, high seas, immersed, powerful, profound, reserved, resonant, sonorous, the drink, vigorous **09** brilliant, cavernous, difficult, engrossed, excessive, full-toned, heart-felt, intensely, recondite, sagacious, unplumbed, very great **10** bottomless, discerning, fathomless, low-pitched, mysterious, passionate, perceptive, profoundly, resounding, unfathomed **11** deep as a well, impassioned, preoccupied, uncrossable **12** immeasurable, intellectual, wholehearted **13** knowledgeable, perspicacious **14** a great distance

deepen
04 grow **06** bump up, dig out, extend, hike up, hollow, step up, worsen **07** build up, magnify **08** excavate, get worse, heighten, increase, mushroom, scoop out **09** intensify, reinforce, scrape out **10** strengthen **11** deteriorate

deeply
04 upsy **05** sadly, upsee, upsey **06** keenly **07** acutely, gravely, greatly, sharply **08** ardently, movingly, severely, strongly, very much **09** earnestly, extremely, feelingly, fervently, intensely, seriously **10** completely, mournfully, profoundly, thoroughly, to the quick, vigorously **12** passionately **13** distressingly

deep-seated
04 deep **05** fixed **07** chronic, settled **08** intimate, Plutonic, profound **09** confirmed, ingrained **10** deep-rooted, entrenched **11** fundamental

deer
03 doe **04** buck, fawn, hart, hind, spay, stag **05** Bambi, spade, spayd **06** cervid, rascal, spayad **07** pricket, spitter **08** staggard

Deer include:

03 elk, hog, red, roe
04 axis, mule, musk, pudu, rusa, sika
05 moose, water
06 chital, fallow, forest, sambar, sambur, tufted, wapiti
07 barking, brocket, caribou, jumping, muntjac, muntjak
08 cariacou, carjacou, Irish elk, reindeer, Virginia
09 barasinga
10 barasingha, chevrotain, Père David's
11 black-tailed, white-tailed
12 Chinese water, Indian sambar
13 Indian muntjac

deface
◇ *head deletion indicator*
03 mar **04** ruin **05** spoil, sully **06** damage, defame, deform, impair, injure **07** blemish, destroy, tarnish **08** mutilate **09** disfigure, vandalize **10** disfeature, obliterate

de facto
04 real **06** actual, in fact, really **08** actually, existing, in effect **10** in practice

defamation
04 slur **05** libel, smear **07** calumny, obloquy, scandal, slander **08** innuendo, slamming **09** aspersion **10** backbiting, derogation, opprobrium **11** badmouthing, denigration, malediction, mud-slinging, slagging-off, traducement **12** vilification **13** disparagement, smear campaign

defamatory
09 aspersory, injurious, insulting, libellous, vilifying **10** calumnious, derogatory, pejorative, scandalous, scurrilous, slanderous **11** denigrating, disparaging, maledictory, mud-slinging **12** contumelious

defame
04 slag, slam **05** cloud, libel, smear **06** deface, infame, infamy, malign, vilify **07** asperse, blacken, blemish, detract, run down, scandal, slag off, slander, traduce **08** badmouth, besmirch, disgrace, infamize **09** bespatter, denigrate, discredit, dishonour, disparage **10** calumniate, sling mud at, stigmatize, throw mud at, vituperate **11** speak evil of **14** cast aspersions

default
04 fail, lack, loss, want **05** dodge, evade, fault, lapse **06** defect **07** absence, defraud, failing, failure, neglect, offence, swindle **08** omission **09** backslide **10** deficiency, negligence, non-payment **11** dereliction

defaulter
04 duck **08** absentee, lame duck, non-payer, offender **11** non-appearer

defeat
03 gub, lam, war **04** balk, beat, best, drub, foil, kill, lick, loss, rout, ruin, tank, tonk, undo, whip **05** annul, block, crush, excel, paste, quell, repel, smash, stump, throw, thump, worst **06** baffle, granny, hammer, outwit, puzzle, reject, subdue, thrash, thwart **07** beating, clobber, conquer, debacle, eclipse, failure, inch out, outplay, pasting, perplex, reverse, setback, surpass, tanking, trounce **08** confound, conquest, crushing, downfall, drubbing, obstruct, outmatch, outscore, outsmart, overcome, squabash, throw out, vanquish, Waterloo, whipping, whupping **09** breakdown, checkmate, defeature,

devastate, discomfort, disfigure, frustrate, marmelize, overmatch, overpower, overthrow, overwhelm, pulverize, rejection, repulsion, shoot down, slaughter, subjugate, thrashing, thwarting, trouncing **10** annihilate, defeasance, disappoint, disconcert, overcoming **11** frustration, subjugation **12** annihilation, pip at the post, vanquishment **13** have the edge on, put to the worse, run rings round **14** disappointment, get the better of **15** make mincemeat of

defeatist
06 gloomy **07** quitter, yielder **08** helpless, hopeless, negative, resigned **09** doomsayer, pessimist **10** despairing, despondent, fatalistic **11** doomwatcher, pessimistic **13** prophet of doom

defecate
03 poo **04** crap, mute, plop, poop **05** egest **07** excrete, scumber, skummer **08** evacuate **11** do number two, pass a motion **12** cover the feet, ease yourself **13** void excrement **14** do your business, move your bowels **15** empty your bowels, relieve yourself

defect
03 bug **04** flaw, lack, snag, spot, want **05** craze, error, fault, rebel, taint **06** desert, hiatus, renege, revolt, wreath **07** abandon, abscond, absence, blemish, default, demerit, failing, frailty, mistake **08** hamartia, omission, psellism, weakness, weak spot **09** deformity, shortfall **10** apostatize, break faith, deficience, deficiency, inadequacy **11** change sides, jump the dyke, loup the dyke, shortcoming, turn traitor **12** imperfection, tergiversate

defection
06 mutiny, revolt **07** perfidy, treason **08** apostasy, betrayal **09** breakaway, desertion, rebellion **10** absconding, disloyalty, renegation **11** abandonment, backsliding, defalcation, dereliction **14** tergiversation

defective
◇ *anagram indicator*
04 bust, duff **05** kaput, trick, wrong **06** broken, faulty, flawed **08** abnormal **09** deficient, imperfect **10** on the blink, on the fritz, out of order **11** in disrepair **12** insufficient **14** malfunctioning

defector
03 rat **05** Judas, rebel **07** traitor **08** apostate, betrayer, deserter, mutineer, quisling, recreant, renegade, turncoat **10** backslider **13** tergiversator

defence
04 army, case, keep, navy, plea, wall **05** alibi, cover, guard **06** excuse, screen, shield, troops **07** apology, bastion, bulwark, outpost, rampart,

shelter, weapons **08** advocacy, air force, apologia, argument, buttress, fortress, garrison, immunity, military, munition, pleading, security, soldiers, weaponry **09** armaments, barricade, deterrent, safeguard, testimony **10** apologetic, deterrence, munificence, protection, resistance, stronghold **11** armed forces, exoneration, explanation, explication, extenuation, vindication **12** propugnation **13** fortification, justification

- **air defence**
02 AD

See also **fortification**

defenceless
04 weak **05** naked, silly **07** exposed, unarmed **08** helpless, impotent **09** guardless, powerless, unguarded **10** undefended, vulnerable **11** susceptible, unprotected **12** open to attack

defend
04 back, fend, hold **05** cover, deter, guard, plead **06** assert, forbid, oppose, resist, screen, secure, shield, uphold **07** bolster, bulwark, contest, endorse, enguard, explain, fortify, justify, protect, shelter, stand by, support, warrant **08** argue for, bestride, buttress, champion, garrison, maintain, preserve, prohibit **09** barricade, exonerate, safeguard, vindicate, watch over, withstand **10** go to bat for, speak up for, stand up for, stick up for **12** keep from harm, make a case for **15** fight your corner, stand your corner

defendant
03 def, dft **07** accused **08** litigant, offender, prisoner **09** appellant **10** respondent

defender
04 back **05** guard **06** backer, keeper, patron **07** bastion, counsel, sponsor, warrant **08** advocate, asserter, assertor, champion, endorser, guardian, upholder **09** apologist, bodyguard, defendant, preserver, promachos, protector, supporter **10** vindicator

defensible
04 safe **05** valid **06** secure **07** tenable **08** arguable **09** plausible **10** pardonable, vindicable **11** impregnable, justifiable, permissible **12** maintainable, unassailable

defensive
04 wary **08** cautious, opposing, watchful **09** defending **10** apologetic, protecting, protective **12** safeguarding **13** Maginot-minded, oversensitive, self-defensive **14** self-justifying

- **defensive ring**
04 laer **06** corral, laager

defer
03 bow **05** delay, waive, yield **06** accede, comply, give in, put off, shelve, submit **07** adjourn, give way,

put back, rejourn, respect, suspend **08** hold over, postpone, prorogue, protract, put on ice, roll over **09** acquiesce, surrender **10** capitulate **13** procrastinate

deference
04 duty **06** esteem, honour, regard **07** respect **08** civility, courtesy, yielding **09** obedience, reverence, servility **10** compliance, politeness, submission **12** acquiescence **13** attentiveness, consideration **14** respectfulness, submissiveness, thoughtfulness

deferential
05 civil **06** humble, polite **07** dutiful **08** obeisant, reverent **09** attentive, courteous, regardful **10** morigerous, obsequious, respectful **11** complaisant, reverential **12** ingratiating

deferment
04 stay **05** delay **07** waiving **08** deferral, shelving **10** moratorium, putting-off, suspension **11** adjournment, holding-over, prorogation **12** postponement **15** procrastination

defiance
08 contempt **09** challenge, contumacy, disregard, insolence **10** opposition, resistance, truculence **12** disobedience **13** confrontation, recalcitrance **14** rebelliousness **15** insubordination

- **expression of defiance**
03 yah **04** nuts **05** ya-boo **06** yah-boo **10** ya-boo sucks **11** yah-boo sucks

defiant
04 bold **08** insolent, militant, roisting, roysting, scornful **09** obstinate, resistant, truculent **10** aggressive, rebellious, refractory **11** challenging, disobedient, provocative **12** antagonistic, contemptuous, contumacious, intransigent, recalcitrant **13** insubordinate, unco-operative

defiantly
05 acock **06** boldly **10** insolently, militantly, scornfully **11** obstinately, truculently **12** aggressively, rebelliously **13** disobediently, provocatively **14** contemptuously, contumaciously, intransigently, recalcitrantly **15** insubordinately, unco-operatively

deficiency
04 flaw, lack, want **05** fault, minus **06** dearth, defect, shorts **07** absence, deficit, failing, frailty, poverty, wantage **08** scarcity, shortage, weakness **10** inadequacy, scantiness **11** shortcoming **12** imperfection **13** insufficiency

10 hypoxaemia
11 hypospadias, sideropenia
14 leucocytopenia, oligocythaemia

deficient

◇ *anagram indicator*
03 low **04** poor, weak **05** minus,
scant, short **06** meagre, scanty, scarce,
skimpy **07** lacking, wanting
08 bankrupt, exiguous, inferior
09 imperfect **10** defectible,
inadequate, incomplete **12** insufficient
14 unsatisfactory

deficit

04 lack, loss **07** arrears, default
08 shortage **09** shortfall **10** deficiency

defile

◇ *anagram indicator*
03 col, ray **04** file, gate, moil, pass, soil
05 dirty, gorge, gully, halse, hause,
hawse, spoil, stain, sully, taint
06 debase, defame, defoul, enseam,
infect, ravine, valley **07** blacken,
corrupt, degrade, passage, pollute,
profane, tarnish, violate, vitiate
08 disgrace, maculate **09** denigrate,
desecrate, dishonour, inquinate
10 make impure **11** contaminate, make
unclean

defilement

04 moil **08** foulness, impurity, staining,
sullying, tainting, tainture **09** pollution,
profanity, violation **10** debasement,
defamation, tarnishing **11** degradation,
denigration, desecration
13 conspurcation, contamination

definable

05 exact, fixed **07** precise
08 definite, specific **10** explicable
11 describable, perceptible
12 determinable, identifiable
13 ascertainable

define

03 fix **05** bound, limit **06** decide,
detail **07** clarify, delimit, explain,
expound, mark out, pin down, specify
08 describe, pinpoint, spell out
09 delineate, demarcate, designate,
determine, elucidate, establish,
interpret **12** characterize, circumscribe

definite

04 firm, hard, sure **05** clear, exact,
fixed **06** marked **07** assured, certain,
decided, obvious, precise, settled
08 clear-cut, distinct, explicit,
positive, specific **10** determined,
guaranteed, noticeable, particular
12 unmistakable

definitely

06 easily, indeed, surely **07** clearly, for
sure, plainly **09** certainly, doubtless,
expressly, no denying, obviously, out-
and-out **10** absolutely, distinctly, in
terminis, positively, undeniably
11 indubitably, undoubtedly
12 unmistakably, without doubt
13 categorically, determinately,
unmistakeably **14** unquestionably
15 without question

definition

03 def **05** focus, sense **07** clarity,
diorism, meaning **08** contrast
09 clearness, precision, sharpness
10 denotation, exposition, visibility
11 description, elucidation,
explanation **12** distinctness,
significance **13** clarification,
determination **14** interpretation

definitive

05 exact, final **07** classic, correct,
perfect **08** absolute, complete,
decisive, positive, reliable, standard,
ultimate **09** classical **10** conclusive,
exhaustive **11** categorical, terminative
13 authoritative

definitively

07 finally **10** absolutely, completely,
decisively **12** conclusively
13 categorically **15** authoritatively

deflate

04 dash, slow, void **05** empty, lower
06 debunk, humble, lessen, reduce,
shrink, squash, subdue **07** chasten,
depress, devalue, exhaust, flatten, let
down, mortify, put down, squeeze
08 collapse, contract, decrease,
diminish, dispirit, puncture, slow down
09 humiliate **10** depreciate,
disappoint, disconcert

deflect

04 bend, draw, turn, veer, wind
05 avert, drift, snick, twist **06** glance,
swerve **07** deviate, diverge, head off,
refract **08** ricochet, withdraw
09 glance off, sidetrack, turn aside
12 change course

deflection

04 bend, veer **05** drift, snick, throw
06 swerve **07** turning **08** ricochet,
twisting **09** deviation, diversion
10 aberration, divergence, refraction
11 glancing-off **12** sidetracking,
turning aside **14** changing course

deflower

03 mar **04** harm, rape, ruin **05** force,
spoil **06** defile, molest, ravish, seduce
07 assault, despoil, violate
09 deflorate, desecrate

deform

◇ *anagram indicator*
03 mar **04** maim, ruin, warp **05** spoil,
twist **06** buckle, damage, deface
07 contort, distort, hideous, malform,
pervert **08** misshape, mutilate
09 disfigure, unshapely

deformation

04 bend, warp **05** curve, twist
06 buckle **08** twisting **10** cataclasis,
contortion, defacement, distortion,
mutilation **11** compression
12 diastrophism, malformation
13 disfiguration, misshapenness

deformed

◇ *anagram indicator*
04 bent **06** camsho, inform, maimed,
marred, ruined, warped **07** buckled,
crooked, defaced, dismayd, gnarled,

mangled, misborn, mishapt, twisted
08 camshoch, crippled
09 camsheugh, contorted, corrupted,
distorted, malformed, miscreate,
misshaped, misshapen, mutilated,
perverted **10** disfigured, miscreated,
out of shape

deformity

06 defect **08** claw-foot, misshape,
ugliness, vileness **09** grossness
10 corruption, defacement, distortion,
misfeature, perversion **11** abnormality,
contracture, crookedness, monstrosity
12 imperfection, irregularity,
malformation **13** disfigurement,
misproportion, misshapenness

defraud

02 do **03** con, rob **04** dupe, fool, nick,
rook, rush, swiz **05** cheat, cozen, lurch,
screw, sting, trick, wrong **06** delude,
diddle, fiddle, fleece, outwit, rip off
07 beguile, deceive, mislead, swindle,
swizzle **08** embezzle, hoodwink

defray

03 pay **04** meet **05** cover, repay
06 refund, settle, square **07** appease,
satisfy **09** discharge, reimburse
10 recompense

defrost

04 melt, thaw **08** defreeze

deft

04 able, feat, neat **05** adept, agile,
handy, natty, nifty **06** adroit, clever,
expert, nimble **07** skilful **09** dexterous
10 proficient

deftly

04 ably **05** slick **06** neatly, nimbly
07 adeptly **08** cleverly, expertly
09 skilfully **12** proficiently

defunct

04 dead, gone **05** passé **06** bygone,
unused **07** disused, expired, extinct,
invalid **08** deceased, departed,
finished, obsolete, outmoded
11 inoperative

defuse

◇ *anagram indicator*
04 calm, cool **06** disarm **07** disable,
quieten, relieve **08** calm down, cool
down, disorder **09** alleviate
10 deactivate, immobilize **11** clear the
air

defy

04 dare, face, foil, mock **05** avoid,
beard, brave, elude, flout, repel, scorn,
spurn **06** baffle, defeat, ignore, resist,
slight, thwart **07** despise, discard,
dislike, disobey, outdare, provoke
08 confront **09** challenge, disregard,
frustrate, stand up to, withstand
10 disrespect **12** rebel against **14** fly in
the face of

degeneracy

08 vileness **09** decadence
10 corruption, debasement,
debauchery, effeteness, fallenness,
immorality, perversion, sinfulness,
wickedness **11** degradation,

depravation 12 degeneration
13 deterioration, dissoluteness

degenerate
3 low, rot **04** base, fail, mean, rake,
oué, sink, slip, vile **05** decay, knave,
apse, rogue, scamp **06** effete, fallen,
ascal, recoil, sinful, sinner, wicked,
worsen, wretch **07** corrupt, dastard,
debased, decline, fall off, go to pot,
ignoble, immoral, regress, villain
8 criminal, decadent, decrease,
degender, degraded, depraved,
derogate, evildoer, vagabond
9 abandoned, debauched, dissolute,
miscreant, perverted, reprobate,
scallywag, scoundrel, wrongdoer
0 bastardize, go downhill, ne'er-do-
well, profligate **11** degenerated,
deteriorate, off the rails
2 deteriorated, troublemaker
3 mischief-maker **14** go down the
ubes

degeneration
3 rot **04** drop, slip **05** decay, lapse,
slide **06** dry rot **07** atrophy, decline,
failure, sinking **08** decrease
9 caseation, steatosis, worsening
0 debasement, falling-off, involution,
regression, retrogress **11** degradation
3 deterioration

degradation
5 shame **07** decline **08** comedown,
demotion, disgrace, ignominy, vileness
9 abasement, decadence, demission,
dishonour **10** corruption, culvertage,
debasement, debauchery, degeneracy,
sullenness, immorality, perversion,
sinfulness, wickedness **11** depravation,
downgrading, humiliation
2 degeneration, immiseration
3 decomposition, deterioration,
dissoluteness, mortification
4 immiserization

degrade
4 sink **05** abase, erode, lower, shame,
sully **06** debase, defile, demean,
demote, depose, embace, embase,
humble, imbase, impair, reduce,
unseat, weaken **07** cashier, cheapen,
corrupt, declass, deprive, devalue,
drum out, embrute, imbrute, mortify,
pervert, put down **08** belittle,
diminish, disgrace, dishonor, relegate
9 brutalize, decompose, discredit,
dishonour, downgrade, humiliate
0 adulterate, disennoble, prostitute
1 deteriorate, lower in rank **12** reduce
in rank

degrading
4 base **07** ignoble **08** debasing,
lowering, shameful, unworthy
9 demeaning **10** belittling,
cheapening, mortifying **11** disgraceful,
humiliating, undignified
2 contemptible, discrediting
3 dishonourable

degree
1 d **02** BA, MA **03** deg, pin **04** mark,
rank, rate, rung, step, unit **05** class,
first, grade, level, limit, order, point,

range, stage, third **06** amount, extent,
second, status **07** Desmond, measure
08 position, standard, standing,
strength **09** intensity **11** double first
13 baccalaureate
See also **qualification**
• **in a high degree**
02 so **03** far **04** much, very **05** great
• **in a lower degree**
04 less
• **in whatever degree**
02 as

dehydrate
03 dry **05** drain, dry up, parch **06** dry
out **09** desiccate, evaporate, exsiccate,
lose water **10** effloresce

dehydration
06 drying **08** parching **11** desiccation,
evaporation **13** dehumidifying
• **treatment for dehydration**
03 ORT

deification
07 worship **08** revering **09** elevation,
extolling, reverence **10** apotheosis,
exaltation, veneration
11 ennoblement, idolization
12 divinization, idealization
13 glorification **14** divinification
15 immortalization

deify
03 god **05** exalt, extol **06** revere
07 elevate, ennoble, glorify, idolize,
worship **08** idealize, venerate
10 aggrandize **11** immortalize

deign
05 daine, stoop **07** consent
10 condescend **13** lower yourself
14 demean yourself

deity
03 god **04** idol **05** numen, power
06 avatar, heaven, spirit **07** demigod,
eternal, goddess, godhead, godhood
08 divinity, immortal, numinous
10 genius loci **11** divine being
12 supreme being
See also **God; god, goddess**

dejected
03 low, sad **04** blue, down, flat, glum
05 amort **06** abattu, dismal, gloomy,
morose **07** alamort, crushed, doleful,
subdued **08** cast down, downcast,
wretched **09** depressed, jaw-fallen,
miserable, sorrowful **10** chopfallen,
despondent, dispirited, melancholy,
spiritless **11** crestfallen, demoralized,
discouraged, downhearted,
melancholic **12** disconsolate,
disheartened **14** down in the dumps

dejectedly
05 sadly **06** glumly **08** dismally,
gloomily, morosely **09** miserably
10 wretchedly **12** despondently
14 disconsolately

dejection
04 crab **05** blues, dumps, gloom
06 misery, sorrow **07** despair, sadness
09 faintness **10** depression,
gloominess, low spirits, melancholy,

moroseness **11** despondence,
despondency, dolefulness,
melancholia, unhappiness
12 wretchedness **14** disconsolation,
discouragement, dispiritedness
15 downheartedness

de jure
05 legal **07** legally **08** rightful
10 rightfully

Delaware
02 DE **03** Del

delay
03 lag, let **04** halt, keep, lull, mora,
slow, stay, stop, wait **05** check, dally,
defer, frist, sit on, stall, stave, tarry
06 dawdle, detain, dilute, dither,
hamper, hang on, hinder, hold up, hold-
up, impede, linger, loiter, put off, retard,
shelve, temper, weaken **07** adjourn,
forsloe, forslow, put back, respite, set
back, setback, suspend, waiving
08 dawdling, foreslow, hang fire,
hesitate, hold back, hold over, interval,
obstruct, postpone, put on ice,
reprieve, restrain, shelving, stalling,
stoppage, tarrying **09** dalliance,
deferment, demurrage, detaining,
detention, faff about, hesitance,
hesitancy, hindrance, lag behind,
lingering, loitering, stonewall, tarriance
10 cunctation, dilly-dally, filibuster,
hesitation, impediment, moratorium,
putting-off, suspension
11 adjournment, holding-over,
obstruction, retardation
12 interruption, postponement
13 dilly-dallying, procrastinate
15 procrastination

delayed
04 late **08** retarded

delectable
05 tasty, yummy **06** dainty, lovely
07 savoury **08** adorable, charming,
engaging, exciting, luscious, pleasant,
pleasing **09** agreeable, beautiful,
delicious, palatable, succulent
10 appetizing, attractive, delightful,
enchanting **11** flavoursome,
scrumptious **13** mouthwatering

delectation
06 relish **07** comfort, delight
08 pleasure **09** amusement, diversion,
enjoyment, happiness **11** contentment,
refreshment **12** satisfaction
13 entertainment, gratification

delegate
03 del **04** give, name **05** agent, envoy,
leave, proxy, vicar **06** assign, charge,
commit, depute, deputy, legate,
ordain, pass on, second, syndic
07 appoint, consign, deputed,
devolve, empower, entrust
08 emissary, hand over, nominate, pass
over **09** authorize, designate,
messenger, secondary, spokesman
10 ambassador, amphictyon,
commission, substitute
11 spokeswoman **12** commissioner,
spokesperson **14** representative

delegation
07 embassy, mission **08** legation
09 committal, passing on
10 assignment, commission,
contingent, deputation, devolution,
entrusting **11** consignment,
empowerment, passing over
12 substitution, transference
15 representatives

delete
01 d **03** cut **04** dele, edit **05** erase
06 cancel, cut out, efface, excise,
remove, rub out, strike **07** blot out,
destroy, edit out, expunge, scratch,
take out **08** cross out, white out
09 strike out **10** blue-pencil, obliterate

deleterious
03 bad **07** harmful, hurtful, noxious,
ruinous **08** damaging **09** injurious,
poisonous, predatory **10** pernicious
11 destructive, detrimental, prejudicial

deliberate
03 set **04** muse, slow **05** think, voulu,
weigh **06** advise, debate, ponder,
steady, wilful, willed **07** advised,
careful, consult, discuss, heedful,
knowing, planned, prudent, reflect,
studied, weigh up, willful, witting
08 cautious, cogitate, consider,
designed, evaluate, measured,
meditate, mull over, propense,
resolute, ruminate, studious, volitive
09 conscious, leisurely, ponderous,
think over, unhurried **10** calculated,
considered, excogitate, methodical,
preplanned, think about, thoughtful,
unwavering **11** circumspect,
considerate, intentional, prearranged
12 preconceived, premeditated,
professional, unhesitating

deliberately
06 slowly **08** by design, steadily,
wilfully **09** carefully, knowingly, on
purpose, pointedly, prudently, wittingly
10 cautiously, studiously
11 consciously, in cold blood,
ponderously, unhurriedly
12 methodically, thoughtfully
13 calculatingly, circumspectly,
coldbloodedly, intentionally

deliberation
04 care **05** study **06** debate, musing
07 caution, counsel, mulling, thought
08 brooding, calmness, coolness,
prudence, slowness **09** pondering
10 advisement, cogitation, conferring,
discussion, evaluation, excogitate,
meditation, reflection, rumination,
steadiness, weighing-up
11 calculation, carefulness,
forethought **12** consultation
13 consideration, unhurriedness
14 circumspection, thoughtfulness

delicacy
04 care, cate, tact **05** goody, taste,
treat **06** dainty, delice, junket, luxury,
nicety, relish, sunket, tidbit, titbit
07 finesse, savoury, trinket
08 elegance, fineness, kickshaw,
niceness, subtlety, weakness
09 diplomacy, fragility, kickshaws,
lightness, precision, sweetmeat
10 daintiness, discretion, morbidezza,
refinement, speciality, tenderness
11 bonne-bouche, sensitivity
12 niminy-piminy **13** consideration,
exquisiteness, luxuriousness
14 discrimination

delicate
04 fine, mild, nesh, nice, pale, soft,
weak **05** bland, dorty, exact, faint,
fairy, frail, light, muted **06** ailing, dainty,
flimsy, friand, gentle, incony, infirm,
luxury, pastel, polite, sickly, slight,
subtle, tender, touchy, tricky, unwell
07 awkward, band-box, brittle, careful,
elegant, fragile, friande, inconie,
precise, subdued, tactful **08** accurate,
critical, delicacy, discreet, graceful,
hothouse, kid-glove, ladylike **09** airy-
fairy, breakable, difficult, exquisite,
fairylike, fingertip, luxurious, precision,
sensitive **10** diaphanous, diplomatic,
fastidious **11** considerate, debilitated,
problematic **12** easily broken, in poor
health, niminy-piminy, softly-softly
13 controversial, easily damaged,
insubstantial

delicately
06 finely, gently, mildly, palely, softly,
subtly **07** blandly, faintly **08** daintily
09 carefully, elegantly, tactfully
10 critically, gracefully **11** exquisitely,
sensitively **14** diplomatically

delicious
04 good **05** juicy, tasty, yummy
06 choice, delish, morish **07** moreish,
savoury, scrummy **08** charming,
pleasant, pleasing, tempting
09 agreeable, ambrosial, enjoyable,
exquisite, palatable, succulent,
toothsome **10** appetizing, delectable,
delightful, enchanting, goloptious,
goluptious, gratifying, nectareous
11 captivating, fascinating, lip-
smacking, pleasurable, scrumptious
12 entertaining **13** mouth-watering

delight
03 joy **04** fain, glee, like, love, rape
05 amuse, bliss, charm, cheer, enjoy,
feast, mirth **06** delice, excite, please,
ravish, relish, savour, thrill, tickle
07 boast of, ecstasy, elation, enchant,
gladden, glory in, gratify, rapture, revel
in **08** bowl over, entrance, euphoria,
felicity, gladness, pleasure, wallow in
09 amusement, captivate, enjoyment,
enrapture, entertain, happiness,
transport **10** appreciate, exultation,
jubilation, tickle pink **11** contentment,
delectation, take pride in
13 entertainment, gratification **14** take
pleasure in **15** give enjoyment to

delighted
04 glad **05** happy **06** elated, joyful,
joyous, made up, stoked **07** charmed,
excited, gleeful, pleased **08** ecstatic,
euphoric, jubilant, thrilled
09 enchanted, entranced, gratified,
overjoyed **10** captivated, enraptured

11 over the moon, tickled pink
12 happy as Larry **14** pleased as Punch
15 happy as a sandboy

delightful
03 ace **04** nice **05** great, magic, super,
sweet **06** divine, groovy, lovely, wizard
07 amusing, darling, the tops
08 charming, engaging, exciting,
glorious, luscious, pleasant, pleasing
09 agreeable, appealing, beautiful,
diverting, enjoyable, ravishing, thrilling
10 attractive, delectable, enchanting,
entrancing, felicitous, gratifying
11 captivating, fascinating,
pleasurable, scrumptious
12 entertaining **14** out of this world
• **something delightful**
03 gas

delimit
03 fix, set **04** mark **05** bound
06 define **09** demarcate, determine,
establish

delineate
03 fix **04** draw, line, mark **05** bound,
chart, stell, trace **06** define, depict,
design, render, sketch **07** outline,
portray **08** describe, set forth
09 determine, establish, represent

delineation
06 sketch **07** tracing **09** depiction,
portrayal, rendering **11** description,
presentment **14** representation

delinquency
05 crime, fault **07** misdeed, offence
10 misconduct, wrongdoing
11 criminality, lawbreaking
12 misbehaviour, misdemeanour
13 transgression

delinquent
03 ned, ted **06** bodgie, guilty, remiss,
vandal, widgie **07** culprit, lawless,
ruffian **08** criminal, culpable, hooligan,
offender **09** miscreant, negligent,
offending, wrongdoer **10** lawbreaker,
malefactor **11** Halbstarker,
lawbreaking **13** young offender

delirious
◊ *anagram indicator*
03 mad **04** gone, wild **05** crazy, light
06 elated, insane, raving **07** frantic
08 babbling, demented, deranged,
ecstatic, euphoric, frenetic, frenzied,
jubilant, rambling, unhinged
09 overjoyed, phrenetic, rapturous,
spaced out, wandering **10** hysterical,
incoherent, irrational **11** carried away,
light-headed, over the moon **13** out of
your mind **14** beside yourself

deliriously
◊ *anagram indicator*
10 jubilantly **11** rapturously
12 ecstatically, hysterically

delirium
03 joy **05** fever **06** frenzy, lunacy,
raving **07** ecstasy, elation, jimjams,
madness, passion, rapture
08 dementia, euphoria, hysteria,
insanity, wildness **09** craziness,

phrenesis **10** excitement, jubilation
11 derangement, incoherence
13 hallucination, irrationality
• **delirium tremens**
03 DTs **05** jumps **07** jimjams **09** Joe
Blakes **10** the horrors **11** the dingbats

deliver
02 do **03** aim, rid **04** bowl, cede,
deal, free, give, hand, make, save, send,
take **05** bring, carry, grant, serve,
speak, utter, voice, yield **06** commit,
convey, direct, fulfil, launch, nimble,
ransom, redeem, render, rescue,
strike, supply **07** declare, entrust,
express, give out, inflict, manumit,
present, provide, release, set free
08 announce, carry out, dispatch,
hand over, liberate, live up to, proclaim,
transfer, turn over **09** enunciate,
implement, pronounce, surrender
10 administer, distribute, emancipate,
relinquish **11** give voice to **15** help give
birth to

deliverance
06 escape, ransom, rescue
07 freedom, release **08** riddance
09 salvation **10** liberation,
redemption **11** extrication
12 emancipation

deliveries
04 over

delivery
04 ball, dlvy, load **05** batch, birth
06 labour, speech, supply **07** travail
08 carriage, dispatch, shipment,
transfer **09** elocution, transport,
utterance **10** childbirth, conveyance,
intonation **11** confinement,
consignment, enunciation, parturition
12 accouchement, articulation,
distribution, transmission
13 pronunciation **14** transportation

Cricket deliveries include:
06 doosra, googly, teesra, yorker
07 bouncer, swinger
08 Chinaman, fastball, leg break, off
break
09 inswinger, leg-cutter, off-cutter
10 outswinger
11 daisy-cutter

• **deliveries**
04 over

dell
04 dale, dean, hole, vale **05** slade, trull
06 dargle, dimble, dingle, hollow,
valley **10** prostitute

delta
01 D

delude
03 kid **04** dupe, fool, hoax **05** blend,
cheat, elude, kiddy, trick **06** cajole,
have on, lead on, take in **07** beguile,
deceive, mislead, two-time
08 hoodwink, misguide
09 bamboozle, misinform **11** double-
cross **12** take for a ride **14** pull a fast
one on, put the change on

deluge
04 rush, soak, wave **05** drown, flood,
spate, swamp **06** drench, engulf
07 barrage, torrent **08** downpour,
inundate, submerge **09** avalanche,
overwhelm, snow under **10** inundation
11 overflowing

delusion
05 error, fancy **07** fallacy **08** illusion,
tricking **09** deception, misbelief
11 false belief **13** hallucination,
misconception **14** misinformation
15 false impression, misapprehension

de luxe, deluxe
04 fine, rich **05** grand, plush, swish
06 choice, costly, lavish, luxury, select
07 elegant, opulent, quality, special
08 palatial, splendid, superior
09 exclusive, expensive, luxurious,
sumptuous

delve
04 cave, hole, poke, root **05** probe
06 burrow, go into, hollow, hunt in,
search **07** dig into, examine, explore,
ransack, rummage **08** look into,
research, scrabble **10** depression
11 hunt through, investigate

demagogue
06 orator **07** speaker **08** agitator
09 firebrand, haranguer **10** tub-
thumper **12** rabble-rouser **13** public
speaker

demand
03 ask, run **04** call, need, plea, sale,
take, tell, urge, want **05** claim, draft,
exact, order **06** ask for, desire, market
07 call for, clamour, command, dictate,
inquire, inquiry, involve, request,
require, solicit **08** exaction, exigency,
insist on, petition, press for, pressure,
question **09** cry out for, necessity,
stipulate, ultimatum **10** hold out for,
insistence **11** interrogate, necessitate,
requirement **13** interrogation
• **in demand**
02 in **03** big **06** trendy **07** desired,
popular **08** asked for **09** requested
11 fashionable, of the moment, sought
after

demanding
04 hard **05** tough **06** taxing, trying,
urgent **07** exigent, nagging, testing,
wearing **08** exacting, pressing
09 difficult, harassing, insistent **10** a tall
order, exhausting **11** challenging
12 back-breaking

demarcate
03 fix **04** mark **05** bound, limit
06 define, divide **07** delimit, mark off,
mark out **08** separate **09** determine,
establish

demarcation
04 line **05** bound, limit **06** fixing,
margin **08** boundary, division
09 enclosure **10** definition, marking
off, marking out, separation
11 distinction **12** delimitation
13 determination, establishment
15 differentiation

demean
03 air **04** bear **05** abase, lower, stoop,
treat **06** behave, debase, demote,
humble **07** bearing, conduct, degrade,
descend **08** belittle, ill-treat
09 deprecate, humiliate, treatment
10 condescend

demeaning
04 base **07** ignoble **08** debasing,
shameful, unworthy **09** degrading
10 belittling, cheapening, mortifying
11 disgraceful, humiliating, undignified
12 contemptible, discrediting
13 dishonourable

demeanour
03 air **04** mien, port **06** manner
07 bearing, conduct **08** carriage,
semblant **09** behaviour **10** deportment
11 comportment, countenance

demented
◊ *anagram indicator*
03 ape, mad **04** bats, gyte, loco, nuts,
wild **05** barmy, batty, buggy, crazy,
daffy, dippy, dotty, flaky, gonzo, loony,
loopy, nutty, potty, wacko, wacky,
wiggy **06** crazed, cuckoo, fruity,
insane, maniac, mental, raving, screwy
07 bananas, barking, berserk, bonkers,
cracked, frantic, lunatic, meshuga
08 crackers, deranged, dingbats,
doolally, frenetic, unhinged
09 disturbed, infuriate, lymphatic, up
the wall **10** bestraught, distracted,
distraught, frantic-mad, off the wall, off
your nut, out to lunch, unbalanced
11 not all there, off the rails, off your
head **12** mad as a hatter, off your
chump, round the bend **13** off your
rocker, out of your head, out of your
mind, out of your tree, round the twist
14 off your trolley, wrong in the head

Demeter
05 Ceres

demigod
04 aitu, hero **05** pagod **06** garuda,
pagoda

demise
03 end **04** fall, ruin **05** death, dying
07 decease, failure, passing
08 collapse, downfall **09** cessation,
departure **10** expiration
11 termination **14** disintegration

demobilize
05 demob **07** break up, disband,
dismiss **08** disperse

democracy
08 autonomy, republic
12 commonwealth **14** self-
government

democratic
01 D **04** left **07** elected, popular
08 populist **10** autonomous,
republican **11** egalitarian
12 Jeffersonian **13** self-governing
14 representative

**Democratic Republic of the
Congo**
03 COD, ZRE

demolish

◇ *anagram indicator*
04 beat, lick, rase, raze, rout, ruin, undo **05** abate, crush, excel, level, quash, quell, repel, wreck **06** hammer, subdue, thrash **07** break up, conquer, destroy, flatten, ruinate, surpass, unbuild **08** bulldoze, knock out, lay waste, massacre, overcome, overturn, pull down, take down, tear down, vanquish **09** break down, devastate, dismantle, knock down, overpower, overthrow, overwhelm, pulverize, slaughter, subjugate, throw down **10** annihilate **14** get the better of

demolition

04 rout, ruin **06** razing **07** beating, licking **08** massacre **09** hammering, levelling, overthrow, slaughter, thrashing **10** breaking-up, clobbering, flattening, surpassing **11** destruction, dismantling, pulling-down, tearing-down **12** annihilation, knocking-down, overpowering, overwhelming

demon

03 ace, imp **04** atua, buff, ogre, Rahu **05** afrit, beast, brute, devil, fiend, freak, ghoul, rogue, satyr **06** addict, afreet, daemon, duende, nicker, savage, wizard **07** dab hand, fanatic, incubus, monster, rakshas, villain, warlock **08** familiar, succubus **09** blue devil, cacodemon **10** evil spirit **11** fallen angel

demonic

03 mad **05** manic **06** crazed **07** frantic, furious, hellish, satanic **08** devilish, fiendish, frenetic, frenzied, infernal, maniacal **09** possessed **10** diabolical

demonstrable

05 clear **07** certain, evident, obvious **08** arguable, positive, provable **09** evincible **10** attestable, verifiable **11** self-evident

demonstrate

04 show **05** march, prove, rally, sit in, teach **06** betray, evince, parade, picket, verify **07** approve, bespeak, betoken, display, exhibit, explain, expound, express, protest **08** describe, indicate, manifest, register, validate **09** determine, establish, make clear, testify to **10** illustrate **11** communicate, remonstrate **12** substantiate **13** bear witness to

demonstration

04 demo, show, test **05** march, proof, rally, sit-in, trial **06** morcha, muster, parade, picket **07** display, protest **08** evidence **09** événement, mass rally, testimony **10** evincement, exhibition, exposition, expression, indication, validation **11** affirmation, description, elucidation, explanation, hunger march **12** confirmation, illustration, presentation, verification **13** communication, manifestation **14** substantiation

demonstrative

04 open, warm **06** loving **07** gushing **08** effusive **09** emotional, expansive, extrovert **10** expressive, scientific, unreserved **12** affectionate

demonstratively

06 openly, warmly **08** lovingly **11** emotionally **12** expressively **14** affectionately

demonstrator

06 shower

demoralize

05 crush, daunt, lower **06** debase, defile, deject, weaken **07** corrupt, deprave, depress, pervert **08** cast down, dispirit **09** undermine **10** disconcert, discourage, dishearten **11** contaminate **14** make despondent

demoralizing

08 daunting **09** weakening **10** depressing **11** dispiriting **12** discouraging **13** disconcerting, disheartening

demote

04 bust **05** break **06** humble **07** cashier, degrade **08** relegate **09** downgrade **12** reduce in rank

demotic

06 vulgar **07** popular **08** enchoric **09** enchorial **10** colloquial, vernacular

demotion

09 degrading **10** relegation **11** downgrading

demur

04 balk, stop **05** cavil, doubt, pause, qualm **06** boggle, object, refuse **07** dispute, dissent, protest, scruple **08** demurral, disagree, hesitate, question **09** misgiving, objection **10** hesitation **11** be unwilling, compunction, reservation **12** disagreement, make question **13** express doubts, take exception

demure

03 coy, mim, shy **04** prim **05** grave, mimsy, quiet, sober, staid, timid **06** chaste, mimsey, modest, prissy **07** primsie, prudish, serious **08** reserved, reticent, retiring **10** unassuming **11** strait-laced

demurely

05 coyly, shyly **06** primly **07** quietly, staidly, timidly **08** modestly **09** seriously **10** reticently **12** unassumingly

den

04 dive, Hell, hole, home, lair, lare, nest **05** haunt, joint, patch, pitch, study **06** bothan, hollow, hotbed, studio **07** hideout, retreat, shelter, spieler **08** hideaway **09** Domdaniel, rock house, sanctuary **12** meeting-place

denial

02 no **03** nay **04** veto **05** denay **06** rebuff **07** démenti, dissent, gainsay, refusal **08** negation, rebuttal, traverse **09** disavowal, dismissal, disowning, forsaking, rejection **10** abjuration, denegation, disclaimer, opposition, refutation **11** prohibition, repudiation **12** disagreement, renunciation **13** contradiction **14** disaffirmation

denigrate

03 bag **05** abuse, decry **06** assail, defame, impugn, malign, revile, vilify **07** blacken, run down, slander **08** belittle, besmirch, fling mud, sling mud, talk down, throw mud, vilipend **09** blackened, criticize, deprecate, disparage **10** calumniate **11** pick holes in

denigration

05 abuse **07** calumny, slander **10** belittling **11** degradation, deprecation **12** vilification **13** disparagement

denizen

07 citizen, dweller, habitué, inhabit **08** habitant, occupant, resident, townsman **10** inhabitant, townswoman

Denmark

02 DK **03** DNK

denomination

04 cult, kind, sect, sort, unit **05** class, creed, faith, grade, order, value, worth **06** belief, Church, parish, school **08** religion **09** communion, face value, tradition **10** persuasion **11** designation **12** constituency **13** religious body **14** religious group

denote

04 mark, mean, note, show **05** imply **06** typify **07** betoken, express, refer to, signify, suggest **08** indicate, stand for **09** be a sign of, designate, represent, symbolize

dénouement

05 close, event **06** climax, finale, finish, pay-off, upshot **07** last act, outcome **08** solution **10** conclusion, resolution **11** culmination, unravelling **13** clarification

denounce

04 post, slag **05** decry, knock, slate **06** accuse, attack, betray, impugn, indict, revile, vilify **07** arraign, censure, condemn, declaim, deplore, rubbish, run down, slag off, thunder, trumpet **08** announce, badmouth, execrate, proclaim **09** castigate, criticize, fulminate, inculpate, pronounce, proscribe **10** denunciate, stigmatize **11** pick holes in **12** pull to pieces, put the boot in, tear to pieces **13** inform against

dense

03 dim **04** dull, dumb, rank, slow **05** close, dopey, heavy, solid, stiff, thick **06** obtuse, opaque, packed, stupid **07** compact, crammed, crowded, intense **08** gormless **09** close-knit, condensed, dim-witted **10** compressed, slow-witted **11** close-packed **12** concentrated, impenetrable **13** tightly packed **14** jammed together

densely
05 close **06** firmly **07** closely, heavily, solidly, thickly, tightly **09** compactly

density
01 d **04** body, bulk, mass **08** solidity **09** closeness, denseness, solidness, thickness, tightness **10** spissitude **11** compactness, consistency **15** impenetrability
• **of little density**
04 thin

dent
03 cut, dip, pit **04** bash, dint, drop, fall **05** gouge **06** crater, damage, dimple, hollow, indent, lessen, push in, reduce, weaken **07** depress **08** diminish **09** concavity, deduction, lessening, reduction **10** depression **11** indentation

dentist
03 BDS, DDS, LDS, MDS **06** doctor **08** odontist **09** gum-digger **13** dental surgeon

denude
04 bare **05** clear, strip **06** divest, expose **07** uncover **08** deforest **09** defoliate

denunciation
03 ban **06** attack, threat **07** censure, decrial, obloquy, thunder **09** criticism, invective **10** accusation **11** castigation, commination, fulmination **12** condemnation, counterblast, denouncement **13** incrimination

deny
03 nay **04** nick, reny, veto **05** denay, rebut, renay, reney, renig, unget **06** abjure, disown, forbid, naysay, negate, oppose, rebuff, recant, refuse, refute, reject, renege **07** decline, disavow, dismiss, gainsay, nullify, renague, renegue, sublate **08** abnegate, disallow, disclaim, disprove, forswear, prohibit, renounce, traverse, turn down, withhold **09** disaffirm, repudiate **10** contradict **12** disagree with **14** turn your back on

deodorant
05 scent **06** roll-on **08** fumigant **09** fumigator **10** deodorizer **12** air-freshener, disinfectant **14** anti-perspirant

deodorize
06 aerate, purify **07** freshen, refresh, sweeten **08** fumigate **09** disinfect, ventilate

depart
02 go **03** dep, die, off **04** blow, exit, fork, part, quit, scat, vade, vary, veer, walk, wend **05** go off, lam it, leave, quite, quyte, scoot, scram, skive, split **06** avaunt, decamp, differ, divide, egress, escape, go away, quight, remove, retire, set off, set out, swerve, vamose, vanish **07** bunk off, deviate, digress, diverge, do a bunk, drop off,

make off, migrate, pull out, push off, retreat, scarper, swan off, take off, tear off, vamoose, walk off **08** check out, clear off, drop away, get going, make wing, separate, shove off, start out, take wing, turn away, up sticks, withdraw **09** branch off, disappear, do a runner, evaporate, push along, skedaddle, turn aside **10** hightail it, hit the road, make tracks **11** hit the trail, take the road **12** shoot through **13** sling your hook, take your leave **14** absent yourself, make a bolt for it, rattle your dags, take it on the lam **15** make a break for it, take to your heels

departed
04 dead, gone, late, lost, went **07** expired **08** deceased **10** passed away

department
01 D **03** Dep, dpt **04** area, Dept, line, nome, part, unit, wing **05** field, realm **06** agency, branch, bureau, domain, office, region, sector, sphere **07** concern, section, station **08** district, division, function, interest, province **10** cost centre, speciality **11** subdivision **12** organization **14** responsibility

Départements of France:

03 Ain, Lot, Var
04 Aube, Aude, Cher, Eure, Gard, Gers, Jura, Nord, Oise, Orne, Tarn
05 Aisne, Doubs, Drôme, Indre, Isère, Loire, Marne, Meuse, Paris, Rhône, Somme, Yonne
06 Allier, Ariège, Cantal, Creuse, Landes, Loiret, Lozère, Manche, Nièvre, Sarthe, Savoie, Vendée, Vienne, Vosges
07 Ardèche, Aveyron, Bas-Rhin, Corrèze, Côte-d'Or, Essonne, Gironde, Hérault, Mayenne, Moselle
08 Ardennes, Calvados, Charente, Dordogne, Haut-Rhin, Morbihan, Val-d'Oise, Vaucluse, Yvelines
09 Finistère, Puy-de-Dôme
10 Corse-du-Sud, Deux-Sèvres, Haute-Corse, Haute-Loire, Haute-Marne, Haute-Saône, Loir-et-Cher, Val-de-Marne
11 Côtes-d'Armor, Eure-et-Loire, Hautes-Alpes, Haute-Savoie, Haute-Vienne, Pas-de-Calais
12 Haute-Garonne, Hauts-de-Seine, Indre-et-Loire, Lot-et-Garonne, Maine-et-Loire, Saône-et-Loire, Seine-et-Marne, Ville de Paris
13 Ille-et-Vilaine, Seine-Maritime, Tarn-et-Garonne
14 Alpes-Maritimes, Bouches-du-Rhône, Hautes-Pyrénées
15 Loire-Atlantique, Seine-Saint-Denis
16 Charente-Maritime, Meurthe-et-Moselle
18 Pyrénées-Orientales
19 Pyrénées-Atlantiques, Territoire de Belfort
20 Alpes-de-Haute-Provence

departs
01 d **03** dep

departure
03 dep **04** exit **05** going, lucky, shift **06** change, egress, escape, exodus **07** forking, leaving, removal, retreat, veering **08** farewell, going off **09** branching, decession, deviation, egression, going away, variation **10** difference, digression, divergence, innovation, retirement, setting-off, setting-out, withdrawal **11** leave-taking **12** branching out

depend
03 lie **04** need, rely, turn **06** bank on, expect, hang on, lean on, lippen, rely on, rest on, ride on, turn on **07** cling to, count on, hinge on, trust in **08** reckon on **09** be based on, build upon **11** be decided by, be subject to, calculate on **13** be dependent on, revolve around **14** be contingent on, be determined by

dependable
04 sure **06** honest, stable, steady, trusty **07** certain **08** faithful, reliable **09** rock-solid, steadfast, unfailing **11** responsible, trustworthy **13** conscientious **14** tried and tested

dependant
04 ward **05** child, minor **06** charge, client, feeder, minion, vassal **07** protégé, relying **08** creature, hanger-on, henchman, parasite, relative, retainer **09** pensioner **10** contingent **11** subordinate

dependence
04 need **05** abuse, faith, trust **08** reliance **09** addiction, vassalage **10** attachment, confidence, dependency **11** expectation **12** helplessness, subservience **13** subordination

dependency
05 abuse, habit **06** colony **07** support **08** dominion, pendicle, province, reliance, weakness **09** addiction, satellite, territory **10** attachment, immaturity **12** helplessness, protectorate, subservience **13** subordination **14** submissiveness

dependent
04 weak **05** based **07** decided, leaning, reliant, relying, subject **08** dictated, helpless, immature, relative **09** adjective, supported, sustained **10** contingent, controlled, determined, influenced, vulnerable **11** conditional, subordinate

depict
04 draw, show **05** paint, trace **06** detail, devise, record, render, sketch **07** depaint, impaint, outline, picture, portray, present, recount **08** describe, resemble **09** delineate, represent, reproduce **10** illustrate **12** characterize

depiction
05 image **06** sketch **07** drawing, outline, picture **08** likeness

09 detailing, portrayal, rendering
10 caricature 11 delineation,
description 12 illustration
14 representation

deplete
05 drain, empty, erode, spend, use up
06 expend, lessen, reduce, weaken
07 consume, eat into, exhaust, run
down 08 bankrupt, decrease,
diminish, evacuate 09 attenuate
10 impoverish 11 whittle away

depletion
07 using-up 08 decrease, lowering
09 dwindling, lessening, reduction,
shrinkage, weakening 10 deficiency,
diminution, evacuation, exhaustion
11 attenuation, consumption,
expenditure 14 impoverishment

deplorable
◇ *anagram indicator*
03 sad 04 dire 05 woful 06 rueful,
woeful 07 chronic, ghastly
08 criminal, grievous, pitiable,
shameful, wretched 09 appalling,
miserable 10 abominable, despicable,
disastrous, lamentable, melancholy,
outrageous, scandalous
11 blameworthy, disgraceful,
distressing, regrettable, unfortunate
12 disreputable 13 dishonourable,
heartbreaking, reprehensible

deplorably
08 shocking 09 miserably
10 abominably, despicably, lamentably,
shamefully 11 appallingly
12 outrageously, scandalously
13 disgracefully, unfortunately

deplore
03 cry, rue 04 pine, slam, weep
05 blame, mourn, slate 06 bemoan,
berate, bewail, lament, regret, revile
07 censure, condemn, reprove,
upbraid 08 denounce, reproach
09 castigate, criticize, deprecate,
disparage, grieve for, reprehend, shed
tears 12 disapprove of

deploy
◇ *anagram indicator*
03 use 04 open 06 extend, unfold
07 arrange, dispose, scatter, station,
utilize 08 position 09 make use of,
spread out 10 distribute

depopulate
05 empty 08 unpeople 09 dispeople

deport
03 act 04 bear, hold, oust 05 carry,
exile, expel 06 acquit, banish, behave,
manage 07 comport, conduct,
perform 09 extradite, ostracize,
transport 10 repatriate

deportation
05 exile 07 ousting 09 expulsion,
ostracism 10 banishment 11 extradition
12 repatriation 14 transportation

deportment
03 air 04 gait, mien, port, pose
06 aspect, manner, stance 07 address,
bearing, conduct, manners, posture

08 behavior, carriage 09 behaviour,
demeanour, etiquette 10 appearance
11 comportment

depose
04 fire, oust, sack 05 swear 06 attest,
demote, remove, topple, unseat
07 degrade, dismiss, unfrock
08 dethrone, displace, down with
09 discharge, downgrade, overthrow
12 disestablish

deposit
◇ *hidden indicator*
03 bed, dep, dew, fan, lay, put, set, sit
04 bank, bung, drop, dump, file, gage,
land, lees, park, save, silt, soot, stow,
ware, warp 05 amass, dregs, hoard,
lay-by, lodge, pay in, place, plant, put
by, stake, store 06 depone, locate,
margin, pledge, settle, tophus
07 consign, earnest, entrust, fall-out,
lay down, put away, put down, reposit,
saburra, set down, sublime
08 alluvium, oviposit, retainer,
security, sediment, stratify
10 deposition, hypostasis, instalment
11 down payment, part payment,
precipitate 12 accumulation

deposition
07 ousting, removal 08 evidence,
sediment, toppling 09 affidavit,
dismissal, overthrow, statement,
testimony, unseating 11 attestation,
declaration, illuviation, information
12 dethronement, displacement
13 sedimentation

depository
05 cache, depot, store 07 arsenal
09 warehouse 10 repository,
storehouse 15 bonded warehouse

depot
04 camp 05 cache, store 06 garage
07 arsenal, station 08 terminal,
terminus 09 barracoon, warehouse
10 depository, repository, storehouse
14 receiving-house

deprave
04 warp 06 debase, defile, infect,
seduce 07 corrupt, debauch, degrade,
pervert, pollute, subvert, viciate, vitiate
10 demoralize, lead astray
11 contaminate

depraved
04 base, evil, vile 06 sinful, warped,
wicked 07 bestial, corrupt, debased,
immoral, obscene, vicious 08 criminal
09 debauched, dissolute, felonious,
graceless, perverted, reprobate,
shameless 10 degenerate, iniquitous,
licentious

depravity
04 evil, vice 08 baseness, iniquity,
vileness 09 reprobacy, turpitude
10 corruption, debasement,
debauchery, degeneracy, immorality,
perversion, sinfulness, wickedness
13 dissoluteness

deprecate
04 slam 05 blame, knock, slate

06 berate, reject, revile 07 censure,
condemn, deplore, reprove, rubbish,
run down, upbraid 08 denounce,
object to, reproach 09 castigate,
criticize, disparage, protest at,
reprehend 12 disapprove of

deprecatory
09 regretful 10 apologetic,
censorious, dismissive, protesting
11 reproachful 12 condemnatory,
disapproving

depreciate
04 drop, fall 05 lower, slump
06 defame, lessen, malign, reduce,
revile, slight 07 decline, deflate,
devalue, disable, run down 08 belittle
09 denigrate, disparage, downgrade,
underrate 10 undervalue 11 fall in
value, make light of 13 go down in
value, underestimate 15 decrease in
value

depreciation
04 fall 05 slump 08 mark-down,
ridicule 09 deflation 10 cheapening,
depression, derogation, detraction
11 denigration, devaluation
12 belittlement 13 disparagement
15 underestimation

depredation
04 prey 05 theft 06 damage
07 looting, pillage, plunder, raiding,
robbery 08 hardship, harrying,
ravaging 09 marauding
10 denudation, desolation, despoiling,
plundering, ransacking 11 destruction,
devastation, laying waste

depress
03 cut, sap 04 down, push, tire
05 daunt, drain, level, lower, press,
slash, upset, weary 06 burden, deject,
hammer, humble, impair, lessen,
reduce, sadden, weaken 07 cheapen,
devalue, exhaust, get down, make sad,
oppress 08 cast down, enervate, hold
down, push down 09 bring down,
press down, undermine, weigh down
10 debilitate, depreciate, discourage,
dishearten, overburden

depressant
06 downer 07 calmant 08 relaxant,
sedative 09 calmative 13 tranquillizer

depressed
03 low, sad 04 blue, down, glum, poor
05 cowed, doomy, fed up, moody,
needy 06 dented, gloomy, hollow,
moping, morose, sunken 07 accablé,
concave, dumpish, humbled, lowered,
run-down, unhappy 08 cast down,
dejected, deprived, downbeat,
downcast, indented, pushed in,
recessed 09 destitute, exanimate,
flattened, heartsick, jaw-fallen,
miserable 10 a peg too low,
despondent, dispirited, distressed,
emarginate, melancholy 11 crestfallen,
discouraged, downhearted, low-
spirited, pessimistic 12 disheartened,
low in spirits, out of spirits, under
hatches 13 broken-hearted,

disadvantaged **14** down in the dumps **15** poverty-stricken

depressing
03 sad **04** grey, grim **05** black, bleak, doomy, grave **06** dismal, dreary, gloomy, leaden, sombre **07** unhappy **08** daunting, downbeat, hopeless **09** cheerless, dejecting, saddening, upsetting **10** melancholy **11** dispiriting, distressing **12** discouraging **13** disheartening, heartbreaking

depressingly
05 sadly **07** bleakly **08** drearily, gloomily **09** unhappily **10** dauntingly **11** cheerlessly **13** dispiritingly, distressingly **14** discouragingly **15** dishearteningly, heartbreakingly

depression
03 col, dip, pit, PND **04** bowl, dent, dint, dish, glen, hole, sink, slot, swag **05** basin, blues, crash, delve, dumps, fossa, gloom, slump **06** cafard, cavity, dimple, downer, hollow, recess, trough, valley **07** cyclone, decline, despair, foveola, foveole, megrims, sadness, sinking **08** black dog, doldrums, glumness, lowering, slowdown **09** baby blues, concavity, dejection, demission, hard times, pessimism, recession, umbilicus **10** desolation, excavation, gloominess, impression, inactivity, low spirits, melancholy, scrobicule, stagnation, standstill, the horrors **11** despondency, indentation, melancholia, unhappiness **12** hopelessness **14** discouragement **15** downheartedness

deprivation
04 lack, loss, need, want **06** denial, penury **07** poverty, removal **08** hardship **09** privation **10** withdrawal **11** bereavement, destitution, withholding **12** disadvantage **13** dispossession **14** impoverishment

deprive
03 rob **04** deny, geld, twin **05** spoil, strip, twine **06** amerce, denude, divest, refuse **07** bereave **08** take away, withhold **09** destitute **10** confiscate, dispossess **11** expropriate

deprived
04 gelt, poor **05** needy **06** bereft, in need **07** lacking **09** destitute **12** impoverished **13** disadvantaged **15** underprivileged
• **be deprived of**
04 lose

depth
01 d **03** bed **04** deep, drop, glow, gulf **05** abyss, floor, midst, range, scope **06** acumen, amount, bottom, extent, middle, vigour, warmth, wisdom **07** fervour, gravity, insight, measure, passion **08** darkness, deepness, richness, severity, strength **09** awareness, intensity, intuition, vividness **10** astuteness, brilliance, cleverness, perception, profundity,

shrewdness **11** discernment, earnestness, penetration, seriousness **12** profoundness, remotest area, thoroughness **13** extensiveness **14** third dimension
• **depth charge**
03 can
• **in depth**
08 in detail, thorough **09** extensive **10** thoroughly **11** extensively **12** exhaustively **13** comprehensive **15** comprehensively

deputation
07 embassy, mission **08** legation **09** committee **10** commission, delegation **15** representatives

depute
06 charge, second **07** appoint, consign, empower, entrust, mandate **08** accredit, delegate, hand over, nominate **09** authorize, designate **10** commission

deputize
05 cover **06** act for, double, sub for **07** relieve, replace **08** take over **09** fill in for, represent **10** stand in for, substitute, understudy **11** pinch-hit for **14** take the place of

deputy
02 TD **03** Dep **04** Dept, mate, vice- **05** agent, envoy, locum, nawab, prior, proxy, vicar **06** commis, -depute, legate, second, vidame **07** stand-in **08** delegate, official, prioress, sidekick, sidesman, Tanaiste, vicaress, viscount **09** alternate, assistant, secondary, surrogate **10** ambassador, commissary, lieutenant, subchanter, substitute, vice-consul, vice-regent **11** locum tenens, subordinate **12** commissioner, spokesperson, under-sheriff, vice-chairman, vice-governor **13** pro-chancellor, sheriff depute, vice-president **14** representative **15** second-in-command, vice-chairperson, vice-chamberlain

derail
05 ditch, upset **06** impede **07** disrupt, disturb, prevent **08** displace, hold back, obstruct **14** throw off course

deranged
◇ *anagram indicator*
03 ape, fey, mad **04** bats, loco, nuts, wild **05** barmy, batty, buggy, crazy, daffy, dippy, dotty, flaky, gonzo, loony, loopy, manic, nutty, potty, wacko, wacky, wiggy **06** crazed, cuckoo, fruity, insane, maniac, mental, raving, screwy, skivie **07** bananas, barking, berserk, bonkers, cracked, frantic, lunatic, meshuga **08** confused, crackers, demented, dingbats, doolally, frenetic, frenzied, maniacal, unhinged, unstable **09** brainsick, delirious, disturbed, lymphatic, psychotic, unsettled, up the wall **10** bestraught, disordered, distracted, distraught, frantic-mad, irrational, off the wall, off your nut, out to lunch, unbalanced

11 not all there, off the rails, off your head **12** mad as a hatter, off your chump, round the bend **13** off your rocker, of unsound mind, out of your head, out of your mind, out of your tree, round the twist **14** off your trolley, wrong in the head **15** non compos mentis, out of your senses

derangement
05 mania **06** frenzy, lunacy **07** madness **08** delirium, dementia, disarray, disorder, insanity, neurosis **09** agitation, confusion **10** aberration **11** dislocation, distraction, disturbance **13** hallucination

Derek
02 Bo **03** Del

derelict
04 hobo **05** jakey, tramp **06** beggar, dosser, no-good, ruined, wretch **07** drifter, no-hoper, outcast, run-down, swagman, vagrant **08** deserted, desolate, forsaken, vagabond **09** abandoned, discarded, neglected **10** down-and-out, ne'er-do-well, ramshackle, tumbledown **11** dilapidated, in disrepair **12** down-and-outer **14** good-for-nothing **15** falling to pieces

dereliction
04 ruin **05** ruins **07** evasion, failure, neglect **08** apostasy, betrayal **09** desertion, disrepair, forsaking **10** abdication, desolation, negligence, remissness, renegation **11** abandonment **12** dilapidation, renunciation **13** faithlessness **14** relinquishment

deride
03 rag **04** gibe, jeer, mock, slag **05** knock, laugh, scorn, taunt, tease **06** bemock, chiack, chyack, insult, jeer at **07** disdain, laugh at, scoff at, slag off, sneer at **08** belittle, pooh-pooh, ridicule, satirize **09** disparage, make fun of

de rigueur
04 done **05** right **06** decent, proper **07** correct, fitting **08** decorous, expected, required **09** necessary **10** compulsory **11** fashionable **12** conventional, the done thing

derision
05 scorn **06** insult, satire **07** disdain, hissing, mockery, ragging, teasing **08** contempt, ridicule, scoffing, sneering, taunting **10** disrespect **13** disparagement
• **expression of derision**
02 ho **03** gup, hoa, hoh, mew, yah **05** sucks!, te-hee, ya-boo **06** tee-hee, yah-boo **07** so there **10** get knotted!, sucks to you!, ya-boo sucks **11** yah-boo sucks

derisive
06 ribald **07** jeering, mocking **08** irrisory, scoffing, scornful, taunting **09** insulting **10** disdainful, irreverent **12** contemptuous **13** disrespectful

derisively
10 scornfully **12** disdainfully, irreverently **14** contemptuously **15** disrespectfully

derisory
04 tiny **05** small **06** absurd, paltry **07** risible **08** pathetic, scoffing **09** insulting, laughable, ludicrous **10** inadequate, outrageous, ridiculous **12** contemptible, insufficient, preposterous

derivation
03 der **04** root **05** basis, deriv **06** origin, source **07** descent **08** ancestry, pedigree **09** beginning, deduction, etymology, genealogy, inference **10** extraction, foundation **13** parasynthesis

derivative
03 der **05** deriv, trite **06** branch, copied **07** cribbed, derived, product, spin-off **08** acquired, borrowed, obtained, offshoot, rehashed **09** by-product, formative, hackneyed, imitative, outgrowth, secondary **10** derivation, descendant, second-hand, unoriginal **11** development, plagiarized

derive
03 get **04** draw, flow, gain, reap, stem, take **05** arise, fetch, infer, issue **06** borrow, deduce, evolve, follow, obtain, spring **07** acquire, descend, develop, emanate, extract, proceed, procure, receive **09** originate **14** have its roots in **15** have as the source, have its origin in
• **derived from**
02 of

derogatory
05 snide **06** snidey **08** critical **09** injurious, insulting, offensive, slighting, vilifying **10** belittling, defamatory, detracting, detractive, detractory, pejorative **11** denigratory, disparaging **12** depreciative, disapproving, unfavourable **15** uncomplimentary

descend
03 dip **04** dive, drop, fall, sink, stem **05** deign, issue, pitch, slope, stoop, storm, swoop **06** alight, arrive, derive, go down, invade, plunge, spring, tumble **07** decline, emanate, go to pot, incline, pancake, plummet, proceed, subside **08** come down, dismount, move down, take over **09** originate, parachute **10** condescend, degenerate, go downhill **11** dégringoler, deteriorate, go to the dogs **13** lower yourself **14** arrive suddenly

descendant
03 son **04** cion, sien, slip, syen **05** child, niece, scion **06** nephew, sprout **08** daughter
• **descendant of**
01 O'

descendants
04 line, race, seed **05** heirs, issue

06 family, scions **07** descent, lineage, progeny **08** children, mokopuna **09** offspring, posterior, posterity **10** generation, posteriors, successors

descended
04 alit

descent
03 dip **04** dive, down, drop, fall, line, raid **05** blood, pitch, slant, slope, stock, stoop **06** origin, plunge **07** decline, incline, lineage, sinking **08** ancestry, comedown, gradient, heredity, invasion, pedigree **09** decadence, declivity, genealogy, going-down, parentage, subsiding **10** debasement, declension, degeneracy, extraction, family tree **11** degradation **12** degeneration, dégringolade **13** deterioration

describe
◇ *containment indicator*
04 call, draw, hail, talk, tell **05** brand, label, style, sweep, think, trace, write **06** define, depict, detail, relate, report, scrive, sketch, strike **07** explain, express, mark out, narrate, outline, portray, present, recount, scrieve, specify **08** consider, descrive **09** character, delineate, designate, elucidate, represent **10** illustrate **12** characterize **13** give details of

description
04 kind, make, sort, type **05** brand, breed, class, order, style **06** report, sketch **07** account, outline, picture, profile, variety **08** category, portrait **09** chronicle, depiction, narration, portrayal, statement **10** commentary, definement, exposition **11** delineation, designation, elucidation, explanation, portraiture **12** presentation **13** particularism, specification **14** representation

descriptive
05 vivid **07** graphic **08** detailed, striking **09** colourful, pictorial **10** blottesque, expressive **11** elucidatory, explanatory **12** illustrative

descry
03 get, see **04** espy, mark, spot **06** detect, notice, reveal **07** discern, glimpse, make out, observe **08** discover, perceive **09** discovery, recognize **11** distinguish **12** catch sight of

desecrate
◇ *anagram indicator*
05 abuse **06** damage, debase, defile, insult **07** pervert, pollute, profane, violate **09** blaspheme, dishallow, dishonour, vandalize **10** unsanctify **11** contaminate

desecration
06 damage, insult **07** impiety **09** blasphemy, pollution, sacrilege, violation **10** debasement, defilement **11** profanation **12** dishonouring

desegregate
04 join **05** blend, merge **08** intermix **09** harmonize, integrate **10** assimilate **11** incorporate

desert
03 dry, due, fly, rat **04** arid, bare, deny, fail, flee, jilt, quit, void, wild **05** empty, leave, merit, rat on, right, waste, wilds, worth **06** barren, betray, bug out, decamp, defect, forhow, give up, go AWOL, lonely, maroon, recant, return, reward, strand, virtue **07** abandon, abscond, cast off, demerit, deserts, dried up, forsake, parched, payment, run away, sterile **08** desolate, dust bowl, renounce, run out on, solitary, solitude **09** infertile, throw over, walk out on, wasteland **10** apostasize, barrenness, chicken out, recompense, relinquish, wilderness **11** change sides, comeuppance, retribution, uninhabited **12** moistureless, remuneration, tergiversate, uncultivated, unproductive **14** turn your back on, what you deserve **15** leave high and dry, leave in the lurch

Deserts include:
04 Gobi, Thar
05 Kavir, Namib, Ordos, Sturt
06 Gibson, Mojave, Nubian, Sahara, Syrian, Ust'-Urt
07 Alashan, Arabian, Atacama, Kara Kum, Simpson, Sonoran
08 Kalahari, Kyzyl Kum
09 Dzungaria
10 Bet-Pak-Dala, Chihuahuan, Great Basin, Great Sandy, Patagonian, Takla Makan
13 Great Victoria
14 Bolson de Mapimi

deserted
01 d **04** left, lorn, void **05** empty **06** bereft, lonely, vacant **08** betrayed, derelict, desolate, forsaken, isolated, solitary, stranded **09** abandoned, neglected **10** unoccupied **11** god-forsaken, uninhabited **14** underpopulated

deserter
03 rat **06** bug-out, truant **07** escapee, runaway, traitor **08** apostate, betrayer, defector, fugitive, renegade, turncoat **09** absconder **10** backslider, delinquent

desertion
06 bug-out, denial, flight, give up **07** jilting, leaving, truancy **08** apostasy, betrayal, giving-up, quitting **09** decamping, defection, forsaking, going AWOL **10** absconding, casting-off, renegation **11** abandonment, dereliction, running-away **12** renunciation **14** relinquishment, tergiversation

deserve
03 win **04** earn, rate **05** incur, merit **07** justify, warrant **10** be worthy of **12** be entitled to, have a right to, have it coming

deserved
03 apt, due 04 fair, just, meet 05 right
06 earned, proper 07 condign, fitting,
merited 08 apposite, rightful, suitable
09 justified, warranted 10 legitimate,
well-earned 11 appropriate, justifiable

deservedly
04 duly 06 fairly, justly 07 rightly
08 by rights, properly, suitably
09 fittingly 10 rightfully 11 justifiably
13 appropriately

deserving
05 worth 06 worthy 07 upright
08 laudable, virtuous 09 admirable,
estimable, exemplary, righteous
11 commendable, meritorious
12 praiseworthy

desiccated
03 dry 04 arid, dead 05 dried
07 drained, dried up, parched, sterile
08 lifeless, powdered 10 dehydrated,
exsiccated

desiccation
07 aridity, dryness 08 parching,
xeransis 09 sterility 11 dehydration,
exsiccation

desideratum
04 must, need, want 09 essential,
necessity, requisite 10 sine qua non
11 requirement 12 prerequisite

design
◇ *anagram indicator*
03 aim, end, lay, map 04 draw, etch,
form, gear, goal, hope, logo, make,
mean, plan, plot, seal, tatu, tool, wish
05 draft, dream, guide, hatch, model,
motif, point, shape, style, think
06 cipher, create, desire, device,
devise, draw up, emblem, figure,
format, intend, intent, invent, make-up,
object, scheme, sketch, slight, tailor,
target, tattoo 07 destine, develop,
diagram, drawing, fashion, meaning,
outline, pattern, project, propose,
purpose, sleight, think up, thought
08 conceive, contrive, indicate,
monogram 09 blueprint, construct,
delineate, fabricate, intention,
objective, originate, prototype,
structure 10 assignment, compassing,
enterprise 11 arrangement,
composition, delineation, destination,
undertaking 12 construction,
contrivement, organization
• by design
08 wilfully 09 knowingly, on purpose,
pointedly, wittingly 11 consciously
12 deliberately 13 calculatingly,
intentionally

designate
03 dub 04 call, name, show, term
05 class, elect, style, title 06 assign,
choose, define, denote, select
07 appoint, earmark, entitle, express,
specify 08 christen, classify, describe,
indicate, nominate, set aside
09 stipulate

designation
03 tag 04 name, term, type 05 label,

style, title 07 epithet, marking
08 category, denoting, election,
nickname 09 selection, sobriquet
10 definition, indication, nomination
11 appellation, appellative,
appointment, description, stipulation
12 denomination 13 specification
14 classification

designer
05 maker 06 author, deccie 07 creator,
deviser, planner, plotter, stylist
08 inventor, producer 09 architect,
contriver, couturier, fashioner
10 originator 11 draughtsman
See also **fashion**

designing
03 sly 04 wily 05 sharp 06 artful,
crafty, shrewd, tricky 07 couture,
cunning, devious 08 guileful, plotting,
scheming 09 deceitful, underhand
10 conspiring, intriguing 11 calculating

desirability
05 merit, worth 06 allure, appeal,
profit 07 benefit 08 sexiness
09 advantage 10 attraction,
excellence, popularity, preference,
usefulness 12 advisability
13 seductiveness 14 attractiveness

desirable
03 fit, hot 04 good, sexy 06 plummy
07 popular, wishful 08 alluring,
beddable, eligible, fetching, in
demand, pleasant, pleasing, sensible,
tempting 09 advisable, agreeable,
appetible, expedient, seductive
10 attractive, beneficial, preferable,
profitable, worthwhile 11 appropriate,
sought-after, tantalizing
12 advantageous

desire
03 ask, yen 04 Cama, earn, envy, erne,
fain, itch, Kama, lech, like, list, lust,
need, salt, urge, vote, want, will, wish
05 bosom, covet, crave, fancy, greed,
mania, yearn 06 ardour, besoin,
demand, libido, take to 07 avidity, burn
for, craving, erotism, gasp for, long for,
longing, passion, wish for 08 appetite,
covetise, feel like, sex drive, yearn for,
yearning 09 cacoëthes, hankering,
hunger for, lust after, sexuality
10 aphrodisia, aspiration, be dying for,
desiderate, preference, proclivity,
sensuality 11 hanker after 12 be crazy
about, ephebophilia, have a crush on,
predilection, take a shine to
13 concupiscence, have designs on
14 have the hots for, have your eyes on,
lasciviousness, predisposition, set your
heart on 15 give the world for

desired
05 exact, right 06 proper, wanted
07 correct, fitting 08 accurate,
expected, in demand, required
09 necessary 10 particular
11 appropriate 13 in great demand

desirous
04 avid, keen 05 eager, ready
06 fervid, hoping, hungry 07 anxious,

burning, craving, fervent, hopeful,
itching, longing, wanting, willing,
wishful, wishing 08 aspiring, yearning
09 ambitious, desirable 10 cupidinous
12 enthusiastic

desist
03 end 04 halt, stay, stop 05 cease,
leave, pause, remit, stash 06 give up
07 abstain, forbear, refrain, suspend
08 break off, have done, leave off, peter
out 09 supersede 11 discontinue

desk
04 ambo 05 desse, table 06 bureau,
carrel, pulpit 07 carrell, lectern,
lecturn, lettern, rolltop 08 prie-dieu,
vargueño 09 davenport, écritoire,
faldstool, secretary 10 secretaire
11 litany-stool, reading-desk
12 writing-table 13 bonheur-du-jour

desolate
03 sad 04 arid, bare, wild 05 bleak,
floor, gaunt, upset, waste 06 barren,
bereft, desert, dismal, dreary, gloomy,
gousty, lonely 07 forlorn, get down,
nonplus, shatter, unhappy
08 confound, dejected, deserted,
downcast, forsaken, isolated, solitary,
unpeeled, wasteful, wretched
09 abandoned, depressed, devastate,
discomfit, miserable, overwhelm, take
aback, wasteland 10 depressing,
despondent, disconcert, distressed,
drearisome, melancholy, unoccupied
11 comfortless, god-forsaken,
heartbroken, uninhabited
12 disheartened, god-forgotten,
unfrequented 13 broken-hearted

desolation
04 ruin 05 gloom, grief, waste
06 misery, sorrow 07 anguish, despair,
ravages, sadness 08 distress, solitude,
wildness 09 bleakness, dejection,
emptiness, isolation 10 barrenness,
depression, loneliness, melancholy,
remoteness, wilderness
11 despondency, destruction,
devastation, forlornness, laying waste,
unhappiness 12 wretchedness

despair
05 gloom 06 give in, give up, misery
07 anguish, wanhope 08 collapse,
distress, lose hope 09 dejection,
dysthymia, lose heart, pessimism,
surrender 10 depression, melancholy
11 desperation, despondency 12 be
despondent, hopelessness,
wretchedness 13 be discouraged, hit
rock bottom 15 throw in the towel

despairing
08 dejected, desolate, dismayed,
downcast, hopeless, suicidal,
wretched 09 anguished, depressed,
desperate, miserable, sorrowful
10 despondent, distraught 11 au
désespoir, desperation, discouraged,
heartbroken, pessimistic
12 disconsolate, disheartened,
inconsolable 13 grief-stricken

despatch *see* **dispatch, despatch**

desperado
04 thug 06 badman, bandit, gunman, mugger, outlaw 07 brigand, hoodlum, ruffian 08 criminal, gangster 09 cut-throat, terrorist 10 lawbreaker

desperate
◇ *anagram indicator*
04 bold, dire, rash, wild 05 acute, dying, grave, great, hasty, risky 06 daring, severe, urgent 07 acharné, crucial, do-or-die, extreme, frantic, furious, lawless, serious, violent 08 critical, dejected, desolate, dismayed, downcast, frenzied, hairless, hopeless, pressing, reckless, suicidal, wretched 09 abandoned, anguished, audacious, dangerous, depressed, foolhardy, hazardous, impetuous, miserable, sorrowful 10 compelling, despondent, determined, distraught, incautious, on the ropes 11 discouraged, heartbroken, in great need, pessimistic, precipitate 12 at rock-bottom, crying out for, disconsolate, disheartened, inconsolable 13 grief-stricken 15 needing very much, wanting very much

desperately
◇ *anagram indicator*
05 badly 07 acutely, gravely, greatly 08 severely, urgently 09 extremely, fearfully, seriously 10 critically, dreadfully, hopelessly 11 à corps perdu, dangerously, frightfully

desperation
04 fury, pain 05 agony, gloom, worry 06 misery, sorrow 07 anguish, anxiety, despair, trouble 08 distress 10 depression, despairing 11 despondency 12 hopelessness, recklessness, wretchedness

despicable
03 bum, low 04 base, mean, vile 05 dirty, spewy 07 caitiff, lowdown, pitiful 08 dwarfish, shameful, wretched 09 dastardly, degrading, loathsome, reprobate, worthless 10 abominable, detestable, disgusting 11 disgraceful 12 contemptible, disreputable 13 reprehensible 15 beneath contempt

despise
04 hate, mock, shun 05 abhor, scorn, sneer, spurn 06 deride, detest, forhow, loathe, revile, slight 07 condemn, conspue, contemn, deplore, disdain, dislike 08 vilipend 10 look down on, undervalue 11 set at naught, set at nought 14 hold in contempt

despite
07 against, defying 09 in spite of 11 in the face of 12 regardless of, undeterred by 15 notwithstanding

despoil
03 rob 04 loot, rape 05 pluck, rifle, spoil, strip, wreck 06 bezzle, denude, divest, maraud, ravage 07 bereave, deprive, destroy, pillage, plunder,

ransack 08 spoliate 09 depredate, devastate, vandalize 10 disgarnish, dispossess, untreasure

despondency
04 hump 05 blues, gloom, grief 06 misery, sorrow 07 despair, sadness 08 distress, glumness 09 dejection, heartache, pessimism 10 depression, melancholy 11 desperation, melancholia 12 hopelessness, wretchedness 14 discouragement, dispiritedness 15 downheartedness, inconsolability

despondent
03 low, sad 04 blue, down, glum 06 gloomy 07 doleful 08 dejected, downcast, mournful, wretched 09 depressed, heartsick, miserable, sorrowful 10 despairing, distressed, melancholy 11 discouraged, heartbroken 12 disheartened, inconsolable 14 down in the dumps

despot
04 boss, czar, tsar, tzar 06 sultan, tyrant 08 autocrat, dictator 09 oppressor 10 absolutist 13 absolute ruler

Despots include:
03 Idi
04 Amin (Idi)
05 Timur
06 Caesar (Julius), Führer, Hitler (Adolf), Stalin (Joseph)
07 Papa Doc
08 Duvalier (François)
09 Ceausescu (Nicolae), Mao Zedong, Tamerlane
10 MaoTse-tung
11 Robespierre (Maximilien de), Tamburlaine
15 Ivan theTerrible

despotic
08 absolute, arrogant 09 arbitrary, imperious, tyrannous 10 autocratic, high-handed, oppressive, tyrannical 11 dictatorial, domineering, overbearing 13 authoritarian

despotism
07 tyranny 09 autocracy 10 absolutism, oppression, repression 11 stratocracy 12 dictatorship 15 totalitarianism

dessert
03 pud 05 sweet 06 afters 07 pudding 09 sweet dish 11 aftersupper, sweet course

Desserts and puddings include:
03 ice, pie
04 flan, fool, sago, tart
05 bombe, jelly, kulfi
06 mousse, mud pie, sorbet, sundae, trifle, yogurt
07 baklava, cobbler, compote, crumble, parfait, pavlova, soufflé, tapioca, tartufo, yoghurt
08 Eton mess, ice cream, pandowdy, plum-duff, syllabub, tiramisu, vacherin, yoghourt

09 clafoutis, cranachan
10 blancmange, Brown Betty, cheesecake, egg custard, frangipane, fruit salad, panna cotta, peach Melba, zabaglione
11 baked Alaska, banana split, banoffee pie, crème brûlée, Eve's pudding, milk pudding, plum pudding, rice pudding, spotted dick
12 crème caramel, crêpe suzette, fruit crumble, profiteroles
13 fruit cocktail, millefeuilles, summer pudding
14 charlotte russe
15 clootie dumpling, queen of puddings, roly-poly pudding

See also **cake**

destabilize
◇ *anagram indicator*
05 upset 08 unsettle

destination
03 aim, end 04 fate, goal, gole, list, stop 06 design, object, target 07 purpose, station 08 ambition, terminus 09 intention, objective 10 aspiration 11 journey's end 12 end of the line, landing place 15 final port of call, jumping-off place

destined
04 born 05 bound, fatal, fated, meant 06 booked, doomed, headed, marked, routed 07 certain, en route, heading 08 assigned, designed, directed, intended, ordained, set apart 09 appointed, scheduled 10 inevitable 11 inescapable, preordained, unavoidable 12 foreordained 13 predetermined

destiny
03 lot 04 doom, fate, luck 05 karma, Moera, Moira 06 future, kismet 07 fortune, portion 09 necessity 10 predestiny 14 predestination

destitute
04 poor 05 broke, needy, skint 06 bereft, hard up, rooked 07 lacking, wanting 08 badly off, bankrupt, depleted, deprived, devoid of, dirt-poor, forsaken, helpless, indigent 09 deficient, penniless, penurious 10 cleaned out, distressed, down-and-out, friendless, innocent of, stony-broke 11 impecunious, necessitous, on the street 12 impoverished 14 on the breadline, on your beam-ends 15 poverty-stricken, strapped for cash

destitution
06 penury 07 beggary, poverty, straits 08 distress 09 indigence, pauperdom 10 bankruptcy, starvation 13 pennilessness 14 impoverishment 15 impecuniousness

destroy
◇ *anagram indicator*
03 eat, end, gut, zap 04 kill, raze, ruin, slay, undo 05 break, crush, erase, fordo, harry, level, smash, spoil, waste, wreck 06 banjax, canker, defeat, delete, finish, perish, quench, ravage,

subdue, thwart, wither **07** attrite, deep-six, flatten, handbag, kill off, nullify, put down, ransack, ruinate, scuttle, shatter, stonker, torpedo, unshape, vitiate **08** decimate, demolish, dispatch, knock out, lay waste, overturn, pull down, sabotage, stamp out, tear down **09** devastate, dismantle, eliminate, eradicate, extirpate, knock down, marmelize, overthrow, pulverize, slaughter, undermine **10** annihilate, do away with, extinguish, obliterate, put to sleep, spiflicate **11** spifflicate

destroyer
06 locust, vandal **07** flivver, ravager, stew-can, wrecker **08** Apollyon **09** desolater, despoiler, ransacker **10** demolisher, destructor **11** annihilator, kiss of death

destruction
◇ *anagram indicator*
03 end **04** bane, loss, rack, ruin **05** death, havoc, stroy, waste, wrack, wreck **06** defeat, murder, razing **07** killing, undoing, wastage **08** crushing, downfall, massacre, smashing, wreckage **09** levelling, overthrow, ruination, shipwreck, slaughter, vandalism **10** demolition, desolation, extinction, killing-off, ravagement, shattering **11** depredation, devastation, dismantling, elimination, eradication, extirpation, liquidation, pulling-down, tearing-down **12** annihilation, depopulation, knocking-down, obliteration **13** extermination, nullification

destructive
05 fatal **06** deadly, lethal **07** adverse, baneful, harmful, hostile, hurtful, killing, noxious, ruinous, vicious **08** contrary, damaging, deathful, negative **09** injurious, malignant, withering **10** derogatory, disastrous, disruptive, nullifying, pernicious, subversive, unfriendly **11** deleterious, denigrating, detrimental, devastating, disparaging, mischievous, undermining **12** antagonistic, catastrophic, discouraging, pestilential, slaughterous, unfavourable

destructively
08 lethally **09** harmfully, hurtfully **12** disastrously **13** detrimentally

desultorily
07 loosely **08** casually, fitfully **09** aimlessly **11** erratically **13** half-heartedly

desultory
◇ *anagram indicator*
05 hasty, loose **06** casual, fitful, random **07** aimless, chaotic, erratic **08** rambling **09** haphazard, irregular, spasmodic **10** capricious, discursive, disorderly, undirected **11** half-hearted **12** disconnected, inconsistent, unmethodical, unsystematic **13** unco-ordinated

detach
04 free, undo **05** calve, draft, sever, split, unfix **06** cut off, divide, loosen, remove, unglue **07** disjoin, divorce, isolate, take off, tear off, unhitch, unloose, unrivet **08** break off, disunite, estrange, separate, take away, uncouple, unfasten, unloosen, withdraw **09** disengage, segregate **10** disconnect, dissociate **11** disentangle

detachable
07 movable **08** moveable **09** removable, separable **10** eradicable, removeable **12** transferable

detached
04 cold, free **05** aloof, loose **06** remote **07** divided, neutral, severed **08** clinical, discreet, discrete, outlying, separate **09** impartial, objective, uncoupled, withdrawn **10** disengaged, impersonal, unattached, undivested, unfastened **11** dissociated, independent, indifferent, unconcerned, unconnected, unemotional **12** disconnected **13** disinterested, dispassionate

detachment
04 unit **05** corps, force, party, squad **06** detail, patrol **07** brigade, removal, reserve, undoing **08** coolness, disunion, fairness, squadron **09** aloofness, isolation, loosening, severance, task force, unconcern **10** dispassion, lack of bias, neutrality, remoteness, separation, uncoupling, withdrawal **11** impassivity, objectivity, unfastening **12** impartiality, indifference, provost guard **13** disconnection, disengagement, disentangling, lack of emotion

detail
◇ *tail deletion indicator*
04 fact, item, list, unit **05** corps, force, point, squad **06** aspect, assign, charge, choose, depict, factor, nicety, patrol, relate, set out **07** appoint, brigade, element, feature, itemize, portray, present, recount, respect, specify **08** allocate, delegate, describe, minutiae, point out, rehearse, specific, spell out, tabulate **09** attribute, catalogue, component, delineate, enumerate, intricacy, precision, task force **10** commission, complexity, ingredient, ins and outs, particular, refinement, triviality **11** elaboration, nitty-gritty **12** circumstance, complication, nuts and bolts, technicality, thoroughness **13** particularity, specification **14** characteristic, meticulousness
• **in detail**
05 fully **07** in depth **08** at length **09** carefully, piecemeal **10** item by item, thoroughly **12** exhaustively, in particular, particularly, point by point **15** comprehensively

detailed
◇ *tail deletion indicator*
04 full **05** close, exact **06** minute, narrow **07** complex, in-depth, precise, special **08** complete, itemized, specific, thorough **09** elaborate, intricate **10** blow-by-blow, convoluted, exhaustive, meticulous, particular **11** complicated, descriptive **13** comprehensive

detain
04 hold, keep, slow, stay, stop **05** check, delay **06** arrest, hinder, hold up, impede, intern, lock up, retard **07** confine, inhibit **08** hold back, imprison, keep back, make late, restrain, withhold **09** detention **11** incarcerate, put in prison **13** hold in custody, keep in custody **15** take into custody

detainee
03 POW

detect
03 spy **04** find, nose, note, spot, take **05** catch, sense, sight, trace **06** accuse, expose, notice, reveal, turn up, unmask **07** discern, find out, make out, nose out, observe, uncover, unearth **08** decipher, disclose, discover, identify, perceive **09** ascertain, deprehend, recognize, track down **11** distinguish **12** bring to light **13** become aware of

detectable
◇ *containment indicator*
05 clear **07** visible **08** apparent, distinct **10** noticeable **11** discernible, perceivable, perceptible **12** discoverable, identifiable, recognizable **14** before your eyes

detection
04 note **06** exposé **08** exposure, noticing, sighting **09** discovery, unmasking **10** disclosure, perception, revelation, uncovering, unearthing **11** discernment, observation, recognition, smelling-out, sniffing-out **12** ascertaining, tracking-down **14** distinguishing, identification

detective
02 DC, DI, DS, PI **03** Det, eye, 'tec **04** busy, dick, jack, tail **05** plant **06** shadow, shamus, sleuth **07** gumshoe **08** prodnose, sherlock **09** operative **10** bloodhound, private eye, thief-taker **11** sleuth-hound **12** investigator, thief-catcher **13** police officer

Detectives include:
03 Zen (Aurelio)
04 Bony (Napoleon Bonaparte), Chan (Charlie), Cuff (Richard), Dean (Sam), Gray (Cordelia), Vane (Harriet)
05 Brown (Father), Drake (Paul), Duffy (Nicholas), Dupin (C Auguste), Ghote (Inspector Ganesh), Grant (Alan), Lewis (Sergeant), Mason (Perry), Morse (Inspector

Endeavour), **Queen** (Ellery), **Rebus**
(John), **Spade** (Sam), **Vance** (Philo),
Wolfe (Nero)
06 **Alleyn** (Roderick), **Archer** (Lew),
Essrog (Lionel), **Hanaud**
(Inspector), **Holmes** (Sherlock),
Marple (Miss Jane), **Pascoe** (Peter),
Poirot (Hercule), **Silver** (Miss
Maude), **Vidocq** (Eugène
Françoise), **Watson** (Dr John),
Wimsey (Lord Peter)
07 **Appleby** (John), **Cadfael** (Brother),
Campion (Albert), **Charles** (Nick),
Columbo (Lieutenant), **Dalziel**
(Andy), **Fansler** (Kate), **Laidlaw**
(Jack), **Maigret** (Inspector),
Marlowe (Philip), **Milhone** (Kinsey),
Moseley (Hoke), **Wexford**
(Reginald)
08 **Bergerac** (Jim), **Lestrade**
(Inspector), **Ramotswe** (Precious)
09 **Bonaparte** (Napoleon), **Dalgliesh**
(Adam), **Hawksmoor** (Nicholas),
Pinkerton (Allan), **Scarpetta** (Kay)
10 **Van Der Valk** (Piet), **Warshawski**
(V I)
13 Continental Op

• **detectives**
03 CID, FBI

detention
05 delay **07** custody, jankers
09 captivity, hindrance, restraint,
slowing-up **10** constraint, detainment,
internment, punishment, quarantine
11 confinement, holding-back
12 imprisonment **13** incarceration

deter
04 stop, warn **05** check, daunt
06 hinder, put off **07** caution, inhibit,
prevent, turn off **08** dissuade, frighten,
prohibit, restrain, scare off **09** talk out
of **10** discourage, disincline, intimidate

detergent
04 soap **07** cleaner **08** cleanser
09 cetrimide, detersive **10** abstergent,
surfactant **13** washing powder
15 washing-up liquid

deteriorate
03 ebb **04** drop, fade, fail, slip, wane
05 decay, go bad, go off, lapse, slide,
spoil **06** go down, starve, weaken,
worsen **07** break up, decline, degrade,
fall off, go to pot, relapse, tail off **08** get
worse, go to seed, tail away
09 decompose, fall apart, grow worse,
run to seed **10** degenerate, depreciate,
go downhill, retrograde, retrogress
11 become worse **12** disintegrate, fall
to pieces **13** go down the tube

deterioration
◇ *anagram indicator*
03 ebb **04** drop **05** decay, lapse, slide
06 waning **07** atrophy, decline, failure,
relapse **08** downturn, senility, slipping
09 corrosion, worsening
10 debasement, falling-off, pejoration
11 degradation, dégringoler
12 degeneration, exacerbation
13 retrogression **14** disintegration

determinate
05 fixed **07** certain, decided, defined,
express, limited, precise, settled
08 absolute, clear-cut, decisive,
definite, distinct, explicit, positive,
specific **09** specified **10** conclusive,
definitive, quantified **11** established

determination
◇ *ends selection indicator*
03 end **04** grit, guts, push, will
05 assay, drive, value **06** decree,
ruling, thrust **07** opinion, purpose,
resolve, stamina, verdict **08** backbone,
decision, firmness, sentence, tenacity
09 fortitude, judgement, willpower
10 conclusion, conviction, dedication,
insistence, resolution, settlement
11 arbitrament, arbitrement,
persistence **12** perseverance,
resoluteness **13** steadfastness

determine
03 fix, set **04** rule **05** check, elect, fix
on, guide, hight, impel, learn, limit,
point, shape **06** affect, assign, choose,
clinch, decide, define, detect, direct,
finish, govern, ordain, prompt, settle,
verify **07** agree on, control, dictate,
find out, purpose, resolve
08 conclude, discover, identify,
regulate **09** ascertain, condition,
establish, influence **12** turn the scale
14 make up your mind

determined
03 out, set **04** bent, dour, firm **05** fixed
06 dogged, gritty, intent, single, strong
07 certain, dead set, decided **08** hell-
bent, resolute, resolved, stubborn
09 convinced, dedicated, insistent,
steadfast, tenacious **10** iron-willed,
persistent, purposeful, unwavering
11 ascertained, persevering, tough-
minded, unflinching, well-defined
12 single-minded, strong-minded,
strong-willed **14** uncompromising

determinedly
06 firmly **08** strongly **09** decidedly
10 resolutely, stubbornly **11** insistently,
steadfastly, tenaciously **12** persistently,
purposefully **13** unflinchingly
14 single-mindedly, strong-mindedly

deterrence
09 avoidance, hindrance, obviation
10 dissuasion, heading-off, prevention,
warding-off **11** elimination

deterrent
03 bar **04** curb **05** block, check
07 barrier **08** obstacle **09** hindrance,
repellent, restraint **10** difficulty,
impediment **11** obstruction
12 disincentive **14** discouragement

detest
04 hate **05** abhor **06** loathe
07 deplore, despise, dislike
08 execrate **09** abominate, can't stand
10 recoil from

detestable
04 vile **06** horrid, odious, sordid
07 hateful, heinous **08** accursed,
horrible, shocking **09** abhorrent,

execrable, loathsome, obnoxious,
offensive, repellent, repugnant,
repulsive, revolting, villanous
10 abominable, despicable,
disgusting, villainous **11** abhominable,
distasteful **12** contemptible,
insufferable, pestilential
13 reprehensible

detestation
04 hate **05** odium **06** hatred
07 dislike **08** anathema, aversion,
loathing **09** animosity, antipathy,
hostility, revulsion **10** abhorrence,
execration, repugnance
11 abomination

dethrone
04 oust **06** depose, topple, unseat
07 uncrown **08** unthrone

detonate
04 pink **05** blast, go off, knock, shoot
06 blow up, ignite, kindle, let off, set off
07 explode **08** spark off **09** discharge,
fulminate

detonation
04 bang, boom **05** blast, burst
06 blow-up, report **08** igniting,
ignition **09** blowing-up, discharge,
explosion **11** fulmination

detour
◇ *anagram indicator*
05 byway **06** bypass, bypath, byroad
09 deviation, diversion **10** digression
11 scenic route **13** indirect route
15 circuitous route, roundabout route

detract
03 mar **04** take **05** abate, lower, spoil
06 defame, lessen, reduce **08** belittle,
derogate, diminish, distract, take away
09 devaluate, disparage **10** depreciate
12 subtract from, take away from

detractor
05 enemy **06** critic **07** defamer, reviler
08 traducer, vilifier **09** backbiter,
belittler, muck-raker, slanderer
10 denigrator, disparager
11 substractor **13** scandalmonger

detriment
03 ill **04** evil, harm, hurt, loss
05 wrong **06** damage, injury
07 empeach, impeach **08** mischief
09 prejudice **10** diminution,
disservice, impairment
12 disadvantage

detrimental
07 adverse, harmful, hurtful
08 damaging, inimical, scathing
09 injurious **10** pernicious
11 deleterious, destructive,
mischievous, prejudicial
15 disadvantageous

detritus
04 junk, scum **05** waste **06** debris,
litter, rubble **07** garbage, remains,
rubbish **08** wreckage **09** fragments

devalue
04 slag, slam **05** knock, lower, slate
06 demean, reduce **07** deflate,

dismiss, run down, slag off **08** decrease, minimize, play down **09** devaluate, disparage, underrate **10** devalorize, undervalue **11** make light of **12** pull to pieces, tear to pieces

devastate
◇ *anagram indicator*
04 raze, ruin, sack **05** floor, level, shock, spoil, waste, wreck **06** ravage **07** despoil, destroy, flatten, nonplus, perturb, pillage, plunder, ransack, shatter **08** confound, demolish, desolate, lay waste, overcome, populate **09** discomfit, overwhelm, take aback **10** discompose, disconcert, traumatize

devastated
◇ *anagram indicator*
05 upset, waste **06** gutted **07** crushed, shocked, stunned **08** appalled, desolate, overcome **09** horrified, in anguish **10** distressed, taken aback **11** heartbroken, overwhelmed, traumatized **13** knocked for six

devastating
05 great **06** lovely **07** harmful, ruinous, wasting **08** crushing, damaging, dazzling, fabulous, gorgeous, incisive, ravaging, shocking, smashing, striking, stunning **09** brilliant, effective, wonderful **10** disastrous, impressive, marvellous, remarkable, shattering, staggering **11** destructive, magnificent, spectacular **12** catastrophic, overwhelming, traumatizing **13** extraordinary

devastation
04 ruin, sack **05** havoc, ruins, waste, wrack **06** damage, ravage **07** pillage, plunder, ravages **08** wreckage **09** wasteness **10** demolition, desolation, spoliation **11** destruction **12** annihilation, fire and sword

develop
◇ *anagram indicator*
03 get **04** grow **05** arise, begin, catch, deduce, ensue, found, hatch, ripen, shape, start **06** create, evolve, expand, follow, foster, happen, invent, mature, pick up, result, set off, spread, unfold **07** acquire, advance, amplify, enhance, enlarge, improve, nurture, open out, produce, prosper, shape up, work out **08** argument, commence, contract, dilate on, disclose, expand on, fetch out, flourish, generate, initiate, progress, set about **09** branch out, come about, elaborate, establish, institute, originate, succumb to **10** go down with **11** fall ill with, materialize, set in motion **13** become ill with

development
◇ *anagram indicator*
04 area, land **05** block, event, issue **06** centre, change, estate, growth, result, spread **07** advance, complex, outcome **08** genetics, incident, increase, maturing, maturity, progress, upgrowth **09** evolution, expansion, extension, happening, promotion, situation, unfolding **10** blossoming, occurrence, phenomenon, prosperity, refinement, upbuilding **11** elaboration, enlargement, flourishing, furtherance, improvement, progression **12** circumstance, turn of events
• **stage of development**
04 pupa

deviance
07 anomaly **08** variance **09** disparity **10** aberration, divergence, perversion **11** abnormality **12** eccentricity, irregularity

deviant
◇ *anagram indicator*
04 bent, geek, goof, kook **05** crank, freak, kinky **06** misfit, oddity, quirky, weirdo **07** bizarre, dropout, oddball, odd sort, pervert, twisted, variant, wayward **08** aberrant, abnormal, freakish, perverse **09** anomalous, disparate, divergent, eccentric, irregular, perverted **13** nonconformist **15** with a screw loose

deviate
◇ *anagram indicator*
03 bag, err, yaw **04** part, seam, turn, vary, veer **05** drift, sheer, sport, stray **06** change, depart, differ, swerve, wander **07** decline, deflect, digress, diverge, incline, oblique, turn off **08** aberrate, go astray, turn away **09** turn aside **11** prevaricate **13** go off the rails

deviation
◇ *anagram indicator*
03 yaw **05** break, drift, error, freak, quirk, sheer, shift **06** change, detour, swerve **07** anomaly, decline, turning **08** variance **09** deflexion, deflexure, departure, disparity, excursion, inflexion, variation **10** aberration, alteration, deflection, difference, digression, divergence, inflection **11** abnormality, declination, discrepancy, fluctuation, inclination **12** eccentricity, inordination, irregularity, turning-aside **13** inconsistency, prevarication

device
04 bomb, logo, plan, plot, ploy, ruse, seal, sign, tool, wile **05** badge, crest, dodge, gizmo, motif, motto, stunt, token, trick, waldo **06** design, emblem, gadget, gambit, masque, scheme, shield, symbol, tactic **07** conceit, machine, slinter, utensil **08** artifice, colophon, insignia, strategy **09** apparatus, appliance, implement, manoeuvre, mechanism, stratagem **10** coat of arms, instrument **11** contraption, contrivance, machination

Devices include:

04 iPod®, Xbox®
05 clock, phone, razor, torch, watch
06 juicer, scales, shaver
07 Game Boy®, lighter, stapler, Walkman
08 CD player, egg timer, Gamecube®, nail file, scissors, tweezers
09 can opener, cell phone, corkscrew, hairdryer, hole punch, magnifier, pedometer, staple gun, stopwatch, telephone, tin opener
10 calculator, coin sorter, fax machine, ice scraper, wine cooler
11 answerphone, baby monitor, electric fan, manicure set, mobile phone, PlayStation®, thermometer
12 bottle opener, curling tongs, games console, kitchen timer, nail clippers
13 remote control, smoke detector, staple remover
14 personal stereo, Swiss army knife

See also **electrical**; **optical**; **rhetorical**

devil
03 div, imp, Pug **04** bogy, fend, Nick, ogre **05** beast, bogey, brute, demon, deuce, fiend, fient, rogue, Satan, sorra, worry **06** Belial, Cloots, daemon, daimon, drudge, Hornie, Mahoun, Old One, pester, ragman, rascal, savage, sorrow, terror, wretch **07** bogyman, Clootie, dickens, Evil One, goodman, incubus, Lucifer, Mahound, monster, Old Nick, Scratch, succuba, the deil **08** Apollyon, bogeyman, firework, goodyear, man of sin, Mephisto, mischief, Old Harry, Old Poker, succubus, the enemy, wirricow, worricow, worrycow **09** Adversary, arch-fiend, Beelzebub, cacodemon, Davy Jones, goodyears, Nickie-ben, yoke-devil **10** cacodaemon, evil spirit, Old Scratch, Ragamuffin, the evil one, the Tempter **11** arch-traitor, the old enemy **12** the wicked one **14** Mephistopheles, Mephistophilis, Mephostophilus

devilish
◇ *anagram indicator*
04 evil, very, vile **05** cruel, jolly **06** highly, knotty, really, thorny, tricky, wicked **07** awfully, awkward, demonic, greatly, hellish, satanic **08** accursed, damnable, delicate, diabolic, dreadful, fiendish, infernal, severely, shocking, terribly, ticklish **09** atrocious, difficult, execrable, extremely, intensely, malignant, nefarious, sensitive, unusually **10** diabolical, disastrous, dreadfully, outrageous, remarkably, thoroughly, uncommonly **11** complicated, exceedingly, excessively, frightfully, problematic **12** excruciating, immoderately, unreasonably **13** exceptionally **15** extraordinarily

devil-may-care
04 rash **06** casual **08** careless, cavalier, flippant, heedless, reckless **09** audacious, easy-going, frivolous, unworried **10** insouciant, nonchalant, swaggering **11** unconcerned **12** happy-go-lucky **13** swashbuckling

devilry
03 sin **04** evil **07** impiety **08** atrocity, enormity, foulness, iniquity, vileness

09 amorality, depravity, diabolism, reprobacy **10** corruption, immorality, sinfulness, wickedness **11** abomination, corruptness, heinousness **12** fiendishness, shamefulness **13** dissoluteness **15** unrighteousness

devious
◊ *anagram indicator*
03 sly **04** wily **06** artful, crafty, erring, subtle, tricky **07** crooked, cunning, erratic, evasive, winding **08** indirect, rambling, scheming, slippery, tortuous **09** deceitful, designing, deviating, dishonest, insidious, insincere, underhand, wandering **10** circuitous, misleading, roundabout **11** calculating, treacherous **12** disingenuous, unscrupulous **13** double-dealing, surreptitious

devise
02 do **04** cast, form, plan, plot, talk, will **05** forge, frame, guess, hatch, hit on, shape, study **06** cook up, create, decoct, depict, design, invent, scheme **07** arrange, compose, concoct, dream up, hit upon, imagine, project, purpose, suppose, think up, work out **08** bequeath, conceive, consider, conspire, contrive, describe, meditate **09** construct, fabricate, formulate, originate **10** come up with **11** put together

devoid
04 bare, free, vain, void **05** empty **06** barren, bereft, vacant **07** lacking, wanting, without **08** deprived **09** deficient, destitute

devolution
09 dispersal **12** distribution

devolve
06 convey, depute, fall to, pass on **07** consign, deliver, entrust, succeed **08** delegate, hand down, pass down, rest with, transfer **10** commission

Devon
02 SW

devote
04 doom, give **05** allot, apply, offer, put in **06** assign, commit, pledge **07** appoint, consign, reserve **08** allocate, dedicate, enshrine, set apart, set aside **09** sacrifice, surrender **10** consecrate **11** appropriate **12** give yourself

devoted
04 fond, true **05** loyal **06** ardent, caring, devout, doomed, loving, sacred **07** staunch, zealous **08** constant, dedicate, faithful, tireless **09** attentive, committed, concerned, dedicated, steadfast **10** unswerving

devotedly
06 fondly **07** loyally **08** ardently, caringly, devoutly, lovingly **09** staunchly **10** faithfully, tirelessly **11** attentively, committedly, dedicatedly, steadfastly **12** unswervingly

devotee
03 bum, fan **04** buff **05** fiend, freak, hound, lover **06** addict, votary, voteen, zealot **07** admirer, fanatic **08** adherent, disciple, follower, merchant **09** supporter **10** aficionado, enthusiast

devotion
04 alms, love, zeal **05** faith, piety **06** ardour, prayer, regard **07** fervour, loyalty, passion, support, worship **08** fidelity, fondness, holiness, sanctity, trueness, warmness **09** adherence, adoration, affection, closeness, constancy, godliness, reverence **10** admiration, allegiance, attachment, commitment, dedication, devoutness, observance, solidarity **11** earnestness, schwärmerei, staunchness **12** consecration, faithfulness, heart-service, spirituality **13** religiousness, steadfastness

• object of devotion
03 god **09** Jugannath **10** Juggernaut

devotional
04 holy **05** pious **06** devout, sacred, solemn **07** dutiful **09** pietistic, religious, spiritual **11** reverential

devour
◊ *insertion indicator*
03 eat **04** bolt, cram, gulp **05** eat up, enjoy, gorge, raven, scarf, scoff, skoff, snarf, stuff, worry **06** absorb, engulf, gobble, guzzle, ravage, relish, take in **07** consume, destroy, drink in, engorge, envelop, feast on, put away, revel in, swallow **08** dispatch, lay waste, tuck into, wolf down **09** depredate, devastate, finish off, knock back, polish off **10** appreciate, gormandize **13** be engrossed in, gourmandize

devout
04 deep, holy **05** godly, pious **06** ardent, solemn **07** devoted, earnest, fervent, genuine, intense, saintly, serious, sincere, staunch, zealous **08** constant, faithful, orthodox, profound, reverent, vehement **09** committed, dedicated, heartfelt, prayerful, religious, steadfast **10** passionate, practising, unswerving **11** church-going **12** wholehearted

devoutly
06 deeply **07** piously **08** ardently **09** earnestly, fervently, sincerely, staunchly, zealously **10** faithfully, reverently **11** prayerfully, religiously, steadfastly **12** passionately **14** wholeheartedly

dewy
05 roral, roric, rorid **06** roscid **07** bedewed **08** blooming, innocent, youthful **10** starry-eyed

dexterity
03 art **05** craft, knack, skill **06** slight **07** ability, address, agility, finesse, mastery, sleight **08** aptitude, artistry, deftness, facility **09** adeptness,

expertise, handiness, ingenuity, readiness **10** adroitness, expertness, nimbleness **11** legerdemain, proficiency, skilfulness **14** effortlessness **15** right-handedness

dexterous
04 able, deft **05** adept, agile, handy, nifty, nippy, ready **06** adroit, artful, clever, expert, facile, habile, nimble, subtle, wieldy **07** featous, skilful **08** feateous, featuous **10** neat-handed, proficient **11** right-handed **12** accomplished **14** nimble-fingered

diabolical
◊ *anagram indicator*
04 evil, vile **05** nasty **06** sinful, wicked **07** demonic, hellish, satanic **08** absolute, complete, damnable, devilish, dreadful, fiendish, infernal, shocking **09** appalling, atrocious, execrable, monstrous **10** disastrous, outrageous **12** excruciating

diacritic
05 acute, breve, grave, haček, tilde **06** accent, macron, umlaut **07** cedilla **08** dieresis, modifier

diadem
05 crown, mitre, round, tiara **07** circlet, circuit, coronet **08** headband

diagnose
06 detect **07** analyse, explain, isolate **08** identify, pinpoint **09** determine, interpret, recognize **11** distinguish, investigate

diagnosis
06 answer **07** opinion, verdict **08** analysis, scrutiny **09** detection, judgement **10** conclusion **11** diagnostics, examination, explanation, recognition **13** investigation **14** identification, interpretation

diagnostic
10 analytical, indicative **11** symptomatic **12** interpretive, recognizable **13** demonstrative **14** distinguishing, interpretative **15** differentiating

diagonal
05 cater, cross **06** angled **07** crooked, oblique, sloping **08** crossing, slanting **09** crosswise **10** cornerways **11** catercorner, catty-corner **13** catercornered, catty-cornered, kitty-cornered

diagonally
05 cater **06** aslant **08** bendwise **09** at an angle, crossways, crosswise, obliquely, on the bias, slantwise **10** cornerways, cornerwise, on the cross, on the slant **11** catercorner, catty-corner **13** catercornered, catty-cornered, kitty-cornered

diagram
03 key **04** abac, plan, plat, tree **05** chart, draft, graph, table **06** figure, layout, schema, scheme, sketch **07** cutaway, drawing, outline,

picture **08** bar chart, isopleth, nomogram, pie chart, run chart **09** floor plan, flow chart, indicator, nomograph, schematic **10** family tree, stereogram **11** delineation **12** exploded view, illustration **14** alignment chart, representation

diagrammatic
07 graphic, tabular **09** schematic **12** illustrative **14** diagrammatical

dial
03 map, pan **04** bass, call, disc, face, mush, ring **05** clock, phone, tuner, watch **06** call up, circle, treble **07** control **09** give a bell, give a buzz, hourplate, telephone
• **compass dial**
04 card

dialect
03 Twi **04** Norn **05** argot, idiom, lingo **06** accent, jargon, patois, speech **07** diction, variety **08** language, localism **10** vernacular **11** regionalism **13** provincialism
• **dialect society**
03 EDS

dialectic
05 logic **06** debate **07** logical **08** analysis, logistic, polemics, rational **09** deduction, deductive, induction, inductive, polemical, rationale, reasoning **10** analytical, contention, dialectics, discussion **11** dialectical, disputation **12** disputatious **13** argumentation, argumentative, ratiocination, rationalistic

dialogue
04 chat, talk **05** lazzo, lines **06** debate, gossip, script **08** colloquy, converse, exchange **09** discourse, tête-à-tête **10** conference, discussion **11** interchange, pastourelle **12** conversation, stichomythia **13** communication, interlocution

diameter
01 d **03** dia **04** diam

diametrically
07 utterly **08** directly **10** absolutely, completely **14** antithetically

diamond
04 bort, pick, rock **05** boart, spark **06** carbon, lasque **07** adamant, paragon, rhombus **08** sparkler **09** brilliant, solitaire **10** Rhinestone

• **diamonds**
01 D **03** ice

Diana
02 Di **07** Artemis

diaphanous
04 fine, thin **05** clear, filmy, gauzy, light, sheer, veily **08** chiffony, cobwebby, delicate, gossamer, pellucid **09** gossamery **10** see-through **11** translucent, transparent

diarrhoea
05 scour **06** scours **07** the runs **08** lientery, the trots, wood-evil **09** dysentery, looseness **10** Delhi belly, gippy tummy, gyppy tummy **12** Aztec two-step, holiday tummy, Spanish tummy, weaning brash

diary
03 log **06** memoir **07** day-book, diurnal, Filofax®, journal, logbook **08** year-book **09** chronicle **13** journal intime **14** engagement book **15** appointment book

diatribe
05 abuse **06** attack, insult, rebuke, tirade **07** reproof, slating **08** harangue, knocking, reviling, slamming **09** criticism, invective, onslaught, philippic, reprimand **10** upbraiding **11** running-down **12** denunciation, vituperation

dice
04 bale **05** bones **09** astragals **11** devil's bones
• **spot on dice**
03 pip **04** peep **05** peepe

dicey
04 iffy **05** dodgy, hairy, risky **06** chancy, tricky **07** dubious **09** dangerous, difficult, uncertain **11** problematic **13** unpredictable

dichotomy
08 conflict, division, variance **09** deviation, disparity, variation **10** difference, divergence, opposition **11** discrepancy **13** dissimilarity **15** differentiation

dicky
◇ *anagram indicator*
03 ass **04** weak **05** frail, shaky **06** ailing, infirm **07** unsound **08** unsteady

dictate
03 law, say **04** dite, read, rule, word **05** edict, order, speak, utter **06** behest, charge, decree, demand, direct, impose, indite, insist, ruling **07** bidding, command, lay down, mandate, precept, read out, set down, statute **08** announce, instruct, transmit **09** direction, ordinance, prescribe, principle, pronounce, read aloud, ultimatum **10** injunction, promulgate **11** requirement **12** give orders to, promulgation

dictator
04 dict, duce **06** despot, tyrant **07** supremo **08** autocrat **09** oppressor **10** autarchist, Big Brother **12** little Hitler **13** absolute ruler

See also **despot**

dictatorial
05 bossy **08** absolute, despotic, dogmatic **09** arbitrary, autarchic, imperious, unlimited **10** autocratic, omnipotent, oppressive, peremptory, repressive, tyrannical **11** all powerful, domineering, magisterial, overbearing **12** totalitarian, unrestricted **13** authoritarian, authoritative

dictatorship
07 fascism, tyranny **09** autocracy, despotism, Hitlerism **11** police state **12** absolute rule **13** reign of terror **15** totalitarianism

diction
05 lexis, style **06** saying, speech **07** fluency **08** delivery, language, locution, phrasing, speaking **09** elocution **10** expression, inflection, intonation **11** enunciation **12** articulation **13** pronunciation

dictionary
03 DNB, OED, TCD **04** dict **06** gradus **07** alveary, lexicon **08** Chambers, glossary, wordbook **09** gazetteer, thesaurus **10** vocabulary **11** concordance, onomasticon, synonymicon **12** encyclopedia, etymologicon, etymologicum

dictum
04 fiat **05** axiom, edict, maxim, order **06** decree, ruling, saying **07** command, dictate, precept, proverb **08** aphorism **09** direction, ipse dixit, utterance **12** proclamation **13** pronouncement

did
01 'd

didactic
05 moral **08** pedantic **09** educative, pedagogic **10** didascalic, moralizing, preceptive, protreptic **11** educational, informative, instructive **12** prescriptive

die

02 go **03** dee, ebb, end, pip **04** ache, cark, exit, fade, fail, kark, long, pass, pine, sink, stop, wane, wilt **05** be mad, choke, croak, decay, drown, go off, lapse, merge, punch, quell, swelt, yearn **06** be nuts, be wild, cut out, depart, desire, expire, famish, finish, go bung, go west, pass on, peg out, perish, pip out, pop off, starve, sterve, vanish, wither **07** be crazy, conk out, decease, decline, dwindle, kick off, kiss off, long for, pass out, pine for, snuff it, subside, succumb **08** be raring, decrease, dissolve, flatline, intaglio, melt away, pass away, pass over, peter out, spark out **09** break down, disappear, go belly up, have had it, lose power **10** hop the twig **11** be desperate, bite the dust, come to an end **12** lose your life, pop your clogs, slip the cable **13** close your eyes, kick the bucket, meet your maker, push up daisies **14** depart this life, give up the ghost, turn up your toes **15** breathe your last, cash in your chips, join the majority

• **die away**
04 fade, fall **07** evanish, fall off **09** disappear **10** become weak **11** become faint

• **die down**
04 drop, stop **05** abate, slake **06** quench **07** decline, quieten, subside **08** blow over, decrease

• **die out**
06 vanish **08** peter out **09** disappear **10** extinguish **11** become rarer

• **soon to die**
03 fay, fey, fie **05** fated

died

01 d **02** ob **05** obiit

diehard

05 blimp **06** zealot **07** fanatic **08** hardline, old fogey, rightist **09** fanatical, hardliner **11** reactionary **12** conservative, intransigent **13** dyed-in-the-wool, stick-in-the-mud **14** traditionalist

diet

04 bant, fare, fast, food, slim, VLCD **06** reduce, regime, viands **07** abstain, cut down, Landtag, rations, regimen **08** fishmeal, victuals **09** nutrition **10** abstinence, conference, foodstuffs, lose weight, provisions, sustenance **11** comestibles, subsistence, weight-watch

differ

04 vary **05** argue, clash **06** debate, oppose **07** contend, deviate, dispute, dissent, diverge, fall out, quarrel **08** be unlike, conflict, contrast, disagree **09** altercate, take issue **10** contradict, depart from, disconsent **11** deviate from **12** be at odds with, be at variance, be dissimilar **14** not see eye to eye

difference

03 row **04** rest, spat, tiff **05** clash, set-to **07** balance, dispute, quarrel, residue, variety **08** argument, conflict,

contrast, variance **09** deviation, dichotomy, disparity, diversity, exception, remainder, variation **10** antithesis, contention, divergence, inequality, unlikeness **11** altercation, controversy, discrepancy, disputation, distinction, incongruity, singularity **12** disagreement, distinctness **13** dissimilarity, dissimilitude **14** discrimination **15** differentiation

different

◊ *anagram indicator*
03 new, odd **04** allo-, many, rare **05** novel, other **06** at odds, sundry, unique, unlike, varied **07** a far cry, another, awkward, bizarre, diverse, opposed, several, special, strange, unusual, variant, various, varying **08** assorted, clashing, discrete, distinct, ill-timed, mixed bag, numerous, original, peculiar, separate, untimely **09** anomalous, deviating, disparate, divergent, otherwise **10** at variance, dissimilar, individual, poles apart, remarkable, unsuitable **11** contrasting, distinctive, inopportune, worlds apart **12** heterologous, inconsistent, inconvenient, poles asunder, streets apart, unfavourable, unmanageable **13** extraordinary, miscellaneous **14** unconventional

differential

03 gap **08** contrast, separate, variance **09** different, disparate, disparity, divergent **10** difference, divergence **11** contrasting, discrepancy, distinctive **14** discriminating

differentiate

06 modify **07** mark off **08** contrast, separate **09** diversify, tell apart **10** specialize **11** distinguish **12** discriminate **13** individualize, particularize

differentiation

08 contrast **10** separation **11** demarcation, distinction **12** modification **14** discrimination, distinguishing

differently

◊ *anagram indicator*
06 at odds **07** a far cry **09** diversely **10** at variance, poles apart **11** worlds apart **12** dissimilarly, incompatibly **13** contrastingly **14** inconsistently

difficult

03 ill **04** dark, hard, high **05** rough, steep, stiff, tough **06** arcane, Augean, badass, gnarly, knotty, thorny, tiring, tricky, trying, uneath, uphill **07** arduous, awkward, complex, Gordian, obscure, onerous, testing **08** abstract, abstruse, badassed, baffling, esoteric, exacting, involved, perverse, puzzling, stubborn, ticklish, tiresome **09** demanding, difficile, gruelling, intricate, laborious, obstinate, recondite, strenuous, wearisome **10** burdensome, exhausting, formidable, perplexing,

refractory **11** complicated, intractable, troublesome **12** back-breaking, hard to please, recalcitrant, unmanageable **13** problematical, unco-operative

difficulty

03 ado, fix, ill, jam, net, rub **04** hole, knot, mess, node, snag, spot, stew **05** bitch, block, devil, nodus, trial **06** aporia, bother, hang-up, hassle, hiccup, hobble, hurdle, labour, pickle, plight, strain **07** barrier, dilemma, nonplus, perplex, pitfall, problem, quarrel, scruple, straits, trouble **08** distress, exigency, hardship, hot water, obstacle, quandary, struggle **09** deep water, hindrance, how-d'you-do, Lob's pound, nineholes, objection, tall order, tight spot **10** cleft stick, disability, impediment, opposition, perplexity, pretty pass, struggling **11** arduousness, awkwardness, dire straits, obstruction, painfulness, predicament, tribulation **12** complication **13** embarrassment, laboriousness, strenuousness **14** stumbling-block

• **get through difficulty**
04 pass

• **in difficulties**
06 in a fix, in a jam **07** in a hole, in a mess, in a stew, stumped, up a tree **08** bunkered **09** in a scrape, in the soup, in trouble **10** hard-pushed, in hot water, up the creek **11** hard-pressed, in deep water, up against it **12** in a tight spot **13** in dire straits **14** having problems, out of your depth

• **with difficulty**
03 ill **04** hard **06** hardly, scarce, uneath **10** at a stretch

diffidence

07 modesty, reserve, shyness **08** humility, meekness, timidity **09** hesitancy, self-doubt **10** inhibition, insecurity, reluctance **11** bashfulness **12** backwardness, self-distrust **14** self-effacement **15** unassertiveness

diffident

03 shy **04** meek **05** timid **06** modest, unsure **07** abashed, bashful, nervous **08** hesitant, insecure, reserved, sheepish **09** inhibited, reluctant, shrinking, tentative, unassured, withdrawn **10** shamefaced **11** distrusting, unassertive **12** self-effacing **13** self-conscious

diffuse

03 ren, rin, run **05** large, vague, wordy **06** prolix, spread, winnow **07** profuse, publish, scatter, send out, verbose **08** diffused, dispense, disperse, permeate, rambling, waffling **09** circulate, dispersed, dissipate, imprecise, propagate, scattered **10** discursive, distribute, long-winded, loquacious, promulgate **11** disseminate **12** disconnected, periphrastic **14** circumlocutory, unconcentrated

ffusion

osmosis **08** bleeding **09** dispersal, tension, spreading **10** permeation, attering **11** circulation, dissipation, opagation **12** distribution, omulgation **13** dissemination

g

get, jab **04** cast, fork, gibe, gird, ub, howk, jeer, mine, poke, prod, it, spud, till, twig, work **05** click, ack, delve, ditch, gouge, graft, grasp, ave, lodge, probe, punch, scoop, eer, spade, taunt **06** burrow, follow, into, grub up, harrow, hollow, insult, erce, plough, quarry, search, take in, rust, trench, tunnel **07** approve, eak up, channel, fossick, grub out, alize, scratch, unearth **08** disinter, trench, excavate, research, turn over cultivate, figure out, make a hole, enetrate, undermine, wisecrack appreciate, compliment, cavation, understand **11** insinuation, vestigate **12** get the hang of

dig up

find **06** exhume, expose **07** root it, uncover, unearth **08** discover, sinter, excavate, retrieve extricate, track down **12** bring to ht

digging implement

ko **04** spud **05** spade

igest

anagram indicator

code **05** endew, endue, grasp, dew, indue, study **06** absorb, codify, onder, précis, reduce, résumé, take in abridge, process, shorten, stomach, mmary **08** abstract, canon law, mpress, condense, consider, ssolve, macerate, meditate, mull er, synopsis **09** break down, duction, summarize **10** assimilate, ompendium, comprehend, derstand **11** abridgement, mpression, contemplate, corporate **12** abbreviation

igestion

eupepsia **09** ingestion absorption, maceration assimilation, breaking-down transformation

igit

toe **05** index, thumb **06** dactyl, ure, finger, hallux, number integer, numeral **10** forefinger, g finger **12** little finger, middle ger

ignified

high **05** grand, grave, lofty, manly, ble **06** august, formal, lordly, sedate, lemn **07** courtly, exalted, stately decorous, handsome, imposing, ajestic, reserved **10** honourable, pressive **11** ceremonious distinguished

ignify

adorn, crown, exalt, grace, raise honour **07** advance, elevate, hance, ennoble, glorify, promote

10 aggrandize **11** apotheosize, distinguish

dignitary

03 VIP **04** dean, name **05** canon **06** big gun, bigwig, high-up, worthy **07** big name, big shot, grandee, notable, provost **08** alderman, luminary, somebody, top brass **09** personage **10** archdeacon

dignity

05 poise, pride, state **06** honour, status **07** decorum, majesty, worship **08** cathedra, eminence, grandeur, nobility, standing **09** elevation, greatness, loftiness, nobleness, propriety, solemnity **10** excellence, importance, preferment, self-esteem **11** courtliness, self-respect, stateliness **13** honourability **14** respectability, self-importance, self-possession

digress

05 drift, stray **06** depart, ramble, wander **07** deviate, diverge, excurse **08** divagate **09** turn aside **13** be sidetracked **15** go off at a tangent, go off the subject

digression

05 aside **06** ecbole, flight, vagary **08** excursus, footnote, straying **09** departure, deviation, diversion, evagation, excursion, wandering **10** apostrophe, divagation, divergence **11** parenthesis **12** extravagance, obiter dictum

digs

03 pad **05** place, rooms **06** billet **08** lodgings, quarters **13** accommodation, boarding-house

dilapidated

◇ *anagram indicator*

05 shaky **06** beat-up, ruined, shabby **07** decayed, in ruins, rickety, run-down, worn-out **08** decaying, decrepit **09** crumbling, neglected **10** broken-down, ramshackle, tumbledown, uncared-for **12** falling apart

dilapidation

04 ruin **05** decay, waste **08** collapse **09** disrepair **10** demolition **11** destruction **13** deterioration **14** disintegration

dilate

04 tent **05** bloat, swell, widen **06** expand, extend, spread **07** broaden, distend, enlarge, inflate, stretch **08** increase **09** spread out

dilatory

04 lazy, slow **05** slack, tardy **08** dawdling, delaying, sluggish, stalling, tarrying **09** lingering, loitering, snail-like **10** postponing, prolixious **11** time-wasting **13** lackadaisical **15** procrastinating

dilemma

03 fix **04** mess, spot **06** plight, puzzle, why-not **07** problem **08** conflict, quandary **10** cleft stick, difficulty,

double bind, perplexity **11** predicament, tight corner **13** embarrassment, vicious circle **14** no-win situation

dilettante

07 amateur, dabbler, trifler **08** aesthete, potterer, sciolist **15** non-professional

diligence

04 care **08** industry **09** assiduity, attention, constancy **10** conscience, dedication, intentness **11** application, earnestness, painstaking, pertinacity **12** perseverance, sedulousness, thoroughness **13** assiduousness, attentiveness, laboriousness

diligent

04 busy **06** eident **07** careful, earnest **08** constant, sedulous, studious, thorough, tireless **09** assiduous, attentive, dedicated **10** meticulous, persistent **11** hard-working, industrious, painstaking, persevering **13** conscientious

dilly-dally

05 dally, delay, hover, tarry, waver **06** dawdle, dither, falter, linger, loiter, potter, trifle **08** hesitate **09** faff about, vacillate, waste time **12** shilly-shally, take your time **13** procrastinate

dilute

03 cut, dil **04** kill, thin **05** allay, delay, lower, small, water **06** lessen, reduce, temper, weaken **07** diffuse, thin out **08** decrease, diminish, mitigate, moderate, tone down, waterish **09** attenuate, water down **10** adulterate, attenuated, make weaker **11** make thinner

diluted

03 cut **04** weak **06** watery **07** thinned **10** thinned out, wishy-washy **11** watered down

dim

04 blur, dark, dull, dumb, dusk, fade, grey, hazy, pale, paly, slow, weak **05** appal, bedim, blear, cloud, dense, dingy, dopey, dusky, faint, foggy, fuzzy, misty, shade, thick, unlit, vague **06** bleary, cloudy, darken, feeble, gloomy, leaden, obtuse, simple, sombre, stupid **07** adverse, becloud, blurred, doltish, obscure, shadowy, tarnish, unclear **08** clouding, confused, gormless, overcast **09** dim-witted, imperfect, make faint, tenebrous **10** caliginous, ill-defined, indistinct, lacklustre, obfuscated, slow-witted **11** become faint, crepuscular, make blurred, unpromising **12** crepusculous, discouraging, inauspicious, simple-minded, unfavourable **13** become blurred

dimension

01 D **03** dim **04** area, bulk, mass, side, size **05** depth, facet, range, scale, scope, width **06** aspect, extent, factor, height, length, volume **07** breadth, element, feature, measure **08** capacity

09 greatness, largeness, magnitude **10** importance **11** measurement, proportions

diminish

03 cut, ebb **04** bate, damp, drop, fade, pare, sink, wane **05** abate, lower, mince **06** defame, die out, impair, lessen, minify, minish, rebate, recede, reduce, shrink, vilify, weaken **07** assuage, attrite, decline, deflate, degrade, detract, devalue, die away, drop off, dwindle, slacken, subside, whittle **08** belittle, contract, decrease, derogate, grow less, minimize, pare down, peter out, retrench, taper off, wear down **09** denigrate, deprecate, disparage **10** become less, deactivate, grow weaker **11** whittle away, whittle down **12** become weaker **14** take the edge off

diminuendo

03 dim **04** fade **11** decrescendo

diminution

03 cut, ebb **04** loss **05** decay, taper **07** atrophy, cutback, decline **08** decrease, drawdown **09** abatement, deduction, detriment, lessening, reduction, shrinkage, weakening **10** shortening, subsidence **11** contraction, curtailment, defalcation **12** retrenchment

diminutive

03 dim, wee **04** mini, tiny **05** dinky, elfin, pigmy, pygmy, small, teeny **06** little, midget, minute, petite, pocket, tottie **07** compact, minikin **08** dwarfish, pint-size **09** miniature, pint-sized **10** contracted, homuncular, hypocorism, small-scale, teeny-weeny, undersized **11** hypocorisma, Lilliputian, microscopic, pocket-sized **13** infinitesimal

dimly

05 dully **06** darkly, feebly, hazily, weakly **07** dingily, faintly, mistily **08** gloomily, sombrely **09** obscurely, unclearly **12** indistinctly

dimness

04 dusk, mist **06** caligo **08** darkness, dullness, greyness, twilight **09** dinginess, half-light **10** cloudiness, crepuscule **12** caliginosity

dimple

04 dint **05** fovea **06** hollow **09** concavity, umbilicus **10** depression **11** indentation

dimwit

03 git **04** berk, clot, dope, dork, fool, geek, prat, twit **05** dumbo, dunce, dweeb, idiot **06** nitwit **07** dullard, halfwit, plonker **08** bonehead, numskull **09** blockhead, ignoramus **10** dunderhead **11** knuckle-head

See also **fool**

din

03 row **04** deen, reel, utis **05** alarm, chirm, clash, crash, noise, noyes, raird, reird, shout **06** babble, hubbub, outcry, racket, randan, stound, stownd, tumult, uproar **07** clamour, clatter, yelling **08** brouhaha, clangour, shouting **09** charivari, commotion, loud noise **10** hullabaloo **11** pandemonium

dine

03 eat, sup **04** feed, mess **05** feast, lunch **06** dinner **07** banquet **10** have dinner

dingy

03 dim, dun **04** dark, drab, dull, fusc, worn **05** dirty, dusky, faded, grimy, murky, oorie, ourie, owrie, seedy **06** dismal, dreary, gloomy, isabel, shabby, soiled, sombre **07** fuscous, obscure, run-down, squalid **08** isabella **09** cheerless **10** colourless, isabelline **11** discoloured **12** disreputable

dinky

04 fine, mini, neat, trim **05** natty, small **06** dainty, little, petite **07** trivial **09** miniature **13** insignificant

dinner

03 tea **04** dine, hall, kail, kale, meal **05** feast **06** repast, spread, supper **07** banquet, blow-out **08** main meal **09** beanfeast, refection, wasegoose, wayzgoose **11** evening meal

• **dinner time**
07 evening

dinosaur

Dinosaurs include:

04 T Rex
06 Raptor
08 Coelurus, Sauropod, Theropod
09 Hadrosaur, Iguanodon, Oviraptor
10 Allosaurus, Anatotitan, Barosaurus, Diplodocus, Megalosaur, Ophiacodon, Torosaurus, Utahraptor
11 Apatosaurus, Ceteosaurus, Coelophysis, Coelurosaur, Deinonychus, Dromaeosaur, Polacanthus, Prosauropod, Saurischian, Stegosaurus, Triceratops, Tyrannosaur
12 Ankylosaurus, Brontosaurus, Camptosaurus, Ceratosaurus, Megalosaurus, Ornithischia, Ornithomimus, Plateosaurus, Titanosaurus, Velociraptor
13 Atlantosaurus, Brachiosaurus, Compsognathus, Corythosaurus, Dwarf Allosaur, Edmontosaurus, Herrerasaurus, Ornitholestes, Styracosaurus, Tyrannosaurus
14 Leaellynasaura
15 Cryolophosaurus, Parasaurolophus

dint

04 blow, dent **05** force **06** hollow, indent, stroke **09** concavity **10** depression, impression **11** indentation

• **by dint of**
09 by means of **10** by virtue of **13** by the agency of

diocese

03 see **04** Ebor, Exon, Oxon **06** Cantab, Dunelm **07** Cantuar, eparchy **09** bishopric, eparchate

Dioceses and archdioceses of the UK:

03 Ely
04 York
05 Derby, Derry, Leeds, Truro
06 Armagh, Bangor, Connor, Durham, Exeter, Hallam, London, Oxford
07 Brechin, Bristol, Cardiff, Chester, Clifton, Clogher, Dromore, Dunkeld, Glasgow, Kilmore, Lincoln, Menevia, Norwich, Paisle, Salford, St Asaph, Wrexham
08 Aberdeen, Bradford, Carlisle, Coventry, Galloway, Hereford, Llandaff, Monmouth, Plymouth, St Albans, St Davids
09 Blackburn, Brentwood, Edinburgh, Guildford, Lancaster, Leicester, Lichfield, Liverpool, Newcastle, Rochester, Salisbury, Sheffield, Southwark, Southwell, Wakefield, Worcester
10 Birmingham, Canterbury, Chelmsford, Chichester, East Anglia, Gloucester, Manchester, Motherwell, Nottingham, Portsmouth, Shrewsbury, Winchester
11 Northampton, Sodor and Man (Anglican), Westminster
12 Bath and Wells, Peterborough
13 Down and Connor, Middlesbrough, Ripon and Leeds
14 Derry and Raphoe, Down and Dromore
16 Swansea and Brecon
17 Aberdeen and Orkney, Argyll and the Isles
18 Arundel and Brighton, Glasgow and Galloway, Hexham and Newcastle
21 Moray, Ross and Caithness, St Andrews and Edinburgh
23 St Edmundsbury and Ipswich
27 St Andrews, Dunkeld and Dunblane

Dionysus

07 Bacchus **10** Liber Pater

dip

03 dap, dib, dim, dop, nod, sag **04** bath, dent, dive, drop, duck, dunk, fall, hole, pawn, plot, sink, soak, swim **05** basin, bathe, cream, delve, douse, lower, merge, ploat, sauce, slope, slump, souse **06** dibble, go down, hollow, plunge, relish **07** baptize, decline, descend, descent, ducking, immerge, immerse, incline, moisten, sloping, soaking, subside, suffuse **08** decrease, dressing, infusion, lowering, mortgage, submerge **09** concavity, drenching, immersion, lessening, reduction **10** depression, pickpocket **11** indentation

• **dip into**
03 use **04** skim **05** spend **06** browse, draw on, look at **10** run through **11** leaf through, look through **12** flick through, thumb through

diplomacy
4 tact 05 craft, skill 07 finesse
8 delicacy, politics, prudence,
subtlety 10 cleverness, discretion,
statecraft 11 manoeuvring,
negotiation, savoir-faire, sensitivity,
tactfulness 12 negotiations
3 judiciousness, statesmanship

diplomat
2 CD, HE 05 envoy 06 consul, legate
7 attaché 08 emissary, mediator
9 go-between, moderator,
statesman 10 ambassador, arbitrator,
negotiator, peacemaker, politician
1 conciliator 12 ambassadress
5 plenipotentiary

diplomatic
6 clever, subtle 07 politic, prudent,
skilful, tactful 08 consular, discreet
9 judicious, sensitive
3 ambassadorial
  diplomatic corps
2 CD
  period of diplomatic service
4 tour

diplomatically
9 prudently, skilfully, tactfully
10 discreetly 11 judiciously, politically,
sensitively 13 by negotiation, with
diplomacy 14 conciliatorily

dipsomaniac
3 sot 04 lush, soak, wino 05 alkie,
bloat, dipso, drunk, souse, toper
6 boozer, sponge 07 Bacchus,
drinker, tippler, tosspot 08 drunkard,
habitual 09 alcoholic, inebriate
10 wine-bibber 11 hard drinker
2 heavy drinker

dire
anagram indicator
4 fell 05 awful, grave, vital 06 urgent
7 crucial, drastic, extreme, ominous
8 alarming, dreadful, horrible,
pressing, shocking, terrible
9 appalling, atrocious, desperate,
frightful 10 calamitous, disastrous,
portentous 11 distressing
2 catastrophic

direct
anagram indicator
3 aim, con, run, set 04 airt, conn,
hold, lead, mean, near, show, tell, turn
05 apply, bluff, blunt, focus, frank,
guide, level, order, point, ready, right,
shape, steer, teach, usher 06 adjure,
candid, charge, escort, govern, handle,
honest, intend, manage, market, target
07 address, command, conduct,
control, incline, non-stop, oversee,
primary, sincere, through, up-front
08 directly, explicit, instruct, organize,
personal, regulate, straight, unbroken
09 first-hand, immediate, outspoken,
supervise 10 administer, face-to-face,
forthright, give orders, mastermind,
point-blank, show the way, unswerving
1 be the boss of, plainspoken, point
the way, preside over, superintend,
unambiguous, undeviating,
unequivocal 12 be in charge of, call the

shots 13 be in control of, uninterrupted
15 straightforward, uninterruptedly
• **directed towards**
02 on
• **direct from**
02 ex

direction
03 set, way 04 airt, goal, lead, line,
path, plan, road 05 brief, drift, route,
rules, tenor, track, trend 06 course,
orders 07 bearing, command, control,
running 08 briefing, guidance,
handling, tendency 10 current aim,
government, guidelines, indication,
leadership, management, overseeing,
regulation 11 inclination, information,
orientation, regulations, supervision
12 instructions 14 administration
15 recommendations,
superintendency
See also **compass**
• **directions**
06 recipe
• **general direction**
03 ren, rin, run
• **in the direction of**
02 on, to 03 for 07 towards
• **in the wrong direction**
03 wry
• **sharp change in direction**
03 zig
• **take a different direction**
07 diverge
• **take a direction**
02 go 04 chop 06 strike

directive
04 fiat 05 edict, order 06 charge,
decree, notice, ruling 07 bidding,
command, concern, dictate, mandate
09 direction, ordinance, speech act
10 imperative, injunction, regulation
11 instruction

directly
03 due 04 bang, dead, full, just, slap,
soon 05 plumb, right, smack 06 at
once, pronto, square 07 bluntly, clearly,
exactly, frankly, plainly, quickly
08 candidly, honestly, outright,
promptly, slap-bang, speedily,
squarely, straight 09 forthwith,
instantly, precisely, presently, right
away, sincerely 10 explicitly, point-
blank, straightly 11 immediately,
straight out, straightway
12 straightaway, straightways,
unswervingly, without delay
13 unambiguously, unequivocally
15 instantaneously

directness
07 honesty 09 bluntness, frankness,
immediacy 10 candidness
13 immediateness, outspokenness
14 forthrightness 15 plainspokenness

director
01 D 03 Dir 04 boss, head 05 chair,
chief 06 auteur, leader, top dog
07 manager 08 chairman, governor,
overseer, Pole Star, producer
09 conductor, corrector, executive,
film-maker, intendant, organizer,

president, principal, régisseur, top
banana 10 chairwoman, controller,
counsellor, supervisor 11 agonothetes,
chairperson, choirmaster, symposiarch
12 chapel master, chorus master,
contributory, manufacturer
13 administrator, kapellmeister
14 chief executive, superintendent
15 Astronomer Royal

Film and theatre directors and
producers include:

03 Cox (Brian), Lee (Spike), May
(Elaine), Ozu (Yasujiro), Ray
(Satyajit), Woo (John)
04 Alda (Alan), Axel (Gabriel), Bond
(Edward), Coen (Ethan), Coen
(Joel), Eyre (Sir Richard), Ford
(John), Gray (Simon), Hall (Sir
Peter), Hare (David), Hart (Moss),
Hill (George Roy), Lang (Fritz),
Lean (Sir David), Nunn (Trevor),
Reed (Sir Carol), Roeg (Nicolas),
Tati (Jacques), Todd (Mike), Weir
(Peter), Wise (Robert)
05 Allen (Woody), Barba (Eugenio),
Boyle (Danny), Brook (Peter), Capra
(Frank), Carné (Marcel), Clair
(René), Craig (Gordon), Cukor
(George Dewey), Dante (Joe),
Demme (Jonathan), Fosse (Bob),
Gance (Abel), Hands (Terry), Hawks
(Howard), Ivory (James), Kazan
(Elia), Kelly (Gene), Korda (Sir
Alexander), Leigh (Mike), Leone
(Sergio), Losey (Joseph), Lucas
(George), Lumet (Sidney), Lynch
(David), Malle (Louis), Mamet
(David), Marsh (Dame Ngaio),
Mayer (Louis B), Miles (Bernard,
Lord), Noble (Adrian), Pabst (Georg
Wilhelm), Perry (Antoinette), Roach
(Hal), Scott (Ridley), Stein (Peter),
Stone (Oliver), Vadim (Roger), Varda
(Agnès), Verdy (Violette), Vidor
(King), Wajda (Andrzej), Wells
(John), Wolfe (George C), Wyler
(William)
06 Abbott (George), Altman (Robert),
Ang Lee, Artaud (Antonin), Arzner
(Dorothy), August (Bille), Badham
(John), Barton (John), Beatty
(Warren), Besson (Luc), Brecht
(Bertolt), Brooks (Mel), Bryden
(Bill), Buñuel (Luis), Burton (Tim),
Callow (Simon), Cooney (Ray),
Copeau (Jacques), Corman (Roger),
Curtiz (Michael), Cusack (Cyril),
Daldry (Stephen), Davies (Howard),
Davies (Terence), De Sica (Vittorio),
Devine (George), Dexter (John),
Disney (Walt), Donner (Richard),
Dunlop (Frank), Dybwad (Johanne),
Ephron (Nora), Forbes (Bryan),
Forman (Milos), Frears (Stephen),
Fugard (Athol), Gibson (Mel),
Godard (Jean-Luc), Godber (John),
Haydee (Marcia), Herzog (Werner),
Hopper (Dennis), Hughes
(Howard), Huston (John), Jarman
(Derek), Jordan (Neil), Jouvet
(Louis), Kantor (Tadeusz), Kasdan
(Lawrence), Landis (John), Lupino

(Ida), **Mendes** (Sam), **Miller** (George), **Miller** (Jonathan), **Moreau** (Jeanne), **Murnau** (F W), **Ophuls** (Max), **Parker** (Alan), **Powell** (Michael), **Prince** (Hal), **Prowse** (Philip), **Quayle** (Sir Anthony), **Reiner** (Carl), **Renoir** (Jean), **Siegal** (Don), **Tairov** (Aleksandr), **Usigli** (Rodolfo), **Warhol** (Andy), **Warner** (Deborah), **Warner** (Jack), **Welles** (Orson), **Wilder** (Billy), **Wilson** (Robert), **Zanuck** (Darryl)

07 **Akerman** (Chantal), **Aldrich** (Robert), **Asquith** (Anthony), **Belasco** (David), **Benigni** (Roberto), **Bennett** (Alan), **Bennett** (Michael), **Bergman** (Ingmar), **Berkoff** (Steven), **Bigelow** (Kathryn), **Boorman** (John), **Branagh** (Kenneth), **Bresson** (Robert), **Cameron** (James), **Campion** (Jane), **Chabrol** (Claude), **Chaikin** (Joseph), **Chaplin** (Charlie), **Clavell** (James), **Clooney** (George), **Clurman** (Harold), **Cocteau** (Jean), **Coppola** (Francis Ford), **Costner** (Kevin), **De Mille** (Cecil Blount), **De Palma** (Brian), **Douglas** (Bill), **Douglas** (Michael), **Fellini** (Federico), **Fleming** (Tom), **Fleming** (Victor), **Forsyth** (Bill), **Gaumont** (Léon), **Gilliam** (Terry), **Goldwyn** (Samuel), **Guthrie** (Sir Tyrone), **Hartley** (Hal), **Heiberg** (Gunnar), **Holland** (Agnieszka), **Jackson** (Peter), **Joffrey** (Robert), **Kaufman** (George S), **Kaufman** (Philip), **Kubrick** (Stanley), **McBride** (Jim), **McGrath** (John), **Nichols** (Mike), **Olivier** (Sir Laurence), **Poitier** (Sidney), **Pollack** (Sydney), **Redford** (Robert), **Resnais** (Alain), **Robbins** (Tim), **Russell** (Ken), **Sellars** (Peter), **Sennett** (Mack), **Stiller** (Mauritz), **Sturges** (Preston), **Webster** (Margaret), **Wenders** (Wim)

08 **Anderson** (Lindsay), **Barrault** (Jean-Louis), **Berkeley** (Busby), **Björnson** (Björnstjerne), **Bogdanov** (Michael), **Brustein** (Robert), **Carrière** (Jean-Claude), **Clements** (Sir John), **Crawford** (Cheryl), **Eastwood** (Clint), **Friedkin** (William), **Griffith** (David Wark), **Houseman** (John), **Jarmusch** (Jim), **Kurosawa** (Akira), **Levinson** (Barry), **Lubitsch** (Ernst), **Luhrmann** (Baz), **Lyubimov** (Yuri), **Marshall** (Penny), **Merchant** (Ismail), **Minnelli** (Vincente), **Mitchell** (Arthur), **Miyazaki** (Hayao), **Ninagawa** (Yukio), **Pasolini** (Pier Paulo), **Piscator** (Erwin), **Polanski** (Roman), **Pudovkin** (Vsevolod), **Schepisi** (Fred), **Scorsese** (Martin), **Selznick** (David Oliver), **Sjöström** (Victor), **Stroheim** (Erich von), **Truffaut** (François), **Visconti** (Luchino), von **Trier** (Lars), **Zemeckis** (Robert)

09 **Alexander** (Bill), **Almodóvar** (Pedro), **Antonioni** (Michelangelo), **Armstrong** (Gillian), **Carpenter** (John), **Chen Kaige**, **Fernández** (Emilio), **Greenaway** (Peter), **Grotowski** (Jerzy), **Hitchcock** (Sir Alfred), **Malkovich** (John), **Meyerhold** (Vsevolod), **Minghella** (Anthony), **Mizoguchi** (Kenji), **Mountford** (Charles P), **Peckinpah** (Sam), **Plowright** (Joan), **Preminger** (Otto), **Spielberg** (Steven), **Stevenson** (Robert), **Strasberg** (Lee), **Streisand** (Barbra), **Tarantino** (Quentin), **Tavernier** (Bertrand), **Von Trotta** (Margarethe), **Wanamaker** (Sam), **Zinnemann** (Fred)

10 **Bertolucci** (Bernardo), **Cronenberg** (David), **Eisenstein** (Sergei), **Fassbinder** (Rainer Werner), **Kaurismäki** (Aki), **Kiarostami** (Abbas), **Kieslowski** (Krzystof), **Littlewood** (Joan), **Makhmalbaf** (Mohsen), **Mankiewicz** (Joseph L), **Mnouchkine** (Ariane), **Rossellini** (Roberto), **Saint-Denis** (Michel), **Sucksdorff** (Arne E), **Vakhtangov** (Evgeny), **Wertmuller** (Lina), **Zeffirelli** (Franco), **Zetterling** (Mai), **Zhang Yimou**

11 **Bogdanovich** (Peter), **Dingelstedt** (Franz von), **Mackendrick** (Alexander), **Pressburger** (Emeric), **Riefenstahl** (Leni), **Roddenberry** (Gene), **Schlesinger** (John)

12 **Attenborough** (Sir Richard), **Espert Romero** (Nuria), **Stanislavsky**, **Von Sternberg** (Josef)

13 **Aguilera Malta** (Demetrio), **Gutiérrez Alea** (Tomás), **Stafford-Clark** (Max)

• directors
05 board

• managing director
02 MD **06** Man Dir

directory
04 list **05** guide, index **06** folder **07** listing, red book, who's who **09** catalogue, inventory **10** court guide **11** Yellow Pages®

dirge
05 elegy **06** dirige, lament, monody **07** requiem **08** coronach, threnody **09** dead-march **11** funeral song

dirk
07 whinger **08** skean-dhu, skene-dhu, whiniard, whinyard **10** skene-occle

dirt
03 mud **04** clay, crap, crud, dust, grot, gunk, loam, mess, mire, muck, pick, smut, soil, soot, yuck **05** bilge, clart, crock, earth, filth, grime, gunge, scuzz, slime, stain **06** clarts, grunge, ordure, scunge, sleaze, sludge, smudge **07** gutters, rubbish, tarnish **08** impurity, lewdness **09** excrement, indecency, obscenity, pollution **10** sordidness **11** pornography **13** salaciousness

dirty
03 bad, mud, ray **04** blue, dark, dull, foul, lewd, mean, mess, miry, poxy, soil, soss **05** bawdy, black, clart, dusty,

grimy, manky, messy, mucky, muddy, nasty, slimy, smear, sooty, spoil, stain, sully, yucky **06** assoil, chatty, clarty, cloudy, coarse, cruddy, defile, filthy, greasy, grotty, grubby, grungy, mess up, mingin', muck up, ribald, risqué, scungy, shabby, skanky, sleazy, smirch, smudge, smutty, soiled, sordid, splash, stormy, unfair, vulgar, X-rated **07** begrime, blacken, clouded, corrupt, defiled, draggle, grufted, immoral, minging, obscene, piggish, pollute, raunchy, scruffy, squalid, stained, sullied, tarnish, unclean **08** bedaggle, besmirch, discolor, enormous, improper, indecent, polluted, unwashed **09** bedraggle, deceitful, discolour, dishonest, salacious, tarnished **10** adulterate, despicable, flea-bitten, insanitary, suggestive, unhygienic, unpleasant **11** contaminate, treacherous, undesirable **12** contaminated, contemptible, pornographic, unscrupulous

disability
04 maim **06** defect, malady **07** ailment, illness **08** disorder, handicap, weakness **09** complaint, inability, infirmity, unfitness **10** affliction, difficulty, impairment, incapacity **11** disablement **12** incapability

disable
04 lame, maim, stop **05** crock, wreck **06** damage, defuse, impair, weaken **07** cripple, invalid **08** enfeeble, handicap, knock out, paralyse **09** disparage, hamstring, make unfit, prostrate **10** deactivate, debilitate, depreciate, disqualify, immobilize, invalidate, undervalue **12** incapacitate **14** put out of action

disabled
04 lame, weak **05** unfit **06** infirm, maimed **07** invalid, wrecked **08** crippled, impaired, weakened **09** bed-ridden, enfeebled, paralysed **10** indisposed **11** debilitated, handicapped, immobilized, out of action **12** hors de combat **13** incapacitated

disabuse
09 enlighten, undeceive **10** disappoint, disenchant **11** disillusion

disadvantage
03 out **04** flaw, harm, hurt, lack, loss, snag **05** catch, minus **06** damage, defect, hang-up, injury **07** own goal, penalty, trouble **08** downside, drawback, handicap, hardship, nuisance, weakness **09** detriment, hindrance, liability, prejudice, privation, weak point **10** disamenity, disbenefit, disservice, disutility, impediment, limitation **11** disinterest **12** Achilles heel **13** inconvenience

disadvantaged
04 poor **06** in need, in want **08** deprived **10** in distress, struggling

11 handicapped **12** impoverished **15** poverty-stricken, underprivileged

disadvantageous
07 adverse, hapless, harmful, hurtful, unlucky **08** damaging, ill-timed **09** injurious **11** deleterious, detrimental, inexpedient, inopportune, prejudicial, unfortunate **12** inconvenient, unfavourable

disaffected
07 hostile **08** disloyal, mutinous **09** alienated, estranged, malignant, seditious **10** rebellious, unfriendly **11** disgruntled, ill-disposed **12** antagonistic, discontented, dissatisfied

disaffection
07 discord, dislike, ill-will **08** aversion, coolness **09** animosity, hostility **10** alienation, antagonism, disharmony, disloyalty, resentment **12** disagreement, estrangement **14** discontentment, disgruntlement, unfriendliness **15** dissatisfaction

disagree
04 vary **05** argue, clash, fight, upset **06** bicker, differ, object, oppose, sicken **07** contend, contest, discord, dispute, dissent, diverge, fall out, quarrel, wrangle **08** conflict, nauseate, squabble **09** be against, disaccord, take issue **10** contradict, make unwell, think wrong **11** beg to differ **12** argue against, be at odds with, cause illness, disapprove of **13** agree to differ, take issue with

disagreeable
03 bad **04** evil, rude, sour **05** cross, nasty, surly **07** awkward, beastly, brusque, grouchy, peevish **08** churlish, contrary, dreadful, horrible, impolite **09** difficult, irritable, obnoxious, offensive, repellent, repugnant, repulsive, unhelpful, unsavoury **10** abominable, disgusting, ill-natured, unfriendly, ungrateful, unpleasant **11** bad-tempered, disobliging, displeasing, distasteful, ill-humoured, unpalatable **12** objectionable

disagreeably
07 nastily **08** horribly **10** dreadfully **11** obnoxiously, offensively, repulsively **12** disgustingly, unpleasantly **13** objectionably

disagreement
03 row **04** flak, tiff **05** clash, fight **06** bust-up, strife **07** discord, dispute, dissent, quarrel, wrangle **08** argument, clashing, conflict, disunion, friction, squabble, variance **09** deviation, disparity, dissensus, diversity **10** conformity, contention, difference, disharmony, dissension, dissidence, dissonance, divergence, falling-out, unlikeness **11** altercation, contretemps, discrepancy, disputation, incongruity **13** dissimilarity, dissimilitude, inconsistency **14** unpleasantness, unsuitableness **15** incompatibility

• expression of disagreement
02 ah, h'm **03** boo, gup, hmm, hum, nah, naw, rot **04** booh, quep, uh-uh **05** arrah **06** hardly **08** nonsense **09** do you mind?

disallow
03 ban **04** veto **05** debar **06** abjure, cancel, disown, forbid, rebuff, refuse, reject **07** disavow, dismiss, embargo, exclude, say no to **08** disclaim, overrule, prohibit **09** disaffirm, dispraise, interdict, proscribe, repudiate, surcharge

disappear
◇ *deletion indicator*
02 go **03** ebb, end, fly **04** exit, fade, flee, hide, melt, pass, walk, wane **05** cease, ghost, slope **06** depart, die out, escape, expire, go cold, perish, recede, retire, vanish **07** die away, drop off, drop out, get lost, pass off, scarper, vamoose **08** dissolve, drop away, evanesce, melt away, peter out, withdraw **09** dissipate, evaporate, go missing **10** make tracks, take flight **12** go out of sight **13** become extinct, dematerialize, pass from sight **14** go like hot cakes **15** take French leave

disappearance
◇ *deletion indicator*
03 end **04** exit, loss **05** going **06** expiry, fading, flight **07** passing **08** dying-out, fade-away **09** departure, desertion, immersion, vanishing **10** extinction, karyolysis, resolution, withdrawal **11** evanescence, evaporation, melting away

disappoint
03 vex **04** fail, foil, mock **06** baffle, betray, defeat, delude, dismay, hamper, hinder, sadden, slip up, thwart **07** deceive, depress, let down **08** dispirit, mistryst **09** devastate, frustrate, mislippen **10** disconcert, discourage, disenchant, disgruntle, dishearten, dissatisfy **11** disillusion, make a fool of

disappointed
04 sick **05** upset, vexed **06** balked, choked, gutted, miffed **07** let-down **08** betrayed, cast down, deflated, saddened, thwarted **09** depressed **10** despondent, devastated, dischuffed, distressed, frustrated, unequipped **11** discouraged, disgruntled, downhearted, ill-equipped **12** disconsolate, disenchanted, disheartened, dissatisfied **13** disillusioned, sick as a parrot

disappointing
03 sad **05** bogus, sorry **07** unhappy **08** inferior, pathetic, unworthy **10** depressing, inadequate **12** disagreeable, discouraging, insufficient **13** anticlimactic, disconcerting, underwhelming **14** unsatisfactory

disappointment
04 balk, blow, sell, swiz **05** baulk, frost, lemon **06** bummer, fiasco, fizzer, regret, suck-in, take-in **07** chagrin, failure, let-down, sadness, setback, swizzle, washout, wipeout **08** calamity, comedown, disaster, distress, non-event **09** damp squib **10** anticlimax, bitter pill, discontent, misfortune **11** cold comfort, despondency, displeasure, frustration **14** discouragement, disenchantment, dispiritedness **15** disillusionment, dissatisfaction

• expression of disappointment
02 aw **04** nuts, pity **05** shoot **06** shucks

disapprobation
05 blame **07** censure, dislike, mislike, reproof **08** reproach **09** criticism, disfavour, exception, objection **11** disapproval, displeasure **12** condemnation, denunciation **13** disparagement, remonstration **14** discountenance **15** dissatisfaction

disapproval
04 veto **05** blame **06** rebuke **07** censure, disgust, dislike, reproof **08** reproach **09** criticism, exception, misliking, objection, rejection **11** displeasure **12** condemnation, denunciation, disallowance **13** disparagement, remonstration, the thumbs-down **14** disapprobation **15** dissatisfaction

• expression of disapproval
01 O **02** oh **03** boo, fie, tut **04** booh, toot, tuts, umph, what **05** humph, toots **06** tut-tut **07** fie upon **10** hoity-toity

• indication of disapproval
03 boo **04** booh, hiss **05** frown **07** catcall, walk out **09** dirty look, raspberry **10** Bronx cheer, thumbs down **12** slow handclap **13** shake your head

disapprove
04 veto **05** blame, spurn **06** reject **07** censure, condemn, deplore, dislike, frown on, mislike **08** denounce, disallow, disfavor, disprove, harrumph, object to **09** be against, deprecate, disesteem, disfavour, disparage, disproove, reprobate **10** animadvert, look down on **11** not hold with **12** think badly of **13** think little of **14** discountenance, hold in contempt, take a dim view of **15** take exception to

disapproving
04 prim **07** killjoy **08** critical, frowning **09** reproving **10** censorious, derogatory, pejorative **11** deprecatory, disparaging, improbative, improbatory, reproachful **12** condemnatory **14** disapprobative, disapprobatory

disarm
05 charm, unarm **07** appease, disable, disband, mollify, placate, unsteel, win over **08** persuade, unweapon **10** conciliate, deactivate, demobilize,

immobilize **11** lay down arms
12 demilitarize **13** make powerless
14 lay down weapons, put out of
action

disarmament
11 arms control **12** deactivation
13 arms reduction **14** arms limitation,
demobilization

disarming
07 winning **08** charming, likeable
10 mollifying, persuasive
12 conciliatory, irresistible

disarmingly
10 charmingly, pleasantly
12 irresistibly, persuasively

disarrange
◇ *anagram indicator*
04 mess, muss **05** musse **06** jumble,
tousle, touzle, untidy **07** confuse,
derange, disturb, shuffle **08** dishevel,
disorder, displace, unsettle
09 dislocate **10** discompose
11 disorganize **13** put out of place

disarray
◇ *anagram indicator*
04 mess, tash **05** chaos, rifle, upset
06 jumble, muddle, tangle **07** clutter,
undress **08** disorder, shambles
09 confusion **10** unruliness, untidiness
11 derangement **12** dishevelment,
indiscipline **13** unsettledness
15 disorganization

disassemble
08 separate **09** dismantle, pull apart,
take apart **12** pull to pieces, take to
pieces

disassociate
05 break **06** cut off, remove
08 separate, withdraw **10** disconnect,
dissociate

disaster
04 blow, flop, ruin **06** fiasco, mishap,
mucker, stroke **07** debacle, failure,
reverse, screw-up, setback, tragedy,
trouble, washout, wipeout
08 accident, act of God, calamity,
reversal **09** adversity, cataclysm,
holocaust, mischance, ruination,
shipwreck, sticky end **10** misfortune,
providence **11** catastrophe, horror
story **12** misadventure

disastrous
◇ *anagram indicator*
04 dire **05** fatal **06** gloomy, tragic
07 adverse, harmful, ruinous, unlucky
08 dreadful, ill-fated, ravaging,
shocking, terrible, tragical
09 appalling, injurious, miserable
10 calamitous, ill-starred
11 cataclysmic, destructive,
devastating, unfortunate
12 catastrophic

disavow
04 deny **06** abjure, disown, reject
08 disvouch, renounce **09** disaffirm,
disavouch, repudiate **10** contradict
15 wash your hands of

disavowal
06 denial **07** dissent **09** rejection
10 abjuration, disclaimer
11 repudiation **12** disclamation,
renunciation **13** contradiction
14 disaffirmation

disband
◇ *anagram indicator*
05 demob **06** disarm, reduce, reform
07 break up, dismiss, scatter
08 disperse, dissolve, separate
10 demobilize **11** part company **14** go
separate ways

disbelief
05 doubt **07** atheism, dubiety, scruple
08 acosmism, distrust, mistrust,
unbelief **09** discredit, rejection,
suspicion **10** infidelity, scepticism
11 incredulity, questioning
• **expression of disbelief**
03 huh, tut **04** as if!, hoot **05** hoots
06 heaven, indeed, phooey, Walker
07 get away, says you **08** honestly,
hoot-toot **09** away you go! **11** away
with you, Betty Martin **12** Hookey
Walker **13** what do you know?

disbelieve
05 doubt **06** reject **07** suspect
08 discount, distrust, mistrust,
question **09** discredit, miscredit,
repudiate **13** be unconvinced

disbeliever
07 atheist, doubter, sceptic, scoffer
08 agnostic **10** questioner, unbeliever
11 non-believer, nullifidian
14 doubting Thomas

disbelieving
07 cynical, infidel **08** doubtful,
doubting **09** sceptical, uncertain
10 suspicious **11** distrustful,
incredulous, unbelieving,
unconvinced

disburse
05 spend **06** expend, lay out, pay out
07 cough up, dish out, fork out **08** shell
out

disbursement
06 outlay **07** payment **08** disposal,
spending **09** disbursal, outgiving
11 expenditure

disc
01 O **02** CD, EP, LP **03** DVD **04** disk,
face, gong, ring **05** album, CD-ROM,
elpee, paten, plate, round, vinyl, wheel
06 button, circle, discus, record, saucer
07 counter, rosette, roundel
08 diskette, hard disk, roundlet
10 floppy disk **11** compact disk,
microfloppy

discard
03 bin **04** cast, defy, drop, dump, jilt,
junk, kill, shed **05** ditch, scrap, trash
06 reject, remove **07** abandon,
cashier, cast off, dismiss, forsake, lay
away, toss out **08** chuck out, get rid of,
jettison, lay aside, throw out **09** cast
aside, chuck away, discharge, dismissal,
dispose of, repudiate, supersede,

throw away, throw over **10** pension off,
relinquish **11** abandonment
12 dispense with

discards
04 crib

discern
03 get, see, wit **04** spot, tell **05** judge
06 descry, detect, notice, scerne
07 make out, observe, pick out
08 discover, perceive, tell from
09 ascertain, determine, recognize
11 distinguish **12** discriminate
13 differentiate

discernible
05 clear, plain **06** patent **07** obvious,
visible **08** apparent, distinct, manifest
10 detectable, noticeable, observable
11 appreciable, conspicuous,
perceptible **12** discoverable,
recognizable **15** distinguishable

discerning
04 wise **05** acute, quick, sharp, sound
06 astute, clever, seeing, shrewd,
subtle **07** prudent, sapient, trained
08 critical, piercing, tasteful **09** clear-
eyed, eagle-eyed, ingenious, judicious,
sagacious, selective, sensitive
10 perceptive, percipient
11 intelligent, penetrating **12** clear-
sighted, eagle-sighted
13 perspicacious, understanding
14 discriminating

discernment
05 flair, sense, taste **06** acumen,
wisdom **07** insight **08** keenness,
sagacity, sapience **09** acuteness,
awareness, good taste, ingenuity,
judgement, sharpness **10** cleverness,
perception, shrewdness
11 penetration, percipience
12 intelligence, perspicacity
13 ascertainment, understanding
14 discrimination, perceptiveness

discharge
02 do **03** arc, axe, pay, pus, ren, rin, run
04 emit, fire, flow, free, gush, leak,
meet, ooze, oust, pass, pour, sack,
vent, void **05** clear, congé, doing,
drain, egest, eject, empty, expel,
exude, issue, let go, loose, rheum,
salvo, shoot, spout **06** acquit, congee,
firing, forbid, fulfil, honour, let fly, let off,
let out, pardon, remove, sanies, set off,
settle, unload **07** absolve, boot out,
discard, dismiss, excrete, explode,
exuding, fire off, fluxion, give off,
ousting, outflow, payment, perform,
release, relieve, removal, sacking,
satisfy, send out, set free, the boot, the
sack, turf out **08** carry out, detonate,
disgorge, dispense, displode, ejection,
emission, evacuate, get rid of, liberate,
settling, the elbow, turn away
09 acquittal, bowler-hat, broadside,
clearance, colluvies, disburden,
dismissal, excretion, exculpate,
execution, exonerate, expulsion,
honouring, quitclaim, repayment,
secretion, unfraught, unloading
10 absolution, cashiering, disburthen,

disembogue, fulfilment, liberation, the heave-ho **11** achievement, carrying-out, exculpation, exoneration, performance, suppuration **12** give the elbow **13** give the boot to **14** accomplishment

disciple
03 son **05** chela, child, pupil **06** votary **07** apostle, convert, devotee, learner, scholar, student **08** adherent, believer, follower, upholder **09** proselyte, supporter
See also **apostle**

disciplinarian
06 despot, ramrod, tyrant **08** autocrat, martinet, stickler **10** taskmaster **13** authoritarian **14** hard taskmaster

discipline
04 bull, curb, judo **05** check, drill, inure, limit, order, teach, train, tutor **06** branch, disple, govern, ground, moguls, punish, rebuke, school **07** break in, chasten, control, correct, educate, regimen, reprove, routine, subject **08** chastise, dressage, exercise, feng shui, instruct, mathesis, penalize, practice, regulate, restrain, restrict, training **09** castigate, direction, inculcate, reprimand, restraint, schooling **10** correction, punishment, regulation, speciality, strictness **11** area of study, castigation, keep in check, orderliness, self-control **12** chastisement, field of study **13** course of study, mortification, self-restraint **14** self-discipline **15** make an example of

disclaim
04 deny **06** abjure, disown, refuse, reject **07** abandon, declaim, decline, disavow **08** renounce **09** repudiate **15** wash your hands of

disclaimer
06 denial **09** disavowal, rejection **10** abjuration, abnegation, disownment, retraction **11** repudiation **12** renunciation **13** contradiction **14** disaffirmation

disclose
04 blab, leak, open, show, tell **05** hatch, let on, unrip **06** betray, evolve, expose, impart, open up, relate, reveal, squeal, unfold, unheal, unhele, unlock, unveil **07** confess, develop, divulge, exhibit, lay bare, let drop, let slip, open out, propale, publish, unclose, uncover **08** blurt out, develope, discover **09** broadcast, make known, tell a tale **10** disclosure, make public **11** blow the gaff, communicate **12** bring to light **13** spill the beans **14** blow the whistle **15** give the game away, take the wraps off

disclosure
04 leak **06** exposé **08** exposure, overture **09** admission, broadcast, discovery **10** apocalypse, confession, divulgence, laying bare, revelation, uncovering **11** declaration, publication

12 announcement **15** acknowledgement, bringing to light

discoloration
04 blot, mark, spot **05** patch, stain **06** blotch, foxing, streak **07** blemish, blue-rot, pink-eye, splotch, tarnish **08** cyanosis, dyschroa, foxiness **09** dyschroia, melanosis **10** ecchymosis **12** acrocyanosis, weather stain **14** xanthochromia

discolour
03 fox, mar **04** fade, mark, rust, soil **05** dirty, stain, tinge **06** bruise, streak **07** tarnish, weather **09** disfigure

discomfit
◇ *anagram indicator*
04 balk, faze, rout **05** abash, shend, throw **06** baffle, defeat, outwit, rattle, ruffle, thwart **07** confuse, fluster, perplex, perturb **08** confound, unsettle **09** embarrass, frustrate **10** demoralize, discompose, disconcert

discomfiture
05 lurch **06** unease **07** chagrin **09** abashment, confusion **10** uneasiness **11** frustration, humiliation **12** discomposure **13** embarrassment **14** demoralization, disappointment

discomfort
04 ache, hell, hurt, pain, pang **05** worry **06** bother, hassle, jet lag, misery, twinge, unease **07** malaise, trouble **08** disquiet, distress, drawback, hardship, nuisance, soreness, vexation **09** annoyance, purgatory **10** cardialgia, difficulty, irritation, tenderness, uneasiness **12** apprehension, disadvantage, restlessness, unpleasantry **13** embarrassment, inconvenience

discompose
◇ *anagram indicator*
06 ruffle **07** agitate, disturb **08** disorder **10** disarrange

discomposure
05 upset **06** unease **07** anxiety, fluster **09** agitation, annoyance **10** inquietude, irritation, uneasiness **11** disquietude, disturbance **12** perturbation, restlessness

disconcert
◇ *anagram indicator*
04 faze **05** abash, alarm, blank, quell, shake, tease, throw, upset **06** baffle, defeat, dismay, put off, put out, rattle, ruffle **07** break up, confuse, disturb, fluster, nonplus, perplex, perturb, startle, stumble, unnerve **08** bewilder, disunion, surprise, throw off, throw out, unsettle **09** discomfit, embarrass, frustrate, knock back, take aback **14** discomboberate, discombobulate **15** throw off balance

disconcerting
◇ *anagram indicator*
07 awkward **08** alarming, baffling,

daunting **09** confusing, dismaying, unnerving, upsetting **10** bothersome, disturbing, off-putting, perplexing, perturbing, unsettling **11** bewildering, distracting **12** embarrassing

disconnect
04 part, undo **05** loose, sever, split **06** cut off, detach, divide, ungear, unhook, unplug **07** disjoin, unhitch **08** disjoint, separate, uncouple **09** disengage **10** de-energize

disconnected
05 loose **06** abrupt **07** garbled, jumbled, mixed-up, scrappy **08** confused, rambling, staccato **09** illogical, separated, wandering **10** disjointed, incoherent, irrational **12** inconsequent **13** unco-ordinated **14** unintelligible

disconnection
07 undoing **08** division **09** severance **10** detachment, separation, uncoupling, unplugging **13** disengagement

disconsolate
03 low, sad **04** down **06** gloomy **07** crushed, forlorn, unhappy **08** dejected, desolate, downcast, hopeless, wretched **09** depressed, miserable **10** despondent, dispirited, melancholy **11** heartbroken, low-spirited **12** heavy-hearted, inconsolable **13** grief-stricken **14** down in the dumps

disconsolately
05 sadly **09** miserably, unhappily **10** dejectedly, desolately, wretchedly **12** despondently, inconsolably **14** heavy-heartedly

discontent
06 misery, regret, unrest **08** disquiet, vexation **09** fed-upness **10** impatience, uneasiness **11** displeasure, fretfulness, unhappiness **12** disaffection, dissatisfied, heartburning, restlessness, wretchedness **15** dissatisfaction

discontented
05 fed up **07** unhappy **08** restless, wretched **09** impatient, miserable, pissed off **10** browned off, cheesed off, displeased, malcontent **11** complaining, disaffected, disgruntled, exasperated **12** dissatisfied

discontinue
03 end **04** drop, halt, quit, stop **05** cease, scrap **06** cancel, finish **07** abandon, abolish, refrain, suspend **08** break off, knock off, withdraw **09** interrupt, terminate **10** do away with **11** come to an end, come to a stop

discontinued
03 dis, off **07** at an end

discontinuity
05 break, comma **06** breach **07** rupture **08** disunion **09** nickpoint **10** disruption, knickpoint

11 incoherence **12** interruption
13 disconnection **14** disjointedness

discontinuous
06 broken, fitful **08** discrete, periodic, sporadic **09** irregular, separated, spasmodic **10** punctuated
11 interrupted **12** disconnected, intermittent

discord
◇ *anagram indicator*
03 row **05** split **06** jangle, strife
07 dispute, dissent, jarring
08 argument, clashing, conflict, disagree, disunity, division, friction, jangling **09** cacophony, disaccord, harshness, wrangling **10** contention, difference, disharmony, dissension, dissonance, opposition, suspension
11 discordance **12** disagreement
13 inharmonicity **15** discord of sounds, incompatibility

discordant
◇ *anagram indicator*
04 flat **05** harsh, sharp **06** at odds, atonal, hoarse, off-key **07** grating, hostile, jarring **08** absonant, clashing, jangling, opposing, strident
09 differing, dissonant **10** at variance, dissenting **11** cacophonous, conflicting, disagreeing, disharmonic, incongruous, unagreeable
12 incompatible, inconsistent, inharmonious **13** contradictory

discount
03 cut **04** agio **05** slash **06** deduct, ignore, rebate, reduce **07** dismiss, take off **08** cut price, knock off, mark down, mark-down, overlook, pass over, pooh-pooh **09** allowance, deduction, disregard, gloss over, reduction
10 concession, disbelieve, rebatement

discourage
04 damp **05** chill, daunt, deter
06 dampen, deject, dismay, hinder, put off **07** depress, prevent, unnerve
08 cast down, choke off, dispirit, dissuade, hold back, restrain **09** talk out of **10** demoralize, disappoint, dishearten **12** put a damper on
13 advise against **14** discountenance
15 pour cold water on

discouraged
04 glum **06** dashed **07** daunted, let down **08** deflated, dejected, dismayed, downcast **09** depressed
10 dispirited **11** crestfallen, demoralized, pessimistic
12 disheartened **14** down in the dumps

discouragement
04 curb, damp **05** gloom **06** damper, dismay, rebuff **07** barrier, despair, setback **08** obstacle **09** dejection, deterrent, hindrance, pessimism, restraint **10** depression, impediment, opposition **11** despondency
12 disincentive, hopelessness
14 disappointment
15 downheartedness

discouraging
08 daunting **09** dampening
10 depressing, dissuasive, dissuasory, off-putting **11** dehortatory, dispiriting
12 demoralizing, inauspicious, unfavourable, unpropitious
13 disappointing, disheartening

discourse
04 chat, tale, talk **05** essay, speak, spell **06** confer, debate, homily, preach, reason, sermon, speech, tongue
07 address, discuss, lecture, oration
08 chit-chat, colloquy, converse, dialogue, exercise, treatise
09 discursus, hold forth, rigmarole
10 discussion, exposition, meditation, preachment **11** exhortation, highfalutin **12** conversation, disquisition, dissertation, exercitation, highfaluting **13** communication, confabulation

discourteous
04 curt, rude **05** gruff, short **06** abrupt
07 boorish, brusque, ill-bred, offhand, uncivil, uncouth **08** ignorant, impolite, impudent, insolent **09** offensive, truculent **10** ungracious, unmannerly, unpleasant **11** bad-mannered, ill-mannered, impertinent
13 disrespectful, unceremonious

discourteously
06 curtly, rudely **07** gruffly
08 abruptly **09** brusquely, uncivilly
10 impolitely, impudently, insolently
11 offensively, offhandedly
12 ungraciously, unpleasantly
13 impertinently **15** disrespectfully, unceremoniously

discourtesy
04 snub **06** insult, rebuff, slight
07 affront **08** curtness, rudeness
09 indecorum, insolence **10** bad manners, disrespect, incivility
11 brusqueness, ill-breeding
12 impertinence, impoliteness
14 indecorousness, ungraciousness, unmannerliness

discover
◇ *anagram indicator*
◇ *hidden indicator*
03 see, spy, sus **04** espy, find, spot, suss, twig **05** dig up, hit on, learn, trace **06** create, descry, detect, devise, fathom, invent, locate, notice, reveal, rumble, sus out, turn up, unmask
07 analyse, compose, discern, discure, exhibit, find out, get onto, hit upon, light on, make out, pioneer, realize, suss out, uncover, unearth, work out
08 disclose, discoure, perceive, smoke out, sound out **09** ascertain, determine, establish, fathom out, ferret out, get wind of, get wise to, originate, recognize, stumble on **10** come across, come to know, excogitate
11 come to light **12** find out about
13 stumble across

discoverer
05 scout **06** author, finder **07** creator, deviser, founder, pioneer **08** explorer,

informer, inventor **09** initiator
10 originator

discovery
04 find **06** descry, eureka **07** finding, heureka **08** devising, findings, learning, location, research
09 detection, invention **10** disclosure, innovation, pioneering, revelation
11 discernment, exploration, origination, realization, recognition
12 breakthrough, introduction
13 determination
• **expression of discovery**
05 bingo, hallo, hello, hullo **06** eureka
07 heureka

discredit
04 deny, slag, slur **05** blame, doubt, shame, slate, smear **06** damage, debunk, defame, infamy, refute, reject, stigma, vilify **07** censure, degrade, discard, explode, rubbish, run down, scandal, slag off, slander, tarnish
08 badmouth, belittle, disgrace, disprove, distrust, ignominy, mistrust, question, reproach **09** aspersion, challenge, dishonour, disparage, disrepute, ill-repute, reflect on
10 disbelieve, invalidate, opprobrium
11 humiliation **14** put in a bad light, reflect badly on

discreditable
06 shabby **08** improper, infamous, shameful, unworthy **09** degrading
10 scandalous **11** blameworthy, disgraceful **12** disreputable
13 dishonourable, reprehensible

discreet
04 wary, wise **05** witty **06** modest
07 careful, guarded, politic, prudent, tactful **08** cautious, delicate, detached, reserved, sensible, separate
09 judicious **10** diplomatic
11 circumspect, considerate
13 unpretentious

discreetly
06 wisely **08** sensibly **09** carefully, prudently, tactfully **10** cautiously, delicately **11** judiciously
13 circumspectly, considerately
14 diplomatically

discrepancy
08 conflict, variance **09** deviation, disparity, variation **10** difference, divergence, inequality **11** discordance, incongruity **12** disagreement
13 contradiction, dissimilarity, inconsistency

discrete
08 abstract, detached, disjunct, distinct, separate **09** disjoined
10 individual, unattached
12 disconnected **13** discontinuous

discretion
04 care, tact, will, wish **06** choice, desire, wisdom **07** caution, freedom, reserve **08** prudence, volition, wariness **09** diplomacy, good sense, judgement **10** preference
11 carefulness, discernment,

discretionary

guardedness, inclination
12 predilection **13** consideration, judiciousness **14** circumspection

discretionary

04 open **08** elective, optional
09 voluntary **12** unrestricted

discriminate

06 secern **07** discern **08** be biased, separate **09** segregate, tell apart, victimize **11** distinguish **12** be intolerant, be prejudiced
13 differentiate, show prejudice, treat unfairly

discriminating

04 keen **05** acute **06** astute, nasute, shrewd **08** critical, delicate, tasteful
09 invidious, selective, sensitive
10 cultivated, discerning, fastidious, particular, perceptive, respective
12 differential, preferential

discrimination

04 bias **05** skill, taste **06** acumen, ageism, racism, sexism, sizism
07 ableism, bigotry, fattism, insight, Jim Crow, lookism, sizeism **08** classism, inequity, judgment, keenness, subtlety
09 acuteness, colour bar, judgement, prejudice **10** astuteness, difference, difference, homophobia, perception, refinement, shrewdness, unfairness
11 discernment, distinction, favouritism, intolerance, penetration, segregation, sensitivity
12 heterosexism, perspicacity **14** male chauvinism

discriminatory

06 biased, loaded, unfair, unjust
07 partial **08** one-sided, partisan, weighted **09** favouring **10** prejudiced
11 inequitable, prejudicial
12 preferential **14** discriminative

discursive

05 wordy **06** prolix **07** diffuse, verbose **08** rambling **09** wandering
10 circuitous, digressing, long-winded, meandering **11** wide-ranging

discuss

03 vex **04** sift, toss **05** argue, study, treat **06** confer, debate, decide, dispel, go into, handle, parley, reason, review, settle, take up **07** agitate, analyse, belabor, beprose, canvass, consult, declare, examine, speak to, weigh up
08 belabour, consider, converse, critique, deal with, question, talk over
09 discourse, kick about, pro and con, talk about, thrash out **10** deliberate, interplead, kick around, knock about, politicize **11** confabulate, expostulate, knock around **12** go into detail
15 exchange views on

discussion

03 rap **04** chat, conf, moot, talk
05 forum, study, talks **06** debate, torero, parley, powwow, review, talk-in
07 gabfest, palaver, seminar
08 analysis, argument, dialogue, exchange, question, scrutiny, speaking, talkfest **09** discourse, symposium,

talkathon **10** colloquium, conference, rap session **11** examination
12 consultation, conversation, deliberation, negotiations
13 consideration

disdain

03 coy **04** snub **05** scorn, sdayn, sdein, spurn **06** deride, ignore, rebuff, reject, sdaine, sdeign, slight
07 contemn, despise, disavow, dislike, sdeigne, sneer at **08** belittle, contempt, derision, pooh-pooh, sneering, turn down **09** arrogance, contumely, disregard **10** look down on, sour grapes, undervalue
11 deprecation, haughtiness **12** cold shoulder, snobbishness, think scorn of
13 disparagement
• **expression of disdain**
04 pooh, tush **06** powwaw
• **show disdain**
04 geck

disdainful

05 aloof, proud, saucy **07** haughty, pompous **08** arrogant, derisive, insolent, scornful, sneering, superior
09 slighting **11** disparaging
12 contemptuous, supercilious

disease

03 bug, pox **05** virus **06** malady
07 ailment, illness **08** disorder, epidemic, sickness **09** complaint, condition, contagion, ill-health, infection, infirmity **10** affliction, disability, uneasiness **13** indisposition, unhealthiness

Diseases and medical conditions include:

02 CF, ME, MS, TB
03 CFS, CJD, DVT, flu, FMS, IBS, PID, PKU, PVS, tic, TSS
04 AIDS, clap, cold, coma, gout, kuru, Lyme, mono, rash, SARS
05 colic, croup, favus, lupus, mumps, polio, Weil's
06 angina, apnoea, asthma, autism, cancer, chorea, Crohn's, dropsy, eczema, emesis, goitre, Grave's, hernia, herpes, oedema, otitis, Paget's, quinsy, rabies, scurvy, stroke, thrush, tumour, typhus
07 abscess, allergy, anaemia, anthrax, anxiety, atrophy, Batten's, bird flu, Bright's, bulimia, cholera, coeliac, kissing, leprosy, lockjaw, malaria, Marburg, measles, myalgia, mycosis, rickets, rubella, sarcoma, scabies, tetanus, typhoid, vertigo
08 Addison's, alopecia, aneurism, anorexia, avian flu, beriberi, botulism, bursitis, cachexia, coxalgia, Cushing's, cynanche, cystitis, dementia, diabetes, embolism, epilepsy, fibroids, gangrene, glaucoma, Hodgkin's, impetigo, jaundice, kala-azar, listeria, lymphoma, melanoma, Ménière's, migraine, necrosis, orchitis, pyelitis, Raynaud's, rhinitis, ringworm, sciatica, shingles,

smallpox, stenosis, syphilis, tapeworm, Tay-Sachs, tinnitus, trachoma, venereal, viraemia
09 arthritis, arthrosis, bilharzia, chlamydia, chlorosis, cirrhosis, cri du chat, distemper, dysentery, eclampsia, emphysema, enteritis, hepatitis, influenza, ketonuria, leukaemia, neoplasia, nephritis, nephrosis, neuralgia, paralysis, parotitis, pertussis, pneumonia, psoriasis, pyorrhoea, silicosis, sinusitis, sunstroke, Sydenham's, toothache, urticaria, varicella
10 acromegaly, Alzheimer's, amoebiasis, asbestosis, Bell's Palsy, Black Death, bronchitis, chickenpox, common cold, depression, diphtheria, gingivitis, gonorrhoea, laryngitis, Lassa fever, meningitis, Parkinson's, rhinorrhea, thrombosis
11 anaphylaxis, brucellosis, cholestasis, consumption, dehydration, dengue fever, farmer's lung, green monkey, haemophilia, haemorrhage, heart attack, Huntington's, hydrophobia, hyperplasia, hypertrophy, hypotension, listeriosis, mastoiditis, motor neuron, myocarditis, peritonitis, pharyngitis, pneumonitis, proteinuria, psittacosis, sarcoidosis, septicaemia, spina bifida, tonsillitis, trench fever, yellow fever
12 appendicitis, athlete's foot, cor pulmonale, encephalitis, endocarditis, foot-and-mouth, heart failure, Legionnaires', liver failure, osteoporosis, pericarditis, scarlet fever, tuberculosis
13 bronchiolitis, bubonic plague, cerebral palsy, coronary heart, Down's syndrome, elephantiasis, endometriosis, German measles, kidney failure, leishmaniasis, mononucleosis, osteomyelitis, poliomyelitis, Rett's syndrome, Reye's syndrome, schizophrenia, toxoplasmosis, varicose veins, West Nile virus, whooping cough
14 angina pectoris, break-bone fever, conjunctivitis, cystic fibrosis, glandular fever, osteoarthritis, pneumoconiosis, rheumatic fever, river blindness, sleepy sickness, thyrotoxicosis
15 anorexia nervosa, atherosclerosis, bipolar disorder, gastro-enteritis, Gulf War syndrome, manic depression, phenylketonuria, schistosomiasis

See also **skin**

Animal diseases include:

03 BSE, FMD, gid, orf
04 gape, gout, loco, roup, wind
05 bloat, braxy, farcy, frush, hoove, pearl, surra, vives
06 canker, Johne's, mad cow, Marek's,

nagana, rabies, spavie, spavin, sturdy

07 anthrax, blue ear, dourine, hard pad, measles, mooneye, moorill, murrain, roaring, rubbers, scrapie, yellows

08 bovine TB, fowl-pest, glanders, pullorum, scaly-leg, seedy-toe, sheep-pox, staggers, swayback, swine-pox, wildfire, wire-heel

09 Aujeszky's, blackhead, distemper, Newcastle, scratches, sheep scab, spauld-ill, St Hubert's, strangles

10 blue tongue, louping-ill, ornithosis, rinderpest, sallenders, swamp fever, swine fever, Texas fever, water-brain

11 blood-spavin, brucellosis, mad staggers, myxomatosis, parrot fever, psittacosis

12 black-quarter, bush sickness, cattle-plague, foot-and-mouth, furunculosis, gall-sickness

13 grass sickness, grass staggers, leptospirosis

14 sleepy staggers

15 Rift Valley fever, stomach staggers

Plant diseases include:

04 bunt, curl, rust, smut

05 ergot

06 blight, blotch, canker, mildew, mosaic, red rot

07 ferrugo, oak wilt, ring rot, rosette, soft rot, yellows

08 blackleg, black rot, clubroot, crown rot, Dutch elm, leaf curl, loose-cut, wheat eel

09 crown gall, potato rot, tulip root

10 fire-blight, leaf mosaic, silver leaf, sooty mould, vine-mildew

11 anthracnose, wheat mildew

12 finger-and-toe, peach-yellows, potato blight

13 powdery mildew

14 psyllid yellows

Disease symptoms include:

04 pain, rash

05 cramp, fever, hives, sniff

06 aching, lesion, tremor

07 anxiety, fatigue, fitting, itching

08 bruising, coughing, deafness, fainting, headache, insomnia, numbness, sickness, sneezing, swelling, tingling, vomiting, weakness

09 blindness, diarrhoea, dizziness, heartburn, impotence, lassitude, nosebleed, paralysis, stiffness, twitching

10 congestion, depression, flatulence, irritation, sore throat, tenderness

11 convulsions, indigestion, loss of voice, trapped wind

12 constipation, incontinence, inflammation, irritability, loss of libido, muscle cramps

13 loss of hearing, stomach cramps, swollen glands

14 loss of appetite, pins and needles

15 high temperature, loss of sensation

• **abatement of disease**
05 lysis

• **infectious diseases**
02 ID

diseased
◊ *anagram indicator*
03 ill **04** poxy, sick **06** ailing, infirm, unwell **07** unsound **08** blighted, infected, soul-sick **09** unhealthy **12** contaminated, distemperate

disembark
04 land **05** leave **06** alight, arrive, debark, get off **07** deplane, detrain, disbark, step off **08** dismount

disembarkation
07 arrival, landing **09** alighting

disembodied
07 ghostly, phantom **08** bodiless, spectral **09** spiritual **10** discarnate, immaterial, intangible **11** incorporeal **12** discorporate

disembowel
◊ *middle deletion indicator*
03 gut **04** draw **06** paunch **07** embowel **08** disbowel, gralloch **09** viscerate **10** eviscerate, exenterate

disenchanted
05 blasé, fed up **06** soured **07** cynical, let down **09** jaundiced **11** discouraged, indifferent **12** disappointed, dissatisfied **13** disillusioned

disenchantment
08 cynicism **09** fed-upness, revulsion **11** disillusion **14** disappointment **15** disillusionment, dissatisfaction

disengage
04 free, slip, undo **05** untie **06** detach, loosen, remove, unhook **07** release, unhitch **08** disunite, liberate, separate, throw off, uncouple, unfasten, withdraw **09** extricate **10** disconnect **11** disentangle

disengaged
04 free **05** clear, freed, loose **08** detached, released, separate **09** liberated, separated, unhitched **10** unattached, unoccupied **11** unconnected **12** disentangled

disengagement
07 release, removal, retreat **09** loosening, releasing **10** detachment, retirement, separating, taking away, withdrawal **13** disconnection **15** disentanglement

disentangle
03 red **04** free, redd, undo **05** loose, ravel **06** detach, unfold, unknot, unwind **07** clarify, release, resolve, unravel, unsnarl, untwist **08** distance, ravel out, separate, simplify, unfasten, untangle **09** debarrass, disengage, extricate **10** disconnect, disinvolve, straighten **11** distinguish **13** straighten out

disfavour
06 oppose **07** disgust, dislike **08** distaste, ignominy **09** discredit,

disesteem, disregard, disrepute, hostility **10** disapprove, low opinion, opprobrium **11** disapproval, displeasure **12** unpopularity **14** disapprobation **15** dissatisfaction

disfigure
◊ *anagram indicator*
03 mar **04** blad, blur, flaw, maim, ruin, scar, tash **05** blaud, spoil **06** agrise, agrize, agryze, beweep, damage, deface, defeat, deform, injure, mangle **07** blemish, distort **08** discolor, make ugly, mutilate **09** defeature, discolour

disfigurement
04 scar, spot, wart **05** stain **06** blotch, defect, injury **07** blemish **08** disgrace **09** defeature, deformity **10** defacement, distortion, impairment, mutilation **12** uglification

disgorge
04 hawk, spew **05** belch, eject, empty, expel, spout, vomit **06** effuse **07** pour out, throw up **09** discharge **11** regurgitate

disgrace
04 blot, slur **05** abase, atimy, blame, shame, shend, smear, stain, sully, taint **06** baffle, debase, defame, ignomy, infamy, stigma **07** attaint, degrade, obloquy, reproof, scandal, villany **08** belittle, contempt, dishonor, ignominy, reproach, ugliness, villainy **09** attainder, black mark, denigrate, discredit, disfavour, dishonour, disparage, disrepute, humiliate, indignify, indignity **10** debasement, defamation, disrespect, disworship, loss of face, opprobrium, put to shame, scandalize, stigmatize **11** degradation, humiliation **12** bring shame on **13** disfigurement **14** disapprobation **15** cause to lose face

disgraced
06 shamed **07** branded **08** degraded **10** humiliated **11** discredited, dishonoured, stigmatized, under a cloud **13** in the doghouse

disgraceful
05 awful **06** indign **08** culpable, dreadful, infamous, shameful, shocking, terrible, unworthy **09** appalling, degrading **10** despicable, inglorious, outrageous, scandalled, scandalous **11** blameworthy, ignominious, opprobrious, reproachful **12** contemptible, dishonorable, disreputable **13** discreditable, dishonourable, reprehensible

disgracefully
07 awfully **08** terribly **10** despicably, dreadfully, shamefully, shockingly **11** appallingly **12** contemptibly, disreputably, outrageously, scandalously **13** dishonourably, ignominiously, reprehensibly

disgruntled
◊ *anagram indicator*
05 fed up, sulky, testy, vexed

06 grumpy, peeved, put out, sullen
07 annoyed, chuffed, peevish
08 petulant **09** hacked off, irritated, resentful **10** brassed off, browned off, cheesed off, displeased, malcontent
11 exasperated **12** discontented, dissatisfied

disguise
◇ anagram indicator
04 face, fake, hide, mask, ring, veil
05 cloak, cloke, color, cover, feign, front, fudge, visor, vizor **06** colour, façade, immask, mantle, screen, shroud, veneer, vizard **07** conceal, costume, cover up, deceive, dress up, falsify, pretend, repress **08** palliate, pretence, suppress, travesty
09 coverture, deception, dissemble, gloss over, whitewash **10** camouflage, masquerade **11** concealment, dissimulate, impersonate **12** be under cover, cook the books, false picture, misrepresent **15** put on a brave face

disguised
◇ anagram indicator
04 fake **05** false **06** covert, hidden, made up, masked, veiled **07** cloaked, feigned **09** incognito **10** under cover
11 camouflaged **14** unrecognizable

disgust
03 irk, pip **04** cloy **05** repel, shock
06 hatred, nausea, offend, put off, revolt, sicken, turn up **07** outrage, scunner, turn off **08** aversion, distaste, gross out, loathing, nauseate, scomfish
09 disfavour, displease, disrelish, repulsion, revulsion **10** abhorrence, repugnance **11** detestation, disapproval, displeasure **15** turn your stomach
• **expression of disgust**
02 aw, fy **03** bah, fie, foh, huh, pah, paw, pho, sis, ugh, wow, yah, yuk
04 damn, phoh, pooh, tush, whow, yech, yuck **05** faugh, shoot, wowee
06 powwaw **07** brother **11** for God's sake **14** for heaven's sake

disgusted
04 sick **06** put off **08** appalled, offended, outraged, repelled, repulsed, revolted, sickened, up in arms
10 cheesed off

disgusting
03 bad **04** foul, vile **05** grody, gross, nasty, slimy, yucky, yukky **06** odious, putrid, ugsome **07** mawkish, noisome, obscene **08** nauseous, shocking
09 appalling, offensive, repellent, repugnant, repulsive, revolting, sickening **10** abominable, detestable, nauseating, off-putting, outrageous, unpleasant **11** disgraceful, distasteful, rebarbative, unpalatable
12 unappetizing **13** objectionable

dish
◇ anagram indicator
04 bowl, fare, food, ruin, tray **05** plate
06 course, recipe, tureen **07** platter
08 delicacy **10** speciality

See also **food**

• **dish out**
◇ anagram indicator
07 dole out, give out, hand out, inflict, mete out **08** allocate, dispense, share out **09** hand round, pass round
10 distribute
• **dish up**
05 ladle, offer, scoop, serve, spoon
07 present **08** dispense

disharmony
05 clash **06** strife **07** discord, dissent
08 conflict, friction **09** disaccord
10 dissonance **11** discordance, incongruity **12** disagreement
15 incompatibility

dishearten
04 dash **05** chill, crush, daunt, deter
06 dampen, deject, dismay
07 depress, unheart **08** cast down, dispirit **09** disparage, weigh down
10 demoralize, disappoint, discourage
12 put a damper on **13** make depressed

disheartened
◇ middle deletion indicator
04 down **07** crushed, daunted
08 dejected, dismayed, downcast
09 depressed **10** dispirited
11 crestfallen, demoralized, discouraged, downhearted
12 disappointed

dishevelled
◇ anagram indicator
04 wild **05** daggy, messy **06** blowsy, blowzy, untidy **07** in a mess, ruffled, rumpled, scruffy, tousled, unkempt
08 slovenly, uncombed **09** windswept
10 bedraggled, disordered
11 disarranged

dishonest
03 sly **04** bent, iffy **05** cross, dirty, dodgy, false, fishy, lying, shady, snide
06 crafty, shifty, untrue **07** corrupt, crooked, cunning, devious, knavish
08 cheating, unchaste **09** deceitful, deceptive, insincere, irregular, swindling **10** fraudulent, mendacious, perfidious, untruthful **11** duplicitous, treacherous **12** disreputable, unprincipled, unscrupulous
13 dishonourable, double-dealing, untrustworthy

dishonestly
05 false **07** falsely **09** corruptly, deviously **10** on the cross
11 deceitfully, deceptively
12 disreputably, fraudulently, perfidiously **13** dishonourably, treacherously **14** unscrupulously

dishonesty
05 fraud **06** deceit **07** falsity, knavery, perfidy **08** cheating, trickery
09 chicanery, duplicity, falsehood, improbity, shadiness, treachery
10 corruption, dirty trick
11 criminality, crookedness, fraudulence, insincerity **12** irregularity
13 double-dealing, sharp practice
14 untruthfulness

dishonour
04 slur **05** abuse, shame, stain, sully, wrong **06** debase, defame, defile, demean, ignomy, infamy, insult, offend, refuse, reject, seduce, slight, stigma
07 affront, debauch, degrade, offence, outrage, scandal **08** disgrace, ignominy, reproach, turn down
09 abasement, aspersion, discredit, disfavour, disparage, disrepute, humiliate, indignity **10** debasement, disworship, opprobrium
11 degradation, discourtesy, humiliation

dishonourable
05 shady **07** corrupt, disleal, ignoble, low-down **08** infamous, shameful, unhonest, unworthy **09** shameless, unethical **10** despicable, perfidious, scandalous **11** disgraceful, ignominious, treacherous
12 contemptible, disreputable, unprincipled, unscrupulous
13 discreditable, untrustworthy

dishy
04 sexy **05** hunky **08** charming, gorgeous, handsome **10** attractive
11 good-looking

disillusion
08 disabuse **09** undeceive
10 disappoint, disenchant
14 disappointment, disenchantment
15 disillusionment

disillusioned
07 let-down **09** disabused
10 undeceived **12** disappointed, disenchanted

disincentive
06 damper **07** barrier, turn-off
08 obstacle **09** determent, deterrent, hindrance, repellent **10** constraint, dissuasion, impediment **11** restriction
14 discouragement

disinclination
07 dislike **08** aversion **09** antipathy, loathness, objection **10** alienation, averseness, hesitation, opposition, reluctance, repugnance, resistance
13 indisposition, unwillingness

disinclined
05 loath **06** averse **07** opposed
08 hesitant **09** reluctant, resistant, unwilling **10** indisposed, undisposed
14 unenthusiastic

disinfect
05 clean, purge **06** bleach, purify
07 cleanse **08** fumigate, sanitize
09 sterilize **13** decontaminate

disinfectant
05 lysol **06** cineol, cresol, phenol
07 cineole **08** fumigant, sheep-dip, terebene **09** germicide, sanitizer
10 antiseptic, sterilizer **11** bactericide
12 methyl violet **13** decontaminant
14 glutaraldehyde

disingenuous
03 sly **04** wily **06** artful, crafty, shifty
07 cunning, devious, feigned

disingenuously

08 guileful, two-faced, uncandid
09 deceitful, designing, dishonest,
insidious, insincere **11** duplicitous

disingenuously

05 slyly **08** artfully **09** cunningly,
deviously **11** deceitfully, dishonestly,
insidiously, insincerely

disinherit

06 cut off, reject **07** abandon
08 renounce **09** repudiate
10 dispossess, exheredate, impoverish
14 turn your back on

disintegrate

◇ *anagram indicator*
03 rot **05** decay, smash **06** reduce
07 break up, crumble, moulder, shatter
08 separate, splinter **09** decompose,
fall apart **10** break apart **12** fall to
pieces, self-destruct

disintegration

◇ *anagram indicator*
03 rot **05** decay **07** breakup
08 biolysis, decaying **09** breakdown,
crumbling **10** karyolysis, separation,
shattering **11** dissolution **12** falling-
apart **13** decomposition, radioactivity,
spondylolysis

disinter

05 dig up **06** exhume, expose, reveal,
unbury **07** uncover, unearth
08 excavate, exhumate **09** disentomb,
disinhume, resurrect **12** bring to light

disinterest

08 fairness **09** unconcern
10 detachment, neutrality
12 disadvantage, impartiality,
unbiasedness

disinterested

04 cool, fair, just **07** neutral
08 detached, generous, unbiased
09 equitable, impartial, objective,
unselfish **10** even-handed, open-
minded, uninvolved **12** unprejudiced
13 dispassionate

disjointed

◇ *anagram indicator*
05 bitty, loose, split **06** abrupt,
broken, fitful **07** aimless, divided
08 confused, rambling **09** displaced,
disunited, separated, spasmodic,
wandering **10** dislocated, disordered,
incoherent **11** unconnected
12 disconnected **13** directionless
14 disarticulated

dislike

04 defy, down, hate, lump, mind, shun
05 abhor, derry, scorn, thing
06 animus, detest, enmity, hatred,
loathe, needle **07** allergy, despise,
disgust, mislike **08** aversion, disfavor,
distaste, dyspathy, execrate, loathing,
object to **09** abominate, animosity,
antipathy, disesteem, disfavour,
disrelish, hostility, objection
10 antagonism, disapprove,
repugnance, resentment
11 detestation, disapproval,
displeasure, take against **12** have a

derry on **14** disapprobation,
disinclination, take a scunner to

dislocate

◇ *anagram indicator*
04 do in, pull, slip **05** shift, twist
06 luxate, put out, sprain, strain
07 confuse, disrupt, disturb
08 disjoint, disorder, displace, disunite,
misplace **09** disengage **10** disconnect
11 disorganize **13** put out of joint, put
out of place

dislocation

◇ *anagram indicator*
04 slip **05** fault **08** disarray, disorder,
luxation **10** disruption **11** disturbance
12 displacement **15** disorganization

dislodge

04 bump, move, oust, tuft **05** eject,
shift **06** remove, uproot **08** displace,
force out, untenant **09** extricate

disloyal

05 false **06** untrue **07** disleal
08 apostate, two-faced **09** deceitful,
faithless **10** perfidious, traitorous, un-
American, unfaithful **11** treacherous,
unpatriotic **13** double-dealing

disloyalty

06 deceit **07** falsity, perfidy, treason
08 adultery, apostasy, betrayal,
sedition **09** falseness, treachery
10 infidelity **11** inconstancy, waka-
jumping **12** disaffection **13** breach of
trust, double-dealing
14 perfidiousness, unfaithfulness

dismal

03 bad, sad **04** blue, dark, drab, dull,
glum, gray, grey, grim, naff, poor, ropy
05 awful, black, bleak, dingy, dowie,
lousy, morne, trist, wormy **06** crummy,
dreary, dreich, gloomy, somber,
sombre, sullen, triste **07** forlorn,
useless **08** desolate, dolesome,
dreadful, funereal, ghastful, hopeless,
terrible **09** cheerless, frightful,
ghastfull, long-faced, miserable,
sorrowful **10** depressing, despondent,
grimlooked, lugubrious, melancholy,
sepulchral **11** low-spirited
12 discouraging, unsuccessful

dismally

05 badly, sadly **06** darkly, drably
08 drearily, gloomily, terribly
09 miserably **10** dreadfully
11 frightfully **12** despondently
14 unsuccessfully

dismantle

◇ *anagram indicator*
05 derig, strip **06** strike **08** demolish,
pull down, separate, take down **09** pull
apart, strip down, take apart
11 disassemble **12** take to pieces

dismay

04 fear **05** alarm, amate, appal, daunt,
dread, scare, shake, shock, upset,
worry **06** bother, fright, horror, put off,
terror **07** concern, depress, disturb,
horrify, perturb, unnerve **08** cast
down, dispirit, distress, frighten,

unsettle **09** agitation, take aback
10 disappoint, disconcert, discourage,
dishearten **11** consternate, disillusion,
heart-strike, trepidation
12 apprehension **13** consternation
14 disappointment, discouragement
● **expression of dismay**
02 ha **03** hah **04** argh, heck, hell,
oops, whew **05** aargh **06** crumbs,
dear me, heaven, oh dear!, wheugh
07 cravens, crivens, deary me, heavens
08 crivvens, dearie me **09** good grief
11 that's done it, that's torn it

dismember

04 limb **05** sever **06** divide **07** break
up, disject, dislimb, dissect, quarter
08 amputate, disjoint, mutilate,
separate **09** dislocate, piecemeal, pull
apart

dismemberment

07 breakup **08** division **10** amputation,
dissection, mutilation, separation

dismiss

◇ *deletion indicator*
04 boot, daff, drop, fire, free, sack
05 chuck, eject, expel, lay by, let go,
spurn **06** banish, bounce, chassé, lay
off, reject, remove, shelve **07** boot out,
cashier, discord, fall out, kick out, kiss
off, put away, release, send off,
suspend, turn off **08** brush off,
discount, dispatch, dissolve, relegate,
send away, set aside **09** bowler-hat,
discharge, disregard, repudiate
10 brush aside, give notice, give the air,
pension off **11** send packing **13** give
the bucket, make redundant **15** pour
cold water on

dismissal

◇ *deletion indicator*
01 b, c **02** ax, hw, ro, st **03** axe, lbw
04 bird, boot, push, road, sack
05 chuck, congé, elbow **06** avaunt,
bounce, bowled, caught, congee,
firing, mitten, notice, papers, run-out
07 discard, heave-ho, kiss-off,
removal, sacking, stumped **08** brush-
off, bum's rush, despatch, dispatch,
mittimus **09** discharge, expulsion, hit
wicket, laying-off **10** cashiering,
redundancy **11** cashierment **12** golden
bowler **13** walking-orders, walking
papers, walking-ticket **14** marching-
orders **15** leg before wicket
● **expression of dismissal**
03 och, out, via **04** poof, pooh, tush
06 avaunt, begone, powwaw
07 voetsak

dismissed

03 out

dismissive

07 off-hand **08** scornful, sneering
10 disdainful, dismissory
12 contemptuous **13** disrespectful,
inconsiderate

dismissively

10 scornfully, sneeringly **11** offhandedly **12** disdainfully
14 contemptuously

dismount
04 lite 05 light 06 alight, get off
07 descend, get down, unmount
09 disembark

disobedience
06 mutiny, revolt 08 defiance
09 contumacy, rebellion 10 infraction,
unruliness, wilfulness 11 contumacity,
waywardness 12 contrariness,
indiscipline 13 recalcitrance
15 insubordination

disobedient
06 unruly, wilful 07 defiant, froward,
naughty, wayward 08 contrary,
recusant 10 disorderly, rebellious,
refractory 11 intractable, mischievous
12 contumacious, obstreperous,
recalcitrant 13 insubordinate

disobey
04 defy 05 flout, rebel 06 ignore,
resist 07 violate 08 infringe, overstep
09 disregard 10 contravene, transgress
13 step out of line

disobliging
04 rude 06 unkind 07 awkward,
uncivil 09 unhelpful, unwilling
11 inofficious 12 bloody-minded,
disagreeable, discourteous 13 unco-
operative 15 unaccommodating

disorder
◇ anagram indicator
03 ADD, OCD, SAD 04 ADHD, mess,
muss, PMDD, PTSD, riot, rout 05 brawl,
chaos, deray, fight, mêlée, musse
06 defuse, fracas, jumble, malady,
muddle, ruffle, rumple, rumpus,
tumble, tumult, unrest, uproar
07 ailment, anarchy, clamour, clutter,
confuse, derange, disease, flutter,
garboil, illness, misrule, overset,
quarrel 08 brouhaha, confound,
disarray, pell-mell, shambles, sickness
09 commotion, complaint, condition,
confusion, mistemper 10 affliction,
disability, disarrange, discompose,
disruption, untidiness
11 derangement, disturbance
12 confusedness 14 disorderliness
15 disorganization

disordered
◇ anagram indicator
03 mad 04 wild 05 messy, mussy,
oncus, onkus, upset 06 turbid, untidy
07 jumbled, muddled, unkempt
08 confused, deranged, madbrain,
troubled 09 betumbled, cluttered,
disturbed 10 madbrained, out of joint,
unbalanced, upside-down
11 distempered, maladjusted
12 disorganized, disreputable

disorderly
◇ anagram indicator
04 wild 05 messy, rough, rowdy
06 ragtag, unruly, untidy 07 chaotic,
jumbled, lawless 08 confused
09 cluttered, irregular, turbulent
10 boisterous, confusedly, in disarray,
ragmatical, rebellious, refractory,
tumultuous 11 disobedient

12 disorganized, hugger-mugger,
obstreperous, unmanageable
13 undisciplined 14 uncontrollable

disorganization
◇ anagram indicator
05 chaos 06 muddle 08 disarray,
disorder, shambles 09 confusion
10 disruption, untidiness
11 dislocation

disorganize
◇ anagram indicator
05 mix up, upset 06 jumble, mess up,
muddle 07 break up, confuse, destroy,
disrupt, disturb 08 disorder, unsettle,
unstring 09 dislocate 10 disarrange,
discompose 11 unmechanize 12 play
hell with 13 play havoc with

disorganized
◇ anagram indicator
07 chaotic, jumbled, muddled
08 careless, confused, unsorted
09 haphazard, shambolic
10 disordered, topsy-turvy, untogether
11 unorganized 12 unmethodical,
unstructured, unsystematic
13 undisciplined 14 unsystematized

disorientate
◇ anagram indicator
04 faze 05 upset 06 muddle, puzzle
07 confuse, mislead, perplex
09 disorient

disorientated
◇ anagram indicator
04 lost 05 at sea, upset 06 adrift,
astray 07 mixed up, muddled, puzzled
08 all at sea, confused 09 perplexed,
unsettled 10 bewildered, unbalanced
11 disoriented

disorientation
◇ anagram indicator
06 muddle 08 lostness 09 confusion
10 perplexity, puzzlement
12 bewilderment

disown
04 deny 05 unget 06 reject
07 abandon, cast off, disavow, forsake
08 abnegate, disallow, disclaim,
renounce 09 reprobate, repudiate
14 disacknowledge, turn your back on

disparage
04 mock, slag, slam, slur 05 decry,
knock, scorn, slate 06 defame, deride,
lessen, malign, vilify 07 cry down,
degrade, disable, disdain, dismiss,
impeach, impeach, rubbish, run
down, slag off, slander, traduce
08 belittle, derogate, disvalue,
minimize, ridicule, vilipend
09 criticize, denigrate, deprecate,
discredit, dishonour, sell short,
underrate 10 calumniate, depreciate,
dishearten, undervalue 11 detract from
13 underestimate

disparagement
04 slur 05 scorn 07 decrial, disdain,
slander 08 contempt, decrying,
derision, ridicule 09 aspersion,
contumely, criticism, discredit

10 debasement, derogation,
detraction 11 degradation,
deprecation 12 belittlement,
condemnation, denunciation,
depreciation, vilification
15 underestimation

disparaging
05 snide 07 mocking 08 critical,
derisive, knocking, scornful
09 insulting 10 derogatory, dismissive,
pejorative 11 deprecating,
deprecatory

disparate
06 unlike 07 diverse, unequal
08 contrary, distinct 09 different
10 discrepant, dissimilar 11 contrasting

disparity
03 gap 04 bias, gulf 08 contrast,
inequity 09 imbalance 10 difference,
inequality, unevenness, unfairness,
unlikeness 11 discrepancy, distinction,
incongruity 13 disproportion,
dissimilarity, dissimilitude,
inconsistency

dispassionate
04 calm, cool, fair 07 neutral
08 composed, detached, unbiased
09 equitable, impartial, objective,
unexcited 10 impersonal
11 unemotional 12 unprejudiced
13 disinterested, self-possessed
14 self-controlled

dispassionately
06 coolly, fairly 09 equitably
11 impartially, objectively, unexcitedly
12 impersonally 13 unemotionally
15 disinterestedly

dispatch, despatch
04 do in, item, kill, mail, news, post,
send, ship 05 haste, piece, remit,
speed 06 convey, finish, letter, murder,
report, settle 07 account, article,
bump off, consign, dépêche, dismiss,
execute, express, forward, mailing,
message, perform, posting, sending,
send off, special 08 alacrity, bulletin,
celerity, conclude, deal with, expedite,
knock off, rapidity, transmit
09 discharge, dismissal, dispose of,
slaughter, swiftness 10 accelerate,
communiqué, expedience,
expedition, forwarding, promptness,
put to death 11 assassinate,
consignment, promptitude, transmittal
13 communication

dispel
◇ anagram indicator
03 rid 04 rout 05 allay, expel 06 assoil,
banish 07 discuss, dismiss, scatter
08 disperse, get rid of, melt away
09 chase away, dissipate, drive away,
eliminate 11 disseminate

dispensable
07 useless 08 needless 10 disposable,
expendable, gratuitous, pardonable
11 inessential, replaceable,
superfluous, unnecessary 12 non-
essential

dispensation
04 plan **05** issue, order **06** relief, scheme, system **07** economy, licence, release **08** bestowal, covenant, immunity, reprieve **09** allotment, authority, direction, discharge, endowment, exception, exemption, provision, remission **10** allocation, handing out, permission, sharing out **11** application, arrangement **12** distribution, organization **13** apportionment **14** administration

dispense
05 allot, apply, issue, share **06** assign, bestow, confer **07** deal out, deliver, dole out, enforce, execute, expense, give out, hand out, mete out, operate **08** allocate, carry out, compound, share out, supplies **09** apportion, discharge, divide out, implement, pass round **10** administer, distribute, effectuate **11** expenditure **12** dispensation
• **dispense with**
02 ax **03** axe **04** omit, want **05** forgo, waive **06** cancel, forego, give up, ignore, revoke **07** abolish, discard, not need, rescind **08** get rid of, renounce **09** dispose of, disregard, do without **10** do away with, relinquish

dispersal
07 breakup **09** dismissal **10** breaking-up, disbanding, scattering, separation **11** segregation **12** distribution

disperse
◊ *anagram indicator*
04 melt, shed **05** break, scail, scale, skail **06** dispel, spread, vanish **07** break up, diffuse, disband, dismiss, resolve, scatter, split up, thin out **08** dissolve, melt away, separate, squander **09** dissipate **10** distribute **11** disseminate

dispersion
◊ *anagram indicator*
07 scatter **08** diaspora **09** broadcast, diffusion, dispersal, spreading **10** scattering **11** circulation, dissipation **12** distribution **13** dissemination

dispirit
04 damp, dash **05** deter **06** dampen, deject, sadden **07** depress **10** demoralize, discourage, dishearten **12** put a damper on

dispirited
03 low, sad **04** down, glum **05** fed up **06** feeble, gloomy, morose **08** cast down, dejected, downcast, sackless **09** depressed **10** brassed off, browned off, cheesed off, despondent, spiritless **11** crestfallen, demoralized, discouraged, pale-hearted **12** disheartened **14** down in the dumps

displace
04 move, oust **05** eject, evict, expel, heave, shift **06** depose, luxate, remove **07** boot out, dismiss, disturb, replace, succeed, turf out **08** dislodge, force

out, misplace, relocate, supplant **09** discharge, dislocate, supersede **10** disarrange

displacement
03 jee **04** warp **05** heave, hitch, shift, throw **06** ectopy, moving, ptosis **07** ectopia, upthrow **08** shifting **09** proptosis **10** aberration, compliance, dislodging **11** dislocation, disturbance, heterotaxis, heterotopia, subluxation, superseding, supplanting **12** misplacement, retroversion **14** Chandler wobble, disarrangement **15** Chandler's wobble

display
03 air, HUD, LCD **04** expo, pomp, shaw, show, wear **05** array, boast, state **06** betray, blazon, evince, expose, flaunt, layout, muster, parade, reveal, set out, splash, unfold, unfurl, unveil **07** airshow, bravura, breathe, étalage, exhibit, pageant, parafle, present, promote, show off, splurge **08** disclose, evidence, flourish, manifest, paraffle, put forth, set forth, showcase **09** advertise, pageantry, publicize, put on show, spectacle, spread out, unfolding **10** disclosure, displaying, evincement, exhibition, exposition, revelation, tournament **11** demonstrate **12** presentation **13** demonstration, manifestation

displease
03 bug, irk, vex **05** anger, annoy, upset **06** offend, put out **07** dislike, disturb, incense, mislike, perturb, provoke **08** irritate **09** aggravate, infuriate, misplease **10** discompose, disgruntle, dissatisfy, exasperate **11** displeasure

displeased
05 angry, cross, upset, vexed **06** peeved, piqued, put out **07** annoyed, furious **08** offended **09** irritated **10** aggravated, dischuffed, infuriated **11** disgruntled, exasperated, out of humour

displeasure
03 ire **05** anger, pique, wrath **07** chagrin, disgust, offence, offense **08** distaste **09** annoyance, disfavour **10** irritation, resentment **11** disapproval, indignation **12** exasperation, perturbation **14** disapprobation, discontentment, disgruntlement **15** dissatisfaction

disport
◊ *anagram indicator*
04 play, romp **05** amuse, cheer, frisk, revel, sport **06** cavort, divert, frolic, gambol **07** delight, get down **09** entertain

disposable
09 throwaway **10** expendable **11** replaceable **13** biodegradable, non-returnable

disposal
05 order **07** command, control, liberty, removal, service **08** bestowal, grouping, ordering, riddance

09 clearance, direction, scrapping **10** deployment, discarding, management **11** arrangement, jettisoning, positioning **12** getting rid of, throwing-away
• **at someone's disposal**
05 on tap, ready **06** at hand, to hand **09** available **10** obtainable

dispose
◊ *anagram indicator*
03 put, set **04** do in, dump, kill, plot, shed, sort **05** align, group, order, place, posit, scrap, see to, sew up, tempt **06** battle, decide, finish, handle, line up, murder, settle, tackle, wrap up **07** arrange, bump off, destroy, discard, dismiss, dispone, incline, situate, sort out **08** attend to, chuck out, clear out, deal with, dispatch, get rid of, jettison, organize, position, throw out **09** clear away, determine, get shot of, look after, polish off, throw away **10** distribute, do away with, put to death, take care of **15** make short work of
• **try to dispose of**
04 hawk

disposed
◊ *anagram indicator*
03 apt **04** bent **05** dight, eager, prone, ready **06** liable, likely, minded **07** subject, willing **08** inclined, pregnant, prepared **11** affectioned, predisposed

disposition
◊ *anagram indicator*
03 lay, lie **04** bent, make, mood, trim **05** cheer, habit, humor, order **06** humour, kidney, layout, line-up, make-up, nature, spirit, system, talent, temper **07** leaning, pattern, placing, stomach **08** disposal, grouping, ordnance, position, sequence, tendency, transfer **09** affection, alignment, character, proneness **10** allocation, conveyance, deployment, giving-over, proclivity, propension, propensity **11** arrangement, inclination, personality, positioning, temperament **12** constitution, distribution, ministration, predilection, propenseness **14** predisposition

dispossess
03 rob **04** oust **05** eject, evict, expel, strip **06** divest **07** deprive **08** dislodge, take away **11** expropriate

disproportion
09 asymmetry, disparity, imbalance **10** inadequacy, inequality, unevenness **11** discrepancy **12** lopsidedness **13** insufficiency

disproportionate
06 uneven **07** unequal **09** excessive **10** inordinate, unbalanced **12** unreasonable **14** incommensurate **15** incommensurable, out of proportion

disproportionately
08 unevenly **11** excessively **12** inordinately, unreasonably

disprove
04 deny 05 rebut, refel 06 debunk, expose, negate, refute 07 confute, reprove 08 blow away 09 discredit 10 contradict, controvert, invalidate, prove false 12 give the lie to

disputable
04 moot 05 dubious 08 arguable, doubtful 09 debatable, litigious, uncertain 12 questionable 13 controversial

disputation
03 act 06 debate 07 dispute, schools 08 argument, diatribe, exercise, polemics 09 quodlibet 10 apposition, discussion, dissension 11 controversy 12 deliberation, kilfud-yoking 13 argumentation

disputatious
08 captious 09 litigious, polemical 10 pugnacious 11 contentious, quarrelsome 12 cantankerous 13 argumentative

dispute
03 row 04 deny, feud, moot, odds, plea, spar, spat, tilt 05 argue, clash, doubt 06 bicker, cangle, debate, differ, strife, threap 07 contend, contest, discept, discuss, gainsay, quarrel, wrangle, wrestle 08 argument, conflict, litigate, question, squabble, traverse, variance 09 altercate, challenge, have words, tug-of-love 10 contention, contradict, controvert, litigation 11 altercation, controverse, controversy, cross swords 12 disagreement, disceptation

disqualification
03 ban, bar 04 veto 10 disability, incapacity, preclusion 11 elimination, prohibition 13 ineligibility 14 disentitlement

disqualified
06 banned 08 debarred 09 incapable, precluded, struck off 10 eliminated, ineligible 11 disentitled

disqualify
03 ban, bar 05 debar, unfit 06 impair 07 disable, rule out, suspend 08 handicap, preclude, prohibit 09 eliminate, strike off 10 debilitate, disentitle, immobilize, invalidate 12 incapacitate 13 dishabilitate

disquiet
03 vex 04 faze, fear, fret 05 alarm, annoy, dread, shake, upset, worry 06 bother, harass, hassle, pester, plague, ruffle, unease, uneasy, unrest 07 agitate, anguish, anxiety, concern, disturb, perturb, trouble, turmoil, unnerve 08 distress, restless, unsettle 09 agitation, incommode 10 discompose, foreboding, inquietude, make uneasy, uneasiness 11 disquietude, disturbance, fretfulness, make anxious, nervousness 12 perturbation, restlessness

disquieting
04 ugly 06 trying 07 anxious 08 worrying 09 unnerving, upsetting 10 disturbing, nail-biting, perturbing, unsettling 11 distressing, troublesome

disquisition
05 essay, paper 06 sermon, thesis 07 descant 08 treatise 09 discourse, monograph 10 exposition 11 explanation 12 dissertation

disregard
◇ deletion indicator
04 bend, omit, pass, shun, snub 05 flout, waive 06 ignore, insult, offend, slight 07 affront, despise, disdain, disobey, neglect, oversee, smile at 08 brush-off, contempt, discount, laugh off, overlook, pass over, set aside 09 denigrate, disesteem, disoblige, disparage, gloss over, oversight, sacrilege 10 brush aside, disrespect, negligence 11 denigration, desperation, inattention, make light of, set at naught, walk all over 12 carelessness, cold shoulder, cold-shoulder, dispense with, indifference 13 give the go-by to, non-regardance, put out of court 14 rule out of court, take no notice of 15 close your eyes to, turn a blind eye to

disrepair
04 ruin 05 decay 08 collapse 10 shabbiness 11 rack and ruin 12 dilapidation 13 deterioration

disreputable
03 low 04 base, mean 05 dodgy, seamy, seedy, shady 06 louche, shabby, shifty, untidy 07 corrupt, dubious, scruffy, unkempt 08 infamous, shameful, shocking, slovenly, unworthy 09 notorious, unsavoury 10 outrageous, scandalous, suspicious 11 disgraceful, dishevelled, ignominious, opprobrious 12 contemptible, unprincipled 13 discreditable, dishonourable, unrespectable

disrepute
05 shame 06 infamy 07 ill fame, obloquy 08 disgrace, ignominy 09 discredit, disesteem, disfavour, dishonour 13 disreputation

disrespect
05 cheek, scorn 08 contempt, rudeness 09 dishonour, disregard, impudence, insolence, misesteem 10 incivility 11 discourtesy, irreverence 12 impertinence, impoliteness

disrespectful
04 rude 05 sassy 06 cheeky 07 uncivil 08 flippant, impolite, impudent, insolent 09 insulting 10 dismissive, irreverent, unmannerly 11 impertinent 12 contemptuous, discourteous 13 inconsiderate

disrespectfully
06 rudely 08 cheekily 09 uncivilly 10 impolitely, impudently, insolently 11 insultingly 12 irreverently 13 impertinently 14 contemptuously, discourteously

disrobe
04 bare, shed 05 strip 06 denude, divest, remove 07 take off, uncover, undress 08 unclothe 10 disapparel

disrupt
◇ anagram indicator
05 burst, split, upset 06 butt in, hamper, impede 07 blemish, break up, confuse, disturb, intrude, screw up 08 sabotage, unsettle 09 dislocate, interrupt 10 disarrange 11 disorganize 13 interfere with

disruption
◇ anagram indicator
05 upset 06 bust-up 07 burst-up, turmoil 08 disarray, disorder, stoppage, upheaval 09 cataclasm, confusion 11 disordering, disturbance 12 interference, interruption 14 disorderliness 15 disorganization

disruptive
05 noisy, rogue 06 unruly 09 turbulent, upsetting 10 boisterous, disorderly, disturbing, unsettling 11 distracting, troublesome 12 obstreperous 13 troublemaking, undisciplined

dissatisfaction
05 anger 06 regret 07 chagrin, dislike 08 vexation 09 annoyance 10 discomfort, discontent, irritation, resentment, uneasiness 11 disapproval, displeasure, frustration, unhappiness 12 disaffection, exasperation, restlessness 14 disappointment, disapprobation
• expression of dissatisfaction
02 oh 03 boo, huh, tut 04 booh, umph, whow 05 humph

dissatisfied
05 angry, fed up 07 annoyed, unhappy 09 irritated, pissed off 10 brassed off, browned off, cheesed off, discontent, displeased, frustrated, malcontent 11 disaffected, disgruntled, exasperated, unfulfilled, unsatisfied 12 disappointed, discontented, disenchanted, malcontented 13 disillusioned

dissatisfy
03 vex 05 anger, annoy 06 put out 07 let down 08 irritate 09 displease, frustrate 10 disappoint, discontent, disgruntle, exasperate

dissect
05 cut up, probe, study 07 analyse, examine, explore, inspect 08 pore over, vivisect 09 anatomize, break down, dismember 10 scrutinize 11 investigate

dissection
05 probe, study 07 anatomy, autopsy, zootomy 08 analysis, necropsy, scrutiny 09 breakdown, cutting up, necrotomy 10 inspection

11 cephalotomy, examination, exploration, vivisection **13** dismemberment, encephalotomy, investigation

dissemble
04 fain, fake, hide, mask, sham
05 cloak, faine, fayne, feign **06** affect
07 conceal, cover up, falsify, pretend
08 disguise, simulate **10** camouflage, play possum **11** counterfeit, dissimulate

dissembler
04 fake, liar **05** fraud **06** con man
07 feigner **08** deceiver, impostor
09 charlatan, hypocrite, pretender, trickster **12** dissimulator **15** whited sepulchre

disseminate
03 sow **05** scale **06** spread **07** diffuse, publish, scatter **08** disperse, proclaim
09 broadcast, circulate, propagate, publicize, scattered **10** distribute, promulgate

dissemination
06 spread **09** broadcast, diffusion, spreading **10** dispersion, publishing
11 circulation, propagation, publication **12** broadcasting, distribution, promulgation

dissension
04 flak **06** square, strife **07** discord, dispute, dissent, faction, quarrel
08 argument, conflict, dispeace, disunion, disunity, friction, variance
10 contention **12** disagreement

dissent
05 demur **06** differ, object, refuse
07 discord, dispute, protest, quibble
08 disagree, friction **09** objection
10 difference, disconsent, disharmony, dissension, opposition, resistance
11 controversy **12** disagreement

dissenter
05 rebel **07** heretic, sectary
08 objector, recusant **09** disputant, dissident, protester, Raskolnik
10 protestant, schismatic, separatist
11 dissentient, Old Believer
12 demonstrator **13** nonconformist, revolutionary

dissentient
08 opposing, recusant **09** differing, dissident, heretical **10** dissenting, protesting, rebellious **11** conflicting, disagreeing **13** nonconformist, revolutionary

dissertation
05 essay, paper **06** thesis **08** critique, excursus, treatise **09** discourse, monograph **10** exposition
11 prolegomena **12** disquisition, propaedeutic

disservice
04 harm, hurt **05** wrong **06** injury
07 bad turn **08** con trick, mischief
09 disfavour, injustice **10** dirty trick, unkindness **13** sharp practice **14** kick in the teeth

dissidence
04 feud **06** schism **07** dispute, dissent, rupture **08** variance **09** recusancy
11 discordance **12** disagreement

dissident
05 rebel **07** heretic **08** agitator, frondeur, objector, opposing, recusant, refusnik **09** differing, dissenter, heretical, heterodox, protester, refusenik **10** discordant, dissenting, protesting, rebellious, schismatic **11** conflicting, disagreeing **13** nonconformist, revolutionary

dissimilar
06 unlike **07** diverse, unalike, various, varying **08** bifacial, distinct
09 deviating, different, disparate, divergent, unrelated **10** mismatched
11 contrasting, hemimorphic
12 incompatible **13** heterogeneous

dissimilarity
07 variety **08** contrast **09** disparity, diversity **10** difference, differency, divergence, inequality, unlikeness
11 discrepancy, distinction
13 dissimilitude, heterogeneity, unrelatedness **15** incomparability, incompatibility

dissimulate
03 lie **04** fake, hide, mask **05** cloak, feign **06** affect **07** conceal, cover up, pretend **08** disguise **09** dissemble
10 camouflage

dissipate
◊ *anagram indicator*
04 blow **05** drain, spend, use up, waste
06 burn up, dispel, expend, lavish, vanish, wanton **07** break up, consume, deplete, diffuse, exhaust, resolve, scatter, splurge **08** disperse, dissolve, melt away, squander **09** disappear, drive away, evaporate **10** get through, run through **11** fritter away

dissipated
◊ *anagram indicator*
03 gay **04** wild **06** rakish, wasted
07 corrupt **08** depraved
09 abandoned, debauched, dissolute
10 degenerate, licentious, profligate
11 intemperate **13** self-indulgent
● **be dissipated**
04 melt **08** peter out

dissipation
06 excess, racket **07** licence
08 pleasure **09** depletion, depravity, diffusion, dispersal **10** corruption, debauchery, immorality
11 abandonment, consumption, evaporation, expenditure, prodigality, squandering **12** extravagance, intemperance **13** disappearance
14 licentiousness, self-indulgence

dissociate
04 quit **05** sever **06** cut off, detach, secede **07** break up, disband, disrupt, divorce, isolate **08** break off, distance, disunite, separate, set apart, withdraw
09 disengage, segregate, separated
10 disconnect **12** disassociate

dissociation
05 break, split **07** divorce **08** disunion, division, severing **09** isolation, severance **10** cutting-off, detachment, distancing, separation **11** dissevering, segregation **12** setting apart
13 disconnection, disengagement
14 disassociation

dissolute
◊ *anagram indicator*
04 fast, lewd, wild **05** loose **06** rakish, wanton **07** corrupt, immoral, outward
08 depraved **09** abandoned, debauched **10** Corinthian, degenerate, dissipated, licentious, profligate **11** Falstaffian, intemperate
12 unrestrained **13** self-indulgent

dissolution
06 ending, Repeal **07** break-up, divorce, melting **08** collapse, dialysis, disposal, division **09** annulment, cessation, loosening, overthrow
10 conclusion, karyolysis, separation, suspension **11** destruction, evaporation, termination, thermolysis
13 decomposition, disappearance
14 disintegration **15** discontinuation

dissolve
03 end **04** melt **05** annul, begin, break, burst, solve, start **06** digest, finish, revoke, vanish, wind up
07 break up, crumble, disband, dismiss, divorce, dwindle, liquefy, nullify, rescind, solvate, unmarry **08** collapse, discandy, disperse, evanesce, melt away, separate **09** disappear, discandie, dissipate, evaporate, terminate **10** deliquesce, invalidate
11 discontinue, lose control **12** bring to an end, disintegrate **14** be overcome with, go into solution

dissonance
03 jar **04** wolf **05** clash **06** jangle
07 discord, grating, jarring **08** variance
09 cacophony, disparity, harshness, stridency **10** difference, disharmony, dissension **11** discordance, discrepancy, incongruity
12 disagreement **13** inconsistency
15 incompatibility

dissonant
◊ *anagram indicator*
05 harsh **07** grating, jarring, raucous
08 clashing, jangling, strident, tuneless
09 anomalous, differing, irregular, unmusical **10** discordant
11 cacophonous, conflicting, disagreeing, incongruous, unmelodious **12** incompatible, inconsistent, inharmonious
13 contradictory **14** irreconcilable

dissuade
04 stop **05** deter **06** dehort, nobble, put off **07** prevent **09** talk out of
10 discounsel, discourage, disincline
13 persuade not to

dissuasion
07 caution **09** deterring **10** deterrence
11 dehortation **12** remonstrance

3 expostulation, remonstration
4 discouragement

istance
3 gap, way **04** span, step **05** break,
epth, lunar, piece, range, reach,
bace, width **06** cut off, detach, extent,
eight, length, remove, secede
7 breadth, faraway, farness, reserve,
tretch **08** coldness, coolness, interval,
eparate, throw out, withdraw
9 aloofness, formality, stiffness
0 detachment, dissociate,
pposition, remoteness, separation
1 mountenance **12** disassociate,
ountenaunce **13** codeclination
4 unfriendliness **15** inaccessibility,
tandoffishness
ee also **measurement**

at a distance
4 afar, wide **06** afield **12** at arm's
ength

short distance
3 wee **06** bittie **11** stone's-throw

distant
3 far, icy **04** cold, cool, deep
5 aloof, blank, stiff **06** abroad,
reamy, far-off, formal, remote, slight,
acant **07** faraway, glacial
8 detached, far-flung, indirect,
olated, not close, outlying, reserved
9 dispersed, withdrawn
0 antisocial, distracted, indistinct,
estrained, unfriendly **11** daydreaming,
ut-of-the-way, preoccupied, stand-
ffish, up the Boohai **12** absent-
inded, back of beyond, unresponsive
4 unapproachable
5 uncommunicative

distantly
5 dimly, miles **06** coldly, coolly
7 faintly, far away, stiffly, vaguely
8 a long way, formally, remotely,
lightly, vacantly **10** not closely
1 imprecisely **12** some distance
3 great distance, unemotionally
4 unresponsively

distaste
6 dégoût, horror, offend **07** disgust,
islike, offence **08** aversion, loathing
9 antipathy, disfavour, disrelish,
evulsion **10** abhorrence, repugnance
1 displeasure
expression of distaste
3 ugh, wow, yuk **04** whow, yech,
uck **05** wowee

distasteful
4 gory, icky **08** god-awful
9 abhorrent, loathsome, obnoxious,
ffensive, repellant, repellent,
epugnant, repulsive, revolting,
nsavoury **10** detestable, disgusting,
ninviting, unpleasant **11** displeasing,
ndesirable, unpalatable
2 disagreeable **13** objectionable

distend
4 puff **05** bloat, bulge, swell, widen
6 dilate, expand **07** balloon, enlarge,
ll out, inflate, stretch **09** intumesce
0 exaggerate

distended
05 puffy **06** astrut, puffed **07** bloated,
dilated, distent, swollen **08** enlarged,
expanded, inflated, varicose
09 puffed-out, stretched, tumescent
10 ventricose, ventricous
13 emphysematous

distension
05 swell **06** spread **07** breadth
08 bloating, dilation, swelling
09 emphysema, expansion, extension
10 flatulence, flatulency, tumescence,
tympanites, wind dropsy
11 enlargement, turgescence
12 intumescence **14** hydronephrosis

distil
04 drip, flow, leak **05** still **06** derive,
purify, refine **07** draw out, express,
extract, rectify, trickle **08** condense,
press out, vaporize **09** evaporate,
sublimate

distillation
◇ *anagram indicator*
06 spirit **07** essence, extract
10 extraction **11** evaporation
12 condensation, purification

distinct
05 clear, plain, sharp **06** marked
07 defined, diverse, evident, obvious,
several **08** apparent, clear-cut,
definite, detached, discrete, manifest,
separate **09** different, disparate,
trenchant **10** dissimilar, individual,
noticeable, variegated
11 unambiguous, unconnected, well-
defined **12** recognizable,
unassociated, unmistakable
13 distinguished **14** differentiated

distinction
04 fame, mark, note **05** éclat, honor,
merit, siege, worth **06** credit, honour,
luster, lustre, renown, repute
07 diorism, feature, quality
08 contrast, division, eminence,
prestige **09** celebrity, greatness
10 difference, excellence, importance,
prominence, reputation, separation
11 consequence, discernment,
peculiarity, superiority **12** distinctness,
significance **13** dissimilarity,
dissimilitude, individuality
14 characteristic, discrimination
15 differentiation, distinguishment
See also **honour**

distinctive
06 unique **07** special, typical
08 original, peculiar, singular
09 different **10** individual, noteworthy,
particular **13** extraordinary,
idiosyncratic **14** characteristic,
distinguishing

distinctiveness
10 uniqueness **11** originality,
peculiarity, singularity **12** idiosyncrasy
13 individuality **14** noteworthiness

distinctly
05 plain **07** clearly, plainly
08 markedly **09** decidedly, evidently,
obviously **10** definitely, manifestly,

noticeably **12** unmistakably
13 unambiguously, unmistakeably

distinguish
03 see **04** dist, mark **05** excel, judge,
stamp **06** descry, detect, divide, do
well, notice, pick up, secern, typify
07 dignify, discern, ennoble, glorify,
make out, mark off, pick out **08** classify,
identify, perceive, set apart, tell from
09 ascertain, determine, recognize,
signalize, single out, tell apart
10 categorize **11** bring fame to
12 characterize, discriminate **13** bring
honour to, differentiate, particularize
14 bring acclaim to

distinguishable
05 clear, plain **07** evident, obvious
08 dividant, manifest **10** noticeable,
observable **11** appreciable,
conspicuous, discernible, perceptible,
plainly seen **12** recognizable

distinguished
04 fine **05** famed, noble, noted
06 famous, marked, of note
07 eminent, notable, refined, shining
08 distinct, especial, esteemed,
eximious, honoured, identify,
renowned, striking **09** acclaimed,
egregious, prominent, well-known
10 celebrated, nameworthy
11 conspicuous, illustrious, outstanding
12 aristocratic **13** extraordinary

distinguishing
06 marked, unique **07** typical
08 peculiar, singular **09** diacritic,
different **10** diagnostic, episematic,
individual **11** diacritical, distinctive
14 characteristic, discriminative,
discriminatory **15** differentiating,
differentiation, individualistic

distort
◇ *anagram indicator*
04 bend, bias, rack, skew, warp
05 color, fudge, slant, thraw, twist,
wrest, wring **06** buckle, colour,
deform, detort, garble, hamper,
jumble, mangle, wrench, writhe
07 contort, falsify, pervert, screw up,
torment, torture **08** misshape
09 disfigure, pull about **10** tamper
with **12** cook the books, misrepresent

distorted
◇ *anagram indicator*
03 wry **04** awry, bent, skew **05** false,
thraw **06** biased, skewed, thrawn,
warped **07** twisted **08** deformed,
tortured **09** falsified, misshapen,
perverted **10** disfigured, out of shape
14 misrepresented

distortion
04 bend, bias, skew, warp **05** slant,
twist **06** buckle **07** warping
08 cinching, garbling, twisting
09 colouring, deformity
10 contortion, perversion
11 crookedness **13** falsification

distract
◇ *anagram indicator*
05 amuse **06** divert, harass, madden,

occupy, put off, puzzle **07** confuse, deflect, detract, disturb, embroil, engross, fluster, perplex **08** bewilder, confound, draw away, forhaile, throw out, turn away **09** entertain, sidetrack, turn aside **10** discompose, disconcert

distracted
◇ *anagram indicator*
03 mad **04** wild **05** crazy, upset **06** éperdu, raving **07** anxious, éperdue, frantic, madding **08** agitated, confused, diverted, dreaming, frenetic, harassed, maddened, worked up **09** miles away, not with it, scattered, up the wall, wandering **10** abstracted, bestraught, bewildered, distraught, distressed, hysterical **11** inattentive, overwrought, preoccupied **12** absent-minded **13** grief-stricken **14** beside yourself

distracting
07 diverse **08** annoying **09** confusing **10** disturbing, irritating, off-putting, perturbing, unsettling **11** bewildering **13** disconcerting

distraction
04 game **05** hobby, sport **07** madness, pastime **09** agitation, amusement, avocation, confusion, diversion **10** perplexity, recreation, relaxation **11** derangement, disturbance, interrupted **12** interference **13** entertainment **14** divertissement
• **drive to distraction**
05 anger, annoy, upset **06** madden **10** drive crazy, exasperate

distraint
03 nam **04** naam **06** stress

distraught
◇ *anagram indicator*
03 mad **04** wild **05** crazy, elvan, elven, het up, upset **06** elfish, elvish, raving **07** anxious, frantic, worried **08** agitated, in a state, worked up, wretched **09** perplexed **10** distracted, distressed, hysterical **11** overwrought **14** beside yourself

distress
03 irk, vex, woe **04** hurt, need, pain, prey **05** agony, cut up, grief, peril, trial, upset, worry **06** danger, grieve, harass, harrow, misery, penury, sadden, sorrow, unease **07** afflict, agonize, anguish, anxiety, disturb, misease, oppress, perturb, poverty, put to it, sadness, torment, torture, trouble **08** aggrieve, calamity, distrain, exigence, exigency, hardship, straiten **09** adversity, extremity, heartache, indigence, privation, suffering **10** affliction, compulsion, desolation, difficulty, discomfort, exhaustion, misfortune **11** destitution, make anxious, tribulation **12** deforciation, difficulties, perturbation, wretchedness **13** make miserable

distressed
03 ill **04** hurt, sore **05** upset **06** pained, put out **07** uptight, worried

08 bothered, dismayed, in a state, perished, troubled, worked up **09** aggrieved, disturbed, heart-sore, on the rack, perturbed, strung out, unsettled **11** discomposed **12** impoverished

distressing
05 sorry **06** crying, tragic, trying, uneath **07** painful **08** alarming, tragical, worrying **09** harrowing, startling, upsetting **10** afflicting, disturbing, off-putting, perturbing, unsettling **11** frightening **13** disconcerting

distribute
◇ *anagram indicator*
04 deal, dish, part **05** allot, carve, issue, ladle, share **06** assort, digest, divide, spread, supply **07** deal out, deliver, diffuse, dish out, dispose, dole out, give out, hand out, mete out, pass out, prorate, scatter **08** allocate, dispense, disperse, ladle out, serve out, transmit **09** apportion, circulate, discharge, pass round **10** measure out, reticulate **11** disseminate

distribution
◇ *anagram indicator*
05 range **06** supply **07** dealing, sharing **08** delivery, division, grouping, handling, position **09** allotment, diffusion, dispersal, giving-out, placement, proration, spreading, transport **10** allocation, conveyance, handing-out, scattering **11** arrangement, circulation, disposition, repartition **12** organization **13** apportionment, dissemination **14** classification, transportation

district
03 gau, way **04** area, belt, hunt, land, leet, pale, ride, side, soke, walk, ward, zila, zone **05** block, patch, place, shire **06** barrio, bounds, circar, county, domain, locale, parish, region, riding, sector, sircar, sirkar, suburb **07** circuit, quarter, section **08** faubourg, highland, locality, precinct, province, quartier, stannary, vicinity **09** community, territory **12** constituency, municipality, neighborhood **13** neighbourhood **15** circumscription

See also **county**; **London**; **New York**; **Paris**

• **District of Columbia**
02 DC
• **outer district**
03 end
• **squalid district**
04 slum

distrust
05 doubt, qualm **07** suspect **08** be wary of, misfaith, mistrust, question, wariness **09** chariness, disbelief, discredit, misgiving, mislippen, suspicion **10** disbelieve, scepticism **11** questioning **12** doubtfulness **14** be suspicious of **15** have doubts about

distrustful
04 wary **05** chary **06** uneasy **07** cynical, dubious **08** doubtful, doubting **09** sceptical **10** suspicious, untrustful, untrusting **11** distrusting, mistrustful **12** disbelieving

disturb
◇ *anagram indicator*
03 jee, vex **04** fret, stir **05** annoy, rouse, shake, sturt, touch, upset, worry **06** affray, beat up, bother, dismay, hassle, infest, muddle, pester, put off, racket, ruffle, tumult, turn up **07** agitate, commove, concern, concuss, confuse, disrupt, fluster, inquiet, mismake, perturb, trouble **08** butt in on, disorder, disquiet, distract, distress, unsettle **09** discomfit, dislocate, interrupt **10** disarrange, discompose, disconcert, distrouble, perturbate **11** disorganize, make anxious

disturbance
◇ *anagram indicator*
03 row **04** dust, fray, muss, riot, rout **05** brawl, broil, musse, sturt, upset **06** bother, cangle, fracas, hassle, hoop-la, kick-up, muddle, racket, ruckus, rumble, rumpus, tumult, turn-up, unrest, uproar, upturn **07** illness, ruction, stashie, stishie, stushie, trouble, turmoil **08** disorder, neurosis, outbreak, sickness, stooshie, stramash, upheaval, williwaw **09** agitation, annoyance, commotion, complaint, confusion, hindrance, intrusion **10** convulsion, disruption, hullabaloo, inquietude, perplexity, rough-house **11** derangement, distraction, embroilment, molestation **12** interference, interruption **13** collieshangie **14** distemperature
• **freedom from disturbance**
04 ease

disturbed
◇ *anagram indicator*
04 vext **05** upset, vexed **06** hung-up, uneasy **07** anxious, inquiet, unquiet, worried **08** bothered, confused, neurotic, paranoid, troubled, unstable **09** concerned, flustered, psychotic, screwed-up, turbulent **10** mistrysted, unbalanced **11** discomposed, maladjusted, mentally ill **12** apprehensive **13** dysfunctional

disturbing

◇ *anagram indicator*
08 alarming, worrying **09** agitating, confusing, dismaying, startling, troubling, troublous, upsetting **10** disturbant, perturbing, unsettling **11** bewildering, disquieting, distressing, frightening, threatening **12** discouraging, disturbative **13** disconcerting

disunited

05 split **07** divided **09** alienated, disrupted, estranged, separated **10** dissevered

disunity

05 split **06** breach, schism, strife **07** discord, dissent, rupture **08** conflict, division **10** alienation, dissension **11** discordance **12** disagreement, estrangement

disuse

05 decay **07** neglect **09** desuetude **11** abandonment, inusitation **14** discontinuance

disused

04 idle **06** unused **07** decayed **08** obsolete **09** abandoned, neglected **12** discontinued

ditch

04 delf, dike, drop, dump, dyke, foss, grip, ha-ha, lode, moat, rean, reen, sike, syke **05** canal, chuck, delph, drain, fosse, graft, gripe, gully, level, rhine, rhyne, scrap, stank **06** derail, furrow, gulley, gutter, haw-haw, sheuch, sheugh, the sea, trench, trough **07** abandon, channel, discard, euripus **08** get rid of, jettison, throw out **09** dispose of, sunk fence, throw away **11** watercourse

dither

◇ *anagram indicator*
04 faff, flap, stew, tizz **05** delay, panic, quake, tizzy, waver **06** bother, dicker, falter, pother, shiver **07** agitate, confuse, fluster, flutter, perturb, tremble **08** hang back, hesitate **09** faff about, vacillate **10** dilly-dally, indecision **12** be in two minds, perturbation, shilly-shally, take your time

ditto

02 do

divan

04 sofa **05** couch, dewan **06** day bed, lounge, settee **07** council, lounger, ottoman, sofa bed **08** assembly **12** chaise-longue, chesterfield

dive

03 bar, dip, fly, ken, pub **04** bolt, club, dart, dash, drop, duck, dump, fall, hole, jump, leap, rush, tear **05** hurry, joint, lunge, pitch, sound, swoop **06** go down, header, plunge, refuge, saloon, spring, subway **07** descend, go under, plummet **08** nose-dive, submerge, tailspin **09** belly-flop, jackknife, nightclub **11** move quickly

diver

04 loom, loon **05** grebe **08** aquanaut, urinator **09** guillemot **10** pickpocket
See also **swimmer**

diverge

04 fork, part, vary **05** clash, drift, split, stray **06** branch, depart, differ, divide, spread, wander **07** deflect, deviate, digress, dissent, radiate **08** conflict, disagree, divagate, separate **09** bifurcate, branch off, spread out, subdivide **10** contradict, divaricate **12** be at variance

divergence

03 gap **05** clash, slant **07** parting **08** conflict **09** departure, deviation, dichotomy, disparity, variation **10** deflection, difference, digression, separation **12** branching-out, disagreement, divarication

divergent

07 diverse, variant, varying **08** separate **09** deviating, different, differing, diverging **10** dissimilar, divaricate, tangential **11** conflicting, disagreeing

divers

04 many, some **06** sundry, varied **07** several, various, varying **08** manifold, numerous **09** different **12** multifarious **13** miscellaneous

diverse

◇ *anagram indicator*
05 mixed **06** sundry, unlike, varied **07** several, various, varying **08** assorted, discrete, distinct, manifold, separate **09** different, differing, multiform **10** all means of, dissimilar **11** contrasting, distracting **13** heterogeneous, miscellaneous

diversification

09 extension, variation **10** alteration **11** variegation **12** branching-out, modification, spreading-out

diversify

03 mix **04** vary **05** alter, paint, spice **06** assort, change, expand, extend, modify **08** sprinkle **09** branch out, spread out, variegate **11** intersperse **13** differentiate **14** bring variety to

diversion

◇ *anagram indicator*
03 fun **04** game, play **05** hobby, sport **06** change, detour **07** pastime **09** amusement, avocation, deviation, switching **10** alteration, recreation, relaxation, rerouteing **11** distraction, redirection **13** divertisement, entertainment **14** divertissement

diversionary

09 divertive **10** deflecting **11** distracting

diversity

05 range **06** medley **07** mixture, variety **08** variance **09** pluralism **10** assortment, difference, embroidery, miscellany **11** variegation **12** biodiversity **13** dissimilarity,

dissimilitude, heterogeneity **15** diversification

divert

◇ *anagram indicator*
04 sway **05** amuse, avert **06** absorb, baffle, occupy, put off, siphon, switch, syphon **07** deflect, delight, engross, hive off, pervert, reroute, turn off **08** call away, distract, draw away, estrange, interest, intrigue, redirect, turn away **09** entertain, sidetrack

diverting

◇ *anagram indicator*
03 fun **05** funny, witty **07** amusing **08** humorous, pleasant **09** enjoyable **11** pleasurable **12** entertaining

divest

04 doff **05** strip **06** denude, remove **07** deprive, despoil, disrobe, undress **08** unclothe **09** disentail **10** dispossess

divide

◇ *insertion indicator*
03 cut, div, gap **04** deal, divi, fork, gulf, part, rank, rift, sort **05** allot, break, cut up, grade, group, order, sever, share, split **06** bisect, branch, breach, cantle, cleave, depart, detach **07** arrange, break up, carve up, deal out, discide, dispart, diverge, dole out, fissure, hand out, opening, sort out, split up **08** alienate, allocate, classify, dispense, disunite, division, estrange, polarize, separate, share out **09** apportion, break down, segregate, watershed **10** categorize, disconnect, distribute, divergence, drive apart, measure out, separation **11** come between, distinguish

• **divide up**
05 allot, share **07** dole out **08** allocate, share out **09** apportion, dismember, parcel out **10** measure out

dividend

03 cut, div, FID **04** divi, gain, perk, plus **05** bonus, divvy, extra, share, whack **07** benefit, portion, surplus **09** advantage **10** percentage, perquisite

divination

05 -mancy **06** augury **07** presage **08** divining, prophecy **10** conjecture, prediction **11** foretelling, hariolation, second sight, soothsaying **14** fortune-telling **15** prognostication

Divination and fortune-telling techniques include:

04 dice
05 runes, tarot
06 I Ching, sortes
07 dowsing, scrying
08 geomancy, myomancy, taghairm, zoomancy
09 aeromancy, astrology, belomancy, ceromancy, gyromancy, oenomancy, palmistry, pyromancy, sortilege, tea leaves, theomancy
10 axinomancy, capnomancy, cartomancy, chiromancy,

cleromancy, dukkeripen, hieromancy, hydromancy, lithomancy, numerology, spodomancy
11 bibliomancy, botanomancy, crithomancy, gastromancy, hepatoscopy, oneiromancy, onychomancy, rhabdomancy, tephromancy
12 clairvoyance, coscinomancy, lampadomancy, omphalomancy, ornithomancy, radiesthesia, scapulomancy
13 Book of Changes, crystal gazing, dactyliomancy, fortune cookie, omoplatoscopy
14 crystallomancy

divine
04 holy, spae **05** godly, guess, infer **06** cleric, deduce, intuit, lovely, parson, pastor, priest, sacred **07** angelic, exalted, godlike, prelate, saintly, suppose, supreme, surmise, suspect **08** charming, foretell, glorious, heavenly, minister, mystical, perceive, reverend, seraphic, splendid **09** apprehend, beautiful, celestial, churchman, clergyman, excellent, prescient, religious, spiritual, wonderful **10** conjecture, delightful, sanctified, superhuman, theologian, understand **11** churchwoman, clergywoman, consecrated **12** ecclesiastic, supernatural, transcendent **13** prognosticate

See also **clergyman, clergywoman**; **religious**

divinely
08 heavenly **10** charmingly, gloriously, mystically **11** angelically, celestially, excellently, spiritually, wonderfully **12** delightfully **14** supernaturally

diviner
04 seer **05** augur, sibyl **06** dowser, oracle **07** prophet **08** haruspex **09** divinator, visionary **10** astrologer, soothsayer **11** clairvoyant, conjecturer, water-finder **12** crystal-gazer

diving *see* **swimming**

divinity
02 RE, RI **03** god **05** deity **06** spirit **07** goddess, godhead, godship **08** holiness, numinous, religion, sanctity, theology **09** godliness **10** divineness

See also **God**; **god, goddess**

division
03 arm, div **04** feud, part, rift, side **05** class, group, limit, share, split, tribe, tuath, world **06** border, branch, breach, divide, region, schism, sector **07** barrier, cutting, discord, parting, portion, rupture, scruple, section, segment, sharing **08** boundary, category, conflict, disunion, disunity, dividing, frontier, scission, scissure, townland **09** allotment, cutting up, detaching, partition, severance **10** alienation, allocation, department,

digitation, dividing up, separation, sharing out, subsection **11** compartment, distinction **12** disagreement, distribution, dividing-line, estrangement **13** apportionment **15** demarcation line

divisive
08 damaging **09** injurious **10** alienating, discordant, disruptive, estranging, schismatic **11** troublesome **12** inharmonious **13** troublemaking

divorce
03 div **04** part **05** annul, sever, split, talak, talaq **06** breach, bust up, detach, divide **07** break up, break-up, isolate, put away, rupture, split up, split-up **08** dissolve, disunion, disunite, division, separate **09** annulment, partition, repudiate, severance **10** disconnect, dissociate, separation **11** dissolution, divorcement **13** diffarreation

divorced
03 div

divorcee
02 ex

divulge
04 leak, talk, tell **05** let on, split **06** babble, betray, bewray, expose, impart, repeat, reveal **07** confess, declare, let slip, publish, uncover **08** disclose, evulgate, proclaim **09** broadcast, make known, unconfine **10** promulgate **11** blow the gaff, communicate **12** break the news **13** spill the beans

dizziness
06 megrim **07** megrims, vertigo **09** faintness, giddiness, mirligoes, wooziness **10** scotodinia **15** light-headedness, vertiginousness

dizzy
◇ *anagram indicator*
04 mazy **05** dazed, ditsy, faint, giddy, shaky, silly, woozy **06** wobbly **07** confuse, extreme, foolish, muddled, reeling **08** confused, Disraeli **09** airheaded, confusing, Gillespie **10** bewildered, off-balance **11** addle-headed, bewildering, light-headed, vertiginous **13** irresponsible, rattle-brained **14** feather-brained, scatterbrained, weak at the knees

Djibouti
03 DJI

do
◇ *anagram indicator*
02 ut **03** act, con, dae, end, fix, put, rob **04** bash, char, comb, cook, dope, do up, dupe, fare, fuss, go at, have, hoax, make, raid, read, take, tidy, tour, wash, work **05** brush, cause, cheat, clean, crack, event, feast, get on, learn, mimic, offer, party, place, put on, reach, serve, solve, study, style, treat, trick, visit **06** adjust, affair, beat up, behave, bestow, come on, confer, create, finish, fleece, fulfil, manage, master, rave-up,

render, rip off, soirée, supply, tackle, tart up, thrash, thrive, tidy up, work as, work at, work on **07** achieve, arrange, assault, clean up, deceive, defraud, develop, dope out, execute, exhaust, explore, furnish, go round, knees-up, major in, perform, prepare, present, proceed, produce, provide, resolve, satisfy, sort out, suffice, swindle, work out **08** activity, be enough, carry out, complete, conclude, deal with, decorate, function, get along, get ready, hoodwink, occasion, organize, progress, sightsee, travel at **09** come along, discharge, figure out, gathering, implement, look after, overreach, prosecute, puzzle out, reception, undertake **10** accomplish, be adequate, effectuate, fit the bill, have as a job, take care of, try to solve **11** celebration, impersonate, travel round **12** be employed as, be in charge of, be sufficient, take for a ride **13** earn a living as, make a bad job of **14** acquit yourself, be satisfactory, make a good job of **15** comport yourself, conduct yourself, find the answer to, put into practice

• **do away with**
04 do in, kill, slay **05** annul, scrap **06** murder, remove **07** abolish, bump off, destroy, discard, nullify **08** get rid of, knock off **09** dispose of, eliminate, finish off, liquidate, slaughter **10** put to death **11** assassinate, discontinue, exterminate

• **do down**
04 slag, slam **05** blame, cheat **06** dump on, subdue **07** censure, condemn, put down, rubbish, slag off **08** badmouth, belittle **09** criticize, disparage **13** find fault with

• **do in**
04 kill, ruin, slay **06** murder **07** bump off, deceive, exhaust **08** knock off **09** slaughter **10** put to death **11** assassinate, exterminate

• **do out of**
06 fleece **08** con out of **09** deprive of **10** cheat out of, trick out of **11** diddle out of **12** swindle out of

• **dos and don'ts**
04 code **05** rules **07** customs **09** etiquette, standards **11** regulations **12** instructions

• **do up**
03 tie **04** lace, pack **05** tie up, zip up **06** button, fasten, repair **07** arrange, restore **08** decorate, renovate **09** modernize, refurbish **10** redecorate **11** recondition

• **do without**
04 miss, want **05** forgo, spare **06** eschew, forego, give up **07** refrain **09** go without **10** relinquish **11** abstain from **12** deny yourself, dispense with **13** manage without

• **that will do**
02 so **03** sae

docile
07 dutiful, willing **08** amenable, flexible, obedient, obliging, yielding

09 childlike, compliant, tractable
10 controlled, manageable,
submissive 11 co-operative
12 controllable

docilely
08 amenably 09 dutifully, willingly
10 obediently, obligingly
11 compliantly 13 co-operatively

docility
07 pliancy 08 meekness 09 ductility,
obedience 10 compliance, pliability
11 amenability 12 biddableness,
complaisance, tractability
13 manageability 14 submissiveness

dock
◇ *tail deletion indicator*
02 dk 03 bob, cut, pen 04 clip, crop,
land, moor, pier, quay, rump 05 basin,
berth, jetty, put in, Rumex, tie up, wharf
06 anchor, deduct, detail, lessen,
marina, reduce, remove, sorrel
07 bistort, curtail, harbour, shorten
08 boat yard, canaigre, decrease,
diminish, patience, quayside, subtract,
truncate, withhold 09 grapetree,
polygonum 10 drop anchor, tidal
basin, waterfront 12 monk's rhubarb,
submarine pen 15 fitting-out basin
• **docked**
02 in
• **in the dock**
07 on trial

docker
04 ship 06 lumper 08 labourer
09 stevedore 11 farmer's wife
12 longshoreman

docket
03 tab, tag 04 bill, chit, file, mark
05 index, label, tally 06 chitty, coupon,
record, ticket 07 receipt, voucher
08 document, register 09 catalogue,
paperwork 10 categorize
11 certificate, counterfoil
13 documentation

doctor
◇ *anagram indicator*
02 Dr 03 doc 04 cook, drug, fake,
lace, load, pill, spay 05 alter, bones,
medic, quack, spike 06 change,
crocus, dilute, fiddle, mganga, neuter,
repair, weaken 07 falsify, massage,
pervert, sangoma 08 castrate,
disguise, marabout, medicate,
medicine, sawbones 09 body-curer,
clinician, physician, sterilize 10 add
drugs to, adulterate, manipulate,
tamper with 11 add poison to,
contaminate, witch-finder
12 misrepresent, sophisticate
13 interfere with

02 BM, GP, MB, MD, MO
03 vet
05 locum
06 intern
07 dentist, surgeon
08 houseman, resident
09 registrar
10 consultant
12 family doctor
14 hospital doctor, medical officer

See also **medical**

03 Who
04 Bell (Sir Charles), Koch (Robert),
Lind (James), Mayo (Charles), Razi
(ar-), Reed (Walter), Ross (Sir
Ronald)
05 Broca (Paul Pierre), Bruce (Sir
David), Galen, Lower (Richard),
Osler (Sir William), Paget (Sir
James), Remak (Robert), Steno
(Nicolaus)
06 Bichat (Marie), Bright (Richard),
Carrel (Alexis), Celsus (Aulus),
Cooper (Sir Astley), Fernel (Jean),
Finsen (Niels), Garrod (Sir
Archibald), Harvey (William),
Hunter (John), Jekyll, Jenner
(Edward), Lister (Joseph, Lord),
Manson (Sir Patrick), Mesmer
(Franz), Watson (John), Willis
(Thomas)
07 Addison (Thomas), Barnard
(Christiaan), Beddoes (Thomas),
Burkitt (Denis), Cushing (Harvey),
Eijkman (Christiaan), Gilbert
(William), Hodgkin (Thomas),
Laënnec (René), Laveran (Charles),
Linacre (Thomas), MacEwen (Sir
William), McIndoe (Sir Archibald),
Nicolle (Charles), Winston (Robert,
Lord)
08 Anderson (Elizabeth Garrett),
Barnardo (Thomas), Beaumont
(William), Billroth (Theodor),
Charnley (Sir John), Duchenne
(Guillaume), Magendie (François),
Morgagni (Giovanni Battista),
Sydenham (Thomas), Tournier
(Paul)
09 Bartholin (Erasmus), Boerhaave
(Hermann), Dutrochet (Henri),
Fabricius (Johannes), Hahnemann
(Samuel), Mackenzie (Sir James),
Parkinson (James)
10 Fracastoro (Girolamo), Paracelsus,
Sanctorius
11 Hippocrates, Ramón y Cajal
(Santiago)
12 Erasistratus

See also **surgeon**

doctrinaire
05 rigid 06 biased 08 armchair,
dogmatic, pedantic 09 fanatical,
insistent 10 inflexible 11 impractical,
opinionated, theoretical

doctrine
03 ism 04 lore 05 canon, credo,
creed, dogma, tenet 06 belief
07 esotery, mystery, opinion, precept
08 teaching 09 principle 10 conviction

See also **philosophy**

document
04 chop, cite, deed, form, list, roll, writ
05 chart, paper, proof, prove 06 back
up, billet, detail, patent, record, report,
verify 07 charter, support, warning,
write up 08 evidence, register, validate
09 affidavit, chronicle, write down
10 chirograph, commission,
instrument 11 certificate, corroborate,
instruction, put on record
12 command paper, commit to film,
give weight to, keep on record,
substantiate 13 commit to paper

documentary
07 charted, factual, written
08 detailed, recorded 09 reportage
10 chronicled, documented, featurette

documentation
06 papers, record 08 evidence
09 authority, paperwork
12 verification 14 qualifications

doddering
◇ *anagram indicator*
04 aged, weak 05 frail 06 feeble,
infirm, senile 07 elderly 08 decrepit
09 tottering

doddery
◇ *anagram indicator*
04 aged, weak 05 shaky 06 feeble,
infirm 07 tottery 08 unsteady
09 doddering, faltering, tottering
10 staggering

dodge
03 tip 04 bolt, dart, dash, dive, duck,
fake, jink, jook, jouk, lurk, ploy, ruse,
rush, shun, veer, wile 05 avoid, elude,
evade, fudge, shift, shirk, trick
06 bypass, device, racket, scheme,
swerve 07 evasion, fend off, quibble,
shuffle, slinter, wrinkle 08 fakement,
get out of, get round, gimcrack,
jimcrack, jump away, side-step
09 deception, manoeuvre, stratagem
10 subterfuge 11 contrivance,
machination 12 move suddenly, steer
clear of 13 sharp practice

dodger
06 evader, skiver 07 avoider, dreamer,
goof-off, shirker, slacker 08 layabout,
slyboots 09 lazybones, trickster
11 goldbricker, lead-swinger

dodgy
◇ *anagram indicator*
04 iffy 05 crook, dicey, fishy, risky
06 artful, chancy, tricky, unsafe
07 dubious, fraught, suspect
08 doubtful, unstable 09 dangerous,
dishonest, uncertain 10 unreliable
12 disreputable 13 problematical

doer
04 hand 05 agent 06 dynamo, factor,
worker 07 bustler 08 achiever,
activist, executor, go-getter, live wire
09 organizer 10 powerhouse
12 accomplisher 14 mover and shaker

doff
03 tip 04 lift, shed, vail 05 avail, avale,
raise, strip, touch 06 availe, lay off,
remove 07 discard, take off, undight
08 throw off

dog
03 cur, pup, tag 04 cock, Fido, mutt,
stag, tail, tike, tyke 05 bitch, harry,

haunt, hound, piper, pooch, puppy, rogue, Rover, stalk, track, trail, worry **06** barker, bitser, canine, follow, infest, plague, pursue, rascal, shadow, touser, towser, wretch, yapper **07** andiron, mongrel, traitor, trouble, villain, whiffet, yapster **08** informer **09** scoundrel **10** tripehound **11** Montmorency, trendle-tail, trindle-tail, trundle-tail

See also **animal**

Dogs include:

03 gun, lab, Pom, pug
04 chow, kuri, Peke, tosa
05 akita, boxer, corgi, dhole, dingo, husky, hyena, laika, spitz
06 badger, bandog, beagle, bitser, borzoi, briard, collie, gun dog, moppet, poodle, saluki, Scotty, setter, vizsla, Westie
07 basenji, bouvier, bulldog, bush dog, coondog, griffon, lurcher, Maltese, mastiff, pitbull, pointer, Samoyed, Scottie, Shar-Pei, sheltie, shih tzu, sloughi, spaniel, terrier, volpino, whippet
08 Airedale, alsatian, chow-chow, coach dog, Doberman, elkhound, foxhound, keeshond, komondor, Labrador, malamute, papillon, Pekinese, Sealyham, sheepdog, warrigal
09 boar-hound, chihuahua, coonhound, dachshund, Dalmatian, Eskimo dog, Great Dane, greyhound, Kerry Blue, lhasa apso, Pekingese, red setter, retriever, schnauzer, St Bernard, wolfhound
10 bloodhound, fox terrier, Iceland-dog, Maltese dog, otter hound, Pomeranian, raccoon dog, Rottweiler, sausage-dog, spotted dog, St Bernard's
11 Afghan hound, basset-hound, bichon frise, bull-mastiff, bull terrier, carriage dog, Irish setter, Jack Russell, kangaroo dog, wishtonwish
12 Border collie, cairn terrier, Irish terrier, Japanese tosa, Newfoundland
13 affenpinscher, bearded collie, Boston terrier, cocker spaniel, Scotch terrier
14 English terrier, German Shepherd, Irish wolfhound, pit bull terrier
15 golden retriever, Scottish terrier, springer spaniel

See also **spaniel**; **terrier**

Dog types include:

02 pi
03 gun, hot, lap, pet, pie, pye, sea, top, toy, war
04 corn, rach, wild
05 guard, guide, house, pooch, rache, ratch, sheep, under, watch, water, zorro
06 kennet, pariah, police, ranger, ratter, sleeve, yellow
07 harrier, hearing, leading, mongrel, tracker, truffle

08 huntaway, turnspit
09 retriever
10 sheep-biter, shin-barker
11 sleuth-hound

Famous dogs include:

03 Lad
04 Lucy, Nana, Odie, Shep, Spot, Toby, Toto
05 Balto, Butch, Flush, Goofy, Laika, Petra, Pluto, Pongo, Sadie, Snowy, Timmy
06 Buster, Droopy, Gelert, Gromit, Hector, Lassie, Missis, Nipper, Sirius, Snoopy
07 Charley, Gnasher, Perdita, Roobarb
08 Bullseye, Cerberus, Dogmatix
09 RinTinTin, Scooby Doo
10 Deputy Dawg, Fred Basset
12 Real Huntsman
13 Master McGrath, Mick the Miller
15 Greyfriars Bobby, The Littlest Hobo

• **dog's breakfast, dog's dinner**
04 mess
• **reproof to dog**
04 rate

dogged
04 firm **06** intent, steady, sullen **07** staunch **08** obdurate, resolute, stubborn, tireless **09** obstinate, steadfast, tenacious **10** determined, persistent, relentless, unflagging, unshakable, unyielding **11** indomitable, persevering, unfaltering, unshakeable **12** pertinacious, single-minded **13** indefatigable

doggedly
06 firmly **09** staunchly **10** resolutely, stubbornly, tirelessly, unshakably **11** obstinately, steadfastly, tenaciously, unshakeably **12** persistently, relentlessly **13** indefatigably **14** single-mindedly

doggedness
08 firmness, tenacity **09** endurance, obstinacy **10** resolution, steadiness **11** persistence, pertinacity **12** perseverance, stubbornness **13** determination, steadfastness, tenaciousness **14** indomitability, relentlessness

doggerel
03 jig **08** nonsense, rat-rhyme **11** crambo clink **12** crambo-jingle

dogma
04 code **05** credo, creed, maxim, tenet **06** belief **07** article, opinion, precept **08** doctrine, teaching **09** principle **10** conviction **12** code of belief **14** article of faith

dogmatic
08 arrogant, emphatic, pontific, positive **09** arbitrary, assertive, canonical, doctrinal, imperious, insistent **10** ex cathedra, intolerant, peremptory, pontifical **11** affirmative, categorical, dictatorial, doctrinaire, domineering, opinionated, overbearing, pragmatical

13 authoritarian, authoritative **14** unquestionable **15** unchallengeable

dogmatically
10 arrogantly **11** assertively, imperiously, insistently **12** emphatically, intolerantly **13** categorically, dictatorially, domineeringly **15** authoritatively

dogmatism
07 bigotry **11** presumption **12** positiveness **13** arbitrariness, assertiveness, imperiousness **14** peremptoriness **15** dictatorialness, opinionatedness

dogsbody
05 gofer, slave **06** drudge, lackey, menial, skivvy **07** doormat **08** factotum **11** galley-slave **12** bottle-washer, man-of-all-work **13** maid-of-all-work

doings
04 acts, work **05** deeds, feats **06** events **07** actions, affairs **08** concerns, dealings, exploits, goings-on **09** handiwork **10** activities, adventures, happenings **11** enterprises, proceedings **12** achievements, transactions

doldrums
05 blues, dumps, ennui, gloom **06** acedia, apathy, tedium, torpor **07** boredom, inertia, malaise, megrims **08** dullness **09** dejection, lassitude **10** depression, melancholy, stagnation **12** listlessness, sluggishness **15** downheartedness, low-spiritedness

dole
03 JSA **04** broo, pain, vail **05** grief, guile, share, vails, vales **06** credit, income **07** benefit, payment, support **08** pittance **09** allowance **12** state benefit **14** social security
• **dole out**
04 deal **05** allot, issue, share **06** assign, divide, ration **07** deal out, dish out, give out, hand out, mete out **08** allocate, dispense, divide up, share out **09** apportion **10** administer, distribute

doleful
03 sad **04** blue **06** dismal, dreary, gloomy, rueful, sombre, woeful **07** forlorn, painful, pitiful **08** dolorous, mournful, pathetic, wretched **09** cheerless, miserable, sorrowful, woebegone **10** depressing, lugubrious, melancholy **11** distressing **12** disconsolate **14** down in the dumps

dolefully
05 sadly **08** dismally, gloomily **09** forlornly, miserably, unhappily **10** mournfully, wretchedly **12** pathetically **14** disconsolately

doll
03 toy **04** babe **05** dolly **06** figure **08** figurine **09** plaything

03 kid, rag, wax
04 baby
05 China, cloth, Dutch, metal, paper, Paris, Sindy®
06 artist, Barbie®, bisque, blow-up, ethnic, fabric, Hamble, kewpie, modern, moppet, poppet, puppet, voodoo, wooden
07 fashion, jointed, kachina, kokeshi, nesting, rag baby, Russian
08 golliwog, gollywog
09 miniature, porcelain, tachibina, Tiny Tears
10 marionette, matryoshka, Raggedy Ann, topsy-turvy
11 composition, papier-mâché, Polly Pocket
12 reproduction
15 Cabbage Patch Kid, frozen Charlotte

• **doll up**
05 preen, primp 06 tart up 07 deck out, dress up, trick up 08 titivate, trick out

dollar
03 cob, dol 04 buck, peso 05 scrip, wheel 06 loonie, single 07 iron man, Mexican, smacker 09 greenback
• **eighth of a dollar**
04 real
• **five dollars**
03 fin 04 spin 05 fiver

dollop
03 gob 04 ball, blob, glob, lump 05 bunch, clump 06 gobbet, slairg

dolly
05 peggy 06 maiden, Parton, Varden

dolorous
03 sad 06 rueful, sombre, woeful 07 doleful, painful 08 grievous, mournful, wretched 09 anguished, harrowing, miserable, sorrowful, woebegone 10 lugubrious, melancholy 11 distressing 12 heart-rending

dolour
04 pain 05 grief 06 misery, sorrow 07 anguish, sadness 08 distress, mourning 09 heartache, suffering 10 heartbreak 11 lamentation

dolphin
06 sea-pig 07 grampus 08 porpoise 09 coryphene, Delphinus, mere swine 10 bottle-nose

dolt
03 ass, git, oaf 04 clot, dope, dork, fool, geek, nerd, twit 05 chump, clunk, golem, idiot, ninny, twerp, wally 06 dimwit, nitwit 07 nutcase, plonker 08 dipstick, imbecile, mooncalf, numskull 09 blockhead, simpleton 10 clodhopper, nincompoop, sheep's-head 11 chuckle-head

domain
04 area 05 arena, bourn, field, lands, realm, reame, reign, world 06 bourne, empire, estate, region, sphere

07 concern, kingdom, section
08 dominion, province, seignory, universe 09 ownership, seigneury, seigniory, territory 10 department, discipline, seigneurie, speciality
12 jurisdiction

See also **classification**

dome
04 tope 05 igloo, mound, stupa, vault 06 bubble, cupola, dagaba, dagoba, tholus 07 rotunda 09 astrodome, macrodome 10 brachydome, hemisphere

domestic
03 dom, pet 04 char, cook, esne, help, home, maid, tame 05 daily, house, local, tamed 06 au pair, broken, family, homely, native 07 cleaner, private, servant 08 broken in, char lady, familiar, fireside, home-bred, home help, internal, national, personal 09 charwoman, daily help, household 10 home-loving, indigenous, stay-at-home 11 domiciliary 12 domesticated, domestic help, housekeeping, house-trained

03 Aga®, hob, Vax®
04 iron, oven, spit
05 grill, mixer, radio, stove
06 cooker, fridge, Hoover®, juicer, kettle, washer
07 blender, fan oven, freezer, griddle, ionizer, toaster
08 barbecue, gas stove, hotplate, wireless
09 deep fryer, Dutch oven, DVD player, steam iron
10 coffee mill, deep-freeze, dishwasher, humidifier, liquidizer, percolator, rotisserie, slow cooker, steam press, television, waffle iron
11 tumble-drier, washer-drier
12 kitchen range, refrigerator, stereo system, trouser press
13 carpet sweeper, electric grill, floor polisher, food processor, fridge-freezer, ice-cream maker, microwave oven, sandwich maker, vacuum cleaner, video recorder
14 electric cooker, juice extractor, upright cleaner, washing machine
15 carpet shampooer, cylinder cleaner

domestically
06 at home 07 locally 08 near home 09 in private 10 internally, nationally

domesticate
04 tame 05 break, train 07 break in 08 accustom 09 habituate 10 assimilate, house-train, naturalize 11 acclimatize, familiarize

domesticated
03 pet 04 tame 05 tamed 06 broken, homely 08 broken in, domestic 10 home-loving, house-proud 11 housewifely, naturalized 12 house-trained

domestication
06 taming 08 training 10 breaking-in 11 habituation 12 assimilation 13 house-training 14 naturalization

domesticity
09 homecraft 10 homemaking, housecraft 12 housekeeping 13 domestication, home economics 15 domestic science

domicile
04 home, live 05 abode, house 06 settle 07 lodging, mansion 08 dwelling, lodgings, quarters 09 establish, residence, residency 10 habitation, settlement 12 make your home, put down roots 15 take up residence

dominance
04 rule, sway 05 power 07 command, control, mastery 08 hegemony 09 authority, supremacy 10 ascendancy, centrality, domination, government, leadership 11 paramountcy, pre-eminence, superiority

dominant
03 key 04 main 05 chief, major, prime 06 ruling, strong 07 central, leading, primary, supreme 08 powerful 09 assertive, besetting, governing, important, paramount, presiding, prevalent, principal, prominent 10 commanding, overriding, pre-eminent, prevailing 11 all-powerful, controlling, influential, outstanding, predominant 13 authoritative, most important

dominate
04 lead, rule 05 dwarf 06 direct, govern, master, rule OK 07 command, control, eclipse, preside, prevail 08 domineer, overbear, overgang, overlook, overrule 09 mesmerize, tower over, tyrannize 10 intimidate, monopolize, overmaster, overshadow, run the show 11 have on toast, predominate 12 hold the floor 15 have over a barrel, wear the trousers

dominating
06 strong 08 dominant, powerful, superior 09 assertive, confident, directing 10 commanding, overruling 11 controlling 12 advantageous 13 authoritative

domination
04 rule, sway 05 power 07 bossism, command, control, mastery, tyranny 09 authority, despotism, influence, prelatism, supremacy 10 ascendancy, government, leadership, militarism, oppression, repression, subjection 11 pre-eminence, superiority, suppression 12 dictatorship, predominance 13 subordination

domineer
04 boss, ride 07 henpeck 08 jackboot

domineering
05 bossy, pushy 07 haughty, kick-ass

08 arrogant, coercive, despotic, forceful, managing **09** imperious, masterful, tyrannous **10** aggressive, autocratic, high-handed, iron-handed, oppressive, peremptory, tyrannical **11** dictatorial, overbearing **13** authoritarian

Dominica
02 WD **03** DJI, DMA

Dominican
03 Dom

Dominican Republic
03 DOM

Dominicans
02 OP

dominion
03 Dom **04** rule, sway **05** power, realm **06** colony, domain, empire **07** command, control, country, kingdom, mastery **08** lordship, province **09** authority, direction, supremacy, territory **10** ascendancy, dependency, domination, government **11** sovereignty **12** jurisdiction, protectorate **14** rangatiratanga

don
◇ *insertion indicator*
04 Juan **05** adept, put on, swell, tutor **06** assume, expert, fellow, reader **07** address, dress in, get into, scholar, teacher **08** academic, Giovanni, lecturer, slip into **09** professor

donate
03 gie **04** give **06** bestow, chip in, confer, pledge **07** cough up, fork out, present **08** bequeath, give away, shell out **09** make a gift, subscribe **10** contribute **12** club together **13** make a donation

donation
04 alms, gift, koha, wakf, waqf **05** grant **07** bequest, charity, largess, present **08** gratuity, largesse, memorial, offering **11** benefaction **12** contribution, presentation, subscription

done
◇ *anagram indicator*
02 OK **04** over **05** baked, crisp, ended, fried, ready, right **06** agreed, boiled, cooked, proper, seemly, stewed, tender **07** browned, correct, decided, fitting, roasted, settled **08** accepted, arranged, complete, decorous, executed, finished, prepared, realized, suitable, well-done **09** completed, concluded, fulfilled **10** absolutely, acceptable, terminated **11** appropriate, consummated **12** accomplished, conventional
• **done for**
04 lost **06** beaten, broken, dashed, doomed, foiled, ruined, undone **07** wrecked **08** defeated, finished, spitcher, washed-up **09** destroyed **10** vanquished **14** for the high jump
• **done in**
04 dead **05** all in, weary **06** bushed,

pooped, zonked **07** whacked, worn out **08** dead beat, dog-tired, fatigued, tired out **09** exhausted, fagged out, fit to drop, flaked out, knackered, pooped out, shattered, stonkered **11** bushwhacked, tuckered out **14** on your last legs, worn to a frazzle
• **have done with**
04 stop **05** cease **06** desist, give up **08** over with **09** throw over **10** finish with, thrash with **12** finished with **13** be through with **15** over and done with, wash your hands of

Don Juan
04 rake **05** lover, romeo **06** gigolo **08** Casanova **09** ladies' man, philander, womanizer **10** lady-killer **11** philanderer

donkey
03 ass **04** moke, mule **05** burro, cuddy, genet, hinny, jenny, neddy **06** cuddie, gennet, jennet **07** jackass **11** cardophagus **13** Jerusalem pony

donnish
07 bookish, erudite, learned, serious **08** academic, pedantic, studious **09** pedagogic, scholarly **10** scholastic **11** formalistic **12** intellectual

donor
05 angel, giver **06** backer **07** donator **08** provider **09** supporter **10** benefactor **11** contributor **14** fairy godmother, philanthropist

doom
03 lot **04** damn, date, dome, fate, ruin **05** death, judge, weird **06** decree, devote **07** condemn, consign, destine, destiny, fortune, portion, verdict **08** disaster, downfall, judgment, sentence **09** destinate, judgement, pronounce, ruination **10** death-knell, predestine **11** catastrophe, destruction, rack and ruin **12** condemnation **13** pronouncement

doomed
03 fay, fey, fie **05** fated **06** cursed, damned, marked, ruined **07** accurst, devoted, unlucky **08** accursed, destined, hopeless, ill-fated, luckless **09** condemned, ill-omened **10** bedevilled, ill-starred **11** star-crossed

door
03 way **04** exit, haik, hake, heck, road, yett **05** entry, hatch, route, way in **06** access, portal **07** doorway, gateway, opening, postern **08** entrance, open door **11** opportunity
• **guard door**
04 tile

doorkeeper
05 tiler, tyler, usher **06** porter **07** doorman, janitor, ostiary **08** huissier **09** caretaker, concierge **10** gatekeeper **14** commissionaire

doorpost
04 dern, durn

dope
01 E **03** gen, git, LSD, oaf, pot, tea **04** acid, berk, clot, coke, dolt, dork, drug, fool, geek, hash, info, lace, prat, twit, weed **05** crack, drugs, dunce, facts, grass, idiot, ninny, opium, speed, spike, twerp **06** dimwit, doctor, heroin, inject, nitwit, opiate, sedate **07** buffoon, details, Ecstasy, halfwit, low-down, plonker, stupefy **08** cannabis, knock out, medicate, narcotic **09** absorbent, blockhead, marijuana, narcotize, simpleton, specifics **10** nincompoop **11** amphetamine, barbiturate, information, particulars **12** anaesthetize, hallucinogen
See also **fool**

dopey
04 daft, dozy **05** silly **06** drowsy, groggy, simple, sleepy, stupid, torpid **07** foolish, muddled, nodding **08** confused, narcotic **09** lethargic, somnolent, stupefied **12** addle-brained **14** not the full quid

dormancy
04 rest **05** sleep **07** latency, slumber **09** inertness **10** estivation, inactivity **11** aestivation, hibernation

dormant
05 inert, joist **06** asleep, fallow, latent, torpid **07** resting **08** comatose, inactive, latitant, sleeping, sluggish **09** crossbeam, lethargic, potential, quiescent **10** slumbering, unrealized **11** hibernating, undeveloped, undisclosed

dormouse
04 loir

dosage
04 dose **06** amount **07** measure, portion **08** quantity

dose
03 fix, hit **04** pill, shot **05** bolus, treat **06** amount, dosage, drench, potion, powder **07** booster, draught, measure, portion **08** dispense, medicate, quantity **09** prescribe **10** administer **11** horse-drench **12** prescription
• **lethal dose**
02 LD

dosh *see* **money**

dossier
04 case, data, file **05** brief, notes **06** folder, papers, report **09** documents, portfolio **11** information

dot
03 dab, dit, hit, jot, set **04** atom, iota, limp, mark, spot, stud, tick **05** fleck, point, prick, speck **06** bullet, circle, pepper, stigme, tittle **07** punctum, scatter, speckle, stipple **08** full stop, particle, pin-point, punctule, sprinkle **09** punctuate **11** bullet point **12** decimal point
• **on the dot**
05 sharp **06** on time **07** exactly

8 promptly **09** precisely
10 punctually **13** exactly on time

dotage
06 old age **07** anility **08** agedness, senility, weakness **09** infirmity
10 feebleness, imbecility
11 decrepitude, elderliness **12** autumn of life **13** evening of life **15** second childhood

dote
• **dote on**
04 love **05** adore, spoil **06** admire, pamper **07** idolize, indulge, worship
08 hold dear, treasure

doting
04 fond, soft **06** loving, tender
07 adoring, devoted **09** indulgent
12 affectionate

dotty
▷ anagram indicator
03 ape **04** bats, loco, nuts **05** barmy, batty, buggy, crazy, daffy, dippy, flaky, gonzo, loony, loopy, nutty, potty, wacko, wacky, weird, wiggy
06 cuckoo, fruity, mental, raving, screwy **07** bananas, barking, bonkers, cracked, meshuga, touched
08 crackers, demented, dingbats, doolally, peculiar, unsteady
09 eccentric, lymphatic, up the wall
10 bestraught, frantic-mad, off the wall, off your nut, out to lunch **11** not all there, off the rails, off your head
12 feeble-minded, mad as a hatter, off your chump, round the bend **13** off your rocker, out of your head, out of your tree, round the twist **14** off your trolley, wrong in the head

double
▷ repetition indicator
02 bi-, di- **03** dbl, twi-, twy- **04** copy, dual, fold, twin **05** clone, duple, image, match, trick, twice **06** binate, clench, do also, duplex, fill in, paired, repeat, ringer, two-ply **07** coupled, doubled, enlarge, magnify, replica, stand in, twofold **08** geminate, geminous, increase, turn down, two-edged
09 ambiguous, bifarious, deceitful, duplicate, equivocal, facsimile, insincere, lookalike **10** ambivalent, substitute, understudy **11** counterpart, deceitfully, double-edged, paradoxical, reduplicate
12 doppelgänger, hypocritical, impersonator **13** double-meaning, have a dual role, multiply by two, spitting image **14** be an understudy, have a second job **15** have a second role
• **at the double**
06 at once **07** quickly **09** right away
11 at full speed, immediately
12 straight away, without delay
• **double back**
04 loop **05** dodge, evade **06** circle, return **07** reverse **09** backtrack

double-cross
03 con **05** cheat, trick **06** betray
07 defraud, mislead, swindle,

two-time **08** hoodwink **12** take for a ride **14** pull a fast one on

double-dealing
07 perfidy **08** betrayal, cheating, tricking **09** duplicity, mendacity, swindling, treachery, two-timing
10 defrauding, misleading
11 crookedness, dissembling, hoodwinking **12** ambidextrous, two-facedness

double entendre
03 pun **08** innuendo, wordplay
09 ambiguity **11** play on words
13 double meaning **14** suggestiveness

doubling
04 fold, loop **05** plait, trick
08 mantling **10** gemination
11 duplicature **12** diplogenesis
13 reduplication

doubly
03 bis **05** again, extra, twice
07 twofold **10** especially

doubt
04 fear **05** demur, qualm, query, waver
06 aporia, danger, mammer, wonder
07 dilemma, dubiety, impeach, problem, scepsis, scruple, skepsis, suspect **08** distrust, dubitate, hesitate, misdoubt, mistrust, quandary, question, wavering **09** ambiguity, be dubious, confusion, hesitance, hesitancy, misgiving, suspicion, vacillate **10** difficulty, disbelieve, hesitation, indecision, perplexity, scepticism, skepticism, uneasiness
11 be uncertain, be undecided, incredulity, reservation, uncertainty
12 apprehension, be suspicious, mixed feeling **14** call in question **15** have qualms about
• **expression of doubt**
02 ha, h'm, um **03** erm, hah, hmm, hum **05** humph
• **in doubt**
04 moot **08** doubtful **09** ambiguous, debatable, uncertain, undecided **10** in question, unreliable, unresolved, up in the air **12** open to debate, questionable **14** open to question
• **no doubt**
04 iwis, ywis **06** surely **08** of course, probably **09** certainly, doubtless, no denying **10** definitely, most likely, presumably, sure enough
11 undoubtedly **12** bang to rights, without doubt **13** in anyone's book
14 unquestionably

doubter
05 cynic **06** Thomas **07** sceptic, scoffer **08** agnostic **10** questioner, unbeliever **11** disbeliever, non-believer, questionist **14** doubting Thomas

doubtful
04 iffy **05** crook, fishy, shady, vague
06 uneasy, unsure **07** dubious, in doubt, obscure, suspect, unclear
08 hesitant, insecure, unlikely, wavering **09** ambiguous, debatable,

sceptical, skeptical, tentative, uncertain, undecided
10 improbable, in two minds, irresolute, suspicious, touch and go
11 distrustful, vacillating
12 apprehensive, inconclusive, questionable **14** open to question

doubtfully
◊ anagram indicator
08 uneasily **10** hesitantly
11 sceptically, uncertainly
12 irresolutely **14** apprehensively

doubtless
04 sure **05** truly **06** surely **07** clearly, no doubt **08** of course, probably
09 assuredly, certainly, dreadless, precisely, seemingly **10** most likely, presumably, supposedly
11 indubitably, undoubtedly **12** bang to rights, indisputably, without doubt
13 in anyone's book
14 unquestionably

dough
04 cake, duff, masa **05** knish, money, pasta, paste **08** kreplach **09** hush puppy
See also **money**

doughnut
05 torus **06** sinker **07** olycook, olykoek **09** friedcake

doughty
04 able, bold, fell, tall **05** brave, gutsy
06 daring, gritty, heroic, plucky, spunky, strong **07** gallant, valiant
08 fearless, intrepid, unafraid, valorous
09 confident, dauntless, unabashed, undaunted **10** courageous, unblinking
11 indomitable, lion-hearted, unblenching, unflinching
14 unapprehensive

doughy
03 sad **04** soft **05** heavy, pasty
06 pallid, sodden

dour
04 grim, hard, sour **05** gruff, harsh, rigid, stern **06** dismal, dreary, gloomy, morose, severe, strict, sullen
07 austere **08** churlish, rigorous
09 obstinate, unsmiling
10 determined, forbidding, inflexible, unfriendly, unyielding

douse, dowse
03 dip, wet **04** duck, dunk, soak
05 flood, snuff, souse, steep
06 deluge, drench, plunge, put out, quench, splash, strike **07** blow out, immerge, immerse, smother
08 saturate, submerge **10** extinguish
13 pour water over

dove
03 doo **06** culver, pigeon, rocker, turtle **07** rockier **10** rock pigeon

dovetail
04 join, link **05** agree, match, tally
06 accord **07** conform **08** coincide
09 harmonize, interlock
10 correspond **11** fit together

dowdy
04 drab **05** dingy, mopsy, tacky, tatty
06 frowsy, frumpy, shabby
08 frumpish, slovenly **10** ill-dressed
12 old-fashioned **13** unfashionable

down
01 d **02** dn **03** ill, low, nap, sad **04** à
bas, blue, bust, fell, flue, fuzz, gulp,
oose, ooze, pile, shag, swig, wool
05 along, bloom, drink, floor, floss,
fluff, kaput, swill, throw, wonky
06 pappus, topple **07** consume,
crashed, depress, descent, floccus, put
away, swallow, toss off, unhappy
08 dejected, downcast, feathers, fine
hair, gulp down, wretched **09** bring
down, conked out, depressed, knock
back, knock down, miserable,
overthrow, prostrate, southward
10 behindhand, dispirited, melancholy,
not working, on the blink, on the fritz,
out of order, to the floor
11 downhearted, inoperative, out of
action, to the bottom, to the ground
12 soft feathers **13** to a lower level
14 down in the dumps, malfunctioning
• **down with**
03 hip **04** à bas **06** depose **07** abolish,
put down, swallow **08** away with, get
rid of **10** in tune with
• **set down**
03 lay **04** drop, dump, land, snub, take
05 judge, state **06** depose, esteem,
record, regard **07** ascribe, deposit,
detrain **09** attribute, discharge
10 disentrain

down-and-out
03 bum **04** hobo, wino **05** caird, jakey,
loser, piker, rogue, tramp **06** dosser,
ruined, toerag, truant, vagrom, walker
07 dingbat, floater, gangrel, tinkler,
vagrant **08** clochard, cursitor,
deadbeat, derelict, homeless, straggle,
stroller, vagabond **09** destitute,
landloper, penniless, sundowner
11 rinthereout, scatterling, Weary
Willie **12** down-and-outer, hallan-
shaker, impoverished, on your uppers
15 knight of the road

down-at-heel
04 drab, poor **05** dingy, dowdy, seedy,
tacky, tatty **06** frayed, frowsy, ragged,
shabby **07** run-down **08** slovenly,
tattered **09** neglected **10** ill-dressed,
ramshackle, tumbledown, uncared for
11 dilapidated, in disrepair

downbeat
03 low **04** calm **06** casual, gloomy
07 cynical, relaxed **08** downcast,
informal, laid-back, negative
09 cheerless, depressed, easy-going,
unhurried, unworried **10** despondent,
insouciant, nonchalant **11** pessimistic
15 fearing the worst

downcast
03 low, sad **04** blue, down, dull, glum
05 fed up **06** gloomy **07** daunted,
hanging, unhappy **08** dejected,
dismayed, wretched **09** depressed,
miserable **10** despondent, dispirited,

downlooked **11** crestfallen,
discouraged, downhearted, low-
spirited **12** disappointed, disconsolate,
disheartened

downfall
04 fall, ruin **05** decay **07** debacle,
failure, undoing **08** collapse, disgrace
09 overthrow **10** debasement
11 degradation, destruction,
humiliation

downgrade
05 decry, lower **06** defame, demote,
depose, do down, humble **07** deflate,
degrade, run down **08** belittle,
minimize, relegate **09** denigrate,
disparage, sell short, underrate
11 lower in rank, make light of
12 reduce in rank

downhearted
03 sad **04** glum **06** gloomy
07 daunted, unhappy **08** dejected,
dismayed, downcast **09** depressed
10 browned off, despondent,
dispirited **11** discouraged, low-spirited
12 disappointed, disconsolate,
disheartened

down-market
04 poor, sale **05** cheap, tacky, tatty
06 budget, cheapo, common, shoddy,
tawdry **07** bargain, economy, low-
cost, reduced **08** cut-price, giveaway,
inferior, low-price, no-frills
09 cheapjack, cheap-rate, knock-
down, throwaway, worthless
10 affordable, discounted,
economical, marked-down,
ramshackle, rock-bottom, second-rate
11 inexpensive **15** bargain-basement

downpour
04 pelt, rain **05** flood, plash **06** deluge
07 torrent **09** rainstorm
10 cloudburst, inundation, waterspout

downright
04 flat **05** clear, plain, plump, sheer,
total, utter **06** arrant, simply
07 brusque, clearly, plainly, totally,
utterly **08** absolute, complete, even-
down, outright, positive, straight,
thorough **09** out-and-out, up-and-
down, wholesale **10** absolutely,
completely, forthright, positively,
thoroughly **11** categorical, plain-
spoken, unequivocal, unqualified
13 categorically

downside
04 flaw, snag **05** minus **06** defect
07 penalty, trouble **08** drawback,
nuisance, weakness **09** liability, weak
point **10** impediment, limitation
12 Achilles heel, disadvantage
13 inconvenience

downsize
04 slim **06** reduce, shrink **08** contract,
diminish, minimize, moderate **11** make
smaller

down-to-earth
04 sane **07** mundane **08** sensible
09 practical, realistic **10** hard-headed,

no-nonsense **11** commonsense, plain-
spoken **12** matter-of-fact **13** plain-
speaking, unsentimental
14 commonsensical

downtrodden
06 abused **07** bullied **08** burdened,
helpless **09** exploited, oppressed,
powerless **10** subjugated, trampled on,
tyrannized, victimized
11 overwhelmed, subservient,
weighed-down

down under
02 Oz **09** Australia

downward
07 sliding **08** downhill, slipping
09 declining, going down
10 descending, moving down

downy
04 fine, soft **05** fuzzy, nappy **06** fleecy,
fluffy, smooth, woolly **07** cottony,
dowlney, knowing, pappose, pappous,
velvety **08** feathery **09** plumulate
10 lanuginose, lanuginous

dowry
03 dot **04** gift **05** share **06** legacy,
talent, tocher **07** faculty, portion
09 endowment, provision
11 inheritance **12** wedding-dower
15 marriage portion

dowse see **douse, dowse**

doxology
04 hymn, song **05** chant, psalm
06 anthem, gloria, praise **07** chorale
08 response **11** recessional **12** hymn of
praise, song of praise **13** glorification

doze
03 kip, nap **04** dare, zizz **05** dover,
go off, sleep **06** catnap, drowse, nod
off, siesta, snooze **07** drop off,
shut-eye **08** drift off, take a nap
10 forty winks
• **doze off**
06 catnap, nod off, snooze **08** drift off
10 fall asleep **14** have forty winks

dozen
02 dz **03** doz, XII **04** twal **06** twelve
07 stupefy

dozy
04 daft **05** dopey, silly, tired, weary
06 dreamy, drowsy, simple, sleepy,
stupid, torpid **07** foolish, nodding,
yawning **09** somnolent **10** half-asleep

drab
04 dull, flat, grey **05** dingy, whore
06 boring, dismal, dreary, gloomy,
isabel, shabby, sombre **07** tedious
08 isabella, lifeless **09** cheerless
10 colourless, isabelline, lacklustre
11 featureless **12** Quaker-colour
13 uninteresting

drabness
05 gloom **08** dullness, greyness
09 dinginess **10** dreariness,
shabbiness, sombreness
12 lifelessness **13** cheerlessness
14 colourlessness

Draconian
04 grim, hard **05** cruel, harsh, stern
06 brutal, savage, severe, strict
07 inhuman **08** abrasive, pitiless,
ruthless **09** merciless, unfeeling
10 iron-fisted, iron-handed
13 unsympathetic

draft
03 dft **04** bill, draw, plan **05** essay,
rough **06** cheque, design, detach,
draw up, scroll, sketch **07** compose,
drawing, ébauche, outline, paste-up
08 abstract, bank-bill, protocol
09 blueprint, delineate, formulate,
treatment **10** money order
11 delineation, postal order, rough
sketch **14** bill of exchange, letter of
credit

drag
03 lag, lug, tow, tug **04** bind, bore,
draw, hale, harl, haul, pain, pest, pull,
rash, shoe, sled, snig, trek, tump, yank
05 crawl, creep, shlep, snake, sweep,
trail, train **06** bother, drogue, schlep,
wear on **07** schlepp, skidpan, trouble
08 go slowly, headache, nuisance
09 annoyance, go on and on, influence
11 go on for ever **12** become boring
13 become tedious, pain in the neck
• **drag on**
04 go on **05** run on **07** persist
08 continue **09** be lengthy **14** be long-
drawn-out
• **drag out**
06 extend, hang on **07** draw out,
persist, prolong, spin out **08** lengthen,
protract
• **drag up**
05 raise **06** rake up, remind, revive
07 bring up, mention **09** introduce

dragon
04 worm **05** Draco, drake
08 lindworm **09** firedrake **12** flying
lizard

dragonfly
05 naiad, nymph **07** Odonata
10 demoiselle

dragoon
05 bully, drive, force, impel **06** coerce,
compel, harass **08** browbeat, pressure
09 constrain, press-gang, strongarm
10 intimidate, pressurize

drain
02 ea **03** dry, eau, pot, sap, sew, tap,
tax **04** buzz, delf, duct, grip, leak, milk,
nala, ooze, pipe, pour, sink, suck, tile,
void **05** bleed, cundy, ditch, drink,
empty, exude, fleet, gripe, gully, ladle,
leach, leech, nalla, nulla, quaff, sewer,
siver, sough, stank, syver, use up
06 condie, effuse, emulge, filter, gutter,
nallah, nullah, outlet, remove, sheuch,
sheugh, sluice, sponge, strain, trench
07 channel, conduit, consume, culvert,
cunette, deplete, dewater, draw off,
drink up, exhaust, extract, flow out,
piscina, pump off, seep out, swallow,
trickle, unwater **08** bleed dry,
evacuate, withdraw **09** depletion,
discharge, lickpenny **10** bleed white,

exhaustion, underdrain **11** common-
shore, consumption, watercourse
12 exsanguinate
• **drained**
05 tired

dram
02 dr **03** tot, wet **04** shot, suck, tiff, tift
06 chasse, drachm **07** caulker,
morning, nobbler, snifter, tickler
08 chota peg, meridian **10** stirrup cup
See also **drink**

drama
02 no **03** noh **04** auto, play, show
05 opera, piece, scene **06** acting,
azione, comedy, crisis, kabuki, thrill
07 dilemma, tension, theater, theatre,
tragedy, turmoil **08** operetta
09 dramatics, melodrama, sensation,
spectacle **10** dramaturgy, excitement,
stagecraft **11** histrionics
See also **play**
• **drama students**
04 RADA

dramatic
05 stage, tense, vivid **06** abrupt,
marked, sudden **07** drastic, graphic
08 distinct, exciting, stirring, striking,
Thespian **09** effective, thrilling
10 artificial, expressive, flamboyant,
histrionic, impressive, noticeable,
theatrical, unexpected
11 exaggerated, personative,
sensational, significant, spectacular,
substantial **12** considerable,
melodramatic

dramatically
07 vividly **08** abruptly, suddenly
10 noticeably, strikingly
12 considerably, expressively,
impressively **13** significantly,
spectacularly, substantially

dramatist
06 writer **08** comedian **09** tragedian
10 dramaturge, playwright, play-writer
12 dramaturgist, screen writer,
scriptwriter
See also **playwright**

dramatization
07 staging **10** adaptation
11 arrangement **12** presentation

dramatize
03 act, ham **05** adapt, ham up, put on,
stage **06** overdo **07** play-act
09 overstate **10** arrange for,
exaggerate **12** lay it on thick **14** present
as a film, present as a play **15** make a
big thing of

drape
◇ *containment indicator*
04 drop, fold, hang, veil, vest, wrap
05 adorn, cloak, cover, droop
06 shroud **07** arrange, envelop,
overlay, suspend **08** decorate

drapery
05 arras, blind, cloth **06** blinds
07 curtain, hanging, valance, valence
08 backdrop, covering, curtains,

hangings, mantling, tapestry
09 coverings **10** jardinière,
lambrequin

drastic
◇ *anagram indicator*
03 bad **04** dire **05** harsh **06** severe,
strong **07** extreme, radical, serious,
violent **08** dramatic, forceful, forcible,
rigorous **09** desperate, Draconian,
swingeing **10** unpleasant **11** far-
reaching

drastically
07 greatly **08** severely, strongly
09 extremely, radically, seriously
10 forcefully, rigorously

draught
03 cup **04** flow, gulp, puff, pull, rush,
swig **05** draft, drink, privy, quaff, swill
06 breath, drench, influx, potion,
waucht, waught **07** current, drawing,
pulling, swallow **08** cesspool,
dragging, movement, potation,
quantity, quencher, traction
10 attraction **12** williewaught

draw
02 go **03** get, lug, tap, tie, tow, tug
04 bait, come, drag, haul, limn, lure,
milk, move, pick, pull, pump, suck,
take, walk **05** chart, drain, drive, frame,
go for, infer, paint, sweep, trace, trail
06 allure, appeal, be even, choose,
come to, deduce, depict, design,
doodle, elicit, entice, gather, infuse,
inhale, map out, obtain, pencil,
prompt, raffle, reason, remove, resort,
select, siphon, sketch, travel
07 advance, attract, be equal, bring in,
extract, inspire, lottery, portray,
proceed, procure, produce, pull out,
receive, respire, take out, tombola
08 approach, bring out, conclude,
dead heat, decide on, describe,
interest, lengthen, persuade, plump for,
progress, scribble, withdraw
09 breathe in, delineate, influence,
magnetism, represent, stalemate,
unsheathe **10** attraction, enticement,
eviscerate, sweepstake **11** be all
square
• **draw back**
04 cock, funk **05** wince **06** boggle,
flinch, recoil, retire, shrink **07** fall off,
retract, retreat **08** withdraw **09** start
back **10** disadvance
• **draw in**
◇ *containment indicator*
04 pull, suck **05** hunch, rough
06 absorb, inhale **07** involve, retract
08 contract
• **draw near**
04 come, nigh **08** approach
• **draw on**
03 use **05** apply, train **06** allure, call
on, employ, induce, lead on, quarry,
rely on **07** exploit, utilize
08 approach, put to use **09** make use
of **14** have recourse to
• **draw out**
04 make, spin, tose, toze **05** educe,
evoke, leave, start, toaze **06** depart,
extend, set out **07** drag out, extract,

move out, prolong, pull out, spin out, stretch **08** continue, elongate, lengthen, protract **09** put at ease **12** induce to talk **13** induce to speak **15** encourage to talk

• **draw together**
04 knit **06** gather **07** close up **08** astringe, contract **10** constringe

• **draw up**
04 halt, stop **05** draft, frame, run in **06** pull up **07** compile, compose, make out, prepare **08** write out **09** formulate **12** put in writing

• **goalless draw**
02 0-0

drawback
03 out **04** flaw, snag **05** catch, fault, hitch **06** damper, defect, hurdle **07** barrier, problem, take-off, trouble **08** handicap, nuisance, obstacle, pullback, weak spot **09** hindrance, liability **10** deficiency, difficulty, disamenity, disbenefit, disutility, impediment, limitation **12** disadvantage, imperfection **14** discouragement, stumbling-block

drawer
02 dr **04** till **07** shottle, shuttle

• **bottom drawer**
08 glory box **09** hope chest

drawing
05 study **06** pencil, pin-man, sketch **07** cartoon, diagram, graphic, outline, picture **08** graffito, portrait, scribble **09** attrahent, depiction, pen-and-ink, portrayal **11** composition, delineation, scenography **12** illustration **14** representation

drawl
03 haw **05** drant, drone, twang **06** dawdle, draunt, haw-haw **08** protract **09** say slowly **11** speak slowly

drawn
◇ *anagram indicator*
04 taut, worn **05** gaunt, tense, tired **06** closed, sapped **07** fraught, haggard, hassled, pinched **08** fatigued, harassed, strained, stressed **09** etiolated, washed out **10** unsheathed **11** eviscerated

dread
03 awe, shy **04** dire, fear, funk, fury **05** alarm, awful, quail, qualm, worry **06** dismay, feared, flinch, fright, grisly, horror, terror **07** dreaded, ghastly, shudder, tremble **08** alarming, blue funk, cringe at, disquiet, dreadful, frighten, gastness, gruesome, horrible, terrible **09** cold sweat, frightful, gastnesse, ghastness, misgiving **10** be afraid of, be scared of, blind panic, shrink from, terrifying **11** fit of terror, frightening, trepidation **12** apprehension, awe-inspiring, perturbation **13** be terrified by **14** be anxious about, be frightened by, be worried about

See also **phobia**

dreadful
◇ *anagram indicator*
04 dern, dire, grim **05** awful, dearn, nasty **06** awsome, tragic **07** awesome, ghastly, heinous, hideous **08** alarming, grievous, horrible, horrific, shocking, terrible, terrific **09** appalling, frightful **10** abortional, calamitous, horrendous, outrageous, terrifying, tremendous, unpleasant **11** frightening

dreadfully
◇ *anagram indicator*
04 very **07** awfully **08** terribly **09** extremely **10** shockingly **11** appallingly, atrociously, exceedingly, frightfully **12** horrendously

dream
03 aim, joy **04** dwam, goal, hope, long, mare, muse, plan, wish **05** crave, dwalm, dwaum, fancy, ideal, mirth, model, music, sound, yearn **06** beauty, design, desire, marvel, superb, sweven, trance, vision **07** aisling, delight, fantasy, imagine, perfect, phantom, reverie, supreme **08** ambition, daydream, delusion, envisage, illusion, somniate, yearning **09** excellent, fantasize, nightmare, pipe dream, switch off, wonderful **10** aspiration, minstrelsy, perfection **11** expectation, hallucinate, imagination, inattention, speculation **12** want very much **13** be lost in space, hallucination **14** phantasmagoria, stare into space **15** castles in the air, not pay attention

• **dream up**
04 spin **05** hatch **06** create, devise, invent **07** concoct, imagine, think up **08** conceive, contrive **09** conjure up, fabricate

• **not dream of**
08 not think **10** not imagine **11** not conceive, not consider

dreamer
07 Utopian **08** idealist, romancer, romantic **09** fantasist, stargazer, theorizer, visionary **10** daydreamer, fantasizer

dreamily
06 gently, softly **08** absently **10** peacefully, pleasantly **12** romantically

dreamlike
06 unreal **07** phantom, surreal **08** ethereal, illusory **09** fantastic, visionary **10** chimerical, trance-like **13** hallucinatory, insubstantial, unsubstantial **14** phantasmagoric

dreamy
03 dim **04** hazy, soft **05** faint, misty, moony, spacy, vague **06** absent, gentle, lovely, musing, spacey, unreal **07** calming, faraway, lulling, pensive, shadowy, unclear **08** ethereal, fanciful, relaxing, romantic, soothing **09** fantastic, imaginary, visionary **10** abstracted, idealistic, indistinct, thoughtful **11** daydreaming, fantasizing, impractical, preoccupied **12** absent-minded **13** wool-gathering

drearily
08 boringly, dismally **09** routinely, tediously **11** monstrously **12** depressingly

dreary
03 sad **04** dark, drab, dull **05** bleak, oorie, ourie, owrie **06** boring, dismal, dreich, gloomy, gousty, sombre **07** humdrum, routine, tedious **08** desolate, ghastful, lifeless, mournful, overcast, unvaried **09** cheerless, ghastfull, wearisome **10** colourless, depressing, monotonous, uneventful **11** commonplace, featureless **12** run-of-the-mill **13** uninteresting

dredge
• **dredge up**
05 dig up, raise **06** drag up, draw up, fish up, rake up **07** scoop up, uncover, unearth **08** discover

dregs
04 lags, lees, scum **05** draff, dross, legge, trash, waste **06** bottom, dunder, faeces, fecula, graves, mother, rabble, tramps, ullage **07** bottoms, deposit, dossers, greaves, grounds, residue, taplash **08** detritus, outcasts, residuum, riff-raff, sediment, tailings, vagrants **09** excrement, scourings, sublimate **10** faex populi **11** down-and-outs, precipitate

drench
03 wet **04** duck, soak **05** douse, drook, drouk, drown, flood, imbue, souse, steep, swamp **06** embrue, imbrue, sluice **07** embrewe, immerse **08** inundate, permeate, saturate **09** milk shake **13** soak to the skin

dress
◇ *anagram indicator*
02 do **03** don, fig, fit, ray, rig, tog **04** boun, busk, comb, deck, doll, draw, garb, gear, gown, rail, robe, tend, tidy, tiff, tift, tire, togs, trim, wear **05** adorn, array, bowne, chide, clean, cover, drape, erect, frock, get-up, groom, guise, habit, preen, primp, put on, style, treat **06** adjust, attire, betrim, bind up, clothe, finish, fit out, graith, manure, outfit, smooth, swathe, thrash **07** apparel, arrange, bandage, bravery, clobber, clothes, costume, deck out, dispose, flatten, garment, garnish, get into, prepare, throw on, turn out **08** accoutre, clothing, decorate, ensemble, garments, get ready, slip into **10** habiliment, straighten **13** put a plaster on **14** wearing-apparel

See also **clothes, clothing**

Dresses include:
03 mob
04 ball, coat, maxi, sack, sari, tent
05 shift, shirt, smock, tasar
06 caftan, dirndl, jumper, kaftan, kimono, muu-muu, sheath, tusser
07 bathing, chemise, evening, gym slip, kitenge, matinee, matinée, tussore, wedding

8 ball-gown, cocktail, gym tunic, negligée, pinafore, princess, sundress
9 cheongsam, farandine, going-away, minidress, slammakin, trollope
0 dinner-gown, farrandine, slammerkin, wraparound
1 d'écolletage, Dolly Varden, riding habit
2 shirtwaister

● **dress down**
5 chide, scold **06** berate, carpet, rebuke, thrash **07** reprove, rouse on, tell off, tick off, upbraid **09** castigate, reprimand **13** dress casually, give a rocket to, tear off a strip, tear strips off
5 dress informally

● **dress up**
▷ *anagram indicator*
4 deck, gild, perk **05** adorn, dizen, tog up **06** buck up, doll up, dude up, jazz up, tart up **07** dandify, improve
8 beautify, decorate, disguise, ornament **09** embellish
0 masquerade **12** dress smartly
3 dress formally

dresser
● **showy dresser**
3 cat **04** beau
● **special dresser**
3 Mod

dressing
▷ *anagram indicator*
3 jus, pad **04** lint **05** gauze, patch, sauce, spica **06** coulis, relish
7 bandage, Band-aid®, clothes, plaster **08** compress, ligature, poultice
9 condiment **10** tourniquet
1 Elastoplast®, vinaigrette
ee also **salad**

dressmaker
6 tailor **07** modiste **09** couturier, midinette, tailoress **10** couturière, seamstress **11** mantua-maker, needlewoman, sewing woman
2 garment-maker

dressy
5 natty, ritzy, sharp, showy, smart, swish **06** classy, formal, ornate
7 elegant, stylish **09** elaborate

dribble
3 run **04** drib, drip, drop, foam, leak, ooze, seep, spit **05** drool, exude, froth, gloop **06** drivel, saliva, slaver
7 droplet, seepage, slobber, trickle
0 sprinkling

dried
4 arid, sear, sere **06** wilted
7 drained, parched, wizened
8 withered **09** mummified
0 dehydrated, desiccated, exsiccated, shrivelled

drier
4 oast **07** tumbler

drift
▷ *anagram indicator*
3 aim, sag **04** bank, core, crab, flow, lord, gist, heap, hull, mass, pile, rack,

roam, rove, rush, vein, waft, wisp
05 amass, coast, drive, drove, float, mound, point, scope, shift, stray, sweep, tenor, trend **06** course, design, gather, heap up, import, leeway, pierce, pile up, stream, thrust, tunnel, wander, wreath **07** current, driving, essence, meaning, purport **08** movement, tendency **09** direction, freewheel, intention, substance, variation
10 accumulate, digression
11 implication **12** accumulation, significance **14** be carried along **15** go with the stream

drifter
04 hobo **05** nomad, rover, tramp
06 drover **07** swagger, swagman, vagrant **08** vagabond, wanderer
09 itinerant, sundowner, traveller
11 beachcomber **12** rolling stone

drill
02 PE, PT **03** awl, bit **04** bore **05** borer, coach, prick, punch, teach, train
06 gimlet, ground, jumper, manual, pierce, reamer, school, seeder
07 routine, tuition, wildcat
08 coaching, exercise, instruct, practice, practise, puncture, rehearse, training **09** exercises, grounding, inculcate, penetrate, perforate, procedure **10** discipline, jackhammer, repetition
11 counterbore, inculcation, instruction, make a hole in, preparation
13 square-bashing **14** indoctrination, manual exercise

drink
03 bib, cup, jar, lap, nip, one, peg, sea, sip, sup, tot **04** brew, down, dram, grog, gulp, have, lush, neck, pint, pull, shot, suck, swig, tass, tiff, tift, tope, toss
05 booze, drain, hooch, juice, plonk, quaff, revel, sauce, smoke, swill, tinct, toast **06** absorb, grog on, guzzle, hootch, imbibe, liquid, liquor, rotgut, salute, swally, tank up, tiddly, tipple
07 alcohol, carouse, draught, drink to, indulge, shicker, spirits, swallow
08 aperitif, beverage, get drunk, infusion **09** firewater, get pissed, hard stuff, knock back, overdrink, partake of, polish off, soft drink, stiffener, the bottle, throw back **10** amber fluid
11 have too much, jungle juice, refreshment, strong drink, the creature, tickle-brain **12** Dutch courage, go on the shout, hit the bottle **13** knock back a few **14** be a hard drinker, drink like a fish, have one too many, thirst-quencher **15** be a heavy drinker, propose a toast to
See also **glass**

02 it
03 ale, dop, gin, kir, mum, nog, rum, rye, tay
04 arak, beer, bull, fine, flip, grog, hock, mead, nipa, ouzo, pils, port, purl, sake, saki, sour, sura, vino, wine

05 cider, G and T, lager, perry, Pimm's®, plonk, stout, vodka
06 arrack, bishop, brandy, bubbly, Cognac, eggnog, grappa, porter, poteen, Scotch, shandy, sherry, whisky
07 alcopop, aquavit, Bacardi®, bourbon, Campari, Gordon's®, liqueur, Marsala, Martell®, martini, oloroso, pink gin, red wine, retsina, sangria, sloe gin, spirits, tequila, vin rosé, whiskey
08 advocaat, Armagnac, Calvados, cold duck, Guinness®, hot toddy, schnapps, Smirnoff®, vermouth, vin blanc, vin rouge
09 badminton, Beefeater®, champagne, cocktails, Laphroaig®, snakebite, white wine, Wincarnis®
10 ginger wine, Remy Martin®
11 black-and-tan, boilermaker, Courvoisier®, gin-and-tonic, Glenfiddich®, Irish coffee, Jack Daniel's®
12 Famous Grouse®, Glenmorangie®, malternative
13 peach schnapps, Scotch and soda
14 Bombay Sapphire®

See also **beer**; **cocktail**; **liqueur**; **spirits**; **wine**

Non-alcoholic drinks include:
03 cha, pop, tea
04 Coke®, cola, kola, milk, soda
05 assai, Assam, cocoa, float, julep, latte, mixer, Pepsi®, tonic, water
06 coffee, Indian, Irn-Bru®, Ribena®, squash, tisane
07 beef tea, cordial, limeade, Perrier®, seltzer
08 café noir, China tea, Coca-Cola®, Earl Grey, espresso, expresso, fruit tea, green tea, Horlicks®, lemonade, lemon tea, Lucozade®, Ovaltine®, root beer, smoothie
09 Aqua Libra®, ayahuasco, Canada Dry®, cherryade, cream soda, ginger ale, herbal tea, milk shake, mint-julep, orangeade, soda water
10 café au lait, café filtre, cappuccino, fizzy drink, fruit juice, ginger beer, rosehip tea, still water, tonic water, Vichy water
11 barley water, bitter lemon, camomile tea
12 hot chocolate, mineral water, sarsaparilla
13 peppermint tea, Turkish coffee
14 sparkling water
15 lapsang souchong

Drinks of the gods include:
06 amrita, nectar
08 ambrosia

Special drinks include:
03 ava
04 kava, soma
05 haoma
09 ayahuasco

● **drink hard**
04 bend, tank **06** bezzle

- **drink in**
05 grasp **06** absorb, digest, imbibe, take in **07** inhaust, realize
10 appreciate

drinkable
04 safe **05** clean **07** potable **10** fit to drink

drinker
03 sot **04** lush, soak, wino **05** alkie, dipso, drunk, toper **06** barfly, boozer, sponge, sucker **07** imbiber, pint-pot, tippler, tosspot **08** drunkard
09 fuddle-cap, inebriate
10 winebibber **11** dipsomaniac, froth-blower, hard drinker **12** heavy drinker
14 serious drinker
- **reformed drinkers**
02 AA

drinking
◇ insertion indicator
- **drinking cup**
03 nut, tig, tot **04** bowl, tass **05** cylix, kylix **06** cotyle, goblet, quaich, quaigh, rhyton **07** chalice, scyphus
09 cantharus **10** parting-cup
- **drinking session**
03 bat, bum **04** bend, bevy, bout, bust, lush, sesh **05** bevvy, binge, blind, booze, drunk, spree **06** beer-up, bender, bottle, fuddle, grog-on, grog-up, razzle, screed **07** blinder, booze-up, carouse, session, wassail
- **expressions relating to drinking**
04 evoe, rivo, skol **05** evhoe, evohe, skoal **06** cheers, prosit **07** slàinte **08** chin-chin **10** good health **12** mud in your eye
- **given to drinking**
03 wet

drip
02 IV **03** wet **04** bead, bore, drop, leak, ooze, plop, tear, weed, weep, wimp **05** gloop, ninny, pansy, sissy, softy **06** filter, splash **07** dewdrop, dribble, drizzle, trickle **08** sprinkle, weakling **09** percolate **10** stillicide
- **dripping**
03 fat

drive
02 ca', Dr, go **03** caa', dig, put, ram, ren, rin, run, tax, vim, zip **04** bear, come, dash, firk, goad, herd, hunt, hurl, lash, lead, move, need, prod, push, rack, rate, ride, road, send, sink, spin, spur, take, trip, turn, urge, will **05** carry, chase, drift, fight, force, guide, impel, jaunt, knock, motor, pilot, power, press, screw, steer, surge, thump, verve **06** action, appeal, avenue, battle, burden, coerce, compel, convey, desire, direct, effort, energy, hammer, handle, incite, manage, oblige, outing, pizazz, plunge, prompt, propel, spirit, strike, thrust, travel, vigour **07** actuate, control, crusade, dragoon, enforce, go by car, impulse, journey, operate, overtax, provoke, resolve, roadway, round up **08** ambition, appetite, approach, campaign, driveway,

instinct, motivate, movement, overdo it, overwork, persuade, pressure, struggle, tenacity **09** chauffeur, come by car, constrain, excursion, transport **10** enterprise, get-up-and-go, initiative, motivation, overburden, pressurize, propulsion **11** give a lift to, travel by car, work too hard **12** be at the wheel, kill yourself, transmission **13** determination **14** propeller shaft **15** be at the controls
- **drive at**
04 hint, mean **05** aim at, get at, imply **06** intend **07** refer to, signify, suggest **08** allude to, indicate, intimate
09 insinuate **10** have in mind
- **drive away**
04 hunt, shoo **05** chase **06** banish, dispel **07** repulse **08** exorcize
- **drive down**
03 ram
- **drive fast**
04 race **05** speed
- **drive inconsiderately**
03 hog
- **drive out**
04 fire **05** expel, wreak **07** turn out **11** exterminate
- **prepare to drive**
03 tee

drivel
03 rot **04** blah, bull, crap, drip, guff **05** balls, bilge, drool, hooey, slush, tripe **06** bunkum, slaver, waffle **07** baloney, dribble, eyewash, garbage, hogwash, maunder, rhubarb, rubbish, slabber, twaddle **08** claptrap, malarkey, nonsense **09** gibberish, poppycock **10** balderdash, mumbo-jumbo **12** gobbledygook

driver
02 Dr **04** Jehu, whip **05** mizen, rider **06** cabbie, jarvey, jarvie, mizzen **07** locoman, taximan, trucker, truckie **08** bullocky, motorist, muleteer, roadsman, truckman **09** chauffeur **12** motorcyclist **15** knight of the road
See also **racing**
- **new driver**
01 L

drivers
02 AA **03** RAC

driving
05 heavy **07** dynamic, violent **08** forceful, sweeping, vigorous **09** energetic **10** compelling, forthright

drizzle
04 drip, drop, mist, pour, rain, smir, smur, spit, spot **05** smirr, spray **06** mizzle, shower **07** dribble, scowder, skiffle, trickle **08** fine rain, scouther, scowther, sprinkle **09** light rain **10** rain finely, Scotch mist **11** rain lightly

droll
03 odd, rum **04** jest, zany **05** comic, funny, queer, witty **06** jester **07** amusing, bizarre, comical, jocular, risible, waggish **08** clownish, farcical,

humorous, peculiar **09** diverting, eccentric, laughable, ludicrous, whimsical **10** ridiculous
12 entertaining

drone
03 dor, hum **04** buzz, dorr, purr **05** chant, drant, drawl, idler, leech, thrum, whirr **06** bumble, bummle, dog-bee, doodle, draunt, intone, loafe **07** bourdon, dreamer, goof-off, slacker, sponger, vibrate **08** hanger-on, layabout, parasite, whirring **09** bombilate, bombinate, go on and on, lazybones, murmuring, scrounger, vibration **10** lazy person **11** goldbricke

drool
04 dote, gush **05** gloat **06** drivel, slave **07** dribble, enthuse, slobber **08** salivate **11** slobber over **15** water at the mouth

droop
03 bow, lob, nod, sag **04** bend, drop, fade, flag, peak, sink, weep, wilt **05** faint, slink, slump, stoop **06** dangle, falter, nutate, slouch, wither **07** decline **08** fall down, hang down, languish, pendency **09** lose heart

droopy
03 lax **04** lank, limp, weak **05** loose, saggy, slack **06** feeble, floppy **07** falling, sagging **08** drooping, dropping

drop
◇ deletion indicator
02 gt **03** bit, can, dab, end, lay, nip, sip, tad, tot **04** bead, blob, cast, dash, dive, drib, drip, fall, fire, glob, gout, jilt, land, leak, omit, plop, quit, sack, shed, sink, spat, spot, stop, take, tear **05** abyss, bring, candy, carry, cease, chasm, chuck, cliff, ditch, droop, forgo, gutta, lapse, let go, lower, pinch, slope, slump, sweet, trace **06** bonbon, bubble, desert, disown, dragée, drappy, finish, forego, give up, goutte, humbug, lessen, little, plunge, put off, reject, splash, tumble, weaken **07** abandon, boot out, cutback, decline, deliver, descend, descent, dismiss, drappie, dribble, driblet, droplet, dwindle, exclude, fall off, forsake, globule, let fall, let go of, lozenge, miss out, modicum, pendant, plummet, smidgen, sweetie, trickle, turf out **08** decrease, diminish, downturn, dribblet, globulet, leave out, lowering, mouthful, pastille, renounce, run out on, spheroid, sprinkle **09** bespatter, declivity, discharge, precipice, reduction, repudiate, terminate, throw over, transport, walk out on **10** falling-off, finish with, relinquish, slacken off **11** devaluation, discontinue **12** depreciation, dispense with **13** deterioration, make redundant
- **drop back**
03 lag **07** retreat **08** fall back **09** lag behind **10** fall behind
- **drop in**
04 call **05** pop in, visit **06** call by, come

by, instil **07** instill **08** come over **09** call round, come round
• **drop off**
04 doze, sink **05** go off **06** catnap, depart, hand in, lessen, nod off, plunge, snooze, unload **07** decline, deliver, deposit, doze off, dwindle, fall off, plummet, set down **08** decrease, diminish, drift off **09** disappear **10** fall asleep, slacken off **14** have forty winks
• **drop out**
04 quit **05** leave **06** cry off, give up **07** abandon, back out, forsake **08** renounce, withdraw
• **drop out of**
04 quit **05** leave **06** opt out, renege **07** abandon, pull out **08** opt out of, renege on, renounce **09** back out of **10** cry off from **12** withdraw from

dropout
05 loner, rebel **06** hippie **07** beatnik, deviant **08** Bohemian, renegade **09** dissenter **10** malcontent **11** dissentient **13** nonconformist

droppings
04 dung, scat, skat **06** egesta, faeces, manure, ordure, stools **07** excreta, spraint **09** excrement

dross
04 junk, lees, rust, scum, slag **05** dregs, lucre, slack, trash, waste **06** debris, refuse, scoria **07** remains, rubbish **08** impurity **09** recrement

drought
04 want **06** drouth, thirst **07** aridity, dryness **08** shortage **11** dehydration, desiccation, parchedness

drove
03 mob **04** herd, host, pack **05** crowd, crush, drift, flock, horde, press, swarm **06** string, throng **07** company **09** gathering, multitude

drown
02 go **03** die **04** sink **05** flood, swamp **06** deluge, drench, engulf, perish **07** founder, go under, howl out, immerse, silence, wipe out **08** drown out, inundate, outvoice, overcome, submerge **09** overpower, overwhelm **10** extinguish **12** lose your life

drowsily
06 dopily, dozily **07** wearily **08** sleepily **10** sluggishly **13** lethargically

drowsiness
06 torpor **08** dopiness, doziness, lethargy, narcosis **09** oscitancy, tiredness, weariness **10** grogginess, sleepiness, somnolence, somnolency **12** sluggishness

drowsy
04 dozy, dull **05** dopey, dozed, heavy, tired, weary **06** bleary, dozing, dreamy, sleepy, torpid **07** nodding, slumbry, yawning **08** comatose, slumbery **09** lethargic, somnolent **10** half-asleep **11** heavy-headed

drubbing
06 defeat **07** beating, licking **08** flogging, pounding, whipping **09** hammering, thrashing, trouncing, walloping **10** clobbering, cudgelling, pummelling

drudge
04 drug, hack, moil, plod, toil, work **05** devil, droil, grind, grunt, scrub, slave, snake, sweat **06** beaver, labour, lackey, menial, skivvy, slavey, stooge, toiler, worker **07** servant **08** dogsbody, factotum, labourer, plug away, slog away, trauchle **09** packhorse **10** after-guard, Cinderella **11** galley-slave

drudgery
03 fag **04** slog, toil **05** chore, grind, sweat, yakka **06** labour, yacker, yakker **07** faggery, slavery **08** hackwork, trauchle **09** skivvying, slaistery, spadework, treadmill **10** collar-work, donkey-work, menial work **13** sweated labour

drug
04 cure, dose, numb **06** deaden, drudge, potion, remedy, sedate **07** stupefy **08** knock out, medicate, medicine, shanghai **09** stimulant **10** medication **12** anaesthetize, tranquillize **15** make unconscious
See also **medicine**

Medicinal drugs include:
03 AZT
04 Soma®
05 Intal®, NSAID, salep, Taxol®, Zyban®
06 opiate, Prozac®, statin, sulpha, Valium®, Viagra®, Zantac®
07 antacid, aspirin, codeine, heparin, insulin, Nurofen®, quinine, Relenza®, Ritalin®, Seroxat®, steroid
08 Antabuse®, diazepam, diuretic, hyoscine, methadon, morphine, narcotic, neomycin, orlistat, Rohypnol®, sedative, warfarin
09 aciclovir, acyclovir, analgesic, co-codamol, cortisone, digitalis, ibuprofen, methadone, oestrogen, stimulant, tamoxifen, temazepam
10 antibiotic, anxiolytic, chloroform, chloroquin, dimorphine, interferon, penicillin, ranitidine, salbutamol
11 allopurinol, amoxycillin, amyl nitrate, anaesthetic, beta-blocker, chloroquine, cyclosporin, haloperidol, ipecacuanha, neuroleptic, paracetamol, propranolol, vasodilator
12 ACE-inhibitor, chlorambucil, methotrexate, progesterone, sleeping pill, streptomycin, sulphonamide, tetracycline
13 antibacterial, anticoagulant, antihistamine, streptokinase, tranquillizer
14 anticonvulsant, antidepressant, azidothymidine, bronchodilator, corticosteroid, erythropoietin, hallucinogenic, hydrocortisone
15 chloramphenicol, vasoconstrictor

Recreational drugs include:
01 C, E, H
03 hop, ice, kef, kif, LSD, PCP, pot, tab
04 acid, bang, barb, blow, coca, coke, dope, dove, gage, hash, hemp, junk, kaif, pill, scag, skag, snow, weed
05 bhang, crack, crank, dagga, horse, jelly, opium, shmek, smack, speed, sugar, upper
06 basuco, charas, downer, heroin, mescal, peyote, pituri, popper
07 charlie, churrus, cocaine, crystal, ecstasy, fantasy, guaraná, pep pill, roofies, schmeck
08 cannabis, freebase, ketamine, laudanum, meconium, mescalin, methadon, moonrock, morphine, nepenthe, Rohypnol, snowball, Special K
09 angel dust, dance drug, marijuana, mescaline, methadone, nose candy, peace pill, ready-wash, speedball, temazepam
10 white stuff
11 amphetamine, barbiturate, purple heart
12 date-rape drug
13 phencyclidine

See also **cannabis**; **cocaine**; **heroin**

• **drug dose**
03 fix **05** bolus
• **drug experience**
04 trip

drug addict
04 head, hype, user **05** freak **06** junkie **07** druggie, hop-head, tripper **08** coke-head, snowbird **09** dope-fiend, mainliner

drugged
04 high **05** doped **06** ripped, stoned, wasted, zonked **07** on a trip **08** comatose, hopped-up, turned on **09** spaced out, stupefied **10** knocked out

drum
03 rap, tap **04** beat, dhol, reel, swag **05** bongo, conga, daiko, house, knock, naker, ridge, tabor, taiko, throb, thrum **06** atabal, barrel, bundle, cannon, kettle, rigger, tabour, tabret, tam-tam, tattoo, timbal, tom-tom, tum-tum, tymbal **07** bodhrán, drumlin, mridang, pulsate, tambour, timpano, tympano **08** mridanga, tympanum **09** mridamgam, mridangam **11** reverberate
• **drum into**
06 hammer, harp on, instil **07** din into **09** drive home, inculcate, reiterate
• **drum out**
05 expel **07** dismiss **08** throw out **09** discharge
• **drum up**
03 get **06** gather, obtain, summon **07** attract, canvass, collect, round up, solicit **08** petition

drumbeat
04 flam, roll, ruff, touk, tuck **05** hurry

06 rafale, rappel, rattan, tattoo
08 assembly **10** paradiddle

drummer
02 Dr **07** swagman **09** timpanist, tympanist

drunk
◇ *anagram indicator*
03 fap, fou, lit, sot, wat, wet **04** full, high, inky, lush, paid, soak, wino
05 alkie, dipso, foxed, happy, inked, lit up, merry, moppy, slued, tight, tipsy, toper, woozy **06** blotto, bombed, boozer, canned, corked, in wine, jagged, jarred, juiced, loaded, mashed, mellow, mortal, ratted, ripped, slewed, soused, sponge, stewed, stinko, stoned, tanked, tiddly, wasted
07 bevvied, bonkers, bottled, crocked, drinker, drunken, ebriose, fairish, half-cut, legless, maggoty, pickled, pie-eyed, shicker, sloshed, smashed, sozzled, squiffy, tiddled, tiddley, tippler, tosspot, trashed, wrecked
08 bibulous, drunkard, footless, hammered, in liquor, juiced up, liquored, moon-eyed, overseen, overshot, sow-drunk, stocious, stotious, tanked up, whiffled, whistled
09 alcoholic, blootered, crapulent, incapable, inebriate, inebrious, paralytic, plastered, saturated, shickered, stonkered, up the pole, well-oiled **10** blind drunk, capernoity, inebriated, obfuscated **11** capernoitie, cappernoity, dipsomaniac, hard drinker, high as a kite, intoxicated, on the tiddly, slaughtered **12** drunk as a lord, drunk as a newt, heavy drinker, roaring drunk **13** drunk as a piper, drunk as a skunk, having had a few, under the table **14** Brahms and Liszt
15 a sheet in the wind, one over the eight, the worse for wear, under the weather
• **getting drunk**
02 on **12** half-seas-over **13** mops and brooms
• **make drunk**
03 cup **05** sew up, souse **07** tipsify
09 inebriate **10** intoxicate

drunkard
03 sot **04** lush, soak, wino **05** alkie, bloat, dipso, drunk, souse, toper
06 boozer, sponge **07** bloater, drinker, fuddler, hophead, shicker, tippler, tosspot **08** bacchant, habitual
09 alcoholic, inebriate **10** wine-bibber **11** dipsomaniac, hard drinker
12 heavy drinker

drunken
◇ *anagram indicator*
03 wat **05** boozy, drunk, happy, lit up, merry, tight, tipsy **06** bombed, boozey, loaded, spongy, stoned, tiddly **07** Bacchic, drucken, riotous, sloshed **08** Bacchian, besotted
09 crapulent, debauched, inebriate, worthless **10** dissipated
11 baccanalian, intemperate, intoxicated

drunkenness
07 ebriety, ivresse **08** methysis
09 ebriosity, inebriety, temulence, tipsiness **10** alcoholism, crapulence, debauchery, dipsomania, insobriety
11 inebriation **12** bibulousness, hard drinking, intemperance, intoxication
13 St Martin's evil **15** serious drinking

dry
02 TT **03** air, sec, xer- **04** arid, brut, dull, fair, flat, kiln, sear, seco, sere, welt, wilt, wipe, xero- **05** baked, drain, droll, husky, parch, secco, witty, xeric
06 barren, boring, clever, dreary, formal, frigid, ironic, low-key, rizzar, rizzer, rizzor, scorch, subtle, torrid, wilted, wither **07** cutting, cynical, deadpan, drouthy, gasping, hirstie, laconic, make dry, parched, precise, shrivel, tedious, thirsty, trocken
08 droughty, rainless, scorched, teetotal, withered **09** abstinent, become dry, dehydrate, desiccate, dry as dust, sarcastic, temperate, unwatered, waterless, wearisome
10 abstemious, dehumidify, dehydrated, desiccated, dry as a bone, monotonous, on the wagon, shrivelled, unbuttered, unexciting **11** alcohol-free
12 moistureless **13** uninteresting
14 prohibitionist
• **dry up**
04 fade, fail, sear, stop, wane **05** arefy
06 die out, ensear, scorch, shut up
07 dwindle **09** desiccate, disappear, exsiccate **11** come to an end, stop talking **15** forget your lines

dryness
06 drouth, thirst **07** aridity, drought, siccity, xerasia, xerosis **08** aridness
09 xerostoma **10** barrenness, xerostomia **11** dehydration, thirstiness

dual
04 twin **06** binary, double, duplex, paired **07** coupled, matched, twofold
08 combined, two-piece **09** duplicate

duality
07 twoness **09** duplicity
10 doubleness, opposition, separation
11 combination, duplication
12 polarization

dub
03 tag **04** call, name, term, trim
05 label, style **06** bestow, confer, puddle **07** entitle **08** christen, nickname **09** designate

dubiety
05 doubt, qualm **08** mistrust
09 misgiving, suspicion **10** hesitation, indecision, scepticism **11** incertitude, uncertainty **12** doubtfulness

dubious
◇ *anagram indicator*
04 iffy **05** crook, fishy, shady **06** shifty, unsure **07** obscure, suspect
08 doubtful, elliptic, hesitant, wavering
09 ambiguous, debatable, sceptical, uncertain, undecided, unsettled
10 backhanded, elliptical, irresolute,

left-handed, suspicious, unreliable
11 vacillating **12** questionable
13 untrustworthy

dubiously
09 debatably **10** hesitantly
11 ambiguously, uncertainly, undecidedly **12** questionably, suspiciously

dubnium
02 Db

duchy
07 dukedom

duck
01 O **03** bob, dip, wet **04** bend, dive, dook, drop, dunk, jook, jouk, shun, zero **05** avoid, dodge, douse, drake, elude, evade, lower, shirk, skive, souse, squat, stoop, yield **06** cringe, crouch, plunge **07** bow down, darling, immerse **08** bankrupt, sidestep, submerge **09** defaulter **10** sweetheart
12 steer clear of, wriggle out of
See also **animal**

Ducks include:
04 blue, musk, smee, smew, surf, teal, wood
05 eider, Pekin, ruddy, scaup
06 burrow, hareld, herald, magpie, Peking, runner, scoter, smeath, smeeth, spirit, tufted, velvet, wigeon
07 crested, gadwall, mallard, moulard, muscovy, old wife, pintail, pochard, steamer
08 garganey, hookbill, mandarin, old squaw, shelduck
09 Cuthbert's, goldeneye, goosander, harlequin, merganser, sheldrake, shielduck, shoveller
10 bufflehead, canvasback, long-tailed, ring-necked
11 ferruginous, St Cuthbert's, white-headed
12 common scoter, Indian runner, velvet scoter
13 ruddy shelduck

• **string of ducks**
04 sord, team
• **two ducks**
02 OO **04** pair

duct
03 vas **04** pipe, tube **05** canal
06 funnel, ureter, vessel **07** channel, conduit, fistula, passage, Venturi, wireway **08** deferent, diffuser
09 emunctory, excretory **11** Venturi tube

ductile
06 pliant **07** plastic, pliable
08 amenable, biddable, flexible, tractile, yielding **09** compliant, malleable, tractable **10** manageable
11 manipulable

dud
03 bum **04** bust, duff, flop **05** kaput
06 broken, failed, faulty, stumer
07 failure, let-down, washout **08** bum steer, nugatory **09** conked out,

lueless, worthless **11** counterfeit,
operative **14** disappointment

ude
cat, fop, Roy **04** buck, lair **05** dandy

udgeon
hilt **05** pique **10** resentment

ue
fee, fit, lot **04** dead, just, levy, owed,
ll **05** ample, owing, right **06** charge,
rect, earned, enough, merits, proper,
ghts, unpaid **07** awaited, charges,
rrect, deserts, dewfull, exactly,
ting, merited, payable, tribute
adequate, deserved, directly,
xpected, plenty of, required, rightful,
raight, suitable **09** appointed, in
rears, justified, precisely, privilege,
payable, requisite, scheduled
birthright, sufficient **11** anticipated,
ppropriate, comeuppance, just
eserts, long-awaited, outstanding,
erogative **12** contribution,
bscription **13** membership fee
due to
owing to **08** caused by **09** because
11 as a result of

uel
tilt **05** clash, fight **06** battle,
ombat, duello **07** contest, rivalry
struggle **09** encounter,
onomachy **10** dependence,
ngagement, monomachia
competition **14** affair of honour
affaire d'honneur

uff
anagram indicator
bad **04** naff, poor, poxy, ropy, rump,
eak **05** awful, dough, lousy, pants
broken, bungle, crummy, faulty
botched, the pits, useless
buttocks, hopeless, inferior,
ediocre, pathetic, terrible
defective, deficient, imperfect,
ird-rate **10** inadequate, mismanaged,
cond-rate **11** incompetent,
effective, poor-quality, substandard
unacceptable **14** a load of garbage,
load of rubbish, unsatisfactory

uffer
git, oaf **04** clod, clot, dolt, dork,
ol, geek, muff, prat **05** fogey, idiot
dimwit **07** bungler, halfwit, plonker,
stler **08** bonehead **09** blunderer,
noramus **11** cattle-thief

ugong
sea cow, sea-pig **08** halicore,
renian

uke
D **04** fist, lord

ulcet
soft **05** sweet **06** gentle, mellow
pleasant, soothing **09** agreeable,
elodious **10** harmonious
mellifluous **13** sweet-sounding

ulcimer
santir, santur **07** cembalo, cymbalo,
ntoor, santour **08** cimbalom
pantaleon

dull
03 dim, dry, mat, sad **04** blah, damp,
dark, dead, dowf, dozy, drab, drug,
dumb, fade, flat, gray, grey, idle, logy,
matt, mild, mull, numb, slow, soft, tame,
weak **05** allay, bland, blunt, cloud,
corny, dense, dingy, dopey, dowdy,
dowie, dusty, faint, gross, heavy, ho-
hum, inert, lower, matte, murky, muted,
plain, prose, prosy, quiet, rusty, slack,
thick, vapid **06** barren, boring, bovine,
cloudy, dampen, darken, deaden,
deject, dismal, dreary, drowsy, feeble,
gloomy, leaden, lessen, mopish,
obtund, obtuse, opaque, opiate,
rebate, reduce, sadden, sleepy, soften,
sombre, sopite, stodgy, stupid, subdue,
sullen, torpid, wooden **07** assuage,
blacken, depress, disedge, doltish,
humdrum, insipid, insulse, lumpish,
muffled, mumpish, obscure, prosaic,
relieve, stupefy, tedious, wash out
08 blockish, Boeotian, decrease,
diminish, downcast, edgeless,
hebetate, inactive, lifeless, mitigate,
moderate, overcast, paralyse, sluggish,
tiresome, tone down, toneless,
workaday **09** alleviate, cheerless,
dead-alive, dimwitted, inanimate,
lethargic, ponderous, prosaical,
wearisome **10** discourage, dishearten,
indistinct, insensible, lackluster,
lacklustre, monochrome,
monotonous, pedestrian, perstringe,
uneventful, unexciting **11** birdbrained,
blunt-witted, desensitize, distressing,
heavy-headed, stereotyped,
stultifying, thick-witted, troublesome,
unsharpened **12** dead-and-alive, thick-
skulled, tranquillize **13** uncomfortable,
unimaginative, unintelligent,
uninteresting **15** slow on the uptake
• **become dull**
04 rust **05** blunt **07** tarnish
08 hebetate

dullard
03 git, oaf, owl **04** clod, clot, dolt,
dope, dork, prat **05** chump, dumbo,
dunce, idiot, moron **06** dimwit, nitwit
07 plonker **08** bonehead, imbecile,
numskull **09** blockhead, ignoramus,
simpleton **10** bufflehead, dunderhead
See also **fool**

dullness
04 drab, yawn **05** cloud **06** fadeur,
tedium, torpor **07** dryness, vacuity
08 flatness, monotony, slowness,
vapidity **09** emptiness, plainness
10 dreariness, oppression
12 sluggishness

duly
05 fitly **08** properly, suitably
09 correctly, fittingly **10** decorously,
deservedly, rightfully, sure enough
11 accordingly, befittingly
13 appropriately

dumb
03 mum **04** dozy, mute **05** dense,
dopey, shtum, stumm, thick
06 shtoom, shtumm, silent, stupid

07 foolish, schtoom **08** gormless
09 brainless, dim-witted, soundless
10 speechless, tongue-tied
12 inarticulate, lost for words
13 unintelligent, without speech **15** at
a loss for words
• **dumb down**
07 deskill **08** simplify

dumbfound
03 wow **04** daze, stun **05** amaze,
floor, shock **07** astound, flummox,
stagger, startle, stupefy **08** astonish,
bewilder, bowl over, confound,
gobsmack, surprise **09** take aback
11 flabbergast, knock for six **12** blow
your mind **15** knock all of a heap

dumbfounded
04 dumb **06** amazed, thrown
07 baffled, floored, stunned, stupent
08 confused, overcome, startled
09 astounded, paralysed, staggered
10 astonished, bewildered, bowled
over, confounded, gobsmacked,
nonplussed, speechless, taken aback
11 overwhelmed **12** lost for words
13 flabbergasted, knocked for six

dumbly
06 mutely **08** silently **11** soundlessly
12 speechlessly **14** inarticulately

dumbo *see* fool

dumbstruck
03 mum **04** dumb, mute **06** aghast,
amazed, silent **07** shocked
09 astounded **10** speechless,
tongue-tied **11** dumbfounded,
obmutescent **12** inarticulate
13 thunderstruck

dummy
03 git, oaf **04** clot, copy, dork, fake,
fool, form, mock, prat, sham, teat
05 bogus, chump, false, idiot, model,
trial **06** dimwit, figure, mock-up,
nitwit, phoney, sample, silent
07 feigned, plonker, soother
08 imbecile, numskull, pacifier,
practice **09** blockhead, comforter,
duplicate, imitation, lay-figure,
mannequin, simulated **10** artificial,
bufflehead, substitute **11** counterfeit
12 reproduction **14** representation
See also **fool**

dump
03 tip **04** bung, drop, hole, jilt, mess,
park, pool, slum **05** chuck, ditch,
hovel, joint, leave, place, plonk, scrap,
shack, shoot, store **06** desert, marble,
midden, pigpen, pigsty, shanty, tip out,
unload **07** abandon, counter, deposit,
discard, forsake, lay down, let fall,
offload, pour out, put down, set down
08 empty out, get rid of, jettison,
junkyard, throw out **09** chuck away,
discharge, dispose of, fling down,
scrapyard, throw away, throw down,
walk out on **10** rubbish tip **11** rubbish
heap **14** give the elbow to
• **down in the dumps**
03 low, sad **04** blue **07** unhappy
08 dejected, downcast **09** depressed,

miserable **10** dispirited, melancholy
11 downhearted
• **dumps**
08 doldrums

dumpling
06 dim sum, perogi, pirogi, won ton
07 gnocchi, knaidel, kneidel, pierogi
08 doughboy, quenelle **09** doughball,
matzo ball **10** corn dodger

dumpster
04 skip

dumpy
05 plump, podgy, pudgy, short, squab,
squat, stout, tubby **06** chubby, chunky,
stubby

dun
04 dull, hill **05** dingy, dusky **06** harass,
pester, plague **11** mud-coloured
12 greyish-brown **13** mouse-coloured

dunce
01 d **03** git **04** dork, fool, nerd, prat,
twit **05** idiot, ninny, twerp, wally
06 dimwit, nitwit **07** dullard, plonker
08 bonehead, dipstick, imbecile,
numskull **09** blockhead
10 bufflehead, loggerhead,
nincompoop

dune *see* **sand dune, sand dunes**
under **sand**

dung
04 chip, cock, dirt, muck, soil, tath
05 argol, dreck, guano, mulch, shard,
sharn, siege **06** cowpat, doo-doo,
faeces, fumets, manure, ordure
07 buttons, fewmets, scumber,
skummer, spraint **08** spraints
09 droppings, excrement, spawn cake
10 spawn brick **11** animal waste
12 album Graecum, buffalo chips
• **devil's dung**
04 hing
• **dog's dung**
04 pure
• **plaster with dung**
04 leep

dung-beetle
03 dor **04** dorr **06** scarab
11 coprophagan

dungeon
04 cage, cell, gaol, jail, keep **05** vault
06 lock-up, prison **09** oubliette

dupe
03 con, gum, mug **04** cony, cull, flat,
fool, geck, gull, hoax, pawn **05** cheat,
coney, cully, shaft, trick **06** chouse,
delude, diddle, outwit, plover, puppet,
rip off, sitter, stooge, sucker, take in,
victim **07** deceive, defraud, dottrel, fall
guy, swindle **08** dotterel, hoodwink,
pushover, soft mark **09** bamboozle,
goldbrick, simpleton **10** instrument
11 make a fool of

duplicate
03 dup, fax **04** copy, echo, fold, like,
mate, twin **05** clone, ditto, match,
model, Roneo®, spare, Xerox®
06 carbon, double, paired, repeat,

ringer **07** do again, forgery, matched,
replica, twofold **08** matching
09 facsimile, identical, imitation,
lookalike, photocopy, Photostat®,
replicate, reproduce **10** carbon copy,
dead ringer, equivalent, transcript
11 alternative, counterpart
12 reproduction **13** corresponding,
spitting image

duplication
04 copy **05** clone **07** cloning, copying
08 doubling **09** photocopy
10 gemination, repetition
11 dittography, replication
12 photocopying, reproduction

duplicity
05 fraud, guile **06** deceit **07** perfidy
08 artifice, betrayal **09** chicanery,
deception, falsehood, hypocrisy,
mendacity, treachery **10** dishonesty,
doubleness **11** insincerity
13 deceitfulness, dissimulation,
double-dealing

durability
04 wear **07** durance, wearing
08 strength **09** constancy, endurance,
longevity, stability **10** permanence
11 durableness, lastingness,
persistence **15** imperishability

durable
04 fast, firm **05** fixed, hardy, pakka,
pucka, pukka, solid, sound, tough
06 robust, stable, strong, sturdy
07 abiding, lasting **08** constant,
enduring, reliable, unfading **09** heavy-
duty, permanent, resistant
10 dependable, persistent, persisting,
reinforced, unchanging **11** hard-
wearing, long-lasting, serviceable,
substantial

duration
04 span, term, time **05** spell **06** extent,
length, period **07** stretch **08** fullness,
standing, time span **09** endurance,
time scale **10** protension
11 continuance, persistence,
persistency, running time
12 continuation, length of time,
perpetuation, prolongation

duress
05 force **06** threat **08** coercion,
exaction, pressure **09** restraint
10 compulsion, constraint **11** arm-
twisting, enforcement
12 imprisonment

during
◇ *insertion indicator*
02 in, of **03** dia-, for **04** over
07 pending **10** throughout **11** all the
while, at the time of, in the time of
12 for the time of **13** in the course of, in
the middle of

dusk
03 dim, eve **04** dark **05** gloom, shade
06 sunset **07** darkish, evening,
shadows, sundown **08** darkness,
gloaming, owl-light, twilight
09 nightfall **10** crepuscule
11 candlelight

dusky
03 dim, dun, sad **04** dark, hazy
05 black, brown, foggy, misty, murky,
swart, tawny **06** cloudy, gloomy,
phaeic, swarth, twilit **07** shadowy,
subfusc, subfusk, swarthy, umbrose
09 tenebrous **10** fuliginous
11 crepuscular, dark-skinned **12** dark
coloured

dust
03 ash, mop **04** bort, clay, coom, culm
dirt, duff, fuzz, grit, mote, seed, smut
soil, soot, wipe **05** ashes, boart, brav
brush, clean, cover, earth, grime, lem
money, smoke, spray, stour **06** bedus
ground, limail, polish, pother, powde
pudder, spread **07** burnish, fallout,
scatter, smother, turmoil **08** bulldust
sprinkle, stardust **09** particles,
pozzolana **10** cryoconite, haemocor
11 disturbance **13** meteor streams
14 micro-meteorite
• **dust storm**
05 devil **06** calima **07** Shaitan

dust-up
05 brawl, brush, fight, scrap, set-to
06 barney, bust-up, fracas, tussle
07 punch-up, quarrel, scuffle
08 argument, conflict, skirmish
09 argy-bargy, commotion, encount∈
11 disturbance **12** disagreement

dusty
03 bad **04** dull **05** dirty, grimy, sandy
sooty **06** chalky, filthy, grubby, stoury
07 crumbly, friable, powdery
08 granular, lifeless **09** pulverous
11 dust-covered **12** contemptible, ol
fashioned

Dutch
01 D **02** Du
• **Cape Dutch**
04 Taal

dutiful
05 pious **06** filial **07** devoted
08 obedient **09** compliant, officious
10 obsequious, respectful, submissiv
thoughtful **11** considerate,
deferential, reverential
13 conscientious

duty
03 job, tax **04** debt, dues, levy, onus,
part, role, task, toll, work **05** chore
06 burden, charge, excise, office, tari
07 calling, customs, loyalty, mission,
respect, service **08** business, fidelity,
function **09** deference, obedience
10 allegiance, assignment, attendanc
commission, obligation
11 requirement **12** faithfulness
14 responsibility
• **active duty**
02 AD
• **duty list**
04 rota
• **off duty**
03 off **04** free **07** off work, resting
08 inactive **09** at leisure, not at work
on holiday **10** not working
• **on duty**
04 busy **06** active, at work, on call,

ied up **07** engaged, working
08 occupied

dwarf
03 elf, toy **04** baby, Mime, mini, tiny,
row **05** check, gnome, pigmy, pygmy,
mall, stunt, troll **06** arrest, droich,
durgan, goblin, little, midget, minute,
petite, pocket, retard **07** atrophy,
manikin, stunted **08** Alberich,
dominate, homuncle, mannikin, Tom
Thumb **09** homuncule, miniature,
power over **10** diminutive,
homunculus, overshadow, undersized
1 Lilliputian

Snow White's dwarfs:

03 Doc
05 Dopey, Happy
06 Grumpy, Sleepy, Sneezy
07 Bashful

dwell
03 won **04** bide, home, live, rest, stay
05 abide, lodge, stall **06** people,
remain, reside, settle, tenant **07** hang
out, inhabit, sojourn **08** populate
1 be domiciled
• **dwell on**
06 harp on **07** brood on **08** mull over
09 elaborate, emphasize, expatiate,
reflect on **10** linger over, meditate on,
ruminate on, think about

dweller
07 denizen **08** occupant, occupier,
resident **10** inhabitant

dwelling
03 cot, dug, hut, won **04** flat, home,
roof, tent, tipi, weem, woon **05** abode,
bothy, bower, donga, gundy, house,
novel, humpy, lodge, place, tepee
06 grange, gunyah, mia-mia, pondok,
shanty, teepee, wurley **07** cottage,
loghole, lodging **08** domicile,
messuage, quarters, tenement
09 apartment, penthouse, residence,
single-end **10** habitation, pied-à-terre
1 continuance **13** dwelling-house,
establishment
See also **accommodation; house**

dwindle
03 ebb **04** fade, fail, fall, wane **06** die
out, lessen, reduce, shrink, vanish,
weaken, wither **07** decline, shrivel,
ubside, tail off **08** decrease, diminish,

fall away, grow less, peter out, taper off
09 disappear, waste away **10** become
less
• **dwindle away**
05 peter

dye
03 hew, hue **04** tint, wash **05** agent,
imbue, shade, stain, tinct, tinge
06 colour, embrue, imbrue
07 embrewe, pigment **09** colouring
See also **colour; pigment**

Dyes include:

04 anil, Saxe, wald, weld, woad
05 chica, eosin, henna, mauve
06 anatto, archil, corkir, flavin, fustic,
indigo, kamala, korkir, madder,
mauvin, orcein, orchel, orchil
07 alkanet, annatto, azurine, cudbear,
flavine, magenta, mauvein, mauvine,
para-red, ponceau, saffron
08 amaranth, fuchsine, mauveine,
orchella, orchilla, safranin, turnsole
09 cochineal, nigrosine, primuline,
safranine, Saxon blue, Turkey red,
Tyrian red
10 carthamine, Saxony blue, tartrazine
12 Tyrian purple

• **dyeing technique**
04 ikat
• **source of dye**
04 chay

dyed-in-the-wool
05 fixed **07** diehard, settled
08 complete, hard-core, hardened,
thorough **09** confirmed **10** deep-
rooted, entrenched, inflexible,
inveterate, unshakable **11** established,
unshakeable **12** card-carrying, long-
standing, unchangeable
14 uncompromising

dying
04 last **05** final, going, waned
06 ebbing, ending, fading, mortal
07 closing, failing, passing
08 expiring, moribund **09** declining,
finishing, perishing, vanishing
10 concluding **11** near to death **12** at
death's door, close to death **14** on your
deathbed, on your last legs

dynamic
◊ *anagram indicator*
05 vital **06** active, causal, lively,

potent, strong **07** driving, go-ahead
08 forceful, powerful, spirited,
vigorous **09** effective, energetic, go-
getting **11** high-powered **12** full of
energy, self-starting

dynamically
07 vitally **08** actively, strongly
10 forcefully, powerfully, vigorously
11 effectively **13** energetically

dynamism
02 go **03** pep, vim, zap, zip **04** push
05 drive **06** energy, spirit, vigour
07 pizzazz **10** enterprise, get-up-and-
go, initiative, liveliness **12** forcefulness

dynasty
04 line, rule **05** house **06** empire,
regime **07** lineage **08** dominion
09 authority **10** government,
succession **11** sovereignty
12 jurisdiction

Dynasties include:

02 Yi
03 Jin, Qin, Sui
04 Asen, Avis, Chin, Lodi, Ming,
Qing, Song, Sung, Tang, Vasa,
Yuan, Zhou
05 Ch'ing, Piast, Qajar, Shang
06 Chakri, Sayyid, Valois, Wettin,
Zangid
07 'Abbasid, Ayyubid, Chakkri, Fatimid,
Romanov, Safavid, Tughlaq
08 Capetian, Habsburg, Ilkhanid
09 Jagiellon
10 Qarakhanid
11 Plantagenet
12 Hohenstaufen, Hohenzollern
14 Petrovic-Njegos

dyspepsia
07 acidity, pyrosis **08** dyspepsy
09 heartburn **10** cardialgia, water-
brash

dyspeptic
04 edgy **05** humpy, ratty, testy
06 crabby, feisty, gloomy, shirty, touchy
07 crabbed, grouchy, in a huff, in a sulk,
peevish, stroppy **08** snappish
09 crotchety, irritable **10** indigested
11 bad-tempered, cacogastric,
indigestive **13** short-tempered

dysprosium
02 Dy

E

E
04 echo 07 epsilon

each
02 ea 03 ilk, per 05 every 06 apiece, singly 07 each one, per head 09 per capita, per person 10 separately 11 every single 12 individually, respectively 15 each and every one, every individual
• **for each**
03 per

eager
04 agog, avid, bore, fain, keen, rath, toey 05 antsy, dying, frack, hasty, prone, rathe, sharp 06 ardent, greedy, gung-ho, hungry, intent, raring, watery 07 anxious, earnest, fervent, longing, thirsty, up for it, willing, wishful, wishing, zealous 08 desirous, diligent, empressé, yearning 09 desperate, impatient, perfervid 12 affectionate, enthusiastic, wholehearted

eagerly
04 sore 06 avidly, keenly 08 ardently, greedily, intently 09 earnestly, fervently, zealously 11 impatiently 14 wholeheartedly

eagerness
03 yen 04 lust, zeal 05 ardor, greed 06 ardour, hunger, thirst 07 avidity, fervour, longing 08 fainness, fervency, keenness, yearning 09 fervidity 10 enthusiasm, greediness, impatience, intentness 11 earnestness, impetuosity

eagle
04 erne 05 harpy 06 Aquila 07 alerion, lectern 08 allerion, bateleur, berghaan 11 king of birds

ear
◇ *homophone indicator*
03 ere, lug 04 heed, till 05 skill, souse, taste 06 notice, plough, regard 07 ability, earhole, hearing, lughole 09 attention, shell-like 10 perception 11 sensitivity 12 appreciation 13 attentiveness 14 discrimination

Ear parts include:
04 drum, lobe
05 anvil, helix, incus, pinna, scala
06 concha, cupola, hammer, stapes, tragus
07 alveary, auricle, cochlea, eardrum, ear lobe, malleus, saccule, stirrup, utricle
08 pavilion, sacculus, tympanum
09 columella, endolymph, labyrinth, perilymph, vestibule

10 oval window
11 Corti's organ, round window
12 organ of Corti
13 auditory canal, auditory nerve
14 columella auris, Eustachian tube
15 vestibular nerve

• **of the ear**
04 otic
• **play it by ear**
05 ad-lib 06 busk it, wing it 09 improvise 11 extemporize 15 think on your feet

earlier
02 ex 06 before 07 already, prior to 08 formerly, previous 10 previously

early
02 am 04 auld, rare, rath, rear, soon 05 first 06 at dawn 07 advance, ancient, forward, initial, morning, opening, too soon 08 advanced, primeval, untimely 09 in advance, premature, primaeval, primitive 10 at daybreak, beforehand, in good time, precocious, primordial 11 ahead of time, prematurely, undeveloped 12 in the morning 13 autochthonous 15 ahead of schedule, with time to spare

earmark
03 tag 05 label 07 mark out, reserve 08 allocate, keep back, lay aside, put aside, set aside 09 designate

earn
03 ern, get, net, win 04 draw, gain, make, rate, reap 05 clear, gross, merit 06 attain, be owed, be paid, curdle, obtain, pocket, pull in, rake in, secure 07 achieve, acquire, bring in, collect, deserve, get paid, realize, receive, warrant 08 take home

earnest
03 sad 04 dear, firm, keen 05 arles, eager, fixed, grave, token, truth 06 ardent, devout, intent, pledge, solemn, steady, urgent 07 deposit, devoted, fervent, forward, intense, promise, serious, sincere, wistful, zealous 08 diligent, resolute, security 09 assiduous, assurance, committed, dedicated, guarantee, heartfelt, sincerity 10 persistent, press-money, resolution, thoughtful 11 down payment, impassioned, seriousness 12 earnest-penny, enthusiastic 13 conscientious, determination
• **in earnest**
07 genuine, serious, sincere, stand-up 08 ardently, intently, steadily 09 not joking, seriously, zealously

10 resolutely 12 passionately, purposefully 14 wholeheartedly 15 conscientiously

earnestly
04 hard 06 dearly, firmly, keenly, warmly, wistly 07 eagerly 08 intently 09 fervently, seriously, sincerely, zealously 10 resolutely

earnestness
04 zeal 06 ardour, warmth 07 fervour, gravity, passion 08 devotion, fervency, keenness 09 eagerness, sincerity, vehemence 10 enthusiasm, intentness, resolution 11 seriousness 13 determination 14 purposefulness

earnings
03 fee, pay 04 gain 05 wages 06 income, net pay, return, reward, salary 07 profits, revenue, stipend 08 gross pay, proceeds, receipts 09 emolument 10 honorarium 11 take home pay 12 remuneration

earring
04 drop, hoop, snap, stud 06 clip-on 07 pendant, pendent, sleeper

earshot
04 hail 05 sound 07 hearing
• **beyond earshot**
10 out of range

earth
01 E 02 Ge 03 orb, sod 04 clay, dirt, dust, eard, Gaea, Gaia, land, loam, mold, soil, turf, yerd, yird 05 globe, humus, mould, world 06 ground, planet, sphere 07 topsoil
• **rammed earth**
04 pisé

earthenware
03 pig, pot 04 delf, pots, waly 05 cloam, delft, delph, wally 07 faience, pottery 08 ceramics, crockery, figuline, maiolica, majolica 09 creamware, ironstone, porcelain, stoneware 10 Samian ware, terracotta 14 terra sigillata

earthly
04 vile 05 human 06 likely, mortal 07 fleshly, mundane, profane, secular, sensual, terrene, worldly 08 feasible, material, physical, possible, sublunar, telluric, temporal 09 slightest, sublunary, tellurian 10 imaginable 11 conceivable, terrestrial 13 materialistic

earthquake
05 quake, seism, shake, shock 06 tremor 07 temblor 08 trembler,

upheaval 10 aftershock, convulsion
11 earth-tremor

earthwork
04 berm, ring **06** cursus, sconce
07 parados **10** breastwork,
embankment, roundabout
12 entrenchment, intrenchment,
maiden castle

earthy
04 blue, rude **05** bawdy, crude, gross,
rough **06** cloddy, coarse, direct, ribald,
simple, vulgar **07** natural, raunchy,
terrene **08** claylike, dirtlike, soil-like
09 earthlike, unrefined **10** indecorous
11 down to earth, uninhibited
15 unsophisticated

ease
04 calm, edge, inch, rest **05** abate,
allay, guide, peace, quiet, relax, salve,
slide, steer **06** lessen, reduce, relent,
repose, smooth, soothe, wealth
07 assuage, comfort, leisure, lighten,
quieten, relieve **08** deftness, diminish,
facility, grow less, mitigate, moderate,
opulence, otiosity, palliate **09** affluence,
alleviate, dexterity, enjoyment,
happiness, manoeuvre **10** adroitness,
ameliorate, become less, bed of roses,
cleverness, easy street, facilitate,
otioseness, prosperity, relaxation
11 contentment, lap of luxury, life of
Riley, naturalness, skilfulness
12 peacefulness **14** effortlessness
• **at ease**
04 calm **06** secure **07** natural, relaxed
08 composed, sans gêne **11** comfortable
• **ease off**
04 wane **05** abate **06** relent **07** die
away, die down, slacken, subside
08 decrease, diminish, moderate, slack
off **10** become less, slacken off

easily
> *anagram indicator*
04 eath, ethe, well **05** by far, eathe
06 simply, surely **07** clearly, readily
08 fluently, probably **09** certainly
10 definitely, far and away, undeniably
11 comfortably, doubtlessly,
undoubtedly **12** effortlessly,
indisputably, without doubt
• **easily handled**
04 yare

east
01 E **04** Asia **06** Levant, Orient
07 sunrise **08** Old World **09** sunrising
11 morning-land
• **East End**
> *dialect indicator*
• **from the east, goes east**
> *reversal indicator*

Easter
04 Pace **05** Pasch

eastern
01 E **06** exotic, Levant, Orient
08 Oriental

East German *see* **German**

East Timor
03 TLS

easy
◊ *anagram indicator*
04 calm, eath, ethe, glib, soft **05** cushy,
eathe **06** a cinch, casual, dégagé,
facile, simple, smooth **07** a doddle,
natural, relaxed, running **08** carefree,
homelike, informal, laid-back, painless,
unforced **09** a cakewalk, a pushover,
easy as ABC, easy as pie, easy-going,
easy-peasy, foolproof, leisurely,
unstudied **10** child's play, effortless,
manageable, unlaboured
11 comfortable, undemanding **12** a
piece of cake **13** uncomplicated **14** a
walk in the park **15** straightforward
• **easy thing**
03 pie **08** pushover
• **take it easy**
04 loll **05** relax

easy-going
04 calm **06** placid, serene **07** equable,
lenient, relaxed **08** amenable,
carefree, indolent, laid-back, tolerant
10 insouciant, nonchalant
11 undemanding **12** even-tempered,
happy-go-lucky **13** imperturbable

eat
◊ *containment indicator*
02 go **03** hog, pig, rot, sup **04** bite,
chew, chop, cram, dine, feed, fret, grub,
guts, mess, nosh, peck, pick, take
05 binge, decay, erode, feast, graze,
hog it, lunch, munch, scoff, snack,
snarf, taste, twist, upset, worry
06 begnaw, devour, gobble, guttle,
ingest, pig out, slairg, tuck in
07 consume, corrode, crumble,
predate, put away, swallow **08** bite
into, bolt down, chow down, demolish,
dissolve, gulp down, irritate, tuck into,
wear away, wolf down **09** breakfast,
have a bite, knock back, manducate,
partake of, polish off, undermine
10 gormandize, have a snack

Eating places include:

04 hall, mess
06 frater, fratry
07 canteen
08 takeaway
09 refectory
10 commissary, dining-hall
11 frater-house

See also **restaurant**
• **eat away**
04 etch, gnaw **05** erode **06** begnaw
07 corrode
• **eat quickly**
04 bolt, cram, gulp

eatable
04 good **06** edible **08** esculent
09 palatable, wholesome
10 comestible, digestible

eavesdrop
03 bug, spy, tap **05** snoop **06** earwig
07 monitor **08** listen in, overhear
10 stillicide

eavesdropper
03 spy **05** snoop **07** monitor, snooper
08 listener

ebb
04 drop, fall, flag, sink, wane **05** abate,
decay, go out **06** lessen, recede,
reflow, reflux, shrink, waning, weaken
07 decline, dwindle, ebb tide, lagging,
low tide, retreat, slacken, subside
08 decrease, diminish, fade away, fall
back, flow back, going-out, low
water, peter out, receding
09 abatement, dwindling, lessening,
refluence, retrocede, subsiding,
weakening **10** degenerate,
slackening, subsidence **11** deteriorate,
flowing-back **12** degeneration
13 deterioration

ebony
03 jet **04** dark, inky **05** black, heben,
jetty, sable, sooty **08** jet-black
09 cocuswood **10** calamander,
coromandel

ebullience
04 zest **07** elation **08** buoyancy,
vivacity **10** breeziness, brightness,
bubbliness, chirpiness, enthusiasm,
excitement, exuberance **11** high spirits
12 effusiveness, exhilaration

ebullient
06 breezy, bright, bubbly, chirpy,
elated **07** buoyant, excited, gushing,
zestful **08** agitated, effusive
09 exuberant, vivacious **11** exhilarated
12 effervescent, enthusiastic
13 irrepressible

eccentric
◊ *anagram indicator*
03 cam, dag, fay, fey, fie, nut, odd, off
04 card, case, cure, ditz, geek, kook,
loon, wack, zany **05** crank, ditsy, ditzy,
dotty, flake, flaky, freak, geeky, kinky,
kooky, loony, loopy, nutty, queer, spacy,
wacko, wacky, weird **06** cranky,
kookie, nutjob, nutter, oddity, quirky,
screwy, spacey, way-out, weirdo,
whacko **07** bizarre, cupcake, dingbat,
erratic, nutcase, oddball, odd fish, offbeat, strange, weirdie **08** aberrant,
abnormal, crackpot, freakish, peculiar,
singular **09** character, ding-a-ling,
screwball **10** loony tunes, off the wall,
outlandish **13** idiosyncratic,
nonconformist **14** fish out of water,
unconventional

eccentricity
01 e **05** quirk **06** oddity **07** anomaly
09 weirdness **10** aberration,
quirkiness, screwiness
11 abnormality, bizarreness,
peculiarity, singularity, strangeness,
unorthodoxy **12** freakishness,
idiosyncrasy **13** nonconformity
14 capriciousness

ecclesiastic
04 abbé, dean **05** canon, padre, vicar
06 bishop, cleric, curate, deacon,
father, lector, parson, pastor, priest,
rector **08** chaplain, man of God,
minister, preacher, reverend
09 churchman, clergyman, deaconess,
presbyter **10** archbishop, woman of
God **11** churchwoman, clergywoman

13 man of the cloth **15** woman of the cloth

See also **clergyman, clergywoman**

ecclesiastical
04 holy **06** church, divine **07** canonic **08** churchly, clerical, pastoral, priestly **09** canonical, religious, spiritual **10** sacerdotal **11** ministerial

echelon
04 rank, rung, tier **05** grade, level, place **06** degree, status **08** position

echinoderm
07 crinoid, cystoid, sea-lily, trepang **08** starfish **09** sea-urchin **10** bêche-de-mer **11** brittlestar, sea-cucumber

echo
01 E **04** copy, hint, ring **05** angel, clone, ditto, image, mimic, reply, trace **06** answer, memory, mirror, parrot, repeat, report **07** imitate, rebound, reflect, remains, resound, respeak, ringing, vestige **08** allusion, imitator, parallel, rebellow, reminder, resemble **09** duplicate, evocation, flashback, imitation, reiterate, repercuss, reproduce **10** reflection, repetition, resounding **11** mirror image, reiteration, remembrance, replication, reverberate **12** reproduction **13** reverberation

éclat
04 fame, show **05** glory, style **06** effect, lustre, renown **07** acclaim, display, success **08** applause, approval, plaudits **09** celebrity, splendour **10** brilliance **11** acclamation, distinction, flamboyance, ostentation, stylishness

eclectic
04 wide **05** broad **06** varied **07** diverse, general, liberal **08** catholic **09** many-sided, selective **11** diversified, wide-ranging **12** all-embracing, multifarious **13** comprehensive, heterogeneous

eclipse
03 dim, ebb **04** fall, loss, veil **05** block, cloud, cover, decay, dwarf, excel, outdo **06** darken, exceed, shroud **07** blot out, conceal, decline, dimming, failure, obscure, shading, surpass, veiling **08** covering, darkness, outshine **09** darkening, deliquium, transcend, weakening **10** concealing, overshadow **11** blotting-out, obscuration **13** overshadowing **14** run rings around **15** cast a shadow over, put into the shade

economic
05 cheap, trade **06** fiscal, viable **08** business, monetary **09** budgetary, financial, pecuniary, rewarding **10** commercial, industrial, productive, profitable **11** moneymaking **12** profit-making, remunerative **13** cost-effective

economical
05 cheap, tight **06** budget, frugal, modest, saving **07** careful, low-cost,

prudent, sparing, thrifty **08** low-price, skimping **09** efficient, low-budget, low-priced, provident, scrimping **10** reasonable **11** inexpensive **12** parsimonious **13** cost-effective **15** bargain-basement

economics

economist
10 chrematist

economize
03 eke **04** save **06** budget **07** cut back, use less **08** cut costs, retrench **10** buy cheaply, cut corners **12** be economical **13** keep down costs, scrimp and save **14** cut expenditure, live on the cheap **15** tighten your belt

economy
04 care **06** saving, thrift, wealth **08** prudence, skimping **09** frugality, husbandry, parsimony, plutology, plutonomy, restraint, scrimping **10** providence **11** carefulness **12** catallactics, retrenchment **13** chrematistics **14** financial state, system of wealth **15** financial system

ecstasy
01 E **03** joy, tab **04** dove **05** bliss **06** frenzy **07** delight, elation, fervour, rapture **08** euphoria, pleasure **09** transport **10** exultation, jubilation **11** sublimation **12** disco biscuit
• **rouse to ecstasy**
04 send

ecstatic
04 rapt, sent **06** elated, joyful, Pythic **07** fervent **08** blissful, euphoric, frenzied, jubilant **09** delirious, overjoyed, rapturous, rhapsodic **10** blissed-out, enraptured, in raptures **11** high as a kite, on cloud nine, over the moon, tickled pink **13** jumping for joy **15** in seventh heaven

Ecuador
02 EC **03** ECU

ecumenical
07 general **08** catholic **09** universal **10** broad-based **12** all-embracing, nonsectarian

eddy
04 curl, pirl, purl, reel, roll, spin, turn, weal, weel, well **05** rotor, swirl, swish, twirl, twist, whirl **06** vortex **07** backset **08** swirling **09** maelstrom, whirlpool, whirlwind

edge
◊ *ends selection indicator*
◊ *head selection indicator*
03 hem, lip, rim **04** bite, brim, ease, head, inch, kerb, lead, line, side, worm, zest **05** bridle, crawl, creep, elbow, force, limit, sidle, steal, sting, verge **06** border, fringe, margin **07** outline **08** acerbity, boundary, frontier, keenness, pungency, severity, whip-hand **09** acuteness, advantage, dominance, extremity, perimeter, periphery, sharpness, threshold, upper hand **10** ascendancy, causticity, outer limit, trenchancy **11** pick your way, superiority **12** incisiveness
• **on edge**
04 edgy, toey **05** jumpy, nervy, tense **06** touchy **07** anxious, keyed-up, nervous, twitchy, uptight **09** ill at ease, irritable **12** apprehensive, highly-strung
• **rough edge**
03 bur **04** burr
• **straight edge**
04 lute, rule

edgy
05 nervy, tense **06** on edge, touchy **07** anxious, brittle, keyed-up, nervous, uptight **09** ill at ease, irritable **12** highly-strung

edible
04 good **07** eatable **08** fit to eat, harmless **09** palatable, safe to eat, wholesome **10** comestible, digestible
• **edible shoots**
03 udo

edict
03 act, law **04** bull, fiat, rule **05** order, ukase **06** decree, ruling **07** command, mandate, process, statute **08** decretal, rescript **09** forbiddal, manifesto, pragmatic **10** golden bull, injunction, regulation **11** forbiddance **12** proclamation **13** pronouncement **14** pronunciamento

edification
07 tuition **08** coaching, guidance, teaching **09** education, elevation, uplifting **10** upbuilding **11** improvement, instruction **13** enlightenment

edifice
08 building, erection **09** structure **12** construction

edify
05 build, coach, guide, teach, tutor **06** inform, school, uplift **07** build up, educate, elevate, improve, nurture **08** instruct **09** enlighten, establish

edit
◇ *anagram indicator*
◇ *deletion indicator*
04 head **05** adapt, amend, check, emend **06** censor, choose, direct, garble, gather, head up, modify, polish, redact, revise, reword, select **07** arrange, collect, compile, correct, reorder, rewrite, subedit **08** annotate, assemble, copy-edit, organize, rephrase **09** proofread, rearrange **10** blue-pencil, bowdlerize **11** put together **12** be in charge of

edition
02 ed **04** Aufl, copy, edit **05** extra, issue, print **06** number, urtext, volume **07** hexapla, omnibus, reprint, version **08** printing, tetrapla, variorum **10** impression **11** publication **12** extra-special, reproduction
• **limited edition**
04 Aufl

editor
02 ed **04** hack **06** journo, writer **07** amender, checker, newsman, reviser **08** director, overseer, reporter, reviewer, rewriter **09** corrector, newswoman, publisher, subeditor **10** copy editor, desk editor, journalist, newscaster, undertaker **11** factchecker, proofreader **12** newspaperman **13** correspondent **14** newspaperwoman
See also **journalist**
• **assistant editor**
03 sub

editorial
06 column

educable
09 teachable, trainable **12** instructible

educate
05 coach, drill, edify, prime, teach, train, tutor **06** inform, school **07** bring up, develop, improve, nourish, nurture, prepare, train up, uptrain **08** hothouse, instruct **09** cultivate, enlighten, inculcate, institute **10** discipline, take in hand **12** indoctrinate

educated
02 ed **04** wise **06** brainy, taught **07** erudite, learned, refined, trained, tutored **08** all there, cultured, informed, lettered, literate, schooled, well-bred, well-read **09** civilized, sagacious **10** cultivated, instructed **11** enlightened **12** clever-clever **13** knowledgeable

education
02 ed **07** culture, letters, nurture, tuition **08** coaching, drilling, guidance, learning, teaching, training, tutoring **09** fostering, informing, knowledge, schooling **10** upbringing **11** cultivation, development, edification, improvement, inculcation, instruction, preparation, scholarship **13** enlightenment **14** indoctrination
• **basic education**
03 RRR
• **education journal**
03 TES
• **further education**
02 FE
• **higher education**
02 HE

educational
08 academic, cultural, didactic, edifying, learning, teaching **09** educative, improving, pedagogic **10** scholastic **11** informative, instructive, pedagogical **12** enlightening **13** instructional **14** institutional

educative
08 didactic, edifying **09** improving **10** catechetic **11** catechismal, catechistic, educational, informative,

instructive **12** enlightening **13** catechistical

educator
05 coach, tutor **06** master, mentor **07** teacher, trainer **08** academic, lecturer, mistress **09** pedagogue, professor, schoolman **10** instructor **11** headteacher **12** schoolmaster **13** schoolteacher **14** educationalist, schoolmistress

educe
05 infer **06** elicit **07** develop, draw out, extract

Edward
02 Ed **03** Ted

eel

• **bait for eel**
03 bob

eerie
05 scary, unked, unket, unkid, weird **06** creepy, spooky **07** ghostly, scaring, strange, uncanny **08** sinister, timorous **09** unearthly, unnatural **10** mysterious **11** frightening **13** bloodcurdling, spine-chilling

eerily
07 weirdly **09** strangely, uncannily **11** unnaturally **12** mysteriously

efface
04 dele **05** erase **06** cancel, delete, excise, remove, rub out **07** blot out, destroy, dislimn, expunct, expunge, wipe out **08** blank out, cross out, wear away **09** eliminate, eradicate, extirpate, strike out **10** obliterate

effect
03 win **04** gear, make **05** carry, cause, drift, force, fruit, goods, issue, power, sense, stuff, tenor **06** action, create, fulfil, impact, import, result, things, thread, upshot **07** achieve, baggage, clobber, execute, luggage, meaning, outcome, perform, produce, purport **08** carry out, chattels, complete, contrive, efficacy, generate, initiate, movables, property, strength **09** aftermath, influence, moveables, repulsion, trappings **10** accomplish, belongings, bring about, conclusion, effectuate, give rise to, impression **11** consequence, possessions **12** significance **13** accoutrements, paraphernalia
• **in effect**
06 in fact, really **07** en effet, in truth **08** actually **09** in reality, virtually **10** in

practice **11** effectively, essentially **12** in actual fact **13** substantially **14** produce results

• **produce an effect**
03 act

• **special effects**
02 FX **03** SFX

• **take effect**
04 bite, take, talk, vest, work **05** begin **06** kick in **07** come off, succeed **08** function **09** become law **11** become valid, be effective **13** be implemented, come into force **14** produce results **15** become operative, come into service

effective
04 home, neat **05** legal, valid **06** active, actual, cogent, potent, superb, useful **07** capable, current, helpful, in force, operant, telling, virtual **08** adequate, exciting, forceful, fruitful, in effect, powerful, striking **09** efficient, energetic, essential, operative, practical **10** attractive, compelling, convincing, impressive, persuasive, prevailing, productive, successful, sufficient, worthwhile **11** devastating, efficacious, energetical, functioning, implemental, in operation, serviceable

effectively
04 home, well **06** in fact, really **07** in truth **08** actually, in effect **09** in reality, virtually **10** fruitfully, in practice **11** efficiently, essentially **12** in actual fact, productively, successfully

effectiveness
03 use **05** clout, force, power **06** vigour, weight **07** ability, cogency, potence, potency, success **08** efficacy, strength, validity **09** influence **10** capability, efficacity, efficiency, usefulness **12** fruitfulness **14** productiveness **15** efficaciousness

effectual
05 legal, sound, valid **06** lawful, proper, useful **07** binding, capable **08** decisive, forcible, powerful **09** authentic, effective, magistral, operative **10** perficient, productive, successful **11** influential, serviceable **13** authoritative

effeminate
04 soft **05** cissy, minty, pansy, sissy **06** prissy, queeny **07** epicene, meacock, unmanly, wimpish, womanly **08** delicate, feminine, womanish **11** limp-wristed

effervesce
04 boil, fizz, foam **05** froth **06** bubble **07** ferment, sparkle **08** be lively **10** be animated **11** be ebullient, be vivacious **13** be exhilarated

effervescence
03 gas, vim, zip **04** fizz, foam, zing **05** froth **07** bubbles, ferment, foaming, sparkle **08** bubbling, buoyancy, frothing, vitality, vivacity **09** animation, fizziness, gassiness

10 ebullience, enthusiasm, excitement, exuberance, liveliness **11** excitedness, high spirits **12** exhilaration, fermentation

effervescent
◊ *anagram indicator*
05 fizzy, gassy, vital **06** bubbly, frothy, lively **07** aerated, buoyant, excited, fizzing, foaming **08** animated, bubbling **09** ebullient, exuberant, sparkling, vivacious **10** carbonated, fermenting **11** exhilarated **12** enthusiastic **13** irrepressible

effete
04 weak **05** spent **06** barren, feeble, used up, wasted **07** corrupt, debased, decayed, drained, shotten, spoiled, sterile, worn out **08** decadent, decrepit, infecund, tired out **09** enervated, enfeebled, exhausted, fruitless, played out **10** degenerate, unfruitful, unprolific **11** debilitated, ineffectual **12** unproductive

efficacious
06 active, potent, strong, useful **07** capable **08** adequate, powerful **09** competent, effective, effectual, operative, potential, sovereign **10** productive, successful, sufficient

efficacy
03 use **04** feck **05** force, power, value **06** effect, energy, virtue **07** ability, potency, success **08** strength **09** influence **10** capability, competence, usefulness **13** effectiveness **14** successfulness

efficiency
05 order, skill **07** ability **09** expertise **10** capability, competence, competency **11** orderliness, proficiency, skilfulness **12** organization, productivity **13** effectiveness

efficient
04 able **05** smart **06** expert, strong **07** capable, skilful, well-run **08** powerful **09** competent, effective, organized, practical **10** methodical, productive, proficient, systematic **11** streamlined, well-ordered, workmanlike **12** businesslike, rationalized **13** well-conducted, well-organized

effigy
03 guy **04** icon, idol, sign **05** dummy, image **06** figure, statue **07** carving, picture **08** likeness, portrait **09** Jack-straw **14** representation

efflorescence
03 reh

effluent
05 waste **06** efflux, sewage **07** outflow **08** emission **09** discharge, effluence, effluvium, emanation, pollutant, pollution **10** exhalation **11** liquid waste

effort
02 go **03** try **04** bash, beef, deed, feat,

opus, push, shot, stab, toil, work **05** crack, essay, force, nisus, pains, power, sweat, whirl **06** energy, labour, result, strain, stress **07** attempt, exploit, muscles, product, travail, trouble **08** creation, exertion, hard work, striving, struggle **09** endeavour **10** attainment, production **11** achievement, application, elbow-grease, muscle power **14** accomplishment **15** sweat of your brow

• **calling for effort**
02 yo

• **sudden effort**
03 fit

• **utmost efforts**
03 all

effortless
04 easy **06** facile, simple, smooth **07** passive **08** painless **10** unexacting **11** undemanding **13** uncomplicated **15** straightforward

effrontery
03 lip **04** face, gall, sass **05** brass, cheek, nerve **07** hutzpah **08** audacity, boldness, brazenry, chutzpah, temerity **09** arrogance, brashness, brass neck, impudence, insolence **10** brazenness, cheekiness, disrespect **11** presumption **12** impertinence **13** shamelessness

effulgent
07 glowing, radiant, shining **08** glorious, splendid **09** brilliant, refulgent **11** resplendent **12** incandescent

effusion
04 gush **06** efflux, stream **07** outflow **08** emission, outburst, shedding, voidance **09** discharge, effluence **10** outpouring

effusive
03 OTT **05** gabby, gassy, gushy **06** lavish **07** fulsome, gushing, lyrical, profuse, voluble **08** all mouth **09** ebullient, expansive, exuberant, rhapsodic, talkative **10** big-mouthed, over the top, unreserved **11** extravagant, overflowing **12** enthusiastic, unrestrained **13** demonstrative

eg
02 as, zB **03** say **06** such as **10** for example, par exemple **11** zum Beispiel **13** exempli gratia

egalitarian
04 fair, just **07** sharing **09** equitable **10** democratic **12** equalitarian

egg
01 O **03** nit **04** blow, bomb, mine, ovum **05** berry, ovule **06** oocyte **08** oosphere

• **egg on**
03 set, tar **04** abet, coax, edge, goad, prod, push, spur, urge **05** drive, prick **06** excite, exhort, incite, prompt, urge on **08** talk into **09** encourage, stimulate

• **egg-supplier** *see* bird

lower half of egg
4 doup, dowp
spot on egg
3 eye

egghead
3 don 05 brain 06 boffin, genius
7 know-all, scholar, thinker
8 academic, bookworm, brainbox,
instein 09 intellect, know-it-all
2 intellectual

eggs
2 OO 03 ova, roe 06 clutch, graine
4 pullet-sperm

ego
1 I 03 sel 04 self, soul 07 egotism
8 identity 09 self-image, self-worth
0 self-esteem 14 self-confidence,
elf-importance 15 sense of identity

egocentric
7 selfish 09 egotistic 11 egotistical,
elf-centred, self-seeking, self-serving
2 narcissistic, self-absorbed 14 self-
nterested

egoism
7 egotism 08 egomania, self-love
0 narcissism, self-regard 11 amour-
propre, selfishness, self-seeking
2 self-interest 13 egocentricity
4 self-absorption, self-importance
5 self-centredness

egoist
7 egotist 09 egomaniac 10 narcissist,
elf-seeker

egoistic
9 egotistic 10 egocentric, egoistical
1 egomaniacal, egotistical, self-
entred, self-seeking 12 narcissistic,
elf-absorbed, self-involved, self-
pleasing 13 self-important

egotism
3 ego 05 pride, swank 06 egoism,
anity 08 egomania, self-love,
elfness, snobbery 10 narcissism, self-
egard 11 braggadocio, self-conceit,
elfishness, superiority
2 boastfulness 13 bigheadedness,
onceitedness, egocentricity 14 self-
dmiration, self-importance 15 self-
entredness

egotist
6 egoist 07 bighead, bluffer, boaster,
how-off 08 big mouth, braggart
9 egomaniac, smart alec, swaggerer
0 clever dick 11 braggadocio, clever
logs, self-admirer

egotistic
4 vain 05 proud 07 selfish
8 boasting, bragging, egoistic,
uperior 09 bigheaded, conceited
0 egocentric 11 self-centred, swell-
eaded 12 narcissistic, self-admiring
3 self-important, swollen-headed

egregious
4 fine, rank 05 gross 06 arrant
7 glaring, heinous 08 flagrant,
rievous, infamous, precious, shocking
9 appalling, monstrous, notorious,

prominent 10 outrageous, scandalous
11 intolerable 12 insufferable
13 distinguished

egress
04 exit, vent 05 issue 06 depart,
escape, exodus, outlet, way out
07 leaving 09 departure, emergence
11 escape route

Egypt
02 ET 03 EGY

Egyptian
07 Thebaic

Ancient Egyptian rulers include:

05 Khufu
06 Ahmose, Cheops
07 Ptolemy, Rameses
08 Berenice, Thutmose
09 Akhenaten, Amenhotep, Cleopatra,
   Nefertiti, Sesostris, Tuthmosis
10 Hatshepsut
11 Tut'ankhamun

See also **god, goddess; pharaoh**

eight
04 VIII 05 octad, octet 06 octave,
octett, ogdoad 07 octette
08 octonary

eighteen
05 XVIII

eighty
04 LXXX

einsteinium
02 Es

ejaculate
03 cry 04 call, come, emit, yell
05 blurt, eject, expel, shout, spurt,
utter 06 cry out, scream 07 call out,
exclaim, release 08 blurt out, shout out
09 discharge

ejaculation
03 cry 04 call, yell 05 shout, spurt
06 climax, coming, scream 07 release
08 ejection, emission 09 discharge,
expulsion, utterance 11 exclamation
12 interjection

eject
04 emit, fire, oust, sack, spew, spit
05 belch, degas, evict, exile, expel,
exude, spout, vomit 06 banish,
bounce, deport, get out, propel,
remove 07 bail out, boot out, dismiss,
exclude, excrete, expulse, kick out,
release, turf out, turn out 08 chuck out,
disgorge, drive out, evacuate, get rid of,
splutter, throw out 09 discharge,
ejaculate, thrust out 11 expectorate

ejection
05 exile 06 firing, ouster, outing
07 ousting, removal, sacking, the boot,
the sack 08 eviction, vomiting
09 discharge, dismissal, exclusion,
expulsion 10 banishment
11 deportation, ejaculation

eke
• **eke out**
03 ech, ich 04 eche, eech 05 add to,
get by 06 scrape 07 fill out, help out,

husband, scratch, spin out, stretch,
survive 08 increase, piece out 10 go
easy with, supplement 11 economize
on 12 feel the pinch 13 scrimp and
save

elaborate
◊ *anagram indicator*
05 exact, fancy, fussy, showy
06 devise, minute, ornate, polish,
quaint, refine, rococo, work up
07 amplify, careful, complex, develop,
enhance, explain, improve, precise,
studied, work out 08 detailed,
develope, expand on, flesh out,
involved, laboured, thorough
09 decorated, enlarge on, expatiate,
extensive, intricate, perfected,
storiated 10 ornamental
11 complicated, extravagant,
highwrought, historiated,
overwrought, painstaking
12 ostentatious

élan
04 brio, dash, zest 05 flair, oomph,
style, verve 06 esprit, pizazz, spirit,
vigour 07 panache, pizzazz
08 flourish, vivacity 09 animation
10 confidence, liveliness
11 impetuosity, stylishness

elapse
02 go 03 ren, rin, run 04 go by, go on,
pass 05 lapse 06 go past, slip by
07 passing 08 overpass, pass away, slip
away

elastic
◊ *anagram indicator*
04 easy 05 buxom, fluid 06 bouncy,
pliant, supple 07 buoyant, plastic,
pliable, rubbery, springy 08 flexible,
stretchy, tolerant, yielding
09 adaptable, compliant, resilient
10 adjustable 11 elasticated,
stretchable 13 accommodating

elasticity
04 give, play 05 tonus 06 bounce,
spring 07 stretch 08 buoyancy
09 tolerance 10 plasticity, pliability,
resilience, suppleness 11 flexibility,
springiness 12 adaptability,
stretchiness 13 adjustability

elated
04 high 05 happy 06 joyful, joyous
07 excited 08 blissful, ecstatic,
euphoric, exultant, glorious, jubilant,
thrilled 09 delighted, overjoyed,
rapturous, rhapsodic 11 exhilarated, on
cloud nine, over the moon

elation
03 joy 04 glee, lift, ruff 05 bliss, ruffe
06 thrill 07 delight, ecstasy, rapture
08 euphoria 09 happiness
10 exaltation, exultation, joyfulness,
joyousness, jubilation 11 high spirits
12 exhilaration, intoxication

elbow
04 bump, push 05 ancon, barge,
crowd, force, knock, nudge, shove
06 jostle, justle 08 shoulder

elbow-grease
04 beef **06** effort, energy **07** muscles
08 exertion, hard work, strength
11 muscle power **15** sweat of your
brow

elbow-room
04 play, room **05** scope, space
06 leeway **07** freedom **08** latitude
10 Lebensraum **14** breathing space

elder
03 OAP **04** aîné, sire **05** aînée, older,
oldie **06** deacon, father, leader, senior
07 ancient, wise man **08** ancestor,
boortree, bountree, bourtree,
kaumatua **09** first-born, old person,
pensioner, presbyter **11** older person

elderly
03 old **04** aged, OAPs **05** aging, hoary
06 ageing, mature, oldies, past it,
senile **07** fossils **08** badgerly, has-
beens **09** old people, senescent,
wrinklies **10** grey-haired, pensioners
11 golden agers, older adults, over the
hill **13** retired people **14** long in the
tooth, senior citizens **15** older
generation

eldest
05 first **06** oldest **09** first-born **13** first-
begotten

elect
03 opt **04** pick, -to-be, vote **05** adopt,
co-opt, élite, voice **06** choose,
chosen, future, opt for, picked, prefer,
return, select, vote in **07** appoint, vote
for **08** decide on, nominate, plump for,
selected **09** cast a vote, chosen few,
designate, determine, preferred
10 hand-picked **11** prospective **12** go
to the polls

elected
02 in

election
04 poll, vote **06** ballot, choice, return,
voting **07** picking, primary
08 choosing, decision, free will,
hustings **09** rectorial, selection
10 preference, referendum
11 appointment **13** determination

electioneering
08 fighting, hustings, lobbying
09 crusading, promotion
10 canvassing, struggling
11 campaigning, championing
13 mainstreeting

elector
05 voter **08** selector **10** electorate
11 constituent

electorate

electric
04 live **05** tense **07** charged, dynamic,
powered, rousing **08** cordless,
exciting, stirring **09** startling, thrilling
11 stimulating **12** electrifying,
rechargeable **13** mains-operated
15 battery-operated, electric-
powered

• **electric fluid**
04 vril

electrical

electrify
04 fire, jolt, stir **05** amaze, rouse,
shock **06** charge, excite, thrill
07 animate, astound, stagger
08 astonish **09** electrize, galvanize,
stimulate **10** invigorate

elegance
04 chic **05** grace, poise, style, taste
06 beauty, luxury, polish **07** dignity
08 grandeur **09** gentility, propriety,
smartness **10** concinnity, politeness,
refinement **11** discernment,
distinction, stylishness
12 gracefulness, tastefulness
13 exquisiteness, sumptuousness
14 sophistication **15** fashionableness

elegant
04 chic, fine, jimp, neat **05** bijou, ritzy,
smart **06** dainty, humane, la-di-da,
lovely, modish, smooth, snazzy,
swanky, urbane **07** genteel, refined,
stylish **08** artistic, charming, cultured,
debonair, delicate, graceful, gracious,
handsome, lah-di-dah, polished,
tasteful **09** beautiful, excellent,
exquisite **10** concinnous, cultivated,
debonnaire **11** fashionable
13 sophisticated

elegiac
03 sad **07** doleful, keening
08 funereal, mournful **09** epicedial,
epicedian, lamenting, plaintive,
threnetic, threnodic **10** threnodial
11 melancholic, threnetical,
valedictory

elegy
05 dirge **06** lament, plaint **07** requiem
08 threnode, threnody **10** burial hymn
11 funeral poem, funeral song

element

03 set **04** hint, part **05** grain, group, haunt, niche, party, piece, touch, trace **06** basics, clique, factor, member, storms, strand **07** climate, faction, feature, habitat, soupçon, weather **08** filament, fragment **09** component, electrode, rudiments, suspicion, territory **10** essentials, individual, ingredient, principles **11** constituent, foundations, individuals, small amount, wind and rain **12** fundamentals **15** first principles

Elements and their symbols include:

01 B (boron), C (carbon), F (fluorine), H (hydrogen), I (iodine), K (potassium), N (nitrogen), O (oxygen), P (phosphorus), S (sulphur), U (uranium), V (vanadium), W (tungsten), Y (yttrium)
02 Ac (actinium), Ag (silver), Al (aluminium), Am (americium), Ar (argon), As (arsenic), At (astatine), Au (gold), Ba (barium), Be (beryllium), Bh (bohrium), Bi (bismuth), Bk (berkelium), Br (bromine), Ca (calcium), Cd (cadmium), Ce (cerium), Cf (californium), Cl (chlorine), Cm (curium), Co (cobalt), Cr (chromium), Cs (caesium), Cu (copper), Db (dubnium), Ds (darmstadtium), Dy (dysprosium), Er (erbium), Es (einsteinium), Eu (europium), Fe (iron), Fm (fermium), Fr (francium), Ga (gallium), Gd (gadolinium), Ge (germanium), Ha (hahnium), He (helium), Hf (hafnium), Hg (mercury), Ho (holmium), Hs (hassium), In (indium), Ir (iridium), Kr (krypton), La (lanthanum), Li (lithium), Lr (lawrencium), Lu (lutetium), Lw (lawrencium), Md (mendelevium), Mg (magnesium), Mn (manganese), Mo (molybdenum), Mt (meitnerium), Na (sodium), Nb (niobium), Nd (neodymium), Ne (neon), Ni (nickel), No (nobelium), Np (neptunium), Os (osmium), Pa (protactinium), Pb (lead), Pd (palladium), Pm (promethium), Po (polonium), Pr (praseodymium), Pt (platinum), Pu (plutonium), Ra (radium), Rb (rubidium), Re (rhenium), Rf (rutherfordium), Rg (roentgenium), Rh (rhodium), Rn (radon), Ru (ruthenium), Sb (antimony), Sc (scandium), Se (selenium), Sg (seaborgium), Si (silicon), Sm (samarium), Sn (tin), Sr (strontium), Ta (tantalum), Tb (terbium), Tc (technetium), Te (tellurium), Th (thorium), Ti (titanium), Tl (thallium), Tm (thulium), Xe (xenon), Yb (ytterbium), Zn (zinc), Zr (zirconium)
03 tin (Sn)
04 gold (Au), iron (Fe), lead (Pb), neon (Ne), zinc (Zn)
05 argon (Ar), boron (B), radon (Rn), xenon (Xe)
06 barium (Ba), carbon (C), cerium (Ce), cobalt (Co), copper (Cu), curium (Cm), erbium (Er), helium (He), indium (In), iodine (I), nickel (Ni), osmium (Os), oxygen (O), radium (Ra), silver (Ag), sodium (Na)
07 arsenic (As), bismuth (Bi), bohrium (Bh), bromine (Br), cadmium (Cd), caesium (Cs), calcium (Ca), dubnium (Db), fermium (Fm), gallium (Ga), hafnium (Hf), hahnium (Ha), hassium (Hs), holmium (Ho), iridium (Ir), krypton (Kr), lithium (Li), mercury (Hg), niobium (Nb), rhenium (Re), rhodium (Rh), silicon (Si), sulphur (S), terbium (Tb), thorium (Th), thulium (Tm), uranium (U), yttrium (Y)
08 actinium (Ac), antimony (Sb), astatine (At), chlorine (Cl), chromium (Cr), europium (Eu), fluorine (F), francium (Fr), hydrogen (H), lutetium (Lu), nitrogen (N), nobelium (No), platinum (Pt), polonium (Po), rubidium (Rb), samarium (Sm), scandium (Sc), selenium (Se), tantalum (Ta), thallium (Tl), titanium (Ti), tungsten (W), vanadium (V)
09 aluminium (Al), americium (Am), berkelium (Bk), beryllium (Be), germanium (Ge), lanthanum (La), magnesium (Mg), manganese (Mn), neodymium (Nd), neptunium (Np), palladium (Pd), plutonium (Pu), potassium (K), ruthenium (Ru), strontium (Sr), tellurium (Te), ytterbium (Yb), zirconium (Zr)
10 dysprosium (Dy), gadolinium (Gd), lawrencium (Lr, Lw), meitnerium (Mt), molybdenum (Mo), phosphorus (P), promethium (Pm), seaborgium (Sg), technetium (Tc)
11 californium (Cf), einsteinium (Es), mendelevium (Md), roentgenium (Rg)
12 darmstadtium (Ds), praseodymium (Pr), protactinium (Pa)
13 rutherfordium (Rf)

• old element

03 air **04** fire **05** earth, water

elemental

05 basic **07** immense, natural, primary, radical **08** forceful, powerful **09** primitive, principal **11** fundamental, rudimentary **12** uncontrolled

elementary

04 easy **05** basic, clear **06** simple **07** primary **09** principal **10** principial **11** fundamental, rudimentary **12** introductory, uncompounded **13** uncomplicated **15** straightforward

elephant

05 Babar, jumbo, rogue **07** mammoth **08** oliphant **09** pachyderm

13 megaherbivore **14** megavertebrate

• elephant carrier

03 roc, rok, ruc **04** rukh

elephantine

04 huge, vast **05** bulky, great, heavy, large **06** clumsy **07** awkward, hulking, immense, massive, weighty **08** enormous **09** lumbering

elevate

◇ *reversal down indicator*
04 lift **05** boost, cheer, exalt, hoist, raise, rouse **06** buoy up, hike up, refine, uplift **07** advance, ennoble, gladden, magnify, promote, upgrade **08** brighten, heighten **09** intensify, sublimate **10** aggrandize, exhilarate **11** give a lift to **12** kick upstairs **14** put on a pedestal **15** move up the ladder

elevated

◇ *anagram indicator*
◇ *reversal down indicator*
04 high **05** grand, great, lofty, moral, noble **06** aerial, lifted, raised, rising **07** exalted, hoisted, stilted, sublime, uplying **08** advanced, lifted up, towering, uplifted **09** dignified, high-flown, high-toned, important **10** high-raised, high-reared **11** exhilarated

elevation

04 back, face, hill, rise, side **05** agger, arsis, front, leg-up, mound, mount, ridge **06** aspect, façade, height, random, uplift **07** dignity, majesty, upright **08** altitude, eminence, foothill, grandeur, monticle, nobility, tallness, upheaval **09** go-getting, loftiness, monticule, promotion, sublimity, upgrading **10** exaltation, monticulus, preferment **11** advancement, sublimation **14** aggrandizement **15** step up the ladder

elevator

04 jack, lift

eleven

02 XI

elf

03 imp **04** peri, puck **05** dwarf, fairy, gnome, pigmy, pixie, pygmy, troll **06** goblin, sprite, urchin **07** banshee, brownie **08** entangle **09** hobgoblin **10** leprechaun

• elf's child

03 auf

elfin

03 fay, fey, fie **05** small **06** dainty, elfish, impish, petite **07** elflike, playful, puckish **08** charming, delicate **09** sprightly **10** frolicsome **11** mischievous

elicit

04 pump, tose, toze **05** cause, educe, evoke, exact, sweep, toaze, wrest **06** derive, extort, obtain **07** draw out, extract, mole out, worm out **08** bring out, outlearn **09** call forth

eligibility

09 allowance, condition **11** entitlement, suitability

12 desirability **13** acceptability, qualification

eligible
03 fit **06** proper, worthy **07** fitting **08** entitled, suitable **09** desirable, qualified **10** acceptable **11** appropriate

eliminate
03 ice, rid **04** beat, cure, do in, drop, kill, lick, omit, wipe **05** expel, whack **06** cancel, cut out, defeat, delete, hammer, murder, reject, remove, rub out, thrash **07** abolish, bump off, conquer, deep-six, exclude, take out, wipe out **08** get rid of, knock out, preclude, stamp out **09** cancel out, dispose of, disregard, eradicate, liquidate, overwhelm **10** annihilate, do away with, extinguish, put an end to, put a stop to **11** exterminate **12** dispense with

elimination
07 quietus, removal **08** deletion, disposal, omission **09** abolition, exclusion, expulsion, rejection **11** eradication

élite
04 best, pick **05** cream, elect, noble **06** choice, gentry, jet set **08** nobility, selected **09** exclusive **10** first-class, upper-class **11** aristocracy, high society **12** aristocratic, upper classes **13** establishment **14** crème de la crème, pick of the bunch

elixir
04 pith **05** daffy, syrup, tinct **06** potion, remedy **07** arcanum, cure-all, essence, extract, mixture, nostrum, panacea **08** solution, tincture **09** principle **11** concentrate **12** quintessence

elliptical
04 oval **05** ovoid, terse **07** concise, cryptic, dubious, laconic, oblique, obscure, oviform, ovoidal **08** abstruse, succinct **09** ambiguous, condensed, egg-shaped, recondite **12** concentrated, unfathomable **13** comprehensive

elocution
06 speech **07** diction, oratory **08** delivery, phrasing, rhetoric **09** eloquence, utterance **11** enunciation **12** articulation **13** pronunciation **15** voice production

elongate
06 extend **07** draw out, prolong, stretch **08** lengthen, protract **10** make longer, stretch out

elongated
04 long, shot **08** extended **09** prolonged, stretched **10** lengthened, protracted

elope
04 bolt, flee **05** leave **06** decamp, escape, run off **07** abscond, do a bunk, make off, run away, scarper, vamoose **08** slip away **09** disappear, do a runner, skedaddle, steal away **10** hightail it, hit

the road **11** hit the trail **14** make a bolt for it **15** make a break for it

eloquence
07 blarney, diction, fluency, oratory **08** facility, rhetoric **09** elocution, facundity, gassiness **10** expression **11** flow of words **12** forcefulness, gift of the gab **14** articulateness, expressiveness, persuasiveness

eloquent
04 glib **05** vivid, vocal **06** fluent, moving **07** voluble **08** forceful, graceful, stirring **09** effective, Mercurial, plausible **10** articulate, Ciceronian, expressive, persuasive, well-spoken **11** Demosthenic **12** honey-tongued **13** silver-tongued, well-expressed

El Salvador
02 ES **03** SLV

elsewhere
06 abroad, absent **07** not here, removed **10** otherwhere **13** somewhere else **14** in another place, to another place

• **and elsewhere**
04 et al **07** et alibi

elucidate
06 fill in, unfold **07** clarify, clear up, explain, expound **08** simplify, spell out **09** exemplify, explicate, interpret, make clear **10** dilucidate, illuminate, illustrate **11** shed light on, state simply **12** throw light on **13** give an example

elucidation
05 gloss **07** comment **08** footnote **10** annotation, commentary, exposition, marginalia **11** explanation, explication **12** illumination, illustration **13** clarification **14** interpretation

elude
◇ *deletion indicator*
04 bilk, duck, flee, foil, jink, slip **05** avoid, dodge, evade, shirk, stump **06** baffle, delude, escape, puzzle, thwart **08** confound, shake off **09** frustrate **10** circumvent **11** get away from

elusive
05 dodgy **06** shifty, slippy, subtle, tricky **07** evasive **08** baffling, puzzling, slippery **09** deceptive, transient **10** intangible, misleading, transitory **11** hard to catch, indefinable **12** unanalysable **15** difficult to find

elusiveness
06 puzzle **08** subtlety **10** transience **11** evasiveness **13** intangibility **14** indefinability, transitoriness

emaciated
04 bony, lean, thin **05** drawn, gaunt **06** meagre, skinny, wasted **07** haggard, pinched, scrawny **08** anorexic, skeletal **10** attenuated, cadaverous, wanthriven **11** thin as a rake **14** all skin and bone

emaciation
07 atrophy **08** boniness, leanness,

thinness **09** gauntness, symptosis **11** haggardness, scrawniness, tabefaction

emanate
04 come, emit, flow, stem **05** arise, exude, issue **06** derive, emerge, exhale, spring, vanish **07** give off, give out, proceed, radiate, send out **09** discharge, originate

emanation
04 aura, flow **06** efflux **08** effluent, effusion, emission **09** discharge, effluence, effluvium, effluxion, radiation **10** exhalation

emancipate
04 free **05** loose, untie **06** unyoke **07** deliver, manumit, release, set free, unchain **08** liberate, set loose, unfetter **09** discharge, unshackle **11** enfranchise **14** forisfamiliate

emancipation
07 freedom, freeing, liberty, release **09** discharge, unbinding **10** liberation, unchaining **11** deliverance, manumission, setting free, unfettering **15** enfranchisement

emasculate
04 geld, spay **06** neuter, soften, weaken **07** cripple **08** castrate, enervate **10** debilitate, impoverish

emasculation
09 abatement, lessening, reduction, weakening **10** moderation **12** debilitation, diminishment **14** impoverishment

embalm
04 balm **05** store **06** balsam, lay out **07** cherish, mummify **08** conserve, enshrine, preserve, treasure **10** consecrate

embankment
03 dam **04** bank, bund **05** levee, mound **06** staith **07** banking, rampart, remblai, seabank, staithe **08** causeway, stopbank **09** earthwork

embargo
03 ban, bar **04** stop, tapu **05** block, check, seize **06** impede **07** barrier, seizure **08** blockage, obstruct, prohibit, restrain, restrict, stoppage **09** hindrance, interdict, proscribe, restraint **10** impediment **11** obstruction, prohibition, restriction **12** interdiction, proscription

embark
04 ship **05** board **06** inship **08** go aboard, take ship **09** board ship

• **embark on**
05 begin, enter, start **06** engage **07** enter on **08** commence, initiate, set about **09** undertake **10** launch into **11** venture into

embarkation
06 vessel **08** boarding, entrance, mounting **09** embussing, emplaning, getting-on **11** entrainment

embarrass

◇ *anagram indicator*
05 shame, upset **06** show up
07 chagrin, confuse, fluster, mortify, perplex **08** distress, encumber, incumber **09** discomfit, humiliate **10** discompose, disconcert **11** make ashamed, make awkward
14 discountenance

embarrassed

◇ *anagram indicator*
03 red **05** upset **06** guilty, shamed, uneasy **07** abashed, ashamed, awkward, shown up **08** confused, sheepish **09** ill at ease, mortified, perplexed, unnatural **10** distressed, humiliated **11** constrained, discomfited **12** disconcerted **13** self-conscious, uncomfortable

embarrassing

06 touchy, tricky **07** awkward, painful, shaming **08** shameful **09** sensitive, upsetting **10** indelicate, mortifying **11** distressing, humiliating
12 compromising, cringe-making, cringeworthy, discomfiting
13 disconcerting, uncomfortable

embarrassment

03 fix, jam **04** gene, mess **05** guilt, shame **06** excess, pickle, plight, scrape, unease **07** chagrin, dilemma, surplus **08** distress, embarras **09** abundance, confusion, profusion **10** constraint, difficulty, perplexity, uneasiness **11** awkwardness, bashfulness, humiliation, predicament **12** difficulties, discomfiture, discomposure, sheepishness
13 mortification, overabundance
14 superabundance

embassy

07 mission **08** legation, ministry **09** consulate, embassade, embassage **10** commission, delegation, deputation

embed

03 bed, fix, lay, set **04** dock, nest, root, sink **05** drive, inlay, plant **06** hammer, insert **07** implant

embellish

03 pan **04** deck, gild, trim, vary **05** adorn, grace **06** bedeck, enrich **07** dress up, enhance, festoon, garnish **08** beautify, decorate, ornament **09** bespangle, elaborate, embroider **10** exaggerate

embellishment

07 garnish, gilding **08** ornament, trimming, vignette **09** adornment, agreement **10** decoration, embroidery, enrichment **11** elaboration, enhancement **13** ornamentation
• **musical embellishment**
04 turn **07** melisma, roulade
09 fioritura, grace note

embers

05 ashes, coals **06** gleeds **07** cinders, clinker, residue **08** charcoal **09** live coals

embezzle

03 nab, rob **04** nick **05** filch, pinch, steal **06** impair, pilfer, rip off
07 purloin, swindle **08** peculate, shoulder **09** defalcate **11** appropriate **14** misappropriate

embezzlement

05 fraud, theft **07** nabbing, nicking, swindle, swizzle **08** filching, stealing **09** pilfering **11** defalcation
13 appropriation

embezzler

05 cheat, crook, fraud, thief **06** con man, robber **07** diddler **08** swindler **09** peculator **10** defalcator

embittered

04 sour **05** angry **06** bitter, piqued, soured **07** rankled **08** enfested **09** rancorous, resentful **11** disaffected, discouraged, exasperated
12 disenchanted, disheartened
13 disillusioned

emblazon

04 laud **05** adorn, extol, paint **06** blazon, colour, depict, praise **07** display, glorify, publish, trumpet **08** decorate, ornament, proclaim **09** celebrate, embellish, publicize **10** illuminate

emblem

04 flag, logo, mark, sign, type **05** badge, crest, image, token, totem **06** device, figure, symbol **08** colophon, insignia **09** symbolize **11** service mark **14** representation
See also **emblem of authority** *under* **authority**

emblematic

07 typical **08** symbolic **10** figurative, symbolical **11** allegorical
12 emblematical, representing
14 representative

embodiment

04 soul, type **05** model **06** vessel **07** epitome, example **10** expression **11** incarnation, realization
12 quintessence **13** concentration, incorporation, manifestation
14 representation, representative
15 exemplification, personification

embody

◇ *containment indicator*
05 shape **06** take in, typify **07** collect, combine, contain, express, include

08 manifest, organize, stand for **09** corporify, exemplify, incarnate, integrate, personify, represent, symbolize **10** assimilate, synonymize **11** encarnalize, impersonate, incorporate **12** substantiate **13** bring together

embolden

04 fire, stir **05** cheer, nerve, rouse **07** animate, hearten, inflame, inspire **08** make bold, reassure, vitalize **09** encourage, make brave, stimulate **10** invigorate, strengthen **13** give courage to

embrace

◇ *containment indicator*
◇ *hidden indicator*
03 hug **04** bind, clip, coll, fold, hold, lock, neck, pash, snog, span, wrap **05** admit, adopt, bosom, brace, clasp, cover, grasp, halse, hause, hawse, inarm **06** abrazo, accept, clinch, cuddle, enfold, enlace, fasten, inclip, infold, inlace, smooch, strain, take in, take up **07** colling, contain, espouse, include, involve, necking, receive, squeeze, welcome **08** accolade, canoodle, complect, compress, comprise **09** embrasure, encompass **10** tangle with **11** incorporate, take on board **13** slap and tickle **14** receive eagerly

embrocation

03 rub **05** cream, salve **06** lotion **07** epithem **08** liniment, ointment

embroider

03 sew **04** darn, purl, work **05** sprig **06** colour, enrich, stitch **07** dress up, enhance, garnish, tambour
08 decorate **09** elaborate, embellish, hemstitch **10** exaggerate **11** cross-stitch

embroidery

04 work **05** braid **06** crewel, sewing **07** apparel, cutwork, orphrey, sampler, tambour, tatting **08** braiding, fagoting, tapestry **09** faggoting, fancywork, stump work **10** canvas-work, needlework **11** needlecraft, needlepoint **13** embellishment, ornamentation

embroil

◇ *anagram indicator*
05 mix up **06** enmesh **07** involve **08** distract, draw into, entangle **09** catch up in, implicate **11** incriminate

embryo
04 germ, root, seed **06** basics, foetus
07 nucleus **08** gastrula, plantule
09 beginning, rudiments **11** unborn child

• **embryo transfer**
02 ET

embryonic
05 early **07** primary **08** emerging, germinal, immature, inchoate, unformed **09** beginning, fledgling, incipient **10** elementary
11 rudimentary, undeveloped

emend
◇ *anagram indicator*
03 fix **04** edit **05** alter, amend
06 polish, redact, refine, repair, revise
07 correct, improve, rectify, rewrite
09 castigate

emendation
◇ *anagram indicator*
07 editing **08** revision
09 amendment, redaction, rewriting
10 alteration, correction, refinement
11 corrigendum, improvement
13 rectification

emerald
07 smaragd

emerge
◇ *anagram indicator*
◇ *hidden indicator*
03 out **04** rise **05** arise, issue
06 appear, cast up, crop up, turn up
07 come out, debouch, develop, emanate, outcrop, proceed, surface, turn out **09** come forth, transpire
10 be revealed **11** become known, come to light, materialize **12** come into view **14** become apparent

emergence
04 dawn, rise **05** issue **06** advent, coming **07** arrival, outcrop
08 disclose, eclosion **09** unfolding
10 appearance, disclosure
11 development, springing-up

emergency
03 fix **04** mess **05** extra, pinch, spare
06 back-up, crisis, crunch, danger, pickle, plight, scrape, strait, urgent
07 dilemma, reserve **08** accident, calamity, disaster, exigence, exigency, fall-back, hot water, quandary
09 extremity, immediate **10** difficulty, substitute **11** alternative, catastrophe, predicament, top-priority
13 extraordinary

emergent
06 coming, rising **07** budding
08 emerging **09** coming out, embryonic, fledgling **10** burgeoning, developing **11** independent

emetic
04 puke **05** puker, vomit **06** emetin, ipecac **07** emetine **08** emetical, vomitary, vomitive, vomitory
11 ipecacuanha, sanguinaria

emigrate
04 move **06** depart **07** migrate

08 relocate, resettle **10** move abroad
13 leave your home

emigration
06 exodus **07** journey, removal
09 departure, migration **10** relocation
12 expatriation, moving abroad

eminence
03 tor **04** berg, fame, hill, knob, note, rank **05** ridge **06** esteem, height, renown **07** dignity, stature **08** altitude, majority, prestige **09** advantage, celebrity, greatness, prelation
10 importance, notability, prominence, promontory, reputation, trochanter **11** distinction, pre-eminence, sovereignty, superiority
14 honourableness **15** illustriousness

eminent
04 high **05** first, grand, great, noted
06 famous **07** notable **08** elevated, esteemed, renowned, superior
09 important, prominent, respected, well-known **10** celebrated, noteworthy, pre-eminent
11 conspicuous, high-ranking, illustrious, outstanding, prestigious, superlative **13** distinguished

eminently
04 high, most, very, well **06** highly
07 greatly, notably **08** signally
09 extremely, obviously
10 remarkably, strikingly
11 exceedingly, prominently
12 surpassingly **13** conspicuously, exceptionally, outstandingly, par excellence

emissary
03 spy **05** agent, envoy, scout
06 deputy, herald **07** courier
08 delegate, diplomat, outgoing
09 go-between, messenger
10 ambassador **12** intermediary
14 representative

emission
04 vent **05** issue **06** escape **07** release
08 effusion, ejection **09** diffusion, discharge, emanation, exudation, giving-off, giving-out, radiation
10 exhalation, outpouring, production
11 ejaculation **12** transmission

emit
03 ren, rin, run, say **04** boak, bock, boke, leak, ooze, pass, shed, spew, vent, void **05** eject, eruct, exude, issue, sound, speak, throw, utter, voice
06 exhale, expire, let out **07** diffuse, emanate, excrete, express, give off, give out, pour out, produce, radiate, release, send out **08** eructate, throw out, vocalize **09** discharge, give forth, send forth, verbalize

emollient
03 oil **04** balm **05** cream, salve
06 lotion **07** calming, lenient, unguent
08 balsamic, lenitive, liniment, ointment, poultice, soap-ball, soothing **09** appeasing, assuaging, assuasive, demulcent, placatory, softening **10** mitigative, mollifying,

palliative **11** moisturizer
12 conciliatory, moisturizing, propitiatory

emolument
03 fee, pay **04** gain, hire **05** wages
06 charge, profit, return, reward, salary
07 benefit, payment, profits, stipend
08 earnings **09** advantage, allowance
10 honorarium, recompense
12 compensation, remuneration

emotion
03 ire, joy **04** envy, fear, hate, pang, turn **05** anger, dread, grief, sense, shock, spasm, whirl **06** affect, ardour, motion, sorrow, spirit, thrill, warmth
07 anoesis, despair, ecstasy, feeling, fervour, passion, sadness, upsurge
08 movement, reaction, surprise
09 affection, happiness, reverence, sensation, sentiment, sublimity, transport, vehemence **10** excitement
11 sensibility

• **expression of emotion**
01 O **02** ha, oh **03** hah, hoo, wow
05 arrah, hoo-oo, wowee

• **sign of emotion**
04 tear

emotional
04 warm **05** fiery, moved, soppy
06 ardent, fervid, heated, loving, moving, red-hot, roused, tender
07 emotive, feeling, fervent, glowing, gushing, radiant, soulful, tearful, zealous **08** effusive, exciting, hysteric, pathetic, poignant, stirring, swelling, touching, white-hot **09** excitable, schmaltzy, sensitive, thrilling **10** hot-blooded, hysterical, passionate, responsive **11** full-hearted, impassioned, overcharged, sentimental, susceptible, tear-jerking, tempestuous **12** enthusiastic, gut-wrenching, heartwarming, soul-stirring **13** demonstrative, psychological, temperamental

emotionally
06 warmly **07** tensely **08** ardently, lovingly, tenderly **09** awkwardly, fervently, nervously, zealously
10 delicately, poignantly, touchingly
11 sensitively **12** passionately
13 sentimentally, under pressure
14 heartwarmingly **15** controversially, demonstratively, psychologically, temperamentally

emotionless
04 cold, cool **05** blank **06** frigid, remote **07** deadpan, distant, glacial, unmoved **08** clinical, cold-fish, detached, toneless **09** impassive, unfeeling **10** antiseptic, impassible, insensible, phlegmatic, unaffected, unblinking **11** cold-blooded, indifferent, unemotional
13 imperturbable **15** undemonstrative

emotive
06 touchy **07** awkward **08** delicate
09 emotional, sensitive
12 inflammatory **13** controversial

empathize
05 share **07** comfort, feel for, support **10** understand **12** have a rapport, identify with

emperor
03 Emp, Imp **04** czar, Inca, king, tsar **05** kesar, tenno **06** kaiser, keasar, mikado, purple, shogun **08** imperial, padishah **09** imperator, sovereign **12** kaisar-i-Hindi

Emperors include:
03 Leo
04 John, Nero, Otho, Otto, Paul, Pu Yi
05 Akbar (the Great), Babur, Basil, Boris, Galba, Henry, Louis, Murad, Nerva, Pedro, Peter, Selim, Titus
06 Caesar (Julius), Conrad, Joseph, Jovian, Julian, Justin, Mehmet, Philip (the Arab), Rudolf, Trajan
07 Agustín (de Itúrbide), Akihito, Alamgir, Alexius, Baldwin, Charles, Charles (the Bald), Charles (the Fat), Francis, Gordian, Hadrian, Leopold, Lothair, Marcian, Michael, Severus, William
08 Augustus, Aurelius, Caligula, Claudius, Commodus, Constans, Domitian, Galerius, Hirohito, Honorius, Jahangir, Licinius, Matthias, Maximian, Napoleon, Nicholas, Süleyman, Tiberius, Valerian
09 Alexander, Antoninus, Atahualpa, Aurangzeb, Caracalla, Carausius, Ferdinand, Frederick, Gallienus, Heraclius, Justinian, Maxentius, Montezuma, Mutsuhito, Shah Jahan, Sigismund, Vespasian, Vitellius, Yoshihito
10 Andronicus, Augustulus, Diocletian, Elagabalus, Kublai Khan, Maximilian, Meiji Tenno, Theodosius
11 Charlemagne, Constantine, Constantius, Jean Jacques, Valentinian
12 Chandragupta, Heliogabalus, John Comnenus, Samudragupta
13 Antoninus Pius, Francis Joseph, Haile Selassie
14 Marcus Aurelius
15 Alexius Comnenus

See also **Roman**

emphasis
04 birr, mark **05** focus, force, power **06** accent, moment, stress, weight **07** urgency **08** priority, strength **09** attention, intensity **10** importance, insistence, prominence **11** pre-eminence **12** accentuation, positiveness, significance, underscoring
• **expression of emphasis**
04 Jeez **05** Jeeze **07** you know

emphasize
06 accent, play up, stress, weight **07** dwell on, enforce, feature, point up **08** heighten, insist on **09** highlight, intensify, press home, punctuate, spotlight, underline **10** accentuate,

foreground, strengthen **11** put stress on **14** bring to the fore **15** call attention to, draw attention to

emphatic
04 firm **05** vivid **06** direct, marked, strong **07** certain, decided, earnest, marcato, telling **08** absolute, decisive, definite, distinct, forceful, forcible, positive, powerful, striking, vehement, vigorous **09** energetic, important, insistent, momentous **10** conclusive, expressive, impressive, pronounced, punctuated **11** categorical, distinctive, significant, unequivocal **12** unmistakable **13** unmistakeable

emphatically
06 firmly **08** in spades, strongly **09** certainly **10** absolutely, definitely, forcefully, vehemently, vigorously **11** insistently **13** categorically, distinctively, unequivocally

empire
03 Emp **04** firm, rule, sway **05** power, realm **06** domain, empery **07** command, company, control, kingdom **08** business, dominion, province **09** authority, supremacy, territory **10** consortium, government **11** corporation, sovereignty **12** commonwealth, conglomerate, jurisdiction, organization **13** multinational

Empires and kingdoms include:
04 Cush, Kush, Moab
05 Akkad, Alban, Media, Mogul, Roman
06 Naples
07 Argolis, Assyria, Bohemia, British, Chinese, Galicia, Ottoman, Persian
08 Dalriada, Lombardy, Sardinia
09 Abyssinia, Byzantine, Holy Roman
10 New Kingdom, Old Kingdom
11 Northumbria
13 Middle Kingdom
15 Austro-Hungarian

See also **classification**
• **part of empire**
04 land

empirical
08 observed **09** practical, pragmatic **11** a posteriori **12** experiential, experimental

empirically
11 practically **13** pragmatically **14** experientially, experimentally

employ
03 ply, use **04** fill, hire **05** apply, exert, spend **06** bestow, draw on, engage, enlist, expend, occupy, retain, sign up, take on, take up **07** appoint, exploit, recruit, service, utilize **08** exercise, put to use **09** make use of **10** apprentice, commission **11** bring to bear **13** bring into play **15** put on the payroll, take advantage of

employed
04 busy, used **05** hired **06** active, in work **07** earning, engaged, working

08 occupied, with a job **11** preoccupied **12** in employment

employee
03 cog, man **04** hand, help **05** gofer, woman **06** casual, worker **08** labourer, munchkin **09** assistant, job-holder, operative, rainmaker **10** wage-earner, waterclerk, working man **12** working woman **13** member of staff, working person

employer
03 guv **04** boss, firm, head, user **05** malik, melik, owner **06** gaffer, master, old man **07** company, manager, padrone, skipper **08** business, director, governor, mistress **09** executive **10** management, proprietor, taskmaster, workmaster **12** entrepreneur, organization, taskmistress, workmistress **13** establishment

employment
03 job, use **04** hire, line, ploy, post, work **05** craft, place, trade **06** employ, hiring, métier **07** calling, pursuit, service **08** business, position, taking-on, vocation **09** signing-up, situation **10** engagement, enlistment, livelihood, occupation, profession **11** application, recruitment **12** exercitation **14** apprenticeship

emporium
04 fair, mart, shop **05** store **06** bazaar, market **08** boutique **11** market-place **13** establishment **15** department store

empower
05 equip **06** enable, permit **07** certify, entitle, license, qualify, set free, warrant **08** accredit, delegate, sanction **09** authorize **10** commission **11** give means to, give power to

empress
03 Emp, Imp **05** queen, ruler **07** czarina, tsarina **08** czaritsa, imperial, kaiserin, tsaritsa **09** imperator, sovereign

Empresses include:
02 Lü, Wu
03 Zoë
04 Anna, Cixi
05 Irene, Livia
06 Helena (St), Tz'u Hsi, Wu Chao, Wu Zhao
07 Eugénie, Wu Zhaov
08 Adelaide (St), Cunegund (St), Faustina, Nur Jahan, Theodora, Victoria
09 Agrippina (the Younger), Alexandra, Catherine, Catherine (the Great), Elizabeth, Joséphine, Kunigundé (St), Messalina, Old Buddha, Theophano
11 Marie Louise
12 Anna Ivanovna, Maria Theresa
13 Livia Drusilla

emptiness
04 void **05** blank **06** hiatus, hollow, hunger, vacuum **07** inanity, vacancy,

vacuity 08 bareness, futility, voidness **09** unreality **10** barrenness, desolation, flatulence, hollowness, vacantness **11** aimlessness, uselessness **13** senselessness, worthlessness **15** ineffectiveness, meaninglessness, purposelessness

empty
◊ *middle deletion indicator*
03 gut **04** bare, boss, free, idle, lade, pump, teem, toom, vain, void **05** addle, blank, clear, drain, go out, inane, issue, leave, strip, use up, waste **06** barren, devoid, frothy, futile, gousty, hollow, hot-air, hungry, unload, unpack, unreal, vacant, vacate **07** aimless, deadpan, deplete, exhaust, flow out, pour out, trivial, turn out, useless, vacuate, vacuous, viduous **08** clear out, deserted, desolate, evacuate, soulless, unfilled **09** available, discharge, fruitless, insincere, pointless, senseless, worthless **10** unoccupied **11** ineffective, ineffectual, meaningless, purposeless, unfurnished, uninhabited **13** insubstantial **14** expressionless, unsatisfactory **15** with nothing in it

empty-headed
04 daft, vain **05** batty, dippy, ditsy, ditzy, dopey, dotty, inane, silly **06** scatty, stupid **07** foolish, vacuous **09** frivolous **13** rattle-brained, unintelligent **14** feather-brained, scatter-brained

emulate
04 copy, echo **05** emule, match, mimic, rival **06** aemule, follow **07** imitate, vie with **09** ambitious, reproduce **11** compete with, contend with **15** model yourself on

emulation
06 strife **07** contest, copying, echoing, mimicry, paragon, rivalry **08** matching **09** challenge, following, imitation, rivalship **10** contention **11** competition **12** contestation

enable
03 fit, let **04** able, help **05** allow, endue, equip **06** permit **07** empower, entitle, further, license, prepare, qualify, warrant **08** accredit, sanction, validate **09** commission, facilitate, make easier **12** make possible **13** pave the way for **14** clear the way for

enact
04 pass, play, rule **05** order **06** act out, decree, depict, ordain, ratify **07** approve, command, make law, perform, portray **08** appear as, sanction **09** authorize, establish, legislate, represent

enactment
03 act, law **04** bill, play, rule **05** edict, order **06** acting, decree **07** command, measure, passing, playing, purview, staging, statute **08** approval, sanction

09 ordinance, portrayal **10** performing, regulation **11** commandment, institution, legislation, performance **12** ratification **13** authorization **14** representation

enamoured
03 mad **04** fond, keen, wild **05** taken **07** charmed, smitten **08** besotted **09** bewitched, enchanted, entranced **10** captivated, enthralled, fascinated, infatuated, in love with

en bloc
05 as one **07** en masse, in a body **08** as a group, as a whole, ensemble **09** all at once, wholesale **11** all together

encampment
04 base, camp, duar, laer **05** douar, dowar, tents **06** laager **07** bivouac, hutment, manyata **08** barracks, campsite, manyatta, quarters **13** camping-ground

encapsulate
◊ *containment indicator*
03 pot **05** sum up **06** digest, précis, take in, typify **07** abridge, capture, contain, include **08** compress, condense **09** epitomize, exemplify, represent, summarize

encapsulation
06 digest, précis **07** summary **10** expression **14** representation **15** exemplification

encase
04 line, wrap **05** bound, cover, frame **07** confine, enclose, envelop **08** surround

enchant
05 charm, spell **06** allure, appeal, thrill **07** attract, becharm, beguile, bewitch, delight, enamour, enthral, glamour **08** entrance, sirenize **09** captivate, enrapture, fascinate, hypnotize, mesmerize, spellbind

enchanter
05 magus, witch **06** wizard **07** warlock **08** conjurer, magician, sorcerer **09** archimage, mesmerist **10** reim-kennar **11** necromancer, spellbinder

enchanting
06 lovely **07** magical, winsome **08** alluring, charming, pleasant **09** appealing, endearing, ravishing, wonderful **10** attractive, bewitching, delightful, entrancing **11** captivating, fascinating, mesmerizing **12** irresistible

enchantment
05 bliss, charm, magic, spell **06** allure, appeal, glamor **07** delight, ecstasy, glamour, gramary, rapture, sorcery **08** gramarye, malefice, witching, wizardry **09** hypnotism, mesmerism **10** allurement, necromancy, witchcraft **11** conjuration, fascination, incantation **14** attractiveness

enchantress
04 vamp **05** Circe, fairy, lamia, siren, witch **07** charmer **08** conjurer, magician **09** sorceress **10** seductress **11** femme fatale, necromancer, spellbinder

encircle
◊ *containment indicator*
04 belt, clip, gird, hoop, pale, ring, wind **05** crowd, girth, hem in, inorb, orbit, twine, wheel **06** circle, embail, enfold, engird, enlace, enring, girdle, inlace, stemme **07** close in, compass, enclose, envelop, environ, enwheel **08** surround **09** encompass **12** circumscribe

enclose
◊ *containment indicator*
02 in **03** box, pen, pin **04** cage, case, coop, hold, ring, seal, tine, womb, wrap **05** bound, bower, clasp, cover, fence, frame, hedge, hem in, pound, put in **06** circle, cocoon, corral, embale, emboss, encase, enfold, enlock, girdle, immure, incase, infold, inhoop, insert, pocket, prison, shut in, take in **07** close in, compass, confine, contain, embound, embowel, embrace, enchase, envelop, include, seclude **08** conclude, encircle, send with, surround **09** encompass, ring-fence **10** comprehend, interclude **12** circumscribe

enclosed
03 enc **04** encl, pend, pent **07** bosomed, recluse **08** included

enclosure
03 box, enc, haw, pen, pit, ree, ren, rin, run, sty **04** area, bawn, boma, cage, camp, encl, fank, fold, hope, lair, pale, peel, pele, reed, ring, town, yard **05** arena, close, court, garth, kraal, pound, sekos, stell **06** corral, runway **07** enclave, fencing, haining, paddock, parrock, pightle, pinfold **08** addition, cloister, compound, enceinte, seraglio, stockade, townland **09** inclusion, insertion **10** encincture

encode
05 ravel **06** cipher, garble **07** encrypt, obscure **08** disguise, encipher, scramble **11** put into code **14** make mysterious

encompass
◊ *containment indicator*
04 gird, hold, ring, span **05** admit, bathe, brace, cover, hem in **06** begird, circle, embody, enfold, infold, shut in, sphere, take in **07** close in, confine, contain, embrace, enclose, envelop, include, involve, procure **08** cincture, comprise, encircle, surround **10** circumvent, comprehend **11** incorporate **12** circumscribe

encore
03 bis **06** ancora, repeat, replay **10** repetition

encounter
04 cope, face, meet, tilt **05** brush, clash, close, fight, joust, match, run-in,

set-to **06** action, battle, combat, engage, oppose, ruffle, strive, tackle, tussle **07** contact, contend, contest, dispute, meeting, run into **08** bump into, conflict, confront, cope with, deal with, happen on, skirmish, struggle **09** clash with, collision, rencontre, run across **10** chance upon, come across, engagement, experience, rencounter, rendezvous **11** be faced with, be up against, compete with, grapple with **12** do battle with **13** come up against, confrontation, passage of arms, stumble across **15** cross swords with

encourage
03 aid **04** abet, back, coax, fuel, help, lift, root, spur, stir, sway, urge **05** boost, cheer, egg on, gee up, jolly, pep up, rally, rouse **06** assist, buck up, buoy up, exhort, favour, foster, incite, induce, prompt, second, spirit, spur on, stroke **07** advance, animate, cheer on, cherish, comfort, console, forward, further, hearten, inspire, promote, support, sustain, upcheer, win over **08** accorage, advocate, convince, embolden, inspirit, motivate, persuade, reassure, talk into **09** accourage, enhearten, influence, stimulate **10** barrack for, strengthen **14** be supportive to

encouragement
03 aid **04** help **05** boost, cheer **06** come-on, urging **07** backing, coaxing, comfort, pep talk, succour, support **08** cheering, stimulus **09** incentive, promotion **10** assistance, heartening, incitement, motivation, persuasion **11** consolation, endorsement, exhortation, furtherance, inspiration, reassurance, stimulation **12** shot in the arm
• **expression of encouragement**
02 ha, on **03** hah, olé, via, yay **04** come, sa sa **05** heigh, hollo, there **06** giddap, now now **07** attaboy, come now **08** attagirl, come come **09** ups-a-daisy, upsy-daisy

encouraging
04 rosy **06** bright **07** hopeful **08** cheerful, cheering **09** hortative, hortatory, incentive, inspiring, promising, uplifting **10** auspicious, comforting, heartening, protreptic, reassuring, supportive **11** cohortative, stimulating **12** satisfactory **14** proceleusmatic

encroach
03 jet **05** pinch, usurp **06** invade, trench **07** impinge, intrude, overrun **08** entrench, infringe, intrench, overstep, trespass **10** infiltrate, muscle in on **11** make inroads

encroachment
06 inroad **08** invasion, trespass **09** incursion, intrusion **11** purpresture, trespassing **12** entrenchment, infiltration, infringement, intrenchment, overstepping

encrypt
05 ravel **06** cipher, encode, garble **07** obscure **08** disguise, encipher, scramble **11** put into code **14** make mysterious

encumber
03 jam **04** cram, load, pack **05** block, check, cramp, stuff **06** accloy, burden, hamper, hinder, impede, retard, saddle, strain, stress **07** bog down, burthen, congest, oppress, overlay, prevent **08** handicap, obstruct, overload, restrain, slow down **09** constrain, embarrass, weigh down **13** inconvenience

encumbrance
04 load **05** cross **06** burden, strain, stress, weight **08** handicap, obstacle **09** albatross, cumbrance, hindrance, liability, millstone, restraint **10** constraint, difficulty, impediment, obligation **11** obstruction **13** inconvenience **14** responsibility

encyclopedia
04 ency **05** encyc

encyclopedic
04 vast **05** broad **07** in-depth **08** complete, thorough **09** universal **10** exhaustive **11** compendious, wide-ranging **12** all-embracing, all-inclusive **13** comprehensive, thoroughgoing **15** all-encompassing

end
◊ *tail selection indicator*
01 Z **03** aim, tip **04** abut, area, butt, doom, edge, fine, goal, part, ruin, side, stop, stub, tail, term **05** cease, close, death, dying, field, issue, limit, omega, point, scrap **06** aspect, be over, border, branch, demise, design, die out, ending, expire, finale, finish, intent, margin, motive, object, period, reason, region, result, run out, target, upshot, wind up **07** abolish, destroy, outcome, purpose, remnant, section, vestige **08** boundary, break off, complete, conclude, dissolve, downfall, epilogue, fade away, fragment, round off **09** cessation, checkmate, culminate, extremity, intention, leftovers, objective, remainder, terminate **10** annihilate, completion, conclusion, dénouement, department, extinction, extinguish **11** come to an end, consequence, culmination, destruction, discontinue, dissolution, exterminate, termination **12** bring to an end **13** extermination
• **at an end**
02 up **03** oer **04** over
• **at the end of**
◊ *juxtaposition indicator*
◊ *tail selection indicator*
• **at the far end**
03 out
• **east end**
04 apse
• **ends**
◊ *ends selection indicator*

• **nearly at an end**
04 late
• **the end**
06 enough **07** too much **08** the limit, the worst **10** unbearable **11** intolerable, unendurable **12** insufferable, the final blow, the last straw **15** beyond endurance

endanger
04 risk **06** expose, hazard, risque **07** imperil **08** threaten **09** prejudice, put at risk **10** compromise, jeopardize **11** periclitate, put in danger **13** put in jeopardy

endearing
04 cute **05** sweet **07** lovable, winsome **08** adorable, charming, engaging, loveable **09** appealing **10** attractive, delightful, enchanting **11** captivating

endearment
04 love **07** pet-name **08** fondness **09** affection, sweet talk **10** attachment, diminutive, hypocorism **12** sweet nothing **15** term of affection
• **term of endearment**
03 bud, hon, luv, pet, pug **04** burd, cony, dear, dove, fool, love, peat **05** chick, chuck, coney, ducks, ducky, heart, hinny, honey, jarta, lovey, mopsy, mouse, popsy, puggy, sugar, yarta, yarto **06** flower, monkey, moppet, pigsny **07** alannah, chuckie, cupcake, pigsney, pigsnie, princox **08** honeybun, precious, princock, treasure **09** pillicock, sugarplum **10** honeybunch, honey-chile, sweetie-pie **11** chick-a-biddy **12** chick-a-diddle

endeavour
02 go **03** aim, try **04** bash, seek, shot, stab **05** assay, crack, Morse **06** aspire, effort, labour, strive **07** attempt, venture, working **08** striving, struggle **09** take pains, undertake **10** do your best, enterprise **11** undertaking **13** try your hand at

ended
02 up **04** over, past

ending
◊ *tail selection indicator*
03 end **04** last **05** close, death, dying **06** climax, finale, finish **07** closing, closure **08** epilogue, terminal **09** cessation, desinence, extremity, finishing **10** completing, completion, concluding, conclusion, dénouement, resolution **11** culmination, termination **12** consummation

endless
◊ *ends deletion indicator*
◊ *tail deletion indicator*
05 whole **06** boring, entire **07** eternal, undying **08** constant, fineless, infinite, termless, unbroken, unending **09** boundless, ceaseless, continual, incessant, limitless, perpetual, Sisyphean, unlimited **10** continuous, monotonous, objectless, without end

11 everlasting, measureless
12 interminable 13 inexhaustible, uninterrupted

endlessly
◇ *tail deletion indicator*
09 eternally 10 constantly, infinitely, unendingly, without end 11 ceaselessly, continually, day after day, day in day out, limitlessly, perpetually
12 continuously, interminably
15 uninterruptedly, without stopping

endmost
◇ *tail selection indicator*
04 last 07 extreme 08 farthest, hindmost

endorse
02 OK 04 back, okay, sign 05 adopt
06 affirm, endoss, favour, ratify, uphold
07 approve, confirm, initial, support, sustain, warrant 08 advocate, be behind, sanction, vouch for
09 authorize, get behind, recommend
11 countersign, subscribe to 15 sign on the back of

endorsement
02 OK 04 okay, visa, visé 07 backing, support, warrant 08 advocacy, approval, sanction, thumbs-up
09 signature 10 green light
11 affirmation, approbation, initialling, testimonial 12 commendation, confirmation, ratification, subscription
13 authorization 14 recommendation, seal of approval

endow
04 fund, gift, give, have, vest, will
05 award, boast, dower, endew, enjoy, found, grant, leave, state 06 bestow, confer, donate, pay for, supply
07 finance, furnish, possess, present, provide, support 08 bequeath, make over 12 be endued with 13 be blessed with

endowment
04 fund, gift, wakf, waqf 05 award, dower, dowry, flair, grant, power
06 genius, income, legacy, talent
07 ability, bequest, faculty, finance, funding, present, quality, revenue
08 aptitude, bestowal, capacity, donation, dotation 09 attribute, character, provision 10 capability, fellowship, settlement 11 benefaction, studentship 13 qualification

endurable
07 lasting 08 bearable, portable
09 tolerable 10 manageable, sufferable 11 supportable, sustainable
13 withstandable

endurance
04 guts, stay 05 spunk 06 bottle
07 lasting, stamina 08 backbone, duration, patience, stoicism, strength, tenacity 09 captivity, fortitude, stability, tolerance 10 durability, resolution, sufferance, toleration
11 continuance, persistence, resignation 12 perseverance, staying power, stickability 13 long-suffering

endure
03 aby 04 abye, bear, bide, dree, dure, face, have, hold, keep, last, live, lump, meet, stay, take, wear 05 abear, abide, allow, brave, brook, stand, stick, thole
06 harden, hold up, permit, remain, suffer 07 abrooke, hold out, perdure, persist, prevail, stick it, stomach, support, survive, sustain, swallow, undergo, weather 08 continue, cope with, outstand, stand for, submit to, tolerate 09 encounter, go through, put up with, withstand 10 experience, sweat it out, tough it out

enduring
04 firm 05 stout 06 stable, steady
07 abiding, chronic, durable, dureful, eternal, lasting 08 immortal, livelong, patience, tolerant 09 permanent, perpetual, remaining, steadfast, surviving 10 continuing, persistent, persisting, prevailing, undergoing, unwavering 11 long-lasting, substantial, unfaltering
12 imperishable, long-standing

enemy
03 foe 04 time 05 Devil, rival
06 foeman 07 anemone, hostile, opposer 08 opponent 09 adversary, other side 10 antagonist, competitor, philistine 13 the opposition 14 the competition

energetic
04 wick 05 brisk, pithy, vital, zappy, zippy 06 active, lively, potent, punchy, strong 07 dynamic, go-ahead, rackety, slammin', zestful 08 animated, bouncing, forceful, forcible, powerful, slamming, spirited, tireless, vigorous
09 effective, go-getting, strenuous
10 boisterous 11 full of beans, high-powered, throughgaun 12 through-going 13 indefatigable

energize
04 stir 05 liven, pep up 06 arouse, excite, fire up, vivify 07 animate, enliven, quicken 08 activate, motivate, vitalize 09 electrify, galvanize, stimulate 10 invigorate

energy
01 E 02 go 03 pep, vim, zip 04 brio, fire, fuel, gism, head, jism, life, push, zeal, zest, zing 05 drive, force, might, power, verve 06 ardour, spirit, vigour
07 pizzazz, potency, sparkle, stamina
08 activity, dynamism, exertion, strength, vitality, vivacity
09 animation, intensity 10 efficiency, enthusiasm, get-up-and-go, liveliness, propellant 11 motive power
12 forcefulness 13 effectiveness, effervescence, kinetic energy
15 potential energy

• **lacking energy**
04 nesh, poky 05 pokey 09 out of curl

• **lose energy**
04 flag, wilt

• **primitive energy**
02 id

• **renewable energy department**
04 ETSU

enervated
04 limp, weak 05 spent, tired
06 beaten, done in, effete, feeble, pooped, sapped 07 run-down, worn out 08 fatigued, unmanned, unnerved, weakened 09 enfeebled, exhausted, paralysed, pooped out, washed-out
10 undermined 11 debilitated, devitalized, tuckered out
13 incapacitated

enervating
04 hard 05 tough 06 taxing, tiring
07 arduous 08 draining, exacting, relaxing, wearying 09 demanding, difficult, fatiguing, laborious, strenuous, wearisome 10 exhausting

enfeeble
03 sap 04 geld 05 waste 06 reduce, weaken 07 deplete, exhaust, fatigue, unhinge, unnerve, wear out
08 diminish, enervate 09 undermine
10 debilitate, devitalize

enfold
◇ *containment indicator*
03 hug, lap 04 fold, hold, wind, wrap
05 clasp, imply 06 clutch, enwrap, inclip, inwrap, plight, shroud, swathe, wimple, wrap up 07 embrace, enclose, envelop, whimple 08 encircle
09 encompass, implicate

enforce
04 urge 05 apply, drive, exact, force
06 coerce, compel, fulfil, impose, lean on, oblige, strive 07 execute, impress, require 08 carry out, insist on, pressure
09 constrain, discharge, emphasize, implement, prosecute, reinforce
10 administer, pressurize
11 necessitate 14 put the screws on

enforced
06 forced 07 binding, imposed, obliged
08 dictated, ordained, required
09 compelled, mandatory, necessary
10 compulsory, obligatory, prescribed
11 constrained, involuntary, unavoidable

enforcement
08 coaction, coercion, pressure
09 discharge, execution
10 compulsion, constraint, fulfilment, imposition, insistence, obligation
11 application, prosecution, requirement 14 administration, implementation

enfranchise
04 free 07 manumit, release
08 liberate 10 emancipate 13 give the vote to 14 give suffrage to

enfranchisement
07 freedom, freeing, release
08 suffrage 10 liberating, liberation
11 manumission 12 emancipation, voting rights

engage
02 do 03 win 04 book, busy, draw, fill, gain, grip, hire, hold, join, lock, mesh,

take **05** catch, charm, enrol, fight, share, tie up **06** absorb, allure, assail, attach, attack, combat, employ, enlist, enmesh, fasten, occupy, pledge, sign on, sign up, take on, take up **07** appoint, attract, betroth, capture, engross, involve, recruit, reserve **08** contract, embark on, entangle, interact, intrigue, practise, take part **09** captivate, clash with, encounter, enter into, guarantee, interlock, partake of, preoccupy, undertake **10** battle with, commission **11** fit together, participate, wage war with **12** interconnect **15** put on the payroll

• **engage in**
◇ *insertion indicator*
04 play, wage **05** enter **07** enter on **08** voutsafe **09** enter upon, prosecute, undertake, vouchsafe

engaged
04 busy **05** in use, taken **06** active, in mesh, tied up **07** pledged **08** absorbed, employed, espoused, immersed, involved, occupied, plighted, promised **09** affianced, betrothed, committed, engrossed, intrigued, spoken for **11** preoccupied, unavailable **12** in conference

engagement
03 gig, vow, war **04** bond, date, snap **05** clash, fight, troth **06** action, attack, battle, combat, pledge, plight, strife **07** assault, booking, contest, fixture, meeting, promise, sharing **08** conflict, contract, espousal, struggle **09** agreement, assurance, betrothal, encounter, interview, offensive, partaking **10** commitment, employment, obligation, rendezvous, taking part **11** appointment, arrangement, assignation, betrothment, hand-promise, involvement, reservation, undertaking **13** confrontation, participation

engaging
05 sweet **07** likable, lovable, winning, winsome **08** adorable, charming, fetching, likeable, loveable, pleasant, pleasing **09** agreeable, appealing **10** attractive, delightful, enchanting **11** captivating, fascinating

engender
04 bear **05** beget, breed, cause **06** arouse, create, effect, excite, incite, induce, kindle, lead to **07** inspire, nurture, produce, provoke **08** generate, occasion **09** encourage, instigate, procreate, propagate **10** bring about, give rise to

engine
03 way **04** tool **05** agent, cause, means, motor, snare, trick **06** device, dynamo, factor, genius, medium, source **07** ability, channel, machine, vehicle **09** apparatus, appliance, generator, implement, ingenuity, machinery, mechanism **10** instrument, locomotive **11** contraption, contrivance

03 air, gas, ion, jet, oil
04 aero, beam, heat
05 motor, steam, water
06 diesel, donkey, petrol, Petter, radial, rocket, rotary, Wankel
07 orbital, turbine, V-engine
08 compound, Stirling, traction, turbojet
09 aerospike, turboprop
10 stationary
11 atmospheric, sleeve-valve
13 fuel-injection, reciprocating
15 linear aerospike

04 pump, sump
05 choke
06 con-rod, gasket, piston, tappet
07 fan belt, oil pump, oil seal, push-rod
08 camshaft, flywheel, radiator, rotor arm
09 air filter, drive belt, oil filter, rocker arm, spark plug
10 alternator, cooling fan, crankshaft, inlet valve, petrol pump, piston ring, thermostat, timing belt
11 carburettor, rocker cover
12 cylinder head, exhaust valve, fuel injector, ignition coil, starter motor, timing pulley, turbocharger
13 camshaft cover, connecting rod, cylinder block, inlet manifold, power-steering
15 exhaust manifold

engineer
◇ *anagram indicator*
02 BE, CE, ME **03** BAI, eng, rig **04** plan, plot **05** cause **06** create, devise, direct, driver, effect, manage, sapper, scheme **07** arrange, builder, control, deviser, greaser, handler, planner **08** contrive, designer, inventor, mechanic, operator **09** architect, machinist, manoeuvre, originate **10** bring about, controller, manipulate, mastermind, originator, technician **11** orchestrate, stage-manage **12** engine driver **13** civil engineer, sound engineer

03 Fox (Sir Charles)
04 Bell (Alexander Graham), Benz (Karl), Eads (James Buchanan), Ford (Henry), Otto (Nikolaus August), Page (Sir Frederick Handley), Watt (James)
05 Baird (John Logie), Baker (Sir Benjamin), Braun (Wernher von), Dodge (Grenville), Gooch (Sir Daniel), Grove (Sir George), Locke (Joseph), Maxim (Sir Hiram Stevens), Reber (Grote), Rolls (Charles Stewart), Royce (Sir Henry), Ruska (Ernst August Friedrich), Smith (William), Tesla (Nikola)
06 Brunel (Isambard Kingdom), Brunel (Sir Marc Isambard), Carnot (Sadi), Cayley (Sir George), Claude

(Georges), **Cugnot** (Nicolas Joseph), **Diesel** (Rudolf Christian Karl), **Donkin** (Bryan), **Eckert** (John Presper), **Edison** (Thomas Alva), **Eiffel** (Gustave), **Fokker** (Anthony Herman Gerard), **Fuller** (Buckminster), **Fulton** (Robert), **Jansky** (Karl Guthe), **Jessop** (William), **Lenoir** (Jean Joseph Étienne), **McAdam** (John Loudon), **Napier** (Robert), **Nipkow** (Paul), **Rennie** (John), **Savery** (Thomas), **Séguin** (Marc), **Sperry** (Elmer Ambrose), **Taylor** (Frederick Winslow), **Vauban** (Sebastien le Prestre de), **Wallis** (Sir Barnes Neville), **Wankel** (Felix), **Wright** (Orville), **Wright** (Wilbur)
07 **Balfour** (George), **Boulton** (Matthew), **Carlson** (Chester Floyd), **Citroën** (André Gustave), **Daimler** (Gottlieb), **Dornier** (Claude), **Eastman** (George), **Fleming** (Sir John Ambrose), **Giffard** (Henri), **Goddard** (Robert Hutchings), **Gresley** (Sir Nigel), **Heinkel** (Ernst), **Houston** (Edwin J), **Junkers** (Hugo), **Keldysh** (Mstislav), **Lesseps** (Ferdinand Marie, Vicomte de), **Nasmyth** (James), **Parsons** (Sir Charles Algernon), **Porsche** (Ferdinand), **Rankine** (William John Macquorn), **Siemens** (Sir William), **Siemens** (Werner von), **Smeaton** (John), **Sopwith** (Sir Thomas Octave Murdoch), **Telford** (Thomas), **Thomson** (Elihu), **Tupolev** (Andrei), **Whittle** (Sir Frank)
08 **Bertrand** (Henri Gratien, Comte), **Bessemer** (Sir Henry), **Brindley** (James), **De Forest** (Lee), **Ericsson** (John), **Ferranti** (Sebastian Ziani de), **Huntsman** (Benjamin), **Ilyushin** (Sergei), **Kennelly** (Arthur Edwin), **Korolyov** (Sergei), **Leonardo** (da Vinci), **Maudslay** (Henry), **Mitchell** (Reginald Joseph), **Poncelet** (Jean Victor), **Reynolds** (Osborne), **Roebling** (John Augustus), **Sikorsky** (Igor), **Sinclair** (Sir Clive), **Zeppelin** (Ferdinand, Graf von)
09 **Armstrong** (Edwin Howard), **Clapeyron** (Emile), **Cockerell** (Sir Christopher Sydney), **Fairbairn** (Sir William), **Fessenden** (Reginald Aubrey), **Issigonis** (Sir Alec), **Trésaguet** (Pierre Marie Jerome), **Whitworth** (Sir Joseph)
10 **Bazalgette** (Sir Joseph William), **Freyssinet** (Marie Eugène Léon), **Hounsfield** (Sir Godfrey Newbold), **Lilienthal** (Otto), **Stephenson** (George), **Stephenson** (Robert), **Trevithick** (Richard)
11 **De Havilland** (Sir Geoffrey), **Montgolfier** (Joseph Michel)
12 **Westinghouse** (George)
13 **Messerschmitt** (Willy)
15 **Leonardo da Vinci**

engineers
02 RE, SE **04** REME **07** sappers

England
03 Eng
See also **county; town**

English
01 E 03 Eng 04 side
See also **alphabet; monarch**

- **early English**
02 EE
- **English as a second language**
03 ESL
- **English language teaching**
03 ELT
- **in English**
03 Ang 07 Anglice

engorged
04 full 05 puffy 07 swollen
08 enlarged, expanded, inflated,
overfull

engrave
03 cut, fix, set 04 etch, mark 05 brand,
carve, chase, embed, inter, lodge,
print, scalp, sculp, stamp, write
06 chisel, incise 07 enchase, engrain,
impress, imprint, insculp 08 inscribe
09 character, mezzotint

engraving
03 cut, eng 04 mark 05 block, plate,
print, steel 06 niello 07 carving,
cutting, etching, imprint, woodcut
08 cerotype, dry-point, glyptics,
intaglio 09 headpiece, mezzotint,
sculpture, tailpiece 10 chiselling,
heliograph, impression, lithoglyph,
photoglyph, xylography 11 inscription,
stylography, zincography
12 glyptography, heliogravure, photo-
etching, photogravure
15 photoxylography

engross
04 grip, hold 05 rivet 06 absorb,
arrest, engage, enwrap, inwrap,
occupy, take up, wrap in 07 enthral,
immerse, involve 08 interest, intrigue
09 captivate, fascinate, preoccupy
10 monopolize

engrossed
04 deep, lost, rapt 06 intent
07 engaged, fixated, gripped, riveted,
taken up, wrapped 08 absorbed,
caught up, immersed, occupied
09 intrigued 10 captivated, enthralled,
fascinated, mesmerized
11 preoccupied 13 up to the elbows

engrossing
08 gripping, riveting 09 absorbing,
consuming 10 compelling, intriguing
11 captivating, enthralling, fascinating,
interesting, suspenseful
12 monopolizing 13 unputdownable

engulf
◇ *containment indicator*
04 bury 05 drown, flood, gulph,
swamp 06 absorb, deluge, devour,
plunge, suck in 07 consume,
engross, envelop, immerse, overrun,
swallow 08 inundate, overtake,
submerge 09 overwhelm,
swallow up

enhance
04 lift 05 add to, boost, exalt, raise,
swell 06 enrich, stress 07 augment,
elevate, improve, magnify, upgrade
08 heighten, increase 09 embellish,
emphasize, intensify, reinforce
10 strengthen

enhancement
05 boost 06 stress 08 emphasis,
increase 09 elevation 10 enrichment
11 heightening, improvement
12 augmentation 13 magnification,
reinforcement 15 intensification

enigma
04 egma 05 poser 06 puzzle, riddle
07 dilemma, mystery, paradox,
problem 08 quandary 09 conundrum
11 brain-teaser 12 brain-twister

enigmatic
◇ *anagram indicator*
06 arcane 07 cryptic, obscure, strange
08 baffling, esoteric, puzzling, riddling
09 recondite 10 mysterious,
mystifying, perplexing, sphinxlike
11 inscrutable, paradoxical
12 inexplicable, unfathomable

enjoin
03 ban, bar 04 urge 05 order
06 advise, charge, decree, demand,
direct, forbid, impose, ordain
07 command, require 08 disallow,
encharge, instruct, prohibit
09 encourage, interdict, prescribe,
proscribe

enjoy
03 joy 04 have, like, love 05 fancy, go
for, taste, wield 06 relish, savour
07 possess, revel in, undergo 08 be
fond of 09 delight in, partake of,
rejoice in 10 appreciate 11 benefit
from, go a bundle on 12 have the use of
13 be blessed with, be endowed with,
get a buzz out of, get a kick out of 14 be
favoured with, take pleasure in

- **enjoy yourself**
03 jol 04 ball, rage 05 party, sport
07 have fun, large it 08 live it up
09 have a ball, make merry 10 have a
blast 11 have it large 12 get your kicks
13 have a good time 14 get your jollies
15 let your hair down, paint the town
red

enjoyable
03 ace, bad, fab, fun 04 cool, fine,
good, mega, neat, nice, wild 05 brill,
rorty, super, triff 06 lekker, lovely,
wicked, wizard 07 amusing, gustful,
kicking, radical, triffic 08 fabulous,
glorious, pleasant, pleasing, smashing,
terrific 09 agreeable, beautiful,
brilliant, delicious, fantastic
10 delectable, delightful, gratifying,
satisfying 11 pleasurable
12 entertaining

enjoyment
03 fun, joy, use 04 glee, zest 05 gusto
06 favour, relish 07 benefit, comfort,
delight 08 blessing, fruition, gladness,
pleasant, pleasure 09 advantage,

amusement, diversion, happiness,
pleasance, privilege 10 indulgence,
possession, recreation, suffisance
11 delectation 12 satisfaction
13 entertainment, gratification

enlarge
03 pan 04 ream, zoom 05 add to,
piece, swell, widen 06 blow up, dilate,
expand, extend, let out 07 amplify,
augment, broaden, develop, distend,
inflate, magnify, stretch 08 dilate on,
elongate, expand on, heighten,
increase, jumboize, lengthen, multiply
09 expatiate, intumesce 10 make
bigger, make larger, supplement
11 elaborate on, expatiate on
12 become bigger, become larger
13 go into details

enlargement
05 swell, tumor 06 blow-up, bouton,
goiter, goitre, growth, oedema, spavin,
tumour 07 release 08 aneurism,
aneurysm, dilation, increase, root-knot
09 exostosis, expansion, extension
10 ampliation, distension, stretching,
varicocele 11 countersink,
development 12 augmentation,
cardiomegaly, hepatomegaly,
intumescence, splenomegaly
13 amplification, magnification
14 multiplication

enlighten
05 edify, teach, tutor 06 advise,
inform, notify 07 apprise, counsel,
educate 08 civilize, instruct
09 cultivate, make aware 10 illuminate,
illustrate 12 open your eyes

enlightened
03 lit 04 wise 05 aware 07 erudite,
learned, liberal, refined 08 cultured,
educated, informed, literate
09 civilized 10 conversant, cultivated,
illuminate, Illuminati, open-minded,
reasonable 11 broad-minded
12 intellectual 13 knowledgeable,
sophisticated

enlightenment
05 light 06 satori, wisdom 07 insight
08 learning, literacy, sapience,
teaching 09 awareness, education,
erudition, eye-opener, knowledge
10 Aufklärung, refinement
11 cultivation, edification, information,
instruction 12 civilization, illumination
13 comprehension, understanding
14 open-mindedness, sophistication
15 broad-mindedness

enlist
03 get, win 04 hire, join, list 05 enrol,
enter, prest 06 employ, engage, enroll,
gather, induct, join up, muster, obtain,
rope in, secure, sign up, take on
07 procure, recruit 08 register
09 conscribe, conscript, volunteer
14 join the colours

enliven
◇ *anagram indicator*
04 fire, jazz 05 cheer, juice, liven, pep
up, rouse, spark 06 buoy up, excite,

ginger, jazz up, kindle, perk up, soup up, vivify, wake up **07** animate, cheer up, gladden, hearten, inspire, juice up, liven up, quicken **08** brighten, ginger up **09** stimulate **10** brighten up, exhilarate, invigorate, revitalize **11** give a lift to

en masse
05 as one **06** en bloc, in sort **07** in a body **08** as a group, as a whole, as one man, ensemble, together **09** all at once, wholesale **10** in the quill **11** all together

enmeshed
07 mixed up **08** caught up, involved **09** concerned, entangled **10** associated

enmity
04 feud, hate **05** venom **06** hatred, malice, needle, rancor, strife **07** discord, ill-will, rancour **08** acrimony, aversion, bad blood, ill blood **09** animosity, antipathy, hostility **10** antagonism, bitterness, ill feeling **11** malevolence **14** unfriendliness

ennoble
05 exalt, raise **06** gentle, honour, uplift **07** dignify, elevate, enhance, glorify, magnify **10** aggrandize, nobilitate **11** distinguish

ennui
04 bore **05** weary **06** acedia, tedium **07** accidie, boredom, languor, malaise **09** lassitude, tiredness **11** the doldrums **12** listlessness **15** dissatisfaction

enormity
04 evil **05** crime **06** horror **07** outrage **08** atrocity, evilness, iniquity, vastness, vileness **09** depravity, violation **10** wickedness **11** abnormality, abomination, immenseness, monstrosity, viciousness **13** atrociousness **14** outrageousness

enormous
04 huge, mega, vast **05** dirty, giant, gross, jumbo **07** immense, mammoth, massive, monster, Titanic, whaling **08** colossal, gigantic, great big, plonking, whacking, whopping **09** abounding, atrocious, ginormous, humongous, humungous, monstrous, walloping **10** astronomic, gargantuan, hellacious, large-scale, monstruous, outrageous, prodigious, stupendous, tremendous **11** God-almighty **12** considerable, hulking great

enormously
04 dead, very, well **05** jolly **06** hugely **08** devilish, terribly **09** extremely, immensely, massively **10** especially **11** exceedingly, God-almighty **12** tremendously **13** exceptionally, to a huge extent, to a vast extent **15** extraordinarily

enormousness
07 expanse **08** hugeness, vastness **09** greatness, immensity, largeness, magnitude **11** immenseness, massiveness **13** extensiveness

enough
04 anow, enow, nuff **05** ample, amply, basta, belay **06** fairly, plenty **08** abundant, adequacy, adequate, passably **09** abundance, amplitude, tolerably **10** adequately, moderately, reasonably, satisfying, sufficient **11** ample supply, sufficience, sufficiency **12** sufficiently **14** satisfactorily

en passant
02 ep **08** by the way **09** cursorily, in passing **12** incidentally **15** parenthetically

enquire, enquirer, enquiring, enquiringly, enquiry *see* inquire, enquire; inquirer, enquirer; inquiring, enquiring; inquiringly, enquiringly; inquiry, enquiry

enrage
03 bug, irk, vex **04** rile **05** anger, annoy **06** incite, madden, needle, wind up **07** agitate, hack off, incense, inflame, provoke **08** irritate **09** enranckle, infuriate, make angry **10** exasperate, push too far

enraged
03 mad **04** wild **05** angry, irate, livid **06** fuming, raging **07** angered, annoyed, furious, horn-mad **08** incensed, inflamed, seething, storming **09** infuriate, irritated, pissed off **10** aggravated, infuriated **11** exasperated

enrapture
05 charm **06** ravish, thrill **07** beguile, bewitch, delight, enchant, enthral **08** enravish, entrance **09** captivate, fascinate, spellbind, translate, transport **10** emparadise, imparadise **13** please greatly

enrich
04 gild, lard **05** add to, adorn, endow, grace **06** fatten, manure, refine **07** augment, develop, enhance, fortify, garnish, improve **08** beautify, decorate, ornament, treasure **09** cultivate, embellish, fertilize **10** aggrandize, ameliorate, supplement

enrol
03 tax **04** list, note **05** admit, enter **06** attest, engage, enlist, enwrap, join up, muster, record, sign on, sign up **07** go in for, put down, recruit **08** inscribe, muster in, register **10** enregister **15** put your name down

enrolment
04 list **09** admission, enlisting, joining up, signing on, signing up **10** acceptance, enlistment **11** recruitment **12** conscription, registration

en route
05 march **08** on the way **09** in transit, on the move, on the road **12** on the journey

ensconce
03 put **05** lodge, niche, place **06** locate, nestle, screen, settle, shield **07** install, protect, shelter **08** entrench **09** establish

ensemble
03 set, sum **04** band, cast, suit, unit **05** get-up, group, total, whole **06** chorus, circle, entity, outfit, rig-out, troupe **07** company, costume **08** entirety **09** aggregate, orchestra **10** collection, whole shoot **11** co-ordinates **12** accumulation **13** corps de ballet, whole caboodle **14** whole bang shoot

enshrine
05 exalt, guard **06** embalm, hallow, revere, shield **07** cherish, enchase, idolize, lay down, protect, set down **08** dedicate, preserve, sanctify, treasure **10** consecrate **11** apotheosize, immortalize

enshroud
04 hide, pall, veil, wrap **05** cloak, cloud, cover **06** enfold, enwrap, shroud **07** conceal, enclose, envelop, obscure

ensign
03 Ens **04** flag, jack, mark, sign, waft **05** badge, color, crest **06** banner, colors, colour, pennon, shield **07** ancient, colours, pennant **08** gonfalon, pavilion, standard **10** coat of arms

enslave
04 bind, trap, yoke **05** thirl **06** thrall **07** enchain, subject **08** bethrall, dominate **09** subjugate **14** disenfranchise

enslavement
07 bondage, dulosis, serfdom, slavery **08** thraldom **09** captivity, servitude, vassalage **10** oppression, repression, subjection **11** enthralment, subjugation

ensnare
◇ *containment indicator*
03 net **04** hook, lime, trap **05** benet, catch, snare, snarl **06** enmesh, entoil, entrap, trepan **07** capture, embroil **08** entangle **09** mousetrap **10** illaqueate

ensue
04 flow, stem **05** arise, issue, occur **06** befall, derive, follow, happen, result **07** develop, proceed, succeed, turn out **08** come next **09** transpire

ensure
05 guard **06** effect, secure **07** betroth, certify, protect, warrant **08** make safe, make sure **09** guarantee, safeguard **11** make certain

entail
03 cut **04** need **05** carve, cause, infer **06** demand, lead to, tailye **07** call for, fashion, involve, produce, require, taillie, tailzie **08** occasion, result in **10** bring about, give rise to **11** necessitate

entangle

◇ *anagram indicator*
03 elf **04** ball, knot, wrap **05** catch, mix up, ravel, snare, twist **06** emmesh, engage, enlace, enmesh, enroot, entoil, entrap, fankle, immesh, inlace, inmesh, jumble, muddle, puzzle, taigle, tangle **07** confuse, embroil, ensnare, ensnarl, involve, perplex, trammel **08** quagmire **09** implicate, interlace **10** complicate, intertwine

entanglement

◇ *anagram indicator*
03 tie **04** knot, mesh, mess, trap **05** mix-up, snare, tie-up **06** affair, jumble, muddle, tangle **07** entrail, liaison, snarl-up **09** confusion **10** difficulty, entrapment, perplexity **11** ensnarement, involvement, predicament **12** complication, relationship **13** embarrassment

entente

04 deal, pact **06** treaty **07** compact **09** agreement **10** friendship **11** arrangement **13** understanding **15** entente cordiale

enter

◇ *insertion indicator*
03 log, ren, rin, run **04** come, go in, join, list, note **05** begin, board, enrol, get in, input, lodge, pop in, start **06** arrive, come in, enlist, go in to, insert, occupy, pierce, record, sign up, submit, take up **07** break in, burst in, get in to, go in for, put down, set down, sneak in **08** come in to, commence, embark on, engage in, inscribe, register, set about, take down, take part **09** introduce, penetrate, undertake, write down **10** embark upon, infiltrate, launch into **11** participate, put on record **12** gain access to **13** get involved in, worm your way in **15** become a member of

enterprise

03 SME **04** firm, plan, push, show, task **05** drive, oomph **06** design, effort, energy, scheme, spirit, voyage **07** company, concern, courage, emprise, project, venture **08** ambition, boldness, business, campaign, gumption, industry, vitality **09** adventure, endeavour, operation, programme, undertake **10** assignment, designment, enthusiasm, expedience, get-up-and-go, initiative **11** imagination, undertaking **13** establishment, strong feeling **15** adventurousness, resourcefulness

enterprising

04 bold, goey, keen **05** eager, pushy **06** active, daring **07** go-ahead, pushful, pushing, zealous **08** aspiring, spirited, vigorous **09** ambitious, energetic, ingenious **11** adventurous, imaginative, resourceful, self-reliant, undertaking, venturesome **12** enthusiastic **13** self-motivated **14** self-motivating **15** entrepreneurial

entertain

◇ *containment indicator*
04 fête, have, host, meet, wine **05** amuse, charm, cheer, put up, treat **06** divert, engage, foster, harbor, junket, occupy, please, regale **07** accourt, ask over, cherish, delight, engross, harbour, imagine, nurture, receive **08** ask round, conceive, consider, distract, interest, maintain **09** captivate, flirt with, have round **10** experience, have guests, invite over, play host to, think about **11** accommodate, contemplate, countenance, invite round

entertainer

04 host **06** diseur **07** diseuse, hostess **09** top banana **10** Amphitryon

See also **actor, actress; comedian; musician; singer**

entertaining

◇ *containment indicator*
03 fun **05** funny, jolly, witty **07** amusing, amusive, comical **08** humorous, pleasant, pleasing **09** diverting, enjoyable **10** delightful **11** interesting, pleasurable **12** recreational

entertainment

03 fun **04** boff, olio, show **05** cheer, drama, hobby, sport, table **07** leisure, pastime, variety **08** activity, pleasure, semblant **09** amusement, diversion, enjoyment, honky-tonk, spectacle **10** confection, recreation **11** distraction, merrymaking, performance **12** extravaganza, presentation **14** divertissement

See also **television; theatrical**

• **entertainment industry**
12 show business
• **undemanding entertainment**
03 pap

enthral

◇ *containment indicator*
04 grip **05** charm, rivet **06** absorb, thrill **07** beguile, bewitch, delight, enchant, engross **08** entrance, intrigue **09** captivate, enrapture, fascinate, hypnotize, mesmerize, spellbind

enthralling

◇ *containment indicator*
08 charming, gripping, mesmeric, riveting **09** beguiling, thrilling **10** compelling, compulsive, enchanting, entrancing, intriguing **11** captivating, fascinating, hypnotizing, mesmerizing **12** spellbinding

enthuse

04 fire, gush, rave **05** drool **06** excite, fire up, praise **07** inspire **08** motivate

10 bubble over, effervesce, wax lyrical
14 go into raptures

enthusiasm
04 brio, buzz, fire, hype, rage, zeal, zest
05 ardor, craze, estro, furor, hobby,
mania, oomph, thing, verve **06** ardour,
frenzy, furore, relish, spirit, warmth
07 ecstasy, fervour, passion, pastime
08 appetite, delirium, devotion,
interest, keenness **09** eagerness,
vehemence **10** commitment,
ebullience, ebulliency, excitement,
fanaticism **11** acclamation,
earnestness, schwärmerei
12 entraînement **13** preoccupation
• **expression of enthusiasm**
03 boy, gee **04** Jeez **05** Jeeze, oh boy!,
whack **06** whacko **10** hubba hubba
• **lose enthusiasm**
04 cool **08** languish

enthusiast
03 bug, fan, nut **04** buff, zeal **05** fiend,
freak, lover **06** maniac, zealot
07 admirer, amateur, devotee, fanatic
08 follower **09** supporter
10 aficionado **11** eager beaver
See also **collector**

enthusiastic
03 mad **04** avid, daft, into, keen, nuts,
rave, warm, wild **05** crazy, eager, potty
06 ardent, gung-ho, hearty, mad for
07 devoted, earnest, excited, fervent,
intense, up for it, zealous **08** empressé,
gaga over, mad about, spirited,
vehement, vigorous **09** committed,
ebullient, exuberant, fanatical, gaga
about **10** passionate **11** rhapsodical
12 rootin'-tootin', wholehearted
13 keen as mustard, self-motivated

entice
04 coax, draw, lure, tice, tole **05** tempt
06 allure, cajole, induce, lead on,
seduce **07** attempt, attract, beguile,
wheedle **08** inveigle, persuade
09 sweet-talk, tantalize

enticement
04 bait, lure, tice **05** decoy **06** allure,
carrot, come-on **07** coaxing
08 cajolery **09** seduction, sweet-talk
10 allurement, attraction, inducement,
invitation, persuasion, temptation
11 beguilement **12** inveiglement
13 blandishments

enticing
08 alluring, charming, inviting,
tempting **09** appealing, seductive
10 attractive **11** captivating **12** irresistible

entire
04 full, meer **05** round, sound, total,
utter, whole **06** intact, within
07 genuine, plenary, untired
08 absolute, complete, integral,
livelong, outright, stallion, thorough
09 sincerely, unmingled
10 unimpaired **11** unmitigated,
unqualified **12** completeness

entirely
03 all **04** inly, only, tout **05** clean, fully,
quite **06** in toto, merely, purely, quight,

solely, wholly **07** all over, totally, utterly
08 every bit, properly **09** every inch,
every whit, perfectly, tout à fait
10 absolutely, altogether, completely,
in every way, thoroughly **11** exclusively
12 unreservedly **14** in every respect

entirety
03 all, sum **05** total, whole **08** fullness,
totality **09** wholeness
12 completeness

entitle
03 dub **04** call, name, term **05** allow,
label, style, title **06** enable, know as,
permit **07** empower, ennoble, license,
qualify, warrant **08** accredit, christen,
sanction **09** authorize, designate
12 give the title, make eligible
• **to be entitled to**
04 bear **07** deserve

entitlement
03 due **05** claim, right, title **07** warrant
09 authority, privilege **11** opportunity,
prerogative

entity
03 ens, Tao **04** body **05** being, thing
06 object, tensor **08** creature,
organism **09** existence, substance
10 individual

entomb
04 bury, tomb **05** inter, inurn, plant
06 inhume, shroud, wall up **07** inearth
09 lay to rest, sepulcher, sepulchre,
sepulture **15** put six feet under

entombment
06 burial **09** interment, sepulture
10 inhumation **12** laying to rest

entourage
04 gang **05** court, posse, staff, suite,
train **06** escort **07** company, cortège,
coterie, retinue **09** followers,
following, hangers-on, retainers
10 associates, attendants, companions

entrails
04 guts **05** offal, tripe **06** bowels,
haslet, inside, quarry, umbles
07 giblets, harslet, humbles, innards,
insides, inwards, numbles, pudding,
viscera **08** chawdron, gralloch,
puddings **10** intestines **11** vital organs
14 internal organs

entrance
03 eye **04** adit, door, gate, hall, ingo,
pend, pipe **05** charm, debut, drive,
entry, foyer, gorge, inlet, lobby, mouth,
porch, start, way in **06** access, atrium,
avenue, dromos, entrée, income,
infare, ingate, portal, ravish **07** arrival,
Avernus, beguile, bewitch, delight,
doorway, enchant, enthral, gateway,
hallway, ingoing, ingress, jawhole,
opening **08** anteroom, approach,
driveway **09** admission, captivate,
closehead, enrapture, fascinate,
hypnotize, introitus, mesmerize,
spellbind, threshold, transport,
vestibule **10** admittance, appearance,
initiation, passageway **12** introduction,
porte-cochère, right of entry

• **narrow entrance**
04 jaws **06** throat

entranced
04 rapt **10** spellbound

entrancing
06 lovely **07** winsome **08** alluring,
charming, pleasant **09** appealing,
endearing, ravishing, wonderful
10 attractive, bewitching, delightful,
enchanting **11** captivating,
fascinating, mesmerizing
12 irresistible

entrant
05 entry, pupil, rival **06** novice, player
07 convert, fresher, learner, starter,
student, trainee **08** beginner,
freshman, initiate, newcomer,
opponent **09** applicant, candidate,
contender **10** apprentice, competitor,
contestant, new arrival **11** participant,
probationer

entrap
03 net **04** lure, trap **05** catch, decoy,
snare, tempt, trick **06** allure, ambush,
delude, enmesh, entice, seduce
07 beguile, capture, deceive, embroil,
ensnare **08** entangle, inveigle
09 crossbite, implicate, underfong

entreat
03 ask, beg, sew, sue **04** pray, prig
05 crave **06** induce, invoke, objure
07 beseech, beseeke, implore,
request, solicit **08** appeal to, petition
09 flagitate, importune, plead with
10 supplicate

entreaty
03 cry **04** plea, suit **06** appeal, prayer
07 beseech, request **08** petition,
pleading **09** exoration **10** cri de coeur,
invocation **11** conjuration
12 solicitation, supplication

entrée
05 entry **06** access **07** ingress,
prelude, starter **08** main dish
09 admission, appetizer
10 admittance, main course **11** first
course **12** introduction, right of entry

entrench
03 fix, set **04** root, seat **05** dig in,
embed, lodge, plant, wound
06 anchor, sconce, settle **07** ingrain,
install **08** ensconce, stop a gap
09 establish **14** take up position

entrenched
03 set **04** firm **05** fixed **06** inbred,
rooted **07** diehard **09** implanted,
indelible, ingrained **10** deep-rooted,
deep-seated, inflexible, unshakable
11 established, unshakeable
12 ineradicable, intransigent **13** dyed-
in-the-wool, stick-in-the-mud **15** well-
established

entrepreneur
05 agent **06** broker, dealer, tycoon
07 magnate, manager **08** promoter
09 financier, middleman
10 contractor, impresario,
moneymaker, speculator, undertaker

11 businessman, enterpriser
13 businesswoman, industrialist

entrepreneurial
05 trade **08** business, economic, monetary **09** budgetary, financial **10** commercial, industrial, managerial **11** contractual **12** professional

entrust
04 aret **05** arett, endow, trust **06** assign, charge, commit, depute, invest, resign **07** commend, confide, consign, deliver, deposit **08** delegate, encharge, hand over, turn over **09** authorize **11** put in charge

entry
04 door, gate, hall, item, note **05** annal, foyer, lobby, porch, rival, way in **06** access, entrée, minute, player, record **07** account, arrival, doorway, entrant, gateway, ingress, listing, opening, passage **08** anteroom, approach, entrance, opponent, register, registry **09** admission, applicant, candidate, contender, statement, threshold, vestibule **10** admittance, appearance, competitor, contestant, memorandum **11** description, participant **12** introduction, right of entry

entwine
◇ *anagram indicator*
04 coil, knit, knot, mesh, warp, wind **05** braid, plait, ravel, twine, twist, weave **06** enlace, inlace **07** embroil, entrail, intwine, wreathe **08** entangle **09** implicate, interlace, interlink **10** intertwine, intervolve, interweave

enumerate
04 cite, list, name, tell **05** count, quote, score **06** detail, number, recite, reckon, relate **07** compute, itemize, mention, recount, specify **08** rehearse, spell out **09** calculate, catalogue **13** particularize

enunciate
03 say **05** sound, speak, state, utter, voice **06** affirm **07** declare, enounce, express, propose **08** announce, proclaim, propound, vocalize **09** pronounce **10** articulate, promulgate, put forward

enunciation
05 sound **06** speech **07** diction **08** sounding **09** statement, utterance **10** expression **11** affirmation, declaration, proposition **12** announcement, articulation, proclamation, promulgation, vocalization **13** pronunciation

envelop
◇ *containment indicator*
04 hide, pack, veil, wrap **05** cloak, cover **06** encase, enfold, engulf, enwrap, muffle, shroud, swathe, wrap up **07** blanket, conceal, enclose, obscure, smother **08** encircle, enshroud, surround **09** encompass, enwreathe, inwreathe

envelope
03 sae **04** case, skin, wrap **05** cover, frank, shell **06** casing, entire, gasbag, holder, jacket, sachet, sheath, sleeve **07** coating, utricle, wrapper **08** covering, Jiffy bag®, wrapping **09** involucre

enviable
04 fine **05** lucky **07** blessed **08** favoured **09** desirable, excellent, fortunate, invidious **10** attractive, privileged **11** sought-after **12** advantageous

envious
05 green **07** jealous **08** covetous, grudging, spiteful **09** green-eyed, jaundiced, resentful **10** begrudging **12** dissatisfied **13** green with envy

enviously
08 with envy **09** jealously **10** covetously, desirously, grudgingly **11** resentfully **12** begrudgingly

environment
04 Gaia, mood **05** earth, scene, world **06** domain, locale, medium, milieu, nature **07** climate, context, element, habitat, setting **08** ambiance, ambience, creation **09** situation, territory **10** atmosphere, background, conditions, influences **11** mother earth **12** mother nature, natural world, surroundings **13** circumstances **15** the lie of the land

Environmental problems include:
06 litter
07 drought
08 acid rain, landfill, oil slick, oil spill
09 pollution
10 extinction, fossil fuel, toxic waste
11 soil erosion
12 air pollution, nuclear waste
13 climate change, deforestation, global dimming, global warming, water shortage
14 light pollution, ozone depletion, water pollution
15 desertification, greenhouse gases

environmentalist
05 green **06** econut **07** greenie **08** ecofreak **09** ecologist **10** tree-hugger **15** conservationist, preservationist
• **environmentalists**
03 FOE **10** Green Party

environs
07 suburbs **08** district, locality, purlieus, vicinage, vicinity **09** outskirts, precincts **12** surroundings **13** neighbourhood **15** circumjacencies, surrounding area

envisage
03 see **05** image **07** foresee, imagine, picture, predict, think of **08** envision **09** see coming, visualize **10** anticipate, conceive of **11** contemplate, preconceive

envision
03 see **07** imagine, picture, think of

08 envisage **09** see coming, visualize **11** contemplate

envoy
05 agent **06** consul, deputy, legate **07** attaché, courier, plenipo **08** delegate, diplomat, emissary, mediator, minister **09** go-between, messenger **10** ambassador **12** intermediary **14** representative **15** plenipotentiary

envy
05 covet, crave, spite **06** desire, grudge, malice, resent **07** ill-will **08** begrudge, jealousy **09** hostility **10** resentment **12** covetousness **13** resentfulness **15** dissatisfaction

enzyme

Enzymes include:
05 DNase, lyase, renin, RNase
06 cytase, kinase, ligase, lipase, papain, pepsin, rennin, zymase
07 amylase, emulsin, erepsin, inulase, lactase, maltase, oxidase, pepsine, plasmin, trypsin, uricase
08 bromelin, catalase, ceramide, elastase, esterase, lysozyme, nuclease, permease, protease, thrombin
09 amylopsin, bromelain, cellulase, coagulase, hydrolase, invertase, isomerase, peptidase, reductase, urokinase
10 insulinase, luciferase, peroxidase, polymerase, sulphatase, telomerase, tyrosinase
11 collagenase, glutaminase, histaminase, hydrogenase, lecithinase, nitrogenase, phosphatase, transferase
12 alpha amylase, asparaginase, chymotrypsin, endonuclease, fibrinolysin, ribonuclease, transaminase
13 decarboxylase, dehydrogenase, DNA polymerase, neuraminidase, penicillinase, phosphorylase, RNA polymerase, streptokinase, thrombokinase, transcriptase
14 cholinesterase, thromboplastin

Eos
06 Aurora

ephemeral
05 brief, short **07** fungous, passing **08** fleeting, flitting **09** fugacious, momentary, temporary, transient **10** evanescent, short-lived, transitory **11** impermanent

epic
04 epos, huge, long, myth, saga, vast **05** grand, great, Iliad, large, lofty **06** epopee, heroic, legend **07** Dunciad, exalted, history, Homeric, Odyssey, romance, sublime **08** colossal, elevated, epopoeia, imposing, Kalevala, long poem, majestic, Ramayana, rhapsody **09** ambitious, colubriad, long story, narrative **10** heroic poem, impressive, large-scale **13** grandiloquent

picure
5 friand 07 friande, glutton, gourmet
8 gourmand, hedonist, Sybarite
9 bon vivant, bon viveur, epicurean
0 gastronome, sensualist, voluptuary
1 connoisseur, gastronomer

picurean
4 lush 07 gourmet, sensual
8 luscious 09 libertine, luxurious,
ybaritic 10 gluttonous, hedonistic,
ensualist, voluptuous 11 gastronomic
2 gormandizing, unrestrained 13 self-
adulgent

pidemic
4 pest, rash, rife, rise, wave 05 spate
6 growth, plague, spread
7 endemic, rampant, scourge,
psurge 08 increase, outbreak,
andemia, pandemic, sweeping
9 extensive, pervasive, prevalent
0 prevailing, widespread 11 wide-
anging

pigram
3 pun 04 quip 05 gnome, maxim
6 bon mot, saying 07 proverb
8 aphorism 09 witticism
0 apophthegm 11 old chestnut, play
n words

pigrammatic
5 brief, pithy, sharp, short, terse, witty
6 ironic 07 concise, laconic, piquant,
ointed, pungent 08 incisive, succinct
0 aphoristic

pilepsy
8 eclampsy, grand mal, petit mal
9 eclampsia 15 falling sickness
sensation before epilepsy
4 aura

pilogue
2 PS 04 coda 08 appendix, swan
ong 09 afterword 10 conclusion,
ostscript

piscopate
3 see

pisode
3 fit 04 bout, part 05 event, scene,
pasm, spell 06 affair, attack, matter,
eriod 07 chapter, passage, section
8 business, incident, occasion
9 adventure, happening
0 experience, instalment, occurrence
2 circumstance

pisodic
8 periodic, sporadic 09 anecdotal,
regular, spasmodic 10 digressive,
isjointed, occasional, picaresque
2 disconnected, intermittent

pistle
2 Ep 04 Epis, line, note 06 letter
7 message, missive, preface
8 bulletin 10 encyclical
3 communication
4 correspondence

pitaph
3 RIP 05 elegy 08 obituary
1 inscription, rest in peace
3 commemoration 14 funeral oration

epithet
03 tag 04 name, term 05 title 06 byname, to-name 08 cognomen,
nickname 09 apathaton, sobriquet
10 expression 11 appellation,
description, designation
12 denomination

epitome
04 type 05 model 06 digest, précis,
résumé 07 essence, example,
outline, summary 08 abstract,
exemplar, synopsis 09 archetype,
prototype 10 abridgment,
embodiment 11 abridgement
12 quintessence 14 representation
15 personification

epitomize
03 cut, pot 05 sum up 06 embody,
précis, reduce, typify 07 abridge,
curtail, shorten 08 abstract,
compress, condense, contract
09 exemplify, incarnate, personify,
represent, summarize, symbolize
10 abbreviate, illustrate
11 encapsulate, incorporate

epoch
03 age, era 04 date, span, time
06 period

See also **geology**

equable
04 calm, even 05 equal 06 placid,
serene, smooth, stable, steady
07 regular, unfazed, uniform
08 composed, constant, laid-back,
moderate, tranquil 09 easy-going,
temperate, unvarying 10 consistent,
even-minded, unchanging 11 level-
headed, unexcitable, unflappable
12 even-tempered 13 imperturbable

equably
06 calmly 08 placidly, serenely
10 tranquilly 11 unexcitably 13 level-
headedly

equal
02 eq 03 fit, par 04 able, egal, even,
fair, fear, feer, fere, just, like, maik,
make, mate, peer, twin, view 05 alike,
feare, fiere, level, match, reach, rival,
total 06 fellow, pheere, strong, suited
07 add up to, balance, capable,
coequal, compeer, contend, emulate,
matched, neutral, peregal, regular, the
same, uniform 08 adequate, amount
to, balanced, come up to, constant,
corrival, equalize, parallel, suitable,
unbiased 09 competent, identical,
impartial, match up to, semblable, tally
with, unvarying 10 be as good as,
comparable, equate with, equivalent,
even-steven, fifty-fifty, keep up with,
square with, sufficient, unchanging
11 be a match for, be level with, be the
same as, compare with, counterpart,
even-stevens, measure up to, neck and
neck, non-partisan, symmetrical 12 be
on a par with, coincide with,
commensurate, correspond to, well
balanced 13 corresponding, evenly
matched 14 be equivalent to

equality
03 par, tie 05 match 06 owelty,
parage, parity 07 balance, egality,
justice 08 evenness, fairness, identity,
likeness, rivality, sameness, symmetry
10 neutrality, proportion, similarity,
uniformity 11 equal rights, equivalence,
parallelism 12 impartiality, partisanship
13 comparability 14 correspondence,
egalitarianism

equalization
08 matching 09 balancing, levelling
10 evening-out 12 compensation
15 standardization

equalize
05 equal, level, match 06 equate, even
up, smooth, square 07 balance, even
out 08 keep pace, make even 09 draw
level 10 compensate, regularize
11 standardize

equally
02 as 05 alike 06 evenly, fairly, just as,
justly 07 ex aequo 08 likewise
09 similarly, uniformly 11 as important
12 in like manner, in the same way, on
equal terms 14 by the same token,
proportionally 15 correspondingly,
proportionately

equanimity
04 calm, ease 05 poise 06 aplomb
07 dignity 08 calmness, coolness,
serenity 09 assurance, composure,
placidity, sangfroid 10 confidence
11 impassivity, self-control
12 tranquillity 13 self-assurance
14 self-possession, unflappability
15 level-headedness

equate
06 offset 07 balance, be equal,
compare, liken to 08 equalize, link
with, pair with, parallel 09 agree with,
compare to, match with, tally with
10 square with 11 compare with,
connect with 12 correspond to,
identify with 13 juxtapose with
14 correspond with 15 bracket
together, regard as the same

equation
02 eq 05 cubic, match 07 pairing
08 equality, identity, likeness,
matching, parallel 09 agreement,
balancing, quadratic 10 comparison,
similarity 11 calculation, equivalence
13 juxtaposition 14 correspondence,
identification

equator
07 the line 11 aclinic line
• **near the equator**
03 low

Equatorial Guinea
03 GNQ

equestrian
05 rider 06 cowboy, equine, herder,
hussar, jockey, knight, riding
07 courier, cowgirl, mounted, rancher,
trooper 08 cavalier, horseman
10 cavalryman, horse-rider,
horsewoman 11 horse-riding

Equestrians and showjumpers include:

03 Hoy (Andrew), **Hoy** (Bettina)
04 Anne (Princess), **Leng** (Virginia), Tait (Blyth),**Todd** (Mark)
05 Green (Lucinda), **Meade** (Richard), Smith (Harvey)
06 Astley (Philip), **Broome** (David), D'Inzeo (Raimondo), Klimke (Reiner), **Smythe** (Pat)
07 Winkler (Hans-Günther)
08 Phillips (Mark),**Whitaker** (John), Whitaker (Michael)

See also **horseman, horsewoman**

equilibrium
05 poise **06** aplomb, stasis
07 balance, dignity **08** calmness, coolness, evenness, serenity, symmetry **09** assurance, composure, equipoise, sangfroid, stability
10 confidence, equanimity, steadiness
11 self-control **12** counterpoise, tranquillity **13** self-assurance **14** self-possession, unflappability **15** level-headedness

equip
03 arm, fit, rig **04** tool **05** array, dight, dress, endow, fit up, issue, rig up, stock
06 aguise, aguize, clothe, fit out, kit out, outfit, supply **07** apparel, appoint, bedight, deck out, furnish, prepare, provide **08** accouter, accoutre, equipage **10** accomplish

equipment
03 kit, rig **04** gear **05** stock, stuff, tools
06 doings, graith, outfit, rig-out, tackle, things **07** baggage, battery, clobber, fixings, luggage **08** articles, hardware, material, materiel, supplies
09 apparatus, furniture, inventory
10 appliances **11** accessories, apparelment, furnishings
12 appointments **13** accoutrements, paraphernalia

See also **farm**; **gardening**; **laboratory**; **medical**; **office**; **photographic**; **plumbing**; **sport**

equipoise
05 poise **07** balance, ballast
08 evenness, symmetry **09** libration, stability **10** steadiness **11** equibalance, equilibrium **12** counterpoise
13 counter-weight **14** counterbalance, equiponderance

equitable
03 due **04** fair, just **05** equal, right
06 honest, proper, square **07** ethical
08 rightful, unbiased **09** impartial, objective **10** even-handed, legitimate, reasonable **12** unprejudiced
13 disinterested, dispassionate, fair-and-square

equitably
06 fairly, justly **07** ex aequo
08 honestly **09** ethically
10 reasonably, rightfully **11** impartially
12 even-handedly **15** disinterestedly, dispassionately

equity
05 right **06** square **07** honesty, justice
08 fairness, fair play, justness
09 integrity, rectitude **11** objectivity, uprightness **12** impartiality
13 equitableness, righteousness
14 even-handedness, fair-mindedness, reasonableness

equivalence
06 amount, parity **08** equality, identity, likeness, parallel, sameness
09 agreement **10** conformity, similarity **11** correlation
13 comparability, identicalness
14 correspondence

equivalent
02 eq **04** even, like, peer, same, twin
05 alike, equal, match, value
06 double, fellow **07** similar
08 parallel **09** homologue, identical
10 comparable, homologous, tantamount **11** alternative, correlative, counterpart, equipollent
12 commensurate **13** correspondent, corresponding, substitutable
14 opposite number
15 interchangeable

equivocal
05 fishy, vague **07** dubious, evasive, oblique, obscure **08** oracular
09 ambiguous, confusing, oraculous, uncertain **10** ambivalent, homonymous, indefinite, misleading, suspicious **12** questionable

equivocate
05 dodge, evade, fence, hedge, mudge
06 boggle, palter, waffle, weasel
07 mislead **09** pussyfoot, vacillate
11 prevaricate **12** shilly-shally, tergiversate **13** chop and change, hedge your bets **14** change your mind, change your tune

equivocation
06 waffle **07** evasion, flannel, hedging
08 shifting **09** quibbling, shuffling
10 double talk **11** weasel words
12 pussyfooting **13** prevarication
14 tergiversation **15** dodging the issue

era
03 age, day **04** aeon, date, days, time
05 cycle, epoch, stage, times
06 period, season **07** century
10 generation

See also **geology**
• **bygone era**
02 BC
• **common era**
02 CE
• **current era**
02 AD

eradicate
04 root, wipe **05** erase **06** efface, remove, uproot **07** abolish, destroy, expunge, root out, weed out, wipe out
08 get rid of, stamp out, suppress
09 eliminate, extirpate **10** annihilate, do away with, extinguish, obliterate
11 crack down on, exterminate

eradication
07 removal **08** riddance **09** abolition
10 effacement, expunction, extinction
11 destruction, elimination, extirpation, suppression
12 annihilation, deracination, obliteration **13** extermination

erasable
08 washable **09** removable
10 effaceable, eradicable

erase
03 rub, zap **04** race, rase, raze
06 cancel, delete, efface, excise, remove, rub off, rub out, scrape
07 blot out, destroy, expunge, rub away, scratch, wipe out **08** get rid of
09 eradicate **10** obliterate, scratch out

erasure
06 rasure, razure **07** removal
08 deletion **09** cleansing, erasement, wiping-out **10** effacement, expunction, rubbing-out **11** blotting-out, elimination, eradication
12 cancellation, obliteration

erbium
02 Er

erect
04 firm, form, hard, lift, rear **05** build, dress, found, mount, on end, pitch, prick, put up, raise, right, rigid, set up, stiff **06** create, raised **07** elevate, prick up, stand-up, upright **08** assemble, initiate, organize, standing, straight, vertical **09** construct, displayed, establish, institute, tumescent
10 upstanding **11** orthostatic, put together **13** perpendicular, straight-pight

erection
04 pile **07** edifice, raising **08** assembly, building, creation, priapism, rigidity
09 elevation, stiffness, structure
10 tumescence **11** fabrication, manufacture **12** construction
13 establishment

ergo
02 so **04** then, thus **05** argal, hence
09 therefore **11** accordingly
12 consequently **13** for this reason, in consequence

Erica
04 ling **07** heather

Eritrea
03 ERI

erode
05 spoil **06** abrade **07** consume, corrode, degrade, deplete, destroy, eat away, eat into **08** fragment, wear away, wear down **09** excoriate, grind down, undermine **11** deteriorate
12 disintegrate

Eros
05 Cupid

erosion
04 wash, wear **07** wash-out
08 abrasion, scouring, wash-away

09 attrition, corrosion **10** denudation
11 degradation, destruction,
excoriation, undermining, wearing
away **13** deterioration
14 disintegration

erotic
03 hot **04** blue, go-go, sexy **05** adult,
dirty, horny **06** carnal, steamy
07 amatory, amorous, lustful, raunchy,
sensual **08** erogenic, venereal
09 erogenous, seductive **10** lascivious,
suggestive, voluptuous
11 Anacreontic, aphrodisiac,
stimulating, titillating **12** pornographic

erotically
08 steamily **09** raunchily, sensually
10 explicitly **11** seductively
12 suggestively **15** anacreontically

err
◇ *anagram indicator*
03 sin **04** boob, flub, goof **05** fluff
06 cock up, duff it, goof up, mess up,
offend, slip up, wander **07** be wrong,
blunder, deviate, do wrong, louse up,
mistake, screw up, stumble **08** go
astray, misjudge **09** make a slip,
misbehave **10** transgress **11** be
incorrect, make a booboo,
misconstrue **12** come a cropper, drop
a clanger, make a mistake, miscalculate
13 fall from grace, misunderstand
15 put your foot in it

errand
03 job **04** duty, task **05** chore
06 charge **07** message, mission
10 assignment, commission
11 undertaking
• **person who runs errands**
03 cad **05** caddy, cadee, cadie
06 caddie **07** express, galopin
10 message-boy **11** message-girl
13 printer's devil

errant
◇ *anagram indicator*
05 loose, stray, wrong **06** erring,
roving, sinful **07** deviant, lawless,
nomadic, peccant, roaming, sinning,
wayward **08** aberrant, criminal,
quixotic, rambling, straying, thorough
09 itinerant, offending, wandering
10 journeying **11** disobedient,
peripatetic

erratic
◇ *anagram indicator*
06 fitful **07** vagrant, varying
08 aberrant, abnormal, shifting,
sporadic, unstable, unsteady, variable,
volatile **09** desultory, eccentric,
irregular, planetary, unsettled,
wandering **10** capricious, changeable,
inconstant, meandering, unbalanced,
unreliable **11** fluctuating
12 inconsistent, intermittent
13 unpredictable

erratically
◇ *anagram indicator*
08 fitfully, variably **10** changeably,
unreliably **11** irregularly
12 inconstantly, sporadically

13 unpredictably **14** inconsistently,
intermittently

erring
◇ *anagram indicator*
05 loose, stray, wrong **06** errant, guilty,
sinful **07** deviant, devious, lawless,
peccant, sinning, wayward
08 criminal, culpable, straying
09 misguided, offending, wandering
11 disobedient

erroneous
◇ *anagram indicator*
05 false, wrong **06** erring, faulty,
flawed, untrue **07** inexact, invalid
08 mistaken, specious, spurious,
straying **09** illogical, incorrect,
misguided, misplaced, unfounded,
wandering **10** fallacious, inaccurate

error
◇ *anagram indicator*
04 boob, flaw, flub, goof, slip, typo
05 fault, fluff, gaffe, lapse, mix-up,
wrong **06** booboo, cock-up, foul-up,
glitch, hickey, howler, slip-up
07 blooper, blunder, clanger, erratum,
fallacy, faux pas, jeofail, literal, miscopy,
mistake, own goal **08** delusion,
mesprize, misprint, omission, solecism
09 oversight **10** aberration, inaccuracy,
misjudgment **12** misjudgement
13 misconception **14** miscalculation
15 misapprehension, slip of the
tongue, spelling mistake
• **errors excepted**
02 EE
• **in error**
03 out **07** falsely, wrongly **08** unfairly,
unjustly **09** by mistake **10** mistakenly
11 erroneously, incorrectly,
misguidedly **12** fallaciously,
inaccurately **15** inappropriately
• **sign of error**
01 X

ersatz
04 fake, sham **05** bogus **06** phoney
07 man-made **09** imitation, simulated,
synthetic **10** artificial, substitute
11 counterfeit

erstwhile
02 ex **03** old **04** late, once, past
06 bygone, former **07** one-time
08 previous, sometime

erudite
04 wise **06** brainy **07** learned
08 academic, cultured, educated,
highbrow, lettered, literate, profound,
well-read **09** scholarly **12** intellectual,
well-educated **13** knowledgeable

erudition
05 facts **06** wisdom **07** culture, letters
08 learning **09** education, knowledge
10 profundity **11** learnedness,
scholarship **13** reconditeness,
scholarliness

erupt
◇ *anagram indicator*
04 emit, gush, spew, vent **05** belch,
burst, eject, expel, spout **06** blow up
07 come out, explode, flare up

08 break out, emit lava **09** burst open,
discharge, pour forth **13** discharge
lava, pour forth lava

eruption
◇ *anagram indicator*
04 rash, spot **06** blow-up, eczema,
lichen, red gum, tetter **07** ecthyma,
flare-up, morphew, prurigo, Purpura,
venting **08** ejection, emission,
empyesis, exanthem, malander,
outbreak, outburst, rose drop
09 discharge, emphlysis, exanthema,
explosion, mallander, mallender,
pompholyx, salt rheum
12 inflammation

erysipelas
04 rose **10** sideration **14** St Anthony's
fire

escalate
04 grow, rise, soar **05** climb, mount,
raise **06** ascend, expand, extend,
rocket, spiral, step up **07** amplify,
develop, enlarge, magnify, shoot up
08 heighten, increase, mushroom
09 intensify **10** accelerate, hit the roof

escalation
04 rise **06** growth **07** soaring
08 increase **09** expansion, extension
11 development, heightening,
mushrooming **12** acceleration
13 magnification **15** intensification

escalator
04 lift **08** elevator **10** travelator,
travolator **13** moving walkway
15 moving staircase

escapable
08 eludible, evadable **09** avertible,
avoidable

escapade
04 hoot, lark, ploy, romp **05** antic,
caper, fling, prank, scape, spree, stunt,
trick **06** escape, frolic, scheme, splore
07 exploit **08** escapado, fredaine
09 adventure, excursion **10** skylarking
11 monkey shine

escape
03 esc, fly, lam, out **04** bolt, bunk,
duck, flee, flit, flow, go-by, gush, hole,
leak, ooze, pass, scat, seep, shun, skip,
slip, vent **05** avoid, break, ditch, dodge,
drain, elope, elude, evade, issue, lam it,
leg it, prank, sally, scape, scoot, scram,
spurt **06** blower, decamp, efflux, flight,
forget, get off, outlet **07** abscond, bail
out, do a bunk, dodging, ducking,
evasion, fantasy, get away, getaway,
leakage, not know, outflow, outpour,
overrun, pastime, pour out, run away,
scarper, seepage, trickle, wilding
08 break out, breakout, dreaming,
emission, escapism, loophole, not
place, run for it, shake off, sidestep, slip
away **09** avoidance, breakaway, break
free, cut and run, discharge, diversion,
do a runner, emanation, jailbreak, pour
forth **10** absconding, break loose,
circumvent, decampment, have it
away, hop the twig, Houdini act,
recreation, relaxation **11** distraction,

fantasizing, safety-valve **12** steer clear of **13** circumvention, extravasation, not be recalled, transgression **14** make a bolt for it, make your escape, run for your life, take it on the lam, take to the boats **15** make a break for it, make your getaway, not be remembered, take to your heels, wishful thinking

• **allow to escape**
03 let **04** vent

• **means of escape**
04 hole, loop **08** loophole

• **way of escape**
03 out **04** mews, muse **05** meuse **06** get-out **08** bolthole

escapee
06 truant **07** escaper, refugee, runaway **08** defector, deserter, fugitive **09** absconder **11** jailbreaker

escapism
07 fantasy, pastime **08** dreaming **09** diversion **10** recreation, relaxation **11** distraction, fantasizing, pie in the sky, safety-valve **15** castles in the air, wishful thinking

escapist
07 dreamer, ostrich **09** Billy Liar **10** daydreamer, Don Quixote, fantasizer, non-realist **11** Walter Mitty **14** wishful thinker

eschew
04 shun **05** avoid, forgo, spurn **06** abjure, forego, give up **07** abandon, disdain **08** forswear, renounce **09** repudiate **11** abstain from, keep clear of, refrain from

escort
03 see, set **04** aide, beau, date, hand, lead, take, tend, wait, walk **05** bring, guard, guide, suite, train, usher **06** convoy, defend, gigolo, squire **07** company, conduct, cortège, esquire, janizar, partner, protect, retinue, take out **08** attend on, chaperon, come with, defender, janizary, shepherd, take down **09** accompany, attendant, bodyguard, chaperone, companion, entourage, janissary, protector **10** attendance, attendants, javelin-man **13** come along with, guard of honour

esoteric
05 inner **06** arcane, hidden, inside, mystic, occult, Orphic, secret **07** cryptic, obscure, private **08** abstruse, mystical, rarefied **09** recondite **10** acroamatic, mysterious **11** inscrutable **12** acroamatical, confidential

esparto grass
04 alfa **05** halfa

especial
06 marked, signal, unique **07** express, notable, special, unusual **08** peculiar, singular, specific, striking, uncommon **09** exclusive, principal **10** noteworthy, particular, pre-eminent, remarkable **11** distinctive, exceptional, outstanding **13** distinguished, extraordinary

especially
03 esp **04** very **05** espec **06** mainly, mostly, namely **07** chiefly, largely, notably **08** above all, markedly, uniquely **09** expressly, in special, most of all, primarily, specially, supremely, unusually **10** remarkably, strikingly, uncommonly **11** exclusively, principally **12** in particular, particularly, pre-eminently **13** exceptionally, outstandingly **15** extraordinarily

espionage
05 scout **06** spying **07** bugging, probing **08** snooping **10** tradecraft **11** fifth column, penetration, wiretapping **12** infiltration, intelligence, intercepting, surveillance **13** investigation, secret service **14** reconnaissance, undercover work

espousal
06 choice **07** backing, defence, support, wedding **08** adoption, advocacy, taking-up **09** embracing, promotion **11** championing, maintenance **12** championship

espouse
04 back **05** adopt **06** choose, defend, opt for, take up **07** embrace, support **08** advocate, champion, maintain **09** patronize **10** stand up for

esprit de corps
10 team spirit **12** group loyalty, mutal respect, public spirit **13** mutual feeling

espy
03 see, spy **04** spot **05** sight, watch **06** behold, descry, detect, notice **07** discern, glimpse, make out, observe **08** discover, perceive **11** distinguish **12** catch sight of

essay
02 go **03** try **04** bash, push, shot, stab, test **05** assay, crack, go for, offer, paper, piece, study, theme, tract, trial **06** leader, review, sketch, strain, strive, tackle, take on, thesis **07** article, attempt, have a go, venture **08** causerie, critique, struggle, treatise **09** discourse, endeavour, have a bash, have a stab, prolusion, undertake **10** assignment, commentary, experiment, have a crack **11** composition **12** disquisition, dissertation

essayist

Essayists include:

04 Greg (William Rathbone), Hunt (Leigh), Lamb (Charles), Lynd (Robert), Rodó (José Enrique)
05 Bacon (Francis), Gould (Stephen Jay), Lucas (Edward Verrall), Pater (Walter Horatio), Smith (Sydney), White (E B)
06 Borges (Jorge Luis), Breton (André), Orwell (George), Ruskin (John), Steele (Sir Richard)
07 Addison (Joseph), Calvino (Italo), Carlyle (Thomas), Chapone (Hester), Emerson (Ralph Waldo),

Hayward (Abraham), Hazlitt (William), Lazarus (Emma), Meynell (Alice Christiana Gertrude), Montagu (Lady Mary Wortley), Thoreau (Henry David)
08 Beerbohm (Sir Max), Macaulay (Thomas Babington, Lord)
09 De Quincey (Thomas), Dickinson (Goldsworthy Lowes), Montaigne (Michel Eyquem de)
10 Chesterton (G K), Crèvecoeur (Michel Guillaume Jean de)
12 Quiller-Couch (Sir Arthur)

essence
03 nub **04** alma, core, crux, esse, life, otto, pith, soul **05** being, heart, juice, point, stuff **06** centre, entity, kernel, marrow, nature, spirit **07** alcohol, extract, meaning, quality, quiddit, ratafia, reality, spirits **08** bergamot, quiddity, whatness **09** actuality, character, principle, substance **10** attributes, distillate, heart-blood, hypostasis, ylang-ylang **11** concentrate, heart's-blood **12** distillation, quintessence, significance **13** concentration, individuation, ylang-ylang oil **15** characteristics, sum and substance

• **in essence**
07 in grain **08** at bottom **09** basically **11** essentially **13** fundamentally, substantially

• **of the essence**
05 vital **06** needed **07** crucial **08** required **09** essential, important, necessary, requisite **13** indispensable

essential
03 key **04** gist, main, must, pure **05** basic, vital **06** formal, innate, needed **07** central, crucial, typical **08** inherent, key point, required, rudiment **09** important, intrinsic, key points, main point, necessary, necessity, principal, principle, requisite **10** definitive, main points, sine qua non, underlying **11** constituent, fundamental, requirement, substantial **12** all-important, constitutive, prerequisite **13** indispensable **14** characteristic

essentially
05 per se **07** at heart **08** deep down **09** basically, in essence, primarily **10** inherently **13** fundamentally, intrinsically

establish
03 fix **04** base, form, haft, make, open, seat, show **05** begin, build, edify, erect, found, lodge, pitch, plant, prove, raise, set up, start, state, stell **06** affirm, attest, create, ordain, ratify, secure, settle, verify **07** certify, confirm, install, start up **08** nail down, organize, validate **09** institute, introduce **10** constitute, inaugurate **11** corroborate, demonstrate **12** authenticate, substantiate **14** bring into being

established
03 est, set 05 fixed 06 proved, proven, rooted, secure, stable, stated
07 settled 08 accepted, radicate, ratified, standing 09 ensconced, radicated, respected, steadfast
10 entrenched 11 experienced, traditional 12 conventional 14 tried and tested
• **to be established**
04 root 06 obtain

establishment
03 fix 04 firm, shop, them 05 store
07 company, concern, forming
08 business, creation, founding
09 formation, inception, institute, setting up, the system 10 enterprise, foundation 11 corporation, down-sitting, institution, ruling class
12 inauguration, installation, organization 13 the government
14 the authorities 15 the powers that be

estate
03 pen 04 alod, area, land, odal, park, rank, site, udal 05 allod, class, goods, lands, manor, place, state, taluk, tract, trust 06 assets, centre, domain, entail, having, realty, region, status
07 demesne, effects, grounds, havings
08 allodium, executry, hacienda, holdings, position, property, standing
09 condition, patrimony, princedom, situation 10 belongings, latifundia, personalty, plantation, real estate
11 development, landholding, possessions 14 conditional fee

estate agent
07 realtor 09 land agent 13 property agent 15 real-estate agent

esteem
03 way 04 deem, have, hold, love, pass, rate, view 05 compt, count, favor, izzat, judge, prise, prize, set by, store, think, value 06 admire, credit, favour, honour, make of, reckon, regard, revere 07 account, adjudge, believe, cherish, respect, set down
08 consider, judgment, treasure, venerate 09 judgement, reckoning, reverence 10 admiration, estimation, veneration 11 approbation, good opinion 12 appreciation, regard highly
13 consideration, put a premium on

esteemed
06 prized, valued, worthy 07 admired, revered 08 favorite, honoured, precious 09 admirable, excellent, favourite, of warrant, reputable, respected, treasured, venerated
10 honourable 11 prestigious, respectable 13 distinguished, of good warrant, well-respected, well-thought-of 14 highly regarded

estimable
04 good 06 valued, worthy
07 notable 08 esteemed, laudable, valuable 09 admirable, excellent, reputable, respected 10 creditable, honourable, noteworthy, worthwhile

11 commendable, meritorious, respectable, warrantable
12 praiseworthy 13 distinguished

estimate
03 aim 04 cost, gage, rate, view
05 carat, gauge, guess, judge, level, value, weigh 06 assess, belief, carrat, reckon, strike 07 compute, opinion
08 appraise, evaluate, judgment, thinking 09 calculate, judgement, quotation, reckoning, valuation
10 appreciate, assessment, conclusion, conjecture, estimation, evaluation, reputation, rough guess
11 calculation, computation, guesstimate 13 approximation, consideration 14 ballpark figure
15 approximate cost

estimated
03 est

estimation
04 rate, view 05 guess, honor, sight, stock 06 belief, credit, esteem, honour, regard 07 account, feeling, opinion, respect 08 estimate, judgment, thinking 09 judgement, reckoning, valuation 10 assessment, conception, conclusion, conjecture, evaluation, importance, reputation, rough guess 11 calculation, computation 12 appreciation
13 consideration, way of thinking
15 approximate cost

Estonia
03 EST

estrange
04 part 05 alien, sever 06 cut off, divide, remove 07 break up, divorce, split up 08 alienate, disunite, separate, withdraw, withhold 09 disaffect
10 antagonize, drive apart, set against
13 set at variance

estranged
05 alien, apart, fraim, fremd 06 fremit
07 aliened, divided 08 alienate, divorced, separate 09 alienated, separated 11 antagonized, disaffected

estrangement
05 split 06 breach 07 break-up, parting 08 disunion, disunity, division
09 antipathy, hostility, severance
10 alienation, antagonism, separation, withdrawal 11 withholding
12 disaffection, dissociation
14 unfriendliness

estuary
03 arm, bay, Est 04 cove 05 creek, firth, fiord, fjord, inlet, mouth 07 sea-loch

et cetera
01 &c 03 etc 04 et al 07 and so on
10 and all that, and so forth, and the like, and the rest, or whatever 11 and suchlike, and whatever 14 and what have you

etch
03 cut, dig 04 bite, burn 05 carve, eat in, stamp 06 furrow, groove, incise

07 corrode, eat away, engrave, impress, imprint, ingrain 08 inscribe

etching
03 cut 05 print 06 sketch 07 carving, imprint 08 aquatint 09 aquatinta, engraving 10 aqua fortis, impression
11 inscription

eternal
07 abiding, aeonian, endless, lasting, non-stop, undying 08 constant, enduring, immortal, infinite, timeless, unending 09 ceaseless, deathless, eviternal, incessant, limitless, perennial, perpetual 10 continuous, persistent, relentless, unchanging
11 everlasting, never-ending, remorseless, unremitting
12 imperishable, interminable, unchangeable 14 indestructible

eternally
04 ever 06 always 07 for ever
09 endlessly, lastingly 10 constantly
11 ceaselessly, continually, incessantly, permanently, perpetually
12 interminably 13 everlastingly
14 indestructibly

eternity
03 age, eon 04 aeon, ages 05 yonks
06 heaven 07 forever 08 Ewigkeit, infinity, long time, paradise 09 after-life, hereafter, next world 10 perpetuity
11 ages and ages, endlessness, everlasting, immortality, world to come 12 donkey's years, immutability, timelessness 13 deathlessness
15 everlasting life, everlastingness, imperishability, world without end

ethereal
04 airy, fine 05 light 06 dainty, subtle
07 refined, tenuous 08 delicate, empyreal, empyrean, gossamer, heavenly, rarefied 09 airy-fairy, celestial, elemental, exquisite, spiritual, unearthly, unworldly 10 diaphanous, immaterial, impalpable, intangible
13 insubstantial

ethical
04 fair, good, just 05 moral, noble, right 06 decent, honest, proper, seemly 07 correct, fitting, upright
08 decorous, virtuous 09 righteous
10 high-minded, honourable, principled 11 commendable, responsible 13 above reproach

ethically
05 nobly 06 justly 07 morally, rightly
08 honestly 09 reputably
10 honourably, virtuously
11 responsibly 12 high-mindedly, respectfully 13 ideologically
14 moralistically

ethics
04 code 05 rules 06 equity, morals, values 07 beliefs 08 morality
09 moral code, propriety, standards
10 conscience, deontology, principles
11 moral values 13 descriptivism, moral theology 14 moral standards
15 moral philosophy, moral principles

Ethiopia
03 ETH

ethnic
04 folk 06 exotic, native, racial, tribal
07 foreign 08 cultural, national,
societal 10 aboriginal, indigenous
11 traditional 12 ethnological
13 autochthonous
15 anthropological

ethnically
08 racially, socially, tribally
10 culturally, societally 13 traditionally
14 humanistically

ethos
04 code 05 tenor 06 ethics, spirit
07 beliefs, flavour, manners
08 attitude, morality 09 character,
rationale, standards 10 atmosphere,
principles 11 disposition

etiquette
04 code, form, kawa 05 rules
07 customs, decency, decorum,
manners 08 ceremony, civility,
courtesy, good form, protocol
09 propriety, standards 10 politeness
11 convenances, conventions,
correctness, formalities, good manners
12 unwritten law 13 code of conduct
14 code of practice 15 code of
behaviour

etymology
03 ety 06 origin, source 08 word-lore
09 philology, semantics 10 derivation,
lexicology 11 linguistics, word history,
word origins

eucalyptus
03 box, gum 05 karri, marri, sally, tuart
06 jarrah, mallee, red gum, sallee,
tewart, tooart, wandoo 07 blue gum,
gum tree 08 coolabah, coolibah,
coolibar, ghost gum, ironbark, sugar
gum 09 black butt, bloodwood, fever
tree 10 tallow wood, woollybutt
11 mountain ash

eulogize
04 hype, laud, plug 05 exalt, extol
06 honour, praise 07 acclaim,
applaud, approve, commend, glorify,
magnify 09 celebrate, rave about
10 compliment, panegyrize, wax
lyrical 12 congratulate

eulogy
04 laud 05 paean 06 praise
07 acclaim, plaudit, tribute
08 accolade, applause, encomion,
encomium 09 laudation, laudative,
laudatory, panegyric 10 compliment,
exaltation 11 acclamation
12 commendation 13 glorification

euphemism
07 evasion 09 softening
10 genteelism, politeness, polite term,
substitute 12 substitution
14 understatement 15 mild alternative
See also **oath**

euphemistic
04 mild 05 vague 06 polite
07 evasive, genteel, neutral 08 indirect

09 soft-toned 10 substitute
11 understated

euphonious
04 soft 05 clear, sweet 06 dulcet,
mellow 07 melodic, musical, silvery,
tuneful 08 canorous, euphonic,
pleasant 09 consonant, melodious
10 harmonious, sweet-toned
11 dulcifluous, mellifluous,
symphonious 12 dulciloquent
13 sweet-sounding

euphoria
03 joy 04 glee, high, rush 05 bliss
07 ecstasy, elation, rapture
08 buoyancy 09 happiness, transport,
wellbeing 10 enthusiasm, exaltation,
exultation, jubilation 11 high spirits
12 cheerfulness, exhilaration,
intoxication

euphoric
04 high 05 happy 06 elated, joyful,
joyous 07 buoyant, exulted, gleeful
08 blissful, cheerful, ecstatic, exultant,
jubilant 09 rapturous 10 enraptured
11 exhilarated, intoxicated
12 enthusiastic

Europe

European countries include:

02 UK
05 Italy, Malta, Spain
06 Cyprus, France, Greece, Latvia,
Monaco, Norway, Poland, Russia,
Sweden, Turkey
07 Albania, Andorra, Austria, Belarus,
Belgium, Croatia, Denmark,
Estonia, Finland, Germany, Hungary,
Iceland, Ireland, Moldova, Romania,
Ukraine, Vatican
08 Bulgaria, Portugal, Slovakia,
Slovenia
09 Lithuania, Macedonia, San Marino
10 Luxembourg
11 Switzerland, Vatican City
13 Czech Republic, Liechtenstein,
United Kingdom
14 The Netherlands
19 Serbia and Montenegro
20 Bosnia and Herzegovina

European landmarks include:

02 Po
04 Alps, Arno, Como, Etna, Lido, Main,
Oder
05 Delos, Eiger, Garda, Loire, Prado,
Rhine, Rhône, Seine, Somme, Tiber,
Urals, Volga
06 Azores, Dachau, Danube, Delphi,
Fátima, Geysir, Liffey, Rhodes, Tatras,
Tivoli
07 Algarve, Kremlin, Lapland, La Scala,
Madeira, Moselle, Pompeii,
Shannon, Siberia
08 Alhambra, Ardennes, Auvergne,
Canaries, Caucasus, Dordogne,
Jungfrau, Lake Como, Legoland,
Oude Kerk, Pantheon, Provence,
Pyrenees, St Peter's, Strokkur,
Tenerife, Vesuvius
09 Acropolis, Balearics, Bantry Bay,
Campanile, Colosseum,

Connemara, Dolomites, Dublin Bay,
Keukenhof, Lake Garda, Lanzarote,
Menin Gate, Mont Blanc, Mount
Etna, Notre Dame, Parc Güell,
Parthenon, Red Square, Reichstag,
Temple Bar, Zuider Zee
10 Bran Castle, Grand Canal,
IJsselmeer, Interlaken, Julian Alps,
Lake Geneva, Lenin's tomb,
Matterhorn, Nieuwe Kerk, Pont du
Gard, Rubenshuis, Schönbrunn,
Versailles, Wienerwald
11 Afsluitdijk, Black Forest, Eiffel
Tower, Königsplatz, Manneken Pis,
Mount Elbrus, Rijksmuseum,
Simplon Pass, Vatican City, Vienna
Woods
12 Abbey Theatre, Bavarian Alps,
Blarney Stone, Frauenkirche, Lake
Maggiore, Leaning Tower, Mont St
Michel, Mount Olympus, Mozart's
House, Ponte Vecchio, Rialto
Bridge, Rubens's House, Summer
Palace, Tower of Belém, Winter
Palace
13 Anne Frank Huis, Arc de Triomphe,
Bridge of Sighs, Canary Islands,
Ha'penny Bridge, Lake Constance,
Little Mermaid, Massif Central,
Millau Viaduct, Mount Vesuvius,
Museo del Prado, Oresund Bridge,
Sistine Chapel, St Mark's Square,
Uffizi Gallery, Ural Mountains,
Vatican Palace
14 Bolshoi Theatre, Mount Parnassus,
O'Connell Street, Palazzo Vecchio,
Piazza San Marco, Potsdamer Platz,
Sagrada Familia, Trinity College
15 Anne Frank's house, Balearic
Islands, Brandenburg Gate, Dingle
Peninsula, Hermitage Museum,
Rock of Gibraltar, Stedelijk Museum

European
◇ *foreign word indicator*
01 E 03 Eur 04 Euro

Europeans include:

04 Balt, Brit, Dane, Esth, Finn, Flem,
Lapp, Pict, Pole, Scot, Serb, Slav, Turk
05 Angle, Czech, Croat, Greek, Latin,
Vlach, Swede, Swiss
06 Almain, Basque, Briton, German,
Nordic, Sabine, Salian, Teuton,
Zyrian
07 Belgian, Bosnian, Cypriot, Fleming,
Iberian, Italian, Latvian, Lombard,
Maltese, Manxman, Monacan,
Russian, Samnite, Serbian, Walloon
08 Albanian, Andorran, Austrian,
Croatian, Dutchman, Estonian,
Irishman, Moldovan, Romanian,
Scotsman, Siberian, Silurian,
Spaniard, Welshman
09 Britisher, Bulgarian, Englander,
Englisher, Frenchman, Hungarian,
Icelander, Manxwoman,
Norwegian, Sardinian, Slovakian,
Slovenian, Ukrainian
10 Anglo-Saxon, Belarusian,
Dutchwoman, Englishman,
Irishwoman, Lithuanian,
Macedonian, Monégasque,

Portuguese, Welshwoman
11 Belarussian, Frenchwoman,
Montenegrin, Sammarinese
12 Luxembourger, Scandinavian
13 Englishwoman, Herzegovinian
15 Liechtensteiner

• **European Union**
02 EU

*European Union member
countries include:*

05 Italy, Malta, Spain
06 Cyprus, France, Greece, Latvia,
Poland, Sweden
07 Austria, Belgium, Denmark, Estonia,
Finland, Germany, Hungary, Ireland
08 Portugal, Slovakia, Slovenia
09 Lithuania
10 Luxembourg
13 Czech Republic, United Kingdom
14 The Netherlands

europium
02 Eu

euthanasia
07 quietus, release 12 happy release,
mercy killing 15 assisted suicide,
merciful release

evacuate
04 ease, quit, void 05 clear, eject,
empty, expel, leave, purge, stool
06 decamp, depart, desert, getter,
remove, vacate 07 abandon, excrete,
forsake, nullify, relieve, retreat, vacuate
08 clear out, defecate, withdraw
09 discharge, eliminate, make empty,
move out of, pull out of 10 go away
from, relinquish, retire from, stercorate

evacuation
06 exodus, flight 07 Dunkirk, leaving,
purging, removal, retreat 08 ejection,
emptying, quitting, vacating
09 clearance, departure, desertion,
discharge, expulsion, forsaking,
gettering, urination, vacuation
10 defecation, retirement, withdrawal
11 abandonment, elimination
14 relinquishment

evade
04 balk, duck, shun 05 avoid, blink,
burke, dodge, elude, fence, fudge,
hedge, parry, sheer, shift, shirk, skive,
waive 06 baffle, bludge, bypass, cop
out, escape 07 fend off, quibble,
shuffle, wriggle 08 get round, sidestep,
skive off 09 back out of, duckshove,
gold brick, weasel out 10 chicken out,
circumvent, equivocate, scrimshank,
skrimshank 11 prevaricate 12 steer
clear of, wriggle out of

evaluate
04 rank, rate 05 gauge, judge, value,
weigh 06 assess, reckon, size up
07 compute, measure 08 appraise,
estimate 09 calculate, determine
15 get the measure of

evaluation
05 audit 06 rating 07 opinion
08 estimate, judgment 09 appraisal,
judgement, reckoning, valuation

10 assessment, estimation
11 calculation, computation
13 determination

evanescent
05 brief 06 fading 07 passing
08 fleeting, unstable 09 ephemeral,
momentary, temporary, transient,
vanishing 10 perishable, short-lived,
transitory 11 evaporating, impermanent
12 disappearing 13 insubstantial

evangelical
03 Sim 06 Marist 07 zealous
08 biblical, orthodox, Stundist
09 crusading, High-flier, High-flyer,
Simeonite 10 converting, missionary,
Morisonian, scriptural 11 campaigning
12 Bible-bashing, enthusiastic,
evangelistic, propagandist 13 Bible-
punching, Bible-thumping,
proselytizing 14 Bible-believing,
fundamentalist, propagandizing

• **Evangelical Union**
02 EU

evangelist
04 John, Luke, Mark 07 Matthew
08 crusader, preacher 09 gospeller,
missioner 10 campaigner, missionary,
revivalist 12 hot gospeller, proselytizer
13 televangelist

evangelize
06 preach 07 baptize, convert,
crusade 08 campaign 09 gospelize
10 missionize 11 proselytize
12 missionarize, propagandize
13 spread the word

evaporate
03 dry, end 04 fade, melt 05 steme,
vapor 06 depart, dispel, distil, exhale,
vanish, vapour 08 boil away, disperse,
dissolve, evanesce, melt away, vaporize
09 dehydrate, desiccate, disappear,
dissipate 10 volatilize 13 dematerialize

evaporation
06 drying, fading 07 melting
09 vanishing 10 exhalation
11 dehydration, desiccation,
dissolution 12 condensation,
distillation, vaporization

evasion
04 go-by 05 dodge, fudge, quirk
06 cop-out, deceit, escape, excuse,
put-off 07 dodging, ducking, elusion,
fencing, fig leaf, fudging, hedging,
quibble, shuffle, skiving 08 go-around,
shirking, shunning, trickery
09 avoidance, deception, quibbling,
shuffling 10 scrimshank, skrimshank,
subterfuge 12 equivocation
13 circumvention, prevarication
14 tergiversation 15 steering clear of

evasive
03 coy 05 cagey, vague 06 shifty,
slippy, tricky 07 cunning, devious,
elusive, elusory, fudging, oblique
08 indirect, slippery, waffling
09 deceitful, deceptive, quibbling,
secretive, shuffling 10 misleading
12 equivocating 13 prevaricating,
unforthcoming

evasiveness
06 deceit 07 cunning, fudging,
secrecy 08 caginess 09 quibbling,
vagueness 12 equivocation,
indirectness 13 deceptiveness,
prevarication

eve
03 e'en 04 edge 05 brink, verge, vigil
09 day before, threshold 10 time
before 12 period before

even
◇ *hidden alternately indicator*
03 all, e'en, too, yet 04 also, calm, cool,
eevn, fair, flat, just, like, more, same,
true 05 align, alike, at all, clean, drawn,
eeven, equal, exact, flush, level, match,
oddly, plain, plane, quits, still 06 as
well, hardly, indeed, in fact, nearly,
placid, serene, smooth, square, stable,
steady 07 balance, compare, eevning,
equable, exactly, flatten, neutral,
regular, similar, uniform 08 actually,
balanced, composed, constant,
equalize, likewise, matching, parallel,
scarcely, so much as, straight, tranquil
09 equitable, identical, impartial,
make equal, stabilize, still more,
unexcited, unruffled, unusually,
unvarying 10 all the more, balance out,
consistent, even-handed, fifty-fifty,
horizontal, regularize, side by side,
straighten, unchanging, unwavering
11 make uniform, more exactly, neck
and neck, non-partisan, symmetrical,
unexcitable, unflappable 12 even-
tempered, surprisingly, unexpectedly
13 evenly matched, more precisely,
unperturbable 14 strike a balance

• **even so**
03 but, yet 05 still 07 however 10 all
the same 11 despite that, nonetheless
12 nevertheless 13 in spite of that

• **get even**
05 repay 06 avenge 07 pay back,
requite 11 have revenge, reciprocate
12 settle a score 14 get your own
back 15 revenge yourself, take your
revenge

• **not even**
06 odd 06 uneven

even-handed
04 fair, just 06 square 07 neutral
08 balanced, unbiased 09 equitable,
impartial 10 reasonable
12 unprejudiced 13 disinterested,
dispassionate, fair and square

evening
03 e'en, ene, eve 04 dusk, eevn, even
05 eeven, night 06 sunset, vesper
07 eevning, sundown 08 eventide,
twilight 09 forenight, nightfall 10 close
of day

evenly
◇ *hidden alternately indicator*
04 flat 06 calmly, square, stably
07 equally 08 placidly, serenely,
steadily 09 regularly, similarly,
uniformly 10 constantly, tranquilly
12 consistently 13 evenly matched,
symmetrically

event
03 end **04** case, fact, fate, gala, game, item, meet, pass, race **05** issue, match, round **06** affair, effect, matter, result, upshot **07** contest, episode, fixture, fortune, meeting, ongoing, outcome **08** business, incident, occasion **09** adventure, aftermath, happening, milestone **10** conclusion, engagement, experience, occurrence, proceeding, tournament **11** competition, consequence, eventuality, possibility, termination **12** circumstance
• **in any event**
06 anyhow, anyway **09** in any case **11** whether or no **12** no matter what, whether or not **15** whatever happens

even-tempered
04 calm, cool **06** placid, serene, stable, steady **07** equable, unfazed **08** composed, laid-back, peaceful, tranquil **09** peaceable **11** level-headed, unflappable **13** imperturbable

eventful
04 busy, full **06** active, lively **07** crucial, notable **08** critical, exciting, historic **09** checkered, chequered, important, memorable, momentous **10** noteworthy, remarkable **11** interesting, ripsnorting, significant **12** action-packed **13** unforgettable

eventual
04 last **05** final, later **06** future **07** closing, ensuing, planned **08** ultimate **09** impending, projected, resulting **10** concluding, subsequent **11** prospective

eventuality
04 case **05** event **06** chance, crisis, mishap **07** outcome **09** emergency, happening, incidence **10** likelihood, occurrence **11** contingency, possibility, probability **12** circumstance, happenstance

eventually
06 at last, in time **07** finally **08** after all, at length, in the end **10** ultimately **11** in due course **12** in the long run, subsequently **13** sooner or later

ever
02 ay **03** aye, e'er **05** at all **06** always **07** for ever **08** evermore **09** at any time, endlessly, eternally, in any case **10** at all times, constantly **11** continually, incessantly, permanently, perpetually **12** on any account, till doomsday **13** on any occasion
• **ever so**
04 very **05** jolly **06** really **07** awfully **08** terribly, very much **09** extremely, immensely **11** exceedingly, frightfully **12** tremendously **13** exceptionally

evergreen *see* pine; tree

everlasting
07 endless, eternal, non-stop, undying **08** cat's-foot, constant, immortal, infinite, timeless, unending **09** continual, deathless, incessant, permanent, perpetual, unceasing **10** continuous, immortelle, perdurable, persistent, relentless **11** Helichrysum, never-ending, remorseless, sempiternal, strawflower, unremitting, xeranthemum **12** imperishable, interminable **14** indestructible

evermore
04 ever **06** always **07** for ever **09** eternally, ever after, hereafter **10** henceforth **11** in perpetuum, unceasingly **12** in perpetuity, till doomsday **14** for ever and a day, for ever and ever, to the end of time

every
03 all, per **04** each, full, tout **05** total **06** entire **08** complete **11** all possible, every single **15** every individual

everybody
03 all **05** a'body **07** each one **08** everyman, everyone **09** one and all **10** each person **11** all the world, every person, tout le monde **12** all and sundry, every man Jack **13** the whole world

everyday
05 basic, daily, plain, stock, usual **06** common, folksy, modern, normal, simple **07** average, regular, routine **08** day-to-day, familiar, frequent, habitual, informal, ordinary, standard, workaday **09** customary, quotidian **10** accustomed, monotonous **11** commonplace **12** conventional, run-of-the-mill **13** unimaginative **14** common-or-garden

everyone
03 all **07** each one **08** universe **09** allcomers, everybody, one and all **10** each person **11** every person **12** all and sundry, every man Jack **13** the whole world

everything
03 all **04** lock **06** a'thing, the lot, the sum **08** the total, the works **09** all things, each thing **11** all the world, the entirety, the whole lot **12** the aggregate **14** stock and barrel **15** the whole shebang

everywhere
04 left **06** a'where, passim, ubique **07** all over **09** all around, eachwhere **10** every place, far and near, far and wide, high and low, near and far, throughout, ubiquitous **11** at every turn, in all places, in each place, to all places, to each place **12** the world over **14** right and centre

evict
04 oust **05** eject, expel **06** put out, remove **07** cast out, kick out, turf out, turn out **08** chuck out, dislodge, force out, throw out **10** dispossess **11** expropriate **12** force to leave

eviction
07 removal, the boot, the push **08** ejection, the elbow **09** clearance, expulsion **11** the bum's rush **12** dislodgement **13** dispossession, expropriation **14** defenestration

evidence
04 data, deed, hint, mark, show, sign, test **05** proof, prove, stamp, title, token, trace, vouch **06** affirm, assert, attest, avouch, betray, denote, evince, reveal **07** bespeak, confirm, display, exhibit, grounds, signify, support, symptom, witness **08** argument, document, indicate, instance, manifest, surrebut, warranty **09** adminicle, affidavit, establish, guarantee, testimony **10** indication, smoking gun, suggestion **11** affirmation, attestation, credentials, declaration, demonstrate **12** compurgation, confirmation, precognition, verification **13** corroboration, demonstration, documentation, manifestation **14** substantiation
• **in evidence**
05 clear, plain **06** patent **07** obvious, visible **08** apparent, clear-cut **10** noticeable **11** conspicuous **12** unmistakable

evident
05 clear, naked, overt, plain **06** patent **07** confest, obvious, visible **08** apparent, clear-cut, distinct, manifest, sensible, tangible **09** confessed, undoubted **10** noticeable **11** conspicuous, discernible, perceptible, transparent **12** indisputable, unmistakable **13** incontestable

evidently
07 clearly, plainly, visibly **08** patently **09** doubtless, obviously, outwardly, seemingly, so it seems **10** apparently, manifestly, ostensibly **11** doubtlessly, so it appears, undoubtedly **12** indisputably **13** as it would seem, on the face of it **15** as it would appear

evil
03 bad, ill, sin, woe **04** bale, base, blow, dire, eale, foul, harm, hurt, pain, ruin, vice, vile **05** amiss, black, cruel, curse, hydra, nasty, wrong **06** deadly, injury, misery, sinful, sorrow, wicked **07** adverse, badness, corrupt, demonic, disease, harmful, heinous, hurtful, illness, immoral, noisome, noxious, ruinous, unlucky, vicious **08** baseness, calamity, depraved, devilish, diabolic, disaster, distress, iniquity, mischief, sinister, stinking, vileness **09** adversity, depravity, injurious, malicious, malignant, malignity, nefarious, offensive, poisonous, suffering **10** affliction, calamitous, corruption, disastrous, immorality, iniquitous, malevolent, misconduct, misfortune, pernicious, sinfulness, wickedness, wrongdoing **11** catastrophe, deleterious, destructive, detrimental, heinousness,

nischievous, unfortunate, viciousness
2 catastrophic, devilishness,
nauspicious, unfavourable,
inpropitious **13** reprehensible

evildoer
5 rogue **06** sinner **07** badmash,
udmash, villain **08** criminal, offender
9 bad person, miscreant, reprobate,
coundrel, wrongdoer **10** delinquent,
malefactor **12** transgressor

evildoing
3 sin **07** badness, cruelty **08** iniquity,
ileness **09** depravity, nastiness
10 corruption, immorality, sinfulness,
vickedness **11** malefaction,
malfeasance

evince
4 show **06** attest, betray, reveal
7 bespeak, betoken, confess, declare,
lisplay, exhibit, express, signify,
vitness **08** evidence, indicate,
manifest, overcome **09** establish,
make clear, overpower **11** demonstrate

eviscerate
3 gut **04** draw **06** paunch
8 gralloch **10** disembowel,
exenterate

evocation
4 echo **06** recall **07** arousal, calling
8 inducing, kindling, stirring
10 activation, excitation, invocation,
suggestion **11** elicitation, stimulation,
summoning-up

evocative
5 vivid **07** graphic **08** redolent
9 memorable **10** expressive,
ndicative, suggestive **11** reminiscent

evoke
4 call, draw, stir **05** cause, raise,
vaken **06** arouse, awaken, call up,
elicit, excite, induce, invoke, kindle,
ecall, summon **07** provoke
8 summon up **09** call forth, conjure
up, stimulate **10** bring about, call to
mind **11** bring to mind

evolution
> anagram indicator
6 growth **07** biogeny, descent
8 increase, progress, ripening
9 expansion, phytogeny, unfolding,
inrolling **10** derivation, noogenesis,
opening-out, working-out
1 development, progression,
inravelling **12** cladogenesis, Neo-
Darwinism, orthogenesis,
phytogenesis, transformism

evolve
> anagram indicator
4 grow **06** derive, emerge, expand,
nature, result, unfold, unroll
7 advance, descend, develop,
enlarge, open out, unravel, work out
8 develope, disclose, generate,
ncrease, progress **09** elaborate

ewe
3 keb, yow **04** yowe **05** crone, yowie
6 gimmer, lamber, theave

ex
01 X **03** old **04** dead, late **06** former
07 outside, without

exacerbate
03 vex **06** deepen, enrage, worsen
07 inflame, provoke, sharpen
08 embitter, heighten, increase, irritate
09 aggravate, infuriate, intensify, make
worse **10** exaggerate, exasperate
12 fan the flames **15** make things worse

exacerbation
09 worsening **10** irritation
11 aggravation **12** embitterment,
exaggeration, exasperation
15 intensification

exact
04 even, flat, just, milk, true **05** bleed,
claim, close, force, right, wrest, wring
06 bang on, compel, dead on, demand,
extort, impose, insist, minute, spot on,
square, strict **07** call for, careful,
command, correct, estreat, express,
extract, factual, literal, orderly, perfect,
precise, require, squeeze **08** accurate,
definite, detailed, exacting, explicit,
faithful, finished, flawless, insist on,
punctual, rigorous, specific, thorough,
unerring **09** faultless, identical, on the
nail, religious, veracious **10** blow-by-
blow, consummate, methodical,
meticulous, on the money, particular,
scrupulous **11** on the button,
painstaking, point-device, point-
devise, punctilious, word-perfect

exacting
04 firm, hard **05** harsh, stern, tough
06 severe, strict, taxing, tiring
07 arduous, exigent, onerous
08 exigeant, rigorous **09** demanding,
difficult, exigeante, laborious,
stringent, unsparing **10** fastidious,
unyielding **11** challenging, painstaking

exactitude
04 care **05** print **06** detail, rigour
08 accuracy **09** exactness, precision
10 strictness **11** carefulness,
correctness, orderliness
12 rigorousness, thoroughness
13 faultlessness, perfectionism
14 meticulousness, scrupulousness
15 painstakingness

exactly
02 on **03** due, e'en, yes **04** dead, even,
flat, jump, just, to a T, true **05** plumb,
quite, right, smash, spang, truly
06 agreed, bang on, dead on, indeed,
just so, spot on, to a tee **07** quite so, to a
hair **08** of course, on the dot, strictly,
verbatim, you got it **09** carefully,
certainly, correctly, expressly, literally,
on the nail, precisely **10** absolutely,
accurately, definitely, explicitly,
faithfully, rigorously, that's right,
unerringly **11** faultlessly, on the button,
religiously, to the letter, veraciously
12 methodically, particularly,
scrupulously, specifically, without error
13 point for point, unequivocally
• **exactly what's looked for**
02 it

exactness
04 care **06** rigour **08** accuracy,
justness **09** precision **10** exactitude,
strictness **11** carefulness, correctness,
orderliness **12** rigorousness,
thoroughness **13** faultlessness
14 meticulousness, scrupulousness

exaggerate
05 color **06** bounce, colour, overdo,
stress **07** amplify, distend, enhance,
enlarge, lay it on, magnify, stretch
08 overdo it, overdraw, overplay,
oversell, pile it on **09** dramatize,
embellish, embroider, emphasize,
intensify, overstate **10** aggrandize,
goliathize, shoot a line **11** overstretch
12 come it strong, lay it on thick,
overdo things **13** make too much of,
overdramatize, overemphasize, pile it
on thick **15** stretch the truth

exaggerated
04 camp, tall **05** steep **07** exalted
08 inflated, overdone **09** amplified,
bombastic, excessive, overblown
10 burlesqued, cartoonish, euphuistic,
hyperbolic, overstated, theatrical
11 caricatured, embellished,
extravagant, overcharged, pretentious
12 overstrained **13** overestimated
14 larger than life

exaggeration
06 excess, parody **07** stretch
08 emphasis **09** burlesque,
hyperbole, stretcher **10** caricature
11 enlargement **12** extravagance,
overemphasis **13** amplification,
embellishment, magnification,
overstatement **14** overestimation
15 pretentiousness

exalt
04 laud **05** adore, bless, deify, elate,
erect, extol, honor, raise, set up
06 excite, honour, praise, prefer, refine,
revere, throne, uplift **07** acclaim,
advance, applaud, delight, dignify,
elevate, enliven, glorify, magnify,
overjoy, promote, sublime, upgrade,
upraise, worship **08** enthrone,
eulogize, venerate **09** reverence,
subtilize, transport **10** aggrandize,
enthronize, exhilarate

exaltation
03 joy **05** bliss, glory, larks **06** eulogy,
honour, praise **07** acclaim, ecstasy,
elation, raising, rapture, worship
08 erection **09** adoration, elevation,
promotion, rejoicing, reverence
10 enthusiasm, excitement, jubilation,
veneration **11** advancement, high
spirits **12** exhilaration **13** glorification
14 aggrandizement

exalted
04 haut, high **05** elate, grand, happy,
hault, lofty, moral, noble, regal
06 elated, haught, joyful, lordly
07 eminent, stately, sublime
08 blissful, ecstatic, elevated, exultant,
jubilant, magnific, supernal, virtuous
09 dignified, rapturous **10** idealistic,
magnifical **11** exaggerated **13** high and

mighty, in high spirits **15** in seventh heaven

exam, examination
02 ex **03** bac, CSE, GCE, MOT, mug **04** exam, GCSE, mods, oral, quiz, scan, test, viva **05** audit, check, final, paper, probe, study, trial **06** Abitur, A-level, biopsy, Greats, higher, O-level, prelim, review, search, survey **07** canvass, check-up, great go, inquiry, perusal **08** analysis, concours, critique, little go, necropsy, once-over, research, scrutiny, viva voce **09** appraisal, exercises, going-over, practical, questions **10** agrégation, assessment, inspection, post-mortem **11** exploration, inquisition, observation, preliminary, questioning **13** baccalaureate, interrogation, investigation
• **reject at examination**
04 fail, plow, spin **06** plough

examine
03 eye, pry, try, vet **04** case, jerk, palp, pump, quiz, scan, seek, sift, test, view, viva **05** assay, audit, check, grill, probe, quote, study **06** appose, assess, depose, go into, go over, jerque, look at, peruse, ponder, reason, review, revise, search, survey **07** analyse, canvass, check up, collate, discuss, dissect, explore, eyeball, inquire, inspect, observe, palpate, process, weigh up **08** appraise, check out, cognosce, consider, look into, look over, overhale, overhaul, pore over, question, research, traverse, viva voce, work over **09** catechize, check over, check up on, overhaile, speculate **10** go to town on, scrutinize **11** interrogate, investigate **12** cross-examine **13** cross-question **14** put the screws on

examinee
07 entrant **09** applicant, candidate **10** competitor, contestant **11** interviewee

examiner
05 judge, juror **06** censor, critic, marker, reader, tester **07** analyst, arbiter, assayer, auditor **08** assessor, external, reviewer **09** examinant, inspector, moderator, scrutator **10** questioner, scrutineer **11** adjudicator, interviewer, scrutinizer **12** interlocutor

example
02 ex **04** case, lead, type **05** guide, ideal, model, peach, pearl, piece, thing **06** corker, lesson, mirror, muster, sample **07** caution, epitome, exemple, pattern, warning **08** ensample, exemplar, exemplum, exponent, instance, monument, paradigm, specimen, standard **09** archetype, criterion, exemplify, footsteps, precedent, prototype, role model **10** admonition, apotheosis, assay-piece, peacherino, punishment **11** case in point, typical case **12** illustration

14 representative **15** exemplification
• **for example**
02 as, eg, zb **03** say **04** like **06** such as **10** par exemple **11** as an example, for instance, zum Beispiel **12** as an instance, to illustrate **13** exempli gratia

exasperate
03 bug, irk, vex **04** bait, gall, goad, rile **05** anger, annoy, get to, rouse **06** enrage, madden, needle, rankle, wind up **07** incense, provoke **08** irritate **09** aggravate, infuriate, irritated **14** drive up the wall

exasperated
05 angry, fed up, irked, riled, vexed **06** bugged, galled, goaded, peeved, piqued **07** angered, annoyed, needled, nettled **08** incensed, maddened, provoked **09** indignant, irritated **10** aggravated, infuriated

exasperating
06 vexing **07** galling, irksome **08** annoying, infernal **09** maddening, provoking, vexatious **10** bothersome, confounded, irritating, pernicious **11** aggravating, infuriating, troublesome **12** disagreeable

exasperation
04 fury, rage **05** anger **07** chagrin **09** annoyance **10** discontent, irritation **11** aggravation, indignation, stroppiness **12** exulceration **14** disgruntlement

excavate
03 cut, dig **04** mine, sink **05** delve, dig up, drive, gouge, navvy, scoop, stope **06** burrow, dig out, exhume, hollow, quarry, reveal, tunnel **07** uncover, unearth **08** disinter **09** hollow out

excavation
03 cut, dig, pit **04** delf, hole, mine **05** delph, ditch, drift, graft, heuch, heugh, shaft, stope **06** burrow, cavity, crater, dugout, hollow, mining, quarry, trench, trough **07** cutting, digging, sondage **08** catacomb, colliery, diggings, open-cast **09** burrowing, glory hole, hollowing **10** digging out, exhumation, tunnelling, unearthing **11** countermine, side cutting **12** hollowing out

exceed
03 cap, top **04** beat, pass **05** excel, outdo **06** better, go over, outrun, overdo, overgo **07** eclipse, o'ergang, outrace, overtop, surpass **08** go beyond, outreach, outshine, outstrip, outweigh, overgang, overpass, overstep, overtake **09** outnumber, overshoot, transcend **10** be more than, transgress **12** be larger than, be superior to **13** be greater than

exceedingly
04 main, very **05** amain, dooms **06** damned, highly, hugely, proper, vastly **07** greatly, not half, passing **08** almighty, devilish, heavenly, powerful, very much, wondrous **09** amazingly, extremely, immensely,

monstrous, unusually, vengeance **10** consumedly, enormously, especially **11** excessively **12** inordinately, out of all nick, surpassingly **13** astonishingly, exceptionally, superlatively **14** with a vengeance **15** extraordinarily, unprecedentedly

excel
03 war **04** beat, ring **05** outdo, shine **06** better, exceed, outtop, overdo **07** eclipse, outpeer, outrank, succeed, surpass **08** outclass, outrival, overpeer, stand out **09** be skilful **10** outperform **11** be excellent, go one better, predominate **12** be better than, be pre-eminent, be superior to **13** be outstanding **15** go one better than

excellence
05 merit, skill, value, worth **06** purity, virtue, worthy **07** quality **08** eminence, fineness, goodness, nobility **09** greatness, supremacy **10** choiceness, perfection **11** distinction, high quality, pre-eminence, superiority **13** transcendence

excellent
02 A1, ME **03** ace, def, exc, fab, rad **04** best, boss, cool, fine, good, high, mean, mega, neat, pure, rare, tops **05** beaut, boffo, brave, bravo, brill, bully, crack, dicty, dilly, great, hunky, jammy, lummy, noble, noted, prime, socko, triff, wally **06** beauty, beezer, bonzer, castor, cushty, dickty, divine, famous, goodly, groovy, grouse, peachy, purler, ripper, select, spot-on, superb, way-out, whizzo, whizzy, wicked, worthy **07** capital, classic, corking, cracker, crucial, elegant, eminent, kicking, notable, perfect, radical, ripping, shining, stellar, supreme, tipping, topping, triffic, trimmer, Utopian **08** champion, clinking, cracking, eximious, fabulous, flawless, heavenly, inspired, jim-dandy, knockout, smashing, spiffing, splendid, sterling, stonking, stunning, superior, terrific, top-notch, very good, whizbang **09** admirable, brilliant, copacetic, copasetic, exemplary, fantastic, faultless, first-rate, hunky-dory, kopasetic, matchless, righteous, top-drawer, whizz-bang, wonderful **10** first-class, marvellous, noteworthy, not half bad, pre-eminent, remarkable, surpassing, unequalled **11** commendable, exceptional, high-quality, magnificent, outstanding, sensational, superlative **12** praiseworthy, second to none, the bee's knees, unparalleled **13** above reproach, distinguished **14** out of this world **15** unexceptionable

excellently
04 well **06** goodly **08** champion, divinely, superbly **09** admirably, capitally, eminently, first-rate, perfectly **10** remarkably, splendidly **11** brilliantly, commendably, wonderfully

2 marvellously, terrifically
3 exceptionally, fantastically, sensationally, superlatively

except
02 ex, sa' **03** bar, but, exc **04** less, omit, only, save, than **05** minus **06** bating, but for, nobbut, reject **07** barring, besides, exclude, outtake, rule out, short of, without **08** leave out, omitting, pass over **09** apart from, aside from, except for, excepting, excluding, other than, outside of **10** leaving out **11** not counting

exception
02 ex **03** exc **05** freak, quirk **06** oddity, rarity **07** anomaly, offence **09** departure, deviation, exclusion, objection **11** abnormality, peculiarity, special case **12** irregularity **13** inconsistency
• **take exception**
05 argue, demur, rebut **06** object, oppose, refuse, resist **07** protest **08** complain **09** challenge, repudiate, take issue, withstand **10** disapprove **11** beg to differ, expostulate, remonstrate
• **with the exception of**
03 bar, but **04** less, save **05** minus **07** barring, besides **08** omitting **09** apart from, except for, excepting, excluding, other than **10** leaving out **11** not counting

exceptionable
09 abhorrent, offensive, repugnant **10** deplorable, disgusting, unpleasant **12** disagreeable, unacceptable **13** objectionable

exceptional
03 odd **04** rare **06** way-out **07** notable, special, strange, unusual **08** aberrant, abnormal, atypical, peculiar, singular, superior, uncommon **09** anomalous, brilliant, excellent, irregular **10** marvellous, noteworthy, phenomenal, prodigious, remarkable, unequalled **11** outstanding **13** extraordinary, one in a million **14** one in a thousand

exceptionally
05 extra **06** rarely **07** notably **09** amazingly, extremely, unusually **10** abnormally, especially, remarkably, uncommonly **11** irregularly, wonderfully **13** outstandingly **15** extraordinarily

excerpt
04 clip, part **05** piece, quote, scrap **07** cutting, extract, passage, portion, section **08** citation, clipping, fragment, pericope **09** quotation, selection

excess
04 glut, rest **05** extra, spare **06** gutful, spilth **07** backlog, nimiety, o'ercome, residue, surfeit, surplus, too much **08** bellyful, left-over, overcome, overflow, overkill, owrecome, plethora, residual **09** leftovers, redundant, remainder, remaining

10 additional, debauchery, oversupply **11** dissipation, exorbitance, exorbitancy, prodigality, superfluity, superfluous, unrestraint **12** extravagance, immoderation, intemperance **13** dissoluteness, overabundance, supernumerary **14** immoderateness, more than enough, overindulgence, superabundance
• **in excess of**
04 over **05** above **08** more than

excessive
03 OTT **04** deep, over, rank **05** steep, stiff, undue **06** lavish **07** burning, extreme, fulsome, too much **08** needless, overdone, unneeded **09** exceeding, overblown **10** exorbitant, immoderate, inordinate, over the top **11** extravagant, superfluous, uncalled-for, unnecessary, unwarranted **12** overabundant, unreasonable **13** superabundant

excessively
06 overly, troppo, unduly **07** too much **08** overmuch, to a fault, woundily **09** extremely, needlessly **11** God-almighty **12** exorbitantly, immoderately, inordinately, out of all cess, unreasonably **13** beyond measure, exaggeratedly, extravagantly, intemperately, superfluously, unnecessarily

exchange
◇ *anagram indicator*
02 ex **04** chat, chop, cope, exch, swap, swop **05** bandy, bazar, swits, trade, trock, troke, truck **06** barter, bazaar, change, excamb, market, niffer, scorse, switch **07** bargain, commute, convert, dealing, replace, traffic **08** argument, commerce, dialogue, trade-off **09** transpose **10** discussion, stand in for, substitute **11** give and take, interchange, reciprocate, reciprocity, replacement **12** conversation, substitution

excise
03 cut, GST, tax, VAT **04** duty, levy, toll **05** erase **06** cut off, cut out, delete, impost, remove, tariff **07** customs, destroy, expunge, extract, rescind **09** eradicate, expurgate, extirpate, surcharge **11** exterminate

excision
◇ *deletion indicator*
03 cut **07** removal **08** deletion **10** expunction **11** destruction, eradication, expurgation, extirpation **13** extermination

excitable
04 edgy **05** fiery, hasty, nappy, nervy **06** feisty **07** nervous, rackety **08** choleric, volatile **09** emotional, hot-headed, irascible, mercurial, sensitive **10** passionate **11** combustible, hot-tempered, susceptible **12** highly-strung **13** quick-tempered, temperamental

excite
◇ *anagram indicator*
04 fire, move, stir, sway, urge, wake, warm, whet, yerk **05** evoke, flush, hop up, impel, rouse, steer, stire, styre, touch, upset, waken **06** accite, aerate, arouse, awaken, emmove, enmove, fire up, ignite, incite, induce, kindle, stir up, thrill, tickle, turn on, wind up, work up **07** agitate, animate, commove, disturb, enliven, ferment, impress, inflame, inspire, provoke, upraise **08** blow away, energize, engender, enkindle, generate, irritate, motivate **09** electrify, galvanize, instigate, sensitize, set on edge, stimulate, suscitate, titillate **10** bring about, intoxicate

excited
◇ *anagram indicator*
02 up **03** het, hot **04** high, warm, wild **05** antsy, astir, eager, hyper, moved, nervy, proud, radge, randy **06** elated, juiced, randie, roused **07** aroused, fevered, fired up, flushed, frantic, hyped up, sexed-up, stirred, uptight **08** agitated, animated, frenzied, hopped-up, restless, revved-up, thrilled, turned on, worked up **09** delirious, red-headed, wrought-up **10** corybantic, stimulated, up in the air **11** exhilarated, overwrought **12** enthusiastic **13** in high spirits, on tenterhooks **14** beside yourself, thrilled to bits

excitement
03 ado, rut, tew **04** fume, fuss, kick, ruff, spin, stir **05** fever, furor, kicks, pride, ruffe **06** action, didder, dither, flurry, furore, hoop-la, thrill, tumult, unrest **07** arousal, elation, emotion, ferment, passion **08** activity, brouhaha, delirium, erethism, flat spin, hilarity, pleasure **09** adventure, agitation, animation, commotion, eagerness, fleshment, rousement, sensation **10** enthusiasm, salutation **11** fun and games, stimulation **12** discomposure, exhilaration, Hobson-Jobson, intoxication, perturbation, restlessness
• **expression of excitement**
04 whee **05** yahoo **06** yippee **07** way to go! **08** hey-go-mad
• **seeking excitement**
04 fast
• **state of excitement**
10 fever pitch

exciting
03 hot **04** sexy **05** heady, magic **06** moving **07** rousing **08** dramatic, excitant, gripping, stirring, striking **09** inspiring, thrilling **10** nail-biting **11** aphrodisiac, enthralling, hair-raising, interesting, provocative, sensational, stimulating **12** action-packed, breathtaking, cliff-hanging, electrifying, exhilarating, intoxicating **13** swashbuckling
• **something exciting**
03 gas

exclaim

03 cry **04** call, roar, yell **05** blurt, shout, utter **06** bellow, cry out, outcry, shriek **07** declare **08** blurt out, proclaim **09** ejaculate, interject **10** vociferate **11** come out with, exclamation

exclamation

02 ho, wo **03** boo, cry, fen, hip, olé, pah, tut, ugh, woe, wow, yah, yay **04** call, go on, hech, I say!, oops, phew, pish, poof, pooh, push, roar, sa sa, shoo, skol, upsy, when, yell **05** bingo, fancy, house, hurra, my hat!, shout, skoal, upsee, upsey, yahoo **06** banzai, bellow, by Jove, hooray, hurrah, hurray, outcry, phooey, shriek, shucks, walker, whoops, zounds **07** bless me!, crivens, good egg, good-now, heigh-ho, hosanna, right on, whoopee **08** crivvens, hear hear!, here goes!, man alive, stroll on! **09** expletive, fancy that, good grief, unberufen, utterance **10** ecphonesis, epiphonema, Great Scott!, hoity-toity, how dare you!, upon my soul! **11** bless my soul!, bumpsadaisy, ejaculation, good heavens, marry come up **12** boomps-a-daisy, Hookey Walker, interjection, strike a light! **15** shiver my timbers

• **exclamation mark**
05 pling **06** shriek **08** screamer

exclude

03 ban, bar **04** drop, omit, skip, veto **05** debar, eject, evict, expel, hatch **06** delete, except, forbid, ice out, ignore, refuse, reject, remove **07** boot out, boycott, keep out, kick out, lock out, miss out, push out, rule out, shut off, shut out, turf out **08** count out, disallow, leave out, preclude, prohibit, throw out **09** blacklist, eliminate, freeze out, interdict, ostracize **10** include out **13** excommunicate **14** send to Coventry

excluding

◇ *deletion indicator*
06 except **07** barring **08** omitting **09** debarring, except for, excepting, ruling out **10** leaving out **11** exclusive of, not counting **12** not including

exclusion

03 ban, bar **04** veto **07** boycott, embargo, refusal, removal **08** ejection, eviction, omission **09** exception, expulsion, interdict, rejection, ruling out **10** preclusion **11** elimination, prohibition, repudiation **12** proscription

exclusive

03 few **04** chic, coup, only, posh, sole **05** plush, ritzy, scoop, swish, total, whole **06** choice, classy, cliquy, closed, clubby, exposé, narrow, select, single, snazzy, unique **07** cliquey, elegant, limited, private **08** boutique, cliquish, complete, peculiar, rarefied, snobbish, unshared, up-market **09** high-class, sectarian, sensation, undivided

10 individual, restricted, revelation, upper-crust **11** fashionable, inside story, restrictive **12** incompatible **14** discriminative

• **exclusive of**
06 except **07** barring **08** omitting **09** debarring, except for, excepting, excluding, ruling out **10** leaving out **11** not counting **12** not including

excommunicate

03 ban, bar **05** curse, debar, eject, expel **06** banish, outlaw, remove **07** exclude **08** denounce, execrate, unchurch **09** blacklist, proscribe, repudiate **12** anathematize **13** disfellowship

excommunication

07 banning, barring **08** ejection **09** exclusion, expulsion, outlawing **10** banishment **11** unchurching **12** denunciation **13** disfellowship

excoriate

03 nag **04** carp, slam **05** blame, decry, knock, slate, snipe **06** attack **07** censure, condemn, nit-pick, run down **08** denounce **09** denigrate, disparage **10** animadvert, come down on, vituperate **12** disapprove of **13** find fault with

excrement

03 poo **04** crap, crud, dung, flux, mess, poop **05** frass, guano, scats, stool **06** doo-doo, egesta, faeces, ordure **07** droppings, excretion **11** waste matter **12** rejectamenta, sir-reverence

excrescence

03 bur, pin **04** blot, boil, bump, burr, knob, lump, moss, nail, nurl, wart, wolf **05** knurl **06** cancer, growth, tumour, wattle **07** eyesore, rat-tail, sarcoma, twitter **08** rat's-tail, swelling **09** appendage, carnosity, misgrowth, outgrowth **10** projection, prominence, proud flesh **11** monstrosity, twitter-bone **12** intumescence, protuberance **13** disfigurement

excrete

03 poo **04** crap, pass, void **05** eject, expel, exude **07** secrete, urinate **08** defecate, evacuate **09** discharge

excretion

03 poo **04** crap, dung **05** stool **06** faeces, ordure **07** excreta **09** discharge, droppings, excrement, urination **10** defecation, evacuation **12** perspiration

excruciate

◇ *anagram indicator*
04 rack **07** torture **08** irritate

excruciating

05 acute, sharp **06** bitter, savage, severe **07** burning, extreme, intense, painful, racking **08** piercing **09** agonizing, atrocious, harrowing, torturing **10** tormenting, unbearable **11** intolerable **12** cringe-making, cringeworthy, insufferable

excruciatingly

07 acutely **08** severely **09** extremely, intensely, painfully **10** unbearably **11** atrociously, intolerably

exculpate

04 free **05** clear **06** acquit, excuse, let off, pardon **07** absolve, deliver, forgive, justify, release **09** discharge, exonerate, vindicate

excursion

02 ex **03** exc **04** raid, ride, tour, trip, walk **05** drive, jaunt, jolly, sally, visit **06** airing, detour, junket, outing, picnic, ramble, sashay, sortie, vagary **07** day trip, journey, outleap **08** breather, escapade, straying **09** departure, diversion, wandering **10** digression, expedition **11** mystery tour **12** pleasure trip

excusable

05 minor **06** slight, venial **09** allowable **10** defensible, forgivable, pardonable **11** explainable, justifiable, permissible **14** understandable

excuse

04 faik, free, hook, plea **05** alibi, front, salvo, scuse, shift, spare **06** acquit, cop-out, defend, essoin, exempt, get-out, ignore, let off, pardon, reason **07** absolve, apology, condone, cover-up, defence, essoyne, evasion, explain, forgive, grounds, indulge, justify, pretext, release, relieve **08** liberate, mitigate, occasion, overlook, palliate, pretence, tolerate **09** allowance, discharge, exculpate, exonerate, vindicate **10** indulgence, mitigation, substitute **11** exoneration, explanation, forgiveness, vindication **12** apologize for **13** justification **14** whittie-whattie

execrable

04 foul, vile **05** awful **06** odious **07** hateful, heinous **08** accursed, damnable, dreadful, horrible, nauseous, shocking **09** abhorrent, appalling, atrocious, loathsome, obnoxious, offensive, repulsive, revolting **10** abominable, deplorable, despicable, detestable, disgusting

execrate

04 damn, hate **05** abhor, blast, curse **06** detest, loathe, revile, vilify **07** condemn, deplore, despise **08** denounce **09** abominate, excoriate, fulminate, imprecate **10** denunciate **12** anathematize **14** inveigh against

execute

02 do **03** cut, fry, run **04** hang, kill, take **05** dance, enact, serve, shoot, stage, throw **06** behead, effect, finish, fulfil, render **07** achieve, crucify, deliver, enforce, garotte, garrote, perform, produce, realize **08** bring off, carry out, complete, despatch, dispatch, engineer, expedite, garrotte, validate **09** discharge, implement, liquidate **10** accomplish, administer, consummate, decapitate, guillotine, erpetrate, put to death **11** electrocute **B** put into effect **15** put into practice

xecution
3 run **04** mode **05** style **06** effect, **i**anner **07** killing, staging **08** delivery, **i**spatch **09** discharge, effecting, **i**actment, operation, rendering, **i**ndition, technique **10** completion, **i**lfilment **11** achievement, carrying-**i**ut, enforcement, performance, **e**alization **12** consummation, death **e**nalty, presentation **13** death **e**ntence **14** accomplishment, **d**ministration, implementation, **i**utting to death

Execution methods include:
6 noyade
7 burning, gassing, hanging, stoning
8 lynching, shooting
9 beheading
) garrotting
I crucifixion, firing squad, stringing up
2 decapitation, guillotining
3 electric chair, electrocution
5 lethal injection

xecutioner
6 axeman, hit man, killer, slayer **7** hangman **08** assassin, carnifex, **e**adsman, murderer **09** deathsman, **i**ck Ketch, tormenter, tormentor **)** liquidator **11** firing squad **2** exterminator **15** Monsieur de Paris

xecutive
2 ex **04** exec, suit **06** leader **07** big **i**uns, guiding, leading, manager **08** big **i**ots, chairman, director, governor, **f**ficial, superior, top brass **9** directing, governing, hierarchy, **i**wmaking, organizer **10** chairwoman, **i**ntroller, government, leadership, **i**anagement, managerial, organizing, **e**gulating **11** chairperson, controlling, **i**rectorial, ministerial, supervisory **3** administrator **14** administration, **d**ministrative, decision-making, **i**ganizational, superintendent

xegesis
9 opening-up **10** exposition, **i**pounding **11** explanation, **i**plication **13** clarification **4** interpretation

xemplar
4 copy, type **05** ideal, model **7** epitome, example, paragon, **i**ttern, sampler **08** instance, **i**radigm, specimen, standard **9** archetype, criterion, prototype, **i**rdstick **10** embodiment **2** illustration **15** exemplification

xemplary
4 good **05** ideal, model **06** worthy **7** correct, perfect, warning **8** flawless, laudable **09** admirable, **i**timable, excellent, faultless **)** admonitory, cautionary, **i**nourable **11** commendable, **i**eritorious **12** praiseworthy

exemplify
03 sum **04** cite, show, type **06** depict, embody, typify **07** display, example, exhibit **08** instance, manifest **09** epitomize, personify, represent **10** illustrate, synonymize **11** demonstrate **12** characterize **13** be an example of

exempt
04 free **05** clear, exeem, exeme, spare, waive **06** excuse, immune, let off, spared **07** absolve, dismiss, exclude, excused, release, relieve **08** absolved, excluded, liberate, released **09** discharge, dismissed, exonerate, liberated, not liable **10** discharged, not subject **11** grandfather **15** grant immunity to, make an exception

exemption
07 freedom, release **08** immunity, variance **09** discharge, exception, exclusion, indemnity, privilege **10** absolution, indulgence, indulgency, overslaugh **11** exoneration **12** dispensation

exercise
◇ *anagram indicator*
02 PE, PT **03** gym, jog, try, use, vex **04** task, work **05** annoy, apply, drill, exert, sport, theme, train, upset, wield, worry **06** burden, effort, employ, labour, lesson, sports, warm up, warm-up **07** afflict, agitate, concern, disturb, exploit, perturb, problem, project, running, trouble, utilize, work out, workout **08** activity, ceremony, distress, exertion, movement, practice, practise, pump iron, training, warm down, warm-down **09** discharge, discourse, implement, make use of, operation, preoccupy, quodlibet **10** assignment, discipline, employment, fulfilment, gymnastics, isometrics **11** application, bring to bear, do exercises, piece of work, utilization **12** exercitation **13** bring into play, exert yourself **14** accomplishment, implementation

Exercises include:
04 yoga
05 Medau
06 qigong, t'ai chi
07 aquafit, chi kung, jogging, keep fit, Pilates, press-up
08 aerobics
09 boxercise, hatha yoga
10 aquarobics, daily dozen, dancercise
11 Callanetics, eurhythmics
12 body-building, calisthenics, step aerobics
13 callisthenics, cross-training, physical jerks
15 circuit training

exert
02 do **03** use **05** apply, spend, wield **06** employ, expend, extend, put out **07** utilize **08** exercise, put forth **11** bring to bear **13** bring into play
• **exert yourself**
04 hump, pull, toil, work **05** sweat

06 labour, pingle, strain, strive **07** try hard **08** go all out, slog away, struggle **09** endeavour, take pains **10** do your best **11** give your all **12** do your utmost **13** apply yourself **15** make every effort

exertion
03 use **04** toil, work **05** graft, pains, trial **06** action, effort, labour, pingle, strain, stress **07** attempt, travail, trouble **08** endeavor, exercise, industry, striving, struggle **09** diligence, endeavour, hard graft, operation **10** employment **11** application, utilization **12** perseverance **13** assiduousness

exhalation
04 mist **06** meteor, vapour **08** emission, fumosity, mephitis **09** discharge, effluvium, emanation, expulsion **10** expiration **11** evaporation, respiration **12** breathing-out

exhale
04 blow, emit, reek **05** expel, issue, smoke, steam **06** expire, vanish **07** blow out, breathe, emanate, give off, respire **08** perspire **09** discharge, evaporate, transpire **10** breathe out

exhaust
02 do **03** beg, dry, sap, tax **04** do in, jade, kill, poop, suck, tire, wear **05** drain, empty, fordo, fumes, smoke, spend, steam, use up, waste, weary, whack **06** expend, fag out, finish, strain, vapour, weaken **07** consume, deplete, fatigue, knacker, overrun, overtax, play out, tire out, wash out, wear out, work out **08** bankrupt, emission, enervate, forspend, forswink, knock out, overlive, override, overteem, overtire, overwork, squander, weary out **09** discharge, dissipate, emanation, forespend, overshoot, overspend, overweary, overwrite, tucker out **10** almost kill, exhalation, impoverish, nearly kill, run through **11** take it out of

exhausted
03 dry **04** done, mate, shot, void, weak, worn **05** all in, empty, jaded, spent, tired, weary **06** all out, beaten, bushed, done in, effete, pooped, used up, wabbit, wasted, zonked **07** at an end, drained, emptied, euchred, fainted, fordone, puggled, shagged, shotten, waygone, whacked, worn out **08** a cot case, burnt out, consumed, dead-beat, depleted, dog-tired, fatigued, finished, forfairn, half-dead, jiggered, tired out, wiped out **09** burned out, dead tired, enervated, enfeebled, fagged out, knackered, played-out, pooped out, prostrate, shattered, stonkered, washed-out, zonked out **10** clapped-out, euchred out, forfeuchen, forfoughen, shagged out **11** bush whacked, forfoughten, ready to drop, stressed-out, tuckered out

exhausting
04 hard **06** severe, taxing, tiring
07 arduous, killing, testing, wearing
08 draining, grueling, wearying
09 depletion, gruelling, laborious, punishing, strenuous **10** enervating, formidable **12** backbreaking, debilitating

exhaustion
06 jet-lag **07** fatigue **08** distress, lethargy, weakness **09** tiredness, weariness **10** enervation, feebleness

exhaustive
04 full **05** total **06** all-out **07** in-depth **08** complete, detailed, sweeping, thorough **09** extensive, full-scale, intensive **10** definitive **11** far-reaching **12** all-embracing, all-inclusive, encyclopedic **13** comprehensive

exhaustively
05 fully **07** totally **10** completely, thoroughly **11** extensively, intensively **12** definitively **14** all-inclusively **15** comprehensively

exhibit
03 air **04** hang, shew, show, wear **05** array, exude, model, offer, sport **06** expose, flaunt, parade, reveal, set out, unveil **07** display, express, present, propose, showing **08** disclose, discover, indicate, manifest, set forth, showcase **09** make clear, make plain, showpiece **10** exhibition **11** demonstrate **12** illustration, presentation, put on display **13** demonstration

exhibition
04 demo, expo, fair, gift, show **05** grant, rodeo, Salon, simul **06** airing **07** academy, diorama, display, exhibit, ice show, preview, showing **08** aquacade, pavilion, showcase, sideshow, waxworks **09** allowance, spectacle **10** cattle show, disclosure, exposition, expression, flower show, indication, panopticon, puppet show, revelation **11** performance **12** presentation, simultaneous **13** cinematograph, demonstration, manifestation, retrospective **14** representation

exhibitionism
09 dramatics, flaunting, staginess **10** overacting, showing-off **11** flamboyance, histrionics, self-display **12** boastfulness

exhibitionist
05 poser **06** poseur **07** show-off **09** extrovert **14** self-advertiser

exhilarate
04 lift **05** cheer, elate **06** excite, perk up, thrill **07** animate, cheer up, delight, elevate, enliven, gladden **08** brighten, vitalize **09** inebriate, make happy, stimulate **10** intoxicate, invigorate, revitalize **11** make excited

exhilarating
05 heady, sapid **06** breezy

08 cheerful, cheering, exciting **09** heartsome, thrilling **10** delightful, enlivening, gladdening **11** mind-blowing, stimulating **12** breathtaking, intoxicating, invigorating, revitalizing **13** heart-stirring

exhilaration
03 joy **04** dash, élan, glee, zeal **05** gusto, mirth **06** ardour, gaiety, thrill **07** delight, elation **08** euphoria, gladness, hilarity, vivacity **09** animation, happiness **10** enthusiasm, exaltation, excitement, joyfulness, joyousness, liveliness **11** high spirits, stimulation **12** cheerfulness, invigoration **14** revitalization

exhort
03 bid **04** goad, spur, urge, warn **05** press **06** advise, call on, enjoin, incite, prompt **07** beseech, caution, counsel, entreat, implore, inflame, inspire **08** admonish, call upon, persuade **09** encourage, instigate

exhortation
04 call **06** advice, appeal, sermon, urging **07** bidding, caution, counsel, goading, lecture, warning **08** entreaty **09** enjoinder, parenesis **10** admonition, allocution, beseeching, incitement, injunction, invitation, paraenesis, persuasion, protreptic **13** encouragement

exhumation
10 excavation, unearthing **12** disinterment **13** disentombment

exhume
05 dig up **06** unbury **07** unearth **08** disinter, excavate **09** disentomb, disinhume, resurrect

exigency
04 need, turn **06** crisis, demand, plight, stress **07** urgency **08** distress, pressure, quandary **09** emergency, necessity **10** difficulty **11** predicament, requirement **12** criticalness **14** imperativeness

exigent
06 urgent **07** crucial **08** critical, exacting, pressing **09** demanding, extremity, insistent, necessary, stringent

exiguous
04 bare, slim **05** scant **06** meagre, scanty, slight, sparse **07** slender **10** inadequate, negligible **12** insufficient

exile
03 ban, bar **04** exul, oust **05** eject, expat, expel, Galut **06** banish, deport, émigré, Galuth, outlaw, pariah, uproot, wretch **07** Babylon, cast out, outcast, refugee **08** deportee, Diaspora, drive out, fugitive, separate **09** expulsion, extradite, ostracism, ostracize, uprooting **10** banishment, expatriate, repatriate, separating, separation **11** deportation **12** expatriation

13 excommunicate **14** transportation **15** displaced person

exist
02 be **04** last, live **05** abide, occur, stand **06** endure, happen, remain **07** be alive, be found, breathe, consist, persist, prevail, subsist, survive **08** continue, have life **09** be present, have being **10** have breath **11** be available **13** eke out a living, have existence

existence
03 ens **04** esse, fact, life **05** being, thing **06** breath, entity, living **07** inbeing, reality **08** creation, creature, survival, the world **09** actuality, endurance, lifestyle, way of life **11** continuance, subsistence, way of living **12** continuation, mode o[ ] living **13** individuation
• **loss of independent existence**
03 LIE

existent
04 real **05** alive **06** actual, around, extant, living **07** abiding, current, present **08** enduring, existing, standing **09** obtaining, remaining, surviving **10** prevailing **11** in existence

exit
02 go **03** die **04** door, gate, vent **05** death, going, go out, issue, leave **06** depart, egress, exodus, flight, log off, log out, outlet, retire, way out **07** doorway, leaving, off-ramp, outgate, retreat **08** farewell, withdraw **09** departure **10** going forth, retirement, withdrawal **11** leave-taking **13** take your leave

exodus
02 Ex **04** exit, Exod **06** escape, flight, hegira **07** fleeing, leaving, retreat **09** departure, long march, migration **10** evacuation, retirement, withdrawal **13** mass departure **14** mass evacuation

exonerate
04 free **05** clear, spare **06** acquit, excuse, exempt, let off, pardon **07** absolve, justify, release, relieve **08** liberate **09** discharge, exculpate, vindicate **15** declare innocent

exoneration
06 pardon, relief **07** amnesty, freeing, release **08** clearing, excusing, immunity **09** acquittal, discharge, dismissal, exemption, indemnity **10** absolution, liberation **11** exculpation, vindication **13** justification

exorbitant
05 steep, undue **07** a rip-off **08** enormous **09** excessive, monstrous **10** immoderate, inordinate **11** extravagant, unwarranted **12** extortionate, preposterous, unreasonable **15** daylight robbery

exorbitantly
06 unduly **11** excessively **12** immoderately, inordinately,

unreasonably **13** extravagantly
14 extortionately, through the nose

exorcism
07 freeing **09** expulsion **10** adjuration, casting out **11** deliverance
12 exsufflation, insufflation, purification

exorcize
03 lay **04** free **05** expel **06** adjure, purify **07** cast out **08** drive out
10 exsufflate, insufflate

exotic
◇ *anagram indicator*
05 alien **06** ethnic, way-out
07 bizarre, curious, foreign, strange, unusual **08** external, imported, peculiar, striking, tropical
09 colourful, different, glamorous, non-native, recherché **10** impressive, introduced, outlandish, outrageous, remarkable, unfamiliar **11** extravagant, fascinating, sensational
13 extraordinary

exotically
09 curiously, strangely, unusually
10 remarkably, strikingly, tropically
12 impressively, outlandishly
13 sensationally **15** extraordinarily

expand
03 pad **04** grow **05** swell, widen
06 blow up, dilate, extend, fatten, intend, put out, spread, unfold, unfurl, work up **07** amplify, broaden, develop, distend, enlarge, fill out, inflate, magnify, open out, puff out, stretch, thicken **08** dispread, enlargen, escalate, increase, lengthen, multiply, mushroom **09** branch out, diversify, intensify, intumesce **10** decompress, make bigger, make larger **12** become bigger, become larger
• **expand on**
08 dilate on, flesh out **09** embroider, enlarge on **11** elaborate on, expatiate on **13** go into details

expanse
03 sea **04** area, main, mass, moor, muir, vast **05** field, ocean, plain, range, sheet, space, sweep, tract, vague, waste **06** extent, region, spread **07** breadth, stretch
08 vastness **09** champaign, immensity, outspread **11** immenseness
13 extensiveness

expansion
04 boom **06** growth, spread
07 expanse **08** dilation, increase, swelling **09** diffusion, explosion, extension, inflation, unfolding, unfurling **10** broadening, dilatation, distension, thickening
11 development, enlargement, lengthening **12** augmentation
13 amplification, decompression, magnification **14** multiplication
15 diversification

expansive
04 open, warm, wide **05** broad
06 genial **07** affable, growing

08 effusive, friendly, outgoing, sociable, sweeping, thorough
09 diffusive, enlarging, expanding, extensive, talkative **10** developing, increasing, loquacious, magnifying, widespread **11** expatiative, expatiatory, forthcoming, multiplying, uninhibited, wide-ranging **12** all-embracing, diversifying **13** communicative, comprehensive

expatiate
06 dilate, expand **07** amplify, develop, dwell on, enlarge, expound
08 enlargen **09** elaborate, embellish, give forth **11** hold forth on

expatriate
04 oust **05** exile, expat, expel
06 banish, deport, émigré, exiled, uproot **07** outcast, refugee
08 banished, deported, drive out, emigrant, expelled, uprooted
09 extradite, ostracize, proscribe
10 repatriate **15** displaced person

expect
04 hope, look, wait, want, ween, wish
05 await, guess, think, trust **06** ask for, assume, bank on, demand, lippen, look to, reckon, rely on **07** believe, call for, count on, foresee, hope for, imagine, look for, predict, presume, project, require, suppose, surmise
08 envisage, figure on, forecast, insist on, think for, watch for **09** bargain on, look after **10** anticipate, bargain for, conjecture **11** contemplate **13** look forward to

expectancy
04 hope **07** waiting **08** suspense
09 curiosity, eagerness **10** conjecture
11 expectation **12** anticipation

expectant
05 eager, great, quick, ready **06** gravid
07 anxious, curious, excited, hopeful
08 awaiting, carrying, enceinte, preggers, pregnant, watchful
09 expecting, in the club, in trouble, with child **10** big-bellied, in suspense
11 open-mouthed **12** anticipating, apprehensive **13** on tenterhooks
14 in the family way, looking forward
15 with bated breath

expectantly
07 eagerly **09** hopefully **10** in suspense **11** expectingly
14 apprehensively, in anticipation, optimistically

expectation
04 hope, view, want, wish **05** trust
06 belief, demand **07** outlook, promise, suppose, surmise
08 forecast, optimism, prospect, reliance, suspense, tendance
09 assurance, eagerness
10 assumption, confidence, conjecture, insistence, looking-for, prediction, projection **11** calculation, possibility, presumption, probability, requirement, supposition
12 anticipation

expecting
05 great, quick **06** gravid **08** carrying, enceinte, preggers, pregnant
09 expectant, in the club, in trouble, with child **10** big-bellied **14** in the family way

expedience
05 haste **07** aptness, benefit, fitness, utility **08** despatch, dispatch, prudence **09** advantage, propriety
10 enterprise, expediency, pragmatism, properness, usefulness
11 convenience, helpfulness, suitability
12 advisability, desirability, practicality
13 effectiveness, judiciousness, profitability **14** profitableness, utilitarianism **15** appropriateness

expedient
04 plan, ploy **05** dodge, means, salvo, shift, trick **06** device, method, scheme, tactic, useful **07** fitting, measure, politic, prudent, stopgap
08 artifice, resource, sensible, suitable, tactical **09** advisable, manoeuvre, opportune, practical, pragmatic, stratagem **10** beneficial, convenient, profitable **11** appropriate, contrivance, expeditious **12** advantageous

expedite
05 hurry, press, quick **06** assist, hasten, prompt, step up **07** further, promote, quicken, speed up **08** despatch, dispatch **09** discharge **10** accelerate, facilitate **11** precipitate **12** hurry through, unencumbered

expedition
03 dig **04** crew, hike, raid, sail, team, tour, trek, trip **05** group, haste, party, quest, shoot, speed **06** outing, ramble, safari, voyage **07** company, crusade, hosting, journey, mission, project, warpath **08** alacrity, campaign
09 adventure, excursion, field trip, swiftness **10** enterprise, pilgrimage, promptness **11** exploration, undertaking

expeditious
04 fast **05** alert, brisk, hasty, quick, rapid, ready, swift **06** active, prompt, speedy **07** express, instant **08** diligent, meteoric **09** efficient, expedient, immediate

expel
03 ban, bar, rid **04** hoof, oust, void
05 belch, eject, evict, exile **06** banish, deport, let out, outlaw, put out, reject
07 boot out, cast out, dismiss, drum out, expulse, extrude, fire out, kick out, read out, spew out, turn out **08** chuck out, drive out, evacuate, send down, sideline, throw out **09** discharge, eliminate, proscribe, turn forth
10 expatriate

expend
03 buy, pay, sap, use **04** blow **05** drain, empty, spend, use up, waste **06** afford, employ, lay out, outlay, pay out
07 consume, deplete, dispend, exhaust, fork out, fritter, procure, utilize

08 disburse, purchase, shell out, squander **09** dissipate, go through, overspend, splash out **10** get through

expendable
09 throwaway **10** disposable
11 dispensable, inessential, replaceable, unimportant, unnecessary **12** non-essential

expenditure
03 use **04** mise **05** costs, outgo, waste **06** outlay, output **07** expense, payment, sapping **08** dispense, draining, expenses, outgoing, spending **09** goings-out, outgoings **10** employment **11** application, consumption, dissipation, squandering, utilization **12** disbursement
• **reduction of expenditure**
02 ax **03** axe **06** saving
11 economizing

expense, expenses
03 fee **04** cost, harm, loss, rate **05** costs, price **06** charge, outlay **07** payment **08** spending **09** detriment, outgoings, overheads, paying-out, sacrifice **11** expenditure, incidentals **12** disadvantage, disbursement
• **share of expense**
03 law

expensive
04 dear, posh, salt **05** fancy, pricy, steep **06** costly, lavish, pricey **07** sky-high **08** high-cost, splendid **09** big-ticket, chargeful, excessive, executive **10** exorbitant, high-priced, overpriced **11** costing a lot, extravagant **12** costing a bomb, extortionate **15** costing the earth, daylight robbery

experience
03 see, try **04** case, face, feel, find, have, know, meet, pass, spin **05** event, skill, taste **06** affair, endure, expert, ordeal, suffer **07** contact, episode, knowhow, receive, sustain, undergo **08** exposure, incident, learning, perceive, practice, training **09** adventure, encounter, go through, happening, knowledge **10** occurrence **11** familiarity, involvement, live through, observation, pass through **12** circumstance **13** participate in, participation, understanding
• **cause to experience**
04 lead
• **irritating experience**
03 rub **06** rubber
• **lacking experience**
05 green, naive
• **painful experience**
03 fit

experienced
03 old **04** wise **05** adept, suave, tried **06** around, au fait, expert, mature **07** capable, skilful, skilled, trained, veteran, weighed **08** familiar, schooled, seasoned, traveled **09** au courant, competent, practised, qualified, travailed, travelled

10 proficient, streetwise, well-versed **11** worldly wise **12** accomplished, experimented, professional **13** knowledgeable, sophisticated

experiment
03 exp, try **04** test **05** assay, essay, proof, trial **06** dry run, sample, try out, try-out, verify **07** attempt, examine, explore, inquiry, observe, testing, venture **08** analysis, dummy run, piloting, research, trial run **09** procedure **10** conclusion, experience, pilot study **11** examination, investigate, observation **13** carry out tests, demonstration, investigation, trial and error **15** experimentation

experimental
03 exp **04** test **05** pilot, trial **09** empirical, peirastic, tentative **10** scientific **11** exploratory, preliminary, provisional, speculative **13** investigative, observational, trial-and-error **15** at the trial stage

experimentally
11 empirically, tentatively **12** innovatively, provisionally **13** by rule of thumb, speculatively **14** scientifically **15** by trial and error, investigatively

experimentation
07 zoopery **08** research **10** empiricism, pragmatism **11** exploration, rule of thumb **12** verification **13** inventiveness, investigation

expert
03 ace, dab, don, gun, pro, sly **04** able, buff, nark, oner, up on **05** adept, crack, fundi, maven, mavin, one-er, whizz **06** boffin, master, pundit, wunner **07** dab hand, egghead, hotshot, maestro, old hand, skilful, skilled, wise guy **08** dextrous, masterly, top-notch, virtuoso, well up on **09** authority, brilliant, dexterous, excellent, old master, practised, qualified **10** experience, past master, proficient, specialist **11** cognoscente, connoisseur, experienced **12** accomplished, practitioner, professional **13** knowledgeable

expertise
05 knack, skill **07** ability, command, finesse, knowhow, mastery **08** deftness, facility **09** dexterity, knowledge **10** cleverness, expertness, tradecraft, virtuosity **11** proficiency, savoir-faire, skilfulness **13** understanding **15** professionalism

expertly
04 ably **07** capably **08** masterly **09** skilfully **11** competently, efficiently, excellently **12** proficiently **14** professionally

expiate
05 atone, purge **06** attone, pay for **07** redress, work out **08** atone for **09** make up for **12** do penance for **13** make amends for

expiation
06 amends, ransom, shrift **07** penance, redress **09** atonement **10** recompense, redemption, reparation

expire
03 die, end **04** emit, stop **05** cease, close, lapse **06** depart, finish, pass on, peg out, perish, pop off, run out **07** decease, snuff it **08** conclude, pass away, pass over **09** have had it, terminate **11** bite the dust, come to an end, discontinue **12** lose your life, pop your clogs **13** kick the bucket, meet your maker **14** depart this life, give up the ghost **15** be no longer valid, breathe your last, cash in your chips

expiry
03 end, exp, ish **05** close, lapse **06** finish **09** cessation **10** conclusion, expiration **11** termination **15** discontinuation

explain
04 tell **05** gloze, solve, teach **06** decode, defend, define, excuse, open up, set out, unfold **07** clarify, expound, justify, resolve, unravel **08** decipher, describe, disclose, simplify, spell out, untangle **09** delineate, elaborate, elucidate, enucleate, explicate, interpret, lie behind, make clear, translate, vindicate **10** account for, illustrate **11** demonstrate, explain away, rationalize, shed light on **12** throw light on **14** give a reason for

explanation
04 note **05** alibi, gloss **06** answer, excuse, motive, reason, report **07** account, comment, defence, meaning, warrant **08** apologia, decoding, exegesis, footnote, solution **09** unfolding **10** annotation, commentary, definition, exposition, expounding **11** deciphering, delineation, description, elucidation, explication, vindication **12** illustration **13** clarification, demonstration, justification **14** interpretation, reconciliation, simplification **15** éclaircissement, rationalization

explanatory
08 exegetic **10** exegetical, expositive, expository, justifying **11** declaratory, descriptive, elucidative, elucidatory, explicative **12** illustrative, interpretive **13** demonstrative **14** interpretative

expletive
04 cuss, oath **05** curse **08** anathema, cussword **09** blasphemy, obscenity, profanity, swear-word **10** execration **11** bad language, imprecation **14** four-letter word

explicable
08 solvable **09** definable, exponible **10** resolvable **11** accountable, explainable, justifiable **12** determinable, intelligible **13** interpretable **14** understandable

plicate
define, unfold **07** clarify, develop,
plain, expound, unravel, work out
describe, set forth, spell out,
tangle **09** elucidate, interpret, make
ear **10** illustrate **11** demonstrate

plication
exposition **11** description,
cidation, explanation **12** illustration
clarification **14** interpretation

plicit
open **05** adult, bawdy, clear, dirty,
act, frank, plain **06** candid, direct,
hy, full-on, smutty, stated, X-rated
certain, express, obscene, pointed,
ecise **08** absolute, declared,
finite, detailed, distinct, hard-core,
sitive, shocking, specific
offensive, outspoken **10** forthright,
censored, unreserved
categorical, near the bone, plain-
oken, unambiguous, unequivocal,
inhibited **12** pornographic,
restrained **14** near the knuckle
straightforward

plicitly
barely **07** clearly, in terms, overtly,
ainly **08** directly **09** expressly
definitely **12** specifically **13** in so
any words, unambiguously,
equivocally

plode
anagram indicator
blow, boom, go up, leap **05** blast,
rst, erupt, go off, rebut, surge
blow up, debunk, go bang, refute,
cket, see red, set off, spring **07** flare
08 boil over, burst out, detonate,
plode, disprove, escalate,
ushroom **09** blow a fuse, discharge,
scredit, do your nut, fulminate,
oudiate **10** accelerate, hit the roof,
validate **11** blow your top, go up the
all, grow rapidly, lose your rag
blow your cool, fly into a rage, give
e lie to, lose your cool **13** hit the
iling **14** lose your temper **15** fly off
e handle, go off the deep end

cause to explode
fire **06** spring **08** detonate
fulminate

ploit
act, tap, use **04** deed, feat, gest,
lk, mine **05** abuse, apply, bleed,
ste, stunt **06** action, draw on,
nploy, fleece, misuse, rip off
oppress, utilize **08** activity, cash in
, ill-treat, impose on, profit by
adventure, make use of, profiteer
attainment, manipulate
achievement, walk all over
capitalize on, put to good use, take
a ride **13** take liberties, turn to
count **14** accomplishment, play off
ainst, pull a fast one on **15** take
vantage of

ploitation
use **05** abuse **06** misuse, rip-off
milking **08** bleeding, fleecing
employment, oppression

11 application, cashing in on, making
use of, utilization **12** manipulation
14 taking for a ride **15** taking
advantage

exploration
04 tour, trip **05** probe, study **06** safari,
search, survey, travel, voyage
07 inquiry **08** analysis, research,
scrutiny **10** expedition, inspection
11 examination, observation
13 investigation **14** reconnaissance

exploratory
05 pilot, trial **07** probing, wildcat
08 analytic **09** searching, tentative
11 fact-finding **12** experimental
13 investigative

explore
02 do **04** feel, palp, tour **05** probe,
scout, study **06** review, search, survey,
travel **07** analyse, examine, inspect
08 consider, look into, prospect,
research, traverse **10** scrutinize
11 inquire into, investigate,
reconnoitre, see the world

explorer
05 scout **06** tourer **08** surveyor
09 navigator, traveller **10** discoverer,
prospector **11** bandeirante
12 reconnoitrer

Explorers and pioneers include:

03 Cam, Caõ, Rae (John)
04 Byrd (Richard Evelyn), Cano (Juan
 Sebastian del), Cook (James), Diaz
 (Bartolomeu), Eyre (Edward John),
 Gama (Vasco da), Park (Mungo),
 Polo (Marco), Ross (Sir James
 Clark), Soto (Fernando de), Soto
 (Hernando de)
05 Barth (Heinrich), Beebe (Charles
 William), Boone (Daniel), Bruce
 (James), Cabot (John), Clark
 (William), Drake (Francis), Fuchs
 (Sir Vivian Ernest), Hanno, Lewis
 (Meriwether), Newby (Eric), Oates
 (Lawrence), Peary (Robert Edwin),
 Scott (Robert Falcon), Speke (John
 Hanning)
06 Baffin (William), Balboa (Vasco
 Núñez de), Bering (Vitus), Burton
 (Sir Richard), Cabral (Pedro
 Alvares), Carson (Kit), Nansen
 (Fridtjof), Tasman (Abel Janszoon),
 Torres (Luis de)
07 Andrews (Roy Chapman), Fiennes
 (Sir Ranulph), Fleming (Peter),
 Hillary (Sir Edmund), La Salle
 (Robert Cavelier, Sieur de), Pytheas,
 Raleigh (Sir Walter), Stanley (Sir
 Henry Morton)
08 Amundsen (Roald), Columbus
 (Christopher), Cousteau (Jacques),
 Flinders (Matthew), Franklin (Sir
 John), Linnaeus (Carolus),
 Magellan (Ferdinand), Standish
 (Myles), Thesiger (Sir Wilfred),
 Vespucci (Amerigo), Williams
 (Roger)
09 Emin Pasha, Frobisher (Sir Martin),
 Heyerdahl (Thor), Rasmussen
 (Knud), Vancouver (George)

10 Erik the Red, Oglethorpe (James
 Edward), Shackleton (Sir Ernest
 Henry), Van der Post (Sir Laurens)
11 Livingstone (David)
12 Leif Eriksson, Younghusband (Sir
 Francis)
14 Bellingshausen (Fabian Gottlieb
 von), Blashford-Snell (Colonel
 John), Hanbury-Tenison (Robin
 Airling)

explosion
03 fit, pop **04** bang, boom, chug, clap,
leap, rage, roll **05** blast, burst, crack,
pluff, surge **06** blow-up, report,
rumble **07** Big Bang, flare-up, tantrum,
thunder **08** airburst, eruption,
outbreak, outburst, paroxysm
09 discharge **10** detonation,
displosion **14** dramatic growth,
sudden increase

explosive
◇ *anagram indicator*
02 HE **04** bomb, mine, wild **05** angry,
fiery, jelly, rapid, tense **06** abrupt,
raging, stormy, sudden, touchy
07 charged, fraught, violent **08** critical,
dramatic, meteoric, perilous,
powerful, unstable, volatile, volcanic,
worked-up **09** dangerous, fulminant,
hazardous, initiator, plastique,
rocketing, sensitive **10** burgeoning,
propellant, unexpected
11 exponential, mushrooming,
overwrought **12** nerve-racking,
unrestrained

Explosives include:

03 RDX, TNT
04 ANFO
06 amatol, dualin, Semtex®, tonite
07 ammonal, cordite, dunnite, lyddite,
 plastic
08 cheddite, dynamite, melinite,
 roburite, xyloidin
09 cyclonite, gelignite, guncotton,
 gunpowder, xyloidine
11 nitrocotton
14 nitrocellulose, nitroglycerine,
 trinitrotoluol
15 trinitrotoluene

explosively
06 wildly **07** angrily, fierily, rapidly,
tensely **08** suddenly, unstably
09 violently **10** critically, powerfully
11 dangerously, hazardously
12 dramatically, unexpectedly,
volcanically **13** destructively,
exponentially

exponent
05 adept, index, power **06** backer,
expert, master, player **08** adherent,
advocate, champion, defender,
promoter, upholder **09** performer,
proponent, spokesman, supporter
10 specialist **11** spokeswoman
12 practitioner, spokesperson

export
02 ex **03** exp **05** trade **08** deal with,
Klondike, Klondyke, re-export, transfer
09 traffic in, transport **10** sell abroad

12 foreign trade, sell overseas
13 exported goods **15** exported product

expose
03 ope **04** open, risk, show **05** flash, strip **06** betray, detect, hazard, reveal, show up, unmask, unveil **07** display, divulge, exhibit, imperil, lay bare, lay open, present, uncover, unearth **08** denounce, disclose, endanger, manifest **09** lay open to, make known, put at risk, subject to **10** jeopardize **11** introduce to, present with **12** acquaint with, bring to light **13** put in jeopardy, take the lid off **14** blow the whistle, make vulnerable **15** familiarize with

exposé
07 account, article **08** exposure **10** disclosure, divulgence, revelation, uncovering

exposed
03 out **04** bare, open **05** naked, shown **06** object, on show, on view **07** subject **08** laid bare, revealed **09** exhibited, in the open, on display **10** vulnerable **11** susceptible, unprotected

exposition
04 expo, fair, show **05** moral, paper, study **06** aperçu, exposé, theory, thesis **07** account, display, exposal, Midrash, working **08** analysis, critique, exegesis **09** discourse, monograph, unfolding **10** commentary, enarration, exhibition **11** description, elucidation, explanation, explication **12** illumination, illustration, presentation **13** clarification, demonstration **14** interpretation

expository
08 exegetic **11** declaratory, descriptive, elucidative, explanatory, explicatory, hermeneutic **12** illustrative, interpretive **14** interpretative

expostulate
05 argue, claim, plead **06** reason **07** protest **08** disagree, dissuade **11** remonstrate

exposure
03 air **04** hype, plug, risk **05** flash **06** airing, danger, exposé, hazard **07** contact, display, exposal, showing **08** jeopardy **09** awareness, detection, discovery, exposture, knowledge, notoriety, promotion, publicity, unmasking, unveiling **10** disclosure, divulgence, exhibition, experience, revelation, uncovering **11** advertising, familiarity **12** acquaintance, denunciation, presentation **13** manifestation, vulnerability **14** susceptibility **15** public attention

expound
04 open, read, rede **06** open up, preach, set out, unbolt, unfold **07** analyse, clarify, dissect, explain, unravel **08** describe, prophesy, set

forth, spell out, untangle **09** comment on, elucidate, explicate, interpret, sermonize **10** illuminate, illustrate **11** demonstrate

express
02 ex **03** air, exp, put, say **04** emit, fast, have, show, sole, tell, vent, word **05** brisk, clear, couch, exact, plain, quick, rapid, speak, state, swift, utter, voice **06** assert, convey, denote, depict, embody, intend, report, reveal, speedy, stated, strain **07** certain, declare, divulge, exhibit, get over, non-stop, precise, put over, signify, special, testify **08** announce, clear-cut, conceive, definite, disclose, distinct, explicit, indicate, intimate, manifest, point out, positive, register, specific, stand for **09** designate, enunciate, estafette, formulate, high-speed, pronounce, put across, represent, specially, symbolize, ventilate, verbalize **10** articulate, particular **11** categorical, communicate, demonstrate, expeditious, give voice to, unambiguous, unequivocal, well-defined **12** put into words

expression
◇ homophone indicator
03 air **04** look, mien, show, sign, term, tone, word **05** adage, axiom, depth, force, idiom, maxim, power, scowl, style, voice **06** aspect, phrase, saying, speech, symbol, vigour **07** diction, emotion, feeling, gesture, grimace, passion, proverb, voicing, wording **08** aphorism, artistry, delivery, language, locution, phrasing **09** assertion, intensity, set phrase, statement, utterance, verbalism, vividness **10** appearance, creativity, embodiment, exhibition, indication, intimation, intonation, modulation **11** countenance, declaration, enunciation, imagination **12** announcement, articulation, illustration, proclamation, turn of phrase, vocalization **13** communication, demonstration, manifestation, pronouncement, verbalization **14** representation
• **prevent free expression**
03 gag

expressionless
04 dull **05** blank, empty **06** glassy, glazed **07** deadpan, vacuous **08** toneless **09** impassive, unmeaning **10** poker-faced **11** emotionless, inscrutable, meaningless **13** straight-faced

expressive
05 vivid **06** lively, moving **07** showing, telling **08** animated, eloquent, emphatic, forceful, poignant, striking **09** evocative, revealing, speechful **10** articulate, indicative, meaningful, suggesting, suggestive, thoughtful **11** informative, significant, sympathetic **13** communicative, demonstrating, demonstrative

expressively
07 vividly **09** meaningly **10** eloquently, espressivo **11** evocatively **12** emphatically, meaningfully, suggestively **13** informatively **15** demonstratively

expressiveness
09 poignancy, vividness **10** articulacy **13** evocativeness **14** articulateness, meaningfulness

expressly
◇ homophone indicator
06 solely **07** clearly, exactly, plainly **09** decidedly, on purpose, pointedly, precisely, purposely, specially **10** absolutely, definitely, distinctly, especially, explicitly, manifestly **12** particularly, specifically **13** categorically, intentionally, unambiguously, unequivocally

expropriate
04 take **05** annex, seize, usurp **06** assume **07** impound, unhouse **08** arrogate, disseise, take away **09** sequester **10** commandeer, confiscate, dispossess **11** appropriate, requisition

expropriation
07 seizure **10** arrogation, impounding, taking-away **12** confiscation **13** appropriation, dispossession, sequestration

expulsion
05 exile, purge **07** removal, sacking, the boot, the sack, voiding **08** belching, ejection, eviction **09** discharge, dismissal, ejectment, exclusion, excretion, extrusion, ostracism, rejection **10** banishment, evacuation **11** throwing out

expunge
04 raze **05** annul, erase **06** cancel, delete, efface, remove, rub out **07** abolish, blot out, destroy, wipe out **08** cross out, get rid of **09** eradicate, extirpate **10** annihilate, extinguish, obliterate **11** exterminate

expurgate
03 cut **04** geld **05** emend, purge **06** censor, purify **07** clean up **08** sanitize **10** blue-pencil, bowdlerize

exquisite
04 fine, keen, pink, rare **05** acute, sharp **06** choice, dainty, lovely, picked, pretty, too-too **07** elegant, fragile, intense, perfect, refined **08** abstruse, charming, cultured, delicate, flawless, piercing, pleasing, poignant, precious **09** beautiful, delicious, excellent, sensitive **10** attractive, cultivated, delightful, discerning, far-fetched, fastidious, impeccable, meticulous **11** outstanding **14** discriminating

exquisitely
06 finely **08** daintily **09** elegantly **10** charmingly, delicately, pleasingly **11** beautifully **12** attractively, delightfully

ex-serviceman
03 vet 07 veteran

extant
05 alive 06 living 08 existent, existing
09 remaining, surviving 10 subsistent,
subsisting 11 in existence 13 still
existing

extempore
05 ad-lib 07 offhand 08 suddenly
09 ad libitum, impromptu, unplanned
10 improvised, off the cuff,
unprepared, unscripted
11 spontaneous, unrehearsed
13 spontaneously 14 extemporaneous

extemporize
04 pong 05 ad-lib 06 make up, wing it
09 improvise 11 play it by ear 15 speak
off the cuff, think on your feet

extend
02 go 03 lap, run 04 draw, give, grow,
last, pass, span 05 cover, grant, offer,
range, reach, renew, seize, value,
widen 06 assess, bestow, come to,
confer, deploy, expand, go up to,
impart, intend, put out, spread, step up,
take in, unfold, unwind 07 amplify,
augment, broaden, carry on, develop,
drag out, draw out, embrace, enlarge,
hold out, include, involve, present,
produce, proffer, prolong, spin out,
stretch 08 come up to, continue,
elongate, go down to, increase,
lengthen, protract, put forth, reach out
09 go as far as, intensify 10 come
down to, comprehend

extendable
07 elastic 08 stretchy 09 dilatable,
extensive 10 expandable
11 enlargeable, magnifiable,
stretchable

extended
04 long, wide 06 spread 07 distent,
lengthy 08 at length, enlarged,
expanded 09 amplified, continued,
developed, expansive, increased,
prolonged 10 diastaltic, lengthened

extension
03 ext 04 wing 05 add-on, delay
06 annexe 07 adjunct, stretch
08 addendum, addition, appendix,
deferral, increase, more time, protense,
quantity, widening 09 diffusion,
expansion 10 broadening, elongation,
production, stretching, supplement
11 development, enhancement,
enlargement, lengthening, protraction
12 continuation, postponement,
prolongation 13 proliferation
14 additional time

extensive
04 huge, long, main, vast, wide
05 broad, large, roomy 07 general, in
depth, lengthy 08 complete,
extended, far-flung, sizeable, spacious,
thorough 09 boundless, capacious,
fair-sized, pervasive, prevalent,
universal, unlimited, wholesale
10 commodious, large-scale,
voluminous, widespread

11 far-reaching, substantial, wide-
ranging 12 all-inclusive
13 comprehensive

extensively
06 widely 07 greatly, largely
09 generally, wholesale 10 completely,
thoroughly 11 boundlessly
13 substantially 15 comprehensively

extent
04 area, bulk, play, size, span, term,
time 05 level, limit, range, reach,
scope, sweep, width 06 amount,
attack, bounds, degree, length, sphere,
spread, volume 07 breadth, compass,
expanse, lengths, measure, seizure,
stretch 08 coverage, duration, quantity
09 dimension, magnitude
10 dimensions
• **to full extent**
04 hard, much
• **to some extent**
◇ *hidden indicator*
• **to that extent**
02 as
• **to the extent of**
02 by 03 for

extenuate
06 excuse, lessen, modify, soften
07 qualify 08 diminish, minimize,
mitigate, palliate

extenuating
08 excusing 09 lessening, modifying,
softening 10 justifying, minimizing,
mitigating, moderating, palliating,
palliative, qualifying 11 diminishing,
exculpatory, extenuative, extenuatory

exterior
03 ext 04 face, skin 05 glaze, outer,
shell 06 façade, finish 07 coating,
foreign, outside, outward, surface
08 covering, external 09 externals,
extrinsic, objective, outermost
10 appearance, peripheral
11 superficial, surrounding 12 outer
surface 15 external surface

exterminate
04 do in, kill 06 kill up 07 abolish,
bump off, destroy, kill off, wipe out
08 knock off, massacre 09 eliminate,
eradicate, extirpate, liquidate,
slaughter 10 annihilate, do away with

extermination
07 killing 08 genocide, massacre
09 ethnocide 11 destruction,
elimination, eradication, extirpation
12 annihilation

external
03 ext, out 05 outer 07 foreign,
outside, outward, surface, visible
08 apparent, cortical, exterior, visiting
09 extrinsic, outermost 10 accidental,
extramural, extraneous, peripheral
11 independent, non-resident,
superficial

externally
03 ext 07 visibly 09 outwardly
10 apparently 12 extraneously,
peripherally 13 superficially

extinct
03 ext, old, out 04 dead, gone, lost
05 ended, passé 06 bygone, former
07 defunct, died out, expired, invalid
08 burnt out, inactive, obsolete,
outmoded, quenched, squashed,
vanished, wiped out 09 abolished
10 antiquated, terminated 11 non-
existent 12 exterminated, extinguished

extinction
05 death 07 quietus 08 dying-out,
excision 09 abolition, vanishing
11 destruction, eradication,
termination 12 annihilation,
obliteration 13 disappearance,
extermination

extinguish
03 end 04 dout, kill 05 choke, douse,
dowse, drown, erase, quash, quell,
slake 06 die out, put out, quench,
remove, rub out, sloken, stifle
07 abolish, blow out, destroy, expunge,
slocken, smother, stub out 08 snuff
out, suppress 09 eliminate, eradicate,
extirpate 10 annihilate, dampen down
11 exterminate

extirpate
04 root 05 erase 06 cut out, remove,
uproot 07 abolish, destroy, expunge,
root out, weed out, wipe out 08 stamp
out 09 eliminate, eradicate
10 annihilate, deracinate, extinguish
11 exterminate

extol
04 laud, puff 05 exalt, raise 06 lift up,
praise 07 acclaim, advance, applaud,
commend, glorify, magnify
08 eulogize 09 celebrate
10 rhapsodize, wax lyrical

extort
04 milk, rack 05 bleed, bully, exact,
force, screw, wrest, wring 06 coerce
07 extract, squeeze 08 get out of,
outwrest 09 blackmail, shake down

extortion
05 chout, force 06 demand
07 milking 08 chantage, coercion,
exaction 09 blackmail 10 oppression
12 malversation, racketeering

extortionate
04 hard 05 harsh 06 severe
08 exacting, grasping, grinding
09 excessive, rapacious 10 exorbitant,
immoderate, inordinate, oppressive,
outrageous 12 preposterous,
unreasonable

extortionist
05 screw, shark 06 yakuza 07 bleeder,
exacter, exactor, menacer
09 exactress, exploiter, profiteer,
racketeer 11 blackmailer, bloodsucker,
extortioner

extra
01 w 02 ex, lb, nb 03 bye, ext, new,
odd, too 04 also, gash, more, over,
wide 05 added, bonus, fresh, other,
spare, super- 06 as well, excess, leg
bye, no ball, unused, walk-on

07 adjunct, and so on, another, besides, further, reserve, surplus **08** addendum, addition, additive, buckshee, left-over, let alone, unneeded **09** accessory, along with, ancillary, appendage, auxiliary, bit player, excessive, extension, extremely, minor role, redundant, unusually **10** additional, attachment, complement, especially, in addition, remarkably, subsidiary, supplement, uncommonly, walk-on part **11** superfluous, unnecessary **12** additionally, not to mention, particularly, spear-carrier, together with **13** exceptionally, extraordinary, not forgetting, supernumerary, supplementary **14** above and beyond, into the bargain **15** extraordinarily

extract
◊ *anagram indicator*
◊ *hidden indicator*
03 ext, get, gut, try **04** cite, clip, copy, cull, draw, grog, milk, pick, pull, suck, worm **05** educe, exact, glean, juice, pluck, prise, quote, wrest, wring **06** choose, cut out, decoct, derive, distil, elicit, extort, gather, get out, gobbet, obtain, quarry, remove, render, select, uproot, wrench **07** cutting, derived, draw out, essence, estreat, excerpt, extrait, logwood, passage, pull out, recover, spirits, take out **08** abstract, boil down, citation, clipping, euonymin, pericope, withdraw **09** decoction, enucleate, quotation, reproduce, selection **10** deracinate, distillate **11** concentrate **12** distillation

extraction
04 race **05** birth, blood, brood, stock **06** family, origin **07** descent, drawing, extreat, lineage, pulling, removal **08** ancestry, pedigree **09** obtaining, parentage, retrieval, taking-out, uprooting **10** derivation, drawing-out, separation, withdrawal

extradite
05 exile, expel **06** banish, deport **08** hand over, send back, send home **10** repatriate

extradition
05 exile **08** handover **09** expulsion **10** banishment **11** deportation, sending back **12** repatriation

extraneous
05 alien, extra, inapt **07** foreign, strange **08** exterior, external, needless, unneeded **09** extrinsic, redundant, unrelated **10** additional, immaterial, inapposite, incidental, irrelevant, peripheral, tangential **11** inessential, superfluous, unconnected, unessential, unnecessary **12** inapplicable, non-essential **13** inappropriate, supplementary

extraordinarily
◊ *anagram indicator*
05 oddly **07** notably **08** uniquely **09** amazingly, bizarrely, curiously,

specially, strangely, unusually **10** remarkably, uncommonly **12** astoundingly, particularly, unexpectedly **13** exceptionally, significantly

extraordinary
◊ *anagram indicator*
03 odd **04** rare **06** unique **07** amazing, bizarre, curious, notable, special, strange, unusual **08** peculiar, singular, uncommon **09** by-ordinar, emergency, fantastic, wonderful **10** astounding, marvellous, noteworthy, particular, portentous, remarkable, surprising, tremendous, unexpected **11** astonishing, exceptional, outstanding, significant **13** unprecedented **14** out of this world, unconventional

extrapolate
04 plan **05** gauge **06** expect, reckon, sample **07** project **08** estimate **09** calculate **11** approximate

extraterrestrial
02 ET **05** alien

extravagance
05 extra, folly, treat, waste **06** excess, luxury, vanity **07** riotise, splurge **08** wildness **09** profusion **10** digression, enthusiasm, imprudence, lavishness, ornateness, profligacy **11** dissipation, ostentation, prodigality, squandering **12** exaggeration, immoderation, improvidence, overspending, recklessness, wastefulness **13** excessiveness **14** outrageousness, thriftlessness **15** pretentiousness

extravagant
◊ *anagram indicator*
03 OTT **04** dear, wild **05** outré, steep **06** costly, flashy, lavish, ornate, pricey, rococo **07** baroque, bizarre, profuse, sky-high **08** fanciful, prodigal, reckless, romantic, wasteful **09** excessive, expensive, fanatical, fantastic, high-flown, imprudent, irregular, wasterful **10** exorbitant, extra modum, flamboyant, high-flying, immoderate, outrageous, overpriced, over the top, profligate, thriftless **11** exaggerated, improvident, pretentious, spendthrift, squandering **12** costing a bomb, extortionate, ostentatious, preposterous, unrestrained **15** churrigueresque, costing the earth, daylight robbery

extravaganza
04 show **06** féerie **07** display, pageant **09** spectacle **11** spectacular

extreme
◊ *head selection indicator*
◊ *tail selection indicator*
◊ *ends selection indicator*
03 end, top **04** acme, apex, dire, edge, last, line, mark, peak, pink, pole, wack **05** acute, depth, final, great, gross, harsh, limit, rigid, stern, ultra, utter **06** climax, excess, far-off, height,

red-hot, severe, strict, utmost, zenith **07** distant, drastic, endmost, faraway, highest, intense, maximum, outside, radical, serious, supreme, zealous **08** farthest, greatest, hardline, outlying, pinnacle, remotest, terminal, ultimate **09** desperate, downright, Draconian, excessive, extremist, extremity, fanatical, out-and-out, outermost, stringent, uttermost **10** immoderate, inordinate, iron-fisted, iron-handed, most remote, pre-eminent, remarkable, unyielding **11** exceptional, termination, unrelenting **12** unreasonable **13** extraordinary **14** uncompromising
• **in the extreme**
04 very **06** highly **07** awfully, greatly, utterly **08** terribly **09** intensely **10** dreadfully, remarkably, uncommonly **11** exceedingly, excessively, frightfully **12** immoderately, inordinately, terrifically **13** exceptionally **15** extraordinarily
• **opposite extreme**
04 pole

extremely
◊ *ends selection indicator*
03 too **04** high, mega, very **05** jolly **06** deuced, highly, mighty, mortal, pretty, really **07** acutely, awfully, greatly, majorly, only too, parlous, utterly **08** deucedly, severely, terribly **09** decidedly, intensely, seriously, unusually **10** dreadfully, remarkably, thoroughly, uncommonly **11** exceedingly, excessively, frightfully **12** immoderately, inordinately, terrifically, tremendously, unreasonably **13** exceptionally **15** extraordinarily

extremism
04 zeal **08** zealotry **09** terrorism **10** fanaticism, radicalism **13** excessiveness

extremist
05 ultra **06** zealot **07** diehard, fanatic, Jacobin, radical **08** militant **09** hardliner, terrorist **11** merveilleux **12** merveilleuse **14** fundamentalist

extremity
03 arm, end, fix, jam, leg, tip, toe, top **04** acme, apex, edge, foot, hand, hole, limb, mess, peak, pole, spot, tail **05** bound, brink, depth, limit, point, verge **06** apogee, border, crisis, danger, ending, excess, finger, height, margin, pickle, plight, zenith **07** exigent, extreme, maximum, minimum, trouble **08** boundary, exigency, frontier, hardship, outrance, pinnacle, terminal, terminus, ultimate **09** adversity, emergency, indigence, periphery, tight spot, utterance **10** misfortune **11** dire straits, termination

extricate
04 free **05** clear **06** detach, get out, remove, rescue **07** deliver, extract,

outwind, release, relieve, set free
08 let loose, liberate, withdraw
09 disengage **11** disentangle

extrinsic
05 alien **06** exotic **07** foreign, outside
08 exterior, external, imported
10 extraneous, forinsecal

extrovert
03 lad **05** mixer **06** joiner **07** mingler
08 outgoing **10** socializer **14** outgoing
person, sociable person

extroverted
06 hearty **07** amiable **08** amicable,
friendly, outgoing, sociable
09 exuberant **13** demonstrative
14 outward-looking

extrude
05 expel, mould **08** force out, press
out, protrude, put forth **09** thrust out
10 squeeze out

exuberance
04 life, zest **05** pride **06** energy, vigour
07 elation, pizzazz **08** buoyancy,
lushness, outburst, rankness, richness,
vitality, vivacity **09** abundance,
animation, eagerness, plenitude,
profusion **10** ebullience, enthusiasm,
excitement, lavishness, liveliness,
luxuriance, luxuriancy, redundancy
11 copiousness, fulsomeness, high
spirits, joie de vivre, prodigality
12 cheerfulness, effusiveness,
exaggeration, exhilaration
13 effervescence, excessiveness
14 superabundance

exuberant
03 mad **04** lush, rank, rich **06** elated,
lavish, lively, skippy **07** buoyant,
excited, fulsome, profuse, zestful
08 abundant, animated, cheerful,
effusive, spirited, thriving, vigorous
09 ebullient, energetic, luxuriant,
luxurious, plenteous, plentiful,
sparkling, vivacious **10** boisterous, full
of life **11** exaggerated, exhilarated,
overflowing **12** effervescent,
enthusiastic, high-spirited,
rambunctious, unrestrained
13 irrepressible **15** on top of the world

exude
03 gum **04** emit, leak, ooze, seep,
show, weep, well **05** bleed, issue, still,
sweat, swelt **07** display, emanate,
excrete, exhibit, flow out, give off, give
out, guttate, radiate, secrete, swelter,
trickle **08** manifest, perspire
09 discharge

exult
03 joy **04** crow **05** gloat, glory, revel
06 relish **07** delight, rejoice, triumph
08 be joyful, jubilate **09** celebrate
10 tripudiate **11** be delighted **13** be
over the moon

exultant
06 elated, joyful, joyous **07** gleeful
08 exulting, jubilant, thrilled **09** cock-
a-hoop, delighted, overjoyed,
rejoicing, revelling **10** enraptured,
triumphant **11** on cloud nine, over the
moon **12** transporting **15** in seventh
heaven

exultation
03 joy **04** glee, pean **05** glory, paean
06 eulogy **07** crowing, delight,
elation, triumph **08** gloating, glorying
09 jubilance, jubilancy, merriness,
rejoicing, revelling, transport
10 joyfulness, joyousness, jubilation
11 celebration

eye
02 ee **03** aim, orb, see **04** glim, glom,
lamp, mind, ogle, peep, scan, view
05 brood, light, optic, sight, study,
taste, watch **06** appear, assess, belief,
gaze at, keeker, look at, notice, ocular,
peeper, peruse, regard, survey, vision,
winker **07** blinker, examine, goggler,
inspect, lookout, observe, ocellus,
opinion, pigsney, stare at **08** eyesight,
glance at, ommateum **09** attention,
awareness, judgement, viewpoint,
vigilance, water pump **10** estimation,
perception, scrutinize **11** contemplate,
discernment, observation, point of
view, recognition, sensitivity
12 appreciation, surveillance,
watchfulness **13** look up and down,
power of seeing, way of thinking
14 discrimination, faculty of sight

Eye parts include:
03 rod
04 cone, irid, iris, lens, uvea
05 fovea, pupil, white
06 areola, cornea, eyelid, retina, sclera
07 choroid, eyeball, eyelash, papilla,
vitreum
08 chorioid, tear duct
09 blind spot, optic disc
10 optic nerve
11 ciliary body, conjunctiva, lower
eyelid, upper eyelid
12 chorioid coat, lacrimal duct, ocular
muscle
13 aqueous humour, lachrymal duct,
sclerotic coat

14 lachrymal gland, vitreous humour
15 anterior chamber, crystalline lens,
hyaloid membrane

• **black eye**
05 mouse **06** keeker, shiner
• **keep an eye on**
04 mind **07** monitor **08** attend to
09 look after **10** keep tabs on, take
care of **12** watch closely
• **reflection in eye**
04 baby
• **see eye to eye**
05 agree **06** concur, go with **07** be at
one **11** be of one mind, go along with
• **set eyes on**
03 see **04** meet **06** behold, notice
07 observe **08** come upon
09 encounter, lay eyes on **10** clap eyes
on, come across
• **up to your eyes**
04 busy **06** tied up **08** involved,
occupied **09** engrossed, inundated
11 overwhelmed, snowed under
13 overstretched **14** fully stretched

eyebrow
04 bree

eye-catching
05 showy **08** gorgeous, imposing,
striking, stunning **09** arresting,
beautiful, prominent **10** attractive,
impressive, noticeable **11** captivating,
conspicuous, spectacular

eye-opener
06 wonder **10** disclosure, revelation
14 quite something, surprising fact
15 surprising thing

eyes
03 een **04** eine, eyne

eyeshadow
04 kohl

eyesight
04 view **05** sight **06** vision
10 perception **11** observation
13 power of seeing **14** faculty of sight

eyesore
03 sty **04** blot, mess, scar, stye
06 blight, horror **07** blemish
08 atrocity, disgrace, ugliness
09 carbuncle **10** defacement
11 monstrosity **13** disfigurement

eyewitness
06 viewer **07** watcher, witness
08 looker-on, observer, onlooker,
passer-by **09** bystander, spectator

F

F
02 ef **07** foxtrot

fable
03 lie **04** epic, myth, saga, tale, yarn
05 feign, story **06** invent, legend
07 fiction, Märchen, parable, untruth
08 allegory, apologue **09** falsehood,
invention, moral tale, tall story
11 fabrication **12** old wives' tale

Fable writers include:

03 Ade (George), Fay (András), Gay
(John)
04 Esop, Ruiz (Juan)
05 Aesop, Boner (Ulrich), Torga
(Miguel)
06 Bidpai, Dryden (John), Halévy (Lon),
Krylov (Ivan), Ramsay (Allan), Tessin
(Carl-Gustaf)
07 Arreola (Juan José), Babrius,
Fénelon (François de Salignac de la
Mothe), Gellert (Christian
Fürchtegott), Iriarte (Tomás de),
Kipling (Rudyard), Sologub
(Fyodor)
08 Andersen (Hans Christian), de
France (Marie), Phaedrus, Saltykov
(Michail)
09 Furetière (Antoine)
10 La Fontaine (Jean de)
15 Iriarte y Oropesa (Tomás de)

fabled
05 famed **06** famous **07** feigned
08 mythical, renowned **09** legendary
10 celebrated, remarkable

fabric
03 web **05** cloth, frame, stuff
06 make-up **07** textile, texture
08 material **09** construct, framework,
structure **10** contexture
11 foundations **12** constitution,
construction, organization
14 infrastructure

Fabrics include:

03 aba, abb, kid, net, rep, rug, say, tat
04 abba, aida, baft, buff, ciré, cord,
drab, duck, ecru, felt, harn, ikat,
jean, kelt, lace, lamé, lawn, leno,
line, lyne, mull, nude, pall, piña,
puke, repp, reps, roan, silk, wool
05 abaya, baize, batik, beige, braid,
camel, chino, crape, crash, crêpe,
denim, dhoti, doily, doyly, drill,
duroy, foulé, gauze, gazar, gunny,
jaspé, kente, khaki, linen, lisle,
llama, loden, Lurex®, Lycra®,
moire, ninon, nylon, Orlon®,
panne, piqué, plaid, plush, rayon,
satin, scrim, serge, suede, surah,
tabby, tamin, tammy, terry, Tibet,
toile, tulle, tweed, twill, voile, wigan
06 alpaca, angora, armure, barège,
Bengal, bouclé, broché, burlap,
burnet, burrel, byssus, calico,
camlet, canvas, chintz, cloqué,
coburg, cotton, coutil, cubica,
Dacron®, damask, dévoré, dowlas,
doyley, Dralon®, duffel, durant,
durrie, faille, fleece, frieze, gloria,
harden, jersey, kersey, kincob,
linsey, madras, merino, mohair,
moreen, muslin, Oxford, plissé,
poplin, rateen, ratine, russet,
samite, satara, sateen, saxony,
sendal, shoddy, sindon, Tactel®,
tamine, tartan, Thibet, tissue, tricot,
tusser, velour, velvet, vicuña,
wadmal, wincey, winsey
07 alepine, baracan, batiste, brocade,
buckram, bunting, cambric,
camelot, caracul, challis, chamois,
Cheviot, chiffon, cramesy, cypress,
doeskin, dornick, drabbet, droguet,
drugget, duvetyn, façonné, fake fur,
flannel, foulard, fustian, gingham,
Gore-Tex®, grogram, hessian,
holland, hopsack, jaconet, karakul,
khaddar, kidskin, leather, lockram,
Mexican, mockado, morocco,
nacarat, nankeen, oil silk, organza,
orleans, paisley, percale, rabanna,
raschel, raw silk, sagathy, scarlet,
schappe, seating, silesia,
Spandex®, stammel, suiting,
tabaret, taffeta, ticking, veiling,
Viyella®, webbing, woolsey,
worsted
08 barathea, barracan, bayadère, box-
cloth, buckskin, cashmere,
casimere, chambray, chenille,
corduroy, coutille, cramoisy,
cretonne, diamanté, drilling,
frocking, gambroon, gossamer,
homespun, jacquard, lambskin,
marcella, mazarine, moleskin,
oilcloth, organdie, osnaburg,
pashmina, plaiding, pleather,
quilting, sarsenet, shagreen,
shalloon, shantung, sheeting,
shirting, spun silk, suedette,
swanskin, Terylene®, toilinet,
waxcloth, whipcord
09 astrakhan, baldachin, bombasine,
calamanco, carmelite, cassimere,
Chantilly, Crimplene®, crinoline,
farandine, folk-weave, fur fabric,
gaberdine, georgette, grenadine,
grosgrain, haircloth, horsehair,
huckaback, interlock, kalamkari,
macintosh, matelassé,
Moygashel®, open-weave,
organzine, paramatta, petersham,
pinstripe, polyester, raven-duck,
sackcloth, sailcloth, satinette,
sharkskin, sheepskin, stockinet,
swans-down, tarpaulin, velveteen
10 Balbriggan, broadcloth, brocatelle,
candlewick, farrandine, florentine,
grass cloth, habit-cloth, hop-
sacking, kerseymere, mackintosh,
microfibre, monk's cloth,
mousseline, mummy-cloth,
needlecord, paper-cloth, peau-de-
soie, pilot cloth, polycotton,
seersucker, sicilienne, Tattersall,
toilinette, winceyette
11 cheesecloth, flannelette, Harris
tweed®, interfacing, Kendal green,
marquisette, mutton cloth, nettle-
cloth, sempiternum, stockinette
12 bolting cloth, Brussels lace, butter-
muslin, cavalry twill, crêpe de
chine, leather-cloth, Lincoln green,
Shetland wool
13 boulting cloth, casement cloth,
foundation-net, linsey-woolsey
14 heather mixture, terry towelling

See also **cotton**

fabricate
◇ *anagram indicator*
04 coin, fake, form, make **05** build,
erect, forge, frame, hatch, shape,
weave **06** cook up, create, devise,
invent, make up **07** concoct, falsify,
fashion, produce, trump up
08 assemble **09** construct
11 counterfeit, manufacture, put
together

fabrication
03 fib, lie, web **04** fake, myth **05** fable,
story **06** mock-up **07** coinage, fiction,
figment, forgery, untruth **08** assembly,
building, erection **09** falsehood,
invention **10** assemblage, concoction,
fairy story, production **11** manufacture
12 construction

fabulous
03 def, fab, rad **04** cool, mean, mega,
neat **05** false, great, magic, super, triff
06 divine, fabled, grouse, made-up,
mythic, superb, unreal, way-out,
wicked **07** amazing, cracker, crucial,
feigned, immense, radical **08** heavenly,
invented, mythical, stonking, top-
notch **09** excellent, fantastic, fictional,
imaginary, legendary, wonderful
10 apocryphal, astounding, fictitious,
incredible, marvellous, mythologic,
not half bad, phenomenal, remarkable,

tremendous **11** astonishing, sensational, spectacular **12** breathtaking, mythological, unbelievable, unimaginable **13** inconceivable **14** out of this world

façade
04 face, mask, show, veil **05** cloak, cover, front, guise **06** veneer **07** frontal **08** disguise, exterior, frontage, pretence **09** semblance **10** appearance, storefront

face
◇ *head selection indicator*
03 air, jib, mug, pan **04** clad, coat, dare, defy, dial, form, head, line, look, meet, mien, moue, name, phiz, pout, puss, side, trim **05** anger, brave, clock, cover, dress, flank, front, frown, looks, pitch, scowl **06** aspect, esteem, façade, favour, honour, kisser, nature, oppose, polish, resist, smooth, tackle, veneer, visage **07** affront, grimace, outside, overlay, profile, respect, surface **08** boldness, confront, cope with, deal with, exterior, face up to, features, frontage, give on to, look onto, overlook, presence, prestige, standing **09** demeanour, encounter, look out on, withstand **10** admiration, appearance, be opposite, effrontery, experience, expression, reputation **11** countenance, look towards, physiognomy **13** come up against

03 ear, eye, gum, jaw, lip
04 brow, chin, hair, iris, jowl, lips, neck, nose, skin
05 beard, cheek, mouth, pupil, teeth
06 eyelid, sclera, septum, temple, tongue
07 earlobe, eyeball, eyebrow, eyelash, freckle, jawbone, nostril, wrinkle
08 philtrum
09 cheekbone, moustache
10 complexion, double chin

See also **hair**

• **face to face**
06 facing **07** vis-à-vis **08** eye to eye, in person, opposite **09** confronté, tête-à-tête **11** confronting **12** a quattr'occhi **14** across-the-table **15** in confrontation
• **face up to**
04 nose **06** accept **08** confront, cope with, deal with **09** recognize, stand up to **10** meet head-on **11** acknowledge **15** come to terms with
• **flat face**
04 pane
• **fly in the face of**
04 defy **05** clash **06** insult, oppose **08** be at odds, conflict, contrast, disagree **09** go against **10** contradict **12** be at variance, be in conflict
• **on the face of it**
07 clearly, plainly **08** patently **09** obviously, outwardly, reputedly, seemingly **10** apparently, manifestly, ostensibly **12** on the surface **13** superficially

• **pull a face**
03 moe, mow **04** girn, gurn, lour, pout, sulk **05** fleer, frown, scowl **06** glower **07** grimace **13** knit your brows
• **tilted face**
04 cant

facelift
05 refit **08** makeover **10** renovation **11** restoration **12** redecoration, rhytidectomy **13** refurbishment **14** plastic surgery, transformation **15** cosmetic surgery

facet
04 face, side **05** angle, plane, point, slant **06** aspect, factor **07** element, feature, surface **10** ommatidium **14** characteristic

facetious
04 glib **05** comic, droll, funny, witty **06** jocose, joking **07** amusing, comical, jesting, jocular, playful, waggish **08** flippant, humorous **09** frivolous **12** light-hearted **13** tongue-in-cheek

facile
04 easy, glib **05** hasty, light, quick, ready, slick **06** fluent, simple, smooth **07** affable, shallow **09** yielding **09** plausible **10** simplistic **11** superficial **13** uncomplicated

facilitate
04 ease, help **06** assist, grease, smooth **07** advance, forward, further, promote, speed up **08** expedite **09** encourage, lubricate **10** accelerate, make easier **12** smooth the way

facilitation
07 helping **09** promotion **10** assistance, expediting, forwarding, furthering **12** acceleration **13** encouragement

facility
03 aid **04** ease, gift **05** knack, means, skill **06** mod con, talent **07** ability, amenity, feature, fluency, pliancy, service, utility **08** aptitude, resource **09** advantage, appliance, dexterity, eloquence, equipment, provision, quickness, readiness **10** affability **11** convenience, opportunity, proficiency, skilfulness **12** prerequisite **14** articulateness, effortlessness

facing
06 façade, lining, veneer **07** coating, overlay, surface **08** cladding, covering, dressing, trimming **09** revetment **10** false front **13** reinforcement

facsimile
03 fax **04** copy **05** image, print, repro, Xerox® **06** carbon **07** replica, telefax **09** duplicate, imitation, photocopy, Photostat®, reproduce **10** carbon copy, mimeograph, transcript **11** electrotype **12** reproduction **13** telefacsimile

fact
03 act, gen **04** deed, info, item, poop **05** datum, event, point, score, thing,

truth **06** detail, factor **07** element, feature, low-down, reality **08** incident, specific **09** actuality, certainty, component, happening **10** factuality, ins and outs, occurrence, particular **11** information **12** circumstance, fait accompli
• **in fact**
03 e'en, nay, yes **04** even **05** truly **06** indeed, really **07** de facto, en effet, in truth **08** actually **09** in reality **10** come to that, in practice **12** in actual fact **13** in point of fact **15** as a matter of fact

faction
03 set **04** band, camp, ring, side **05** cabal, group, junta, junto, lobby, party **06** caucus, clique, sector, strife **07** coterie, discord, section, trouble **08** argument, conflict, division, fraction, friction, grouplet, minority, quarrels, tendency **10** contention, contingent, disharmony, dissension, infighting **11** ginger group **12** disagreement **13** pressure group, splinter group

factious
05 rival, split **06** at odds **07** divided, warring **08** clashing, divisive, mutinous, partisan **09** dissident, sectarian, seditious, turbulent **10** discordant, rebellious, refractory, tumultuous **11** conflicting, contentious, quarrelling, quarrelsome **12** disputatious **13** at loggerheads, troublemaking **15** insurrectionary

factitious
04 made, sham **05** bogus, false **09** contrived, imitation, pretended, unnatural **10** artificial, fabricated **11** counterfeit

factor
04 fact, gene, item, part **05** cause, facet, point **06** aspect, detail **07** divisor, element, feature **09** component, influence **10** ingredient **11** constituent, contingency, determinant, submultiple **12** circumstance **13** consideration **14** characteristic
• **unknown factor**
01 x, y, z

factory
04 mill, yard **05** plant, works **07** foundry **08** workshop **09** shop floor **11** manufactory **12** assembly line, assembly shop

factotum
05 do-all **06** circar, sircar, sirkar **07** famulus **08** handyman **09** Man Friday, odd-jobman **10** Girl Friday **12** bottle-washer **13** maid-of-all-work **15** jack-of-all-trades

facts
04 data, poop **05** truth **09** bare bones

factual
04 real, true **05** close, exact **06** actual, strict **07** correct, genuine, literal, precise **08** accurate, detailed, faithful,

truthful, unbiased **09** authentic, objective, realistic **10** historical, true-to-life **12** unprejudiced

factually
05 truly **06** really **08** actually **09** genuinely, in reality **10** truthfully **12** historically

faculties
04 wits **06** powers, reason, senses **12** capabilities, intelligence

faculty
03 ear, wit **04** bent, bump, gift, nose **05** flair, knack, power, sight, skill, taste **06** school, talent **07** ability, licence, section **08** aptitude, capacity, division, facility, function **10** capability, department **11** proficiency **12** organization

fad
04 buzz, cult, mode, rage, whim **05** craze, fancy, mania, trend, vogue **06** maggot **07** fashion **10** enthusiasm **11** affectation **14** passing fashion

faddy
05 exact, fussy, picky **06** choosy **07** finicky **10** fastidious, nit-picking, particular, pernickety **11** persnickety **12** hard-to-please

fade
03 die, dim, ebb **04** dull, fail, fall, flag, melt, miff, pale, vade, wane, weak, wilt **05** appal, droop, faint **06** blanch, bleach, blench, die out, perish, recede, vanish, wallow, weaken, whiten, wither **07** decline, die away, dwindle, ebb away, shrivel, wash out **08** diminish, dissolve, etiolate, evanesce, grow pale, melt away, peter out, tone down, wear away **09** disappear, discolour, fizzle out, waste away **10** become pale, lose colour **11** become paler **12** become weaker

faeces
04 crap, crud, dung, flux, mute, poop, pure **05** frass, guano, scats, stool **06** doo-doo, egesta, ordure, stools **07** excreta, motions **09** body waste, droppings, excrement, number two **11** waste matter **12** rejectamenta, sir-reverence

fag
03 cig, tab **04** bind, bore, drag, pest, slog **05** chore, ciggy, grind, joint, smoke, weary, whiff **06** bother, ciggie, dog end, fag end, gasper, low-tar, roll-up **07** high-tar **08** drudgery, king-size, nuisance **09** cigarette, filter-tip **10** coffin-nail, irritation **11** cancer-stick, roll-your-own **13** inconvenience

fagged
04 beat, done **05** all in, jaded, weary **06** beaten, bushed, done in, pooped, wasted, zonked **07** euchred, whacked, worn out **08** burnt out, dead-beat, dog-tired, fatigued, jiggered **09** exhausted, knackered, pooped out **10** euchred out **11** ready to drop, tuckered out **14** on your last legs

fail
02 go **03** die, ebb, mis, sod **04** bomb, fade, feal, flag, flop, fold, lose, miss, omit, plow, sink, stop, turf, wane **05** abort, crash, decay, droop, flunk, fudge, leave, smash **06** blow it, cut out, desert, falter, forget, go bung, go bust, go phut, pack up, play up, plough, weaken **07** abandon, conk out, crap out, deceive, decline, dwindle, forsake, founder, go broke, go kaput, go under, go wrong, let down, misluck, neglect, not work **08** bottle it, collapse, diminish, fall down, fall flat, miscarry, not start **09** break down, come short, fall apart, fizzle out, go belly-up, not make it **10** come undone, disappoint, draw a blank, get nowhere, go bankrupt, not come off **11** bite the dust, come a gutser, come to grief, come unglued, come unstuck, dégringoler, deteriorate, fall through, go to the wall, malfunction **12** come a cropper, come to naught, go into the red, go on the blink, go on the fritz, underachieve **13** come to nothing **14** be unsuccessful, not do something, score an own goal **15** become insolvent, blow your chances

• **without fail**
08 reliably **09** regularly **10** constantly, dependably, faithfully, punctually **11** predictably, religiously, unfailingly **13** like clockwork **15** conscientiously

failing
03 sin **04** flat, flaw **05** error, fault, lapse **06** defect, foible **07** blemish, default, failure, lacking, wanting, without **08** drawback, on the ebb, weakness, weak spot **10** deficiency **11** in default of, shortcoming **12** imperfection **14** in the absence of

failure
03 dud **04** flop, hash, mess, miss, no go, no-no, ruin **05** botch, crash, decay, flunk, loser **06** cock-up, defeat, demise, ebbing, fading, fiasco, misfit, reject, slip-up, victim, waning **07** also-ran, burst-up, debacle, decline, default, dropout, flivver, folding, has-been, let-down, neglect, no-hoper, screw-up, sinking, washout, wipeout **08** abortion, calamity, collapse, dead loss, disaster, downfall, flagging, meltdown, omission, shambles, shutdown, stalling, stopping, write-off **09** born loser, breakdown, disregard, oversight, packing-up, unsuccess, weakening **10** bankruptcy, conking-out, cutting-out, foundering, going under, ill success, insolvency, misfortune, negligence, non-starter, remissness **11** dereliction, frustration, malfunction, miscarriage **12** waste of space **13** deterioration, forgetfulness, lack of success **14** disappointment, going to the wall, malfunctioning **15** coming to nothing

faint
03 dim, low, wan **04** drop, dull, fade, gone, hazy, mild, pale, soft, weak

05 decay, dizzy, droop, faded, giddy, light, muted, queer, quiet, sound, swarf, swelt, swerf, swoon, swoun, vague, woozy **06** feeble, hushed, slight, stanck, swarve, swerve, swound, vanish **07** blurred, ghostly, languid, muffled, obscure, pass out, subdued, syncope, unclear **08** black out, blackout, bleached, collapse, flake out, keel over, unsteady **09** exhausted **10** indistinct, oppressive **11** half-hearted, lightheaded **14** unenthusiastic **15** unconsciousness

faint-hearted
04 soft, weak **05** timid, wussy **06** craven, scared, yellow **07** chicken, fearful, gutless, jittery, wimpish **08** cowardly, timorous **09** diffident, spineless, weak-kneed **10** hen-hearted, irresolute, spiritless **11** half-hearted, lily-livered **12** weak-spirited, white-livered **13** pusillanimous, yellow-bellied **14** chicken-hearted, chicken-livered

faintly
04 a bit **06** feebly, softly, weakly **07** a little, vaguely **08** slightly, somewhat

fair
02 OK **03** dry **04** even, expo, fete, fine, full, gaff, gala, good, just, mela, open, pale, pure, show, so-so, warm **05** blond, civil, clean, clear, cream, ivory, legit, light, quite, right, sunny, tryst, white, woman **06** bazaar, beauty, blonde, bright, decent, flaxen, golden, honest, kosher, lawful, likely, market, modest, not bad, proper, square, yellow **07** upright **08** adequate, all right, carnival, detached, directly, exchange, festival, handsome, mediocre, middling, moderate, passable, pleasing, specious, sporting, unbiased **09** beautiful, cloudless, craft fair, equitable, impartial, objective, out-and-out, plausible, tolerable, trade fair, unclouded, veritable **10** above board, acceptable, even-handed, exhibition, exposition, fair-haired, fair-headed, favourable, honourable, legitimate, on the level, prosperous, reasonable, straight up, sufficient **11** light-haired, respectable, trustworthy **12** satisfactory, unobstructed, unprejudiced **13** disinterested, dispassionate, done by the book **14** going by the book **15** played by the book

fairground
• **fairground attraction**
04 ride

06 hoop-la
07 Dodgems®
08 carousel, waltzers
10 bumper cars, coconut shy, ghost train, swing boats
11 Ferris wheel, wall of death
12 bouncy castle, chair-o-planes, merry-go-round, tunnel of love
13 helter-skelter, rollercoaster

airly
3 gay, gey **05** fully, quite **06** enough, .ently, justly, neatly, pretty, quight, .ather, really, square **07** legally, plainly **8** honestly, lawfully, middling, .assably, properly, somewhat **9** equitably, neutrally, tolerably, .eritably **10** absolutely, adequately, .noderately, positively, reasonably, .nbiasedly **11** beautifully, impartially, .bjectively

air-minded
4 fair, just **05** right **06** honest, proper, .quare **07** upright **08** detached, .nbiased **09** equitable, impartial, .bjective **10** even-handed, .nonourable, on the level, straight up **1** trustworthy **12** unprejudiced **3** disinterested, dispassionate

airness
6 equity, square **07** decency, justice **9** rightness **10** legitimacy **1** uprightness **12** impartiality, .ghtfulness, unbiasedness **3** equitableness **14** even-handedness, .nonourableness, legitimateness

airy
3 elf, fay, fée, hob, imp, Mab **04** peri, .ixy, Puck **05** faery, nymph, pisky, .ixie, pouke **06** faerie, sprite **7** brownie, rusalka, sandman **8** delicate, fanciful **09** hobgoblin, .uck-hairy, whimsical **10** leprechaun **1** enchantress **15** Robin Goodfellow

airy tale
3 fib, lie **04** myth **07** fantasy, fiction, .omance, untruth **08** folk-tale **9** invention, tall story **10** fairy story **1** fabrication

Fairy tales include:
7 Aladdin, Ali Baba, The Bell **8** MomoTaro, Peter Pan, Rapunzel, Snowdrop, The Angel, The Daisy, The Raven, TomThumb **9** Ashputtel, Bluebeard, Briar Rose, Pinocchio, Snow White, The Shadow, The Storks **10** Cinderella, Clever Hans, Goldilocks, Hans in Luck, The Fir Tree, The Rose-Elf, Thumbelina **11** Clever Elsie, Hop o' myThumb, Little Thumb, Mother Elder, Mother Goose, Puss in Boots, The Old House, The Red Shoes **12** Holger Danske, Little Red-Cap, The Elderbush, The Goose Girl, The Pied Piper, The Snow Queen, The Tinderbox, The Wild Swans, UrashimaTaro **13** Chicken Licken, Red Riding Hood, The Frog Prince, The Golden Bird, The Neighbours, The Tin Soldier, The White Snake, The Wizard of Oz **14** Babes in the Wood, Sleeping Beauty, The Flying Trunk, The Golden Goose, The Juniper Tree, The Nightingale, The Seven Ravens, The Water of Life **15** Dick Whittington, Hansel and Gretel, Rumpelstiltskin, The Elfin

Hillock, The Little Lovers, Three Little Pigs, The Ugly Duckling

Fairy tale characters include:
03 Cat, Dog **04** Duck, Jack, John, Liza, Nana, Nibs **05** Beast, Curly, Wendy **06** Beauty, Conrad, Donkey, Falada, Gretel, Hansel **07** Michael, Rooster, Rose Red, The King, The Ogre, The Wolf, Tootles **08** Baby Bear, Foxy Loxy, Geppetto, Peter Pan, Rapunzel, Slightly, The Elves, The Giant, The Queen, The Troll, The Twins, TomThumb **09** Briar Rose, Daddy Bear, Good Fairy, Mummy Bear, Pinocchio, Snow White, The Miller, The Mirror, The Prince **10** Cinderella, Ducky Lucky, Goldilocks, Henny Penny, Stepmother, The Emperor, Thumbelina, Tinker Bell **11** Captain Hook, Grandmother, Pedlar Woman, Puss in Boots, The Huntsman, The Lost Boys, The Princess, Ugly Sisters, Wicked Fairy, Wicked Witch **12** Goosey Loosey, The Goose Girl, The Shoemaker **13** Band of Robbers, Chicken Licken, Red Riding Hood **14** Fairy Godmother, The Golden Goose, The Seven Dwarfs **15** Alice Fitzwarren, Billy Goats Gruff, Dick Whittington, Fairy Godmothers, Mr and Mrs Darling, Rumpelstiltskin, The Little Red Hen, The Rich Merchant, The Ugly Duckling, Three Little Pigs

faith
03 fay, lay **04** faix, sect **05** creed, dogma, fides, troth, trust **06** belief, church, credit, fealty, honour, indeed **07** believe, honesty, loyalty **08** credence, devotion, doctrine, fidelity, reliance, religion, teaching **09** assurance, obedience, sincerity **10** allegiance, commitment, confidence, conviction, dedication, dependence, persuasion **12** denomination, faithfulness, truthfulness
• **in faith**
04 fegs

faithful
04 feal, leal, true **05** afald, close, exact, loyal **06** aefald, afawld, strict, trusty **07** aefauld, devoted, precise, staunch **08** accurate, brethren, constant, obedient, reliable, soothful, truthful **09** adherents, believers, believing, committed, dedicated, followers, soothfast, steadfast **10** dependable, supporters, unflagging, unswerving, unwavering **11** true-hearted, trustworthy **12** communicants, congregation

faithfully
04 true **05** truly **06** firmly **07** closely, exactly, loyally **08** reliably, solemnly,

strictly **09** devotedly, precisely, staunchly **10** accurately, constantly, dependably **11** steadfastly

faithfulness
05 truth **06** fealty **07** loyalty **08** accuracy, devotion, fidelity **09** closeness, constancy, exactness **10** allegiance, commitment, dedication, strictness **11** reliability, staunchness **13** dependability, steadfastness **14** scrupulousness **15** trustworthiness

faithless
05 false **06** fickle, untrue **08** agnostic, disloyal, doubting **09** atheistic, deceptive **10** adulterous, inconstant, perfidious, traitorous, unfaithful, unreliable, untruthful **11** nullifidian, treacherous, unbelieving **12** disbelieving, false-hearted **13** untrustworthy

faithlessness
06 deceit **07** perfidy **08** adultery, apostasy, betrayal **09** treachery **10** disloyalty, fickleness, infidelity **11** inconstancy **14** unfaithfulness

fake
◇ *anagram indicator*
03 rob **04** coil, cook, copy, faux, fold, hoax, mock, sham **05** bogus, dodge, false, feign, filch, flake, forge, fraud, fudge, phony, pseud, put on, quack **06** affect, assume, attack, bodgie, doctor, ersatz, forged, phoney, pirate, pseudo **07** assumed, forgery, hyped-up, imitate, pretend, replica, swindle **08** affected, impostor, simulate, spurious **09** charlatan, fabricate, imitation, simulated **10** artificial, fraudulent, mountebank, simulation **11** counterfeit **12** reproduction

falcon

Falcons include:
05 hobby, saker **06** gentle, lanner, merlin **07** Iceland, kestrel **08** duck-hawk **09** gerfalcon, gyrfalcon, jerfalcon, peregrine, stone hawk **11** tassell-gent **12** falcon-gentil, falcon-gentle, tassel-gentle, tercel-gentle, tercel-jerkin

Falkland Islands
03 FLK

fall
◇ *anagram indicator*
◇ *reversal indicator*
02 fa **03** cut, die, ebb, get, lot, sin **04** dive, drip, drop, grow, hang, purl, rain, ruin, rush, sink, slip, soss, trap, trip, turn **05** abate, chute, crash, falls, lapse, occur, onset, pitch, slant, slide, slope, slump, souse, spill, yield **06** alight, autumn, become, be lost, chance, dangle, defeat, demise, give in, go down, gutzer, happen, lessen, perish, plunge, recede, revert, shower, submit, topple, tumble **07** be slain, be taken,

cadence, capture, cascade, decline, descend, descent, dwindle, failure, fall off, fall-off, fortune, impinge, incline, offence, plummet, stumble, subside, torrent **08** be killed, cataract, collapse, come down, come to be, conquest, decrease, diminish, down-come, downfall, fall down, giving-in, grow into, keel over, nose-dive, yielding **09** come about, declivity, dwindling, lessening, overthrow, reduction, surrender, take place, terminate, waterfall **10** be defeated, capitulate, plummeting, submission, topple over, wrongdoing **11** be conquered, come a gutser, destruction, keeling-over, lose control, original sin, precipitate, resignation **12** be vanquished, capitulation, come a cropper, disobedience, lose your life, pitch forward, precipitance, precipitancy **13** loss of control, transgression
• **fall apart**
03 rot **04** fail **05** break, decay **06** divide **07** break up, crack up, crumble, shatter **08** collapse, come away, dissolve, disunite, go to bits **09** break down, decompose **10** fall to bits, go to pieces **11** lose control **12** come to pieces, disintegrate, fall to pieces **15** break into pieces
• **fall asleep**
04 doze **06** get off, nod off, pop off **07** doze off, drop off **08** crash out, drift off, flake out, spark out **13** pass into sleep **15** go out like a light
• **fall away**
04 drop, fail **05** lapse **06** go down, revolt **07** decline, drop off, dwindle, relapse **08** drop away, languish **09** slope away, slope down
• **fall back**
06 depart, recoil, recule, revert **07** back off, give way, recoyle, recuile, relapse, retreat **08** draw back, pull back, withdraw **09** disengage **10** give ground, lose ground
• **fall back on**
03 use **06** call on, employ, look to, turn to **08** resort to **09** make use of **12** call into play **14** have recourse to
• **fall behind**
03 lag **05** trail **08** drop back, straggle **09** lag behind, not keep up
• **fall down**
04 fail, flop **07** founder **08** collapse **09** break down **11** come unglued, come unstuck **12** come a cropper **13** come to nothing **14** be unsuccessful
• **fall for**
03 buy **05** fancy **06** accept, desire, take to **07** swallow **10** be fooled by **11** be taken in by **12** be attached to, be crazy about, be deceived by, have a crush on **14** fall in love with
• **fall in**
04 sink **05** array, crash **06** cave in, line up, revert **07** give way, subside **08** collapse, come down **11** stand in line **14** get in formation
• **fall in with**
06 accept **07** support **08** assent to,

hang with **09** agree with **10** comply with **11** go along with, hang out with **12** go around with **13** co-operate with, hang about with **14** hang around with **15** get involved with
• **fall off**
04 drop, shed, slow **05** crash, slump **06** lessen, perish, worsen **07** decline, die away, drop off, slacken, slip off **08** decrease, draw back **11** deteriorate
• **fall on**
04 meet **06** assail, attack, snatch **07** assault, lay into, set upon **08** pounce on **09** descend on
• **fall out**
05 argue, clash, fight **06** bicker, differ, happen **07** dismiss, quarrel **08** disagree, squabble
• **fall slightly**
04 ease
• **fall through**
04 fail **05** abort **07** founder, go wrong **08** collapse, miscarry **11** come to grief **13** come to nothing
• **fall to**
05 begin, set to, start **07** stand to **08** commence, set about **10** get stuck in **11** be the duty of, be the task of **13** apply yourself

fallacious
05 false, wrong **06** untrue **07** inexact **08** delusive, delusory, illusory, mistaken, spurious **09** deceptive, erroneous, illogical, incorrect, sophistic **10** fictitious, inaccurate, misleading **11** casuistical, sophistical

fallacy
04 flaw, myth **05** error **06** idolon, idolum **07** idolism, mistake, sophism **08** delusion, illusion **09** deception, falsehood, false idea, sophistry **12** equivocation, misjudgement **13** deceitfulness, inconsistency, misconception **14** miscalculation, mistaken belief **15** misapprehension

fallen
04 dead, died, lost **05** loose, slain **06** killed, ruined, shamed **07** immoral, seduced **08** murdered, perished **09** disgraced **10** degenerate, overthrown **11** promiscuous, slaughtered

fallibility
07 failing **08** weakness **09** mortality **10** inaccuracy **12** imperfection **13** unreliability

fallible
04 weak **05** frail, human **06** errant, erring, flawed, mortal **08** ignorant **09** imperfect, uncertain **10** unreliable

fallow
03 lay, lea, ley **04** idle **06** barren, unsown, unused **07** dormant, resting **08** inactive **09** unplanted **10** unploughed **11** undeveloped **12** uncultivated, unproductive

false
◊ *anagram indicator*
03 bum **04** fake, faux, mock, sham

05 bogus, lying, pseud, wrong **06** faulty, forged, phoney, pseudo, untrue **07** assumed, bastard, feigned, inexact, invalid, pretend **08** disloyal, fabulous, illusive, illusory, invented, mistaken, postiche, pseudish, recrean **09** deceitful, dishonest, erroneous, faithless, imitation, incorrect, insincer pretended, simulated, synthetic, trumped-up **10** artificial, fabricated, fallacious, fictitious, fraudulent, inaccurate, misleading, perfidious, traitorous, unfaithful, ungrounded, unreliable **11** counterfeit, double-faced, duplicitous, treacherous **12** hypocritical **13** double-dealing, untrustworthy

falsehood
03 fib, lie **04** flam **05** fable, porky, story **06** deceit **07** fiction, leasing, perfidy, perjury, untruth, whopper **09** deception, duplicity, hypocrisy, invention, mendacity, tall story, treachery **10** dishonesty, fairy story **11** fabrication, insincerity **12** two-facedness **13** deceitfulness, double dealing **14** untruthfulness

falsely
07 in error, untruly, wrongly **09** by mistake, deviously **10** mistakenly, wrongfully **11** deceitfully, dishonestly, erroneously, incorrectly, insincerely **12** artificially, fallaciously, fraudulently **13** counterfeitly, treacherously **14** hypocritically

falsetto
04 alto **08** high note **09** high pitch, hig voice **10** shrillness **12** head register

falsification
06 change, deceit **07** forgery **08** adultery **09** tampering **10** alteration, distortion, perversion **12** adulteration **13** dissimulation

falsify
◊ *anagram indicator*
03 lie, rig **04** cook, fake, rort **05** alter, belie, false, feign, forge, twist **06** diddle, doctor, fiddle, garble, wangle **07** distort, massage, pervert **08** misstate **10** adulterate, manipulate tamper with **11** counterfeit **12** misrepresent, sophisticate

falter
04 fail, flag **05** delay, quail, shake, waver **06** flinch, hiccup, totter **07** be shaky, stammer, stoiter, stumble, stutter, tremble **08** hesitate, hiccough **09** vacillate **10** be unsteady, dilly-dally **12** be in two minds, drag your feet, shilly-shally, take your time, unsteadiness **13** sit on the fence **14** fluff your lines

faltering
◊ *anagram indicator*
04 weak **05** timid **06** broken **07** failin **08** flagging, hesitant, unsteady **09** stumbling, tentative, uncertain **10** irresolute, stammering

fame
04 name, note **05** glory, kudos
06 esteem, honour, renown, report, repute, rumour **07** stardom
08 eminence **09** celebrity, greatness
10 importance, notability, prominence, reputation **11** distinction
15 illustriousness

famed
05 noted **06** famous **08** esteemed, renowned **09** acclaimed, prominent, well-known **10** celebrated, recognized **11** widely known

familiar
03 fam, old **04** bold, dear, easy, free, maty, near, open **05** aware, close, known, matey, pally, privy, usual **06** au fait, casual, chummy, common, homely, smarmy, versed, well up
07 abreast, clued up, forward, natural, relaxed, routine **08** everyday, fireside, frequent, friendly, genned up, habitual, homelike, informal, intimate, ordinary, repeated, sociable **09** au courant, customary, household, up to speed, well-known **10** accustomed, acquainted, conversant, recognized, unreserved **11** comfortable, commonplace, free-and-easy, impertinent **12** confidential, conventional, over-familiar, over-friendly, presumptuous, recognizable, run-of-the-mill, unmistakable
13 disrespectful, knowledgeable, unceremonious

familiarity
04 ease **05** grasp, habit, skill
07 liberty, mastery **08** boldness, intimacy, nearness, openness
09 awareness, closeness, impudence, knowledge, liberties, palliness, pushiness **10** casualness, chumminess, consuetude, disrespect, experience, inwardness **11** conversance, conversancy, forwardness, informality, naturalness, presumption, sociability
12 acquaintance, friendliness, impertinence **13** comprehension, intrusiveness, understanding **15** over-familiarity

familiarize
05 brief, coach, gen up, prime, teach, train **06** clue up, school **08** accustom, acquaint, instruct **09** habituate, make aware **11** acclimatize **12** get up to speed, indoctrinate, make familiar
13 keep up to speed **14** make acquainted

family
03 fam, kin **04** clan, folk, gens, kids, kind, line, name, race, stem, type
05 birth, blood, brood, class, flesh, genus, group, house, issue, order, stock, tribe **06** kinred, people, scions, stirps, strain, whanau **07** descent, dynasty, kiddies, kindred, kinsmen, lineage, parents, progeny, species
08 ancestry, children, pedigree, subclass **09** ancestors, forebears, household, next of kin, offspring, parentage, relations, relatives
10 extraction, generation, little ones
11 descendants, you and yours
13 nuclear family **14** classification, extended family **15** one-parent family
• **member of family**
08 relation, relative
See also **relative**
• **family tree**
04 line **06** stemma **07** descent, lineage **08** ancestry, pedigree
09 genealogy, whakapapa
10 background, extraction

famine
04 lack, want **05** death **06** dearth, hunger **08** scarcity **10** starvation
11 deprivation, destitution
12 exiguousness, malnutrition
14 shortage of food

famished
06 hungry **07** starved **08** ravenous, starving **09** famishing, voracious
14 undernourished

famous
04 name **05** famed, great, noted
06 legend, signal **07** eminent, notable, popular **08** esteemed, glorious, honoured, infamous, renowned
09 acclaimed, celebrity, excellent, legendary, notorious, prominent, respected, venerable, well-famed, well-known **10** celebrated, remarkable **11** illustrious, world-famous **13** distinguished

famously
04 well **07** greatly, happily, notably
08 superbly **09** eminently, popularly
10 infamously, splendidly, swimmingly
11 brilliantly, notoriously, prominently, wonderfully **13** conspicuously

fan
◇ *anagram indicator*
03 air, nut **04** blow, buff, cone, cool, vane, wing **05** fiend, freak, lover, punka, rouse **06** addict, aerate, arouse, backer, blower, Colmar, cooler, excite, groupy, ignite, incite, kindle, punkah, stir up, whip up, winnow, work up **07** admirer, agitate, air-cool, devotee, flutter, freshen, groupie, provoke, refresh **08** adherent, follower, increase **09** air cooler, extractor, flabellum, instigate, intensify, propeller, rhipidion, stimulate, supporter, ventilate **10** aficionado, enthusiast, ventilator **11** afficionado **12** air-condition, extractor fan **14** air-conditioner
• **fan out**
04 open **06** spread, unfold, unfurl
07 move out, open out **09** spread out

fanatic
03 nut **05** bigot, fiend, freak **06** addict, maniac, zealot **07** devotee, radical
08 activist, militant **09** extremist, visionary **10** enthusiast
14 fundamentalist

fanatical
03 mad **04** wild **05** rabid **07** bigoted, burning, extreme, fervent, radical, zealous **08** activist, dogmatic, frenzied, militant **09** extremist, obsessive **10** immoderate, passionate
11 extravagant **12** narrow-minded, single-minded **14** fundamentalist

fanaticism
04 zeal **06** frenzy **07** bigotry, fervour, madness **08** activism, wildness, zealotry **09** dogmatism, extremism, militancy, monomania **10** dedication, enthusiasm **11** infatuation, schwärmerei **13** obsessiveness
14 fundamentalism

fancier
03 fan **05** fiend, freak **06** keeper
07 breeder, devotee **08** follower
10 enthusiast

fanciful
◇ *anagram indicator*
04 wild **05** fairy **06** exotic, ornate, quaint, unreal **07** curious, flighty
08 chimeric, creative, fabulous, illusory, mythical, notional, romantic, vaporous **09** airy-fairy, decorated, elaborate, fairytale, fantastic, imaginary, legendary, visionary, whimsical **10** chimerical
11 extravagant, fantastical, imaginative, make-believe, unrealistic
12 metaphysical

fancy
◇ *anagram indicator*
03 yen **04** flam, idea, itch, like, love, urge, want, ween, whim, wish
05 covet, dream, go for, guess, humor, showy, taste, think **06** desire, fangle, favour, humour, lavish, liking, notion, ornate, prefer, raving, reckon, rococo, take to, vision **07** adorned, baroque, believe, caprice, chimera, dream of, elegant, fantasy, imagine, impulse, long for, longing, not mind, opinion, picture, suppose, surmise, thought, wish for
08 chimaera, conceive, crotchet, delusion, fanciful, fantasia, feel like, fondness, illusion, penchant, phantasy, superior, yearn for, yearning
09 decorated, elaborate, expensive, fantastic, lust after **10** be mad about, conception, conjecture, creativity, far-fetched, have in mind, impression, not say no to, ornamented, preference
11 be wild about, embellished, extravagant, have eyes for, imagination, inclination **12** be crazy about, have a crush on, ostentatious, predilection, take a shine to **13** be attracted to, particoloured, take a liking to **14** be interested in, find attractive, have the hots for **15** think the world of

fanfare
04 fuss, show **05** trump **06** parade, sennet, tucket **07** display **08** flourish
09 fanfarade, pageantry, publicity, tarantara **11** flamboyance, ostentation, taratantara, trumpet call

fang
04 claw, grip, tang, tusk **05** catch, prong, talon, tooth **10** venom-tooth

fantasize

05 dream **06** invent **07** imagine, romance **08** daydream **11** hallucinate **12** live in a dream

fantastic

◊ *anagram indicator*

03 ace, odd **04** cool, mega, neat, wild **05** antic, brill, fancy, great, magic, outré, super, weird **06** absurd, antick, exotic, superb, unreal, wicked **07** amazing, anticke, antique, bizarre, extreme, foppish, radical, strange **08** enormous, fabulous, fanciful, illusory, romantic, smashing, terrific, top-notch **09** brilliant, eccentric, excellent, first-rate, grotesque, imaginary, storybook, visionary, whimsical, wonderful **10** capricious, impressive, incredible, marvellous, outlandish, phenomenal, remarkable, tremendous **11** extravagant, imaginative, sensational **12** overwhelming, transcendent, unbelievable **14** out of this world

fantastically

09 amazingly, extremely **10** incredibly **12** phenomenally, terrifically, tremendously, unbelievably

fantasy

03 GBH, GHB **04** idol, love, myth **05** dream, fancy **06** mirage, vision, whimsy **07** caprice, reverie, whimsey **08** daydream, delusion, fantasia, illusion **09** fantasque, invention, moonshine, nightmare, pipe dream, unreality **10** apparition, creativity **11** imagination, inspiration, originality, pie in the sky, speculation **12** fancifulness **13** flight of fancy, hallucination, inventiveness, misconception **15** cloud-cuckoo-land, imaginativeness, resourcefulness

far

03 way **04** away, much **05** miles, other **06** far-off, remote **07** distant, faraway, further, greatly, removed **08** a good way, a long way, far-flung, markedly, opposite, outlying, secluded, very much **09** decidedly, distantly, extremely **10** far-removed **11** back o' Bourke, godforsaken, nowhere near, out-of-the-way, up the Boohai **12** considerably, immeasurably, inaccessible, incomparably, in the boonies, in the wop-wops, some distance **13** great distance, significantly, the black stump **14** in the boondocks

• **as far as**
02 to, up **04** up to

• **far and wide**
06 widely **07** broadly **08** all about **09** worldwide **10** everywhere, far and near **11** extensively, in all places **13** from all places

• **far end, far side**
◊ *tail selection indicator*

• **far out**
05 weird **06** exotic, way out **07** bizarre, extreme, radical, strange, unusual **10** outlandish, unorthodox **14** unconventional

• **go far**
05 get on **06** arrive **07** succeed **08** go places **12** be successful, make your mark **14** achieve success **15** get on in the world

• **not far**
02 nl

• **so far**
02 as **03** als **06** to date **07** thus far, till now, up to now **08** hitherto **12** to some extent, within limits **13** up to this point

faraway

03 far **04** lost **06** absent, dreamy, far-off, remote **07** distant **08** far-flung, outlying **10** abstracted **11** preoccupied **12** absent-minded

farce

03 jig **04** cram, joke, mime, sham **05** exode, lazzo, stuff **06** comedy, parody, satire **07** mockery **08** burletta, nonsense, shambles, stuffing, travesty **09** absurdity, burlesque, forcemeat, pantomime, slapstick **10** buffoonery **11** opera bouffe **14** ridiculousness

farcical

05 comic, silly **06** absurd, stupid **08** derisory **09** diverting, laughable, ludicrous **10** ridiculous **11** nonsensical **12** preposterous

fare

02 be, do, go **03** fee **04** cost, diet, eats, food, go on, menu, nosh, tack, what **05** board, cheer, get on, meals, price, speed, table **06** charge, course, happen, manage, ticket, travel, viands **07** make out, passage, proceed, prosper, rations, succeed, turn out **08** eatables, get along, progress, victuals **09** nutriment, passenger **10** provisions, sustenance **11** nourishment **12** passage-money

farewell

02 BV **03** bye **04** ciao, ta-ta, vale **05** adieu, adios, aloha, later, leave **06** bye-bye, cheers, see you, so long, valete **07** cheerio, goodbye **08** au revoir, take care **10** all the best **11** arrivederci, be seeing you, leave-taking, see you later, valediction, valedictory **12** have a nice day, mind how you go, see you around **14** auf Wiedersehen

• **expression of farewell**
03 bye **04** ciao, ta-ta, vale **05** addio, adieu, adiós, aloha, later **06** hooray, hooroo, see you, shalom, sheers, so long **07** cheerio, goodbye **08** au revoir, chin-chin, sayonara, toodle-oo **11** arrivederci, be seeing you, see you later **14** auf Wiedersehen, shalom aleichem

far-fetched

05 crazy **06** forced **07** dubious **08** fanciful, unlikely **09** exquisite, fantastic, recherché, unnatural **10** improbable, incredible **11** implausible, unrealistic **12** preposterous, unbelievable, unconvincing

farm

03 mas **04** ferm, land, sted, till **05** acres, mains, plant, ranch **06** bowery, grange, plough, shamba **07** acreage, holding, mailing, operate, station **08** farmland, hacienda, property **09** cultivate, farmstead, homestead **11** co-operative, work the land

Farms and farming types include:

03 dry, ley, pig **04** deer, fish, hill, stud, wind **05** croft, dairy, mixed, store, trash, trout **06** arable, estate, salmon, turkey **07** factory, organic, ostrich, poultry **09** extensive, free-range, intensive **10** collective, plantation **11** cattle ranch, monoculture, subsistence **12** sheep station, smallholding, stock station

Farm animals include:

02 ox **03** ass, cow, ewe, hen, pig, ram, sow **04** bull, calf, cock, duck, foal, goat, lamb, mare, mule **05** goose, horse, sheep **06** cattle, donkey, piglet, rabbit, turkey **07** chicken, rooster **08** cockerel, stallion **09** billy goat

Farming equipment includes:

03 ard, ATV, axe, hoe, saw **04** fork, plow, rake, wain **05** baler, drill, flail, gambo, mower, share, spade **06** harrow, plough, ricker, ripple, scythe, shovel, sickle, tanker, tedder **07** combine, draw hoe, grubber, hayfork, hayrake, mattock, scuffle, sprayer, tractor, trailer **08** buckrake, chainsaw, hay knife, haymaker, scuffler, spreader **09** corn drill, drop-drill, harvester, irrigator, pitchfork, power lift, rotary hoe, Rotavator®, Rotovator®, scarifier, seed drill, whetstone **10** cropduster, cultivator, disc harrow, disc plough, earth-board, flail mower, seed-harrow **11** bale wrapper, broadcaster, chaff-cutter, chaff-engine, drill-harrow, hedgecutter, mole drainer, reaping hook, wheelbarrow, wheel plough **12** muckspreader, slurry tanker **13** fork-lift truck, potato planter, slurry sprayer **14** field sprinkler, front end loader, milking machine

• **farm out**
08 delegate **09** outsource **11** contract out, subcontract **12** give to others, pass to others

• **farm worker**
03 dey **04** peon **06** sheepo **07** orra man **08** farmhand

• **healthy farm animal**
04 doer

farmer
04 Boer, ryot **05** cocky, colon, gebur **06** cockie, mailer, raiyat, yeoman **07** crofter, grazier, métayer, rancher **08** cockatoo **09** campesino, cowcockie, sodbuster **10** agronomist, estanciero, husbandman **11** flockmaster, share-milker, smallholder, stock-farmer, store farmer **12** sharecropper **13** agriculturist **15** agriculturalist

farming
06 arable **07** tilling **08** agronomy, crofting **09** geoponics, husbandry **11** agriculture, agroscience, cultivation **12** agribusiness, share-milking

Faroe Islands
02 FO **03** FRO

far-off
03 far **06** remote **07** distant, faraway **08** far-flung, outlying

farrago
04 hash **06** jumble, medley **07** mélange, mixture **08** mishmash **09** pot-pourri **10** dog's dinner, hodgepodge, hotchpotch, miscellany, salmagundi **11** gallimaufry **13** dog's breakfast

far-reaching
04 wide **05** broad **06** global **08** profound, sweeping, thorough **09** extensive, important, momentous **10** widespread **11** significant, wide-ranging **13** comprehensive

far-sighted
04 wise **05** acute, canny **06** shrewd **07** politic, prudent **08** cautious **09** far-seeing, judicious, prescient, provident **10** discerning **11** circumspect **14** forward-looking

farther
07 further, remoter **11** more distant, more extreme

farthest
08 furthest, remotest **11** most distant, most extreme

farthing
01 f **03** rag **06** farden **07** farding

fascia
04 band, sign **05** board, front, panel **06** fillet **07** console **08** platband **09** dashboard **15** instrument panel

fascinate
04 draw, lure **05** charm, rivet, witch **06** absorb, allure, entice **07** attract, beguile, bewitch, delight, enchant, engross, enthral **08** intrigue, transfix **09** captivate, enrapture, hypnotize, mesmerize, spellbind

fascinated
06 hooked **07** charmed, curious, enticed, smitten **08** absorbed, beguiled **09** bewitched, delighted, engrossed, entranced, intrigued **10** captivated, enthralled, hypnotized, infatuated, mesmerized, spellbound

fascinating
04 sexy **07** killing **08** alluring, charming, engaging, enticing, exciting, fetching, gripping, riveting, tempting, witching **09** absorbing, seductive **10** bewitching, compelling, compulsive, delightful, enchanting, engrossing, intriguing **11** captivating, interesting, mesmerizing, stimulating **12** irresistible

fascination
04 draw, lure, pull **05** charm, magic, spell **06** allure, appeal **07** delight, sorcery **08** interest, witchery **09** magnetism **10** attraction, compulsion **11** captivation, enchantment **13** preoccupation

fascism
09 autocracy, Falangism, Hitlerism **10** absolutism, Sinarchism **12** dictatorship **15** totalitarianism

fascist
04 duce, Nazi **08** autocrat **09** Falangist, Hitlerist, Hitlerite **10** absolutist, autocratic, Blackshirt, Brownshirt, sinarchist **12** totalitarian **13** authoritarian

fashion
◇ *anagram indicator*
03 cut, fad, fit, ton, way **04** fain, feat, form, kind, line, look, make, mode, rage, sort, suit, turn, twig, type, wear, work **05** adapt, alter, build, craze, faine, fayne, feign, model, mould, shape, smith, style, trend, vogue **06** adjust, aguise, aguize, create, custom, design, entail, latest, manner, method, system, tailor **07** clothes, couture, entayle, in thing, pattern **08** approach, practice, rag trade, tendency **09** construct **10** appearance, convention **11** high fashion, manufacture **12** haute couture **13** designer label **15** clothes industry, fashion business

• **after a fashion**
08 in a sense **11** not very well **12** to some extent
• **current fashion**
02 go
• **out of fashion**
03 out **05** dated, passé **06** démodé, old hat, square **08** dismoded, obsolete, outmoded **09** out of date, unpopular **10** antiquated **12** old-fashioned **13** unfashionable

fashionable
02 in **03** fly, hip, hot **04** chic, cool, tony **05** culty, flash, funky, natty, ritzy, smart, toney, vogue **06** chichi, glitzy, latest, modern, modish, snappy, snazzy, swanky, trendy, with it **07** à la mode, cultish, current, elegant, genteel, in vogue, mondain, popular, stylish, swagger **08** all the go, designer, fantoosh, mondaine, swinging, up-to-date **09** exclusive, happening, high-toned **10** all the rage, prevailing **11** in the groove **12** contemporary **13** up-to-the-minute

fast
03 pdq **04** diet, firm, pacy, rash, shut, slim, wild **05** apace, brisk, faced, fiery, fixed, fleet, fully, hasty, nippy, pacey, quick, rapid, sound, swift, thick, tight **06** closed, deeply, firmly, flying, presto, secure, speedy, starve **07** abstain, express, fasting, fixedly, hastily, hurried, immoral, like mad, quickly, rapidly, refrain, riotous, swiftly, tightly **08** cracking, doggedly, exciting, fastened, go hungry, immobile, in a hurry, securely, speedily **09** breakneck, dissolute, fortified, high-speed, hurriedly, immovable, immovably, indelible, like a shot, like crazy, permanent, shameless, thrilling, turbulent **10** abstinence, blistering, boisterous, dissipated, like a flash, resolutely, starvation, stubbornly **11** accelerated, double-quick, lickety-spit, like the wind, ripsnorting **12** action-packed, deny yourself, dissipatedly, exhilarating, hunger strike, like the devil **13** extravagantly, like lightning, self-indulgent, unflinchingly **14** at a rate of knots, hell for leather **15** like the clappers

09 Ember-days, Tisha Baav, Tisha be'Ab, Tisha Be'Av, Tishah b'Ab, Tishah B'Av, Yom Kippur
10 Holy Friday
12 Golden Friday

fasten
03 aim, bar, fix, pin, tag, tie **04** bind, bolt, clip, do up, grip, join, lace, link, lock, moor, nail, seal, shut, spar, tack, zero **05** affix, chain, clamp, close, focus, hitch, latch, point, rivet, steek, unite, zip up **06** anchor, attach, buckle, button, direct, secure, take up, tether **07** connect **09** interlock **11** concentrate

fastened
02 to **05** bound

fastener, fastening

Fasteners include:

03 bar, fly, pin, tie, zip
04 bond, clip, frog, hasp, hook, knot, lace, link, lock, loop, nail, stud, tach, tack
05 catch, clasp, hinge, latch, morse, rivet, screw, tache
06 buckle, button, clinch, cotter, eyelet, holder, staple, stitch, tassel, toggle, Velcro®, zipper
07 padlock, tacking
08 cufflink, shoelace, split pin
09 paperclip, press stud, strapping
10 collar stud, hook-and-eye
11 bulldog clip, Chelsea clip, treasury tag
12 espagnolette
13 alligator clip, crocodile clip

fast food *see* food; restaurant

fastidious
04 nice **05** chary, faddy, fussy, picky **06** choosy, dainty, quaint, queasy, queazy, spruce **07** choosey, finicky, precise **08** delicate, overnice, precious **09** difficult, exquisite, niff-naffy, squeamish, superfine **10** meticulous, niffy-naffy, particular, pernickety, scrupulous **11** persnickety, punctilious **12** hard-to-please **13** hypercritical **14** discriminating

fat
02 OS **03** big, ghi, oil, pot, wax **04** bard, bulk, flab, fozy, ghee, lard, oily, rich, spek, suet, wide **05** beefy, broad, buxom, cream, dumpy, fatty, gross, heavy, keech, large, money, obese, plump, podgy, porky, pursy, round, solid, sonsy, speck, squab, stout, thick, tubby **06** butter, cheese, chubby, creesh, degras, flabby, fleshy, grease, greasy, lipoid, paunch, portly, rotund, tallow **07** adipose, blubber, fatness, fleshed, fulsome, in flesh, lanolin, obesity, paunchy, pinguid, sizable, tubbish **08** dripping, fruitful, generous, handsome, palmitin, pot belly, sizeable **09** animal fat, corpulent, fat as a pig, margarine, plumpness, sebaceous, solidness, spare tyre, stoutness **10** chubbiness, corpulence,

deutoplasm, gor-bellied, kitchen-fee, oleaginous, overweight, pot-bellied, profitable **11** chylomicron, lipomatosis, substantial, well-endowed **12** considerable, saturated fat, steatopygous, vegetable fat **15** well-upholstered

fatal
05 final, vital **06** deadly, lethal, mortal **07** fateful, killing **08** critical, decisive, destined, terminal **09** incurable, malignant **10** calamitous, disastrous **11** destructive, mortiferous, unavoidable **12** catastrophic

fatalism
08 stoicism **09** endurance, passivity **10** acceptance **11** resignation

fatalistic
07 passive, patient, stoical **08** resigned, yielding **09** defeatist **10** reconciled, submissive **11** acquiescent **13** long-suffering, philosophical

fatality
04 dead, loss **05** death **08** casualty, disaster **09** lethality, mortality **10** deadliness **11** catastrophe

fate
03 end, lot **04** doom, joss, luck, Norn, ruin **05** cavel, death, event, issue, karma, Moera, Moira, Norna, stars, weird **06** chance, defeat, future, kismet **07** destiny, fortune, outcome **08** disaster, God's will **09** horoscope **10** ill-fortune, predestiny, providence **11** catastrophe, destruction **14** predestination

The Greek Fates:

06 Clotho
07 Atropos
08 Lachesis

The Norse Fates:

03 Urd
05 Skuld
08 Verdande

fated
03 fay, fey, fie **04** sure **06** doomed **07** certain **08** destined **09** enchanted **10** inevitable **11** ineluctable, inescapable, predestined, preordained, unavoidable **12** foreordained, predestinate

fateful
05 fatal **07** crucial, pivotal **08** critical, decisive **09** important, momentous, prophetic **10** portentous **11** significant

fatefully
09 crucially **10** critically, decisively **11** importantly, momentously **13** significantly

father
02 da, Fr, pa **03** dad, gov, guv, pop **04** abba, abbé, bapu, curé, male, papa, père, pops, sire **05** adopt, beget, daddy, elder, maker, padre, pappy, pater **06** author, invent, leader, old

man, parent, parson, pastor, patron, priest **07** creator, founder, genitor, produce **08** ancestor, beau-pere, begetter, engender, forebear, governor, inventor, minister **09** architect, clergyman, initiator, originate, patriarch, procreate **10** forefather, give life to, originator, prime mover, procreator, progenitor **11** birth father, predecessor **12** guiding light **13** paterfamilias

Father Christmas
05 Santa **06** St Nick **10** Santa Claus **11** Kris Kringle **12** Kriss Kringle
See also **reindeer**

fatherland
04 home **08** homeland **10** motherland, native land, old country **13** mother-country **15** land of your birth

fatherly
04 kind **06** benign, kindly, tender **08** paternal **09** avuncular, indulgent **10** benevolent, forbearing, protective, supportive **11** patriarchal **12** affectionate

fathom
01 f **02** fm **03** fth, get, see **04** fthm, twig **05** gauge, grasp, plumb, probe, sound **06** rumble **07** measure, plummet, suss out, work out **08** estimate, perceive **09** interpret, latch onto, penetrate, search out **10** comprehend, understand **12** get the hang of

fathomless
04 deep **07** complex, endless **08** infinite **09** enigmatic, intricate **10** bottomless, mysterious **11** complicated **12** immeasurable, impenetrable

fatigue
02 ME **03** CFS, sap, tax **04** do up, PVFS, tire, toil **05** drain, weary **06** overdo, weaken **07** exhaust, wear out **08** debility, enervate, lethargy, overwork, weakness **09** lassitude, tiredness, weariness, yuppie flu **10** debilitate, enervation, exhaustion **11** take it out of **12** listlessness **13** wearisomeness

fatigued
04 beat **05** all in, jaded, tired, weary **06** beaten, bushed, done in, fagged, pooped, swink't, wasted, zonked **07** euchred, swinked, wappend, whacked **08** dead-beat, jiggered, tired out **09** exhausted, fagged out, knackered, overspent, overtired, pooped out **10** euchred out **11** tuckered out

fatness
04 bulk, flab **06** grease **07** obesity **08** richness **09** bulkiness, fertility, grossness, heaviness, largeness, plumpness, podginess, rotundity, stoutness, tubbiness **10** corpulence, corpulency, overweight, pinguidity, pinguitude, portliness

fatten
04 cram, feed, lard, soil 05 bloat, flesh, frank, stuff, swell, widen 06 batten, battle, enrich, expand, feed up, spread 07 broaden, build up, engross, fill out, nourish, nurture, thicken 08 overfeed, pinguefy, saginate 09 stall-feed

fatty
03 fat 04 oily, waxy 05 oleic, suety 06 creamy, fleshy, greasy, lipoid, suetty 07 adipose, buttery, pinguid 08 unctuous 09 aliphatic, sebaceous 10 oleaginous

fatuous
04 daft, gaga 05 dense, inane, moony, silly 06 absurd, stupid 07 asinine, foolish, idiotic, lunatic, moronic, puerile, vacuous, witless 08 imbecile, mindless 09 brainless, ludicrous 10 ridiculous, weak-minded

fault
◇ *anagram indicator*
03 bug, nag, sin 04 beam, boob, carp, flaw, flub, gall, goof, slam, slip, trap, vice 05 blame, error, fluff, hitch, judge, knock, lapse, pinch, scold, slate, wrong 06 booboo, defect, foible, glitch, impugn, nibble, slip-up 07 blemish, blunder, censure, default, demerit, failing, impeach, misdeed, mistake, offence, quarrel 08 omission, weakness 09 criticize, inculpate, liability, oversight, reprehend, weak point 10 culpa levis, deficiency, negligence, peccadillo, wrongdoing 11 culpability, delinquency, pick holes in, shortcoming 12 imperfection, indiscretion, misdemeanour, pull to pieces 13 answerability, call to account, find fault with 14 accountability, responsibility 15 blameworthiness
• at fault
◇ *anagram indicator*
03 out 05 wrong 06 guilty 07 at a loss, to blame 08 culpable 10 in the wrong 11 accountable, blameworthy, responsible
• to a fault
06 unduly 07 too much 09 extremely 10 over the top, to extremes 11 excessively 12 immoderately, inordinately, in the extreme 13 unnecessarily

fault-finding
04 crab 07 carping, nagging 08 captious, critical, niggling 09 cavilling, complaint, criticism, grumbling, querulous, quibbling 10 censorious, nit-picking 11 complaining 12 captiousness, pettifogging 13 hair-splitting, hypercritical 14 finger-pointing, hypercriticism

faultless
04 pure 05 model 07 correct, perfect 08 accurate, flawless, spotless 09 blameless, exemplary, lily-white, unsullied 10 immaculate, impeccable 11 unblemished 13 unimpeachable 14 irreproachable, without blemish

faulty
◇ *anagram indicator*
03 bad 04 bust, duff, weak 05 kaput, wonky, wrong 06 broken, flawed 07 damaged, invalid, vicious 08 culpable 09 casuistic, conked out, defective, erroneous, illogical, imperfect, incorrect, playing up 10 fallacious, inaccurate, not working, on the blink, out of order 11 inoperative, out of action 14 malfunctioning

Faunas
03 Pan

faux pas
04 boob, goof 05 error, gaffe 06 booboo, howler, slip-up 07 blunder, clanger, mistake 08 solecism 11 impropriety 12 indiscretion

favour
03 aid 04 back, boon, gree, help, like, pick 05 go for, grace, spoil 06 assist, choose, esteem, opt for, pamper, prefer, select 07 aggrace, approve, backing, benefit, endorse, indulge, make for, promote, service, succour, support 08 advocate, approval, befriend, champion, courtesy, good deed, good turn, goodwill, kindness, plump for, resemble, sanction, sympathy 09 advantage, encourage, patronage, recommend 10 acceptance, act of grace, assistance, attraction, indulgence, obligation, partiality, preference 11 approbation, countenance, favouritism 12 commendation, friendliness, take kindly to 13 act of kindness
• in favour of
03 for, pro 06 all for, behind 07 backing 10 supporting 11 on the side of
• obtain favour
03 win

favourable
04 fair, good, kind 05 white 06 benign, toward 08 amicable, Favonian, friendly, pleasing, positive, suitable, towardly 09 agreeable, approving, benignant, effective, opportune, promising 10 auspicious, beneficial, convenient, heartening, propitious, reassuring 11 appropriate, encouraging, meliorative, sympathetic 12 advantageous, enthusiastic, well-disposed 13 complimentary, understanding

favourably
04 well 09 agreeably, helpfully 10 in good part, positively, profitably 11 approvingly, fortunately, opportunely 12 auspiciously, conveniently, propitiously 14 advantageously 15 sympathetically

favoured
05 élite, fa'ard, faurd 06 chosen, graced 07 blessed, fancied 08 selected 09 favourite, predilect,

preferred 10 advantaged, privileged 11 predilected, recommended

favourite
03 nap, pet 04 fave, idol, peat, pick 05 great 06 choice, chosen, minion, winger 07 beloved, best boy, darling, dearest, nostrum, special 08 Benjamin, best girl, esteemed, favoured, gracioso, white boy 09 best-loved, boyfriend, certainty, form horse, golden boy, most-liked, number one, preferred, treasured 10 girlfriend, particular, preference 11 blue-eyed boy, first choice, teacher's pet 12 likely winner 13 fair-haired boy 14 apple of your eye, white-headed boy 15 odds-on favourite

favouritism
04 bias 08 inequity, nepotism 09 injustice, prejudice 10 inequality, partiality, preference, unfairness 12 one-sidedness, partisanship

fawn
04 buff, claw 05 beige, court, crawl, creep, khaki, kotow, sandy, smalm, smarm, toady 06 cosy up, cozy up, cringe, crouch, grovel, kowtow 07 adulate, cervine, flatter, spaniel 08 bootlick, butter up, cosy up to, pay court, soft-soap, suck up to 09 pale brown 10 cozy up with 11 curry favour 12 bow and scrape, sand-coloured 14 be obsequious to, yellowish-brown

fawning
06 abject, supple 07 servile, spaniel 08 crawling, cringing, toadying, toadyish, unctuous 10 flattering, grovelling, obsequious, oleaginous 11 bootlicking, deferential, sycophantic 12 ingratiating, knee-crooking

fay *see* fairy

faze
03 rub 04 beat, rush, stun 05 drive, shake, shock, worry 06 dismay, put off, put out, puzzle, rattle 07 disturb, fluster, perturb, startle, unnerve 08 disquiet, drive off, surprise, unsettle 09 dumbfound, take aback 10 disconcert 12 perturbation

FBI member
03 Fed 04 G-man

fear
03 awe 04 risk 05 alarm, doubt, dread, panic, scope, worry 06 adread, affray, chance, dismay, expect, fright, honour, horror, phobia, qualms, regret, revere, terror, unease, wonder 07 anxiety, concern, foresee, phobism, redoubt, respect, shaking, suspect, terrify 08 aversion, be afraid, disquiet, distress, freak out, prospect, venerate, wonder at 09 agitation, bête noire, fear of God, nightmare, quivering, reverence, shudder at, suspicion, tremble at, trembling 10 anticipate, be afraid of, be scared of, foreboding, heart-quake, likelihood, likeliness, misgivings, shrink from, solicitude,

tremble for, uneasiness, veneration
11 expectation, fearfulness,
pantophobia, possibility, probability,
trepidation **12** affrightment,
apprehension, get the wind up, stand in
awe of, take fright at **13** be in a blue
funk, be uneasy about, consternation,
have a horror of, lose your nerve **14** be
anxious about, be in a cold sweat, lose
your bottle, your heart melts **15** have
qualms about, hold in reverence
• **for fear that**
04 lest

fearful
04 dire, grim **05** adred, afear, awful,
ferly, nervy, tense, timid **06** afraid,
aghast, hunted, scared, uneasy, yellow
07 alarmed, anxious, ghastly, hideous,
in dread, nervous, panicky, shaking
08 affrayed, agitated, dreadful,
effraide, fearsome, gruesome,
hesitant, horrible, horrific, shocking,
terrible, timorous **09** appalling,
atrocious, frightful, harrowing,
monstrous, petrified, quivering,
spineless, trembling, tremulous
10 frightened **11** distressing, in a blue
funk **12** apprehensive, faint-hearted, in
a cold sweat **13** having kittens, scared
to death

fearfully
04 most, very, well **05** jolly **06** highly
07 awfully, timidly **08** terribly, uneasily
09 anxiously, extremely, intensely,
nervously, unusually **10** dreadfully,
hesitantly, incredibly **11** exceedingly,
frightfully **12** terrifically, unbelievably
13 exceptionally **14** apprehensively

fearless
04 bold, game **05** brave, gutsy, proud
06 ballsy, daring, feisty, gritty, heroic,
plucky, spunky **07** aweless, doughty,
gallant, impavid, valiant **08** intrepid,
unafraid, valorous **09** confident,
dauntless, unabashed, undaunted
10 courageous, unblinking
11 indomitable, lion-hearted,
unblenching, unflinching
14 unapprehensive

fearsome
04 unco **05** awful **07** awesome,
dreaded **08** alarming, daunting,
horrible, horrific, menacing, terrible
09 appalling, dismaying, frightful,
unnerving **10** formidable, horrendous,
horrifying, terrifying **11** frightening,
hair-raising **12** awe-inspiring

feasibility
09 viability **10** expedience
11 possibility, workability
12 practicality **13** achievability
14 practicability, reasonableness

feasible
02 on **06** doable, likely, viable
08 possible, probable, workable
09 expedient, practical, realistic
10 achievable, attainable, realizable,
reasonable **11** practicable
14 accomplishable

feast
02 do **03** ale, pig **04** fest, fete, gala,
luau, wake, Yule **05** agape, beano,
binge, gaudy, gorge, hangi, Purim,
revel, treat **06** bridal, dinner, double,
Isodia, junket, kaikai, Lammas, pig out,
regale, repast, revels, spread, Sukkot,
wealth **07** banquet, blow-out,
convive, holiday, holy day, lamb-ale,
name day, potlach, Rood Day, Shavuot,
Sukkoth **08** carnival, carousal, feast
day, festival, Id al-Adha, Id al-Fitr,
Passover, potlatch, Shabuoth,
Shavuoth, Shevuoth **09** abundance,
Eid al-Adha, Eid al-Fitr, entertain,
epulation, Hallowmas, indulge in,
junketing, love-feast, Martinmas,
Martlemas, partake of, Pentecost,
profusion, saint's day **10** cornucopia,
jour de fête, Roodmas Day, slap-up
meal **11** celebration, eat your fill,
festivities, Holy-rood Day, wine and
dine **13** All-hallowmass

feat
03 act, art **04** deed **05** point, skill
06 action, henner, splits, stroke
07 exploit **08** hat trick, shanghai
09 keepy-uppy **10** attainment,
Houdini act **11** achievement,
performance, tour de force,
undertaking **14** accomplishment

feather
03 pen **04** down, tuft **05** crest, egret,
penna, pinna, plume, quill, wedge
06 covert, fletch, hackle, manual,
pinion, sickle **07** plumage, plumula,
plumule, primary, rectrix, tectrix
08 aigrette, standard, tertiary, vibrissa
09 condition, filoplume, secondary,
semiplume
• **coil of feathers**
03 boa
• **part of feather**
04 harl, herl

feathery
04 soft **05** downy, light, plumy, wispy
06 fledgy, fleecy, flimsy, fluffy, plumed
07 plumate, plumose, plumous
08 delicate **09** feathered, penniform
10 pennaceous **11** featherlike

feature
03 act, mug, pan **04** chin, dial, face,
form, item, mark, nose, phiz, show,
side, star **05** clock, facet, focus, looks,
piece, point, shape, story, trait
06 appear, aspect, beauty, column,
factor, figure, kisser, phizog, play up,
report, visage **07** article, comment,
perform, phantom, present, promote,
quality **08** hallmark, property
09 attribute, character, emphasize,
highlight, lineament, spotlight
10 accentuate, attraction, focal point,
lineaments, speciality **11** centrepiece,
countenance, participate, peculiarity,
physiognomy **14** characteristic **15** call
attention to, draw attention to

featureless
04 dull **05** bland, blank, plain, vague
07 anaemic, insipid, vanilla **08** ordinary

11 commonplace, nondescript,
uninspiring **12** cookie cutter, run of the
mill, unattractive, unclassified,
unremarkable **13** indeterminate,
undistinctive, unexceptional,
uninteresting **14** common or garden
15 undistinguished

febrile
03 hot **05** fiery **07** burning, fevered,
flushed, pyretic **08** feverish, inflamed
09 delirious

February
03 Feb

feckless
03 wet **04** weak **06** feeble, futile, no-
good **07** aimless, useless, wimpish
08 helpless, hopeless **09** shiftless,
worthless **11** incompetent, ineffectual
13 irresponsible

fecund
07 fertile, teeming **08** fruitful, prolific
09 feracious, fructuous **10** productive
12 fructiferous

fecundity
08 feracity **09** fertility **12** fruitfulness
14 productiveness

federal
03 Fed **06** allied, united **07** unified
08 combined, in league **10** associated,
integrated **11** amalgamated
12 confederated

federate
04 ally **05** unify, unite **06** league
07 combine **09** associate, integrate,
syndicate **10** amalgamate
11 confederate **12** confederated, join
together

federation
05 union **06** league **08** alliance,
federacy **09** coalition, syndicate
11 association, combination,
confederacy **12** amalgamation
13 confederation, copartnership

fed up
03 ate **04** blue, down, glum, jack
05 bored, jaded, sated, tired, weary
06 dismal, gloomy **07** annoyed,
chocker, pig sick **09** depressed,
hacked off, pissed off **10** brassed off,
browned off, cheesed off
11 disgruntled **12** discontented,
dissatisfied, sick and tired **13** have had
enough

fee
03 due, pay, sub **04** bill, cost, fine, hire,
rent, toll, wage **05** money, price, terms,
tithe, tythe **06** cattle, charge, hirage,
mouter, reward, salary, towage
07 account, faldage, footing, hireage,
moorage, multure, payment, premium,
service, tuition **08** chummage,
pilotage, property, retainer
09 emolument, livestock, obvention,
ownership, refresher, vassalage
10 bell-siller, honorarium, possession,
recompense **11** inheritance
12 remuneration, subscription
15 appearance money

feeble

03 wet 04 lame, poor, puny, tame, thin, weak 05 faint, frail, silly, sober, washy, versh, wussy 06 ailing, debile, effete, flabby, flimsy, futile, infirm, sickly, slight, weakly 07 failing, rickety, wastrel, wearish, wimpish 08 daidling, decrepit, delicate, feckless, helpless, listless, pathetic, sackless 09 enervated, exhausted, graspless, powerless, weak-kneed 10 dispirited, izzenless, foisonless, impuissant, inadequate, indecisive, namby-pamby, spiritless, wishy-washy 11 debilitated, cushionless, incompetent, ineffective, ineffectual, vacillating 12 unconvincing, unsuccessful

feeble-minded

04 dumb 05 dotty, silly 06 simple, stupid 07 idiotic, moronic 08 imbecile, retarded 09 deficient, dim-witted, imbecilic 10 half-witted, indecisive, slow-witted, weak-minded 11 not all there 13 soft in the head 14 mouth breathing, not the full quid 15 slow on the uptake

feebly

06 lamely, sickly, weakly 07 faintly 08 slightly 10 helplessly 11 powerlessly 12 dispiritedly, indecisively, pathetically 13 ineffectively

feed

> insertion indicator
03 eat, put 04 crop, dine, food, fuel, give, paid, slip, soil, tire 05 graze, slide 06 battle, browse, dine on, fodder, forage, foster, insert, repast, silage, stooge, suckle, supply, take in, tuck-in 07 consume, deliver, fortify, gratify, nourish, nurture, pasture, provide, support, victual 08 cater for, ruminate 09 encourage, foodstuff, introduce, partake of, provender 10 give food to, provide for, strengthen

feedback

05 reply 06 answer 08 comeback, response 11 respondence

feel

02 be 03 air, paw, rub 04 aura, bear, bent, deem, gift, hand, hold, know, look, maul, mood, palp, poke, seem 05 enjoy, flair, grasp, grope, judge, knack, nurse, sense, skill, think, touch, vibes 06 appear, caress, clutch, detect, endure, finger, finish, fondle, fumble, handle, notice, reckon, stroke, suffer, talent 07 ability, believe, contact, discern, faculty, feeling, harbour, massage, observe, quality, realize, surface, texture, undergo 08 ambience, aptitude, consider, instinct, perceive 09 be aware of, give way to, go through 10 atmosphere, experience, impression, manipulate, understand 11 consistency, live through 12 be overcome by 15 feel in your bones

• **feel for**
04 pity 07 weep for 09 be moved by,

grieve for 10 be sorry for, sympathize 11 commiserate 13 empathize with 14 sympathize with 15 commiserate with

• **feel like**
04 want, wish 05 fancy 06 desire 09 would like

feeler

04 horn, palp 05 probe 06 palpus 07 advance, antenna 08 approach, overture, tentacle 09 overtures 10 sense organ 12 ballon d'essai, trial balloon

feeling

03 air, ego 04 aura, bent, care, feel, gift, idea, love, mood, pity, view 05 flair, hunch, knack, sense, skill, touch, vibes 06 ardour, belief, motion, notion, spirit, talent, theory, warmth 07 ability, concern, emotion, fervour, inkling, opinion, passion, pitying, quality, thought 08 aptitude, emotions, esthesia, fondness, instinct, passions, sympathy 09 aesthesia, aesthesis, affection, intensity, intuition, sensation, sentience, sentiment, suspicion 10 affections, atmosphere, compassion, Empfindung, impression, perception, self-esteem, tenderness 11 point of view, sensibility, sensitivity, sympathetic 12 appreciation 13 compassionate, sensibilities, sensitivities, understanding, way of thinking 14 natural ability, sentimentality, susceptibility

• **show feeling**
05 emote

• **with no feeling**
04 numb

feign

03 act 04 fain, fake, sham 05 fable, faine, false, fayne, forge, put on, shape 06 affect, assume, gammon, invent, make up 07 falsify, fashion, imagine, imitate, pretend, put it on 08 misfeign, simulate 09 dissemble, fabricate 11 counterfeit, dissimulate, make a show of, make believe

feint

04 play, ruse, sham, wile 05 blind, bluff, dodge, dummy 06 gambit 08 artifice, pretence 09 deception, expedient, manoeuvre, stratagem 10 subterfuge 11 distraction, make-believe, mock-assault 12 dissemblance

feisty

04 bold 05 brave, gutsy, tough 06 gritty, lively, plucky, spunky, touchy 08 spirited 09 excitable, irritable 10 courageous, determined

feldspar, felspar

06 albite 08 adularia, andesine, sanidine, sunstone 09 anorthite, moonstone 10 hyalophane, oligoclase, orthoclase 11 anorthosite, labradorite, peristerite, plagioclase

felicitous

03 apt 05 happy 06 timely 07 apropos, fitting 08 apposite,

inspired, suitable 09 fortunate, opportune, well-timed 10 delightful, propitious, prosperous, well-chosen, well-turned 11 appropriate 12 advantageous

felicity

03 joy 05 bliss 07 aptness, delight, ecstasy, rapture 08 blessing, euphoria 09 eloquence, happiness, propriety 11 delectation, suitability 12 suitableness 13 applicability 15 appropriateness

feline

03 cat, tom 04 eyra, puss 05 catty, felid, manul, moggy, ounce, pussy, queen, quoll, rumpy, sleek, tabby 06 kitten, malkin, mouser, ocelot, serval, slinky, smooth, Tibert, tomcat 07 catlike, cattish, leonine, sensual, sinuous, wildcat 08 alleycat, baudrons, graceful, stealthy 09 grimalkin, sealpoint, seductive 10 jaguarundi
See also **cat**

fell

02 ax, KO 03 axe, hew, lit, log 04 alit, dire, gall, hide, hill, keen, moor, pelt, raze, skin, very 05 cruel, felon, floor, great, level 06 deadly, fierce, lay low, mighty, poleax 07 cut down, doughty, flatten, poleaxe, pungent 08 chop down, demolish, felonous, membrane, ruthless 09 knock down, overthrow, prostrate 10 bitterness, strike down 15 raze to the ground

fellow

01 F, m 02 bo, co-, he 03 boy, bud, cat, cod, don, guy, Joe, lad, man, pal, sod, wag 04 bozo, chap, chum, cove, dean, dude, gent, like, male, mate, oppo, peer, twin 05 bloke, buddy, crony, devil, equal, match 06 buffer, callan, double, friend, person, rascal, sister 07 callant, compeer, comrade, partner, related, similar 08 confrère, co-worker 09 associate, boyfriend, character, colleague, companion, semblable 10 associated, compatriot, individual 11 counterpart 12 contemporary
See also **boy**

• **little fellow**
03 elf, imp

fellow feeling

04 care 07 empathy, feeling 08 sympathy 10 compassion 13 commiseration, understanding

fellowship

04 club 05 guild, order, union 06 league 07 society 08 intimacy, matiness, sodality, sorority 09 communion, palliness 10 affability, amiability, chumminess, consortium, fraternity, friendship, sisterhood 11 affiliation, association, brotherhood, camaraderie, comradeship, familiarity, sociability 13 companionship, compatibility

felon see criminal

felspar see feldspar, felspar

felt
03 bat **04** batt

female
01 f **03** doe, -ess, gal, hen, her, pen, rib, she **04** bird, girl, hind, miss **05** woman **06** maiden **07** girlish, womanly **08** feminine, ladylike, womanish **09** petticoat **10** carpellate, pistillate

See also **animal; girl**

feminine
01 f **03** fem **04** weak **05** cissy, girly **06** female, gentle, pretty, tender **07** girlish, unmanly, wimpish, womanly **08** delicate, graceful, ladylike, womanish **09** petticoat **10** effeminate

femininity
08 delicacy **09** sissiness, womanhood **10** effeminacy, gentleness, muliebrity, prettiness, tenderness **11** girlishness, womanliness **12** feminineness, gracefulness, womanishness

feminism
09 women's lib **12** women's rights **14** women's movement

Feminists include:

04 Daly (Mary), Hite (Shere), Mott (Lucretia), Shaw (Anna Howard), Wolf (Naomi)
05 Abzug (Bella), Astor (Nancy), Beale (Dorothea), Greer (Germaine), Stone (Lucy)
06 Callil (Carmen), Cixous (Hélène), Faludi (Susan), Friday (Nancy), Fuller (Margaret), Gilman (Charlotte Perkins), Grimké (Sarah Moore), Orbach (Susie), Rankin (Jeannette), Stopes (Marie), Weldon (Fay)
07 Anthony (Susan B), Davison (Emily), Dworkin (Andrea), Egerton (Sarah), Fawcett (Dame Millicent), Friedan (Betty), Goldman (Emma), Kennedy (Helena, Baroness), Lenclos (Ninon de), Steinem (Gloria), Tennant (Emma)
08 Beauvoir (Simone de), Brittain (Vera), MacPhail (Agnes), Rathbone (Eleanor)
09 Blackwell (Elizabeth), Pankhurst (Adela), Pankhurst (Christabel), Pankhurst (Emmeline), Pankhurst (Sylvia)
11 Burgos Seguí (Carmen de)
14 Wollstonecraft (Mary)

femme fatale
04 vamp **05** Circe, siren **06** Sirens **07** charmer, Delilah, Lorelei **08** Mata Hari **09** temptress **10** seductress **11** enchantress

fen
03 bog **04** moss, quag, wash **05** marsh, swamp **06** morass, slough **08** quagmire

fence
◊ *containment indicator*
03 hay, pen **04** coop, oxer, pale, rail, wall, wear, weir, wire **05** bound, dodge, evade, guard, hedge, parry

06 defend, fraise, paling, pusher, rasper, rustic, secure, shield, shut in **07** barrier, confine, defence, enclose, fortify, inclose, protect, quibble, railing, rampart **08** encircle, palisade, palisado, restrict, separate, sepiment, stockade, surround **09** barricade, enclosure, pussyfoot, stonewall, vacillate, windbreak **10** digladiate, equivocate, trafficker **11** prevaricate **12** circumscribe, shilly-shally, tergiversate

• **sit on the fence**
06 dither **08** be unsure **09** vacillate **11** be uncertain, be undecided **12** be irresolute, shilly-shally **13** be uncommitted **14** blow hot and cold

fencing
07 railing **08** guarding **09** defending, swordplay

Fencing terms include:

03 bib, cut, hit
04 bout, épée, foil, pass, pink, volt, ward
05 allez, appel, carte, feint, forte, lunge, parry, piste, prime, punto, sabre, sixte, touch, volte
06 attack, button, come in, doigté, faible, flèche, foible, octave, parade, puncto, quarte, quinte, remise, thrust, tierce, touché
07 barrage, counter, en garde, on guard, passado, reprise, riposte, seconde, septime, stop hit
08 back edge, balestra, coquille, plastron, tac-au-tac, traverse
09 disengage, repechage
10 flanconade, imbroccata, time-thrust
11 corps à corps, punto dritto
12 colichemarde, counter-parry, punto reverso
14 counter-riposte

fend
05 avert, parry, repel **06** defend, divert, resist **07** beat off, deflect, head off, keep off, provide, repulse, shut out, support, sustain, ward off **08** maintain, stave off **09** hold at bay, look after, turn aside **10** take care of

feral
04 wild **06** animal, brutal, deadly, fierce, savage **07** bestial, brutish, untamed, vicious **08** funereal, unbroken **09** ferocious **12** uncultivated **14** undomesticated

ferment
◊ *anagram indicator*
04 boil, brew, foam, fret, fuss, heat, rise, stew, stir, work, zyme **05** cause, fever, froth, mould, rouse, yeast **06** arouse, bubble, enzyme, excite, fester, foment, frenzy, furore, hubbub, incite, leaven, seethe, stir up, tumult, unrest, uproar, work up **07** agitate, inflame, provoke, ptyalin, turmoil **08** bacteria, brouhaha, smoulder **09** agitation, commotion, confusion **10** disruption, effervesce, excitement, turbulence

fermium
02 Fm

fern

Ferns include:

03 oak
04 hard, lady, male, tree
05 beech, brake, chain, crown, holly, marsh, royal, sword, water
06 Boston, ribbon, shield, silver, tongue
07 bladder, bracken, buckler, Dickie's, elkhorn, Goldie's, leather, ostrich, parsley, rockcap, wall rue, woodsia
08 aspidium, cinnamon, climbing, hairy lip, licorice, moonwort, pillwort, polypody, staghorn
09 asparagus, asplenium, bird's nest, hare's foot, rusty-back, sensitive
10 Asian chain, Korean rock, maidenhair, soft shield, spleenwort
11 hart's tongue, rabbit's foot
12 broad buckler, elephant's ear, resurrection
13 crested ribbon, Japanese holly, scolopendrium, squirrel's foot
14 brittle bladder
15 Japanese painted

ferocious
04 deep, grim, wild **05** cruel, feral **06** bitter, brutal, fierce, savage, severe, strong **07** extreme, inhuman, intense, salvage, untamed, vicious, violent **08** barbaric, pitiless, ruthless, sadistic, Tartarly, vigorous **09** barbarous, merciless, murderous **12** bloodthirsty, catamountain, cat o' mountain

ferocity
06 sadism **07** cruelty **08** savagery, severity, violence, wildness **09** barbarity, brutality, extremity, intensity **10** fierceness, inhumanity **11** viciousness **12** ruthlessness

ferret
03 hob **04** gill, hunt, jill **05** rifle, scour **06** forage, search **07** rummage **09** go through

• **ferret out**
04 find **05** dig up, trace **06** elicit **07** extract, nose out, root out, suss out, unearth, worm out **08** discover, hunt down **09** search out, track down **10** fossick out, run to earth

ferry
03 ply, run **04** boat, move, pont, ro-ro, ship, take, taxi **05** carry, drive, shift **06** convey, packet, ponton, vessel **07** passage, pontoon, shuttle, traject, tranect **08** car ferry **09** ferry-boat, transport **10** packet boat **12** flying bridge **13** Interislander®, roll-on roll-off

fertile
04 rich **06** battle, broody, fecund, potent, virile **08** abundant, creative, fruitful, inspired, pregnant, prolific **09** ingenious, inventive, luxuriant, visionary **10** generative, productive **11** imaginative, resourceful **12** reproductive

fertility

07 fatness, potency **08** richness, virility **09** abundance, fecundity **10** luxuriance **12** fruitfulness, prolificness **14** generativeness, productiveness

fertilization

03 IVF **04** ICSI **07** selfing **10** conception **11** fecundation, pollination, procreation, propagation, siphonogamy **12** implantation, impregnation, insemination **13** palmification, superfetation

fertilize

04 dung, feed, self **05** dress, mulch **06** enrich, manure **07** compost **08** fructify, top-dress **09** fecundate, pollinate, procreate **10** impregnate, inseminate **12** make fruitful, make pregnant

fertilizer

04 dung, marl **05** guano, humus, mulch **06** manure **07** compost, humogen, kainite, nitrate, tankage **08** bone meal, dressing **09** cyanamide, plant food, soda nitre **10** fish-manure **11** top-dressing **13** sodium nitrate **14** superphosphate **15** ammonium nitrate

fervent

03 hot **04** warm **05** eager, fiery **06** ardent, devout **07** earnest, excited, intense, sincere, zealous **08** spirited, vehement, vigorous **09** emotional, energetic, heartfelt **10** passionate **11** full-blooded, impassioned **12** enthusiastic, wholehearted

fervently

07 eagerly **08** ardently **09** earnestly, excitedly, intensely, sincerely **10** vigorously **11** emotionally **12** passionately **13** energetically **14** wholeheartedly

fervour

04 fire, heat, hwyl, zeal **05** verve **06** ardour, energy, spirit, vigour, warmth **07** emotion, passion **09** animation, eagerness, intensity, sincerity, vehemence **10** enthusiasm, excitement **11** earnestness

fester

03 irk, rot **04** brew, gall **05** anger, annoy, chafe, decay, go bad **06** gather, infect, perish, rankle **07** moulder, putrefy **08** maturate, smoulder, ulcerate **09** decompose, discharge, suppurate

festival

03 ale **04** fair, fete, gala, play, tide, wake **05** feast, festa, party, revel **06** double, fiesta, pardon **07** gala day, high day, holiday, jubilee **08** carnival, high tide, panegyry **10** merry-night, semi-double **11** anniversary, celebration, festivities, merrymaking **13** commemoration, entertainment

See also **celebration; service**

Ancient festivals and celebrations include:

03 Bon, Mod
04 feis, Lots, Yule
05 Purim, Saman, Weeks, Wesak
06 Advent, Diwali, Easter, Floria, Lammas, May Day, Oimelc, Opalia, Pesach, Plebii
07 Beltane, Equiria, Feralia, Fugalia, holy-ale, Imbolic, Lady Day, Lemuria, Mop Fair, Navrati, Palilia, Parilia, Ramadan, Samhain, Sukkoth, Sullani, Theseia, Vinalia
08 Agonalia, Cerealia, Fasching, Faunalia, Floralia, Hanukkah, Hogmanay, Homstrom, Hull Fair, Id ul-Adha, Id ul-Fitr, Lucia Day, Lugnasad, Mahayana, Matralia, Nit de foc, Passover, Samhuinn, Setsubun, Shabuoth, Stow Fair, Tanabata, Vestalia
09 Baishakhi, Boxing Day, Christmas, church-ale, Floralies, Goose Fair, Hallowe'en, Hallowmas, Ides of Mar, Liberalia, Ludi Magni, Lugnasadh, Magalesia, Magha-puja, Mardi Gras, Martinmas, Nemoralia, Paganalia, Pentecost, Puanepsia, Robigalia, Thargelia, Ullambana, Up-Helly-Aa, Wakes Week, Yom Kippur
10 Allhallows, Ambarvalia, Barnet Fair, Fordicidia, Fornicalia, Good Friday, Larentalia, La Tomatina, Lee Gap Fair, Ludi Romani, Lupercalia, Matronalia, Mother's Day, Neptunalia, Palm Sunday, Pancake Day, Parentalia, Portunalia, Quirinalia, Regifugium, Saturnalia, Swan Upping, Terminalia, Volcanalia
11 Acension Day, All Fools' Day, All Souls' Day, Bacchanalia, Carmentalia, Epulum Jovis, Hina Matsuri, Lady Luck Day, Oktoberfest, Oskhophoria, Panathenaea, Quinquatrus, Semo Sanctus, St David's Day, Tabernacles
12 All Saints' Day, Annunciation, Armilustrium, Ash Wednesday, Barranquilla, Day of the Dead, Doll Festival, Holy Wells Day, Kanda Matsuri, Ludi Merceruy, Mahashivrati, Meditrinalia, Moon Festival, Nutters Dance, Rosh Hashanah, St Andrew's Day, St George's Day, Thanksgiving, Tubilustrium, Twelfth Night, Well-dressing
13 April Fool's Day, Haxey Hood Game, Ludi Consualia, Ludi Martiales, Midsummer's Eve, Raksha Bandhan, Shrove Tuesday, St Patrick's Day, The Furry Dance, Water Festival, Widecombe Fair
14 Chinese New Year, Maundy Thursday, St Nicholas's Day, Vinalia Rustica, Walpurgis Night
15 Festival of Light, Harvest Festival, Lares Praestites, Ludi Apollinares, Mahavira Jayanti, Mothering Sunday, Priddy Sheep Fair, St Valentine's Day

---

Modern festivals and celebrations include:

05 VE Day, VJ Day, WOMAD
08 Anzac Day, Earth Day, Labor Day
09 Canada Day, Labour Day
10 Burns Night, Eisteddfod
11 Bastille Day, Cinco de Mayo, Glastonbury, Republic Day, Waitangi Day
12 Armistice Day, Australia Day, Bonfire Night, Glyndebourne, Groundhog Day
13 New Zealand Day
14 Guy Fawkes' Night, Remembrance Day
15 Edinburgh Fringe, Edinburgh Tattoo, Independence Day

Religious festivals include:

02 Id
03 Eid
04 Holi, Lent, Lots, mela, Obon, Oram, puja, Yule
05 Litha, Pesah, Purim
06 Advent, Bakrid, Basant, Dhamma, Divali, Diwali, Easter, Lammas, Pesach, Sukkot
07 Baisaki, Beltane, holy day, matsuri, New Year, Ramadan, Samhain, Shavuot, Sukkoth
08 All Souls, Baisakhi, Dipavali, Dusserah, Epiphany, feast day, Hanukkah, Id-al-Adha, Id al-Fitr, Id-ul-Zuha, Muharram, Passover
09 All Saints, Ascension, Candlemas, Christmas, Deepavali, Dolayatra, Durga-puja, Easter Day, Eid-al-Adha, Eid al-Fitr, Mardi Gras, Navaratri, Oshogatsu, Pentecost, Up-Helly-Aa, Yom Kippur
10 All Hallows, Assumption, Good Friday, Lughnasadh, Lupercalia, Michaelmas, Palm Sunday, Ramanavami, Rathayatra, Saturnalia, Vulcanalia, Whit Sunday
11 All Souls' Day, Bacchanalia, Lakshmi-puja, Milad-un-Nabi, Panathenaea, Rosh Hashana
12 All Saints' Day, Annunciation, Ascension Day, Ash Wednesday, Christmas Day, Easter Sunday, Holy Saturday, Holy Thursday, Night of Power, Ohinamatsuri, Prakash Utsav, Rosh Hashanah, Simchat Torah, Star Festival, Tango no Sekku
13 Buddha Purnima, Corpus Christi, Holy Innocents, Night of Ascent, Passion Sunday, spring equinox, Trinity Sunday, vernal equinox
14 Chinese New Year, Day of Atonement, Easter Saturday, Maundy Thursday, summer solstice, winter solstice
15 autumnal equinox, Lantern Festival, Tanabata Matsuri, Transfiguration

• **day before a festival**
03 eve
• **octave of a festival**
04 utas

festive

04 gala **05** happy, jolly, merry

06 cheery, festal, hearty, jovial, joyful, joyous **07** cordial, holiday **08** carnival, cheerful, feastful, jubilant **09** convivial **11** celebratory **12** light-hearted

festivity
03 fun, rag **04** gala, gaud **05** party, revel, sport **06** fiesta, gaiety, let-off **07** jollity, joyance, revelry, triumph **08** carousal, feasting, festival, pleasure **09** amusement, enjoyment, joviality, junketing, merriment **10** banqueting, cheeriness, joyfulness, jubilation **11** celebration, fun and games, merrymaking **12** cheerfulness, conviviality **13** entertainment, glorification, jollification

festoon
04 deck, hang, swag **05** adorn, array, drape **06** bedeck, swathe, wreath **07** bedizen, chaplet, garland, garnish, wreathe **08** decorate, encarpus, ornament

fetch
03 fet, get **04** earn, fett, make, take **05** bring, carry, ghost, go for, reach, yield **06** arrive, attain, convey, derive, double, escort **07** bring in, collect, conduct, deliver, realize, sell for **08** go and get **09** stratagem, transport **10** apparition
• **fetch up**
05 end up, vomit **06** arrive, show up, turn up, wind up **07** recover **08** finish up **11** materialize

fetching
04 cute **05** sweet **06** pretty **07** winsome **08** adorable, alluring, charming **09** appealing **10** attractive, enchanting **11** captivating, fascinating

fête, fete
04 fair, gala **05** treat **06** bazaar, honour, regale **07** holiday, lionize, welcome **08** carnival, festival **09** entertain **10** sale of work **11** garden party

fetid, foetid
04 foul, rank **05** pongy **06** filthy, rancid, sickly, smelly, whiffy **07** humming, noisome, noxious, odorous, reeking **08** mephitic, stinking **09** offensive **10** disgusting, graveolent, malodorous, nauseating

fetish
03 obi **04** idol, ju-ju, obia **05** charm, image, mania, obeah, thing, totem **06** amulet **08** fixation, idée fixe, talisman **09** obsession **10** cult object

fetter
03 tie **04** bind, curb, gyve, iron **05** chain, tie up, truss **06** hamper, hinder, hobble, impede **07** confine, hopples, leg-iron, manacle, shackle **08** encumber, obstruct, restrain, restrict **09** constrain, entrammel, hamstring **10** hamshackle

fetters
05 bands, bonds, curbs, irons **06** chains, checks, slangs **07** bondage **08** manacles, shackles **09** bracelets,

captivity, handcuffs **10** hindrances, restraints **11** constraints, inhibitions **12** obstructions, restrictions

fettle
◊ *anagram indicator*
• **in fine fettle**
03 fit **04** trim **05** sound **06** on form, strong **07** healthy, in shape **09** shipshape **10** in fine form, in good nick **11** in good shape **12** in good health **13** hale and hearty **15** in good condition

feud
03 row, war **04** duel, food **05** argue, brawl, clash, fight **06** bicker, enmity, strife **07** contend, discord, dispute, ill will, quarrel, rivalry, wrangle **08** argument, bad blood, be at odds, conflict, squabble, vendetta **09** altercate, animosity, bickering, hostility **10** antagonism, bitterness **12** disagreement

fever
04 heat **06** frenzy, unrest **07** ecstasy, ferment, passion, pyrexia, turmoil **08** delirium **09** agitation, calenture **10** excitement **11** temperature **12** feverishness, restlessness **15** high temperature

Fevers include:
01 Q
03 hay, tap
04 ague, camp, gaol, gold, jail, Rock, ship, tick, worm
05 brain, cabin, dandy, Lassa, Malta, marsh, stage, swamp, swine, Texas
06 dengue, dumdum, hectic, jungle, parrot, plague, rabbit, spring, trench, typhus, valley, yellow
07 biliary, enteric, gastric, malaria, measles, ratbite, sandfly, scarlet, splenic, spotted, typhoid, verruga
08 childbed, kala-azar, undulant
09 breakbone, calenture, East Coast, glandular, phrenitis, puerperal, relapsing, remittent, rheumatic
10 blackwater, Rift Valley, scarlatina, yellow Jack
12 African coast
13 cerebrospinal, leptospirosis, Mediterranean
14 kissing disease
15 acute rheumatism

fevered
03 hot, red **07** burning, excited, febrile, flushed, frantic, nervous **08** feverish, frenzied, restless, worked up **09** impatient **10** passionate

feverish
◊ *anagram indicator*
03 hot, red **05** hasty **06** hectic, rushed **07** burning, excited, febrile, flushed, frantic, hurried, in a tizz, nervous **08** agitated, bothered, febrific, frenzied, in a tizzy, restless, troubled, worked up **09** delirious, flustered, impatient, in a dither **10** passionate **11** overwrought **12** in a kerfuffle **14** hot and bothered

few
04 rare, some, thin **05** scant, wheen **06** meagre, scanty, scarce, sparse **07** a couple, handful, not many, several **08** one or two, sporadic, uncommon **09** a minority, exclusive, hardly any **10** inadequate, infrequent, negligible, scattering, sprinkling, two or three **11** scarcely any **12** insufficient **13** short supply **14** a small number of, inconsiderable **15** thin on the ground

fey
03 fay, fie, odd, shy **05** dotty, droll, elfin, funny, weird **06** doomed, quaint, quirky **07** curious, playful, unusual **08** childish, fanciful, peculiar **09** eccentric, impulsive, whimsical **10** capricious **11** mischievous **12** supernatural **13** unpredictable

fiancé, fiancée
08 intended, wife-to-be **09** betrothed, bride-to-be **10** future wife **11** husband-to-be **13** future husband **14** bridegroom-to-be **15** prospective wife

fiasco
04 bomb, flop, mess, rout, ruin **05** flask **06** bottle, fizzer, lash-up **07** cropper, debacle, failure, screw-up, washout **08** calamity, collapse, disaster **09** damp squib **11** catastrophe

fiat
02 OK **05** edict, order **06** decree, dictum, diktat **07** command, dictate, mandate, precept, warrant **08** sanction **09** directive, ordinance **10** injunction, permission **12** proclamation **13** authorization

fib
03 gag, lie **04** tale, yarn **05** evade, fable, porky, punch, story **06** invent, pummel **07** evasion, falsify, fantasy, fiction, untruth, whopper **08** sidestep, white lie **09** dissemble, fabricate, falsehood, fantasize, invention **10** concoction, taradiddle **11** prevaricate, tarradiddle **13** prevarication

fibre
04 coir, hair, pile, pita, silk **05** cloth, nerve, sinew, stuff, viver **06** fibril, make-up, nature, strand, thread **07** calibre, courage, funicle, resolve, stamina, tendril, texture **08** backbone, filament, firmness, material, roughage, strength **09** character, substance, toughness, willpower **10** resolution **11** disposition, temperament **12** resoluteness **13** determination

fibres
03 tow **04** pons

fickle
◊ *anagram indicator*
06 kittle, labile, volage **07** flighty, mutable **08** disloyal, unstable, unsteady, variable, volatile **09** choiceful, faithless, mercurial, volageous **10** capricious, changeable, inconstant, irresolute, unfaithful, unreliable **11** treacherous,

vacillating **12** inconsistent, wind-changing **13** unpredictable
• **be fickle**
04 turn

fickleness
06 change, levity **09** treachery
10 disloyalty, fitfulness, mutability, volatility **11** flightiness, inconstancy, instability **12** unsteadiness
13 changeability, faithlessness, unreliability **14** capriciousness, changeableness, unfaithfulness

fiction
03 fib, lie **04** myth, pulp, tale, yarn
05 fable, story **06** legend, novels
07 fantasy, parable, romance, stories, untruth **08** chick lit, noveldom, pretence **09** falsehood, invention, tall story **10** concoction **11** fabrication
12 splatterpunk, storytelling
15 creative writing
See also **literature**; **non-fiction**
• **science fiction**
02 SF **05** sci-fi **09** cyberpunk

fictional
06 made-up, unreal **08** fabulous, invented, literary, mythical
09 imaginary, legendary **11** make-believe, non-existent **12** mythological
See also **literary**; **novel**

fictitious
04 fake, sham **05** bogus, false
06 made-up, mythic, untrue
07 assumed, feigned, fictive
08 invented, mythical, romantic, spurious, supposed **09** concocted, imaginary **10** apocryphal, artificial, fabricated, improvised **11** counterfeit, non-existent

fiddle
02 do, gu **03** con, fix, gju, gue, kit, toy
04 fuss, play, rasp, rote, scam **05** cheat, fraud, graft, viola **06** diddle, fidget, juggle, meddle, racket, rip-off, scrape, tamper, tinker, trifle, violin **07** falsify, sultana, swindle **08** gold brick, interfere, manoeuvre, racketeer
10 fool around, mess around **12** cook the books **13** sharp practice

fiddling
05 petty **06** fiddly, paltry **07** trivial
08 trifling **10** negligible
13 insignificant

fidelity
05 faith, fides, troth, trust **07** honesty, loyalty **08** accuracy, devotion
09 adherence, closeness, constancy, exactness, precision **10** allegiance, strictness **11** devotedness, reliability
12 authenticity, faithfulness
13 dependability **15** trustworthiness

fidget
03 toy **04** fike, fret, fuss, jerk, jump
05 hotch **06** bustle, fiddle, footer, hirsle, jiggle, niggle, squirm, tamper, tinker, trifle, twitch, writhe **07** shuffle, twiddle, wriggle **09** mess about
10 play around **11** toss and turn
12 restlessness

fidgety
05 jumpy **06** on edge, uneasy
07 excited, jittery, nervous, restive, twitchy, uptight **08** agitated, restless
09 impatient

field
03 lea, ley **04** area, lawn, line, mead, play, slip, stop **05** catch, champ, close, forte, glebe, green, parry, pitch, put up, range, sawah, scene, scope, sward
06 answer, bounds, domain, ground, handle, lea-rig, limits, meadow, padang, pick up, regime, return, select, sphere **07** deflect, paddock, pasture, present, runners, send out, stubble
08 ball park, confines, cope with, deal with, entrants, province, retrieve
09 grassland, opponents, possibles, territory **10** applicants, candidates, contenders, department, discipline, opposition, speciality **11** competition, competitors, contestants, environment
12 choose to play, participants, playing-field
See also **athletics**; **cricket**
• **stubble field**
05 arish **06** arrish

Field Marshal
02 FM **13** velt-mareschal

fiend
03 fan, nut **04** buff, ogre **05** beast, brute, demon, devil, fient, freak, ghoul
06 addict, savage **07** devotee, fanatic, monster **10** aficionado, enthusiast, evil spirit

fiendish
05 cruel **06** brutal, clever, savage, wicked **07** complex, cunning, inhuman, obscure, vicious
08 barbaric, devilish, infernal, involved, ruthless **09** difficult, ferocious, ingenious, intricate, monstrous **10** aggressive, diabolical, horrendous, malevolent
11 challenging, complicated, imaginative, resourceful, unspeakable
12 bloodthirsty **14** Mephistophelic
15 Mephistophelean, Mephistophelian

fierce
03 hot, wud **04** fell, grim, keen, wild, wood **05** angry, breem, breme, cruel, felon, grave, stern, stout **06** brutal, raging, savage, severe, strong, wrathy
07 furious, intense, rampant, vicious, violent **08** menacing, powerful, ruthless, terrible, walleyed **09** cut-throat, dangerous, ferocious, merciless, murderous, truculent
10 aggressive, passionate, relentless
11 frightening, tempestuous, threatening **12** bloodthirsty, uncontrolled

fiercely
06 keenly, wildly **07** cruelly, sternly
08 bitterly, brutally, savagely, severely, strongly, terribly **09** furiously, intensely, viciously, violently **10** implacably, menacingly, powerfully, ruthlessly
11 dangerously, fanatically, ferociously, mercilessly, murderously

12 aggressively, passionately, relentlessly, tooth and nail
13 tempestuously, threateningly

fiery
03 hot **05** afire, aglow, sharp, spicy **06** ablaze, aflame, ardent, fierce, heated, red-hot, spiced, spunky, sultry, torrid **07** blazing, burning, fervent, flaming, flushed, frampal, glowing, piquant, pungent, violent **08** frampold, inflamed, seasoned **09** excitable, hot-headed, impatient, impetuous, impulsive, irritable **10** passionate, phlogistic, sulphurous **11** empassioned, high-mettled, impassioned

fiesta
04 gala **05** feast, party **07** holiday, jubilee **08** carnival, festival **09** festivity **11** celebration, merrymaking

fifteen
02 XV

fifty
01 L
• **fifty per cent**
02 so

fight
03 box, hit, row, wap, war **04** blue, bout, camp, curb, defy, duel, feud, fray, grit, guts, mill, riot, rout, ruck, spar, stem, yike **05** aggro, argue, bandy, brawl, brush, clash, drive, fence, joust, mêlée, mix-in, pluck, punch, rammy, scrap, set-to, spunk, yikes **06** action, attack, barney, battle, bicker, bottle, bovver, bundle, combat, debate, dust-up, engage, fracas, meddle, medley, oppose, repugn, resist, ruckus, ruffle, rumble, scrape, shindy, spirit, stifle, stoush, strike, strive, take on, thwart, tussle **07** bashing, be at war, contend, contest, crusade, discord, dispute, fall out, grapple, lay into, make war, pasting, punch-up, quarrel, repress, resolve, ruction, scuffle, smother, tuilyie, tuilzie, wage war, warfare, wrangle, wrestle **08** argument, be at odds, bottle up, campaign, champion, conflict, ding-dong, do battle, dogfight, exchange, firmness, gunfight, have a row, hold back, keep back, militate, movement, object to, pell-mell, restrain, set about, skirmish, squabble, struggle, suppress, tenacity **09** altercate, bloodshed, cockfight, duke it out, encounter, force back, monomachy, skiamachy, stand up to, weigh into, willpower, withstand **10** aggression, bandy words, digladiate, dissension, Donnybrook, engagement, fisticuffs, free-for-all, graplement, will to live **11** altercation, come to blows, cross swords, disturbance, hostilities, snickersnee, work against **12** disagreement, resoluteness **13** confrontation, determination, measure swords, take issue with **14** hold out against **15** campaign against, do battle against, struggle against

• **fight back**
04 curb **05** check, reply **06** resist, retort **07** contain, control, repress **08** bottle up, hold back, restrain, suppress **09** force back, retaliate **11** put up a fight **13** counter-attack **14** defend yourself, hold out against
• **fight off**
04 rout **05** repel **06** rebuff, resist **07** beat off, hold off, ward off **08** stave off **09** hold at bay, keep at bay **11** put to flight
• **incite to fight**
03 tar **05** tarre

fighter
01 F **03** EFA, MiG **05** rival **07** bruiser, chetnik, fechter, jump jet, soldier, trouper, warrior **08** attacker, hired gun, opponent **09** adversary, combatant, contender, disputant, man-at-arms, mercenary **10** antagonist, contestant **11** bushwhacker **13** Messerschmitt **15** sparring partner

Fighters include:
05 boxer, pugil
06 fencer, hitman, knight
07 matador, picador, sworder
08 pugilist, toreador, wrestler
09 gladiator, kick boxer, spadassin, swordsman
10 rejoneador
11 bullfighter, digladiator
12 banderillero, prizefighter

See also **aeroplane**

figment
• **figment of your imagination**
05 fable, fancy **07** fiction **08** delusion, illusion **09** deception, falsehood, invention **10** concoction **11** fabrication **13** improvisation

figurative
03 fig **07** typical **08** symbolic, tropical **09** parabolic, pictorial **10** emblematic **11** allegorical, descriptive **12** metaphorical, naturalistic **14** representative

figure
03 fig, sum **04** body, form, icon, idol, ikon, sign, sums **05** build, digit, frame, guess, image, judge, maths, price, shape, think, torso, total, value **06** amount, appear, crop up, design, emblem, leader, number, person, reckon, sketch, symbol, worthy **07** believe, diagram, drawing, feature, integer, notable, numeral, outline, passage, pattern, picture, suppose **08** conclude, consider, estimate, foreshow, physique **09** authority, celebrity, character, dignitary, horoscope, personage, symbolize **10** appearance, silhouette, statistics **11** mathematics, personality **12** be included in, calculations, illustration **13** be mentioned in **14** representation

Figures include:
04 cone, cube, kite, oval
05 prism
06 circle, cuboid, oblong, sector,

sphere, square
07 decagon, diamond, ellipse, hexagon, nonagon, octagon, polygon, pyramid, rhombus
08 crescent, cylinder, heptagon, pentagon, quadrant, tetragon, triangle
09 chiliagon, dodecagon, rectangle, trapezium, undecagon
10 hemisphere, hendecagon, octahedron, polyhedron, quadrangle, semicircle
11 pentahedron, tetrahedron
13 parallelogram, quadrilateral
15 scalene triangle

See also **circle**; **triangle**

• **figure of speech**
05 image, trope **06** flower, simile, zeugma **07** imagery, meiosis **08** diallage, metaphor, oxymoron **09** prolepsis **10** abscission, antithesis, hyperbaton, synecdoche **11** parenthesis **12** antimetabole, turn of phrase
• **figure on**
04 plan **06** expect **07** plan for **08** depend on, reckon on **10** bargain for **13** be prepared for **15** take into account
• **figure out**
03 see **04** dope, make, twig **05** count **06** fathom, reason, reckon **07** compute, dope out, make out, resolve, work out **08** decipher, estimate, tumble to **09** calculate, latch onto, puzzle out **10** understand **13** get the picture

figurehead
04 bust, name **05** dummy, image, token **06** figure, puppet **07** carving **08** front man **10** man of straw, mouthpiece **11** nominal head, titular head

Fiji
03 FJI

filament
04 cord, hair, pile, wire **05** cable, fiber, fibre, seton **06** cirrus, elater, sleave, strand, string, thread **07** fimbria, tendril, whisker **08** fibrilla, tentacle **09** microwire, protonema **10** paraphysis **11** gonimoblast

filch
03 nab, rob **04** crib, drib, fake, lift, nick, palm, prig, take **05** lurch, pinch, steal, swipe **06** nobble, pilfer, rip off, smouch, snitch, thieve **07** purloin, snaffle **08** embezzle, knock off, peculate **09** knock down **14** misappropriate

file
03 ask, box, row, rub **04** case, data, hone, line, list, make, note, rake, rasp, risp, roll, sand, text, whet **05** apply, enter, grate, march, plane, put in, queue, scour, shape, shave, store, trail, train, troop **06** abrade, binder, column, folder, format, papers, parade, polish, record, scrape, smooth, stream, string

submit, thread **07** box file, cortège, data set, details, dossier, pollute, process, program, Rolodex®, rub down **08** classify, document, organize, register **09** catalogue, crocodile, lever arch, portfolio **10** categorize, pickpocket, pigeonhole, procession, put in place, walk in line **11** information, particulars

filial
04 fond **05** loyal **06** loving **07** devoted, dutiful **10** daughterly, respectful **12** affectionate

filibuster
05 delay, stall **06** hinder, impede, pirate, put off **07** prevent **08** obstruct, perorate **09** buccaneer, hindrance, speechify, waste time **10** impediment, peroration **11** obstruction **12** postponement, speechifying **13** procrastinate **15** delaying tactics, procrastination

filigree
04 lace **07** lattice, tracery **08** fretwork, lacework, wirework **09** interlace **10** scrollwork **11** latticework

fill
◊ *insertion indicator*
04 brim, bung, clog, cork, cram, glut, hold, line, pack, plug, seal, soak, stop **05** ample, block, close, crowd, imbue, prime, stack, stock, stuff **06** bishop, charge, englut, enough, fulfil, occupy, plenty, riddle, stop up, supply, take up **07** congest, furnish, implete, perform, pervade, provide, satisfy, suffuse **08** complete, make full, permeate, saturate **09** abundance, replenish **10** all you want, impregnate, sufficient **11** sufficiency **13** all you can take **14** more than enough
• **fill in**
05 brief, write **06** act for, advise, answer, inform **07** cover in, fill out, replace, stand in **08** acquaint, complete, deputize **09** represent **10** substitute, understudy **11** pinch-hit for **13** bring up to date
• **fill out**
06 answer, fill in **08** complete **10** gain weight, grow fatter **11** put on weight **12** become fatter **13** become plumper **14** become chubbier

fillet
04 list **05** label **06** anadem, fascia, reglet, regula **07** annulet, cloison **09** sphendone, tournedos

filling
◊ *insertion indicator*
03 big **04** full, rich **05** ample, heavy, large, solid **06** filler, hearty, inside, square, stodgy **07** padding, wadding **08** contents, generous, stuffing **09** impletion, substance **10** nutritious, satisfying **11** substantial

fillip
04 goad, prod, push, spur **05** boost, flick, shove **06** incite, snitch **07** impetus **08** stimulus **09** incentive,

stimulant, stimulate **10** inducement, motivation **11** stimulation **13** encouragement

film
03 cel, ISO, pic, web **04** cell, cine-, coat, epic, haze, kell, mist, reel, skin, veil, weft **05** cloud, cover, flick, glaze, layer, movie, sheet, shoot, short, spool, video **06** cinema, deepie, screen, silent, tissue **07** blanket, coating, dusting, feature, footage, picture **08** cassette, covering, membrane, pellicle, televise **09** blue movie, cartridge, mistiness, skinflick, videogram, videotape **10** featurette, horse opera, photograph, screenplay, video nasty **11** documentary, feature film **12** record on film **13** motion picture, video cassette

See also **director**

Films include:

02 ET, If...
03 Big, JFK, Kes, Ran
04 Antz, Babe, Dr No, Gigi, Heat, Jaws, MASH, Reds
05 Alfie, Alien, Bambi, Bugsy, Crash, Dumbo, Fargo, Ghost, Giant, Rocky, Shrek
06 Aliens, Amélie, Batman, Ben-Hur, Blow-Up, Casino, Gandhi, Grease, Heimat, Lolita, Mad Max, Misery, Psycho, The Fly, Top Gun, Top Hat
07 Amadeus, Big Fish, Cabaret, Das Boot, Die Hard, Dracula, Rain Man, Rebecca, Robocop, Titanic, Tootsie, Traffic, Vertigo
08 Apollo 13, Body Heat, Born Free, Cape Fear, Chocolat, Duck Soup, Fantasia, High Noon, Insomnia, Key Largo, Kill Bill, King Kong, Scarface, Star Wars, The Birds, The Piano, The Sting, The Thing, The Tramp, Toy Story
09 12 Monkeys, A Bug's Life, Annie Hall, Betty Blue, Cat Ballou, Chinatown, City of God, Easy Rider, Excalibur, Funny Girl, Get Shorty, Gladiator, GoldenEye, Home Alone, Local Hero, Manhattan, Moonraker, Nosferatu, Octopussy, Pinocchio, Rio Grande, Spartacus, Spider-Man, Stand by Me, Vera Drake
10 Blue Velvet, Braveheart, Casablanca, Chicken Run, Cry Freedom, Dirty Harry, East of Eden, Goldfinger, GoodFellas, Grand Hotel, High Sierra, Men in Black, Metropolis, My Fair Lady, My Left Foot, Now Voyager, Paris Texas, Raging Bull, Rear Window, Stagecoach, Taxi Driver, The Big Easy, The Hustler, The Postman, The Shining, The Wild One, Unforgiven, Wall Street
11 A Few Good Men, All About Eve, American Pie, Beetlejuice, Blade Runner, Citizen Kane, Deliverance, Don't Look Now, Finding Nemo, Forrest Gump, Gosford Park, Heaven's Gate, La Dolce Vita, Mary

Poppins, Mean Streets, Monsters, Inc, Mystic River, Notting Hill, Out of Africa, Pretty Woman, Public Enemy, Pulp Fiction, The 400 Blows, The Big Sleep, The Evil Dead, The Exorcist, The Fugitive, The Gold Rush, The Graduate, The Lion King, The Red Shoes, The Third Man, Thunderball, Wayne's World, Wild at Heart
12 A View to a Kill, Brighton Rock, Casino Royale, Cool Hand Luke, Eyes Wide Shut, Frankenstein, Ghostbusters, Gregory's Girl, Groundhog Day, Jurassic Park, Lethal Weapon, Philadelphia, Prizzi's Honor, Roman Holiday, Rome, Open City, Salaam Bombay!, Seven Samurai, Sleepy Hollow, The Apartment, The Godfather, The Searchers, The Wicker Man, The Wild Bunch, Whisky Galore!, Withnail and I
13 Apocalypse Now, Basic Instinct, Batman Forever, Batman Returns, Burnt by the Sun, Death in Venice, Die Another Day, Doctor Zhivago, Educating Rita, Eight and a Half, His Girl Friday, Licence to Kill, Live and Let Die, Mildred Pierce, Raining Stones, Reservoir Dogs, Scent of a Woman, Some Like It Hot, The Crying Game, The Dam Busters, The Deer Hunter, The Dirty Dozen, The Fisher King, The Jazz Singer, The Jungle Book, The Right Stuff, The Terminator, To Catch a Thief, Trainspotting, West Side Story, Wings of Desire, Zorba the Greek
14 A Day at the Races, American Beauty, American Psycho, As Good as it Gets, Blazing Saddles, Bonnie and Clyde, Brief Encounter, Bringing Up Baby, Central Station, Chariots of Fire, Cinema Paradiso, Dial M for Murder, Empire of the Sun, Enter the Dragon, Erin Brockovich, Five Easy Pieces, Gangs of New York, Goodbye Mr Chips, Jean de Florette, LA Confidential, Midnight Cowboy, Minority Report, Muriel's Wedding, Schindler's List, Secrets and Lies, The Big Lebowski, The Commitments, The Elephant Man, The Great Escape, The Ladykillers, The Last Emperor, The Life of Brian, The Lost Weekend, The Mask of Zorro, The Music Lovers, The Seventh Seal, Un Chien Andalou
15 Annie Get Your Gun, A Passage to India, Back to the Future, Crocodile Dundee, Dog Day Afternoon, Do the Right Thing, Fatal Attraction, For Your Eyes Only, Full Metal Jacket, Gone With the Wind, Good Will Hunting, Heart of Darkness, Independence Day, Life Is Beautiful, Manon des Sources, Meet Me in St Louis, On the Waterfront, Return of the Jedi, Road to Perdition, Singin' in the Rain, Sunset Boulevard, Tarzan the Ape Man, The African Queen,

The Bicycle Thief, Thelma and Louise, The Piano Teacher, The Seven Samurai, The Sound of Music, Thirty-nine Steps

Film types include:

03 spy, war

04 blue, cult, epic, noir

05 adult, anime, buddy, crime, farce, heist, short, spoof, vogue, weepy

06 action, auteur, biopic, B-movie, comedy, Disney, erotic, family, horror, murder, police, re-make, rom-com, silent, weepie

07 Carry-on, cartoon, classic, diorama, fantasy, musical, neo-noir, new wave, passion, realist, robbery, slasher, tragedy, war hero, western

08 animated, disaster, escapist, film noir, gangster, newsreel, romantic, space-age, thriller

09 adventure, Bollywood, burlesque, chopsocky, detective, film à clef, flashback, Hitchcock, Hollywood, James Bond, love story, low-budget, melodrama, political, road movie, satirical, skin flick, Spielberg, whodunnit

10 avant-garde, bonkbuster, gay-lesbian, neo-realist, period epic, snuff movie, surrealist, tear-jerker, travelogue

11 black comedy, blockbuster, cliff-hanger, documentary, kitchen sink, period drama, tragicomedy, underground

12 cinéma-vérité, Ealing comedy, ethnographic, fly-on-the-wall, mockumentary, pornographic, rockumentary, social comedy

13 comic-book hero, expressionist, multiple-story, murder mystery, nouvelle vague, sexploitation, sexual fantasy, social problem

14 blaxploitation, Charlie Chaplin, comedy thriller, police thriller, rites of passage, romantic comedy, science-fiction

15 animated cartoon, cowboy and Indian, romantic tragedy, screwball comedy

• **film classification**
01 A, U, X **02** AA, PG
• **film company**
05 indie **06** studio
• **film over**
03 fog **04** blur, dull **05** glaze **08** mist over **09** cloud over **13** become blurred
• **horror film** *see* horror
• **part of film**
04 reel

filmy
04 fine, thin **05** gauzy, light, sheer **06** flimsy, floaty **07** clouded, fragile **08** chiffony, cobwebby, delicate, gossamer **09** gossamery **10** diaphanous, see-through, shimmering **11** translucent, transparent **13** insubstantial

filter
04 leak, mesh, ooze, seep, sift

05 drain, gauze, leach, sieve **06** purify, refine, riddle, screen, sifter, strain **07** clarify, dribble, netting, trickle **08** colander, filtrate, membrane, strainer **09** percolate

filth
03 mud **04** crap, crud, dirt, dung, gore, grot, gunk, mire, muck, porn, smut, soil, yuck **05** addle, bilge, dreck, dross, grime, gunge, slime, trash **06** faeces, grunge, manure, refuse, sewage, sleaze, sludge, wallow **07** garbage, rubbish, squalor, sullage **08** effluent, foulness, hard porn, impurity **09** blue films, colluvies, excrement, indecency, obscenity, pollution, vulgarity **10** coarseness, corruption, defilement, dirty books, sordidness **11** pornography, putrescence, raunchiness, uncleanness **12** putrefaction **13** contamination, sexploitation

filthy
03 bad, low, wet **04** base, blue, foul, lewd, mean, vile, wild **05** adult, angry, bawdy, black, cross, dirty, grimy, gross, manky, mucky, muddy, nasty, rainy, ratty, rough, slimy, sooty, yucky **06** Augean, coarse, crabby, cruddy, faecal, grubby, impure, putrid, rotten, shirty, smutty, soiled, sordid, stormy, vulgar, X-rated **07** corrupt, obscene, raunchy, squalid, stroppy, swinish, unclean **08** decaying, depraved, explicit, indecent, polluted, unwashed, wretched **09** irritable, offensive, worthless **10** despicable, putrefying, suggestive **11** bad-tempered, foul-mouthed **12** contaminated, contemptible, disagreeable, pornographic

fin
03 arm **04** hand, skeg, tail, vane **05** fiver, pinna, skegg **06** dorsal **07** Finland, ventral **08** pectoral

final
◊ *tail selection indicator*
03 end, net **04** last, nett **05** dying **06** latest **07** closing, settled, supreme **08** decisive, definite, eventual, farewell, terminal, ultimate **09** finishing **10** concluding, conclusive, conclusory, definitive, last-minute, peremptory **11** determinate, irrefutable, irrevocable, terminating, unalterable **12** indisputable
• **final word**
04 amen

finale
◊ *tail selection indicator*
03 end **05** close **06** climax, ending **07** curtain **08** epilogue, final act **10** conclusion, dénouement **11** culmination **13** crowning glory

finality
08 firmness, ultimacy **09** certitude **10** conviction, resolution **11** decidedness **12** decisiveness, definiteness **13** inevitability **14** conclusiveness, inevitableness,

irrevocability, unavoidability **15** irreversibility

finalize
03 end **05** agree, close, sew up **06** clinch, decide, finish, settle, wrap up **07** resolve, work out **08** complete, conclude, round off

finally
◊ *tail selection indicator*
04 last **06** at last, in fine, lastly **07** for ever, for good **08** at length, in the end **10** decisively, definitely, eventually, to conclude, ultimately **11** irrevocably, permanently **12** conclusively, in conclusion, irreversibly **13** for good and all, once and for all

finance
04 back, cash, fund **05** float, funds, means, money, set up, trade **06** assets, budget, income, pay for, wealth **07** affairs, banking, capital, funding, revenue, savings, sponsor, subsidy, support **08** accounts, bankroll, business, commerce **09** economics, guarantee, liquidity, resources, subsidize **10** accounting, capitalize, habilitate, investment, underwrite **11** bank account, sponsorship, stock market, wherewithal **15** money management

financial
05 money **06** fiscal **08** economic, monetary **09** budgetary, pecuniary **10** commercial **15** entrepreneurial
• **financial expert**
09 economist **10** monetarist

financier
05 bania, gnome **06** banian, banker, banyan, trader **07** swindle **08** investor **10** moneymaker, speculator **11** stockbroker, white knight **12** financialist, Wall-Streeter **13** industrialist

finch
05 spink, twite **06** canary, linnet, siskin, towhee, whidah, whydah **07** bunting, chewink, manikin, redbird, waxbill **08** grosbeak, mannikin, snowbird, wheatear **09** brambling, crossbill, grassquit **10** fallow-chat, indigo bird, marsh-robin, weaver bird, whidah bird, whydah bird **11** green linnet, tree sparrow **12** cardinal-bird **13** indigo bunting

find
02 be **03** get, try, win **04** boon, coup, deem, earn, gain, meet, rate, rule, spot **05** asset, catch, exist, gauge, judge, learn, occur, reach, think, trace **06** attain, come by, decree, detect, dig out, expose, locate, notice, obtain, regain, reveal, review, secure, turn up, umpire **07** achieve, acquire, adjudge, bargain, believe, declare, examine, get back, godsend, good buy, mediate, observe, procure, realize, recover, referee, uncover, unearth **08** come upon, consider, discover, perceive, retrieve, sentence **09** arbitrate, be

resent, discovery, encounter,
cognize, stumble on, track down
adjudicate, chance upon, come
cross, experience, happen upon, lay
ands on, run to earth, trouvaille
acquisition **12** bring to light, pass
entence **13** give a sentence, stumble
cross **14** sit in judgement **15** deliver a
erdict

find in
anagram indicator
hidden indicator
insertion indicator

find out
see, sus **04** note, suss, take, twig
catch, get at, learn **06** detect,
xpose, gather, reveal, rumble, show
, unmask **07** extract, lay bare,
bserve, realize, suss out, uncover
disclose, discover, identify,
erceive, pinpoint, tumble to
ascertain, establish, expiscate, get
ind of **10** cotton on to, understand
make certain **12** bring to light
make certain of

nding
find **05** award, order **06** decree
verdict **08** decision, judgment
discovery, judgement
conclusion, innovation
breakthrough **13** pronouncement
recommendation

ne
F **02** A1, OK **03** A-OK, dry, end, fit,
g, oke, yes **04** braw, eric, fair, good,
ke, keen, mooi, nice, pawn, phat,
ure, safe, slim, thin, well **05** beaut,
onny, clear, dandy, exact, gauzy, great,
ght, mulct, nifty, right, sharp, sheer,
owy, smart, sound, sting, sunny,
nlaw **06** agreed, amerce, assess,
onnie, bright, choice, dainty, flimsy,
odly, ground, incony, lovely, minute,
rrow, on form, pledge, punish, purify,
fine, sconce, select, slight, strong,
btle **07** clement, crushed, damages,
egant, forfeit, fragile, gradely, healthy,
mense, inconie, in shape, penalty,
wdery, precise, radical, refined,
ender, stylish **08** accurate, all right,
itical, delicate, gossamer, graithly,
andsome, jim-dandy, narrowly,
nalize, precious, properly, splendid,
riking, superior, very good, very well,
gorous **09** admirable, agreeable,
eautiful, brilliant, cloudless, correctly,
regious, excellent, expensive,
xquisite, first-rate, sensitive,
ipshape, temperate **10** acceptable,
cceptably, amercement, attractive,
aphonous, discerning, first-class,
rfeiture, punishment, remarkable,
cketty-boo **11** americiament,
cceptional, fashionable, fine-grained,
urishing, in good shape, lightweight,
agnificent, outstanding, pretentious,
ckettyboo, up to scratch **12** in good
ealth, satisfactory, successfully
distinguished, hair-splitting, hale
nd hearty **14** satisfactorily **15** in good
ndition

fine-looking
04 waly **05** wally

finely
05 wally **06** nicely, subtly, thinly
07 exactly, lightly, sharply **08** minutely
09 admirably, precisely **10** critically,
delicately, splendidly **11** brilliantly,
excellently **12** attractively
13 magnificently

finery
07 bravery, gaudery, regalia, wallies
08 frippery, glad rags **09** jewellery,
ornaments, showiness, splendour,
trappings **10** rattletrap, Sunday best
11 bedizenment, best clothes,
decorations

finesse
◊ *anagram indicator*
04 tact **05** bluff, evade, flair, skill, trick
06 polish **07** knowhow **08** deftness,
delicacy, elegance, neatness, strategy,
subtlety **09** adeptness, diplomacy,
expertise, manoeuvre, quickness
10 adroitness, cleverness, discretion,
manipulate, refinement **11** savoir-faire,
tactfulness **12** gracefulness
14 sophistication

finger
03 paw **04** feel, name **05** pinky, share,
talon, touch **06** agency, caress, fondle,
handle, medius, paddle, pilfer, pinkie,
stroke **07** annular, toy with **08** interest,
virginal **09** prepollex **10** fiddle with,
manipulate, meddle with **13** play
about with

• put your finger on
05 place **06** locate, recall **07** find out,
hit upon, isolate, pin down
08 discover, identify, indicate,
pinpoint, remember

fingerhole
04 lill, lilt, stop **07** ventage, ventige

finial
03 tee **04** crop **06** pommel
09 pineapple, poppy-head

finicky
◊ *anagram indicator*
05 faddy, fussy, picky **06** choosy, fiddly,
tricky **08** critical, delicate **09** difficult,
finickety, intricate, selective
10 fastidious, meticulous, nit-picking,
particular, pernickety, scrupulous
11 persnickety **13** hypercritical
14 discriminating

finish
◊ *tail selection indicator*
02 do **03** eat, end, use **04** coat, coda,
down, rout, ruin, stop **05** apply, cease,
close, crush, drain, drink, empty, glaze,
gloss, grain, scoff, sew up, shine, use up
06 attain, be over, defeat, devour,
ending, expend, finale, fulfil, guzzle,
lustre, pack in, polish, settle, topple,
veneer, wind up, wind-up, wrap up
07 absolve, achieve, coating, conquer,
consume, deplete, destroy, exhaust,
lacquer, outwork, perfect, surface,
texture, varnish, wipe out **08** carry out,
complete, conclude, curtains, deal

with, get rid of, overcome, round off,
run out of **09** be through, bring down,
cessation, culminate, discharge, get
shot of, overpower, overthrow,
overwhelm, polish off, put paid to,
terminate, winding-up **10** accomplish,
annihilate, appearance, be done with,
call it a day, completion, conclusion,
consummate, do away with, fulfilment,
get through, lamination, perfection,
smoothness **11** achievement, come to
an end, culmination, destruction,
discontinue, exterminate, termination
12 bring to an end
14 accomplishment, get the better of

• finish off
03 end, ice, top **04** do in, slay **05** drain,
mop-up, quash, quell, still, use up
06 defeat, murder **07** bump off,
destroy, execute, put down, wipe out
08 despatch, dispatch, knock off
09 dispose of, eliminate, eradicate,
liquidate, polish off, slaughter
10 annihilate, do away with,
extinguish, put an end to, put to death,
put to sleep **11** assassinate, exterminate

finished
02 up **04** arch, dead, done, lost, neat,
over, past, ripe **05** empty, exact, spent
06 doomed, expert, made up, ruined,
sewn up, undone, urbane, zonked
07 all done, at an end, defunct, done
for, drained, perfect, refined, rounded,
through, useless **08** complete,
defeated, flawless, masterly, polished,
unwanted, virtuoso **09** completed,
concluded, dealt with, exhausted,
faultless, played out, unpopular,
wrapped up **10** consummate,
impeccable, proficient **11** all over with,
consummated **12** accomplished,
professional **13** sophisticated **15** over
and done with

• before it is finished
03 yet

finite
05 fixed **07** bounded, limited
08 numbered **09** countable, definable
10 calculable, demarcated,
measurable, restricted, terminable

Finland
03 FIN

fire
03 axe, can, fan **04** bake, flak, heat,
hurl, kiln, life, sack, stir, whet, zeal
05 blame, blaze, eject, let go, light,
rouse, salvo, shoot, start, stick, torch,
verve **06** ardour, arouse, attack,
energy, excite, firing, flames, heater,
ignite, incite, kindle, launch, let off, set
off, spirit, stir up, vigour **07** animate,
barrage, bombing, bonfire, boot out,
burning, censure, dismiss, enliven,
explode, feeling, fervour, gunfire,
inferno, inflame, inspire, kick out,
passion, reproof, slating, sniping,
sparkle, trigger **08** brickbat, detonate,
dynamism, get rid of, knocking,
motivate, radiance, radiator, shelling,
slamming, spark off, vivacity
09 animation, cannonade, cauterize,

convector, criticism, discharge, eagerness, electrify, fusillade, galvanize, holocaust, intensity, lightning, set ablaze, set alight, set fire to, set on fire, stimulate **10** combustion, creativity, enthusiasm, excitement, liveliness, trigger off **11** bombardment, disapproval, put a match to **12** condemnation, fault-finding **13** conflagration, disparagement, inventiveness
• **fire up**
06 arouse
• **on fire**
03 lit **05** eager, fiery **06** ablaze, aflame, alight, ardent **07** blazing, burning, excited, flaming, ignited **08** creative, in flames, inspired **09** energetic, inventive, sparkling **10** passionate **12** enthusiastic

firearm
03 gun **04** heat **05** rifle **06** musket, pistol, weapon **07** handgun, shotgun **08** revolver **09** automatic **10** self-cocker **12** breech-loader, muzzle-loader, shooting iron, single-action **13** semi-automatic
See also **gun**; **weapon**

firebrand
05 rebel **07** fanatic, radical **08** agitator, militant **09** extremist, insurgent **10** incendiary **12** rabble-rouser, troublemaker **13** revolutionary **15** insurrectionist

fireplace

Fireplaces include:
04 kiln, oven
05 forge, grate, ingle, range, stove
06 boiler, hearth
07 bonfire, brazier, firebox, furnace, gas fire
08 campfire, open fire
09 wood stove
10 backboiler
11 incinerator
12 electric fire
13 paraffin stove

firepower
04 ammo

fireproof
10 flameproof **12** non-flammable **13** fire-resistant, incombustible **14** flame-resistant, non-inflammable

fireside *see* **fireplace**

firewater *see* **drink**

fireworks
03 fit **04** rage, rows **05** storm **06** frenzy, sparks, temper, uproar **07** trouble **08** outburst **09** hysterics **10** explosions **12** pyrotechnics **13** feux d'artifice, illuminations

Fireworks include:
04 cake, mine, pioy
05 devil, flare, gerbe, peeoy, pioye, shell, squib, wheel
06 banger, fisgig, fizgig, maroon, petard, rocket

07 cracker, serpent, volcano
08 flip-flop, fountain, pinwheel, slap-bang, sparkler, whizbang
09 firedrake, girandola, girandole, sky-rocket, throw-down, waterfall, whizz-bang
10 golden rain, Indian fire, tourbillon
11 firecracker, firewriting, jumping-jack, roman candle, tourbillion
14 Catherine wheel, Chinese cracker, indoor firework
15 Pharaoh's serpent, Waterloo cracker

firm
02 Co, OK **03** Cie, oke, set **04** boon, fast, good, hard, oaky, sure, true **05** close, crisp, dense, fixed, house, rigid, solid, stiff, tight **06** dogged, secure, siccar, sicker, stable, stanch, steady, steeve, stieve, strict, strong, sturdy, trusty **07** adamant, compact, company, concern, decided, riveted, secured, settled, staunch, unmoved **08** anchored, business, constant, definite, embedded, fastened, forceful, hardened, obdurate, resolute, resolved, stubborn, unshaken, vigorous **09** committed, immovable, inelastic, obstinate, rock-solid, sclerotic, steadfast, syndicate, tenacious **10** compressed, dependable, determined, enterprise, inflexible, motionless, solidified, stationary, unchanging, unshakable, unswerving, unwavering, unyielding **11** association, corporation, established, institution, long-lasting, partnership, substantial, substantive, unalterable, unfaltering, unflinching, unshakeable **12** close-grained, concentrated, conglomerate, long-standing, organization, unchangeable **13** establishment

firmament
03 sky **05** ether, skies, space **06** heaven, welkin **07** expanse, heavens, the blue **08** empyrean **10** atmosphere

firmly
04 fast **06** fastly, stably, steeve, stieve, surely **07** tightly **08** doggedly, robustly, securely, steadily, strictly, strongly, sturdily **09** immovably, staunchly **10** decisively, definitely, enduringly, inflexibly, resolutely, unshakably **11** steadfastly, unalterably **12** determinedly, unchangeably, unwaveringly **13** unflinchingly

firmness
06 fixity, fixure **07** density, resolve, tension **08** fixation, hardness, obduracy, rigidity, solidity, strength, sureness, tautness **09** constancy, stability, stiffness, tightness, willpower **10** conviction, doggedness, resistance, resolution, steadiness, strictness **11** compactness, reliability, staunchness **12** immovability, inelasticity **13** dependability, determination, inflexibility,

steadfastness **14** changelessness, indomitability, strength of will
• **body firmness**
04 tone

first
◇ *head selection indicator*
◇ *juxtaposition indicator*
01 A **03** 1st, key, one, top **04** arch-, best, head, main **05** basic, chief, prim, prime, primo, prior, proto-, start **06** eldest, oldest, origin, outset, prim, rather, ruling, senior, sooner **07** at fir, earlier, firstly, highest, initial, leading, opening, origins, premier, primary, supreme **08** cardinal, champion, earliest, foremost, greatest, original, paravant, première, primeval **09** beginning, inaugural, inception, initially, paramount, paravaunt, primaeval, primitive, principal, prototype, sovereign, square one, the word go, unveiling, uppermost **10** beforehand, elementary, first of al, originally, pre-eminent, primordial **11** at the outset, fundamental, predominant, preliminary, rudimentary, to begin with, to start with **12** commencement, in preference, introduction, introducto **14** at the beginning **15** in the first place
• **at first**
◇ *head selection indicator*
04 erst **07** at first **09** initially **10** first all **11** at the outset, to begin with, to start with **15** in the first place
• **come first**
◇ *juxtaposition indicator*
04 lead **05** outdo **07** precede
• **first lady**
03 Eve

first-born
04 aîné **05** aînée, eigne, elder, older **06** eldest, oldest, senior **10** primoger **12** primogenital **13** primogenitary, primogenitive

first-class
01 A **02** A1 **03** ace, top **04** cool, fine, mean, mega **05** crack, prime, super **06** slap-up, superb, way-out, wicked **07** crucial, leading, premier, radical, supreme, top-hole **08** fabulous, peerless, splendid, superior, top-note **09** admirable, excellent, first-rate, matchless, top-flight **11** exceptional, outstanding, superlative **12** second-to-none **14** out of this world

firsthand
06 direct **07** hands-on, primary **08** directly, on the job, personal **09** immediate, in service **10** persona **11** immediately

firstly
04 once **07** at first **09** initially **10** firs of all **11** at the outset, to begin with, t start with **15** in the first place

first name
08 forename **09** given name **13** baptismal name, Christian name

first-rate

01 A **02** A1 **03** ace, top **04** cool, fine, rake, mean, mega **05** crack, prime, super **06** superb, way-out, wicked **07** crucial, leading, premier, radical, supreme **08** fabulous, peerless, splendid, superior, top-notch **09** admirable, excellent, matchless, top-flight **10** first-class **11** excellently, exceptional, outstanding, superlative **12** second-to-none **14** out of this world

firth

03 Tay
04 Lorn, Wide
05 Clyde, Forth, Lorne, Moray
06 Beauly, Solway, Thames
07 Dornoch, Westray
08 Cromarty, Pentland, Stronsay, Szczecin
09 Inverness
14 North Ronaldsay

fiscal

03 tax **05** money **06** bursal **07** capital **08** economic, monetary, treasury **09** budgetary, financial, pecuniary, treasurer
● **procurator fiscal**
02 PF

fiscally

09 moneywise **11** financially, pecuniarily **12** economically

fish

03 ask, bob, dap, dib, dip, fry, jig, net **04** harl, hunt, look, sean, seek, spin, rot **05** angle, catch, delve, grope, otter, seine, spoon, trawl, troll, whiff **06** guddle, ledger, search **07** counter, ransack, skitter, snigger, sniggle **08** hand line, try to get **09** go fishing **11** try to obtain
see also **animal**

02 ai, id
03 aua, ayu, bar, bib, cod, dab, eel, gar, ged, hag, ide, lax, par, ray, sar, sei, tai
04 barb, bass, blay, bley, brit, carp, chad, char, chub, chum, clam, coho, crab, cray, cusk, dace, dare, dart, dory, fugu, gade, goby, hake, hoki, huso, huss, kelt, keta, kina, lant, ling, luce, lump, moki, opah, orfe, parr, paua, pawa, peal, peel, pike, pipi, pope, pout, pupu, rudd, scad, scar, scat, scup, seer, shad, sild, slip, snig, sole, spot, tang, tope, tuna, tusk
05 ablet, allis, basse, bleak, bream, brill, bully, cohoe, coley, danio, flake, guppy, koura, lance, loach, molly, perch, platy, porgy, prawn, roach, shark, skate, smelt, sprat, squid, tench, tetra, torsk, trout, tunny, whelk, yabby, zebra
06 allice, angler, barbel, blenny, braise, braize, cockle, doctor, dorado, gadoid, groper, hapuku, jilgie, kipper, kokopu, launce, marlin, marron, minnow, mullet, mussel, oyster, piraña, plaice, porgie, puffer, red cod, red-eye, salmon, saurel, shrimp, tailor, turbot, wrasse
07 abalone, anchovy, bloater, blue cod, catfish, cavalla, cavally, cichlid, cobbler, codfish, cowfish, dhufish, dogfish, garfish, gourami, grouper, gurnard, haddock, halibut, herring, kahawai, lamprey, lobster, morwong, mudfish, octopus, piranha, sardine, scallop, sea bass, snapper, toheroa, warehou, whiting
08 blowfish, bluefish, bluenose, brisling, calamari, characid, crawfish, crayfish, dragonet, flathead, flounder, goldfish, grayling, ichthyic, John Dory, kingfish, luderick, mackerel, monkfish, Moray eel, pilchard, pipefish, rockfish, sailfish, scuppaug, sea bream, seahorse, skipjack, stingray, sturgeon, tarakihi, toadfish, trevally, tuna fish
09 allis shad, angel-fish, barracuda, conger eel, Dover sole, greenling, grenadier, king prawn, lemonfish, lemon sole, Murray cod, neon tetra, red mullet, sea urchin, stonefish, swordfish, trumpeter, tunnyfish, whitebait, wobbegong, zebrafish
10 angler fish, Balmain bug, barracouta, barramundi, bluebottle, Bombay duck, brown trout, butterfish, cuttlefish, damsel fish, flying fish, grey mullet, gummy shark, jellied eel, mossbunker, parrot-fish, puffer fish, red snapper, rock salmon, tommy rough
11 electric eel, rock lobster, stickleback
12 jellyblubber, orange roughy, rainbow trout, scorpion fish, skipjack tuna
13 butterfly fish, horse mackerel, leatherjacket, Moreton Bay bug, sergeant-major
14 Arbroath smokie

See also **crustacean; mollusc; shark; seafood**

● **fish out**
04 find **07** extract, haul out, produce, pull out, take out **08** dredge up, retrieve **10** come up with
● **fish tank**
04 stew **08** aquarium
● **queer fish**
04 cure

fisherman

03 rod **05** liner **06** angler, banker, codder, fisher, rodman, Walton **07** crabber, drag-man, drifter, rodsman, rodster **08** peter-man, piscator, shareman **09** cockleman, rodfisher, sharesman, Waltonian, trawlerman **11** piscatorian

fishing

07 angling **08** trawling **09** piscatory **11** piscatorial **12** catching fish

03 fly, net, rod, tag, tie
04 bait, barb, bite, cast, drag, gimp, hook, lead, line, lure, reel, sean, weel, weir, whip
05 angle, baker, catch, clean, creel, seine, snell, troll
06 angler, bob-fly, coarse, dry-fly, fly-rod, leader, sagene, sinker, tackle, waders, wet-fly
07 angling, bycatch, drifter, dropper, flyline, fly reel, harpoon, keepnet, piscary, setline, spinner
08 backcast, drift net, roll cast, trotline
09 brandling, drabbling, false cast, hairy Mary, halieutic, indicator, leger line, night-line, piscatory
10 bait bucket, casting arc, casting-net, fly casting, fly fishing, halieutics, landing net, ledger bait, ledger line, net-fishing, sea-fishing, weigh sling
11 forward cast, game fishing, line-fishing, paternoster
12 drift fishing, night crawler, night-fishery, shooting line
13 bottom-fishing, coarse fishing
15 catch-and-release

See also **fly**

fishy

◇ *anagram indicator*
03 odd **05** funny, queer, shady **06** unsafe **07** dubious, piscine, suspect **08** doubtful, fish-like **09** equivocal, irregular, piscatory **10** improbable, suspicious **11** implausible, piscatorial **12** questionable

fission

06 schism **07** parting, rending, rupture **08** breaking, cleavage, cleaving, division, scission **09** severance, splitting

fissure

03 gap **04** chop, gape, gash, hole, rent, rift, rime, slit, vein **05** break, chasm, chink, cleft, crack, fault, grike, gryke, porta, shake, split, zygon **06** breach, cleave, cranny, divide, groove, sulcus **07** crevice, foramen, opening, rupture **08** cleavage, crevasse, fracture, scissure, sink hole **10** interstice **11** swallow hole

fist

03 paw, pud **04** dook, duke, hand, mitt, neif, nief, palm **05** index, neafe, neive, nieve, puddy **06** neaffe **08** knuckles **11** handwriting **12** bunch of fives, clenched hand

fit

◇ *anagram indicator*
02 A1, go **03** apt, arm, cry, due, fix, gee, jag, pet, rig, sit **04** able, ague, bout, hard, huff, join, lune, mate, meet, song, sort, suit, well **05** adapt, agree, alter, burst, canto, coach, equal, equip, exies, flaky, gapes, groom, hardy, ictus, match, place, prime, put in, queme, ready, right, shape, sharp, sound,

spasm, spell, surge, tally, train
06 access, adjust, attach, attack, belong, change, concur, crisis, didder, dither, dueful, follow, habile, insert, in trim, modify, passus, proper, robust, seemly, square, strong, sturdy, tailor, worthy **07** arrange, be right, capable, chipper, conform, connect, correct, debauch, dewfull, fashion, fitting, get into, gradely, healthy, in shape, install, prepare, provide, qualify, seizure, tantrum, trained **08** decorous, dovetail, eligible, equipped, eruption, graithly, outbreak, outburst, paroxysm, position, prepared, regulate, suitable, vigorous **09** agreement, befitting, competent, condition, explosion, harmonize, interlock, make ready, pertinent, qualified **10** able-bodied, be a good fit, be suitable, conformity, conniption, convenient, convulsion, correspond, good enough, in good form, put in place, the shivers **11** accommodate, appropriate, be consonant, concurrence, correlation, equivalence, flourishing, in good shape, put together **12** be consistent, in good health, make suitable, relationship **13** be appropriate, fit like a glove, hale and hearty, put in position **14** correspondence **15** in good condition

• **fit for use**
04 ripe

• **fit in**
◇ *insertion indicator*
04 slot **05** agree, match **06** accord, belong, concur, square **07** conform, squeeze **10** correspond

• **fit out, fit up**
03 arm, rig **04** trim **05** equip, frame **06** kit out, outfit, rig out, supply **07** furnish, prepare, provide **08** accoutre

• **fit together**
04 nest

• **in fits and starts**
08 brokenly, fitfully, off and on, unevenly **11** erratically, irregularly **12** occasionally, sporadically **13** spasmodically **14** intermittently

fitful
06 broken, catchy, patchy, uneven **07** erratic **08** sporadic **09** disturbed, haphazard, irregular, spasmodic **10** occasional **12** disconnected, intermittent

fitfully
08 unevenly **11** erratically, haphazardly, irregularly **12** occasionally, sporadically **13** spasmodically **14** intermittently **15** by fits and starts, in fits and starts

fitness
04 trim **05** shape **06** health, vigour **07** aptness **08** adequacy, aptitude, haleness, property, strength **09** condition, edibility, readiness **10** capability, competence, competency, edibleness, good health, pertinence, robustness **11** eligibility, healthiness, opportunity, suitability

12 preparedness **13** applicability **14** qualifications **15** appropriateness
• **condition of fitness**
04 form

fitted
03 fit **05** armed, fixed, right **06** cut out, shaped, suited **07** built-in **08** equipped, integral, prepared, provided, suitable, tailored **09** appointed, furnished, permanent, qualified, rigged out **10** integrated

fitting
03 apt, fit **04** meet, part, unit **05** piece, right **06** extras, liable, proper, seemly, square **07** condign, correct, fitment, fixture **08** decorous, deserved, fitments, fixtures, suitable, wise-like **09** accessory, component, desirable, equipment, furniture **10** attachment, connection, convenable **11** accessories, appropriate, furnishings **12** appointments **13** accoutrements, installations

fittings
04 trim **09** trimmings **11** furnishings

five
01 V **06** pentad **07** quinary, quintet **08** quintett **09** quintette **10** quintuplet
• **one of five**
04 quin

five hundred
01 D

fix
◇ *anagram indicator*
02 do **03** aim, hit, jam, pin, rig, set, tie **04** bang, bind, comb, cook, dose, draw, fake, glue, hang, hold, hole, join, link, make, mend, mess, nail, name, root, scam, seat, shoo, shot, slug, sort, spay, spot, tidy, turn **05** affix, clamp, dress, embed, emend, focus, groom, level, lodge, order, plant, point, rivet, score, screw, see to, set up, set-up, stell, stick **06** adjust, anchor, answer, assign, attach, cement, corner, couple, decide, define, direct, fasten, fiddle, freeze, harden, locate, muddle, neaten, pickle, plight, remedy, repair, scrape, secure, settle, strike, way out **07** agree on, appoint, arrange, attract, connect, correct, destine, dilemma, falsify, implant, install, knock up, patch up, prepare, rectify, resolve, restore, rigging, situate, specify, station, stiffen, the soup **08** arrive at, castrate, chastise, finalize, get ready, position, put right, quandary, solidify, solution, valorize **09** destinate, determine, establish, injection, manoeuvre, stabilize, tight spot **10** difficulty, manipulate, put in order, resolution, straighten, tamper with **11** concentrate, predicament, put together **12** manipulation **13** throw together
• **fix up**
04 clew, clue, plan **05** equip, lay on, plant **06** settle, supply **07** agree on, arrange, furnish, produce, provide, sort out **08** organize **10** bring about

fixated
03 set **06** phobic **07** gripped **08** hung up on, neurotic, obsessed **09** dominated **10** compulsive, infatuated **11** preoccupied **12** pathological

fixation
05 mania, thing **06** fetich, fetish, hang-up, phobia **07** complex, fetiche, setting **08** firmness, idée fixe, neurosis **09** obsession **10** compulsion, steadiness **11** infatuation **13** preoccupation

fixed
◇ *anagram indicator*
03 set **04** fake, fast, firm **05** false, rigid, tight **06** phoney, rooted, secure, steady **07** decided, lasting, planned, pretend, settled, well-set **08** arranged, constant, definite, immobile, standing **09** appointed, insincere, permanent, pretended **10** determined, entrenched, inflexible, persistent, set in stone, stationary **11** cast in stone, determinate, established

fixedly
04 hard **07** closely **08** intently, steadily **09** staringly **10** watchfully **11** attentively, searchingly

fixity
09 constancy, fixedness, stability **10** permanence, steadiness **11** persistence **12** immutability

fixture
04 game, race, unit **05** event, match, round **06** fixing **07** contest, fitting, meeting **09** equipment, furniture **11** competition, furnishings **13** installations

fizz
03 gas, vim, zip **04** foam, hiss, zing **05** froth **06** bubble, fizzle **07** bubbles, ferment, foaming, sparkle **08** bubbling, buoyancy, frothing, vitality, vivacity **09** animation, champagne, fizziness, gassiness **10** effervesce, enthusiasm, excitement, exuberance, liveliness **11** excitedness, high spirits **12** exhilaration, fermentation **13** effervescence

fizzle
• **fizzle out**
04 fail, flop, fold, stop **07** die away, die down, subside **08** collapse, peter out, taper off **09** disappear, dissipate, evaporate **11** come to grief, fall through **13** come to nothing

fizzy
05 gassy **06** bubbly, frothy **07** aerated, foaming **08** bubbling **09** sparkling **10** carbonated **12** effervescent

flab
03 fat, pot **04** bulk **06** paunch **07** blubber, fatness, obesity **08** pot belly **09** plumpness, solidness, spare tyre, stoutness **10** chubbiness, corpulence, overweight

flabbergasted
◇ *anagram indicator*
05 dazed **06** amazed **07** stunned
08 overcome **09** astounded, blown
away, staggered **10** astonished,
bowled over, confounded,
gobsmacked, nonplussed, speechless
11 dumbfounded, overwhelmed
13 knocked for six

flabby
03 fat, lax **04** limp, soft **05** loose,
plump, slack **06** feeble, flaggy, fleshy,
floppy, sloppy **07** flaccid, hanging,
sagging **08** drooping, wasteful,
yielding **09** lymphatic, nerveless
10 overweight **11** inefficient
12 disorganized, uneconomical

flaccid
03 lax **04** lank, limp, soft, weak
05 loose, slack **06** clammy, droopy,
flabby, floppy **07** relaxed, sagging
08 drooping, toneless **09** nerveless

flag
03 die, ebb, rag, sag, tag **04** fade, fail,
fall, flop, hail, iris, jade, mark, note,
sink, slow, tire, waft, wane, wave, wilt
05 abate, color, droop, faint, label,
slump, weary **06** Acorus, colors, colour,
falter, lessen, marker, motion, salute,
weaken **07** calamus, decline, dwindle,
fall off, slacken, subside **08** diminish,
hang down, indicate, languish, peter
out, taper off, wave down **09** grow
tired, reed-grass **12** signal to stop

• **flags**
07 bunting

flagellation
07 beating, flaying, lashing, whaling
08 flogging, whipping **09** scourging,

thrashing **10** vapulation **11** castigation,
verberation, vice anglais
12 chastisement

flagging
06 ebbing, fading, tiring, waning
07 abating, failing, languid, sagging,
sinking, slowing, wilting **08** drooping,
pavement **09** declining, dwindling,
faltering, lessening, subsiding,
weakening **10** decreasing
11 diminishing

flagon
03 jug **04** ewer **05** flask, half-g, peter
06 bottle, carafe, vessel **07** pitcher
08 decanter **09** container

flagrant
04 bold, open, rank **05** gross, naked,
overt **06** arrant, brazen, raging
07 blatant, burning, glaring, heinous
08 blattant, dreadful, enormous,
infamous **09** atrocious, audacious,
barefaced, egregious, notorious,
shameless, unashamed **10** outrageous,
scandalous **11** conspicuous,
disgraceful, undisguised
12 ostentatious

flagstaff
03 pin

flail
◇ *anagram indicator*
04 beat, whip **06** batter, strike, thrash,
thresh **08** threshel, thresher **11** swing
wildly

flair
04 bent, feel, gift, nose **05** knack, skill,
style, taste **06** acumen, genius, talent
07 ability, faculty, mastery, panache
08 aptitude, elegance, facility
11 discernment, stylishness **14** natural
ability

flak
02 AA **05** abuse, blame, stick
07 censure, panning **08** bad press,
knocking **09** brickbats, criticism,
hostility, invective **10** aspersions,
complaints, opposition **11** disapproval
12 condemnation, fault-finding
13 disparagement **14** animadversions,
disapprobation

flake
◇ *anagram indicator*
03 bit **04** chip, flaw, peel, smut
05 flash, scale, scurf, shark, spark,
wafer **06** furfur, paring, shiver, sliver,
squama **07** blister, flaught, peeling,
shaving, spangle **08** fragment,
particle, splinter **09** eccentric,
exfoliate, flocculus **10** desquamate
11 exfoliation **12** desquamation

• **flake out**
04 drop **05** faint **07** pass out
08 collapse, keel over **10** fall asleep
15 relax completely

flaky
◇ *anagram indicator*
03 dry **05** crazy, inept, scaly **06** scurfy,
stupid **07** laminar, layered
08 scabrous, squamate, squamose,

squamous **09** eccentric **10** flocculent
11 exfoliative, incompetent
12 desquamative, desquamatory,
furfuraceous

flamboyance
04 dash, élan **05** style **06** colour
07 glamour, panache, pizzazz
09 showiness **10** brilliance
11 ostentation **12** extravagance
13 theatricality

flamboyant
04 rich **05** gaudy, showy **06** bright,
flashy, florid, ornate, rococo
07 baroque, dashing **08** dazzling,
exciting, striking **09** brilliant, colourful,
elaborate, glamorous **10** theatrical
11 extravagant **12** ostentatious

flame
03 low **04** beam, burn, fire, glow, heat,
lowe, lunt, rage, zeal **05** blaze, flake,
flare, flash, flush, glare, gleam, go red,
light, lover, shine **06** ardour, redden,
warmth **07** fervour, partner, passion,
radiate, sparkle, turn red **08** fervency,
flammule, keenness, radiance
09 become red, boyfriend, catch fire,
eagerness, intensity **10** brightness,
enthusiasm, excitement, girlfriend,
sweetheart **13** conflagration **15** burst
into flames
• **in flames**
06 ablaze, aflame, alight, on fire
07 blazing, burning, flaming, ignited
• **old flame**
02 ex

flameproof
09 fireproof **12** non-flammable
13 fire-resistant, incombustible
14 flame-resistant, non-inflammable

flaming
03 mad **04** vile **05** angry, fiery, gaudy,
vivid **06** aflame, alight, bloody, bright,
cursed, damned, darned, dashed,
odious, on fire, raging, red-hot
07 blasted, blazing, burning, enraged,
furious, glowing, hateful, intense,
violent **08** annoying, blinking,
blooming, dratting, fiendish, flipping,
incensed, infamous, infernal, in flames,
wretched **09** brilliant, execrable,
loathsome **10** abominable,
confounded, detestable, infuriated,
pernicious, unpleasant **11** smouldering
13 scintillating

flammable
08 burnable **09** ignitable
11 combustible, inflammable

flank
◇ *containment indicator*
03 hip **04** edge, line, lisk, loin, side,
wall, wing **05** bound, skirt, thigh
06 border, fringe, haunch, screen
07 confine, quarter

flannel
03 rot **05** spiel **06** waffle **07** blarney,
flatter, rubbish, washrag **08** flattery,
nonsense, soft soap **09** facecloth,
sweet talk, washcloth **10** smooth talk
13 blandishments

flap
◇ *anagram indicator*
03 fly, lap, lug, tab, tag, wag, wap
04 beat, fall, flag, flip, fold, fuss, loma, slat, stew, sway, tail, waff, wave
05 apron, flaff, lapel, panic, shake, skirt, state, swing, swish, tizzy, tuner, visor
06 dither, elevon, lappet, thrash, thresh, tiswas, tizwas, tongue, waggle, wallop, winnow **07** agitate, aileron, flacker, fluster, flutter, overlap, tent-fly, vibrate **08** aventail, barn-door, covering, epiploon, overhang
09 agitation, aventaile, commotion
10 clack valve, epiglottis, fluttering
12 great omentum **13** move up and down

flare
04 beam, burn, glow, Very **05** blaze, burst, erupt, flame, flash, glare, gleam, light, splay, torch, widen **06** beacon, dazzle, flanch, rocket, signal, spread
07 broaden, explode, flaunch, flicker, glimmer, glitter, sparkle **08** flare out, widening **09** spread out, Very light
10 broadening, Verey light **13** warning signal **14** distress signal
• **flare out**
04 bell
• **flare up**
05 blaze, erupt, go ape, go mad
06 blow up **07** explode **08** boil over, break out, burst out, freak out **09** blow a fuse, do your nut, go berserk **10** go to market, hit the roof **11** blow your top, do your block, flip your lid, go ballistic, go up the wall, lose control, lose your rag **12** fly into a rage, lose your cool, throw a wobbly **14** foam at the mouth, lose your temper **15** fly off the handle, go off the deep end

flare-up
04 rash **07** venting **08** ejection, emission, eruption, outbreak, outburst
09 discharge, explosion
12 inflammation

flash
◇ *anagram indicator*
02 mo **03** fly, ray **04** beam, bolt, dart, dash, fork, pond, pool, race, rush, show, tear, zoom **05** blaze, blink, bound, burst, dance, flake, flare, gaudy, glaik, glare, gleam, glint, quick, shaft, shine, shoot, showy, smart, spark, speed **06** career, flaunt, glaiks, glance, kitsch, moment, streak, strobe, sudden, vulgar **07** bluette, display, flaught, flicker, glimmer, glisten, glitter, instant, lighten, light up, shimmer, show off, sparkle, twinkle **08** brandish, concetto, fire-flag, flourish, green ray, outbreak, outburst **09** coruscate, expensive, fulgurate, fulminate, glamorous, lightning **10** exhibition
11 coruscation, fashionable, fire-flaught, fulguration, pretentious, scintillate **12** ostentatious
13 scintillation **14** expose yourself
• **in a flash**
03 pdq **06** pronto **08** in a jiffy, in a trice, in no time **09** in a moment,

instantly **11** in an instant **12** in a twinkling **13** in no time at all **14** in a split second

flashy
04 bold, loud **05** brash, cheap, flash, gaudy, jazzy, lairy, showy, tacky, vapid
06 garish, glitzy, kitsch, snazzy, tawdry, vulgar **07** buckeye, raffish, tigrish
08 tigerish **09** glamorous, tasteless
10 bling-bling, flamboyant
11 pretentious **12** meretricious, ostentatious
• **flashy person**
04 lair, raff

flask
04 cask, mick **05** dewar, micky
06 bottle, carafe, coffin, fiasco, flagon, mickey, retort, vessel **07** ampulla, balloon, canteen, costrel, flacket, matrass, Thermos® **08** decanter, lekythos **09** aryballos, container, livery pot **10** powder horn **12** pocket-pistol

flat
03 low, OYO, pad, set **04** bust, dead, down, duff, dull, even, firm, flew, flue, fool, slow, tame, true, unit, weak
05 banal, bland, burst, empty, exact, final, fixed, haugh, kaput, level, plain, plane, prone, quiet, rigid, rooms, sheer, slack, stale, still, stock, suite, total, utter, vapid **06** bedsit, boring, callow, direct, evenly, planar, sleepy, smooth, supine, used up, watery **07** exactly, flatlet, insipid, not deep, not tall, plainly, planned, regular, shallow, tedious, totally, uniform, utterly **08** absolute, arranged, blown-out, complete, defeated, definite, deflated, dejected, directly, downcast, entirely, explicit, finished, home unit, inactive, levelled, lifeless, not thick, outright, positive, ruptured, sluggish, stagnant, standard, straight, tenement, toneless, unbroken
09 apartment, bedsitter, collapsed, depressed, downright, miserable, out-and-out, penthouse, pointless, precisely, prostrate, punctured, reclining, recumbent, unvarying
10 absolutely, completely, despondent, homaloidal, horizontal, lacklustre, maisonette, monotonous, point-blank, spiritless, unexciting
11 categorical, discouraged, maisonnette, unequivocal, unqualified
12 outstretched, spread-eagled
13 categorically, no longer fizzy, unconditional, uninteresting **14** flat as a pancake
• **flat out**
04 hard **06** all out **10** at top speed **11** at full speed
• **flat place**
04 plat

flatly
10 absolutely, completely, point-blank, positively **12** peremptorily
13 categorically **14** unhesitatingly
15 unconditionally

flatness
06 tedium **07** boredom, languor

08 dullness, evenness, monotony, vapidity **09** emptiness, levelness, platitude, staleness **10** insipidity, smoothness, uniformity
13 horizontality, tastelessness

flatten
02 KO **04** fell, iron, raze, roll
05 amaze, crush, dress, floor, level, plane, press **06** defeat, smooth, squash, subdue **07** even out, planish
08 compress, demolish, knock out, make even, make flat, tear down
09 knock down, overwhelm, prostrate

flatter
04 claw, coax, fawn, soap, suit, word
05 befit, court, creep, gloze, grace, toady **06** become, butter, cozy up, cringe, fleech, humour, kowtow, phrase, praise, sawder, smooth, soothe, stroke **07** adulate, enhance, flannel, gratify, lay it on, palaver, show off, soother, wheedle **08** beslaver, blandish, butter up, collogue, eulogize, inveigle, make up to, play up to, smooth it, soft-soap, suck up to **09** beslobber, embellish, sweet-talk **10** bear in hand, compliment, cozy up with, look good on, overpraise, pay court to, soft sawder, soft sowder **12** sycophantize
14 tickle the ear of **15** curry favour with, make fair weather, show to advantage

flatterer
05 carny, creep, toady **06** carney, earwig, fawner, lackey, minion, yes-man **07** crawler, creeper, proneur
08 adulator, incenser, incensor, smoother **09** encomiast, eulogizer, groveller, sycophant **10** bootlicker, foot-licker **11** lickspittle **12** court-dresser **13** back-scratcher

flattering
04 kind **06** honied, sugary
07 candied, fawning, fulsome, honeyed, servile, sugared
08 becoming, effusive, unctuous
09 adulatory, enhancing, gnathonic, laudatory **10** favourable, gratifying, obsequious **11** gnathonical, soft-soaping, sycophantic **12** honey-tongued, ingratiating, smooth-spoken, sweet-talking **13** complimentary, smooth-talking, smooth-tongued

flattery
04 fawn, soap **05** carny, sugar, taffy
06 butter, carney, eulogy, praise, sawder **07** blarney, fawning, flannel, glozing, mamaguy **08** cajolery, soft soap, toadyism **09** adulation, fair words, fleeching, laudation, servility, sweet talk **10** cajolement, flapdoodle, fleechment, soft sawder, soft sowder, sycophancy **11** compliments, fulsomeness **12** blandishment, ingratiation **13** blandishments **14** back scratching, court holy water

flatulence
03 gas **04** wind **06** flatus **07** farting
09 gassiness, ventosity, windiness
10 eructation **11** borborygmus

flatulent
05 gassy, windy **07** ventose

flaunt
03 air **05** boast, flash, skyre, sport, strut, vaunt, wield **06** dangle, parade, strout **07** display, disport, exhibit, show off **08** brandish, flourish

flavour
03 hop **04** feel, gust, hint, lace, race, soul, tack, tang, tone, zest, zing **05** aroma, flava, imbue, lemon, odour, sapor, savor, smack, spice, style, taste, tinge, touch, twang **06** aspect, infuse, nature, palate, pepper, relish, savour, season, spirit **07** essence, feeling, liqueur, quality, spice up **08** ginger up, piquancy, property **09** character **10** atmosphere, impression, indication, suggestion

flavouring
04 hops, miso, sage, tang, zest, zing **05** caper, shoyu, spice **06** borage, Bovril®, cassis, cloves, relish, savory **07** bay leaf, bitters, caramel, essence, extract, flavour, ratafia, saffron, vanilla **08** additive, costmary, piquancy, rosemary, tarragon **09** coriander, fenugreek, pistachio, seasoning, spearmint **10** peach-water **11** citronellal, malt-extract, wintergreen **12** bouquet garni, butterscotch
See also **herb**

flaw
04 chip, gall, mark, rent, rift, slip, spot, tear **05** brack, break, cleft, crack, craze, error, fault, flake, lapse, speck, split, thief **06** defect, foible, uproar **07** blemish, crevice, failing, fallacy, fissure, mistake **08** fracture, fragment, hamartia, splinter, weakness, weak spot **09** windshake **11** shortcoming **12** Achilles' heel, imperfection

flawed
◇ *anagram indicator*
06 broken, faulty, marked, marred, spoilt **07** chipped, cracked, damaged, unsound **09** blemished, defective, erroneous, imperfect **10** fallacious

flawless
05 sound, whole **06** intact **07** perfect **08** spotless, unbroken **09** faultless, stainless, undamaged **10** immaculate, impeccable, unimpaired **11** unblemished **12** indefectible **14** without blemish

flax
03 tow **04** harl, herl, line, lint **05** hards, hurds **06** byssus **07** allseed **08** Phormium **12** mill-mountain

flay
03 pan **04** flog, skin, slam **05** knock, slate **06** attack, flench, flense, flinch, revile, uncase **07** condemn, lambast, run down, scourge, upbraid **08** denounce, execrate, frighten **09** castigate, criticize, excoriate, pull apart, skin alive, tear apart **12** pull to pieces **13** find fault with, tear a strip off

flea
05 Pulex **06** chigoe, chigre, jigger **07** chigger, Daphnia, daphnid **09** turnip fly **11** Aphaniptera **12** Siphonaptera

fleck
03 dot **04** dust, mark, spot **05** point, speck, stain **06** dapple, mottle, streak **07** freckle, spatter, speckle, stipple **08** sprinkle

fledgling
03 new **04** tiro **05** squab **06** coming, novice, rising, rookie **07** budding, learner, nascent, recruit, trainee **08** beginner, emergent, emerging, neophyte, newcomer **09** coming out, embryonic, greenhorn, novitiate **10** apprentice, burgeoning, developing, tenderfoot **11** independent

flee
03 fly, lam, ren, rin, run **04** bolt, bunk, loup, quit, rush, scat **05** lam it, leave, scoot, scram, skive, split **06** decamp, depart, escape, get out, vanish **07** abscond, bunk off, do a bunk, get away, make off, push off, retreat, run away, scarper, take off, vamoose **08** clear off, shove off, up sticks, withdraw **09** cut and run, disappear, do a runner, push along, skedaddle **10** hightail it, hit the road, make tracks, take flight **11** hit the trail **13** sling your hook **14** make a bolt for it **15** make a break for it, take to your heels

fleece
02 do **03** con, jib, rob, teg **04** bilk, coat, down, gull, plot, rook, skin, tegg, wool **05** bleed, cheat, mulct, ploat, pluck, shave, shear, steal, sting **06** diddle, fiddle, rip off, toison **07** defraud, plunder, squeeze, swindle **08** fetch off **09** shearling, toison d'or **10** overcharge **11** string along **12** pull a fast one, put one over on, take for a ride **13** have someone on

fleecy
04 soft **05** downy, hairy, nappy **06** fluffy, pilose, shaggy, woolly **07** velvety **08** floccose **10** flocculate, lanuginose **11** eriophorous

fleet
02 RN **04** fast, flit, flow, navy **05** agile, flitt, float, flota, quick, rapid, swift **06** armada, flying, marine, nimble, speedy, winged **07** caravan **08** flotilla, meteoric, navarchy, squadron **09** mercurial, task force, transient **10** naval force **11** expeditious, light-footed

fleeting
04 flit **05** brief, flitt, quick, short **06** bubble, flying, hollow, rushed, sudden **07** passing **08** fugitive, volatile **09** ephemeral, fugacious, momentary, temporary, transient **10** evanescent, short-lived, transitory

fleetingly
07 briefly, quickly **08** casually **10** for a

moment, for a second **11** momentarily **12** for an instant

flesh
03 fat **04** boar, body, meat, pith, pulp, skin **05** brawn, braxy, stuff **06** matter, muscle, tissue, weight **08** solidity **09** carnality, sexuality, substance **10** sensuality **11** human nature, physicality **12** carnal nature, corporeality, significance, sinful nature **14** physical nature

• **flesh and blood**
03 kin **04** rels **05** folks **06** family **07** kindred, rellies **08** relative **09** relations

• **flesh out**
08 expand on **09** elaborate **10** add details **11** elaborate on, give details **12** make complete

• **flesh round jaw**
04 gill

• **in the flesh**
05 alive **06** bodily **08** in person **09** incarnate **10** in real life **12** in actual life

fleshly
05 human **06** animal, bodily, carnal, earthy, erotic, sexual **07** bestial, brutish, earthly, lustful, sensual, worldly **08** corporal, material, physical **09** corporeal

fleshy
03 fat **05** ample, beefy, hefty, meaty, obese, plump, podgy, pulpy, stout, tubby **06** brawny, chubby, chunky, flabby, portly, rotund **07** carnose, paunchy **08** carneous **09** corpulent, succulent **10** overweight, well-padded

flex
03 bow, ply **04** bend, cord, lead, wire **05** angle, cable, crook, curve **07** stretch, tighten **08** contract, double up

flexibility
04 give **06** spring **07** flexion, pliancy **09** tensility **10** elasticity, pliability, resilience, suppleness **11** amenability, bendability, springiness **12** adaptability, agreeability, complaisance **13** adjustability

flexible
◇ *anagram indicator*
04 open **05** agile, bendy, lithe, withy **06** docile, floppy, limber, lissom, mobile, pliant, supple **07** elastic, flexile, lissome, plastic, pliable, springy, willowy **08** amenable, bendable, stretchy, variable, yielding **09** adaptable, compliant, complying, malleable, mouldable, open-ended, tractable **10** adjustable, changeable, manageable **13** accommodating, double-jointed

flick
03 dab, hit, rap, tap **04** flip, jerk, lash, lick, snap, whip **05** click, flirt, swish, touch **06** fillip, strike

• **flick through**
04 scan, skim, skip **08** glance at

10 glance over, run through 11 flip through, leaf through 12 thumb through 13 browse through

flicker
03 bat 04 atom, drop, iota, jump, lick, play, wink 05 blink, flare, flash, gleam, glint, spark, trace, waver 06 gutter, quiver, yucker 07 flaught, flutter, glimmer, glitter, shimmer, sparkle, twinkle, vibrate 08 lambency 09 flaughter 10 indication

flier
02 FO, PO 07 handout, leaflet 08 brochure, bulletin, circular, pamphlet 09 statement 10 literature 12 press release

See also **bird**

• **expert flier**
03 ace
• **non-flier** *see* **flightless birds** *under* **bird**

fliers
03 RAF

flight
03 fly, guy, lam, set 04 exit, pair, rout, rush, trap, trip, wing 05 steps 06 escape, exodus, flying, roding, stairs, voyage 07 fleeing, getaway, journey, retreat, roading, runaway, shuttle, soaring 08 aviation, stairway 09 air travel, breakaway, departure, skedaddle, staircase 10 absconding, exaltation, running off, volitation, withdrawal 11 aeronautics, running away 12 air transport 13 globetrotting
• **take flight**
03 fly, run 04 bolt, flee, quit, rush, scat 05 lam it, leave, leg it, scoot, scram, skive, split 06 decamp, depart, escape, vanish 07 abscond, bunk off, do a bunk, get away, make off, push off, retreat, run away, scarper, take off, vamoose 08 clear off, shove off, up sticks, withdraw 09 cut and run, disappear, do a runner, push along, skedaddle 10 hightail it, hit the road, make tracks 11 hit the trail 13 sling your hook 14 make a bolt for it, take it on the lam 15 make a break for it, take to your heels

flighty
◊ *anagram indicator*
04 wild 05 giddy, silly, swift 06 fickle, volage 07 erratic, flyaway 08 fanciful, hellicat, skipping, skittish, unstable, unsteady, volatile 09 butterfly, frivolous, impetuous, impulsive, mercurial, volageous 10 bird-witted, capricious, changeable, inconstant, unbalanced 11 birdbrained, flirtatious, hare-brained, lightheaded, loup-the-dyke, thoughtless, unballasted 12 bubble-headed, rattle-headed, whisky-frisky 13 irresponsible, rattle-brained, weather-headed 14 scatterbrained
• **flighty type**
04 bird

flimsy
04 fine, poor, thin, weak 05 filmy, light, shaky, sheer, wispy 06 feeble, meagre, slight, slimsy 07 band-box, fragile, rickety, shallow, trivial 08 banknote, delicate, ethereal, gossamer, trifling, vaporous 09 airy-fairy, cardboard, gossamery, makeshift, paper-thin 10 inadequate, jerry-built, ramshackle 11 implausible, lightweight, superficial 12 unconvincing 13 insubstantial

flinch
04 balk, duck, flay, flee, funk 05 avoid, cower, dodge, quail, quake, shake, shirk, start, wince 06 blench, cringe, crouch, falter, recoil, shiver, shrink 07 retreat, shudder, shy away, tremble 08 draw back, pull back, withdraw 10 shrink back

fling
02 go 03 lob, shy, try 04 cast, dart, dash, hurl, jerk, jibe, rush, send, shot, toss, turn 05 amour, binge, chuck, crack, heave, lance, lanch, pitch, sling, spang, spree, taunt, throw, trial, whirl 06 affair, gamble, launce, launch, let fly, propel 07 affaire, attempt, carry-on, flounce, liaison, romance, venture 08 catapult, good time, intrigue, spanghew, throw out 10 indulgence, love affair, send flying 12 relationship 13 affaire d'amour, grande passion

flinty
03 icy 04 cold, hard 05 blank, cruel, stern, stony 06 chilly, frigid, frosty, severe, steely 07 adamant, callous, deadpan, hostile 08 obdurate, pitiless 09 heartless, merciless, unfeeling 10 inexorable, poker-faced 11 emotionless, indifferent, unforgiving 12 unresponsive 14 expressionless

flip
◊ *reversal indicator*
04 cast, flap, jerk, pert, snap, spin, toss, turn 05 click, flick, pitch, throw, twirl, twist 09 pitch-pole, pitch-poll
• **flip through**
04 scan, skim, skip 08 glance at 10 glance over 11 leaf through 12 flick through, thumb through 13 browse through

flippancy
05 cheek 06 levity 08 glibness, pertness 09 frivolity, sauciness 10 cheekiness, disrespect, persiflage 11 irreverence, shallowness 12 impertinence 13 facetiousness 14 superficiality 15 thoughtlessness

flippant
04 flip, glib, pert, rude 05 saucy 06 cheeky, nimble 07 offhand, playful, shallow 08 impudent 09 facetious, frivolous 10 insouciant, irreverent 11 impertinent, superficial, thoughtless 12 light-hearted 13 disrespectful, irresponsible

flippantly
06 glibly, rudely 11 facetiously, frivolously 12 irreverently

13 impertinently, irresponsibly, superficially, thoughtlessly 14 light-heartedly 15 disrespectfully

flipping
06 cursed, damned, darned, dashed 07 blasted 08 annoying, blinking, blooming, dratting, fiendish, infernal, wretched 10 confounded, unpleasant

flirt
03 rap, toy 04 jerk, mash, ogle, vamp 05 dally, eye up, flick, hussy, tease 06 chat up, chippy, coquet, gillet, lead on, masher, wanton 07 carry on, pickeer, trifler 08 coquette, make up to 09 gillflirt, philander 10 make eyes at 11 make a pass at, philanderer 12 heart-breaker
• **flirt with**
03 try 04 mash 05 hit on 06 coquet 07 carry on, hit upon, toy with 08 consider, coquette, dabble in, play with 09 entertain 10 trifle with

flirtation
05 amour, sport 06 affair, come-on, lumber, toying 07 teasing 08 coquetry, dallying, intrigue, trifling 09 dalliance 10 chatting up 12 philandering

flirtatious
05 loose 06 come-on, flirty, wanton 07 amorous, flighty, teasing 08 flirtish, sportive 10 come-hither, coquettish 11 promiscuous, provocative

flit
◊ *anagram indicator*
03 bob, fly 04 dart, dash, pass, rush, skim, skip, slip, wing 05 dance, flash, fleet, light, speed, whisk 07 flitter, flutter 08 fleeting

float
03 bob 04 cart, cork, hang, hull, pram, sail, swim, waft 05 balsa, camel, drift, fleet, glide, hover, quill, set up, slide, table 06 bobber, launch, smooth, submit, wander 07 oropesa, pontoon, present, promote, propose, suggest, suspend 08 get going, initiate, levitate, lifebuoy 09 be buoyant, establish, recommend 10 come up with, put forward, stay afloat 13 pneumatophore 15 get off the ground

floating
◊ *anagram indicator*
04 free 06 afloat, natant 07 bobbing, buoyant, movable, sailing, wafting 08 drifting, hovering, swimming, variable 09 migratory, unsettled, wandering 10 indecisive, transitory, unattached, unsinkable 11 fluctuating, uncommitted

flock
03 mob 04 band, bevy, fold, game, herd, host, mass, mill, pack, rout, sord, trip, tuft, walk, wing, wisp, wool 05 bunch, charm, chirm, covey, crowd, drove, flush, group, shoal, skein, swarm, troop, watch 06 flight, gaggle, gather, huddle, school, spring, throng

▼ cluster, collect, company, dopping
8 assemble, assembly, converge,
addling **09** flocculus, gathering,
multitude **10** collection, congregate,
nkindness **11** murmuration **12** come
•gether, congregation

log
anagram indicator
3 tan, tat, taw **04** beat, belt, cane,
rub, flay, hawk, hide, lash, sell, whip
5 birch, knout, strap, swish, trade,
•hack, whang **06** breech, deal in,
andle, larrup, peddle, punish, strike,
•rash, wallop **07** scourge, sjambok
8 chastise, urticate, vapulate
9 horsewhip **10** flagellate **12** offer for
•le, put up for sale

logging
6 caning, hiding **07** beating, belting,
aying, lashing **08** birching, whacking,
•hipping **09** scourging, strapping,
•rashing, walloping **10** vapulation
2 flagellation **13** horsewhipping,
•hipping-cheer

lood
4 bore, eger, fill, flow, glut, gush, pour,
•ge, rush, soak, tide **05** drown, eager,
•agre, spate, speat, surge, swamp,
•vell **06** deluge, drench, engulf,
•xcess, series, stream **07** debacle,
•eshet, immerse, smother, torrent
8 alluvion, brim over, diluvion,
•luvium, downpour, inundate,
•verflow, plethora, saturate, submerge
9 abundance, cataclysm, overwhelm,
•rofusion **10** flash flood, inundation,
•utpouring, spring tide, succession,
•ansgress **11** superfluity **13** Ogygian
•eluge

loor
2 fl, KO **04** area, base, beat, dais,
•eck, fell, loft, tier **05** attic, basis,
•tage, level, stage, stump, throw
6 baffle, defeat, ground, planch,
•uzzle, storey **07** flummox, landing,
•onplus, perplex **08** basement, bel
•tage, bewilder, confound, entresol,
•ooring, platform **09** discomfit,
•umbfound, frustrate, knock down,
•verwhelm, prostrate **10** disconcert,
•ownstairs, strike down **11** piano
•obile

first floor
1 ground level

floor material
4 lino, pisé, rung

loozy *see* **tart**

lop
anagram indicator
3 sag **04** bomb, drop, fail, fall, fold,
•ang, sink, swap, swop **05** crash,
•roop, flump, slump **06** dangle, fiasco,
•o bust, pack up, slip-up, topple,
•mble **07** also-ran, debacle, failure,
•under, go broke, has-been, misfire,
•o-hoper, washout **08** collapse,
•isaster, fall flat, lay an egg, shambles
•0 non-starter **11** go to the wall
•2 come a cropper, go into the red
•4 be unsuccessful

• **flop down**
03 wop **04** whap, whop **05** plump

floppy
◇ *anagram indicator*
04 limp, soft **05** baggy, loose
06 droopy, flabby **07** flaccid, hanging,
sagging **08** dangling, diskette, flexible
12 flexible disk

flora
06 botany, Cybele, plants **07** herbage
08 plantage **09** plant life **10** vegetation

floral emblem *see* **emblem**

florid
03 red **04** high **05** Asian, fussy, ruddy
06 ornate, purple, rococo **07** baroque,
flowery, flushed, pompous, reddish,
taffeta, verbose **08** beetroot, blushing,
figurate, red-faced, rubicund,
sanguine, taffetas **09** bombastic,
elaborate, high-flown **10** coloratura,
flamboyant, melismatic **11** embellished,
extravagant **12** high-sounding
13 grandiloquent, overelaborate

Florida
02 FL **03** Fla

flotsam
04 junk **05** dreck **06** debris, jetsam
07 flotage, rubbish **08** detritus,
floatage, oddments, wreckage **11** odds
and ends

flounce
03 bob **04** jerk, toss **05** fling, frill,
stamp, storm, throw, twist **06** bounce,
fringe, ruffle, spring **07** falbala, valance
08 furbelow, trimming

flounder
◇ *anagram indicator*
05 fluke, grope, slosh **06** dither, falter,
fumble, jumble, tolter, wallop, wallow
07 blunder, go under, stagger, stumble
08 struggle **10** be confused, flail about
11 thresh about **12** lose the place

flour
04 meal **06** red-dog **07** cribble,
pollard **08** tailings **09** wheatmeal
11 strong wheat

flourish
◇ *anagram indicator*
03 wag, wax **04** boom, élan, grow, lick,
mort, show, wave **05** bloom, get on,
serif, shake, swash, sweep, swing, swirl,
swish, twirl, twist, vaunt, wield **06** do
well, flaunt, flower, parade, paraph,
rubric, swinge, thrive, tucket
07 blossom, burgeon, cadenza,
develop, display, exhibit, fanfare,
gesture, panache, pizzazz, prosper,
show off, succeed, wampish **08** be
strong, brandish, curlicue, increase,
ornament, progress **09** bear fruit
10 decoration

flourished
◇ *anagram indicator*
02 fl **04** flor

flourishing
◇ *anagram indicator*
04 pert **05** green, palmy **06** bloomy

07 booming **08** blooming, thriving
10 blossoming, burgeoning,
prosperous, successful **11** going strong

flout
04 defy, gibe, jibe, lout, lowt, mock
05 break, scorn, scout, spurn **06** jeer
at, reject **07** disdain, disobey, laugh at,
scoff at, sneer at, violate **08** ridicule
09 disregard, go against **11** set at
nought **15** show contempt for

flow
◇ *anagram indicator*
02 go **03** jet, ren, rin, run **04** drip, flux,
gush, leak, make, melt, move, ooze,
pour, rail, roll, rush, seep, slip, spew,
stem, teem, tide, well, wend **05** arise,
drift, flood, glide, issue, raile, rayle,
slide, spate, spill, spout, spurt, surge,
sweep, swirl, whirl **06** babble, bubble,
course, deluge, derive, emerge, gurgle,
morass, plenty, result, ripple, spring,
squirt, stream **07** cascade, current,
emanate, passage, proceed, trickle
08 effusion, movement, overflow,
plethora, recourse **09** abundance,
circulate, originate, quicksand
10 outpouring

flower
03 bud **04** acme, best, grow, open,
peak, pick **05** bloom, cream, élite,
prime **06** choice, finest, floret, height,
heyday, mature, select, sprout, thrive,
zenith **07** blossom, burgeon, come
out, develop, prosper, succeed **08** best
part, flourish, floweret, maturity,
pinnacle **10** perfection **11** culmination,
florescence **13** efflorescence,
inflorescence **14** crème de la crème

See also **birth; river**

Flower parts include:

05 calyx, ovary, ovule, petal, sepal,
     spike, stalk, style, torus, umbel
06 anther, carpel, corymb, pistil,
     raceme, spadix, stamen, stigma
07 corolla, nectary, panicle, pedicel
08 filament, thalamus
09 capitulum, dichasium, gynoecium
10 receptacle
11 monochasium

Garden flowers include:

04 lis
04 aloe, daff, flag, glad, iris, lily, pink,
     rose, sego
05 aster, daisy, lotus, lupin, pansy,
     phlox, poppy, stock, tulip, viola
06 allium, azalea, crocus, dahlia,
     orchid, salvia, squill, violet, zinnia
07 alyssum, anemone, begonia,
     campion, day-lily, freesia, fuchsia,
     lobelia, nemesia, nigella, petunia,
     primula, verbena
08 arum lily, asphodel, bluebell,
     cyclamen, daffodil, dianthus,
     foxglove, gardenia, geranium,
     gladioli, hyacinth, marigold, pond
     lily, primrose, snowdrop, sweet pea
09 amaryllis, aubrietia, calendula,
     candytuft, carnation, digitalis,
     gladiolus, hollyhock, narcissus,

nicotiana, regal lily, sunflower, tiger lily, torch lily
10 agapanthus, busy lizzie, cornflower, delphinium, Easter lily, fleur-de-lis, fleur-de-lys, fritillary, nasturtium, poinsettia, polyanthus, ragged-lady, snake's head, snapdragon, wallflower
11 African lily, antirrhinum, forget-me-not, gillyflower, love-in-a-mist, Madonna-lily, naked ladies, red-hot poker, tiger flower
12 devil-in-a-bush, flower of Jove, rose geranium, Solomon's seal, sweet william, wild hyacinth, Zantedeschia
13 African violet, butcher's broom, chrysanthemum, grape hyacinth, lily of the Nile, winter aconite
14 belladonna lily, glory of the snow, Ithuriel's spear
15 dog's tooth violet, lily of the valley, star of Bethlehem

See also **lily**

Wild flowers include:
03 kex, meu
04 daff, geum, ling, nard, woad
05 clary, daisy, gowan, laser, poppy
06 clover, oxslip, teasel, violet, yarrow
07 ale hoof, bistort, campion, comfrey, cowslip, dog rose, goldcup, heather, spignel
08 bluebell, crowfoot, dog daisy, foxglove, harebell, lungwort, primrose, rock rose, self-heal, spicknel, toadflax, wild iris
09 Aaron's rod, baldmoney, birth-wort, broomrape, buttercup, celandine, columbine, edelweiss, goldenrod, horsetail, moneywort, stonecrop, water lily, wild pansy
10 crane's bill, goatsbeard, heartsease, lady's smock, marguerite, masterwort, oxeye daisy, pennyroyal, wild endive, wild orchid
11 ragged robin, wild chicory, wood anemone
12 common mallow, cuckoo flower, great mullein, lady's slipper, solomon's seal, white campion, yellow rocket
13 butter-and-eggs, field cow-wheat, shepherd's club, wild gladiolus
14 black-eyed susan, bladder campion, common toadflax, multiflora rose
15 New England aster

● **garland of flowers**
03 lei **05** toran **06** torana
● **mass of flowers**
04 head

flowery
05 fancy **06** bloomy, floral, florid, ornate **07** baroque, chintzy, pompous, verbose **08** blossomy **09** bombastic, elaborate, high-flown **10** euphuistic, rhetorical **13** grandiloquent

flowing
04 easy, flux **05** loose **06** floppy, fluent, liquid, moving, oozing, smooth

07 current, cursive, falling, flaccid, gushing, hanging, natural, pouring, rolling, running, rushing, seeping, surging, welling **08** bubbling, sweeping, unbroken **09** cascading, streaming **10** continuous, effortless **11** loose-bodied, overflowing **12** hanging loose **13** hanging freely, uninterrupted

fluctuate
◊ *anagram indicator*
04 sway, trim, vary, yo-yo **05** alter, float, range, shift, swing, waver **06** change, differ, seesaw **07** balance **08** hesitate, undulate **09** alternate, come and go, oscillate, vacillate **10** ebb and flow **11** go up and down, rise and fall **13** chop and change

fluctuation
05 range, shift, swing **06** change, seiche **08** floating, nutation, wavering **09** variation **10** fickleness **11** alternation, ambivalence, inconstancy, instability, oscillation, vacillation, variability **12** irresolution, unsteadiness **14** capriciousness

flue
03 fur **04** duct, flat, pipe, vent **05** shaft, tewel **06** flared, tunnel, uptake **07** channel, chimney, passage, shallow, splayed **08** fluework **09** influenza

fluency
04 ease, flow **07** command, control **08** facility, glibness **09** assurance, eloquence, facundity, flippancy, readiness, slickness **10** outpouring, smoothness, volubility **12** flippantness **13** copia verborum **14** articulateness

fluent
04 easy, glib **05** fluid, ready, slick **06** facile, smooth **07** elegant, flowing, natural, voluble **08** eloquent, graceful **10** articulate, effortless **11** free-flowing, mellifluous **13** silver-tongued

fluently
03 pat **05** patly **06** easily, glibly **08** smoothly **09** elegantly, naturally **10** eloquently, gracefully **12** articulately, effortlessly

fluff
◊ *anagram indicator*
03 fug, nap **04** blow, boob, dowl, down, dust, flue, fuzz, lint, muff, oose, ooze, pile **05** botch, dowle, flosh, floss, spoil **06** bungle, cock up, foul up, fumble, mess up, muck up, muddle **07** do badly, screw up **09** dust bunny, mismanage **11** make a mess of **13** make a bad job of **15** put your foot in it

fluffy
04 soft **05** downy, furry, fuzzy, hairy, silky **06** fleecy, pluffy, shaggy, woolly **07** velvety **08** feathery

fluid
◊ *anagram indicator*
02 fl **03** gas **04** easy, open **05** chyle, grume, juice, runny **06** liquid, liquor,

melted, mobile, molten, smooth, vapour, watery **07** aqueous, elegant, flowing, natural, protean, running **08** atrament, flexible, graceful, shifting, solution, unstable, unsteady, variable **09** adaptable, diffluent, liquefied, unsettled **10** adjustable, changeable, effortless, inconstant, karyolymph **11** fluctuating, free-flowing **12** unsolidified

fluke
03 fan **04** barb, worm **05** break, freak quirk **06** chance, stroke, upcast **07** killick, killock, scratch **08** accident blessing, flounder, fortuity, windfall **09** trematode **10** lucky break **11** coincidence, serendipity **12** stroke of luck

fluky
05 jammy, lucky **06** chance **08** freakish **09** fortunate, uncertain **10** accidental, fortuitous **12** coincidental, incalculable **13** serendipitous

flummox
03 fox **04** faze **05** floor, stump **06** baffle, defeat, puzzle, stymie **07** confuse, mystify, nonplus, perplex **08** bewilder, confound **09** bamboozle

flummoxed
05 at sea, fazed, foxed **07** at a loss, baffled, floored, puzzled, stumped, stymied **08** confused **09** mystified, perplexed **10** bamboozled, bewildered, confounded, nonplussed

flunk
04 bomb, fail, flop, fold **06** blow it **07** failure, founder **08** fall flat **09** not make it **10** come undone, not come off **11** bite the dust, come to grief, come unglued, come unstuck **12** come a cropper **14** be unsuccessful **15** blow your chances

flunkey
05 slave, toady, valet **06** drudge, Jeames, lackey, menial, minion, yes-man **07** cringer, footman, servant, steward **08** hanger-on **09** assistant, underling **10** bootlicker, manservant

fluorine
01 F

flurried
◊ *anagram indicator*
05 fazed, upset **07** in a flap, in a tizz, rattled **08** in a tizzy, unnerved **09** disturbed, flustered, perturbed, unsettled **12** all of a lather **13** having kittens

flurry
◊ *anagram indicator*
04 bout, flap, fuss, gust, stir, to-do **05** blast, burst, hurry, spell, spurt, swirl upset, whirl **06** bother, bustle, hassle, hubbub, hustle, rattle, ruffle, scurry, shower, squall, tumult **07** agitate, confuse, disturb, fluster, flutter, perturb swither **08** bewilder, outbreak, unsettle **09** agitation, commotion

flush (continued)

10 disconcert, excitement
11 disturbance **12** perturbation
14 discountenance

flush
03 rud **04** burn, even, flat, full, gild, glow, hose, rich, swab, true, wash
05 bloom, blush, clear, eject, elate, empty, expel, flame, go red, level, plane, rinse, rouse, scour, start
06 colour, hectic, heyday, lavish, puddle, redden, sluice, smooth, square, vigour **07** cleanse, crimson, disturb, moneyed, redness, replete, suffuse, turn red, uncover, wealthy, well-off **08** abundant, colour up, discover, drive out, evacuate, force out, generous, rosiness, well-to-do
09 abounding, abundance, freshness, reddening, ruddiness **10** prosperous, run to earth, well-heeled
11 overflowing

flushed
03 hot, red **04** pink, rosy **05** aglow, rosed, ruddy **06** ablaze, aflame, blowsy, blowzy, elated, florid, hectic
07 aroused, burning, crimson, excited, glowing, scarlet **08** animated, blushing, enthused, exultant, inspired, rubicund, sanguine, thrilled
11 embarrassed, exhilarated, intoxicated

fluster
◇ *anagram indicator*
04 faze, flap, heat, tizz **05** panic, state, tizzy, upset **06** bother, bustle, dither, flurry, pother, pudder, put off, rattle, ruffle **07** agitate, confuse, disturb, perturb, turmoil, unnerve
08 confound, distract, hurrying, unsettle **09** agitation, commotion, confusion, embarrass, flustrate
10 discompose, disconcert
11 disturbance, flustration, make nervous **12** perturbation
13 embarrassment

flute
04 fife **05** quena, tibia **06** poogye, zufolo **07** chamfer, piccolo, poogyee, zuffolo **08** recorder **09** flageolet
10 shakuhachi

fluted
06 ribbed, ridged **07** grooved
08 furrowed **10** channelled, corrugated

flutter
◇ *anagram indicator*
03 bat, bet, fan, fly **04** beat, flap, play, punt, risk, toss, waff, wave **05** dance, flaff, hover, shake, wager, waver
06 gamble, quiver, ripple, ruffle, shiver, tremor, twitch, winnow **07** agitate, flacker, flaffer, flicker, flitter, pulsate, shudder, tremble, twitter, vibrate
08 flapping, flichter, volitate
09 agitation, confusion, flaughter, fluctuate, palpitate, vibration
11 palpitation, speculation

flux
04 flow, fuse, melt **05** issue

06 change, motion, unrest **08** fluidity, movement, mutation **10** alteration, transition **11** development, fluctuation, instability **12** modification
13 changeability

• **electric flux displacement**
01 D

• **magnetic flux density**
01 B

fly
◇ *anagram indicator*
03 jet, run, sly **04** bolt, dart, dash, flap, flee, flit, quit, race, rise, rush, scat, show, soar, tear, wave, wily, wing, zoom
05 alert, canny, float, glide, guide, hover, hurry, leave, mount, pilot, scoot, scram, sharp, shoot, skive, smart, speed, split, steer **06** artful, ascend, astute, career, decamp, depart, escape, flight, get out, hasten, reveal, shrewd, slip by, sprint, stream, vanish, winnow **07** abscond, careful, control, cunning, display, do a bunk, exhibit, flutter, get away, go by air, make off, operate, present, prudent, push off, retreat, run away, scarper, stylish, take off, vamoose **08** clear off, shove off, volitate, withdraw **09** cut and run, disappear, do a runner, golden-eye, go quickly, manoeuvre, on the ball, push along, sagacious, skedaddle **10** hit the road, make tracks, take flight
11 fashionable, hit the trail, nobody's fool, pass quickly, travel by air **14** make a bolt for it **15** make a break for it, take to your heels

Flies include:
03 bee, bot, day, dor, gad, hop, ked, may, med
04 beet, blow, boat, bulb, bush, cleg, corn, deer, dung, fire, frit, gnat, gout, kade, lamp, meat, pium, sand
05 alder, birch, black, crane, drone, flesh, froth, fruit, horse, house, hover, march, midge, onion, sedge, snake, snipe, water, wheat
06 blowie, caddis, carrot, cuckoo, forest, motuca, muscid, mutuca, pomace, robber, stable, tipula, tsetse, turnip, tzetse, tzetze, warble
07 blister, brommer, cabbage, cluster, diptera, dolphin, harvest, Hessian, lantern, sciarid, smother, Spanish, vinegar
08 glossina, ruby-tail, scorpion, sheep ked, simulium, tachinid
09 cantharis, ichneumon, screw-worm
10 bluebottle, Cecidomyia, drosophila, spittle bug
11 biting midge, buffalo gnat, cabbage-root, greenbottle
12 cheesehopper
13 cheese skipper, spittle insect

Fishing flies include:
03 bob
04 harl, herl, tail
05 sedge
06 doctor, hackle, palmer, salmon
07 watchet

09 hairy Mary, Jock Scott
10 cock-a-bondy

• **fly at**
03 hit **05** go for **06** attack, charge, let fly, strike **07** assault, lay into **08** fall upon **09** have a go at, lash out at

• **fly open**
◇ *anagram indicator*
05 burst **15** burst at the seams

fly-by-night
05 shady **06** cowboy **07** dubious
09 ephemeral **10** short-lived, unreliable **12** disreputable, questionable, undependable
13 discreditable, irresponsible, untrustworthy

flyer *see* **flier**

flying
04 fast **05** brief, hasty, rapid
06 mobile, rushed, speedy, volant, winged **07** gliding, hurried, soaring, winging **08** airborne, flapping, fleeting, flighted, floating, hovering, volitant **09** on the wing, wind-borne
10 fluttering, volitation **11** upon the wing, whistle-stop

foam
03 fry **04** boil, fizz, head, scum, suds, surf **05** froth, spume, yeast
06 befoam, bubble, lather, mousse, seethe **07** aerogel, bubbles **08** sea froth **10** effervesce **13** effervescence

foamy
05 spumy, sudsy **06** bubbly, frothy, yeasty **07** foaming, lathery
10 spumescent

fob
• **fob off**
04 dump **05** foist **06** impose, put off, unload **07** deceive, inflict, palm off, pass off **08** get rid of

focus
03 aim, fix, hub **04** axis, core, crux, join, meet, turn **05** heart, hinge, pivot
06 accent, center, centre, direct, home in, kernel, stress, target, weight, zero in, zoom in **07** nucleus **08** converge, emphasis, linchpin, pinpoint, priority
09 attention, spotlight **10** focal point, importance, metropolis, prominence
11 concentrate, pre-eminence
12 accentuation, significance, underscoring **13** concentration
14 bring into focus

• **in focus**
05 clear, crisp, sharp **08** distinct
11 well-defined

• **out of focus**
04 hazy **05** fuzzy, muzzy **06** blurry
07 blurred **10** ill-defined, indistinct

fodder
02 ti **03** hay **04** feed, food, milo
05 grass, vetch **06** eatage, forage, fother, lucern, luzern, silage, stover
07 alfalfa, lucerne, pabulum, provand, provend, rations, soilage, timothy
08 browsing, goat's-rue, oat grass, proviant, rye grass, sainfoin, teosinte

09 foodstuff, milk vetch, milo maize, provender, sago grass, saintfoin **10** cow parsnip, serradella, serradilla, Sudan grass **11** nourishment, white clover **12** meadow fescue, timothy grass **13** kangaroo grass

foe
05 enemy, rival **08** opponent, wrangler **09** adversary, combatant, ill-wisher **10** antagonist

foetid *see* **fetid, foetid**

foetus
06 embryo **10** unborn baby **11** unborn child

fog
◇ *anagram indicator*
03 dim **04** blur, daze, dull, haar, haze, mist, moss, smog **05** befog, brume, cloud, gloom, smoke **06** baffle, darken, muddle, stupor, trance **07** aerosol, confuse, obscure, pea-soup, perplex, sea fret, steam up **08** bewilder, haziness **09** confusion, mistiness, murkiness, obfuscate, obscurity, pease-soup, pea-souper, vagueness **10** bafflement, perplexity, puzzlement **12** bewilderment **14** disorientation

foggy
03 dim **04** damp, dark, grey, hazy **05** misty, muggy, murky, thick, vague **06** cloudy, gloomy, smoggy, stupid **07** brumous, clouded, muddled, obscure, shadowy, unclear **08** overcast **10** indistinct

foible
05 fault, habit, quirk **06** defect, faible, oddity **07** failing, oddness **08** penchant, weakness **09** weak point **11** peculiarity, shortcoming, strangeness **12** eccentricity, idiosyncrasy, imperfection

foil
03 pip **04** balk, stop **05** baulk, block, chaff, check, elude, foyle, stump **06** baffle, defeat, hamper, hinder, outwit, relief, set-off, thwart, window **07** balance, counter, fleuret, nullify, paillon, prevent, repulse, scupper, scuttle, setting **08** contrast, obstruct **09** frustrate **10** antithesis, background, beauty spot, circumvent, complement **11** frustration, silver paper

foist
03 fob **05** force **06** fob off, impose, saddle, thrust, unload, wish on **07** palm off, pass off **08** get rid of **09** introduce

fold
03 hug, lap, pen, ply **04** bend, cuff, dart, fail, fake, flop, hood, line, lirk, purl, ring, ruck, tuck, turn, wrap, yard **05** clasp, close, court, crash, crimp, flock, kraal, layer, paper, pleat, plica, pouch, pound, prank, quill, quire **06** church, crease, crista, diapir, dog-ear, double, enfold, furrow, gather, go bust, mantle, middle, pack up, pleach,

plight, pranck, pucker, ruffle, rumple, wimple, wrap up **07** company, crinkle, crumple, dog's-ear, embrace, enclose, entwine, envelop, flexion, folding, go broke, go under, omentum, overlap, paddock, prancke, squeeze, whimple, wrinkle **08** assembly, collapse, compound, doubling, patagium, shut down, stockade, syncline, turn down, turn over **09** community, duplicate, enclosure, gathering, gill cover, inflexure, knife-edge, mesentery, monocline, plication, plicature, replicate, turn under **10** epicanthus, fellowship, go bankrupt, intertwine **11** convolution, corrugation, duplicature, go to the wall **12** congregation, parishioners **14** hospital corner **15** go out of business

folder
04 file **05** folio **06** binder, holder, jacket, pocket, wallet **08** envelope **09** directory, matchbook, portfolio **13** lever arch file

foliage
06 canopy, leaves **07** boscage, boskage, leafage, verdure **08** greenery **09** foliation, foliature, vernation **10** vegetation **12** frondescence

folio
01 f **02** fo **03** fol

folios
02 ff

folk
03 kin, men **04** clan, race **05** tribe **06** ethnic, family, humans, nation, native, people, public, tribal, tupuna **07** kindred, parents, persons, popular, society **08** kinsfolk, national **09** ancestral, relations, relatives **10** indigenous, population **11** ethnic group, traditional
See also **singer**

folklore
04 lore **05** myths, tales **06** fables **07** beliefs, customs, legends, stories **09** folktales, mythology, tradition **13** superstitions

folksy
04 fond, kind, maty, warm **05** basic, close, crude, matey, pally, plain, thick, tight **06** chummy, genial, kindly, rustic, simple **07** affable, amiable, cordial, helpful, natural **08** amicable, everyday, familiar, friendly, intimate, ordinary, outgoing, sociable **09** comradely, convivial, receptive **10** hospitable **11** good-natured, inseparable, neighbourly, sympathetic, traditional **12** affectionate, approachable, time-honoured **13** companionable **15** unsophisticated

follow
◇ *juxtaposition indicator*
03 ape, dog, ren, rin, run, sew, sue, use **04** copy, flow, heed, heel, hunt, mind, note, obey, stag, suss, tail, twig **05** arise, catch, chase, ensue, grasp,

hound, issue, mimic, stalk, track, trail, watch **06** accept, attend, escort, fathom, go with, pursue, repeat, result, second, shadow, spring, take in **07** develop, emanate, emulate, go after, imitate, observe, proceed, replace, stick to, succeed, support, suss out, yield to **08** adhere to, be a fan of, carry out, come next, go behind, practise, run after, supplant, tag along **09** accompany, come after, conform to, give chase, latch onto, supersede **10** appreciate, come behind, comply with, comprehend, keep up with, understand, walk behind **11** be devoted to, go along with, tread behind **14** be a supporter of, be interested in, take the place of **15** take your cue from
• **follow slavishly**
04 echo
• **follow through**
06 finish, fulfil, pursue **08** complete, conclude, continue **09** implement **10** see through
• **follow up**
06 pursue **07** succeed **08** check out, continue, look into, research **09** prosecute, reinforce **11** consolidate, investigate

follower
03 fan, man **04** buff **05** freak, pupil **06** backer, cohort, escort, helper, lackey, voteen **07** acolyte, acolyth, admirer, Anthony, apostle, convert, devotee, janizar, lacquey, sectary **08** adherent, believer, disciple, emulator, hanger-on, imitator, janizary, retainer, sidekick **09** attendant, companion, janissary, poodle-dog, satellite, supporter **10** aficionado, enthusiast, pursuivant, running dog **11** afficionado

following
◇ *juxtaposition indicator*
01 f **03** fol **04** fans, next **05** later, suite **06** circle, public **07** backers, backing, coterie, ensuing, patrons, retinue, sequent, support **08** admirers, audience, secundum **09** adherents, clientèle, entourage, favorable, followers, hereunder, patronage, resulting **10** consequent, favourable, subsequent, succeeding, succession, successive, supporters **13** body of support
• **following pages**
02 ff

folly
03 sin **04** whim **05** folie, moria, tower **06** gazebo, idiocy, lunacy, vanity **07** foolery, foppery, idiotcy, inanity, madness **08** insanity, monument, nonsense, rashness **09** absurdity, belvedere, craziness, silliness, stupidity **10** imbecility, imprudence **11** fatuousness, foolishness **12** illogicality, indiscretion, recklessness **13** foolhardiness, ludicrousness, senselessness **14** ridiculousness

foment

04 brew, goad, spur **05** raise, rouse
06 arouse, excite, foster, incite, kindle,
prompt, stir up, whip up, work up
07 agitate, promote, provoke, quicken
08 activate, incubate **09** encourage,
instigate, stimulate

fond

03 hot, try **04** daft, dote, vain, warm
05 basis, naive **06** absurd, caring,
doting, keen on, liking, loving, nuts on,
spoony, tender **07** adoring, amatory,
amorous, attempt, deluded, devoted,
foolish, proceed **08** hooked on, mad
about **09** credulous, daft about,
indulgent, nuts about, partial to
10 addicted to, attached to,
background, crazy about, dotty about,
foundation **11** enamoured of,
impractical **12** affectionate **14** over-
optimistic

fondle

03 hug, pat, pet **05** grope **06** caress,
cocker, cosset, cuddle, dandle, stroke
07 smuggle, touch up

fondly

06 warmly **08** lovingly, tenderly
09 amorously **14** affectionately
• **speak fondly**
03 coo **04** bill

fondness

04 love **05** fancy, taste **06** dotage,
liking, tender, tendre **07** leaning
08 devotion, kindness, penchant, soft
spot, weakness **09** affection,
engoûment, tendresse **10** attachment,
engouement, enthusiasm, partiality,
preference, tenderness, well-liking
11 inclination **12** predilection
14 susceptibility

font

08 bénitier, delubrum

food

03 kai **04** chow, diet, dish, eats, fare,
feed, feud, grub, meal, menu, nosh,
tack, tuck **05** board, meals, scoff,
scran, table **06** fodder, kaikai, staple,
stores, tucker, viands **07** aliment,
cooking, cuisine, pabulum, pasture,
rations **08** delicacy, eatables, victuals
09 nutriment, nutrition, provender,
repasture **10** foodstuffs, provisions,
speciality, sustenance **11** comestibles,
nourishment, subsistence
12 refreshments

03 dal, dip, ham, pie, poi
04 dhal, eddo, flan, fool, hash, luau,
mash, olio, olla, pâté, rice, soss,
soup, stew, taco, tart, tofu, wrap
05 balti, bhaji, boxty, brose, broth,
champ, chips, crêpe, curry, daube,
dolma, grits, gumbo, jelly, kebab,
kofta, laksa, latke, pasta, pasty,
pesto, pilau, pizza, Quorn®, roast,
salad, salmi, salsa, satay, sauce,
sushi, tapas, tikka, toast
06 bhajee, borsch, burger, canapé,
caviar, cheese, cookie, faggot,

fajita, fondue, fu yung, gratin,
haggis, hotpot, hummus, kipper,
mousse, paella, pakora, panini,
pastry, pilaff, quiche, ragout,
samosa, scampi, sorbet, tahina,
tamale, trifle, waffle
07 biryani, biscuit, borscht, burrito,
chowder, chutney, cobbler,
compote, cracker, crowdie,
crumble, fajitas, falafel, felafel,
fritter, friture, galette, gnocchi,
goulash, gravlax, lasagne, oatcake,
pancake, pavlova, polenta,
pudding, rarebit, risotto, rissole,
sashimi, sausage, seafood, soufflé,
stir fry, stovies, tempura, terrine,
timbale, tostada
08 barbecue, biriyani, calamari, chop
suey, chow mein, cocktail, coleslaw,
consommé, coq au vin, couscous,
dolmades, dumpling, fishcake,
fricasee, gado-gado, gazpacho, ice
cream, kedgeree, meringue,
moussaka, nut roast, omelette,
porridge, pot-roast, raclette,
sandwich, souvlaki, syllabub,
tandoori, teriyaki, tortilla, turnover,
tzatziki, vindaloo, yakitori
09 casserole, cassoulet, charlotte,
colcannon, croquette, enchilada,
fricassée, galantine, gravadlax,
guacamole, Irish stew, jambalaya,
macedoine, meatballs, nut cutlet,
souvlakia, succotash, tabbouleh
10 blancmange, cannelloni,
cheesecake, corned beef, cottage
pie, enchiladas, fish-finger, fruit
salad, Greek salad, green salad,
minestrone, mixed grill,
peperonata, quesadilla,
salmagundi, salmagundy,
sauerkraut, spring roll, stroganoff
11 baba ganoush, caesar salad,
cockaleekie, French fries, fritto
misto, gefilte fish, potato salad,
ratatouille, rumblethump,
smorgasbord, vichyssoise, winter
salad
12 eggs Benedict, fish and chips,
mulligatawny, pease pudding,
rumblethumps, Russian salad,
shepherd's pie, taramasalata,
Waldorf salad, welsh rarebit
13 bouillabaisse, fisherman's pie,
prawn cocktail, salade niçoise,
toad-in-the-hole
14 chilli con carne, macaroni cheese,
pickled herring
15 bubble-and-squeak, Wiener
schnitzel

See also **bean**; **biscuit**; **bread**; **cake**;
cheese; **fruit**; **herb**; **meat**; **mushroom**;
nut; **pasta**; **pastry**; **sauce**; **sausage**;
sweet; **vegetable**

03 KFC®
04 taco, wrap
05 bagel, chips, donut, fries, kebab,
pizza
06 Big Mac®, burger, hot dog,
nachos

07 burrito, chalupa, falafel, noodles,
shwarma, Whopper®
08 doughnut, sandwich
09 bacon roll, chip butty, hamburger,
Happy Meal®, milkshake
10 beanburger, beefburger, doner
kebab, fish 'n' chips, fish supper,
onion rings, shish kebab
11 bacon burger, baked potato, French
fries, sausage roll
12 cheeseburger, chicken wings, club
sandwich, fish and chips, tortilla
wrap, veggie burger
13 chicken burger, sausage supper
14 chicken nuggets, quarter pounder

See also **restaurant**

• **provide food**
05 cater

fool

04 goof, hoax, jest, joke **05** bluff,
cheat, feign, tease, trick **06** delude,
diddle, have on, play up, take in, trifle
07 beguile, carry on, deceive, mislead,
pretend, swindle **08** hoodwink
09 bamboozle, lark about, mess
about, play about **10** mess around, play
around, play tricks **11** horse around,
monkey about, string along **12** monkey
around, put one over on

02 bf
03 ass, auf, con, fon, git, kid, mug, nit,
nut, oik, sap, sot, yap
04 berk, bête, bozo, burk, butt, cake,
calf, clot, cony, coof, coot, cuif, dill,
dope, dork, dupe, geek, goat, goof,
goon, goop, gouk, gowk, gull,
gump, hash, jerk, kook, loon, lump,
lunk, muck, mutt, nana, nerd, nerk,
nong, ouph, poop, prat, punk, putz,
sham, shmo, simp, soft, tony, twit,
yo-yo
05 chump, clown, cluck, comic, coney,
divvy, droll, dumbo, dunce, dweeb,
eejit, galah, idiot, moron, neddy,
nelly, ninny, patch, patsy, prick,
purée, schmo, snipe, softy, twerp,
wally
06 bampot, bauble, cretin, dimwit,
donkey, doofus, dottle, drongo,
dum-dum, jester, josser, madcap,
monkey, motley, muppet, nitwit,
nutter, sawney, schmoe, stooge,
sucker, turkey, wallie, wigeon, Yorick
07 airhead, barmpot, bourder,
buffoon, Charley, Charlie, dingbat,
fat-head, God's ape, gubbins,
halfwit, haverel, jackass, jughead,
lemming, muggins, pillock, plonker,
saphead, tomfool, want-wit,
wazzock, widgeon
08 boofhead, dipstick, flathead,
fondling, Fred Nerk, imbecile, Jack-
fool, lunkhead, merryman,
mooncalf, omadhaun, shlemiel,
Tom-noddy, Trinculo
09 April fool, birdbrain, blockhead,
capocchia, chipochia, cloth head,
court fool, dumb-cluck, ignoramus,
joculator, lack-brain, lamebrain,

mumchance, philander, schlemiel, schlemihl, simpleton
10 head-banger, nincompoop, silly-billy, Touchstone
11 chowderhead, knuckle-head,
13 laughing-stock, poisson d'avril, proper Charlie

• **play the fool**
03 fon **04** daff **07** act dido **09** fool about, mess about, muck about **10** act the fool, fool around, mess around, muck around **11** clown around, horse around **12** monkey around

foolery
05 farce, folly, larks **06** antics, capers, pranks **07** carry-on, daffing, fooling, waggery, zanyism **08** clowning, drollery, mischief, nonsense, trumpery **09** high jinks, horseplay, silliness **10** buffoonery, tomfoolery **11** shenanigans **12** childishness, monkey tricks **14** practical jokes

foolhardiness
08 boldness, rashness **10** imprudence **12** recklessness **13** impulsiveness

foolhardy
04 bold, rash **06** daring **08** kamikaze, reckless **09** daredevil, imprudent, impulsive **10** ill-advised, incautious **11** temerarious **13** irresponsible

foolish
◇ anagram indicator
03 mad, twp **04** daft, dumb, fond, fool **05** barmy, batty, crazy, dilly, divvy, doilt, dotty, glaik, goofy, inane, inept, nutty, potty, seely, silly, wacky **06** absurd, doiled, dottle, insane, paltry, simple, stupid, unwise **07** dottled, étourdi, fatuous, glaiket, glaikit, goatish, gudgeon, idiotic, moronic, peevish, risible, sottish, tomfool, unwitty, vacuous **08** étourdie, gormless, ignorant, imbecile, overfond **09** half-baked, idiotical, ill-judged, ludicrous, pointless, senseless **10** half-witted, idle-headed, ill-advised, pea-brained, ridiculous **11** hare-brained, injudicious, nonsensical **12** crack-brained, short-sighted, simple-minded, unreasonable **13** cockle-brained, ill-considered, out of your mind, rattle-brained, unintelligent

foolishly
◇ anagram indicator
05 fonly, madly **06** daftly **07** crazily, ineptly, wackily **08** absurdly, stupidly, unwisely **09** fatuously, shallowly **10** mistakenly **11** idiotically, imprudently, senselessly **12** ill-advisedly, incautiously, indiscreetly, ridiculously **13** injudiciously **14** short-sightedly

foolishness
03 rot **04** bunk, crap **05** balls, bilge, folly **06** bunkum, lunacy, piffle **07** baloney, foolery, hogwash, inanity, madness, rubbish **08** claptrap, cobblers, daftness, nonsense, unreason, unwisdom, weakness

09 absurdity, craziness, incaution, meshugaas, mishegaas, niaiserie, poppycock, silliness, stupidity **10** imprudence, ineptitude **12** indiscretion **13** senselessness

foolproof
04 safe, sure **07** certain **08** fail-safe, sure-fire **09** unfailing **10** dependable, guaranteed, idiot-proof, infallible **11** trustworthy

foot
01 f **02** ft **03** end, leg, pad, paw, pes, toe **04** base, heel, hoof, kick, sole **05** dance, limit, paeon **06** border, bottom, dactyl, far end, iambus, tarsus **07** anapest, paeonic, pyrrhic, spondee, tootsie, trochee, trotter **08** anapaest, bacchius, choriamb, dochmius, molossus, tribrach **09** extremity **10** amphibrach, amphimacer, choriambus, foundation **12** antibacchius, tootsy-wootsy

• **discomfort of foot**
04 corn

• **division of foot**
04 inch

• **model of foot**
04 last

• **part of foot**
03 toe **04** arch, vola **06** instep

football
02 RL, RU **04** camp **06** soccer

See also **American football**; **Australian football**

15 Bayer Leverkusen, Red Star Belgrade, Steaua Bucharest

02 O's, R's, U's
03 Ton
04 Bees, Boro, City, Dale, Dons, Gers, Jags, Owls, Pars, Pool, Posh, Rams, Reds, Sons, Well
05 Arabs, Bhoys, Binos, Blues, Foxes, Gills, Gulls, Hoops, Irons, Lions, Loons, Shire, Spurs, Stags, Swans, Villa, Wasps
06 Accies, Albion, Bairns, Blades, County, Eagles, Fifers, Hibees, Jambos, Killie, Latics, Pompey, Robins, Rovers, Royals, Saints, Tigers, United, Whites, Wolves
07 Addicks, Baggies, Bantams, Buddies, Clarets, Glovers, Gunners, Hammers, Hatters, Hornets, Magpies, Pirates, Potters, Quakers, Red Imps, Shakers, Silkmen, Spiders, Terrors, Toffees, Villans
08 Blue Toon, Bully Wee, Canaries, Cherries, Citizens, Cobblers, Diamonds, Filberts, Harriers, Jam Tarts, Mariners, Pilgrims, Saddlers, Seagulls, Sky Blues, Terriers, Trotters, Valiants, Villains, Warriors
09 Black Cats, Bluebirds, Borderers, Chairboys, Cottagers, Cumbrians, Dark Blues, Honest Men, Red Devils, Seasiders, Shrimpers, Spireites, Throstles, Toffeemen, Wee Rovers
10 Blue Brazil, Doonhamers, Light Blues, Lilywhites, Livvy Lions, Minstermen, Railwaymen, Tangerines, Teddy Bears
11 Gable Endies, Red Lichties, Tractor Boys
12 Caley Thistle, Merry Millers
13 Blue and Whites
14 Black and Whites

03 box, cap, lob, net
04 back, dive, foul, goal, half, head, hole, loan, mark, pass, post, save, shot, trap, wall, wing
05 bench, chest, pitch
06 assist, corner, double, futsal, goalie, handle, header, keeper, libero, nutmeg, one-two, soccer, tackle, treble, volley, winger
07 booking, caution, dribble, far post, forward, kick-off, offside, own goal, penalty, red card, referee, stopper, sweeper, throw-in, whistle
08 back heel, crossbar, dead ball, defender, free kick, friendly, full back, goal kick, goal line, half time, hand ball, hat-trick, left back, linesman, midfield, near post, outfield, play-offs, set piece, transfer, wall pass, wingback
09 extra time, five-a-side, formation, give-and-go, goalmouth, promotion, right back, touchline
10 centre back, centre half, centre spot, corner flag, corner kick,

goalkeeper, golden goal, half volley, injury time, man marking, midfielder, off-the-ball, penalty box, possession, relegation, sending off, silver goal, substitute, suspension
11 bicycle kick, half-way line, keepie-uppie, obstruction, offside trap, penalty area, penalty kick, penalty spot, six-yard area, straight red, time wasting
12 back-pass rule, Bosman ruling, centre circle, overhead kick, stoppage time
13 centre forward, dangerous play, technical area
14 fourth official, goal difference, relegation zone
15 eighteen-yard box

footballer

03 Fry (Charles Burgess), Law (Denis)
04 Best (George), Dean (Dixie), Didi, Figo (Luis), Hall (Sir John), Owen (Michael), Pelé, Rush (Ian), Zico, Zoff (Dino)
05 Adams (Tony), Banks (Gordon), Busby (Sir Matt), Carey (Johnny), Giggs (Ryan), Greig (John), Henry (Thierry), Hurst (Sir Geoff), James (Alex), Moore (Bobby), Revie (Don), Rimet (Jules), Rossi (Paolo), Stein (Jock), Young (George)
06 Baggio (Roberto), Baresi (Franco), Barnes (John), Baxter (Jim), Bosman (Jean-Marc), Clough (Brian), Cruyff (Johann), Finney (Sir Tom), Ginola (David), Graham (George), Gullit (Ruud), Haynes (Johnny), Hoddle (Glenn), Keegan (Kevin), Lawton (Tommy), McColl (Robert Smyth), McStay (Paul), Mercer (Joe), Morton (Alan Lauder), Müller (Gerd), Puskas (Ferenc), Ramsey (Sir Alf), Robson (Sir Bobby), Robson (Bryan), Rooney (Wayne), Seaman (David), Stiles (Nobby), St John (Ian), Walker (Tommy), Wenger (Arsene), Wright (Billy), Wright (Ian), Yashin (Lev), Zidane (Zinedine)
07 Ardiles (Osvaldo), Beckham (David), Bremner (Billy), Butcher (Terry), Cantona (Eric), Charles (John), DiCanio (Paolo), Eastham (George), Edwards (Duncan), Eusebio (Silva), Greaves (Jimmy), Lineker (Gary), Macleod (Ally), Mannion (Wilfred), McCoist (Ally), McNeill (Billy), Paisley (Bob), Platini (Michel), Rivaldo, Ronaldo, Shankly (Bill), Shearer (Alan), Shilton (Peter), Souness (Graeme), Toshack (John), Waddell (Willie)
08 Bergkamp (Dennis), Charlton (Sir Bobby), Charlton (Jack), Dalglish (Kenny), Docherty (Tommy), Ferguson (Sir Alex), Fontaine (Just), Harkness (Jack), Jennings (Pat), Johnston (Maurice), Maradona

(Diego), Matthaus (Lothar), Matthews (Sir Stanley), Mourinho (José), Nicholls (Sir Douglas Ralph), Rivelino (Roberto)
09 Batistuta (Gabriel), Collymore (Stan), DiStefano (Alfredo), Garrincha, Gascoigne (Paul 'Gazza'), Greenwood (Ron), Johnstone (Jimmy), Klinsmann (Jurgen), Lofthouse (Nat), Van Basten (Marco)
10 Schmeichel (Peter)
11 Beckenbauer (Franz)
12 Blanchflower (Danny)

• **footballers**
02 FA **03** SFA

footing
04 base, cost, grip, rank, trod **05** basis, coast, coste, dance, grade, state, terms, track, tread, troad, trode **06** ground, status, troade **07** balance, support, surface **08** foothold, position, roothold, standing **09** relations **10** conditions, foundation **12** relationship

footling
05 minor, petty **06** paltry **07** trivial **08** piffling, trifling **10** irrelevant **13** insignificant

footloose
04 free **09** available, fancy-free **10** unattached, uninvolved **11** uncommitted

footnote
04 note **05** gloss **07** comment, subtext **08** scholium **10** annotation, commentary, marginalia **12** marginal note

footnotes
04 note **05** gloss **07** scholia **10** annotation, commentary, marginalia **12** marginal note

footprint
03 pad, pug **04** mark, seal, step **05** prick, spoor, trace, track, trail, tread **07** ichnite, vestige **08** footmark, footstep **09** ichnolite **13** ornithichnite

footprints
04 slot

footstep
04 plod, step **05** track, tramp, tread **06** trudge **08** footfall, footmark

footwear

03 dap, tie
04 boot, clog, geta, mule, pump, shoe, vibs
05 jelly, sabot, tacky, thong, wader, welly
06 bootee, brogue, casual, galosh, lace-up, loafer, Oxford, patten, sandal, slip-on
07 gumboot, slipper, sneaker, tap shoe, trainer
08 boat shoe, deck shoe, flip-flop, jazz shoe, Mary Jane, moccasin,

overshoe, pantofle, plimsoll, snow-shoe
09 court shoe, Derry boot, rugby boot, slingback, wedge heel
10 ballet shoe, combat boot, Doc Martens®, espadrille, hiking-boot, kitten-heel, riding boot, tennis shoe
11 bowling shoe, Chelsea boot, Hush Puppies®, walking boot
12 climbing boot, football boot, platform heel, stiletto heel
13 beetle-crusher
14 beetle-crushers, brothel creeper, wellington boot
15 brothel-creepers

See also **boot; clothes, clothing**

fop
04 beau, dude, toff **05** dandy, swell **07** coxcomb, peacock **08** muscadin, popinjay, skipjack **09** exquisite, fantastic **10** Jack-a-dandy **11** petit maître **12** barber-monger

foppish
04 vain **05** apish, natty **06** dainty, dapper, dressy, fallal, la-di-da, spruce **07** fangled, finical **08** affected, dandyish, preening, swellish **09** coxcombic, dandified, fantastic **10** coxcomical **11** coxcombical, fantastical, overdressed

for
03 pro

forage
04 feed, food, guar, hunt, loot, prog, raid, seek **05** étape, foray, scour **06** fodder, invade, ladino, ravage, search **07** assault, pickeer, plunder, ransack, rummage, scratch **08** mung bean, scavenge **09** cast about, gama grass, pasturage, provender **10** foodstuffs, provisions

foray
04 raid **05** sally, swoop **06** attack, creach, creagh, forray, inroad, ravage, sortie **07** assault, attempt, journey, spreagh, venture **08** invasion **09** incursion, offensive **14** reconnaissance

forbear
04 hold, omit, stay, stop **05** avoid, cease, pause **06** desist, eschew **07** abstain, decline, refrain **08** ancestor, hesitate, hold back, keep from, withhold

forbearance
05 mercy **06** pardon **08** clemency, leniency, mildness, patience **09** avoidance, endurance, restraint, tolerance **10** abstinence, indulgence, indulgency, moderation, refraining, self-denial, sufferance, temperance, toleration **11** longanimity, resignation, self-control **13** long-suffering

forbearing
04 easy, mild **07** clement, lenient, patient **08** merciful, moderate, tolerant **09** forgiving, indulgent **10** restrained **13** long-suffering **14** self-controlled

forbid
03 ban, bar **04** deny, tabu, veto, warn **05** block, debar, taboo **06** defend, enjoin, forsay, hinder, not let, outlaw, refuse **07** exclude, foresay, forwarn, inhibit, prevent, rule out **08** disallow, forewarn, forspeak, not allow, preclude, prohibit, restrain **09** blacklist, discharge, forespeak, interdict, proscribe **13** excommunicate **14** contraindicate

forbidden
02 nl **04** tabu, tapu, tref **05** not on, taboo, trefa, treif **06** banned, vetoed **07** illicit, profane **08** debarred, defended, excluded, outlawed, unlawful, verboten **10** contraband, prohibited, proscribed, restrained **11** out of bounds

forbidding
04 grim **05** harsh, stern **06** severe **07** awesome, hostile, ominous **08** daunting, menacing, sinister **09** repulsive **10** Acherontic, foreboding, formidable, off-putting, unfriendly, uninviting **11** frightening, hard-grained, prohibitory, threatening **15** unprepossessing

force
◊ *anagram indicator*
01 F **02** od **03** put, vis, zap **04** army, body, care, cops, dint, gist, make, odyl, pull, push, sway, unit, urge **05** blast, bully, corps, crack, drive, exact, group, impel, might, odyle, power, press, prise, sense, squad, stuff, troop, wrest, wring **06** coerce, compel, duress, dynamo, effort, energy, extort, impose, lean on, muscle, oblige, patrol, propel, ravish, stress, strive, thrust, vigour, wrench **07** cogency, essence, extract, impetus, impulse, inflict, meaning, passion, platoon, stamina **08** armament, bulldoze, coercion, division, dynamism, emphasis, exertion, momentum, pressure, railroad, regiment, squadron, strength, validity, vehement, violence, vitality **09** battalion, break open, constrain, force open, influence, intensity, necessity, pressgang, substance, the screws, vehemence, waterfall **10** aggression, compulsion, constraint, detachment, pressurize **11** arm-twisting, enforcement **12** significance **13** determination, effectiveness, put pressure on **14** persuasiveness, put the screws on, the third degree

See also **army; police**

• in force
05 valid **07** binding, current, working **08** in crowds, in droves, in flocks **09** effective, operative **10** in strength **11** functioning, in operation **14** in great numbers, in large numbers

forced
◊ *anagram indicator*
02 sf **03** sfz **05** false, stiff **06** wooden **07** binding, feigned, stilted **08** affected, enforced, laboured,

overdone, sforzato, strained **09** compelled, contrived, excessive, insincere, mandatory, sforzando, unnatural **10** artificial, compulsory, far-fetched, non-natural, obligatory **11** constrained, involuntary

forceful
05 gutty, valid **06** cogent, mighty, potent, strong, urgent **07** dynamic, telling, weighty **08** emphatic, forcible, powerful, vehement, vigorous **09** assertive, effective, energetic **10** compelling, convincing, impressive, persuasive **11** high-powered **12** high-pressure

forcefully
07 con brio **08** strongly **10** powerfully, vehemently, vigorously **11** assertively, effectively **12** convincingly, emphatically, persuasively **13** energetically

forcible
04 vive **05** pithy **06** cogent, forced, mighty, potent, strong **07** by force, drastic, marrowy, telling, violent, weighty **08** coercive, forceful, powerful, vehement **09** effective, energetic **10** aggressive, compelling, compulsory, impressive, using force **11** energetical

forcibly
03 out **04** hard **07** by force **09** vi et armis, violently **10** using force, vehemently, vigorously, willy-nilly **11** under duress **12** compulsorily, emphatically, obligatorily **15** against your will, under compulsion

ford
04 rack, wade **05** drift **06** Model T **08** causeway, crossing **09** tin lizzie **11** Irish bridge **13** crossing place

forebear
06 father, tupuna **08** ancestor **10** antecedent, forefather, forerunner, progenitor **11** predecessor **12** primogenitor

foreboding
04 fear, omen, sign **05** dread, token, worry **06** hoodoo **07** anxiety, feeling, presage, warning **09** abodement, intuition, misgiving, suspicion **10** prediction, sixth sense **11** premonition **12** apprehension, presentiment **15** prognostication

forecast
03 tip **04** omen, perm **05** augur, guess **06** augury, divine, expect, tip off **07** foresee, metcast, outlook, portend, predict, presage, project **08** estimate, foretell, forewarn, prophecy, prophesy **09** calculate, prognosis **10** anticipate, conjecture, prediction, projection **11** calculation, expectation, extrapolate, forewarning, guesstimate, permutation, second-guess, speculation **13** extrapolation, prognosticate, weather report **15** prognostication

See also **shipping**

forefather
06 father **08** ancestor, forebear
10 ancestress, antecedent, forerunner, progenitor **11** predecessor
12 primogenitor

forefront
03 van **04** fore, head, lead **05** front
06 vaward **08** vanguard **09** front line, spearhead **10** avant-garde, firing line
11 leading edge **15** leading position

forego, forgo
05 leave, waive, yield **06** abjure, eschew, give up, pass up, resign
07 abandon, forfeit, precede
08 renounce **09** do without, go without, sacrifice, surrender
10 relinquish **11** abstain from, refrain from

foregoing
05 above, prior **06** former **07** earlier
08 previous **09** aforesaid, precedent, preceding **10** antecedent
14 aforementioned

foregone
• **foregone conclusion**
04 fact **09** certainty, sure thing
10 inevitable **13** inevitability

foreground
04 fore **05** front **06** centre
09 forefront, limelight **10** prominence
15 leading position

forehead
04 brow **05** front **06** metope, temple
07 temples **08** audacity
10 confidence

foreign
◇ *anagram indicator*
◇ *foreign word indicator*
03 odd **05** alien, fraim, fremd
06 ethnic, exotic, forane, forren, fremit
07 distant, faraway, migrant, outside, strange, unknown **08** borrowed, étranger, exterior, external, imported, overseas, peculiar **09** barbarian, étrangère, extrinsic, immigrant
10 extraneous, forinsecal, outlandish, tramontane, unfamiliar
11 unconnected **12** adventitious
13 international
See also **nationality**

foreigner
05 alien **06** gaijin, taipan **07** incomer, visitor **08** étranger, newcomer, outsider, stranger **09** Ausländer, barbarian, étrangère, immigrant, outlander, uitlander **10** tramontane

foreknowledge
09 foresight, prevision **10** prescience
11 forewarning, premonition, second sight **12** clairvoyance, precognition
15 prognostication

foreleg
04 gamb

foreman
04 bo's'n, boss **05** bosun **06** gaffer, ganger, honcho, induna, leader
07 manager, overman, steward,

topsman **08** gangsman, overseer
09 boatswain, straw boss
10 chancellor, charge hand, supervisor
14 superintendent

foremost
◇ *head selection indicator*
03 top, van **04** main **05** chief, first, front, prime **07** central, highest, leading, premier, primary, supreme, up front **08** advanced, cardinal, vanguard **09** paramount, principal, uppermost **10** pre-eminent **13** most important

foreordained
05 fated **08** destined **09** appointed, predevote **10** foredoomed
11 prearranged, predestined, preordained **12** predestinate
13 predetermined

forerunner
04 omen, sign **05** envoy, token
06 herald **08** ancestor **09** harbinger, messenger, precurrer, precursor
10 antecedent, forefather
11 forewarning, predecessor **12** vaunt-courier
• **be a forerunner**
04 lead, pace

foresee
06 divine, expect, prevue **07** predict, preview, previse **08** envisage, forebode, forecast, foreknow, foretell, prophesy **10** anticipate
13 prognosticate

foreshadow
04 bode, mean, type **05** augur
06 signal **07** portend, predict, presage, promise, signify, suggest **08** indicate, prophesy **09** adumbrate, forepoint, prefigure **13** prognosticate

foreshore
04 hard

foresight
04 care **06** vision **07** caution
08 forecast, planning, prudence
09 prevision, provision, readiness
10 precaution, prescience, providence
11 discernment, forethought, prospection **12** anticipation, perspicacity, preparedness
13 judiciousness **14** circumspection, discrimination, far-sightedness
15 forward planning

forest
04 bosk, wood **05** Arden, trees, woods **06** rustic, sylvan, timber
07 boscage **08** Sherwood, tree farm, woodland **09** backwoods

Forests and woods include:
04 bush, gapó
05 brush, igapò, monte, selva, taiga, urman
06 boreal, jungle, mallee, maquis, pinery
07 coastal, garigue, lowland, macchie, wetland
08 caatinga, garrigue, littoral, mangrove

09 broadleaf, chaparral, deciduous, evergreen, greenwood, temperate
10 coniferous, equatorial, peat forest, plantation, rainforest
11 cloud forest, heath forest, lignum-scrub, lignum-swamp, mallee scrub, moist forest
12 vàrzea forest
13 ancient forest, gallery forest, mangrove swamp, savanna forest
14 moist evergreen

forestall
03 bar **04** balk, beat, stop **05** avert, lurch, parry **06** hinder, impede, thwart
07 head off, obviate, pre-empt, prevent, ward off **08** obstruct, preclude, stave off **09** frustrate, intercept **10** anticipate, get ahead of
11 second-guess

forested
05 bosky **06** wooded **12** reafforested

forester
06 foster, walker **08** woodsman

forestry
09 woodcraft **10** dendrology
11 forestation, woodmanship
12 silviculture, sylviculture
13 afforestation, arboriculture

foretaste
05 whiff **06** prevue, sample, taster
07 earnest, example, pre-echo, preview, trailer, warning **08** antepast, specimen **09** appetizer, avant-goût, foretoken **10** anticipate, indication
11 forewarning, prelibation, premonition **12** anticipation, pregustation

foretell
04 bode, spae **05** augur, write
06 divine **07** bespeak, foresay, foresee, predict, presage, signify
08 forebode, forecast, foreread, forewarn, indicate, prophesy, soothsay
10 foreshadow **13** prognosticate

forethought
07 caution **08** planning, prudence
09 foresight, provision **10** precaution
11 discernment, preparation
12 anticipation, perspicacity
13 judiciousness **14** circumspection, far-sightedness **15** forward planning

forever
02 ay **03** aye **04** ever **06** always **07** à jamais, for good **08** evermore
09 endlessly, eternally **10** all the time, constantly, for all time **11** continually, incessantly, permanently, perpetually
12 interminably, persistently, till doomsday **13** everlastingly **15** till kingdom come

forewarn
04 warn **05** alert, weird **06** advise, forbid, tip off **07** apprise, caution, previse **08** admonish, dissuade **10** give notice, precaution **11** preadmonish

forewarning
06 tip-off **10** forerunner
11 premonition **12** early warning

13 advance notice 14 advance warning

foreword
07 preface, prelims 08 prologue 11 frontmatter 12 introduction, prolegomenon

forfeit
04 fine, lose, loss 05 cheat, forgo 06 forego, give up, pass up, sconce 07 abandon, damages, penalty 08 hand over, renounce 09 sacrifice, surrender 10 amercement, confiscate, relinquish, rue-bargain 12 confiscation 13 sequestration 14 relinquishment

forfeiture
04 loss 07 escheat 08 forgoing, giving up 09 attainder, déchéance, foregoing, sacrifice, surrender 12 confiscation 13 sequestration 14 relinquishment

forge
◇ *anagram indicator*
04 cast, copy, fake, form, make, tilt, work 05 build, feign, found, frame, mould, shape, smith 06 create, devise, invent, smithy, stithy 07 beat out, falsify, fashion, imitate, stiddie 08 simulate 09 construct, hammer out 11 counterfeit, put together, rivet hearth 13 beat into shape
• **forge ahead**
07 advance 08 progress 09 go forward 11 make headway, move forward, push forward 12 make progress, move steadily

forged
◇ *anagram indicator*
04 fake, sham 05 bogus, faked, false, pseud, snide 06 copied, phoney, pirate, pseudo 07 feigned, simular 08 borrowed, spurious 09 imitation, pretended, simulated 10 artificial, fraudulent 11 counterfect, counterfeit

forger
05 faker 06 coiner, framer 09 contriver, falsifier 10 fabricator 13 counterfeiter

forgery
03 dud 04 copy, fake, sham 05 fraud 06 deceit, faking, phoney 07 replica 09 imitation 11 counterfeit, falsi crimen 12 reproduction 13 falsification 14 counterfeiting 15 counterfeisance, counterfesaunce

forget
04 fail, omit, wipe 05 dry up 06 corpse, ignore 07 dismiss, let slip, neglect, unlearn 08 not place, overlook, put aside 09 disregard 11 disremember, leave behind, lose sight of, misremember 12 put behind you, slip your mind 13 think no more of 14 fail to remember
• **forget yourself**
09 be naughty, misbehave 11 behave badly

forgetful
03 lax 06 dreamy, remiss 08 careless, heedless 09 negligent, oblivious, unheeding 10 abstracted, distracted, neglectful 11 inattentive, not all there, preoccupied 12 absent-minded 14 scatterbrained

forgetfulness
05 lapse 07 amnesia, laxness, neglect 08 oblivion 10 dreaminess 11 abstraction, inattention 12 carelessness, heedlessness, obliviscence 13 obliviousness, woolgathering

forgivable
05 minor, petty 06 slight, venial 08 innocent, trifling 09 excusable 10 condonable, pardonable

forgive
05 clear, remit, spare 06 acquit, excuse, let off, pardon 07 absolve, condone, let it go 08 overlook 09 exculpate, exonerate, shake on it 10 shake hands 13 think no more of 14 bury the hatchet

forgiveness
05 mercy 06 excuse, pardon 07 amnesty 08 clemency, leniency, oblivion 09 acquittal, remission 10 absolution, misericord 11 condonation, exoneration, misericorde

forgiving
04 kind, mild 06 humane 07 clement, lenient, pitying 08 merciful, placable, tolerant 09 indulgent, remissive 10 forbearing 11 magnanimous, softhearted 13 compassionate

forgo *see* **forego, forgo**

forgotten
04 gone, lost, past 06 buried, bygone 07 ignored, omitted 09 neglected, oblivious, out of mind 10 blotted out, in the shade, left behind, overlooked, past recall, unrecalled 11 disregarded, obliterated, unretrieved 12 unremembered 13 irrecoverable, irretrievable 15 in the wilderness

fork
01 Y 04 part 05 grain, graip, prong, spear, split, twist 06 branch, crotch, divide 07 diverge, furcate, toaster 08 division, junction, separate 09 bifurcate, branching, branch off, furcation, tormenter, tormentor 10 divaricate, divergence, separation 11 bifurcation 12 divarication, intersection, toasting iron 14 go separate ways
• **fork out**
03 pay 04 give 05 pay up 06 pony up 07 cough up, stump up 08 shell out

forked
05 split, tined 06 furcal 07 divided, furcate, pronged, Y-shaped 08 biramous, branched, furcated, furcular 09 bifurcate, branching, deceitful, forficate, insincere, separated 10 trifurcate 11 divaricated

forlorn
◇ *anagram indicator*
03 sad 04 lost 06 bereft, lonely 07 unhappy 08 deserted, desolate, forsaken, helpless, homeless, hopeless, pathetic, pitiable, wretched 09 abandoned, cheerless, desperate, destitute, forgotten, miserable, neglected 10 despairing, drearisome, friendless, uncared-for 12 disconsolate

forlornly
05 sadly 06 in vain 09 miserably, to no avail, unhappily 10 hopelessly 11 desperately, pointlessly 12 despondently 14 unsuccessfully

form
◇ *anagram indicator*
03 cut, set 04 cast, face, grow, kind, make, mode, rite, sort, trim, turn, type, year 05 bench, build, class, forge, found, frame, genre, genus, grade, guise, model, mould, order, paper, set up, shape, sheet, style, usage 06 appear, beauty, create, custom, design, devise, draw up, fettle, figure, format, health, line up, make up, manner, nature, ritual, show up, stream, system 07 acquire, arrange, compose, develop, fashion, fitness, manners, outline, pattern, produce, serve as, species, spirits, variety 08 assemble, ceremony, comprise, conceive, contrive, document, organize, planning, protocol 09 be a part of, behaviour, character, condition, construct, establish, etiquette, formation, formulate, framework, structure, take shape 10 appearance, constitute, convention, regularity, silhouette 11 application, arrangement, crystallize, description, disposition, manufacture, materialize, put together 12 construction, organization, the done thing 13 become visible, configuration, manifestation, questionnaire 15 application form, correct practice, polite behaviour

formal
03 dry, set 04 prim, sane 05 aloof, exact, fixed, rigid, stiff 06 proper, pusser, remote, ritual, solemn, starch, strict 07 correct, ordered, orderly, outward, precise, regular, starchy, stately, stilted 08 academic, approved, arranged, black tie, literary, methodic, official, orthodox, reserved, standard 09 customary, essential, organized, unbending 10 ceremonial, controlled, inflexible, methodical, prescribed 11 ceremonious, established, perfunctory, punctilious, ritualistic, strait-laced, symmetrical, traditional 12 conventional

formality
03 ice 04 form, rite, rule 06 custom, ritual, starch 07 decorum, red tape, wiggery 08 ceremony, pedantry, protocol 09 etiquette, procedure, propriety, punctilio, sociality, stiffness

10 convention, politeness
11 bureaucracy, correctness **12** matter of form **13** spit and polish
15 ceremoniousness, conventionality

formalization
08 ordering **09** arranging
11 arrangement, structuring
12 arrangements, confirmation, organization **15** standardization, systematization

formalize
03 fix, set **05** order **06** affirm, ordain, ratify **07** arrange, confirm, stylize
08 organize **09** ritualize, structure
10 make formal, regularize
11 standardize, systematize **12** make official

formally
06 primly **07** exactly, rigidly
08 properly, ritually, solemnly
09 correctly, precisely **10** formaliter, inflexibly, officially **12** ceremonially, methodically **13** punctiliously
14 conventionally

format
03 GIF, PDF, PNG, RTF, ZIP **04** form, JPEG, look, plan, TIFF, type **05** order, shape, style **06** design, layout, make-up **07** pattern, tabloid **08** portrait
09 landscape, letterbox, structure
10 appearance, dimensions, widescreen **11** arrangement
12 construction, presentation
13 configuration

formation
04 make **05** order **06** design, figure, format, layout, make-up, making, series **07** pattern, phalanx, shaping
08 building, creation, founding, grouping, starting **09** emergence, structure **10** appearance, generation, production **11** arrangement, composition, development, disposition, institution, manufacture
12 constitution, construction, inauguration, organization
13 configuration, establishment

formative
06 creant, pliant **07** growing, guiding, plastic, shaping **08** dominant, moulding **09** malleable, mouldable, sensitive, teachable **11** controlling, determining, influential, susceptible
13 determinative, developmental
14 impressionable

former
02 ex- **03** old **04** auld, fore, late, once, onst, past **05** above, first, olden, prior
06 bygone, of yore, whilom
07 ancient, earlier, long ago, old-time, one-time, quondam **08** ci-devant, departed, long-gone, previous, pristine, sometime **09** erstwhile, foregoing, preceding **10** antecedent, historical **14** first-mentioned

formerly
04 erst, once, onst **05** as was, earst, of old **06** before **07** earlier, whilere
08 ci-devant, erewhile, hitherto,

sometime, while-ere **09** at one time, erstwhile, in the past, yesterday
10 heretofore, previously
12 historically **15** at an earlier time

formidable
04 huge **05** great, scary, stiff, stoor, stour, sture **06** gorgon, no mean, shrewd, spooky, stowre **07** awesome, fearful, mammoth, onerous
08 alarming, colossal, daunting, dreadful, horrific, menacing, powerful, terrific **09** frightful, leviathan
10 horrifying, impressive, prodigious, staggering, terrifying, tremendous
11 challenging, frightening, mind-blowing, redoubtable, threatening
12 intimidating, overwhelming

formidably
07 awfully **09** fearfully **10** dreadfully, menacingly, shockingly **11** frightfully
12 horrifically, tremendously
14 overwhelmingly

formless
05 vague **06** inform **07** chaotic
08 confused, inchoate, indigest, nebulous, unformed, unshaped
09 amorphous, shapeless
10 incoherent, indefinite
12 disorganized, invertebrate
13 indeterminate

formula
03 mix, way **04** code, form, rule
05 spell **06** method, recipe, rubric
07 precept, wording **08** equation, exorcism, fog index, proposal, protocol **09** blueprint, principle, procedure, technique **10** convention
12 prescription **13** set expression
15 fixed expression
• **Formula One** *see* **racing**

formulate
04 cast, form, plan **05** found, frame, state **06** create, define, design, detail, devise, draw up, evolve, invent, map out **07** compose, develop, express, formate, itemize, lay down, prepare, propose, put down, set down, specify, think up, work out **08** conceive
09 originate, symbolize **10** articulate

formulation
07 formula, framing, product
08 creating, devising **10** conception, definition, expression, production
11 composition, development, preparation **13** specification

fornication
06 affair **07** avoutry, liaison
08 adultery, cheating, idolatry **09** two-timing **10** flirtation, infidelity, unchastity **12** entanglement **13** a bit on the side, playing around
14 unfaithfulness **15** extramarital sex, playing the field

forsake
04 jilt, quit **05** chuck, ditch, forgo, leave, waive **06** desert, disown, forego, give up, reject **07** abandon, cast off, discard, forlese **08** jettison, renounce, set aside **09** destitute, repudiate,

surrender, throw over **10** relinquish
12 have done with **14** turn your back on **15** leave in the lurch

forsaken
04 lorn **06** dreary, jilted, lonely, remote
07 cast off, forlorn, ignored, outcast, shunned **08** derelict, deserted, desolate, disowned, isolated, lasslorn, lovelorn, marooned, rejected, solitary
09 abandoned, destitute, discarded, neglected **10** friendless
11 godforsaken **14** left in the lurch

forswear
03 lie **04** deny, drop, reny **05** forgo, renay, reney **06** abjure, cut out, disown, forego, give up, jack in, pack in, recant, reject, renege **07** abandon, disavow, forsake, retract **08** disclaim, renounce **09** do without, repudiate
15 perjure yourself

fort
02 Ft, pa **03** pah **04** camp, keep, rath
05 tower **06** castle, donjon, turret
07 citadel, parapet, redoubt, station
08 fortress, garrison, martello, pentagon **09** castellum
10 blockhouse, stronghold, watchtower **11** battlements
13 fortification, martello tower

forte
01 f **04** bent, gift, loud **05** skill
06 métier, talent **08** aptitude, strength
10 speciality **11** strong point

forth
02 on **03** off, out **04** away **05** furth
06 abroad, onward **07** forward, onwards, outside **08** forwards, into view **13** into existence

forthcoming
04 open **05** frank, on tap, ready
06 chatty, coming, direct, future
07 voluble **08** expected, friendly, imminent, sociable, upcoming
09 available, expansive, impending, projected, talkative **10** accessible, loquacious, obtainable, up for grabs **11** approaching, informative, in the offing, prospective
13 communicative **14** at your disposal, conversational

forthright
04 bold, open **05** blunt, frank, plain
06 at once, candid, direct, honest
07 up-front **09** outspoken, trenchand, trenchant **10** four-square **11** plain-spoken **15** straightforward

forthwith
03 eft **04** asap, away **06** at once, pronto **07** quickly **08** directly, eftsoons **09** instantly, right away
11 immediately **12** straightaway, there and then, without delay

fortification
08 munition **09** munitions
10 munifience, protection, stronghold **12** embattlement, entrenchment **13** reinforcement, strengthening

Fortifications include:

02 pa
03 pah
04 bawn, fort, gate, keep, laer, moat, wall
05 ditch, fence, hedge, limes, tower
06 abatis, castle, glacis, laager, sconce, trench, Vauban
07 barrier, bastion, bulwark, citadel, defence, flanker, moineau, outwork, parapet, pillbox, rampart, redoubt, sandbag
08 buttress, cavalier, fortress, outworks, palisade, stockade
09 barricade, earthwork, fieldwork, fortalice, gabionade, gatehouse, razor wire
10 barbed wire, bridgehead, fieldworks, trou de loup
11 battlements, buttressing, crémaillère
13 cheval-de-frise, Martello tower
14 motte-and-bailey
15 circumvallation, contravallation

fortify

04 fort, load, wall **05** boost, brace, cheer, cover, fence, guard, mound **06** buoy up, castle, defend, munify, munite, revive, secure **07** bulwark, hearten, protect, rampart, shore up, support, sustain **08** buttress, embattle, energize, entrench, garrison, intrench, reassure **09** encourage, reinforce **10** invigorate, strengthen

fortitude

04 grit, guts **05** nerve, pluck, spine **06** mettle, valour **07** bravery, courage **08** backbone, firmness, patience, stoicism, strength, tenacity **09** endurance, hardihood, willpower **10** resolution **11** forbearance **12** perseverance **13** determination **14** strength of mind

fortress

04 burg, fort, keep **05** guard, place, tower **06** casbah, castle, kasbah **07** alcázar, citadel, defence **08** bastille, fastness, garrison **09** fortalice **10** stronghold **11** battlements **13** fortification

fortuitous

05 fluky, lucky **06** casual, chance, random **09** arbitrary, fortunate, haphazard, unplanned **10** accidental, incidental, unexpected, unforeseen **12** providential **13** unintentional

fortuitously

07 luckily **08** at random, by chance, casually, randomly **11** arbitrarily, fortunately, haphazardly **12** accidentally, incidentally, unexpectedly **13** inadvertently **15** unintentionally

Fortuna

05 Tyche

fortunate

04 rich, well **05** canny, happy, lucky, seely **06** timely **07** blessed, well-off

08 favoured **09** fairytale, opportune, promising, well-timed **10** auspicious, convenient, favourable, felicitous, fortuitous, profitable, propitious, prosperous, successful **11** encouraging, flourishing **12** advantageous, providential

fortunately

07 happily, luckily **10** thankfully **12** conveniently **13** encouragingly **14** providentially

fortune

03 cup, hap, lot **04** bomb, doom, fall, fate, life, luck, mint, pile, seal, seel, seil, sele **05** means, speed **06** assets, befall, bundle, chance, estate, future, income, packet, riches, wealth **07** destiny, heiress, history, portion, success **08** accident, big bucks, opulence, position, property, treasure **09** affluence, condition, megabucks, situation, substance **10** experience, prosperity, providence **11** coincidence, possessions, serendipity **13** circumstances **14** state of affairs
- **loss of fortune**
  04 ruin **05** decay
- **sudden good fortune**
  08 windfall

fortune-teller

04 seer **05** augur, sibyl **06** oracle **07** diviner, prophet, psychic **08** telepath **09** visionary **10** prophetess, soothsayer **11** clairvoyant

fortune-telling *see* divination

forty

02 XL
- **forty winks**
  03 nap **04** rest **05** sleep

forum

03 BBS **05** arena, stage **06** debate **07** meeting, rostrum **08** assembly **09** gathering, symposium **10** conference, discussion **12** meeting-place

forward

02 on, to **03** aid, out **04** back, bold, fore, head, help, mail, post, send, ship **05** ahead, brash, cocky, early, first, forth, fresh, front, hurry, pushy, ready, speed **06** assist, avanti, brazen, cheeky, favour, foster, future, hasten, onward, pass on, send on, step up **07** advance, deliver, earnest, frontal, further, go-ahead, leading, onwards, promote, speed up, support **08** advanced, dispatch, expedite, familiar, foremost, forwards, impudent, into view, long-term, redirect **09** advancing, assertive, audacious, barefaced, confident, encourage, long-range, officious, premature, presuming, readdress, thrusting, transport **10** accelerate, aggressive, facilitate, medium-term, precocious **11** impertinent, into the open, medium-range, progressing, progressive, prospective

12 enterprising, overfamiliar, presumptuous, well-advanced **13** over-assertive, over-confident, progressively, well-developed **14** forward-looking

forward-looking

04 goey **06** modern **07** dynamic, go-ahead, liberal **09** go-getting, reforming **10** avant-garde, far-sighted, innovative **11** enlightened, progressive **12** enterprising

forwardness

04 neck **05** cheek **08** audacity, boldness, pertness **09** brashness, brass neck, impudence, pushiness **10** brazenness, cheekiness, confidence **11** presumption **12** forth-putting, impertinence **14** aggressiveness, over-confidence

forwards

02 on **03** out **04** pack **05** ahead, forth **06** onward **07** forward, onwards **13** progressively

fossil

05 relic **07** remains, remnant **09** reliquiae **10** antiquated

Fossils include:

04 bone, cast
05 amber, shell
06 burrow
07 bivalve, crinoid
08 ammonite, baculite, dinosaur, echinoid, nautilus, skeleton
09 belemnite, coccolith, coprolite, fish teeth, steinkern, trilobite
10 cast fossil, gastrolith, graptolite, snakestone
11 ichnofossil, microfossil, mould fossil, resin fossil, sharks' teeth, trace fossil
12 Burgess shale, stromatolite

fossilized

04 dead **05** passé, stony **07** archaic, extinct **08** hardened, obsolete, ossified, outmoded **09** out of date, petrified **10** antiquated **11** prehistoric **12** antediluvian, old-fashioned **13** anachronistic

foster

03 aid **04** back, feed, help, hold, rear **05** boost, nurse, raise **06** assist, foment, mother, nousle, nuzzle, uphold **07** advance, bring up, care for, cherish, further, harbour, nourish, noursle, nousell, nurture, promote, support, sustain **08** forester, incubate **09** cultivate, encourage, entertain, look after, stimulate **10** make much of, take care of

foster-child

04 dalt **05** dault

foul

◇ *anagram indicator*
03 bad, jam, low, paw, wet **04** base, blue, clog, edgy, lewd, mean, rank, soil, ugly, vile, wild **05** angry, black, block, catch, choke, cross, dirty, fetid, gross, humpy, mucky, muddy, narky, nasty,

putid, rainy, ratty, reeky, rough, snarl, stain, sully, taint, testy, twist **06** coarse, crabby, defile, dreggy, feisty, filthy, foetid, foul up, grumpy, impure, odious, pawpaw, putrid, reekie, ribald, rotten, shirty, smelly, smutty, snappy, soiled, stingy, stormy, tangle, tetchy, unfair, untidy, virose, vulgar, wicked **07** abusive, bilious, blacken, collide, crabbed, decayed, defiled, ensnare, gnarled, grouchy, heinous, obscene, peppery, pollute, prickly, profane, rotting, squalid, squally, stroppy, tainted, unclean, vicious **08** blustery, choleric, entangle, feculent, harlotry, horrible, indecent, infected, obstruct, polluted, shameful, stagnant, stinking **09** abhorrent, crotchety, dyspeptic, entangled, execrable, fractious, impatient, inclement, irritable, loathsome, nefarious, off-colour, offensive, repellent, repulsive, revolting, sickening, splenetic, technical **10** abominable, capernoity, despicable, detestable, disfigured, disgusting, indelicate, iniquitous, nauseating, putrescent, unpleasant **11** bad-tempered, blasphemous, carnaptious, contaminate, disgraceful **12** contaminated, contemptible, disagreeable, foul-smelling, putrefactive, unfavourable **13** quick-tempered
• **foul play**
05 crime **06** murder **08** violence **09** deception, dirty work **13** double-dealing, funny business, sharp practice **15** unfair behaviour

foul-mouthed
06 coarse, ribald, ribaud **07** abusive, obscene, profane, rybauld **09** offensive **10** foul-spoken **11** blasphemous

foul-smelling stuff
04 hing **10** asafoetida

found
03 fix, met, set **04** base, cast, rest, root **05** build, endow, erect, merit, plant, raise, set up, start **06** bottom, create, ground, locate, settle **07** develop **08** initiate, organize, position **09** construct, establish, institute, originate **10** constitute, inaugurate **14** bring into being
• **found in**
◊ anagram indicator
◊ containment indicator
◊ hidden indicator

foundation
◊ tail selection indicator
03 key **04** base, call, core, crib, fond, foot, fund, rock, root **05** basis, cause, heart, score **06** bottom, excuse, ground, motive, reason, rip-rap, thrust **07** account, bedrock, charity, essence, footing, grounds, keynote, premise, reasons, roadbed, support **08** argument, creation, cribwork, founding, grillage, occasion, pitching **09** endowment, essential, grounding, institute, principle, rationale,

setting-up, substance **10** essentials, grass-roots, groundwork, hypostasis, inducement, initiation, stereobate, substratum **11** fundamental, institution, vindication **12** constitution, fundamentals, inauguration, organization, quintessence, substructure, underpinning **13** alpha and omega, establishment, justification, starting-point **14** main ingredient, understructure **15** first principles

founder
◊ anagram indicator
04 fail, fall, sink **05** abort, maker **06** author, father, go down, mother, oecist, oikist **07** builder, capsize, creator, endower, go wrong, misfire, stumble, subside **08** belleter, collapse, designer, inventor, miscarry, submerge **09** architect, break down, developer, initiator, organizer, patriarch **10** benefactor, discoverer, institutor, originator, prime mover, progenitor **11** come to grief, constructor, establisher, fall through **13** come to nothing, go to the bottom **14** be unsuccessful

foundling
04 waif **05** stray **06** orphan, urchin **07** outcast **12** enfant trouvé **15** abandoned infant

fount
04 font, rise, well **05** birth, cause **06** origin, source, spring **08** wellhead **09** beginning, inception **10** mainspring **12** commencement, fountainhead

fountain
03 jet **04** fons, font, pant, rise, well **05** birth, cause, fount, gerbe, laver, spout, spray, spurt **06** origin, source, spring **07** bubbler, conduit, jet d'eau **08** Aganippe, wellhead **09** beginning, Castalian, inception, reservoir **10** Hippocrene, mainspring, waterworks, wellspring **11** Aonian fount, scuttlebutt, scuttle cask **12** commencement, fountainhead

four
02 IV **04** IIII, mess **06** tetrad **07** quartet **08** quartett **09** quartette **10** quaternary, quaternion, quaternity
• **one of four**
04 quad

four-square
05 frank **06** firmly, honest **07** frankly, solidly **08** honestly, squarely **10** forthright, resolutely

fourteen
03 XIV

fowl
03 hen **04** bird, cock, coot, duck **05** chook, goose, poult **06** bantam, boiler, Brahma, houdan, rumkin, sultan, turkey **07** chicken, Hamburg, leghorn, pintado, poultry **08** Hamburgh, pheasant, rose comb, wildfowl **09** wyandotte **10** chittagong,

spatchcock **11** brissel-cock **14** Rhode Island red

fox
03 pug, tod **05** cheat, puggy, vixen, zerda, zorro **06** baffle, corsac, fennec, Lowrie **07** Charley, Charlie, deceive, Reynard **09** Lowrie-tod, Tod-lowrie **10** Basil Brush

foxglove
09 digitalis **13** dead-men's bells **14** witches' thimble

foxtrot
01 F

foxy
03 fly, sly **04** wily **05** canny, sharp **06** artful, astute, crafty, shrewd, tricky **07** cunning, devious, knowing, vulpine **08** guileful

foyer
04 hall **05** lobby **07** hallway **08** anteroom **09** reception, vestibule **11** antechamber **12** entrance hall

fracas
03 row **04** riot, rout, spat **05** aggro, brawl, fight, mêlée, scrap, set-to **06** affray, barney, bust-up, ruckus, ruffle, rumpus, shindy, uproar **07** quarrel, ruction, scuffle, trouble **10** Donnybrook, free-for-all **11** disturbance

fraction
03 bit **04** half, part **05** ratio, third **06** amount **07** decimal, ligroin, quarter **08** repeater, tailings **10** proportion, sexagenary **11** sexagesimal, subdivision

fractional
04 tiny **05** small **06** little, minute, slight, subtle **07** partial **10** negligible **13** imperceptible, insignificant, insubstantial

fractious
05 cross, testy **06** crabby, grumpy, touchy, unruly **07** awkward, fretful, grouchy, peevish **08** captious, choleric, petulant **09** crotchety, irritable, querulous **10** refractory **11** bad-tempered, quarrelsome **12** recalcitrant

fracture
◊ anagram indicator
03 gap **04** chip, rent, rift, slit, snap **05** break, cleft, crack, fault, split **06** breach, schism **07** fissure, opening, rupture **08** aperture, breakage, breaking, splinter **09** splitting **10** microcrack

fragile
04 fine, weak **05** frail **06** dainty, feeble, flimsy, infirm, slight, tender **07** brittle **08** delicate, unstable **09** breakable, frangible **13** insubstantial

fragility
07 frailty **08** delicacy, weakness **09** infirmity **10** feebleness **11** brittleness **12** frangibility **13** breakableness

fragment

◇ *hidden indicator*
02 fr **03** bit, end, ort **04** blad, chip, flaw, mite, part, rift, snip, spar **05** blaud, break, chink, crumb, frust, patch, piece, scrap, shard, shred, split **06** cinder, divide, morsel, sheave, shiver, sliver, snatch **07** break up, cantlet, crumble, flinder, flitter, fritter, morceau, portion, remains, remnant, shatter, snippet, split up **08** disunite, fraction, particle, potshard, potshare, potsherd, quantity, splinter, xenolith **09** come apart, remainder **10** sequestrum, smithereen **11** smithereens **12** come to pieces, disintegrate **13** smash to pieces

fragmentary

05 bitty **06** broken, snippy, uneven **07** partial, scrappy, sketchy **08** separate, snippety **09** piecemeal, scattered **10** disjointed, incoherent, incomplete **11** fractionary **12** disconnected **13** discontinuous

fragmentation

07 break-up **08** division **09** crumbling, splitting **10** separation, shattering **11** atomization, splitting-up **13** decomposition **14** disintegration

fragmented

06 broken, in bits **07** divided **08** in pieces, separate **09** disunited **10** disjointed, incomplete **13** disintegrated

fragrance

04 balm, otto **05** aroma, attar, odour, scent, smell **07** bouquet, perfume **09** redolence **10** sweet smell

fragrant

04 nosy **05** balmy, nosey, spicy, sweet **07** balsamy, odorous, savoury, scented **08** aromatic, perfumed, redolent **09** ambrosial **10** suaveolent **11** odoriferous **12** sweet-scented **13** sweet-smelling

frail

04 puny, rush, weak **05** shaky **06** feeble, flimsy, infirm, slight, slimsy, unwell **07** brittle, fragile, unsound **08** delicate **09** breakable, frangible **10** vulnerable **11** susceptible **12** easily broken **13** insubstantial

frailty

04 flaw **05** fault **06** defect, foible **07** blemish, failing **08** delicacy, weakness **09** fragility, infirmity, weak point **10** deficiency **11** brittleness, fallibility, shortcoming **12** imperfection **13** vulnerability **14** susceptibility

frame

◇ *containment indicator*
◇ *ends selection indicator*
03 set **04** body, case, draw, edge, form, husk, loom, make, plan, plot, sash, size, tent, trap **05** adapt, box in, build, draft, erect, fit up, forge, model, mould, mount, pin on, plant, set up, shape, shell **06** adjust, border, casing, cook up, create, devise, draw up, encase,

fabric, figure, map out, redact, sketch **07** carcase, chassis, compose, concoct, enclose, fashion, monture, pretend, setting, support, taboret **08** assemble, bodywork, conceive, contrive, mounting, physique, skeleton, stitch up, surround, tabouret **09** construct, establish, fabricate, formulate, framework, structure **10** articulate, foundation **11** incriminate, manufacture, put together, scaffolding **12** construction, substructure **13** cook up a charge

• frame of mind

04 mood, tune **05** state **06** humour, spirit, temper **07** outlook **08** attitude **09** condition **11** disposition, state of mind

frame-up

03 fix **04** plot, trap **05** fit-up **08** put-up job **10** conspiracy **11** fabrication **15** trumped-up charge

framework

◇ *containment indicator*
04 grid, plan, rack **05** frame, shell **06** casing, cradle, fabric, scheme **07** lattice, outline, tressel, trestle **08** scaffold, skeleton **09** bare bones, structure **10** foundation, groundwork, parameters **11** constraints, trestlework **12** substructure

France

01 F **02** Fr **03** FRA **04** Gaul

See also **department**

• in France

◇ *foreign word indicator*

• South of France

04 Midi **07** Riviera **09** Côte d'Azur

franchise

05 right **07** candour, charter, consent, freedom, liberty, licence, warrant **08** immunity, suffrage **09** exemption, frankness, privilege **10** concession, permission **11** prerogative **13** authorization **15** enfranchisement

francium

02 Fr

frank

04 free, mark, open **05** bluff, blunt, plain, stamp **06** cancel, candid, direct, honest, pigsty **07** genuine, liberal, sincere, up-front **08** explicit, postmark, straight, truthful **09** downright, ingenuous, outspoken, Ripuarian **10** forthright, four-square **11** hard-hitting, open-hearted, plain-spoken, transparent, undisguised **12** unrestrained **13** simple-hearted **15** straightforward

frankincense

04 thus **08** olibanum

frankly

06 freely, openly **07** bluntly, in truth, plainly **08** candidly, directly, eye to eye, honestly, straight **09** to be blunt, to be frank **10** explicitly, to be honest, truthfully **11** straight out **14** without reserve

frankness

06 candor **07** candour, freedom, honesty **08** openness **09** bluntness, franchise, sincerity **10** directness **12** truthfulness **13** ingenuousness, outspokenness, plain speaking **14** forthrightness

frantic

◇ *anagram indicator*
03 mad **04** wild **06** hectic, raging, raving **07** berserk, fraught, furious **08** agitated, frenetic, frenzied **09** desperate **10** distracted, distraught, distressed **11** overwrought **12** out of control **13** at your wits' end, panic-stricken **14** beside yourself

frantically

◇ *anagram indicator*
05 madly **06** wildly **09** furiously **11** desperately **12** hysterically, out of control **13** at your wits' end **14** beside yourself

fraternity

03 set **04** clan, club **05** guild, order, union **06** circle, fratry, league **07** company, fratery, kinship, society **08** sodality **10** fellowship **11** association, brotherhood, camaraderie, comradeship **13** companionship

fraternize

03 mix **04** move **05** unite **06** hobnob, mingle **07** consort **08** go around **09** affiliate, associate, forgather, hang about, pal up with, socialize **10** cordialize, foregather, gang up with, sympathize **11** keep company **12** rub shoulders

fraud

03 con, fix **04** fake, hoax, scam, sham, swiz **05** cheat, guile, phony, quack, snare, trick **06** con man, deceit, diddle, hoaxer, humbug, hustle, phoney, racket, riddle, rip-off, take-in **07** bluffer, forgery, roguery, swindle, swizzle **08** cheating, fraus pia, impostor, pia fraus, swindler, trickery **09** charlatan, chicanery, deception, duplicity, embezzler, fraudster, gold brick, imposture, pretender, swindling, trickster **10** mountebank **11** counterfeit, fraudulence, stellionate, supercherie **12** double-dealer, embezzlement **13** double-dealing, sharp practice **15** salami technique

fraudulent

04 sham **05** bogus, cronk, false, quack, shady **06** phoney **07** crooked, knavish **08** cheating, covinous, criminal **09** deceitful, deceptive, dishonest, shameless, swindling **11** counterfeit, duplicitous **12** exploitative, unscrupulous **13** double-dealing, surreptitious

fraudulently

07 falsely **09** corruptly, illegally **11** deceitfully, dishonestly, shamelessly **14** unscrupulously

fraught

04 full, load **05** cargo, laden, tense **06** filled **07** anxious, charged, freight, replete, uptight, worried **08** agitated, attended **09** abounding, bristling, freighted **10** distraught, distressed **11** accompanied, overwrought, stressed out, under stress

fray

03 rag, row, tax, vex **04** riot, wear **05** aggro, brawl, clash, fight, scrap, set-to **06** affray, battle, bovver, combat, dust-up, fridge, rumpus, scrape, strain, stress **07** bashing, frazzle, overtax, pasting, punch-up, quarrel, scuffle, unravel, wear out **08** conflict, frighten, irritate, wear thin **09** challenge, make tense, put on edge **10** excitement, free-for-all, push too far **11** disturbance, make nervous **12** become ragged **14** wigs on the green

frayed

04 thin, worn **06** ragged **08** tattered, worn thin **10** threadbare, unravelled

freak

◇ *anagram indicator*
03 fan, nut, odd **04** buff, geek, turn, whim **05** fiend, fluky, queer, quirk, twist **06** addict, chance, mutant, oddity, vagary, weirdo **07** anomaly, bizarre, caprice, devotee, erratic, fanatic, monster, oddball, unusual **08** aberrant, abnormal, atypical, mutation, surprise **09** curiosity, deformity, eccentric **10** aberration, aficionado, capricious, enthusiast, fortuitous, unexpected **11** abnormality, exceptional, monstrosity **12** irregularity, lusus naturae, malformation **13** freak of nature, unpredictable

• **freak out**
◇ *anagram indicator*
06 go wild, wig out **07** explode, go crazy **09** go bananas, go berserk **11** lose control **12** throw a wobbly **15** go off the deep end, go out of your mind

freakish

03 odd **05** weird **06** fitful, freaky **07** erratic, strange, unusual **08** aberrant, abnormal, fanciful, peculiar **09** arbitrary, fantastic, grotesque, malformed, monstrous, whimsical **10** capricious, changeable, outlandish **13** unpredictable **14** unconventional

freckle

04 spot **07** ephelis, lentigo **08** heatspot **09** fernticle **10** ferniticle, ferntickle, fernyticle **11** fairniticle, fairnyticle, fernitickle, fernytickle **12** fairnitickle, fairnyticle

free

◇ *anagram indicator*
03 ope, out, rid **04** bold, easy, idle, open, quit, save **05** broad, clear, empty, fluid, let go, loose, rough, spare, unmew, untie, vague **06** acquit, casual, except, excuse, exempt, freely, giving, gratis, lavish, let out, ransom, redeem, rescue, smooth, solute, svelte, unbind, vacant **07** absolve, acquite, at large, clear of, deliver, for free, for love, general, inexact, lacking, liberal, natural, off duty, relaxed, release, relieve, set free, unbowed, unchain, unleash, untaken, without **08** acquight, at no cost, buckshee, devoid of, generous, immune to, indecent, laid-back, lavishly, liberate, safe from, set loose, unburden **09** at liberty, autarchic, available, copiously, debarrass, disburden, discharge, disengage, easy-going, extricate, imprecise, liberally, liberated, sovereign, turn loose, unblocked, unimpeded, unsecured, voluntary **10** abundantly, autonomous, charitable, democratic, disburthen, emancipate, exempt from, for nothing, generously, hospitable, munificent, on the house, on the loose, open-handed, self-ruling, unattached, unconfined, unemployed, unfastened, unhampered, unoccupied, unstinting **11** Anacreontic, disentangle, emancipated, free as a bird, independent, requiteless, spontaneous, uninhibited **12** free of charge, unaffected by, unobstructed, unrestrained, unrestricted **13** at no extra cost, complimentary, extravagantly, make available, self-governing, without charge **15** with compliments

• **free and easy**
06 casual **07** relaxed **08** carefree, informal, laid-back, tolerant **09** easy-going **11** spontaneous **12** happy-go-lucky **15** unconstrained

• **free hand**
05 power, scope **07** freedom, liberty, licence **08** free rein, latitude **09** authority **10** discretion, permission **12** carte blanche

• **setting free**
03 lib **07** release **09** unbinding **10** liberation

freebooter

07 cateran, pindari **08** pindaree **09** snaphance **10** snaphaunce, snaphaunch

freedom

04 ease, play **05** power, range, right, scope **06** leeway, margin **07** liberty, licence, release **08** autarchy, autonomy, free hand, free rein, home rule, immunity, impunity, latitude **09** democracy, exemption, frankness, privilege **10** separation **11** deliverance, flexibility, open slather, opportunity, prerogative, sovereignty **12** emancipation, independence **13** outspokenness **14** self-government

free-for-all

03 row **04** fray **05** brawl, broil, clash, fight, mêlée, rammy, scrap **06** affray, bust-up, dust-up, fracas, fratch, ruckus, rumpus, stoush **07** bagarre, brabble, brangle, dispute, punch-up, quarrel, scuffle, tuilyie **08** argument, disorder, skirmish, squabble **10** Donnybrook, fisticuffs **11** altercation, open slather

freely

◇ *anagram indicator*
05 ad-lib, amply **06** easily, openly **07** bluntly, frankly, loosely, plainly, readily **08** candidly, lavishly, smoothly **09** liberally, naturally, willingly **10** abundantly, generously **11** voluntarily **12** unreservedly **13** extravagantly, spontaneously **14** frictionlessly, without jerking **15** in all directions

freeman

05 ceorl, thete **07** burgess, burgher, citizen **09** liveryman

freethinker

05 deist **07** doubter, infidel, sceptic **08** agnostic **09** libertine **10** esprit fort, unbeliever **11** independent, rationalist **13** nonconformist

freethinking

07 liberal **08** agnostic **09** sceptical **10** open-minded **11** broad-minded, independent, rationalist **13** nonconformist **14** unconventional

free will

07 autarky, freedom, liberty **08** autonomy, election, volition **11** spontaneity **12** independence **15** self-sufficiency

• **of your own free will**
06 freely **08** by choice **09** purposely, willingly **11** consciously, voluntarily **12** deliberately **13** intentionally, spontaneously **15** of your own accord

freeze

03 fix, ice, peg, set **04** cool, halt, hold, stay, stop, take **05** chill, frost, ice up **06** fixing, harden, quiver, shiver **07** congeal, embargo, get cold, ice over, stiffen, suspend **08** cold snap, enfreeze, freeze-up, glaciate, preserve, shutdown, solidify, stoppage **09** freeze-dry, stabilize **10** deep-freeze, immobilize, moratorium, stand still, standstill, suspension **11** catch a chill, refrigerate **12** anaesthetize, interruption, postponement **15** become paralysed

• **freeze out**
03 cut **04** snub **05** eject, evict, expel **06** ice out, ignore, remove **07** boot out, boycott, exclude, kick out, lock out, turf out **08** brush off, throw out **09** ostracize **13** excommunicate **14** send to Coventry

freezing

03 icy, raw **04** cold, numb **05** polar **06** arctic, baltic, biting, bitter, chilly, frosty, wintry **07** cutting, glacial, numbing **08** piercing, Siberian, stinging **09** perishing **10** frigorific **11** penetrating **12** bitterly cold, brass monkeys

freight

04 hire, load **05** cargo, goods **06** lading, let out **07** fraught, haulage, payload, portage **08** carriage, contents, shipment **10** conveyance, freightage **11** consignment, merchandise **14** transportation

French
◇ *foreign word indicator*
02 Fr
See also day; month; number; shop
• **Old French**
02 OF

French Guiana
03 GUF

Frenchman
01 M

French first names include:

03 Luc
04 Jean, Léon, Rémi, Rémy, René, Yves,
05 Alain, André, Denis, Émile, Henri, Jules, Louis, Serge
06 Claude, Didier, Gaston, Gérard, Honoré, Jérôme, Marcel, Michel, Pascal, Pierre, Xavier
07 Antoine, Édouard, Étienne, Georges, Gustave, Jacques, Laurent, Olivier, Patrice, Thibaut, Thierry, Vincent
08 Frédéric, Matthieu, Philippe, Stéphane, Thibault
09 Guillaume

French Revolutionary Calendar
see month

frenetic
◇ *anagram indicator*
03 mad **04** wild **05** manic **06** hectic, insane, madman **07** berserk, excited, frantic **08** demented, frenzied, maniacal **09** delirious, obsessive **10** distracted, distraught, hysterical, unbalanced **11** hyperactive, overwrought

frenetically
◇ *anagram indicator*
05 madly **06** wildly **09** excitedly, intensely, manically **10** hectically **11** frantically **12** hysterically

frenzied
03 mad **04** amok, wild **05** manic **06** crazed, hectic, raving **07** berserk, frantic, furious **08** demented, feverish, frenetic **09** desperate, obsessive, phrenetic, raving mad **10** distracted, distraught, hysterical **11** overwrought **12** out of control, uncontrolled **13** at your wits' end, panic-stricken **14** beside yourself

frenzy
◇ *anagram indicator*
03 fit **04** bout, fury, must, rage **05** burst, fever, mania, musth, spasm **06** lunacy **07** madness, oestrum, oestrus, passion, seizure, turmoil **08** delirium, hysteria, insanity, outburst, paroxysm, tailspin, wildness **09** agitation, phrenesis, transport **10** convulsion **11** derangement, distraction, nympholepsy **13** furor poeticus
• **expression of frenzy**
04 euoi, evoe **05** evhoe, evohe, yahoo

frequency
01 f **06** resort **09** constancy, incidence, oftenness **10** commonness, prevalence, recurrence, repetition **11** commonality, periodicity **12** frequentness

frequent
05 daily, haunt, lobby, often, thick, usual, visit **06** attend, common, hourly, normal, weekly **07** crowded, regular **08** addicted, constant, everyday, familiar, habitual, numerous, practise, repeated **09** continual, countless, customary, habituate, hang out at, incessant, patronize, prevalent, recurrent, recurring **10** accustomed, persistent, prevailing, visit often **11** commonplace, hang about at, predominant **13** associate with, go to regularly **14** go to frequently, happening often

frequenter
06 client, patron **07** habitué, haunter, regular **08** customer, resorter **14** regular visitor

frequently
02 fr **03** oft **04** much **05** daily, often, thick **06** hourly, weekly **08** commonly **09** many a time, many times, regularly **10** habitually, oftentimes, repeatedly **11** continually, customarily, half the time, over and over **12** persistently

fresh
◇ *anagram indicator*
03 hot, new, raw **04** bold, cool, fair, firm, just, keen, more, pert, pink, pure, rosy, span, warm **05** alert, brisk, clean, clear, cocky, crisp, crude, extra, green, newly, other, right, sassy, saucy, spick, sweet, vital, windy **06** afresh, brazen, bright, caller, cheeky, chilly, direct, latest, lively, maiden, modern, recent, rested **07** bracing, forward, freshly, further, glowing, healthy, natural, renewed, revived, span new, uncured, undried, unfaded, unusual, vibrant **08** blooming, bouncing, brand-new, dewy-eyed, exciting, familiar, impudent, insolent, original, pristine, restored, straight, up-to-date, vigorous, youthful **09** different, energetic, refreshed, virescent **10** additional, a new person, innovative, new-fangled, raring to go, refreshing, stimulated, unpolluted **11** impertinent, invigorated, unpreserved, unprocessed **12** enthusiastic, invigorating, overfamiliar, presumptuous, ready for more **13** disrespectful, fresh as a daisy, inexperienced, revolutionary, supplementary, yourself again **14** healthy-looking, unconventional
• **remain fresh**
04 keep, last

freshen
◇ *anagram indicator*
03 air **05** clean, clear, liven, rouse **06** purify, refill, revive, tart up

07 enliven, liven up, refresh, restore **09** deodorize, stimulate, ventilate, vernalize **10** revitalize **12** reinvigorate
• **freshen up**
09 get washed, have a wash **12** get spruced up, wash yourself **14** tidy yourself up

freshly
◇ *anagram indicator*
04 anew, just **05** newly **06** barely, lately, of late **08** recently **10** not long ago **13** a short time ago

freshman
05 bajan, frosh **06** bejant, pennal **07** fresher **08** newcomer **09** first-year **13** underclassman

freshness
04 glow **05** bloom, flush, shine **06** vigour, youths **07** May-morn, newness, novelty, sparkle, verdure **09** cleanness, clearness, fraîcheur, immediacy, vernality **10** brightness, May-morning **11** originality **13** wholesomeness
• **early freshness**
03 dew

fret
03 rub, vex **04** mope, pine, rile, stop **05** anger, annoy, brood, chafe, grate, worry **06** bother, nettle, ripple **07** agonize, anguish, be upset, concern, corrode, disturb, torment, trouble, whittle **08** irritate **09** be anxious, infuriate, make a fuss, variegate **10** exasperate **12** be distressed **15** concern yourself

fretful
04 edgy **05** tense, upset **06** uneasy **07** anxious, fearful, peevish, unhappy, uptight, worried **08** restless, troubled **09** disturbed, impatient **10** distressed

fretfully
06 edgily **07** tensely **08** uneasily **09** anxiously, fearfully, worriedly **10** restlessly

friable
05 crisp, crump **07** brittle, crumbly, powdery **12** pulverizable

friar
02 Fr **03** fra **04** monk **05** abbot, frate, frier, minim, prior **06** frater **07** brother, limiter **08** Capuchin, récollet **09** Carmelite, Cordelier, Dominican, mendicant, Observant, predicant, recollect, religieux, religious **10** Franciscan, religioner **12** Observantine **13** Redemptionist

friction
06 strife **07** arguing, chafing, discord, dispute, erosion, gnawing, grating, jarring, rasping, rivalry, rubbing **08** abrading, abrasion, bad blood, clashing, conflict, disunity, scraping, traction **09** animosity, attrition, hostility **10** antagonism, bad feeling, disharmony, dissension, ill feeling, irritation, opposition, resentment, resistance **11** disputation, excoriation,

uarrelling, wearing away, xerotripsis
 disagreement

riday
 Fr **03** Fri

ridge
 rub **04** fray, frig **06** cooler, icebox
 minibar **12** refrigerator
 refrigeratory

riend
 ami, bud, pal **04** ally, amie, chum,
noa, mate, tosh **05** amigo, buddy,
rony, ingle, lover **06** backer, belamy,
on ami, cobber, co-mate, gossip,
ossip, inward, mucker, patron **07** best
oy, comrade, goombah, paisano,
artner, privado, sponsor **08** alter ego,
est girl, compadre, familiar, intimate,
laymate, sidekick, soul mate
 associate, belle amie, bonne amie,
oyfriend, companion, confidant,
onfident, paranymph, pen friend,
upporter **10** back-friend, benefactor,
est friend, better half, buddy-buddy,
onfidante, girlfriend, good friend,
ubscriber, well-wisher **11** bosom
iend, cater-cousin, close friend,
ondisciple **12** acquaintance, fidus
chates, schoolfriend **15** sparring
artner
  mans' best friend
 dog

riendless
 alone **06** lonely **07** forlorn,
hunned, unloved **08** deserted,
orsaken, isolated, lonesome, solitary
 abandoned, destitute, unbeloved,
npopular **10** by yourself, ostracized,
nattached **11** lonely-heart
 unbefriended **13** companionless
 cold-shouldered

riendliness
 warmth **08** bonhomie, kindness,
natiness **09** geniality, palliness
0 affability, amiability, chumminess,
indliness **11** sociability
 congeniality, conviviality
 Gemütlichkeit **15** approachability,
eighbourliness

riendly
 fond, kind, maty, nice, tosh, warm
 close, matey, pally, thick, tight
 chummy, couthy, folksy, genial,
indly **07** affable, amiable, cordial,
outhie, helpful **08** amicable, down-
ome, familiar, informal, intimate,
utgoing, pleasant, sociable
 agreeable, comradely, congenial,
onvivial, favorable, peaceable,
eceptive, welcoming **10** favourable,
ospitable **11** forthcoming, good-
atured, inseparable, neighbourly,
ympathetic **12** affectionate,
pproachable, well-disposed
 companionable

riendship
 love **05** amity, amour **06** warmth
 company, concord, harmony,
apport **08** affinity, alliance, fondness,
oodwill, intimacy, mateship

09 affection, closeness **10** amiability,
attachment, fellowship, kindliness
11 camaraderie, comradeship,
familiarity **12** friendliness
13 companionship, confraternity,
understanding

fright
04 fear, fleg, funk **05** alarm, dread, gliff,
glift, panic, scare, shock, skrik
06 creeps, dismay, horror, terror, tirrit
07 jitters, shivers, willies **08** affright,
blue funk, disquiet **09** bombshell, cold
sweat **10** blind panic **11** fearfulness,
trepidation **12** affrightment,
apprehension, perturbation
13 consternation, heebie-jeebies,
knocking knees **15** bolt from the blue
 • **expression of fright**
03 eek **04** yike **05** yikes

frighten
03 awe **04** dare, flay, fleg, fley, fray,
gast, shoo **05** afear, alarm, appal,
daunt, dread, ghast, panic, scare,
shock, spook, unman **06** affear, affray,
boggle, dismay, gallow, rattle
07 affeare, horrify, petrify, scarify,
startle, terrify, unnerve **08** affright
09 terrorize **10** affrighten, intimidate,
scare silly, scare stiff **12** put the wind up

frightened
04 frit **05** cowed, feart, windy
06 afraid, frozen, scared **07** alarmed,
chicken, panicky, quivery, trembly
08 dismayed, startled, unnerved
09 petrified, terrified **10** terrorized
11 in a blue funk, scared stiff **13** having
kittens, panic-stricken, scared to death
14 terror-stricken

frightening
04 eery, grim **05** eerie, hairy, scary
06 creepy, scarey, spooky
08 alarming, daunting, fearsome,
terrific **09** traumatic **10** forbidding,
formidable, petrifying, terrifying
11 hair-raising **12** white-knuckle
13 bloodcurdling, spine-chilling

frightful
◇ *anagram indicator*
04 dire, grim, huge, ugly **05** awful,
great, nasty **06** grisly, horrid, odious
07 fearful, ghastly, hideous, macabre,
very bad **08** alarming, dreadful,
fearsome, gruesome, horrible, horrific,
shocking, terrible **09** abhorrent,
appalling, harrowing, loathsome,
repulsive, revolting **10** frightsome,
horrendous, unbearable, unpleasant
11 affrightful, schrecklich, unspeakable
12 disagreeable

frightfully
◇ *anagram indicator*
04 much, very **07** awfully, beastly,
greatly **08** terribly **09** decidedly,
extremely **10** dreadfully, ghastfully,
thoroughly **11** desperately,
exceedingly

frigid
03 dry, icy **04** cold, cool **05** aloof, chill,
polar, stiff, stony **06** arctic, bitter, chilly,

formal, frosty, frozen, remote, wintry
07 distant, glacial, passive, unmoved
08 clinical, freezing, lifeless, reserved,
Siberian, unloving, very cold
09 unfeeling **10** impersonal,
unanimated **11** indifferent, passionless,
standoffish, unemotional, unexcitable
12 unresponsive **13** unsympathetic

frigidity
05 chill **07** iciness **08** coldness
09 aloofness, passivity, stiffness
10 chilliness, frostiness **11** impassivity
12 lifelessness **15** cold-heartedness

frill
04 fold, ruff, tuck **05** extra, jabot,
ruche **06** finery, fringe, purfle, ruffle
07 armilla, flounce, orphrey, ruching,
valance **08** addition, frippery,
furbelow, trimming **09** accessory,
fanciness, fandangle, gathering,
trimmings **10** decoration, frilliness
11 chitterling, ostentation, superfluity
13 embellishment, ornamentation

frilly
◇ *anagram indicator*
04 lacy **05** fancy **06** ornate
07 crimped, frilled, ruffled, trimmed
08 flounced, gathered

fringe
◇ *ends selection indicator*
03 hem, rim **04** bang, edge, fall, loma,
purl, trim **05** bangs, frill, limit, skirt,
thrum, verge **06** border, edging,
margin, pelmet, tassel **07** bullion,
enclose, fimbria, macramé, macrami,
off-beat, valance **08** frisette, surround,
trimming **09** left-field, outskirts,
perimeter, periphery, peristome
10 avant-garde, borderline, unofficial,
unorthodox **11** alternative
12 experimental **14** unconventional

fringed
05 edged **06** fringy, hemmed
07 trimmed **08** bordered, tasselly
09 fimbriate, tasselled **10** fimbriated

frippery
05 froth **06** finery, frills, trivia
07 baubles, foppery, gewgaws, trifles,
useless **08** glad rags, nonsense, trifling,
trinkets **09** fanciness, fussiness,
gaudiness, nick-nacks, ornaments,
showiness **10** adornments,
fandangles, flashiness, frilliness,
tawdriness, triviality **11** decorations,
knick-knacks, ostentation
15 pretentiousness

frisk
03 hop **04** fisk, jump, leap, play, romp,
skip, trip **05** caper, check, dance, sport
06 bounce, cavort, curvet, frolic,
gambol, prance, search **07** inspect
09 shake down **10** body-search

friskily
08 actively **09** playfully **10** spiritedly
11 exuberantly

frisky
◇ *anagram indicator*
04 high **05** hyper **06** active, bouncy,

fritter

lively, wanton **07** buckish, coltish, dashing, playful, romping **08** skittish, spirited **09** exuberant **10** frolicsome, rollicking **11** full of beans **12** high-spirited **13** in high spirits **15** alive and kicking

fritter
04 blow, idle **05** waste **06** misuse **07** beignet, friture **08** fragment, misspend, squander **09** dissipate, go through, overspend **10** get through **14** spend like water

frivolity
03 fun **04** jest **05** folly, froth **06** gaiety, levity **07** inanity **08** nonsense **09** flippancy, pettiness, silliness **10** triviality **11** foolishness **13** facetiousness, senselessness **14** superficiality

frivolous
04 idle, vain **05** inane, light, petty, silly **06** futile **07** étourdi, foolish, jocular, puerile, shallow, trivial **08** étourdie, flippant, juvenile, skittish, trifling **09** airheaded, facetious, pointless, senseless **11** empty-headed, giddy-headed, light-minded, superficial, unimportant **12** bubble-headed, light-hearted **13** irresponsible **14** featherbrained
• **frivolous person**
09 butterfly

frivolously
04 idly **06** vainly **09** foolishly, jocularly **11** pointlessly, senselessly, whimsically **13** irresponsibly **14** light-heartedly

frizzle
03 fry **04** bend, coil, curl, hiss, kink, loop, purl, roll, spit, tong, turn, wave, wind **05** crimp, curve, frizz, twine, twirl, twist **06** becurl, scorch, scroll, sizzle, spiral **07** crackle, crimple, crinkle, sputter, wreathe

frizzy
04 wiry **05** crisp, curly **06** curled **07** crimped, frizzed **10** corrugated

frock
04 gown, robe **05** dress
See also **dress**

frog
04 hyla, Rana **05** frush **06** peeper **07** paddock, puddock **08** platanna, tree toad **12** spring peeper **15** Cape nightingale

frolic
◊ *anagram indicator*
03 fun, hop, rig **04** game, lark, leap, play, rant, romp, skip **05** caper, dance, frisk, merry, mirth, prank, revel, sport, spree **06** antics, bounce, buster, cavort, curvet, gaiety, gambol, prance, pranky, razzle, splore, wanton **07** disport, gambado, gammock, jollity, May-game, rollick, skylark, stashie, stishie, stushie **08** escapade, stooshie **09** amusement, galravage, gilravage, high jinks, make merry, merriment **10** galravitch, gillravage,

gilravitch, lark around **11** fun and games, gillravitch, merrymaking **12** razzle-dazzle **13** barnsbreaking

frolicsome
◊ *anagram indicator*
03 gay **05** ludic, merry **06** frisky, lively, skippy **07** coltish, kitteny, playful **08** skittish, sportive **09** kittenish, sprightly **10** rollicking

from
◊ *anagram indicator*
◊ *hidden indicator*
01 à **02** ab-, ex, of, on **03** fro, off, out **04** frae **05** out of, since

front
◊ *head selection indicator*
03 air, bow, top, van **04** face, fore, head, lead, look, mask, meet, prow, show **05** blind, cover, first **06** aspect, façade, facing, manner, oppose, vaward **07** cover-up, leading, obverse, outside, pretext **08** confront, disguise, exterior, foremost, forepart, frontage, look over, overlook, pretence, vanguard **09** forefront, front line, look out on **10** appearance, battle zone, expression, firing line, foreground **11** countenance
• **in front**
◊ *juxtaposition indicator*
04 fore **05** ahead, first **06** before, en face **07** leading **08** anterior, paravant **09** in advance, paravaunt, preceding, to the fore
• **in front of**
◊ *juxtaposition indicator*
06 before, facing **07** ahead of **11** in advance of **14** under the nose of **15** in the presence of

frontier
04 edge **05** limit, verge **06** border, bounds **07** marches **08** boundary, confines **09** bordering, partition, perimeter **10** borderline

front-runner
03 nap **07** top seed **08** finalist **09** certainty, favourite, form horse **12** likely winner **15** odds-on favourite

frost
03 ice, mat **04** rime **06** freeze **08** coldness, freeze-up **09** hoar-frost, Jack Frost

frostily
06 coldly, coolly **07** stiffly

frosty
03 icy **04** cold, cool, rimy **05** aloof, chill, frore, frorn, nippy, parky, polar, stiff **06** arctic, chilly, frigid, froren, frorne, frozen, wintry **07** glacial, hostile **08** freezing, Siberian **10** unfriendly **11** standoffish, unwelcoming **12** bitterly cold, discouraging

froth
03 pap **04** barm, fizz, foam, head, mill, ream, scum, suds **05** spume, yeast **06** bubble, lather, mantle, trivia **07** bubbles, chatter, ferment, sea foam,

trifles **10** cuckoo-spit, effervesce **12** trivialities **13** cuckoo-spittle, effervescence, irrelevancies

frothy
04 vain **05** barmy, empty, fizzy, foamy, light, nappy, reamy, spumy, sudsy **06** bubbly, slight, yeasty **07** foaming, spumous, trivial **08** bubbling, trifling **09** frivolous **10** spumescent **11** lightweight **13** insubstantial

frown
03 mow **04** lour, moue, pout **05** glare, scowl **06** glower **07** frounce, grimace **09** dirty look **13** look daggers at, raise eyebrow
• **frown on**
05 glare, scowl **06** glower **07** dislike, grimace **08** object to **10** discourage **12** disapprove of, think badly of **14** take a dim view of **15** not take kindly to

frowsty
05 fuggy, fusty, musty **06** stuffy **07** airless **12** unventilated

frowsy
05 dirty, fusty, messy **06** frumpy, sloppy, stuffy, untidy **07** scruffy, unkempt **08** frumpish, slovenly, sluttish, unwashed **09** offensive, ungroomed **10** slatternly **11** dishevelled

frozen
03 icy, raw **04** hard, iced, numb **05** fixed, frore, frorn, glacé, polar, rigid, stiff **06** arctic, frigid, froren, frorne, frosty **07** chilled, frosted, glacial, ice-cold **08** freezing, icebound, Siberian **10** ice-covered, solidified **11** frozen-stiff **12** bitterly cold

frugal
05 spare **06** meagre, paltry, saving, scanty, stingy **07** careful, miserly, prudent, sparing, spartan, thrifty **09** husbandly, niggardly, penny-wise, provident **10** economical, inadequate **12** parsimonious **13** penny-pinching

frugality
06 saving, thrift **07** economy **08** prudence **09** husbandry, parsimony **11** carefulness **12** conservation

frugally
05 spare **08** meagrely, scantily **09** carefully, prudently, thriftily **12** economically, inadequately **14** parsimoniously

fruit
03 haw, hep, hip, nut, pod **04** crop **05** acorn, berry, yield **06** effect, profit, result, return, reward **07** benefit, harvest, outcome, produce, product, rosehip **08** fruitage **09** advantage **11** consequence

Fruits include:
03 bel, Cox, fig
04 bael, bhel, Cox's, date, gage, kaki, lime, pear, plum, sloe, Ugli®

05 apple, carob, galia, grape, guava, Jaffa, lemon, mango, melon, olive, peach, prune

06 banana, cherry, damson, loquat, litchi, lychee, medlar, orange, papaya, pawpaw, pippin, pomelo, quince, raisin, russet, tomato, wampee

07 acerola, apricot, avocado, bramble, Bramley, chayote, kumquat, mineola, rhubarb, satsuma, Seville, soursop, tangelo, William

08 bilberry, Braeburn, date plum, googoosog, honeydew, kalumpit, mandarin, minneola, mulberry, muscatel, physalis, Pink Lady, rambutan, sebesten, sunberry, tamarind

09 beach plum, blueberry, cantaloup, carambola, cherimoya, crab apple, cranberry, greengage, Juneberry, kiwi fruit, nectarine, persimmon, pineapple, raspberry, rose apple, sapodilla, saskatoon, shadberry, star-apple, star fruit, tangerine, ugli®fruit

10 blackberry, breadfruit, cantaloupe, clementine, Conference, damask plum, elderberry, gooseberry, granadilla, grapefruit, loganberry, mangosteen, redcurrant, salal berry, sour cherry, spiceberry, strawberry, watermelon

11 blood orange, boysenberry, eating apple, Granny Smith, Jaffa orange, navel orange, pomegranate, sallal berry, sharon fruit, sweet cherry

12 blackcurrant, buffalo-berry, cooking apple, costard apple, custard apple, passion fruit, Red Delicious, serviceberry, victoria plum, whitecurrant, winter cherry

13 kangaroo-apple, morello cherry, sapodilla plum, Seville orange

14 Cape gooseberry, pink grapefruit

15 Golden Delicious

• **fruit juice**
03 oil 05 mobby 06 mobbie
• **fruit refuse**
04 marc
• **fruit stone**
03 pip, pit 06 pyrene 07 putamen
• **fruit syrup**
03 rob

fruitful
03 fat 04 rich 06 fecund, useful 07 fertile, teeming 08 abundant, fructive, pregnant, prolific 09 effective, effectual, feracious, fructuous, plenteous, plentiful, rewarding, well-spent 10 beneficial, productive, profitable, successful, worthwhile 11 conceptious, efficacious, increaseful 12 advantageous, fruit-bearing

fruitfully
08 usefully 10 profitably 11 effectively 12 beneficially, productively, successfully 14 advantageously

fruitfulness
06 uberty 08 feracity 09 fecundity,

fertility 10 usefulness 11 fecundation 13 profitability 14 productiveness

fruition
07 success 08 maturity, ripeness 09 enjoyment 10 attainment, completion, fulfilment, maturation, perfection 11 achievement, realization 12 consummation 13 actualization

fruitless
04 idle, vain 06 barren, futile 07 sterile, useless 08 abortive, hopeless 09 pointless, worthless 11 ineffectual, infructuous 12 unproductive, unsuccessful

fruitlessly
06 in vain, vainly 09 uselessly 10 hopelessly 11 pointlessly 14 unproductively, unsuccessfully

fruity
03 low 04 blue, deep, full, racy, rich, sexy 05 bawdy, crazy, juicy, saucy, spicy 06 mellow, risqué, smutty, vulgar 07 naughty 08 indecent, resonant 09 salacious 10 indelicate, suggestive 11 titillating

frumpy
04 drab 05 dated, dingy, dowdy 06 dreary 08 frumpish 09 out of date 10 ill-dressed 12 badly dressed

frustrate
03 bug 04 balk, beat, crab, dash, foil, miff, nark, rile, stop 05 anger, annoy, baulk, block, check, get at, spike, stimy 06 baffle, balked, blight, defeat, hamper, hinder, hogtie, impede, needle, nobble, scotch, stimie, stymie, thwart, wind up 07 counter, depress, inhibit, nullify, scupper, useless 08 drive mad, embitter, irritate, obstruct 09 aggravate, forestall, infuriate 10 disappoint, disconcert, discourage, dishearten, dissatisfy, drive crazy, exasperate, neutralize 11 ineffectual

frustrated
05 angry 06 dished 07 annoyed 08 blighted, thwarted 09 repressed, resentful 10 embittered 11 discouraged 12 disappointed, discontented, disheartened, dissatisfied

frustrating
08 annoying 09 maddening 10 irritating 11 infuriating 12 discouraging, exasperating 13 disappointing, disheartening

frustration
04 balk, foil 05 anger, baulk 06 defeat, thwart 07 balking, curbing, failure, foiling 08 blocking, vexation 09 annoyance, thwarting 10 irritation, resentment 11 obstruction 12 exasperation 13 circumvention, contravention, non-fulfilment 14 disappointment, discouragement 15 dissatisfaction
• **expression of frustration**
11 for God's sake 12 for pete's sake

14 for Christ's sake, for heaven's sake 15 for goodness sake

fry
04 burn, foam 05 sauté, spawn 06 scorch, sizzle 07 frizzle, skegger 09 whitebait

frying-pan
03 wok 06 spider 07 skillet

fuddled
◊ anagram indicator
03 fap 04 hazy 05 drunk, mused, muzzy, tipsy, woozy 06 addled, groggy, swipey, tavert 07 bemused, muddled, sozzled, taivert 08 confused 09 overtaken, stupefied 10 inebriated, tossicated, tosticated 11 intoxicated

fuddy-duddy
04 prim 06 fossil, square, stuffy 07 carping 08 old fogey 10 back number, censorious, conformist 11 museum piece, old-fogeyish 12 buttoned-down, conservative, old-fashioned, stuffed shirt 13 stick-in-the-mud 14 traditionalist

fudge
◊ anagram indicator
03 fix 04 cook, fail, fake 05 avoid, cheat, dodge, evade, hedge, stall, stuff 06 fiddle, humbug 07 distort, evasion, falsify, shuffle 08 nonsense 10 distortion, equivocate 12 misrepresent

fuel
03 fan 04 feed, fire 05 boost 06 incite 07 goading, inflame, nourish, stoke up, sustain 08 material, stimulus 09 encourage, incentive, stimulate 10 ammunition, incitement, propellant 11 combustible, motive power, provocation 13 encouragement

Fuels include:

03 gas, LNG, LPG, MOX, oil, RDF
04 coal, coke, derv, logs, peat, slug, SURF, wood
05 argol, eldin, fagot, vraic
06 benzol, billet, borane, butane, diesel, elding, faggot, gas oil, hydyne, petrol, smudge, Sterno®
07 astatki, benzine, benzole, biofuel, Coalite®, eilding, gasahol, gasohol, mesquit, methane, propane, uranium
08 calor gas®, charcoal, firewood, gasoline, kerosene, kerosine, kindling, mesquite, paraffin, tan balls, triptane
09 acetylene, biodiesel, Campingaz®, cane-trash, diesel oil, hydrazine, plutonium, red diesel
10 anthracite, atomic fuel, fossil fuel, natural gas, Orimulsion®
11 electricity, North Sea gas, nuclear fuel
12 buffalo chips, nitromethane, nuclear power, vegetable oil
13 smokeless fuel
14 aviation spirit

See also **petrol**

fug
04 reek **05** stink **09** fetidness, fustiness, staleness **10** foetidness, stuffiness **11** frowstiness

fuggy
04 foul **05** close, fetid, fusty, stale **06** foetid, stuffy **07** airless, frowsty, noisome, noxious **11** suffocating **12** unventilated

fugitive
04 AWOL **05** brief, exile, short **06** flying, maroon, runner **07** elusive, escapee, fleeing, passing, refugee, runaway **08** deserter, fleeting, hideaway, runagate **09** ephemeral, fugacious, momentary, temporary, transient **10** evanescent, short-lived, transitory

fulfil
04 fill, keep, meet, obey **05** honor **06** answer, effect, finish, honour **07** achieve, act up to, execute, live out, observe, perfect, perform, qualify, realize, satisfy **08** carry out, complete, conclude, live up to, make good **09** conform to, discharge, implement, stand up to **10** accomplish, comply with, consummate **15** come up to scratch

fulfilled
05 happy **07** content, pleased **09** gratified, satisfied

fulfilling
08 pleasing **10** comforting, completion, completory, gratifying, satisfying **12** satisfactory **14** accomplishment

fulfilment
04 pass **07** success **08** enacture, fruition **09** discharge, execution, impletion **10** completion, observance, perfection **11** achievement, performance, realization **12** consummation, satisfaction **14** accomplishment, implementation

full
◇ *anagram indicator*
03 fat, fed, top **04** bang, busy, deep, loud, rich, vast, walk, warm, wauk, wide **05** ample, baggy, broad, buxom, clear, drunk, flush, laden, large, loose, obese, plump, quite, right, round, sated, smack, stout, total, truly, waulk, whole **06** active, chubby, entire, filled, fruity, gorged, hectic, intact, jammed, lively, loaded, packed, rotund, strong, tiring, utmost **07** bulging, chocker, copious, crammed, crowded, exactly, filling, frantic, highest, intense, maximum, perfect, profuse, replete, rounded, shapely, stuffed, swelled, vibrant, well fed **08** abundant, bursting, chockers, chockful, complete, detailed, directly, distinct, eventful, exciting, generous, greatest, resonant, satiated, sonorous, squarely, straight, thorough **09** abounding, chock-full, corpulent, extensive,

packed out, plentiful, satisfied **10** exhaustive, full-bodied, overweight, sufficient, thoroughly, unabridged, voluminous **11** chock-a-block, overflowing, protuberant, well-rounded, well-stocked **12** all-inclusive, loose-fitting, unexpurgated **13** comprehensive, full to the brim

• **be full**
04 teem

• **in full**
05 fully, uncut **06** wholly **07** at large, in pleno, in total **08** at length, in detail **10** completely **13** in its entirety

• **to the full**
05 fully **07** utterly **08** entirely **10** completely, thoroughly **11** to the utmost

full-blooded
06 hearty **07** devoted **08** thorough, vigorous **09** committed, dedicated, out-and-out **11** sanguineous **12** enthusiastic, wholehearted

full-blown
04 full **05** major, total **06** all-out **07** intense **08** complete, thorough **09** full-scale, out-and-out **11** full-fledged

full-bodied
03 fat **04** deep, full, rich **06** fruity, strong **07** amoroso, intense

full-frontal
05 total **06** direct, strong **08** absolute, complete, forceful, thorough **09** out-and-out **12** unexpurgated, unrestrained

full-grown
04 ripe **05** adult, of age **06** mature, seeded **07** grown-up **09** developed, full-blown, full-scale **10** fully grown **12** fully fledged **14** fully developed

fullness
04 body, fill, glut **05** depth, force, power, width **06** growth, plenty, wealth **07** breadth, fatness, pleroma, satiety **08** dilation, loudness, plethora, richness, solidity, strength, swelling, totality, vastness **09** abundance, ampleness, greatness, impletion, intensity, largeness, plenitude, plumpness, profusion, repletion, resonance, satedness, satiation, wholeness **10** complement, congestion, tumescence **11** enlargement, repleteness, shapeliness **12** completeness, inflammation, satisfaction, thoroughness **13** extensiveness **14** curvaceousness, voluptuousness

• **in the fullness of time**
06 in time **07** finally **08** in the end **10** eventually, ultimately **11** in due course

full-scale
05 major **06** all-out **07** in-depth **08** complete, sweeping, thorough **09** extensive, intensive **10** exhaustive **11** wide-ranging **13** comprehensive, thoroughgoing **15** all-encompassing

fully
02 up **05** quite **06** fairly, wholly **07** totally, utterly **08** entirely **09** perfectly **10** altogether, completely positively, thoroughly, to the nines **12** sufficiently, unreservedly **13** in all respects **14** satisfactorily, without reserve

fully fledged
06 mature, senior **07** trained **08** graduate **09** full-blown, qualified **10** proficient **11** experienced **12** professional **14** fully developed

fulminate
04 fume, rage, rail, slam **05** curse, decry, flash, slate **07** condemn, declaim, inveigh, protest, thunder **08** denounce, detonate **09** criticize **10** animadvert, vituperate

fulmination
06 tirade **07** decrial, obloquy, slating **08** brickbat, diatribe **09** criticism, invective, philippic **10** detonation, thundering **11** thunderbolt **12** condemnation, denunciation

fulsome
03 fat, OTT **05** gross, slimy **06** smarmy **07** buttery, cloying, fawning **08** effusive, luscious, nauseous, overdone, unctuous **09** adulatory, excessive, insincere, offensive, sickening **10** immoderate, inordinate, nauseating, obsequious, over the top, saccharine **11** extravagant, sycophantic, well-rounded **12** enthusiastic, ingratiating **13** well-developed

fulsomely
10 effusively, over the top **11** excessively, insincerely, sickeningly **12** immoderately, inordinately, nauseatingly **13** extravagantly

fumble
◇ *anagram indicator*
04 faff, feel **05** botch, grope, spoil **06** bobble, bungle, huddle, mumble **07** blunder **08** flounder, scrabble **09** faff about, feel about, mishandle, mismanage

fume
04 boil, rage, rant, rave, reek, stum **05** go mad, nidor, smoke, steam, storm, vapor **06** blow up, seethe, vapour **07** be livid, explode **08** boil over, smoulder **09** be furious **10** hit the roof **11** blow your top, lose your rag, rant and rave **12** blow your cool, fly into a rage, lose your cool **15** fly off the handle, go off the deep end

fumes
03 fog, gas **04** haze, reek, smog **05** gases, smell, smoke, stink **06** stench, vapour **07** exhaust, vapours **09** pollution **10** exhalation

fumigate
05 smoke **06** purify, smudge **07** cleanse, incense, perfume **08** sanitize **09** deodorize, disinfect, sterilize

fumigation
09 cleansing, purifying
12 disinfecting, purification, sanitization 13 sterilization

fuming
03 mad 05 angry, livid 06 raging
07 boiling, enraged, furious, smoking, uptight 08 incensed, seething, up in arms 09 in a lather, raving mad, seeing red, steamed up, ticked off 10 hopping mad 11 disgruntled

fun
03 gig, joy 04 game, hoax, jest, joke, lark, play, romp 05 bourd, crack, craic, mirth, music, sport, trick, witty
06 joking, laughs, lekker, lively
07 amusing, foolery, gammock, jesting, jollity 08 gladness, hilarity, laughter, pleasure 09 amusement, diversion, diverting, enjoyable, enjoyment, frivolity, horseplay, merriment 10 buffoonery, delightful, jocularity, recreation, relaxation, skylarking, tomfoolery 11 celebration, distraction, merrymaking, pleasurable
12 cheerfulness, entertaining, recreational 13 entertainment
• **for fun**
08 for kicks 09 for a laugh 12 for enjoyment 14 for the hell of it
• **in fun**
06 in jest 07 as a joke, playful, to tease
08 jokingly 09 for a laugh, playfully, teasingly 11 mischievous
13 mischievously, tongue in cheek
• **make fun of**
03 cod, guy, rib 04 goof, jeer, joke, mock 05 get at, jolly, sport, taunt, tease 06 banter, deride, jeer at, send up 07 laugh at, scoff at, sneer at
08 ridicule 09 humiliate, poke fun at
11 have a shot at, poke borak at 13 take the mickey 15 pull someone's leg

function
02 do, go 03 act, cos, cot, job, log, run, sec, sin, tan, use 04 cosh, coth, duty, part, post, role, sech, sine, sinh, tanh, task, work 05 chore, cosec, party, serve 06 affair, behave, charge, cosech, cosine, dinner, office, result, upshot 07 concern, mission, operate, perform, purpose, tangent 08 activity, business, capacity, luncheon
09 corollary, deduction, gathering, induction, inference, reception, situation 10 conclusion, employment, occupation 11 concomitant, consequence, social event 12 have the job of 13 play the part of
14 responsibility

See also **dance**

functional
05 plain 06 useful 07 running, utility, working 08 clinical 09 operative, practical 11 hard-wearing, operational, serviceable, utilitarian

functionally
08 usefully 11 efficiently, practically
13 operationally

functionary
07 officer 08 employee, official
09 dignitary 10 bureaucrat 12 office-bearer, office-holder

fund
03 box, IMF 04 back, bank, cash, dosh, gelt, loot, mine, pool, well
05 brass, bread, cache, dough, endow, float, fonds, grant, gravy, hoard, kitty, lolly, means, money, rhino, stack, stock, store 06 assets, greens, moolah, pay for, source, supply, wealth 07 backing, capital, finance, jackpot, promote, readies, reserve, savings, shekels, sponsor, support, tracker 08 treasury
09 endowment, megabucks, reservoir, resources, slate club, subsidize
10 capitalize, collection, foundation, investment, repository, storehouse, underwrite 11 spondulicks
12 accumulation, the necessary
14 community chest
• **reserve fund**
04 rest
• **transfer funds**
04 vire

fundamental
03 key 04 main, root 05 basal, basic, chief, first, prime, vital 06 bottom, primal 07 bedrock, central, crucial, initial, organic, primary, radical
08 cardinal, integral, original, profound, ultimate 09 elemental, essential, important, necessary, primitive, principal 10 elementary, underlying 11 rudimentary
12 foundational 13 indispensable

fundamentalist
05 fundy, rigid, Talib 06 fundie, strict
08 orthodox, rigorous
14 uncompromising

fundamentally
05 à fond 06 deeply 07 acutely, at heart 08 at bottom, deep down
09 basically, crucially, in essence, primarily, radically 10 cardinally, critically, inherently, profoundly
11 essentially 13 intrinsically, substantially

fundamentals
04 laws 05 facts, rules 06 basics
09 rudiments 10 brass tacks, essentials
11 necessaries, nitty-gritty 12 nuts and bolts 14 practicalities 15 first principles

fundraising *see* **charity**

funeral
04 obit, wake 05 tangi 06 burial
08 exequies 09 cremation, interment, obsequies 10 entombment, inhumation

funereal
03 sad 04 dark 05 feral, grave
06 dismal, dreary, gloomy, solemn, sombre, woeful 07 serious
08 exequial, funeral, mournful
09 deathlike, funebrial, lamenting
10 depressing, lugubrious, sepulchral

fungus
11 thallophyte

See also **mushroom**

funk
04 fear, flap, fuss, stew 05 alarm, dodge, panic, spark, state, tizzy
06 balk at, blench, cop out, dither, flinch, frenzy, fright, terror, tiswas, tizwas 07 fluster 08 blue funk
09 agitation, cold sweat, commotion, duck out of, shirk from, touchwood
10 flinch from, recoil from 12 chicken out of

funnel
02 go 04 flue, horn, move, pass, pipe, pour, tube, vent 05 guide, shaft, stack
06 choana, convey, direct, drogue, filter, siphon 07 channel, chimney, tundish 08 sink hole, transfer, windsail
10 smokestack 11 swallow hole
12 infundibulum

funnily
◇ *anagram indicator*
09 amazingly 10 incredibly, remarkably 12 surprisingly
13 astonishingly

funny
◇ *anagram indicator*
03 odd, rum 04 rich 05 a hoot, comic, corny, droll, queer, shady, silly, wacky, weird, witty 06 absurd, way-out
07 amusing, a scream, bizarre, comical, curious, dubious, killing, oddball, off-beat, riotous, risible, strange, unusual 08 farcical, humorous, peculiar, puzzling
09 diverting, facetious, hilarious, laughable 10 hysterical, mysterious, perplexing, remarkable, ridiculous, suspicious, uproarious 12 entertaining, knee-slapping 13 side-splitting
• **something funny**
04 hoot, yell

fur
03 boa 04 coat, down, fell, flue, hair, hide, mane, muff, pane, pean, pelt, skin, wool 06 fleece, pelage
07 necklet

07 blue fox, caracal, caracul, crimmer, fitchet, fitchew, genette, karakul, krimmer, minever, miniver, muskrat, opossum, raccoon
08 cony-wool, kolinsky, moleskin, musquash, ponyskin, sealskin, sea otter, zibeline
09 broadtail, silver fox, wolverene, wolverine, zibelline
10 chinchilla
11 beech marten, Persian lamb, stone marten

furbish
04 do up **05** refit, renew **06** polish, purify, reform, repair, revamp
07 improve, remodel, restore
08 overhaul, renovate **09** modernize, refurbish **10** redecorate
11 recondition **12** rehabilitate
15 give a facelift to

furious
◇ *anagram indicator*
03 mad, wud **04** wild, wood, yond
05 angry, irate, livid **06** fierce, fuming, raging, savage, stormy **07** acharné, boiling, enraged, flaming, frantic, in a huff, in a stew, intense, salvage, violent
08 brainish, frenzied, in a paddy, incensed, inflamed, maenadic, seething, sizzling, up in arms, vehement, vigorous **09** desperate, in a lather, indignant **10** boisterous, hopping mad, infuriated, outrageous
11 tempestuous **12** incandescent
14 purple with rage

furiously
05 madly **06** wildly **07** angrily, crossly, in anger, irately, like mad **08** fiercely, in a paddy, stormily, up in arms
09 intensely, seeing red, violently
10 like blazes, vehemently, vigorously
11 indignantly **12** passionately
13 infuriatingly, tempestuously **15** avec acharnement

furnace *see* **oven**

furnish
03 fit, rig **04** gird, give, suit **05** besee, endue, equip, grant, offer, plant, stock, stuff, yield **06** afford, bestow, fit out, kit out, purvey, supply **07** appoint, bedight, garnish, present, provide
08 decorate, minister

furniture
06 things **07** effects **08** fitments, fittings, movables **09** equipment, moveables **10** appliances
11 accessories, furnishings, possessions **12** appointments
14 household goods

Furniture items include:

03 bed, cot
04 bunk, desk, sofa
05 chair, chest, couch, divan, stool, suite, table, trunk, wagon
06 buffet, bureau, carver, coffer, cradle, daybed, fender, lowboy, mirror, pouffe, settee, waggon
07 armoire, beanbag, bunkbed, cabinet, camp-bed, commode,

dresser, ottoman, sofa bed, tallboy, whatnot
08 armchair, bar chair, bedstead, bookcase, cupboard, end table, hatstand, recliner, toy chest, tub chair, wall unit, wardrobe, water bed
09 bed-settee, card table, coatstand, easy chair, fireplace, footstool, hallstand, high-chair, lamp table, sideboard, side table, step-stool, washstand, wine table
10 blanket box, chiffonier, dumb-waiter, encoignure, escritoire, firescreen, four-poster, secretaire, truckle bed, vanity unit
11 coffee table, dining chair, dining table, mantelpiece, room-divider, swivel chair
12 bedside table, chaise-longue, chesterfield, china cabinet, computer desk, folding table, gateleg table, kitchen chair, kitchen table, magazine rack, nest of tables, rocking chair, Welsh dresser
13 dressing table, four-poster bed, umbrella stand
14 chest of drawers, display cabinet, extending table, refectory table
15 bathroom cabinet, butcher's trolley, occasional chair, occasional table

See also **office**

Furniture styles include:

04 Adam, buhl
06 boulle, Empire, Gothic, rococo, Shaker
07 Art Deco, Baroque, Regency, Windsor
08 Colonial, Georgian, Sheraton
09 Charles II, Edwardian, Queen Anne, Shibayama, Victorian, William IV
10 Art Nouveau, Mackintosh, provincial
11 Anglo-Indian, Biedermeier, Chippendale, Cromwellian, Hepplewhite, Louis-Quinze, Restoration
12 Gainsborough, Transitional, Vernis Martin
13 Anglo-Colonial, Arts and Crafts, Dutch Colonial, Louis Philippe, Louis-Quatorze
14 William and Mary

furore
04 flap, fury, fuss, rage, stir, to-do
05 craze, stink, storm **06** frenzy, outcry, tumult, uproar **08** outburst
09 commotion **10** excitement, hullabaloo **11** disturbance

furrow
03 fur, rut **04** furr, knit, line, list, mill, plow, rill, seam **05** flute, gouge, stria, track **06** crease, feerin, groove, gutter, hollow, plough, sulcus, trench, trough
07 chamfer, channel, crinkle, feering, wrinkle **08** engroove, ingroove
09 corrugate, crow's foot, vallecula
11 canaliculus, lister ridge **12** draw together

• **draw first furrow**
04 feer

furry
04 soft **05** downy, fuzzy, hairy
06 fleecy, fluffy, woolly

further
03 aid, als, new, too **04** agen, also, ease, help, more, push **05** again, extra, fresh, other, speed **06** assist, as well, foster, hasten **07** advance, besides, develop, farther, forward, promote, remoter, speed up **08** champion, expedite, moreover **09** encourage, what's more **10** accelerate, additional, facilitate, in addition
11 furthermore, more distant, more extreme **12** additionally
13 supplementary

furtherance
04 help **07** backing, pursuit
08 advocacy, boosting, speeding
09 advancing, promoting, promotion **10** preferment
11 advancement, carrying-out, championing **12** facilitation
13 encouragement

furthermore
03 too **04** also **06** as well **07** besides, further **08** moreover **09** what's more
10 in addition **12** additionally **14** into the bargain

furthermost
06 utmost **07** extreme, outmost
08 farthest, furthest, remotest, ultimate **09** outermost, uttermost

furthest
06 utmost **07** extreme, outmost
08 farthest, remotest, ultimate
09 outermost, uttermost
11 furthermost

furtive
03 sly **06** covert, hidden, secret, shifty, sneaky, veiled **07** cloaked **08** stealthy, thievish, weaselly **09** secretive, underhand **11** clandestine
13 surreptitious

furtively
05 slyly **08** covertly, secretly
11 secretively **15** surreptitiously

fury
03 ire **04** rage **05** anger, dread, force, furor, power, wrath **06** Erinys, frenzy
07 madness, passion **08** ferocity, severity, violence, wildness
09 Eumenides, intensity, vehemence
10 fierceness, turbulence
11 desperation

The Furies:

06 Alecto, Megara
07 Megaera
09 Tisiphone

furze
04 whin **05** gorse

fuse
03 ren, rin, run **04** flux, join, meld, melt, weld **05** blend, fusee, fuzee, merge, smelt, unite **06** mingle, solder
07 combine **08** ankylose, coalesce, conflate, intermix **09** anchylose,

fusillade

commingle, integrate, interfuse
10 amalgamate, colliquate, synthesize
11 agglutinate, intermingle, put
together

fusillade
04 fire, hail **05** burst, salvo **06** volley
07 barrage **08** outburst **09** broadside,
discharge

fusion
05 blend, union **06** merger
07 melting, running, welding
08 blending, smelting **09** ankylosis,
synthesis **10** anchylosis, conflation,
federation **11** coalescence,
integration **12** amalgamation,
colliquation

fuss
02 do **03** ado, row **04** coil, faff, flap,
fret, rout, song, stir, to-do, work
05 hoo-ha, hurry, panic, tizzy, upset,
worry **06** bother, bustle, chichi, create,
fidget, fikery, flurry, furore, hassle, hoo-
hah, pother, pudder, racket **07** agitate,
carry-on, fluster, grumble, palaver,
parafle, stashie, stishie, stushie,
tamasha, trouble **08** ballyhoo,
brouhaha, complain, paraffle,
squabble, stooshie **09** agitation, be all
over, commotion, confusion, kerfuffle,
pantomime, take pains **10** be in a tizzy,
excitement, make a thing **11** piece of
work **13** a song and dance **14** storm in
a teacup

fussiness
08 busyness, niceness, niggling
09 finicking **10** choosiness, finicality
11 finicalness **13** particularity,
perfectionism **14** meticulousness,
pernicketiness

fusspot
06 fantod, fidget **07** old maid, worrier
08 old woman, stickler **09** nit-picker
10 fussbudget **11** hyper-critic
13 perfectionist

fussy
◊ *anagram indicator*
04 busy **05** faddy, fancy, picky, tatty
06 chichi, choosy, ornate, prissy,
rococo, spoffy **07** baroque, finical,
finicky **08** niggling, pedantic, spoffish
09 cluttered, demanding, difficult,
elaborate, quibbling, selective
10 fastidious, nit-picking, old-maidish,
particular, pernickety, scrupulous
11 old-womanish, persnickety
12 fiddle-faddle, hard to please,
pettifogging **13** grandmotherly,
overdecorated **14** discriminating

fusty
04 damp, dank, rank **05** fuggy, musty,
passé, stale **06** fousty, frowsy, frowzy,
mouldy, stuffy **07** airless, archaic,
frowsty **08** outdated **09** out-of-date
10 antiquated, malodorous,
mouldering **11** ill-smelling, old-
fogeyish **12** old-fashioned,
unventilated

futile
04 idle, no go, vain **05** empty, inept
06 barren, hollow, in vain, no good,
otiose, wasted **07** forlorn, useless
08 abortive, feckless, nugatory,
tattling, trifling **09** fruitless, pointless,
to no avail, worthless **10** profitless,
sleeveless, unavailing **11** ineffective,
ineffectual, meaningless
12 unproductive, unprofitable,
unsuccessful

futility
05 waste **06** vanity **07** mockery
08 vainesse **09** emptiness
10 barrenness, hollowness
11 aimlessness, uselessness
12 nugatoriness **13** fruitlessness,
pointlessness, worthlessness
15 ineffectiveness, meaninglessness

future
03 fut **04** next, to be **05** fated, later
06 avenir, coming, to come, unborn
07 by-and-by, outlook, planned
08 destined, eventual, expected,
imminent, tomorrow **09** designate,
hereafter, impending, prospects
10 subsequent, time to come
11 approaching, coming times,
forthcoming, in the offing, prospective
12 expectations
• **in future**
04 once **05** hence **09** after this, from
now on, hereafter **10** henceforth
11 hereinafter **12** henceforward
13 from this day on **14** from this time
on

fuzz
03 fug, nap **04** blur, down, hair, lint,
pile **05** fibre, flock, floss, fluff
06 police

fuzzy
◊ *anagram indicator*
04 hazy **05** downy, faint, foggy, furry,
linty, muzzy, vague **06** fleecy, fluffy,
frizzy, napped, woolly **07** blurred,
fuddled, muffled, shadowy, unclear,
velvety **08** confused **09** distorted,
unfocused **10** ill-defined, indefinite,
indistinct

G

G
03 gee 04 golf

gab
03 jaw, yak 04 blab, brag, buzz, chat, jest, talk 05 boast, prate, vaunt 06 babble, drivel, gossip, jabber, tattle 07 blabber, blarney, blather, blether, chatter, mockery, prattle 08 chitchat 09 loquacity, prattling, small talk 10 blethering, yackety-yak 12 conversation, tittle-tattle 13 tongue-wagging

gabble
04 blab 05 spout 06 babble, cackle, drivel, gaggle, gibber, jabber, patter, rabble, rattle, waffle 07 blabber, blether, chatter, prattle, sputter, twaddle 08 cackling, nonsense, splutter 09 gibberish 10 blethering 12 gibble-gabble, ribble-rabble

Gabon
01 G 03 GAB

gad
• **gad about**
04 fisk, roam, rove 05 jaunt, range, stray 06 ramble, travel, wander 07 traipse 08 dot about 09 flit about, gallivant, run around

gadabout
05 rover 07 rambler 08 runabout, wanderer 10 stravaiger 11 gallivanter 14 pleasure-seeker

gadget
03 toy 04 tool 05 gismo, gizmo, thing, waldo 06 device, doodad, doodah, hickey, jimjam, widget 07 gimmick, gubbins, novelty, whatnot, whatsit 08 thingamy 09 apparatus, appliance, doohickey, implement, invention, jigamaree, jiggumbob, mechanism, thingummy 10 instrument 11 contraption, contrivance, thingamybob 12 executive toy, thingummyjig 14 what-d'you-call-it

gadolinium
02 Gd

Gaelic
04 Erse

gaffe
◇ anagram indicator
04 boob, flub, goof, slip 05 brick, error 06 boo-boo, howler, slip-up 07 bloomer, blunder, clanger, faux pas, mistake 08 solecism 09 gaucherie 12 indiscretion

gaffer
03 gov, guv 04 boss 06 bigwig, ganger, honcho 07 foreman, manager, overman 08 overseer 09 big cheese 10 supervisor 14 superintendent

gag
03 pun 04 clog, curb, hoax, jest, joke, plug, pong, quip 05 block, check, choke, crack, funny, heave, quiet, retch, still 06 muffle, muzzle, stifle, wheeze 07 deceive, silence, smother 08 one-liner, restrain, suppress, throttle 09 put a gag on, wisecrack, witticism 11 nearly vomit

gaga
03 mad 04 nuts 05 barmy, batty, crazy, dotty, loony, loopy, potty 06 cuckoo, insane, raving 07 fatuous 08 demented, deranged, doolally, unhinged 09 disturbed 10 distracted, unbalanced 11 not all there, off the rails 12 mad as a hatter 13 off your rocker 14 wrong in the head

Gaia
05 Terra

gaiety
03 fun, joy 04 glee, show 05 mirth 06 colour, frolic, racket 07 daffing, delight, frolics, gayness, glitter, jollity, joyance, revelry, sparkle 08 buoyancy, gladness, hilarity, pleasure, vivacity 09 festivity, happiness, joviality, merriment, showiness 10 blitheness, brightness, brilliance, exuberance, good humour, liveliness 11 celebration, galliardise, high spirits, joie de vivre, merrymaking 12 cheerfulness 13 colourfulness

gaily
07 happily, merrily 08 blithely, brightly, joyfully 10 cheerfully 11 brilliantly, colourfully 12 flamboyantly 14 light-heartedly

gain
03 add, ern, get, nab, net, win 04 earn, make, near, nett, reap, rise 05 bunce, carry, clear, get to, gross, put on, reach, yield 06 attain, collar, come to, gather, growth, income, obtain, pick up, profit, rake in, return, reward, secure 07 achieve, acquire, advance, benefit, bring in, capture, collect, harvest, headway, improve, procure, produce, realize, revenue, takings 08 addition, arrive at, dividend, earnings, increase, interest, pickings, proceeds, progress, straight, winnings 09 accretion,

advantage, emolument, increment 10 attainment, chevisance, convenient 11 achievement, acquisition, advancement, improvement 12 augmentation
• **gain on**
07 catch up 08 approach, overtake 09 catch up on, close in on, close with, level with 11 catch up with, get closer to, get nearer to, outdistance 12 narrow the gap
• **gain time**
05 delay, stall 09 temporize 10 dilly-dally 11 play for time 12 drag your feet 13 procrastinate
• **seek to gain**
03 woo 09 cultivate

gainful
04 paid 06 paying, useful 08 fruitful 09 fructuous, lucrative, rewarding 10 beneficial, productive, profitable, worthwhile 11 moneymaking 12 advantageous, remunerative

gainfully
08 usefully 10 profitably 11 lucratively 12 beneficially, productively 14 advantageously

gainsay
04 deny 06 oppose 07 dispute 09 challenge, disaffirm 10 contradict, contravene, controvert 12 disagree with

gait
03 get 04 brat, gyte, pace, step, walk 05 child, going, tread 06 allure, manner, stride 07 bearing 08 carriage 10 deportment

gaiter
04 spat 06 hogger 07 cutikin, spattee 08 cootikin, cuitikin 11 spatterdash

gala
04 fair, fete 05 party 07 jubilee, pageant 08 carnival, festival, jamboree 09 festivity 10 procession 11 celebration

galaxy
04 host, mass 05 array, stars 06 blazar, nebula 07 cluster 09 gathering, multitude 10 collection, star system 11 solar system 13 constellation, group assembly

Galaxies include:

03 Leo
04 Arp's, Lost, Mice
05 Bode's, Helix, Malin
06 Baade's, Carafe, Hydra A, Maffei, Spider, Virgo A, Zwicky

Cannon's, Cygnus A, Pancake, Sextans, Spindle, The Eyes
8 Antennae, Barnard's, Bear's Paw, Black Eye, Milky Way, Papillon, Perseus A, Pinwheel, Seashell, Sombrero
9 Andromeda, Bear's Claw, Cartwheel, Centaurus, Hercules A, Sunflower, Whirlpool
0 Draco Dwarf, Silver Coin, The Garland, Triangulum
Carina Dwarf, Hardcastle's, Pisces Cloud, Pisces Dwarf, The Ringtail
2 Atom For Peace, Integral Sign, Pegasus Dwarf, Siamese Twins, Virgo Cluster
3 Aquarius Dwarf, Sculptor Dwarf, Serpens Sextet, Virgo Pinwheel
4 Capricorn Dwarf, Copeland Septet, Reticulum Dwarf, Ursa Minor Dwarf
5 Exclamation Mark, Horologium Dwarf, Magellanic Cloud, Miniature Spiral

ale
3 fit **04** wind **05** blast, burst, storm **6** Myrica, squall, wester **07** cyclone, orther, sea turn, snorter, souther, ornado, typhoon **08** eruption, outbreak, outburst **09** bog myrtle, xplosion, hurricane, sou'wester **0** ripsnorter **11** equinoctial, sweet villow

all
3 irk, nag, vex **04** bile, dyke, fell, flaw, eck, rile **05** annoy, brass, cheek, fault, et to, nerve, peeve, scoff, spite, venom **6** animus, bother, enmity, harass, nalice, nettle, oak-nut, pester, plague, ankle, ruffle **07** ill-will, provoke, ancour **08** acrimony, bedeguar, hutzpah, irritate, oak apple, sourness, acahout **09** aggravate, animosity, ntipathy, assurance, brass neck, ostility, impudence, insolence, sage pple, sauciness, virulence **0** bitterness, brazenness, effrontery, xasperate **11** malevolence, resumption **12** impertinence, nycodomatium **13** get on your wick, et up your nose, get your back up, put our back up

allant
3 fop, gay **04** beau, bold **05** brave, andy, lover, manly, noble **06** daring, eroic, plucky, polite **07** amorous, ourtly, dashing, valiant **08** cavalier, icisbeo, fearless, gracious, intrepid, plendid **09** attentive, audacious, hamberer, chevalier, chivalric, courteous, dauntless **10** chivalrous, ourageous, honourable, thoughtful **1** considerate, gentlemanly, nagnificent

allantly
5 nobly **07** bravely **08** politely **9** valiantly **10** fearlessly, graciously, eroically, honourably, intrepidly **1** audaciously, courteously, auntlessly **12** chivalrously,

courageously, thoughtfully **13** considerately

gallantry
04 game **05** pluck **06** daring, honour, spirit, valour **07** bravery, courage, heroism **08** audacity, boldness, chivalry, courtesy, nobility, valiance **09** manliness **10** politeness **11** courtliness, intrepidity **12** fearlessness, graciousness **13** attentiveness, consideration, courteousness, dauntlessness **14** courageousness, thoughtfulness **15** gentlemanliness

gallery
04 brow, gods, loft, mine, pawn, walk **05** alure, level **06** arcade, circle, dedans, museum **07** balcony, passage, terrace, veranda **08** bartisan, bartizan, brattice, brattish, brettice, casemate, rood loft, traverse, verandah **09** choir loft, triforium **10** art gallery, earthhouse, hall of fame, pinakothek, scaffolage, spectators **11** display room, dress circle, pinacotheca, scaffoldage **14** exhibition area

See also **museum**

galley *see* ship

galling
06 bitter, vexing **07** irksome **08** annoying, nettling, plaguing, rankling **09** harassing, provoking, vexatious **10** bothersome, irritating **11** aggravating, embittering, humiliating, infuriating **12** exasperating

gallium
02 Ga

gallivant
04 roam, rove **05** range, stray **06** ramble, travel, wander **07** traipse **08** dot about, gad about, stravaig **09** flit about, run around

gallon
01 g **03** gal **04** cong, gall **07** congius

gallop
03 fly, run **04** bolt, dart, dash, race, rush, tear, zoom **05** burst, hurry, shoot, speed **06** canter, career, hasten, scurry, sprint, wallop **07** cariere

gallows
03 nub **04** tree, wild **05** bough, cheat, perky, saucy **06** daring, gallus, gibbet, plucky, woodie **07** stifler, the rope **08** damnably, dule-tree, impudent, scaffold, spirited, tiresome **09** sprightly **10** Tyburn-tree, villainous **11** mischievous **12** confoundedly, nubbing-cheat, unmanageable

galore
06 lots of, plenty, tons of **07** aplenty, heaps of, to spare **08** stacks of **09** in numbers **10** everywhere, millions of **11** in abundance, in profusion

galvanize
04 fire, jolt, move, prod, spur, stir, urge, zinc **05** rouse, shock **06** arouse,

awaken, excite **07** animate, enliven, inspire, provoke, quicken, startle **08** energize, vitalize **09** electrify, stimulate **10** invigorate

Gambia
03 GMB, WAG

gambit
04 move, play, ploy, ruse, wile **05** trick **06** device, tactic **07** tactics **08** artifice **09** manoeuvre, stratagem **11** machination

gamble
03 bet **04** back, dice, gaff, game, jeff, play, punt, risk, spec **05** stake, wager **06** chance, hazard, plunge, toss-up **07** flutter, lottery, pot luck, venture **08** chance it **09** speculate, take a risk **10** put money on **11** speculation, take a chance, try your luck **12** have a flutter, play for money **13** leap in the dark, play the horses

gambler
06 better, punter **07** plunger, tinhorn, tipster **08** gamester **09** bookmaker, daredevil, desperado, risk-taker, throwster **14** turf accountant

gambling
04 play **07** betting **10** risk-taking **11** speculation **15** playing for money

Gambling-related terms include:
03 hit, lay, pot
04 back, bust, dice, hold, odds, punt, shoe, tout
05 bingo, cards, craps, jeton, lotto, motza, poker, pools, stake, stick, wager, welsh
06 bookie, casino, chip in, fan-tan, fulham, gaming, jetton, lay off, motser, punter
07 flutter, lottery, tipster
08 levanter, long shot, outsider, roulette, teetotum
09 blackjack, bookmaker, card shark, dog racing, favourite, place a bet, vingt-et-un
10 put-and-take, put money on, sweepstake
11 card-sharper, find the lady, go one better, horse racing, numbers game, rouge-et-noir, slot machine
12 break the bank, card counting, debt of honour, pitch-and-toss, scoop the pool
13 hedge your bets, shoot the works, spread betting
14 shove-halfpenny, three-card trick, wheel of fortune
15 cash in your chips, disorderly house, greyhound racing, make a clean sweep

See also **bet**

• **gambling place**
04 hell **06** arcade, casino

gambol
◊ *anagram indicator*
03 hop **04** jump, leap, romp, skip **05** bound, caper, dance, frisk **06** bounce, cavort, frolic, prance,

spring **07** disport **09** cut a caper, cut capers **15** kick up your heels

game
03 bag, fun, jeu, pit, tie **04** ball, bold, bout, jest, joke, lame, meat, meet, play, prey, romp **05** brave, eager, event, flesh, match, prank, ready, round, sport, trick, up for **06** daring, frolic, gamble, plucky, quarry, spoils **07** contest, gallant, meeting, pastime, valiant, willing **08** activity, business, desirous, fearless, inclined, intrepid, prepared, resolute, spirited, wild fowl **09** amusement, diversion, gallantry, merriment, operation **10** courageous, interested, recreation, tournament **11** competition, distraction, lion-hearted, unflinching **12** enthusiastic **13** entertainment, practical joke

Game animals and birds include:

03 elk, fox
04 bear, boar, coot, deer, duck, guan, hare, lion, stag, teal, wolf
05 bison, goose, hyena, moose, quail, scaup, snipe, tiger, zebra
06 curlew, grouse, plover, rabbit, wigeon
07 buffalo, caribou, giraffe, mallard, moorhen, muntjac, pintail, pochard, red deer, roe deer, widgeon
08 antelope, elephant, kangaroo, pheasant, sika deer, squirrel, wild boar, woodcock
09 blackcock, blackgame, crocodile, partridge, ptarmigan, waterfowl
10 fallow deer, guinea fowl, tufted duck, wild turkey, wood grouse, woodpigeon
11 Canada goose
12 capercaillie, capercailzie, hippopotamus, mountain lion

See also **poultry**

Games include:

03 loo, nap
04 brag, crib, dice, faro, I-spy, ludo, pool, snap
05 bowls, chess, clubs, craps, darts, halma, jacks, Jenga®, poker, rummy, whist
06 bridge, Cluedo®, quinze
07 bezique, bowling, canasta, hangman, mah-jong, marbles, old maid, picquet, pinball, pontoon, snooker
08 baccarat, card game, charades, checkers, cribbage, dominoes, draughts, forfeits, gin rummy, Kim's game, Monopoly®, napoleon, patience, ping pong, reversis, roulette, sardines, Scrabble®
09 bagatelle, billiards, blackjack, board game, draw poker, hopscotch, newmarket, Pelmanism, Simon says, solitaire, solo whist, stud poker, tic-tac-toe, twenty-one, vingt-et-un
10 backgammon, Balderdash®, fivestones, jackstraws, Pictionary®, spillikins

11 battleships, beetle drive, chemin de fer, hide-and-seek, table tennis, tiddlywinks
12 consequences, partner whist, shove ha'penny
13 blind man's buff, clock patience, happy families, musical chairs, pass the parcel, postman's knock, spin the bottle, table football, ten-pin bowling
14 contract bridge, follow-my-leader, hunt-the-thimble, nine men's morris, Trivial Pursuit®
15 Chinese checkers, Chinese whispers, duplicate bridge

Board games include:

02 go
04 ludo, Risk®, siga
05 chess, darts, goose, halma, lurch, marls, nyout, senet, shogi, Sorry®
06 Boggle®, Cluedo®, gobang, gomuku, merels, merils, morals, morris, tables, tabula, uckers
07 Cranium®, mah-jong, mancala, marrels, merells, pachisi, petteia, reverse, reversi, Yahtzee
08 checkers, chequers, cribbage, Dingbats®, draughts, miracles, Monopoly®, parchesi, Rummikub®, Scrabble®
09 bagatelle, Buccaneer®, Operation®, Parcheesi®, solitaire, tic-tac-toe
10 backgammon, Go for Broke®, latrunculi, Mastermind®, Pictionary®
11 Battleships®, fox and geese, Frustration®
12 pente grammai
13 Concentration®, table skittles, The Game of Life®
14 nine men's morris, Trivial Pursuit®
15 Chinese checkers, Chinese chequers, duodecim scripta, fivepenny morris, ninepenny morris, three men's morris

See also **sport**

Card games include:

03 don, nap, pig, war
04 brag, bust, faro, fish, golf, king, loba, may I?, phat, pits, push, rook, scat, skat, snap, solo, spit, tunk, tute, ugly
05 blitz, cheat, cinch, crash, flush, knack, nerts, pairs, pedro, pitch, poker, ronda, rummy, samba, shoot, speed, tarok, tarot, whist
06 big two, boodle, bridge, casino, church, crates, cuckoo, dakota, deuces, écarté, euchre, fan tan, five up, go fish, hearts, henway, kaiser, knaves, oh hell!, palace, pepper, piquet, pounce, red dog, sevens, spades, spoons, squeal, stitch, switch, tarock, taroky, trumps, turtle, valets
07 auction, authors, bezique, bone ace, canasta, clabber, last one, mah jong, old maid, pontoon, quartet, setback, spitzer, whipsaw

08 ace-deuce, all fives, all fours, anaconda, baccarat, bid whist, blackout, carousel, cribbage, drunkard, elevator, gin rummy, high five, Michigan, napoleon, patience, pinochle, Pope Joan, sequence, shanghai, Welsh don
09 abyssinia, bid euchre, blackjack, catch five, golden ten, king pedro, king rummy, let it ride, newmarket, Pelmanism, poker bull, president, quadrille, racehorse, solitaire, solo whist, stud poker, tic-tac-toe, tile rummy, vingt-et-un
10 black maria, buck euchre, capitalism, chinese ten, cincinnati, crazy nines, dirty clubs, German solo, parliament, preference, ride the bus, sheepshead, strip poker, three in one, Wall Street
11 cat and mouse, chase the ace, chemin de fer, chicken foot, crazy eights, English stud, find the lady, French tarot, French whist, German whist, high-low-jack, Indian poker, Mexican stud, nine-card don, Oklahoma gin, racing demon, Russian bank, six-card brag, speculation, Texas hold 'em
12 Chinese poker, devil's bridge, draw dominoes, five-card brag, five-card draw, four-card brag, high-card pool, kings corners, Mexican sweat, Mexican train, nine-card brag, one and thirty, pick a partner, ruff and trump, Russian poker, shoot pontoon
13 concentration, contract rummy, contract whist, happy families, knockout whist, lame-brain Pete, Michigan rummy, Romanian whist, sergeant major, seven-card brag, Shanghai rummy, three-card brag
14 Caribbean poker, contract bridge, five hundred rum, fives and threes, follow the queen, good, better, best, jack the shifter, Liverpool rummy, Minnesota whist, rich man poor man, ruff and honours, second hand high, spite and malice, spit in the ocean, three-card monte, trust—don't trust
15 back alley bridge, cut-throat euchre, double solitaire, nomination whist, railroad canasta, stealing bundles

- **end to game**
04 draw, mate **09** checkmate, stalemate
- **point out game**
03 set
- **preliminary to game**
04 toss
- **right to begin game**
04 pose

gamekeeper
06 keeper, warden **07** venerer

gamely
06 boldly **07** bravely **09** valiantly **10** fearlessly, intrepidly, resolutely **12** courageously **13** unflinchingly

gamut
04 area **05** field, gamme, range, scale, scope, sweep **06** series **07** compass, variety **08** sequence, spectrum

gang
02 go **03** lot, mob, set **04** band, club, core, crew, crue, ging, herd, nest, pack, push, ring, team **05** coven, crowd, group, horde, party, posse, shift, squad **06** circle, clique, coffle, outfit, troupe **07** company, coterie, massive, ratpack **09** gathering **11** tribulation
• **gang up on, gang up against**
12 unite against **13** team up against **15** conspire against

gangling
04 bony, tall **05** gawky, lanky, rangy **06** gangly, gauche, skinny **07** angular, awkward, spindly **08** raw-boned, ungainly **12** loose-jointed

gangrene
07 mortify **08** necrosis **09** phagedena **10** phagedaena, thanatosis

gangster
02 Al **04** hood, thug **05** crook, heavy, rough, tough **06** bandit, Capone, robber, yakuza, Yardie **07** brigand, gangsta, goombah, greaser, hoodlum, mobster, ruffian, steamer, tumbler, wise guy **08** criminal, enforcer **09** desperado, goodfella, racketeer, terrorist

gangway
04 brow **05** aisle **07** passage, walkway **08** corridor **10** passageway

gannet
04 guga **05** booby, solan **10** solan goose

gaol, gaoler *see* jail, gaol; jailer, gaoler

gap
04 gulf, hole, lack, leap, lull, rent, rift, rima, slap, void **05** blank, break, chasm, chink, cleft, crack, gorge, musit, notch, pause, shard, sherd, space **06** breach, bunker, cavity, cranny, divide, hiatus, lacuna, recess, spread, street, window **07** crevice, opening, orifice, passage, saw gate, saw kerf, vacancy, vacuity **08** aperture, distance, fontanel, fracture, interval, sliprail **09** disparity, interlude **10** difference, divergence, fontanelle, interstice, separation **12** intermission, interruption **13** discontinuity, node of Ranvier **14** expansion joint

gape
04 bawl, gaup, gawk, gawp, gaze, open, part, yawn **05** crack, gerne, split, stare **06** goggle, rictus, wonder **07** dehisce **10** rubberneck

gaper
03 Mya **06** comber

gaping
04 open, vast, wide **05** broad, hiant **06** rictus **07** ringent, yawning

09 cavernous, fatiscent, interrupt **11** open-mouthed **12** fissirostral

garage
04 barn **06** lock-up **07** car port **10** gas station **11** muffler shop **13** petrol station **14** service station

garb
03 rig **04** form, gear, look, robe, togs, vest, wear **05** array, cover, dress, get-up, guise, robes, style **06** aspect, attire, clothe, livery, outfit, rig out, rig-out **07** apparel, clobber, clothes, costume, fashion, garment, raiment, regalia, uniform, vesture **08** clothing **09** semblance, vestiment, vestments **10** appearance, habiliment, habilitate

garbage
03 rot **04** blah, bosh, bull, bunk, cock, crap, guff, junk, muck **05** balls, bilge, dross, filth, hooey, slops, swill, trash, tripe, waste **06** bunkum, debris, drivel, hot air, litter, piffle, refuse, scraps **07** baloney, eyewash, hogwash, remains, rhubarb, rubbish, twaddle **08** claptrap, cobblers, detritus, malarkey, nonsense, tommyrot **09** gibberish, leftovers, moonshine, poppycock, scourings, sweepings **10** codswallop **11** odds and ends **13** bits and pieces

garble
◇ *anagram indicator*
04 edit, sift, warp **05** mix up, slant, twist **06** doctor, jumble, mangle, muddle **07** cleanse, confuse, corrupt, distort, falsify, pervert **08** mutilate, scramble **10** tamper with **12** misinterpret, misrepresent

garbled
◇ *anagram indicator*
07 jumbled, mixed-up, muddled **08** confused **09** scrambled **14** undecipherable, unintelligible

garden
03 erf **04** bagh, park, plot, yard **05** garth **06** herbar **08** backyard, paradise **09** curtilage

Gardens include:
03 Kew
04 Eden, Ness
05 Stowe
06 Het Loo, Monet's, Suzhou, Tivoli, Wisley
07 Alnwick, Bodnant, Boxwood, Giverny, Heligan, Kane'ohe, Motsuji, Urakuen
08 Alhambra, Biltmore, Blenheim, Claymont, Ermitage, Hopewood, Hyde Hall, Longwood, Mt Vernon, Nanzenji, Pleasure, Rikugien, Rosedown, Rosemoor, Sankeien
09 Bagatelle, Claremont, Lingering, Lion Grove, Stourhead, Tuileries
10 Capel Manor, Chatsworth, Harlow Carr, Kensington, Levens Hall, Schönbrunn, Versailles
11 Chanticleer, Eden Project, Ji Chang Yuan
12 Castle Howard, Hampton Court, Hidcote Manor, Jingshan Park,

Katsura Rikyu, Royal Botanic, Sissinghurst, Studley Royal
13 Dumbarton Oaks, Harewood House, Orange Botanic, Vaux le Vicomte
14 Biddulph Grange, Drummond Castle, Hua Ching Palace, Stone Lion Grove
15 Arnold Arboretum

Garden types include:
03 tea
04 beer, herb, knot, lawn, rock, roof, rose
05 arbor, fruit, water
06 alpine, arbour, border, flower, herbar, indoor, market, physic, rosary, rosery, sunken, walled, winter
07 cottage, hanging, Italian, kitchen, olitory, orchard, rockery, rose bed
08 chinampa, Japanese, kailyard, rosarium
09 allotment, arboretum, botanical, cole-garth, flower bed, kailyaird, raised bed, shrubbery, terrarium, truck-farm, window box
10 ornamental, rose arbour
13 plantie-cruive, vegetable plot

gardener
03 Eve **04** Adam, mali **06** mallee **07** trucker

Gardeners include:
03 Don (Monty)
04 Kent (William), Page (Russell)
05 Brown (Lancelot 'Capability'), Gavin (Diarmuid), Lloyd (Christopher), Monet (Claude), Wilde (Kim)
06 Gilpin (William Sawrey), Ingram (Collingwood 'Cherry'), Jekyll (Gertrude), Paxton (Sir Joseph), Repton (Humphry)
07 Clusius (Carolus), Dimmock (Charlie), Le Nôtre (André), Thrower (Percy)
08 Hamilton (Geoff), Jellicoe (Sir Geoffrey), Robinson (William)
10 Titchmarsh (Alan), Tradescant (John, the Elder), Tradescant (John, the Younger)
13 Sackville-West (Vita)

garden flower *see* flower

gardening
Gardening tools include:
03 axe, hoe
04 fork, pots, rake
05 Flymo®, spade
06 cloche, gloves, scythe, shears, trowel
07 fan rake, hatchet, kneeler, loppers, netting, pruners, trellis, wellies
08 chainsaw, clippers, hosepipe, shredder, strimmer
09 cold frame, fruit cage, garden saw, lawn edger, lawnmower, lawn raker, secateurs, sprinkler, water butt
10 compost bin, cultivator, fertilizer, garden cart, greenhouse, lawn

roller, soil tester, weedkiller
11 incinerator, watering can,
wheelbarrow
12 hedge trimmer, potting table
13 garden sprayer, lawn scarifier
14 rotary spreader

Gardening-related terms include:

03 bed
04 bulb, clay, loam, plot, seed, soil,
tree, weed
05 bower, graft, hedge, mulch, plant,
shrub
06 annual, hoeing, hybrid, manure,
raking
07 climber, compost, cutting, digging,
growing, organic, produce,
pruning, staking, topiary, topsoil,
weeding
08 gardener, layering, planting,
thinning, watering
09 deciduous, germinate, leaf-mould,
perennial, pesticide
10 coniferous, fertilizer, hardy plant
11 cultivation, green manure, ground
cover, hydroponics, potting shed,
propagation
12 bedding plant, conservatory,
horticulture, hybrid vigour
13 double digging, growing season,
transplanting
15 window gardening

Gardner
03 Ava

gargantuan
03 big **04** huge, vast **05** giant, large
07 immense, mammoth, massive,
titanic **08** colossal, enormous,
gigantic, towering **09** ginormous,
humongous, humungous, leviathan,
monstrous **10** monumental,
prodigious, tremendous
11 elephantine **14** Brobdingnagian

garish
04 heal, loud, rory **05** cheap, flash,
gaudy, jazzy, lurid, roary, rorie, showy
06 criant, flashy, glitzy, roarie, tawdry,
vulgar **07** glaring, raffish **08** luminous,
tinselly **09** flaunting, tasteless
10 glittering **12** meretricious

garishly
06 loudly **07** gaudily, jazzily, luridly
08 glitzily **09** glaringly **11** tastelessly

garland
03 lei **04** bays, deck **05** adorn, crown,
glory, toran **06** crants, stemma, torana,
wreath **07** chaplet, coronal, coronet,
festoon, flowers, girlond, honours,
laurels, wreathe **08** decorate,
headband, ornament **09** engarland
10 decoration, naval crown

garments
04 garb, gear, togs, wear **05** dress, get-
up **06** attire, outfit **07** apparel, clothes,
costume, uniform **08** clothing,
menswear
See also **clothes, clothing**

garner
04 cull, heap, save **05** amass, hoard,

lay up, put by, store **06** gather, pile up
07 collect, deposit, granary, husband,
reserve, stack up **08** assemble, stow
away, treasure **09** stockpile
10 accumulate

garnet
06 pyrope **08** melanite **09** almandine,
andradite, carbuncle, demantoid,
grossular, pyreneite, rhodolite,
uvarovite **10** alabandine, topazolite
11 schorlomite, spessartine,
spessartite **12** grossularite
13 cinnamon stone **14** Uralian
emerald

garnish
04 deck, lard, trim **05** adorn, grace
06 kit out, relish, set off, supply
07 deck out, enhance, festoon, furnish
08 beautify, decorate, ornament,
trimming **09** adornment, embellish,
gremolata **10** decoration
11 enhancement **13** embellishment,
ornamentation

garret
04 loft **05** attic, roost, solar **06** turret
07 mansard **09** roof space
10 watchtower

garrison
03 man **04** base, camp, fort, post, unit
05 guard, mount, place, stuff
06 assign, casern, defend, occupy,
troops, zareba **07** command, furnish,
protect, station **08** barracks, fortress,
position **10** armed force, detachment,
encampment, engarrison, stronghold
13 fortification

garrulous
04 glib **05** gabby, gassy, windy, wordy
06 chatty, mouthy, prolix **07** gushing,
prating, verbose, voluble, wordish
08 babbling, effusive, gaggling
09 gossiping, prattling, talkative,
yabbering **10** chattering, long-winded,
loquacious

garrulousness
09 loquacity, prolixity, verbosity
10 mouthiness, volubility
11 verboseness, wordishness
13 talkativeness **14** long-windedness,
loquaciousness

gas

Gases include:

02 CS
03 air, LNG, LPG
04 neon, tear, town
05 ether, marsh, nerve, niton, ozone,
radon, xenon
06 butane, helium, ketene
07 ammonia, krypton, methane,
mustard, natural, propane
08 cyanogen, ethylene, firedamp,
laughing
09 acetylene, black damp, chokedamp
10 chloroform
12 nitrous oxide
13 carbon dioxide, dimethylamine
14 carbon monoxide

See also **talk**

gash
03 cut **04** hack, nick, rend, rent, slit,
tear **05** extra, gouge, score, slash,
spare, split, wound **06** incise, scotch,
tattle **07** ghastly, hideous **08** incision,
lacerate **09** talkative **10** laceration

gasp
04 blow, gulp, kink, pant, puff
05 chink, choke, heave **06** breath,
wheeze **07** breathe **11** exclamation
15 catch your breath

gassy
06 bubbly, frothy **07** aerated, foaming,
gaseous, verbose **08** bubbling
09 sparkling **10** carbonated
12 effervescent

gastric
07 coeliac, enteric, stomach
09 abdominal, stomachic **10** intestinal

gastropod *see* **mollusc**

gate
03 way **04** door, exit, goat, path, port,
yate, yett **05** hatch, koker **06** access,
portal, street, vimana, wicket
07 barrier, caisson, channel, doorway,
gateway, opening, passage, pontoon,
postern, shutter **08** aboideau,
aboiteau, entrance, sliprail
See also **circuit**

gatecrash
04 sorn

gateway
04 arch, port **05** pylon, toran, torii
06 torana **08** propylon **09** sallyport
10 propylaeum

gather
◇ *containment indicator*
02 in **03** add **04** camp, club, crop, cull,
draw, fold, gain, grow, heap, hear, mass,
meet, pick, pull, rake, reap, tuck
05 amass, build, crowd, flock, get in,
glean, group, hoard, infer, learn, pleat,
pluck, rally, shirr **06** assume, deduce,
garner, muster, pick up, pile up, pucker,
pull in, rake in, ruffle, select, summon,
throng **07** accrete, advance, attract,
believe, build up, cluster, collect,
convene, develop, harvest, hoard up,
improve, marshal, round up, surmise
08 assemble, conclude, converge,
increase, progress **09** stash away,
stockpile, suppurate **10** accumulate,
congregate, understand **12** come
together **13** bring together

gathering
◇ *containment indicator*
03 bee, hui, lek, mob **04** band, feis,
fest, mass, meet, rave, rout, ruck, shir
05 coven, crowd, flock, group, hangi,
horde, party, rally, salon, shirr, spree
06 huddle, love-in, muster, rabble,
social, throng **07** company, gabfest,
husking, Kommers, meeting, reunion,
round-up, turnout **08** assembly,
conclave, function, jamboree,
musicale, singsong, tea party
09 wapenshaw, wapinshaw
10 assemblage, collective, convention,

orroboree, logrolling, wapenschaw,
vapinschaw, wappenshaw
11 convocation, gallimaufry, get-
gether, wappenschaw
12 congregation **14** belle assemblée

gauche
03 shy **05** gawky, inept **06** clumsy
07 awkward, ill-bred **08** farouche,
gnorant, tactless, ungainly
09 graceless, inelegant, maladroit
10 uncultured, ungraceful, unpolished
11 ill-mannered, insensitive
15 unsophisticated

gaudiness
08 loudness **09** harshness, showiness
10 brightness, brilliance, flashiness,
garishness, tawdriness **11** raffishness
13 tastelessness

gaudy
03 gay **04** loud **05** flash, harsh, merry,
showy, stark, tacky **06** bright, flashy,
garish, glitzy, kitsch, snazzy, tawdry,
tinsel, vulgar **07** flaming, glaring,
raffish **08** tinselly **09** brilliant,
colourful, flaunting, shrieking,
tasteless, too bright **12** meretricious,
ostentatious **13** multicoloured

gauge
04 area, bore, norm, rate, rule, size,
span, test **05** basic, check, count,
depth, guess, guide, judge, meter,
model, scale, scope, sizer, value,
weigh, width **06** assess, degree,
extent, figure, height, reckon, sample
07 apprise, calibre, compute, example,
measure, pattern, scantle **08** capacity,
estimate, evaluate, exemplar, standard
09 ascertain, benchmark, calculate,
criterion, determine, guideline,
indicator, magnitude, marijuana,
scantling, thickness, yardstick
11 guesstimate

gaunt
04 bare, bony, grim, lank, lean, thin,
lawn **05** bleak, harsh, stark **06** barren,
dismal, dreary, skinny, wasted
07 angular, forlorn, haggard, rawbone,
scraggy, scrawny, spindly **08** desolate,
rawboned, skeletal **09** emaciated
10 cadaverous, forbidding, hollow-
eyed **12** skin and bones

Gauss
01 G **02** gs

gauze
04 film **07** tiffany **08** illusion
11 cheesecloth

gauzy
04 thin **05** filmy, light, sheer **06** flimsy
08 delicate, gossamer **10** diaphanous,
see-through **11** transparent
13 insubstantial, unsubstantial

gawk
04 gape, gawp, gaze, look, ogle
05 stare **06** goggle

gawky
05 inept, lanky **06** clumsy, gauche,
oafish **07** awkward, loutish
08 gangling, ungainly **09** graceless,
lumbering, maladroit **13** unco-
ordinated

gawp
04 gape, gawk, gaze, look, ogle
05 stare **06** goggle

gay
04 camp, pink, rich **05** gaudy, happy,
jolly, merry, nitid, riant, showy, sunny,
vivid **06** blithe, bright, flashy, garish,
joyful, lively, wanton **07** festive, gallant,
lesbian, playful, sapphic, spotted
08 animated, bisexual, carefree,
cheerful, debonair, speckled
09 brilliant, colourful, exuberant, fun-
loving, homophile, sparkling, sprightly,
vivacious **10** dissipated, flamboyant,
homosexual **12** light-hearted **13** in
good spirits, in high spirits **15** pleasure-
seeking

gaze
03 eye **04** gape, gawk, look, moon,
muse, pore, view **05** stare, watch
06 goggle, regard, wonder
08 aftereye, gazement, outstare, wait
upon **09** fixed look, moon about
10 moon around **11** contemplate
12 look vacantly, stare fixedly **13** stare
intently

gazebo
03 hut **07** shelter **08** pavilion
09 belvedere **11** summerhouse

gazelle
03 goa **04** mohr **05** ariel, mhorr
07 chikara **08** chinkara

gazette
03 gaz **05** organ, paper **06** notice
07 journal, tabloid **08** despatch,
dispatch, magazine **09** newspaper,
news-sheet **10** broadsheet, periodical

gear
03 cog, fit, kit, low, top **04** garb, togs
05 adapt, dress, drugs, first, get-up,
shift, stuff, third, tools, works **06** affair,
armour, attire, design, devise, doings,
matter, outfit, second, tackle, tailor,
things **07** apparel, baggage, clobber,
clothes, effects, gearing, harness,
luggage, prepare, ratchet, reverse,
threads **08** business, clothing,
cogwheel, garments, organize,
supplies, utensils **09** apparatus,
engrenage, equipment, gearwheel,
machinery, mechanism **10** appliances,

belongings, implements, link-motion,
tooth-wheel, underdrive
11 accessories, instruments,
possessions, synchromesh
12 contrivances, toothed wheel
13 accoutrements, paraphernalia

See also **clothes, clothing**; **garments**

geegee
02 GG

See also **horse**

geezer
03 man **04** chap, cove **05** bloke
06 fellow

gel, jell
03 set **04** form **06** harden **07** congeal,
stiffen, thicken **08** finalize, solidify
09 coagulate, take shape **11** crystallize,
materialize **12** come together

gelatinous
05 gluey, gooey, gummy **06** sticky,
viscid **07** jellied, rubbery, viscous
09 congealed, glutinous, jelly-like
12 mucilaginous

geld
03 cut, lib, tax **04** sort, spay
05 unman, unsex **06** neuter
07 deprive **08** castrate, enfeeble
09 expurgate **10** emasculate

gem
03 bud **04** rose **05** cameo, jewel,
prize, stone **06** scarab **08** gemstone,
marquise, sparkler, treasure
09 bespangle, brilliant, scaraboid
11 masterpiece, pride and joy **12** the
bee's knees **13** precious stone
14 crème de la crème

gen
04 data, dope, info **05** facts **07** details,
low-down **09** knowledge
10 background **11** information
• **gen up on**
05 study **08** bone up on, read up on,
research, swot up on **09** brush up on
12 find out about

gene *see* **genetics**

genealogy
04 line **05** birth **06** family **07** dynasty
08 breeding **09** parentage,
whakapapa **10** derivation, extraction
11 generations **13** family history

Genealogy-related terms include:

03 DSP, IGI, née
04 AGRA, clan, deed, heir, late, race,
will
05 issue, trace, widow
06 census, degree, estate, legacy, relict
07 archive, bastard, bequest, consort,
descent, divorce, epitaph, kinship,
lineage, peerage, probate, progeny,
removed, surname, testate, trustee,
widower, witness
08 ancestor, ancestry, bachelor,
bequeath, canon law, deceased,
decedent, emigrant, forebear,
maternal, paternal, pedigree,
relation, spinster
09 ascendant, given name, immigrant,
indenture, intestate, necrology,
offspring, sine prole, testament
10 ahnentafal, descendant, family
name, family tree, forefather,
generation, maiden name,
onomastics, progenitor, succession
11 beneficiary, genealogist, record
agent
12 burial record, census record,
cousin-german, Domesday Book,
illegitimate, primogenitor, vital
records
13 Christian name, consanguinity,
pedigree chart, primogeniture
14 cemetery record, common
ancestor, marriage record
15 vital statistics

general
05 broad, loose, mixed, rough, total,
usual, vague **06** common, global,
normal, public, varied **07** blanket,
diverse, inexact, overall, popular,
regular, typical **08** accepted, all-round,
assorted, everyday, habitual, ordinary,
standard, sweeping **09** customary,
extensive, imprecise, panoramic,
prevalent, universal **10** ill-defined,
indefinite, prevailing, unspecific,
variegated, widespread
11 approximate, wide-ranging **12** all-
inclusive, conventional
13 comprehensive, heterogeneous,
miscellaneous **14** across-the-board

Generals include:

03 Doe (Samuel K), Ike, Lee (Robert E),
Ney (Michel)
04 Alba (Ferdinand Alvarez de Toledo,
Duke of), Alva (Ferdinand Alvarez
de Toledo, Duke of), Asad
(Hafez al-), Dyer (Reginald), Haig
(Alexander), Prem (Tinsulanonda)
05 Assad (Hafez al-), Booth (William),
Clive (Robert, Lord), Gates
(Horatio), Grant (Ulysses S), Scott
(Winfield), Soult (Nicolas Jean de
Dieu), Wolfe (James)
06 Anders (Wladyslaw), Caesar

(Julius), Custer (George
Armstrong), Franco (Francisco),
Moreau (Jean Victor), Napier (Sir
Charles), Powell (Colin), Rommel
(Erwin), Scipio (the Younger),
Sharon (Ariel), Zhukov (Georgi)
07 Agrippa (Marcus Vipsanius),
Atatürk (Mustapha Kemal), Fairfax
(Thomas, Lord), Masséna (André),
Spínola (António de)
08 Agricola (Gnaeus Julius), Badoglio
(Pietro), Brisbane (Sir Thomas
Makdougall), Camillus (Marcus
Furius), Cardigan (James Thomas
Brudenell, Earl of), de Gaulle
(Charles), Hamilton (Sir Ian
Standish Monteith), Hannibal,
Montrose (James Graham, Marquis
of)
09 Antigonus, Aristides, Boulanger
(Georges), MacArthur (Douglas),
Omar Pasha, Santander (Francisco
de Paula), Townshend (George,
Viscount and Marquess),
Townshend (Sir Charles Vere
Ferrers)
10 Abercromby (Sir Ralph),
Eisenhower (Dwight D 'Ike'),
Oglethorpe (James Edward),
Timoshenko (Semyon)
11 Baden-Powell (Robert, Lord), Jiang
Jieshi, Schwarzkopf (H Norman)
12 Clive of India
13 Chiang Kai-shek
14 Osman Nuri Pasha

General Electric
02 GE **03** GEC

generality
03 run **04** bulk, many, most
07 breadth, the many **08** majority
09 broadness, looseness, nearly all,
vagueness **10** commonness, larger
part, popularity, prevalence
11 catholicity, ecumenicity, greater
part, inexactness **12** more than half,
universality **13** extensiveness,
impreciseness, miscellaneity
14 generalization, indefiniteness
15 approximateness

generalization
09 looseness, vagueness
11 inexactness **12** axioma medium,
inexactitude **13** impreciseness
14 indefiniteness **15** approximateness

generalize
05 infer **06** assume, deduce
08 conclude, theorize **11** standardize

generally
06 mainly, mostly **07** as a rule, at large,
broadly, chiefly, largely, overall, usually
08 commonly, normally **09** in general
10 by and large, habitually, more or
less, on the whole, ordinarily
11 customarily, in most cases,
universally **13** predominantly **14** for
the most part

generate
◊ *anagram indicator*
04 form, make **05** breed, cause, spawn

06 arouse, create, evolve, gender, wh’
up **07** produce **08** engender, initiate
occasion **09** originate, procreate,
propagate **10** bring about, give
rise to **11** give birth to **14** bring into
being

generation
03 age, era **04** days, kind, race, time
05 class, epoch **06** family, period
07 descent, genesis, progeny **08** age
group, breeding, creation
09 engendure, formation, offspring
10 engendrure, production
11 engendering, origination,
procreation, propagation
12 reproduction

generic
04 wide **06** common **07** blanket,
general **08** superior, sweeping
09 inclusive, unbranded, universal
10 collective **12** all-inclusive
13 comprehensive, non-registered,
untrademarked **14** non-proprietary,
non-trademarked **15** all-
encompassing

generically
08 commonly **09** generally
11 inclusively, universally **14** all-
inclusively **15** comprehensively

generosity
06 bounty **07** charity, largess
08 goodness, kindness, largesse
10 lavishness, liberality
11 benevolence, magnanimity,
munificence **12** philanthropy,
selflessness **13** unselfishness **14** big-
heartedness, open-handedness

generous
03 big **04** free, full, good, kind, rich
05 ample, large, lofty, noble, plump,
roomy **06** giving, lavish **07** copious,
liberal **08** abundant, handsome,
menseful, selfless, sporting
09 bounteous, bountiful, plentiful,
unselfish, unsparing **10** altruistic,
beneficent, benevolent, big-hearted,
charitable, courageous, free-handed,
high-minded, munificent, open-
handed, unstinting **11** gentlemanly,
magnanimous, open-hearted,
overflowing, soft-hearted, warm-
hearted **12** large-hearted,
wholehearted **13** disinterested,
philanthropic **14** public-spirited

generously
05 amply, fully, nobly **06** freely, richly
08 lavishly **09** copiously, liberally
10 abundantly, charitably, handsomely
selflessly **11** bountifully, plentifully,
unselfishly **12** open-handedly
13 magnanimously

genesis
03 Gen **04** dawn, root **05** birth, start
06 origin, outset, source **08** creation,
founding **09** beginning, formation,
inception **10** foundation, generation,
initiation, production **11** developmen
engendering, propagation
12 commencement

genetic
07 genomic 09 inherited 10 biological, hereditary 11 chromosomal

genetics
06 origin 11 development

Geneticists include:

05 Brown (Michael S), Jones (Steve), Leder (Philip), Ochoa (Severo), Sager (Ruth), Snell (George Davis)
06 Beadle (George Wells), Biffen (Sir Rowland Harry), Bodmer (Sir Walter), Boveri (Theodor Heinrich), Cantor (Charles), Fisher (Sir Ronald Aylmer), Galton (Sir Francis), Gurdon (Sir John), Morgan (Thomas Hunt), Müller (Hermann Joseph), Zinder (Norton David)
07 Bateson (William), Correns (Carl), De Vries (Hugo Marie), Gehring (Walter), Hopwood (Sir David), Lysenko (Trofim)
08 Auerbach (Charlotte), Lewontin (Richard), Yanofsky (Charles)
09 Baltimore (David), Goldstein (Joseph), Lederberg (Joshua)
10 Darlington (Cyril Dean), Dobzhansky (Theodosius), Kettlewell (Henry Bernard David), McClintock (Barbara), Sturtevant (Alfred Henry), Waddington (C H), Weatherall (Sir David)
12 Maynard Smith (John)

Genetics-related terms include:

02 GM
03 DNA, PCR, RNA
04 base, gene
05 allel, clone, codon, helix, sperm
06 allele, gamete, genome, hybrid, intron, vector, zygote
07 diploid, meiosis, mitosis
08 autosome, dominant, heredity, mutation, promoter, sequence
09 amino acid, homologue, inversion, karyotype, offspring, recessive, repressor, variation
10 adaptation, chromosome, generation, geneticist, homozygous, nucleosome, nucleotide, polymerase, speciation
11 double helix, epigenetics, genetic code, inheritance, nucleic acid, polypeptide, X-chromosome, Y-chromosome
12 cell division, heterozygous, reproduction
13 DNA sequencing, fertilization, recombination, transcription, translocation

genial
04 kind, maty, mild, warm 05 happy, human, jolly, matey, pally, sunny 06 chummy, hearty, jovial, kindly, mellow 07 affable, amiable, cordial 08 amicable, cheerful, cheering, friendly, pleasant, sociable, sunshiny 09 agreeable, convivial, easy-going, healthful 11 good-natured, sympathetic, warm-hearted 12 good-humoured

geniality
06 warmth 07 jollity 08 bonhomie, gladness, kindness, sunshine 09 happiness, joviality 10 affability, amiability, cheeriness, cordiality, good nature, kindliness 12 cheerfulness, conviviality, friendliness, pleasantness 13 agreeableness, congenialness 15 warm-heartedness

genially
06 warmly 07 affably, amiably 08 amicably, heartily 09 cordially 10 cheerfully, pleasantly 13 warm-heartedly

genie
04 jann 05 demon, fairy, jinni 06 djinni, jinnee, spirit

genitals
08 privates 09 genitalia 12 private parts, sexual organs

genius
04 bent, gift, nous, sage 05 adept, brain, demon, flair, knack 06 boffin, brains, daemon, daimon, engine, expert, ingine, master, talent, wisdom, wizard 07 ability, egghead, faculty, maestro, prodigy 08 aptitude, capacity, fine mind, ingenium, virtuoso 09 bel esprit, intellect 10 brightness, brilliance, cleverness, grey matter, mastermind, past master, propensity, time spirit 11 inclination 12 intellectual, intelligence 15 little grey cells

genocide
08 massacre 09 ethnocide, slaughter 13 extermination 15 ethnic cleansing

genre
04 epic, form, kind, sort, type 05 brand, class, conte, genus, group, novel, sci-fi, style 06 comedy, satire, school, strain 07 fantasy, fashion, romance, variety 08 category, intimism, pastoral, prog rock 09 character, chopsocky, cyberpunk, reality TV 10 rare groove, whodunitry 11 fête galante, pastourelle, tragicomedy, whodunnitry 12 splatterpunk 13 fête champêtre 14 science fiction 15 progressive rock

gent *see* **gentleman**

genteel
05 civil 06 dainty, formal, polite, urbane 07 courtly, elegant, refined, stylish 08 cultured, graceful, ladylike, mannerly, polished, well-bred 09 courteous 10 cultivated 11 comme il faut, fashionable, gentlemanly, respectable 12 aristocratic, well-mannered

gentile
03 goy 06 ethnic 13 uncircumcised

gentility
04 rank 05 élite 06 gentry, nobles 07 culture, decorum, manners 08 breeding, civility, courtesy, elegance, nobility, poshness, urbanity 09 blue blood, etiquette, formality,

high birth, propriety 10 good family, politeness, refinement, upper class 11 aristocracy, courtliness, gentle birth 12 mannerliness 14 respectability

gentle
04 calm, easy, gent, kind, meek, mild, slow, soft, tame 05 balmy, bland, canny, light, milky, quiet, sweet 06 benign, humane, kindly, placid, serene, slight, smooth, tender 07 amiable, clement, ennoble, gradual, lenient 08 delicate, lamb-like, maidenly, mansuete, merciful, moderate, peaceful, pleasant, soothing, tranquil, well-born 10 charitable, low-pitched 11 soft-hearted, sympathetic 13 compassionate, imperceptible, tender-hearted

gentleman
02 Mr 03 rye, sir 04 gent 05 Señor 06 gemman, knight, Signor, squire, stalko, yeoman 07 esquire, hidalgo, Signior, Signore, younker 08 cavalier 09 caballero, Signorino 10 duniwassal, pukka sahib 11 duniewassal, gentilhomme 12 dunniewassal 13 grand seigneur

gentlemanly
04 gent 05 civil, janty, noble, suave 06 jantee, jaunty, polite, urbane 07 gallant, genteel, jauntee, refined 08 generous, mannerly, obliging, polished, well-bred 09 civilized, courteous, reputable 10 chivalrous, cultivated, honourable 12 well-mannered 13 gentlemanlike

gentleness
05 mercy 06 warmth 08 calmness, kindness, meekness, mildness, softness, sympathy 09 sweetness 10 compassion, humaneness, tenderness

gently
01 p 04 soft 05 small 06 calmly, fairly, mildly, slowly, stilly, warmly 07 lightly 08 serenely, slightly, tenderly 09 gradually 10 charitably, moderately, pleasantly, sordamente, tranquilly 14 hooly and fairly 15 compassionately, sympathetically

gentry
05 élite 06 nobles 08 nobility, squirage 09 gentility, squireage, top drawer 10 upper class, upper crust 11 aristocracy

gents *see* **toilet**

genuflect
03 bow 05 kneel 11 bend the knee 12 pay obeisance 13 make obeisance 14 humble yourself 15 pay your respects

genuine
04 echt, good, open, pure, real, true 05 frank, legal, pakka, pucka, pukka, right, sound 06 actual, candid, dinkum, entire, honest, kosher, lawful, native, pusser 07 dinky-di, earnest,

factual, natural, sincere **08** bona fide, dinky-die, original, sterling, truthful, unartful **09** authentic, intrinsic, real McCoy, simon-pure, undoubted, veritable **10** fair dinkum, legitimate, ridgy-didge, sure-enough **11** honest-to-God, intrinsical **12** unadulterate **13** unadulterated, with integrity **14** unsophisticate **15** unsophisticated

genuinely
04 echt **06** dinkum, really **07** dinky-di **08** actually, dinky-die, honestly **09** earnestly, sincerely

genus
03 set **04** kind, race, sort, type **05** breed, class, genre, group, order, taxon **07** species **08** category, division **11** subdivision

geography

Geographical regions include:

04 veld
05 basin, coast, heath, plain, polar, veldt
06 Arctic, desert, forest, jungle, orient, pampas, steppe, tundra
07 outback, prairie, riviera, savanna, seaside, tropics
08 lowlands, midlands, occident, savannah, woodland
09 Antarctic, grassland, green belt, marshland, scrubland, wasteland
10 Third World, wilderness
11 countryside
13 Mediterranean, rural district, urban district
14 developed world
15 developing world

Geography terms include:

03 bay, col, cwm
04 arid, crag, mesa, tail, veld, wadi, wady
05 butte, delta, shott, taiga, veldt
06 canyon, cirque, corrie, tundra, valley
07 aggrade, caldera, equator, glacial, hachure, isthmus, tropics, volcano
08 alluvium, altitude, landmass, landslip, latitude, meridian, prograde
09 accretion, antipodes, base level, billabong, deviation, ethnology, landslide, longitude, metroplex, relief map
10 co-ordinate, demography, glaciation, landlocked, topography
11 archipelago, cartography, chorography, conurbation, demographic, hydrography, triangulate, vulcanology
13 hanging valley, Ordnance Datum, shield volcano
14 plate tectonics, roche moutonnée

Geographers include:

03 Dee (John)
04 Cary (John), Mela (Pomponius)
05 Barth (Heinrich), Cabot (Sebastian), Darby (Clifford), Guyot (Arnold), Hedin (Sven), Penck

(Albrecht), **Sauer** (Carl), **Stamp** (Sir Lawrence Dudley)
06 Batuta, Behaim (Martin), Bowman (Isaiah), Clüver (Phillip), Gmelin (Johann Georg), Harvey (David), Idrisi, Ritter (Karl), Strabo
07 Haggett (Peter), Hakluyt (Richard), Markham (Sir Clements), Ogilvie (Alan), Ptolemy
08 Büsching (Anton Friedrich), Filchner (Wilhelm), Humboldt (Alexander, Baron von), Mercator (Gerhardus), Ortelius (Abraham Ortel), Robinson (Arthur)
09 Kropotkin (Pyotr), Mackinder (Sir Halford John), Muqaddasi, Pausanias
10 Hartshorne (Richard), Huntington (Ellsworth), Richthofen (Ferdinand Baron von), Wooldridge (Sydney)
11 Christaller (Walter), Hägerstrand (Torsten), Kingdon-Ward (Frank)
12 Eratosthenes, Leo Africanus
15 Eudoxus of Cnidus, Vidal de la Blache (Paul)

geology

Geological time periods include:

06 Eocene (Epoch)
07 Miocene (Epoch), Permian (Period)
08 Cambrian (Period), Cenozoic (Era), Devonian (Period), Holocene (Epoch), Jurassic (Period), Mesozoic (Era), Pliocene (Epoch), Silurian (Period), Tertiary (Period), Triassic (Period)
09 Oligocene (Epoch)
10 Cretaceous (Period), Ordovician (Period), Palaeocene (Epoch), Palaeozoic (Era), Quaternary (Period)
11 Phanerozoic (Eon), Pleistocene (Epoch), Precambrian (Era), Proterozoic (Eon)
13 Carboniferous (Period), Mississippian (Epoch), Pennsylvanian (Epoch)

Geology-related terms include:

02 aa
03 bar, cwm, mya, ore
04 clay, dome, dune, fold, lava, limb, lode, Moho, Riss, till, trap, tuff, vein, wadi
05 agate, atoll, basin, butte, chert, delta, epoch, esker, fault, fiord, fjord, focus, gorge, gully, guyot, horst, joint, Karst, lahar, levee, magma, plain, P-wave, ridge, S-wave, talus
06 albite, arkose, arroyo, basalt, bolson, canyon, cirque, corrie, debris, gabbro, geyser, gneiss, graben, mantle, oolite, quartz, runoff, schist, scoria, stress, tephra, trench, uplift
07 aquifer, barchan, bauxite, bed-load, blowout, breccia, caldera, drumlin, glacier, granite, hogback, igneous, isograd, lapilli, meander, mineral, moraine, orogeny, outwash, plateau, pothole, vesicle, volcano

08 A-horizon, alluvium, backwash, basement, B-horizon, C-horizon, feldspar, fumarole, isostasy, leaching, lopolith, monolith, mountain, obsidian, oilfield, oil shale, pahoehoe, pediment, regolith, rhyolite, syncline, xenolith
09 alabaster, batholith, carbonate, deflation, epicentre, flood tide, hot spring, intrusion, laccolith, landslide, limestone, Mohs scale, monadnock, monocline, oxidation, peneplain, rock cycle, rockslide, sandstone, slip fault, striation, tableland, viscosity, volcanism
10 anthracite, astrobleme, block fault, cinder cone, deposition, depression, earthquake, flood plain, kettle hole, mineralogy, rift valley, subsidence, topography, travertine, water table, weathering
11 alluvial fan, central vent, exfoliation, geosyncline, groundwater, maar volcano, metamorphic, normal fault, sublimation, swallow hole, thrust fault, volcanic ash
12 artesian well, coastal plain, fringing reef, magma chamber, pyroclastics, stratigraphy, unconformity, volcanic bomb, volcanic cone, volcanic dome, volcanic pipe
13 angle of repose, barrier island, drainage basin, geomorphology, hanging valley, recumbent fold, shield volcano, stratovolcano, U-shaped valley, V-shaped valley
14 bituminous coal, eustatic change, lateral moraine, longshore drift, stratification, subduction zone, transform fault, wave-cut terrace
15 million years ago, sedimentary rock, strike-slip fault, terminal moraine

Georgia
02 GA, GE **03** GEO

germ
03 bud, bug, wog **04** root, seed, zyme **05** cause, shoot, spark, start, virus **06** embryo, origin, source, sprout **07** microbe, nucleus **08** bacillus, fountain, rudiment **09** bacterium, beginning, inception, swarm-cell **10** seminality, swarm-spore **12** commencement **13** micro-organism

German
◇ *foreign word indicator*
01 G **03** Ger, Hun **04** Jute, Ossi **05** boche, Gerry, Jerry, Wessi **06** Almain, bosche, Teuton

German first names include:

03 Jan, Max, Uwe
04 Dirk, Eric, Erik, Jens, Jörg, Ralf, Sven, Swen
05 Bernd, Erich, Fritz, Jonas, Klaus, Lukas, Ralph
06 Dieter, Jürgen, Markus, Niklas, Stefan, Tobias, Ulrich
07 Andreas, Dominik, Mathias, Steffen, Stephan, Torsten

Kristian, Matthias, Thorsten,
Wolfgang

e also **day**; **month**; **number**
East German
Ost

ermane
apt **04** akin **06** allied, proper
apropos, fitting, related
apposite, material, relevant,
itable **09** connected, pertinent
applicable **11** appropriate

ermanium
Ge

ermany
D **03** DDR, DEU, FDR, FRG, GDR,
er **05** Reich **06** Almany **07** Almaine
Alemaine
in Germany
foreign word indicator

erminal
seminal **09** embryonic
developing, generative
preliminary, rudimentary,
ndeveloped

erminate
bud **04** grow **05** shoot, swell
sprout **07** burgeon, develop
spring up, take root **09** originate

estation
drafting, planning, ripening
evolution, pregnancy
conception, incubation, maturation
development

esticulate
sign, wave **06** motion, signal
gesture **08** indicate **09** make a sign

esticulation
sign, wave **06** motion, signal
gesture **08** movement
chironomy **10** indication **12** body
nguage

esture
act **04** geck, gest, mint, sign, wave
geste, point, snook **06** action,
eckon, motion, signal **08** dumbshow,
idicate, movement **09** beau geste,
ehaviour, chirology, reverence
indication **11** gesticulate
gesticulation

et
juxtaposition indicator
go **03** bug, buy, cop, fix, hit, nab,
e, vex, wax, win **04** brat, bust, coax,
ome, cook, earn, gain, grab, grow,
ave, hear, kill, land, make, move, nick,
e, suss, sway, take, trap, turn, twig,
rge **05** annoy, bring, catch, child,
ear, fetch, get it, go for, grasp, learn,
ach, seize, snare **06** answer, arrest,
rive, attain, baffle, become, bother,
ollar, come by, descry, fathom, follow,
duce, manage, obtain, pick up,
ecure, take in, travel, wangle, wind up,
ork it **07** achieve, acquire, arrange,
e given, bring in, capture, collect,
evelop, discern, make out, prepare,
rocure, provoke, realize, receive,

succeed, suss out, win over, work out
08 come to be, contract, convince,
find a way, get ready, hunt down,
irritate, organize, persuade, purchase,
rustle up, talk into **09** aggravate,
apprehend, figure out, influence,
infuriate, lay hold of, recognize,
succumb to **10** comprehend, drive
crazy, exasperate, go down with,
understand **11** get the point, prevail
upon, put together **12** come down
with, get the hang of **13** be afflicted
by

• **get about**
02 go **06** travel **08** go widely **09** move
about **10** move around **12** travel
widely

• **get across**
06 convey, impart **07** express, get over,
put over **08** transmit **09** make clear,
put across **11** bring home to,
communicate

• **get ahead**
05 get on **06** do well, make it, thrive
07 advance, prosper, succeed
08 flourish, get there, go places, make
good, progress **11** go great guns **12** get
somewhere, make your mark **14** go up
in the world, make the big time

• **get along**
04 cope, fare **05** agree, get by, get on
06 giddap, giddup, manage, relate
07 develop, giddy-up, make out,
survive **08** hit it off, progress, rub along
09 harmonize

• **get around**
◇ containment indicator
04 coax, move, sway **05** avoid, evade
06 bypass, cajole, induce, travel
07 win over **08** persuade **09** talk
round **10** circumvent **11** prevail upon

• **get at**
04 find, hint, mean, slam **05** begin,
bribe, imply, knock, reach, slate, touch
06 areach, attack, attain, intend,
nobble, obtain, pick on, suborn
07 corrupt, suggest **08** discover
09 criticize, influence, insinuate, make
fun of **11** pick holes in **12** gain access to
13 find fault with

• **get away**
04 flee, scat **05** be off, leave, never!,
scoot, scram **06** begone, depart,
escape, get out **07** do a bunk, run away,
scarper **08** break out, run for it
09 break away, break free, do a runner
13 sling your hook **14** make a bolt for
it, run for your life **15** make a break for
it, take to your heels

• **get back**
06 go back, go home, recoup, recure,
redeem, regain, return **07** pay back,
recover **08** come back, come home,
retrieve **09** repossess, retaliate **11** get
even with **13** take revenge on **15** take
vengeance on

• **get by**
04 cope, fare **05** exist **06** hang on,
manage **07** subsist, survive **08** get
along **12** make ends meet, see it
through **13** scrape through **15** weather
the storm

• **get down**
06 alight, get off, sadden **07** depress,
descend, make sad **08** dismount,
dispirit **09** disembark **10** dishearten

• **get in**
◇ insertion indicator
04 come, land **05** enter **06** arrive,
embark **09** penetrate **10** infiltrate

• **get into**
◇ insertion indicator
05 enjoy, enter, put on **06** arrive
09 penetrate **10** infiltrate

• **get off**
04 shed **05** learn, leave **06** alight,
detach, escape, get out, remove
07 descend, get down **08** climb off,
dismount, get out of, memorize,
separate **09** disembark **10** alight from

• **get on**
03 age **04** cope, fare **05** agree, board,
get in, mount, shift **06** ascend, embark,
manage, relate, thrive **07** advance,
climb on, get into, make out, press on,
proceed, prosper, succeed
08 continue, get along, hit it off,
progress **09** harmonize **12** hit it off
with

• **get on well**
03 gee

• **get out**
04 away, flee, quit, scat **05** leave,
scoot, scram **06** depart, escape,
spread, vacate **07** come out, do a
bunk, extract, leak out, produce,
scarper, take out **08** be leaked, break
out, clear off, clear out, evacuate, run
for it, withdraw **09** circulate, do a
runner **11** become known **12** become
public, free yourself **14** make a bolt for
it, run for your life **15** make a break for
it, take to your heels

• **get out of**
05 avoid, dodge, evade, shirk, skive
06 escape, outwin **07** goof off
09 gold-brick

• **get over**
06 convey, defeat, impart, master
07 explain, get well, put over, survive
08 complete, deal with, get round,
overcome, shake off, surmount **09** get
across, get better, make clear **10** be
restored **11** communicate, pull
through, recover from **14** recuperate
from

• **get ready**
04 boun **05** bowne, fix up, ready
06 set out **07** arrange, prepare
08 rehearse

• **get round**
◇ containment indicator
04 coax, move, sway **05** avoid, evade
06 bypass, cajole, induce, travel
07 win over **08** persuade **09** talk
round **10** circumvent **11** prevail upon

• **get there**
06 arrive, make it **07** advance, prosper,
succeed **08** go places, make good

• **get through**
04 pass

• **get together**
04 join, meet **05** rally, unite **06** finish,
gather **07** collect **08** assemble,

organize **10** congregate **11** collaborate

• **get up**
03 fig **04** rise, stir **05** arise, climb, mount, scale, stand **06** ascend, huddup **07** stand up **08** show a leg **11** get out of bed

getaway
05 break, start **06** escape, flight **08** breakout **10** absconding, decampment

get-together
02 do **04** bash **05** party, rally **06** social, soirée **07** meeting, reunion **08** assembly, function, sing-sing **09** gathering, reception

get-up
03 kit, set **04** gear, togs **06** make-up, outfit, rig-out **07** clobber, clothes, threads, turnout **08** clothing, garments **09** equipment

Ghana
02 GH **03** GHA

ghastliness
08 grimness **09** awfulness, nastiness **11** hideousness **12** dreadfulness, gruesomeness **13** frightfulness

ghastly
03 bad, ill **04** gash, grim, ropy, sick **05** awful, grave, lousy, lurid, nasty, ropey **06** grisly, horrid, poorly, rotten, unwell **07** greisly, griesly, hideous, macabre, serious **08** critical, dreadful, gruesome, horrible, shocking, terrible **09** appalling, dangerous, deathlike, frightful, loathsome, off colour, repellent **10** deplorable, horrendous, terrifying **11** frightening **12** unrepeatable **15** under the weather

ghost
04 hint, soul, waff **05** duppy, fetch, haunt, jumby, larva, lemur, shade, spook, trace, umbra **06** duende, jumbie, shadow, spirit, wraith **07** gytrash, phantom, specter, spectre **08** manifest, presence, revenant, visitant **09** semblance **10** apparition, astral body, impression, suggestion **11** poltergeist

ghostly
05 eerie, faint, spook, weird **06** creepy, spooky **07** phantom, shadowy **08** chthonic, illusory, spectral **09** chthonian, ghostlike, religious, spiritual, sprightly, unearthly **10** wraith-like **12** supernatural

ghoulish
04 sick **06** grisly, morbid **07** macabre **08** gruesome **09** revolting, unhealthy **11** unwholesome

giant
04 eten, huge, ogre, vast **05** ettin, jotun, jumbo, large, titan, troll **06** jötunn, ogress **07** immense, mammoth, massive, monster, titanic **08** behemoth, Briarean, colossal, colossus, cyclopic, enormous, gigantic, great big, king-size, titaness,

whopping **09** cyclopean, cyclopian, ginormous, humongous, humungous, leviathan, rounceval **10** gargantuan, monumental, Patagonian, prodigious, tremendous **11** gigantesque **14** Brobdingnagian

Giants include:

03 Gog
04 Gaia, Gerd, Grid, Loki, Rhea, Ymir
05 Aegir, Arges, Argus, Atlas, Grawp, Hymir, Jotun, Magog, Orion, Pan Gu, Skadi, Theia, Thrym
06 Albion, Bestla, Cronus, Hagrid, Phoebe, Tethys, Themis, Thiazi, Titans
07 Cyclops, Geirrod, Goliath, Iapetus, Oceanus, Suttung
08 Angrboda, Cyclopes, Gigantes, Gogmagog, Hrungnir, Hyperion, Jarnsaxa, Morgante, Nephilim, Panoptes, Steropes
09 Angerboda, Bergelmir, Enceladus, Gandareva, Gargantua, Mnemosyne, Olentzero
10 Angerbotha, Epimetheus, Paul Bunyan, Prometheus
11 Finn MacCool, Galligantus, Gog and Magog, Utgardaloki
12 Giant Despair, Vafthruthnir
15 Cerne Abbas Giant, Fionn MacCumhail

gibber
04 blab, cant **05** stone **06** babble, cackle, gabble, jabber **07** blabber, blather, boulder, chatter, prattle

gibberish
04 blah, bosh, guff **05** hooey **06** bunkum, drivel, jargon, linsey, yammer **07** baloney, eyewash, hogwash, prattle, ravings, rhubarb, rubbish, twaddle **08** cobblers, malarkey, nonsense, tommyrot **09** moonshine, poppycock **10** balderdash, codswallop, jabberwock, mumbo-jumbo **11** abracadabra, jabberwocky **12** gobbledygook **13** linsey-woolsey

gibbet
05 crook, cross **07** gallows, potence

gibbon
06 wou-wou, wow-wow **07** hoolock, siamang **08** hylobate

gibe, jibe
03 bob, dig, shy **04** gird, goof, jeer, mock, poke, quip, wipe, yerk **05** crack, fleer, fling, flout, gleek, scoff, slant, sneer, taunt, tease **06** deride **07** brocard, mockery, sarcasm, teasing **08** derision, outfling, ridicule **09** make fun of, wisecrack, witticism

Gibraltar
03 GBZ, GIB

giddily
◊ anagram indicator
06 wildly **07** dizzily, woozily **09** excitedly **10** restlessly, unsteadily **11** frantically **12** euphorically **13** lightheadedly

giddiness
06 frenzy, nausea, thrill **07** vertigo **08** staggers **09** animation, dizziness, faintness, wooziness **10** excitement, wobbliness **11** glaikitness **12** exhilaration **15** lightheadedness

giddy
◊ anagram indicator
04 high, wild **05** dizzy, faint, light, queer, silly, woozy **06** elated, sturdy, volage **07** excited, flighty, glaiket, glaikit, reeling, stirred **08** frenzied, hellicat, skipping, thrilled, unsteady **09** volageous **10** capernoity, hoity-toity, stimulated **11** capernoitie, cappernoity, exhilarated, hair-brained, hare-brained, lightheaded, vertiginou

gift
03 foy, tip **04** bent, boon, give, koha, turn **05** bonus, bribe, flair, grant, knack, offer, power, skill **06** befana, bestow, bounty, confer, donate, geniu hansel, legacy, talent **07** ability, aptness, beffana, bequest, cumshaw, étrenne, faculty, fairing, freebie, handsel, minding, present, pressie, prezzie, propine **08** aptitude, capaci donation, donative, facility, gratuity, largesse, offering, thankyou **09** attribute, book token, endowmen **10** capability, contribute, exhibition **11** beneficence, inheritance, proficiency **12** Christmas box, contribution

See also **Christmas**

gifted
04 able **05** adept, sharp, smart **06** bright, clever, expert **07** capable, endowed, skilful, skilled **08** masterly, talented **09** brilliant **10** proficient **11** intelligent **12** accomplished

gig
03 fun **04** moze **05** buggy, sport **06** dennet, whisky **07** whiskey **11** hurly-hacket

gigantic
04 huge, mega, vast **05** giant, jumbo **07** immense, mammoth, massive, monster, titanic **08** colossal, enormous, great big, king-size, whopping **09** Atlantean, ginormous, Herculean, humongous, humungous, leviathan, rounceval **10** Babylonian, gargantuan, monumental, Patagonian **14** Brobdingnagian

giggle
05 laugh **06** titter **07** chortle, chuckle snicker, snigger

gilbert
02 Gb

• **Gilbert and Sullivan**
05 G and S

gild
04 coat, deck, trim **05** adorn, array, grace, paint **06** bedeck, enrich, golde **07** dress up, enhance, festoon, garnish **08** beautify, brighten, ornament **09** elaborate, embellish, embroider

gilded
04 gilt, gold 06 golden 07 aureate
08 inaurate 10 gold-plated 11 gold-
layered

gill
04 glen 05 brook 06 noggin, ravine
08 branchia 09 ctenidium

gilt
03 elt

gimcrack
05 cheap, dodge, tacky, trick 06 fisgig,
fizgig, shoddy, tawdry, trashy
08 rubbishy, trumpery 10 jerry-built

gimmick
04 hype, ploy, ruse 05 dodge, stunt,
trick 06 device, gadget, scheme
07 novelty 09 publicity, stratagem
10 attraction 11 contrivance

gimmickry
07 novelty 09 modernity 10 innovation

gin
02 by, if 03 max 04 ruin, trap 05 snare
06 geneva, Old Tom, scheme, spring
07 schnaps, springe, twankay
08 artifice, blue ruin, Hollands,
schiedam, schnapps 10 square-face
11 contrivance, mother's ruin
• **gin and tonic**
02 gt 05 g and t

ginger
▷ anagram indicator
03 pop 04 race, rase, raze 05 bluey,
sandy 06 amomum, asarum, mettle
07 curcuma, enliven, reddish
08 cardamom, cardamon, cardamum,
turmeric, zingiber 09 galingale
10 cassumunar 11 stimulation

gingerbread
05 parly 06 parkin, parley, perkin
10 parliament, pepper-cake
14 parliament-cake

gingerly
06 warily 07 charily 09 carefully,
prudently 10 cautiously, delicately,
hesitantly, watchfully 11 attentively,
judiciously, tentatively, with caution

Gipsy *see* **Gypsy, Gipsy**

gird
03 pen 04 belt, bind, girr, hoop, ring
05 brace, hem in, ready, steel, taunt
06 enfold, fasten, girdle 07 accinge,
enclose, fortify, prepare 08 cincture,
encircle, get ready, surround
09 encompass

girder
04 beam, spar 05 H-beam, I-beam
06 rafter 07 box beam

girdle
03 hem 04 band, belt, bind, gird, ring,
sash, zona, zone 05 bound, mitre,
waist 06 cestos, cestus, circle, corset
07 enclose, go round, griddle, zonulet
08 ceinture, cincture, cingulum,
encircle, surround 09 encompass,
surcingle, waistband 10 cummerbund,
encincture 15 cingulum Veneris

girl
03 bit, cub, gal, gel, gig, hen, her, kid,
mor, tit 04 babe, baby, bint, bird, chit,
dell, gill, jill, Judy, lass, maid, mawr,
minx, miss, peat, puss, romp, tart
05 belle, chick, child, cutie, cutty, dolly,
fille, filly, flirt, gerle, gilpy, hussy,
madam, peach, popsy, quean, randy,
tabby, wench 06 au pair, blowze,
chokri, cummer, damsel, female, fizgig,
gamine, geisha, giglet, kimmer, lassie,
maiden, moppet, mousmé, nipper,
number, pigeon, sheila, shiksa, tawpie,
tomboy, tottie 07 blushet, chapess,
chicken, colleen, flapper, mauther,
mawther, mousmee, nymphet
08 chappess, daughter, grisette, jail-
bait, princess, teenager 09 backfisch,
dolly bird, maid-child, young lady,
youngster 10 adolescent, bit of fluff, bit
of skirt, bit of stuff, bobbysoxer,
Cinderella, girlfriend, jeune fille,
schoolgirl, sweetheart, young woman
11 beauty queen, kinchin-mort,
maidservant, teeny-bopper
12 bachelorette, bobby-dazzler

Girls' names include:

02 Di, Jo, Mo, Vi
03 Ada, Ali, Amy, Ann, Ava, Bab, Bea,
Bee, Bel, Bet, Cis, Con, Deb, Dee,
Die, Dot, Edy, Emm, Ena, Eva, Eve,
Fay, Flo, Gay, Ida, Ina, Isa, Ivy, Jan, Jay,
Jen, Joe, Joy, Kay, Kim, Kit, Lea, Lee,
Liv, Liz, Lou, Mae, Mag, Mat, May,
Meg, Mia, Nan, Pam, Pat, Peg, Pen,
Pia, Pru, Rae, Ray, Ria, Ros, Roz, Sal,
Sue, Una, Val, Viv, Win, Zoë
04 Abby, Addy, Afra, Aggy, Alex, Ally,
Alma, Alme, Angy, Anna, Anne,
Asma, Babs, Bell, Bess, Beth, Cara,
Caro, Cass, Ceri, Cher, Cleo, Cora,
Dana, Dawn, Dian, Dora, Edel, Edie,
Edna, Ella, Elma, Elsa, Elva, Emma,
Emmy, Enid, Erin, Evie, Faye, Floy,
Fred, Gabi, Gaea, Gaia, Gail, Gale,
Gaye, Gene, Gert, Gill, Gina, Gita,
Gwen, Hope, Ibby, Ines, Inez, Inga,
Inge, Iona, Iris, Irma, Isla, Jade, Jane,
Jean, Jess, Jill, Joan, Jodi, Jody, Joey,
Joni, Joss, Jozy, Jude, Judy, June, Kate,
Kath, Katy, Kaye, Lara, Leah, Lena,
Lian, Lily, Lina, Lisa, Lise, Livy, Liza,
Lois, Lola, Lucy, Lynn, Maev, Mary,
Maud, Meta, Mina, Moll, Mona,
Myra, Nell, Nina, Nita, Noel, Nola,
Nona, Nora, Olga, Page, Phyl, Poll,
Prue, Rana, Rene, Rita, Rona, Rosa,
Rose, Ruby, Ruth, Sara, Sian, Sìne,
Siri, Suke, Suky, Susy, Suzy, Tess,
Thea, Tina, Toni, Trix, Vera, Vita, Zara,
Zena, Zola
05 Addie, Adela, Adèle, Aggie, Agnes,
Ailie, Ailsa, Aisha, Alexa, Alice,
Allie, Amber, Amina, Anaïs, Angel,
Angie, Anila, Anita, Annie, Annis,
Annot, Aphra, April, Areta, Aruna,
Avril, Aysha, Becky, Bella, Belle,
Beryl, Bessy, Betsy, Betty, Biddy,
Bride, Brona, Bunny, Bunty, Candy,
Carla, Carly, Carol, Carys, Cathy,
Celia, Cerys, Chère, Chloe, Chris,
Ciara, Cindy, Cissy, Clara, Clare,

Coral, Daisy, Debby, Debra, Delia,
Della, Diana, Diane, Dilys, Dinah,
Dolly, Donna, Doris, Edith, Effie,
Eliza, Ellen, Ellie, Elsie, Emily, Emmie,
Erica, Essie, Ethel, Ethna, Ethne,
Faith, Fanny, Farah, Ffion, Fiona,
Fleur, Flora, Freda, Freya, Gabby,
Gauri, Gayle, Geeta, Gemma,
Gerda, Ginny, Golda, Golde, Grace,
Greta, Haley, Hatty, Hazel, Heidi,
Helen, Helga, Hetty, Hilda, Holly,
Honor, Ilana, Ilona, Irena, Irene,
Isbel, Isold, Ivana, Jaime, Jamie,
Janet, Janis, Jemma, Jenna, Jenny,
Jessy, Jinny, Jodie, Joely, Josie, Joyce,
Judie, Julia, Julie, Kanta, Karen, Karin,
Karla, Kathy, Katie, Katya, Kelly,
Kenna, Kerry, Kiera, Kitty, Kylie, Lalla,
Lally, Laura, Leigh, Leila, Leona,
Letty, Liana, Libby, Linda, Lindy,
Lorna, Lorne, Louie, Lubna, Lucia,
Lydia, Lynda, Lynne, Mabel, Madge,
Maeve, Magda, Máire, Màiri,
Mamie, Mandy, Margo, Maria,
Marie, Matty, Maude, Maura,
Mavis, Meena, Megan, Mercy,
Meryl, Moira, Molly, Morag,
Morna, Moyra, Myrna, Nabby,
Nadia, Nance, Nancy, Nelly, Nerys,
Nessa, Nesta, Netta, Netty, Ngaio,
Niamh, Nicky, Noele, Norah,
Norma, Nuala, Olive, Olwen, Olwin,
Olwyn, Onora, Oprah, Paddy,
Padma, Paige, Pansy, Patsy, Patty,
Paula, Pearl, Peggy, Penny, Petra,
Pippa, Polly, Priya, Raine, Rajni,
Renée, Rhian, Rhoda, Rhona, Robin,
Robyn, Rosie, Sacha, Sadie, Sally,
Sarah, Sasha, Senga, Shona, Shula,
Sibyl, Sindy, Sonia, Sonya, Sophy,
Stacy, Sukie, Susan, Susie, Sybil,
Tamar, Tammy, Tania, Tanya, Terry,
Tessa, Thora, Tibby, Tilda, Tilly, Tracy,
Trina, Trish, Trixy, Trudy, Unity, Viola,
Wanda, Wendy, Wilma, Zahra,
Zelda, Zowie
06 Adella, Agatha, Aileen, Alexia,
Alexis, Alicia, Alison, Althea,
Amabel, Amanda, Amelia, Andrea,
Angela, Anneka, Annika, Anthea,
Aphrah, Aretha, Ashley, Astrid,
Audrey, Auriel, Auriol, Aurora,
Aurore, Averil, Ayesha, Babbie,
Barbie, Beatty, Bertha, Bertie,
Bessie, Bianca, Biddie, Blanch,
Bonnie, Brenda, Bridie, Brigid, Brigit,
Briony, Bryony, Bunnie, Caddie,
Candia, Carina, Carlie, Carmel,
Carmen, Carola, Carole, Carrie,
Cassie, Cathie, Cecily, Celina,
Cherie, Cherry, Cheryl, Cicely,
Cissie, Claire, Connie, Daphne,
Davina, Deanna, Deanne, Debbie,
Delyth, Denise, Dervla, Dianne,
Dionne, Dolina, Doreen, Dorrie,
Dottie, Dulcie, Dympna, Eartha,
Edwina, Eileen, Eilidh, Eirian, Eirlys,
Eithna, Eithne, Elaine, Elinor, Eloisa,
Eloise, Elspet, Eluned, Elvira, Esther,
Eunice, Evadne, Evelyn, Evonne,
Fatima, Fedora, Felice, Finola, Flavia,
Freddy, Frieda, Gaynor, Gertie,

Gladys, Glenda, Glenys, Gloria, Glynis, Goldie, Gracie, Grania, Granya, Gudrun, Gwenda, Hannah, Hattie, Hayley, Helena, Hermia, Hester, Hilary, Honora, Honour, Imelda, Imogen, Indira, Ingrid, Isabel, Iseult, Ishbel, Isobel, Isolda, Isolde, Jamila, Jancis, Janice, Janina, Janine, Jeanie, Jemima, Jennie, Jessie, Joanie, Joanna, Joanne, Joelle, Joleen, Jolene, Judith, Juliet, Kamala, Karena, Karina, Kathie, Kirsty, Kittie, Kumari, Lalage, Lalita, Lallie, Laurel, Lauren, Laurie, Leanne, Leonie, Lesley, Lettie, Lianna, Lianne, Lilian, Lilias, Linnet, Lisbet, Lizzie, Lolita, Lottie, Louisa, Louise, Lynsey, Madhur, Maggie, Maisie, Marcia, Marian, Marina, Marion, Marsha, Martha, Mattie, Maxine, Melody, Meriel, Millie, Minnie, Miriam, Monica, Morven, Muriel, Myriam, Myrtle, Nabila, Nadine, Nellie, Nessie, Nettie, Nicola, Nicole, Noelle, Noreen, Odette, Olivia, Olwyne, Paloma, Pamela, Pattie, Petula, Phemie, Phoebe, Rachel, Rajani, Raquel, Regina, Renata, Rhonda, Robina, Rodney, Roisin, Roshan, Rosina, Rowena, Roxana, Roxane, Rubina, Sabina, Sabine, Salome, Sandra, Saskia, Selina, Seonag, Serena, Sharon, Shashi, Sheela, Sheena, Sheila, Sherry, Sheryl, Silvia, Simone, Sinéad, Sophia, Sophie, Stacey, Stella, Suhair, Sydney, Sylvia, Tamara, Tammie, Tamsin, Teenie, Teresa, Thelma, Tibbie, Tracey, Tricia, Trisha, Trixie, Ulrica, Ursula, Vanora, Verity, Vijaya, Vinaya, Violet, Vivian, Vivien, Vyvian, Vyvyan, Winnie, Winona, Wynona, Xanthe, Yasmin, Yvette, Yvonne, Zainab, Zaynab

07 Abigail, Aisling, Allegra, Allison, Andrina, Annabel, Annette, Antonia, Anushka, Ariadne, Augusta, Barbara, Beatrix, Belinda, Bernice, Bethany, Bettina, Bharati, Blanche, Bridget, Bronach, Bronagh, Bronwen, Caitlín, Camilla, Candace, Candice, Candida, Carolyn, Cecilia, Chandra, Chantal, Charity, Charley, Chelsea, Christy, Clarice, Claudia, Colette, Colleen, Corinna, Corinne, Crystal, Cynthia, Daniela, Deborah, Deirdre, Désirée, Dolores, Dorothy, Eleanor, Elspeth, Emerald, Estella, Estelle, Eugenia, Eugénie, Felicia, Fenella, Floella, Florrie, Flossie, Frances, Francie, Frankie, Freddie, Georgia, Georgie, Gillian, Giselle, Gwennie, Gwenyth, Gwyneth, Harriet, Heather, Heloise, Isadora, Isidora, Jacinta, Jacinth, Janetta, Janette, Jasmine, Jeannie, Jessica, Jillian, Jocasta, Jocelin, Jocelyn, Johanna, Jonquil, Josette, Juliana, Justina, Justine, Kathryn, Katrina, Katrine, Kirstie, Kirstin, Lakshmi, Lavinia, Leonora, Letitia, Lettice, Lillian, Lillias, Lindsay, Lindsey,

Linette, Lisbeth, Lisette, Lizbeth, Loretta, Lucilla, Lucille, Lucinda, Lynette, Madonna, Margery, Marilyn, Marjory, Marlene, Martina, Martine, Matilda, Maureen, Melanie, Melissa, Mildred, Miranda, Myfanwy, Nanette, Natalia, Natalie, Natasha, Nichola, Nigella, Ninette, Ophelia, Pandora, Parvati, Pascale, Paulina, Pauline, Phyllis, Queenie, Rachael, Rebecca, Roberta, Rosabel, Rosalie, Rosanna, Rosetta, Roxanne, Sabrina, Saffron, Sharifa, Shelagh, Shelley, Shirley, Sidonie, Silvana, Siobhán, Surayya, Susanna, Sybilla, Tabitha, Theresa, Tiffany, Valerie, Vanessa, Venetia, Yolanda, Zuleika

08 Adelaide, Adrianne, Adrienne, Angelica, Angelina, Angharad, Arabella, Ashleigh, Beatrice, Berenice, Beverley, Caroline, Catriona, Charlene, Charmian, Chrissie, Clarinda, Clarissa, Claudine, Cordelia, Cornelia, Courtney, Cressida, Daniella, Danielle, Dorothea, Eleanore, Emmeline, Euphemia, Felicity, Florence, Francine, Georgina, Germaine, Gertrude, Griselda, Grizelda, Gurinder, Hermione, Isabella, Jacintha, Jacinthe, Jeanette, Jennifer, Joceline, Joscelin, Katerina, Kathleen, Kimberly, Kirsteen, Lauretta, Lorraine, Madeline, Magdalen, Margaret, Marigold, Marjorie, Mathilda, Meredith, Michaela, Michelle, Morwenna, Ottoline, Patience, Patricia, Paulette, Penelope, Philippa, Primrose, Prudence, Prunella, Rhiannon, Rosalind, Rosamond, Rosamund, Roseanna, Roseanne, Rosemary, Samantha, Scarlett, Susannah, Theodora, Tomasina, Veronica, Victoria, Virginia, Winifred

09 Albertina, Alexandra, Anastasia, Annabella, Annabelle, Cassandra, Catharine, Catherina, Catherine, Charlotte, Charmaine, Christina, Christine, Claudette, Cleopatra, Constance, Elisabeth, Elizabeth, Frederica, Gabrielle, Genevieve, Georgette, Georgiana, Geraldine, Ghislaine, Guinevere, Gwendolen, Henrietta, Jaqueline, Jeannette, Josephine, Katharine, Katherine, Kimberley, Madeleine, Magdalene, Mélisande, Millicent, Nicolette, Parminder, Priscilla, Rosemarie, Sigourney, Silvestra, Stephanie, Sylvestra, Thomasina, Valentine

10 Antoinette, Bernadette, Christabel, Clementina, Clementine, Jacqueline, Shakuntula, Wilhelmina

---

• **society girl**
03 deb **09** débutante

girlfriend
03 mot **04** babe, baby, bint, bird, date, girl, lady, lass, moll **05** chick, lover, woman **06** steady **07** fiancée, partner,

squeeze **08** best girl, mistress, old flame **09** cohabitee, young lady **10** sweetheart **11** live-in lover **15** common-law spouse

girlish
08 childish, immature, innocent, youthful **09** childlike **10** adolescent **11** unmasculine

girth
04 band, bulk, size **05** strap **06** asylum **07** compass, measure **08** encircle **09** perimeter, sanctuary, surcingle **13** circumference

gist
03 nub **04** core, crux, idea, pith **05** drift, point, sense **06** import, marrow, matter, thrust **07** essence, keynote, meaning, nucleus, purport **09** direction, substance **12** quintessence, significance **15** sum and substance

give
◇ *juxtaposition indicator*
02 do **03** aim, gie **04** bend, cede, fall, gift, have, lead, lend, make, move, play, show, sink, slip, tell, turn, will, yeve **05** admit, allow, award, break, cause, endow, focus, grant, lay on, leave, offer, put on, slack, throw, utter, yield **06** accord, afford, bestow, buckle, commit, confer, convey, create, devote, direct, donate, fetter, give up, impart, induce, permit, prompt, render, reveal, supply **07** arrange, concede, declare, deliver, display, dispose, entrust, exhibit, furnish, give way, incline, perform, present, produce, proffer, provide, publish, shackle, stretch **08** announce, bequeath, carry out, collapse, estimate, hand over, indicate, make over, manifest, occasion, organize, set forth, transfer, transmit, turn over, yielding **09** break down, fall apart, pronounce, surrender **10** administer, contribute, distribute, elasticity, give rise to **11** cause to have, communicate, concentrate, springiness **12** stretchiness, take charge of **14** cause to undergo, let someone have

• **give away**
04 leak, shed, tell **06** betray, expose, let out, reveal **07** concede, divulge, let slip, uncover **08** disclose, inform on
• **give in**
04 quit **05** yield **06** give up, jack in, submit **07** chuck up, concede, give way, succumb **08** pack it in **09** chuck in, surrender **10** call it a day, capitulate, knock under **11** admit defeat **13** concede defeat **15** throw in the cards, throw in the towel, throw up the cards
• **give off**
04 emit, fume, vent **05** exude **06** evolve, exhale **07** give out, pour out, produce, release, send out **08** liberate, throw out **09** discharge
• **give on to**
06 lead to **08** open on to, overlook
• **give out**
04 deal, emit, vent **05** allot, exude,

yield **06** exhale, impart, notify, pack up, report, run out **07** conk out, declare, dish out, dole out, give off, hand out, mete out, pour out, produce, publish, release, send out **08** announce, depleted, disperse, share out, throw out, transmit **09** advertise, be mixed up, break down, broadcast, circulate, discharge, make known **10** be depleted, distribute, pass around, relinquish **11** be exhausted, come to an end, communicate, disseminate, stop working **12** be all mixed up

• **give over**
03 lin **07** chuck it **08** transfer

• **give up**
03 cut **04** cede, quit, stop **05** cease, forgo, remit, waive **06** cut out, forego, give in, render, resign, turn in **07** abandon, chuck in, chuck up, concede, crap out, deliver, forbear, forgive, lay down, put down, respite, throw up **08** abdicate, forswear, leave off, renounce **09** sacrifice, surrender **10** capitulate, relinquish **11** admit defeat, discontinue **13** concede defeat **14** drop your bundle **15** throw in the towel

give-and-take
08 goodwill **10** compliance, compromise **11** co-operation, flexibility, negotiation, willingness **12** adaptability

given
05 prone **06** liable, likely, stated **08** assuming, definite, disposed, distinct, inclined, in view of, specific **09** specified **10** individual, particular **11** considering **12** in the light of **13** bearing in mind

giver
05 angel, donor **06** backer, friend, helper, patron **07** sponsor **08** promoter, provider **09** supporter **10** benefactor, subscriber, subsidizer, well-wisher **11** contributor **14** fairy godmother, philanthropist

glacial
03 icy, raw **04** cold **05** chill, gelid, polar, stiff **06** arctic, biting, bitter, chilly, frigid, frosty, frozen, wintry **07** brumous, distant, hostile **08** freezing, inimical, piercing, Siberian **10** unfriendly **12** antagonistic

glaciation stage
04 Günz, Riss, Würm **06** Mindel

glad
04 fain, keen **05** eager, happy, merry, ready **06** bright, cheery, elated, joyful **07** chuffed, gleeful, pleased, welcome, willing **08** cheerful, disposed, gladsome, inclined, prepared, thrilled **09** contented, delighted, gratified, overjoyed, satisfied **11** over the moon, tickled pink

gladden
05 cheer, elate **06** buck up, please **07** delight, enliven, gratify, hearten,

rejoice **08** brighten **09** encourage **10** exhilarate

glade
03 gap **04** dell, land **05** laund, space **07** opening **08** clearing **09** cock-shoot

gladiator
07 Samnite, sworder **09** retiarius, Spartacus

gladly
04 fain **06** fainly, freely **07** happily, readily **09** willingly **10** cheerfully, gladsomely **12** with pleasure **13** with good grace

gladness
03 joy **04** glee **05** mirth **06** gaiety **07** delight, jollity **08** felicity, hilarity, pleasure **09** happiness **10** brightness, joyousness **11** high spirits **12** cheerfulness

glamorous
04 glam **05** ritzy, smart **06** exotic, flashy, glammy, glitzy, glossy, lovely **07** elegant **08** alluring, charming, dazzling, exciting, gorgeous **09** appealing, beautiful, colourful, thrilling **10** attractive, bewitching, enchanting, glittering **11** captivating, fascinating, well-dressed

glamour
02 it, SA **04** gilt, Ritz **05** charm, magic **06** allure, appeal, beauty, thrill **07** glitter **08** elegance, prestige, witchery **09** magnetism **10** attraction, excitement **11** captivation, enchantment, fascination **14** attractiveness

• **sentimental glamour**
04 halo

glance
03 dip, ray **04** flip, leaf, leer, look, ogle, peek, peep, scan, skim, view **05** blink, dekko, eliad, flash, flick, glide, slant, squiz, thumb, tweer, twire **06** amoret, aspect, browse, eyliad, gander, gledge, illiad, shufti, shufty, skelly, squint, vision **07** deflect, eye-beam, eyeliad, eyeshot, eye-wink, glimpse, skellie **08** butcher's, oeillade, ricochet **09** brief look, quick look **10** redruthite **13** look briefly at, look quickly at **15** catch a glimpse of

• **at first glance**
09 outwardly, seemingly **10** apparently, ostensibly, prima facie **12** at first sight, on the surface **13** on the face of it, superficially

• **glance off**
07 rebound **08** ricochet **09** bounce off **10** spring back

gland

Glands include:

05 lymph, ovary **06** cortex, pineal, thymus **07** adrenal, eccrine, mammary, medulla, parotid, thyroid **08** apocrine, exocrine, pancreas, prostate, testicle

09 endocrine, holocrine, lachrymal, lymph node, merocrine, pituitary, sebaceous **11** parathyroid

glare
04 beam, glow, look, lour **05** blaze, flame, flare, frown, lower, scowl, shine, stare **06** dazzle, glassy, glower **07** daggers, reflect **08** iceblink **09** black look, dirty look, limelight, look frown, spotlight **10** brightness, brilliance

glaring
04 open **05** glary, gross, lurid, overt **06** garish, patent **07** blatant, obvious **08** flagrant, manifest, walleyed **10** outrageous **11** conspicuous

glaringly
06 openly **07** overtly **08** patently **09** blatantly, obviously **10** flagrantly, manifestly **13** conspicuously

glass
04 lens, opal, pony **05** loupe, poney, specs **06** beaker, copita, cullet, goblet, mirror, psyche, rummer **07** brimmer, crystal, monocle, opaline, sleever, tumbler, vitrail, vitrics **08** pince-nez **09** barometer, glassware, lorgnette **10** aventurine, aventurine, dildo-glass, eyeglasses, spectacles **12** opera-glasses, supernaculum **13** contact lenses

Glass sizes include:

03 pot, six, ten **04** pint **05** bobby, middy, seven **06** handle **07** butcher, sleever **08** half pint, schooner

• **flaw in glass**
04 tear

• **substitute for glass**
04 mica

glassy
03 icy **04** cold, dull **05** blank, clear, dazed, empty, fixed, glare, shiny **06** glazed, glazen, glossy, smooth, vacant **07** deadpan, hyaline, vacuous **08** lifeless, polished, slippery, unmoving, vitreous **09** glasslike **10** mirrorlike **11** transparent **12** crystal clear **14** expressionless

glaze
04 ciré, coat **05** aspic, cover, glass, gloss, shine, smear **06** enamel, finish, luster, lustre, polish, sancai **07** burnish, celadon, coating, eggwash, lacquer, varnish **08** tiger eye **09** peach-blow, tiger's eye

gleam
03 ray **04** beam, glow, leam, leme **05** blink, flame, flare, flash, glint, gloss, light, shaft, sheen, shine **06** glance, lustre **07** flicker, glimmer, glimpse, glisten, glitter, radiate, shimmer, sparkle **08** sun-blink **10** brightness, shimmering **11** scintillate

glean
04 cull, pick, reap **05** amass, learn, lease **06** garner, gather, pick up, select **07** collect, find out, harvest **10** accumulate

glee
03 fun, joy **04** gley **05** mirth, verve **06** gaiety, squint **07** delight, elation, jollity, triumph **08** gladness, hilarity, pleasure **09** joviality, merriment **10** exuberance, exultation, jocularity, joyfulness, joyousness, liveliness **12** cheerfulness, exhilaration **13** gratification

gleeful
05 happy, merry **06** elated, jovial, joyful, joyous **07** pleased **08** cheerful, exultant, jubilant, mirthful **09** cock-a-hoop, delighted, exuberant, gratified, overjoyed **10** triumphant **11** over the moon **14** beside yourself

gleefully
07 happily, merrily **08** joyfully, joyously **10** cheerfully, jubilantly **11** exuberantly **12** triumphantly

glen
03 cwm **04** gill **05** ghyll **10** depression

glib
04 easy **05** gabby, gassy, quick, ready, slick, suave **06** facile, fluent, smooth **07** voluble **08** castrate **09** insincere, plausible, talkative **10** loquacious **13** silver-tongued, smooth-talking, smooth-tongued

glibly
05 patly, slick **06** easily **07** quickly, slickly **08** fluently, smoothly **11** insincerely

glide
03 fly, run **04** cost, flow, pass, roll, sail, skim, slip, slur, soar, swan, swim **05** coast, coste, drift, float, lapse, skate, sleek, slide **06** vanish **07** scrieve **08** volplane **10** portamento **12** move smoothly

glimmer
03 ray **04** glow, hint, wink **05** blink, flash, gleam, glint, grain, shine, stime, styme, trace **07** flicker, glimpse, glisten, glitter, inkling, shimmer, sparkle, twinkle **10** suggestion

glimmering
04 clue, hint, idea, sign **06** notion **07** inkling, pointer, whisper **08** allusion, faintest, foggiest, innuendo **09** suspicion **10** indication, intimation, suggestion **11** insinuation

glimpse
03 spy **04** espy, glim, look, peek, peep, spot, view, waff **05** blink, flash, gliff, glift, glisk, sight, stime, styme, whiff **06** aperçu, glance, gledge, squint **08** sighting **09** brief look, foregleam, quick look **12** catch sight of

glint
05 flash, gleam, shine **07** glimmer, glisten, glitter, reflect, shimmer,

sparkle, twinkle **10** glistening, reflection **11** scintillate

glisten
05 flash, gleam, glint, shine **07** flicker, glimmer, glitter, shimmer, sparkle, twinkle **09** coruscate

glitch
04 snag **05** block, catch, check, delay **06** hiccup, hold-up, mishap **07** barrier, problem, setback, trouble **08** drawback, obstacle **09** hindrance **10** difficulty, impediment **11** obstruction

glitter
04 gilt, glee **05** flare, flash, gleam, glint, glitz, sheen, shine **06** bicker, dazzle, lustre, tinsel **07** flicker, glamour, glimmer, glisten, glister, shimmer, spangle, sparkle, twinkle **08** radiance **09** coruscate, showiness, splendour **10** brightness, brilliance, flashiness, razzmatazz **11** coruscation, scintillate **12** razzle-dazzle **13** scintillation

glitz
05 swank **07** glitter, pizzazz **09** gaudiness, showiness **10** flashiness, garishness, razzmatazz **11** flamboyance, ostentation **12** razzle-dazzle **13** tastelessness **14** attractiveness **15** pretentiousness

glitzy
04 loud, posh **05** cheap, fancy, flash, gaudy, ritzy, showy, vivid **06** flashy, garish, ornate, swanky, tawdry **07** pompous **09** brilliant, tasteless **10** flamboyant, glittering **11** pretentious **12** ostentatious

gloat
04 crow **05** boast, exult, glory, vaunt **06** relish **07** rejoice, revel in, rub it in, triumph **09** delight in

global
05 total **07** general **08** thorough **09** spherical, universal, worldwide **10** exhaustive **11** wide-ranging **12** all-inclusive, encyclopedic **13** comprehensive, encyclopaedic, international **15** all-encompassing

globally
09 generally, worldwide **10** everywhere **11** in every land, under the sun, universally **12** in every place **14** in every country **15** internationally

globe
03 orb **04** ball, pome **05** earth, round, world **06** planet, sphere **08** roundure

globular
05 round **07** globate **08** spheroid **09** orbicular, spherical **10** ball-shaped

globule
04 ball, bead, blob, drop, pill **05** pearl **06** bubble, pellet **07** droplet, vesicle **08** globulet, particle, vesicula

gloom
03 woe **04** damp, dark, dusk, mirk, mood, murk **05** cloud, drere, grief,

scowl, shade **06** dreare, misery, shadow, sorrow **07** despair, dimness, sadness **08** darkness, dullness, glumness, the blues, twilight **09** blackness, dejection, murkiness, obscurity, pessimism **10** cloudiness, depression, desolation, low spirits, melancholy, sullenness **11** despondency, unhappiness **12** hopelessness **14** discouragement

gloomily
05 sadly **06** glumly **08** dismally, drearily, morosely **09** miserably **11** cheerlessly **12** depressingly, despondently **13** downheartedly **15** pessimistically

gloomy
03 dim, low, sad, wan **04** dark, down, dull, glum, grim, mirk, murk **05** dingy, drear, dusky, heavy, morne, murky, sable, unlit **06** cloudy, dismal, dreary, drumly, morose, somber, sombre **07** obscure, shadowy, Stygian **08** darksome, dejected, desolate, downbeat, downcast, frowning, overcast **09** cheerless, Cimmerian, depressed, dyspeptic, miserable, saturnine, sorrowful, tenebrose, tenebrous **10** Acherontic, depressing, despondent, disastrous, dispirited, downlooked, melancholy, sepulchral, tenebrious **11** crepuscular, downhearted, dyspeptical, pessimistic **12** disconsolate, in low spirits **14** down in the dumps
• **gloomy appearance**
04 lour

glorification
06 avatar, praise **07** lauding, worship **08** doxology, thanking **09** adoration, extolling, gratitude, honouring, reverence **10** apotheosis, veneration **11** celebration, idolization, lionization **13** magnification **15** romanticization, transfiguration

glorify
04 hail, laud **05** adore, bless, exalt, extol, thank **06** honour, praise, revere **07** elevate, heroize, idolize, lionize, magnify, worship **08** emblazon, enshrine, eulogize, sanctify, venerate **09** celebrate **10** panegyrize **11** immortalize, romanticize, transfigure

glorious
04 fine **05** famed, grand, great, noble, noted, super, tipsy **06** bright, elated, famous, superb **07** eminent, perfect, radiant, shining, supreme **08** boastful, dazzling, gorgeous, heavenly, honoured, majestic, renowned, splendid, terrific **09** beautiful, brilliant, excellent, wonderful **10** celebrated, delightful, marvellous, triumphant, victorious **11** illustrious, magnificent **13** distinguished

glory
03 sun **04** crow, fame, halo, pomp **05** boast, crown, exult, gloat, kudos, revel, strut **06** beauty, diadem, gloire,

gloria, homage, honour, praise, relish, renown **07** acclaim, aureola, delight, dignity, garland, majesty, preface, rejoice, tribute, triumph, worship **08** accolade, blessing, doxology, eminence, gloriole, grandeur, prestige, radiance **09** adoration, celebrity, gratitude, greatness, splendour **10** brightness, brilliance, exaltation, veneration **11** distinction, recognition **12** magnificence, resplendence, thanksgiving **13** pride yourself **14** impressiveness **15** illustriousness

gloss
04 mask, note, show, veil **05** front, gleam, sheen, shine **06** define, façade, luster, lustre, polish, postil, veneer **07** comment, explain, shimmer, sparkle, surface, varnish **08** annotate, construe, disguise, footnote, scholion **09** elucidate, interpret, semblance, translate **10** annotation, appearance, brightness, brilliance, camouflage, commentary, definition **11** elucidation, explanation, explication, translation **12** add glosses to **14** interpretation, window-dressing

• **gloss over**
04 fard, gild, hide, mask, veil **05** avoid, evade **06** ignore, soothe **07** conceal, cover up **08** disguise **09** whitewash **10** camouflage, double-gild, smooth over **11** explain away **13** draw a veil over **15** deal with quickly

glossary
05 index **06** clavis **07** lexicon **08** wordbook, word list **09** thesaurus **10** dictionary **11** concordance

glossy
05 glacé, shiny, silky, sleek, slick **06** bright, glassy, glazed, polite, sheeny, silken, smooth **07** shining, wet-look **08** gleaming, lustrous, polished **09** brilliant, burnished, enamelled, sparkling **10** shimmering

glove
03 kid **04** gage, left, mitt **05** right **06** beaver, cestus, mitten, muffle **07** caestus, chevron **08** cheveron, gauntlet **09** oven glove

glow
04 burn, leam, leme, rose **05** bloom, blush, flush, gleam, glory, light, shine **06** ardour, colour, redden, warmth **07** burning, fervour, glimmer, passion, radiate, redness, sunglow **08** grow pink, look pink, outflush, pinkness, radiance, richness, rosiness, smoulder **09** afterglow, corposant, happiness, intensity, reddening, splendour, vividness **10** brightness, brilliance, enthusiasm, excitement, luminosity **11** gegenschein, St Elmo's fire **12** satisfaction **13** incandescence **15** phosphorescence

glower
04 look **05** frown, glare, scowl, stare **09** black look, dirty look **11** look daggers

glowing
03 red **04** rave, rich, warm **05** ruddy, vivid **06** bright, fervid **07** candent, flaming, flushed, lambent, radiant, vibrant **08** ecstatic, luminous, rutilant **09** laudatory, rhapsodic **10** candescent, eulogistic, favourable **11** noctilucent, noctilucous, panegyrical, smouldering **12** enthusiastic, incandescent **13** complimentary **14** phosphorescent

glue
03 fix, gum **04** bond, grip, seal, size **05** affix, epoxy, paste, rivet, stick **06** absorb, cement, compel, engage, mortar **07** engross, gelatin **08** adhesive, Araldite®, fixative, gelatine, propolis **09** hypnotize, mesmerize **11** agglutinate **12** conglutinate, ichthyocolla **14** impact adhesive

gluey
05 gummy **06** sticky, viscid **07** viscous **08** adhesive **09** glutinous

glum
03 low, sad **04** down, sour **05** gruff, moody, sulky, surly **06** gloomy, grumpy, morose, solemn, sullen **07** crabbed, doleful, forlorn, unhappy **08** churlish, dejected **09** depressed, miserable **10** despondent **11** crestfallen, ill-humoured, pessimistic **14** down in the dumps

glumly
05 sadly **06** sourly **08** gloomily, gruffily, grumpily, morosely, sullenly **09** forlornly, miserably, unhappily **10** dejectedly **12** despondently

glut
04 clog, cram, fill, sate **05** choke, flood, gorge, stuff **06** deluge, excess **07** engorge, satiate, surfeit, surplus **08** inundate, overfeed, overflow, overload, saturate **10** oversupply, saturation **11** superfluity **13** overabundance **14** superabundance

glutinous
04 limy, ropy **05** gluey, gummy, ropey **06** mucous, sticky, viscid **07** viscous **08** adhesive, cohesive **09** emplastic **12** mucilaginous

• **glutinous formation**
04 rope

glutton
03 pig **06** gorger, gutser, gutzer **07** gobbler, guzzler, lurcher **08** belly-god, carcajou, gourmand **09** cormorant, free-liver, wolverine **10** greedy guts **11** gormandizer

gluttonous
05 gutsy **06** greedy **07** hoggish, piggish **08** edacious, esurient, gourmand, ravenous **09** rapacious, voracious **10** gluttonish, insatiable, omnivorous **12** gormandizing

gluttony
05 greed **07** edacity, surfeit **08** gulosity, voracity **09** esurience

10 gormandize, greediness **11** gourmandism, piggishness **13** insatiability

G-man
03 fed

gnarled
◊ *anagram indicator*
05 bumpy, lumpy, rough **06** gnarly, knotty, knurly, rugged **07** gnarred, knarred, knotted, twisted **08** leathery, wrinkled **09** contorted, distorted **13** weather-beaten

gnash
04 grit **05** grate, grind **06** scrape

gnaw
03 eat, nag **04** bite, chew, fret, prey, wear **05** erode, harry, haunt, munch, worry **06** crunch, devour, harass, nibble, niggle, plague **07** consume, eat away, torment, trouble **09** masticate

gnome
03 saw **05** adage, dwarf, maxim, motto **06** goblin, kobold, saying **07** proverb **08** aphorism **09** financier

go
03 act, bet, bid, die, fit, gae, gee, get, pep, run, try, zip **04** bash, bout, cark, deal, emit, fail, fare, gang, go by, grow, hark, head, kark, lead, life, move, pass, push, quit, scat, shot, span, stab, suit, turn, walk, work, yead, yede, yeed, zing **05** begin, blend, crack, croak, drive, drown, end up, fit in, force, lapse, leave, match, occur, oomph, reach, ready, scoot, scram, sound, spell, stake, start, whirl **06** accord, affair, beat it, be axed, become, be kept, belong, cark it, depart, effort, elapse, energy, expire, extend, go away, kark it, manage, matter, pan out, pass by, pass on, peg out, perish, pop off, repair, result, roll on, set off, set out, slip by, spirit, spread, starve, travel, unfold, vanish, vigour **07** advance, attempt, bargain, be fired, be found, be given, be spent, carry on, decease, develop, give off, journey, make for, operate, perform, pizzazz, proceed, release, retreat, send out, snuff it, stretch, success, turn out, urinate, work out **08** activity, be sacked, be used up, clear off, come to be, continue, dynamism, function, get rid of, melt away, pass away, progress, slip away, tick along, vitality, withdraw **09** animation, be donated, be given to, be located, be pledged, be spent on, disappear, endeavour, eventuate, harmonize **10** be consumed, be finished, be situated, complement, co-ordinate, correspond, get-up-and-go, go together, make a sound, make tracks **11** be awarded to, be discarded, be dismissed, be exhausted, be presented, bite the dust **12** be allotted to, be assigned to, be thrown away, lose your life, pop your clogs, shoot through **13** be changed into, close your eyes, kick the bucket, push up daisies, take your leave **14** be given the push, be given the sack, be shown the door,

depart this life, give up the ghost **15** be made redundant, breathe your last, cash in your chips, go with each other

• go about
◊ *containment indicator*
02 do **04** stir **05** begin **06** tackle **07** address, perform **08** approach, attend to, embark on, engage in, set about **09** undertake

• go ahead
04 move **05** begin **07** advance, carry on, precede, proceed **08** continue, fire away, progress **12** make progress

• go along with
04 obey **06** accept, follow **07** abide by, support **09** accompany, agree with **10** comply with, concur with, fall in with

• go and get
03 fet **05** fetch

• go around, go round
◊ *anagram indicator*
◊ *containment indicator*
◊ *reversal indicator*
04 reel, spin, turn **05** swirl, twirl, twist, wheel, whirl, whirr **06** bypass, circle, gyrate, rotate, swivel **07** go about, revolve **09** circulate, pirouette, turn round **13** be passed round, be talked about **14** be spread around

• go at
05 argue, blame **06** attack, tackle **08** set about **09** criticize

• go away
04 scat **05** choof, hence, imshi, imshy, leave, scoot, scram, swith **06** begone, depart, vanish **07** abscond, do a bunk, gertcha, nick off, rack off, retreat **08** choof off, run for it, withdraw **09** disappear, do a runner **10** get knotted **13** sling your hook **14** make a bolt for it, run for your life **15** make a break for it, take to your heels

• go back
◊ *reversal indicator*
06 return, revert **07** regress, retreat **09** backslide

• go back on
◊ *reversal indicator*
04 deny **05** break **08** renege on **09** default on

• go by
04 flow, heed, obey, pass **05** lapse **06** elapse, follow **07** observe **10** comply with

• go down
03 dip, set **04** drop, fail, fall, fold, lose, sink **07** decline, descend, founder, go under, sustain **08** be beaten, collapse, decrease, fall down **09** be met with, be reduced **10** be defeated, be honoured, be received, be recorded, degenerate **11** be reacted to, be submerged, deteriorate **12** be recognized, be remembered, come a cropper, suffer defeat **15** have as a response

• go down with
05 catch **06** pick up **07** develop **08** contract **09** succumb to **12** come down with **13** be afflicted by

• go for
04 like **05** enjoy **06** admire, aim for,

assail, attack, choose, favour, prefer, rush at, select **07** assault, lunge at **08** set about

• go forward
03 rip

• go freely
03 run

• go in for
05 adopt, enter **06** follow, go into, pursue, take up **07** embrace, espouse **08** engage in, practise **09** undertake **10** take part in **13** participate in

• go into
◊ *insertion indicator*
05 probe, study **06** review **07** analyse, discuss, dissect, examine **08** check out, consider, look into, research **09** delve into **10** scrutinize **11** inquire into, investigate

• go off
◊ *anagram indicator*
03 rot **04** quit, sour, turn **05** blast, burst, go bad, leave **06** blow up, depart, go bang, set out, vanish **07** abscond, be fired, explode, go stale **08** detonate **09** disappear **11** deteriorate **12** be discharged

• go on
03 gab, gas, hup **04** last, stay **05** occur **06** endure, happen, natter, rabbit, remain, witter **07** carry on, chatter, persist, proceed **08** continue, ramble on **09** take place

• go out
03 ebb **04** date, exit **05** court, leave **06** depart, go with **07** go round **08** go around, go steady, withdraw **11** be turned off **12** see each other **13** be switched off **14** be extinguished

• go over
04 list, read, scan **05** check, study **06** peruse, repeat, review, revise **07** discuss, examine, inspect **08** look over, rehearse **10** think about

• go quickly
03 cut, run, zap **04** hare, race, spin

• go round
04 ring, turn **06** rotate

• go slow
04 lose

• go through
04 bear, face, hunt **05** check, spend, stand, use up **06** endure, search, suffer **07** consume, examine, exhaust, explore, undergo **08** be passed, be signed, rehearse, squander, tolerate **09** be adopted, be carried, withstand **10** be accepted, be approved, experience, get through **11** be confirmed, investigate, look through **12** be authorized **13** be subjected to

• go together
◊ *juxtaposition indicator*
03 fit **04** suit **05** blend, match **06** accord **09** harmonize **10** complement, co-ordinate

• go under
◊ *juxtaposition down indicator*
03 die **04** fail, flop, fold, sink **05** drown **06** go bust, go down **07** default, founder, succumb **08** collapse, submerge **09** close down **10** go

bankrupt **11** go to the wall **15** go out of business

• go with
03 fit **04** suit, take **05** blend, match, usher **06** escort **09** accompany, harmonize **10** complement, co-ordinate, correspond

• go without
04 lack, want **05** forgo **06** forego **07** abstain **09** do without **12** deny yourself **13** manage without

• tell to go
04 send

goad
03 gad, nag, vex **04** brod, jolt, prod, push, spur, urge **05** ankus, annoy, drive, hound, impel, prick, sound, sting, taunt **06** arouse, harass, incite, induce, needle, prompt **07** inspire, provoke **08** irritate, motivate **09** instigate, stimulate **10** cattle prod, pressurize

go-ahead
02 OK **05** pushy **06** assent **07** consent, dashing, dynamic, forward **08** approval, sanction, thumbs-up, vigorous, warranty **09** agreement, ambitious, clearance, energetic, go-getting **10** aggressive, green light, permission, pioneering **11** opportunist, progressive, resourceful, up-and-coming **12** confirmation, enterprising **13** authorization **14** forward-looking

goal
03 aim, end **04** cage, dool, dule, hail, home, mark, race **05** bourn, grail, ideal, limit **06** bourne, design, object, target **07** purpose **08** ambition, boundary, terminus **09** direction, equalizer, intention, objective **10** aspiration **11** competition, destination

• prevent goal
04 save

goat
03 bok, kid **04** gate, ibex, tahr, tehr, thar **05** nanny **06** Angora, butter, caprid, lecher, Saanen **07** bucardo, markhor **09** Capricorn

goat-antelope
05 goral, serow **07** chamois

goatsucker
06 evejar **07** bullbat, dorhawk, fern-owl **08** churn-owl, nightjar, poorwill **09** nighthawk **10** moth-hunter, night-churr **11** screech-hawk **12** mosquito hawk, whippoorwill **15** chuck-will's-widow

gobble
◊ *containment indicator*
04 bolt, cram, gulp, wolf **05** gorge, scoff, snarf, stuff **06** devour, guzzle **07** consume, put away, slabber, slubber, swallow **10** eat quickly

gobbledygook
06 drivel, jargon **07** prattle, rubbish, twaddle **08** nonsense **09** buzz words, gibberish **10** balderdash, journalese

11 computerese, officialese
12 psychobabble

go-between
05 agent **06** broker, dealer, factor, medium **07** contact, liaison **08** mediator **09** messenger, middleman **10** love-broker **11** ring-carrier **12** intermediary

goblet
03 cup **05** glass, hanap **06** beaker **07** chalice, stem cup, tumbler

goblin
03 elf, imp, nis, pug **04** bogy, puck **05** bogey, bogle, demon, fiend, gnome, nisse, nixie, pooka, pouke, troll **06** bodach, duende, Empusa, kelpie, kobold, redcap, spirit, sprite **07** bargest, brownie, gremlin, knocker, red-cowl **08** barghest **09** barghaist, gobbeline, hobgoblin **10** leprechaun, shellycoat **11** lubber fiend **12** esprit follet

gobsmacked
04 dumb **06** amazed, thrown **07** baffled, floored, shocked, stunned **08** confused, overcome, startled **09** astounded, paralysed, staggered **10** astonished, bewildered, bowled over, confounded, nonplussed, speechless, taken aback **11** dumbfounded, overwhelmed **12** lost for words **13** flabbergasted, knocked for six

God
01 D **02** od **03** dod, dog, gad, Gog, gum, Jah, odd **04** Dieu, gosh, King, Lord, Zeus **05** Allah, Deity, Judge, Maker, monad **06** Brahma, Elohim, Father, Yahweh **07** all-seer, Bhagwan, Creator, Eternal, Godhead, Holy One, Jehovah, Saviour **08** all-giver, Almighty, gracious, infinite **09** All-father **10** first cause, prime mover, Providence **11** Divine Being, Everlasting, king of kings **12** Supreme Being

• **God willing**
02 DV **09** inshallah **10** Deo volente, volente Deo

god, goddess
02 as **04** aitu, cock, deus, deva, Fate, faun, icon, idol, kami, Muse, Norn **05** deify, deity, Grace, Norna, power **06** spirit, sylvan **08** divinity **09** promachos **11** divine being, graven image

Babylonian gods include:
02 Ea
03 Anu, Bel, Sin
04 Adad, Apsu, Baal, Enki, Nabu
05 Ellil, Enlil, Hadad, Mummu
06 Anshar, Dumuzi, Marduk, Nergal, Tammuz
07 Ninurta, Shamash, Thammuz

Babylonian goddesses include:
03 Aja
04 Antu
05 Antum, Belit, Nintu

06 Ishtar, Kishar, Ningal, Ninlil, Nintur, Tiamat
07 Anunitu, Damkina
10 Ereshkigal

Central and South American gods include:
04 Chac, Inti
06 Tlaloc
07 Huang-ti, Hunab Ku, Itzamma
08 Catequil, Kukulkan
09 the Bacabs, Viracocha, Xipe Totec
10 Apu Punchau, Manco Capac, Pachacamac, Xochipilli
12 Quetzalcoatl, Tezcatlipoca, Xiuhtecuhtli
15 Huitzilopochtil

Central and South American goddesses include:
05 Aknah
06 Ixchel
09 Coatlicue, Ixazaluoh, Mama Oella, Pachamama
10 Mama Quilla
11 Tlazolteotl
12 Xochiquetzal
15 Chalchiuhtlicue

Egyptian gods include:
02 Ra, Re
03 Bes, Geb, Nut
04 Apis, Aten, Atum, Ptah, Seth
05 Horus, Thoth
06 Amun-Re, Anubis, Osiris
07 Khonsou, Sarapis, Serapis

Egyptian goddesses include:
03 Nut
04 Isis, Maat
05 Khnum
06 Hathor, Sakmet, Sekmet
07 Nepthys, Sakhmet, Sekhmet
08 Nephthys

Greek gods include:
03 Pan
04 Ares, Atys, Eros, Zeus
05 Atlas, Attis, Hades
06 Adonis, Aeolus, Apollo, Boreas, Cronus, Helios, Hermes, Hypnos, Nereus
07 Oceanus
08 Dionysus, Ganymede, Morpheus, Poseidon, Thanatos
09 Asclepius
10 Hephaestus
11 Aesculapius

Greek goddesses include:
03 Eos, Nyx
04 Gaea, Gaia, Hebe, Hera, Iris, Nike, Rhea
05 Tyche
06 Athene, Cybele, Hecate, Hestia, Hygeia, Selene, Themis, Thetis
07 Alphito, Artemis, Demeter, Erinyes, Nemesis
08 Arethusa, the Fates, the Horae, the Muses
09 Aphrodite, the Furies, the Graces
10 Persephone

Hindu gods include:
04 Agni, Kama, Rama, Siva, Soma, Yama
05 Indra, Kurma, Radha, Rudra, Shani, Shiva, Surya
06 Brahma, Ganesa, Ganesh, Garuda, Iswara, Narada, Pushan, Ravana, Skanda, Varuna, Vishnu
07 Ganesha, Hanuman, Krishna, Savitri
08 Ganapati, Nataraja
09 Kartikeya, Lakshmana, Narasimha, Prajapati
10 Jagannatha

Hindu goddesses include:
03 Uma
04 Devi, Kali, Maya, Sita
05 Aditi, Durga, Gauri, Radha, Sakti
06 Shakti
07 Lakshmi, Parvati
09 Sarasvati

Maori gods include:
02 Tu
03 Uru
04 Maui, Tane
05 Rangi, Rongo
06 Haumia
07 Tawhiri
08 Ranginui, Ruaumoko, Tangaroa
10 Tane Mahuta
11 Rongomatane, Tumatauenga
12 Tawhiri Matea

Maori goddesses include:
04 Papa
10 Hinetitama
11 Hinenuitepo, Papatuanuku

Norse gods include:
03 Bor, Otr, Tyr, Ull
04 Frey, Logi, Loki, Odin, Thor
05 Aegir, Aesir, Alcis, Bragi, Donar, Freyr, Hoder, Mimir, Njord, Vanir, Vidar, Woden, Wotan
06 Balder, Fafnir, Hermod, Hoenir, Kvasir, Weland
07 Volundr, Wayland, Weiland
08 Heimdall

Norse goddesses include:
03 Hel, Ran, Sif
04 Hela
05 Frigg, Idunn, Nanna, Norns, Sigyn
06 Freyja, Gefion
07 Nerthus
08 Fjorgynn
09 Valkyries
10 Nehallenia

Roman gods include:
04 Mars
05 Cupid, Fides, Janus, Lares, Orcus, Picus, Pluto
06 Apollo, Consus, Faunus, Genius, Mithra, Saturn, Vulcan
07 Bacchus, Jupiter, Mercury, Mithras, Neptune, Penates
08 Portunus, Silvanus
09 Vertumnus
10 Liber Pater

Roman goddesses include:

03 Ops
04 Juno, Luna, Maia
05 Ceres, Diana, Epona, Fauna, Flora, Pales, Venus, Vesta
06 Pomona, Rumina
07 Bellona, Egreria, Feronia, Fortuna, Minerva
08 Libitina, Victoria
10 Proserpina

Gods and goddesses of other regions and cultures include:

03 Rod, Wak
04 Amma, Kane, Tane
05 Epona, Pan Gu, Perun
06 Guan Di, Inanna, Kuan Ti, Mithra, Modimo, Moloch, Shango, Svarog, Tengri, Teshub, Vahagn
07 Anahita, Astarte, Kumarbi, Taranis, Triglav, Zanhary
08 Rosmerta, Skyamsen, Sucellus, Teutates
09 Amaterasu, Sventovit
10 Ahura Mazda
11 Thunderbird
15 Izanagi no Mikoto, Izanami no Mikoto

god-forsaken
05 bleak **06** dismal, dreary, gloomy, lonely, remote **07** forlorn **08** deserted, desolate, isolated, wretched **09** abandoned, miserable **10** depressing

godless
03 bad **04** evil **05** pagan **06** sinful, unholy, wicked **07** atheous, heathen, immoral, impious, profane, ungodly **08** agnostic **09** atheistic, faithless **10** irreverent **11** irreligious, nullifidian, unrighteous **12** sacrilegious

godlessness
07 atheism, impiety **08** paganism **10** irreligion, wickedness **11** agnosticism, irreverence, ungodliness **13** faithlessness **14** unfaithfulness

godlike
04 holy **06** divine, sacred **07** deiform, exalted, perfect, saintly, sublime **08** heavenly, Olympian **09** celestial **10** superhuman **11** theomorphic **12** transcendent

godliness
05 piety **06** belief, purity **08** holiness, morality, religion, sanctity **10** devoutness **13** righteousness

godly
04 good, holy, pure, wise **05** moral, pious **06** devout **07** saintly **08** innocent, virtuous **09** believing, religious, righteous **10** God-fearing

godsend
04 boon **07** bonanza, miracle **08** blessing, windfall **11** benediction **12** stroke of luck

goggle
04 gawk, gawp, gaze, ogle **05** stare **06** wonder **08** protrude

going-over
03 row **05** check, study **06** attack, rebuke, review, survey **07** beating, check-up, chiding, pasting **08** analysis, scolding, scrutiny, whipping **09** criticism, reprimand, thrashing, trouncing **10** inspection **11** castigation, examination **12** chastisement, dressing-down **13** investigation

goings-on
06 events, scenes **07** affairs **08** business, mischief **09** behaviour **10** activities, happenings **11** occurrences **12** misbehaviour **13** funny business

gold
02 Au, or **03** bar, Sol **04** gool, gule, leaf **05** goold, ingot **06** nugget, riches, yellow **07** bullion **12** king of metals **13** precious metal
• **yield gold**
03 pan

golden
03 red **04** fair, gilt, gold, rosy **05** blond, happy, sunny **06** blonde, bright, flaxen, gilded, gilden, gylden, joyful, yellow **07** aureate, goldish, luteous, shining **08** aurelian, dazzling, gleaming, glorious, inaurate, lustrous, precious **09** brilliant, excellent, promising, rewarding, Saturnian, treasured **10** auspicious, delightful, favourable, millennial, propitious, prosperous, successful **11** flourishing, hyacinthine, resplendent **12** gold-coloured

goldfinch
06 redcap **09** goldspink, gowdspink **10** yellowbird

golf
01 G **04** gowf

Golf courses include:

04 Deal, Eden
05 Troon
06 Manito, Merion, Skokie
07 Balgove, Buffalo, Hoylake, Jubilee, Medinah, Newport, Oak Hill, Oakmont, Oak Tree, Prince's, Sahalee
08 Bethesda, Birkdale, Blue Hill, Glen View, Portland, Sandwich, Valhalla
09 Aronimink, Baltimore, Baltusrol, Bellerive, Brookline, Englewood, Hazeltine, Inverness, Minikahda, Muirfield, New Course, Old Course, Onwentsia, Pinehurst, Prestwick, St Andrews, The Belfry, Turnberry
10 Canterbury, Carnoustie, Garden City, Royal Troon, Shoal Creek, Tanglewood, Winged Foot
11 Cherry Hills, Kemper Lakes, Miami Valley, Musselburgh, Olympic Club, Pebble Beach, Strathtyrum
12 Crooked Stick, Laurel Valley, Oakland Hills
13 Northwood Club, Olympia Fields, Royal Birkdale, Royal Portrush, Southern Hills
14 Keller Golf Club, Myopia Hunt Club, NCR Country Club, Pelham Golf Club
15 Augusta National, Chicago Golf Club, Shinnecock Hills

golf club

Golf clubs include:

04 iron, wood
05 baffy, blade, cleek, mashy, spoon, wedge
06 brassy, bulger, driver, jigger, mashie, putter
07 blaster, brassie, midiron, niblick
08 long iron
09 midmashie, sand wedge, short iron
10 mashie iron
11 belly putter, driving iron, fairway wood, spade mashie
12 putting-cleek
13 mashie-niblick, pitching wedge, two-ball putter
15 pitching niblick

golfer
06 gowfer, yipper

Golfers include:

03 Els (Ernie)
04 Lyle (Sandy), Webb (Karrie)
05 Braid (James), Brown (Ken), Duval (David), Faldo (Nick), Floyd (Raymond), Hagen (Walter), Hogan (Ben), Jones (Bobby), Locke (Bobby), Lopez (Nancy), Singh (Vijay), Snead (Sam Jackson), Woods (Tiger)
06 Alliss (Peter), Cotton (Sir Henry), Davies (Laura), Garcia (Sergio), Langer (Bernhard), Nelson (Byron), Norman (Greg), O'Meara (Mark), Palmer (Arnold), Player (Gary), Taylor (John), Vardon (Harry), Watson (Tom)
07 Charles (Bob), Couples (Fred), Jacklin (Tony), Sarazen (Gene), Stewart (Payne), Strange (Curtis), Thomson (Peter), Trevino (Lee Buck), Woosnam (Ian), Zoeller (Fuzzy)
08 Crenshaw (Ben), Nicklaus (Jack), Olazábal (Jose Maria), Torrance (Sam), Westwood (Lee), Zaharias (Babe)
09 Mickelson (Phil), Sorenstam (Annika), Whitworth (Kathy)
11 Ballesteros (Severiano), Montgomerie (Colin)

gone
◊ *anagram indicator*
03 ago, ygo **04** away, dead, done, gane, lost, over, past, used, ygoe **05** agone, spent **06** absent, astray **07** defunct, elapsed, extinct, missing, worn-out **08** departed, finished, vanished **11** disappeared **15** over and done with

goo
03 mud **04** crud, grot, gunk, mire, muck, ooze, scum, slop, yuck

05 gloop, grime, gunge, slime, slush
06 grease, grunge, matter, sludge
10 stickiness **14** sentimentality

good

01 g **02** OK **03** bad, bon, fab, fit, rum,
top, use **04** able, best, dear, fair, fine,
gain, kind, mega, neat, nice, safe, sake,
true, well **05** adept, avail, beaut,
bewdy, bonne, bosom, brill, bully,
close, great, large, lucky, merit, moral,
nasty, noble, pakka, pious, pucka,
pukka, right, sound, super, valid,
whole, worth **06** agreed, behalf,
bonzer, bosker, castor, clever, corker,
cushty, ethics, expert, gifted, honest,
honour, indeed, just so, loving, morals,
polite, profit, ripper, strong, superb,
useful, virtue, wicked, worthy
07 awesome, benefit, capable, ethical,
fitting, genuine, healthy, helpful,
honesty, perfect, purpose, service,
sizable, skilful, skilled, upright, welfare
08 adequate, all right, budgeree,
cheerful, complete, cracking, fabulous,
faithful, friendly, goodness, gracious,
interest, intimate, morality, obedient,
passable, pleasant, pleasing, reliable,
sensible, sizeable, smashing, suitable,
superior, talented, terrific, thorough,
very well, vigorous, virtuous
09 admirable, advantage, agreeable,
bodacious, brilliant, competent,
compliant, desirable, dexterous,
efficient, enjoyable, excellent,
exemplary, fantastic, first-rate,
fortunate, integrity, in the pink,
rectitude, righteous, tolerable,
wellbeing, wonderful **10** acceptable,
altruistic, auspicious, beneficial,
benevolent, charitable, convenient,
convincing, dependable, favourable,
first-class, good as gold, honourable,
marvellous, persuasive, proficient,
profitable, propitious, prosperity,
reasonable, respectful, satisfying,
sufficient, thoughtful, usefulness,
worthwhile **11** appropriate,
commendable, considerate,
convenience, exceptional, kind-
hearted, pleasurable, serviceable,
substantial, sympathetic, trustworthy,
uprightness, well-behaved
12 accomplished, advantageous,
bewdy bottler, considerable, fit as a
fiddle, professional, satisfactory, under
control, well-disposed, well-
mannered **13** hale and hearty,
philanthropic, righteousness **14** salt of
the earth
• **for good**
04 ever **06** always **07** for ever
08 evermore, for keeps **09** eternally
10 for all time **11** irrevocably,
permanently **15** till kingdom come
• **make good**
02 do **04** abet **05** go far **06** arrive,
effect, fulfil, make it, recoup, repair,
supply **07** justify, perform, restore,
succeed, support **08** carry out, get
ahead, live up to, progress, put right,
retrieve **09** establish **10** compensate
12 be successful **13** compensate for,

make amends for, put into action
15 get on in the world
• **neither good nor bad**
04 so-so **14** comme çi comme ça
• **no good**
02 ng **03** bad, bum **04** duff **06** futile,
no chop **07** useless **09** worthless
• **pretty good**
04 fair, tidy **06** decent, not bad
08 middling **09** tolerable **14** fair to
middling
• **unusually good**
04 gear **10** incredible
• **very good**
02 OK, so, vg **03** sae, top **04** keen,
mega **05** bonza, grand **06** bangin',
beezer, bonzer, boshta, bosker, grouse,
peachy **07** banging, boshter, crucial,
immense, ripping **08** all right,
cracking, terrific **09** brilliant
10 marvellous, tremendous

goodbye

03 bye **04** ciao, ta-ta **05** addio, adieu,
adiós, later **06** bye-bye, cheers,
hooray, hooroo, kia ora, haere ra, see
you, so long, valete **07** bonsoir,
cheerio, good-day, good-den, good-
e'en, parting **08** au revoir, chin-chin,
farewell, good-even, sayonara, swan
song, take care, toodle-oo **09** bon
voyage, good night, toodle-pip **10** all
the best, a rivederci, good morrow
11 arrivederci, be seeing you, good
evening, good morning, leave-taking,
see you later, valediction, valedictory
12 have a nice day, mind how you go,
see you around **13** good afternoon
14 auf Wiedersehen

See also **farewell**

good-for-nothing

03 bum **04** idle, lazy **05** idler, lorel,
losel, stiff **06** donnat, donnot, loafer,
lozell, no-good, skiver, waster
07 bludger, lorrell, sculpin, slacker,
useless, vaurien, wastrel **08** feckless,
indolent, layabout, scalawag
09 lazybones, reprobate, scallawag,
scallywag, worthless **10** black sheep,
ne'er-do-weel, ne'er-do-well,
profligate **11** scant-o'-grace
13 irresponsible

good-humoured

05 happy **06** genial, jovial **07** affable,
amiable **08** cheerful, friendly, pleasant
09 congenial **12** approachable, good-
tempered

good-looking

04 fair **05** dishy **06** comely, goodly,
lovely, pretty **08** handsome, weel-
far'd, weel-far't **09** beautiful, weel-
faird, weel-faur'd, weel-faurt
10 attractive, personable
11 presentable **12** well-favoured

goodly

04 fine, good, tidy **05** ample, large
06 comely, proper **07** sizable
08 sizeable **09** excellent **10** sufficient
11 good-looking, significant,
substantial **12** considerable

good-natured

04 kind, nice **05** sonsy **06** clever,
gentle, kindly, sonsie **07** helpful,
patient **08** friendly, generous, tolerant
10 benevolent **11** kind-hearted,
neighbourly, sympathetic, warm-
hearted **12** approachable, good-
tempered

goodness

02 my **03** boy, law, wow **05** mercy,
value **06** virtue **07** benefit, honesty,
probity **08** altruism, goodwill, kindness
09 integrity, rectitude **10** compassion,
excellence, generosity **11** beneficence,
benevolence, helpfulness, uprightness
12 friendliness, graciousness
13 righteousness, unselfishness,
wholesomeness

goods

04 bona, gear **05** lines, stock, stuff,
wares **06** taonga, things **07** effects,
freight **08** chattels, products, property
10 belongings **11** commodities,
merchandise, possessions
13 accoutrements, appurtenances,
paraphernalia
• **package of goods**
04 bale, wrap

good-tempered

04 kind **06** gentle, kindly **07** helpful,
patient **08** friendly, generous, tolerant
10 benevolent **11** good-natured, kind-
hearted, neighbourly, sympathetic,
warm-hearted **12** approachable

goodwill

04 gree, zeal **05** amity, favor **06** favour
08 kindness **10** compassion,
friendship, generosity **11** benevolence,
well-wishing **12** friendliness

goody-goody

05 pious **08** priggish, unctuous
13 sanctimonious, self-righteous, ultra-
virtuous

gooey

04 soft **05** gluey, gucky, gungy, gunky,
tacky, thick **06** gloopy, sickly, sloppy,
slushy, sticky, syrupy, viscid **07** cloying,
maudlin, mawkish, squidgy, viscous
09 glutinous **10** nauseating
11 sentimental **12** mucilaginous

goose

04 nene, wavy **05** roger, wavey
06 gander, goslet **07** gosling, grey-lag
08 barnacle **09** whitehead
10 saddleback **13** brent barnacle
See also **fool**
• **goose's lungs**
04 soul

gooseberry

06 groser, groset **07** grosert
08 goosegob, goosegog, grossart
09 honey-blob **14** worcesterberry

goosefoot

04 beet **05** blite, orach **06** fat hen,
kochia, orache, quinoa, saxaul
07 pigweed, saksaul **08** saltbush,
saltwort, seablite **10** greasewood,
Mexican tea **13** good-King-Henry

gore
02 Al **04** cloy, gair, horn, stab **05** blood, cruor, filth, grume, skirt, spear, stick, wound **06** engore, impale, pierce **07** carnage **08** butchery **09** bloodshed, penetrate, slaughter **10** bloodiness

gorge
03 gap **04** bolt, cram, feed, fill, glut, gulp, pass, rift, sate, wolf **05** abyss, cañon, chasm, cleft, gully, stuff **06** canyon, defile, devour, gobble, guzzle, ravine, stodge **07** crevice, fissure, overeat, surfeit, swallow **08** barranca
See also **ravine**

gorgeous
04 fine, good, rich, sexy **05** grand, showy, sweet **06** lovely, pretty, superb **07** opulent **08** dazzling, glorious, handsome, pleasing, splendid, stunning **09** beautiful, brilliant, enjoyable, glamorous, luxurious, ravishing, splendent, sumptuous, wonderful **10** attractive, delightful, impressive, marvellous **11** good-looking, magnificent, resplendent **15** pulchritudinous

gorgeously
06 richly **08** superbly **10** gloriously, splendidly **11** brilliantly, luxuriously, sumptuously, wonderfully **12** delightfully, impressively, marvellously **13** magnificently

gorilla
04 thug **05** pongo **08** King Kong **10** silverback

gorse
04 ulex, whin **05** furze, gosse

gory
05 goary **06** bloody, brutal, grisly, savage **07** violent **09** murderous **10** sanguinary **11** blood-soaked, distasteful **12** bloodstained

gospel
04 fact, John, Luke, Mark **05** credo, creed, truth **06** verity **07** evangel, kerygma, Matthew **08** doctrine, good news, teaching **09** certainty **12** life of Christ, New Testament **14** Protevangelium **15** message of Christ
See also **Bible**

gossamer
04 airy, fine, thin **05** gauzy, light, sheer, silky **06** flimsy **08** cobwebby, delicate **10** diaphanous, see-through, shimmering **11** translucent, transparent **13** insubstantial

gossip
03 ana, gab, gas, gup, jaw **04** aunt, buzz, chat, dirt, goss, talk **05** clash, crack, rumor, yenta **06** babble, claver, cummer, gabble, jabber, kimmer, natter, rabbit, report, rumour, tatler, tattle, tittle, waffle **07** babbler, blather, blether, chatter, chinwag, clatter, hearsay, prattle, scandal, shmoose,

shmooze, tattler, whisper **08** busybody, causerie, chitchat, clatters, idle talk, prattler, rabbit on, schmooze, tell-tale **09** reportage, tell tales, whisperer **10** chatterbox, chew the fat, chew the rag, clish-clash, newsmonger, talebearer **11** mud-slinging, Nosey Parker, scuttlebutt, sweetie-wife **12** gossip-monger, spread gossip, tittle-tattle **13** bush telegraph, clishmaclaver, scandal-bearer, scandalmonger, smear campaign, spread a rumour **14** clash-ma-clavers

gouge
03 cut, dig **04** claw, gash, hack **05** scoop, score, slash, wench **06** chisel, groove, hollow, incise **07** extract, scratch, swindle

gourd
05 guiro, loofa, luffa **06** bryony, cacoon, loofah **07** pumpkin **08** calabash **11** white bryony **12** Hercules' club

Gourde
01 G **03** Gde

gourmand
03 hog, pig **06** gorger **07** glutton, guzzler **08** omnivore **09** voracious **10** gluttonous **11** gormandizer

gourmet
06 foodie **07** epicure **09** bon vivant, epicurean **10** gastronome **11** connoisseur

gout
04 drop, spot **05** taste **06** relish **07** podagra **08** chiragra **09** arthritis **10** cephalagra **12** hamarthritis

govern
03 run **04** curb, head, lead, rein, rule, sway, tame **05** check, guide, order, pilot, quell, reign, steer **06** bridle, direct, manage, master, rein in, subdue **07** command, conduct, contain, control, oversee, preside **08** dominate, hold back, keep back, regulate, restrain **09** be in power, constrain, determine, influence, supervise **10** administer, discipline, hold office **11** keep in check, superintend **12** be in charge of

governess
05 guide **06** duenna, mentor **07** teacher, tutress **08** fräulein, tutoress **09** companion **11** gouvernante **12** instructress, mademoiselle

governing
06 ruling **07** guiding, leading, supreme **08** dominant, reigning **09** kingcraft, uppermost **10** commanding, dominative, overriding, prevailing, regulatory **11** controlling, predominant **12** transcendent

government
01 g **03** Gov, HMG, raj **04** Govt, rule, sway **05** power, state **06** charge, circar, papacy, policy, régime, sircar, sirkar **07** cabinet, command, conduct, control, council, regence, regency,

regimen, serkali **08** congress, dominion, guidance, ministry, politics, steerage **09** archology, authority, direction, executive, restraint **10** domination, governance, leadership, management, parliament, regulation **11** authorities, sovereignty, supervision **12** powers that be, surveillance **13** Establishment **14** administration **15** superintendence

05 junta **06** empire **07** kingdom **08** monarchy, republic **09** autocracy, communism, democracy, despotism, theocracy **10** absolutism, federation, hierocracy, plutocracy **11** triumvirate **12** commonwealth, dictatorship

• member of government
02 in

governor
02 Pa **03** Ban, beg, bey, Dad, dey, gov, guv **04** boss, head, khan, naik, vali, wali **05** chief, guide, hakim, mudir, pilot, ruler, tutor **06** eparch, exarch, grieve, leader, legate, master, Pilate, rector, satrap, tuchun, warden **07** alcaide, alcayde, catapan, harmost, manager, nomarch, podestà, rectrix, subadar, vaivode, viceroy, voivode **08** alderman, burgrave, director, ethnarch, gospodar, hospodar, kaimakam, overseer, pentarch, provedor, providor, resident, subahdar **09** beglerbeg, castellan, commander, corrector, directrix, dominator, executive, governess, intendant, president, proconsul, provedore, regulator **10** adelantado, controller, directress, gubernator, Lord Warden, proveditor, stadholder, supervisor **11** proveditore, stadtholder **12** commissioner **13** administrator **14** chief executive, superintendent

04 King (Captain Philip Gidley) **05** Bligh (Captain William), Gipps (Sir George) **06** Bourke (Major-General Richard), Hunter (Captain John) **07** Darling (Lieutenant-General Ralph), Denison (Sir William), FitzRoy (Sir Charles), Phillip (Captain Arthur) **08** Brisbane (Sir Thomas) **09** Macquarie (Colonel Lachlan)

04 Kerr (Sir John), Slim (Field-Marshal Sir William) **05** Casey (Richard Gardiner, Baron), Cowen (Sir Zelman), Deane (Sir William) **06** Denman (Thomas, Baron), Dudley (William Humble Ward, Earl of), Gowrie (Alexander Hore-Ruthven,

Baron), **Hayden** (William), **Isaacs** (Sir Isaac), **McKell** (Sir William)
07 De L'Isle (William,Viscount), **Forster** (Henry William, Baron), **Hasluck** (Sir Paul), **Stephen** (Sir Ninian)
08 Hopetoun (John Adrian Louis Hope, Earl of),**Tennyson** (Hallam, Baron)
09 Dunrossil (William,Viscount), **Northcote** (Henry, Baron)
10 Gloucester (Prince Henry, Duke of), **Stonehaven** (Sir John Lawrence Baird, Baron)
12 Hollingworth (Dr Peter)
13 Munro-Ferguson (Sir Ronald)

Governors-general of New Zealand:

06 Cobham (Charles George Lyttleton), **Galway** (Earl of), **Newall** (Cyril Louis Norton), **Norrie** (Lord), **Reeves** (Paul Alfred),**Tizard** (Catherine)
07 Beattie (David Stuart), **Porritt** (Arthur Espie)
08 Blundell (Edward Denis), **Freyberg** (Bernard Cyril), **Holyoake** (Keith Jacka), **Jellicoe** (John Henry Rushworth)
09 Bledisloe (Charles Bathurst), **Fergusson** (Bernard), **Fergusson** (Charles), **Liverpool** (Earl of)
10 Hardie Boys (Michael)

Governors of New Zealand:

04 Grey (George),**Weld** (Frederick Aloysius)
05 Bowen (Charles Ferguson)
06 Browne (Thomas Robert Gore), **Gordon** (Arthur Hamilton), **Hobson** (William), **Onslow** (Earl of), **Onslow** (William Hillier)
07 FitzRoy (Robert), **Glasgow** (Earl of), **Jervois** (William Francis Drummond), **Plunket** (Lord)
08 Normanby (Marquess of), **Ranfurly** (Earl of), **Robinson** (Hercules George Robert)
09 Fergusson (James), **Islington** (Lord), **Liverpool** (Earl of)

gown
04 garb, robe, sack, silk **05** bania, dress, frock, habit, manto, shift, stole **06** banian, banyan, kirtle, mantua, sacque **07** costume, garment, manteau, negligé **08** mazarine, negligee, peignoir **09** sack dress, slammakin **10** slammerkin **12** bearing cloth, dressing-gown **13** Mother Hubbard

grab
◊ *containment indicator*
03 bag, nab, rap **04** grip, nail, take **05** annex, catch, grasp, pluck, seize, swipe, usurp **06** arrest, clutch, collar, nobble, snap up, snatch **07** capture, impress **08** interest **09** lay hold of **10** commandeer, take hold of **11** appropriate, catch hold of
See also **steal**

• **up for grabs**
06 at hand **07** to be had **09** available **10** obtainable **12** for the asking

grace
04 ease, trim **05** adorn, charm, honor, mense, mercy, poise,Venus **06** beauty, become, enrich, favour, honour, pardon, polish, prayer, set off, virtue **07** aggrace, charity, decency, decorum, dignify, enhance, finesse, fluency, garnish, manners, quarter, unction **08** beautify, blessing, breeding, clemency, courtesy, decorate, elegance, goodness, goodwill, kindness, leniency, ornament, reprieve **09** bethankit, embellish, etiquette, good taste, propriety **10** benedicite, comeliness, compassion, generosity, indulgence, kindliness, loveliness, refinement, smoothness **11** benediction, beneficence, benevolence, cultivation, distinguish, forgiveness, shapeliness **12** gracefulness, mercifulness, tastefulness, thanksgiving **13** consideration **14** attractiveness, prayer of thanks

The Three Graces:

06 Aglaia,Thalia
10 Euphrosyne

graceful
04 deft, easy, fine, kind **05** agile, fluid, genty, suave **06** comely, fluent, gainly, nimble, polite, smooth, supple, svelte **07** elegant, flowing, genteel, natural, refined, slender, tactful, willowy **08** charming, cheerful, cultured, generous, gracious, grazioso, pleasant, polished, sylphine, sylphish, tasteful **09** agreeable, appealing, beautiful, courteous, sylphlike **10** attractive, cultivated, diplomatic, respectful

gracefully
06 deftly, nimbly **08** grazioso, politely, smoothly **09** agreeably, elegantly, naturally, tactfully **10** cheerfully, generously, graciously, pleasantly, tastefully **11** beautifully, courteously **12** attractively, respectfully **14** diplomatically

graceless
04 rude **05** crude, gawky, rough **06** clumsy, coarse, forced, gauche, vulgar **07** awkward, uncouth **08** impolite, improper, ungainly **09** barbarous, inelegant, menseless, shameless **10** indecorous, ungraceful, unmannerly **11** ill-mannered **12** unattractive **15** unsophisticated

gracelessly
06 rudely **07** roughly **08** clumsily **09** awkwardly **10** impolitely **11** inelegantly **12** ungracefully

gracious
04 hend, kind, mild **05** sweet **06** benign, kindly, polite **07** affable, clement, elegant, lenient, refined **08** friendly, generous, handsome, menseful, merciful, obliging, pleasant, tasteful **09** benignant, courteous, forgiving, indulgent, luxurious, sumptuous **10** acceptable, beneficent,

benevolent, charitable, favourable, hospitable **11** comfortable, considerate, kind-hearted, magnanimous **12** well-mannered **13** accommodating, compassionate, condescending

graciously
06 goodly, kindly **07** civilly **08** politely **09** tactfully **10** handsomely, pleasantly **11** courteously **12** respectfully **14** diplomatically

gradation
04 mark, rank, step **05** array, cline, level, stage **06** ablaut, change, degree, series **07** grading, shading, sorting **08** ordering, progress, sequence **10** succession **11** arrangement, progression

grade
03 gon **04** mark, rank, rate, rung, size, sort, step, type **05** brand, class, group, label, level, notch, order, place, range, stage, value **06** assess, degree, rating, status **07** arrange, echelon, quality, station **08** category, classify, evaluate, position, standard, standing **09** condition **10** categorize, pigeonhole **14** classification
• **equivalent grade**
02 EG
• **first grade**
05 alpha
• **fourth grade**
05 delta
• **make the grade**
04 pass **07** succeed **10** win through **11** come through **13** cut the mustard **15** come up to scratch
• **second grade**
04 beta
• **third grade**
05 gamma

gradient
04 bank, hill, rise **05** grade, lapse, slope **07** incline **09** acclivity, declivity

gradual
04 easy, even, slow **05** grail **06** gentle, steady **07** regular **08** measured, moderate **09** leisurely, unhurried **10** continuous, step-by-step **11** progressive

gradually
06 evenly, gently, slowly **08** bit by bit, gingerly, steadily **09** by degrees, piecemeal, regularly **10** cautiously, inch by inch, moderately, step by step **11** unhurriedly **12** continuously, successively **13** imperceptibly, progressively **14** little by little

graduate
02 BA, MA **04** grad, pass, rank, sort **05** grade, group, order, ovate, range **06** alumna, doctor, expert, fellow, master, member, move up **07** advance, alumnus, arrange, go ahead, mark off, qualify **08** bachelor, classify, graduand, progress, whizz kid **09** calibrate **10** promoted, categorize, consultant, forge ahead, licentiate, measure out,

proportion, specialist **11** make headway, move forward **12** professional **13** skilled person, valedictorian **15** complete studies, qualified person

See also **qualification**

graft
03 bud, dig, imp **04** join, scam, slog, take, toil **05** affix, ditch, graff, plant, scion, shoot, sting **06** branch, effort, growth, inarch, insert, labour, rip-off, sleaze, splice, sprout, sucker **07** bribery, cuckold, engraft, implant **08** exertion, hard word **09** allograft, autograft, con tricks, extortion, homograft, inoculate, xenograft **10** corruption, dishonesty, excavation, transplant **11** dirty tricks, heterograft **12** implantation **13** dirty dealings, shady business **14** sharp practices **15** sweat of your brow

grain
02 gr **03** bit, jot, nap, rye **04** atom, corn, curn, fork, hint, iota, mite, oats, ragi, rice, seed **05** berry, crumb, emmer, fibre, grits, maize, minim, piece, prong, scrap, speck, trace, weave, wheat **06** barley, branch, fabric, groats, kernel, maslin, morsel **07** cereals, graddan, granule, marking, mashlam, mashlim, mashlin, mashlum, modicum, pattern, soupçon, surface, texture **08** fragment, mashloch, molecule, particle **09** scintilla **10** suggestion
• **soften grain**
04 cree

gram
01 g **02** gm, gr **03** urd **05** anger, grief, pulse **07** trouble **08** chickpea

grammar
05 Donat, Donet, style, usage **06** syntax **11** good English **14** correct English **15** linguistic rules

See also **speech**

grammatical
07 correct **09** syntactic **10** acceptable, linguistic, structural, well-formed **11** appropriate, syntactical **14** well-structured

See also **tense**

grand
01 G **03** fab **04** arch, cool, fine, head, main, mega **05** chief, final, great, large, lofty, noble, regal, showy, super **06** in full, lavish, lordly, pretty, senior, superb, wicked **07** exalted, highest, leading, opulent, pompous, stately, sublime, supreme **08** complete, exalting, glorious, imposing, majestic, palatial, precious, smashing, splendid, striking, terrific, thousand **09** ambitious, dignified, enjoyable, excellent, fantastic, first-rate, grandiose, inclusive, luxurious, mausolean, principal, sumptuous, wonderful **10** delightful, impressive, marvellous, monumental, pre-eminent **11** illustrious, magnificent,

outstanding, pretentious **12** all-inclusive, ostentatious **13** comprehensive

grandchild
02 oe, oy **03** oye

grandeur
04 fame, pomp **05** state **06** renown **07** dignity, majesty **08** eminence, nobility, opulence, vastness **09** greatness, splendour **10** importance, lavishness, prominence **11** stateliness **12** magnificence **13** luxuriousness **14** impressiveness **15** illustriousness, pretentiousness

grandfather
04 oupa, papa **06** gramps, granda **07** grandad, grandpa, granfer, gutcher **08** goodsire, granddad, gudesire **09** grandaddy, grandpapa, grandsire, luckie-dad **10** granddaddy **11** grandparent

grandiloquent
06 rotund, turgid **07** flowery, fustian, orotund, pompous, swollen **08** inflated **09** bombastic, high-flown, ororotund **10** euphuistic, rhetorical **11** exaggerated, pretentious **12** high-sounding, magniloquent **13** grandiloquous

grandiose
04 long **05** grand, lofty, showy **07** pompous, stately **08** imposing, majestic, splendid, striking **09** ambitious, bombastic, high-flown, mausolean **10** flamboyant, impressive, monumental, over-the-top **11** extravagant, magnificent, pretentious **12** high-sounding, magniloquent, ostentatious

grandly
07 regally **09** pompously **10** gloriously, strikingly **11** excellently **12** impressively, majestically **13** magnificently, pretentiously

grandmother
03 nan **04** gran, nana, ouma **05** nanna, nanny **06** beldam, granny **07** beldame, grandam, grandma, grannam, grannie **08** babushka, good-dame, gude-dame **09** grandmama **10** grandmamma **11** grandparent

grandparental
04 aval **06** avital

granite
07 greisen **08** resolute **09** pegmatite, protogine **10** china stone, unyielding **11** luxulianite, luxulyanite **12** luxullianite

grant
03 aid, fee, feu, let **04** Cary, gift, give, lend, send **05** admit, allot, allow, award, feoff, yield **06** accept, accord, assign, bestow, beteem, confer, donate, impart, permit, supply **07** agree to, annuity, appoint, bequest, beteeme, bursary, charter, concede, consent,

furnish, licence, license, pension, present, provide, subsidy **08** accede to, allocate, dispense, donation, granting, transmit **09** allowance, apportion, consent to, endowment, vouchsafe **10** concession, condescend, contribute, exhibition, honorarium, subvention **11** acknowledge, benefaction, expectative, scholarship **12** contribution
• **granted**
06 agreed

granular
04 corn **05** curny, lumpy, rough, sandy **06** curney, grainy, gritty **07** crumbly, friable **10** granulated

granule
03 jot **04** atom, bead, iota, seed **05** crumb, grain, pearl, piece, scrap, speck **06** pellet **07** plastid **08** bioblast, fragment, molecule, particle **09** chondrule, microsome

grape
03 uva

See also **wine**

grapefruit
06 pomelo **07** pompelo **10** pompelmous, pumple-nose **11** pampelmoose, pampelmouse, pompelmoose, pompelmouse

grapeskins
04 marc

graph
04 grid, plot **05** chart, curve, ogive, table **07** diagram, profile **08** bar chart, bar graph, nomogram, pie chart, waveform **09** histogram, nomograph, waveshape **10** carpet plot **11** demand curve, supply curve **13** learning curve **14** scatter diagram

graphic
05 clear, drawn, lucid, vivid **06** cogent, lively, visual **07** telling **08** detailed, explicit, specific, striking, symbolic **09** effective, pictorial, realistic **10** blow-by-blow, expressive **11** delineative, descriptive, well-defined **12** diagrammatic, illustrative

graphically
07 clearly, vividly **10** explicitly, strikingly **12** expressively **13** descriptively, realistically

graphite
04 kish, lead **08** plumbago **09** blacklead, pencil-ore **10** pencil-lead

grapple
04 face, grab, grip, hold, lock **05** clash, clasp, close, fight, grasp, seize **06** battle, clinch, clutch, combat, craple, engage, snatch, tackle, tussle **07** address, contend, wrestle **08** confront, cope with, deal with, struggle **09** encounter, lay hold of **14** get to grips with

grasp

◇ *containment indicator*

03 get, see **04** clat, grab, grip, have, hend, hent, hold, holt, rule **05** catch, clamp, clasp, claut, gripe, power, seize, sense **06** clench, clutch, follow, graple, griple, master, rumble, snatch, strain, take in **07** catch on, command, compass, control, embrace, grapple, gripple, mastery, prehend, realize, squeeze **08** clutches, conceive, dominion, handgrip, perceive **09** apprehend, awareness, knowledge, latch onto, lay hold of **10** comprehend, perception, possession, understand **11** familiarity **12** apprehension, get a handle on, get the hang of **13** comprehension, understanding

grasping

◇ *containment indicator*

04 mean **06** grabby, greedy, griple, stingy **07** griping, gripple, miserly, seizing, selfish **08** covetous **09** mercenary, niggardly, rapacious **10** avaricious **11** acquisitive, close-fisted, large-handed, tight-fisted **12** parsimonious **13** money-grubbing

grass

03 fog, hay, lea, pot, rat, rip **04** blab, lawn, mead, nark, shop, tell, turf, veld **05** dob in, downs, field, green, rough, split, sward, veldt **06** betray, common, inform, snitch, squeal, steppe, tell on **07** foggage, pasture, prairie, savanna, stool on **08** denounce, informer, stitch up **09** asparagus, grassland **11** incriminate

See also **cannabis**

Grasses include:

03 nit, nut, oat, poa, rye, sea, seg, tef **04** alfa, bent, cane, cord, corn, crab, dari, diss, doob, dura, gama, holy, kans, knot, lyme, moor, nard, oats, ragi, reed, rice, rusa, sago, sand, star, tape, tath, teff **05** alang, arrow, beard, brome, bunch, canna, chess, China, couch, doura, float, grama, halfa, lemon, maize, melic, paddy, panic, plume, quack, quick, ragee, raggy, roosa, spear, spike, starr, stipa, Sudan, wheat **06** bamboo, barley, canary, cotton, darnel, dhurra, fescue, finger, fiorin, guinea, kikuyu, lalang, marram, marrum, meadow, melick, millet, pampas, panick, quitch, raggee, rattan, redtop, rescue, scutch, sesame, switch, twitch, vernal **07** Bermuda, bristle, buffalo, cannach, esparto, feather, pannick, papyrus, quaking, sacaton, sorghum, timothy, wild oat **08** cat's-tail, cockspur, dog's-tail, Flinders, kangaroo, moss-crop, ryegrass, spinifex, teosinte **09** bluegrass, buckwheat, cocksfoot, danthonia, hare's-tail, marijuana, porcupine, sugar cane **10** citronella

12 creeping bent, Kentucky blue, squirrel-tail **13** meadow foxtail **15** English ryegrass, Italian ryegrass

• **grass after hay**
03 fog **07** foggage

• **handful of grass**
03 rip **04** ripp

• **stem of grass**
04 cane, culm

grasshopper

04 grig, weta **09** wart-biter

grate

03 irk, jar, rub, vex **04** bray, cage, gall, grid, grit, rasp, risp **05** annoy, chirk, creak, gride, grind, gryde, mince, peeve, shred, stove **06** rankle, scrape, squeak **07** scratch, screech **08** irritate **09** aggravate, pulverize, triturate **10** exasperate **12** kitchen-range **15** get on your nerves

grateful

07 obliged, pleased **08** beholden, indebted, thankful **09** obligated **12** appreciative

gratefully

10 thankfully **13** with gratitude **14** appreciatively

gratification

03 joy, tip **04** glee, gust **05** bribe, feast, kicks **06** relish, thrill **07** delight, elation **08** easement, pleasure **09** enjoyment **10** indulgence, indulgency, recompense **11** contentment **12** satisfaction

gratify

03 pay **05** charm, cheer, flesh, humor, spoil **06** arride, cosset, favour, fulfil, humour, pamper, please, thrill **07** aggrate, delight, flatter, gladden, indulge, placate, satiate, satisfy **08** pander to, recreate **09** make happy

grating

04 grid, hack, haik, hake, heck, iron, rack **05** frame, grate, grill, harsh, siver, syver **06** grille **07** braying, galling, grizzly, irksome, jarring, lattice, rasping, raucous, squeaky, trellis **08** annoying, cancelli, creaking, grinding, gritting, mort-safe, scrannel, scraping, scratchy, strident **09** fire-grate, graticule, offensive **10** discordant, irritating, portcullis, scratching, screeching, unpleasant **12** disagreeable, exasperating

gratis

04 free **08** at no cost, buckshee **10** for nothing, on the house **12** free of charge **13** complimentary, without charge

gratitude

06 thanks **10** obligation **11** recognition **12** appreciation, gratefulness, indebtedness, thankfulness **15** acknowledgement

• **expression of gratitude**
02 ta **06** thanks **07** thankee **08** bless you!, gramercy, thank you

09 God-a-mercy **10** grand merci **11** God bless you!

gratuitous

04 free **06** gratis, unpaid, wanton **08** buckshee, needless **09** unfounded, unmerited, voluntary **10** for nothing, groundless, unasked-for, undeserved, unprovoked, unrewarded **11** superfluous, uncalled-for, unjustified, unnecessary, unsolicited, unwarranted **12** free of charge **13** complimentary, without reason

gratuitously

10 needlessly **12** undeservedly **13** unjustifiably, unnecessarily

gratuity

03 tip **04** boon, dash, gift, mags, perk **05** bonus, maggs **06** bounty, reward **07** bansela, cumshaw, present, primage **08** bonsella, donation, donative, lagnappe, largesse **09** backshish, bakhshish, baksheesh, beer-money, lagniappe, pourboire **10** backsheesh, drink-money, glove-money, gratillity, perquisite, recompense

grave

03 dig, pit, sad **04** bass, bury, dust, grim, high, lair, loss, tomb **05** acute, cairn, count, crypt, death, graff, heavy, mouls, quiet, sober, staid, vault, vital **06** barrow, demise, gloomy, moulds, sedate, severe, solemn, sombre, urgent **07** austere, crucial, decease, earnest, exigent, passing, pensive, prefect, serious, subdued, tumulus, weighty **08** Catonian, critical, curtains, fatality, long home, matronal, menacing, perilous, pressing, reserved **09** dangerous, departure, dignified, hazardous, important, long-faced, mausoleum, momentous, plague-pit, saturnine, sepulchre **10** burial site, expiration, loss of life, restrained, thoughtful **11** bed of honour, burial mound, burial place, destruction, passing away, significant, threatening **12** last farewell

gravel

04 grit **05** grail **06** chesil, chisel, graile, grayle, hoggin, murram, stones **07** channel, channer, hogging, pebbles, shingle

• **layer of gravel**
04 hard

gravelly

05 gruff, harsh, rough, thick **06** grainy, gritty, hoarse, pebbly **07** grating, shingly, throaty **08** glareous, granular, guttural, sabulose, sabulous

gravely

07 acutely, quietly **08** gloomily, severely, solemnly, urgently **09** crucially, earnestly, pensively, seriously **10** critically **11** dangerously, importantly **12** thoughtfully **13** significantly

gravestone

05 stone, table **08** memorial **09** headstone, tombstone

graveyard
08 cemetery, God's acre **10** burial site, churchyard, necropolis **11** burial place **12** burial ground, charnel house **13** burying ground

gravitas
06 weight **07** gravity **09** solemnity **10** importance **11** earnestness, seriousness

gravitate
04 drop, fall, lean, move, sink, tend **05** drift **06** settle **07** descend, head for, incline **09** be drawn to **11** precipitate **12** be attached to

gravity
01 g **04** pull **05** peril, state **06** danger, hazard, weight **07** dignity, reserve, urgency **08** exigency, grimness, severity, sobriety **09** acuteness, graveness, heaviness, restraint, soberness, solemnity **10** attraction, gloominess, importance, sombreness **11** consequence, earnestness, gravitation, seriousness, weightiness **12** significance **13** momentousness **14** thoughtfulness

gray
02 Gy
See also **grey**

graze
03 rub **04** crop, feed, kiss, rake, rase, raze, skim, skin **05** brush, chafe, gride, gryde, scuff, shave, touch **06** abrade, browse, bruise, crease, fodder, scrape **07** pasture, scratch **08** abrasion, ruminate **09** depasture, glance off

grease
03 fat, oil **04** dope, lard, seam **05** bribe, seame, smear **06** creesh, dubbin, enlard, enseam, tallow **07** dubbing **08** dripping **09** lubricate **10** facilitate **11** lubrication

greasy
04 oily, waxy **05** fatty, lardy, oleic, slimy **06** smeary, smooth **07** adipose, buttery, obscene, shearer **08** slippery, unctuous **09** sebaceous **10** oleaginous **12** ingratiating
• **greasy substance**
04 glit

great
02 gt **03** ace, big, fit, gay, gey **04** able, bulk, cool, fell, fine, gran, huge, main, mass, mega, neat, tall, unco, up on, vast, well **05** adept, brill, chief, crack, eager, famed, grand, jumbo, large, major, noted, stoor, stour, sture, super, titan, vital, whole **06** august, awsome, bangin', cushty, expert, famous, grouse, lively, mickle, muckle, stowre, superb, wicked **07** awesome, banging, crucial, eminent, extreme, healthy, immense, leading, mammoth, massive, notable, primary, rousing, salient, serious, sizable, skilful, skilled, sublime, tearing, teeming, weighty **08** colossal, cracking, critical, dextrous, enormous, fabulous, gigantic, glorious, great big, habitual, imposing, masterly, powerful,

pregnant, renowned, sizeable, smashing, spacious, splendid, terrific, top-notch, virtuoso, well up on, whopping **09** admirable, boundless, brilliant, dexterous, energetic, essential, excellent, excessive, extensive, fantastic, favourite, first-rate, ginormous, humongous, humungous, important, momentous, paramount, practised, principal, prominent, qualified, swingeing, wholesale, wonderful **10** celebrated, impressive, inordinate, marvellous, noteworthy, proficient, pronounced, remarkable, specialist, successful, tremendous **11** experienced, illustrious, magnificent, outstanding, significant, substantial **12** accomplished, considerable, enthusiastic, professional **13** distinguished, knowledgeable

Great Britain
02 GB, UK **03** GBR

greatly
04 much **06** highly, hugely, sorely, vastly **07** big-time, majorly, notably **08** markedly, mightily, very much **09** extremely, immensely **10** abundantly, enormously, noticeably, powerfully, remarkably **11** exceedingly **12** considerably, impressively, tremendously **13** significantly, substantially

greatness
04 fame, note **05** glory, power **06** genius, renown, weight **07** heroism, success **08** eminence, grandeur, muchness **09** intensity, magnitude **10** excellence, excellency, importance, mightiness **11** distinction, seriousness **12** significance **13** momentousness **14** successfulness **15** illustriousness

Greece
02 GR **03** GRC

greed
06 desire, hunger **07** avarice, avidity, craving, edacity, longing **08** bingeing, cupidity, gluttony, rapacity, voracity **09** eagerness, esurience, pleonexia **10** impatience **11** gourmandise, gourmandism, hoggishness, itching palm, piggishness, selfishness **12** covetousness, ravenousness **13** insatiability **15** acquisitiveness

greedily
06 avidly **07** eagerly **09** selfishly **10** esuriently, ravenously **11** impatiently, rapaciously **12** avariciously

greedy
04 avid, gare **05** eager **06** grabby, griple, having, hungry **07** craving, gripple, hoggish, piggish, selfish **08** covetous, desirous, edacious, esurient, grabbing, grasping, ravenous, starving **09** impatient, on the make, rapacious, voracious **10** avaricious, cupidinous, gluttonous, insatiable,

omnivorous, pleonectic **11** acquisitive, itchy-palmed, open-mouthed **12** gormandizing **13** money-grubbing

Greek
02 Gk, Gr

See also **alphabet**; **god, goddess**; **muse**; **mythology**; **seven**

green
03 eco, lea, new, raw **04** lawn, long, lush, pine, sage, turf **05** field, fresh, grass, leafy, naive, sward, virid, yearn, young **06** common, grassy, meadow, recent, simple, tender, unripe, virent **07** budding, envious, growing, healthy, jealous, pasture, undried, verdant **08** blooming, covetous, glaucous, grudging, gullible, ignorant, immature, inexpert, unversed, vigorous **09** grassland, resentful, untrained, verdurous, virescent **10** ecological, olivaceous, porraceous, smaragdine, unseasoned **11** eco-friendly, flourishing, unqualified, viridescent **13** environmental, inexperienced **15** conservationist, preservationist, unsophisticated

greenery
04 vert **07** foliage, verdure **08** verdancy, viridity **09** greenness **10** vegetation, virescence **12** viridescence

greenhorn
03 put **04** putt, tiro **06** newbie, novice, rookie **07** learner, recruit **08** beginner,

nitiate, neophyte, newcomer
9 fledgling, Johnny-raw
0 apprentice, tenderfoot

greenhouse
6 vinery **08** hothouse, orangery,
pavilion **09** coldhouse, coolhouse
0 glasshouse **12** conservatory

greenland
3 GRL

greet
3 bid, bow **04** hail, kiss, meet, weep,
vish **05** halse, hongi, nod to
6 accost, salute, wave to **07** address,
receive, regret, weeping, welcome
8 congreet, remember **10** say hello
o, shake hands, tip your hat
1 acknowledge, doff your hat
4 shake hands with **15** give someone
ive

greeting
3 bow, nod **04** kiss, wave **05** hongi
6 abrazo, accost, salute **07** accoast,
address, air kiss, namaste **08** glad
hand, high five, namaskar
9 handshake, reception, time of day
0 how-do-you-do, salutation **12** the
ime of day **15** acknowledgement
• **expression of greeting**
2 hi, yo **03** ave, how **04** ciao, g'day,
hail, heil!, hiya **05** aloha, chimo, hallo,
hello, holla, howdy, hullo, jambo, salve,
koal **06** salaam, shalom, wotcha
7 all-hail, bonjour, bonsoir, good-day,
good-den, good-e'en, salaams,
salvete, save you, welcome, well met,
votcher **08** chin-chin, good-even,
haeremai **09** how are you?, son of a
gun, what cheer? **10** benedicite, good-
morrow, how do you do? **11** good-
evening, good-morning **13** good
afternoon **14** shalom aleichem

greetings
4 love **05** salve **07** regards, regreet,
salaams **08** regreets, respects **10** best
wishes, good wishes **11** compliments,
kind regards, salutations, warm regards
2 remembrances **15** congratulations

gregarious
4 warm **06** social **07** affable, cordial
8 friendly, outgoing, sociable
9 convivial, extrovert **10** hospitable
3 companionable

Grenada
2 WG **03** GRD

grenade
9 Mills bomb, pineapple **15** Molotov
cocktail

grey
2 gr **03** dim, old, wan **04** dark, dull,
gris, pale **05** ashen, bleak, foggy, grise,
grisy, misty, murky **06** cloudy, dismal,
dreary, gloomy, gryesy, leaden, mature,
pallid **07** griesie, neutral, unclear
8 bloncket, doubtful, griseous,
grizzled, overcast **09** ambiguous,
anonymous, canescent, cheerless,
cinereous, debatable, uncertain
0 colourless, depressing,

dove-colour **13** uninteresting **14** open
to question

Greys include:
03 ash
04 drab
05 liard, liart, lyart, perse, stone,
taupe
06 isabel, pewter, silver
07 grizzle
08 charcoal, dove grey, feldgrau,
graphite, gridelin, platinum
09 field grey, pearl-grey, slate-grey,
steel-grey
10 dapple-grey, dove-colour

• **greyish-brown**
03 dun **04** ecru **05** mousy **06** mousey
07 chamois
• **greyish-white**
04 hoar, hore

greyhound
04 grew **07** lurcher, sapling, whippet
08 long-tail **09** deerhound,
grewhound

grid
05 frame, grate, grill **06** grille
07 grating, lattice, network, trellis
08 gridiron **09** framework, graticule

grief
02 wo **03** vex, woe **04** dole, dool,
gram, pain, sore, teen, tene **05** agony,
dolor, doole, grame, teene **06** bother,
dolour, misery, regret, sorrow, tsuris
07 anguish, despair, remorse, sadness,
thought, trouble, tsouris, wayment
08 distress, mourning **09** bemoaning,
dejection, grievance, heartache,
suffering, tristesse **10** affliction,
depression, desiderium, desolation,
heartbreak **11** bereavement,
despondency, lamentation, tribulation,
unhappiness **12** dolorousness
• **come to grief**
04 bomb, flop, fold **05** crash, spill
06 mucker **07** founder, go wrong,
miswend **08** collapse, fall down, fall
flat **09** break down **10** not come off
11 bite the dust, come unglued, come
unstuck, fall through **12** come a
cropper **13** come to nothing **14** be
unsuccessful
• **emblem of grief**
03 yew
• **expression of grief**
02 io, oh **03** wow **04** alas **05** ohone,
waugh, wowee **06** dear me, ochone,
oh dear! **07** deary me **08** dearie me
• **feel grief**
04 earn **05** yearn

grief-stricken
03 sad **06** broken **07** crushed,
unhappy **08** dejected, desolate,
grieving, mourning, overcome,
troubled, wretched **09** afflicted,
anguished, depressed, sorrowful,
sorrowing, woebegone **10** despairing,
despondent, devastated, distressed
11 heartbroken, overwhelmed
12 disconsolate, inconsolable
13 broken-hearted

grievance
04 beef, moan **05** grief, gripe, peeve,
score, trial, wrong **06** charge, damage,
grouse, injury **07** grumble, offence,
protest, trouble **08** distress, gravamen,
hardship **09** complaint, injustice,
objection **10** affliction, bone to pick,
resentment, unfairness **11** tribulation

grieve
03 cry, rue, sob, vex **04** ache, hone,
hurt, mope, pain, wail, weep **05** brood,
crush, mourn, shock, upset, wound
06 bemoan, dismay, lament, offend,
sadden, sorrow, suffer **07** afflict,
condole, horrify, sheriff, wayment
08 distress, engrieve, governor, pine
away

grievous
04 dear, sore **05** deare, deere, grave,
heavy **06** noyous, severe, strong,
tragic **07** careful, glaring, harmful,
hurtful, painful **08** damaging,
dolorous, dreadful, flagrant, shameful,
shocking, wounding **09** appalling,
atrocious, dolorific, injurious,
monstrous, plightful, sorrowful
10 afflicting, burdensome, calamitous,
deplorable, outrageous, unbearable
11 devastating, distressing, intolerable
12 doloriferous, overwhelming

grievously
04 sore **06** dernly **07** dearnly
08 severely **10** dolorously, dreadfully,
shockingly, tragically, unbearably
11 appallingly, intolerably
12 outrageously

grill
04 cook, grid, heat, pump **05** bar-b-q,
broil, frame, roast, toast **06** grille,
wicket **07** grating, lattice, scallop
08 barbecue, barbeque, gridiron
09 charbroil **10** flame-grill

grim
◇ *anagram indicator*
03 ill **04** dire, dour **05** awful, grisy,
gurly, harsh, stern, surly **06** dismal,
dogged, fierce, gloomy, griesy, grisly,
grysie, horrid, morose, severe, sullen
07 ghastly **08** dreadful, fearsome,
gruesome, horrible, menacing,
obdurate, resolute, shocking, sinister,
stubborn, terrible **09** appalling,
ferocious, harrowing, repellent,
tenacious **10** depressing, determined,
forbidding, formidable, horrendous,
inexorable, persistent, unpleasant,
unshakable, unyielding **11** frightening,
threatening, unappealing, unshakeable,
unspeakable **12** unattractive

grimace
03 moe, mop, mou, mow, mug
04 face, girn, moue, mump, pout
05 frown, mouth, scowl, smirk, sneer
07 murgeon **09** make a face, pull a
face **12** fit of the face

grime
03 mud **04** coom, crud, dirt, dust, grot,
muck, soot, yuck **05** filth, gunge
06 grunge, smutch

grimly
07 harshly, sternly **08** fiercely, gloomily, morosely, sullenly

grimy
05 dirty, dusty, mucky, muddy, sooty **06** filthy, grubby, rechie, reechy, smudgy, smutty, soiled **07** reechie, stained **10** besmirched

grin
04 beam, girn, gren, leer, trap **05** gerne, laugh, risus, smile, smirk, snare, sneer **06** giggle, titter **07** chuckle, snigger

grind
03 pug, rub **04** bray, chew, file, grit, meal, mill, rasp, sand, task, toil, whet **05** chore, crush, gnash, grate, pound, round, slime, stamp, sweat **06** abrade, crunch, kibble, labour, polish, powder, scrape, smooth **07** chamfer, crumble, graunch, routine, sharpen, slavery **08** drudgery, exertion, levigate **09** comminute, granulate, masticate, pulverize, triturate
• grind down
05 crush, harry, hound **06** harass, plague **07** afflict, oppress, torment, trouble **08** wear down **09** persecute, tyrannize

grip
◇ *containment indicator*
03 bag, get, hug **04** bite, case, fang, grab, hold, vice, vise **05** catch, clasp, cling, ditch, drain, grasp, power, rivet, sally, seize **06** absorb, clench, clutch, compel, engage, graple, griple, kitbag, strain, thrill, trench, valise **07** command, control, embrace, engross, enthral, fingers, grapple, gripple, holdall, involve, mastery **08** clutches, entrance, foothold, handfast, suitcase, traction **09** fascinate, get hold of, hypnotize, influence, latch onto, mesmerize, spellbind **10** domination, grab hold of **11** catch hold of, shoulder bag **12** overnight bag **13** travelling bag
• come to grips with, get to grips with
◇ *containment indicator*
05 grasp **06** handle, tackle, take on **08** confront, cope with, deal with, face up to **09** encounter, look after **10** take care of

gripe
03 nag **04** beef, carp, moan **05** bitch, ditch, drain, groan, whine **06** grouch, grouse, trench, whinge **07** griffin, griping, grumble, protest, vulture **08** complain **09** bellyache, complaint, grievance, objection **15** have a bone to pick

gripping
◇ *containment indicator*
06 griple **07** gripple **08** exciting, riveting **09** absorbing, thrilling **10** compelling, compulsive, enchanting, engrossing, entrancing **11** enthralling, fascinating, suspenseful **12** spellbinding **13** unputdownable

• gripping instrument
04 grip, vice, vise **05** clamp **08** tweezers

grisly
04 gory, grim **05** awful, grisy **06** griesy, grysie, horrid **07** ghastly, hideous, macabre **08** dreadful, gruesome, horrible, shocking, terrible **09** abhorrent, appalling, frightful, loathsome, repulsive, revolting **10** abominable, disgusting, horrifying

gristly
04 hard **05** chewy, tough **06** sinewy **07** fibrous, rubbery, stringy **08** leathery **13** cartilaginous

grit
04 dust, guts, rasp, sand **05** gnash, grate, great, grind, swarf **06** clench, gravel, mettle, scrape **07** bravery, courage, pebbles, resolve, shingle **08** backbone, hardness, strength, tenacity **09** endurance, toughness **10** doggedness, resolution **12** perseverance **13** determination, steadfastness

gritty
05 brave, dusty, gutsy, gutty, hardy, rough, sandy, tough **06** dogged, feisty, grainy, pebbly, plucky, spunky **07** powdery, shingly **08** abrasive, granular, gravelly, resolute, sabuline, sabulose, sabulous, spirited **09** steadfast, tenacious **10** courageous, determined, mettlesome **14** uncompromising

grizzle
03 cry **04** fret, moan **05** whine **06** snivel, whinge **07** grumble, sniffle, snuffle, whimper **08** complain

grizzled
04 grey, hoar **05** hoary **07** greying **08** griseous **09** canescent **10** grey-haired, grey-headed **13** pepper-and-salt

groan
03 cry **04** beef, moan, sigh, wail **05** whine **06** grouch, grouse, lament, object, outcry, whinge **07** griping, grumble, protest, whimper **08** complain **09** bellyache, complaint, grievance, objection

grocer
06 dealer **07** épicier **08** pepperer, purveyor, supplier **10** victualler **11** greengrocer, storekeeper, supermarket

groggy
◇ *anagram indicator*
04 weak **05** dazed, dizzy, dopey, faint, muzzy, shaky, woozy **06** wobbly **07** reeling, stunned **08** confused, unsteady **09** befuddled, stupefied **10** bewildered, punch-drunk, staggering

groin
04 lisk **05** growl, grunt **06** crotch, crutch **07** grumble **08** genitals

groom
◇ *anagram indicator*
02 do **03** fix **04** sice, syce, tidy **05** brush, clean, coach, curry, dress, drill, preen, prime, prink, saice, teach, train, tutor **06** adjust, neaten, school, smooth, spouse, tidy up **07** arrange, educate, husband, prepare, smarten, turn out **08** coistrel, coistril, instruct, newly-wed, spruce up, strapper **09** make ready, stableboy, stable lad, stableman **10** bridegroom, palfrenier, put in order, stable hand, stable lass **11** honeymooner, husband-to-be **15** marriage partner

groove
03 cut, pod, rut **04** kerf, mark, oche, race, sipe, slot **05** canal, chase, croze, ditch, flute, gouge, quirk, ridge, rigol, score, slide, track **06** cullis, furrow, gutter, hollow, keyway, rabbet, raggle, rebate, riffle, scrobe, sulcus, throat, trench, trough **07** chamfer, channel, diglyph, fissure, fossula, key-seat **09** cannelure, vallecula **11** indentation

grooved
06 fluted, rutted, scored, sulcal **07** exarate, sulcate **08** furrowed, rabbeted, sulcated **09** chamfered **10** channelled **12** canaliculate, scrobiculate **13** canaliculated

grope
04 feel, fish, hunt, pick, poke, ripe **05** abuse, probe, touch **06** feel up, fondle, fumble, molest, search **07** grabble, touch up **08** flounder, scrabble **09** cast about **13** abuse sexually, interfere with

gross
◇ *anagram indicator*
02 gr **03** big, fat **04** blue, dull, earn, foul, huge, lewd, make, rank, rude, slow, take **05** bawdy, bulky, crass, crude, dirty, heavy, large, nasty, obese, plain, sheer, solid, thick, total, utter, whole, yucky **06** coarse, earthy, entire, filthy, odious, pull in, rake in, ribald, risqué, smutty, strong, stupid, vulgar **07** blatant, boorish, bring in, extreme, glaring, hulking, immense, lumpish, massive, obscene, obvious, sensual, serious **08** colossal, complete, enormous, flagrant, grievous, improper, indecent, manifest, material, nauseous, outright, palpable, shameful, shocking **09** aggregate, before tax, corpulent, egregious, inclusive, offensive, repugnant, repulsive, revolting, sickening, tasteless, unrefined **10** accumulate, disgusting, earthbound, nauseating, off-putting, outrageous, overweight, salt-butter, uncultured, unpleasant **11** disgraceful, distasteful, insensitive, unpalatable **12** all-inclusive, pornographic, unappetizing, unrepeatable **13** coarse-grained, comprehensive **15** unsophisticated

grossly
04 very **05** fatly **06** highly, really
07 acutely, awfully, greatly, utterly
08 severely, terribly **09** decidedly,
extremely, intensely, unusually
10 dreadfully, remarkably, thoroughly,
uncommonly **11** exceedingly,
excessively, frightfully
12 immoderately, inordinately,
terrifically, unreasonably
13 exceptionally **15** extraordinarily

grotesque
◇ anagram indicator
03 odd **04** ugly **05** antic, black, weird
06 absurd, antick, Gothic, rococo
07 anticke, antique, bizarre, hideous,
macabre, strange, surreal, twisted
08 deformed, fanciful, freakish,
peculiar **09** distorted, fantastic,
ludicrous, malformed, misshapen,
monstrous, unnatural, unsightly,
whimsical **10** outlandish, ridiculous
11 extravagant

grotesquely
09 bizarrely, hideously, strangely
11 unnaturally **12** outlandishly,
unpleasantly

grotto
04 cave, grot **05** speos **06** cavern
07 chamber **08** catacomb, Lupercal
09 Mithraeum, nymphaeum
10 subterrane

grotty
03 ill **04** sick, ugly **05** dirty, grody,
mangy, rough, seedy, tatty **06** ailing,
crummy, groggy, poorly, shabby, sleazy,
untidy, unwell **07** run-down, scruffy,
squalid **08** decaying **09** off-colour
10 out of sorts **11** dilapidated **15** under
the weather

grouch
04 moan **05** gripe, grump, sulks
06 griper, grouse, kvetch, moaner,
sulker, whiner, whinge **07** grouser,
grumble, whinger **08** grumbler,
kvetcher, murmurer, mutterer,
sourpuss **09** complaint, grievance,
objection **10** bellyacher, complainer,
crosspatch, malcontent **11** fault-finder

grouchy
05 cross, sulky, surly, testy **06** grumpy
07 peevish **08** captious, churlish,
petulant **09** crotchety, grumbling,
irascible, irritable, querulous, truculent
11 bad-tempered, complaining, ill-
tempered **12** cantankerous,
discontented, dissatisfied

ground
◇ anagram indicator
03 fix, set, sod **04** base, call, clay, dirt,
dust, eard, land, lees, loam, marl, park,
plot, soil, yerd, yird **05** acres, arena,
basis, cause, coach, dregs, drill, earth,
field, found, lawns, pitch, score, teach,
terra, train, tutor, yeard **06** bottom,
campus, domain, estate, excuse, fields,
inform, motive, reason, settle
07 account, deposit, dry land,
educate, gardens, holding, prepare,

residue, stadium, surface, terrain
08 argument, initiate, instruct,
occasion, position, property, sediment
09 advantage, background, establish,
introduce, principle, scourings,
territory **10** foundation, inducement,
terra firma **11** precipitate, vindication
12 acquaint with, surroundings
13 justification **15** familiarize with
See also **stadium**
• **leave the ground**
04 yump
• **patch of ground**
03 lot, tee **04** area
• **run along ground**
04 taxi

groundbait
04 chum **06** berley, burley

groundless
05 empty, false **08** baseless, illusory
09 imaginary, unfounded
10 unprovoked **11** uncalled-for,
unjustified, unsupported, unwarranted
13 without reason **15** unsubstantiated

grounds
04 lees **05** dregs

groundwork
04 base **05** basis **06** bottom
07 footing **08** homework, research
09 spadework **10** essentials,
foundation, metaphysic
11 cornerstone, preparation
12 fundamentals **13** preliminaries,
underpinnings

group
03 lot, mob, set **04** band, body, club,
crew, gang, knot, link, mass, pack,
pool, rank, sort, team, unit **05** batch,
bunch, class, clump, crowd, flock,
genus, grade, guild, order, party, range,
squad, troop, unite **06** circle, clique,
cohort, family, gather, huddle, league,
line up, school **07** arrange, bracket,
cluster, collect, company, coterie,
element, faction, marshal, society,
species **08** assemble, assembly,
category, classify, grouping, organize
09 associate, formation, gathering
10 categorize, collection, congregate,
contingent, detachment
11 association, combination
12 congregation, organization
14 classification, conglomeration
See also **singer**
• **group of women**
02 WI **05** coven
• **unit group**
04 cell

grouse
04 beef, carp, good, moan, neat
05 bitch, gripe, groan, peeve, whine
06 grouch, whinge **07** grumble,
protest **08** complain **09** bellyache,
complaint, excellent, find fault,
grievance, objection

Grouse include:

03 red
04 sage, sand

05 black, hazel
06 ruffed, willow
07 gorcock, greyhen, pintail, prairie,
red game
08 hazel hen, heath-hen, moorcock,
moorfowl, moor-poot, moor-pout,
muir-poot, muir-pout, pheasant,
sage cock
09 blackcock, blackgame, heathbird,
heathcock, heath-fowl, partridge,
ptarmigan
10 heath-poult, prairie hen
11 prairie fowl, sharp-tailed
12 capercaillie, capercailzie
14 prairie chicken

See also **game**
• **grouse-shooters' lair**
04 butt

grove
03 Gro **04** tope, wood **05** copse, hurst
06 arbour, avenue, covert, lyceum
07 coppice, spinney, thicket
08 woodland **10** plantation

grovel
04 fawn **05** cower, crawl, creep, defer,
kneel, kotow, stoop, toady **06** cheese,
cringe, crouch, kowtow, lie low, suck
up **07** bow down, flatter, lie down
08 kiss up to **12** bow and scrape
14 demean yourself **15** butter
someone up, fall on your knees

grow
02 go **03** bud, get, sow, wax **04** farm,
rise, stem, turn **05** arise, breed, issue,
plant, raise, shoot, swell, widen
06 become, change, deepen, expand,
extend, flower, mature, spread, spring,
sprout, thrive **07** advance, broaden,
burgeon, develop, enlarge, fill out,
harvest, improve, produce, prosper,
stretch, succeed, thicken
08 bourgeon, come to be, elongate,
escalate, flourish, increase, lengthen,
multiply, mushroom, progress
09 cultivate, germinate, get bigger, get
taller, originate, propagate **11** make
headway, proliferate **12** become
bigger, become larger, become taller
14 increase in size
• **grow up**
03 age **06** mature

growl
03 yap **04** bark, gnar, gurl, howl, roar,
roin, snap, snar, yelp **05** groin, royne,
snarl **06** rumble **07** grumble

grown-up
03 big, man **05** adult, of age, woman
06 mature **09** full-grown **10** fully
grown **12** fully fledged **14** fully
developed

growth
04 crop, gall, lump, rise **05** plant
06 antler, flower, spread, tumour
07 advance, budding, flowers,
headway, success **08** greenery,
increase, progress, shooting, swelling
09 deepening, evolution, expansion,
extension, flowering, outgrowth,
springing, sprouting **10** burgeoning,

maturation, prosperity
11 development, enlargement, excrescence, germination, improvement **12** augmentation, intumescence, protuberance **13** amplification, magnification, proliferation **14** aggrandizement, multiplication
• **halt growth**
03 nip

grub
03 dig, eat, wog **04** eats, food, hunt, nosh, pupa, root, rout, stub, tuck, worm **05** delve, grout, larva, meals, probe, scour, wroot **06** burrow, ferret, forage, gru-gru, maggot, muddle, rootle, search, tucker **07** explore, rummage, snuzzle, uncover, unearth **08** bookworm, excavate, flag-worm, groo-groo, muck-worm **09** chrysalis, nutrition, provision, witchetty **10** gru-gru worm, sustenance **11** caterpillar, refreshment **12** refreshments **13** leatherjacket

grubby
05 dirty, grimy, messy, mucky, seedy **06** filthy, shabby, soiled, thumby **07** scruffy, squalid **08** unwashed

grudge
04 envy, hate, mind **05** covet, pique, score, spite, venom **06** animus, enmity, grutch, hatred, malice, malign, murmur, repine, resent **07** dislike, ill-will, rancour **08** aversion, begrudge, jealousy, object to **09** animosity, antipathy, grievance **10** antagonism, bitterness, resentment **11** be jealous of, malevolence **12** hard feelings **15** take exception to

grudging
07 envious, jealous **08** hesitant **09** reluctant, resentful, unwilling **11** half-hearted **12** heartburning **14** unenthusiastic

gruel
05 kasha **06** congee, conjee, skilly **07** brochan **08** loblolly **10** punishment **11** skilligalee, skilligolee

gruelling
04 hard **05** harsh, tough **06** severe, taxing, tiring, trying **07** arduous **08** crushing, draining, grinding **09** demanding, difficult, laborious, punishing, strenuous **10** exhausting **12** backbreaking

gruesome
04 grim, sick **05** awful **06** grisly, grooly, horrid **07** ghastly, hideous, macabre **08** dreadful, horrible, horrific, shocking, terrible **09** abhorrent, appalling, frightful, loathsome, monstrous, repellent, repugnant, repulsive, revolting, sickening **10** abominable, disgusting

gruesomely
06 grimly **08** horribly, terribly **09** hideously **10** dreadfully **11** frightfully, monstrously, repulsively

gruff
04 curt, rude, sour **05** blunt, harsh, husky, rough, surly, testy, thick **06** abrupt, grumpy, hoarse, sullen, tetchy **07** brusque, crabbed, rasping, throaty **08** churlish, croaking, guttural, impolite **09** crotchety **10** unfriendly **11** bad-tempered **12** discourteous

gruffly
06 curtly, rudely **07** harshly, huskily, roughly **08** abruptly, hoarsely **09** brusquely **10** gutturally, impolitely **14** discourteously

grumble
04 beef, carp, moan, mump, nark, roar **05** bitch, bleat, croak, gripe, groin, growl, grump, whine **06** grouch, grouse, gurgle, mumble, murmur, mutter, object, rumble, whinge **07** chunder, chunner, chunter, grizzle, maunder, protest **08** chunter, complain **09** bellyache, complaint, find fault, grievance, muttering, objection

grumbler
04 moan **06** grouch, moaner, whiner **07** croaker, fusspot, grouser, niggler, whinger **09** nit-picker **10** bellyacher, complainer, fussbudget **11** fault-finder

grumpily
07 crossly, in a huff, in a sulk, sulkily **08** sullenly **09** grouchily **10** churlishly

grumpy
05 crabby, cross, moany, ratty, sulky, surly **06** snappy, sullen, tetchy **07** crabbed, grouchy, in a huff, in a sulk **08** churlish, grumpish, petulant **09** crotchety, irritable **11** bad-tempered, ill-tempered **12** cantankerous, discontented

grunt
03 ugh **04** oink, rasp **05** cough, croak, grate, groin, power, snore, snort **06** drudge, grumph **07** pig-fish, soldier **08** labourer

Guadeloupe
03 GLP

Guam
03 GUM

guarantee
04 back, bond, gage, oath **05** swear, token **06** assure, avouch, engage, ensure, insure, pledge, secure, surety **07** certify, earnest, endorse, promise, protect, sponsor, support, warrant **08** contract, covenant, guaranty, make sure, security, vouch for, warranty **09** answer for, assurance, insurance, stipulate, undertake, vouchsafe **10** collateral, underwrite, warrandice, warrantise **11** endorsement, make certain, testimonial **12** word of honour **15** give an assurance

guarantor
05 angel **06** backer, surety **07** referee, sponsor, voucher **08** bailsman, bondsman **09** guarantee, supporter,

warrantor **10** covenantor **11** underwriter

guard
◊ *containment indicator*
03 pad **04** care, keep, mind, rail, save, wait, wall, ward, wear, weir **05** check, cover, fence, garda, hedge, scout, watch **06** beware, buffer, bumper, captor, charge, defend, escort, fender, keeper, minder, patrol, picket, police, screen, secure, sentry, shield, warden, warder **07** barrier, be alert, control, cushion, defence, enguard, look out, lookout, oversee, protect, shelter, watcher **08** bostangi, defender, fortress, guardian, preserve, savegard, scrutiny, security, sentinel, splasher, take care, watchman **09** bodyguard, conductor, custodian, direction, keep watch, protector, safeguard, supervise, vigilance **10** inspection, monitoring, protection, regulation **11** observation, stewardship, supervision **12** guardianship, surveillance **15** superintendence
• **officer of the Guard**
04 exon
• **off your guard**
06 unwary **07** napping, unaware, unready **08** careless, unawares **09** red-handed, surprised **10** unprepared **11** inattentive **12** unsuspecting
• **on your guard**
04 wary **05** alert, ready **07** careful **08** cautious, excubant, prepared, vigilant, watchful **09** attentive, wide awake **10** on the alert **11** circumspect **12** on the lookout

guarded
04 wary **05** cagey, chary **07** careful, striped, trimmed **08** cautious, defended, discreet, reserved, reticent, watchful **09** reluctant, secretive **10** restrained **11** circumspect **12** non-committal

guardedly
06 warily **07** charily **09** carefully **10** cautiously **11** reluctantly, secretively **13** circumspectly **14** non-committally

guardian
05 angel, guard, Janus, tutor **06** custos, escort, gryfon, keeper, patron, warden, warder **07** curator, Granthi, griffin, griffon, gryphon, steward, trustee, tutelar **08** Cerberus, champion, curatrix, defender, tutelary **09** attendant, caretaker, custodian, preserver, protector **10** depositary, depository, protecting **11** conservator **12** conservatrix
• **guardian of women**
04 Juno

guardianship
04 care, ward **05** aegis, guard, hands, trust **07** custody, defence, keeping, tuition **08** guidance, tutelage, wardenry, wardship **09** patronage **10** attendance, protection, wardenship **11** curatorship, safekeeping,

stewardship, trusteeship
12 preservation, protectorate
13 custodianship

Guatemala
03 GCA, GTM

Guernsey
03 GBG

guerrilla
03 Che **06** haiduk, maquis, sniper
07 chetnik, fedayee, heyduck
08 komitaji, partisan, Viet Cong
09 irregular, terrorist, Zapatista
10 Tamil tiger **11** bushwhacker, franc-tireur, guerrillero **14** freedom fighter

guess
03 aim, bet **04** feel, idea, shot
05 aread, arede, augur, fancy, hunch, judge, level, think **06** assume, belief, devise, divine, notion, reckon, theory
07 arreede, believe, feeling, imagine, opinion, predict, suppose, surmise, suspect, work out **08** consider, estimate **09** guesswork, intuition, judgement, postulate, reckoning, speculate, suspicion **10** assumption, conjecture, hypothesis, make a guess, prediction **11** guesstimate, hypothesize, speculation, supposition
13 shot in the dark **14** a shot in the dark, a stab in the dark, ballpark figure, put something at

guessing-game
04 mora **05** morra

guesstimate
05 guess **09** judgement, quotation, reckoning, valuation **10** assessment, estimation, evaluation, rough guess
11 computation **13** approximation
14 ballpark figure **15** approximate cost

guesswork
06 theory **07** surmise **09** intuition, reckoning **10** assumption, conjecture, estimation, hypothesis, prediction
11 guesstimate, speculation, supposition

guest
02 PG **05** umbra **06** caller, lodger, patron **07** boarder, invitee, regular, visitor **08** manuhiri, resident, symphile, visitant **09** synoecete, synoekete

guesthouse
03 inn **05** hotel **06** hostel **07** Gasthof, hospice, pension, taverna
08 Gasthaus, hostelry, minshuku
11 xenodochium **12** rooming-house
13 boarding-house **15** bed-and-breakfast

guff
03 rot **04** blah, bosh, bull, bunk, cock, crap **05** balls, bilge, hooey, smell, stink, trash, tripe **06** bunkum, drivel, hot air, humbug, piffle **07** baloney, eyewash, hogwash, rhubarb, rubbish, twaddle
08 claptrap, cobblers, malarkey, nonsense, tommyrot **09** gibberish, moonshine, poppycock
10 codswallop

guffaw
04 hoot, roar **05** laugh, whoop
06 bellow, cackle, haw-haw, shriek
09 loud laugh **11** laugh loudly

guidance
03 tip **04** help, hint, lead, rule, tips
05 hints **06** advice, charge
07 conduct, control, counsel, leading, pointer **08** pointers, teaching
09 direction **10** assistance, directions, guidelines, indication, leadership, management, suggestion
11 counselling, indications, information, instruction, suggestions
12 instructions **14** recommendation
15 recommendations
• **Parental Guidance**
02 PG

guide
03 ABC, key **04** guru, lead, mark, norm, rule, show, sign, wise **05** abcee, absey, gauge, maxim, model, pilot, point, steer, teach, train, tutor, usher, weise, weize **06** advise, attend, beacon, direct, escort, govern, leader, manage, manual, marker, mentor, ranger, signal **07** adviser, command, conduct, control, counsel, courier, educate, example, inspire, labarum, measure, oversee, pattern, pointer, red book, shikari, teacher, waymark
08 Bradshaw, chaperon, cicerone, cynosure, director, engineer, exemplar, Good Food, handbook, helmsman, instruct, landmark, navigate, Pole Star, regulate, road book, shikaree, signpost, standard **09** accompany, archetype, attendant, benchmark, catalogue, chaperone, companion, conductor, criterion, directory, guidebook, guideline, influence, manoeuvre, navigator, sightsman, steersman, supervise, tombstone, yardstick **10** counsellor, indication, instructor, show the way **11** preside over, superintend **12** be in charge of, valet de place **14** Tyrian cynosure
• **weaver's guide**
04 card

guidebook
03 ABC **04** A to Z® **05** guide
06 manual **08** Baedeker, handbook
09 companion **10** prospectus
15 instruction book

guideline
04 rule **05** terms **06** advice
07 measure, road map **08** standard
09 benchmark, criterion, direction, framework, parameter, principle, procedure, yardstick **10** constraint, indication, regulation, suggestion, touchstone **11** information, instruction
14 recommendation

guild
03 WAG **04** club, tong **05** artel, lodge, order, union **06** chapel, league
07 basoche, company, mistery, mystery, society **08** alliance, sorority
10 federation, fellowship, fraternity
11 association, brotherhood,

corporation **12** organization
13 incorporation

guile
04 dole, ruse **05** craft, fraud, trick
06 deceit **07** cunning, knavery, slyness
08 artifice, trickery, wiliness
09 deception, duplicity, stratagem, treachery **10** artfulness, cleverness, craftiness, trickiness **11** deviousness
12 gamesmanship **13** double-dealing

guileless
04 open **05** frank, naive **06** candid, direct, honest, simple **07** artless, genuine, natural, sincere **08** innocent, sackless, straight, trusting, truthful
09 ingenuous, unworldly
10 unreserved **11** transparent
13 simple-hearted **15** straightforward, unsophisticated

guilt
03 sin **05** blame, shame, wrong
06 regret **07** remorse **08** disgrace
09 dishonour, guilt trip, penitence
10 blood-guilt, conscience, contrition, misconduct, repentance, sinfulness, wrongdoing **11** compunction, criminality, culpability **12** self-reproach, unlawfulness
14 responsibility, self-accusation
15 blameworthiness

guiltily
07 at fault, to blame, wrongly
09 illegally, illicitly **10** contritely, shamefully, unlawfully, with sorrow
11 regretfully, responsibly
12 remorsefully, unforgivably
13 penitentially, reprehensibly, without excuse **14** caught in the act **15** caught red-handed

guiltless
04 free, pure **05** clean, clear **07** sinless
08 innocent, spotless **09** blameless, faultless, stainless, undefiled, unspotted, unsullied, untainted **10** immaculate, impeccable, inculpable, unblamable
11 untarnished **13** above reproach, unimpeachable **14** irreproachable

guilty
03 bad **04** evil **05** sorry, wrong
06 faulty, nocent, sinful, wicked
07 ashamed, at fault, illegal, illicit, to blame **08** blamable, contrite, criminal, culpable, infamous, penitent, sheepish, unlawful **09** condemned, convicted, offending, regretful, repentant
10 delinquent, flagitious, remorseful, shamefaced **11** blameworthy, guilt-ridden, responsible **12** bloodstained, compunctious

guinea
02 Ls, RG **03** GIN **04** quid **06** canary, George **07** Geordie
• **guineas**
02 gs

Guinea-Bissau
03 GNB, RGB

guinea pig
04 cavy, paca **05** aguti **06** agouti,

agouty **08** capybara **09** do-nothing, triallist

Guinness
04 Alec

guise
03 air **04** face, form, mask, show
05 dress, front, shape **06** aspect, custom, façade, manner **07** purport
08 disguise, features, likeness, pretence **09** behaviour, demeanour, semblance **10** appearance

guitar
02 ax **03** axe, uke **04** bass
05 Dobro®, sanko **06** sancho
07 gittern, samisen, ukulele
08 shamisen **09** humbucker
• **play guitar**
05 strum

gulf
03 bay, gap, maw **04** cove, hole, rift, void **05** abyss, basin, bight, chasm, cleft, gorge, inlet, split **06** breach, canyon, divide, hollow, ravine, vorago
07 crevice, fissure, opening
08 division **09** whirlpool
10 separation

Gulfs include:
04 Aden, Huon, Lion, Moro, Oman, Riga, Siam, Suez
05 Ancud, Aqaba, Càdiz, Davao, Dulce, Gabes, Gaeta, Genoa, Kutch, Lions, Maine, Panay, Papua, Penas, Ragay, Saros, Sidra, Sirte, Tunis
06 Aegina, Alaska, Cambay, Chania, Darien, Gdansk, Guinea, Kavala, Mannar, Mexico, Naples, Nicoya, Orosei, Panama, Parita, Patras, St Malo, Tonkin, Triste, Venice
07 Almeria, Arabian, Asinara, Boothia, Bothnia, Cazones, Corinth, Edremit, Exmouth, Finland, Fonseca, Hauraki, Kachchh, Lepanto, Obskaya, Persian, Salerno, San Blas, Saronic, Spencer, Taranto, The Gulf, Trieste, Udskaya
08 Amundsen, Batabano, Cagliari, Campeche, Chiriqui, Honduras, Khambhat, Liaotung, Lingayen, Martaban, Mosquito, Oristano, Papagayo, San Jorge, Taganrog, Thailand, Valencia
09 Buor-Khaya, Corcovado, Dvinskaya, Guayaquil, Queen Maud, San Matias, San Miguel, St Florent, St Vincent, Van Diemen, Venezuela
10 California, Chaunskaya, Cheshskaya, Coronation, Kyparissia, Policastro, St Lawrence, Tazovskaya, Thermaikos
11 Carpentaria, Guacanayabo, Manfredonia, Pechorskaya, Strymonikos, Tehuantepec
12 los Mosquitos, Penzhinskaya
13 Baydaratskaya, Santa Catalina
15 Joseph Bonaparte

gull
04 dupe, fool, hoax **05** cheat
07 deceive
See also **bird**; **fool**

gullet
03 maw **04** craw, crop, gula **06** throat
07 Red Lane, weasand **09** esophagus
10 oesophagus

gullibility
07 naivety **09** credulity, innocence
10 simplicity **11** foolishness
12 trustfulness

gullible
05 green, naive **07** foolish, verdant
08 innocent, trustful, trusting
09 credulous, ingenuous **11** suggestible
12 overtrusting, unsuspecting
13 inexperienced **14** easily deceived, impressionable **15** unsophisticated

gully
03 geo, gio, goe **05** ditch, donga, gorge, gulch **06** canyon, grough, gutter, ravine, valley **07** channel, couloir **11** watercourse
See also **ravine**

gulp
◇ *containment indicator*
04 bolt, slug, swig, wolf **05** gulch, quaff, stuff, swill, swipe **06** devour, gobble, gollop, guzzle **07** draught, swallow **08** mouthful, tuck into
09 knock back

gum
03 fix, God, jaw **04** clog, dupe, glue, guar, seal **05** affix, cheat, myrrh, paste, resin, stick **06** acajou, angico, balata, cement, chewie, chicle, chuddy, humbug, mastic **07** benzoin, deceive, dextrin, gamboge, mastich
08 adhesive, bdellium, benjamin, dextrine, fixative, galbanum, mucilage, nonsense, olibanum, opopanax, scammony **09** courbaril, insolence, sagapenum, tacamahac, tacmahack
10 ammoniacum, asafoetida, caoutchouc, euphorbium, sarcocolla, tragacanth
• **gum tree**
04 arar **05** karri **06** tupelo
08 sandarac **10** eucalyptus
• **gum up**
04 clog **05** choke **06** hinder, impede
08 obstruct

gummy
05 gluey, gooey, tacky **06** sticky, viscid
07 viscous **08** adhesive **09** toothless

gumption
03 wit **04** nous **05** savvy, sense
06 acumen **07** ability, courage
08 sagacity **09** acuteness
10 astuteness, cleverness, enterprise, initiative, shrewdness **11** common sense, discernment **15** resourcefulness

gumshoe *see* **detective**

gun
03 rod **05** piece, shoot **06** expert, heater, weapon **07** firearm, shooter
10 pre-eminent **12** shooting iron

Guns include:
02 MG
03 air, dag, gas, gat, ray, six, Uzi

04 AK-47, Bren, burp, Colt®, hand, pump, punt, shot, sten, stun
05 baton, field, fusil, Lewis, Maxim, rifle, siege, spear, tommy
06 airgun, Archie, Bofors, cannon, mortar, musket, needle, pistol, pom-pom, Purdey®, Quaker, turret
07 bazooka, carbine, chopper, gatling, Long Tom, machine, pounder, scatter
08 air rifle, arquebus, elephant, falconet, firelock, howitzer, pederero, revolver, starting, Sterling
09 Archibald, Big Bertha, flintlock, harquebus
10 black Maria, demi-cannon, six-shooter, submachine, Winchester®
11 blunderbuss, four-pounder, half-pounder, Kalashnikov
12 fowling-piece, mitrailleuse, three-pounder

• **gun's catch**
04 sear
• **row of guns**
04 tier

gunfire
04 flak **05** salvo **06** firing
08 gunshots, pounding, shelling, shooting **09** cannonade
11 bombardment

gunman
04 thug **05** bravo **06** bandit, gunsel, hit man, killer, sniper **07** mobster
08 assassin, gangster, murderer, shootist **09** desperado, terrorist
10 gunslinger, hatchet man **11** armed robber

gurgle
03 lap **04** crow **05** brawl, clunk, plash
06 babble, bubble, buller, burble, guggle, murmur, ripple, ruckle, splash
08 bubbling

guru
04 sage **05** swami, tutor **06** expert, gooroo, leader, master, mentor, pundit
07 Bhagwan, teacher, tohunga
08 luminary, Svengali **09** authority, maharishi **10** instructor **12** guiding light

gush
03 goo, jet, run **04** boak, bock, boke, emit, flow, fuss, go on, pour, rail, rave, rush, tide, well **05** burst, flood, issue, raile, rayle, slush, spate, spout, spurt, surge **06** babble, drivel, effuse, jabber, stream **07** blather, cascade, chatter, enthuse, outflow, regorge, torrent
08 fountain, outburst **10** bubble over, effervesce, outpouring **11** regurgitate
12 effusiveness **14** sentimentality

gushing
05 gushy **06** sickly, too-too
07 cloying, fulsome, mawkish
08 effusive **09** emotional, excessive
10 saccharine, scaturient
11 sentimental

gust
03 fit **04** blow, flaw, gale, puff, rush, scud, wind **05** blast, blore, burst,

erupt, storm, surge 06 breeze, flurry, relish, squall 07 bluster, flaught, flavour 08 burst out, eruption, outbreak, outburst, williwaw 13 gratification

gustily
06 wildly 07 windily 08 breezily, stormily 13 tempestuously

gusto
04 élan, zeal, zest 05 verve 06 energy, relish 07 delight, fervour, unction 08 pleasure 09 enjoyment 10 enthusiasm, exuberance 12 appreciation, exhilaration

gusty
05 blowy, windy 06 breezy, stormy 07 savoury, squally 08 blustery 10 blustering 11 tempestuous

gut
◇ middle deletion indicator
03 rob 04 draw, gill, grit, lane, loot, sack 05 balls, basic, belly, clean, clear, dress, empty, nerve, pluck, rifle, spunk, strip 06 bottle, bowels, innate, mettle, paunch, ravage, strong 07 bravery, courage, destroy, enteron, innards, insides, natural, plunder, ransack, stomach, viscera 08 audacity, backbone, boldness, clean out, clear out, entrails, tenacity 09 devastate, emotional, fortitude, heartfelt, intuitive 10 deep-seated, disembowel, eviscerate, exenterate, intestines, mesenteron, unthinking 11 archenteron, instinctive, involuntary, spontaneous, vital organs 14 internal organs

gutless
◇ middle deletion indicator
04 nesh, weak 05 timid 06 abject, craven, feeble 07 chicken 08 cowardly 09 spineless 10 irresolute 11 lily-livered 12 faint-hearted 14 chicken-hearted, chicken-livered

gutsily
06 boldly 07 bravely 08 spunkily 10 resolutely, staunchily 11 indomitably 12 courageously, passionately

gutsy
04 bold, game 05 brave, gutty, lusty 06 ballsy, plucky, spunky 07 gallant, staunch 08 resolute, spirited

10 courageous, determined, gluttonous, mettlesome, passionate 11 indomitable

gutter
04 duct, grip, pipe, roan, rone, tube 05 ditch, drain, gripe, gully, rhone, rigol, sewer, swale, swayl, sweal, sweel 06 cullis, gulley, kennel, rigoll, runnel, sluice, strand, trench, trough 07 channel, conduit, culvert, passage 08 downpipe, roanpipe, ronepipe 09 guttering

guttersnipe
04 waif 05 gamin 06 urchin 07 mudlark 10 ragamuffin 14 tatterdemalion

guttural
03 low 04 deep 05 gruff, harsh, husky, rough, thick 06 hoarse 07 grating, rasping, throaty 08 croaking, gravelly

guy
02 bo 03 boy, lad, man, sod 04 boyo, chap, cove, dude, joke, lark, stay, vang 05 bloke, bucko, fella, youth 06 decamp, Fawkes, fellow, flight, geezer, person 09 character, decamping 10 individual

Guyana
03 GUY

guzzle
04 bolt, cram, gulp, soak, swig, wolf 05 quaff, scoff, stuff, swill 06 devour, gobble 07 put away, swallow 08 tuck into 09 knock back, polish off 10 gormandize

gymnastics
02 PE, PT 03 gym

Gymnastics disciplines include:

04 ball, beam, hoop 05 clubs, floor, rings, vault 06 ribbon 07 high bar 08 tumbling 10 horse vault, uneven bars 11 balance beam, pommel horse 12 parallel bars, trampolining 13 horizontal bar 14 asymmetric bars, floor exercises, side horse vault, sports aerobics

Gymnastics-related terms include:

04 beam, pike, tuck

05 cross, floor, giant, rings, salto, stick, twist, vault 06 aerial, bridge, layout 07 element, flyaway, Gaylord 08 dismount, flic-flac, rotation, round-off, straddle, walkover, whip back 09 all-around, apparatus, cartwheel, execution, handstand, Yurchenko 10 double back, handspring, somersault, uneven bars 11 balance beam, double twist, pommel horse, Swedish fall 12 compulsories, parallel bars 13 horizontal bar, inverted cross 14 asymmetric bars

Gymnasts include:

03 Kim (Nellie), Ono (Takashi) 06 Korbut (Olga Valentinovna), Miller (Shannon), Retton (Mary Lou) 07 Scherbo (Vitaly), Tweddle (Beth) 08 Comaneci (Nadia), Ditiatin (Aleksandr), Latynina (Larissa Semyonovna), Shakhlin (Boris Anfiyanovich) 09 Andrianov (Nikolai Yefimovich), Cáslavská (Vera) 10 Boginskaya (Svetlana), Turischeva (Lyudmila Ivanovna)

gym shoe
03 dap 08 plimsole, plimsoll, sandshoe

Gypsy, Gipsy
03 chi, faw, rom, rye 04 chai, chal, Roma 05 caird, nomad, rover 06 gipsen, gitana, gitano, hawker, roamer, Romani, Romany, tinker 07 rambler, Rommany, tinkler, tsigane, tzigany, Zincala, Zincalo, Zingana, Zingano, Zingara, Zingaro 08 Bohemian, diddicoy, Egyptian, huckster, wanderer, Zigeuner 09 out-of-door, traveller 14 unconventional

gyrate
04 gyre, spin, turn 05 swirl, twirl, wheel, whirl 06 circle, rotate, spiral, swivel 07 revolve 09 pirouette

gyration
04 spin, turn 05 swirl, twirl, twist, whirl, whorl 06 circle, spiral, swivel 08 rotation, spinning, wheeling, whirling 09 pirouette 10 revolution 11 convolution

H

H
05 aitch, hotel **07** hydrant

habit
03 way, won **04** bent, cowl, gear, mode, robe, rule, togs, ways, wont **05** dress, ethos, get-up, knack, quirk, trick, usage **06** custom, manner, monkey, outfit, policy **07** costume, garment, leaning, routine, uniform **08** clothing, fixation, practice, tendency, vestment, weakness **09** addiction, assuetude, mannerism, obsession, procedure **10** dependence, proclivity, propensity **11** familiarity, inclination **12** second nature **14** accustomedness, matter of course

See also **clothes, clothing**

• **bad habit**
04 vice **09** cacoethes

habitable
07 livable **08** liveable **09** livable in **10** liveable in **11** fit to live in, inhabitable

habitat
04 home **05** abode, niche **06** domain **07** element, station, terrain **08** dwelling, locality **09** territory **10** metropolis **11** environment **12** surroundings

habitation
03 hut, pad **04** digs, flat, gaff, home **05** abode, house, joint **06** biding **07** cottage, housing, lodging, mansion, tenancy **08** domicile, dwelling, quarters, tenement **09** apartment, occupancy, residence, residency **10** occupation **11** inhabitance, inhabitancy **12** inhabitation **13** accommodation, dwelling-place **14** living quarters

habitual
03 set **05** fixed, great, usual **06** common, normal, wonted **07** chronic, natural, regular, routine **08** addicted, constant, familiar, hardened, ordinary, standard **09** confirmed, customary, dependent, obsessive, recurrent **10** accustomed, inveterate, persistent, systematic **11** established, intemperate, traditional **12** pathological, systematical

habitually
06 mainly, mostly **07** as a rule, chiefly, usually **08** commonly, normally **09** generally, in the main, on average, regularly, routinely, typically **10** by and large, on the whole, ordinarily **13** traditionally **14** for the most part

habituate
03 use **04** tame **05** adapt, break, enure, inure, train **06** harden, school, season, settle **07** break in **08** accustom, make used, settle in **09** condition **10** discipline **11** acclimatize, familiarize

habitué
06 patron **07** denizen, regular **10** frequenter **15** frequent visitor, regular customer

hack
03 cut, hag, hew, saw **04** chop, fell, gash, hash, kick, pick, rack **05** clear, cough, hired, notch, slash, slave **06** drudge, mangle, writer **07** grating, hackney, mattock **08** lacerate, mediocre, mutilate, reporter, tomahawk **09** hackneyed, mercenary, scribbler **10** journalist **11** hedge-writer, penny-a-liner

See also **horse**

• **hack it**
04 cope **05** get by, get on **06** manage **07** carry on, make out **08** get along **10** get through **13** muddle through

hackle
• **make someone's hackles rise**
03 bug, irk, vex **04** gall, miff, nark, rile **05** anger, annoy, get at **06** bother, enrage, hassle, heckle, madden, needle, nettle, offend, ruffle, wind up **07** affront, hatchel, incense, outrage, provoke **08** flax-comb, irritate **09** aggravate, infuriate, make angry **10** antagonize, exasperate **13** make sparks fly **15** get on your nerves

hackneyed
03 old **04** hack, worn **05** banal, corny, hoary, stale, stock, tired, trite **06** common **07** cliché'd, percoct, worn-out **08** clichéed, overused, time-worn **09** twice-told **10** overworked, pedestrian, prostitute, threadbare, uninspired, unoriginal, yawn-making **11** commonplace, stereotyped, wearing thin **12** cliché-ridden, run-of-the-mill **13** platitudinous, unimaginative

had
01 'd

haddock
05 capon, scrod, smoky **06** finnan, rizzar, rizzer, rizzor, smokie **07** findram, speldin **08** spelding, speldrin **09** speldring **14** Arbroath smokie

Hades
05 Pluto

hafnium
02 Hf

haft
04 grip, hilt, knob **05** shaft, stock **06** handle **07** dudgeon **08** handgrip

hag
03 hew **04** fury, hack **05** crone, harpy, rudas, shrew, vixen, witch **06** beldam, gorgon, virago **07** beldame, hellcat **08** harridan **09** battle-axe, termagant

haggard
03 wan **04** lean, pale, thin **05** drawn, gaunt, Rider **06** pallid, wasted **07** drained, ghastly, pinched, untamed **08** careworn, shrunken **10** cadaverous **11** intractable **13** hollow-cheeked

haggle
04 prig **05** cavil **06** barter, bicker, dicker, higgle, mangle, niffer, palter **07** bargain, chaffer, dispute, quarrel, quibble, wrangle **08** beat down, huckster, squabble **09** negotiate

hahnium
02 Ha

hail
03 ave **04** ahoy, beat, come, goal, hale, heil, laud, pelt, rain, skol **05** cheer, exalt, greet, nod to, salve, score, skoal, sleet, sound, speak, storm **06** accost, assail, attack, batter, health, honour, praise, salute, shower, volley, wave to, what ho **07** acclaim, address, applaud, barrage, bombard, earshot, torrent, welcome **08** be born in, flag down, greeting, signal to, wave down, whoa-ho-ho **09** call out to, frozen ice, hail-storm, originate, whoa-ho-hoa **10** frozen rain, hailstones, say hello to **11** acknowledge, bombardment, communicate **13** precipitation **14** have your home in **15** have your roots in

hail-fellow-well-met
05 jolly, merry **06** genial, hearty, jovial, lively **07** affable, cordial, festive **08** cheerful, friendly, sociable **09** convivial, fun-loving

hair
03 fur, mop **04** coat, hide, pelt, pile, type, wool **05** fibre, locks, pilus, shock **06** fibril, fleece, lanugo, thatch, villus **07** bristle, tresses **08** strammel, strummel **09** character

Hair-related terms include:

3 bob, cue, cut, dod, dye, gel, wax, wig
4 bald, body, clip, coif, comb, crop, curl, down, fine, grip, hank, kesh, lank, lice, lock, mane, perm, pouf, tête, tint, tong, trim, tuft, wavy, wiry
5 bangs, black, blond, bluey, braid, brown, brush, crimp, curly, frizz, henna, layer, moult, mousy, queue, quiff, rinse, roots, sandy, serum, shade, shaft, shine, short, slick, slide, snood, tease, thick, tress
6 auburn, barber, barnet, blonde, bobble, brunet, coarse, colour, crinal, fillet, flaxen, fringe, frizzy, ginger, greasy, hairdo, kangha, mousey, mousse, peruke, pomade, pompom, pompon, pouffe, ribbon, roller, silver, tangle, titian
7 balding, bandeau, blow-dry, cowlick, crinate, flyaway, frizzle, greying, haircut, hair gel, hair net, hair oil, hirsute, keratin, lacquer, parting, periwig, pin curl, rat-tail, redhead, ringlet, shampoo, streaks, stylist, tonsure, topknot, tow-head, tressed, wet-look, xerasia
8 alopecia, ash-blond, back-comb, baldpate, barrette, bar slide, bouffant, brunette, canities, chestnut, clippers, coiffeur, coiffure, combover, cow's lick, crinated, dandruff, diffuser, elflocks, fixature, follicle, forelock, grizzled, hair band, hairless, hairline, headring, kisscurl, lovelock, peroxide, rat's-tail, receding, roulette, scrunchy, side comb, sidelock, split end, straight
9 Alice band, ash-blonde, bandoline, blue rinse, Brylcreem®, capillary, chevelure, coiffeuse, colourant, curlpaper, finger-dry, fright wig, hairbrush, hairdryer, hairpiece, hair slide, hairspray, hairstyle, headdress, Kirbigrip®, lowlights, madarosis, mop-headed, papillote, redheaded, scalp lock, scrunchie, tow-headed, trichosis, water wave
10 bad hair day, bald-headed, detangling, extensions, fair-haired, fair-headed, finger wave, hair-powder, highlights, leiotrichy, long-haired, perruquier, piliferous, pocket-comb, scrunch-dry, trichology, widow's peak
11 conditioner, flame-haired, hairdresser, hairstylist, side-parting, tow-coloured, white-haired, white-headed
12 bottle-blonde, brilliantine, Cain-coloured, close-cropped, curling tongs, cymotrichous, hair restorer, leiotrichous, straightener, trichologist
13 centre-parting, corkscrew curl, Judas-coloured, lissotrichous, pepper-and-salt, permanent wave, platinum-blond
14 shoulder-length
15 strawberry blond, styling products

Facial hair-related terms include:

05 beard, pluck, razor
06 goatee, tweeze, waxing
07 epilate, eyelash, goateed, shaving, stubble
08 bumfluff, depilate, stubbled, sugaring, tweezers
09 depilator, moustache, sideburns
10 aftershave, depilation, depilatory, face-fungus, pogonotomy, shaving gel
11 clean-shaven, shaving foam, shaving-soap
12 electrolysis, shaving-brush, shaving-stick, side whiskers
13 eyebrow pencil, eyelash curler
15 designer stubble

• **let your hair down**
05 relax **08** chill out, loosen up
09 hang loose **13** have a good time, let yourself go **15** let it all hang out
• **make someone's hair stand on end**
03 jar **04** daze, jolt, numb, stun
05 amaze, appal, repel, shake, shock, upset **06** dismay, revolt **07** agitate, astound, disgust, horrify, outrage, perturb, stagger, startle, stupefy, terrify, unnerve **08** bewilder, confound, disquiet, distress, frighten, paralyse, unsettle **09** dumbfound, take aback
10 scandalize, traumatize
• **not turn a hair**
04 calm **08** stay cool **10** remain calm
11 see it coming **12** keep your cool
14 not bat an eyelid, remain composed
• **piece of hair**
03 cue **04** lock **05** tress
• **split hairs**
05 cavil **07** nit-pick, quibble
08 pettifog **09** find fault **10** over-refine

haircut, hairdo *see* hairstyle

hairdresser
06 barber **07** crimper, friseur, stylist
08 coiffeur **09** coiffeuse **11** hairstylist
12 trichologist

Hairdressers include:

06 Clarke (Nicky), **Sorbie** (Trevor)
07 Grateau (Marcel), **Sassoon** (Vidal)
08 Collinge (Andrew), **Mitchell** (Paul)
10 Teazy Weazy, Toni and Guy
11 Worthington (Charles)

hairless
04 bald **05** shorn **06** shaven, smooth
08 glabrate, glabrous, tonsured
09 beardless, desperate **10** bald-headed **11** clean-shaven

hairpiece
03 jiz, rug, tie, wig **04** gizz, jasy, jazy
05 caxon, jasey, major, syrup
06 bagwig, bobwig, Brutus, merkin, peruke, tie-wig, toupee, toupet
07 buzz-wig, periwig, Ramilie, scratch, spencer **08** postiche, Ramilies, Ramillie **09** fright wig, Ramillies
10 full-bottom, scratch-wig
12 Gregorian wig **14** transformation

hair-raising
05 eerie, scary **06** creepy
08 alarming, exciting, shocking
09 startling, thrilling **10** horrifying, petrifying, terrifying **11** frightening
13 bloodcurdling, spine-chilling

hair's-breadth
03 jot **04** hair, inch **07** whisker
08 fraction

hairstyle
03 cut, set **05** style **06** barnet, hairdo
07 haircut **08** coiffure

Hairstyles include:

02 DA
03 bob, bun, wig
04 Afro, crop, perm, shed
05 bangs, braid, plait, quiff, weave
06 curled, dreads, fringe, mullet, pouffe, toupee
07 beehive, bunches, chignon, cowlick, crewcut, crimped, mohican, pageboy, pigtail, shingle, tonsure, topknot
08 bouffant, combover, corn rows, Eton crop, frizette, ponytail, ringlets, skinhead, undercut
09 duck's arse, hair-piece, Hoxton fin, number one, pompadour, sideburns
10 backcombed, dreadlocks, extensions, marcel wave, sideboards
11 French pleat
13 hair extension

hairy
◇ *anagram indicator*
05 bushy, dicey, dodgy, furry, fuzzy, grave, nasty, risky **06** chancy, daring, fleecy, pilose, pilous, severe, shaggy, unsafe, woolly **07** bearded, crinite, crinose, exposed, hirsute, ominous, serious **08** alarming, critical, high-risk, insecure, menacing, perilous, reckless, unshaven **09** breakneck, dangerous, hazardous **10** precarious, vulnerable
11 crinigerous, frightening, susceptible, threatening, treacherous
• **hairy person**
04 Esau

Haiti
02 RH **03** HTI

halcyon
04 calm, mild **05** balmy, happy, quiet, still **06** gentle, golden, placid, serene
07 pacific **08** carefree, peaceful, tranquil **10** kingfisher, prosperous
11 flourishing, undisturbed

hale
03 fit **04** drag, hail, well **05** sound
06 hearty, raucle, robust, strong
07 healthy **08** athletic, blooming, vigorous, youthful **09** in the pink
10 able-bodied **11** flourishing **12** in fine fettle

half
◇ *deletion indicator*
◇ *insertion indicator*
02 hf **04** demi-, hemi-, part, semi-
05 share **06** barely, halved, moiety,

partly, slight **07** à moitié, divided, limited, partial, portion, section, segment **08** bisected, fraction, moderate, slightly **09** bisection, equal part, partially **10** equal share, fractional, hemisphere, incomplete, moderately, semicircle **11** imperfectly **12** divided in two, fifty per cent, inadequately, incompletely **13** hemispherical **14** insufficiently

• **by half**

03 too **04** very **11** excessively **12** considerably

• **by halves**

05 à demi **07** à moitié **11** imperfectly **12** inadequately, incompletely **14** insufficiently

• **not half**

04 very **06** indeed, really **08** not at all, very much **09** not nearly **11** exceedingly

• **other half**

04 wife **06** spouse **07** husband, partner **08** alter ego

• **too ... by half**

03 too **04** over **06** unduly **11** excessively **12** immoderately, inordinately, unreasonably **13** unjustifiably, unnecessarily

half-baked

05 crazy, crude, silly **06** stupid **07** foolish **08** crackpot, immature **09** ill-judged, senseless, underdone, unplanned **10** half-witted, incomplete **11** harebrained, impractical, undeveloped **12** ill-conceived, short-sighted

half-caste

05 griff, metif, Métis, sambo **06** Creole, griffe, mestee **07** mestiza, mestizo, Métisse, mongrel, mulatta, mulatto **08** miscegen, quadroon **09** miscegene, miscegine, quintroon **10** mulattress, quarteroon **12** quarter-blood

half-cough

03 hem

half-hearted

◇ *middle deletion indicator*
04 cool, weak **05** tepid **06** feeble **07** neutral, passive **08** listless, lukewarm **09** apathetic, Laodicean **10** lacklustre **11** indifferent, unconcerned **12** uninterested **14** unenthusiastic

half-heartedly

◇ *middle deletion indicator*
06 feebly **09** neutrally **10** listlessly **13** apathetically

half-moon

04 lune **08** demilune

halfpenny

03 mag, meg, rap **04** maik, mail, make, posh **05** maile **06** bawbee, magpie, obolus **07** patrick **10** portcullis

halfway

03 mid **04** mean **06** barely, median, middle, midway **07** central **08** slightly **09** centrally **11** equidistant,

imperfectly, in the middle, to the middle **12** intermediate

• **meet someone halfway**

09 make a deal, negotiate **10** compromise **11** give and take **15** make concessions

halfwit

03 ass, git, mug, nit **04** berk, butt, clot, dill, dope, dork, dupe, fool, geek, nerk, nong, prat, twit **05** chump, clown, comic, dumbo, dunce, eejit, galah, idiot, moron, ninny, prick, twerp, wally **06** cretin, dimwit, doofus, jester, nitwit, numpty, stooge, sucker **07** airhead, buffoon, fat-head, pillock, plonker **08** imbecile **09** birdbrain, blockhead, ignoramus, simpleton **10** nincompoop **13** laughing-stock

half-witted

04 dull, dumb **05** barmy, batty, crazy, dotty, nutty, potty, silly, wacky **06** simple, stupid **07** foolish, idiotic, moronic **08** crackpot **09** dim-witted **12** crack-brained, feeble-minded, simple-minded **14** not the full quid

hall

02 ha' **04** aula, gild **05** foyer, guild, lobby, odeon, salle **06** atrium, exedra **07** apadana, chamber, citadel, commons, exhedra, hallway, megaron, passage **08** basilica, corridor **09** concourse, Domdaniel, longhouse, vestibule **10** auditorium, passageway **11** concert hall **12** assembly hall, assembly room, entrance-hall **14** conference hall

See also **college**

hallmark

04 mark, sign **05** badge, stamp **06** device, emblem, symbol **09** brand-name, indicator, platemark, trademark **10** indication **12** official mark **13** official stamp **14** typical quality

hallo

02 hi **04** g'day **05** chimo, hello, hillo, hullo **06** holloa **07** welcome **09** greetings **11** good evening, good morning **13** good afternoon

hallowed

04 holy, tapu **06** age-old, sacred **07** blessed, revered **08** honoured **09** dedicated, venerable **10** inviolable, sacrosanct, sanctified **11** consecrated, established

hallucinate

04 trip **05** dream **07** imagine **08** daydream, freak out **09** fantasize, see things **10** see visions **13** imagine things

hallucination

04 trip **05** dream **06** mirage, vision **07** fantasy, figment **08** daydream, delirium, delusion, freak-out, illusion **09** autoscopy **10** apparition **14** phantasmagoria **15** hypnagogic image, hypnogogic image

halo

01 O **04** aura, ring **05** crown, glory

06 corona, gloria, nimbus **07** aureola, aureole **08** gloriole, halation, radiance **12** vesica piscis **13** circle of light

halt

03 alt, end **04** curb, lame, limp, quit, rest, stem, stop, wait **05** block, break, cease, check, close, crush, pause **06** arrest, desist, draw up, finish, impede, pull up **07** limping, respite **08** break off, crippled, deadlock, full stop, hold back, interval, obstruct, stoppage **09** cessation, stalemate, terminate, vacillate **10** call it a day, come to rest, desistance, put an end to, standstill **11** come to a rest, come to a stop, discontinue, termination **12** bring to a stop, draw to a close, interruption **13** bring to a close **14** breathing space, discontinuance **15** discontinuation

halting

06 broken **07** awkward **08** hesitant, laboured, unsteady **09** faltering, imperfect, stumbling, uncertain **10** stammering, stuttering

halve

◇ *insertion indicator*
05 sever, share, split **06** bisect, divide, lessen, reduce **07** cut down **09** cut in half **10** split in two **11** dichotomize **13** divide equally

halved

03 cut **05** split **06** shared **07** divided **08** bisected **09** dimidiate

ham

◇ *anagram indicator*
04 hock **05** hough **06** clumsy, coarse **07** amateur, overact, pigmeat **08** inexpert **10** prosciutto

ham-fisted

03 ham **05** gawky, inept **06** clumsy, thumby **07** awkward, unhandy **08** bungling **09** all thumbs, lumbering, maladroit, two-fisted, unskilful **10** blundering, cack-handed **11** heavy handed **13** accident-prone, unco-ordinated

hamlet

05 aldea, thorp **06** thorpe

hammer

◇ *anagram indicator*
02 ax **03** axe, din, hit **04** bang, bash, beat, drum, form, lick, make, mall, maul, pane, pean, peen, pein, pene, pick, plug, rout, slam, slap, slog **05** blame, bully, decry, dolly, drive, force, forge, gavel, grind, knock, madge, mould, pound, rivet, shape, slate **06** attack, batter, beetle, defeat, drudge, instil, keep on, labour, mallet, martel, monkey, oliver, plexor, sledge, strike, thrash **07** censure, clobber, condemn, dog-head, fashion, malleus, Mjölnir, outplay, persist, plessor, run down, trounce **08** malleate, Mjöllnir, overcome, trouncer, work away **09** criticize, denigrate, drive home, overwhelm, percussor, persevere, reiterate, slaughter **10** annihilate, claw hammer, sheep's-foot, tack hammer,

lt-hammer, trip hammer **11** about-
ledge, steam hammer, stone hammer,
walk all over, water hammer
2 sledgehammer **13** run rings round,
ear a strip off **14** knapping-hammer
5 make mincemeat of

hammer out
 anagram indicator
6 finish, settle **07** produce, resolve,
ort out, work out **08** complete
9 negotiate, thrash out
0 accomplish, bring about **12** carry
hrough

ammered
 anagram indicator
6 incuse **07** excudit

ammerhead
4 pane, pean, peen, pein, pene
5 umbre **07** Zygaena **08** umbrette
9 umber-bird

ammock support
4 clew, clue

amper
 anagram indicator
 containment indicator
3 box, pad, ped **04** curb, foil, stop,
uck **05** baulk, block, bribe, cabin,
heck, cramp, creel, pinch, seron
6 basket, bridle, fetter, hinder, hobble,
old up, impede, retard, seroon,
tymie, tangle, thwart **07** curtail,
istort, inhibit, pannier, prevent,
hackle **08** encumber, handicap,
ncumber, obstruct, restrain, restrict,
low down **09** container, frustrate,
amstring

amstring
3 hox **04** foil, hock, stop **05** baulk,
lock, check, cramp, hough
6 hinder, hold up, impede, stymie,
hwart **07** cripple, disable
8 encumber, handicap, paralyse,
estrain, restrict **09** frustrate
2 incapacitate

and
3 aid, fin, paw, pud **04** care, doer, fist,
ive, help, hond, mitt, palm, part, pass,
ide **05** arrow, manus, offer, power,
kill, style, touch, yield **06** author,
harge, convey, marker, needle,
ledge, script, stroke, submit, worker
7 acclaim, command, conduct,
ontrol, custody, deliver, ovation,
ointer, present, quarter, succour,
upport, workman, writing
8 applause, cheering, clapping,
lutches, employee, farm-hand,
andclap, hand over, hireling, labourer,
roducer, transmit **09** authority,
irection, handiwork, indicator,
nfluence, operative, performer,
ignature, workwoman **10** assistance,
nanagement, penmanship, possession
1 calligraphy, handwriting, helping
and, supervision **12** manual worker
3 participation **14** responsibility
5 instrumentality, round of applause
• **at hand**
4 near, nigh **05** close, handy, ready
6 to hand, toward **08** imminent

09 available, to the fore **10** accessible
11 forthcoming, in the offing **13** about
to happen
• **by hand**
07 à la main **08** manually **13** with your
hands **14** using your hands
• **from hand to mouth**
09 in poverty **10** insecurely
11 dangerously, uncertainly **12** au jour
le jour, from day to day, precariously
14 on the breadline
• **hand down**
04 give, will **05** grant, leave **06** pass on
07 devolve **08** bequeath, pass down,
transfer
• **hand in glove**
09 in cahoots **11** very closely
• **hand in hand**
12 holding hands **13** with hands held
14 closely related **15** closely together,
with hands joined
• **hand on**
04 give **06** pass on, supply **08** transfer,
transmit **09** surrender **14** let someone
have
• **hand out**
04 dole **07** deal out, dish out, give out,
mete out, pass out **08** dispense, share
out **10** distribute **11** disseminate
• **hand over**
04 give, pass, turn **05** yield **06** donate,
give up, render **07** consign, deliver,
present, release **08** transfer, turn over
09 surrender **10** relinquish
• **hollow of hand**
04 vola
• **in hand**
05 put by, ready, spare **07** à la main
08 under way **09** available, in reserve
10 attended to, considered **12** under
control **14** being dealt with
• **on the other hand**
03 but **04** then **05** again
12 contrariwise
• **out of hand**
◇ *anagram indicator*
06 at once **11** immediately **12** out of
control
• **to hand**
04 near **05** close, handy, ready **06** at
hand, nearby **07** ad manum
08 imminent **09** available
10 accessible **13** about to happen
• **try your hand**
03 try **04** seek **06** strive **07** attempt,
have a go **09** have a shot, have a stab
10 have a crack **13** see if you can do
• **win hands down**
09 win easily **15** win effortlessly
• **winning hand**
04 post

handbag
04 caba, grip **05** cabas, purse
07 holdall **08** handgrip, reticule
09 clutch bag, flight bag, vanity bag
10 pocketbook **11** shoulder bag

handbill
05 flier **06** letter, notice **07** leaflet
08 circular, flysheet, pamphlet
09 throwaway **12** announcement
13 advertisement

handbook
03 ABC **05** guide **06** manual
08 Baedeker **09** companion,
guidebook, vade-mecum
10 prospectus **11** enchiridion
12 encheiridion **15** instruction book

handcuff
03 tie **04** cuff **06** fasten, fetter, secure
07 manacle, shackle **08** bracelet,
snitcher, wristlet

handcuffs
05 cuffs, snaps **07** darbies, fetters,
mittens, nippers **08** manacles,
shackles, snippers **09** bracelets,
snitchers, wristlets

handful
03 few, rip **04** hank, pain, pest, ripp
05 bunch, pugil **06** bother, little
07 fistful, loofful **08** nieveful, nuisance
10 scattering, smattering, sprinkling
11 small amount, small number
13 pain in the neck **15** thorn in the
flesh

handgun
03 gat, gun, rod **04** iron **05** piece
06 pistol **07** sidearm **08** culverin,
revolver **09** derringer **10** six-shooter
11 blunderbuss
See also **gun**

handicap
03 hcp **04** curb **05** block, check, limit
06 bridle, burden, defect, hamper,
hinder, impair, impede, retard
07 barrier, disable, half-one, penalty
08 drawback, encumber, hold back,
obstacle, obstruct, restrict
09 hindrance **10** constraint, disability,
impairment, impediment, limitation
11 abnormality, encumbrance,
obstruction, restriction, shortcoming
12 disadvantage **14** stumbling-block
• **concede as handicap**
03 owe
• **with adverse handicap**
04 plus
• **with a handicap of**
03 off

handicapped
08 disabled **10** challenged
13 disadvantaged, incapacitated

handicraft
03 art **05** craft, skill **08** artifice,
handwork **09** craftwork, handiwork,
scrimshaw **11** scrimshandy,
workmanship **12** scrimshander
13 craftsmanship

handily
06 at hand, nearly, to hand **07** adeptly,
readily **08** adroitly, cleverly, usefully
09 helpfully, skilfully **10** accessibly
11 practically, within reach
12 conveniently

handiwork
03 art **04** hand, work **05** craft, doing,
skill **06** action, design, result
07 product **08** creation **09** craftwork,
invention **10** handicraft, production
11 achievement, artisanship,

workmanship **13** craftsmanship **14** responsibility

handkerchief
03 rag **04** wipe **05** blind, fogle, hanky, romal, rumal **06** hankie, napkin, tissue **07** bandana, foulard, Kleenex®, nose-rag, orarium, snotrag **08** kerchief, monteith, mouchoir **09** muckender
• **keep in a handkerchief**
04 mail

handle
03 bow, lug, paw **04** bail, feel, grip, haft, hilt, hold, knob, name, work **05** brake, drive, grasp, shaft, staff, stale, steal, steel, steer, steil, stele, stock, sweep, touch, treat, wield **06** behave, deal in, finger, fondle, manage, market, pick up, steale, tackle **07** control, discuss, operate, trade in, traffic **08** cope with, deal with, handgrip **09** handstaff, supervise **10** plough-tree, take care of **11** plough-stilt **12** be in charge of, do business in

handling
07 conduct, running **08** approach, managing **09** direction, operation, treatment **10** discussion, management **11** transaction **12** manipulation **14** administration

handout
04 alms, dole **05** gifts, issue, share **07** charity, freebie, leaflet **08** brochure, bulletin, circular, largesse, pamphlet **09** statement **10** free sample, literature **12** press release

handover
04 move **05** shift **06** change **07** removal **08** transfer **10** assignment, changeover, conveyance, relocation **12** displacement, transference, transmission **13** transposition

hand-picked
05 elect, élite **06** choice, chosen, picked, select **08** screened, selected **09** recherché

hands
02 hh

handsome
04 fair, fine **05** ample, brave, dishy, hunky, large, noble **06** comely, lavish, seemly **07** elegant, featous, liberal, sizable, stately **08** abundant, becoming, feateous, featuous, generous, gorgeous, gracious, sizeable, suitable **09** bountiful, dignified, featurely, goodfaced, plentiful, unsparing **10** attractive, convenient, personable, unstinting **11** good-looking, magnanimous **12** considerable

handsomely
05 amply **06** richly **08** lavishly **09** carefully, liberally **10** abundantly, generously, graciously **11** bountifully, plentifully, unsparingly **12** munificently, unstintingly **13** magnanimously

handwriting
03 paw **04** fist, hand **05** Neski

06 Naskhi, Neskhi, niggle, scrawl, script **07** writing **08** half-text, join-hand, printing, scribble **09** autograph, character, court hand, scripture **10** penmanship **11** calligraphy, chirography, copperplate, running hand **13** secretary hand **15** Lombardic script

handy
04 deft, near **05** adept, gemmy, jemmy, ready **06** adroit, at hand, clever, expert, nearly, nimble, to hand, useful **07** helpful, skilful, skilled **08** handsome **09** available, dexterous, practical **10** accessible, convenient, functional, proficient **11** practicable, within reach

handyman
05 DIYer **08** factotum **09** odd-jobber, odd-jobman **10** bluejacket **15** Jack-of-all-trades

hang
03 fix, nub, sag **04** bend, damn, drop, flit, flop, glue, kill, kilt, lean, loll, pend **05** affix, cling, drape, drift, droop, float, hover, lynch, paste, put up, run up, scrag, stick, strap, swing, trail, truss **06** append, attach, cement, dangle, fasten, impend, linger, remain, string **07** execute, flutter, justify, meaning, stretch, suspend, turn off **08** hang down, string up **09** declivity **10** put to death **11** be suspended **13** suspercollate **15** send to the gibbet
• **get the hang of**
04 twig **05** grasp, learn **06** fathom, master **10** comprehend, understand **13** get the knack of
• **hang about**
04 lime, mike, stay **05** haunt **06** dawdle, linger, loiter, remain **07** hang out, persist **08** frequent **09** waste time **10** hang around **13** associate with **15** keep company with
• **hang back**
05 demur, stall **06** recoil **07** shy away **08** hesitate, hold back **10** shrink back, stay behind **11** be reluctant
• **hang down loosely**
03 lop
• **hang fire**
04 stop, wait **05** delay, stall, stick **06** hold on **08** hang back, hesitate, hold back **09** vacillate **13** procrastinate
• **hang on**
04 grip, wait **05** cling, grasp **06** append, clutch, endure, hold on, remain, rest on, turn on **07** carry on, hinge on, hold out, persist **08** continue, depend on, hold fast **09** persevere **14** be contingent on, be determined by **15** be conditional on
• **hang over**
04 loom **06** impend, menace **08** approach, threaten **10** be imminent, overshadow

hangdog
05 cowed **06** abject, guilty **07** furtive **08** cringing, defeated, downcast,

sneaking, wretched **09** miserable **10** browbeaten, shamefaced

hanger-on
05 toady **06** client, lackey, minion, sponge **07** flunkey, sponger **08** follower, henchman, parasite **09** courtling, dependant, dependent, sycophant **10** freeloader

hanging
04 drop **05** drape, loose, tapis **06** dossal, dossel, floppy **07** curtain, drapery, draping, frontal, pendant, pendent, pending, pensile **08** dangling, downcast, drooping, flapping, flopping, parament, swingin **09** drop-scene, pendulous, suspende **10** suspending, unattached **11** antependium, unsupported

hangman
07 lockman, topsman **08** rascally **09** Jack Ketch **11** nubbing-cove

hang-out
03 den **04** dive, home **05** haunt, join local, patch **12** meeting-place, watering-hole **14** stamping-ground

hangover
08 survival **10** crapulence **12** after-effects, katzenjammer, morning after

hang-up
05 block, thing **06** phobia **07** probler **08** fixation, idée fixe, neurosis **09** obsession **10** difficulty, inhibition **11** mental block **13** preoccupation

hank
04 coil, fank, loop, roll, tuft **05** catch, piece, skein, twist **06** length **07** handful **08** selvagee

hanker
06 linger
• **hanker after, hanker for**
04 want **05** covet, crave **06** desire **07** itch for, long for, pine for, wish for **08** yearn for **09** hunger for, thirst for **10** be dying for **14** set your heart on

hankering
04 ache, itch, urge, wish **06** desire, hunger, pining, thirst **07** craving, longing **08** yearning

hankie, hanky *see* **handkerchief**

hanky-panky
05 fling **06** affair, tricks **07** carry-on, devilry **08** adultery, cheating, mischie nonsense, trickery **09** chicanery, deception **10** dishonesty, subterfuge **11** shenanigans **12** bit on the side, machinations **13** fooling around, funn business, jiggery-pokery, slap and tickle **14** how's-your-father, monkey business

haphazard
◊ *anagram indicator*
04 wild **06** casual, chance, random, randon **07** aimless, wildcat **08** careless, slapdash, slipshod **09** arbitrary, hit-or-miss, irregular, orderless, unplanned **10** disorderly, hitty-missy, tumultuary, willy-nilly

1 promiscuous **12** disorganized, unmethodical, unsystematic **14** indiscriminate, rough-and-tumble

haphazardly
◊ *anagram indicator*
6 wildly **08** by chance, randomly **10** carelessly, willy-nilly **11** arbitrarily, irregularly **14** unmethodically

hapless
6 cursed, jinxed **07** unhappy, unlucky **8** ill-fated, luckless, wretched **9** miserable **10** ill-starred **11** star-crossed, unfortunate

happen
2 be **03** hap **04** come, fall, find, go on, pass, tide **05** arise, ensue, hit on, occur, worth **06** appear, arrive, befall, chance, crop up, follow, result, turn up **7** develop, light on, perhaps, turn out **8** become of, bump into, chance on, come true, discover **09** come about, eventuate, run across, stumble on, supervene, take place, transpire **10** come across, come to pass **11** be the fate of, eventualize, materialize **3** come into being, present itself

happening
4 case **05** event, scene, thing, weird **6** action, affair, chance **07** episode **8** accident, business, incident, occasion **09** adventure, événement, occurrent **10** experience, occurrence, phenomenon **11** eventuality, fashionable, proceedings **2** circumstance

happily
6 gladly **07** luckily, merrily, perhaps **8** by chance, heartily, joyfully, joyously **09** agreeably, feliciter, fittingly, gleefully, willingly **0** cheerfully **11** contentedly, delightedly, fortunately, opportunely **2** auspiciously, propitiously **4** providentially

happiness
3 joy **04** glee, life, seal, seel, seil, sele **5** bliss **06** gaiety, heaven **07** delight, ecstasy, elation **08** delirium, euphoria, felicity, gladness, pleasure **9** beatitude, enjoyment, eudaemony, jog heaven, merriment, merriness **0** blitheness, cheeriness, eudaemonia, exuberance, joyfulness **1** contentment, good spirits, high spirits **12** cheerfulness

happy
◊ *anagram indicator*
3 apt, gay **04** glad **05** blest, jolly, lucky, merry, seely **06** blithe, elated, golden, jovial, joyful, joyous, proper **7** blessed, chuffed, content, exalted, fitting, gleeful, halcyon, helpful, pleased, radiant, smiling **08** apposite, carefree, cheerful, ecstatic, euphoric, gruntled, thrilled **09** cock-a-hoop, confident, contented, delighted, delirious, exuberant, fortunate, gratified, high-blest, opportune, overjoyed, rapturous, satisfied,

unworried **10** auspicious, beneficial, convenient, favourable, felicitous, propitious, starry-eyed, untroubled **11** appropriate, in a good mood, on cloud nine, over the moon, tickled pink, unconcerned **12** advantageous, happy as a clam, happy as Larry, light-hearted, walking on air **13** floating on air, in good spirits, in high spirits **15** happy as a sandboy, in seventh heaven, on top of the world
• **be happy**
03 ave

happy-go-lucky
06 blithe, casual **08** carefree, cheerful, heedless, reckless **09** easy-going, unworried **10** insouciant, nonchalant, untroubled **11** improvident, unconcerned **12** devil-may-care, light-hearted **13** irresponsible

harangue
05 orate, spout **06** lay off, preach, sermon, speech, spruik, tirade **07** address, declaim, lecture, oration **08** diatribe, perorate **09** hold forth, speechify **10** peroration, talky-talky **11** exhortation, paternoster **12** talkee-talkee

harass
◊ *anagram indicator*
03 dun, nag, vex **04** bait, cark, fret, tire **05** annoy, chevy, chivy, grind, harry, hound, pinch, press, trash, weary, worry **06** argufy, badger, bother, chivvy, harrow, hassle, infest, overdo, pester, pingle, plague, pursue, stress **07** afflict, disturb, dragoon, exhaust, fatigue, provoke, torment, trouble, trounce, turmoil, wear out **08** distract, distress, irritate **09** importune, persecute **10** antagonize, exasperate **11** have it in for **12** put the wind up

harassed
◊ *anagram indicator*
05 vexed **06** hunted **07** harried, hassled, hounded, plagued, uptight, worried **08** careworn, pestered, strained, stressed, troubled **09** pressured, tormented **10** distracted, distraught, distressed **11** pressurized, stressed-out, under stress **13** under pressure

harassment
05 grief **06** bother, hassle, molest **07** mobbing, torment, trouble **08** distress, nuisance, vexation **09** annoyance, badgering, pestering **10** irritation, pressuring **11** aggravation, bedevilment, molestation, persecution

harbinger
04 host, omen, sign **06** herald **07** pioneer, portent, warning **09** foretoken, messenger, precursor **10** forerunner, indication **12** avant-courier

harbour
◊ *containment indicator*
04 bear, dock, herd, hide, hold, keep, mole, port, quay **05** basin, haven,

house, lodge, nurse, reset, wharf **06** foster, marina, refuge, retain, shield, take in **07** believe, cherish, cling to, conceal, imagine, lodging, mooring, nurture, protect, receive, shelter **08** maintain **09** anchorage, entertain

hard
01 H **03** bad, raw, set **04** bony, busy, cold, firm, grim, keen, live, near, real, sore, true **05** badly, close, cruel, dense, flint, harsh, heavy, horny, irony, rigid, sharp, solid, stern, stiff, stony, tough **06** actual, bitter, busily, crusty, deeply, flinty, keenly, knotty, marble, potent, severe, stingy, strict, strong, tiring, wooden **07** acutely, arduous, austere, callous, certain, closely, compact, complex, eagerly, harmful, harshly, heavily, hornish, intense, onerous, painful, sharply, violent, zealous **08** baffling, definite, diligent, exacting, forceful, forcibly, freezing, intently, involved, narcotic, obdurate, pitiless, powerful, puzzling, reliable, rigorous, ruthless, scleroid, sedulous, severely, steadily, strongly, toilsome, uneasily, verified, vigorous **09** addictive, arduously, assiduous, carefully, compacted, condensed, difficult, earnestly, energetic, intensely, intricate, laborious, merciless, niggardly, resistant, strenuous, unfeeling, unpliable, unsparing, violently **10** compressed, critically, diligently, exhausting, forcefully, hard as iron, hard as rock, implacable, inflexible, oppressive, perplexing, powerfully, tyrannical, undeniable, unpleasant, unyielding, vigorously **11** assiduously, attentively, bewildering, cold-hearted, complicated, constrained, distressing, hard as flint, hard as stone, hard-hearted, hard-working, industrious, insensitive, intractable, laboriously, strenuously, troublesome, unrelenting **12** backbreaking, disagreeable, enthusiastic, habit-forming, impenetrable, indisputable **13** conscientious, energetically, industriously, reverberating, uncomfortable, unsympathetic **14** after a struggle, unquestionable, with difficulty **15** conscientiously
• **hard and fast**
03 set **05** fixed, rigid **06** strict **07** binding **08** definite **09** immutable, stringent **10** inflexible, invariable, unchanging **11** unalterable **12** unchangeable **14** uncompromising
• **hard black**
02 HB
• **hard up**
04 bust, poor, puir **05** broke, short, skint **07** boracic, lacking **08** bankrupt, dirt-poor, in the red, strapped **09** penniless **10** cleaned out, stony broke **11** impecunious, near the bone **12** impoverished, on your uppers **14** on your beam ends **15** strapped for cash
• **very hard**
02 HH

hard-bitten
05 tough **06** inured, shrewd
07 callous, cynical **08** ruthless
09 hard-nosed, practical, realistic,
toughened **10** hard-boiled, hard-
headed **11** down-to-earth **12** case-
hardened, matter-of-fact
13 unsentimental

hard-boiled
05 tough **06** brazen **07** callous,
cynical **09** practical **10** hard-headed
11 down-to-earth **13** unsentimental

hard-core
05 rigid **07** blatant, diehard, extreme,
staunch **08** explicit **09** dedicated,
obstinate, steadfast **12** intransigent
13 dyed-in-the-wool

harden
03 set **04** bake, cake, geal, gird
05 brace, chill, enure, flesh, inure,
nerve, steel, train **06** anneal, bronze,
deaden, endure, freeze, season,
temper **07** calcify, congeal, fortify,
petrify, stiffen, toughen **08** accustom,
buttress, concrete, indurate, sclerose,
solidify **09** habituate, reinforce,
vulcanize **10** case-harden, sclerotize,
strengthen, work-harden

hardened
03 set **06** inured **07** bronzed, callous,
chilled, chronic, coctile, steeled
08 habitual, obdurate, scleroid,
seasoned **09** reprobate, shameless,
toughened, unfeeling **10** accustomed,
habituated, inveterate **12** incorrigible,
irredeemable

hard-headed
05 sharp, tough **06** astute, shrewd
08 pitiless, rational, sensible **09** hard-
nosed, practical, pragmatic, realistic
10 cool-headed, hard-bitten, hard-
boiled **11** down-to-earth, level-
headed, tough-minded **12** businesslike
13 clear-thinking, unsentimental

hard-hearted
04 cold, hard **05** cruel, stony
06 unkind **07** callous, inhuman
08 pitiless, uncaring **09** heartless,
merciless, unfeeling **10** flint-heart
11 cold-blooded, unconcerned
12 stony-hearted **13** unsympathetic
14 marble-breasted

hard-hitting
04 bold **05** blunt, frank, tough
06 direct **08** critical, forceful, straight,
vigorous **09** unsparing **10** forthright
12 condemnatory **13** no-holds-barred
14 uncompromising

hardihood
04 grit, guts, risk **05** pluck **06** bottle,
daring, valour **07** bravery, courage
08 audacity, boldness, rashness
10 enterprise, robustness **11** intrepidity
12 fearlessness, recklessness
13 dauntlessness **15** adventurousness

hardiness
06 valour **07** courage **08** boldness
09 fortitude, toughness **10** resilience,

resolution, robustness, ruggedness,
sturdiness **11** intrepidity

hardline
05 tough **06** strict **07** extreme
08 militant **10** immoderate, inflexible,
unyielding **11** undeviating
12 intransigent **14** uncompromising

hardly
04 jimp, just **06** barely, jimply, uneath
07 harshly, none too **08** not at all, not
quite, only just, scarcely, severely
09 almost not, by no means **14** with
difficulty

hardness
06 rigour **07** granite **08** coldness,
firmness, rigidity, severity
09 harshness, sternness, toughness
10 difficulty, inhumanity
12 pitilessness **13** insensitivity,
laboriousness

hard-nosed
05 tough **08** ruthless **09** practical,
realistic **10** hard-bitten, hard-boiled,
hard-headed, no-nonsense
13 unsentimental

hard-pressed
06 pushed, strait **07** hard put, harried
08 harassed **09** in a corner, overtaxed
10 hard-pushed **11** under stress, up
against it **12** in a tight spot,
overburdened **13** under pressure

hardship
04 need, pain, want **05** trial **06** misery,
murder, rigour, strait, stress
07 burdens, penance, poverty, trouble
08 distress **09** adversity, austerity,
grievance, privation, suffering
10 affliction, difficulty, misfortune
11 depredation, deprivation,
destitution, tribulation
12 depredations

hardware
03 kit **04** gear **05** stuff, tools **06** outfit,
rig-out, tackle, things **08** articles,
supplies **09** apparatus, equipment,
furniture **10** appliances **11** accessories,
apparelment, ironmongery
13 accoutrements, paraphernalia

hard-wearing
05 stout, tough **06** rugged, strong,
sturdy **07** durable, lasting **08** well-
made **09** resilient **10** made to last
11 built to last

hard-working
04 busy, keen **07** zealous **08** diligent,
sedulous **09** assiduous, energetic
11 industrious **12** enthusiastic
13 conscientious

hardy
03 fit **04** bold, Olly **05** brave, sound,
stout, tough **06** daring, heroic, plucky,
robust, strong, sturdy, trusty
07 durable, healthy, spartan, stoical
08 fearless, impudent, indurate,
intrepid, resolute, stalwart, vigorous
09 confident, heavy-duty, indurated,
iron-sided, undaunted **10** courageous
11 indomitable **12** stout-hearted

hare
03 doe, wat **04** baud, bawd, buck,
mara, pika, puss, scut **06** hasten,
malkin, mawkin **07** leveret
08 baudrons **10** Dolichotis, jack
rabbit, sage rabbit, springhaas
14 snowshoe rabbit
See also **rabbit**

hare-brained
04 daft, rash, wild **05** giddy, inane, sill
06 scatty, stupid **07** foolish
08 careless, crackpot, headlong,
heedless, reckless **09** half-baked **12** il
conceived **14** scatterbrained

harem
05 serai **06** zenana **08** seraglio
• **room in a harem**
03 oda

hark
04 hear, mark, note **06** listen, notice
07 give ear, hearken, pay heed,
whisper **12** pay attention
• **hark back**
06 go back, hoicks, recall, revert
07 regress, try back **08** remember,
turn back **09** recollect

harlequin
04 fool, zany **05** clown, comic, joker
06 jester **07** buffoon **10** variegated

harlot
03 pro **04** base, lewd, loon, lown, slag
tart **05** hussy, lowne, tramp, whore
06 hooker **07** slapper, trollop, wagtail
08 callgirl, scrubber, strumpet
10 loose woman, prostitute **11** fallen
woman, working girl **12** streetwalker

harm
◇ *anagram indicator*
03 ill, mar **04** bane, evil, hurt, loss,
pain, ruin **05** abuse, annoy, scath, spoi
touch, wound, wreak, wrong
06 damage, impair, injure, injury,
misuse, molest, scathe **07** blemish,
destroy **08** ill-treat, maltreat
09 adversity, detriment, prejudice,
suffering, vengeance **10** disservice,
impairment, misfortune
11 destruction, work against **12** do
violence to **15** be detrimental to

harmful
03 bad, ill **04** evil **05** toxic **06** wicked
07 hurtful, noxious **08** damaging,
wounding **09** dangerous, hazardous,
injurious, poisonous, unhealthy
10 pernicious **11** deleterious,
destructive, detrimental,
unwholesome

harmless
04 mild, safe **05** silly **06** gentle
07 anodyne **08** -friendly, hurtless,
innocent, non-toxic **09** blameless,
innocuous, woundless **11** inoffensive

harmonious
06 dulcet, in sync, mellow **07** amiable
cordial, in synch, musical, tuneful
08 amicable, balanced, friendly,
matching, peaceful, pleasant, rhythmi
09 according, agreeable, congruous,

consonant, consonous, melodious, peaceable **10** Apollonian, compatible, concinnous, concordant, concordial, consistent, euphonious, like-minded **11** co-ordinated, harmonizing, mellifluous, sympathetic, symphonious **13** sweet-sounding

harmoniously
08 amicably **09** agreeably, cordially **10** compatibly, peacefully **11** congruously **12** consistently **13** symmetrically **14** in a balanced way **15** sympathetically

harmonization
08 matching **09** agreement, balancing **10** adaptation **11** arrangement **12** co-ordination **13** accommodation **14** correspondence, reconciliation

harmonize
02 go **03** mix **04** mesh, rime, suit, tone **05** adapt, agree, atone, blend, fit in, match, rhyme, salve **06** accord, attone **07** arrange, balance, compose, concord **08** coincide **09** get on with, reconcile **10** co-ordinate, correspond, go together **11** accommodate, be congruent, be congruous

harmony
04 tone, tune **05** amity, chime, music, peace, unity **06** accord, assent, melody, unison **07** balance, chiming, concent, concert, concord, euphony, keeping, oneness, rapport **08** blending, diapason, eurythmy, laburden, goodwill, symmetry, sympathy, symphony **09** agreement, concentus, eurhythmy, unanimity **10** concinnity, conformity, consonance, consonancy **11** amicability, concurrence, consistence, consistency, co-operation, tunefulness **12** co-ordination, friendliness, thorough bass **13** compatibility, melodiousness, understanding **14** correspondence, correspondency, like-mindedness **15** mellifluousness
• **in harmony**
08 together **15** never a cross word
• **out of harmony**
04 ajar

harness
03 use **04** gear, tack, team **05** apply, hitch, put to, trace **06** employ, straps, tackle **07** channel, control, exploit, gearing, hitch up, utilize **08** mobilize, tackling **09** equipment, make use of **10** baby-jumper **11** baby-bouncer **13** accoutrements
• **in harness**
04 busy **06** active, at work **07** working **08** employed, together **11** co-operating **13** collaborating, in co-operation

harp
04 kora, lyre **05** nebel **06** trigon **07** sambuca **08** clarsach **09** harmonica **10** mouth organ
• **harp on**
03 nag **05** grind, press, renew **06** labour, repeat **07** dwell on **09** go

on about, reiterate **11** flog to death, keep on about **14** go on and on about

harpoon
03 peg **04** barb, dart **05** arrow, spear **06** fisgig, fizgig, grains **07** fishgig, trident **10** toggle iron

harpsichord
06 spinet **07** cembalo, spinnet **08** clavecin, spinette, virginal **09** virginals **12** clavicembalo **15** pair of virginals

harridan
03 hag, nag **04** fury **05** harpy, scold, shrew, vixen, witch **06** dragon, gorgon, tartar, virago **07** hell-cat **09** battle-axe, termagant, Xanthippe

harried
05 beset **07** anxious, hassled, plagued, ravaged, worried **08** agitated, bothered, harassed, troubled **09** pressured, tormented **10** distressed **11** hard-pressed, pressurized

harrow
04 drag, haro **05** brake, herse, wring **09** pitch-pole, pitch-poll
• **point of harrow**
04 tine

harrowing
05 rough **08** alarming, daunting, lacerant **09** agonizing, traumatic, upsetting **10** disturbing, perturbing, terrifying, tormenting **11** distressing, frightening **12** excruciating, heart-rending, nerve-racking

harry
03 nag, vex **05** annoy, hound, worry **06** badger, bother, chivvy, harass, hassle, molest, pester, plague, ravage **07** destroy, disturb, oppress, plunder, torment, trouble **09** persecute **10** pressurize

harsh
03 raw **04** bold, grim, hard, iron, rude, wild **05** asper, bleak, cruel, gaudy, gruff, lurid, rough, sharp, showy, stark, stern, stoor, stour, sture **06** barren, bitter, bright, brutal, coarse, flashy, garish, hoarse, savage, severe, shrill, stowre, strict, unkind **07** acerbic, austere, cracked, glaring, grating, hostile, inhuman, jarring, rasping, raucous, spartan **08** abrasive, croaking, dazzling, desolate, gravelly, grinding, guttural, jangling, metallic, pitiless, rigorous, ruthless, scabrous, strident **09** barbarian, barbarous, dissonant, Draconian, inclement, merciless, unfeeling, untunable **10** discordant, unpleasant, untuneable **11** comfortless, ear-piercing **12** inhospitable **13** unsympathetic

harshly
04 hard **06** grimly, hardly **07** cruelly, gruffly, roughly, sharply, sternly **08** brutally, hoarsely, severely, unkindly **10** pitilessly, ruthlessly, stridently **11** mercilessly **12** discordantly, unpleasantly

harshness
06 rigour **07** tyranny **08** acerbity, acrimony, asperity, hardness, severity, sourness **09** austerity, brutality, ill-temper, roughness, starkness, sternness **10** bitterness, coarseness, strictness **12** abrasiveness

harum-scarum
04 rash, wild **05** hasty **06** scatty **07** erratic **08** careless, reckless **09** haphazard, impetuous, imprudent **11** hare-brained, precipitate **12** disorganized **13** ill-considered, irresponsible **14** scatterbrained

harvest
02 in **03** mow **04** crop, gain, kirn, pick, rabi, reap **05** amass, glean, horde, pluck, stock, store, yield **06** autumn, effect, fruits, garner, gather, hairst, hockey, obtain, result, return, secure, silage, supply **07** acquire, collect, hopping, produce, product, reaping, returns **08** gather in, ingather, Spätlese, vendange **10** accumulate, collection, harvesting **11** consequence, harvest-home, harvest-time, ingathering **12** accumulation **13** tattie-howking, tattie-lifting

has
◇ *juxtaposition indicator*
01 's **04** hath
• **has not, hasn't**
03 an't

hash
◇ *anagram indicator*
04 hack, mash, mess, stew **05** botch, mince, mix-up **06** bungle, hachis, hotpot, jumble, muddle, scouse **07** goulash, hashish **08** mishmash **09** confusion, lobscouse, pound sign **10** hotchpotch, lob's course **11** olla-podrida **13** mismanagement

hashish
03 pot **04** dope, hash, hemp, weed **05** bhang, ganja, grass **08** cannabis **09** marijuana **12** electric puha

hassium
02 Hs

hassle
03 bug **04** fuss **05** aggro, annoy, fight, harry, hound, trial, upset **06** badger, bother, chivvy, harass, mither, moider, pester, strife **07** dispute, moither, problem, quarrel, trouble, wrangle **08** argument, nuisance, squabble, struggle **09** bickering **10** difficulty **11** altercation **12** disagreement **13** inconvenience

hassled
05 vexed **07** harried, hounded, plagued, uptight, worried **08** careworn, harassed, pestered, strained, stressed, troubled **09** pressured, tormented **10** distraught, distressed **11** pressurized, stressed-out, under stress **13** under pressure

hassock
04 pouf 06 pouffe 07 kneeler
09 footstool

haste
03 hie 04 post, rush 05 hurry, speed
06 bustle, hasten, hustle, scurry
07 urgency 08 alacrity, celerity,
despatch, dispatch, fastness, rapidity,
rashness, velocity 09 briskness,
quickness, swiftness 10 expedience
11 impetuosity 12 carelessness,
precipitance, precipitancy,
recklessness 13 foolhardiness,
impulsiveness, precipitation
15 expeditiousness
• in haste
04 fast, rash 05 apace 06 subito
07 hotfoot, quickly, rapidly 08 in a
hurry, promptly, speedily
12 straightaway

hasten
03 aid, fly, hie, ren, rin, run 04 bolt,
dash, help, race, rush, spur, tear, urge
05 boost, hurry, press, speed 06 assist,
bustle, go fast, hustle, sprint, step up
07 advance, be quick, forward, hurry
up, quicken, speed up 08 despatch,
dispatch, expedite, step on it 09 go
quickly, hotfoot it, make haste
10 accelerate, get a move on
11 precipitate, push forward 12 step on
the gas 15 put your foot down

hastily
04 fast 05 apace 06 rashly 07 quickly,
rapidly 08 chop-chop, promptly,
speedily 09 hurriedly 10 heedlessly,
recklessly 11 double-quick,
impetuously, impulsively
12 straightaway 13 precipitately

hasty
04 fast, rash 05 brief, brisk, eager,
quick, rapid, short, swift 06 prompt,
rushed, speedy, sudden 07 cursory,
hurried, running 08 careless, fleeting,
headlong, heedless, reckless
09 desultory, festinate, hotheaded,
impatient, impetuous, impulsive,
irritable 10 transitory 11 expeditious,
perfunctory, precipitant, precipitate,
subitaneous, thoughtless

hat
03 lid, nab 04 tile 06 titfer
09 headpiece 10 upper crust

Hats include:

03 cap, fez, sun, taj, tam, tin, top, toy
04 doek, hard, hood, kepi, poke, tall
05 beret, Bronx, busby, derby, mitre,
   mutch, opera, shako, snood, straw,
   tammy, toque, tuque
06 beanie, beaver, biggin, boater,
   bobble, bonnet, bowler, chapka,
   cloche, fedora, helmet, kalpak,
   mob-cap, panama, pileus, sailor,
   trilby, turban
07 bicorne, biretta, bycoket, Cossack,
   flat-cap, Homburg, leghorn,
   montero, picture, pill-box, pork-
   pie, stetson, tricorn
08 balmoral, bearskin, chaperon, fool's

cap, nightcap, skullcap, sombrero,
tricorne, yarmulka
09 Balaclava, cock's-comb, dunce's
   cap, forage cap, glengarry, jockey
   cap, muffin-cap, peaked cap,
   school cap, sou'wester, stovepipe,
   sun bonnet, ten-gallon
10 cockernony, college cap, hunting-
   cap, Kilmarnock, pith helmet,
   poke-bonnet
11 baseball cap, crash helmet,
   deerstalker, mortar-board, tam-o'-
   shanter, trencher cap
12 cheesecutter, hummle bonnet,
   Scotch bonnet

See also **straw hat** *under* **straw**
• **shade attached to hat**
04 ugly

hatch
◇ *anagram indicator*
04 plan, plot 05 breed, brood, cleck,
covey, sit on 06 clutch, design, devise,
invent, scheme 07 concoct, develop,
dream up, exclude, guichet, project,
think up 08 conceive, contrive,
disclose, incubate 09 formulate,
originate

hatchet
03 axe 07 chopper, cleaver, machete,
mattock, pickaxe 08 tomahawk
09 battle-axe, hedgebill 11 hedging-
bill

hate
02 ug 04 whit 05 abhor, spite
06 detest, enmity, grudge, hatred,
loathe, regret 07 be loath, be sorry,
despise, dislike, ill-will, rancour
08 aversion, execrate, loathing, not
stand 09 abominate, animosity,
apologize, hostility 10 abhorrence,
antagonism, bitterness, recoil from,
resentment 11 abomination, be
reluctant, be unwilling 15 feel
revulsion at
• **pet hate**
04 bane, bogy 05 bogle, dread, fiend,
poker 06 horror 07 bugbear, rawhead
08 anathema 09 bête noire, nightmare

hateful
04 evil, foul, loth, vile 05 loath, nasty
06 cursed, damned, goddam, horrid,
odious 07 goddamn, heinous
08 damnable, horrible 09 abhorrent,
execrable, goddamned, loathsome,
obnoxious, offensive, repellent,
repugnant, repulsive, revolting
10 abominable, despicable,
detestable, disgusting, unpleasant
11 abhominable 12 contemptible,
disagreeable

hating
04 miso-

hatred
04 hate 05 odium, spite 06 animus,
enmity, grudge, phobia 07 despite,
disgust, dislike, ill-will, phobism,
rancour 08 aversion, haterent, loathing
09 animosity, antipathy, hostility,
malignity, revulsion 10 abhorrence,

antagonism, bitterness, execration,
repugnance, resentment
11 abomination, detestation

haughtily
07 proudly 08 snootily 10 arrogantly,
cavalierly, scornfully 11 imperiously
12 disdainfully 14 contemptuously,
superciliously

haughtiness
04 airs 05 pride 06 hubris, morgue
07 conceit, disdain, hauteur
08 contempt 09 aloofness, arrogance,
insolence, loftiness, pomposity
10 hogen-mogen, snootiness
12 snobbishness

haughty
04 bold, haut, high, vain 05 hault, lofty,
proud, surly 06 haught, lordly, snooty,
superb 07 paughty, stuck-up
08 arrogant, assuming, cavalier,
fastuous, orgulous, scornful, snobbish,
stomachy, superior, toplofty
09 conceited, imperious, orgillous
10 disdainful, hoity-toity, stomachful,
stomachous 11 cavalierish, egotistical,
overbearing, patronizing, stiff-necked,
toploftical 12 contemptuous,
supercilious 13 condescending, high
and mighty, self-important, swollen-
headed 14 proud-stomached 15 on
your high horse

haul
03 lug, rug, tow, tug 04 cart, drag,
draw, find, gain, harl, hump, loot, mess,
move, pull, push, ship, swag, wind
05 booty, bouse, bowse, brail, carry,
catch, heave, scoop, slack, touse,
touze, towse, towze, trail, trice, wince,
winch, yield 06 convey, convoy, spoils
07 plunder, takings 09 transport

haunches
04 hips, rump 05 hucks, nates
06 thighs 07 huckles, hunkers, rear
end 08 buttocks

haunt
03 den 04 houf, howf, walk 05 beset,
curse, ghost, harry, houff, howff, local,
recur, spook, visit, worry 06 burden,
obsess, plague, prey on, resort, show
up 07 disturb, hangout, inhabit,
oppress, possess, spright, torment,
trouble 08 frequent 09 honky-tonk,
patronize 10 rendezvous 11 hang
about in, materialize, spend time in
12 hang around in, meeting-place
13 appear often in, favourite spot
14 stamping-ground, visit regularly

haunted
05 eerie 06 cursed, jinxed, spooky
07 ghostly, plagued, worried
08 infested, obsessed, troubled
09 hag-ridden, possessed, tormented
10 frequented 11 preoccupied

haunting
08 poignant 09 evocative,
memorable, nostalgic, recurrent
10 persistent 11 atmospheric
13 unforgettable

auteur
4 airs 05 pride 06 hubris 07 conceit,
isdain 08 contempt 09 aloofness,
rrogance, insolence, loftiness,
omposity 10 snootiness
1 haughtiness 12 snobbishness

ave
2 ha', 've 03 ask, bid, con, eat, get,
ae, han, own, put, use 04 bear, down,
upe, feel, find, fool, gain, gulp, hold,
eep, know, make, meet, must, show,
ke, tell 05 abide, allow, beget, brook,
heat, drink, enjoy, force, order, ought,
and, trick 06 accept, assert, coerce,
ompel, devour, diddle, embody,
ndure, enjoin, esteem, guzzle, oblige,
btain, permit, secure, should, suffer,
ke in 07 acquire, arrange, be given,
ause to, command, consume, contain,
eceive, develop, display, embrace,
xhibit, express, include, possess,
rocure, put away, receive, request,
equire, swallow, swindle, undergo
8 be forced, comprise, contract,
anifest, organize, persuade, submit
o, talk into, tolerate, tuck into, wolf
own 09 be obliged, consist of,
ncounter, go through, knock back,
artake of, put up with, succumb to
0 be required, bring forth,
omprehend, experience, suffer from,
ke part in 11 be compelled,
emonstrate, give birth to, incorporate,
revail upon 13 be delivered of, be
ubjected to, participate in
  have had it
6 be lost 10 be defeated, have no
ope 11 be exhausted, be in trouble,
ite the dust
  have on
3 kid, rag 04 hoax, wear 05 chaff,
ease, trick 11 be clothed in, be
ressed in, have planned, play a joke on
2 have arranged, take for a ride
3 wind someone up 15 pull
omeone's leg

aven
3 bay 04 dock, port 05 basin, hithe,
asis 06 asylum, harbor, refuge
7 harbour, retreat, shelter
9 anchorage, sanctuary

aversack
6 kitbag 08 backpack, knapsack,
ucksack

avoc
anagram indicator
4 Hell, ruin 05 chaos, waste, wreck
6 damage, mayhem 08 disorder,
avaging, shambles, wreckage
9 confusion, ruination 10 desolation,
isruption 11 destruction, devastation,
ack and ruin 12 depopulation,
espoliation

Hawaii
2 HI

awk
3 cry 04 bark, eyas, kite, nyas, sell,
oar, sore, tout, vend 05 offer, soare,
ant 06 falcon, keelie, market, peddle,
arcel, tarsal, tarsel, tassel, tercel

07 buzzard, goshawk, haggard, harrier,
tassell, tiercel 08 brancher, huckster
10 eyas-musket 11 sparrowhawk
12 honey buzzard, offer for sale
• **accustom hawk to handling**
03 man

hawker
04 spiv 05 crier 06 auceps, cadger,
coster, dealer, mugger, pedlar, seller,
sutler, trader, vendor 07 camelot,
chapman, slanger, tranter 08 huckster
09 barrow-boy, cheap-jack, cheap
John 10 colporteur 11 speech-crier
12 costermonger
• **hawker's round**
04 walk

hawseholes
04 eyes

hawthorn
05 quick, thorn 07 may tree
08 cockspur 09 albespine, albespyne,
mayflower, thornbush, thorntree
10 quickthorn, whitethorn

hay
• **bundle of hay**
03 wad, wap 04 wise, wisp 06 bottle
• **pile of hay**
03 mow 04 cock, rick 05 stack
07 haycock 08 haystack

haywire
◇ *anagram indicator*
03 mad 04 wild 05 crazy, wrong
07 chaotic, tangled 08 confused
10 disordered, topsy-turvy
12 disorganized, out of control

hazard
04 jump, luck, risk, wage 05 offer,
peril, stake, wager 06 bunker, chance,
danger, gamble, menace, niffer, risque,
submit, threat 07 pitfall, suggest,
venture 08 accident, endanger,
jeopardy 09 deathtrap, hazardize, put
at risk, speculate 10 jeopardize, put
forward 12 endangerment 13 put in
jeopardy 14 expose to danger

hazardous
04 nice 05 hairy, risky 06 chancy,
queasy, queazy, tricky, unsafe
07 chancey 08 insecure, menacing,
perilous 09 dangerous, difficult,
uncertain 10 jeopardous, precarious
11 threatening 13 unpredictable

hazardously
07 riskily 10 insecurely, perilously
11 dangerously, uncertainly
12 jeopardously, precariously
13 unpredictably

haze
03 fog, rag 04 blur, daze, film, mist,
smog 05 bully, cloud, steam
06 muddle, vapour 07 dimness
09 confusion, fogginess, mistiness,
obscurity, smokiness, vagueness
10 cloudiness 11 uncertainty
12 bewilderment 14 indistinctness

hazelnut
03 cob 06 cobnut 07 filberd, filbert
12 Barcelona nut

hazy
◇ *anagram indicator*
03 dim 05 faint, foggy, fuzzy, milky,
misty, muzzy, smoky, vague 06 cloudy,
veiled, woolly 07 blurred, clouded,
misting, obscure, unclear
08 confused, nebulous, overcast
09 uncertain 10 ill-defined, indefinite,
indistinct

head
◇ *head selection indicator*
03 cop, nab, nob, nut, pow, ras, ren, rin,
run, tip, top, van, wit 04 apex, bean,
bent, boss, cape, conk, face, fizz,
foam, fore, gift, lead, loaf, main, mind,
ness, pash, pate, peak, poll, rise, rule,
suds, tête, wits 05 bonce, brain, caput,
chair, chief, crest, crown, first, flair,
fount, front, froth, guide, knack, onion,
power, prime, ruler, sense, skill, skull,
steer, title 06 bigwig, brains, charge,
climax, crisis, crunch, direct, genius,
govern, height, lather, leader, manage,
mazard, napper, noddle, noggin,
noodle, origin, source, spring, summit,
talent, vertex, wisdom 07 ability,
aptness, bubbles, captain, command,
control, cranium, crumpet, dilemma,
faculty, go first, heading, headway,
highest, leading, manager, obverse,
oversee, premier, supreme, thought,
topknot, topmost 08 aptitude,
calamity, capacity, chairman, controls,
director, dominant, facility, foremost,
governor, headland, pressure, strength,
vanguard, wellhead 09 attribute, be
first in, big cheese, capitulum,
commander, emergency, endowment,
forefront, intellect, mentality,
president, principal, reasoning,
supervise, top banana 10 administer,
capability, chairwoman, controller,
grey matter, headmaster, leadership,
management, pre-eminent,
supervisor, upper crust, upperworks,
wellspring 11 catastrophe,
chairperson, common sense, head
teacher, proficiency, superintend,
supervision, upper storey 12 be in
charge of, directorship, headmistress,
intelligence 13 administrator, be in
control of, critical point, understanding
14 be at the front of, superintendent
15 little grey cells, mental abilities

See also **toilet**

• **fox's head**
04 mask
• **go to your head**
06 puff up 08 befuddle 09 inebriate,
make dizzy, make drunk, make proud,
make woozy 10 intoxicate 12 make
arrogant 13 make conceited
• **head for**
06 aim for 07 make for, point to, turn
for 08 steer for 09 go towards
11 move towards 13 direct towards,
travel toward
• **head off**
◇ *head deletion indicator*
04 stop 05 avert 06 cut off, divert
07 deflect, fend off, prevent, ward off

09 forestall, intercept, interpose, intervene, turn aside

• **head over heels**
◇ *reversal down indicator*
06 wildly **07** utterly **08** headlong
09 intensely **10** completely, recklessly, thoroughly **14** uncontrollably, wholeheartedly

• **head up**
04 lead **06** direct, manage **12** be in charge of, take charge of

• **keep your head**
08 keep calm **12** keep your cool

• **lose your head**
◇ *head deletion indicator*
04 flap **05** panic **08** freak out **12** lose your cool

• **muffle head**
03 mob

• **top of head**
04 nole, noll, noul, nowl **05** noule

headache
04 bane, head, pest **05** worry
06 bother, hassle **07** problem, trouble
08 migraine, nuisance, splitter, vexation **09** neuralgia **10** hemicrania
11 cephalalgia **13** inconvenience, pain in the neck

headdress

Headdresses include:

03 cap, taj
04 coif, head, kell, tête, tire
05 mitre, tower
06 cornet, modius, pinner, turban
07 commode, coronet, kufiyah
08 coiffure, fontange, fool's cap, head-tire, joncanoe, junkanoo, kaffiyeh, keffiyeh, ship-tire, stephane
09 John Canoe, John Kanoo, porrenger, porringer, war bonnet
10 lappet-head
11 tire-valiant
13 feather-bonnet

See also **hat**; **helmet**; **scarf**

headgear
03 hat, jiz, lid, wig **04** call, caul, gizz, hood, tiar **05** crown, tiara **07** coronet
08 silly-how

See also **hat**; **helmet**; **scarf**

heading
◇ *head selection indicator*
04 head, name, text **05** class, point, title **06** header, rubric **07** bearing, caption, section, subject **08** category, division, headline **09** direction
10 capitulary, descriptor, letterhead
14 classification

See also **compass**

headland
03 ras **04** cape, head, naze, ness, noup, scaw, skaw **05** morro, point
07 headrig **08** foreland
10 promontory

headless
◇ *head deletion indicator*
07 trunked **10** acephalous, leaderless
11 decapitated

headlong
04 rash **05** ahead, hasty, steep
06 rashly, wildly **07** hastily, ramstam, tantivy **08** careless, full tilt, pell-mell, proclive, reckless **09** breakneck, dangerous, head first, hurriedly, impetuous, impulsive **10** carelessly, heedlessly, recklessly **11** hair-brained, hare-brained, impetuously, impulsively, precipitate, prematurely **12** hand over head **13** precipitately, thoughtlessly
15 without thinking

headman
05 chief, ruler **06** ataman, leader, sachem **07** captain **08** caboceer, mocuddum, mokaddam, muqaddam, starosta **09** chieftain

head-on
06 direct **08** straight **10** straight-on
11 full-frontal

headquarters
02 HQ **04** base, hall **05** depot, SHAPE
06 armory, Temple **07** station **08** base camp, Pentagon **10** head office, main office, officialty, praetorium
11 command post, nerve centre, officiality

headstone
06 plaque **08** memorial
09 tombstone **10** gravestone
11 cornerstone

headstrong
06 unruly, wilful **07** wayward, willful
08 contrary, obdurate, perverse, stubborn **09** obstinate, pigheaded
10 refractory, self-willed **11** intractable
12 intransigent, recalcitrant, ungovernable

headway
03 way **06** ground **07** advance
08 distance, movement, progress
11 development, improvement

headwear *see* **headgear**

heady
04 rash **05** nappy **06** potent, strong
07 huff-cap, rousing, violent
08 ecstatic, euphoric, exciting, inflamed **09** thrilling **11** stimulating
12 exhilarating, intoxicating, invigorating, overpowering

heal
04 cure, hide, mend, sain **05** cover, salve, treat **06** balsam, garish, physic, recure, remedy, settle, soothe
07 assuage, comfort, conceal, guarish, improve, patch up, restore **08** make good, make well, palliate, put right, set right **09** cicatrize, incarnate, reconcile
10 make better **12** conglutinate

healer
03 Asa

See also **doctor**

health
04 form, heal, tone, trim **05** shape, state, toast **06** fettle, sanity, vigour
07 fitness, welfare **08** strength
09 condition, good shape,

soundness, wellbeing **10** robustness
11 healthiness **12** constitution **13** goo condition

• **good health**
04 tope **06** cheers, kia-ora
07 cheerio, slàinte, wassail **08** chin-chin, waes hail **09** bene vobis, drink hail **10** Gesundheit **12** mud in your e

healthily
04 well **07** soundly **08** robustly, strongly **10** vigorously **11** in conditio in good shape **12** in fine fettle

healthy
03 fit **04** fine, good, hale, well, wise
05 hardy, jolly, lusty, sound **06** robust strong, sturdy **07** bracing, lustick, prudent **08** blooming, lustique, sensible, thriving, vigorous
09 healthful, in the pink, judicious, wholesome **10** able-bodied, beneficial, hartie-hale, healthsome, nourishing, nutritious, refreshing, salubrious, successful **11** flourishing, condition, in good shape, right as rair stimulating **12** considerable, fit as a fiddle, in fine fettle, invigorating, well-disposed **13** hale and hearty

heap
03 lot, mow, pit, pot **04** a lot, bank, bing, bulk, cock, load, lots, mass, pile pots, raff, raft, rick, ruck, ruin, tass, tor
05 amass, build, cairn, clamp, drift, hoard, loads, mound, stack, store
06 bestow, bundle, burden, confer, gather, lavish, lumber, midden, oodle pile up, plenty, quarry, rickle, scores, shower, stacks, supply, toorie
07 collect, company, congest, cumulus, store up, uphoard
08 assemble, cumulate, dunghill, lashings, millions, molehill, mountain
09 abundance, congeries, embroglio great deal, imbroglio, stockpile
10 accumulate, acervation, assemblage, coacervate, collection, quantities **12** accumulation
13 agglomeration, kitchen midden
14 clearance cairn

hear
◇ *homophone indicator*
03 get, try **04** heed **05** catch, judge, learn **06** be told, gather, listen, pick u take in **07** examine, find out, inquire, make out **08** consider, discover, overhear, perceive **09** ascertain, eavesdrop, latch onto **10** adjudicate, be informed, understand **11** investiga
12 pay attention **13** be in touch with, pass judgement

• **hearer**
03 ear

hearing
◇ *homophone indicator*
03 ear **04** case, news, oyer **05** audit, range, reach, sound, trial **06** review
07 earshot, inquest, inquiry
08 audience, audition, scolding
09 interview, judgement
10 perception **11** examination, inquisition **12** adjudication **13** chanc

o speak, investigation **15** hearing
*istance

hearsay
homophone indicator
*4 buzz, talk **05** on-dit, rumor,
ay-so **06** gossip, report, rumour
*0 common talk **11** word of mouth
*2 tittle-tattle **15** common
nowledge

heart
◇ *middle selection indicator*
*3 hub, nub **04** core, crux, guts, love,
nind, pith, pity, soul **05** bosom, pluck,
punk **06** bottle, centre, kernel,
narrow, middle, nature, spirit, vigour,
varmth **07** bravery, concern, courage,
motion, essence, feeling, heroism,
ucleus, passion, stomach
*8 boldness, keenness, kindness,
ympathy **09** affection, character,
agerness, fortitude, sentiment,
ubstance **10** compassion, cordiality,
nthusiasm, resolution, tenderness
* disposition, intrepidity,
emperament **12** fearlessness,
uintessence **13** determination,
*ssential part **14** responsiveness

Heart parts include:
*4 vein
*5 aorta, valve
*6 artery, atrium, AV node, muscle, SA
node
*7 auricle
*8 vena cava
*9 sinus node, ventricle
*0 epicardium, left atrium,
myocardium
* aortic valve, endocardium, mitral
valve, pericardium, right atrium
*3 bicuspid valve, carotid artery, left
ventricle
*4 ascending aorta, pulmonary valve,
Purkinje fibres, right ventricle, sino-
atrial node, tricuspid valve
*5 papillary muscle

* **at heart**
* *insertion indicator*
* *middle selection indicator*
*6 really **08** at bottom **09** basically, in
ssence **11** essentially
*3 fundamentally
* **by heart**
*3 pat **06** by rote, off pat **08** verbatim
*9 memoriter **10** from memory
*1 word for word **13** parrot-fashion
* **change of heart**
*7 rethink **12** change of mind
*4 second thoughts
* **from the bottom of your
*eart**
*6 deeply **08** devoutly **09** earnestly,
ervently, sincerely **10** profoundly
*2 passionately
* **heart and soul**
*6 gladly **07** eagerly **08** entirely,
*eartily **09** devotedly **10** absolutely,
ompletely **12** unreservedly
*4 wholeheartedly
* **hearts**
*1 H **10** black Maria

* **lose heart**
◇ *middle deletion indicator*
08 collapse **13** be discouraged
* **set your heart on**
05 crave, yearn **06** desire **07** long for,
wish for
* **take heart**
05 rally **06** buck up, perk up, revive
07 cheer up **10** brighten up **12** be
encouraged
* **take to heart**
09 be moved by, be upset by **12** be
affected by **13** be disturbed by

heartache
04 pain **05** agony, grief, worry
06 sorrow **07** anguish, anxiety,
despair, remorse, torment, torture
08 distress **09** dejection, suffering
10 affliction, bitterness, heartbreak
11 despondency

heartbreak
04 pain **05** agony, grief **06** misery,
sorrow **07** anguish, despair, sadness
08 distress **09** dejection, suffering
10 crève-coeur, desolation

heartbreaking
03 sad **05** cruel, harsh **06** bitter,
crying, tragic **07** painful, pitiful
08 grievous, poignant **09** agonizing,
harrowing **11** distressing
12 excruciating, heart-rending
13 disappointing

heartbroken
03 sad **07** crushed, grieved
08 dejected, desolate, downcast
09 anguished, miserable, sorrowful,
suffering **10** despondent, dispirited
11 crestfallen **12** disappointed,
disheartened, in low spirits **13** broken-
hearted

heartburn
05 brash **07** pyrosis **09** cardialgy,
dyspepsia **10** cardialgia **11** indigestion

hearten
05 boost, cheer, pep up, rouse
06 buck up **07** animate, cheer up,
comfort, console, inspire **08** energize,
reassure **09** encourage, stimulate
10 invigorate, revitalize

heartening
06 moving **08** cheering, pleasing,
touching **09** affecting, rewarding,
uplifting **10** gladdening, gratifying,
satisfying **11** encouraging
12 heartwarming

heartfelt
04 deep, warm **06** ardent, devout,
honest **07** earnest, fervent, genuine,
sincere **08** profound **09** unfeigned
12 wholehearted **13** compassionate

heartily
◇ *middle selection indicator*
04 upsy, very **05** agood, upsee, upsey
06 deeply, gladly, warmly **07** cheerly,
eagerly, hartely, lustily, totally **08** con
amore, entirely **09** cordially, earnestly,
extremely, feelingly, genuinely,
sincerely, staunchly, zealously

10 absolutely, completely, profoundly,
resolutely, thoroughly, upsey Dutch,
vigorously **11** unfeignedly, upsey Friese
12 upsey English **13** warm-heartedly

heartless
◇ *middle deletion indicator*
04 cold, hard **05** cruel, harsh
06 brutal, unkind **07** callous, inhuman,
unmoved **08** pitiless, ruthless,
sardonic, uncaring **09** merciless,
unfeeling **11** cold-blooded, cold-
hearted, hard-hearted
13 inconsiderate, unsympathetic

heartlessly
◇ *middle deletion indicator*
06 coldly **07** cruelly, harshly
08 brutally **09** callously **10** pitilessly
11 mercilessly **13** cold-heartedly, hard-
heartedly

heart-rending
03 sad **06** moving, tragic **07** piteous,
pitiful **08** pathetic, poignant
09 affecting, agonizing, harrowing
11 distressing **13** heartbreaking

heartsick
03 sad **04** glum **08** dejected,
downcast **09** depressed
10 despondent, melancholy
12 disappointed, heavy-hearted

heart-throb
04 hunk, idol, star **05** pin-up
09 dreamboat

heart-to-heart
08 cosy chat **09** tête-à-tête **10** honest
talk **12** friendly talk

heartwarming
06 moving **08** cheering, pleasing,
touching **09** affecting, rewarding,
uplifting **10** gladdening, gratifying,
heartening, satisfying **11** encouraging

hearty
04 maty, warm **05** ample, bluff, eager,
hardy, large, lusty, matey, solid, sound
06 blokey, jovial, robust, stanch, strong
07 affable, cordial, filling, genuine,
healthy, sincere, sizable, staunch
08 abundant, blokeish, bouncing,
cheerful, effusive, friendly, generous,
sizeable, stalwart, vigorous
09 ebullient, energetic, exuberant,
heartfelt, unfeigned **10** boisterous,
nourishing, nutritious, unreserved
11 substantial, warm-hearted
12 enthusiastic, unrestrained,
wholehearted

heat
◇ *anagram indicator*
03 hot **04** bake, boil, cook, fire, fury,
glow, race, rost, stir, warm, zeal
05 anger, annoy, beath, fever, flush,
roast, rouse, toast **06** ardour, arouse,
calefy, enrage, excite, fervor, reheat,
sizzle, warmth, warm up **07** agitate,
animate, fervour, firearm, hotness,
inflame, passion, swelter, trouble
08 fervency **09** closeness, eagerness,
fieriness, heaviness, intensity,
microwave, stimulate, vehemence

10 enthusiasm, excitement, sultriness, torridness **11** calefaction, earnestness, impetuosity **12** feverishness **15** high temperature
• **dead heat**
03 tie **04** draw

heated
05 angry, fiery, fired **06** bitter, fierce, raging, roused, stormy **07** enraged, excited, furious, intense, stirred, violent **08** animated, frenzied, inflamed, vehement, worked-up **10** passionate, stimulated **11** impassioned, tempestuous

heatedly
07 angrily **08** bitterly, fiercely **09** excitedly, furiously, intensely, violently **10** vehemently **12** passionately

heater
03 gun **04** fire **06** boiler, pistol **08** Califont®, radiator **09** convector, fan heater, gas heater, immersion **11** solar heater **12** electric fire **13** storage heater **14** central heating, electric heater **15** immersion heater

heath
03 Ted **04** bent, fell, ling, moor, muir **05** briar, brier, erica **06** kalmia, manoao, upland **07** arbutus, heather **08** moorland **09** andromeda, bearberry **10** gaultheria

heathen
05 pagan **06** ethnic, paynim, savage **07** Gentile, godless, infidel, nations **08** barbaric, idolater **09** barbarian **10** idolatress, idolatrous, philistine, unbeliever **11** irreligious, nullifidian, unbelieving, uncivilized **13** unenlightened

heather
04 ling **05** erica **07** calluna **08** foxberry **11** Labrador tea

heave
◇ *deletion indicator*
03 cat, gag, tug **04** barf, boke, cast, drag, give, haul, honk, hump, hurl, lift, puke, pull, rise, send, sigh, spew, toss **05** chuck, fling, heeze, hitch, hoist, lever, pitch, raise, retch, sling, surge, swell, throw, utter, vomit **06** be sick, let fly, let out, popple, sick up, wallow **07** breathe, bring up, chuck up, chunder, cough up, express, fetch up, throw up, upchuck **08** disgorge, parbreak, swelling **10** egurgitate

heaven
03 joy, sky **04** Zion **05** bliss, ether, glory, skies **06** Asgard, on high, Svarga, Swarga, Swerga, utopia, welkin **07** delight, ecstasy, Elysium, nirvana, Olympus, rapture, the blue, up there **08** empyrean, holy city, paradise, Valhalla **09** afterlife, firmament, happiness, hereafter, home of God, next world, Shangri-La **10** abode of God, life to come **12** Land o' the Leal, New Jerusalem, promised land, upper regions **13** elysian fields,

fiddler's green, seventh heaven, vault of heaven
• **the heavens**
03 sky **04** pole **06** region **08** empyrean **12** upper regions

heavenly
04 holy, pure **06** cosmic, divine, lovely **07** angelic, blessed, godlike, perfect, sublime, Uranian **08** beatific, blissful, cherubic, empyreal, empyrean, ethereal, etherial, glorious, immortal, seraphic **09** ambrosial, beautiful, celestial, enjoyable, excellent, exquisite, rapturous, spiritual, unearthly, wonderful **10** delightful, enchanting, marvellous **12** other-worldly, supernatural **14** out of this world

heaven-sent
05 happy **06** bright, timely **09** fortunate, opportune **10** auspicious, favourable

heavily
04 hard, upsy **05** thick, upsee, upsey **06** slowly **07** closely, densely, roundly, solidly, soundly, thickly, too much, utterly **08** clumsily, to excess, woodenly **09** awkwardly, compactly, copiously, painfully, weightily **10** abundantly, completely, decisively, sluggishly, thoroughly, upsey Dutch **11** excessively, laboriously, ponderously, upsey Friese **12** immoderately, upsey English **14** with difficulty

heaviness
04 bulk **05** depth, gloom **06** weight **07** density, languor, sadness **08** deadness, severity, solidity **09** dejection, greatness, heftiness, intensity, lassitude, thickness **10** depression, drowsiness, gloominess, melancholy, oppression, sleepiness, somnolence **11** despondency, onerousness, seriousness, weightiness **12** sluggishness **13** ponderousness **14** burdensomeness, oppressiveness

heavy
03 big, dry, sad **04** dark, deep, dowf, dull, full, grey, hard, rich, sour, thug **05** bulky, close, dense, Dutch, grave, great, harsh, hefty, humid, laden, large, muggy, sharp, solid, tense, thick, tough **06** clammy, cloudy, clumpy, doughy, drowsy, gloomy, hearty, leaden, loaded, severe, sombre, steamy, sticky, stodgy, strong, sultry, taxing, trying, wooden **07** arduous, awkward, crushed, extreme, filling, hulking, intense, irksome, lumping, lumpish, massive, onerous, pesante, pompous, serious, starchy, tedious, violent, weighty **08** burdened, crushing, downcast, exacting, forceful, grievous, groaning, highbrow, overcast, pedantic, powerful, profound, strained **09** abounding, burdenous, demanding, depressed, difficult, emotional, excessive, important,

laborious, miserable, ponderous, sorrowful, squabbish, strenuous, wearisome **10** burdensome, cumbersome, despondent, encumbered, immoderate, inordinate, oppressive, unbearable **11** discouraged, heavy as lead, intemperate, intolerable, substantial, troublesome, weighed down **12** considerable, indigestible, sodden-witted, weighing a ton **13** overindulgent, uninteresting

heavy-duty
02 HD **05** solid, sound, tough **06** robust, strong, sturdy **07** abiding, durable, lasting **08** enduring **09** resistant **10** reinforced **11** hard-wearing, long-lasting, substantial

heavy-handed
05 harsh, inept, stern **06** clumsy, severe **07** awkward **08** bungling, despotic, forceful, tactless, unsubtle **09** ham-fisted, maladroit **10** autocratic, blundering, cack-handed, oppressive **11** domineering, insensitive, overbearing, thoughtless

heavy-hearted
03 sad **04** glum **06** gloomy, morose **07** crushed, forlorn **08** downcast, mournful **09** depressed, heartsick, miserable, sorrowful **10** despondent, melancholy **11** discouraged, downhearted **12** disappointed, disheartened

Hebe
08 Juventas

Hebrew
03 Heb, Jew
See also **alphabet**

Hebrew alphabet *see* **alphabet**

Hecate
06 Trivia

heckle
04 bait, gibe, jeer **05** taunt **06** needle, pester **07** barrack, catcall, disrupt **09** interrupt, shout down

hectare
02 ha

hectic
◇ *anagram indicator*
04 busy, fast, wild **06** heated, rushed **07** chaotic, excited, flushed, frantic, furious **08** agitated, bustling, feverish, frenetic, frenzied **09** turbulent **10** tumultuous **11** consumptive

hector
03 nag **04** huff **05** annoy, bully, worry **06** badger, chivvy, harass, menace **07** bluster, provoke **08** browbeat, bulldoze, bullyrag, threaten **09** blusterer **10** intimidate

hedge
◇ *containment indicator*
03 haw, hay, low **04** duck, dyke, edge **05** cover, dodge, evade, fence, guard, hem in, limit, mound, stall **06** insure, lay off, raddle, screen, shield, waffle,

zareba, zariba, zereba, zeriba
07 barrier, confine, debased, enclose, fortify, ox-fence, protect, quibble, shuffle, wayside, zareeba
08 boundary, encircle, hedgerow, obstruct, quickset, restrict, sepiment, sidestep, surround **09** safeguard, temporize, windbreak **10** equivocate, protection **11** prevaricate **13** sit on the fence
• **escape through hedge**
04 mews, muse **05** meuse

hedgehog
06 urchin **08** herisson **11** tiggywinkle

hedonism
09 dolce vita, epicurism
10 sensualism, sensuality, sybaritism
12 Epicureanism **13** gratification, luxuriousness **14** self-indulgence, voluptuousness **15** pleasure-seeking

hedonist
07 epicure **08** sybarite **09** bon vivant, bon viveur, epicurean **10** sensualist, voluptuary **14** pleasure-seeker

hedonistic
09 epicurean, luxurious, sybaritic
10 voluptuous **13** self-indulgent
15 pleasure-seeking

heed
03 ear **04** care, gaum, gorm, mark, mind, note, obey, reak, reck, tent
06 follow, listen, notice, regard
07 caution, hearken, observe, respect, thought **08** attend to, consider
09 attention **10** bear in mind, observance, take note of
11 heedfulness **12** take notice of, watchfulness **13** animadversion, consideration **14** pay attention to
15 take into account

heedful
04 wary **05** chary **07** careful, jealous, mindful, prudent **08** cautious, vigilant, watchful **09** advertent, attentive, observant, regardful **10** respective
11 circumspect

heedless
04 rash **06** blithe, remiss, unwary
08 careless, reckless, tactless, uncaring
09 foolhardy, forgetful, negligent, oblivious, unguarded, unmindful
10 incautious, indiscreet, insouciant, regardless, unthinking **11** hair-brained, hare-brained, inattentive, inobservant, precipitate, thoughtless, unconcerned, unobservant **12** absent-minded
13 inconsiderate, irresponsible

heedlessly
06 rashly **09** blindfold **10** carelessly, recklessly **11** negligently
12 neglectly, unthinkingly
13 inattentively, thoughtlessly

heel
03 cad, cow, rat, tip **04** bank, hele, hide, knob, lean, list, puke, seel, spur, sway, tilt **05** angle, cover, slant, slope
06 ratbag, toerag, wretch **07** conceal, incline, ratfink **08** lean over, stiletto

hefty
03 big **04** hard, huge, very **05** ample, beefy, bulky, burly, heavy, large, solid, stout **06** brawny, robust, strong
07 awkward, hulking, immense, massive, sizable, violent, weighty
08 abundant, colossal, forceful, generous, muscular, powerful, sizeable, unwieldy, vigorous
09 strapping **11** substantial
12 considerable

Hegira
• **in the year of Hegira**
02 AH

heifer
04 quey

height
01 H **02** ht **03** alp, sum, top, tor
04 apex, hill, peak, torr **05** crest, crown, level, limit, pitch **06** apogee, climax, summit, vertex, zenith
07 ceiling, hill top, maximum, stature
08 altitude, eminence, highness, pinnacle, tallness, ultimate
09 elevation, extremity, loftiness, uttermost **10** perfection
11 culmination, mountain top, sublimation

heighten
04 lift **05** add to, boost, elate, exalt, raise **07** amplify, augment, build up, elevate, enhance, improve, magnify, sharpen **08** increase **09** intensify
10 strengthen

heinous
04 evil **05** awful, grave **06** odious, wicked **07** hateful, hideous, vicious
08 flagrant, infamous, shocking
09 abhorrent, atrocious, execrable, loathsome, monstrous, nefarious, revolting, unnatural **10** abominable, despicable, detestable, facinorous, iniquitous, outrageous, villainous
11 unspeakable **12** contemptible

heir, heiress
03 her **05** scion **06** co-heir, tanist
07 fortune, legatee **08** apparent, atheling, parcener **09** inheritor, successor **10** cesarevich, cesarewich, coparcener, fellow-heir, inheritrix, next in line, substitute **11** beneficiary, cesarevitch, cesarewitch, coinheritor, crown prince, inheritress, tsesarevich, tsesarewich **12** tsesarevitch, tsesarewitch **13** crown princess

heist *see* **robbery**

held
• **held by, held in**
◇ *insertion indicator*
◇ *hidden indicator*

helicopter
05 hover **06** copter **07** chopper, medevac **08** sikorsky **09** egg beater
10 rotorcraft, rotor plane, whirlybird
12 air ambulance

Helios
03 Sol

helium
02 He

helix
04 coil, curl, loop **05** screw, twist, whorl **06** spiral, volute **07** wreathe
08 curlicue **09** corkscrew

hell
03 Dis, pit **04** Ades, fire, heck, hele, ruin **05** abyss, agony, below, Hades, havoc, Sheol **06** Erebus, misery, ordeal, Tophet, uproar **07** Abaddon, Acheron, anguish, Gehenna, inferno, the heck, torment, torture **08** Tartarus, the deuce **09** commotion, down there, Malebolge, nightmare, perdition, suffering, the blazes
10 other place, the dickens, underworld **11** netherworld, tribulation **12** lower regions, wretchedness **13** bottomless pit, nether regions **15** abode of the devil, infernal regions
• **give someone hell**
03 vex **04** beat, flog **05** annoy, scold
06 harass, pester, punish **07** tell off, torment, trouble **08** chastise
09 criticize **13** tear off a strip
• **hell for leather**
06 rashly, wildly **07** quickly, rapidly, swiftly **08** very fast **09** hurriedly, like crazy, post-haste **10** recklessly **11** very quickly **13** precipitately **15** like the clappers
• **raise hell**
07 run riot **09** be furious **10** hit the roof
11 be very angry, make trouble
13 object noisily, protest loudly
15 cause a commotion

hell-bent
03 set **04** bent **05** fixed **06** dogged, intent **07** settled **08** obdurate, resolved **09** tenacious **10** determined, inflexible, unwavering **12** intransigent, unhesitating

hellish
◇ *anagram indicator*
04 very **05** cruel, nasty **06** savage, wicked **07** awfully, demonic, satanic, Stygian **08** accursed, barbaric, damnable, devilish, dreadful, fiendish, infernal **09** atrocious, execrable, extremely, immensely, intensely, monstrous, nefarious **10** abominable, diabolical, dreadfully, unpleasant
12 disagreeable, unpleasantly
13 exceptionally

hello
02 hi, yo **04** g'day **05** hallo, hillo, howdy, hullo **06** holloa **07** bonjour, welcome **08** chin-chin **09** greetings
10 buon giorno **11** good evening, good morning **13** good afternoon

helm
05 steer, stern, timon, wheel **06** direct, helmet, rudder, tiller
• **at the helm**
07 leading **08** in charge **09** directing, in command, in control **11** in the saddle
15 holding the reins

helmet
03 pot, top **04** topi **05** armet, salet, topee **06** basnet, casque, heaume, morion, murren, murrin, sallet, tin hat **07** basinet, hard hat, morrion, murrin, pith hat, skid lid, sola hat **08** burganet, burgonet, knapscal, sola topi **09** Balaclava, headpiece, knapscull, knapskull, sola topee **11** pickelhaube

helmsman
03 cox **08** coxswain, timoneer **09** cockswain, steersman **10** steersmate

help
03 aid, use **04** back, balm, cure, ease, heal **05** avail, boost, guide, nurse, salve, serve, stead **06** advice, assist, backup, helper, Mrs Mop, oblige, relief, remedy, soothe, worker **07** assuage, backing, benefit, be of use, bestead, charity, cleaner, further, healing, improve, promote, relieve, service, stand by, succour, support, utility **08** adjuvant, employee, guidance, home help, mitigate **09** advantage, alleviate, charwoman, co-operate, do your bit, encourage, lend a hand, moderator **10** ameliorate, assistance, contribute, facilitate, mitigation, rally round **11** alleviation, collaborate, co-operation, helping hand, improvement, restorative **12** amelioration, contribute to, give a boost to, shot in the arm **13** collaboration, encouragement **14** be of assistance, do something for **15** tower of strength
• **call for help**
03 SOS **06** mayday **09** au secours **14** distress signal
• **cannot help**
14 be unable to stop

helper
02 PA **03** aid **04** aide, ally, maid, mate **06** deputy, second, worker **07** partner, servant **08** adjutant, co-worker, employee, helpmate, treasure **09** assistant, associate, attendant, auxiliary, colleague, man Friday, paraclete, supporter **10** accomplice, girl Friday, subsidiary **11** subordinate **12** collaborator, right-hand man **14** right-hand woman **15** second-in-command

helpful
04 kind **05** of use **06** caring, second, useful **08** friendly, obliging, valuable **09** of service, practical **10** beneficial, benevolent, charitable, profitable, supportive, worthwhile **11** considerate, co-operative, furthersome, neighbourly, sympathetic **12** advantageous, constructive, instrumental **13** accommodating

helpfully
06 kindly **08** usefully **10** obligingly **12** conveniently, reassuringly **13** considerately **15** sympathetically

helping
05 order, piece, share **06** aidant, amount, dollop, ration **07** bowlful, portion, serving **08** adjuvant, plateful, spoonful **09** assistant, auxiliary **12** contributive

helpless
04 weak **06** feeble, infirm **07** exposed, forlorn **08** clueless, desolate, disabled, feckless, impotent **09** abandoned, dependent, destitute, incapable, paralysed, powerless **10** friendless, high and dry, vulnerable **11** debilitated, defenceless, incompetent, unprotected

helplessly
06 feebly, weakly **10** desolately, impotently, vulnerably **11** powerlessly **13** defencelessly

helpmate
04 wife **06** helper, spouse **07** consort, husband, partner, support **08** helpmeet **09** assistant, associate, companion, other half **10** better half

helter-skelter
◇ *anagram indicator*
06 random, rashly, wildly **07** hastily, jumbled, muddled **08** confused, headlong, pell-mell **09** haphazard, hit-or-miss, hurriedly **10** carelessly, confusedly, disordered, recklessly, topsy-turvy **11** impulsively **12** disorganized, like hey-go-mad, tumultuously, unsystematic

hem
04 bind, edge, fold, trim **05** frill, skirt **06** border, edging, fringe, margin **07** fimbria, flounce, valance **08** trimming **09** fimbriate
• **hem in**
04 trap **05** box in, limit, pen in **06** pocket, shut in **07** close in, confine, enclose, hedge in **08** restrict, surround **09** constrain

hemispherical
04 domy **07** rose-cut

hemlock
05 Tsuga **07** cowbane **10** insane root **13** water dropwort

hemp
03 tow **04** pita, sida, sunn **05** abaca, bhang, dagga, ganja, hards, hurds, murva **06** fimble, moorva **07** boneset, hashish **08** agrimony, cannabis, hasheesh, henequen, henequin, heniquin, love-drug, neckweed **09** marihuana, marijuana, true dagga **10** crotalaria **13** Pantagruelion
See also **cannabis**

hen
04 balk **05** biddy, chook, layer, poule **06** Cochin, eirack, female, pullet **07** chookie, clocker, Partlet, poulard **08** Langshan **09** incubator **10** Australorp **11** Cochin-China, Spanish fowl
See also **chicken**

hence
04 away!, ergo, thus **06** begone! **09** therefore **11** accordingly **12** consequently **13** for this reason **14** as a consequence

henceforth
05 hence **09** from now on, hereafter **11** hereinafter, in the future **12** henceforward **14** from this time on

henchman, henchwoman
04 aide, page **05** crony, heavy **06** hit man, lackey, minder, minion **07** servant **08** follower, sidekick **09** associate, attendant, bodyguard, supporter, underling **10** hatchet man, led captain **11** subordinate **12** right-hand man **14** right-hand woman

henna
08 camphire

henpecked
04 meek **05** timid **07** bullied **08** badgered, harassed, pestered **09** dominated, hag-ridden, tormented **10** browbeaten, criticized, subjugated, woman-tired **11** intimidated

Henry
01 H, O **03** Hal

Hephaestus
06 Vulcan

her
04 elle

Hera
04 Juno

herald
04 Lyon, omen, show, sign **05** augur, crier, token, usher **06** augury, Hermes, signal **07** courier, fanfare, portend, portent, precede, presage, promise, trumpet, usher in **08** announce, blazoner, indicate, Lord Lyon, proclaim **09** advertise, announcer, broadcast, harbinger, make known, messenger, precursor, publicize **10** forerunner, foreshadow, indication, king-at-arms, king-of-arms, Lyon-at-arms, make public, pave the way, proclaimer, promulgate **14** Lyon King of arms

heraldry

Heraldry terms include:

02 or **04** arms, fess, lion, orle, pall, pile, semé, urdé, vert **05** azure, badge, crest, eagle, eisen, fesse, field, gules, motto, sable, tawny, tenné, undee **06** argent, bezant, blazon, canton, centre, charge, dexter, emblem, ensign, helmet, impale, mullet, murrey, sejant, shield, volant, wivern **07** annulet, bordure, cendreé, chevron, dormant, griffin, gyronny, lozenge, martlet, passant, phoenix, quarter, rampant, regalia, roundel, saltire, statant, tierced, unicorn, urinant

08 addorsed, antelope, caboched, couchant, insignia, mantling, sanguine, sinister, tincture
09 carnation, displayed, hatchment
10 camelopard, cinquefoil, coat of arms, cockatrice, emblazonry, escutcheon, fleur-de-lis, quatrefoil, supporters
11 bleu celeste, compartment
15 regaliamantling

herb
04 forb, weed, wort **07** olitory

Herbs and spices include:

03 bay, nep, nip
04 balm, dill, mace, mint, sage
05 anise, basil, cumin, curry, thyme
06 borage, cassia, chilli, chives, cloves, fennel, garlic, ginger, hyssop, lovage, nutmeg, pepper, savory, sesame, sorrel
07 catmint, chervil, comfrey, mustard, oregano, paprika, parsley, pimento, saffron, vanilla
08 allspice, angelica, bergamot, camomile, cardamom, cardamum, cinnamon, lavender, marjoram, rosemary, tarragon, turmeric
09 chamomile, coriander, fenugreek, hypericum, lemon balm
10 gaillardia
12 caraway seeds
13 cayenne pepper

• **magic herb**
04 moly **13** Pantagruelion

herbal tea *see* tea

herbicide
06 diquat **08** paraquat, simazine
10 glyphosate **11** glufosinate, graminicide

herculean
04 hard, huge **05** great, heavy, large, tough **06** strong **07** arduous, mammoth, massive, onerous
08 colossal, daunting, enormous, exacting, gigantic, powerful, toilsome
09 demanding, difficult, gruelling, laborious, strenuous **10** exhausting, formidable, tremendous

herd
03 mob **04** band, goad, host, lead, mass, pack, race, rout, tail, urge
05 crowd, crush, drive, drove, flock, force, guide, horde, meiny, plebs, press, rally, swarm, troop **06** gather, huddle, meiney, meinie, menyie, muster, proles, rabble, throng **07** collect, round up, sounder, wrangle
08 assemble, riff-raff, shepherd
09 look after, multitude, the masses
10 congregate, take care of **11** get together

herdsman
06 cowman, drover **07** cowherd, grazier, vaquero **08** shepherd, stockman, wrangler **10** stock rider

here
02 in **03** ici, now **05** adsum **06** around **07** present **10** at this time **11** at this place, at this point, at this stage, in this place, to this place

• **here is**
04 ecco

hereabouts
04 here **08** near here **10** around here **11** in this place **12** in these parts

hereafter
05 hence, later **06** beyond, heaven
08 paradise **09** afterlife, from now on, next world **10** eventually, henceforth, life to come **11** in the future
12 henceforward **13** elysian fields
14 life after death

here and there
05 about, among **06** thinly **08** to and fro **11** irregularly **12** sporadically **15** in various places

hereditary
04 left **06** family, inborn, inbred, innate, willed **07** genetic, natural
08 inherent **09** ancestral, inherited
10 bequeathed, congenital, handed down **11** transferred **13** transmissible

• **hereditary factor**
02 id **04** gene

heredity
03 DNA **04** gene **05** genes
08 genetics **11** chromosomes, inheritance **13** genetic make-up

herein
◇ *containment indicator*
06 within **11** contained in **13** in this respect

heresy
05 error **06** schism **07** atheism, dissent **08** apostasy, Docetism, unbelief **09** blasphemy, Montanism, recusance **10** dissension, dissidence, heterodoxy, scepticism, separatism
11 agnosticism, revisionism, unorthodoxy **12** free-thinking, sectarianism **13** nonconformity

heretic
06 zendik **07** atheist, sceptic
08 agnostic, apostate, recusant, renegade **09** dissenter, dissident, miscreant, sectarian **10** schismatic, separatist, unbeliever **11** free-thinker, revisionist **13** nonconformist

heretical
07 impious **08** agnostic, recusant, renegade **09** atheistic, dissident, heterodox, sceptical, sectarian
10 dissenting, irreverent, schismatic, separatist, unorthodox
11 blasphemous, revisionist, unbelieving **12** free-thinking, iconoclastic **13** rationalistic

heritage
03 due, lot **04** past **05** share **06** estate, family, legacy **07** bequest, culture, descent, dynasty, history, lineage, portion **08** ancestry, cultural
09 endowment, tradition
10 background, birthright, extraction, traditions **11** inheritance
See also **world**

hermaphrodite
08 bisexual **09** androgyne, polygamic
10 monoecious **11** androgynous, monoclinous, protogynous
12 heterogamous **13** gynodioecious, male and female **14** androdioecious

Hermes
07 Mercury

hermetic
04 shut **06** sealed **07** magical, obscure **08** abstruse, airtight
10 hermetical, watertight

hermit
04 monk **05** loner, Peter **07** ancress, ascetic, eremite, pagurid, recluse, stylite **08** beadsman, marabout, pagurian, sannyasi, solitary
09 anchoress, anchorite, pillarist
10 robber crab, solitarian
11 Hieronymite, pillar-saint, soldier crab

hermitage
05 haven **06** ashram, asylum, refuge
07 hideout, retreat, shelter **08** cloister, hideaway **09** sanctuary **11** hiding-place

hero
03 cid, god **04** idol, lead, lion, star
05 ideal, pin-up, sheik **06** eponym, sheikh, victor **07** demigod, good guy, paragon **08** cavalier, champion, male lead **09** celebrity, conqueror, lead actor, superstar **10** heart-throb
11 brave person, demigoddess, protagonist **12** leading actor
15 leading male part, leading male role, person of courage

Heroes include:

04 Ajax, Bond (James), Dare (Dan), Hood (Robin)
05 Bruce (Robert), El Cid, Jason, Jones (Indiana), Kelly (Ned), Zorro
06 Arthur, Barton (Dick), Batman, Brutus (Lucius Junius), Rogers (Buck), Sharpe (Richard), Tarzan
07 Beowulf, Biggles, Glyn Dwr (Owain), Ivanhoe, Perseus, Theseus, Wallace (William)
08 Achilles, Heracles, Hercules, Lancelot, Odysseus, Superman
09 Churchill (Sir Winston), D'Artagnan, Glendower (Owain), MacGregor (Rob Roy), Schindler (Oskar), Spiderman
10 Coriolanus, Cú Chulainn, Hornblower (Horatio), Little John, Lone Ranger, Richthofen (Manfred von 'the Red Baron')
11 Bellerophon, Finn MacCool, Wilberforce (William)
14 Finn MacCumhail, Robert the Bruce
15 Three Musketeers

heroic
04 bold, epic **05** brave, noble
06 daring **07** doughty, gallant, Homeric, valiant **08** fearless, intrepid, selfless, valorous **09** dauntless, undaunted **10** chivalrous, courageous,

determined **11** adventurous, lion-hearted **12** stout-hearted

heroically
05 nobly **06** boldly **07** bravely
09 valiantly **10** fearlessly, selflessly
11 dauntlessly **12** courageously

heroin
01 H **04** junk, scag, skag, snow
05 horse, shmek, smack, sugar
07 schmeck **10** white stuff
11 diamorphine

heroine
04 diva, idol, lead, star **05** ideal, pin-up
06 Amazon, victor **07** goddess,
paragon **08** champion **09** celebrity,
conqueror, lead actor, superstar
10 brave woman, female lead, prima
donna **11** leading lady, protagonist
14 leading actress, prima ballerina,
woman of courage

Heroines include:

04 Lane (Lois)
05 Croft (Lara), Szabo (Violette)
06 Cavell (Edith), Judith, Ripley (Ellen)
07 Ariadne, Darling (Grace), Deirdre
08 Antigone, Atalanta, Boadicea,
Boudicca, Penelope
09 Cassandra, Joan of Arc, Macdonald
(Flora), Snow White
10 Cinderella
11 Helen of Troy, Nightingale
(Florence), Wonderwoman

heroism
06 daring, valour **07** bravery,
courage, prowess **08** boldness,
chivalry **09** fortitude, gallantry
11 doughtiness, intrepidity
12 fearlessness, selflessness
13 dauntlessness, determination
14 courageousness **15** lion-heartedness

heron
04 hern **05** Ardea, egret **07** bittern,
squacco **08** boatbill, hernshaw,
heronsew **09** heronshaw

hero-worship
07 worship **09** adoration, adulation
10 admiration, exaltation, veneration
11 deification, idolization
12 idealization **13** glorification

herring
04 brit, sild **05** capon **06** kipper,
matjes, mattie **07** anchovy, bloater,
clupeid, maatjes, rollmop, soldier
08 buckling, clupeoid, menhaden, sea
stick **09** gaspereau **10** mossbunker
12 Norfolk capon
• **measure of herring**
04 cran, maze, warp **05** maise, maize,
mease

hesitancy
05 delay, demur, doubt, qualm
08 scruples, wavering **09** misgiving
10 indecision, reluctance, stammering
11 reservation, uncertainty
12 doubtfulness, irresolution
13 unwillingness **14** disinclination

hesitant
03 shy **04** wary **05** timid **06** unsure
07 dubious, halting **08** delaying,
doubtful, stalling, wavering
09 demurring, reluctant, sceptical,
tentative, uncertain, unwilling
10 hesitating, indecisive, irresolute,
stammering, stuttering **11** disinclined,
half-hearted, vacillating

hesitate
04 halt, wait **05** delay, demur, doubt,
pause, stall, waver **06** boggle, dicker,
dither, falter, mammer, tarrow, teeter
07 balance, scruple, stammer, stumble,
stutter, swither, um and ah **08** dubitate,
hang back, hang fire, hold back
09 hum and haw, vacillate **10** dilly-
dally, shrink from, think twice **11** be
reluctant, be uncertain, be unwilling
12 shilly-shally **13** be disinclined

hesitation
05 delay, demur, doubt, dwell, pause,
qualm **06** demure, qualms **07** scruple,
waiting **08** misdoubt, scruples, stalling,
wavering **09** faltering, hesitance,
stumbling **10** cunctation, indecision,
misgivings, reluctance, scepticism,
stammering, stuttering, unsureness
11 hanging-back, holding-back,
uncertainty, vacillation **12** doubtfulness,
irresolution **13** dilly-dallying,
unwillingness **14** disinclination, second
thoughts **15** shilly-shallying
• **expression of hesitation**
02 er, ha, um, ur **03** erm, hah **04** well

Hestia
05 Vesta

heterodox
07 unsound **09** dissident, heretical
10 dissenting, schismatic, unorthodox
11 revisionist **12** free-thinking,
iconoclastic

heterogeneous
05 mixed **06** motley, unlike, varied
07 diverse, opposed, piebald, pyebald
08 assorted, catholic, contrary
09 different, disparate, divergent,
multiform, unrelated **10** contrasted,
discrepant, dissimilar **11** diversified,
incongruous, polymorphic
13 miscellaneous

heterogeneously
09 diversely **10** contrarily
11 differently, disparately, divergently
12 dissimilarly **13** incongruously

heterosexual
03 het **06** hetero **07** breeder
08 straight

het up
05 angry, tense, upset **07** anxious, in a
rage, uptight, worried, wound up
08 agitated, offended, stressed,
worked up **09** indignant, pissed off,
resentful **11** stressed-out **14** beside
yourself

hew
03 axe, cut, dye, hag, hue, lop, saw
04 chip, chop, fell, form, hack, make,

tint, trim **05** carve, model, prune,
sever, shape, split **06** chisel, colour,
hammer, sculpt **07** fashion, whittle
09 sculpture **10** appearance

heyday
04 peak **05** bloom, flush, prime
06 summer **08** boom time, pinnacle
09 flowering, golden age
11 culmination

hiatus
03 gap **04** lull, rest, rift, void **05** blank,
break, chasm, lapse, pause, space
06 breach, defect, lacuna **07** opening
08 aperture, interval **10** suspension
12 interruption **13** discontinuity
14 discontinuance

hibernate
06 winter

hibernating
06 torpid **07** dormant **08** latitant

hibiscus
04 okra **07** roselle, rozelle **10** cotton
tree, rose mallow **12** rose of Sharon

hiccup
03 hic, yex **04** snag, yesk **05** block,
catch, check, delay, hitch **06** glitch,
hold-up, mishap **07** barrier, problem,
setback, trouble **08** drawback,
obstacle **09** hindrance **10** difficulty,
impediment **11** obstruction

hick *see* **bumpkin**

hickory
05 pecan **08** shagbark **09** scaly-bark,
shellbark

hidden
◇ *hidden indicator*
04 dark, dern **05** close, dearn
06 arcane, covert, latent, masked,
occult, secret, unseen, veiled
07 covered, cryptic, obscure,
unknown **08** abstruse, mystical,
shrouded, ulterior **09** concealed,
disguised, invisible, recondite
10 indistinct, mysterious, out of sight,
under wraps **11** camouflaged,
clandestine **12** subterranean, under
hatches

hide
◇ *containment indicator*
◇ *hidden indicator*
03 fur **04** buff, bury, coat, fell, flog,
heal, heel, hele, hell, lurk, mask, pell,
pelt, robe, skin, stow, veil, whip, wrap
05 cache, cloak, cloud, cover, earth,
slink, store **06** darken, encave, fleece,
hole up, incave, lie low, screen, shadow,
shroud, spetch **07** abscond, conceal,
eclipse, envelop, flaught, leather,
obscure, secrete, shelter, tappice
08 bottle up, disguise, keep dark, lie
doggo, lock away, obstruct, suppress,
withhold **09** dissemble, stash away,
take cover **10** camouflage, go to
ground, keep secret **12** go into hiding
13 draw a veil over, put out of sight
14 keep out of sight, keep under wraps,
lay a false scent **15** conceal yourself,
cover your tracks, keep a low profile

hideaway
03 den **04** hole, lair, nest **05** haven
06 refuge **07** hideout, retreat, shelter
08 cloister, fugitive **09** hermitage,
sanctuary **11** hiding-place

hidebound
03 set **05** fixed, rigid **06** narrow
07 bigoted **08** stubborn **09** obstinate
10 entrenched, intolerant
11 Biedermeier, intractable,
reactionary, strait-laced
12 conventional, narrow-minded
14 uncompromising

hideous
◊ *anagram indicator*
04 gash, grim, huge, ugly **05** awful
06 deform, horrid, ugsome **07** ghastly,
loathly, macabre **08** dreadful,
gruesome, horrible, shocking, terrible
09 appalling, frightful, grotesque,
monstrous, repellent, repulsive,
revolting, unsightly **10** abominable,
disgusting, horrendous, horrifying,
monstrous, outrageous, terrifying

hideously
08 horribly, horridly, terribly
10 abominably, dreadfully, gruesomely,
shockingly **11** frightfully, grotesquely,
repulsively **12** disgustingly,
horrendously, outrageously, terrifyingly

hideout
03 den **04** hole, lair, nest **05** haven
06 refuge **07** retreat, shelter
08 cloister, hideaway **09** hermitage,
sanctuary **11** hiding-place

hiding
◊ *containment indicator*
04 dern, mask, veil **05** cover, dearn
06 caning, shroud **07** beating, belting,
licking, tanning, veiling **08** disguise,
drubbing, flogging, spanking,
whacking, whipping **09** battering,
screening, thrashing, walloping
10 camouflage **11** concealment

hiding-place
03 den, mew **04** hide, hole, lair, nest
05 cache, cover, haven, stash
06 refuge **07** hideout, hidling, hidlins,
retreat, shelter **08** cloister, hideaway,
hidlings, hidy-hole **09** glory hole,
hidey-hole, sanctuary

hierarchy
05 scale **06** ladder, series, strata,
system **07** grading, ranking
08 echelons **09** structure **12** pecking
order

hieroglyphics
04 code **05** runes, signs **06** cipher
07 scratch, symbols **08** scrabble,
scribble, squiggle **10** bad writing,
cacography, pictograms **13** secret
symbols **14** picture writing

higgledy-piggledy
◊ *anagram indicator*
06 anyhow, untidy **07** jumbled,
muddled **08** confused, pell-mell,
untidily **09** any old how, haphazard
10 confusedly, disorderly, topsy-turvy

11 haphazardly **12** disorganized,
through-other **14** indiscriminate

high
◊ *anagram indicator*
03 bad, off, top **04** dear, fine, gamy,
good, haut, loud, peak, tall, trip
05 acute, aloft, angry, chief, doped,
drunk, great, gusty, lofty, moral, nervy,
noble, sharp, steep, tinny, wired
06 bombed, choice, classy, costly, de
luxe, elated, height, loaded, piping,
putrid, rancid, record, select, senior,
severe, shrill, smelly, stoned, stormy,
strong, summit, tiptop, treble, turn-on,
wasted, worthy, zenith, zonked
07 blasted, blitzed, complex, decayed,
eminent, ethical, exalted, extreme,
haughty, intense, leading, notable, on a
trip, out of it, perfect, quality, rotting,
shrilly, soaring, soprano, squally,
upright, violent **08** abstruse, admiring,
advanced, arrogant, blue-chip,
blustery, elevated, falsetto, forceful,
freak-out, high-tech, inflated, piercing,
positive, powerful, smelling, superior,
top-class, towering, turned on,
vigorous, virtuous **09** admirable,
agreeable, approving, difficult,
dignified, elaborate, eminently,
excellent, excessive, exemplary,
expensive, extremely, first-rate, gilt-
edged, high-level, important,
luxurious, principal, prominent,
spaced out **10** arrogantly, exorbitant,
favourable, first-class, freaked out,
honourable, inebriated, noteworthy,
powerfully, surpassing, unequalled
11 anticyclone, commendable,
high-pitched, high-ranking,
inebriation, influential, intoxicated,
luxuriously, outstanding, penetrating,
progressive, superlative, tempestuous,
ultra-modern **12** altitudinous,
appreciative, extortionate,
intoxication, unparalleled,
unreasonable, well-disposed
13 complimentary, distinguished,
hallucinating, hallucination, high-
frequency
• **high and dry**
06 bereft, dumped **07** ditched
08 helpless, marooned, stranded
09 abandoned, destitute
• **high and low**
07 all over **09** all around **10** every
place, everywhere, far and near,
throughout **11** in all places, in each
place **12** in every place
• **high and mighty**
05 proud **06** swanky **07** exalted,
haughty, stuck-up **08** arrogant,
cavalier, snobbish, superior, toplofty
09 conceited, egotistic, imperious
10 disdainful, hogen-mogen
11 overbearing, overweening,
patronizing, toploftical
13 condescending, self-important
• **hit high**
03 lob, sky
• **on high**
02 up **05** ahigh, aloft **07** aheight
08 supernal **10** in excelsis

high-born
05 noble **08** well-born **09** patrician
11 blue-blooded **12** aristocratic,
thoroughbred

highbrow
04 deep **05** heavy **06** boffin, brains,
brainy, genius **07** bookish, egghead,
scholar, serious **08** academic,
brainbox, cultured, long-hair, profound
09 classical, know-it-all, scholarly
10 cultivated, long-haired,
mastermind **11** clever clogs
12 intellectual **13** sophisticated
14 third-programme

high-class
01 U **04** posh **05** dicty, élite, pakka,
pucka, pukka, super **06** choice, classy,
de luxe, dickty, select **07** elegant,
quality **08** superior, top-class
09 excellent, exclusive, first-rate,
luxurious, top-flight **10** upper-class
11 high-quality

highest
03 top **04** best **05** chief **07** supreme,
topmost **08** crowning **09** uppermost

highfalutin, highfaluting
05 lofty **06** la-di-da, swanky
07 pompous **08** affected
09 bombastic, grandiose, high-flown
11 pretentious **12** high-sounding,
magniloquent, supercilious

high-flown
05 lofty **06** florid, la-di-da, ornate,
turgid **07** pompous, stilted
08 affected, elevated **09** bombastic,
elaborate, grandiose **10** artificial,
flamboyant **11** exaggerated,
extravagant, highfalutin, pretentious
12 high-sounding, ostentatious,
supercilious **13** grandiloquent, grand-
sounding

high-handed
05 bossy **07** haughty **08** arrogant,
despotic **09** arbitrary, imperious
10 autocratic, oppressive, peremptory,
tyrannical **11** dictatorial, domineering,
overbearing

high-handedness
09 arrogance, bossiness
13 arbitrariness, imperiousness,
inflexibility **14** peremptoriness

high jinks
06 antics, capers, pranks **07** foolery,
fooling, jollity **08** clowning
09 horseplay **10** buffoonery,
skylarking, tomfoolery **11** fun and
games **13** fooling around **14** monkey
business, practical jokes, rough-and-
tumble

highland
04 hill, rise **05** mound, mount, ridge
06 height, upland **07** plateau
08 mountain **09** elevation

Highlander
04 Gael **06** Gadhel, Goidel **07** nainsel'
08 nainsell, plaidman, teuchter **09** Irish
Scot

highlight

04 best, peak **05** cream, focus **06** accent, climax, play up, set off, show up, stress **07** feature, focus on, point up **08** high spot **09** emphasize, high point, spotlight, underline **10** accentuate, illuminate **11** main feature **13** put emphasis on **15** call attention to

highly

04 most, very, well **06** hugely, really, thrice, vastly, warmly **07** greatly **08** very much **09** certainly, decidedly, extremely, immensely **10** favourably, thoroughly **11** approvingly **12** considerably, tremendously **13** exceptionally **14** appreciatively **15** extraordinarily

highly-strung

04 edgy **05** jumpy, nervy, tense **06** on edge **07** nervous, uptight, wound up **08** neurotic, restless, stressed **09** excitable, sensitive **11** easily upset, overwrought **13** temperamental

high-minded

04 fair, good, pure **05** lofty, moral, noble **06** worthy **07** ethical, upright **08** elevated, virtuous **09** righteous **10** honourable, idealistic, principled **14** high-principled

high-pitched

05 acute, sharp, steep, tinny **06** piping, shrill, treble **07** orthian, soprano **08** falsetto, piercing **11** penetrating

high-powered

05 pushy, valid **06** mighty, potent, strong, urgent **07** dynamic, go-ahead, telling, weighty **08** emphatic, forceful, forcible, powerful, vehement, vigorous **09** assertive, effective, energetic **10** compelling, convincing, impressive, persuasive

high-priced

04 dear, high **05** steep, stiff **06** costly, pricey **09** excessive, expensive **10** exorbitant **12** extortionate, unreasonable

high-sounding

06 florid **07** orotund, pompous, stilted **08** affected, imposing, strained **09** bombastic, grandiose, high-flown, overblown, ponderous **10** altisonant, artificial, flamboyant **11** extravagant, pretentious **12** magniloquent, ostentatious **13** grandiloquent

high-speed

05 brisk, fleet, hasty, quick, rapid, swift **06** flying, speedy **07** express, hurried **11** accelerated

high-spirited

04 bold **05** proud **06** active, bouncy, daring, lively **07** dashing, dynamic, mettled, playful, rampant, vibrant **08** animated, cheerful, spirited, vigorous **09** ebullient, energetic, exuberant, sparkling, vivacious **10** boisterous, frolicsome, hot-blooded, mettlesome **11** full of beans,

high-mettled **12** effervescent, great-hearted, thoroughbred

high spirits

06 bounce, capers, energy, heyday, spirit **07** elation, sparkle **08** boldness, buoyancy, hilarity, vivacity **09** animation, good cheer **10** ebullience, exuberance, liveliness **11** high feather, joie de vivre **12** exhilaration **14** boisterousness

highway

04 road, rode **05** grove, route **06** avenue, bypass **07** flyover, freeway, roadway, tollway **08** Autobahn, broadway, clearway, main road, motorway, ring road, toll road, turnpike **09** autoroute, boulevard, trunk road **10** autostrada, camino real, expressway, high street, interstate **11** carriageway **12** arterial road, primary route, thoroughfare **15** dual carriageway

highwayman

03 pad **05** scamp **06** bandit, hold-up, robber **07** footpad **08** hijacker **09** bandolero, rank-rider, road agent **10** bushranger, highjacker, land-pirate **15** knight of the road

Highwaymen include:

04 King (Tom)
05 Duval (Claude)
06 Turpin (Dick)
07 Brennan (Willie), Nevison (John), Nevison (William)
08 MacHeath
09 Abershawe (Jerry), Swift Nick
12 Mack the Knife

hijack

05 seize **07** carjack, skyjack **08** take over **10** commandeer **11** expropriate

hike

03 tug **04** jack, jerk, lift, plod, pull, ramp, trek, walk, yank **05** hitch, hoist, march, put up, raise, tramp **06** jack up, pull up, push up, ramble, trudge, wander **08** bushwalk, increase

hilarious

05 funny, jolly, merry, noisy **06** jovial **07** amusing, a scream, comical, killing, riotous, risible **08** farcical, humorous **09** laughable **10** boisterous, hysterical, rollicking, uproarious **12** entertaining **13** side-splitting

hilariously

09 comically, laughably **10** farcically, humorously **12** boisterously, hysterically, uproariously

hilarity

03 fun **05** mirth **06** comedy, gaiety, levity **07** jollity **08** laughter **09** amusement, frivolity, merriment **10** exuberance **11** high spirits **12** conviviality, exhilaration **14** boisterousness

hill

03 dod, dun, how, kip, kop, law, low, man, pap, tel, tor **04** berg, cone, down,

drop, dune, fell, holt, howe, knot, loma, mesa, pike, ramp, rise, tell, toot, torr **05** butte, coast, jebel, knoll, kopje, morro, mound, mount, slope **06** ascent, barrow, cuesta, djebel, height, koppie, pimple, rising **07** descent, hillock, hilltop, hummock, incline, mamelon **08** eminence, foothill, gradient, mountain **09** acclivity, declivity, elevation, monadnock, monticule, sugarloaf **10** prominence, saddleback **12** rising ground

Rome's seven hills:

07 Caelian, Viminal
08 Aventine, Palatine, Quirinal
09 Esquiline
10 Capitoline

• over the hill

03 old **04** gone **06** past it **09** getting on **13** past your prime

hillbilly

03 oaf **04** boor, hick, lout **06** rustic **07** bumpkin, hawbuck, hayseed, hoedown, peasant **08** clodpoll **10** clodhopper, provincial **11** bushwhacker **12** country yokel **14** country bumpkin

hill fort

04 rath

hillock

04 dune, knap, knob, toft, tump **05** knoll, knowe, mound **06** barrow **07** hommock, hummock **08** monticle **10** monticulus

hill-slope

04 brae

hilltop

03 dod, nab **05** crest

hilt

04 grip, haft, heft **05** helve, shaft **06** basket, handle **08** coquille, handgrip

• to the hilt

05 fully **06** wholly **07** utterly **08** entirely, to the end **09** all the way, to the full **10** completely, thoroughly **14** in every respect **15** from first to last

him

02 un

hind

04 back, rear, rump, tail **05** after, stern **06** caudal, hinder **09** posterior

hinder

03 bar, let **04** balk, curb, foil, halt, hind, last, rear, stay, stop **05** block, check, crimp, debar, delay, deter, dwarf, embar, estop, imbar, stunt **06** arrest, cumber, hamper, hold up, impede, oppose, resist, retard, stymie, taigle, thwart **07** empeach, forelay, impeach, inhibit, keep off, porlock, prevent, set back, trammel **08** encumber, handicap, hold back, obstruct, preclude, slow down **09** forestall, frustrate, hamstring, interrupt, throw back, withstand **10** overslaugh **13** interfere with

hindmost
03 lag **04** last, tail **05** final **07** aftmost, endmost **08** furthest, rearmost, remotest, terminal, trailing, ultimate **09** aftermost **10** concluding **12** furthest back **14** farthest behind

hindrance
03 bar, let **04** curb, drag, foil, snag, stop **05** block, check, delay, hitch **06** hold-up, thwart **07** barrier, empeach, impeach, shackle **08** drawback, handicap, obstacle, pullback, stoppage **09** cumbrance, deterrent, impedance, restraint, thwarting **10** difficulty, impediment, limitation, prevention **11** encumbrance, obstruction, obstructive, restriction **12** disadvantage, interference, interruption **13** inconvenience **14** stumbling-block

hindsight
06 review, survey **10** reflection, retrospect **11** remembrance **12** afterthought, recollection, thinking back **13** re-examination

Hindu *see* god, goddess; month

Hindustani
04 Hind, Urdu **05** Hindi

hinge
◇ *reversal indicator*
04 hang, rest, turn **05** gemel, pivot **06** centre, depend, garnet **07** revolve **09** ginglymus **11** cross-garnet **12** be contingent

hint
03 cue, tip **04** clue, dash, help, mint, note, sign, tang, wind, wink, word **05** hunch, imply, light, point, savor, speck, taste, tinge, touch, trace, whiff **06** advice, allude, moment, nuance, office, prevue, prompt, savour, signal, squint, tip off, tip-off **07** glimmer, inkling, let fall, mention, pointer, preview, soupçon, suggest, thought, whisper, wrinkle **08** allusion, indicate, innuendo, intimate, reminder **09** insinuate, scintilla, suspicion **10** indication, intimation, sprinkling, suggestion **11** implication, insinuation, opportunity, subindicate

hinterland
08 backveld, interior **10** back-blocks, hinderland **11** back-country

hip
02 in **03** hep **04** cool, huck, loin, rump **05** croup, funky, thigh **06** dog-hep, dog-hip, groovy, haunch, huckle, modish, pelvis, trendy, with it **07** stylish, voguish **08** buttocks **09** happening, posterior **10** all the rage **11** fashionable **12** hindquarters, hypochondria **13** up to the minute
• **hip bone**
04 coxa **10** huckle-bone **14** innominate bone

hippie, hippy
05 loner, rebel **07** beatnik, deviant, dropout **08** bohemian **10** long-haired **11** flower child

hire
03 fee, job, let, pay **04** book, cost, lend, rent, wage **05** lease, price **06** charge, employ, engage, enlist, rental, retain, salary, sign on, sign up, take on **07** appoint, charter, freight, reserve **11** commission

hire-purchase
02 HP **09** easy terms **10** never-never **14** instalment plan

hirsute
05 hairy, rough **06** crinal, hispid, shaggy **07** bearded, bristly, crinate, crinite, crinose **08** unshaven **11** bewhiskered, crinigerous

hiss
03 boo **04** buzz, hish, hizz, hoot, jeer, mock **05** goose, scorn, taunt, whiss, whizz **06** deride, fizzle, shrill, siffle, sizzle **07** catcall, hissing, mockery, scoff at, the bird, whistle **08** contempt, derision, ridicule, scoffing, sibilant, sibilate, taunting **09** raspberry, shout down, sibilance **10** assibilate, effervesce, sibilation **15** blow raspberries

historian
07 diarist **08** annalist, narrator, recorder **09** archivist **10** chronicler **11** chronologer **15** historiographer

historic
05 famed **06** famous **07** notable **08** renowned **09** important, memorable, momentous, red-letter **10** celebrated, remarkable **11** epoch-making, outstanding, significant **13** consequential, extraordinary

historical
03 old **04** past, real **05** prior **06** actual, bygone, former, of yore **07** ancient, factual **08** attested, recorded, verified **09** authentic, confirmed **10** chronicled, documented, verifiable

historically
04 once **07** long ago **08** formerly **09** in the past, yesterday **10** originally **11** some time ago **13** in former times, in years gone by

history
04 life, saga, tale **05** story, study **06** annals, family, record, report **07** account, memoirs, records, reports, the past **08** archives **09** antiquity, biography, chronicle, days of old, education, narrative, olden days, yesterday **10** background, bygone days, chronology, days of yore, experience, the old days, yesteryear **11** credentials, former times **13** autobiography, circumstances **14** qualifications, the good old days

histrionic
03 ham **05** bogus, stagy **06** forced **08** affected, dramatic, operatic

09 insincere, unnatural **10** artificial, theatrical **11** exaggerated, sensational **12** hypocritical, melodramatic

histrionics
05 scene **08** tantrums **09** dramatics, melodrama, staginess, theatrics **10** overacting **11** affectation, insincery, performance **13** artificiality, theatricality, unnaturalness **14** sensationalism

hit
◇ *anagram indicator*
03 bat, bop, box, cue, dod, dot, fit, get, hay, pat, tap, tip, wow, zap **04** bang, bash, beat, belt, biff, blow, boff, bonk, bump, clip, club, cuff, daud, dawd, harm, hurt, move, polt, shot, skit, slap, slew, slog, sock, suit, swap, swat, tonk **05** catch, clonk, clout, crash, knock, pound, prang, punch, smack, smash, smite, thump, touch, upset, whack **06** affect, batter, buffet, come to, damage, dawn on, impact, strike, stroke, thrash, wallop, winner **07** beating, clobber, disturb, occur to, perturb, run into, success, triumph, trouble **08** knockout **09** collision, crash into, devastate, overwhelm, smash into, thrashing **10** clobbering, come to mind, meet head-on, plough into **11** be thought of, blockbuster, collide with, knock for six **12** be remembered **13** enter your mind **14** have an effect on
See also **kill**

• **hit back**
06 return **07** respond **09** retaliate **10** strike back **11** reciprocate **13** counter-attack

• **hit it off**
05 agree, click, fadge **06** warm to **09** get on with **10** grow to like **12** get along with **13** become friends, get on well with **14** be friendly with

• **hit on**
05 guess **06** invent **07** light on, realize, think of, uncover **08** arrive at, chance on, discover **09** stumble on

• **hit out**
04 rail **05** flail **06** assail, attack, strike, vilify **07** condemn, inveigh, lash out **08** denounce **09** criticize, strike out

hitch
03 rub, tie, tug **04** bind, hike, hook, jerk, join, limp, pull, snag, yank, yoke **05** block, catch, check, delay, heave, hoist, hotch, stick, unite **06** attach, couple, fasten, glitch, hiccup, hike up, hobble, hold-up, mishap, tether **07** barrier, cat's-paw, connect, harness, problem, setback, trouble **08** drawback, obstacle **09** hindrance **10** difficulty, impediment **11** contretemps, obstruction

hitherto
03 yet **05** so far **07** thus far, till now, up to now **08** formerly, until now **10** beforehand, heretofore, previously

hitman
03 gun **06** ice man **08** assassin

hit-or-miss
06 casual, hobnob, random, uneven **07** aimless, cursory, offhand **08** careless **09** apathetic, haphazard, unplanned **10** undirected **11** perfunctory **12** disorganized **13** lackadaisical, trial-and-error **14** indiscriminate

hive
03 gum **04** skep **07** alveary, bee-skep

hoard
04 fund, heap, keep, mass, pile, pose, save **05** amass, buy up, cache, hoord, hutch, lay in, lay up, plant, put by, spare, stash, store, uplay **06** coffer, gather, heap up, mucker, pile up, supply **07** collect, put away, reserve, stack up, stock up, uphoard **08** hoarding, salt away, set aside, squirrel, treasure **09** reservoir, stash away, stockpile **10** accumulate, collection **11** aggregation **12** accumulation, squirrel away **13** treasure-trove **14** conglomeration

hoarder
05 miser, saver **06** magpie **07** niggard **08** gatherer, squirrel **09** collector

hoarse
05 gruff, harsh, husky, raspy, roopy, rough **06** croaky, roopit **07** grating, rasping, raucous, throaty **08** croaking, gravelly, growling, guttural **10** discordant

hoarsely
07 gruffly, harshly, huskily, roughly **08** croakily **09** raucously **10** gutturally

hoarseness
04 roop, roup

hoary
03 old **04** aged, grey **05** banal, trite, white **06** old-hat **07** ancient, antique, archaic, cliché'd, silvery **08** clichéed, familiar, grizzled **09** canescent, senescent, venerable **10** antiquated, grey-haired **11** predictable, white-haired **12** overfamiliar

hoax
02 do **03** bam, cod, con, fun, gag, hum, kid **04** dupe, fake, fool, gull, jest, joke, josh, quiz, ruse, scam, sham, skit **05** bluff, cheat, fraud, kiddy, prank, put-on, spoof, stuff, trick **06** canard, delude, gammon, have on, humbug, pigeon, string, take in **07** deceive, fast one, frame-up, leg-pull, mystify, swindle, two-time **08** hoodwink, put-up job **09** April-fish, April fool, bamboozle, deception, gold brick **10** huntiegowk **11** double-cross, hunt-the-gowk, supercherie **12** take for a ride **13** practical joke **14** pull a fast one on

hoaxer
05 joker **06** humbug **07** sharper, spoofer **09** mystifier, prankster, trickster **10** bamboozler, hoodwinker **14** practical joker

hobble
04 clog, limp, reel **05** hilch, hitch **06** dodder, falter, fetter, hamper, scrape, totter **07** pastern, perplex, shackle, shuffle, spancel, stagger, stumble, trammel **10** walk lamely **13** walk awkwardly, walk with a limp

hobbling
04 game, lame **06** lamish

hobby
03 fad **04** game **05** sport **07** pastime, pursuit **08** interest, play-mare, sideline **09** amusement, avocation, diversion **10** recreation, relaxation **13** entertainment **14** divertissement, leisure pursuit **15** leisure activity

Hobbies and pastimes include:
05 batik, chess
06 acting, baking, bonsai, hiking, poetry, raffia
07 camping, CB radio, collage, cookery, crochet, dancing, drawing, macramé, mosaics, origami, pottery, quizzes, reading, singing, tatting, topiary, weaving, writing
08 basketry, cat shows, dog shows, draughts, feng shui, knitting, knotting, lacework, lapidary, marbling, painting, quilling, quilting, spinning, tapestry
09 astrology, astronomy, decoupage, gardening, genealogy, marquetry, millinary, model cars, philately, rug-making, sketching, strawwork, toy-making, train sets
10 beekeeping, board games, crosswords, doll-making, embroidery, kite-flying, lace-making, pub quizzes, pyrography, renovating, upholstery, wine-making
11 archaeology, beadworking, bell-ringing, book-binding, calligraphy, card playing, cat breeding, cross-stitch, dog breeding, dressmaking, home brewing, model-making, model trains, needlepoint, numismatics, ornithology, paper crafts, papier-mâché, photography, wine-tasting, woodcarving, woodworking
12 amateur radio, basketmaking, candle-making, games playing, phillumenism
13 bungee jumping, egg decorating, toy collecting
14 book collecting, coin collecting, cruciverbalism, doll collecting, flower pressing, herpetoculture, metal detecting
15 aquarium keeping, ballroom dancing, flower arranging, jewellery making, model aeroplanes, stamp collecting

hobgoblin
03 elf, imp **05** bogey, dwarf, gnome **06** buggan, buggin, goblin, spirit, sprite **07** bugaboo, bugbear, buggane,

spectre **08** wirricow, worricow, worrycow **10** apparition, bull-beggar, evil spirit

hobnob
03 mix **06** mingle **07** consort **08** go around **09** associate, hang about, hit-or-miss, pal around, socialize **10** fraternize **11** keep company

hock
03 ham, hox **04** pawn **07** gambrel, Rhenish **09** Rhine wine **11** Rhenish wine

See also **pawn**

hockey

Hockey-related terms include:

01 D
03 hit
04 ball, feet, goal, push
05 flick, scoop
06 aerial, tackle
07 dribble, free hit, red card, striker, sweeper
08 back line, bully-off, left back, left half, left wing
09 corner hit, drag flick, field goal, green card, right back, right half, right wing
10 centre half, centre pass, goal circle, goalkeeper, inside left, long corner, yellow card
11 field player, hockey stick, inside right, obstruction, short corner
12 penalty flick, reverse stick
13 centre forward, penalty corner, penalty stroke
14 shooting circle, striking circle

hocus-pocus
04 cant, hoax **05** cheat, spell **06** deceit, humbug, jargon, juggle **07** juggler, swindle **08** artifice, delusion, hoky-poky, nonsense, trickery **09** chicanery, conjuring, deception, gibberish, imposture, rigmarole **10** hokey-pokey, magic words, mumbo-jumbo **11** abracadabra, legerdemain, trompe-l'oeil **12** gobbledygook **13** sleight of hand

hodgepodge
03 mix **04** mess **06** jumble, medley **07** melange, mixture **08** mishmash **09** confusion **10** collection, hotchpotch, miscellany

hoe
04 clat **05** claut **06** pecker **07** scuffle **10** promontory

hog
03 pig **04** boar **05** swine **06** corner, porker **07** control, grunter **08** babirusa, dominate, shilling, take over, wild boar **09** babirussa **10** babiroussa, monopolize **14** keep to yourself

hogshead
04 muid
• **two hogsheads**
04 pipe

hogwash
03 rot **04** blah, bosh, bunk, crap, guff, tosh **05** balls, bilge, hooey, swill, trash, tripe **06** bunkum, drivel, hot air, piffle **07** baloney, eyewash, rubbish, twaddle **08** claptrap, cobblers, malarkey, nonsense, tommyrot **09** gibberish, moonshine, poppycock **10** balderdash

hoi polloi
07 the herd **08** riff-raff, the plebs, varletry **09** the masses, the proles, the rabble **11** the peasants, the populace **14** the proletariat, the third estate **15** the common people

hoist
04 jack, lift, rear, sway, wind **05** crane, erect, heave, hoise, raise, steal, wince, winch **06** jack up, pulley, tackle, teagle, uplift, wind up **07** capstan, elevate, winch up **08** elevator, windlass

hoity-toity
05 giddy, huffy, lofty, noisy, proud **06** snooty, uppity **07** haughty, pompous, stuck-up **08** arrogant, scornful, snobbish **09** conceited **10** disdainful **11** overweening, toffee-nosed **12** supercilious **13** high and mighty

hold
◇ *containment indicator*
02 ho **03** aim, bet, hoa, hoh, hug, own, ren, rin, run **04** bear, bind, bulk, call, curb, deem, fill, go on, grip, have, holt, hook, keep, last, soft, stay, stop, sway, take, view **05** apply, belay, brace, carry, catch, check, clasp, cling, clout, grasp, gripe, judge, power, rivet, seize, stick, think, treat **06** absorb, adhere, arrest, assume, clutch, detain, direct, endure, enfold, engage, esteem, fulfil, hold up, keep up, lock up, nelson, occupy, prop up, reckon, regard, remain, retain, summon, suplex, take up **07** adjudge, armlock, bear hug, believe, carry on, clauch, claught, cling to, conduct, confine, contain, control, convene, custody, embrace, enclose, engross, enthral, holding, impound, mastery, observe, persist, possess, presume, reserve, soft you, support, suppose, sustain, toehold **08** assemble, buttress, consider, continue, dominion, headlock, hold down, imprison, leverage, maintain, organize, purchase, restrain, scissors, tenacity **09** authority, be in force, captivate, celebrate, dominance, fascinate, influence **10** Boston crab, compromise, full nelson, half nelson, hammerlock, monopolize, remain true, stronghold **11** accommodate, backbreaker, have room for, incarcerate, preside over, remain valid, scissor hold **12** have space for, stranglehold **13** be in operation, hold in custody, remain in force **14** have in your hand **15** have a capacity of, have in your hands

See also **wrestling**

• **get hold of**
◇ *containment indicator*
03 get **05** reach **06** obtain **07** acquire, contact, speak to **12** get through to **14** get in touch with, get your hands on **15** communicate with
• **hold back**
03 bar **04** curb, hang, pull, stop **05** check, delay, pause **06** desist, impede, refuse, retain, retard, shrink, stifle **07** contain, control, forbear, inhibit, prevent, refrain, repress **08** hesitate, keep back, obstruct, restrain, strangle, suppress, withhold
• **hold down**
03 pin **04** have, keep **06** occupy **07** oppress **08** dominate, keep down, restrain, suppress **09** tyrannize **10** continue in
• **hold fast**
03 pin **04** clip, nail **05** avast, stick **07** enchain, pin down
• **hold forth**
04 show, talk **05** orate, speak, spout **06** preach **07** declaim, lecture **08** harangue **09** discourse **12** talk at length **13** speak at length
• **hold off**
04 wait **05** avoid, defer, delay, repel **06** put off, rebuff, resist **07** fend off, hang off, keep off, ward off **08** fight off, postpone, stave off **09** keep at bay
• **hold on**
04 grip, stop, wait **05** clasp, cling, grasp, seize **06** clutch, endure, hang on, remain **07** carry on, cling to, survive **08** continue **09** keep going, persevere
• **hold out**
04 give, last, stay **05** offer, reach **06** endure, extend, hang on, resist **07** carry on, last out, persist, present, proffer, protend, subsist **08** continue **09** persevere, stand fast, stand firm, withstand
• **hold over**
05 defer, delay **06** put off, shelve **07** adjourn, put back, suspend **08** postpone
• **hold up**
◇ *reversal down indicator*
03 mug, rob **04** bear, lift, rear, show, slow, stay **05** apply, brace, carry, delay, raise **06** burgle, detain, endure, hinder, impede, nobble, prop up, remain, retard, upbear, uphold **07** bolster, display, exhibit, present, put back, set back, shore up, stick up, support, sustain **08** hold high, knock off, obstruct **09** be in force, break into, knock over, steal from **10** burglarize, remain true **11** remain valid **13** be in operation, remain in force
• **hold with**
06 accept **07** support **09** agree with, approve of **11** countenance, go along with, subscribe to
• **hold your own**
06 resist **07** survive **09** stand fast, stand firm, withstand **15** stand your ground

- **put on hold**
05 defer, delay 06 put off 07 hold off
08 postpone

holder
04 case, rest 05 cover, haver, owner,
stand 06 bearer, casing, keeper,
sheath 07 housing 08 occupant
09 container, custodian, incumbent,
possessor, purchaser 10 proprietor,
receptacle

holdings
04 land 05 bonds 06 assets, estate,
shares, stocks, tenure 08 property
09 resources 10 real estate, securities
11 investments, possessions

hold-up
03 jam 04 raid, snag, wait 05 delay,
heist, hitch, theft 07 break-in,
mugging, problem, robbery, setback,
stick-up, trouble 08 burglary, stoppage
10 bottleneck, difficulty, stick-up job,
traffic jam 11 obstruction

hole
03 cup, den, eye, fix, gap, jam, pit, set,
tip 04 bind, bore, cave, dent, drop,
dump, flaw, gash, geat, lair, mess, mine,
nest, pore, rent, rift, slit, slot, slum,
snag, spot, stab, stew, tear, vent
05 break, chasm, crack, delve, error,
fault, hovel, notch, scoop, shack, shaft,
space, spike, split, thirl, whole
06 breach, burrow, cavern, cavity,
corner, covert, crater, defect, dimple,
eyelet, hollow, outlet, pickle, pierce,
pigpen, pigsty, plight, pocket, recess,
scrape 07 chamber, fissure, mistake,
opening, orifice, pothole 08 aperture,
hot water, loophole, puncture,
quandary, weakness 09 deep water,
perforate 10 depression, difficulty,
excavation, pretty pass, subterfuge
11 discrepancy, perforation,
predicament 13 inconsistency

See also **fingerhole**

- **hole in one**
03 ace

- **hole up**
04 hide 06 lie low 09 take cover 10 go
to ground 12 go into hiding 15 conceal
yourself

- **pick holes in**
04 slag 05 slate 07 nit-pick, run down,
slag off 09 criticize 12 pull to pieces
13 find fault with

hole-and-corner
06 covert, secret, sneaky 07 furtive
08 back-door, hush-hush, stealthy
09 secretive, underhand 10 backstairs
11 clandestine 13 surreptitious
15 under-the-counter

holiday
03 vac 04 fete, play, rest, trip, wake
05 break, festa, leave, wakes 06 day
off, fiesta, recess 07 half-day, high day,
holy day, play-day, time off 08 feast
day, festival, fly-drive, furlough, half-
term, leisure, vacation 09 honeymoon,
minibreak, saint's day 11 anniversary,
bank holiday, celebration, package tour

12 legal holiday, long vacation
13 public holiday 14 leave of absence

National holidays include:
05 UN Day
07 Flag Day
08 Anzac Day, Unity Day
09 Labour Day, Women's Day
10 Culture Day, Freedom Day, Martyrs'
Day, Mothers' Day, Victory Day
11 Bastille Day, National Day, Republic
Day
12 Armistice Day, Australia Day,
Children's Day, Discovery Day,
Thanksgiving
13 King's Birthday, Liberation Day,
Revolution Day
14 Armed Forces Day, Queen's
Birthday, Remembrance Day,
Unification Day
15 Constitution Day, Emancipation
Day, Independence Day

holier-than-thou
04 smug 05 pious 08 priggish,
unctuous 09 pietistic, religiose
10 complacent, goody-goody
13 sanctimonious, self-approving, self-
righteous, self-satisfied

holiness
05 piety 06 purity 07 halidom
08 divinity, goodness, sanctity
09 godliness 10 dedication,
devoutness, perfection, sacredness,
sanctimony 11 blessedness,
saintliness, sinlessness
12 consecration, spirituality,
virtuousness 13 religiousness,
righteousness

holler
03 cry 04 bawl, call, howl, roar, yell,
yelp, yowl 05 cheer, shout, whoop
06 bellow, shriek 07 clamour

hollow
03 cup, dig, dip, how, lap, low, pan, pit
04 boss, bowl, cave, comb, dale, deaf,
deep, dell, dent, dish, dull, flat, glen,
hole, howe, khud, nook, sham, vain,
vale, void, vola, well 05 basin, chasm,
clean, combe, coomb, delve, empty,
false, gorge, gouge, niche, scoop,
womby 06 burrow, cavern, cavity,
cirque, coombe, cranny, crater, dimple,
dingle, furrow, futile, groove, indent,
ravine, recess, sunken, trough, tunnel,
unreal, vacant, valley 07 caved-in,
channel, concave, deep-set, dishing,
echoing, muffled, Pyrrhic, unsound,
useless, vacuity 08 coreless, excavate,
fleeting, fossette, indented, inflated,
rumbling, unfilled 09 cavernous,
concavity, deceitful, deceptive,
depressed, emptiness, fruitless,
incurvate, insincere, of no avail,
pointless, pretended, valueless,
worthless 10 artificial, completely,
depression, excavation, profitless,
semicirque, unavailing 11 indentation,
meaningless, reverberant
12 hypocritical

- **beat someone hollow**
04 lick, rout 05 crash 06 hammer,

thrash 07 clobber, trounce
09 devastate, overwhelm, slaughter
10 annihilate 13 defeat soundly

holly
04 holm, ilex, mate 06 yaupon
13 Aquifoliaceae

holmium
02 Ho

holocaust
05 Shoah 06 flames, pogrom
07 carnage, inferno 08 disaster,
genocide, hecatomb, massacre
09 cataclysm, sacrifice, slaughter
10 extinction, immolation, mass
murder 11 catastrophe, destruction,
devastation 12 annihilation
13 conflagration, extermination
15 ethnic cleansing

holy
02 pi 04 good, pure 05 godly, moral,
pious, saint 06 devout, divine, sacred
07 blessed, perfect, revered, saintly,
sinless 08 faithful, hallowed, virtuous
09 dedicated, pietistic, religious,
righteous, spiritual, venerated 10 God-
fearing, sacrosanct, sanctified
11 consecrated 13 sanctimonious

- **holy book** *see* Bible

holy of holies
05 altar 06 shrine 07 sanctum
12 inner sanctum 13 most holy place

homage
03 awe 06 esteem, honour, manred,
praise, regard 07 incense, manrent,
respect, service, tribute, worship
08 devotion 09 adoration, adulation,
deference, reverence 10 admiration,
veneration 11 knee-tribute,
recognition 15 acknowledgement

home
02 in 03 den, pad 04 base, digs, flat,
goal, nest, semi 05 abode, fount,
house, local, place, roots, villa
06 asylum, centre, cradle, family,
hostel, inland, libken, native, refuge,
source 07 address, blighty, cottage,
element, habitat, retreat 08 bungalow,
domestic, domicile, dwelling, fireside,
homeland, home town, interior,
internal, national 09 apartment,
effective, household, residence, safe
place, searching 10 birthplace,
fatherland, habitation, motherland,
native town 11 effectively, institution,
nursing home 13 children's home,
dwelling-place, mother country, native
country, place of origin 14 old people's
home, retirement home 15 country of
origin, residential home, somewhere
to live

See also **animal**

- **at home**
02 in 06 at ease, well up, within
07 relaxed, skilled 08 familiar
09 competent, confident
10 conversant 11 comfortable,
experienced 13 knowledgeable

- **at home of**
04 chez

- **bring home**
05 prove **06** instil **07** impress
08 convince **09** emphasize, inculcate
- **home improvements**
03 DIY
- **home in on**
03 aim **05** focus **06** direct **08** pinpoint,
zero in on, zoom in on **11** concentrate
- **not at home**
03 out **04** away
- **nothing to write home about**
02 OK **04** drab, dull **06** boring
08 inferior, mediocre, ordinary **11** not
exciting, predictable **13** no great
shakes **14** not interesting

homecoming
06 return **07** arrival **10** coming-back,
return home **13** arrival at home

homeland
04 home **10** fatherland, motherland,
native land **13** mother country, native
country **15** country of origin

homeless
06 exiled, tramps **07** dossers, dossing,
evicted, nomadic, outcast, vagrant
08 forsaken, rootless, vagrants
09 abandoned, derelicts, destitute,
displaced, itinerant, squatters,
unsettled, vagabonds, wandering
10 down-and-out, travellers, travelling
11 down-and-outs, on the street
12 dispossessed, on the streets **13** on
the pavement, sleeping rough **14** of no
fixed abode
- **homeless person**
04 hobo, waif **05** skell

homelessness
07 dossing **08** vagrancy
11 abandonment, destitution
12 displacement, no fixed abode,
rootlessness **13** sleeping rough

homely
04 cosy, homy, snug, ugly **05** homey,
mumsy, plain **06** folksy, modest, russet,
simple **07** natural, relaxed
08 cheerful, domestic, everyday,
familiar, friendly, homelike, homespun,
informal, intimate, ordinary, unlovely
09 welcoming **10** hospitable,
unassuming **11** comfortable
12 unattractive **13** unpretentious
15 not much to look at,
unprepossessing, unsophisticated

homer
03 cor **09** Maeonides

homespun
04 rude **05** crude, plain, rough
06 coarse, folksy, homely, russet,
rustic, simple **07** artless, raploch
08 home-made **09** inelegant,
unadorned, unrefined **10** amateurish,
unpolished **13** uncomplicated
15 unsophisticated

homestead
04 toft

homework
04 prep **09** spadework
10 groundwork **11** preparation

homey
04 cosy, snug **07** relaxed **08** cheerful,
familiar, friendly, homelike, informal,
intimate **09** welcoming **10** hospitable
11 comfortable

homicidal
06 bloody, deadly, lethal, mortal
07 violent **08** maniacal **09** murderous
10 sanguinary **12** bloodthirsty, death-
dealing

homicide
06 murder **07** killing, slaying
09 bloodshed, slaughter **12** chance-
medley, manslaughter **13** assassination

homily
04 talk **05** prone, spiel **06** postil,
sermon, speech **07** address, lecture,
oration **08** harangue **09** discourse,
preaching

homogeneity
07 oneness **08** likeness, sameness
09 agreement **10** consonancy,
similarity, similitude, uniformity
11 consistency, resemblance
13 analogousness, comparability,
identicalness **14** correspondence

homogeneous
04 akin **05** alike **07** cognate, kindred,
similar, the same, uniform **08** of a
piece, unvaried **09** analogous,
identical, unvarying **10** all the same,
comparable, compatible, consistent,
harmonious, indiscrete **11** all of a piece,
correlative **13** corresponding, of the
same kind

homogeneously
07 the same **09** similarly, uniformly
10 all the same **11** all of a piece,
identically **12** consistently **13** of the
same kind **15** correspondingly

homogenize
04 fuse **05** blend, merge, unite
07 combine **08** coalesce
10 amalgamate **11** make similar, make
uniform

homologous
04 like **07** related, similar
08 matching, parallel **09** analogous
10 comparable, equivalent
13 correspondent, corresponding

homosexual
03 gay **04** pink **07** lesbian, same-sex
08 bisexual
See also **gay**

Honduras
02 HN **03** HND

hone
04 edge, file, whet **05** grind, point
06 polish **07** develop, sharpen

honest
04 fair, jake, just, open, real, true
05 afald, blunt, clean, frank, legal,
moral, plain, round, white **06** aefald,
afawld, candid, chaste, dinkum, direct,
lawful, seemly, simple, single, square,
trusty **07** aefauld, dinky-di, ethical,
genuine, sincere, up-front, upright

08 bona fide, dinky-die, even-down,
outright, reliable, soothful, straight,
truthful, virtuous, yeomanly
09 equitable, impartial, ingenuous,
objective, outspoken, reputable,
righteous, soothfast **10** above-board,
dependable, fair dinkum, forthright,
four-square, high-minded,
honourable, law-abiding, legitimate,
on the level, principled, scrupulous,
upstanding **11** respectable, right-
minded, trustworthy **12** on the up and
up, plain-hearted **13** fair and square,
incorruptible, plain-speaking,
unpretentious **14** straight as a die
15 straightforward

honestly
04 true **05** truly **06** dinkum, direct,
fairly, justly, really, simply, square
07 dinky-di, frankly, legally, morally,
plainly, up-front, upright **08** dinky-die,
directly, lawfully, straight **09** equitably,
ethically, no messing, sincerely,
uprightly **10** above board, honourably,
on the level, straight up, to be honest,
truthfully **11** impartially, in good faith,
objectively, on the square
12 legitimately **13** fair and square

honesty
05 faith **06** equity, ethics, honour,
lunary, morals, square, virtue
07 balance, candour, decorum,
probity, realtie **08** chastity, fairness,
fidelity, justness, legality, moonwort,
morality, openness, veracity
09 bluntness, frankness, integrity,
rectitude, sincerity **10** legitimacy,
principles **11** genuineness, objectivity,
uprightness **12** explicitness,
impartiality, truthfulness
13 outspokenness, plain-speaking,
righteousness **14** even-handedness,
forthrightness, scrupulousness
15 trustworthiness

honey
03 hon, mel, sis **04** babe **05** sweet
06 nectar **07** sweeten
- **honey buzzard**
04 pern **07** bee-kite
- **honey guide**
03 tui
- **honey possum**
04 tait **08** Tarsipes

honeyed
04 cute, dear, kind **05** sweet **06** lovely,
pretty, tender **07** winning
08 charming, engaging, pleasant,
pleasing, precious, unctuous
09 agreeable, appealing, beautiful,
seductive **10** attractive, delightful,
flattering **11** mellifluous
12 affectionate

honeysuckle
06 abelia **08** Lonicera, rewarewa,
suckling, woodbind, woodbine
09 anthemion, caprifoil, caprifole,
eglantine, snowberry, wolfberry
14 Caprifoliaceae

Hong Kong
02 HK **03** HGK

honorarium
03 fee, pay **06** reward, salary
07 payment **09** emolument
10 recompense **12** remuneration

honorary
03 Hon **06** formal, unpaid **07** nominal,
titular **09** ex officio, honorific **10** in
name only, unofficial

honour
01 A, J, K, Q **03** pay **04** fame, keep, take
05 adorn, award, clear, crown, exalt,
glory, izzat, pride, prize, title, value
06 accept, admire, credit, esteem,
ethics, favour, fulfil, homage, laurel,
morals, praise, purity, regard, renown,
repute, revere, reward, trophy, virtue,
worthy **07** acclaim, applaud,
commend, decency, dignity, execute,
glorify, honesty, modesty, observe,
perform, probity, respect, tribute,
worship **08** accolade, applause, be
true to, carry out, celibacy, chastity,
decorate, good name, goodness,
morality, remember, venerate
09 adoration, celebrate, discharge,
innocence, integrity, privilege,
recognize, rectitude, reverence,
virginity **10** abstinence, admiration,
compliment, continence, continency,
decoration, estimation, maidenhood,
principles, reputation, singleness,
veneration **11** acclamation,
acknowledge, commemorate,
distinction, pay homage to,
recognition, self-respect, uprightness
12 commendation, pay tribute to,
truthfulness **13** righteousness,
temperateness **14** immaculateness,
unmarried state **15** acknowledgement,
trustworthiness

Honours include:

02 GC, KG, OM, VC
03 CBE, DBE, DSC, DSO, GBE, KBE,
MBE, OBE
09 Iron Cross
10 Bronze Star, Grand Cross,
knighthood, Silver Star
11 George Cross, Purple Heart
12 Order of Merit
13 Croix de Guerre, Legion of Merit,
Medal for Merit, Victoria Cross,
Victoria Medal
14 Légion d'Honneur

• in honour of
02 to **05** after **11** celebrating

honourable
03 Hon **04** fair, good, just, true
05 great, moral, noble, noted, right,
white **06** decent, family, famous,
honest, trusty, worthy **07** eminent,
ethical, notable, sincere, worthful
08 reliable, renowned, straight,
truthful, virtuous, worthful
09 admirable, ingenuous, reputable,
respected, righteous **10** dependable,
high-minded, principled, upstanding
11 illustrious, prestigious, respectable,
trustworthy **13** distinguished **14** high-
principled

honourably
04 well **05** nobly, truly **07** morally
08 decently, honestly, worthily
09 ethically, reputably, sincerely
10 virtuously **11** respectably

hood
02 Al **04** cowl **05** amice, blind, Robin,
scarf, snood, visor, vizor **06** almuce,
biggin, bonnet, calash, domino, mantle
07 bashlik, capouch, capuche,
hoodlum, surtout **08** calyptra,
capeline, capuccio, chaperon, trot-
cozy **09** calyptera, capelline,
chaperone, condition, Nithsdale, trot-
cosey

hoodlum
03 yob **04** hood, lout, thug **05** brute,
felon, rowdy, tough **06** gunman,
mugger, vandal **07** mobster, ruffian
08 criminal, gangster, hooligan,
offender **09** bovver boy **10** lawbreaker
11 armed robber

hoodoo
04 jinx **05** magic, spell **06** voodoo
07 bewitch, sorcery **08** wizardry
09 occultism, the occult **10** black
magic, divination, necromancy,
witchcraft **11** conjuration,
enchantment, incantation, the black
art

hoodwink
03 con **04** dupe, fool, gull, hide, hoax,
rook, seel **05** blear, cheat, trick
06 baffle, delude, have on, outwit, take
in **07** deceive, defraud, mislead,
swindle **09** bamboozle, blindfold
12 take for a ride **14** get the better of,
pull a fast one on

hoof
04 foot, kick **05** cloot, expel
06 ungula **07** trotter **10** cloven hoof

hoofed
08 ungulate **10** horn-footed
11 unguligrade **12** cloven-footed,
cloven-hoofed

hook
03 arc, bag, bow, box, dog, fix, hit,
peg, rap **04** barb, bend, blow, clip, cuff,
curl, gaff, grab, hasp, loop, snig, trap
05 angle, catch, chape, clasp, cleek,
clout, crome, crook, curve, elbow,
hinge, hitch, knock, punch, snare,
thump, uncus **06** attach, becket,
enmesh, entrap, excuse, fasten, griple,
scythe, secure, sickle, strike, stroke,
tenter, wallop **07** attract, cantdog,
capture, ensnare, gripple, hamulus,
pretext, sniggle **08** crotchet,
crummock, entangle, fastener
09 goose-neck, tenaculum
10 tenterhook **13** grappling-iron

• by hook or by crook
07 somehow **10** by any means **11** by
some means, come what may **15** one
way or another

• hook, line and sinker
05 fully, quite **06** in full, wholly
07 solidly, totally, utterly **08** entirely
09 every inch, perfectly **10** absolutely,

altogether, completely, thoroughly
12 heart and soul **13** root and branch
14 in every respect **15** from first to last

• off the hook
07 cleared **08** scot free **09** acquitted,
ready-made **10** exonerated, in the
clear, vindicated

hookah
06 kalian **07** chillum, nargile, nargily
08 narghile, narghily, nargileh, nargilly
09 narghilly, water pipe **12** hubble-
bubble

hooked
04 bent **05** adunc, beaky **06** barbed,
beaked, curled, curved, hamate,
hamose, hamous, uncate **07** devoted,
falcate, hamular **08** addicted,
aduncate, aduncous, aquiline,
hamulate, obsessed, unciform,
uncinate **09** aduncated, dependent,
enamoured **10** enthralled **12** sickle-
shaped

hooligan
03 ned, yob **04** hoon, lout, thug
05 droog, rough, rowdy, tough
06 apache, mugger, skolly, tsotsi,
vandal **07** hoodlum, mobster, ruffian,
skollie **08** larrikin, tough guy
09 bovver boy, roughneck
10 delinquent

hoop
04 bail, band, gird, girr, loop, ring, tire
05 round, wheel **06** basket, circle,
girdle **07** circlet, sleeper, stirrup,
trochus, trundle **08** encircle, hula-
hoop **10** laggen-gird

hoot
03 boo, cry, jot, wit **04** beep, call, care,
hiss, hoop, howl, jeer, mock, riot, toot,
yell **05** blare, comic, joker, laugh,
shout, sneer, taunt, whoop **06** scream,
shriek **07** screech, ululate, whistle
08 howl down, ridicule **09** character
12 tu-whit tu-whoo **13** amusing
person

• not give a hoot
12 not care a toss, not give a damn
13 not be bothered **15** not give a
monkey's

hooter
03 owl **04** horn, nose **05** siren
• little hooter
05 owlet

hop
03 fly, nip, pop **04** jump, leap, limp,
skip, step, trip **05** bound, dance, disco,
frisk, jaunt, opium, party, vault
06 bounce, flight, hobble, prance,
social, spring **07** journey, knees-up,
shindig **09** excursion **10** fly quickly
11 quick flight

• caught on the hop
07 unready **11** ill-equipped **14** caught
in the act, caught unawares

• stem of hop
04 bind, bine

hope
03 aim **04** fear, long, pray, rely, wish
05 await, combe, crave, dream, faith,

let, trust, yearn **06** aspire, assume,
elief, desire, expect **07** believe,
raving, foresee, longing, promise
8 ambition, optimism, prospect,
eckon on, yearning **09** assurance, be
opeful, enclosure, esperance, pipe
ream **10** anticipate, aspiration,
ssumption, confidence, conviction,
xpectance, expectancy **11** be
mbitious, contemplate, expectation,
opefulness **12** anticipation **13** look
orward to **14** have confidence, pin
our hopes on **15** hope against
ope

hopeful
4 rosy **06** bright **07** assured, bullish,
uoyant **08** aspirant, aspiring,
heerful, pleasant, positive, sanguine
9 confident, expectant, promising
0 auspicious, favourable, gladdening,
eartening, optimistic, propitious,
eassuring **11** encouraging

hopefully
5 I hope **07** eagerly **08** probably,
ith hope, with luck **09** bullishly
0 expectedly, sanguinely
1 conceivably, confidently,
xpectantly **12** all being well **13** if all
oes well **14** optimistically

hopefulness
4 wish **05** faith, trust **06** belief, desire
7 craving, longing **08** ambition,
ptimism, prospect, yearning
9 assurance **10** aspiration,
ssumption, confidence, conviction
1 expectation **12** anticipation

hopeless
◇ anagram indicator
3 bad **04** lost, poor, vain, weak **05** all
p, awful, bleak, grave, lousy **06** futile,
loomy, no-hope **07** foolish, forlorn,
seless **08** dejected, downcast,
elpless, negative, pathetic, wretched
9 all up with, defeatist, desperate,
ncurable, pointless, worthless
0 despairing, despondent,
mpossible **11** demoralized,
ownhearted, incompetent,
reparable, pessimistic **12** beyond
emedy, beyond repair, irremediable,
reversible, unachievable,
nattainable **13** impracticable **14** past
raying for

hopelessly
◇ anagram indicator
5 badly **06** weakly **07** awfully
8 gloomily **09** unhappily, uselessly
0 dejectedly, negatively
1 desperately **12** despairingly,
espondently, pathetically
3 incompetently, inefficiently
5 pessimistically

hopelessness
5 blues, dumps, gloom **06** misery
7 despair, wanhope **09** dejection,
essimism **10** gloominess
1 despondency, forlorn hope
2 wretchedness **14** discouragement

hophead *see* addict

horde
03 mob **04** army, band, crew, gang,
herd, host, mass, pack **05** crowd,
drove, flock, swarm, troop **06** throng
09 multitude

horizon
05 range, scope, verge, vista
07 compass, outlook, skyline
08 prospect **10** experience,
perception **11** perspective **13** range of
vision
• **on the horizon**
04 near **05** close **06** at hand, coming
07 brewing, looming **08** imminent, in
the air, menacing, on the way
09 impending **11** approaching,
forthcoming, in the offing, threatening
13 about to happen, almost upon you
15 fast approaching

horizontal
04 flat **05** level, plane **06** smooth,
supine **08** levelled, straight **09** on its
side

hormone
Hormones include:
05 kinin
07 gastrin, insulin, relaxin
08 abscisin, androgen, autacoid,
estrogen, florigen, glucagon,
oxytocin, secretin, thyroxin
09 adrenalin, cortisone, melatonin,
oestrogen, pituitrin, prolactin,
thyroxine
10 adrenaline, calcitonin
11 thyrotropin, vasopressin
12 androsterone, melanotropin,
noradrenalin, progesterone,
somatostatin, somatotropin,
testosterone, thyrotrophin
14 erythropoietin, glucocorticoid

horn
04 butt, cusp, gore, push **05** bugle,
corno, cornu **06** klaxon **07** keratin
08 cornicle, oliphant **09** telephone
10 corniculum **15** corno di bassetto
• **horn band**
04 frog
• **horn sound**
03 mot **04** beep, honk, hoot, parp
05 blast
• **part of horn**
03 bay, bez **04** tray, trey, trez **07** bay-
tine, bez-tine **08** brow-tine, trey-tine
09 bay-antler, bez-antler **10** brow-
antler, trey-antler

hornless
05 mooly, muley, poley **06** dodded,
humble, hummel, mulley, polled

horny
04 hard, sexy **05** corny, randy
06 ardent **07** aroused, callous, lustful,
ruttish **08** ceratoid, corneous
09 lecherous **10** keratinous, lascivious,
libidinous **12** concupiscent

horrendous
08 dreadful, horrible, horrific,
shocking, terrible **09** appalling, frightful
10 horrifying, terrifying **11** frightening

horrible
◇ anagram indicator
04 foul, grim, ugly **05** awful, black,
grisy, nasty, scary **06** griesy, grisly,
grysie, horrid, unkind **07** ghastly,
hideous **08** dreadful, gruesome,
horrific, shocking, terrible
09 appalling, frightful, harrowing,
loathsome, monstrous, obnoxious,
offensive, repulsive, revolting
10 abominable, detestable, disgusting,
horrendous, horrifying, monstruous,
terrifying, unpleasant **11** frightening,
hair-raising **12** disagreeable
13 bloodcurdling

horribly
◇ anagram indicator
03 ill **06** grimly **07** awfully **08** terribly
09 hideously **10** dreadfully,
gruesomely **11** appallingly, frightfully,
repulsively **12** disagreeably,
horrifically, unpleasantly

horrid
◇ anagram indicator
04 grim, mean **05** awful, cruel, nasty,
rough **06** shaggy, unkind **07** beastly,
ghastly, hateful, hideous **08** dreadful,
gruesome, horrific, shocking, terrible
09 appalling, bristling, frightful,
harrowing, obnoxious, repellent,
repulsive, revolting **10** abominable,
detestable, horrifying, terrifying
11 frightening, hair-raising
13 bloodcurdling

horrific
◇ anagram indicator
05 awful, scary **07** ghastly
08 dreadful, gruesome, shocking,
terrible **09** appalling, frightful,
harrowing **10** horrifying, terrifying
11 frightening **13** bloodcurdling

horrifically
07 awfully **08** terribly **10** dreadfully,
shockingly **11** appallingly, frightfully,
repulsively **12** disagreeably

horrify
05 abhor, alarm, appal, panic, repel,
scare, shock, spook **06** agrise, agrize,
agryze, dismay, offend, revolt, sicken
07 disgust, outrage, startle, terrify
08 frighten, nauseate **09** terrorize
10 intimidate, scandalize **12** put the
wind up, scare to death

horror
04 fear, hate **05** alarm, dread, panic,
shock **06** dismay, fright, terror
07 disgust, outrage **08** distaste,
loathing **09** awfulness, revulsion
10 abhorrence, raggedness,
repugnance, shagginess, shuddering
11 abomination, detestation,
ghastliness, hideousness, trepidation
12 apprehension **13** consternation,
frightfulness **14** unpleasantness
• **horror film**
07 chiller **10** hair raiser

horror-struck
06 aghast **07** shocked, stunned
08 appalled **09** horrified, petrified,

terrified **10** frightened **11** scared stiff **14** horror-stricken

hors d'oeuvre
04 meze **05** mezze **06** hummus, matjes **07** ceviche, maatjes, zakuska **08** crudités **09** antipasto, carpaccio **11** smörgåsbord

horse
01 H **02** GG **03** pad **04** crib, hack, hoss, moke, pony, prad, yaud **05** filly, mount, neddy **06** dobbin, gee-gee, heroin, keffel, sorrel **07** broncho, cavalry, centaur, charger, trotter **08** yarraman

See also **animal; heroin; pony**

Horses and ponies include:

03 Don
04 Arab, Barb, Fell
05 Dales, Iomud, Lokai, Pinto, Shire, Toric, Waler, Welsh
06 Auxois, Breton, Brumby, Exmoor, Morgan, Nonius, Tersky
07 Comtois, Criollo, Finnish, Furioso, Hackney, Hispano, Jutland, Masuren, Muraköz, Murgese, Mustang, Salerno
08 Budyonny, Danubian, Dartmoor, Friesian, Highland, Holstein, Kabardin, Karabair, Karabakh, Lusitano, Palomino, Paso Fino, Poitevin, Shetland, Welsh Cob
09 Akhal-Teké, Alter-Réal, Anglo-Arab, Appaloosa, Ardennias, Brabançon, Calabrese, Connemara, Falabella, Groningen, Kladruber, Knabstrup, Kustanair, Maremmana, New Forest, New Kirgiz, Oldenburg, Percheron, Sardinian, Tchenaran, Trakehner, Welsh Pony
10 Andalusian, Boulonnais, Clydesdale, Einsiedler, Freiberger, Gelderland, Hanoverian, Lipizzaner, Mangalarga, Shagya Arab
11 Anglo-Norman, Døle Trotter, Irish Hunter, Mecklenburg, Przewalski's, Trait du Nord, Württemberg
12 Cleveland Bay, Dutch Draught, East Friesian, French Saddle, Irish Draught, Metis Trotter, North Swedish, Orlov Trotter, Suffolk Punch, Thoroughbred
13 East Bulgarian, Frederiksborg, French Trotter, German Trotter, Welsh Mountain
14 American Saddle, Latvian Harness, Plateau Persian
15 American Quarter, American Trotter, Swedish Halfbred

Points of a horse include:

03 ear, eye, hip
04 back, chin, dock, face, head, heel, hock, hoof, knee, lips, mane, neck, nose, poll, ribs, rump, shin, tail
05 atlas, belly, canon, cheek, chest, crest, croup, elbow, ergot, flank, girth, loins, mouth, thigh
06 breast, cannon, gaskin, haunch, muzzle, sheath, stifle, temple, throat
07 abdomen, brisket, buttock, coronet, crupper, fetlock, forearm, hind leg, pastern, quarter, shannon, tendons, withers
08 chestnut, forefoot, forehead, forelock, lower jaw, lower lip, nostrils, shoulder, under lip, upper lip, windpipe
09 hamstring, hock joint, nasal peak
10 chin groove, point of hip, wall of foot
11 back tendons, point of hock, stifle joint
12 fetlock joint, hindquarters, hollow of heel, point of elbow
13 dock of the tail, flexor tendons, jugular groove, root of the tail
14 Achilles tendon, crest of the neck
15 point of shoulder

Horses' tack includes:

03 bit
05 arson, cinch, girth, hames, reins
06 bridle, cantle, collar, halter, numnah, pommel, saddle, traces
07 alforja, crupper, housing, stirrup
08 backband, blinders, blinkers, noseband, shabrack
09 bellyband, breeching, hackamore, headstall, saddlebag, saddlebow, saddlepad, surcingle
10 martingale, saddletree, shabracque, throatlash
11 bearing rein, saddlecloth, saddle-girth, throatlatch
13 saddle blanket

See also **bridle**

Horse-related terms include:

03 bay, cob, dun, hie, hup, nag, shy
04 bolt, buck, colt, foal, gait, grey, mare, roan, stud, trot, walk
05 break, forge, gee up, groom, hands, lunge, mount, nappy, pinto, steed
06 bronco, brumby, canter, equine, gallop, hippic, livery, manège, riding, stable
07 astride, blanket, gelding, giddy-up, hacking, nosebag, paddock, passade, piebald
08 chestnut, dismount, horse box, skewbald, stallion
09 horseshoe, roughshod
10 blood horse, draft horse, en cavalier, equestrian, heavy horse, side-saddle
11 riding habit
12 broken-winded, pony-trekking, thoroughbred
13 champ at the bit, mounting block, put out to grass
14 strawberry roan

Racehorses include:

05 Arkle, Cigar, Pinza
06 Nearco, Red Rum, Sir Ken
07 Alleged, Dawn Run, Eclipse, Phar Lap, Sceptre, Shergar, Sir Ivor
08 Aldaniti, Best Mate, Corbiere, Esha Ness, Hyperion, Istabraq, Mill Reef, Nijinsky
09 John Henry, L'Escargot, Oh So Sharp
10 Night Nurse, Persian War, Seabiscuit, See You Then, Sun Chariot
11 Cottage Rake, Never Say Die, Pretty Polly
12 Dancing Brave, Desert Orchid, Golden Miller, Hatton's Grace

See also **racecourse; racing**

• **call to horse**
03 hie, hup **04** high, proo, pruh
• **inferior horse**
03 nag, rip **04** moke
• **pair of horses**
04 span
• **shying horse**
03 jib **06** jibber
• **thin horse**
04 rake
• **working horse**
03 cut
• **worn-out horse**
03 tit **04** jade, plug **07** knacker

horsefly
04 cleg

horseman, horsewoman
05 rider **06** hussar, jockey, knight **07** dragoon, hobbler, pricker **08** stradiot, wrangler **09** caballero **10** cavalryman, equestrian **12** horse soldier

Horseriders, jockeys and trainers include:

04 Anne (Princess), Hern (Major Dick), Leng (Virginia), Pipe (Martin), Tait (Blyth), Todd (Mark)
05 Cecil (Henry), Green (Lucinda), Krone (Julie), Lukas (D Wayne), McCoy (Tony), Meade (Richard), Smith (Harvey), Smith (Robyn)
06 Arcaro (Eddie), Archer (Fred), Carson (Willie), Eddery (Pat), Fallon (Keiren), O'Brien (Vincent), O'Neill (Jonjo), Pitman (Jenny)
07 Dettori (Frankie), Francis (Dick), Gifford (Josh), Piggott (Lester), Winkler (Hans Günter)
08 Champion (Bob), Donoghue (Steve), Dunwoody (Richard), Phillips (Captain Mark), Richards (Sir Gordon)
09 Scudamore (Peter), Shoemaker (Willie)

See also **equestrian**

horseplay
03 rag **06** antics, capers, pranks **07** foolery, fooling **08** clowning **09** high jinks **10** buffoonery, skylarking, tomfoolery **11** fun and games **13** fooling around **14** monkey business, practical jokes, rough-and-tumble

horsepower
02 CV, hp, PS

horseradish tree
03 ben

horsewoman *see* horseman, horsewoman

hortatory
03 pep 08 didactic, edifying, inciting
09 homiletic, hortative, practical
10 heartening, preceptive
11 encouraging, exhortative, exhortatory, inspiriting, instructive, stimulating

horticulture
09 gardening 11 agriculture, cultivation 12 floriculture
13 arboriculture

hosanna
06 praise, save us 07 worship
08 alleluia 09 laudation

hose
03 sox 04 duct, pipe, tube 05 socks
06 piping, trunks, tubing 07 airline, channel, conduit 08 chausses
09 stockings 12 galligaskins

hosiery
04 hose 05 socks 06 tights 07 hold-ups, stay-ups 08 leggings
09 stockings 12 leg-coverings

hospitable
04 kind, warm 05 cadgy 06 genial, kidgie 07 cordial, helpful, liberal
08 amicable, friendly, generous, gracious, sociable 09 bountiful, congenial, convivial, receptive, welcoming 10 open-handed 11 kind-hearted, neighbourly

hospital
01 H 03 CHE, san 04 GOSH, Guy's, home, lock, MASH 05 Bart's
06 clinic, spital 07 hospice, spittle
08 clinique, nuthouse, snake-pit
09 ambulance, funny farm, hôtel-Dieu, infirmary, institute, leprosery 10 booby hatch, leproserie, polyclinic, sanatorium 11 nursing home 12 health centre 13 lunatic asylum, medical centre
• **hospital department**
03 ENT 04 gyny 05 A and E
08 casualty

hospitality
05 cheer 06 warmth 07 welcome
08 kindness 09 open house
10 generosity, liberality, philoxenia
11 helpfulness, sociability
12 congeniality, conviviality, friendliness, housekeeping
13 accommodation, entertainment
14 open-handedness, tea and sympathy 15 neighbourliness

host
◇ *containment indicator*
02 MC 03 mob 04 army, band, give, herd, mass, pack 05 array, crowd, crush, emcee, horde, swarm, troop
06 anchor, myriad, throng
07 compère, linkman, present
08 landlady, landlord, publican
09 anchorman, announcer, harbinger, innkeeper, introduce, multitude, presenter 10 party-giver, proprietor
11 anchorwoman, entertainer
12 proprietress

hostage
04 pawn 06 pledge, surety 07 captive
08 detainee, prisoner, security

hostel
01 Y 03 inn 04 hall, YMCA, YWCA
05 entry, hotel, motel 07 hospice, pension 08 hospital 09 dormitory, dosshouse, flophouse, residence
10 guesthouse 11 youth hostel
13 boarding-house 15 bed-and-breakfast

hostelry
03 bar, inn, pub 05 hotel, motel
06 tavern 07 canteen, pension
09 public bar 10 guesthouse 11 public house 13 boarding-house

hostile
03 icy 05 enemy 06 averse, infest, wintry 07 adverse, glacial, opposed, warlike, wintery 08 contrary, inimical, opposite 09 bellicose, oppugnant
10 aggressive, inveterate, malevolent, unfriendly 11 adversarial, belligerent, disinclined, ill-disposed
12 antagonistic, antipathetic, disapproving, inauspicious, inhospitable, unfavourable
13 unsympathetic 14 at daggers drawn
• **become hostile**
04 rise

hostilities
03 war 04 arms 06 action, battle, strife
07 warfare 08 conflict, fighting
09 bloodshed

hostility
03 war 04 envy, hate 05 anger
06 animus, enmity, hatred, malice
07 cruelty, dislike, ill-will 08 aversion, disfavor 09 animosity, antipathy, disfavour, militancy, prejudice
10 abhorrence, aggression, antagonism, bitterness, opposition, resentment 11 bellicosity, malevolence
12 belligerence, estrangement, hard feelings 14 unfriendliness, unpleasantness

hot
01 h 02 in 03 het, hip, new, red
04 chic, cool, keen, warm 05 angry, balmy, eager, fiery, fresh, funky, livid, quick, ritzy, sharp, spicy 06 ardent, baking, fervid, fierce, fuming, glitzy, heated, latest, modern, piping, raging, recent, red hot, snazzy, spiced, stolen, strong, sultry, swanky, torrid, trendy, uncool, with it 07 boiling, burning, candent, current, devoted, earnest, enraged, flushed, furious, illicit, intense, in vogue, lustful, peppery, piquant, popular, pungent, searing, stylish, summery, violent, zealous
08 animated, diligent, exciting, feverish, incensed, inflamed, parching, pilfered, powerful, roasting, scalding, seething, sizzling, steaming, swinging, toasting, tropical, up-to-date, vehement 09 cut-throat, dangerous, delirious, dog-eat-dog, ill-gotten, indignant, scorching 10 all the rage, blistering, candescent, contraband,

passionate, prevailing, sweltering
11 fashionable 12 contemporary, enthusiastic, incandescent 13 up-to-the-minute

See also **warm**
• **be hot**
04 boil
• **blow hot and cold**
04 sway 05 haver, waver 08 hesitate, hum and ha 09 fluctuate, hum and haw, oscillate, temporize, vacillate
10 dilly-dally 12 shilly-shally
• **feel hot**
04 burn
• **hot air**
03 gas 04 bosh, bunk, crap, foam
05 bilge, froth 06 bunkum, piffle, vapour 07 baloney, blather, blether, bluster, bombast, eyewash, vapours
08 blethers, claptrap, cobblers, nonsense, verbiage 09 bullswool, emptiness, empty talk, mere words
10 balderdash, codswallop

hotbed
03 den 04 hive, nest 06 cradle, school 07 nursery, seedbed 08 seed plot 12 forcing-house 14 breeding-ground

hot-blooded
04 bold, rash, wild 05 eager, fiery, lusty
06 ardent, heated 07 fervent, lustful, sensual 08 spirited 09 excitable, impetuous, impulsive, irritable, perfervid 10 passionate 11 precipitate
12 high-spirited, homothermous
13 temperamental

hotchpotch
◇ *anagram indicator*
03 mix, pie 04 mess 06 jumble, medley 07 melange, mixture
08 mishmash 09 confusion, potpourri
10 collection, hodgepodge, miscellany

hotel
01 H 03 inn, pub 04 Ritz 05 botel, hydro, motel 06 boatel, hostel, tavern
07 Gasthof, pension 08 Gasthaus, hostelry 09 flophouse 10 aparthotel, guesthouse, trust house
11 hydropathic, public house
13 boarding-house, sporting house
15 bed and breakfast
• **hotel employee**
04 chef, page 05 boots 06 porter
07 bell boy, bell hop 11 chambermaid

hotfoot
07 flat out, hastily, in haste, quickly, rapidly, swiftly 08 pell-mell, speedily
09 hurriedly, posthaste 10 at top speed
11 at the double 12 lickety-split, without delay 13 helter-skelter 14 at a rate of knots, hell for leather 15 like the clappers
• **hotfoot it**
04 belt, dash, pelt, race, rush, tear, zoom 05 hurry, speed 06 career, gallop, hurtle, sprint 07 quicken
08 step on it 09 bowl along
10 accelerate 15 put your foot down

hothead
06 madcap, madman, terror
07 hotspur **08** cacafogo, tearaway
09 cacafuego, daredevil, desperado

hotheaded
04 rash, wild **05** fiery, hasty
08 reckless, volatile, volcanic
09 excitable, explosive, foolhardy,
impetuous, impulsive, irascible
10 headstrong **11** hot-tempered
13 quick-tempered, short-tempered

hothouse
05 stove **06** vinery **07** brothel
08 orangery **10** glasshouse,
greenhouse **12** conservatory, forcing-
house

hotly
04 near, nigh **06** keenly, nearly
07 closely, tightly **08** ardently, fiercely,
narrowly, strongly **09** fervently,
intensely **10** forcefully, vehemently,
vigorously **12** at close range,
passionately **15** at close quarters

hot-tempered
05 fiery, hasty, ratty, testy **07** crabbit,
stroppy, violent **08** choleric, petulant,
volcanic **09** explosive, irascible,
irritable **10** splenative **13** quick-
tempered, short-tempered

hound
03 dog, nag **04** goad, hunt, lime, lyam,
lyme, prod, urge **05** brach, bully, chase,
drive, force, harry, stalk, track, trail
06 badger, basset, beagle, chivvy,
follow, harass, jowler, pester, pursue,
talbot, tufter **07** coondog, disturb,
provoke **08** hunt down **09** persecute
• **pack of hounds**
03 cry **04** hunt **06** kennel

hour
01 h **02** hr

Hours include:

04 rush
05 flexi, happy, lunch, small
06 dinner, golden, office, waking
07 trading, working
08 business, eleventh, midnight,
unsocial, visiting, witching

See also **canonical**
• **early hours**
02 am
• **outside hours**
04 kerb

house
◇ *containment indicator*
02 ho **03** Hse, inn, ken, mas, pad
04 body, casa, clan, door, firm, gaff,
hame, hold, home, keep, line, race
05 bingo, blood, board, cover, crowd,
guard, lodge, place, put up, store, tribe
06 billet, family, ménage, reside, strain,
take in **07** chamber, company, contain,
convent, dynasty, harbour, kindred,
lineage, protect, quarter, sheathe,
shelter, turnout, viewers **08** ancestry,
assembly, audience, building, business,
congress, domestic, domicile, dwelling
09 gathering, household, listeners,

onlookers, residence **10** auditorium,
enterprise, habitation, parliament,
spectators **11** accommodate,
corporation, have room for, legislature
12 family circle, have space for,
organization **13** establishment

Houses include:

03 hut
04 flat, hall, semi, weem
05 croft, igloo, lodge, manor, manse,
shack, villa, whare
06 bedsit, chalet, duplex, grange, mia-
mia, pondok, prefab, shanty, studio,
wurley
07 cottage, mansion, rectory
08 bungalow, detached, hacienda, log
cabin, terraced, vicarage
09 apartment, but and ben,
farmhouse, homestead, parsonage,
penthouse, single-end, town
house, treehouse, villa home, villa
unit
10 granny flat, maisonette, pied-à-
terre, ranch house, state house
11 condominium
12 council house, semi-detached
14 chalet bungalow
15 thatched cottage

See also **accommodation**; **building**;
zodiac
• **House of Commons**
02 HC
• **House of Lords**
02 HL
• **on the house**
04 free **06** gratis **08** at no cost **10** for
nothing **11** without cost **12** free of
charge **13** at no extra cost, without
charge **14** without payment

household
04 home **05** house, plain, set-up
06 common, family, famous, ménage,
people **08** domestic, everyday,
familiar, ordinary **09** well-known
11 established **12** family circle
13 establishment

Household items include:

03 bin, mop
04 comb, hook, pram, vase
05 broom, brush, diary, match, potty,
range, towel
06 basket, candle, duster, pet bed,
sponge
07 ashtray, coaster, dustpan, flannel,
key rack, key ring, wash bag
08 aquarium, bassinet, birdcage,
calendar, coat hook, dish rack, fish
tank, flatiron, hat stand, hip flask,
ornament, place mat, shoe rack,
soap dish, suitcase, tea towel, waste
bin, wine rack
09 cat basket, dishcloth, dog basket,
door wedge, fireguard, hairbrush,
hearth rug, highchair, memo board,
phone book, pushchair, sponge
bag, stair gate, stepstool, towel rail,
washboard, washcloth
10 baby bottle, baby walker,
coathanger, laundry bag, letter
rack, oven gloves, photo album,

photo frame, stepladder, storage
box, toothbrush
11 address book, candlestick,
changing mat, first aid kit,
paperweight, toilet brush
12 clothes airer, clothes-brush, clothes
horse, ironing board, magazine
rack, perambulator, picnic basket,
thermos flask
13 feather duster, laundry basket,
satellite dish, soap dispenser,
umbrella stand, washing-up bowl
14 hot water bottle, phone directory
15 draught excluder, photograph
album, photograph frame

householder
05 owner **06** tenant **07** goodman,
gude-man **08** landlady, landlord,
occupant, occupier, resident
09 home-owner **10** freeholder,
proprietor **11** leaseholder **13** owner-
occupier

housekeeping
08 domestic **10** homemaking
11 hospitality, housewifery
12 domestic work, running a home
13 home economics **15** domestic
matters, domestic science

houseman
05 valet **06** butler, doctor, intern
07 interne, servant **08** resident,
retainer **10** manservant **12** house-
surgeon, junior doctor **14** house-
physician

house-trained
04 tame **05** tamed **11** house-broken
12 domesticated, well-mannered

housing
◇ *containment indicator*
04 case **05** cover, guard, homes
06 casing, holder, houses, jacket,
sheath **07** shelter **08** covering,
shabrack **09** container, dwellings
10 habitation, protection, shabracque
13 accommodation

hovel
03 hut **04** dump, hole, shed, slum
05 cabin, shack, whare **06** kennel,
shanty **07** shelter

hover
03 fly **04** flap, hang, hove, wave
05 drift, float, hoove, pause, poise,
waver **06** linger, loiter, seesaw
07 flutter **08** hesitate **09** alternate,
fluctuate, hang about, oscillate,
vacillate **10** helicopter **11** be
suspended

however
03 but, yet **05** howbe, still **06** anyhow,
even so, though **07** howbeit
08 actually **09** as it comes,
howsoever, in any case, leastways,
leastwise **10** howsomever,
leastaways, regardless
11 howsomdever, just the same,
nonetheless **12** nevertheless
13 at the same time
15 notwithstanding

howl
03 bay, cry, wow **04** bawl, gowl, hoot, moan, roar, wail, yawl, yell, yelp, yowl **05** groan, laugh, shout **06** bellow, scream, shriek

howler
04 boob, flub, goof **05** boner, error, fluff, gaffe **07** bloomer, blunder, clanger, mistake, Mycetes **08** solecism **11** malapropism

HQ *see* **headquarters**

hub
03 hob **04** axis, boss, core, nave **05** focus, heart, pivot **06** centre, middle **08** linchpin **10** focal point **11** nerve centre

hubbub
03 din, row **04** coil, riot **05** chaos, noise **06** racket, rumpus, tumult, uproar **07** clamour, whoobub **08** disorder, hubbuboo, rowdedow, rowdydow **09** commotion, confusion, level-coil **10** hullabaloo, hurly-burly **11** disturbance, pandemonium

hubris
05 nerve, pride, scorn **06** vanity **07** conceit, disdain, egotism, hauteur **08** boasting, contempt **09** arrogance, contumely, insolence, lordiness, pomposity **11** haughtiness, overweening, presumption, superiority **12** snobbishness **13** condescension, imperiousness **14** high-handedness, self-importance

huckster
04 hawk **06** barker, dealer, hawker, kidder, peddle, pedlar, tinker, trader, vendor **07** haggler, kiddier, packman, pitcher **11** salesperson

huddle
04 cram, heap, herd, knot, mass, meet, pack, ruck **05** clump, crowd, flock, hunch, press **06** bundle, crouch, cuddle, curl up, fumble, gather, hustle, jumble, muddle, nestle, pester, powwow, throng **07** cluster, meeting, snuggle, squeeze **08** conclave, converge **09** confusion, gravitate **10** conference, congregate, discussion **12** consultation

hue
03 dye, hew **04** tint, tone **05** color, light, shade, tinge **06** aspect, chroma, colour, nuance **07** clamour **08** shouting **10** appearance, complexion

hue and cry
03 ado **04** fuss, to-do **05** chase, hoo-ha, tizzy **06** furore, outcry, rumpus, uproar **07** carry-on, clamour, ruction **08** ballyhoo, brouhaha **09** commotion, kerfuffle **10** hullabaloo **13** a song and dance

huff
03 pet **04** mood, rage, stew, tiff **05** anger, bully, paddy, pique, snuff, sulks **06** hector, strunt **07** bad mood, bluster, passion **09** blusterer

huffily
07 angrily, crossly, in a huff **08** in a paddy, in a strop, morosely, snappily **09** in a temper, irritably, peevishly **11** resentfully

huffy
05 angry, cross, moody, short, sulky, surly, testy **06** crusty, grumpy, miffed, moping, morose, shirty, snappy, snuffy, touchy **07** crabbed, peevish, stroppy, waspish **08** offended, petulant **09** crotchety, irritable, querulous, resentful **10** hoity-toity **11** disgruntled

hug
◇ *containment indicator*
01 O **04** coll, grip, hold **05** clasp, press **06** clinch, clutch, cuddle, enfold **07** cherish, cling to, embrace, enclose, snuggle, squeeze **08** stay near **09** hold close **11** keep close to, stay close to **13** follow closely

huge
02 OS **03** big **04** mega, vast **05** bulky, enorm, giant, great, heavy, jumbo, large **06** immane **07** hideous, hugeous, immense, mammoth, massive, socking, titanic **08** colossal, enormous, gigantic, unwieldy **09** cavernous, extensive, frightful, gigantean, ginormous, Herculean, humongous, humungous, monstrous, swingeing **10** Babylonian, gargantuan, monumental, prodigious, stupendous, tremendous **11** mountainous, stupendious

hugely
04 very **06** highly, really, vastly **07** awfully, greatly, largely **08** terribly, very much **09** extremely, immensely, massively **10** enormously, thoroughly **11** frightfully **12** terrifically, tremendously **15** extraordinarily

hugger-mugger
03 sly **06** closet, covert, hidden, secret, sneaky, untidy **07** chaotic, furtive, jumbled, mixed-up, muddled, private, secrecy **08** backroom, confused, stealthy **09** concealed, confusion, underhand **10** behind-door, disordered, disorderly, fraudulent, out of order, undercover **11** clandestine, disarranged, underground **12** disorganized **13** surreptitious **14** cloak-and-dagger **15** under-the-counter

Hughes
03 Ted

hulk
03 oaf **04** clod, hull, lout, lump **05** frame, shell, wreck **06** lubber **07** remains **08** derelict **09** shipwreck **10** clodhopper

hulking
03 big **05** bulky, heavy, large **06** clumsy **07** awkward, massive, weighty **08** ungainly, unwieldy **09** lumbering **10** cumbersome

hull
03 pod **04** body, bulk, husk, pare, peel, rind, skin, trim **05** frame, shell, shuck, strip **06** casing, legume **07** capsule, epicarp **08** covering, skeleton **09** framework, monocoque, structure

hullabaloo
03 din, hue **04** fuss, to-do **05** hoo-ha, noise, tizzy **06** furore, hubbub, outcry, racket, rumpus, tumult, uproar **07** carry-on, palaver, ruction, turmoil **08** ballyhoo, brouhaha, razmataz **09** commotion, hue and cry, kerfuffle **10** razzmatazz **11** disturbance, pandemonium, razzamatazz **13** a song and dance

hum
03 bum **04** buzz, hoax, lilt, purr, sing **05** chirm, croon, drone, pulse, sough, throb, thrum, whirr **06** be busy, mumble, murmur **07** applaud, buzzing, purring, vibrate **08** whirring **09** bombilate, bombinate, pulsation, throbbing, vibration **10** imposition
• **hum and haw**
04 sway **05** waver **06** dither **08** hesitate **09** fluctuate, oscillate, vacillate **10** dilly-dally **12** be indecisive, shilly-shally **14** blow hot and cold

human
03 man **04** body, kind, soul, weak **05** child, woman **06** genial, humane, mortal, person **07** fleshly **08** fallible, physical, rational, tolerant **09** anthropic **10** anthropoid, human being, individual, reasonable, vulnerable **11** anthropical, considerate, Homo sapiens, susceptible, sympathetic **13** compassionate, flesh and blood, understanding
• **human affairs**
04 life

humane
04 good, kind, mild **06** benign, gentle, kindly, loving, polite, tender **07** elegant, lenient **08** generous, merciful **09** classical, forgiving **10** benevolent, charitable, forbearing, humanizing, thoughtful **11** considerate, good-natured, kind-hearted, sympathetic **12** humanitarian **13** compassionate, understanding

humanely
06 gently, kindly, mildly **08** lovingly, tenderly **10** generously, mercifully **12** thoughtfully **13** kind-heartedly **15** compassionately, sympathetically

humanitarian
04 kind **06** humane **07** welfare **08** altruist, do-gooder, generous **09** unselfish **10** altruistic, benefactor, benevolent, charitable **11** considerate, sympathetic **13** compassionate, good Samaritan, philanthropic, understanding **14** philanthropist, public-spirited

humanitarianism
07 charity **08** goodwill, humanism
10 generosity **11** beneficence,
benevolence **12** philanthropy
14 charitableness, loving-kindness

humanities
04 arts **08** classics **10** literature,
philosophy **11** liberal arts

humanity
03 man **04** pity **05** mercy
06 mandom, people, ubuntu
07 mankind, mortals **08** goodness,
goodwill, kindness, sympathy
09 humankind, human race, mortality,
tolerance, womankind **10** compassion,
generosity, gentleness, humaneness,
tenderness **11** benevolence, Homo
sapiens **13** brotherly love, fellow-
feeling, understanding
14 thoughtfulness **15** kind-
heartedness

humanize
04 tame **05** edify **06** better, polish,
refine **07** educate, improve **08** civilize
09 cultivate, enlighten **11** domesticate

humankind
03 man **06** people **07** mankind,
mortals **08** humanity **09** human race,
mortality, womankind **11** Homo
sapiens

humanness
08 goodness, goodwill, humanity,
kindness, sympathy **09** tolerance
10 compassion, generosity, gentleness,
tenderness **11** benevolence, human
nature **14** understanding
14 thoughtfulness **15** kind-
heartedness

humble
03 low **04** base, mean, meek, poor,
sink **05** abase, crush, lower, lowly,
plain, pluck, shame, silly, small
06 abased, common, demean, demiss,
hummel, modest, polite, simple,
subdue **07** afflict, awnless, chasten,
deflate, degrade, depress, mortify,
servile **08** belittle, bring low, disgrace,
hornless, inferior, ordinary, yeomanly
09 afflicted, bring down, demissive,
discredit, disparage, humiliate,
prideless, unrefined **10** low-ranking,
obsequious, put to shame, respectful,
submissive, unassuming
11 commonplace, deferential,
subservient, sycophantic, unassertive,
unimportant **12** self-effacing,
supplicatory **13** cut down to size,
insignificant, unpretentious
14 unostentatious **15** undistinguished

humbleness
07 modesty **08** humility, meekness
09 deference, lowliness, servility
10 diffidence **13** self-abasement
14 self-effacement, submissiveness,
unassumingness **15** unassertiveness

humbly
03 low **06** meekly, simply **08** docilely,
modestly **09** cap in hand, servilely
10 sheepishly **11** diffidently

12 obsequiously, respectfully,
submissively, unassumingly
13 deferentially, subserviently
15 unpretentiously

humbug
03 con, gum, rot **04** bunk, cant, fake,
gaff, guff, hoax, sham **05** actor, balls,
bluff, cheat, fraud, fudge, poser, rogue,
trick **06** barney, berley, blague,
bunkum, burley, cajole, con man,
deceit, gammon, string **07** baloney,
bluffer, deceive, eyewash, rubbish,
swindle **08** buncombe, cheating,
claptrap, cobblers, flummery,
impostor, nonsense, pretence,
swindler, trickery **09** charlatan,
deception, gold brick, hypocrisy,
kidstakes, poppycock, trickster
10 balderdash, hollowness

humdrum
04 dull **05** banal, prosy **06** boring,
dreary **07** droning, mundane, routine,
tedious **08** everyday, monotony,
ordinary, tiresome, unvaried
09 bourgeois **10** monotonous,
uneventful **11** commonplace,
repetitious **12** run-of-the-mill
13 uninteresting

humid
03 wet **04** damp, dank **05** close,
heavy, mochy, moist, muggy
06 clammy, mochie, steamy, sticky,
sultry **10** oppressive

humidity
03 dew **04** damp, mist **07** wetness
08 dampness, dankness, moisture
09 closeness, heaviness, humidness,
moistness, mugginess, sogginess
10 clamminess, steaminess, stickiness,
sultriness, vaporosity **12** vaporousness

humiliate
05 abase, abash, break, crush, shame
06 demean, humble, wither
07 chasten, deflate, degrade, mortify,
put down **08** bring low, confound,
disgrace, take down **09** discomfit,
discredit, embarrass **11** make a fool of
12 bring shame on, take down a peg

humiliating
07 shaming **08** crushing, humbling,
snubbing **09** deflating, degrading,
humiliant, withering **10** chastening,
disgracing, inglorious, mortifying
11 disgraceful, humiliative, humiliatory,
ignominious **12** discomfiting,
embarrassing

humiliation
04 snub **05** shame **06** ignomy, rebuff
07 affront, put-down **08** crushing,
disgrace, downfall, humbling,
ignominy, take-down **09** abasement,
deflation, discredit, dishonour, humble
pie, indignity **10** chastening, loss of
face **11** confounding, degradation
12 discomfiture **13** embarrassment,
mortification

humility
07 modesty **08** meekness
09 deference, lowlihead, lowliness,

servility **10** diffidence, humbleness
13 self-abasement **14** self-effacement,
submissiveness, unassumingness
15 unassertiveness

humming see smelly

hummingbird
05 sylph, topaz **06** hermit, hummer
07 colibri, jacobin, rainbow
08 coquette **09** sabrewing, swordbill,
trochilus **10** racket-tail, rubythroat,
sicklebill **11** whitethroat **12** sapphire-
wing

hummock
04 hump **05** knoll, mound **06** barrow
07 hillock **09** elevation
10 prominence

humorist
03 wag, wit **05** clown, comic, joker
06 gagman, jester **08** comedian,
satirist **10** cartoonist **12** caricaturist

humorous
04 zany **05** comic, droll, funny, pawky,
witty **06** absurd **07** amusing, comical,
giocoso, jocular, playful, risible,
waggish **08** farcical **09** facetious,
funny ha-ha, hilarious, irregular,
laughable, ludicrous, satirical,
whimsical **10** capricious, Gilbertian,
humoristic, ridiculous **11** Falstaffian,
Rabelaisian **12** entertaining, knee-
slapping **13** side-splitting

humour
03 fun, wit **04** coax, gags, mood, vein
05 jokes, jolly, spoil **06** comedy,
cosset, favour, kidney, pamper, pecker,
permit, please, temper **07** flatter,
gratify, indulge, jesting, mollify,
observe, satisfy, spirits **08** badinage,
drollery, hilarity, pander to, repartee,
tolerate **09** absurdity, amusement,
wittiness **10** comply with, jocularity,
wisecracks **11** accommodate,
acquiesce in, disposition, frame of
mind, go along with, state of mind,
temperament **13** facetiousness
14 ridiculousness

The four bodily humours include:
05 blood
06 choler, phlegm
09 black bile
10 melancholy, yellow bile

Humour includes:
03 dry
04 blue, sick
05 black
07 gallows, surreal
08 farcical
09 satirical, slapstick
10 lavatorial
11 barrack-room, Pythonesque
12 Chaplinesque

humourless
02 po **03** dry **04** dour, dull, glum, grim
05 grave **06** boring, morose, solemn,
sombre **07** earnest, po-faced, serious,
tedious **09** long-faced, unsmiling
10 unlaughing

hump

03 hog, lug, pip, vex **04** arch, bend, bump, haul, knob, lift, lump, mass, ramp **05** annoy, bulge, bunch, carry, crook, curve, heave, hoist, humph, hunch, hurry, mound, ridge **08** shoulder, swelling **09** outgrowth, speed bump **10** projection, prominence, protrusion **11** excrescence **12** intumescence, protuberance

• **get the hump**
04 mope, sulk **09** be annoyed, get the pip **11** be irritated **13** be exasperated

• **give someone the hump**
03 bug, irk, nag, vex **04** gall, rile **05** anger, annoy, tease **06** bother, harass, hassle, madden, pester, plague, ruffle, wind up **07** disturb, hack off, provoke, tick off, trouble **08** brass off, irritate **09** aggravate, cheese off **10** exasperate **13** make sparks fly **14** drive up the wall **15** get someone's goat

• **over the hump**
12 over the worst **13** past the crisis

hump-backed

06 humped **07** crooked, gibbose, gibbous, hunched, stooped **08** deformed, kyphotic **09** misshapen **11** bunch-backed, crookbacked, hunchbacked

humped

04 bent **06** arched, curved **07** bunched, crooked, gibbose, gibbous, hunched

humus

03 mor **04** mull **05** moder

hunch

04 arch, bend, bump, hint, hump, idea, knob, lump, mass, ramp **05** bulge, curve, guess, mound, squat, stoop **06** crouch, curl up, draw in, huddle **07** feeling, inkling **08** swelling **09** intuition, outgrowth, suspicion **10** impression, projection, prominence, protrusion, sixth sense **11** premonition **12** presentiment, protuberance

hundred

01 C **04** cent **05** centi- **06** centum **07** cantred, cantref **09** centenary

hundredweight

03 cwt **07** quintal

Hungary

01 H **03** HUN **04** Hung

hunger

03 yen **04** ache, itch, long, need, pine, want, wish **05** crave, greed, raven, yearn **06** desire, famine, hanker, pining, starve, thirst **07** bulimia, craving, longing **08** appetite, voracity, yearning **09** emptiness, esurience, esuriency, hankering **10** famishment, greediness, hungriness, starvation **12** malnutrition, ravenousness **15** have a craving for, have a longing for

hungrily

06 avidly **07** eagerly **08** greedily **09** longingly **10** covetously, insatiably, ravenously

hungry

04 avid, lean, mean, poor, yaup **05** eager, empty, sharp **06** aching, greedy, hollow, pining, stingy **07** craving, itching, longing, needing, peckish, thirsty **08** covetous, desirous, esurient, famished, hungerly, ravenous, sharp-set, starving, underfed, yearning **09** ahungered, hankering, hungerful, voracious **10** insatiable **12** malnourished **14** could eat a horse, undernourished

hunk

04 base, clod, dish, goal, lump, mass, safe, slab, stud **05** block, chunk, he-man, piece, wedge **06** dollop, gobbet, secure **08** beefcake, macho man **09** dreamboat, strong man **10** studmuffin

hunt

03 cub, dog, rat, ren, rin, run **04** fish, hawk, meet, seal, seek, slug **05** chase, chevy, chivy, drive, hound, mouse, quest, scour, stalk, track, trail **06** battue, beagle, chivvy, course, ferret, follow, forage, halloo, prey on, pursue, rabbit, search, shadow, turtle **07** dismiss, look for, predate, pursuit, ransack, rummage, scare up **08** scouring, scrounge, stalking, tire down, tracking, venation **09** persecute, rummaging, still-hunt, try to find **11** investigate, run to ground **12** ride to hounds **13** investigation

hunter

05 hound, jäger **06** chaser, hawker, jaeger, Nimrod, ratter, shikar, wolfer **07** Actaeon, beagler, montero, shikari, turtler, venator, venerer, woodman **08** chasseur, free-shot, huntsman, rabbiter, shikaree, woodsman **10** lion-hunter, seal-fisher **11** still-hunter **13** rabbit trapper

hunting

05 chase **06** shikar, venery **07** birding, cubbing, ducking, lamping, ratting, wolfing, wolving **08** beagling, coursing, falconry, stalking, trapping, turtling, venation **11** field sports

• **expressions relating to hunting**
04 alew, so-ho **05** chevy, chivy **06** chivvy, halloa, halloo, hoicks, yoicks **07** tally-ho, tantivy

• **hunting-coat**
04 pink

• **hunting-cry**
04 alew **05** chevy, chivy **06** chivvy, halloa, halloo

• **hunting ground**
04 walk

• **hunting group**
04 meet

huntsman

04 Peel **05** jäger, yager **06** jaeger **07** montero, skirter, venator, woodman **08** chasseur, woodsman

hurdle

03 bar **04** doll, jump, snag, wall **05** fence, flake, hedge **06** raddle, wattle **07** barrier, problem, railing **08** handicap, obstacle **09** barricade, hindrance **10** difficulty, impediment **11** obstruction **12** complication **14** stumbling-block

hurl

◇ *anagram indicator*
03 bum, put **04** cast, dart, dash, fire, pelt, putt, send, toss **05** chuck, fling, heave, lanch, pitch, sling, swing, throw, wheel **06** hurtle, launch, let fly, propel **07** project **08** catapult **11** precipitate

hurly-burly

05 chaos **06** bedlam, bustle, frenzy, furore, hassle, hubbub, hustle, racket, tumult, unrest, uproar **07** trouble, turmoil **08** brouhaha, disorder, upheaval **09** agitation, commotion, confusion **10** disruption, turbulence **11** distraction, pandemonium

hurricane

04 gale, rout **05** storm **06** baguio, squall, tumult **07** cyclone, tempest, tornado, typhoon **09** commotion, whirlwind

hurried

03 ran **04** fast **05** brief, hasty, quick, rapid, short, swift **06** hectic, rushed, speedy **07** cursory, offhand, passing, rush job, shallow **08** careless, fleeting, slapdash **09** breakneck, festinate, transient **10** transitory **11** perfunctory, precipitate, superficial

hurriedly

07 flat out, hastily, hotfoot, in haste, quickly, rapidly, swiftly **08** pell-mell, speedily **09** posthaste **10** at top speed **11** at the double **12** lickety-split, without delay **13** helter-skelter **14** at a rate of knots, hell for leather **15** like the clappers

hurry

03 fly, hie, ren, rin, run **04** belt, dash, hare, hump, push, race, rush, tear **05** chase, drive, haste, mosey, press, pronto, speed **06** buck up, bustle, flurry, giddap, hasten, hubbub, hustle, scurry **07** press on, quicken, speed up, urgency, vamoose **08** celerity, chop-chop, despatch, dispatch, expedite, fastness, go all out, jump to it!, rapidity, step on it **09** beetle off, commotion, confusion, cut and run, festinate, hastiness, look alive, look smart, make haste, quickness, swiftness **10** accelerate, expedition, hightail it, look slippy, look snappy **11** run like hell **12** get a wiggle on, make it snappy, step on the gas **13** precipitation

hurt

◇ *anagram indicator*
03 ake, cut, hit, mar, noy, sad **04** ache, burn, gall, harm, maim, pain, sore **05** abuse, annoy, grief, smart, spoil, sting, throb, upset, wound, wring **06** aching, be sore, blight, bruise,

hurtful

damage, grazed, grieve, impair, injure, injury, lesion, maimed, misery, offend, sadden, sorrow, tingle **07** afflict, annoyed, blemish, bruised, burning, disable, injured, painful, sadness, scarred, scratch, torture, wounded **08** distress, ill-treat, lacerate, maltreat, mischief, nuisance, offended, saddened, smarting, soreness, tingling **09** affronted, aggrieved, be painful, in anguish, lacerated, miserable, sorrowful, suffering, throbbing **10** affliction, debilitate, discomfort, distressed **12** cause sadness **13** grief-stricken

hurtful

03 bad, ill **04** mean **05** catty, cruel, nasty **06** naught, nocent, shrewd, unkind **07** baleful, cutting, harmful, nocuous, noysome, ruinous, vicious **08** damaging, grievous, scathing, spiteful, wounding **09** injurious, malicious, obnoxious, offensive, pestilent, scatheful, upsetting **10** derogatory, maleficent, maleficial, pernicious **11** deleterious, destructive, detrimental, distressing, malefactory

hurtle

03 fly **04** belt, dash, dive, hurl, pelt, race, rush, spin, tear **05** clash, crash, shoot, speed **06** career, charge, plunge, rattle **08** brandish, step on it **12** step on the gas **14** step on the juice **15** put your foot down

husband

01 h **03** man **04** lord, mate, save **05** baron, groom, hoard, hubby, put by, store **06** budget, eke out, manage, master, old boy, old man, ration, save up, spouse **07** consort, goodman, manager, partner, reserve **08** conserve, preserve, put aside **09** cultivate, economize, other half **10** better half, hoddy-doddy, married man **12** gander-mooner, use carefully, use sparingly **15** mari complaisant
• **husband and wife**
04 pair **06** couple
• **without husband or wife**
04 sole

husbandry

06 saving, thrift **07** economy, farming, tillage **08** agronomy **09** frugality **10** agronomics, management **11** agriculture, cultivation, thriftiness **12** agribusiness, conservation **14** farm management, land management

hush

04 calm **05** peace, quiet, still **06** repose, settle, silent, soothe, subdue **07** be quiet, bestill, compose, mollify, quieten, silence **08** calmness, serenity **09** quietness, stillness **12** peacefulness, tranquillity
• **hush up**
03 gag **04** smug **06** huddle, stifle **07** conceal, cover up, smother **08** keep dark, suppress **10** keep secret

hush-hush

06 secret **09** top-secret **10** classified, restricted, under wraps **12** confidential

husk

03 pod **04** bran, case, coir, hull, peel, pill, rind, skin **05** chaff, shale, sheal, sheel, shell, shiel, shill, shuck, strip **06** legume **07** capsule, epicarp **08** covering **09** corn shuck

huskily

06 deeply **07** gruffly, harshly **08** croakily, gravelly, hoarsely **10** gutturally

husky

03 dry, low **04** deep **05** beefy, burly, gruff, harsh, hefty, Inuit, rough, thick **06** brawny, coarse, croaky, hoarse, strong **07** rasping, throaty **08** croaking, gravelly, guttural, muscular **09** strapping, well-built

hussy

04 minx, slag, slut, tart, vamp **05** huzzy, tramp **06** hussif, limmer **07** floozie **08** scrubber **09** housewife, temptress **10** loose woman

hustle

03 fly, tew **04** dash, fuss, push, rush, sell, stir **05** crowd, elbow, force, fraud, hurry, nudge, shove **06** bounce, bundle, bustle, hasten, huddle, jostle, justle, rustle, thrust, tumult **07** swindle **08** activity **09** agitation, commotion, manhandle **10** hurly-burly, pressurize

hut

03 den **04** shed, skeo, skio, tilt **05** banda, booth, bothy, cabin, hogan, humpy, shack, sheal, shiel, whare **06** bothan, bothie, chalet, gunyah, lean-to, mia-mia, pondok, rancho, saeter, shanty, succah, sukkah, wiltja, wurley **07** caboose, shelter, wickiup **08** log cabin, rondavel, shealing, shieling **09** pondokkie, rancheria

hybrid

◇ *anagram indicator*
05 cross, mixed **06** mosaic **07** amalgam, bigener, mixture, mongrel **08** combined, compound **09** composite, crossbred, half-blood, half-breed **10** crossbreed **11** combination, single-cross **13** heterogeneous **14** conglomeration

Hybrids include:

02 zo **03** dso, dzo, zho **04** dzho, mule, OEIC, Ugli® **05** oxlip, topaz **06** oxslip **07** beefalo, Bourbon, cattabu, cattalo, Jersian, lurcher, plumcot, tangelo, tea rose **08** citrange, noisette, sunberry, tayberry **09** perpetual, tiger tail, triticale **10** clementine, loganberry, polyanthus **11** boysenberry, bull-mastiff, Jacqueminot, marionberry, miracle rice **13** polecat-ferret

hybridize

05 cross **10** bastardize, crossbreed, interbreed

hydrant

01 H **02** FP **08** fireplug

hydrocarbon

Hydrocarbons include:

03 wax **05** halon **06** aldrin, alkane, alkene, alkyne, butane, cetane, decane, ethane, hexane, indene, nonane, octane, olefin, picene, pyrene, retene **07** benzene, heptane, methane, olefine, pentane, propane, styrene, terpene **08** camphane, camphene, diphenyl, isoprene, pristane, stilbene **09** butadiene **10** benzpyrene, mesitylene **11** hatchettite, naphthalane **12** cyclopropane

hydrogen

01 H

hyena

09 tiger wolf **10** strandwolf

hygiene

06 purity **09** sterility **10** sanitation **11** cleanliness **12** disinfection, sanitariness **13** wholesomeness

hygienic

04 pure **05** clean **07** aseptic, healthy, sterile **08** germ-free, sanitary **09** wholesome **10** salubrious, sterilized **11** disinfected

hymn

03 air **04** song **05** carol, chant, dirge, motet, paean, psalm **06** anthem, choral, chorus, mantra, Te Deum **07** cantata, chorale, introit, mantram, Sanctus **08** canticle, cathisma, dies irae, doxology, hymeneal, sequence **09** dithyramb, offertory, spiritual, sticheron, trisagion, troparion **10** paraphrase, procession, Tantum ergo **11** recessional, Stabat Mater **12** Marseillaise, processional, song of praise

hype

04 fuss, plug, puff **06** racket, talk up **07** build up, build-up, promote, puffery **08** ballyhoo, plugging **09** advertise, deception, promotion, publicity, publicize **10** razzmatazz **11** advertising **13** advertisement

hyped up

04 fake, high, wild **05** eager, hyper, moved **06** elated **07** anxious, excited, fired up, frantic, stirred, uptight **08** agitated, animated, frenzied, restless, thrilled, worked up **09** wrought-up **10** artificial, stimulated **11** exhilarated, overwrought **12** enthusiastic **13** in high spirits, on tenterhooks **14** beside yourself, thrilled to bits

hyperbole

06 excess **07** auxesis **08** overkill **12** exaggeration, extravagance **13** magnification, overstatement

hypercritical
05 fussy, picky 06 choosy, strict
07 carping, finicky 08 captious,
niggling, pedantic 09 cavilling,
quibbling 10 censorious, nit-picking,
pernickety 11 persnickety 12 fault-
finding 13 hair-splitting 14 over-
particular

hypnos
06 Somnus

hypnotic
07 numbing 08 magnetic, sedative
09 soporific 10 compelling,
magnetical 11 fascinating,
mesmerizing, somniferous
12 irresistible, spellbinding,
stupefactive 13 sleep-inducing

hypnotism
08 Braidism, hypnosis 09 mesmerism
10 suggestion 12 neurypnology
14 auto-suggestion, electrobiology,
neurohypnology 15 animal
magnetism

hypnotize
06 dazzle 07 beguile, bewitch,
enchant 08 entrance 09 captivate,
fascinate, magnetize, mesmerize,
spellbind 10 put to sleep

hypochondria
03 hip, hyp 08 neurosis
15 hypochondriasis

hypochondriac
08 neurotic 10 melancholy,
phrenesiac 11 atrabilious
14 hypochondriast, valetudinarian
15 hypochondriacal

hypocrisy
04 cant 06 deceit 07 falsity
08 pretence 09 deception, duplicity
10 dishonesty, double-talk, lip service,
pharisaism, phoneyness
11 dissembling, insincerity 12 two-
facedness, wearing a mask
13 deceitfulness, dissimulation,
double-dealing

hypocrite
05 fraud, Janus, pseud 06 canter,
mucker, phoney, pseudo 08 deceiver,
impostor, Pharisee, Tartuffe
09 charlatan, Pecksniff, pretender
10 dissembler, Holy Willie,
mountebank 15 whited sepulchre

hypocritical
05 false, lying 06 double, hollow,
phoney 08 specious, spurious, two-
faced 09 deceitful, deceptive,
dishonest, insincere, pharisaic, self-
pious, Tartufian, Tartufish 10 false-
faced, fraudulent, histrionic, Janus-
faced, perfidious, Tartuffian, Tartuffish
11 dissembling, double-faced,
duplicitous, Janian-faced, pharisaical
12 histrionical, Pecksniffian 13 double-
dealing, sanctimonious, self-righteous

hypothesis
03 hyp 05 axiom 06 notion, theory,
thesis 07 premise, theorem
09 postulate 10 assumption,
conjecture 11 presumption,
proposition, speculation, supposition

hypothetical
03 hyp 07 assumed 08 imagined,

notional, presumed, proposed,
supposed 09 imaginary
11 conjectural, speculative, theoretical
13 suppositional

hypothetically
07 ideally 08 in theory 10 supposedly
13 conjecturally, speculatively,
theoretically

hysteria
05 mania, panic 06 frenzy, mother
07 habdabs, madness 08 delirium,
neurosis 09 agitation, hysterics 15 fits
of the mother

hysterical
03 mad 04 rich 06 crazed, raving
07 berserk, frantic 08 demented,
farcical, frenzied, in a panic, neurotic
09 delirious, hilarious, ludicrous,
priceless 10 ridiculous, uproarious
11 overwrought 12 out of control
13 side-splitting 14 beside yourself,
extremely funny, uncontrollable

hysterically
05 madly 08 absurdly, in a panic
10 farcically 11 frantically, hilariously,
ludicrously, screamingly
12 neurotically, out of control,
ridiculously, uproariously 13 out of
your mind 14 beside yourself,
uncontrollably

hysterics
05 mania, panic 06 frenzy
07 habdabs, madness 08 delirium,
hysteria, neurosis 09 agitation 12 crise
de nerfs

I

I
02 ch, me **03** aye, che, ego, ich, one, yes **05** India **06** indeed, iodine
• **I am**
02 I'm **03** sum

ice
04 cool, kill **05** chill, frost, glaze
06 freeze, harden **07** diamond, iciness, reserve **08** coldness, coolness, diamonds, distance, enfreeze
09 formality **10** freeze over, frostiness
11 frozen water, refrigerate

• **ice cream**
04 cone **05** bombe, kulfi **06** bucket, cornet, gelato, ripple, slider, sorbet, sundae **07** cassata, choc-bar, granita, sherbet, spumone, spumoni, tortoni
08 hoky-poky, macallum **10** hokey-pokey, Neapolitan **11** tutti-frutti
• **put on ice**
05 defer, delay **06** put off, shelve
07 suspend **08** postpone **14** hold in abeyance **15** leave in abeyance

iceberg
04 berg, calf **07** growler

ice-cold
03 icy, raw **04** hard, iced, numb
05 algid, fixed, gelid, polar, rigid, stiff
06 arctic, baltic, frigid, frosty, frozen
07 chilled, frosted, glacial **08** freezing, icebound, Siberian **10** solidified
11 frozen-stiff **12** bitterly cold

ice hockey

Iceland
02 IS **03** ISL

ice skating

icily
06 coldly, coolly, rudely **07** stiffly
08 formally, morosely **12** forbiddingly

icon
04 idol **05** image **06** figure, smiley, sprite, symbol **08** likeness, portrait
09 portrayal **14** representation

iconoclast
05 rebel **06** critic **07** heretic, radical, sceptic **08** opponent **09** denouncer, dissenter, dissident **10** questioner, unbeliever **11** denunciator **12** image-breaker

iconoclastic
07 impious, radical **08** critical
09 dissident, heretical, sceptical
10 innovative, irreverent, rebellious, subversive **11** dissentient, questioning
12 denunciatory

icy
03 raw **04** cold, cool, rimy, rude
05 aloof, chill, gelid, polar, stiff, stony
06 arctic, biting, bitter, chilly, formal, frigid, frosty, frozen, glassy, morose, slippy **07** distant, glacial, hostile, ice-cold **08** chilling, freezing, icebound, reserved, Siberian, slippery
10 forbidding, frostbound, restrained, unfriendly **11** indifferent

id
04 orfe

Idaho
02 ID

idea
03 aim, end **04** clou, clue, goal, idée, plan, view **05** fancy, guess, image, point **06** belief, design, notion, object, reason, scheme, target, theory, vision
07 conceit, concept, feeling, inkling, opinion, purpose, thought, wrinkle
08 proposal **09** brainwave, intention, judgement, objective, obsession, suspicion, viewpoint **10** conception, conjecture, hypothesis, impression, perception, suggestion **11** abstraction, connotation, inspiration, proposition
13 understanding **14** interpretation, recommendation

ideal
04 acme, best, type **05** cause, dream, image, model **06** ethics, morals, unreal, Utopia **07** eidolon, epitome, example, highest, optimal, optimum, paragon, pattern, perfect, supreme, utopian **08** absolute, abstract, complete, exemplar, fanciful, notional, romantic, standard **09** archetype, benchmark, criterion, imaginary, nonpareil, principle, prototype, visionary, yardstick **10** archetypal, conceptual, consummate, idealistic, perfection **11** impractical, moral values, theoretical **12** hypothetical, unattainable **13** ethical values, philosophical **14** moral standards, quintessential
• **ideal state**
06 Utopia **07** nirvana

idealism
09 mentalism **10** utopianism
11 romanticism **13** perfectionism
14 impracticality

idealist
07 dreamer **08** optimist, romantic
09 visionary **11** romanticist
13 perfectionist

idealistic
07 utopian **08** quixotic, romantic
09 visionary **10** optimistic, starry-eyed
11 impractical, unrealistic
13 impracticable, perfectionist

idealization
07 worship **10** apotheosis, exaltation
11 ennoblement, idolization
13 glamorization, glorification,
romanticizing **15** romanticization

idealize
05 exalt **07** glorify, idolize, worship
09 glamorize **10** utopianize
11 romanticize

ideally
06 at best **08** in theory, mentally
09 perfectly **13** theoretically
14 hypothetically, in an ideal world
15 in a perfect world

idée fixe
06 hang-up **07** complex **08** fixation
09 fixed idea, leitmotiv, monomania,
obsession

identical
04 like, same, self, twin **05** alike, equal,
right **06** cloned **07** identic, numeric,
precise, similar **08** matching, selfsame **09** analogous, congruent,
duplicate, syngeneic **10** coincident,
consistent, equivalent **11** a dead ringer
12 doppelgänger **13** corresponding,
one and the same, spitting image
15 interchangeable

identically
05 alike **07** equally **09** similarly
11 analogously, congruently, just the
same **12** consistently, equivalently, in
the same way **15** correspondingly,
interchangeably

identifiable
05 known **10** detectable, noticeable
11 discernible, perceptible
12 recognizable, unmistakable
13 ascertainable **15** distinguishable

identification
02 ID **03** tie **04** bond, link **05** badge,
label **06** naming, papers **07** empathy,
rapport **08** passbook, passport,
relation, spotting, sympathy
09 biometric, detection, diagnosis,
documents, labelling **10** connection
11 association, correlation, credentials,
involvement, pointing-out,
recognition **12** dactyloscopy, identity
card, relationship **13** fellow feeling,
interrelation **14** classification, driving
licence, fingerprinting

identify
03 tag **04** know, name, spot **05** label,
place **06** couple, detect, finger, notice,
relate **07** connect, discern, feel for, find
out, involve, make out, pick out, pin
down, specify **08** classify, diagnose,
discover, perceive, pinpoint, point out,
relate to **09** ascertain, associate,
catalogue, establish, recognize,
respond to, single out **11** distinguish
13 associate with, empathize with
14 put the finger on, sympathize with
15 think of together

identity
02 ID **03** ego **04** face, name, self
05 image, roots, seity, unity
07 oneness, profile **08** equality,
likeness, property, sameness, selfhood
09 character, closeness, existence
10 appearance, background,
impression, personhood, public face,
similarity, uniqueness **11** equivalence,
personality, resemblance, singularity
12 selfsameness **13** individuality,
particularity, public persona
14 correspondence **15** distinctiveness

ideologist
07 teacher, thinker **08** theorist
09 ideologue, visionary **11** doctrinaire,
philosopher

ideology
05 credo, creed, dogma, faith, ideas
06 belief, tenets, theory, thesis
07 beliefs, opinion **08** doctrine,
opinions, teaching **09** doctrines,
world-view **10** philosophy, principles
11 convictions, metaphysics

See also **political**

idiocy
05 folly **06** lunacy **07** inanity
08 daftness, insanity **09** absurdity,
craziness, silliness, stupidity
10 imbecility **11** fatuousness
13 foolhardiness, senselessness

idiom
04 talk **05** style, usage **06** jargon,
phrase, speech, Syrism **07** Arabism,
dialect, Grecism, Pahlavi, Pehlevi,
Persism, Slavism, Syriasm
08 Aramaism, Graecism, Hebraism,
idiotism, Irishism, language, Latinism,
locution, parlance, polonism,
prosaism, Saxonism, Semitism,
Sinicism **09** anglicism, Celticism,
Chaldaism, Gallicism, Germanism,
Gothicism, Hellenism, Italicism,
Scoticism, Syriacism, Syrianism
10 classicism, cockneyism,
Englishism, expression, femininism,
Italianism, Johnsonese, Scotticism,
vernacular, Yiddishism
11 Americanism, Hibernicism,
phraseology **12** classicalism,
Hibernianism, turn of phrase
13 Australianism, colloquialism,
vernacularism

idiomatic
06 native **07** correct, natural
08 everyday **09** dialectal
10 colloquial, idiolectal, vernacular
11 dialectical, grammatical

idiosyncrasy
03 way **05** freak, habit, quirk, trait
06 oddity **07** feature, quality
09 mannerism **10** speciality
11 peculiarity, singularity
12 eccentricity **13** individuality
14 characteristic

idiosyncratic
03 odd **06** quirky **08** peculiar,
personal, singular **09** eccentric
10 individual **11** distinctive
14 characteristic

idiot
03 ass, mug, nit, nut, oaf **04** berk, clod,
clot, dill, dope, dork, fool, geek, jerk,
nana, nerd, nerk, nong, prat, putz, twit
05 chump, clown, divvy, dumbo,
dunce, eejit, galah, klutz, moron, nelly,
ninny, prick, schmo, twerp, wally
06 bammer, bampot, cretin, dimwit,
doofus, drongo, dum-dum, muppet,
nidget, nitwit, numpty, sucker
07 airhead, barmpot, dumb-ass, fat-
head, halfwit, jughead, natural, pillock,
plonker, schmuck, wazzock
08 boofhead, dipstick, flathead,
imbecile, innocent, numskull, pea-
brain **09** birdbrain, blockhead, cloth
head, ignoramus, lame brain, malt-
horse, simpleton, thickhead
10 bufflehead, nincompoop
11 chowderhead, knuckle-head

See also **fool**

idiotic
◊ *anagram indicator*
03 mad, twp **04** daft, dozy, dumb
05 barmy, batty, crazy, dorky, dotty,
goofy, inane, inept, nutty, potty, silly,
wacky **06** absurd, insane, oafish,
simple, stupid, unwise **07** asinine,
dumb-ass, fatuous, foolish, moronic,
risible **08** gormless, ignorant **09** dim-
witted, half-baked, ludicrous,
pointless, senseless **10** half-witted, ill-
advised, ridiculous **11** hare-brained,
injudicious, nonsensical, thick-headed
12 crack-brained, short-sighted,
simple-minded, unreasonable **13** ill-
considered, knuckle-headed,
unintelligent

idle
03 lig **04** dead, doss, laze, lazy, loaf,
mike, move, vain **05** dally, empty, light,
petty, relax, shirk, skive, slack, waste,
while **06** bludge, casual, daidle,
dawdle, fester, fiddle, futile, loiter,
lollop, lounge, potter, putter, unused,
wanton **07** dormant, dronish, foolish,
fritter, goof off, jobless, loafish, shallow,
sit back, trivial, useless, work-shy
08 baseless, bone-idle, inactive,
indolent, kill time, lallygag, lollygag,
slothful, sluggish, sod about, tick over,
trifling **09** bum around, do nothing,
fruitless, gold-brick, lethargic, on the
dole, pointless, redundant, while away,
worthless **10** mothballed, not
working, take it easy, unedifying,
unemployed, unoccupied, whip the
cat **11** fiddle about, horse around,

idleness

ineffective, ineffectual, inoperative, unimportant **12** be ready to run, fiddle around, fiddle-faddle, unproductive, unsuccessful **13** be operational, be ready to work, insignificant, lackadaisical

idleness

04 ease **05** sloth **06** lazing, torpor **07** idlesse, inertia, leisure, loafing, skiving, vacancy, vacuity **08** inaction, laziness, otiosity **09** indolence, pottering **10** inactivity, otioseness, vegetating **12** slothfulness, sluggishness, unemployment **13** shiftlessness **14** dolce far niente

idler

04 slob, spiv **05** drone, sloth **06** bumble, bummle, dodger, donnat, donnot, dosser, loafer, skiver, truant, waster **07** bludger, dawdler, goof-off, laggard, Lollard, lounger, shirker, slacker, wastrel **08** do-naught, fine lady, layabout, sluggard **09** do-nothing, gold brick, lazybones **10** malingerer **11** couch potato **12** carpet-knight, clock-watcher **13** fine gentleman **14** good-for-nothing

idol

03 god, pet **04** hero, icon, joss, sham, star, wood **05** deity, image, pagod, pin-up, swami **06** effigy, fetish, figure, mammet, maumet, mawmet, mommet, pagoda **07** beloved, darling, fantasy, goddess, heroine, phantom **08** Baphomet, impostor, likeness **09** favourite, semblance, superstar **11** blue-eyed boy, graven image

idolater

06 adorer, votary **07** admirer, devotee, idolist **10** iconolater, idolatress, worshipper **14** idol-worshipper

idolatrous

05 pagan **07** adoring **09** adulatory, heretical, idolizing, lionizing **10** glorifying, uncritical **11** reverential, worshipping **15** idol-worshipping

idolatry

07 idolism **08** mammetry, maumetry, mawmetry, paganism, whoredom **09** adoration, adulation, fetishism, idolizing, reverence **10** admiration, exaltation, heathenism, iconolatry **11** deification, fornication, hero-worship, icon worship, worshipping **13** glorification

idolize

04 love **05** adore, deify, exalt **06** admire, dote on, revere **07** adulate, glorify, lionize, worship **08** venerate **09** reverence **11** hero-worship **14** put on a pedestal

idyllic

05 happy **06** rustic **07** perfect **08** blissful, charming, heavenly, pastoral, peaceful, romantic **09** idealized, unspoiled, wonderful **10** delightful **11** picturesque, Theocritean

ie

02 so

if

02 an **03** and, gin **06** though **07** suppose, whether **08** as long as, assuming, in case of, provided, so long as, whenever **09** condition, providing, supposing **11** supposition, uncertainty **12** assuming that, in the event of **13** supposing that **15** on condition that

• **even if**

03 and, tho **04** albe **05** albee, all-be **06** albeit, though **07** suppose

• **if it**

03 an't

iffy

04 suss **05** dodgy, risky **07** dubious **08** doubtful, low-grade **09** defective, imperfect, tentative, uncertain, undecided, unsettled **10** second-rate **11** substandard **13** disappointing **14** not up to scratch, unsatisfactory

ignite

04 burn, fire **05** light, torch **06** kindle **07** flare up, inflame **08** spark off, touch off **09** catch fire, set alight, set fire to, set on fire **11** conflagrate, put a match to **15** burst into flames

ignoble

03 low **04** base, mean, vile **05** petty, small **06** vulgar **07** heinous **08** infamous, shameful, unworthy, wretched **09** worthless **10** despicable **11** disgraceful **12** contemptible **13** dishonourable

ignobly

06 meanly, vilely **07** pettily **10** despicably, infamously, shamefully, wretchedly **12** contemptibly **13** disgracefully, dishonourably, without honour

ignominious

04 base **05** sorry **06** abject **08** infamous, shameful **09** degrading **10** despicable, mortifying, scandalous **11** disgraceful, humiliating, undignified **12** contemptible, disreputable, embarrassing **13** discreditable, dishonourable

ignominiously

10 despicably, shamefully **12** disreputably, scandalously **13** disgracefully, dishonourably

ignominy

05 odium, shame **06** infamy, stigma **07** obloquy, scandal **08** contempt, disgrace, reproach **09** discredit, dishonour, disrepute, indignity **10** opprobrium **11** degradation, humiliation **13** mortification

ignoramus

03 ass **04** dolt, fool **05** dunce **06** dimwit, duffer, ignaro **07** dullard, halfwit **08** bonehead, ignorant, imbecile, numskull **09** blockhead, simpleton **10** illiterate **11** know-nothing

ignorance

05 night **07** naivety **08** oblivion **09** greenness, innocence, nescience, stupidity, thickness **10** illiteracy **11** unawareness **12** inexperience **13** obliviousness, unfamiliarity **14** unintelligence **15** unconsciousness

ignorant

04 dumb, lewd, rude **05** blind, dense, naive, thick **06** ingram, ingrum, stupid, unread **07** ill-bred, redneck, unaware, unknown **08** backward, clueless, innocent, inscient, nescient, untaught **09** benighted, in the dark, lack-Latin, oblivious, unknowing, unlearned, untrained, unwitting **10** analphabet, illiterate, innumerate, uneducated, unfamiliar, uninformed, unschooled **11** analphabete, ill-educated, ill-informed, know-nothing, unconfirmed, unconscious, uninitiated **12** discourteous, having no idea, unacquainted **13** inexperienced, unenlightened

ignore

◊ *deletion indicator*

03 cut **04** balk, omit, snub **05** baulk, blank, blink, spurn, waive **06** bypass, pass by, reject, slight **07** cut dead, high-hat, neglect, tune out **08** brush off, discount, overlook, pass over, set aside, shrug off **09** disregard **10** brush aside, scrub round, slight over **11** not listen to, run away from **12** cold-shoulder **13** be oblivious to, keep in the dark **14** shut your eyes to, take for granted, take no notice of, turn a deaf ear to, turn your back on **15** close your eyes to, look the other way, turn a blind eye to

ilk

04 each, kind, make, same, sort, type, ylke **05** brand, breed, class, stamp, style **07** variety **09** character **11** description

ill

◊ *anagram indicator*

03 bad **04** down, evil, harm, hurt, pain, sick, weak **05** amiss, badly, cronk, crook, dicky, frail, harsh, rough, seedy, trial **06** ailing, barely, crummy, feeble, groggy, grotty, hardly, infirm, injury, laid up, naught, poorly, queasy, severe, sorrow, trials, unkind, unweal, unwell, wicked **07** adverse, ailment, cruelty, grieved, harmful, hostile, hurtful, ominous, peevish, problem, ruinous, run down, trouble, unlucky **08** critical, damaging, disaster, diseased, scantily, scarcely, sinister, unkindly **09** adversely, afflicted, bedridden, by no means, difficult, in a bad way, incorrect, injurious, off-colour, resentful, suffering, unhealthy, unluckily **10** affliction, broken-down, distressed, indisposed, misfortune, out of sorts, unfriendly, unpleasant, wickedness, wrongfully **11** belligerent, deleterious, destruction, destructive, detrimental, incompetent, peelie-wally, threatening, tribulation,

unfortunate, unpromising
12 antagonistic, inadequately,
inauspicious, infelicitous,
unfavourable, unfavourably,
unpropitious **13** reprehensible,
unfortunately **14** disapprovingly,
inauspiciously, insufficiently,
unpleasantness, unsuccessfully,
valetudinarian **15** under the weather

ill at ease
> anagram indicator
04 edgy **05** tense **06** on edge, uneasy,
unsure **07** anxious, awkward, fidgety,
nervous, strange, worried **08** farouche,
hesitant, restless **09** disturbed,
unrelaxed, unsettled **10** disquieted
11 embarrassed **13** on tenterhooks,
self-conscious, uncomfortable

speak ill of
03 nag, pan **04** carp, slag, slam
05 blame, cut up, decry, knock, roast,
score, slash, slate, trash **06** attack,
hammer, impugn, niggle, peck at, tilt at
07 censure, condemn, nit-pick,
rubbish, run down, scarify, slag off,
snipe at **08** backbite, badmouth,
denounce, wade into **09** castigate,
criticize, denigrate, disparage,
excoriate, have a go at, misreport, pull
apart, take apart, tear apart
10 animadvert, come down on, go to
town on, vituperate **11** pick holes in
12 disapprove of, pull to pieces, put the
boot in, tear to shreds **13** find fault
with, tear a strip off **15** do a hatchet job
on, pass judgement on

ill-advised
04 rash **05** hasty **06** unwise **07** foolish
08 careless, overseen, reckless **09** ill-
judged, imprudent, misguided
11 injudicious, thoughtless **12** short-
sighted **13** ill-considered,
inappropriate

ill-assorted
> anagram indicator
08 unsuited **09** misallied
10 discordant, mismatched
11 incongruous, uncongenial
12 incompatible, inharmonious

ill-bred
> anagram indicator
04 rude **05** crass, crude, ocker
06 coarse, vulgar **07** boorish, loutish,
uncivil, uncouth **08** ignorant, impolite,
unseemly **10** indelicate, misbehaved,
unmannerly, unnurtured **11** bad-
mannered, ill-mannered, uncivilized
12 discourteous

ill-considered
04 rash **05** hasty **06** unwise **07** foolish
08 careless, heedless **09** ill-judged,
imprudent, overhasty **10** ill-advised
11 improvident, injudicious, precipitate
12 misconceived

ill-defined
03 dim **04** hazy **05** fuzzy, vague
06 blurry, woolly **07** blurred, mongrel,
shadowy, unclear **08** nebulous
09 imprecise, shapeless **10** indefinite,
indistinct

ill-disposed
04 anti **06** averse **07** against, hostile,
opposed **08** inimical **10** malevolent,
unfriendly **11** disaffected,
unwelcoming **12** antagonistic
13 unco-operative, unsympathetic

illegal
05 wrong **06** banned, barred
07 bootleg, crooked, illicit
08 criminal, outlawed, unlawful,
wrongful, wrongous **09** felonious,
forbidden **10** adulterine, fraudulent,
prohibited, proscribed **11** black-
market, interdicted **12** criminalized,
illegitimate, unauthorized **15** under-
the-counter

illegality
05 crime, wrong **06** felony
09 wrongness **11** criminality, illicitness,
lawlessness, malfeasance
12 illegitimacy, unlawfulness,
wrongfulness

illegally
07 wrongly **08** guiltily **09** illicitly
10 criminally, unlawfully, wrongfully
13 against the law, disobediently
14 illegitimately

illegible
05 faint **07** obscure **08** scrawled
10 hard to read, indistinct, unreadable
12 hieroglyphic **14** indecipherable,
unintelligible

illegitimacy
08 bastardy **10** bastardism **12** bend-
sinister **13** baton-sinister
14 fatherlessness

illegitimate
04 base, love **07** bastard, illegal, illicit,
invalid, lawless, natural, unsound
08 base-born, improper, misbegot,
nameless, spurious, unlawful
09 illogical, incorrect **10** adulterine,
fatherless, unfathered, unlicensed
11 misbegotten, unwarranted
12 inadmissible, unauthorized

ill-equipped
07 exposed **10** unprovided,
unsupplied **11** ill-supplied,
underfunded, undermanned,
unprotected **12** disappointed,
understaffed **13** underfinanced, under
strength, unprovided for **14** under-
resourced

ill-fated
06 doomed **07** hapless, unhappy,
unlucky **08** blighted, luckless **09** ill-
omened, star-crost **10** ill-starred
11 star-crossed, unfortunate

ill-favoured
04 ugly **05** plain **06** homely
07 hideous **08** unlovely **09** repulsive,
unsightly **12** unattractive
15 unprepossessing

ill-feeling
05 anger, odium, pique, spite, wrath
06 animus, enmity, grudge, malice
07 dudgeon, ill-will, offence, rancour
08 bad blood, sourness **09** animosity,

hostility **10** antagonism, bitterness,
resentment, unkindness **11** frustration,
indignation **12** hard feelings
14 disgruntlement **15** dissatisfaction

ill-founded
07 unsound **08** baseless
10 groundless **11** unconfirmed,
unjustified, unsupported
15 unsubstantiated

ill-gotten
03 hot **04** bent **05** dodgy, taken
06 nicked, stolen, swiped **07** nobbled
08 pilfered **09** purloined, ripped off
10 knocked off

ill-humour
03 dod **04** bile, dump **05** dumps,
rheum **06** spleen **09** distemper

ill-humoured
04 tart **05** cross, huffy, moody, ratty,
sharp, sulky, testy **06** crabby, grumpy,
morose, shirty, snappy, sullen
07 crabbed, grouchy, peevish, stroppy,
waspish **08** petulant, snappish
09 crotchety, impatient, irascible,
irritable **11** acrimonious, bad-
tempered, distempered
12 cantankerous, disagreeable
13 quick-tempered

illiberal
04 mean **05** petty, tight **06** stingy
07 bigoted, miserly **08** verkramp
09 hidebound, niggardly **10** intolerant,
prejudiced, ungenerous **11** close-
fisted, reactionary, small-minded, tight-
fisted **12** narrow-minded,
parsimonious, uncharitable
13 unenlightened

illicit
03 sly **05** black, wrong **06** banned,
barred, shonky **07** bootleg, furtive,
illegal **08** criminal, improper, stealthy,
unlawful **09** forbidden, ill-gotten,
secretive **10** contraband, prohibited,
unlicensed **11** black-market,
clandestine **12** illegitimate,
unauthorized **13** surreptitious, under-
the-table **15** under-the-counter

illicitly
07 wrongly **08** guiltily **09** illegally
10 criminally, unlawfully, wrongfully
13 against the law, disobediently
14 illegitimately

Illinois
02 IL **03** Ill

illiteracy
09 ignorance **15** inability to read, lack
of education, lack of schooling

illiterate
08 ignorant, untaught **09** benighted,
unlearned, untutored **10** letterless,
uncultured, uneducated, unlettered,
unschooled **12** analphabetic

ill-judged
04 daft, rash **05** hasty **06** unwise
07 foolish **08** mistaken, reckless
09 foolhardy, impolitic, imprudent,
misguided, overhasty, unadvised

10 ill-advised, incautious, indiscreet **11** injudicious, wrong-headed **12** short-sighted **13** ill-considered

ill-mannered
04 rude **05** crude **06** coarse **07** boorish, cubbish, ill-bred, loutish, uncivil, uncouth **08** churlish, impolite, insolent **10** ill-behaved, unmannerly **11** bad-mannered, insensitive **12** badly behaved, discourteous

ill-natured
03 wry **04** acid, mean, ugly **05** cross, nasty, sulky, surly **06** crabby, gnarly, shrewd, sullen, unkind **07** crabbed, vicious **08** churlish, perverse, petulant, shrewish, spiteful **09** malicious, malignant **10** malevolent, unfriendly, unpleasant, vindictive **11** bad-tempered **12** disagreeable

illness
03 wog **04** bout, evil, tout, towt, weed, weid **05** touch **06** attack, malady **07** ailment, disease **08** disorder, sickness **09** complaint, condition, ill health, infirmity **10** affliction, disability, poor health **13** indisposition
See also **disease**

illogical
05 crazy, wrong **06** absurd, faulty **07** invalid, unsound **08** fallible, specious, spurious **09** casuistic, incorrect, senseless, untenable **10** fallacious, irrational **11** meaningless, sophistical **12** inconsequent, inconsistent, unreasonable, unscientific, woolly minded

illogicality
07 fallacy **08** unreason **09** absurdity **10** invalidity **11** unsoundness **12** speciousness **13** inconsistency, irrationality, senselessness **14** fallaciousness

ill-starred
06 doomed **07** hapless, unhappy, unlucky **08** blighted, ill-fated **09** star-crost **11** star-crossed, unfortunate **12** inauspicious

ill-tempered
04 curt **05** cross, curst, ratty, sharp, testy **06** crabby, cranky, girnie, grumpy, morose, shirty, tetchy, touchy **07** crabbed, grouchy, stroppy, vicious **08** choleric, spiteful **09** crotchety, impatient, irascible, irritable **10** ill-natured **11** acrimonious, bad-tempered, ill-humoured **12** cantankerous

ill-timed
05 crass, inept **07** awkward **08** mistimed, tactless, untimely **09** unwelcome **10** wrong-timed **11** inopportune, unfortunate **12** inconvenient, unseasonable **13** inappropriate

ill-treat
◇ *anagram indicator*
04 harm **05** abuse, wrong **06** damage, demean, injure, misuse **07** neglect,

oppress **08** maltreat, misguide, mistreat **09** mishandle

ill-treatment
04 harm **05** abuse **06** damage, ill-use, injury, misuse **07** neglect **11** manhandling, mishandling **12** maltreatment, mistreatment

illuminate
04 limn **05** adorn, edify, light **07** clarify, clear up, explain, lighten, light up, miniate, shine on **08** brighten, decorate, illumine, instruct, ornament, twilight **09** back-light, elucidate, embellish, enlighten, limelight, overshine **10** floodlight, illustrate **12** throw light on

illuminating
07 helpful **08** edifying **09** revealing **10** revelatory **11** explanatory, informative, instructive **12** enlightening

illumination
03 ray **04** beam **05** flash, light **06** lights **07** insight **08** learning, lighting, radiance **09** adornment, awareness, education, miniature, theosophy **10** brightness, decoration, perception, revelation **11** candlelight, elucidation, instruction, irradiation **12** illustration **13** clarification, embellishment, enlightenment, ornamentation, understanding, zodiacal light

illusion
04 maya **05** error, fancy **06** déjà vu, mirage **07** chimera, fallacy, fantasy, mocking, phantom, spectre **08** delusion, phantasm, prestige **09** deception, phantosme **10** apparition, fata Morgana **12** misjudgement, will-o'-the-wisp **13** hallucination, misconception **15** false impression, misapprehension

illusory
04 sham **05** false **06** unreal, untrue **07** fancied, phantom, seeming **08** apparent, deluding, delusive, delusory, illusive, imagined, mistaken, specious **09** deceptive, erroneous, imaginary **10** chimerical, fallacious, misleading **11** illusionary **13** unsubstantial

illustrate
04 draw, show **05** adorn **06** depict, sketch **07** clarify, exhibit, explain, miniate, picture **08** decorate, instance, ornament, renowned **09** elucidate, embellish, enlighten, exemplify, interpret **10** illuminate **11** demonstrate

illustrated
08 miniated **09** decorated, pictorial **11** embellished, illuminated **12** with drawings, with pictures

illustration
04 case, note **05** bleed, chart, gloss, plate, quote **06** blow-up, design, figure, remark, sample, sketch **07** analogy, artwork, comment,

diagram, drawing, example, graphic, picture **08** exemplar, exponent, half-tone, instance, specimen, vignette **09** adornment, hors texte, quotation, sidelight **10** decoration, photograph **11** case in point, elucidation, explanation, observation **12** frontispiece **13** clarification, demonstration, embellishment, ornamentation **14** interpretation, representation **15** exemplification

illustrative
06 sample **07** graphic, typical **08** specimen **09** pictorial **10** expository **11** delineative, descriptive, explanatory, explicatory **12** diagrammatic, exemplifying, illustratory **14** illustrational, interpretative, representative

illustrious
04 dull **05** famed, great, noble, noted **06** bright, famous **07** eminent, exalted, notable **08** esteemed, glorious, honoured, luminous, renowned, splendid **09** acclaimed, brilliant, excellent, prominent, well-known **10** celebrated, honourable, pre-eminent, remarkable **11** magnificent, outstanding **13** distinguished

ill-will
04 envy, gall **05** anger, odium, spite, wrath **06** animus, enmity, grudge, hatred, malice, maugre **07** dislike, envying, maulgre, rancour **08** aversion, bad blood **09** animosity, antipathy, hostility, maltalent **10** antagonism, ill-feeling, resentment **11** indignation, malevolence **12** disaffection, hard feelings **14** unfriendliness

image
03 pic **04** bust, copy, doll, face, icon, idea, idol, tiki, twin **05** clone, fancy, match **06** double, effigy, figure, idolor idolum, mirror, notion, reflex, ringer, shadow, simile, statue, typify, vision **07** concept, eidolon, fantasy, imagery, imagine, persona, picture, portray, profile, replica, thought **08** figurine, identity, likeness, metaphor, phantasy, portrait **09** depiction, duplicate, facsimile, lookalike, portrayal, statuette **10** appearance, conception, dead ringer, impression, perception, photograph, projection, public face, reflection **11** graven image, resemblance **12** doppelgänger, reproduction, turn of phrase **13** public persona, spitting image **14** figure of speech, representation

imaginable
06 likely **08** credible, feasible, possible, probable **09** plausible, thinkable **10** believable, supposable **11** conceivable

imaginary
06 dreamy, made-up, unreal **07** assumed, fancied, fictive, ghostly, phantom, pretend, shadowy **08** fabulous, fanciful, illusory,

imagination

magined, invented, mythical, notional, spectral, supposed **09** fantastic, fictional, legendary, visionary **10** chimerical, fictitious **11** fantastical, make-believe, non-existent **12** hypothetical, mythological **13** hallucinatory, insubstantial

imagination

03 wit **05** dream, fancy **06** schema, vision **07** chimera, fantasy, imagery, insight, project **08** illusion, mind's eye, phantasy **09** dreamland, ingenuity **10** creativity, enterprise, mental view **11** inspiration, originality **12** fancifulness **13** contemplation, flight of fancy, ingeniousness, inventiveness **15** imaginativeness, resourcefulness

imaginative

05 vivid **06** clever, poetic **07** lyrical **08** creative, fanciful, inspired, original, poetical **09** fantastic, ingenious, inventive, visionary, whimsical **10** innovative **11** full of ideas, resourceful **12** enterprising

imagine

03 see **04** deem, plan, ween **05** dream, fancy, feign, guess, image, judge, think **06** assume, create, devise, figure, gather, ideate, invent, reckon, scheme, take it, vision **07** believe, conceit, dream up, picture, presume, pretend, project, propose, suppose, surmise, think up **08** conceive, contrive, daydream, envisage **09** conjure up, fantasize, visualize **10** conjecture **11** make believe **14** form a picture of

imbalance

04 bias **08** inequity, variance **09** disparity **10** inequality, partiality, unevenness, unfairness **13** disproportion

imbecile

◇ anagram indicator
03 ass, mug, nit **04** berk, clot, daft, dope, dork, dumb, fool, geek, jerk, nana, nerd, nerk, nong, prat, putz, twit **05** anile, barmy, batty, chump, crazy, dorky, dotty, dumbo, dunce, eejit, goofy, idiot, inane, klutz, moron, ninny, nutty, potty, silly, twerp, wacky, wally **06** absurd, bammer, bampot, cretin, dimwit, doofus, dum-dum, nitwit, numpty, stupid, sucker **07** asinine, bungler, fatuous, foolish, halfwit, idiotic, jughead, moronic, pillock, plonker, wazzock, witless **08** flathead, innocent, numskull **09** birdbrain, blockhead, cloth head, lame brain, ludicrous, simpleton, thickhead **10** nincompoop **11** chowderhead, knuckle-head, thick-headed **12** crack-brained **13** knuckle-headed

imbecility

06 idiocy **07** amentia, fatuity, idiotcy, inanity **08** daftness **09** asininity, craziness, cretinism, stupidity **11** foolishness **12** childishness, incompetence

imbibe

◇ containment indicator
03 sip **04** gain, gulp, suck, swig **05** drink, lap up, quaff **06** absorb, gather, ingest, soak up, take in **07** acquire, consume, drink in, receive, swallow **09** knock back **10** assimilate

imbroglio

04 mess **06** muddle, scrape, tangle **07** dilemma **08** quandary **09** confusion **10** difficulty **11** embroilment, involvement **12** complication, entanglement

imbue

04 fill, tint **05** embay, steep, taint, tinct, tinge **06** charge, infuse, inject, instil, season **07** breathe, ingrain, inspire, moisten, pervade, possess, suffuse **08** permeate, saturate, tincture **09** inbreathe, inculcate, inoculate, transfuse **10** impregnate **12** indoctrinate

imitate

03 act, ape, hit **04** copy, echo, fake, mock **05** feign, forge, mimic, spoof **06** follow, hit off, mirror, parody, parrot, repeat, send up **07** copycat, emulate, take off **08** simulate **09** duplicate, replicate, reproduce **10** caricature, do likewise, follow suit **11** counterfeit, impersonate **12** take as a model

imitation

04 copy, echo, -ette, fake, faux, mock, sham **05** apery, aping, dummy, spoof **06** ersatz, parody, phoney, pseudo, send-up **07** forgery, man-made, mimesis, mimicry, mockery, mocking, replica, take-off **08** knock-off, likeness, parrotry, travesty **09** burlesque, duplicate, emulation, simulated, synthetic **10** artificial, caricature, impression, reflection, simulation **11** counterfeit, resemblance **12** reproduction **13** impersonation

imitative

04 mock **05** apish, me-too, mimic **07** copying, mimetic, servile **09** emulating, mimetical, mimicking, simulated **10** derivative, parrot-like, second-hand, unoriginal **11** plagiarized **12** onomatopoeic

imitator

03 ape **04** echo **05** mimic **06** copier, epigon, parrot **07** copycat, copyist, epigone **08** emulator, follower, parodist **10** plagiarist **12** impersonator **13** impressionist

immaculate

04 pure **05** clean **07** perfect, sinless **08** flawless, innocent, pristine, spotless, unsoiled **09** blameless, faultless, guiltless, incorrupt, stainless, undefiled, unstained, unsullied, untainted **10** impeccable **11** unblemished **12** spick and span, squeaky clean

immaculately

06 purely **09** perfectly, sinlessly **10** flawlessly, impeccably, innocently, spotlessly, without sin **11** blamelessly, faultlessly, guiltlessly, incorruptly **12** to perfection, without blame, without guilt

immanent

06 innate **08** inherent **09** ingrained, intrinsic, pervading **10** permeating, ubiquitous **11** omnipresent **12** all-pervading

immaterial

05 minor, petty **07** trivial **08** trifling **10** irrelevant **11** incorporeal, inessential, of no account, unessential, unimportant **13** insignificant **15** inconsequential

immature

◇ tail deletion indicator
03 raw **05** crude, green, naive, vealy, young **06** callow, jejune, unripe **07** babyish, budding, puerile, unbaked, unready **08** childish, juvenile, under-age, unformed, untimely **09** beardless, embryonic, fledgling, half-baked, infantile, ingenuous, unfledged, unsizable **10** adolescent, incomplete, unmellowed, unprepared, unsizeable **11** undeveloped **13** inexperienced

immaturity

05 youth **07** crudity, rawness **09** crudeness, greenness, puerility **10** callowness, juvenility, unripeness **11** adolescence, babyishness **12** childishness, immatureness, imperfection, inexperience **14** unpreparedness

immeasurable

04 vast **07** endless, immense **08** infinite **09** boundless, limitless, unbounded, unlimited **10** bottomless, fathomless **11** illimitable, inestimable, never ending **12** immensurable, incalculable, interminable, unfathomable **13** inexhaustible

immeasurably

06 vastly **09** endlessly, immensely **10** infinitely **11** boundlessly, illimitably, inestimably, limitlessly **12** incalculably, interminably **13** beyond measure, inexhaustibly

immediacy

07 urgency **08** instancy **09** freshness, imminence, swiftness **10** directness, importance, promptness **11** spontaneity **12** criticalness, simultaneity **13** instantaneity

immediate

04 main, near, next **05** basic, chief, close, swift, vital **06** direct, prompt, recent, speedy, sudden, urgent **07** closest, crucial, current, instant, nearest, present, primary, soonest **08** abutting, adjacent, critical, existing, next-door, pressing **09** adjoining, first-time, important, posthaste, principal, proximate **11** fundamental, top-priority **12** high-priority, without delay **13** instantaneous

immediately
03 now, pdq **04** anon, ASAP, next, stat, then, tite **06** at once, belive, pronto, statim, subito **07** bang off, quickly **08** as soon as, directly, promptly, right now, speedily, straight, urgently **09** at a glance, forthwith, instantly, like a shot, on the spot, out of hand, presently, right away, thereupon, yesterday **10** this minute **11** incessantly, incontinent, in the wake of, on the morrow, straightway, therewithal, this instant, tout de suite **12** lickety-split, no sooner than, on the instant, on the knocker, straight away, straightways, there and then, without delay **13** incontinently, straightforth **14** unhesitatingly, without more ado **15** before you know it, instantaneously, without question

immemorial
05 fixed, hoary **06** age-old, of yore **07** ancient, archaic **08** timeless **09** ancestral **11** traditional **12** long-standing, time-honoured

immense
04 fine, huge, mega, vast **05** enorm, giant, great, jumbo **06** bumper, cosmic, myriad **07** mammoth, massive, titanic **08** colossal, cyclopic, enormous, fabulous, gigantic, whopping **09** cyclopean, cyclopian, extensive, ginormous, herculean, humungous, limitless **10** monumental, tremendous **11** Brobdingnag, elephantine **14** Brobdingnagian, extremely large

immensely
04 very **05** jolly **06** highly, really, vastly **07** acutely, awfully, greatly, utterly **08** severely, terribly **09** decidedly, extremely, intensely, massively, unusually **10** dreadfully, enormously, remarkably, uncommonly **11** exceedingly, excessively, frightfully **12** immoderately, inordinately, terrifically, unreasonably **13** exceptionally **15** extraordinarily

immensity
04 bulk **07** expanse **08** hugeness, infinity, vastness **09** expansion, greatness, magnitude **11** massiveness **12** enormousness, giganticness **13** extensiveness, limitlessness

immerse
◇ *hidden indicator*
03 dip **04** bury, duck, dunk, sink, soak **05** bathe, douse, souse **06** absorb, blanch, drench, engage, engulf, occupy, plunge, wallow **07** baptize, demerge, demerse, embathe, engross, imbathe, immerge, involve **08** saturate, submerge, submerse, wrap up in **09** preoccupy

immersed
◇ *hidden indicator*
04 busy, deep, rapt, sunk **06** buried **07** taken up **08** absorbed, consumed, involved, occupied **09** engrossed, wrapped up **11** preoccupied

immersion
03 dip **05** bathe **07** baptism, dipping, dousing, ducking, dunking, sinking, soaking **08** plunging **09** drenching **10** absorption, engagement, engrossing, saturation, submersion **11** involvement **13** concentration, preoccupation

immigrant
03 pom **04** Balt **05** alien, issei, pommy **06** merino **07** greener, incomer, migrant, new chum, settler, wetback **08** newcomer, outsider **09** foreigner, Pakistani **10** Aussiedler, new arrival, overstayer **13** new Australian

immigrate
06 come in, move in, remove, settle **07** migrate **08** resettle

imminence
06 menace, threat **08** approach, instancy, nearness **09** closeness, immediacy **11** propinquity

imminent
04 near **05** close **06** at hand, coming **07** brewing, in store, jutting, looming **08** in the air, menacing, on the way, upcoming **09** impending **11** approaching, forthcoming, in the offing, overhanging, threatening **12** on the horizon **13** about to happen, almost upon you **14** round the corner **15** fast approaching

immobile
05 fixed, rigid, stiff, still **06** at rest, frozen, rooted, static **07** riveted **08** moveless, unmoving **09** immovable **10** motionless, stationary, stock-still **11** immobilized

immobility
06 fixity **08** catatony, firmness **09** catatonia, fixedness, inertness, stability, stillness **10** disability, steadiness **12** immovability **14** motionlessness

immobilize
04 halt, stop **05** Taser® **06** freeze **07** cripple, disable **08** paralyse, transfix **10** deactivate, inactivate **14** put out of action

immoderate
03 OTT **05** steep, undue **06** lavish, wanton **07** extreme, fulsome **08** enormous, uncurbed **09** egregious, excessive, hubristic, unbridled, unlimited **10** exorbitant, inordinate, outrageous, over the top, profligate **11** exaggerated, extravagant, intemperate, overweening, uncalled-for, unjustified, unwarranted **12** distemperate, uncontrolled, unreasonable, unrestrained, unrestricted **13** self-indulgent **14** unconscionable

immoderately
06 unduly **08** to excess, wantonly **09** extremely **11** excessively **12** exorbitantly, inordinately, out of all cess, unreasonably **13** exaggeratedly,

extravagantly, unjustifiably **14** unrestrainedly, without measure

immoderation
06 excess **08** unreason **10** inordinacy, lavishness **11** dissipation, exorbitance, prodigality, unrestraint **12** extravagance, intemperance **13** excessiveness **14** immoderateness, overindulgence

immodest
04 bold, lewd **05** cocky, fresh, saucy **06** brazen, cheeky, coarse, risqué **07** forward, immoral, obscene **08** boastful, improper, impudent, indecent **09** revealing, shameless **10** indecorous, indelicate

immodesty
04 gall **05** brass **08** audacity, boldness, impurity, lewdness, temerity **09** bawdiness, impudence, indecorum, obscenity **10** coarseness, impudicity, indelicacy **11** forwardness **13** shamelessness **14** indecorousness

immolate
04 burn, kill **05** offer **07** offer up **09** sacrifice

immoral
03 bad **04** base, blue, evil, lewd, vile **05** juicy, loose, wrong **06** impure, naught, sinful, wanton, wicked **07** corrupt, godless, obscene, raunchy, vicious **08** depraved, indecent, unhonest **09** debauched, dishonest, dissolute, nefarious, reprobate, unethical **10** degenerate, iniquitous, licentious **11** promiscuous **12** pornographic, questionable, unprincipled, unscrupulous **13** against nature
• **immoral act**
03 sin

immorality
03 sin **04** evil, vice **05** wrong **07** badness **08** impurity, iniquity, lewdness, vileness **09** depravity, indecency, obscenity, turpitude **10** corruption, debauchery, dishonesty, profligacy, sinfulness, wickedness, wrongdoing **11** pornography **12** indiscretion **13** dissoluteness **14** licentiousness

immortal
03 god **04** hero **05** deity, great **06** famous, genius **07** abiding, ageless, endless, eternal, goddess, lasting, undying **08** constant, divinity, enduring, fadeless, honoured, Olympian, timeless, unfading **09** amarantin, ambrosial, ceaseless, deathless, memorable, perennial, perpetual, well-known **10** celebrated, ever-living **11** divine being, everlasting, sempiternal **12** imperishable **13** distinguished, unforgettable **14** indestructible

immortality
04 fame **05** glory **06** honour, renown **08** eternity **09** celebrity, greatness **10** amritattva, perpetuity

distinction, endlessness, eternal life gloriousness, timelessness deathlessness, glorification everlasting life, imperishability

nmortalize
laud **07** glorify **08** enshrine, eternize celebrate **10** eternalize, perpetuate commemorate, memorialize

nmovable
set **04** fast, firm, real **05** fixed, stuck dogged, jammed, moored, rooted, cure, stable **07** adamant, riveted anchored, constant, immobile, solute, stubborn **09** impassive, stinate, steadfast **10** determined, flexible, motionless, unshakable, nswerving, unwavering, unyielding unalterable, unshakeable intransigent **14** marble-constant, ncompromising

nmune
free, safe **05** clear, proof exempt, secure, spared **07** excused absolved, released, relieved protected, resistant **12** invulnerable unsusceptible

nmunity
right **06** safety **07** freedom, liberty, ence, release **08** impunity exception, exemption, franchise, demnity, privilege **10** permission, otection, resistance **11** exoneration, oculation, vaccination immunization, mithridatism

nmunization
jab **09** injection **10** protection inoculation, vaccination

nmunize
salt **06** inject, shield **07** protect inoculate, safeguard, vaccinate

nmure
cage, jail **06** enwall, shut up, wall in confine, enclose **08** cloister, prison **11** incarcerate **13** put behind rs

nmutability
constancy, fixedness, stability durability, permanence immutableness, invariability changelessness **15** unalterableness

nmutable
fixed **06** stable **07** abiding, lasting constant, enduring **09** permanent, rpetual, steadfast **10** changeless, flexible, invariable, sacrosanct unalterable **12** unchangeable

np
elf **04** brat, limb, minx, puck, ympe demon, devil, gamin, gnome, graft, lph, rogue, scamp, scion, shoot goblin, rascal, sprite, urchin hobgoblin, prankster, trickster troublemaker **13** mischief-maker flibbertigibbet

npact
act, fix, hit **04** bang, belt, blow, mp, dush, jolt, work **05** brunt, clash,

crash, crush, force, knock, poise, power, shock, smash, souse **06** affect, effect, glance, strike **07** apply to, collide, contact, impinge, meaning, results **09** collision, influence **10** impression, percussion **12** consequences, significance **13** press together, repercussions **14** have an effect on, reverberations

impair
◇ *anagram indicator*
03 mar **04** harm, rust **05** alloy, blunt, craze, decay, spoil, wrong **06** damage, hinder, injure, lessen, reduce, weaken, worsen **07** cripple, disable, empeach, impeach, tarnish, vitiate, wear out **08** decrease, diminish, embezzle, emperish, enervate, enfeeble, wear away, wear down **09** undermine **10** debilitate **11** deteriorate

impaired
◇ *anagram indicator*
04 poor, weak **05** rusty, stale **06** faulty, flawed, spoilt **07** damaged, unsound, vicious **08** disabled, vitiated, weakened **09** defective, imperfect **10** challenged **11** handicapped

impairment
04 flaw, harm, hurt, ruin, wear **05** allay, fault, spoil **06** damage, injury **07** empeach, impeach **08** handicap, weakness **09** paralogia, reduction, vitiation **10** disability **11** disablement, dysfunction **13** deterioration
See also **sight**

impale
04 spit, stab **05** ganch, lance, prick, spear, spike, stick **06** gaunch, pierce, skewer **08** puncture, transfix **09** perforate **10** disembowel, run through

impalpable
04 airy, fine, thin **06** subtle **07** elusive, shadowy, tenuous **08** delicate **10** indistinct, intangible **11** incorporeal, indefinable **13** imperceptible, insubstantial, unsubstantial **15** inapprehensible

impart
04 give, lend, shed, tell **05** break, grant, offer **06** accord, assign, bestow, confer, convey, pass on, relate, report, reveal **07** divulge **08** disclose, transmit **09** make known **10** contribute **11** communicate

impartial
04 fair, just **05** equal **06** candid **07** neutral **08** detached, judicial, unbiased **09** equitable, objective **10** crossbench, even-handed, fair-minded, open-minded **11** non-partisan, uncommitted, unconcerned **12** unprejudiced **13** disinterested, dispassionate

impartiality
06 candor, equity **07** candour, justice **08** equality, fairness **10** detachment, dispassion, neutrality **11** disinterest, objectivity **12** unbiasedness

14 even-handedness, open-mindedness **15** non-partisanship

impassable
06 closed **07** blocked, invious **08** pathless **09** trackless **10** invincible, obstructed, unpassable **11** insuperable, unnavigable **12** impenetrable, unassailable, unvoyageable **13** untraversable **14** insurmountable

impasse
04 halt **06** log jam **07** dead end **08** cul-de-sac, deadlock **09** checkmate, stalemate **10** blind alley, standstill **15** Mexican standoff

impassioned
05 eager, fiery **06** ardent, fervid, heated **07** blazing, earnest, excited, fervent, furious, glowing, intense, rousing, violent **08** animated, forceful, inflamed, inspired, spirited, stirring, vehement, vigorous **09** emotional, heartfelt **10** passionate **12** enthusiastic

impassive
04 calm, cool **05** bland **06** stolid **07** stoical, unmoved **08** composed, laid-back **09** apathetic, immovable, unfeeling, unruffled **10** impassible, phlegmatic **11** emotionless, indifferent, unconcerned, unemotional, unemotioned, unexcitable, unflappable **13** dispassionate, imperturbable **14** expressionless

impassively
06 calmly, coolly **11** unfeelingly **13** apathetically, emotionlessly, imperturbably, unemotionally **14** phlegmatically **15** dispassionately

impatience
05 haste **07** anxiety **08** curtness, edginess, keenness, rashness **09** agitation, dysphoria, eagerness, shortness, tenseness **10** abruptness, indignance, uneasiness **11** brusqueness, impetuosity, intolerance, nervousness **12** excitability, irritability, restlessness
• **expression of impatience**
03 ach, dam, och, poh, tut **04** chut, damn, phew, pish, push, toot, tush, tuts, when **05** damme, devil, pshaw, toots **06** dammit, tut-tut **07** crimine, crimini **10** tilly-fally, tilly-vally **12** Donnerwetter, tilley-valley

impatient
04 curt, edgy, keen **05** angry, eager, hasty, narky, ratty, short, tense, testy **06** abrupt, snappy **07** anxious, brusque, fidgety, fretful, jittery, nervous **08** restless **09** excitable, impetuous, irritable, querulous **10** intolerant **11** hot-tempered **13** on tenterhooks, quick-tempered

impeach
05 blame **06** accuse, attack, charge, damage, hinder, impair, impede, impugn, indict, revile **07** arraign, censure, prevent **08** denounce **09** criticize, detriment, disparage, hindrance **10** impairment, prevention

impeachment
06 appeal, charge **10** accusation, indictment **11** arraignment **13** disparagement

impeccable
04 pure **05** exact **06** just so **07** correct, perfect, precise, upright **08** flawless, innocent **09** blameless, exemplary, faultless, stainless **10** immaculate **11** unblemished **12** squeaky clean **14** irreproachable

impecunious
04 poor **05** broke, needy, skint **07** boracic **08** dirt-poor, indigent, strapped **09** destitute, insolvent, penniless, penurious **10** cleaned out, stony-broke **12** impoverished, on your uppers **15** poverty-stricken

impedance
01 Z **09** hindrance
• **measure of impedance**
03 ohm

impede
03 bar, rub **04** clog, curb, slow, stop **05** block, check, delay **06** hamper, hinder, hogtie, hold up, retard, thwart **07** disrupt, empeach, impeach, trammel **08** encumber, handicap, hold back, incumber, obstruct, restrain, slow down, strangle

impediment
03 bar, bur, log, rub **04** burr, clog, curb, halt, snag **05** block, check **06** burden, defect, rubber **07** barrier, setback, stammer, stutter **08** handicap, obstacle **09** hindrance, restraint **10** difficulty **11** encumbrance, obstruction, restriction **14** stumbling-block

impedimenta
04 gear **05** stuff **06** things **07** baggage, effects, luggage **09** equipment **10** belongings **12** encumbrances **13** accoutrements, bits and pieces, paraphernalia

impel
03 put **04** goad, move, prod, push, spur, urge **05** drive, force, press **06** compel, excite, incite, oblige, prompt, propel, strike **07** inspire **08** get going, motivate, pressure **09** constrain, instigate, stimulate **10** pressurize

impending
04 near **05** close **06** at hand, coming, toward **07** brewing, looming **08** imminent, in the air, menacing, on the way, upcoming **11** approaching, forthcoming, in the offing, threatening **12** on the horizon **13** about to happen

impenetrable
04 dark **05** dense, solid, thick **07** cryptic, obscure **08** abstruse, airtight, baffling, puzzling **09** enigmatic, overgrown, recondite **10** adamantine, impassable, impervious, mysterious, soundproof **11** inscrutable **12** unfathomable **13** indiscernible **14** unintelligible

impenitence
08 defiance, obduracy **11** impenitency **12** stubbornness **15** hard-heartedness, incorrigibility

impenitent
07 defiant **08** hardened, obdurate **09** unabashed, unashamed **10** uncontrite, unreformed **11** remorseless, unrepentant **12** incorrigible, unregenerate, unremorseful **13** without regret **14** without remorse

imperative
05 vital **06** urgent **07** crucial **08** critical, pressing **09** essential, necessary **10** compulsory, obligatory, peremptory **13** authoritative, indispensable

imperceptible
04 fine, tiny **05** faint, small, vague **06** minute, slight, subtle **07** gradual, muffled, obscure, unclear **09** inaudible, minuscule **10** impalpable, indefinite, indistinct, negligible, unapparent **11** microscopic **12** undetectable, unnoticeable **13** inappreciable, indiscernible, infinitesimal

imperceptibly
06 slowly, subtly, unseen **08** bit by bit **09** gradually **10** insensibly **12** unnoticeably **13** inappreciably, indiscernibly, unobtrusively **14** little by little

imperfect
◇ *anagram indicator*
04 lame **06** broken, faulty, flawed **07** chipped, damaged, sketchy **08** impaired **09** blemished, defective, deficient, embryonic, unperfect **10** inadequate, incomplete **12** insufficient

imperfection
03 cut **04** blot, dent, flaw, kink, spot, tear **05** break, crack, fault, stain, taint **06** blotch, defect, foible, hickey, mackle **07** blemish, failing, scratch **08** weakness **09** deformity **10** deficiency, impairment, inadequacy **11** shortcoming **13** insufficiency **15** malconformation

imperial
03 Imp **05** grand, great, lofty, noble, regal, royal **06** august, kingly **07** queenly, stately, supreme **08** absolute, glorious, majestic, splendid **09** sovereign **10** commanding **11** magnificent, monarchical

imperialism
10 flag-waving **11** adventurism, colonialism, flag-wagging **12** expansionism **14** empire-building **15** acquisitiveness

imperil
04 harm, risk **06** expose, hazard, injure **08** endanger, threaten **10** compromise, jeopardize **11** put in

danger, take a chance **12** expose to ri **13** put in jeopardy

imperious
06 lordly **07** haughty **08** arrogant, despotic **09** assertive, masterful **10** autocratic, commanding, high-handed, peremptory, tyrannical **11** dictatorial, domineering, overbearing, overweening

imperishable
07 abiding, eternal, undying **08** enduring, immortal, unfading **09** deathless, perennial, permanent, perpetual **11** everlasting **13** immarcescible, incorruptible, unforgettable **14** indestructible

impermanence
09 briefness **10** transience, transienc **11** elusiveness, inconstancy **12** ephemerality **13** temporariness **14** transitoriness

impermanent
05 brief **06** flying, mortal **07** elusive, passing, unfixed **08** fleeting, fugitive, unstable **09** ephemeral, fugacious, momentary, temporary, transient, unsettled **10** evanescent, fly-by-nigh inconstant, perishable, short-lived, transitory

impermeable
05 proof **06** sealed **08** airtight, hermetic **09** damp-proof, non-porous, resistant **10** impassable, impervious, waterproof, watertight **11** greaseproof **12** impenetrable **14** water-repellent, water-resistant

impersonal
04 cold, cool **05** aloof, stiff **06** forma frigid, remote, stuffy **07** distant, neutr **08** clinical, detached, official, unbiased **09** objective, unfeeling **11** unemotional **12** businesslike, unprejudiced **13** dispassionate

impersonally
06 fairly, justly **09** equitably, neutrally **11** objectively, without bias **12** open-mindedly **14** with an open mind **15** dispassionately

impersonate
02 do **03** act, ape **04** mock **05** mimi **06** embody, parody, pose as, send up **07** imitate, portray, present, take off **09** incarnate, pass off as **10** caricature **12** masquerade as

impersonation
05 apery, aping, fraud, spoof **06** parody, send-up **07** mimicry, take off **09** burlesque, imitation **10** caricature, impression

impertinence
03 lip **04** face, gall, sass **05** brass, cheek, crust, mouth, nerve, sauce, snash **08** attitude, audacity, backchat boldness, chutzpah, rudeness **09** brass neck, flippancy, impudence, insolence, intrusion **10** brazenness, disrespect, effrontery **11** discourtesy, forwardness, presumption

12 flippantness, impoliteness
13 shamelessness

impertinent
04 bold, pert, rude 05 brash, fresh,
assy, saucy 06 brazen, cheeky
07 forward 08 impolite, impudent,
insolent 09 audacious, intrusive,
shameless 10 unmannerly 11 ill-
mannered 12 discourteous,
presumptuous 13 disrespectful

imperturbability
04 cool 08 calmness, coolness
09 composure, sangfroid
10 equanimity 11 complacency
12 tranquillity 14 self-possession

imperturbable
04 calm, cool 06 serene 07 unfazed,
unmoved 08 composed, laid-back,
tranquil 09 collected, impassive,
supercool, unruffled 10 complacent,
unruffable, untroubled 11 unexcitable,
unflappable 12 even-tempered
13 self-possessed 15 cool as a
cucumber

impervious
05 proof, tight 06 closed, immune,
opaque, sealed 07 unmoved 08 gas-
tight, hermetic 09 damp-proof,
dustproof, non-porous, rainproof,
resistant, star-proof, untouched
10 light-proof, smokeproof,
smoketight, steamtight, unaffected,
waterproof, watertight 11 adiathermic,
impermeable, showerproof
12 impenetrable, invulnerable

impetuosity
04 birr, dash, élan, rush 05 haste
08 rashness 09 hastiness, vehemence
10 impatience 11 spontaneity
12 recklessness 13 foolhardiness,
impetuousness, impulsiveness
15 precipitateness, thoughtlessness

impetuous
04 rash 05 brash, fiery, hasty 06 sturdy
07 violent 08 headlong, reckless,
tearaway 09 foolhardy, hot-headed,
impatient, impulsive, unplanned
10 bull-headed, unreasoned,
unthinking 11 precipitate,
spontaneous, thoughtless 12 ill-
conceived, uncontrolled
14 unpremeditated 15 spur-of-the-
moment

impetuously
06 rashly 10 recklessly, vehemently
11 impulsively 12 passionately,
unthinkingly 13 precipitately,
spontaneously

impetus
04 birr, goad, push, send, spur 05 boost,
drive, force, power, sweep, swing
06 energy, travel, urging 07 impulse
08 momentum, stimulus 09 actuation,
incentive, influence 10 motivation
11 inspiration 13 encouragement

impiety
06 hubris 08 iniquity 09 blasphemy,
profanity, sacrilege 10 irreligion,

sinfulness, unholiness, wickedness
11 godlessness, irreverence,
profaneness, ungodliness
15 unrighteousness

impinge
03 hit 04 beat, fall 05 souse, touch
06 affect, invade, strike 07 intrude,
touch on 08 encroach, infringe,
trespass 09 influence

impious
06 sinful, unholy, wicked 07 godless,
profane, ungodly 09 hubristic
10 iniquitous, irreverent
11 blasphemous, irreligious,
unrighteous 12 sacrilegious

impish
05 elfin, gamin 07 naughty, puckish,
roguish, tricksy, waggish 08 devilish,
rascally, sportive 09 pranksome,
tricksome 10 frolicsome
11 mischievous

implacability
12 pitilessness, ruthlessness,
vengefulness 13 inexorability,
inflexibility, intransigence,
mercilessness, rancorousness
14 implacableness, intractability,
relentlessness 15 remorselessness,
unforgivingness

implacable
05 cruel 06 deadly, mortal
07 adamant 08 pitiless, ruthless,
vengeful 09 heartless, impacable,
merciless, rancorous 10 inexorable,
inflexible, relentless, unyielding
11 intractable, remorseless,
unforgiving, unrelenting
12 intransigent, unappeasable
14 irreconcilable, uncompromising

implant
03 fix, put, sow 04 root 05 embed,
graft, inset, place, plant 06 enrace,
enroot, insert, instil 07 embosom,
engraft, imbosom 09 inculcate,
introduce 10 inseminate, transplant

implausible
04 lame, thin, weak 06 flimsy
07 dubious, suspect 08 doubtful,
unlikely 10 far-fetched, improbable,
incredible 11 transparent
12 questionable, unbelievable,
unconvincing 13 hard to believe,
inconceivable

implausibly
10 doubtfully, improbably, incredibly
12 questionably, unbelievably
13 inconceivably

implement
02 do 04 celt, comb, loom, rake, tool
05 apply, brush, dolly, flail, raker, razor,
steel, whisk 06 anchor, device, effect,
eolith, fulfil, gadget, pusher, ricker,
ripple, sickle, taster, tedder 07 enforce,
execute, grubber, perform, realize,
utensil 08 carry out, complete, fly
whisk, scuffler, shoehorn, spreader,
squeegee, squilgee, tint tool
09 apparatus, appliance, discharge,

fire-stick, fish slice, microlith, poop
scoop, requisite, scarifier
10 accomplish, bring about, cultivator,
extirpator, fish-carver, fish-trowel,
gold-washer, instrument, loggerhead,
snowplough, sucket fork, wheel brace
11 contrivance, road scraper, sucket
spoon, turfing iron 13 pooper-
scooper, put into action, put into effect
14 rostrocarinate

implementation
06 action 09 discharge, effecting,
execution, operation 10 completion,
fulfilling, fulfilment, performing
11 application, carrying-out,
enforcement, performance, realization
14 accomplishment

implicate
◇ anagram indicator
05 imply 06 enfold 07 concern,
connect, embroil, include, involve
08 entangle 09 associate, be a part of,
be party to, inculpate 10 be a party to,
compromise 11 incriminate

implicated
◇ anagram indicator
07 party to 08 included, involved
09 concerned, connected, embroiled,
entangled, suspected 10 associated,
inculpated 11 compromised,
responsible 12 incriminated

implication
06 effect 07 meaning 08 overtone
09 deduction, inference, undertone
10 conclusion, connection, suggestion
11 association, consequence,
embroilment, inculpation, insinuation,
involvement 12 entanglement,
ramification, repercussion,
significance 13 incrimination
15 subintelligitur

implicit
04 full 05 sheer, tacit, total, utter
06 entire, hidden, hinted, latent, unsaid
07 implied, perfect 08 absolute,
complete, indirect, inferred, inherent,
positive, unspoken, unstated
09 deducible, entangled, steadfast,
suggested 10 insinuated, understood,
unreserved 11 intertwined,
unexpressed, unqualified
12 unhesitating, wholehearted
13 unconditional, unquestioning

implicitly
06 firmly 07 totally, utterly
10 absolutely, completely
11 steadfastly 12 unreservedly
14 unhesitatingly, wholeheartedly
15 unconditionally, unquestioningly

implied
05 tacit 06 hinted 07 assumed
08 implicit, indirect, inherent,
unspoken, unstated 09 suggested
10 insinuated, undeclared, understood
11 unexpressed

implore
03 ask, beg 04 pray 05 crave, plead,
press 06 appeal, invoke 07 beseech,
beseeke, conjure, entreat, request,

solicit **09** importune, obsecrate
10 supplicate

imply
04 hint, mean **05** infer, state
06 denote, enfold, entail, signal
07 connote, involve, point to, require,
signify, suggest, suppose **08** indicate,
intimate **09** implicate, insinuate,
predicate **10** presuppose, understand
13 say indirectly

impolite
04 rude **05** crude, rough **06** abrupt,
cheeky, coarse, vulgar **07** boorish, ill-
bred, loutish, uncivil **08** insolent
09 unrefined **10** indecorous,
ungracious, unladylike, unmannerly
11 bad-mannered, ill-mannered,
impertinent, uncivilized
12 discourteous **13** disrespectful,
inconsiderate, ungentlemanly

impolitely
06 rudely **07** crudely **09** uncivilly
10 insolently **12** indecorously,
ungraciously **13** impertinently
14 discourteously **15** disrespectfully,
inconsiderately

impoliteness
08 rudeness **09** crassness, gaucherie,
indecorum, insolence, roughness
10 abruptness, bad manners,
coarseness, disrespect, incivility,
indelicacy **11** boorishness, discourtesy
12 churlishness, impertinence
14 indecorousness, unmannerliness

impolitic
04 daft, rash **06** unwise **07** foolish
09 ill-judged, imprudent, maladroit,
misguided **10** ill-advised, indiscreet,
unpolicied **11** inexpedient, injudicious
12 short-sighted, undiplomatic **13** ill-
considered

import
03 nub **04** gist **05** buy in, drift, sense,
state **06** amount, behove, convey,
moment, ship in, thrust, weight
07 bring in, content, essence,
meaning, message, portend, purport,
signify **08** reimport, tendency
09 importing, intention, introduce,
substance **10** importance
11 consequence, implication,
seriousness **12** foreign goods, foreign
trade, significance **13** buy from
abroad, imported goods **14** foreign
product **15** imported product

importance
04 mark, note, pith **05** power, state,
value, worth **06** esteem, import,
matter, status, weight **07** concern,
urgency **08** eminence, gravitas,
interest, prestige, standing
09 graveness, influence, magnitude,
substance **10** prominence, usefulness
11 consequence, distinction
12 criticalness, significance
13 consideration, momentousness,
signification **14** noteworthiness
• **anything of importance**
04 much

• **anything of minor
importance**
02 by **03** bye
• **be of importance**
04 mean **06** matter

important
03 big, key, top **04** main **05** chief,
grave, heavy, major, noted, vital
06 mighty, urgent, valued **07** big-time,
capital, central, crucial, eminent,
fateful, leading, notable, pivotal,
pompous, primary, salient, seminal,
serious, weighty **08** critical, esteemed,
foremost, historic, material, powerful,
priority, relevant, ultimate, valuable
09 essential, front-page, high-level,
momentous, number one, of warrant,
paramount, principal, prominent
10 meaningful, noteworthy, pre-
eminent **11** epoch-making, far-
reaching, fundamental, high-ranking,
influential, outstanding, prestigious,
significant, substantial **12** world-
shaking **13** consequential,
distinguished, of good warrant
15 world-shattering

importunate
06 dogged, urgent **08** annoying,
pressing **09** impatient, insistent,
tenacious **10** burdensome, persistent
11 inopportune, troublesome
12 pertinacious

importune
03 beg, dun, ply **04** prig, urge
05 annoy, beset, hound, press
06 appeal, badger, cajole, harass,
import, pester, plague, urgent
07 besiege, request, signify, solicit
08 untimely **09** flagitate, plead with
10 burdensome, lay siege to, resistless,
supplicate **11** inopportune

importunity
06 urging **07** urgency **08** cajolery,
hounding, pressing **09** harassing,
pestering **10** entreaties, harassment,
importance, insistence **11** persistence
12 solicitation

impose
03 fix, lay, put, set **04** levy, palm
05 abuse, apply, clamp, exact, foist,
force, lay on, place, put on **06** burden,
butt in, charge, decree, enjoin, impone,
saddle, thrust **07** break in, command,
enforce, exploit, inflict, intrude,
mislead, obtrude, place on, presume,
put over, put upon **08** encroach,
encumber, trespass **09** establish,
institute, introduce **13** force yourself,
take liberties **14** thrust yourself **15** take
advantage of

imposing
05 grand, lofty **06** august **07** stately
08 majestic, matronly, specious,
splendid, striking **09** deceptive,
dignified, grandiose, mausolean
10 commanding, impressive,
statuesque **12** high-sounding

imposition
03 hum, tax **04** bite, duty, levy, load,

task, toll **05** impot **06** burden, charge
decree, fixing, hassle, pensum, tariff
07 levying, setting **08** exaction,
pressure, trickery **09** intrusion
10 constraint, infliction, punishment
11 application, encumbrance,
enforcement, institution, trespassing
12 encroachment, introduction
13 establishment
See also **tax**

impossibility
04 no-no **09** absurdity, inability
10 non-starter **11** unviability
12 hopelessness, untenability
13 ludicrousness **14** ridiculousness
15 unacceptability

impossible
03 out **06** absurd **08** hopeless
09 beyond you, insoluble, ludicrous
10 incredible, outlandish, ridiculous,
unbearable, unworkable
11 intolerable, prohibitive,
unthinkable **12** pigs might fly,
preposterous, unacceptable,
unachievable, unattainable,
unbelievable, unimaginable,
unobtainable, unrealizable,
unreasonable **13** anybody's guess,
impracticable, inconceivable **15** and
pigs might fly

impostor
04 fake, idol, sham **05** cheat, fraud,
quack, rogue **06** bunyip, con man,
faitor, phoney, ringer **07** deluder,
faitour **08** deceiver, phantasm,
swindler **09** charlatan, defrauder,
pretender, trickster **10** hoodwinker,
mountebank **12** impersonator

imposture
03 con **04** hoax, sham **05** cheat,
fraud, trick **07** swindle **08** artifice, con
trick, pretence, quackery
09 deception **10** imposition
11 counterfeit **13** impersonation

impotence
07 frailty **08** ligature, weakness
09 inability, infirmity, paralysis
10 disability, enervation, feebleness,
inadequacy, incapacity, inefficacy
11 impuissance, uselessness
12 helplessness, incompetence
13 powerlessness **15** ineffectiveness

impotent
04 weak **05** frail **06** feeble, futile,
infirm, unable **07** useless, worn out
08 crippled, disabled, helpless
09 enervated, exhausted, incapable,
paralysed, powerless, worthless
10 impuissant, inadequate
11 debilitated, incompetent,
ineffective **12** unrestrained
13 incapacitated

impound
04 cage **05** hem in, pen in, poind, seize
06 coop up, immure, keep in, lock up,
remove, shut up **07** confine, pinfold
08 take away **10** commandeer,
confiscate **11** appropriate, expropriate
incarcerate

impoverish
04 ruin 05 break, drain, waste
06 beggar, denude, reduce, weaken
07 deplete, exhaust 08 bankrupt,
diminish, distress, make poor
09 pauperize 11 depauperate

impoverished
04 bare, bust, dead, poor 05 broke,
empty, needy, skint, waste 06 barren,
ruined 07 boracic, decayed, drained,
reduced 08 bankrupt, desolate, dirt-
poor, indigent, weakened
09 destitute, exhausted, penniless,
penurious 10 cleaned out, distressed,
down-and-out, stony-broke
11 depauperate, impecunious
12 on your uppers, without a bean
14 on your beam ends 15 poverty-
stricken

impracticability
08 futility 11 unviability, uselessness
12 hopelessness 13 impossibility,
infeasibility, unworkability
14 unsuitableness

impracticable
04 wild 07 useless 08 unviable, wild-
eyed 09 non-viable, visionary
10 impossible, inoperable, unfeasible,
unworkable 11 unrealistic
12 unachievable, unattainable,
unmanageable 13 unpracticable,
unserviceable

impractical
05 crazy 07 awkward 08 academic,
romantic 09 visionary 10 idealistic,
impossible, ivory-tower, starry-eyed,
unworkable 11 doctrinaire, unrealistic
12 inconvenient 13 impracticable,
unserviceable

impracticality
08 idealism 11 romanticism
12 hopelessness 13 impossibility,
infeasibility, unworkability
14 unworkableness

imprecation
04 oath, pize 05 abuse, curse
08 anathema, goodyear
09 blasphemy, goodyears, profanity
10 execration 11 malediction
12 denunciation, vilification,
vituperation

imprecise
04 hazy 05 loose, rough, vague
06 sloppy, woolly 07 blurred, inexact
09 ambiguous, equivocal, estimated
10 ill-defined, inaccurate, indefinite,
inexplicit 11 approximate

imprecision
04 haze 08 estimate 09 ambiguity,
vagueness 10 inaccuracy, sloppiness
11 inexactness 12 inexactitude
13 approximation

impregnable
04 safe 05 solid 06 secure, strong
09 fortified 10 adamantine, invincible,
inviolable, unbeatable 11 irrefutable
12 impenetrable, inexpugnable,
invulnerable, unassailable

13 unconquerable 14 indestructible,
unquestionable

impregnate
03 pad 04 fill, melt, milt, soak
05 imbue, stain, steep 06 drench,
infuse 07 pervade, suffuse
08 permeate, saturate 09 fecundate,
fertilize, penetrate 10 inseminate
12 make pregnant

impregnation
07 imbuing 10 saturation
11 fecundation, fertilizing, fructifying
12 insemination 13 fertilization
14 fructification

impresario
07 manager, showman 08 director,
producer, promoter 09 exhibitor,
organizer

impress
03 gas, wow 04 drum, grab, mark,
move, slay, stir, sway 05 knock, press,
prest, print, rouse, stamp, touch
06 affect, deboss, emboss, excite,
incuse, indent, instil, stress, strike
07 enforce, engrave, impresa, imprint,
inspire, possess 08 astonish, bowl
over, knock out 09 beglamour, bring
home, emphasize, fix deeply, go over
big, highlight, inculcate, influence,
overwhelm, pressgang, underline,
watermark 10 bear in upon, hammer
home, prepossess 11 knock for six
13 go over big with

impressed
05 moved, taken, wowed 06 marked,
struck 07 excited, grabbed, stamped,
stirred, touched 08 affected,
overawed 10 bowled over, influenced,
knocked out 13 knocked for six

impression
04 dent, feel, idea, mark, note, ring,
seal, sway 05 fancy, hunch, power,
print, sense, sound, spoof, stamp, vibes
06 belief, effect, impact, memory,
notion, parody, repute, send-up
07 control, feeling, imprint, mimicry,
opinion, outline, tableau, take-off,
thought 08 illusion, pressure, printing
09 awareness, burlesque, imitation,
influence, sensation, suspicion
10 caricature, conviction, gut feeling
11 indentation 12 funny feeling,
recollection 13 consciousness,
impersonation
• **confused impression**
04 blur
• **give false impression**
03 lie
• **make an impression**
03 let 08 register 10 come across

impressionability
07 naivety 09 greenness 11 gullibility,
receptivity, sensitivity
13 ingenuousness, receptiveness,
vulnerability 14 suggestibility,
susceptibility

impressionable
04 open, waxy 05 naive 07 pliable
08 gullible 09 ingenuous, mouldable,

receptive, sensitive 10 responsive,
vulnerable 11 persuadable, susceptible

impressive
04 epic 05 grand, noble 06 awsome,
killer, moving, rotund, solemn, superb,
whizzo, whizzy 07 awesome, rousing,
stately 08 dazzling, dramatic,
emphatic, exciting, imposing, lapidary,
powerful, stirring, stonking, striking,
touching 09 affecting, effective,
inspiring 10 commanding, emphatical,
monumental, portentous
11 magnificent, spectacular 12 awe-
inspiring, breathtaking 13 scintillating

impressively
07 grandly 09 awesomely
10 powerfully, strikingly 11 effectively
12 emphatically 13 magnificently,
spectacularly

imprint
03 fix 04 etch, logo, mark, sign, tool
05 badge, brand, power, press, print,
stamp 06 burn in, effect, emblem,
emboss 07 engrave, impress,
meaning, results 08 colophon
09 character, establish, influence
10 impression 11 indentation, rubber-
stamp 12 consequences, significance
13 repercussions 14 reverberations
See also **publisher**

imprison
◇ *containment indicator*
03 jug, lag, pen 04 cage, gaol, jail,
quad, quod, shop 06 bang up, cage in,
detain, immure, intern, lock up, lumber,
shut in, shut up 07 confine, put away
08 restrain, send down 11 incarcerate,
put in prison 12 send to prison

imprisoned
◇ *insertion indicator*
05 caged 06 inside, jailed 07 captive,
immured, put away 08 banged up,
confined, locked up, sent down
09 doing bird, doing time 10 behind
bars 12 incarcerated 13 doing
porridge 15 under lock and key

imprisonment
04 bird, life 05 bonds 06 duress
07 custody, durance, duresse
08 porridge 09 captivity, committal,
detention 10 commitment, internment
11 confinement 13 incarceration

improbability
05 doubt 07 dubiety 11 dubiousness,
uncertainty 12 doubtfulness,
unlikelihood, unlikeliness 14 far-
fetchedness, implausibility,
ridiculousness

improbable
06 farfet 07 dubious 08 doubtful,
unlikely 09 uncertain 10 far-fetched,
incredible, marvellous, ridiculous
11 implausible 12 preposterous,
questionable, unbelievable,
unconvincing

impromptu
05 ad-lib 07 offhand 09 ad libitum,
extempore, makeshift 10 improvised,

off the cuff, unprepared, unscripted **11** spontaneous, unrehearsed **13** spontaneously **14** extemporaneous

improper

◇ *anagram indicator*
04 rude **05** false, unfit, wrong
06 risqué, vulgar **07** immoral
08 immodest, indecent, shocking, unlawful, unseemly **09** erroneous, incorrect, irregular, unfitting
10 inadequate, indecorous, indelicate, indiscreet, out of place, unbecoming, unsuitable **11** incongruous, inopportune **12** illegitimate
13 inappropriate

improperly

◇ *anagram indicator*
05 amiss, wrong **06** rudely **07** falsely, wrongly **09** immorally **10** immodestly, indecently, unlawfully, unsuitably
11 erroneously, incorrectly, irregularly, unfittingly **12** indecorously, indiscreetly **13** incongruously
15 inappropriately

impropriety

04 slip **05** gaffe, lapse **07** blunder, faux pas, mistake **08** bad taste, solecism
09 gaucherie, immodesty, indecency, indecorum, vulgarity **11** incongruity
12 unseemliness **13** unsuitability
14 indecorousness

improve

04 beet, bete, do up, file, grow, help, mend, rise **05** amend, do for, emend, fix up, rally **06** better, buck up, enrich, look up, occupy, perk up, pick up, polish, reform, revamp, revise, uplift, work on **07** advance, correct, develop, enhance, perfect, recover, rectify, touch up, upgrade **08** increase, progress, put right, set right, work upon **09** get better, meliorate, modernize **10** ameliorate, convalesce, make better, recuperate, streamline
11 make headway **12** gain strength, mend your ways, rehabilitate
14 be on the up and up **15** give a facelift to

improvement

04 gain, rise **05** rally **06** growth, pick-up, profit, reform **07** advance, headway, upswing **08** increase, progress, recovery, revision
09 amendment, bettering, upgrading
10 betterment, correction, rectifying, refinement **11** development, enhancement, furtherance, modernizing, reformation
12 amelioration **13** rectification
14 rehabilitation

improvident

06 wastry **07** wastery **08** careless, heedless, prodigal, reckless, wasteful
09 imprudent, negligent, shiftless, unthrifty **10** profligate, thriftless, unprepared **11** extravagant, inattentive, Micawberish, spendthrift, thoughtless **12** uneconomical
13 underprepared

improvisation

04 vamp **05** ad-lib **06** improv, lash-up
08 ad hocery **09** ad-libbing, expedient, impromptu, invention, makeshift **11** spontaneity
13 autoschediasm, extemporizing
15 extemporization

improvise

03 jam **04** vamp, wing **05** ad-lib, rig up, run up **06** busk it, devise, invent, make do, noodle, wing it **07** concoct, knock up **08** contrive **09** play by ear
11 extemporize, play it by ear **13** throw together **14** cobble together, have a brainwave **15** speak off the cuff
• **improvise on**
04 ride

improvised

◇ *anagram indicator*
05 ad-lib, scrub **06** sudden **07** scratch
08 drumhead, on the fly
09 extempore, impromptu, makeshift
10 off-the-cuff, unprepared, unscripted **11** spontaneous, unrehearsed **12** extemporized
14 extemporaneous

imprudence

05 folly, haste **08** rashness
12 carelessness, heedlessness, recklessness **13** foolhardiness
15 thoughtlessness

imprudent

04 rash **05** hasty **06** unwise **07** foolish
08 careless, heedless, reckless
09 foolhardy, ill-judged, impolitic
10 ill-advised, incautious, indiscreet, unthinking **11** improvident, injudicious, thoughtless **12** short-sighted **13** ill-considered, inconsiderate, irresponsible

impudence

03 lip **04** face, gall, neck, sass
05 cheek, front, mouth, nerve, snash
06 bronze **07** hutzpah **08** attitude, boldness, chutzpah, pertness, rudeness **09** brass neck, insolence, sauciness **10** brazenness, effrontery
11 presumption **12** impertinence, impertinency

impudent

04 bold, calm, cool, pert, rude
05 bardy, cocky, fresh, hardy, nervy, sassy, saucy **06** brazen, cheeky, gallus
07 forward, gallows **08** immodest, impolite, insolent, malapert, petulant
09 audacious, barefaced, boldfaced, out of line, shameless **10** brass-faced, unblushing **11** impertinent
12 presumptuous **13** disrespectful

impugn

06 assail, attack, berate, oppose, resist, revile, vilify **07** censure, dispute, traduce **08** question, vilipend
09 challenge, criticize **10** vituperate
14 call in question

impulse

04 push, send, urge, whim, wish
05 drive, force, nisus, pulse, spike, surge **06** desire, impact, motion,

motive, notion, signal, thrust
07 caprice, conatus, feeling, impetus, passion **08** instinct, momentum, movement, pressure, stimulus
09 brainwave, impulsion, incentive, premotion **10** compulsion, incitement, inducement, motivation, propulsion
11 inclination, stimulation, thought-wave
• **on impulse**
06 rashly **07** hastily **08** suddenly
10 recklessly **11** impatiently, impetuously, impulsively, intuitively
13 automatically, instinctively, irresponsibly, spontaneously, thoughtlessly **15** without thinking

impulsive

04 rash **05** hasty, quick **06** madcap, sudden **08** reckless **09** automatic, emotional, foolhardy, ill-judged, impatient, impetuous, intuitive
10 headstrong, passionate, unthinking
11 instinctive, precipitate, spontaneous, thoughtless **13** ill-considered

impulsively

06 rashly **07** hastily **08** suddenly
09 on impulse **10** recklessly
11 impatiently, impetuously, intuitively
13 automatically, instinctively, irresponsibly, spontaneously, thoughtlessly **15** without thinking

impulsiveness

05 haste **07** emotion, passion
08 instinct, rashness **09** hastiness, quickness **10** impatience, suddenness
11 impetuosity, spontaneity
12 recklessness **13** foolhardiness, impetuousness, intuitiveness, precipitation **15** precipitateness, thoughtlessness

impunity

07 amnesty, excusal, freedom, liberty, licence **08** immunity, security
09 exemption **10** permission
12 dispensation
• **with impunity**
06 freely, safely **08** in safety **11** without risk

impure

04 foul, lewd, sexy **05** bawdy, crude, dirty, mixed **06** coarse, drossy, erotic, filthy, ribald, risqué, smutty, vulgar
07 alloyed, blended, corrupt, debased, defiled, diluted, immoral, lustful, obscene, sullied, tainted, unclean, vicious **08** combined, depraved, immodest, improper, indecent, infected, polluted, unchaste
09 lecherous, offensive, shameless, unrefined **10** licentious, suggestive
11 adulterated, promiscuous
12 contaminated, pornographic

impurity

04 dirt, mark, smut, spot **05** blend, donor, dross, filth, grime, taint
07 crudity, mixture **08** dilution, foulness, lewdness **09** dirtiness, eroticism, immodesty, indecency, infection, looseness, obscenity,

pollutant, pollution, vulgarity
10 coarseness, corruption,
debasement, immorality, unchastity
11 contaminant, foreign body,
impropriety, lustfulness, pornography,
promiscuity **12** adulteration
13 contamination, offensiveness,
shamelessness **14** licentiousness

impute
03 lay, put **05** refer **06** assign, charge,
credit, object **07** ascribe **08** accredit
09 attribute, put down to

in
◇ *hidden indicator*
◇ *insertion indicator*
01 i′ **02** at, by, of, on **03** hip, per
04 cool, each, into, with **05** abode,
among, every, funky, smart **06** alight,
during, inside, modish, trendy, within
07 current, enclose, in vogue, popular,
stylish, through **10** all the rage,
enclosed by, throughout **11** fashionable
12 surrounded by **15** during the time of
• **in for**
12 due to receive **13** going to suffer
• **in itself**
04 in se **05** per se **13** intrinsically
• **in on**
07 aware of **09** clued up on
10 involved in **14** acquainted with
• **in with**
07 liked by **12** friendly with **15** on
good terms with

inability
08 handicap, weakness **09** impotence
10 disability, inadequacy, incapacity,
ineptitude **11** uselessness
12 incapability, incompetence
13 powerlessness **15** ineffectiveness

inaccessibility
08 distance **09** isolation
10 remoteness, separation
15 unattainability

inaccessible
06 remote **08** isolated **10** out of reach
11 beyond reach, god-forsaken, out of
the way, unavailable, uncomatable,
unget-at-able, unreachable
12 impenetrable, unattainable,
uncomeatable, unfrequented
14 inapproachable, unapproachable

inaccuracy
04 flub, goof, slip **05** error, fault, gaffe
06 boo-boo, defect, howler, slip-up
07 blunder, clanger, erratum, mistake
11 corrigendum, imprecision,
inexactness **12** mistakenness
13 erroneousness, unreliability
14 fallaciousness, miscalculation

inaccurate
◇ *anagram indicator*
03 out **05** false, loose, wrong
06 adrift, faulty, flawed, untrue
07 inexact, unsound **08** mistaken
09 defective, erroneous, imperfect,
imprecise, incorrect **10** fallacious,
unfaithful, unreliable
• **be inaccurate**
03 err

inaccurately
06 wildly **07** falsely, loosely, wrongly
08 clumsily **09** inexactly **10** carelessly,
unreliably **11** defectively, erroneously,
imperfectly, imprecisely, incorrectly
12 unfaithfully

inaction
04 rest **06** torpor **07** inertia
08 idleness, lethargy, slowness
09 passivity **10** immobility, inactivity,
stagnation **12** lifelessness, sluggishness
14 motionlessness

inactivate
04 stop **07** cripple, disable, scupper
08 mothball, paralyse **09** stabilize
10 deactivate, immobilize

inactive
04 dead, idle, lazy, slow **05** inert, still
06 shadow, sleepy, torpid, unused
07 dormant, passive **08** immobile,
indolent, lifeless, slothful, sluggish,
stagnant, unactive **09** dead-alive,
lethargic, quiescent, sedentary
10 motionless, stationary,
unemployed, vegetating
11 hibernating, inoperative **12** dead-
and-alive

inactivity
04 rest **05** sloth **06** stasis, torpor
07 inertia, languor, vacancy
08 abeyance, dormancy, dullness,
idleness, inaction, laziness, lethargy
09 heaviness, indolence, inertness,
lassitude, passivity **10** immobility,
quiescence, quiescency, stagnation,
vegetation **11** hibernation
12 dilatoriness, lifelessness,
sluggishness, unemployment

inadequacy
04 flaw, lack, want **05** fault **06** dearth,
defect, foible **07** deficit, failing,
paucity, poverty **08** scarcity,
shortage, weakness **09** inability
10 deficiency, inefficacy, inequality,
meagreness, scantiness
11 shortcoming **12** imperfection,
incapability, incompetence
13 defectiveness, insufficiency
15 ineffectiveness

inadequate
03 bad **04** poor **05** scant, short, unfit
06 faulty, meagre, scanty, scarce,
skimpy, sparse, too few **07** sketchy,
unequal, wanting **08** careless,
derisory, inexpert, pathetic
09 defective, deficient, imperfect,
incapable, niggardly, too little
11 incompetent, ineffective,
ineffectual, substandard, unqualified
12 insufficient, unproficient
13 disappointing, inefficacious, not
good enough **14** incommensurate, not
up to scratch, unsatisfactory **15** thin on
the ground

inadequately
05 badly **06** poorly, thinly
08 meagrely, scantily, skimpily, sparsely
09 sketchily **10** carelessly
11 imperfectly **14** insufficiently

inadmissible
08 improper **09** precluded
10 disallowed, immaterial, inapposite,
irrelevant, prohibited **11** unallowable
12 unacceptable **13** inappropriate

inadvertent
06 chance **08** careless **09** negligent,
unadvised, unguarded, unplanned,
unwitting **10** accidental, unintended
11 inattentive, involuntary,
thoughtless, unconscious
12 uncalculated **13** unintentional
14 unpremeditated

inadvertently
08 by chance, remissly **09** by mistake
10 by accident, carelessly, heedlessly,
mistakenly **11** negligently, unwittingly
12 accidentally, unthinkingly
13 involuntarily, thoughtlessly,
unconsciously **15** unintentionally

inadvisable
05 silly **06** unwise **07** foolish **09** ill-
judged, imprudent, misguided **10** ill-
advised, indiscreet **11** inexpedient,
injudicious **13** ill-considered

inalienable
08 absolute, inherent **09** permanent
10 inviolable, sacrosanct
11 unremovable **12** unassailable
13 non-negotiable **14** untransferable
15 imprescriptible, non-transferable

inane
04 vain, void **05** empty, silly, vapid
06 absurd, drippy, futile, stupid, vacant
07 fatuous, foolish, idiotic, puerile,
vacuous **08** mindless, trifling
09 frivolous, ludicrous, senseless,
worthless **10** ridiculous **11** nonsensical
13 characterless, unintelligent

inanely
08 absurdly, futilely, stupidly
09 fatuously, foolishly, vacuously
11 idiotically, ludicrously
12 ridiculously **13** nonsensically

inanimate
04 dead, dull, lazy **05** inert **06** torpid,
wooden **07** abiotic, defunct, dormant,
extinct **08** immobile, inactive, lifeless,
stagnant **09** apathetic, insensate,
lethargic **10** insentient, spiritless
11 unconscious

inanity
05 folly **06** waffle **07** fatuity, vacancy,
vacuity **08** daftness, vapidity
09 absurdity, asininity, emptiness,
frivolity, puerility, silliness, stupidity
10 imbecility **11** foolishness
13 ludicrousness, senselessness
14 ridiculousness

inapplicable
05 inapt **08** unsuited **09** unrelated
10 immaterial, inapposite, irrelevant,
unsuitable **11** unconnected
12 inconsequent **13** inappropriate

inapposite
10 immaterial, irrelevant, out of place,
unsuitable **13** inappropriate

inappreciable
04 fine, tiny 05 faint, small, vague
06 minute, slight, subtle 07 gradual,
muffled, obscure, unclear
09 inaudible, minuscule, priceless
10 impalpable, indefinite, indistinct,
negligible, unapparent 11 microscopic
12 undetectable, unnoticeable
13 imperceptible, indiscernible,
infinitesimal

inappropriate
05 inapt, undue 08 ill-timed,
improper, tactless, unseemly, untimely
09 facetious, ill-fitted, ill-suited,
tasteless, unfitting 10 inapposite,
indecorous, irrelevant, malapropos,
out of place, unbecoming, unsuitable
11 incongruous, inopportune
12 infelicitous 13 unappropriate

inappropriately
07 unfitly 08 off topic 10 malapropos,
out of place, tactlessly, unsuitably 11 off
the point, tastelessly 12 irrelevantly
13 incongruously, inopportunely
14 beside the point, infelicitously

inapt
05 unfit 07 unhappy 08 ill-timed,
unsuited 09 ill-fitted, ill-suited
10 inapposite, irrelevant, malapropos,
out of place, unsuitable
11 inopportune, unfortunate,
unqualified 12 infelicitous
13 inappropriate

inarticulacy
08 mumbling 09 hesitancy, stumbling
10 stammering, stuttering
11 incoherence 14 indistinctness,
speechlessness, tongue-tiedness

inarticulate
04 dumb, mute 07 blurred, halting,
muffled, mumbled, quavery, shaking,
unclear 08 hesitant 09 faltering,
gibbering, soundless, stumbling,
trembling, voiceless 10 disjointed,
hesitating, incoherent, indistinct,
speechless, stammering, stuttering,
tongue-tied 14 unintelligible

inattention
07 absence 09 disregard, misregard
10 dreaminess, negligence
11 daydreaming, distraction
12 carelessness, heedlessness,
unobservance 13 forgetfulness,
preoccupation, unmindfulness
15 inattentiveness, thoughtlessness

inattentive
04 deaf 05 loose, slack 06 absent,
asleep, dreamy, remiss 08 careless,
distrait, heedless 09 forgetful,
incurious, miles away, negligent,
unmindful 10 distracted, neglectful,
regardless 11 daydreaming,
inadvertent, preoccupied, thoughtless
12 absent-minded, disregarding,
unrespective 13 somewhere else,
wool-gathering

inaudible
03 low 04 dull, soft 05 faint, muted
06 silent 07 muffled, mumbled, stifled

08 murmured, muttered 09 noiseless,
whispered 10 indistinct
13 imperceptible

inaugural
05 first 06 maiden 07 initial, opening
08 exordial, original 09 launching
12 introductory

inaugurate
04 open 05 begin, set up, start
06 hansel, induct, invest, launch,
ordain 07 handsel, install, instate,
swear in, usher in 08 commence,
dedicate, enthrone, get going, initiate
09 auspicate, institute, introduce,
originate 10 commission, consecrate
11 set in motion 13 admit to office
14 open officially

inauguration
06 launch 07 opening 08 starting
09 induction, launching, setting up
10 initiation, installing, ordination,
swearing-in 11 institution, investiture
12 commencement, consecration,
enthronement, installation

inauspicious
03 bad 05 black 07 ominous, unlucky
08 ill-fated, sinister, untimely 09 ill-
boding, ill-omened 10 ill-starred,
sinistrous 11 threatening, unfortunate,
unpromising 12 discouraging,
infelicitous, unfavourable,
unpropitious

inborn
06 inbred, innate, native 07 connate,
natural 08 inherent, untaught
09 ingrained, inherited, intuitive
10 congenital, hereditary, ingenerate
11 instinctive, in the family

inbred
03 sib 06 innate, native 07 connate,
natural 08 inherent 09 incrossed,
ingrained 10 ingenerate
14 constitutional

inbuilt
05 basic 07 built-in 08 inherent,
integral 09 elemental, essential
11 constituent, fundamental

incalculable
04 vast 06 untold 07 endless,
immense, sumless 08 enormous,
infinite 09 boundless, countless,
limitless, unlimited 10 numberless
11 inestimable, innumerable,
measureless 12 immeasurable
13 unpredictable, without number

incandescence
04 fire, glow, leam 05 gleam, glory
07 glimmer, sunglow 08 outflush,
radiance, richness 09 afterglow,
splendour, vividness 10 brightness,
brilliance, luminosity
15 phosphorescence

incandescent
03 mad 05 aglow, angry, irate, livid
06 bright, fuming, raging 07 boiling,
enraged, furious, glowing, shining
08 dazzling, frenzied, gleaming,
incensed, inflamed, seething, sizzling,

up in arms, white-hot 09 brilliant, in a
lather, indignant 10 hopping mad,
infuriated 14 purple with rage

incantation
03 hex 04 rune 05 chant, charm, spell
06 mantra 07 formula, karakia,
mantram 10 invocation
11 abracadabra, conjuration 12 magic
formula

incapable
◇ anagram indicator
04 weak 05 drunk, inept, unfit
06 feeble, unable 07 useless
08 helpless, impotent, unfitted,
unsuited 09 powerless 10 inadequate
11 incompetent, ineffective,
ineffectual, unqualified
12 disqualified, not hacking it 14 not
up to scratch 15 out of your league

incapacitate
05 lay up 07 cripple, disable, scupper
08 paralyse 10 debilitate, disqualify,
immobilize 14 put out of action

incapacitated
05 drunk, tipsy, unfit 06 laid up, unwell
08 crippled, disabled 09 hamstrung,
paralysed, prostrate, scuppered
10 indisposed 11 immobilized, out of
action 12 disqualified

incapacity
08 weakness 09 impotence, inability,
unfitness 10 disability, feebleness,
inadequacy, ineptitude, non-ability
11 uselessness 12 incapability,
incompetence, incompetency
13 powerlessness 14 ineffectuality
15 ineffectiveness

incarcerate
04 cage, gaol, jail 06 bang up, commit,
coop up, detain, encage, immure,
intern, lock up, wall in 07 confine,
impound, put away 08 imprison,
restrain, restrict, send down 09 put in
jail, put inside 11 put in prison

incarceration
04 jail 07 bondage, custody
09 captivity, detention, restraint
10 internment 11 confinement,
restriction 12 imprisonment

incarnate
04 heal 05 human 07 fleshly
08 embodied, typified 09 corporeal,
made flesh, personify 10 in the flesh
11 impersonate, incardinate, in human
form, personified

incarnation
06 avatar 09 human form
10 embodiment 13 impersonation,
manifestation 15 personification

Incarnations include:
04 Rama
07 Krishna
09 Jugannath
10 Juggernaut

incautious
04 rash 05 hasty 06 unwary
07 foolish 08 careless, cavalier,

eckless, wareless **09** foolhardy, ill-
udged, imprudent, impulsive,
unguarded **10** ill-advised, unthinking,
unwatchful **11** inattentive, injudicious,
precipitate, thoughtless, unobservant
13 ill-considered, inconsiderate,
uncircumspect

incendiary
04 bomb, mine **06** charge **07** carcase,
carcass, firebug, grenade **08** agitator,
arsonist, fireball, firebomb, inciting,
stirring **09** demagogue, explosive,
firebrand, flammable, insurgent,
pétroleur, seditious **10** fire-raiser,
petrol bomb, pétroleuse, pyromaniac,
rick-burner, subversive **11** combustible,
dissentious, fire-raising, provocative
12 inflammatory, rabble-rouser
13 rabble-rousing, revolutionary
14 proceleusmatic **15** Molatov cocktail

incense
03 irk, vex **04** balm, rile, thus, urge
05 anger, aroma, myrrh, scent
06 enrage, excite, hassle, homage,
incite, kindle, madden, nettle, stacte
07 agitate, benzoin, bouquet, inflame,
perfume, provoke **08** irritate, pastille
09 adulation, aggravate, fragrance,
infuriate, joss-stick **10** exasperate
12 frankincense **14** drive up the wall

incensed
03 mad **04** waxy **05** angry, cross, irate,
ratty, spewy **06** choked, fuming, ireful
07 crooked, enraged, furious, ropable,
stroppy, uptight **08** burned up,
furibund, hairless, in a paddy, in a strop,
maddened, up in arms, wrathful **09** in a
rather, indignant, pissed off, raving
mad, seeing red, steamed up, ticked off
10 aggravated, hopping mad,
infuriated **11** disgruntled, exasperated,
fit to be tied **12** on the warpath

incentive
04 bait, goad, lure, spur **06** carrot,
motive, reason, reward **07** impetus
08 igniting, inciting, stimulus
09 stimulant, sweetener
10 enticement, incitation, incitement,
inducement, motivation
11 encouraging **13** encouragement

inception
04 dawn, rise **05** birth, start **06** origin,
outset **07** kick-off, opening
09 beginning **10** initiation
12 commencement, inauguration,
installation **13** establishment

incessant
07 endless, eternal, non-stop
08 constant, unbroken, unending
09 ceaseless, continual, perpetual,
recurrent, unceasing, weariless
10 continuous, persistent
11 everlasting, never-ending,
unremitting **12** interminable
13 uninterrupted

incessantly
07 for ever **09** endlessly, eternally
10 constantly, unendingly **11** at every
turn, ceaselessly, immediately,

unceasingly **12** continuously,
interminably **13** everlastingly,
unremittingly **14** for ever and ever
15 twenty-four seven, uninterruptedly

incidence
04 rate **05** range **06** amount, degree,
extent, to-fall **09** frequency
10 commonness, occurrence,
prevalence

incident
03 bar, row **04** baur, bawr, page
05 brush, clash, event, fight, scene,
upset **06** affair, comedy, fracas, matter,
mishap, period **07** affaire, episode,
falling, passage, subject **08** conflict,
instance, occasion, skirmish
09 adventure, commotion, happening
10 consequent, experience,
occurrence, proceeding
11 disturbance **12** circumstance
13 confrontation **14** unpleasantness

incidental
05 minor, petty, small **06** casual,
chance, random **07** passing, related,
trivial **08** by chance, striking
09 ancillary, attendant, impinging,
occurrent, secondary **10** accidental,
background, fortuitous, occasional,
peripheral, subsidiary **11** concomitant,
contingency, facultative, subordinate
12 accompanying, contributory, non-
essential **13** supplementary

incidentally
07 apropos, by the by **08** by chance,
by the way, casually **09** as an aside, en
passant, in passing **10** by accident
11 secondarily **12** accidentally,
digressively, episodically, fortuitously,
unexpectedly **13** as a digression
14 coincidentally **15** parenthetically

incinerate
04 burn **07** cremate **09** carbonize
13 reduce to ashes

incineration
07 burning **09** cremation
13 carbonization **14** turning to ashes

incipient
07 nascent, newborn **08** inchoate,
starting **09** beginning, embryonic,
impending, inaugural, inceptive
10 commencing, developing
11 originating, rudimentary

incise
03 cut **04** etch, gash, nick, slit
05 carve, notch, slash **06** chisel,
scribe, sculpt **07** cut into, engrave
09 sculpture

incision
03 cut **04** gash, nick, slit **05** notch,
slash, wound **07** coupure, cutting,
opening **08** colotomy, incisure,
lobotomy, oncotomy **09** cystotomy,
insection, iridotomy **10** craniotomy,
discission, enterotomy, episiotomy,
nephrotomy, phlebotomy, pleurotomy,
sclerotomy, trenchancy
11 hysterotomy, myringotomy,
thoracotomy, tracheotomy,

venesection, venisection
12 pharyngotomy, tonsillotomy

incisive
04 acid, keen **05** acute, sharp
06 astute, biting, shrewd **07** caustic,
cutting, mordant, pungent
08 piercing, stinging, surgical
09 sarcastic, trenchant **10** perceptive
11 penetrating **13** perspicacious

incisively
06 keenly, tartly **07** acutely, sharply
08 astutely **09** mordantly, pungently
10 piercingly **11** caustically,
trenchantly **13** penetratingly,
sarcastically

incisiveness
04 bite, edge **07** acidity, sarcasm
08 astucity, keenness, pungency,
tartness **09** acuteness, sharpness
10 astuteness, trenchancy
11 penetration **12** perspicacity

incite
03 egg, hoi, hoy, put, set, sic, tar
04 abet, fuel, goad, poke, prod, sick,
spur, urge, whet **05** drive, egg on,
impel, prick, put on, rouse, tarre
06 arouse, excite, fillip, foment,
induce, kindle, prompt, stir up, whip
up, work up **07** actuate, agitate,
animate, incense, inflame, premove,
provoke, solicit **09** encourage,
instigate, stimulate **13** stir the possum

incitement
04 goad, prod, spur, whet **05** drive,
sting **06** motive, urging **07** impetus,
rousing **08** stimulus **09** agitation,
animation, incentive, onsetting,
prompting **10** inducement,
motivation, suggestion **11** instigation,
provocation, stimulation
13 encouragement

inciting
08 stirring **09** hortative, hortatory,
incentive, seditious **10** incendiary,
subversive **11** provocative
12 inflammatory **13** rabble-rousing
14 proceleusmatic

incivility
08 rudeness **09** indignity, roughness,
vulgarity **10** bad manners, coarseness,
disrespect, inurbanity **11** boorishness,
discourtesy, ill-breeding
12 impoliteness **14** unmannerliness

inclemency
07 rawness **08** foulness, severity
09 harshness, roughness **10** bitterness,
storminess **15** tempestuousness

inclement
03 raw, wet **04** cold, foul **05** harsh,
nasty, rough **06** bitter, severe, stormy
07 squally **08** blustery **11** intemperate,
tempestuous

inclination
03 bow, maw, nod, set **04** bank, bend,
bent, bias, cant, kant, lift, list, mind,
rake, ramp, tilt **05** angle, pitch, slant,
slope, study, taste, trend **06** ascent,
liking, notion **07** incline, leaning

08 affinity, fondness, gradient, penchant, tendency **09** acclivity, affection, declivity, deviation, steepness **10** attraction, partiality, preference, proclivity, propension, propensity **11** disposition **12** predilection, propenseness **14** predisposition
• **with inclination towards**
02 on

incline
03 bow, dip, kip, nod, tip **04** bank, bend, bias, hade, heel, hill, lean, list, peck, rake, ramp, rise, slip, stay, sway, tend, tilt, veer **05** curve, offer, slant, slope, stoop, swell, swing, tempt, verge **06** affect, ascent, direct, prefer, shelve, steeve **07** descent, deviate, dispose, diverge, propend, recline **08** gradient, persuade **09** acclivity, declivity, influence, prejudice

inclined
03 apt **04** bent, wont **05** given, ready **06** liable, likely, minded **07** oblique, of a mind, sloping, tending, willing **08** disposed, proclive, propense **10** well-minded **11** predisposed
• **be inclined**
04 care
• **inclined to**
01 -y

include
◇ *containment indicator*
◇ *hidden indicator*
03 add **04** hold, span **05** add in, admit, carry, cover, enter, put in **06** embody, insert, reckon, rope in, take in **07** connote, contain, count in, embrace, enclose, involve, let in on, subsume, throw in **08** allow for, classify, comprise, conclude **09** encompass, introduce **10** comprehend **11** incorporate **15** take into account

including
◇ *containment indicator*
03 inc **04** incl, with **08** as well as, counting, included **11** inclusive of **12** together with

inclusion
08 addition **09** insertion **10** embodiment **11** involvement, subsumption **12** encompassing **13** comprehension, incorporation

inclusive
03 inc **04** full, incl **05** all-in **07** blanket, general, overall **08** catch-all, included, sweeping **09** enclosing **12** all-embracing, all-inclusive **13** comprehensive **14** across-the-board

incognito
06 masked, veiled **07** unknown **08** nameless, unmarked **09** disguised **10** in disguise **11** camouflaged **12** unidentified **14** unidentifiable, unrecognizable **15** under a false name

incognizant
07 unaware **08** ignorant **09** unknowing **10** uninformed

11 inattentive, unconscious, unobservant **12** unacquainted **13** unenlightened

incoherence
05 mix-up **06** jumble, muddle, mumble, mutter **07** stammer, stutter **08** wildness **09** confusion **10** brokenness **11** garbledness **12** illogicality **13** inconsistency **14** disjointedness

incoherent
05 loose **06** broken **07** garbled, jumbled, mixed-up, muddled, mumbled, unclear **08** confused, muttered, rambling, wandered **09** illogical, rigmarole, scrambled, unjointed, wandering **10** disjointed, disordered, stammering, stuttering **11** unconnected **12** disconnected, inarticulate, inconsistent **14** skimble-skamble, unintelligible

incombustible
09 fireproof **10** flameproof, unburnable **12** non-flammable **13** fire-resistant **14** flame-resistant, flame-retardant, non-inflammable

income
03 pay **05** gains, means, rente, wages **06** inflow, profit, salary **07** arrival, profits, returns, revenue, takings **08** benefice, earnings, entrance, interest, proceeds, receipts, rent roll **09** allowance, comings-in, penny-rent **10** emoluments **12** independency, remuneration

incoming
03 new **04** next **06** coming **07** ensuing, revenue **08** accruing, arriving, entering, homeward **09** returning **10** succeeding **11** approaching

incommensurate
07 extreme, unequal **09** excessive **10** inadequate, inordinate **11** extravagant, inequitable **12** insufficient **15** incommensurable

incommunicable
09 ineffable **11** unspeakable, unutterable **12** unimpartable **13** indescribable, inexpressible

incomparable
06 superb **07** supreme **08** peerless **09** brilliant, matchless, nonpareil, paramount, unmatched **10** inimitable, unequalled, unrivalled **11** superlative, unsurpassed **12** second to none, unparalleled, without equal **13** beyond compare **15** without parallel

incomparably
05 by far **06** easily **08** superbly **09** eminently, supremely **10** far and away, infinitely **11** brilliantly **12** immeasurably **13** beyond compare, superlatively

incompatibility
05 clash **08** conflict, mismatch, variance **09** antipathy, disparity **10** antagonism, difference

11 discrepancy, incongruity **12** disagreement **13** contradiction, disparateness, inconsistency **14** uncongeniality

incompatible
05 alien, wrong **06** at odds **08** clashing, unsuited **09** disparate, dissonant, exclusive, repugnant **10** at variance, discordant, ill-matched, in conflict, insociable, mismatched **11** conflicting, disagreeing, ill-assorted, incongruous, uncongenial **12** antagonistic, inconsistent **13** contradictory **14** irreconcilable

incompetence
08 bungling **09** inability, ineptness, stupidity, unfitness **10** inadequacy, ineptitude, inequality **11** uselessness **12** incapability, inefficiency **13** insufficiency, unsuitability **14** ineffectuality **15** ineffectiveness, ineffectualness

incompetent
03 ill **04** naff, poxy, ropy **05** awful, flaky, lousy, pants, ropey, unfit **06** clumsy, crummy, stupid, unable **07** awkward, botched, the pits, useless **08** bungling, fumbling, handless, hopeless, inexpert, pathetic, schleppy, terrible **09** deficient, incapable, unskilful **10** amateurish, inadequate, unsuitable **11** a load of crap, ineffective, inefficient, unqualified **12** insufficient **14** a load of garbage, a load of rubbish

incomplete
◇ *tail deletion indicator*
04 half, part **05** short **06** broken, patchy **07** lacking, partial, pendant, pendent, scrappy, sketchy, wanting **08** abridged **09** defective, deficient, embryonic, half-baked, imperfect, piecemeal, shortened **10** catalectic, unfinished **11** fragmentary, rudimentary, undeveloped **14** unaccomplished

incomprehensible
04 deep **06** opaque **07** complex, obscure, unaware **08** abstruse, baffling, involved, profound, puzzling **09** enigmatic, limitless, recondite **10** mysterious, perplexing, unfamiliar, unreadable **11** complicated, double Dutch, inscrutable **12** impenetrable, mind-boggling, over your head, unfathomable **13** above your head, all Greek to you, inconceivable **14** unintelligible

incomprehension
09 ignorance, obscurity **10** complexity, profundity **11** unawareness **12** incognizance **13** unfamiliarity **14** inscrutability, mysteriousness **15** impenetrability

inconceivable
06 absurd **08** shocking **09** ludicrous, unheard-of **10** impossible, incredible, outrageous, ridiculous, staggering **11** implausible, unthinkable **12** mind-boggling, unbelievable, unimaginable

inconclusive
04 open, weak **05** vague
09 ambiguous, uncertain, undecided, unsettled **10** indecisive, indefinite, up in the air **11** left hanging
12 unconvincing, unsatisfying
13 indeterminate **14** open to question

incongruity
05 clash **08** conflict **09** disparity, inaptness **10** disharmony
11 discrepancy **13** contradiction, inconsistency, unsuitability
14 dissociability **15** dissociableness, incompatibility

incongruous
03 odd **06** absurd, at odds, patchy
07 jarring, strange **08** clashing, contrary, out of key **09** dissonant
10 out of place, unsuitable
11 conflicting, disharmonic, dissociable **12** incompatible, inconsistent, out of keeping
13 contradictory, inappropriate
14 irreconcilable

incongruously
08 off topic **10** out of place, unsuitably
11 off the point **12** irrelevantly
13 inopportunely **14** beside the point, infelicitously **15** inappropriately

inconsequential
05 minor, petty **07** trivial **08** trifling
09 small beer **10** immaterial, negligible
11 unimportant **13** inappreciable, insignificant **14** of no importance

inconsiderable
04 mean, weak **05** minor, petty, small
06 slight **07** nominal, trivial **08** trifling
10 negligible **11** unimportant
13 insignificant

inconsiderate
04 rash, rude **06** unkind **07** selfish
08 careless, heedless, tactless, uncaring **09** egotistic, imprudent
10 dismissive, intolerant, regardless, unthinking, unweighing **11** insensitive, light-minded, self-centred, thoughtless, unconcerned **12** light-hearted, uncharitable, undiscerning

inconsiderateness
08 rudeness **09** unconcern
10 unkindness **11** intolerance, selfishness **12** carelessness, tactlessness **13** insensitivity **15** self-centredness, thoughtlessness

inconsistency
04 odds **07** paradox **08** conflict, variance **09** disparity **10** divergence, fickleness, repugnance **11** contrariety, discrepancy, gallimaufry, incongruity, inconstancy, instability
12 disagreement, unsteadiness
13 contradiction, unreliability
14 changeableness **15** incompatibility

inconsistent
05 alien **06** at odds, fickle, spotty
07 erratic, jarring, varying **08** contrary, in and out, unstable, unsteady, variable
09 differing, irregular, mercurial,

repugnant **10** at variance, capricious, changeable, discordant, dissimilar, inconstant, out of place **11** conflicting, incongruent, incongruous, unagreeable **12** incompatible, in opposition, out of keeping
13 contradictory, self-repugnant, unpredictable **14** disconformable, irreconcilable

inconsolable
08 desolate, wretched **09** miserable
10 despairing, devastated
11 heartbroken **12** disconsolate
13 broken-hearted, grief-stricken

inconspicuous
05 plain, quiet **06** hidden, low-key, modest **07** obscure **08** discreet, ordinary, retiring **09** concealed
10 indistinct, unassuming
11 camouflaged, unobtrusive
12 unremarkable **13** insignificant **15** in the background, undistinguished

inconspicuously
07 faintly, quietly **08** modestly
12 unassumingly **13** unobtrusively
15 insignificantly, in the background

inconstancy
05 range, shift, swing **06** change
08 wavering **09** variation **10** fickleness
11 alternation, ambivalence, fluctuation, instability, oscillation, vacillation, variability **12** irresolution, unsteadiness, variableness

inconstant
06 fickle, giglet, giglot **07** erratic, moonish, mutable, Protean, vagrant, varying, wayward **08** strumpet, unstable, unsteady, variable, volatile, wavering **09** changeful, faithless, fluxional, mercurial, uncertain, unsettled **10** capricious, changeable, fluxionary, irresolute, unfaithful, unreliable **11** fluctuating, vacillating
12 inconsistent, undependable

incontestable
04 sure **05** clear **07** certain, evident, obvious **08** cast-iron **10** undeniable
11 indubitable, irrefutable, self-evident
12 indisputable **14** unquestionable

incontinent
04 lewd **05** loose **06** wanton
07 lustful **08** unchaste **09** debauched, dissolute, lecherous, unbridled, unchecked **10** dissipated, lascivious, licentious, ungoverned, unstanched
11 immediately, promiscuous, unstaunched **12** uncontrolled, ungovernable, unrestrained
14 uncontrollable

incontrovertible
05 clear **07** certain **10** undeniable
11 beyond doubt, indubitable, irrefutable, self-evident
12 indisputable **13** incontestable
14 beyond question, unquestionable

incontrovertibly
07 clearly **09** certainly **10** undeniably
11 beyond doubt, indubitably,

irrefutably **12** indisputably **14** beyond question, unquestionably

inconvenience
03 irk **04** bind, bore, burr, drag, fuss, pain **05** annoy, upset, worry
06 bother, burden, hassle, put out
07 disrupt, disturb, problem, trouble, turn-off **08** drawback, flea-bite, headache, nuisance, vexation
09 annoyance, disoblige, hindrance, incommode **10** difficulty, discommode, disruption, disutility, impose upon **11** awkwardness, disturbance, incommodity
12 disadvantage, discommodity

inconvenient
06 ungain **07** awkward **08** annoying, ill-timed, untimely, untoward, unwieldy
09 difficult **10** bothersome, cumbersome, unhandsome, unsuitable
11 inexpedient, inopportune, troublesome **12** embarrassing, incommodious, unmanageable, unseasonable **13** inappropriate

incorporate
◇ *containment indicator*
03 mix **04** fuse **05** blend, merge, unify, unite **06** absorb, embody, imbody, take in **07** build in, combine, contain, embrace, include, piece up, subsume
08 coalesce, incorpse **09** integrate, multiplex **10** amalgamate, assimilate
11 consolidate

incorporated
03 inc

incorporation
05 blend, union **06** fusion, merger
07 company, society **08** unifying
09 inclusion, subsuming
10 absorption, assumption, embodiment, federation
11 association, coalescence, combination, integration, unification
12 amalgamation, assimilation

incorporeal
04 aery **05** aerie **06** unreal **07** ghostly
08 bodiless, ethereal, illusory, spectral, unfleshy **09** spiritual, unfleshly
10 immaterial, intangible, phantasmal, phantasmic

incorrect
◇ *anagram indicator*
03 bad, ill **05** false, wrong **06** faulty, untrue **07** inexact, off beam
08 improper, mistaken, not right
09 erroneous, imprecise **10** fallacious, inaccurate, unsuitable, way off beam
12 illegitimate **13** inappropriate, ungrammatical

incorrectly
05 false, wrong **07** falsely, in error, wrongly **08** unfairly, unjustly **09** by mistake **10** mistakenly **11** erroneously, misguidedly **12** fallaciously, inaccurately **15** inappropriately

incorrectness
05 error **07** fallacy **09** falseness, wrongness **10** faultiness, inaccuracy

11 imprecision, inexactness, unsoundness **12** inexactitude, mistakenness, speciousness **13** erroneousness, impreciseness, unsuitability

incorrigible
08 hardened, hopeless **09** incurable **10** beyond hope, inveterate **12** irredeemable **13** dyed-in-the-wool, irreclaimable

incorruptibility
06 honour, virtue **07** honesty, probity **08** justness, morality, nobility **09** integrity **11** uprightness **15** trustworthiness

incorruptible
04 just **05** moral **06** honest **07** ethical, upright **08** straight, virtuous **10** honourable, unbribable **11** trustworthy **14** high-principled

increase
02 up **03** add, ech, eik, eke, ich, wax **04** eche, eech, gain, go up, grow, hike, rise, soar, wave **05** add to, boost, breed, bulge, climb, mount, raise, surge, swell, widen **06** bump up, deepen, expand, extend, flow-on, gather, growth, hike up, mark-up, profit, pump up, rocket, spiral, spread, step up, step-up, uplift, upturn **07** advance, augment, broaden, build up, build-up, develop, enhance, enlarge, further, improve, inflate, magnify, produce, progeny, prolong, scale up, upsurge **08** addition, escalate, heighten, interest, maximize, multiply, mushroom, progress, redouble, snowball **09** expansion, extension, increment, intensify, propagate, rocketing, skyrocket **10** accumulate, escalation, strengthen **11** development, enlargement, heightening, mushrooming, proliferate, snowballing **12** augmentation, bring to a head **13** become greater, proliferation **14** bring to the boil **15** be on the increase, intensification

increasingly
06 more so **10** all the more **11** more and more **12** cumulatively **13** exponentially, on the increase, progressively

incredible
04 tall **05** great, steep **06** absurd, unreal **07** amazing **08** smashing, terrific **09** fantastic, wonderful **10** astounding, cockamamie, far-fetched, formidable, impossible, improbable, marvellous, past belief, remarkable, surprising, tremendous **11** astonishing, cock-and-bull, exceptional, implausible, jaw-dropping, magnificent, unthinkable **12** beyond belief, mind-boggling, preposterous, unbelievable, unimaginable **13** extraordinary, inconceivable **14** out of this world

incredibly
04 very **06** highly **07** greatly **09** amazingly, extremely **10** impossibly, remarkably **11** unspeakably, wonderfully **12** marvellously, surprisingly, terrifically, tremendously, unbelievably, unimaginably **13** exceptionally, fantastically, inconceivably, inexpressibly **15** extraordinarily

incredulity
05 doubt **08** cynicism, distrust, mistrust, unbelief **09** amazement, disbelief, suspicion **10** scepticism

incredulous
07 cynical, dubious **08** doubtful, doubting **09** sceptical, uncertain **10** suspicious **11** distrustful, distrusting, unbelieving, unconvinced **12** disbelieving, unbelievable

increment
04 gain **06** growth, step-up **07** accrual **08** addendum, addition, increase **09** accretion, accrument, expansion, extension **10** growth ring, supplement **11** advancement, enlargement **12** augmentation

incriminate
05 blame, set up **06** accuse, charge, indict **07** arraign, impeach, involve **08** stitch up **09** implicate, inculpate **13** put the blame on

inculcate
03 fix **05** teach **06** infuse, instil, preach **07** din into, engrain, implant, impress, imprint **08** drum into **09** drill into **10** hammer into **12** indoctrinate

inculpate
05 blame **06** accuse, charge, indict **07** arraign, censure, impeach, involve **09** implicate **11** incriminate, recriminate **13** put the blame on

incumbent
04 up to **05** right **06** bearer, holder, member, parson **07** binding, officer **08** official **09** mandatory, necessary, overlying **10** compulsory, obligatory, prescribed **11** functionary, overhanging **12** office-bearer, office-holder **15** perpetual curate

incur
03 ren, rin, run **04** earn, gain, risk **05** run up **06** arouse, suffer **07** provoke, sustain **08** contract, meet with **10** experience

incurable
05 fatal **08** hardened, hopeless, terminal **10** beyond hope, inoperable, inveterate, remediless, unhealable, unrecuring **11** immedicable, untreatable **12** incorrigible **13** dyed-in-the-wool, unmedicinable

incurably
07 fatally **10** beyond hope, hopelessly, inoperably, terminally **12** incorrigibly, inveterately

incursion
04 raid, road, rode **05** foray, sally **06** attack, inroad, razzia, sortie **07** assault, inroads **08** invasion **09** intrusion, irruption, onslaught **11** penetration **12** infiltration

indebted
05 owing **07** obliged **08** beholden, grateful, thankful **09** obligated **12** appreciative
• **be indebted**
03 owe

indebtedness
09 gratitude **10** obligation **12** appreciation **15** debt of gratitude

indecency
07 crudity **08** foulness, impurity, lewdness **09** grossness, immodesty, indecorum, obscenity, vulgarity **10** coarseness **11** pornography **13** offensiveness **14** licentiousness

indecent
◇ *anagram indicator*
04 blue, foul, free, lewd, ripe **05** bawdy, crude, dirty, gross, nasty **06** coarse, filthy, fruity, impure, ribald, risqué, sleazy, smutty, sultry, vulgar **07** corrupt, immoral, obscene, raunchy **08** depraved, immodest, improper, scabrous, shocking, uncomely, unhonest, unseemly **09** off colour, offensive, perverted **10** degenerate, indecorous, indelicate, licentious, outrageous, suggestive, unbecoming, unsuitable **11** near the bone, Rabelaisian **12** pornographic, unrepeatable **13** inappropriate **14** close to the bone, near the knuckle

indecipherable
04 tiny **07** crabbed, cramped, unclear **09** illegible **10** indistinct, unreadable **14** unintelligible

indecision
05 doubt **07** swither **08** suspense, wavering **09** hesitancy **10** hesitation **11** ambivalence, fluctuation, uncertainty, vacillation **12** irresolution **13** tentativeness **14** indecisiveness **15** shilly-shallying

indecisive
04 open **06** unsure **07** unclear **08** doubtful, hesitant, wavering **09** faltering, tentative, uncertain, undecided, unsettled **10** ambivalent, hesitating, indefinite, in two minds, irresolute, undecisive, up in the air, weak-willed, wishy-washy **11** fluctuating, vacillating **12** feeble-minded, inconclusive, pussyfooting, undetermined **13** indeterminate **15** shilly-shallying

indecorous
04 rude **05** crude, rough **06** coarse, vulgar **07** boorish, ill-bred, naughty, uncivil, uncouth **08** churlish, immodest, impolite, improper, indecent, seemless, unseemly, untoward **09** graceless, tasteless, unfitting **10** high-kilted, in bad taste,

eemelesse, unladylike, unmannerly, unsuitable **11** ill-mannered, indignified **13** inappropriate, ungentlemanly

ndecorum
07 crudity **08** bad taste, rudeness **09** immodesty, indecency, roughness, vulgarity **10** coarseness, incivility **11** impropriety **12** impoliteness, unseemliness **13** tastelessness

ndeed
01 I 02 ay, la **03** aye, e'en, nay, yah, yea, yes **04** deed, even, faix, just **05** faith, haith, marry, quite, sooth, truly **06** atweel, in fact, quotha, rather, really **07** for sure, insooth, in truth, quite so, soothly **08** actually, forsooth, to be sure **09** certainly, soothlich **10** absolutely, definitely, in good time, positively, undeniably **11** doubtlessly, undoubtedly **12** without doubt **13** for that matter, in anyone's book, in point of fact

ndefatigable
06 dogged **07** patient, undying **08** diligent, tireless, untiring **09** unfailing, unresting, unwearied **10** relentless, unflagging, untireable, unwearying **11** indomitable, persevering, unremitting, unweariable **13** inexhaustible

ndefatigably
08 doggedly **09** patiently **10** diligently, tirelessly **11** indomitably, unfailingly, unrestingly **12** relentlessly, unflaggingly **13** unremittingly

ndefensible
05 wrong **06** faulty, flawed **07** exposed, unarmed **08** disarmed, specious **09** unguarded, untenable **10** unshielded, vulnerable **11** defenceless, ill-equipped, inexcusable, unfortified, unprotected **12** undefendable, unforgivable, unpardonable **13** insupportable, unjustifiable

ndefinable
03 dim **04** hazy **05** vague **06** subtle **07** obscure, unclear **08** nameless **10** impalpable, indistinct, unrealized **13** indescribable, inexpressible

ndefinite
04 hazy **05** fuzzy, loose, vague **07** blurred, general, inexact, obscure, unclear, unfixed, unknown **08** confused, doubtful, twilight **09** ambiguous, equivocal, imprecise, uncertain, undecided, undefined, unlimited, unsettled **10** ambivalent, ill-defined, indistinct, unresolved **11** nondescript, unspecified **12** inconclusive, undetermined **13** indeterminate

ndefinitely
06 always **07** for ever **09** endlessly, eternally **11** ad infinitum, continually, permanently **12** without limit

indelible
04 fast **07** lasting **08** enduring, unfading **09** ingrained, permanent **12** imperishable, ineffaceable, ineradicable **14** indestructible

indelibly
10 enduringly **11** permanently **12** ineradicably **14** indestructibly

indelicacy
07 crudity **08** bad taste, rudeness **09** grossness, immodesty, indecency, obscenity, vulgarity **10** coarseness, smuttiness **11** impropriety **13** offensiveness, tastelessness **14** suggestiveness

indelicate
03 low **04** blue, rude, warm **05** crude, gross **06** coarse, risqué, sultry, vulgar **07** obscene **08** immodest, improper, indecent, tactless, unseemly, untoward **09** off-colour, offensive, tasteless **10** in bad taste, indecorous, suggestive, unbecoming **12** embarrassing

indemnify
03 pay **04** free **05** repay **06** exempt, insure, recoup, repair, secure **07** endorse, protect, requite, satisfy **09** guarantee, reimburse **10** compensate, remunerate, underwrite

indemnity
07 amnesty, redress **08** immunity, requital, security **09** assurance, exemption, guarantee, insurance, repayment, safeguard **10** protection, reparation **11** restitution **12** compensation, remuneration **13** reimbursement

indent
03 cut **04** dent, dint, mark, nick, pink **05** notch, order **06** ask for, crenel, demand, recess **07** bargain, impress, request, scallop, serrate **08** apply for, crenelle **09** penetrate **10** apprentice **11** requisition

indentation
03 cut, dip, pit **04** dent, nick **05** gouge, notch, sinus **06** crenel, dimple, furrow, groove, hollow, recess **08** crenelle **09** serration **10** depression **11** engrailment

indenture
04 bond, deal, deed **08** contract, covenant **09** agreement **10** commitment, settlement **11** certificate

independence
01 I 05 uhuru **06** swaraj **07** autarky, freedom, liberty **08** autonomy, home rule, self-rule **10** competency, separation **11** nationalism, sovereignty **12** independency, self-reliance **13** individualism **14** decolonization, self-government **15** self-sufficiency

independent
01 I 03 Ind **04** fair, free, just **07** neutral, private, unaided **08** absolute, autarkic, discrete, distinct, separate, unbiased

09 autarchic, freelance, impartial, liberated, objective, sovereign, unrelated **10** autogenous, autonomous, crossbench, individual, non-aligned, self-ruling, unattacked **11** self-reliant, unconnected **12** free-standing, free-thinking, self-standing, unprejudiced, unrestrained **13** autocephalous, disinterested, dispassionate, individualist, self-contained, self-governing, unconstrained **14** self-sufficient, self-supporting, unconventional **15** going your own way, individualistic, self-determining, self-legislating

independently
04 solo **05** alone **07** unaided **09** on your own, on your tod **10** by yourself, separately **12** autonomously, individually

indescribable
07 amazing **08** nameless **09** ineffable **10** incredible **11** exceptional, indefinable, inenarrable, undefinable, unspeakable, unutterable **13** extraordinary, inexpressible

indescribably
04 very **06** highly **07** greatly **09** amazingly, extremely **10** incredibly **11** unspeakably, unutterably **13** exceptionally, inexpressibly **15** extraordinarily

indestructible
05 tough **06** strong **07** abiding, durable, endless, eternal, lasting **08** enduring, immortal **09** permanent **10** undecaying **11** everlasting, infrangible, unbreakable **12** imperishable **15** tough as old boots

indeterminate
04 hazy **05** vague **07** inexact, unclear, unfixed, unknown **08** unstated, variable **09** ambiguous, equivocal, imprecise, open-ended, uncertain, undecided, undefined **10** ambivalent, ill-defined, indefinite **11** unspecified **12** inconclusive, undetermined **13** unpredictable

index
03 BMI, key, RPI **04** clue, dial, hand, hint, list, mark, nose, rate, sign **05** guide, power, ratio, scale, style, table, token **06** alidad, gnomon, needle, number **07** average, formula, pointer, preface, symptom **08** card file, exponent, fraction, prologue **09** catalogue, directory, indicator **10** difference, forefinger, indication, percentage, proportion **11** concordance **12** introduction **13** card catalogue **14** correspondence

India
01 I 03 IND
See also **state**

Indian *see* **American; Asian**

Indiana
02 IN **03** Ind

indicate

03 put, say, tip **04** mark, mean, note, read, shew, show, sign, tell **05** argue, arrow, imply, point, spell, state, utter, voice **06** affirm, assert, denote, evince, record, report, reveal, set out **07** declare, display, divulge, express, point to, present, signify, specify, suggest **08** announce, disclose, evidence, manifest, point out, register **09** designate, formulate, make known, represent **10** articulate **11** communicate **15** be symptomatic of

indicated

06 marked, needed **08** required **09** advisable, called-for, desirable, necessary, suggested **11** recommended

indication

03 nod **04** clue, hint, lead, mark, note, omen, shew, show, sign **05** token, trace **06** augury, oracle, record, signal **07** glimpse, pointer, portent, symptom, warning **08** endeixis, evidence, monument, register, signpost **10** denotement, expression, intimation, suggestion **11** explanation **13** demonstration, manifestation

indicative

07 typical **08** indicant, symbolic, telltale **10** denotative, exhibitive, indicatory, suggestive **11** significant, symptomatic **13** demonstrative, significative **14** characteristic

indicatively

07 as a sign **09** as a symbol, typically **10** as evidence **12** symbolically **13** significantly **14** as an expression **15** symptomatically

indicator

04 dial, hand, mark, sign **05** bezel, gauge, guide, index, meter, token **06** gnomon, marker, needle, signal, symbol **07** display, flasher, pointer **08** signpost **09** barometer **10** litmus test, turn signal

indict

04 dite **06** accuse, charge, summon **07** arraign, article, impeach, summons, trounce **09** inculpate, prosecute **10** put on trial **11** incriminate

indictment

06 charge, dittay **07** summons **10** accusation, allegation **11** arraignment, impeachment, inculpation, prosecution **13** incrimination, recrimination

indifference

06 apathy, phlegm, slight **08** coldness, coolness **09** disregard, unconcern **10** negligence, neutrality **11** impassivity, inattention, nonchalance **12** heedlessness **13** lack of concern, lack of feeling **14** lack of interest

indifferent

02 OK **03** bad **04** cold, cool, easy, fair, so-so **05** aloof, blasé **06** medium **07** average, callous, distant, easy-osy, neutral, not good, unmoved **08** adequate, careless, detached, heedless, inferior, jack easy, mediocre, middling, moderate, ordinary, passable, uncaring **09** apathetic, impassive, incurious, unexcited, unfeeling **10** insouciant, nonchalant, uninvolved **11** cold-hearted, pococurante, unconcerned, unemotional **12** could be worse, run of the mill, uninterested, unresponsive **13** could be better, disinterested, dispassionate, uninteresting, unsympathetic **14** unenthusiastic **15** all the same to you, undistinguished

indigence

04 need, want **06** penury **07** poverty **08** distress **09** necessity, privation **11** deprivation, destitution

indigenous

05 local **06** native **08** original **09** home-grown **10** aboriginal, vernacular **13** autochthonous

indigent

04 bust, poor **05** broke, needy, skint **06** in need, in want **08** dirt-poor **09** destitute, penniless, penurious **10** cleaned out, down and out, stony-broke **11** impecunious, necessitous, up against it **12** impoverished, on your uppers **13** in dire straits **14** on your beam ends **15** poverty-stricken

indigestion

07 acidity, apepsia, pyrosis **08** dyspepsy, apepsia **09** dyspepsia, heartburn **10** cardialgia, water-brash **13** grass staggers **15** stomach staggers

indignant

03 mad **05** angry, cross, irate, livid, riled **06** bitter, fuming, heated, miffed, narked, peeved **07** annoyed, enraged, furious, in a huff **08** in a strop, incensed, outraged, up in arms, wrathful **09** aggrieved, resentful, steamed up **10** got the hump, infuriated **11** acrimonious, disgruntled, exasperated

indignantly

07 angrily, crossly, in a huff, irately **08** bitterly, up in arms **09** furiously, steamed up **11** resentfully **13** acrimoniously, reproachfully

indignation

03 ire **04** fury, rage **05** anger, pique, scorn, wrath **06** furore **07** dudgeon, outrage **08** contempt **09** annoyance **10** resentment **12** exasperation **15** saeva indignatio

indignity

04 snub **05** abuse, shame **06** injury, insult, slight **07** affront, obloquy, offence, outrage, putdown **08** contempt, disgrace, reproach **09** contumely, dishonour **10** disrespect, incivility, opprobrium **11** humiliation **12** cold shoulder, mistreatment, unworthiness **13** slap in the face **14** kick in the teeth

indigo

04 anil

indirect

02 by **03** bye **06** remote, squint, ungain, zigzag **07** curving, devious, mediate, oblique, winding **08** allusive, rambling, tortuous **09** ancillary, divergent, secondary, wandering **10** back-handed, circuitous, discursive, incidental, meandering, roundabout, subsidiary, unintended **11** subordinate **12** periphrastic **14** circumlocutory

indirectly

05 round **09** deviously, hintingly, obliquely **10** allusively, second-hand **12** at second hand, incidentally, roundaboutly

indiscernible

04 tiny **06** hidden, minute **07** obscure, unclear **09** invisible, minuscule **10** impalpable, indistinct, unapparent **11** microscopic **12** undetectable, unnoticeable **13** imperceptible, undiscernible

indiscreet

04 rash **05** hasty **06** unwary, unwise **07** foolish **08** careless, heedless, immodest, reckless, tactless **09** foolhardy, ill-judged, impolitic, imprudent, shameless **10** ill-advised, indelicate, unthinking **11** injudicious, insensitive **12** undiplomatic **13** ill-considered

indiscreetly

06 rashly **08** unwisely **09** foolishly **10** carelessly, heedlessly, immodestly, recklessly, tactlessly **11** shamelessly **12** indelicately **13** insensitively

indiscretion

04 boob, flub, slip **05** error, folly, gaffe, lapse **06** slip-up **07** blunder, faux pas, mistake **08** rashness **09** immodesty **10** imprudence, indelicacy **11** foolishness **12** carelessness, recklessness, tactlessness **13** shamelessness

indiscriminate

◊ *anagram indicator*
05 mixed **06** motley, random, varied **07** aimless, chaotic, diverse, general **08** careless, confused, pell-mell, sweeping **09** haphazard, hit or miss, wholesale **10** hit and miss **11** promiscuous, scattershot, unselective **12** unmethodical, unrespective, unsystematic **13** miscellaneous

indiscriminately

08 randomly **09** aimlessly, generally, in the mass, wholesale **10** carelessly **11** haphazardly **13** unselectively **14** unmethodically **15** indistinctively

indispensable

03 key **05** basic, vital **06** needed **07** crucial, needful **08** required **09** essential, important, necessary, requisite **10** absolutely, imperative **11** fundamental

indisposed
03 ill **04** sick **05** crook, loath **06** ailing, averse, groggy, laid up, poorly, unwell **09** reluctant, unwilling **10** not of a mind, not willing, out of sorts **11** disinclined **12** not of a mind to **13** confined to bed, incapacitated **15** under the weather

indisposition
03 ail **06** malady **07** ailment, disease, dislike, illness **08** aversion, disorder, distaste, sickness **09** bad health, complaint, hesitancy, ill health **10** reluctance **13** unwillingness **14** disinclination, distemperature

indisputable
04 sure **06** liquid **07** certain, dead set **08** absolute, definite, positive **10** inarguable, unarguable, undeniable, undisputed **11** indubitable, irrefutable **13** incontestable **14** beyond question, uncontrollable, unquestionable

indissoluble
05 fixed, solid **07** abiding, binding, eternal, lasting **08** enduring **09** permanent **10** inviolable **11** inseparable, sempiternal, unbreakable **12** imperishable **13** incorruptible **14** indestructible

indistinct
03 dim, low **04** hazy, pale **05** blear, faded, faint, fuzzy, misty, muted, vague **06** grainy, woolly **07** blurred, clouded, distant, muffled, obscure, shadowy, unclear **08** confused, muttered **09** ambiguous, undefined **10** ill-defined, indefinite, out of focus **14** indecipherable, unintelligible
• **indistinct appearance**
04 blur, loom

indistinctly
05 dimly **06** hazily **07** fuzzily, vaguely **09** obscurely, unclearly **10** out of focus **14** unintelligibly

indistinguishable
04 same, twin **05** alike **06** cloned **09** identical **10** tantamount **13** indiscernible **15** interchangeable

indium
02 In

individual
03 one, own **04** body, idio-, lone, poll, sole, sort, soul, type, unit **05** being, party **06** fellow, mortal, person, proper, single, unique, versal **07** private, several, special, typical **08** creature, distinct, isolated, original, peculiar, personal, separate, singular, solitary, specific **09** character, exclusive **10** human being, particular, respective, subjective **11** distinctive, inseparable **12** personalized **13** idiosyncratic **14** characteristic

individualism
06 egoism **09** anarchism **11** freethought, originality **12** eccentricity, freethinking,

independence, self-interest, self-reliance **13** egocentricity, self-direction **14** libertarianism

individualist
05 loner **06** egoist **08** bohemian, lone wolf, maverick, original **09** anarchist, eccentric **10** egocentric, free spirit **11** freethinker, independent, libertarian **13** nonconformist

individualistic
06 unique **07** special, typical **08** bohemian, egoistic, original **09** eccentric **10** egocentric, individual, particular, unorthodox **11** anarchistic, independent, libertarian, self-reliant **13** idiosyncratic, nonconformist **14** unconventional

individuality
07 oneness **08** identity, property **09** character, propriety **10** uniqueness **11** distinction, originality, peculiarity, personality, singularity **12** separateness **15** distinctiveness

individually
06 singly **08** one by one **09** in several, severally **10** one at a time, personally, separately **12** in particular, particularly **13** independently

indivisible
10 impartible **11** inseparable, intrenchant, undividable **12** indissoluble **14** indiscerptible

indoctrinate
05 drill, teach, train **06** ground, instil, school **07** impress **08** instruct **09** brainwash, inculcate **12** propagandize

indoctrination
08 drilling, teaching, training **09** grounding, schooling **10** catechesis, instilling **11** catechetics, inculcation, instruction **12** brainwashing

Indo-European
02 IE

See also **European**

indolence
05 sloth **06** apathy, torpor **07** inertia, languor **08** idleness, laziness, lethargy, shirking, slacking **09** heaviness, inertness, torpidity, torpitude **10** inactivity, torpidness **11** languidness **12** do-nothingism, listlessness, sluggishness

indolent
04 idle, lazy, slow **05** inert, slack **06** otiose, supine, torpid **07** languid, lumpish **08** bone-idle, fainéant, inactive, listless, slothful, sluggard, sluggish **09** apathetic, do-nothing, easy-going, lethargic, shiftless **13** lackadaisical

indomitable
04 bold, firm **05** brave **07** staunch, valiant **08** fearless, intrepid, resolute, stalwart **09** steadfast, undaunted **10** courageous, determined, invincible,

unbeatable, unyielding **11** impregnable, lion-hearted, unflinching **12** intransigent, unassailable, undefeatable **13** unconquerable

Indonesia
02 RI **03** IDN

indubitable
04 sure **07** certain, evident, obvious **08** absolute **09** undoubted **10** unarguable, undeniable **11** beyond doubt, irrefutable, undoubtable **12** indisputable, irrebuttable, irrefragable, unanswerable **13** beyond dispute, incontestable **14** unquestionable

indubitably
05 truly **06** surely **07** clearly, no doubt **08** of course, probably **09** assuredly, certainly, doubtless, precisely **10** most likely, presumably **11** undoubtedly **12** indisputably, without doubt **14** unquestionably

induce
03 get **04** coax, draw, lead, move, urge **05** cause, force, impel, press, tempt **06** effect, incite, lead to, prompt, seduce **07** actuate, bring on, entreat, inspire, intreat, procure, produce, provoke **08** generate, motivate, occasion, persuade, talk into **09** encourage, influence, instigate, originate **10** bring about, give rise to **11** prevail upon, set in motion

inducement
04 bait, goad, lure, spur **05** bribe, cause, drink **06** carrot, motive, reason, reward **07** impetus **08** stimulus **09** incentive, influence, sweetener **10** attraction, back-hander, enticement, incitement, persuasion **11** seditionary **13** encouragement

induct
05 admit, place, stall **06** enlist, invest, ordain **07** install, swear in **08** enthrone, initiate **09** conscript, introduce **10** consecrate, inaugurate

inductance
01 L
• **measure of inductance**
01 H **05** henry

induction
07 epagoge, prelude **09** deduction, inference **10** conclusion, initiation, ordination **11** institution, investiture **12** consecration, enthronement, inauguration, installation, introduction **14** generalization

indulge
03 pet **05** allow, spoil, treat **06** cocker, cosset, cuiter, favour, humour, pamper, pettle, regale **07** cater to, gratify, revel in, satisfy, yield to **08** give in to, pander to, wallow in **09** give way to, make merry **11** go along with, luxuriate in, mollycoddle **14** give free rein to

indulgence
03 law **04** luxe, riot **05** favor, swing, treat **06** excess, excuse, favour, luxury,

indulgent
pardon **08** lenience, spoiling
09 pampering, remission, tolerance
10 fulfilment, generosity, sensualism,
sensuality **11** dissipation, forbearance
12 extravagance, immoderation,
intemperance, satisfaction
13 dissoluteness, gratification,
mollycoddling

indulgent
04 fond, kind **06** humane, tender
07 lenient, liberal, patient
08 generous, merciful, spoiling,
tolerant **09** compliant, cosseting, easy-
going, forgiving, humouring,
pampering **10** forbearing, permissive
11 sympathetic **13** compassionate,
mollycoddling, understanding

indulgently
06 fondly, kindly **08** humanely,
tenderly **09** leniently, liberally,
patiently, with mercy **10** generously,
mercifully, tolerantly **12** with sympathy
14 with compassion
15 compassionately, sympathetically

industrial
05 trade **08** business **09** technical
10 commercial **13** manufacturing

industrialist
05 baron **06** tycoon **07** magnate
08 producer **09** financier **10** capitalist
12 manufacturer

industrious
04 busy, hard **05** deedy **06** active,
dogged, steady **07** notable, on the go,
skilful, workful, zealous **08** diligent,
sedulous, studious, tireless, vigorous,
worksome **09** assiduous, dedicated,
energetic, laborious **10** busy as a bee,
determined, persistent, productive
11 hard-working, persevering
13 conscientious, indefatigable

industriously
04 hard **08** doggedly, steadily
10 diligently, sedulously **11** assiduously
13 perseveringly **15** conscientiously

industry
04 line, toil, zeal **05** field, trade
06 effort, energy, labour, vigour
07 service **08** activity, business,
commerce, hard work, sedulity
09 assiduity, diligence **10** enterprise,
intentness, production, steadiness
11 application, persistence
12 perseverance, sedulousness,
stickability, tirelessness
13 assiduousness, concentration,
determination, laboriousness,
manufacturing **14** productiveness
15 industriousness

inebriated
◇ *anagram indicator*
04 full, high, inky **05** drunk, happy,
inked, lit up, merry, moppy, tight, tipsy,
woozy **06** blotto, bombed, canned,
corked, jarred, juiced, loaded, mortal,
pished, ripped, rotten, soused, stewed,
stinko, stoned, tiddly, wasted
07 bevvied, bonkers, bottled, crocked,
drunken, half-cut, legless, maggoty,

pickled, pie-eyed, sloshed, smashed,
sozzled, squiffy, tiddled, wrecked
08 bibulous, footless, hammered, in
liquor, juiced up, liquored, moon-
eyed, ossified, sow-drunk, steaming,
stocious, tanked up, whiffled, whistled
09 bladdered, crapulent, paralytic,
plastered, shickered, up the pole, well-
oiled **10** blind drunk, obfuscated
11 intoxicated, off your face **12** drunk
as a lord, drunk as a newt, roaring
drunk **13** drunk as a piper, drunk as a
skunk, having had a few, under the
table **14** Brahms and Liszt **15** one over
the eight, the worse for wear, under
the weather

inedible
03 bad, off **05** stale **06** deadly, rancid,
rotten **07** harmful, noxious
09 poisonous, uneatable **10** inesculent
11 not fit to eat, unpalatable
12 indigestible, unconsumable

ineducable
08 indocile **11** unteachable
12 incorrigible

ineffable
07 fearful **10** remarkable **11** beyond
words, unspeakable, unutterable
12 unimpartible **13** indescribable,
inexpressible **14** incommunicable

ineffably
09 fearfully **10** absolutely, remarkably
11 beyond words, unspeakably,
unutterably **13** indescribably,
inexpressibly

ineffective
03 dud **04** idle, lame, vain, weak
05 inept **06** feeble, futile **07** useless
08 abortive, impotent **09** burned out,
fruitless, powerless, to no avail,
toothless, worthless **10** inadequate,
profitless, unavailing, unpregnant
11 incompetent, ineffectual
12 unproductive, unsuccessful

ineffectiveness
08 futility, weakness **10** feebleness,
inadequacy **11** uselessness
13 fruitlessness, worthlessness

ineffectual
03 wet **04** lame, vain, void, weak
05 inept, resty, wimpy **06** feeble, futile,
unable **07** useless **08** abortive,
chinless, feckless, impotent
09 fruitless, frustrate, powerless,
worthless **10** inadequate, unavailing
11 incompetent **12** unproductive
13 inefficacious, lackadaisical

ineffectually
06 feebly, in vain, lamely, weakly **09** to
no avail, uselessly **11** fruitlessly, to no
purpose **14** unproductively,
unsuccessfully

inefficacy
08 futility **10** inadequacy
11 uselessness **14** ineffectuality
15 ineffectiveness, ineffectualness

inefficiency
05 waste **06** laxity, muddle

09 slackness **10** ineptitude,
negligence, sloppiness
12 carelessness, incompetence,
wastefulness **15** disorganization

inefficient
03 lax **05** inept, slack **06** flabby,
sloppy **08** careless, inexpert, slipshod,
wasteful **09** negligent, shiftless
10 uneconomic **11** incompetent,
ineffective, time-wasting, unorganized
12 disorganized, money-wasting
13 unworkmanlike

inelegant
04 ugly **05** crude, rough **06** clumsy,
gauche, vulgar **07** awkward, ill-bred,
uncouth **08** homespun, laboured,
ungainly, unpolite **09** graceless,
unrefined **10** uncultured, unfinished,
ungraceful, unpolished
12 uncultivated **15** unsophisticated

ineligible
05 unfit **08** ruled out, unfitted,
unworthy **10** unequipped, unsuitable
11 incompetent, undesirable,
unqualified **12** disqualified,
unacceptable

ineluctable
04 sure **05** fated **07** assured, certain
08 destined **10** ineludible, inevitable,
inexorable **11** inescapable,
irrevocable, unalterable, unavoidable

inept
◇ *anagram indicator*
04 void **05** flaky, lousy, silly **06** clumsy,
stupid **07** awkward, foolish, useless
08 bungling, inexpert, pathetic
09 appalling, ham-fisted, incapable,
maladroit, unskilful **10** cack-handed,
inadequate, unsuitable **11** heavy-
handed, incompetent **12** unsuccessful

ineptitude
07 fatuity **08** bungling **09** crassness,
gaucherie, ineptness, stupidity,
unfitness **10** clumsiness, gaucheness,
incapacity **11** awkwardness,
glaikitness, unhandiness, uselessness
12 incapability, incompetence,
inexpertness **13** unskilfulness

inequality
03 rub **04** bias, odds, wave **05** whelk
08 contrast, imparity **09** disparity,
diversity, imbalance, prejudice,
roughness, variation **10** difference,
inadequacy, unevenness
11 discrepancy, unequalness
12 incompetence, irregularity
13 disproportion, dissimilarity,
nonconformity **14** discrimination

inequitable
06 biased, unfair, unjust **07** bigoted,
partial, unequal **08** one-sided,
partisan, wrongful **10** intolerant,
prejudiced **12** preferential
14 discriminatory

inequity
04 bias **05** abuse **09** injustice,
prejudice **10** inequality, partiality,
unfairness, unjustness

maltreatment, mistreatment, one-
ledness, wrongfulness
discrimination

ert
cold, dead, dull, idle, lazy **05** slack,
ll **06** leaden, sleepy, static, supine,
rpid **07** dormant, languid, passive,
stive **08** comatose, immobile,
active, indolent, lifeless, listless,
ıggish, stagnant, thowless, unmoving
apathetic, inanimate, lethargic,
rveless **10** motionless, stationary,
ck-still **12** unresponsive

ertia
sloth **06** apathy, torpor **07** languor
idleness, inaction, laziness, lethargy
indolence, inertness, passivity,
llness **10** immobility, inactivity,
blomovism, stagnation
listlessness, slothfulness
motionlessness

escapable
sure **05** fated **07** assured, certain
destined **10** ineludible, inevitable,
exorable **11** ineluctable, irrevocable,
alterable, unavoidable

escapably
surely **09** assuredly, certainly
definitely, inevitably, inexorably
irrevocably, necessarily, unavoidably
automatically

essential
extra, spare **06** luxury **07** surplus
needless, optional, trimming
accessory, appendage, extrinsic,
dundant, secondary **10** accidental,
pendable, extraneous, immaterial,
elevant, unasked-for **11** dispensable,
perfluity, superfluous, uncalled-for,
nessential, unimportant, unnecessary
extravagance, non-essential

estimable
vast **06** untold **07** immense
infinite, precious **09** priceless,
nlimited **10** invaluable, prodigious
measureless, uncountable
immeasurable, incalculable,
computable, mind-boggling,
nfathomable **13** worth a fortune

evitability
fact **05** truth **07** reality, safe bet
dead cert, validity **09** certainty,
ıre thing **14** matter of course

evitable
sure **05** fated, fixed **07** assured,
ertain, decreed, fateful, settled,
nshun'd **08** definite, destined,
rdained **09** automatic, necessary,
navoided, unshunned **10** inexorable,
fallible **11** ineluctable, inescapable,
revocable, predestined, unalterable,
navoidable **13** unpreventable

evitably
surely **09** assuredly, certainly,
tefully, presently **10** definitely,
exorably, infallibly, willy-nilly
inescapably, irrevocably, necessarily,
navoidably **13** automatically

inexact
03 lax **05** fuzzy, loose **06** untrue,
woolly **07** muddled, of a sort, of sorts
09 erroneous, imprecise, incorrect
10 fallacious, inaccurate, indefinite,
indistinct **11** approximate
13 indeterminate

inexactitude
05 error **07** blunder, mistake
09 looseness **10** inaccuracy,
woolliness **11** imprecision, inexactness
13 approximation, impreciseness,
incorrectness **14** indefiniteness,
miscalculation

inexcusable
08 shameful **10** outrageous
11 blameworthy, intolerable
12 indefensible, unacceptable,
unforgivable, unpardonable
13 reprehensible, unjustifiable

inexcusably
10 shamefully **12** indefensibly,
outrageously, unacceptably
13 reprehensibly, unjustifiably

inexhaustible
07 endless **08** abundant, infinite,
tireless, untiring **09** boundless,
limitless, unbounded, unfailing,
unlimited, unwearied, weariless
10 unflagging, unwearying
11 illimitable, measureless, never-
ending **12** unrestricted
13 indefatigable

inexorable
04 sure **05** fated **07** certain
08 definite, destined, ordained
09 immovable, incessant, unceasing
10 implacable, inevitable, relentless,
unyielding **11** ineluctable, inescapable,
irrevocable, remorseless, unalterable,
unavertable, unfaltering, unrelenting,
unstoppable **12** intransigent,
irresistible **13** unpreventable

inexorably
06 surely **09** certainly **10** definitely,
implacably, inevitably, pitilessly
11 ineluctably, inescapably, irrevocably,
mercilessly **12** irresistibly, relentlessly,
resistlessly **13** remorselessly

inexpedient
05 wrong **06** unwise **07** foolish
09 ill-chosen, ill-judged, impolitic,
imprudent, misguided, senseless
10 ill-advised, indiscreet, unsuitable
11 detrimental, impolitical,
impractical, inadvisable, injudicious,
unadvisable, undesirable
12 inconvenient, undiplomatic,
unfavourable **13** inappropriate
15 disadvantageous

inexpensive
05 a snip, cheap **06** a steal, budget,
modest **07** bargain, cut-rate, low-cost,
reduced **08** dog-cheap, low-price,
uncostly **09** dirt-cheap, low-priced,
ten a penny **10** discounted,
economical, reasonable **13** going for a
song, on a shoestring

inexperience
07 newness, rawness **09** freshness,
ignorance, innocence, naiveness
10 immaturity **11** strangeness
12 inexpertness **13** unfamiliarity

inexperienced
03 new, raw **04** puny **05** fresh, green,
naive, young **06** callow, rookie,
unseen **07** amateur **08** farouche,
ignorant, immature, inexpert,
innocent, unsifted, wide-eyed
09 fledgling, unfledged, unskilled,
untrained, untutored **10** apprentice,
fledgeling, unfamiliar, uninformed,
unseasoned **11** new to the job,
unexperient, unpractised, unqualified
12 probationary, unaccustomed,
unacquainted **14** out of your depth,
unsophisticate **15** unsophisticated
• **inexperienced person**
03 cub **04** baby **09** fledgling
10 fledgeling

inexpert
03 ham **05** inept **06** clumsy
07 amateur, awkward, unhandy
08 bungling, untaught **09** ham-fisted,
maladroit, unskilful, unskilled, untrained,
untutored **10** amateurish, blundering,
cack-handed **11** incompetent,
unpractised, unqualified
13 unworkmanlike **14** unprofessional

inexplicable
05 weird **07** strange **08** abstruse,
baffling, puzzling **09** enigmatic,
insoluble **10** incredible, miraculous,
mysterious, mystifying, perplexing
11 bewildering, inscrutable
12 inextricable, unbelievable,
unfathomable **13** inexplainable,
unaccountable, unexplainable
14 unintelligible

inexplicably
09 strangely **10** bafflingly, incredibly,
puzzlingly **12** miraculously,
mysteriously, mystifyingly
13 unaccountably, unexplainably

inexpressible
08 nameless, termless **09** ineffable,
unsayable **10** untellable **11** indefinable,
unspeakable, unutterable
12 inexpressive **13** indescribable,
undescribable **14** incommunicable

inexpressibly
09 ineffably **11** beyond words,
unspeakably, unutterably
13 indescribably

inexpressive
04 cold, dead **05** blank, empty
06 vacant **07** deadpan **08** lifeless
09 impassive **10** poker-faced
11 emotionless, inscrutable
12 unexpressive **14** expressionless

inextinguishable
07 eternal, lasting, undying
08 enduring, immortal **09** deathless
11 everlasting, unquellable
12 imperishable, unquenchable
13 irrepressible, unconquerable
14 indestructible, unsuppressible

inextricable
08 confused **09** intricate **11** indivisible, inescapable, inseparable
12 indissoluble, inexplicable, irreversible **13** irretrievable

inextricably
11 indivisibly, inescapably, inseparably, intricately, irresolubly
12 indissolubly, irreversibly
13 irretrievably

infallibility
06 safety **08** accuracy, sureness
09 inerrancy, supremacy
10 perfection **11** omniscience, reliability **12** inerrability, unerringness
13 dependability, faultlessness, impeccability **14** irrefutability
15 trustworthiness

infallible
04 sure **05** sound **07** certain, perfect
08 accurate, fail-safe, flawless, reliable, sure-fire, unerring **09** faultless, foolproof, inerrable, unfailing
10 dependable, impeccable, inevitable **11** trustworthy

infamous
03 bad **04** base, evil, vile **06** wicked
07 hateful **08** ill-famed, shameful, shocking **09** dastardly, egregious, nefarious, notorious **10** abominable, detestable, iniquitous, outrageous, scandalous **11** disgraceful, ignominious, opprobrious
12 disreputable **13** discreditable, dishonourable

infamy
04 evil **05** shame **06** defame, ignomy
08 baseness, disgrace, ignominy, vileness, villainy **09** depravity, discredit, dishonour, disrepute, notoriety, turpitude **10** opprobrium, wickedness

infancy
04 dawn, rise **05** birth, roots, seeds, start, youth **06** cradle, nonage, origin, outset **07** genesis, origins, silence
08 babyhood **09** beginning, childhood, emergence, inception
11 early stages **12** commencement
14 speechlessness

infant
03 new, tot **04** babe, baby **05** bairn, child, early, sprog, young **07** dawning, growing, initial, nascent, newborn, toddler **08** emergent, immature, juvenile, nursling, youthful
09 beginning, fledgling, little one, nurseling **10** babe in arms, burgeoning, developing
11 rudimentary

infantile
05 young **07** babyish, puerile
08 childish, immature, juvenile, youthful **10** adolescent
11 undeveloped

infantry
02 LI **03** inf **06** pultan, pulton, pultun, tercio, tertia **07** phalanx, pultoon

infantryman
04 kern, naik, peon **05** grunt, kerne, Turco **06** ensign, evzone, Zouave
07 dragoon, footman, hoplite, pandoor, pandour **08** chasseur, doughboy **10** voetganger **11** foot soldier, landsknecht **13** beetle-crusher

infatuated
03 mad **06** assott, entêté, in love, sold on **07** entêtée, far gone, smitten, sweet on, wild for **08** assotted, besotted, mad about, obsessed, ravished
09 bewitched, daft about, enamoured, nuts about, wild about **10** bowled over, captivated, crazy about, enraptured, fascinated, lovestruck, mesmerized, potty about, spellbound
11 carried away **12** having a crush, having a thing, love-stricken

infatuation
04 love, mash, pash, rave **05** craze, crush, mania, shine, thing **07** passion
08 fixation, fondness **09** engoûment, obsession **10** engouement
11 fascination **12** besottedness

infect
03 mar, pox **04** clap, move, smit
05 spoil, taint, touch **06** affect, blight, canker, defile, excite, measle, pass on, poison **07** animate, corrupt, inspire, overrun, pervert, pollute, tainted
08 spread to, ulcerate **09** influence, stimulate, syphilize **10** parasitize
11 contaminate, tuberculize

infection
03 bug, wog **04** cold, germ, smit
05 taint, virus **06** blight, poison, sepsis
07 disease, fouling, illness **08** bacteria, epidemic, spoiling, tainting
09 complaint, condition, contagion, influence, pollution **10** corruption, defilement, pestilence
13 contamination
See also **disease**

infectious
05 toxic **06** deadly, septic, taking
07 noxious, smittle **08** catching, defiling, epidemic, virulent
09 infective, polluting, spreading
10 compelling, contagious, corrupting
12 communicable, irresistible
13 contaminating, transmissible, transmittable

infelicitous
03 sad **05** inapt **07** unhappy, unlucky
08 untimely, wretched **09** miserable, sorrowful, unfitting **10** despairing, unsuitable **11** incongruous, inopportune, unfortunate
13 inappropriate **15** disadvantageous

infer
05 educe, imply **06** allude, assume, deduce, derive, gather, induce, reason, render **07** conster, presume, surmise
08 conclude, construe **09** figure out
10 conjecture, generalize, understand
11 extrapolate

inference
07 reading, surmise **08** illation

09 corollary, deduction, reasoning
10 assumption, conclusion, conjectur
11 consequence, presumption
12 construction **13** extrapolation
14 contraposition, interpretation

inferior
03 bad, dog, inf, low **04** less, naff, poc
ropy, weak **05** awful, cheap, crook, grody, lousy, lower, lowly, minor, rope
06 coarse, crummy, faulty, grotty, humble, impair, junior, lesser, menial, minion, ornery, second, shoddy, vassa
07 low-rent, of a sort, of sorts, provan
rubbish, shilpit, tinhorn, useless
08 hopeless, mediocre, paravail, pathetic, slipshod, underman
09 ancillary, cheap-jack, defective, deficient, imperfect, secondary, underling, underrate **10** fourth-rate, inadequate, low-quality, second-best
second-rate, subsidiary
11 incompetent, indifferent, second-class, subordinate, subservient, substandard, under-sawyer
12 unacceptable **14** unsatisfactory

inferiority
08 meanness, ropiness **09** lowliness
10 bad quality, crumminess, faultiness
grottiness, humbleness, inadequacy, low quality, mediocrity, shoddiness
11 poor quality **12** imperfection, incompetence, slovenliness, subservience **13** defectiveness, subordination **14** insignificance

infernal
04 evil, vile **06** cursed, damned, darned, dashed, Hadean, wicked
07 blasted, demonic, fecking, flaming
hellish, satanic, Stygian **08** accursed, all-fired, blinking, blooming, devilish, fiendish, flipping, wretched
09 atrocious, execrable
10 confounded, diabolical, malevolent, outrageous, sulphurous

infertile
04 arid **06** barren, effete **07** dried-up
parched, sterile **08** infecund
09 childless **10** unfruitful
11 unfructuous **12** unproductive
13 non-productive

infertility
07 aridity **08** aridness **09** sterility
10 barrenness, effeteness
11 infecundity **14** unfruitfulness

infest
03 dog **04** teem **05** beset, crawl, flood, swarm **06** harass, invade, peste
plague, ravage, throng **07** bristle, disturb, overrun, pervade
08 permeate, take over **09** penetrate
10 infiltrate, overspread, parasitize, trichinize **13** spread through

infestation
04 pest **05** crabs **06** blight, plague
07 scourge **09** pervasion, taeniasis
10 affliction, ascariasis, giardiasis, pestilence, visitation **11** molestation, overrunning, parasitosis, phthiriasis, shigellosis **12** infiltration, strongylosis,

ncinariasis 13 cysticercosis,
elminthiasis, verminousness
14 trichinization

nfested
04 mity **05** alive, batty, beset, buggy,
ousy, midgy, mousy, ratty **06** chatty,
grubby, mousey, ridden **07** haunted,
overrun, plagued, rattish, ravaged,
eeming, verminy, weevily
08 crawling, pervaded, swarming,
hievish, vermined, weeviled, weevilly
09 bristling, permeated, verminous,
veevilled **10** overspread, stylopized
11 helminthous, infiltrated
12 pestilential

nfidel
05 pagan **06** giaour **07** atheist,
heathen, heretic, sceptic
09 miscreant, sceptical **10** unbeliever
11 disbeliever, freethinker, nullifidian,
unbelieving **13** irreligionist

nfidelity
05 amour **06** affair **07** liaison, perfidy,
romance **08** adultery, betrayal,
cheating, intrigue **09** duplicity,
falseness, treachery **10** disloyalty
12 relationship **13** faithlessness,
fooling around, playing around
14 unfaithfulness

nfiltrate
04 seep, slip, soak **05** enter **06** filter,
nvade **07** intrude, pervade
08 permeate **09** creep into, insinuate,
penetrate, percolate

nfiltration
07 entrism **08** entryism, invasion
09 intrusion, pervasion **10** permeation
11 insinuation, penetration,
percolation

nfiltrator
03 spy **07** entrist **08** entryist, intruder
09 subverter **10** insinuator, penetrator,
subversive **11** seditionary **14** fifth
columnist

nfinite
03 all **04** huge, vast **05** total **06** untold
07 endless, immense **08** absolute,
enormous **09** boundless, countless,
extensive, limitless, unbounded,
unlimited **10** bottomless, fathomless,
numberless **11** illimitable, inestimable,
innumerable, never-ending,
uncountable **12** immeasurable,
incalculable, interminable,
unfathomable **13** inexhaustible,
unconditioned, without number
14 indeterminable

nfinitely
03 all **09** endlessly, immensely
10 absolutely, enormously, without
end **11** ad infinitum, boundlessly,
inestimably, limitlessly
12 interminably, without limit
13 inexhaustibly

nfinitesimal
03 wee **04** tiny **05** teeny **06** minute
08 trifling **09** minuscule **10** negligible
11 microscopic **13** imperceptible,

inappreciable, insignificant
14 inconsiderable

infinitesimally
06 tinily **08** minutely **10** negligibly
13 imperceptibly, inappreciably
15 insignificantly, microscopically

infinity
07 allness **08** eternity, vastness
09 immensity **10** perpetuity
11 endlessness **12** enormousness
13 boundlessness, countlessness,
extensiveness, limitlessness

infirm
03 ill, old **04** lame, weak **05** frail, shaky
06 ailing, feeble, poorly, sickly, unwell,
wobbly **07** doddery, failing
08 decrepit, disabled, unstable,
unsteady **09** faltering **11** debilitated

infirmity
06 malady **07** ailment, disease, failing,
frailty, illness **08** debility, disorder,
frailtee, senility, sickness, weakness
09 complaint, frailness, ill health
10 feebleness, sickliness
11 decrepitude, dodderiness,
instability **13** vulnerability

inflame
03 fan **04** fire, fuel, heat, rile, stir
05 anger, rouse **06** arouse, enrage,
excite, foment, ignite, incite, kindle,
madden, stir up, whip up, work up,
worsen **07** agitate, incense, provoke
08 enkindle, increase **09** aggravate,
impassion, infuriate, intensify, make
worse, stimulate **10** exacerbate,
exasperate

inflamed
03 het, hot, raw, red **04** sore **05** angry,
heady **06** heated, septic **07** fevered,
flushed, glowing, swollen **08** festered,
feverish, infected, poisoned, reddened
11 carbuncular

inflammable
06 ardent **07** piceous **08** burnable
09 flammable, ignitable **10** tinder-like
11 combustible, combustious

inflammation
04 fire, heat, rash **07** burning, hotness,
redness **08** eruption, soreness,
swelling **09** festering, infection
10 irritation, tenderness **11** painfulness

Inflammations include:
03 RSI, sty
04 acne, boil, bubo, sore, stye
05 croup, felon, mange
06 ancome, angina, bunion, canker,
otitis, quinsy, sepsis, thrush, ulitis
07 abscess, colitis, empyema, pink-
eye, sycosis, tylosis, whitlow
08 bursitis, carditis, cynanche, cystitis,
erythema, mastitis, myelitis,
neuritis, orchitis, prunella, rhinitis,
windburn
09 arthritis, carbuncle, enteritis,
fasciitis, frostbite, gastritis, glossitis,
hepatitis, keratitis, laminitis,
nephritis, phlebitis, retinitis,
septicity, sinusitis, vaginitis

10 bronchitis, cellulitis, dermatitis,
erysipelas, gingivitis, intertrigo,
laryngitis, meningitis, sore throat,
tendinitis, tonsilitis, tracheitis,
vasculitis
11 mad staggers, myocarditis,
peritonitis, pharyngitis,
pneumonitis, prickly heat, shin
splints, spondylitis, tennis elbow,
thyroiditis, tonsillitis
12 appendicitis, encephalitis,
endocarditis, pancreatitis,
pericarditis, vestibulitis
13 jogger's nipple, labyrinthitis
14 conjunctivitis, diverticulitis,
housemaid's knee, sleepy staggers
15 gastroenteritis

inflammatory
04 sore **05** fiery, rabid **06** septic,
tender **07** painful, riotous, swollen
08 allergic, anarchic, inciting, infected
09 demagogic, explosive, festering,
inflaming, insurgent, seditious
10 incendiary, incitative, phlogistic
11 instigative, intemperate,
provocative **13** rabble-rousing

inflate
05 blast, bloat, boost, elate, raise, swell
06 aerate, blow up, dilate, expand,
extend, hike up, puff up, pump up, push
up, step up **07** amplify, augment,
balloon, bombast, distend, enlarge,
magnify, puff out **08** escalate, increase,
overrate, sufflate **09** intensify, overstate
10 aggrandize, daisy-chain,
exaggerate **11** fill with air
12 overestimate

inflated
04 tall **05** tumid **06** puffed, raised,
turgid **07** bloated, blown up, bombast,
bullate, dilated, pompous, swollen,
upblown **08** extended, puffed up,
rhetoric, tumefied **09** ballooned,
bombastic, distended, escalated, high-
blown, increased, overblown, puffed
out **10** euphuistic, rhetorical
11 exaggerated, intensified,
overweening **12** magniloquent,
ostentatious **13** grandiloquent

inflation
04 rise **08** afflatus, cost push, increase
09 expansion, turgidity **10** escalation
11 inspiration **14** hyperinflation
• **measure of inflation**
03 RPI

inflection
04 tone **05** pitch **06** ending, rhythm,
stress **07** bending, cadence
08 emphasis **09** deviation
10 comparison, modulation
11 conjugation **12** change of tone

inflexibility
06 fixity **08** hardness, obduracy,
rigidity **09** obstinacy, stiffness
10 stringency **12** immovability,
immutability, incompliance,
inelasticity, stubbornness,
unsuppleness **13** immutableness,
intransigence **14** intractability

inflexible
03 set **04** fast, firm, hard, iron, taut **05** fixed, rigid, solid, stern, stiff **06** ramrod, steely, strict **07** adamant, uniform **08** obdurate, pitiless, resolute, rigorous, standard, stubborn, unsupple **09** calcified, immovable, immutable, merciless, obstinate, stringent, tramlined, unbending, unelastic, unvarying **10** entrenched, implacable, intolerant, relentless, unbendable, unyielding **11** hard and fast, intractable **12** intransigent, standardized, unchangeable **13** dyed-in-the-wool **14** uncompromising **15** unaccommodating

inflict
03 hit, lay **04** deal, levy **05** apply, exact, lay on, wreak **06** burden, impose, strike, thrust **07** deal out, deliver, enforce, mete out **10** administer, perpetrate

infliction
05 worry **06** burden **07** penalty, trouble **08** delivery, exaction, wreaking **10** affliction, imposition, punishment **11** application, castigation, enforcement, retribution **12** chastisement, perpetration **14** administration

influence
03 say **04** bias, drag, hand, hold, mark, move, pull, rule, stir, sway, toll **05** alter, clout, force, guide, impel, mould, power, reign, rouse, shape **06** affect, arouse, change, colour, direct, effect, impact, incite, induce, inflow, modify, prompt, weight **07** control, dispose, holding, impress, incline, mastery **08** ambiance, ambience, dominate, guidance, impact on, interest, motivate, persuade, pressure, prestige, standing **09** authority, condition, determine, direction, dominance, have clout, instigate, manoeuvre, operation, prejudice, pull wires, restraint, supremacy, transform **10** domination, importance, manipulate **11** carry weight, pull strings **12** wheel and deal **14** have an effect on **15** hold over a barrel
- **easily influenced**
09 malleable
- **unlucky influence**
04 jinx

influential
06 moving, potent, strong **07** guiding, leading, telling, weighty **08** dominant, powerful **09** effective, important, inspiring, momentous **10** compelling, convincing, meaningful, persuasive **11** charismatic, controlling, far-reaching, heavyweight, prestigious, significant, substantial **12** instrumental **13** authoritative

influx
04 flow, rush, salt **05** flood **06** inflow, inrush, stream **07** arrival, ingress **08** invasion **09** accession, avalanche, incursion, influence, intrusion

10 inundation, visitation **11** instreaming

inform
◇ *homophone indicator*
03 rat **04** blab, blow, fink, leak, mark, nark, shop, sing, tell **05** avail, brand, brief, cue in, dob in, grass, peach, split, stamp **06** advise, betray, clue in, clue up, direct, fill in, impart, notify, relate, rumble, snitch, squeak, squeal, tell on, tip off, typify, wise up **07** animate, apprise, certify, educate, inspire, let know, partake, possess, put wise, resolve, sing out, stool on **08** acquaint, announce, deformed, denounce, formless, identify, instruct, permeate, unformed **09** advertise, advertize, enlighten, misshapen, recommend **10** give notice, illuminate, keep posted **11** blow the gaff, communicate, distinguish, incriminate **12** characterize **13** spill the beans **15** put in the picture, sing like a canary

informal
03 inf **04** easy, free **06** candid, casual, simple **07** invalid, natural, relaxed **08** everyday, familiar, friendly, unsolemn **09** easy-going, officious **10** colloquial, unofficial, vernacular **12** off the record **13** go-as-you-please, unceremonious, unpretentious

informality
04 ease **07** freedom **08** cosiness **10** casualness, homeliness, relaxation, simplicity **11** familiarity, naturalness **12** congeniality **15** approachability

informally
06 easily, freely, simply **08** casually **09** privately **10** familiarly, on the quiet **12** colloquially, off the record, unofficially **13** sans cérémonie **14** confidentially **15** unceremoniously, without ceremony

information
02 SP **03** gen, inf, wit **04** bumf, data, dope, file, info, news, poop, word **05** clues, facts, input, score **06** advice, notice, record, report **07** counsel, details, dossier, good oil, low-down, message, tidings, witting **08** briefing, bulletin, databank, database, evidence, izvestia **09** hard stuff, izvestiya, knowledge **10** communiqué, propaganda **11** instruction, particulars **12** intelligence **13** enlightenment
- **measure of information**
03 bit, nit **05** field, nepit, qubit **08** location **11** binary digit

informative
05 newsy **06** chatty, useful **07** gossipy, helpful **08** edifying **09** revealing **11** educational, forthcoming, instructive **12** constructive, enlightening, illuminating **13** communicative

informed
02 up **03** hep, hip **05** aware **06** au fait, expert, posted, primed, sussed, versed **07** abreast, briefed, clued-up, erudite,

knowing, learned **08** educated, familiar, up to date, well-read **09** au courant, in the know, in the loop, up to speed **10** acquainted, conversant, well-versed **11** enlightened, intelligent, well-briefed **12** well-informed **13** authoritative, knowledgeable **14** well-researched

informer
03 dog, rat, spy **04** fink, mole, nark, nose, stag **05** grass, Judas, shelf, sneak, snout **06** dobber, canary, finger, fizgig, moiser, singer, snitch **07** fizzgig, grasser, peacher, pentito, stoolie, traitor **08** animator, approver, betrayer, inspirer, promoter, snitcher, squeaker, squealer, tell-tale **09** informant, sycophant, whisperer **10** discoverer, supergrass **11** stool pigeon **13** whistle blower

infraction
06 breach **08** breaking **09** violation **12** encroachment, infringement **13** contravention, transgression

infrared
02 ir

infrequent
04 rare **06** scanty, seldom, sparse **07** unusual **08** sporadic, uncommon **09** spasmodic **10** occasional **11** exceptional **12** intermittent, like gold dust

infringe
04 defy **05** break, flout **06** ignore, invade **07** disobey, impinge, infract, intrude, violate **08** encroach, overstep, trespass **10** contravene, transgress

infringement
06 breach, piracy **07** evasion **08** breaking, defiance, invasion, trespass **09** intrusion, violation **10** infraction **12** disobedience, encroachment **13** contravention, non-compliance, non-observance, transgression

infuriate
03 bug, vex **04** miff, nark, rile **05** anger, annoy, get at, rouse **06** enrage, madden, needle, nettle, wind up **07** incense, inflame, provoke **08** drive mad, irritate **09** aggravate **10** antagonize, drive crazy, exasperate **12** drive bananas **13** make sparks fly **14** drive up the wall

infuriated
03 mad **04** wild **05** angry, cross, irate, radge, ratty, spewy, vexed **06** choked, heated, miffed, narked, peeved, roused **07** crooked, enraged, flaming, furious, ropable, stroppy, uptight, violent **08** agitated, burned up, hairless, in a paddy, incensed, maddened, provoked, up in arms **09** in a lather, irritated, pissed off, raving mad, seeing red, ticked off **10** aggravated, apoplectic, hopping mad **11** disgruntled, exasperated, fit to be tied **12** on the warpath **14** beside yourself

infuriating
05 pesky **07** galling **08** annoying
09 maddening, provoking, thwarting,
vexatious **10** irritating, unbearable
11 aggravating, frustrating, intolerable
12 exasperating

infuse
◇ *insertion indicator*
04 brew, draw, fill, mash, mask, pour,
shed, soak **05** imbue, immit, steep
06 inject, instil **07** implant, inspire,
pervade **08** impart to, saturate
09 inculcate, introduce **11** breathe into

infusion
03 tea **04** brew, mate **06** saloop,
tisane **07** malt tea, sage tea, soaking,
uva-ursi **08** infusing, senna tea,
steeping, tar water **09** sassafras
10 capillaire **11** inculcation, inspiration
12 implantation, instillation

ingenious
03 sly **04** neat, wily **05** adept, natty,
nifty, sharp, slick, smart, witty
06 adroit, astute, bright, clever, crafty,
gifted, patent, pretty, quaint, shrewd
07 cunning, skilful **08** creative,
masterly, original, talented **09** brilliant,
inventive **10** artificial, innovative
11 imaginative, resourceful

ingeniously
07 niftily **08** cleverly **09** cunningly,
skilfully **10** originally **11** brilliantly
13 imaginatively

ingenuity
03 wit **04** gift **05** flair, knack, skill
06 engine, genius, ingine **07** cunning,
faculty, slyness **08** deftness
09 invention, nattiness, niftiness,
sharpness, slickness **10** adroitness,
astuteness, cleverness, shrewdness
11 originality, skilfulness
12 creativeness **13** ingeniousness,
ingenuousness, inventiveness
14 innovativeness **15** resourcefulness

ingenuous
04 open **05** frank, naive, plain
06 candid, direct, honest, simple
07 artless, genuine, sincere
08 freeborn, innocent, trustful, trusting
09 guileless **10** forthright, honourable
11 transparent **12** single-minded
13 undissembling **14** unsophisticate
15 unsophisticated

ingenuously
06 openly, simply **07** naively, plainly
08 directly, honestly **09** artlessly,
genuinely, sincerely **10** innocently,
trustingly **11** guilelessly **12** without
guile

ingenuousness
07 candour, honesty, naiveté, naivety
08 openness **09** frankness, innocence,
unreserve **10** directness **11** artlessness,
genuineness **12** trustfulness
13 guilelessness **14** forthrightness

inglorious
06 unsung **07** ignoble, obscure,
unknown **08** infamous, shameful,

unheroic **10** irrenowned, mortifying,
unhonoured **11** blameworthy,
disgraceful, humiliating, ignominious
12 disreputable, unsuccessful
13 discreditable, dishonourable

ingrain
03 dye, fix **04** root **05** embed, imbue,
infix **06** instil **07** build in, engrain,
implant, impress, imprint **08** entrench
09 establish, ingrained

ingrained
05 fixed **06** inborn, inbred, rooted
07 built-in, inbuilt **08** embedded,
inherent **09** immovable, implanted,
permanent **10** deep-rooted, deep-
seated, entrenched **11** established
12 ineradicable **13** thorough-going

ingratiate
04 fawn, sook **05** crawl, creep, toady
06 cozy up, grovel **07** flatter **08** play
up to, soft-soap, suck up to **09** get in
with **10** cozy up with **11** curry favour
12 bow and scrape **15** butter someone
up

ingratiating
05 suave, sweet **06** greasy, silken
07 fawning, servile **08** crawling,
toadying, unctuous **09** flattering,
obsequious **11** bootlicking,
sycophantic, time-serving **13** smooth-
tongued

ingratitude
13 thanklessness **14** ungraciousness,
ungratefulness, unthankfulness

ingredient
◇ *anagram indicator*
04 base, item, part, unit **05** basis
06 bottom, factor **07** amalgam,
element, feature **09** component
11 constituent
See also **salad**

• **little boy ingredients**
05 frogs, snips **06** snails **14** puppy
dogs' tails
• **little girl ingredients**
05 sugar, spice **13** all things nice
14 everything nice

ingress
05 entry **06** access **08** entrance
09 admission **10** admittance **12** means
of entry, right of entry **15** means of
approach

inhabit
05 dwell, haunt **06** live in, occupy,
people, settle, stay in **07** denizen,
dwell in, possess **08** colonize,
populate, reside in **14** make your home
in

inhabitable
09 habitable **11** fit to live in

inhabitant
03 son **05** child, towny **06** inmate,
lodger, native, tenant **07** citizen,
denizen, dweller, settler **08** habitant,
occupant, occupier, resident
09 indweller **10** residenter
12 residentiary

inhabited
04 held **07** lived-in, peopled, settled
08 occupied, populate, populous,
tenanted **09** colonized, developed,
populated, possessed

inhalation
05 whiff **06** breath **07** suction
08 inhaling **09** breathing, spiration
11 inspiration, respiration

inhale
04 draw, take, toot, tout **05** whiff
06 draw in, suck in **07** inspire, respire
09 breathe in, inbreathe

inharmonious
03 out **04** sour **05** harsh **06** atonal,
patchy **07** grating, jarring, raucous
08 clashing, jangling, perverse,
strident, tuneless **09** dissonant,
unmusical, untuneful **10** discordant,
out of place, unfriendly
11 cacophonous, conflicting,
disagreeing, inconsonant,
quarrelsome, unmelodious
12 antipathetic, incompatible,
unharmonious **13** contradictory,
unsympathetic **14** irreconcilable

inherent
05 basic **06** inborn, inbred, innate,
native, natura **07** built-in, inbuilt,
natural, radical **08** immanent, resident
09 essential, ingrained, inherited,
intrinsic **10** hereditary, inexistant,
inexistent, in the blood, subsistent
11 fundamental, intrinsical

inherently
08 inwardly **09** basically, centrally
10 integrally **11** essentially
13 constituently, fundamentally,
intrinsically

inherit
04 heir **06** assume, be left
07 receive, succeed **08** accede to,
be heir to, come into, take over
09 succeed to **10** fall heir to **12** be
bequeathed

inheritance
03 fee **06** legacy **07** bequest, descent
08 heredity, heritage **09** accession,
endowment, patrimony **10** birthright,
proportion, succession
13 primogeniture **15** secundogeniture

inheritor
04 heir **05** scion **06** co-heir, tanist
07 devisee, heiress, heritor, legatee
08 heritrix, legatary **09** heritress,
recipient, successor **10** fellow-heir,
inheritrix, next in line, substitute
11 beneficiary, inheritress
12 reversionary

inhibit
04 balk, curb, stem, stop **05** baulk,
check **06** bridle, hamper, hinder, hold
in, impede, rein in, stanch, thwart
07 prevent, repress, staunch **08** hold
back, obstruct, restrain, restrict, slow
down, suppress **09** constrain, frustrate
10 discourage **12** put a damper on,
straitjacket **13** interfere with

inhibited
03 shy **06** wooden **07** guarded, subdued, uptight **08** reserved, reticent **09** repressed, withdrawn **10** frustrated, restrained **11** constrained, embarrassed, introverted **13** self-conscious **14** self-restrained

inhibition
03 bar **04** curb **05** check **06** hang-up **07** coyness, reserve, shyness **09** hampering, hindrance, restraint, reticence, thwarting **10** impediment, repression **11** frustration, obstruction, restriction **12** interference **13** embarrassment

inhospitable
04 bare, cold, cool, wild **05** aloof, bleak, empty **06** barren, lonely, unkind **07** hostile, uncivil **08** desolate, inimical **09** hostilesse **10** antisocial, forbidding, unfriendly, ungenerous, uninviting, unsociable, xenophobic **11** uncongenial, unreceptive, unwelcoming **12** unfavourable **13** uninhabitable, unneighbourly

inhuman
03 odd **05** cruel, harsh **06** animal, brutal, savage **07** bestial, strange, vicious **08** barbaric, fiendish, non-human, ruthless, sadistic **09** barbarous, merciless **10** diabolical **11** cold-blooded

inhumane
05 cruel, harsh **06** brutal, unkind **07** callous **08** pitiless, uncaring **09** heartless, unfeeling **11** cold-hearted, dehumanized, hard-hearted, insensitive **13** inconsiderate, unsympathetic

inhumanity
06 sadism **07** cruelty **08** atrocity **09** barbarism, barbarity, brutality **10** savageness, unkindness **11** brutishness, callousness, viciousness **12** pitilessness, ruthlessness **13** heartlessness **15** cold-bloodedness, cold-heartedness, hard-heartedness

inimical
07 adverse, harmful, hostile, hurtful, noxious, opposed **08** contrary **09** injurious, repugnant **10** intolerant, pernicious, unfriendly **11** destructive, disaffected, ill-disposed, unwelcoming **12** antagonistic, antipathetic, inhospitable, unfavourable

inimitable
06 unique **07** sublime, supreme **08** peerless **09** matchless, nonpareil, unmatched **10** consummate, unequalled, unexampled, unrivalled **11** distinctive, exceptional, superlative, unsurpassed **12** incomparable, unparalleled **13** unsurpassable

iniquitous
04 base, evil **05** awful **06** sinful, unjust, wicked **07** heinous, immoral, vicious **08** accursed, criminal, dreadful, infamous **09** atrocious,

nefarious, reprobate **10** abominable, facinorous, flagitious, outrageous **11** unrighteous **13** reprehensible

iniquity
03 sin **04** evil, vice **05** crime, wrong **06** infamy **07** misdeed, offence **08** baseness, enormity **09** evil-doing, injustice **10** sinfulness, wickedness, wrongdoing **11** abomination, heinousness, lawlessness, ungodliness, viciousness **13** transgression **15** unrighteousness

initial
◇ *head selection indicator*
04 sign **05** basic, early, first, prime **07** bloomer, endorse, opening, primary **08** inchoate, original, starting **09** autograph, beginning, formative, inaugural, inceptive, incipient **10** commencing, elementary **11** countersign **12** foundational, introductory

initially
◇ *head selection indicator*
05 first **07** at first, firstly **08** first off **10** at the start, first of all, originally **11** at the outset, to begin with, to start with **14** at the beginning

initiate
04 open, tiro **05** admit, begin, blood, cause, crash, drill, enrol, enter, lanch, let in, set up, start, teach, train, tutor **06** accept, induce, induct, instil, invest, launch, novice, ordain, prompt, rookie, sign up **07** convert, entrant, install, kick off, learner, pioneer, receive, recruit, start up, trigger, welcome **08** activate, beginner, bejesuit, commence, instruct, neophyte, newcomer **09** auspicate, establish, greenhorn, inculcate, instigate, institute, introduce, new member, novitiate, originate, proselyte, stimulate **10** bring about, catechumen, inaugurate, tenderfoot **11** get under way, probationer, set in motion **13** sow the seeds of **15** get off the ground, get things moving

initiation
05 debut, entry, start **07** baptism, opening **08** entrance **09** admission, beginning, enrolment, inception, induction, launching, reception, setting-up **10** admittance, enlistment, ordination **11** investiture, origination **12** inauguration, installation, introduction **13** rite of passage
• **initiation rite**
04 bora

initiative
02 go **04** lead, plan, push **05** drive **06** action, energy, scheme **07** lead-off **08** ambition, démarche, dynamism, gumption, proposal **09** first move, first step **10** creativity, enterprise, get-up-and-go, suggestion **11** opening move, originality **12** introductory **13** inventiveness **14** innovativeness, recommendation **15** resourcefulness

inject
03 add, hit, jab **04** bang, hype **05** bring, immit, shoot, spike **06** hype up, infuse, insert, instil **07** bring in, crank up, hit it up, inspire, shoot up, skin-pop, syringe **08** immunize, mainline **09** inoculate, introduce, vaccinate

injection
03 fix, jab, jag **04** bang, dose, shot **06** needle **07** skin-pop **08** addition, infusion **09** insertion **10** hypodermic, instilling **11** inoculation, vaccination **12** immunization, introduction **13** a shot in the arm

injudicious
04 rash **05** hasty **06** stupid, unwise **07** foolish **08** ill-timed **09** ill-judged, impolitic, imprudent, misguided **10** ill-advised, incautious, indiscreet, unthinking **11** inadvisable, inexpedient, wrong-headed **13** inconsiderate

injunction
05 order **06** dictum, ruling **07** command, dictate, mandate, precept **09** direction, directive **10** admonition **11** conjunction, exhortation, instruction

injure
◇ *anagram indicator*
03 cut, get, mar **04** bomb, burn, dere, harm, hurt, kill, lame, maim, maul, ruin, skin **05** abuse, annoy, break, chill, choke, deare, misdo, rifle, scald, scath, shend, spoil, touch, upset, waste, wound, wring, wrong **06** accloy, blight, damage, deface, deform, impair, mangle, nobble, offend, poison, put out, scaith, scathe, skaith, strain, weaken **07** blemish, carve up, cripple, disable, outrage, shoot up **08** aggrieve, fracture, ill-treat, maltreat, mutilate, override **09** disfigure, disoblige, humiliate, overshoot, prejudice, undermine **10** vitriolize **11** hospitalize **13** stab in the back

injured
◇ *anagram indicator*
03 bad **04** hurt, lame, sore **05** upset **06** abused, harmed, pained, put out, tender **07** bruised, damaged, defamed, grieved, misused, unhappy, unsound, wounded, wronged **08** crippled, disabled, insulted, maligned, offended, weakened **09** aggrieved **10** displeased, ill-treated, maltreated, vulnerable **11** disgruntled, wither-wrung **13** cut to the quick
• **easily injured**
04 nice

injurious
03 bad **06** malign, noyous, unjust **07** adverse, baneful, harmful, hurtful, noxious, ruinous **08** damaging, wrongful **09** insulting, libellous, unhealthy **10** calumnious, corrupting, defamatory, derogatory, iniquitous,

injury

offenceful, pernicious, slanderous
11 deleterious, destructive, detrimental, mischievous, prejudicial, unconducive **15** disadvantageous

injury
03 cut, ill, RSI **04** bale, dere, gash, harm, hurt, maim, ruin, sore, teen, tene, tort **05** abuse, deare, teene, wound, wrong **06** bruise, damage, insult, lesion, scathe, trauma **07** offence, offense, outrage **08** abrasion, fracture, mischief, violence **09** annoyance, contusion, grievance, injustice, prejudice **10** affliction, contrecoup, disservice, impairment, laceration, mutilation, traumatism
12 endamagement, ill-treatment
13 disfigurement
• **after injury**
◊ *anagram indicator*

injustice
04 bias **05** abuse, wrong **06** injury **07** offence, unright **08** inequity, iniquity, unreason **09** disparity, prejudice **10** inequality, oppression, partiality, unfairness, unjustness
11 favouritism **12** ill-treatment, one-sidedness, partisanship
14 discrimination

inkling
04 clue, hint, idea, sign **06** notion **07** glimmer, pointer, umbrage, whisper **08** allusion, faintest, foggiest, innuendo **09** suspicion
10 glimmering, indication, intimation, suggestion **11** insinuation

inky
◊ *anagram indicator*
03 jet **05** black, drunk, sooty **08** dark-blue, jet-black **09** coal-black **10** pitch-black
• **inky blotch**
04 monk

inlaid
03 set **05** inset, lined, tiled **06** mosaic **07** studded **08** enchased
09 empaestic, enamelled
10 damascened **11** tessellated

inland
05 inner **06** upland **07** central, midland, refined **08** domestic, interior, internal, landward **09** up-country
10 within land **13** sophisticated

inlay
05 embed, inset **06** enamel, insert, lining, mosaic, tiling **07** emblema, setting **08** damaskin, studding
09 damascene, damaskeen, damasquin **10** damasceene **12** tessellation

inlet
03 arm, bay **04** cove, hope **05** bight, creek, fiord, firth, fjord, haven, sound **06** infall, ingate **07** opening, passage **08** entrance

inmate
03 zek **04** case **06** client, intern **07** convict, patient **08** detainee, prisoner **09** collegian **10** collegiate

inmost
04 deep **05** basic **06** buried, hidden, secret **07** central, closest, dearest, deepest, private **08** esoteric, intimate, personal **09** essential, innermost
12 confidential

inn
03 bar, pub **04** khan **05** abode, hotel, house, howff, local, lodge, put up **06** boozer, hostel, imaret, posada, public, ryokan, shanty, tavern
07 albergo, auberge, canteen, potshop **08** bona fide, groggery, hostelry **09** free house, gin palace, lush-house, posthouse, roadhouse **11** caravansary, change-house, public house
12 caravansarai, caravanserai, halfway house **13** watering-house

innards
◊ *middle selection indicator*
04 guts **05** works **06** entera, organs, umbles, vitals **07** giblets, insides, viscera **08** entrails, interior
09 mechanism **10** intestines **13** inner workings **14** internal organs

innate
06 inborn, inbred, native **07** connate, natural **08** inherent, original
09 inherited, intrinsic, intuitive
10 congenital, hereditary, indigenous, ingenerate **11** instinctive

innately
08 inwardly **09** basically, centrally
10 inherently, integrally **11** essentially **13** constituently, fundamentally, intrinsically

inner
04 deep **06** entire, hidden, inside, inward, mental, middle, secret
07 central, obscure, private
08 esoteric, interior, internal, intimate, personal, profound **09** concealed, emotional, innermost, spiritual
10 restricted **13** psychological

innermost
04 deep **05** basic **06** buried, hidden, inmost, secret **07** central, closest, dearest, deepest, private **08** esoteric, intimate, personal **09** essential
12 confidential

innkeeper
04 host **07** hostess, manager, padrone **08** boniface, hotelier, landlady, landlord, mine host, publican
09 barkeeper, innholder
10 aubergiste, proprietor **11** hotel-keeper **12** restaurateur

innocence
06 purity, safety, virtue **07** honesty, naivety **08** chastity, openness
09 credulity, frankness, ignorance, integrity, naiveness, virginity
10 simplicity **11** artlessness, gullibility, naturalness, playfulness, sinlessness **12** harmlessness, inexperience, spotlessness, trustfulness **13** blamelessness, childlikeness, faultlessness, guilelessness, guiltlessness,

impeccability, inculpability, ingenuousness, innocuousness, righteousness, stainlessness, unworldliness **14** immaculateness **15** inoffensiveness

innocent
04 babe, lamb, naif, open, pure, safe **05** bland, canny, child, clear, frank, fresh, green, idiot, naive, seely, white **06** benign, chaste, gentle, honest, infant, novice, simple **07** angelic, anodyne, artless, ingénue, natural, playful, sinless, upright **08** Arcadian, beginner, dewy-eyed, dovelike, gullible, harmless, imbecile, lamblike, neophyte, sackless, spotless, trustful, trusting, virginal, virtuous
09 blameless, childlike, credulous, crimeless, faultless, greenhorn, guileless, guiltless, incorrupt, ingenuous, innocuous, righteous, stainless, unsullied, untainted, unworldly **10** babe in arms, immaculate, impeccable, inculpable, tenderfoot **11** inoffensive, offenceless, unblemished, uncorrupted
12 prelapsarian, simple-minded, unsuspecting, unsuspicious
13 inexperienced, unblameworthy, unimpeachable **14** above suspicion, irreproachable, uncontaminated
15 unsophisticated

innocently
06 simply **07** naively **09** artlessly **10** harmlessly, trustfully, trustingly **11** blamelessly, credulously, ingenuously, innocuously
13 inoffensively, unoffendingly
14 unsuspiciously

innocuous
04 mild, safe **05** bland **07** anodyne, playful **08** harmless, innocent
11 inoffensive, unobtrusive
15 unobjectionable

innovation
06 change, novity, reform **07** newness, novelty **08** novation, novelism, progress **09** departure, neologism, new method, variation **10** alteration, new product **12** introduction
13 modernization

innovative
03 new **04** bold **05** fresh **06** daring **07** go-ahead **08** creative, original **09** inventive, reforming **10** avant-garde, Promethean **11** adventurous, imaginative, progressive, resourceful **12** enterprising, trail-blazing
14 groundbreaking

innovator
06 source **07** creator, deviser, pioneer **08** novelist, reformer **09** developer **10** modernizer, originator
11 progressive, trailblazer **12** fresh thinker

innuendo
04 hint, slur **07** whisper **08** allusion, overtone **09** aspersion **10** intimation, suggestion **11** implication, insinuation

innumerable
04 many, tons **05** heaps, loads, piles
06 dozens, masses, oodles, stacks,
untold **07** umpteen **08** hundreds,
infinite, millions, numerous
09 countless, thousands
10 numberless, unnumbered
11 uncountable **12** incalculable

inoculate
05 graft, imbue **06** inject **07** protect
08 immunize **09** safeguard, syphilize,
vaccinate, variolate **10** give a jab to
11 give a shot to

inoculation
03 jab, jag **04** shot **09** injection
10 protection **11** vaccination,
variolation **12** immunization

inoffensive
04 mild, safe **05** bland, quiet
07 anodyne **08** harmless, innocent,
pleasant, retiring **09** innocuous,
peaceable **11** unassertive, unobtrusive
15 unexceptionable, unobjectionable

inoperable
05 fatal **06** deadly **08** hopeless,
terminal **09** incurable **10** unhealable
11 intractable, irremovable,
unremovable, untreatable

inoperative
04 bust, duff, idle **05** kaput, resty
06 broken, futile, kaputt, silent, unused
07 invalid, useless **08** nugatory
09 defective, worthless **10** broken-
down, inadequate, not working, on the
blink, on the fritz, out of order,
unworkable **11** ineffective, ineffectual,
inefficient, inofficious, out of action
12 not operative, out of service
13 inefficacious, unserviceable
14 non-functioning **15** out of
commission

inopportune
06 clumsy **08** ill-timed, mistimed,
tactless, untimely **09** ill-chosen,
importune **10** unsuitable, wrong-
timed **11** importunate, out of season,
unfortunate **12** inauspicious,
inconvenient, infelicitous,
intempestive, unpropitious,
unseasonable **13** inappropriate

inordinate
◊ *anagram indicator*
03 OTT **05** great, undue **07** extreme
08 vaulting **09** excessive
10 exorbitant, immoderate,
outrageous, over the top **11** God-
almighty, unwarranted
12 preposterous, unmeasurable,
unreasonable, unrestrained,
unrestricted **14** unconscionable

inorganic
04 dead **07** mineral **08** lifeless
09 inanimate **10** artificial, non-natural

input
04 code, data, load **05** enter, facts, key
in, put in, store **06** feed in, insert
07 capture, details, figures, process
08 material **09** resources **10** statistics
11 information, particulars
12 contribution

inquest
07 hearing, inquiry **10** inspection,
post-mortem **11** examination
13 investigation

inquietude
05 worry **06** unease **07** anxiety
08 disquiet **09** agitation, jumpiness
10 solicitude, uneasiness
11 disquietude, disturbance,
nervousness **12** apprehension,
discomposure, perturbation,
restlessness

inquire, enquire
03 ask, see **04** call, quiz, scan, seek
05 probe, query, snoop, speer, speir,
study **06** quaere, search **07** examine,
explore, inquere, inspect **08** look into,
question, research **10** scrutinize
11 interrogate, investigate

inquirer, enquirer
06 seeker **07** querist, student
08 explorer, searcher **10** inquisitor,
questioner, researcher **12** interrogator,
investigator

inquiring, enquiring
04 nosy **05** eager, nosey **06** prying
07 curious, probing, zetetic
08 doubtful **09** sceptical, searching,
wondering **10** analytical, interested
11 inquisitive, questioning
13 interrogatory, investigative,
investigatory **14** outward-looking

inquiringly, enquiringly
06 keenly **07** eagerly **09** curiously
11 wonderingly **12** analytically
13 inquisitively, questioningly

inquiry, enquiry
04 poll **05** probe, query, quest, study
06 demand, quaere, search, survey
07 hearing, inquest, inquire
08 etiology, question, scrutiny,
sounding **09** aetiology **10** inspection
11 examination, exploration,
inquisition, star chamber
12 perquisition **13** interrogation,
interrogatory, investigation
14 reconnaissance

inquisition
07 inquest, inquiry **08** grilling,
quizzing **09** witch hunt **10** Holy Office
11 examination, questioning
13 interrogation, investigation **14** the
third degree

inquisitive
04 nosy **05** nosey **06** prying, snoopy,
spying **07** curious, peeping, peering,
probing **08** snooping **09** inquiring,
intrusive, searching **10** meddlesome
11 interfering, questioning
12 scrutinizing

inquisitively
06 keenly **07** eagerly **09** curiously
11 inquiringly, searchingly
12 meddlesomely **13** interferingly,
questioningly

inquisitor
04 Deza **07** Ximenes **10** Torquemada

inroad
04 raid **05** foray, sally **06** attack,
charge, infall, sortie **07** advance,
assault **08** invasion, progress, trespass
09 incursion, intrusion, irruption,
offensive, onslaught, sea breach
11 impingement, trespassing
12 encroachment

insane
◊ *anagram indicator*
03 ape, fey, mad **04** bats, daft, gyte,
loco, nuts, wild, wood, yond **05** barmy,
batty, buggy, crazy, daffy, dippy, dotty,
flaky, gonzo, loony, loopy, manic, nutty,
potty, queer, wacko, wacky, wiggy
06 absurd, crazed, cuckoo, dement,
fruity, maniac, mental, raving, red-mad,
screwy, stupid **07** bananas, barking,
berserk, bonkers, cracked, foolish,
frantic, horn-mad, idiotic, lunatic,
meshuga **08** bughouse, crackers,
crackpot, demented, deranged,
dingbats, doolally, frenetic, frenzied,
maniacal, unhinged, unstable
09 delirious, disturbed, half-baked,
lymphatic, psychotic, senseless, up the
wall **10** bestraught, distracted,
distraught, frantic-mad, off the wall, off
your nut, out to lunch, ridiculous,
stone-crazy, unbalanced **11** hare-
brained, impractical, nonsensical, not
all there, off the rails, off your head
12 crackbrained, mad as a hatter, off
your chump, round the bend **13** off
your rocker, of unsound mind, out of
your head, out of your mind, out of
your tree, round the twist **14** off your
trolley, wrong in the head **15** non
compos mentis, out of your senses

insanely
◊ *anagram indicator*
05 madly **08** absurdly **09** foolishly
11 ludicrously, senselessly
12 outrageously, ridiculously

insanitary
04 foul **05** dirty **06** filthy, impure
07 dirtied, noisome, noxious, unclean
08 feculent, infected, infested,
polluted **09** unhealthy **10** unhygienic,
unsanitary **11** unhealthful, unsanitized
12 contaminated, insalubrious
13 disease-ridden

insanity
◊ *anagram indicator*
05 craze, folie, folly, mania **06** frenzy,
lunacy **07** madness **08** daftness,
delirium, dementia, neurosis
09 absurdity, craziness, psychosis,
stupidity **10** insaneness
11 derangement, foolishness,
hebephrenia, psychopathy **13** mental
illness, senselessness
14 ridiculousness

See also **lunacy**

insatiable
04 avid **06** greedy, hungry **07** craving
08 ravenous, sateless **09** rapacious,

oracious **10** gluttonous, immoderate, ordinate **12** unappeasable, nquenchable **13** unsatisfiable

nscribe
3 cut **04** etch, mark, sign **05** brand, arve, enrol, enter, print, stamp, write **6** endoss, enlist, incise, record, scrive **7** address, engrave, impress, imprint, crieve **08** dedicate, register **9** autograph

nscription
4 ogam **05** ogham, title, words **6** legend **07** caption, epitaph, tching, message, trigram, wording, vriting **08** colophon, epigraph, akemono **09** autograph, engraving, ettering, signature, tetragram **0** chronogram, dedication **1** insculpture **15** circumscription

nscrutable
4 deep **06** arcane, hidden, invis'd **7** cryptic **08** baffling, puzzling **9** enigmatic **10** mysterious, nreadable **12** impenetrable, hexplicable, unfathomable, nsearchable **13** unexplainable **4** unintelligible

nsect

Insects include:

3 ant, bee, bug, fly, ked, nit
4 cleg, flea, frit, gnat, kade, moth, tick, wasp
5 aphid, aphis, cimex, emmet, louse, midge, ox-bot, roach, sedge
6 bedbug, beetle, bembex, capsid, cicada, cootie, drongo, earwig, gadfly, gru-gru, hornet, jigger, locust, maggot, mantis, may bug, mayfly, muscid, red ant, sawfly, thrips, tipula, tsetse, tzetse, tzetze, weevil
7 antlion, blowfly, buzzard, chigger, cornfly, cricket, deer fly, fire ant, gallfly, gold-bug, hive bee, June bug, katydid, lace bug, lady bug, lamp fly, pill bug, rose bug, soldier, termite, wood ant
8 berry bug, birch fly, blackfly, bookworm, cornworm, crane fly, fruit fly, gall wasp, glowworm, greenfly, honey bee, horse fly, house fly, hoverfly, lacewing, ladybird, mealy bug, mosquito, onion fly, sand wasp, sedge fly, snake fly, stink bug, white ant, whitefly, woodworm
9 amazon ant, ant weaver, bumblebee, butterfly, caddis fly, carpet bug, cochineal, cockroach, coffee bug, damselfly, doodlebug, dragonfly, golden-eye, humble-bee, leaf miner, mason wasp, mining bee, mud dauber, paper wasp, shield bug, squash bug, stable fly, tsetse fly, tzetse fly, tzetze fly, velvet ant, wax insect, woodlouse
0 blister fly, bluebottle, boll weevil, bulldog ant, cabbage-fly, cockchafer, dolphin-fly, drosophila,

froghopper, grapelouse, kissing bug, leaf-cutter, leaf insect, Pharoah ant, pondskater, silverfish, vinegar-fly, web spinner
11 backswimmer, biting louse, biting midge, bristletail, bush cricket, caterpillar, froth-hopper, grasshopper, greenbottle, harvest mite, harvest tick, honeypot ant, stick insect, umbrella-ant, vine-fretter, walking leaf, walking twig
12 house cricket, lightning bug, walking stick, water boatman
13 daddy longlegs, diamond-beetle, leatherjacket, praying insect, praying mantis, water measurer, water scorpion

See also **animal; beetle; butterfly; invertebrate; moth**

Insect parts include:

03 eye, jaw, leg
04 head, vein, wing
06 cercus, feeler, scutum, thorax
07 abdomen, antenna, cuticle, maxilla, ocellus, pedicel, segment
08 antennae, forewing, hindwing, mandible, peduncle, spiracle, tympanum
09 mouthpart, proboscis
10 epicuticle, integument, ovipositor
11 compound eye

• **study of insects**
03 ent **10** entomology

insecticide

Insecticides include:

02 Bt
03 BHC, DDT
05 timbó, zineb
06 aldrin, derris
07 cinerin, safrole
08 camphene, carbaryl, chlordan, chromene, diazinon, dieldrin, flyspray, rotenone
09 chlordane, Gammexane®, Malathion®, parathion, toxaphene
10 carbofuran, dimethoate, Paris green, piperazine
15 organophosphate

insectivore
04 mole, tody **05** shrew **06** agouta, desman, tanrec, tenrec, Tupaia **08** hedgehog, serotine **09** solenodon, tree shrew **10** golden mole, otter shrew **11** diamond bird, gnatcatcher **13** elephant shrew

• **insectivorous plant**
06 sundew **07** Dionaea, drosera **10** butterwort, sarracenia **11** gobe-mouches **12** pitcher plant, Venus flytrap **13** Venus's flytrap

insecure
◇ *anagram indicator*
04 weak **05** frail, loose, shaky **06** afraid, flimsy, tickle, unsafe, unsure **07** anxious, exposed, fearful, nervous, worried **08** doubtful, hesitant, perilous, unstable, unsteady **09** dangerous, hazardous, unassured,

uncertain, unguarded **10** precarious, vulnerable **11** defenceless, unprotected **12** apprehensive, open to attack

insecurity
04 fear **05** peril, worry **06** danger, hazard **07** anxiety **08** unsafety, weakness **09** frailness, shakiness **10** flimsiness, uneasiness, unsafeness, unsureness **11** instability, nervousness, uncertainty **12** apprehension, unsteadiness **13** vulnerability **14** precariousness **15** defencelessness

insensate
04 deaf, numb **05** blind **07** unaware **08** comatose, ignorant **09** inanimate, oblivious, senseless, unfeeling, unmindful **10** insensible, insentient **11** unconscious **12** unresponsive **13** anaesthetized

insensible
03 out **04** cold, deaf, dull, hard, numb **05** aloof, blind, faint **06** marble, slight, stupid, wooden, zonked **07** callous, distant, unaware, unmoved **08** comatose, detached, ignorant **09** oblivious, senseless, unfeeling, unmindful, untouched **10** insentient, iron-witted, knocked out, unaffected, unapparent **11** emotionless, hard-hearted, insensitive, unconscious **12** undetectable, unresponsive **13** anaesthetized, imperceptible, indiscernible **14** dead to the world, out for the count

insensitive
04 dead, hard, iron **05** crass, tough **06** immune, obtuse **07** callous, unmoved **08** hardened, tactless, uncaring **09** anomalous, heartless, impassive, oblivious, resistant, unfeeling, untouched **10** hypalgesic, impervious, unaffected **11** hard-hearted, indifferent, thoughtless, unconcerned **12** case-hardened, impenetrable, thick-skinned, unresponsive **13** unsusceptible, unsympathetic **14** pachydermatous

insensitivity
08 hardness, hypalgia, immunity **09** bluntness, crassness, toughness, unconcern **10** crassitude, hypalgesia, obtuseness, resistance **11** callousness **12** indifference, tactlessness **14** hard-headedness, imperviousness **15** hard-heartedness, impenetrability

inseparable
05 bosom, close **07** devoted **08** constant, intimate **10** individual **11** individuate, indivisible, undividable **12** indissoluble, inextricable

inseparably
05 as one **06** firmly **07** closely **08** arm in arm, together **10** hand in hand, intimately **11** indivisibly **12** indissolubly, inextricably

insert
03 cue, put, set **04** sink **05** embed, enter, immit, infix, inlay, inset, let in,

place, plant, press, put in, stick
06 notice, push in, slip in **07** enchase, enclose, engraft, implant, ingraft, slide in, stick in **08** addition, circular, intromit, thrust in **09** enclosure, insertion, interject, interpose, introduce **10** interleave, supplement **11** intercalate, interpolate **13** advertisement

insertion
05 entry, inset, miter, mitre **06** insert **07** implant **08** addition **09** inclusion, intrusion **10** supplement **12** introduction, intromission **13** intercalation, interpolation

inside
◊ *hidden indicator*
◊ *insertion indicator*
04 core, guts **05** belly, heart, inner **06** centre, indoor, inward, middle, secret, within **07** content, indoors, private **08** contents, hush-hush, implicit, inherent, interior, internal, intromit, inwardly, reserved, secretly **09** innermost, intrinsic, privately **10** classified, internally, restricted **12** confidential

insider
06 member **07** one of us **08** co-worker **11** participant, staff member **15** one of the in-crowd

insides
04 guts **05** belly, tummy **06** bowels, organs **07** abdomen, giblets, innards, stomach, viscera **08** entrails **10** intestines **14** internal organs

insidious
03 sly **04** wily **06** artful, crafty, sneaky, subtle, tricky **07** cunning, devious, furtive **08** sneaking, stealthy **09** cautelous, deceitful, deceptive, dishonest, insincere **10** perfidious **11** duplicitous, treacherous **13** Machiavellian, surreptitious

insidiously
05 slyly **06** subtly **09** cunningly

insight
05 grasp, sight **06** acumen, aperçu, vision, wisdom **08** epiphany **09** awareness, furniture, intuition, judgement, knowledge, sharpness **10** perception, shrewdness **11** discernment, observation, penetration, realization, sensitivity **12** apprehension, intelligence, perspicacity **13** comprehension, enlightenment, understanding

insightful
04 wise **05** acute, sharp **06** astute, seeing, shrewd **07** prudent **08** inscient **09** observant, sagacious **10** discerning, perceptive, percipient **11** intelligent, penetrating **13** knowledgeable, perspicacious, understanding

insignia
03 tab **04** arms, logo, mark, sign, type **05** armor, badge, brand, clasp, crest,

eagle, order, signs **06** armour, emblem, ensign, ribbon, symbol **07** regalia **08** hallmark **09** hallmarks, medallion, trademark **10** coat of arms, decoration **11** cap and bells

insignificance
08 meanness, tininess **09** pettiness, smallness **10** paltriness, triviality **11** irrelevance, nothingness **12** nugatoriness, unimportance **13** immateriality, inconsequence, negligibility, worthlessness **15** meaninglessness

insignificant
04 tiny **05** C-list, dinky, minor, petit, petty, scrub, small **06** insect, meagre, paltry, puisne, puisny, scanty, slight **07** minimal, nebbich, scrubby, trivial **08** marginal, nugatory, piddling, trifling **09** jerkwater, no-account, small beer, small-time **10** fractional, immaterial, irrelevant, negligible, peripheral **11** meaningless, Mickey Mouse, unimportant **12** cutting no ice, non-essential **13** hole-in-the-wall, insubstantial, no great shakes **14** inconsiderable **15** inconsequential

insincere
04 jive **05** false, lying **06** double, forked, hollow, phoney, untrue **07** devious, feigned, lip-deep **08** disloyal, rhetoric, two-faced **09** deceitful, dishonest, faithless, mouth-made, pretended, underhand, unnatural **10** backhanded, mendacious, perfidious, rhetorical, unfaithful, untruthful **11** dissembling, duplicitous, pretentious, treacherous **12** disingenuous, hypocritical, meretricious **13** double-dealing

insincerely
07 falsely **09** deviously **10** disloyally **11** deceitfully, dishonestly **12** perfidiously, unfaithfully, untruthfully **13** duplicitously, pretentiously, treacherously **14** hypocritically

insincerity
04 cant **06** humbug **07** falsity, perfidy **08** bad faith, pretence **09** duplicity, falseness, hypocrisy, mendacity, phoniness **10** dishonesty, hollowness, lip service **11** deviousness, dissembling, evasiveness **13** artificiality, deceitfulness, dissimulation, faithlessness **14** untruthfulness **15** pretentiousness

insinuate
04 hint, wind **05** get at, imply **06** allude **07** mention, suggest, whisper **08** indicate, innuendo, intimate, work into **10** serpentine
• **insinuate yourself**
04 work, worm **05** crawl, sidle **07** wriggle **09** get in with **10** ingratiate **11** curry favour

insinuation
04 hint, slur **05** slant **08** allusion, innuendo **09** aspersion, inference

10 insinuendo, intimation, suggestion **11** implication **12** introduction

insipid
03 dry **04** blah, drab, dull, fade, flat, lash, tame, thin, weak **05** banal, bland, trite, vapid, wersh **06** boring, pallid, watery **07** anaemic, insulse, mawkish, missish, shilpit, tedious, wearish **08** lifeless, waterish **09** inanimate, sapidless, tasteless, unsavoury, wearisome **10** albuminous, colourless, monotonous, spiritless, wishy-washy **11** flavourless **12** milk-and-water, unappetizing **13** characterless, unimaginative, uninteresting

insist
03 vow **04** aver, hold, urge **05** claim, press, swear **06** assert, demand, harp on, repeat, strain, stress, threap **07** contend, declare, dwell on, entreat, persist, require, stand on **08** maintain **09** emphasize, reiterate, stand firm, stipulate **10** hang out for **11** state firmly, stick out for **12** ask for firmly **15** put your foot down, stand your ground, stick to your guns

insistence
05 claim **06** demand, stress, urging **08** emphasis, entreaty, firmness **09** assertion **10** contention, repetition, resolution **11** declaration, exhortation, maintenance, persistence, reiteration, requirement **13** assertiveness, determination

insistent
06 dogged, urgent **07** adamant, exigent **08** constant, emphatic, forceful, pressing, repeated, resolute **09** assertive, demanding, incessant, tenacious **10** determined, inexorable, persistent, relentless, unyielding **11** importunate, persevering, unrelenting, unremitting

insobriety
09 inebriety, tipsiness **10** crapulence **11** drunkenness, inebriation **12** hard drinking, intemperance, intoxication

insolence
03 gum, lip **04** gall, sass **05** abuse, cheek, mouth, nerve, sauce, snash **06** hubris, hybris **07** insults **08** attitude, audacity, boldness, chutzpah, defiance, pertness, rudeness **09** arrogance, contumely, impudence, sauciness **10** cheekiness, disrespect, effrontery, incivility **11** forwardness, presumption **12** impertinence **13** offensiveness **15** insubordination

insolent
04 bold, rude **05** bardy, brash, fresh, lairy, lippy, sassy, saucy **06** brazen, cheeky, mouthy, wanton **07** abusive, defiant, forward **08** arrogant, impudent **09** audacious, insulting **10** purse-proud **11** ill-mannered, impertinent **12** contemptuous, contumelious, presumptuous **13** disrespectful, insubordinate

insoluble

07 complex, obscure **08** baffling, involved, puzzling **09** enigmatic, intricate **10** mysterious, mystifying, perplexing, unsolvable **11** inscrutable **12** impenetrable, inexplicable, unfathomable **13** unexplainable **14** indecipherable

insolvency

04 ruin **07** default, failure **10** bankruptcy **11** destitution, liquidation, queer street **12** indebtedness **13** impecuniosity, pennilessness **14** impoverishment

insolvent

04 bust **05** broke, skint **06** failed, in debt, ruined **07** boracic **08** bankrupt, in the red, strapped **09** destitute, gone under, penniless **10** liquidated, on the rocks **11** impecunious **12** impoverished **13** gone to the wall, in queer street **14** on your beam ends **15** strapped for cash

insomnia

11 wakefulness **12** insomnolence, restlessness **13** sleeplessness
• **insomnia drug**
06 Ativan® **07** Mogadon® **08** Rohypnol® **09** lorazepam, Temazepam **10** nitrazepam

insouciance

04 ease **08** airiness **09** flippancy, unconcern **10** breeziness, jauntiness **11** nonchalance **12** carefreeness, heedlessness, indifference

insouciant

04 airy **06** breezy, casual, jaunty **07** buoyant **08** carefree, flippant, heedless **09** apathetic, easy-going, unworried **10** nonchalant, untroubled **11** free and easy, indifferent, unconcerned **12** happy-go-lucky, light-hearted

inspect

03 vet **04** case, scan, tour, view **05** audit, check, study, visit **06** assess, go over, review, search, survey **07** examine, oversee, see over **08** appraise, check out, look into, look over, pore over **09** supervise **10** scrutinize **11** investigate, perlustrate, reconnoitre, superintend

inspection

04 scan, tour, view **05** audit, check, dekko, recce, study, visit **06** alnage, muster, review, search, survey **07** autopsy, check-up, inspect, rag-fair, vetting, vidimus **08** analysis, autopsia, look-over, once-over, overview, scrutiny **09** appraisal, Cook's tour, look-round **10** assessment **11** examination, perspective, supervision **12** tracheoscopy **13** investigation

inspector

06 conner, critic, exarch, keeker, tester, viewer **07** alnager, auditor, checker, officer, scanner, visitor **08** assessor, examiner, overseer, provedor,

providor, reviewer, searcher, surveyor **09** appraiser, provedore **10** controller, proveditor, scrutineer, supervisor **11** proveditore **12** investigator **14** superintendent

inspiration

04 goad, hoop, hwyl, idea, muse, spur **05** estro, whoop **06** breath, duende, fillip, genius **07** insight **08** afflatus, Aganippe, arousing, inflatus, infusion, stimulus, stirring, taghairm **09** afflation, awakening, brainwave, inflation, influence, theosophy **10** brainstorm, bright idea, creativity, enthusiasm, incitement, motivation, revelation **11** imagination, originality, stimulation, theopneusty **12** illumination **13** encouragement, enlightenment, inventiveness **14** stroke of genius

inspirational

09 emotional, inspiring, spiritual **10** devotional, heartening, motivating, suggestive **11** encouraging, influential, instinctive **13** psychological

inspire

04 fire, goad, spur, stir **05** guide, imbue, rouse **06** arouse, enamor, excite, inform, infuse, inject, kindle, prompt, thrill **07** animate, breathe, embrave, enamour, enliven, enthral, enthuse, hearten, impress, inflame, produce, provoke, quicken, trigger **08** energize, instruct, motivate, spark off, touch off **09** encourage, galvanize, infatuate, influence, instigate, stimulate **10** bring about, exhilarate

inspired

05 vatic **08** afflated, creative, daemonic, daimonic, dazzling, exciting, splendid, talented, visioned **09** brilliant, memorable, thrilling, wonderful **10** impressive, marvellous, remarkable, theopneust **11** enthralling, exceptional, imaginative, outstanding, superlative **12** theopneustic

inspiring

06 moving **07** rousing **08** exciting, stirring **09** affecting, memorable, thrilling, uplifting **10** heartening, impressive **11** encouraging, enthralling, interesting, stimulating **12** enthusiastic, exhilarating, invigorating **13** inspirational

inspirit

04 fire, move **05** cheer, nerve, rouse **06** incite **07** animate, enliven, gladden, hearten, inspire, quicken, refresh **08** embolden **09** encourage, galvanize, stimulate **10** exhilarate, invigorate **12** reinvigorate

instability

07 frailty **08** wavering **09** lubricity, shakiness **10** fickleness, fitfulness, flimsiness, insecurity, transience, unsafeness, volatility **11** flightiness, fluctuation, inconstancy, oscillation, temperament, uncertainty, unsoundness, vacillation, variability **12** impermanence, irresolution,

unsteadiness **13** unreliability **14** capriciousness, changeableness, precariousness

install

03 fit, fix, lay, put **04** site **05** lodge, place, plant, put in, set up, state **06** induct, insert, invest, locate, nestle, ordain, settle **07** instate, plumb in, situate, station, swear in **08** ensconce, enthrone, entrench, position **09** establish, institute, introduce **10** consecrate, inaugurate

installation

02 HQ **04** base, camp, post, site **05** plant **06** centre, siting, system **07** artwork, fitting, placing, station **08** location **09** apparatus, equipment, induction, insertion, machinery **10** ordination, settlement, swearing-in **11** instatement, investiture, positioning **12** consecration, headquarters, inauguration **13** establishment

instalment

02 HP **04** call, heft, part **06** lesson **07** chapter, episode, payment, portion, section, segment, tranche **08** division, rhapsody **09** repayment **11** part payment **12** continuation, hire purchase **13** the never-never

instance

04 case, cite, give, name, suit **05** cause, proof, quote **06** adduce, behest, demand, motive, sample, urging **07** example, mention, point to, process, refer to, request, specify **08** citation, entreaty, evidence, occasion, pressure **09** exemplify, prompting **10** incitement, initiative, insistence, occurrence, particular **11** case in point, exhortation, importunity, instigation **12** illustration, solicitation **15** exemplification
• **for instance**
02 as, eg, zB **10** for example **13** exempli gratia

instant

02 mo **03** sec **04** fast, jiff, tick, time, whip **05** flash, jiffy, quick, rapid, swift, trice **06** direct, minute, moment, prompt, second, urgent **07** current, present **08** juncture, occasion **09** immediate, on-the-spot, twinkling **10** ready mixed **11** convenience, pre-prepared, split second **12** unhesitating **13** instantaneous **14** easily prepared **15** quickly prepared

instantaneous

05 rapid **06** direct, prompt, snappy, sudden **07** instant **09** immediate, momentary, on-the-spot **12** momentaneous, unhesitating

instantaneously

03 pdq **04** anon, ASAP **06** at once, pronto **07** quickly, rapidly **08** directly, in a jiffy, promptly, speedily **09** forthwith, instantly, on the spot, right away **11** immediately **12** straight away, there and then, without delay **14** unhesitatingly

instantly
03 now, pdq **04** ASAP **06** at once, pronto **08** directly, in a jiffy, on the dot **09** forthwith, like a shot, on the spot, right away, zealously **11** immediately **12** straight away, there and then, without delay **13** importunately **15** instantaneously

instead
04 else **06** rather **10** by contrast, in contrast, preferably, substitute **11** replacement **13** alternatively **15** as an alternative
- **instead of**
04 vice **07** against **08** in lieu of **09** in place of **10** in favour of, on behalf of, rather than **11** as opposed to **12** in contrast to **14** in preference to

instigate
04 goad, move, prod, spur, urge **05** begin, cause, impel, press, rouse, set on, spark, start **06** excite, foment, incite, induce, kindle, prompt, stir up, whip up **07** inspire, provoke **08** generate, initiate, persuade **09** encourage, influence, stimulate **10** bring about

instigation
06 behest, motion, urging **07** bidding **09** incentive, prompting, prompture **10** incitement, inducement, initiation, initiative, insistence **11** fomentation **13** encouragement

instigator
04 goad, spur **06** leader **07** inciter **08** agitator, fomenter, incensor, provoker, putter-on **09** firebrand, initiator, motivator **10** incendiary, prime mover, ringleader **12** troublemaker **13** mischief-maker

instil
05 drill, imbue, plant, teach **06** infuse, inject **07** breathe, din into, implant, impress, ingrain **09** inculcate, insinuate, introduce, transfuse

instinct
04 bent, feel, gift, urge **05** drive, flair, hunch, knack, moved **06** imbued, nature, talent **07** ability, charged, faculty, feeling, impulse, incited **08** animated, aptitude, tendency **09** intuition, principle **10** gut feeling, instigated, sixth sense **11** gut reaction **14** inbred response, predisposition **15** natural response

instinctive
03 gut **06** inborn, innate, native, reflex **07** natural **08** inherent, knee-jerk, primeval, untaught, visceral **09** automatic, immediate, impulsive, intuitive, primaeval, unlearned **10** mechanical, unthinking **11** involuntary, spontaneous **13** unintentional **14** seat-of-the-pants, unpremeditated

instinctively
09 naturally **11** intuitively **12** mechanically, unthinkingly

13 automatically, involuntarily, spontaneously **15** without thinking

institute
01 I **03** law **04** Inst, open, rule **05** begin, enact, found, order, raise, set up, start **06** create, custom, decree, induct, invest, launch, ordain, school **07** academy, appoint, college, develop, educate, install, precept **08** commence, initiate, organize, seminary **09** establish, introduce, originate, principle **10** foundation, inaugurate, regulation **11** institution, put in motion, set in motion **12** conservatory, organization

Institutes include:
02 IA, IM, WI
03 BFI, CGI, CIB, CMI, EMI, ICA, MIT
04 NICE, RIBA, RNIB, RNID, RTPI
05 C and G, UMIST, UWIST
07 Caltech

institution
03 law **04** club, home, rule **05** guild, usage **06** center, centre, custom, league, ritual, system **07** college, concern, society **08** creation, founding, hospital, practice, starting **09** enactment, formation, inception, institute, setting-up, tradition **10** convention, foundation, initiation **11** association, corporation **12** commencement, installation, introduction, organization **13** establishment

institutional
03 set **04** cold, drab, dull **06** dreary, formal **07** orderly, routine, uniform **08** accepted, clinical, orthodox **09** cheerless, customary, organized **10** forbidding, impersonal, methodical, monotonous, regimented, systematic **11** established, ritualistic, uninspiring, unwelcoming **12** bureaucratic, conventional **13** establishment

instruct
03 bid **04** shew, show, tell, warn **05** brief, coach, drill, guide, order, prime, study, teach, train, tutor **06** advise, charge, demand, direct, enjoin, gospel, ground, inform, lesson, notify, school, taught **07** call out, command, counsel, educate, inspire, lecture, mandate, prepare, require **09** catechize, enlighten, make known **10** discipline **12** indoctrinate

instruction
03 key **05** brief, order, rules **06** advice, charge, legend, lesson, manual, orders, ruling **07** classes, command, lecture, lessons, mandate, priming, telling, tuition **08** briefing, coaching, drilling, guidance, handbook, lectures, pedagogy, teaching, training, tutelage, tutoring **09** direction, directive, education, grounding, knowledge, schooling **10** directions, discipline, guidelines, injunction **11** book of words, edification, information,

inspiration, preparation, requirement **13** enlightenment **14** indoctrination, recommendation **15** recommendations

instructive
06 useful **07** helpful **08** didactic, edifying, teaching **09** doctrinal, educative, improving, uplifting **10** didactical **11** educational, informative, informatory **12** enlightening, illuminating

instructor
04 guru **05** coach, guide, swami, tutor **06** master, mentor, sensei **07** adviser, teacher, trainer **08** educator, exponent, lecturer, mistress **09** maharishi, pedagogue, preceptor **10** counsellor, instituter, institutor **11** preceptress **12** demonstrator

instrument
03 act, way **04** mean, rule, tool **05** agent, cause, gauge, gismo, means, meter, organ **06** agency, device, factor, gadget, medium **07** channel, measure, utensil, vehicle **09** apparatus, appliance, guideline, implement, indicator, mechanism, yardstick **11** contraption, contrivance

See also **measurement**; **optical**; **scientific**; **torture**; **writing**

Musical instruments include:
02 gu
03 gju, gue, lur, oud, sax, saz, uke, zel
04 alto, bass, bell, drum, erhu, fife, gong, harp, horn, kora, koto, lure, lute, lyre, Moog®, oboe, pipe, rote, sang, tuba, vibe, vina, viol, zeze
05 Amati, banjo, bells, bongo, bugle, cello, chime, crwth, flute, gusla, gusle, gusli, hi-hat, kazoo, mbira, organ, piano, pipes, rebec, shalm, shawm, sitar, strad, tabla, tabor, vibes, viola, zanze, zirna, zurna
06 carnyx, cither, citole, cornet, cymbal, Fender, fiddle, guitar, rattle, spinet, tom-tom, tympan, vielle, violin, zither
07 alphorn, bagpipe, bandore, bandura, baryton, bassoon, bazouki, bodhran, buccina, celeste, cembalo, cithara, cithern, cittern, clarion, clavier, cowbell, hautboy, lyricon, maracas, marimba, ocarina, pandora, Pianola®, piccolo, sackbut, sambuca, sarangi, saxhorn, serpent, sistrum, tambura, theorbo, timpani, trumpet, ukulele, vihuela, whistle, zithern
08 angklung, bagpipes, barytone, bass drum, bass viol, bouzouki, calliope, carillon, charango, cimbalom, clappers, clarinet, clarsach, cornpipe, crumhorn, dulcimer, handbell, hornpipe, humstrum, jew's harp, keyboard, mandolin, manzello, melodeon, Pan-pipes, polyphon, psaltery, recorder, side-drum, spinette, Steinway, surbahar, tamboura, theramin, theremin, timbales, triangle, trombone,

virginal, vocalion, zambomba
accordion, alpenhorn, balalaika, banjolele, bugle-horn, castanets, chime bars, decachord, euphonium, flageolet, harmonica, harmonium, Mellotron®, polyphone, saxophone, snare-drum, tenor-drum, wood block, Wurlitzer®, xylophone
arpeggione, bass guitar, bird-scarer, bongo-drums, bullroarer, clavichord, concertina, cor anglais, didgeridoo, double bass, eolian harp, flugelhorn, French horn, grand piano, hurdy-gurdy, kettle-drum, mouth organ, oboe d'amore, pentachord, pianoforte, sousaphone, squeeze-box, tambourine, thumb piano, tin whistle, vibraphone
aeolian harp, barrel organ, harpsichord, phonofiddle, player-piano, sleigh bells, synthesizer, violoncello
glockenspiel, harmonichord, penny whistle, stock and horn, Stradivarius, tubular bells, viola da gamba
contra-bassoon, Ondes Martenot, panharmonicon, slide trombone, Swanee whistle
acoustic guitar, electric guitar, jingling Johnny
Moog synthesizer®, wind synthesizer

instrumental
active, useful 07 helpful, organic 08 involved 09 auxiliary, conducive, important 10 subsidiary implemental, influential, ministerial, significant, subservient 12 contributory

insubordinate
04 rude 06 unruly 07 defiant, riotous 08 impudent, mutinous 09 insurgent, seditious, turbulent 10 disorderly, rebellious, refractory 11 disobedient, impertinent 12 contumacious, recalcitrant, ungovernable 13 undisciplined

insubordination
06 mutiny, revolt 08 defiance, rudeness, sedition 09 impudence, rebellion 11 riotousness 12 disobedience, impertinence, indiscipline, insurrection, mutinousness 13 recalcitrance 15 ungovernability

insubstantial
04 idle, poor, thin, weak 05 false, frail, wispy 06 bubble, feeble, flimsy, frothy, meagre, slight, unreal, yeasty 07 tenuous 08 fanciful, illusory, tenuous, vaporous 09 airy-fairy, cardboard, ephemeral, imaginary, moonshine 10 chimerical, immaterial, intangible 11 incorporeal

insufferable
08 dreadful, shocking 09 loathsome, repugnant, revolting 10 detestable,

impossible, outrageous, unbearable 11 intolerable, unendurable 13 insupportable, too much to bear

insufferably
10 impossibly, shockingly, unbearably 11 intolerably, repugnantly 12 outrageously

insufficiency
04 lack, need, want 06 dearth 07 paucity, poverty 08 scarcity, shortage 10 deficiency, inadequacy 11 short supply 14 inadequateness

insufficient
05 scant, short 06 meagre, scanty, scarce, sparse 07 lacking, wanting 09 defective, deficient, not enough 10 inadequate 13 in short supply

insular
05 aloof, petty 06 biased, closed, cut off, narrow, remote 07 bigoted, limited 08 detached, isolated, separate, solitary 09 blinkered, insulated, parochial, withdrawn 10 prejudiced, provincial, restricted, xenophobic 12 narrow-minded, short-sighted 13 inward-looking

insularity
04 bias 07 bigotry 09 isolation, pettiness, prejudice 10 detachment, xenophobia 12 parochiality, solitariness 13 parochialness

insulate
03 lag, pad 04 wrap 05 cover 06 cocoon, cut off, detach, encase, shield 07 cushion, envelop, exclude, isolate, protect, shelter 08 separate 09 segregate, sequester

insulation
05 cover 06 shield 07 lagging, padding, shelter 08 asbestos, cladding, covering, sleeving, stuffing, wrapping 09 cocooning, corkboard, exclusion, fibrefill, foam glass, isolation 10 cushioning, detachment, fiberglass, fibreglass, protection, separation, Thermalite® 11 segregation 12 foam plastics 13 building paper, double-glazing, triple glazing 14 foamed plastics, Willesden paper 15 contour feathers, vulcanized fibre

insulator

Insulators include:

03 lag
04 mica
07 bushing, tea cosy
08 rock wool
09 pink batts®
10 dielectric
11 vermiculite
12 friction tape
14 insulating tape, Willesden paper

insult
04 bait, barb, gibe, hurt, slur, snub 05 abuse, libel, taunt, wound 06 damage, impugn, injure, injury, malign, mud pie, offend, rebuff, revile, slight, verbal 07 affront, mortify,

offence, outrage, put-down, slander, traduce, trample, triumph 08 derogate, repriefe, ridicule, rudeness 09 call names, contumely, disparage, indignity, insolence 10 aspersions, calumniate, defamation, fling mud at, insultment, revilement, sling mud at, throw mud at 11 triumph over 13 disparagement, slap in the face 14 fly in the face of, kick in the teeth

insulting
04 rude 07 abusive, hurtful 08 insolent, reviling 09 degrading, injurious, libellous, offensive, slighting 10 affronting, derogatory, outrageous, scurrilous, slanderous 11 disparaging, opprobrious 12 contemptuous, contumelious

insuperable
10 formidable, impassable, invincible 12 overwhelming, unassailable 13 unconquerable 14 insurmountable

insupportable
07 hateful 08 dreadful 09 loathsome, untenable 10 detestable, unbearable 11 intolerable, unendurable 12 indefensible, insufferable, irresistible, unacceptable 13 unjustifiable

insuppressible
06 lively, unruly 09 energetic, go-getting 11 unstoppable, unsubduable 12 incorrigible, obstreperous, ungovernable 13 irrepressible 14 uncontrollable

insurance
02 NI 03 ins 05 cover 06 policy, surety 07 premium 08 security, warranty 09 assurance, guarantee, indemnity, provision, safeguard 10 protection 15 indemnification

insure
05 cover 06 assure, ensure 07 protect, warrant 08 reinsure 09 guarantee, indemnify 10 overinsure, underwrite

insurer
07 assurer 09 abandonee, guarantor, protector, warrantor 11 indemnifier, underwriter

insurgence
04 coup, riot 06 mutiny, putsch, revolt, rising 08 sedition, uprising 09 coup d'état, rebellion 10 revolution 12 insurrection

insurgent
05 pandy, rebel 06 rioter, rising 07 riotous 08 Camisard, mutineer, mutinous, partisan, resister, revolted, revolter 09 revolting, seditious 10 rebellious 11 disobedient, seditionist 13 insubordinate, revolutionary, revolutionist 15 insurrectionary, insurrectionist

insurmountable
08 hopeless 10 impossible, invincible 11 insuperable 12 overwhelming, unassailable 13 unconquerable

insurrection
04 coup, riot **06** mutiny, putsch, revolt, rising, uproar **08** sedition, uprising **09** coup d'état, rebellion **10** insurgence, insurgency, revolution

intact
05 sound, whole **06** entire, unhurt **07** perfect **08** complete, flawless, integral, unbroken, unharmed **09** faultless, undamaged, uninjured, unscathed, untouched **10** in one piece, unimpaired **12** undiminished **13** all in one piece

intangible
04 airy **05** vague **06** subtle, unfelt, unreal **07** elusive, obscure, shadowy, unclear **08** abstract, fleeting **09** invisible, touchless **10** impalpable, indefinite **11** incorporeal, indefinable, undefinable **12** immeasurable, imponderable **13** indescribable, insubstantial

integer
04 unit **05** digit, whole **06** figure, number **07** numeral **11** whole number

integral
04 full **05** basic, total, whole **06** entire, intact **07** built-in, inbuilt, unitary **08** complete, inherent **09** component, elemental, essential, intrinsic, necessary, requisite, undivided **10** integrated, unimpaired **11** constituent, fundamental **13** indispensable

integrate
03 mix **04** fuse, join, knit, mesh **05** blend, merge, unite, whole **06** mingle **07** combine **08** coalesce, complete, intermix **09** harmonize **10** amalgamate, assimilate, co-ordinate, homogenize, mainstream **11** consolidate, desegregate, incorporate

integrated
05 fused, mixed **06** hybrid, joined, merged, meshed, united **07** blended, mingled, mongrel, unified **08** cohesive, combined, joined-up **09** coalesced, connected, one-nation, tight-knit **10** harmonious, harmonized **11** amalgamated, assimilated, tightly knit, unseparated **12** consolidated, desegregated, incorporated, interrelated **13** part and parcel

integration
03 mix **05** blend, unity **06** fusion, merger **07** harmony **11** combination, unification **12** amalgamation, assimilation **13** consolidation, desegregation, incorporation **14** homogenization

integrity
05 honor, unity **06** honour, purity, virtue **07** decency, honesty, justice, probity **08** cohesion, entirety, fairness, goodness, morality, totality **09** coherence, principle, rectitude, sincerity, wholeness **10** entireness **11** unification, uprightness

12 completeness, impartiality, truthfulness **13** righteousness

intellect
04 mind, nous **05** brain, sense **06** brains, genius, noesis, reason, wisdom **07** egghead, noology, thinker, thought **08** academic, brainbox, highbrow **09** judgement **10** brainpower, brilliance, mastermind **12** intellectual, intelligence **13** comprehension, understanding

intellectual
04 blue **05** titan **06** boffin, brainy, far-out, genius, mental, noetic **07** bookish, egghead, erudite, learned, logical, thinker **08** academic, brainbox, cerebral, cultural, good mind, highbrow, studious, well-read **09** intellect, scholarly **10** mastermind, noematical, thoughtful **11** intelligent **12** bluestocking, pointy-headed, well-educated **13** rocket scientist

intellectually
08 mentally **10** cerebrally, culturally, studiously **12** academically, conceptually, noematically

intelligence
01 G **02** IQ **03** gen, wit **04** data, dope, news, nous, wits **05** brain, facts **06** acumen, advice, brains, notice, reason, report, rumour, spying, tip-off **07** account, low-down, thought, warning **08** aptitude, findings **09** alertness, espionage, intellect, knowledge, quickness, sharpness **10** brainpower, brightness, brilliance, cleverness, grey matter, perception **11** discernment, information, observation **12** notification, surveillance **13** comprehension, understanding **15** little grey cells
- **intelligence service**
02 MI **03** CIA, KGB, SIS **05** Stasi **06** Mossad

intelligent
05 acute, alert, quick, sharp, smart **06** brainy, bright, clever **07** knowing **08** all there, educated, informed, rational, sensible, thinking **09** brilliant, sagacious **10** discerning, perceptive **11** quick-witted **12** apprehensive, knowledgable, pointy-headed, well-informed **13** communicative, knowledgeable, perspicacious, understanding, using your loaf

intelligently
07 quickly **08** all there, cleverly, sensibly **09** knowingly **10** rationally **11** sagaciously **12** discerningly, perceptively **13** using your loaf **15** perspicaciously

intelligentsia
06 brains **08** eggheads, literati **09** academics, highbrows **10** illuminati **11** cognoscenti **13** intellectuals

intelligibility
07 clarity **08** lucidity **09** clearness, lucidness, plainness, precision

10 legibility, simplicity **11** exotericism **12** distinctness, explicitness

intelligible
04 open **05** clear, lucid, plain **07** legible **08** distinct, exoteric, explic **10** exoterical, fathomable, penetrable **12** decipherable **14** comprehensible, understandable

intemperance
06 excess **07** licence **10** crapulence, debauchery, insobriety **11** drunkenness, inebriation, unrestraint **12** extravagance, immoderation, intoxication **14** overindulgence, self-indulgence

intemperate
03 OTT **04** wild **06** severe, strong **07** drunken, extreme, violent **08** prodigal **09** dissolute, excessive, unbridled **10** immoderate, inebriated, inordinate, licentious, over the top, passionate, profligate **11** dissipation, distempered, extravagant, incontinent intoxicated, tempestuous **12** uncontrolled, ungovernable, unreasonable, unrestrained **13** self-indulgent **14** irrestrainable, uncontrollable

intend
03 aim **04** mean, plan, plot, turn **05** ettle, hight, think **06** choose, design, devise, direct, expand, expect extend, scheme, strain **07** be going, destine, earmark, express, mark out, project, propose, purport, purpose, resolve **08** foremean, meditate, set apart **09** be looking, calculate, destinate, determine, have a mind, intensify **10** have in mind **11** contemplate **12** be determined

intended
06 fiancé, future **07** fiancée, planned **08** destined, proposed, purposed, wife-to-be **09** betrothed, designate **10** deliberate, designated, future wife **11** husband-to-be, intentional, prospective **13** future husband
- **as intended**
15 according to plan

intense
04 deep, full, keen **05** acute, dense, eager, great, harsh, heavy, sharp, tense vivid **06** ardent, fervid, fierce, opaque potent, severe, strong **07** burning, earnest, excited, extreme, fervent, nervous, serious, violent, zealous **08** blinding, electric, forceful, powerful, profound, strained, vehement, vigorous **09** consuming, emotional, energetic, exquisite, intensive **10** heightened, passionate, thoughtful **11** impassioned **12** concentrated, enthusiastic

intensely
04 deep, very **06** deeply **07** greatly **08** ardently, fiercely, strongly **09** extremely, fervently, like stink **10** profoundly **12** passionately **14** with a vengeance

intensification

05 boost **07** build-up **08** emphasis, increase **09** deepening, intension, worsening **10** building-up, escalation, stepping-up **11** aggravation, enhancement, heightening **12** acceleration, augmentation, exacerbation **13** concentration, magnification, reinforcement, strengthening **14** exacerbescence

intensify

03 fan **04** fire, fuel, whet **05** add to, boost, hot up, raise, widen **06** bump up, deepen, fester, hike up, intend, step up, worsen **07** augment, broaden, build up, enhance, magnify, quicken, sharpen **08** compound, escalate, heighten, increase, maximize **09** aggravate, emphasize, reinforce **10** exacerbate, exaggerate, strengthen **11** concentrate **12** bring to a head

intensity

04 fire, zeal **05** depth, force, power **06** accent, ardour, energy, strain, vigour **07** emotion, fervour, passion, potency, tension **08** fervency, fullness, keenness, severity, strength **09** acuteness, eagerness, extremity, greatness, intension, vehemence **10** enthusiasm, fanaticism, fierceness, profundity **11** earnestness, intenseness **13** concentration

intensive

04 full **05** total **06** all-out **07** in-depth, intense **08** detailed, rigorous, strained, thorough **10** exhaustive **11** unremitting **12** concentrated **13** comprehensive, thoroughgoing

intensively

05 fully **07** closely, totally **09** intensely **10** completely, rigorously, thoroughly **11** extensively **12** exhaustively **15** comprehensively

intent

03 aim, end, set **04** bent, firm, goal, hard, idea, keen, plan, rapt, view **05** alert, close, eager, ettle, fixed, point **06** design, enrapt, object, steady, target **07** earnest, focused, meaning, purpose, wistful **08** absorbed, occupied, resolved, watchful **09** attentive, committed, engrossed, intention, objective, searching, wrapped up **10** determined **11** connotation, preoccupied **13** concentrating

• **to all intents and purposes**
06 almost, nearly **07** morally **08** as good as, in effect **09** in essence, just about, virtually **10** more or less, pretty much, pretty well **11** effectively, practically

intention

03 aim, end **04** goal, hent, idea, plan, view, wish **05** point **06** animus, design, intent, object, target **07** concept, meaning, purpose, thought **08** ambition **09** objective **10** aspiration, attendment, designment **11** attendement

intentional

03 set **05** meant **06** wilful **07** planned, studied, willful, willing **08** designed, intended, prepense, purposed **09** conscious, on purpose, voluntary, weighed-up **10** calculated, considered, deliberate, purposeful, systematic **11** prearranged **12** preconceived, premeditated, systematical

intentionally

08 by design, wilfully **09** advisedly, knowingly, meaningly, on purpose, purposely, willingly **10** designedly, prepensely **11** in cold blood **12** deliberately

intently

04 hard **06** keenly **07** closely, fixedly **08** steadily **09** carefully, earnestly, staringly **10** diligently, watchfully **11** attentively, searchingly

inter

04 bury **05** earth, inurn **06** entomb, inhume **07** inearth **08** inhumate **09** lay to rest, sepulchre

interbreed

03 mix **05** cross **09** hybridize **10** crossbreed, mongrelize **11** miscegenate **14** cross-fertilize

interbreeding

07 syngamy **08** crossing **13** cross-breeding, hybridization, miscegenation

intercede

05 plead, speak **07** beseech, entreat, mediate **08** moderate, petition **09** arbitrate, interpose, intervene, negotiate

intercept

◇ *insertion indicator*
04 stop, take **05** block, catch, check, cut in, delay, seize **06** ambush, arrest, cut off, impede, thwart, waylay **07** deflect, head off **08** obstruct **09** frustrate, interrupt **10** commandeer

interception

◇ *insertion indicator*
06 ambush **07** seizure **08** blocking, checking, stopping **10** cutting-off, deflection, heading-off **11** obstruction

intercession

04 plea **06** agency, prayer **08** advocacy, entreaty, pleading **09** mediation **10** beseeching **11** arbitration, good offices, negotiation **12** intervention, solicitation, supplication **13** interposition **14** interpellation

intercessor

04 mean **05** agent **06** broker, prayer **08** advocate, mediator **09** go-between, middleman, moderator, paraclete **10** arbitrator, negotiator **12** intermediary

interchange

04 swap **05** trade **06** barter, switch **07** permute, replace, reverse, trading **08** crossing, exchange, junction **09** alternate, crossfire, crossroad, interplay, permutate, transpose **10** alternance, crossroads, substitute **11** alternation, give-and-take, reciprocate **12** intersection **13** reciprocation

interchangeability

04 swap **06** barter **08** exchange, synonymy **10** congruence, similarity **11** equivalence, interaction, parallelism, reciprocity **13** comparability, reciprocation **14** correspondence **15** exchangeability, transposability

interchangeable

07 similar, the same **08** fungible, standard **09** identical **10** comparable, equivalent, permutable, reciprocal, synonymous **11** commutative **12** exchangeable, transposable **13** corresponding

interconnect

04 join, link **06** join up **07** network **09** interlink, interlock **10** interweave **11** communicate, interrelate

intercourse

05 trade, trock, troke, truck **07** contact, traffic **08** commerce, congress, converse, dealings **10** connection **11** association **12** conversation **13** communication **14** correspondence

interdependent

06 mutual, two-way **10** correlated, reciprocal **11** interlinked **12** interlocking, interrelated **13** complementary **14** interconnected

interdict

03 ban, bar **04** tabu, veto **05** debar, taboo **06** forbid, outlaw **07** embargo, prevent, rule out **08** disallow, preclude, prohibit **09** proscribe **10** injunction, preclusion **11** prohibition **12** disallowance, interdiction, proscription

interest

03 fad, int **04** care, gain, good, grip, heed, move, note, part, side **05** amuse, bonus, charm, claim, hobby, rivet, share, stake, stock, touch, value **06** absorb, allure, appeal, divert, engage, equity, moment, notice, occupy, profit, regard, return, weight **07** attract, benefit, concern, credits, engross, gravity, involve, pastime, portion, premium, pursuit, revenue, urgency **08** activity, appeal to, business, dividend, intrigue, priority, proceeds, receipts **09** advantage, amusement, attention, captivate, curiosity, diversion, fascinate, magnitude, relevance **10** attraction, engagement, importance, investment, percentage, prominence, recreation **11** consequence, fascination, involvement, seriousness **12** partisanship, significance

13 attentiveness, consideration, participation **15** inquisitiveness
• **in the interests of**
10 on behalf of **12** for the sake of **15** for the benefit of
• **lack of interest**
06 apathy **07** boredom
• **object of interest**
04 lion

interested
04 into, keen **05** hot on **06** intent **07** curious, devoted, engaged, gripped, riveted **08** absorbed, affected, involved **09** attentive, attracted, concerned, engrossed, intrigued **10** captivated, enthralled, fascinated, implicated **12** enthusiastic, having the bug

interesting
05 tasty **07** amusing, amusive, curious, unusual **08** engaging, exciting, gripping, readable, riveting, viewable **09** absorbing, appealing **10** attractive, compelling, compulsive, engrossing, intriguing **11** captivating, fascinating, stimulating **12** entertaining **13** unputdownable

interestingly
09 curiously **10** poignantly **11** ingeniously **12** intriguingly

interfere
03 jam, mar, pry **04** balk, rape **05** abuse, block, check, choke, clash, cramp, grope, upset **06** attack, butt in, feel up, hamper, hinder, impede, meddle, molest, tamper, thwart **07** assault, barge in, inhibit, intrude, touch up, trammel **08** conflict, handicap, intromit, mess with, obstruct, trespass **09** interpose, interrupt, intervene, mess about **10** mess around, muscle in on **11** intermeddle **12** put your bib in, put your oar in **13** get in the way of, poke your bib in, touch sexually **14** poke your nose in, stick your bib in, stick your oar in **15** sexually assault, stick your nose in

interference
03 EMI **05** noise, shash **06** prying, static **07** clutter, trammel **08** blocking, checking, clashing, conflict, handicap, meddling, trammels **09** cross-talk, hampering, hindrance, intrusion, thwarting **10** antagonism, impediment, inhibiting, opposition **11** disturbance, obstruction **12** interruption, intervention, intromission **13** interposition **14** meddlesomeness **15** intermodulation

interfering
04 nosy **05** nosey **06** prying **08** meddling **09** intruding, intrusive **10** meddlesome

interim
06 acting, pro tem **07** stand-in, stopgap **08** interval, meantime **09** caretaker, makeshift, meanwhile,

temporary **10** improvised **11** interregnum, provisional

interior
03 int **04** core, home **05** heart, inner, local **06** centre, depths, hidden, inland, innate, inside, inward, mental, middle, remote, secret **07** central, innards, nucleus, private **08** domestic, internal, intimate, personal **09** emotional, impulsive, innermost, intrinsic, intuitive, spiritual, up-country **10** inside part **11** instinctive, involuntary, spontaneous **13** psychological

interject
03 cry **04** call **05** shout, utter **06** insert, pipe up **07** exclaim, throw in **09** ejaculate, interpose, interrupt, introduce **11** interpolate

interjection
03 cry **04** call **05** shout **09** utterance **11** ejaculation, exclamation **12** interruption **13** interpolation, interposition

interlace
04 knit **05** braid, cross, plait, twine, weave **06** enlace, inlace **07** entrail, entwine, intwine **08** intermix **09** interlock **10** intertwine, interweave, reticulate **11** intersperse **12** interwreathe

interlink
04 knit, link, mesh **07** network **09** intergrow, interlock **10** intertwine, interweave **12** interconnect, link together, lock together **13** clasp together

interlock
04 link, mesh **05** pitch, tooth **06** engage **10** intertwine **12** interconnect, link together, lock together **13** clasp together, interdigitate

interloper
07 invader **08** intruder **10** encroacher, trespasser **11** gatecrasher **14** uninvited guest

interlude
03 jig **04** halt, rest, stop, wait **05** break, delay, let-up, pause, spell **06** hiatus, kyogen, recess, verset **07** respite **08** antimask, breather, entr'acte, interact, interval, stoppage **09** interrupt **10** antimasque **11** parenthesis **12** intermission **14** breathing space, divertissement

intermediary
05 agent **06** broker **08** linguist, mediator **09** comprador, go-between, in-between, middleman **10** arbitrator, compradore, contact man, negotiator

intermediate
03 mid **04** mean **05** mesne **06** medial, median, medium, middle, midway **07** halfway **09** in-between **11** intervening **12** intermediary, transitional

interment
06 burial **07** burying, funeral, obsequy **08** exequies **09** obsequies, sepulture **10** inhumation

interminable
04 dull, long **06** boring, prolix **07** endless, eternal, tedious **08** dragging, infinite **09** boundless, ceaseless, limitless, perpetual, unlimited, wearisome **10** long-winded, loquacious, monotonous, without end **11** everlasting, never-ending **12** long-drawn-out

intermingle
03 mix **04** fuse, lace **05** blend, merge, mix up **06** commix **07** combine **08** intermix **09** commingle, interlace **10** amalgamate, interweave **11** mix together

intermission
04 halt, lull, rest, stop **05** break, let-up, pause **06** recess **07** respite **08** apyrexia, breather, interval, stoppage, suspense, vacation **09** cessation, interlude, remission **10** suspension **12** interruption **14** breathing space

intermittent
06 broken, cyclic, fitful **07** erratic **08** off and on, on and off, periodic, sporadic **09** irregular, spasmodic **10** occasional **11** spasmodical **13** discontinuous

intermittently
08 off and on, on and off **09** sometimes **11** erratically, irregularly **12** occasionally, periodically, sporadically **13** spasmodically **14** from time to time **15** by fits and starts, discontinuously, in fits and starts

intern
04 hold, jail, tiro **05** cadet, pupil **06** detain, inmate, novice **07** confine, learner, recruit, starter, student, trainee **08** beginner, graduate, imprison, newcomer, prentice **10** apprentice **11** probationer **13** hold in custody

internal
03 int **04** home **05** civil, inner, local **06** inside, inward, mental **07** in-house, private **08** domestic, interior, intimate, personal **09** emotional, intrinsic, spiritual **10** subjective **13** psychological

internally
06 inside, within **07** at heart, locally **08** deep down, inwardly, secretly **09** privately **10** to yourself **12** domestically, subjectively **13** deep inside you

international
01 I **03** cap, int **06** global, public **07** general **09** test match, universal, worldwide **12** cosmopolitan

internecine
05 civil, fatal **06** bloody, deadly, family, fierce, mortal **07** ruinous, violent **08** internal **09** murderous **11** destructive **13** exterminating

ternet *see* **computer**

terplay
exchange **11** alternation, give-and-
ke, interaction, interchange
reciprocation, transposition

terpolate
add **05** put in **06** insert
interject, interpose, intersert,
troduce **10** spatchcock
intercalate

terpolation
gag **05** aside **06** insert **08** addition
insertion **12** interjection,
troduction **13** intercalation

terpose
add **05** cut in, put in **06** butt in, chip
horn in, insert, step in, strike
barge in, intrude, mediate, stickle
interlay, intermit, muscle in, strike in,
rust in **09** arbitrate, intercede,
terfere, interject, interpone,
terrupt, intervene, introduce **10** put
tween **11** come between,
terpolate **12** place between, put
ur oar in **14** poke your nose in

terpret
read, scan, take **05** aread, arede,
lve **06** decode, define, open up,
nder, unfold **07** arreede, clarify,
nster, explain, expound
construe, decipher **09** elucidate,
plicate, make clear, translate
paraphrase, understand **11** make
nse of, rationalize, shed light on
interpretate, throw light on

terpretation
read, rede, spin, take **05** sense
anagoge, anagogy, meaning,
pinion, reading, version **08** analysis,
nstrue, decoding, exegesis
rendering **10** exposition,
pounding, paraphrase
deciphering, elucidation,
planation, explication, performance,
anslation **12** construction
clarification, understanding

terpretative
exegetic **10** expository
explanatory, explicatory,
rmeneutic **12** interpretive
clarificatory

terpreter
lawyer, munshi **07** dobhash,
egete, Latiner **08** dragoman,
ponent, lingster, linguist, linkster,
oonshee, truchman **09** annotator,
positor, expounder **10** elucidator,
guister, textualist, translator
commentator, expositress
hermeneutist, oneirocritic
interpretress, oneiroscopist

terrelate
link **09** interlink, interlock
interweave **11** communicate
interconnect

terrogate
pump, quiz **05** grill **07** debrief,
amine **08** question **12** cross-examine

13 cross-question, give a roasting
14 give a going-over

interrogation
04 quiz **07** inquest, inquiry, pumping
08 grilling, question, quizzing
09 going-over **11** examination,
inquisition, questioning, third degree
14 the third degree

interrogative
07 curious, probing **08** erotetic
09 inquiring, quizzical **11** inquisitive,
questioning **12** catechetical
13 inquisitional, inquisitorial,
interrogatory

interrupt
◇ *insertion indicator*
03 cut, end **04** halt, stop **05** block,
break, cut in, delay **06** butt in, cancel,
chip in, chop in, cut off, heckle, hold up,
snap up, take up **07** barge in, barrack,
break in, chequer, disrupt, disturb,
intrude, suspend **08** cut short,
obstruct, postpone **09** intercept,
interject, interlude, interpose,
intervene, punctuate, take short
10 disconnect **11** interpolate, take up
short **12** put your oar in **13** interfere
with, interjaculate

interruption
◇ *insertion indicator*
03 cut **04** halt, stop **05** break, delay,
hitch, let-up, pause **06** cesure, hiatus,
recess, remark **07** wipeout
08 blocking, breather, interval,
obstacle, power cut, question
09 abatement, barging-in, butting-in,
cessation, cutting-in, hindrance,
interlude, intrusion **10** disruption,
impediment, suspension **11** breaking-
off, disturbance, obstruction
12 interference, interjection,
intermission, solarization
13 disconnection, interpolation
14 discontinuance, interpellation

intersect
03 cut **04** meet **05** cross **06** bisect,
divide **07** overlap **08** converge **09** cut
across, decussate, intervein **10** criss-
cross

intersection
04 edge, meet **06** carfax, carfox,
chiasm, vertex **07** chiasma, meeting
08 crossing, junction **10** crossroads,
roundabout **11** box junction,
interchange **13** traffic circle **15** railway
crossing

intersperse
03 dot **06** pepper, spread **07** scatter
08 dispense, intermix, sprinkle
09 diversify, interlard, interpose,
punctuate **10** distribute

interstice
03 gap **04** gulf, hole, pore, rent, rift,
void **05** blank, chink, cleft, crack,
space **06** areola, breach, cavity,
cranny, divide, lacuna **07** crevice,
opening, orifice **08** aperture,
fracture

intertwine
03 mix **04** coil, knit, lace **05** blend,
braid, cross, plait, pleat, twine, twirl,
twist, weave **06** pleach, writhe
07 connect, entwine **08** empleach,
impleach **09** interlace, interlink,
interwind **10** interweave **12** link
together

interval
03 gap **04** leap, lull, rest, time, wait
05 break, comma, delay, pause, space,
spell **06** period, recess, season
07 interim, opening **08** breather,
distance, meantime **09** in-between,
interlude, meanwhile **10** interspace
11 intervallum, parenthesis
12 intermission **14** breathing space

intervene
04 pass **05** arise, occur **06** befall,
elapse, happen, step in **07** intrude,
mediate **08** separate **09** arbitrate,
intercede, interfere, interrupt,
negotiate **10** come to pass
• **intervene boldly**
02 up

intervening
06 middle **07** between, mediate
09 in-between **11** interjacent,
interposing **12** intercurrent,
intermediate, intervenient

intervention
06 agency **09** intrusion, mediation
10 stepping-in **11** arbitration,
involvement, negotiation
12 intercession, interference,
interruption **13** interposition

interview
03 vet **04** talk, viva **05** grill **06** assess,
talk to **07** examine, meeting
08 audience, dialogue, evaluate, one-
to-one, question, sound out
09 appraisal, encounter, tête-à-tête
10 assessment, conference,
discussion, evaluation **11** interrogate
12 consultation, cross-examine
13 cross-question **15** oral
examination, press conference

interviewer
08 assessor, examiner, reporter
09 appraiser, evaluator **10** inquisitor,
questioner **11** interrogant
12 interlocutor, interrogator,
investigator **13** correspondent

interweave
03 mat, mix **04** coil, knit **05** blend,
braid, cross, plash, twine, twist, weave
06 raddle, splice, tissue **07** connect,
entwine, perplex **08** complect
09 interlace, interlink, interlock,
interwind, interwork **10** criss-cross,
intertwine, intertwist, reticulate
11 intermingle, intertangle
12 interconnect, interwreathe, link
together

intestinal
05 ileac **07** coeliac, enteric, gastric
08 duodenal, internal, visceral
09 abdominal, stomachic
10 splanchnic

intestines
04 guts 05 colon, offal 06 bowels, casing, vitals 07 innards, insides, viscera 08 entrails 09 chidlings, chitlings 11 chitterling 12 chitterlings

intimacy
06 warmth 07 privacy 09 affection, closeness, connexion, knowledge 10 confidence, connection, friendship, inwardness 11 camaraderie, familiarity 13 understanding

intimate
03 pal 04 boon, chum, cosy, cozy, dear, deep, hint, mate, maty, near, pack, snug, tell, tosh, warm 05 bosom, buddy, chief, china, close, crony, imply, matey, pally, palsy, privy, state, thick, tight 06 allude, belamy, chummy, friend, impart, intime, inward, secret, signal, strict, throng 07 Achates, comrade, declare, gremial, in-depth, private, special, suggest 08 alter ego, announce, detailed, familiar, friendly, indicate, informal, internal, personal, profound, thorough 09 associate, cherished, confidant, gemütlich, innermost, insinuate, make known, welcoming 10 best friend, better half, confidante, deep-seated, exhaustive, give notice, palsy-walsy 11 bosom friend, cater-cousin, close friend, communicate, penetrating 12 affectionate, confidential, fidus Achates, heart-to-heart, let it be known 13 boon companion 14 well-acquainted

See also **friend**

intimately
04 well 05 fully 06 deeply, nearly, warmly 07 closely 08 commonly, in detail, tenderly 09 inside out, privately 10 familiarly, personally, thoroughly 11 confidingly, hand in glove 12 exhaustively, hand and glove, particularly 14 affectionately, confidentially

intimation
04 hint, note 05 sniff 06 notice, signal 07 inkling, warning 08 allusion, innuendo, reminder 09 reference, statement 10 indication, suggestion 11 declaration, implication, insinuation 12 announcement 13 communication

intimidate
03 cow 05 alarm, appal, bully, daunt, get at, scare 06 coerce, compel, dismay, extort, lean on, menace, subdue 07 overawe, terrify, warn off 08 ballyrag, browbeat, bulldoze, bullyrag, domineer, frighten, pressure, psych out, threaten 09 blackmail, terrorize, tyrannize 10 pressurize 13 turn the heat on 14 put the screws on

intimidation
04 fear 06 screws, terror 07 menaces, threats 08 big stick, bullying, coercion, pressure 10 compulsion, terrifying 11 arm-twisting, browbeating,

domineering, frighteners, frightening, terrorizing, threatening 12 scare tactics 13 sabre-rattling, terrorization, tyrannization

intolerable
05 awful 06 the end, too bad 08 dreadful, the limit 09 loathsome 10 detestable, impossible, unbearable 11 unendurable 12 insufferable, the last straw, unacceptable 13 beyond the pale, insupportable

intolerably
10 impossibly, shockingly, unbearably 11 repugnantly 12 insufferably, outrageously

intolerance
06 ageism, racism, sexism 07 bigotry 08 jingoism 09 dogmatism, extremism, prejudice, racialism 10 chauvinism, fanaticism, impatience, insularity, narrowness, xenophobia 12 anti-Semitism, illiberality 14 discrimination 15 small-mindedness

intolerant
06 ageist, biased, narrow, racist, sexist 07 bigoted, insular, redneck 08 dogmatic, one-sided, partisan 09 extremist, fanatical, illiberal, impatient, parochial, racialist 10 jingoistic, prejudiced, provincial, xenophobic 11 anti-Semitic, opinionated, persecuting, small-minded 12 chauvinistic, incompatible, narrow-minded, uncharitable 14 discriminating

intonation
02 Om 04 lilt, tone 05 pitch, twang 06 stress, timbre 07 cadence 08 emphasis 10 expression, inflection, modulation 12 accentuation

intone
03 say 04 sing 05 chant, croon, speak, utter, voice 06 chaunt, incant, recite 07 declaim 08 intonate, monotone 09 enunciate, pronounce 10 cantillate

intoxicate
◇ *anagram indicator*
04 corn 05 elate 06 excite, fuddle, poison, sozzle, thrill 07 animate, enthuse, inflame, inspire, stupefy 08 befuddle, disguise 09 inebriate, make drunk, stimulate 10 exhilarate

intoxicated
◇ *anagram indicator*
04 full, high, inky, winy 05 drunk, happy, inked, lit up, merry, moppy, moved, tight, tipsy, winey, woozy 06 blotto, bombed, canned, corked, elated, groggy, in wine, jarred, juiced, loaded, mortal, ripped, soused, stewed, stinko, stoned, tiddly, wasted, zonked 07 bevvied, blasted, blitzed, bonkers, bottled, coked-up, crocked, drunken, ebriate, ebriose, excited, half-cut, in drink, legless, maggoty, pickled, pie-eyed, sloshed, smashed, sozzled, squiffy, stirred, tiddled, wrecked 08 besotted, bibulous, ebriated,

footless, hammered, in liquor, juiced up, liquored, moon-eyed, sow-drunk, steaming, stocious, tanked up, thrilled, whiffled, whistled, worked up 09 crapulent, inebriate, paralytic, pixilated, plastered, shickered, up the pole, well-oiled, zonked out 10 blind drunk, inebriated, obfuscated, pixillated, stimulated, whiskified 11 carried away, exhilarated, whiskeyfied 12 drunk as a lord, drunk as a newt, enthusiastic, roaring drunk 13 drunk as a piper, having had a few, i high spirits, under the table 14 Brahms and Liszt 15 one over the eight, the worse for wear, under the weather

See also **drunk**

intoxicating
05 heady 06 moving, strong 07 rousing 08 dramatic, exciting, stirring 09 alcoholic, inebriant, inspiring, methystic, stimulant, thrillin 11 enthralling, stimulating 12 exhilarating 15 going to your head

intoxication
06 fuddle, thrill 07 elation, rapture 08 euphoria, methysis, pleasure 09 animation, inebriety, poisoning, temulence, temulency, tipsiness 10 alcoholism, crapulence, debauchery, dipsomania, enthusiasm, excitement, insobriety 11 drunkenness, inebriation, stimulation 12 bibulousness, exhilaration, hard drinking, intemperance 15 serious drinking

intractability
08 obduracy 09 obstinacy 10 perversity 11 awkwardness, waywardness 12 contrariness, indiscipline, perverseness, stubbornness 13 pig-headedness, unamenability 15 incorrigibility, ungovernability

intractable
04 hard, wild 05 tough 06 kittle, unruly, wilful 07 awkward, frampal, haggard, problem, unwayed, wayward 08 contrary, frampold, obdurate, perverse, stubborn 09 difficult, fractious, obstinate, pig-headed, unbending 10 headstrong, monolithic refractory, self-willed, unamenable, unyielding 11 disobedient, untreatabl 12 cantankerous, cross-grained, intransigent, ungovernable, unmanageable 13 unco-operative, undisciplined 14 uncontrollable

intransigence
08 obduracy, tenacity 09 toughness 10 obstinacy 12 stubbornness 13 determination, implacability, inflexibility, pig-headedness 14 intractability, relentlessness

intransigent
05 rigid, tough 06 uppity 08 hardline, obdurate, stubborn 09 immovable, obstinate, pig-headed, tenacious, unbending 10 determined,

mplacable, inexorable, inflexible, relentless, unamenable, unyielding **11** intractable, unbudgeable, unrelenting **12** bloody-minded **13** unpersuadable **14** irreconcilable, uncompromising

intrepid
04 bold **05** brave, gutsy **06** daring, gritty, heroic, plucky, spunky **07** doughty, gallant, valiant **08** fearless, spirited, stalwart, unafraid, valorous **09** audacious, dauntless, undaunted **10** courageous, undismayed **11** lion-hearted, unflinching **12** stout-hearted

intrepidness
04 grit, guts **05** nerve, pluck **06** daring, spirit, valour **07** bravery, courage, heroism, prowess **08** audacity, boldness **09** fortitude, gallantry **11** doughtiness, intrepidity **12** fearlessness **13** dauntlessness, undauntedness **15** lion-heartedness

intricacy
06 enigma **09** obscurity **10** complexity, involution, knottiness, perplexity **11** complexness, convolution, involvement **12** complication, convolutions, entanglement **13** complexedness, elaborateness, intricateness **14** sophistication

intricate
◊ *anagram indicator*
05 dedal, fancy **06** daedal, knotty, ornate, rococo, twisty **07** complex, finicky, Gordian, tangled **08** baffling, intrince, involved, puzzling, ravelled, tortuous **09** Byzantine, contrived, difficult, elaborate, enigmatic, entangled **10** convoluted, perplexing **11** complicated **12** intrinsicate, tirlie-wirlie **13** sophisticated

intrigue
03 web **04** draw, pack, plot, pull, ruse, wile **05** amour, cabal, charm, dodge, junta, rivet **06** absorb, affair, brigue, puzzle, scheme **07** affaire, attract, connive, consult, liaison, romance, traffic **08** artifice, collogue, conspire, interest, intimacy, trickery **09** captivate, collusion, conniving, fascinate, gallantry, machinate, manoeuvre, stratagem, tantalize, undermine **10** conspiracy, courtcraft, dirty trick, love affair, manipulate **11** beguilement, machination **12** machinations **13** double-dealing, sharp practice, work the oracle **15** practise against

intriguer
06 Jesuit **07** plotter, schemer, wangler **08** conniver **09** intrigant, trinketer **10** intrigante, machinator, politician, wire-puller **11** conspirator **12** collaborator **13** Machiavellian, wheeler-dealer

intriguing
07 politic **08** charming, exciting, puzzling, riveting **09** absorbing, appealing, beguiling, diverting, stairwork **10** attractive, compelling **11** captivating, fascinating, interesting, tantalizing, titillating

intrinsic
05 basic **06** inborn, inbred, inward, native **07** built-in, central, genuine, in-built, natural, radical **08** inherent, integral, interior, internal **09** elemental, essential **10** congenital, indigenous, underlying **11** fundamental **14** constitutional

intrinsically
08 in itself, inwardly **09** basically, centrally **10** inherently, integrally **11** essentially **12** by definition **13** constituently, fundamentally

introduce
◊ *containment indicator*
03 add **04** open **05** begin, float, found, immit, offer, plant, put in, start **06** induct, inject, insert, launch, lead in, prolog, submit **07** advance, bring in, develop, precede, preface, present, propose, suggest, usher in **08** acquaint, announce, commence, initiate, intromit, lead into, organize, prologue **09** establish, instigate, institute, originate **10** inaugurate, put forward **11** familiarize, put in motion, set in motion
• **be introduced to**
04 meet

introduction
◊ *head selection indicator*
05 debut, intro, proem, start **06** basics, entrée, launch, lead-in **07** baptism, opening, preface, prelude **08** exordium, foreword, overture, preamble, prologue **09** beginning, knock-down, rudiments **10** essentials, initiation **11** acquainting, development, front matter, institution, origination, prolegomena **12** announcement, commencement, fundamentals, inauguration, intromission, organization, presentation, prolegomenon **13** establishment, preliminaries **15** familiarization, first principles

introductory
05 basic, early, first **07** initial, opening **08** exordial, isagogic, starting **09** beginning, essential, inaugural, prefatory, prelusory **10** elementary, initiative, initiatory, precursory **11** fundamental, preliminary, preparatory, rudimentary

introspection
08 brooding **11** navel-gazing, pensiveness **12** introversion, self-analysis **13** contemplation, soul-searching **14** heart-searching, thoughtfulness **15** self-centredness, self-examination, self-observation

introspective
06 musing **07** pensive **08** brooding, reserved **09** withdrawn **10** meditative, subjective, thoughtful **11** introverted,

self-centred **12** self-absorbed **13** contemplative, inward-looking, self-analysing, self-examining, self-observing

introverted
03 shy **05** quiet **08** reserved **09** withdrawn **11** self-centred **12** self-absorbed **13** introspective, inward-looking, self-examining

intrude
04 sorn **05** abate **06** butt in, chip in, invade, meddle, thrust **07** aggress, barge in, impinge, obtrude, violate **08** encroach, infringe, trespass **09** gatecrash, interfere, interject, interlope, interrupt

intruder
05 thief **06** raider, robber **07** burglar, invader, prowler **08** Derby dog, pilferer **10** interloper, trespasser **11** gatecrasher, infiltrator **12** housebreaker **14** unwelcome guest

intrusion
04 vein **08** invasion, lopolith, meddling, trespass **09** incursion, obtrusion, phacolith, violation **12** encroachment, gatecrashing, impertinence, impertinency, infringement, interference, interruption

intrusive
04 nosy **05** nosey, pushy **06** prying **07** forward **08** annoying, intruded, invasive, snooping, unwanted **09** go-getting, obtrusive, officious, uninvited, unwelcome **10** disturbing, irritating, meddlesome **11** impertinent, importunate, interfering, trespassing, troublesome, uncalled-for **12** interrupting, presumptuous

intuition
03 ESP **05** hunch **06** belief **07** feeling, insight **08** instinct **10** gut feeling, perception, sixth sense **11** discernment, premonition **12** anticipation, presentiment **13** light of nature

intuitive
06 inborn, innate **08** untaught, visceral **09** automatic, unlearned **11** instinctive, intuitional, involuntary, spontaneous

intuitively
08 innately **10** by instinct **13** automatically, instinctively, spontaneously

inundate
04 bury, soak **05** drown, flood, swamp **06** deluge, engulf **07** immerse, overrun **08** overflow, saturate, submerge **09** overwhelm **10** overburden

inundation
04 glut **05** flood, spate, swamp **06** deluge, excess **07** surplus, torrent **08** diluvian, diluvium, overflow **09** land-flood, tidal wave **10** water flood

inure
03 use **05** flesh, train **06** commit, harden, season, temper **07** toughen **08** accustom, practise **09** habituate **10** strengthen **11** acclimatize, desensitize, familiarize

invade
◇ *insertion indicator*
04 raid **05** enter, seize, storm **06** attack, infest, maraud, occupy **07** assault, burst in, conquer, intrude, obtrude, overrun, pervade, pillage, plunder, violate **08** encroach, infringe, take over, trespass **09** descend on, interrupt, march into, penetrate, swarm over **10** infiltrate **12** enter by force

invader
04 Dane **06** raider **08** attacker, intruder, marauder, pillager **09** aggressor, assailant, infringer, plunderer **10** trespasser

invalid
◇ *anagram indicator*
03 ill **04** null, sick, void, weak **05** false, frail, wrong **06** ailing, feeble, infirm, poorly, sickly, unwell **07** chronic, expired, illegal, patient, quashed, revoked, unsound **08** baseless, disabled, informal, mistaken, sufferer **09** abolished, bedridden, cancelled, erroneous, illogical, incorrect, nullified, rescinded, unfounded, untenable, worthless **10** fallacious, groundless, ill-founded, irrational, overturned **11** debilitated, inoperative, null and void, unjustified, unwarranted **12** convalescent, unacceptable, unscientific **14** valetudinarian **15** unsubstantiated

invalidate
04 undo, veto, void **05** annul, avoid, quash **06** cancel, negate, revoke, weaken **07** nullify, rescind, vitiate **08** abrogate, overrule **09** discredit, overthrow, terminate, undermine

invalidity
07 fallacy, falsity, sophism **08** voidness **11** unsoundness **12** illogicality, speciousness **13** inconsistency, incorrectness, irrationality **14** fallaciousness

invaluable
06 costly, useful **07** crucial **08** critical, precious, valuable **09** priceless **11** inestimable **12** incalculable **13** indispensable

invariable
03 set **05** fixed, rigid **06** stable, steady **07** regular, uniform **08** constant, habitual **09** immutable, invariant, permanent, unvarying **10** changeless, consistent, inflexible, unchanging, unwavering **11** unalterable **12** unchangeable

invariably
06 always **09** regularly **10** constantly, habitually, inevitably, repeatedly **11** unfailingly, without fail **12** consistently

invasion
04 raid **05** foray **06** attack, breach, sepsis **07** descent **08** Overlord, storming **09** incursion, intrusion, irruption, offensive, onslaught, violation **10** occupation **11** penetration **12** encroachment, infiltration, infringement, interference, interruption

invective
05 abuse **06** rebuke, satire, tirade, verbal **07** censure, obloquy, sarcasm **08** berating, diatribe, reproach, scolding **09** contumely, philippic, reprimand **10** revilement **11** castigation, fulmination **12** denunciation, vilification, vituperation **13** recrimination, tongue-lashing

inveigh
04 rail **05** blame, scold **06** berate, revile **07** censure, condemn, lambast, thunder, upbraid **08** denounce, reproach, sound off **09** castigate, criticize, fulminate **10** tongue-lash, vituperate **11** expostulate, recriminate

inveigle
03 con **04** coax, lure, wile **05** decoy **06** allure, cajole, entice, entrap, lead on, seduce **07** beguile, ensnare, wheedle **08** persuade **09** bamboozle, manoeuvre, sweet-talk **10** manipulate

invent
04 coin, fain, find, mint, plan **05** fable, faine, fayne, feign, frame **06** cook up, create, design, devise, father, make up **07** concoct, dream up, hit upon, imagine, pioneer, think up, trump up **08** conceive, contrive, discover, innovate **09** fabricate, formulate, improvise, originate **10** come up with **11** confabulate, manufacture **12** swing the lead

invented
03 inv **06** made up **09** trumped-up **10** fictitious

invention
◇ *anagram indicator*
03 fib, lie, wit **04** baby, fake, gift, idea, myth **05** skill **06** deceit, design, device, gadget, genius, system, talent **07** coinage, coining, concept, fantasy, fiction, figment, forgery, machine, untruth **08** artistry, creation **09** discovery, falsehood, ingenuity, tall story **10** brainchild, concoction, contriving, creativity, innovation **11** contrivance, development, fabrication, imagination, inspiration, originality, origination **12** construction, contrivement, excogitation **13** falsification, inventiveness **15** resourcefulness

inventive
06 clever, devise, gifted **07** fertile, skilful **08** artistic, contrive, creative, inspired, original, pregnant, talented **09** ingenious **10** innovative **11** imaginative, resourceful

inventiveness
04 gift **05** power, skill **06** talent **10** creativity, enterprise, innovation **11** imagination, inspiration, originality **13** ingeniousness **14** innovativeness **15** imaginativeness, resourcefulness

inventor
05 maker **06** author, coiner, father, framer, mother **07** creator, deviser **08** designer, engineer, producer **09** architect, developer, innovator, scientist, sloganeer **10** discoverer, mind, master, originator **11** emblematist **12** palindromist

Inventors include:

03 Sax (Antoine Joseph)
04 Abel (Sir Frederick), Bell (Alexander Graham), Benz (Karl), Biro (Laszlo), Colt (Samuel), Davy (Sir Humphry), Hood (Thomas), Jobs (Steve), Land (Edwin Herbert), Moon (William), Otis (Elisha Graves), Swan (Sir Joseph Wilson), Tull (Jethro), Watt (James), Yale (Linus)
05 Baird (John Logie), Boehm (Theobald), Boyle (Robert), Cyril (St), Dyson (James), Hertz (Heinrich), Kilby (Jack S), Maxim (Sir Hiram Stevens), Monge (Gaspard), Morse (Samuel), Nobel (Alfred), Rubik (Ernö), Sousa (John Philip), Tesla (Nikola), Volta (Alessandro, Count), Zeiss (Carl)
06 Ampère (André Marie), Brunel (Isambard Kingdom), Brunel (Sir Marc Isambard), Bunsen (Robert Wilhelm), Diesel (Rudolf), Dunlop (John Boyd), Eckert (J Presper), Edison (Thomas Alva), Frisch (Otto), Hansom (Joseph Aloysius), Hornby (Frank), Hubble (Edwin Powell), Lenoir (Jean Joseph Étienne), Lister (Samuel, Lord), McAdam (John Loudon), Napier (John), Newton (Sir Isaac), Pascal (Blaise), Pitman (Sir Isaac), Schick (Jacob), Singer (Isaac Merritt), Sperry (Elmer Ambrose), Talbot (William Henry Fox), Wallis (Sir Barnes), Wright (Orville), Wright (Wilbur)
07 Babbage (Charles), Blériot (Louis), Carlson (Chester Floyd), Daimler (Gottlieb), Drebbel (Cornelis), Eastman (George), Faraday (Michael), Gaumont (Léon), Giffard (Henri), Goddard (Robert Hutchings), Huygens (Christiaan), Jacuzzi (Candido), Janssen (Zacharias), Lumière (Auguste), Lumière (Louis Jean), Marconi (Guglielmo), Mauchly (John W), Maxwell (James Clerk), Pasteur (Louis), Pullman (George Mortimer), Thomson (Elihu), Whitney (Eli), Whittle (Sir Frank)
08 Bessemer (Sir Henry), Birdseye (Clarence), Daguerre (Louis Jacques Mandé), De Forest (Lee), Ericsson (John), Ferranti (Sebastian Ziani de), Franklin (Benjamin), Gillette (King Camp), Goodyear

(Charles), **Huntsman** (Benjamin), **Newcomen** (Thomas), **Sandwich** (John Montagu, Earl), **Sinclair** (Sir Clive), **Zamenhof** (Lazarus Ludwig), **Zeppelin** (Ferdinand von, Count)
09 **Arkwright** (Sir Richard), **Armstrong** (Edwin Howard), **Butterick** (Ebenezer), **Cockerell** (Sir Christopher Sydney), **Ctesibius**, **Fessenden** (Reginald Aubrey), **Gutenberg** (Johannes), **Hollerith** (Herman), **Macmillan** (Kirkpatrick), **McCormick** (Cyrus Hall), **Pinchbeck** (Christopher), **Remington** (Philo), **Whitworth** (Sir Joseph)
10 **Archimedes**, **Berners-Lee** (Tim), **Cristofori** (Bartolommeo), **Fahrenheit** (Gabriel), **Lilienthal** (Otto), **Pilkington** (Sir Alastair), **Senefelder** (Aloys), **Stephenson** (George), **Torricelli** (Evangelista), **Trevithick** (Richard)
11 **Montgolfier** (Jacques), **Montgolfier** (Joseph)
12 **Friese-Greene** (William)

inventory
04 file, list, roll **05** stock, sum up, tally **06** record, roster, scroll, supply **07** account, listing, terrier **08** register, schedule **09** catalogue, checklist, equipment **11** description, stocktaking

inverse
05 other **07** counter, obverse, reverse **08** contrary, converse, inverted, opposite, reversed **10** reciprocal, retrograde, transposed, upside down **12** antistrophic

inversion
◇ *reversal indicator*
07 reverse **08** contrary, converse, opposite, reversal **09** entropion, entropium **10** anastrophe, antithesis, transposal **11** contrariety **13** transposition **14** antimetathesis, contraposition

invert
◇ *reversal indicator*
05 upset **06** turn up, upturn **07** capsize, reverse **08** overturn, turn down **09** transpose **10** homosexual, turn around, turn turtle **11** transsexual **13** turn inside out **14** turn upside down **15** turn back to front

invertebrate
> *Invertebrates include:*
05 coral, fluke, hydra, leech
06 chiton, insect, spider, sponge
07 bivalve, crinoid, mollusc, sea lily, sea wasp
08 arachnid, flatworm, nematode, sea pansy, starfish, tapeworm
09 arthropod, centipede, earthworm, gastropod, jellyfish, millipede, planarian, roundworm, sea spider, sea urchin, spoonworm, trilobite, water bear
10 cephalopod, crustacean, echinoderm, sand dollar, sea anemone, tardigrade
11 annelid worm, brittle star, chaetognath, feather star, sea cucumber
12 box jellyfish, coelenterate, Venus's girdle
13 crown-of-thorns, horseshoe crab, sea gooseberry
15 dead-men's fingers

See also **animal; butterfly; crustacean; insect; mollusc; moth; spider; worm**

invest
◇ *hidden indicator*
◇ *insertion indicator*
03 put **04** belt, fund, give, gown, robe, sink, vest **05** admit, adorn, cover, crown, endow, endue, frock, grant, imbue, place, put in, spend, tie up **06** bestow, clothe, confer, create, devote, enrobe, induct, lay out, lock up, ordain, supply **07** besiege, dignify, empower, entrust, install, mandate, provide, swear in **08** dedicate, sanction, surround **09** authorize, beglamour, subsidize **10** contribute, inaugurate

investigate
03 spy, sus **04** case, comb, feel, sift, suss **05** probe, study, trawl **06** go into, muzzle, nuzzle, pry out, search **07** analyse, check up, examine, explore, inspect, suss out **08** check out, consider, look into, research **09** delve into **10** scrutinize **11** inquire into **15** give the once-over

investigation
05 probe, quest, study **06** review, search, survey **07** enquiry, hearing, inquest, inquiry, sifting, zetetic **08** analysis, research, scrutiny **10** inspection **11** examination, exploration, inquisition **13** consideration
• **bear investigation**
04 wash

investigative
07 zetetic **08** research **09** heuristic **10** analytical, inspecting **11** exploratory, fact-finding, researching **13** investigating

investigator
02 PI **04** dick **06** ferret, prober, sleuth **07** analyst **08** analyser, examiner, explorer, inquirer, quaestor, reviewer, searcher **09** detective, inspector **10** private eye, questioner, researcher, scrutineer **11** scrutinizer

investiture
09 admission, induction, investing **10** coronation, investment, ordination, swearing-in **11** instatement **12** enthronement, inauguration, installation

investment
04 cash, gilt, risk, spec **05** asset, funds, money, stake, stock **06** outlay, wealth **07** capital, finance, reserve, savings, venture **08** blockade, property **09** principal, resources **11** expenditure, investiture,

speculation, transaction **12** contribution **14** venture capital

inveterate
05 sworn **06** inured **07** chronic, diehard **08** addicted, habitual, hard-core, hardened, stubborn **09** confirmed, incurable, obstinate **10** double-dyed, entrenched **11** established **12** incorrigible, irreformable, long-standing **13** dyed-in-the-wool

invidious
06 odious **07** awkward, hateful **08** enviable **09** difficult, obnoxious, offensive, repugnant, slighting **10** unpleasant **11** undesirable **13** objectionable **14** discriminating, discriminatory

invigilate
05 watch **06** direct **07** inspect, monitor, oversee **09** look after, supervise, watch over **11** keep an eye on, superintend **12** be in charge of **13** be in control of

invigilation
04 care **06** charge **07** control, running **08** guidance **09** direction, oversight **10** inspection **11** supervision **12** surveillance **15** superintendence

invigilator
07 monitor, proctor **08** director, examiner, overseer **09** inspector **10** supervisor **14** superintendent

invigorate
04 buck **05** brace, pep up, renew, rouse **06** buck up, excite, perk up, soup up **07** animate, enliven, fortify, freshen, inspire, liven up, quicken, refresh **08** energize, motivate, vitalize **09** stimulate **10** exhilarate, rejuvenate, revitalize, strengthen

invigorating
05 brisk, fresh, tonic, vital **07** bracing **08** generous **09** animating, healthful, uplifting, vivifying **10** energizing, fortifying, life-giving, quickening, refreshing, salubrious **11** inspiriting, restorative, stimulating **12** exhilarating, rejuvenating

invincibility
05 force, power **08** strength **13** inviolability **14** impregnability, insuperability **15** impenetrability, invulnerability, unassailability

invincible
08 almighty **10** unbeatable, unshakable, unyielding **11** all-powerful, impregnable, indomitable, insuperable, unshakeable **12** impenetrable, invulnerable, unassailable, undefeatable **13** unconquerable **14** indestructible, unsurmountable

inviolability
08 holiness, sanctity **09** inviolacy **10** sacredness **14** inalienability, inviolableness, sacrosanctness **15** invulnerability

inviolable
04 holy **06** sacred **08** hallowed
10 intemerate, sacrosanct
11 inalienable, unalterable, untouchable

inviolate
04 pure **05** whole **06** entire, intact,
sacred, unhurt, virgin **08** complete,
unbroken, unharmed **09** stainless,
undamaged, undefiled, uninjured,
unspoiled, unstained, unsullied,
untouched **10** intemerate, unpolluted,
unprofaned **11** undisturbed

invisible
05 blind **06** hidden, unseen
08 viewless **09** concealed, disguised,
imaginary, occulting, sightless,
unnoticed, unseeable **10** evaporated,
out of sight, unobserved
11 microscopic, non-existent
12 undetectable **13** imperceivable,
imperceptible, inconspicuous,
indiscernible, infinitesimal,
microscopical **14** dematerialized

invitation
04 bait, call, draw, lure **06** appeal,
come-on, invite **07** bidding, request,
summons, welcome **08** overture,
petition **09** challenge **10** allurement,
attraction, come-hither, enticement,
incitement, inducement, temptation
11 proposition, provocation
12 solicitation **13** encouragement

invite
03 ask, bid, woo **04** call, draw, lead,
seek, will **05** press, tempt **06** allure,
appeal, ask for, entice, summon
07 attract, bring on, look for, provoke,
request, solicit, welcome **08** have
over, petition **09** encourage, entertain,
have round **15** give the come-on to

inviting
07 winning **08** alluring, engaging,
enticing, pleasant, pleasing, tempting
09 agreeable, appealing, beguiling,
seductive, welcoming **10** attractive,
bewitching, come-hither, delightful,
enchanting, entrancing, intriguing
11 captivating, fascinating, tantalizing
12 irresistible

invocation
04 call **05** curse **06** appeal, prayer
07 request, summons **08** entreaty,
petition **09** epiclesis **10** beseeching
11 benediction, conjuration,
imploration **12** solicitation, supplication
• **expression of invocation**
02 io

invoice
03 inv **04** bill **07** account, charges
08 manifest, pro forma **09** reckoning

invoke
03 beg **04** cite, wish **05** curse, swear
06 call on, pray to, rabbit, turn to
07 beseech, conjure, entreat, implore,
refer to, request, solicit, swear by
08 appeal to, call down, call upon,
petition, resort to **09** deprecate,
imprecate, make use of **10** supplicate
14 have recourse to

involuntary
05 blind **06** forced, reflex **07** coerced
08 knee-jerk, unwilled **09** automatic,
compelled, impulsive, mandatory,
reluctant, unwilling **10** compulsory,
mechanical, obligatory, unthinking
11 conditioned, instinctive,
spontaneous, unconscious
12 uncontrolled **13** unintentional

involve
◇ *anagram indicator*
◇ *insertion indicator*
03 mix **04** cost, grip, hold, mean, wind,
wrap **05** cover, imply, infer, mix up,
rivet **06** absorb, affect, assume,
commit, denote, draw in, engage,
entail, mess in, occupy, take in
07 concern, connect, connote, count
in, dip into, embrace, embroil, engross,
immerse, include, require **08** entangle,
interest, mess with, walk into
09 associate, embarrass, encompass,
implicate, inculpate, preoccupy
10 complicate, comprehend,
compromise, presuppose
11 incorporate, incriminate,
necessitate **15** cause to take part

involved
◇ *anagram indicator*
04 deep, held, in on **06** implex, knotty
07 complex, engaged, gripped,
jumbled, mixed up, riveted, tangled
08 absorbed, caught up, confused,
immersed, intorted, involute,
occupied, plighted, tortuous
09 concerned, confusing, difficult,
elaborate, engrossed, intricate
10 associated, convoluted, implicated,
inculpated, interested, taking part
11 anfractuous, complicated,
preoccupied **12** incriminated,
inextricable **13** participating
• **involved with**
◇ *insertion indicator*
02 in

involvement
04 part **05** share **06** action
07 concern **08** interest **09** immersion
10 attachment, connection
11 association, implication
12 contribution, entanglement
13 participation **14** responsibility

invulnerability
05 proof **06** safety **08** security,
strength **13** invincibility, inviolability
14 impregnability **15** impenetrability,
unassailability

invulnerable
04 safe **05** proof **06** secure
09 woundless **10** impervious,
invincible **12** impenetrable,
unassailable **14** indestructible

inward
02 in **05** inner **06** entire, hidden, infelt,
inmost, inside, secret, toward
07 private **08** entering, homefelt,
incoming, interior, internal, intimate,
introrse, involute, personal, turned-in
09 heartfelt, incurrent, innermost,
intrinsic **11** intrinsical **12** confidential

inwardly
04 inly **06** inside, within **07** at heart
08 deep down, secretly **09** privately
10 to yourself **13** deep inside you

inwards
06 inside, inward, within **07** indoors
08 inwardly

iodine
01 I

iota
03 bit, jot, tad **04** atom, hint, mite, whit
05 grain, scrap, speck, trace **06** morsel
08 fraction, particle

Iowa
02 IA

Iran
02 IR **03** IRN

Iraq
03 IRQ

irascibility
06 choler **08** edginess **09** bad temper,
crossness, fieriness, ill-temper,
petulance, shortness, testiness
10 crabbiness, impatience, irritation,
touchiness **12** irritability,
snappishness

irascible
05 cross, hasty, narky, ratty, testy
06 crabby, touchy **07** crabbed,
iracund, prickly, toustie **08** choleric,
petulant **09** irritable, querulous **10** ill-
natured **11** bad-tempered, hot-
tempered, ill-tempered
12 cantankerous, iracundulous
13 quick-tempered, short-tempered

irate
03 mad **04** waxy **05** angry, livid, vexed
06 fuming, raging **07** annoyed,
enraged, furious, ranting **08** incensed,
up in arms, worked up **09** indignant,
irritated, pissed off, steamed up
10 hopping mad, infuriated
11 exasperated

irately
07 angrily, crossly, in a huff **08** bitterly
09 furiously **11** indignantly, resentfully
13 acrimoniously, reproachfully

ire
04 fury, rage **05** anger, wrath
06 choler **07** passion **09** annoyance
11 displeasure, indignation
12 exasperation

Ireland
03 IRL **04** Éire, Erin **08** Hibernia
09 Green Isle **11** blarney-land, Emerald
Isle

*Irish cities and notable towns
include:*

04 Cork
05 Sligo
06 Dublin, Galway
07 Dundalk
08 Drogheda, Limerick
09 Waterford

See also **county**; **province**

ridescent

4 shot 06 flambé, pearly 07 rainbow
8 dazzling 09 chatoyant, prismatic,
sparkling 10 glittering, opalescent,
shimmering, variegated 11 rainbow-
ke 13 multicoloured, polychromatic
5 rainbow-coloured

ridium

2 Ir

ris

3 lis, seg 04 flag, irid, ixia 05 orris,
edge 07 gladdon 09 water flag
0 fleur-de-lis, fleur-de-lys 12 flower-
elice, flower-deluce 13 flower-de-
euce 14 roast-beef plant

rish

2 Ir 04 Erse 08 Milesian
9 Hibernian
ee also **Ireland**

Irish first names include:

3 Ena, Kit, Pat, Una
4 Aine, Cait, Colm, Edel, Elva, Eoin,
Erin, Euan, Ewan, Ewen, Finn, Kath,
Kyra, Liam, Maev, Maud, Mona,
Neal, Neil, Nola, Nora, Nora, Owen,
Rory, Ryan, Sean, Sine, Tara
5 Aidan, Aiden, Barry, Brona, Cahal,
Ciara, Colum, Conor, Duane,
Dwane, Elvis, Ethna, Ethne, Fionn,
Kelly, Kerry, Kevan, Kevin, Kiera,
Maeve, Maire, Maude, Maura,
Moira, Moyra, Neale, Niall, Niamh,
Norah, Norah, Nuala, Oscar, Paddy,
Ronan, Rowan, Shane, Shaun,
Shawn, Ultan
6 Aileen, Ailish, Arthur, Cathal, Ciaran,
Connor, Declan, Dervla, Dympna,
Eamonn, Eamunn, Eileen, Eithna,
Eithne, Finbar, Fingal, Finola, Finola,
Fintan, Garret, Grania, Granya,
Kieran, Kieron, Kilian, Lorcan,
Noreen, Noreen, Roisin, Seamas,
Seamus, Shamus, Sheila, Sinead,
Sorcha, Tyrone
7 Aisling, Brendan, Bronach, Bronagh,
Caitlin, Christy, Clodagh, Colleen,
Deirdre, Desmond, Dymphna,
Feargal, Finbarr, Grainne, Killian,
Mairead, Maureen, Padraic,
Padraig, Patrick, Shannon, Shelagh,
Siobhan
8 Kathleen, Ruaidhri
9 Fionnuala, Fionnuala

rk

3 bug, get, vex 04 gall, miff, rile
5 anger, annoy, get at, get to, weary
6 needle, nettle, put out, ruffle, wind
up 07 disgust, incense, provoke
8 distress, drive mad, irritate
9 aggravate, infuriate 10 drive crazy,
exasperate 12 drive bananas 13 make
sparks fly 14 drive up the wall, piss
someone off

rksome

6 boring, trying, vexing 07 painful,
tedious 08 annoying, infernal,
tiresome 09 vexatious, wearisome
10 bothersome, burdensome,
confounded, irritating, ungrateful

11 aggravating, infuriating,
troublesome 12 disagreeable,
exasperating

iron

02 Fe 04 airn, firm, hard, Mars
05 harsh, press, rigid, stern, tough
06 fetter, pistol, robust, smooth, steely,
strong 07 adamant, flatten, grating,
stirrup 08 decrease, revolver, strength
10 determined, inflexible 11 insensitive
14 uncompromising

• iron out

06 settle 07 clear up, resolve, sort out
08 deal with, get rid of, put right
09 eliminate, eradicate, harmonize,
reconcile 13 straighten out

ironic, ironical

03 wry 04 rich 05 bland 07 mocking
08 derisive, sardonic, scoffing,
scornful, sneering 09 sarcastic,
satirical 10 ridiculing, ridiculous
11 paradoxical 12 antiphrastic,
contemptuous 14 antiphrastical

irons

05 bonds 06 chains 07 fetters
08 manacles, shackles, trammels

irony

04 hard 05 scorn 06 satire 07 asteism,
mockery, paradox, sarcasm 08 ridicule
10 enantiosis 11 antiphrasis,
incongruity 12 contrariness 14 sting in
the tail

irradiate

06 expose, illume 07 lighten, light up,
radiate, shine on 08 brighten, illumine
09 enlighten 10 illuminate

irrational

04 surd, wild 05 brute, crazy, silly
06 absurd, phobic, unwise 07 brutish,
foolish, invalid, unsound 08 paranoid
09 arbitrary, beastlike, illogical,
senseless 10 groundless, ridiculous
11 implausible, nonsensical,
unreasoning 12 inconsistent,
unreasonable 14 beside yourself

irrationality

06 lunacy 07 madness 08 insanity,
unreason 09 absurdity
11 unsoundness 12 illogicality
13 senselessness 14 groundlessness,
ridiculousness

irreconcilable

05 alien 06 at odds 07 opposed
08 clashing, contrary, frondeur,
hardline, opposite 10 implacable, in
conflict, inexorable, inflexible,
unatonable 11 conflicting,
incongruous 12 incompatible,
inconsistent, intransigent
13 contradictory, intransigeant
14 uncompromising

irrecoverable

04 lost 09 unsavable 11 irreparable
12 irredeemable, irremediable
13 irreclaimable, irretrievable,
unrecoverable, unsalvageable

irredeemable

08 past hope 09 incurable 10 beyond

hope 11 irreparable, irrevocable
12 incorrigible 13 irretrievable

irrefutable

04 sure 07 certain 08 decisive,
definite, positive 10 unarguable,
undeniable 11 beyond doubt,
indubitable 12 indisputable,
unanswerable 13 incontestable
14 beyond question, unquestionably

irregular

◇ *anagram indicator*
03 odd 04 bent, iffy 05 bumpy, false,
fishy, freak, lumpy, rough, shady, shaky
06 fitful, haiduk, jagged, patchy, pitted,
ragged, random, rugged, shifty, sniper,
uneven 07 corrupt, crooked, devious,
erratic, lawless, scraggy, snatchy,
strange, unusual, wayward
08 aberrant, abnormal, cheating,
improper, indecent, lopsided, partisan,
peculiar, scraggly, sporadic, unsteady,
variable, wavering 09 anomalous,
deceitful, dishonest, guerrilla,
haphazard, incondite, maquisard,
spasmodic, terrorist 10 asymmetric,
asyntactic, disorderly, fraudulent,
immoderate, mendacious, occasional,
out of order, perfidious, scraggling,
unofficial, unorthodox 11 anomalistic,
bushwhacker, duplicitous, exceptional,
extravagant, fluctuating, fragmentary,
franc-tireur, guerrillero, heteroclite
12 disorganized, disreputable,
immethodical, inconsistent,
intermittent, unmethodical,
unprincipled, unscrupulous,
unsystematic 13 against the law,
anomalistical, dishonourable,
extraordinary, unsymmetrical
14 freedom fighter, unconventional
15 against the rules

irregularity

05 fraud, freak, spasm 06 breach,
deceit, oddity 07 anomaly, falsity,
perfidy 08 cheating, trickery, wavering
09 arhythmia, asymmetry, bumpiness,
chicanery, deviation, duplicity,
falsehood, improbity, lumpiness,
obliquity, roughness, shadiness,
treachery 10 aberration, arrhythmia,
corruption, dirty trick, dishonesty,
fitfulness, jaggedness, misconduct,
patchiness, raggedness, randomness,
unevenness 11 abnormality,
criminality, crookedness, fluctuation,
fraudulence, impropriety, inconstancy,
insincerity, lawlessness, malpractice,
obliqueness, peculiarity, singularity,
uncertainty, unorthodoxy,
unusualness, variability
12 eccentricity, inordination,
lopsidedness, perturbation,
unsteadiness 13 double-dealing,
haphazardness, inconsistency,
intermittence, sharp practice,
unpunctuality 14 disorderliness,
occasionalness, untruthfulness
15 disorganization

irregularly

06 anyhow 07 jerkily 08 fitfully, off
and on, unevenly 11 erratically,

haphazardly, now and again **12** here and there, occasionally **13** eccentrically, interruptedly, spasmodically **14** disconnectedly, intermittently, unmethodically **15** by fits and starts, in fits and starts

irrelevance
07 tangent **09** inaptness **10** digression, red herring **11** irrelevancy **12** unimportance **13** inconsequence, unrelatedness **14** extraneousness, inappositeness **15** inapplicability

irrelevant
05 inapt, inept **09** not matter, ungermane, unrelated **10** extraneous, immaterial, inapposite, irrelative, out of place, peripheral, tangential **11** off the point, unconnected, unimportant **12** inapplicable, inconsequent **13** beside the mark, inappropriate **14** beside the point **15** having no bearing, not coming into it

irreligious
05 pagan **06** sinful, unholy, wicked **07** godless, heathen, impious, profane, ungodly **08** agnostic, undevout **09** atheistic, heretical, sceptical **10** heathenish, irreverent **11** blasphemous, nullifidian, unbelieving, unreligious, unrighteous **12** free-thinking, iconoclastic, sacrilegious **13** rationalistic

irremediable
05 fatal, final **06** deadly, mortal **08** hopeless, terminal **09** incurable **10** inoperable, remediless **11** irreparable **12** incorrigible, irredeemable, irreversible **13** irrecoverable, irretrievable, unmedicinable

irremovable
03 set **04** fast **05** fixed, stuck **06** rooted **07** durable **08** obdurate **09** immovable, ingrained, obstinate, permanent **10** inoperable, persistent **12** ineradicable **14** indestructible

irreparable
09 incurable **12** irremediable, irreversible, unrepairable **13** irreclaimable, irrecoverable, irretrievable

irreplaceable
05 vital **06** unique **07** special **08** peerless, precious **09** essential, matchless, priceless, unmatched **13** indispensable

irrepressible
06 bubbly, lively **07** buoyant **08** animated **09** ebullient, energetic, resilient, vivacious **10** boisterous **11** uninhibited, unstoppable **12** effervescent, ungovernable **13** uncontainable **14** insuppressible, uncontrollable, unrestrainable

irreproachable
04 pure **07** perfect, sinless **08** flawless, innocent, spotless **09** blameless, faultless, guiltless,

stainless **10** immaculate, impeccable, unblamable **11** unblemished **13** unimpeachable **14** beyond reproach **15** irreprehensible

irresistible
06 potent, urgent **07** killing **08** alluring, almighty, charming, enticing, forceful, pressing, tempting **09** ravishing, seductive **10** compelling, compulsive, enchanting, imperative, importable, inevitable, inexorable, opposeless, resistless **11** captivating, fascinating, inescapable, tantalizing, unavoidable **12** overpowering, overwhelming **13** insupportable, irrepressible, overmastering, unpreventable **14** uncontrollable

irresolute
04 weak **06** fickle, unsure **07** dubious **08** doubtful, hesitant, shifting, unstable, unsteady, variable, wavering **09** dithering, tentative, uncertain, undecided, unsettled **10** ambivalent, hesitating, indecisive, in two minds, on the fence, unresolved, weak-willed, wishy-washy **11** fluctuating, half-hearted, vacillating **12** faint-hearted, invertebrate, pussyfooting, undetermined **15** shilly-shallying

irrespective
- **irrespective of**
07 however, whoever **08** ignoring, no matter, whatever **09** never mind, whichever **12** disregarding, not affecting, regardless of **15** notwithstanding

irresponsible
04 rash, wild **06** unwise **07** erratic, flighty **08** carefree, careless, heedless, immature, reckless **09** negligent **10** fly-by-night, unreliable **11** injudicious, thoughtless **12** light-hearted **13** ill-considered, untrustworthy **14** scatterbrained

irretrievable
04 lost **06** damned **08** hopeless **11** irreparable, irrevocable **12** irredeemable, irremediable, irreversible, unrecallable **13** irrecoverable, unrecoverable, unsalvageable

irretrievably
10 hopelessly **11** irreparably, irrevocably **12** irredeemably, irreversibly **13** irrecoverably

irreverence
05 cheek, sauce **06** heresy, levity **07** impiety, mockery **08** rudeness **09** blasphemy, flippancy, impudence, insolence, profanity, sacrilege **10** cheekiness, disrespect, irreligion **11** discourtesy, godlessness, ungodliness **12** impertinence, impoliteness

irreverent
04 rude **05** saucy **06** cheeky **07** godless, impious, mocking, profane, ungodly **08** flippant, impolite, impudent, insolent

09 heretical **10** unreverend **11** blasphemous, impertinent, irreligious **12** discourteous, sacrilegious **13** disrespectful

irreversible
05 final **07** lasting **08** hopeless **09** incurable, permanent **11** irreparable, irrevocable, unalterab **12** irremediable **13** irretrievable, unrectifiable

irrevocable
05 final, fixed **07** settled **09** immutable **10** changeless, invariable **11** unalterable **12** irreversible, unchangeable **13** irretrievable, predetermined

irrevocably
07 for good **10** hopelessly, inevitably **11** inescapably, insuperably, irreparab unavoidably **13** for good and all

irrigate
03 wet **04** soak **05** drink, flood, spra water **06** dampen, deluge **07** moiste **08** inundate, sprinkle

irritability
04 bile, edge **08** edginess, erethism **09** bad temper, crossness, hastiness, temper, petulance, rattiness, testiness **10** crabbiness, grumpiness, impatience, tetchiness, touchiness **11** fretfulness, peevishness, pricklines stroppiness **12** irascibility **13** fractiousness

irritable
04 edgy, sore **05** cross, fiery, gusty, hasty, humpy, narky, ratty, riley, short, spiky, techy, testy **06** chippy, crabby, crusty, feisty, grumpy, livery, on edge, shirty, snappy, tetchy, touchy **07** bilious, crabbit, fretful, gustful, peckish, peevish, peppery, prickly, stroppy **08** liverish, scratchy, snappis **09** crotchety, fractious, impatient, irascible, splenetic **10** capernoity, ho blooded, nettlesome **11** bad-tempered, capernoitie, cappernoity, ill-tempered, out of temper, thin-skinned **12** cantankerous **13** quick-tempered, short-tempered **14** hypersensitive

irritant
04 gall, goad, pain **05** CS gas, savin **06** bother, menace, savine **07** trouble **08** nuisance, urushiol, vexation **09** annoyance **11** provocation **15** thorn in the flesh

irritate
03 bug, eat, get, irk, jar, rub, try, vex **04** fret, gall, goad, grig, hurt, itch, miff nark, rile **05** anger, annoy, chafe, get a grate, peeve, rouse, tease **06** bother, emboil, enrage, excite, gravel, harass, jangle, needle, nettle, niggle, put out, rattle, ruffle, tickle, wind up **07** enchafe, incense, inflame, provoke **08** acerbate, drive mad **09** aggravate displease, drive nuts, infuriate, stimulate **10** drive crazy, exasperate, excruciate **12** drive bananas **13** get

your back up, make sparks fly **14** drive up the wall, piss someone off, rub the wrong way **15** get on your nerves, give the needle to

irritated
◇ *anagram indicator*
03 mad **04** edgy, sore **05** angry, cross, irked, raggy, ratty, riled, spewy, vexed **06** choked, miffed, narked, peeved, piqued, put out, roused **07** annoyed, crooked, in a huff, nettled, ropable, ruffled, stroppy, uptight **08** bothered, harassed, in a paddy, in a strop, up in arms **09** flappable, flustered, impatient, in a lather, irritable, pissed off, raving mad, seeing red, splenetic, ticked off **10** aggravated, displeased, exasperate, hopping mad **11** discomposed, disgruntled, exacerbated, exasperated, fit to be tied **12** on the warpath

irritating
04 sore **05** itchy, pesky **06** thorny, trying, vexing **07** chafing, galling, grating, irksome, nagging, rubbing **08** abrasive, annoying, infernal, ticklish, tiresome, urticant **09** maddening, provoking, upsetting, vexatious, worrisome **10** bothersome, confounded, disturbing **11** aggravating, displeasing, infuriating, troublesome **12** excruciating

irritation
03 rub **04** bind, drag, fret, fury, pain, pest **05** anger, pique **06** bother **07** scunner, trouble **08** nuisance, pinprick, vexation **09** annoyance, crossness, testiness **10** impatience, snappiness **11** aggravation, displeasure, disturbance, indignation, provocation, running sore, stimulation **12** exasperation, excruciation, heeby-jeebies, irritability **13** heebie-jeebies, pain in the neck **15** dissatisfaction, thorn in the flesh
See also **itch**

• **display of irritation**
04 tiff, tift

is
01 's **03** est

Islamic *see* **month**

island
01 I **02** Is **03** ait, cay, île, Isl, key **04** eyot, holm, inch, isle **05** atoll, islet **06** skerry **07** isolate **11** archipelago

Islands and island groups include:

03 Cos, Ely, Fyn, Hoy, IOM, Ios, IOW, Man, Rab, Rum
04 Bali, Coll, Cook, Corn, Cuba, Eigg, Elba, Fiji, Gozo, Guam, Holy, Iona, Java, Jura, Line, Long, Mahe, Maui, Muck, Mull, Nias, Niue, Oahu, Rota, Sado, Sark, Skye, Uist, Wake
05 Arran, Barra, Bioko, Bonin, Capri, Chios, Cocos, Coney, Corfu, Crete, Delos, Éfaté, Ellis, Farne, Faroe, Handa, Hondo, Hydra, Ibiza, Islay, Kauai, Kuril, Lanai, Lundy, Luzon,

Malta, Melos, Nauru, Naxos, North, Öland, Orust, Palau, Paros, Pearl, Pemba, Samoa, Samos, South, Sunda, Timor, Tiree, Tonga, Wight
06 Aegean, Aegina, Andros, Azores, Baffin, Bikini, Borneo, Caicos, Canary, Chagos, Comino, Cyprus, Devil's, Easter, Euboea, Flores, Flotta, Hainan, Harris, Hawaii, Honshu, Icaria, Ionian, Jersey, Kodiak, Komodo, Kosrae, Kyushu, Lemnos, Lesbos, Midway, Orkney, Patmos, Penghu, Rhodes, Scilly, Sicily, Skiros, Staffa, Staten, Tahiti, Taiwan, Tinian, Tobago, Tubuai, Tuvalu, Virgin
07 Anjouan, Anthony, Antigua, Bahamas, Bahrain, Bermuda, Bonaire, Cabrera, Celebes, Channel, Chatham, Comoros, Corsica, Curaçao, Frisian, Gilbert, Gotland, Grenada, Iceland, Ireland, Iwo Jima, Jamaica, La Digue, Leeward, Lofoten, Loyalty, Madeira, Majorca, Mayotte, Menorca, Mikonos, Mindoro, Minorca, Molokai, Nicobar, Norfolk, Oceania, Okinawa, Palawan, Phoenix, Praslin, Rathlin, Réunion, Siberut, Society, Solomon, Stewart, St Kilda, St Lucia, Sumatra, Surtsey, Tokelau, Vanuatu, Visayan, Westman, Wrangel, Zealand
08 Aleutian, Anglesey, Anguilla, Balearic, Bornholm, Colonsay, Coral Sea, Cyclades, Dominica, Falkland, Guernsey, Hawaiian, Hebrides, Hokkaido, Hong Kong, Jan Mayen, Johnston, Kiribati, Lord Howe, Maldives, Marshall, Mindanao, Moluccas, Pitcairn, Sakhalin, Sandwich, São Tiago, Sardinia, Shetland, Skiathos, Sri Lanka, Sulawesi, Svalbard, Tenerife, Trinidad, Victoria, Viti Levu, Windward, Zanzibar
09 Admiralty, Ascension, Australia, Benbecula, Cape Verde, Christmas, Ellesmere, Galápagos, Greenland, Halmahera, Indonesia, Irian Jaya, Isle of Man, Kárpathos, Lanzarote, Las Palmas, Macquarie, Manhattan, Marquesas, Mascarene, Mauritius, Melanesia, Nantucket, New Guinea, North Uist, Rodrigues, Santorini, Singapore, South Seas, South Uist, Stromboli, Vanua Levu, Zacynthus
10 Ahvenanmaa, Basse-Terre, Cape Breton, Cephalonia, Cook Strait, Dodecanese, Formentera, Heligoland, Hispaniola, Ile d'Oléron, Kalimantan, Kiritimati, Madagascar, Martinique, Micronesia, Montserrat, New Britain, New Ireland, Puerto Rico, Samothrace, Seychelles, Vesterålen, West Indies
11 Gran Canaria, Grand Bahama, Grand Cayman, Grande-Terre, Guadalcanal, Iles d'Hyères, Iles du Salut, Isla Cozumel, Isle of Wight,

North Island, Philippines, Saint Helena, Scilly Isles, South Island, South Orkney
12 Bougainville, Grande Comore, Great Britain, Isla de Pascua, Newfoundland, Novaya Zemlya, Prince Edward, Prince Rupert, South Georgia
13 American Samoa, British Virgin, Inner Hebrides, Isla Contadora, Isles of Scilly, New Providence, Outer Hebrides, South Shetland
14 Oki Archipelago, Papua New Guinea, The Philippines, Tierra del Fuego, Tristan da Cunha, Turks and Caicos
15 French Polynesia, Lewis with Harris, Martha's Vineyard, Wallis and Futuna

See also **Channel Islands** *under* **channel**
• **reef island**
04 motu

Isle of Man
03 GBM, IMN **11** Ellan Vannin

isn't
03 nis, nys **04** ain't

isolate
06 cut off, detach, enisle, inisle, island, maroon, remove, strand **07** divorce, exclude, seclude, shut out **08** abstract, alienate, insulate, separate, set apart, shut away **09** keep apart, ostracize, segregate, sequester **10** disconnect, quarantine **11** marginalize **12** cold-shoulder **14** send to Coventry

isolated
04 lone **05** alone, apart, freak, stray **06** cut off, lonely, remote, single, unique **07** insular, special, unusual **08** abnormal, atypical, deserted, detached, outlying, secluded, solitary, uncommon **09** anomalous, separated, unrelated, untypical **10** segregated **11** exceptional, god-forsaken, in the sticks, out-of-the-way **12** unfrequented

isolation
05 exile **08** solitude **09** aloneness, seclusion **10** alienation, detachment, insulation, loneliness, quarantine, remoteness, retirement, separation, withdrawal **11** abstraction, segregation **12** dissociation, separateness, solitariness **13** disconnection, sequestration **15** marginalization

Israel
02 IL **03** ISR
See also **tribe**

issue
03 ish, jet, son **04** come, copy, emit, fall, fine, flow, flux, gush, mark, ooze, rise, rush, seed, seep, stem, turn **05** ensue, equip, exude, fit up, heirs, point, proof, spurt, topic, young **06** affair, debate, derive, effect, embryo, emerge, escape, family, finale, fit out, follow, kit out, matter, number, outlet, pay-off, put out, result, rig out, scions, spread, spring, stream, supply,

upshot 07 concern, deal out, debouch, deliver, develop, dispute, edition, emanate, give out, handout, outcome, outflow, problem, proceed, produce, profits, progeny, provide, publish, release, send out, subject, version **08** announce, argument, children, daughter, delivery, effusion, emission, printing, proclaim, question **09** broadcast, discharge, effluence, offspring, originate, supplying, terminate **10** break forth, burst forth, conclusion, dénouement, distribute, impression, instalment, promulgate, successors **11** circulation, consequence, controversy, descendants, disseminate, publication **12** announcement, distribution, promulgation **13** dissemination

• **at issue**
10 in question **12** being debated **14** being discussed **15** under discussion

• **final issue**
04 fate

• **side issue**
02 by **03** bye

• **take issue**
05 argue, fight **06** object **07** contest, dispute, protest, quarrel **08** be at odds, disagree **09** challenge **12** be at odds with **13** take exception

• **violent issue**
04 gush

• **without issue**
02 sp **03** dsp, osp **09** sine prole

it
01 a, 't **02** SA **05** oomph **08** vermouth **09** sex appeal

• **it is not**
05 'taint, 'tisn't **06** aikona

• **it's**
03 'tis

• **on it**
03 an't

Italian
◊ *foreign word indicator*
01 I **02** It **03** Sig **04** Ital, trat **05** Roman, tratt **08** Ausonian, Sicilian, Venetian **09** trattoria **10** Neapolitan

See also **day**; **month**; **number**

• **Italian family**
06 Medici

Italy
01 I **03** ITA **04** Ital

itch
03 die, euk, ewk **04** ache, burn, long, pine, yeuk, youk, yuck, yuke **05** crave, crawl, psora, yearn **06** desire, hanker, hunger, thirst, tickle, tingle **07** burning, craving, longing, passion, prickle, scabies **08** irritate, keenness, pruritus, tingling, yearning **09** cacoethes, eagerness, hankering, itchiness, prickling **10** irritation

itching
03 euk, ewk **04** avid, yeuk, youk, yuck, yuke **05** dying, eager **06** aching, greedy, raring **07** burning, longing **08** prurient, pruritus **09** hankering, impatient **11** inquisitive

item
03 job **04** also **05** entry, issue, piece, point, story, thing **06** aspect, detail, factor, matter, notice, number, object, report **07** account, article, element, feature **08** bulletin, likewise **09** component, paragraph **10** accidental, ingredient, particular **12** circumstance **13** consideration

itemize
04 list **05** count **06** detail, number, record **07** mention, specify **08** document, instance, overname, tabulate **09** catalogue, enumerate **13** particularize **15** make an inventory

itinerant
◊ *anagram indicator*
03 faw **04** hobo, Roma **05** caird, Gypsy, nomad, rover **06** gitano, hawker, pedlar, roamer, Romani, Romany, roving, tinker **07** chapman, didakai, didakei, didicoi, didicoy, nomadic, rambler, roadman, roaming, running, swagman, tzigany, vagrant, Zincalo, Zingaro **08** Bohemian, diddicoy, drifting, huckster, minstrel, preacher, rambling, rootless, stroller, vagabond, wanderer, Zigeuner **09** itinerary, migratory, muffin man, piepowder, strolling, sundowner, traveller, unsettled, wandering, wayfaring **10** evangelist, journeying, revivalist, travelling **11** gandy dancer, peripatetic, Scotch cuddy **12** on the wallaby, Scotch draper **15** New-Age Traveller, strolling player

itinerary
03 way **04** plan, tour **05** route **06** course **07** circuit, journey **08** schedule **09** itinerant, programme, timetable **10** travelling **12** arrangements

itself
• **of itself**
03 sui

ivory
07 dentine **08** eburnean **09** eburneous **10** whale's bone

IVR code *see* **vehicle**

ivy
03 tod, udo **04** gill **06** aralia, fatsia, Hedera **07** ale-hoof **08** cat's-foot

Ivy League *see* **university**

izzard
01 Z **03** zed

J

J
03 jay **06** Juliet

jab
03 box, dig, tap **04** poke, prod, push, shot, stab **05** elbow, lunge, nudge, punch **06** thrust **09** injection

jabber
03 gab, jaw, yap **05** prate **06** babble, gabble, mumble, rabbit, ramble, rattle, tattle, witter, yabber, yatter **07** blather, blether, chatter, prattle, sputter

jack
01 J **02** AB **03** Dee, jak, nob, pam, pur, tar **04** Jock, John, mark **05** bower, fed up, kitty, knave, makar, money, noddy, tired, winch **06** hopper, runner, sailor **07** pantine, sticker **08** mistress, sawhorse, turnspit **09** detective, handscrew
• **jack up**
04 hike, lift **05** hoist, put up, raise **06** hike up, push up, refuse, resist **07** elevate, inflate **08** increase

jackal
04 dieb **13** lion's provider

jackass
04 fool **09** blockhead **10** kookaburra

jackdaw
02 ka **03** daw, kae **04** jack **07** dawcock

jacket
02 DJ **03** tux **04** baju, beat, case, skin, wrap **05** acton, bania, cover, duvet, gilet, grego, jupon, polka, sayon, shell, tunic **06** anorak, banian, banyan, Basque, blazer, bolero, casing, dolman, folder, jerkin, railly, sheath, tuxedo, Zouave **07** Barbour®, Mae West, spencer, vareuse, wrapper **08** camisole, covering, envelope, water box, wrapping **09** night-rail, shortgown, slip cover **10** bodywarmer, bumfreezer, duffel coat, sports coat, windjammer **11** Barbour® coat, windcheater

jackpot
03 pot **04** mess, pool **05** award, kitty, prize **06** reward, stakes **07** big time, bonanza **08** winnings **10** first prize
• **hit the jackpot**
05 score **06** arrive, make it **07** clean up, get rich, succeed **08** rake it in **09** make a pile **11** make a bundle, make a packet **13** hit the big time

jade
02 yu **03** nag **06** limmer **08** axe-stone, nephrite **11** spleenstone

jaded
04 done **05** all in, bored, fed up, spent, tired, weary **06** bushed, done in, dulled, fagged, pooped **07** wearied, whacked, worn out **08** fatigued, jiggered, tired out **09** disjaskit, exhausted, knackered, played-out, pooped out, shattered **10** cheesed off **11** ready to drop, tuckered out **14** unenthusiastic

jag
03 dag, fit **04** barb, cart, load, snag, spur **05** cleft, notch, point, prick, slash, spell, spree, tooth **06** bundle, dentil, Jaguar, pierce **08** denticle, division, quantity **09** injection, saddlebag **10** projection, protrusion **11** inoculation

jagged
◇ anagram indicator
04 rag'd **05** drunk, ragde, rough **06** barbed, broken, craggy, hackly, nicked, ragged, ridged, snaggy, spiked, uneven **07** notched, pointed, snagged, toothed **08** indented, saw-edged, serrated **09** irregular **11** denticulate

jaggedness
09 roughness, serration, serrature **10** brokenness, raggedness, unevenness **12** irregularity

jaguar
03 Jag **05** ounce, tiger **07** leopard, tigress **10** leopardess **13** American tiger

jail, gaol
03 bin, can, jug, pen **04** nick, poky, quad, quod, stir **05** choky, clink, kitty, pokey **06** cooler, detain, immure, inside, intern, lock up, lock-up, prison **07** confine, custody, hoosgow, impound, put away, slammer **08** big house, hoosegow, imprison, porridge, send down **09** bridewell, jailhouse **10** guardhouse **11** incarcerate **12** penitentiary, send to prison **15** detention centre

See also **prison**

jailbird *see* **prisoner**

jailer, gaoler
04 Adam **05** guard, screw **06** captor, keeper, warden, warder **07** alcaide, alcayde, turnkey **09** dungeoner **12** under-turnkey **13** prison officer

jake
02 OK **04** fine, okay **05** yokel **06** honest **07** correct **09** first-rate

jam
03 fix, mob, ram **04** bind, clog, cram, herd, hole, lock, pack, push, spot, stew **05** block, close, crowd, crush, force, horde, jeely, jelly, press, seize, stall, stick, stuff, swarm, wedge **06** hold-up, insert, jeelie, konfyt, pickle, plight, scrape, spread, squash, throng, thrust **07** confine, congest, seize up, squeeze, straits, the soup, trouble **08** close off, conserve, gridlock, obstruct, preserve, quandary **09** confiture, interfere, marmalade, multitude, tight spot **10** bottleneck, congestion **11** obstruction, predicament **12** damson cheese

Jamaica
02 JA **03** JAM

jamb
04 dern, durn, pole, post, prop **05** frame, shaft **06** greave, pillar **07** support, upright **08** doorpost, side post **09** stanchion **10** ingle-cheek

jamboree
04 fête **05** party, rally, spree **06** frolic, junket **07** carouse, jubilee, revelry, shindig **08** carnival, festival, field day **09** festivity, gathering, merriment **10** convention **11** celebration, get-together

jammy
05 lucky **06** timely **07** charmed **08** favoured **09** excellent, expedient, fortunate, opportune **10** auspicious, fortuitous, propitious, prosperous, successful **12** providential

jangle
◇ anagram indicator
03 din, jar **05** chime, clang, clank, clash, clink, upset **06** bother, jingle, racket, rattle **07** clatter, discord, disturb, jarring, quarrel, stridor, trouble, vibrate, wrangle **08** clangour, irritate **09** cacophony **10** contention, dissonance **11** make anxious **13** reverberation

janitor
06 porter **07** doorman, ostiary **08** servitor **09** attendant, caretaker, concierge, custodian **10** doorkeeper, servitress

January
03 Jan

japan
01 J **03** JPN **07** lacquer

Japanese
03 eta **07** Japonic **09** Nipponese
See also **Asian**

02 no
03 noh
04 raku
05 haiku, Hizen, Imari, kendo
06 gagaku, kabuki, nogaku, saikei, ukiyo-e
07 bunraku, chanoyu, ikebana, nihonga, origami
08 kakemono, kakiemon, tsutsumu
11 linked verse, tea ceremony

• **Japanese title**
03 san **04** sama

jar
◊ *anagram indicator*
03 irk, jug, mug, pot, urn **04** jerk, jolt, olla, pint, rasp, turn, vase
05 annoy, caddy, clash, crock, cruet, flask, grate, grind, shake, stave, upset
06 bicker, carafe, dolium, flagon, jampot, jangle, jostle, justle, kalpis, nettle, offend, pithos, rattle, tinaja, tureen, vessel **07** agitate, amphora, disturb, pitcher, quarrel, stamnos, terrine, trouble, vibrate **08** be at odds, canister, conflict, disagree, irritate
09 albarello, bell-glass, container, greybeard **10** receptacle **11** water monkey **12** be at variance, be in conflict

jargon
04 cant, jive **05** argot, Greek, idiom, lingo, slang, usage **06** patois, patter, pidgin **07** chatter, Kennick, twitter
08 legalese, nonsense, parlance, pig Latin **09** baragouin, buzz words, Europspeak, gibberish **10** Eurobabble, greenspeak, journalese, mumbo-jumbo, twittering, vernacular
11 computerese, diplomatese, lingoa geral, officialese, sociologese, technospeak **12** gobbledegook, gobbledygook, lingua franca, psychobabble, technobabble, telegraphese **13** commercialese, computerspeak, pidgin English

jarring
04 ajar **05** harsh, shock **06** off-key
07 grating, jolting, rasping
08 backlash, clashing, friction, jangling, strident **09** dissonant, troubling, upsetting **10** discordant, disturbing, irritating **11** cacophonous

jasmine
07 jessamy **09** gelsemium, gessamine, jessamine **10** frangipani

jaundiced
05 jaded **06** biased, bitter **07** bigoted, cynical, envious, hostile, jealous
09 distorted, resentful, sceptical
10 prejudiced, suspicious
11 distrustful, icteritious, pessimistic
12 disbelieving, misanthropic, preconceived **14** unenthusiastic

jaunt
04 ride, spin, tour, trip **05** drive, sally
06 outing, ramble, stroll **07** holiday
09 excursion

jauntily
06 airily **07** perkily, smartly
08 brightly, cheekily **10** cheerfully
13 energetically **15** self-confidently

jaunty
◊ *anagram indicator*
04 airy, pert, trim **05** perky, showy, smart **06** bouncy, breezy, cheeky, dapper, flashy, lively, rakish, spruce
07 buoyant, stylish **08** carefree, cheerful, debonair, sparkish
09 energetic, sprightly **11** gentlemanly, Micawberish **12** high-spirited **13** self-confident

javelin
04 dart, pile **05** jerid, pilum, spear
06 jereed **07** harpoon **08** gavelock
09 handstaff

jaw
03 gum, rap **04** chap, chat, chaw, chop, dash, jole, joll, jowl, talk, trap
05 chaft, chops, claws, grasp, mouth, power, scold, visit, wongi **06** babble, chafts, confab, gabble, gossip, jabber, muzzle, natter, rabbit **07** chatter, chinwag, control, lecture, maxilla
08 clutches, mandible, rabbit on, schmooze **09** threshold **10** discussion, masticator **12** conversation
13 talkativeness
• **front of jaw**
04 chin

jay
01 J **10** whisky jack, whisky john

jazz
◊ *anagram indicator*

03 bop, hot, rag
04 acid, Afro, cool, jive, soul, trad
05 bebop, blues, funky, kwela, modal, spiel, swing
06 fusion, groove, modern
07 classic, hard bop, New Wave, post-bop, ragtime
08 free-form, high life
09 Afro-Cuban, bossa nova, Dixieland, gutbucket, West Coast
10 avant-garde, improvised, mainstream, neo-classic, New Orleans
11 barrelhouse, third stream, traditional
12 boogie-woogie

See also **singer**
• **jazz fan**
03 cat
• **jazz up**
07 enliven, liven up **08** ginger up
09 smarten up **10** brighten up

jazzy
04 bold, wild **05** fancy, gaudy, smart
06 bright, flashy, lively, snazzy
07 stylish, zestful **08** spirited, swinging
09 vivacious

jealous
04 wary **05** green **07** anxious, careful, envious, gealous, mindful
08 covetous, desirous, doubting, grudging, insecure, vigilant, watchful
09 defensive, green-eyed, jaundiced, resentful **10** begrudging, possessive, protective, solicitous, suspicious
11 distrustful

jealously
08 with envy **09** enviously
10 covetously, desirously **11** resentfully
12 possessively **13** distrustfully

jealousy
04 envy **05** doubt, spite **06** gelosy, grudge **07** envying, ill-will **08** distrust, gealousy, mistrust, wariness
09 emulation, suspicion, vigilance, zelotypia **10** bitterness, insecurity, resentment, yellowness **11** carefulness, mindfulness **12** covetousness, grudgingness, watchfulness
13 defensiveness **14** possessiveness, protectiveness

jeans
05 Levis®

jeer
03 boo, dig **04** gibe, gird, goof, hiss, hoot, jest, jibe, mock, razz, twit
05 abuse, chaff, fleer, flout, frump, geare, knock, scoff, scorn, sneer, taunt, tease **06** banter, chiack, deride, heckle
07 barrack, catcall, mockery, teasing
08 derision, ridicule **09** make fun of, shout down **10** sling off at **11** have a shot at, poke borak at **12** laugh to scorn

jejune
03 dry **04** arid, dull **05** banal, empty, naive, silly, trite, vapid **06** barren, boring, callow, meagre, simple
07 insipid, prosaic, puerile **08** childish, immature, juvenile **09** senseless
10 colourless, spiritless, unoriginal, wishy-washy **13** uninteresting
15 unsophisticated

jell *see* **gel, jell**

jelly
03 gel **04** agar, jeel **05** aspic, jeely, shape **06** jeelie, kanten, napalm, Sterno® **07** congeal **08** agar-agar, quiddany, Vaseline® **09** calf's-foot, gelignite **10** petrolatum **14** liquid paraffin

jellyfish
05 jelly **06** medusa **07** acaleph, aurelia, blubber, sea wasp
08 acalephe, sea jelly **09** sea nettle
10 nettle-fish, scyphozoan, sea blubber

jeopardize
04 risk **05** stake **06** chance, expose, gamble, hazard, menace **07** imperil, venture **08** endanger, threaten **09** put at risk **11** take a chance **13** put in jeopardy **14** expose to danger

jeopardy
04 risk **05** peril **06** danger, hazard, menace, threat **07** venture
08 exposure **09** liability **10** insecurity
12 endangerment **13** vulnerability
14 precariousness

erk
▸ *anagram indicator*
3 ass, bob, git, jar, jig, jog, mug, nit, ap, tug **04** berk, cant, clot, coot, lope, dork, fool, geek, goat, goof, goop, hoik, hoik, jolt, jump, kick, kook, nerd, nerk, peck, prat, pull, toss, twit, yank **5** braid, chump, dumbo, dweeb, flirt, aitch, hoick, idiot, lurch, neddy, ninny, pluck, prick, quirk, shrug, surge, throw, twerp, wally **06** bounce, dum-dum, fillip, jiggle, josser, nitwit, sawney, sucker, switch, thrust, turkey, twitch, wrench **07** Charlie, charqui, gubbins, pillock, plonker, saphead, tosspot, wazzock **08** dipstick **09** birdbrain, cloth head, schlemiel **10** headbanger, nincompoop, silly-billy **11** kangaroo hop **13** proper Charlie

erkily
07 bumpily, jumpily, roughly **08** fitfully, unevenly **13** spasmodically

erky
▸ *anagram indicator*
5 bumpy, jumpy, rough, shaky **06** bouncy, fitful, uneven **07** charqui, jolting, shaking, twitchy **08** lurching, saccadic **09** spasmodic **10** convulsive, incoherent **12** disconnected, uncontrolled **13** unco-ordinated

erry-built
04 Lego® **05** cheap **06** faulty, flimsy, shoddy **07** rickety **08** slipshod, unstable **09** cheapjack, defective, slop-built **10** ramshackle **12** quickly built **13** insubstantial, unsubstantial **14** thrown together **15** built on the cheap

ersey
03 GBJ, top **04** polo **05** frock **06** gansey, jumper, woolly, zephyr **07** maillot, sweater **08** guernsey, polo neck, pullover **10** sweatshirt

Jerusalem
04 Zion

jest
03 cod, fun, gab, gag, jig, kid, toy **04** fool, game, hoax, jape, jeer, joke, mock, quip **05** bourd, crack, droll, gleek, prank, taunt, tease, trick **06** banter **07** fooling, kidding, leg-pull **08** drollery **09** Joe Miller, tell jokes, wisecrack, witticism **13** practical joke
• **in jest**
05 in fun **07** as a joke, to tease **08** jokingly **09** playfully **13** mischievously

jester
03 wag, wit **04** fool, scop, zany **05** clown, comic, droll, joker, patch **06** gagman, motley, mummer **07** bourder, buffoon, juggler **08** comedian, humorist, merryman, quipster **09** court-fool, harlequin, joculator, pantaloon, prankster **11** Jack-pudding, merry-andrew

Jesuits
02 SJ **09** Ignatians

jet
03 fly, jut **04** flow, gush, inky, jeat, rush, zoom **05** black, ebony, jumbo, raven, sable, shoot, sooty, spirt, spout, spray, spurt, strut **06** Airbus®, candle, career, douche, spring, squirt, stream **07** sprayer **08** encroach, fountain **09** delta wing, sprinkler **10** pitch-black, tankbuster
See also **aircraft**

jettison
04 drop, dump **05** chuck, ditch, eject, expel, heave, scrap **06** jetsam, unload **07** abandon, discard, offload **08** get rid of **09** throw away

jetty
04 dock, mole, pier, quay **05** jutty, wharf **06** groyne **07** harbour **10** breakwater **12** landing-place, landing-stage

jewel
03 gem **04** find, rock **05** bijou, pearl, prize **06** rarity **07** navette, paragon **08** gemstone, ornament, sparkler, treasure **09** jewellery, showpiece **10** ferronière **11** ferronnière, masterpiece, pride and joy **13** precious stone **14** crème de la crème

jewellery
03 tom **04** gems **05** gauds **06** bijoux, finery, jewels **07** gemmery, regalia **08** treasure, trinkets **09** ornaments **10** bijouterie, tomfoolery **13** paraphernalia

> *Jewellery types include:*

04 prop, ring, stud
05 beads, bindi, cameo, chain, tiara
06 amulet, anklet, bangle, brooch, choker, corals, diadem, hatpin, locket, pearls, tiepin, torque
07 armilla, coronet, earring, necklet, pendant, rivière, sautoir, toe ring
08 bracelet, cufflink, necklace, negligee, nose ring, wristlet
09 medallion, navel ring
10 signet ring
11 mangalsutra
12 eternity ring
13 charm bracelet, solitaire ring
15 belly-button ring

Jewish calendar *see* **month**

Jezebel
04 jade, tart, vamp **05** hussy, whore, witch **06** harlot, wanton **07** Delilah **08** man-eater, scrubber **09** temptress **10** loose woman, seductress **11** femme fatale **12** scarlet woman

jib
03 shy **04** balk, face, stop **05** baulk, genoa, stall, strip **06** boggle, fleece, recoil, refuse, shrink **07** back off, retreat **09** stop short **10** standstill

jibe *see* **gibe**

jiffy
02 mo **03** bit, sec **04** tick **05** flash, trice, whiff **06** minute, moment, no

time, second **07** instant **08** two ticks **09** twinkling **11** split second

jig
◇ *anagram indicator*
03 bob, hop **04** jerk, jest, jump, leap, skip **05** caper, prank, shake **06** bounce, jingle, prance, twitch, wiggle, wobble

jigger
04 damn, jerk, ruin **05** blast, break, shake, spoil, wreck **06** chigoe, chigre, jolley, kibosh **07** botch up, chigger, destroy, louse up, scupper, vitiate **08** sand flea **09** undermine **14** make a pig's ear of

jiggery-pokery
05 fraud **06** deceit **08** mischief, trickery **09** chicanery, deception **10** dishonesty, hanky-panky, subterfuge **13** funny business **14** monkey business

jiggle
◇ *anagram indicator*
03 jig, jog **04** jerk, jump **05** shake, shift **06** bounce, fidget, joggle, twitch, waggle, wiggle, wobble **07** agitate

jilt
04 drop, dump **05** chuck, ditch, leave, spurn **06** begunk, betray, desert, pack in, reject **07** abandon, discard **08** brush off **09** cast aside, throw over, walk out on

jingle
03 jig **04** ding, poem, ring, song, tune **05** carol, chant, chime, chink, clang, clink, ditty, rhyme, verse **06** chorus, jangle, melody, rattle, slogan, tinkle **07** clatter, refrain, ringing **08** clangour, doggerel, limerick **14** tintinnabulate

jingoism
10 chauvinism, flag-waving, insularity, patriotism **11** imperialism, nationalism **13** sabre-rattling

jinx
03 hex, moz **04** doom, mozz **05** charm, curse, spell **06** hoodoo, plague, voodoo **07** bad luck, bedevil, bewitch, evil eye, gremlin **10** affliction, black magic, Indian sign **11** malediction **12** cast a spell on

jitters
◇ *anagram indicator*
06 nerves **07** anxiety, fidgets, habdabs, jimjams **08** edginess **09** agitation, tenseness, the creeps, the shakes, trembling **10** the shivers, the willies, uneasiness **11** nervousness **12** collywobbles **13** heebie-jeebies

jittery
◇ *anagram indicator*
04 edgy **05** het up, jumpy, nervy, shaky **06** on edge, uneasy **07** anxious, fidgety, in a stew, keyed up, nervous, panicky, quaking, shivery, twitchy, uptight, wound up **08** agitated, in a sweat, in a tizzy **09** flustered, perturbed, quivering, screwed-up, trembling

job

04 char, darg, duty, part, peck, post, prod, role, spot, task, work **05** berth, chore, place, punch, share, stint, trade **06** affair, career, charge, errand, métier, office, thrust **07** calling, concern, mission, project, pursuit, venture **08** activity, business, capacity, function, position, province, sinecure, vocation **09** situation, soft thing **10** assignment, commission, employment, enterprise, line of work, livelihood, occupation, proceeding, profession **11** appointment, consignment, piece of work, undertaking **12** contribution **14** line of business, responsibility

See also **burglary**; **occupation**

- **have a job doing something**
14 find it a problem
- **just the job**
12 just the thing **13** just the ticket

jobless

04 idle **07** laid off **08** inactive, workless **09** on the dole, out of work, redundant **10** unemployed **11** without work

jock

02 DJ **03** Mac **04** jack **06** deejay **08** Scotsman **10** disc jockey

jockey

◇ *anagram indicator*
04 coax, ease, edge **05** rider **06** cajole, induce, manage **07** wheedle **08** engineer, horseman, inveigle, jockette **09** manoeuvre, negotiate **10** equestrian, horsewoman, jump-jockey, manipulate

See also **equestrian**; **horseman, horsewoman**

jocose

05 droll, funny, lepid, merry, witty **06** jovial, joyous **07** comical, jesting, playful, teasing, waggish **08** humorous, mirthful, pleasant, sportive **09** facetious **11** mischievous

jocular

05 comic, droll, funny, witty **06** jocose, joking, jovial **07** amusing, comical, jesting, playful, roguish, scurril, teasing, waggish **08** humorous, scurrile **09** facetious, hilarious, whimsical **12** entertaining

jocularity

03 wit **05** sport **06** gaiety, humour **07** fooling, jesting, teasing **08** drollery, hilarity, jocosity, laughter **09** amusement, funniness, jolliness, joviality, merriment **10** comicality, desipience, jocoseness, pleasantry **11** playfulness, roguishness, waggishness **12** sportiveness, whimsicality **13** entertainment, facetiousness

jog

◇ *anagram indicator*
03 hod, jar, run **04** bump, jerk, jolt, poke, prod, push, rock, shog, stir, trot, whig **05** dunch, dunsh, elbow, hotch,

mosey, nudge, shake, shove **06** arouse, bounce, canter, jig-jog, joggle, jostle, prompt, remind **08** activate **09** stimulate

john

02 WC **03** bog, can, lat, lav, loo **04** jack, rear **08** lavatory

See also **toilet**

joie de vivre

03 joy **04** zest **05** gusto, mirth **06** bounce, esprit, gaiety, relish **08** buoyancy, pleasure **09** enjoyment, merriment **10** blitheness, ebullience, enthusiasm, exuberance, get-up-and-go, joyfulness **12** cheerfulness

join

◇ *juxtaposition indicator*
03 add, mix, oop, oup, sew, tie, wed **04** abut, ally, bind, fuse, glue, knit, link, meet, weld, yoke **05** annex, enrol, enter, marry, merge, touch, unify, unite **06** adhere, adjoin, attach, border, cement, couple, enlist, fasten, sign up, solder, splice **07** combine, conjoin, connect, injoint, verge on **08** border on, coincide, converge, splinter **09** accompany, affiliate, associate, co-operate, interjoin, march with **10** amalgamate, team up with **11** collaborate, compaginate **15** become a member of

- **join in**
04 help **06** chip in, muck in **07** chime in, get in on, partake, pitch in **08** take part **09** co-operate, lend a hand **10** contribute, take part in **11** participate
- **join up**
04 link **05** enrol, enter **06** accede, enlist, sign up

joint

01 J **03** bar, fit, pub **04** club, dive, join, knot, lith, seam, weld **05** carve, cut up, haunt, hinge, nexus, place, roach, sever, stick, union, unite **06** common, couple, divide, fasten, joined, mutual, reefer, shared, spliff, united **07** connect, dissect, joining, segment **08** combined, communal, conjunct, coupling, junction, juncture **09** cigarette, concerted, dismember, ginglymus, nightclub **10** articulate, collective, commissure, connection, cup-and-ball **11** amalgamated, co-operative, co-ordinated, enarthrosis **12** articulation, consolidated, intersection

See also **bone**

jointly

08 together, unitedly **09** in cahoots, in harmony **11** in agreement **13** co-operatively, in co-operation, in partnership **15** in collaboration

joke

03 bar, cod, fun, gag, guy, kid, one, pun, rot **04** baur, bawr, fool, hoax, hoot, jape, jest, josh, lark, mock, play, quip, yarn **05** chaff, clown, crack, farce, funny, kiddy, laugh, prank, spoof, sport,

stunt, tease, trick **06** banter, frolic, gambol, parody, wheeze, whimsy **07** leg-pull, mockery **08** chestnut, nonsense, one-liner, repartee, shambles, travesty **09** absurdity, booby trap, fool about, tell jokes, throwaway, wisecrack, witticism **10** break a jest, crack a joke, fool around, funny story, rib-tickler, running gag, whip the cat **11** apple-pie bed, old chestnut **12** take for a ride **13** have someone on, practical joke **14** pull a fast one on, ridiculousness

joker

03 wag, wit **04** card **05** clown, comic, droll, laugh, sport **06** gagman, hoaxer, jester, kidder **07** buffoon, farceur, funster **08** comedian, farceuse, humorist, quipster **09** character, prankster, trickster **11** wisecracker **14** practical joker

jollity

05 mirth **08** gladness **09** happiness, high jinks, merriment **11** high spirits, merrymaking **12** cheerfulness

jolly

02 RM **03** gay **04** coax, dead, glad, spur, trip, urge, very, well **05** buxom, egg on, gaucy, gawcy, gawsy, happy, merry, party, plump **06** bootee, cheery, ever so, gaucie, hearty, highly, jovial, joyful, lively, outing, prompt, titupy **07** awfully, festive, gleeful, greatly, healthy, playful, tittupy **08** cheerful, mirthful, persuade, splendid, terribly **09** certainly, convivial, encourage, enjoyable, extremely, exuberant, influence, intensely **10** delightful **11** celebration, pleasurable, royal marine **12** entertaining **13** exceptionally **15** extraordinarily

jolt

◇ *anagram indicator*
03 hit, jar, jog **04** bang, blow, bump, jerk, push, stun **05** amaze, floor, knock, lurch, nudge, shake, shock, shove, start, upset **06** bounce, hotter, impact, jostle, jounce, jumble **07** astound, disturb, perturb, setback, shake up, startle **08** astonish, reversal, surprise **09** bombshell **10** discompose, disconcert **11** knock for six, thunderbolt **15** bolt from the blue

Jordan

03 HKJ, JOR

jostle

◇ *anagram indicator*
03 jog, vie **04** bang, bump, jolt, push, tilt **05** crowd, elbow, fight, joust, shake, shove **06** battle, hustle, jockey, joggle, throng **07** collide, compete, contend, squeeze **08** shoulder, struggle **11** hog, shouther

jot

03 ace, bit, dot, fig **04** atom, hint, hoot, iota, mite, whit **05** aught, gleam, grain, scrap, speck, stime, styme, trace

detail, morsel, tittle, trifle
  glimmer, smidgen **08** fraction,
  rticle **09** scintilla

jot down

list, note **05** enter **06** record **07** put
wn **08** note down, register, scribble,
ke down **09** write down

tting

line, memo, note **05** lines, notes
  comment, message **08** reminder,
ribble **10** memorandum

urnal

J **03** log **04** blog **05** diary, e-zine,
per **06** record, review, weekly
account, daybook, diurnal, fanzine,
zette, logbook, monthly
magazine, register **09** chronicle,
hemeris, newspaper, waste book
periodical, trade paper
  publication

e also **newspaper**

urnalism

press **09** reportage, reporting
copy-writing, e-journalism, gutter
ess **12** broadcasting, fourth estate,
ws coverage **13** sportswriting, web
urnalism **14** correspondence,
ature-writing, telejournalism

ournalism-related terms include:

cub, cut, NPA, run, tip
blat, bump, copy, deck, desk, kill,
  leak, news, op-ed
angle, blatt, blurb, break, extra,
  local, media, pitch, quote, radio,
  scoop, squib, story, tie in
anchor, Balaam, byline, column,
  editor, impact, kicker, leader, leg-
  man, rookie, source
advance, article, caption, compact,
  editing, feature, journal, kill fee,
  spoiler, subhead, tabloid, topical,
  writing
causerie, follow-up, headline,
  magazine, masthead, national,
  newshawk, news item, reporter,
  revision, stringer
broadcast, columnist, editorial,
  exclusive, freelance, freesheet,
  front-page, interview, newshound,
  newspaper, paragraph, pull quote,
  reportage, scare-head, scare-line,
  soundbite, statement, stop-press,
  strapline
broadsheet, centrefold, credit line,
  daily paper, journalist, leaderette,
  multimedia, newsreader,
  periodical, publishing, retraction,
  standfirst, television
Fleet Street, Sunday paper
breaking news, centre spread, press
  council, press release, scare-heading
correspondent, human interest,
  middle article
banner headline, blind interview,
  current affairs, leading article
photojournalism, press conference

urnalist

2 Ed **03** man, sub **04** hack **06** editor,
urno, scribe **07** diarist, wireman

08 hackette, pressman, reporter,
reviewer, stringer **09** columnist,
freelance, gazetteer, ink-jerker,
newshound, paparazzo, sob sister,
subeditor, thunderer **10** diurnalist,
hatchet man, ink-slinger, news-writer,
presswoman **11** broadcaster,
commentator, contributor, e-journalist
12 gossip-writer, newspaperman,
sportswriter **13** correspondent,
feature-writer, web journalist
14 newspaperwoman, telejournalist

Journalists and editors include:

03 Day (Sir Robin), Mee (Arthur)
04 Adie (Kate), Bell (Martin), Birt
  (John, Lord), Ford (Anna), Gall
  (Sandy), Hogg (Sarah, Baroness),
  Jane (Frederick), Marr (Andrew),
  Neil (Andrew), Rook (Jean), Self
  (Will), Snow (Jon), Snow (Peter),
  Wade (Rebekah), Wark (Kirsty)
05 Brown (Helen Gurley), Buerk
  (Michael), Cooke (Alistair), Dacre
  (Paul), Ensor (Sir Robert), Evans (Sir
  Harold), Frost (Sir David), Green
  (Charlotte), Hardy (Bert), James
  (Clive), Junor (Sir John), Laski
  (Marghanita), Levin (Bernard),
  Lewis (Martyn), Reith (John, Lord),
  Scott (C P), Waugh (Auberon),
  Wolfe (Tom), Young (Toby)
06 Bailey (Trevor), Barron (Brian),
  Bierce (Ambrose), Burnet (Sir
  Alastair), Deedes (Bill, Lord), Fisher
  (Archie), Forman (Sir Denis), Gallup
  (George), Gordon (John), Greene
  (Sir Hugh), Hislop (Ian), Hulton (Sir
  Edward), Hutton (Will), Isaacs (Sir
  Jeremy), Martin (Kingsley), Morgan
  (Charles), Morgan (Piers), Murrow
  (Edward R), O'Brien (Conor Cruise),
  Paxman (Jeremy), Pilger (John),
  Proops (Marjorie), Reuter (Paul
  Julius von, Lord), Rippon (Angela),
  Stuart (Moira), Wilkes (John)
07 Alagiah (George), Barclay
  (William), Boycott (Rosie), Bradlee
  (Ben), Brunson (Michael), Buckley
  (William F, Jnr), Cameron (James),
  Camrose (William Berry, Viscount),
  Cobbett (William), Dunnett (Sir
  Alastair), Edwards (Huw), Fairfax
  (John), Fleming (Peter), Gardner
  (Frank), Hellyer (Arthur George
  Lee), Ingrams (Richard), Jackson
  (Dame Barbara), Johnson (Boris),
  Kennedy (Helena, Baroness),
  Kennedy (Sir Ludovic), Leeming
  (Jan), Malcolm (Derek), Mencken
  (H L), Perkins (Brian), Rowland
  (Tiny), Simpson (John), Sissons
  (Peter), Stanley (Sir Henry Morton),
  Thomson (Robert)
08 Burchill (Julie), Cronkite (Walter),
  Dimbleby (David), Dimbleby
  (Jonathan), Dimbleby (Richard),
  Douglass (Frederick), Drawbell
  (James Wedgwood), Gellhorn
  (Martha), Hanrahan (Brian),
  Hobhouse (Leonard), Horrocks (Sir
  Brian), Humphrys (John), Lippmann
  (Walter), McCarthy (John),
  McDonald (Sir Trevor), Naughtie
  (James), Nevinson (Henry Wood),
  Rees-Mogg (William, Lord),
  Robinson (Henry Crabb),
  Thompson (Hunter S), Woodward
  (Bob)
09 Bernstein (Carl), Bosanquet
  (Reginald), Hopkinson (Sir Tom),
  Macdonald (Gus, Lord), MacGregor
  (Sue), Mackenzie (Kelvin),
  Magnusson (Magnus), Plekhanov
  (Georgi), Streicher (Julius),
  Trethowan (Sir Ian)
10 Greenslade (Roy), Guru-Murthy
  (Krishnan), Muggeridge
  (Malcolm), Rusbridger (Alan),
  Waterhouse (Keith), Worsthorne
  (Sir Peregrine)
12 Street-Porter (Janet)

See also **newspaper**

journey

02 go, OE **03** fly, ren, rin, run, way
04 eyre, hike, mush, raik, rake, ride,
  roam, rove, sail, step, tour, trek, trip,
  went **05** drive, foray, jaunt, range,
  route, shlep, tramp **06** bummel,
  cruise, flight, outing, ramble, roving,
  safari, schlep, travel, voyage, wander
07 milk run, odyssey, passage, proceed,
  sailing, schlepp, stretch, travels
08 campaign, crossing, progress
09 excursion, gallivant, walkabout
10 expedition, pilgrimage, wanderings
11 peregrinate **13** globetrotting,
  peregrination
• **good journey, safe journey**
08 godspeed **09** bon voyage
• **journey regularly**
03 ply **07** commute

journeyer

07 pilgrim, rambler, tourist, trekker,
  tripper, voyager **08** wanderer, wayfarer
09 traveller **12** peregrinator

joust

03 vie **04** just, spar, tilt **05** fight, giust,
  trial **06** jostle, justle **07** compete,
  contest, quarrel, tourney, wrangle
08 skirmish **09** encounter, pas d'armes
10 engagement, tournament

jovial

03 gay **04** boon, glad **05** happy, jolly,
  merry **06** cheery, genial, joyous, lively,
  wanton **07** affable, Bacchic, buoyant,
  cordial, gleeful **08** animated, Bacchian,
  cheerful, mirthful, sociable
09 convivial **11** Falstaffian **13** in good
spirits

joviality

03 fun **04** glee **05** mirth **06** gaiety
07 jollity **08** buoyancy, gladness,
  hilarity **09** happiness, merriment
10 affability, cheeriness, ebullience
12 cheerfulness

joy

03 gem **04** dear, glee, list, nuts
05 bliss, cheer, dream, exult, prize,
  treat **06** thrill **07** delight, ecstasy,
  elation, rapture, rejoice, success,
  victory **08** felicity, gladness, pleasure,

treasure **09** cloud nine, enjoyment, happiness, rejoicing, transport **10** exultation, joyfulness, jubilation **11** achievement **12** entrancement, satisfaction **13** gratification, seventh heaven **14** accomplishment, positive result

• **expression of joy**
02 ah, ha, ho, io **03** aha, hah, hey, hoa, hoh, ooh, rah, say, wow, yay **04** I say!, whee **05** heigh, hurra, huzza, oh boy!, tra-la, wowee, yahoo, yummy, zowie **06** banzai, gotcha, heyday, hooray, hurrah, hurray, yippee, yum-yum **07** whoopee

joyful
04 fain, glad **05** happy, merry **06** elated **07** festive, gleeful, pleased **08** cheerful, ecstatic, euphoric, feastful, gleesome, jubilant, pleasing, thrilled **09** delighted, gratified, overjoyed **10** exhilarant, triumphant **11** on cloud nine, over the moon, tickled pink **15** in seventh heaven, on top of the world

joyfully
06 gladly **07** happily **09** gleefully **10** cheerfully, jubilantly **12** ecstatically, euphorically, triumphantly

joyless
03 sad **04** dour, glum, grim **05** bleak, sober **06** dismal, dreary, gloomy, sombre **07** doleful, forlorn, serious, unhappy **08** dejected, downcast **09** cheerless, miserable **10** depressing, despondent, dispirited **12** discouraging

joyous
04 glad **05** happy, merry **06** festal, jovial, joyful **07** festive, gleeful **08** cheerful, ecstatic, frabjous, gladsome, jubilant **09** rapturous **10** blithesome, rollicking

joyously
06 gladly **07** happily, merrily **08** joyfully **10** cheerfully, jubilantly **11** rapturously **12** ecstatically

jubilant
06 elated, joyful **07** excited **08** ecstatic, euphoric, exultant, thrilled **09** delighted, exuberant, overjoyed, rejoicing, rhapsodic **10** triumphant **11** on cloud nine, over the moon, tickled pink **15** in seventh heaven, on top of the world

jubilation
03 joy **07** ecstasy, elation, jubilee, triumph **08** euphoria, jamboree **09** festivity, rejoicing **10** excitement, exultation **11** celebration **13** jollification

jubilee
04 fete, gala **07** holiday **08** carnival, feast day, festival **09** festivity **11** anniversary, celebration **13** commemoration **14** semi-centennial

Judas
07 traitor **08** betrayer, deceiver, quisling, renegade, turncoat **11** backstabber **13** tergiversator

judder
◇ *anagram indicator*
05 quake, shake **06** quiver **07** shudder, tremble, vibrate

judge
01 J **03** lud, ref, see, try, ump, wig **04** beak, damn, deem, doom, find, lord, rate, rule, scan **05** award, gauge, hakim, think, value, weigh **06** assess, critic, decern, decide, decree, expert, puisne, puisny, reckon, review, syndic, umpire **07** account, adjudge, arbiter, believe, censure, condemn, convict, coroner, discern, examine, her nibs, his nibs, justice, Law Lord, mediate, referee, set down, sheriff, weigh up **08** appraise, assessor, conclude, consider, doomsman, estimate, evaluate, mediator, recorder, reviewer, sentence **09** arbitrate, ascertain, authority, criticize, determine, evaluator, judiciary, justiciar, moderator, ombudsman, seneschal, syndicate **10** adjudicate, arbitrator, dijudicate, magistrate **11** adjudicator, connoisseur, distinguish **12** pass sentence **13** form an opinion, give a sentence **14** sit in judgement **15** deliver a verdict

Judges include:

04 Coke (Sir Edward)
05 Allen (Florence Ellinwood), Burgh (Hubert de), Draco, Minos, Solon
06 Aeacus, Burger (Warren Earl), Gideon, Holmes (Oliver Wendell), Irvine (Alexander, Lord), Mackay (James, Lord), Warren (Earl)
07 Brennan (William J), Denning (Alfred, Lord), Erskine (Thomas, Lord), O'Connor (Sandra Day), Scarman (Leslie, Lord)
08 Gardiner (Gerald, Lord), Ginsburg (Ruth Bader), Hailsham (Quintin McGarel Hogg, Viscount), Jeffreys (George, Lord), Marshall (John), Marshall (Thurgood)
09 Rehnquist (William), Vyshinsky (Andrei)
10 Elwyn-Jones (Frederick, Lord)
11 Butler-Sloss (Dame Elizabeth), Montesquieu (Charles-Louis de Secondat, Baron de)
12 Rhadamanthus

judgement
04 doom, fate, mind, view **05** award, order, sense, sight, taste **06** acumen, belief, decree, result, ruling, wisdom **07** decreet, finding, opinion, verdict **08** decision, estimate, prudence, sagacity, sapience, sentence, thinking **09** appraisal, criticism, damnation, diagnosis, good sense, mediation, reckoning, sentiment **10** assessment, judication, misfortune, perception, punishment, shrewdness

11 arbitration, common sense, discernment, penetration, retribution **12** adjudication, condemnation, intelligence, perspicacity **13** enlightenment, judiciousness, understanding **14** discrimination

judgemental
07 carping **08** critical, scathing **10** censorious, derogatory **11** disparaging **12** condemnatory, disapproving, fault-finding **13** hypercritical

judicial
05 legal **08** critical, forensic, official **09** decretory, impartial, judiciary, magistral **14** discriminating

judicially
07 legally **10** officially **11** impartially **12** forensically

judiciary
06 judges, the law **07** justice **08** the bench **10** magistracy **11** court system, legal system

judicious
04 wise **05** smart, sound **06** astute, clever, shrewd **07** careful, prudent **08** cautious, discreet, informed, rational, sensible, wise-like **09** sagacious, well-timed **10** considered, discerning, reasonable, thoughtful, well-judged **11** circumspect, common-sense, intelligent, well-advised **14** discriminating

judiciously
06 wisely **08** astutely, sensibly, shrewdly **09** carefully, prudently **10** cautiously **11** sagaciously **12** discerningly, thoughtfully **13** circumspectly

judo see **martial art**

jug
03 jar, urn **04** ewer, olpe, Toby **05** crock **06** carafe, flagon, pourie, prison, vessel **07** bombard, creamer, growler, pitcher, Toby jug **08** decanter, imprison **09** blackjack, container **10** aquamanale, aquamanile, bellarmine, receptacle **11** Enghalskrug
See also **prison**

juggle
◇ *anagram indicator*
03 rig **04** cook, fake **05** alter **06** adjust, change, doctor, fiddle, tamper **07** balance, conjure, falsify, massage **08** disguise, equalize **09** rearrange **10** hocus-pocus, manipulate, tamper with **12** misrepresent

juice
03 jus, oil, sap **04** must **05** fluid, serum **06** cremor, liquid, liquor, nectar, succus, walnut **07** enliven, essence, extract **08** piquancy, vitality **09** secretion **10** pancreatin

juicy
03 hot, wet **04** lush, racy **05** lurid, moist, sappy, spicy, vivid **06** risqué,

watery **07** flowing **08** exciting **09** colourful, succulent, thrilling **10** profitable, scandalous, suggestive **11** interesting, sensational

jujube
04 jube **05** lotus **08** zizyphus **12** Christ's-thorn

Juliet
01 J

July
02 Jy **03** Jul

jumble
◇ *anagram indicator*
02 pi **03** mix, pie, pye **04** jolt, junk, mess **05** chaos, mix up, mix-up **06** garble, huddle, jabble, jumbal, medley, mingle, muddle, raffle, tangle, tumble, wuzzle **07** clutter, confuse, jolting, mixture, rummage, shuffle **08** cast-offs, disarray, disorder, hotchpot, mishmash, mixy-maxy, oddments, pastiche, shambles **09** bric-à-brac, confusion, pasticcio, potpourri, praiseach **10** disarrange, hodgepodge, hotchpotch, miscellany, mixty-maxty **11** disorganize, printer's pie **12** mingle-mangle, mixter-maxter, mixtie-maxtie **14** conglomeration

jumbled
◇ *anagram indicator*
06 untidy **07** chaotic, garbled, huddled, mixed-up, muddled, tangled, tumbled **08** confused, shuffled, unsorted **10** disarrayed, disordered **11** farraginous **12** disorganized, mingle-mangle **13** miscellaneous

jumbo
02 OS **04** huge, mega, vast **05** giant **07** immense, mammoth, massive, outsize, Titanic **08** colossal, elephant, enormous, gigantic, whopping **09** ginormous, walloping **10** extra-large

jump
◇ *anagram indicator*
03 gap, hop, jar, lep, mug **04** axel, gain, gate, go up, hike, jerk, jolt, leap, lutz, miss, omit, rail, rise, risk, romp, skip **05** avoid, boost, bound, break, caper, clear, fence, frisk, halma, hedge, lapse, lurch, mount, ollie, quail, shake, shock, shoot, space, spasm, sport, start, surge, throb, vault, wince **06** ascend, attack, beat up, bounce, breach, bypass, cavort, cut out, do over, flinch, frolic, gambol, go over, hazard, hiatus, hurdle, ignore, lacuna, leap up, pounce, prance, quiver, recoil, shiver, spiral, spring, switch, twitch, upturn **07** advance, assault, barrier, digress, exactly, flicker, salchow, set upon, shoot up, swoop on, toe loop, upsurge, venture **08** batterie, bunny hop, escalate, go across, increase, interval, leave out, mounting, obstacle, omission, overlook, pass over, pounce on, spring on **09** barricade, disregard, elevation, increment, stage-dive **10** appreciate, escalation, quersprung,

trampoline **12** Becher's Brook, interruption

• **jump at**
04 grab **05** seize **06** accept, leap at, snatch **07** agree to, fall for, seize on, swallow **08** pounce on **13** accept eagerly, accept quickly

• **jump on**
05 blame, chide, fly at, scold **06** berate, rebuke, revile **07** censure, reprove, tick off, upbraid **08** reproach **09** castigate, criticize, reprimand

• **jump the gun**
10 act hastily, act too soon, anticipate **13** start too early **14** act prematurely

jumper
03 roo **04** euro, flea **05** lammy **06** jersey, lammie, woolly **07** sweater **08** kangaroo, pullover, wallaroo **10** churn-drill, sweatshirt

jumpy
04 edgy **05** bumpy, het up, jerky, nappy, nervy, rough, shaky, tense **06** bouncy, fitful, on edge, uneasy **07** anxious, fidgety, in a stew, jittery, jolting, keyed up, nervous, panicky, restive, shaking, twitchy, uptight, wound up **08** agitated, in a sweat, in a tizzy, lurching **09** spasmodic, squirrely **10** convulsive, incoherent, squirrelly **12** apprehensive, disconnected, uncontrolled **13** unco-ordinated

junction
01 T **04** bond, cove, join, link, node, seam, toll **05** close, crown, graft, joint, raphe, union **06** circus, collar, infall, suture **07** cornice, joining, linking, meeting, welding **08** abutment, coupling, crossing, juncture, knitting **09** interface, symphysis, T-junction **10** confluence, connection, crossroads, match-joint **11** box junction, combination, interchange **12** intersection, meeting-point

juncture
04 crux, time **05** point, stage, union **06** crisis, minute, moment, period **07** article, joining **08** occasion **09** emergency, situation **11** predicament

June
03 Jun

jungle
03 web **04** bush, heap, mass, maze **05** chaos, shola, snarl **06** growth, medley, tangle **07** clutter **08** disarray, disorder, mishmash **09** confusion, labyrinth **10** hotchpotch, miscellany, rainforest **14** tropical forest

junior
02 Jr **03** Jnr, Jun, lad **04** fils, Junr **05** chota, lower, minor, young **06** lesser, minion, puisne, puisny, rating **07** servant, younger **08** dogsbody, inferior, under-boy **09** assistant, associate, secondary, underling **10** subsidiary **11** subordinate

junk
◇ *anagram indicator*
◇ *deletion indicator*
04 dump, spam **05** chuck, chunk, ditch, dregs, scrap, trash, waste **06** debris, litter, refuse **07** clutter, discard, garbage, rubbish, rummage **08** cast-offs, get rid of, jettison, leavings, narcotic, nonsense, oddments, throw out, wreckage **09** bric-à-brac, dispose of, leftovers, throw away, worthless

junket
02 do **04** bash, trip **05** beano, feast, spree, visit **06** outing, picnic, regale **07** banquet, journey **09** entertain **11** celebration

Juno
04 Hera

junta
03 set **04** gang, ring **05** cabal, group, party **06** cartel, clique, league **07** coterie, council, faction, meeting **08** conclave **09** camarilla **11** confederacy

Jupiter
04 Zeus

jurisdiction
04 area, bail, rule, soke, sway, zone **05** field, orbit, power, range, reach, right, scope, soken, verge **06** bounds, region, sphere **07** command, control, mastery **08** capacity, district, dominion, province **09** authority, influence, territory **10** cognizance, competence, domination, judicature, leadership **11** prerogative, sovereignty **14** administration

jury
04 pais **05** panel, quest **06** assize, jurors **07** jurymen **09** grand jury, jurywomen, party-jury, petit jury, petty jury

just
03 all, apt, due **04** egal, even, fair, good, only, to a T **05** equal, exact, joust, legal, moral, quite, right, sound, valid **06** bang on, barely, earned, hardly, honest, indeed, lately, lawful, merely, normal, proper, purely, simply, spot-on **07** ethical, exactly, fitting, merited, neutral, sincere, upright **08** deserved, recently, rightful, scarcely, suitable, truthful, unbiased, virtuous **09** equitable, impartial, justified, objective, perfectly, precisely, righteous **10** absolutely, a moment ago, completely, even-handed, fair-minded, honourable, legitimate, nothing but, principled, reasonable, upstanding **11** appropriate, well-founded **12** unprejudiced, well-deserved, well-grounded **13** a short time ago, disinterested, incorruptible, true-disposing **14** irreproachable

• **just about**
06 all but, almost, nearly **08** as good as, well-nigh **09** virtually **10** more or less **11** practically

- **just after**
02 on

justice
01 J 02 CJ, JP, LJ 03 law 05 judge, right
06 amends, equity, ethics, honour,
morals 07 honesty, nemesis, penalty,
redress, sheriff 08 fairness, fair play,
justness, legality, validity 09 integrity,
propriety, rectitude, rightness,
soundness 10 lawfulness, legitimacy,
magistrate, neutrality, punishment,
recompense, reparation 11 objectivity,
uprightness 12 compensation,
impartiality, rightfulness, satisfaction
13 equitableness, righteousness
14 even-handedness, fair-
mindedness, reasonableness
15 justifiableness

justifiable
03 fit 05 legal, right, sound, valid
06 lawful, proper 07 tenable
08 sensible 09 excusable, justified,
plausible, warranted 10 acceptable,
defensible, explicable, forgivable,
legitimate, pardonable, reasonable
11 explainable, supportable,
sustainable, warrantable, well-founded
12 within reason 14 understandable

justifiably
07 legally, rightly, validly 08 lawfully,
properly 09 excusably, plausibly

10 acceptably, defensibly, reasonably
12 legitimately, within reason
14 understandably

justification
04 plea 05 basis 06 excuse, reason
07 apology, defence, defense,
grounds, warrant 08 warranty
10 absolution, mitigation
11 explanation, vindication
12 confirmation, verification
15 rationalization

justify
04 aver, avow 05 clear, prove
06 acquit, defend, excuse, pardon,
punish, uphold, verify 07 absolve, bear
out, confirm, darrain, darrayn, deraign,
deserve, explain, forgive, support,
sustain, warrant 08 darraign, darraine,
maintain, make good, validate
09 authorize, darraigne, establish,
exculpate, exonerate, vindicate
10 stand up for 11 rationalize
12 substantiate 13 show to be right
14 give grounds for, give reasons for

justly
04 duly 05 right 06 fairly 07 equally,
rightly 08 honestly, lawfully, properly
09 equitably 10 rightfully, with reason
11 deservingly, impartially, justifiably,
objectively 12 even-handedly,
legitimately

jut, jut out
03 jet 04 butt 05 jetty, jutty, stick
06 beetle, extend 07 extrude, project
08 overhang, protrude, stick out
10 projection

jute
03 tow 05 gunny, kenaf, urena
06 burlap 07 Hessian, hopsack
09 Corchorus 10 hop-sacking, Jews'
mallow

juvenile
03 boy, juv, kid 04 girl 05 child, green,
minor, young, youth 06 callow, infant,
junior 07 babyish, puerile, teenage
08 childish, immature, teenager,
youthful 09 infantile, youngster
10 adolescent 11 young person
13 inexperienced 15 unsophisticated

Juventus
04 Hebe

juxtapose
06 empale, impale 11 put together
13 place together, put side by side
15 place side by side

juxtaposition
07 contact 08 nearness, vicinity
09 closeness, immediacy, proximity
10 apposition, contiguity, impalement

K

3 Kay 04 kara, kesh, kilo 06 kaccha, kangha, kirpan

kaleidoscopic
05 fluid 06 motley 08 manifold 10 changeable, poikilitic, polychrome, variegated 11 fluctuating 12 ever-hanging, many-coloured, multifarious 13 multicoloured, parti-coloured, polychromatic 15 many-splendoured

kame
02 ås 05 eskar, esker

kangaroo
03 roo 04 euro, joey 06 boomer, old man 07 steamer, wallaby 08 forester, wallaroo

Kansas
02 KS 04 Kans

kaput
04 bust, phut 06 broken, ruined, undone 07 defunct, extinct, smashed, wrecked 08 finished 09 conked out, destroyed

karate
08 Shotokan

Shotokan belts include:
03 red
05 black, brown, green, white
06 orange, purple, yellow
20 brown with white stripe
21 purple with white stripe
24 brown with two white stripes
see also **martial art**

• **karate costume**
02 gi 03 gie

kay
01 K

Kazakhstan
02 KZ 03 KAZ

keel
04 back, base, cool, ship, skeg
05 barge, skegg 06 bottom, carina, puddle 07 keelson 08 backbone
10 stabilizer 11 centreboard
12 cheesecutter
• **keel over**
◇ *reversal down indicator*
04 drop, fall 05 faint, swoon, upset
07 capsize, founder, pass out, stagger
08 black out, collapse, overturn
10 topple over, turn turtle 14 turn upside down

keen
03 cry, mad, sob 04 acid, avid, cold, deep, fell, fine, gleg, howl, moan, nuts, wail, weep, wild, wise, yowl 05 acute, breem, breme, crazy, eager, groan, mourn, potty, quick, razor, sharp, smart, snell 06 argute, astute, biting, caring, clever, fierce, fond of, grieve, intent, lament, liking, loving, narrow, severe, shrewd, shrill, strong 07 anxious, devoted, earnest, fervent, hawking, hawkish, intense, mordant, nipping, pointed, pungent, sharpen, ululate 08 diligent, incisive, piercing, ruthless, stinging 09 assiduous, cut-throat, devoted to, dog-eat-dog, enamoured, impatient, quick-eyed, razor-like, sagacious, sensitive, trenchant, wide awake, wonderful 10 attached to, discerning, double-eyed, perceptive, razor-sharp 11 heavily into, industrious, lamentation, penetrating, quick-witted, sharp-witted 12 enthusiastic 13 conscientious, keen as mustard, perspicacious 14 discriminating

keenly
06 deeply, shrewd 07 acutely, eagerly, quickly, sharply 08 astutely, cleverly, fiercely, shrewdly, strongly 09 earnestly, fervently, intensely 10 diligently, incisively 11 assiduously, sensitively 12 perceptively 13 penetratingly

keenness
03 eye 04 edge 06 wisdom 08 industry, sagacity, sapience, sedulity 09 diligence, eagerness, sharpness 10 astuteness, cleverness, enthusiasm, shrewdness, trenchancy 11 discernment, earnestness, penetration, sensitivity 12 incisiveness 15 industriousness

keep
◇ *containment indicator*
◇ *hidden indicator*
03 own, run 04 curb, feed, food, fort, have, heap, hold, last, mark, mind, obey, pile, rear, save, stay, tend 05 amass, block, board, breed, carry, check, delay, deter, guard, hoard, limit, means, place, raise, stack, stock, store, tower, watch 06 arrest, castle, deal in, defend, detain, donjon, endure, foster, fulfil, hamper, hinder, hold up, honour, impede, keep at, keep on, keep up, living, manage, pile up, remain, retain, retard, shield, upkeep 07 abide by, care for, carry on, citadel, collect, conduct, confine, control, deposit, dungeon, furnish, inhibit, nurture, observe, perform, persist, possess, prevent, protect, refrain, reserve, respect, shelter, store up, support, sustain 08 adhere to, carry out, conserve, continue, fortress, hang on to, hold back, hold on to, keep back, maintain, obstruct, preserve, restrain, withhold 09 celebrate, constrain, look after, persevere, recognize, safeguard, solemnize, subsidize, watch over 10 accumulate, comply with, effectuate, livelihood, perpetuate, provide for, stronghold, sustenance, take care of 11 commemorate, keep waiting, maintenance, not part with, nourishment, subsistence, superintend 12 be in charge of, have charge of 13 have custody of, interfere with, keep faith with 15 keep in good order
• **for keeps**
06 always 07 for ever, for good 10 for all time
• **keep at**
03 nag 04 last, stay, toil 05 grind 06 badger, drudge, endure, finish, labour, remain, slog at 07 carry on, persist, stick at 08 complete, continue, fight off, maintain 09 persevere 10 plug away at 11 be steadfast 12 beaver away at
• **keep back**
◇ *reversal indicator*
04 curb, hide, save, stop 05 check, delay, hoard, limit, store 06 censor, hinder, hold up, hush up, impede, retain, retard, stifle 07 conceal, control, inhibit, repress, reserve 08 hold back, keep down, lay aside, prohibit, restrain, restrict, set aside, suppress, withhold 09 constrain, stockpile 10 accumulate, keep secret
• **keep from**
04 halt, help, stop 06 desist, resist 07 forbear, prevent, refrain 08 restrain
• **keep in**
04 hide 05 quell 06 coop up, detain, shut in, stifle, stop up 07 conceal, confine, control, inhibit, repress 08 bottle up, keep back, restrain, suppress
• **keep off**
05 avoid, expel, fence, parry 07 stay off 08 hands off, keep away 09 not go near 10 keep-swerve 12 stay away from, steer clear of 14 avoid going near
• **keep on**
04 go on, last, stay 06 endure, hold on, remain, retain 07 carry on, persist 08 continue, keep at it, maintain 09 persevere, soldier on, stick at it 13 stay the course 14 continue to hire
• **keep on at**
03 nag 05 harry 06 badger, chivvy, go

on at, harass, pester, plague, pursue
09 importune
- **keep secret**
04 hide **07** conceal **08** keep back,
keep dark, suppress **09** dissemble
14 keep under wraps
- **keep to**
04 obey **06** fulfil **07** observe, respect,
stick to **08** adhere to **10** comply with
- **keep up**
03 vie **05** equal, match, rival **06** retain
07 compete, contend, emulate, persist,
support, sustain **08** continue, keep
pace, maintain, preserve **09** entertain,
persevere **10** keep tabs on **11** go along
with **13** keep abreast of **15** keep in
touch with

keeper
03 nab **05** guard **06** custos, escort,
gaoler, jailer, mahout, minder, parker,
parkie, warden, warder **07** curator,
granger, marshal, steward **08** defender,
governor, guardian, overseer, surveyor,
vesturer **09** archivist, attendant,
bodyguard, caretaker, castellan,
constable, custodian, guard ring,
inspector **10** austringer, châtelaine,
proprietor, supervisor **11** conservator,
park-officer **13** administrator
14 superintendent

keep fit
02 PE, PT

keeping
04 care, cure, hand, ward **05** aegis,
hands, store, trust **06** accord, charge
07 balance, custody, harmony, support
08 auspices, tutelage **09** agreement,
congruity, patronage, retention
10 compliance, conformity,
observance, proportion, protection
11 consistency, maintenance,
reservation, safe-keeping,
supervision **12** guardianship,
preservation, surveillance
14 correspondence

keepsake
05 relic, token **06** emblem, pledge
07 memento **08** reminder, souvenir
11 remembrance

keg
02 kg **03** tun, vat **04** butt, cask, drum
06 barrel, firkin **08** hogshead

kelvin
01 K

ken
04 know **05** field, grasp, range, reach,
scope **06** notice **07** compass
09 awareness, knowledge
10 cognizance, perception
11 realization **12** acquaintance,
appreciation **13** comprehension,
understanding

Kent
02 SE

Kentucky
02 KY

Kenya
03 EAK, KEN

kerfuffle
03 ado **04** flap, fuss, to-do **05** hoo-ha,
tizzy **06** bother, bustle, flurry, furore
07 agitate, carry-on, fluster, palaver
08 ballyhoo, brouhaha, disorder
09 agitation, commotion

kernel
03 nub, nut **04** core, corn, crux, germ,
gist, seed **05** copra, gland, grain, heart,
stone **06** almond, centre, marrow,
nutmeg **07** essence, innards, nucleus
08 pichurim **09** pistachio, substance
11 nitty-gritty, quandong-nut **12** nuts
and bolts, quintessence

kestrel
06 keelie **07** staniel, stannel, stanyel
08 stallion **09** windhover

key
01 A, B, C, D, E, F, G, H **03** cue **04** clue,
code, crib, kaie, main, mood, note,
sign, tone **05** basic, chief, gloss, guide,
index, major, means, pitch, style, table,
vital, wedge **06** answer, clavis, legend,
secret, timbre, winder **07** central,
crucial, leading, pointer, spanner
08 decisive, glossary, solution
09 character, essential, important,
indicator, necessary, principal
11 explanation, explication,
fundamental, translation **12** passe-
partout **14** interpretation
See also **island**

*Keys on a computer keyboard
include:*

03 alt, del, end, esc, ins, tab
04 ctrl, home, pg dn, pg up
05 alt gr, enter
06 delete, insert, page up
07 num lock
08 caps lock, page down

- **key stem**
03 pin

keynote
01 C **04** core, gist, mese, pith **05** final,
heart, point, theme, tonic **06** accent,
centre, marrow, stress **07** essence
08 emphasis **09** substance

keystone
04 base, core, crux, root **05** basis,
quoin **06** ground, motive, source,
spring **07** sagitta **08** linchpin
09 principle **10** foundation,
mainspring **11** cornerstone

kick
◇ *anagram indicator*
03 fun, hit, pep, toe, zip **04** bite, blow,
boot, buzz, chip, foot, hack, heel, high,
hoof, jolt, knee, lark, lift, punt, quit,
shin, spur, stop, tang, yerk, zing
05 break, fling, pause, power, punce,
punch, react, shoot, spurn, wince
06 effect, falter, give up, jack in, let out,
pack in, recoil, strike, thrill
07 abandon, dropout, fly-kick,
grubber, lash out, misfire, penalty,
potency, project, rebound, spurn at,
tap-kick **08** back-heel, drop-kick, free
kick, goal kick, grub kick, high kick,

jump back, leave off, move back,
pleasure, pungency, set piece,
sixpence, spot kick, stimulus, strength,
striking **09** boomerang, cross-kick,
garryowen, place kick **10** desist from,
excitement, pile-driver, point after,
resilience, resistance, spring back
11 stimulation **12** recalcitrate, spurn
against
- **kick against**
04 defy **05** rebel, spurn **06** oppose,
resist **07** protest **09** withstand **14** hold
out against
- **kick around**
03 use **05** abuse **07** discuss, exploit,
toy with **08** ill-treat, maltreat, play
with **09** mess about, push about, talk
about, trample on **10** mess around,
push around **15** take advantage of
- **kick off**
03 die **04** open **05** begin, start
08 commence, initiate **09** introduce
10 inaugurate **11** get under way
- **kick out**
04 oust, sack, spur **05** eject, evict,
expel **06** reject, remove **07** boot out,
dismiss, turf out **08** chuck out, get rid
of, throw out **09** discharge **13** give the
boot to, give the push to, give the sack
to **14** give the elbow to

kickback
05 bribe **06** pay-off, recoil
07 rebound **08** backlash, reaction
09 incentive, sweetener **10** back-
hander, inducement

kick-off
02 KO **05** start **06** outset, word go
07 opening **09** beginning, inception
12 commencement, introduction

kid
03 boy, con, imp, lad, rib, tot **04** brat,
dupe, fool, girl, gull, hoax, jest, joke,
wean **05** bairn, child, kiddy, sprog,
tease, trick, youth **06** delude, faggot,
have on, humbug, infant, nipper, rug
rat, wind up **07** deceive, littlin, littl 'un,
pretend, tiny tot, toddler, young 'un
08 cheverel, cheveril, hoodwink,
juvenile, littling, teenager, yeanling,
young one **09** bamboozle, deception,
kiddywink, littleane, little boy, little
one, youngster **10** adolescent, ankle-
biter, little girl **11** young person

kidnap
05 seize, steal **06** abduct, hijack,
snatch **07** capture **08** carry off **12** hold
to ransom **13** hold as hostage, take as
hostage

kill
03 axe, bag, end, ice, pip, sap, top, use,
zap **04** ache, do in, dull, ease, fill, hang,
hurt, pass, prey, ruin, slay **05** death,
drain, mop-up, napoo, pound, quash,
quell, shoot, smart, smite, spend, spoil,
still, sting, throb, total, use up, waste,
weary, whack **06** behead, be sore,
climax, deaden, defeat, dilute, fag out,
finish, lay low, muffle, murder, occupy,
reject, rub out, settle, soothe, stifle,
strain, suffer, twinge, weaken

07 abolish, bump off, butcher, cut down, destroy, discard, execute, exhaust, fatigue, kiss off, knacker, nullify, put down, relieve, scupper, smother, stonker, take out, tire out, wipe out **08** blow away, decimate, despatch, dispatch, knock off, massacre, moderate, ring-bark, shoot-out, suppress **09** alleviate, be painful, cause pain, death-blow, devastate, dispose of, do to death, eliminate, eradicate, finish off, liquidate, overexert, polish off, shoot dead, slaughter, while away **10** annihilate, conclusion, decapitate, dénouement, do away with, extinguish, guillotine, neutralize, put an end to, put to death, put to sleep **11** assassinate, coup de grâce, electrocute, exterminate, stab to death, take it out of

killer
03 gun, orc **04** orca **06** gunman, hit-man, ice man, slayer **07** butcher, matador, shooter **08** assassin, hired gun, homicide, murderer **09** cut-throat, destroyer **10** hatchet man, liquidator, man-queller, stupendous **11** axe murderer, executioner, slaughterer **12** exterminator, mass murderer, serial killer, woman-queller
• **natural killer**
02 NK

killing
03 hit **04** coup, gain, hard **05** booty, death, funny **06** absurd, big hit, deadly, murder, profit, taxing, tiring **07** amusing, arduous, a scream, bonanza, carnage, clean-up, comical, fortune, slaying, success, wearing **08** butchery, draining, fatality, genocide, homicide, massacre, windfall **09** bloodshed, execution, fatiguing, gruelling, hilarious, ludicrous, mactation, matricide, patricide, predation, slaughter, uxoricide **10** enervating, exhausting, fratricide, hysterical, lucky break, sororicide, uproarious **11** destruction, destructive, elimination, fascinating, infanticide, liquidation, rib-tickling **12** back-breaking, debilitating, irresistible, manslaughter, stroke of luck **13** assassination, extermination, side-splitting

killjoy
05 cynic **06** damper, grouch, misery, moaner, whiner **07** sceptic **08** buzzkill, dampener **09** pessimist **10** complainer, spoilsport, wet blanket **11** Weary Willie **12** trouble-mirth **13** prophet of doom

kiln
04 oast **05** stove **06** muffle

kilo
01 K

kilt
07 filabeg, filibeg **08** fillibeg, philabeg, philibeg **09** phillabeg, phillibeg **10** fustanella

kilter
• **out of kilter**
04 awry **05** askew **08** confused, lopsided **09** skew-whiff **10** misaligned, unbalanced **12** out of balance

kin
04 clan **05** blood, catty, stock, tribe **06** family, people **07** cousins, kindred, lineage, related **08** affinity **09** relations, relatives **10** extraction **12** relationship **13** consanguinity, flesh and blood

kina
01 K

kind
03 ilk, set **04** form, good, mild, nice, race, sort, type, warm **05** beget, brand, breed, class, genre, genus, stamp, style **06** benign, family, genial, gentle, giving, humane, kindly, loving, manner, nature, strain **07** amiable, cordial, helpful, lenient, patient, pitying, species, tactful, variety **08** amicable, category, friendly, generous, gracious, merciful, obliging, selfless, tolerant **09** agreeable, bounteous, character, congenial, courteous, indulgent, unselfish **10** altruistic, benevolent, big-hearted, charitable, forbearing, persuasion, thoughtful **11** considerate, description, good-hearted, good-natured, kind-hearted, magnanimous, neighbourly, soft-hearted, sympathetic, temperament, warm-hearted **12** affectionate, humanitarian **13** compassionate, philanthropic, tender-hearted, understanding
• **in kind**
08 in return, in specie **09** similarly, tit for tat **10** in exchange **12** in like manner
• **kind of**
◊ anagram indicator
04 a bit **05** kinda, quite **06** fairly, pretty, rather, sort of **07** a little **08** slightly, somewhat **10** moderately, relatively **12** to some degree, to some extent

kind-hearted
04 kind, warm **06** benign, humane, kindly **07** helpful **08** amicable, generous, gracious, obliging **10** altruistic, big-hearted **11** considerate, good-hearted, good-natured, sympathetic, warm-hearted **12** humanitarian **13** compassionate, philanthropic, tender-hearted

kindle
03 fan **04** blow, fire, lunt, stir, tind, tine, tynd **05** brood, light, rouse, spark, teend, tynde **06** accend, arouse, awaken, excite, ignite, incite, induce, litter, thrill **07** enlight, incense, inflame, inspire, provoke **09** set alight, set fire to, set on fire, stimulate

kindliness
06 nature, warmth **07** charity **08** kindness, sympathy **09** benignity **10** amiability, compassion, generosity

11 beneficence, benevolence **12** friendliness **14** loving-kindness

kindly
04 fond, good, kind, mild, nice, warm **06** benign, couthy, genial, gentle, gently, giving, goodly, humane, native, please, polite, tender, warmly **07** benefic, cordial, couthie, helpful, natural, patient **08** amicable, benignly, friendly, generous, humanely, lovingly, pleasant **09** agreeable, avuncular, helpfully, indulgent, patiently, tactfully **10** benevolent, big-hearted, charitable, charitably, favourable, generously, mercifully, selflessly, thoughtful, tolerantly **11** considerate, courteously, good-natured, kind-hearted, magnanimous, neighbourly, sympathetic, unselfishly **12** benevolently, thoughtfully **13** compassionate, considerately, grandfatherly, kind-heartedly, magnanimously, understanding **14** affectionately, altruistically **15** compassionately, sympathetically

kindness
03 aid **04** help, love **05** grace **06** favour, warmth **07** aggrace, benefit, candour, charity, service **08** altruism, courtesy, good deed, goodness, good turn, goodwill, humanity, leniency, mildness, niceness, patience, sympathy **09** affection, benignity, tolerance **10** assistance, benignancy, compassion, generosity, gentleness, humaneness, indulgence, kindliness **11** beneficence, benevolence, helpfulness, hospitality, magnanimity **12** friendliness, philanthropy, pleasantness **13** consideration, fellow feeling, Gemütlichkeit, understanding **14** loving-kindness, thoughtfulness **15** considerateness, humanitarianism, warm-heartedness

kindred
03 kin, sib **04** akin, clan, folk, hapu, like **05** flesh, house, stock **06** allied, common, family, people **07** cognate, lineage, related, similar **08** affinity, kinsfolk, matching **09** congenial, connected, relations, relatives **10** affiliated, similarity **11** connections **12** relationship **13** consanguinity, corresponding, flesh and blood

king
01 K, R **02** HM **03** Rex, Roi **04** Inca, lord, shah, star **05** chief, ruler **06** bigwig, kaiser, leader, master, prince, top dog **07** big shot, emperor, kingpin, majesty, monarch, supremo **08** big noise **09** big cheese, chieftain, sovereign **11** head of state, the greatest **12** leading light

Kings include:

03 Ban, Ida, Ine, Lot, Zog
04 Ahab, Cnut, Cole, Edwy, Erik, Fahd, Ivan, Ivan (the Terrible), John, John (the Blind), Karl, Knut, Lear, Offa, Olaf, Olav, Otto, Paul, Quin, Saud, Saul, Zeus

05 Boris, Brian, Bruce (Robert), Capet (Hugo or Hugh), Carol, Creon, David, Edgar, Edred, Edwin (St), Henri, Henry, Henry (the Fowler), Herod (the Great), Hiero, Ixion, James, Louis, Midas, Murat (Joachim), Penda, Pepin (the Short), Priam, Svein, Sweyn

06 Alaric, Albert, Alboin, Alfred, Alonso, Arthur, Attila, Baliol (Edward de), Canute, Cheops, Clovis, Darius, Donald, Duncan, Edmund, Edmund (Ironside), Edward, Edward (the Confessor), Edward (the Elder), Edward (the Martyr), Egbert, Faisal, Farouk, George, Gustav, Haakon, Harald, Harold, Harold (Harefoot), Hassan, Khalid, Magnus, Oberon, Oswald (St), Philip, Ramses, Robert, Robert (the Bruce), Rudolf, Sargon, Xerxes

07 Alfonso, Aragorn, Balliol (John de), Cepheus, Charles, Croesus, Emanuel, Francis, Fredrik, Humbert, Hussein, Ibn Saud, Kenneth, Leopold, Macbeth, Malcolm, Michael, Odoacer, Perseus, Ptolemy, Pyrrhus, Rameses, Richard, Romulus, Solomon, Stephen, Tarquin, Umberto, Wilhelm, William, William (the Conqueror), William (the Silent)

08 Baudouin, Birendra, Ethelred, Ethelred (the Unready), Frederik, Gaiseric, Gustavus, Jeroboam, Leonidas, Matthias, Ramesses, Sihanouk (Norodom), Thutmose

09 Aethelred, Akhenaten, Alexander, Alexander (the Great), Amenhotep, Antigonus, Antiochus, Athelstan, Christian, Cuchulain, Cymbeline, Ethelbert, Ethelwulf, Ferdinand, Frederick, Hammurabi, Hardaknut, Nadir Shah, Sigismund, Stanislaw, Taufa'ahau, Theodoric, Tuthmosis, Vortigern, Wenceslas, Wladyslaw, Zahir Shah (Mohammed)

10 Aethelbert, Aethelstan, Aethelwulf, Artaxerxes, Carl Gustaf, Esarhaddon, Fisher King, Juan Carlos, Moshoeshoe, Ozymandias, Tarquinius, Wenceslaus

11 Charlemagne, Constantine, Franz Joseph, Hardacanute, Hardicanute, Mithridates, Old King Cole, Sennacherib, Shalmaneser, Tut'ankhamun

12 Assurbanipal, Boris Godunov, Herod Agrippa

13 Chulalongkorn, Louis-Philippe

14 Nebuchadnezzar, Philip Augustus, Victor Emmanuel

15 Artaxerxes Ochus, Norodom Sihanouk

• **Three Kings** *see* **wise man** *under* **wise**

See also **Roman**

kingdom
04 land **05** realm, reign, state **06** domain, empire, nation, sphere

07 country, dynasty **08** division, dominion, grouping, monarchy, province **09** territory **11** sovereignty **12** commonwealth, principality
See also **classification**; **empire**

kingfisher
07 halcyon **10** kookaburra

kingly
05 grand, noble, regal, royal **06** august, lordly **07** stately, sublime, supreme **08** glorious, imperial, imposing, majestic, splendid **09** dignified, grandiose, imperious, sovereign **11** monarchical

Kingsley
03 Ben **04** Amis

kink
◊ *anagram indicator*
03 bug **04** bend, coil, curl, dent, flaw, gasp, knot, loop, null, whim **05** chink, cough, crick, crimp, curve, hitch, quirk, twirl, twist **06** defect, fetish, foible, glitch, tangle **07** blemish, caprice, crinkle, failing, wrinkle **08** weakness **09** deviation, weak point **10** deficiency, perversion **11** indentation, peculiarity, shortcoming **12** eccentricity, entanglement, idiosyncrasy, imperfection

kinkajou
05 potto **09** honey bear

kinky
◊ *anagram indicator*
03 odd **04** wavy **05** crazy, curly, funky, queer, weird **06** coiled, curled, frizzy, quirky, warped **07** bizarre, crimped, deviant, strange, tangled, twisted, unusual **08** abnormal, crumpled, depraved, freakish, peculiar, wrinkled **09** eccentric, perverted, unnatural, whimsical **10** capricious, degenerate, licentious, outlandish **13** idiosyncratic **14** unconventional

kinsfolk
03 kin **04** clan, hapu **06** family **07** cousins, kindred **09** relations, relatives **11** connections

kinship
03 kin, sib, tie **04** ties **05** blood **06** family **07** kindred, lineage **08** affinity, alliance, ancestry, likeness, relation **09** community **10** conformity, connection, similarity **11** association, equivalence **12** relationship **13** consanguinity **14** correspondence

kinsman
03 sib **04** ally **06** cousin **07** brother

kiosk
03 box **05** booth, cabin, stall, stand **07** counter **09** bandstand, bookstall, news-stand

Kiribati
03 KIR

Kirkpatrick
01 K

kismet
03 lot **04** doom, fate **05** karma **07** destiny, fortune, portion **10** predestiny, providence

kiss
01 X **03** fan, lip, pax **04** buss, lick, neck, pash, peck, snog **05** brush, cross, graze, mouth, smack, touch **06** caress, scrape, smooch, smouch **07** plonker, smacker **08** canoodle, deep kiss, osculate, suck face **09** baisemain, glance off **10** bill and coo, contrecoup, French kiss, osculation **11** touch gently **12** touch lightly **13** butterfly kiss

kit
03 rig, set **04** gear, togs **05** get-up, strip, stuff, tools **06** kitten, outfit, rig-out, tackle, things **07** baggage, clobber, clothes, colours, effects, luggage **08** clothing, supplies, utensils **09** apparatus, equipment, trappings **10** implements, provisions **11** instruments **13** accoutrements, appurtenances, paraphernalia
• **kit out**
03 arm **05** dress, equip, fix up **06** fit out, outfit, rig out, supply **07** deck out, furnish, garnish, prepare, provide

kitchen
03 but **06** galley **07** caboose, cookery, cuisine **08** scullery **10** percussion
See also **utensil**

kite
04 gled **05** belly, glede **06** dragon, elanet, Milvus, paunch **07** puttock, rokkaku **08** aircraft

kittenish
04 cute **05** ludic **06** frisky **07** playful **08** skittish, sportive **09** fun-loving **10** coquettish, frolicsome **11** flirtatious

kittiwake
06 haglet **07** hacklet

kitty
04 fund

knack
03 art, toy **04** bent, feel, gift, hang, turn **05** flair, forte, habit, quirk, skill, trick **06** genius, talent **07** ability, faculty **08** aptitude, capacity, facility, ornament **09** dexterity, expertise, handiness, quickness, technique **10** adroitness, capability, competence, propensity **11** proficiency, skilfulness

knapsack
03 bag **04** pack **06** kitbag **07** holdall, musette **08** backpack, rucksack **09** duffel bag, haversack

knave
01 J **03** boy, cad, nob, pam, pur **04** jack **05** cheat, drôle, rogue, scamp, swine **06** fripon, rascal, rotter, varlet **07** bounder, custrel, dastard, villain **08** blighter, coistrel, coistril, swindler **09** reprobate, scallywag, scoundrel

knavery
05 fraud **06** deceit, ropery **07** devilry, roguery **08** mischief, patchery,

rickery, villainy **09** chicanery,
deception, duplicity, imposture
10 corruption, dishonesty, hanky-
panky **11** caddishness, friponnerie,
knavishness **13** double-dealing
14 monkey business

knavish
06 rascal, wicked **07** caddish,
corrupt, roguish **08** devilish, fiendish,
rascally **09** dastardly, deceitful,
deceptive, dishonest, reprobate
10 fraudulent, villainous
11 mischievous, scoundrelly
12 contemptible, unprincipled,
unscrupulous **13** dishonourable

knead
◊ anagram indicator
03 ply, rub **04** form, mold, work
05 malax, mould, pound, press, shape
06 conche, puddle, pummel
07 knuckle, massage, squeeze
08 malaxate **09** masticate
10 manipulate

kneel
03 bow **04** bend **05** stoop **06** curtsy,
kowtow, revere **07** bow down, defer to
09 genuflect **13** make obeisance
15 fall to your knees

knees
03 lap

knell
03 end **04** peal, ring, toll **05** chime,
knoll, sound **07** ringing

knickers
05 pants, thong **06** briefs, smalls
07 drawers, g-string, panties
08 bloomers, frillies, lingerie, scanties
09 underwear **10** underpants **12** bikini
briefs, camiknickers
14 knickerbockers

knick-knack
04 quip **05** knack **06** bauble, gewgaw,
imjam, pretty, trifle **07** bibelot,
rangam, trinket **08** gimcrack,
imcrack, nick-nack, ornament
09 bagatelle, bric-à-brac, plaything
11 whigmaleery **12** pretty-pretty,
whigmaleerie

knife
03 cut, rip **04** stab **05** blade, slash,
wound **06** cutter, pierce **08** lacerate

Knives include:
02 da
03 dah, hay, pen
04 bolo, case, chiv, dirk, fish, jack,
moon, shiv, simi
05 bowie, bread, clasp, craft, cutto,
flick, fruit, gully, kukri, panga, paper,
putty, skean, skene, spade, steak,
table
06 barong, butter, carver, chakra,
cradle, cuttle, cuttoe, dagger, gulley,
oyster, parang, pocket, sheath,
trench
07 bayonet, carving, catling, drawing,
dudgeon, hunting, leather,
machete, palette, pruning, scalpel,
Stanley®, whittle

08 bistoury, chopping, scalping,
skean-dhu, skene-dhu,
tranchet
09 butterfly, jockteleg, Swiss army,
toothpick
10 skene-occle
11 snickersnee, switchblade
13 Kitchen Devils®, pusser's dagger

See also **dagger; sword**

• knife stand
03 nef **05** block

knight
01 K, N **02** AK, Kt **03** dub, Sir
07 gallant, soldier, warrior, younker
08 champion, horseman **09** freelance,
man-at-arms **10** cavalryman,
equestrian **12** carpet-knight, knight-
errant

Knights include:
04 grey
05 black, white
06 Bayard, carpet, errant, kemper,
ritter
07 paladin
08 bachelor, banneret, cavalier,
douzeper, vavasour
09 chevalier, doucepere, valvassor
10 kempery-man
14 knight-bachelor, preux chevalier

*Knights of the Round Table in
Arthurian legend include:*
03 Kay
05 Lucan, Safer
06 Degore, Gareth
07 Alymere, Dagonet, Galahad,
Gawaine, Lamorak, Lionell,
Mordred, Pelleas, Tristan
08 Bedivere, Tristram
09 Bleoberis, Palomedes, Percivale
10 King Arthur
11 Bors de Ganis
12 Brunor le Noir, Ector de Maris
13 Lancelot Du Lac
15 La Cote Male Taile

knightly
04 bold **05** noble **06** heroic
07 courtly, gallant, valiant **08** gracious,
intrepid, valorous **09** dauntless,
soldierly **10** chivalrous, courageous,
honourable

knit
03 set, tie **04** ally, bind, join, knot, link,
loop, mend **05** unite, weave
06 crease, fasten, furrow, gather,
secure **07** connect, tighten,
wrinkle **08** contract, crotchet
09 interlace **10** intertwine **12** draw
together

Knitting-related terms include:
03 rib, row
04 aran, purl, wool
05 chart, pearl, plain
06 cast on, marker, needle, stitch
07 cast off, chevron, four-ply, tension,
twin rib
08 ball band, fair isle, intarsia
09 box stitch, double rib, fingering,
garter rib, single rib

10 double knit, French heel, moss
stitch, rice stitch, row counter, seed
stitch, tricoteuse
11 basketweave, cable needle, cable
stitch, drop a stitch, plain stitch,
thumb method
12 basket-stitch, garter-stitch, stitch
holder
13 fisherman's rib, stocking frame
14 circular needle, double knitting,
knitting needle, stocking stitch
15 knitting machine, knitting
pattern

knob
03 bur, nub **04** ball, boll, boss, bump,
burr, heel, knop, knot, knub, lump,
node, noop, snub, stop, stud, umbo
05 berry, gnarl, knurl, mouse, offer,
plook, plouk, rowel, swell, tuber, tuner
06 button, croche, handle, pommel,
snubbe, switch, toorie, tourie, tumour
07 chesnut **08** chestnut, doorstop,
eminence, pulvinar, register, swelling,
tubercle **10** doorhandle, projection,
protrusion, push-button
12 protuberance

knock
◊ anagram indicator
02 ca' **03** box, caa', con, dod, hit, pan,
rap, tap **04** bang, bash, belt, blow,
bump, chap, clip, cuff, dash, daud,
dawd, daze, ding, jole, joll, jolt, jowl,
pink, punt, slag, slam, slap, stun
05 clock, clour, clout, crash, joule,
pound, punch, shock, slate, smack,
stamp, swipe, thump, whack
06 attack, batter, defeat, nubble,
rebuff, strike, wallop, whammy **07** bad
luck, banging, censure, collide,
condemn, failure, innings, knobble,
knubble, rubbish, run down, setback,
slag off **08** bump into, confound,
pounding, reversal **09** criticism,
criticize, deprecate, disparage,
hammering, pull apart, rejection
10 misfortune **11** collide with, pick
holes in **12** pull to pieces, tear to
pieces **13** bad experience, find fault
with

See also **beat**

• knock about
03 gad, hit **04** bash, hurt, roam, rove
05 abuse, punch, range, wound
06 bang up, batter, beat up, bruise,
buffet, damage, injure, ramble, strike,
travel, wander **07** consort, saunter,
traipse **08** go around, maltreat,
mistreat **09** associate, gallivant,
hang about, manhandle **10** hang
around

• knock back
◊ reversal indicator
04 cost, down, gulp, swig **05** drink,
scoff, shock **06** devour, guzzle, rebuff,
reject **07** swallow **08** gulp down
10 disconcert

• knock down
03 hit **04** fell, prop, raze **05** clout,
floor, level, lower, pound, smash,
wreck **06** batter, reduce, wallop
07 destroy, run down, run over, skittle

08 bowl over, decrease, demolish, pull down, take down **09** bring down, knock over

• **knocked down**
02 KD

• **knock off**
03 rob **04** do in, kill, lift, nick, slay, stop, whip **05** cease, filch, pinch, steal, swipe, waste **06** deduct, finish, murder, pack in, pilfer, pirate, rip off, snitch **07** bump off, snaffle **08** clock off, clock out, get rid of, pack it in, stop work, take away **09** polish off, terminate **10** do away with, finish work **11** assassinate, discontinue

• **knock out**
02 KO **04** beat, fell, kayo, rout, stun **05** amaze, crush, floor, level, shock **06** defeat, hammer, thrash **07** astound, destroy, disable, flatten, impress, startle **08** astonish, bowl over, demolish, overcome, surprise **09** eliminate, overwhelm, prostrate **10** strike down **11** knock for six **13** run rings round **14** get the better of **15** make unconscious

• **knock over**
◊ *anagram indicator*
04 fell **05** floor, level **07** run down, run over

• **knock up**
04 call, stir **05** awake, rouse, waken **06** awaken, wake up **07** wear out **09** improvise **10** impregnate, jerry-build **11** make quickly **12** build quickly, make pregnant, put in the club

knockout
02 KO **03** hit **04** coup, kayo **05** smash, socko **06** winner **07** king-hit, stunner, success, triumph **08** smash-hit **09** sensation **10** attraction

knoll
04 hill, rise **05** knell, knowe, mound **06** barrow, koppie **07** hillock, hummock **09** elevation

knot
◊ *anagram indicator*
02 kn, kt **03** bud, nur **04** band, bind, bond, boss, gnar, hill, knag, knar, knit, knob, knub, knur, lash, lump, node, nurr, ring, tags **05** bunch, clump, crowd, gnarl, group, joint, knurl, knurr, leash, mouse, ravel, snarl, twist, weave **06** circle, gaggle, nodule, secure, splice, tangle, tether **07** chignon, cluster, entwine **08** entangle, ligature, swelling **09** fastening, gathering **10** concretion, difficulty **14** marriage-favour

Knots include:

03 bow, tie
04 bend, flat, loop, love, reef, wale, wall
05 blood, chain, hitch, plait, thief, thumb, turle
06 Domhof, granny, lover's, prusik, square

07 bowline, Gordian, running, seizing, weaver's, Windsor
08 overhand, slipknot, spade-end, surgeon's, true-love
09 half hitch, lark's head, sheet bend, swab hitch, Turk's head
10 clove hitch, common bend, fisherman's, Flemish eye, sheepshank, true-lover's
11 carrick bend, donkey hitch, double blood, Englishman's, Hunter's bend, timber hitch
12 marling hitch, rolling hitch, simple sennit, weaver's hitch
13 drummer's chain, figure of eight, slippery hitch
14 Blackwall hitch, common whipping, double Cairnton, double-overhand, double-overhang, Englishman's tie, fisherman's bend, Matthew Walker's, running bowline

knotty
◊ *anagram indicator*
04 hard **05** bumpy, nirly, rough **06** knaggy, knobby, nirlie, nodose, nodous, rugged, thorny, tricky **07** complex, gnarled, gnarred, knarred, knobbly, knotted, nodular **08** baffling, puzzling **09** Byzantine, difficult, intricate **10** mystifying, perplexing **11** anfractuous, complicated, troublesome **13** problematical

know
03 con, ken, kon, see, wis, wit, wot **04** have, tell, weet, wish, wist **05** conne, savey, savvy, sense, weete **06** fathom, notice, savvey, weeten **07** approve, be aware, discern, make out, realize, undergo **08** identify, perceive **09** apprehend, be clued up, go through, have taped, recognize, tell apart **10** comprehend, experience, understand **11** distinguish, know by sight **12** be au fait with, discriminate **13** associate with, be cognizant of, be conscious of, be friends with, differentiate **14** be familiar with, be well-versed in

• **I don't know**
04 pass

know-all
06 Jowett **07** wise guy **08** polymath, wiseacre **09** know-it-all, smart alec **10** clever dick **11** clever clogs, smartypants

know-how
04 bent **05** flair, knack, savey, savvy, skill **06** savvey, talent **07** ability, faculty **08** aptitude, cum-savvy, gumption **09** adeptness, dexterity, expertise, ingenuity, knowledge **10** adroitness, capability, competence, experience **11** proficiency, savoir-faire

knowing
03 fly, hep, hip **05** aware, canny, downy **06** astute, shrewd, sussed **07** cunning, gnostic, skilful

08 informed **09** conscious, up to snuff **10** deliberate, discerning, expressive, meaningful, perceptive **11** intelligent, significant, worldly-wise

knowingly
08 by design, scienter, wilfully **09** on purpose, purposely, studiedly, willingly, wittingly **10** designedly **11** consciously **12** calculatedly, deliberately **13** intentionally

knowledge
03 art, gen, sus **04** data, suss **05** facts, grasp, jnana, light, skill, truth **06** gnosis, wisdom **07** ability, cunning, insight, knowhow, letters, tuition, witting **08** intimacy, learning, pansophy **09** awareness, cognition, education, erudition, expertise, judgement, schooling **10** cognizance **11** conversance, discernment, familiarity, information, instruction, proficiency, recognition, savoir-faire, scholarship **12** acquaintance, apprehension, intelligence **13** comprehension, consciousness, encyclopedism, enlightenment, understanding

• **full knowledge**
11 omniscience

• **range of knowledge**
03 ken

knowledgeable
02 up **05** aware, savey, savvy **06** au fait, expert, savvey **07** clued-up, erudite, learned **08** educated, familiar, genned up, informed, lettered, well-read, well up in **09** conscious, in the know, scholarly, up to speed **10** acquainted, conversant, well-versed **11** enlightened, experienced, intelligent **12** well-informed

known
04 kent **05** couth, noted, plain **06** avowed, famous, patent **07** obvious **08** admitted, familiar, revealed **09** confessed, published, well-known **10** celebrated, proclaimed, recognized **11** commonplace **12** acknowledged

• **also known as**
03 aka **05** alias

knuckle

• **knuckle down**
10 buckle down **12** begin to study **15** start to work hard

• **knuckle under**
05 defer, yield **06** accede, give in, submit **07** give way, succumb **09** acquiesce, surrender **10** capitulate **11** buckle under

Koran
05 Qoran, Quran **07** Alcoran

• **chapter of the Koran**
04 sura **05** surah

Korea
02 KP, KR 03 KOR, PRK, ROK

kosher
• **not kosher**
04 tref 05 trefa, treif

kowtow
04 fawn 05 defer, kneel, toady
06 cringe, grovel, pander, suck up
07 flatter 08 pay court 11 curry favour
12 bow and scrape

krypton
02 Kr

kudos
04 fame, mana 05 glory 06 cachet,
credit, esteem, honour, praise, regard,
renown, repute 07 acclaim, laurels
08 applause, plaudits, prestige
09 laudation 10 reputation
11 distinction

Kuwait
03 KWT

Kyrgyzstan
02 KS 03 KGZ

L

L
02 el 04 Lima

label
03 dub, tab, tag 04 call, logo, make, mark, name, seal, term 05 badge, brand, class, flash, stamp, tally, title 06 define, docket, marker, number, sticky, ticket 07 address, crowner, epithet, sticker 08 classify, describe, identify, nickname 09 bookplate, brand name, designate, dripstone, trademark 10 categorize, identifier, pigeonhole 11 description, designation 12 characterize 13 bumper sticker 14 attach a label to, categorization, classification, identification 15 proprietary name

laboratory

Laboratory apparatus includes:

05 clamp, flask, slide, stand, still, U-tube
06 beaker, Bunsen, funnel, Gilson®, mortar, pestle, retort, tripod, trough
07 bell jar, burette, cuvette, dropper, pipette, spatula, stirrer
08 crucible, cylinder, fume hood, glove box, test tube
09 autoclave, condenser, Petri dish, power pack, steam bath, stop clock
10 centrifuge, desiccator, ice machine, microscope, PCR machine, Petri plate, watchglass
11 boiling tube, filter flask, filter paper, fume chamber, thermometer
12 Bunsen burner, cloud chamber, conical flask, fume cupboard, heating block, test tube rack, Woulfe bottle
13 bubble chamber, Büchner funnel, top-pan balance
14 Kipp's apparatus
15 Erlenmeyer flask, evaporating dish, laminar flow hood, Liebig condenser, volumetric flask

laborious
04 hard 05 heavy, tough 06 tiring, uphill 07 arduous, careful, onerous, operose, painful, slavish, tedious 08 diligent, tiresome, toilsome, wearying 09 assiduous, difficult, fatiguing, Sisyphean, strenuous, wearisome 10 laboursome, working-day 11 hard-working, industrious, painstaking 12 backbreaking 13 indefatigable

laboriously
09 arduously, operosely, slavishly 10 drudgingly, tiresomely, toilsomely

11 strenuously, wearisomely 14 with difficulty

labour
◇ *anagram indicator*
03 job, Lab 04 hard, moil, plod, roll, slog, task, toil, toss, turn, work 05 begar, birth, chore, grind, hands, pains, pangs, pitch, slave, sweat, yakka 06 drudge, duties, effort, overdo, strain, strive, suffer, throes 07 dwell on, katorga, travail, try hard, workers, workmen 08 belabour, be misled, delivery, drudgery, drudgism, exertion, go all out, hard work, struggle, work hard 09 be blinded, diligence, do to death, elaborate, employees, endeavour, hard yakka, labourers, reiterate, servitude, workforce 10 be deceived, childbirth, do your best, employment, overstress 11 flog to death, give your all, harp on about, labour pains, parturition 12 contractions, kill yourself 13 exert yourself, labor improbus, overemphasize 14 go on and on about 15 industriousness

laboured
◇ *anagram indicator*
05 heavy, stiff 06 forced, leaden, worked 07 awkward, stilted, studied 08 affected, overdone, strained 09 contrived, difficult, effortful, ponderous, unnatural 10 cultivated 11 complicated, overwrought

labourer
03 boy 04 hand, jack, peon 05 churl, cooly, grunt, navvy 06 bohunk, coolie, docker, drudge, hodman, Kanaka, menial, worker 07 culchie, Grecian, hobbler, pioneer, redneck, seagull, wharfie, workman 08 cottager, dataller, daytaler, farm hand, hireling 09 field hand, operative 10 hod carrier, roustabout 11 gandy dancer 12 manual worker 15 unskilled worker

labyrinth
03 web 04 maze 06 enigma, jungle, puzzle, riddle, tangle, warren 07 mizmaze, network, winding 09 confusion, intricacy 10 complexity, perplexity 12 complication, entanglement

labyrinthine
◇ *anagram indicator*
04 mazy 06 knotty 07 complex, tangled, winding 08 confused, involved, mazelike, puzzling, tortuous 09 Byzantine, intricate 10 convoluted, perplexing 11 complicated

lace
◇ *anagram indicator*
03 net, tat, tie 04 bind, cord, do up 05 add to, blend, close, mix in, point, spike, thong, twine 06 attach, fasten, lacing, secure, string, tawdry, thrash, thread 07 crochet, flavour, fortify, latchet, netting 08 bobbinet, bootlace, filigree, mesh-work, open work, shoelace, stay tape 09 bobbin net 10 intertwine, interweave, strengthen 11 intermingle

Lace types include:

04 bone, gold
05 blond, filet, jabot, orris, point
06 blonde, bobbin, pillow, thread, trolly
07 footing, galloon, guipure, Honiton, Mechlin, pearlin, tatting, torchon, trolley
08 Brussels, dentelle, duchesse, net orris, pearling
09 Chantilly, reticella
10 Colbertine, mignonette
12 Valenciennes

lacerate
03 cut, rip 04 claw, gash, hurt, maim, rend, rent, tear, torn 05 ganch, slash, wound 06 gaunch, harrow, injure, mangle 07 afflict, cut open, scarify, torment, torture 08 distress, mutilate 09 lancinate

laceration
03 cut, rip 04 gash, maim, rent, tear 05 slash, wound 06 injury 10 mutilation

lachrymose
03 sad 05 teary, weepy 06 crying, woeful 07 maudlin, sobbing, tearful, weeping 08 dolorous, mournful 10 lugubrious, melancholy

lack
◇ *deletion indicator*
03 gap 04 miss, need, void, want 06 dearth, defect, penury 07 absence, not have, paucity, require, vacancy 08 scarcity, shortage 09 emptiness, privation 10 deficiency, have need of, scantiness 11 deprivation, destitution 12 be clean out of, be fresh out of 13 deficient in, insufficiency 15 not have enough of

lackadaisical
04 dull, idle, lazy, limp 05 inert 06 dreamy 07 languid 08 careless, indolent, listless, lukewarm 09 apathetic, enervated, lethargic 10 abstracted, languorous, spiritless 11 half-hearted, indifferent

lackey
04 page, pawn, tool **05** gofer, guide, toady, valet **06** fawner, menial, minion, monkey, poodle, vassal, yes-man **07** doormat, equerry, footman, servant, steward **08** hanger-on, parasite, retainer **09** attendant, flatterer, sycophant **10** instrument, manservant, skip-kennel

lacking
◇ *deletion indicator*
03 shy **04** poor **05** minus **06** absent, flawed, to seek, wanted **07** missing, needing, short of, wanting, without **09** defective, deficient **10** inadequate

lacklustre
03 dim, dry **04** drab, dull, flat **05** vapid **06** boring, leaden **07** insipid, tedious **08** lifeless **10** spiritless, uninspired **11** commonplace **12** run-of-the-mill **13** unimaginative, uninteresting

laconic
04 curt **05** blunt, brief, crisp, pithy, short, terse **06** abrupt **07** concise, spartan **08** incisive, succinct, taciturn **10** economical, to the point **12** monosyllabic

laconically
07 bluntly, briefly, in a word, in brief, pithily, tersely **08** abruptly **09** concisely **10** incisively, succinctly, to the point

lacquer
05 japan **07** varnish **09** hairspray **12** vernis martin **14** Coromandel work

lacuna
03 gap **04** void **05** blank, break, space **06** cavity, hiatus **08** omission

lad
03 boy, guy, kid, son, tad **04** boyo, chap, sort, type **05** bloke, bucko, chiel, whelp, youth **06** callan, chield, fellow, nipper **07** callant, gossoon **08** juvenile, spalpeen **09** character, schoolboy, stripling, youngster **10** individual **13** gillie-wetfoot **14** whippersnapper **15** gillie-white-foot

ladder
03 run, sty **04** rank, rung, trap **05** level, point, rungs, scala, scale, steps **06** étrier, series, stairs **07** fish-way, grading, potence, ranking **08** echelons **09** companion, hierarchy **10** set of steps **12** pecking order

laden
04 full **05** heavy, taxed **06** jammed, loaded, packed **07** charged, fraught, gestant, stuffed **08** burdened, hampered, pregnant, weighted **09** chock-full, oppressed **10** encumbered **11** weighed down

la-di-da
04 posh **05** put-on **06** snooty **07** foppish, stuck-up **08** affected, mannered, snobbish **09** conceited **11** highfalutin, over-refined, pretentious, toffee-nosed

ladies *see* **toilet**

ladle
03 dip **04** bail, bale, dish, lade **05** scoop, shank, spoon **06** dipper, shovel **07** divider
• **ladle out**
07 bail out, bale out, dish out, dole out, hand out **08** disburse **10** distribute

lady
01 L **04** burd, dame, miss **05** begum, lakin, siren, woman **06** damsel, duenna, female, khanum, matron, Señora **07** hidalga, ladykin, old dear, sheikha, Signora **08** countess, Señorita **09** Signorina **10** demoiselle, grande dame, noblewoman, young woman **11** gentlewoman
See also **girl; woman**
• **lady's fingers**
04 okra **05** gumbo
• **lot of ladies**
04 bevy
• **organized ladies**
02 WI **15** Women's Institute

ladylike
04 soft **06** modest, polite, proper **07** courtly, elegant, genteel, queenly, refined **08** cultured, decorous, delicate, matronly, polished, well-bred **09** courteous **11** respectable **12** well-mannered

lag
04 drag, idle, late **05** dally, delay, steal, tardy, tarry, trail **06** arrest, dawdle, linger, loiter, lounge, retard **07** convict, saunter, shuffle **08** hang back, hindmost, imprison, straggle **10** behindhand, fall behind, retardment **11** retardation **12** drag your feet, shilly-shally **13** kick your heels **14** bring up the rear
See also **prisoner**

lager *see* **beer**

laggard
05 idler, snail **06** loafer **07** dawdler, lounger **08** lingerer, loiterer, sluggard **09** saunterer, slowcoach, straggler

lagoon
03 bog, fen **04** haff, lake, pond, pool **05** bayou, marsh, swamp **06** lagune, salina **08** shallows

laid-back
04 calm, cool **06** at ease, casual **07** relaxed **09** easy-going, leisurely, unhurried, unworried **10** untroubled **11** free and easy, unflappable **13** imperturbable

laid up
03 ill **04** sick **05** crook **07** injured **08** disabled **09** bedridden **10** housebound **11** immobilized, out of action **12** hors de combat **13** confined to bed, incapacitated, on the sick list

lair
03 den, lie **04** mire **05** couch **07** retreat
See also **animal**

laissez-faire
09 free-trade **10** free-market, permissive **14** free-enterprise, live and let live, non-interfering

laity
03 lay **06** people **08** amateurs **09** lay people, outsiders **10** temporalty, unordained **12** parishioners **14** the non-ordained

lake
01 L **03** dam, lac, sea **04** loch, meer, mere, pond, pool, tarn **05** basin, bayou, cowal, lough, playa, shott, water **06** lagoon, lagune, nyanza, salina **07** carmine **09** everglade, reservoir, saltchuck

The Great Lakes:
04 Erie
05 Huron
07 Ontario
08 Michigan, Superior

Lakes, lochs and loughs include:
03 Awe, Van
04 Abbé, Bala, Biwa, Bled, Chad, Como, Derg, Earn, Erie, Eyre, Kivu, Ness, Tana
05 Foyle, Garda, Great, Huron, Leven, Morar, Neagh, Nyasa, Ohrid, Onega, Patos, Poopó, Tahoe, Taupo, Volta
06 Albert, Baikal, Corrib, Crater, Finger, Geneva, Ladoga, Lomond, Louise, Malawi, Nasser, Saimaa, Taimyr, Taymyr, Vänern, Zurich
07 Aral Sea, Balaton, Chapala, Dead Sea, Katrine, Lucerne, Ontario, Rannoch, Scutari, Torrens, Turkana
08 Balkhash, Bodensee, Chiemsee, Issyk Kul, Lac Léman, Loch Earn, Loch Ness, Lough Awe, Maggiore, Michigan, Superior, Tiberias, Titicaca, Tonlé Sap, Victoria, Winnipeg
09 Constance, Great Bear, Great Salt, Kammer See, Loch Leven, Loch Morar, Lough Derg, Maracaibo, Neuchâtel, Nicaragua, Ullswater, Willandra, Zeller See
10 Caspian Sea, Great Slave, Loch Lomond, Lough Foyle, Lough Neagh, Okeechobee, Tanganyika, Windermere, Wörther See
11 Great Bitter, Loch Katrine, Lough Corrib
12 Derwent Water, Kielder Water
13 Bassenthwaite, Coniston Water

lam
03 hit **04** bash, beat, belt, pelt **05** clout, knock, pound, thump, whack **06** batter, escape, pummel, strike, thrash, wallop **07** leather

lamb
04 cade, Elia, yean **08** yeanling

lambast, lambaste
03 tan **04** beat, belt, drub, flay, flog, slag, whip **05** clout, roast, scold, thump, whack **06** batter, berate, rebuke, strike, thrash, wallop

07 censure, clobber, leather, reprove, rubbish, slag off, upbraid **08** badmouth **09** castigate, criticize, reprimand

lambert
01 L

lame
04 game, halt, hurt, maim, main, poor, tame, thin, weak **05** gammy **06** feeble, flimsy, maimed, mained, poorly **07** cripple, halting, injured, limping **08** crippled, disabled, hobbling, spavined **09** defective, hamstring, hamstrung **10** inadequate **11** handicapped **12** unconvincing **13** incapacitated **14** unsatisfactory
• **lame person**
04 gimp

lamely
06 feebly, tamely, weakly **07** shakily **09** with a limp **10** hobblingly, unsteadily **12** inadequately **14** unconvincingly

lament
03 cry, sob **04** howl, keen, mean, mein, mene, moan, wail, weep **05** dirge, dumka, elegy, groan, meane, mourn, plain, tears **06** bemoan, bewail, beweep, crying, grieve, regret, repine, sorrow, yammer **07** deplore, requiem, sobbing, ululate, wayment, weeping **08** complain, grieving, threnody **09** complaint **11** lamentation

lamentable
◇ *anagram indicator*
03 low, sad **04** mean, poor **05** lousy **06** crying, funest, grotty, meagre, measly, tragic, woeful **07** moanful, pitiful **08** grievous, mournful, terrible, wretched **09** miserable, niggardly, sorrowful, worthless **10** deplorable, inadequate **11** distressing, regrettable, unfortunate **12** insufficient **13** disappointing **14** unsatisfactory

lamentably
08 woefully **09** miserably, pitifully **10** deplorably, tragically **11** regrettably **12** inadequately **14** insufficiently **15** disappointingly

lamentation
03 cry **04** keen, moan **05** dirge, elegy, grief **06** lament, plaint, sorrow **07** keening, sobbing, wailing, wayment, weeping **08** grieving, jeremiad, mourning, threnody **09** ululation **11** deploration

laminate
04 coat, face **05** cover, flake, layer, plate, split **06** veneer **07** foliate, overlay **08** separate, stratify **09** exfoliate

lamp
03 eye **04** bulb, Davy **05** crusy, light, torch **06** argand, crusie, Leerie, sconce **07** cruisie, Geordie, lantern, lucigen, pendant, pendent, scamper **08** arc-light, fog light, torchier **09** light bulb,

moderator, spotlight, torchière, veilleuse **10** Anglepoise®, Kleig light, Klieg light, night-light, photoflood **11** searchlight

lampoon
04 mock, skit **05** spoof, squib **06** parody, satire, send up, send-up **07** Pasquil, Pasquin, take off, take-off **08** ridicule, satirize, travesty **09** burlesque, make fun of **10** caricature, pasquinade

lampooner
07 Pasquil, Pasquin **08** parodist, satirist **09** pasquiler **10** pasquilant **11** pasquinader **12** caricaturist

lance
03 cut **04** pike, slit **05** lanch, prick, rejón, shaft, spear **06** incise, lancet, launch, pierce **07** bayonet, cut open, harpoon, javelin **08** puncture, white arm

land
03 bag, get, hit, nab, net, tax, win **04** area, deal, dock, drop, gain, give, loam, lord, moor, soil **05** acres, berth, catch, earth, end up, fetch, manor, reach, realm, state, tract **06** alight, anchor, arrive, burden, direct, domain, estate, fields, ground, lumber, nation, obtain, people, region, saddle, secure, settle, turn up, unload, whenua, wind up **07** achieve, acquire, acreage, capture, country, deliver, deplane, deposit, dry land, grounds, inflict, oppress, procure, terrain, trouble **08** dismount, district, encumber, farmland, finish up, go ashore, property, province, take down **09** bring down, disembark, get hold of, open space, rural area, territory, touch down, weigh down **10** administer, come to rest, fatherland, motherland, real estate, terra firma **11** countryside, terrestrial **12** come in to land, find yourself **13** bring in to land, native country

See also **country; continent**
• **amount of land**
03 are, lot, rod, ure **04** acre, shot **07** hectare
• **arable land**
03 lay, lea, ley

landing
04 dock, pier, quay **05** jetty, wharf **07** arrival, greaser, harbour **08** coming in **09** alighting, belly flop, deplaning, touchdown **12** landing-place, landing-stage, three-pricker **13** putting ashore **14** coming in to land, coming to ground, disembarkation

landing-stair
04 ghat **05** ghaut

landlady, landlord
04 host **05** owner **06** lessor **07** hostess, Rachman **08** hotelier, mine host, publican, slumlord **09** innkeeper, landowner **10** freeholder, proprietor **11** hotel-keeper **12** proprietress, restaurateur

landmark
05 cairn, meith **06** beacon, crisis **07** feature **08** boundary, milepost, monument, signpost **09** milestone, watershed **12** turning-point

See also **Africa; Asia; Australia; Canada; Europe; London; Middle East; New York; New Zealand; United Kingdom; United States of America**

landscape
04 view **05** scene, vista **06** aspect, saikei **07** outlook, paysage, scenery **08** panorama, prospect **11** countryside, perspective

landslide
04 slip **07** runaway **08** decisive, emphatic, landslip, rockfall **09** avalanche, earthfall **10** éboulement **12** overwhelming

lane
02 La **03** gut, way **04** loan, loke, lone, path, wynd **05** alley, byway, entry, track **06** avenue, boreen, byroad, ruelle, vennel **07** bikeway, channel, footway, loaning, passage, pathway, sea road, towpath, twitten **08** alleyway, driveway, footpath, twitting **10** backstreet, passageway

language
03 bat **04** cant, talk **05** argot, lingo, style **06** jargon, speech, tongue **07** diction, wording **08** converse, parlance, phrasing, rhetoric, speaking, swearing, uttering **09** discourse, utterance **10** expression, vocabulary, vocalizing **11** phraseology, terminology, verbalizing **12** conversation **13** communication

Languages include:

02 Wu
03 ASL, BSL, Edo, Gan, Giz, Ibo, Kru, Lao, Mam, Mon, Twi, Yue
04 Chad, Cree, Crow, Dari, Erse, Fang, Gaul, Inca, Lapp, Manx, Maya, Moto, Nupe, Pali, Susu, Thai, Tshi, Urdu, Xosa, Zulu
05 Attic, Aztec, Bantu, Cajun, Carib, Creek, Croat, Czech, Doric, Dutch, Farsi, Greek, Hindi, Inuit, Ionic, Iraqi, Irish, Karen, Kazak, Khmer, Latin, Malay, Maori, Masai, Norse, Osean, Punic, Saxon, Scots, Shona, Sioux, Tamil, Uzbek, Welsh, Xhosa, Yakut
06 Arabic, Bangla, Basque, Berber, Bokmål, Celtic, Coptic, Creole, Dakota, Danish, French, Gaelic, German, Gothic, Hebrew, Lydian, Magyar, Micmac, Mohawk, Mongol, Polish, Romany, Sherpa, Slovak, Tartar
07 Afghani, Amharic, Aramaic, Ayamará, Bengali, Bosnian, Catalan, Chinese, Chinook, Cornish, English, Euskera, Finnish, Flemish, Frisian, Guaraní, Italian, Kalmuck, Lappish, Latvian, Maltese, Mohican, Nynorsk, Punjabi, Quechua, Russian, Semitic, Siamese, Slovene, Spanish, Swahili, Swedish, Tagálog,

Turkish, Umbrian, Volapük, Walloon, Yiddish, Zapotec
08 Albanian, Armenian, Cherokee, Croatian, Demotiki, Estonian, Etruscan, Georgian, Japanese, Malagasy, Mandarin, Moldovan, Phrygian, Pilipino, Romanian, Romansch, Sanskrit, Setswana
09 Aborigine, Afrikaans, Algonquin, Bulgarian, Cantonese, Castilian, Dalmatian, Ethiopian, Hungarian, Icelandic, Kiswahili, Malayalam, Norwegian, Provençal, Sardinian, Ukrainian
10 Anglo-Saxon, Babylonian, Belarusian, Hindustani, Lithuanian, Macedonian, Malayaalam, Phoenician, Portuguese, Serbo-Croat, Vietnamese
12 ancient Greek, Katharevousa, Sign Language
13 Middle English
14 Lëtzebuergesch

Invented languages include:
03 Ido, Neo
06 Novial
07 Volapük
08 Newspeak
09 Esperanto
10 Occidental
11 Interglossa, Interlingua
12 Idiom Neutral

Computer programming languages include:
01 C
03 ADA, AWK, C++, XML
04 HTML, Java, Perl
05 BASIC, COBOL
06 Delphi, Pascal, Python
07 FORTRAN
10 Postscript

Language terms include:
02 RP
03 ASR, NLP
04 cant
05 argot, idiom, lingo, slang, usage
06 accent, brogue, creole, jargon, patois, patter, pidgin, syntax, tongue
07 dialect, grammar
08 buzz word, localism, Newspeak, standard
09 etymology, phonetics, semantics
10 journalese, vernacular, vocabulary
11 doublespeak, linguistics, non-standard, orthography, regionalism
12 gobbledygook, lexicography, lingua franca, vulgar tongue
13 colloquialism

• **bad language**
04 cuss, oath **05** curse **07** cussing
08 swearing **09** expletive, swearword
• **language unit**
04 word **07** phoneme

languid
04 dull, lazy, limp, slow, weak **05** faint, heavy, inert, slack, weary **06** feeble, pining, sickly, torpid **07** relaxed

08 drooping, flagging, inactive, listless, sluggish **09** enervated, lethargic
10 languorous, spiritless **11** debilitated, indifferent **12** uninterested
13 lackadaisical **14** unenthusiastic

languidly
05 dully **06** feebly, lazily, slowly, weakly **07** heavily, inertly **08** torpidly
10 inactively, listlessly **13** lethargically

languish
03 die, rot **04** fade, fail, flag, long, mope, pine, sigh, sink, want, wilt
05 brood, droop, faint, quail, waste, yearn **06** desire, grieve, hanker, hunger, sicken, sorrow, weaken, wither
07 decline **08** fall away **09** waste away
11 deteriorate

languor
04 calm, lull **05** ennui, sloth **06** pining, torpor **07** fatigue, frailty, inertia, silence **08** debility, laziness, lethargy, weakness **09** faintness, heaviness, indolence, lassitude, stillness, weariness **10** affliction, dreaminess, drowsiness, enervation, feebleness, relaxation, sleepiness **12** listlessness
14 oppressiveness

languorous
04 lazy, weak **05** weary **06** dreamy, feeble, sleepy, torpid **07** relaxed
08 listless **09** lethargic

lank
04 lean, limp, long, slim, tall, thin
05 gaunt, lanky **06** skinny **07** flaccid, scraggy, scrawny, slender
08 drooping, lifeless, rawboned
09 emaciated, slab-sided **10** lustreless, straggling

lanky
04 lean, slim, tall, thin **05** gaunt, rangy, weedy **06** gangly **07** scraggy, scrawny, slender **08** gangling

lantern
04 buat, glim, lamp **05** bowat, bowet, crown, darky **06** cupola, darkey, sconce **08** bull's-eye **09** Aldis lamp, belvedere **12** stereopticon

lanthanum
02 La

Laos
03 LAO

lap
03 leg, lip, rag, sip, sup **04** beat, dash, flap, flow, fold, lick, loop, roll, rush, slop, tour, wash, wind, wrap **05** ambit, break, cover, drink, knees, orbit, round, slosh, stage, swish, twine **06** circle, course, encase, enfold, hollow, lappet, splash, swathe, thighs **07** circuit, compass, envelop, overlap, scoop up, section, stretch, swaddle **08** distance, surround
• **lap up**
06 absorb, relish, savour **08** listen in
09 delight in **13** accept eagerly

lapse
03 end, gap **04** drop, fail, fall, go by, go on, lull, pass, sink, slip, stop, trip

05 blank, break, cease, drift, error, fault, glide, pause, slide **06** course, elapse, expire, hiatus, run out, slip by, worsen **07** blunder, decline, descent, failing, go to pot, mistake, passage, relapse, resolve, stumble
08 downturn, interval, omission, slip away, slipping **09** backslide, oversight, prescribe, terminate, worsening
10 aberration, become void, degenerate, go downhill, negligence
11 backsliding, dereliction, deteriorate, go to the dogs **12** degeneration, indiscretion, intermission, interruption
13 become invalid, deterioration, fall from grace **14** go down the tubes
15 go to rack and ruin

lapsed
04 once, void **05** ended **06** former, run out **07** expired, invalid
08 finished, obsolete, outdated
09 out of date, unrenewed
11 backslidden **12** discontinued
13 non-practising

lapwing
05 pewit, tewit **06** peewit, tewhit
07 teuchat **08** teru-tero

larceny
05 heist, theft **06** piracy **07** robbery
08 burglary, stealing **09** pilfering
10 purloining **13** expropriation

lard
04 load, saim, seam **05** enarm, seame, strew, stuff **06** fatten **07** garnish
14 interpenetrate

larder
06 pantry, spence **08** scullery
09 storeroom **11** springhouse, storage room

large
02 lg, OS **03** big, lge **04** full, high, huge, mega, tall, vast **05** ample, broad, bulky, giant, grand, great, heavy, jumbo, roomy **06** bumper **07** copious, diffuse, immense, liberal, mammoth, massive, monster, outsize, sizable
08 abundant, colossal, enormous, generous, gigantic, sizeable, spacious, spanking, sweeping, whopping
09 extensive, ginormous, good-sized, grandiose, humungous, king-sized, monstrous, plentiful **10** commodious, dirty great, exhaustive, monumental, prodigious, stupendous, voluminous
11 far-reaching, importantly, magnanimous, prominently, substantial, wide-ranging
12 considerable **13** comprehensive, wide-stretched **14** Brobdingnagian, ostentatiously
• **at large**
03 out **04** free **06** abroad, mainly
07 chiefly **08** on the run **09** at liberty, generally, in general, in the main **10** by and large, on the loose, on the whole, unconfined **11** independent
• **by and large**
06 mainly, mostly **07** as a rule
09 generally **10** on the whole **14** for the most part

largely

06 mainly, mostly, widely **07** chiefly, greatly **09** generally, in the main, primarily **10** by and large, especially **11** extensively, principally **12** considerably **13** predominantly **14** for the most part, to a large extent

largeness

04 bulk, size **08** vastness, wideness **09** ampleness, amplitude, broadness, grandness, greatness, heaviness, immensity **11** sizableness **12** enormousness, macrocephaly, sizeableness **13** expansiveness **14** stupendousness, voluminousness

large-scale

04 epic, mega, vast, wide **05** broad **06** global **08** sweeping **09** expansive, extensive, universal, wholesale **10** nationwide **11** country-wide, far-reaching, wide-ranging **12** wide-reaching

largesse

03 aid **04** alms, gift **05** grant **06** bounty **07** bequest, charity, handout, present **08** donation, kindness **09** allowance, endowment **10** generosity, liberality **11** benefaction, munificence **12** philanthropy **14** open-handedness

lark

◇ *anagram indicator*
03 guy, job **04** game, play, romp, task **05** antic, caper, chore, fling, prank, revel, sport, thing **06** cavort, frolic, gambol **07** fooling, gammock, have fun, rollick, skylark **08** activity, business, escapade, mischief **09** cavorting, fool about, horseplay, mess about **10** fool around, play tricks

larva

04 grub, moth, spat **05** ghost, naiad, ox-bot **06** caddis, chigoe, chigre, measle **07** budworm, chigger, hydatid, planula, pluteus, spectre, tadpole, veliger **08** army worm, bookworm, coenurus, cornworm, mealworm, wireworm, woodworm **09** auger-worm, bloodworm, doodlebug, glass-crab, joint-worm, screw-worm, sporocyst, strawworm, xylophage **10** bipinnaria, caddis-worm, cankerworm, miracidium, woolly bear **11** cabbage-worm, caterpillar, corn earworm, hellgramite **12** hellgrammite **13** leptocephalus, spruce budworm
• **larval stage**
04 zoea **08** cercaria

lascivious

04 blue, lewd **05** bawdy, crude, dirty, horny, randy, saucy **06** coarse, ribald, smutty, vulgar, wanton **07** lustful, obscene, Paphian, sensual, Sotadic **08** indecent, petulant, prurient, Sotadean, unchaste **09** lecherous, offensive, salacious **10** libidinous, licentious, scurrilous, suggestive **12** pornographic

lash

03 cat, hit, tie, wag **04** beat, belt, bind, blow, dash, flog, join, rope, rush, slow, soft, stop, welt, whip, wire **05** affix, break, flail, flick, horse, pound, scold, seize, slack, slash, smash, strap, swipe, swish, thong, whack **06** attack, batter, berate, buffet, fasten, gammon, lavish, rebuke, secure, strike, stripe, stroke, swinge, switch, tether, thrash, wallop **07** bawl out, censure, insipid, lay into, reprove, scourge **08** bullwhip, make fast, squander **09** bullwhack, criticize, fulminate, horsewhip **12** tear to shreds **13** tear a strip off
• **lash out**
04 yerk **06** thrash **07** lay into, run down **08** hit out at **09** have a go at **11** splash out on **12** tear to pieces, tear to shreds **13** tear a strip off, tear strips off **14** attack strongly **15** speak out against, spend a fortune on

lashings

04 lots, tons **05** heaps, loads, piles **06** masses, oodles, stacks **11** large amount **13** great quantity

lass

03 hen **04** bird, girl, miss **05** chick, filly, Jenny, popsy **06** damsel, lassie, maiden **10** schoolgirl, sweetheart, young woman **11** maid-servant
See also **girl**

lassitude

06 apathy, torpor **07** fatigue, languor **08** dullness, lethargy, weakness **09** faintness, heaviness, tiredness, weariness **10** drowsiness, enervation, exhaustion **11** spring fever **12** listlessness, sluggishness

lasso

04 lazo, rope **05** noose, reata, riata **06** lariat

last

◇ *tail selection indicator*
03 end, ult **04** back, dure, go on, hind, keep, live, load, stay, take, wear **05** abide, after, cargo, close, dying, exist, final **06** behind, ending, endure, finish, hold on, keep on, latest, live on, remain, utmost, yester **07** carry on, closing, dernier, endmost, extreme, finally, hold out, persist, stand up, subsist, survive, tail-end **08** at the end, continue, farthest, furthest, hindmost, previous, rearmost, remotest, terminal, ultimate **09** at the back, at the rear, finishing **10** completion, concluding, conclusion, get through, lattermost, most recent, stick it out, ultimately **11** least likely **12** most unlikely **13** least suitable **14** coming at the end, most improbable, most unsuitable
• **at last**
◇ *tail selection indicator*
07 finally **08** at length, in the end **10** eventually, ultimately **11** in due course **12** in conclusion
• **last word**
04 amen, best, pick, rage **05** cream, vogue **06** latest **08** final say, ultimate

09 ultimatum **10** dernier cri, perfection **11** ne plus ultra **12** quintessence **13** final decision **14** crème de la crème, final statement **15** definite comment

last-ditch

04 wild **05** final **06** all-out, heroic **07** frantic **08** frenzied, last-gasp **09** desperate, straining **10** last-chance, struggling **12** eleventh-hour

lasting

05 fixed **07** abiding, durable, dureful, undying **08** enduring, external, lifelong, long-term, unending **09** ceaseless, endurable, long-lived, permanent, perpetual, surviving, unceasing **10** continuing, monumental, persisting, unchanging **11** everlasting, never-ending **12** interminable, long-standing

lastly

◇ *tail selection indicator*
07 finally, to sum up **08** in the end **10** ultimately **12** in conclusion

last-minute

04 late **05** hasty **06** forced, rushed **07** overdue **11** superficial **12** eleventh-hour

latch

03 bar **04** bolt, hasp, hook, lock, mire **05** catch, clink, sneck **06** fasten **07** clicket **09** fastening **10** make secure
• **latch on to**
04 twig **05** grasp, learn **06** follow **07** realize **09** apprehend **10** comprehend, understand **14** not want to leave

late

03 lag, new, old **04** dead, past, slow **05** fresh, tardy **06** behind, former, latest, recent, slowly, whilom **07** current, defunct, delayed, overdue, tardily **08** backward, deceased, departed, formerly, overtime, previous, recently, sometime, umquhile, up-to-date **09** belatedly, in arrears, preceding **10** after hours, behindhand, behind time, dilatorily, last-minute, unpunctual **12** unpunctually **13** up-to-the-minute **14** behind schedule
• **of late**
05 newly **06** lately **08** latterly, recently **10** not long ago

lately

05 alate, newly **06** of late **08** latterly, recently **09** now of late **10** not long ago

lateness

05 delay **09** tardiness **11** belatedness, retardation **12** dilatoriness **13** unpunctuality

latent

06 hidden, secret, unseen, veiled **07** dormant, lurking, passive **08** inactive, possible **09** concealed, invisible, potential, quiescent **10** underlying, unrealized, unrevealed

delitescent, undeveloped,
nexpressed **12** undiscovered

ater

4 next, syne **05** after **06** latter
7 goodbye, later on **08** in a while
9 following, posterior **10** afterwards,
ventually, subsequent, succeeding
1 in due course, in the future **12** at a
ater time, subsequently, successively
3 at a future date, at a future time,
ome other time **15** in the near future

ateral

3 lat **04** side **05** fresh **06** clever
7 oblique **08** creative, edgeways,
anking, indirect, inspired, marginal,
riginal, sideward, sideways, slanting
9 brilliant, illogical, ingenious
0 unorthodox **11** alternative,
maginative **13** outside the box
4 unconventional

aterally

8 edgeways, sideways **09** obliquely
0 creatively, originally **11** illogically,
geniously **13** imaginatively, outside
ne box

atest

2 in **03** hip, now **04** last **05** funky
6 modern, newest, trendy, with it
7 current **08** ultimate, up-to-date
0 most recent **11** fashionable **13** up-
-the-minute

ather

3 rub **04** flap, foam, fuss, soap, stew,
uds **05** fever, froth, panic, state, sweat,
zzy **06** dither, whip up **07** anxiety,
ubbles, fluster, flutter, shampoo
8 soapsuds **09** agitation

atin

foreign word indicator
1 L **03** Lat

*Latin words and expressions
include:*

3 sic
4 idem, pace
5 ad hoc, circa
6 gratis, ibidem, passim
7 alumnus, a priori, de facto, erratum,
floruit, in vitro, sub rosa
8 addendum, emeritus, ex gratia,
gravitas, infra dig, mea culpa, nota
bene, subpoena
9 ad nauseam, alma mater, carpe
diem, et tu, Brute, ex officio, inter
alia, ipso facto, per capita, status
quo, sub judice, vox populi
0 anno Domini, ante-bellum, ex
cathedra, in absentia, in extremis,
magnum opus, post mortem, prima
facie, quid pro quo, sine qua non,
tabula rasa
1 ad infinitum, memento mori, non
sequitur, tempus fugit
2 ante meridiem, caveat emptor,
compos mentis, habeas corpus,
post meridiem
3 camera obscura, deus ex machina,
modus operandi
4 annus mirabilis, in loco parentis, pro
bono publico, terra incognita

15 annus horribilis, curriculum vitae,
delirium tremens, persona non
grata

See also **day**; **month**; **number**

latitude

01 l **03** lat **04** play, room, span **05** field,
range, reach, scope, space, sweep,
width **06** extent, laxity, leeway, spread
07 breadth, freedom, liberty, licence
09 allowance, clearance
10 indulgence **11** flexibility **12** carte
blanche

latter

03 end **04** last **05** final, later
06 modern, recent, second
07 closing, ensuing **10** concluding,
succeeding, successive **13** last-
mentioned

latter-day

06 modern, recent **07** current
10 present-day **12** contemporary

latterly

06 lately, of late **08** hitherto, recently
12 most recently

lattice

03 web **04** grid, mesh **05** grate, grill
06 grille, jacket **07** grating, network,
tracery, trellis **08** espalier, fretwork,
openwork **10** portcullis **11** latticework
12 reticulation

Latvia

02 LV **03** LVA

laud

04 hail **05** extol **06** admire, honour,
praise **07** acclaim, applaud, approve,
glorify, magnify **09** celebrate

laudable

06 of note, worthy **08** sterling
09 admirable, estimable, excellent,
exemplary **10** creditable
11 commendable, meritorious
12 praiseworthy

laudation

05 glory, kudos, paean **06** eulogy,
homage, praise **07** acclaim, tribute
08 accolade, blessing, devotion,
encomion, encomium **09** adulation,
celebrity, extolment, panegyric,
reverence **10** veneration
11 acclamation **12** commendation
13 glorification

laudatory

06 eulogy **09** adulatory, approving
10 eulogistic, glorifying
11 acclamatory, approbatory,
celebratory, encomiastic, panegyrical
12 commendatory **13** complimentary,
encomiastical **14** congratulatory

laugh

03 fun, wag, wit, yok **04** boff, card, ha-
ha, he-he, hoax, hoot, howl, jest, joke,
lark, peal, peel, play, roar, yock
05 clown, comic, joker, lauch, prank,
risus, snirt, sport, te-hee, trick
06 cackle, giggle, guffaw, haw-haw,
hoaxer, jester, nicher, nicker, scream,
tee-hee, titter **07** break up, buffoon,

chortle, chuckle, snicker, snigger,
snirtle **08** comedian, crease up,
humorist, irrision, quipster
09 character, fall about, prankster,
trickster **10** belly-laugh, cachinnate,
horse laugh **11** wisecracker **12** be in
stitches, cachinnation **14** practical
joker, shake your sides, split your sides
15 laugh like a drain

• **laugh at**

04 jeer, mock **05** scorn, taunt
06 deride **07** scoff at **08** ridicule
09 make fun of, poke fun at **11** make a
fool of **14** make jokes about

• **laugh off**

06 ignore **07** dismiss **08** belittle,
minimize, pooh-pooh, shrug off
09 disregard **10** brush aside **12** make
little of

laughable

05 comic, droll, funny **06** absurd
07 amusing, comical **08** derisive,
derisory, farcical, humorous
09 diverting, hilarious, ludicrous
10 ridiculous, uproarious
11 nonsensical **12** entertaining,
preposterous **13** side-splitting

laughably

08 absurdly **10** farcically **11** ludicrously
12 ridiculously **14** preposterously

laughing-stock

04 butt, dupe **05** sport **06** stooge,
target, victim **08** derision, fair game
09 Aunt Sally **10** outspeckle **11** figure
of fun

laughter

03 haw **04** glee, ha-ha **05** mirth
06 cackle, haw-haw, tee-hee **07** fou
rire, hooting **08** cackling, giggling,
hilarity, irrision, laughing, paroxysm
09 amusement, chortling, chuckling,
guffawing, happiness, hysterics,
merriment, tittering **10** risibility,
sniggering **11** convulsions
12 cachinnation, cheerfulness

launch

04 dart, fire, hurl, open, shot **05** begin,
float, found, lance, set up, shoot, start,
throw **06** attack, propel **07** lancing,
project, rollout, send off, unstock
08 commence, dispatch, embark on,
initiate, organize **09** discharge,
establish, instigate, institute, introduce,
set afloat **10** inaugurate **11** set in
motion **12** presentation

launder

◇ *anagram indicator*
04 wash **05** clean **06** trough
07 cleanse **09** washerman
11 washerwoman

laundry

04 wash **07** bagwash, clothes,
steamie, washing **08** lavatory
10 Laundromat® **11** dry cleaner's,
launderette **12** dirty clothes, dirty
washing

laurel

03 bay **04** Stan **06** aucuba, daphne,
kalmia, Laurus **08** pichurim, sweet bay

09 sassafras, spicebush **10** greenheart, mock orange

lava
04 bomb, slag **05** lahar **06** cinder, coulée, pumice, scoria **07** clinker, lapilli **08** pahoehoe **09** toadstone **10** palagonite **12** volcanic bomb **13** volcanic glass

lavatory
02 WC **03** bog, can, lav, loo **04** dike, dyke, john, kazi, rear, toot **05** dunny, Elsan®, gents', heads, karsy, karzy, khazi, lavvy, privy, rears **06** carsey, karsey, ladies', lavabo, lotion, office, throne, toilet, urinal **07** cludgie, cottage, crapper, latrine **08** bathroom, dunnakin, Portaloo®, rest room, superloo, washroom **09** cloakroom, necessary **10** facilities, powder room, reredorter, thunderbox **11** convenience, earth-closet, water closet **12** smallest room **14** comfort station, little boys' room

lavish
04 free, heap, lash, lush, pour, rich, wild **05** grand, spend, waste **06** bestow, deluge, expend, lordly, shower, slap-up **07** copious, fulsome, liberal, profuse **08** abundant, generous, gorgeous, princely, prodigal, prolific, splendid, squander, wasteful **09** bountiful, dissipate, excessive, expensive, exuberant, luxuriant, plentiful, profusion, sumptuous, unlimited, unsparing **10** give freely, immoderate, open-handed, profligate, thriftless, unstinting **11** extravagant, intemperate, spendthrift **12** unrestrained **13** unwithdrawing

lavishly
06 freely, lushly, richly, wildly **07** grandly **09** liberally, profusely **10** abundantly, generously, splendidly **11** excessively, luxuriously, sumptuously, unsparingly **13** extravagantly, intemperately

law
03 act, lay, lex **04** code, cops, pigs, rule **05** axiom, canon, edict, maxim, order, tenet **06** decree **07** charter, command, coppers, formula, lawsuit, precept, rozzers, statute, the Bill, the fuzz **08** standard, the force **09** criterion, determine, direction, directive, enactment, guideline, ordinance, principle, the police **10** boys in blue, expedite, indulgence, litigation, regulation **11** commandment, instruction, legal action, legislation **12** constitution **13** jurisprudence, pronouncement **14** police officers, the police force

Laws and Acts include:

04 DORA
07 Riot Act, Test Act
08 Corn Laws, Poor Laws, Stamp Act, Sugar Act
10 Act of Union, Magna Carta, Patriot Act, Reform Acts

11 Abortion Act, Equal Pay Act
12 Bill of Rights, Homestead Act
13 Act of Congress, Enclosure Acts, Parliament Act
14 Act of Supremacy, Cat and Mouse Act, Civil Rights Act, Corporation Act, Declaratory Act, Native Title Act, Taft–Hartley Act
15 Act of Parliament, Act of Settlement, Act of Succession, Habeas Corpus Act

Scientific and other laws include:

04 Ohm's, Oral, Sod's
05 lemon, Roman, Salic
06 Boyle's, Hooke's, Mosaic, Snell's, Stoke's
07 Dalton's, Hubble's, Kepler's, Murphy's, natural
08 Charles's
09 Avogadro's
10 Parkinson's
13 inverse square

• by law
04 iure, jure

law-abiding
04 good **06** decent, honest, lawful **07** dutiful, orderly, upright **08** obedient, virtuous **09** complying, righteous **10** honourable, upstanding **15** whiter than white

lawbreaker
05 crook, felon **06** outlaw, sinner **07** convict, culprit **08** criminal, offender **09** infractor, miscreant, wrongdoer **10** delinquent, trespasser **11** perpetrator **12** transgressor

lawcourt
03 bar **05** bench, court, trial **07** assizes, session **08** tribunal **09** judiciary **10** court of law

lawful
04 just **05** legal, legit, licit, valid **06** proper **08** rightful **09** allowable, legalized, warranted **10** authorized, legitimate, recognized, sanctioned **11** permissible **14** constitutional

lawfully
05 by law **07** legally, validly **08** by rights, properly **10** rightfully **11** permissibly **12** legitimately

lawless
◊ *anagram indicator*
04 wild **05** rowdy **06** unruly **07** chaotic, illegal, riotous, rulesse **08** anarchic, criminal, mutinous, reckless, ruleless **09** insurgent, seditious, unsettled **10** anarchical, disorderly, rebellious, ungoverned, wrongdoing **11** lawbreaking **12** unrestrained **13** revolutionary, wild and woolly **15** insurrectionary

lawlessness
05 chaos **06** mob law, piracy **07** anarchy, mob rule **08** disorder, rent-a-mob, lynch-law, sedition **09** mobocracy, rebellion **10** insurgency, ochlocracy, revolution **12** insurrection, racketeering

lawman
03 Ohm **05** Boyle, Hooke, Mufti **09** Parkinson

Lawrence
02 DH, TE

lawrencium
02 Lr, Lw

lawsuit
04 case, plea, suit **05** cause, trial **06** action **07** contest, dispute, process **08** argument **10** indictment, litigation **11** legal action, proceedings, prosecution

lawyer
02 Av, BL **03** Att **04** Atty, silk **05** brief **06** jurist **07** counsel, mukhtar, shyster, templar **08** advocate, attorney, green-bag, Man of Law **09** lawmonger **10** legal eagle **12** legal adviser

See also **barrister**

Lawyer types include:

02 DA, KC, QC
05 avoué, judge
06 avocet
07 bencher, coroner, counsel, justice, sheriff
08 Recorder
09 barrister, solicitor
11 conveyancer, crown lawyer
12 circuit judge, jurisconsult, Lord Advocate
13 attorney at law, Crown attorney, district judge, Queen's Counsel, sheriff depute
14 criminal lawyer, deputy recorder, High Court judge, Lord Chancellor, public defender, Vice-Chancellor
15 ambulance-chaser, Attorney-General

Lawyers include:

04 Hill (Anita), John (Otto), Reno (Janet)
05 Booth (Cherie), Finch (Atticus), Mason (Perry), Mills (Dame Barbara Jean Lyon), Nader (Ralph), Slovo (Joe), Vance (Cyrus R)
06 Bailey (F Lee), Butler (Benjamin Franklin), Carton (Sydney), Darrow (Clarence), Devlin (Patrick, Lord), Holmes (Oliver Wendell), Martin (Richard)
07 Acheson (Dean), Clinton (Hillary Rodham), Haldane (Richard, Viscount), Kennedy (Helena, Baroness), Mondale (Walter), O'Connor (Sandra Day)
08 Kunstler (William), Marshall (Thurgood), Mortimer (Sir John)
09 La Guardia (Fiorello H), Shawcross (Hartley William, Baron)
10 Birkenhead (Frederick Edwin Smith, Earl of), Dershowitz (Alan)
11 Hore-Belisha (Leslie, Lord)
12 Guicciardini (Francesco)
14 Brillat-Savarin (Anthelme)

• lawyers
03 bar

lax

◇ anagram indicator
04 wide **05** broad, loose, slack, vague
06 casual, remiss, salmon, sloppy
07 flaccid, general, inexact, lenient
08 careless, heedless, laid-back, slipshod, tolerant, wide-open
09 easy-going, imprecise, indulgent, negligent **10** inaccurate, indefinite, neglectful, permissive **11** inattentive
14 latitudinarian

laxative

05 purge, salts, senna **06** ipecac, saline
07 cascara, Gregory **08** aperient, evacuant, lenitive, loosener, relaxant, solutive **09** aperitive, cathartic, purgative, taraxacum **10** eccoprotic, Epsom salts **11** health salts, ipecacuanha **14** cascara sagrada, Gregory's powder, liquid paraffin, Seidlitz powder **15** Gregory's mixture

laxity

07 freedom, neglect **08** latitude, leniency, softness **09** looseness, slackness, tolerance **10** indulgence, negligence, sloppiness **11** imprecision, inexactness, nonchalance
12 carelessness, heedlessness, indifference, laissez-faire, slovenliness
14 indefiniteness, permissiveness

lay

03 bet, ode, put, set **04** bear, bung, drop, laic, make, plan, poem, risk, song
05 allot, apply, beset, breed, civil, cover, embed, imbed, leave, lodge, lyric, offer, place, plant, plonk, posit, stick, wager **06** arable, assign, ballad, burden, chance, charge, design, devise, gamble, hazard, impose, impute, locate, meadow, saddle, set out, settle, submit, thrust, waylay
07 amateur, arrange, ascribe, deposit, dispose, inflict, oppress, pasture, prepare, present, produce, secular, set down, station, work out **08** encumber, engender, exorcize, madrigal, oviposit, position **09** attribute, establish, weigh down **10** make it with, put forward
11 give birth to, **12** non-qualified
13 non-specialist **15** non-professional
• lay aside
04 keep, save, void **05** defer, store
06 put off, reject, shelve **07** abandon, discard, dismiss **08** postpone, put aside, set aside **09** cast aside
• lay bare
04 show **05** scale, strip, unrip
06 expose, reveal, uncase, unveil
07 divulge, exhibit, explain, uncover
08 disclose, manifest
• lay down
04 drop, give **05** couch, plant, plonk, state, store, yield **06** affirm, assert, depone, give up, ordain, record, submit
07 deposit, discard **09** establish, formulate, postulate, prescribe, stipulate, surrender **10** relinquish
• lay down the law
07 dictate **09** crack down, dogmatize, emphasize **11** pontificate **12** rule the roost **14** read the riot act

• lay hands on
03 get **04** find, grab, grip **05** bless, catch, clasp, grasp, seize, set on
06 attack, beat up, clutch, locate, obtain, ordain **07** acquire, assault, confirm, lay into, unearth **08** discover
09 get hold of, lay hold of
10 consecrate **12** bring to light
• lay in
05 amass, glean, hoard, store
06 gather **07** build up, collect, stock up, store up **09** stockpile
10 accumulate
• lay into
06 assail, attack **08** hit out at, let fly at, set about, tear into **09** have a go at, lash out at, pitch into
• lay it on
07 flatter **08** butter up, overdo it, soft-soap **09** sweet-talk **10** exaggerate, overpraise
• lay off
04 doff, drop, quit, sack, stop
05 cease, hedge, let go, let up
06 desist, give up, pay off **07** dismiss, refrain **08** leave off **09** discharge
10 leave alone **11** discontinue **13** make redundant
• lay on
04 give **05** cater, pound, set up
06 impose, supply **07** furnish, inflict, provide **08** organize
• lay out
03 pay **04** fell, give, plan **05** floor, spend **06** design, expend, invest, put out, set out, streek **07** arrange, display, exhibit, flatten, fork out, stretch
08 demolish, disburse, knock out, shell out, straucht, straught **09** spread out
10 contribute
• lay up
04 hive, keep, save **05** amass, hoard, set by, store **07** deposit, put away, store up **08** mothball **10** accumulate
• lay waste
04 rape, raze, ruin, sack **05** havoc, spoil **06** locust, ravage **07** despoil, destroy, estrepe, pillage **08** demolish, desolate **09** depredate, devastate, vandalize

layabout

05 idler **06** loafer, skiver, waster
07 goof-off, laggard, lounger, shirker, wastrel **09** corner-boy, corner-man, lazybones, sundowner **10** ne'er-do-well **14** good-for-nothing

layer

01 E **03** bed, hen, lie, ply, row **04** band, coat, film, seam, skin, tier, vein
05 cover, flake, plate, sheet, table
06 course, lamina, mantle, scrape
07 blanket, coating, deposit, lamella, stratum **08** covering **09** mesoblast, thickness **10** lamination **11** superficies

See also **atmosphere**
• layers
06 strata

layman, layperson, laywoman

04 laic **07** amateur, secular
08 exhorter, outsider, tertiary
11 parabolanus, parishioner, terrestrial
12 impropriator **13** local preacher, unordained man **15** non-professional, unordained woman

lay-off

05 cards **06** firing, papers **07** jotters, sacking, the boot, the push, the sack
08 the elbow **09** discharge, dismissal
10 redundancy **12** unemployment

layout

◇ anagram indicator
03 map, set **04** plan, unit **05** draft
06 design, format, outfit, sketch
07 display, outline **09** blueprint, geography **11** arrangement
12 organization **13** comprehensive

layperson *see* **layman, layperson, laywoman**

laze

03 veg **04** idle, loaf, loll, lusk **05** chill, relax **06** bludge, lounge, unwind, veg out **08** chill out **09** bum around, lie around, sit around

lazily

◇ anagram indicator
04 idly **06** slowly **07** slackly
10 sluggishly **13** lethargically

laziness

05 sloth **07** languor **08** idleness, lethargy, slowness **09** fainéance, indolence, slackness, tardiness
10 inactivity, Oblomovism
12 dilatoriness, slothfulness, sluggishness

lazy

04 idle, lusk, slow **05** inert, slack, tardy
06 laesie, lither, torpid **07** dronish, languid, luskish, work-shy **08** bone-idle, fainéant, inactive, indolent, slothful, sluggish **09** lethargic
10 languorous, slow-moving **14** good-for-nothing

lazybones

04 lusk, slob, slug **05** drone, idler
06 loafer, lubber, skiver, slouch
07 goof-off, laggard, lounger, lubbard, mollusc, shirker **08** do-nought, fainéant, layabout, slowback, sluggard
09 do-nothing, sundowner
10 bedpresser, ne'er-do-well, sleepyhead **14** good-for-nothing

leach

04 seep **05** drain **06** filter, osmose, strain **07** extract **08** filtrate
09 lixiviate, percolate

lead

◇ head selection indicator
02 Pb **03** gap, tip, top, van **04** clue, cord, edge, hand, have, head, hint, hold, line, live, main, move, pass, rein, rule, shot, show, slip, star, sway
05 balls, cause, chain, chief, excel, first, guide, leash, model, outdo, pilot, plumb, prime, slugs, spend, start, steer, usher **06** convey, direct, escort, exceed, govern, induce, manage, margin, minium, outrun, prompt, sinker, string, tether, tip-off, weight
07 bring on, bullets, command,

conduct, dispose, eclipse, example, incline, leading, officer, pattern, pellets, plummet, pointer, precede, premier, primary, produce, provoke, running, surpass, undergo **08** foremost, guidance, interval, outstrip, persuade, priority, regulate, result in, star role, vanguard **09** advantage, be in front, call forth, come first, direction, extension, forefront, indicator, influence, precedent, principal, supervise, supremacy, title role, transcend **10** ammunition, bring about, experience, first place, indication, initiative, leadership, leading man, precedence, suggestion **11** be in the lead, heavy weight, leading lady, leading role, outdistance, pre-eminence, preside over, tend towards **12** be in charge of, call the shots, contribute to, starring part **13** be at the head of, principal part **15** advance position, leading position

• **lead gradually**
04 drib

• **lead off**
04 open **05** begin, start **07** kick off **08** commence, get going, initiate, start off **10** inaugurate

• **lead on**
04 dupe, lure **05** tempt, trail, trick **06** draw on, entice, seduce **07** beguile, deceive, mislead **08** persuade **11** string along **12** put one over on, take for a ride **14** pull a fast one on

• **lead the way**
04 show **05** guide **07** go first, pioneer **09** go in front, set a trend **10** be a pioneer, pave the way, show the way **11** blaze a trail **14** break new ground

• **lead up to**
05 usher **07** prepare **08** approach **09** introduce **10** open the way, pave the way, prepare for **13** make overtures

leaden
04 dull, grey, lead **05** ashen, dingy, heavy, inert, stiff **06** boring, cloudy, dismal, dreary, gloomy, sombre, wooden **07** greyish, humdrum, languid, onerous, stilted **08** laboured, lifeless, listless, overcast, plodding, sluggish **09** plumbeous **10** burdensome, cumbersome, depressing, lacklustre, oppressive, spiritless

leader
◊ *head selection indicator*
02 PM **03** dux, gov, guv **04** boss, cock, head, imam **05** ariki, chief, guide, ruler, sheik, usher **06** bigwig, escort, expert, honcho, sachem, sheikh, top dog, zaddik **07** big shot, captain, coryphe, courier, founder, general, khalifa, kingpin, mahatma, manager, pioneer, skipper, tsaddik, tsaddiq, tzaddik, tzaddiq **08** big noise, caudillo, director, governor, inventor, khalifah, mocuddum, mokaddam, muqaddam, overseer, superior **09** architect, authority, big cheese, chieftain, commander, conductor, developer,

editorial, innovator, liturgist, principal **10** coryphaeus, discoverer, figurehead, head honcho, pathfinder, ringleader, supervisor **11** front-runner, trailblazer **12** guiding light, leading light **13** groundbreaker **14** mover and shaker, superintendent

See also **governor**; **emperor**; **empress**; **king**; **leader**; **Maori**; **president**; **queen**; **Roman**; **ruler**

leaderless
◊ *head deletion indicator*
08 headless **10** acephalous

leadership
◊ *head selection indicator*
04 lead, rule, sway **07** command, control **08** guidance, headship, hegemony **09** authority, captaincy, direction **10** apostolate, domination, management **11** generalship, pre-eminence, premiership, supervision **12** directorship, governorship **14** administration, rangatiratanga **15** superintendency

lead-in
05 debut, intro, proem, start **06** launch **07** opening, preface, prelude **08** exordium, foreword, overture, preamble, prologue **09** beginning **11** front matter **12** inauguration, introduction, presentation, prolegomenon **13** preliminaries

leading
◊ *head selection indicator*
03 top **04** main, star **05** chief, first, front **06** ruling, staple **07** guiding, highest, premier, primary, supreme, top-rank **08** dominant, foremost, greatest, guidance, mistress, superior **09** directing, governing, number one, paramount, preceding, principal **10** pre-eminent **11** outstanding

leaf
01 f, p **03** pad **04** flip, page, skim **05** bract, calyx, folio, frond, sepal, sheet, thumb **06** browse, folium, glance, needle, troely **07** foliole, leaflet, troelie, troolie **09** cataphyll, clinquant, cotyledon, marijuana **11** sclerophyll **12** thumb through

Leaf parts include:

03 tip
04 back, lobe, vein
05 blade, lobus, stoma, thorn
06 margin, midrib, sheath, stipel
07 petiole, stipule, stomata
08 leaf axil
09 epidermis, leaf cells
11 axillary bud, chloroplast

Leaf shapes include:

04 oval
05 acute, lobed, ovate
06 cusped, entire, linear, lyrate
07 acerose, ciliate, cordate, crenate, dentate, falcate, hastate, obovate, palmate, peltate, pinnate, ternate
08 digitate, elliptic, reniform, subulate

09 orbicular, runcinate, sagittate
10 lanceolate, pinnatifid, spathulate, trifoliate
13 doubly dentate
15 abruptly pinnate

• **turn over a new leaf**
05 amend, begin **06** change, reform **07** improve **10** begin again, start again **11** start afresh **12** mend your ways **14** better yourself, change your ways **15** improve yourself, make a fresh start, pull your socks up

leaflet
04 bill **05** flier, flyer, pinna, tract **06** dodger, mailer **07** booklet, foliole, handout **08** brochure, circular, handbill, pamphlet

leafy
05 bosky, green, shady, woody **06** bowery, leafed, leaved, shaded, wooded **07** foliose, verdant **08** frondent, frondose **11** frondescent **12** dasyphyllous

league
01 I **03** cup **04** ally, band, bond, Bund, link **05** class, group, guild, Hansa, Hanse, level, union, unite **06** cartel **07** combine, compact, consort, contest **08** alliance, category, conspire, division **09** associate, coalition, co-operate, syndicate **10** amalgamate, consortium, federation, fellowship, join forces, tournament **11** affiliation, amphictyony, association, collaborate, combination, competition, confederacy, confederate, co-operative, corporation, partnership **12** band together, championship, conglomerate, Holy Alliance **13** confederation

See also **Australian football**; **baseball**; **football**; **rugby**

• **in league**
06 allied, linked **08** in tandem **09** in cahoots **10** conspiring, in alliance **11** co-operating, hand in glove, in collusion **13** collaborating, in co-operation, in partnership

leak
03 cut, ren, rin, run **04** blab, drip, hole, ooze, seep, tell, weep **05** break, chink, crack, exude, let in, let on, spill **06** escape, exposé, impart, let out, oozing, pass on, relate, reveal, run out, squeal **07** crevice, divulge, fissure, leakage, leaking, let slip, opening, seepage, seeping, trickle, urinate **08** disclose, exposure, give away, overflow, puncture, spillage **09** discharge, make known, make water, percolate **10** disclosure, divulgence, make public, revelation, uncovering **11** percolation **12** blow the gaffe **13** spill the beans **15** bringing to light

leaky
05 holey, split **06** gizzen, porous **07** cracked, leaking **08** dripping

495

leave

9 permeable, punctured
10 perforated, unstanched
11 unstaunched

ean
03 lie **04** abut, arid, bank, bare, bend,
bony, hard, heel, lank, list, poor, prop,
rest, slim, tend, thin, tilt **05** gaunt,
lanky, slant, slink, slope, spare, tough
06 barren, favour, hungry, meagre,
prefer, repose, scanty, skinny, slinky,
sparse **07** angular, austere, haggard,
incline, minceur, recline, scraggy,
scrawny, slender **09** difficult,
emaciated, fleshless, gravitate,
rigwiddie, rigwoodie **10** inadequate,
unfruitful, unpleasant **11** be at an angle
12 insufficient, unproductive,
unprofitable, unsuccessful
13 uncomfortable **15** all skin and
bones
• **lean on**
04 rest **05** force **06** bank on, coerce,
rely on **07** trust in **08** depend on,
persuade **10** intimidate, pressurize
13 put pressure on **14** put the screws
on

eaning
04 bent, bias **06** liking **08** aptitude,
fondness, penchant, tendency
10 attraction, partiality, preference,
proclivity, propensity **11** disposition,
inclination **12** predilection

eanness
08 boniness, lankness, slimness,
thinness **09** gauntness, lankiness
11 scragginess, scrawniness,
slenderness

ean-to
03 hut **04** pent, shed **05** shack
06 garage, lock-up **08** outhouse,
skilling, skillion **09** penthouse

eap
◊ *anagram indicator*
03 hop, lep **04** jeté, jump, lope, loup,
over, rise, romp, salt, skip, soar, volt
05 bound, caper, clear, dance, fence,
flier, flyer, frisk, mount, pronk, salto,
sault, spang, surge, vault, volte
06 basket, bounce, breach, cavort,
curvet, frolic, gambol, rocket, spring
07 échappé, falcade, soaring, upsurge,
upswing **08** assemblé, cabriole,
capriole, croupade, escalate, fish-dive,
increase, jump over, overskip,
somerset **09** elevation, entrechat, pas
de chat, skyrocket **10** escalation,
pigeon-wing, somersault
11 summersault
• **by leaps and bounds, in leaps
and bounds**
07 quickly, rapidly, swiftly **08** in no
time **13** in no time at all
• **leap at**
04 grab **05** seize **06** jump at, snatch
07 agree to, fall for, swallow
08 pounce on **13** accept eagerly

earn
03 con, get, kon, see **04** cram, hear,
larn, lear, leir, lere, read **05** conne,
glean, grasp, leare, study, train

06 absorb, detect, digest, gather, get
off, master, pick up, take in **07** acquire,
discern, find out, gen up on, prepare,
realize, receive, suss out **08** discover,
memorize, remember **09** ascertain,
determine, get wind of **10** assimilate,
comprehend, have off pat, understand
12 get the hang of, learn by heart
13 become aware of **14** acquire skill in,
commit to memory **15** gain knowledge
of

learned
04 cond, read, wise **06** savant,
versed **07** erudite, savante
08 academic, cultured, lettered,
literary, literate, pedantic, scienced,
studious, well-read **09** scholarly
10 widely read **11** literatured
12 intellectual, well-educated,
well-informed **13** knowledgeable

learner
01 L **04** tiro, tyro **05** pupil
06 conner, intern, novice, rookie
07 scholar, student, trainee
08 beginner, neophyte
09 greenhorn **10** apprentice
11 abecedarian

See also **beginner**

learning
04 lear, leir, lere, lore **05** leare, study
06 wisdom **07** conning, culture,
letters, tuition **08** pedantry, research
09 education, erudition, intellect,
knowledge, schooling **11** edification,
information, scholarship, schoolcraft
• **basic learning**
03 RRR

lease
03 let, set **04** farm, hire, loan, rent, tack
05 glean **06** let out, rental, sublet
07 chapter, charter, hire out, pasture,
rent out, tenancy **08** contract
09 agreement

leash
03 lym **04** bind, cord, curb, hold, lead,
lime, lyam, lyme, rein, slip **05** check,
trash **06** string, tether **07** control
09 restraint **10** discipline

See also **three**

• **strain at the leash**
07 be dying, be eager **09** be anxious,
be itching, be longing **11** be impatient

least
06 fewest, lowest **07** minimum,
poorest **08** smallest **09** slightest
• **at least**
06 anyhow **07** however **09** at any rate,
in any case **10** as a minimum, at the
least, for all that, in any event, no less
than **12** nevertheless, no matter what
14 at the very least, nothing short of
15 nothing less than, whatever
happens
• **to say the least**
13 to put it mildly **14** at the very least

leather
03 taw **04** beat, butt **06** levant, spetch,
thrash **08** studwork

03 kid
04 buff, calf, napa, roan, shoe, wash,
yuft
05 grain, Mocha, nappa, neat's, plate,
split, suede, waxed, white
06 chrome, Nubuck, patent, Rexine®,
Russia, shammy, skiver, spruce
07 chamois, cowhide, dogskin, hog-
skin, kidskin, kipskin, morocco,
pigskin, saffian
08 buckskin, cabretta, calfskin,
capeskin, cheverel, cheveril,
cordovan, cordwain, deerskin,
goatskin, lambskin, maroquin,
shagreen
09 crocodile, lacquered, sheepskin,
slinkskin, snakeskin
10 artificial
11 aqualeather, cuir-bouilli,
whiteleather

leathery
04 hard **05** rough, tough **06** rugged
07 corious, durable, wizened
08 hardened, leathern, wrinkled
10 coriaceous

leave
◊ *deletion indicator*
02 go, OK **03** let, vac **04** drop, dump,
exit, jilt, levy, lose, miss, move, park,
part, quit, will **05** allot, avoid, break,
cause, cease, chuck, congé, ditch,
endow, go off, raise, say-so, scoot, split
06 assign, commit, congee, create, day
off, decamp, depart, desert, desist,
devise, forget, give up, go away, hook
it, lead to, mislay, resign, retire, set out,
vamose **07** abandon, consent,
consign, deliver, do a bunk, entrust,
forsake, freedom, holiday, liberty,
licence, license, produce, pull out,
push off, retreat, take off, time off,
vamoose, walk off, warrant
08 bequeath, choof off, clear off, come
away, emigrate, farewell, furlough,
generate, give over, hand down, hand
over, holidays, make over, misplace,
occasion, renounce, result in, run
along, run out on, sanction, shove off,
transmit, up sticks, vacation, withdraw
09 allowance, disappear, push along,
sick leave, surrender **10** bring about,
concession, give rise to, green light, hit
the road, indulgence, make tracks,
permission, relinquish, sabbatical
11 leave behind **12** dispensation, shoot
through **13** authorization, sling your
hook, take your leave **14** leave of
absence, turn your back on **15** leave
high and dry, take French leave
• **leave off**
03 end **04** halt, omit, quit, stop
05 cease **06** desist, lay off **07** abstain,
refrain **08** break off, give over, knock
off **09** terminate **11** discontinue
• **leave out**
03 bar, cut **04** miss, omit **06** bypass,
cut out, except, ignore, reject
07 exclude, miss out, neglect **08** count
out, overlook, pass over, suppress
09 cast aside, disregard, eliminate

leaven

• **leave quickly**
08 light out

leaven
04 barm, work, zyme **05** imbue, raise, swell, yeast **06** expand, puff up **07** enliven, ferment, inspire, lighten, pervade, quicken, suffuse **08** permeate **09** sourdough, stimulate **11** cause to rise **12** raising agent

leaves
03 tea **04** atap **05** attap

leavings
04 bits **05** dregs, dross, spoil, waste **06** debris, pieces, refuse, relics, scraps **07** remains, residue, rubbish **08** detritus, oddments, remnants **09** alms-drink, fragments, leftovers, remainder, sweepings **11** broken meats

Lebanon
02 RL **03** LBN

lecher
04 gate, goat, lech, perv, rake, roué, wolf **05** Romeo, satyr **06** wanton **07** Don Juan, flasher, seducer **08** Casanova, Lothario, Lovelace **09** adulterer, debauchee, libertine, womanizer **10** fornicator, libidinist, profligate, sensualist **11** dirty old man, whoremonger

lecherous
04 lewd **05** horny, pervy, randy **06** carnal, wanton **07** codding, leering, lustful, rammish, raunchy **08** prurient, unchaste **09** debauched, dissolute, lickerish, liquorish, salacious **10** degenerate, dissipated, lascivious, libidinous, licentious, womanizing **11** promiscuous **12** concupiscent

lechery
04 lust **08** lewdness, salacity **09** carnality, prurience, randiness **10** debauchery, rakishness, sensuality, wantonness, womanizing **11** libertinism, lustfulness, raunchiness **13** concupiscence, lickerishness, salaciousness **14** lasciviousness, libidinousness, licentiousness

lectern
04 ambo, desk **05** eagle, stand, table **07** lettern, oratory **11** reading-desk

lecture
03 act, jaw **04** read, talk **05** chide, class, scold, speak, teach **06** berate, homily, lesson, rebuke, rocket, sermon, speech **07** address, censure, chiding, expound, jawbone, prelect, reproof, reprove, tell off **08** admonish, berating, extender, harangue, instruct, reproach, scolding, travelog **09** chalk talk, discourse, give a talk, hold forth, reprimand, talking-to **10** conférence, prelection, rollicking, telling-off, travelogue, upbraiding **11** instruction, make a speech, pick holes in **12** disquisition, dressing-down, pull to pieces, tear to pieces **13** give lessons in **14** curtain lecture

lecturer
01 L **03** don **04** lect **05** tutor **06** docent, lector, orator, reader, talker **07** scholar, speaker, teacher **08** academic, preacher **09** declaimer, expounder, haranguer, pedagogue, preceptor, prelector, professor **10** instructor, sermonizer, theologian **11** speechifier, speechmaker **12** conférencier, extensionist, instructress

ledge
04 berm, lode, sill, step, vein **05** altar, bench, linch, ridge, shelf, stock **06** gradin, mantel, offset, settle, shelve **07** gradine, linchet, lynchet **08** fire-step, overhang **10** buttery-bar, firing-step, projection, scarcement **11** mantelpiece, mantelshelf

ledger
05 books **07** journal **08** accounts, register **09** inventory **10** record book **11** account book

lee
05 cover, river **06** arable, meadow, refuge **07** pasture, shelter **09** sanctuary **10** protection

leech
05 drain, toady **06** usurer **07** clinger, sponger **08** hanger-on, parasite **09** physician, scrounger, sycophant **10** freeloader **11** bloodsucker, extortioner

leer
03 eye **04** grin, ogle, perv, wink **05** gloat, smirk, sneer, stare, tweer, twire **06** colour, goggle, squint **07** glad eye **10** complexion **13** lecherous look

leery
04 wary **05** chary **06** unsure **07** careful, dubious, guarded **08** cautious, doubting **09** sceptical, uncertain **10** suspicious **11** distrustful, on your guard

lees
05 draff, dregs, grout **06** dunder, refuse **07** deposit, grounds, residue **08** sediment **09** settlings **11** precipitate

leeway
04 play, room **05** drift, scope, slack, space **06** margin **07** freedom **08** latitude **09** elbow-room **11** flexibility

left
◇ *deletion indicator*
01 L **03** red **04** gone, lorn, near, over, port, quit, went **06** Maoist **07** liberal, Marxist, radical **08** larboard, left-hand, left-wing, Leninist **09** communist, sinistral, socialist, Stalinist **10** Bolshevist, Spartakist, Trotskyist, Trotskyite **11** progressive, revisionist **12** collectivist **13** revolutionary
• **turn left**
03 hie **04** high

left-handed
06 clumsy, gauche **07** awkward, dubious, unlucky **08** southpaw **09** ambiguous, equivocal, insincere, sinistral **10** backhanded, cack-handed, kack-handed **12** corrie-fisted, hypocritical

left-hander
05 lefty **06** leftie **08** southpaw **09** sinistral **11** cackyhander, molly-dooker

left-over
04 orra **06** excess, unused **07** oddment, settled, surplus, uneaten **09** remaining **11** superfluous

leftovers
05 dregs **06** excess, refuse, scraps **07** remains, residue, surplus **08** leavings, remnants **09** remainder, sweepings

left-wing
04 left **06** Maoist **07** liberal, Marxist, radical **08** Leninist **09** communist, socialist, Stalinist **10** Bolshevist, Spartakist, Trotskyist, Trotskyite **11** progressive, revisionist **12** collectivist **13** revolutionary
• **left-winger**
04 trot

leg
02 on **03** bit, gam, lap, peg, pin **04** crus, gamb, limb, part, prop **05** brace, shank, stage, stump **06** member, timber **07** pleopod, portion, section, segment, stretch, support, upright **08** swindler **10** sheepshank **12** underpinning
• **leg it**
03 run **04** walk **05** hurry **06** hoof it **07** scarper **08** go by foot
• **not have a leg to stand on**
10 be unproved **11** lack support **12** lack an excuse **13** be unjustified
• **on its last legs**
04 weak **06** ailing **07** failing **10** fading fast, near to ruin **11** about to fail, near to death **12** at death's door **15** about to collapse, nearing collapse
• **pull someone's leg**
03 kid, rib **04** fool, joke **05** tease, trick **06** have on, wind up **07** deceive **09** make fun of **11** play a joke on **12** take for a ride **14** pull a fast one on

legacy
04 gift **06** estate **07** bequest **08** heirloom, heritage **09** endowment, heritance, patrimony **10** bequeathal, birthright **11** inheritance

legal
03 leg **05** legit, licit, right, sound, valid **06** lawful, proper **07** allowed **08** forensic, judicial, licensed, rightful **09** allowable, judiciary, legalized, permitted, statutory, warranted **10** above-board, acceptable, admissible, authorized, legitimate, sanctioned **11** permissible **12** within the law **14** constitutional
See also **court**; **crime**

egal terms include:

2 JP, QC
3 bar, DPP, sue
4 ASBO, bail, deed, dock, fine, jury, oath, plea, will, writ
5 alibi, asset, bench, brief, by-law, claim, felon, grant, judge, juror, lease, party, proof, proxy, title, trial
6 appeal, arrest, bigamy, charge, client, demand, equity, estate, guilty, lawyer, legacy, pardon, parole, patent, remand, repeal, the bar, waiver
7 accused, alimony, amnesty, caution, charter, codicil, convict, coroner, custody, damages, defence, divorce, hearing, inquest, inquiry, Law Lord, lawsuit, mandate, penalty, probate, sheriff, statute, summons, tenancy, verdict, warrant, witness
8 act of God, adultery, advocate, civil law, contract, covenant, criminal, easement, eviction, evidence, executor, freehold, hung jury, innocent, judgment, juvenile, legal aid, mortgage, offender, prisoner, receiver, reprieve, sanction, sentence, subpoena, tribunal
9 accessory, acquittal, affidavit, agreement, annulment, barrister, common law, copyright, court case, defendant, endowment, fee simple, indemnity, intestacy, judgement, judiciary, leasehold, liability, plaintiff, precedent, probation, solicitor, testimony, trademark
0 accomplice, allegation, confession, conveyance, decree nisi, indictment, injunction, liquidator, magistrate, settlement
1 adjournment, arbitration, extradition, foreclosure, inheritance, local search, maintenance, plea bargain, plead guilty, proceedings, ward of court
2 age of consent, Bill of Rights, constitution, court martial, cross-examine, Lord Advocate, misadventure, notary public
3 King's evidence, public inquiry, Queen's Counsel, young offender
4 decree absolute, Lord Chancellor, plead not guilty, Queen's evidence
5 Act of Parliament, Attorney General, clerk of the court, contempt of court, power of attorney

legal document
4 deed, writ

egality
8 validity **09** rightness, soundness
0 lawfulness, legitimacy
2 rightfulness **14** admissibleness, ermissibility

egalize
5 admit, allow **06** accept, permit, tify **07** approve, license, warrant
8 sanction, validate **09** authorize, ake legal **10** legitimize
3 decriminalize

legally
05 by law **07** validly **08** by rights, lawfully, properly **10** rightfully
11 permissibly **12** legitimately

legate
03 leg **05** agent, envoy **06** deputy, exarch, nuncio **08** delegate, emissary
09 messenger **10** ambassador
12 commissioner **14** representative

legatee
04 heir **06** co-heir **07** devisee
08 legatary, receiver **09** co-heiress, inheritor, recipient **10** inheritrix
11 beneficiary

legation
07 embassy, mission **08** ministry
09 consulate **10** commission, delegation, deputation
14 representation

legend
03 key, VIP **04** myth, name, saga, star, tale **05** celeb, fable, motto, story
06 bigwig, cipher, legion, worthy
07 big name, big shot, caption, fiction, notable, romance **08** folk tale, luminary **09** celebrity, dignitary, narrative, personage, superstar, underline **11** explanation, inscription, personality **12** famous person, living legend **13** household name

See also **mythology**

See also **knight**

legendary
06 fabled, famous **07** popular
08 fabulous, fanciful, glorious, honoured, immortal, mythical, renowned **09** acclaimed, fictional, storybook, well-known **10** celebrated, fictitious, remembered **11** illustrious, traditional

legerdemain
05 feint **06** tricky **07** cunning
08 artifice, jugglery, juggling, trickery
09 chicanery, deception, sophistry
10 artfulness, craftiness, hocus-pocus, subterfuge **11** contrivance, logodaedaly, manoeuvring
12 manipulation **13** sleight of hand, thaumaturgics

legibility
07 clarity **08** lucidity **09** clearness, lucidness, plainness, precision
10 simplicity **11** readability
12 distinctness, explicitness, readableness **15** intelligibility

legible
04 neat **05** clear, lucid, plain **06** simple
07 precise **08** distinct, explicit, readable **10** easy to read
12 decipherable, intelligible
14 comprehensible

legibly
06 simply **07** clearly, lucidly, plainly
08 readably **09** precisely **10** easily read, explicitly **12** intelligibly
14 comprehensibly

legion
04 army, host, mass, unit **05** drove, force, horde, swarm, troop **06** cohort, legend, myriad, number, throng
07 brigade, company **08** division, numerous, regiment **09** battalion, countless, multitude **10** numberless
11 illimitable, innumerable
13 multitudinous
• **British Legion**
03 BL

legislate
05 enact, order 06 codify, decree, ordain 08 make laws, pass laws 09 authorize, establish, formulate, prescribe

legislation
03 act, law, leg 04 bill, code 05 legis, rules 06 ruling 07 charter, measure, statute 09 enactment, lawmaking, ordinance 10 regulation 11 formulation 12 codification, prescription 13 authorization

legislative
03 leg 05 legis 08 judicial 09 lawgiving, lawmaking 10 senatorial 12 jurisdictive 13 congressional, parliamentary

legislator
02 MP 06 deputy 07 senator 08 lawgiver, lawmaker 09 nomothete 10 nomothetes 11 congressman 13 congresswoman 15 parliamentarian

legislature
03 leg 05 house, legis 06 senate, states 07 chamber 08 assembly, congress 10 parliament

See also **parliament**

legitimacy
08 fairness, legality, validity 09 rightness, soundness 10 lawfulness 11 credibility, rationality 12 plausibility, rightfulness, sensibleness 13 acceptability, admissibility 14 admissibleness, justifiability, permissibility, reasonableness

legitimate
04 fair, real, true 05 legal, legit, licit, loyal, sound, valid 06 kosher, lawful, proper 07 correct, genuine, logical, natural 08 credible, rational, rightful, sensible, true-born 09 competent, justified, plausible, statutory, warranted 10 acceptable, admissible, authorized, reasonable, sanctioned 11 justifiable, well-founded 12 acknowledged

legitimize
05 allow 06 permit 07 charter, entitle, license, warrant 08 legalize, sanction, validate 09 authorize 10 legitimate 13 decriminalize

leisure
04 ease, rest, time 05 break, R and R, space 06 by-time 07 freedom, holiday, leasure, liberty, respite, time off, time out, vacancy 08 free time, off-hours, vacation 09 spare time 10 recreation, relaxation, retirement
• **at your leisure**
11 unhurriedly 13 in your own time, when you want to 14 when it suits you 15 in your spare time

leisurely
04 easy, lazy, slow 05 loose 06 gentle 07 relaxed, restful, unhasty 08 carefree, laid-back, tranquil 09 easy-going, unhurried 10 leisurable 11 comfortable

lemur
05 indri, loris 06 aye-aye, colugo, galago, indris, macaco, sifaka 07 half-ape, meercat, meerkat, nagapie 08 mongoose, mungoose 09 babacoote, mangouste 10 angwantibo 12 Cynocephalus 13 Galeopithecus

lend
03 add, sub 04 give, loan, spot 05 grant, prest 06 bestow, confer, credit, donate, impart, on-lend, supply 07 advance, furnish, provide 08 overlend, put forth 10 allow to use, contribute 11 allow to have 13 let someone use
• **lend a hand**
03 aid 04 help 06 assist 07 help out, pitch in 09 do your bit 14 give assistance
• **lend an ear**
04 heed 06 listen 07 give ear, hearken 10 take notice 12 pay attention
• **lend itself to**
13 be suitable for 15 be easily used for

length
01 l 04 span, term 05 piece, reach, space 06 extent, period 07 measure, portion, section, segment, stretch 08 distance, duration 09 prolixity
• **at length**
05 fully 06 at last, in full 07 finally 10 eventually, thoroughly 11 in due course 12 exhaustively, for a long time 13 in great detail 14 after a long time 15 comprehensively
• **go to any lengths**
10 do anything 11 try very hard 12 go to extremes

lengthen
03 eik, eke 04 draw 06 eke out, expand, extend, pad out 07 draw out, prolong, spin out, stretch 08 continue, elongate, increase, protract 10 grow longer, prolongate

lengthwise
05 along 07 endlong, endways, endwise 10 fore-and-aft, lengthways, vertically 12 horizontally

lengthy
04 long 05 wordy 06 prolix 07 diffuse, tedious, verbose 08 drawn-out, extended, overlong, rambling 09 prolonged 10 lengthened, long-winded, protracted 12 interminable, long-drawn-out

leniency
05 mercy 08 clemency, kindness, lenience, mildness, softness 09 tolerance 10 compassion, generosity, gentleness, humaneness, indulgence, moderation, tenderness 11 forbearance, forgiveness, magnanimity 14 permissiveness 15 soft-heartedness

lenient
04 kind, mild 06 gentle, humane, tender 07 liberal, sparing 08 generous, merciful, moderate,

soothing, tolerant 09 emollient, forgiving, indulgent, softening 10 forbearing, permissive 11 magnanimous, soft-hearted 13 compassionate

lenitive
06 easing 07 calming 08 laxative, soothing 09 assuaging, relieving 10 mitigating, mollifying, palliative 11 alleviating

lens
03 eye 05 glass, optic, power 06 finder, lentil, pebble, peeper 07 aplanat, contact 08 achromat, bull's-eye, eyeglass, eyepiece, meniscus 09 amplifier, condenser, magnifier, telephoto 10 anastigmat, apochromat, pantoscope 11 object-glass 12 burning-glass

Lent
04 fast 06 carême, spring

leopard
04 pard 05 ounce, tiger 06 pardal 07 libbard, panther, pardale 08 pardalis 12 catamountain, cat o' mountain

leper
05 lazar, mesel 06 meazel, pariah 07 leprosy, outcast 11 undesirable, untouchable 13 social outcast

leprechaun
03 elf, imp 04 puck 05 bogey, demon, fiend, gnome, nixie, pooka, troll 06 goblin, kelpie, kobold, red-cap, spirit, sprite 07 brownie, gremlin 09 hobgoblin

lesbian
03 gay 07 Sapphic 08 sapphist 10 homosexual

lesion
03 cut 04 gash, hurt, sore 05 wound 06 bruise, injury, scrape, trauma 07 scratch 08 abrasion 09 contusion 10 impairment, laceration

Lesotho
02 LS 03 LSO

less
03 bar 04 meno, save 05 fewer, minor, minus 06 except 07 short of, smaller, wanting, without, younger 08 inferior 09 excepting, excluding, not as many, not as much, not so many, not so much 13 smaller amount 15 to a lesser degree, to a lesser extent

lessen
03 cut, dip, ebb 04 alay, bate, dull, ease, fail, flag, wane 05 abate, aleye, allay, erode, let up, lower, slack 06 absorb, deaden, go down, impair, narrow, plunge, reduce, shrink, weaken 07 abridge, curtail, decline, die down, dwindle, ease off, lighten, plummet, relieve, slacken, subside, tail off 08 belittle, come down, contract, decrease, derogate, diminish, minimize, mitigate, moderate,

osedive, peter out, slow down, tail
vay **09** disparage, extenuate **10** de-
calate

ssening
 dip **05** allay, let-up **06** easing,
bing, waning **07** cutting, decline,
osion, failure **08** batement,
crease, flagging **09** abatement,
eadening, dwindling, reduction,
rinkage, weakening **10** derogation,
minution, imminution, mitigation,
oderation, slackening **11** contraction,
rtailment, extenuation, petering out
 de-escalation, minimization

sser
 lower, minor **07** smaller **08** inferior,
ghter **09** secondary **11** subordinate
 less important

sson
 lear, leir, lere, task, text **05** class,
ill, leare, model, moral, train
 course, period, rebuke, sermon
 example, lection, lecture, reading,
minar, warning **08** coaching,
ercise, homework, instruct, liripipe,
poop, practice, teaching, tutorial,
orkshop **09** deterrent, practical,
ripture **10** assignment, recitation,
hoolwork **11** application, instruction,
aster-class **12** Bible reading
 demonstration

st
 in case, listen **07** for fear **11** for fear
at **14** in order to avoid

t
 OK **03** net **04** hire, make, rent
 allow, cause, check, grant, lease
 enable, hinder, let out, permit
 agree to, hire out, prevent, rent out
 assent to, obstacle, sanction,
lerate **09** authorize, consent to, give
ave, give the OK, hindrance, restraint
 constraint, give the nod,
pediment, obstructed
obstruction, prohibition, restriction
 interference **14** give permission,
ve the go-ahead **15** say the magic
ord

let alone
 also **08** as well as **09** apart from,
ver mind **12** not to mention **13** not
rgetting

let down
 fail, vail **05** lower **06** betray, desert
 abandon, depress **09** fall short
 disappoint, disenchant, dissatisfy
disillusion **14** disappointment
 leave in the lurch

let fly
 hit **05** fling, fly at, go for, shoot
 attack, charge, strike **07** assault, lay
to **08** fall upon **09** discharge, have a
 at, lash out at

let go
 drop, free, omit, quit, sack **06** give
, unhand **07** dismiss, hang off,
anumit, release, set free, slacken,
leash **08** liberate, released
 relinquish **11** stop holding **13** make
dundant

• let in
04 sink **05** admit, greet **06** accept,
insert, take in **07** enchase, include,
receive, welcome **11** incorporate
12 allow to enter
• let in on
04 tell **06** inform **07** include, let know
11 allow to know **14** allow to share in
• let off
04 emit, fire **05** spare **06** acquit,
excuse, exempt, ignore, pardon
07 absolve, explode, forgive, give off,
release **08** detonate, liberate, reprieve
09 discharge, exonerate
• let on
04 blab, tell **06** impart, pass on,
relate, reveal, squeal **07** divulge,
let slip **08** disclose, give away
09 make known **10** make public
13 spill the beans **15** give the game
away
• let out
03 job **04** blab, emit, free, leak **05** let
go, utter, widen **06** betray, reveal,
squeal **07** enlarge, freight, let slip,
release, slacken **08** disclose
09 discharge, make known **13** spill the
beans
• let up
03 end **04** ease, halt, stop **05** abate,
cease **06** lessen **07** die down, ease off,
slacken, subside **08** decrease,
diminish, moderate

let-down
04 sell **07** setback, washout
08 betrayal **09** desertion
10 anticlimax **14** disappointment
15 disillusionment

lethal
05 fatal, toxic **06** deadly, mortal
07 deathly, noxious, ruinous, vicious
08 venomous **09** dangerous,
murderous, poisonous **10** disastrous
11 destructive, devastating **12** death-
dealing

lethally
07 fatally **08** mortally **09** noxiously,
toxically **11** dangerously
12 disastrously **13** destructively,
devastatingly

lethargic
04 dull, idle, lazy, logy, slow **05** heavy,
inert, weary **06** drowsy, sleepy, torpid
07 dormant, languid, passive
08 hebetant, inactive, lifeless, listless,
slothful, sluggish **09** apathetic,
enervated, somnolent **11** debilitated

lethargically
04 idly **05** dully **06** lazily, slowly
07 heavily, inertly, wearily **08** drowsily,
sleepily, torpidly **09** languidly
10 inactively, lifelessly, listlessly,
slothfully, sluggishly **11** somnolently
13 apathetically

lethargy
05 sloth **06** apathy, stupor, torpor
07 inertia, languor **08** dullness,
idleness, inaction, laziness, slowness
09 lassitude, weariness **10** drowsiness,
inactivity, sleepiness, somnolence

12 indifference, lifelessness,
listlessness, sluggishness

let-out
04 cure **06** escape, excuse, get-out,
remedy, way out **08** loophole **09** legal
flaw **11** safety valve, way of escape
12 escape clause, technicality **13** error
in the law, means of escape

letter
02 Ep **03** dak **04** chit, dawk, Epis, line,
note, sign, sort, type **05** books, hirer,
reply **06** device, figure, italic, lettre,
scrawl, symbol, uncial **07** bloomer,
capital, culture, epistle, message,
missive, notelet, screeve, writing
08 academia, circular, dispatch,
grapheme, learning, pastoral
09 character, education, epistolet,
erudition, rune-stave **10** aerogramme,
billet-doux, humanities, literature,
round robin, semi-uncial
11 scholarship **13** belles-lettres,
communication **14** correspondence
15 acknowledgement

Letters include:

03 ash, edh, eth, wen, wyn
04 aesc, ogam, wynn, yogh
05 thorn

See also **alphabet; typeface**

• to the letter
07 exactly **08** strictly **09** by the book,
literally, precisely **10** accurately
11 religiously, word for word **13** in
every detail, punctiliously

lettered
06 versed **07** erudite, learned, studied
08 academic, cultured, educated,
highbrow, informed, literary, literate,
well-read **09** scholarly **10** cultivated,
widely read **12** accomplished, well-
educated **13** knowledgeable

letter-opener
04 Dear

letters
04 mail, post

lettuce
07 Lactuca

Lettuce varieties include:

03 cos
04 flat
05 lamb's, round
06 frisée
07 cabbage, Chinese, iceberg,
romaine
08 Batavian
09 little gem
10 butterhead, lollo rosso

let-up
03 end **04** lull **05** break, pause
06 recess, relief **07** ceasing, respite
08 breather, interval **09** abatement,
cessation, lessening, remission
10 slackening

level
03 aim **04** avow, calm, even, flat, mark,
rank, rase, raze, size, tell, tier, zone

05 admit, class, drawn, equal, flush, focus, grade, guess, layer, plain, plane, plumb, point, range, stage, train **06** amount, degree, direct, even up, extent, height, on a par, open up, smooth, stable, status, steady, storey, volume **07** abreast, aligned, be frank, confess, destroy, divulge, echelon, even out, flatten, gallery, horizon, measure, regular, station, stratum, tell all, uniform **08** altitude, balanced, bulldoze, composed, constant, demolish, equalize, estimate, highness, lay waste, make flat, matching, position, pull down, quantity, standard, standing, tear down, zero in on **09** be upfront, champaign, come clean, devastate, elevation, knock down, magnitude, make level, stabilize **10** horizontal, unchanging **11** concentrate, neck and neck, unemotional, unflappable **12** level pegging, speak plainly, well-balanced **13** self-possessed **14** tell it like it is **15** keep nothing back, raze to the ground

• **on the level**
04 fair, open **06** candid, honest **07** jannock, up-front **08** straight **10** above board, fair dinkum, straight-up **12** on the up and up **13** fair and square

level-headed
04 calm, cool, sane **06** steady **07** prudent **08** balanced, composed, rational, sensible **09** practical **10** cool-headed, dependable, reasonable **11** circumspect, unflappable **12** even-tempered **13** imperturbable, self-possessed

lever
03 bar, key, pry **04** lift, move, pull **05** brake, crank, force, heave, hoist, jemmy, peavy, pedal, pinch, prise, raise, shift **06** handle, peavey, switch, tiller **07** control, crowbar, treadle, treddle, trigger **08** backfall, crossbar, dislodge, joystick, knee-stop, throttle, tommy bar, water key **09** bell crank, handspike, knee-swell, rocker arm, whipstaff **10** pump-handle, tremolo arm **11** walking-beam

leverage
04 grip, hold, pull, rank **05** clout, force, grasp, power, prise, prize **06** weight **08** purchase, strength **09** advantage, authority, influence **10** ascendancy

leviathan
04 hulk **05** giant, Satan, Titan, whale **07** mammoth, monster **08** behemoth, colossus, gigantic **10** formidable, sea monster

levitate
03 fly **04** hang, waft **05** drift, float, glide, hover **07** suspend

levitation
06 flying **07** gliding, hanging, wafting **08** drifting, floating, hovering **10** suspension **11** yogic flying

levity
03 fun **08** hilarity **09** flippancy, frivolity, silliness, whifflery **10** fickleness, triviality **11** glaikitness, irreverence **12** carefreeness, flippantness **13** facetiousness **15** light-mindedness, thoughtlessness

levy
03 due, fee, tax **04** duty, rate, toll **05** exact, leave, raise, stent, tithe, tythe **06** charge, demand, duties, excise, gather, impose, impost, tariff **07** collect, customs, estreat, militia, precept, tallage **10** assessment, collection **12** contribution, subscription

lewd
03 bad **04** bare, blue **05** bawdy, randy **06** carnal, harlot, impure, smutty, vulgar, wanton **07** Cyprian, lustful, obscene, raunchy, sensual, unclean **08** ignorant, indecent, unchaste **09** debauched, dissolute, lecherous, lubricous, salacious **10** degenerate, lascivious, libidinous, licentious, lubricious, suggestive **11** promiscuous **12** concupiscent, pornographic

lewdly
07 randily **08** impurely, smuttily, vulgarly **09** lustfully, obscenely, raunchily **10** indecently **11** dissolutely, lecherously **12** degenerately **13** promiscuously

lewdness
04 smut **07** crudity, lechery **08** impurity, priapism **09** bawdiness, carnality, depravity, indecency, lubricity, obscenity, randiness, vulgarity **10** debauchery, smuttiness, unchastity, wantonness **11** lustfulness, pornography **13** concupiscence, salaciousness **14** lasciviousness, licentiousness

lexicographer
10 vocabulist

Lexicographers and philologists include:

04 Bopp (Franz)
05 Pliny (Gaius 'the Elder'), Sapir (Edward), Skeat (Walter William)
06 Bierce (Ambrose), Brewer (Ebenezer Cobham), Fowler (Henry Watson), Freund (Wilhelm), Hornby (A S), Murray (Sir James Augustus Henry), Onions (Charles Talbut), Trench (Richard Chenevix)
07 Chomsky (Noam), Craigie (Sir William Alexander), Diderot (Denis), Johnson (Samuel, 'Dr'), Mencken (H L), Tolkien (J R R), Ventris (Michael George Francis), Webster (Noah)
08 Chambers (Ephraim), Chambers (Robert), Chambers (William), Larousse (Pierre Athanase), Saussure (Ferdinand de)
09 Furnivall (Frederick James),

Jespersen (Otto Harry), Partridge (Eric)
10 Amarasimha, Burchfield (Robert)

lexicon
03 lex, OED, TCD **08** glossary, wordbook, word-list **10** dictionary, phrase book, vocabulary **12** encyclopedia

Leytonstone
03 E11

liability
04 drag, dues, duty, onus **05** debit **06** burden, charge **07** arrears **08** drawback, nuisance **09** hindrance **10** impediment, obligation **11** culpability, encumbrance **12** disadvantage, indebtedness **13** answerability, inconvenience **14** accountability, responsibility **15** blameworthiness

liable
03 apt **04** open **05** prone **06** likely **07** at fault, exposed, fitting, subject, tending, to blame **08** amenable, disposed, inclined, suitable **10** answerable, changeable, vulnerable **11** accountable, predisposed, responsible, susceptible

liaise
07 contact, network **08** relate to **09** co-operate, interface **11** collaborate, communicate **12** work together

liaison
04 link **05** agent, amour, fling, union **06** affair, broker **07** affaire, carry-on, contact, romance **08** intrigue, mediator **09** go-between, middleman, two-timing **10** arbitrator, connection, flirtation, love affair, negotiator **11** co-operation, interchange **12** bit on the side, entanglement, intermediary, relationship **13** collaboration, communication **15** working together

liar
05 leear **06** falser, fibber **07** Ananias, bouncer **08** deceiver, fabulist, perjure **09** falsifier **11** pseudologue, storyteller **12** false witness, prevaricator

libation
08 oblation **09** sacrifice **13** drink offering

libel
04 slur **05** abuse, smear **06** defame, malign, revile, vilify **07** calumny, slander, traduce **08** badmouth **09** aspersion, denigrate, disparage **10** calumniate, defamation, muck-raking, throw mud at **11** denigration, false report, mudslinging **12** vilification **13** disparagement **15** untrue statement

libellous
05 false **06** untrue **07** abusive **09** injurious, maligning, traducing, vilifying **10** defamatory, derogatory, scurrilous, slanderous **11** denigratory, disparaging **12** calumniatory

liberal

◇ *anagram indicator*
1 L **03** Lib **04** free, left, whig
05 ample, broad, frank **06** candid,
giving, lavish, verlig **07** copious, leftish,
lenient, profuse, radical **08** abundant,
advanced, catholic, flexible, generous,
handsome, left-wing, moderate,
tolerant, unbiased **09** bountiful,
impartial, plentiful, reformist,
unsparing **10** altruistic, big-hearted,
broad-based, free-handed,
munificent, open-handed, open-
minded **11** broad-minded,
enlightened, free-hearted, libertarian,
magnanimous, open-hearted,
progressive, wide-ranging **12** large-
hearted, unprejudiced
13 philanthropic, unwithdrawing
14 forward-looking, latitudinarian

liberalism

07 leftism **10** radicalism **12** free-
thinking **13** progressivism
14 libertarianism **15** humanitarianism

liberality

06 bounty **07** breadth, candour,
charity **08** altruism, kindness, largesse
09 tolerance **10** generosity, liberalism,
toleration **11** beneficence,
benevolence, catholicity, flexibility,
magnanimity, munificence, prodigality
12 generousness, impartiality,
magnificence, philanthropy
13 progressivism **14** free-handedness,
libertarianism, open-handedness,
open-mindedness, permissiveness
15 broad-mindedness, open-
heartedness

liberalize

04 ease **05** relax **06** loosen, reduce,
soften **07** ease off, slacken
08 moderate **10** deregulate **14** lift
controls on

liberate

04 free **05** let go, steal **06** let out,
ransom, redeem, rescue, uncage
07 deliver, manumit, release, set free,
unchain **08** let loose, set loose,
unfetter **09** discharge, disimmure,
unshackle **10** emancipate
11 appropriate

liberation

03 lib **07** freedom, freeing, liberty,
loosing, release **08** uncaging
09 discharge, ransoming, releasing,
unpenning **10** liberating, redemption,
unchaining **11** deliverance,
manumission, unfettering, unshackling
12 emancipation, risorgimento
13 franchisement **15** enfranchisement

liberator

05 freer **07** rescuer, saviour
08 ransomer, redeemer **09** deliverer
10 manumitter **11** emancipator

Liberia

02 LB **03** LBR

Liber Pater

07 Bacchus

libertine

04 rake, roué **05** Romeo **06** lecher
07 Don Juan, lustful, seducer
08 Casanova, freedman, Lothario,
Lovelace, palliard **09** debauched,
debauchee, dissolute, lecherous,
reprobate, salacious, womanizer
10 degenerate, licentious, profligate,
sensualist, voluptuary, womanizing
11 gay deceiver, promiscuous
See also **womanizer**

liberty

03 ish **05** leave, right **07** freedom,
leisure, licence, release **08** autonomy,
boldness, disposal, sanction, self-rule
09 franchise, impudence, insolence,
privilege **10** discretion, disrespect,
indulgence, liberation, permission
11 deliverance, entitlement, familiarity,
impropriety, manumission,
prerogative, presumption, sovereignty
12 dispensation, emancipation,
impertinence, independence
13 authorization **14** self-government
15 overfamiliarity

• **at liberty**
04 free **05** loose **07** allowed, at large
08 entitled **09** available, permitted
10 disengaged, unhindered,
unoccupied **11** not confined
12 unrestrained, unrestricted
13 unconstrained

• **take the liberty**
08 make bold **10** be impudent **12** be
so bold as to **13** be impertinent
14 show disrespect

libidinous

04 lewd **05** horny, loose, randy
06 carnal, impure, wanton, wicked
07 lustful, ruttish, sensual **08** prurient,
unchaste **09** debauched, lecherous,
salacious **10** cupidinous, lascivious
11 promiscuous **12** concupiscent
13 whoremasterly

libido

04 lust **06** ardour **07** passion, the hots
08 sex drive **09** eroticism, randiness
10 sexual urge **12** erotic desire, sexual
desire **14** sexual appetite

libra

01 l **02** lb

librarian

03 ALA, lib

library

02 BL, PL, RL **03** lib

libretto

04 book, text **05** lines, words
06 lyrics, script

Librettists include:

04 Hart (Lorenz), Jouy (Étienne), Rice
(Sir Tim), Stow (Randolph)
05 Swann (Donald)
06 Berlin (Irving), Lerner (Alan Jay),
Malouf (David), Porter (Cole)
07 Gilbert (Sir W S), Harwood (Gwen)
08 Gershwin (Ira), Sondheim (Stephen)
11 Hammerstein (Oscar, II)

See also **composer**

Libya

03 LAR, LBY

licence

04 gale, pass **05** grant, leave, right,
slang **06** excess, indult, permit, ticket
07 abandon, anarchy, charter, consent,
faculty, freedom, liberty, warrant
08 approval, disorder, document,
sanction, warranty **09** authority,
decadence, deviation, exemption,
franchise, privilege **10** creativity,
debauchery, immorality, imprimatur,
indulgence, permission, unruliness
11 certificate, dissipation, entitlement,
impropriety, inspiration, lawlessness,
libertinage, miner's right, originality,
prerogative **12** carte blanche,
dispensation, exaggeration,
fancifulness, immoderation,
independence, intemperance
13 accreditation, authorization,
certification, dissoluteness, ticket of
leave **14** letter-of-marque,
licentiousness, self-indulgence
15 imaginativeness, letters-of-marque

license

03 let **05** allow **06** permit **07** certify,
consent, dismiss, empower, entitle,
warrant **08** accredit, sanction
09 authorize, franchise, privilege
10 commission **14** give permission

licentious

03 lax **04** lewd, wild **05** large, loose,
randy **06** impure, ribald, ribaud,
wanton **07** Cyprian, immoral, liberal,
lustful, raunchy, rybauld **08** decadent,
depraved, unchaste **09** abandoned,
debauched, dissolute, lecherous,
libertine **10** disorderly, dissipated,
lascivious, profligate **11** promiscuous

licentiousness

04 lust **07** abandon, lechery, licence,
license **08** impurity, lewdness,
priapism, salacity **09** prurience,
randiness **10** debauchery, immorality,
wantonness **11** dissipation, libertinism,
lustfulness, promiscuity, raunchiness
13 dissoluteness, salaciousness
14 cupidinousness

lichen

10 consortium
See also **alga, algae**

licit

04 real **05** legal, legit **06** lawful,
proper **07** correct, genuine **08** rightful
09 allowable, statutory, warranted
10 authorized, legitimate, sanctioned
12 acknowledged

lick

03 bit, dab, lap, tad, wag, wet **04** beat,
blow, dart, fawn, hint, spot, wash
05 brush, clean, flick, slake, smear,
speck, taste, touch **06** defeat,
hammer, little, ripple, sample, stroke,
thrash, tongue **07** conquer, flicker,
moisten, trounce **08** demolish, play
over, smidgeon, vanquish **09** slaughter
13 run rings round **15** make mincemeat
of

- **lick your lips**
05 enjoy **06** relish, savour **09** drool over **10** anticipate

licking
06 defeat, hiding **07** beating, lambent, tanning **08** drubbing, flogging, smacking, spanking, whipping **09** thrashing

lid
03 cap, hat, top **05** cover, slide **07** scuttle, stopper **08** covering, screw cap **09** operculum

lie
02 be **04** cram, keep, lair, laze, lean, rest, stay **05** abide, couch, dwell, exist, lodge, press, reach, stand **06** belong, bounce, deceit, depend, extend, invent, lounge, remain, repose **07** be found, consist, falsify, perjure, perjury, recline, romance, stretch **08** be placed, continue, tell a lie, white lie **09** be located, dissemble, fabricate, sprawl out **10** equivocate, stretch out **11** dissimulate, prevaricate **12** be positioned, make up a story, misrepresent

Lies include:

03 bam, fib, gag
04 cram, crap, flam, oner, whid
05 fable, one-er, porky, story
06 deceit, unfact, wunner, yanker
07 cretism, falsity, fiction, leasing, swinger, thumper, untruth, whacker, whopper
08 porkypie, strapper, white lie
09 fairy tale, falsehood, half-truth, invention, mendacity, tall story
10 concoction, fairy story, taradiddle
11 fabrication, made-up story, out-and-outer, pseudologia, tarradiddle
13 dissimulation, falsification, prevarication

- **give the lie to**
05 rebut **08** disprove **10** contradict, invalidate, prove false
- **lie about**
03 lig
- **lie in sun**
04 bask
- **lie in wait for**
04 lurk, trap **06** ambush, attack, waylay **08** surprise **09** ambuscade **10** lie at lurch **11** lay a trap for
- **lie low**
04 hide, lurk **05** skulk **06** hole up **07** hide out, tappice **08** hide away, lie doggo **09** go to earth, take cover **12** go into hiding **15** conceal yourself, keep a low profile

Liechtenstein
02 FL **03** LIE

liege
04 king, lord **05** chief **06** master, vassal **07** subject **08** nobleman, overlord, superior **09** liege-lord **10** feudal lord

lieutenant
02 DL, LL, Lt **04** loot **05** Lieut **06** deputy, guider, legate **09** assistant,

number one, scavenger **11** subordinate **12** right-hand man **14** right-hand woman **15** second-in-command

life
03 bio, man, pep, zip **04** élan, soul, span, time, vita, zest, zing **05** being, child, diary, fauna, flora, oomph, plant, verve, woman **06** breath, career, course, energy, entity, person, spirit, vigour **07** diaries, journal, memoirs, pizzazz, sparkle **08** activity, duration, lifespan, lifetime, vitality, vivacity **09** aliveness, animation, biography, existence, human life, life story, viability **10** animal life, enthusiasm, excitement, experience, exuberance, human being, individual, liveliness, travelling **11** continuance, high spirits **12** cheerfulness, living things **13** autobiography, effervescence, fauna and flora, meeting people **14** life expectancy, wide experience
- **come to life**
04 rise **06** wake up **09** come alive **12** become active, become lively **14** become exciting
- **enjoy life**
04 live
- **give your life**
06 die for **14** give up your life **15** offer up your life
- **in present life**
04 here
- **term of life**
04 date

life-and-death
05 vital **07** crucial, serious **08** critical **09** important **12** all-important

lifeblood
04 core, soul **05** heart **06** centre, lethee, spirit **09** life-force **11** inspiration **13** essential part **15** essential factor

lifeless
04 arid, bare, cold, dead, dull, flat, gone, lank, slow **05** dusty, empty, stark, stiff **06** barren, wooden **07** defunct, insipid, key-cold, passive, sterile **08** clay-cold, deceased, desolate, listless, sluggish, soulless **09** apathetic, bloodless, cauldrife, exanimate, inanimate, lethargic, stone-dead **10** colourless, insensible, lacklustre, uninspired **11** unconscious, unemotional, uninhabited, uninspiring **12** unproductive

lifelike
04 real, true **05** exact, vivid **06** lively **07** ad vivum, graphic, natural **08** faithful, speaking **09** authentic, breathing, realistic **10** true-to-life

lifelong
07 abiding, lasting **08** constant, enduring, lifetime **09** permanent **10** persistent **11** long-lasting **12** long-standing **14** for all your life

lifestyle
04 life **08** position **09** situation, way of life **11** way of living **14** manner of living

lifetime
03 day **04** days, life, span, time **06** career, course, period **08** anthesis, duration, lifespan **09** existence **10** pilgrimage

lift
02 up **03** air, end, fly, run, sky **04** copy, crib, jack, move, nick, pick, ride, rise, spur, stop **05** annul, arsis, boost, clear, dig up, drive, elate, exalt, hitch, hoist, mount, press, raise, relax, shift, spout, steal **06** arrest, borrow, buoy up, cancel, convey, fillip, hold up, pick up, pull up, remove, revoke, snatch, teagle, uplift, vanish **07** airlift, elevate, heavens, relieve, rescind, root out, scatter, support, thin out, unearth, upraise **08** disperse, dissolve, elevator, hold high, increase, pick-me-up, transfer, withdraw **09** disappear, encourage, escalator, terminate, transport **10** plagiarize **11** paternoster, reassurance **12** shot in the arm **13** encouragement

See also **steal**

- **lift off**
04 rear **05** climb **06** ascend, depart **07** take off **08** blast off

lift-off
05 climb **06** ascent **07** take-off **08** blast-off **09** departure

lift-shaft
04 well

ligament
03 ACL, tie **04** bond **06** frenum **07** fraenum, urachus

ligature
03 tie **04** aesc, band, bond, cord, link, rope, slur **05** strap, thong **06** string **07** bandage, binding, funicle **08** ligament **09** diphthong **10** connection, deligation, tourniquet

light
◇ *anagram indicator*
03 day, eye, gay, ray, way **04** airy, beam, bulb, clue, dawn, deft, easy, fair, fine, fire, flit, glow, hint, idle, lamp, lyte, mild, pale, rest, side, soft, thin, weak **05** agile, angle, blaze, blond, cheer, faded, faint, flash, funny, glare, gleam, glint, happy, loose, match, merry, petty, put on, quick, shaft, shine, slant, small, style, sunny, taper, torch, witty **06** active, aspect, beacon, blithe, blonde, bright, candle, cheery, facile, flimsy, floaty, gentle, ignite, kindle, lively, lustre, manner, modest, nimble, pastel, porous, scanty, settle, slight, turn on **07** amusing, animate, buoyant, cheer up, cresset, crumbly, daytime, friable, glowing, insight, lantern, lenient, lighten, lighter, light up, shining, sunrise, trivial, well-lit, whitish **08** approach, bleached, brighten, carefree, cheerful, cockcrow, daybreak, daylight, delicate, dismount, feathery, graceful, humorous, lambency, luminous, moderate, pleasing, portable, radiance, switch on,

rifling, unchaste, untaxing **09** brilliant,
imension, diverting, easily dug,
rivolous, irradiate, knowledge, set
light, set fire to, unheeding, worthless
0 brightness, brilliance, digestible,
ffortless, effulgence, first light,
ashlight, floodlight, illuminate,
iminosity, set burning, unexacting,
veightless **11** crack of dawn, easily
noved, elucidation, explanation,
luminated, lightweight, point of view,
uperficial, undemanding,
nimportant **12** easy to digest,
ntertaining, illumination, light-
earted, luminescence, make cheerful
3 comprehension, enlightenment,
ncandescence, insubstantial,
nderstanding **14** inconsiderable
5 inconsequential

bring to light
4 rout **06** exhume, expose, notice,
eveal **07** uncover, unearth
8 disclose, discover, disinter,
xhumate **09** make known

come to light
9 be exposed, be noticed, transpire
1 be made known, be uncovered
2 be discovered **13** become obvious

in the light of
8 in view of **09** because of
1 considering, remembering
3 bearing in mind, keeping in mind
4 being mindful of

light on, light upon
4 find, spot **05** hit on **06** notice
8 chance on, discover **09** encounter,
tumble on **10** come across, happen
pon

**shed light on, throw light on,
ast light on**
7 clarify, enlight, explain **09** elucidate,
nake clear, make plain **10** illuminate

speck of light
4 peep

ighten
4 calm, ease, glow, lift **05** allay, cheer,
late, shine **06** buoy up, lessen, perk
p, reduce, revive, unload, uplift
7 assuage, cheer up, gladden,
earten, inspire, light up, relieve,
estore **08** brighten, illumine, inspirit,
evigate, mitigate **09** alleviate,
ncourage **10** illuminate **11** make
ghter **12** make brighter

lighten up
4 cool **05** chill, relax **06** unwind
8 calm down, chill out **09** hang loose
0 take it easy **13** let yourself go, put
our feet up

ighter
4 pram **05** barge, praam, Zippo
7 gondola, pontoon

ight-fingered
3 sly **06** crafty, shifty **07** crooked,
urtive **08** filching, stealing, thieving,
hievish **09** dishonest, pilfering
1 shoplifting

ight-footed
4 deft, spry **05** agile, lithe, swift
6 active, nimble **08** graceful
9 sprightly

light-headed
04 airy **05** dizzy, faint, giddy, silly,
woozy **07** flighty, foolish, shallow,
vacuous **08** flippant, trifling, unsteady
09 airheaded, delirious, frivolous
11 empty-headed, superficial,
thoughtless, vertiginous **14** feather-
brained, scatter-brained

light-hearted
03 gay **04** glad, high **05** happy, jolly,
merry, sunny **06** blithe, bouncy, bright,
chirpy, elated, jovial, joyful
07 amusing, playful **08** carefree,
cheerful **10** frolicsome, untroubled
12 entertaining, happy-go-lucky
13 inconsiderate, in good spirits, in
high spirits, irresponsible

• **light-heartedness**
06 levity

lighthouse
05 fanal, phare, tower **06** beacon,
pharos **12** danger signal **13** warning
signal

lightly
05 gaily **06** airily, easily, gently, mildly,
softly, thinly **07** faintly, readily
08 breezily, casually, facilely, gingerly,
slightly, sparsely **09** leniently,
sparingly **10** carelessly, delicately,
flippantly, heedlessly **11** frivolously,
slightingly **12** effortlessly
13 thoughtlessly

lightness
05 grace **06** gaiety, levity **07** agility
08 airiness, buoyancy, deftness,
delicacy, mildness, porosity, thinness
09 animation, frivolity, litheness,
sandiness **10** blitheness, cheeriness,
fickleness, flimsiness, gentleness,
liveliness, nimbleness, porousness,
slightness, triviality **11** crumbliness
12 cheerfulness, delicateness,
gracefulness **14** weightlessness

lightning
04 fire **05** levin **08** fireball, wildfire
11 fulguration, thunderbolt,
thunderclap, thunderdart
12 thunderstorm **13** ball lightning, clap
of thunder, electric storm **14** chain
lightning, sheet lightning **15** forked
lightning, lightning strike, summer
lightning, zigzag lightning

• **like lightning**
07 a rocket, hastily, quickly, rapidly
08 speedily, wildfire **11** immediately

lightweight
02 oz **04** thin **05** light, petty **06** flimsy,
paltry, slight **07** trivial **08** delicate,
feathery, nugatory, trifling
09 worthless **10** negligible, weightless
11 unimportant **13** insignificant,
insubstantial **15** inconsequential

likable, likeable
04 nice **06** genial **07** amiable, lovable,
winning, winsome **08** charming,
engaging, friendly, loveable, pleasant,
pleasing **09** agreeable, appealing,
congenial **10** attractive, personable
11 sympathetic

like
02 as **03** à la, dig **04** akin, love, mate,
peer, same, true, twin, want, wish
05 adore, alike, enjoy, equal, fancy, go
for, match, prize, usual **06** admire,
allied, choose, desire, esteem, fellow,
normal, prefer, relish, select, such as,
take to **07** approve, care for, cherish, of
a kind, related, revel in, similar, suiting,
typical, welcome **08** appeal to, be
fond of, be keen on, decide on, hold
dear, parallel, relating **09** analogous,
befitting, delight in, identical, similar to
10 appreciate, comparable,
equivalent, for example, resembling
11 counterpart, for instance, go a
bundle on, much the same, would
rather, would sooner **12** feel inclined,
find pleasant, on the lines of, take a
shine to, take kindly to
13 approximating, corresponding, find
enjoyable **14** by way of example,
characteristic, find attractive, in the
same way as, opposite number, take
pleasure in **15** along the lines of, find
interesting

likeable *see* **likable**

likelihood
06 chance **08** prospect **09** liability
10 likeliness **11** possibility, probability

likely
03 apt, fit **04** fair **05** prone, right
06 liable, odds-on, proper **07** fitting,
hopeful, in order, no doubt, tending
08 credible, expected, feasible,
inclined, pleasing, possible, probable,
probably **09** in the wind, plausible,
promising **10** acceptable, believable,
calculated, on the cards, presumably,
reasonable **11** anticipated,
appropriate, doubtlessly, foreseeable,
likely as not, predictable **12** to be
expected **13** as likely as not

like-minded
08 agreeing, in accord **09** in harmony,
in rapport, of one mind, unanimous
10 compatible, harmonious **11** in
agreement **13** of the same mind

liken
04 like, link **05** match **06** equate,
relate **07** compare **08** parallel, similize
09 analogize, associate, correlate,
juxtapose, set beside

likeness
04 bust, copy, form, icon **05** guise,
image, shape, study **06** effigy, sketch,
statue **07** analogy, drawing, picture,
replica **08** affinity, painting, portrait
09 depiction, facsimile, sculpture,
semblance **10** appearance, caricature,
comparison, expression, photograph,
similarity, similitude, simulacrum
11 counterpart, parallelism,
personation, portraiture, resemblance
12 reproduction **14** correspondence,
representation

likewise
02 do, so **03** als, eke, too **04** also, item
05 ditto **06** as also, to boot **07** besides,

further **08** moreover, same here
09 similarly **10** in addition
11 furthermore **12** in like manner, in the
same way **14** by the same token **15** in
the same manner

liking
04 bent, bias, broo, brow, love
05 fancy, taste, thing **06** desire, notion,
palate **07** leaning **08** affinity, fondness,
penchant, soft spot, tendency,
weakness **09** affection, proneness
10 attraction, partiality, preference,
proclivity, propensity **11** inclination
12 appreciation, predilection,
satisfaction

lilac
07 laylock, syringa **08** pipe-tree

lilt
03 air, hum **04** beat, lill, song, sway
05 swing **06** rhythm **07** cadence,
measure **10** fingerhole **11** rise and fall

lily

Lilies include:

03 day, may
04 aloe, arum, pond, sego
05 calla, camas, lotus, regal, tiger,
torch, yucca
06 camash, camass, Canada, crinum,
Easter, Nuphar, scilla, smilax
07 candock, day-lily, Madonna, may-
lily, quamash, Tritoma
08 asphodel, galtonia, gloriosa,
hyacinth, martagon, nenuphar,
Phormium, trillium, Turk's cap,
victoria
09 amaryllis, grass tree, herb-Paris,
kniphofia, Richardia
10 agapanthus, aspidistra, belladonna,
fritillary
11 cabbage-tree, Convallaria,
Madonna-lily, red-hot poker,
spatterdock
12 Annunciation, Hemerocallis,
Solomon's seal, zantedeschia
13 butcher's broom, lily of the Nile
15 lily of the valley, star of Bethlehem

• **lily leaf**
03 pad

lily-white
04 pure **06** chaste, virgin **08** innocent,
spotless, virtuous **09** blameless,
faultless, incorrupt, milk-white,
uncorrupt, unsullied, untainted
11 uncorrupted, untarnished
14 irreproachable

Lima
01 L

limb
03 arm, leg **04** edge, fork, part, spur,
wing **05** bough, spald, spall, spaul
06 border, branch, member, spalle,
spauld **07** flipper, quarter, section
08 offshoot **09** appendage, extension,
extremity, pterygium **10** projection
• **out on a limb**
07 exposed **08** isolated **10** vulnerable
15 in a weak position

limber
05 agile, lithe **06** lissom, pliant, supple
07 elastic, plastic, pliable **08** flexible,
graceful **11** loose-limbed **12** loose-
jointed
• **limber up**
06 warm up **07** prepare, work out
08 exercise, loosen up

limbo
• **in limbo**
10 in abeyance, up in the air **11** left
hanging **12** left in the air **14** awaiting
action **15** on the back burner

lime
04 bass, bast, lind, line, teil, trap
05 leash, Tilia **06** linden, loiter, temper,
viscum **07** ensnare **08** basswood

limelight
04 fame **06** notice, renown
07 stardom **08** eminence
09 attention, celebrity, public eye,
publicity, spotlight **10** notability,
prominence **11** recognition

limestone
03 cam **04** calm, calp, caum
06 kunkar, kunkur, oolite **07** coquina,
scaglia **08** Coral Rag, dolomite
09 caen-stone, coral-rock, cornbrash,
cornstone **10** Kentish rag, stinkstone,
travertine **11** cement-stone,
rottenstone, sarcophagus **12** Forest
Marble, Purbeck stone **13** Purbeck
marble **15** coralline oolite, Kentish
ragstone, landscape-marble

limit
◊ *containment indicator*
◊ *tail deletion indicator*
◊ *ends selection indicator*
03 cap, end, lid, rim, tie **04** brim, curb,
edge, goal, gole, line, mete, pale, rein,
roof, term **05** bound, brink, check,
hem in, stint, Thule, verge **06** border,
bounds, bridle, hinder, impede,
margin, ration, reduce, region, tropic,
utmost **07** appoint, ceiling, compass,
confine, contain, control, delimit,
extreme, margent, maximum, outside,
specify **08** boundary, confines,
deadline, division, frontier, outgoing,
restrain, restrict, terminus, ultimate
09 condition, constrain, demarcate,
determine, extremity, perimeter,
prescribe, restraint, threshold
10 constraint, limitation, parameters
11 cut-off point, demarcation,
demarkation, hold in check, keep in
check, restriction, termination, ultima
Thule **12** circumscribe **14** greatest
amount, greatest extent **15** saturation
point
• **extend beyond limit**
03 lap
• **the limit**
06 enough, the end, utmost **07** too
much **08** the worst **11** intolerable, the
final bow **12** the final blow, the last
straw

limitation
04 curb, snag, tail **05** block, check
06 burden, defect **07** control, reserve

08 drawback, tail male, weakness
09 condition, hindrance, inability,
restraint, weak point **10** constraint,
impediment, inadequacy
11 demarcation, reservation,
restriction, shortcoming
12 delimitation, disadvantage,
imperfection, incapability
13 qualification **15** circumscription

limited
◊ *ends deletion indicator*
03 Ltd **04** tail, tyde **05** basic, borné,
fixed, small **06** finite, narrow, scanty
07 checked, defined, minimal
08 confined **09** imperfect, qualified
10 controlled, inadequate,
incomplete, restricted **11** constrained,
determinate **12** insufficient
13 circumscribed

limitless
◊ *ends deletion indicator*
◊ *head deletion indicator*
◊ *tail deletion indicator*
04 vast **06** untold **07** endless,
immense **08** infinite, unending
09 boundless, countless, illimited,
unbounded, undefined, unlimited
10 bottomless **11** measureless, never-
ending, unspecified **12** immeasurable,
incalculable, interminable
13 inexhaustible

limp
03 dot, hop, lax **04** flop, gimp, halt,
lank, soft, weak **05** frail, hilch, hitch,
loose, slack, spent, tired, weary
06 falter, feeble, flabby, flaggy, floppy,
hamble, hobble, limber, totter
07 flaccid, pliable, relaxed, shamble,
shuffle, stagger, stumble, worn out
08 drooping, fatigued, flexible,
lameness **09** enervated, exhausted,
lethargic, out of curl **10** uneven walk
11 debilitated, out of energy
12 claudication, walk unevenly
13 walk with a limp

limpid
04 pure **05** clear, lucid, plain, still
06 bright, glassy **07** flowing
08 coherent, pellucid **09** unruffled
10 untroubled **11** translucent,
transparent **12** crystal-clear, intelligible
14 comprehensible

limply
06 softly **07** loosely, slackly
08 flabbily, flexibly **09** flaccidly

limpness
06 laxity **09** looseness, slackness
10 flabbiness, flaccidity **11** flaccidness,
flexibility **12** claudication

Lincoln
03 Abe

line
01 l **03** bar, job, ley, pad, rew, rim,
row, way **04** area, axis, back, band,
bank, belt, book, card, ceil, ciel,
cord, dash, draw, edge, face, file,
fill, firm, flax, kind, lind, make,
mark, memo, note, oche, part, path,
race, rank, role, rope, rule, seam,

de, sort, talk, text, tier, type, wire,
vord, work **05** bound, brand, breed,
able, canon, chain, cover, e-mail,
eld, forte, front, hatch, inlay, limit,
anel, pitch, queue, route, score,
hape, skirt, slash, spiel, stock, story,
rip, stuff, style, track, trade, trail,
wine, verge, words **06** avenue, belief,
order, career, column, course, crease,
ncase, family, figure, fringe, furrow,
roove, letter, margin, method, parade,
atter, policy, report, scheme, script,
eries, strain, strand, streak, string,
tripe, stroke, system, thread
7 calling, channel, company, contour,
escent, lineage, message, outline,
attern, profile, pursuit, scratch, variety,
vrinkle **08** activity, ancestry,
pproach, attitude, boundary,
usiness, defences, filament, frontier,
eritage, ideology, inscribe, interest,
bretto, pedigree, position, postcard,
ractice, province, sequence, vocation
9 crow's feet, direction, formation,
ront line, parentage, perimeter,
eriphery, procedure, reinforce, sales
alk, specialty, technique, underline
0 appearance, battle zone,
orderline, department, employment,
xtraction, firing-line, line of work,
nemorandum, occupation,
rocession, profession, silhouette,
pecialism, speciality, strengthen,
uccession, trajectory, underscore
1 battlefield, corrugation, delineation,
lemarcation, information
2 battleground **13** configuration,
nodus operandi **14** course of action,
ne of business, specialization
5 draughtsmanship

ee also **poetry; railway**

• curved line
3 tie
• draw the line
5 limit **06** refuse, reject **07** exclude,
ule out, say no to **08** say not to
9 stand firm **11** stop short of **15** put
our foot down
• fishing line
4 gimp, gymp **05** guimp
• in line
3 due **06** in a row, in step, likely **08** in
ccord, in a queue, in series **09** in a
olumn, in harmony **10** on the cards
1 in agreement **12** in the running
5 being considered
• lay on the line, put on the line
4 risk **07** imperil **08** endanger
0 jeopardize **13** put in jeopardy
• line up
5 align, array, group, lay on, order,
queue, range **06** fall in, obtain, secure
7 arrange, marshal, prepare, procure,
roduce, queue up **08** assemble,
organize, regiment **09** form ranks
0 form a queue, straighten, wait in line
1 stand in line
• new line
3 zag
• toe the line
7 conform **12** keep the rules **14** be
conventional, follow the rules

lineage
04 line, race **05** birth, breed, house,
stock **06** family, parage **07** descent,
lignage, progeny **08** ancestry, heredity,
pedigree **09** ancestors, forebears,
genealogy, offspring, whakapapa
10 descending, extraction, succession
11 descendants

lineaments
04 face **05** lines **06** aspect, traits,
visage **07** outline, profile **08** features,
outlines **10** appearance
11 countenance, physiognomy
13 configuration

lined
04 worn **05** feint, ruled **07** creased,
wizened **08** furrowed, wrinkled

linen
04 duck, ecru, harn, lawn, line, lint,
snow **05** crash, drill, toile **06** byssus,
damask, dowlas, napery, sendal,
sheets, sindon, whites **07** byssine,
cambric, dornick, drabbet, holland,
lockram, napkins, silesia **08** bed linen,
drilling, gambroon, marcella, osnaburg
09 huckaback, Moygashel®, tea
towels **10** seersucker, table linen,
white goods **11** pillowcases,
tablecloths
• measure of linen
03 lay, lea, ley
• strip of linen
04 amis **05** amice

liner
04 boat, ship **07** steamer **10** cruise
ship

linesman
04 poet **06** author, writer

line-up
03 row **04** bill, cast, line, list, team
05 array, queue **09** selection
11 arrangement

linger
03 lag **04** hang, hove, idle, last, lurk,
stay, stop, wait **05** dally, delay, hoove,
hover, tarry **06** dawdle, endure, hang
on, hanker, loiter, remain, taigle
07 hold out, persist, survive
08 continue, smoulder, straggle
10 dilly-dally, hang around **11** stick
around **12** take your time
13 procrastinate
• linger on scent
03 tie

lingerie
03 bra **04** slip **05** teddy **06** smalls,
undies **07** panties **08** camisole, frillies,
half-slip, knickers, scanties
09 brassiere, underwear **11** panty
girdle **12** body stocking, camiknickers,
underclothes **13** suspender belt,
underclothing, undergarments
14 inexpressibles, unmentionables

lingering
04 slow **08** dragging **09** prolonged,
remaining, surviving **10** persistent,
persisting, protracted **11** languishing
12 long-drawn-out

lingo
03 bat **04** cant, talk **05** argot, idiom
06 jargon, patois, patter, speech,
tongue **07** dialect **08** language,
parlance **10** mumbo-jumbo,
vernacular, vocabulary
11 terminology

liniment
04 balm, wash **05** cream, salve
06 balsam, lotion **07** unguent
08 ointment **09** carron oil, emollient,
opodeldoc **11** embrocation
14 camphorated oil

lining
◇ *insertion indicator*
03 lag **04** cush **05** inlay, stean, steen,
stein **06** casing, facing, fettle
07 backing, cushion, furring, padding,
sarking, tubbing **08** brattice, brattish,
brettice, doublure, steaning, steening,
steining, wainscot **09** alignment,
panelling **10** encasement,
incasement, stiffening **11** interfacing
13 reinforcement

link
03 map, tie **04** ally, bind, bond, join,
knot, loop, part, ring, yoke **05** cleek,
joint, merge, piece, tie-up, torch,
union, unite **06** attach, bridge, couple,
fasten, hook up, liaise, member, relate,
swivel, team up **07** bracket, connect,
element, enchain, hot line, liaison,
network, shackle **08** division, identify,
osculate **09** air-bridge, associate,
carabiner, component, interlink,
karabiner **10** amalgamate, attachment,
connection, join forces **11** association,
concatenate, constituent, partnership
12 relationship **13** communication,
concatenation
• link up
04 ally, dock, join **05** merge, unify
06 bridge, hook up, join up, meet up,
team up **07** connect, network
10 amalgamate, join forces

linkage
03 tie **04** bond, knot **05** joint, tie-in,
tie-up, union **06** merger **07** liaison
08 alliance **09** valve gear
10 attachment, connection
11 association, partnership
12 amalgamation, relationship
13 communication

link-up
05 tie-in, union **06** merger **08** alliance
10 connection **11** association,
partnership **12** amalgamation,
relationship

lion
03 Leo **05** Aslan **12** king of beasts
• lion's share
04 bulk, mass, most **08** main part,
majority **09** almost all, nearly all
11 largest part **12** greatest part
13 preponderance

lion-hearted
04 bold **05** brave **06** daring, heroic
07 gallant, valiant **08** fearless, intrepid,
resolute, stalwart, valorous

09 dauntless, dreadless
10 courageous **12** stout-hearted

lionize
04 fête **05** exalt **06** honour, praise
07 acclaim, adulate, glorify, idolize,
magnify **08** eulogize **09** celebrate
10 aggrandize **11** hero-worship
12 treat as a hero **14** put on a pedestal

lip
03 jib, lap, rim **04** brim, edge, flew, kiss,
lave **05** brink, cheek, mouth, sauce,
spout, verge **06** border, fipple, helmet,
labium, labrum, ligula, margin, muffle
07 corolla, hare-lip **08** attitude,
backchat, labellum, rudeness,
underlip **09** impudence, insolence,
submentum **10** effrontery
12 impertinence

lippy
04 pert **05** fresh, sassy, saucy
06 brazen, cheeky, lippie, mouthy
07 forward **08** impudent, insolent
09 audacious **11** impertinent
12 overfamiliar **13** disrespectful

liquefaction
06 fusion **07** melting, thawing
08 solation, syntexis **10** dissolving,
karyolysis, liquefying **11** dissolution
13 deliquescence

liquefy
03 run **04** flux, fuse, melt, thaw
05 smelt **08** dissolve, fluidize, liquesce
09 liquidize **10** deliquesce

liqueur

Liqueurs include:

04 ouzo
05 Aurum®, noyau
06 Glayva, Kahlúa®, kirsch, kümmel,
Malibu®, Midori®, pastis,
Pernod®
07 Baileys®, curaçao, ratafia, sambuca
08 absinthe, advocaat, amaretto,
Drambuie®, Galliano®, Tia Maria®
09 Cointreau®, mirabelle, Triple sec
10 Chartreuse®, limoncello,
maraschino
11 Benedictine
12 cherry brandy, crème de cacao,
Grand Marnier®, kirschwasser,
Parfait Amour
13 crème de cassis, crème de menthe,
Cuarenta y Tres
15 Southern Comfort®

See also **cocktail**; **spirits**

liquid
02 aq **03** sap, wet **04** even, pure, thin
05 clear, drink, fluid, juice, moist, runny
06 liquor, lotion, mellow, melted,
molten, sloppy, smooth, steady,
thawed, watery **07** aqueous, flowing,
hydrous, regular, running, unfixed
08 solution, unbroken **09** liquefied,
melodious **12** indisputable
13 uninterrupted
• **coloured liquid**
03 dye, ink
• **liquid for washing**
03 lye

liquidate
03 pay **04** kill, sell **05** clear **06** cash in,
murder, pay off, remove, rub out, wind
up **07** abolish, break up, destroy,
disband, sell off, wipe out **08** dispatch,
dissolve, massacre **09** close down,
discharge, eliminate, finish off,
terminate **10** annihilate, do away with,
put an end to **11** assassinate,
exterminate **13** convert to cash

liquidize
03 mix **05** blend, cream, crush, purée
07 process **10** synthesize

liquor
03 liq **04** bree, broo, grog, malt, vino
05 boose, booze, bouse, broth, drink,
gravy, hogan, hogen, hooch, juice,
plonk, sauce, stock, tinct **06** hootch,
liquid, porter, rotgut, strunt, tiddly,
tipple **07** alcohol, essence, extract,
hokonui, shicker, spirits **08** infusion,
potation **09** firewater, hard stuff,
stiffener, stimulant, the bottle
10 intoxicant **11** aguardiente, jungle
juice, strong drink, the creature, tickle-
brain **12** Dutch courage
See also **drink**

• **liquor house** *see* **public house**

liquorice
07 nail-rod, pomfret **09** jequirity,
sugarally **10** sugarallie

lissom
05 agile, light, lithe **06** limber, nimble,
pliant, supple **07** pliable, willowy
08 flexible, graceful **09** lithesome
11 loose-limbed **12** loose-jointed

list
◊ *homophone indicator*
03 tip **04** bill, book, cant, file, heel,
lean, leet, menu, note, roll, roon, rota,
tilt **05** enrol, enter, index, slant, slate,
slope, strip, table, tally **06** agenda,
border, fillet, litany, recipe, record,
roster, scroll, series, stripe **07** compile,
incline, invoice, itemize, listing,
scedule, selvage, set down
08 boundary, calendar, classify,
contents, heel over, lean over, register,
schedule, syllabus, tabulate
09 catalogue, checklist, directory,
enumerate, inventory, programme,
write down **10** tabulation
11 alphabetize, enumeration
See also **lean**

listen
◊ *homophone indicator*
04 hark, hear, heed, lest, list, mind
05 lithe **06** attend, intend **07** give ear,
hearken, monitor **09** eavesdrop, lend
an ear **10** auscultate, get a load of, take
notice **12** pay attention **15** prick up
your ears
• **listen in**
◊ *homophone indicator*
03 bug, tap **07** monitor, wiretap
08 overhear **09** eavesdrop **15** pin back
your ears, prick up your ears

listener
03 ear

listless
04 dull, limp, waff **05** bored, heavy,
inert **06** mopish, torpid, vacant
07 languid, passive **08** inactive,
indolent, lifeless, sluggish, thowless,
toneless **09** apathetic, depressed,
enervated, impassive, lethargic,
upsitting **10** spiritless **11** indifferent,
languishing **12** uninterested
13 lackadaisical

listlessly
05 dully **06** limply **07** inertly
09 passively **10** inactively, lifelessly,
sluggishly **11** impassively **12** spiritlessly
13 apathetically, lacking energy,
lethargically

listlessness
05 ennui, sloth **06** acedia, apathy,
torpor **07** languor, vacuity **08** lethargy
09 indolence, torpidity, upsitting
10 enervation, supineness
11 inattention, languidness
12 indifference, lifelessness,
sluggishness **14** spiritlessness

lit
◊ *anagram indicator*
02 in **05** drunk, light, merry, tight, tipsy
06 ablaze, blotto, rested, soused
07 drunken, legless, pickled, settled,
sloshed, sozzled, squiffy **09** crapulent
paralytic, plastered **10** dismounted,
inebriated **11** intoxicated

litany
04 list **06** prayer **07** account, recital,
synapte **08** devotion, irenicon,
petition **09** catalogue, eirenicon
10 invocation, procession, recitation,
repetition **11** enumeration
12 supplication

literacy
07 culture **08** learning **09** education,
erudition, knowledge **10** articulacy
11 cultivation, learnedness, proficiency
scholarship **12** intelligence **13** ability
to read **14** ability to write, articulateness

literal
03 lit **04** dull, true, typo **05** clear,
close, error, exact, plain **06** actual,
boring, strict, verbal **07** erratum,
factual, genuine, humdrum, mistake,
precise, prosaic, tedious **08** accurate,
faithful, misprint, verbatim
10 colourless, uninspired
11 corrigendum, down-to-earth,
undistorted, unvarnished, word-for-
word **12** matter-of-fact **13** printing
error, unembellished, unexaggerated,
unimaginative

literalism
06 letter **09** biblicism, verbalism
10 textualism **13** scripturalism
14 exact rendering, fundamentalism,
letter of the law

literally
03 lit **05** truly **06** really **07** closely,
exactly, plainly **08** actually, strictly,
verbatim **09** certainly, precisely
10 faithfully **11** to the letter, word for
word

terary

3 lit **06** formal, poetic **07** bookish,
ʳudite, learned, refined, written
8 cultured, educated, lettered,
ˀerate, literose, well-read **09** scholarly
ɔ cultivated, epistolary, widely-read
˞ old-fashioned

iterary characters include:

2 Pi

3 Eva (Little), Fox (Brer), Jim (Lord),
Kaa, Kim, Lee (Lorelei), Pan (Peter),
Pip, Roo, Tom (Uncle), Una

4 Ahab (Captain), Bede (Adam),
Bond (James), Budd (Billy), Dent
(Arthur), Eyre (Jane), Finn
(Huckleberry), Fogg (Phileas),
Gamp (Sarah), Gray (Charlotte),
Gray (Dorian), Gunn (Ben), Haze
(Dolores), Heep (Uriah), Hood
(Robin), Hook (Captain), Hyde
(Mister), Jack, Mole, Mole (Adrian),
Pooh, Pope (Giant), Ridd (John),
Slop (Doctor), Tigg (Montague),
Toad (Mister), Trim (Corporal), Troy
(Sergeant Francis), Tuck (Friar), Wilt
(Henry)

5 Akela, Aslan, Athos, Avery (Shug),
Baloo, Bates (Miss), Bloom
(Leopold), Bloom (Molly), Boxer,
Brown (Father), Celie, Chips
(Mister), Clare (Angel), Darcy
(Fitzwilliam), Darcy (Mark), Doone
(Lorna), Drood (Edwin), Flint
(Captain), Geste (Beau), Jones
(Bridget), Jones (Tom), Kanga,
Kipps (Arthur), Loman (Willy),
Lucky, March (Amy), Maria (Mad),
Mitty (Walter), Moore (Mrs),
Mosca, Nancy, O'Hara (Kimball),
O'Hara (Scarlett), Parry (Will),
Piggy, Polly (Alfred), Porgy, Pozzo,
Price (Fanny), Quilp (Daniel), Ralph,
Ratty, Rebus (Inspector John),
Remus (Uncle), Rudge (Barnaby),
Satan, Sharp (Becky), Sikes (Bill),
Slope (Reverend Obadiah), Sloth,
Smike, Smith (Winston), Spade
(Sam), Stubb, Tarka (the Otter),
Titus, Topsy, Trent (Little Nell), Twist
(Oliver), Wonka (Willy), Yahoo

6 Aramis, Archer (Isabel), Arthur
(King), Badger, Barkis, Belial,
Bennet (Elizabeth), Bourgh (Lady
Catherine de), Bovary (Emma),
Brodie (Miss Jean), Brooke
(Dorothea), Bucket (Charlie),
Bumble (Mister), Bumppo (Natty),
Bunter (Billy), Butler (Rhett),
Carton (Sydney), Crusoe
(Robinson), Dombey (Paul), Dorrit
(Amy), Dorrit (William), Du Bois
(Blanche), Eeyore, Friday (Man),
Gamgee (Sam), Gatsby (Jay),
Gawain, Gollum, Grimes, Hagrid
(Rubeus), Hannay (Richard),
Holmes (Sherlock), Jeeves
(Reginald), Jekyll (Doctor Henry),
Legree (Simon), Little (Vernon
Gregory), Lolita, Marley (Jacob),
Marner (Silas), Marple (Jane),
Moreau (Doctor), Mowgli,
Omnium (Duke of), Pickle

(Gamaliel), Piglet, Pinkie, Pliant
(Dame), Poirot (Hercule), Potter
(Harry), Rabbit, Rabbit (Brer),
Random (Roderick), Rob Roy,
Salmon (Susie), Sawyer (Bob),
Sawyer (Tom), Shandy (Tristram),
Silver (Long John), Subtle, Tarzan,
Tigger, Tybalt, Tyrone (James),
Varden (Dolly), Wadman (Widow),
Watson (Doctor John), Weller
(Samuel), Wimsey (Lord Peter),
Wopsle (Mister), Yahoos

07 Andrews (Pamela), Ayeesha,
Baggins (Bilbo), Baggins (Frodo),
Beowulf, Biggles, Bramble
(Matthew), Brer Fox, Bromden
(Chief), Clinker (Humphry), Corelli
(Captain Antonio), Crackit (Toby),
Danvers (Mrs), Dawkins (Jack),
Dedalus (Stephen), Deronda
(Daniel), Despair (Giant), Don Juan,
Dorigen, Dorothy, Dracula (Count),
Estella, Fairfax (Jane), Gandalf,
Gargery (Joe), Granger
(Hermione), Grendel, Harding
(Reverend Septimus), Harlowe
(Clarissa), Hawkins (Jim), Higgins
(Professor Henry), Hopeful,
Humbert (Humbert), Ishmael,
Jaggers (Mister), Jellyby (Mrs), Le
Fever (Lieutenant), Maigret (Jules),
Marlowe (Philip), Mellors (Oliver),
Newsome (Chad), Obadiah,
Orlando, Peachum (Thomas),
Pierrot, Porthos, Prefect (Ford),
Proudie (Doctor), Raffles, Rebecca,
Scarlet (Will), Scrooge (Ebenezer),
Shalott (Lady of), Shipton
(Mother), Slumkey (Samuel),
Squeers (Wackford), Surface
(Charles), Surface (Joseph), Tiny
Tim, Weasley (Ron), Wemmick
(Mister), Wickham (George),
William, Witches (The Three),
Wooster (Bertie), Would-be (Sir
Politic)

08 Absolute (Captain), Anderson
(Pastor Anthony), Backbite (Sir
Benjamin), Bagheera, Bedivere
(Sir), Belacqua (Lyra), Black Dog,
Casaubon (Reverend Edward),
Cratchit (Bob), Criseyde, Dalloway
(Mrs Clarissa), Dashwood (Elinor),
Dashwood (Marianne), de Winter
(Max), de Winter (Rebecca),
Everdene (Bathsheba), Faithful,
Flanders (Moll), Flashman,
Gloriana, Griselda (Patient),
Gulliver (Lemuel), Havisham (Miss),
Hrothgar, Jarndyce (John),
Kowalski (Stanley), Kowalski
(Stella), Ladislaw (Will), Lancelot
(Sir), Lestrade (Inspector),
MacHeath (Captain), Magwitch
(Abel), Malaprop (Mrs), McMurphy
(Randle Patrick), Micawber
(Wilkins), Moriarty (Dean),
Moriarty (Professor James),
Napoleon, Nickleby (Nicholas),
Paradise (Sal), Peggotty (Clara),
Peterkin, Pickwick (Samuel),
Queequeg, Ramotswe (Precious),

Snowball, Starbuck, Svengali,
Tashtego, Thatcher (Becky), The
Clerk, The Friar, The Reeve,
Trotwood (Betsey), Tulliver
(Maggie), Twitcher (Jemmy),
Vladimir

09 Archimago, Bounderby (Josiah),
Britomart, Bulstrode (Nicholas),
Caulfield (Holden), Cheeryble
(Charles), Christian, Churchill
(Frank), Constance, D'Artagnan,
Doolittle (Eliza), Fezziwigg
(Mister), Golightly (Holly),
Gradgrind (Thomas), Grandison
(Sir Charles), Harlequin, Knightley
(George), Lismahago (Obadiah),
Lochinvar, Minnehaha, Pecksniff
(Seth), Pendennis (Arthur),
Pollyanna, Robin Hood, Rochester
(Edward Fairfax), Scudamour (Sir),
Shere Khan, The Knight, The Miller,
The Squire, The Walrus, Tiger Lily,
Trelawney (Squire), Van Winkle
(Rip), Voldemort (Lord),
Woodhouse (Emma), Yossarian
(Captain John), Zenocrate

10 Allan-a-Dale, Big Brother, Brer
Rabbit, Challenger (Professor),
Chatterley (Lady Constance),
Chuzzlewit (Martin), Dumbledore
(Albus), Evangelist, Fauntleroy
(Little Lord), Great-heart (Mister),
Heathcliff, Hornblower (Horatio),
Houyhnhnms, Little John, Little
Nell, Maid Marian, Quatermain
(Allan), The Red King, The Tar Baby,
Tinkerbell, Tweedledee,
Tweedledum

11 Copperfield (David), D'Urberville
(Alec), Durbeyfield (Tess), Mickey
Mouse, Mutabilitie, Pumblechook
(Mister), The Dormouse, The
Franklin, The Man of Law, The
Merchant, The Pardoner, The
Prioress, The Red Queen, The
Summoner, Tiggy-Winkle (Mrs)

12 Blatant Beast, Chaunticleer,
Frankenstein (Victor), Humpty-
Dumpty, Lilliputians, Osbaldistone
(Francis), Rip Van Winkle,
Silvertongue (Lyra), The Carpenter,
The Mad Hatter, The March Hare,
The Pied Piper (of Hamelin), The
Red Knight, The Scarecrow

13 The Jabberwock, The Mock Turtle,
The Tin Woodman, The Wife of
Bath, Winnie-the-Pooh

14 Mephistopheles, Rikki-Tikki-Tavi,
The White Rabbit, Worldly
Wiseman (Mister)

15 The Artful Dodger, The Cowardly
Lion, The Three Witches, Valiant-for-
Truth

See also **Shakespeare**

Literary critics include:

04 Bell (Clive), Blum (Léon), Frye
(Northrop)

05 Hicks (Granville), Lodge (David),
Stead (C K)

06 Arnold (Matthew), Calder (Angus),
Empson (Sir William), Leavis (F R),

Leavis (Q D), Lukacs (Georg), Sontag (Susan), Wilson (Edmund)
07 Ackroyd (Peter), Alvarez (A), Barthes (Roland), Daiches (David), Derrida (Jacques), Hoggart (Richard), Kermode (Frank)
08 Bradbury (Sir Malcolm), Eagleton (Terry), Longinus, Nicolson (Sir Harold), Richards (I A), Trilling (Lionel), Williams (Raymond)
10 Saintsbury (George Edward Bateman)
11 Matthiessen (F O), Sainte-Beuve (Charles Augustin)
• **literary work**
04 book, poem **05** essay **07** article

literate
07 learned **08** cultured, educated **09** scholarly **10** able to read, proficient **11** able to write, intelligent **12** intellectual, well-educated **13** knowledgeable
• **Literate in Arts**
02 LA **03** LLA

literati
06 brains **08** eggheads **09** academics, highbrows **10** illuminati, the erudite, the learned **11** cognoscenti, the studious **12** men of letters, the scholarly **13** intellectuals **14** intelligentsia, women of letters **15** the well-informed

literature
03 lit **04** bumf, data, page **05** facts, paper **06** papers **07** hand-out, leaflet, letters **08** brochure, circular, hand-outs, leaflets, pamphlet, writings **09** brochures, circulars, pamphlets **11** information **12** printed works **13** printed matter **14** published works

Literature types include:

04 epic, play, saga
05 drama, essay, novel, prose, verse
06 comedy, parody, poetry, satire, thesis
07 aga-saga, epistle, fantasy, fiction, lampoon, novella, polemic, tragedy, trilogy
08 allegory, chick lit, libretto, pastiche, treatise
09 anti-novel, biography, children's, novelette
10 magnum opus, non-fiction, roman à clef, short story, travelogue
11 black comedy, Gothic novel, pulp fiction
12 bodice-ripper, crime fiction
13 autobiography, belles-lettres, Bildungsroman, penny dreadful, travel writing
14 science fiction
15 epistolary novel, historical novel, picaresque novel

lithe
05 agile **06** limber, lissom, listen, pliant, supple, svelte **07** lissome, pliable **08** flexible **09** lithesome **11** loose-limbed **12** loose-jointed **13** double-jointed

lithium
02 Li

Lithuania
02 LT **03** LTU **04** Lith

litigant
05 party **08** claimant, opponent **09** contender, disputant, litigator, plaintiff **10** contestant **11** complainant

litigate
03 sue

litigation
03 law **04** case, suit **06** action **07** dispute, lawsuit, process **09** legal case **10** contention **11** legal action, prosecution

litigious
10 disputable **11** belligerent, contentious, quarrelsome **12** disputatious **13** argumentative

litter
03 bed, hay **04** grot, junk, mess, muck, team, teme **05** brood, chaff, issue, sedan, straw, strew, trash, wagon, waste, young **06** debris, doolie, family, farrow, jumble, kindle, mahmal, mess up, refuse, shreds **07** bedding, bracken, cacolet, clutter, garbage, progeny, rubbish, scatter **08** brancard, detritus, disarray, disorder, shambles **09** confusion, fragments, offspring, palankeen, palanquin, stretcher **10** light couch, make untidy, untidiness **11** make a mess of, odds and ends

little
03 bit, dab, sma, wee **04** baby, curn, cute, dash, drop, hint, leet, lite, lyte, mini, nice, poco, some, spot, tine, tiny, tyne, whit **05** brief, chota, dwarf, minor, petty, pinch, scant, short, small, speck, sweet, taste, teeny, touch, trace, young **06** barely, hardly, junior, meagre, midget, minute, paltry, petite, rarely, seldom, skimpy, slight, sparse, trifle **07** faintly, modicum, nominal, not much, passing, peanuts, shortly, slender, soupçon, trickle, trivial, younger **08** exiguous, fleeting, fragment, nugatory, particle, pint-size, pleasant, scarcely, skerrick, slightly, trifling **09** ephemeral, miniature, momentary, pint-sized, transient **10** attractive, diminutive, negligible, short-lived, smattering, transitory **11** Lilliputian, microscopic, small amount, unimportant **12** infrequently, insufficient **13** infinitesimal, insignificant, next to nothing **14** inconsiderable **15** a drop in the ocean
See also **small**
• **a little**
03 tad **04** some
• **little by little**
04 Eric **06** slowly **08** bit by bit, inchmeal **09** by degrees, gradually, piecemeal, poco a poco **10** step by step **13** imperceptibly, progressively
• **take a little**
04 drib

liturgical
06 formal, ritual, solemn **08** hieratic **10** ceremonial, sacerdotal **11** eucharistic, sacramental

liturgy
04 form, rite **05** usage **06** office, ritual **07** formula, service, worship **08** ceremony **09** ordinance, sacrament **10** observance **11** celebration

livable, liveable
08 adequate, bearable **09** endurable, habitable, tolerable **10** acceptable, worthwhile **11** comfortable, inhabitable, supportable **12** satisfactory
• **livable with, liveable with**
08 bearable, passable, sociable **09** congenial, gemütlich, tolerable **10** compatible, harmonious **13** companionable

live
02 be **03** hot **04** hard, last, lead, pass, stay **05** abide, alert, alive, dwell, exist, lodge, spend, squat, vital, vivid **06** active, alight, behave, bodily, endure, lively, living, public, red hot, remain, reside, urgent **07** animate, be alive, blazing, breathe, burning, charged, comport, conduct, current, dynamic, flaming, glowing, have fun, ignited, inhabit, persist, see life, subsist, survive, topical, undergo **08** continue, existent, have life, in person, live it up, personal, pressing, real-time, relevant, stirring, unstable, vigorous, volatile **09** be settled, breathing, connected, energetic, enjoy life, explosive, important, pertinent, unwrought **10** applicable, draw breath, experience, having life, in the flesh, unexploded, unquarried **11** electrified, not recorded **12** have your home **13** controversial, enjoy yourself **14** earn your living, not prerecorded, with an audience **15** support yourself
• **live it up**
05 revel **09** celebrate, have a ball, make merry **10** go on a spree **11** make whoopee **12** push the boat out **15** paint the town red
• **live on**
04 feed, last **05** exist **06** rely on **07** live off, subsist **08** continue **09** subsist on
• **live wire**
06 dynamo **08** go-getter, whizz kid **10** ball of fire **11** eager beaver, self-starter

liveable *see* **livable**

livelihood
03 job **04** keep, work **05** bread, crust, means, trade **06** income, living, upkeep **07** livelod, support **08** livelood **09** existence **10** daily bread, employment, livelihead, occupation, profession, sustenance **11** maintenance, subsistence **13** means of living **14** bread-and-butter, means of support, source of income

liveliness
04 brio, life, salt 05 oomph 06 energy, esprit, spirit, vigour 07 entrain, pizzazz 08 activity, dynamism, vitality, vivacity 09 animation, briskness, quickness, smartness 10 livelihead 11 refreshment 13 animal spirits, sprightliness, vivaciousness 14 boisterousness

livelong
04 full, long 05 whole 06 entire, orpine 08 complete, enduring 10 protracted

lively
◇ anagram indicator
03 gay 04 busy, cant, go-go, keen, pacy, racy, spry, vive, vivo, warm, wick 05 agile, alert, alive, brisk, buxom, canty, cobby, kedge, kedgy, kidge, light, ludic, merry, pacey, peart, perky, piert, quick, rapid, vital, vivid, zappy, zippy 06 active, blithe, bouncy, breezy, bright, bubbly, chirpy, crouse, frisky, heated, hectic, jaunty, living, nimble, snappy, sporty, strong, titupy, vivace 07 buckish, buoyant, buzzing, crowded, dynamic, graphic, mettled, playful, slammin', teeming, tittupy, vibrant 08 animated, brushing, bustling, cheerful, eventful, exciting, friskful, galliard, lifesome, rattling, skittish, slamming, spirited, stirring, striking, swarming, vigorous 09 colourful, energetic, lightsome, sparkling, sprightly, vivacious 10 frolicsome, mettlesome, mouvementé, refreshing 11 imaginative, interesting, stimulating 12 effervescent, enthusiastic, high-spirited, invigorating

liven
04 stir 05 cheer, hot up, pep up, rouse, spice 06 buck up, jazz up, perk up, stir up 07 animate, cheer up, enliven, spice up 08 brighten, energize, vitalize 10 invigorate 11 put life into

liverish
05 testy 06 crabby, crusty, grumpy, snappy, tetchy 07 crabbed, peevish 09 crotchety, irascible, irritable, splenetic 11 ill-humoured 12 disagreeable 13 quick-tempered

livery
04 garb, gear, suit, togs 05 dress, get-up, habit 06 attire 07 apparel, clobber, clothes, costume, regalia, uniform 08 clothing, garments 09 irritable, vestments 11 habiliments

livid
03 mad, wan 04 blae, blue, pale, waxy 05 angry, ashen, irate, pasty, white 06 fuming, leaden, pallid, purple, raging 07 bruised, enraged, furious, ghastly, greyish 08 blanched, incensed, outraged, purplish, seething 09 bloodless, indignant 10 infuriated 11 deathly pale, discoloured, exasperated, Hippocratic 12 black-and-blue

living
03 job 04 life, live, true, work 05 alive, being, bread, close, crust, exact, in use, trade, vital 06 active, extant, income, lively, strong 07 animate, current, genuine, precise, support 08 animated, benefice, existing, faithful, property, vigorous 09 animation, breathing, existence, identical, lifestyle, operative, surviving, way of life 10 continuing, daily bread, livelihood, occupation, profession, sustenance 11 going strong, maintenance, subsistence 13 means of living 14 bread-and-butter, means of support, source of income
• **mode of living**
04 diet

living room
06 lounge 07 day room, parlour 09 front room 11 drawing room, sitting room 13 reception room

lizard

| Lizards include: |

03 eft
04 evet, gila, sand, seps, tegu, wall, worm
05 blind, Draco, fence, gecko, skink
06 agamid, dragon, flying, goanna, horned, iguana
07 bearded, frilled, monitor, perenty
08 basilisk, perentie, slowworm, teguexin
09 chameleon
10 blue-tongue, chamaeleon
11 gila monster
12 Komodo dragon

See also **animal**

llama
06 alpaca 07 guanaco, huanaco

load
03 arm, jag, put, tax, tod 04 a lot, cram, duty, fill, haul, heap, lade, lard, lots, onus, pack, pile, plug, seam, slot, tons 05 cargo, enter, equip, goods, heaps, miles, piles, prime, put in, scads, slide, stack, stuff, todde, worry 06 burden, charge, dozens, fill up, hordes, insert, lading, masses, oodles, scores, stacks, strain, weight 07 fraught, freight, oppress, prepare, put into, trouble 08 a million, contents, encumber, hundreds, incumber, lashings, millions, pressure, shipment 09 abundance, albatross, great deal, millstone, overwhelm, thousands, weigh down 10 commitment, obligation, oppression, overburden, saddle with 11 consignment, encumbrance, large amount, tribulation 13 prepare to fire 14 responsibility

loaded
◇ anagram indicator
03 fap, fou 04 full, high, inky, paid, rich 05 drunk, fixed, flush, foxed, happy, inked, laden, lit up, merry, moppy, piled, set up, tight, tipsy, woozy 06 biased, blotto, bombed, canned, corked, filled, heaped, jagged, juiced, mellow, mortal, packed, rigged, ripped, soused, stewed, stinko, stoned, tiddly, wasted 07 bevvied, bonkers, bottled, charged, crocked, drunken, ebriose, fairish, half-cut, legless, maggoty, pickled, pie-eyed, sloshed, smashed, sozzled, squiffy, stacked, tiddled, trashed, wealthy, well-off, wrecked 08 affluent, bibulous, burdened, footless, in liquor, juiced up, liquored, moon-eyed, overseen, overshot, pregnant, sow-drunk, stotious, tanked up, weighted, whiffled, whistled 09 blootered, crapulent, incapable, paralytic, plastered, shickered, up the pole, well-oiled 10 blind drunk, capernoity, inebriated, in the money, obfuscated, well-heeled 11 intoxicated, made of money, rolling in it, snowed under 12 drunk as a lord, drunk as a newt, on easy street, roaring drunk 13 drunk as a piper, having had a few, under the table 14 Brahms and Liszt 15 a sheet in the wind, one over the eight, the worse for wear, under the weather

loaf
03 bum, tin, veg 04 cake, cube, head, idle, laze, loll, lump, mass, mind, nous, pone, slab 05 block, brick, miche, mooch, relax, sense, slosh 06 bludge, brains, coburg, loiter, lounge, noddle, stotty, unwind, veg out 07 bloomer, brioche, challah, manchet, Panagia, stottie 08 baguette, corn pone, focaccia, gumption, Panhagia, scrapple 09 barmbrack, lie around, sit around 10 corn dodger, hang around, stand about, take it easy 11 common sense, French stick, spotted dick 12 lounge around

See also **bread**; **head**

• **loaf about**
04 laze 06 lounge

loafer
03 yob 04 slob 05 idler 06 bummer, skiver 07 goof-off, lounger, shirker, wastrel 08 layabout, sluggard 09 corner-boy, corner-man, lazybones, sundowner 10 ne'er-do-well 11 beachcomber

See also **footwear**

loam
04 clay, core, lome, malm, sand, soil 05 earth 09 brickclay, malmstone 10 brick-earth

loan
03 len', sub 04 lane, lend 05 allow, prest 06 credit, on-lend 07 advance, finance, imprest, lending 08 mortgage, overlend, put forth 09 allowance 12 floating debt, respondentia 13 accommodation

loath
04 ugly 05 laith 06 averse 07 against, hateful, opposed 08 grudging, hesitant 09 reluctant, repulsive,

resisting, unwilling **10** indisposed
11 disinclined

loathe
02 ug **04** hate **05** abhor **06** detest
07 despise, dislike **08** execrate,
nauseate, not stand **09** abominate
10 recoil from **15** feel revulsion at

loathing
04 hate **05** odium **06** hatred, horror,
nausea **07** disgust, dislike, ill-will
08 aversion **09** antipathy, repulsion,
revulsion **10** abhorrence, execration,
repugnance **11** abomination,
detestation

loathsome
04 foul, vile **05** nasty **06** odious
07 hateful, mawkish, obscene
08 horrible, nauseous **09** abhorrent,
execrable, lothefull, obnoxious,
offensive, repellent, repugnant,
repulsive, revolting **10** abominable,
despicable, detestable, disgusting,
nauseating **12** contemptible,
disagreeable

lob
03 shy **04** hurl, lift, loft, lout, lump,
puck, toss **05** chuck, droop, fling,
heave, pitch, throw **06** launch
07 lobworm, pollack

lobby
04 hall, urge **05** entry, foyer, porch
06 demand **07** call for, faction, hallway,
passage, promote, push for, solicit
08 anteroom, box-lobby, campaign,
corridor, entrance, persuade, press for,
pressure **09** influence, lobbyists,
vestibule **10** passageway **11** campaign
for, ginger group, waiting room
12 entrance hall **13** pressure group

lobster
04 cock **08** crawfish, crayfish
09 langouste **11** langoustine
• **lobster cage**
04 corf

local
◇ *foreign word indicator*
03 bar, inn, pub **04** city, town **05** place,
urban **06** boozer, narrow, native,
number, parish, saloon, tavern
07 citizen, limited, topical, vicinal,
village **08** district, hostelry, regional,
resident **09** community, municipal,
parochial, small-town **10** inhabitant,
parish-pump, provincial, restricted,
vernacular **11** anaesthetic,
examination, public house
12 watering-hole **13** neighbourhood
See also **public house**
• **local worker**
06 barman **09** bartender

locale
04 area, site, spot, zone **05** locus,
place, scene, venue **07** setting
08 locality, location, position
11 environment **13** neighbourhood

locality
04 area, site, spot **05** locus, place,
scene **06** locale, region **07** setting

08 district, position, vicinity
11 environment **12** neighborhood
13 neighbourhood **15** surrounding
area

localize
05 limit **06** assign **07** ascribe, confine,
contain, delimit, specify **08** identify,
pinpoint, restrain, restrict, zero in on
10 delimitate, narrow down
11 concentrate **12** circumscribe

locate
03 fix, lay, put, set **04** find, seat, site,
spot **05** build, place, plant **06** access,
detect, finger, settle **07** hit upon, pick
out, situate, station, uncover, unearth
08 allocate, discover, identify,
pinpoint, position **09** establish, track
down **10** come across, run to earth
14 lay your hands on
• **be located**
03 sit

location
04 farm, seat, site, spot **05** locus,
place, point, scene, venue **06** locale,
ubiety **07** setting **08** bearings,
position **09** situation **11** whereabouts

loch
01 L **03** dam, sea **04** lake, mere, pond,
pool, tarn **05** basin, lough, water
09 reservoir
See also **lake**

lock
03 bar, hug, jam, tag **04** curl, join, link,
mesh, seal, shut, snap, trap, tuft
05 catch, clasp, grasp, latch, plait,
sasse, stick, tress, unite **06** clench,
clutch, engage, fasten, secure, strand
07 embrace, enclose, entwine,
grapple, ringlet **08** encircle, entangle
09 certainty, fastening, interlock
12 scalping-tuft

Locks include:
03 rim
04 dead, Yale®
05 child, Chubb®, wagon
06 safety, spring
07 mortice, mortise, padlock
08 cylinder
10 night latch
11 combination

Lock parts include:
03 bit, key, pin
04 bolt, hasp, knob, post, rose, sash,
ward
05 latch, talon
06 barrel, keyway, spring, staple
07 key card, keyhole, spindle, tumbler
08 cylinder, dead bolt, sash bolt
09 face plate, latch bolt
10 escutcheon, latch lever, push
button
11 mortise bolt, spindle hole, strike
plate
12 cylinder hole
13 latch follower

• **lock out**
03 bar **05** debar **07** exclude, keep out,
shut out

• **lock up**
◇ *containment indicator*
◇ *hidden indicator*
03 pen **04** cage, jail **06** detain,
secure, shut in, shut up, wall in
07 close up, confine, put away
08 imprison **11** incarcerate **13** put
behind bars
• **open lock**
04 pick

locker
07 cabinet **08** cupboard **09** container
11 compartment

lock-up
03 can, jug **04** cell, gaol, jail, quod
05 choky, clink **06** chokey, cooler,
garage, prison **07** slammer
09 storeroom, warehouse
10 depository, roundhouse, watch
house **12** penitentiary, station house

locomotion
06 action, motion, moving, travel
07 headway, walking **08** movement,
progress **10** ambulation, travelling
11 progression **13** perambulation

locus
04 site **05** place, point, polar, venue
06 locale, spiral **08** centrode,
conchoid, envelope, locality, location,
parabola, position, roulette
09 directrix, situation, wavefront
10 lemniscate **11** radical axis,
whereabouts **14** director circle

locust
08 devourer **10** devastator,
voetganger

locution
04 term **05** idiom, style **06** accent,
cliché, phrase **07** diction, talking,
wording **08** phrasing, speaking
10 expression, inflection, intonation
11 collocation **12** articulation, turn of
phrase

lode
04 reef

lodge
03 box, cup, den, dig, fix, hut, inn, lay,
lie, put **04** bank, club, file, host, keep,
lair, live, make, nest, room, stay, stow,
tent **05** board, bower, cabin, dwell,
group, grove, haunt, house, imbed,
infix, layer, place, put in, put up
06 billet, branch, chalet, grange, hand
in, harbor, loggia, record, reside, show
up, submit, teepee **07** barrack,
chapter, cottage, deposit, hang out,
harbour, implant, quarter, retreat,
section, shelter, society, sojourn
08 campfire, get stuck, register **09** be
settled, gatehouse, get caught,
longhouse **10** habitation, put forward
11 accommodate, association
12 accumulation, have your home,
hunting-lodge, meeting-place

lodger
02 PG **05** guest **06** inmate, roomer,
tenant **07** boarder **08** resident
11 paying guest

lodgings
03 pad **04** digs, ferm **05** abode, board, place, rooms **06** bedsit, billet **07** flea-bag **08** dwelling, quarters **09** bedsitter, residence **13** accommodation, boarding house **14** bedsitting-room

loftily
07 proudly, stately **08** snootily **09** haughtily **10** arrogantly **12** disdainfully **14** superciliously

lofty
04 high, tall **05** brent, grand, noble, proud, steep, wingy **06** aerial, lordly, raised, skyish, snooty, winged **07** exalted, haughty, sky-high, soaring, stately, sublime **08** arrogant, elevated, esteemed, imperial, imposing, majestic, renowned, superior, towering **09** dignified **10** disdainful **11** illustrious, patronizing, toffee-nosed **12** supercilious **13** condescending, distinguished, high and mighty, high-stomached

log
04 book, clog, file, note **05** block, chart, chock, chunk, diary, piece, stock, tally, trunk **06** billet, loggat, record, timber **07** account, daybook, journal, logbook, set down, write up **08** register **09** logarithm

logbook
03 log **05** chart, diary, tally **06** record **07** account, daybook, journal **08** register

loggerheads
• **at loggerheads**
◊ anagram indicator
06 at odds **10** in conflict **11** disagreeing, quarrelling **12** in opposition **13** like cat and dog **14** at daggers drawn

logic
05 sense **06** reason **08** argument **09** coherence, deduction, judgement, rationale, reasoning, redecraft **10** dialectics **13** argumentation, ratiocination

See also **circuit**

logical
04 wise **05** clear, sound, valid **06** cogent **07** Boolean **08** coherent, rational, reasoned, relevant, sensible, thinking **09** deducible, deductive, dialectic, inductive, judicious **10** consistent, convergent, methodical, reasonable, sequacious **11** consecutive, dialectical, intelligent, syllogistic, well-founded **12** well-reasoned **13** well-organized **14** well-thought-out

logically
07 clearly, validly **08** sensibly **10** coherently, rationally, relevantly **11** deductively, inductively **12** consistently, methodically **13** consecutively, dialectically, intelligently

logistics
05 plans **07** tactics **08** planning, strategy **09** direction **10** management **11** arrangement, engineering **12** co-ordination, organization **13** masterminding, orchestration

logo
04 mark, sign **05** badge, image **06** device, emblem, figure, symbol **08** insignia **09** trademark **14** representation

loiter
03 lag **04** hove, idle, lime, loaf, lurk, mike **05** dally, delay, hoove, mooch, mouch, tarry **06** dawdle, linger, lounge, taigle **07** saunter **08** lallygag, lollygag **09** hang about, waste time **10** dilly-dally, hang around **12** take your time
• **loitering with intent**
03 sus **04** suss

loll
03 sag **04** drop, flap, flop, hang, lill, loaf **05** droop, relax, slump **06** dangle, lounge, slouch, sprawl **07** recline

lollop
03 run **04** idle, lope **05** bound **06** canter, gallop, lounge, spring, stride

lolly
05 money **06** sucker **07** lulibub **08** ice block, lollipop, Popsicle®
See also **money**

London
03 wen **08** great wen

London boroughs:
05 Brent
06 Barnet, Bexley, Camden, Ealing, Harrow, Merton, Newham, Sutton
07 Bromley, Croydon, Enfield, Hackney, Lambeth
08 Haringey, Havering, Hounslow, Lewisham
09 Greenwich, Islington, Redbridge, Southwark
10 Hillingdon, Wandsworth
12 Tower Hamlets
13 Waltham Forest
17 City of Westminster
18 Barking and Dagenham, Kingston upon Thames, Richmond upon Thames
20 Hammersmith and Fulham, Kensington and Chelsea

Other districts of London include:
02 EC
03 Bow, Kew, Lee
04 Bank, Oval, Soho
05 Acton, Angel, Erith, Hayes, Penge
06 Arkley, Balham, Barnes, Debden, Eltham, Epping, Euston, Fulham, Hendon, Heston, Hoxton, Ilford, Kenton, Leyton, Malden, Morden, Pinner, Poplar, Purley, Putney, Temple, Waddon
07 Aldgate, Archway, Barking, Beckton, Belmont, Borough, Brixton, Catford, Chelsea, Clapham, Cranham, Dalston, Dulwich, East End, East Ham, Edgware, Elm Park, Feltham, Hampton, Hanwell, Holborn, Hornsey, Kilburn, Mayfair, Mile End, Mitcham, Neasden, Norwood, Old Ford, Olympia, Peckham, Pimlico, Selsdon, Stepney, The City, Tooting, Wapping, Welling, Wembley, West End, West Ham, Yeading
08 Alperton, Bankside, Barbican, Brockley, Brompton, Chiswick, Coulsdon, Crayford, Dagenham, Deptford, Edmonton, Elmstead, Finchley, Finsbury, Grays Inn, Hanworth, Hatch End, Heathrow, Highbury, Highgate, Holloway, Homerton, Hyde Park, Ickenham, Kingston, Mill Hill, Mortlake, New Cross, Nine Elms, Northolt, Osterley, Perivale, Plaistow, Richmond, Shadwell, Southall, Stanmore, Surbiton, Sydenham, Tolworth, Uxbridge, Vauxhall, Victoria, Walworth, Wanstead, Waterloo, Woodford, Woolwich
09 Abbey Wood, Addington, Barnsbury, Battersea, Bayswater, Beckenham, Becontree, Belgravia, Blackwall, Brentford, Brimsdown, Canonbury, Chalk Farm, Chingford, Colindale, Crouch End, Docklands, Fitzrovia, Foots Cray, Gant's Hill, Gidea Park, Gipsy Hill, Goodmayes, Gospel Oak, Greenford, Green Park, Hampstead, Harefield, Harlesden, Harringay, Herne Hill, Isleworth, Kidbrooke, Kingsbury, Kingsland, Limehouse, Maida Vale, Mark's Gate, Newington, Northwood, Orpington, Park Royal, Petts Wood, Plumstead, South Bank, Southgate, Stockwell, St Pancras, Stratford, Streatham, Tottenham, Tower Hill, Tulse Hill, Upminster, Whetstone, White City, Whitehall, Willesden, Wimbledon, Wood Green
10 Addiscombe, Albany Park, Arnos Grove, Beddington, Bellingham, Bermondsey, Blackheath, Bloomsbury, Brent Cross, Camberwell, Chase Cross, Collier Row, Creekmouth, Dollis Hill, Earls Court, Earlsfield, Embankment, Farringdon, Forest Gate, Forest Hill, Goddington, Green Lanes, Haggerston, Harlington, Harold Hill, Harold Wood, Horse Ferry, Isle of Dogs, Kennington, Kensington, King's Cross, Manor House, Marylebone, Mottingham, Paddington, Piccadilly, Queensbury, Raynes Park, Seven Dials, Seven Kings, Shad Thames, Shoreditch, Silvertown, Smithfield, Teddington, Thamesmead, Totteridge, Twickenham, Wallington, Wealdstone
11 Bedford Park, Belsize Park, Bexleyheath, Blackfriars, Bounds Green, Brondesbury, Canada Water, Canary Wharf, Canning Town,

Chessington, Clerkenwell, Cockfosters, Cricklewood, East Dulwich, Fortis Green, Gunnersbury, Hammersmith, Highams Park, Holland Park, Kensal Green, Kentish Town, Leytonstone, Lincoln's Inn, Little Italy, Ludgate Hill, Muswell Hill, Notting Hill, Pentonville, Regent's Park, Rotherhithe, Snaresbrook, St John's Wood, Surrey Quays, Tufnell Park, Walthamstow, Westminster, Whitechapel

12 Bethnal Green, Billingsgate, Bromley-by-Bow, Charing Cross, City of London, Colliers Wood, Covent Garden, Crossharbour, Epping Forest, Finsbury Park, Golders Green, Hatton Garden, Havering Park, London Bridge, London Fields, Palmers Green, Parsons Green, Pool of London, Primrose Hill, Seven Sisters, Sloane Square, Stamford Hill, Swiss Cottage

13 Ardleigh Green, Chadwell Heath, Crystal Palace, Harmondsworth, Knightsbridge, Ladbroke Grove, Lancaster Gate, North Woolwich, Petticoat Lane, Shepherd's Bush, Thornton Heath, Tottenham Hale, Wanstead Flats, Winchmore Hill

14 Angel Islington, Becontree Heath, Hackney Marshes, Stoke Newington, Tottenham Green, Wormwood Scrubs

15 Alexandra Palace, Leicester Square, Westbourne Green

Gerrard Street, Grosvenor Road, Knightsbridge, Lombard Street, Ludgate Circus, New Bond Street, New Fetter Lane, Newgate Street, Old Bond Street, Petticoat Lane, Portland Place, Portman Square, Russell Square, Wardour Street

14 Belgrave Square, Berkeley Square, Coventry Street, Earl's Court Road, Earnshaw Street, Exhibition Road, Gloucester Road, Holborn Viaduct, Horseferry Road, Hyde Park Square, Kensington Road, Marylebone Road, Mayfair Gardens, Portobello Road, Stamford Street

15 Albemarle Street, Blackfriars Road, Clerkenwell Road, Grosvenor Square, Horse Guards Road, Leicester Square, Liverpool Street, New Bridge Street, Pentonville Road, Southwark Street, St John's Wood Road, Trafalgar Square, Whitechapel Road

British Library, Hayward Gallery, Hermitage Rooms, Lancaster House, London Aquarium, Millennium Dome, Museum of London, Portobello Road, Speakers' Corner, St Clement Danes, St James's Palace, Waterloo Bridge, Wellington Arch

15 Bankside Gallery, Banqueting House, Brompton Oratory, Burlington House, Cabinet War Rooms, National Gallery, Royal Albert Hall, Royal Opera House, Temple of Mithras, Trafalgar Square, Westminster Hall

Water, Canary Wharf, Canning Town, Chorleywood, Cockfosters, Custom House, Edgware Road, Gunnersbury, Hammersmith, Holland Park, Kensal Green, Kentish Town, Kilburn Park, Latimer Road, Leytonstone, North Ealing, Northfields, Regent's Park, Rotherhithe, Royal Albert, South Ealing, Southfields, St John's Wood, Surrey Quays, Tufnell Park, Wembley Park, Westminster, Whitechapel
2 Bethnal Green, Bromley-by-Bow, Cannon Street, Chancery Lane, Charing Cross, Chiswick Park, Clapham North, Clapham South, Colliers Wood, Covent Garden, Dagenham East, Ealing Common, East Finchley, Elverson Road, Euston Square, Finchley Road, Finsbury Park, Golders Green, Goldhawk Road, Goodge Street, Holloway Road, Lambeth North, London Bridge, Mansion House, New Cross Gate, Oxford Circus, Parsons Green, Prince Regent, Putney Bridge, Seven Sisters, Sloane Square, Stepney Green, St James's Park, Swiss Cottage, Tower Gateway, Turnham Green, Turnpike Lane, Warren Street, West Brompton
3 Clapham Common, Gallions Reach, Hendon Central, Island Gardens, Knightsbridge, Ladbroke Grove, Lancaster Gate, Rickmansworth, Royal Victoria, Russell Square, Shepherd's Bush, Stamford Brook, Tottenham Hale, Warwick Avenue, West Hampstead, West India Quay, Wimbledon Park
4 Blackhorse Road, Caledonian Road, Deptford Bridge, Ealing Broadway, Fulham Broadway, Gloucester Road, Hyde Park Corner, North Greenwich, South Wimbledon, Westbourne Park, West Kensington, Willesden Green
15 Finchley Central, Harrow-on-the-Hill, Hounslow Central, Leicester Square, Liverpool Street, Notting Hill Gate, Pudding Mill Lane, Ravenscourt Park, South Kensington, Stonebridge Park, Tooting Broadway

one
▪3 one 04 lane, only, sole 05 alone
▪6 barren, remote, single
07 widowed 08 deserted, desolate, divorced, forsaken, isolated, secluded, separate, solitary
09 abandoned, on your own, separated, unmarried 10 by yourself, unattached 11 out-of-the-way, uninhabited 12 unfrequented
15 without a partner

oneliness
08 solitude 09 aloneness, isolation, seclusion 10 desolation
12 lonesomeness, solitariness

lonely
03 sad 04 lone 05 alone, unked, unket, unkid 06 barren, remote
07 outcast, unhappy 08 deserted, desolate, forsaken, isolated, lonesome, rejected, secluded, solitary, wretched
09 abandoned, destitute, miserable, reclusive 10 friendless 11 god-forsaken, out-of-the-way, uninhabited
12 solitudinous, unfrequented
13 companionless, unaccompanied

loner
06 hermit 07 recluse 08 lone wolf, solitary 09 introvert 13 individualist
14 solitudinarian

lonesome
03 sad 04 lone 05 alone 06 barren, lonely, remote 07 outcast, unhappy
08 deserted, desolate, forsaken, isolated, rejected, secluded, solitary, wretched 09 abandoned, destitute, miserable, reclusive 10 friendless
11 out-of-the-way, uninhabited
12 unfrequented 13 companionless, unaccompanied

long
01 L 03 ake, die, far, yen 04 ache, hope, itch, lang, leng, lust, pant, pine, side, slow, tall, want, wish 05 covet, crave, dream, longa, tardy, yearn
06 desire, hanker, hunger, thirst
07 lengthy, spun out, tedious, verbose
08 expanded, extended, marathon, overlong 09 diuturnal, elongated, expansive, extensive, prolonged, spread out, stretched, sustained
10 protracted 11 far-reaching
12 interminable, long-drawn-out, stretched out
See also **want**

• **before long**
04 soon 07 by and by, shortly 09 in a moment, presently 12 in a short time
14 in a minute or two 15 in the near future
• **long ago**
03 eld 04 yore
• **Long Island**
02 LI
• **long live**
04 viva, vive 05 vivat 08 zindabad

long-drawn-out
06 prolix 07 lengthy, spun out, tedious
08 long-spun, marathon, overlong
09 long-drawn, prolonged
10 dragging on, long-winded, protracted 12 interminable, overextended

longer
04 more
• **no longer**
02 ex

longing
03 yen 04 avid, earn, erne, hope, itch, lust, urge, wish 05 brame, crave, dream, eager, greed, yearn 06 ardent, desire, hunger, hungry, pining, thirst
07 anxious, craving, wanting, wishful, wistful 08 ambition, appetent,

coveting, desirous, yearning
09 breathing, cacoethes, hankering, hungering 10 aspiration, desiderium
11 languishing

longingly
06 avidly, wistly 07 eagerly
08 ardently 09 anxiously, wishfully, wistfully 10 yearningly

long-lasting
07 abiding, chronic 08 enduring, unfading 09 lingering, permanent, prolonged 10 continuing, protracted, unchanging 12 imperishable, long-standing

long-lived
07 durable, lasting 08 enduring
09 longevous, macrobian, vivacious
11 long-lasting, macrobiotic 12 long-standing

long-standing
07 abiding 08 enduring 09 long-lived
11 established, long-lasting, traditional
12 time-honoured 15 long-established, well-established

long-suffering
07 patient, stoical 08 resigned, tolerant 09 easy-going, forgiving, indulgent 10 forbearant, forbearing
13 uncomplaining

long-winded
05 wordy 06 prolix 07 diffuse, lengthy, tedious, verbose, voluble 08 overlong, rambling 09 garrulous, prolonged
10 discursive, protracted
11 repetitious 12 long-drawn-out

long-windedness
08 longueur 09 garrulity, macrology, prolixity, verbosity, wordiness
10 volubility 11 diffuseness, lengthiness, tediousness
14 discursiveness 15 repetitiousness

loo
02 WC 03 bog, lav 04 john, kazi, love, toot 05 dunny, Elsan®, gents', privy
06 ladies', throne, toilet, urinal
07 crapper, latrine 08 bathroom, lavatory, Portaloo®, rest room, superloo, washroom 09 cloakroom, lanterloo 10 facilities, powder room
11 convenience, water closet
12 smallest room 14 comfort station, little boys' room 15 little girls' room
See also **toilet**

look
02 hi, la, lo, oi 03 air, eye, ray, see, spy
04 deek, ecce, ecco, face, gape, gawp, gaze, geek, keek, leer, mien, peek, peep, peer, quiz, scan, seem, show, view, vise, vizy 05 check, decko, dekko, focus, front, frown, glout, guise, scowl, sight, squiz, stare, study, visie, watch 06 appear, aspect, behold, blench, effect, eyeful, façade, gander, give on, glance, gledge, manner, regard, review, shufti, shufty, squint, survey, take in, vision, vizzie
07 bearing, belgard, display, examine, exhibit, eyeball, front on, glimpse,

inspect, observe **08** butcher's, consider, features, give on to, look onto, once-over, overlook, scrutiny **09** eyeglance, semblance, take a look **10** appearance, be opposite, complexion, expression, get a load of, impression, inspection, scrutinize **11** contemplate, countenance, examination, observation **12** butcher's hook, take a dekko at **13** contemplation, get an eyeful of, take a gander at, take a shufti at, take a squint at **14** give a going-over **15** give the once-over, run your eyes over

• **look after**
03 sit **04** heed, keep, mind, seek, tend **05** guard, nurse, see to, watch **06** expect **07** babysit, care for, protect **08** attend to, maintain **09** childmind, supervise, watch over **10** take care of **11** keep an eye on **12** take charge of

• **look back**
06 recall **08** remember **09** reminisce, think back **10** retrospect

• **look down on**
05 scorn, spurn **07** despise, disdain, sneer at **08** overpeer, pooh-pooh **09** disparage, patronize **10** talk down to **14** hold in contempt

• **look for**
04 seek **05** await, quest **06** expect **07** hunt for, hunt out **08** scavenge **09** forage for, search for, try to find **10** fossick out

• **look forward to**
05 await **06** expect **07** count on, hope for, long for, look for, wait for **08** envisage, envision **09** apprehend **10** anticipate

• **look into**
03 dig **05** delve, plumb, probe, study **06** fathom, go into **07** examine, explore, inspect **08** ask about, check out, look over, research **10** scrutinize, search into **11** investigate **12** inquire about

• **look like**
08 resemble **09** take after **11** be similar to, remind you of

• **look on, look upon**
03 eye **04** deem, hold, view **05** count, judge, think **06** regard **07** overeye **08** consider, spectate

• **look out**
04 mind **06** beware **07** Achtung, be alert **08** watch out **09** be careful **11** mind your eye **12** keep an eye out, pay attention **13** be on your guard, guard yourself **14** be on the qui vive

• **look over**
04 scan, view **05** check **07** examine, inspect, monitor, surview **08** check out **09** go through **11** look through, read through **13** cast an eye over, give a once-over **15** cast your eye over

• **look to**
05 await, besee, watch **06** expect, regard, rely on, turn to **07** count on, hope for, respect **08** consider, reckon on, resort to **10** anticipate, fall back on, think about **13** give thought to

• **look up**
04 find, seek **05** visit **06** call on, come on, drop by, perk up, pick up, stop by **07** advance, consult, develop, hunt for, improve **08** drop in on, look in on, progress, research **09** come along, get better, search for, track down **10** ameliorate **11** make headway, pay a visit to **12** make progress

• **look up to**
06 admire, esteem, honour, revere **07** respect **12** regard highly **13** think highly of

lookalike
04 spit, twin **05** clone, image **06** double, ringer **07** replica **10** dead ringer **11** living image **12** doppelgänger **13** exact likeness, spitting image

lookout
03 nit **04** huer, post, ward **05** guard, tower, watch, worry **06** affair, conder, conner, pigeon, sentry **07** concern, problem **08** business, cockatoo, prospect, sentinel, watchman, watch-out **10** speculator, watch-tower **14** responsibility **15** observation post

• **keep a lookout**
05 watch **09** keep guard **10** be vigilant **11** remain alert **14** be on the qui vive

loom
04 loon, rise, soar, tool **05** frame, mount, tower **06** appear, emerge, impend, menace **07** overtop **08** dominate, hang over, jacquard, overhang, threaten **09** implement, take shape **10** be imminent, overshadow, receptacle **13** become visible

loony
◇ *anagram indicator*
03 mad, nut **04** daft, hook, wild **05** barmy, crank, crazy, loopy, nutty, potty, silly **06** crazed, insane, madman, maniac, nutter, psycho, stupid **07** berserk, bonkers, foolish, frantic, idiotic, lunatic, nutcase, oddball, strange **08** crackpot, demented, deranged, headcase, imbecile, madwoman, unhinged **09** disturbed, eccentric, fruitcake, psychotic, screwball **10** basket case, distracted, distraught, psychopath, unbalanced

See also **madman, madwoman**

loop
01 O **03** eye, lug, tab, tie, tug **04** bend, coil, curl, fold, hank, hoop, join, kink, knop, knot, oval, purl, ring, roll, turn, wind **05** braid, curve, noose, pearl, picot, sling, snare, twirl, twist, whorl **06** becket, cannon, circle, eyelet, fasten, lasket, runner, spiral, stitch **07** connect, latchet **08** carriage, écraseur, encircle, loophole, surround **09** billabong, eye splice **10** curve round, rubber band **11** convolution, elastic band, jubilee clip

loophole
04 plea **06** escape, excuse, eyelet, get-out, let-out, wicket **07** evasion,

mistake, pretext **08** omission, pretence **09** ambiguity **12** escape clause

loose
◇ *anagram indicator*
03 lax, off **04** ease, fast, free, lose, open, undo **05** baggy, broad, let go, losen, lowse, relax, shaky, shoot, slack, solve, unpen, untie, vague **06** detach, flabby, lessen, loosen, reduce, solute, unbind, undone, unhook, unknit, unlock, unmoor, untied, wanton, weaken, wobbly **07** at large, corrupt, escaped, flowing, general, hanging, immoral, inexact, movable, relaxed, release, sagging, set free, slacken, unbound, unclasp, unleash **08** diffused, diminish, insecure, liberate, moderate, rambling, released, unchaste, uncouple, unfasten, unlocked, unpicked, unsteady **09** abandoned, debauched, desultory, discharge, disengage, dissolute, imprecise, shapeless, uncoupled **10** degenerate, disconnect, ill-defined, inaccurate, incoherent, indefinite, indistinct, licentious, unattached, unconfined, unfastened, untethered **11** inattentive, light-heeled, promiscuous **12** disreputable, loose-fitting, unrestrained

• **at a loose end**
04 idle **05** bored, fed up **07** aimless, off duty **09** désoeuvré **11** out of action, purposeless **14** with time to kill **15** with nothing to do

• **on the loose**
04 free **07** at large, escaped **08** on the run **09** at liberty **10** unconfined

loosely
◇ *anagram indicator*
06 freely **07** baggily, broadly, movably, slackly, vaguely **09** generally, inexactly **10** insecurely, unsteadily **11** imprecisely, shapelessly **12** inaccurately

loosen
04 ease, free, undo **05** let go, loose, relax, untie **06** let out, unbind, unglue, weaken **07** deliver, release, set free, shake up, slacken, unscrew, work out **08** diminish, moderate, set loose, unfasten, unthread

• **loosen up**
05 let up, relax **06** cool it, ease up, go easy, lessen, unwind, warm up **07** prepare, work out **08** chill out, exercise, limber up, warm down **09** hang loose

loot
03 let, rob **04** haul, raid, sack, swag **05** booty, money, prize, rifle, steal **06** burgle, maraud, ravage, riches, spoils **07** despoil, pillage, plunder, ransack **08** pickings **09** steal from **10** lieutenant **11** stolen goods, stolen money

lop
03 cut **04** chop, clip, crop, dock, hack, sned, trim **05** prune, sever, shrub, trash **06** cut off, detach, reduce, remove,

hroud **07** curtail, shorten, take off
8 truncate **10** detruncate

ope
3 run **05** bound **06** canter, gallop,
ollop, spring, stride

opsided
5 askew **06** squint, uneven
7 crooked, slanted, sloping, tilting,
nequal **08** one-sided **09** skew-whiff
0 off balance, unbalanced
2 asymmetrical

oquacious
5 gabby, gassy, wordy **06** chatty
7 gossipy, voluble **08** babbling
9 garrulous, speechful, talkative
0 blathering, chattering
2 multiloquent, multiloquous

oquacity
9 garrulity, gassiness **10** chattiness,
nultiloquy, volubility **12** effusiveness
3 multiloquence, talkativeness

ord
1 D **02** Ld **03** Dom, God, lud
4 duke, earl, Herr, kami, king, land,
osh, peer, sire, tuan **05** baron, chief,
ount, Maker, noble, omrah, ruler
6 bishop, Christ, Father, leader,
naster, prince, Yahweh **07** captain,
Creator, emperor, Eternal, Holy One,
ehovah, Messiah, monarch, Saviour,
he Word **08** Almighty, governor,
nobleman, overlord, Redeemer,
eigneur, seignior, Son of God, Son of
Man, superior, suzerain, viscount
9 commander, patrician, sovereign
0 aristocrat **11** Jesus Christ, King of
Kings **13** grand seigneur
ee also **nobility**

• **lord it over**
6 act big **07** oppress, repress,
wagger **08** domineer, pull rank
9 put on airs, tyrannize **10** boss
around, overoffice **11** order around,
queen it over **13** be overbearing

ordliness
5 pride **07** disdain, majesty
9 arrogance, grandness, nobleness
1 haughtiness, imperiality
2 magnificence, splendidness **13** big-
eadedness, condescension,
mperiousness **14** high-handedness,
mpressiveness, overconfidence

ordly
5 grand, lofty, noble, proud **06** lavish,
ppity **07** haughty, stately, stuck-up
8 arrogant, imperial, majestic,
plendid **09** big-headed, dignified,
grandiose, hubristic, imperious
0 disdainful, high-handed, hoity-toity,
mpressive, peremptory, tyrannical
1 dictatorial, domineering,
nagnificent, overbearing, patronizing,
offee-nosed **12** aristocratic,
upercilious **13** condescending, high
nd mighty, overconfident

ore
4 lair, lare, lear, leir, lere **05** leare,
nyths, thong **06** cabala, kabala,

wisdom **07** beliefs, cabbala, kabbala,
legends, qabalah, sayings, stories
08 folklore, kabbalah, learning,
teaching **09** erudition, knowledge,
mythology **10** traditions
11 scholarship **13** superstitions

lorry
03 rig **04** drag **05** artic, float, truck,
wagon **06** camion, pick-up, tipper
07 flatbed, trailer, vehicle **09** dump
truck, Jugannath, semi-truck
10 juggernaut, removal van **11** dumper
truck, semi-trailer **12** curtain-sider,
double-bottom, flatbed truck,
pantechnicon, trailer truck **13** drawbar
outfit

lose
◇ *deletion indicator*
04 drop, fail, miss, tine, tyne **05** drain,
elude, evade, leese, loose, losen,
spend, use up, waste **06** expend,
forget, go down, ignore, mislay, outrun
07 confuse, consume, deplete,
exhaust, forfeit, fritter, get lost, neglect,
not find **08** be beaten, bewilder, go
astray, misplace, shake off, squander,
throw off **09** disregard, dissipate, fall
short, stray from **10** be defeated,
depart from, escape from, stop having,
wander from **11** be conquered, be
taken away, come to grief, fail to grasp,
leave behind **12** be bereaved of, be
deprived of, be divested of, come a
cropper, no longer have, suffer defeat
14 be unsuccessful **15** throw in the
towel

• **lose out**
06 suffer **07** miss out **08** be beaten
14 be unsuccessful **15** be
disadvantaged

• **lose yourself in something**
11 be riveted by **12** be absorbed in, be
occupied in **13** be engrossed in, be
taken up with **14** be captivated by, be
enthralled by, be fascinated by **15** be
preoccupied in

loser
04 flop **07** also-ran, failure, has-been,
no-hoper, washout **08** dead loss,
runner-up, write-off **10** non-starter
11 the defeated

loss
04 dead, debt, harm, hurt, miss
05 traik, waste **06** damage, defeat,
tinsel **07** default, deficit, missing,
undoing, wastage, wounded
08 casualty, decrease, deprival,
dropping, fatality **09** death toll,
detriment, disprofit, mislaying,
privation **10** deficiency, diminution,
forfeiture, forgetting, impairment
11 bereavement, deprivation,
destruction **12** disadvantage,
endamagement, misplacement
13 disappearance, dispossession

• **at a loss**
03 out **04** will, wull **07** at fault,
baffled, puzzled **09** mystified,
perplexed **10** bewildered,
nonplussed

lost
◇ *anagram indicator*
04 dead, gone, lore, lorn, past, tint
05 stray, tyned **06** astray, bygone,
cursed, damned, doomed, dreamy,
fallen, former, missed, ruined, wasted,
way-out **07** at a loss, baffled, defunct,
extinct, forlorn, mislaid, missing,
puzzled, riveted, strayed, wrecked
08 absorbed, amissing, confused,
occupied, vanished **09** condemned,
destroyed, engrossed, misplaced,
neglected, off course, perplexed
10 bewildered, captivated,
demolished, enthralled, fascinated,
nonplussed, spellbound, squandered
11 disappeared, disoriented, out of the
way, preoccupied, taken up with,
untraceable **12** absent-minded,
irredeemable **13** disorientated,
frittered away, long-forgotten,
unrecoverable **14** gone for a Burton

• **be lost**
04 tine, tyne

• **lost cause**
04 flop **07** also-ran, has-been, no-
hoper, washout **08** dead loss, write-off
10 non-starter **12** hopeless case
14 hopeless person

lot, lots
03 cut, due, erf, set, tax **04** fall, fate,
gobs, luck, many, part, plot, raft, scad,
sort, tons **05** batch, bunch, cavel,
crowd, group, heaps, loads, miles,
piece, piles, quota, scads, share, weird
06 bundle, dozens, masses, oodles,
parcel, ration, shower, stacks **07** destiny,
fortune, portion **08** heritage, hundreds,
jingbang, lashings, millions, quantity
09 a good deal, allotment, allowance, a
quantity, gathering, shedloads,
situation, sortilege, thousands **10** a
great deal, assortment, collection,
divination, percentage **11** bucketloads,
consignment, great number, large
amount, piece of land
13 circumstances, piece of ground
See also **fate**; **number**

• **a lot**
04 much, scad, slew, slue **05** loads,
often **06** barrel **09** any amount **10** a
great deal, frequently **12** for a long time
14 to a great degree, to a great extent

• **throw in your lot with**
06 muck in **07** pitch in **10** join forces,
take part in, team up with **11** combine
with **14** join forces with

lotion
04 balm, wash **05** cream, salve, scrub,
toner **06** balsam, tanner **07** eyewash,
washing **08** aftersun, cleanser, eye-
water, lavatory, liniment, ointment
09 blackwash, collyrium, emollient,
sunscreen **10** aftershave, astringent,
witch-hazel, yellow wash
11 arquebusade, embrocation,
fomentation **12** hairdressing, retinoic
acid

lottery
04 draw, luck, risk **05** bingo, lotto, Tatts
06 chance, gamble, hazard, raffle

07 tombola, venture **08** art union
10 Golden Kiwi, sweepstake
11 speculation **12** gambling game

loud
01 f **02** ff **03** big **04** bold, high
05 brash, flash, forte, gaudy, lairy, noisy, rowdy, showy **06** brassy, brazen, flashy, garish, shrill, vulgar **07** blaring, booming, glaring, raucous, roaring **08** emphatic, gorblimy, piercing, plangent, resonant, strident, vehement **09** clamorous, deafening, gorblimey, insistent, obtrusive, tasteless **10** aggressive, flamboyant, fortissimo, resounding, stentorian, streperous, strepitant, thundering, vociferous **11** ear-piercing, full-mouthed, loud-mouthed, penetrating **12** ear-splitting, ostentatious **13** reverberating
• **very loud**
02 ff

loudly
01 f **02** ff **03** out **05** aloud, forte **07** lustily, noisily, shrilly **08** strongly **10** fortissimo, stridently, vehemently, vigorously **11** clamorously, deafeningly **12** resoundingly, streperously, strepitantly, uproariously, vociferously
• **very loudly**
02 ff

loudmouth
04 brag **06** gasbag **07** boaster, windbag **08** big mouth, blowhard, braggart **09** blusterer, swaggerer **11** braggadocio

loud-mouthed
04 bold **05** noisy **06** brazen, coarse, vulgar **08** boasting, bragging **10** aggressive, blustering

loudness
• **unit of loudness**
04 phon, sone

loudspeaker
06 woofer **07** tweeter **09** subwoofer

lough *see* lake

Louisiana
02 LA

lounge
04 hawm, idle, laze, loll **05** daker, relax, slump **06** dacker, daiker, lollop, repose, sprawl **07** day room, lie back, parlour, recline **08** kill time, lie about **09** front room, lie around, loll about, waste time **10** living room, take it easy **11** drawing room, sitting room **13** reception room
See also laze

lour, lower
04 loom **05** frown, glare, scowl **06** darken, glower, impend, menace **07** blacken **08** threaten **09** be brewing, cloud over **11** look daggers **14** give a dirty look

louring, lowering
04 dark, grey, grim **05** black, gurly, heavy **06** cloudy, gloomy **07** ominous **08** menacing, overcast **09** darkening,

impending **10** forbidding, foreboding **11** threatening

louse
03 nit
See also **contemptible**

lousy
◇ *anagram indicator*
03 bad, ill, low **04** crap, poor, ropy, sick **05** awful, mingy, pants, ropey, rough, seedy **06** chatty, mouldy, no good, poorly, queasy, rotten, unwell **07** rubbish **08** below par, crawling, inferior, pathetic, terrible **09** miserable, off-colour, pedicular **10** inadequate, out of sorts, pediculous, second-rate **12** contemptible **14** unsatisfactory **15** under the weather

lout
03 bow, hob, lob, oaf, oik, yob **04** boor, calf, clod, coof, cuif, dolt, gawk, hick, hoon, jake, slob, swad **05** flout, loord, stoop, yahoo, yobbo **06** lubber **07** bumpkin, hallian, hallion, hallyon, lumpkin **08** bull-calf, loblolly **09** barbarian, roughneck **10** clodhopper **11** bushwhacker, chuckle-head, hobbledehoy

loutish
04 rude **05** crude, gawky, gruff, rough **06** coarse, oafish, rustic, vulgar **07** boorish, doltish, ill-bred, uncouth, yobbish **08** churlish, clownish, ignorant, impolite **09** unrefined **10** uneducated, unmannerly **11** clodhopping, ill-mannered, uncivilized

lovable, loveable
04 cute, dear **05** sweet **06** lovely, taking **07** amiable, likable, winsome **08** adorable, charming, engaging, fetching, likeable, pleasing **09** appealing, endearing **10** attractive, bewitching, delightful, enchanting **11** captivating

love
01 O **03** lo'e, loo, luv, nil, pet **04** amor, care, dear, doat, dote, Eros, lust, zeal, zero **05** adore, agape, amour, angel, Cupid, enjoy, fancy, honey, prize, sugar, taste **06** ardour, desire, dote on, liking, nought, poppet, regard, relish, savour, warmth **07** acushla, asthore, beloved, be mad on, care for, charity, cherish, concern, darling, dearest, dear one, delight, idolize, long for, machree, nothing, passion, rapture, sweetie, worship **08** amorance, be daft on, be fond of, be nuts on, be sold on, devotion, fondness, hold dear, intimacy, kindness, pleasure, precious, soft spot, sympathy, treasure, weakness **09** adoration, adulation, affection, be sweet on, delight in, enjoyment, favourite, Platonics, tendresse **10** appreciate, attachment, compassion, friendship, jeune amour, mavourneen, partiality, sweetheart, tenderness **11** amorousness, be

devoted to, be partial to, brotherhood, inclination, infatuation, Platonicism **12** appreciation, belle passion, Frauendienst, have a crush on, like very much **13** amour courtois, be attracted to **14** have a liking for, have the hots for, take pleasure in **15** think the world of
• **fall in love with**
05 fancy **06** take to **07** fall for **09** have it bad **12** be crazy about, have a crush on, take a shine to **13** have a thing for **15** burn with passion, lose your heart to
• **in love with**
06 doting, hooked, soft on **07** charmed, smitten, stuck on, sweet on **08** besotted, mad about, mashed on **09** enamoured, nuts about, wild about **10** crazy about, infatuated, potty about **11** attracted to, enamoured of **12** have a crush on
• **love affair**
05 amour, fling **06** affair **07** carry-on, liaison, passion, romance **08** amour fou, intrigue **12** relationship **13** grande passion
• **make love**
09 philander, sleep with **11** go to bed with, have sex with **13** sleep together

loveable *see* lovable

loveless
03 icy **04** cold, hard **06** frigid **07** unloved **08** disliked, forsaken, unloving, unvalued **09** heartless, unfeeling **10** friendless, unfriendly **11** cold-hearted, insensitive, passionless, uncherished **12** unresponsive **13** unappreciated

lovelorn
06 pining **07** longing **08** desiring, lovesick, yearning **10** infatuated **11** languishing

lovely
04 fair **05** nasty, super, sweet **06** dreamy, pretty **07** amorous, winning **08** adorable, charming, handsome, pleasant, pleasing **09** agreeable, beautiful, enjoyable, exquisite, ravishing, wonderful **10** attractive, delightful, enchanting, marvellous **11** beautifully, good-looking **12** delightfully

lover
03 fan, lad **04** beau, bird, buff, date **05** fella, fiend, flame, freak, leman **06** fiancé, friend, suitor, toy boy **07** admirer, amorist, amoroso, beloved, devotee, fanatic, fiancée, partner, servant **08** amoretto, follower, lady love, loved one, mistress, other man, paramour, Platonic **09** boyfriend, man friend, philander, supporter **10** enthusiast, girlfriend, lady friend, other woman, sweetheart **11** woman friend **12** bit on the side **13** live-in partner

Lovers include:

04 Bess, Dido, Eros, Eyre (Jane), Hera, Hero, Ilsa, Joan, Lamb (Lady Caroline), Rick, Sand (George), Zeus

05 Byron (Lord), Cathy, Clyde, Dante, Darby, Darcy (Mr), Harry, Helen, Laura, O'Hara (Scarlett), Paris, Porgy, Pwyll, Romeo, Sally,Tracy (Spencer)
06 Aeneas, Antony, Bacall (Lauren), Bogart (Humphrey), Bonnie, Burton (Richard), Butler (Rhett), Caesar, Chopin, Isolde, Juliet, Marian (Maid), Nelson (Lord), Psyche, Samson,Taylor (Elizabeth), Thisbe
07 Abelard, Barrett (Elizabeth), Bennett (Elizabeth), Delilah, Don Juan, Héloïse, Hepburn (Katharine), Leander, Louis XV, Mellors, Orlando, Orpheus, Pyramus, Rimbaud, Simpson (Mrs),Tristan, Troilus,Vronsky (Count)
08 Beatrice, Benedick, Browning (Robert), Casanova (Giacomo Girolamo), Cressida, Eurydice, Hamilton (Lady Emma), Karenina (Anna), Lancelot, Lothario, Napoleon, Nell Gwyn, Odysseus, Penelope, Petrarch, Rhiannon, Rosalind,Verlaine
09 Charles II, Cleopatra, Guinevere, Joséphine, Launcelot, Pompadour (Madame de), Robin Hood, Rochester (Mr),Valentino (Rudolph)
10 Chatterley (Lady), Edward VIII, Heathcliff

lovesick
06 pining **07** longing **08** desiring, lovelorn, yearning **10** infatuated
11 languishing

love story
07 romance

loving
04 fond, kind, warm **06** ardent, caring, doting, lovely, tender **07** adoring, amorous, devoted **08** beloving, friendly **10** passionate **11** sympathetic, warmhearted **12** affectionate

lovingly
06 fondly, warmly **08** ardently, tenderly **12** passionately
14 affectionately **15** sympathetically

low
03 bad, law, moo, sad **04** base, bass, blue, deep, down, dull, evil, flat, glum, hill, late, mean, meek, mild, poor, rich, sale, slow, soft **05** a snip, blaze, cheap, early, fed up, flame, hedge, lowly, muted, nadir, nasty, plain, quiet, scant, short, small, squat **06** a steal, bellow, bottom, coarse, common, gentle, gloomy, humble, humbly, hushed, junior, little, meagre, modest, paltry, ribald, ribaud, scanty, scarce, shabby, simple, smutty, sparse, sunken, vulgar, wicked **07** adverse, debased, foolish, heinous, hostile, immoral, low-born, muffled, obscene, obscure, peasant, reduced, rybauld, shallow, slashed, stunted, subdued, tumulus, unhappy **08** degraded, dejected, depraved, dog-cheap, downcast, indecent,

inferior, low-lying, low point, mediocre, moderate, negative, opposing, ordinary, plebeian, resonant, sea-level, sonorous, trifling **09** dastardly, deficient, depressed, dirt-cheap, knock-down, miserable, quietened, ten a penny, whispered **10** all-time low, cheesed off, despicable, despondent, inadequate, low-pitched, low-ranking, reasonable, rock-bottom, submissive
11 downhearted, ground-level, inexpensive, lowest point, low-spirited, subordinate, unimportant
12 antagonistic, contemptible, disconsolate, disheartened, insufficient, low-watermark, unfavourable **13** below standard, dishonourable, going for a song, insignificant, unintelligent **14** down in the dumps, unsatisfactory

low-born
04 poor **05** lowly **06** humble
07 obscure, peasant, plebean, villain
08 mean-born, plebeian **09** unexalted
10 low-ranking

lowbrow
04 rude **05** crude **07** tabloid
08 ignorant **09** unlearned, unrefined
10 downmarket, mass-market, uncultured, uneducated, unlettered
11 unscholarly **12** uncultivated

lowdown
03 gen **04** base, data, dope, info, mean, news, vile **05** facts **07** caitiff
08 shameful, wretched **09** dastardly, degrading, loathsome, reprobate, worthless **10** abominable, despicable, detestable, disgusting **11** disgraceful, information, inside story
12 contemptible, disreputable, intelligence **13** dishonourable, reprehensible

lower
03 cow, cut, dip **04** drop, hush, sink, vail **05** abase, abate, couch, demit, lowly, minor, slash, stoop, under
06 bottom, debase, demean, dilute, embace, embase, humble, imbase, junior, lessen, lesser, nether, reduce, settle, submit **07** beneath, cheapen, curtail, degrade, depress, descend, let down, let fall, quieten, set down
08 belittle, bring low, decrease, diminish, disgrace, inferior, look down, low-level, move down, take down
09 bring down, dishonour, disparage, secondary, undermost **10** nethermore, underneath **11** second-class, subordinate **12** speak quietly **13** move downwards
See also **lour, lower**

• **lower in estimation**
04 less

lowering
03 ebb **04** dark, drop, duck, grey, grim
05 black, gurly, heavy **06** cloudy, gloomy **07** ominous, sinking
08 menacing, overcast, reducing
09 darkening, degrading, demission,

impending, reduction **10** depression, forbidding, foreboding
11 degradation, letting down, threatening
See also **louring, lowering**

lowest
03 net **04** nett

low-grade
03 bad **04** naff, poor, poxy, ropy
05 awful, lousy, pants, ropey
06 crummy **07** botched, the pits, useless **08** inferior, pathetic, terrible
09 cheap-jack, third-rate **10** second-rate **11** a load of crap, poor-quality, second-class, substandard **13** below standard **14** a load of garbage, a load of rubbish, not up to scratch

low-key
04 soft **05** muted, quiet **06** slight, subtle **07** relaxed, subdued **09** easy-going **10** restrained, undramatic
11 understated

lowliness
07 modesty, poverty **08** humility, meekness, mildness **09** obscurity
10 commonness, simplicity
11 inferiority **12** ordinariness, unimportance **14** submissiveness
15 subordinateness

lowly
04 base, mean, meek, mild, poor
05 plain **06** common, humble, junior, modest, simple **07** low-born, obscure, peasant **08** inferior, ordinary, plebeian
10 low-ranking, submissive
11 subordinate, unimportant

low-pitched
03 low **04** bass, deep, rich
08 resonant, sonorous

low-spirited
03 low, sad **04** down, glum **05** dowie, fed up, moody **06** gloomy
07 unhappy **08** dejected, downcast
09 depressed, miserable **10** cheesed off, despondent **11** discouraged, downhearted **12** heavy-hearted
14 down in the dumps

loyal
04 feal, firm, leal, true **06** stanch, trusty
07 devoted, sincere, staunch
08 constant, faithful, reliable
09 committed, dedicated, patriotic, steadfast **10** dependable, supportive, unchanging **11** true-hearted, trustworthy **12** well-affected

loyalty
06 fealty, lealty **08** devotion, fidelity
09 constancy, sincerity **10** allegiance, commitment, dedication, patriotism
11 reliability, staunchness
12 faithfulness **13** dependability, esprit de corps, steadfastness
15 trustworthiness

lozenge
05 rhomb **06** cachou, jujube, rustre, tablet, troche **07** gumdrop, rhombus
08 pastille, trochisk **09** cough drop
10 trochiscus

LSD
04 acid
• **LSD experience**
04 trip

lubber
03 oaf, yob 04 boor, clod, dolt, gawk, hick, lout, slob, swab 05 yahoo, yobbo 07 bumpkin 09 barbarian 10 clodhopper 11 hobbledehoy

lubberly
05 crude, dense, gawky 06 clumsy, coarse, oafish 07 awkward, doltish, loutish, lumpish, uncouth 08 bungling, churlish, clownish, ungainly 09 lumbering 10 blundering 11 clodhopping, heavy-handed

lubricant
03 fat, oil 04 lard, lube 06 ben-oil, grease 07 K-Y® jelly 08 oil of ben, ointment, Vaseline® 11 lubrication 14 petroleum jelly

lubricate
03 oil, wax 04 ease, help, lard, lube 05 bribe, smear 06 assist, grease, polish, smooth 07 advance, forward, further, promote, speed up 08 expedite 09 encourage 10 accelerate, facilitate, make easier, make smooth 12 smooth the way

luce
03 ged

lucid
04 pure, sane 05 clear, plain, sober, sound 06 bright, glassy, limpid 07 beaming, evident, obvious, radiant, shining 08 distinct, explicit, gleaming, luminous, pellucid, rational, sensible 09 brilliant, effulgent 10 diaphanous, reasonable 11 clear-headed, crystalline, of sound mind, perspicuous, resplendent, translucent, transparent 12 compos mentis, intelligible 14 comprehensible

lucidity
06 sanity 07 clarity 09 plainness, soundness 11 rationality 12 compos mentis 14 reasonableness 15 clear-headedness, intelligibility

lucidly
07 clearly, plainly 09 evidently, obviously 10 explicitly 12 intelligibly 14 comprehensibly

luck
03 hap 04 fate, joss, seal, seel, seil, sele 05 break, fluke 06 chance, hazard 07 destiny, fortune, godsend, success 08 accident, fortuity, good luck, the stars 10 prosperity, providence 11 good fortune, serendipity 14 predestination
• **bad luck**
06 hoodoo, mishap, mozzle 07 ambs-ace, ames-ace 08 deuce-ace 09 hard lines, mischance 10 hard cheese, ill fortune 12 misadventure
• **bring bad luck**
03 hex 04 jinx

• **good luck**
05 sonce, sonse 06 prosit 07 wassail 08 godspeed, waes hail 09 drink hail 11 bonne chance
• **in luck**
05 happy, jammy 06 timely 08 favoured 09 fortunate, opportune 10 advantaged, auspicious, successful
• **out of luck**
07 hapless, unlucky 08 luckless 11 unfortunate 12 inauspicious, unsuccessful 13 disadvantaged 14 down on your luck

luckily
07 happily 08 by chance 10 by accident, by good luck, mercifully 11 fortunately 12 fortuitously, propitiously 14 providentially

luckless
06 cursed, doomed, jinxed 07 hapless, unhappy, unlucky 08 hopeless, ill-fated 09 miserable 10 calamitous, disastrous, ill-starred 11 fortuneless, star-crossed, unfortunate 12 catastrophic, unpropitious, unsuccessful

lucky
05 canny, happy, jammy, tinny 06 chancy, in luck, spawny, timely 07 chancey, charmed 08 favoured 09 departure, expedient, fortunate, opportune, promising 10 auspicious, fortuitous, just as well, propitious, prosperous, successful 12 providential
• **lucky chance**
03 hit

lucrative
07 gainful 08 well-paid 10 high-paying, productive, profitable, worthwhile 11 moneymaking 12 advantageous, profit-making, remunerative

lucratively
09 gainfully 10 profitably 12 productively 14 advantageously, remuneratively

lucre
03 pay 04 cash, dosh, gain 05 brass, bread, dough, dross, gains, lolly, money, ready 06 income, mammon, profit, riches, spoils, wealth 07 profits, readies 08 greenies, proceeds, winnings 11 spondulicks 12 remuneration

ludicrous
◊ anagram indicator
03 odd 04 zany 05 comic, crazy, droll, funny, silly 06 absurd 07 amusing, comical, risible 08 farcical, humorous, sportive 09 burlesque, eccentric, grotesque, hilarious, laughable 10 outlandish, ridiculous 11 nonsensical 12 preposterous
• **something ludicrous**
04 jest

ludicrously
08 absurdly 09 laughably 11 grotesquely, hilariously

12 outlandishly, ridiculously 13 nonsensically 14 preposterously

lug
03 ear, tow, tug 04 bear, drag, haul, hump, lift, loop, pole, pull, tote 05 carry, heave, stick 06 handle

luggage
04 gear 05 stuff, traps 06 things 07 baggage, clobber 10 belongings 11 impedimenta 13 paraphernalia

Luggage includes:
03 bag, box
04 case, grip
05 chest, trunk
06 basket, hamper, kitbag, valise
07 holdall, satchel
08 backpack, knapsack, rucksack, suitcase
09 briefcase, flight bag, haversack, portfolio, travel bag
10 vanity-case
11 attaché case, hand-luggage, portmanteau
12 Gladstone bag, overnight bag

lugubrious
03 sad 04 glum 06 dismal, dreary, gloomy, morose, sombre, woeful 07 baleful, doleful, serious 08 funereal, mournful 09 sorrowful, woebegone 10 lachrymose, melancholy, sepulchral

lugworm
03 lob 07 lobworm

lukewarm
03 lew 04 cool 05 tepid 07 coolish, warmish 09 apathetic, impassive, Laodicean 11 half-hearted, indifferent, unconcerned 12 slightly warm, uninterested, unresponsive 14 unenthusiastic

lull
04 calm, ease, hush 05 abate, allay, let-up, pause, peace, quell, quiet, still 06 pacify, soothe, sopite, subdue 07 assuage, compose, silence, subside 08 calmness 09 stillness 11 quieten down 12 tranquillity

lullaby
05 baloo 07 hushaby 08 berceuse 10 cradle song

lumber
04 junk, land, load, pawn, plod, wood 05 clump, stamp, stump, trash 06 burden, charge, hamper, impose, jumble, prison, raffle, refuse, rumble, saddle, timber, trudge 07 clutter, rubbish, shamble, shuffle, stumble, trundle 08 encumber, imprison, pawnshop 10 flirtation 11 odds and ends 13 bits and pieces

lumbering
05 heavy 06 bovine, clumsy 07 awkward, hulking, lumpish, massive 08 bumbling, ungainly, unwieldy 09 ponderous 10 blundering 11 elephantine, heavy-footed

lumen
02 lm, lu

luminary
03 VIP 04 star 05 celeb 06 bigwig, candle, expert, leader, worthy 07 big name, notable 09 authority, celebrity, dignitary, personage, superstar 12 leading light

luminence
01 L
• **amount of luminence**
03 nit

luminescent
06 bright 07 glowing, radiant, shining 08 luminous 09 effulgent 10 luciferous 11 fluorescent 14 phosphorescent

luminosity
04 glow 05 light 06 lustre 08 radiance 10 brightness, brilliance 12 fluorescence, illumination

luminous
03 lit 05 clear, lucid 06 bright 07 glowing, lighted, radiant, shining 08 dazzling, lustrous 09 brilliant, effulgent 11 fluorescent, illuminated, illustrious, luminescent

lump
03 bur, cob, dab, dad, dod, gob, lob, nub, nut, pat, wad 04 ball, bear, bees, bump, burr, cake, clat, clod, core, daud, dawd, fuse, hunk, knob, knot, knub, loaf, mass, nirl, node, pool, rock, slub, slug, take 05 blend, block, bolus, brook, bulge, bunch, chuck, chump, chunk, claut, clump, crowd, gnarl, group, hunch, knarl, lunch, piece, plook, plouk, slump, stand, thole, tuber, unite, wedge, wodge 06 bruise, bunion, dallop, dollop, endure, gather, gobbet, growth, nodule, nubble, nugget, suffer, tumour 07 cluster, collect, combine, dislike, knubble, pustule, stomach, swallow 08 bear with, coalesce, swelling, tolerate 09 carbuncle, put up with 10 concretion, protrusion, tumescence 11 consolidate, mix together, put together 12 conglomerate, protuberance

lumpish
04 dull 05 gawky, gross, heavy 06 clumsy, oafish, obtuse, stolid, stupid, sullen 07 awkward, boorish, doltish, hulking 08 bungling, ungainly 09 lethargic, lumbering 10 dull-witted 11 elephantine

lumpy
04 slub 05 bumpy 06 cloggy, grainy, nodose, nodous 07 bunched, clotted, curdled, grumose, grumous, knobbly 08 granular 09 congealed 10 coagulated

Luna
06 Selene

lunacy
05 folly, mania 06 idiocy 07 inanity, madness 08 dementia, insanity, nonsense 09 absurdity, craziness, silliness, stupidity 10 aberration, imbecility 11 derangement, foolishness, moon-madness 12 dementedness, illogicality 13 irrationality, senselessness 14 outrageousness, ridiculousness
• **fit of lunacy**
04 lune

lunar see **Moon**

lunatic
◊ anagram indicator
03 mad 04 daft, nuts 05 barmy, crazy, inane, loony, loopy, nutty, potty, silly 06 absurd, insane, madman, maniac, nutter, psycho, stupid 07 bonkers, foolish, idiotic, nutcase, oddball 08 crackpot, demented, deranged, headcase, imbecile, madwoman, neurotic 09 disturbed, fruitcake, illogical, psychotic, senseless 10 irrational, moonstruck, psychopath, unbalanced 11 hare-brained, nonsensical 12 insane person, moon-stricken, round the bend 13 off your rocker, round the twist

lunch
04 tiff, tift 05 piece, snack 06 brunch, dinner, nacket, nocket, tiffin 07 tiffing 08 luncheon, nuncheon 10 light lunch, midday meal 11 packed lunch, Sunday lunch
• **out to lunch**
◊ anagram indicator
05 crazy

lunge
03 cut, hit, jab 04 dart, dash, dive, grab, leap, pass, poke, stab 05 bound, hit at 06 charge, grab at, plunge, pounce, spring, strike, thrust 08 fall upon, strike at 09 pitch into

lungs
• **goose lungs**
04 soul

lurch
04 list, reel, rock, roll, sway, swee, swey, veer, wait 05 filch, pitch, stoit 06 ambush, swerve, totter 07 defraud, stagger, stumble 09 forestall, overreach 11 weather roll 12 discomfiture
• **leave in the lurch**
04 fail 06 desert 07 abandon, let down 10 disappoint 13 leave stranded 15 leave high and dry

lure
03 jig 04 bait, draw, tole, toll 05 decoy, Devon, squid, stale, stool, tempt, train, troll 06 allure, carrot, entice, induce, lead on, seduce, trepan 07 attract, beguile, ensnare 08 inveigle 09 decoy-duck, honey-trap, seduction, spoonbait, spoonhook 10 allurement, attraction, enticement, inducement, temptation, trout-spoon 11 Devon minnow 12 trolling-bait 13 trolling-spoon 14 take a rise out of

lurid
04 gory, loud 05 showy, vivid 06 garish, Gothic, grisly, sultry 07 ghastly, glaring, graphic, intense, macabre 08 dazzling, explicit, gruesome, horrific, shocking 09 brilliant, brimstony, revolting, startling 11 exaggerated, sensational 12 melodramatic

luridly
07 vividly 08 garishly 09 intensely 10 explicitly, gruesomely, shockingly 11 brilliantly, graphically, revoltingly

lurk
04 dare, hide 05 dodge, prowl, skulk, slink, sneak, snoke, snook, snoop, snowk 06 crouch, lie low, loiter 07 swindle 09 lie in wait 15 conceal yourself

luscious
04 sexy 05 juicy, sweet, tasty, yummy 06 morish 07 cloying, fulsome, moreish, savoury 08 gorgeous, sensuous, smashing, stunning 09 beautiful, delicious, desirable, ravishing, succulent 10 appetizing, attractive, delectable, delightful, voluptuous 11 pleasurable, scrumptious 13 mouthwatering

lush
03 sot 04 posh, rich, soak, wino 05 alkie, dense, dipso, drink, drunk, grand, green, plush, ritzy, souse, toper 06 boozer, classy, glitzy, lavish, ornate, sponge, swanky 07 alcohol, bloater, drinker, fuddler, opulent, profuse, shicker, teeming, tippler, tosspot, verdant 08 abundant, drunkard, habitual, palatial, prolific 09 alcoholic, inebriate, luxuriant, luxurious, overgrown, sumptuous 10 wine-bibber 11 dipsomaniac, extravagant, flourishing, hard drinker 12 heavy drinker

lust
04 lech, will 05 greed 06 desire, hunger, libido, relish 07 avidity, craving, lechery, longing, passion, the hots 08 appetite, cupidity, lewdness, pleasure, yearning 09 horniness, prurience, randiness 10 greediness, sensuality 11 raunchiness, sexual drive 12 covetousness, sexual desire 13 concupiscence 14 lasciviousness, licentiousness
• **lust after**
04 need, want 05 covet, crave 06 desire, lecher, slaver 07 long for 08 yearn for 09 hunger for, thirst for

lustful
03 hot 04 lewd, rank 05 horny, radge, randy 06 carnal, randie, wanton 07 craving, goatish, rammish, raunchy, ruttish, sensual 08 prurient, unchaste 09 hankering, lecherous, lickerish, luxurious, salacious, venereous 10 cupidinous, lascivious, libidinous, licentious, passionate 12 concupiscent

lustily
04 hard 06 loudly 07 stoutly 08 heartily, robustly, strongly 10 forcefully, powerfully, vigorously

lustiness
05 power **06** energy, health, vigour
08 haleness, strength, virility
09 hardiness, stoutness, toughness
10 robustness, sturdiness
11 healthiness

lustre
04 fame, gaum, glow, gorm, silk
05 glare, gleam, glint, glory, gloss,
merit, sheen, shine, water **06** credit,
honour, renown **07** burnish, glitter,
shimmer, sparkle, varnish
08 lambency, prestige, radiance,
schiller **09** lovelight, splendour
10 brightness, brilliance, refulgence
11 distinction **12** resplendence
15 illustriousness

lustreless
03 mat **04** matt **05** matte

lustrous
05 glacé, shiny **06** bright, glossy,
sheeny **07** glowing, lambent, radiant,
shining **08** dazzling, gleaming,
luminous **09** brilliant, burnished,
sparkling, twinkling **10** glistening,
glittering, shimmering

lusty
03 fit **04** hale, rank **05** beefy, bulky,
frack, gutsy, stout, tough **06** hearty,
lively, robust, rugged, strong, sturdy,
virile **07** healthy, lustick **08** blooming,
forceful, lustique, pleasant, pleasing,
powerful, skelping, vigorous
09 energetic, strapping **13** hale and
hearty

lute
03 oud **04** pipa **06** cither **07** bandura,
cithern, cittern, dichord, pandora,
pandore, theorbo **08** archlute,
polyphon **09** orpharion, polyphone
10 chitarrone

lutetium
02 Lu

Luxembourg
01 L **03** LUX

luxuriance
06 excess **08** lushness, rankness,
richness **09** abundance, denseness,
fecundity, fertility, profusion
10 exuberance, exuberancy,
lavishness, overgrowth **11** copiousness
13 sumptuousness

luxuriant
04 lush, rank, rich **05** ample, dense,
fancy **06** fecund, florid, lavish, ornate,
rococo **07** baroque, copious, fertile,
flowery, opulent, profuse, riotous,
teeming **08** abundant, prolific,
thriving, tropical **09** elaborate,
excessive, exuberant, plenteous,
plentiful, sumptuous **10** flamboyant,
productive **11** extravagant,
overflowing **12** overabundant
13 superabundant

luxuriate
04 bask, grow **05** bloom, enjoy, revel
06 abound, frowst, relish, savour,
thrive, wallow **07** burgeon, delight,
indulge, prosper, relax in **08** flourish
09 have a ball **12** live in clover

luxurious
04 high, lush, posh, rich **05** cushy,
grand, plush, ritzy **06** costly, de luxe,
glitzy, lavish, plushy, silken, swanky
07 Apician, elegant, lustful, opulent
08 affluent, delicate, feastful,
pampered, splendid **09** expensive,
sumptuous **10** Babylonian, mollitious
11 comfortable, magnificent **13** self-
indulgent, well-appointed

luxuriously
04 high **06** poshly **07** plushly
08 glitzily, lavishly, swankily
09 opulently **10** affluently
11 comfortably, deliciously,
sumptuously **13** magnificently

luxury
03 pie **04** luxe, Ritz **05** extra, treat
06 dainty **07** comfort **08** delicacy,
delicate, grandeur, hedonism,
opulence, pleasure, richness
09 affluence, grand luxe, grandness,
splendour **10** costliness, indulgence,
wantonness **11** lap of luxury
12 extravagance, magnificence, milk
and honey, satisfaction
13 expensiveness, gratification,
sumptuousness **14** self-indulgence

lying
05 false **06** deceit **07** crooked, falsity,
fibbing, leasing, perjury **08** two-faced
09 deceitful, dishonest, duplicity,
falsehood, invention, white lies
10 dishonesty, mendacious, untruthful
11 crookedness, dissembling,
fabrication, pseudologia
13 dissimulating, double-dealing,
falsification **14** untruthfulness

lynch
04 hang, kill **06** dewitt **07** execute
08 string up **10** put to death **13** hang
by the neck

lyre string
04 mese, nete **05** trite **06** hypate

lyric
03 lay, ode **04** lied, pean, song
05 melic, paean **06** poetic
07 melodic, musical **08** personal
09 emotional **10** passionate,
subjective

lyrical
04 odic **06** poetic **07** musical
08 ecstatic, effusive, inspired, romantic
09 emotional, rapturous, rhapsodic
10 expressive, passionate **11** carried
away, impassioned **12** enthusiastic

lyrically
09 musically **10** effusively, poetically
11 emotionally, rapturously
12 ecstatically, expressively,
passionately, romantically

lyricist *see* **songwriter**

lyrics
04 book, text **05** words **08** libretto

M

M
02 em **04** Emma, Mike

macabre
◇ *anagram indicator*
04 gory, grim, sick **05** eerie, sicko
06 Gothic, grisly, morbid **07** ghastly,
ghostly, hideous **08** chilling, dreadful,
gruesome, horrible, horrific, shocking
09 frightful **10** terrifying **11** frightening

Macao
03 MAC

macaroni
04 zite, ziti **05** dandy **06** medley
10 rockhopper

mace
03 rod **04** club, maul **05** poker, staff,
stick **06** cudgel

mace-bearer
05 bedel **06** beadle

Macedonia
02 MK **03** MKD

macerate
04 mash, pulp, soak **05** blend, steep
06 soften, squash **07** liquefy, mortify
08 marinade

Machiavellian
03 sly **04** foxy, wily **06** artful, astute,
crafty, shrewd **07** cunning, devious
08 guileful, scheming **09** deceitful,
designing, underhand **10** intriguing,
perfidious **11** calculating, opportunist
12 unscrupulous **13** double-dealing

machination
04 plot, ploy, ruse, wile **05** cabal,
dodge, trick **06** design, device,
scheme, tactic **08** artifice, intrigue
09 manoeuvre, stratagem
10 conspiracy **11** shenanigans

machine
04 tool **05** motor, organ, robot
06 agency, device, engine, gadget,
system, zombie **07** android, vehicle
08 catalyst, hardware, workings
09 apparatus, appliance, automaton,
influence, mechanism, structure
10 instrument **11** contraption,
contrivance **12** organization

machine-gun
02 MG **04** Bren **05** Maxim **07** Bren
gun **08** Lewis gun, Maxim-gun
12 mitrailleuse

machinery
04 gear **05** tools **06** agency, system,
tackle **07** channel **08** channels,
gadgetry, workings **09** apparatus,

equipment, mechanism, procedure,
structure **11** instruments
12 organization

Machinery includes:

03 Cat®, JCB®
05 crane, dozer
06 digger, dumper, grader, jigger
07 dredger, grapple, gritter, skidder,
tractor
08 dragline, dustcart, fork lift, jib crane
09 bulldozer, calfdozer, dump truck,
excavator
10 angledozer, earthmover, pile-
driver, road roller, snowplough,
tower crane, tracklayer, truck crane,
water crane
11 Caterpillar®, dumper truck, gantry
crane, road-sweeper, wheel loader
12 cherry picker, crawler crane, luffing
crane, pick-up loader
13 concrete mixer, floating crane, fork-
lift truck, grabbing crane, platform
hoist
14 container crane, crawler tractor,
tractor-scraper
15 hydraulic shovel, luffing-jib crane,
walking dragline

machinist
06 worker **08** mechanic, operator
09 operative **11** factory hand

machismo
08 maleness, strength, virility
09 manliness, toughness
11 masculinity

macrocosm
05 world **06** cosmos, entity, planet,
system **07** culture, society **08** creation,
humanity, totality, universe
09 community, structure **11** solar
system **12** civilization, single entity

mad
◇ *anagram indicator*
03 ape, fay, fey, fie, wud **04** avid, bats,
daft, fond, gyte, keen, loco, nuts, wild,
wood, wowf, yond **05** angry, barmy,
batty, berko, buggy, crazy, cross, daffy,
dippy, dotty, flaky, gonzo, hasty, irate,
livid, loony, loopy, manic, nutty, potty,
queer, rabid, rapid, ratty, silly, spewy,
wacko, wacky, wiggy **06** absurd,
ardent, choked, crazed, cuckoo, fruity,
fuming, insane, locoed, maniac,
mental, raging, raving, red-mad, red-
wud, screwy, stupid, troppo, whacko
07 bananas, barking, berserk, blazing,
bonkers, cracked, crooked, devoted,
enraged, excited, flipped, foolish,
frantic, furious, hurried, idiotic, intense,

lunatic, meshuga, red-wood, ropable,
stroppy, uptight, violent, zealous
08 burned up, choleric, crackers,
crackpot, demented, deranged,
dingbats, doolally, frenetic, frenzied,
hairless, in a paddy, in a strop, incensed,
maniacal, meshugga, meshugge,
reckless, unhinged, unstable, up in
arms **09** abandoned, disturbed,
energetic, fanatical, foolhardy, illogical,
in a lather, infuriate, ludicrous,
lymphatic, psychotic, raving mad,
seeing red, ticked off, up the wall
10 aggravated, bestraught, distracted,
distraught, frantic-mad, hopping mad,
infatuated, infuriated, irrational, off the
wall, off your nut, out to lunch,
passionate, stone-crazy, unbalanced
11 disgruntled, fit to be tied, hare-
brained, nonsensical, not all there, off
the rails, off your head
12 crackbrained, enthusiastic, mad as a
hatter, off your chump, on the warpath,
preposterous, round the bend,
uncontrolled, unreasonable,
unrestrained **13** off your rocker, of
unsound mind, out of your head, out of
your mind, out of your tree, round the
twist **14** off your trolley, wrong in the
head **15** non compos mentis, out of
your senses
• **go mad**
04 flip **05** go ape **06** blow up, wig out
07 go crazy **09** go bananas **11** flip
your lid, go ballistic **15** lose your
marbles
• **like mad**
06 avidly, wildly **07** quickly
09 furiously, hurriedly, zealously
11 fanatically, frantically
13 energetically

Madagascar
02 RM **03** MDG

madcap
04 cake, fury, rash, wild **05** crazy, silly
06 lively **07** flighty, hothead
08 crackpot, heedless, reckless,
tearaway **09** daredevil, desperado,
eccentric, firebrand, foolhardy,
hotheaded, imprudent, impulsive
10 adventurer, ill-advised
11 birdbrained, hare-brained,
thoughtless

madden
◇ *anagram indicator*
03 bug, irk, vex **05** anger, annoy,
bemad, upset **06** enrage, hassle
07 agitate, incense, inflame, provoke
08 distract, irritate **09** aggravate, drive

nuts, infuriate **10** drive crazy, exasperate **13** get on your wick, get up your nose, get your back up **14** drive up the wall **15** get on your nerves, get your dander up

maddening
◇ *anagram indicator*
07 galling **08** annoying **09** upsetting, vexatious **10** disturbing, irritating **11** aggravating, infuriating, troublesome **12** exasperating

madder
04 chay **05** chaya, Rubia, shaya **07** alizari **08** gardenia **10** buttonbush

made
• **made it**
02 ff
• **recently made**
03 new

made-up
◇ *anagram indicator*
05 false **06** done up, unreal, untrue **07** painted **08** invented, mythical, powdered, specious **09** fairytale, fictional, imaginary, trumped-up **10** fabricated **11** make-believe **13** wearing make-up

madhouse
05 Babel, chaos **06** asylum, bedlam, mayhem, uproar **07** turmoil **08** disarray, disorder, loony bin, nuthouse **09** funny farm **11** pandemonium **13** lunatic asylum **14** mental hospital

madly
◇ *anagram indicator*
04 fast, very **06** wildly **07** crazily, hastily, rapidly, utterly **08** insanely **09** devotedly, excitedly, extremely, fervently, furiously, hurriedly, intensely, violently **10** completely, dementedly, frenziedly, recklessly **11** deliriously, exceedingly, frantically **12** distractedly, hysterically, irrationally, unreasonably **13** energetically, exceptionally

madman, madwoman
03 nut **04** gelt, kook **05** crank, loony **06** bedlam, maniac, nutter, psycho **07** cupcake, furioso, lunatic, nutcase, oddball **08** crackpot, frenetic, headcase, imbecile **09** bedlamite, fruitcake, psychotic, screwball **10** basket case, psychopath, Tom o' Bedlam

madness
◇ *anagram indicator*
03 ire **04** fury, rage, riot, zeal **05** anger, craze, folie, folly, mania, wrath **06** ardour, frenzy, lunacy, raving, uproar **07** abandon, inanity, passion **08** daftness, delusion, dementia, hysteria, insanity, keenness, nonsense, wildness **09** absurdity, agitation, craziness, furiosity, meshugaas, mishegaas, psychosis, silliness, stupidity, theomania **10** deliration, enthusiasm, excitement, fanaticism, insaneness **11** derangement, distraction, foolishness, infatuation,

lycanthropy, unrestraint **12** exasperation, intoxication **13** foolhardiness, irrationality

madrigal
04 fa-la

madwoman *see* **madman, madwoman**

Mae
04 West

maelstrom
04 mess **05** chaos **06** bedlam, tumult, uproar, vortex **07** turmoil **08** disorder **09** Charybdis, confusion, whirlpool **10** turbulence **11** pandemonium

maestro
03 ace **06** expert, genius, master, wizard **07** prodigy **08** director, virtuoso **09** conductor

Mafia
06 the Mob **10** Cosa Nostra
• **Mafia boss**
03 don **04** capo **09** godfather
• **Mafia code**
06 omertà
• **Mafia member**
07 made man, pentito, soldier **09** goodfella

magazine
03 mag **04** pulp, zine **05** comic, depot, e-zine, paper, slick **06** glossy, lad mag, weekly **07** arsenal, fanzine, journal, monthly **08** carousel, ordnance **09** carousel, quarterly **10** periodical, powder room, repository, storehouse, supplement **11** fortnightly, publication **12** contemporary **14** ammunition dump

See also **newspaper**

maggot
03 bot, fad **04** bott, mawk, whim, worm **06** gentle **09** fleshworm

Magi *see* **wise man** *under* **wise**

magic
03 ace, art **04** cool, mega, mojo, pull **05** brill, charm, curse, goety, great, spell, wicca **06** allure, hoodoo, occult, voodoo, wicked, wonder **07** conjury, demonic, glamour, gramary, mystery, sorcery **08** black art, charming, diablery, gramarye, hermetic, illusion, magnetic, prestige, romantic, smashing, spellful, stardust, terrific, trickery, wizardry **09** conjuring, deception, diablerie, excellent, magnetism, occultism, wonderful **10** allurement, bewitching, black magic, enchanting, enticement, entrancing, marvellous, mysterious, necromancy, tremendous, witchcraft **11** captivating, enchantment, fascinating, fascination, incantation, legerdemain, thaumaturgy **12** irresistible, metaphysical, spellbinding, supernatural **13** magical powers, sleight of hand, wonder-working

magical
05 magic **06** occult **07** demonic **08** charming, hermetic, spellful, stardust **09** wonderful **10** enchanting, hermetical, marvellous, mysterious **11** captivating, fascinating **12** spellbinding, supernatural

magician
03 ace **05** magus, pawaw, witch **06** expert, genius, master, powwow, wizard **07** juggler, maestro, warlock, wise man **08** conjurer, conjuror, sorcerer, virtuoso **09** archimage, enchanter **11** enchantress, illusionist, necromancer, spellbinder, spellworker, thaumaturge, witch doctor **12** wonder-worker **13** miracle-worker

magisterial
05 bossy **06** lordly **08** arrogant, despotic **09** assertive, imperious, masterful **10** commanding, high-handed, peremptory **11** dictatorial, domineering, overbearing **13** authoritarian, authoritative

magistrate
02 JP, RM **04** beak, cadi, doge, foud, kadi, qadi **05** amman, edile, judge, jurat, mayor, prior, reeve **06** aedile, amtman, avoyer, bailie, bailli, censor, cotwal, kotwal, pretor, sharif, sherif, syndic **07** alcalde, bailiff, baillie, burgess, justice, podestà, praetor, prefect, provost, shereef, tribune **08** dictator, landdros, mittimus, praefect, quaestor **09** landamman, landdrost, Lord Mayor, novus homo, portreeve, proconsul **10** corregidor, landammann, propraetor **11** baron bailie, burgomaster, field cornet, gonfalonier, stipendiary

magnanimity
05 mercy **07** charity **08** altruism, kindness, largesse, nobility **10** generosity, liberality **11** beneficence, benevolence, munificence **12** generousness, philanthropy, selflessness **13** bountifulness, unselfishness **14** big-heartedness, charitableness, high-mindedness, open-handedness

magnanimous
03 big **04** kind **05** large, noble **06** kindly **07** liberal **08** generous, merciful, selfless **09** bountiful, forgiving, unselfish **10** altruistic, beneficent, benevolent, big-hearted, charitable, munificent, open-handed, ungrudging **11** large-minded **12** great-hearted **13** philanthropic

magnate
05 baron, mogul, noble **06** bigwig, fat cat, leader, tycoon **07** big shot, notable **08** big noise, big timer **09** big cheese, executive, financier, moneybags, personage, plutocrat **12** entrepreneur **13** industrialist

See also **newspaper**

magnesium
02 Mg

magnet
04 bait, draw, lure 05 charm, focus
06 appeal, needle 08 solenoid
09 loadstone, lodestone
10 allurement, attraction, enticement, focal point

magnetic
03 mag 08 alluring, charming, engaging, gripping, hypnotic, tempting 09 absorbing, appealing, seductive 10 attractive, bewitching, enchanting, entrancing 11 captivating, charismatic, enthralling, fascinating, mesmerizing, tantalizing
12 irresistible

magnetism
02 it 03 mag 04 draw, grip, lure, pull 05 charm, magic, oomph, power, spell 06 allure, appeal, duende, glamor 07 glamour 08 charisma
09 hypnotism, mesmerism
10 attraction, temptation
11 captivation, enchantment, fascination 12 drawing power
13 seductiveness

magnification
05 boost 07 build-up 08 dilation, increase 09 deepening, expansion, extolling, extolment, hyperbole, inflation, overdoing 10 embroidery
11 enhancement, enlargement, heightening, lionization
12 augmentation, exaggeration, overemphasis 13 amplification, dramatization, embellishment, overstatement 14 aggrandizement
15 intensification

magnificence
04 pomp 05 glory, pride 06 luxury 07 majesty 08 grandeur, nobility, opulence, splendor 09 splendour, sublimity 10 brilliance, excellence, lavishness 11 stateliness
12 gorgeousness, resplendence
13 luxuriousness, sumptuousness
14 impressiveness

magnificent
04 fine, rich 05 grand, noble, royal, state 06 august, lavish, lordly, superb 07 elegant, exalted, gallant, opulent, stately, sublime 08 dazzling, glorious, gorgeous, imposing, majestic, princely, splendid, striking 09 brilliant, excellent, grandiose, luxurious, splendent, sumptuous, wonderful
10 impressive, marvellous
11 resplendent

magnify
05 boost 06 blow up, deepen, dilate, expand, extend, overdo 07 amplify, broaden, build up, enhance, enlarge, greaten, signify 08 heighten, increase, multiply, overplay 09 dramatize, embellish, embroider, intensify, overstate 10 exaggerate 13 overemphasize

magniloquence
07 bombast, fustian 08 euphuism,

rhetoric 09 loftiness, pomposity, turgidity 10 orotundity
14 grandiloquence 15 pretentiousness

magniloquent
05 lofty 06 turgid 07 exalted, fustian, orotund, pompous, stilted 08 elevated, sonorous 09 bombastic, high-flown, overblown 10 euphuistic, rhetorical
11 declamatory, pretentious 12 high-sounding 13 grandiloquent

magnitude
03 mag 04 bulk, fame, mass, note, size 05 space 06 amount, extent, import, moment, volume, weight 07 expanse, measure 08 capacity, eminence, muchness, quantity, strength
09 amplitude, greatness, intensity, largeness 10 dimensions, importance
11 consequence, distinction, proportions 12 significance
13 absolute value

magnolia
03 bay 05 yulan 07 champac, champak 08 sweet bay 09 star anise, tulip tree 10 beaver-tree, beaver-wood 12 cucumber tree, umbrella tree

magnum opus
10 masterwork 11 chef d'oeuvre, masterpiece

magpie
03 mag, pie 04 Pica, piet, pyat, pyet, pyot 05 madge 06 maggie 09 organ-bird 10 piping crow

mahogany
04 toon 05 carap, khaya 06 acajou 07 Cedrela 10 chinaberry
14 chittagong wood

maid
03 may 04 ayah, girl, lass 05 bonne, daily, wench 06 au pair, maiden, Mrs Mop, skivvy, slavey, tweeny, virgin 07 abigail, dresser, Mrs Mopp, pucelle, servant 08 bonibell, charlady, domestic, home help, spinster, suivante, tabby cat, waitress
09 bonnibell, charwoman, housemaid, lady's maid, soubrette, tire-woman
10 bowerwoman, Cinderella, handmaiden 11 chambermaid, kitchenmaid, maidservant, serving-maid 12 cleaning lady, kitchen-wench 13 maid-of-all-work 14 femme de chambre

maiden
01 M 03 new 04 burd, girl, kore, lass, miss, pure, wili 05 first, nymph, popsy, unwed 06 chaste, damsel, decent, demure, female, gentle, lassie, modest, proper, seemly, vestal, virgin 07 girlish, initial 08 celibate, decorous, reserved, virginal, virtuous 09 inaugural, undefiled, unmarried, unsullied, young girl, young lady 10 initiatory, unbroached, young woman
12 bachelorette, introductory

maidenhood
06 honour, purity, virtue 08 chastity
10 chasteness, maidenhead

maidenly
04 pure 05 unwed 06 chaste, decent, demure, female, gentle, modest, proper, seemly, vestal, virgin 07 girlish 08 becoming, decorous, reserved, virginal, virtuous 09 undefiled, unmarried, unsullied 10 immaculate, unbroached

maidservant
03 may 04 amah, girl, maid 05 daily 06 au pair, maiden, skivvy, slavey 07 abigail, dresser, Mrs Mopp, pucelle, servant 08 charlady, domestic, suivante, waitress 09 bonnibell, charwoman, housemaid, lady's maid, soubrette 10 bowerwoman, handmaiden 11 chambermaid, kitchenmaid, parlour-maid, serving-maid 13 maid-of-all-work

mail
03 dak 04 dawk, post, rent, send, spam, spot 05 armor, e-mail
06 armour 07 airmail, fan mail, forward, junk fax, letters, packets, panoply, parcels, payment 08 delivery, dispatch, hate mail, junk mail, packages 09 chain mail, habergeon, halfpenny, snail mail 10 cataphract, direct mail, Post Office 11 chain armour, general post, surface mail 12 all-up service, iron-cladding, postal system, recorded mail 13 postal service
14 communications, correspondence, electronic mail, first-class mail, registered mail 15 second-class mail, special delivery
• **Royal Mail**
02 RM

mail-coach
04 drag

maim
03 mar 04 hurt, lame, main 05 wound 06 impair, injure, injury, scotch
07 cripple, cut down, disable
08 crippled, mutilate, truncate
09 disfigure 10 disability
12 incapacitate 14 put out of action

main
03 key, sea 04 duct, head, lame, lead, line, maim, pipe 05 cable, chief, first, grand, great, major, prime, sheer, vital 06 staple, strong 07 capital, central, channel, conduit, crucial, general, leading, pivotal, premier, primary, purpose, supreme 08 cardinal, critical, dominant, foremost, strength 09 essential, extensive, important, necessary, paramount, principal 10 pre-eminent
11 exceedingly, fundamental, outstanding, predominant 13 most important
• **in the main**
06 mostly 07 as a rule, chiefly, largely, usually 08 commonly 09 generally, in general 10 by and large, especially, on the whole 14 for the most part

Maine
02 ME

mainly

04 much **06** mostly **07** as a rule, chiefly, largely, overall, usually **08** above all, commonly **09** generally, in general, in the main, primarily **10** by and large, especially, on the whole **11** principally **13** predominantly **14** for the most part

mainspring

05 cause **06** motive, origin, reason, source **07** impulse **09** generator, incentive **10** motivation, prime mover, wellspring **11** inspiration **12** driving force, fountainhead

mainstay

04 base, prop **05** basis **06** anchor, pillar **07** bulwark, support **08** backbone, buttress, linchpin **09** key player **10** foundation **11** cornerstone **12** right-hand man **14** right-hand woman **15** tower of strength

mainstream

06 normal **07** average, central, general, regular, typical **08** accepted, mainline, orthodox, received, standard **11** established **12** conventional

maintain

04 aver, avow, feed, hold, keep **05** carry, claim, escot, state **06** affirm, assert, avouch, defend, insist, keep up, retain, supply, uphaud, uphold **07** believe, care for, carry on, contend, declare, finance, nourish, nurture, observe, possess, profess, stand by, support, sustain **08** announce, conserve, continue, fight for, practise, preserve **09** keep going, look after **10** asseverate, perpetuate, provide for, take care of

maintenance

04 care, keep **05** title **06** living, upkeep **07** aliment, alimony, defence, feeding, keeping, nurture, repairs, running, support **08** altarage, appanage **09** allowance, financing **10** carrying-on, livelihood, protection, sustenance **11** continuance, nourishment, subsistence, traineeship **12** conservation, continuation, perpetuation, preservation

maize

03 Zea **04** corn, maze, samp **05** maise, mealy, mease, stamp **06** hominy, mealie **07** mealies, popcorn **09** flint corn, sweetcorn **10** Indian corn, Indian meal, masa harina **12** corn on the cob

- **maize dough**
  04 masa
- **maize loaf**
  04 pone
- **styles of maize**
  04 silk

majestic

05 grand, lofty, noble, regal, royal **06** august, kingly, lordly, superb **07** awesome, exalted, pompous, queenly, stately, sublime **08** elevated, glorious, imperial, imposing, princely, splendid **09** dignified **10** impressive, marvellous, monumental **11** magnificent, resplendent **13** distinguished

majestically

05 nobly **07** grandly, regally, royally, stately **08** maestoso, superbly **09** pompously, sublimely **10** gloriously, imperially, splendidly **12** impressively, marvellously **13** magnificently, resplendently

majesty

04 pomp **05** glory **06** beauty, Tuanku **07** dignity, royalty **08** grandeur, nobility, regality **09** grandness, loftiness, nobleness, splendour, sublimity **11** awesomeness, exaltedness, stateliness **12** magnificence, majesticness, resplendence **14** impressiveness, majesticalness

- **Her Majesty**
  02 ER, HM **06** Brenda
- **His Majesty**
  02 HM

major

03 key, Maj **04** best, main **05** chief, great, older, prime, vital **06** bigger, higher, larger, senior **07** crucial, greater, highest, keynote, largest, leading, notable, serious, supreme, weighty **08** greatest, superior **09** important, paramount, uppermost **10** pre-eminent **11** outstanding, significant

majority

04 bulk, many, mass, most **07** general, manhood, the many **08** legal age, maturity **09** adulthood, nearly all, plurality, womanhood **10** generality, larger part, lion's share **11** coming of age, greater part, pre-eminence **12** age of consent, larger number, more than half **13** greater number, preponderance **15** reaching full age

make

◇ *anagram indicator*

02 do **03** fix, get, mag, net, win **04** cook, earn, flow, form, gain, give, kind, maik, mark, mate, name, sort, tell, tend, turn, type, urge, vote **05** act as, add up, brand, build, cause, clear, drive, elect, equal, erect, force, frame, gross, impel, model, mould, offer, press, put up, reach, score, shape, start, state, style, total, write **06** become, coerce, come to, commit, compel, convey, create, devise, draw up, effect, impart, marque, matter, oblige, obtain, ordain, reckon, render, result, secure, select, settle, vote in, wrap up **07** achieve, acquire, add up to, appoint, arrange, attempt, bring in, chalk up, compose, compute, consort, convert, declare, deliver, dragoon, execute, fashion, install, notch up, perform, prepare, proceed, produce, promote, realize, require, serve as, shuffle, texture, think up, turn out, variety, work out **08** amount to, arrive at, assemble, bulldoze, carry out, comprise, conclude, contract, engender, estimate, generate, get ready, nominate, occasion, pressure, reckon up, set forth, take home **09** calculate, character, constrain, construct, designate, determine, discharge, establish, fabricate, formation, formulate, get down to, halfpenny, originate, pronounce, strongarm, structure, undertake **10** accomplish, bring about, constitute, contribute, function as, give rise to, perpetrate, pressurize **11** communicate, disposition, manufacture, mass-produce, prevail upon, put together **12** be to blame for **13** play the part of, play the role of **14** put the screws on **15** deliver the goods

See also **halfpenny**

- **make away with**
  03 nab, rid **04** do in, kill, lift, nick **05** pinch, seize, steal, swipe **06** kidnap, murder, remove, snatch **07** bump off, destroy **08** carry off, fetch off, knock off **09** slaughter **10** do away with, run off with **11** assassinate, walk off with
- **make believe**
  03 act **04** play **05** dream, enact, feign **07** imagine, play-act, pretend **09** fantasize
- **make do**
  04 cope **05** get by **06** manage **07** make out, survive **08** get along, scrape by **09** improvise **13** muddle through
- **make for**
  06 aim for, favour, lead to **07** forward, further, head for, produce, promote **09** go towards **10** facilitate **11** move towards **12** contribute to **13** be conducive to
- **make it**
  05 get on, reach **06** arrive **07** prosper, succeed, survive **11** come through, pull through **12** be successful
- **make of**
  04 rate **05** judge **06** assess, regard **07** think of, weigh up **08** consider, evaluate
- **make off**
  03 fly **04** bolt **05** brush, leave, mosey, truss **06** beat it, decamp, depart, hook it, pop off, run off **07** run away, scarper **08** clear off, up sticks **09** cut and run, shemozzle, skedaddle **12** make a getaway **15** take to your heels
- **make off with**
  03 nab **04** flog, nick, take **05** filch, pinch, steal, swipe **06** abduct, kidnap, pilfer **07** purloin **08** carry off, knock off **10** run off with **11** appropriate, walk off with
- **make out**
  03 get, see, spy **04** aver, bang, bonk, cope, espy, fare, read, scan, shag **05** claim, get by, get on, grasp, imply, prove, screw, spell **06** affirm, assert, descry, detect, divine, draw up, fathom, fill in, follow, manage **07** achieve, declare, discern, fill out, succeed, work out **08** complete, decipher, describe, discover, get along, maintain, make love, perceive,

progress, write out **09** establish, recognize **10** bear in hand, comprehend, understand **11** demonstrate, distinguish, manage to see **12** manage to hear **13** sleep together **14** get your leg over

• **make over**
05 leave **06** assign, convey **07** dispone, dispose **08** bequeath, sign over, transfer

• **make the rounds of**
02 do

• **make up**
◇ *anagram indicator*
04 fill, form, meet **05** feign, frame, hatch, paint, rouge **06** create, decide, devise, doll up, invent, parcel, powder, render, repair, repent, settle, supply, tart up **07** arrange, collect, compose, concoct, dream up, perfume, provide, think up **08** complete, compound, comprise, round off **09** construct, fabricate, formulate, make peace, originate **10** constitute, shake hands, supplement **11** call it quits, put make-up on **12** be reconciled **13** Birminghamize, put on your face **14** bury the hatchet

• **make up for**
06 offset **07** redress **08** atone for **13** compensate for, make amends for

• **make up to**
03 eik, eke **05** court **06** chat up, cozy up, fawn on **07** toady to **08** butter up, suck up to **10** compensate, cozy up with **15** curry favour with, make overtures to

• **make way**
06 gather **07** advance, gangway **11** allow to pass, clear the way, make room for **12** make space for, stand back for **14** allow to succeed

make-believe
04 mock, sham **05** dream **06** made-up, unreal **07** charade, fantasy, feigned, pretend **08** dreaming, imagined, imitated, pretence, pretense, role-play **09** imaginary, pretended, simulated, unreality **10** fantasized, masquerade, play-acting **11** daydreaming, fabrication, imagination

maker
06 author, wright **07** builder, creator, deviser **08** director, producer, repairer **09** architect **10** fabricator **11** constructor **12** manufacturer

makeshift
06 cutcha, make-do **07** Band-aid®, fig leaf, stand-by, stopgap **08** pis aller **09** expedient, impromptu, temporary, timenoguy **10** improvised, substitute **11** provisional, rudimentary **13** rough and ready **14** thrown together **15** cobbled together

make-up
◇ *anagram indicator*
04 form, slap **05** get-up, paint, style **06** format, nature, powder, temper **07** pancake **08** assembly, panstick, war paint **09** blackface, character, cosmetics, formation, structure,

whiteface **10** foundation, maquillage **11** arrangement, composition, disposition, greasepaint, personality, temperament **12** constitution, construction, organization **13** configuration

making
04 form **06** income **07** forging, profits, promise, returns, revenue, takings **08** assembly, building, capacity, creating, creation, earnings, moulding, proceeds **09** materials, modelling, potential, producing, qualities, structure **10** beginnings, capability, production **11** composition, fabrication, ingredients, manufacture **12** construction, potentiality **13** possibilities

• **in the making**
06 coming **07** budding, nascent **08** emergent **09** incipient, potential, promising **10** burgeoning, developing **11** up and coming

maladjusted
◇ *anagram indicator*
04 gaga **05** dotty **06** psycho, schizo **08** confused, neurotic, unstable **09** alienated, disturbed, estranged, screwed-up **10** disordered **12** round the bend

maladministration
07 misrule **08** bungling **09** stupidity **10** blundering, corruption, dishonesty, misconduct **11** malfeasance, malpractice, misfeasance, mishandling **12** incompetence, inefficiency, malversation **13** misgovernment, mismanagement

maladroit
05 inept **06** clumsy, gauche **07** awkward, unhandy **08** bungling, ill-timed, inexpert, tactless, untoward **09** graceless, ham-fisted, inelegant, unskilful **10** cack-handed **11** insensitive, thoughtless **12** undiplomatic **13** inconsiderate

maladroitness
10 clumsiness, inelegance, ineptitude **11** awkwardness **12** tactlessness **13** gracelessness, insensitivity, unskilfulness **15** thoughtlessness

malady
07 ailment, disease, illness, malaise **08** disorder, sickness **09** breakdown, complaint, infirmity **10** affliction **13** indisposition
See also **disease**

malaise
05 angst **06** unease **07** anguish, anxiety, disease, illness **08** disquiet, doldrums, sickness, weakness **09** lassitude, weariness **10** depression, discomfort, discontent, enervation, melancholy, uneasiness **11** unhappiness **12** restlessness **13** indisposition

malapropism
06 misuse **08** slipslop, solecism **09** wrong word **10** infelicity

11 Dogberryism **14** misapplication **15** slip of the tongue

malapropos
05 inapt **07** inaptly **08** ill-timed, tactless, unseemly, untimely **10** inapposite, misapplied, tactlessly, unsuitable, unsuitably **11** inopportune, uncalled-for **12** inappositely, unseasonably **13** inappropriate, inopportunely **15** inappropriately

malaria
04 ague

Malawi
02 MW **03** MWI

Malaysia
03 MAL, MYS

malcontent
05 fed up, rebel **06** grouch, moaner, morose **07** aginner, grouser, restive, unhappy, whinger **08** agitator, grumbler **09** nit-picker, resentful **10** bellyacher, cheesed off, complainer, rebellious **11** bellyaching, disaffected, disgruntled, dissentious, ill-disposed, unsatisfied **12** discontented, dissatisfied, fault-finding, troublemaker **13** mischief-maker

Maldives
03 MDV

male
01 m **02** he **03** dog, man, tom **04** bull, cock, mail, stag **05** macho, manly **06** armour, boyish, virile **07** laddish, manlike **09** masculine, staminate
See also **animal**

malediction
04 oath, wish **05** curse **07** cursing, damning, malison **08** anathema **09** damnation **10** execration **11** imprecation **12** denunciation

malefactor
05 crook, felon **06** outlaw **07** convict, culprit, villain **08** criminal, evildoer, offender **09** miscreant, misfeasor, wrongdoer **10** delinquent, lawbreaker **12** transgressor

malevolence
04 hate **05** spite, venom **06** hatred, malice **07** cruelty, ill-will, rancour **09** hostility, malignity **10** bitterness, fierceness, malignancy **11** viciousness **12** spitefulness, vengefulness **13** maliciousness **14** unfriendliness, vindictiveness

malevolent
05 cruel **06** bitter, fierce, malign **07** baleful, hostile, vicious **08** spiteful, vengeful, venomous **09** malicious, rancorous, resentful **10** evil-minded, ill-natured, maleficent, pernicious, unfriendly, vindictive

• **malevolent being**
04 peri

malevolently
07 cruelly **08** bitterly, fiercely **09** viciously **10** spitefully, vengefully,

venomously **11** maliciously, resentfully **13** vindicatively

malformation
04 warp **09** deformity **10** distortion **12** irregularity **13** disfigurement, misshapenness

malformed
◇ *anagram indicator*
04 bent **06** warped **07** crooked, twisted **08** deformed **09** distorted, irregular, misshapen **10** disfigured

malfunction
◇ *anagram indicator*
04 fail, flaw **05** crash, fault **06** defect, glitch, go phut, hiccup, pack up **07** conk out, failure, go kaput, go wrong **08** disorder, hiccough **09** break down, breakdown **11** stop working

Mali
03 MLI, RMM

malice
04 hate **05** spite, venom **06** animus, enmity, hatred, spleen **07** despite, ill-will, rancour **08** bad blood **09** animosity, hostility **10** bitchiness, bitterness, bone to pick, resentment **11** malevolence **13** maliciousness **14** vindictiveness

malicious
04 evil, mean **05** snide **06** bitchy, bitter, malign **07** baleful, hostile, vicious **08** narquois, spiteful, vengeful, venomous **09** poisonous, rancorous, resentful **10** dispiteous, evil-minded, ill-natured, malevolent, pernicious **11** mischievous

maliciously
08 bitterly **09** unhappily, viciously **10** spitefully, venomously **11** resentfully **12** malevolently, perniciously

malign
03 bad **04** bait, evil, harm, slur **05** abuse, libel, smear **06** defame, injure, insult, vilify **07** baleful, envenom, harmful, hostile, hurtful, run down, slander, traduce **08** badmouth, sinister **09** disparage, injurious, malignant, misintend, poor-mouth **10** calumniate, malevolent **11** destructive **13** stab in the back **14** kick in the teeth

malignancy
08 fatality **09** lethality, mortality, virulence **12** incurability

malignant
04 evil **05** black, fatal, swart **06** deadly, lethal, malign, sullen, swarth **07** baleful, harmful, hostile, hurtful, vicious **08** cankered, Cavalier, devilish, Royalist, spiteful, venomous, viperous, virulent **09** cancerous, dangerous, incurable, injurious, malicious, poisonous, rancorous **10** malevolent, pernicious, rebellious **11** destructive, disaffected **14** uncontrollable **15** life-threatening

malignity
04 gall, hate **05** spite, venom **06** animus, hatred, malice, taking **07** ill-will, rancour **08** bad blood **09** animosity, hostility, virulence **10** bitterness, deadliness, wickedness **11** balefulness, harmfulness, hurtfulness, malevolence, viciousness **12** vengefulness **13** maliciousness **14** perniciousness, vindictiveness **15** destructiveness

malinger
04 loaf **05** dodge, shirk, skive, skulk, slack **07** pretend, put it on **09** gold-brick **12** swing the lead **14** pretend to be ill

malingerer
06 dodger, loafer, skiver **07** shirker, slacker **11** lead-swinger

mall
04 beat, maul, mell, walk **05** plaza **06** arcade **08** galleria, precinct **13** outlet village **14** shopping centre **15** shopping complex

mallard
08 wild duck

• **mallard flock**
04 sord

malleability
07 pliancy **08** softness **10** compliance, plasticity, pliability, suppleness **11** ductileness, flexibility **12** adaptability **13** manageability, receptiveness, tractableness **14** susceptibility

malleable
◇ *anagram indicator*
04 soft **06** pliant, supple **07** ductile, plastic, pliable **08** biddable, flexible, tractile, workable, yielding **09** adaptable, compliant, receptive, tractable **10** governable, manageable **11** persuadable, susceptible **14** impressionable

mallow
04 sida

malnourished
06 hungry **07** starved **08** anorexic, underfed **09** anorectic **14** undernourished

malnutrition
06 hunger **08** anorexia **09** inanition **10** starvation **12** underfeeding **13** unhealthy diet **15** anorexia nervosa

malodorous
04 rank **05** fetid, niffy **06** foetid, putrid, smelly **07** miasmal, miasmic, noisome, reeking **08** mephitic, miasmous, stinking **09** miasmatic, offensive **10** infragrant, miasmatous, nauseating **12** evil-smelling, foul-smelling

malpractice
05 abuse **07** misdeed, offence **10** misconduct, negligence, wrongdoing **11** impropriety **12** carelessness **13** mismanagement

malt
04 wort

Malta
01 M **03** MLT

maltreat
◇ *anagram indicator*
04 harm, hurt, maul **05** abuse, bully, hound **06** damage, injure, misuse **07** torture **08** ill-treat, mistreat **09** mishandle, victimize **10** rough-house, treat badly **11** assassinate

maltreatment
04 harm, hurt **05** abuse **06** damage, ill-use, injury, misuse **07** torture **08** bullying, ill-usage **12** ill-treatment, mistreatment **13** victimization

mammal
Mammals include:

03 ape, ass, bat, cat, cow, dog, elk, fox, gnu, pig, rat, yak
04 bear, boar, cavy, deer, goat, hare, ibex, kudu, lion, lynx, mink, mole, paca, puma, seal, soor, tahr, vole, wolf, zebu
05 aguti, bison, camel, civet, coney, coypu, dingo, eland, genet, hippo, horse, human, hyena, hyrax, koala, lemur, llama, loris, moose, mouse, okapi, otter, ounce, panda, potto, rhino, sheep, shrew, skunk, sloth, stoat, takin, tapir, tiger, whale, zebra
06 aye-aye, baboon, badger, beaver, beluga, bobcat, cattle, colugo, cougar, coyote, cuscus, dassie, dugong, duiker, ermine, ferret, galago, gerbil, gibbon, gopher, hacker, impala, jackal, jaguar, jerboa, langur, marmot, marten, monkey, numbat, ocelot, possum, rabbit, racoon, reebok, rhebok, sea cow, serval, tenrec, vicuna, walrus, wapiti, weasel, wombat
07 ant-bear, bosvark, buffalo, caracal, caribou, chamois, cheetah, dolphin, echidna, fur seal, gazelle, gerenuk, giraffe, gorilla, grampus, grizzly, guanaco, guereza, gymnura, hamster, lemming, leopard, macaque, manatee, meercat, meerkat, mole rat, muntjac, muskrat, narwhal, opossum, pack rat, panther, peccary, polecat, primate, raccoon, red deer, roe deer, sea lion, sun bear, tamarin, tarsier, wallaby, warthog, wild ass, wildcat
08 aardvark, aardwolf, anteater, antelope, bushbaby, bushbuck, capybara, chipmunk, dormouse, duckbill, elephant, fruit bat, grey wolf, harp seal, hedgehog, house bat, kangaroo, mandrill, mangabey, marmoset, mongoose, musk deer, pacarana, pangolin, platypus, porpoise, reedbuck, reindeer, sea otter, sewer rat, squirrel, steenbok, steinbok, talapoin, wild goat
09 Arctic fox, armadillo, bamboo rat, bandicoot, black bear, blue sheep, blue whale, brown bear, dromedary, flying fox, grey whale, grindhval, guinea pig, jungle cat,

mouse-deer, orang utan, palm civet, phalanger, polar bear, porcupine, springbok, steinbuck, thylacine, waterbuck, wolverine

10 Barbary ape, chevrotain, chimpanzee, chinchilla, coatimundi, common seal, fallow deer, field mouse, giant panda, hartebeest, house mouse, human being, jack rabbit, kodiak bear, pilot whale, pine marten, prairie dog, rhinoceros, sperm whale, springbuck, springhare, vampire bat, white whale, wildebeest

11 beaked whale, flying lemur, green monkey, grizzly bear, honey badger, killer whale, muntjac deer, pipistrelle, rat kangaroo, red squirrel, snow leopard

12 Arabian camel, barbary sheep, elephant seal, grey squirrel, harvest mouse, hippopotamus, leaf-nosed bat, mountain goat, mountain lion, rhesus monkey, river dolphin, spider monkey, two-toed sloth, vervet monkey, water buffalo

13 American bison, Bactrian camel, colobus monkey, dwarf antelope, elephant shrew, European bison, hanuman monkey, howling monkey, humpback whale, marsupial mole, mouse-eared bat, spiny anteater, Tasmanian wolf

14 capuchin monkey, edible dormouse, flying squirrel, Indian elephant, marsupial mouse, mountain beaver, Patagonian hare, squirrel monkey, Tasmanian devil, three-toed sloth

15 African elephant, black rhinoceros, brushtail possum, hamadryas baboon, humpbacked whale, proboscis monkey, ring-tailed lemur, Thomson's gazelle, white rhinoceros

See also **animal; ape; cat; cattle; deer; dog; horse; marsupial; monkey; pig; rodent; sheep; whale**

mammoth

04 huge, vast **05** giant, jumbo **06** bumper, mighty **07** immense, massive **08** colossal, enormous, gigantic, whopping **09** ginormous, herculean, leviathan **10** gargantuan, monumental, prodigious, stupendous **14** Brobdingnagian

man

01 b, k, m, n, p, q, r **02** bo, he, Mr, ou **03** boy, guy, IOM, lad, mun, pin **04** chap, crew, gent, hand, homo, jack, king, male, page, pawn, rook, work **05** adult, bloke, cairn, human, lover, piece, queen, staff, valet **06** bishop, castle, fellow, fiancé, geezer, helper, knight, Mister, mortal, occupy, people, person, spouse, toy boy, vassal, worker **07** chequer, draught, husband, mankind, mortals, operate, partner, servant, soldier, workman **08** employee, factotum, follower, houseboy, houseman, humanity,

labourer **09** attendant, boyfriend, gentleman, humankind, human race, odd-jobman **10** human being, individual, manservant, sweetheart **11** Homo sapiens, human beings **12** be in charge of, man-of-all-work, take charge of **15** jack-of-all-trades

See also **boy; chess**

• **first man**
04 Adam

• **good man**
01 S **02** St **04** sant **05** Saint

• **old man** *see* **old man**

• **to a man**
05 as one **07** bar none **09** one and all **11** unanimously **12** with one voice

• **wise man**
04 mage, sage **05** magus

manacle

03 tie **04** bind, curb **05** chain, check **06** fetter, hamper, secure **07** inhibit, shackle **08** handcuff, restrain **11** put in chains

manacles

05 bonds, cuffs, gyves, irons **06** chains **07** darbies, fetters, mittens, nippers **08** shackles **09** bracelets, handcuffs, snitchers, wristlets

manage

03 ren, rin, run, use **04** boss, cope, fare, head, keep, lead, play, rule, work **05** cut it, get by, get on, guide, shift, wield **06** direct, effect, govern, handle, head up, honcho, make do, manure, master **07** achieve, carry on, command, conduct, control, make out, operate, oversee, solicit, succeed, survive **08** be head of, bring off, contrive, deal with, engineer, get along, maneuver, navigate, organize **09** influence, manoeuvre, negotiate, supervise **10** accomplish, administer, bring about, manipulate **11** preside over, superintend **12** be in charge of

manageable

04 yare **05** handy **06** doable, docile, pliant, viable, wieldy **07** pliable **08** amenable, feasible, flexible, yielding **09** compliant, easy-to-use, tolerable, tractable **10** acceptable, attainable, functional, governable, reasonable, submissive **11** practicable **12** controllable **13** accommodating

management

04 care **05** admin, board **06** bosses, charge, owners, ruling **07** command, conduct, control, dispose, running **08** disposal, handling, managers, ordering **09** direction, directors, employers, executive, governall, governors, husbandry, stewardry, treatment **10** executives, government, intendance, intendancy, leadership, overseeing **11** directorate, proprietors, stewardship, supervision, supervisors **12** organization **14** administration **15** superintendence

manager

02 GM **03** guv, Mgr **04** boss, head, suit

05 agent, chair, chief **06** gaffer, honcho, serang **07** amildar, husband, planter, proctor **08** chairman, director, employer, governor, hotelier, landlady, landlord, motelier, overseer **09** conductor, contriver, directrix, executive, intendant, organizer, president, régisseur **10** chairwoman, controller, directress, head-bummer, head serang, impresario, manageress, procurator, supervisor **11** businessman, chairperson, comptroller, land-steward **12** commissioner, maître d'hôtel, manufacturer **13** administrator, businesswoman **14** chief executive, superintendent

managerial

09 executive **10** industrial **11** legislative, supervisory **12** departmental, governmental **14** administrative, organizational, superintendent **15** entrepreneurial

mandate

02 OK **03** law, let **04** okay **05** allow, edict, order **06** charge, decree, enable, permit, ratify, ruling **07** approve, bidding, command, confirm, dictate, empower, entitle, licence, precept, statute, warrant **08** legalize, sanction, validate **09** authority, authorize, consent to, direction, directive, make legal, ordinance **10** commission, injunction, king's brief **11** instruction **13** authorization **15** give authority to

mandatory

07 binding **08** required **09** essential, necessary, requisite **10** compulsory, imperative, obligatory

manful

04 bold **05** brave, hardy, manly, noble, stout **06** daring, heroic, strong **07** gallant, valiant **08** intrepid, powerful, resolute, stalwart, vigorous **09** steadfast **10** courageous, determined **11** indomitable, lion-hearted, noble-minded, unflinching **12** stout-hearted

manfully

04 hard **05** nobly **06** boldly **07** bravely, man-like, stoutly **08** pluckily, strongly **09** gallantly, valiantly **10** heroically, intrepidly, powerfully, resolutely, stalwartly, vigorously **11** desperately, steadfastly **12** courageously, determinedly **13** unflinchingly

manganese

02 Mn

• **manganese ore**
03 wad **04** wadd, wadt

manger

04 crib **06** cratch, feeder, trough **13** feeding trough

mangle

◇ *anagram indicator*
03 cut, mar **04** hack, maim, maul, rend, ruin, tear **05** botch, crush, mouth, spoil, twist, wreck **06** bungle, deform, garble, haggle, mess up **07** butcher, destroy, distort, mammock, screw up

08 calender, lacerate, mutilate
09 disfigure **11** make a hash of, make a mess of

mangy
04 mean, worn **05** dirty, seedy, tatty
06 filthy, scabby, shabby, shoddy
07 roynish, scruffy **08** cowardly
09 moth-eaten

manhandle
03 tug **04** haul, hump, maul, pull, push
05 abuse, heave, shove **06** jostle, misuse **07** rough up **08** maltreat, mistreat **10** knock about **13** handle roughly

manhood
08 machismo, maleness, maturity, virility **09** adulthood, manliness
10 manfulness **11** masculinity

mania
03 fad **04** rage, urge **05** craze, thing
06 desire, fetish, frenzy, lunacy, raving
07 craving, madness, passion
08 dementia, disorder, fixation, hysteria, insanity, wildness
09 craziness, gold-fever, obsession, psychosis, tarantism **10** aberration, compulsion, enthusiasm
11 derangement, fascination, infatuation **13** preoccupation

Manias include:
08 egomania
09 cynomania, demomania, ergomania, infomania, logomania, melomania, monomania, oenomania, opsomania, pyromania, theomania, tomomania, xenomania
10 anthomania, dipsomania, erotomania, hippomania, hydromania, methomania, metromania, mythomania, narcomania, necromania, nostomania
11 ablutomania, acronymania, ailuromania, bibliomania, cleptomania, demonomania, etheromania, graphomania, hedonomania, kleptomania, megalomania, nymphomania, technomania, toxicomania
12 arithmomania, balletomania, pteridomania, thanatomania, theatromania
13 flagellomania, morphinomania
14 eleutheromania

maniac
03 fan, nut **04** buff, kook **05** crank, fiend, freak, loony **06** madman, nutter, psycho **07** cupcake, fanatic, lunatic, nutcase, oddball **08** crackpot, headcase, madwoman **09** fruitcake, psychotic, screwball **10** enthusiast, psychopath **14** deranged person

manic
◊ *anagram indicator*
03 mad **04** amok, wild **05** barmy, batty, crazy, daffy, dippy, loopy **06** crazed, hectic, insane, raving **07** berserk, frantic, furious **08** demented,

deranged, feverish, frenetic, frenzied
09 desperate, obsessive **10** distracted, distraught, hysterical **11** overwrought
12 uncontrolled **13** panic-stricken
14 beside yourself

manically
◊ *anagram indicator*
05 madly **06** wildly **09** excitedly, intensely **10** hectically **12** frenetically, hysterically

manifest
◊ *anagram indicator*
04 open, shew, show **05** clear, plain, prove **06** appear, attest, evince, expose, patent, reveal **07** blatant, confess, declare, display, evident, exhibit, express, glaring, obvious, present, visible **08** apparent, distinct, indicate, set forth **09** establish, extrovert, make clear, make plain, show forth **10** illustrate, noticeable
11 conspicuous, demonstrate, perceptible, transparent, unconcealed
12 be evidence of, unmistakable
13 unmistakeable

manifestation
◊ *anagram indicator*
04 mark, mode, show, sign **05** gleam, glory, token **06** avatar, reflex **07** display
08 Epiphany, evidence, exposure
09 theophany **10** appearance, disclosure, exhibition, exposition, expression, indication, revelation
11 angelophany, declaration, incarnation **12** illustration, presentation **13** demonstration
14 representation **15** exemplification

manifesto
08 platform, policies **09** programme, statement **11** declaration, publication
12 announcement, proclamation
14 pronunciamento

manifold
04 many **06** varied **07** copious, diverse, several, various
08 abundant, multiple, multiply, numerous **09** aggregate
12 multifarious **13** kaleidoscopic, multitudinous

manipulate
◊ *anagram indicator*
03 cog, ply, rig, use **04** cook, hand, milk, tong, work **05** fit up, frame, guide, knead, nurse, steer, wield
06 direct, doctor, employ, fiddle, handle, juggle, manage, wangle
07 control, exploit, falsify, finesse, massage, operate, process, shuffle, utilize **08** cash in on, engineer
09 influence, manoeuvre, negotiate
10 juggle with, tamper with, thimblerig
11 gerrymander, pull strings
12 capitalize on, wheel and deal
15 have over a barrel

manipulation
◊ *anagram indicator*
05 using **07** control, massage, milking, rigging, working **08** fiddling, guidance, handling, juggling, kneading, steering,

wangling, wielding **09** directing, doctoring, influence, massaging, operation **11** manoeuvring, negotiation, utilization **12** exploitation, mobilization **13** falsification **14** pulling strings **15** cooking the books

manipulative
03 sly **04** foxy, wily **06** artful, crafty, tricky **07** cunning, devious
08 scheming, slippery **09** conniving, deceitful, designing, insidious, underhand **11** calculating, duplicitous
12 unscrupulous **13** Machiavellian

manipulator
04 user **05** slave **06** worker **07** handler, schemer, smoothy, wielder
08 director, engineer, operator, smart guy **09** exploiter **10** controller, influencer, manoeuvrer, negotiator, wirepuller **13** wheeler-dealer

Manitoba
02 MB

mankind
03 man **05** flesh **06** Bimana, people, public **07** mortals **08** humanity
09 humankind, human race **11** Homo sapiens, human beings

manliness
06 mettle, valour, vigour **07** bravery, courage, heroism, manhood
08 boldness, firmness, machismo, maleness, strength, virility
09 fortitude, hardihood
10 manfulness, resolution
11 intrepidity, masculinity
12 fearlessness, independence, resoluteness, stalwartness

manly
04 bold, firm, male **05** brave, macho, noble, tough **06** heroic, manful, robust, rugged, strong, sturdy, virile
08 fearless, intrepid, powerful, vigorous **09** dignified, masculine
10 courageous, determined

man-made
04 faux, mock **06** ersatz **09** imitation, simulated, synthetic **10** artificial
12 manufactured

manna
07 trehala **08** honeydew

manner
03 air, how, way **04** form, look, mien, mode **05** means, style **06** aspect, custom, mainor, method, stance
07 bearing, conduct, decorum, fashion, posture, process, p's and q's, routine, variety **08** approach, attitude, courtesy, good form, practice, protocol
09 behaviour, character, demeanour, etiquette, procedure, propriety, technique **10** appearance, deportment, politeness **11** formalities
12 social graces, the done thing **13** way of behaving
• **in the manner of**
02 as, of **03** à la, per
• **unconstrained manner**
04 ease

mannered
5 posed, put-on 06 pseudo, thewed
7 stilted 08 affected, precious
0 artificial, euphuistic 11 pretentious
ee also **bad-mannered**

mannerism
5 habit, quirk, trait, trick 06 foible
7 feature 10 foreignism 11 peculiarity,
tiltedness 12 idiosyncrasy
4 characteristic

mannerly
5 civil 06 formal, polite 07 civilly,
genteel, refined 08 decorous,
gracious, ladylike, polished, well-bred
9 civilized, courteous 10 respectful
1 deferential, gentlemanly, well-
behaved 12 well-mannered

mannish
5 butch 07 laddish, mankind
9 Amazonian, masculine, tomboyish,
unwomanly, viragoish 10 unfeminine,
unladylike, viraginian, viraginous
1 virilescent

mannishness
8 virilism 09 butchness
1 masculinity 12 unfemininity,
virilescence 13 unwomanliness
4 unladylikeness

manoeuvre
◇ *anagram indicator*
4 dock, ease, loop, move, pick, plan,
plot, ploy, roll, ruse, turn 05 berth, cut
in, dodge, drive, guide, pilot, stall, steer,
trick 06 action, device, devise, direct,
gambit, handle, jockey, manage,
desade, scheme, tactic, wangle
7 wheelie 08 alley-oop, artifice,
contrive, engineer, exercise, intrigue,
movement, navigate, snap roll,
wingover 09 chandelle, checkmate,
lecursion, half board, negotiate,
operation, stratagem 10 deployment,
manipulate, subterfuge
1 machination, pull strings, skilful plan,
victory roll 12 countermarch,
manipulation, renversement
3 Immelmann turn

manor
3 Hof 04 hall, seat, vill 05 house, villa
6 barony 07 château, Schloss
2 country house

manpower
5 staff 07 workers 09 employees,
personnel, workforce 14 human
resources, skilled workers

manse
7 deanery, rectory 08 vicarage
9 parsonage 10 glebe-house

manservant
5 valet 06 butler, Jeeves 08 retainer
9 attendant

mansion
4 casa, hall, home, seat 05 abode,
house, manor, place, villa 06 castle
7 château, Schloss 08 dwelling
9 residence 10 habitation, manor-
house

manslaughter
06 murder 07 carnage, killing, slaying
08 butchery, fatality, genocide, homicide,
massacre 09 bloodshed, execution,
matricide, patricide, slaughter, uxoricide
10 fratricide, sororicide 11 destruction,
elimination, infanticide, liquidation
13 assassination, extermination

mantle
04 cape, hide, hood, mask, pall, veil,
wrap 05 blush, cloak, cloud, cover,
froth, layer, palla, shawl, vakas
06 bubble, capote, dolman, rochet,
screen, shroud 07 blanket, conceal,
envelop, obscure, pallium, pelisse,
pluvial 08 covering, disguise, envelope
13 asthenosphere

manual
03 ABC 05 bible, guide, human 06 by
hand 07 cambist, positif
08 handbook, physical 09 companion,
guidebook, portolano, vade-mecum
10 directions, mechanical, prospectus
11 book of words, enchiridion
12 encheiridion, hand-operated,
instructions 13 with your hands
15 instruction book

manually
06 by hand 10 physically 13 with your
hands

manufacture
◇ *anagram indicator*
04 form, make 05 build, forge, frame,
model 06 create, devise, invent, make
up, making 07 concoct, dream up,
fashion, forming, process, produce,
think up, turn out 08 assemble,
assembly, building, creation
09 construct, fabricate, formation,
modelling 10 fashioning, processing,
production 11 fabrication, mass-
produce, put together 12 construction
14 mass-production

manufacturer
05 maker 07 builder, chemist, creator
08 producer 09 fabricant 10 paper-
maker, soap boiler 11 chocolatier,
constructor, tobacconist 12 factory-
owner 13 industrialist
See also **car**

manure
04 dung, hold, lime, muck, soil, tath
05 dress, guano, vraic 06 bedung, hen-
pen, manage, occupy, ordure
07 compost 08 dressing 09 cultivate,
droppings, fish-guano 10 compost,ure,
fertilizer 11 top-dressing 12 animal
faeces, police-manure 15 animal
excrement

manuscript
02 MS 04 text 05 codex, paper
06 scroll, uncial, vellum 07 papyrus
08 document 09 autograph,
minuscule, parchment 10 Mabinogion,
palimpsest, typescript
12 opisthograph

Manx
◇ *tail deletion indicator*
08 tailless

many
01 C, D, K, L, M 04 a lot, lots, tons, wads
05 a mass, heaps, loads, piles, scads
06 a lot of, a wheen, hantle, lots of,
masses, oodles, plenty, scores, stacks,
sundry, varied 07 copious, diverse,
several, umpteen, various 08 billions,
hundreds, manifold, millions, multiple,
numerous, zillions 09 countless, hoi
polloi, thousands 10 a multitude 11 any
number of, innumerable 12 a large
number 13 multitudinous 14 a large
number of

Maori

05 Ngata (Sir Apirana Turupa)
06 Cooper (Dame Whina), Mahuta
(Sir Robert), O'Regan (Sir Tipene),
Pomare (Sir Maui), Ratana
(Tuhupotiki Wiremu)
07 Te Kooti (Arikirangi Te Turuki)
09 Heke Potai (Hone Wiremu), Hongi
Hika, Rua Kenana (Hepetipa)
11 Te Rauparaha
14 Te Heuheu Tukino (Sir Hepi)

See also **god, goddess; mythology**

map
04 card, face, mark, plan, plot 05 atlas,
chart, graph, inset 06 sketch 07 road-
map 08 town plan 09 cartogram,
delineate, gazetteer, horoscope,
mappemond 10 projection, street plan
11 carte du pays, hypsography,
planisphere, street guide 12 weather
chart

• **map out**
04 draw 05 draft 06 draw up, sketch
07 outline, work out

maple
04 acer 05 mazer, plane 08 box elder,
sycamore

mapmakers
02 OS

mar
◇ *anagram indicator*
04 harm, hurt, maim, ruin, scar
05 spoil, stain, sully, taint, wreck
06 damage, deface, deform, impair,
injure, mangle, poison 07 blemish,
tarnish 08 mutilate 09 disfigure,
misguggle 10 mishguggle
11 contaminate, detract from

maraud
04 loot, raid, sack 05 foray, harry
06 forage, ravage 07 despoil, pillage,
plunder, raiding, ransack 08 spoliate
09 depredate 10 plundering

marauder
05 rover 06 bandit, looter, mugger,
outlaw, pirate, raider, robber
07 brigand, ravager, rustler 08 pillager,
predator 09 buccaneer, plunderer
10 freebooter, highwayman

marble
03 taw 04 ally, bool, bowl, dump, marl,
onyx 05 agate, alley, bonce, touch
06 nicker, Parian 07 cipolin, knicker,
paragon, plonker, plunker

08 commoney, onychite **09** cipollino, pavonazzo, scagliola **10** nero-antico **11** ophicalcite

march
03 Mar **04** demo, file, gait, hike, Lide, pace, step, trek, walk, yomp **05** étape, hikoi, stalk, strut, tramp, tread, troop **06** border, defile, parade, stride **07** advance, debouch, en route, forward, headway, passage, swagger **08** boundary, footslog, progress **09** evolution, paso doble **10** procession, route-march, walk-around **11** development, make headway **12** countermarch **13** demonstration
- **March 15**
04 Ides
- **section of march**
04 trio

marches
06 border **08** boundary, frontier, protests **10** borderland **14** border district

mare
04 yaud

margarine
04 oleo

margin
03 rim **04** brim, curb, edge, kerb, marg, play, rand, room, side, tail **05** bound, brink, extra, limit, marge, scope, skirt, space, verge **06** border, leeway, limits, spread **07** confine, surplus, whisker **08** boundary, confines, frontier, latitude **09** allowance, perimeter, periphery **10** difference **12** differential **15** demarcation line

marginal
03 low **04** marg, tiny **05** minor, small **06** minute, slight **07** minimal **08** doubtful **09** on the edge **10** borderline, negligible, peripheral **11** subordinate **13** insignificant
- **marginal note**
03 k'ri
- **of marginal value**
04 lean

marginalization
05 exile **08** solitude **09** aloneness, isolation, seclusion **10** alienation, detachment, loneliness, remoteness, retirement, separation, withdrawal **11** abstraction, segregation **12** dissociation, separateness, solitariness **13** disconnection, sequestration

marginalize
06 cut off, detach, maroon, remove, strand **07** divorce, exclude, isolate, seclude, shut out **08** abstract, alienate, separate, set apart, shut away **09** keep apart, ostracize, segregate, sequester **10** disconnect **12** cold-shoulder

margosa
03 nim **04** neem, nimb **05** Melia, neemb

marijuana *see* cannabis

marina
04 dock, port **07** harbour, mooring **12** yacht station

marinade
04 soak **05** imbue, souse, steep **06** infuse **07** immerse **08** marinate, permeate, saturate **09** chermoula, escabeche

marine
02 RM **03** sea **05** jolly, naval **06** bootee **07** aquatic, oceanic, pelagic **08** maritime, nautical, seagoing, seascape, seawater **09** saltwater, seafaring, thalassic **10** ocean-going, thalassian **11** leatherneck

mariner
02 AB **03** tar **04** salt **05** limey, matlo **06** matlow, sailor, sea dog, seaman **07** Jack Tar, matelot **08** deckhand, seafarer **09** navigator
See also **sailor**

marital
06 wedded **07** married, nuptial, spousal, wedding **08** conjugal, marriage **09** connubial **11** matrimonial

maritally
09 by wedlock, in wedlock, nuptially **10** by marriage, conjugally, in marriage **11** connubially **13** matrimonially

maritime
03 sea **05** naval **06** marine **07** coastal, oceanic, pelagic, seaside **08** littoral, nautical, sea-coast, seagoing, sea-trade **09** seafaring

mark
01 m **02** DM, mk, NB **03** aim, cut, dot, end, see, tag, tee, zit **04** blot, butt, chip, clue, dash, dent, dool, dule, flag, goal, heed, hint, keep, line, ling, logo, mind, name, nick, norm, note, scar, seal, sign, spot, stop, tatu, tick, tika, type **05** badge, brand, gauge, grade, issue, label, level, limit, model, motto, notch, patch, point, print, proof, scale, score, smear, speck, stage, stain, stamp, tally, token, trace, track **06** accent, assess, blotch, bruise, caract, denote, device, emblem, honour, listen, notice, object, picket, pimple, piquet, record, regard, smudge, smutch, stigma, symbol, target, tattoo, tattow, tittle, tracks, typify **07** blemish, correct, discern, feature, freckle, imprint, jot down, measure, observe, picquet, purpose, quality, scratch, signify, specify, symptom **08** appraise, boundary, bull's-eye, evaluate, evidence, identify, indicate, monogram, note down, remember, standard **09** attribute, birthmark, celebrate, character, criterion, designate, discolour, footprint, idiograph, intention, objective, recognize, represent, trademark, write down, yardstick **10** assessment, bear in mind, evaluation, impression, indication, percentage, take heed of, take note of **11** acknowledge, commemorate, distinguish, fingerprint, take to heart **12** characterize,

fingerprints, pay tribute to **13** put your name on **14** characteristic, noteworthiness, pay attention to
- **encircling mark**
03 rim **04** ring
- **make your mark**
05 get on **06** make it **07** prosper, succeed **12** be successful, make the grade **13** hit the big time **14** make the big time
- **mark down**
03 cut **05** lower, slash **06** reduce **08** decrease
- **mark out**
03 fix **04** line **07** delimit, destine, measure **08** set apart **09** delineate, demarcate, designate, draw lines, single out, tell apart **11** distinguish **12** discriminate **13** differentiate
- **mark up**
05 put up, raise **06** hike up, jack up **08** increase
- **mark well**
02 nb **08** nota bene
- **miss mark**
03 err
- **up to the mark**
02 OK **10** acceptable, good enough **11** up to scratch **12** satisfactory
- **wide of the mark**
04 gone, wild **06** abroad, far out **09** imprecise, incorrect, off target **10** inaccurate, irrelevant **14** beside the point

marked
05 clear, noted, thick **06** doomed, pimply, signal, spotty, strong **07** blatant, blotchy, bruised, decided, evident, glaring, marcato, obvious, scarred, spotted, stained, watched **08** apparent, blotched, distinct, emphatic, freckled, striking **09** blemished, condemned, indicated, prominent, scratched, suspected **10** noticeable, pronounced, remarkable **11** conspicuous **12** considerable, unmistakable

markedly
07 clearly **08** signally **09** blatantly, decidedly, evidently, glaringly, obviously **10** distinctly, noticeably, remarkably, strikingly **11** prominently **12** considerably, emphatically, unmistakably **13** conspicuously

marker
03 dan, tag **04** buck, flag, goal **07** counter **08** bookmark, gybe mark, milepost, tidemark **09** milestone, stake boat

market
03 AIM, mkt, USM **04** call, fair, hawk, kerb, mall, mart, need, sale, sell, shop, souk, vent, want **05** agora, trade, valu **06** bazaar, buying, demand, desire, outlet, peddle, retail **07** bargain, promote, selling, trading **08** business, dealings, exchange, industry, occasion, shambles **09** advertize **10** Smithfield **11** market-place, requirement **12** Billingsgate, Covent Garden, offer for sale **14** shopping centre

on the market
5 on sale 07 for sale 09 available, up
or sale

marketable
5 wanted 08 in demand, saleable,
sellable, vendible 11 sought after
2 merchantable

marketing
4 hype 05 sales 07 pushing
8 plugging 09 promotion, publicity
advertising 12 distribution
8 merchandizing

market-place
3 suk 04 sook, souk, sukh, tron

marksman, markswoman
4 shot 06 sniper 07 deadeye 08 dead
shot, free-shot, shootist, wing shot
9 crack shot 12 sharpshooter

mark-up
4 hike, leap, rise 07 upsurge
8 increase 10 escalation 13 price
increase

Marlowe
3 Kit

marmoset
4 mico 07 jacchus, wistiti

marmot
5 bobac, bobak 08 whistler
9 woodchuck

maroon
5 leave 06 desert, strand
7 abandon, forsake, isolate 08 cast
way 09 put ashore 11 leave behind
4 turn your back on 15 leave high and
ry, leave in the lurch

marriage
4 link 05 match, noose, union
5 fusion, merger 07 spousal,
wedding, wedlock 08 alliance,
coupling, nuptials, shidduch,
spousage, spousals 09 espousals,
matrimony 10 connection
1 affiliation, association, combination,
handfasting, partnership, unification
2 amalgamation, married state
8 confederation

Marriage- and wedding-related
erms include:

3 vow, wed
4 ring, veil, wife
5 aisle, altar, banns, bride, dowry,
elope, groom, in-law, usher, vicar
6 beenah, bigamy, digamy, favour,
fiancé, garter, huppah, prenup,
priest, speech, spouse
7 best man, betroth, bouquet,
chuppah, consort, divorce,
espouse, exogamy, fiancée,
husband, Ketubah, marital,
merchet, Mr Right, nuptial, page
boy, propose, punalua, trigamy,
wedding
8 bedright, best maid, confetti,
conjugal, endogamy, hen night,
jointure, levirate, maritage,
minister, monogamy, monogyny,
polygamy

09 annulment, coemption, common-
law, communion, connubial,
honeymoon, hope chest,
horseshoe, hypergamy, love match,
matrimony, other half, reception,
registrar, stag night, trousseau
10 better half, bridesmaid, buttonhole,
consortium, consummate,
engagement, first dance, first night,
flower girl, her indoors, him
indoors, honeymoon, invitation,
Lucy Stoner, maiden name,
matrilocal, morganatic, patrilocal,
separation, settlement, uxorilocal,
wedding day
11 deuterogamy, dissolution, Gretna
Green, handfasting, misalliance,
morning gift, mother in-law,
outmarriage, wedding cake,
wedding list
12 bottom drawer, bridal shower,
concubitancy, mariage blanc, open
marriage, prothalamion, something
new, something old, wedding dress,
wedding march, wedding night
13 church service, civil marriage,
hedge-marriage, holy matrimony,
marriage-lines, something blue
14 matron of honour, pop the
question, steal a marriage
15 chief bridesmaid, going-away outfit,
marriage-licence, plight one's troth

• **promise of marriage**
04 hand

married
01 m 03 wed 05 wived, yoked
06 joined, united, wedded, wifely
07 hitched, marital, nuptial, spliced,
spousal 08 conjugal 09 connubial,
husbandly 11 matrimonial

marrow
03 nub 04 core, gist, like, mate, pith,
soul 05 equal, heart, match, quick,
stuff 06 centre, couple, kernel, spirit
07 essence, medulla, nucleus
08 zucchini 09 companion, courgette,
substance 11 nitty-gritty 12 nuts and
bolts, quintessence

marry
03 wad, wed 04 ally, fuse, join, knit,
link, mate, weld, wive 05 cleek, elope,
match, merge, unite 06 couple,
indeed!, spouse 07 combine, connect,
hitch up 08 forsooth! 09 affiliate,
associate 10 amalgamate, get hitched,
get married, get spliced, intermarry,
take to wife, tie the knot 12 go to the
world, join together 13 take the
plunge 14 become espoused, lead to
the altar, lead up the aisle 15 join in
matrimony

Mars
04 Ares

marsh
03 bog, fen 04 mire, salt, wash
05 bayou, swamp 06 marish, morass,
muskeg, salina, slough 07 corcass
08 quagmire 09 everglade, marshland
10 Everglades

marshal
◇ *anagram indicator*
04 lead, rank, take 05 align, array,
group, guide, order, usher 06 deploy,
draw up, escort, gather, line up, muster,
parade 07 arrange, collect, conduct,
dispose, farrier 08 assemble, organize,
shepherd 09 mareschal, marischal
10 put in order 13 velt-mareschal
14 gather together

Marshals include:

03 Ney (Michel)
04 Earp (Wyatt), Foch (Ferdinand),
Saxe (Maurice, Comte de), Tito
06 Hickok (Wild Bill), Pétain (Philippe),
Tedder (Arthur, Lord), Zhukov
(Georgi)
08 MacMahon (Patrice de)

See also **Field Marshal**

Marshall Islands
03 MHL

marshy
03 wet 04 miry 05 boggy, fenny,
moory, muddy 06 quaggy, slumpy,
spongy, swampy 07 fennish, moorish,
paludal 08 paludine, paludose,
paludous, squelchy 09 paludinal
10 paludinous 11 waterlogged

marsupial

Marsupials include:

03 roo
04 euro, tuan
05 koala, quoll
06 boodie, cuscus, glider, numbat,
possum, quokka, tammar, wombat
07 bettong, dasyure, dibbler, dunnart,
opossum, potoroo, wallaby
08 kangaroo, macropod, tarsiped,
wallaroo
09 bandicoot, boodie-rat, koala bear,
native cat, pademelon, petaurist,
phalanger, thylacine, wambenger
10 native bear, Notoryctes
11 diprotodont, honey possum, rat
kangaroo, rock wallaby
12 marsupial rat, pouched mouse, tree
kangaroo
13 brush kangaroo, marsupial mole,
Tasmanian wolf
14 marsupial mouse, Tasmanian devil,
vulpine opossum
15 flying phalanger

See also **animal**

mart
04 fair, mall, souk 06 bazaar, market,
outlet, staple 08 emporium, exchange
10 repository 11 market-place
14 shopping centre

marten
05 pekan, sable 06 fisher 07 Mustela
09 woodshock

martial
04 army 05 brave 06 heroic
07 hawkish, warlike 08 militant,
military 09 bellicose, combative,
soldierly 10 aggressive, pugnacious
11 belligerent

martial art

Martial arts and forms of self-defence include:

04 judo
05 lai-do, sambo, wushu
06 aikido, karate, kung fu, t'ai chi
07 capuera, ju-jitsu
08 capoeira, jiu-jitsu, ninjitsu, ninjutsu, Shotokan
09 tae kwon do
10 kick boxing
11 self-defence, t'ai chi ch'uan

• **martial art expert**
03 dan

martinet
06 martin, tyrant **08** stickler
09 formalist **10** taskmaster **11** slave-driver **12** taskmistress **14** disciplinarian

Martinique
03 MTQ

martyr
05 stone **06** victim **07** crucify, torment, torture **09** persecute **10** put to death
12 give the works, put on the rack
13 make a martyr of **14** burn at the stake **15** throw to the lions

martyrdom
05 agony, death, stake **06** ordeal
07 anguish, passion, torment, torture, witness **09** suffering **11** persecution
12 excruciation **13** baptism of fire
14 baptism of blood

marvel
04 gape, gawp, gaze, marl **05** marle, stare **06** genius, goggle, wonder
07 miracle, portent, prodigy **08** be amazed, surprise **09** eye-opener, fairy tale, not expect, sensation, spectacle
10 fairy story, phenomenon
12 astonishment, be astonished
14 quite something **15** be flabbergasted

marvellous
03 ace, bad, def, fab, rad **04** cool, mean, mega, neat, phat **05** brill, great, magic, super **06** superb, wicked
07 amazing, awesome, crucial, épatant, mirific, radical, wondred
08 glorious, selcouth, splendid, terrific, wondered **09** bodacious, excellent, fantastic, mirifical, wonderful
10 astounding, improbable, incredible, miraculous, out of sight, remarkable, stupendous, super-duper, surprising
11 astonishing, fantabulous, magnificent, merveilleux, sensational, spectacular **12** merveilleuse, unbelievable **13** extraordinary

marvellously
04 very **06** highly, really **07** acutely, awfully, greatly, utterly **08** severely, terribly **09** decidedly, extremely, intensely, to a wonder, unusually
10 dreadfully, remarkably, thoroughly, uncommonly **11** exceedingly, excessively, frightfully **12** inordinately, terrifically **13** exceptionally
15 extraordinarily

Maryland
02 MD

masculine
01 m **02** he **03** mas **04** bold, male, masc **05** brave, butch, macho, manly
06 heroic, robust, rugged, strong, virile
07 gallant, manlike, mannish
08 fearless, muscular, powerful, resolute, vigorous **09** confident, strapping **10** determined, red-blooded
12 stout-hearted

masculinity
06 mettle, valour, vigour **07** bravery, courage, heroism, manhood
08 boldness, firmness, machismo, maleness, strength, virility
09 fortitude, hardihood, manliness
10 manfulness, resolution
11 intrepidity **12** fearlessness, independence, stalwartness

mash
◊ *anagram indicator*
03 pap **04** beat, hash, mush, pulp
05 champ, crush, grind, paste, pound, purée, smash **06** bungle, infuse, muddle, pummel, squash **09** pulverize

mask
04 hide, show, veil **05** blind, cloak, cover, front, guise, matte, steep, visor, vizor **06** domino, façade, immask, infuse, masque, screen, shield, veneer, vizard **07** conceal, cover up, cover-up, goggles, inhaler, obscure, persona
08 disguise, joncanoe, junkanoo, pretence **09** dissemble, false face, gas helmet, John Canoe, John Kanoo, semblance **10** camouflage, gorgoneion, masquerade, respirator
11 concealment

masquerade
◊ *anagram indicator*
03 mum **04** mask, mumm, play, pose
05 cloak, cover, front, guise
06 masque **07** cover-up, dress up, pretend, profess **08** disguise, pretence
09 deception **10** masked ball
11 costume ball, counterfeit, dissimulate, impersonate **14** fancy dress ball **15** fancy dress party, pass yourself off

mass
01 m **03** lot, mob, ped, sea, sum, wad
04 bags, ball, band, body, bulk, clod, hang, heap, herd, hunk, load, lots, lump, most, nest, pile, size, tons
05 amass, batch, block, bolus, bunch, chaos, chunk, crowd, group, heaps, horde, loads, piece, piles, plebs, rally, stack, swarm, total, troop, whole, wodge **06** dallop, dollop, gather, huddle, medley, muster, oodles, rabble, scores, tangle, throng, weight, welter
07 blanket, cluster, clutter, collect, general, popular **08** assemble, capacity, coagulum, entirety, indigest, majority, pandemic, quantity, riff-raff, sweeping, totality **09** abundance, aggregate, Communion, dimension, Eucharist, extensive, hoi polloi, immensity, magnitude, multitude,

rotundity, universal, wholesale
10 accumulate, assemblage, collection, concretion, congregate, large-scale, Lord's Table, widespread
11 combination, greater part, large number, Lord's Supper, proletariat
12 accumulation, come together, common people, draw together, lower classes, working class **13** agglutination, bring together, comprehensive, Holy Communion, preponderance
14 across-the-board, conglomeration, indiscriminate, the rank and file, working classes

Massachusetts
02 MA **04** Mass

massacre
04 kill, slay **05** purge **06** murder, pogrom **07** butcher, carnage, killing, kill off, mow down, wipe out
08 butchery, decimate, genocide, homicide **09** bloodbath, holocaust, liquidate, slaughter **10** annihilate, blood purge, decimation
11 exterminate, liquidation
12 annihilation **13** extermination
15 ethnic cleansing

Massacres include:

04 Hama, Lari
05 Ambon, Katyn, My Lai, Paris, Sabra
06 Bezier, Boston, Cataví, Herrin, Kanpur, Lidice, Rishon
07 Amboyna, Babi Yar, Badajoz, Baghdad, Chatila, Glencoe, Halabja, Nanking, Tianjin
08 Amritsar, Cawnpore, Drogheda, El Mozote, Kishinev, Novgorod, Peterloo, Tientsin
09 Fetterman, Innocents, Jerusalem, Sand Creek, September, Trebizond
10 Addis Ababa, Fort Pillow, Myall Creek, Paxton Boys, Sack of Rome, Srebrenica, Tlatelolco
11 Janissaries, Sharpeville, Wounded Knee
12 Bloody Sunday, Sabra/Chatila
15 Oradour-sur-Glane, Sicilian Vespers, St Valentine's Day, Tiananmen Square

massage
◊ *anagram indicator*
03 rub **04** an mo, cook, do-in **05** alter, knead, reiki, tui na **06** doctor, fiddle, pummel **07** falsify, Jacuzzi®, rubbing, rub down, rub-down, shampoo, shiatsu, shiatzu, tripsis **08** aerotone, kneading **10** manipulate, osteopathy, percussion, petrissage, pummelling, tamper with **11** acupressure, reflexology **12** aromatherapy, manipulation, misrepresent
13 interfere with, physiotherapy
15 Reichian therapy, thalassotherapy

massive
03 big **04** bull, gang, huge, vast
05 beamy, bulky, great, heavy, hefty, jumbo, large, solid **06** mighty
07 hulking, immense, mammoth, popular, weighty **08** colossal, enormous, gigantic, timbered,

whopping **09** extensive, ginormous, ponderous **10** large-scale, monolithic, monumental, successful **11** substantial

massively
06 vastly **07** greatly, heavily **08** very much **09** immensely **10** enormously **11** extensively **12** monumentally **13** substantially

mast
03 bar, rod **04** boom, heel, nuts, pole, post, spar, yard **05** shaft, staff, stick **06** acorns, jigger **07** pannage, support, upright **10** topgallant

master
01 M **02** MA, PM, RM **03** ace, Dan, guv, Mas, Mes, pro **04** baas, beak, boss, buff, curb, guru, head, Herr, lord, main, Mass, Mess, rule, sire, tame, tuan **05** adept, bwana, check, chief, grand, grasp, great, guide, learn, maven, mavin, owner, prime, quell, ruler, tutor **06** bridle, defeat, expert, gaffer, genius, govern, honcho, leader, manage, mentor, pick up, pundit, season, subdue, temper **07** acquire, captain, conquer, control, dab hand, egghead, leading, maestro, manager, skilful, skilled, skipper, teacher, wise guy **08** director, employer, foremost, governor, masterly, overcome, overlord, overseer, suppress, vanquish, virtuoso **09** commander, dexterous, overpower, pedagogue, practised, preceptor, principal, Signorino, subjugate **10** controller, instructor, past master, proficient **11** controlling, experienced, grand master, predominant, symposiarch, triumph over **12** get the hang of, professional, schoolmaster **13** most important, schoolteacher **14** schoolmistress, superintendent

masterful
05 bossy, pithy **08** arrogant, despotic, powerful **09** imperious **10** autocratic, dominating, high-handed, peremptory, tyrannical **11** controlling, dictatorial, domineering, overbearing **13** authoritative

masterly
03 ace **05** adept, crack **06** adroit, artful, expert, superb **07** skilful, skilled, supreme **08** polished, superior, top-notch **09** dexterous, excellent, first-rate, magistral **10** consummate **11** overbearing **12** accomplished, professional

mastermind
04 mind, plan **05** forge, frame, hatch **06** brains, design, devise, direct, genius, manage **07** control, creator, dream up, inspire, manager, planner, think up **08** be behind, conceive, contrive, director, engineer, organize, virtuoso **09** architect, authority, initiator, intellect, organizer, originate **10** originator, prime mover

masterpiece
05 jewel **08** creation **09** work of art

10 magnum opus, masterwork **11** chef d'oeuvre

masterstroke
04 coup, feat **07** success, triumph, victory **10** attainment **11** achievement **12** coup de maître **14** accomplishment

mastery
04 grip, rule **05** grasp, skill **07** ability, command, control, knowhow, prowess, triumph, victory **08** dominion **09** authority, dexterity, direction, expertise, knowledge, supremacy, upper hand **10** ascendancy, capability, domination, virtuosity **11** familiarity, proficiency, sovereignty, superiority **13** comprehension, understanding

• **strive for mastery**
04 kemp

masticate
03 eat **04** chew **05** champ, chomp, knead, munch **06** crunch **08** ruminate **09** manducate **10** chew the cud

mastication
06 eating **07** chewing **08** champing, munching **10** rumination **11** manducation

mat
03 rug **04** dull, felt, knot, mass, matt, taut, tawt **05** frost, matte, tatty, twist **06** carpet, felter, paunch, tangle, tatami **07** cluster, coaster, doormat, drugget **08** place mat, table mat, underlay **09** underfelt **10** interweave, lustreless

match
03 fit, pit, tie, vie **04** ally, bout, copy, fuse, game, join, link, main, mate, meet, pair, peer, spar, suit, team, test, twin, yoke **05** adapt, agree, amate, blend, equal, event, fusee, fuzee, light, marry, rival, spill, tally, taper, trial, union, unite, vesta **06** accord, besort, couple, double, fellow, go with, marrow, merger, oppose, pair up, relate **07** combine, compact, compare, compete, connect, contend, contest, hitch up, Lucifer, pairing, paragon, pattern, replica **08** alliance, bonspiel, coupling, locofoco, marriage, parallel, tone with **09** accompany, companion, duplicate, encounter, harmonize, lookalike **10** competitor, complement, co-ordinate, correspond, dead ringer, equivalent, go together, keep up with, one of a pair, pit against, Promethean, tournament **11** affiliation, combination, competition, counterpart, measure up to, partnership, safety match **13** be in agreement

See also **game**; **sport**

• **match up to**
04 meet **05** reach **08** approach, come up to, live up to **11** compare with, measure up to **12** make the grade

• **start of match, start the match**
02 KO **05** break, bully **06** tee off **07** face-off, kick-off **13** break the balls

matching
04 like, same, twin **06** double, in sync, paired **07** coupled, in synch, similar **08** blending, parallel **09** analogous, duplicate, identical **10** comparable, equivalent **11** correlative, harmonizing **12** co-ordinating **13** complementary, complementing, corresponding

matchless
06 unique **07** perfect **08** makeless, peerless **09** nonpareil, unmatched **10** inimitable, unequalled, unexcelled, unrivalled **11** unsurpassed **12** incomparable, unparalleled, without equal **13** beyond compare

mate
03 fit, pal, wed, wus **04** chum, feer, fere, join, leap, line, maik, make, nick, oppo, pair, twin, wack, wife **05** breed, buddy, china, crony, cully, equal, feare, fiere, marry, match, rival **06** baffle, buffer, cobber, co-mate, couple, deputy, fellow, friend, gender, helper, hubbie, marrow, missis, missus, mucker, pheere, spouse, subdue **07** baffled, compeer, comrade, consort, daunted, husband, Mr Right, oldster, paragon, partner **08** confound, copulate, co-worker, sidekick, workmate **09** assistant, associate, boyfriend, checkmate, colleague, companion, exhausted, other half **10** accomplice, apprentice, better half, checkmated, china plate, confounded, equivalent, girlfriend **11** counterpart, subordinate **12** fellow worker **14** opposite number

material
03 gen, key **04** body, data, info, work **05** cloth, facts, gross, ideas, notes, stuff, vital **06** bodily, fabric, matter, medium **07** details, earthly, germane, low-down, numbers, serious, textile, weighty, worldly **08** apposite, concrete, evidence, palpable, physical, relevant, tangible **09** corporeal, essential, important, momentous, pertinent, substance **10** meaningful **11** information, particulars, significant, substantial **12** constituents **13** consequential, indispensable **15** facts and figures

See also **art**; **building**; **fabric**

• **set material in position**
03 lay

materialism
05 greed **06** hylism **08** hylicism, somatism **11** consumerism, worldliness **12** corporealism **15** acquisitiveness

materialistic
07 worldly **08** banausic **09** bourgeois, mammonist, mercenary **11** acquisitive, consumerist, mammonistic **13** money-grabbing **14** bread-and-butter

materialize
05 arise, occur, reify **06** appear, happen, turn up **08** take place, take shape **12** show yourself **13** become visible, come into being **14** reveal yourself

materially

04 much **07** gravely, greatly
09 basically, seriously **11** essentially
12 considerably **13** fundamentally,
significantly, substantially

maternal

04 fond, kind, warm **05** mumsy
06 caring, doting, gentle, loving,
tender **08** motherly, vigilant
09 nurturing **10** comforting,
motherlike, nourishing, protective
12 affectionate **13** understanding

matey *see* **maty, matey**

mathematics

Branches of mathematics include:

06 conics
07 algebra, applied, fluxion
08 calculus, geometry
09 set theory
10 arithmetic, game theory, statistics
11 games theory, group theory
12 number theory, trigonometry
13 combinatorics
14 biomathematics
15 metamathematics, pure
mathematics

Mathematics terms include:

02 pi
03 arc, set
04 apex, area, axes, axis, base, cube,
edge, face, line, mean, mode, plus,
root, side, sine, skew, unit, zero
05 angle, chaos, chord, curve, depth,
equal, graph, group, helix, locus,
minus, ogive, point, ratio, solid,
speed, total, width
06 binary, chance, convex, cosine,
degree, factor, height, length,
linear, matrix, median, number,
origin, radian, radius, sample,
secant, sector, spiral, square,
subset, vector, vertex, volume
07 algebra, average, bearing,
bounded, breadth, chaotic,
concave, decimal, divisor, formula,
fractal, integer, mapping,
maximum, measure, minimum,
modulus, oblique, product,
segment, tangent
08 addition, analysis, antipode,
argument, bar chart, bar graph,
binomial, calculus, capacity,
constant, converse, cube root,
diagonal, diameter, discrete,
dividend, division, equation,
exponent, fraction, function,
geometry, gradient, identity,
infinity, latitude, less than, multiple,
parabola, pie chart, quadrant,
quartile, quotient, rotation,
symmetry, variable, variance,
velocity, vertical
09 algorithm, Cartesian, congruent,
factorial, frequency, histogram,
hyperbola, iteration, logarithm,
longitude, numerator, odd number,
operation, parameter, perimeter,
remainder
10 acute angle, arithmetic,

complement, continuous,
coordinate, covariance, derivative,
even number, horizontal,
hypotenuse, percentage,
percentile, place value, proportion,
protractor, Pythagoras, real
number, reciprocal, reflection,
regression, right-angle, square root,
statistics, subtractor
11 approximate, coefficient,
combination, coordinates,
correlation, denominator,
determinant, enlargement,
equidistant, exponential, greater
than, integration, magic square,
mirror image, Möbius strip, obtuse
angle, permutation, plane figure,
prime number, probability,
Pythagorean, real numbers, reflex
angle, translation, Venn diagram,
whole number
12 asymmetrical, cross section,
distribution, random sample,
straight line, trigonometry, universal
set
13 circumference, complex number,
Mandelbrot set, mixed fraction,
natural number, ordinal number,
parallel lines, perpendicular,
quadrilateral, scalar segment,
triangulation
14 axis of symmetry, cardinal number,
common fraction, directed number,
mirror symmetry, multiplication,
negative number, parallel planes,
positive number, rational number,
transformation, vulgar fraction
15 conjugate angles, differentiation,
imaginary number, scalene triangle

Mathematicians include:

03 Dee (John), Lie (Sophus)
04 Abel (Niels Henrik), Hero (of
Alexandria), Hopf (Heinz), Kerr
(Roy), Pell (John), Tait (Peter
Guthrie), Thom (René), Venn (John),
Weil (André), Weyl (Hermann)
05 Bayes (Thomas), Boole (George),
Dirac (Paul), Euler (Leonhard),
Gauss (Carl Friedrich), Gödel (Kurt),
Green (George), Hardy (Godfrey),
Hoyle (Sir Fred), Klein (Felix),
Monge (Gaspard), Peano
(Giuseppe), Serre (Jean-Pierre),
Snell (Willebrod), Vieta (Franciscus)
06 Ampère (André), Argand (Jean-
Robert), Bessel (Friedrich), Briggs
(Henry), Cantor (Georg), Cauchy
(Augustin Louis, Baron), Cayley
(Arthur), Euclid, Fermat (Pierre de),
Fields (J C), Fisher (Sir Ronald),
Galois (Évariste), Halley (Edmond),
Jacobi (Carl), Jordan (Camille),
Kelvin (William Thomson, Lord),
Lorenz (Edward), Markov (Andrei),
Möbius (August Ferdinand), Moivre
(Abraham de), Napier (John),
Newton (Sir Isaac), Pappus (of
Alexandria), Pascal (Blaise), Picard
(Émile), Stokes (Sir George), Turing
(Alan), Wallis (John), Wiener
(Norbert)

07 Alhazen, Babbage (Charles),
Cardano (Girolamo), Carroll
(Lewis), Eudoxus (of Cnidus),
Fourier (Joseph, Baron de), Galileo,
Germain (Sophie), Hilbert (David),
Laplace (Pierre, Marquis de),
Leibniz (Gottfried), Penrose
(Roger), Poisson (Siméon),
Riemann (Bernhard), Russell
(Bertrand, Earl), Shannon (Claude)
08 Alembert (Jean le Rond d'),
Birkhoff (George David), Dedekind
(Julius), De Morgan (Augustus),
Guldberg (Cato), Hamilton (Sir
William Rowan), Lagrange (Joseph
de, Comte), Legendre (Adrien-
Marie), Lovelace (Ada, Countess
of), Mercator (Nicolaus), Playfair
(John), Poincaré (Jules)
09 Bernoulli (Daniel), Bernoulli
(Jacques), Bronowski (Jacob),
Descartes (René), Dirichlet
(Lejeune), Fibonacci (Leonardo),
Minkowski (Hermann), Whitehead
(Alfred)
10 Apollonius (of Perga), Archimedes,
Diophantus, Hipparchus,
Maupertuis (Pierre Louis de),
Pythagoras, Sierpinski (Wactaw),
Torricelli (Evangelista), Zeno of
Elea
11 al-Khwarizmi
12 Eratosthenes

mating

06 fusing **07** coition, joining, pairing,
uniting **08** breeding, coupling,
matching, twinning **10** copulating,
copulation

matriarch

04 nana

matrimonial

06 wedded **07** marital, married,
nuptial, spousal, wedding **08** conjugal
marriage
• **matrimonial duties**
03 bed

matrimony

05 union **07** wedlock **08** marriage,
nuptials, spousage **09** espousals
12 married state

matrix

03 gel, mat **04** cast, form, mold, womb
05 array, frame, mould, plasm, table
06 stroma **07** context, matrice
08 analysis, chondrin, Jacobian,
template **09** composite, framework,
transpose **11** arrangement

matron

04 dame

matted

05 taggy **06** tangly **07** knotted,
tangled, tousled **08** uncombed
09 entangled **11** dishevelled **13** blood-
boltered

matter

02 go **03** pus **04** body, case, hyle, note
05 count, event, issue, point, stuff,
thing, topic, upset, value, worry

6 affair, bother, import, medium, weight **07** concern, content, episode, problem, subject, trouble **08** business, distress, incident, interest, material, nuisance, question, weakness **9** discharge, happening, make a stir, make waves, purulence, secretion, situation, substance **10** be relevant, difficulty, importance, occurrence, proceeding **11** be important, carry weight, consequence, shortcoming, suppuration **12** circumstance, cut a lot of ice, significance **13** have influence, inconvenience, mean something, momentousness **14** be of importance **15** make a difference

◦ as a matter of fact
5 truly **06** in fact, really **08** actually **11** as it happens **12** in actual fact
◦ matter of no importance
3 toy **10** triviality
◦ no matter
9 never mind **15** it does not matter, it is unimportant

matter-of-fact
3 dry **04** dull, flat **05** sober **06** thingy **7** deadpan, prosaic **08** lifeless, positive **09** practical, pragmatic, prosaical **10** pedestrian **11** down-to-earth, emotionless, pragmatical, unemotional **13** unimaginative, unsentimental **15** straightforward

matting
3 tat **04** bast

mattress
3 bed **04** Lilo® **05** futon **06** airbed, pallet **07** biscuit **08** crash-mat, water bed **09** paillasse, palliasse **10** feather bed

maturation
6 growth **08** fruition, ripening **9** seasoning **11** development

mature
3 age **04** bold, gray, grey, ripe, wise **5** adult, bloom, grown, of age, ready, ripen **06** evolve, grow up, mellow, nubile, season **07** concoct, develop, fall due, grown-up, perfect, prepare, ripened **08** balanced, complete, finished, joined-up, maturate, seasoned, sensible **09** come of age, finalized, full-grown, perfected **10** become ripe, precocious **11** become adult, draw to a head, experienced, responsible **12** become mellow, fully fledged **13** well-developed **14** become sensible, well-thought-out

maturity
3 age **06** summer, wisdom **7** manhood, puberty **08** majority, ripeness **09** adulthood, readiness, womanhood **10** experience, full growth, mellowness, perfection **11** coming of age **12** sensibleness **14** responsibility **15** age of discretion

matweed
4 nard

maty, matey
04 kind, warm **05** close, pally, thick, tight **06** blokey, chummy, folksy, genial **07** affable, cordial, helpful **08** amicable, blokeish, familiar, friendly, intimate, outgoing, sociable **09** agreeable, comradely, convivial, peaceable, receptive **10** favourable **11** good-natured, inseparable, neighbourly, sympathetic **12** affectionate, approachable, well-disposed **13** companionable

maudlin
05 drunk, gushy, mushy, soppy, tipsy, weepy **06** sickly, sloppy, slushy **07** fuddled, mawkish, tearful, weeping **09** emotional, half-drunk, schmaltzy **10** lachrymose **11** sentimental

maul
◊ *anagram indicator*
03 mug, paw **04** beat, belt, claw, mall, mell **05** abuse **06** attack, batter, beat up, do over, mangle, molest, thrash, wallop **07** assault, rough up **08** ill-treat, lacerate, maltreat, mutilate **09** manhandle **10** knock about

maunder
04 ease, inch, laze, roam, rove **05** amble, mooch, mosey, stray **06** babble, beggar, drivel, gabble, jabber, mutter, natter, rabbit, ramble, stroll, waffle, wander, witter **07** blather, chatter, grumble, meander, prattle, shuffle **08** rabbit on

Maureen
02 Mo

Mauritania
03 MRT, RIM

Mauritius
02 MS **03** MUS

mausoleum
04 mole, tomb **05** crypt, vault **08** catacomb, Taj Mahal **09** sepulchre **10** undercroft **13** burial chamber

maverick
05 rebel **08** agitator, outsider **09** odd one out **13** individualist, nonconformist **14** fish out of water

maw
04 gulf, jaws **05** abyss, chasm, mouth **06** gullet, throat **07** seagull, stomach **08** appetite **11** inclination

mawkish
04 flat, foul **05** gushy, mawky, mushy, soppy **06** feeble, gloopy, sickly, slushy **07** insipid, maggoty, maudlin **08** nauseous **09** emotional, loathsome, offensive, schmaltzy, squeamish **10** disgusting, nauseating **11** sentimental

mawkishly
06 feebly **07** mushily, soppily **11** emotionally, loathsomely **12** nauseatingly **13** sentimentally

maxim
03 saw **04** rule **05** adage, axiom, gnome, motto **06** byword, dictum,

saying **07** epigram, precept, proverb **08** aphorism, apothegm, moralism, sentence **09** principle, sentiment, watchword **10** apophthegm, prudential

maximize
05 add to, boost, breed, raise, widen **06** bump up, deepen, expand, extend, hike up, spread, step up **07** advance, augment, broaden, build up, develop, enhance, enlarge, further, magnify, prolong, scale up **08** heighten, increase **09** intensify, propagate **10** accumulate, strengthen

maximum
03 max, top **04** acme, full, high, most, peak **06** apogee, height, summit, utmost, zenith **07** biggest, ceiling, highest, largest, supreme, topmost **08** greatest, pinnacle, top point, ultimate **09** extremity, uttermost **10** upper limit

may
04 mote **08** hawthorn
• may it do
04 dich

maybe
◊ *anagram indicator*
07 could be, perhaps **08** possibly **09** perchance **11** conceivably, possibility **12** peradventure **13** for all you know

mayfly
06 day-fly **08** ephemera **09** caddis fly, ephemerid **10** green-drake **11** Plectoptera, turkey brown

mayhem
◊ *anagram indicator*
04 mess, riot **05** chaos, havoc **06** bedlam, tumult, uproar **07** anarchy, maiming **08** disorder, madhouse **09** confusion **10** disruption **11** lawlessness **15** disorganization

mayor
02 LM **05** maire **07** alcalde

Mayotte
03 MYT

maze
◊ *anagram indicator*
03 web **04** mesh **05** maise, maize, mease **06** jungle, puzzle, tangle, warren **07** complex, meander, network **09** confusion, honeycomb, intricacy, labyrinth

me
02 mi, us **03** moi

meadow
03 ing, lay, lea, lee, ley **04** inch, mead **05** field, grass, green, haugh **06** leasow, saeter **07** paddock, pasture, salting **09** grassland **11** pastureland

meadow-grass
03 poa

meagre
03 bar **04** arid, bony, lean, poor, puny, thin, weak **05** gaunt, mingy, small,

spare **06** barren, frugal, jejune, Lenten, maigre, measly, paltry, scanty, skimpy, skinny, slight, sparse, stingy **07** scraggy, scrawny, slender **08** exiguous, roncador, scrannel **09** deficient, emaciated, niggardly **10** inadequate, negligible, threadbare **12** insufficient **13** insubstantial

meagreness
07 poverty **08** puniness **09** smallness **10** deficiency, inadequacy, measliness, scantiness, slightness, sparseness, stinginess **13** insufficiency

meal
03 kai **04** fare, feed, kail, kale, meat, mess, mush **05** grout, scoff, skoff **06** farina, repast **07** meltith, surfeit **08** freeload, racahout **09** collation, raccahout, refection, scambling **12** refreshments

Meals include:
03 BBQ, tea
04 bite
05 feast, lunch, snack
06 barbie, brunch, buffet, dinner, nosh-up, picnic, repast, spread, supper, tiffin
07 banquet, blow-out, high tea
08 barbecue, cream tea, luncheon, takeaway, tea break, tea party, TV dinner
09 breakfast, cold table, collation, elevenses
10 fork supper, midday meal, slap-up meal
11 dinner party, evening meal
12 afternoon tea, safari supper
13 harvest supper

• before a meal
02 ap

mealy-mouthed
04 glib, prim **07** mincing **08** indirect, reticent **09** equivocal, hestitant, plausible **10** flattering **11** euphemistic **12** overdelicate **13** over-squeamish, smooth-tongued

mean
03 ace, aim, low, rad **04** base, cool, fate, fine, mega, mein, mene, mode, neat, norm, plan, poor, rare, show, vile, wish, wont **05** boffo, brill, cause, crack, cross, cruel, dirty, footy, imply, lowly, mangy, meane, mingy, nasty, prime, scall, slink, snide, tight **06** abject, aspire, common, convey, crabby, denote, design, dismal, divine, effect, entail, humble, intend, lament, lead to, mangey, matter, maungy, median, medium, middle, normal, ordain, ornery, paltry, ribald, ribaud, shabby, simple, skimpy, snotty, sordid, stingy, superb, unkind, way-out **07** appoint, average, beastly, betoken, caitiff, chintzy, connote, crucial, destine, express, grouchy, halfway, involve, mesquin, miserly, niggard, obscure, perfect, piggish, produce, propose, purport, purpose, radical, roynish, rybauld, selfish, signify, skilful, spaniel,

squalid, suggest, think of **08** beggarly, complain, fabulous, grasping, heavenly, indicate, intimate, mesquine, middling, mid-point, moderate, ordinary, result in, smashing, sneaking, spiteful, splendid, stand for, stunning, terrific, top-notch, very good, whoreson, wretched **09** admirable, brilliant, crotchety, cullionly, designate, earth-bred, excellent, fantastic, first-rate, malicious, matchless, middle way, miserable, niggardly, represent, symbolize, wonderful **10** base-minded, bring about, compromise, contracted, despicable, fast-handed, first-class, give rise to, golden mean, have in mind, ill-natured, marvellous, not half bad, predestine, remarkable, surpassing, threepenny, unequalled, unfriendly, ungenerous, unpleasant **11** bad-tempered, be important, carry weight, close-fisted, close-handed, exceptional, happy medium, high-quality, magnificent, near the bone, necessitate, outstanding, sensational, superlative, tight-fisted **12** cheese-paring, disagreeable, intermediate, middle course, parsimonious, second to none, unparalleled **13** have influence, penny-pinching, uncomfortable **14** inconsiderable, out of this world **15** make a difference

• mean time
02 MT

meander
04 bend, ease, inch, laze, maze, roam, rove, turn, wind **05** amble, curve, mooch, mosey, snake, stray, twist **06** ramble, stroll, wander, wimple, zigzag **07** shuffle, turning, whimple **09** sinuosity **10** perplexity

meandering
◇ *anagram indicator*
07 sinuous, snaking, turning, winding **08** indirect, rambling, tortuous, twisting **09** meandrous, wandering **10** circuitous, convoluted, roundabout, serpentine

meaning
03 aim **04** feck, gist, goal, hang, idea, plan, wish **05** drift, point, sense, trend, value, worth **06** import, letter, object, spirit, thrust **07** essence, message, purpose **08** sentence **09** intention, objective, substance **10** aspiration, definition, expression, usefulness **11** connotation, elucidation, explanation, explication, implication **12** construction, significance **13** signification **14** interpretation

meaningful
05 valid **06** useful **07** pointed, serious, telling, warning **08** eloquent, material, pregnant, relevant, speaking **09** effective, important **10** expressive, purposeful, suggestive, worthwhile **11** significant

meaningfully
08 usefully **09** pointedly **10** eloquently, relevantly **11** effectively,

importantly **12** expressively, purposefully, suggestively **13** significantly

meaningless
04 vain **05** empty **06** absurd, futile, hollow **07** aimless, trivial, useless, vacuous **08** trifling, unsensed **09** gibberish, pointless, senseless, worthless **10** irrational, motiveless **11** nonsensical, purposeless **13** insignificant, insubstantial **14** expressionless, unintelligible

• meaningless word, meaningless refrain
05 nonny **07** ducdame, mirbane **08** falderal, fal de rol, folderol, rumbelow, rum-ti-tum **09** expletive **11** rumti-iddity **12** rumpti-iddity

meaninglessly
06 in vain, vainly **08** futilely **09** aimlessly, uselessly **11** pointlessly, senselessly **12** irrationally **13** purposelessly **14** unintelligibly

meanly
06 poorly, slight **07** cruelly, nastily **08** beggarly, commonly, scurvily, shabbily, unkindly **09** miserably, niggardly, selfishly **10** graspingly, spitefully **12** contemptibly, ungenerously, unpleasantly

meanness
09 parsimony **10** niggardise, niggardize, stinginess **11** mesquinerie, miserliness **12** illiberality **13** niggardliness, penuriousness **15** close-fistedness, close-handedness, tight-fistedness

means
03 way **04** mode **05** funds, money **06** agency, assets, avenue, course, income, manner, medium, method, riches, wealth **07** capital, channel, fortune, process, vehicle **08** property **09** affluence, resources, substance **10** instrument **11** wherewithal

• by all means
06 surely **08** of course **09** certainly, naturally **10** of all loves **11** à toute force **12** with pleasure

• by means of
03 per, via **04** with **05** using **07** through **08** by dint of **11** as a result o **12** with the aid of **13** with the help of

• by no means
04 none **05** never, no way **07** in no way **08** not at all **11** anything but **12** certainly not

• having enough means
04 able

meantime, meanwhile
05 among **06** for now **07** interim **12** concurrently, for the moment, in the interim **13** at the same time, in the interval, in the meantime **14** in the meanwhile, simultaneously **15** for the time being

measly
04 mean, poor, puny **05** mingy, petty **06** meagre, paltry, scanty, skimpy,

potty, stingy **07** miserly, pitiful, trivial
8 beggarly, pathetic, piddling
9 miserable, niggardly **10** ungenerous
2 contemptible

measurable
8 material, mensural, moderate
9 gaugeable **10** assessable,
omputable, fathomable, mensurable,
oticeable **11** appreciable, perceptible,
ignificant **12** determinable,
uantifiable, quantitative

measure
2 be **03** act, cut, lot, pit **04** area, bill,
ulk, deed, gage, line, mass, mete,
orm, pace, part, rate, read, rule, size,
tep, tape, test, time, unit **05** depth,
auge, judge, level, limit, means, meter,
netre, piece, plumb, quota, range,
uler, scale, scope, share, sound, units,
alue, weigh, width **06** action, amount,
ssess, course, degree, extent, fathom,
eight, length, method, ration, record,
hythm, size up, strain, survey, system,
olume, weight **07** compute, expanse,
ortion, rake-off, statute **08** acid test,
ppraise, capacity, division, estimate,
valuate, quantify, quantity, standard,
averse **09** allotment, barometer,
enchmark, calculate, criterion,
etermine, dimension, enactment,
xpedient, magnitude, procedure,
estraint, treatment, yardstick
0 allocation, dimensions, litmus test,
neasure off, measure out, moderation,
roceeding, proportion, resolution,
ouchstone **11** proportions

ee also **measurement**

beyond measure
8 out of cry **09** endlessly, immensely
0 extra modum, infinitely
1 excessively, inestimably, limitlessly
2 beyond belief, incalculably

for good measure
6 as well **07** besides **08** as a bonus
0 in addition **11** furthermore **12** over
nd above

**get the measure of, take the
neasure of**
4 rate **05** gauge, judge, value
6 assess, handle, reckon, size up
8 appraise, estimate, evaluate
9 calculate, determine **12** get a
andle on

measure off
3 fix **05** limit **07** delimit, lay down,
nark out, pace out **09** demarcate,
letermine **10** measure out
2 circumscribe

measure out
5 allot, issue **06** assign, divide **07** deal
ut, dole out, hand out, mete out, pour
ut **08** dispense, share out
9 apportion, parcel out **10** distribute,
roportion

measure up
2 do **07** shape up, suffice **10** fit the
ill, pass muster **11** fill the bill **12** make
he grade **15** come up to scratch

measure up to
4 meet **05** equal, match, rival, touch
7 satisfy **08** come up to, live up to

09 match up to **11** compare with
12 make the grade

measured
04 slow **06** steady **07** careful, planned,
precise, regular, studied **08** reasoned
09 unhurried **10** calculated,
considered, deliberate, mensurable,
restrained, rhythmical
12 premeditated **14** well-thought-out

measureless
04 vast **07** endless, immense
08 infinite **09** boundless, limitless,
unbounded **10** bottomless
11 inestimable, innumerable
12 immeasurable, incalculable

measurement
04 area, bulk, gage, mass, size, tare,
unit **05** depth, range, width
06 amount, extent, height, length,
sizing, survey, volume, weight
07 expanse, gauging, reading
08 capacity, quantity, weighing
09 amplitude, appraisal, dimension,
judgement, magnitude **10** assessment,
estimation, evaluation, proportion
11 calculation, calibration,
computation, proportions
12 appreciation **14** quantification

Measurement units include:

01 f, g, k, l, m, t, y
02 as, cg, cm, ct, dg, em, en, ft, gm, gr,
hg, kg, lb, li, mg, mm, oz, pt, st, yd
03 amp, are, bar, bel, bit, cab, cor, cup,
cwt, day, ell, erg, gal, grt, hin, kat,
kin, kip, kos, lay, lea, ley, log, lux,
mho, mil, mna, nit, ohm, oke, pin,
rem, rod, tod, ton, tun, wey
04 acre, aune, barn, bath, baud, boll,
bolt, butt, cell, cord, coss, cran,
demy, dyne, epha, foot, gill, gram,
hand, hour, inch, kati, khat, knot,
link, mile, mill, mina, mole, muid,
nail, obol, omer, peck, pica, pint,
pipe, pole, pood, ream, rood, rope,
seer, sone, span, tael, thou, tola,
torr, vara, volt, watt, week, yard, year
05 cable, caneh, catty, chain, cubit,
ephah, farad, henry, hertz, joule,
kaneh, katti, litre, lumen, metre,
month, ounce, perch, point, pound,
quart, stere, stone, tesla, therm,
tonne, weber
06 ampere, barrel, bushel, decade,
degree, fathom, firkin, gallon,
gramme, kelvin, league, minute,
newton, parsec, pascal, radian,
second
07 calorie, candela, century, coulomb,
decibel, fresnel, furlong, hectare,
long ton, siemens, volt amp
08 angstrom, cord foot, hogshead,
kilogram, millibar, short ton
09 becquerel, board foot, centigram,
cubic foot, cubic inch, cubic yard,
decimetre, foot-pound, kilolitre,
kilometre, light year, metric ton,
milligram, steradian
10 atmosphere, barleycorn, centilitre,
centimetre, cubic metre, fluid
ounce, hectolitre, hoppus foot,

horsepower, kilogramme,
micrometre, millennium, millilitre,
millimetre, millistere, square foot,
square inch, square mile, square yard
11 centigramme, milligramme,
newton metre, square metre
12 cable's length, nautical mile
13 degree Celsius, hundredweight,
volts per metre
14 cubic decimetre, farads per metre,
henrys per metre
15 cubic centimetre, metres per
second, newtons per metre, square
decimetre, square kilometre

See also **measurement of pressure**
under **pressure**; **timber**; **unit of weight**
under **weight**; **wood**

• **Old Measurement**
02 OM

measuring instrument

Measuring instruments include:

04 rule
05 gauge, meter
06 octant
07 ammeter, balance, burette, pipette,
sextant
08 luxmeter, odometer, ohmmeter,
quadrant
09 altimeter, barometer, callipers,
cryometer, dosimeter, flowmeter,
focimeter, hodometer, hourglass,
manometer, milometer, optometer,
pedometer, plumb line, pyrometer,
rheometer, steelyard, stopwatch,
vinometer, voltmeter, volumeter,
wattmeter, wavemeter
10 anemometer, audiometer,
bathometer, clinometer,
cyclometer, gravimeter,
hydrometer, hyetometer,
hygrometer, hypsometer,
micrometer, mileometer,
multimeter, ombrometer,
photometer, planimeter, protractor,
pulsimeter, radiosonde,
tachometer, tachymeter,
theodolite, vibrograph, vibrometer,
viscometer
11 calorimeter, chronometer,
colorimeter, dynamometer,
pluviometer, pyranometer,
salinometer, seismograph,
seismometer, speedometer,
spherometer, tape measure,
tensiometer, thermometer,
vaporimeter, velocimeter,
weighbridge
12 Breathalyser®, densitometer,
evaporimeter, galvanometer,
inclinometer, magnetometer,
psychrometer, respirometer,
spectrometer, sphygmometer,
trundle wheel, viscosimeter
13 accelerometer, decelerometer,
Geiger counter, saccharometer
14 geothermometer, interferometer

See also **gauge**

meat
03 nub **04** core, crux, eats, fare, food,
gist, grub, nosh, pith, tuck **05** flesh,

heart, point, scran **06** kernel, marrow, tucker, viands **07** essence, nucleus, rations **08** eatables, victuals **09** substance **10** provisions, sustenance **11** comestibles, nourishment, subsistence **12** fundamentals

Cold meats include:

03 ham
04 beef, game, pâté, pork, Spam®
06 salami, tongue, turkey
07 biltong, chicken, chorizo, kabanos, pork pie, sausage, terrine, venison
08 bresaola, Cervelat, cold cuts, cured ham, meat loaf, ox tongue, parma ham, pastrami, salt beef
09 Bierwurst, glazed ham, liver paté, Mettwurst, pepperoni, rillettes, saucisson, scotch egg
10 breaded ham, corned beef, crumbed ham, liverwurst, mortadella, prosciutto, Serrano ham
11 sausage roll
12 Ardennes pâté, Brunswick ham, Brussels pâté, jamón serrano, liver sausage, luncheon meat, peppered beef, Wiltshire ham
13 chicken breast, garlic sausage, honey roast ham, Schinkenwurst, smoked sausage
15 luncheon sausage

Meat cuts include:

03 leg, rib, sey
04 chop, clod, hand, hock, loin, neck, rack, rump, shin
05 baron, chine, chuck, flank, hough, round, scrag, shank
06 breast, collar, cutlet, fillet, saddle
07 best end, brisket, buttock, knuckle, sirloin, topside
08 escalope, forehock, noisette, popeseye, shoulder, spare rib
09 aitchbone, médaillon
10 silverside
11 filet mignon, porterhouse

Meats and meat products include:

03 ham, MRM, red
04 beef, bush, duck, hare, lamb, loaf, pâté, pork, Spam®, spek, veal
05 bacon, brawn, goose, heart, liver, mince, offal, quail, speck, steak, tripe, vifda, vivda, white
06 brains, burger, faggot, gammon, grouse, haggis, haslet, kidney, mutton, oxtail, pigeon, polony, rabbit, tongue, turkey
07 biltong, chicken, fatback, griskin, harslet, long pig, pemican, poultry, rissole, sausage, variety, venison
08 bushmeat, foie gras, fricadel, luncheon, meat loaf, pemmican, pheasant, scrapple, trotters
09 forcemeat, frikkadel, hamburger, partridge, rillettes
10 beefburger, horseflesh, minced beef, sweetbread
11 pig's knuckle, sausage meat
12 black pudding, luncheon meat

13 shield of brawn
14 mousse de canard

meaty

04 rich **05** beefy, burly, heavy, hunky, pithy, solid **06** brawny, fleshy, hearty, sturdy **08** muscular, profound **09** strapping **10** meaningful **11** interesting, significant, substantial

mechanic

07 artisan **08** engineer, operator **09** artificer, grauncher, groundman, machinist, operative, repairman, tradesman **10** groundsman, millwright, technician **11** card-sharper, mechanician, tradeswoman **12** grease monkey

mechanical

04 cold, dead, dull **06** manual, reflex **07** organic, routine **08** electric, habitual, lifeless, soulless **09** automated, automatic, dynamical, technical, unfeeling **10** impersonal, mechanized, unthinking **11** emotionless, instinctive, involuntary, machine-like, mechanistic, perfunctory, power-driven, unconscious, unemotional **12** matter-of-fact **14** machine-powered

mechanically

09 routinely **10** as a machine, by a machine, habitually **11** intuitively, on autopilot **12** unthinkingly **13** automatically, instinctively, involuntarily, unconsciously **14** electronically

mechanism

04 guts, tool **05** gears, means, motor, works **06** action, agency, device, engine, gadget, medium, method, system **07** channel, machine, process **08** gimcrack, jimcrack, movement, workings **09** apparatus, appliance, interlock, machinery, operation, procedure, propeller, structure, technique **10** components, instrument, propelment **11** contraption, contrivance, functioning, performance

mechanize

07 program **08** automate **11** computerize

medal

04 gold, gong **05** award, cross, model, prize **06** bronze, honour, reward, ribbon, silver, trophy **08** contorno, vernicle **09** gold medal, medallion **10** decoration, touch-piece **11** bronze medal, contorniate, silver medal

See also **military**

meddle

◊ *anagram indicator*
03 mix, pry **04** mell, mess **05** medle, snoop **06** butt in, fiddle, kibitz, tamper, temper, tinker **07** intrude **09** interfere, intervene **10** stickybeak **12** put your oar in **14** poke your nose in, stick your oar in **15** stick your nose in

meddlesome

04 nosy **05** nosey **06** prying

08 meddling, snooping **09** intruding, intrusive, pragmatic **11** interfering, mischievous, pragmatical

mediaeval *see* **medieval, mediaeval**

mediate

06 convey, middle, settle, step in, umpire **07** referee, resolve, stickle **08** indirect, moderate, transmit **09** arbitrate, intercede, interpose, intervene, negotiate, reconcile **10** conciliate **11** intervening **12** intermediate **13** act as mediator **15** act as peacemaker

mediation

11 arbitration, good offices, negotiation, peacemaking **12** conciliation, intercession, intervention **13** interposition **14** reconciliation

mediator

04 mean **05** judge **06** priest, umpire **07** arbiter, referee **08** stickler **09** go-between, middleman, moderator, Ombudsman, thirdsman **10** arbitrator, interceder, intervener, negotiator, peacemaker, reconciler **11** conciliator, intercessor, interventor **12** honest broker, intermediary

medical

03 med

See also **disease**

Medical and surgical equipment includes:

03 ECG, MRI
05 clamp, swabs
06 canula, scales
07 cannula, curette, dilator, forceps, inhaler, scalpel, scanner, syringe
08 catheter, iron lung, speculum, tweezers, X-ray unit
09 aspirator, auriscope, autoclave, CT scanner, endoscope, incubator, inhalator, nebulizer, retractor
10 audiometer, CAT scanner, ear syringe, hypodermic, kidney dish, microscope, MRI scanner, oxygen mask, rectoscope, respirator, rhinoscope, sterilizer, ultrasound
11 body scanner, first aid kit, laparoscope, stethoscope, stomach pump, thermometer
12 bronchoscope, isolator tent, laryngoscope, resuscitator, surgical mask, urethroscope
13 aural speculum, defibrillator, specimen glass
14 oesophagoscope, operating table, ophthalmoscope, oxygen cylinder
15 instrument table

Medical specialists include:

07 dentist
08 optician
09 dietician, homeopath
10 homoeopath, oncologist, orthoptist, pharmacist
11 audiologist, chiropodist, neurologist, optometrist, pathologist, radiologist

2 anaesthetist, cardiologist,
chiropractor, embryologist,
geriatrician, immunologist,
obstetrician, orthodontist,
orthopaedist, psychiatrist,
psychologist, toxicologist
3 dermatologist, gerontologist,
gynaecologist, haematologist,
paediatrician, vaccinologist
4 bacteriologist, microbiologist,
pharmacologist, rheumatologist
5 endocrinologist, ophthalmologist,
physiotherapist

see also **doctor**; **nurse**

medical man *see* **doctor**
medical records
4 case

medicinal
6 physic 07 healing, medical
8 curative, physical, remedial
9 restorative, therapeutic 12 health-
giving

medicinally
9 medically 10 curatively, remedially
13 restoratively 15 therapeutically

medicine
3 med 04 cure, drug 05 trade
6 remedy 07 panacea 09 analeptic,
physician 10 medicament, medication
2 prescription 14 pharmaceutical

see also **drug**

Branches of medicine include:
5 ob-gyn
7 otology, urology
8 nosology, obs/gynae, oncology,
pharmacy
9 andrology, audiology, chiropody,
dentistry, neurology, optometry,
pathology, radiology
0 cardiology, embryology, geriatrics,
immunology, obstetrics,
osteopathy, pediatrics, psychiatry,
psychology, toxicology
1 dermatology, diagnostics,
gerontology, gynaecology,
haematology, paediatrics,
physiatrics
2 anaesthetics, bacteriology,
kinesiatrics, microbiology,
orthodontics, orthopaedics,
perinatology, pharmacology,
radiotherapy, rheumatology
3 cytopathology, endocrinology,
ophthalmology, physiotherapy,
psychotherapy
4 electrotherapy, neuropathology,
neuroradiology, sports medicine
5 neuropsychiatry

*Branches of complementary
medicine include:*
4 yoga
5 reiki
7 massage, Pilates, Rolfing, shiatsu
8 Ayurveda
9 herbalism, iridology
0 art therapy, autogenics,
homeopathy, meditation,
osteopathy

11 acupressure, acupuncture, aura
therapy, kinesiology, moxibustion,
naturopathy, reflexology, t'ai chi
ch'uan
12 aromatherapy, Bach remedies,
chiropractic, hydrotherapy,
hypnotherapy, macrobiotics
14 autosuggestion, crystal healing,
herbal medicine
15 Chinese medicine, thalassotherapy

Medicine types include:
04 pill
05 tonic
06 arnica, emetic, gargle, tablet
07 antacid, capsule, inhaler, linctus,
lozenge, pessary, steroid
08 diuretic, ear drops, eye drops,
hypnotic, laxative, narcotic,
ointment, pastille, sedative
09 analgesic, paregoric, stimulant
10 antibiotic, antiseptic, gripe-water,
nasal spray, painkiller
11 anaesthetic, neuroleptic,
suppository
13 antibacterial, anticoagulant,
antihistamine, tranquillizer
14 anticonvulsant, antidepressant,
bronchodilator, hallucinogenic

See also **antibiotic**; **drug**

• **medicine box**
04 inro

medieval, mediaeval
03 med, old 07 antique, archaic
08 historic, obsolete, old-world,
outmoded 09 primitive 10 antiquated
12 antediluvian, old-fashioned 13 of
the Dark Ages, unenlightened 15 of the
Middle Ages

mediocre
04 hack, so-so 06 medium 07 average
08 adequate, inferior, middling,
ordinary, passable 09 tolerable 10 not
much cop, pedestrian, second-rate,
uninspired 11 bog standard,
commonplace, indifferent, not up to
much, respectable 12 run-of-the-mill
13 insignificant, no great shakes,
unexceptional 14 fair to middling
15 middle-of-the-road,
undistinguished

mediocrity
06 nobody 07 no-hoper, nothing
08 adequacy, dead loss, poorness
09 nonentity 10 non-starter
11 averageness, inferiority
12 indifference, ordinariness,
passableness, unimportance
14 insignificance

meditate
04 chew, muse, plan 05 brood, study,
think 06 design, devise, intend,
ponder, scheme 07 reflect
08 cogitate, consider, mull over,
ruminate 09 speculate, think over
10 chew the cud, deliberate, have in
mind 11 concentrate, contemplate

meditation
02 TM 05 study, zazen 06 musing

07 reverie, thought 08 brooding
09 pondering 10 brown study,
cogitation, reflection, ruminating,
rumination 11 cerebration, mulling
over, speculation 12 deliberation,
excogitation 13 concentration,
contemplation

meditative
07 museful, pensive 08 ruminant,
studious 09 prayerful 10 cogitative,
reflective, ruminative, thoughtful
12 deliberative 13 contemplative

Mediterranean
03 Med

medium
01 m 03 med, way 04 fair, form, mean,
mode, norm 05 ether, means, organ,
stuff 06 agency, avenue, centre,
medial, median, middle, midway,
milieu 07 average, channel, element,
habitat, midsize, psychic, setting,
vehicle 08 ambience, material,
middling, midpoint, moderate,
standard 09 middle way, spiritist,
substance 10 atmosphere,
compromise, conditions, golden
mean, influences, instrument
11 clairvoyant, environment, happy
medium, necromancer
12 intermediate, middle ground,
sound-carrier, spiritualist,
surroundings 13 circumstances,
fortune-teller 15 instrumentality, way
of expressing

• **by the medium of**
02 in

medley
◇ *anagram indicator*
03 mix 04 mess, olio, olla 05 fight,
mêlée 06 jumble, mingle 07 farrago,
melange, mixture, variety
08 macaroni, mishmash, mixed bag,
pastiche 09 confusion, macédoine,
patchwork, potpourri, quodlibet
10 assortment, collection,
hodgepodge, hotchpotch, miscellany,
salmagundi, salmagundy
11 gallimaufry, smorgasbord 13 helter-
skelter 14 conglomeration, omnium-
gatherum

meek
04 mild, tame, weak 05 lowly, quiet,
timid 06 docile, gentle, humble,
modest 07 patient 08 peaceful,
resigned, yielding 09 compliant,
spineless 10 forbearing, spiritless,
submissive, unassuming 11 deferential
13 long-suffering, unpretentious

meekly
06 gently, humbly, mildly 07 quietly
08 modestly 09 patiently
12 submissively 13 deferentially

meekness
07 modesty 08 docility, humility,
mildness, patience, softness, tameness,
timidity, weakness 09 deference,
lowliness 10 compliance, gentleness,
humbleness, submission
11 forbearance, resignation,

wimpishness **12** acquiescence, peacefulness **13** long-suffering, self-abasement, spinelessness **14** self-effacement, spiritlessness, submissiveness

meet
◊ *juxtaposition indicator*
03 get, pay, see **04** abut, bear, even, face, fill, game, give, hear, join, link, race, take **05** abide, cross, equal, event, greet, match, quits, rally, round, touch, unite **06** adjoin, answer, endure, fulfil, gather, handle, honour, hook up, link up, manage, muster, pay for, settle, suffer, tackle **07** balance, collect, connect, contest, convene, convoke, execute, fitting, fixture, meeting, perform, react to, receive, run into, satisfy, undergo **08** assemble, bump into, chance on, come upon, come up to, converge, cope with, deal with, listen to **09** discharge, encounter, fittingly, forgather, go through, intersect, look after, qualified, respond to, run across **10** come across, comply with, congregate, engagement, experience, foregather, happen upon, join up with, rencounter, rendezvous, tournament **11** competition, get together, measure up to **12** come together, intersection **14** get to grips with **15** make contact with
• **failure to meet**
04 gape

meeting
03 AGM, EGM, hui **04** date, meet, moot **05** rally, tryst, union, venue **07** cabinet, contact, gorsedd, session **08** abutment, assembly, camporee, concours, consulta, exercise, junction, wardmote **09** concourse, encounter, gathering, interface, interview **10** chautauqua, conference, confluence, convention, engagement, rencounter, rendezvous, watersmeet **11** appointment, assignation, conjunction, conventicle, convergence **12** intersection, introduction **13** confrontation **14** point of contact
See also **greeting**

meeting-place
04 gild, moot, Pnyx **05** guild, house, joint, lodge, marae, venue **06** baraza, centre **07** cenacle **10** confluence, rendezvous, vestry-room **11** senate-house **12** chapterhouse

megalomania
13 conceitedness **14** overestimation, self-importance **15** folie de grandeur

meitnerium
02 Mt

melancholy
03 low, sad **04** blue, down, glum **05** adust, blues, dumps, gloom, moody **06** dismal, gloomy, hipped, misery, rueful, somber, sombre, sorrow, spleen, woeful **07** doleful, pensive, sadness, unhappy **08** dejected, doldrums, downcast, mournful

09 allicholy, dejection, depressed, miserable, pessimism, sorrowful, splenetic, surliness, tristesse, woebegone **10** allycholly, deplorable, depression, despondent, dispirited, low spirits, lugubrious, pensieroso **11** atrabilious, despondency, downhearted, low-spirited, melancholia, melancholic, the black dog, unhappiness **12** disconsolate, heavy-hearted **13** hypochondriac, in the doldrums **14** down in the dumps
• **make melancholy**
03 hip, hyp

melange
◊ *anagram indicator*
03 mix **06** jumble, medley **07** farrago, mixture, variety **08** mishmash, mixed bag, pastiche **09** confusion, patchwork, potpourri **10** assortment, collection, hodgepodge, hotchpotch, miscellany, salmagundi **11** gallimaufry, smorgasbord **14** conglomeration, omnium-gatherum

mêlée
◊ *anagram indicator*
04 fray, mess **05** brawl, broil, chaos, fight, mix-up, rally, scrum, set-to **06** affray, fracas, jumble, medley, mellay, muddle, ruckus, rumpus, tangle, tussle **07** clutter, ruction, scuffle **08** disorder, dogfight, stramash **09** confusion, scrimmage, scrummage **10** free-for-all **11** battle royal **15** disorganization

Melia
03 nim **04** neem, nimb **05** neemb

mellifluous
04 soft **05** sweet **06** dulcet, mellow, smooth **07** honeyed, silvery, tuneful **08** canorous, soothing **10** euphonious, harmonious **13** sweet-sounding

mellow
04 full, kind, mild, rich, ripe, soft **05** happy, jolly, juicy, ripen, sweet **06** dulcet, fruity, genial, gentle, jovial, mature, placid, season, serene, smooth, soften, temper, tender **07** affable, amiable, cordial, improve, perfect, relaxed, rounded, sweeten, tuneful **08** amicable, cheerful, luscious, pleasant, resonant, tranquil **09** easy-going, melodious **10** euphonious, harmonious, pear-shaped **11** good-natured, kind-hearted **13** full-flavoured **15** make less extreme

melodic
05 sweet **06** dulcet **07** musical, silvery, tuneful **09** melodious **10** euphonious, harmonious **13** sweet-sounding

melodically
07 sweetly **09** musically, tunefully **11** melodiously **12** harmoniously

melodious
05 sweet **06** dulcet, pretty **07** melodic, musical, Orphean, silvery, songful, tuneful **09** cantabile **10** euphonious, harmonious **13** sweet-sounding

melodrama
07 tragedy **09** dramatics, high drama, staginess **10** overacting **11** histrionics, performance, tragicomedy **13** theatricality

melodramatic
03 OTT **05** hammy, stagy **06** stagey **08** overdone, theatric **10** histrionic, over-the-top, theatrical **11** exaggerated, extravagant, sensational **12** histrionical, overdramatic, overstrained, transpontine **13** overemotional **15** blood-and-thunder

melody
03 air **04** aria, ayre, part, song, tune **05** canto, chant, music, theme **06** cantus, rhythm, strain **07** euphony, harmony, melisma, musette, refrain **08** carillon, cavatina, part-song **09** cabaletta, cantilena, plainsong, sweetness **10** canto fermo, musicality **11** musicalness, tunefulness **12** augmentation, counterpoint **13** ranz-des-vaches **14** harmoniousness

melon
04 pepo **06** casaba **07** cassaba **09** cantaloup, musk melon, Ogen melon, rock melon **10** cantaloupe, Charentais, Galia melon **11** winter melon **13** honeydew melon

melt
◊ *anagram indicator*
03 ren, rin, run **04** blow, calm, flow, flux, fuse, move, thaw **05** smelt, touch **06** affect, relent, render, soften, spleen **07** defrost, liquate, liquefy, resolve **08** discandy, dissolve, moderate, unfreeze **09** discandie, uncongeal **10** colliquate, deliquesce, impregnate, make tender **12** become tender
• **melt away**
04 fade **06** dispel, vanish **08** disperse, dissolve, evanesce, fade away **09** disappear, evaporate

meltdown
06 defeat, fiasco **07** debacle, failure **08** abortion, calamity, collapse, disaster, downfall **09** breakdown **11** frustration, miscarriage **15** coming to nothing

member
01 M **02** MP **03** arm, leg, MBE, Mem **04** limb, part **05** organ **06** clause, fellow **07** comrade, dumaist, element **08** adherent **09** appendage, associate, extremity, stretcher **10** subscriber **12** incorporator **14** representative

membership
04 body, seat **07** fellows, members **08** comrades **09** adherence, adherents, enrolment **10** allegiance, associates, fellowship **11** affiliation, subscribers **13** participation **15** representatives

membrane
03 haw, rim **04** fell, film, kell, skin, veil **05** hymen, layer, sheet, velum

06 mucosa, septum, tissue
08 patagium **09** arachnoid,
diaphragm, partition **10** integument

memento
03 mem **04** Goss **05** relic, token
06 record, trophy **07** vestige
08 keepsake, memorial, reminder,
souvenir **11** remembrance

memo
03 fax **04** note **05** e-mail **06** letter
07 jotting, message **08** reminder
10 memorandum **11** aide-mémoire,
remembrance **12** memory-jogger

memoir
04 life **05** essay **06** record, report
07 account, journal **08** register
09 biography, chronicle, monograph,
narrative **13** autobiography

memoirs
05 diary **06** annals **07** diaries, records
08 journals, memories **09** life story
10 chronicles **11** confessions,
experiences **13** autobiography,
recollections, reminiscences

memorable
06 catchy, unique **07** notable, special
08 eventful, historic, striking
09 important, momentous
10 impressive, noteworthy,
remarkable **11** distinctive, outstanding,
significant **13** consequential,
distinguished, extraordinary,
unforgettable

memorandum
03 fax, mem **04** memo, note, slip **05** e-
mail, jurat **06** letter **07** jotting, message
08 memorial, reminder **09** bordereau
11 aide-mémoire, remembrance
12 memory-jogger

memorial
03 mem **05** brass, relic, stone, stupa
06 dagaba, dagoba, marker, memory,
plaque, record, shrine, statue, trophy,
Yizkor **07** memento, relique
08 cenotaph, ebenezer, monument,
Pantheon, souvenir **09** altar-tomb,
mausoleum, tombstone
10 gravestone, memorandum,
monumental, remembered
11 celebratory, Norman cross,
remembrance, testimonial
13 commemorative
See also **monument**

memorize
05 learn **06** get off, record
08 remember **09** celebrate **11** learn by
rote **12** learn by heart **14** commit to
memory

memory
03 RAM, ROM **04** mind, rote
06 honour, recall **07** tribute
09 retention, sovenance
10 observance **11** recognition,
remembrance **12** recollection,
reminiscence **13** commemoration
14 powers of recall
• **memory block**
04 page

men
02 OR
See also **man**
• **excluding men**
03 hen

menace
04 loom, lour, pain, pest, risk **05** alarm,
appal, bully, daunt, peril, press, scare,
shore **06** bother, coerce, danger,
dismay, hazard, screws, threat
07 terrify, warning **08** big stick,
browbeat, bullying, coercion, frighten,
jeopardy, nuisance, pressure, threaten
09 annoyance, terrorism, terrorize
10 intimidate, pressurize
11 browbeating, frighteners,
ominousness, public enemy,
terrorizing **12** intimidation,
troublemaker **13** tyrannization
15 thorn in your side

menacing
04 grim **07** looming, louring, ominous,
warning **08** alarming, minatory, sinister
09 Damoclean, dangerous,
impending, minacious, threatful
10 portentous **11** frightening,
threatening **12** intimidating,
intimidatory

mend
03 fix, sew, toe **04** beet, bete, cure,
darn, heal **05** amend, clout, emend,
patch, plash, refit, renew, run up, stick
06 bushel, cobble, reform, remedy,
repair, revise, solder **07** correct,
improve, patch up, recover, rectify,
restore **08** put right, renovate, solution
09 get better, make whole
10 ameliorate, put in order, recuperate,
supplement **14** mend your fences
15 put back together
• **mend your ways**
06 reform **15** improve yourself, make a
fresh start
• **on the mend**
07 healing **08** reviving **09** improving
10 recovering **12** convalescent,
convalescing, recuperating

mendacious
05 false, lying **06** untrue **08** perjured
09 deceitful, deceptive, dishonest,
insincere **10** fallacious, fictitious,
fraudulent, perfidious, untruthful
11 duplicitous

mendacity
03 lie **05** lying **06** deceit **07** perfidy,
perjury, untruth **09** duplicity,
falsehood **10** dishonesty, distortion,
inveracity **11** fraudulence, insincerity
13 deceitfulness, falsification
14 untruthfulness

mendelevium
02 Md

mendicant
03 bum **04** hobo **05** fakir, frate, friar,
sadhu, tramp **06** beggar, cadger,
canter, craver, pauper, saddhu, toerag
07 begging, bludger, cadging, jarkman,
moocher, sponger, vagrant
08 besognio, blighter, calender,

vagabond, whipjack **09** scrounger
10 down-and-out, freeloader,
panhandler, scrounging, supplicant
11 beachcomber, petitionary

menial
03 eta, low **04** base, dull **05** lowly, slave
06 boring, drudge, humble, minion,
ribald, skivvy **07** humdrum, routine,
servant, servile, slavish, waister
08 dogsbody, domestic, labourer
09 attendant, degrading, demeaning,
underling, unskilled **10** after-guard
11 ignominious, subservient

menstruation
04 flow **06** menses, period **07** courses
08 the curse, the usual **09** monthlies
10 menorrhoea **11** monthly flow
14 menstrual cycle, time of the month

mensuration
06 metage, survey **09** measuring,
surveying, valuation **10** assessment,
estimation, evaluation, planimetry
11 calculation, calibration,
computation, measurement

mental
◊ *anagram indicator*
03 ape, fey, mad **04** bats, gyte, loco,
nuts, wild **05** barmy, batty, buggy,
crazy, daffy, dippy, dotty, flaky, gonzo,
loony, loopy, manic, nutty, potty, queer,
wacko, wacky, wiggy **06** crazed,
cuckoo, fruity, insane, maniac, raving,
red-mad, screwy, troppo **07** bananas,
barking, berserk, bonkers, cracked,
frantic, lunatic, meshuga **08** abstract,
cerebral, crackers, demented,
deranged, dingbats, doolally, frenetic,
frenzied, maniacal, rational, unhinged,
unstable **09** cognitive, disturbed,
lymphatic, psychotic, up the wall
10 bestraught, conceptual, distracted,
distraught, frantic-mad, off the wall, off
your nut, out to lunch, ridiculous,
stone-crazy, unbalanced **11** not all
there, off the rails, off your head,
theoretical, unconscious
12 intellectual, mad as a hatter, off your
chump, round the bend **13** off your
rocker, of unsound mind, out of your
head, out of your mind, out of your
tree, round the twist **14** off your trolley,
wrong in the head **15** non compos
mentis, out of your senses
• **mental health workers**
15 men in white coats

mentality
04 mind **06** brains, make-up
07 faculty, mindset, outlook
08 attitude, ingenium **09** character,
intellect **10** grey matter, psychology
11 disposition, frame of mind,
personality, rationality **12** intelligence
13 comprehension, understanding,
way of thinking **14** mental attitude
15 little grey cells

mentally
07 ideally **08** inwardly **09** in the mind
10 rationally **11** emotionally
12 subjectively **14** intellectually
15 psychologically, temperamentally

mention
03 say **04** cite, hint, mind, name, note, talk **05** hight, mensh, quote, speak, state **06** bename, broach, cast up, drag up, exhume, hint at, impart, notice, remark, report, reveal, speech **07** bring up, declare, divulge, let fall, refer to, speak of, specify, touch on, tribute **08** allude to, allusion, citation, disclose, instance, intimate, nominate, point out, remember **09** introduce, make known, reference, statement **10** indication, particular **11** acknowledge, communicate, observation, recognition **12** announcement, notification **14** condescend upon **15** acknowledgement
• **don't mention it**
05 bitte **08** forget it, not at all **09** don't worry **12** it's a pleasure, it was nothing
• **not to mention**
05 let be **06** let-a-be **07** besides **08** as well as, let alone, much less **12** not including **13** not forgetting **14** to say nothing of

mentioned
05 cited **06** quoted, stated **08** foresaid, reported **09** aforesaid, fore-cited, forenamed **10** fore-quoted **13** forementioned **14** above-mentioned, aforementioned

mentor
03 rav **04** guru **05** coach, guide, swami, tutor **07** adviser, advisor, teacher, trainer **09** confidant, pedagogue, therapist **10** confidante, counsellor, instructor

menu
04 card, list **06** tariff **10** bill of fare **11** carte du jour

mercantile
05 trade **07** salable, trading **08** saleable **09** mercenary **10** commercial, marketable **12** merchantable

mercenary
04 hack, merc, paid **05** hired, venal **06** greedy, rutter, sordid **07** Hessian, pindari, Switzer **08** covetous, grasping, hired gun, hireling, huckster, pindaree **09** freelance, on the make, warmonger **10** avaricious, galloglass, lansquenet, mercantile, prostitute **11** acquisitive, condottiere, landsknecht, mammonistic **12** hired soldier, professional **13** free companion, materialistic, money-grubbing **15** money-orientated

merchandise
04 ware **05** cargo, goods, stock, trade, wares **07** dealing, freight, produce **08** products, shipment **09** vendibles **11** commodities

merchandize
04 hype, plug, push, sell, vend **05** carry, trade **06** deal in, market, peddle, retail, supply **07** promote **09** advertise, publicize, traffic in **10** buy and sell, distribute

merchant
05 agent, bunia, trade **06** broker, bunnia, dealer, factor, jobber, seller, trader, vendor **07** Antonio **08** hoastman, retailer, salesman **09** bourgeois, négociant **10** commercial, marcantant, saleswoman, shopkeeper, supercargo, trafficker, wholesaler **11** distributor, salesperson **14** sales executive

merciful
04 kind, mild **06** humane **07** clement, lenient, liberal, pitying, sparing **08** generous, gracious, tolerant **09** forgiving, merciable **10** forbearing **11** soft-hearted, sympathetic **12** humanitarian **13** compassionate, tender-hearted

mercifully
06 kindly **07** luckily **10** generously, graciously, thankfully, tolerantly **11** fortunately **15** compassionately, sympathetically, tender-heartedly

merciless
04 hard **05** cruel, harsh, rigid, stern **06** severe, wanton **07** callous, inhuman **08** inhumane, pitiless, ruthless **09** barbarous, heartless, unfeeling, unpitying, unsparing **10** implacable, inexorable, intolerant, relentless, unmerciful **11** hard-hearted, remorseless, unforgiving **13** unsympathetic

mercilessly
07 cruelly, harshly, sternly **08** severely **09** callously **10** implacably, inexorably, pitilessly, ruthlessly **11** heartlessly **12** relentlessly **13** hard-heartedly, remorselessly

mercurial
06 active, fickle, lively, mobile **07** erratic, flighty **08** spirited, unstable, variable, volatile **09** impetuous, impulsive, sprightly **10** capricious, changeable, inconstant **11** quicksilver **12** light-hearted **13** irrepressible, temperamental, unpredictable

mercury
02 Hg **06** Hermes

mercy
04 boon, pity **05** grace **06** favour, relief **07** godsend, quarter **08** blessing, clemency, good luck, kindness, leniency, mildness, sympathy **10** compassion, generosity, humaneness, misericord, tenderness **11** forbearance, forgiveness, misericorde **14** loving-kindness **15** humanitarianism
• **at the mercy of**
09 exposed to, prostrate **11** at the whim of **12** in the power of, vulnerable to **14** in the control of, unarmed against

mere
04 bare, lake, meer, meri, pool, poor, pure, very **05** bound, petty, plain, sheer, stark, utter **06** common, paltry, simple **07** unmixed **08** absolute, boundary, complete **10** absolutely, no

more than **13** pure and simple, unadulterated

merely
03 but **04** just, only **06** barely, hardly, purely, simply **08** scarcely **10** nothing but

meretricious
04 bold, loud **05** cheap, flash, gaudy, jazzy, showy, tacky **06** flashy, garish, glitzy, kitsch, made up, tawdry, vulgar **09** glamorous, insincere, tasteless **10** flamboyant **11** pretentious **12** ostentatious

merganser
04 smew

merge
03 die, dip, mix **04** fuse, join, meet, meld, sink **05** blend, unite, verge **06** mingle, plunge, team up **07** collate, combine, run into **08** coalesce, converge, intermix, liquesce, melt into **10** amalgamate, be engulfed, join forces **11** consolidate, incorporate **12** become lost in, come together **13** bring together **15** be assimilated in, be swallowed up in

merger
05 blend, union **06** fusion **08** alliance **09** coalition **11** combination, convergence **12** amalgamation, assimilation **13** confederation, consolidation, incorporation

merit
03 due **04** earn, good, plus **05** asset, claim, found, value, worth **06** credit, desert, praise, reward, talent, virtue **07** be worth, deserts, deserve, justify, quality, warrant **08** goodness **09** advantage **10** be worthy of, excellence, excellency, recompense, worthiness **11** distinction, high quality, strong point **12** be entitled to, have a right to **13** justification

merited
03 due **04** just **06** earned, worthy **07** condign, fitting **08** deserved, entitled, rightful **09** justified, warranted **11** appropriate **12** well-deserved

meritorious
04 good **05** right **06** worthy **08** laudable, virtuous, worthful **09** admirable, deserving, estimable, excellent, exemplary, righteous **10** creditable, honourable **11** commendable **12** praiseworthy

mermaid
05 siren **06** undine **07** seamaid **08** sea nymph, seawoman **11** water-spirit, water sprite

merrily
06 gladly **07** happily **08** blithely, chirpily, jovially **10** cheerfully, pleasantly

merriment
03 fun **05** mirth **06** frolic, gaiety **07** jollity, revelry, waggery **08** buoyance, carnival, hilarity, laughter

merry

09 amusement, festivity, jocundity, jolliment, joviality 10 blitheness, joyfulness, liveliness 11 high spirits 12 carefreeness, cheerfulness, conviviality, mirthfulness 13 jollification

merry

◇ anagram indicator
03 gay 04 cant, daft, gean, glad 05 gaudy, happy, jolly, nitid, riant, tipsy, vogie 06 blithe, cheery, chirpy, frolic, jocose, jocund, jovial, joyful, lively, tiddly 07 amusing, festive, gleeful, squiffy 08 carefree, cheerful, gleesome, mirthful, pleasant, sportful, sportive 09 convivial, heartsome, hilarious 10 frolicsome 11 saturnalian 12 high-spirited, light-hearted 13 in good spirits, slightly drunk 15 one over the eight

• **make merry**
04 gaud, rant, sing 05 dance, drink, revel 07 carouse, have fun, rejoice 09 celebrate 10 have a party 13 enjoy yourself

merry-andrew

05 clown 07 buffoon 11 Jack-pudding 13 pickle-herring

merry-go-round

08 carousel, galloper, joy-wheel 09 carrousel, gallopers, whirligig 10 roundabout

merrymaking

03 fun 05 party, revel 06 frolic, gaiety 07 revelry 08 carousal, merimake 09 carousing, festivity, galravage, gilravage, junketing, merriment 10 galravitch, gillravage, gilravitch, rejoicings 11 celebration, gillravitch 12 conviviality 13 jollification

mesh

03 net, web 04 trap 05 gauze, match, snare 06 engage, enmesh, inmesh, tangle 07 combine, connect, entwine, lattice, netting, network, tracery, trellis 08 dovetail, entangle 09 harmonize, interlock 10 co-ordinate, go together 11 fit together, latticework 12 come together, entanglement

mesmerize

04 grip 06 benumb 07 enthral, stupefy 08 entrance, transfix 09 captivate, fascinate, hypnotize, magnetize, spellbind 14 hold spellbound

mess

◇ anagram indicator
03 fix, jam, mix, mux, tip 04 dine, dirt, dump, hash, hole, meal, muck, muss, soss, spot, stew 05 botch, chaos, farce, filth, mix-up, musse, slosh 06 bungle, cock-up, course, guddle, hiccup, jumble, lash-up, litter, medley, midden, mucker, muddle, pickle, plight 07 balls-up, clutter, dilemma, failure, jackpot, pig's ear, screw-up, squalor, trouble, turmoil 08 disarray, disorder, hot water, quandary, shambles, slaister, whoopsie 09 confusion, deep water, dirtiness, praiseach, shemozzle,

shimozzle, tight spot 10 difficulty, dog's dinner, filthiness, pretty pass, schemozzle, shlemozzle, untidiness 11 predicament 13 dog's breakfast, embarrassment, pig's breakfast 15 disorganization

• **make a mess of**
04 flub, goof

• **mess about, mess around**
04 goof, play 05 upset 06 piddle, puddle, putter 09 faff about, goof about, muck about, play about 10 faff around, fool around, goof around, play around 11 potter about 12 fiddle around

• **mess about with, mess around with**
05 bother 07 trouble 08 play with 10 meddle with, tamper with, treat badly 13 fool about with, inconvenience, interfere with, play about with 14 fool around with, play around with

• **mess up**
04 foul, muff, ruin 05 bitch, bodge, botch, dirty, fluff, spoil 06 bungle, cock up, foul up, jumble, muck up, muddle, tangle, untidy 07 confuse, disrupt, louse up, screw up 08 dishevel 09 clutter up 10 disarrange 11 make a hash of, make a mess of

message

03 fax 04 gist, idea, memo, news, note, task, wire, word 05 cable, drift, e-mail, moral, point, sense, telex, theme 06 errand, import, letter, notice, report, thrust 07 dépêche, epistle, essence, express, meaning, missive, purport, tidings 08 aerogram, bulletin, dispatch, irenicon, mailgram, telegram, Teletype® 09 autoreply, eirenicon, telegraph, telepheme 10 communiqué, intimation, memorandum 11 implication, marconigram, Telemessage® 12 significance 13 communication

• **end message**
07 sign off

• **get the message**
03 see 04 twig 05 get it, grasp 06 follow, take in 07 catch on, latch on 08 cotton on, tumble to 09 latch onto 10 comprehend, cotton on to, get the hang, get the idea, understand 11 get the point 13 catch the drift, get the picture

messenger

04 page, peon, post, send 05 agent, angel, caddy, cadee, cadie, envoy 06 beadle, bearer, caddie, herald, Hermes, nuncio, runner 07 carrier, courier, express, Mercury, missive 08 dispatch, emissary, footpost 09 chaprassi, chaprassy, chuprassy, errand-boy, go-between, harbinger, woman post 10 ambassador, errand-girl, forerunner, pursuivant, shellycoat 11 internuncio 12 ambassadress, valet de place 13 gillie-wetfoot, secretary-bird 14 commissionaire 15 corbie-messenger, gillie-white-foot

messy

◇ anagram indicator
05 dirty, gungy, yucky, yukky 06 filthy, grubby, grungy, sloppy, untidy 07 chaotic, muddled, unkempt 08 bungling, confused, littered, slobbish, slovenly 09 cluttered, shambolic 10 disordered, in disarray 11 dishevelled 12 disorganized

metal

Metals include:

01 K (potassium), U (uranium), V (vanadium), W (tungsten), Y (yttrium)
02 Ac (actinium), Ag (silver), Al (aluminium), Am (americium), Au (gold), Ba (barium), Be (beryllium), Bi (bismuth), Bk (berkelium), Ca (calcium), Cd (cadmium), Ce (cerium), Cf (californium), Cm (curium), Co (cobalt), Cr (chromium), Cs (caesium), Cu (copper), Dy (dysprosium), Er (erbium), Es (einsteinium), Eu (europium), Fe (iron), Fm (fermium), Fr (francium), Ga (gallium), Gd (gadolinium), Ge (germanium), Hf (hafnium), Hg (mercury), Ho (holmium), In (indium), Ir (iridium), La (lanthanum), Li (lithium), Lr (lawrencium), Lu (lutetium), Md (mendelevium), Mg (magnesium), Mn (manganese), Mo (molybdenum), Na (sodium), Nb (niobium), Nd (neodymium), Ni (nickel), No (nobelium), Np (neptunium), Os (osmium), Pa (protactinium), Pb (lead), Pd (palladium), Pm (promethium), Po (polonium), Pr (praseodymium), Pt (platinum), Pu (plutonium), Ra (radium), Rb (rubidium), Re (rhenium), Rh (rhodium), Ru (ruthenium), Sb (antimony), Sc (scandium), Sm (samarium), Sn (tin), Sr (strontium), Ta (tantalum), Tb (terbium), Tc (technetium), Th (thorium), Ti (titanium), Tl (thallium), Tm (thulium), Yb (ytterbium), Zn (zinc), Zr (zirconium)
03 tin (Sn)
04 gold (Au), iron (Fe), lead (Pb), zinc (Zn)
06 barium (Ba), cerium (Ce), cobalt (Co), copper (Cu), curium (Cm), erbium (Er), indium (In), nickel (Ni), osmium (Os), radium (Ra), silver (Ag), sodium (Na)
07 bismuth (Bi), cadmium (Cd), caesium (Cs), calcium (Ca), fermium (Fm), gallium (Ga), hafnium (Hf), holmium (Ho), iridium (Ir), lithium (Li), mercury (Hg), niobium (Nb), rhenium (Re), rhodium (Rh), terbium (Tb), thorium (Th), thulium (Tm), uranium (U), yttrium (Y)
08 actinium (Ac), antimony (Sb), chromium (Cr), europium (Eu),

francium (Fr), lutetium (Lu), nobelium (No), platinum (Pt), polonium (Po), rubidium (Rb), samarium (Sm), scandium (Sc), tantalum (Ta), thallium (Tl), titanium (Ti), tungsten (W), vanadium (V)

09 aluminium (Al), americium (Am), berkelium (Bk), beryllium (Be), germanium (Ge), lanthanum (La), magnesium (Mg), manganese (Mn), neodymium (Nd), neptunium (Np), palladium (Pd), plutonium (Pu), potassium (K), ruthenium (Ru), strontium (Sr), ytterbium (Yb), zirconium (Zr)

10 dysprosium (Dy), gadolinium (Gd), lawrencium (Lr), molybdenum (Mo), promethium (Pm), technetium (Tc)

11 californium (Cf), einsteinium (Es), mendelevium (Md)

12 praseodymium (Pr), protactinium (Pa)

Metal alloys include:

03 pot
04 type
05 brass, Dutch, Invar®, Muntz, potin, steel, terne, white
06 Alnico®, billon, bronze, latten, occamy, ormolu, oroide, pewter, solder, tambac, tombac, tombak, Y-alloy
07 amalgam, Babbit's, chromel, Nitinol, prince's, shakudo, similor, tutania, tutenag
08 Babbitt's, cast iron, gunmetal, Manganin®, Nichrome®, orichalc, speculum, zircaloy, Zircoloy®
09 Britannia, Duralumin®, Dutch gold, Dutch leaf, magnalium, pinchbeck, shibuichi, white gold
10 constantan, ferro-alloy, iridosmine, iridosmium, mischmetal, Monel metal®, mosaic gold, osmiridium, white brass
11 chrome steel, cupro-nickel, nicrosilial, white copper
12 German silver, nickel silver
14 high-speed steel, phosphor-bronze, stainless steel

- **design on metal**
04 etch
- **join metal**
04 weld
- **metal after heating**
04 calx
- **metal bar**
03 zed **05** ingot
- **piece of metal**
03 gib
- **precious metal**
03 ore
- **thin metal**
04 foil

metallic
03 tin **04** gold, iron, lead **05** harsh, rough, shiny, steel, tinny **06** copper, nickel, silver **07** grating, jarring

08 gleaming, jangling, polished **09** dissonant **10** unpleasant

metamorphose
◇ *anagram indicator*
05 alter **06** change, modify, mutate, remake **07** convert, remodel, reshape **09** transform, translate, transmute **11** transfigure **12** transmogrify

metamorphosis
◇ *anagram indicator*
06 change **07** rebirth **08** mutation **09** staminody **10** alteration, changeover, conversion, metabolism **12** modification, regeneration **13** transmutation **14** holometabolism, transformation **15** transfiguration

metaphor
03 met **05** image, trope **06** emblem, metaph, symbol, visual **07** analogy, picture **08** allegory **10** emblematic **12** transumption **14** figure of speech, representation

metaphorical
03 met **06** metaph, visual **08** symbolic **10** analogical, emblematic, figurative **11** allegorical

metaphysical
04 deep **05** basic, ideal **06** unreal **07** eternal, general **08** abstract, abstruse, esoteric, fanciful, profound **09** essential, high-flown, recondite, spiritual, universal **10** immaterial, impalpable, intangible, subjective **11** fundamental, incorporeal, speculative, theoretical **12** intellectual, supernatural **13** insubstantial, philosophical, unsubstantial **14** transcendental

mete
- **mete out**
05 allot **06** assign **07** deal out, dole out, hand out, portion **08** dispense, share out **09** apportion, divide out, ration out **10** administer, distribute, measure out

meteor
05 comet, drake **06** bolide **08** aerolite, aerolith, fireball **09** meteorite, meteoroid **10** exhalation **11** falling star **12** shooting star

Meteor showers include:

06 Lyrids, Ursids
07 Leonids, Taurids
08 Geminids, Orionids, Perseids
11 Quadrantids
12 Eta Aquariids
14 Alpha-Scorpiids, Delta Aquariids

meteoric
04 fast **05** brief, quick, rapid, swift **06** speedy, sudden **08** dazzling, flashing **09** brilliant, lightning, momentary, overnight, transient **11** spectacular **13** instantaneous

meteorologist
06 met man **10** weatherman **11** weathergirl, weatherlady **13** climatologist **14** weather prophet

meteorology

Meteorology-related terms include:

04 calm, eddy, flux, haar, haze, ITCZ, rime
05 flood, front, frost, Q-code, radar, ridge, SIGWX, solar, taiga, virga
06 arctic, el Niño, flurry, haboob, isobar, Kelvin, oxygen
07 Celsius, chinook, climate, cyclone, drizzle, drought, graupel, mistral, monsoon, rainbow, thunder, tornado, typhoon, weather
08 acid rain, blizzard, dewpoint, doldrums, forecast, humidity, isotherm, millibar, rainfall, windsock, wind vane
09 advection, aerograph, altimeter, barograph, barometer, cold front, hurricane, hyetology, jet stream, lightning, Met Office, nephology, radiation, rain gauge, satellite, sub-arctic, trade wind, warm front, wind chill, wind speed
10 aerography, air quality, anemometer, atmosphere, baroclinic, barotropic, cloud cover, conduction, convection, depression, Fahrenheit, Gulf stream, Hadley Cell, hemisphere, hyetograph, hyetometer, hygrometer, nephograph, nephoscope, nowcasting, ozone layer, rain shadow, rain shower, visibility, waterspout, wavelength
11 air pressure, anticyclone, climatology, evaporation, ground frost, hyetography, pollen count, temperature, thermograph, thermometer, thermopause, troposphere, ultra violet, water vapour, wave cyclone
12 cloud seeding, condensation, cyclogenesis, meteorograph, microclimate, pilot balloon, thunderstorm, weather chart, weather watch
13 ball lightning, Beaufort scale, boundary layer, climate change, fork lightning, frontogenesis, magnetosphere, occluded front, onshore breeze, precipitation
14 air temperature, continentality, horse latitudes, offshore breeze, prevailing wind, sheet lightning, transmissivity, weather station
15 hyetometrograph, stationary front, weather forecast, wind-chill factor

method
03 art, how, way **04** form, line, mode, plan, rule **05** means, order, route, style **06** course, design, manner, scheme, system **07** fashion, pattern, process, routine **08** approach, modality, planning, practice **09** procedure, programme, structure, technique **10** regularity **11** arrangement, orderliness **12** organization **13** modus operandi **14** classification

methodical

04 neat, tidy 06 formal 07 logical, ordered, orderly, planned, precise, regular 09 efficient, organized 10 deliberate, meticulous, scrupulous, structured, systematic 11 disciplined, painstaking, well-ordered 12 businesslike, systematical

methodically

06 neatly, tidily 07 in place, orderly 08 formally 09 as planned, by the book, logically, precisely, regularly, to the rule, uniformly 11 efficiently 12 meticulously, scrupulously 13 painstakingly 14 systematically

metical

02 Mt 03 MZM

meticulous

05 exact, fussy, timid 06 strict 07 careful, precise 08 accurate, detailed, rigorous, thorough 10 fastidious, particular, scrupulous 11 overcareful, painstaking, punctilious 13 conscientious

meticulously

07 exactly 08 strictly 09 carefully, precisely 10 accurately, rigorously, thoroughly 12 scrupulously 13 painstakingly, punctiliously 15 conscientiously

métier

03 job 04 line 05 craft, field, forte, trade 06 sphere 07 calling, pursuit 08 business, vocation 09 specialty 10 occupation, profession, speciality 14 line of business

metro *see* underground

metropolis

04 city 07 capital 08 main city 09 large city 10 cosmopolis 11 capital city, megalopolis 12 municipality 14 cultural centre

See also city

mettle

04 guts, pith 05 nerve, pluck, pride, spunk 06 daring, ginger, make-up, nature, spirit, valour, vigour 07 bravery, calibre, courage, resolve, smeddum 08 backbone, boldness 09 character, endurance, fortitude, gallantry 11 disposition, intrepidity, personality, temperament 12 fearlessness 13 determination, sprightliness 14 indomitability

mettlesome

04 bold 05 brave 06 ardent, daring, lively, plucky, spunky 07 gallant, valiant 08 fearless, intrepid, resolute, spirited 10 courageous 11 lion-hearted, unflinching 12 high-spirited, stout-hearted

mew

04 cast, coop, gull, meow, mewl, shed 05 miaow, miaul, moult, whine 07 confine, retreat 09 caterwaul

mewl

03 cry 05 whine 06 snivel, whinge 07 blubber, grizzle, whimper

Mexican

03 Mex

Mexico

03 MEX

miaow

03 mew 04 meow, mewl 05 miaul, whine 09 caterwaul

miasma

04 reek 05 fetor, odour, smell, stink 06 stench 07 malaria 08 mephitis 09 effluvium, pollution

miasmal

04 foul 05 fetid 06 foetid, putrid, smelly 07 miasmic, noisome, noxious, reeking 08 mephitic, miasmous, polluted, stinking 09 miasmatic 10 malodorous, miasmatous 11 unwholesome 12 foul-smelling

mica

03 mic 04 daze 07 biotite

Michigan

02 MI 04 Mich

microbe

03 bug 04 germ 05 virus 08 bacillus, pathogen 09 bacterium 13 micro-organism

Micronesia

03 FSM

microphone

03 bug

microscope

03 SEM, TEM

microscopic

04 tiny 06 minute 09 minuscule 10 negligible 13 imperceptible, indiscernible, infinitesimal 14 extremely small

microscopically

08 minutely 09 extremely 13 imperceptibly 15 infinitesimally

midday

01 m, n 04 noon 06 twelve 07 noonday 08 meridian, noontide, noontime 09 lunchtime 10 meridional, twelve noon 12 twelve o'clock

middle

◇ *middle selection indicator* 03 med, mid 04 core, mean, noon 05 belly, heart, inner, midst, tummy, waist 06 centre, inside, medial, median, medium, mesial, midway, paunch 07 central, halfway, mediate, midriff, stomach 08 bull's eye, midpoint 11 bread basket, equidistant, intervening 12 halfway point, intermediate

• in the middle of

05 among, while 06 during 08 busy with 09 engaged in 12 in the midst of, occupied with, surrounded by 14 in the process of

middle-class

08 suburban 09 bourgeois 10 gentrified 11 white-collar 12 conventional, professional

Middle East

05 Kabaa 06 Qumran, Red Sea, Tigris 07 Dead Sea, Ephesus 08 Bosporus 09 Bosphorus, Gallipoli 10 Persepolis 11 Grand Mosque, Hagia Sophia, River Jordan, Via Dolorosa, Wailing Wall, Western Wall 12 Sea of Galilee 13 Dome of the Rock 15 Elburz Mountains

middleman

05 fixer 06 broker 08 bummaree, regrater, regrator, retailer 09 go-between 10 negotiator 11 distributer, distributor 12 entrepreneur, intermediary

Middlesex

02 Mx

middling

02 OK 04 fair, so-so 06 fairly, medium, modest 07 average 08 adequate, mediocre, moderate, ordinary, passable 09 tolerable 10 not much cop 11 indifferent, not up to much 12 intermediate, run-of-the-mill, unremarkable 13 no great shakes, unexceptional 14 fair to middling

midget

03 toy 04 baby, tiny 05 dwarf, gnome, pygmy, small, teeny 06 little, minute, pocket 07 manikin 08 mannikin, Tom Thumb 09 itsy-bitsy, miniature 10 diminutive, homunculus, teeny-weeny 11 Lilliputian, pocket-sized, small person

midpoint

11 middle point 12 central point, halfway point

midshipman

03 mid 04 Easy 05 middy 06 reefer, snotty 07 oldster, snottie 11 midshipmate 12 brass-bounder

midst

03 hub 04 core 05 bosom, heart, thick 06 centre, depths, middle 07 nucleus 08 interior, midpoint

• in the midst

04 amid 05 among 06 during 12 in the thick of, surrounded by 13 in the middle of

midway

07 halfway 11 in the centre, in the middle 13 at the midpoint

midwife

05 howdy 06 granny, howdie, Lucina 07 grannie 09 wise woman 10 accoucheur 11 accoucheuse

mien

03 air 04 aura, look 06 allure, aspect, manner 07 bearing 08 carriage, presence 09 demeanour, semblance 10 appearance, complexion,

deportment, expression
11 countenance

miffed
04 hurt **05** irked, upset, vexed
06 narked, peeved, piqued, put out
07 annoyed, in a huff, nettled
08 offended **09** aggrieved, chagrined,
irritated, resentful **10** cheesed off,
displeased **11** disgruntled

might
04 sway **05** clout, force, power
06 energy, muscle, valour, vigour
07 ability, potency, prowess, stamina
08 capacity, efficacy, strength
09 heftiness, puissance **10** capability
11 muscularity **12** forcefulness,
powerfulness

mightily
04 much, very **06** highly, hugely
07 greatly, lustily **08** manfully, strongly,
very much **09** decidedly, extremely,
intensely **10** forcefully, powerfully,
vigorously **11** exceedingly, strenuously
13 energetically

mighty
04 fell, huge, vast, very **05** bulky, felon,
grand, great, hardy, hefty, large, lusty,
stout, tough **06** highly, manful, potent,
really, robust, strong **07** awfully,
doughty, greatly, immense, massive,
titanic, utterly, valiant **08** almighty,
colossal, dominant, enormous,
forceful, gigantic, mightful, muscular,
powerful, puissant, stalwart, terribly,
towering, vigorous **09** extremely,
important, intensely, strapping,
unusually, wonderful **10** dreadfully,
monumental, prodigious, remarkably,
stupendous, thoroughly, tremendous
11 exceedingly, excessively, frightfully,
indomitable, influential **12** terrifically,
unreasonably **13** exceptionally
15 extraordinarily

mignonette
04 wald, weld **06** Reseda

migrant
05 Gypsy, nomad, rover **06** roving,
tinker **07** drifter, nomadic, swagger,
swagman, vagrant **08** drifting,
emigrant, shifting, wanderer
09 immigrant, itinerant, migratory,
transient, traveller, wandering
10 travelling **11** peripatetic
12 Gastarbeiter, globetrotter,
transmigrant **13** globetrotting

migrate
04 hike, move, roam, rove, trek **05** drift
06 travel, voyage, wander **07** journey
08 emigrate, relocate, resettle

migration
03 ren, rin, run **04** trek **05** shift
06 roving, travel, voyage **07** journey,
passage **08** diaspora, movement
09 walkabout, wandering
10 emigration **12** transhumance
15 Völkerwanderung

migratory
05 Gypsy **06** roving **07** migrant,

nomadic, vagrant **08** drifting, shifting
09 immigrant, itinerant, transient,
wandering **10** travelling **11** peripatetic
13 globetrotting

mike
01 M

mild
04 calm, fair, kind, meek, soft, warm,
weak **05** balmy, bland, faint, vague
06 feeble, gentle, humane, mellow,
modest, placid, slight, smooth, subtle,
tender **07** amiable, clement, insipid,
lenient, pacific **08** gall-less, mansuete,
merciful, moderate, pleasant, soothing
09 easy-going, peaceable, sensitive,
tasteless, temperate **10** forbearing
11 flavourless, good-natured, soft-
hearted, sympathetic, warm-hearted
13 compassionate, imperceptible,
tender-hearted

mildewy
05 fetid, fusty, mucid, musty **06** foetid,
rotten **10** mucedinous

mildly
06 calmly, gently, meekly, softly, subtly,
warmly, weakly **07** faintly, vaguely
08 slightly, tenderly **10** mercifully
11 sensitively **13** imperceptibly
15 compassionately

mildness
05 mercy **06** lenity, warmth
08 calmness, clemency, docility,
kindness, leniency, meekness, softness,
sympathy **09** blandness, milkiness,
passivity, placidity **10** compassion,
gentleness, indulgence, mellowness,
moderation, smoothness, tenderness
11 forbearance, insipidness
12 tranquillity **13** tastelessness,
temperateness

mile
01 m **02** mi, ml, nm **05** n mile

milieu
05 arena, scene **06** locale, medium,
sphere **07** element, setting **08** location
10 background **11** environment
12 surroundings

militancy
08 activism **09** extremism
12 belligerence, vigorousness
13 assertiveness **14** aggressiveness,
British disease

militant
07 fighter, soldier, warring, warrior
08 activist, fighting, partisan, vigorous
09 aggressor, assertive, combatant,
combative, embattled, struggler
10 aggressive, pugnacious
11 belligerent, Black Muslim **12** Black
Panther, militaristic

militantly
10 vigorously **11** assertively
12 aggressively **13** belligerently

military
03 mil **04** army, navy **05** armed, milit
06 forces **07** martial, militia, service,
soldier, warlike **08** air force, services,

soldiers, soldiery **09** soldierly
11 armed forces, disciplined

• **military equipment**
05 train
• **military life**
04 camp
• **military men** *see* **soldiers** *under*
soldier
• **military police**
02 MP

militate
• **militate against**
04 hurt **06** damage, oppose, resist
07 contend, counter **09** go against,
prejudice **10** act against, counteract,
discourage **11** be harmful to, tell
against, work against **12** count against
weigh against **15** be detrimental to
• **militate for**
03 aid **04** back, help **07** advance,
further, promote **08** speak for

militia
02 SA, TA **04** fyrd **06** Milice **07** reserve
08 yeomanry **09** fencibles, home
guard, minutemen, trainband
10 reservists **13** National Guard
15 Territorial Army

milk
03 tap, use **04** draw, pump, skim, whig
05 bleed, drain, press, screw, wring
06 rip off, siphon, stroke **07** draw off,
exploit, express, extract, oppress,
squeeze **08** impose on, moo-juice
10 manipulate **11** semi-skimmed
15 take advantage of
• **milk producer**
03 cow **04** teat
• **not yielding milk**
04 eild, yeld, yell

milk-can
04 kirn 05 churn

milking
• place for milking
04 loan 07 loaning

milkman's cart
04 pram 05 float 09 milkfloat

milksop
04 wimp, wuss 05 cissy, molly, pansy
06 coward, jessie 07 meacock
08 weakling 09 mummy's boy
10 namby-pamby

milk-strainer
03 sye

milky
04 soft, weak 05 white 06 chalky,
cloudy, gentle, opaque 07 clouded
08 lacteous 09 milk-white, snow-
white, spineless

mill
◇ anagram indicator
03 box 04 nurl, roll, shop 05 crush,
grate, grind, knurl, plant, pound, press,
quern, works 06 crunch, powder, roller
07 crusher, factory, foundry, grinder
08 snuffbox, spinnery, workshop
09 comminute, pulverize 11 boxing
match, molendinary 15 processing
plant
• mill around
05 swarm 06 stream, throng 09 move
about 11 crowd around, press around

millet
04 dari, dura, ragi 05 bajra, bajri,
doura, durra, proso, ragee, raggy, whisk
06 bajree, dhurra, raggee 09 broom-
corn 10 guinea corn

million
01 m

millstone
04 duty, load, onus 06 burden, ligger,
runner, weight 07 trouble 09 buhrstone,
burrstone 10 affliction, dead-weight,
grindstone, obligation, quernstone
11 cross to bear, encumbrance
• millstone support
04 rind

millstream
04 lade

Milne
02 AA

mime
05 mimic 06 act out, signal
07 buffoon, charade, gesture, imitate,
mimicry, mummery 08 dumb show,
indicate, simulate 09 chironomy,
pantomime, represent 11 impersonate

mimic
02 do 03 ape 04 copy, echo, mime,
mina, mock, myna, play 05 mynah
06 mirror, monkey, parody, parrot, send
up 07 copycat, copyist, emulate,
imitate, mimetic, minnick, minnock,
take off 08 imitator, look like,
mimicker, resemble, simulate,
starling 09 mimetical, personate

10 caricature 11 impersonate
12 caricaturist, impersonator
13 impressionist

mimicry
05 aping 06 parody 07 copying,
mimesis, mockery, take-off
09 burlesque, imitating, imitation
10 caricature, impression, simulation
13 impersonation

minatory
04 grim 07 looming, ominous, warning
08 menacing, sinister 09 impending,
minacious 10 cautionary, foreboding
11 threatening 12 inauspicious,
intimidatory

mince
◇ anagram indicator
03 cut 04 chop, dice, hash, pose
05 grind, ponce 06 prance, simper
07 crumble, posture 11 strike a pose
12 attitudinize 14 walk affectedly
• not mince your words
11 talk plainly 13 speak directly

mincing
04 camp, nice 05 cissy, poncy 06 chichi, dainty, la-di-da 07 foppish, minikin
08 affected, chee-chee, precious
09 coxcombic 10 effeminate
11 coxcombical, pretentious 12 niminy-
piminy

mind
03 wit 04 care, head, heed, mark, note,
obey, soul, tend, urge, view, will, wish,
wits 05 brain, fancy, guard, sense,
watch 06 attend, belief, brains, desire,
expert, follow, genius, memory, notion,
object, psyche, reason, recall, record,
resent, sanity, spirit 07 dislike,
egghead, feeling, mention, observe,
opinion, outlook, purpose, respect,
scholar, thinker, thought 08 academic,
attend to, attitude, brainbox, listen to,
remember, take care, tendency,
thinking, thoughts, watch out
09 attention, intellect, intention,
judgement, look after, mentality,
retention, sentiment, viewpoint
10 grey matter, mastermind
11 application, disposition, inclination,
keep an eye on, personality, point of
view, remembrance 12 intellectual,
intelligence, pay attention,
recollection, subconscious
13 commemoration, comprehension,
concentration, consciousness,
ratiocination, understanding, way of
thinking 15 little grey cells
• bear in mind, keep in mind
04 note 06 retain 08 consider,
remember 10 take note of 13 give
thought to 15 take into account
• be in two minds
05 waver 06 dither 08 be unsure,
hesitate 09 vacillate 10 be hesitant,
dilly-dally 11 be uncertain, be
undecided 12 shilly-shally 13 sit on the
fence
• cross your mind
03 hit 06 come to, strike 07 occur to,
think of 08 remember

• have in mind
03 aim 04 plan, talk, want 06 design,
intend 07 think of 11 contemplate
• make up your mind
06 choose, decide, settle 07 resolve
09 determine 13 make a decision
14 reach a decision 15 come to a
decision
• mind out
05 watch 06 beware 07 look out
08 take care, watch out 09 be careful
12 pay attention 13 be on your guard
• mind's eye
04 head 06 memory 11 imagination,
remembrance 12 recollection
13 contemplation
• never mind
03 too 04 also 06 skip it! 08 as well as,
forget it, let alone 09 apart from, don't
worry 10 nix my dolly 12 not to
mention 13 not forgetting 14 not
bother about, take no notice of
• out of your mind
03 mad 04 nuts 05 barmy, batty, crazy,
daffy, dippy, loony, loopy, manic, nutty,
potty 06 crazed, cuckoo, insane,
maniac, mental, raving, screwy
07 bananas, bonkers, flipped, lunatic
08 crackers, demented, deranged,
doolally, frenzied, maniacal, unhinged,
unstable 09 psychotic, up the wall
10 barking mad, distracted, distraught,
off the wall, unbalanced 11 not all
there, off the rails, off your head
12 mad as a hatter, off your chump,
round the bend 13 off your rocker, of
unsound mind, round the twist 14 off
your trolley, wrong in the head 15 non
compos mentis, out of your senses
• put you in mind of
06 prompt, remind 10 call to mind
11 bring to mind 14 make you think of
• put your mind to
09 persevere, take pains 10 buckle
down 13 concentrate on, exert
yourself
• sharpness of mind
04 edge
• speak your mind
11 talk plainly 14 tell it like it is
• to my mind
04 heed, mark, note, obey 05 guard,
watch 06 ensure, follow, I think, object,
regard, resent 07 dislike, observe,
respect 08 as I see it, attend to, I
believe, in my view, listen to, make sure,
object to, remember, take care, watch
out 09 be careful, disapprove, look
after, not forget, pay heed to, watch
over 10 comply with, disapprove,
personally, take care of 11 be annoyed
by, in my opinion, keep an eye on, make
certain, take offence 12 be bothered
by, be offended by, be troubled by, have
charge of, pay attention 13 concentrate
on, take offence at

mind-boggling
07 amazing 10 astounding, formidable,
impossible, incredible, surprising
11 astonishing, exceptional, unthinkable
12 unbelievable, unimaginable
13 extraordinary, inconceivable

mindful

04 wary **05** alert, alive, aware, chary **07** alive to, careful, heedful **08** inclined, sensible, watchful **09** attentive, cognizant, conscious, observant

mindless

04 dull, dumb **05** dopey, thick **06** stupid **07** foolish, robotic, routine, tedious, witless **08** knee-jerk **09** automatic, illogical, negligent, senseless **10** gratuitous, irrational, mechanical **11** birdbrained, instinctive, involuntary, thoughtless **13** unintelligent

mindlessly

08 stupidly **09** foolishly, routinely **11** illogically, senselessly **12** irrationally, mechanically **13** automatically, instinctively, involuntarily, thoughtlessly

mine

02 my **03** dig, egg, pit, win **04** bomb, fund, lode, seam, vein, well **05** delve, dig up, hoard, shaft, stock, store, wheal **06** burrow, dig for, duffer, quarry, remove, search, source, supply, trench, tunnel, wealth **07** bonanza, coalpit, deposit, extract, reserve, unearth **08** claymore, colliery, excavate, landmine, treasury **09** coalfield, explosive, reservoir, undermine **10** excavation, repository, storehouse **11** depth charge
• **mine opening**
03 eye **04** adit
• **mine tunnel**
04 head
• **mining licence**
04 gale
• **surface over a mine**
03 day

mine-passage

04 road

miner

06 digger, hatter, pitman, tinner **07** collier, faceman **08** tributer **09** coalminer **10** faceworker, gold-digger, honeyeater, mineworker

mineral

Minerals include:

03 jet
04 alum, mica, ruby, salt, spar, talc **05** beryl, borax, emery, flint, fluor, topaz, umber **06** albite, blende, cerite, galena, gangue, garnet, glance, gypsum, halite, haüyne, humite, illite, jasper, kermes, lithia, maltha, natron, nosean, pyrite, quartz, rutile, silica, sphene, spinel, talcum, zircon **07** anatase, apatite, axinite, azurite, barytes, biotite, bornite, brucite, calcite, cassite, crystal, cuprite, desmine, diamond, dysodil, epidote, jacinth, jadeite, jargoon, kandite, leucite, nacrite, olivine, pennine, peridot, pyrites, realgar, syenite, thorite, uralite, uranite,

zeolite, zincite, zoisite
08 allanite, ankerite, asbestos, autunite, blue john, boracite, brookite, calamine, calcspar, chlorite, chromite, cinnabar, corundum, crocoite, cryolite, diallage, diaspore, dolomite, dysodyle, epsomite, erionite, euxenite, feldspar, fluorite, goethite, graphite, gyrolite, hematite, hyacinth, idocrase, ilmenite, iodyrite, lazulite, lewisite, melilite, mimetite, nephrite, orpiment, plumbago, prehnite, pyroxene, rock salt, sanidine, sapphire, sardonyx, siderite, smaltite, sodalite, stannite, stibnite, stilbite, titanite, wurtzite **09** alabaster, amphibole, anhydrite, aragonite, atacamite, bentonite, blacklead, cairngorm, celestite, cobaltite, elaterite, evaporite, fibrolite, fluorspar, fool's gold, goslarite, grossular, haematite, kaolinite, lodestone, magnesite, magnetite, malachite, marcasite, margarite, microlite, muscovite, nepholine, niccolite, olivenite, pearl spar, quartzite, saltpetre, scheelite, soapstone, sylvanite, tantalite, turquoise, uraninite, vulpinite, wavellite **10** antimonite, aquamarine, aventurine, bloodstone, chalcedony, chrysolite, glauconite, hornblende, meerschaum, microcline, orthoclase, polyhalite, pyrolusite, samerskite, serpentine, sphalerite, tourmaline **11** alexandrite, amphibolite, chrysoberyl, French chalk, lapis lazuli, pitchblende, sal ammoniac, smithsonite, vesuvianite **12** chalcanthite, chalcopyrite, hemimorphite **13** arsenopyrites **14** hydroxyapatite, sodium chloride, yttro-columbite **15** gooseberry-stone

mineral water *see* **water**

Minerva

06 Athene

mingle

03 mix **04** fuse, join, mell **05** alloy, blend, go out, merge, unite **06** hobnob, medley **07** combine, mixture **08** coalesce, compound, intermix **09** associate, circulate, commingle, interfuse, socialize **10** amalgamate **11** intermingle, run together **12** rub shoulders

mingy

04 mean, poor, puny **05** close **06** meagre, measly, paltry, scanty, skimpy, stingy **07** miserly, pitiful, sparing, trivial **08** grudging, pathetic, piddling, ungiving **09** miserable, niggardly **10** hard-fisted, ungenerous **11** close-fisted, close-handed, tight-fisted **12** cheese-paring, parsimonious

miniature

03 toy, wee **04** baby, mini, tiny **05** cameo, dwarf, small, teeny, young **06** little, midget, minute **07** diorama, reduced **08** pint-size **09** microcosm, pint-sized **10** diminutive, scaled-down, small-scale **11** microcosmic, pocket-sized, rubrication

minimal

05 least, token **06** minute **07** minimum, nominal **08** littlest, smallest **09** slightest **10** negligible

minimize

03 cut **05** decry, slash **06** lessen, reduce, shrink **07** curtail **08** belittle, decrease, diminish, discount, laugh off, play down **09** deprecate, disparage, soft-pedal, underrate **10** trivialize **11** make light of **12** make little of **13** underestimate

minimum

◇ *head selection indicator*
03 min **05** least, nadir **06** bottom, lowest **07** minimal, tiniest **08** littlest, smallest **09** slightest **11** lowest point **12** lowest number

minion

05 leech **06** drudge, fawner, lackey, menial, stooge, yes-man **07** darling, flunkey, servant **08** follower, hanger-on, henchman, hireling, parasite **09** attendant, dependant, favourite, flatterer, sycophant, underling **10** bootlicker, henchwoman **11** henchperson

minister

02 PM **03** Min, Rev **04** aide, dean, tend **05** agent, dewan, diwan, elder, envoy, nurse, padre, serve, vezir, vicar, vizir **06** attend, cleric, consul, curate, deacon, divine, leader, legate, parson, pastor, priest, rector, supply, verger, visier, vizier, wait on, wizier **07** cater to, furnish, Mas-John, Mes-John, servant **08** chaplain, delegate, diplomat, emissary, Mass-John, Mess-John, official, preacher **09** churchman, clergyman, dignitary, executive, look after, presbyter **10** administer, ambassador, chancellor, politician, take care of **11** accommodate, clergywoman, Grand Vizier **12** ecclesiastic, office-holder, parish priest **13** administrator **14** representative **15** cabinet minister

See also **prime minister**

ministration

03 aid **04** care, help **06** favour, relief **07** backing, service, succour, support **09** patronage **10** assistance **11** disposition, supervision

ministry

03 Min, MOD, MOH **04** MAFF, METI **06** bureau, clergy, office **07** cabinet, service **08** the cloth **09** the church, the clergy **10** department, government, holy orders **13** the priesthood **14** administration

Minnesota
02 MN 04 Minn

minnow
04 pank, pink

minor
03 boy, kid, son, tot 04 baby, girl, less
05 child, light, lower, petty, small
06 infant, junior, lesser, nipper, slight
07 nominal, smaller, tiny tot, toddler,
trivial, unknown, younger 08 daughter,
inferior, juvenile, marginal, trifling,
young one 09 little one, secondary,
youngster 10 negligible, peripheral,
subsidiary 11 little known, second-
class, subordinate, unimportant, young
person 12 unclassified 13 insignificant
14 inconsiderable
• **minor item**
02 by 03 bye

minstrel
04 bard, scop 05 rimer 06 rhymer,
singer 07 gleeman 08 jongleur,
musician 09 hamfatter, joculator
10 troubadour

mint
◇ *anagram indicator*
03 aim, nep, new, nip 04 bomb, cast,
coin, fake, heap, hint, make, pile 05 as
new, forge, fresh, hatch, punch, stack,
stamp 06 bundle, catnep, catnip,
devise, invent, make up, packet, riches,
strike, unused, wealth 07 attempt,
billion, concoct, falsify, fashion,
fortune, million, mint-new, monarda,
perfect, produce, purpose, trump up,
venture 08 bergamot, billions, brand-
new, millions 09 bugle-weed,
construct, excellent, fabricate,
megabucks, undamaged 10 first-class,
immaculate, pennyroyal 11 king's
ransom, loadsamoney, manufacture,
unblemished

minus
03 bar 04 less, save 06 except
07 short of, without 08 negative
09 excepting, excluding 10 deficiency
11 subtraction

minuscule
04 fine, tiny 05 teeny 06 little, minute
09 itsy-bitsy, miniature, very small
10 diminutive, teeny-weeny
11 Lilliputian, microscopic
13 infinitesimal

minute
01 m 02 mo 03 min, sec 04 note,
tick, tiny 05 close, exact, flash, jiffy,
minim 06 moment, second, slight,
strict 07 instant, precise, trivial
08 accurate, as soon as, critical,
detailed, directly, no sooner, the point,
trifling 09 miniature, minuscule, short
time, the moment, very small
10 diminutive, exhaustive,
meticulous, negligible, the instant
11 immediately, Lilliputian,
microscopic, painstaking, punctilious
13 infinitesimal, insignificant,
microscopical 14 circumstantial,
inconsiderable

• **in a minute**
04 anon, soon 06 pronto 07 in a tick,
shortly 08 in a flash, in a jiffy, very soon
09 in a moment 10 before long 15 in
the near future
• **this minute**
03 now 04 next, then 06 at once,
pronto 07 quickly 08 as soon as,
directly, promptly, right now, speedily
09 forthwith, instantly, like a shot, right
away, yesterday 11 immediately, this
instant 12 no sooner than, straight
away, there and then, without delay
14 unhesitatingly, without more ado
15 before you know it, instantaneously,
without question
• **up to the minute**
02 in 03 now 06 latest, newest, with it
09 happening 10 all the rage, most
modern, most recent 11 fashionable

minutely
07 closely, exactly 08 in detail
09 precisely 10 critically
12 exhaustively, meticulously,
scrupulously 13 painstakingly
14 systematically

minutes
04 acta 05 notes, tapes 06 record
07 details, records 10 memorandum,
transcript 11 proceedings
12 transactions

minutiae
07 details, trifles 08 niceties 10 small
print, subtleties 11 fine details, finer
points, intricacies, particulars
12 complexities, trivialities

miracle
04 sign 06 marvel, wonder 07 prodigy
10 phenomenon, wonderwork

miraculous
07 amazing 09 monstrous, unnatural,
wonderful 10 astounding, incredible,
marvellous, monstruous, phenomenal,
remarkable, superhuman, surprising,
unexpected 11 astonishing
12 inexplicable, supernatural,
unbelievable 13 extraordinary,
unaccountable

miraculously
09 amazingly 10 incredibly,
remarkably 11 wonderfully
12 inexplicably, superhumanly,
surprisingly, unbelievably,
unexpectedly 13 unaccountably
14 supernaturally 15 extraordinarily

mirage
04 loom 07 fantasy 08 illusion,
phantasm 11 fata Morgana
13 hallucination 14 phantasmagoria
15 optical illusion

mire
03 bog, fen, fix, jam, mud 04 dirt, hole,
lair, mess, muck, ooze, quag, sink, spot,
stew 05 glaur, latch, letch, marsh,
slime, swamp 06 deluge, morass,
pickle, slough, sludge 07 bog down,
trouble 08 loblolly, quagmire
09 marshland, overwhelm
12 difficulties

mirror
03 ape 04 copy, echo, show, twin
05 clone, glass, image, mimic, stone
06 depict, double, follow, parrot
07 emulate, imitate, reflect
08 busybody, likeness, speculum
09 coelostat, condenser, hand-glass,
pier-glass, reflector, represent 10 dead
ringer, reflection, siderostat, wing
mirror 11 cheval-glass, pocket-glass,
tiring-glass, toilet glass 12 keeking-
glass, laryngoscope, looking-glass
13 driving-mirror, exact likeness,
spitting image 14 rear-view mirror

mirth
03 fun 04 glee 05 dream, sport
06 gaiety, spleen 07 delight, frolics,
jollity, revelry 08 buoyancy, hilarity,
laughter, pleasure 09 amusement,
enjoyment, merriment, merriness
10 blitheness, jocularity 11 high spirits
12 cheerfulness

mirthful
03 gay 04 glad 05 funny, happy, jolly,
ludic, merry 06 amused, blithe,
cheery, jocund, jovial 07 amusing,
buoyant, festive, playful 08 cheerful,
gladsome, laughful, laughing, sportive
09 hilarious, laughable, vivacious
10 frolicsome, uproarious
11 pleasurable 12 light-hearted
13 light-spirited

mirthless
03 sad 04 glum, sour 05 gruff, moody,
sulky, surly 06 gloomy, grumpy,
morose, sullen 07 doleful, unhappy
08 churlish, dejected, unamused
09 depressed, miserable
10 despondent, humourless
11 crestfallen, ill-humoured, pessimistic

miry
04 oozy 05 boggy, dirty, fenny, mucky,
muddy, slimy 06 glaury, marshy, sludgy,
swampy

misadventure
06 mishap 07 bad luck, debacle,
failure, ill luck, problem, reverse,
setback, tragedy 08 accident,
calamity, disaster, hard luck
09 cataclysm, misaunter, mischance
10 ill fortune, misfortune
11 catastrophe

misanthrope
05 cynic, loner, miser, Timon
06 hermit, meanie 07 recluse
08 solitary 14 unsocial person

misanthropic
05 surly 08 egoistic, inhumane
10 antisocial, malevolent, unfriendly,
unsociable 13 unsympathetic

misanthropy
06 egoism 08 cynicism 10 inhumanity
11 malevolence 13 antisociality
14 unsociableness

misapply
05 abuse 06 misuse 07 exploit,
pervert 09 misemploy 11 use unwisely
13 use unsuitably 14 misappropriate

misapprehend
07 misread, mistake 11 misconceive,
misconstrue 12 misinterpret
13 miscomprehend, misunderstand
15 get the wrong idea

misapprehension
05 error, mix-up 07 fallacy, mistake
08 delusion 09 wrong idea
10 misreading 13 misconception
15 false impression

misappropriate
03 nab, rob 04 nick 05 abuse, filch,
pinch, steal 06 misuse, pilfer, pocket,
thieve 07 pervert, swindle
08 embezzle, misapply, misspend,
peculate 09 defalcate, knock down

misappropriation
05 theft 06 misuse 07 robbing
08 stealing 09 pilfering, pocketing
10 peculation 11 defalcation
12 embezzlement 14 misapplication

misbegotten
05 shady 06 stolen 07 bastard, illicit,
natural 08 abortive, unlawful
09 dishonest, ill-gotten, ill-judged,
imprudent, monstrous, purloined,
unadvised 10 ill-advised, monstrous
11 hare-brained 12 contemptible,
disreputable, ill-conceived, illegitimate

misbehave
◇ anagram indicator
05 act up, lapse 06 be rude, offend,
play up 07 carry on, disobey
08 trespass 09 be naughty, fool about,
mess about, misdemean, muck about
10 fool around, transgress 11 behave
badly 15 be beyond the pale, get up to
mischief

misbehaviour
◇ anagram indicator
08 mischief, misguide 10 bad manners,
carrying-on, misconduct
11 impropriety, naughtiness 12 bad
behaviour, disobedience,
misdemeanour, mucking about
15 insubordination

misbelief
05 error 06 heresy 07 fallacy, mistake
08 delusion, illusion 10 heterodoxy
11 unorthodoxy, wrong belief
13 misconception 15 misapprehension

miscalculate
03 err 04 boob 06 slip up 07 blunder,
go wrong, miscast 08 get wrong,
miscount, misjudge 09 misreckon
12 make a mistake, overestimate
13 underestimate

miscalculation
04 boob, slip 05 error, fault, gaffe,
lapse 06 booboo, howler, slip-up
07 bloomer, blunder, clanger, mistake
08 miscount 09 oversight
10 aberration, inaccuracy
12 misjudgement, overestimate
13 underestimate 14 miscomputation
15 misapprehension

miscarriage
05 error 06 mishap 07 failure, misdeed

08 aborting, abortion 09 breakdown,
ruination 10 misconduct, perversion
13 mismanagement
14 disappointment

miscarry
04 fail, flop, fold, warp 05 abort, slink
07 founder, go amiss, go wrong,
misfire, miswend 10 not come off
11 bite the dust, come to grief, fall
through, lose the baby 12 come a
cropper 13 come to nothing

miscellaneous
04 chow 05 mixed 06 motley, sundry,
varied 07 diverse, jumbled, mingled,
various 08 assorted, eclectic
10 variegated 11 diversified,
farraginous 12 multifarious
13 heterogeneous

• **miscellaneous lot**
04 raft

miscellany
03 mix 04 olio, olla 06 jumble, medley
07 farrago, mixture, variety
08 mishmash, mixed bag, pastiche
09 anthology, diversity, patchwork,
potpourri 10 assortment, collection,
hotchpotch, salmagundi, salmagundy
11 collectanea, gallimaufry,
miscellanea, smorgasbord
14 conglomeration, omnium-
gatherum

mischance
04 blow 06 mishap 07 ill luck, tragedy
08 accident, bad break, calamity,
disaster 09 ill-chance 10 ill fortune,
infelicity, misfortune 11 contretemps
12 misadventure

mischief
03 Ate, elf, hob, imp, wag 04 bale,
bane, dido, evil, harm, hurt, lark, limb,
pest, puck, tyke 05 cutty, devil, gamin,
rogue, scamp 06 damage, gamine,
injury, monkey, nickum, pranks, rascal,
terror, tricks, urchin 07 carry-on,
hellion, malicho, pliskie, stirrer,
trouble, varmint, villain 08 diablery,
escapade, makebate, nuisance,
spalpeen 09 devilment, diablerie,
scallywag, vengeance 10 cockatrice,
disruption, disservice, hanky-panky,
impishness, shenanigan, wrongdoing
11 limb of Satan, monkey shine,
naughtiness, roguishness, shenanigans
12 bad behaviour, esprit follet,
misbehaviour, monkey tricks
13 barnsbreaking, funny business,
jiggery-pokery 14 monkey business
15 flibbertigibbet

mischievous
◇ anagram indicator
03 bad 04 arch, evil 05 elfin, elvan,
elven, rogue 06 elfish, elvish, impish,
shrewd, wicked 07 gallows, harmful,
hurtful, naughty, playful, roguish,
teasing, tricksy, unhappy, vicious,
waggish 08 litherly, rascally, spiteful
09 ill-deedly, injurious, malicious,
malignant, pestilent 10 frolicsome,
pernicious, up to no good
11 destructive, detrimental,

disobedient, misbehaving,
troublesome 12 badly behaved

mischievously
◇ anagram indicator
08 impishly, wickedly 09 harmfully,
naughtily, playfully, roguishly, teasingly,
viciously, waggishly 10 spitefully
11 injuriously, maliciously
13 destructively, disobediently

misconceive
07 misread, mistake, suspect
08 misjudge 11 misconstrue
12 misapprehend, misinterpret
13 misunderstand

misconception
05 error 07 fallacy, mistake
08 delusion 09 wrong idea
10 misconceit, misreading 15 false
impression, misapprehension

misconduct
◇ anagram indicator
08 adultery, misusage 10 wrongdoing
11 impropriety, malpractice,
miscarriage 12 bad behaviour,
misbehaviour, misdemeanour
13 mismanagement

misconstrue
◇ anagram indicator
07 misread, mistake, pervert
08 misjudge 09 misreckon
10 misconster 11 misconceive
12 misapprehend, misinterpret,
mistranslate 13 misunderstand 15 take
the wrong way

miscreant
05 knave, rogue, scamp 06 rascal,
sinner, wicked, wretch 07 dastard,
heretic, infidel, villain 08 criminal,
evildoer, vagabond 09 reprobate,
scallywag, scoundrel, wrongdoer
10 malefactor, profligate, villainous
11 misbeliever, scoundrelly,
unbelieving 12 troublemaker
13 mischief-maker

misdeed
03 sin 05 amiss, crime, error, fault,
wrong 06 felony 07 offence
08 trespass, villainy 10 misconduct,
peccadillo, wrongdoing
11 delinquency, miscarriage,
misdemeanor, mistreading
12 misdemeanour 13 transgression

misdemeanour
05 error, fault, lapse, wrong
07 misdeed, offence 08 trespass
10 misconduct, peccadillo,
wrongdoing 11 malfeasance
12 indiscretion, infringement,
misbehaviour 13 transgression

misdirect
◇ anagram indicator
05 avert 06 divert, misuse 07 mislead
08 misapply, misguide 09 misinform
10 misaddress 13 give a bum steer
14 misappropriate

miser
04 carl 05 hunks 06 meanie, wretch
07 niggard, save-all, Scrooge

08 muckworm, tightwad **09** skinflint **10** cheapskate, curmudgeon, scrapegood **11** cheeseparer, scrapepenny **12** money-grubber, penny-pincher

05 Burns (Montgomery)
06 Mammon, Marner (Silas)
07 Scrooge (Ebenezer)
08 Nickleby (Ralph), Trabois
10 Fardorough, Van Swieten
(Ghysbrecht)
11 Earlforward (Henry)

miserable
◇ *anagram indicator*
03 low, miz, sad **04** base, blue, down, glum, mean, mizz, poor, punk, vile **05** lousy, sorry, surly **06** dismal, dreary, gloomy, grumpy, meagre, measly, mouldy, paltry, rotten, scanty, shabby, sullen **07** crushed, forlorn, grouchy, joyless, pitiful, squalid, unhappy **08** dejected, desolate, downcast, pathetic, pitiable, shameful, wretched **09** cheerless, crotchety, depressed, irritable, niggardly, sorrowful, worthless **10** deplorable, depressing, despicable, despondent, detestable, distressed, unpleasant **11** bad-tempered, disgraceful, downhearted, god-forsaken, heartbroken, ignominious, ill-tempered, low-spirited, melancholic **12** contemptible, disagreeable, disconsolate, god-forgotten, impoverished **14** down in the dumps

miserably
◇ *anagram indicator*
05 sadly **06** glumly, poorly **07** greatly **08** gloomily, markedly, paltrily, scantily, stingily, very much **09** niggardly, pitifully, unhappily **10** desolately **11** dangerously, desperately, sorrowfully **12** despondently, pathetically **14** disconsolately

miserliness
07 avarice **08** meanness **09** frugality, minginess, parsimony, tightness **10** stinginess **12** cheeseparing, covetousness **13** niggardliness, penny-pinching, penuriousness **15** close-fistedness, tight-fistedness

miserly
04 gare, mean **05** close, mingy, tight **06** stingy **07** chintzy, sparing **08** beggarly **09** niggardly, penurious **11** close-fisted, close-handed, tight-fisted **12** candle-paring, cheeseparing, parsimonious **13** money-grubbing, penny-pinching

misery
02 wo **03** miz, woe **04** bale, hell, mizz, want **05** agony, gloom, grief **06** grouch, misère, moaner, penury, sorrow, whiner **07** anguish, avarice, despair, killjoy, poverty, sadness, whinger **08** buzzkill, distress, hardship, Jeremiah, sourpuss **09** adversity, indigence, perdition, pessimist,

privation, suffering, the depths **10** affliction, complainer, depression, desolation, discomfort, melancholy, misfortune, oppression, spoilsport, wet blanket **11** deprivation, destitution, living death, melancholia, unhappiness **12** wretchedness **13** prophet of doom **14** dog in the manger

misfire
04 fail, flop **05** abort **06** go awry **07** founder, go amiss, go wrong **08** miscarry **09** fizzle out **10** not come off **11** bite the dust, come to grief, fall through **12** come a cropper

misfit
◇ *anagram indicator*
04 geek **05** freak, loner **06** weirdo **07** dropout, oddball, sad sack **08** lone wolf, maverick **09** eccentric, odd one out **13** individualist, nonconformist **14** fish out of water

misfortune
02 wo **03** ill, woe **04** blow, evil, ruth, woes **05** trial **06** mishap, sorrow, wroath **07** bad luck, failure, ill luck, misfare, misluck, reverse, setback, tragedy, trouble **08** accident, calamity, casualty, disaster, distress, hard luck, hardship, judgment **09** adversity, judgement, mischance, mishanter **10** affliction, infelicity, mischanter **11** catastrophe, tribulation **12** misadventure

• **expression of misfortune**
02 ah, ay, oh **03** out **04** alas, ay me, haro, waly **06** harrow **07** welaway **08** waesucks, welladay, wellaway **09** alack-a-day, wellanear **10** alas the day **12** alas the while

misgiving
04 fear **05** doubt, qualm, worry **06** niggle, unease **07** anxiety, scruple **08** distrust, misdoubt, mistrust **09** suspicion **10** hesitation **11** reservation, uncertainty **12** apprehension **14** second thoughts

misguided
◇ *anagram indicator*
04 rash **05** wrong **06** erring, misled **07** deluded, foolish, off-beam **08** mistaken **09** erroneous, ill-judged, imprudent, misplaced **10** fallacious, ill-advised **11** injudicious, misdirected, misinformed **12** misconceived **13** ill-considered

mishandle
◇ *anagram indicator*
04 muff **05** botch, fluff **06** bungle, fumble, mess up **07** balls up, screw up **08** maltreat, misjudge **09** mismanage **11** make a hash of, make a mess of **12** make a balls of **14** make a balls-up of, make a pig's ear of

mishap
◇ *anagram indicator*
04 blow **05** drere, shunt, trial **06** dreare, mucker **07** reverse, setback, trouble **08** accident, calamity, disaster, incident **09** adversity, misaunter,

mischance **10** ill fortune, misfortune **11** catastrophe, disaventure, tribulation **12** disadventure, misadventure **15** stroke of bad luck

mishit
04 duff, thin **05** flier, flyer **06** sclaff

mishmash
04 hash, mess, olio, olla **05** salad **06** jumble, medley, muddle **07** farrago **08** pastiche **09** potpourri **10** hodgepodge, hotchpotch, salmagundi **11** gallimaufry **14** conglomeration

misinform
05 bluff **07** deceive, mislead **08** hoodwink, misguide **09** misdirect **12** take for a ride **13** give a bum steer

misinformation
04 dope, guff, hype, lies **05** bluff **07** baloney, eyewash **08** bum steer, nonsense **09** deception **10** misleading **12** misdirection **14** disinformation

misinterpret
◇ *anagram indicator*
04 warp **05** wrest **06** garble **07** distort, misread, mistake **08** misjudge **11** misconceive, misconstrue **12** misapprehend **13** misunderstand **15** take the wrong way

misinterpretation
10 misreading **12** misjudgement **13** misconception **14** misacceptation **15** false impression, misapprehension, misconstruction

misjudge
07 mistake **08** miscount **11** misconstrue **12** miscalculate, misinterpret, overestimate **13** misunderstand, underestimate

misjudgement
07 mistake **09** wrong idea **10** misdeeming **12** wrong opinion **14** miscalculation **15** wrong conclusion

mislay
04 lose, miss **07** misfile **08** misplace **11** lose sight of, lose track of **14** be unable to find

mislead
◇ *anagram indicator*
04 fool, snow **05** put on **06** delude **07** deceive **08** fool into, hoodwink, impose on, misguide **09** blindfold, misdirect, misinform **10** impose upon, lead astray **12** misrepresent, take for a ride **13** give a bum steer, lead into error **14** pull a fast one on, put off the scent

misleading
◇ *anagram indicator*
06 biased, loaded, tricky **07** evasive **08** delusive, illusive, illusory, sinister **09** ambiguous, confusing, deceiving, deceptive, equivocal **10** fallacious, unreliable

mismanage
◇ *anagram indicator*
03 mar **04** muff **05** botch, waste

06 bungle, foul up, mess up **07** balls up, blunder, misrule, screw up **08** misjudge, misspend **09** mishandle **11** make a hash of, make a mess of **12** make a balls of **14** make a balls-up of, make a pig's ear of

mismanagement
◊ *anagram indicator*
04 hash, mess **05** farce **06** bungle, cock-up, muddle **07** balls-up, failure, pig's ear **08** bungling, shambles **11** mishandling **12** misjudgement **13** pig's breakfast **14** misgovernaunce

mismatched
08 clashing, mismated, unsuited **09** disparate, irregular, misallied **10** discordant, unmatching **11** ill-assorted, incongruous **12** antipathetic, incompatible **14** unreconcilable

misogynist
03 MCP **06** sexist **10** woman-hater **12** anti-feminist **14** male chauvinist **15** male supremacist

misogyny
06 sexism **12** anti-feminism **13** male supremacy **14** male chauvinism

misplace
◊ *anagram indicator*
04 lose, miss **06** mislay **07** misfile **08** misapply **09** misassign **11** lose sight of, lose track of **14** be unable to find

misprint
◊ *anagram indicator*
04 typo **05** error **07** erratum, literal, mistake **11** corrigendum **12** literal error **13** printing error

misquote
05 twist **06** garble, muddle **07** distort, falsify, pervert **08** misstate **09** misreport **11** misremember **12** misrepresent

misread
◊ *anagram indicator*
06 garble **07** distort, mistake **08** misjudge **11** misconceive, misconstrue **12** misapprehend, misinterpret **13** misunderstand **15** take the wrong way

misrepresent
◊ *anagram indicator*
05 abuse, belie, color, slant, twist **06** colour, garble **07** distort, falsify, pervert **08** disguise, minimize, miscolor, misquote, misstate **09** miscolour, misreport **10** exaggerate, manipulate **11** misconstrue **12** misinterpret

misrepresentation
◊ *anagram indicator*
08 twisting **10** distortion, perversion **12** exaggeration, manipulation, misreporting **13** falsification **15** misconstruction

misrule
04 riot **05** chaos **06** tumult **07** anarchy, turmoil **08** disorder, unreason **09** confusion **10** turbulence

11 lawlessness **12** indiscipline **13** misgovernment, mismanagement **15** disorganization

miss
02 Ms **03** err **04** beat, blow, fail, flop, flub, girl, lack, lass, lose, maid, Mlle, muff, need, omit, skip, slip, trip, want, wish **05** avoid, dodge, error, evade, fault, forgo, let go, Mdlle **06** bypass, damsel, escape, fiasco, forego, kumari, lament, maiden, not see, pass up, regret **07** ache for, blunder, failure, let slip, long for, mistake, neglect, not go to, not spot, pine for **08** fräulein, leave out, miscarry, omission, overlook, pass over, Señorita, sidestep, teenager, yearn for **09** disregard, fail to get, fail to hit, grieve for, not notice, oversight, Signorina, sorrow for, young lady **10** be away from, circumvent, desiderate, not go to see, schoolgirl, young woman **11** fail to catch, fail to seize, not be part of **12** be absent from, be too late for, fail to attend, fail to notice, mademoiselle **13** feel the loss of, misunderstand, not take part in

See also **girl**; **woman**

• **miss out**
04 jump, omit, skip **06** bypass, ignore **07** exclude **08** leave out, pass over **09** disregard **12** dispense with

missal
08 breviary, mass-book, Triodion **09** formulary **10** office-book, prayerbook **11** euchologion, servicebook

misshapen
◊ *anagram indicator*
04 bent, ugly **06** inform, warped **07** crooked, dismayd, twisted **08** crippled, deformed **09** contorted, distorted, grotesque, malformed, monstrous **15** misproportioned

missile
04 bomb, dart, shot **05** arrow, shaft, shell **06** rocket, weapon **07** grenade, torpedo **10** flying bomb, projectile

Missiles include:
02 MX, V-2
03 AAM, ABM, AGM, ASM, ATM, SAM, SSM
04 ALCM, ASBM, ICBM, IRBM, MIRV, MRBM, Scud, SLBM, TASM
05 smart
06 AMRAAM, cruise, Exocet®, guided
07 Polaris, Trident
08 Maverick
09 ballistic, minuteman
10 sidewinder, wire-guided
11 heat-seeking
12 surface-to-air

• **missile container**
04 silo

missing
◊ *deletion indicator*
04 gone, lost **06** absent, astray

07 lacking, mislaid, strayed, wanting **08** awanting **09** misplaced **10** gone astray **11** disappeared **14** gone for a Burton, unaccounted-for

mission
02 op **03** aim, job **04** duty, goal, raid, task, work **05** chore, quest **06** action, charge, errand, office, sortie **07** calling, crusade, embassy, purpose, pursuit **08** business, campaign, exercise, legation, ministry, vocation **09** manoeuvre, operation, task force **10** assignment, commission, delegation, deputation **11** raison d'être, undertaking

missionary
05 envoy **07** apostle **08** champion, crusader, emissary, minister, preacher, promoter **09** converter **10** ambassador, campaigner, evangelist **12** propagandist, proselytizer

Missionaries include:
03 Fox (George), Huc (Evariste Régis)
04 Luke (St), Mark (St), Paul (St)
05 Carey (William), David (Père Armand), Eliot (John), Ellis (William), Moody (Dwight L), Ricci (Matteo), Smith (Eli)
06 Damien (Father Joseph), Graham (Billy), Teresa (Mother), Wesley (John)
07 Aylward (Gladys), Columba (St), Liddell (Eric), ten Boom (Corrie)
08 Boniface (St), Crowther (Samuel)
09 McPherson (Aimee Semple), Southwell (Robert)
10 Huddleston (Trevor), Macpherson (Annie), Schweitzer (Albert)
11 Livingstone (David)
13 Francis Xavier (St)

Mississippi
02 MS **04** Miss

missive
04 line, memo, note, sent **06** letter, report **07** epistle, message, missile **08** bulletin, dispatch **09** messenger **10** communiqué, memorandum **13** communication

Missouri
02 MO

misspell
◊ *anagram indicator*

misspent
04 idle **06** wasted **07** misused **08** prodigal **09** idled away **10** dissipated, misapplied, profitless, squandered, thrown away **12** unprofitable **13** frittered away

misstate
05 twist **06** garble **07** distort, falsify, pervert **08** misquote **09** misrelate, misreport **11** misremember **12** misrepresent

mist
03 dew, fog **04** drow, film, haar, haze, murk, rack, roke, smog, veil **05** cloud,

spray, steam 06 mizzle, nimbus, vapour 07 dimness, drizzle 10 exhalation 12 condensation

• **mist over, mist up**
03 dim, fog 04 blur, veil 05 fog up, glaze 07 obscure, steam up 09 cloud over 10 become hazy 12 become cloudy 13 become blurred

mistake
◇ *anagram indicator*
03 err 04 bish, blue, boob, boss, flaw, flub, goof, muff, slip, take, typo 05 error, fault, fluff, gaffe, lapse, mix up, mix-up 06 booboo, cock up, domino, duff it, foul up, foul-up, goof up, howler, mess up, miscue, muddle, ricket, slip up, slip-up, stumer 07 bad move, balls up, bloomer, blooper, blunder, botch-up, clanger, clinker, confuse, erratum, fallacy, faux pas, go wrong, louse up, misread, misstep, own goal, screw up, take for 08 confound, get wrong, mesprize, misfield, misjudge, misprint, misprise, misprize, muddle up, omission, solecism 09 make a slip, oversight 10 aberration, inaccuracy, misprision, misreading 11 corrigendum, make a booboo, misconceive, misconstrue, misspelling 12 come a cropper, drop a clanger, indiscretion, misapprehend, miscalculate, misjudgement 13 misunderstand 14 miscalculation 15 misapprehension, put your foot in it, slip of the tongue

mistaken
◇ *anagram indicator*
03 wet 05 false, wrong 06 faulty, misled, untrue 07 at fault, deluded, in error, inexact, off base, off-beam, vicious 08 deceived, overseen 09 erroneous, ill-judged, incorrect, misguided, misprised, unfounded 10 fallacious, inaccurate, up the booay 11 inauthentic, misinformed 13 inappropriate, wide of the mark 15 got the wrong idea

mistakenly
◇ *anagram indicator*
07 falsely, in error, wrongly 08 unfairly, unjustly 09 by mistake 11 erroneously, incorrectly, misguidedly 12 fallaciously, inaccurately 15 inappropriately

Mister
02 Mr

mistimed
08 ill-timed, tactless, untimely 10 malapropos 11 inopportune, unfortunate 12 inconvenient, infelicitous, unseasonable 14 unsynchronized

mistiness *see* mist

mistreat
◇ *anagram indicator*
04 harm, hurt, maul 05 abuse, bully 06 batter, beat up, ill-use, injure, misuse, molest 08 ill-treat, maltreat, walk over 09 mishandle 10 knock about, treat badly 11 walk all over

mistreatment
04 harm, hurt 05 abuse 06 ill-use, injury, misuse 07 cruelty, mauling 08 bullying, ill-usage 09 battering 10 unkindness 11 manhandling, mishandling, molestation 12 ill-treatment, maltreatment 13 brutalization

mistress
04 amie, dame, doxy, lady, miss, wife 05 lover, tutor, wench, woman 06 ruling 07 Aspasia, herself, hetaera, leading, partner, stepney, teacher 08 goodwife, lady-love, paramour 09 belle amie, concubine, courtesan, courtezan, governess, housewife, inamorata, kept woman, principal 10 canary-bird, châtelaine, fancy woman, girlfriend, school dame 11 live-in lover 12 bit on the side 13 schoolteacher

mistrust
04 fear 05 doubt, qualm 06 beware 07 caution, suspect 08 be wary of, distrust, wariness 09 chariness, hesitancy, misgiving, suspicion 10 scepticism 11 uncertainty 12 apprehension, reservations 13 have no faith in 14 be suspicious of, have misgivings 15 have doubts about

mistrustful
03 shy 04 wary 05 chary, leery 07 cynical, dubious, fearful 08 cautious, doubtful, hesitant 09 sceptical, uncertain 10 suspicious 11 distrustful 12 apprehensive

misty
03 dim 04 hazy 05 foggy, fuzzy, murky, smoky, vague 06 cloudy, opaque, veiled 07 blurred, clouded, obscure, tearful, unclear 08 nebulous 10 indistinct

misunderstand
07 mishear, misknow, misread, mistake 08 get wrong, misjudge 11 misconstrue, misperceive 12 misapprehend, misinterpret, miss the point 13 miscomprehend 15 get the wrong idea

misunderstanding
03 row 04 rift, tiff 05 clash, error, mix-up 06 breach 07 discord, dispute, mistake, quarrel 08 argument, conflict, squabble 09 wrong idea 10 difference, falling-out, malentendu, misreading 12 crossed wires, disagreement, misjudgement 13 misconception 15 false impression, misapprehension, misintelligence

misunderstood
07 misread 08 misheard, mistaken 09 ill-judged, misjudged 12 misconstrued, unrecognized 13 unappreciated 14 misappreciated, misinterpreted, misrepresented

misuse
◇ *anagram indicator*
04 harm, hurt 05 abuse, waste, wrong

06 ill-use, injure, injury 07 abusion, corrupt, deceive, distort, exploit, pervert 08 ill-treat, misapply, mistreat, squander, wrong use 09 dissipate, misemploy 10 corruption, perversion, treat badly 11 mishandling, squandering 12 exploitation, ill-treatment, maltreatment, mistreatment 13 misemployment 14 malappropriate, misapplication, misappropriate

mite
03 bit, jot, tad 04 atom, iota, whit, worm 05 grain, ounce, scrap, spark, touch, trace 06 acarus, lepton, morsel, varroa 07 modicum, smidgen 08 berry bug 09 red spider, Sarcoptes 11 trombiculid, tyroglyphid

mitigate
04 calm, dull, ease, help 05 abate, allay, blunt, check, mease, quiet, remit, slake, still 06 aslake, lenify, lessen, modify, pacify, reduce, soften, soothe, subdue, temper, weaken 07 appease, assuage, lighten, mollify, placate, qualify, relieve, sweeten 08 decrease, diminish, moderate, palliate, tone down 09 alleviate, extenuate

mitigating
08 lenitive, mitigant 09 assuasive, modifying, tempering 10 justifying, palliative, qualifying 11 extenuating, vindicating, vindicatory

mitigation
06 relief 07 remorse 08 allaying, decrease, easement 09 abatement, lessening, reduction, remission, tempering 10 diminution, moderation, palliation 11 alleviation, appeasement, assuagement, extenuation 13 mollification, qualification

mitre
04 tiar 05 tiara

mix
◇ *anagram indicator*
04 card, fuse, hash, join, mash, mell, meng, mess, ming, olio, stir, suit 05 agree, alloy, blend, cross, get on, menge, merge, union, unite, whisk 06 caudle, fold in, fusion, hobnob, jumble, meddle, medley, merger, mingle, muddle 07 amalgam, combine, consort, farrago, involve, mixture, shake up, swizzle 08 coalesce, compound, confound, emulsify, get along, intermix, mingling, mishmash, pastiche 09 associate, coalition, composite, harmonize, interfuse, introduce, potpourri, socialize, synthesis 10 amalgamate, assortment, complement, fraternize, go well with, hodgepodge, homogenize, hotchpotch, infiltrate, interbreed, meet others, salmagundi, synthesize 11 combination, gallimaufry, incorporate, intermingle, interpolate, olla-podrida, put together 12 amalgamation, be compatible, conglomerate

- **mix in**
◇ *anagram indicator*
05 add in, blend, merge **09** introduce
10 infiltrate **11** incorporate, interpolate

- **mix up**
◇ *anagram indicator*
05 upset **06** garble, jumble, muddle,
puzzle **07** confuse, disturb, involve,
mistake, perplex, snarl up **08** bewilder,
confound, muddle up **09** implicate
10 complicate **12** get jumbled up

mixed
◇ *anagram indicator*
02 pi **03** pie, pye **04** chow, ment
05 fused, meint, meynt **06** hybrid,
menged, minged, motley, united,
unsure, varied **07** alloyed, blended,
diverse, mingled, mongrel
08 assorted, combined, compound,
confused **09** composite, crossbred,
equivocal, half-caste, interbred,
uncertain **10** ambivalent
11 amalgamated, conflicting,
diversified, promiscuous
12 incorporated, through-other
13 contradicting, miscellaneous

- **mixed up**
◇ *anagram indicator*
04 in on **05** upset **06** hung up
07 chaotic, muddled, puzzled
08 caught up, confused, involved,
messed up **09** disturbed, embroiled,
entangled, perplexed, screwed up
10 bewildered, désorienté, disordered,
distracted, distraught, implicated,
inculpated **11** complicated,
disoriented, maladjusted
12 incriminated

mixer
05 whisk **06** beater, joiner **07** blender,
meddler, stirrer **08** busybody,
makebate **09** disrupter, extrovert
10 interferer, liquidizer, socializer,
subversive **12** troublemaker **13** food
processor, mischief-maker

mixing
05 cross, union **06** fusion **08** blending,
mingling **09** interflow, synthesis
10 commixtion, commixture,
confection, minglement
11 association, coalescence,
combination, socializing
12 amalgamation **13** hybridization,
interbreeding, intermingling,
miscegenation **14** fraternization

mixture
◇ *anagram indicator*
03 mix **04** brew, mong, olio, olla, wash
05 alloy, blend, cross, union **06** fusion,
hybrid, jumble, medley, mingle
07 amalgam, compost, farrago,
melange, variety **08** compound,
mishmash, mixed bag, pastiche
09 composite, patchwork, potpourri,
synthesis **10** assortment, composture,
concoction, hodgepodge,
hotchpotch, miscellany
11 coalescence, combination, olla-
podrida, smorgasbord, temperature
12 amalgamation **14** conglomeration

mix-up
◇ *anagram indicator*
04 mess **05** chaos, snafu **06** foul-up,
jumble, muddle, tangle **07** balls-up,
mistake, snarl-up **08** disorder,
nonsense **09** confusion
12 complication

moan
03 sob **04** beef, carp, hone, howl,
mean, mein, mene, sigh, wail, weep
05 bleat, gripe, groan, meane, mourn,
whine **06** bemoan, charge, grieve,
grouse, lament, whinge **07** beefing,
carping, censure, grumble, whimper
08 bleating, complain, grumbler
09 annoyance, bellyache,
complaint, criticism, grievance,
whingeing **10** accusation
11 bellyaching, kick up a fuss,
lamentation **12** fault-finding
14 representation **15** dissatisfaction

moaner
06 whiner **07** fusspot, grouser, niggler,
whinger **08** grumbler **09** nit-picker
10 bellyacher, complainer, fussbudget
11 fault-finder

mob
03 set **04** body, crew, fill, gang, herd,
host, mass, pack **05** brood, crowd,
drove, flock, group, horde, plebs,
press, swarm, tribe, troop **06** attack,
charge, jostle, masses, mobile, pester,
proles, rabble, throng **07** besiege,
company, king mob, overrun, set upon
08 canaille, fall upon, mobility,
populace, riff-raff, surround
09 descend on, gathering, hoi polloi,
multitude **10** assemblage, collection,
common herd, crowd round, faex
populi, rabble rout, swarm round
11 gather round, proletariat, rank and
file **12** common people, ribble-rabble
13 great unwashed **15** many-headed
beast

mobile
◇ *anagram indicator*
04 thin **05** agile, quick **06** active,
lively, motile, moving, nimble,
roving, supple **07** migrant, movable,
roaming **08** changing, flexible,
moveable, portable **09** adaptable,
energetic, itinerant, revealing,
wandering **10** able to move, adjustable,
ambulatory, changeable, expressive,
locomotive, suggesting, travelling
11 peripatetic **12** ever-changing
13 transportable

mobility
06 motion **07** agility **08** motility,
motivity, vivacity **09** animation
10 locomotion, movability, suppleness
11 flexibility, movableness, portability
12 locomobility, locomotivity
14 expressiveness

mobilization
08 assembly **09** mustering,
summoning **10** activation
11 marshalling, preparation
12 organization

mobilize
◇ *anagram indicator*
05 rally, ready **06** call up, enlist, muster,
summon **07** animate, marshal, prepare
08 activate, assemble, get ready,
organize **09** conscript, galvanize,
make ready **14** call into action

mob rule
06 mob law **08** lynch law
09 mobocracy **10** ochlocracy
13 kangaroo court, Reign of Terror

mobster
04 thug **05** crook, heavy, rough, tough
06 bandit, robber **07** brigand,
hoodlum, ruffian **08** criminal, gangster,
hooligan, skinhead **09** bovver boy,
desperado, racketeer, terrorist

mock
03 ape, cod, dor, kid, rag, rib **04** fake,
geck, gibe, goof, jape, jeer, rail, sham,
slag **05** bogus, chaff, dummy, faked,
false, fleer, flout, knock, mimic, scoff,
scorn, scout, sneer, taunt, tease
06 bemock, deride, ersatz, forged,
insult, parody, phoney, pseudo, send up
07 emulate, feigned, imitate, lampoon,
laugh at, murgeon, pretend, slag off,
take off **08** ridicule, satirize, simulate,
spurious **09** burlesque, disparage,
imitation, imitative, make fun of, poke
fun at, pretended, simulated, synthetic
10 artificial, caricature, fraudulent,
substitute **11** counterfeit, poke borak at
13 poke mullock at
See also **imitation**

mocker
05 tease **06** critic, jeerer **07** clothes,
derider, flouter, reviler, scoffer, scorner,
sneerer **08** bellbird, satirist, vilifier
09 detractor, lampooner, ridiculer,
tormentor **10** iconoclast, lampoonist
11 pasquinader

mockery
03 dor, gab **04** jeer, quiz, sham
05 farce, fleer, scoff, scorn, serve,
sneer, spoof, sport **06** banter, parody,
satire, send-up **07** apology, disdain,
horning, jeering, kidding, lampoon,
mimicry, ragging, ribbing, sarcasm,
take-off, teasing **08** contempt,
derision, raillery, ridicule, scoffing,
sneering, taunting, travesty
09 burlesque, charivari, contumely,
emulation, imitation **10** caricature,
disrespect **12** mickey-taking
13 disparagement

mocking
03 wry **05** snide **07** cynical
08 derisive, derisory, illusion,
impudent, irrisory, narquois, sardonic,
scoffing, scornful, sneering, taunting
09 insulting, quizzical, sarcastic,
satirical **10** disdainful, irreverent, wry-
mouthed **12** contemptuous
13 disrespectful

mock-up
04 copy **05** dummy, image, model
07 replica **09** facsimile, imitation
11 fabrication **14** representation

mode
03 fad, way **04** form, kind, look, mood, plan, rage, rate **05** craze, modus, style, trend, vogue **06** custom, Dorian, lastic, Ionian, Lydian, manner, method, system **07** Aeolian, fashion, Locrian, process **08** approach, modality, Phrygian, practice **09** condition, procedure, technique **10** convention, dernier cri **11** latest thing **13** manifestation **15** fashionableness

model
◇ *anagram indicator*
01 T **03** sit, toy **04** base, cast, copy, form, kind, make, mark, mode, mold, plan, pose, sort, type, wear, work **05** carve, dummy, ideal, image, medal, mould, poser, shape, sport, style **06** byword, create, design, lovely, mirror, mock-up, module, sample, sculpt, sitter **07** cutaway, display, epitome, example, exemple, fashion, paragon, pattern, perfect, reduced, replica, show off, subject, typical, variety, version **08** bozzetto, exemplar, original, paradigm, specimen, standard, template **09** archetype, dress form, exemplary, facsimile, imitation, mannequin, miniature, prototype, superwaif **10** archetypal, embodiment, small-scale, stereotype **11** guiding star **12** artist's model, fashion model, guiding light, prototypical, reproduction **14** perfect example, representation

moderate
03 mod **04** calm, cool, curb, ease, fair, just, mean, mild, soft, so-so, tame **05** abate, allay, chair, check, slake, sober **06** decent, direct, gentle, lessen, medium, modest, modify, pacify, relent, soften, steady, subdue, temper **07** appease, assuage, average, chasten, control, die down, dwindle, fairish, liberal, qualify, repress, slacken, subside **08** adequate, attemper, centrist, chastise, decrease, diminish, don't know, mediocre, middling, mitigate, modulate, muscadin, ordinary, palliate, passable, play down, regulate, restrain, sensible, suppress, tone down **09** alleviate, attenuate, Menshevik, Octobrist, soft-pedal, soft-shell, supervise, temperate, tolerable, treatable **10** controlled, measurable, not much cop, reasonable, restrained **11** indifferent, keep in check, not up to much, preside over, soft-shelled **12** act as chair at, conservative, nonextremist **13** neutral person, no great shakes, well-regulated **14** fair to middling **15** act as chairman at, middle-of-the-road

moderately
05 mezzo, quite **06** fairly, rather **08** passably, slightly, somewhat **10** reasonably **12** to some extent, within reason **13** within measure **14** conservatively

moderation
02 ho **03** hoa, hoh **06** reason

07 caution, control, curbing, measure **08** chastity, decrease, sobriety **09** abatement, composure, lessening, reduction, restraint **10** golden mean, mitigation, regulation, relaxation, subsidence, temperance **11** alleviation, attenuation, self-control **13** self-restraint, temperateness **14** abstemiousness, reasonableness

• **in moderation**
10 moderately **12** within bounds, within limits, within reason **15** with self-control

modern
02 AD, in **03** hip, mod, new, now **04** cool, late **05** fresh, novel **06** latest, latter, modish, recent, trendy, with it **07** current, faddish, go-ahead, in style, in vogue, present, stylish, voguish **08** advanced, everyday, existing, neoteric, space-age, up-to-date **09** in fashion, inventive, latter-day, newfangle, the latest **10** all the rage, avant-garde, futuristic, innovative, neoterical, newfangled, present-day **11** commonplace, cutting edge, fashionable, modernistic, progressive, spanking new **12** contemporary **13** state-of-the-art, up-to-the-minute **14** forward-looking, hot off the press

modernity
07 newness, novelty **09** freshness **10** innovation, recentness **11** originality **14** innovativeness **15** contemporaneity, fashionableness

modernization
07 renewal **08** redesign, updating **09** revamping **10** renovation **11** improvement, remodelling **12** modification, regeneration **13** refurbishment **14** transformation

modernize
04 do up **05** fix up, renew **06** do over, modify, reform, remake, revamp, update **07** improve, refresh, remodel **08** progress, redesign, renovate **09** get with it, refurbish, transform **10** make modern, regenerate, rejuvenate, streamline **13** bring up-to-date

modest
03 coy, shy **04** fair, pure **05** lowly, plain, prude, pudic, quiet, small, timid **06** chaste, decent, demure, humble, proper, pudent, seemly, simple **07** bashful, limited, prudent **08** adequate, decorous, discreet, maidenly, moderate, ordinary, passable, reserved, retiring, verecund, virtuous **09** chastened, diffident, shamefast, tolerable **10** reasonable, shamefaced, unassuming **11** inexpensive, unobtrusive **12** satisfactory, self-effacing, unpretending **13** self-conscious, unexceptional, unpretentious **15** self-deprecating

modestly
05 coyly, shyly **06** humbly, purely **07** quietly, timidly **08** chastely, decently, demurely **09** bashfully

10 adequately, discreetly, moderately, reasonably, virtuously **11** diffidently **12** unassumingly **14** satisfactorily **15** self-consciously, unpretentiously

modesty
05 aidos, shame **07** coyness, decency, decorum, pudency, reserve, shyness **08** humility, pudicity, timidity **09** plainness, propriety, quietness, reticence **10** chasteness, demureness, humbleness, seemliness, simplicity **11** bashfulness **13** shamefastness **14** self-effacement, shamefacedness **15** inexpensiveness, self-deprecation

modicum
03 bit, tad **04** atom, dash, drop, hint, inch, iota, mite **05** crumb, grain, ounce, pinch, scrap, shred, speck, tinge, touch, trace, woman **06** degree, little **08** fragment, molecule, particle **09** little bit **10** suggestion **11** small amount

modification
◇ *anagram indicator*
05 tweak **06** change **08** mutation, revision **09** recasting, reworking, tempering, variation **10** adaptation, adjustment, alteration, limitation, moderation, modulation, refinement, remoulding **11** improvement, reformation, restriction **13** qualification **14** reorganization, transformation

modify
◇ *anagram indicator*
04 dash, dull, vary **05** abate, adapt, alter, limit, touch, tweak, vowel **06** adjust, change, invert, lessen, recast, reduce, reform, revise, rework, sculpt, soften, temper, umlaut **07** convert, improve, qualify, remould, reshape **08** attemper, decrease, diminish, mitigate, moderate, overrule, redesign, retrofit, tone down, vowelize **09** diversify, transform **10** assimilate, reorganize **11** explain away **13** differentiate, trim your sails

modish
02 in **03** hip, mod, now **04** chic, cool **05** jazzy, smart, vogue **06** latest, modern, tonish, trendy, with it **07** à la mode, current, stylish, tonnish, voguish **10** all the rage, avant-garde **11** fashionable, modernistic **12** contemporary **13** up-to-the-minute

modulate
04 tune, vary **05** alter, lower **06** adjust, change, modify, soften, temper **07** balance, inflect **08** moderate, regulate **09** harmonize

modulation
04 tone **05** shade, shift **06** accent, change, tuning **07** balance, cadence **08** lowering **09** inflexion, softening, variation **10** adjustment, alteration, inflection, intonation, moderation, regulation **12** modification **13** harmonization

module

02 LM **03** bug, LEM **04** item, part, SIMM, unit **05** image, model, piece **06** factor, plug-in **07** element, section **09** component

modus operandi

02 MO **03** way **04** plan, rule **06** manner, method, praxis, system **07** process **08** practice **09** operation, procedure, technique **11** rule of thumb

mogul

03 VIP **05** baron, Mr Big **06** big gun, big pot, bigwig, Mughal, top dog, tycoon **07** big shot, magnate, notable, supremo **08** big noise, big wheel, padishah **09** big cheese, personage, potentate

moist

03 wet **04** damp, dank, dewy **05** humid, juicy, muggy, rainy, soggy, washy **06** clammy, hydric, liquid, marshy, watery **07** drizzly, tearful, wettish **08** dripping **09** drizzling, humectant, hygrophil **12** hygrophilous

moisten

03 dew, dip, wet **04** damp, lick, soak, wash **05** bathe, bedew, bewet, imbue, latch, slake, water **06** dampen, embrue, humect, humefy, humify, imbrue, madefy, sloken, sparge **07** embrewe, make wet, slocken, spairge **08** humidify, irrigate **09** humectate **10** moisturize

moisture

03 dew, wet **04** damp, rain **05** humor, spray, steam, sweat, water **06** humour, liquid, vapour **07** drizzle, soaking, wetness **08** dampness, dankness, humidity **09** mugginess **10** wateriness **11** humectation, precipitate **12** condensation, perspiration **13** precipitation

molar

04 wang **08** jaw-tooth **09** mill-tooth

Moldova

02 MD **03** MDA

mole

03 mol, spy **04** dyke, mark, pier, spot, want **05** agent, jetty, Talpa **06** blotch, groyne **07** barrier, blemish, freckle, speckle **08** causeway **09** mouldwarp, mowdiwort **10** breakwater, embankment, moudiewart, moudiewort, mowdiewart, Notoryctes **11** double agent, infiltrator, secret agent

molest

03 bug, nag, vex **04** harm, hurt, rape **05** abuse, annoy, harry, hound, tease, upset, worry **06** accost, assail, attack, badger, bother, chivvy, harass, hassle, injure, needle, pester, plague, ravish **07** agitate, assault, disturb, fluster, provoke, torment, trouble **08** ill-treat, irritate, maltreat, mistreat **09** aggravate, persecute

10 exasperate **13** interfere with **15** sexually assault

molestation

04 harm, rape **05** abuse **06** attack, injury **07** assault **11** disturbance, infestation **12** interference

molester

06 abuser, rapist **08** attacker, ravisher **09** assaulter

mollify

04 calm, ease, lull **05** abate, allay, blunt, quell, quiet, relax **06** lessen, mellow, modify, pacify, soften, soothe, temper **07** appease, assuage, compose, cushion, placate, quieten, relieve, sweeten **08** mitigate, moderate **10** conciliate, propitiate

mollusc

Molluscs include:

03 Mya
04 clam, slug, Unio
05 conch, cowry, snail, spoot, squid, whelk
06 chiton, cockle, cowrie, cuttle, dodman, limpet, loligo, mussel, nerite, oyster, winkle
07 abalone, octopus, piddock, scallop, sea slug
08 escargot, nautilus, sea snail, shipworm, wallfish
09 cone shell, hodmandod, land snail, pond snail, razorclam, razorfish, tusk shell, wing shell, wing snail
10 cuttlefish, giant squid, nudibranch, periwinkle, razor shell, Roman snail
11 horse mussel, marine snail
12 sea butterfly
13 great grey slug, keyhole limpet, ramshorn snail, slipper limpet
15 freshwater snail

See also **animal; crustacean**

• **mollusc's tongue**
04 rasp

mollycoddle

03 pet **04** baby, ruin **05** spoil **06** coddle, cosset, mother, pamper **07** indulge **08** pander to **09** spoonfeed **11** overprotect

molten

05 fusil **06** fusile, melted **07** flowing **08** magmatic **09** liquefied **12** circumfusile

molybdenum

02 Mo

moment

02 mo **03** sec **04** hint, note, tick **05** flash, gliff, glift, jiffy, point, punto, trice, twink, value, worth **06** import, minute, puncto, second, stound, stownd, weight **07** concern, gravity, instant **08** as soon as, directly, gliffing, interest, occasion, the point, two ticks **09** short time, substance, the minute, twinkling **10** importance, the instant **11** consequence, immediately, little while, point in time, seriousness, split

second, weightiness **12** significance **13** very short time **14** less than no time

• **a moment ago**
04 enow

momentarily

07 briefly **10** fleetingly, for a moment, for a second **11** temporarily **12** for an instant **13** for a short time **15** instantaneously

momentary

05 brief, hasty, quick, short **07** passing **08** fleeting **09** ephemeral, momentany, spasmodic, temporary, transient **10** evanescent, short-lived, transitory **12** momentaneous **13** instantaneous

momentous

05 grave, major, vital **07** crucial, fateful, pivotal, serious, weighty **08** critical, decisive, eventful, historic, pregnant **09** important **11** epoch-making, significant **12** earth-shaking, of importance **13** consequential **14** of significance **15** earth-shattering, world-shattering

momentum

04 push, urge **05** drive, force, poise, power, speed **06** energy, impact, thrust **07** impetus, impulse **08** stimulus, strength, velocity **09** incentive **10** propulsion **12** driving-power

• **angular momentum**
01 L

Monaco

02 MC **03** MCO

monarch

01 K, Q, R **02** ER, GR, HM, VR **03** rex, roi **04** Cole, czar, Inca, king, ksar, tsar, tzar **05** queen, ruler **06** Caesar, prince, regina **07** czarina, emperor, empress, tsarina **08** autocrat, czarevna, czaritsa, princess, the Crown, tsarevna, tsaritsa **09** cesarevna, czarevich, potentate, sovereign, tsarevich **10** cesarevich, cesarewich, czarevitch, tsesarevna, tsarevitch **11** cesarevitch, cesarewitch, crowned head, king of kings, tsesarevich, tsesarewich **12** tsesarevitch, tsesarewitch

See also **king; prince; princess; queen**

Anglo-Saxon and English monarchs:

04 Cnut ('the Great'), Edwy, Grey (Lady Jane), John (Lackland), Mary (I, Tudor), Offa
05 Edgar, Edred, Henry (I, II, III, IV, V, VI, VII, VIII), Svein (I Haraldsson, 'Fork-Beard')
06 Alfred ('the Great'), Canute, Edmund (I, II Ironside'), Edward (I, II 'the Martyr', III 'the Confessor', IV, V, VI, 'the Elder'), Egbert, Harold (I Knutsson, 'Harefoot', II)
07 Richard (I 'the Lion Heart', II, III), Stephen, William (I 'the Conqueror', II 'Rufus')
08 Ethelred (I, II 'the Unready')
09 Athelstan, Elizabeth (I), Ethelbald, Ethelbert, Ethelwulf

11 Hardicanute
13 Edgar Atheling, Knut Sveinsson

monarchy
05 realm **06** domain, empire
07 kingdom, royalty, tyranny
08 dominion, kingship, royalism
09 autocracy, despotism, monocracy
10 absolutism **11** sovereignty
12 principality **14** sovereign state

monastery
03 wat **04** cell **05** abbey, gompa
06 friary, priory, vihara **07** convent, minster, nunnery **08** cloister, lamasery
09 coenobium, lamaserai
12 Charterhouse

See also **abbey**; **religious**

monastic
07 ascetic, austere, monkish, recluse
08 celibate, eremitic, secluded, solitary **09** canonical, reclusive, withdrawn **10** anchoritic, cloistered, coenobitic, meditative **11** sequestered
13 contemplative

See also **religious**

monasticism
07 monkery **08** monkhood
09 austerity, eremitism, monachism, reclusion, seclusion **10** asceticism
11 coenobitism, recluseness

Monday
03 Mon

monetary
04 cash **05** money **06** fiscal **07** capital
08 economic **09** budgetary, financial, pecuniary

money
01 L, M, P **03** fat, LSD, oof, tin, utu
04 cash, cent, coin, dibs, dosh, dust, gelt, gilt, hoot, jack, kail, kale, loot, pelf
05 blunt, brass, bread, bucks, chink, dough, dumps, funds, gravy, lolly, means, Oscar, purse, ready, rhino, smash, sugar, wonga **06** argent, assets, greens, moolah, riches, stumpy, wealth
07 capital, dingbat, ooftish, readies, savings, scratch, shekels **08** currency, finances, greenies **09** affluence, banknotes, megabucks, resources
10 big bikkies, prosperity **11** legal tender, spondulicks **12** the necessary

See also **coin**; **currency**

• **get money from**
03 tap

• **hand over money**
03 pay

• **in the money**
04 rich **05** flush **06** loaded **07** wealthy, well-off **08** affluent, well-to-do
10 prosperous, well-heeled **11** rolling in it **12** stinking rich

• **large amount of money**
03 wad **04** mint, pile, pots, scad

• **money collection**
03 cap **04** whip **09** whip-round

• **provide with money**
03 pay **04** fund

• **quantity of money**
03 sum

money-box
04 safe **05** chest **06** coffer **07** cash box, poor box **08** penny-pig **09** piggy-bank

money-changing
04 agio

moneyed
04 rich **05** flush **06** loaded **07** opulent, wealthy, well-off **08** affluent, well-to-do **10** prosperous, well-heeled
11 comfortable, rolling in it

money-grubbing
07 miserly **08** grasping
09 mammonish, mercenary
10 quaestuary **11** acquisitive, mammonistic

moneymaking
06 paying **09** lucrative **10** commercial, profitable, quaestuary, successful
12 profit-making, remunerative

Mongolia
03 MGL, MNG

mongoose
04 urva

mongrel
◊ *anagram indicator*
03 cur **04** kuri, mong, mutt **05** cross, mixed, pooch **06** bitser, hybrid
07 bastard **08** half-bred **09** crossbred, half-breed, yellow dog **10** crossbreed, ill-defined, mixed breed **12** of mixed breed

monicker
04 name **05** alias **07** pen name
08 nickname **09** false name, pseudonym, sobriquet, stage name
10 soubriquet **11** assumed name

monitor
03 VDU **04** CCTV, note, plot, scan
05 check, trace, track, varan, watch
06 detect, follow, goanna, iguana, leguan, marker, record, screen, survey, worral, worrel **07** adviser, advisor, display, head boy, leguaan, observe, oversee, perenty, prefect, scanner, Varanus **08** detector, head girl, observer, overseer, perentie, recorder, watchdog **09** supervise **10** supervisor
11 invigilator, keep an eye on, keep track of **12** dragon lizard, Komodo dragon, Komodo lizard **14** security camera

monk
03 Dan, Dom **04** lama **05** abbot, friar, prior **06** beguin, frater, hermit
07 brother **08** cenobite, monastic, talapoin **09** anchorite, bullfinch, coenobite, Dalai Lama, gyrovague, mendicant, religieux, religious
10 cloisterer, conventual, religioner
11 abbey-lubber, religionary
13 contemplative, possessionate

Bonivard (François de), Duchesne (St Rose Philippine), Foucauld (Charles de), Houedard (Dom Sylvester), Pelagius, Rabelais (François), Rasputin (Grigori)
09 Bonnivard (François de), MacKillop (Mary), Skobtsova (Maria)
10 Bernadette (St), Fra Diavolo, Montfaucon (Bernard de), Torquemada (Tomás de), Walsingham (Thomas), Willibrord (St)
11 Bodhidharma, Ponce de León (Luis), Scholastica (St)
12 Guido d'Arezzo
13 The Singing Nun
14 Francis of Paola (St), Marianus Scotus, Peter the Hermit
15 Bernard of Morval

See also **religious**

monkey
03 imp, tup 04 brat, fool, mess, muck, play, tyke 05 anger, clown, mimic, rogue, scamp, sheep 06 fiddle, fidget, footle, lackey, meddle, potter, rascal, simian, tamper, tinker, trifle, urchin 07 primate 09 interfere, scallywag 10 jackanapes 13 mischief-maker

Monkeys include:

03 ape, pug, sai
04 douc, leaf, mico, mona, saki, titi, zati
05 Diana, drill, green, magot, night, sajou, Satan, toque
06 baboon, bandar, bonnet, coaita, grivet, guenon, howler, langur, malmag, rhesus, sagoin, saguin, spider, tee-tee, uakari, vervet, woolly
07 cacajou, colobus, guereza, hanuman, jacchus, macaque, sagouin, saimiri, sapajou, tamarin, tarsier, wistiti
08 capuchin, durukuli, entellus, mandrill, mangabey, marmoset, squirrel, talapoin, wanderoo
09 proboscis
10 Barbary ape, moustached
11 douroucouli, platyrrhine, white-eyelid
13 platyrrhinian

See also **animal**; **ape**

• **monkey business**
06 pranks 07 carry-on, foolery
08 clowning, mischief, trickery
09 chicanery 10 dishonesty, hanky-panky, tomfoolery 11 legerdemain, shenanigans, skulduggery 12 monkey tricks 13 funny business, jiggery-pokery, sleight-of-hand
• **monkey puzzle**
09 araucaria, Chile pine 11 Chilean pine

monochrome
05 sepia 08 monotone, unicolor
09 unicolour 10 monochroic, monotonous 11 unicolorate, unicolorous, unicoloured 13 black-and-white, monochromatic

monocle
04 quiz 05 glass 08 eyeglass
13 quizzing-glass

monogamous
09 monogamic 10 monandrous, monogynous

monogamy
08 monandry, monogyny

monolingual
08 monoglot 10 unilingual

monolith
05 shaft 06 menhir, sarsen 08 megalith
13 standing stone

monolithic
04 huge, vast 05 giant, rigid, solid
07 massive 08 colossal, faceless, gigantic, immobile, unmoving, unvaried 09 hidebound, immovable
10 fossilized, inflexible, monumental, unchanging 11 intractable

monologue
03 rap 05 spiel 06 homily, sermon, speech 07 address, lecture, oration
09 soliloquy

monomania
05 mania, thing 06 fetish 08 fixation, idée fixe, neurosis 09 fixed idea, obsession 10 fanaticism, hobby-horse 13 ruling passion 15 bee in your bonnet

monopolize
03 hog 05 tie up 06 corner, occupy, take up 07 control, engross
08 dominate, take over 09 preoccupy
11 appropriate 14 have sole rights, have to yourself, keep to yourself

monopoly
05 régie 06 corner 07 appalto, control
09 franchise, monopsony, privilege, sole right 10 ascendancy, domination, sole rights 14 exclusive right
15 exclusive rights

monotonous
04 drab, dull, flat 05 ho-hum, samey
06 boring, deadly 07 humdrum, routine, tedious, uniform 08 plodding, tiresome, toneless, unvaried
09 unvarying, wearisome 10 all the same, colourless, mechanical, monochrome, repetitive, unchanging, uneventful, unexciting 11 repetitious
12 run-of-the-mill 13 uninteresting
14 soul-destroying

monotony
06 tedium 07 boredom, humdrum, routine, taedium 08 ding-dong, dullness, flatness, sameness
10 repetition, uniformity
11 routineness 12 tiresomeness
13 wearisomeness 14 repetitiveness, uneventfulness

monster
04 huge, mega, vast 05 alien, beast, brute, devil, fiend, freak, giant, jumbo
06 mutant, savage 07 immense, mammoth, massive, villain 08 colossal, colossus, enormous, gigantic, teratism,

whopping 09 barbarian, ginormous, monstrous 10 tremendous
11 miscreation, monstrosity
12 malformation 13 freak of nature
14 Brobdingnagian

Monster types include:

03 orc, roc
04 cete, gila, ogre
05 alien, gulon, harpy, lamia, phoca, troll, yowie, zombi
06 ajatar, bunyip, dragon, gorgon, kraken, nicker, ogress, sphinx, wivern, wyvern, zombie
07 cyclops, griffin, griffon, gryphon, prodigy, satyral, taniwha, triffid, wendigo, windigo, ziffius
08 basilisk, behemoth, bogeyman, dinosaur, lindworm, mooncalf, mushussu, seahorse
09 leviathan, manticore, marakihau, rosmarine, sea satyre, wasserman, whirlpool
10 chupacabra, cockatrice, crio-sphinx, salamander, sea monster
11 amphisbaena, hippocampus

Monsters include:

02 ET
05 Hydra, Smaug, snark
06 Balrog, Duessa, Empusa, Fafnir, Geryon, Medusa, Nazgul, Nessie, Python, Scylla, Shelob, Sphinx, Stheno, Typhon
07 Bathies, Caliban, Cecrops, Chimera, Cyclops, Dracula, Echidna, Euryale, Grendel
08 Cerberus, Chimaera, Godzilla, King Kong, Minotaur, Typhoeus
09 Charybdis
10 Black Annis, jabberwock, Jormangund, jubjub bird, Polyphemus
12 bandersnatch, Blatant Beast, Count Dracula, Frankenstein
13 Cookie Monster, Hecatonchires, Questing Beast
14 Incredible Hulk, Midgard serpent
15 Glatysaunt Beast, Loch Ness monster

See also **mythical**; **mythology**

monstrosity
04 evil 05 freak, teras 06 horror, mutant 07 eyesore, monster
08 atrocity, enormity, ugliness
09 carbuncle, obscenity
11 abnormality, heinousness, hellishness, hideousness, miscreation
12 dreadfulness 13 frightfulness, loathsomeness

monstrous
04 evil, foul, huge, vast, vile 05 cruel, nasty 06 grisly, savage, wicked
07 heinous, hideous, immense, inhuman, mammoth, massive, vicious 08 abnormal, colossal, criminal, deformed, dreadful, enormous, freakish, gigantic, gruesome, horrible, misbegot, shocking, teratoid, terrible
09 abhorrent, atrocious, frightful,

grotesque, malformed, misshapen, unnatural **10** abominable, horrifying, miraculous, outrageous, prodigious, scandalous, tremendous **11** disgraceful, misbegotten **12** preposterous

monstrously
06 hugely, vastly **08** terribly **09** immensely, massively **10** colossally, dreadfully, enormously, shockingly **11** atrociously, frightfully **12** gigantically, outrageously, scandalously, tremendously

Montana
02 MT **04** Mont

month
01 m **02** mo

Months:
02 Jy
03 Apr, Aug, Dec, Feb, Jan, Jul, Jun, Mar, May, Nov, Oct, Sep
04 July, June, Sept
05 April, March
06 August
07 January, October
08 December, February, November
09 September

French month names:
02 Av
03 mai
04 août, juin, mars
05 avril
07 février, janvier, juillet, octobre
08 décembre, novembre
09 septembre

French Revolutionary calendar month names:
06 Nivôse
07 Floréal, Ventôse
08 Brumaire, Frimaire, Germinal, Messidor, Pluviôse, Prairial
09 Fructidor, Thermidor
11 Vendémiaire

German month names:
03 Mai
04 Juli, Juni, März
05 April
06 August, Januar
07 Februar, Oktober
08 Dezember, November
09 September

Hindu calendar month names:
05 Magha, Pausa
06 Asadha, Asvina
07 Chaitra, Sravana
08 Jyaistha, Karttika, Phalguna, Vaisakha
10 Bhadrapada, Margasirsa
13 Dvitiya Asadha
14 Dvitiya Sravana

Islamic calendar month names:
05 Rabi I, Rajab, Safar
06 Rabi II, Shaban
07 Jumada I, Ramadan, Shawwal
08 Jumada II, Muharram

10 Dhu al-Qadah
11 Dhu al-Hijjah

Italian month names:
05 marzo
06 agosto, aprile, giugno, luglio, maggio
07 gennaio, ottobre
08 dicembre, febbraio, novembre
09 settembre

Jewish calendar month names:
02 Ab, Av
04 Abib, Adar, Elul, Iyar
05 Iyyar, Nisan, Sivan, Tebet, Tevet, Tisri
06 Hesvan, Kisleu, Kislev, Shebat, Shevat, Tammuz, Tebeth, Tishri, Veadar
07 Chislev, Heshvan
09 Adar Sheni

Latin month names:
05 Maius
06 Julius, Junius
07 Aprilis, Martius, October
08 Augustus, December, November, Sextilis
09 Januarius, Quintilis, September
10 Februarius

Spanish month names:
04 mayo
05 abril, enero, julio, junio, marzo
06 agosto
07 febrero, octubre
09 diciembre, noviembre
10 septiembre

• in the last month
03 ult **04** ulto **06** ultimo
• the present month
04 inst **07** instant

Montserrat
03 MSR

monument
04 tomb **05** cairn, cross, folly, relic, token, trace **06** barrow, column, heroon, marker, pillar, record, shrine, statue **07** hogback, martyry, memento, obelisk, prodigy, pyramid, talayot, trilith, witness **08** cenotaph, evidence, memorial, reminder, sacellum **09** headstone, mausoleum, testament, tombstone, trilithon **10** gravestone, immortelle, indication **11** remembrance, war memorial **13** commemoration

Monuments and memorials include:
04 Eros, Homo
05 Grant, Scott
06 Albert, Sphinx
07 Lincoln, Martyr's
08 Boadicea, Cenotaph, Daibutsu, Lion Gate, Taj Mahal, Victoria
09 Charminar, Menin Gate, Qutb Minar, Tsar's Bell
10 Berlin Wall, Broken Ring, Ishtar Gate, Kutab Minar, London Wall, Marble Arch, Mt Rushmore, Navigators', Stonehenge, Washington

11 Civil Rights, Eiffel Tower, Grande Arche, Great Sphinx, Machu Picchu, Madara Rider, Silbury Hill, Voortrekker
12 Antonine Wall, Eleanor Cross, Glass Pyramid, Great Pyramid, Hadrian's Wall, Spanish Steps, Statue of Zeus, Tower of Babel
13 Admiralty Arch, Arc de Triomphe, Great Zimbabwe, Mount Rushmore, Nelson's Column, People's Heroes, Trajan's Column, Trevi Fountain
14 Albert Memorial, Eleanor Crosses, Gateway of India, Glastonbury Tor, Hands of Victory, Hiroshima Peace, Lenin Mausoleum, Spasskaya Tower, Stone of Destiny, Tomb of Mausolus, Wayland's Smithy, Wright Brothers
15 Brandenburg Gate, Lincoln Memorial, Nubian monuments, Rollright Stones, Statue of Liberty, Thatta monuments

monumental
04 huge, vast **05** great **07** abiding, amazing, awesome, classic, immense, lasting, massive, notable **08** colossal, enduring, enormous, historic, immortal, imposing, majestic, memorial, striking **09** important, memorable, permanent **10** impressive, remarkable, tremendous **11** celebratory, epoch-making, exceptional, magnificent, outstanding, significant **12** awe-inspiring, overwhelming **13** commemorative, extraordinary, unforgettable

monumentally
06 hugely, vastly **09** immensely, massively **10** colossally, enormously **12** gigantically, tremendously

mood
03 fit, tid **04** feel, mode, sulk, tone, vein, whim **05** anger, blues, dumps, pique, tenor **06** humour, plight, spirit, temper **07** bad mood, climate, feeling, spirits **08** ambience, doldrums, optative, the sulks **09** bad temper, potential **10** atmosphere, depression, imperative, indicative, infinitive, low spirits, melancholy **11** conjunctive, disposition, frame of mind, state of mind, subjunctive
• in the mood for
06 keen on, keen to **07** eager to **08** ready for **09** willing to **10** disposed to, inclined to **11** feeling like, wanting to do **13** wanting to have

moody
04 glum, mopy **05** angry, faked, mopey, sulky, testy **06** broody, crabby, crusty, fickle, gloomy, morose, sullen, touchy **07** doleful, flighty, in a huff, in a mood **08** downcast, petulant, unstable, volatile **09** crotchety, impulsive, irascible, irritable, miserable, pretended **10** capricious, changeable, in a bad mood, melancholy **11** bad-tempered **12** cantankerous **13** short-tempered, temperamental, unpredictable

moon

04 idle, loaf, mope, pine **05** brood, dream, month, mooch **06** Lucina, Phoebe **08** daydream, languish **09** fantasize, satellite **13** Paddy's lantern **15** MacFarlane's buat

Lunar seas:

08 Bay of Dew
09 Moscow Sea, Sea of Cold, Smyth's Sea
10 Bay of Heats, Central Bay, Eastern Sea, Foaming Sea, Mare Nubium, Sea of Waves, Sinus Medii, Sinus Roris
11 Lacus Mortis, Lake of Death, Mare Crisium, Mare Humorum, Mare Imbrium, Mare Ingenii, Mare Smythii, Mare Spumans, Mare Undarum, Mare Vaporum, Marginal Sea, Palus Somnii, Sea of Clouds, Sea of Crises, Sea of Nectar, Sinus Iridum, Southern Sea
12 Humboldt's Sea, Lake of Dreams, Mare Australe, Mare Frigoris, Mare Marginis, Mare Nectaris, Marsh of Decay, Marsh of Mists, Marsh of Sleep, Sea of Showers, Sea of Vapours, Sinus Aestuum
13 Bay of Rainbows, Mare Orientale, Ocean of Storms, Sea of Geniuses, Sea of Moisture, Sea of Serenity
14 Lacus Somniorum, Palus Nebularum, Sea of Fertility
15 Mare Moscoviense, Mare Serenitatis, Palus Putredinis
16 Mare Fecunditatis, Marsh of Epidemics, Palus Epidemiarum
17 Mare Humboldtianum, Sea of Tranquillity
18 Oceanus Procellarum
19 Mare Tranquillitatis

Moons include:

02 Io
04 Moon, Rhea
05 Ariel, Dione, Mimas, Titan
06 Charon, Deimos, Europa, Nereid, Oberon, Phobos, Tethys, Triton
07 Iapetus, Miranda, Proteus, Titania, Umbriel
08 Callisto, Cruithne, Ganymede, Hyperion
09 Enceladus

Moon-related terms include:

05 lunar, phase
06 waning, waxing
07 far side, gibbous, new moon
08 blue moon, crescent, dark side, full moon, half-moon, lunation, near side
09 blood moon, moonlight, moonscape, moonshine
11 harvest moon, hunter's moon, last quarter, quarter moon
12 first quarter, man in the moon, synodic month, third quarter

• **once in a blue moon**
06 seldom **08** not often **10** hardly ever, very rarely **11** almost never

• **over the moon**
06 elated, joyful **07** fervent **08** blissful, ecstatic, euphoric, frenzied, jubilant **09** delighted, delirious, overjoyed, rapturous, rhapsodic **10** enraptured **11** high as a kite, on cloud nine, tickled pink **13** jumping for joy **15** in seventh heaven, on top of the world

moonlike

05 lunar, moony **06** lunate **07** lunular, selenic **08** crescent **09** meniscoid **10** crescentic, moon-shaped

moonshine

03 rot **04** bosh, bunk, crap, guff, tosh **05** hooch, month, stuff, tripe **06** bunkum, hootch, hot air, liquor, piffle, poteen **07** baloney, blather, blether, bootleg, eyewash, fantasy, hogwash, hokonui, potheen, rubbish, spirits, twaddle **08** blathers, blethers, bodiless, claptrap, nonsense, tommyrot **09** bull's wool

moor

03 fix **04** bind, dock, fell, lash, muir **05** berth, heath, hitch, tie up **06** anchor, fasten, secure, upland **07** Moresco, Morisco, mudéjar, Saracen **08** make fast, moorland **09** fix firmly **10** drop anchor

• **tightly moored**
04 girt

moot

04 open, pose, stir **05** argue, plead, raise, vexed **06** broach, debate, knotty, submit **07** advance, bring up, crucial, discuss, dispute, meeting, propose, suggest **08** academic, arguable, disputed, doubtful, propound **09** debatable, difficult, insoluble, introduce, undecided, unsettled **10** discussion, disputable, put forward, unresolved **11** contestable, problematic **12** open to debate, questionable, undetermined, unresolvable **13** controversial

mop

03 mat **04** mane, mass, soak, swab, wash, wipe **05** clean, dwile, shock, wiper **06** absorb, malkin, mawkin, sponge, tangle, thatch **07** grimace, swabber **08** squeegee **10** head of hair

• **mop up**
04 swab, wash **06** absorb, secure, soak up, sponge, tidy up, wipe up **07** clean up, round up **08** deal with **09** dispose of, eliminate, finish off **10** account for, neutralize, take care of

mope

04 fret, mump, peak, pine, sulk **05** boody, brood, droop, grump, moper **06** grieve, grouch, misery, moaner **07** despair, killjoy **08** languish **09** introvert, pessimist **10** depressive **11** be miserable, melancholic **12** melancholiac

• **mope about**
04 idle, loll, moon **05** mooch **06** lounge, wander **08** languish

moral

03 tag **04** good, just, pure **05** adage, maxim, noble, point, right **06** chaste, decent, dictum, honest, lesson, proper, saying, symbol **07** epigram, ethical, meaning, message, precept, proverb, upright **08** aphorism, straight, teaching, virtuous **09** blameless, certainty, emotional, righteous **10** high-minded, honourable, principled, upstanding **11** application, clean-living, encouraging **12** significance **13** incorruptible, psychological

morale

04 mood **05** heart **06** spirit **07** spirits **08** optimism **10** confidence, self-esteem **11** hopefulness, state of mind **13** esprit de corps **14** self-confidence

moralistic

04 smug **05** pious **08** priggish, superior **09** pietistic **10** complacent, goody-goody **11** pharisaical **12** hypocritical **13** sanctimonious, self-righteous **14** holier-than-thou

morality

04 good **06** ethics, ideals, morale, morals, purity, virtue **07** conduct, decency, honesty, justice, manners **08** chastity, goodness, moralism **09** integrity, principle, propriety, rectitude, standards **10** principles **11** moral values, uprightness **12** Sittlichkeit **13** righteousness

moralize

05 edify **06** preach **07** lecture **08** ethicize **09** discourse, preachify, sermonize **11** pontificate

morally

05 nobly **06** justly **08** properly, socially **09** ethically **10** honourably **11** practically **13** behaviourally

morals

06 ethics, habits, ideals **07** conduct, manners **08** morality, scruples **09** behaviour, integrity, moral code, standards **10** principles **11** moral values **12** Sittlichkeit **13** right and wrong

• **lax in morals**
04 wide

morass

03 bog, fen, jam **04** flow, mess, mire, moss, quag **05** chaos, marsh, mix-up, swamp **06** jumble, muddle, slough, tangle **07** clutter **08** quagmire **09** confusion, marshland, quicksand **10** can of worms

moratorium

03 ban **04** halt, stay **05** delay **06** freeze **07** embargo, respite **08** stoppage **10** standstill, suspension **12** postponement

morbid

04 down, grim, sick **06** ailing, gloomy, grisly, horrid, morose, sickly, sombre **07** ghastly, hideous, macabre, peccant, vicious **08** dejected, diseased, dreadful, ghoulish, gruesome, horrible **09** unhealthy **10** lugubrious, melancholy **11** pessimistic,

unwholesome **12** insalubrious
14 down in the dumps

morbidly
06 grimly **08** horribly, horridly
09 hideously **10** dreadfully, ghoulishly, gruesomely

mordant
04 acid, base **05** edged, harsh, sharp
06 biting, bitter **07** acerbic, caustic, cutting, mixtion, pungent, vicious, waspish **08** critical, incisive, scathing, stinging, venomous, wounding
09 sarcastic, trenchant **10** astringent, iron-liquor **11** acrimonious

more
02 mo **03** mae, moe, new, più **04** root
05 added, again, extra, fresh, other, plant, spare, stump **06** better, longer, rather **07** another, further
08 moreover, repeated **09** increased
10 additional **11** alternative **13** greater
number, supplementary **15** greater
quantity
• **more or less**
04 some **06** mainly, mostly **07** broadly
09 generally, in general, just about
10 by and large, on the whole, pretty
much, pretty well **11** in most cases
13 predominantly **14** for the most part
• **more than**
04 plus
• **yet more**
03 nay

moreover
03 eft **04** also **06** as well, at that, either
07 besides, further **08** likewise **10** in
addition, what is more **11** furthermore
12 additionally

mores
04 ways **06** custom, habits, usages
07 customs, manners **09** etiquette,
practices **10** procedures, traditions,
ways of life **11** conventions **14** ways of
behaving

morgue
08 mortuary **09** arrogance,
deadhouse **11** haughtiness **12** charnel
house **14** funeral parlour

moribund
04 weak **05** dying **06** doomed,
ebbing, fading, feeble, senile, waning
07 failing **08** comatose, expiring,
lifeless, stagnant **09** crumbling,
declining, dwindling **10** collapsing, in
extremis, stagnating **11** obsolescent,
on the way out, wasting away **14** on
your last legs

morning
02 am **04** dawn, morn **05** matin
07 sunrise **08** cock-crow, daybreak,
daylight, forenoon **10** before noon,
break of day, first light **11** crack of dawn
• **morning star**
05 Venus **07** daystar, Lucifer
08 Phosphor **09** precursor
10 Phosphorus **11** morgenstern

Morocco
02 MA **03** MAR, Mor

moron
03 ass, git, mug, nit **04** berk, butt, clot,
dolt, dope, dork, dupe, fool, geek,
goof, jerk, kook, nerd, nerk, prat, twit
05 chump, clown, comic, dumbo,
dunce, dweeb, idiot, neddy, ninny,
prick, twerp, wally **06** cretin, dimwit,
jester, muppet, nitwit, stooge, sucker
07 buffoon, Charlie, fat-head, halfwit,
pillock, plonker, tosspot **08** dipstick,
imbecile **09** birdbrain, blockhead,
cloth head, ignoramus, simpleton
10 nincompoop, silly-billy **13** laughing-
stock, proper Charlie

moronic
03 mad **04** daft, dumb **05** barmy, batty,
crazy, dotty, inane, inept, nutty, potty,
silly, wacky **06** absurd, insane, simple,
stupid, unwise **07** foolish, idiotic
08 gormless, ignorant **09** half-baked,
ludicrous, pointless, senseless **10** half-
witted, ill-advised, ridiculous **11** hare-
brained, nonsensical **12** crack-brained,
shortsighted, simple-minded,
unreasonable **13** ill-considered, out of
your mind, unintelligent **14** with a tile
loose **15** with a screw loose

morose
04 acid, glum, grim, grum, sour
05 gruff, moody, sulky, surly **06** crabby,
gloomy, severe, sombre, sullen
07 grouchy **08** mournful, taciturn
09 depressed, saturnine **10** lugubrious
11 bad-tempered, ill-tempered,
melancholic, pessimistic

morosely
06 sourly **07** gruffly, moodily
08 gloomily, sullenly **10** mournfully
12 lugubriously

morse
06 walrus **09** Endeavour, iddy-umpty

morsel
03 bit **04** atom, bite, part **05** crumb,
grain, piece, scrap, slice, taste
06 dainty, nibble, sippet, titbit
07 modicum, morceau, segment,
soupçon **08** fraction, fragment,
mouthful, particle **11** bonne bouche

mortal
◊ *anagram indicator*
03 man **04** body, dire, Yama **05** awful,
being, cruel, dying, fatal, grave, great,
human, woman **06** bitter, bodily,
deadly, lethal, person, severe
07 earthly, extreme, fleshly, intense,
killing, worldly **08** creature, deathful,
temporal, terrible, vengeful
09 corporeal, earthling, ephemeral,
extremely, murderous, transient,
worldling **10** human being,
implacable, individual, perishable,
relentless, thoroughly, unbearable
11 unrelenting **12** irremissible,
unforgivable, unpardonable
• **first mortal**
04 Adam, Yama

mortality
05 death **07** carnage, killing
08 casualty, fatality, humanity **09** death

rate, slaughter **10** loss of life, transience
11 earthliness, worldliness
12 ephemerality, impermanence
13 perishability

mortally
07 awfully, fatally, finally, gravely,
greatly **08** lethally, severely, terribly
09 extremely, intensely **12** disastrously

mortgage
03 dip **04** bond, lien, loan **06** pledge,
wadset **07** wadsett **08** home loan,
security **09** debenture
11 hypothecate, impignorate

mortification
05 shame **06** denial **07** chagrin,
control **08** disgrace, ignominy,
vexation **09** abasement, annoyance,
dishonour, sphacelus **10** asceticism,
chastening, conquering, discipline,
loss of face, punishment, self-denial
11 confounding, humiliation, self-
control, subjugation **12** discomfiture
13 embarrassment

mortified
04 sick **06** shamed **07** ashamed,
crushed, humbled **08** defeated
09 disgraced, horrified
10 confounded, gangrenous,
humiliated **11** dishonoured,
embarrassed

mortify
03 die **04** deny, kill **05** abash, annoy,
crush, shame **06** humble, offend,
subdue, wither **07** affront, chagrin,
chasten, conquer, control, crucify,
deflate, horrify **08** bring low, chastise,
confound, disgrace, gangrene,
macerate, restrain, suppress
09 discomfit, dishonour, embarrass,
humiliate **10** disappoint, discipline, put
to shame

mortifying
07 shaming **08** crushing, humbling,
salutary **09** punishing, thwarting
10 chastening **11** humiliating,
ignominious **12** discomfiting,
embarrassing, overwhelming

mortuary
06 morgue **09** deadhouse **12** charnel
house **14** funeral parlour

mosaic
06 musive, screen **08** terrazzo
10 pietra dura, pietre dure **11** opus
musivum

moss
03 hag **04** hagg **05** Musci

Mosses include:

03 bog, bur, cup, fog
04 burr, club, long, peat, tree
05 fairy, usnea
06 hypnum
07 acrogen, foggage, lycopod
08 sphagnum, staghorn
09 wolf's claw, wolf's foot
10 fontinalis, ground pine

• **stalk of moss capsule**
04 seta

most

◇ *tail deletion indicator*
04 bulk, mass **08** majority **09** almost all, nearly all **10** lion's share **11** largest part **12** greatest part **13** preponderance

mostly

◇ *deletion indicator*
06 feckly, mainly **07** as a rule, chiefly, largely, overall, usually **08** above all **09** generally, in general, in the main **10** especially, on the whole **11** principally **13** predominantly **14** for the most part

moth

> *Moths include:*

01 Y
02 Io
03 pug, wax
04 goat, hawk, luna, puss
05 ghost, gypsy, tiger
06 bogong, bugong, burnet, carpet, kitten, lackey, lappet, magpie, sphinx, turnip, winter
07 buff-tip, clothes, emerald, emperor, hook-tip, silver-Y, six-spot, tussock
08 cinnabar, peppered, silkworm
10 death's-head
11 garden tiger, pale tussock, swallowtail
12 Kentish glory, peach blossom, red underwing
13 processionary

See also **animal**; **butterfly**; **insect**

moth-eaten

03 old **04** worn **05** dated, mangy, musty, seedy, stale **06** mouldy, ragged, shabby **07** ancient, archaic, decayed, outworn, worn-out **08** decrepit, moribund, obsolete, outdated, tattered **10** antiquated, threadbare **11** dilapidated **12** old-fashioned

mother

02 ma **03** dam, mam, mom, mum **04** baby, base, bear, mama, rear, scum, tend **05** cause, dregs, fount, mamma, mammy, mater, mommy, mummy, mumsy, nanny, nurse, raise, roots, spoil **06** foster, matron, minnie, origin, pamper, parent, source, spring, venter **07** care for, cherish, indulge, nurture, old lady, produce **08** ancestor, fuss over, hysteria, old woman **09** look after, matriarch **10** bring forth, derivation, foundation, procreator, take care of, wellspring **11** birth mother, give birth to, overprotect **12** progenitress **13** materfamilias

See also **dregs**

motherly

04 fond, kind, warm **06** caring, gentle, loving, tender **08** maternal, matronal **09** nurturing **10** comforting, motherlike, protective **12** affectionate

motif

04 form, idea, logo **05** shape, theme, topic **06** design, device, emblem,

figure **07** concept, pattern **08** ornament **10** decoration

motion

03 act, bid, nod **04** flow, plan, sign, wave **05** going, offer, usher **06** action, beckon, change, direct, moving, puppet, scheme, signal, travel **07** feeling, gesture, passage, passing, project, transit **08** activity, mobility, motility, movement, progress, proposal **09** agitation, manifesto, prompting **10** indication, locomotion, suggestion, travelling **11** gesticulate, inclination, instigation, proposition **12** presentation **13** changing place, gesticulation **14** changing places, recommendation

• **in motion**
◇ *anagram indicator*
03 off **05** about, astir, going **06** agoing, moving **07** on the go, running **08** under way **09** on the move, on the wing **10** in progress, travelling **11** functioning, operational, upon the wing

• **set in motion**
04 move, open, stir **05** begin, found, start, steer, stire, styre **06** set off, winnow **07** actuate, kick off, promote, start up **08** activate, commence, embark on, get going, initiate, set about **09** instigate, institute, introduce **10** launch into **11** get cracking **13** begin to happen, take the plunge

motionless

03 set **05** fixed, inert, rigid, still **06** at rest, frozen, halted, static **07** resting **08** becalmed, immobile, lifeless, moveless, sleeping, stagnant, standing, unmoving **09** immovable, inanimate, paralysed, unmovable **10** stationary, stock-still, transfixed **13** at a standstill

motivate

04 draw, goad, lead, move, push, spur, stir, urge **05** bring, cause, drive, impel **06** arouse, excite, incite, induce, kindle, prompt, propel **07** actuate, inspire, provoke, trigger **08** activate, initiate, persuade **09** encourage, kick-start, stimulate

motivation

04 push, spur, urge, wish **05** drive **06** desire, hunger, motive, reason **07** impulse **08** ambition, interest, momentum, stimulus **09** incentive, prompting **10** incitement, inducement, persuasion **11** inspiration, instigation, provocation

motive

03 aim **04** goad, lure, spur, urge **05** basis, cause, motif **06** design, desire, ground, moment, object, reason **07** grounds, impulse, pretext, purpose **08** instance, occasion, sanction, stimulus, thinking **09** incentive, influence, intention, rationale **10** attraction, incitement, inducement, mainspring, motivation, persuasion, propellent **11** inspiration **13** consideration, encouragement

motley

04 pied **05** mixed, tabby **06** jester, varied **07** dappled, diverse, mottled, piebald, pyebald, spotted, striped **08** assorted, brindled, many-hued, streaked **09** colourful, patchwork **10** variegated **11** diversified **12** multifarious **13** heterogeneous, miscellaneous, multicoloured, particoloured

motor club *see* **motoring organization**

motorcyclists *see* **racing**

motoring *see* **car**

motoring organization

02 AA **03** AAA, BSM, FIA, RAC

motor racing *see* **racing**

motor vehicle *see* **car**; **vehicle**

motorway

01 M **02** AB, M1 **07** freeway, thruway **08** Autobahn, turnpike **09** autopista, autoroute **10** autostrada, expressway, throughway **12** superhighway

mottled

04 marl **05** chiné, jaspe, pinto, tabby **06** dapple **07** blotchy, brinded, brindle, dappled, flecked, marbled, piebald, spotted **08** blotched, brindled, freckled, speckled, splotchy, stippled, streaked **10** poikilitic, variegated

motto

03 cry, mot, saw **04** posy, rule **05** adage, axiom, gnome, maxim, poesy **06** byword, device, dictum, legend, saying, slogan, truism **07** epigram, formula, ich dien, ichthys, impresa, imprese, precept, proverb **08** aphorism, epigraph **09** catchword, watchword **10** golden rule **13** e pluribus unum **15** per ardua ad astra

mould

◇ *anagram indicator*
03 cut, die, mix, rot **04** cast, form, fust, kind, line, make, must, sort, type, work **05** brand, build, carve, earth, forge, frame, knead, model, plasm, print, shape, stamp, style **06** affect, blight, create, design, direct, figure, format, fungus, matrix, mildew, nature, sculpt **07** calibre, casting, chessel, control, dariole, fashion, outline, pattern, quality, ramakin, ramekin **08** meringue, ramequin, template **09** character, construct, formation, framework, influence, mustiness, sculpture, structure **10** mouldiness **11** arrangement, blister pack **12** construction **13** configuration

moulder

03 rot **05** decay, waste **06** humify, perish **07** corrupt, crumble **09** decompose **10** turn to dust **12** disintegrate

moulding

◇ *anagram indicator*
04 ogee, tore **05** torus

mouldy

anagram indicator

3 bad **04** fust, hoar **05** fusty, lousy, mochy, mucid, muggy, musty, stale **6** fousty, mochie, putrid, rotten **7** corrupt, foughty, spoiled, vinewed **8** blighted, decaying, mildewed **9** miserable **10** mucedinous

moult

3 mew **04** cast

mound

3 but, dun, hog, lot, orb, tel **04** bank, arp, butt, dike, dune, dyke, heap, hill, note, pile, rise, tell, tump **05** agger, airn, hoard, knoll, mogul, motte, mount, pingo, ridge, stack, store **6** barrow, bundle, kurgan, supply, uffet **07** hillock, hummock, rampart, umulus **08** mine dump, mountain **9** abundance, earthwork, elevation, monticule, stockpile, whaleback **0** collection, embankment **1** termitarium **12** accumulation

mound-bird

5 lowan **08** megapode **09** mallee-en **10** junglefowl, mallee-bird, mallee-fowl **11** brush turkey

mount

reversal down indicator

2 Mt **03** set, sty **04** back, base, go up, row, lift, ride, rise, soar, stie, stye **5** build, climb, erect, frame, get on, get p, horse, put on, raise, scale, set up, rage, stand, steed, swell, tot up **6** accrue, ascend, jump on, launch, ile up, saddle, step up **07** arrange, acking, build up, climb on, climb up, isplay, exhibit, fixture, install, prepare, roduce, support **08** escalade, escalate, ncrease, jump on to, mounting, ultiply, organize, override, saddle up **9** clamber up, climb on to, inselberg, ntensify, take horse **10** accumulate, get stride **12** passe-partout

mountain

3 alp, ben, lot, tor **04** berg, fell, heap, ill, mass, peak, pike, pile **05** guyot, ebel, mound, mount, stack **06** djebel, eight, massif **07** backlog **08** pinnacle **9** abundance, elevation **2** accumulation

Mountains and mountain ranges include:

2 K2
3 Apo, Dom, Tai
4 Alai, Alps, Blue, Cook, Etna, Fuji, Jura, Meru, Ossa, Rila, Sion, Ural
5 Altai, Andes, Atlas, Coast, Downs, Eiger, Ghats, Halti, Huang, Kamet, Kékes, Kenya, Logan, Matra, Ozark, Qogir, Rocky, Sinai, Snowy, Table, Tatra
6 Ararat, Cho Oyu, Deccan, Denali, Egmont, Elbert, Elbrus, Haltia, Hoggar, Lhotse, Makalu, Mourne, Musala, Pindus, Taurus, Vosges, Zagros
7 Ahaggar, Belukha, Beskids, Everest, Fuji-san, Hua Shan, Lebanon, Manaslu, Nilgiri, Olympus, Rainier, Rhodope, Rockies, Roraima, Scafell, Skiddaw, Snowdon, Stanley, Tai Shan, Troödos
08 Ben Nevis, Cameroon, Catskill, Caucasus, Cévennes, Damavand, Five Holy, Fujiyama, Heng Shan, Jungfrau, Kinabalu, Mauna Kea, Mauna Loa, McKinley, Pennines, Pyrenees, Rushmore, song Shan, St Helens, Taranaki
09 Aconcagua, Allegheny, Altai Shan, Annapurna, Apennines, Blue Ridge, Broad Peak, Cotswolds, Dolomites, Grampians, Helvellyn, Himalayas, Hindu Kush, Inyangani, Karakoram, Kosciusko, Lenin Peak, Mont Blanc, Muz Tag Ata, Nanda Devi, Rakaposhi, Tirichmir, Tirol Alps, Zugspitze
10 Adirondack, Cader Idris, Cairngorms, Cantabrian, Carpathian, Chimborazo, Dhaulagiri, Gasherbrum, Gosainthan, Great Smoky, MacDonnell, Matterhorn, Pobedy Peak, Puncak Jaya, Sagarmatha
11 Appalachian, Arthur's Pass, Black Forest, Chomolungma, Drakensberg, Kilimanjaro, Mendip Hills, Mongo-Ma-Loba, Nanga Parbat, Pico Bolívar, Siula Grande
12 Bavarian Alps, Cascade Range, Cheviot Hills, Darling Range, Dufourspitze, Kanchenjunga, Popocatepetl, Sierra Nevada, Southern Alps, Tibet Plateau, Ulugh Muztagh, Victoria Peak, Vinson Massif
13 Carrantuohill, Chiltern Hills, Communism Peak, Great Dividing, Haltiatunturi, Kangchenjunga, Ojos del Salado, Stirling Range
14 Australian Alps, Bavarian Forest, Bohemian Forest, Fichtelgebirge, Flinders Ranges, Grand St Bernard, Hamersley Range, Mackenzie Range, Musgrave Ranges, Qomolangma Feng, Thadentsonyane, Trans-Antarctic
15 Guiana Highlands, Nevado de Illampu

See also **volcano**

• mountain pass
04 ghat

Mountain passes include:

04 Ofen
05 Haast, Lewis, South
06 Khyber, Lindis, Shipka
07 Arthur's, Brenner, Oberalp, Plöcken, Simplon, Wrynose
08 Hongshan, Yangguan
09 Khunjerab, St Bernard
10 St Gotthard
12 Roncesvalles
13 Cilician Gates, San Bernardino
14 Grand St Bernard
15 Little St Bernard

• mountain peak
03 ben

• mountain range
04 tier

mountaineering

Mountaineers include:

04 Hunt (John, Lord)
05 Brown (Joe), Bruce (C G), Munro (Sir Hugh), Scott (Doug), Tabei (Junko)
06 Haston (Dougal), Herzog (Maurice), Irvine (Andrew), Smythe (Frank), Tilman (Bill), Uemura (Naomi)
07 Hillary (Sir Edmund), Mallory (George), Messner (Reinhold), Shipton (Eric), Simpson (Myrtle), Tazieff (Haroun), Tenzing (Sherpa), Whymper (Edward)
08 Coolidge (W A B), MacInnes (Hamish), Whillans (Don)
09 Bonington (Sir Chris)
10 Hargreaves (Alison)
13 Tenzing Norgay

mountainous

04 high, huge, mega, vast **05** giant, hilly, jumbo, lofty, rocky, steep **06** alpine, craggy, upland **07** immense, mammoth, massive, soaring **08** colossal, enormous, gigantic, highland, towering **09** ginormous, humongous

mountebank

04 fake **05** antic, cheat, fraud, pseud, quack, rogue **06** antick, con man, phoney **07** anticke, antique, buffoon **08** impostor, jongleur, swindler **09** charlatan, pretender, trickster **11** saltimbanco

mourn

04 keen, miss, wail, weep **06** bemoan, bewail, grieve, lament, regret, sorrow **07** deplore

mourner

04 mute **06** keener, saulie, weeper **07** griever **08** bereaved, sorrower

mournful

03 sad **06** dismal, gloomy, rueful, sombre, tragic, woeful **07** dernful, doleful, elegiac, funèbre, unhappy **08** cast-down, dearnful, dejected, desolate, downcast, funereal **09** depressed, miserable, plaintive, sorrowful **10** lachrymose, lugubrious, melancholy **11** heartbroken, melancholic **12** disconsolate, heavy-hearted **13** broken-hearted, grief-stricken

mournfully

05 sadly **08** dismally, gloomily, ruefully, sombrely **09** con dolore, dolefully, miserably, unhappily **10** desolately **11** plaintively, sorrowfully **15** broken-heartedly

mourning

05 grief **06** sorrow **07** keening, sadness, wailing, weeping **08** grieving **09** sorrowing **10** desolation **11** bereavement, lamentation **13** sorry business

mouse
03 Mus **06** muscle, shiner **07** dunnart, Muridae, waltzer **08** black eye **09** Zapodidae

mousey, mousy
03 shy **04** drab, dull, meek **05** plain, quiet, timid **07** greyish **08** brownish, timorous **09** diffident, shrinking, withdrawn **10** colourless **11** unassertive **12** self-effacing **13** unforthcoming, uninteresting

moustache
04 tash **05** tache **06** walrus **07** Charley, Charlie **08** whiskers **09** excrement, mustachio **10** face fungus **15** zapata moustache

mousy *see* mousey, mousy

mouth
◇ *head selection indicator*
03 cry, gab, gam, gas, gob, gub, mou, mug, say **04** door, form, gall, jaws, kiss, rant, trap, vent **05** bazoo, bocca, cheek, chops, delta, hatch, inlet, nerve, sauce, stoma, utter, voice **06** babble, cavity, hot air, kisser, oscule, outlet, portal **07** debouch, declaim, doorway, estuary, gateway, grimace, opening, orifice, speaker, whisper **08** aperture, backchat, boasting, bragging, cakehole, entrance, idle talk, rudeness, traphole **09** brass neck, empty talk, enunciate, impudence, insolence, pronounce, utterance **10** articulate, blustering, disrespect, effrontery, embouchure, potato trap, rattletrap **12** impertinence, laughing gear

Mouth parts and features include:
03 gum, jaw, lip
04 lips
05 uvula
06 tongue, tonsil
07 hare lip
08 lower lip, upper lip
10 hard palate, soft palate
11 cleft palate
13 alveolar ridge
15 isthmus of fauces

See also **teeth**

• **keep your mouth shut**
06 clam up, shut up **07** cover up, keep mum **08** pipe down **09** keep quiet **10** say nothing **14** hold your tongue **15** not breathe a word
• **sew up mouth**
04 cope

mouthful
03 bit, gag, gob, sip, sup **04** bite, drop, gulp, slug **05** taste **06** gobbet, morsel, nibble, sample, titbit **07** forkful, swallow **08** spoonful **11** bonne-bouche

mouthpiece
04 horn **05** agent, organ, voice **07** journal **08** delegate **09** spokesman **10** periodical **11** publication, spokeswoman **12** propagandist, spokesperson **14** representative

movable
06 mobile **08** flexible, portable **09** alterable, portative **10** adjustable, changeable **12** transferable **13** transportable

movables
04 gear **05** goods, stuff **06** things **07** clobber, effects **08** chattels, property **09** furniture **10** belongings **11** impedimenta, plenishings, possessions

move
◇ *anagram indicator*
02 go **03** act, mix, wag **04** draw, lead, nose, pass, push, sell, step, stir, tack, take, urge, walk **05** bring, budge, carry, cause, drive, fetch, impel, leave, pal up, rouse, shift, shunt, swing, touch, upset **06** action, affect, arouse, change, decamp, depart, device, excite, gang up, go away, hobnob, incite, induce, mingle, motion, prompt, propel, remove, strike, submit, switch, travel **07** actuate, advance, agitate, consort, develop, disturb, gesture, hang out, impress, incline, inspire, measure, migrate, proceed, propose, provoke, quinche, removal, request, suggest **08** activity, advocate, go around, motivate, move away, movement, persuade, progress, relocate, transfer **09** associate, circulate, hang about, influence, instigate, manoeuvre, migration, move house, recommend, socialize, stimulate, stratagem, transport, transpose **10** fraternize, initiative, proceeding, put forward, relocation, take action **11** keep company, make strides, zwischenzug **12** rub shoulders **13** gesticulation, repositioning **15** change of address
• **get a move on**
07 hurry up, speed up **08** step on it **09** make haste, shake a leg **11** get cracking **12** step on the gas **15** put your foot down
• **make a move**
02 go **05** frame, leave, split **06** depart **07** push off **08** clear off, get going **10** make tracks **11** do something, get cracking **13** take the plunge, take your leave
• **move aimlessly**
04 mope
• **move around**
04 stir **05** steer, stire, styre
• **move gradually**
04 ease, edge
• **move in some direction**
04 tend
• **move lightly**
04 flit
• **move on**
03 gee, jee **06** avaunt
• **move quickly**
03 hop **04** tear, whid, whip, zoom
• **move round**
04 eddy, turn
• **move sideways**
04 crab

• **move silently**
06 tiptoe
• **move slowly**
03 lag **04** inch
• **move unsteadily**
03 yaw
• **move up and down**
03 bob **04** yo-yo
• **move violently**
04 tear
• **on the move**
05 astir **06** active, around, moving **07** on the go **08** under way **09** advancing, on the hoof, walkabou **10** journeying, travelling **11** progressir **13** moving forward **14** making progre

movement
◇ *anagram indicator*
03 act, bit **04** fall, flow, guts, move, pace, part, play, rise, stir, wing **05** dri drive, group, party, piece, shift, swing tempo, trend, works **06** action, change, moving, system **07** advance, crusade, current, emotion, faction, gesture, impulse, passage, portion, section **08** activity, campaign, divisio progress, shifting, stirring, tendency, transfer, workings **09** agitation, coalition, evolution, machinery, mechanism, variation **10** relocation **11** development, improvement, progression **12** breakthrough, organization **13** gesticulation, repositioning **14** transportation

See also **art**, **poetry**

• **rapid eye movement**
03 REM
• **sudden movement**
04 dart, volt

movie
04 film **05** flick, video **06** cinema, talkie **07** fleapit, picture **09** multiplex **10** silent film **11** feature film, film theat **12** movie theatre, picture-house **13** motion picture, picture-palace

See also **film**

moving
◇ *anagram indicator*
05 astir **06** active, mobile, motile, urging **07** driving, dynamic, emotive, flowing, kinetic, leading **08** arousing, exciting, in motion, pathetic, poignan stirring, touching, worrying **09** affecting, emotional, inspiring, thrilling, upsetting **10** disturbing, impressive, motivating, persuasive **11** influential, stimulating **12** manoeuvrable **13** inspirational

movingly
10 poignantly, touchingly **11** with emotion, with feeling **12** expressively, pathetically **15** inspirationally

mow
03 cut, moe **04** barb, clip, crop, tass, trim **05** shear **06** scythe
• **mow down**
04 kill **07** butcher, cut down, gun dow **08** decimate, massacre **09** shoot down, slaughter **11** cut to pieces

mowing
04 math

Mozambique
03 MOC, MOZ

much
04 a lot, lots, many 05 ample, great, heaps, loads, molto, often, piles, scads 06 masses, mickle, muckle, oodles, plenty, stacks 07 copious, greatly 08 abundant, lashings 09 extensive, plentiful 10 a great deal, frequently, widespread 11 substantial 12 considerable, considerably 14 a great number of, to a great degree, to a great extent
• **by so much**
03 the
• **how much**
03 the
• **not so much**
04 less
• **too much**
03 OTT 04 over
• **very much**
03 far 04 sore

muck
03 mud 04 crud, dirt, dung, gold, guck, mess, mire, scum, yuck 05 filth, grime, guano, gunge, slime 06 debris, faeces, grunge, manure, ordure, rubble, scunge, sewage, sludge 09 excrement
• **muck about, muck around**
05 upset 06 bother, meddle, mess up, potter, tamper, untidy 07 trouble 08 dishevel, disorder 09 fool about, goof about, interfere, lark about, mess about, play about 10 disarrange, fool around, goof around, lark around, mess around, play around 13 inconvenience 15 lead a merry dance, make life hell for
• **muck up**
04 ruin 05 botch, spoil, wreck 06 bungle, cock up, mess up 07 louse up, screw up 11 make a mess of

mucky
04 miry, oozy 05 dirty, grimy, gucky, messy, muddy, nasty, slimy 06 filthy, scungy, soiled, sticky 08 begrimed, mud-caked 11 bespattered

mucous
05 gummy, slimy 06 snotty, viscid 07 viscous 09 glutinous 10 gelatinous 12 mucilaginous

mud
03 dub 04 clay, dirt, dubs, mire, moya, ooze, silt, slab, soil 05 abuse, clart, slake, slush 06 clarts, sleech, sludge 07 clabber, slander 12 vilification
• **cover with mud**
04 lair

muddle
◇ anagram indicator
03 mix 04 daze, mash, mess, mull, muzz, stir 05 chaos, mix up, mix-up 06 bemuse, bungle, cock-up, fankle, guddle, jumble, mess up, pickle, puddle, puzzle, tangle 07 blunder, clutter, confuse, perplex 08 befuddle,

bewilder, confound, disarray, disorder, jumble up, scramble, shambles 09 confusion 11 disorganize 12 bewilderment 15 disorganization
• **muddle through**
04 cope 05 get by 06 make do, manage 08 get along

muddled
◇ anagram indicator
05 addle, at sea, dazed, loose, messy, vague 06 tavert, woolly 07 chaotic, jumbled, mixed-up, taivert, tangled, unclear 08 confused 09 befuddled, perplexed, scrambled, stupefied 10 bewildered, disarrayed, disordered, incoherent 11 addle-headed, disoriented, muddy-headed 12 disorganized 13 disorientated

muddy
◇ anagram indicator
04 dull, foul, hazy, miry, oozy, soil 05 boggy, cloud, dingy, dirty, fuzzy, grimy, mix up, mucky, murky, slimy, smear, smoky 06 bedash, bedaub, cloudy, dreggy, drumly, filthy, grouty, grubby, jumble, limous, marshy, muddle, opaque, puddle, quaggy, slabby, sloppy, sludgy, slushy, smirch, stupid, swampy, tangle, turbid 07 begrime, blurred, confuse, obscure, splashy, trouble 08 confused, jumble up, scramble 09 befuddled, bespatter, make muddy 10 indistinct 11 disorganize, make unclear, waterlogged

muff
◇ anagram indicator
04 miss, mitt 05 botch, fluff, spoil 06 bungle, duffer, mess up, mishit 07 bungler 09 mishandle, mismanage

muffle
03 gag, mob 04 dull, hush, kill, mute, wrap 05 cloak, cover, moble 06 dampen, deaden, mobble, muzzle, soften, stifle, swathe, wrap up 07 cover up, envelop, quieten, silence, smother, swaddle 08 suppress 09 blindfold

mug
03 can, cup, pot, rob, sap 04 bash, bock, dupe, exam, face, fool, gull, jump, mush, phiz, swot, Toby 05 chump, clock, mouth, stein, tinny 06 attack, batter, beaker, beat up, do over, jump on, kisser, noggin, sconce, sucker, tinnie, visage, waylay 07 assault, muggins, rough up, set upon, tankard 08 features 09 simpleton, soft touch, steal from 10 knock about 11 countenance, physiognomy
See also **face; fool**
• **mug up**
03 con 04 cram, swot 05 get up, study 06 bone up

muggy
04 damp 05 close, foggy, humid, mochy, moist 06 clammy, mochie, sticky, stuffy, sultry 07 airless 10 oppressive, sweltering

mulberry
04 upas 05 Morus, mvule 06 murrey 07 cowtree 08 cecropia, sycamine 10 artocarpus 11 contrayerva, Osage orange

mule
04 moyl, muil 05 moyle 06 hybrid 07 slipper, sumpter 09 dziggetai

mulish
05 rigid 06 wilful 07 defiant 08 perverse, stubborn 09 difficult, obstinate, pig-headed 10 headstrong, inflexible, refractory, self-willed 11 intractable, stiff-necked, wrong-headed 12 intransigent, recalcitrant, unreasonable

mull
• **mull over**
05 study 06 muse on, ponder 07 examine, weigh up 08 chew over, consider, meditate, ruminate 09 reflect on, think over 10 deliberate, think about 11 contemplate

multicoloured
04 pied 06 motley 07 dappled, piebald, spotted, striped 08 brindled 09 colourful 10 variegated 11 psychedelic 13 kaleidoscopic, particoloured

multifarious
04 many 06 legion, sundry, varied 07 diverse 08 manifold, multiple, numerous 09 different, multiform 10 variegated 11 diversified 13 miscellaneous, multitudinous

multiple
04 many 06 sundry 07 several, various 08 compound, manifold, numerous, repeated 10 collective, multiplied

multiplicity
03 lot 04 host, lots, mass, tons 05 array, heaps, loads, piles 06 myriad, number, oodles, scores, stacks 07 variety 09 abundance, diversity, profusion 12 manifoldness, numerousness

multiplied with
01 x 02 by

multiply
04 grow 05 boost, breed 06 double, expand, extend, spread 07 augment, build up, decuple, octuple 08 centuple, increase, manifold, septuple, sextuple 09 intensify, propagate, quadruple, quintuple, reproduce 10 accumulate 11 proliferate

multipurpose
05 handy 08 all-round, flexible, variable 09 adaptable, many-sided, versatile 10 adjustable, all-purpose, functional 11 resourceful 12 multifaceted 14 general-purpose

multitude
03 lot, mob 04 army, herd, hive, host, lots, mass, ruck 05 crowd, horde, plebs, shoal, swarm 06 hirsel, legion, number, people, public, rabble, throng

07 king mob **08** assembly, canaille, populace, riff-raff **09** hoi polloi **10** common herd, the million **11** rank and file **12** common people, congregation **13** great unwashed

multitudinous
04 many **05** great **06** legion, myriad **07** copious, profuse, teeming, umpteen **08** abundant, infinite, manifold, numerous, swarming **09** abounding, countless **11** innumerable **12** considerable

mum
02 ma **04** dumb, ma'am, mama, marm, mute **05** mummy, quiet **06** mother, silent **07** silence **08** reticent **09** secretive **10** masquerade **11** close-lipped, tight-lipped **12** close-mouthed **13** chrysanthemum, unforthcoming **15** uncommunicative

mumble
04 moop, moup, mump, slur **06** fumble, murmur, mutter, rumble **07** grumble, stutter **08** splutter **11** speak softly **14** speak unclearly, talk to yourself

mumbo-jumbo
04 cant, rite **05** chant, charm, magic, spell **06** humbug, jargon, ritual **07** mummery **08** claptrap, nonsense **09** gibberish, rigmarole **10** double talk, hocus-pocus **11** abracadabra, conjuration, incantation **12** gobbledygook, superstition

mummer
05 actor **06** guiser, guizer **07** guisard, scudler, skudler **09** scuddaler **11** masquerader

munch
03 eat **04** chew, moop, moup, mump **05** champ, chomp **06** crunch **09** masticate

mundane
04 dull **05** banal, stale, trite, usual **06** boring, common, cosmic, normal **07** earthly, fleshly, humdrum, prosaic, regular, routine, secular, terrene, typical, worldly **08** everyday, ordinary, temporal, workaday **09** customary, hackneyed **11** commonplace, terrestrial

municipal
04 city, town **05** civic, civil, urban **06** public **07** borough **09** community **12** metropolitan

municipality
04 city, town **05** burgh **07** borough, council **08** district, precinct, township **10** department **11** département **15** local government

munificence
06 bounty **08** altruism, largesse **10** generosity, liberality **11** beneficence, benevolence, hospitality **12** generousness, philanthropy **13** bounteousness, bountifulness **14** charitableness, open-handedness **15** magnanimousness

munificent
04 rich **06** lavish **07** liberal **08** generous, princely **09** bounteous, bountiful **10** altruistic, beneficent, benevolent, big-hearted, charitable, free-handed, hospitable, open-handed, unstinting **11** magnanimous **15** philanthropical

munitions
03 kit **04** gear, guns **05** bombs, tools **06** shells, tackle **08** armament, materiel, ordnance, supplies **09** apparatus, equipment, materials **10** provisions

murder
03 hit, ice, rid **04** beat, do in, hell, kill, lick, rout, ruin, slay **05** agony, blood, botch, burke, spoil, stiff, waste, whack, wreck **06** fill in, hammer, mess up, misery, ordeal, outwit, rub out, rubout, thrash **07** anguish, bump off, butcher, clobber, destroy, execute, killing, murther, outplay, removal, slaying, take out, torment, torture, trounce, wipe out **08** blow away, butchery, dispatch, filicide, foul play, homicide, knock off, massacre, outsmart **09** bloodshed, do to death, eliminate, execution, liquidate, matricide, nightmare, overwhelm, parricide, patricide, slaughter, suffering, uxoricide **10** annihilate, fratricide, put to death, sororicide **11** assassinate, infanticide, liquidation, make a mess of **12** defeat easily, manslaughter, petty treason, wretchedness **13** assassination

See also **kill**

murderer
04 Cain **06** killer, slayer **07** butcher **08** assassin, filicide, homicide **09** bluebeard, cut-throat, matricide, murtherer, patricide **10** man-queller **11** slaughterer **12** serial killer

Murderers, alleged murderers and assassins include:

03 Ray (James Earl)
04 Aram (Eugene), Cain, Edny (Clithero), Hare (William), Kray (Reggie), Kray (Ronnie), Retz (Gilles de Laval, Baron), Ruby (Jack), Todd (Sweeney), West (Fred), West (Rosemary)
05 Beane (Sawney), Booth (John Wilkes), Brady (Ian), Bundy (Ted), Burke (William), Craig (Christopher), Ellis (Ruth), Haigh (John), Havoc (Jack), Rudge
06 Barrow (Clyde), Borden (Lizzie), Corday (Charlotte), Dahmer (Jeffrey), Lecter (Dr Hannibal), Manson (Charles), Misfit (the), Nilsen (Dennis), Oswald (Lee Harvey), Parker (Bonnie), Sirhan (Sirhan)
07 Bathori (Elizabeth), Bentley (Derek), Bianchi (Kenneth), Chapman (Mark), Crippen (Hawley Harvey), Hindley (Myra), Macbeth, Manston (Aeneas), Neilson (Donald), Shipman (Harold)

08 Barabbas, Christie (John Reginald Halliday), Claudius, Dominici (Gaston), Hanratty (James), Son of Sam, Thompson (Edith)
09 Berkowitz (David), Bluebeard, Harmodius, McNaghten (Daniel), Sutcliffe (Peter)
10 McNaughten (Daniel), McNaughton (Daniel), Nirdlinger (Phyllis)
11 Anckarström (Johan Jakob), Quare Fellow (the)
13 Jack the Ripper
14 Moors Murderers
15 Yorkshire Ripper

murderous
05 cruel, fatal **06** bloody, brutal, carnal, deadly, lethal, mortal, savage **07** arduous, killing **09** barbarous, butcherly, cut-throat, dangerous, difficult, ferocious, gruelling, homicidal, punishing, strenuous **10** exhausting, unpleasant **11** internecine, internecive **12** bloodthirsty, slaughterous

murderously
06 grimly **07** fatally **09** ominously **10** alarmingly, menacingly, sinisterly **11** dangerously, homicidally **12** portentously, unpleasantly **13** threateningly **14** bloodthirstily

murk
04 dark, dusk, mirk **05** gloom, night, shade **06** gloomy **07** dimness, obscure, shadows **08** darkness, twilight **09** blackness, half-light, murkiness, shadiness, tenebrity **10** cloudiness, gloominess **11** sunlessness, tenebrosity

murky
03 dim, sus **04** dark, dull, grey **05** dingy, dirty, fishy, foggy, misty, muddy, rooky, shady **06** cloudy, dismal, dreary, gloomy, secret, turbid, veiled **07** obscure **08** overcast **09** cheerless, tenebrose, tenebrous **10** mysterious, suspicious, tenebrious **12** questionable

murmur
◊ *homophone indicator*
03 bur, coo, hum **04** beef, burr, buzz, carp, fuss, moan, purl, purr **05** brawl, brool, bruit, drone, gripe, mourn, thrum, whine **06** babble, burble, grouse, grudge, intone, mumble, mutter, object, repine, rumble, rumour, rustle, whinge **07** beefing, carping, censure, croodle, grumble, humming, protest, purring, whisper **08** complain, rumbling, syllable **09** annoyance, bellyache, complaint, criticism, criticize, find fault, grievance, muttering, objection, undertone, whingeing **11** bellyaching **12** fault-finding **15** dissatisfaction

murmuring
04 buzz, purl, purr **05** drone **06** babble, mumble, mutter, rumble **07** buzzing, droning, humming,

urring, souffle, whisper
8 mumbling, rumbling, susurrus
9 murmurous, muttering
0 whispering **11** murmuration

Murphy
4 spud **05** praty, tater, tatie **06** potato,
ratie, tattie

muscle
4 beef, thew **05** brawn, clout, force,
night, power, sinew **06** mussel,
endon, weight **07** potency, stamina
8 ligament, strength **10** sturdiness
2 forcefulness

Muscles include:
2 ab
3 pec
4 delt
5 glute, psoas
6 biceps, rectus, soleus
7 cardiac, deltoid, gluteus, iliacus,
omohyid, triceps
8 detrusor, masseter, platysma,
pronator, risorius, scalenus,
splenius
9 abdominal, complexus, eye-string,
perforans, sartorius, stapedius,
supinator, trapezius
0 buccinator, quadriceps
1 ciliary body, rhomboideus
3 gastrocnemius
4 xiphihumeralis
5 latissimus dorsi, pectoralis major,
pectoralis minor, peroneal muscles

• **muscle in**
5 shove **06** butt in, jostle, push in
9 strongarm **13** interfere with
4 elbow your way in, force your way
n, impose yourself

muscular
5 beefy, burly, hefty, husky, thewy
6 brawny, potent, robust, rugged,
inewy, strong, sturdy, thewed
7 fibrous **08** athletic, powerful,
talwart, vigorous **09** strapping
5 powerfully built

muse
4 mews **05** brood, dream, meuse,
tudy, think, weigh **06** ponder, review
7 reflect **08** chew over, cogitate,
onsider, meditate, mull over, ruminate
9 speculate, think over **10** deliberate
1 contemplate **13** contemplation

The Greek Muses:
4 Clio
5 Erato
6 Thalia, Urania
7 Euterpe
8 Calliope, Polymnia
9 Melpomene
0 Polyhymnia
1 Terpsichore

• **the Muses**
7 the nine

museum
3 mus **07** palazzo **10** art gallery,
collection, repository **14** heritage
entre

Museums and galleries include:
02 BM, RA
03 ICA
04 MoMA, MOMI, Tate
05 Prado, Terme, V and A
06 Correr, London, Louvre, Uffizi
07 British, Fogg Art, Hofburg,
Mankind, Pushkin, Russian, Science,
Vatican
08 Bargello, Borghese, National,
Pergamum
09 Accademia, Albertina, Arnolfini,
Ashmolean, Belvedere, Cloisters,
Deutsches, Hermitage, Holocaust,
Modern Art, Sans Souci, Tretyakov
10 Guggenheim, Pinakothek, Pitt-
Rivers, Serpentine, Tate Modern
11 Fitzwilliam, Imperial War,
Mauritshuis, Musée d'Orsay, Pitti
Palace, Rijksmuseum, Tate Britain
12 Royal Academy, Whitworth Art
13 Jean Paul Getty, Peace Memorial,
Royal Pavilion
14 Barbican Centre, Natural History,
State Hermitage
15 Centre Beaubourg, Frick
Collection, South Bank Centre

mush
03 pap **04** corn, glop, mash, pulp
05 cream, dough, gloop, notch, paste,
purée, slush, swill **07** rubbish, scallop,
shmaltz **08** schmaltz, umbrella
11 mawkishness **14** sentimentality

mushroom
04 boom, grow **06** expand, spread,
sprout **07** burgeon, shoot up, upstart
08 flourish, increase, spring up,
umbrella **09** luxuriate, pixy-stool
11 proliferate

*Mushrooms and toadstools
include:*
03 cep
04 base, ugly, wood
05 brain, field, gypsy, horse, magic,
march, morel, naked
06 agaric, blewit, button, elf cup, ink
cap, meadow, mower's, oyster,
satan's, winter
07 amanita, blewits, blusher, boletus,
Caesar's, griping, parasol, porcini,
truffle
08 death cap, deceiver, hedgehog,
penny bun, shiitake, sickener
09 cramp ball, earth ball, fairy ring, fly
agaric, St George's, stinkhorn
10 champignon, false morel, lawyer's
wig, liberty cap, panther cap,
sweetbread, wood agaric
11 chanterelle, clean mycena,
common morel, dingy agaric,
honey fungus, stout agaric, sulphur
tuft, velvet shank
12 common ink cap, dryad's saddle,
false blusher, horn of plenty, larch
boletus, lurid boletus, purple
blewit, shaggy ink cap, slippery
jack, white truffle, winter fungus,
wood hedgehog
13 buckler agaric, clouded agaric,
copper trumpet, devil's boletus,

emetic russula, firwood agaric,
honey mushroom, Jew's ear
fungus, purple boletus, satan's
boletus, shaggy milk cap, shaggy
parasol, summer truffle, trumpet
agaric, woolly milk cap, yellow
stainer
14 common grisette, common
laccaria, common puffball, fairies'
bonnets, man on horseback,
penny-bun fungus, saffron milk cap,
yellow staining
15 beefsteak fungus, chestnut boletus,
common earthball, common
stinkhorn, destroying angel, garlic
marosmius, périgord truffle,
stinking parasol, stinking russula,
verdigris agaric

See also **fungus**

mushy
◇ *anagram indicator*
03 wet **04** soft **05** pappy, pulpy, soppy,
weepy **06** doughy, sloppy, slushy,
sugary, syrupy **07** maudlin, mawkish,
pulpous, squashy, squidgy **08** squelchy
09 schmaltzy **10** saccharine
11 sentimental

music
03 fun, mus **04** note, tune **05** dream
06 melody **07** harmony

Music types include:
03 AOR, MOR, pop, rai, rap, ska
04 folk, funk, jazz, jive, mood, raga,
rock, Romo, soca, soul, zouk
05 bebop, blues, cajun, dance, disco,
house, indie, muzak, R and B, salsa,
samba, sokah, swing, world
06 atonal, ballet, choral, doo-wop,
fusion, garage, gospel, grunge, hip-
hop, jungle, lounge, reggae, sacred,
techno, trance
07 ambient, baroque, bhangra, Big
Beat, calypso, chamber, gamelan,
gangsta, karaoke, nu-metal,
ragtime, skiffle, trip-hop
08 acid jazz, ballroom, folk rock, glam
rock, hardcore, hard rock, jazz-
funk, jazz-rock, operatic, oratorio,
punk rock, soft rock
09 acid house, bluegrass, classical,
Dixieland, honky-tonk
10 electronic, gangsta rap, heavy
metal, incidental, orchestral,
twelve-tone
11 country rock, drum and bass, rock
and roll, thrash metal
12 boogie-woogie, instrumental
13 easy listening
14 rhythm and blues
15 middle-of-the-road

See also **jazz; opera**

• **compose music to**
03 set

musical
03 mus **06** dulcet, mellow **07** lyrical,
melodic, tuneful **09** melodious
10 euphonious, harmonious
11 mellifluous **13** sweet-sounding
See also **instrument; note**

Musicals include:

04 Cats, Fame, Hair, Rent
05 Annie, Blitz, Chess, Evita, Fosse, Zorba
06 Grease, Joseph, Kismet, Oliver!, The Wiz
07 Cabaret, Camelot, Chicago, Company, Follies
08 Carnival, Carousel, Fiorello!, Godspell, Mamma Mia!, Oklahoma!, Peter Pan, Show Boat
09 Brigadoon, Funny Girl, Girl Crazy, On the Town
10 Hello Dolly!, Kiss Me Kate, Miss Saigon, My Fair Lady
11 A Chorus Line, Babes in Arms, Billy Elliot, Bitter Sweet, Carmen Jones, Mary Poppins, Me and My Girl, Sweeney Todd, The King and I, The Lion King, The Music Man
12 Anything Goes, Bombay Dreams, Bye Bye Birdie, Guys and Dolls, Martin Guerre, South Pacific, The Boy Friend, The Producers
13 Aspects of Love, Blood Brothers, Les Miserables, Man of La Mancha, The Pajama Game, West Side Story
14 Babes in Toyland, Victor/Victoria
15 Annie Get Your Gun, La Cage aux Folles, Mister Wonderful, Sunset Boulevard, The Sound of Music, The Woman in White

Songs from musicals include:

03 One
04 Fame
05 Maria
06 Do-Re-Mi, Memory, People
07 America, Bali Ha'i, Cabaret, Camelot, Tonight
08 Aquarius, Day by Day, Oklahoma!, Time Warp, Tomorrow
09 Edelweiss, Evergreen, Footloose, Somewhere, Superstar, Tradition
10 42nd Street, Be Our Guest, Big Spender, Friendship, Hello, Dolly, I Am What I Am, I Got Rhythm, Matchmaker, Night Fever, Ol' Man River, Too Darn Hot, Willkommen
11 76 Trombones, All That Jazz, Luck, Be a Lady, Night and Day, Old Man River, Summer Lovin', Where is Love?, You're The Top
12 All I Ask of You, Broadway Baby, Circle of Life, Dancing Queen, Easter Parade, Hakuna Matata, Mack the Knife, Makin' Whoopee, Rich Man's Frug, Shall We Dance?, Sound of Music, Staying Alive, Summer Nights, There She Goes, We Go Together
13 Skimbleshanks, Sunrise, Sunset
14 Ain't Misbehavin', Any Dream Will Do, Chim Chim Cher-ee, Close Every Door, I Dreamed a Dream, I Know Him So Well, Lonely Goatherd, Mr Mistoffelees, New York, New York, So Long, Farewell, They All Laughed, We're in the Money
15 A Bushel and a Peck, Bells Are Ringing, Greased Lightnin',

Honeysuckle Rose, I Am the Starlight, If I Were a Rich Man, Music of the Night, Put On a Happy Face, Send in the Clowns, Singin' in the Rain, Sunset Boulevard, Tell Me on a Sunday, The Lady is a Tramp, Till There Was You

People associated with musicals include:

04 Bart (Lionel), Hart (Lorenz), Kaye (Danny), Kern (Jerome), Nunn (Trevor), Rice (Tim)
05 Black (Don), Donen (Stanley), Fosse (Bob), Kelly (Gene), Lenya (Lotte), Loewe (Frederick)
06 Berlin (Irving), Coward (Sir Noel), Gaynor (Mitzi), Jolson (Al), Lerner (Alan Jay), Merman (Ethel), Porter (Cole), Prince (Hal), Rogers (Ginger), Steele (Tommy)
07 Astaire (Fred), Burnett (Carol), Garland (Judy), Gilbert (Sir W S), Novello (Ivor), Rodgers (Richard)
08 Berkeley (Busby), Gershwin (George), Gershwin (Ira), Minnelli (Liza), Robinson (Bill 'Bojangles'), Sondheim (Stephen), Ziegfeld (Florenz, Jnr)
09 Bernstein (Leonard), Macintosh (Cameron), Offenbach (Jacques)
10 D'Oyly Carte (Richard)
11 Hammerstein (Oscar, II), Lloyd Webber (Andrew, Lord)

Musical composition types include:

03 jig, lay, rag
04 aria, duet, hymn, lied, opus, raga, song, trio, tune
05 canon, carol, étude, fugue, gigue, march, opera, piece, polka, rondo, round, suite, tango, track, waltz
06 aubade, ballad, bolero, lieder, masque, minuet, number, pavane, shanty, sonata
07 ballade, bourrée, cantata, fanfare, gavotte, mazurka, partita, prelude, quartet, requiem, scherzo, toccata
08 berceuse, cavatina, chaconne, concerto, fandango, fantasia, galliard, hornpipe, madrigal, nocturne, operetta, overture, rhapsody, saraband, serenade, sonatina, symphony, zarzuela
09 allemande, arabesque, bagatelle, cabaletta, capriccio, écossaise, farandole, impromptu, invention, pastorale, polonaise, sarabande, spiritual, voluntary
10 barcarolle, bergamasca, concertino, humoresque, intermezzo, opera buffa, tarantella
11 bacchanalia, ballad opera, composition, pastourelle, sinfonietta
12 divertimento, extravaganza
13 missa solemnis
14 chorale fantasy, chorale prelude, concerto grosso

See also **song**

Musical compositions include:

04 Saul
05 Rodeo
06 Boléro, Elijah, Études, Façade, Images
07 Epitaph, Jephtha, Mazeppa, Messiah
08 Ballades, Caprices, Creation, Drum Mass, Ode to Joy, Peer Gynt
09 Capriccio, Fantaisie, Finlandia, Jerusalem, Nocturnes
10 Arabesques, Bacchanale, Bagatelles, Concertino, Nelson Mass, The Planets, The Seasons, Water Music
11 Curlew River, Gymnopédies, Harmony Mass, Minute Waltz, Requiem Mass, Stabat Mater, Winterreise
12 A Sea Symphony, Danse Macabre, Golden Sonata, Karelia Suite, Kinderscenen, Linz Symphony, Piano Fantasy, Schéhérazade, Trout Quintet
13 Alpensinfonie, Carmina Burana, Choral Fantasy, Ebony Concerto, Faust Symphony, Fêtes Galantes, German Requiem, Israel in Egypt, Metamorphoses, Missa Solemnis, On Wenlock Edge, The Art of Fugue
14 Canticum Sacrum, Choral Symphony, Colour Symphony, Eroica Symphony, Glagolitic Mass, Prague Symphony, Rhapsody in Blue, Slavonic Dances, The Four Seasons
15 A Child of our Time, Alexander's Feast, Children's Corner, Emperor Concerto, Haffner Symphony, Hungarian Dances, Italian Concerto, Judas Maccabaeus, Jupiter Symphony, Kossuth Overture, Manfred Symphony, Peter and the Wolf, Sicilian Vespers

See also **opera**; **oratorio**; **song**

Musical terms include:

03 bar, bis, cue, key, tie
04 a due, alto, arco, bass, beat, clef, coda, fine, flat, fret, hold, mode, mute, note, part, rest, root, slur, solo, tone, tune, turn
05 ad lib, breve, buffo, chord, dolce, drone, forte, grave, largo, lento, lyric, major, metre, minim, minor, molto, pause, piano, piece, pitch, scale, score, senza, shake, sharp, staff, stave, swell, tacet, tanto, tempo, tenor, theme, triad, trill, tutti
06 adagio, al fine, a tempo, da capo, duplet, encore, finale, legato, manual, medley, melody, octave, phrase, presto, quaver, rhythm, sempre, subito, tenuto, timbre, treble, tuning, unison, upbeat, vivace
07 agitato, allegro, al segno, amoroso, andante, animato, attacca, bar line, cadence, con brio, concert, con moto, descant, harmony, langsam, marcato, mediant, middle C, mordent, natural, recital,

refrain, soprano, tremolo, triplet, vibrato
8 acoustic, alto clef, arpeggio, baritone, bass clef, col canto, con fuoco, crotchet, diatonic, doloroso, dominant, downbeat, ensemble, interval, maestoso, moderato, movement, ostinato, perdendo, ritenuto, semitone, semplice, sequence, staccato, vigoroso, virtuoso
9 alla breve, cantabile, cantilena, chromatic, contralto, crescendo, glissando, harmonics, imitation, larghetto, mezza voce, microtone, non troppo, obbligato, orchestra, pizzicato, semibreve, sextuplet, sforzando, smorzando, sostenuto, sotto voce, spiritoso, tablature, tenor clef
10 accidental, affettuoso, allargando, allegretto, consonance, diminuendo, dissonance, dotted note, dotted rest, double flat, double stop, expression, fortissimo, intonation, ledger line, mezzo forte, modulation, pedal point, pentatonic, pianissimo, quadruplet, quintuplet, resolution, semiquaver, simple time, submediant, supertonic, tonic sol-fa, treble clef, two-two time
1 accelerando, arrangement, decrescendo, double sharp, double trill, fingerboard, leading note, quarter tone, rallentando, rinforzando, subdominant, syncopation
2 acciaccatura, alla cappella, appoggiatura, compound time, counterpoint, four-four time, key signature, six-eight time
3 accompaniment, double bar line, fifth interval, improvisation, major interval, minor interval, orchestration, sixth interval, sul ponticello, third interval, three-four time, time signature, transposition
4 cross-fingering, demisemiquaver, fourth interval, second interval
5 perfect interval, seventh interval

musician

Musician types include:
3 duo
4 band, bard, diva, duet, trio
5 choir, griot, group, nonet, octet, piper, waits
6 bugler, busker, folkie, jazzer, oboist, player, sextet, singer
7 cellist, drummer, fiddler, harpist, maestro, Orphean, pianist, quartet, quintet, soloist
8 clarsair, composer, ensemble, flautist, lutenist, minstrel, organist, virtuoso, vocalist
9 balladeer, conductor, guitarist, itinerant, orchestra, performer, trumpeter, violinist
10 one-man band, prima donna, trombonist
1 accompanist, saxophonist

12 backing group, clarinettist
13 percussionist, session singer
15 instrumentalist, session musician

See also **composer**; **conductor**; **libretto**; **pianist**; **singer**; **songwriter**

Classical musicians include:
02 Ax (Emmanuel), Ma (Yo-Yo)
03 Mae (Vanessa), Pré (Jacqueline du)
04 Bell (Joshua), Hahn (Hilary), Hess (Dame Myra), Lupu (Radu), Mork (Truls), Wild (Earl)
05 Boehm (Theobald), Borge (Victor), Bream (Julian), Bülow (Hans von), Chung (Kyung-Wha), Dupré (Marcel), Elman (Mischa), Grove (Sir George), Isbin (Sharon), Ogdon (John), Sharp (Cecil), Stern (Isaac)
06 Casals (Pablo), Czerny (Karl), Galway (James), Gitlis (Ivry), Kissin (Evgeny), Köchel (Ludwig von) Rizzio (David), Schiff (András)
07 Blondel, Glennie (Evelyn), Heifetz (Jascha), Kennedy (Nigel), Menuhin (Yehudi), Mutter (Anne-Sophie), Perahia (Murray), Perlman (Itzhak), Pollini (Maurizio), Richter (Sviatoslav), Russell (David), Segovia (Andrés), Shankar (Ravi), Starker (Janos)
08 Argerich (Martha), Bronfman (Yefim), Browning (John), Goossens (Léon), Helfgott (David), Holliger (Heinz), Horowitz (Vladimir), Kreisler (Fritz), Paganini (Niccolò), Sarasate (Pablo), Steinway (Henry), Vengerov (Maxim), Williams (John)
09 Ashkenazy (Vladimir), Barenboim (Daniel), Benedetti (Nicola), Boulanger (Nadia), Broadwood (John), Dolmetsch (Arnold), Guarnieri, Tortelier (Paul)
10 Cristofori, de Larrocha (Alicia), Paderewski (Ignacy), Rubinstein (Anton), Rubinstein (Artur), Stradivari (Antonio), Villa-Lobos (Heitor), Williamson (Malcolm)
11 Theodorakis (Mikis)
12 Guido d'Arezzo, Rostropovich (Mstislav)
14 Jaques-Dalcroze (Emile)

musing
05 study **07** reverie **08** dreaming, studying, thinking **10** brown study, cogitation, meditation, ponderment, reflection, rumination **11** abstraction, cerebration, daydreaming **13** contemplation, introspection, wool-gathering

musk
04 must **05** civet, moust, muist, scent **07** mimulus

musket
05 fusee, fusil **06** gingal, jezail, jingal **07** caliver, dragoon, gingall **08** Biscayan **09** brown Bess, queen's-arm **10** musquetoon

musketeer
12 mousquetaire

Musketeers include:
05 Athos
06 Aramis
07 Porthos
09 D'Artagnan

Muslim

Muslims include:
04 Shia
05 Shiah, Sunni
06 Senusi, Shiite
07 Alawite, dervish, Mevlevi, Senussi, Sonnite, Sunnite
08 Senoussi
10 Karmathian
11 Black Muslim
15 whirling dervish

muslin
04 leno, mull **05** sails **06** canvas, gurrah, mulmul **07** jamdani, mulmull, organdy **08** coteline, nainsook, organdie, tarlatan **09** persienne **10** mousseline

muss
◇ *anagram indicator*
03 row **04** mess **06** ruffle, tousle **08** dishevel, disorder, scramble **09** confusion **10** disarrange, make untidy **11** disturbance, make a mess of

mussel
04 Unio **06** muscle, muskle **07** Modiola, Mytilus **08** deer horn, Modiolus **09** clabby-doo, clappy-doo, date-shell

must
◇ *anagram indicator*
03 man, mun **04** amok, duty, maun, mote, musk, stum **05** amuck, basic, mould **06** frenzy, powder **09** essential, necessity, provision, requisite **10** imperative, obligation, sine qua non **11** fundamental, requirement, stipulation **12** fermentation, prerequisite

mustard
05 runch, senvy **08** charlock, flix-weed **09** praiseach **10** sauce-alone **14** jack-by-the-hedge

muster
04 mass, meet **05** enrol, group, rally **06** call up, gather, number, parade, review, summon, throng **07** collect, convene, convoke, display, example, hosting, marshal, meeting, round up, round-up, turnout **08** assemble, assembly, mobilize, register, summon up **09** concourse, gathering, march past **10** assemblage, collection, congregate, convention, inspection **11** convocation **12** call together, come together, congregation, mobilization **13** bring together, demonstration **14** gather together
• **pass muster**
07 shape up **09** measure up **10** be accepted, fit the bill **11** fill the bill **12** be

musty
◇ *anagram indicator*
04 amok, damp, dank **05** amuck, frowy, funky, fusty, mucid, stale **06** fousty, frowie, mochie, mouldy, smelly, stuffy **07** airless, decayed, foughty, froughy, mildewy, vinewed **08** decaying, mildewed

mutability
09 variation **11** variability **12** alterability **13** permutability **14** changeableness

mutable
06 fickle **08** changing, flexible, unstable, unsteady, variable, volatile, wavering **09** adaptable, alterable, uncertain, unsettled **10** changeable, inconstant, irresolute, permutable, unreliable **11** vacillating **12** inconsistent, undependable **15** interchangeable

mutate
◇ *anagram indicator*
05 alter, morph **06** change, evolve, modify, remake **07** convert, remodel, reshape **09** transform, translate, transmute **11** transfigure **12** metamorphose, transmogrify

mutation
◇ *anagram indicator*
06 change **07** anomaly **09** deviation, evolution, inversion, variation **10** adaptation, alteration, revolution **11** vicissitude **12** modification **13** metamorphosis **14** transformation

mute
03 mum **04** dull, dumb, stop **05** lower **06** dampen, damper, deaden, muffle, shtoom, silent, soften, stifle, subdue **07** aphasic, plosive, quieten, silence, smother, sordino **08** moderate, sourdine, suppress, taciturn, tone down, unspoken, wordless **09** noiseless, soft-pedal, voiceless **10** speechless **11** unexpressed **12** unpronounced **15** uncommunicative

muted
04 dull, soft **05** faint, quiet, sorda, sordo **06** low-key, subtle **07** muffled, stifled, subdued **08** dampened, discreet, softened **10** restrained, suppressed

mutely
06 dumbly **08** silently **09** in silence **10** taciturnly **11** noiselessly, voicelessly **12** speechlessly

mutilate
◇ *anagram indicator*
03 cut, mar **04** hack, lame, maim, ruin **05** cut up, spoil **06** censor, damage, garble, hack up, hamble, impair, injure, mangle **07** butcher, concise, cripple, disable, distort **08** lacerate **09** disfigure, dismember **10** bowdlerize, detruncate **11** cut to pieces

mutilation
◇ *anagram indicator*
06 damage **07** maiming **10** amputation **12** detruncation, dismembering **13** disfigurement

mutinous
◇ *anagram indicator*
06 unruly **07** bolshie, riotous **09** insurgent, seditious **10** disorderly, rebellious, refractory, subversive **11** anarchistic, disobedient **12** contumacious, ungovernable, unsubmissive **13** insubordinate, revolutionary **14** uncontrollable

mutiny
04 defy, riot **05** rebel **06** resist, revolt, rise up, rising, strife, strike, tumult **07** disobey, protest **08** defiance, uprising **09** rebellion **10** insurgence, resistance, revolution **12** disobedience, insurrection **15** insubordination

mutt
03 cur, dog **04** dolt, fool, kuri **05** bitch, hound, idiot, moron, pooch **07** mongrel **08** imbecile **09** blockhead, ignoramus, thickhead **10** dunderhead

mutter
◇ *homophone indicator*
04 beef, carp, fuss, mump, roin **05** gripe, royne, whine **06** grouse, mumble, murmur, object, rumble, whinge, witter **07** chunder, chunner, chunter, grumble, maunder, protest, stutter, whitter **08** chounter, complain, splutter **09** bellyache, criticize, find fault, murmuring, mussitate **14** talk to yourself, whittie-whattie

mutton
02 em **05** gigot, macon, sheep, traik **07** haricot **09** Irish stew, Southdown **10** Fanny Adams **13** colonial goose

mutual
05 joint **06** common, shared **09** commutual, exchanged **10** collective, commonable, reciprocal **12** interchanged **13** complementary **15** interchangeable

muzzle
03 gag **04** mute **05** check, choke, snout **06** censor, fetter, stifle **07** inhibit, silence **08** gunpoint, restrain, suppress

muzzy
04 hazy **05** dazed, faint, fuzzy, mused, tipsy **06** addled, groggy **07** blurred, muddled, unclear **08** confused **09** befuddled, unfocused **10** bewildered, indistinct

my
01 m' **02** ha **03** cor, gad, lor **04** gosh **08** well, well

Myanmar
03 BUR, MMR, MYA

myopic
06 narrow, unwise **08** purblind **09** half-blind, imprudent, localized, parochial,

short-term **11** near-sighted, thoughtless **12** narrow-minded, short-sighted **13** ill-considered, unadventurous, uncircumspect, unimaginative

myriad
03 sea **04** army, host **05** flood, horde, swarm, toman **06** scores, throng, untold **08** millions, mountain, zillions **09** boundless, countless, limitless, multitude, thousands **10** numberless **11** innumerable **12** immeasurable, incalculable **13** multitudinous

mysterious
◇ *anagram indicator*
04 dark **05** shady, weird **06** arcane, creepy, hidden, mystic, occult, secret, veiled **07** cryptic, curious, furtive, obscure, shadowy, strange **08** abstruse, baffling, esoteric, mystical, puzzling, reticent, sinister **09** enigmatic, insoluble, recondite, secretive **10** mystifying, perplexing **11** as if by magic, inscrutable **12** inexplicable, unfathomable, unsearchable **13** surreptitious

mysteriously
◇ *anagram indicator*
08 arcanely, in secret, secretly **09** curiously, magically, obscurely, strangely **10** abstrusely, mystically, puzzlingly **11** cryptically, inscrutably **12** esoterically, inexplicably **13** enigmatically **15** surreptitiously

mystery
06 enigma, puzzle, riddle, secret **07** arcanum, problem, secrecy **08** mystique, question **09** ambiguity, conundrum, curiosity, obscurity, reticence, sacrament, weirdness **10** closed book **11** concealment, furtiveness, miracle play, strangeness **12** question mark **14** inscrutability **15** inexplicability, unfathomability

mystic
04 Sofi, Sufi **05** swami **07** psychic **09** occultist, spiritist **11** allegorical, esotericist **12** spiritualist **13** metaphysicist **15** supernaturalist

mystical
05 weird **06** arcane, hidden, mystic, occult **07** obscure, strange **08** abstruse, baffling, esoteric **09** recondite, spiritual **10** mysterious, paranormal **12** inexplicable, metaphysical, other-worldly, supernatural, unfathomable **13** preternatural **14** transcendental

mysticism
05 deism **06** theism **07** mystery **09** occultism, spiritism **10** arcaneness **11** esotericism **12** spirituality **14** mysteriousness **15** inexplicability, supernaturalism

mystification
03 awe, fog **04** daze **06** muddle **08** surprise **09** confusion **10** perplexity, puzzlement

uncertainty **12** bewilderment,
ɹpefaction **13** disconcertion
disorientation

ystify
hoax **06** baffle, puzzle **07** confuse,
ɹrplex **08** bewilder, confound
bamboozle **10** take to town
metagrabolize, metagrobolize

ystique
awe **05** charm, magic, spell
appeal **07** glamour, mystery,
mance, secrecy **08** charisma
adventure **11** fascination

yth
fib, lie **04** saga, tale **05** fable, fancy,
ɔry **06** legend **07** fallacy, fantasy,
tion, parable, untruth **08** allegory,
ɔstiary, delusion, folk tale, pretence
fairy tale, invention, tall story
fairy story **11** fabrication
misconception
book of myths
Edda **09** Elder Edda, Prose Edda
Younger Edda

ythical
put-on **06** fabled, made-up,
ɹoney, unreal, untrue **07** fantasy,
etend **08** fabulous, fanciful, invented
fairytale, fantastic, imaginary,
gendary, pretended **10** chimerical,
ɔricated, fictitious **11** make-believe,
ɔn-existent **12** mythological

*lythical creatures and spirits
include:*

elf, hob, imp, orc, roc
faun, fury, jinn, ogre, peri, pixy,
puck, yeti
afrit, demon, devil, djinn, dobby,
dryad, dwarf, fairy, genie, ghost,
ghoul, giant, gnome, golem, harpy,
kelpy, lamia, naiad, nymph, oread,
pixie, satyr, shade, Siren, sylph, troll,
yowie
afreet, bunyip, dobbie, dragon,
dybbuk, Fafnir, Furies, Geryon,
goblin, Gorgon, kelpie, kobald,
kraken, Lilith, Medusa, merman,
nereid, ogress, Scylla, selkie,
Sphinx, sprite, wivern, yaksha
banshee, Bigfoot, brownie,
Cecrops, centaur, Chimera,
Cyclops, Echidna, Erinyes, gremlin,
Grendel, griffin, Harpies, incubus,
lorelei, mermaid, Pegasus, phoenix,
sandman, taniwha, unicorn,
vampire, windigo
basilisk, Cerberus, Gigantes,
lindworm, Minotaur, seahorse,
succubus, werewolf
Charybdis, hamadryad, hobgoblin,
mermaiden, sasquatch
cockatrice, hippogriff, leprechaun,
salamander, sea serpent, tooth fairy
hippocampus
Loch Ness monster

e also **bird**; **monster**

lythical places include:

Dis, Hel
Hell, Styx

05 Argos, Babel, Hades, Lethe, Pluto,
Thule
06 Albion, Anghar, Asgard, Avalon,
Heaven, Heorot, Nedyet, Utgard
07 Acheron, Agartha, Alfheim,
Alpheus, Arcadia, Bifrost, Boeotia,
Elysium, Lemuria, Nirvana, Pohjola,
Tuonela
08 Amazonia, Archeron, Atlantis, El
Dorado, Niflheim, Paradise, Tir-na-
nOg, Tlalocan, Valhalla, Vanaheim
09 Cockaigne, Fairyland, Purgatory,
River Styx, Yggdrasil
10 River Lethe, Stymphalos
11 Ultima Thule
12 River Acheron, River Alpheus
13 Jewel Mountain, River Archeron,
The Underworld
14 Lake Stymphalos
15 Cloudcuckooland, The Garden of
Eden, The Isle of Avalon, The Tower
of Babel

See also **mythology**; **river**

mythological
06 fabled, mythic **08** fabulous,
mythical **09** fairytale, folkloric,
legendary **10** fictitious **11** traditional

mythology
04 lore **05** myths, tales **06** legend
07 stories **08** folklore, Pantheon
09 folk tales, tradition **10** traditions

See also **god, goddess**; **fate**; **fury**; **grace**;
muse; **mythical**; **sage**

*Characters from Celtic mythology
include:*

03 Anu, Lug
04 Badb, Bran, Danu, Lugh, Medb,
Ogma
05 Balor, Boann, Dagda, Macha,
Maeve, Neman, Nuada, Oisin, Pwyll
06 Brigit, Danaan, Deidre, Imbolc,
Isolde, Ogmios, Ossian
07 banshee, Beltane, Branwen, Brighid,
Deirdre, Samhain, Tristan
08 Manannan, Morrigan, Rhiannon,
The Dagda, Tir nan-Og
09 Bean Sidhé, Cernunnos, Conchobar
10 Cú Chulainn, Lughnasadh
11 Finn mac Cool
13 Bendigeidfran, Finn mac Cumhal
14 Bran the Blessed, Finn mac Cumhail,
Tuatha dé Danaan

*Characters from Greek
mythology include:*

02 Io
04 Ajax, Dido, Echo, Eris, Hero, Leda,
Leto, Rhea
05 Atlas, Chloe, Circe, Creon, Danae,
Helen, Horae, Hydra, Irene, Ixion,
Jason, Kreon, Laius, Lamia, Medea,
Midas, Minos, Niobe, Orion, Paris,
Priam, Rheia
06 Aeneas, Aeolus, Alecto, Amazon,
Atreus, Cadmus, Castor, Charon,
Chiron, Cronus, Danaoi, Daphne,
Dryads, Europa, Europe, Furies,
Graiae, Hecabe, Hector, Hecuba,
Hellen, Icarus, Iolaus, Kronos,
Latona, Medusa, Megara,

Memnon, Naiads, Nessus, Nestor,
Nymphs, Oreads, Peleus, Pelops,
Phoebe, Pollux, Python, Satyrs,
Scylla, Semele, Sileni, Sirens,
Stheno, Syrinx, Titans, Triton, Typhon
07 Actaeon, Alcyone, Arachne,
Ariadne, Calchas, Calypso,
Cecrops, Cepheus, Chimera,
Cyclops, Danaans, Daphnis,
Diomede, Echidna, Electra, Epigoni,
Erinyes, Euryale, Galatea, Gorgons,
Griffin, Gryphon, Harpies, Iapetus,
Jocasta, Kekrops, Laocoon, Lapiths,
Leander, Maenads, Marsyas,
Nereids, Oceanus, Oedipus,
Orestes, Orpheus, Pandora,
Pegasus, Perseus, Phaedra, Silenus,
Theseus, Titania, Troilus, Ulysses
08 Achilles, Alcestis, Alcmaeon,
Anchises, Antigone, Arethusa,
Atalanta, Basilisk, Centaurs,
Cerberus, Chimaera, Cressida,
Cyclopes, Daedalus, Diomedes,
Endymion, Eteocles, Eurydice,
Ganymede, Gigantes, Halcyone,
Heracles, Hyperion, Iphicles,
Lycurgus, Meleager, Menelaus,
Minotaur, Nausicaa, Oceanids,
Odysseus, Pasiphae, Penelope,
Pentheus, Phaethon, Pleiades,
Sarpedon, Sisyphus, Tantalus,
Thyestes, Tiresias, Typhoeus
09 Aegisthus, Agamemnon,
Andromeda, Argonauts, Autolycus,
Cassandra, Charybdis, Deucalion,
Idomeneus, Lotophagi,
Mnemosyne, Myrmidons,
Narcissus, Patroclus, Polynices,
Pygmalion, Semiramis, Tisiphone
10 Amphitryon, Andromache,
Cassiopeia, Cockatrice,
Erechtheus, Hamadryads,
Hesperides, Hippolytus,
Iphigeneia, Polyneices,
Polyphemus, Procrustes,
Prometheus, Telemachus
11 Bellerophon, Lotus-eaters,
Neoptolemus, Philoctetes
12 Clytemnestra, Hyperboreans,
Rhadamanthus, Rhadamanthys

*Characters from Maori mythology
include:*
04 Kupe, Maui, Rona
05 Pania
07 Hinemoa, Mahuika
09 Tutanekai

*Characters from Norse
mythology include:*
03 Lif
06 Gudrun, Sigurd
09 Berserker
10 Lifthrasir

*Characters from Roman
mythology include:*
05 Lamia, Lares, Manes, Remus, Sibyl
07 Danaans, Latinus, Lemures,
Lucrece, Penates, Romulus, Sibylla,
Tarpeia
08 Anchises, Callisto, Hercules,
Lucretia, Verginia

09 Androcles
10 Coriolanus, Rhea Silvia, Rhea
    Sylvia

Other mythological and
legendary characters include:

03 Qat
04 Tell (William)
05 Adapa, El Cid, Faust, Frost (Jack)
06 Anansi, Arthur, Bunyan (Paul),

    Enkidu, George (St), Godiva (Lady),
    Kraken, Weland
07 Aladdin, Ali Baba, Beowulf,
    Grendel, Wayland, Weiland,
    Weyland
08 Baba Yaga, Brunhild, Hang Tuah,
    Hiawatha, Parsifal
09 Appleseed (Johnny), Bluebeard,
    Lohengrin

10 Yu the Great
11 Old King Cole
12 Lemminkainen, Rip Van Winkle,
    Scheherazade, Will-o'-the-
    Wisp
14 Flying Dutchman
15 Father Christmas

See also **fate**; **fury**; **god, goddess**; **grad**
monster; **muse**; **sage**

N

N
02 en **08** November

nab
03 hat **04** bone, grab, head, nail, nick **05** catch, run in, seize **06** arrest, collar, nobble, pull in, snatch **07** capture, **hilltop 09** apprehend **10** projection, promontory

nabob
03 VIP **05** celeb, nawab **06** bigwig, tycoon **07** magnate **08** luminary **09** celebrity, financier, personage **11** billionaire, millionaire

nadir
04 zero **06** bottom, depths **07** minimum **08** low point **10** all-time low, rock bottom **11** lowest point **12** low-watermark

nag
03 bug, rip, tit, vex **04** carp, hack, jade, moan, moke, plug, yaff **05** annoy, harry, horse, scold, tease, worry **06** badger, berate, bother, grouse, harass, hassle, keep at, keffel, niggle, pester, pick on, plague, rouncy **07** earbash, henpeck, torment, trouble, upbraid **08** complain, ding-dong, irritate, keep on at **09** aggravate, Rosinante, Rozinante

nagging
06 aching **07** moaning, painful **08** critical, niggling, scolding, shrewish, worrying **09** upsetting **10** continuous, irritating, nit-picking, persistent, tormenting **11** distressing

nail
03 fix, nab, pin, toe **04** brad, brod, claw, grab, join, nick, stub, stud, tack, trap **05** catch, clout, rivet, screw, seize, spick, spike, sprig, talon **06** arrest, attach, collar, corner, detect, expose, fasten, hammer, nipper, nobble, pierce, pincer, reveal, secure, skewer, snatch, tingle, unguis, unmask **07** capture, clinker, pin down, toenail, uncover, unearth **08** fastener, holdfast, identify, panel pin, sparable **09** apprehend **10** fingernail, tenterhook
• **hit the nail on the head**
10 be accurate **14** be exactly right, score a bull's eye

naïve
04 naif, open **05** frank, green **06** candid, jejune, simple **07** artless, natural **08** gullible, immature, innocent, trusting, wide-eyed **09** childlike, credulous, guileless, ingenuous, primitive, simpliste, small-town, unworldly **10** simplistic, unaffected **11** unrealistic **12** having no idea, pollyannaish, unsuspecting, unsuspicious **13** born yesterday, inexperienced, unpretentious **14** bread-and-butter **15** unsophisticated

naively
06 simply **08** gullibly **09** artlessly, naturally **10** immaturely, innocently **11** guilelessly, ingenuously **14** simplistically, unsuspiciously

naivety
08 openness **09** credulity, frankness, innocence **10** candidness, immaturity, simplicity **11** artlessness, gullibility, naturalness **12** inexperience **13** childlikeness, guilelessness, ingenuousness

naked
03 raw **04** bald, bare, nude, open, weak **05** overt, plain, stark **06** Adamic, barren, patent, simple **07** artless, blatant, denuded, evident, exposed, glaring, skyclad, unarmed **08** Adamical, disrobed, flagrant, helpless, in the raw, starkers, stripped, treeless, undraped **09** au naturel, grassless, in the buff, in the scud, powerless, unadorned, unclothed, uncovered, undressed, unguarded **10** stark-naked, start-naked, unprovided, vulnerable **11** defenceless, mother-naked, unconcealed, undisguised, unprotected, unqualified, unvarnished **12** not a stitch on **13** with nothing on **15** in the altogether

nakedness
06 nature, nudity **07** the buff, undress **08** baldness, bareness, openness **09** plainness, starkness **10** barrenness, simplicity **13** the altogether

namby-pamby
03 wet **04** prim, weak **05** cissy, soppy, vapid, weedy, wussy **06** feeble, prissy **07** anaemic, insipid, maudlin, mawkish, wimpish **09** spineless, white-shoe **10** colourless, wishy-washy **11** sentimental **12** pretty-pretty

name
01 n **03** dub, nom, tag, VIP **04** call, cite, clan, fame, hero, nemn, note, noun, pick, star, term **05** celeb, label, state, style, title, utter **06** behalf, bigwig, choose, esteem, expert, family, famous, handle, honour, renown, repute, select **07** appoint, baptize, big name, entitle, epithet, mention, specify **08** big noise, christen, classify, cognomen, eminence, identify, luminary, monicker, nominate, prestige, somebody, standing **09** authority, celebrity, character, designate, dignitary, well-known **10** commission, denominate, give name to, popularity, prominence, reputation **11** appellation, designation, distinction **12** denomination, leading light

Names include:
03 pen, pet
04 code, full, last
05 alias, brand, false, first, given, place, stage
06 anonym, eponym, exonym, family, maiden, middle, proper, second
07 agnomen, allonym, assumed, autonym, surname, toponym
08 nickname
09 baptismal, Christian, cryptonym, pseudonym, sobriquet, trademark
10 diminutive, nom de plume, soubriquet
11 nom de guerre

See also **boy**; **cinema**; **French**; **German**; **girl**; **Irish**; **public house**; **Scottish**; **Welsh**
• **in name only**
07 titular
• **list of names**
04 roll
• **name unknown**
02 NU

named
03 dit, hot **04** hote **05** cited, nempt **06** called, chosen, dubbed, picked, styled, termed, titled **07** known as **08** baptized, entitled, labelled, selected **09** appointed, mentioned, nominated, specified **10** christened, classified, designated, identified, singled out **11** by the name of, denominated **12** commissioned

nameless
07 obscure, unknown, unnamed **08** untitled **09** anonymous, titleless, unheard-of **10** innominate, unlabelled **11** unspeakable, unspecified, unutterable **12** illegitimate, undesignated, unidentified **13** indescribable, inexpressible, unmentionable **15** undistinguished

namely
02 ie, sc **03** viz **04** scil, sciz **05** to wit **06** famous, that is **08** scilicet **09** videlicet **10** especially **11** that is to say **12** in other words, specifically

Namibia
03 NAM

nanny
03 nan, pet 04 amah, ayah, baby, nana
05 nanna, nurse, spoil 06 au pair,
coddle, cosset, mother, pamper
07 indulge, she-goat 08 pander to,
wet-nurse 09 governess, nursemaid,
spoon-feed 11 childminder,
grandmother, mollycoddle, mother's
help, overprotect

nanosecond
02 ns

nap
03 kip, nod, ziz 04 down, doze, fuzz,
oose, ooze, pile, rest, shag, zizz
05 fibre, grain, seize, sleep, steal,
weave 06 catnap, nod off, siesta,
snooze 07 bedding, bedroll, doze off,
drop off, lie down, lie-down, surface,
texture 08 meridian, napoleon
09 downiness 10 forty winks, light
sleep 12 sleep lightly 14 get some shut-
eye, have forty winks

napkin
05 doily, doyly, nappy 06 doyley
09 muckender, serviette
12 handkerchief

nappy
04 oosy, oozy 05 downy, heady, jumpy,
terry, tipsy, towel 06 diaper, frothy,
hippen, hippin, napkin, shaggy, strong
07 hipping, nervous 09 excitable,
serviette 10 disposable

narcissism
06 vanity 07 conceit, egotism
08 egomania, self-love 10 self-regard
11 self-conceit 13 egocentricity, self-
obsession 15 self-centredness

narcissistic
04 vain 09 conceited, egotistic
10 egocentric, self-loving
11 egomaniacal, self-centred 12 self-
absorbed, self-obsessed

narcotic
03 hop 04 dopy, drug 05 dopey, upper
06 downer, opiate 07 anodyne,
calming, dulling, numbing
08 hypnotic, sedative 09 analgesic,
somnolent, soporific 10 painkiller,
palliative, stupefying 11 anaesthetic,
pain-dulling, painkilling 12 sleeping
pill, stupefacient 13 sleep-inducing,
tranquillizer 14 tranquillizing

Narcotics include:

03 ava
04 bang, benj, coca, dope, kava
05 bhang, dagga
06 charas, datura, pituri
07 churrus, narceen
08 narceine
10 belladonna
11 Indian berry, laurel-water
15 cocculus indicus

See also **drug**

• **packet of narcotic**
04 deck

narked
05 irked, riled, vexed 06 bugged,
galled, miffed, peeved, piqued
07 annoyed, in a huff, nettled
08 bothered, in a paddy, provoked
09 irritated 10 brassed off, cheesed off,
got the hump 11 exasperated

narrate
◇ *homophone indicator*
04 read, tell 05 state 06 detail, recite,
record, relate, report, set out, unfold
07 explain, portray, recount
08 describe, rehearse, set forth
09 chronicle

narration
04 tale 05 story 06 detail, report,
sketch 07 account, history, reading,
recital, telling 09 chronicle, portrayal,
recountal, rehearsal, statement, voice-
over 11 description, explanation
12 storytelling

narrative
04 saga, tale 05 fable, novel, prose,
récit, story 06 detail, report, sketch
07 account, history, process, reading,
romance 08 allegory, anecdote,
periplus, relation 09 chronicle,
portrayal, statement 10 short story
11 description

narrator
06 author, writer 07 relater, relator,
sagaman 08 annalist, reporter
09 describer, raconteur, recounter
10 anecdotist, chronicler, tale-teller
11 commentator, storyteller
12 mythographer

narrow
03 set 04 fine, keen, slim, thin, true
05 close, cramp, exact, limit, petty,
rigid, scant, small, spare, taper, tight
06 biased, meagre, reduce, strait,
strict 07 bigoted, confine, cramped,
insular, limited, literal, precise, slender,
tighten 08 confined, contract,
detailed, diminish, dogmatic, exiguous,
original, restrict, simplify, squeezed,
straiten, tapering, thorough
09 attenuate, coarctate, constrict,
hidebound, illiberal 10 attenuated,
contracted, intolerant, prejudiced,
restricted 11 close-minded,
constricted, incapacious, reactionary,
small-minded, strait-laced
12 circumscribe, conservative,
incommodious, narrow-minded,
parsimonious 13 circumscribed, dyed-
in-the-wool

narrowing
06 intake 08 stenosis, tapering,
thinning 09 gathering, reduction,
reductive 10 emaciation, rebatement
11 attenuation, compression,
contraction, curtailment
12 constipation, constriction

narrowly
04 fine, just, near 06 barely, strait
07 closely, exactly 08 only just,
scarcely, straitly, strictly 09 carefully,
precisely 10 by a whisker 11 attentively

12 by a short head 13 painstakingly
14 scrutinizingly

narrow-minded
03 set 05 borné, petty, rigid 06 biased,
warped 07 bigoted, diehard, insular,
redneck, twisted 08 blimpish,
verkramp 09 claustral, exclusive,
hidebound, illiberal, jaundiced,
parochial 10 entrenched, inflexible,
intolerant, prejudiced, provincial
11 close-minded, opinionated, petty-
minded, reactionary, small-minded,
strait-laced 12 conservative,
unreasonable 13 dyed in the wool

narrow-mindedness
04 bias 07 bigotry 08 rigidity
09 prejudice 12 parochialism
13 exclusiveness, inflexibility 15 close-
mindedness, petty-mindedness, small-
mindedness

narrowness
04 bias 07 bigotry 08 nearness,
rigidity, thinness 09 closeness,
pettiness, prejudice, tightness
10 insularity, limitation, meagreness
11 attenuation, intolerance,
slenderness 12 conservatism,
constriction, parochialism
13 exclusiveness, provincialism
14 restrictedness 15 small-mindedness

narrows
05 sound 07 channel, passage, straits
08 waterway

nascent
05 young 06 rising 07 budding,
growing 08 evolving, naissant
09 advancing, beginning, embryonic,
incipient 10 burgeoning, developing

nastily
◇ *anagram indicator*
11 obnoxiously, offensively, repulsively
12 disagreeably, disgustingly,
unpleasantly 13 objectionably

nastiness
04 porn 05 filth, spite 06 malice
07 squalor 08 foulness, impurity,
meanness 09 dirtiness, indecency,
obscenity, pollution 10 defilement,
filthiness, smuttiness 11 malevolence,
pornography, viciousness
12 horribleness, spitefulness
13 offensiveness, repulsiveness,
uncleanliness, unsavouriness
14 unpleasantness

nasty
◇ *anagram indicator*
03 wet 04 blue, foul, good, mean, rank,
sore, vile, wild 05 awful, crook, cruel,
dirty, dodgy, foggy, grave, mucky, rainy,
ribby, rough, yucky 06 filthy, grotty,
horrid, lovely, odious, ribald, smutty,
stormy, tricky, unkind 07 awkward,
hateful, noisome, obscene, serious,
squalid, vicious 08 alarming,
annoying, critical, delicate, horrible,
indecent, nauseous, polluted, spiteful,
ticklish, worrying 09 dangerous,
difficult, loathsome, malicious,
obnoxious, offensive, repellent,

epugnant, repulsive, revolting,
ickening **10** disgusting, ill-natured,
nalevolent, malodorous, unpleasant
 bad-tempered, disquieting,
istasteful, threatening
2 disagreeable, exasperating,
ornographic **13** objectionable

ation
 folk, land, race, volk **05** realm, state,
ibe **06** people, public, vassal
 country, kingdom, society
 republic **09** community
 population
ee also **Africa; America; Asia; country;
urope**

ational
1 N **03** Nat **05** civic, civil, state
 native, public, social **07** citizen,
ederal, general, subject **08** domestic,
nternal, resident **10** inhabitant,
ationwide, widespread
 countrywide **12** governmental
 comprehensive
ee also **park**

ationalism
 loyalty **08** jingoism **10** allegiance,
hauvinism, patriotism, xenophobia

ationalist
1 N **03** Nat **07** patriot **08** jingoist,
oyalist **09** flag-waver, xenophobe
 chauvinist

ationalistic
 loyal **09** patriotic **10** jingoistic,
enophobic **12** chauvinistic
 ethnocentrist

ationality
 clan, race **05** birth, tribe **06** nation
 citizenship, ethnic group

 Lao
 Kiwi, Thai
 Bajan, Congo, Cuban, Czech, Dutch,
Greek, Iraqi, Irish, Omani, Saudi,
Swazi, Swiss, Tajik, Uzbek, Welsh
 Afghan, Danish, Fijian, French,
German, Indian, Kenyan, Kyrgyz,
Libyan, Malian, Polish, Qatari,
Samoan, Somali, Syrian, Tongan,
Yapese, Yemeni
7 Angolan, Basotho, Belgian, Bosnian,
British, Burmese, Chadian, Chilean,
Chinese, Comoran, Cypriot, Emirati,
English, Finnish, Gambian, Guinean,
Haitian, Iranian, Israeli, Italian,
Ivorian, Kosraen, Kuwaiti, Laotian,
Latvian, Maltese, Mexican,
Monacan, Mosotho, Nauruan,
Palauan, Russian, Rwandan,
Sahrawi, Serbian, Spanish, Swedish,
Tadzhik, Turkish, Turkmen, Ugandan,
Zambian
 Albanian, Algerian, American,
Andorran, Antiguan, Armenian,
Austrian, Bahamian, Bahraini,
Barbudan, Batswana, Belizean,
Beninese, Bolivian, Bruneian,
Canadian, Chuukese, Croatian,
Egyptian, Eritrean, Estonian, Filipina,

Filipino, Gabonese, Georgian,
Ghanaian, Grenadan, Guyanese,
Honduran, Jamaican, Japanese,
Lebanese, Liberian, Malagasy,
Malawian, Moldovan, Moroccan,
Motswana, Namibian, Nepalese,
Nevisian, Nigerian, Nigerien,
Peruvian, Romanian, Sahraoui,
Scottish, St Lucian, Sudanese,
Timorese, Togolese, Tunisian,
Tuvaluan
09 Argentine, Barbadian, Bhutanese,
Brazilian, Bulgarian, Burkinabé,
Burundian, Cambodian,
Colombian, Congolese, Dominican,
Ethiopian, Grenadian, Hungarian,
Icelandic, I-Kiribati, Jordanian,
Kittitian, Malaysian, Maldivian,
Mauritian, Mongolian, Ni-Vanuatu,
Norwegian, Pakistani, Pohnpeian,
Sahrawian, Santoméan, São
Toméan, Singapore, Slovakian,
Slovenian, Sri Lankan, Taiwanese,
Tanzanian, Ukrainian, Uruguayan
10 Australian, Belarusian, Costa Rican,
Djiboutian, Ecuadorean,
Ecuadorian, Guatemalan,
Indonesian, Lithuanian,
Luxembourg, Macedonian,
Monégasque, Mozambican,
Myanmarese, New Zealand,
Nicaraguan, Panamanian,
Paraguayan, Philippine, Portuguese,
Sahraouian, Salvadoran,
Senegalese, Surinamese,
Tobagonian, Venezuelan,
Vietnamese, Vincentian,
Zimbabwean
11 Argentinian, Azerbaijani,
Bangladeshi, Cameroonian, Cape
Verdean, Kazakhstani, Marshallese,
Mauritanian, Micronesian,
Montenegrin, North Korean,
Sammarinese, Seychellois,
Singaporean, South Korean,
Tajikistani, Trinidadian
12 Luxembourger, Saudi Arabian,
South African, St Vincentian
13 Equatoguinean, Herzegovinian,
Liechtenstein, Sierra Leonean
14 Central African, Guinea-Bissauan
15 Liechtensteiner, Papua New
Guinean, Solomon Islander

nationally
09 generally **10** nationwide
11 countrywide **15** comprehensively

National Trust
02 NT

nationwide
05 state **07** general, overall **08** national
09 extensive **10** widespread
11 countrywide **12** coast-to-coast
13 comprehensive

native
03 nat, son **04** home **05** local, natal
06 inborn, inbred, innate, mother,
oyster **07** built-in, citizen, connate,
dweller, genuine, natural **08** domestic,
home-born, home-bred, indigene,
inherent, national, original, resident

09 aborigine, home-grown, ingrained,
inherited, intrinsic, intuitive
10 aboriginal, autochthon, congenital,
hereditary, indigenous, inhabitant,
vernacular **11** instinctive
13 autochthonous, tangata whenua
15 unsophisticated
See also **African; American; Asian;
European**

nativity
04 putz **05** birth **06** jataka **08** delivery
09 horoscope **10** childbirth
11 parturition

NATO

02 UK
03 USA
05 Italy, Spain
06 Canada, France, Greece, Latvia,
Norway, Poland, Turkey
07 Belgium, Denmark, Estonia,
Germany, Hungary, Iceland,
Romania
08 Bulgaria, Portugal, Slovakia,
Slovenia
09 Lithuania
10 Luxembourg
13 Czech Republic, United Kingdom
14 The Netherlands
21 United States of America

• **NATO phonetic alphabet** see
alphabet

natron
04 urao

natter
03 gab, jaw **04** chat, talk **06** confab,
gabble, gossip, jabber, rabbit, witter
07 blather, blether, chatter, chinwag,
prattle **08** chit-chat, rabbit on **10** chew
the fat **11** confabulate **12** conversation
14 shoot the breeze

nattily
06 neatly **07** smartly **09** elegantly,
stylishly **11** fashionably

natty
04 chic, deft, neat, trim **05** ritzy, smart
06 clever, dapper, snazzy, spruce,
swanky **07** elegant, stylish, varment,
varmint **09** ingenious **11** fashionable,
well-dressed

natural
03 nat, raw **04** open, pure, real
05 frank, idiot, plain, usual, whole
06 candid, common, inborn, inbred,
innate, kindly, native, normal, physic,
simple, virgin **07** artless, built-in,
connate, genuine, organic, regular,
relaxed, routine, sincere, typical,
unmixed **08** everyday, inherent,
lifelike, ordinary, standard, unforced
09 authentic, certainty, guileless,
ingenuous, ingrained, inherited,
intuitive, unrefined, unstudied
10 congenital, indigenous, unaffected,
unlaboured, unstrained **11** instinctive,
spontaneous, unprocessed
12 additive-free, chemical-free,
illegitimate, run-of-the-mill,

unregenerate **13** unpretentious
15 unsophisticated
See also **fool**

- **natural order**
02 NO

naturalist
08 botanist **09** biologist, Darwinist,
ecologist, zoologist **11** creationist
12 evolutionist **13** life scientist **14** plant
scientist
See also **biology**

naturalistic
07 factual, graphic, natural **08** lifelike,
real-life **09** realistic **10** true-to-life
12 photographic

naturalize
05 adapt, adopt **06** accept
08 accustom **09** acclimate, endenizen,
habituate, introduce **10** assimilate
11 acclimatize, acculturate,
domesticate, enfranchise, familiarize,
incorporate, nationalize

naturally
05 natch **06** simply **07** clearly, frankly
08 candidly, normally, of course
09 artlessly, certainly, genuinely,
logically, obviously, sincerely, typically
10 absolutely **11** ingenuously,
simpliciter **13** instinctively,
spontaneously

naturalness
04 ease **06** purity **07** realism
08 openness, pureness **09** frankness,
plainness, sincerity, wholeness
10 candidness, simpleness, simplicity
11 artlessness, genuineness, informality,
spontaneity **13** ingenuousness
14 unaffectedness **15** spontaneousness

nature
04 Gaia, kind, mood, sort, type
05 being, class, earth, stamp, style,
world **06** cosmos, humour, make-up,
temper **07** country, essence, outlook,
quality, scenery, species, variety
08 category, creation, features, identity,
universe **09** character, chemistry,
landscape, nakedness **10** attributes,
complexion, kindliness **11** countryside,
description, disposition, environment,
mother earth, personality,
temperament **12** constitution, mother
nature **14** characteristic, natural history
15 characteristics

- **according to nature**
02 sn
- **of nature**
04 akin

naught
01 O **03** bad, ill, nil **04** evil, nowt, zero
05 zilch **06** cipher, cypher, foiled,
nought, ruined **07** hurtful, immoral,
nothing, sweet FA **09** worthless
10 wickedness **11** nothingness
15 sweet Fanny Adams

naughtily
06 lewdly **07** bawdily **08** coarsely,
vulgarly **09** defiantly, obscenely,
playfully, waywardly **10** indecently,

perversely **12** badly behaved
13 disobediently, mischievously

naughtiness
08 defiance, lewdness, mischief
09 bawdiness, indecency, obscenity,
vulgarity **10** coarseness, smuttiness
11 playfulness, waywardness **12** bad
behaviour, disobedience,
misbehaviour

naughty
◊ *anagram indicator*
03 bad **04** blue, bold, lewd **05** bawdy
06 coarse, ribald, risqué, smutty, unruly,
vulgar, wicked **07** defiant, obscene,
playful, roguish, wayward **08** indecent,
perverse **09** off-colour, worthless
10 refractory **11** disobedient,
misbehaving, mischievous, titillating
12 badly behaved, exasperating,
incorrigible **13** undisciplined

Nauru
03 NAU, NRU

nausea
06 hatred, puking, wamble **07** disgust,
gagging **08** aversion, distaste, loathing,
retching, sickness, vomiting
09 revulsion **10** queasiness,
repugnance, throwing up
11 airsickness, biliousness, carsickness,
detestation, seasickness **12** sick
headache **14** motion sickness, travel
sickness **15** morning sickness

nauseate
04 turn **05** repel **06** loathe, offend,
revolt, sicken **07** disgust, scunner, turn
off **08** gross out, make sick **14** turn the
stomach **15** turn your stomach

nauseating
06 odious **08** nauseous **09** abhorrent,
loathsome, offensive, repellent,
repugnant, repulsive, revolting,
sickening **10** chunderous, detestable,
disgusting **11** distasteful **14** stomach-
turning **15** stomach-churning

nauseous
03 ill **04** puky, sick **05** nasty, pukey
06 queasy **07** airsick, carsick, seasick
09 loathsome, nauseated
10 disgusting, travel sick **14** about to
throw up **15** under the weather

nautical
05 naval **07** boating, oceanic, sailing
08 maritime, seagoing, yachting
09 seafaring

naval
03 nav, sea **06** marine **08** maritime,
nautical, seagoing **09** seafaring

navel
03 hub **06** centre, middle **07** nombril
08 omphalos **09** umbilicus **11** belly-
button, tummy-button

navigable
03 nav **04** open **05** clear **08** passable,
sailable **09** crossable, dirigible,
unblocked **10** negotiable, voyageable
11 traversable **12** surmountable,
unobstructed

navigate
04 helm, plan, plot, sail **05** cross, drive
guide, pilot, steer **06** cruise, direct,
handle, voyage **07** journey, skipper
09 manoeuvre, negotiate **11** plan a
course

navigation
03 nav **05** canal **06** voyage **07** guiding
nautics, sailing **08** cruising, guidance,
pilotage, piloting, seacraft, steering,
voyaging **09** directing, direction
10 seamanship **11** manoeuvring
12 helmsmanship **13** contact flight

*Navigational aids and systems
include:*

03 gee, GPS, INS, log, Vor
05 chart, loran, pilot, radar
07 compass, navarho, sextant
08 bell buoy, dividers, VHF radio
09 lightship, omnirange
10 depth gauge, lighthouse, marker
buoy
11 chronometer, conical buoy, echo-
sounder, gyrocompass
13 nautical table, parallel ruler
15 astronavigation, flux-gate compass
magnetic compass

navigator
03 nav **05** navvy, pilot **06** master,
sailor, seaman **07** mariner
08 helmsman **09** steersman

navvy
06 digger, ganger, worker **07** workman
08 labourer **09** navigator **12** manual
worker **14** common labourer

navy
01 N **02** RN **03** RAN **05** fleet, ships
06 armada **08** flotilla, warships
10 naval fleet, naval force **12** merchant
navy **15** merchant service
See also **rank**

nay
02 no **03** nae **06** denial, indeed, in fac
07 in truth **08** actually, not at all, or
rather **09** not really **11** of course not
12 certainly not **13** absolutely not, in
point of fact

near
02 by, nr, ny, to **03** nie, nye **04** akin,
come, dear, inby, left, like, nigh
05 alike, close, ewest, forby, handy,
inbye, local **06** almost, at hand, beside
come by, coming, nearby, nearly, next
to, stingy **07** cling to, close by, closely,
close to, looming, related, similar
08 adjacent, approach, familiar,
imminent, intimate, left-hand, narrowl
09 adjoining, alongside, bordering,
close in on, immediate, impending,
proximate, thriftily **10** accessible,
adjacent to, close-range, come closer,
come nearer, comparable, contiguous
convenient, draw near to, not far away
11 approaching, bordering on, come
towards, forthcoming, get closer to, in
the offing, move towards, surrounding
within cooee, within range, within
reach **12** contiguous to, draw nearer to
neighbouring, parsimonious

13 corresponding, within reach of
14 advance towards, closely related,
parsimoniously 15 at close quarters
• **draw near**
04 come
• **near thing**
08 near miss 09 close call 10 close
shave 11 nasty moment 12 narrow
escape, narrow squeak

nearby
04 near 05 close, handy 06 beside
07 close by 08 adjacent 09 adjoining
10 accessible, convenient, not far away
11 close at hand, within cooee, within
reach 12 neighbouring 13 in the
vicinity 14 on your doorstep 15 at close
quarters

nearly
◊ deletion indicator
◊ tail deletion indicator
02 ny 03 e'en, nie, nye 04 even, nigh
05 about, close 06 all but, almost,
feckly, nigh on 07 closely, close on,
close to, roughly 08 à peu près, as
good as, nigh-hand, well-nigh 09 just
about, verging on, virtually
10 intimately, more or less
11 practically 13 approximately
14 parsimoniously, scrutinizingly
15 close but no cigar

nearness
06 degree 08 affinity, dearness,
intimacy, vicinity 09 closeness,
handiness, immediacy, imminence,
proximity 10 chumminess, contiguity
11 familiarity, propinquity
12 availability, neighborhood
13 accessibility, appropinquity,
neighbourhood

near-sighted
06 myopic 08 purblind 09 half-blind
12 short-sighted

neat
02 ox 03 apt, cow, net 04 bull, cool,
deft, dink, feat, good, mega, nett, nice,
oxen, pure, smug, snod, tidy, tosh, trig,
trim 05 clean, clear, crisp, dinky, genty,
great, handy, jemmy, jimpy, natty, nifty,
short, slick, smart, super, tight
06 adroit, cattle, clever, dainty, dapper,
donsie, expert, nimble, pretty, simple,
spruce, superb, wicked 07 band-box,
cleanly, compact, elegant, featous,
ordered, orderly, shining, skilful,
unmixed 08 clean-cut, fabulous,
feateous, featuous, finished, sensible,
smashing, straight, terrific, well-made
09 admirable, dexterous, effective,
efficient, excellent, fantastic,
ingenious, organized, practised,
shipshape, undiluted, wonderful
10 convenient, marvellous,
tremendous 11 well-groomed, well-
ordered 12 spick-and-span,
undiminished, user-friendly, well-
designed 13 unadulterated, well-
organized 15 in apple-pie order

neaten
◊ anagram indicator
04 edge, prim, tidy, trim 05 clean,

groom 06 tidy up 07 arrange, clean up,
smarten 08 round off, spruce up
09 smarten up 10 square away,
straighten 11 put to rights

neatly
04 jimp 05 aptly 06 deftly, fairly, featly,
jimply, nicely, nimbly, tidily 07 adeptly,
agilely, handily, smartly 08 adroitly,
cleverly, daintily, expertly, prettily,
sprucely 09 elegantly, precisely,
skilfully, stylishly 10 accurately,
feateously, gracefully 11 dexterously,
efficiently 12 conveniently, effortlessly,
methodically 14 systematically

neatness
05 grace, skill, style 06 nicety
07 agility, aptness 08 accuracy,
deftness, elegance, niceness, tidiness,
trimness 09 adeptness, dexterity,
handiness, jemminess, precision,
smartness 10 adroitness, cleverness,
daintiness, efficiency, expertness,
nimbleness, spruceness 11 orderliness,
preciseness, skilfulness, stylishness
12 gracefulness, straightness
14 methodicalness

Nebraska
02 NE 04 Nebr

nebulous
03 dim 04 hazy 05 fuzzy, misty, vague
06 cloudy 07 obscure, shadowy,
unclear 08 abstract, confused,
formless, unformed 09 ambiguous,
amorphous, imprecise, shapeless,
uncertain 10 indefinite, indistinct
13 indeterminate

necessarily
04 thus 06 needly 08 no remedy,
obligate, of course, perforce
09 certainly, naturally, therefore
10 inevitably, inexorably, willy-nilly
11 accordingly, ineluctably,
inescapably, of necessity, unavoidably
12 by definition, compulsorily,
consequently, nolens volens
13 automatically, axiomatically,
indispensably

necessary
04 sure 05 money, needy, vital
06 needed, toilet 07 certain, crucial,
needful 08 enforced, required 09 de
rigueur, essential, mandatory, requisite
10 compulsory, imperative, inevitable,
inexorable, obligatory 11 ineluctable,
inescapable, predestined, unavoidable
13 indispensable

necessitate
04 mean, need, take 05 exact, force
06 compel, demand, entail, oblige
07 call for, involve, require
09 constrain 13 make necessary

necessity
04 fate, must, need, want 06 ananke,
demand, mister, need-be, penury
07 destiny, poverty 08 exigence,
exigency, extremes, hardship
09 certainty, emergency, essential,
indigence, privation, requisite
10 compulsion, obligation, sine qua

non 11 deprivation, desideratum,
destitution, fundamental, needfulness,
requirement 12 prerequisite
13 indispensable, inevitability,
inexorability 14 inescapability
• **of necessity**
05 needs 08 no remedy, perforce
09 certainly 10 inevitably, inexorably
11 inescapably, unavoidably 12 by
definition, compulsorily
13 automatically, indispensably

neck
03 col, pet 04 crag, kiss, nape, snog
05 drink, halse, hause, hawse, scrag
06 caress, cervix, scruff, smooch
08 audacity, canoodle 09 impudence
• **neck and neck**
04 even 05 drawn, equal, level 06 on a
par 07 aligned, uniform 08 balanced,
matching 10 nip and tuck, side by side
12 level pegging

necklace
04 band, torc 05 beads, chain
06 choker, corals, gorget, jewels,
locket, pearls, string, torque
07 negligé, pendant, rivière, sautoir
08 carcanet, negligee 10 lavallière
11 mangalsutra

necromancer
05 witch 06 wizard 07 diviner, warlock
08 conjurer, magician, sorcerer
09 sorceress, spiritist 11 thaumaturge
12 spiritualist 13 thaumaturgist

necromancy
05 magic 06 hoodoo, voodoo
07 sorcery 08 black art, witchery,
wizardry 09 spiritism 10 black magic,
demonology, divination, nigromancy,
witchcraft 11 conjuration,
enchantment, thaumaturgy
12 spiritualism 13 magical powers,
wonder-working

necropolis
08 cemetery, God's acre 09 graveyard
10 burial site, churchyard 11 burial
place 12 burial ground, charnel house

need
04 call, lack, miss, must, want, wish
05 crave 06 besoin, demand, desire,
egence, egency, have to, mister, rely on
07 call for, pine for, poverty, require
08 depend on, exigency, occasion,
shortage, yearn for 09 cry out for,
essential, necessity, neediness,
requisite 10 have need of,
inadequacy, obligation 11 be obliged
to, be reliant on, desideratum,
necessitate, requirement
12 prerequisite 13 be compelled to, be
dependent on, insufficiency,
justification 14 be desperate for
15 have occasion for
• **in need**
04 poor 05 needy 06 hard up
08 deprived, dirt-poor, indigent
09 destitute, penniless, penurious
11 impecunious 12 impoverished
13 disadvantaged 14 on the breadline
15 poverty-stricken, underprivileged

needed
06 wanted **07** desired, lacking
08 required **09** called for, essential, necessary, requisite **10** compulsory, obligatory

needful
05 needy, vital **06** needed **08** required **09** essential, necessary, requisite **10** stipulated **13** indispensable

needle
03 bug, irk, nag, nib, pin, sew **04** bait, barb, gall, goad, hand, hype, hypo, miff, nark, prod, rile, spud, spur **05** annoy, arrow, briar, get at, point, prick, quill, sharp, spike, spine, sting, taunt, thorn **06** bodkin, darner, enmity, harass, heckle, marker, nettle, niggle, pester, pierce, ruffle, stylus, thread, wind up **07** bramble, bristle, dislike, obelisk, pointer, prickle, provoke, spicule, syringe, torment **08** drive mad, dry-point, irritate, splinter **09** aggravate, indicator, penetrate **10** drive crazy **11** microneedle **12** drive bananas **13** darning-needle, make sparks fly, packing-needle **14** drive up the wall, knitting needle

needless
06 luxury **07** useless **08** unwanted **09** pointless, redundant, undesired **10** expendable, gratuitous **11** dispensable, purposeless, superfluous, uncalled-for, unnecessary
- **needless to say**
06 surely **07** no doubt **08** of course **09** certainly, naturally **10** by all means, definitely **11** doubtlessly, indubitably, undoubtedly **13** without a doubt

needlessly
09 uselessly **11** dispensably, pointlessly, redundantly **13** superfluously, unnecessarily

needlework
06 sewing **07** tatting **08** tapestry, woolwork **09** drawn work, fancywork, hemstitch, patchwork, piqué work, plainwork, stitching, white seam **10** crocheting, embroidery **11** cross-stitch, needlepoint, seamstressy, stitchcraft, worsted-work **12** saddle stitch

needy
04 poor **06** hard up, in need, strait **07** needful, wanting **08** deprived, dirt-poor, indigent **09** destitute, necessary, penniless, penurious **11** impecunious **12** impoverished **13** disadvantaged **14** on the breadline **15** poverty-stricken, underprivileged

ne'er-do-well
04 spiv **05** idler **06** dodger, dosser, loafer, skelum, skiver, waster **07** bludger, goof-off, lounger, shirker, skellum, slacker, wastrel **08** layabout, schellum **09** do-nothing **10** black sheep **14** good-for-nothing

nefarious
04 base, evil, foul, vile **06** odious,
sinful, unholy, wicked **07** heinous, satanic, vicious **08** criminal, depraved, dreadful, horrible, infamous, infernal, shameful, terrible **09** atrocious, execrable, loathsome, monstrous **10** abominable, detestable, horrendous, iniquitous, outrageous, villainous **11** opprobrious

negate
04 deny, undo, void **05** annul, quash **06** cancel, oppose, refute, reject, repeal, revoke, squash **07** explode, gainsay, nullify, rescind, retract, reverse, wipe out **08** abrogate, disprove, renounce **09** discredit, repudiate **10** contradict, invalidate, neutralize **11** countermand

negation
04 veto **06** denial, repeal **07** inverse, reverse **08** contrary, converse, opposite **09** disavowal, rejection **10** abrogation, antithesis, disclaimer **12** cancellation, renunciation **13** contradiction, nullification **14** countermanding, neutralization

negative
03 bad, neg **04** acid, deny, veto, weak **05** minus **06** denial, gloomy **07** adverse, counter, cynical, denying, harmful, hostile, hurtful, opposed, refusal, unlucky **08** contrary, critical, opposing, opposite, refusing, saying no **09** annulling, defeatist, injurious, rejection, spineless, unhelpful, unwilling **10** censorious, dissension, dissenting, gainsaying, neutralize, nullifying, unfriendly **11** conflicting, destructive, detrimental, obstructive, pessimistic, subtractive, uncongenial, unfortunate **12** antagonistic, inauspicious, invalidating, neutralizing, unfavourable, uninterested, unpropitious **13** contradiction, laevorotatory, unco-operative **14** unconstructive, unenthusiastic **15** disadvantageous

negativity
08 cynicism **09** defeatism, pessimism **10** gloominess **12** criticalness **13** unhelpfulness, unwillingness **14** lack of interest

neglect
◇ *anagram indicator*
04 fail, omit **05** abuse, scorn, shirk, skimp, spurn **06** disuse, fail in, forget, ignore, laxity, pass by, pass up, pigeon, rebuff, slight **07** abandon, default, disdain, disobey, failure, forsake **08** ignoring, incivism, infringe, leave out, let slide, omission, overlook, spurning **09** desuetude, disregard, disrepair, mislippen, oversight, slackness **10** be lax about, culpa levis, disrespect, leave alone, misprision, negligence, remissness **11** inattention, rack and ruin, shortcoming **12** carelessness, heedlessness, indifference **13** forgetfulness **14** non-performance

neglected
◇ *anagram indicator*
04 waif **07** forlorn, run-down, squalid **08** derelict, deserted, forsaken, stranded, unheeded, untended, untilled, unweeded **09** abandoned, overgrown **10** uncared-for **11** dilapidated, disregarded, undervalued, unhusbanded **12** uncultivated, unmaintained **13** unappreciated

neglectful
03 lax **06** remiss, sloppy **08** careless, derelict, heedless, uncaring **09** forgetful, negligent, oblivious, slighting, unmindful **11** inattentive, indifferent, thoughtless **12** disregardful

négligé dress
03 mob

negligence
◇ *anagram indicator*
06 laches, laxity, slight **07** default, failure, neglect **08** omission **09** culpa lata, disregard, oversight, slackness **10** remissness, sloppiness **11** inattention, shortcoming **12** carelessness, heedlessness, inadvertence, inadvertency, indifference **13** forgetfulness **15** inattentiveness, thoughtlessness

negligent
◇ *anagram indicator*
03 lax **05** slack **06** casual, remiss, sloppy **07** cursory, offhand **08** careless, dilatory, heedless, uncaring **09** forgetful, unmindful **10** neglectful, neglecting, nonchalant **11** inattentive, indifferent, thoughtless

negligible
04 tiny **05** minor, petty, small **06** minute, paltry **07** minimal, trivial **08** trifling **09** off the map **11** neglectable, unimportant **13** imperceptible, inappreciable, insignificant

negotiable
03 neg **04** open **05** clear **08** arguable, passable **09** crossable, debatable, navigable, unblocked, undecided, unsettled **11** contestable, traversable **12** questionable, surmountable, unobstructed **14** open to question

negotiate
◇ *anagram indicator*
04 deal, pass, talk **05** agree, broke, clear, cross, float, treat **06** broker, confer, debate, fulfil, haggle, manage, parley, settle **07** arrange, bargain, consult, discuss, execute, mediate, pull off, resolve, traffic, work out **08** complete, conclude, contract, get round, pass over, surmount, transact, traverse **09** arbitrate, hammer out, intercede, intervene, thrash out **11** pass through **12** wheel and deal

negotiation
◇ *anagram indicator*
05 talks, treat **06** debate, parley, treaty **08** haggling, practice **09** diplomacy, mediation, parleying **10** bargaining,

conference, discussion, pulling-off
11 arbitration, transaction
12 hammering-out, thrashing-out

negotiator
06 broker **07** haggler **08** diplomat,
mediator, parleyer **09** bargainer, go-
between, moderator **10** ambassador,
arbitrator **11** adjudicator, intercessor
12 intermediary **13** wheeler-dealer

neigh
04 bray **05** hinny **06** nicher, nicker,
whinny **07** snicker, whicker

neighbour
03 bor **04** abut

neighbourhood
04 area, hood, part **06** locale, region
07 quarter **08** confines, district,
environs, locality, precinct, presence,
purlieus, vicinage, vicinity
09 community, proximity, voisinage
11 convicinity **12** surroundings
• **in the neighbourhood of**
04 near, up to **05** about, round
06 almost, around, nearby, next to
07 close to, roughly **13** approximately

neighbouring
04 near, next **05** local **06** nearby
07 nearest, vicinal **08** abutting,
adjacent, next-door **09** adjoining,
bordering, sistering **10** connecting,
contiguous, near at hand **11** close at
hand, surrounding

neighbourly
04 kind, warm **06** genial, social
07 affable, amiable, cordial, helpful
08 friendly, generous, obliging,
sociable **10** hospitable **11** considerate
13 companionable

nemesis
04 fate, ruin **07** destiny **08** downfall
09 vengeance **10** punishment
11 destruction, retribution **14** just
punishment

neodymium
02 Nd

neologism
07 coinage, new term, new word,
novelty **09** new phrase, vogue word
10 innovation **13** new expression

neon
02 Ne

neophyte
01 L **04** tiro **06** newbie, novice, rookie
07 learner, recruit, trainee **08** beginner,
newcomer **09** greenhorn, new
member, noviciate, novitiate
10 apprentice, raw recruit
11 probationer

Nepal
03 NEP, NPL

nephrite
02 yu

nepotism
04 bias **10** partiality **11** favouritism
12 old school tie **13** Old Boy network
14 jobs for the boys

Neptune
08 Poseidon

neptunium
02 Np

nerd see **fool**

nerk see **fool**

nerve
03 lip **04** face, gall, grit, guts, neck, will
05 brace, cheek, force, mouth, pluck,
sauce, sinew, spunk, steel **06** bottle,
daring, mettle, spirit, valour, vigour
07 bolster, bravery, courage, fortify,
hearten, prepare **08** audacity,
boldness, chutzpah, embolden,
firmness, strength, temerity
09 bowstring, brass neck, encourage,
endurance, fortitude, hardihood,
impudence, insolence **10** brazenness,
effrontery, invigorate, resolution,
strengthen **11** intrepidity, presumption
12 fearlessness, impertinence
13 determination, steadfastness
14 cool-headedness, self-confidence

Nerves include:
05 optic, ulnar, vagus
06 facial, lumbar, medial, median,
radial, sacral, tibial
07 femoral, phrenic, plantar, sciatic
08 axillary, brachial, peroneal, thoracic
09 cutaneous, laryngeal, occipital,
olfactory
10 splanchnic, trigeminal
11 intercostal
12 suboccipital
15 lesser occipital, spinal accessory

nerveless
04 calm, weak **05** inert, slack, timid
06 afraid, feeble, flabby **07** nervous
08 cowardly, unnerved **09** enervated,
spineless **11** debilitated

nerve-racking
05 tense **06** trying **07** anxious
08 worrying **09** difficult, harrowing,
maddening, stressful **10** nail-biting
11 disquieting, distressing, frightening

nerves
05 shock, worry **06** strain, stress,
wobbly **07** anxiety, jitters, tension,
twitter, willies **11** butterflies,
fretfulness, nervousness
12 collywobbles, crise de nerfs
13 heebie-jeebies **14** nervous
tension
• **get on someone's nerves**
03 bug, irk, nag, vex **04** fash, gall, rile
05 anger, annoy, tease **06** bother,
harass, hassle, madden, molest, pester,
plague, ruffle, wind up **07** disturb, hack
off, provoke, tick off, trouble **08** brass
off, irritate **09** aggravate, cheese off,
displease, drive nuts **10** drive crazy,
exasperate **12** drive bananas **13** make
sparks fly **14** drive up the wall **15** get
someone's goat, get your dander up

nervous
◊ *anagram indicator*
03 shy **04** edgy, toey **05** het up, jumpy,
nappy, nervy, shaky, tense, timid **06** on

edge, sinewy, strong, uneasy
07 anxious, fearful, fidgety, fretful, in a
stew, jittery, keyed up, quaking, twitchy,
uptight, worried, wound up
08 agitated, in a sweat, in a tizzy,
neurotic, skittish, strained, timorous,
vigorous **09** excitable, flustered,
perturbed, screwed-up, squirrely,
tremulous **10** disquieted, squirrelly
11 overwrought **12** all of a dither,
apprehensive, highly-strung **13** having
kittens, on tenterhooks

nervous breakdown
06 crisis **08** neurosis **10** cracking-up,
depression **11** melancholia **15** mental
breakdown, nervous disorder

nervously
◊ *anagram indicator*
06 edgily, on edge **07** in a stew, timidly
08 in a sweat, in a tizzy, uneasily
09 anxiously, fearfully, fretfully,
twitchily **13** having kittens
14 apprehensively

nervousness
05 worry **06** strain, stress **07** anxiety,
fluster, habdabs, tension, willies
08 disquiet, edginess, timidity
09 agitation **10** touchiness, uneasiness
11 stage fright **12** excitability,
perturbation, restlessness,
timorousness **13** heebie-jeebies,
tremulousness

nervy
04 cool, edgy, high **05** het up, jumpy,
shaky, tense **06** on edge, uneasy
07 anxious, fearful, fidgety, jittery,
keyed up, twitchy, uptight, worried,
wound up **08** agitated, impudent,
neurotic, strained **09** audacious,
excitable, flustered **12** apprehensive,
highly-strung **13** having kittens

nescient
05 dense, thick **06** stupid, unread
07 unaware **08** backward, clueless,
ignorant, untaught **09** unlearned,
untrained, unwitting **10** illiterate,
innumerate, uneducated, unfamiliar,
uninformed, unschooled **11** ill-
informed, uninitiated **12** unacquainted
13 inexperienced, unenlightened

ness
04 naze
See also **headland**

nest
03 den, mew, nid **04** aery, bike, bink,
byke, cage, cote, dray, drey, eyry, lair,
nide **05** aerie, ayrie, eyrie, haunt,
lodge, nidus, perch, roost **06** refuge,
settle, wurley **07** cabinet, hideout,
retreat, shelter **08** hideaway, hive-nest,
vespiary **09** bird-house, formicary,
termitary **10** nesting-box
11 formicarium, hiding-place,
termitarium **12** accumulation,
nidification **14** breeding-ground
See also **animal**

nest egg
04 fund **05** cache, funds, store

07 deposit, reserve, savings
08 reserves **12** bottom drawer

nestle
06 cuddle, curl up, huddle, nuzzle
07 cherish, snuggle **08** cuddle up
09 snuggle up **14** huddle together

nestling
04 baby **05** chick **08** suckling,
weanling **09** fledgling

net
◇ *containment indicator*
03 bag, end, get, let, nab, web **04** caul,
drag, earn, gain, lace, leap, make, mesh,
neat, nett, nick, pure, sean, take, toil,
trap, trim **05** broad, catch, clean, clear,
drift, final, raise, seine, snare, toils, total,
trawl **06** bright, cobweb, collar,
enmesh, lowest, obtain, pocket, pull in,
rake in, sagene, tunnel **07** bring in,
capture, dragnet, drop-net, ensnare,
fishnet, general, lattice, netting,
network, overall, realize, receive,
tracery, trammel, unmixed, webbing
08 after tax, drift-net, entangle, filigree,
meshwork, open work, seine net, take
home, take-home, ultimate **09** inclusive,
reticulum **10** accumulate, after taxes,
conclusive, difficulty **11** latticework,
take captive **15** after deductions

nether
03 low **05** basal, below, lower, under
06 bottom **07** beneath, hellish, Stygian
08 inferior, infernal **09** Plutonian
10 lower-level, underworld
11 underground

Netherlands
02 NL **03** NLD **04** Neth

Netherlands Antilles
02 NA **03** ANT

netherworld
03 pit **04** fire, hell **05** abyss, below,
Hades, Sheol **06** Erebus, Tophet
07 Abaddon, Acheron, Gehenna,
inferno **08** Tartarus **09** down there,
Malebolge, perdition **10** other place,
underworld **12** lower regions
13 bottomless pit **15** abode of the
devil, infernal regions

nettle
03 bug, vex **04** fret, goad, miff, nark,
rami, rile **05** annoy, chafe, get at, pique,
ramee, ramie, sting, tease, upset
06 harass, hassle, hen-bit, needle,
ruffle, urtica, wind up **07** incense,
provoke, torment **08** drive mad, irritate
09 aggravate, archangel, pellitory
10 drive crazy, exasperate **12** drive
bananas **13** make sparks fly
14 artillery-plant, discountenance,
drive up the wall **15** yellow archangel

nettled
05 angry, cross, got at, huffy, riled,
stung, vexed **06** bugged, galled,
goaded, miffed, narked, peeved,
piqued **07** annoyed, needled, rattled,
ruffled, wound up **08** harassed,
incensed, offended, provoked
09 aggrieved, driven mad, irritable,

irritated **10** aggravated **11** driven crazy,
exasperated **13** driven bananas
15 driven up the wall

network
03 CNN, LAN, MAN, net, PCN, WAN,
web **04** fret, grid, ISDN, lace, maze,
mesh, PSTN, rete **05** grill, nexus
06 matrix, plexus, sagene, system,
tracks **07** complex, lattice, netting,
tracery, webbing **08** channels, filigree,
gridiron, meshwork, open work
09 circuitry, grapevine, labyrinth,
reticulum, structure **10** Eurovision
11 arrangement, convolution,
latticework **12** old school tie,
organization, reticulation **13** bush
telegraph, Old Boy network

neurosis
05 mania **06** phobia **08** disorder,
fixation **09** deviation, obsession
10 affliction **11** abnormality,
derangement, disturbance, instability
13 maladjustment **14** mental disorder

neurotic
05 manic **06** phobic **07** anxious,
deviant, nervous **08** abnormal,
deranged, paranoid, unstable
09 disturbed, obsessive, unhealthy
10 compulsive, hysterical, irrational
11 maladjusted, overanxious,
overwrought **14** hypersensitive

neuter
01 n **03** fix, gib **04** geld, neut, spay
05 dress **06** agamic, clonal, doctor,
gib-cat **07** agamous, asexual, neutral,
sexless **08** caponize, castrate, conidial
09 castrated, sterilize **10** emasculate
11 monogenetic **12** intransitive

neutral
04 drab, dull, fawn, gray, grey, pale
05 beige, bland, white **06** neuter,
pastel **07** anaemic, anodyne, insipid
08 detached, ordinary, unbiased
09 anonymous, impartial, objective,
undecided **10** colourless, even-
handed, indefinite, indistinct, non-
aligned, open-minded, uninvolved
11 indifferent, inoffensive, nondescript,
non-partisan, unassertive,
uncommitted **12** non-combatant, non-
committal, unprejudiced,
unremarkable **13** disinterested,
dispassionate, uninteresting
14 expressionless **15** unexceptionable

neutrality
10 detachment **11** disinterest
12 impartiality, non-alignment,
unbiasedness **13** impartialness
14 non-involvement **15** non-
intervention

neutralize
04 kill, undo **05** annul **06** cancel,
negate, offset **07** balance, nullify
08 negative **09** cancel out, frustrate,
make up for **10** counteract, invalidate
12 incapacitate **13** compensate for
14 counterbalance

Nevada
02 NV **03** Nev

never
03 not **04** nary, ne'er **05** no way **07** not
ever, Tib's Eve **08** at no time, not at all,
Tibb's Eve **09** St Tib's Eve **10** St Tibb's
Eve **11** on no account, when pigs fly
13 not for a moment, not on your life
15 not on your nellie

never-ending
◇ *tail deletion indicator*
07 endless, eternal, non-stop
08 constant, infinite, unbroken,
unending **09** boundless, incessant,
limitless, permanent, perpetual,
unceasing **10** continuous, persistent,
relentless, unchanging, without end
11 everlasting, unremitting
12 interminable **13** uninterrupted

nevertheless
03 but, tho, yet **05** still **06** algate,
anyhow, anyway, at that, even so,
howe'er, though, withal **07** algates,
however **08** after all **09** in any case,
quand même **10** all the same, by any
means, for all that, in any event, malgré
tout, not but what, regardless, still and
on, tout de même **11** by some means,
just the same, none but what,
nonetheless, still and all **13** at the same
time **15** notwithstanding

new
◇ *anagram indicator*
01 N **04** mint, more, span **05** added,
alien, extra, fresh, green, novel, young
06 latest, maiden, modern, modish,
recent, trendy, unused, virgin, way out
07 altered, another, changed, current,
further, newborn, nouveau, renewed,
resumed, strange, topical, unknown,
unusual **08** advanced, brand-new,
creative, ignorant, improved, nouvelle,
original, reformed, restored, unversed,
up-to-date **09** a stranger, born-again,
different, fledgling, ingenious,
refreshed **10** additional, avant-garde,
fledgeling, futuristic, innovative,
modernized, newfangled, pioneering,
present-day, redesigned, remodelled,
unfamiliar **11** imaginative, regenerated,
resourceful, spanking-new, ultra-
modern **12** contemporary,
experimental, unaccustomed,
unacquainted **13** inexperienced,
reinvigorated, revolutionary, state-of-
the-art, supplementary, up-to-the-
minute **14** ground-breaking,
unconventional **15** newly discovered

New Brunswick
02 NB

newcomer
04 tiro **05** alien, pupil **06** blow-in,
gryfon, newbie, novice, rookie **07** arrival,
griffin, griffon, gryphon, incomer,
learner, pilgrim, recruit, settler, trainee
08 beginner, colonist, freshman, intruder,
jackaroo, jackeroo, jillaroo, neophyte,
outsider, stranger **09** foreigner,
greenhorn, immigrant **10** apprentice,
new arrival, tenderfoot **11** probationer

newfangled
03 new **05** novel **06** modern, recent,

trendy **08** gimmicky **10** futuristic
11 fashionable, modernistic, ultra-
modern **12** contemporary **13** state-of-
the-art

Newfoundland and Labrador
02 NL

New Hampshire
02 NH

New Jersey
02 NJ

newly
◇ *anagram indicator*
04 anew, just **05** fresh **06** afresh, lately,
of late **07** freshly **08** latterly, recently

New Mexico
02 NM **04** N Mex

newness
06 novity, oddity **07** novelty, recency
09 freshness **10** innovation,
uniqueness **11** originality, strangeness,
unusualness **13** unfamiliarity

news
03 gen, oil **04** data, dope, info, word
05 facts, story **06** advice, budget,
exposé, gossip, latest, report, rumour
07 account, hearing, hearsay,
lowdown, message, scandal, tidings
08 bulletin, dispatch, izvestia,
newscast, news item **09** izvestia,
newsflash, speerings, speirings,
statement **10** communiqué, disclosure,
revelation **11** information
12 announcement, developments,
intelligence, press release
13 advertisement, communication

News agencies include:

02 AP, PA
03 AAP, AFP, UPI
04 NZPA, Tass
07 Reuters
08 ITAR-Tass
15 Associated Press

• **piece of news**
04 item, unco

newspaper
03 rag **04** blat, post **05** blatt, daily,
local, organ, paper, press, print, sheet
06 weekly **07** evening, gazette,
journal, quality, tabloid, tribune
08 magazine, national, regional
09 telegraph **10** broadsheet, local
paper, periodical, provincial
11 publication **12** evening paper,
morning paper **13** national paper,
regional paper **15** provincial paper

*Newspapers and magazines
include:*

02 FT, GQ, Ms, OK!
03 FHM, NME, Red, She, Sun, TES, TLS,
Viz
04 Best, Chat, Chic, Elle, Heat, Judy,
Life, Mail, Mind, Mizz, Mojo, More!,
Real, THES, Time
05 Bella, Bliss, Bunty, Hello!, Mandy,
Maxim, Prima, Punch, Times, Vogue,
Which?, Wired, Woman
06 Forbes, Granta, Lancet, Loaded,

Mirror, Nature, The Sun, War Cry
07 Company, Esquire, Express,
Fortune, Glamour, Hustler, Le
Monde, Mayfair, Men Only,
Newsday, Options, Playboy,
Science, The Chap, The Face, The
Lady, The Star, Time Out, Tribune, TV
Times
08 Campaign, Die Woche, Gay Times,
Guardian, Le Figaro, Newsweek,
New Woman, Scotsman, The
Beano, The Dandy, The Eagle, The
Field, The Month, The Oldie, The
Times, USA Today
09 Daily Mail, Daily Star, Ideal Home,
Penthouse, Q Magazine, Red
Pepper, Smash Hits, Telegraph, The
Friend, The Grocer, The Herald, The
Mirror, The People, The Tablet, The
Tatler, Woman's Own
10 Asian Times, Daily Sport, Irish Times,
Private Eye, Racing Post, Radio
Times, Sunday Post, Take a Break,
Vanity Fair
11 Church Times, Country Life, Daily
Record, Marie Claire, Melody
Maker, Morning Star, Sunday Sport,
The Big Issue, The European, The
Guardian, The Observer, The
Universe, Woman's Realm
12 Angling Times, Cosmopolitan, Daily
Express, Family Circle, Fortean
Times, History Today, Mail on
Sunday, New Scientist, New
Statesman, Poetry Review, Sunday
Mirror, The Economist, The Pink
Paper, The Spectator, Time
Magazine, Woman's Weekly
13 Catholic Times, Daltons Weekly,
Farmers Weekly, Homes and Ideas,
Horse and Hound, Just Seventeen,
Mother and Baby, People's Friend,
Reader's Digest, Sunday Express,
The Bookseller, The Watchtower,
Woman's Journal
14 Caribbean Times, Catholic Herald,
Financial Times, House and
Garden, Literary Review, News of
the World, The Boston Globe, The
Independent, The New York Post,
The Sunday Times, The Times
Higher, Washington Post
15 Evening Standard, Exchange and
Mart, Harpers and Queen, Homes
and Gardens, Sunday Telegraph,
The Boston Herald, The Mail on
Sunday, The New York Times

*Newspaper proprietors and
magnates include:*

04 King (Cecil Harmsworth), Ochs
(Adolph Simon), Shah (Eddy)
05 Astor (John Jacob, Lord), Astor
(William Waldorf, Viscount), Black
(Conrad, Lord)
06 Aitken (Sir Max), Graham
(Katherine Meyer), Hearst (William
Randolph), Packer (Sir Frank),
Ridder (Bernard H, Jnr), Walter (John)
07 Barclay (Sir David), Barclay (Sir
Frederick), Camrose (William Ewert
Berry, Viscount), Kemsley (James

Gomer Berry, Viscount), Maxwell
(Robert), Murdoch (Rupert),
Pearson (Sir Cyril Arthur), Riddell
(George, Lord), Scripps (Edward
Wyllis), Thomson (D C), Thomson
(Roy, Lord)
08 Pulitzer (Joseph)
10 Berlusconi (Silvio), Harmsworth
(Alfred, Viscount), Harmsworth
(Harold, Viscount)
11 Beaverbrook (Max, Lord)

See also **journalist**

newspaperman *see* **journalist**

newsreader
06 anchor **07** newsman **08** reporter
09 anchorman, announcer,
newswoman, presenter **10** journalist,
newscaster **11** anchorwoman,
commentator **13** correspondent

newsworthy
07 notable, topical, unusual
09 arresting, important **10** noteworthy,
remarkable, reportable **11** interesting,
significant, stimulating

newt
03 ask, eft **05** asker

New York
◇ *dialect indicator*
02 NY

New York boroughs include:

06 Queens
08 Brooklyn, The Bronx
09 Manhattan
12 Staten Island

*Other districts of New York
include:*

04 Noho, Soho
06 Corona, Harlem, Hollis, Inwood,
Nolita, Queens
07 Astoria, Chelsea, Clifton, Kips Bay,
Midtown, Midwood, Tribeca
08 Brooklyn, Canarsie, East Side, El
Barrio, Elmhurst, Flatbush, Flatiron,
Flushing, Gramercy, Rego Park,
Steinway, The Bronx, West Side
09 Briarwood, Chinatown, Flatlands,
Manhattan, Ozone Park, Park Slope,
Princeton, Ridgewood, The Bowery,
Turtle Bay, Woodhaven, Yorkville
10 Cobble Hill, Douglaston,
Greenpoint, Ground Zero, Kew
Gardens, Marble Hill, Sunset Park
11 Borough Park, Central Park, Coney
Island, East Village, Ellis Island,
Forest Hills, Howard Beach, Little
Italy, Little Korea, New Brighton,
West Village
12 Alphabet City, Crown Heights,
Cypress Hills, Hell's Kitchen, South
Jamaica, Staten Island, Williamsburg
13 Brighton Beach, Lower East Side,
Spanish Harlem, Upper East Side,
Upper West Side
14 Jackson Heights, Long Island City,
Lower Manhattan, Manhattan
Beach, Stuyvesant Town
15 Brooklyn Heights, Garment
District, Roosevelt Island

New Zealand
02 NZ **03** NZL

See also **electorate; governor; premier; prime minister; province; team**

next
04 syne, then **05** along, later **06** beside
07 closest, ensuing, nearest
08 adjacent **09** adjoining, alongside, bordering, following, immediate, proximate **10** afterwards, contiguous, subsequent, succeeding, successive, tangential, thereafter **11** approximate
12 neighbouring, subsequently
13 after that time

next-door
08 adjacent

nibble
03 bit, eat **04** bite, gnaw, knap, moop, moup, nosh, peck, pick **05** crumb, munch, piece, snack, taste **06** morsel, pick at, titbit **07** knapple

Nicaragua
03 NIC

nice
03 bad, coy **04** cute, fine, good, kind **05** canny, civil, close, exact, sweet **06** dainty, decent, genial, kindly, lovely, minute, polite, strict, subtle, tickle, wanton **07** amiable, amusing, careful, likable, precise, refined, welcome **08** accurate, careless, charming, critical, delicate, friendly, likeable, pleasant, ticklish **09** agreeable, appealing, courteous, endearing, enjoyable, hazardous **10** acceptable, attractive, delectable, delightful, fastidious, meticulous, particular, satisfying, scrupulous **11** good-natured, pleasurable, respectable, sympathetic **12** entertaining, good-humoured, satisfactory, well-mannered **13** understanding
14 discriminating

nicely
04 well **07** civilly **08** politely, properly **09** agreeably **10** pleasantly, pleasingly **11** courteously, pleasurably, respectably **12** attractively, delightfully **14** satisfactorily

niceness
05 charm **08** kindness **10** amiability, politeness **11** likableness **12** friendliness, likeableness, pleasantness **13** agreeableness **14** attractiveness, delightfulness, respectability

nicety
06 nuance **07** coyness, finesse, quiddit **08** accuracy, delicacy, quiddity, subtlety **09** exactness, fine point, precision, punctilio **10** choiceness, minuteness, perjinkity, refinement **11** distinction **14** fastidiousness, meticulousness, scrupulousness

niche
04 nook, slot **05** place **06** alcove, corner, cranny, exedra, hollow, métier, mihrab, recess, shrine **07** calling, exhedra, opening **08** position, vocation **09** cubbyhole **10** fenestella, pigeonhole, tabernacle **11** columbarium **14** specialist area **15** specialized area

nick
02 do **03** can, cut, jug, lag, nab, rob **04** bust, chip, dent, deny, form, jail, mark, nail, quod, scar, snip, take **05** catch, choky, clink, Devil, notch, pinch, run in, score, shape, sneck, snick, state, steal, swipe **06** arrest, collar, cooler, damage, fettle, groove, health, indent, inside, pick up, pilfer, pocket, prison, pull in, snitch **07** capture, defraud, scratch, slammer **08** knock off, porridge **09** apprehend, condition, jailhouse **11** indentation **13** police station

See also **prison; steal**

nickel
02 Ni

nickname
06 byname, to-name **07** epithet, moniker, pet name **08** cognomen, monicker **09** sobriquet **10** diminutive, soubriquet **12** familiar name

See also **Australian football; football; state; team**

nifty
03 apt **04** chic, deft, fine, neat **05** agile, nippy, quick, sharp, slick, smart **06** adroit, clever, spruce **07** skilful, stylish **08** pleasing **09** enjoyable, excellent

Niger
02 RN **03** NER

Nigeria
03 NGA, NGR, WAN

Nigerian
03 Ibo, Tiv **04** Efik, Igbo, Nupe **05** Hausa

niggardliness
08 meanness, scarcity **09** closeness, parsimony, smallness **10** inadequacy, meagreness, paltriness, scantiness, skimpiness, stinginess **11** miserliness **12** cheeseparing, grudgingness **13** insufficiency **14** ungenerousness **15** tight-fistedness

niggardly
04 hard, mean **05** close, mingy, nippy, nirly, small **06** meagre, measly, niding, nirlie, paltry, scanty, skimpy, stingy **07** miserly, nithing, sparing **08** grudging, near-gaun, nidering, ungiving **09** illiberal, miserable, niddering, niderling, penny-wise, penurious **10** hard-fisted, inadequate, near-begaun, nidderling, ungenerous **11** tight-fisted **12** cheeseparing, insufficient, parsimonious

niggle
03 bug, nag **04** carp, gnaw, moan **05** annoy, cavil, query, upset, worry **06** bother, hassle, pick on, potter, trifle **07** henpeck, nit-pick, protest, quibble, trouble **08** complain, irritate, keep on at **09** complaint, criticism, criticize, objection **10** nit-picking **12** equivocation, pettifogging **13** prevarication

night

04 dark, evil, nite **05** death **06** sorrow **07** evening **08** darkmans, darkness **09** ignorance, night-time, obscurity **10** affliction **11** dead of night **15** hours of darkness

• **pass the night**
03 lie

nightclub

04 club **05** disco **06** nitery **07** cabaret, hot spot, niterie **09** nightspot **11** boîte de nuit, discotheque

nightfall

04 dark, dusk **06** sunset **07** evening, sundown **08** gloaming, twilight **10** crepuscule

nightingale

04 Lind **06** bulbul, Progne **08** Philomel **09** Philomela, Philomene

• **sound of nightingale**
03 jug

nightly

07 at night **09** after dark, each night **10** every night **11** nocturnally **15** night after night

nightmare

05 agony, trial **06** horror, ordeal **07** anguish, incubus, torment, torture **08** bad dream, calamity **09** cacodemon, cauchemar, ephialtes **10** cacodaemon **11** oneirodynia **13** hallucination **15** awful experience

nightmarish

06 creepy, unreal **07** ghostly, scaring **08** alarming, dreadful, horrible, horrific **09** agonizing, harrowing **10** disturbing, terrifying **11** frightening

night-time

04 dark **05** night **08** darkness **11** dead of night **15** hours of darkness

nihilism

06 denial **07** anarchy, atheism, nullity **08** cynicism, disorder, negation, oblivion **09** disbelief, emptiness, pessimism, rejection, terrorism **10** abnegation, negativism, scepticism **11** agnosticism, lawlessness, nothingness, repudiation **12** non-existence, renunciation

nihilist

05 cynic **07** atheist, sceptic **08** agitator, agnostic **09** anarchist, extremist, pessimist, terrorist **10** antinomian, negativist **11** disbeliever, negationist **13** revolutionary

Nike

08 Victoria

nil

01 O **04** duck, love, none, nowt, zero **05** zilch **06** cipher, cypher, naught, nought **07** nothing

nimble

04 deft, spry, yald **05** agile, alert, brisk, fleet, light, lithe, nippy, quick, ready, smart, swack, swift, wanle, wight, yauld **06** active, clever, lissom, lively, prompt, quiver, volant, wandle,

wannel, wimble **07** deliver, lissome, springe **08** flippant, graceful **09** fleetfoot, sharp-eyed, sprightly **10** sure-footed **11** light-footed, quick-moving, quick-witted, sharp-witted **13** quick-thinking

nimbleness

05 grace, skill **07** agility, finesse **08** alacrity, deftness, legerity, spryness **09** alertness, dexterity, lightness, niftiness, nippiness, smartness **10** adroitness **13** sprightliness

nimbly

04 fast **06** deftly, easily, spryly **07** agilely, alertly, briskly, lightly, quickly, readily, sharply, smartly, swiftly **08** actively, promptly, snappily, speedily **11** dexterously **12** proficiently **13** quick-wittedly

nincompoop

04 clot, dolt, fool, nerd, poop, twit **05** chump, dunce, idiot, twerp, wally **06** dimwit, nitwit **07** plonker **08** numskull **09** blockhead, ignoramus, simpleton

nine

02 IX **06** ennead **08** nonuplet, novenary, Pierides

nineteen

03 XIX

ninety

02 XC

ninny *see* fool

niobium

02 Nb

nip

02 go **03** fly, lop, nep, pop, ren, rin, run, sip **04** bite, clip, dart, dash, dock, dram, drop, grip, rush, shot, snip, tear **05** catch, chack, check, hurry, pinch, smart, sneap, steal, taste, tweak **06** arrest, nibble, snatch **07** catmint, draught, portion, squeeze, swallow **08** cutpurse, mouthful

• **nip in the bud**
04 curb, halt, stem, stop **05** block, check **06** arrest, impede **08** obstruct **09** frustrate

nipple

03 dug, pap, tit **04** teat **05** diddy, udder **06** breast **07** mamilla, papilla **08** mammilla

nippy

03 icy, raw **04** cold, fast, spry **05** agile, brisk, quick, sharp **06** active, biting, chilly, frosty, nimble, speedy **07** nipping, pungent **08** piercing, stinging, waitress **09** niggardly, sprightly

nirvana

03 joy **05** bliss, peace **06** heaven **07** ecstasy **08** paradise, serenity **10** exaltation **12** tranquillity **13** enlightenment

nit-picking

05 fussy **07** carping, finicky

08 captious, pedantic **09** cavilling, quibbling **12** pettifogging **13** hair-splitting, hypercritical

nitrogen

01 N **02** az- **03** azo-

nitty-gritty

06 basics **09** key points **10** bottom line, brass tacks, essentials, main points **12** fundamentals, nuts and bolts

nitwit

03 ass **04** clot, dope, fool, jerk, prat, twit **05** chump, dumbo, idiot, neddy, ninny, wally **06** dimwit, drongo **07** pillock, plonker **09** birdbrain, blockhead, simpleton **10** nincompoop, silly-billy

Niue

03 NIU

no

◇ *deletion indicator*
01 O **02** na **03** nae, nay, non, not **04** none, nope, uh-uh, zero **05** no way **06** aikona, denial, never a **07** refusal **08** not at all, no thanks **09** not really **11** of course not **12** certainly not, nothing doing **13** absolutely not, not on your life **14** not on your nelly, over my dead body

nob

03 VIP **04** head, toff **06** bigwig, fat cat **07** big shot **09** personage **10** aristocrat

nobble

◇ *anagram indicator*
02 do **03** buy, nab **04** bust, dope, drug, foil, grab, nail, nick, take **05** bribe, catch, check, get at, pinch, run in, seize, steal, swipe **06** arrest, buy off, collar, defeat, hinder, pick up, pilfer, pull in, snitch, thwart **07** disable, swindle, warn off **08** knock off, threaten **09** frustrate, hamstring, influence **10** intimidate **12** incapacitate **13** interfere with

nobelium

02 No

Nobel Prize

Nobel Prize winners include:

02 Fo (Dario), Oë (Kenzaburo)
03 Lee (Tsung-Dao), Orr (Lord Boyd), Paz (Octavio), Tum (Rigoberta Menchú)
04 Belo (Carlos), Bohr (Aage), Bohr (Niels), Böll (Heinrich), Born (Max), Buck (Pearl S), Cela (Camilo José), Duve (Christian de), Gide (André), Hume (John), Hunt (Tim), Katz (Sir Bernard), King (Martin Luther), Koch (Robert), Mann (Thomas), Mott (Sir Nevill F), Nash (John), Rabi (Isidor Isaac), Rous (Peyton), Shaw (George Bernard), Tutu (Desmond), Urey (Harold C)
05 Annan (Kofi), Bethe (Hans), Bloch (Felix), Bragg (Sir Lawrence), Bragg (Sir William), Bunin (Ivan), Camus (Albert), Chain (Sir Ernst), Crick (Francis), Curie (Marie), Curie

(Pierre), **Debye** (Peter), **Dirac** (Paul A M), **Ebadi** (Shirin), **Eliot** (T S), **Euler** (Ulf von), **Fermi** (Enrico), **Golgi** (Camillo), **Grass** (Günter), **Haber** (Fritz), **Hesse** (Hermann), **Jerne** (Niels), **Klerk** (F W de), **Krebs** (Sir Hans), **Kroto** (Sir Harold), **Lewis** (Sinclair), **Libby** (Willard F), **Lwoff** (André), **Monod** (Jacques), **Nurse** (Sir Paul), **Pauli** (Wolfgang), **Peres** (Shimon), **Rabin** (Yitzhak), **Sachs** (Nelly), **Salam** (Abdus), **Simon** (Claude), **Soddy** (Frederick), **Stern** (Otto), **Yeats** (W B)

06 Arafat (Yasser), **Baeyer** (Adolf von), **Bellow** (Saul), **Bordet** (Jules), **Calvin** (Melvin), **Carrel** (Alexis), **Cronin** (James Watson), **Debreu** (Gerard), **Enders** (John F), **Florey** (Howard, Lord), **France** (Anatole), **Frisch** (Ragnar), **Glaser** (Donald A), **Hamsun** (Knut), **Heaney** (Seamus), **Hevesy** (George von), **Hewish** (Antony), **Huxley** (Andrew F), **Lorenz** (Konrad), **Myrdal** (Gunnar), **Nernst** (Walther), **Neruda** (Pablo), **O'Neill** (Eugene), **Pavlov** (Ivan), **Perutz** (Max F), **Planck** (Max), **Porter** (George, Lord), **Sanger** (Frederick), **Sartre** (Jean-Paul), **Singer** (Isaac Bashevis), **Tagore** (Rabindranath), **Walesa** (Lech), **Watson** (James), **Wiesel** (Elie), **Wilson** (Robert)

07 Akerlof (George A), **Alferov** (Zhores I), **Alvarez** (Luis), **Axelrod** (Julius), **Banting** (Sir Frederick G), **Beckett** (Samuel), **Behring** (Emil von), **Brenner** (Sydney), **Brodsky** (Joseph), **Canetti** (Elias), **Coetzee** (JM), **Dae-jung** (Kim), **Ehrlich** (Paul), **Feynman** (Richard P), **Fleming** (Sir Alexander), **Glashow** (Sheldon), **Golding** (William), **Hershey** (Alfred), **Hodgkin** (Dorothy), **Hodgkin** (Sir Alan L), **Jelinek** (Elfriede), **Jiménez** (Juan Ramón), **Kendrew** (John), **Kertész** (Imre), **Khorana** (H Gobind), **Kipling** (Rudyard), **Laxness** (Halldór), **Maathai** (Wangari), **Mahfouz** (Naguib), **Mandela** (Nelson), **Marconi** (Guglielmo), **Márquez** (Gabriel García), **Mauriac** (François), **Medawar** (Sir Peter), **Mistral** (Frédéric), **Mommsen** (Theodor), **Naipaul** (VS), **Pauling** (Linus), **Penzias** (Arno), **Röntgen** (Wilhelm Konrad), **Rotblat** (Joseph), **Russell** (Bertrand, Earl), **Seaborg** (Glen T), **Seifert** (Jaroslav), **Soyinka** (Wole), **Thomson** (J J), **Trimble** (David), **Waksman** (Selman A), **Walcott** (Derek), **Whipple** (George H), **Wilkins** (Maurice)

08 Appleton (Sir Edward V), **Asturias** (Miguel Angel), **Chadwick** (Sir James), **Delbrück** (Max), **Einstein** (Albert), **Faulkner** (William), **Friedman** (Milton), **Gajdusek** (D Carleton), **Gell-Mann** (Murray), **Gordimer** (Nadine), **Hartwell**

(Leland H), **Langmuir** (Irving), **Leontief** (Wassily), **Meyerhof** (Otto), **Millikan** (Robert A), **Milstein** (Cesar), **Morrison** (Toni), **Mulliken** (Robert S), **Northrop** (John H), **Sakharov** (Andrei), **Saramago** (José), **Shockley** (William B), **Tiselius** (Arne), **Tonegawa** (Susumu), **Weinberg** (Steven), **Xingjian** (Gao)

09 Arrhenius (Svante), **Becquerel** (Henri), **Cherenkov** (Pavel), **Churchill** (Sir Winston), **Dalai Lama**, **Gorbachev** (Mikhail), **Hemingway** (Ernest), **Kissinger** (Henry), **Markowitz** (Harry M), **Mechnikov** (Ilya), **Michelson** (Albert A), **Nirenberg** (Marshall W), **Pasternak** (Boris), **Prudhomme** (Sully), **Rainwater** (James), **Roosevelt** (Theodore), **Sholokhov** (Mikhail), **Steinbeck** (John), **Tinbergen** (Jan), **Tinbergen** (Nikolaas)

10 Galsworthy (John), **Heisenberg** (Werner), **Hofstadter** (Robert), **Lagerkvist** (Pär), **McClintock** (Barbara), **Modigliani** (Franco), **Pirandello** (Luigi), **Ramos-Horta** (José), **Rutherford** (Ernest, Lord), **Szymborska** (Wislawa)

11 Joliot-Curie (Frédéric), **Joliot-Curie** (Irène), **Kantorovich** (Leonid), **Landsteiner** (Karl), **Maeterlinck** (Maurice), **Ramón y Cajal** (Santiago), **Schrödinger** (Erwin), **van der Waals** (Johannes Diderik), **Zinkernagel** (Rolf M)

12 Hammarskjöld (Dag), **Mother Teresa**, **Solzhenitsyn** (Aleksandr), **Szent-Györgyi** (Albert)

13 Aung San Suu Kyi, **Chandrasekhar** (Subrahmanyan), **García Márquez** (Gabriel)

14 Levi-Montalcini (Rita)

---

nobility

04 nobs, rank **05** élite, glory, lords, peers, toffs **06** family, gentry, honour, nobles, virtue **07** dignity, majesty, peerage **08** eminence, grandeur, noblesse **09** grandness, integrity, nobilesse, nobleness, splendour **10** excellence, generosity, worthiness **11** aristocracy, high society, magnanimity, stateliness, superiority, uprightness **12** generousness, magnificence **14** impressiveness **15** illustriousness

The nobility includes:

01 d, E, P
02 Bt, Kt, Pr
03 Dom, Don, Duc
04 Bart, dame, duke, earl, jarl, lady, lord, Marq, peer
05 baron, count, laird, liege, nawab, noble, ruler, thane
06 daimio, Junker, knight, squire, vidame
07 baronet, dowager, duchess, marquis, peeress, vicomte
08 baroness, countess, governor, life peer, margrave, marquess,

nobleman, seigneur, starosta, toiseach, vavasour, viscount
09 grand duke, liege lord, magnifico, patrician
10 aristocrat, noblewoman
11 marchioness, viscountess
12 grand duchess
13 grand seigneur

noble

04 fine, gent, high, lady, lord, peer **05** brave, grand, great, lofty, manly **06** gentle, landed, manful, titled, vidame, worthy **07** eminent, exalted, gallant, grandee, magnate, stately **08** atheling, douzeper, elevated, generous, glorious, handsome, high-born, honoured, imposing, majestic, nobleman, splendid, virtuous **09** dignified, doucepere, excellent, patrician, unselfish, venerated **10** aristocrat, honourable, impressive, noblewoman **11** blue-blooded, high-ranking, illustrious, magnanimous, magnificent, noble-minded **12** aristocratic, great-hearted **13** distinguished **15** self-sacrificing
See also **nobility**

nobly

07 bravely **08** manfully, worthily **09** gallantly **10** generously, honourably, virtuously **11** unselfishly

nobody

04 Nemo **05** no one **06** cipher, menial, Pooter **07** naebody, nothing **09** nonentity **10** mediocrity **11** lightweight

nocturnal

05 night **09** night-time **13** active at night

nod

03 bow, dip, nap **04** beck, doze, sign **05** agree, sleep **06** accept, assent, beckon, drowse, nid-nod, noddle, nutate, salute, signal **07** approve, doze off, drop off, gesture, incline, support **08** greeting, indicate, say yes to **10** fall asleep, indication **11** acknowledge **15** acknowledgement

• **give the nod to**
02 OK **03** buy **04** back, pass **05** adopt, allow, carry **06** accept, permit, ratify, second, uphold **07** agree to, approve, confirm, endorse, mandate, support **08** assent to, hold with, sanction, validate **09** authorize, consent to **11** rubber-stamp

• **nod off**
03 nap **04** doze **05** sleep **06** drowse **07** doze off, drop off, slumber **10** fall asleep

node

03 bud **04** bump, knob, knot, lump **05** joint, nodus **06** growth, nodule **08** junction, swelling **09** carbuncle **11** convergence **12** protuberance

noise

◇ *homophone indicator*
03 cry, din, pop, row **04** bang, boom, chug, clap, coil, roar, talk, wham, zoom

05 blare, clash, clunk, sound, whang
06 babble, bicker, clamor, hubbub, jangle, outcry, racket, report, rumble, rumour, tumult, uproar **07** brattle, clamour, clangor, clatter, discord, thunder **08** announce, clangour **09** circulate, commotion, publicize **11** pandemonium
• **amount of noise**
02 dB **03** bel, dBA **04** phon, PNdB **07** decibel

noiseless
04 mute, soft **05** mousy, quiet, still **06** hushed, mousey, silent **07** catlike **09** inaudible, soundless

noiselessly
06 softly **07** quietly **08** silently **09** inaudibly **11** soundlessly

noisily
06 loudly, wallop **07** rowdily **10** fortissimo **11** deafeningly **12** boisterously, resoundingly, tumultuously, vociferously

noisome
03 bad **04** foul **05** fetid **06** foetid, putrid, smelly **07** harmful, hurtful, noxious, reeking **08** mephitic, stinking **09** injurious, obnoxious, offensive, poisonous, repulsive, unhealthy **10** disgusting, malodorous, nauseating, pernicious **11** deleterious, pestiferous, unwholesome **12** disagreeable, pestilential

noisy
01 f **02** ff **04** loud **05** roary, rowdy, vocal **06** roarie **07** blaring, blatant, booming, rackety, roaring **08** blasting, blattant, boastful, piercing, plangent, strepent **09** clamorous, deafening, turbulent **10** blusterous, boisterous, hoity-toity, strepitant, strepitoso, thundering, tumultuous, vociferous **11** rumbustious **12** ear-splitting, obstreperous
• **not too noisy**
02 mf

nomad
03 San **04** Bedu **05** rover **06** Beduin, roamer, Tuareg **07** Bedouin, Bushman, migrant, rambler, Saracen, swagger, swagman, vagrant **08** Khoikhoi, vagabond, wanderer **09** Hottentot, itinerant, transient, traveller

nomadic
05 Gypsy **06** Beduin, roving, Tuareg **07** Bedouin, migrant, roaming, vagrant **08** drifting, Khoikhoi, Scythian **09** itinerant, migratory, unsettled, wandering **10** travelling **11** peripatetic **13** peregrinating

nom-de-plume
05 alias **07** pen-name **09** pseudonym **11** assumed name

nomenclature
06 naming **08** locution, taxonomy **10** vocabulary **11** phraseology, terminology **12** codification **14** classification

nominal
03 nom **04** tiny **05** nomin, small, token **06** formal, puppet **07** minimal, titular, trivial **08** so-called, supposed, symbolic, trifling **09** professed, purported **10** figurehead, in name only, ostensible, peppercorn, self-styled **11** theoretical **13** insignificant

nominally
08 formally **10** in name only, ostensibly **12** symbolically **13** theoretically

nominate
04 name, term **05** elect, put up, voice **06** assign, choose, select, submit **07** appoint, elevate, present, propose, suggest **09** designate, postulate, recommend **10** commission, substitute

nomination
06 choice, naming **08** election, proposal **09** selection **10** submission, suggestion **11** appointment, designation **14** recommendation

nominative
01 n **03** nom

nominee
06 runner **07** entrant **08** assignee **09** appointee, candidate **10** contestant

nomogram
04 abac

non-alcoholic drink *see* **drink**

non-aligned
07 neutral **09** impartial, undecided **10** uninvolved **11** independent, non-partisan, uncommitted **13** disinterested

nonchalance
04 calm, cool **06** aplomb **08** calmness, coolness **09** composure, sangfroid, unconcern **10** detachment, equanimity **11** insouciance **12** indifference **13** pococurantism **14** pococuranteism, self-possession

nonchalant
04 calm, cool **05** blasé **06** casual **07** offhand **08** careless, detached, laid-back **09** apathetic, collected, easy-going **10** insouciant **11** indifferent, pococurante, unconcerned **13** dispassionate, imperturbable **15** cool as a cucumber

non-combatant
06 dovish **07** conchie, neutral **08** civilian, pacifist **10** non-aligned, non-violent **11** non-fighting, peacemaking **12** conciliatory, unaggressive **14** non-belligerent **15** passive resister

non-committal
04 wary **05** vague **07** careful, evasive, guarded, neutral, politic, prudent, tactful **08** cautious, discreet, reserved **09** ambiguous, equivocal, tentative **10** diplomatic, indefinite **11** circumspect, unrevealing

non compos mentis
03 ape, fey, mad **04** bats, gyte, loco, nuts, wild **05** barmy, batty, buggy, crazy, daffy, dippy, dotty, flaky, gonzo,

loony, loopy, manic, nutty, potty, queer, wacko, wacky, wiggy **06** crazed, cuckoo, fruity, insane, maniac, mental, raving, red-mad, screwy **07** bananas, barking, berserk, bonkers, cracked, frantic, lunatic, meshuga **08** crackers, demented, deranged, dingbats, doolally, frenetic, frenzied, maniacal, unhinged, unstable **09** disturbed, lymphatic, psychotic, up the wall **10** bestraught, distracted, distraught, frantic-mad, off the wall, off your nut, out to lunch, stone-crazy, unbalanced **11** not all there, off the rails, off your head **12** mad as a hatter, off your chump, round the bend **13** off your rocker, of unsound mind, out of your head, out of your mind, out of your tree, round the twist **14** off your trolley, wrong in the head **15** out of your senses

nonconformist
05 rebel **06** chapel **07** heretic, oddball, radical, seceder **08** maverick **09** dissenter, dissident, eccentric, heretical, protester **10** iconoclast **11** dissentient **12** secessionist **13** individualist, unco-operative **14** fish out of water

nonconformity
06 heresy **07** dissent **09** deviation, secession **10** heterodoxy **11** originality **12** eccentricity

nondescript
04 dull **05** bland, plain, vague **07** anaemic, insipid, vanilla **08** ordinary **11** commonplace, featureless, uninspiring **12** cookie-cutter, run of the mill, unattractive, unclassified, unremarkable **13** indeterminate, no great shakes, undistinctive, unexceptional, uninteresting **14** common or garden **15** undistinguished

non-drinking
02 TT **03** dry **10** on the wagon

none
01 O **02** no **03** nil **04** zero **05** no one, zilch **06** nobody, not any, not one **07** nothing **08** not a soul **10** not even one **13** not a single one
• **none the …**
02 no **07** not a bit **08** not at all **10** to no extent

nonentity
06 cipher, cypher, menial, nobody **07** nothing **08** shlepper **09** non-person, schlepper **10** mediocrity **11** lightweight

non-essential
08 unneeded **09** accessory, excessive, redundant **10** expendable, extraneous, peripheral **11** dispensable, inessential, superfluous, unimportant, unnecessary **13** supplementary

nonetheless
03 but, yet **05** still **06** anyhow, anyway, even so, though **07** however **08** after all **09** in any case **10** all the same, by

any means, for all that, in any event, regardless **11** by some means, just the same **12** nevertheless **13** at the same time **15** notwithstanding

non-event
04 no-no **06** fiasco **07** let-down **08** comedown **09** damp squib **10** anticlimax **14** disappointment

non-existence
05 fancy **07** absence, chimera, unbeing **08** illusion **09** unreality **11** nothingness **12** illusiveness

non-existent
04 null **06** unborn, unreal **07** fancied, fantasy, missing, phantom, unbeing **08** fanciful, illusory, imagined, mythical **09** fictional, imaginary, legendary **10** chimerical, fictitious, immaterial **11** incorporeal **12** hypothetical **13** hallucinatory, insubstantial, suppositional

non-fiction

Non-fiction works include:

06 Walden
07 Capital, Who's Who
08 Self-Help
09 Kama Sutra, Leviathan, On Liberty, Table Talk, The Phaedo
10 Das Kapital, The Annales, The Gorgias, The Poetics, The Timaeus
11 Down the Mine, Mythologies, The Agricola, The Analects, The Germania, The Phaedrus, The Republic
12 Novum Organum, Silent Spring, The City of God, The Second Sex, The Symposium
13 The Story of Art
14 A Room of One's Own, Birds of America, Eudemian Ethics, Inside the Whale, Modern Painters, Past and Present, Sartor Resartus, The Age of Reason, The Golden Bough, The Life of Jesus, The Rights of Man, The Selfish Gene
15 Lives of the Poets, The Essays of Elia, The Female Eunuch, The Sleepwalkers

non-flammable
09 fireproof **10** flameproof **12** not flammable **13** fire-resistant, incombustible, uninflammable **14** flame-resistant

non-intervention
06 apathy **07** inertia **08** inaction **09** passivity **12** laissez-faire, non-alignment **14** hands-off policy, non-involvement **15** non-interference

non-Jew
03 goy **07** gentile

nonpareil
06 unique **09** matchless **10** inimitable, unequalled, unrivalled **12** incomparable, unparalleled, without equal **13** beyond compare

non-partisan
07 neutral **08** detached, unbiased

09 impartial, objective **10** even-handed **11** independent **12** unprejudiced **13** dispassionate

nonplus
04 faze, stun **05** sew up, stick, stump **06** baffle, dismay, puzzle **07** astound, confuse, flummox, mystify, perplex, stagger **08** astonish, bewilder, confound **09** discomfit, dumbfound, embarrass, take aback **10** disconcert, perplexity **11** flabbergast **14** discountenance

nonplussed
05 blank, fazed **07** at a loss, baffled, floored, puzzled, stumped, stunned **08** dismayed **09** astounded, flummoxed, perplexed **10** astonished, bewildered, confounded, taken aback **11** dumbfounded, embarrassed **12** disconcerted **13** flabbergasted **14** out of your depth

non-professional
03 lay **04** laic **07** amateur

nonsense
03 gum, rot **04** blah, bosh, bull, bunk, cack, cock, crap, gaff, guff, jazz, junk, kack, pulp, punk, tosh **05** balls, bilge, borak, borax, folly, fudge, haver, hooey, pants, squit, stuff, trash, tripe **06** blague, bunkum, drivel, faddle, footle, gammon, havers, hoop-la, humbug, kibosh, kybosh, piffle, waffle **07** baloney, blather, blether, boloney, doggrel, eyewash, flannel, garbage, hogwash, malarky, pisheog, rhubarb, rubbish, twaddle **08** all my eye, blah-blah, blathers, blethers, bumfluff, claptrap, cobblers, doggerel, flimflam, malarkey, pishogue, tommyrot, trifling, unreason **09** absurdity, bull's wool, fandangle, gibberish, kidstakes, moonshine, mouthwash, poppycock, silliness, stupidity **10** balderdash, clamjamfry, codswallop, flapdoodle, galimatias, jabberwock, mumbo-jumbo, taradiddle, tomfoolery **11** clanjamfray, double Dutch, fiddle-de-dee, fiddlestick, foolishness, jabberwocky, tarradiddle **12** blah-blah-blah, clamjamphrie, fiddle-faddle, fiddlesticks, gobbledegook, gobbledygook **13** gas and gaiters, horsefeathers, senselessness **14** how's your father, ridiculousness

See also **rubbish**

nonsensical
◊ *anagram indicator*
05 barmy, crazy, dotty, inane, nutty, potty, silly, wacky **06** absurd, stupid **07** fatuous, foolish **08** crackpot **09** gibberish, ludicrous, senseless **10** irrational, ridiculous **11** hare-brained, meaningless **12** preposterous **14** unintelligible

nonsmoker
02 ns

non-stop
07 endless, ongoing **08** constant, steadily, unbroken, unending

09 ceaseless, endlessly, incessant, unceasing **10** constantly, continuous, persistent, relentless, unbrokenly, unendingly **11** ceaselessly, incessantly, never-ending, unceasingly, unfaltering **12** continuously, interminable, interminably, relentlessly **13** round-the-clock, unfalteringly, uninterrupted, unrelentingly, unremittingly **15** uninterruptedly

non-violent
06 dovish, irenic **07** passive **08** pacifist, peaceful **09** peaceable

noodle
04 head, udon **05** moony, Sammy **09** blockhead, improvise, simpleton
See also **head**

nook
03 den **04** neuk **05** angle, niche **06** alcove, cavity, corner, cranny, recess, refuge **07** hideout, opening, retreat, shelter **08** hideaway **09** cubbyhole

noon
01 m, n **06** midday, middle **08** twelve pm **09** lunchtime **10** meridional, twelve noon **12** twelve o'clock

noose
04 fank **05** snare **06** twitch **07** necktie **08** marriage, rope's end **12** hempen caudle

norm
03 par **04** mean, rule, type **05** gauge, model, scale **07** average, measure, pattern **08** standard **09** benchmark, criterion, principle, reference, usual rule, yardstick **10** touchstone

normal
05 usual **06** common **07** average, general, natural, popular, regular, routine, typical **08** accepted, everyday, habitual, ordinary, rational, standard, straight **10** accustomed, mainstream, reasonable, regulation **11** bog standard, commonplace **12** conventional, run of the mill, twenty-twenty, well-adjusted **13** perpendicular

normality
06 reason **07** balance, routine **08** normalcy **09** usualness **10** adjustment, commonness, regularity, typicality **11** averageness, naturalness, rationality **12** ordinariness **14** reasonableness **15** conventionality

normally
07 as a rule, as usual, usually **08** commonly **09** generally, naturally, regularly, routinely, typically **10** ordinarily **14** conventionally

Norse
01 N
See also **god, goddess**

north
01 N

North Atlantic Treaty Organization *see* NATO

North America see America;
Canada; United States of America

North Carolina
2 NC

North Dakota
2 ND 04 N Dak

north-east, north-eastern
2 NE

northern
1 N 05 north, polar 06 Arctic, boreal
9 northerly 11 hyperborean
3 septentrional

Northern Ireland see district; town

north-west, north-western
2 NW

Northwest Territories
2 NT

Norway
1 N 03 NOR

nose
03 neb, pry, pug 04 beak, bill, boko,
conk, ease, edge, feel, inch, push, snub
05 aroma, flair, nudge, scent, sense,
smell, snoot, snout 06 hooter, nozzle,
nuzzle, schnoz, snitch 08 informer,
instinct 09 proboscis, schnozzle
10 move slowly, perception, projection
• **get up your nose**
3 bug, irk, nag, vex 04 fash, gall, rile
05 anger, tease 06 bother, harass, hassle,
madden, molest, pester, plague, ruffle,
wind up 07 disturb, hack off, provoke,
tick off, trouble 08 brass off, irritate
09 aggravate, cheese off, displease,
drive nuts 10 drive crazy, exasperate
11 get your goat 12 drive bananas 13 get
on your wick, get your back up, make
sparks fly 14 drive up the wall, get your
blood up, give you the hump 15 get on
your nerves, get your dander up
• **nose around**
03 pry 05 snoop 06 search 10 poke
around, rubberneck 14 poke your nose
in
• **nose out**
06 detect, reveal 07 find out, inquire,
uncover 08 discover, sniff out
• **poke your nose into**
03 pry 05 pry in, snoop 06 butt in,
fiddle, tamper 07 intrude 08 meddle in
09 interfere, intervene 10 stickybeak,
tamper with 11 interfere in 12 put your
oar in 14 stick your oar in
• **under your nose**
07 clearly, plainly 09 obviously 10 plain
to see 11 for all to see 12 in front of you

nosedive
04 dive, drop 05 swoop 06 go down,
header, plunge, purler 07 decline,
plummet 08 get worse, submerge

nosegay
04 posy 05 bunch, spray 07 bouquet

nosey, nosy
06 prying 07 curious, probing
08 fragrant, snooping 10 meddlesome
11 inquisitive, interfering
13 eavesdropping

• **Nosey Parker**
08 busybody

nosh
03 eat, kai 04 diet, dish, eats, fare, feed,
food, grub, menu, tuck 05 board,
meals, scran, table 06 fodder, nibble,
stores, tucker, viands 07 cooking,
cuisine, rations 08 delicacy, eatables,
victuals 09 nutriment, nutrition
10 bush tucker, foodstuffs, provisions,
speciality, sustenance 11 comestibles,
nourishment, subsistence
12 refreshments

nosiness
06 prying 08 snooping 11 curiousness
12 interference 13 intrusiveness
14 meddlesomeness
15 inquisitiveness

nostalgia
06 pining, regret 07 longing, regrets
08 yearning 09 mal du pays
11 remembrance, wistfulness
12 homesickness, recollection,
reminiscence 13 recollections,
regretfulness, reminiscences

nostalgic
06 pining 07 longing, wistful
08 homesick, yearning 09 emotional,
regretful 11 reminiscent, sentimental

nostril
04 nare

nostrum
04 cure, drug, pill 06 elixir, potion,
remedy, secret 07 cure-all, panacea
08 medicine 13 universal cure
14 cure for all ills 15 universal
remedy

nosy see nosey, nosy

not
◊ anagram indicator
◊ deletion indicator
02 na, ne, no, -n't 03 non 04 nary, ne'er
05 never 06 polled
• **and not**
03 nor
• **has not**
03 nas 04 ain't, ha'n't
• **is not**
03 nis, nys 04 ain't
• **not out**
02 in, no

notability
03 VIP 04 fame, note 05 celeb
06 bigwig, esteem, renown, worthy
07 big shot, magnate, notable,
someone 08 big noise, eminence,
luminary, somebody, top brass 09 big
cheese, celebrity, dignitary, personage
10 importance 11 distinction,
heavyweight 12 significance
14 impressiveness, noteworthiness,
observableness

notable
03 VIP 04 rare, star 05 celeb, great
06 bigwig, clever, famous, marked,
signal, worthy 07 big shot, capable,
eminent, serious, someone, special,
unusual 08 big noise, luminary,

renowned, somebody, striking,
terrible, top brass, uncommon 09 big
cheese, celebrity, dignitary, important,
memorable, momentous, notorious,
personage, well-known 10 celebrated,
impressive, notability, noteworthy,
noticeable, observable, particular, pre-
eminent, remarkable 11 heavyweight,
illustrious, outstanding, significant
12 considerable 13 distinguished,
extraordinary, unforgettable

notably
08 above all, markedly, signally
09 eminently 10 distinctly, especially,
noticeably, remarkably, strikingly,
uncommonly 12 impressively, in
particular, particularly
13 conspicuously, outstandingly,
significantly 15 extraordinarily

notation
04 code 05 Romic, signs 06 cipher,
noting, record, script, system
07 symbols 08 alphabet 09 shorthand,
tablature 10 characters 11 Laban
system 13 hieroglyphics,
orchesography

notch
01 V 03 cut, gap, jag, lip 04 dent, gash,
gimp, hack, kerf, mark, mush, nick,
nock, snip, step 05 cleft, crena, gouge,
grade, level, score, sinus, stage, tally
06 degree, groove, indent, joggle,
raffle 07 achieve, scratch, serrate,
vandyke 08 incision, nail-hole, swan-
mark, undercut 09 insection
11 indentation
• **notch up**
04 gain, make 05 score 06 attain,
record 07 achieve, chalk up 08 register

notched
05 erose, jaggy 06 eroded, jagged,
nicked, pinked 07 dentate, serrate
08 dentated, serrated 09 serrulate
10 crenellate, emarginate, serrulated
11 crenellated, denticulate
12 denticulated

note
01 A, B, C, D, E, F, G, H, n 02 NB 03 log,
see 04 bill, care, chit, fame, heed, item,
line, long, mark, memo, mese, nete,
oner, show, tone, tune 05 breve, drone,
e-mail, enter, entry, fiver, gloss, large,
minim, music, one-er, token 06 chitty,
denote, detect, letter, minute, notice,
postil, quaver, record, regard, remark,
renown, signal, single, sticky, stigma,
symbol, tenner, twenty, wunner
07 account, apostil, comment,
element, epistle, jot down, jotting,
mention, message, middle c, missive,
observe, put down, receipt, refer to,
touch on, voucher, witness 08 allude
to, annotate, Bradbury, crotchet,
eminence, footnote, indicate,
perceive, prestige, register, reminder,
sforzato 09 apostille, attention,
greatness, non placet, semibreve,
sforzando, write down 10 annotation,
cognizance, commentary, fortepiano,
importance, impression, indication,

inflection, intimation, marginalia, memorandum, notability, reputation, semiquaver, stigmatize **11** consequence, distinction, explanation, explication, mindfulness, observation, pre-eminence **12** acciaccatura, put in writing, significance **13** attentiveness, become aware of, communication, consideration **14** characteristic, demisemiquaver **15** illustriousness

Musical notes of the sol-fa scale:
02 do (first), fa (fourth), la (sixth), me (third), mi (third), re (second), si (seventh), so (fifth), te (seventh), ti (seventh), ut (first) **03** doh (first), fah (fourth), lah (sixth), ray (second), soh (fifth), sol (fifth)

See also **strings of a lyre** *under* **string**

• **highest note**
03 e-la
• **of note**
04 some
• **take note**
02 NB **03** dig

notebook
03 log **05** diary **06** cahier, jotter, record **07** daybook, journal, logbook, notepad **09** field book, table-book **10** index rerum, pocket-book **11** address book **12** exercise book

noted
05 great **06** famous, marked, of note **07** eminent, notable **08** renowned **09** acclaimed, notorious, prominent, respected, well-known **10** celebrated, pre-eminent, recognized **11** illustrious **13** distinguished

notes
05 draft **06** record, report, sketch **07** minutes, outline **08** jottings, synopsis **10** adversaria, commentary, personalia, transcript **11** impressions

noteworthy
06 marked **07** notable, unusual **08** striking **09** important, memorable **10** impressive, particular, remarkable **11** exceptional, outstanding, significant **13** extraordinary

nothing
01 O **03** nil, nix, zip **04** love, nada, nowt, void, zero **05** nihil, squat, zilch, zippo **06** cipher, cypher, menial, naught, nix-nie, nobody, nought, sod all, trifle, vacuum **07** nullity, sweet FA **08** naething, oblivion **09** emptiness, nonentity, not an iota, not a thing, worthless **10** mediocrity **11** diddly-squat, lightweight, nothingness **12** non-existence **15** sweet Fanny Adams
• **doing nothing**
04 idle
• **for nothing**
04 free **06** gratis, in vain **08** at no cost, futilely **09** to no avail **10** as a freebie, needlessly, on the house **12** free of charge, with no result **13** complimentary, without charge **14** unsuccessfully

• **nothing but**
04 just, only **06** merely, simply, solely **11** exclusively
• **nothing more**
04 mere

nothingness
04 nada, void **06** vacuum **07** nullity, vacuity **08** nihilism, nihility, oblivion **09** emptiness **12** non-existence **13** worthlessness **14** insignificance

notice
02 ad **03** see **04** bill, crit, espy, gaum, gorm, heed, mark, mind, news, note, sign, spot, tent **05** order **06** advert, advice, behold, detect, poster, regard, remark, review, si quis **07** comment, discern, leaflet, make out, mention, observe, thought, warning, write-up **08** appraisal, bulletin, circular, civility, critique, handbill, interest, monition, pamphlet, perceive **09** attention, awareness, criticism **10** cognizance, intimation, take heed of, take note of **11** declaration, distinguish, information, instruction, observation **12** announcement, intelligence, notification, watchfulness **13** advertisement, become aware of, communication, consideration **14** pay attention to
• **give in your notice**
04 quit **05** leave **06** resign **07** walk out **08** step down **09** stand down **13** pack in your job **14** chuck in your job
• **give someone notice**
03 axe **04** fire, sack, warn **05** eject **07** boot out, dismiss, kick out **08** get rid of **09** discharge

noticeable
04 bold **05** clear, plain **06** marked, patent **07** evident, notable, obvious, visible **08** distinct, manifest, powerful, striking **10** detectable, impressive, measurable, observable, pronounced **11** appreciable, conspicuous, discernible, distinction, perceptible, significant **12** unmistakable **15** distinguishable

noticeably
07 clearly, notably, plainly, visibly **08** markedly, patently **09** evidently, obviously **10** distinctly, strikingly **11** discernibly, perceptibly **12** unmistakably **13** conspicuously, significantly

notification
05 aviso **06** advice, notice **07** message, telling, warning **09** informing, statement **10** disclosure, divulgence **11** declaration, information, publication **12** announcement, intelligence **13** communication **14** acknowledgment **15** acknowledgement

notify
04 tell, warn **05** alert **06** advise, inform, reveal **07** apprise, caution, declare, divulge, placard, publish **08** acquaint, announce, disclose **09** broadcast, make known **11** communicate

notion
04 idea, mind, view, whim, wish **05** fancy, vapor **06** belief, desire, liking, notice, revery, theory, vapour **07** caprice, concept, impulse, inkling, opinion, project, reverie, thought, wrinkle **08** crotchet, supposal, whim-wham **10** assumption, conception, conviction, hypothesis, impression **11** abstraction, inclination **12** anticipation, apprehension **13** understanding

notional
05 ideal **06** unreal **07** fancied **08** abstract, fanciful, illusory, thematic **09** imaginary, unfounded, visionary **10** conceptual, ideational **11** speculative, theoretical **12** hypothetical **14** classificatory

notionally
08 in theory **10** putatively **12** conceptually **13** conjecturally, theoretically **14** hypothetically

notoriety
06 infamy **07** obloquy, scandal **08** disgrace, ignominy **09** celebrity, dishonour, disrepute, esclandre, publicity **10** opprobrium

notorious
05 noted **06** arrant, notour **07** blatant, glaring **08** flagrant, ill-famed, infamous **09** egregious, well-known **10** proverbial, scandalous **11** disgraceful, ignominious, of ill repute, opprobrious **12** disreputable **13** dishonourable

notoriously
06 openly **07** notably, overtly **08** arrantly, patently **09** blatantly, glaringly, obviously **10** flagrantly, infamously **11** egregiously **12** disreputably, particularly, scandalously **13** disgracefully, dishonourably, ignominiously, opprobriously, spectacularly

notwithstanding
03 for, yet **05** howbe **06** even so, for all, maugre, though **07** despite, howbeit, however, maulgre **08** although, nathless, naythles **09** in spite of, natheless **10** for all that, nathelesse **11** nonetheless, non obstante **12** nevertheless, regardless of **13** at the same time

nought
01 O **03** nil, nix **04** nada, nowt, null, zero **05** zilch **06** cipher, cypher, naught **07** nothing **11** nothingness
See also **nothing**

noun
01 n **06** aptote, gerund **11** substantive

nourish
03 aid **04** feed, have, help, rear, tend **05** boost, nurse **06** assist, foster, suckle **07** advance, bring up, care for, cherish, educate, forward, further, nurture, promote, support, sustain **08** attend to, maintain **09** cultivate, encourage,

stimulate **10** provide for, strengthen, take care of

nourishing
04 good **06** battle **08** nutrient
09 healthful, nutritive, wholesome
10 beneficial, nutritious **11** substantial
12 alimentative, health-giving, invigorating **13** strengthening

nourishment
04 diet, eats, food, grub, nosh, tuck
05 juice, scran **07** aliment, ingesta, pabulum **08** goodness **09** nouriture, nutriment, nutrition **10** nourriture, sustenance **11** subsistence

nouveaux riches
08 parvenus, upstarts **10** arrivistes, the new rich

Nova Scotia
02 NS

novel
◇ *anagram indicator*
03 new **04** book, epic, rare, tale
05 fresh, roman, story **06** modern, unique **07** Aga saga, fiction, romance, strange, unusual **08** creative, hardback, original, uncommon
09 different, ingenious, inventive, narrative, paperback **10** innovative, pioneering, unfamiliar, unorthodox, yellowback **11** imaginative, resourceful, three-decker **12** bodice-ripper, double-decker, nouveau roman
13 Bildungsroman, unprecedented
14 ground-breaking, unconventional

Novels and fictional works include:

03 Kim, She, USA
04 Emma, Jazz, Nana, Voss
05 Kipps, Money, Porgy, Scoop, Sybil
06 Ben Hur, Carrie, Herzog, Lolita, Nausea, Pamela, Rob Roy, The Sea, Trilby, Utopia, Walden
07 Babbitt, Beloved, Candide, Catch-22, Cat's Eye, Dracula, Erewhon, Euphues, Ivanhoe, Justine, Lord Jim, Orlando, Rebecca, Shirley, The Bell, The Fall, Ulysses
08 Adam Bede, Birdsong, Clarissa, Cranford, Disgrace, Germinal, Jane Eyre, Lavengro, Lucky Jim, Moby Dick, Newcomes, Nostromo, Oroonoko, Peter Pan, Rasselas, The Idiot, The Trial, The Waves, The Years, Tom Jones, Tom Thumb, Villette, Waverley
09 About a Boy, Amsterdam, Beau Geste, Billy Budd, Billy Liar, Dead Souls, Dubliners, Gargantua, Hard Times, Kidnapped, L'Étranger, On the Road, Rogue Male, The Devils, The Egoist, The Hobbit, The Warden, Tom Sawyer, White Fang
10 A Man in Full, Animal Farm, Bleak House, Cancer Ward, Cannery Row, Clayhanger, Don Quixote, East of Eden, Edwin Drood, Fever Pitch, Goldfinger, Howards End, Kenilworth, Labyrinths, Lorna Doone, Persuasion, Rural Rides, The Leopard, The Rainbow, The Tin Drum, Titus Alone, Titus Groan, Uncle Remus, Vanity Fair, Westward Ho!, White Teeth
11 A Tale of a Tub, Black Beauty, Burmese Days, Cakes and Ale, Daisy Miller, Gormenghast, Greenmantle, Little Women, Middlemarch, Mrs Dalloway, Oliver Twist, Silas Marner, Steppenwolf, The Big Sleep, The Hireling, The Outsider, The Talisman, The Third Man, War and Peace, Women in Love
12 Anna Karenina, A Severed Head, A Suitable Boy, Barnaby Rudge, Brighton Rock, Casino Royale, Dombey and Son, Fear of Flying, Frankenstein, Little Dorrit, Madame Bovary, Moll Flanders, Of Mice and Men, Old Mortality, Rip Van Winkle, Room at the Top, The Go-Between, The Golden Ass, The Lost World, Volsungasaga
13 A Kind of Loving, Arabian Nights, Brave New World, Call of the Wild, Daniel Deronda, Doctor Zhivago, Finnegans Wake, Joseph Andrews, Just So Stories, Les Misérables, Mansfield Park, Metamorphosis, New Grub Street, North and South, Schindler's Ark, Sketches By Boz, Smiley's People, Sons and Lovers, Tarka the Otter, The Awkward Age, The Bostonians, The Golden Bowl, The Jungle Book, The Last Tycoon, The Mabinogion, The Naked Lunch, The Odessa File, Thérèse Raquin, The Virginians, Under Milk Wood, Winnie-the-Pooh, Zuleika Dobson
14 A Handful of Dust, A Room with a View, A Town Like Alice, Cider with Rosie, Death on the Nile, Decline and Fall, Fathers and Sons, Humphry Clinker, Jude the Obscure, Le Morte d'Arthur, Lord of the Flies, Lord of the Rings, Robinson Crusoe, Roderick Random, The Ambassadors, The Coral Island, The Da Vinci Code, The First Circle, The Forsyte Saga, The Great Gatsby, The Human Comedy, The Kraken Wakes, The Long Goodbye, The Lovely Bones, The Secret Agent, The Time Machine, The Water-Babies, The Woodlanders, Treasure Island, Tristram Shandy, Tropic of Cancer, Uncle Tom's Cabin, What Maisie Knew
15 A Christmas Carol, A Farewell to Arms, A Passage to India, Cold Comfort Farm, Daphnis and Chloe, Flaubert's Parrot, Gone with the Wind, Huckleberry Finn, Le Rouge et le Noir, Northanger Abbey, Our Mutual Friend, Peregrine Pickle, Tarzan of the Apes, The African Queen, The Invisible Man, The Little Prince, The Old Wives' Tale, The Secret Garden, The Woman in White, Three Men in a Boat, To the Lighthouse, Under the Volcano, Vernon God Little, Where Eagles Dare

novelist
06 author, fabler, writer **09** innovator
10 newsmonger, news-writer
11 storyteller **12** man of letters
13 fiction writer **14** creative writer, woman of letters
See also **author**

novelty
06 bauble, gadget, trifle **07** gimmick, memento, newness, primeur, trinket
08 gimcrack, rareness, souvenir
09 curiosity, freshness **10** creativity, difference, innovation, knick-knack, uniqueness **11** originality, strangeness, unusualness **13** unfamiliarity
15 imaginativeness

November
01 N **03** Nov

novice
01 L **03** cub, kyu **04** tiro, tyro **05** chela, pupil **06** gryfon, newbie, rookie
07 amateur, griffin, griffon, grommet, gryphon, learner, new chum, recruit, student, trainee **08** beginner, neophyte, newcomer **09** greenhorn, noviciate, novitiate **10** apprentice, raw recruit **11** probationer

noviciate
06 novice **08** training **09** novitiate, probation **10** initiation **11** trial period
13 trainee period **14** apprenticeship

now
02 AD **04** next, then **05** today **06** at once **07** just now, present **08** directly, nowadays, promptly, right now **09** at present, currently, instantly, presently, right away, these days **10** at this time
11 at the moment, immediately
12 straight away, without delay **15** for the time being

• **now and then**
07 at times **08** on and off
09 sometimes **10** on occasion
11 desultorily, now and again
12 infrequently, occasionally, once in a while, periodically, sporadically
13 spasmodically **14** from time to time, intermittently

nowadays
02 AD **03** now **05** today **09** at present, currently, presently, these days **10** at this time **11** at the moment **15** in this day and age

noxious
04 foul **05** toxic **06** deadly **07** harmful, nocuous, noisome, ruinous
08 damaging, menacing **09** injurious, malignant, obnoxious, poisonous, unhealthy **10** contagious, disgusting, pernicious **11** deleterious, destructive, detrimental, pestiferous, threatening, unwholesome

nozzle
03 jet **04** nose, rose **05** snout, spout,

tweer, twier, twire, twyer **06** stroup, tuyère, twyere **07** ajutage, sparger, sprayer **08** adjutage **09** nosepiece, sprinkler **10** projection **13** sprinkler head

nuance
04 hint **05** shade, tinge, touch, trace **06** degree, nicety **07** shading **08** overtone, subtlety **09** gradation, suspicion **10** refinement, suggestion **11** distinction **15** fine distinction

nub
04 core, crux, gist, hang, knob, lump, meat, pith **05** chunk, focus, heart, pivot, point **06** centre, kernel, marrow **07** essence, gallows, nucleus **12** central point, protuberance

nubile
04 sexy **05** adult **06** mature **09** desirable **10** attractive, voluptuous **12** marriageable

nuclear
01 N

nucleus
◇ *middle selection indicator*
03 nub **04** core, crux, meat **05** basis, focus, heart, pivot **06** centre, kernel, marrow **08** eucaryon, eukaryon, heartlet, nucellus **09** karyosome

nude
03 raw **04** bare **05** naked **06** Adamic **07** denuded, exposed, skyclad **08** disrobed, in the raw, starkers, stripped, undraped **09** butt-naked, in the buff, in the scud, unclothed, uncovered, undressed **10** start-naked **11** mother-naked **12** not a stitch on **13** with nothing on **15** in the altogether
See also **bare**; **naked**

nudge
03 dig, jab, jog **04** bump, knee, poke, prod, push **05** dunch, dunsh, elbow, shove **06** prompt

nudity
04 scud **06** nudism **07** undress **08** bareness **09** nakedness **10** déshabillé, dishabille **14** state of undress **15** in the altogether

nugatory
04 vain **06** futile **07** invalid, trivial, useless **08** trifling **09** valueless, worthless **10** inadequate, negligible, unavailing **11** ineffectual, inoperative, null and void **13** insignificant **15** inconsequential

nugget
03 wad **04** hunk, lump, mass **05** chunk, clump, piece, wodge

nuisance
04 bore, chiz, drag, hoha, hoop, hurt, pain, pest **05** chizz, trial **06** bother, burden, hoop-la, injury, plague, weight **07** problem, scunner, trouble **08** drawback, irritant, vexation **09** annoyance **10** affliction, difficulty, irritation **11** tribulation **13** inconvenience **15** thorn in your side

null
04 kink, vain, void, zero **05** annul, empty, knurl **06** cipher, cypher, nought **07** invalid, nullify, revoked, useless **08** annulled **09** abrogated, cancelled, nullified, powerless, worthless **11** ineffectual, inoperative, invalidated

nullify
04 kill, null, void **05** abate, annul, quash **06** cancel, negate, offset, repeal, revoke **07** abolish, rescind, reverse **08** abrogate, evacuate, renounce, set aside **10** counteract, invalidate, neutralize **11** countermand, discontinue **12** bring to an end

nullity
08 voidness **10** invalidity **11** uselessness **12** non-existence **13** immateriality, powerlessness, worthlessness **14** incorporeality **15** ineffectualness

numb
04 daze, dead, drug, dull, stun **05** dazed **06** benumb, deaden, freeze, frozen, torpid **07** drugged, in shock, stunned, stupefy, torpefy **08** benumbed, deadened, paralyse, sleeping **09** insensate, paralysed, stupefied, unfeeling **10** immobilize, insensible **11** immobilized, insensitive **12** anaesthetize **13** anaesthetized **14** without feeling

number
01 C, D, K, L, M, n **02** no **03** act, add, num, sum **04** copy, data, item, many, song, tale, turn, unit **05** count, crowd, dance, digit, group, horde, issue, limit, local, score, tally, total, track **06** amount, cipher, figure, reckon, sketch, throng, volume **07** add up to, company, compute, decimal, delimit, edition, imprint, include, integer, numeral, ordinal, routine, several, specify **08** cardinal, estimate, fraction, printing, quantity, restrain, restrict **09** aggregate, apportion, calculate, character, enumerate, multitude **10** collection, impression, statistics **11** anaesthetic, performance **12** anaesthetist, piece of music

Numbers include:
02 pi
03 one, six, ten, two
04 five, four, half, nine, zero
05 eight, fifty, forty, seven, sixty, three
06 eighty, eleven, googol, ninety, thirty, twelve, twenty
07 billion, chiliad, fifteen, hundred, million, seventy, sixteen
08 eighteen, fourteen, nineteen, thirteen, thousand, trillion
09 decillion, nonillion, octillion, seventeen
10 centillion, googolplex, one hundred, septillion, sextillion
11 quadrillion, quintillion

French numbers include:
02 un
03 dix, six

04 cent, cinq, deux, huit, neuf, onze, sept, zéro
05 douze, mille, seize, trois, vingt
06 quatre, quinze, treize, trente
07 dix-huit, dix-neuf, dix-sept
08 quarante, quatorze, soixante
09 cinquante, deux mille, un million
10 un milliard
11 soixante-dix
12 quatre-vingts

German numbers include:
03 elf
04 acht, drei, eins, fünf, neun, null, vier, zehn, zwei
05 sechs, zwölf
06 sieben
07 achtzig, Billion, fünfzig, hundert, Million, neunzig, sechzig, siebzig, tausend, vierzig, zwanzig
08 achtzehn, dreissig, dreizehn, fünfzehn, neunzehn, sechzehn, siebzehn, vierzehn
09 Milliarde
10 einhundert, eintausend

Italian numbers include:
03 due, sei, tre, uno
04 nove, otto
05 cento, dieci, sette, venti
06 cinque, dodici, sedici, trenta, undici
07 novanta, ottanta, quattro, tredici
08 diciotto, quaranta, quindici, sessanta, settanta
09 cinquanta
10 diciannove
11 diciassette, quattordici

Latin numbers include:
03 duo, nil, sex
04 octo, tres, unus
05 decem, mille, novem
06 centum, septem
07 quinque, sedecim, undecim, viginti
08 duodecim, quattuor, tredecim, trigenta
09 nonaginta, octoginta, sexaginta
11 quadraginta, septendecim, septuaginta, undeviginti
12 duodeviginti, quinquaginta, quinquedecim
13 quattuordecim

Spanish numbers include:
03 dos, mil, uno
04 diez, doce, ocho, once, seis, tres
05 cinco, nueve, siete, trece
06 ciento, cuatro, quince, veinte
07 catorce, noventa, ochenta, sesenta, setenta, treinta
08 cuarenta, un millón
09 cincuenta, dieciocho, dieciséis
10 diecinueve, diecisiete, quinientos
11 mil millones

- **any number**
01 n
- **large number**
01 n **03** lot, ten **04** army, host, raft, slew, slue
See also **many**

numberless

04 many **06** myriad, untold **07** endless **08** infinite, unsummed **09** countless, uncounted **10** unnumbered **11** innumerable **12** immeasurable **13** multitudinous, without number

numbness

06 stupor, torpor **08** deadness, dullness **09** paralysis **10** night-palsy **12** stupefaction **13** insensateness, insensibility, insensitivity, unfeelingness

numeral

03 num **04** unit **05** digit **06** cipher, figure, number **07** integer **09** character

Roman numerals include:

01 C (hundred), D (five hundred), I (one), L (fifty), M (thousand), V (five), X (ten)
02 II (two), IV (four), IX (nine), VI (six), XI (eleven), XV (fifteen), XX (twenty)
03 III (three), VII (seven), XII (twelve), XIV (fourteen), XIX (nineteen), XVI (sixteen)
04 VIII (eight), XIII (thirteen), XVII (seventeen)
05 XVIII (eighteen)

numerical

05 whole **06** graded, ranked, scalar **07** digital, figural **08** integral **09** identical **11** statistical **12** hierarchical **13** computational

numerically

07 in order **09** digitally **10** measurably **12** quantifiably **13** algebraically, exponentially **14** arithmetically, mathematically

numerous

04 many **05** great **06** a lot of, legion, strong, sundry, untold **07** copious, endless, profuse, several, various **08** abundant, a good few, manifold, populous **09** countless, plentiful, quite a few **10** rhythmical **11** innumerable **13** great in number, multitudinous

numerousness

06 number **08** multeity **09** abundance, plurality, profusion **10** numerosity **11** copiousness **12** manifoldness, multiplicity **13** countlessness, plentifulness

numinous

04 holy **05** deity, numen **06** divine, sacred **08** divinity, mystical **09** religious, spiritual **10** mysterious **12** supernatural, transcendent

numskull

03 ass, git, mug, nit, sap **04** berk, clot, coot, dill, dope, dork, fool, geek, goat, goof, goop, jerk, kook, nana, nerd, nerk, nong, prat, putz, twit, yo-yo **05** chump, dumbo, dunce, dweeb, galah, neddy, ninny, prick, schmo, twerp, wally **06** bampot, dimwit, doofus, dum-dum, josser, muppet, nignog, nitwit, sawney, sucker, turkey **07** Charlie, dingbat, gubbins, jughead, pillock, plonker, saphead, tosspot, wazzock **08** boofhead, dipstick,

lunkhead **09** birdbrain, blockhead, cloth head, schlemiel, simpleton **10** headbanger, nincompoop, silly-billy **11** chowderhead **13** proper Charlie

nun

03 top **06** abbess, sister, vestal, vowess **07** ancress, blue tit, zelator **08** canoness, prioress, zelatrix **09** anchoress, deaconess, zelatrice **10** cloistress, conventual, religieuse **14** mother superior

See also **monk**

Nunavut

02 NU

nuncio

05 envoy **06** legate **09** messenger **10** ambassador **14** representative

nunnery

05 abbey **06** priory **07** convent, nunship **08** cloister

nuptial

06 bridal, wedded **07** marital, spousal, wedding **08** conjugal, hymeneal **09** connubial **11** epithalamic, matrimonial **12** epithalamial

nuptials

06 bridal **07** wedding **08** espousal, marriage, spousals **09** hymeneals, matrimony

nurse

◇ *containment indicator*
03 aid **04** feed, help, keep, tend **05** angel, boost, shark, treat **06** assist, cradle, foster, suckle **07** advance, care for, cherish, dogfish, further, harbour, nourice, nourish, nurture, promote, support, sustain **08** attend to, preserve **09** encourage, entertain, look after **10** breast-feed, take care of

Nurse types include:

02 EN, RN
03 aia, CNN, dry, pro, RGN, SEN, SRN, wet
04 amah, ayah, home, maid, sick
05 nanny, night, staff, tutor
06 charge, dental, matron, school, sister
07 midwife, nursery
08 district
09 auxiliary, children's, community, Macmillan
10 consultant, Iain Rennie, ward sister
11 night sister, psychiatric
12 practitioner
13 health visitor, State Enrolled, theatre sister
15 locality manager, State Registered

Nurses include:

05 Kenny (Elizabeth)
06 Barton (Clara), **Cavell** (Edith), Rayner (Claire), **Sanger** (Margaret)
07 Seacole (Mary)
08 Pattison (Dorothy Wyndlow)
10 Stephenson (Elsie)
11 Nightingale (Florence)
14 Queen Alexandra

See also **medical**

nurture

03 aid **04** care, diet, eats, feed, food, grub, help, nosh, rear, tend, tuck **05** boost, coach, nurse, scran, train, tutor **06** assist, cradle, foster, school **07** advance, bring up, care for, cherish, develop, educate, feeding, further, nourish, promote, rearing, support, sustain, tending **08** boosting, instruct, training **09** cultivate, education, fostering, nouriture, nutrition, promotion, schooling, stimulate **10** assistance, discipline, nourriture, sustenance, upbringing **11** cultivation, development, environment, furtherance, nourishment, stimulation, subsistence **13** encouragement

nut

02 en **03** fan, pip **04** buff, butt, head, seed **05** crank, fiend, freak, loony, stone **06** kernel, madman, maniac, nutter, psycho, zealot **07** admirer, devotee, fanatic, lunatic, nutcase, oddball **08** crackpot, follower, headcase, madwoman **09** fruitcake, screwball, supporter **10** aficionado, basket-case, enthusiast, psychopath **12** insane person

Nuts include:

03 ben, oak, pig
04 cola, horn, kola, pará, pili, pine, shea, wing
05 acorn, areca, arnut, beech, betel, cedar, cream, earth, ivory, lichi, pecan, tiger
06 almond, Brazil, cashew, castle, cobnut, cohune, corozo, ginger, hognut, illipe, lichee, litchi, lychee, monkey, oilnut, peanut, physic, poison, sleeve, souari, walnut
07 babassu, bladder, buffalo, chesnut, coconut, filberd, filbert, gallnut, hickory, leechee, locknut, marking, palmyra, pilinut, saouari
08 chestnut, clearing, cocoanut, cokernut, coquilla, hazelnut, quandong, sapucaia, thumbnut
09 Barcelona, beech mast, butterfly, butternut, groundnut, macadamia, mockernut, pistachio, sassafras, scaly-bark
10 locking-nut, Queensland, St Anthony's
11 Molucca bean
13 earth-chestnut, horse chestnut

See also **head**

● **do your nut**
05 go mad **06** blow up, see red **07** explode **08** boil over, freak out **09** blow a fuse, go berserk, raise hell **11** blow your top, flip your lid, go ballistic, go up the wall, have kittens, lose your rag **12** blow your cool, fly into a rage, lose your cool, throw a wobbly **13** hit the ceiling, throw a tantrum **14** foam at the mouth **15** fly off the handle, go off the deep end

nutriment

04 diet, eats, food, grub, nosh, tuck

05 scran **09** nutrition **10** sustenance **11** nourishment, subsistence

nutrition
04 diet, eats, food, grub, nosh, tuck **05** scran **08** eutrophy **09** nutriment **10** sustenance **11** nourishment, subsistence

nutritious
04 good **09** healthful, nutritive, wholesome **10** beneficial, nourishing, sustaining **11** substantial **12** body-building, health-giving, invigorating **13** strengthening

nuts
◇ *anagram indicator*
03 mad **04** avid, bats, daft, fond, keen, loco, mast, wild **05** barmy, batty, crazy, daffy, dippy, loony, loopy, nutty, potty

06 ardent, crazed, insane **07** berserk, bonkers, devoted, lunatic, smitten, zealous **08** demented, deranged, doolally, unhinged **09** disturbed, enamoured, fanatical **10** infatuated, out to lunch, passionate, unbalanced **12** enthusiastic, round the bend **13** off your rocker, out of your mind, round the twist **14** off your trolley
See also **mad**

nuts and bolts
06 basics **07** details **10** components, essentials **11** nitty-gritty **12** fundamentals **13** bits and pieces **14** practicalities

nutty
03 mad **04** nuts, wild **05** barmy, batty, crazy, daffy, dippy, loony, loopy, potty

06 crazed, insane **07** berserk, bonkers, lunatic **08** demented, deranged, doolally, unhinged **09** disturbed **10** out to lunch, unbalanced **12** round the bend **13** off your rocker, out of your mind, round the twist **14** off your trolley

nuzzle
03 pet, rub **04** nose, poke, root **05** nudge, press, sniff, train **06** burrow, caress, cuddle, fondle, foster, nestle **07** bring up, snoozle, snuggle, snuzzle

nymph
04 Echo, girl, lass, maid, pupa **05** dryad, houri, naiad, oread, sylph **06** damsel, maelid, maiden, nereid, sprite, Tethys, undine **07** mermaid, oceanid, rusalka **09** hamadryad

o

O
05 Oscar 06 nought 07 nothing,
spangle

oaf
03 auf, oik 04 boor, clod, dolt, gawk,
hick, hoon, lout, ouph, slob 05 idiot,
ocker, ouphe, yahoo, yobbo 06 lubber
07 bumpkin 09 barbarian, roughneck
10 changeling, clodhopper
11 hobbledehoy

oafish
05 gawky, gross, ocker, rough
06 clumsy, coarse, lumpen, stolid
07 boorish, doltish, idiotic, ill-bred,
loutish, lumpish, swinish, uncouth,
yobbish 08 bungling, churlish,
lubberly 10 unmannerly
11 clodhopping, ill-mannered

oak
04 holm, ilex 05 roble 06 cerris,
kermes 07 durmast, Quercus
08 corktree, flittern, wainscot
10 quercitron 13 partridge-wood
15 king of the forest
• **oak bark**
03 tan

oar
03 row 05 blade, scull, spoon, sweep
06 bow-oar, paddle, stroke 09 stroke
oar
• **oar blade**
04 peel

oasis
05 haven 06 island, refuge, spring
07 hideout, retreat, sanctum
08 hideaway 09 sanctuary
12 watering-hole

oath
03 vow 04 bond, cuss, word 05 curse
06 avowal, pledge 07 promise
08 cussword 09 assurance, blasphemy,
curse-word, expletive, obscenity,
profanity, sacrament, swear-word
11 affirmation, attestation, bad
language, imprecation, malediction
12 word of honour 14 four-letter
word
• **oaths and euphemisms**
02 od 03 dod, dog, gad, gee, Gog, odd
04 drat, ecod, egad, gosh, heck,hell,
igad, life, odso, oons, rats, 'slid, 'zbud
05 bedad, begad, gadso, nouns, 'sfoot,
'slife, zooks 06 cricky, crikey, 'sblood,
'sdeath, 'sheart, 'snails 07 begorra, by
Jingo, crickey, jabbers, odzooks,
strewth 08 begorrah, bejabers,
gadzooks 09 bismillah, 'sbodikins
10 sapperment, 'sbuddikins

obduracy
08 firmness, tenacity 09 obstinacy
10 doggedness, mulishness, perversity,
wilfulness 11 frowardness, persistence,
pertinacity 12 perseverance,
resoluteness, stubbornness
13 inflexibility, intransigence,
pigheadedness 14 relentlessness
15 hard-heartedness,
wrongheadedness

obdurate
04 firm, hard, iron 05 stony
06 dogged, flinty, wilful 07 adamant
08 hardened, stubborn 09 immovable,
obstinate, pigheaded, steadfast,
tenacious, unbending, unfeeling
10 determined, headstrong,
implacable, inflexible, persistent, self-
willed, unyielding 11 hard-hearted,
intractable, stiff-necked, unrelenting
12 bloody-minded, intransigent,
strong-minded

obedience
04 duty 07 respect 08 docility
09 agreement, deference, obeisance,
passivity, reverence 10 accordance,
allegiance, compliance, observance,
submission 11 amenability, dutifulness
12 acquiescence, amenableness,
malleability, subservience, tractability
14 conformability, submissiveness

obedient
04 bent, obdt 06 docile 07 duteous,
dutiful, pliable 08 amenable, biddable,
yielding 09 compliant, malleable,
observant, tractable 10 bridle-wise,
conforming, law-abiding, obsequious,
respectful, submissive 11 acquiescent,
deferential, disciplined, subservient,
well-trained

obeisance
03 bow 06 cringe, curtsy, homage,
kowtow, salaam, salute 07 curtsey,
respect 09 deference, obedience,
reverence 10 salutation, submission,
veneration 12 genuflection

obelisk
06 column, dagger, needle, obelus,
pillar 08 memorial, monument

obese
03 big, fat 05 beefy, bulky, gross, heavy,
hefty, large, plump, podgy, porky,
round, stout, tubby 06 chubby, flabby,
fleshy, portly, rotund 07 outsize,
paunchy 08 roly-poly 09 corpulent,
ponderous 10 overweight
11 Falstaffian, well-endowed 15 well-
upholstered

obesity
04 bulk 07 fatness 09 grossness,
plumpness, podginess, stoutness,
tubbiness 10 chubbiness, corpulence,
flabbiness, overweight, portliness,
rotundness

obey
04 heed, keep, mind 05 bow to, defer,
yield 06 comply, follow, fulfil, keep to,
submit 07 abide by, act upon, conform,
defer to, execute, give way, observe,
perform, respect, respond 08 adhere
to, carry out 09 be ruled by, consent to,
discharge, surrender 10 come to heel,
toe the line 11 acquiesce in, go by the
book 14 do as you are told, take orders
from 15 stick to the rules

obfuscate
◇ *anagram indicator*
04 blur, hide, mask, veil 05 cloak,
cloud, cover, shade 06 darken,
muddle, shadow, shroud 07 conceal,
confuse, obscure 08 bewilder,
disguise 10 complicate, overshadow

obfuscation
06 muddle 08 disguise 09 confusion,
obscurity 11 concealment
12 complication

obituary
04 obit 06 eulogy 09 necrology
11 death notice

object
03 aim, end, jib 04 body, butt, goal,
idea, item, sake 05 argue, cavil, demur,
focus, point, rebut, thing 06 adduce,
design, device, entity, gadget, impute,
intent, motive, oddity, oppose, reason,
recuse, refuse, resist, target, victim
07 article, exposed, opposed, present,
protest, purpose 08 ambition, artefact,
complain 09 challenge, intention,
objective, recipient, repudiate,
something, take issue, withstand
10 disapprove, interposed,
phenomenon 11 beg to differ,
expostulate, remonstrate
12 recalcitrate 13 interposition, take
exception
• **provisional object**
02 it
• **with the object of**
02 to

objection
02 ob 03 but 05 cavil, demur
06 boggle 07 dislike, dissent, protest,
quarrel, scruple 08 argument,
demurrer, question 09 challenge,
complaint, exception, grievance

10 difficulty, opposition, recusation **11** disapproval **13** expostulation, recalcitrance, remonstrance, unwillingness **15** dissatisfaction

objectionable
04 pert **05** nasty **07** hateful **09** abhorrent, loathsome, obnoxious, offensive, repellent, repugnant, repulsive, revolting, sickening **10** deplorable, despicable, detestable, nauseating, unpleasant **11** distasteful, intolerable **12** contemptible, disagreeable, unacceptable **13** exceptionable, reprehensible

objective
03 aim, end, obj **04** fair, goal, idea, just, mark, real, true **05** point **06** actual, design, intent, object, target, thingy **07** factual, genuine, neutral, purpose **08** ambition, clinical, detached, unbiased **09** authentic, equitable, impartial, intention **10** even-handed, impersonal, open-minded, uninvolved **12** unprejudiced **13** disinterested, dispassionate

objectively
06 fairly, justly **09** equitably, neutrally **11** impartially **12** even-handedly **14** with an open mind **15** disinterestedly, dispassionately

objectivity
07 justice **08** fairness, justness, open mind **10** detachment, thinginess **11** disinterest, outwardness, thinginess **12** impartiality **13** equitableness **14** even-handedness, open-mindedness

objector
05 rebel **07** opposer, striker **08** agitator, opponent **09** dissenter, dissident, protester **10** complainer **12** demonstrator

obligate
04 bind, make **05** force, impel, press **06** coerce, compel, oblige **07** require **08** pressure **09** constrain **10** pressurize **11** necessitate

obligation
03 job, tie **04** bond, cess, debt, deed, duty, must, onus, task **05** trust **06** burden, charge, demand, duress, favour **07** astrict, burthen, command **08** contract, covenant, function, pressure **09** agreement, liability **10** assignment, commitment, compulsion, incumbency **11** obstriction, requirement **12** indebtedness **14** accountability, responsibility

obligatory
03 set **05** usual **06** normal **07** binding, bounden, regular, routine **08** accepted, enforced, familiar, habitual, ordinary, required **09** customary, essential, incumbent, mandatory, necessary, requisite, statutory **10** compulsory, imperative **11** established, fashionable, traditional, unavoidable **12** conventional

oblige
03 put, tie **04** bind, help, make **05** force, impel, press, serve **06** assist, coerce, compel, please **07** gratify, require **08** astringe, obligate, pressure **09** constrain **10** pressurize **11** accommodate, necessitate **15** be given no option

obliged
05 bound **06** debted, forced, in debt **08** beholden, grateful, having to, indebted, in debt to, required, thankful **09** compelled, duty-bound, gratified, obligated **11** constrained, having got to, honour-bound **12** appreciative **15** under compulsion

obliging
04 kind **05** civil **06** polite **07** helpful, willing **08** friendly, generous, pleasant **09** agreeable, courteous, indulgent, officious **11** complaisant, considerate, co-operative, good-natured **13** accommodating

obligingly
07 civilly **08** politely **09** agreeably, helpfully, willingly **10** generously **11** courteously **13** considerately

oblique
◇ *anagram indicator*
03 obl **04** skew **05** cross, slant, slash **06** angled, squint, stroke, tilted, zigzag **07** awkward, devious, sloping, solidus, virgule, winding **08** bevelled, diagonal, inclined, indirect, rambling, sidelong, sideways, slanting, tortuous, traverse **09** divergent, skew-whiff, underhand **10** circuitous, discursive, meandering, roundabout **12** forward slash, periphrastic **14** circumlocutory, slantendicular, slantindicular

obliquely
05 askew **06** askant, aslant, aslope, squint **07** askance, asquint **08** sidelong **09** at an angle, evasively, slantwise, slopewise **10** diagonally, indirectly **12** circuitously

obliterate
04 blot **05** erase **06** deface, delete, efface, rub out **07** blot out, destroy, expunge, wipe out **08** black out, vaporize, wash away **09** eliminate, eradicate, extirpate, overscore, strike out **10** annihilate

obliteration
04 blot **06** rasure, razure **07** erasure **08** deletion **10** effacement, expunction **11** blotting out, destruction, elimination, eradication, extirpation **12** annihilation

oblivion
04 void **05** Lethe, limbo **06** disuse, pardon, stupor **07** amnesty, silence **08** darkness, deafness **09** blankness, blindness, ignorance, obscurity **11** forgiveness, nothingness **12** carelessness, non-existence **13** forgetfulness, insensibility, unmindfulness **15** inattentiveness, unconsciousness

oblivious
04 deaf **05** blind **07** unaware **08** careless, heedless, ignorant **09** forgetful, forgotten, negligent, unheeding, unmindful **10** insensible **11** inattentive, preoccupied, unconcerned, unconscious **12** absent-minded

obliviousness
07 naivety **09** greenness, ignorance, innocence, stupidity, thickness **10** illiteracy **11** unawareness **12** inexperience **13** unfamiliarity **14** unintelligence **15** unconsciousness

obloquy
05 abuse, blame, odium, shame **06** attack, stigma **07** calumny, censure, slander **08** bad press, disgrace, ignominy, reproach **09** aspersion, contumely, criticism, discredit, disfavour, dishonour, invective **10** defamation, detraction, opprobrium **11** humiliation **12** vilification **13** animadversion

obnoxious
04 vile **05** nasty **06** horrid, odious **07** exposed, hateful, hurtful, noxious **08** horrible **09** abhorrent, loathsome, offensive, repellent, repugnant, repulsive, revolting, sickening **10** deplorable, detestable, disgusting, nauseating, unpleasant **11** intolerable **12** contemptible, disagreeable, unacceptable **13** objectionable

obscene
03 paw **04** blue, foul, lewd, rude, sexy, vile **05** bawdy, dirty, gross, nasty **06** carnal, coarse, filthy, fruity, greasy, impure, pawpaw, risqué, sleazy, smutty, vulgar, X-rated **07** immoral, raunchy **08** hard-core, immodest, improper, indecent, prurient, shocking, unchaste **09** loathsome, off-colour, offensive, repellent, shameless **10** disgusting, licentious, lubricious, outrageous, scandalous, scurrilous, suggestive **11** disgraceful, near the bone **12** pornographic **14** near the knuckle

obscenity
04 cuss, dirt, evil, smut **05** curse, filth **06** sleaze **07** offence, outrage **08** atrocity, cussword, foulness, impurity, lewdness, ribaldry, ribaudry, vileness **09** bawdiness, carnality, dirtiness, eroticism, expletive, grossness, immodesty, indecency, lubricity, profanity, prurience, rybaudrye, scatology, swear-word, vulgarity **10** balderdash, coarseness, filthiness, immorality, indelicacy, wickedness **11** bad language, heinousness, imprecation, impropriety, malediction, pornography, raunchiness **12** unchasteness **13** salaciousness, shamelessness **14** four-letter word, lasciviousness, licentiousness, scurrilousness, suggestiveness

obscure
◇ *anagram indicator*
03 dim, fog **04** blur, dark, deep, hazy,

ide, mask, mist, veil, wrap **05** cloak,
cloud, cover, dusky, faint, fuzzy, lowly,
minor, misty, murky, shade, shady,
vague **06** arcane, cloudy, darken,
fogged, gloomy, hidden, humble,
muddle, occult, opaque, remote,
screen, shadow, shroud, unsung
07 blurred, complex, conceal, confuse,
cryptic, eclipse, shadowy, unclear,
unknown **08** abstruse, block out,
darkness, disguise, doubtful, esoteric,
involved, nameless, oracular, puzzling,
riddling, twilight **09** concealed,
confusing, enigmatic, obfuscate,
oraculous, recondite, uncertain,
unheard-of **10** complicate, indefinite,
indistinct, mysterious, overshadow,
perplexing **11** god-forsaken, little-
known, out-of-the-way, unexplained,
unimportant **12** impenetrable,
inexplicable, unfathomable,
unrecognized **13** inconspicuous,
insignificant **14** indistinctness
15 undistinguished

obscurity
03 fog **05** depth, night, shade
07 mystery **09** ambiguity, confusion,
intricacy, lowliness, murkiness,
mysticism **10** complexity, lack of fame
11 unclearness **12** abstruseness,
namelessness, unimportance
13 reconditeness **14** insignificance
15 impenetrability
▶ bring out of obscurity
04 fish

obsequies
04 wake **06** burial **07** funeral
08 exequies **09** cremation, interment
10 entombment, inhumation

obsequious
04 oily **06** abject, creepy, menial,
smarmy **07** dutiful, fawning, fulsome,
kiss-ass, servile, slavish **08** crawling,
cringing, obedient, toadying, toadyish,
unctuous **10** flattering, grovelling,
submissive **11** bootlicking, deferential,
subservient, sycophantic
12 ingratiating, knee-crooking

observable
04 open **05** clear **06** patent
07 evident, notable, obvious, visible
08 apparent **09** scrutable
10 detectable, measurable, noticeable
11 appreciable, discernible,
perceptible, significant
12 recognizable

observance
04 Lent, puja, rite **06** custom, maying,
notice, ritual **07** heeding, keeping,
service, trinket, triumph **08** ceremony,
festival, practice **09** adherence,
attention, discharge, execution,
following, formality, honouring,
obedience, punctilio, reverence,
sabbatism, tradition **10** compliance,
fulfilment **11** celebration, performance
13 lectisternium

observant
05 alert, sharp **06** seeing **07** devoted,
dutiful, heedful, mindful, on guard

08 hawk-eyed, obedient, orthodox,
vigilant, watchful **09** attentive, beady-
eyed, committed, eagle-eyed, sharp-
eyed, wide-awake **10** perceptive,
percipient, practising **11** observative
12 card-carrying, on the lookout, on
the qui vive

observation
04 data, note **05** study **06** espial,
notice, regard, remark, result, review,
seeing **07** comment, finding, opinion,
thought, viewing **08** eyesight,
noticing, scrutiny, watching
09 attention, criticism, statement,
utterance **10** annotation, cognizance,
inspection, monitoring, perception,
reflection **11** declaration, description,
discernment, examination,
information **13** consideration,
pronouncement

observatory
06 orrery **09** viewpoint
11 planetarium, planisphere

Observatories include:
04 Keck
05 Royal, Tower
06 Gemini
07 Arecibo, Palomar, Paranal
08 Kitt Peak, Mauna Kea
09 Greenwich
11 Jodrell Bank, Mount Wilson
12 Herstmonceux
13 Tower of London
14 Royal Greenwich

observe
02 la, lo **03** eye, say, see, spy, use
04 espy, heed, hold, keep, mark, note,
obey, spot, take, twig, view **05** clock,
smoke, state, study, utter, watch
06 behold, detect, follow, fulfil,
honour, notice, regard, remark
07 abide by, comment, declare,
discern, examine, execute, inspect,
look you, mention, monitor, perform,
respect **08** adhere to, maintain,
perceive, remember, take note
09 celebrate, conform to, discharge,
recognize, speculate, surveille
10 animadvert, comply with, keep tabs
on, take notice **11** commemorate,
contemplate, keep an eye on, keep
watch on, miss nothing **12** catch sight
of **14** watch like a hawk

observer
06 looker, viewer **07** watcher, witness
08 beholder, looker-on, onlooker,
reporter **09** bystander, sightseer,
spectator **10** eyewitness
11 commentator, speculation

obsess
04 grip, rule **05** beset, eat up, haunt,
hound **06** plague, prey on **07** bedevil,
besiege, consume, control, engross,
possess, torment **08** dominate
09 preoccupy **10** monopolize **11** have
a grip on, have a hold on

obsessed
05 beset **06** hipped **07** gripped,
haunted, hounded, plagued **08** hung

up on **09** dominated **10** bedevilled,
immersed in, infatuated **11** in the grip
of, preoccupied

obsession
03 bug **05** mania, siege, thing **06** fetish,
hang-up, phobia **07** complex
08 fixation, idée fixe, neurosis
09 monomania **10** compulsion,
enthusiasm, hobby-horse
11 fascination, infatuation **12** one-track
mind **13** preoccupation, ruling passion
15 bee in your bonnet

obsessive
04 anal **05** fixed **08** gripping,
haunting, neurotic **09** consuming,
maddening **10** compulsive, tormenting
12 all-consuming, trainspotter

obsolescence
06 disuse **07** failure **09** rejection,
scrapping **10** redundancy
12 obsoleteness **13** disappearance

obsolescent
05 aging, dated **06** ageing, fading, old
hat, waning **08** dying out, moribund,
outdated **09** declining, on the wane,
out of date, redundant **10** on the shelf
11 on the way out, out of the ark
12 antediluvian, disappearing, old-
fashioned, on the decline, past its
prime

obsolete
03 obs, old **04** dead **05** dated, passé
06 bygone, old hat **07** ancient, antique,
disused, expired, extinct, outworn
08 in disuse, outdated, outmoded
09 discarded, out of date
10 antiquated, on the shelf **11** on the
way out, out of the ark **12** antediluvian,
discontinued, old-fashioned, out of
fashion, past its prime
13 superannuated **14** behind the times

obstacle
03 bar **04** boyg, curb, drag, gate, jump,
oxer, rock, snag, stay, stop **05** catch,
check, hitch, mogul **06** hazard, hiccup,
hurdle, remora **07** barrier
08 blockade, blockage, drawback,
handicap, stoppage, stubborn, tank
trap **09** barricade, deterrent,
hindrance **10** difficulty, hinderance,
impediment **11** obstruction
12 Becher's Brook, entanglement,
interference, interruption
14 stumbling-block

obstinacy
08 firmness, obduracy, self-will,
tenacity **10** doggedness, mulishness,
perversity, wilfulness **11** frowardness,
persistence, persistency, pertinacity
12 perseverance, resoluteness,
stubbornness **13** inflexibility,
intransigence, pigheadedness
14 relentlessness **15** hard-heartedness,
wrongheadedness

obstinate
04 dour, firm **05** rusty, stoor, stour,
sture **06** cussed, dogged, kittle, mulish,
stowre, sturdy, thrawn, wilful
07 adamant, bullish, diehard, hard-set,

restive, willful **08** camelish, stubborn, thraward, thrawart **09** hidebound, immovable, pigheaded, steadfast, unbending **10** bull-headed, determined, headstrong, inflexible, persistent, refractory, refractory, self-willed, stomachful, unyielding **11** hard-hearted, intractable, persevering, stiff-necked, unrelenting, wrongheaded **12** bloody-minded, contumacious, intransigent, pertinacious, pervicacious, recalcitrant, stiff-hearted, strong-minded **13** high-stomached, intransigeant

See also **stubborn**

- **obstinate person**
04 mule

obstreperous
◇ *anagram indicator*
04 loud, wild **05** noisy, radge, rough, rowdy **06** unruly **07** bolshie, raucous, restive, riotous, stroppy **09** clamorous, out of hand, turbulent **10** boisterous, disorderly, disruptive, refractory, rip-roaring, tumultuous, uproarious, vociferous **11** intractable, tempestuous **12** bloody-minded, uncontrolled, unmanageable **13** undisciplined

obstruct
◇ *containment indicator*
03 bar **04** clog, crab, curb, foul, halt, stap, stop **05** block, brake, check, choke, cross, delay, hedge, limit, stall, stimy, stuff **06** arrest, bridle, cut off, hamper, hinder, hold up, impede, retard, stimie, stymie, thwart, waylay **07** blanket, inhibit, obscure, prevent, sandbag, shut off **08** encumber, restrict, slow down **09** barricade, frustrate, hamstring, interfere, interrupt **10** portcullis **13** interfere with

obstruction
03 bar, let **04** clog, stop, veil **05** block, check, ileus, trump **07** barrier, embargo **08** blockade, blockage, obstacle, sanction, stoppage, traverse **09** barricade, body-check, deterrent, hindrance, roadblock **10** bottleneck, difficulty, filibuster, impediment, prevention **11** restriction **14** stumbling-block

obstructive
07 awkward **08** blocking, delaying, negative, stalling **09** difficult, hindering, hindrance, unhelpful **10** inhibiting **11** restrictive **12** interrupting **13** unco-operative

obtain
03 cop, get, pan **04** earn, gain, have, hold, make, rule, snag, take **05** exist, reach, reign, seize, stand **06** attain, come by, come to, derive, occupy, secure **07** achieve, acquire, be in use, compass, possess, prevail, procure, realize **08** hold sway **09** be in force, be the case, get hold of **11** be effective, be prevalent **14** get your hands on

obtainable
05 on tap, ready **06** at hand, on call

07 to be had **09** available **10** accessible, achievable, attainable, procurable, realizable

obtrude
04 sorn **05** abuse, foist **06** butt in, impose **07** break in, exploit, intrude, mislead, presume, put upon **08** encroach, protrude **13** force yourself **14** thrust yourself **15** take advantage of

obtrusive
04 bold, loud, nosy **05** nosey, pushy **06** prying **07** blatant, forward, obvious **08** flagrant, meddling **09** intrusive, prominent **10** noticeable, projecting, protruding **11** conspicuous, interfering

obtuse
03 dim **04** dozy, dull, dumb, slow **05** blunt, crass, dense, dopey, thick **06** stolid, stupid **09** dim-witted **10** dull-witted, slow-witted **11** insensitive **12** thick-skinned **13** unintelligent **15** slow on the uptake

obverse
05 cross, heads **07** inverse, reverse **08** contrary, converse, opposite **10** antithesis **12** complemental

obviate
04 save **05** avert **06** divert, remove **07** counter, prevent **08** preclude **09** forestall **10** anticipate, counteract

obvious
04 bald, open, rank **05** broad, clear, plain **06** patent **07** blatant, evident, glaring, visible **08** apparent, clear-cut, distinct, manifest, palpable, pregnant **09** prominent, writ large **10** detectable, noticeable, pronounced, undeniable, well-marked **11** conspicuous, open-and-shut, perceptible, self-evident, transparent, unconcealed **12** crystal clear, recognizable, unmistakable **14** self-explaining **15** self-explanatory, straightforward

obviously
03 duh **07** clearly, plainly **08** of course, patently **09** certainly, eminently, evidently **10** distinctly, manifestly, noticeably, undeniably **11** undoubtedly **12** unmistakably, without doubt

occasion
02 do **04** bash, call, case, gala, hour, make, need, rise, room, time, turn **05** breed, cause, event, evoke, party, point, throw **06** affair, chance, create, effect, elicit, excuse, ground, induce, lead to, prompt, reason **07** bring on, episode, grounds, inspire, pretext, produce, provoke **08** accustom, engender, function, generate, incident, instance, juncture, persuade **09** encheason, happening, influence, originate, situation **10** bring about, experience, give rise to, occurrence **11** celebration, get-together, opportunity, requirement, social event **12** circumstance **13** justification

See also **event**; **party**

occasional
03 odd **04** orra, rare **06** casual, daime **08** fugitive, off and on, on and off, periodic, sometime, sporadic, uncommon **09** irregular **10** incidental infrequent **12** intermittent

occasionally
07 at times **08** casually, off and on, on and off **09** sometimes **10** now and then, once in a way, on occasion **11** at intervals, irregularly, now and again **12** every so often, infrequently, once in a while, periodically, sporadically **14** from time to time, intermittently

occlude
◇ *containment indicator*
03 bar **04** clog, fill, halt, plug, seal, sto **05** block, check, choke, close, cover, dam up **06** absorb, arrest, bung up, clog up, hinder, impede, retain, stop u thwart **08** obstruct

occlusion
03 jam **04** clot **05** block **06** log jam **08** blockage, blocking, stoppage **09** hindrance **10** congestion, impediment **11** obstruction

occult
03 art **04** arts **05** magic **06** arcane, hidden, secret, veiled **07** magical, obscure, unknown **08** abstruse, esoteric, mystical **09** black arts, concealed, mysticism, recondite **10** mysterious **12** metaphysical, supernatural **13** preternatural **14** transcendental **15** supernaturalism, the supernatural

Occult- and supernatural-related terms include:

03 ESP, obi
04 jinx, juju, omen, rune
05 charm, coven, curse, relic, spell, totem, witch
06 amulet, déjà vu, fetish, hoodoo, medium, séance, shaman, spirit, trance, vision, voodoo
07 cabbala, diviner, evil eye, palmist, psychic, satanic, sorcery, warlock
08 black cat, exorcism, exorcist, familiar, Satanism, Satanist, sorcerer, talisman
09 astrology, black mass, ectoplasm, Hallowe'en, horoscope, influence, palmistry, pentagram, tarot card
10 astrologer, black magic, broomstick, chiromancy, divination, evil spirit, hydromancy, necromancy, Ouija board®, paranormal, planchette, possession, sixth sense, white magic, witchcraft
11 chiromancer, clairvoyant, crystal ball, divining-rod, hydromancer, incantation, necromancer, oneiromancy, poltergeist, premonition, psychometer, psychometry, second sight, witch doctor
12 clairvoyance, oneiromancer, spiritualism, spiritualist,

supernatural, superstition, tarot reading
13 fortune-teller, witch's sabbath
14 Walpurgis Night

occupancy
03 use **04** term **06** tenure **07** holding, tenancy **09** ownership, residence **10** habitation, occupation, possession **11** inhabitancy **13** domiciliation **14** owner-occupancy

occupant
04 user **05** owner **06** holder, inmate, lessee, renter, tenant **08** occupier, resident, squatter **09** homeowner, incumbent **10** inhabitant **11** householder, leaseholder **13** owner-occupier

occupation
03 job, use **04** line, post, work **05** craft, field, trade **06** billet, career, employ, métier, tenure **07** calling, capture, control, holding, pursuit, seizure, tenancy **08** activity, business, conquest, interest, invasion, province, takeover, vocation **09** occupancy, overthrow, residence, residency **10** employment, habitation, possession, profession, walk of life **11** foreign rule, subjugation

Occupations include:

02 AM, DJ, GP, MD, MP, PA
03 MSP, nun, spy, vet
04 aide, chef, cook, dean, dyer, hack, maid, monk, page, poet
05 abbot, actor, agent, baker, boxer, buyer, caddy, clerk, coach, diver, envoy, friar, guide, judge, juror, mason, mayor, medic, miner, model, nanny, nurse, pilot, smith, tawer, tutor, usher, valet, vicar
06 abbess, artist, au pair, author, banker, barber, barman, bishop, bookie, bowyer, brewer, broker, butler, cabbie, cleric, cooper, copper, coster, cowboy, critic, curate, dancer, dealer, doctor, draper, driver, editor, eggler, factor, farmer, fitter, forger, gaffer, glazer, grocer, herald, hermit, hosier, hunter, jailer, jester, jockey, joiner, lawyer, mercer, miller, ostler, packer, parson, pastor, pig-man, pirate, player, porter, potter, priest, ragman, ranger, roofer, sailor, salter, server, singer, skater, sniper, sparks, spicer, tailor, tanner, teller, tinner, trader, tycoon, typist, vendor, verger, waiter, warden, warder, weaver, welder, writer
07 acrobat, actress, actuary, admiral, adviser, almoner, analyst, artisan, artiste, athlete, attaché, auditor, aviator, bailiff, barista, barmaid, bellboy, bellhop, bottle-o, breeder, builder, butcher, cashier, chemist, cleaner, climber, coalman, cobbler, collier, coroner, courier, cowherd, crofter, curator, cyclist, dentist, doorman, dresser, drummer, equerry, farrier, fiddler, fighter,

fireman, florist, footman, foreman, frogman, general, glazier, gymnast, hangman, haulier, hostess, janitor, junkman, lace-man, lineman, lorimer, luthier, magnate, manager, marshal, masseur, midwife, milkman, oculist, officer, orderly, painter, partner, pianist, planner, plumber, poacher, popstar, postman, prefect, printer, rancher, referee, saddler, scholar, senator, servant, shearer, sheriff, showman, soldier, spinner, stapler, steward, student, surgeon, teacher, trainee, trainer, trapper, vintner, warrior, woolman, workman
08 advocate, animator, armourer, attorney, banksman, botanist, bottle-oh, brakeman, callgirl, cardinal, chairman, chandler, chaplain, comedian, compiler, composer, conjurer, conjuror, corporal, costumer, coxswain, croupier, dairyman, deckhand, designer, diplomat, director, druggist, educator, embalmer, engineer, engraver, essayist, executor, factotum, farmhand, ferryman, film star, fishwife, forester, gangster, gardener, goatherd, governor, gunsmith, handyman, henchman, herdsman, hireling, home help, hotelier, huntsman, inventor, jeweller, labourer, landlady, landlord, lecturer, linguist, lyricist, magician, maltster, mapmaker, masseuse, mechanic, merchant, milkmaid, milliner, minister, minstrel, muleteer, musician, novelist, operator, optician, organist, pardoner, perfumer, pig-woman, polisher, preacher, producer, promoter, publican, quarrier, recorder, reporter, retailer, reviewer, salesman, sales rep, satirist, scrapman, sculptor, seedsman, sergeant, shepherd, showgirl, smuggler, sorcerer, spaceman, spurrier, stockman, stripper, stuntman, supplier, surveyor, thatcher, upholder, waitress, watchman, wet nurse, wig-maker, woodsman, wrangler
09 alchemist, anatomist, announcer, antiquary, architect, archivist, art critic, art dealer, assistant, associate, astronaut, attendant, barperson, barrister, biologist, bodyguard, bookmaker, brinjarry, buccaneer, bus driver, cab driver, caretaker, carpenter, charwoman, chauffeur, clergyman, coal miner, collector, columnist, commander, concierge, conductor, constable, cosmonaut, costumier, couturier, cricketer, decorator, detective, dietician, dramatist, ecologist, economist, executive, financier, fisherman, fruiterer, gas fitter, geologist, goldsmith, governess, guitarist, gutter-man, harvester,

herbalist, historian, homeopath, horologer, housemaid, HR manager, hypnotist, innkeeper, inspector, ironsmith, jacksmith, landowner, launderer, laundress, librarian, lifeguard, locksmith, machinist, messenger, musketeer, navigator, newsagent, nursemaid, osteopath, outfitter, paralegal, paramedic, performer, physician, physicist, plasterer, ploughman, policeman, pop singer, poulterer, professor, publicist, publisher, puppeteer, registrar, robe maker, sailmaker, scientist, secretary, shoemaker, signaller, signalman, songsmith, spokesman, stagehand, stationer, staymaker, stevedore, subeditor, subtitler, swineherd, therapist, towncrier, tradesman, traveller, trumpeter, usherette, van driver, violinist, volunteer, whittawer, yachtsman, zookeeper, zoologist
10 accountant, advertiser, air hostess, air steward, amanuensis, apothecary, apprentice, archbishop, astrologer, astronomer, auctioneer, baby sitter, bank teller, beautician, bellringer, bill-broker, biochemist, biographer, blacksmith, bookbinder, bookkeeper, bookseller, bricklayer, bureaucrat, campaigner, cartoonist, cartwright, chairmaker, clockmaker, coastguard, compositor, consultant, controller, copywriter, corn-dealer, corn-factor, councillor, counsellor, disc jockey, dishwasher, dramaturge, dressmaker, dry cleaner, equestrian, fellmonger, fishmonger, footballer, forecaster, frame-maker, fundraiser, gamekeeper, game warden, gatekeeper, geneticist, geochemist, geographer, glassmaker, handmaiden, headhunter, headmaster, highwayman, horologist, instructor, ironmonger, journalist, junk-dealer, keyboarder, legislator, librettist, lumberjack, magistrate, manageress, manicurist, manservant, midshipman, millwright, missionary, naturalist, negotiator, newscaster, newsmonger, nurseryman, obituarist, pallbearer, park ranger, pawnbroker, peltmonger, perruquier, pharmacist, piano tuner, playwright, podiatrist, politician, postmaster, private eye, programmer, proprietor, prospector, railwayman, removal man, researcher, ringmaster, roadmender, sales clerk, saleswoman, sempstress, shipbroker, shipwright, shopfitter, shopkeeper, signwriter, songstress, stewardess, stock agent, stockinger, stonemason, supervisor, taxi driver, technician, translator, typesetter, undertaker, unguentary,

wainwright, wharfinger, whitesmith, wholesaler, woodcarver, woodcutter

11 accompanist, antiquarian, art director, astrologist, audio typist, bank manager, bingo caller, broadcaster, bullfighter, burn-the-wind, businessman, candlemaker, car salesman, chambermaid, cheerleader, chiropodist, clergywoman, commentator, coppersmith, delivery man, distributor, draughtsman, electrician, entertainer, estate agent, etymologist, executioner, firefighter, foot soldier, fund manager, glass blower, grave digger, greengrocer, haberdasher, hairdresser, hair stylist, head teacher, horse-dealer, illustrator, interpreter, interviewer, lifeboatman, linen-draper, lollipop man, lorry driver, metalworker, money broker, mountaineer, music-seller, neurologist, optometrist, panel beater, parlourmaid, pathologist, philatelist, philologist, philosopher, policewoman, proofreader, radiologist, relic-monger, secret agent, set designer, sociologist, sharebroker, ship builder, silversmith, steelworker, stockbroker, taxidermist, telephonist, ticket agent, tobacconist, travel agent, tree surgeon, truck driver, underwriter, upholsterer, vitraillist, wagonwright, wax-chandler, web designer, wheelwright, wool-stapler, youth worker

12 anaesthetist, broker-dealer, cabinet maker, calligrapher, cartographer, cheesemonger, chimney sweep, chiropractor, churchwarden, civil servant, coal merchant, corn-merchant, costermonger, demonstrator, dramaturgist, entomologist, entrepreneur, event manager, fent-merchant, film director, garret-master, hotel manager, immunologist, IT consultant, longshoreman, maitre d'hotel, make-up artist, media planner, metallurgist, mineralogist, nutritionist, obstetrician, orthodontist, photographer, physiologist, ploughwright, postal worker, practitioner, PR consultant, press officer, prison warder, psychologist, radiographer, receptionist, restaurateur, sales manager, schoolmaster, screenwriter, scriptwriter, ship chandler, slink butcher, social worker, spokesperson, stage manager, statistician, stenographer, toxicologist, urban planner, veterinarian, warehouseman, wine merchant, wood engraver

13 administrator, antique dealer, archaeologist, charity worker, choreographer, civil engineer, crane operator, criminologist, dental surgeon, food scientist, groundskeeper, gynaecologist, harbour master, health visitor, home economist, industrialist, lab technician, lexicographer, lollipop woman, mathematician, meteorologist, nightwatchman, oceanographer, old-clothesman, police officer, prison officer, rag-and-bone-man, rent collector, retail manager, scrap merchant, security guard, ship's chandler, shop assistant, sound engineer, streetcleaner, streetsweeper, support worker, traffic warden, window cleaner

14 anthropologist, camera operator, claims assessor, draughtsperson, market gardener, marriage-broker, merchant tailor, microbiologist, music therapist, naval architect, pharmacologist, pharmacopolist, store detective, superintendent, systems analyst, tallow chandler

15 biotechnologist, business analyst, commission agent, computer analyst, conservationist, costume designer, dental hygienist, fashion designer, flight attendant, funeral director, graphic designer, marine biologist, military officer, ophthalmologist, personal trainer, physiotherapist, police constable, refuse collector, speech therapist, stock controller, ticket collector

occupational
04 work **05** trade **06** career **08** business **10** employment, job-related, vocational **12** professional

occupied
04 busy, full **05** in use, taken **06** tied up **07** engaged, taken up, working **08** absorbed, employed, hard at it, immersed, tenanted **09** engrossed **11** preoccupied, unavailable

occupier
04 user **06** dealer, holder, inmate, lessee, renter, tenant **08** occupant, resident, squatter **09** homeowner, incumbent **10** inhabitant **11** householder, leaseholder **13** owner-occupier

occupy
◇ *insertion indicator*
03 own, use **04** busy, fill, have, hold, nest, rent, tire **05** amuse, beset, seize, trade, use up **06** absorb, divert, embusy, employ, engage, fill in, invade, live in, manure, move in, obsess, obtain, people, settle, stay in, take up, tenant **07** capture, cohabit, dwell in, engross, entreat, immerse, improve, inhabit, involve, overrun, possess **08** interest, occupate, overbusy, reside in, take over **09** entertain, preoccupy, stimulate **14** make your home in

occur
03 hit **04** fall, meet **05** arise, exist **06** appear, befall, chance, crop up, dawn on, happen, obtain, result, sink in, strike, turn up **07** be found, develop, turn out **09** be present, come about, come to you, eventuate, take place, transpire **10** come to mind, come to pass **11** materialize **12** have its being, spring to mind **13** cross your mind, enter your head, present itself, suggest itself **14** manifest itself

occurrence
04 case **05** event **06** action, affair **07** arising, episode **08** incident, instance **09** existence, happening, incidence **10** appearance **11** development, proceedings, springing-up **12** circumstance **13** manifestation
• **trying occurrence**
03 cow

ocean
03 sea **04** main **05** briny **07** the deep **08** high seas, millpond, profound, the drink **11** herring pond

Oceans include:

06 Arctic, Indian
07 Pacific
08 Atlantic, Southern
12 North Pacific, South Pacific
13 North Atlantic, South Atlantic

See also **sea**

Ocean trenches include:

03 Yap
04 Java
05 Japan, Kuril, Palau, Tonga
06 Cayman, Ryukyu
07 Atacama, Mariana
08 Aleutian, Izu Bonin, Kermadec, Marianas, Mindanao, Romanche
09 Peru-Chile
10 Philippine, Puerto Rico
11 Nansei Shoto
12 Bougainville, West Caroline
13 Middle America, South Sandwich

ocean-going
05 naval **06** marine **07** sailing **08** maritime, nautical, seagoing **09** seafaring

ochre
04 keel

octave
04 utas

October
03 Oct

octopus
05 polyp, poulp **06** polype, poulpe **07** octopod **08** Octopoda **09** devilfish

odd
◇ *anagram indicator*
◇ *hidden alternately indicator*
03 god, rum **04** fent, orra, rare, wild, zany **05** barmy, drôle, droll, extra, funny, kinky, queer, spare, wacky, weird **06** casual, far-out, freaky, quaint, quirky, random, single, sundry, way-out, whimsy **07** bizarre, curious, deviant, oddball, odd-like, strange,

surplus, uncanny, unusual, various,
whimsey **08** abnormal, atypical,
crackers, freakful, freakish, left-over,
original, part-time, peculiar, periodic,
seasonal, singular, uncommon,
unpaired **09** different, eccentric,
haphazard, irregular, remaining,
temporary, unmatched, whimsical
10 additional, fortuitous, incidental,
mismatched, occasional, off the wall,
outlandish, remarkable **11** exceptional,
superfluous **13** extraordinary,
idiosyncratic, miscellaneous
14 unconventional

• **odd one out**
04 case, cure **05** freak **06** odd bod,
weirdo **07** oddball, odd fish
09 eccentric, odd man out, queer fish,
tall poppy **11** odd woman out
13 nonconformist **14** fish out of water

oddball
◇ *anagram indicator*
03 dag, nut, rum **04** card, case, geek,
kook, loon, wack **05** crank, flake, freak
06 nutter, oddity, weirdo **07** cupcake,
dingbat, oddfish, strange **08** crackpot,
peculiar **09** character, eccentric, queer
fish **13** nonconformist **14** fish out of
water

oddity
03 dag, nut, rum **04** card, case, geek,
kook, loon, wack **05** flake, freak, quirk,
twist **06** jimjam, misfit, nutter, object,
rarity, weirdo **07** anomaly, cupcake,
dingbat, oddball, odd fish
08 crackpot, queerity **09** character,
curiosity, queer fish, queerness
10 phenomenon **11** abnormality,
peculiarity, singularity, strangeness
12 eccentricity, idiosyncrasy **14** fish out
of water

odd-looking person
04 quiz

oddly
◇ *anagram indicator*
◇ *hidden alternately indicator*
07 weirdly **09** curiously, strangely,
unusually **10** abnormally, remarkably
11 irregularly

oddment
03 bit, end **04** fent **05** patch, piece,
scrap, shred **06** offcut **07** remnant,
snippet **08** fragment, leftover

odds
02 SP **04** edge, lead, line **05** price
06 scraps **07** chances, dispute, the line
09 advantage, supremacy
10 ascendancy, inequality, likelihood
11 probability, superiority **13** starting
price

• **at odds**
06 at outs **07** arguing **08** clashing
09 differing, out of step **10** at variance,
in conflict **11** disagreeing, quarrelling
13 at loggerheads **14** in disagreement

• **ignore the odds**
◇ *hidden alternately indicator*

• **odds and ends**
03 tat **04** bits, junk, tatt **06** debris, job-
lot, litter, scraps **07** rubbish

08 cuttings, leavings, oddments,
remnants, snippets **09** bric-à-brac
11 bits and bobs, odds and sods, this
and that **13** bits and pieces, odd-
come-shorts

ode
04 awdl **06** monody, threne
07 epicede, threnos **08** Pindaric,
stasimon, threnode, threnody
09 epicedium, epinicion, epinikion
12 genethliacon

odious
04 foul, vile **06** horrid **07** hateful,
heinous **08** horrible **09** abhorrent,
execrable, loathsome, obnoxious,
offensive, repugnant, repulsive,
revolting **10** abominable, despicable,
detestable, disgusting, unpleasant
12 contemptible, disagreeable
13 objectionable

odium
05 blame, shame **06** hatred, infamy
07 censure, dislike, obloquy
08 contempt, disgrace **09** animosity,
antipathy, discredit, disfavour,
dishonour, disrepute **10** abhorrence,
execration, opprobrium **11** detestation,
disapproval, reprobation
12 condemnation **13** offensiveness
14 disapprobation

odorous
05 balmy **07** pungent, scented
08 aromatic, fragrant, perfumed,
redolent **11** odoriferous **13** sweet-
smelling

odour
02 bo **04** niff, pong, sent, waff
05 aroma, savor, scent, smell, stink,
whiff **06** repute, savour, stench
07 bouquet, perfume **09** fragrance,
redolence

odourless
09 inodorous, unscented
10 deodorized **12** without smell
13 having no smell

odyssey
04 trek **06** voyage **07** journey, travels
09 adventure, wandering
13 peregrination

of
01 o' **02** de, du, on, to

off
◇ *anagram indicator*
03 bad, far, ill, out **04** away, from, gone,
high, kill, sick, sour **05** apart, aside,
right, rough, seedy, slack, wrong
06 absent, depart!, mouldy, poorly,
queasy, rancid, rotten, spoilt, turned,
unwell **07** dropped, off form, shelved
08 below par, scrapped
09 abandoned, called off, cancelled,
elsewhere, incorrect, off-colour,
postponed **10** decomposed,
indisposed, out of sorts **11** at a
distance, substandard, unavailable
12 unobtainable **13** disappointing
14 unsatisfactory **15** under the
weather

offal
03 fry **05** gurry, heart, liver **06** kidney,
refuse, tongue **07** garbage **08** entrails,
lamb's fry **11** variety meat

offbeat
05 kooky, wacky, weird **06** far-out,
freaky, way-out **07** bizarre, oddball,
strange, unusual **08** abnormal
09 eccentric **10** unorthodox
13 untraditional **14** unconventional

off-colour
◇ *anagram indicator*
03 ill **04** blue, foul, lewd, rude, sexy,
sick **05** crook, crude, dirty, gross,
rough, seedy **06** coarse, crummy, filthy,
impure, poorly, queasy, risqué, sleazy,
smutty, unwell, vulgar **07** immoral,
obscene, off form, run down
08 depraved, immodest, improper,
indecent **09** offensive, perverted
10 degenerate, indelicate, indisposed,
licentious, out of sorts, suggestive
11 peelie-wally **12** pornographic
15 under the weather

offence
03 ire, sin **04** hurt, snub **05** anger,
crime, fault, pique, wrong **06** injury,
insult, slight **07** affront, assault,
misdeed, outrage, umbrage
08 atrocity, trespass **09** annoyance,
antipathy, exception, indignity,
stumbling, violation **10** illegal act,
infraction, resentment, wrongdoing
11 disapproval, displeasure, indignation
12 exasperation, hard feelings,
infringement, misdemeanour
13 transgression **14** breach of the
law

See also **crime**

• **take offence**
04 huff, miff **06** be hurt, resent **07** be
angry, be upset **08** be miffed, be put
out, get huffy **09** be annoyed **10** be
insulted, be offended, feel put out, get
the hump **11** be indignant, go into a
huff, take umbrage **13** be exasperated,
take exception **14** take personally

offend
03 err, hip, hyp, sin **04** hurt, miff, snub
05 anger, annoy, repel, upset, wound,
wrong **06** injure, insult, kittle, needle,
put off, put out, revolt, sicken
07 affront, disgust, do wrong, incense,
outrage, provoke, umbrage, violate
08 distaste, go astray, gross out,
nauseate **09** disoblige, displease
10 exasperate, transgress **11** break the
law, displeasure

offended
04 hurt **05** huffy, stung, upset
06 hipped, miffed, pained, piqued, put
out **07** angered, annoyed, in a huff,
wounded **08** incensed, outraged,
smarting **09** affronted, disgusted,
resentful **10** displeased **11** disgruntled,
exasperated

offender
07 culprit **08** criminal **09** defaulter,
miscreant, wrongdoer **10** delinquent,

lawbreaker, malefactor **11** guilty party, probationer **12** transgressor

offensive

03 bad **04** foul, push, raid, rude, vile **05** alien, drive, grody, nasty **06** attack, charge, frowsy, frowzy, odious, sortie, thrust, wicked **07** abusive, assault, hostile, hurtful **08** annoying, impolite, indecent, insolent, invading, invasion, stinking, wounding **09** abhorrent, attacking, incursion, insulting, loathsome, obnoxious, onslaught, repellent, repugnant, revolting, sickening, unsavoury, upsetting **10** abominable, affronting, aggressive, detestable, disgusting, nauseating, outrageous, unpleasant **11** belligerent, displeasing, impertinent **12** antagonistic, disagreeable, discourteous, disrelishing, exasperating **13** disrespectful, objectionable

offensively

10 detestably **12** disagreeably, disgustingly, nauseatingly, unpleasantly **13** objectionably

offer

03 bid, try **04** bode, give, make, sell, show **05** essay, shore **06** afford, extend, prefer, submit, supply, tender **07** advance, attempt, bidding, express, hold out, offer up, present, proffer, propine, propose, provide, suggest, worship **08** approach, dedicate, overture, proposal, propound **09** celebrate, put in a bid, recommend, sacrifice, volunteer **10** consecrate, put forward, submission, suggestion **11** come forward, proposition, show willing **12** presentation **13** make available **14** put on the market

offering

03 IPO **04** gift **05** tithe **06** ex voto, xenium **07** handout, present **08** donation, oblation **09** sacrifice **10** dedication **11** celebration **12** consecration, contribution, subscription **13** heave-shoulder

offhand

04 airy, curt, rude, snap **05** ad lib, blasé, terse **06** abrupt, at once, casual **07** brusque, cursory **08** careless, cavalier, informal, laid-back **09** brevi manu, extempore, impromptu **10** cavalierly, nonchalant, off the cuff **11** free-and-easy, immediately, indifferent, perfunctory, unconcerned **12** at first blush, discourteous, happy-go-lucky, uninterested **13** unceremonious **14** currente calamo **15** at the first blush, take-it-or-leave-it, without checking

office

03 aid **04** base, duty, help, hint, part, post, role, wing, word, work **05** aegis, place **06** agency, back-up, branch, bureau, charge, favour, tenure **07** backing, cockpit, section, service, support **08** advocacy, auspices, business, division, function, lavatory,

position, referral, workroom **09** affiliate, mediation, patronage, situation, workplace **10** assistance, commission, department, employment, obligation, occupation, subsection, subsidiary **11** appointment, local office, subdivision **12** intercession, intervention **14** recommendation, regional office, responsibility **15** place of business

See also **toilet**

Offices include:

02 CO, FO, PO, TO, WO
03 box, COI, CRO, DLO, EPO, FCO, GAO, GPO, IIP, IRO, Met, NAO, OFT, OME, ONS, OPW, ORR, OSS, OST, pay, PRO, RLO, SFO, War
04 back, BFPO, fire, HMSO, Holy, Home, land, loan, Pipe, Post
05 Assay, Crown, front, Ofcom, Offer, Ofgas, Ofgem, Oflot, Oftel, Ofwat, paper, press, stamp
06 Ofsted, Patent, Pat Off, police, Record, ticket
07 booking, Foreign, sorting
08 Chancery, Colonial, Eurostat, incident, printing, register, registry, Scottish
09 personnel, receiving, telegraph
10 dead-letter, employment, Quai d'Orsay, registered, Stationery
11 general post, left-luggage, victualling
12 Commonwealth, Serious Fraud
13 Inland Revenue, National Audit
14 European Patent, Meteorological, returned letter
15 Criminal Records

Office furniture includes:

04 desk, safe
07 lectern
08 desk lamp, fire safe
09 partition, plan chest, stepstool, work table
11 storage unit, swivel chair, workstation
12 computer desk, drawing-board, fire cupboard, printer stand, typist's chair
13 executive desk, filing cabinet, filing trolley
14 boardroom table, display cabinet, executive chair, filing cupboard, reception chair
15 conference table, secretarial desk

Office equipment includes:

03 OHP, VDU
05 mouse
06 inkpad, screen, tacker
07 cash box, monitor, planner, printer, scanner, stapler, trimmer
08 computer, intercom, keyboard, mouse mat, plan file, shredder
09 date-stamp, dust cover, laminator, telephone, textphone, time clock, wages book
10 calculator, comb binder, copy holder, Dictaphone®, duplicator,

fax machine, guillotine, letter tray, monitor arm, paper punch, printwheel, typewriter
11 comb binding, hole puncher, noticeboard, photocopier, switchboard
12 acoustic hood, letter opener, letter scales, message board, parcel scales, screen filter, telex machine, visitors' book, wire bindings
13 data cartridge, desk organizer, microcassette, planning board, reference book, staple-remover, thermal binder, waste-paper bin, word processor
14 adhesive binder, diskette mailer, flip-chart easel, laptop computer, slide projector, telephone index

See also **stationery**

- **branch office**
02 bo
- **in office**
02 in
- **office of bishop**
03 see
- **office of cardinal**
03 hat
- **out of office**
04 late

officer

03 col, off **04** lead **05** agent, envoy, polis **06** deputy, fantad, fantod, non-com, pusser, schout, varlet **07** command **08** dog's-body, official **09** appointee, dignitary, executive, inspector, messenger, subaltern **10** bureaucrat **11** board member, functionary **12** office-bearer, office-holder **13** administrator, public servant **14** representative **15** committee member

See also **police officer; rank; religious; ship**

official

03 off **05** legal **06** Bumble, formal, kosher, lawful, proper, pusser, ritual, solemn **07** officer, stately **08** accepted, approved, bona fide, endorsed, licensed **09** authentic, certified, dignified, validated **10** accredited, authorized, ceremonial, legitimate, recognized, sanctioned **11** functionary **12** Jack-in-office, office-bearer, office-holder **13** authenticated, authoritative

Officials include:

02 JP, MP
05 agent, chief, clerk, druid, elder, envoy, hakim, mayor, reeve, usher
06 atabeg, atabek, consul, Euro-MP, notary, purser, pusser
07 bailiff, captain, coroner, equerry, manager, marshal, monitor, prefect, proctor, senator, sheriff, steward, vaivode, voivode
08 chairman, delegate, diplomat, director, Eurocrat, executor, governor, mandarin, mayoress, minister, mud-clerk, nipcheese, overseer, provedor, providor
09 commander, commissar, executive,

Gauleiter, inspector, ombudsman, president, principal, provedore, registrar
10 ambassador, bureaucrat, chairwoman, chancellor, councillor, magistrate, proprietor, proveditor, railroader, supervisor
11 chairperson, congressman, proveditore
12 baron-officer, borough-reeve, civil servant, commissioner
13 administrator, congresswoman, fonctionnaire
14 representative, superintendent

officialdom
04 them **08** ministry **09** mandarins, officials, the system **10** government
11 bureaucracy **12** civil service
13 administrator, civil servants
14 administration, the authorities
15 local government

officialese
06 jargon **07** rubbish **08** nonsense
09 buzz words, gibberish
10 journalese **11** computerese
12 gobbledygook, psychobabble

officially
08 formally, properly **09** correctly
11 on the record **12** managerially, procedurally **13** authentically
15 authoritatively

officiate
03 run **05** chair **06** manage
07 conduct, oversee, preside **10** be in charge, take charge **11** superintend
12 take the chair

officious
05 bossy, pushy **06** prying, spoffy
07 dutiful, forward **08** bustling, informal, meddling, obliging, overbusy, spoffish **09** diplomacy, intrusive, obtrusive **10** meddlesome
11 dictatorial, domineering, importunate, inquisitive, interfering, opinionated, over-zealous, pragmatical **13** self-important

officiously
07 bossily, pushily **13** dictatorially, over-zealously **15** self-importantly, with importunity

offing
• **in the offing**
04 near **06** at hand **07** in sight
08 coming up, imminent, on the way
10 coming soon, on the cards **11** close at hand **12** on the horizon
13 happening soon

offish
04 cool **05** aloof **07** haughty, stuck-up
10 unsociable **11** standoffish

off-key
07 jarring **09** dissonant, out of tune
10 discordant, unsuitable
11 conflicting **12** inharmonious, out of keeping **13** inappropriate

offload
04 drop, dump, palm **05** chuck, shift
06 unload **07** deposit **08** get rid of,

jettison, unburden **09** disburden, discharge

off-putting
08 daunting **09** unnerving, upsetting
10 disturbing, formidable, unpleasant, unsettling **11** dispiriting, frightening, unappealing **12** demoralizing, discomfiting, discouraging, intimidating **13** disconcerting, disheartening

offset
06 cancel **07** balance **09** cancel out, make up for **10** balance out, counteract, neutralize **11** countervail
12 counterpoise **13** compensate for
14 counterbalance

offshoot
03 arm **04** limb, sien **05** bayou, plant, scion, swarm **06** branch, reform, result
07 outcome, product, spin-off
08 shoulder, sideslip **09** apophysis, appendage, billabong, by-product, outgrowth **11** consequence, development

offspring
03 get, kid, son **04** baby, burd, kids, seed, sons **05** breed, brood, child, heirs, issue, spawn, young **06** babies, family, infant, nipper, source **07** infants, nippers, product, progeny **08** ancestry, children, daughter, young one
09 daughters, little one, young ones, youngster **10** generation, little ones, successors, youngsters **11** descendants

often
03 oft **04** much **08** commonly, frequent, ofttimes **09** generally, many a time, many times, regularly
10 frequently, repeatedly **11** day in day out **12** time and again **13** again and again, time after time, week in week out **15** month in month out

ogle
03 eye **04** leer, look **05** eliad, eye up, stare **06** eyliad, illiad **07** eyeliad, glad eye **08** oeillade **10** make eyes at

ogre
03 orc **04** boyg **05** beast, bogey, brute, demon, devil, fiend, giant, troll
06 savage **07** monster, villain
08 bogeyman **09** barbarian

Ohio
02 OH

oik *see* **cad**

oil
03 fat **04** balm, news, oint **05** cream, salve, smear **06** anoint, grease, lotion
07 unguent **08** liniment, ointment
09 lubricant, lubricate **10** impregnate, make smooth **11** information

Oils include:

03 ben, gas, nim, nut, til
04 baby, cade, coal, corn, crab, derv, dika, fish, fuel, hair, neem, nimb, otto, palm, poon, rape, rock, rose, rusa, seed, tall, tung, wood, wool, zest

05 attar, carap, crude, grass, heavy, macaw, neemb, niger, olive, ottar, poppy, pulza, rosin, salad, savin, shale, shark, snake, sperm, spike, sweet, thyme, train, whale
06 ajowan, almond, canola, castor, chrism, cloves, cohune, diesel, illipe, jojoba, macoya, neroli, peanut, savine, Seneca, sesame
07 arachis, cajuput, camphor, coconut, gingili, jinjili, linseed, lumbang, mineral, mirbane, mustard, myrrhol, spindle, verbena, vitriol
08 ambrosia, bergamot, camphine, cinnamon, cod-liver, creosote, gingelly, kerosene, kerosine, lavender, macahuba, macassar, North Sea, paraffin, pristane, rapeseed, rosewood
09 black gold, candlenut, grapeseed, neat's-foot, patchouli, patchouly, safflower, sassafras, spikenard, sunflower, vanaspati, vegetable
10 citronella, eucalyptus, peppermint, petit grain, turpentine, ylang-ylang
11 camphorated, chaulmoogra, wintergreen
12 brilliantine
15 evening primrose

• **oil platform**
03 rig
• **oil receptacle**
04 sump

oily
03 fat **04** glib **05** fatty, slimy, suave
06 greasy, smarmy, smooth, urbane
07 buttery, servile **08** slippery, unctuous **10** flattering, obsequious, oleaginous **11** subservient
12 ingratiating **13** smooth-talking

ointment
03 gel **04** balm **05** cream, salve
06 balsam, cerate, lotion, pomade
07 pomatum, unction, unguent
08 eye-salve, liniment, lipsalve, Vaseline® **09** basilicon, cold cream, collyrium, emollient, inunction, lubricant, Tiger balm®
11 embrocation, preparation
• **ointment base**
07 lanolin

OK
03 A-OK, oke, yes **04** fair, fine, good, jake, okay, pass, so-so, sure, well
05 right **06** agreed, not bad, righto
07 agree to, approve, consent, correct, go-ahead, in order, up to par
08 accurate, adequate, all right, approval, okey-doke, passable, passably, sanction, say yes to, thumbs-up, very good, very well
09 agreement, authorize, certainly, consent to, no worries, okey-dokey, permitted, tolerable, tolerably
10 acceptable, all correct, convenient, good as gold, green light, no problems, permission, reasonable, reasonably
11 approbation, endorsement, rubber-stamp, up to scratch **12** satisfactory,

she'll be right **13** authorization, Bob's your uncle, she'll be apples **14** satisfactorily

Oklahoma
02 OK **04** Okla

okra
05 gumbo **06** bhindi **11** lady's finger **12** lady's fingers

old
◇ *archaic word indicator*
01 O **02** ex- **03** eld, set **04** aged, auld, folk, gaga, gray, grey, oral, torn, wise, worn **05** aging, banal, corny, early, fixed, passé, stale, stock, tired, trite, usual **06** ageing, age-old, bygone, common, former, mature, past it, primal, senile, shabby **07** ancient, antique, archaic, cast-off, classic, cliché'd, decayed, earlier, elderly, lasting, one-time, quondam, routine, veteran, vintage, worn-out **08** clichéed, decaying, decrepit, earliest, enduring, habitual, historic, obsolete, original, outdated, overused, previous, primeval, pristine, sensible, sometime, time-worn **09** crumbling, customary, erstwhile, getting on, hackneyed, long-lived, out of date, primaeval, primitive, senescent, unwritten, worm-eaten **10** accustomed, antiquated, broken down, ceremonial, Dickensian, overworked, pedestrian, primordial, ramshackle, threadbare, tumbledown, uninspired, unoriginal, yawn-making **11** commonplace, established, on the way out, out of the ark, over the hill, prehistoric, stereotyped, traditional, wearing thin **12** antediluvian, cliché-ridden, conventional, long-standing, old-fashioned, run-of-the-mill, time-honoured **13** old as the hills, past your prime, platitudinous, unfashionable, unimaginative **14** behind the times, long in the tooth **15** advanced in years, long-established, no spring chicken

old age
03 age, eld **04** hoar, hore **05** years **06** dotage **07** oldness **08** agedness, senility **09** antiquity **10** senescence **11** elderliness, vale of years **14** advancing years, declining years **15** second childhood

old-fashioned
◇ *archaic word indicator*
03 old **04** dead, past **05** corny, dated, dusty, fusty, mumsy, passé, steam **06** antick, bygone, old hat, past it, Podunk, quaint, rococo, square, uncool **07** ancient, antique, archaic, arriéré, old-time **08** medieval, obsolete, outdated, outmoded, shmaltzy, vieux jeu **09** mediaeval, moth-eaten, out of date, primitive, rinky-dink, schmaltzy **10** antiquated, auld-farand, fuddy-duddy, oldfangled, written off **11** auld-farrant, Neanderthal, obsolescent, on the way out, out of the ark **12** antediluvian, out of fashion **13** unfashionable **14** behind the times

old maid
08 spinster

old man
02 pa **03** OAP **04** boss, koro **05** elder, oldie **06** bodach, father, gaffer, geezer, Nestor **07** grandad, husband, oldster **08** employer, granddad, old-timer, presbyte **09** greybeard, old codger, old stager, patriarch, pensioner **10** fuddy-duddy, golden ager, white-beard **11** grandfather **12** coffin-dodger **13** senior citizen **14** elder statesman **15** old-age pensioner

See also **father**; **old woman**

old-time
03 old **04** past **05** dated, passé **06** bygone **07** archaic **08** obsolete, outdated, outmoded **09** out of date **10** antiquated **12** old-fashioned, out of fashion **13** unfashionable **14** behind the times

old woman
03 bag, hag, OAP **04** aunt, kuia, trot, wife **05** biddy, crone, fagot, oldie **06** beldam, faggot, gammer, granny, grouch, mother **07** beldame, carline, fusspot, grandma, grannie, old dear **08** caillach, grumbler **09** cailleach, cailliach, grandmama, pensioner **10** complainer, golden ager, grandmamma **11** grandmother **12** coffin-dodger **13** senior citizen **15** old-age pensioner

See also **mother**; **old man**

old-world
04 past **06** bygone, quaint **07** archaic **09** auld-warld **10** antiquated, olde-worlde **11** picturesque, traditional **12** old-fashioned

olio
04 olla **06** medley **07** mixture **10** miscellany

olive
04 Olea **05** wolly **08** oleaster

Olympics

Olympians include:

03 Coe (Sebastian)
04 Clay (Cassius), Dean (Christopher), Ewry (Ray), Otto (Kristin), Papp (Laszlo), Todd (Mark), Witt (Katarina)
05 Blair (Bonnie), Bubka (Sergei), Chand (Dhyan), Cranz (Christl), Curry (John), Henie (Sonja), Killy (Jean-Claude), Lewis (Carl), Lewis (Denise), Longo (Jeannie), Meade (Richard), Nurmi (Paavo), Ottey (Merlene), Owens (Jesse), Popov (Aleksandr), Savon (Felix), Spitz (Mark), Tomba (Alberto)
06 Aamodt (Kjetil), Beamon (Bob), Bikila (Abebe), Biondi (Matt), Button (Dick), D'Inzeo (Raimondo), Fraser (Dawn), Heiden (Eric), Holmes (Dame Kelly), Korbut (Olga), Oerter (Al), Phelps (Michael), Ritola (Ville), Sailer (Toni), Thorpe (Ian), Thorpe (Jim)

07 Ainslie (Ben), Boitano (Brian), Cousins (Robin), Daehlie (Bjorn), Edwards (Jonathan), Fischer (Birgit), Johnson (Michael), Klammer (Franz), Mathias (Bob), Nykänen (Matti), Pinsent (Sir Matthew), Scherbo (Vitaly), Schmidt (Birgit), Torvill (Jayne), Voronin (Mikhail), Zatopek (Emil), Zelezny (Jan)
08 Christie (Linford), Comaneci (Nadia), Cuthbert (Betty), De Bruijn (Inge), Dityatin (Aleksandr), Elvstrøm (Paul), Gerevich (Aladár), Jernberg (Sixten), Latynina (Larissa), Louganis (Greg), Redgrave (Sir Steve), Stenmark (Ingemar), Thompson (Daley), Zijlaard (Leontien)
09 Andrianov (Nikolay), Babashoff (Shirley), Cáslavská (Vera), Egerszegi (Krisztina), Gräfström (Gillis), Schneider (Vreni), Seizinge (Katja), Stevenson (Teófilo)
10 Linsenhoff (Liselott), Moser-Proll (Annemarie), van Moorsel (Leontien)
11 Mangiarotti (Edouardo), Weissmuller (Johnny)
12 Blankers-Koen (Fanny), Gebrselassie (Haile), Germeshauser (Bernhard), Joyner-Kersee (Jackie), Suleymanoglu (Naim)
13 Longo-Ciprelli (Jeannie)
14 Griffith-Joyner (Florence)

Oman
03 OMN

omelette
08 frittata, tortilla

omen
04 sign **05** freet, freit, purse, token **06** augury, boding **07** auspice, portent, presage, warning **08** bodement, dead-fire, forecast, prodrome, soothsay **09** abodement, harbinger, night-crow, prodromus, prognosis **10** foreboding, forerunner, indication, night-raven, prediction, prognostic **11** premonition, presagement **12** corpse candle, presentiment

ominous
07 bodeful, fateful, unlucky **08** menacing, minatory, sinister **10** foreboding, portentous **11** threatening, unpromising **12** inauspicious, unfavourable, unpropitious

ominously
06 grimly **10** alarmingly **11** dangerously **13** frighteningly

omission
03 gap, out **04** balk, lack **05** baulk **06** lacuna **07** default, elision, erasure, failure, neglect **08** deletion **09** avoidance, disregard, exception, exclusion, haplology, oversight **10** expunction, leaving-out, lipography, negligence **11** dereliction

omit
03 let **04** drop, fail, miss, pass, skip

erase **06** delete, except, forget, rub
…t **07** edit out, exclude, expunge, miss
…t, neglect **08** cross out, leave out,
…erlook, overskip, pass over, white
…t **09** disregard, eliminate, pretermit
leave undone **13** fail to mention

mnibus
… anthology, inclusive **10** collection,
…mpendium **11** compendious,
…mpilation, wide-ranging **12** all-
…mbracing, encyclopedia,
…cyclopedic **13** comprehensive

mnipotence
mastery **09** supremacy **10** total
…wer **11** divine right, sovereignty
almightiness, plenipotence
absolute power, invincibility **15** all-
…werfulness

mnipotent
supreme **08** almighty **10** invincible
all-powerful, plenipotent

mnipresent
… infinite **09** limitless, pervasive,
…iversal **10** all-present, ubiquitary,
…iquitous **12** all-pervasive

mniscient
… all-wise **09** all-seeing, pansophic
… all-knowing

mnivorous
… gluttonous **12** all-devouring,
…antophagous **14** eating anything,
…discriminate

n
anagram indicator
juxtaposition down indicator
… o **02** an, by, in, of, re, to **03** leg, sur
… atop, over, side, upon **05** about, tipsy
… beside, tiddly **07** against, forward!,
…roceed!, stuck to, towards **08** feasible,
…uching **09** apropos of, as regards,
…garding, resting on **10** acceptable,
…tached to, concerning, relating to
… dealing with, practicable, referring
… **12** with regard to **13** concerned
…ith, connected with, in contact with,
…the matter of, with respect to **14** on
…e subject of **15** with reference to
on and off
… fitfully, off and on, sporadic
… sometimes **10** now and then,
…ccasional, on occasion **11** at intervals,
…regularly, now and again **12** every so
…ften, intermittent, occasionally,
…eriodically, sporadically
… spasmodically **14** from time to time,
…termittently **15** discontinuously
on and on
… e'er **04** ever **06** always **07** forever,
…on-stop **09** endlessly, eternally,
…gularly **10** all the time, constantly,
…equently, habitually, repeatedly
… ceaselessly, continually, incessantly,
…erpetually, recurrently
… interminably, persistently
… everlastingly

nce
archaic word indicator
… ance, onst, when **05** after
… former **07** firstly, long ago, on a time,

one time **08** as soon as, formerly **09** at
one time, in the past, upon a time **10** at
one point, previously **11** in times past
12 in the old days **13** in times gone by,
once upon a time, on one occasion
• **at once**
03 now, tit **04** tite, tyte **05** alike, atone,
ek dum, swith, tight **06** attone, presto,
pronto, statim, titely **07** at a word,
attonce, attones, offhand **08** directly,
promptly, right now, together
09 forthwith, hey presto, instantly, like a
shot, on the spot, right away, yesterday
10 forthright **11** immediately, tout de
suite **12** straightaway, without delay **13** at
the same time **14** simultaneously **15** at
the same moment, before you know it
• **more than once**
04 anew, over **05** again **10** repeatedly
• **once and for all**
07 finally, for good **10** decisively,
positively **11** permanently
12 conclusively, definitively **14** for the
last time
• **once in a while**
07 at times **08** off and on, on and off
09 sometimes **10** now and then, on
occasion **11** now and again
12 infrequently, occasionally,
periodically, sporadically **14** from time
to time, intermittently **15** once in a blue
moon

once-over
04 gape, gaze, look, peek, peep, test
05 audit, check, dekko, probe, stare
06 eyeful, gander, glance, shufti, squint
07 checkup, glimpse, inquiry
08 analysis, butcher's, research,
scrutiny **10** inspection, monitoring
11 examination **12** confirmation,
verification **13** investigation

oncoming
07 looming, nearing **08** approach,
upcoming **09** advancing, gathering,
onrushing **11** approaching

one
01 a, I **02** ae, us **03** ace, ane, yin
04 lone, only, sole, tane, unit **05** alike,
bound, equal, fused, monad, unity,
whole **06** entire, joined, single, united,
wedded **07** married **08** complete,
solitary **09** identical, undivided
10 harmonious, individual, like-
minded
• **French one**
02 un **03** une
• **German one**
03 ein **04** eine, eins
• **Italian one, Spanish one**
03 uno

oneness
05 unity **07** unicity **08** identity,
sameness **09** wholeness **10** singleness,
uniqueness **11** consistency,
homogeneity, singularity
12 completeness **13** identicalness,
individuality

onerous
04 hard **05** heavy **06** taxing, tiring
07 arduous, exigent, weighty

08 crushing, exacting, wearying
09 demanding, difficult, fatiguing,
laborious, strenuous **10** burdensome,
exhausting, oppressive **11** troublesome
12 back-breaking

oneself
• **by oneself**
04 solo **05** alone **06** lonely, singly
07 forlorn, unaided **08** deserted,
desolate, forsaken, isolated, lonesome
09 abandoned, on your own, on your
tod **10** by yourself, unassisted,
unattended, unescorted **11** without
help **12** single-handed
13 independently, unaccompanied
15 on your Pat Malone

one-sided
06 biased, one-way, uneven, unfair,
unjust **07** bigoted, partial, unequal
08 lopsided, partisan, separate
09 separated **10** prejudiced,
unbalanced, unilateral **11** independent,
inequitable **12** disconnected, narrow-
minded **14** discriminatory

one-time
02 ex- **03** old **04** late, past **06** former
07 quondam **08** previous, sometime
09 erstwhile

ongoing
05 event **07** current, growing, non-
stop **08** constant, evolving, unbroken,
unending **09** advancing, incessant,
unfolding **10** continuing, continuous,
developing, in progress, unfinished
11 progressing **13** uninterrupted

onion
04 head, moly, ramp, sybo **05** cibol,
ingan, syboe, sybow **06** chibol, shalot
07 shallot **08** scallion
See also **head**

onlooker
06 gawper, viewer **07** watcher, witness
08 beholder, looker-on, observer
09 bystander, sightseer, spectator
10 eyewitness, rubberneck

only
03 but, one **04** just, lone, sole **05** alone
06 anerly, at most, barely, except,
merely, nobbut, purely, simply, single,
singly, solely, unique **07** onliest
08 solitary **09** allenarly, exclusive
10 individual, no more than, nothing
but, one and only **11** exclusively, not
more than

onrush
04 flow, push, rush **05** flood, onset,
surge, sweep **06** career, charge, stream
07 cascade **08** stampede
09 onslaught

onset
04 dash, fall, push, raid, rush **05** break,
start **06** access, affret, attack, charge,
onding, onrush, outset **07** assault, kick-
off **08** outbreak, storming
09 beginning, inception, onslaught
12 commencement

onslaught
04 push, raid **05** blitz, drive, foray,

onset, swoop **06** attack, charge,
dismay, onfall, onrush, thrust
07 assault, dead-set **08** storming
09 offensive **11** bombardment

Ontario
02 ON

onus
04 duty, load, task **06** burden, charge,
weight **09** albatross, liability, millstone
10 obligation **11** encumbrance
14 responsibility

onward
04 away

onwards
02 on **05** ahead, forth **06** beyond
07 forward, in front **08** forwards

oodles
04 bags, lots, tons **05** heaps, loads
06 masses **08** lashings **09** abundance

oomph
02 it, SA **03** pep **04** zing **06** bounce,
energy, vigour **07** pizzazz, sparkle
08 sexiness, vitality, vivacity
09 animation, sex-appeal
10 enthusiasm, exuberance, get-up-
and-go

ooze
03 mud, nap, sap, sew **04** drip, drop,
emit, flow, leak, mire, muck, seep, silt,
sipe, slob, spew, spue, sype, weep
05 bleed, drain, exude, fluff, slime
06 escape, exhale, filter, sludge
07 deposit, dribble, excrete, secrete,
seepage, trickle **08** alluvium, filtrate,
sediment **09** discharge, percolate,
pour forth **12** overflow with

oozy
04 dewy, miry **05** moist, mucky,
muddy, slimy, weepy **06** sloppy, sludgy,
sweaty **07** weeping **08** dripping
09 uliginose, uliginous

opacity
04 body, onyx **06** nebula **07** density,
leucoma **08** dullness **09** filminess,
milkiness, murkiness, obscurity
10 cloudiness, opaqueness
11 obfuscation, unclearness
14 impermeability **15** impenetrability

opal
07 girasol, hyalite **08** girasole
09 cacholong **10** hydrophane

opalescence
05 prism **07** glitter, rainbow
08 dazzling **09** sparkling **10** glittering,
shimmering **11** iridescence,
multicolour **14** rainbow colours

opalescent
04 shot **06** pearly **07** rainbow
08 dazzling **09** prismatic, sparkling
10 glittering, iridescent, shimmering,
variegated **11** cymophanous, rainbow-
like **13** multicoloured, polychromatic
15 rainbow-coloured

opaque
03 dim **04** dark, dull, hazy **05** dense,
dingy, misty, muddy, murky, shady,

thick **06** cloudy, turbid **07** blurred,
clouded, cryptic, doltish, intense,
muddied, obscure, unclear
08 abstruse, baffling, esoteric,
puzzling **09** confusing, difficult,
enigmatic, recondite **12** as clear as
mud, impenetrable, unfathomable
14 unintelligible

OPEC

04 Iran, Iraq
05 Libya, Qatar
06 Kuwait
07 Algeria, Nigeria
09 Indonesia, Venezuela
11 Saudi Arabia
18 United Arab Emirates

open
03 dup **04** agee, airy, ajar, ajee, bare,
fair, free, moot, undo, wide **05** apert,
begin, blunt, broad, clear, crack, frank,
holey, loose, overt, plain, split, start,
unlid, unrip, untie **06** broach, candid,
deploy, direct, expose, extend, flower,
gaping, honest, launch, liable, ouvert,
patent, porous, public, reveal, simple,
spread, spring, unbolt, uncork, unfold,
unfurl, unlock, unpack, unroll, unseal,
unshut, vacant **07** blatant, divulge,
evident, explain, exposed, general,
kick off, lay bare, lidless, natural,
obvious, ouverte, subject, topless,
unblock, unclasp, unclose, uncover,
unlatch, unscrew, upbreak, visible,
yawning **08** apparent, arguable,
cellular, commence, disclose,
disposed, flagrant, initiate, manifest,
openwork, passable, push open,
separate, unbarred, unbolted,
unclosed, unfasten, unfenced,
unfolded, unfrozen, unhidden,
unlocked, unripped, unsealed, wide
open **09** available, break open, burst
open, champaign, come apart,
coverless, debatable, fenceless, force
open, guileless, ingenuous, navigable,
prise open, receptive, slide open,
spread out, unblocked, uncovered,
undecided, unlatched, unsettled,
unstopped, well known **10** above-
board, accessible, forthright,
inaugurate, noticeable, obtainable,
spongelike, unenclosed, unfastened,
unoccupied, unreserved, unresolved,
up in the air, vulnerable
11 conspicuous, get cracking,
honeycombed, problematic, set in
motion, susceptible, unconcealed,
undisguised, unprotected,
unsheltered, widely known
12 approachable, loosely woven,
unobstructed, unrestricted **13** take the
plunge **15** open to the risk of
• **opening words**
06 sesame
• **open onto**
04 face **06** lead to **08**. give onto,
overlook **14** command a view of
• **open up**
03 win

open-air
06 afield **07** outdoor, outside
08 alfresco, plein-air **10** out-of-doors

open-and-shut
05 clear **06** simple **07** obvious
12 easily solved **13** easily decided
15 straightforward

opener
◇ *head selection indicator*

open-handed
04 free **06** lavish **07** liberal
08 generous **09** bounteous, bountiful
10 munificent, unstinting
11 magnanimous **12** eleemosynary,
large-hearted

opening
◇ *head selection indicator*
02 os **03** gap, gat, job **04** adit, anus,
bole, cave, dawn, gape, gate, hole,
pore, port, rent, scye, slit, slot, vent,
yawn **05** birth, break, chasm, chink,
cleft, crack, early, first, inlet, onset,
place, space, split, start, stoma, thirl
06 breach, chance, hiatus, launch,
outlet, outset, window **07** crevice,
fissure, foramen, initial, kick-off, orifice
ostiole, portage, primary, rupture,
undoing, vacancy **08** aperture,
fenestra, occasion, position, starting
09 beginning, first base, inaugural,
inception, mouse hole, square one, the
word go **10** commencing, fenestella,
interstice **11** opportunity, possibility
12 inauguration, introductory

openly
06 barely **07** bluntly, frankly, overtly,
plainly, up front **08** brazenly, candidly,
directly, honestly, in public, patently,
publicly **09** blatantly, glaringly
10 above board, flagrantly, immodestly
in full view **11** on the square,
shamelessly, unashamedly
12 forthrightly, unreservedly

open-minded
04 free **05** broad **07** liberal
08 catholic, tolerant, unbiased
09 impartial, objective, receptive
10 reasonable **11** broad-minded,
enlightened **12** unprejudiced
13 dispassionate **14** latitudinarian

open-mindedness
06 equity **07** justice **08** equality,
fairness **10** detachment, dispassion,
neutrality **11** disinterest, objectivity
12 impartiality, unbiasedness **14** even-
handedness **15** non-partisanship

open-mouthed
06 amazed, gaping, greedy
07 shocked **08** wide-eyed
09 astounded, clamorous, expectant,
surprised **10** astonished, spellbound
11 dumbfounded, widechapped
13 flabbergasted, thunderstruck

openwork
04 mode

opera
03 ENO **05** works **08** burletta
09 pastorale **10** music drama

13 dramma giocoso **15** dramma per musica

See also **singer**

Operas and operettas include:

04 Aïda
05 Faust, Manon, Norma, Tosca
06 Carmen, Otello, Salome
07 Elektra, Fidelio, Macbeth, Nabucco, Thespis, The Ring, Werther, Wozzeck
08 Falstaff, Idomeneo, Iolanthe, La Bohème, Parsifal, Patience, Turandot
09 Billy Budd, Capriccio, Don Carlos, King Priam, Lohengrin, Rigoletto, Ruddigore, Siegfried, The Mikado, Véronique
10 Cinderella, Die Walküre, I Pagliacci, La Traviata, Oedipus Rex, Tannhäuser
11 Don Giovanni, Don Pasquale, HMS Pinafore, Il Trovatore, La Périchole, Peter Grimes, Princess Ida, The Sorceror, Trial by Jury, William Tell
12 Boris Godunov, Cosí Fan Tutte, Das Rheingold, Eugene Onegin, Manon Lescaut, Nixon in China, Porgy and Bess, The Grand Duke, The Huguenots, The Rhinegold, The Valkyries
13 Albert Herring, Der Freischütz, Dido and Aeneas, Die Fledermaus, La Belle Hélène, Moses and Aaron, Powder Her Face, The Fairy Queen, The Gondoliers, The Knot Garden, The Magic Flute, Utopia Limited
14 Le Grand Macabre, Samson et Dalila
15 Ariadne auf Naxos, Götterdämmerung, Hansel and Gretel, Le Nozze di Figaro, Madama Butterfly, Madame Butterfly, Orfeo ed Euridice, Simon Boccanegra, The Beggar's Opera, The Pearl Fishers

Opera houses include:

03 Met, ROH
05 Cairo, Lyric, Royal, State
06 De Munt, Sydney, the Met, Zurich
07 La Scala
08 La Fenice, San Carlo
09 La Monnaie
10 Mussorgsky, Semper Oper
11 Oper Leipzig, Teatro Liceo, Verona Arena
12 Glyndebourne, Komische Oper, Metropolitan, Opéra-Comique
13 Kennedy Center, Muziektheater, Opera Bastille, Teatro Massimo
14 Bolshoi Theatre, Estates Theatre, Hungarian State, Kungliga Operan, London Coliseum, Unter den Linden
15 Gothenburg Opera, Teatro alla Scala, Zheng Yici Peking

Opera characters include:

03 Eva, Liu
04 Aïda, Bess, Budd (Billy), Erda, Froh, Iago, Il Re, Loge, Luna (Il Conte di), Mime, Mimì, Pang, Pike (Florence),

Ping, Pong, Tito, Vere (Captain)
05 Caius (Dr), Calaf, Falke (Dr), Faust, Freia, Gilda, Herod, Jeník, Kecal, Porgy, Rocco, Sachs (Hans), Titus, Tosca, Vasek, Wotan
06 Alcina, Alzira, Carmen, Donner, Emilia, Fafner, Fasolt, Figaro, Fricka, Gretel, Grimes (Peter), Hänsel, Isolde, Lockit (Lucy), Mantua (Duke of), Onegin (Eugene), Otello, Pamina, Pogner (Veit), Rosina, Salome, Tamino, Valery (Violetta), Wagner
07 Bartolo (Dr), Bastien, Billows, Despina, Don José, Douphol (Baron), Germont (Alfredo), Godunov (Boris), Gunther, Gutrune, Herring (Albert), Hunding, Jocasta, Leonora, Manrico, Marenka, Micaëla, Musetta, Oedipus, Peachum (Polly), Pelléas, Quickly (Mistress), Radamès, Rodolfo, Scarpia (Baron), Susanna, Tristan, Wozzeck
08 Alberich, Almaviva (Count), Almaviva (Countess), Azeucena, Claggart (John), Falstaff (Sir John), Ferrando, Herodias, Hoffmann, Lucretia, Macheath, Marcello, Mercédès, Orlofsky (Prince), Papagena, Papageno, Parsifal, Roderigo, Sarastro, Siegmund, Turandot, Valentin, Woglinde, Yamadori (Prince)
09 Angelotti (Cesare), Bastienne, Butterfly (Madame), Cherubino, Cio-Cio-San, Desdemona, Donna Anna, Dorabella, Escamillo, Esmerelda, Florestan, Guglielmo, Leporello, Lohengrin, Maddalena, Mélisande, Narraboth, Pinkerton (Lieutenant), Rigoletto, Sharpless, Siegfried, Sieglunde, Vogelsang (Kunz), Waltraute
10 Beckmesser (Sixtus), Brünnhilde, Don Alfonso, Don Basilio, Don Ottavio, Eisenstein (Gabriele von), Eisenstein (Rosalinde von), Fiordiligi, Marcellina, Monostatos, Prince Igor, Tannhäuser
11 Cavaradossi (Mario), Don Giovanni, Donna Elvira, Marschallin, Sparafucile, The Dutchman
14 Henry the Fowler, John the Baptist, Mephistopheles
15 Queen of the Night

---

operate

◇ *anagram indicator*

02 go **03** act, fly, ren, rin, run, set, use **04** play, trip, work **05** drive, pilot, serve **06** direct, employ, handle, make go, manage **07** actuate, conduct, control, perform, utilize **08** function, tick over **09** manoeuvre **12** be in charge of

operation

02 op **03** job, ure, use **04** deal, game, play, raid, task **05** using **06** action, affair, agency, attack, charge, effect, effort, motion **07** assault, control, process, running, surgery, working **08** activity, business, campaign,

exercise, handling, movement **09** influence, manoeuvre, procedure **10** enterprise, management, proceeding **11** functioning, performance, transaction, undertaking, utilization **12** manipulation

• **combined operations**
02 CO

• **in operation**
02 on **04** live **05** going, valid **06** active, viable **07** in force, working **08** in action, in effect, prepared, workable **09** effective, efficient, in service **10** functional **11** functioning, operational, serviceable **12** taking effect

operational

05 going, in use, ready **06** usable, viable **07** running, working **08** in action, prepared, workable **09** in service **10** functional **11** functioning **12** up and running **14** in working order

operative

03 key, spy **04** dick, hand, mole **05** agent, valid, vital **06** active, shamus, sleuth, viable, worker **07** artisan, crucial, gumshoe, in force, operant, ouvrier, working, workman **08** employee, in action, in effect, labourer, mechanic, operator, ouvrière, relevant, workable **09** detective, effective, efficient, important, machinist **10** functional, private eye **11** double agent, efficacious, functioning, in operation, operational, secret agent, serviceable, significant **12** investigator

operator

02 op **05** mover **06** dealer, driver, punter, trader, worker **07** functor, handler, manager, operant, shyster **08** director, mechanic **09** machinist, operative **10** contractor, machinator, manoeuvrer, speculator, technician **11** manipulator **12** practitioner **13** administrator, wheeler-dealer

operetta *see* **opera**

opiate

04 drug, dull **06** downer **07** anodyne, bromide **08** narcotic, nepenthe, pacifier, sedative **09** soporific **10** depressant **12** stupefacient **13** tranquillizer

opine

03 say **05** guess, judge, think **07** believe, declare, presume, suggest, suppose, surmise, suspect, venture **08** conceive, conclude **09** volunteer **10** conjecture

opinion

03 bet **04** deem, doxy, idea, mind, view, vote **05** sense, tenet **06** belief, notion, stance, theory **07** feeling, thought **08** attitude, feelings, suffrage, thoughts **09** arrogance, judgement, sentiment, viewpoint **10** assessment, assumption, conception, conviction, estimation, impression, perception, persuasion, reputation, standpoint **11** point of view, supposition **13** way of thinking **15** school of thought

• **in my opinion**
03 IMO **06** I think **08** à mon avis, as I see it, I believe, in my book, in my view, me judice **10** for my money, if you ask me, personally

• **opinion tester**
04 kite

opinionated
06 biased, entêté **07** adamant, bigoted, entêtée, pompous **08** arrogant, cocksure, dogmatic, stubborn **09** obstinate, pigheaded, pragmatic **10** inflexible, pontifical, prejudiced **11** dictatorial, doctrinaire, pragmatical **12** single-minded **13** self-important **14** uncompromising

opium
03 hop

opossum
04 joey **05** yapok **06** yapock **07** marmose **09** phalanger **12** Didelphyidae

opponent
03 foe **04** anti **05** enemy, rival **07** opposer **08** objector, opposite **09** adversary, contender, dissenter, dissident, oppugnant **10** antagonist, challenger, competitor, contestant, opposition **11** dissentient

• **opponents**
02 NE, SW

opportune
03 apt, fit **04** good **05** happy, lucky **06** proper, timely **07** fitting, in place **08** suitable **09** fortunate, pertinent, well-timed **10** auspicious, convenient, favourable, felicitous, propitious, seasonable **11** appropriate **12** advantageous, providential

opportunism
07 realism **10** expediency, pragmatism **12** exploitation **15** taking advantage

opportunity
03 ren, rin, run **04** hour, pick, room, roum, turn **05** break, power, scope, space **06** chance, look-in, moment **07** fitness, opening, vantage **08** occasion, overture, prospect **09** privilege **11** possibility **14** crack of the whip

• **alive to opportunity**
04 go-go

oppose
03 bar, opp **04** defy, face **05** check, fight, match **06** attack, breast, combat, hinder, impugn, offset, oppugn, repugn, resist, thwart **07** balance, compare, contest, counter, dispute, play off, prevent **08** confront, contrary, contrast, disfavor, obstruct, traverse **09** be against, challenge, disfavour, encounter, juxtapose, stand up to, withstand **10** contradict, contravene, controvert, set against **11** take against **12** argue against, disagree with, disapprove of **13** take

issue with **14** counterbalance, fly in the face of

opposed
03 opp **04** anti **06** averse, object **07** adverse, against, hostile **08** clashing, contrary, inimical, opposing, opposite **09** toto caelo **11** conflicting, disagreeing **12** antagonistic, incompatible, in opposition

• **as opposed to**
01 v **02** vs **06** versus **09** as against, instead of **10** rather than **12** in contrast to

opposing
05 enemy, rival **06** at odds **07** counter, hostile, opposed, warring **08** clashing, contrary, fighting, opponent, opposite **09** combatant, differing, oppugnant **10** at variance, contending **11** conflicting, contentious **12** antagonistic, antipathetic, disputatious, incompatible **14** irreconcilable

opposite
02 op **03** opp **06** at odds, en face, facing, unlike **07** adverse, counter, hostile, inverse, opposed, reverse **08** clashing, contrary, converse, flip side, fronting, opponent, opposing **09** different, differing, dissident **10** antipathic, antithesis, at variance, contrasted, face to face, overthwart, poles apart **11** conflicting, over against **12** antagonistic, antithetical, inconsistent **13** contradiction, contradictory, corresponding **14** irreconcilable

opposition
03 foe **05** enemy, rival **06** syzygy **07** dislike **08** clashing, contrast, distance, opponent **09** adversary, collision, hostility, other side **10** antagonism, antagonist, antithesis, reluctance, resistance **11** competition, contrariety, counter-time, counter-view, disapproval **12** colluctation, counter-stand, opposing side **13** confrontation **14** unfriendliness **15** obstructiveness

• **set in opposition**
04 play

oppress
03 vex **04** ride **05** abuse, bully, crush, grind, gripe, press, quash, quell, tread **06** burden, deject, hang on, harass, ravish, sadden, subdue, weight **07** afflict, depress, enslave, overset, repress, smother, torment, trample **08** desolate, dispirit, distress, hang over, maltreat, suppress **09** overpower, overpress, overwhelm, persecute, subjugate, suffocate, tyrannize, weigh down **10** discourage, dishearten, lie heavy on **11** walk all over **12** bear hard upon **13** treat like dirt, use as a doormat **15** bear heavily upon

oppressed
06 abused **07** crushed, misused, subject **08** burdened, enslaved,

harassed, troubled **09** repressed **10** maltreated, persecuted, subjugated, tyrannized **11** downtrodden **13** disadvantaged **15** underprivileged

oppression
05 abuse **07** cruelty, tyranny **08** hardship **09** brutality, despotism, harshness, injustice **10** repression, subjection **11** persecution, subjugation, suppression **12** maltreatment, overpowering, overwhelming, ruthlessness

oppressive
05 close, cruel, faint, harsh, heavy, muggy **06** brutal, leaden, stuffy, sultry, unjust **07** airless, inhuman, onerous, sweltry **08** crushing, despotic, pitiless, ruthless, stifling **09** burdenous, Draconian, merciless, troubling, tyrannous **10** broodiness, burdensome, iron-fisted, repressive, tyrannical **11** domineering, heavy-handed, intolerable, overbearing, suffocating **12** extortionate, overpowering, overwhelming

oppressor
05 bully, tyran **06** despot, tyrant **08** autocrat, dictator, torturer **09** tormentor **10** persecutor, subjugator, taskmaster **11** intimidator, slave-driver **14** hard taskmaster

opprobrious
07 abusive **08** damaging, infamous, insolent, venomous **09** insulting, invective, offensive, vitriolic **10** calumnious, defamatory, derogatory, scandalous, scurrilous **11** disgraceful, dyslogistic, reproachful **12** calumniatory, contemptuous, contumelious, vituperative

opprobrium
04 slur **05** odium, shame **06** infamy, stigma **07** calumny, censure, obloquy **08** disgrace, ignominy, reproach **09** contumely, discredit, disfavour, dishonour, disrepute **10** debasement, scurrility **11** degradation

Ops
04 Rhea

opt
04 pick **05** elect, go for **06** choose, decide, prefer, select **08** decide on, plump for, settle on **09** single out

optical

Optical instruments and devices include:

05 laser
06 camera
07 sextant
08 spyglass
09 endoscope, periscope, telescope
10 binoculars, microscope, opera-glass, theodolite
12 field-glasses, stereocamera
13 film projector
14 slide projector
15 magnifying glass, photomicroscope, telescopic sight, telestereoscope

optimism

5 cheer **06** morale **08** buoyancy, idealism **10** brightness, confidence, expectancy **11** hopefulness **12** cheerfulness, sanguineness **13** Leibnizianism **14** feel-good factor, Leibnitzianism

optimistic

06 bright, upbeat **07** assured, bullish, buoyant, hopeful **08** cheerful, positive, sanguine **09** confident, expectant **10** idealistic, Panglossic **11** Panglossian, pollyannish **12** happy-go-lucky, pollyannaish

optimum

03 opt, top **04** best **05** ideal, model **06** choice **07** highest, optimal, perfect, supreme, utopian **08** flawless **11** superlative **14** most favourable

option

03 put **04** call, wish **06** choice **07** refusal **08** swaption **09** privilege, election **10** preference **11** alternative, possibility

optional

03 opt **04** free **08** elective, unforced **09** voluntary **10** permissive **11** facultative **13** discretionary

options

04 menu

opulence

06 luxury, plenty, riches, wealth **07** fortune **08** fullness, richness **09** abundance, affluence, profusion **10** cornucopia, easy street, lavishness, luxuriance, prosperity **11** copiousness **13** sumptuousness **14** superabundance

opulent

04 posh, rich **05** plush, pluty **06** lavish **07** copious, moneyed, profuse, wealthy, well-off **08** abundant, affluent, prolific, well-to-do **09** luxuriant, luxurious, plentiful, sumptuous **10** prosperous, well-heeled **11** rolling in it **13** superabundant

opus

02 op **04** work **05** piece **06** oeuvre **08** creation **10** brainchild, production **11** composition

or

04 gold **05** ossia **06** before, yellow **10** conversely **13** alternatively **14** in reference to, on the other hand **15** as an alternative
see also **gold**

oracle

04 guru, sage, seer, Urim **05** augur, sibyl **06** answer, augury, expert, mentor, pundit, vision, wizard **07** adviser, prophet, Thummin **08** forecast, prophecy **09** authority **10** divination, forecaster, high priest, mastermind, prediction, prophetess, revelation, soothsayer, specialist **13** fortune teller **14** Urim and Thummim **15** prognostication

oracular

04 sage, wise **05** grave, vatic **06** arcane **07** cryptic, Delphic, obscure, ominous **08** abstruse, dogmatic, positive, two-edged **09** ambiguous, equivocal, prescient, prophetic, venerable **10** auspicious, haruspical, mysterious, portentous, predictive **11** dictatorial, significant **13** authoritative

oral

◇ *homophone indicator*
04 quiz, said, viva **05** vocal **06** buccal, lively, spoken, verbal **07** uttered **08** viva voce **09** unwritten **11** nuncupative

orally

◇ *homophone indicator*
07 by mouth, vocally **08** verbally, viva voce

orange

11 hesperidium

Oranges include:

04 gold **05** amber, chica, chico, coral, henna, tawny, tenné, tenny **06** anatta, anatto, aurora, chicha, kamala, kamela, kamila, roucou, salmon, tawney **07** annatta, annatto, apricot, arnotto, jacinth, nacarat, paprika, saffron **08** croceate, croceous, mandarin **09** bilirubin, tangerine **13** cadmium yellow, canthaxanthin

Orange varieties include:

04 mock, Ruta, sour **05** blood, Jaffa, navel, sweet, topaz **06** bitter **07** cumquat, kumquat, naartje, nartjie, satsuma, Seville **08** bergamot, bigarade, mandarin **09** clockwork, mandarine, tangerine **10** clementine

• **segment of orange**
03 pig

orate

04 talk **05** speak **07** declaim, lecture **08** harangue **09** discourse, hold forth, sermonize, speechify **11** pontificate

oration

05 éloge, elogy, spiel **06** eulogy, homily, korero, sermon, speech **07** address, elogium, lecture **08** eulogium, harangue **09** discourse, set speech **11** declamation

orator

06 Cicero, rhetor **07** speaker, spieler **08** lecturer **09** Boanerges, declaimer, demagogue, spokesman, thunderer **10** petitioner **11** Demosthenes, rhetorician, spellbinder **12** phrasemonger, prevaricator **13** public speaker

oratorical

08 eloquent, rhetoric, sonorous **09** bombastic, high-flown **10** Ciceronian, rhetorical **11** declamatory, Demosthenic

12 elocutionary, magniloquent **13** grandiloquent, silver-tongued, smooth-tongued

oratorio

Oratorios include:

04 Saul **06** Elijah, Esther, Joshua, Samson, Semele, St Paul **07** Athalia, Deborah, Jephtha, Messiah, Solomon, Susanna **08** Christus, Giuseppe, Hercules, Theodora **09** Christmas **10** Belshazzar, Oedipus Rex, The Seasons **11** The Creation **13** Israel in Egypt **14** Alexander Balus, La Resurrezione **15** Judas Maccabaeus

oratory

04 hwyl **06** chapel, speech **07** diction **08** rhetoric **09** elocution, eloquence, proseucha, proseuche **11** chapel royal, declamation **12** speechifying, speechmaking **14** grandiloquence, public speaking

orb

03 eye **04** ball, pome, ring **05** globe, mound, orbit, round, world **06** circle, sphere **07** eyeball, globule **08** bereaved, spherule

orbit

03 orb **04** path **05** ambit, cycle, range, reach, scope, sweep, track **06** circle, course, domain, sphere **07** circuit, compass, revolve **08** encircle, rotation **09** eye socket, influence **10** revolution, trajectory **11** circumgyration, circumnavigate

• **point in orbit**
04 apse **05** apsis **06** apogee **07** apolune, perigee **08** aphelion, perilune **10** perihelion **12** pericynthion, periselenium

orchestra

Orchestras include:

03 LPO, NSO, OAE, OSM, RPO **04** ASMF, CBSO, RLPO, RSNO **05** Hallé **06** Ulster **09** Minnesota **11** BBC Symphony, NBC Symphony **12** Milan La Scala, Philadelphia, San Francisco **13** Concertgebouw, Staatskapelle **14** Boston Symphony, English Chamber, LA Philharmonic, London Symphony, Sydney Symphony, Vienna Symphony **15** BBC Philharmonic, Chicago Symphony, Detroit Symphony, New York Symphony, Scottish Chamber, Seattle Symphony, The Philharmonia, Toronto Symphony

orchestrate

03 fix **05** score **07** arrange, compose, prepare, present **08** organize **09** integrate **10** co-ordinate, mastermind **11** put together, stage-manage

orchestration
05 score **07** running, scoring, setting, version **08** planning **10** adaptation, management **11** arrangement, engineering, preparation **12** co-ordination, organization **13** harmonization, masterminding, stage-managing **14** interpretation **15** instrumentation

orchid

Orchids include:

03 bee, bog, bug, fen, fly, man, sun **04** blue, disa, frog, king, kite, lady, moth, musk, wasp **05** burnt, clown, comet, ghost, giant, pansy, queen, tiger, tulip **06** lizard, monkey, spider **07** leopard, slipper, vanilla **08** calanthe, cattleya, crucifix, fragrant, military, oncidion **09** bee-orchis, birds-nest, chocolate, Christmas, coralroot, cymbidium, false musk, fly orchis, pyramidal, twayblade **10** early marsh, epidendrum, late spider, small white **11** cockleshell, cypripedium, dancing lady, early purple, early spider, epidendrone, green-winged, helleborine **12** black vanilla, heath spotted, ladys' tresses, Lapland marsh, narrow-leaved, one-leaved bog, western marsh **13** Chinese ground, common spotted, dense-flowered, elder-flowered, ladies' tresses, loose-flowered, orange blossom, southern marsh **14** moccasin flower, violet birds-nest **15** lesser butterfly

ordain
03 fix, set **04** call, fate, rule, will **05** elect, frock, japan, order **06** anoint, assign, decree, invest, priest **07** appoint, arrange, destine, dictate, dispose, foresay, lay down, require **08** instruct, ordinate **09** destinate, establish, preordain, prescribe, pronounce **10** consecrate, foreordain, lay hands on, predestine **12** predetermine

ordeal
04 pain, test **05** agony, trial **07** anguish, torment, torture, trouble **08** distress, troubles **09** bier right, gruelling, nightmare, suffering **10** affliction **11** persecution, tribulation **12** tribulations **13** baptism of fire

order
◇ anagram indicator
02 OM **03** bid, law, OBE, ord **04** book, call, calm, chit, club, fiat, form, kind, line, nick, plan, rank, rota, rule, sect, sort, tell, type, writ **05** array, caste, class, cycle, edict, genus, grade, group, guild, level, lodge, peace, quiet, set-up, shape, state, union **06** codify, decree,

degree, demand, direct, enjoin, family, fettle, kilter, lay out, layout, league, line-up, manage, method, ordain, system, tidy up **07** arrange, booking, call for, command, company, conduct, control, dictate, dispose, harmony, mandate, marshal, pattern, precept, request, require, reserve, society, sort out, species, station, summons, variety, warrant **08** apply for, classify, grouping, instruct, neatness, organize, position, practice, regulate, sequence, sorority, symmetry, tidiness **09** authorize, catalogue, community, condition, direction, directive, hierarchy, legislate, ordinance, prescribe, structure **10** commission, discipline, fellowship, fraternity, injunction, lawfulness, regularity, regulation, sisterhood, uniformity **11** application, arrangement, association, brotherhood, disposition, instruction, law and order, orderliness, requirement, requisition, reservation, send away for, stipulation, systematize, write off for **12** codification, denomination, notification, organization, pecking order, tranquillity, working order **13** secret society **14** categorization, classification

See also **command; honour; religious**

• **in order**
02 OK **04** done, neat, tidy **05** right **06** lawful, likely, mended, proper **07** allowed, correct, fitting, ordered, orderly, regular, working **08** all right, arranged, suitable **09** operative, organized, permitted, shipshape **10** acceptable, classified, good as gold, in sequence, methodical, systematic **11** appropriate, categorized, functioning **13** well-organized **15** secundum ordinem

• **in order that**
02 so

• **in order to**
02 to **05** for to **06** so that **11** intending to, with a view to **13** with the result **14** with the purpose

• **order around**
05 bully **07** lay down **08** browbeat, bulldoze, dominate, domineer **09** push about, tyrannize **10** boss around, order about, push around **13** lay down the law

• **out of order**
◇ anagram indicator
04 bust **05** amiss, kaput, messy, wrong **06** broken, untidy **07** haywire, muddled **08** confused, gone phut, improper, unlawful, unseemly **09** conked out, incorrect, irregular, off kilter **10** broken down, disordered, not working, on the blink, on the fritz, out of sorts, out of whack, unsuitable **11** inoperative, out of course, out of kilter, uncalled-for **12** disorganized, unacceptable **13** inappropriate, out of sequence **14** not functioning **15** out of commission

• **set in order**
02 do **03** red **04** redd, trim **05** dress, prank, right **06** betrim, fettle, pranck, snod up **07** dispone, prancke

• **special order, standing order**
02 SO

orderliness
08 neatness, tidiness, trimness **09** smartness **10** regularity, spruceness **12** organization, straightness **14** methodicalness

orderly
◇ anagram indicator
04 neat, ruly, tidy, trim **05** quiet **06** cosmic **07** in order, ordered, regular **09** chaprassi, chaprassy, chuprassy, efficient, regularly **10** controlled, law-abiding, methodical, restrained, systematic **11** disciplined, well-behaved **12** businesslike, methodically **13** well-organized, well-regulated **15** in apple-pie order

ordinance
03 law **04** fiat, rite, rule **05** canon, edict, order **06** bye-law, decree, dictum, ritual, ruling **07** command, statute **08** ceremony, planning, practice **09** directive, enactment, equipment, prescript, sacrament **10** dead-letter, injunction, observance, regulation **11** appointment, institution, preparation

ordinarily
07 as a rule, usually **08** commonly, normally **09** generally, in general **10** familiarly, habitually **11** customarily **14** conventionally

ordinary
01 O **03** ord **04** dull, fair **05** banal, bland, blunt, plain, usual **06** canton, common, cotise, modest, normal, simple **07** average, cottise, mundane, prosaic, quarter, regular, routine, typical, vanilla **08** everyday, familiar, habitual, mediocre, standard, workaday **09** customary, plain-Jane, quotidian **10** mainstream, pedestrian, working-day **11** bog standard, commonplace, indifferent, nondescript, unmemorable **12** conventional, run-of-the-mill, unremarkable **13** penny-farthing, unexceptional, uninteresting, unpretentious **14** bread-and-butter, common-or-garden **15** undistinguished

• **out of the ordinary**
04 rare **05** kinky **06** unique **07** unusual **09** different, left-field, memorable **10** noteworthy, remarkable, surprising, unexpected **11** exceptional, out of the way, outstanding **13** extraordinary

ordnance
03 ord **04** arms, guns **06** cannon **07** big guns, pelican, weapons **09** artillery, munitions **14** field artillery

ordure
03 poo **04** crap, dirt, dung, poop

5 filth, frass, guano, scats, stool **6** egesta, faeces **09** droppings, excrement, excretion **11** waste matter

ore
03 o'er **04** over **06** tangle **07** mineral, seaweed **09** sea tangle

Ores include:
3 wad
4 wadd, wadt
6 bog-ore, coltan, galena, rutile
7 bauxite, bog-iron, bornite, cuprite, iron ore, oligist, schlich, uranite, wood tin
8 beauxite, braunite, calamine, enargite, hematite, limonite, siderite, sinopite, stibnite, taconite, tenorite
9 anglesite, blackband, coffinite, haematite, hedyphane, ironstone, kidney ore, lodestone, magnetite, malachite, manganite, minestone, morass ore, proustite, tantalite
10 erubescite, melaconite, peacock-ore, pyrolusite, ruby silver, sphalerite, stephanite
11 cassiterite, chloanthite, pyrargyrite, tetradymite
12 babingtonite, chalcopyrite, pyromorphite, tetrahedrite
13 copper pyrites, horseflesh ore
15 stilpnosiderite

See also **seaweed**

• **vein of ore**
04 rake

Oregon
02 OR **04** Oreg

organ
04 part, tool, unit **05** forum, paper, pedal, regal, voice **06** agency, device, medium, member **07** element, journal, process, vehicle **08** magazine, melodeon, melodion **09** component, harmonium, implement, newspaper, structure **10** instrument, mouthpiece, periodical **11** apollonicon, constituent, publication **13** kist o' whistles

Organs include:
03 ear, eye
04 lung, nose, skin
05 bowel, brain, colon, liver, lungs, lymph, penis, vulva
06 cervix, rectum, spleen, testes, throat, thymus, ureter, uterus, vagina
07 bladder, kidneys, ovaries, oviduct, pharynx, scrotum, stomach, thyroid, tonsils, trachea, urethra
08 adenoids, appendix, bronchus, clitoris, pancreas, prostate, windpipe
09 diaphragm, pituitary, taste buds
10 epididymis, intestines, lymph nodes, oesophagus, spinal cord
11 gall bladder, parathyroid, vas deferens
12 hypothalamus, thymus glands, thyroid gland
13 adrenal glands, nervous system

14 fallopian tubes, large intestine, small intestine
15 ejaculatory duct, seminal vesicles

Organ stops include:
04 echo, oboe, sext, tuba
05 dolce, gamba, quint
06 cornet, nasard, octave, tierce
07 bombard, bourdon, clarino, clarion, fagotto, mixture, piccolo, salicet, trumpet
08 carillon, crumhorn, diapason, diaphone, dulciana, gemshorn, krumhorn, register, waldhorn
09 fifteenth, furniture, krummhorn, principal, pyramidon, vox humana, waldflute
10 clarabella, fourniture, salicional
11 superoctave, voix céleste
12 sesquialtera
15 corno di bassetto

organic
06 biotic, GM-free, living **07** animate, natural, ordered **08** coherent **09** organized **10** biological, harmonious, mechanical, structural, structured **11** non-chemical **12** additive-free, chemical-free, instrumental **13** not artificial, pesticide-free

organism
04 body, cell **05** being, biont, plant, set-up, unity, whole **06** animal, entity, system **08** creature **09** bacterium, structure **11** living thing **12** organization

See also **animal; cell; classification**

organization
◊ *anagram indicator*
04 body, club, firm, plan **05** group, order, set-up, union, unity, whole **06** design, layout, league, method, outfit, system **07** company, concern, council, pattern, running, society **08** grouping, planning **09** authority, formation, institute, operation, structure, syndicate **10** consortium, federation, management, regulation **11** arrangement, association, composition, corporation, development, institution, methodology **12** co-ordination **13** confederation, configuration, establishment **14** administration, classification, conglomeration

Organization of Petroleum Exporting Countries *see* **OPEC**

organize
◊ *anagram indicator*
03 ren, rin, run **04** form **05** begin, found, frame, group, mould, order, see to, set up, shape, start **06** create, embody, imbody, manage, obtain **07** arrange, develop, dispose, marshal, prepare, sort out **08** assemble, classify, regiment, tabulate **09** catalogue, construct, establish, institute, lemmatize, originate, structure **10** administer, co-ordinate, put in order **11** orchestrate, put together,

rationalize, standardize, systematize **12** be in charge of

organized
◊ *anagram indicator*
04 neat, tidy **07** in order, ordered, orderly, organic, planned, regular **08** arranged **09** efficient **10** methodical, structured, systematic **11** well-ordered **12** businesslike **13** well-organized, well-regulated

orgiastic
04 wild **05** orgic **07** Bacchic **09** debauched, Dionysiac **12** bacchanalian

orgy
04 bout, riot **05** binge, party, revel, spree **06** excess, frenzy, revels **07** debauch, revelry, splurge **08** carousal, Dionysia **09** wild party **10** indulgence, Saturnalia **11** bacchanalia

orient
01 E **04** East **05** adapt, align **06** adjust, attune, rising **07** eastern, sunrise, the East **08** accustom **09** habituate, orientate **11** acclimatize, accommodate, familiarize **15** get your bearings

oriental
01 E **05** Asian **07** Asiatic, Eastern **10** Far Eastern

See also **Asian**

orientation
07 guiding, leading **08** attitude, bearings, location, position, training **09** alignment, direction, induction, placement, situation **10** adaptation, adjustment, initiation, settling-in **11** inclination, positioning **15** acclimatization, familiarization

orifice
03 gap **04** hole, pore, rent, rift, slit, slot, vent **05** break, cleft, crack, inlet, mouth, space, trema **06** breach, orifex **07** crevice, fissure, opening **08** aperture, spiracle **09** micropyle **10** blastopore **11** perforation

origin
04 base, dawn, germ, line, rise, root **05** basis, birth, cause, fount, roots, start, stock **06** family, launch, source, spring **07** dawning, descent, genesis, lineage **08** ancestry, creation, fountain, genetics, heritage, pedigree **09** beginning, emergence, etymology, inception, parentage, paternity, principle **10** conception, derivation, extraction, foundation, provenance, well-spring **12** commencement, fountainhead, inauguration **13** line of descent

original
◊ *anagram indicator*
02 ur- **03** new **04** real, true, type **05** early, first, fresh, model, novel, prime **06** actual, innate, master, primal, unique **07** genuine, initial, opening, pattern, primary, radical, unusual

08 creative, earliest, paradigm, primeval, pristine, standard, starting **09** archetype, authentic, embryonic, first-hand, ingenious, inventive, primaeval, primitial, primitive, prototype **10** archetypal, commencing, indigenous, innovative, pioneering, primordial, protoplast, unborrowed, unorthodox **11** imaginative, primigenial, resourceful, rudimentary **13** autochthonous **14** ground-breaking, unconventional

originality
06 daring **07** newness, novelty **08** boldness **09** freshness, ingenuity **10** cleverness, creativity, innovation **11** imagination, singularity, unorthodoxy **12** creativeness, eccentricity **13** individuality, inventiveness **14** creative spirit, innovativeness **15** imaginativeness, resourcefulness

• **lacking originality**
07 clichéd **08** clichéed **09** hackneyed

originally
05 first **07** at first, by birth **08** in origin **09** initially **10** at the start **11** at the outset, to begin with **12** by derivation **14** in the beginning **15** in the first place

originate
04 come, flow, form, head, rear, rise, seed, stem **05** arise, begin, found, hatch, issue, plant, set up, start **06** be born, create, derive, emerge, evolve, father, invent, launch, result, source, spring **07** develop, emanate, pioneer, proceed, produce **08** commence, conceive, discover, generate, take rise **09** establish, institute, introduce, set on foot **10** inaugurate, mastermind **11** give birth to, set in motion **13** be the father of, be the mother of

origination
07 forming **08** creation **09** invention, paternity **10** conception, generation, production **11** development

originator
06 author, father, mother **07** creator, founder, pioneer **08** designer, inventor **09** architect, developer, generator, initiator, innovator, the brains **10** discoverer, prime mover **11** establisher

ornament
04 deck, fall, gaud, gild, knob, ouch, spar, tiki, trim **05** adorn, crown, décor, frill, gnome, jewel, mense, spray, sprig, wally **06** almond, bauble, bedeck, fallal, gewgaw, gorget, griffe, labret, relish, set-off **07** dress up, emblema, figgery, fleuron, frigger, frounce, garland, garnish, hei-tiki, lunette, netsuke, pattern, pendant, pendent, rellish, trinket, twiddle **08** barrette, bar slide, beautify, brighten, carcanet, decorate, furbelow, rocaille, sunburst, trimming **09** accessory, adornment, arabesque, dog collar, embellish, fandangle, medallion, multifoil,

scalework **10** decoration, escutcheon, Japanesery, knick-knack **11** garden gnome, garnishment **12** curliewurlie, jingle-jangle **13** embellishment

ornamental
05 fancy, showy **06** florid **08** adorning **10** attractive, decorative **12** embellishing, embroidering

ornamentation
04 fret, seam **06** frills **07** barbola, die-work **09** adornment, fallalery, garniture, strap work **10** decoration, embroidery, enrichment, figuration, ornateness **11** barbola work, elaboration, whigmaleery **12** whigmaleerie **13** embellishment

ornate
◇ *anagram indicator*
04 busy, fine **05** adorn, fancy, flash, fussy, showy **06** florid, rococo **07** baroque, elegant, flowery **08** barbaric, mandarin **09** barbarian, decorated, elaborate, grandiose, luxuriant, sumptuous **10** flamboyant, ornamented **11** embellished **12** ostentatious

orotund
04 deep, full, loud, rich **05** round **06** ornate, strong **07** booming, pompous **08** imposing, powerful, sonorous, strained **09** dignified **10** resonating **11** pretentious **12** magniloquent **13** grandiloquent

orthodox
04 true **05** sound, usual **06** devout, square, strict **07** canonic, correct, regular **08** accepted, catholic, faithful, official, received **09** canonical, customary, hardshell **10** conformist, recognized **11** bien pensant, established, traditional **12** conservative, conventional **13** authoritative **14** fundamentalist **15** well-established

orthodoxy
05 canon, credo, creed, dogma, tenet **06** belief **07** precept **08** devotion, doctrine, teaching, trueness **09** principle, soundness **10** conformism, conformity, conviction, devoutness, properness, strictness **11** correctness **12** conservatism, faithfulness **13** inflexibility **14** fundamentalism, received wisdom, traditionalism **15** conventionality

oscar
01 O

oscillate
03 wag **04** hunt, sway, vary, yo-yo **05** pitch, squeg, swing, waver **06** seesaw, wigwag **07** librate, vibrate **09** fluctuate, vacillate **12** move to and fro

oscillation
05 surge, swing **07** flutter **08** sine wave, swinging, wavering **09** seesawing, squegging, variation,

vibration **10** swing-swang **11** fluctuation, instability, vacillation **15** shilly-shallying

osmium
02 Os

osprey
07 Pandion **08** fish-hawk **09** ossifrage

ossify
06 harden **07** petrify **08** indurate, make hard, rigidify, solidify **09** fossilize, make fixed **10** become hard **11** become fixed

ostensible
07 alleged, claimed, feigned, outward, seeming **08** apparent, presumed, so-called, specious, supposed **09** ostensive, pretended, professed, purported **11** superficial

ostensibly
09 allegedly, outwardly, reputedly, seemingly **10** apparently, supposedly **11** professedly, purportedly **12** on the surface **13** superficially

ostentation
03 dog **04** dash, fuss, pomp, puff, show **05** flash, pride, swank **06** ostent, parade, splash, tinsel, vanity **07** display **08** boasting, flourish, pretence, pretense, vaunting **09** flaunting, pageantry, showiness, trappings **10** flashiness, peacockery, phylactery, pretension, showing-off **11** affectation, fanfaronade, flamboyance **13** exhibitionism **14** window-dressing **15** pretentiousness

ostentatious
03 OTT **04** loud **05** flash, gaudy, showy **06** flashy, garish, glitzy, kitsch, vulgar **07** splashy **08** affected, barbaric, fastuous **09** barbarian, barbarous, flaunting, obtrusive **10** flamboyant, over the top **11** conspicuous, extravagant, pretentious **13** demonstrative

ostentatiously
03 OTT **05** large **06** loudly **07** showily **08** flashily, garishly **10** over the top **11** obtrusively **12** flamboyantly **13** conspicuously, extravagantly, pretentiously **15** demonstratively

ostracism
04 tabu **05** exile, taboo **07** barring, boycott **09** avoidance, exclusion, expulsion, isolation, rejection **10** banishment **12** cold-shoulder, proscription **13** disfellowship **15** excommunication

ostracize
03 bar, cut **04** shun, snub **05** avoid, exile, expel **06** banish, outlaw, reject **07** boycott, exclude, isolate **09** blackball, proscribe, segregate **12** cold-shoulder **13** excommunicate **14** send to Coventry

ostrich
04 rhea **05** nandu **06** nandoo, nhandu **07** estrich **08** estridge, oystrige, Struthio

OT *see* **Bible**

other
» *anagram indicator*
04 else, left, more **05** extra, spare
06 second, unlike **07** further, variant
08 distinct, separate **09** alternate,
different, disparate, remaining
10 additional, dissimilar **11** alternative,
contrasting **13** supplementary
» **all others**
04 rest

otherwise
» *anagram indicator*
02 or **03** aka **04** else **05** alias, if not
06 or else, unless **09** different **11** also
known as, differently, failing that **12** in
another way **15** in a different way, in
other respects

otherworldly
03 fey **04** rapt **06** dreamy **07** bemused
08 ethereal **11** preoccupied **12** absent-
minded

otiose
05 extra, spare **06** excess, futile
07 surplus, to spare **08** indolent,
needless, unneeded, unwanted
09 excessive, redundant, remaining
10 gratuitous, unoccupied
11 superfluous, uncalled-for,
unnecessary, unwarranted
12 functionless **13** supernumerary

ottoman
04 pouf **05** squab

ounce
02 oz **03** jot, tad **04** atom, drop, fl oz,
iota, lynx, spot, tael, unce, whit
05 crumb, grain, liang, scrap, shred,
peck, touch, trace **06** jaguar, morsel
07 cheetah, modicum **08** particle
11 snow leopard

oust
04 fire, sack **05** eject, evict, expel
06 depose, put out, topple, unseat
07 boot out, dismiss, kick out, replace,
turn out **08** dislodge, displace, drive
out, force out, get rid of, supplant,
throw out **09** overthrow, thrust out
10 disinherit, dispossess **13** show the
door to

out
» *anagram indicator*
» *deletion indicator*
02 to **03** KO'd, set **04** alas, away, bent,
dead, gone **05** dated, forth, known,
passé, ready **06** abroad, absent,
démodé, doused, intent, old hat,
public, remote, used up **07** evident,
expired, exposed, in bloom, in print,
out cold, outside, without
08 blooming, comatose, divulged,
drawback, excluded, external,
finished, forcibly, in flower, manifest,
outlying, revealed, seawards
09 available, disclosed, dismissed,
elsewhere, forbidden, insistent, in the
open, not at home, out-of-date,
published, unwelcome **10** antiquated,
blossoming, completely, determined,
disallowed, impossible, insensible,

knocked out, not burning, not shining,
obtainable, thoroughly, unsuitable **11** in
full bloom, unconscious, undesirable
12 disadvantage, extinguished,
inadmissible, old-fashioned,
unacceptable, unreservedly
13 inappropriate, unfashionable
• **not out**
02 no
• **out of**
04 frae, from, hors
• **out upon it**
04 haro **06** harrow

out-and-out
04 fair, flat, rank **05** plumb, stark, total,
utter **06** arrant, full-on, proper
07 perfect, regular **08** absolute,
complete, outright, positive, teetotal,
thorough, whole-hog **09** bald-faced,
downright, right-down, up and down
10 consummate, definitely, heart-
whole, inveterate **11** honest-to-God,
straight-out, unmitigated, unqualified
12 unreservedly **13** dyed-in-the-wool,
thoroughgoing **14** hundred-per-cent,
uncompromising

outbreak
04 rash **05** burst, clash, flash, storm
06 putsch **07** flare-up, upbreak,
upsurge **08** epidemic, eruption,
hysteria, outburst **09** explosion
10 ebullition **11** disturbance,
excrescence, sudden start
13 recrudescence

outburst
03 fit, rag **04** flaw, gale, gush, gust, song
05 blurt, burst, flaky, spasm, storm,
surge **06** attack, escape, outcry, volley
07 boutade, flare-up, ovation, passion,
seizure **08** eruption, mouthful,
outbreak, paroxysm, sunburst
09 explosion **10** exuberance,
exuberancy, outpouring, solar flare
11 fit of temper

outcast
05 cagot, exile, leper **06** abject,
outlaw, pariah, reject, wretch
07 evacuee, quarrel, refugee
08 castaway, outsider, rejected
11 untouchable **15** persona non grata

outclass
03 top **04** beat **05** outdo **07** eclipse,
outrank, surpass **08** outrival, outshine,
outstrip **09** excel over, transcend
10 overshadow **11** outdistance
13 leave standing, put in the shade

outcome
05 issue, proof **06** answer, effect, pay-
off, result, sequel, upcome, upshot,
wash-up **07** proceed, product
08 proceeds **09** end result, outspring
10 conclusion, dénouement **11** after-
effect, consequence

outcry
03 cry, row **04** fuss **05** noise
06 clamor, racket, rumour, steven,
tumult, uproar, yammer **07** clamour,
dissent, exclaim, protest **08** outburst
09 commotion, complaint, hue and cry,

objection **10** hullabaloo, humdudgeon
11 exclamation, indignation
12 protestation, vociferation

outdated
03 obs **05** dated, mumsy, passé, steam
06 démodé, old hat, past it, square,
uncool **07** antique, archaic
08 obsolete, outmoded **09** out of date
10 antiquated, fuddy-duddy,
oldfangled, superseded
11 obsolescent, old-fogeyish, on the
way out, out of the ark **12** antediluvian,
old-fashioned, out of fashion
13 unfashionable **14** behind the times

outdistance
04 pass **06** outrun **07** outpace, surpass
08 outstrip, overhaul, overtake, shake
off **11** leave behind, pull ahead of
13 leave standing

outdo
03 cap **04** beat, best, whip **05** excel,
lurch **06** defeat, exceed **07** eclipse,
surpass **08** outclass, out-Herod,
outshine, outstrip, overcome, superate
09 come first, transcend
10 outperform **11** outdistance **12** walk
away from **13** knock spots off, put in
the shade, run rings round **14** get the
better of **15** go one better than, run
circles round

outdoors
03 out **06** abroad **07** outside
08 alfresco **10** en plein air, out-of-
doors **12** in the open air

outer
06 fringe, remote **07** distant, faraway,
further, outside, outward, surface
08 exterior, external, outlying
09 outermost **10** peripheral
11 superficial

outface
04 defy **05** beard, brave **08** confront,
outbrave, outstare **09** brazen out,
stand up to, stare down

outfit
03 kit, rig, set **04** crew, firm, gang, garb,
gear, suit, team, togs, unit, weed
05 dress, equip, fit up, get-up, group,
samfu, set-up, squad, stock, tools
06 attire, clique, fit out, fit-out, kit out,
layout, rig-out, samfoo, setout, supply
07 apparel, appoint, bloomer, clothes,
company, costume, coterie, furnish,
provide, sunsuit, turn out, turnout
08 accoutre, business, ensemble
09 apparatus, equipment, provision,
separates, trappings **10** sailor suit
11 bag of tricks, corporation
12 organization **13** accoutrements,
paraphernalia, shalwar-kameez

outfitter
06 sartor, tailor **07** modiste **08** clothier,
costumer **09** costumier, couturier
10 couturière, dressmaker
11 haberdasher

outflow
03 ebb, jet **04** gush, rush **05** spout
06 efflux, spring **07** outfall, outrush

08 drainage, effluent, effusion
09 discharge, effluence, effluvium, effluxion, emanation, emergence
10 outpouring **11** debouchment
14 disemboguement

outflowing
07 emanant, gushing, leaking, rushing
08 effluent, spurting **10** debouching
11 discharging

outfox
03 con, kid **04** beat, best, dupe
05 trick **06** have on, outwit **07** deceive
08 outsmart, out-think **10** outperform
12 outmanoeuvre, take for a ride **14** get the better of, pull a fast one on

outgoing
02 ex- **04** last, open, past, warm
06 former, genial **07** affable, amiable, cordial, leaving **08** emissary, friendly, retiring, sociable **09** departing, easy-going, expansive, extrovert, talkative
10 gregarious, unreserved
11 expenditure, sympathetic, uninhibited **12** affectionate, approachable **13** communicative, demonstrative

outgoings
04 exes **05** costs **06** outlay
08 expenses, spending **09** disbursal, overheads **11** expenditure
12 disbursement

outgrowth
03 ala **04** aril, hair, horn **05** shoot
06 air-sac, effect, sprout, stolon
07 enation, product, spin-off, verruca
08 caruncle, offshoot, root hair, swelling, trichome **09** apophysis, appendage, by-product, emanation, emergence, flocculus, propagule, rostellum **10** osteophyte, pollen tube, propagulum **11** consequence, excrescence **12** appressorium, effiguration, protuberance

outhouse
04 shed

outing
03 out **04** hike, romp, spin, tour, trip
05 jaunt, jolly, sally **06** junket, picnic
08 ejection **09** coach tour, excursion
10 expedition **11** mystery tour
12 pleasure trip

outlandish
◇ *anagram indicator*
03 odd **05** alien, wacky, weird
06 exotic, far-out, freaky, quaint, way-out **07** bizarre, curious, foreign, oddball, strange, unknown, unusual
08 peculiar **09** barbarous, eccentric, grotesque, peregrine, unheard-of, uplandish **10** unfamiliar
12 preposterous, unreasonable
13 extraordinary **14** unconventional

outlandishness
07 oddness **09** queerness, weirdness
10 exoticness, quaintness
11 bizarreness, peregrinity, strangeness, unusualness
12 eccentricity **13** grotesqueness

outlast
04 ride **07** outdure, outlive, outstay, survive, weather **11** come through

outlaw
03 ban, bar **04** horn, Tory **05** debar, exile **06** badman, bandit, banish, forbid, pirate, robber **07** brigand, condemn, embargo, exclude, outcast
08 criminal, disallow, fugitive, marauder, prohibit **09** broken man, desperado, interdict, proscribe, Robin Hood **10** bushranger, highwayman
12 put to the horn **13** excommunicate

outlay
04 cost, mise **05** price **06** charge, expend **07** expense, payment
08 expenses, spending **09** outgoings
11 expenditure **12** disbursement

outlet
04 duct, exit, port, shop, vent **05** issue, store, valve **06** egress, escape, let-off, market, nozzle, sluice, way out
07 channel, conduit, culvert, opening, outfall, release, sea gate **08** débouché, emissary, femerall, retailer, supplier
10 going forth **11** safety valve **12** retail outlet **14** means of release

outline
03 map **04** edge, form, plan, trim
05 braid, chart, draft, dress, shape, trace, trick **06** aperçu, design, figure, fringe, layout, précis, résumé, schema, sketch **07** balloon, contour, croquis, diagram, keyline, profile, skyline, summary, tracing **08** abstract, chalk out, contorno, esquisse, rough out, scenario, skeleton, synopsis
09 adumbrate, bare bones, bare facts, delineate, framework, lineament, programme, rough idea, sketch out, summarize, waterline **10** ground plan, main points, prospectus, silhouette
11 delineation **12** underdrawing
13 configuration **15** thumbnail sketch

outlive
07 outlast, outwear, survive, weather
08 overwear **11** come through, live through

outlook
04 view **05** angle, slant **06** aspect, future **07** mindset, opinion, picture
08 attitude, forecast, panorama, prospect **09** prognosis, prospects, viewpoint, world-view **10** standpoint
11 frame of mind, perspective, point of view **12** expectations
14 interpretation, Weltanschauung

outlying
03 out **05** outby, outer **06** far-off, forane, outbye, remote **07** distant, far-away, outland **08** detached, far-flung, isolated **10** provincial **11** out-of-the-way **12** inaccessible

outmanoeuvre
04 beat **05** outdo **06** outfox, outwit
07 sandbag **08** outflank, outsmart, outthink **10** circumvent, outgeneral
14 get the better of

outmoded
05 dated, passé, steam **06** démodé, old hat, past it, square, uncool
07 archaic **08** obsolete, outdated, shmaltzy **09** out of date, schmaltzy
10 antiquated, fuddy-duddy, oldfangled, superseded
11 obsolescent, old-fogeyish, on the way out, out of the ark **12** antediluvian, old-fashioned, out of fashion
13 unfashionable **14** behind the times

out of date
03 old **05** dated, passé, steam
06 démodé, old hat, passée, past it, square, uncool **07** archaic, belated, vintage **08** obsolete, outdated, outmoded, overworn **09** overdated
10 antiquated, behindhand, fuddy-duddy, oldfangled, superseded
11 obsolescent, old-fogeyish, on the way out, out of the ark, prehistoric
12 antediluvian, old-fashioned, out of fashion **13** horse-and-buggy, prehistorical, unfashionable **14** behind the times
See also **outdated**

out-of-the-way
03 odd **04** lost **05** outer **06** far-off, hidden, lonely, remote **07** distant, far-away, obscure, unusual **08** far-flung, isolated, outlying, secluded, singular, uncommon **10** outlandish, peripheral
11 god-forsaken, little-known
12 inaccessible, unfrequented

out of work
04 idle **07** jobless, laid off, resting
08 workless **09** on the dole, out of a job, redundant **10** unemployed
11 between jobs

outpace
04 beat, pass **05** outdo **06** outrun
07 surpass **08** outstrip, overhaul, overtake **11** outdistance

outpouring
04 flow, flux **05** blast, flood, spate, spurt **06** deluge, efflux, lavish, strain, stream **07** cascade, outflow, torrent, welling **08** effusion **09** effluence, emanation, word salad
11 debouchment **14** disemboguemen

output
◇ *anagram indicator*
04 gain **05** yield **06** fruits, return
07 harvest, outturn, product, turnout
10 production, throughput
11 achievement, manufacture, performance **12** productivity
14 accomplishment

outrage
04 evil, fury, rage, rape **05** abuse, anger, appal, crime, shock, wrath
06 defile, enrage, horror, injure, injury, madden, offend, ravage, ravish
07 abusion, affront, assault, disgust, horrify, incense, offence, scandal, violate **08** atrocity, enormity, violence
09 barbarism, brutality, desecrate, infuriate, sacrilege, violation
10 scandalize **11** indignation

outrageous

◇ *anagram indicator*

04 foul, rich, vile, wild **05** enorm, gross **06** unholy **07** furious, ghastly, heinous, obscene, ungodly, violent **08** dreadful, enormous, flagrant, gruesome, horrible, infernal, shocking, terrible **09** atrocious, egregious, excessive, monstrous, offensive, turbulent **10** abominable, diabolical, exorbitant, immoderate, inordinate, monstrous, scandalous, unbearable **11** disgraceful, extravagant, intolerable, unchristian, unspeakable **12** extortionate, insufferable, preposterous, unacceptable, unreasonable **14** unconscionable

outrageously

08 horribly, terribly **09** obscenely **10** dreadfully, unbearably **11** intolerably, unspeakably **12** scandalously, unacceptably **13** disgracefully

outré

◇ *anagram indicator*

03 odd **05** weird **06** far-out, freaky, way-out **07** bizarre, oddball, strange, unusual **08** shocking **09** eccentric, fantastic **10** outrageous **11** extravagant **13** extraordinary **14** unconventional

outrider

05 guard **06** escort, herald **08** vanguard **09** attendant, bodyguard, precursor **12** advance guard

outright

04 pure **05** clear, total, utter **06** at once, direct, openly, wholly **07** perfect, totally, utterly **08** absolute, complete, definite, directly, entirely, thorough **09** downright, instantly, out-and-out **10** absolutely, completely, explicitly, positively, thoroughly, undeniable **11** categorical, immediately, unequivocal, unmitigated, unqualified **12** straight away, there and then, unmistakable, unreservedly **13** categorically, thoroughgoing, unconditional, undisguisedly **15** instantaneously, straightforward

outrun

04 beat, lose, pass **05** excel, outdo **06** exceed **07** outpace, surpass **08** outstrip, overhaul, overtake, shake off **11** leave behind, outdistance, spread-eagle **13** run faster than

outset

05 onset, start **07** kick-off, opening **09** beginning, inception, threshold **12** commencement, inauguration

outshine

03 top **04** beat, best **05** dwarf, excel, outdo **07** eclipse, outrank, put down, surpass, upstage **08** outclass, outstrip **09** outlustre, transcend **10** overshadow, put to shame **13** put in the shade

outside

◇ *anagram indicator*

◇ *containment indicator*

03 exo- **04** ecto-, face, hors, rind, rine, slim **05** cover, extra, faint, front, outer, small, vague **06** casual, façade, remote, slight **07** distant, extreme, furth of, neutral, outdoor, outward, slender, surface, without **08** exterior, external, marginal, unbiased, unlikely, visiting **09** impartial, objective, outermost, temporary **10** appearance, consulting, extramural, extraneous, improbable, negligible **11** independent, non-resident, peripatetic, superficial **12** outer surface, self-employed **13** subcontracted

outsider

05 alien **06** émigré, layman, misfit, ringer **07** outlier, roughie, visitor **08** emigrant, intruder, newcomer, stranger **09** foreigner, immigrant, non-member, odd one out, outlander **10** interloper **11** gatecrasher, non-resident

outsize

02 OS **04** huge, mega, vast **05** giant, great, jumbo **07** immense, mammoth, massive, titanic, very big **08** colossal, enormous, gigantic **09** extensive, frightful, ginormous, humongous, monstrous, very large **10** gargantuan, prodigious, stupendous, tremendous

outskirts

04 edge **05** edges, limit **06** margin **07** borders, fringes, suburbs **08** boundary, environs, frontier, purlieus, suburbia, vicinity **09** perimeter, periphery **13** neighbourhood

outsmart

03 con, kid **04** beat, best, dupe **05** trick **06** have on, outfox, outwit **07** deceive **08** out-think **10** outperform **12** outmanoeuvre, take for a ride **14** get the better of, pull a fast one on

outsource

07 farm out **08** delegate **11** contract out **12** give to others, pass to others

outspoken

04 free, rude **05** bluff, blunt, broad, frank, plain, vocal **06** candid, direct **07** brusque **08** explicit, straight **10** forthright, unreserved **11** plain-spoken, Rabelaisian, unequivocal **13** unceremonious **15** straightforward

outspokenness

07 freedom **08** rudeness **09** bluffness, bluntness, frankness, plainness **10** candidness, directness **11** brusqueness **14** forthrightness

outspread

04 open, wide **06** flared, opened **08** expanded, extended, unfolded, unfurled, wide-open **09** fanned out, spread out, stretched **12** outstretched

outstanding

03 ace, due **04** cool, some **05** brill, chief, famed, great, owing **06** famous, golden, superb, unpaid, wicked **07** eminent, notable, ongoing, payable, pending, radical, salient, special **08** left-over, renowned, smashing, striking, superior, to be done, top-notch **09** arresting, brilliant, excellent, important, memorable, prominent, remaining, unsettled, well-known **10** celebrated, impressive, noteworthy, pre-eminent, prosilient, remarkable, unfinished, unresolved **11** exceptional, superlative, uncollected **13** distinguished, extraordinary **14** extraordinaire, out of this world

outstandingly

07 greatly, notably **09** amazingly, extremely **10** especially, remarkably, strikingly **12** impressively **13** exceptionally **15** extraordinarily

outstrip

03 top **04** beat, cote, pass **05** outdo, outgo, strip **06** better, exceed, gain on, outrun **07** eclipse, outfoot, outpace, surpass **08** outshine, overtake **09** transcend **11** leave behind, outdistance **12** go faster than **13** leave standing

outward

05 outer **06** carnal, extern, formal, public **07** evident, externe, obvious, outside, seeming, surface, visible, worldly **08** apparent, exterior, external, supposed **09** dissolute, outermost, posticous, professed **10** accidental, additional, noticeable, observable, ostensible **11** discernible, perceptible, superficial, without-door **13** superficially

outwardly

07 visibly, without **09** seemingly **10** apparently, exteriorly, externally, supposedly **12** at first sight, on the outside, on the surface **13** on the face of it, superficially

outweigh

06 exceed **07** surpass **08** overcome, override **09** cancel out, make up for, overpoise **10** be more than, outbalance **11** predominate, prevail over **12** be superior to, preponderate **13** be greater than, compensate for

outwit

03 con, fox, kid **04** beat, best, dish, dupe **05** cheat, trick **06** better, euchre, have on, outfox **07** deceive, defraud, swindle **08** outsmart, outthink **09** crossbite, overreach **10** circumvent **12** outmanoeuvre, take for a ride **14** be cleverer than, get the better of, pull a fast one on

outwork

04 moon

outworn

05 stale **06** old hat, past it **07** ancient, archaic, defunct, disused **08** obsolete, outdated, outmoded, rejected

09 abandoned, exhausted, hackneyed, moth-eaten, out of date **10** antiquated **11** discredited, obsolescent **12** old-fashioned **14** behind the times

oval
05 ovate, ovoid **07** navette, obovate, oviform **08** elliptic **09** egg-shaped, vulviform **10** elliptical **11** ellipsoidal

ovation
06 bravos, cheers, praise **07** acclaim, bouquet, praises, tribute **08** accolade, applause, cheering, clapping, plaudits **09** laudation, rejoicing **11** acclamation **12** handclapping

oven
03 Aga, oon, umu **04** kiln, lear, leer, lehr, oast **05** hangi, micro, stove **06** calcar, cooker **07** furnace, tandoor **09** microwave **11** copper Maori **13** microwave oven

over
◇ *containment indicator*
◇ *juxtaposition down indicator*
◇ *reversal down indicator*
02 of, on, re, up **03** o'er, ore **04** gone, left, ower, owre, past, upon **05** about, above, aloft, along, ended, extra, upper **06** across, beyond, closed, during, excess, no more, on high, unused **07** at an end, on top of, settled, surplus **08** done with, finished, in excess, left over, more than, overhead, superior, unwanted **09** apropos of, as regards, completed, concluded, exceeding, excessive, forgotten, in the past, regarding, remaining, unclaimed **10** concerning, higher than, in addition, in charge of, in excess of, relating to, superior to, terminated, throughout **11** dealing with, in command of, referring to, superfluous **12** accomplished, with regard to **13** concerned with, connected with, in the matter of, with respect to **14** ancient history, on the subject of **15** over and done with, with reference to
• **over and above**
04 plus **06** beside **07** added to, besides, on top of **08** as well as, let alone **09** along with **12** in addition to, not to mention, together with
• **over and over**
05 often **09** ad nauseam, endlessly **10** frequently, repeatedly **11** ad infinitum, continually **12** time and again **13** again and again

overabundance
04 glut **06** excess **07** surfeit, surplus **08** plethora **09** profusion **10** oversupply **11** superfluity **14** superabundance **15** embarras de choix

overact
03 ham **04** hoke **06** overdo **07** lay it on **08** overplay, pile it on **10** exaggerate **12** lay it on thick **13** pile it on thick

overall
05 broad, pinny, total **06** global, pinnie

07 all-over, blanket, broadly, crawler, general, save-all, tablier **08** complete, dustcoat, out to out, pinafore, sweeping, umbrella **09** dungarees, inclusive, in general, siren suit, universal **10** altogether, boiler suit, by and large, everywhere, on the whole **12** all-embracing, all-inclusive **13** comprehensive **15** broadly speaking

overalls
06 jumper, pinnie **07** crawler, save-all, tablier **08** coverall, dust-coat, fatigues, pinafore, workwear **09** dungarees **10** boiler suit

overawe
03 awe, cow **05** abash, alarm, daunt, scare **06** dismay **07** buffalo, petrify, terrify, unnerve **08** browbeat, frighten **10** disconcert, intimidate

overbalance
04 slip, trip **05** upset **06** topple, tumble **07** capsize, tip over **08** fall over, keel over, overturn **10** somersault, topple over, turn turtle **15** lose your balance, lose your footing

overbearing
05 bossy, proud **06** la-di-da, lordly, snobby, snooty, snotty **07** haughty, stuck-up **08** arrogant, cavalier, despotic, dogmatic, masterly, smartass **09** imperious, officious, smartarse **10** autocratic, disdainful, dogmatical, high-handed, oppressive, tyrannical **11** dictatorial, domineering, toffee-nosed **12** contemptuous, presumptuous, supercilious

overblown
03 OTT **07** exalted **08** inflated, overdone **09** amplified, bombastic, excessive **10** burlesqued, overstated, over the top **11** caricatured, embellished, extravagant, overcharged, pretentious **13** overestimated, self-important

overcast
04 dark, dull, grey, hazy, whip **05** foggy, misty, shade **06** cloudy, dismal, dreary, gloomy, leaden, sombre **07** clouded, louring, recover, sunless **08** darkened **11** clouded over

overcharge
02 do, o/c **04** clip, rook, rush, soak **05** cheat, sting **06** diddle, extort, fleece, rip off **07** swindle **09** surcharge **11** short-change

overcoat *see* coat

overcome
04 beat, best, lick, rout **05** break, cover, force, fordo, moved, outdo, worst **06** broken, byword, defeat, evince, excess, expugn, hammer, master, mither, moider, outwit, subdue, thrash **07** beat off, clobber, conquer, consume, moither, outplay, overget, prevail, refrain, surplus, trounce **08** affected, choked up, convince, dead-beat, knock out,

outsmart, superate, surmount, vanquish, wear down **09** exhausted, hit for six, overmatch, overpower, overthrow, overwhelm, rise above, slaughter, subjugate, underfong **10** bowled over, speechless, surmounted **11** knock for six, overpowered, overwhelmed, triumph over **12** lost for words, put on the foil **13** have the edge on **14** get the better of

over-confident
04 rash **05** brash, cocky **06** secure, uppish, uppity **08** arrogant, cocksure, sanguine **09** foolhardy, hubristic **10** blustering, incautious, swaggering **11** overweening, self-assured, temerarious **12** presumptuous **14** over-optimistic

overcook
04 burn, char **05** singe **07** blacken

overcritical
06 purist **07** carping, Zoilean **08** captious, over-nice, pedantic **09** cavilling **10** nit-picking, pernickety **11** persnickety **12** fault-finding, hard to please **13** hair-splitting, hypercritical **14** overparticular

overcrowded
06 packed **07** chocker, overrun, teeming **08** swarming **09** chock-full, congested, jam-packed, packed out **10** overloaded **11** chock-a-block, crammed full **13** overpopulated

overdo
05 excel **06** harass **07** fatigue, ham it up, lay it on, overact **08** camp it up, go too far, overplay, pile it on **09** overstate **10** exaggerate **11** cut it too fat, go overboard, overindulge **12** lay it on thick **13** carry to excess, pile it on thick, stretch a point
• **overdo it**
07 crack up **08** overwork **09** do too much **10** sweat blood **11** work too hard **14** strain yourself **15** burn yourself out

overdone
03 OTT **05** burnt, hokey, undue **07** charred, dried up, fulsome, gushing, percoct, spoiled **08** effusive, overshot **09** excessive, overbaked **10** histrionic, immoderate, inordinate, overcooked, overplayed, overstated, over the top **11** exaggerated, overwrought, unnecessary **13** overelaborate **14** burnt to a cinder **15** burnt to a frazzle

overdose
02 OD

overdraft
02 OD **04** debt **07** arrears, deficit **10** borrowings **11** liabilities **13** unpaid amounts

overdue
03 due **04** late, slow **05** owing, tardy **06** unpaid **07** belated, delayed, payable, pending **09** unsettled **10** behindhand, unpunctual **14** behind schedule

overeat
05 binge, gorge **06** guzzle, pig out
10 eat too much, go on a binge,
gormandize **11** overindulge **13** stuff
yourself

overeating
07 bulimia **08** bingeing, gluttony,
guzzling **10** gormandise, gormandism
11 gourmandise, gourmandism,
hyperphagia **14** overindulgence

overemphasize
06 labour **08** belabour **10** exaggerate,
overstress **13** make too much of,
overdramatize

overexert
• **overexert yourself**
07 fatigue **08** overdo it, overwork
11 work too hard **14** strain yourself
15 overtax yourself, wear yourself out

overfeed
04 cram, glut, sate

overflow
03 lip, ren, rin, run **04** ream, soak, teem
05 cover, flood, spill, surge, swamp,
water **06** back-up, deluge, shower
07 overrun, redound, run over, surplus
08 brim over, flow over, inundate,
outswell, pour over, spillage, submerge,
surround, well over **09** discharge,
overspill, spill over **10** bubble over,
inundation **13** overabundance

overflowing
04 full, rife **05** flush **06** filled
07 brimful, copious, crowded, profuse,
teeming **08** inundant, overfull,
swarming, thronged **09** abounding,
bountiful, exuberant, land-flood,
plenteous, plentiful, redundant
13 superabundant

overgrown
04 rank

overgrowth
05 naeve, nevus **06** naevus
09 gigantism **10** escalation, luxuriance,
luxuriancy, rhinophyma **11** gliomatosis,
hyperplasia, hypertrophy
13 overabundance
14 superabundance
15 overdevelopment

overhang
03 jut **04** loom, poke **05** bulge
06 beetle, extend, impend, jut out
07 poke out, project **08** bulge out,
protrude, stand out, stick out

overhanging
06 beetle, shelvy **07** bulging, jutting,
pendant, pendent, pensile
08 beetling, imminent **09** incumbent,
pendulous, prominent **10** bulging out,
jutting out, projecting, protruding
11 standing out, sticking out
14 superincumbent

overhaul
03 fix **04** mend, pass **05** check **06** gain
on, go over, repair, revamp, survey
07 check up, check-up, examine,
inspect, outpace, rummage, service

08 outstrip, overtake, renovate
09 check over, going-over, re-examine
10 get ahead of, inspection, renovation
11 examination, investigate,
outdistance, pull ahead of, recondition
14 reconditioning

overhead
03 air **05** above, aloft **06** aerial, on
high, raised, upward **07** average,
general, up above **08** all-round,
elevated **11** overhanging

overheads
06 burden, oncost **07** oncosts
08 expenses **09** outgoings **10** fixed
costs **11** expenditure **12** disbursement,
regular costs, running costs
14 operating costs

overheated
05 angry, fiery **06** roused **07** excited,
flaming **08** agitated, inflamed
10 passionate **11** impassioned,
overexcited, overwrought
• **overheated state**
04 stew

overindulge
03 pet **04** lush, sate **05** binge, booze,
gorge, spoil **06** cosset, guzzle, pamper,
pander, pig out **07** debauch, satiate
09 spoon-feed **10** eat too much,
gluttonize, gormandize **11** mollycoddle
12 drink too much

overindulgence
05 binge **06** excess **07** debauch,
surfeit **10** overeating **12** immoderation,
intemperance

overjoyed
04 rapt **06** elated, joyful **08** ecstatic,
euphoric, jubilant, thrilled
09 delighted, rapturous **10** enraptured,
in raptures **11** high as a kite, on cloud
nine, over the moon, tickled pink
14 pleased as Punch **15** in seventh
heaven, on top of the world

overlap
03 lap **04** ride **05** cover **07** overlay,
overlie, shingle **08** coincide, flap over,
override **09** imbricate

overlay
04 ceil, face, line, span, whip, wrap
05 adorn, belay, cover, inlay, patch
06 spread, veneer **07** blanket, envelop,
surface, varnish **08** covering, decorate,
encumber, laminate, ornament

overload
03 tax **04** glut **06** burden, excess,
lumber, saddle, strain **07** oppress,
overtax, surfeit, surplus **08** encumber,
plethora **09** surcharge, weigh down
10 overburden, overcharge,
oversupply **11** hypercharge,
overfreight, superfluity
13 overabundance
14 superabundance

overlook
04 face, miss, omit **05** leave **06** excuse,
forget, ignore, pardon, pass by, slight,
wink at **07** condone, forgive, let pass,
let ride, neglect, oversee **08** look onto,

look over, open onto, overskip, pass
over **09** disregard, front onto,
mislippen **11** have a view of,
superintend **14** command a view of,
take no notice of **15** take no account of,
turn a blind eye to

overlooked
07 unnoted **08** unheeded, unprized,
unvalued **10** in the shade, unhonoured,
unregarded, unremarked
12 unconsidered

overly
03 too **04** over **06** casual, unduly
08 casually, superior **11** exceedingly,
excessively **12** immoderately,
inordinately, supercilious,
unreasonably **13** unnecessarily
14 superciliously

overmuch
06 unduly **07** too much **11** excessively
12 immoderately, inordinately,
unreasonably **13** unnecessarily

overnice
07 finical **08** kid glove **10** nit-picking,
oversubtle, pernickety **11** overprecise,
persnickety **13** oversensitive
14 overfastidious, over-meticulous,
overparticular, overscrupulous

overplay
06 colour, overdo, stress **07** amplify,
enhance, enlarge, lay it on, magnify
08 oversell, pile it on **09** dramatize,
embellish, embroider, emphasize,
overstate **10** aggrandize, exaggerate,
shoot a line **12** lay it on thick **13** make
too much of, overdramatize,
overemphasize, pile it on thick
15 stretch the truth

overpopulated
06 packed **07** overrun, teeming
08 swarming **09** chock-full, congested,
jam-packed, packed out
10 overloaded **11** crammed full,
overcrowded

overpower
04 beat, daze, move, rout **05** crush,
floor, quash, quell, swelt, touch, whelm
06 dazzle, defeat, evince, master,
overgo, subdew, subdue **07** confuse,
conquer, perplex, stagger, swelter,
trounce **08** bedazzle, bowl over,
overbear, overcome, vanquish
09 dumbfound, hit for six, hypnotize,
overthrow, overwhelm, subjugate, take
aback **10** immobilize, overmaster
11 flabbergast, knock for six **12** affect
deeply **14** affect strongly **15** gain
mastery over, leave speechless

overpowering
06 strong **07** extreme **08** forceful,
powerful, stifling **09** sickening,
tyrannous **10** compelling, nauseating,
oppressive, unbearable, undeniable
11 irrefutable, suffocating
12 irresistible, overwhelming
14 uncontrollable

over-productive
04 rank

overrate
06 blow up **07** magnify **09** overprize, overvalue **10** overpraise
12 overestimate **13** make too much of

overreach
• **overreach yourself**
08 go too far, overdo it **14** strain yourself, try to do too much **15** burn yourself out

override
05 annul, quash **06** cancel, exceed, ignore **07** nullify, overlap, rescind, reverse, surpass **08** abrogate, outweigh, overcome, overrule, overtake, set aside, vanquish
09 disregard, supersede
11 countermand, prevail over, trample over **12** be superior to **13** be greater than

overriding
05 final, first, major, prime, prior **06** ruling **07** pivotal, primary, supreme **08** cardinal, dominant, ultimate **09** essential, number one, paramount, principal **10** compelling, overruling, prevailing **11** determining, predominant **13** most important **15** most significant

overrule
05 annul **06** cancel, reject, revoke **07** nullify, outvote, prevail, rescind, reverse **08** abrogate, disallow, overbear, override, oversway, overturn, set aside, vote down **10** invalidate **11** countermand

overrun
03 lip **05** bleed, storm, swamp **06** attack, exceed, go over, infest, invade, occupy, ravage **07** besiege, run riot **08** inundate, overgrow, overstep, permeate **09** overreach, overshoot, overwhelm, penetrate, surge over, swarm over **10** depopulate, spread over

overseas
06 abroad, exotic, remote, widely **07** distant, faraway, foreign **08** external, outremer **10** far and wide **11** ultramarine **13** international **14** in foreign parts, to foreign parts **15** in foreign climes, out of the country, to foreign climes

oversee
03 ren, rin, run **05** guide, watch **06** direct, manage **07** conduct, control, inspect **09** disregard, look after, supervise, watch over **10** administer **11** keep an eye on, preside over, superintend **12** be in charge of **13** be in control of

overseer
03 guv **04** baas, boss **05** chief **06** bishop, critic, editor, gaffer, grieve, guv'nor, induna **07** captain, foreman, manager, overman, steward **08** banksman, decurion, oversman, surveyor **09** forewoman, woodreeve **10** foreperson, manageress, supervisor, workmaster **11** flock-master, mine-captain **12** workmistress **14** superintendent

overshadow
◇ *containment indicator*
03 dim, mar **04** veil **05** cloud, dwarf, excel, shade, spoil **06** blight, darken **07** eclipse, obscure, protect, shelter, surpass **08** bescreen, dominate, hang over, outshine **09** adumbrate, obumbrate, rise above **10** tower above **12** be superior to, put a damper on **13** put in the shade **14** take the edge off

oversight
04 boob, care, flub **05** error, fault, lapse **06** charge, howler, slip-up **07** blunder, control, custody, keeping, mistake, neglect **08** handling, omission **09** direction **10** management, parablepsy **11** dereliction, parablepsis, supervision **12** carelessness, inadvertence, inadvertency, surveillance **14** administration, responsibility **15** superintendence

oversize
04 huge, mega, vast **05** giant, great, jumbo **07** immense, mammoth, massive, titanic, very big **08** colossal, enormous, gigantic **09** extensive, frightful, ginormous, humongous, monstrous, very large **10** gargantuan, monumental, prodigious, stupendous, tremendous

overstate
06 colour, overdo, stress **07** amplify, enhance, enlarge, lay it on, magnify **08** oversell, pile it on **09** dramatize, embellish, embroider, emphasize **10** aggrandize, exaggerate, shoot a line **12** lay it on thick **13** make too much of, overdramatize, overemphasize, pile it on thick **15** stretch the truth

overstatement
06 excess, parody **08** emphasis **09** burlesque, hyperbole **10** caricature **11** enlargement **12** exaggeration, extravagance, overemphasis **13** amplification, embellishment, magnification **14** overestimation **15** pretentiousness

overt
04 open **05** plain **06** patent, public **07** evident, obvious, visible **08** apparent, manifest **09** professed **10** noticeable, observable **11** conspicuous, unconcealed, undisguised

overtake
03 lap **04** pass **05** catch **06** befall, engulf, gain on, go past, strike **07** forhent, run past **08** come upon, forehent, happen to, outstrip, overhaul, ride down **09** drive past, overcatch, overwhelm **10** come up with **11** catch up with, leave behind, outdistance, pull ahead of **13** catch unawares, draw level with **14** take by surprise

over the top *see* **over the top** *under* **top**

overthrow
◇ *anagram indicator*
03 end **04** beat, best, down, fall, oust, rout, ruin **05** crush, quash, quell, smite, spill, upset, whelm, worst **06** defeat, depose, invert, lay low, master, subdue, topple, tumble, unseat, upturn **07** abolish, conquer, ousting, put down, run down, run over, stonker, subvert, tip over, trounce, undoing, whemmle, whomble, whommle, whummle **08** bear down, confound, dethrone, displace, downfall, keel over, overcast, overcome, overturn, ride down, supplant, turn over, vanquish **09** bring down, confusion, knock over, overpower, overwhelm, prostrate, unseating, upsetting **10** deposition, subversion **11** destruction, humiliation, labefaction, overbalance, suppression, vanquishing **12** dethronement **13** labefactation **14** bouleversement

overtly
06 openly **07** clearly, plainly **08** patently **09** obviously **10** in full view, manifestly, noticeably **11** for all to see **13** conspicuously

overtone
04 hint **05** sense **06** nuance **07** feeling, flavour **08** harmonic, innuendo **10** intimation, suggestion **11** association, connotation, implication, insinuation **12** undercurrent **13** hidden meaning

overture
04 move **05** moves, offer **06** feeler, gambit, motion, signal **07** advance, feelers, opening, prelude, toccata **08** advances, aperture, approach, proposal **09** beginning **10** invitation, suggestion **11** opening move, opportunity, proposition **12** introduction **13** opening gambit

Overtures include:
05 Cuban, Herod, Wasps
06 Adonis, Choral, Comedy, Esther, French, Heroic, Solemn, Spring, Thalia, Tragic
07 Aladdin, Euterpe, Festive, Holiday, Idyllic, Jubilee, Leonora, Maytime, Othello
08 Carnival, Columbus, Coriolan, Hebrides, Hyperion, In Autumn, King Lear, Romantic, Waverley
09 Britannia, Children's, Fairy Land, In Bohemia, Pinocchio, The Naiads
10 Amid Nature, In the South, Salutatory
11 East and West, Fingal's Cave, Pickwickian, Shéhérazade, The Faithful, William Tell
12 Fair Melusina, In London Town, Rip van Winkle, Street Corner, The Rehearsal
13 In the Highland, Shadowy Waters, The Wood-Nymphs
14 Eighteen Twelve, Eighteen-Twelve, In Nature's Realm, In the Mountains, Romeo and Juliet
15 Comes Autumn Time, Portsmouth Point, The Fair Melusina

overturn
◊ *anagram indicator*
◊ *reversal down indicator*
03 tip **04** beat, coup, cowp, oust, veto **05** annul, crush, quash, spill, upset, whelm **06** cancel, defeat, depose, invert, repeal, revoke, topple, unseat, upturn **07** abolish, capsize, conquer, destroy, nullify, rescind, reverse, skittle, subvert, tip over, whemmle, whomble, whommle, whummle **08** abrogate, confound, dethrone, displace, keel over, overcome, override, overrule, set aside, turn over, vanquish **09** bring down, knock over, overpower, overthrow, overwhelm **11** overbalance

overused
04 worn **05** stale, tired, trite **07** cliché'd **08** bromidic, clichéed **09** hackneyed, played out **10** overworked, threadbare, unoriginal **11** commonplace, stereotyped **13** platitudinous

overview
05 study **06** review, survey **08** panorama, scrutiny **09** appraisal, valuation **10** assessment, inspection **11** examination, measurement **13** consideration

overweening
04 vain **05** cocky, proud **06** hubris, hybris, lordly **07** haughty, pompous, swollen **08** arrogant, cavalier, cocksure, inflated, insolent, vaulting **09** conceited, excessive, hubristic, overblown, upsetting **10** high-handed, immoderate **11** egotistical, extravagant, opinionated **12** presumptuous, supercilious, vainglorious **13** outrecuidance, over-confident, self-confident

overweight
03 fat **04** huge **05** ample, bulky, buxom, gross, heavy, hefty, obese, plump, podgy, stout, tubby **06** chubby, chunky, flabby, fleshy, portly **07** massive, outsize **09** corpulent **10** pot-bellied, voluptuous, well-padded **13** preponderance **15** well-upholstered

overwhelm
04 beat, best, bury, daze, kill, lick, move, rout **05** amaze, crush, floor, quash, quell, swamp, touch, worst **06** defeat, deluge, engulf, hammer, ingulf, outwit, subdue, thrash **07** clobber, confuse, destroy, engulph,

ingulph, oppress, outplay, overrun, prevail, stagger, trounce **08** bowl over, inundate, knock out, outsmart, overbear, overcome, submerge, vanquish **09** devastate, hit for six, overpower, overthrow, slaughter, snow under, subjugate **10** overburden **11** knock for six **12** affect deeply **13** have the edge on, knock sideways **14** affect strongly, get the better of

overwhelming
04 huge, vast **05** great, large **06** strong **07** banging, extreme, immense, massive, runaway **08** crashing, enormous, forceful, powerful, stifling **09** sickening **10** compelling, formidable, foudroyant, nauseating, oppressive, unbearable, undeniable **11** irrefutable, suffocating **12** irresistible, overpowering **14** uncontrollable

overwork
05 weary **06** burden, strain **07** crack up, exhaust, exploit, oppress, overtax, overuse, wear out **08** overdo it, overload **09** do too much **10** overstrain, sweat blood **11** work too hard **14** strain yourself **15** burn yourself out

overworked
04 worn **05** stale, tired, trite **07** cliché'd, worn out **08** bromidic, clichéed, forswunk **09** exhausted, forswonck, hackneyed, overtaxed, played out **10** threadbare, unoriginal **11** commonplace, stereotyped, stressed out **12** overstrained **13** platitudinous

overwrought
04 edgy **05** nervy, tense **06** highly, on edge, strung **07** excited, frantic, keyed up, nervous, uptight, wound up **08** agitated, worked up **10** distraught **11** overcharged, overexcited **14** beside yourself

owe
10 be in debt to, be in the red, run up debts **11** be overdrawn, get into debt **12** be indebted to **13** be in arrears to

owing
03 dew, due **04** owed **06** unpaid **07** overdue, payable **09** imputable, in arrears, unsettled **11** outstanding
• **owing to**
02 of **05** due to **08** thanks to **09** because of **11** as a result of, on account of **15** in consequence of

owl
04 Bubo, ruru **05** madge **06** hooter, howlet, mopoke, strich **07** boobook, dullard, smuggle **08** longhorn, mopehawk, morepork, wiseacre **09** screecher **11** glimmer-gowk

own
03 ain, use **04** have, hold, keep, nain, nown **05** admit, enjoy **06** occupy, proper, retain **07** concede, confess, have got, possess, private **08** peculiar, personal **09** authentic, recognize **10** individual, monopolize, particular **11** acknowledge **12** be the owner of **13** idiosyncratic **14** have to yourself
• **on your own**
05 alone **06** singly **07** unaided **08** isolated **09** on your tod **10** by yourself, unassisted **13** independently, off your own bat, unaccompanied
• **own up**
05 admit **07** confess **09** come clean **11** acknowledge, plead guilty **12** tell the truth

owner
05 malik, melik **06** holder, keeper, master **08** landlady, landlord, mistress **09** homeowner, possessor **10** freeholder, proprietor **11** householder, proprietary **12** proprietress

ownership
04 uses **05** title **06** domain, rights **08** dominion, freehold, property **10** possession **11** proprietary **14** proprietorship

owning
02 of

ox
03 ure, yak **04** anoa, bull, gaur, gyal, mart, neat, urus, zebu **05** bison, bugle, gayal, steer, stirk **06** rother **07** aurochs, banteng, banting, buffalo, bullock **08** bull-beef, sapi-utan **09** sapi-outan
• **team of oxen**
04 span

Oxford University *see* college

oxygen
01 O

oyster
05 plant **06** native, Ostrea **07** spondyl **08** seedling
• **oyster bed**
04 stew

P

P
03 pee 04 papa

pace
04 gait, pass, rate, step, walk 05 amble, march, pound, speed, tempo, tramp, tread 06 flight, motion, patrol, stride 07 mark out, measure, passage, running 08 celerity, movement, progress, rapidity, velocity 09 quickness, swiftness 13 walk up and down 14 rate of progress

pacific
04 calm, mild 05 quiet, still 06 dovish, gentle, irenic, placid, serene, smooth 07 equable, halcyon 08 dovelike, friendly, irenical, pacifist, peaceful, tranquil 09 appeasing, peaceable, placatory, unruffled 10 diplomatic, non-violent 11 complaisant, peace-loving, peacemaking 12 conciliatory, pacificatory, propitiatory 14 nonbelligerent

pacification
07 calming 08 soothing 09 placating, silencing 10 moderating, moderation, quietening 11 appeasement, peacemaking 12 conciliation, propitiation 14 quietening down

pacifism
10 pacificism, satyagraha 11 non-violence, peacemaking

pacifist
02 CO 04 dove 06 conchy 08 peacenik 10 pacificist, peace-lover, peacemaker 11 peace-monger

pacify
04 calm, lull, tame 05 allay, crush, quell, quiet, still 06 defuse, soften, soothe, subdue 07 appease, assuage, compose, mollify, placate, put down, quieten, silence, sweeten 08 calm down, moderate 09 reconcile 10 conciliate, propitiate

pack
03 bag, box, jam, mob, ram, set, tin 04 bale, band, cram, crew, fill, gang, herd, load, plot, rout, stow, swag, wrap 05 bluey, bunch, cover, crate, crowd, drove, flock, group, press, put in, stock, store, stuff, tie up, troop, truss, wedge 06 bundle, burden, carton, charge, fardel, kitbag, packet, parcel, steeve, throng, wrap up 07 compact, company, dismiss, envelop, matilda, package, prepack, squeeze 08 backpack, canister, compress, intrigue, knapsack, rucksack 09 container, haversack 10 collection 11 blister card, canisterize

• **pack in**
03 end, jam, mob, ram 04 fill, load, stop 05 chuck, crowd, leave, press, stuff, wedge 06 charge, cram in, give up, jack in, resign, throng 07 squeeze, throw in
• **pack off**
04 send 07 dismiss 08 dispatch 09 bundle off
• **pack round**
04 tamp
• **pack up**
03 end 04 fail, stop 05 crash, truss 06 bundle, finish, give up, go phut, jack in, tidy up, wrap up 07 clear up, conk out, go kaput, put away, seize up, throw in 08 empacket, tidy away 09 break camp, break down 10 call it a day 11 malfunction, stop working 12 go on the fritz 13 put things away

package
03 box, lot, set 04 bale, pack, roll, unit, wrap 05 batch, group, whole 06 bundle, carton, entity, packet, pack up, parcel, wrap up 08 gift-wrap, parcel up 09 container 10 collection, shrink-wrap 11 consignment, package deal

packaging
03 box 06 packet 07 packing, wrapper 08 wrappers, wrapping 09 container, wrappings 12 presentation
• **without packaging**
03 net 04 nett

packed
04 full 05 thick 06 filled, jammed 07 brimful, chocker, crammed, crowded, serried 08 thronged 09 chockfull, congested, jam-packed 10 overloaded 11 chock-a-block, overflowing

packet
03 bag, box 04 a lot, bomb, case, deck, lots, mint, pack, pile, post, pots 06 bundle, carton, parcel, sachet 07 fortune, package, packing, tidy sum, wrapper 08 envelope, Jiffy bag®, wrapping 09 a bob or two, container, megabucks, padded bag 11 king's ransom, loadsamoney, pretty penny 12 small fortune 14 padded envelope

packhorse load
04 seam

packing-ring
04 lute

pact
04 bond, deal 06 cartel, treaty 07 bargain, compact, concord, entente 08 alliance, contract, covenant 09 agreement, concordat 10 convention, settlement 11 arrangement 13 understanding

pad
03 paw, ren, rin, run, wad 04 fill, flat, foot, home, line, lope, move, mute, pack, path, roll, room, sole, step, sunk, walk, wase, wrap 05 block, guard, inker, place, print, quilt, rooms, squab, stuff, tramp, tread 06 buffer, hamper, jotter, pillow, shield, tiptoe, trudge 07 blotter, bolster, bombast, bum roll, cushion, hang-out, memo pad, notepad, padding, pannier, pillion, protect, wadding 08 compress, dressing, leg-guard, notebook, quarters, stuffing 09 apartment, flip chart, footprint, penthouse 10 impregnate, protection, writing pad
• **pad out**
06 expand 07 amplify, augment, bolster, fill out, inflate, spin out, stretch 08 flesh out, increase, lengthen, protract 09 elaborate

padding
06 hot air, lining, waffle 07 bombast, filling, packing, wadding 08 crashpad, stuffing, verbiage 09 prolixity, verbosity, wordiness 10 cotton wool, cushioning, protection 11 verboseness

paddle
03 oar, row 04 pull, punt, slop, wade 05 canoe, scull, steer, sweep 06 dabble, finger, plunge, propel, splash, trifle 10 lumpsucker

paddock
03 pen 04 fold, frog, park, toad, yard 05 field, pound 06 corral 07 parrock 08 birdcage, compound, stockade 09 enclosure

paddy
03 pet 04 bate, fury, rage, tiff 05 sawah, strop 06 taking, temper 07 passion, tantrum 08 manrider 11 fit of temper 14 manriding train

padlock
03 bar 04 bolt, lock, seal, shut 05 catch, clasp, latch 06 fasten, secure 09 fastening 10 spring lock 11 mortise lock

padre
05 vicar 06 cleric, curate, deacon, father, parson, pastor, priest, rector 08 chaplain, minister, reverend 09 churchman, clergyman, deaconess

paean
04 hymn 05 psalm 06 anthem, eulogy

ovation **08** doxology, encomium,
le to joy **09** dithyramb, panegyric
exultation **12** song of praise

gan
paynim **07** atheist, Gentile, godless,
athen, infidel, ungodly **08** idolater
atheistic **10** idolatrous, unbeliever
irreligious, nonbeliever, nullifidian,
ntheistic

ge
p **02** ro, vo **03** bid, era **04** call, leaf,
le **05** epoch, event, folio, phase,
cto, sheet, stage, title, verso **06** ask
r, period, summon **07** bellboy,
ellhop, chapter, episode, footman,
ageboy, send for, servant
announce, henchman, incident,
ginate **08** attendant, messenger,
arsheet **10** henchwoman
henchperson
pages
pp
two pages
leaf

ageant
play, show **05** antic, scene
antick, parade **07** anticke, antique,
splay, tableau, triumph **08** specious
cavalcade, spectacle **10** procession
extravaganza **14** representation

ageantry
pomp, show **05** drama **06** parade
display, glamour, glitter
ceremony, flourish, grandeur
melodrama, showiness, spectacle,
lendour **12** extravagance,
agnificence **13** theatricality

ageboy
page **07** bellboy, bellhop, footman,
rvant **09** attendant, messenger

aid-up
loyal **06** active, red-hot **07** devoted,
rvent, zealous **08** involved
committed, dedicated
evangelical **12** card-carrying,
thusiastic

ail
can, kit, tub **04** bail, dixy **05** churn,
xie **06** bucket, leglan, leglen, leglin,
ggin, vessel **07** pitcher, scuttle
slop bucket

ain
wo **03** ake, gip, gyp, mal, woe
ache, bore, dole, dool, drag, hurt,
ang, pest, rack, stab, sten, teen, tene
agony, cramp, dolor, doole, grief,
ipe, shoot, smart, spasm, stend,
ing, teene, thraw, throb, throe, throw,
oset, worry **06** aching, be sore,
other, bummer, burden, cramps,
olour, grieve, misery, sadden, sorrow,
itch, throwe, twinge **07** afflict,
gonize, ailment, anguish, anxiety,
enalty, torment, torture, trouble
be tender, distress, headache,
ritate, nuisance, smarting, soreness,
xation **09** annoyance, causalgia,
eartache, suffering, throbbing
affliction, desolation, discomfort,

heartbreak, irritation, tenderness
11 indigestion, lancination, make
anxious, tribulation **12** collywobbles,
wretchedness **13** make miserable, pain
in the neck
• **expression of pain**
01 O **02** oh, ow **04** argh, ouch
05 aargh
• **freedom from pain**
04 ease

pained
03 sad **04** hurt **05** stung, upset, vexed
06 piqued **07** grieved, injured,
unhappy, worried, wounded
08 offended, saddened **09** aggrieved
10 distressed **11** reproachful

painful
03 bad **04** achy, hard, sore **05** tough
06 aching, bitter, guilty, tender, touchy,
trying **07** arduous, awkward, baleful,
hurting, irksome, panging, pungent,
shaming, tedious **08** exacting,
grievous, inflamed, poignant, rigorous,
shameful, smarting, stabbing, tortured,
wretched **09** agonizing, difficult,
harrowing, laborious, miserable,
saddening, sensitive, strenuous,
throbbing, traumatic, upsetting
10 disturbing, irritating, mortifying,
unpleasant **11** disquieting, distressing,
humiliating **12** disagreeable,
discomfiting, embarrassing,
excruciating **13** disconcerting,
uncomfortable
• **be painful**
04 tine, tyne, work

painfully
◇ *anagram indicator*
04 sore **05** sadly **07** clearly
08 markedly, pitiably, terribly, woefully
09 pitifully **10** alarmingly, deplorably,
dreadfully, wretchedly **11** agonizingly,
excessively **13** distressingly,
unfortunately **14** excruciatingly

painkiller
04 bute, drug **06** remedy **07** anodyne,
metopon, morphia, Nurofen®
08 lenitive, morphine, sedative
09 analgesia, analgesic **10** palliative
11 aminobutene, anaesthetic
See also **anaesthetic**; **analgesic**

painless
04 easy **05** cushy **06** simple **08** pain-
free **10** child's play, effortless
11 comfortable, trouble-free,
undemanding **12** a piece of cake, plain
sailing

painlessly
06 easily, simply **11** comfortably
12 effortlessly **13** undemandingly

pains
04 care, fash, teen, tene **05** labor,
teene **06** bother, effort, labour, rheums
07 trouble **09** diligence **10** rheumatics
13 assiduousness
• **be at pains**
06 bother **07** try hard **08** take care
09 be anxious **11** be concerned **14** put
yourself out **15** make every effort

painstaking
07 careful, devoted **08** diligent,
sedulous, studious, thorough
09 assiduous, attentive, dedicated,
searching **10** meticulous, scrupulous
11 hardworking, industrious,
persevering, punctilious
13 conscientious

paint
03 dye **04** bice, coat, daub, draw, fard,
gaud, limn, tell, tint, wash **05** adorn,
apply, brush, color, cover, evoke, smear,
stain **06** bister, bistre, colour, depict,
finish, sketch, tipple **07** narrate,
picture, pigment, plaster, portray,
priming, recount, respray, stipple,
topcoat **08** colorant, decorate,
depeinct, describe **09** colouring,
delineate, depicture, diversify, oil
colour, represent, vinyl wash
10 redecorate **11** boot-topping

Paints include:

03 oil
04 matt, oils
05 glaze, gloss, satin, spray
06 enamel, fabric, pastel, poster,
primer
07 acrylic, gouache, lacquer, masonry,
scumble, shellac, stencil, tempera,
varnish
08 eggshell, emulsion
09 anti-climb, distemper, undercoat,
whitewash
10 colourwash, egg tempera
11 watercolour

• **paint the town red**
04 rave **05** binge, go out **07** have fun,
rejoice **08** live it up **09** celebrate, have
a ball, whoop it up **10** have a party
11 throw a party **13** enjoy yourself, go
on the razzle **14** go out on the town,
push the boat out, put the flags out

painted
• **painted woman**
04 pict

painter
02 RA **06** artist, dauber, limner
07 Zeuxian **08** depicter **09** colourist,
old master, paysagist, primitive,
tactilist, vedutista **10** delineator, oil
painter, miniaturist,
plein-airist **13** watercolorist
14 watercolourist

*Painters, printmakers and other
artists include:*

03 Arp (Jean), Dix (Otto), Ray (Man)
04 Bell (Vanessa), Dali (Salvador), Doré
(Gustave), Dufy (Raoul), Eyck (Jan
van), Goya (Francisco de), Gris
(Juan), Hals (Frans), Hunt (Holman),
John (Augustus), Klee (Paul), Lely (Sir
Peter), Long (Richard), Marc
(Franz), Miró (Joan), Nash (Paul)
05 Bacon (Francis), Bakst (Léon), Blake
(Peter), Blake (William), Bosch
(Hieronymus), Brown (Ford
Madox), Burra (Edward), Clark
(Kenneth, Lord), Corot (Camille),

David (Jacques Louis), **Degas** (Edgar), **Dürer** (Albrecht), **Ernst** (Max), **Freud** (Lucian), **Gorky** (Arshile), **Greco** (El), **Grosz** (George), **Hirst** (Damien), **Homer** (Winslow), **Hooch** (Pieter de), **Johns** (Jasper), **Kahlo** (Frida), **Kitaj** (R B), **Klimt** (Gustav), **Kline** (Franz), **Léger** (Fernand), **Lewis** (Wyndham), **Lippi** (Filippino), **Lippi** (Fra Filippo), **Lowry** (L S), **Lucas** (Sarah), **Manet** (Edouard), **Monet** (Claude), **Mucha** (Alphonse), **Munch** (Edvard), **Nolan** (Sir Sidney), **Peake** (Mervyn), **Piper** (John), **Riley** (Bridget), **Sarto** (Andrea del)

06 Braque (Georges), **Bratby** (John), **Cassat** (Mary), **Claude**, **Derain** (André Louis), **Escher** (Maurits Cornelis), **Fuseli** (Henri), **Giotto**, **Gordon** (Douglas), **Ingres** (Jean), **Jarman** (Derek), **Knight** (Dame Laura), **Mabuse**, **Marini** (Marino), **Martin** (John), **Massys** (Quentin), **Millet** (Jean François), **Morley** (Malcolm), **Moroni** (Giovanni Battista), **Morris** (William), **Newman** (Barnett), **O'Keefe** (Georgia), **Orozco** (José), **Palmer** (Samuel), **Peploe** (Samuel John), **Pisano** (Nicola), **Ramsay** (Allan), **Renoir** (Pierre Auguste), **Rivera** (Diego), **Rothko** (Mark), **Rubens** (Sir Peter Paul), **Scarfe** (Gerald), **Searle** (Ronald), **Seurat** (Georges), **Sisley** (Alfred), **Strong** (Sir Roy), **Stubbs** (George), **Tanguy** (Yves), **Tissot** (James), **Titian**, **Turner** (J M W), **Warhol** (Andy), **Wilkie** (Sir David), **Wright** (Joseph)

07 Attwell (Mabel Lucie), **Bellini** (Giovanni), **Bonnard** (Pierre), **Boucher** (François), **Cézanne** (Paul), **Chagall** (Marc), **Chirico** (Giorgio de), **Christo**, **Cimabué**, **Courbet** (Gustave), **Cranach** (Lucas, the Elder), **Daumier** (Honoré), **Delvaux** (Paul), **Duchamp** (Marcel), **El Greco**, **Gauguin** (Paul), **Hobbema** (Meindert), **Hockney** (David), **Hodgkin** (Sir Howard), **Hogarth** (William), **Hokusai** (Katsushika), **Holbein** (Hans), **Keating** (Tom), **Martini** (Simone), **Matisse** (Henri), **Millais** (Sir John Everett), **Morisot** (Berthe), **Pevsner** (Sir Nikolaus), **Picabia** (Francis), **Picasso** (Pablo), **Pollock** (Jackson), **Poussin** (Nicolas), **Rackham** (Arthur), **Raeburn** (Sir Henry), **Raphael**, **Sargent** (John Singer), **Schiele** (Egon), **Sickert** (Walter), **Spencer** (Sir Stanley), **Tenniel** (Sir John), **Thurber** (James), **Tiepolo** (Giovanni), **Uccello** (Paolo), **Utrillo** (Maurice), **Van Eyck** (Jan), **Van Gogh** (Vincent), **Vermeer** (Jan), **Watteau** (Antoine), **Wearing** (Gillian)

08 Angelico (Fra), **Annigoni** (Pietro), **Auerbach** (Frank), **Breughel** (Pieter), **Brueghel** (Pieter), **cummings** (e e), **Delaunay** (Robert),

Dubuffet (Jean), **Goncourt** (Edmond de), **Gossaert** (Jan), **Hamilton** (Richard), **Hilliard** (Nicholas), **Landseer** (Sir Edwin), **Leonardo**, **Magritte** (René), **Malevich** (Kasimir), **Mantegna** (Andrea), **Masaccio**, **Mondrian** (Piet), **Perugino**, **Piranesi** (Giambattista), **Pissarro** (Camille), **Reynolds** (Sir Joshua), **Rossetti** (Dante Gabriel), **Rousseau** (Henri, 'Le Douanier'), **Rousseau** (Théodore), **Ruisdael** (Jacob van), **Ruysdael** (Jacob van), **Topolski** (Feliks), **Vasarely** (Victor), **Veronese** (Paolo), **Vlaminck** (Maurice de), **Whistler** (James McNeill)

09 Beardsley (Aubrey), **Canaletto**, **Constable** (John), **Correggio**, **De Kooning** (Willem), **Delacroix** (Eugène), **Fergusson** (John Duncan), **Fragonard** (Jean), **Friedrich** (Caspar David), **Géricault** (Théodore), **Giorgione**, **Greenaway** (Kate), **Greenaway** (Peter), **Grünewald** (Matthias), **Kandinsky** (Wasily), **Kokoschka** (Oskar), **Lancaster** (Sir Osbert), **Nicholson** (Ben), **Nollekens** (Joseph), **Pisanello**, **Rembrandt**, **Rodchenko** (Alexander), **Velázquez** (Diego)

10 Alma-Tadema (Sir Lawrence), **Botticelli** (Sandro), **Burne-Jones** (Sir Edward), **Caravaggio** (Michelangelo), **Giacometti** (Alberto), **Modigliani** (Amedeo), **Motherwell** (Robert), **Parmigiano**, **Sutherland** (Graham), **Tintoretto**

12 Bairnsfather (Bruce), **Fantin-Latour** (Henri), **Gainsborough** (Thomas), **Lichtenstein** (Roy), **Michelangelo**

13 Piero di Cosimo

14 Andrea del Sarto, **Lucas van Leyden**

15 Leonardo da Vinci, **Toulouse-Lautrec** (Henri de)

painting

03 art, oil **04** daub, oils **08** likeness **09** cerograph, portrayal **11** delineation, scenography **13** belle peinture **14** representation

See also **art**

04 icon, tint, tone, wash
05 bloom, brush, easel, gesso, mural, paint, pieta, secco, tondo
06 canvas, fresco, frieze, primer, sketch
07 atelier, aureola, aureole, cartoon, collage, diptych, drawing, facture, gallery, gouache, impasto, limning, montage, palette, pastels, paysage, picture, pigment, scumble, sfumato, stipple, tempera
08 abstract, aquatint, bleeding, charcoal, esquisse, fixative, frottage, hard edge, hatching, paintbox, pastoral, portrait, seascape, skyscape, thinners, triptych, vignette
09 alla prima, aquarelle, brushwork,

capriccio, encaustic, flat brush, grisaille, grotesque, landscape, mahlstick, maulstick, miniature, polyptych, scumbling, sgraffito, still life
10 art gallery, craquelure, dead colour, figurative, hair-pencil, monochrome, paint-brush, pentimento, pochade box, round brush, sable brush, silhouette, turpentine
11 canvas board, chiaroscuro, composition, fête galante, foreshorten, found object, illusionism, objet trouvé, oil painting, perspective, pointillism, trompe l'oeil, watercolour
12 anamorphosis, brush strokes, camera lucida, filbert brush, illustration, palette knife, pencil sketch
13 fête champêtre, genre painting, underpainting
14 foreshortening

04 Flag
05 Manga, Pietà, Trees
06 Spring
07 Bubbles, Erasmus, Gin Lane, Olympia, Targets, The Kiss
08 Guernica, L'Estaque, Maja Nude, Mona Lisa, The Dream
09 Bacchanal, Black Iris, Haystacks, Henry VIII, Jerusalem, L'Escargot, Night Café, Primavera, The Scream, The Tailor
10 Adam and Eve, Assumption, Beer Street, Blue Horses, Las Meninas, Sunflowers, The Angelus, The Hay Wain
11 100 Soup Cans, Arthur's Tomb, A Shrimp Girl, Crucifixion, Limp Watches, Maja Clothed, Starry Night, The Gleaners, View of Delft, Water Lilies
12 Beata Beatrix, Black on Black, Los Caprichos, Peasant Dance, The Nightmare, The Scapegoat, The Umbrellas
13 A Bigger Splash, Christ in Glory, Isenheim Altar, Man with a Glove, Sleeping Gypsy, The Last Supper, The Night Watch
14 A Rake's Progress, Disasters of War, Peasant Wedding, Random Sketches, Rouen Cathedral, Sistine Madonna, The Ambassadors, The Card Players, The Four Seasons, The Rokeby Venus, The Turkish Bath, View on the Stour
15 Absinthe Drinker, Commodore Keppel, Flight into Egypt, Madonna and Child, Madonna del Prato, Marriage à la Mode, The Annunciation, The Birth of Venus, The Charnel House, The Dance of Death, The Death of Marat, The Flagellation, The Potato Eaters, The Raft of Medusa, The Rape of Europa, Triumph of Caesar

pair

02 OO, pr **03** duo, set, twa, two, wed
04 duad, duet, join, link, mate, pack, team, twae, tway, twin, yoke **05** brace, marry, match, twain, twins, unite
06 couple, geminy, join up, link up, splice, team up **07** bracket, couplet, match up, partner, twosome **10** two of a kind **11** put together **14** arrange in pairs

paired

05 mated, yoked **06** double, in twos, joined, jugate, linked **07** coupled, matched, twinned **09** bracketed
10 associated

Pakistan

02 PK **03** PAK

pal

04 chum, mate **05** buddy, crony, cully
06 cobber, friend, winger **07** comrade, partner **08** intimate, sidekick, soul mate **09** companion, confidant
10 buddy-buddy, confidante
• **pal up**
06 chum up, gang up, join up **11** get together, make friends **13** become friends

palace

04 dome **05** court, hôtel **06** castle
07 alcázar, château, mansion, palazzo, schloss **08** basilica, seraglio **11** stately home

Palaces include:

05 Pitti, Royal, Savoy
06 Louvre, Mirror, Potala, Winter
07 Bishop's, Crystal, People's, Sultan's, Vatican
08 Alhambra, Blenheim, Borghese, Imperial, National, St James's, Valhalla, Walhalla
09 Episcopal, Maharaja's, Sans Souci, Tuileries, Whitehall
10 Buckingham, El Escorial, Fishbourne, Generalife, Kensington, Linlithgow, President's, Qusayr Amra, Quseir Amra, Schönbrunn, Versailles
11 Archbishop's, Westminster
13 Forbidden City, Holyrood House, Royal Pavilion, Tower of London, Windsor Castle
14 Charlottenburg
15 Palais de l'Elysée

paladin

04 peer

palaeontologist

Palaeontologists include:

04 Cope (Edward Drinker), Owen (Sir Richard)
05 Gould (Stephen Jay), Marsh (O C)
06 Dubois (Eugène), Forbes (Edward), Kurtén (Björn), Leakey (Louis), Leakey (Mary), Leakey (Richard), Osborn (Henry Fairfield), Zittel (Karl von)
07 Colbert (Ned), Mantell (Gideon), Simpson (George Gaylord)
08 Guettard (Jean Étienne), Johanson (Donald)

palanquin

04 kago **05** palki, sedan **06** doolie, litter, palkee **07** norimon

palatable

04 nice **05** tasty, yummy **06** delish, edible, morish **07** eatable, moreish, savoury, scrummy **08** pleasant, pleasing **09** agreeable, delicious, enjoyable, flavorous, succulent, toothsome **10** acceptable, appetizing, attractive, delectable **11** done to a turn, flavoursome, scrumptious
12 satisfactory **13** mouthwatering

palate

04 gout **05** heart, taste, velum
06 liking, relish **07** stomach
08 appetite **09** enjoyment, taste buds
10 enthusiasm **12** appreciation, sense of taste

palatial

04 posh **05** grand, plush, regal, ritzy
06 de luxe **07** opulent, stately
08 imposing, majestic, spacious, splendid **09** grandiose, luxurious, sumptuous **11** magnificent

Palau

03 PLW

palaver

04 flap, fuss, talk, to-do **05** hoo-ha
06 bother, bustle **07** carry-on, flatter, fluster **08** activity, business
09 commotion, kerfuffle, procedure, rigmarole **10** conference, discussion
12 song and dance

pale

03 dim, wan **04** ashy, fade, gray, grey, lily, melt, pall, pole, post, thin, waxy, weak **05** appal, ashen, blank, crown, faded, faint, fence, green, light, limit, livid, lurid, mealy, muted, pasty, peaky, shaft, stain, stake, vapid, verge, waxen, white **06** blanch, bleach, chalky, column, feeble, lessen, low-key, mealie, pallid, pastel, sallow, whiten
07 anaemic, drained, dwindle, high-key, insipid, upright, whitely, whitish
08 bleached, delicate, diminish, encircle, etiolate, grow pale, maid-pale
09 bloodless, enclosure, etiolated, grow white, washed-out, whey-faced
10 colourless, pallescent, pasty-faced, restrained, wishy-washy **11** peelie-wally **12** change colour
14 complexionless
• **beyond the pale**
08 improper, unseemly **10** unsuitable
11 intolerable **12** inadmissible, unacceptable, unreasonable
13 inappropriate

paleness

04 pale **06** pallor **07** anaemia, wanness **09** pastiness, whiteness
10 sallowness **11** pallescence
14 colourlessness

palindromic

07 Sotadic **08** cancrine, Sotadean

palisade

05 fence **06** fraise, paling **07** barrier,

bulwark, defence, stacket **08** stockade
09 barricade, enclosure
13 fortification

pall

04 cloy, jade, pale, sate, tire, veil
05 cloak, cloud, daunt, gloom, weary
06 damper, mantle, shadow, shroud, sicken, weaken **07** curtain, frontal, pallium, satiate, wear off **08** corporal, covering **09** mortcloth **11** become bored, become tired, hearse-cloth
• **cast a pall over**
03 mar **04** harm, ruin **05** spoil, upset, wreck **06** impair **07** destroy

palladium

02 Pd

palliate

04 ease **05** abate, allay, cloak, cover
06 excuse, lenify, lessen, soften, soothe, temper **07** assuage, conceal, lighten, mollify, relieve **08** diminish, disguise, minimize, mitigate, moderate
09 alleviate, extenuate

palliative

07 anodyne, calming **08** lenitive, sedative, soothing **09** analgesic, assuasive, calmative, demulcent, paregoric **10** mitigating, mitigative, mitigatory, mollifying, painkiller
11 alleviating, alleviative, extenuative, extenuatory **13** tranquillizer

pallid

03 wan **04** ashy, dull, pale, tame, waxy, weak **05** ashen, bland, lurid, pasty, tired, vapid, waxen, white **06** boring, doughy, sallow, sickly **07** anaemic, insipid, sterile, whitish **08** lifeless
09 bloodless, etiolated, whey-faced
10 colourless, pallescent, pasty-faced, spiritless, unexciting, uninspired
11 peelie-wally **13** uninteresting
14 complexionless

pallor

07 anaemia, wanness **08** paleness
09 whiteness **10** chalkiness, etiolation, pallidness, sallowness **11** pallescence
13 bloodlessness

pally

04 warm **05** close, thick, tight
06 chummy, folksy **08** familiar, friendly, intimate **12** affectionate

palm

03 fob, paw **04** grab, hand, loof, mitt, take, vola **05** bribe **06** snatch, thenar
11 appropriate

Palms include:

03 dum, ita, oil, wax
04 atap, coco, date, doom, doum, hemp, nipa, sago
05 areca, assai, bussu, macaw, nikau, peach, royal, Sabal, sugar, toddy
06 buriti, cohune, corozo, Elaeis, gomuti, gru-gru, jupati, kentia, kittul, miriti, raffia, Raphia, rattan, troely
07 babassu, cabbage, calamus, coconut, coquito, Corypha, Euterpe, moriche, palmyra,

paxiuba, pupunha, talipat, talipot, troelie, troolie
08 carnauba, coco-tree, date-tree, groo-groo, palmetto
10 Chamaerops
12 chiquichiqui, Washingtonia
15 cabbage-palmetto

• **have someone in the palm of your hand**
13 have power over **15** have control over

• **palm off**
05 foist **06** fob off, impose, pass on, put off, thrust, unload **07** offload, pass off, work off **08** get rid of, pass upon

palmist
10 palm reader **11** clairvoyant
13 chirographist, fortune-teller

palmistry
10 chirognomy, chiromancy **11** palm reading **12** clairvoyancy **14** fortune-telling

palmy
05 happy **06** golden, joyous
07 halcyon **08** carefree, glorious, thriving **09** fortunate, luxurious
10 prosperous, successful, triumphant
11 flourishing

palpable
04 real **05** clear, gross, plain, solid
06 patent **07** blatant, evident, glaring, obvious, visible **08** apparent, concrete, manifest, material, tangible
09 touchable **11** conspicuous, perceptible, substantial
12 unmistakable **13** unmistakeable

palpably
07 clearly, plainly, visibly **08** patently
09 blatantly, evidently, glaringly, obviously **10** apparently, manifestly
12 unmistakably **13** conspicuously, unmistakeably

palpitate
04 beat, thud **05** pound, pulse, quake, shake, throb, thump **06** pit-pat, quiver, shiver **07** flutter, pitapat, pulsate, tremble, twitter, vibrate **08** pitty-pat

palpitation
05 shake, throb **06** quiver, shakes
07 flutter, shaking **08** pounding
09 quivering, throbbing, trembling, vibration **10** fluttering

paltry
03 low, tin **04** bald, bare, mean, poor, puny, vile, waff **05** cheap, minor, petty, scald, small, sorry, woful **06** jitney, meagre, measly, shabby, slight, tinpot, trashy, two-bit, vulgar, woeful
07 foolish, miserly, pelting, pimping, piteous, trivial **08** derisory, piddling, rubbishy, trifling, wretched
09 miserable, worthless **10** negligible, shoestring **11** unimportant
12 contemptible, pettifogging
13 insignificant **14** inconsiderable

pamper
03 pet **04** baby **05** spoil **06** cocker, coddle, cosher, cosset, cuiter, fondle,

humour, pander, pompey **07** gratify, indulge **09** spoon-feed **10** featherbed
11 mollycoddle, overindulge

pampered
06 petted, spoilt **07** coddled, high-fed, overfed **08** cosseted, indulged, spoon-fed **10** lust-dieted **12** mollycoddled

pamphlet
03 pam **05** flyer, sheet, tract **06** folder, notice **07** booklet, handout, leaflet
08 brochure, chapbook, circular
10 mazarinade

pan
03 pit, pot, wok **04** bowl, cake, cave, face, flay, hole, lead, move, scan, slag, slam, turn, well **05** basin, betel, frier, fryer, knock, ladle, roast, scale, slate, sweep, swing, track, yield **06** cavern, cavity, circle, crater, Faunus, follow, hammer, hollow, obtain, spider, vessel
07 censure, channel, goat-god, rubbish, skillet, slag off **08** pancheon, panchion, pannikin, saucepan, traverse
09 bed-warmer, casserole, concavity, container, criticize, frying-pan, saltworks **10** corn popper, depression, excavation **11** calefactory **12** pull to pieces **13** find fault with

• **pan out**
05 yield **06** happen, result **07** turn out, work out **09** culminate, eventuate
11 be exhausted, come to an end

panacea
06 elixir, tutsan **07** allheal, cure-all, nostrum **10** catholicon, parkleaves
12 panpharmacon **13** diacatholicon
15 universal remedy

panache
04 brio, dash, élan, zest **05** flair, plume, style, verve **06** energy, pazazz, pizazz, spirit, vigour **07** pazzazz, pizzazz, swagger **08** flourish **10** enthusiasm
11 flamboyance, ostentation

Panama
02 PA **03** PAN

pancake
04 flam, taco **05** blini, crêpe, flamm, flawn, latke, rösti, wafer **06** blintz, flaune, fraise, froise, roesti, waffle
07 bannock, blintze, crumpet, pikelet
08 flapjack, omelette, tortilla **09** drop scone **10** battercake, spring roll
11 griddle-cake **12** crêpe suzette, dropped scone

pandemic
04 rife **06** common, global **07** general
09 extensive, pervasive, prevalent, universal **10** widespread **11** far-reaching

pandemonium
03 din **04** to-do **05** chaos **06** bedlam, hubbub, rumpus, tumult, uproar
07 turmoil **08** disorder **09** commotion, confusion, hue and cry, shemozzle
10 hullabaloo, turbulence

pander
04 bawd, pimp **06** broker **07** procure
08 procurer **11** whoremonger

• **pander to**
06 fulfil, humour, pamper, please
07 cater to, gratify, indulge, provide, satisfy

pane
04 pean, peen, pein, pene **05** glass, panel **06** window **07** quarrel
10 windowpane

panegyric
05 éloge, elogy, paean **06** eulogy, homage, praise **07** elogium, glowing, tribute **08** accolade, citation, encomium, eulogium, praising
09 laudation, laudatory, praiseful
10 eulogistic, favourable, flattering
11 encomiastic, panegyrical
12 commendation, commendatory
13 complimentary **14** speech of praise

panel
03 orb **04** beam, jury, mola, pane, sign, slab, team, unit **05** array, board, dials, knobs, plank, plate, sheet, table
06 coffer, levers, screen, tablet, timber
07 buttons, console, council, inn sign, lacunar, valance, valence **08** controls, mandorla, switches, trustees
09 cartouche, committee, dashboard, faceplate, headboard, medallion
10 commission, focus group, patchboard **11** compartment, directorate, instruments **13** advisory group **15** instrument panel

panelling
04 dado **06** coffer **07** lacunar, reredos
08 wainscot **09** panelwork, reredorse, reredosse **11** wainscoting
12 wainscotting

pang
04 ache, cram, pain, stab **05** agony, gripe, prick, qualm, spasm, sting, stuff, thraw, throe, throw, tight **06** shower, stitch, stound, stownd, throwe, twinge
07 anguish, crammed, crowded, scruple, stuffed **08** distress
09 misgiving **10** discomfort, uneasiness

pangolin
05 Manis **08** anteater **13** scaly anteater

panic
◊ *anagram indicator*
04 fear, flap, funk **05** alarm, amaze, scare **06** dismay, frenzy, fright, horror, panick, terror **07** pannick, unnerve
08 disquiet, flat spin, hysteria, tailspin
09 agitation, overreact, run scared
10 amazedness, go to pieces **11** have kittens, trepidation **12** get the shakes, lose your cool, lose your head, perturbation, sauve qui peut
13 consternation, get the jitters, get the willies, lose your nerve **14** lose your bottle

panic-stricken
06 aghast, scared **07** alarmed, frantic, panicky **08** frenzied, in a tizzy
09 horrified, perturbed, petrified, terrified **10** frightened, hysterical **11** in a blue funk, in a flat spin, scared stiff
12 in a cold sweat **14** terror-stricken

pannier
3 pad, ped 06 dosser 07 cacolet, ajawah 09 ambulance

panoply
4 garb, gear, show 05 array, dress, get-p, range 06 armour, attire 07 raiment, egalia, turn-out 08 insignia 9 equipment, trappings

panorama
4 view 05 scene, vista 06 survey 7 scenery 08 overview, prospect, vide view 09 broad view, cyclorama, landscape, spectacle 11 perspective 2 bird's-eye view

panoramic
4 wide 05 broad 06 scenic 7 general, overall 08 sweeping 9 extensive, universal 10 widespread 1 far-reaching, wide-ranging 3 comprehensive

pansy
5 pance, viola 06 kiss-me, paunce, pawnce 10 effeminate, heart's-ease, homosexual 11 herb-trinity, kiss-me-quick 14 love-in-idleness

pant
3 yen 04 ache, blow, gasp, huff, long, pech, pegh, pine, puff, sigh, want 5 covet, crave, flaff, heave, throb, yearn 06 desire, hanker, thirst, wheeze 7 breathe 09 palpitate 11 huff and puff

panting
5 eager 06 puffed, winded 7 anxious, craving, gasping, longing, puffing 09 hankering, impatient, puffed out 10 breathless 11 out of breath, short-winded

pantomime
4 mime, show 05 farce, panto 6 masque 07 charade 08 dumbshow 2 harlequinade

pantry
05 ambry, awmry 06 almery, aumbry, awmrie, larder, spence 07 butlery 08 scullery 09 stillroom, storeroom

pants
05 jeans, loons, teddy, thong 06 briefs, shorts, slacks, smalls, trunks, undies 07 drawers, joggers, panties, rubbish, Y-fronts 08 frillies, knickers, nonsense, trousers 10 underpants 11 boxer shorts, panty girdle 12 camiknickers

pap
03 goo, rot 04 crap, mash, mush, pulp 05 purée, trash 06 breast, drivel, hot air, nipple 07 rubbish, twaddle 08 claptrap, nonsense, soft food 09 gibberish, poppycock 14 semi-liquid food

papa
01 P
See also **father**

paper
03 rag 04 ream, work 05 daily, essay, organ, study 06 report, thesis, weekly 07 article, journal, tabloid 08 analysis, magazine, treatise 09 monograph, newspaper 10 broadsheet, periodical 11 composition, examination 12 dissertation
See also **newspaper**

10 pasteboard
11 greaseproof

• **on paper**
07 ideally 08 in theory, recorded 09 in writing, seemingly 10 officially, supposedly 11 on the record, written down 13 theoretically 14 hypothetically, in your mind's eye 15 in black and white

• **paper over**
04 hide 07 conceal, cover up, obscure 08 disguise 10 camouflage 13 put out of sight

• **paper size**
03 pot 04 demy, pott

papers
02 ID 04 bumf 05 bumph, deeds, sheaf 07 records 08 document, evidence, passbook, passport 10 despatches, dispatches 11 credentials 12 certificates, identity card 13 authorization, documentation 14 driving licence, identification, qualifications

papery
04 thin 05 frail, light 06 flimsy 07 fragile 08 delicate 09 paper-thin 10 glumaceous, membranous 11 chartaceous, lightweight, membraneous, papyraceous, translucent 13 insubstantial, membranaceous

Papua New Guinea
03 PNG

par
04 mean, norm, parr 05 level, usual 06 median, parity 07 average, balance 08 equality, standard 09 paragraph 10 accordance, similarity 11 equilibrium, equivalence 12 equal footing 14 correspondence

• **below par**
05 lousy, rough, tired 06 unwell 08 inferior, under par 10 inadequate, not up to par, out of sorts 11 at a discount 12 below average 14 not up to scratch, unsatisfactory 15 under the weather

• **deviation from par**
04 agio

• **on a par with**
07 equal to 08 as good as 12 equivalent to

• **par for the course**
05 usual 06 normal 07 typical 08 standard 11 predictable

• **up to par**
02 OK 04 fine 08 adequate 10 acceptable 11 up to scratch 12 satisfactory

parable
05 fable, story 06 lesson 07 proverb 08 allegory 09 discourse, moral tale 10 comparison, similitude 15 story with a moral

parachute
04 pack 05 chute 06 drogue, pappus 08 parafoil, patagium 09 aeroshell, parabrake

parade
03 row **04** file, pass, shew, show
05 array, march, parry, train, vaunt
06 column, flaunt, line-up, prance,
review **07** display, exhibit, pageant,
process, show off, stand-to
08 brandish, ceremony, file past
09 cavalcade, decursion, motorcade,
spectacle **10** appearance, exhibition,
procession **11** ostentation, progression
13 demonstration

paradigm
05 ideal, model **07** example, pattern
08 exemplar, original **09** archetype,
framework, prototype

paradise
03 joy **04** Eden **05** bliss **06** heaven,
parvis, Svarga, Swarga, Swerga, utopia
07 delight, ecstasy, Elysium, rapture
08 felicity **09** afterlife, cloud nine,
happiness, hereafter, home of God,
next world, Shangri-La **10** life to come
12 Garden of Eden **13** Elysian Fields,
seventh heaven

paradox
06 enigma, oddity, puzzle, riddle
07 anomaly, mystery **09** absurdity
11 incongruity **13** contradiction,
inconsistency

paradoxical
06 absurd **08** baffling, puzzling
09 anomalous, enigmatic, illogical
10 impossible, improbable, mysterious
11 conflicting, incongruous
12 inconsistent **13** contradictory

paraffin
07 coal oil **08** earthwax, kerosene,
kerosine, photogen **09** ozocerite,
ozokerite, photogene **10** mineral wax
14 petroleum jelly

paragon
04 mate, rose **05** equal, ideal, match,
model, pearl, rival **07** compare,
epitome, paladin, pattern, phoenix,
surpass **08** exemplar, standard
09 archetype, criterion, emulation,
nonpareil, prototype **10** comparison
11 competition, masterpiece
12 quintessence, the bee's knees
14 crème de la crème, perfect example

paragraph
03 par **04** item, para, part **05** piece
06 clause **07** article, passage, portion,
section, segment **08** causerie, te igitur
10 stand first, subsection
11 subdivision

Paraguay
02 PY **03** PRY

parallel
03 par **04** echo, like, twin **05** agree,
equal, liken, match **06** be like
07 aligned, analogy, compare,
conform, similar, uniform **08** analogue,
likeness, matching, resemble
09 alongside, analogous, correlate,
duplicate **10** co-existing, collateral,
comparable, comparison, correspond,
equivalent, homologous, resembling,

side by side, similarity **11** be analogous,
be similar to, coextensive, correlation,
counterpart, equidistant, equivalence,
resemblance **12** be equivalent
13 corresponding **14** correspondence

paralyse
04 dull, halt, lame, numb, stop **05** palsy,
scram, shock **06** benumb, deaden,
freeze **07** cripple, disable, terrify,
torpefy **08** transfix **10** deactivate,
debilitate, immobilize **12** anaesthetize,
incapacitate

paralysed
04 lame, numb **08** crippled, disabled
09 paralytic **10** paraplegic
11 immobilized **12** quadriplegic
13 incapacitated

paralysis
04 halt **05** palsy, shock **07** paresis
08 deadness, diplegia, numbness,
shutdown, stoppage **09** breakdown
10 Bell's palsy, hemiplegia, immobility,
monoplegia, paraplegia, sideration,
standstill **11** cycloplegia, paraparesis
12 debilitation, quadriplegia
13 cerebral palsy, powerlessness
15 ophthalmoplegia

paralytic
04 lame, numb **05** drunk **06** blotto,
canned, soused, stewed, stoned,
wasted **07** legless, palsied, pie-eyed,
sloshed, smashed, sozzled, wrecked
08 crippled, disabled, immobile
09 incapable, paralysed, plastered
10 hemiplegic, inebriated, monoplegic
11 immobilized, intoxicated
12 quadriplegic **13** incapacitated **15** a
sheet in the wind

parameter
05 limit **06** factor **08** boundary,
variable **09** criterion, framework,
guideline **10** indication, limitation
11 restriction **13** figure of merit,
specification **14** limiting factor

paramilitaries
04 sena

paramount
04 main **05** chief, first, prime
07 highest, primary, supreme, topmost
08 cardinal, foremost, superior,
suzerain **09** principal **10** pre-eminent
11 outstanding, predominant **13** most
important

paramour
04 beau **05** leman, lover, woman
07 beloved, franion, hetaera, hetaira
08 copemate, fancy man, mistress
09 concubine, copes-mate, courtesan,
inamorata, inamorato, kept woman
10 bit of fluff, fancy woman **12** bit on
the side

paranoia
09 delusions, monomania, obsession,
psychosis **11** megalomania

paranoid
05 fazed **06** afraid **07** fearful
08 confused **10** bewildered,
suspicious **11** distrustful

paranormal
◊ *anagram indicator*
05 eerie, magic, weird **06** hidden,
mystic, occult **07** ghostly, magical,
phantom, psychic **08** abnormal,
mystical **09** spiritual, unnatural
10 miraculous, mysterious
12 metaphysical, otherworldly,
supernatural **13** preternatural

parapet
03 top **04** rail, wall **05** fence, guard
06 flèche, paling, parpen **07** barrier,
bastion, bulwark, defence, parpane,
parpend, parpent, perpend, perpent,
railing, rampart **08** barbican, bartisan,
bartizan, parpoint, traverse
09 barricade **10** balustrade, battlement,
embankment **13** fortification

paraphernalia
04 gear **05** stuff, tools **06** tackle, things
07 baggage, effects **09** apparatus,
equipment, materials, trappings
10 belongings, implements
11 accessories, odds and ends,
possessions **13** accoutrements, bits
and pieces

paraphrase
05 gloss **06** rehash, render, reword,
Targum **07** restate, version **08** rephrase
09 interpret, rendering, rewording,
translate **10** rephrasing **11** restatement,
translation **14** interpretation **15** put in
other words

parasite
03 bum, fly **05** drone, leech **06** cadger,
ligger, sponge, sucker **07** bludger,
epizoan, epizoon, moocher, sponger,
vampire **08** endozoon, entozoon,
epiphyte, hanger-on, quandang,
quandong, quantong **09** endophyte,
passenger, scrounger, sycophant
10 freeloader **11** bloodsucker **12** lick-
trencher **14** trencher-friend, trencher-
knight

Parasites include:
03 bot, ked, nit
04 bott, chat, crab, flea, kade, mite,
tick
05 fluke, louse
06 chigoe, chigre, cootie, jigger
07 argulus, ascarid, ascaris, Babesia,
bonamia, cestode, chalcid, chigger,
Giardia, pinworm
08 hookworm, itch-mite, lungworm,
nematode, sheep ked, strongyl,
tapeworm, toxocara, whipworm
09 Bilharzia, bird louse, crab louse, fish
louse, fluke-worm, head louse,
pediculus, roundworm, sheep tick,
sporozoan, strongyle, trematode
10 Guinea worm, Plasmodium,
threadworm
11 biting louse, sarcocystis, scabies
mite, trichomonad, trypanosome
12 echinococcus, ectoparasite,
endoparasite, semiparasite
13 hyperparasite

parasitic
07 cadging, epizoan, epizoic

8 sponging **09** biogenous, leechlike
0 scrounging **11** freeloading,
arasitical **12** bloodsucking

arasol
4 veil **05** shade **06** shield **07** shelter
8 marquise, sunshade, umbrella
9 en tout cas **10** protection
See also **umbrella**

arcel
3 box, dak, lot, mob, set **04** area,
and, crew, dawk, deal, gang, herd,
tem, pack, plot, sort, wrap **05** bunch,
crowd, flock, group, patch, piece, put
p, tie up, tract, troop **06** bundle,
carton, make up, packet, pack up,
partly, wrap up **07** company, package,
portion **08** bundle up, gift-wrap,
quantity **09** allotment **10** collection
1 transaction
● **parcel out**
5 allot, whack **06** divide **07** carve up,
deal out, dole out, hand out, mete out
8 allocate, dispense, share out
9 apportion, divide out **10** distribute

parch
03 dry **04** bake, burn, sear **05** dry up,
roast **06** scorch, wither **07** blister,
shrivel, torrefy **09** dehydrate, desiccate

parched
03 dry **04** arid, sear, sere **05** baked
06 burned, seared **07** dried up,
gasping, thirsty **08** scorched, withered
09 blistered, waterless **10** dehydrated,
desiccated, dry as a bone, shrivelled

parchment
04 pell, roll **05** forel, panel **06** mezuza,
scroll, vellum **07** charter, diploma,
mezuzah **08** document, membrane
09 sheepskin **10** palimpsest,
phylactery **11** certificate

pardon
02 eh? **04** free, what? **05** bitte, grace,
mercy, remit, sorry **06** acquit, excuse,
let off **07** absolve, amnesty, condone,
forgive, release, you what?
08 clemency, excuse me, lenience,
liberate, oblivion, overlook, reprieve,
say again?, tolerate **09** acquittal, come
again?, discharge, exculpate,
exonerate, remission, vindicate
10 absolution, act of grace, indulgence
11 condonation, cry you mercy,
exculpation, exoneration, forbearance,
forgiveness **13** let off the hook, what
did you say? **14** I beg your pardon

pardonable
05 minor **06** slight, venial
09 allowable, excusable
10 condonable, forgivable
11 dispensable, justifiable, permissible,
warrantable **14** understandable

pare
03 cut, lop **04** chip, clip, crop, dock,
peel, skin, trim **05** prune, shave, shear,
skive **06** reduce **07** cut back, whittle
08 clip coin, decrease

parent
02 ma, pa **03** dad, dam, mam, mom,

mum, pop **04** papa, rear, root, sire
05 beget, cause, daddy, folks, mamma,
mammy, mommy, mummy, mumsy,
raise, teach, train **06** author, create,
father, foster, mother, old man, origin,
source **07** bring up, creator, educate,
genitor, nurture **08** begetter, generant,
genetrix, genitrix, guardian, old
woman, relative **09** architect,
bioparent, look after, procreate,
prototype **10** forerunner, originator,
procreator, progenitor, solo parent,
step-parent, take care of **11** birth
mother, birth parent, empty-nester,
progenitrix **12** foster parent,
progenitress, single parent **13** be the
father of, be the mother of **14** adoptive
parent **15** custodial parent

parentage
04 line, race **05** birth, brood, stock
06 family, origin, source, stirps
07 descent, lineage, origins
08 ancestry, pedigree **09** filiation,
paternity, whakapapa **10** derivation,
extraction **11** affiliation

parenthetical
08 inserted **09** as an aside, bracketed
10 extraneous, incidental, interposed,
qualifying **11** elucidative, explanatory,
intervening **13** in parenthesis

parenthetically
03 btw **08** by the way **09** as an aside
11 secondarily **12** incidentally **13** as a
digression

par excellence
02 A1 **03** ace **04** best, cool, fine, mean,
neat, rare **05** brill, great, noted, prime
06 divine, select, superb, wicked
07 eminent, notable, perfect, shining
08 fabulous, flawless, heavenly,
smashing, splendid, stunning, superior,
terrific, top-notch, very good
09 brilliant, excellent, exemplary,
fantastic, faultless, first-rate, matchless,
wonderful **10** first-class, marvellous,
noteworthy, pre-eminent, remarkable,
surpassing, unequalled
11 commendable, exceptional, high-
quality, magnificent, outstanding,
sensational, superlative **12** praiseworthy,
second to none, unparalleled
13 distinguished **14** out of this world

pariah
05 exile, leper, pi-dog **06** outlaw, pie-
dog, pye-dog **07** Ishmael, outcast
08 castaway, unperson **10** black sheep
11 undesirable, untouchable
15 persona non grata

paring
04 peel, rind, skin **05** flake, shave,
shred, slice **06** sliver **07** cutting,
flaught, peeling, shaving, snippet
08 clipping, fragment, trimming
09 flaughter

Paris

07 Pigalle
08 Bastille, Chaillot, Left Bank,
Sorbonne
09 Chinatown, La Défense, Les Halles,
Right Bank, Trocadero, Tuileries
10 Belleville, La Villette, Montmartre,
Rive Droite, Rive Gauche, Tour Eiffel
11 Batignolles
12 Latin Quarter, Les Invalides,
Montparnasse, Place d'Italie
13 Champs Élysées, Quartier Latin

parish
03 par **04** fold, town **05** flock, title
06 church, county **07** village
08 district, parishen, parochin,
peculiar, township **09** community,
parischan, parochine **10** parischane
11 churchgoers **12** congregation,
denomination, parishioners

Parisian
◇ *foreign word indicator*

parity
03 par **05** unity **07** analogy **08** affinity,
equality, likeness, sameness

09 agreement, congruity, semblance **10** conformity, congruence, consonance, similarity, similitude, uniformity **11** consistency, equivalence, parallelism, resemblance **14** correspondence

park
01 P **02** Pk **03** put, set, zoo **04** bung, stop **05** field, leave, place, plonk, stand, walks **06** domain, draw up, pull up **07** deposit, grounds, reserve **08** paradise, position, woodland **09** grassland

Parks include:

04 Hyde, West
05 Green, Güell, Kings
06 Albert, Domain
07 Battery, Central, Phoenix, Regent's, Stanley
08 Gramercy, Richmond, St James's, Victoria
09 Battersea, Tuileries
10 Tiergarten
11 Champ de Mars, Vienna Woods
13 Madison Square, Tivoli Gardens
14 Bois de Boulogne
15 Bois de Vincennes

National parks in the UK:

06 Exmoor
08 Dartmoor
09 New Forest, Snowdonia, The Broads
10 Cairngorms
12 Lake District, Peak District
13 Brecon Beacons
14 Northumberland, North York Moors, Yorkshire Dales
18 Pembrokeshire Coast
25 Loch Lomond and the Trossachs

parking
01 P

parlance
04 cant, talk **05** argot, idiom, lingo **06** jargon, speech, tongue **07** diction **08** language, speaking **11** phraseology **12** conversation

parley
04 talk **05** parle, parly, speak, talks, treat **06** confab, confer, emparl, imparl, powwow **07** consult, council, discuss, meeting **08** colloquy, dialogue **09** negotiate, tête-à-tête **10** conference, deliberate, discussion, parliament **11** get together, get-together, negotiation **12** deliberation **14** parliament-cake

parliament
05 house, parly **06** parley **07** chamber **11** convocation, legislature

Parliament types include:

04 diet, duma, moot
05 boule, douma, gemot, jirga
06 majlis, senate
07 commons, council
08 assembly, congress
09 volksraad
10 consistory, lower house, upper house

12 lower chamber, upper chamber
14 Council of State
15 House of Assembly

Parliaments and political assemblies include:

02 EP, HK, HP
04 Dáil, Diet, Duma, Keys, Long, Pnyx, Rump, Sejm
05 boule, Forum, gemot, Lords, Porte
06 Cortes, kgotla, Majlis, Mejlis, Seanad, Senate, Senato, Soviet
07 Althing, comitia, Commons, Knesset, Lagting, Landtag, Rigsdag, Riksdag, Tynwald, zemstvo
08 Assembly, Congress, ecclesia, European, folkmoot, Imperial, Lagthing, Lok Sabha, Scottish, Sobranje, Sobranye, Stannary, Storting
09 Bundesrat, Bundestag, Directory, Eduskunta, Folketing, Landsting, Loya Jirga, Odelsting, Reichsrat, Reichstag, Skupstina, Ständerat, State Duma
10 Bundesrath, Convention, Landsthing, lower house, Odelsthing, Oireachtas, Rajya Sabha, Reichsrath, Skupshtina, St Stephen's, upper house
11 Dáil Eireann, Folketinget, House of Keys, Nationalrat, Star Chamber, Volkskammer, Westminster
12 House of Lords
13 House of States, Seanad Eireann, States General, Supreme Soviet, Welsh Assembly
14 Council of State, Estates General, House of Commons, Long Parliament, Rump Parliament, Staten-Generaal
15 Council of States, House of Assembly, People's Assembly, People's Congress

parliamentary
05 civil **07** elected, popular **08** decorous, official **09** lawgiving, lawmaking **10** democratic, republican, senatorial **11** legislative **12** governmental **13** congressional, legislatorial **14** representative

parlour
06 lounge, spence **09** front room **10** living room **11** drawing room, keeping-room, morning room, sitting room

parlous
04 dire **05** awful, grave **08** alarming, dreadful, horrible, perilous, shocking, terrible **09** appalling, atrocious, desperate, frightful **10** calamitous, disastrous **11** distressing **12** catastrophic

parochial
04 hick **05** petty **06** narrow **07** insular, limited **08** confined **09** blinkered, small-town **10** parish-pump, provincial, restricted **11** small-minded **12** narrow-minded **13** inward-looking **14** denominational

parochialism
09 pettiness **10** insularity, narrowness, parish pump **13** provincialism **15** small-mindedness

parody
03 ape **04** skit **05** mimic, spoof **06** satire, send up, send-up **07** imitate, lampoon, mimicry, take off, take-off **08** satirize, travesty **09** burlesque, imitation **10** caricature, corruption, distortion, pasquinade, perversion

paroxysm
03 fit **05** spasm, storm, thraw, throe, throw **06** attack, frenzy, throwe **07** flare-up, rapture, seizure **08** eruption, outbreak, outburst **09** explosion **10** convulsion

parrot
03 ape **04** copy, echo, Poll **05** mimic, Polly **06** repeat **07** copycat, imitate, phraser **08** imitator, popinjay, rehearse, repeater **09** reiterate

Parrots include:

03 fig, kea
04 grey, kaka, lory
05 galah, macaw, pygmy
06 Amazon, budgie, conure, kakapo, Nestor
07 corella, hanging, rosella
08 cockatoo, lorikeet, lovebird, parakeet, paroquet, Pesquet's, Strigops
09 cockateel, cockatiel, green leek, owl-parrot, paraquito, parrakeet, parroquet, parrotlet, Psittacus, Stringops
10 budgerigar, ring-necked
11 African grey, night-parrot, shell-parrot
13 Major Mitchell, zebra parakeet
14 shell parrakeet

parrot-fashion
06 by rote **10** mindlessly **12** mechanically, unthinkingly **13** automatically

parrot-wrasse
04 scar

parry
04 duck, shun, ward **05** avert, avoid, block, dodge, evade, field, put by, repel, sixte **06** parade, rebuff **07** counter, deflect, fend off, keep off, repulse, ward off **08** sidestep, stave off, tac-au-tac **09** hold at bay, keep at bay, turn aside **10** bodyswerve, circumvent **12** steer clear of

parsimonious
04 mean, near **05** close, mingy, tight **06** frugal, narrow, saving, scanty, stingy **07** miserly, scrimpy, sparing **08** grasping, stinting **09** niggardly, penurious **10** Aberdonian **11** close-fisted, close-handed, tight-fisted **12** candle-paring, cheeseparing **13** penny-pinching

parsimony
08 meanness **09** frugality, minginess, tightness **10** stinginess **11** miserliness

cheeseparing **13** niggardliness, penny-pinching **15** tight-fistedness

arson
Rev **05** padre, vicar **06** cleric, curate, deacon, pastor, priest, rector holy Joe **08** minister, preacher, reverend **09** churchman, clergyman, soul-curer **10** Jack-priest

arson-bird
tui

art
hidden indicator
hidden alternately indicator
insertion indicator
by, pt **03** bit, bye, job **04** area, book, duty, gift, half, hand, quit, role, shed, side, some, task, tear, twin, wing, work **05** break, chore, facet, leave, organ, party, piece, scene, scrap, sever, share, skill, slice, split, twine **06** aspect, branch, charge, cleave, depart, detach, divide, factor, genius, member, module, office, region, sector, talent, volume **07** ability, break up, calibre, chapter, concern, disband, disjoin, diverge, element, episode, excerpt, extract, faculty, limited, partial, passage, persona, portion, push off, quarter, scarper, scatter, section, segment, split up, take off **08** capacity, clear off, disperse, district, division, fraction, fragment, function, get going, interest, locality, particle, separate **09** attribute, character, come apart, component, dimension, direction, dismantle, endowment, expertise, imperfect, intellect, keep apart, portrayal, push along, take apart, territory **10** capability, depart from, department, disconnect, distribute, go away from, hit the road, ingredient, instalment, make tracks, percentage, proportion, restricted, say goodbye, unfinished **11** constituent, divorce from, fragmentary, hit the trail, involvement, not complete, split up from **12** intelligence, separate from, withdraw from **13** neighbourhood, participation, take your leave **14** accomplishment, representation, responsibility **15** get divorced from, part company with

act the part of
come

assign part
cast

even parts
hidden alternately indicator

for the most part
mainly, mostly **07** as a rule, chiefly, largely, overall, usually **08** above all, commonly **09** generally, in general, in the main **10** by and large, especially, on the whole **11** principally, predominantly

in part
hidden indicator
half **06** parcel, partim, partly slightly, somewhat **10** up to a point **12** to some degree, to some extent

• **in the part of**
02 as

• **odd parts**
◇ *hidden alternately indicator*

• **on the part of**
02 by **08** caused by **10** on behalf of **12** carried out by **13** from the side of

• **part of**
◇ *hidden indicator*

• **part with**
04 drop **05** forgo, yield **06** forego, give up **07** abandon, discard, let go of **08** jettison, renounce **09** surrender **10** relinquish

• **principal part**
04 lead, main, mass

• **take part in**
◇ *hidden indicator*
05 opt in **06** join in **07** go in for, partake, share in **08** assist in, engage in, help with **11** play a part in, play a role in **12** be involved in, contribute to **13** participate in

partake
05 enter, share **06** engage, inform **07** indulge **08** take part **10** be involved **11** participate

• **partake of**
03 eat **04** have, show, take **05** drink, evoke, share, taste **06** evince **07** consume, receive, suggest, undergo **08** manifest **11** demonstrate

partial
04 half, part **06** biased, in part, unfair, unjust **07** ex parte, limited **08** affected, coloured, one-sided, partisan, twilight **09** component, imperfect **10** incomplete, prejudiced, restricted, unfinished **11** fragmentary, inequitable, predisposed, subordinate **12** preferential **14** discriminatory

• **partial to**
06 fond of, keen on, liking, loving **08** mad about **09** taken with **10** crazy about

partiality
04 bias, love **05** favor **06** favour, liking **07** respect **08** fondness, inequity **09** injustice, prejudice **10** preference, proclivity, unfairness **11** inclination **12** partisanship, predilection **14** discrimination, predisposition **15** inequitableness

partially
05 slack **06** in part, partly **08** halflins, not fully, somewhat **09** halflings **12** fractionally, incompletely

participant
05 party **06** helper, member, sharer, worker **07** entrant, partner, sharing **09** associate **10** competitor, contestant, co-operator **11** contributor, shareholder **12** participator

participate
◇ *insertion indicator*
04 be in, help **05** enter, opt in, share **06** assist, be in it, engage, join in, muck in **07** partake **08** take part **09** co-operate, play a part, play a role **10** be involved, contribute **12** be associated

participation
04 part **07** sharing **09** mucking in, partaking **10** assistance **11** association, co-operation, involvement, partnership **12** contribution

particle
03 bit, jot, tad **04** atom, corn, curn, drop, iota, mite, spot, whit **05** crumb, grain, piece, scrap, shred, spark, speck, stime, styme, touch, trace **06** morsel, prefix, sliver, suffix, tittle **07** globule, granule, smidgen **08** fragment, molecule, ribosome **09** inclusion **11** conjunction **12** interjection

Particles include:

01 W, X, Z
03 ion, psi
04 kaon, muon, pion
05 anion, boson, gluon, meson, omega, quark, sigma
06 baryon, cation, hadron, kation, lambda, lepton, parton, photon, proton
07 neutron, nucleon, upsilon
08 electron, neutrino, positron, thermion
09 carbanion, gravitron, tau lepton
10 anti-proton, gauge boson, zwitterion
11 anti-neutron
12 anti-neutrino

parti-coloured
06 motley **07** piebald **10** variegated **11** polychromic **13** polychromatic, versicoloured

particular
04 fact, item **05** exact, faddy, fussy, picky, point **06** choosy, detail, marked **07** certain, feature, finicky, minutia, notable, precise, respect, several, special, unusual **08** accurate, definite, detailed, distinct, especial, exacting, faithful, peculiar, specific, thorough, uncommon **09** favourite, selective **10** fastidious, individual, meticulous, noteworthy, pernickety, remarkable **11** exceptional, outstanding, painstaking, persnickety **12** circumstance **14** discriminating

• **in particular**
07 exactly **08** in detail **09** in special, precisely, severally **10** especially, in especial **12** individually, particularly, specifically, to be specific

particularity
04 fact, item **05** point, quirk, trait **06** detail **07** feature **08** instance, property **10** uniqueness **11** peculiarity, singularity **12** circumstance, idiosyncrasy **13** individuality **14** characteristic **15** distinctiveness

particularize
06 detail **07** itemize, specify **09** enumerate, stipulate **11** individuate **13** individualize

particularly
07 notably **08** markedly **09** expressly, severally, unusually **10** distinctly, especially, explicitly, intimately, remarkably, uncommonly

12 individually, in particular,
specifically, surprisingly
13 exceptionally **15** extraordinarily

parting
◇ *insertion indicator*
04 last, rift, shed **05** adieu, dying, final,
going, leave, split **06** depart **07** closing,
divorce, goodbye, leaving, rupture
08 breaking, division, farewell
09 departing, departure, partition,
partitive **10** breaking-up, concluding,
divergence, separation **11** leave-taking,
valediction, valedictory **12** disseverance,
disseverment **13** disseveration

See also **farewell**

partisan
03 fan **06** backer, biased, unfair, unjust,
votary **07** devotee, partial
08 adherent, champion, disciple,
follower, henchman, loyalist, one-
sided, party man, queenite, sidesman,
stalwart, upholder **09** factional,
guerrilla, irregular, sectarian, supporter
10 henchwoman, prejudiced
11 henchperson, imperialist,
inequitable, out-and-outer,
predisposed **14** discriminatory,
freedom fighter

partisanship
04 bias **08** interest, partyism
09 prejudice **10** partiality
12 factionalism, sectarianism

partition
03 bar **04** wall, with **05** panel, score,
sever, share, shoji, withe **06** divide,
hallan, parpen, replum, screen,
septum, tabula, travis, trevis **07** barrier,
break up, break-up, cloison, divider,
eardrum, grating, parpane, parpend,
parpent, parting, perpend, perpent,
split up, treviss, wall off **08** brattice,
brattish, brettice, divide up, division,
fence off, parpoint, separate, traverse
09 dashboard, diaphragm, parcel out,
screen off, segregate, separator,
severance, splitting, subdivide
10 rood screen, separation
11 dissepiment, false bottom, room-
divider, segregation, separate off,
subdivision **12** dividing wall
14 dividing screen

partly
04 half, semi- **06** in part, parcel **07** a
little **08** slightly, somewhat, to a point
09 partially **10** moderately, relatively,
up to a point **12** fractionally,
incompletely, to some degree, to some
extent **13** in some measure

partner
03 man, pal, SOP **04** ally, lady, mate,
oppo, pair, pard, wife **05** butty, catch,
rival, woman **06** fiancé, friend, helper,
lumber, sharer, spouse **07** comrade,
consort, fiancée, husband, kept man,
pardner **08** cavalier, copemate, co-
worker, sidekick, teammate, yoke-
mate **09** associate, boyfriend,
cohabitee, colleague, companion,
copesmate, kept woman, other half

10 accomplice, better half, co-
operator, girlfriend, yoke-fellow
11 confederate, live-in lover **12** bit on
the side, collaborator **13** common-law
wife **14** opposite number
• **former partner**
02 ex
• **partners**
02 EW, NS

partnership
04 firm **05** stand, union **06** cahoot
07 company, consort, sharing, society
08 alliance **09** symbiosis, syndicate
10 fellowship, fraternity **11** affiliation,
association, brotherhood,
combination, co-operation, co-
operative, corporation
12 conglomerate **13** collaboration,
confederation, participation

partridge
05 quail **06** chikor, chukar, chukor
07 chikhor, flapper, tinamou
08 paitrick, percolin

part-song
04 glee

party
03 jol **04** band, body, camp, crew, fest,
gang, rage, rort, rout, sect, side, team,
unit **05** binge, cabal, go out, group,
posse, quest, squad **06** league, parted,
person, thrash **07** carouse, company,
divided, faction, have fun, large it
08 alliance, function, grouping,
litigant, live it up, party-goer
09 celebrate, defendant, festivity,
gathering, have a ball, plaintiff, whoop
it up **10** contingent, detachment, have
a party, individual **11** affiliation,
association, celebration, combination,
get-together, have it large, throw a
party **13** enjoy yourself, go on the
razzle **14** go out on the town, push the
boat out, put the flags out **15** paint the
town red

Parties include:

02 do
03 hen, tea
04 bash, drum, foam, luau, orgy, rave,
    stag, toga, wine, wrap
05 beano, disco, hangi, house
06 at-home, beer-up, bottle, dinner,
    drinks, garden, grog-on, grog-up,
    hooley, Kneipe, picnic, pyjama,
    rave-up, shivoo, social, soirée, supper
07 blow-out, ceilidh, cookout, knees-
    up, leaving, new year, potluck,
    reunion, shindig, slumber
08 barbecue, birthday, bunfight,
    clambake, cocktail, farewell, tea
    fight, wingding
09 acid-house, beanfeast, Christmas,
    Hallowe'en, hootnanny, reception,
    sleepover, welcoming
10 baby shower, fancy dress,
    hootenanny, whist drive
11 cookie-shine, discotheque, flat-
    warming, muffin-fight, muffin-worry
12 bridal shower, house-warming
13 cheese and wine, coffee klatsch,
    fête champêtre, small-and-early

Political parties in the UK include
01 L
03 BNP, Con, DUP, Lab, Lib, PUP, SNP
04 SDLP, Tory, Whig
05 Green
06 Labour
07 Liberal
08 Alliance, Sinn Féin
09 Communist
10 Democratic, Plaid Cymru,
    Republican, UK Unionist
11 Co-operative
12 Conservative
13 National Front, Parliamentary
14 UK Independence, Ulster Unionis
15 British National, Liberal Democra

*Political parties worldwide
include:*
02 AN, FN, PP
03 ALP, CDU, NDP, NPD, RPR
05 Green, Labor
06 Labour
07 Worker's
08 Batasuna, Democrat, Fine Gael,
    National, Sinn Féin
09 One Nation, Socialist
10 Fianna Fáil, Republican
12 Workers' Party
13 Bloc Québécois, Front National,
    National Front
14 Partido Popular

• **be a party to**
09 know about **12** be involved in
• **dancing party**
03 hop

party-goer
09 socialite

parvenu
07 climber, new rich, upstart
09 arriviste, pretender, vulgarian
12 nouveau riche **13** social climber

pascal
02 Pa

pasha
03 dey **06** bashaw

pass
02 go, OK **03** col, die, gap, hit, lap, ne
ren, rin, run, say, sit, tip, way **04** beat,
chit, drag, emit, fill, flow, ghat, give, g
by, hand, jark, kick, live, lose, make,
move, okay, omit, pace, path, play, sla
turn, visa **05** adopt, allow, botte, cros
drive, enact, event, expel, ghaut,
gorge, halse, hause, hawse, issue,
lunge, notch, occur, outdo, poort,
punto, reach, route, serve, sling, spea
spend, stand, state, swing, throw, use
up, utter, voice **06** accept, assert,
become, befall, be left, canyon, chala
change, chitty, decree, defile, devote
elapse, employ, esteem, evolve,
exceed, go over, go past, happen, let
out, occupy, parade, permit, puncto,
ratify, ravine, slip by, take up, thrust,
ticket, travel **07** advance, agree to,
approve, be given, challan, declare,
deliver, develop, excrete, express, fae
out, get over, licence, passage,

proceed, qualify, release, run past, succeed, surpass, undergo, vote for, warrant **08** advances, announce, approach, be willed, currency, go across, go beyond, graduate, outstrip, overhaul, overtake, overture, passport, proclaim, progress, sanction, slip away, transfer, transmit, traverse, validate **09** authorize, be endowed, be granted, circulate, come about, condition, disappear, discharge, disregard, drive past, get across, go through, pronounce, take place, transpire, while away **10** adjudicate, be made over, experience, fulfilment, get through, permission, protection, reputation, suggestion **11** be consigned, be inherited, go unnoticed, leave behind, make your way, outdistance, predicament, proposition, pull ahead of, sail through **12** be bequeathed, be handed down, consummation **13** authorization, be transferred, breeze through, draw level with, laissez-passer, scrape through **14** be successful in, identification, let someone have

See also **mountain pass** under **mountain**

• **pass as, pass for**
10 appear to be, be taken for **12** be regarded as **13** be mistaken for
• **pass away**
02 go **03** die **04** vade **05** forgo **06** elapse, expire, forego, pass on, peg out, pop off **07** decease **08** blow over **13** kick the bucket **14** depart this life, give up the ghost **15** breathe your last
• **pass degree**
04 poll
• **pass off**
04 fake **05** feign, go off, occur **06** happen, vanish **07** die down, palm off, put over, wear off **08** fade away, wear away **09** disappear, take place **11** counterfeit **12** misrepresent
• **pass out**
03 die **04** dole, drop **05** allot, faint, swoon **07** deal out, dole out, give out, hand out **08** allocate, black out, collapse, flake out, keel over, share out, spark out **10** distribute
• **pass over**
02 go **03** die **04** balk, miss, omit, skim **05** baulk, leave **06** forget, ignore, overgo, voyage **07** neglect **08** look over, overjump, overlook, overpass, override, overskip **09** disregard **14** take no notice of, turn a deaf ear to **15** turn a blind eye to
• **pass quickly**
03 fly, hie, ren, rin, run
• **pass the ball to**
04 feed
• **pass up**
04 miss **06** ignore, refuse, reject **07** let slip, neglect **08** renounce

passable
02 OK **04** fair, open, so-so **05** clear **06** decent **07** average **08** adequate, all right, mediocre, moderate, ordinary, pervious **09** allowable, navigable,

tolerable, unblocked **10** acceptable, not much cop **11** practicable, presentable, respectable, traversable **12** run of the mill, satisfactory, unobstructed **13** no great shakes, unexceptional

passably
05 quite **06** fairly, rather **08** somewhat **09** tolerably **10** moderately, reasonably, relatively **13** after a fashion, indifferently

passage
03 cut, gap, gut, way **04** adit, coda, duct, exit, fare, flow, gate, hall, lane, lick, loan, main, neck, pace, pass, path, pend, pore, road, slap, text, tour, trek, trip **05** aisle, alley, alure, break, canal, chute, creep, cundy, entry, flume, fogou, gully, lapse, lento, lobby, locus, piano, piece, route, shaft, shoot, shute, sound, track, verse, vista **06** access, avenue, burrow, change, clause, condie, course, dromos, furrow, groove, gullet, gutter, legato, narrow, presto, screed, strait, street, throat, trance, transe, travel, trough, tunnel, voyage **07** advance, archway, cadenza, channel, conduit, doorway, episode, excerpt, extract, fistula, gallery, hallway, journey, offtake, opening, orifice, passing, prelude, running, sea lane, section, snicket, stretto, traffic, turning **08** adoption, alleyway, approval, citation, corridor, crossing, division, entrance, incident, longueur, movement, mutation, pericope, progress, ritenuto, sanction, southing, spiccato, staccato, straight, streight, thorough, transfer, waterway **09** admission, breezeway, enactment, migration, paragraph, quotation, ventiduct, vestibule **10** acceptance, occurrence, passageway, pianissimo, ritardando, scherzando, transition, tremolando, validation **11** development, safe conduct, watercourse **12** deambulatory, ratification, thoroughfare, transmission **13** authorization, metamorphosis

Passages include:
04 Mona
05 Drake, Gaspé, Umnak
06 Akutan, Amukta, Burias, Caicos, Colvos, Mompog, Seguam, Unimak
07 Oronsay, Palawan
08 Amchitka, Dominica, Fenimore, Mouchoir, Saratoga, Windward
09 Deception, Mayaguana, St Vincent
10 Backstairs, Guadeloupe, Martinique, Mira Por Vos, Silver Bank
11 Turks Island, Verde Island
13 Crooked Island
14 Jacques Cartier

passageway
03 way **04** exit, hall, lane, path, port **05** aisle, alley, lobby, track **06** arcade, runway **07** gangway, hallway, passage **08** corridor, entrance **11** back passage

passé
03 out **05** dated, faded **06** démodé, groovy, old hat, past it **07** outworn **08** obsolete, outdated, outmoded **09** out-of-date **10** antiquated **11** on the way out, past its best **12** old-fashioned **13** unfashionable

passenger
04 fare **05** drone, rider **07** outside, shirker, voyager **08** commuter, hanger-on **09** fare-payer, traveller **10** freeloader, hitchhiker **11** strap-hanger
• **turn away passenger**
04 bump

passer-by
06 gawper **07** witness **08** looker-on, observer, onlooker **09** bystander, spectator **10** eyewitness, rubberneck

passing
03 end **04** flow, loss, very **05** brief, death, hasty, march, quick, rapid, short **06** casual, course, demise, elapse, finish, slight **07** advance, cursory, decease, diadrom, passage, quietus, shallow **08** fleeting, movement **09** departure, ephemeral, momentary, perishing, temporary, transient **10** evanescent, expiration, incidental, short-lived **11** exceedingly, passing away, superficial, termination **12** transitional
• **in passing**
07 by the by **08** by the bye, by the way **09** en passant **12** incidentally **15** parenthetically

passion
03 fit, wax **04** fire, fury, heat, love, lust, pash, rage, zeal, zest **05** anger, brame, craze, mania, wrath **06** ardour, dander, desire, spirit, temper, warmth **07** avidity, craving, emotion, feeling, fervour, tantrum **08** fondness, keenness, outburst **09** adoration, affection, altitudes, eagerness, explosion, intensity, obsession, vehemence **10** enthusiasm, fanaticism **11** fascination, indignation, infatuation **12** sexual desire
• **burst of passion**
04 gust

passionate
03 hot, mad **04** avid, keen, nuts, sexy, warm, wild **05** crazy, eager, fiery, gutsy, horny, Latin, potty, randy **06** ardent, erotic, fervid, fierce, loving, stormy, strong, sultry, torrid, wilful **07** aroused, excited, fervent, intense, lustful, sensual, violent, zealous **08** choleric, frenzied, inflamed, turned on, vehement **09** emotional, excitable, fanatical, hotheaded, impetuous, impulsive, irritable, obstinate **10** headstrong, hot-blooded, self-willed **11** impassioned, tempestuous, warm-blooded **12** affectionate, enthusiastic **13** quick-tempered, waspish-headed

passionately
05 hotly **06** keenly **08** ardently, fiercely, lovingly, strongly **09** con

calore, fervently, intensely, lustfully, sensually, violently, zealously **10** erotically **11** fanatically **14** affectionately

passionless

03 icy **04** calm, cold **06** frigid, frosty **07** callous, neutral **08** detached, uncaring, unloving **09** apathetic, impartial, impassive, unfeeling, withdrawn **10** insensible, restrained, uninvolved **11** cold-blooded, cold-hearted, emotionless, indifferent, unemotional **12** unresponsive **13** dispassionate

passive

05 aloof, inert **06** docile, remote, supine **07** distant, patient, subdued, unmoved **08** detached, inactive, lifeless, resigned, yielding **09** apathetic, compliant, lethargic, receptive, suffering **10** effortless, non-violent, submissive, uninvolved **11** emotionless, indifferent, unassertive, unemotional, unresisting **13** dispassionate, long-suffering **14** unenterprising

passively

09 patiently **10** lifelessly **12** submissively **13** emotionlessly, unassertively

passport

02 ID **03** key, way **04** door, pass, path, visa **05** entry, route **06** avenue, papers, permit **07** doorway **09** admission **12** identity card **13** authorization, laissez-passer, means of access **15** travel documents

password

03 key **04** word **06** parole, signal **07** tessera **09** watchword **10** open sesame, shibboleth **11** countersign

past

02 by, pa, pt **03** ago, ygo **04** done, gone, last, late, life, near, over, ygoe, yore **05** after, agone, early, ended, forby, olden, round, since **06** behind, beside, beyond, bygone, by-past, former, gone by, latter, no more, recent, record **07** ancient, defunct, elapsed, extinct, history, long ago, one-time, worn-out **08** finished, foregone, overworn, preterit, previous, sometime **09** antiquity, completed, erstwhile, foregoing, forgotten, olden days, preceding, preterite, too old for, yesterday **10** background, bygone days, days gone by, days of yore, experience, olden times **11** bygone times, former times, good old days, track record **12** too mature for **15** over and done with

pasta

Pasta types include:

04 orza, ziti
05 penne, ruoti
06 anelli, ditali, noodle, trofie
07 fusilli, gnocchi, lasagna, lasagne, lumache, mafalde, maruzze,

mezzani, noodles, pennine, ravioli
08 bucatini, farfalle, fedelini, linguini, macaroni, rigatoni, stelline
09 agnolotti, angel hair, casarecci, crescioni, fiochetti, manicotti, spaghetti
10 angel's hair, bombolotti, cannelloni, conchiglie, farfalline, fettuccine, strangozzi, tagliarini, taglierini, tortellini, vermicelli
11 cappelletti, pappardelle, tagliatelle
12 lasagne verde
13 elbow macaroni

paste

03 fix, gum, pap **04** glue, miso, mush, pack, pâté, pulp **05** blend, purée, putty, stick **06** cement, cerate, fasten, mastic, slurry, spread, thrash **07** mixture **08** adhesive

pastel

04 pale, soft, woad **05** chalk, faint, light, muted, quiet **06** crayon, low-key, sketch, subtle **07** drawing, subdued **08** delicate, discreet, pastille, soft-hued, vignette **11** sauce-crayon **13** light-coloured

pastiche

◇ *anagram indicator*
03 mix **04** olio **06** jumble, medley **07** farrago, melange, mixture, variety **08** mishmash, mixed bag **09** confusion, pasticcio, patchwork, potpourri **10** assortment, collection, hodgepodge, hotchpotch, miscellany, salmagundi **11** gallimaufry, olla-podrida, smorgasbord **14** conglomeration, omnium-gatherum

pastille

05 sweet **06** jujube, pastel, tablet, troche **07** lozenge **09** cough drop **10** confection, cough sweet

pastime

03 fun **04** game, play **05** hobby, sport **08** activity, pastance **09** amusement, avocation, diversion **10** abridgment, recreation, relaxation, suppliance **11** abridgement, distraction **12** Zeitvertreib **13** entertainment **14** leisure pursuit **15** leisure activity
See also **hobby**

past master

02 PM **03** ace **05** adept **06** artist, expert, wizard **07** dab hand, old hand **08** virtuoso **10** proficient

pastor

01 P **05** canon, vicar **06** cleric, deacon, divine, parson, priest, rector **08** minister, shepherd **09** churchman, clergyman **10** prebendary **12** ecclesiastic

pastoral

03 oat **04** idyl **05** idyll, rural **06** rustic, simple **07** bucolic, country, crosier, crozier, eclogue, idyllic **08** agrarian, Arcadian, clerical, priestly, serenata **09** bucolical, siciliano **11** ministerial, Theocritean **12** agricultural **14** ecclesiastical

pastry

Pastry types include:

04 filo, flan, puff
05 choux, flaky, plain, short, sweet
06 cheese, Danish
07 pork-pie
08 one-stage, piecrust
09 rough-puff, suetcrust
10 pâte brisée, pâte frolle, pâte sablée, pâte sucrée, shortcrust, wholewheat
12 biscuit-crumb, pâte à savarin
13 American crust, hot-water crust
14 rich shortcrust
See also **cake**

pasture

03 alp, lay, lea, lee, ley, tie, tye **04** feed, fell, food, gang, mead, raik, rake, soum, sowm, walk **05** downs, field, grass, graze, lease, leaze, range **06** leasow, meadow, saeter **07** feeding, grazing, leasowe, paddock **08** mountain, shealing, shieling **09** grassland, pasturage, sheepwalk **11** grazing land

• **pasture grass**
04 bent **05** grama **06** fescue **07** timothy **08** paspalum, rye grass **09** bent grass **10** grama grass **12** meadow fescue, sheep's fescue, timothy grass **13** dog's-tail grass, Flinders grass

pasty

03 wan **04** pale, waxy **06** doughy, pallid, sallow, sickly **07** anaemic **08** empanada **09** unhealthy **10** pasty-faced **11** oyster-patty

pat

03 dab, pet, pot, tap **04** ball, burp, clap, easy, glib, lump, mass, slap, tick **05** bepat, chunk, print, ready, slick, touch **06** caress, facile, fluent, fondle, patter, simple, smooth, stroke **07** exactly **08** coquille, fluently **09** perfectly, precisely **10** flawlessly, simplistic **11** faultlessly, word-for-word
• **pat someone on the back**
06 praise **10** compliment **12** congratulate **13** say well done to

patch

03 bed, fix, lot, sew **04** area, mend, plot, snip, spot, term, time, zona **05** botch, cloth, clout, cover, phase, piece, scrap, spell, tract **06** parcel, period, plaque, pocket, repair, shield, stitch **07** stretch **08** covering, dressing, fragment, material **09** reinforce **10** protection

patchwork

04 hash **06** jumble, medley, motley **07** farrago, mixture **08** mishmash, pastiche **10** assortment, hotchpotch **11** gallimaufry

patchy

◇ *anagram indicator*
05 bitty **06** fitful, random, spotty, uneven **07** blotchy, erratic, macular, sketchy, varying **08** variable

9 centonate, irregular **10** incomplete
11 incongruous **12** inconsistent,
1harmonious

atent
3 pat **04** open **05** clear, overt, plain,
1ght **07** blatant, charter, evident,
1aring, licence, obvious, visible
8 apparent, flagrant, manifest,
1alpable **09** copyright, expanding,
1genious, invention, privilege,
1preading **10** undeniable **11** certificate,
1onspicuous, self-evident, transparent,
1nequivocal **12** crystal clear,
1nmistakable **13** unmistakeable
5 clear as daylight

atently
6 openly **07** clearly, plainly, visibly
8 palpably **09** blatantly, glaringly,
1bviously **10** manifestly
12 unmistakably **13** conspicuously,
1nequivocally, unmistakeably

aternal
8 fatherly, vigilant **09** concerned
10 benevolent, fatherlike, protective

ath
12 go **03** pad, sty, way **04** berm, gate,
1ne, road, trod, walk, went **05** allée,
1rbit, route, track, trail, troad, trode
16 avenue, course, troade **07** circuit,
1ighway, passage, pathway, slidder,
1owpath, walkway **08** approach,
1ycleway, footpath **09** bridleway,
1irection, footsteps **10** bridle-road,
1rthright

athetic
anagram indicator
3 sad **04** poor **05** sorry **06** dismal,
1eeble, meagre, moving, tender,
1oeful **07** pitiful, useless **08** derisory,
1itiable, poignant, touching, wretched
19 affecting, miserable, plaintive,
1orthless **10** deplorable, inadequate,
1mentable **11** distressing
12 contemptible, heart-rending
13 heartbreaking **14** unsatisfactory

athetically
5 sadly **08** dismally, pitiably, woefully
19 miserably, pitifully **10** deplorably,
1mentably, wretchedly
12 contemptibly, inadequately

athological
7 chronic **08** addicted, habitual,
1ardened **09** confirmed, dependent,
1bsessive **10** compulsive, inveterate,
1ersistent

athos
6 misery **07** sadness, tragedy **08** sob
1tuff **09** poignancy **10** inadequacy
14 pitifulness **12** pitiableness
13 plaintiveness

atience
14 cool **07** bistort **08** calmness,
1londike, Klondyke, serenity, stoicism,
1enacity **09** composure, diligence,
1ndurance, fortitude, restraint,
1olitaire, tolerance **10** doggedness,
1quanimity, submission, sufferance
11 forbearance, persistence,

resignation, self-control **12** monk's
rhubarb, perseverance, stickability,
tranquillity **13** long-suffering
14 inexcitability, unflappability

patient
04 calm, case, cool, kind, mild
06 client, extern, serene, tender
07 externe, invalid, lenient, stoical,
subject **08** ambulant, composed,
enduring, laid-back, resigned,
resolute, sufferer, tolerant **09** easy-
going, forgiving, indulgent, leisurely,
unhurried **10** forbearant, forbearing,
out-patient, persistent, restrained,
submissive **11** persevering,
susceptible, unflappable **12** even-
tempered, patient as Job
13 accommodating, imperturbable,
long-suffering, philosophical, self-
possessed, uncomplaining,
understanding **14** hanging in there,
self-controlled
• **be patient**
04 bear
• **hospital patients**
04 ward

patiently
06 calmly, kindly, mildly **08** tenderly
09 leisurely **10** enduringly, resolutely,
tolerantly **11** unflappably, unhurriedly
12 persistently **13** considerately,
perseveringly

patois
04 cant **05** argot, Gumbo, lingo, slang
06 Creole, jargon, patter **07** dialect
08 Guernsey **10** vernacular **11** local
speech **12** lingua franca **13** local
parlance

patriarch
04 pope, sire **05** abuna, elder **06** father
07 founder **09** greybeard **10** Catholicos
11 grandfather, grand old man
13 paterfamilias

Patriarchs include:

04 Levi, Noah
05 Aaron, Abram, Enoch, Isaac, Jacob
06 Joseph
07 Abraham, Ishmael
10 Methuselah, Theophilus

patrician
03 nob **04** peer **05** noble **06** gentle,
lordly, patron **07** grandee **08** high-
born, nobleman, well-born
09 gentleman, high-class **10** aristocrat,
upper-crust **11** blue-blooded
12 aristocratic, thoroughbred

patrimony
05 share **06** estate, legacy **07** bequest,
portion, revenue **08** heritage, property
10 birthright **11** inheritance, possessions

patriot
05 jingo **08** jingoist, loyalist **09** flag-
waver **10** chauvinist **11** nationalist

patriotic
05 loyal **08** loyalist **10** flag-waving,
jingoistic **11** nationalist **12** chauvinistic
13 nationalistic

patriotism
07 loyalty **08** jingoism **10** chauvinism,
flag-waving **11** nationalism

patrol
04 beat, tour **05** guard, round, vigil,
watch **06** defend, picket, piquet,
police, sentry **07** defence, inspect,
monitor, picquet, protect **08** defender,
policing, sentinel, sentry-go,
watchman **09** milk train, patrolman
10 patrolling, protection **11** be on the
beat, do the rounds, go the rounds,
keep guard on, keep watch on,
patrolwoman, perambulate
12 surveillance **13** keep watch over,
make the rounds, night-watchman,
perambulation, police officer, security
guard **14** make your rounds

patron
05 angel, buyer, stoop, stoup, Venus
06 Apollo, backer, client, fautor, friend,
helper, Hermes **07** pattern, regular,
shopper, sponsor **08** advocate,
champion, customer, defender,
guardian, Maecenas, promoter,
upholder **09** protector, purchaser,
supporter **10** benefactor, frequenter,
subscriber **11** sympathizer
12 benefactress **13** guardian angel
14 fairy godmother, philanthropist

patronage
05 aegis, trade **06** buying, custom
07 backing, funding, support
08 auspices, business, commerce,
shopping **09** promotion **10** protection,
purchasing **11** countenance,
sponsorship **12** financial aid,
subscription **13** encouragement,
financial help

patronize
03 aid **04** back, fund, help **05** scorn
06 assist, foster, shop at **07** buy from,
despise, finance, promote, protect,
sponsor, support **08** champion, deal
with, empatron, frequent, maintain
09 disparage, encourage **10** look down
on, talk down to **12** be a regular at

patronizing
05 lofty **06** snooty **07** haughty, stuck
up **08** scornful, snobbish, stooping,
superior **10** disdainful, high-handed
11 overbearing, toffee-nosed
12 contemptuous, supercilious
13 condescending, high-and-mighty
14 holier-than-thou **15** on your high
horse

patter
03 pat, rap, tap, yak **04** beat, drum, line,
pelt, trip **05** lingo, pitch, pound, spiel
06 bicker, gabble, gammon, jabber,
jargon, pit-pat, scurry, verbal
07 beating, chatter, pitapat, scuttle,
tapping, verbals **08** pitty-pat
09 monologue, pattering **12** pitter-
patter

pattern
03 key **04** copy, form, mold, norm,
plan, trim, type **05** guide, ideal, match,
model, motif, mould, order, shape,

style, whirl **06** design, device, dicing, figure, follow, method, sample, stripe, swatch, system **07** emulate, example, fashion, Gestalt, grecque, imitate, stencil, tracery **08** decorate, Greek key, markings, original, ornament, parallel, standard, template **09** blueprint, criterion, influence, prototype, scantling **10** craquelure, decoration **11** arrangement, instruction **13** ornamentation

patterned
05 moiré **07** figured, printed, watered **09** decorated **10** ornamented

paucity
04 lack, want **06** dearth, rarity **07** fewness, poverty **08** scarcity, shortage, sparsity **09** smallness **10** deficiency, meagreness, paltriness, scantiness, slightness, sparseness **11** slenderness **12** exiguousness **13** insufficiency

paunch
03 gut, pod **04** kite, kyte **05** belly, rumen, tripe **07** abdomen, beer gut **08** pot-belly **09** beer belly **10** eviscerate, fat stomach **11** corporation

paunchy
03 fat **05** podgy, pudgy, tubby **06** portly, rotund **07** adipose **08** stomachy **09** corpulent **10** pot-bellied

pauper
06 beggar **07** have-not **08** bankrupt, indigent **09** insolvent, mendicant **10** down-and-out **11** church mouse

pause
03 gap **04** halt, hold, kick, lull, rest, stay, stop, wait **05** break, cease, close, delay, demur, dwell, let up, let-up, limma **06** cesura, desist **07** adjourn, breathe, caesura, fermata, respite, sit down, time out **08** break off, breather, dieresis, hesitate, hold back, interval, stoppage, take five **09** cessation, diaeresis, interlude, interrupt, take a rest **10** hesitation, take a break **11** discontinue, freeze-frame **12** intermission, interruption **13** take a breather **14** breathing space

pave
03 tar **04** flag, tile **05** cover, floor, pitch **06** cobble, tarmac **07** asphalt, surface **08** concrete **10** macadamize, tessellate **11** cobblestone
• **pave the way for**
08 lead up to **09** introduce, take steps **10** prepare for **11** get ready for **12** make ready for, take measures **14** clear the ground

pavement
03 bed, way **04** path **05** floor **07** footway, walkway **08** causeway, flagging, footpath, platform, sidewalk, trottoir **11** plainstanes, plainstones

pavilion
04 flag, tent **05** kiosk **06** canopy,

ensign, houdah, howdah **09** belvedere **14** jingling Johnny

paving-block
03 set **04** sett

paw
03 pad, pah, pud **04** foot, foul, hand, maul, poke **05** mouse, puddy, touch **06** molest, stroke **07** obscene, touch up **08** forefoot **09** manhandle, mishandle

pawn
01 P **03** dip, pan, pop, toy **04** dupe, fine, hock, paan, pown, tool **05** betel, powin, spout, stake **06** impawn, lumber, pledge, puppet, stooge, wadset **07** cat's paw, deposit, gallery, peacock, wadsett **08** mortgage **09** pignerate, pignorate, plaything **10** instrument **11** impignorate, oppignerate, oppignorate **13** lay in lavender

pawnbroker
05 uncle **06** lender, sheeny, usurer **07** pop-shop **08** lumberer, pawnshop **10** gombeen-man **11** money-lender, mont-de-piété **12** monte di pietà

pay
02 do **03** fee **04** ante, bung, foot, give, make, pony, sold **05** atone, grant, offer, remit, repay, solde, spend, wages, yield **06** afford, answer, ante up, bestow, defray, expend, extend, income, invest, lay out, net pay, outlay, pay off, pay out, profit, rake in, refund, return, reward, salary, settle, square, suffer, supply **07** benefit, bring in, cough up, fork out, imburse, pay back, payment, produce, proffer, stipend, stump up **08** disburse, earnings, gross pay, hand over, settle up, shell out **09** discharge, indemnify, reimburse **10** be punished, commission, compensate, emoluments, honorarium, make amends, recompense, remunerate **11** foot the bill, take-home pay **12** compensation, pick up the tab, remuneration, satisfaction **13** meet the cost of, reimbursement **14** be beneficial to, be worthwhile to, let someone have
• **pay back**
05 repay **06** pay off, punish, refund, return, settle, square **08** give back **09** reimburse, retaliate **10** recompense **11** get even with, reciprocate, take revenge **13** counter-attack **14** get your own back
• **pay for**
04 take **05** atone, escot, prize, pryse **06** suffer **09** answer for **10** compensate, cost dearly, make amends **12** count the cost, face the music **13** be punished for **14** count the cost of, get your deserts, pay a penalty for, pay the price for
• **pay off**
03 fix **04** fire, meet, sack, work **05** bribe, clear, repay **06** buy off, grease, honour, lay off, settle, square, suborn **07** dismiss, requite, succeed

08 amortize **09** discharge, pay in full **10** extinguish, get results, take care of **12** be successful **13** make redundan‹
• **pay out**
04 veer **05** remit, spend **06** ante up, expend, lay out **07** cough up, dispen‹ fork out **08** disburse, hand over, part with, shell out

payable
03 due **04** owed **05** owing **06** matur‹ unpaid **08** to be paid **09** in arrears **10** profitable **11** outstanding **13** contributable

payload
04 haul, load **05** cargo, goods **06** lading **07** baggage, freight, tonnag‹ **08** contents, shipment **11** consignment, merchandise

payment
03 fee, pay, sub **04** ante, dole, fare, farm, hire, mail, rent, scot, shot, toll, wage **05** arles, modus **06** amount, hansel, outlay, payola, reward **07** advance, annuity, deposit, expens‹ handsel, pension, premium, primage **08** danegeld, danegelt, donation, sou‹ scat, soul-scot, soul-shot **09** allowance, clearance, discharge **10** instalment, prestation, punishmen‹ quarterage, recompense, remittance, settlement **12** compensation, contribution, remuneration, satisfaction **13** consideration
• **demand payment**
03 dun

pay-off
03 fee, pay **05** bribe, wages **06** crunc‹ income, net pay, result, reward, salary upshot **07** benefit, outcome, paymen‹ stipend **08** earnings, gross pay **09** advantage, hush money, punchline slush fund, sweetener **10** allurement, back-hander, commission, dénouement, emoluments, enticement, honorarium, inducemen‹ recompense, settlement **11** consequence, take-home pay **12** compensation, remuneration **13** moment of truth, reimbursement **15** protection money

PC *see* **police officer**

pea
03 dal **04** daal, dahl, dhal **05** dholl, pease **06** legume **08** kaka beak, kak‹ bill **09** chickling, mangetout, marrowfat, parrot-jaw, rounceval **10** parrot-beak, parrot-bill **14** chicklir vetch

peace
03 pax **04** calm, ease, hush, pact, rest **05** amity, frith, olive, quiet, still, truce **06** accord, repose, shalom, treaty **07** concord, harmony, silence **08** calmness, goodwill, serenity **09** agreement, armistice, ceasefire, composure, placidity, quietness, stillness **10** friendship, relaxation **11** contentment, law and order, non-violence, peace treaty, restfulness

12 amicableness, conciliation, peacefulness, tranquillity 13 non-aggression

peaceable
04 mild 05 douce 06 dovish, gentle, irenic, placid 07 cordial, pacific 08 amicable, friendly 09 easy-going, unwarlike 10 harmonious, non-violent 11 good-natured, inoffensive, peace-loving 12 conciliatory, even-tempered 13 non-aggressive

peaceably
06 gently, mildly 08 amicably, placidly 09 cordially 11 pacifically 12 harmoniously 13 inoffensively

peaceful
04 calm 05 quiet, still 06 gentle, irenic, placid, serene, sleepy 07 halcyon, pacific, restful 08 amicable, friendly, in repose, relaxing, tranquil 09 peaceable, reposeful, unruffled 10 harmonious, untroubled 11 undisturbed

peacefully
06 calmly, gently 07 quietly 08 amicably, placidly, serenely, sleepily 09 restfully 12 harmoniously

peacemaker
04 dove 06 broker 08 appeaser, mediator, pacifier, pacifist, revolver 09 make-peace 10 arbitrator 11 conciliator, intercessor, pacificator, peace-monger

peacemaking
06 irenic 07 pacific 09 appeasing, mediating, mediative, mediatory 11 mediatorial 12 conciliatory, pacification

peach
03 dob 06 accuse, betray, inform 07 sing out, whittle 08 quandang, quandong, quantong 09 melocoton, nectarine, victorine 10 melicotton, melocotoon 11 malakatoone

peacock
03 pea 04 Pavo, pawn, pown 05 powin 06 paiock, pajock, pavone 07 paiocke, pajocke

peak
02 pk 03 ben, nib, pin, tip, top 04 apex, hill, mope, peag, rise 05 crest, crise, crown, droop, mount, pique, point, prick, spike, spire, visor, vizor 06 apogee, climax, height, summer, summit, zenith 07 maximum 08 aiguille, high noon, mountain, pinnacle 09 culminate, elevation, high point 11 come to a head, culmination

peaky
03 ill, wan 04 pale, sick 05 dicky, seedy 06 crummy, pallid, poorly, queasy, sickly, unwell 09 off-colour, washed-out 10 out of sorts 15 under the weather

peal
04 boom, clap, howl, ring, roar, roll, toll

05 chime, clang, crash, knell 06 firing, grilse, rumble, triple 07 resound, ringing, ring out 08 carillon, resonate 10 resounding 11 reverberate 13 reverberation

peanut
05 arnut 06 goober 07 arachis 08 earth-nut, earth-pea 09 goober pea, groundnut, monkey nut

pear
04 tuna 05 nashi, nelis, nopal 06 Colmar, comice, nelies, pepino, seckel, seckle, warden 07 avocado, poperin 08 aguacate, bergamot, blanquet, muscadel, muscatel 09 Indian fig, poppering 10 Conference, jargonelle 11 bon chrétien, queez-maddam 12 cuisse-madame

pearl
04 purl, Unio 05 nacre, union 06 barock, orient 07 barocco, baroque, granule, paragon 10 granulated
• **string of pearls**
04 rope

peasant
03 oaf 04 boor, hick, kern, lout, rude, ryot 05 churl, kerne, kisan, kulak, mujik, rural, swain, yokel 06 carlot, cottar, cotter, fellah, jungli, moujik, muzhik, raiyat, rustic 07 bumpkin, Cossack 09 campesino, contadina, contadino 10 blue-bonnet, clodhopper, provincial 13 country person 14 country bumpkin

pebble
04 chip, pelt, pumy, rock 05 agate, chuck, pumie, stone 06 gallet 07 chuckie 09 pumy stone 10 dreikanter, pumie stone 12 chuckie-stane, chuckie-stone

peccadillo
04 boob, slip 05 error, fault, lapse 06 slip-up 07 misdeed 10 infraction 11 delinquency 12 indiscretion, minor offence, misdemeanour

peck
02 pk 03 dab, hit, jab, job, nip, rap, tap 04 bite, food, jerk, kiss, pick 05 pitch, prick 06 pickle, strike

peculiar
◇ *anagram indicator*
03 ill, odd, own 04 sick 05 dizzy, droll, ferly, funny, queer, weird 06 exotic, poorly, proper, quaint, queasy, unique, unwell, way-out 07 bizarre, curious, oddball, offbeat, special, strange, unusual 08 abnormal, distinct, freakish, personal, singular, specific 09 eccentric, grotesque, preserved 10 individual, outlandish, out of sorts, particular, remarkable 11 distinctive, exceptional 12 appropriated 13 extraordinary, idiosyncratic 14 characteristic, distinguishing, unconventional 15 individualistic, under the weather
• **peculiar to**
04 like 08 unique to 09 typical of

11 belonging to 12 indicative of 13 in keeping with

peculiarity
04 mark 05 quirk, trait 06 foible, jimjam, oddity 07 feature, quality 08 hallmark, property 09 attribute, exception, mannerism, weirdness 10 shibboleth 11 abnormality, bizarreness, singularity 12 eccentricity, idiosyncrasy 13 individuality, particularity 14 characteristic 15 distinctiveness

peculiarly
◇ *anagram indicator*
05 oddly 08 quaintly, uniquely 09 bizarrely, curiously, strangely, unusually 10 distinctly, remarkably, singularly 12 particularly 13 distinctively, exceptionally 15 extraordinarily

pecuniary
06 fiscal 07 nummary 08 monetary 09 financial, nummulary 10 commercial

pedagogic
08 academic, didactic, teaching 09 tuitional 10 scholastic 11 educational 13 instructional

pedagogue
03 don 05 teach 06 master, pedant 07 dominie, teacher 08 educator, mistress 09 dogmatist, preceptor 10 instructor 12 educationist, schoolmaster 13 schoolteacher 14 educationalist, schoolmistress

pedagogy
07 tuition 08 teaching, training, tutelage 09 didactics 10 pedagogics 11 instruction

pedal
01 P

pedant
06 purist 07 academe, casuist, egghead 08 academic, highbrow, quibbler 09 dogmatist, Dryasdust, formalist, nit-picker, pedagogue, precisian 10 literalist, scholastic, schoolmarm 11 doctrinaire, pettifogger 12 hair-splitter, intellectual, precisionist, schoolmaster 13 perfectionist

pedantic
04 blue 05 exact, fussy, heavy 06 purist, stuffy 07 bookish, erudite, finical, inkhorn, pompous, precise, stilted 08 academic 09 formalist, quibbling 10 literalist, meticulous, nit-picking, particular, scholastic, scrupulous 11 pretentious, punctilious, sesquipedal 12 intellectual 13 hair-splitting, perfectionist, schoolmarmish 14 schoolmasterly, sesquipedalian

pedantry
09 cavilling, dogmatism, exactness, pedantism, pomposity, quibbling 10 finicality, nit-picking, pedagogism, stuffiness 11 bookishness 12 academicness 13 hair-splitting

14 meticulousness 15 intellectualism, pedagoguishness, pretentiousness, punctiliousness

peddle
◇ *anagram indicator*
04 flog, hawk, push, sell, tout, vend
05 trade 06 market, smouch, trifle
07 traffic 08 huckster 12 offer for sale
14 present for sale

pedestal
04 base, dado, foot 05 basis, stand, trunk 06 column, pillar, plinth, podium
07 acroter, support 08 mounting, platform 09 axle-guard, stylobate
10 acroterion, acroterium, foundation
11 pillow-block
• **put on a pedestal**
05 exalt 06 admire, revere 07 adulate, idolize 08 look up to 11 hero-worship

pedestrian
03 ped 04 dull, flat 05 banal, hiker
06 boring, hicker, stodgy, turgid, walker
07 humdrum, mundane, prosaic
08 mediocre, ordinary, plodding
09 jaywalker 10 unexciting, uninspired, voetganger
11 commonplace, indifferent, not up to much, peripatetic 12 matter-of-fact, run-of-the-mill 13 foot-traveller, no great shakes, unimaginative

pedigree
03 set 04 line, race, tree 05 blood, breed, stirp, stock 06 family, series, stemma, stirps, strain 07 descent, lineage 08 ancestry, breeding, pure-bred 09 genealogy, parentage, phylogeny 10 derivation, extraction, family tree, succession 11 full-blooded
12 aristocratic, phylogenesis, thoroughbred 13 line of descent

pediment
07 frontal, fronton 08 frontoon
09 fastigium 12 frontispiece

pedlar
06 bodger, cadger, hawker, jagger, pedder, pether, seller, smouch, smouse, vendor, walker, yagger
07 camelot, chapman, packman, smouser 08 huckster 09 boxwallah, cheap-jack, gutter-man, itinerant
10 colporteur 12 street-trader
14 gutter-merchant

pee
01 P
See also **urinate**

peek
03 spy 04 look, peep, peer 05 blink, dekko, squiz 06 gander, glance, shufti, squint 07 glimpse, look-see 11 have a gander 12 have a look-see

peel
◇ *ends deletion indicator*
04 bark, pale, pare, peal, pill, rind, skin, zest 05 flake, scale, shell, shuck, stake, strip 06 grilse, remove, shovel
07 epicarp, exocarp, peeling, pillage, plunder, take off, undress 08 flake off

10 desquamate, integument
11 decorticate
• **keep your eyes peeled**
07 be alert, monitor, observe 12 watch closely 15 keep a lookout for

peep
03 cry, eye, pip, pry, spy 04 cook, keek, kook, look, peek, peer, pink, pipe, slit, toot, word 05 blink, cheep, chirp, dekko, issue, noise, sound, speck, tweet 06 appear, emerge, gander, glance, shufti, squeak, squint, warble
07 chatter, chirrup, glimpse, look-see, twitter 09 quick look, utterance

peephole
04 hole, slit 05 chink, cleft, crack, slink
07 crevice, eyehole, fissure, keyhole, opening, pinhole, spyhole 08 aperture
09 Judas hole 10 interstice 11 Judas window

peer
03 pry, spy 04 dick, duke, earl, gaze, lady, like, look, lord, peep, pink, scan, toot 05 baron, count, equal, match, noble, snoop, stime, styme, trier, tweer, twire 06 appear, fellow, squint, squiny
07 compeer, examine, inspect, Law Lord, marquis, peeress, squinny
08 confrère, marquess, nobleman, protrude, viscount 09 patrician
10 antagonist, aristocrat, equivalent, scrutinize 11 counterpart
12 backwoodsman
See also **nobility**

peerage
07 Debrett, red book 08 nobility
09 top drawer 10 upper crust
11 aristocracy 14 lords and ladies

peeress
04 dame, lady 05 noble 07 duchess
08 baroness, countess 10 aristocrat, noblewoman 11 marchioness, viscountess

peerless
06 unique 07 supreme 09 excellent, matchless, nonpareil, paramount, unmatched 10 incompared, unbeatable, unequalled, unexcelled, unrivalled 11 outstanding, superlative, unsurpassed 12 incomparable, second to none, unparalleled, without equal
13 beyond compare

peeve
03 bug, irk, vex 04 gall, rile 05 annoy
06 grouse, hassle, wind up 07 hack off, tick off 08 brass off, irritate
09 aggravate, cheese off, drive nuts, grievance 10 drive crazy, exasperate
12 drive bananas 13 make sparks fly
14 drive up the wall

peeved
04 sore 05 irked, riled, upset, vexed
06 bugged, galled, miffed, narked, piqued, put out, shirty 07 annoyed, hassled, in a huff, nettled, stroppy 08 in a paddy 09 irritated, ticked off
10 brassed off, cheesed off, driven nuts, got the hump 11 driven crazy, exasperated

peevish
03 ill 04 sour 05 cross, moody, ratty, sulky, surly, testy 06 crusty, franzy, girnie, grumpy, hipped, snappy, sullen, tetchy, touchy 07 crabbed, foolish, frabbit, frampal, fretful, grouchy, nattery, pettish, wayward 08 captious, churlish, frampold, nattered, perverse, petulant 09 crotchety, fractious, irritable, querulous, splenetic, vexatious 10 capernoity, in a bad mood
11 capernoitie, cappernoity, complaining, ill-tempered, out of temper 12 cantankerous 13 short-tempered

peevishly
07 crossly 08 grumpily, sullenly
09 fretfully, irritably 10 churlishly, in a bad mood, petulantly 11 fractiously

peevishness
03 dod, pet 05 pique 08 acrimony, fretting 09 curstness, ill-temper, petulance, testiness 10 perversity, protervity 12 captiousness, irritability 13 querulousness

peg
03 fix, key, leg, nog, pin, set, tap
04 brad, hook, join, knag, knob, mark, nail, plug, poke, post, step 05 dowel, limit, perch, piton, score, screw, spike, stake, theme, thole, throw 06 attach, degree, fasten, freeze, hatpeg, marker, picket, piquet, secure, spigot, target, thrust 07 control, picquet, tent pin
08 cheville, hold down, thole pin
09 soft spile, stabilize, tuning pin
• **peg away**
06 hang in 07 persist 08 keep at it, plug away, work away, work hard
09 persevere, plod along, stick at it
10 beaver away 13 apply yourself
• **take down a peg or two, bring down a peg or two**
06 humble 09 humiliate 13 cut down to size 15 bring down to size

pejorative
03 bad 08 negative 09 slighting
10 belittling, derogatory, unpleasant
11 deprecatory, disparaging
12 depreciating, unflattering
15 uncomplimentary

pellet
04 ball, drop, pill, shot, slug 05 prill
06 bullet 07 capsule, granule, lozenge
08 pithball 09 coprolite, paintball

pell-mell
◇ *anagram indicator*
06 rashly 07 hastily 08 disorder, headlong 09 hurriedly, posthaste 10 at full tilt, confusedly, feverishly, heedlessly, recklessly, vehemently
11 hurry-scurry, impetuously 13 helter-skelter, precipitously 14 indiscriminate

pellucid
04 pure 05 clear 06 bright, glassy, limpid 10 diaphanous 11 translucent, transparent

pelt
03 fur, hit, ren, rin, run, zip 04 beat,

...elt, blow, clod, coat, dash, fell, hide,
...rl, pour, race, rush, skin, tear, teem
hurry, scoot, speed, stone, throw
...assail, attack, batter, bucket, career,
...arge, fleece, pebble, pellet, pelter,
...pper, shower, sprint, squail, strike
bombard **08** bearskin, bepepper,
...onskin, downpour, lapidate, squirrel,
...olfskin **10** bucket down **15** rain cats
...d dogs

en

containment indicator
...Bic®, cub, dam, mew, nib, sty
...Biro®, cage, coop, fold, J-pen, note,
...ed, shut, stie, stye, weir **05** crawl,
...uve, draft, fence, hedge, hem in,
...tch, kraal, penne, pound, quill, stall,
...rite **06** author, corral, croove, cruive,
tate, shut up **07** compose, confine,
...sh off, enclose, felt pen, felt-tip,
...adius, jot down, rastrum, writing
...compound, note down, scribble,
...ke down **09** ballpoint, enclosure,
...arker pen, sheepfold, write down
...felt-tip pen, plantation, Rollerball®,
...lf-filler, stylograph **11** fountain pen,
...ghlighter, Magic Marker®
ballpoint pen, penitentiary
...e also **author**

enal

...punitive **10** corrective, vindictive
retaliatory, retributive
disciplinary, penitentiary

enalize

...fine **06** punish **07** correct, forfeit
...chastise, handicap, sanction
...castigate **10** discipline
disadvantage

enal servitude

...lag **04** bird, time **07** katorga, stretch
...porridge **10** hard labour

enalty

...fine, pain, snag **05** minus, mulct
...amende **07** forfeit **08** downside,
...awback, handicap, sentence
...weak point **10** punishment
castigation, retribution
...chastisement, demerit point,
sadvantage
pay penalty
...aby **04** abye

enance

...shrift **07** penalty **08** hardship
...atonement, expiation, penitence
...punishment, reparation, repentance
...mortification, self-abasement
...self-punishment

enchant

...bent, bias **05** taste **06** foible, liking
...leaning **08** affinity, fondness, soft
...ot, tendency, weakness
...proneness **10** partiality, preference,
...oclivity, propensity **11** disposition,
...clination **12** predilection
...predisposition

encil

...cam **04** calm, caum **05** stump
...crayon **09** keelivine, keelyvine,
...rtillon **10** Chinagraph®

pendant

03 bob **04** drop, tika, tiki **05** cross
06 locket, luster, lustre **07** eardrop,
earring, heitiki, necklet, pennant,
sautoir **08** appendix, necklace, pear
drop **09** girandola, girandole, lavaliere,
medallion **10** lavallière, Rouen cross,
stalactite

pendent

06 nutant **07** hanging, pensile
08 dangling, drooping, swinging
09 pendulous, suspended
11 overhanging

pending

02 to **04** near, till **05** until, while
06 before, coming, during, whilst
07 hanging, awaiting, nearing **08** awaiting,
imminent, so long as **09** impending,
uncertain, undecided, unsettled
10 throughout, unresolved, up in the
air **11** approaching, forthcoming, in the
offing **12** in the balance

pendulous

06 droopy **07** hanging, pendent,
sagging, swaying **08** dangling,
drooping, swinging **09** suspended
11 overhanging

penetrable

04 open **05** clear **06** porous
08 passable, pervious **09** permeable
10 accessible, explicable, fathomable
12 intelligible **14** comprehensible,
understandable

penetrate

◊ *insertion indicator*
03 cut, see **04** bite, bore, fill, seep, sink,
stab, twig **05** crack, enter, grasp,
imbue, prick, probe, sease, shear, spike
06 fathom, indent, invade, needle,
pierce, rain in, sink in, strike **07** get into,
make out, pervade, suffuse, suss out,
work out **08** cotton on, permeate,
perviate, puncture, register, saturate
09 perforate **10** comprehend, infiltrate,
understand **11** make your way

penetrating

◊ *insertion indicator*
04 deep, hard, keen, loud, wise
05 acute, clear, sharp **06** biting,
shrewd, shrill **07** cutting, in-depth,
ingoing, intrant, probing **08** carrying,
incisive, invasive, piercing, poignant,
profound, stinging, strident
09 observant, searching **10** discerning,
insightful, perceptive **14** discriminating

penetration

◊ *insertion indicator*
03 wit **05** entry **06** acumen, fathom,
inroad **07** insight **08** entrance, incision,
invasion, keenness, piercing, pricking,
stabbing **09** acuteness, pervasion,
sharpness **10** astuteness, perception,
permeation, puncturing, shrewdness
11 discernment, perforation
12 infiltration, perspicacity

penguin

05 diver **06** gentoo, korora **07** pinguin
08 macaroni **10** rockhopper,
Spheniscus **11** king penguin **12** fairy

penguin **13** little penguin **14** emperor
penguin

peninsula

03 Pen **04** cape, doab, mull **05** point
06 tongue **10** chersonese

04 Ards, Cape, Eyre, Gyda, Huon, Kola
05 Gaspé, Gower, Italy, Lleyn, Malay,
Otago, Qatar, Sinai
06 Alaska, Avalon, Azuero, Balkan,
Carnac, Crimea, Iberia, Istria, Jaffna,
Korean, Recife, Seward, Taymyr,
Wirral
07 Alaskan, Arabian, Cape Cod,
Chukchi, Florida, Furness, Iberian,
Jiulong, Jutland, Kintyre, Kowloon,
Olympic, Yucatàn
08 Apsheron, Cape York, Cotentin,
Musandam, Pinellas, Sorrento,
Yorktown
09 Cape Verde, Gallipoli, Kamchatka,
Paraguana, Peary Land
10 Arnhem Land, Graham Land, Isle of
Dogs, Nova Scotia
11 Peloponnese
12 Scandinavian
14 Baja California, Isle of Portland
15 Rinns of Galloway

See also **cape**

penitence

05 shame **06** regret, sorrow
07 remorse **10** contrition, repentance,
ruefulness **11** compunction **12** self-
reproach

penitent

05 sorry **06** humble, rueful
07 ashamed, mourner **08** contrite
09 regretful, repentant, sorrowful
10 apologetic, remorseful,
shamefaced

pen-name

06 anonym **07** allonym **09** false name,
pseudonym, stage-name **10** nom de
plume **11** assumed name, nom de
guerre

pennant

04 flag, jack **06** banner, burgee, ensign,
guidon, pennon **07** colours, pendant,
pendent **08** banderol, gonfalon,
standard, streamer

penniless

04 bust, poor **05** broke, skint, stony
06 ruined **07** boracic **08** bankrupt,
dirt-poor, indigent **09** destitute
10 cleaned out, down and out, on the
rocks, stone-broke, stony-broke
11 impecunious **12** impoverished, on
your uppers **14** on the breadline, on
your beam-ends **15** poverty-stricken,
strapped for cash

Pennsylvania

02 PA

penny

01 d, p **03** win **04** cent, wing, winn
08 denarius, sterling

penny-pincher

05 miser **06** meanie **07** niggard,

Scrooge 09 skinflint 10 cheapskate
11 cheeseparer 12 money-grubber

penny-pinching
04 mean 05 close, mingy, tight
06 frugal, stingy 07 miserly
09 niggardly, scrimping 10 ungenerous
11 tight-fisted 12 cheeseparing,
parsimonious

pension
04 SIPP 05 board 06 corody, income
07 annuity, benefit, corrody, support,
welfare 09 allowance 11 deferred pay
12 state pension 13 old-age pension
14 company pension, superannuation
15 personal pension

pensioner
03 OAP 07 boarder 09 dependant
12 out-pensioner 13 retired person,
senior citizen 15 gentleman-at-arms,
old-age pensioner

pensive
05 sober 06 dreamy, musing, solemn
07 serious, wistful 08 absorbed,
thinking 09 pondering 10 cogitative,
meditative, melancholy, reflective,
ruminative, thoughtful 11 preoccupied
12 absent-minded 13 contemplative,
lackadaisical

pensively
08 dreamily 09 seriously, wistfully
12 meditatively, thoughtfully
14 absent-mindedly
15 contemplatively

Pentateuch
05 Torah

penthouse
03 cat 04 pent

pent-up
06 curbed, held in 07 bridled, stifled
09 bottled-up, inhibited, repressed
10 restrained, suppressed

penurious
04 bust, mean, poor 05 close, mingy,
tight 06 hard up, scanty, stingy
07 lacking, miserly 08 beggarly,
grudging, indigent 09 destitute, flat
broke, niggardly, penniless
10 inadequate, ungenerous 11 close-
fisted, close-handed, impecunious,
tight-fisted 12 cheeseparing,
impoverished, on your uppers,
parsimonious 14 on your beam-ends
15 poverty-stricken

penury
04 lack, need, want 06 dearth
07 beggary, poverty, straits
09 indigence, mendicity, pauperism
10 deficiency, insolvency 11 destitution
14 impoverishment

people
03 men, mob 04 clan, folk, gens, land,
race 05 folks, laity, ngati, plebs, tribe,
tuath 06 family, hordes, humans,
masses, nation, occupy, proles, public,
rabble, settle, voters 07 inhabit,
mankind, mortals, parents, persons,
punters, society 08 citizens, colonize,

humanity, populace, populate, riff-raff,
servants, subjects 09 community,
employees, followers, hoi polloi,
humankind, relations, relatives, retainers
10 attendants, electorate, kith and kin,
population 11 ethnic group, human
beings, individuals, inhabitants, rank
and file 12 congregation, the human
race 13 general public, great unwashed

Peoples include:
03 Han, Ibo, Jat, Kru, Mam, Mon, San,
   Tiv, Twi
04 Ainu, Cham, Efik, Goth, Hutu, Igbo,
   Jute, Kroo, Lett, Moor, Motu, Nair,
   Nupe, Roma, Saba, Shan, Sulu,
   Susu, Tshi, Zulu
05 Bajau, Bantu, Hausa, Iceni, Inuit,
   Karen, Khmer, Maori, Masai, Nayar,
   Nguni, Oriya, Saxon, Swazi, Taino,
   Tamil, Temne, Tonga, Tutsi, Vedda,
   Wolof, Yakut, Yupik
06 Angles, Aymara, Griqua, Gurkha,
   Herero, Innuit, Kabyle, Kalmyk,
   Kikuyu, Manchu, Nyanja, Ostiak,
   Ostyak, Sherpa, Tswana, Tungus,
   Yoruba, Zyrian
07 Barotse, Basotho, Calmuck,
   Cossack, Goorkha, Hittite,
   Kalmuck, Manchoo, Maratha,
   Pashtun, Quechua, Quichua,
   Samoyed, Swahili, Tagálog, Walloon
08 Khoikhoi, Mahratta, Polabian,
   Yanomami
09 Himyarite, Ostrogoth, Ruthenian,
   Sinhalese, Tocharian, Tokharian

pep
02 go 03 zip 04 life, zing 05 oomph,
verve 06 energy, ginger, spirit, vigour
07 pizzazz, sparkle 08 dynamism,
vitality 10 ebullience, exuberance, get-
up-and-go, liveliness 11 high spirits
13 effervescence

• pep up
06 excite 07 animate, improve, inspire,
liven up, quicken 08 energize, vitalize
09 stimulate 10 exhilarate, invigorate

pepper
03 dot 04 bomb, pelt, stud 05 blitz,
Piper, strew 06 assail, attack, shower
07 bombard, scatter, spatter
08 sprinkle 09 bespatter

Pepper and peppercorns include:
03 ava, red
04 bird, kava, pink
05 black, chile, chili, green, sweet,
   white
06 cherry, chilli, yellow
07 cayenne, Jamaica, paprika, pimento
08 allspice, capsicum, habañero,
   jalapeño, pimiento, piquillo
12 Scotch bonnet

peppermint
06 humbug 07 pan drop 08 bull's-eye

peppery
03 hot 05 fiery, sharp, spicy, testy
06 biting, grumpy, touchy 07 caustic,
piquant, pungent, waspish
08 choleric, incisive, seasoned,

snappish, stinging 09 irascible,
irritable, sarcastic, trenchant
10 astringent 11 hot-tempered
13 quick-tempered

peppy
04 spry 05 agile, alert, alive, brisk,
quick 06 active, lively, nimble
07 dynamic 08 animated, spirited,
vigorous 09 energetic, sprightly,
vivacious 12 enthusiastic, high-spirited

per
01 a 02 by, pr 07 through

perceive
03 see 04 espy, feel, hear, know, note,
spot, twig, view, wind 05 grasp, learn,
sense, smell, taste 06 behold, deduce,
detect, gather, notice, remark, survey
07 believe, discern, glimpse, make out,
observe, realize, suppose
08 conclude, discover, subitize
09 apprehend, be aware of, get wind
of, recognize, undertake
10 appreciate, comprehend,
understand 11 distinguish 12 catch
sight of 13 be cognizant of

perceptible
05 clear, plain 06 patent 07 evident,
obvious, tactile, visible 08 apparent,
distinct, manifest, palpable, sensible,
tangible 10 detectable, noticeable,
observable 11 appreciable,
conspicuous, discernible, perceivable
15 distinguishable

perception
04 idea, view 05 grasp, sense, taste
06 vision 07 feeling, insight, percept
09 awareness, knowledge
10 cognizance, conception,
experience, impression
11 discernment, observation,
recognition, sensitivity
12 appreciation, apprehension
13 consciousness, light of nature,
understanding 14 discrimination,
interpretation, responsiveness

• fine perception
04 tact

perceptive
04 deep, keen 05 acute, alert, aware,
quick, sharp 06 astute, shrewd
08 delicate 09 observant, sensitive,
sharp-eyed 10 discerning, insightful,
percipient, responsive 11 penetrating,
quick-witted 13 perspicacious,
understanding 14 discriminating

perceptively
06 keenly 07 sharply 08 astutely
11 observantly, sensitively
12 insightfully 15 perspicaciously

perch
03 bar, lug, rod, sit 04 bass, land, perk,
pole, rest, rood, ruff 05 basse, gaper,
Perca, roost, ruffe 06 alight, anabas,
comber, darter, fogash, sander, sauger,
settle, zander, zingel 07 balance,
kahawai, walleye 09 blackfish,
overperch, stone bass, wreckfish
12 walleyed pike

perchance
05 maybe 07 percase, perhaps
08 feasibly, possibly 11 conceivably

percipience
07 insight 08 sagacity 09 acuteness,
alertness, awareness, intuition,
judgement 10 astuteness, perception
11 discernment, penetration,
sensitivity 12 perspicacity
13 understanding

percipient
05 alert, alive, aware, sharp 06 astute
07 knowing 09 judicious, observant,
wide-awake 10 discerning, perceptive
11 intelligent, penetrating, quick-witted
13 perspicacious 14 discriminating

percolate
03 sop 04 drip, leak, ooze, perk, seep,
sift 05 drain, leach, sieve 06 filter, strain
07 pervade 08 filtrate, permeate
09 penetrate 11 pass through
13 spread through 14 trickle through

perdition
04 doom, hell, loss, ruin 08 downfall,
hellfire 09 confusion, damnation,
ruination 11 destruction
12 annihilation, condemnation

peregrination
04 tour, trek, trip 06 roving, travel,
voyage 07 journey, odyssey, roaming
08 trekking 09 excursion, wandering,
wayfaring 10 expedition, pilgrimage,
travelling 11 exploration
13 globetrotting

peremptory
04 curt 05 bossy, final, utter 06 abrupt,
lordly 07 summary 08 absolute,
dogmatic 09 arbitrary, assertive,
imperious 10 autocratic,
commanding, high-handed,
imperative, tyrannical 11 dictatorial,
domineering, irrefutable, overbearing
13 authoritative

perennial
07 abiding, endless, eternal, lasting,
undying 08 constant, enduring,
immortal, unending 09 ceaseless,
continual, incessant, permanent,
perpetual, unceasing, unfailing
10 persistent, unchanging
11 everlasting, never-ending
12 imperishable 13 uninterrupted

perfect
04 full, mint, perf, pure, true 05 exact,
ideal, model, prize, right, sheer, total,
utter 06 better, entire, expert, finish,
fulfil, mature, polish, refine, superb,
triple 07 certain, correct, improve,
precise, sinless, skilful 08 absolute,
accurate, complete, copybook,
faithful, finished, flawless, peerless,
spotless, textbook, thorough, ultimate,
unmarred 09 blameless, completed,
convinced, downright, elaborate,
excellent, exemplary, faultless,
matchless, out-and-out, wonderful
10 consummate, immaculate,
impeccable, just the job, to the nines
11 experienced, superlative,

unblemished 12 accomplished,
incomparable

perfection
04 acme, best 05 bloom, crown, ideal,
model, prime 06 flower 07 paragon
08 maturity, pinnacle, ripeness,
ultimate 09 polishing 10 betterment,
completion, excellence, refinement
11 improvement, ne plus ultra, point-
device, point-devise, realization,
roundedness, superiority
12 consummation, flawlessness
13 faultlessness, impeccability, one in a
million 14 immaculateness

perfectionism
06 purism 08 idealism, pedantry
09 formalism 10 Utopianism

perfectionist
06 pedant, purist 08 idealist, stickler
09 formalist, Free-lover 12 precisionist

perfectly
04 very 05 fully, quite 06 à point,
wholly 07 down pat, exactly, ideally,
totally, utterly 08 entirely, superbly
09 correctly 10 absolutely, altogether,
completely, flawlessly, impeccably, like
a charm, thoroughly 11 faultlessly,
wonderfully 12 consummately,
immaculately, to perfection 14 without
blemish

perfidious
05 false, Punic 07 corrupt 08 disloyal,
two-faced 09 deceitful, dishonest,
faithless 10 traitorous, treasonous,
unfaithful 11 double-faced,
duplicitous, treacherous 13 double-
dealing, Machiavellian, untrustworthy

perfidy
06 deceit 07 falsity, treason
08 betrayal 09 duplicity, treachery
10 disloyalty, infidelity 13 double-
dealing, faithlessness
14 perfidiousness, traitorousness

perforate
04 bore, gore, hole, stab, tear 05 burst,
drill, prick, punch, spike, split 06 pierce
07 rupture 08 puncture, trephine
09 penetrate 11 make holes in

perforated
05 bored, holed 06 porous 07 drilled,
ethmoid, pierced, punched
09 fenestral, punctured 10 cribriform,
fenestrate, fenestrial, foraminous
11 fenestrated

perforation
04 bore, hole 05 prick 06 pierce
07 foramen 08 fenestra, puncture
10 dotted line 12 fenestration

perforce
10 inevitably, willy-nilly 11 necessarily,
of necessity, unavoidably

perform
◇ anagram indicator
02 do, go 03 act, cut, run 04 make,
play, sing, take, work 05 dance, enact,
put on, stage, throw 06 behave, effect,
fulfil, recite, render 07 achieve, conduct,

execute, operate, portray, present,
produce, pull off, satisfy 08 appear as,
atchieve, bring off, carry out, complete,
despatch, dispatch, function, make
good, transact 09 discharge,
implement, represent 10 accomplish,
bring about 12 give effect to

performance
03 act 04 deed, duet, play, show, solo,
spot, trio 05 doing, going, house
06 acting, action, acture, ballet, try-out
07 account, benefit, concert, conduct,
recital, running, showing, working
08 hierurgy, première, set piece
09 behaviour, discharge, effecting,
execution, happening, operation,
portrayal, prolusion, rendering,
rendition 10 appearance, completion,
conducting, fulfilling, fulfilment, last
hurrah, peroration, production
11 achievement, carrying-out,
functioning, presentment, tour de
force 12 presentation
14 accomplishment, implementation,
interpretation, representation

performer
04 doer, hand, moke, star, turn
05 actor, clown, comic 06 artist,
author, dancer, player, singer
07 actress, artiste, old hand, ripieno,
trouper 08 achiever, comedian,
executor, Fancy Dan, film star,
musician, operator, star turn, Thespian,
topliner 09 ecdysiast, executant
10 rope-walker 11 entertainer
12 improvisator, vaudevillean,
vaudevillian 15 jerry-come-tumble

performers
04 cast

perfume
04 balm, musk, otto, sent 05 aroma,
attar, odour, ottar, scent, smell
06 chypre 07 bouquet, cologne,
essence, incense 08 fumigate,
opopanax 09 aromatize, fragrance,
redolence, sweetness 10 frangipane,
frangipani, heliotrope, Jockey Club
11 millefleurs, toilet water 12 eau-de-
cologne 13 eau-de-toilette, lavender
water

perfunctorily
07 quickly 09 cursorily, hurriedly
10 carelessly 13 inattentively,
superficially

perfunctory
05 brief, quick 06 wooden 07 cursory,
hurried, offhand, routine 08 careless,
heedless, slipshod, slovenly
09 automatic, desultory, negligent
10 mechanical 11 inattentive,
indifferent, superficial

perhaps
◇ anagram indicator
03 say 05 haply, maybe 06 ablins,
belike, happen, mayhap 07 aiblins,
could be, happily, percase, yibbles
08 feasibly, possibly 09 perchance
11 conceivably 12 peradventure, you
never know

peril

04 risk **06** danger, hazard, menace, threat **07** apperil **08** apperill, distress, jeopardy **10** insecurity **11** uncertainty **12** endangerment

perilous

04 dire **05** dicey, dodgy, hairy, risky **06** chancy, unsafe, unsure **07** exposed, parlous, perlous **08** high-risk, insecure, menacing **09** dangerous, hazardous **10** precarious, vulnerable **11** threatening

perimeter

04 edge **05** limit **06** border, bounds, fringe, limits, margin **07** circuit **08** boundary, confines, frontier **09** periphery **11** outer limits **13** circumference

period

03 age, end, eon, era, per **04** aeon, date, span, spin, stop, term, time, turn **05** class, cycle, epoch, phase, point, shift, space, spell, stage, stint, while, years **06** finish, lesson, menses, season **07** lecture, seminar, session, stretch **08** duration, full stop, interval, semester, the curse, tutorial **09** full point, monthlies **10** conclusion, end of story, generation **11** instruction **12** menstruation **13** menstrual flow **14** menstrual cycle, time of the month

See also **geological; historical; time**

periodic

05 round **06** cyclic **07** regular **08** cyclical, repeated, seasonal, sporadic **09** recurrent, recurring **10** infrequent, occasional, periodical **12** intermittent, once in a while

periodical

03 mag **05** organ **06** review, weekly **07** etesian, journal, monthly, regular **08** bi-weekly, bulletin, magazine **09** pictorial, quarterly, thunderer, tri-weekly **11** illustrated, publication, semi-monthly **12** trade journal

See also **newspaper**

periodically

07 at times **08** off and on, on and off **09** sometimes **10** now and then, on occasion **11** at intervals, irregularly, now and again **12** every so often, infrequently, occasionally, once in a while, sporadically **14** from time to time, intermittently **15** every now and then

peripatetic

06 mobile, roving **07** migrant, nomadic, roaming, vagrant **08** ambulant, vagabond **09** itinerant, migratory, traveling, wandering **10** ambulatory, journeying, pedestrian, travelling **12** Aristotelian

peripheral

05 add-on, input, minor, outer **06** lesser, output **07** storage, surface **08** computer, marginal, outlying **09** ancillary, auxiliary, disk drive, outermost, secondary, sidelined **10** additional, borderline, incidental, irrelevant, subsidiary, tangential **11** superficial, surrounding, unimportant, unnecessary **14** beside the point, graphics tablet

periphery

03 hem, rim **04** brim, edge **05** ambit, brink, skirt, verge **06** border, fringe, margin **07** circuit **08** boundary **09** outskirts, perimeter **12** outer regions **13** circumference

periphrastic

07 oblique **08** indirect, rambling, tortuous **09** wandering **10** circuitous, discursive, roundabout **12** long-drawn-out **14** circumlocutory

perish

02 go **03** die, rot **04** cark, exit, fail, fall, pass, ruin, tine, tyne, vade **05** choke, croak, decay, drown, go off, quell, swelt **06** depart, expire, famish, go bung, go west, pass on, peg out, pip out, pop off, starve, sterve, vanish **07** crumble, decease, destroy, die away, fall off, forfair, kick off, kiss off, snuff it, succumb **08** collapse, flatline, pass away, spark out **09** decompose, disappear, go belly up, have had it **10** hop the twig **11** bite the dust, come to an end **12** disintegrate, lose your life, pop your clogs, slip the cable **13** close your eyes, kick the bucket, meet your maker, push up daisies **14** depart this life, give up the ghost, turn up your toes **15** breathe your last, cash in your chips

perishable

10 short-lived **12** decomposable, destructible **13** biodegradable

periwinkle

05 vinca **06** winkle **08** Apocynum, dog-whelk **11** pennywinkle **12** strophanthus

perjure

- **perjure yourself**

03 lie **12** lie under oath **13** commit perjury

perjury

09 false oath, mendacity **11** crimen falsi, forswearing **12** false witness, hard swearing, oath-breaking **13** false evidence, false swearing, falsification **14** false statement, false testimony, lying under oath

perk

03 tip **04** plus **05** bonus, brisk, extra, perch **07** benefit, freebie **08** dividend, gratuity **09** advantage, baksheesh, percolate **10** percolator, perquisite **13** fringe benefit **15** golden handshake

- **perk up**

05 pep up, rally **06** buck up, cock up, look up, revive **07** cheer up, improve, liven up, recover **08** brighten **09** take heart **10** brighten up, make lively, revitalize **12** become lively

perky

03 gay **04** pert **05** cocky, peppy, sunny **06** bouncy, bright, bubbly, cheery, gallus, jaunty, lively **07** buoyant, gallows **08** animated, cheerful, spirited **09** ebullient, sprightly, vivacious **12** effervescent

permanence

09 constancy, endurance, fixedness, stability **10** durability, perpetuity **11** persistence **13** steadfastness **15** imperishability

permanent

04 firm **05** fixed, pakka, pucka, pukka, solid **06** stable **07** abiding, durable, eternal, lasting, regular, stative **08** constant, enduring, lifelong, standing, unfading **09** immutable, indelible, perennial, perpetual, steadfast **10** invariable, unchanging **11** established, everlasting, long-lasting **12** imperishable, unchangeable **14** indestructible

permanently

06 always **07** for ever, for good **08** ever more, for keeps **09** endlessly, eternally, indelibly **10** constantly, for all time, unendingly **11** ceaselessly, continually, incessantly, perpetually, unceasingly **12** in perpetuity, till doomsday **13** everlastingly, for good and all, once and for all, unremittingly **14** for ever and ever **15** till kingdom come

permeable

06 porous, spongy **08** passable, pervious **09** absorbent, poromeric **10** absorptive, penetrable

permeate

04 fill **05** imbue **06** leaven **07** diffuse, pervade, suffuse **08** saturate **09** penetrate, percolate **10** impregnate, infiltrate **11** impenetrate, pass through, seep through, soak through, transpierce **13** filter through, spread through

permissible

02 OK **05** legal, legit **06** kosher, lawful, proper, venial **07** allowed **08** all right **09** allowable, permitted, tolerable **10** acceptable, admissible, authorized, legitimate, sanctioned

permission

03 out **04** loan, pass **05** congé, exeat, leave, power **06** access, assent, congee, permit, placet, square **07** consent, freedom, go-ahead, liberty, licence, license, mandate, warrant **08** approval, pratique, sanction, thumbs-up, wayleave **09** admission, agreement, allowance, authority, clearance **10** green light, imprimatur **11** approbation, bill of sight, congé d'élire, permittance **12** dispensation **13** authorization **14** leave of absence, permis de séjour

permissive

03 lax **04** free **07** lenient, liberal **08** optional, tolerant **09** easy-going, indulgent, permitted **10** forbearing **11** broad-minded **13** overindulgent **14** latitudinarian

permit
03 let 04 give, pass, visa 05 admit,
agree, allow, grant, smoke 06 carnet,
docket, enable, suffer, ticket
07 consent, docquet, empower,
indulge, licence, license, placard,
warrant 08 intromit, passport,
sanction, tolerate 09 authorize, green
card 10 permission 11 safe-conduct
12 give the nod to 13 authorization,
laissez-passer 14 permis de séjour
• **it is not permitted**
02 nl

permutation
04 perm 05 shift 06 barter, change
09 obversion, variation 10 alteration
11 commutation 13 configuration,
transmutation, transposition
14 transformation

pernicious
03 bad 04 evil 05 fatal, ready, swift,
toxic 06 deadly, prompt, wicked
07 baneful, harmful, hurtful, noisome,
noxious, ruinous 08 damaging,
damnable, venomous 09 dangerous,
injurious, malicious, malignant,
offensive, pestilent, poisonous,
unhealthy 10 maleficent, malevolent
11 deleterious, destructive,
detrimental, unwholesome

pernickety
04 fine, nice 05 fussy, picky 06 choosy,
niddly, tricky 07 careful, carping,
finical, finicky 08 detailed, exacting
10 fastidious, nit-picking, particular
11 over-precise, painstaking,
persnickety, punctilious 13 hair-
splitting 14 over-particular

peroration
04 talk 06 korero, speech 07 address,
lecture, oration, summary 08 diatribe,
pirlicue, purlicue 09 recapping,
summing-up 10 conclusion
11 declamation, reiteration 14 closing
remarks, recapitulation

perpendicular
04 sine 05 atrip, erect, plumb, right,
sheer, steep 06 abrupt, normal, offset
07 apothem, upright 08 cathetus,
straight, vertical 09 downright,
erectness 10 anticlinal 11 precipitous,
verticality 13 at right angles

perpetrate
02 do 05 wreak 06 commit, effect
07 execute, inflict, perform 08 carry
out 10 accomplish, effectuate 12 be to
blame for

perpetration
05 doing 09 committal, execution
10 commitment 11 achievement,
carrying-out, performance
14 accomplishment, implementation

perpetrator
04 doer, perp 05 agent 08 executor,
offender 09 committer, executant

perpetual
07 abiding, endless, eternal, lasting,
undying 08 constant, enduring,

infinite, repeated, unbroken, unending
09 ceaseless, continual, incessant,
perennial, permanent, recurrent,
unceasing, unfailing, unvarying
10 continuous, persistent, persisting,
unchanging 11 everlasting, never-
ending, unremitting 12 interminable,
intermittent 13 uninterrupted

perpetually
09 endlessly, eternally 10 constantly
11 ceaselessly, continually, incessantly,
permanently, unceasingly
12 interminably, persistently
13 unremittingly

perpetuate
06 keep up 07 sustain 08 continue,
maintain, preserve 09 keep alive, keep
going 10 eternalize 11 commemorate,
immortalize, memorialize

perpetuation
09 extension 10 sustaining
11 lengthening, maintenance,
protraction 12 continuation, keeping
alive, preservation, prolongation
13 commemoration

perpetuity
• **in perpetuity**
06 always 07 for ever 08 ever more
09 endlessly, eternally 10 for all time
11 perpetually 14 for ever and ever

perplex
◇ *anagram indicator*
04 pose 05 beset, stump, throw
06 baffle, bother, feague, fickle, gravel,
hobble, muddle, pother, pudder,
puzzle, tangle, tickle 07 bumbaze,
confuse, flummox, mystify, nonplus
08 bewilder, confound, entangle,
throw off 09 bamboozle, dumbfound,
embarrass, embrangle, imbrangle
10 complicate, difficulty, distrouble,
interweave

perplexed
05 spiny 07 at a loss, baffled, fuddled,
muddled, puzzled, stumped, worried
08 confused 09 flummoxed, mystified,
quizzical 10 bamboozled, bewildered,
confounded, distraught, nonplussed,
tosticated 11 embarrassed
12 disconcerted

perplexing
04 hard 05 weird 06 knotty, taxing,
thorny 07 amazing, complex, strange
08 baffling, involved, puzzling
09 confusing, difficult, enigmatic,
intricate 10 mysterious, mystifying
11 bewildering, complicated,
paradoxical 12 inexplicable,
labyrinthine

perplexity
05 doubt, tweak, worry 06 bother,
enigma, puzzle, taking, tangle
07 dilemma, meander, mystery,
nonplus, paradox 09 confusion,
intricacy, labyrinth, obscurity
10 bafflement, complexity, difficulty,
fickleness, puzzlement 11 distraction,
disturbance, involvement,
obfuscation, tostication

12 bewilderment, complication,
entanglement 13 embarrassment,
mystification 15 incomprehension

perquisite
03 tip 04 lock, perk, plus, vail
05 bonus, extra, vales 07 apanage,
benefit, freebie 08 appanage,
dividend, gratuity 09 advantage,
baksheesh, royal fish 10 emoluments,
kitchen-fee 13 fringe benefit

persecute
04 bait, hunt 05 abuse, annoy, hound,
worry 06 badger, bother, harass,
hassle, martyr, molest, pester, pursue
07 afflict, crucify, oppress, torment,
torture 08 distress, hunt down, ill-treat,
maltreat, mistreat 09 tyrannize,
victimize

persecution
05 abuse 07 torture, tyranny
09 martyrdom 10 dragonnade,
harassment, oppression, punishment
11 crucifixion, molestation,
subjugation, suppression 12 ill-
treatment, maltreatment,
mistreatment 13 victimization
14 discrimination

Persephone
10 Proserpina

perseverance
07 purpose, resolve, stamina
08 tenacity 09 assiduity, constancy,
diligence, endurance
10 commitment, dedication,
doggedness, resolution 11 application,
persistence, persistency, pertinacity
12 stickability 13 determination,
intransigence, steadfastness
14 purposefulness

persevere
04 go on 05 truck 06 bash on, hang on,
hold on, remain 07 carry on, persist,
stick in 08 continue, plug away
09 keep going, prosecute, soldier on,
stand fast, stand firm, stick at it 10 be
resolute, hammer away, struggle on
11 hang in there 12 be determined, be
persistent, mean business 15 stick to
your guns

Persian
04 Babi, Mede 05 Babee, Farsi

persist
04 go on, hold, last 05 abide
06 endure, hang in, hang on, hold on,
insist, keep on, linger, remain 07 carry
on 08 continue, keep at it, plug away
09 hang about, keep going, persevere,
soldier on, stand fast, stand firm, stick at
it 10 be resolute, hang around 11 hang
in there 12 be determined, be
persistent

persistence
04 grit 07 stamina 08 sedulity, tenacity
09 assiduity, constancy, diligence,
endurance, obstinacy 10 doggedness,
resolution 11 pertinacity
12 continuation, perseverance,
stickability, tirelessness

13 assiduousness, determination, steadfastness

persistent
05 fixed 06 dogged, steady, urgent
07 endless, lasting, zealous
08 constant, diligent, enduring, obdurate, repeated, resolute, stubborn, tireless 09 assiduous, ceaseless, continual, incessant, obstinate, perpetual, steadfast, tenacious, unceasing 10 continuous, determined, persisting, purposeful, relentless, unflagging 11 importunate, intractable, never-ending, persevering, unrelenting, unremitting 12 interminable, pertinacious, stick-to-it-ive 13 indefatigable

persistently
10 constantly, diligently, resolutely, stubbornly, tirelessly 11 assiduously, ceaselessly, continually, incessantly, obstinately, tenaciously, unceasingly 12 continuously, interminably, relentlessly

person
03 bod, chi, man, per 04 body, chai, chal, fish, pers, soul, type 05 being, human, woman 06 mortal
07 someone 08 somebody
09 character 10 human being, individual
• **good person**
01 S 02 St 04 sant 05 Saint
• **individual person**
03 one
• **in person**
06 bodily, myself 08 actually 10 face to face, in the flesh, personally 13 as large as life

persona
04 face, mask, part, role 05 front, image 06 façade 09 character
10 public face 11 personality

personable
04 nice, warm 07 affable, amiable, winning 08 charming, handsome, likeable, outgoing, pleasant, pleasing 09 agreeable 10 attractive 11 good-looking, presentable

personage
03 VIP 04 name 05 celeb 06 bigwig, figure, worthy 07 big shot, notable
08 big noise, luminary, somebody
09 big cheese, celebrity, dignitary, headliner 11 personality 12 public figure

personal
03 gut, own 04 live, pers, rude
05 privy 06 bodily, secret, unique
07 abusive, hurtful, private, special
08 critical, in person, intimate, peculiar, wounding 09 exclusive, insulting, offensive, upsetting 10 derogatory, individual, in the flesh, particular, subjective 11 distinctive
12 confidential 13 disrespectful, idiosyncratic 14 characteristic

personality
03 VIP 04 mind, self, star 05 charm

06 figure, make-up, nature, person, psyche, temper, traits, worthy
07 notable 08 charisma, identity, selfhood, selfness 09 celebrity, character, dignitary, magnetism, personage 10 the real you 11 beastly-head, disposition, temperament
12 public figure 13 individuality

personalize
03 fit 04 suit 05 adapt, alter 06 adjust, modify, tailor 07 convert
09 customize, personify, transform

personally
05 alone 06 I think, solely 08 as I see it, I believe, in my book, in my view, in person, uniquely 09 as a slight, ourselves, privately, specially 10 for my money, if you ask me 11 exclusively, in my opinion, insultingly, offensively
12 individually, particularly, subjectively, the way I see it 13 distinctively, independently 14 confidentially

personification
05 image 07 epitome, essence
08 likeness 09 portrayal, semblance
10 embodiment, recreation
11 delineation, incarnation
12 quintessence 13 manifestation
14 representation

personify
06 embody, imbody, mirror, typify
09 epitomize, exemplify, incarnate, personize, represent, symbolize
11 hypostatize, impersonate, personalize

personnel
04 crew 05 staff 06 people
07 members, service, workers
08 liveware, manpower
09 employees, workforce 11 labour force 14 human resources

perspective
04 take, view 05 angle, scene, slant, vista 06 aspect, optics 07 balance, optical, outlook 08 attitude, peepshow, prospect, relation
09 viewpoint 10 inspection, proportion, standpoint 11 equilibrium, frame of mind, point of view
12 vantage point

perspicacious
04 keen 05 alert, aware, quick, sharp
06 astute, shrewd 09 judicious, observant, sagacious, sensitive, sharp-eyed 10 discerning, perceptive, percipient, responsive 11 penetrating, quick-witted 13 understanding
14 discriminating

perspicacity
03 wit 06 acumen, brains 07 insight
08 keenness, sagacity 09 acuteness, sharpness 10 astuteness, cleverness, shrewdness 11 discernment, penetration, percipience, perspicuity
13 sagaciousness 14 discrimination, perceptiveness

perspicuity
07 clarity 08 lucidity 09 clearness,

limpidity, plainness, precision
10 limpidness 12 distinctness, explicitness, transparency
13 penetrability 15 intelligibility

perspicuous
05 clear, lucid, plain 06 limpid
07 obvious 08 apparent, distinct, explicit, manifest 11 self-evident, transparent, unambiguous 12 crystal-clear, intelligible 14 comprehensible, understandable 15 straightforward

perspiration
04 foam 05 sudor, suint, sweat
07 wetness 08 hidrosis, moisture
09 exudation, secretion 11 diaphoresis

perspire
04 drip 05 exude, sweat 06 exhale, sudate 07 secrete, swelter

persuadable
07 pliable 08 amenable, flexible
09 agreeable, compliant, malleable, receptive 10 susceptive
11 acquiescent, persuasible
14 impressionable

persuade
03 con, win 04 coax, lure, move, snow, sway, urge 05 argue, lobby, moody, plead, tempt 06 cajole, coerce, incite, induce, lead on, lean on, nobble, prompt 07 convert, prevail, satisfy, swing it, wheedle, win over
08 convince, fast-talk, get round, inveigle, lamb down, perswade, soft-soap, talk into, talk over 09 argue into, influence, sweet-talk 10 bring round
11 prevail upon, pull strings 13 bring yourself 14 put the screws on

persuasion
04 camp, kind, pull, sect, side, sway, view 05 clout, creed, faith, party, power 06 belief, come-on, school, urging 07 coaxing, faction, opinion, suasion 08 cajolery, coercion, pressure, soft sell 09 influence, prompting, sweet talk, viewpoint, wheedling 10 conversion, conviction, enticement, incitement, inducement, philosophy, prevailing 11 affiliation, arm-twisting, point of view, talking into, winning over 12 denomination, sweet-talking 15 school of thought

persuasive
05 pushy, slick, sound, valid 06 cogent, moving, potent 07 telling, weighty, winning 08 eloquent, forceful, touching 09 effective, effectual, plausible 10 compelling, convincing
11 influential 12 high-pressure, honey-tongued, smooth-spoken 13 smooth-talking, smooth-tongued

persuasively
08 cogently 09 plausibly 10 forcefully, powerfully 11 effectively, effectually
12 compellingly, convincingly
13 influentially

pert
03 gay 04 bold, coxy, flip, open
05 brash, brisk, cocky, fresh, perky,

assy, saucy, smart, tossy **06** adroit,
heeky, cocksy, daring, jaunty, lively
7 forward **08** flippant, impudent,
nsolent, spirited **09** sprightly
1 flourishing, impertinent,
nconcealed **12** presumptuous
3 objectionable

ertain
4 long **05** apply, befit, refer **06** bear
n, belong, regard, relate **07** concern
8 be part of **09** appertain, come
nder **10** be relevant **13** be appropriate
4 have a bearing on

ertinacious
5 stiff **06** dogged, mulish, wilful
8 obdurate, perverse, resolute,
tubborn **09** obstinate, tenacious
0 determined, headstrong, inflexible,
ersistent, purposeful, relentless, self-
villed, unyielding **11** intractable,
ersevering **12** strong-willed
3 inquisitorial **14** uncompromising

ertinent
3 apt **05** ad rem **07** apropos, fitting,
germane, related **08** apposite,
naterial, relating, relevant, suitable
0 applicable, to the point
1 appropriate

ertness
4 face, sass **05** brass, cheek
8 audacity, boldness, chutzpah,
udeness **09** brashness, cockiness,
reshness, impudence, insolence,
assiness, sauciness **10** brazenness,
heekiness, effrontery **11** forwardness,
resumption **12** impertinence

erturb
◇ *anagram indicator*
3 vex **04** faze **05** alarm, feese,
eeze, phase, phese, upset, worry
6 aerate, bother, didder, dither,
heese, pheeze, rattle, ruffle
7 agitate, confuse, disturb, fluster,
rouble **08** disquiet, unsettle
0 discompose, disconcert **11** make
nxious **12** put the wind up

erturbation
4 faze, fear, flap **05** alarm, panic,
care, shock, worry **06** didder, dismay,
dither, fright, horror, terror **07** anxiety
8 disquiet, distress **10** uneasiness
1 nervousness, trepidation
2 apprehension, irregularity
3 consternation

erturbed
◇ *anagram indicator*
5 upset **06** shaken, uneasy
7 alarmed, anxious, fearful, nervous,
worried **08** agitated, flurried,
narassed, restless, troubled
9 disturbed, flustered, unsettled
1 discomposed **12** disconcerted
3 uncomfortable

Peru
2 PE **03** PER

perusal
4 look, read, skim **05** check, sight,
study **06** browse, glance **07** reading

08 scrutiny **10** inspection, run-through
11 examination

peruse
04 read, scan, skim **05** check, study
06 browse, revise **07** examine, inspect
08 pore over **10** run through, scrutinize
11 leaf through, look through **13** glance
through

pervade
04 fill **05** imbue **06** affect, charge,
infuse **07** diffuse, suffuse **08** permeate,
saturate **09** penetrate, percolate
10 impregnate, infiltrate **11** pass
through **13** spread through
14 interpenetrate

pervasive
04 rife **06** common **07** diffuse, general
08 immanent **09** extensive, prevalent,
universal **10** ubiquitous, widespread
11 inescapable, omnipresent

perverse
◇ *anagram indicator*
03 wry **05** balky **06** cussed, donsie,
thrawn, thwart, unruly, wilful
07 adverse, awkward, bolshie,
crabbed, deviant, froward, peevish,
stroppy, wayward **08** alarming,
contrary, improper, obdurate,
stubborn, worrying **09** camstairy,
camsteary, difficult, incorrect,
obstinate, pig-headed, senseless,
unhelpful **10** camsteerie, headstrong,
overthwart, rebellious, refractary,
refractory, unyielding **11** disobedient,
ill-tempered, intractable, obstructive,
troublesome, wrong-headed
12 bloody-minded, cantankerous,
cross-grained, intransigent,
unmanageable, unreasonable
13 unco-operative **14** uncontrollable

perversely
◇ *anagram indicator*
04 awry **09** waywardly **10** alarmingly,
stubbornly, worryingly **11** obstinately,
thwartingly, unhelpfully **12** cross-
grained **13** obstructively **15** unco-
operatively

perversion
◇ *anagram indicator*
04 vice **06** misuse **08** deviance,
travesty, twisting **09** depravity,
deviation, kinkiness **10** aberration,
corruption, debauchery, distortion,
immorality, paraphilia, subversion,
wickedness **11** abnormality
12 irregularity **13** exhibitionism,
falsification **14** misapplication

perversity
◇ *anagram indicator*
03 gee **08** obduracy **09** adversity,
contumacy, obstinacy **10** cussedness,
protervity, unruliness, wilfulness
11 awkwardness, frowardness,
gallowsness, waywardness
12 contrariness, disobedience,
stubbornness **13** intransigence,
senselessness **14** rebelliousness,
refractoriness **15** troublesomeness,
wrong-headedness

pervert
◇ *anagram indicator*
03 wry **04** perv, turn, vert, warp
05 abuse, avert, sicko, twist, wrest
06 debase, divert, garble, misuse,
weirdo **07** corrupt, debauch, deflect,
degrade, deprave, deviant, deviate,
distort, falsify, oddball, subvert, vitiate
08 misapply **09** debauchee, misdirect,
turn aside **10** degenerate, lead astray
11 misconstrue, prevaricate
12 misinterpret, misrepresent

perverted
◇ *anagram indicator*
04 evil **05** kinky, pervy, sicko
06 warped, wicked **07** corrupt,
debased, deviant, immoral, twisted
08 abnormal, depraved, vitiated
09 corrupted, debauched, distorted,
unhealthy, unnatural

pesky
06 thorny, trying, vexing **07** galling,
grating, irksome, nagging **08** annoying,
infernal, tiresome **09** maddening,
provoking, upsetting, vexatious,
worrisome **10** bothersome, confounded,
disturbing, irritating **11** aggravating,
displeasing, infuriating, troublesome

pessimism
05 gloom **07** despair **08** cynicism,
distrust, fatalism, glumness
09 defeatism, dejection, doomwatch
10 depression, gloominess,
melancholy **11** despondency,
Weltschmerz **12** hopelessness

pessimist
05 cynic **07** doubter, killjoy, no-hoper,
worrier **08** alarmist, doomsman,
doomster, fatalist **09** defeatist, saturnist
10 wet blanket **11** crapehanger,
crepehanger, dismal Jimmy,
doomwatcher, gloom-monger,
melancholic **12** doom merchant
13 prophet of doom **14** doubting
Thomas

pessimistic
04 glum **05** bleak, doomy **06** dismal,
gloomy, morose, negate **07** cynical
08 alarmist, dejected, doubting,
hopeless, negative, resigned
09 defeatist, depressed **10** depressing,
despairing, despondent, fatalistic,
melancholy, off-putting, suspicious
11 distrustful, downhearted
12 discouraging

pest
03 bug, fly, nun **04** bane, frit, pain, pize
05 brize, curse, trial **06** blight, bother,
breese, breeze, capsid, May bug,
plague **07** blister, cane rat, fritfly,
scourge **08** irritant, meal moth, mealy
bug, nuisance, onion fly, vexation,
viticide **09** annoyance, capsid bug,
carrot fly, chinch bug, cornborer, May
beetle, squash bug, stable fly
10 cicadellid, cockchafer, codlin moth,
fowl-plague, house mouse, irritation,
spider mite **11** codling moth,
spermophile **13** jointed cactus, pain in
the neck, red spider mite **14** American

blight, Colorado beetle, Japanese beetle **15** thorn in the flesh

pester
03 bug, dun, irk, nag **04** clog, fret **05** annoy, chevy, chivy, devil, get at, hound, worry **06** badger, bother, chivvy, earwig, harass, hassle, huddle, infest, mither, moider, pick on, plague **07** besiege, disturb, moither, provoke, torment **08** doorstep, irritate **09** annoyance, beleaguer **12** rhyme to death **14** drive up the wall

pestilence
04 lues **06** plague **07** cholera, disease, murrain **08** epidemic, pandemic, sickness **09** contagion, infection **11** infestation

pestilent
06 deadly, vexing **07** harmful, irksome, ruinous **08** annoying, catching, diseased, infected, tiresome **09** poisonous, vexatious **10** bothersome, contagious, corrupting, infectious, irritating, pernicious **11** deleterious, destructive, detrimental, infuriating, mischievous, troublesome **12** communicable, contaminated, plague-ridden **13** disease-ridden

pestilential
06 vexing **07** baneful, harmful, irksome, ruinous **08** annoying, diseased, infected, tiresome **09** pestering, poisonous **10** bothersome, contagious, detestable, infectious, irritating, pernicious **11** destructive, infuriating, troublesome **12** contaminated, plague-ridden **13** disease-ridden

pet
04 cade, chou, coax, daut, dawt, dear, huff, hump, idol, kiss, neck, snog, stew, sulk, tame, tiff, tift, tout, towt **05** jewel, paddy, strop, sulks **06** caress, chosen, cosset, cuddle, dautie, dawtie, fondle, grumps, pamper, pettle, prized, smooch, stroke, temper **07** bad mood, darling, dearest, embrace, indulge, special, subdued, tantrum, the pits, trained **08** canoodle, favoured, fondling, indulged, personal, treasure **09** bad temper, cherished, favourite, preferred **10** manageable, particular **11** blue-eyed boy, teacher's pet **12** blue-eyed girl, domesticated, house-trained **14** apple of your eye

Pets include:

03 cat, cow, dog, pig, rat
04 bird, fish, goat, newt, pony
05 goose, horse, llama, mouse, sheep
06 alpaca, canary, donkey, ferret, gerbil, jerboa, lizard, parrot, rabbit, turtle
07 chicken, hamster
08 chipmunk, cyberpet, goldfish, parakeet, terrapin, tortoise
09 guinea pig, tarantula
10 budgerigar, chinchilla, salamander, virtual pet
11 stick insect

See also **cat**; **dog**; **fish**; **horse**; **rabbit**

peter
03 jar, jug **05** half-g **06** flagon
• **peter out**
03 ebb **04** fade, fail, stop, wane **05** cease **06** go cold **07** die away, dwindle **08** diminish, taper off **09** evaporate, fizzle out **11** come to an end **13** come to nothing

petite
05 bijou, dinky, small **06** dainty, little, slight **08** delicate

petition
03 ask, beg, bid, sue **04** boon, plea, pray, suit, urge **05** axiom, crave, plead, press **06** adjure, appeal, prayer **07** beseech, entreat, implore, protest, request, solicit **08** call upon, entreaty **09** postulate, supplicat **10** invocation, round robin, supplicate **11** application, deprecation, memorialize **12** solicitation, supplication **14** representation

pet name
03 mog, nan **04** nana **05** bunny, moggy, nanna, nanny **06** moggie **08** nickname **10** diminutive, endearment, hypocorism **11** hypocorisma

petrel
05 ariel, nelly, prion **06** fulmar **07** pintado, stinker **09** stormbird **10** Cape pigeon, sea swallow **11** Procellaria

petrified
04 numb **05** dazed **06** aghast, frozen **07** shocked, stunned **08** appalled, benumbed **09** horrified, stupefied, terrified **10** speechless, transfixed **11** dumbfounded, in a blue funk, scared stiff **13** having kittens, scared to death **14** horror-stricken, terror-stricken

petrify
04 numb, stun **05** alarm, appal, panic, spook **06** boggle, ossify, rattle **07** horrify, stupefy, terrify **08** frighten, paralyse **09** dumbfound, fossilize **11** turn to stone **12** put the wind up

petrol
03 gas, LRP **05** ethyl, juice, super **08** gasolene, gasoline
See also **fuel**

petticoat
04 coat, slip **05** jupon, woman **06** female, kirtle **07** placket **08** balmoral, basquine, feminine **09** crinoline, wyliecoat **10** underskirt

pettifogging
04 mean **05** petty **06** paltry, subtle **07** trivial **08** captious, niggling **09** casuistic, cavilling, quibbling **10** nit-picking **11** over-refined, sophistical **12** equivocating **13** hair-splitting

pettiness
08 meanness **09** quibbling **10** nit-picking **12** spitefulness **15** small-mindedness

pettish
05 cross, dorty, huffy, sulky **06** grumpy, tetchy, touchy **07** fretful, peevish, waspish **08** petulant, snappish **09** fractious, irritable, querulous, splenetic **11** bad-tempered, ill-humoured, thin-skinned

petty
04 mean **05** minor, petit, potty, small **06** grotty, lesser, little, measly, paltry, poking, puisne, puisny, slight **07** pimping, scantle, trivial **08** grudging, niggling, picayune, piddling, piffling, spiteful, trifling **09** parochial, quibbling, scantling, secondary, small-town **10** negligible, nit-picking, parish-pump, shoestring, ungenerous **11** in a small way, inessential, small-minded, unimportant **12** contemptible, narrow-minded **13** insignificant **14** inconsiderable **15** inconsequential

petulance
05 pique **06** spleen **09** bad temper, ill-humour, ill-temper, procacity, sulkiness **10** crabbiness, sullenness **11** crabbedness, peevishness, waspishness **12** irritability **13** querulousness

petulant
04 sour **05** cross, mardy, moody, ratty, sulky **06** crabby, sullen, touchy, toutie, wanton **07** crabbed, forward, fretful, in a stew, peevish **08** in a paddy, snappish **09** crotchety, impatient, irritable, querulous **10** browned off, humoursome, lascivious, ungracious **11** bad-tempered, complaining, ill-humoured

pew
03 box **04** seat **05** stall **08** horse box

phalanger
04 tait **06** cuscus, glider, possum **07** opossum **08** Tarsipes **09** petaurist **10** honey-mouse **11** honey possum **14** flying squirrel, vulpine opossum

phantasmagorical
06 unreal **07** surreal **08** ethereal, illusory **09** dreamlike, fantastic, visionary **10** chimerical, trance-like **13** hallucinatory, insubstantial, unsubstantial **14** phantasmagoric

phantom
04 idol **05** ghost, spook **06** fantom, spirit, unreal, vision, wraith **07** eidolon, feature, figment, specter, spectre **08** illusion, illusory, revenant, spectral **09** imaginary **10** apparition, Scotch mist **12** Pepper's ghost **13** hallucination

pharaoh
04 faro **11** river-dragon

Pharaohs include:

07 Rameses
08 Thutmose
09 Akhenaten
10 Hatshepsut
11 Tut'ankhamun

pharisaical
6 formal 07 preachy 09 insincere, pietistic 10 goody-goody, moralizing 2 hypocritical 13 sanctimonious, self-righteous 14 holier-than-thou

pharisee
5 fraud 06 humbug, phoney 7 pietist 09 formalist, hypocrite 0 dissembler 12 dissimulator 5 whited sepulchre

phase
4 beat, faze, form, part, step, time 5 drive, morph, point, shape, spell, stage, state, worry 06 aspect, period, season 07 chapter, perturb 8 juncture, position, unsettle 9 condition 11 development
• **phase in**
5 start 06 ease in 07 bring in 8 initiate 09 introduce 10 start using
• **phase out**
4 stop 05 close 06 remove, wind up 7 ease off, run down 08 get rid of, taper off, wind down, withdraw 9 dispose of, eliminate, stop using, terminate

pheasant
5 argus, monal 06 coucal, monaul 8 fireback, lyrebird, tragopan 9 francolin
• **brood of pheasants**
3 eye, nid, nye 04 nide

phenomenal
6 unique 07 amazing, unusual 8 singular 09 fantastic, unheard of, wonderful 10 astounding, incredible, marvellous, remarkable, stupendous 1 astonishing, exceptional, mind-blowing, sensational 12 breathtaking, mind-boggling, unbelievable, unparalleled 13 extraordinary, unprecedented 15 too good to be true

phenomenally
9 amazingly 10 incredibly, remarkably 11 wonderfully 2 astoundingly, marvellously, unbelievably 13 astonishingly, exceptionally, sensationally 5 extraordinarily

phenomenon
4 fact 05 event, sight 06 marvel, phenom, rarity, wonder 07 episode, miracle, prodigy 08 incident 9 curiosity, happening, sensation, spectacle 10 appearance, experience, occurrence 12 circumstance

philander
5 dally, flirt, lover 08 womanize 0 fool around, play around 11 sleep around 12 have an affair, philandering, play the field

philanderer
4 rake, roué, stud, wolf 05 flirt 7 dallier, Don Juan, playboy 8 Casanova 09 ladies' man, libertine, womanizer 10 lady-killer

philanthropic
4 kind 06 humane 07 liberal

08 generous, selfless 09 bounteous, bountiful, unselfish 10 alms-giving, altruistic, benevolent, charitable, munificent, open-handed 11 kind-hearted 12 humanitarian 14 public-spirited

philanthropist
05 donor, giver 06 backer, helper, patron 07 sponsor 08 altruist 09 almsgiver 10 benefactor 11 contributor 12 humanitarian

philanthropy
04 help 06 giving 07 backing, charity 08 altruism, kindness 09 patronage 10 alms-giving, generosity, liberality 11 beneficence, benevolence, munificence, sponsorship 12 selflessness 13 bounteousness, bountifulness, social concern, unselfishness 14 open-handedness 15 humanitarianism, kind-heartedness, social awareness

Philip
04 Phil

philippic
05 abuse 06 attack, insult, rebuke, tirade 07 reproof 08 diatribe, harangue, reviling 09 criticism, invective, onslaught, reprimand 10 upbraiding 12 denunciation, vituperation

Philippines
02 RP 03 PHL

philistine
04 boor, lout 05 crass, enemy, yahoo 06 gigman, unread 07 bailiff, boorish, lowbrow 08 ignorant 09 barbarian, bourgeois, ignoramus, tasteless, unrefined, vulgarian 10 uncultured, uneducated, unlettered 12 uncultivated

Phillip
04 Phil

philologer *see* **lexicographer**

philosopher
04 guru, sage 06 expert 07 scholar, thinker 08 academic, analyser, logician, theorist 09 theorizer 12 dialectician 13 deipnosophist, metaphysician, philosophizer 14 epistemologist

Philosophers include:

04 Ayer (Sir A J), Hume (David), Joad (C E M), Kant (Immanuel), Mach (Ernst), Marx (Karl), Mill (James), Mill (John Stuart), More (Henry), Otto (Rudolf), Ryle (Gilbert), Vico (Giambattista), Weil (Simone)
05 Bacon (Francis), Bacon (Roger), Bayle (Pierre), Benda (Julien), Bodin (Jean), Broad (Charlie Dunbar), Bruno (Giordano), Buber (Martin), Burke (Edmund), Comte (Auguste), Croce (Benedetto), Dewey (John), Dunne (John William), Frege (Gottlob), Gödel (Kurt), Hegel (Georg Wilhelm Friedrich), Hulme

(T E), James (William), Locke (John), Moore (George Edward), Occam (William of), Plato, Smith (Adam), Vivés (Juan Luis)
06 Adorno (Theodor), Anselm (St), Berlin (Sir Isaiah), Bonnet (Charles), Carnap (Rudolf), Celsus, Engels (Friedrich), Fichte (Johann Gottlieb), Goedel (Kurt), Herder (Johann Gottfried von), Hobbes (Thomas), Langer (Suzanne Knauth), Lukács (Georg), Ockham (William of), Palach (Jan), Popper (Sir Karl), Pyrrho, Sartre (Jean-Paul), Strato, Thales
07 Aquinas (St Thomas), Bentham (Jeremy), Buridan (Jean), Derrida (Jacques), Diderot (Denis), Dilthey (Wilhelm), Edwards (Jonathan), Erasmus (Desiderius), Gentile (Giovanni), Gorgias, Haldane (Richard, Viscount), Husserl (Edmund), Hypatia, Jaspers (Karl), Leibniz (Gottfried Wilhelm), Marcuse (Herbert), Mencius, Proclus, Russell (Bertrand, Earl), Sankara, Schlick (Moritz), Spencer (Herbert), Spinoza (Baruch), Steiner (Rudolf), Tillich (Paul)
08 Alcmaeon, Alembert (Jean le Rond d'), Averroës, Avicenna, Beauvoir (Simone de), Berkeley (Bishop George), Boethius (Anicius Manlius Severinus), Buchanan (George), Cassirer (Ernst), Cudworth (Ralph), Epicurus, Foucault (Michel), Habermas (Jürgen), Hamilton (Sir William), Hobhouse (Leonard), Longinus (Dionysius), Plotinus, Porphyry, Ram Singh, Rousseau (Jean Jacques), Sidgwick (Henry), Socrates, Spengler (Oswald)
09 Althusser (Louis), Aristotle, Avicebrón, Bronowski (Jacob), Condorcet (Marie-Jean-Antoine-Nicolas de Caritat, Marquis de), Confucius, Descartes (René), Feuerbach (Ludwig), Heidegger (Martin), Nietzsche (Friedrich), Plekhanov (Giorgiy), Santayana (George), Schelling (Friedrich), Whitehead (Alfred North)
10 Anaxagoras, Aristippus, Democritus, Duns Scotus (John), Empedocles, Heraclitus, Horkheimer (Max), Maimonides (Moses), Parmenides, Posidonius, Protagoras, Pythagoras, Schweitzer (Albert), Xenocrates, Xenophanes, Zeno of Elea
11 Anaximander, Kierkegaard (Sören), Montesquieu (Charles-Louis, Baron de), Reichenbach (Hans), Shaftesbury (Anthony Ashley Cooper, Earl of), Vivekananda
12 Merleau-Ponty (Maurice), Philo Judaeus, Schopenhauer (Arthur), Theophrastus, Wittgenstein (Ludwig), Zeno of Citium
14 Albertus Magnus (St), Schleiermacher (Friedrich)
15 William of Ockham

philosophical
04 calm, cool, wise **05** stoic **06** placid, serene **07** erudite, learned, logical, patient, pensive, stoical **08** abstract, composed, rational, resigned **09** collected, impassive, realistic, unruffled **10** analytical, meditative, phlegmatic, reflective, thoughtful **11** theoretical, unemotional, unflappable **12** metaphysical **13** contemplative, dispassionate, imperturbable, self-possessed
See also **philosophy**

philosophically
06 calmly **08** placidly **09** logically, patiently, stoically **10** abstractly, resignedly **11** impassively, unflappably **12** analytically **13** theoretically, unemotionally **14** metaphysically

philosophy
04 view **06** reason, tenets, values, wisdom **07** beliefs, thought **08** attitude, doctrine, ideology, stoicism, thinking **09** knowledge, reasoning, viewpoint, world-view **10** principles **11** convictions, point of view

Branches of philosophy include:
03 est, law
04 mind, yoga
05 logic, moral
06 ethics
07 biology, eastern, history, Sankhya, science, Vedanta
08 axiology, language, medicine, ontology, politics, religion
09 bioethics, economics, education, semiotics
10 aesthetics, literature, psychology
11 informatics, mathematics, metaphysics
12 epistemology
13 applied ethics, jurisprudence, phenomenology

Philosophical schools, doctrines and theories include:
05 deism
06 egoism, monism, Taoism, theism
07 atheism, atomism, dualism, fideism, Marxism, realism, Thomism
08 altruism, ascetism, cynicism, fatalism, feminism, hedonism, humanism, idealism, nihilism, Stoicism
09 dogmatism, pantheism, Platonism, pluralism, solipsism
10 absolutism, Eleaticism, empiricism, gnosticism, Kantianism, naturalism, nominalism, positivism, pragmatism, Pyrrhonism, relativism, scepticism
11 agnosticism, determinism, Hegelianism, historicism, materialism, objectivism, rationalism, Sankhya-Yoga
12 behaviourism, Cartesianism, Confucianism, Epicureanism, essentialism, Neoplatonism, reductionism, subjectivism
13 antinomianism, conceptualism,

descriptivism, immaterialism, neo-Kantianism, occasionalism, phenomenalism, scholasticism, structuralism
14 existentialism, interactionism, intuitionalism, libertarianism, Nyaya-Vaisesika, prescriptivism, Pythagoreanism, sensationalism, utilitarianism, Vedanta-Mimamsa
15 Aristotelianism, experimentalism, Frankfurt School, instrumentalism

Philosophy terms include:
05 deism, logic, moral
06 egoism, ethics, monism, theism
07 a priori, atheism, atomism, dualism, falsafa, Marxism, realism
08 altruism, ascetism, axiology, cynicism, fatalism, feminism, hedonism, humanism, idealism, identity, nihilism, ontology, stoicism
09 deduction, dogmatism, induction, intuition, pantheism, Platonism, pluralism, sense data, solipsism, substance, syllogism, teleology
10 absolutism, aesthetics, deontology, empiricism, entailment, gnosticism, Kantianism, naturalism, nominalism, positivism, pragmatism, relativism, scepticism
11 agnosticism, a posteriori, determinism, historicism, materialism, metaphysics, objectivism, rationalism
12 behaviourism, Confucianism, Epicureanism, epistemology, Neoplatonism, reductionism, subjectivism
13 antinomianism, conceptualism, immaterialism, jurisprudence, neo-Kantianism, phenomenalism, phenomenology, scholasticism, structuralism
14 existentialism, interactionism, intuitionalism, libertarianism, prescriptivism, sensationalism, utilitarianism
15 Aristotelianism, experimentalism, instrumentalism

phlegmatic
04 calm, cool **06** placid, stolid **07** stoical **08** tranquil **09** impassive, saturnine **11** indifferent, unconcerned, unemotional, unflappable **12** matter-of-fact **13** dispassionate, imperturbable **14** self-controlled

phobia
04 fear **05** dread, thing **06** hang-up, hatred, horror, terror **07** anxiety, dislike **08** aversion, loathing, neurosis **09** antipathy, obsession, repulsion, revulsion **11** detestation **14** irrational fear

Phobias include:
09 apiphobia, neophobia, panphobia, zoophobia
10 acrophobia, algophobia, aquaphobia, autophobia, canophobia, cynophobia,

demophobia, hodophobia, musophobia, nosophobia, pyrophobia, toxiphobia, xenophobia
11 agoraphobia, astraphobia, cnidophobia, cyberphobia, gymnophobia, hippophobia, hydrophobia, hypnophobia, necrophobia, nyctophobia, ophiophobia, photophobia, scotophobia, tachophobia, taphephobia
12 achluophobia, ailurophobia, belonephobia, brontophobia, entomophobia, phasmophobia, technophobia
13 arachnophobia, arithmophobia, bacillophobia, herpetophobia
14 anthropophobia, bacteriophobia, claustrophobia, ereuthrophobia, thalassophobia

Phoebus
03 Sol, sun **05** Titan **06** Apollo, Helio

phoenix
03 fum **04** fung, huma **07** paragon **12** bird of wonder

phone
04 bell, buzz, call, dial, ring **06** blowe call up, mobile, ring up, tinkle **07** contact, handset **08** car phone, receiver **09** cell phone, give a bell, giv a buzz, make a call, phone call, telephone **10** dog and bone, get in touch **11** give a tinkle, mobile phone **13** cordless phone

phonetic alphabet *see* **alphabet**

phoney
◇ *anagram indicator*
04 fake, mock, sham **05** bogus, faker, false, fraud, hokey, pseud, put-on, quack, trick **06** ersatz, forged, humbug, pseudo, unreal **07** assumed feigned, forgery **08** affected, imposto spurious **09** contrived, imitation, pretender, simulated **10** fraudulent, mountebank **11** counterfeit, pretentious

phosphorescent
06 bright **07** glowing, radiant **08** luminous **09** refulgent **11** luminescent, noctilucent, noctilucous

phosphorus
01 P

photocopy
04 copy **05** print, Xerox® **06** run off **09** duplicate, facsimile, Photostat®

photograph
03 pic, pin **04** film, shot, snap, take, X ray **05** image, Kodak®, panel, photo, piccy, print, sepia, shoot, slide, still, video **06** blow up, blow-up, record, retake **07** close-up, enlarge, montage mug shot, picture **08** abstract, exposure, headshot, hologram, likeness, microdot, portrait, seascape skiagram, snapshot, sun print **09** angiogram, ferrotype, karyotype,

landscape, mammogram, microgram, nephogram, photogene, photogram, radiogram, rotograph, skiagraph, visual aid, wirephoto **10** centrefold, chromatype, ferro-print, micrograph, radiograph, sun picture **11** composition, enlargement, heliochrome, platinotype, spectrogram **12** cathodograph, röntgenogram, transparency **13** capture on film, chlorobromide, daguerreotype, encephalogram **14** pyrophotograph, take a picture of **15** microphotograph, take a snapshot of

photographer
07 snapper **09** cameraman, paparazzo **11** camerawoman **14** camera operator

Photographers include:
03 Ray (Man)
04 Capa (Robert), Hill (David Octavius), Penn (Irving)
05 Adams (Ansel), Arbus (Diane), Hardy (Bert), Karsh (Yousuf), Lange (Dorothea), Ritts (Herb), Smith (W Eugene)
06 Arnold (Eve), Avedon (Richard), Bailey (David), Beaton (Sir Cecil), Brandt (Bill), Godwin (Fay), McBean (Angus), Miller (Lee), Newton (Helmut), Niepce (Joseph Nicéphore), Rankin, Talbot (William Henry Fox), Warhol (Andy)
07 Brassaï, Cameron (Julia Margaret), Carroll (Lewis), Dodgson (Charles Lutwidge), Eastman (George), Lumière (Auguste), McCurry (Steve), Salgado (Sebastião), Siskind (Aaron), Snowdon (Antony Armstrong-Jones, Earl of), Waddell (Rankin)
08 Daguerre (Louis), McCullin (Don), Sielmann (Heinz), Steichen (Edward)
09 Leibovitz (Annie), Lichfield (Patrick, Earl of), Muybridge (Eadweard James), Rodchenko (Alexander), Rosenblum (Walter), Stieglitz (Alfred), Winogrand (Garry)
10 Moholy-Nagy (László)
11 Bourke-White (Margaret), Wakabayashi (Yasuhiro)
12 Friese-Greene (William)
13 Ducos du Hauron (Louis)
14 Armstrong-Jones (Antony), Cartier-Bresson (Henri)

photographic
05 exact, vivid **06** filmic, minute, visual **07** graphic, natural, precise **08** accurate, detailed, faithful, lifelike **09** cinematic, pictorial, realistic, retentive **12** naturalistic

Photographic equipment includes:
06 camera, tripod, viewer
08 enlarger, light-box, stop bath
09 camcorder, safelight
10 fixing bath, paper drier, Vertoscope®
11 print washer, slide viewer
13 developer bath, enlarger timer, film projector, flash umbrella
14 contact printer, developing tank, focus magnifier, slide projector
15 negative carrier, print-drying rack

Photographic accessories include:
04 film, lens
06 eye-cup, filter
07 battery, hot shoe, lens cap
08 diffuser, disc film, flashgun, lens hood, zoom lens
09 camera bag, flashbulb, flash card, flashcube, flash unit, macro lens, polarizer, spot meter
10 afocal lens, lens shield, light meter, memory card, slide mount, video light, video mixer, viewfinder
11 close-up lens, fish-eye lens, sepia filter, video editor
12 cable release, colour filter, memory reader
13 auxiliary lens, cartridge film, exposure meter, remote control, teleconverter, telephoto lens, wide-angle lens

Photostat®
04 copy **05** print, Xerox® **06** run off **09** duplicate, facsimile, photocopy

phrase
03 phr, put, say **04** cant, hook, riff, word **05** couch, frame, idiom, style, usage, utter **06** clause, cliché, mantra, remark, saying **07** comment, express, flatter, formula, mantram, present, wheedle **08** laconism, language, locution **09** catchword, formulate, pronounce, utterance **10** expression, laconicism, mondegreen **11** phraseology **12** construction, group of words, put into words **13** way of speaking **15** style of speaking

phraseology
04 cant **05** argot, idiom, style **06** patois, phrase, speech, syntax **07** diction, wording, writing **08** language, parlance, phrasing **10** expression **11** terminology

phrasing
05 idiom, style, words **07** diction, wordage, wording **08** language, verbiage **10** expression **11** phraseology, terminology **13** choice of words

physical
04 real **05** brute, solid **06** actual, bodily, carnal, fleshy, mortal **07** earthly, fleshly, medical, somatic, spatial, visible **08** concrete, material, palpable, tangible **09** corporeal, incarnate, medicinal, wholesome **11** substantial, unspiritual **13** materialistic

physically
06 bodily, really **07** visibly **08** actually, animally, tangibly **10** concretely, in your body, materially **13** substantially **15** physiologically

physician
02 GP **03** doc **05** hakim, leech, medic, Paean, quack **06** doctor, healer, intern, medico **08** external, houseman, medicine **09** internist, mediciner, registrar **10** consultant, medicaster, specialist **11** physicianer **12** school doctor

See also **doctor**

physics

Physics terms include:
03 gas, GUT, ion, law, QCD, QED, TOE
04 area, atom, barn, flux, gate, heat, lens, mass, node, rule, spin, wave, WIMP, work, X-ray
05 chaos, fermi, field, focus, force, laser, lever, light, phase, power, quark, ratio, sound, speed, SQUID, state
06 atomic, charge, couple, energy, engine, liquid, mirror, moment, motion, optics, phonon, photon, proton, scalar, SI unit, string, theory, volume, weight
07 circuit, density, digital, entropy, formula, gravity, inertia, neutron, nuclear, nucleus, orbital, process, statics, tension
08 alpha ray, dynamics, electron, equation, friction, gamma ray, half-life, harmonic, infrared, molecule, momentum, neutrino, particle, polarity, pressure, rest mass, spectrum, velocity
09 acoustics, amplitude, black body, cosmology, dimension, frequency, induction, magnetism, mechanics, Mohs scale, potential, principle, radiation, radio wave, resonance, sound wave, subatomic, substance, vibration, viscosity, white heat
10 efficiency, elasticity, flash point, gauge boson, heavy water, Higgs boson, hydraulics, latent heat, Mach number, microwaves, reflection, refraction, relativity, resistance, separation, shear force, ultrasound, wavelength
11 diffraction, electricity, equilibrium, evaporation, light source, oscillation, periodic law, sensitivity, temperature, ultraviolet
12 absolute zero, acceleration, boiling point, centre of mass, critical mass, hydrostatics, interference, Kelvin effect, laws of motion, luminescence, radioisotope, spectroscopy, speed of light, standing wave, string theory, time dilation, wave property
13 Appleton layer, beta particles, Big Bang theory, bubble-chamber, chain reaction, freezing point, hydrodynamics, incandescence, kinetic energy, kinetic theory, light emission, magnetic field, nuclear fusion, optical centre, quantum theory, radioactivity, semiconductor, supersymmetry, Thomson effect
14 alpha particles, analogue signal,

applied physics, circuit-breaker, Coriolis effect, light intensity, nuclear fission, nuclear physics, parallel motion, states of matter, superconductor, surface tension, thermodynamics, transverse wave
15 angular momentum, capillary action, centre of gravity, charged particle, electric current, electrodynamics, Fourier analysis, moment of inertia, perpetual motion, potential energy, specific gravity, visible spectrum

02 Wu (Chien-Shiung)
03 Lee (Tsung-Dao), Ohm (Georg Simon)
04 Abbe (Ernst), Biot (Jean-Baptiste), Bohr (Niels), Born (Max), Bose (Satyendra Nath), Dick (Robert Henry), Gray (Stephen), Haüy (René Just), Hess (Victor Francis), Katz (Sir Bernard), Kerr (John), Land (Edwin Herbert), Laue (Max Theodor Felix von), Lenz (Heinrich Friedrich Emil), Mach (Ernst), Mott (Sir Nevill Francis), Néel (Louis Eugène Félix), Rabi (Isidor Isaac), Saha (Meghnad),Ting (Samuel Chao Chung),Wien (Wilhelm),Yang (Chen Ning)
05 Aston (Francis William), Auger (Pierre Victor), Bethe (Hans Albrecht), Bloch (Felix), Bondi (Sir Hermann), Boyle (Robert), Bragg (Sir Lawrence), Bragg (Sir William Henry), Braun (Ferdinand), Curie (Marie), Curie (Pierre), Debye (Peter), Dewar (Sir James), Dirac (P A M), Dyson (Freeman), Esaki (Leo), Fermi (Enrico), Fuchs (Klaus), Gabor (Dennis), Gamow (George), Gauss (Carl Friedrich), Gibbs (Josiah Willard), Grove (Sir William Robert), Henry (Joseph), Hertz (Heinrich Rudolf), Higgs (Peter), Hooke (Robert), Jeans (Sir James Hopwood), Joule (James Prescott), Milne (Edward Arthur), Pauli (Wolfgang), Raman (Sir Chandrasekhara Venkata), Rossi (Bruno), Salam (Abdus), Segrè (Emilio), Stern (Otto),Tesla (Nikola), Vleck (John Hasbrouck van),Volta (Alessandro Giuseppe Anastasio, Count),Waals (Johannes van der), Young (Thomas)
06 Ampère (André Marie), Bunsen (Robert Wilhelm), Carnot (Sadi), Dalton (John), Edison (Thomas Alva), Frisch (Otto Robert), Geiger (Hans Wilhelm), Glaser (Donald Arthur), Huxley (Hugh Esmor), Kelvin (William Thomson, Lord), Lorenz (Ludwig Valentin), Newton (Sir Isaac), Pascal (Blaise), Planck (Max), Rohrer (Heinrich), Stokes (Sir George Gabriel),Taylor (Sir Geoffrey Ingram),Teller (Edward), Wigner (Eugene Paul),Wilson (Robert), Zwicky (Fritz)

07 Alferov (Zhores I), Alvarez (Luis Walter), Bednorz (Georg), Broglie (Louis-Victor Pierre Raymond de), Charles (Jacques), Compton (Arthur Holly), Coulomb (Charles Augustin de), Doppler (Christian Johann), Eastman (George), Faraday (Michael), Feynman (Richard Phillips), Fresnel (Augustin Jean), Galilei (Galileo), Galileo, Glashow (Sheldon Lee), Goddard (Robert Hutchings), Hawking (Stephen), Huygens (Christiaan), Langley (Samuel Pierpont), Lorentz (Hendrik Antoon), Marconi (Guglielmo, Marchese), Maxwell (James Clerk), Meitner (Lise), Oersted (Hans Christian), Peierls (Sir Rudolf Ernst), Penzias (Arno Allan), Poisson (Siméon Denis), Réaumur (René Antoine Ferchault de), Richter (Burton), Röntgen (Wilhelm Konrad von), Rotblat (Sir Joseph), Seaborg (GlenTheodore), Szilard (Leo),Thomson (Sir J J), Vernier (Pierre)
08 Ångström (Anders Jonas), Appleton (Sir Edward Victor), Avogadro (Amedeo), Beaufort (Sir Francis), Chadwick (Sir James), Clausius (Rudolf), De Forest (Lee), Delbrück (Max), Einstein (Albert), Foucault (Jean Bernard Léon), Gell-Mann (Murray), Langevin (Paul), Lemaître (Georges Henri), Millikan (Robert Andrews), Mulliken (Robert Sanderson), Oliphant (Sir Mark), Regnault (Henri Victor), Sakharov (Andrei), Shockley (William Bradford),Tomonaga (Sin-Itiro), Van Allen (James Alfred), Weinberg (Steven)
09 Aristotle, Bartholin (Erasmus), Becquerel (Antoine Henri), Birkeland (Kristian Olaf Bernhard), Boltzmann (Ludwig), Cavendish (Henry), Cherenkov (Pavel), Cockcroft (Sir John Douglas), Gay-Lussac (Joseph Louis), Heaviside (Oliver), Helmholtz (Hermann von), Michelson (Albert Abraham)
10 Anaximenes, Fahrenheit (Daniel), Heisenberg (Werner Karl), Rutherford (Ernest, Lord),Torricelli (Evangelista),Weizsäcker (Carl Friedrich, Baron von),Wheatstone (Sir Charles), Xenocrates
11 Chamberlain (Owen), Joliot-Curie (Frédéric), Joliot-Curie (Irène), Leeuwenhoek (Antoni van), Oppenheimer (Robert), Schrödinger (Erwin),Tsiolkovsky (Konstantin),Van de Graaff (Robert Jemison)
13 Chandrasekhar (Subrahmanyan)

physiognomy
03 mug **04** dial, face, look, phiz **05** clock **06** aspect, kisser, phizog, visage **07** visnomy **08** features, fisnomie, phisnomy, visnomie **09** character **11** countenance, craniognomy

physiology

04 Best (Charles Herbert), Dale (Sir Henry Hallett), Hess (Walter Rudolf)
05 Hubel (David Hunter), Kühne (Wilhelm), Lower (Richard), Marey (Etienne-Jules), Mayow (John), Prout (William),Yalow (Rosalyn)
06 Adrian (Edgar Douglas, Lord), Bordet (Jules), Cannon (Walter Bradford), Haller (Albrecht von), Huxley (Sir Andrew), Ludwig (Karl), Müller (Johannes Peter), Pavlov (Ivan), Pincus (Gregory Goodwin)
07 Banting (Sir Frederick Grant), Bayliss (Sir William), Beddoes (Thomas Lovell), Bernard (Claude), Borelli (Giovanni Alfonso), Diamond (Jared Mason), Galvani (Luigi), Haldane (John Scott), Helmont (Johannes Baptista van), Hodgkin (Sir Alan Lloyd), Schwann (Theodor)
08 Flourens (Pierre Jean Marie), Magendie (François), Mariotte (Edmé), Meyerhof (Otto Fritz), Purkinje (Jan Evangelista), Starling (Ernest Henry)
09 Blakemore (Colin), Dutrochet (Henri), Einthoven (Willem), Helmholtz (Hermann von)
11 Sherrington (Sir Charles Scott)

physique
04 body, form **05** build, frame, set-up, shape **06** figure, make-up **09** structure **12** constitution

pi
03 pie, pye **05** pious **09** confusion, religious **13** sanctimonious

pianist

02 Ax (Emmanuel)
04 Bush (Alan), Cole (Nat 'King'), Hess (Dame Myra), John (Sir Elton), Lupu (Radu), Monk (Thelonious Sphere), Wild (Earl)
05 Alkan, Arrau (Claudio), Basie (Count), Beach (Mrs H H A), Blake (Eubie), Bolet (Jorge), Borge (Victor), Bülow (Hans), Corea (Chick), Evans (Bill), Evans (Gil), Field (John), Friml (Rudolf), Gould (Glenn), Hallé (Sir Charles), Harty (Sir Hamilton), Henri (Florence), Hines (Earl), Joyce (Eileen), Lewis (Jerry Lee), Liszt (Franz), Nyman (Michael), Ogdon (John Andrew Howard), Szell (George),Tatum (Art),Tovey (Sir Donald),Weber (Carl Maria von)
06 Albert (Eugen d'), Arnaud (Yvonne), Atwell (Winifred), Busoni (Ferruccio), Chopin (Frédéric), Cortot (Alfred), Cramer (Johann), Curzon (Sir Clifford), Czerny (Karl), Domino (Fats), Dussek (Jan), Garner (Errol), Hummel (Johann), Joplin (Scott), Kenton (Stan), Kissin

(Evgeny), **Koppel** (Herman D),
Lamond (Frederic), **Levine** (James),
Martin (Frank), **Morton** (Jelly Roll),
Powell (Bud), **Schiff** (András),
Serkin (Rudolf), **Sitsky** (Larry),
Stoker (Richard),**Taylor** (Cecil),
Tracey (Stan),**Turina** (Joaquín),
Waller (Fats),**Wilson** (Teddy)
07 **Albéniz** (Isaac), **Bennett** (Sir
William), **Bentzon** (Niels), **Brendel**
(Alfred), **Brubeck** (Dave), **Charles**
(Ray), **Goodman** (Isador), **Hancock**
(Herbie), **Ibrahim** (Abdullah),
Johnson (James P), **Kentner** (Louis),
Lipatti (Dinu), **Malcolm** (George),
Mathias (William), **Matthay**
(Tobias), **Medtner** (Nikolai),
Perahia (Murray), **Richter**
(Svyatoslav), **Solomon**, **Sorabji**
(Kaikhosru),**Taneyev** (Sergei),
Vaughan (Sarah)
08 **Argerich** (Martha), **Bronfman**
(Yefim), **Browning** (John), **Clementi**
(Muzio), **Dohnanyi** (Ernst), **Fou
Ts'ong**, **Franklin** (Aretha),
Godowsky (Leopold), **Grainger**
(Percy), **Henschel** (Sir George),
Horowitz (Vladimir), **Leighton**
(Kenneth), **Lhévinne** (Josef),
Pachmann (Vladimir de), **Peterson**
(Oscar), **Richards** (Henry),
Schnabel (Artur), **Schumann**
(Clara), **Scriabin** (Aleksandr),
Skriabin (Aleksandr),**Thalberg**
(Sigismond),**Williams** (Mary Lou)
09 **Ashkenazy** (Vladimir), **Barenboim**
(Daniel), **Bernstein** (Leonard),
Butterley (Nigel), **Ellington** (Duke),
Gieseking (Walter), **Henderson**
(Fletcher), **Landowska** (Wanda),
MacDowell (Edward), **Moscheles**
(Ignaz), **Stevenson** (Ronald),
Westbrook (Mike)
10 **de Larrocha** (Alicia), **Gottschalk**
(Louis), **Moszkowski** (Moritz),
Paderewski (Ignacy), **Rubinstein**
(Anton), **Rubinstein** (Artur),
Scharwenka (Xaver)
11 **Farren-Price** (Ronald), **Mitropoulos**
(Dimitri), **Reizenstein** (Franz)
12 **Michelangeli** (Arturo),
Moiseiwitsch (Benno),
Shostakovich (Maxim)
13 **Little Richard**

piano
01 p **05** grand **06** flügel, joanna
07 upright **08** music box **09** baby
grand, semi-grand **12** boudoir grand,
concert grand

pick
04 best, bite, cull, hack, open, peck,
pull, wale **05** begin, cause, crack,
cream, elect, élite, fix on, go for, pique,
pluck, prize, start **06** choice, choose,
favour, flower, gather, lead to, nibble,
opt for, option, pickle, pilfer, prefer,
prompt, select, take in **07** collect,
harvest, mandrel, mandril, produce,
provoke **08** choicest, decide on,
decision, plectrum, plump for, settle on
09 break open, force open, prise open,

selection, single out **10** give rise to,
preference **14** crème de la crème,
make up your mind
- **pick at**
04 peck **06** nibble **07** toy with **08** play
with
- **pick off**
03 hit **04** kill **05** shoot, snipe
06 detach, fire at, remove, strike
07 gun down, pull off, take out **08** take
away
- **pick on**
03 nag **04** bait **05** blame, bully, get at
06 needle **07** torment **09** criticize,
have a go at, persecute, victimize
13 find fault with
- **pick out**
04 cull, sort, spot **05** fix on, go for
06 choose, favour, notice, opt for,
prefer, select, single **07** discern, make
out **08** decide on, hand-pick, perceive,
separate, settle on **09** recognize, single
out, tell apart **11** distinguish
12 discriminate **14** make up your
mind
- **pick up**
◊ *reversal down indicator*
03 buy, get, nab **04** bust, find, gain, go
on, hear, lift, nick, peck, pull, tong
05 catch, fetch, glean, grasp, hoist,
learn, pinch, raise, rally, run in **06** arrest,
collar, detect, gather, master, obtain,
perk up, resume, take in, take up
07 acquire, call for, carry on, collect,
improve, receive, recover **08** continue,
contract, discover, purchase
09 apprehend, get better, get to know,
give a lift, give a ride **10** begin again,
chance upon, come across, cop off
with, get off with, go down with, start
again **11** make headway **12** make
progress **13** become ill with **15** take
into custody

picket
03 peg **04** pale, pike, post **05** guard,
rebel, spike, stake, watch **06** paling,
patrol, piquet, sentry **07** boycott,
enclose, lookout, outpost, picquet,
protest, striker, upright **08** blockade,
objector, picketer, surround
09 dissident, protester, stanchion
11 demonstrate **12** demonstrator **15** go
on a picket line

pickings
04 loot, take **05** booty, gravy, yield
06 spoils **07** plunder, profits, returns,
rewards **08** earnings, proceeds

pickle
◊ *anagram indicator*
03 fix, jam **04** bind, cure, mess, peck,
pick, salt, spot **05** achar, pinch, sauce,
souse, steep **06** crisis, muddle, pilfer,
plight, relish, scrape **07** chutney,
dilemma, put down, straits, vinegar
08 conserve, cucumber, exigency, hot
water, marinade, preserve, quandary
09 condiment, seasoning, tight spot
10 difficulty, flavouring, piccalilli
11 predicament

pick-me-up
05 boost, tonic **06** fillip **07** cordial

08 roborant, stimulus **09** stimulant
11 refreshment, restorative **12** shot in
the arm

pickpocket
03 dip **04** bung, file, wire **05** diver, thief
06 dipper, nipper **07** whizzer **08** cly-
faker, cutpurse, snatcher **09** pick-purse
11 bagsnatcher

pick-up
02 PU **03** ute, van **04** gain, rise
05 float, lorry, rally, truck, wagon
06 bakkie, growth, reform **07** advance,
headway, upswing, utility **08** increase,
progress, recovery, revision
09 amendment, humbucker,
reception, upgrading **10** betterment,
correction, rectifying **11** development,
enhancement, furtherance,
improvement, modernizing,
reformation **12** amelioration, utility
truck **13** rectification **14** rehabilitation,
utility vehicle

picky
05 faddy, fussy **06** choosy **07** finicky
08 exacting **09** selective **10** fastidious,
particular, pernickety **11** persnickety
14 discriminating

picnic
05 cinch, gipsy, gypsy **06** doddle,
junket, outing **08** clambake, pushover,
tailgate, walkover, waygoose
09 excursion, wasegoose, wayzgoose
10 child's play **11** outdoor meal, piece
of cake **13** a kettle of fish, fête champêtre

pictorial
05 vivid **06** scenic **07** graphic
08 striking **09** schematic
10 expressive, in pictures **11** illustrated,
picturesque **12** diagrammatic **13** in
photographs

picture
03 pic, see **04** draw, film, show, tale
05 flick, movie, paint, story **06** appear,
cinema, depict, flicks, movies, report
07 account, epitome, essence,
imagine, outlook, portray
08 conceive, describe, envisage,
envision, exemplar **09** archetype,
delineate, depiction, multiplex,
narrative, portrayal, represent,
reproduce, semblance, situation,
visualize **10** call to mind, embodiment,
illustrate, impression, similitude
11 delineation, description, film theatre
12 picture-house, quintessence
13 motion picture, picture-palace
15 personification

Pictures include:
04 E-fit®, icon, ikon, snap
05 cameo, image, mural, pin-up, plate,
print, slide, still, study
06 bitmap, canvas, design, doodle,
effigy, fresco, kit-cat, mosaic,
sketch, veduta
07 cartoon, collage, diptych, drawing,
etching, modello, montage,
mugshot, tableau, tracing, vanitas
08 abstract, anaglyph, graffiti,
graphics, kakemono, likeness,

monotype, negative, painting, panorama, Photofit®, portrait, snapshot, tapestry, transfer, triptych, vignette
09 bricolage, engraving, identikit, landscape, miniature, old master, oleograph, still life
10 altarpiece, caricature, photograph, silhouette
11 oil painting, trompe l'oeil, watercolour
12 illustration, photogravure, reproduction, self-portrait, transparency
13 passport photo
14 action painting, cabinet picture, representation

• **get the picture**
03 see **05** get it, grasp **06** follow, take in **07** catch on, latch on **08** cotton on, tumble to **10** comprehend, get the idea, understand **11** get the point **13** get the message
• **put someone in the picture**
04 tell **06** clue up, fill in, inform, notify, update **07** explain **10** keep posted **11** communicate

pictures
03 pix

picturesque
05 vivid **06** lovely, pretty, quaint, scenic, vulgar **07** graphic, idyllic **08** charming, pleasant, pleasing, romantic, striking **09** beautiful, colourful, depictive **10** attractive, delightful, impressive **11** descriptive

piddling
03 low **04** mean, poor, puny **05** minor, petty, small, sorry **06** meagre, measly, paltry, slight **07** trivial **08** derisory, piffling, trifling, wretched **09** miserable, worthless **10** negligible **11** unimportant **12** contemptible **13** inconsiderate, insignificant

pie
◇ *anagram indicator*
02 pi **03** mag, pye **04** flan, pâté, Pica, piet, pyat, pyet, pyot, tart **05** madge, pasty, patty, pirog **06** chewet, maggie, magpie, pastry **07** cobbler, floater **08** pandowdy **09** chatterer, confusion, coulibiac, croquante, vol-au-vent **10** Florentine, koulibiaca, tarte tatin **11** Banbury cake, oyster-patty
• **pie in the sky**
05 dream **06** hot air, mirage, notion **07** fantasy, reverie, romance **08** daydream, delusion **11** jam tomorrow **13** castle in Spain **14** castle in the air

piebald
04 pied **05** pinto **06** motley **07** dappled, flecked, mottled, spotted **08** brindled, skewbald, speckled **10** variegated **13** black and white, heterogeneous

piece
◇ *anagram indicator*
◇ *hidden indicator*
01 b, k, n, p, q, r **03** bar, bit, cut, die,

dod, écu, end, gun, man, nip, pce **04** bite, chip, daud, dawd, dice, hunk, item, king, lump, opus, part, pawn, peso, rook, slab, snip, solo, unit, work, zack **05** block, cameo, chunk, crown, crumb, dumka, flake, fleck, patch, queen, quota, scrap, shard, share, sherd, shred, slice, small, speck, stick, story, strip, study, wedge **06** bishop, bittie, castle, dollop, jitney, knight, length, lesson, morsel, offcut, report, review, sample, scliff, skliff, sliver, tidbit, titbit **07** allegro, article, combine, element, example, intrada, mammock, mummock, peeling, portion, quarter, scaling, section, segment, snippet **08** creation, division, fraction, fragment, instance, louis-d'or, mouthful, nocturne, particle, picayune, quantity, specimen, splinter **09** allotment, component, dandiprat, dandyprat, interlude, truncheon **10** allegretto, allocation, comedietta, embodiment, percentage, production, smithereen **11** composition, constituent **12** illustration **14** morceau de salon **15** exemplification
• **all in one piece**
05 whole **06** entire, intact, unhurt **08** complete, integral, unbroken, unharmed **09** undamaged, uninjured
• **go to pieces**
05 break **06** blow up **07** break up, crack up, go to pot **08** collapse **09** break down, fall apart **10** be overcome **11** lose control **14** have a breakdown
• **in pieces**
◇ *anagram indicator*
05 kaput **06** broken, in bits, ruined **07** damaged, smashed **09** shattered **13** disintegrated, in smithereens
• **piece together**
03 fit, fix **04** join, mend **05** patch, unite **06** attach, repair **07** compose, restore **08** assemble **10** rhapsodize **11** put together
• **pull to pieces, tear to pieces**
03 nag, pan **04** slag, slam **05** blame, knock, slate, snipe **06** attack, tear up **07** censure, condemn, mammock, rubbish, run down, slag off **08** badmouth, denounce **09** criticize, dismember **10** come down on, go to town on **11** pick holes in **12** disapprove of, put the boot in, tear to shreds **13** find fault with, tear a strip off **15** do a hatchet job on

pièce de résistance
05 jewel, joint, prize **09** showpiece **10** magnum opus, masterwork **11** chef-d'oeuvre, masterpiece

piecemeal
06 patchy, slowly **07** partial **08** bit by bit, discrete, fitfully, in detail, sporadic **09** by degrees, dismember, partially, scattered **10** parcel-wise **11** at intervals, fragmentary, interrupted **12** intermittent, unsystematic **14** intermittently, little by little **15** in dribs and drabs

pied
04 piet, pyat, pyet, pyot **06** motley **07** brindle, dappled, flecked, mottled, piebald, spotted **08** brindled, skewbald, streaked **09** irregular **10** variegated **12** varicoloured **13** multicoloured, parti-coloured

pier
04 dock, mole, pile, post, quay **05** jetty, jutty, wharf **06** column, pillar **07** slipway, support, upright **08** buttress **09** Swiss roll **10** breakwater **12** landing-stage **15** clustered column

pierce
◇ *insertion indicator*
03 jag, peg, ren, rin, run, tap **04** barb, bore, fill, gore, hurt, move, nail, pain, pike, pink, pith, prog, rive, slap, stab **05** drift, drill, enter, gride, gryde, lance, perce, perse, prick, probe, punch, spear, spike, spile, stake, steek, stick, sting, thirl, touch **06** broach, cleave, engore, gimlet, impale, launce, launch, needle, pearce, percen, skewer, thrill, thrust **07** bayonet, emperce, light up **08** empierce, puncture, transfix **09** lancinate, penetrate, perforate, stick into **10** run through **11** pass through, perforation, transpierce **12** burst through **13** cut to the quick, thrill through

pierced
05 grypt, stung **06** pearst, pierst, pinked **07** impaled, pertuse **08** pertused **09** perforate, pertusate, punctured **10** fenestrate, foraminous, penetrated, perforated **11** fenestrated, foraminated

piercing
◇ *insertion indicator*
03 raw **04** cold, keen, loud **05** acute, alert, sharp **06** Arctic, astute, biting, bitter, fierce, frosty, severe, shrewd, shrill, wintry **07** extreme, intense, numbing, painful, probing **08** freezing, perceant, shooting, stabbing **09** agonizing, searching, thrillant **10** discerning, lacerating, perceptive **11** ear-piercing, high-pitched, penetrating, penetrative, sharp-witted **12** ear-splitting, excruciating

piercingly
06 keenly, loudly **07** alertly, sharply, shrilly **08** astutely, bitterly, fiercely, severely **09** extremely, intensely, numbingly, painfully **11** agonizingly **12** discerningly **13** penetratingly **14** excruciatingly

piety
04 fear, pity **05** faith **07** respect **08** devotion, holiness, religion, sanctity **09** deference, fear of God, godliness, piousness, reverence **10** devoutness **11** dutifulness, saintliness **12** spirituality **13** religiousness

piffle
03 rot **04** blah, bosh, bull, bunk, cock, guff, tosh **05** balls, hooey, trash, tripe **06** bunkum, drivel, trifle **07** baloney,

eyewash, hogwash, rhubarb, rubbish, twaddle **08** malarkey, nonsense, tommyrot **09** bull's wool, moonshine, poppycock **10** balderdash, codswallop **11** tarradiddle

piffling
04 idle **05** empty, minor, petty, silly, small **06** paltry, slight **07** foolish, shallow, trivial **08** trifling **09** frivolous, worthless **10** inadequate, negligible **11** superficial, unimportant **12** insufficient **13** insignificant **14** inconsiderable **15** inconsequential

pig
03 elt, hog, sow **04** boar, boor, cram, gilt, runt, slip, wolf, yelt **05** beast, brute, feast, gorge, piggy, scoff, shoat, shote, snarf, stuff, swine **06** animal, gobble, guffie, guzzle, piggie, piglet, porker, sucker, weaner **07** Anthony, glutton, grunter, guzzler, monster, pigling, roaster, tantony **08** gourmand, grumphie, porkling, potsherd, wild boar **09** policeman **10** greedy guts **11** earthenware, gormandizer **13** Captain Cooker

Pigs include:
05 Duroc
07 Old Spot
08 landrace, Pietrain, Tamworth, wild boar
09 Berkshire, Hampshire, Yorkshire
10 Large White, potbellied, saddleback
11 Middle White
15 Chinese Meishian

pigeon
03 nun, owl **04** barb, clay, dove, girl, gull, hoax, kuku, rock, ront, ruff, runt, spot **05** goura, homer, piper, quest, quist, ronte, squab, wonga **06** affair, culver, cushat, pouter, queest, quoist, roller, turbit, zoozoo **07** carrier, concern, cropper, fantail, jacinth, jacobin, laugher, manumea, pintado, tumbler **08** business, capuchin, horseman, ringdove, rock dove, squealer **09** archangel, solitaire, trumpeter **10** bronze-wing, Didunculus, wonga-wonga **12** mourning dove

pigeonhole
03 box, tag **04** file, slot, sort **05** class, defer, label, niche, place **06** locker, put off, shelve **07** cubicle, section **08** category, classify, postpone **09** catalogue, cubby-hole **10** categorize **11** alphabetize, compartment **14** classification

pigeon pea
03 dal **04** daal, dahl, dhal **05** dholl

pig-headed
06 mulish, stupid, wilful **07** froward **08** contrary, perverse, stubborn **09** obstinate **10** bull-headed, headstrong, inflexible, self-willed, unyielding **11** intractable, stiff-necked, wrong-headed **12** intransigent

piglet *see* **pig**

pigment
03 dye, hue **04** tint **05** paint, stain **06** colour, piment **08** tincture **09** colouring

Pigments include:
03 hem
04 haem, heme
05 henna, ochre, sepia, smalt, umber
06 bister, bistre, cobalt, cyanin, lutein, madder, sienna, zaffer, zaffre
07 carmine, etiolin, gamboge, melanin, sinopia, turacin
08 cinnabar, luteolin, orpiment, rose-pink, verditer, viridian
09 anthocyan, bilirubin, colcothar, Indian red, lamp-black, lithopone, phycocyan, quercetin, zinc white
10 Berlin blue, biliverdin, Chinese red, chlorophyl, green earth, lipochrome, madder-lake, Paris-green, pearl white, rhodophane, terre verte, vermillion
11 anthochlore, anthocyanin, chlorophyll, King's-yellow, phycocyanin, phycophaein, phytochrome, ultramarine, Venetian red
12 anthoxanthin, Cappagh-brown, Chinese white, chrome yellow, Naples-yellow, phaeomelanin, phycoxanthin, Prussian blue, turacoverdin, Tyrian purple, xanthopterin
13 cadmium yellow, phycoerythrin, Scheele's green, titanium white, xanthopterine
15 purple of Cassuis

See also **colour**; **dye**

pike
03 gar, ged **04** jack, luce, pick, toll **05** speed **06** renege **07** garfish, walleye **08** jackfish, pickerel, turnpike **11** Lepidosteus

Pikes include:
03 Esk, Red
04 Cold, High
05 Heron, Rispa
06 Causey, Kidsty, Ullock
07 Rossett, Scafell
08 Kentmere, Langdale
09 Angletarn, Grisedale, Sheffield
10 Dollywagon, Nethermost

pilaster
04 anta

pile
03 bar, fur, jam, nap **04** a lot, beam, bing, bomb, cock, down, fuzz, hair, heap, load, lots, mass, mint, pack, post, rush, shag, tons, wool **05** amass, crowd, crush, flock, flood, fluff, heaps, hoard, loads, mound, plush, stack, store **06** bundle, charge, column, fibres, gather, heap up, masses, oodles, packet, piling, riches, stacks, stream, wealth **07** build up, collect, edifice, fortune, mansion, rouleau, squeeze, stack up, support, surface, texture, threads, upright **08** assemble, big bucks, hundreds, lashings, millions,

mountain **09** arrowhead, megabucks, stockpile, thousands **10** accumulate, a great deal, assemblage, assortment, collection, foundation, quantities **11** loadsamoney, soft surface **12** accumulation **13** large building, large quantity

• **pile it on**
06 overdo, stress **07** lay it on, magnify **08** overplay **09** dramatize, emphasize, overstate **10** exaggerate **12** lay it on thick **13** make too much of, overdramatize, overemphasize, pile it on thick

• **pile up**
03 big **04** deck, grow, soar **07** mount up **08** escalate, increase, multiply **10** accumulate

pile-up
04 bump **05** crash, prang, smash, wreck **07** smash-up **08** accident **09** collision

pilfer
03 bag, lag, mag, nim, rob **04** blag, lift, mill, nick, pick, pull, smug, whip **05** boost, filch, heist, hoist, miche, mooch, mouch, pinch, sneak, steal, swipe **06** finger, nobble, pickle, snitch, thieve **07** purloin, snaffle **08** knock off, peculate, shoplift **10** run off with **12** make away with

pilfering *see* **theft**

pilgrim
05 hadji **06** palmer **07** devotee **08** crusader, newcomer, wanderer, wayfarer **09** peregrine, traveller **10** worshipper

pilgrimage
03 haj **04** hadj, hajj, tour, trip **06** wander **07** crusade, journey, mission **08** lifetime **10** expedition **13** peregrination

pill
03 dex, tab **04** ball, husk, peel **05** bolus, upper **06** bomber, cachou, caplet, doctor, pellet, pilula, pilule, tablet **07** capsule, globule, lozenge, plunder **08** goofball, microdot, spansule **09** blackball **10** integument, number nine **12** multivitamin **13** pain in the neck

pillage
03 rob **04** loot, peel, raid, raze, sack **05** booty, rifle, spoil, strip **06** maraud, rapine, ravage, spoils **07** despoil, plunder, ransack, robbery, seizure **08** freeboot, harrying, spoliate **09** depredate, marauding, vandalize **10** spoliation **11** depredation, devastation

pillar
03 lat, man **04** goal, mast, pier, pile, pole, post, prop, rock **05** shaft, stack, stoop, stoup **06** cippus, column **07** bastion, obelisk, respond, support, telamon, trumeau, upright **08** baluster, caryatid, gendarme, lamppost, mainstay, monolith, pilaster, stalwart, standard **09** pillarbox, sandspout,

pillory

stanchion **12** lamp-standard **15** tower of strength

pillory
04 cang, lash, mock **05** brand **06** attack, cangue, show up **07** laugh at, tumbrel, tumbril **08** denounce, ridicule **09** criticize **10** little-ease, stigmatize **11** cast a slur on, pour scorn on **13** hold up to shame

pillow
03 bed, cod **04** rest **07** bolster, cushion **08** headrest, pulvinar

pillowcase
04 bear, beer, bere, slip

pilot
03 fly, run **04** crew, lead, test **05** drive, flier, flyer, guide, model, prune, steer, trial **06** airman, direct, George, handle, leader, manage, sample **07** aircrew, aviator, captain, conduct, control, hobbler, operate, shipman **08** airwoman, aviatrix, coxswain, director, governor, helmsman, lodesman, navigate **09** aviatress, commander, manoeuvre, navigator, rocketeer, steersman **10** cowcatcher, cropduster **12** experimental, first officer **14** flight engineer

pimp
04 bawd, hoon, mack **05** ponce **06** broker, pandar, pander **07** hustler, procure **08** fancy man, mackerel, panderer, procurer **09** solicitor **11** fleshmonger, whoremonger

pimpernel
06 burnet **09** brookweed, wincopipe, wink-a-peep **12** weather glass **14** shepherd's glass

pimple
03 zit **04** boil, quat, spot **05** botch, plook, plouk, whelk **06** button, milium, papula, papule, rum-bud **07** bubukle, pustule **08** swelling **09** blackhead, carbuncle, whitehead **10** rum-blossom

pin
03 fix, lay, leg, nog, peg, put **04** axle, bolt, clip, hold, join, nail, peak, stud, tack **05** affix, dowel, drift, pitch, pivot, place, preen, press, rivet, screw, spike, stage, stick, wrist **06** attach, brooch, cotter, degree, fasten, impute, pintle, secure, skewer, staple **07** ascribe, enclose, gudgeon, skittle, trenail **08** chessman, fastener, hold down, hold fast, restrain, treenail **09** attribute, constrain, thumbtack **10** immobilize
• pin down
03 peg **04** make, nail **05** force, press **06** compel, define **07** specify **08** hold down, hold fast, identify, nail down, pinpoint, restrain **09** constrain, determine **10** pressurize **15** put your finger on

pinafore
04 brat, tire **05** apron, pinny **06** jumper, pinner, pinnie **07** gym slip, overall, save-all **08** gym tunic

pincers
06 forfex **07** forceps, nippers **08** pinchers, tweezers **10** Jaws of Life®

pinch
◇ *containment indicator*
03 bag, bit, jot, nab, nip, tad **04** bite, book, bust, carp, dash, grip, hurt, lace, lift, mite, nail, nick, nirl, pook, pouk, save, shut, spot, tait, tate, whip **05** catch, chack, check, cramp, crush, filch, grasp, gripe, pleat, press, pugil, run in, seize, sneap, snuff, speck, steal, stint, swipe, taste, touch, trace, tweak, wring **06** arrest, budget, collar, crisis, detain, eke out, hamper, harass, narrow, pick up, pilfer, pincer, pull in, snatch, sneesh, stress, twinge, twitch **07** capture, confine, cut back, purloin, smidgen, soupçon, squeeze **08** compress, encroach, half-inch, hardship, knock off, peculate, pressure, restrict, sneeshan, sneeshin, souvenir **09** economize, emergency, sneeshing **10** difficulty **11** appropriate, predicament, walk off with **13** keep costs down, scrape a living, scrimp and save **14** live on the cheap **15** tighten your belt
• at a pinch
11 if necessary **13** in an emergency
• feel the pinch
06 be poor **12** hit a bad patch **13** have a hard time **14** be short of money, scratch a living **15** strike a bad patch, tighten your belt

pinched
04 pale, thin, worn **05** drawn, gaunt, peaky **07** haggard, starved **08** careworn, narrowed, strained **12** straightened

pine
04 ache, fade, fret, hone, long, sigh, wish **05** crave, dwine, mourn, yearn **06** desire, grieve, hanker, hunger, repine, thirst, weaken **08** languish **09** waste away

Pine trees include:
03 nut, red
04 blue, Huon, jack
05 Chile, kauri, pinon, Scots, stone, sugar, white
06 arolla, celery, cembra, Jersey, Korean, limber, Paraná, Scotch, spruce
07 Amboina, Chilean, cluster, Mexican, radiata
08 Japanese, Jeffrey's, knobcone, lacebark, loblolly, longleaf, mountain, Pandanus, pinaster, Scots fir, umbrella
09 lodgepole, Scotch fir
11 bristlecone
12 monkey puzzle
13 Norfolk Island

pineapple
04 bomb, piña, pine **05** anana **06** ananas **07** grenade **10** tillandsia

pining
04 sick

pinion
03 cog, tie **04** bind, wing **05** chain, penne, truss **06** fasten, fetter, hobble, pennon **07** confine, manacle, pin down, shackle **10** immobilize

pink
03 cut, top **04** acme, best, peak, peep, peer, penk, rosy, stab, wink **05** blink, knock, notch, pinky, prick, prime, punch, score, small **06** eyelet, flower, height, incise, minnow, pierce, pinkie, samlet, summit, tiptop **07** extreme, flushed, reddish, roseate, scallop, serrate **08** blinking, detonate **09** chaffinch, exquisite, perforate **10** crenellate, perfection, rose colour **12** rose-coloured

Pinks include:
04 puce, rose
05 coral, peach
06 oyster, salmon, shrimp
07 old rose
08 cyclamen
09 carnation, pompadour, shell pink
12 mushroom pink, shocking pink

• in the pink
03 fit **04** trim, well **07** healthy **08** very well **10** in good nick, in good trim, on good form **11** in good shape, right as rain **12** in fine fettle, in good health **15** in perfect health

pinnacle
03 cap, top **04** acme, apex, cone, peak **05** crest, crown, spire **06** apogee, height, hoodoo, needle, pinnet, summit, turret, vertex, zenith **07** minaret, obelisk, pyramid, steeple, sublime **08** eminence **11** culmination

pinpoint
04 spot **05** exact, place, right **06** define, locate **07** pin down, precise, specify **08** accurate, discover, home in on, identify, nail down, rigorous, zero in on **09** determine **10** meticulous, scrupulous **11** distinguish, punctilious **15** put your finger on

pint
02 pt
• nearly a pint
03 log

pint-size
03 wee **04** mini, tiny **05** dinky, dwarf, pygmy, small, teeny **06** little, midget, pocket **09** miniature, pint-sized **10** diminutive, teeny-weeny **11** pocket-sized

pioneer
05 begin, chips, found, set up, start **06** create, invent, launch, leader, open up **07** develop, founder, planter, settler **08** colonist, discover, explorer, initiate, inventor, labourer, way-maker **09** developer, establish, excavator, harbinger, innovator, instigate, institute, introduce, originate, spearhead **10** discoverer, lead the way, pathfinder, pave the way, sandgroper **11** bandeirante, blaze a trail, trailblazer,

ortrekker **12** First Fleeter,
ontiersman **13** groundbreaker
break new ground, founding father,
ontierswoman

ee also **explorer**

ious
2 pi **03** pia **04** good, holy, wise
5 godly, moral **06** devout **07** devoted,
utiful, saintly **08** faithful, priggish,
everent, unctuous, virtuous
9 dedicated, insincere, religious,
ghteous, spiritual **10** goody-goody,
inctified **12** hypocritical
3 sanctimonious, self-righteous
4 holier-than-thou

iously
7 morally **08** devoutly **10** faithfully,
riggishly, reverently, virtuously
1 insincerely, religiously, righteously,
piritually **14** hypocritically
5 sanctimoniously, self-righteous

ip
3 die **04** hump, kill, peep, roup, seed,
oot, star **05** chirp, peepe, speck,
round **06** acinus, pippin, spleen
7 ailment, disgust, offence **08** fruitlet,
yphilis **09** blackball, distemper
0 grapestone

ipe
3 ait, jet, oat, tap **04** clay, duct, fife,
ue, hose, line, main, peep, play, pule,
eed, sing, take, tube, vent, weep,
vorm **05** aulos, brier, bring, carry,
heep, chirp, crane, cutty, drone, flute,
elly, quill, riser, sound, tibia, trill, tweet
6 convey, dudeen, faucet, funnel,
ookah, kalian, piping, shrike, shrill,
phon, supply, tubing, uptake, warble
7 calumet, channel, chanter, chibouk,
hirrup, cob-pipe, conduct, conduit,
ead-end, deliver, dip-pipe, nargile,
argily, passage, tweedle, twitter,
vhistle **08** aqueduct, bagpipes, blow
ipe, claypipe, conveyor, cornpipe,
ylinder, dry riser, feed-pipe, manifold,
airliton, narghile, narghily, nargileh,
argilly, overflow, pipeline, recorder,
oil pipe, stopcock, tailpipe, transmit
9 blast-pipe, chibouque, drainpipe,
oose-neck, narghilly, peace-pipe,
itch-pipe, standpipe, stovepipe,
entiduct, wastepipe, water pipe
0 chimney pot, gas-bracket, kill
tring, meerschaum **11** clyster-pipe,
xhaust pipe, service pipe, tobacco-
ipe **12** churchwarden, hubble-
ubble, penny whistle, throttle-pipe
3 woodcock's-head **15** injection string

ee also **tobacco**

pipe down
6 shut up **07** be quiet **11** stop talking

ipeclay
3 cam **04** calm, caum

ipe dream
5 dream **06** mirage, notion, vagary
7 chimera, fantasy, reverie, romance
8 daydream, delusion **09** false hope
1 pie in the sky **13** castle in Spain
4 castle in the air

pipeline
04 duct, line, pipe, tube **07** channel,
conduit, passage **08** conveyor
• **in the pipeline**
07 planned **08** on the way, under way
13 in preparation **14** already started

pipsqueak
05 creep, twerp **06** nobody, squirt
07 nothing, upstart **09** nonentity
11 hobbledehoy **14** whippersnapper

piquancy
03 pep, zip **04** bite, edge, kick, race,
salt, tang, zest **05** juice, oomph, punch,
spice **06** colour, ginger, relish, spirit,
vigour **07** flavour, pizzazz **08** interest,
pungency, raciness, vitality
09 sharpness, spiciness **10** excitement,
liveliness **11** pepperiness **13** strong
flavour

piquant
04 racy, tart **05** juicy, salty, sharp, spicy,
tangy, zesty **06** biting, lively
07 peppery, pungent, savoury
08 poignant, seasoned, spirited,
stinging **09** colourful, sparkling
10 appetizing, intriguing
11 fascinating, interesting, provocative,
stimulating **14** highly seasoned

pique
03 bug, get, irk, vex **04** gall, goad, huff,
miff, nark, peak, rile, spur, stir, whet
05 anger, annoy, get at, peeve, point,
rouse, sting, wound **06** arouse, excite,
grudge, kindle, needle, nettle, offend,
put out, wind up **07** affront, dudgeon,
incense, mortify, offence, provoke,
umbrage **08** drive mad, irritate,
vexation **09** aggravate, animosity,
annoyance, displease, galvanize,
punctilio, stimulate **10** drive crazy, ill-
feeling, irritation, resentment
11 displeasure **12** drive bananas
13 make sparks fly **14** drive up the
wall

piqued
03 mad **05** angry, cross, ratty, riled,
vexed **06** choked, miffed, narked,
peeved, put out **07** annoyed, stroppy,
uptight **08** in a paddy, offended, up in
arms **09** in a lather, irritated, raving
mad, resentful, seeing red
10 aggravated, displeased, hopping
mad **11** disgruntled, fit to be tied **12** on
the warpath

piracy
05 theft **06** rapine **07** robbery
08 stealing **09** hijacking, sea-roving
10 plagiarism **11** bootlegging,
freebooting **12** buccaneering,
infringement
• **practise piracy**
04 rove

piranha
05 perai, pirai **06** caribe, piraña, piraya
08 characid, characin

pirate
04 copy, crib, lift, nick **05** pinch, poach,
rover, steal **06** borrow, marque, raider,
sea dog, sea rat, viking **07** brigand,

corsair, sea wolf **08** algerine, knock off,
marauder, picaroon, sea rover, water rat
09 buccaneer, infringer, sallee-man,
sea robber **10** arch-pirate, filibuster,
freebooter, plagiarist, plagiarize, water-
thief **11** appropriate, plagiarizer

Pirates include:

03 Tew (Thomas)
04 Bart (Jean), Gunn (Ben), Hook
(Captain), Kidd (William), Otto,
Read (Mary), Smee
05 Barth (Jean), Bones (Billy), Bonny
(Anne), Bunce (Jack), Drake (Sir
Francis), Every (Henry), Ewart
(Nanty), Flint (Captain), Tache
(Edward), Teach (Edward)
06 Aubery (Jean-Benoit), Conrad,
Jonsen (Captain), Morgan (Sir
Henry), Silver (Long John), Thatch
(Edward), Walker (William)
07 Dampier (William), Lafitte (Jean),
O'Malley (Grace), Rackham (John),
Roberts (Bartholomew), Sparrow
(Captain Jack), Trumpet (Solomon)
08 Altamont (Frederick), Black Dog,
Blackett (Nancy), Blackett (Peggy),
Blind Pew, Redbeard, Ringrose
(Basil)
09 Black Bart, Cleveland (Clement)
10 Barbarossa (Khair-ed-din),
Blackbeard, Calico Jack
14 Long John Silver

pirouette
04 spin, turn **05** pivot, twirl, whirl
06 gyrate **08** gyration **15** turn on a
sixpence

pistol
03 dag, gat, gun, pop, rod **04** Colt®,
iron **05** Luger®, piece **06** barker,
heater, puffer, zip gun **07** handgun,
pistole, sidearm **08** revolver, water gun
09 derringer, squirt gun **10** six-shooter
11 barking iron
See also **gun**

piston
03 ram

pit
03 bed, den, put **04** dent, gulf, hole,
khud, mark, mine, play, scar, silo, sump
05 abyss, chasm, ditch, fossa, fovea,
notch, stone **06** cavity, crater, dimple,
hollow, indent, quarry, trench
07 blemish, depress, measure, moss
hag, pothole **08** alveolus, coalmine,
diggings, moss hagg, pockmark,
punctule, workings **10** depression,
scrobicule **11** excavations, indentation
• **pit against**
05 match **06** oppose **07** compete
10 set against
• **the pits**
04 crap, naff **05** awful, lousy, pants,
spewy **06** cruddy, crummy **07** abysmal
08 dreadful, inferior, pathetic, terrible,
very poor **09** third-rate **10** inadequate,
second-rate **14** a load of rubbish,
unsatisfactory

Pitcairn Island
03 PCN

pitch
03 aim, fix, lob, pin, pop, set, tar, yak **04** bowl, cant, cast, dive, drop, face, fall, fire, hurl, keel, line, list, mark, nets, park, peck, reel, roll, stud, sway, talk, tilt, tone, toss **05** angle, arena, chuck, cover, erect, field, fling, grade, heave, level, lurch, place, plant, point, put up, set up, slant, sling, slope, sound, spiel, throw **06** alight, bounce, degree, direct, encamp, extent, gabble, ground, height, jargon, launch, maltha, patter, plunge, settle, timbre, topple, tumble, wallow, wicket **07** asphalt, bitumen, chatter, descent, incline, plummet, set down, stadium, station **08** flounder, gradient, position, tonality **09** determine, establish, frequency, intensity, interlock, steepness **10** modulation **11** inclination, sports field **12** fall headlong, playing-field **13** move up and down
- **make a pitch for**
05 offer, put up **06** bid for, submit, tender **07** advance, proffer, propose **08** put in for, try to get **09** try to sell **10** put forward **11** try to obtain
- **pitch in**
04 help **06** join in, muck in **07** help out **09** co-operate, do your bit, lend a hand **10** be involved **11** participate
- **too low in pitch, too high in pitch**
04 flat **05** sharp

pitch-black
04 dark, inky **05** black, unlit **08** jet-black **09** coal-black, pitch-dark **13** unilluminated

pitcher
03 can, jar, jug, urn **04** ewer, jack, sett **05** crock **06** bottle, closer, vessel **07** growler **09** container **11** screwballer **13** knuckleballer
- **pitcher plant**
08 nepenthe **09** Nepenthes **10** Sarracenia **12** Darlingtonia

piteous
03 sad **06** moving, paltry, rueful, woeful **07** pitiful, ruthful **08** mournful, pathetic, pitiable, poignant, touching, wretched **09** plaintive, sorrowful **10** lamentable **11** distressing **12** heart-rending **13** compassionate, heartbreaking

pitfall
04 risk, snag, trap **05** catch, peril, snare **06** danger, hazard **08** drawback, trapfall **10** difficulty **14** stumbling-block

pith
03 nub **04** core, crux, gist, meat **05** heart, point, value **06** import, kernel, marrow, matter, mettle, moment, vigour, weight **07** essence, medulla, papyrus **09** substance **10** importance **11** consequence **12** forcefulness, quintessence, salient point, significance **13** essential part

pithead
04 brow

pithily
07 in a word, in brief, tersely **09** compactly, concisely **10** succinctly, to the point **11** in a few words, in a nutshell **12** meaningfully

pithy
05 brief, meaty, short, terse **06** cogent, strong **07** compact, concise, marrowy, pointed, summary, telling **08** forceful, forcible, incisive, lapidary, material, pregnant, succinct **09** condensed, energetic, matterful, trenchant **10** expressive, meaningful

pitiable
03 sad **04** poor **05** silly, sorry **06** woeful **07** doleful, piteous, woesome **08** grievous, mournful, pathetic, wretched **09** miserable **10** distressed, lamentable **11** distressful, distressing **12** commiserable, contemptible **14** compassionable

pitiful
03 low, sad **04** base, mean, poor, vile **05** lousy, seely, sorry, waefu' **06** crummy, meagre, moving, paltry, shabby, waeful, woeful **07** doleful, piteous, ruthful, the pits, woesome **08** hopeless, mournful, pathetic, pitiable, terrible, wretched **09** affecting, miserable, worthless **10** deplorable, despicable, inadequate, lamentable **11** distressing **12** contemptible, heart-rending **13** compassionate, heartbreaking, insignificant

pitifully
05 sadly **08** terribly, woefully **09** miserably, piteously **10** deplorably, despicably, hopelessly, lamentably **12** contemptibly, pathetically **13** distressingly

pitiless
05 cruel, harsh, stony **06** brutal, severe **07** callous, inhuman **08** inhumane, ruthless, uncaring **09** heartless, merciless, unfeeling **10** dispiteous, hard-headed, inexorable, relentless **11** cold-blooded, cold-hearted, hard-hearted, unremitting **13** unsympathetic

pitilessly
07 cruelly, harshly **08** brutally **09** callously **10** ruthlessly **11** mercilessly **13** cold-bloodedly, cold-heartedly, hard-heartedly

pittance
04 dole, drop **05** crumb **06** trifle **07** modicum, peanuts **11** chickenfeed **14** drop in the ocean

pitted
05 holey, rough **06** dented, marked **07** foveate, notched, scarred **08** alveolar, indented, lacunose, potholed, punctate **09** alveolate, blemished, depressed, punctated **10** pockmarked

pity
03 rew, rue, sin **04** ruth **05** bleed, grace, mercy, piety, shame **06** bemoan, bepity, bowels, regret, sorrow **07** bad luck, emotion, feel for, feeling, mercify, remorse, sadness, weep for **08** distress, kindness, sympathy **09** grieve for **10** compassion, condolence, have a heart, misericord, misfortune, tenderness **11** crying shame, forbearance, forgiveness, misericorde **12** feel sorry for **13** commiseration, empathize with, fellow-feeling, understanding **14** disappointment, sympathize with **15** commiserate with
- **take pity on**
03 rue **05** spare **06** pardon **07** feel for **09** show mercy **11** have mercy on **12** feel sorry for **13** empathize with **14** emphathize with, sympathize with **15** commiserate with

pivot
03 hub, lie **04** axis, axle, hang, rely, spin, turn **05** focus, heart, hinge, swing **06** centre, depend, rotate, swivel **07** fulcrum, kingpin, revolve, spindle **08** cardinal, linchpin **10** focal point **12** be contingent, central point

pivotal
05 axial, focal, vital **07** central, crucial **08** critical, decisive **09** climactic, important **11** determining

pixie
03 elf, imp **04** pixy **05** fairy, pisky **06** goblin, sprite **07** brownie **10** leprechaun

pizzazz
04 brio, life **05** oomph **06** energy, esprit, spirit, vigour **07** entrain **08** activity, dynamism, vitality, vivacity **09** animation, briskness, quickness, smartness **10** liveliness **11** refreshment **13** sprightliness, vivaciousness **14** boisterousness

placard
02 ad **04** bill, sign **05** title **06** advert, notice, poster **07** affiche, placcat, placket, sticker **13** advertisement

placate
04 calm, lull **05** quiet **06** disarm, pacify, soothe **07** appease, assuage, mollify, win over **08** calm down **10** conciliate, propitiate

placatory
07 calming **08** soothing **09** appeasing **10** mollifying **11** peace-making **12** conciliatory, pacificatory, propitiative, propitiatory

place
01 P **02** do, Pl **03** fix, job, lay, pad, put, set **04** area, city, digs, duty, flat, home, know, lieu, park, part, pose, post, rank, rest, role, room, seat, site, sort, spot, sted, task, town **05** abode, class, grade, group, hotel, house, leave, locus, lodge, niche, order, plant, point, right, scene, space, stand, state, stead, stedd, stede, steed, topic, venue **06** assign, hamlet, induct, invest, locale, locate, region, settle, square,

status, stedde **07** appoint, arrange, concern, country, deposit, footing, install, lay down, put down, set down, setting, situate, station, village **08** allocate, building, business, classify, district, domicile, dwelling, fortress, function, identify, locality, location, pinpoint, position, property, remember, standing **09** apartment, establish, recognize, residence, situation **10** categorize, restaurant **11** appointment, battlefield, find a job for, institution, whereabouts **13** accommodation, establishment, neighbourhood **14** responsibility

See also **Bible; eating; entertainment; fictional; mythical**

- **all over the place**
◇ *anagram indicator*
04 awry **05** messy **07** muddled **08** confused **09** dispersed, scattered **12** disorganized
- **at the right place**
03 pat
- **at that place**
05 there
- **at this place**
04 here
- **in place**
05 set up **07** in order, working **08** arranged **10** in position
- **in place of**
04 lieu, vice **08** in lieu of **09** instead of **13** in exchange for
- **in the same place**
02 ib **04** ibid **06** ibidem
- **no place**
02 np
- **out of place**
◇ *anagram indicator*
04 away **08** improper, out of key, tactless, unseemly **09** unfitting **10** inapposite, malapropos, unbecoming, unsuitable **12** unseasonable **13** inappropriate
- **put someone in their place**
05 crush, shame **06** humble **07** deflate **08** bring low **09** humiliate
- **take place**
02 be **04** fall **05** occur **06** befall, be held, betide, happen **07** come off **09** come about, transpire **10** come to pass
- **take the place of**
06 act for **07** replace, serve as, succeed **09** supersede **10** stand in for **12** take over from **13** substitute for

placement
03 job **07** placing, ranking, setting **08** locating, location, ordering **10** assignment, deployment, employment, engagement, internship, stationing **11** appointment, arrangement, disposition, emplacement, positioning **12** distribution, installation **14** classification

placid
04 calm, cool, mild **05** quiet, still **06** gentle, serene **07** equable, pacific, restful, unmoved **08** composed,

peaceful, tranquil **09** easy-going, peaceable, unruffled **10** untroubled **11** level-headed, undisturbed, unemotional, unexcitable, unflappable **12** even-tempered **13** imperturbable, self-possessed

placidly
06 calmly, gently, mildly **08** serenely **09** restfully **10** peacefully **11** unflappably **13** imperturbably

plagiarism
04 crib **05** theft **06** piracy **07** copying, lifting **08** cribbing **09** borrowing **12** infringement, reproduction **13** appropriation **14** counterfeiting

plagiarist
05 thief **06** copier, pirate, robber **08** imitator **09** Autolycus

plagiarize
04 copy, crib, lift, nick **05** poach, steal **06** borrow, pirate **07** imitate **09** reproduce **11** appropriate, counterfeit

plague
03 bug, dog, dun, pox, vex **04** bane, blow, pest **05** annoy, curse, death, haunt, hound, swarm, tease, trial, upset, worry, wound **06** bother, hamper, harass, hassle, hinder, influx, pester **07** afflict, bedevil, cholera, disease, disturb, murrain, scourge, torment, torture, trouble **08** calamity, distress, epidemic, goodyear, invasion, irritate, nuisance, pandemic, sickness, vexation **09** aggravate, annoyance, contagion, goodyears, infection, persecute **10** affliction, Black Death, huge number, pestilence **11** infestation **13** bubonic plague, pain in the neck **15** pneumonic plague, thorn in the flesh

04 lice
05 boils, flies, frogs
07 locusts
08 darkness
09 hailstorm
18 disease of livestock
19 death of the firstborn
21 Nile waters turn to blood

plain
04 even, flat, open, ugly **05** basic, blunt, clear, frank, level, lucid, muted, overt, prose, quite, secco, stark, utter **06** candid, direct, homely, honest, lament, modest, patent, rustic, simple, simply, **07** austere, clearly, evident, obvious, plateau, sincere, spartan, totally, unruled, utterly, visible **08** apparent, clinical, complain, flatland, home-bred, home-made, homespun, manifest, ordinary, truthful, uncurled, unlovely **09** downright, grassland, outspoken, plain-Jane, practical, tableland, unadorned **10** accessible, completely, distinctly, forthright, noticeable, restrained, thoroughly, unaffected, unassuming, uncoloured, undeniably **11** discernible,

perceptible, plain-spoken, transparent, unambiguous, undecorated, unelaborate, unpatterned **12** intelligible, self-coloured, unattractive, unmistakable, unobstructed, unvariegated **13** uncomplicated, unembellished, unpretentious **14** understandable **15** clear as daylight, not much to look at, straightforward, undistinguished, unprepossessing, unsophisticated

04 vega
05 carse, lande, llano
06 maidan, pampas, sabkha, steppe, tundra
07 lowland, prairie, sabkhah, sabkhat
08 savannah

plain-spoken
04 open **05** blunt, frank, round **06** candid, direct, honest **08** explicit, outright, truthful **09** downright, outspoken **10** forthright **11** unequivocal **15** straightforward

plaintive
03 sad **06** woeful **07** doleful, piteous, pitiful, unhappy, wistful **08** mournful, wretched **09** lacrimoso, lagrimoso, querulous, sorrowful **10** melancholy **11** heartbroken, high-pitched **12** disconsolate, heart-rending **13** grief-stricken

plaintively
05 sadly **08** woefully **09** dolefully, lacrimoso, lagrimoso, pitifully, unhappily, wistfully **10** mournfully, wretchedly **14** disconsolately

plait
04 plat **05** braid, pedal, pleat, tress **06** plight **07** frounce, leghorn **08** doubling **09** Dunstable

plan
◇ *anagram indicator*
03 aim, lay, map, way **04** case, dart, hang, idea, mean, plat, plot, seek, want, wish **05** block, chart, draft, frame, means, model, shape, trace **06** design, device, devise, intend, invent, layout, map out, method, policy, schema, scheme, sketch, system **07** arrange, complot, concoct, develop, diagram, drawing, foresee, formula, outline, prepare, project, propose, purpose, resolve, think of, work out **08** conspire, contrive, envisage, organize, platform, proposal, scenario, schedule, strategy **09** architect, blueprint, formulate, intention, itinerary, procedure, programme, timetable **10** conception, mastermind, suggestion **11** arrangement, contemplate, contrivance, delineation, ichnography, premeditate, projectment, proposition **12** illustration, scale drawing **14** representation

plane
03 bus, fly, jet **04** even, flat, rank, rung, sail, skim, soar, VTOL, wing **05** class,

flush, glide, jumbo, level, plain, skate, stage **06** bomber, degree, glider, planar, smooth, thrust **07** echelon, fighter, footing, jointer, regular, stratum, uniform **08** aircraft, airliner, airplane, jumbo jet, position, seaplane, sycomore, volplane **09** aeroplane, condition, fillister, swing-wing **10** buttonball, buttonwood, homaloidal, horizontal **11** flat surface **12** level surface

See also **aircraft**

planet
05 world

Planets:

04 Mars
05 Earth, Pluto, Venus
06 Saturn, Uranus
07 Jupiter, Mercury, Neptune

---

plank
04 beam, slab, slat **05** board, panel, sheet **06** planch, timber **08** stringer **09** washboard **12** weatherboard

planner
05 maker **06** author **07** creator, deviser, stylist **08** arranger, designer, inventor, producer **09** architect, contriver, developer, fashioner, organizer **10** mastermind, originator

planning
06 design **07** control, running **09** ordinance **10** management, projection, regulation **11** arrangement, development, preparation **12** co-ordination, organization **13** establishment **14** administration

plant
03 fix, put, set, sow **04** bury, gear, hide, land, mill, post, root, salt, seed, shop, slip, yard **05** found, imbed, inter, lodge, place, scion, stock, works **06** cudgel, insert, instil, locate, settle **07** conceal, cutting, factory, foundry, implant, scatter, secrete, situate, station **08** colonize, disguise, offshoot, position, workshop **09** apparatus, equipment, establish, introduce, machinery **10** transplant **11** put secretly **13** put out of sight

See also **flower; leaf**

Plant types include:

03 air, pot
04 bean, beet, bulb, bush, cane, corm, fern, herb, moss, tree, vine, weed
05 algae, grass, house, sedge, shrub, water
06 annual, cactus, cereal, flower, fungus, hybrid, lichen
07 bedding, climber, foliage, sapling
08 biennial, cultivar, epiphyte, seedling
09 aerophyte, evergreen, perennial, succulent, vegetable
10 herbaceous, wild flower
11 carnivorous
13 insectivorous

See also **alga, algae; bean; bulb; cactus; cereal; crop; disease; grass; herb; lily;**

orchid; **palm; poison; seaweed; sedge; shrub; tree; vegetable; weed**

plantation
03 pen **04** tope **06** bosket **07** bosquet, fazenda, pinetum **08** vineyard **09** cornbrake, salicetum, shrubbery, tea garden, viticetum

plaque
04 sign, slab **05** badge, brass, medal, panel, plate **06** brooch, shield, tablet **07** plateau **09** cartouche, medallion, plaquette

plaster
03 mud **04** coat, daub, leep, teer **05** cover, gesso, grout, parge, patch, smarm, smear **06** bedaub, clatch, gypsum, laying, mortar, parget, peloid, render, screed, spread, stucco **07** bandage, Band-aid®, overlay, pugging **08** dressing, plaister, sinapism **09** beplaster, cataplasm, emplaster, Polyfilla®, rendering, roughcast **10** emplastron, emplastrum **11** Elastoplast®, plasterwork, scratchcoat **12** cover thickly, plasterboard **13** butterfly clip **14** plaster of Paris **15** sticking-plaster

plastered
◊ *anagram indicator*
See **drunk**

plastic
◊ *anagram indicator*
04 soft **05** false **06** phoney, pliant, supple **07** ductile, man-made, pliable, shaping **08** flexible, modeller, sculptor **09** compliant, formative, malleable, mouldable, receptive, shapeable, synthetic, tractable, unnatural **10** artificial, manageable, modifiable **14** impressionable

---

Plastics include:

03 PVC
04 PTFE, uPVC
05 vinyl
06 Biopol®, Teflon®
07 Perspex®
08 Bakelite®, laminate, silicone
09 celluloid®, Plexiglas®, polyester, polythene, Styrofoam®
10 epoxy resin, plexiglass
11 polystyrene
12 polyethylene, polyurethane
13 phenolic resin, polypropylene
14 polynorbornene

---

plasticity
07 pliancy **08** softness **10** pliability, suppleness **11** flexibility, pliableness **12** malleability, tractability

plate
01 L, T **03** seg, tin, web **04** bowl, coat, dish, foil, gild, pane, rove, sign, slab **05** ashet, cover, layer, ortho, panel, paten, print, sheet **06** baffle, lamina, latten, muffin, plaque, remark, salver, silver, tablet, veneer **07** anodize, gravure, helping, lamella, ossicle, overlay, picture, plateau, platter, portion, serving **08** laminate, mazarine, pattress, trencher

09 galvanize, osteoderm, platinize **10** lithograph, photograph, zincograph **11** photo-relief **12** electroplate, illustration, mazarine dish

See also **platter**

plateau
04 mesa, roof **05** grade, level, plane, stage, table **06** meseta, upland **08** highland, platform **09** Altiplano, stability, tableland

platform
03 pad, rig, top **04** aims, bema, dais, deck, kang, plan, site **05** basis, bench, crane, dolly, floor, ideas, stage, stand, stoep, stoop, stump **06** bridge, cradle, device, flotel, gantry, machan, oil rig, pallet, perron, podium, policy, pulpit, scheme, sketch, tenets **07** balcony, decking, estrade, floatel, foretop, maintop, plateau, rostrum, soapbox, sponson, terrace, tribune **08** barbette, flooring, labellum, predella, round top, scaffold, strategy **09** crow's-nest, drillship, footplate, gangboard, manifesto, party line, programme, traverser, turntable **10** dumb waiter, intentions, objectives, principles, roundabout **11** emplacement, entablement, monkey board, paint-bridge **12** landing stage, launching-pad

platinum
02 Pt

platitude
06 cliché, truism **07** bromide, inanity **08** banality, chestnut, flatness **10** generality, stereotype **11** commonplace **15** trite expression

platitudinous
03 set **04** dull, flat **05** banal, corny, inane, stale, stock, tired, trite, vapid **07** cliché'd **08** clichéed, truistic, well-worn **09** hackneyed **10** overworked **11** commonplace, stereotyped

platonic
05 ideal **09** non-sexual, spiritual **10** idealistic **11** incorporeal, non-physical, non-romantic **12** intellectual, transcendent

platoon
04 team, unit **05** group, squad, troop **06** outfit, patrol, volley **07** battery, company **08** squadron

platter
04 dish, lanx, tray **05** graal, grail, plate **06** grayle, salver **07** charger **08** trencher

See also **plate**

plaudits
04 hand **06** praise **07** acclaim, bouquet, hurrahs, ovation **08** accolade, applause, approval, clapping **09** good press **10** rave review **11** acclamation, approbation **12** commendation, pat on the back **15** congratulations, standing ovation

plausible
04 fair, glib **06** cogent, likely **07** logical,

plausibly

roball **08** credible, possible, probable, specious **10** acceptable, believable, colourable, convincing, imaginable, persuasive, reasonable, soft-spoken **11** conceivable, smooth-faced **12** smooth-spoken **13** silver-tongued, smooth-talking, smooth-tongued

plausibly

08 possibly, probably **09** logically **10** imaginably, pleasantly, reasonably **11** commendably, conceivably **12** convincingly, persuasively

play

◇ *anagram indicator*
02 do, no **03** act, fun, noh, pit, ply, toy **04** game, give, jest, laik, lake, plot, romp, room, show, work **05** caper, dance, drama, farce, flash, frisk, gleam, hobby, kicks, laugh, range, revel, rival, scope, slack, space, sport, wield **06** action, cavort, comedy, frolic, gamble, gambol, glance, join in, joking, leeway, margin, nogaku, oppose, take on, trifle **07** compete, flicker, flutter, freedom, have fun, holiday, leisure, liberty, licence, operate, pastime, perform, portray, shimmer, teasing, tragedy, twinkle, vie with **08** activity, exercise, free rein, gambling, latitude, movement **09** amusement, challenge, dalliance, diversion, enjoyment, interplay, looseness, melodrama, operation, play games, represent **10** recreation, take part in **11** flexibility, impersonate, interaction, merrymaking, move lightly, performance, transaction **12** be involved in **13** amuse yourself, enjoy yourself, entertainment, participate in, play the part of **14** compete against, divert yourself, occupy yourself

Plays include:

03 RUR
04 Loot
05 Equus, Faust, Le Cid, Medea, Médée, Roots, Yerma
06 Becket, Phèdre, St Joan
07 Amadeus, Candida, Electra, Endgame, Galileo, La Ronde, Oedipus, Oleanna, Orestes, Volpone, Woyzeck
08 Antigone, Betrayal, Everyman, Hay Fever, Huis Clos, Oresteia, Peer Gynt, Tartuffe, The Birds, The Flies, The Frogs, The Miser, The Price, The Wasps
09 All My Sons, Happy Days, Miss Julie, Party Time, Pygmalion, Saint Joan, The Chairs, The Clouds, The Father, The Rivals, The Vortex
10 A Dream Play, All for Love, Andromache, Andromaque, Lysistrata, Misery Guts, No Man's Land, The Bacchae, The Robbers, The Seagull, Uncle Vanya
11 A Doll's House, Blood and Ice, Hedda Gabler, The Blue Bird, The Crucible, The Wild Duck, Trojan Women
12 Anna Christie, Blithe Spirit, Blood

Wedding, Major Barbara, Private Lives, Punch and Judy, The Alchemist, The Caretaker, The Mousetrap
13 Arms and the Man, A Taste of Honey, Doctor Faustus, Educating Rita, Le Misanthrope, The Homecoming, The Jew of Malta, The White Devil, The Winslow Boy
14 Can't Pay? Won't Pay!, Krapp's Last Tape, Man and Superman, Orlando Furioso, Riders to the Sea, Separate Tables, The Country Wife, The Entertainer, The Silent Woman
15 Bartholomew Fair, Look Back in Anger, Prometheus Bound, The Beggar's Opera, The Iceman Cometh, The Three Sisters, Waiting for Godot

See also **Shakespeare**

• out of play
04 dead

• part of play
03 act

• play around with
◇ *anagram indicator*
07 toy with **08** fool with **09** dally with, flirt with **10** fiddle with, fidget with, meddle with, tamper with, trifle with **12** womanize with **13** interfere with, philander with **14** mess around with

• play at
06 affect **07** make out, pretend **10** put on an act **11** pretend to be

• play down
08 downplay, minimize **09** gloss over, underplay **10** understate, undervalue **11** make light of **13** underestimate

• play harshly
03 saw

• play on
07 exploit, trade on **08** profit by **12** capitalize on **13** turn to account **15** take advantage of

• play out
03 act **04** go on **05** enact **06** act out, unfold **07** carry on, exhaust, wear out **08** continue **10** be revealed

• play the fool
03 fon **04** daff, fool **07** act dido, tomfool

• play up
04 fool, hurt **05** annoy, boost **06** bother, stress **07** go wrong, not work, point up, trouble **09** be naughty, emphasize, highlight, misbehave, spotlight, underline **10** accentuate, exaggerate **11** give trouble, malfunction **12** be on the blink, go on the blink **13** be mischievous **15** call attention to

• play up to
04 fawn **05** toady **06** cozy up **07** flatter **08** blandish, bootlick, butter up, soft-soap, suck up to **15** curry favour with

• play with
◇ *anagram indicator*

play-act
03 act **04** fake, mime, sham **05** bluff, feign, put on **06** affect, assume **07** pretend **08** simulate **09** dissemble,

fabricate **10** put on an act **11** counterfeit, impersonate **15** pass yourself off

playboy
04 rake, roué **09** debauchee, ladies' man, libertine, socialite, womanizer **10** lady-killer **11** philanderer **12** man about town

player
01 E, N, S, W **03** ace, ham, man **04** east, pone, star, west **05** actor, north, south **06** artist **07** actress, artiste, trifler, trouper **08** comedian, musician **09** performer, sportsman **10** all-rounder, competitor, contestant **11** accompanist, entertainer, participant, sportswoman **15** instrumentalist

See also **Australian football**; **baseball**; **basketball**; **chess**; **footballer**; **instrument**; **rugby**; **tennis**

• bit player
05 extra

• opposing player
02 it

players
04 band, cast, wind **05** brass **07** strings
See also **football**; **orchestra**

playful
03 gay, mad **05** funny, ludic **06** frisky, impish, joking, lively, toyish **07** jesting, kitteny, puckish, roguish, teasing, toysome, waggish **08** espiègle, flippant, friendly, gamesome, humorous, skittish, spirited, sportive **09** facetious, fun-loving, kittenish, piacevole **10** frolicsome, rollicking **11** mischievous **12** high-spirited, light-hearted **13** tongue-in-cheek

playfully
06 in jest **08** jokingly **09** piacevole **10** humorously **11** facetiously **14** light-heartedly

playground
04 park **08** play area **12** playing-field **13** amusement park **14** pleasure ground

playmate
03 pal **04** chum, mate **05** buddy **06** friend **07** comrade **09** companion, neighbour **10** playfellow

plaything
03 toy **04** game **05** sport **06** bauble, gewgaw, puppet, trifle **07** pastime, trinket **08** gimcrack **09** amusement

playwright
06 writer **09** dramatist, tragedian **10** dramaturge **12** dramaturgist, screen writer, scriptwriter

Playwrights and screenwriters include:

02 Fo (Dario)
03 Fry (Christopher), Gay (John), Hay (Ian), Kyd (Thomas), May (Elaine)
04 Bolt (Robert), Bond (Edward), Coen (Ethan), Coen (Joel), Dane (Clemence), Ford (John), Hare

(David), Rowe (Nicholas), **Shaw**
(George Bernard), **Vega** (Lope de)
05 Albee (Edward), **Allen** (Woody),
Arden (John), **Bates** (Herbert
Ernest), **Behan** (Brendan), **Dumas**
(Alexandre), **Eliot** (T S), **Frayn**
(Michael), **Friel** (Brian), **Genet**
(Jean), **Gogol** (Nikolai), **Havel**
(Vaclav), **Ibsen** (Henrik), **Lodge**
(Thomas), **Lorca** (Federico García),
Mamet (David), **Nashe** (Thomas),
Odets (Clifford), **Orton** (Joe),
Otway (Thomas), **Sachs** (Hans),
Sachs (Nelly), **Smith** (Dodie), **Stone**
(Oliver), **Synge** (John Millington),
Udall (Nicholas), **Wilde** (Oscar),
Yeats (W B)
06 Barrie (Sir James Matthew), **Brecht**
(Bertolt), **Bridie** (James), **Colman**
(George), **Coward** (Sir Noël),
Dekker (Thomas), **Dryden** (John),
Galdós (Benito Pérez), **Goethe**
(Johann Wolfgang von), **Greene**
(Robert), **Herzog** (Werner), **Hilton**
(James), **Huston** (John), **Jerome**
(Jerome K), **Jonson** (Ben), **Kaiser**
(Georg), **Lerner** (Alan Jay), **Mercer**
(David), **Miller** (Arthur), **Miller**
(Henry), **Musset** (Alfred de),
O'Casey (Sean), **O'Neill** (Eugene),
Pinero (Sir Arthur Wing), **Pinter**
(Harold), **Powell** (Michael), **Racine**
(Jean), **Sardou** (Victorien), **Sartre**
(Jean-Paul), **Steele** (Sir Richard),
Storey (David), **Tagore**
(Rabindranath), **Wesker** (Arnold),
Wilder (Thornton)
07 Anouilh (Jean), **Arrabal** (Fernando),
Beckett (Samuel), **Bennett** (Alan),
Büchner (Georg), **Chapman**
(George), **Chekhov** (Anton),
Cocteau (Jean), **Coppola** (Francis
Ford), **Diderot** (Denis), **Garrick**
(David), **Gregory** (Lady Isabella
Augusta), **Holberg** (Ludvig, Baron),
Ionesco (Eugène), **Klinger**
(Friedrich Maximilian von), **Kubrick**
(Stanley), **Labiche** (Eugène),
Lardner (Ring), **Marlowe**
(Christopher), **Marston** (John),
McGough (Roger), **Mishima**
(Yukio), **Molière**, **Novello** (Ivor),
Osborne (John), **Plautus** (Titus
Maccius), **Richler** (Mordecai),
Rostand (Edmond), **Russell** (Willy),
Shaffer (Peter), **Shepard** (Sam),
Terence, **Ustinov** (Sir Peter), **Vicente**
(Gil), **Walcott** (Derek), **Webster**
(John)
08 Andersen (Hans Christian), **Banville**
(Théodore de), **Beaumont**
(Francis), **Björnson** (Björnstjerne),
Brentano (Clemens), **Burgoyne**
(John), **Congreve** (William),
Davenant (Sir William), **Fielding**
(Henry), **Fletcher** (John), **Hochhuth**
(Rolf), **Lochhead** (Liz), **Menander**,
Mortimer (Sir John), **Polanski**
(Roman), **Rattigan** (Sir Terence),
Schiller (Friedrich), **Shadwell**
(Thomas), **Sheridan** (Richard
Brinsley), **Stoppard** (Sir Tom),

Suckling (Sir John), **Tourneur** (Cyril),
Vanbrugh (Sir John), **Wedekind**
(Frank), **Williams** (Emlyn), **Williams**
(Tennessee)
09 Aeschylus, **Ayckbourn** (Sir Alan),
Corneille (Pierre), **D'Annunzio**
(Gabriele), **Euripides**, **Goldsmith**
(Oliver), **Hauptmann** (Gerhart),
Isherwood (Christopher),
Mankowitz (Wolf), **Marinetti**
(Filippo Tommaso), **Middleton**
(Thomas), **Poliakoff** (Stephen),
Priestley (J B), **Rosenthal** (Jack),
Sophocles, **Wycherley** (William)
10 Galsworthy (John), **Pirandello**
(Luigi), **Strindberg** (August)
11 Maeterlinck (Maurice),
Shakespeare (William)
12 Aristophanes, **Beaumarchais**
(Pierre-Augustin Caron de)

plea
05 alibi, claim, fains **06** appeal, excuse,
fains I, placet, placit, prayer
07 defence, defense, lawsuit, pretext,
request **08** demurrer, entreaty, fainites,
petition, placitum, pleading
10 invocation **11** declinature,
explanation, imploration, vindication
12 supplication **13** justification **14** nolo
contendere

plead
03 ask, beg **04** moot, urge **05** argue,
claim, state **06** adduce, allege, appeal,
assert **07** beseech, entreat, implore,
request, solicit **08** maintain, persuade,
perswade, petition **09** intercede
10 put forward **12** intercede for
• **refusing to plead**
04 mute

pleasant
04 cute, fine, nice **05** amene, lepid,
merry, tipsy **06** genial, groovy, jocund,
lekker, lovely **07** affable, amiable,
amusing, likable, welcome, winsome
08 all roses, charming, cheerful,
friendly, gorgeous, likeable, pleasing,
savorous, sunshiny **09** agreeable,
congenial, enjoyable, piacevole,
toothsome **10** acceptable, delightful,
gratifying, refreshing, salubrious,
satisfying **11** inoffensive
12 entertaining, good-humoured
14 roses all the way

pleasantly
07 nice and **09** enjoyably, piacevole,
plausibly **10** pleasingly **12** delightfully,
refreshingly **14** entertainingly

pleasantry
04 jest, joke, quip **05** sally **06** banter,
bon mot **08** badinage **09** enjoyment,
witticism **10** jocularity **12** casual
remark, pleasantness **13** polite
comment **14** friendly remark

please
04 like, list, suit, want, will, wish
05 agree, amuse, bitte, charm, cheer,
queme **06** arride, choose, desire,
divert, fulfil, humour, kindly, prefer, see
fit, tickle **07** aggrate, attract, cheer up,

content, delight, flatter, gladden,
gratify, indulge, prithee, prythee,
satisfy **08** appeal to, think fit
09 captivate, entertain, make happy
11 if you please **12** je vous en prie
14 give pleasure to
• **hard to please**
04 nice **09** difficult

pleased
04 glad, rapt **05** happy **06** elated
07 chuffed **08** cheerful, euphoric,
grateful, gruntled, thrilled
09 contented, delighted, delirious,
gratified, satisfied **10** complacent **11** on
cloud nine, over the moon, tickled pink

pleasing
04 cute, fair, fine, good, nice **05** lusty
06 comely, liking, taking **07** amusing,
savoury, winning **08** charming,
engaging, pleasant **09** agreeable,
desirable, enjoyable **10** acceptable,
attractive, delectable, delightful,
gratifying, satisfying **11** pleasurable
12 entertaining, heartwarming, honey-
tongued **13** prepossessing

pleasurable
03 fun **04** good, nice **06** groovy, lovely
07 amusing, welcome **08** luscious,
pleasant **09** agreeable, congenial,
diverting, enjoyable **10** delightful,
gratifying **12** entertaining

pleasure
03 fun, gem, joy **04** will, wish **05** glory,
mirth, prize **06** choice, desire, heaven,
solace, thrill **07** command, delight,
elation, leisure, purpose **08** gladness,
treasure **09** amusement, enjoyment,
happiness, hog heaven, pleasance
10 preference, recreation, sensuality
11 complacence, complacency,
contentment, dissipation, inclination
12 satisfaction **13** entertainment,
gratification
• **expression of pleasure**
03 aha, boy, oho, ooh, wow **05** good-
o, oh boy, tra-la, whack, wowee, zowie
06 good-oh, gotcha, whacko **07** way
to go!, whoopee **10** hubba hubba
• **it's a pleasure**
07 any time **08** forget it, not at all **09** no
problem **10** my pleasure **11** it's all right
12 it's no trouble, it was nothing, you're
welcome **13** don't mention it, that's all
right
• **with pleasure**
04 fain **06** gladly **07** happily, readily
08 of course **09** willingly **11** avec plaisir

pleasure-flight
04 flip

pleat
04 fold, kilt, purl, tuck **05** braid, crimp,
flute, pinch, plait, prank **06** crease,
gather, goffer, pranck, pucker
07 folding, gauffer, plicate, prancke
09 plication **10** intertwine

plebeian
03 low **04** base, boor, mean, non-U,
pleb **05** prole **06** coarse, common,
vulgar, worker **07** ignoble, low-born,

plebiscite

peasant, popular **08** commoner, roturier **09** unrefined, vulgarian **10** lower-class, uncultured **11** proletarian **12** common person, uncultivated, working-class **15** undistinguished

plebiscite
04 poll, vote **06** ballot **09** straw poll **10** referendum

pledge
03 vow, wad, wed **04** bail, band, bond, fine, gage, hand, oath, pass, pawn, wage, word **05** swear, vouch, wager **06** borrow, commit, engage, impawn, plight, secure, surety **07** betroth, deposit, earnest, hostage, promise, propine, warrant **08** contract, covenant, impledge, mortgage, security **09** assurance, committal, guarantee, pignorate, sacrament, undertake **10** collateral, commitment, take an oath **11** impignorate, undertaking **12** give your word, word of honour

plenary
04 full, open **05** whole **06** entire **07** general **08** absolute, complete, integral, sweeping, thorough **09** unlimited **11** unqualified **12** unrestricted **13** unconditional

plenipotentiary
05 envoy **06** legate, nuncio **08** absolute, diplomat, emissary, minister **09** dignitary **10** ambassador

plenitude
06 bounty, excess, plenty, wealth **08** fullness, plethora **09** abundance, amplitude, profusion, repletion **10** cornucopia, entireness **11** copiousness **12** completeness **13** plenteousness, plentifulness

plenteous
04 rich **05** ample **06** bumper, lavish **07** copious, fertile, liberal, profuse **08** abundant, fruitful, generous, infinite, prolific **09** abounding, bounteous, bountiful, luxuriant, plentiful **10** productive **11** overflowing **13** inexhaustible

plentiful
04 easy **05** ample, routh, rowth **06** bumper, lavish **07** copious, liberal, profuse, teeming **08** abundant, fruitful, generous, infinite **09** bounteous, bountiful **10** productive **11** overflowing **13** inexhaustible

plentifully
05 amply **08** lavishly **09** copiously, liberally, profusely **10** abundantly, fruitfully, generously **11** bountifully

plenty
04 bags, fund, mass, mine **05** store **06** enough, foison, riches, scouth, scowth, volume, wealth **07** fortune, fulness **08** fullness, plethora, quantity **09** abundance, affluence, profusion, substance **10** abundantly, cornucopia, prosperity **11** copiousness, sufficiency,

wealthiness **12** milk and honey **13** plenteousness **14** stouth and routh
• **plenty of**
04 bags, lots, many **05** heaps, loads, piles **06** enough, masses, stacks **09** shedloads **11** large amount, large number **14** more than enough

plethora
04 glut **06** excess **07** surfeit, surplus **09** abundance, profusion, repletion **11** repleteness, superfluity **12** overfullness **13** overabundance **14** superabundance

pliability
08 docility **09** ductility **10** compliance, elasticity, plasticity **11** amenability, bendability, flexibility **12** adaptability, malleability **13** tractableness **14** suggestibility, susceptibility

pliable
05 bendy, lithe **06** docile, pliant, supple **07** elastic, plastic **08** bendable, biddable, cheverel, cheveril, flexible, yielding **09** adaptable, compliant, malleable, receptive, tractable **10** manageable, responsive **11** persuadable, susceptible **12** superplastic **13** accommodating **14** impressionable

pliant
05 bendy, lithe, swack, swank, wanle **06** docile, limber, supple, wandle, wannel, whippy **07** elastic, plastic, pliable **08** bendable, biddable, flexible, yielding **09** adaptable, compliant, malleable, receptive, tractable **10** manageable, responsive, sequacious **11** persuadable, susceptible **13** accommodating **14** impressionable

plight
03 fix, jam, vow **04** case, fold, hole, mood, risk, trim **05** array, plait, point, state, swear, vouch, weave **06** enfold, engage, liking, pickle, pledge, scrape, secure, taking **07** dilemma, pliskie, promise, propose, straits, trouble **08** affiance, contract, covenant, quandary **09** condition, extremity, guarantee, situation, tight spot **10** difficulty, engagement **11** dire straits, predicament **13** circumstances

plimsoll
03 dap **05** tacky **07** gym shoe **08** sandshoe

plod
04 plot, slog, thud, toil **05** clump, grind, stomp, stump, tramp **06** drudge, labour, lumber, stodge, trudge **07** peg away **08** plug away **09** persevere, policeman, soldier on **11** police force, walk heavily **13** plough through

plodder
03 mug, sap **06** drudge, toiler **07** dullard, slogger

plot
03 bed, erf, lay, lot, map, web **04** area, brew, burn, draw, mark, pack, plan, plod, ruse **05** cabal, chart, draft, frame,

hatch, patch, piece, ploat, scald, story, theme, tract **06** action, cook up, design, devise, fleece, garden, locate, map out, parcel, scheme, scorch, sketch, thread **07** collude, concoct, connive, dispose, outline, project, subject **08** conspire, contrive, intrigue, scenario **09** allotment, calculate, machinate, narrative, storyline, stratagem **10** conspiracy **11** machination

plotter
06 dabble, potter **07** planner, schemer **08** dabbling, designer, paddling **09** intriguer **10** machinator **11** conspirator

plough
◇ *anagram indicator*
03 ard, dig, ear, ere, pip, rib **04** beam, fail, list, plow, rive, sill, till, work **05** break, ridge, spade **06** Dipper, fallow, furrow, lister, pleuch, pleugh, rafter, ridger, triones, turn up **07** break up, scooter, tractor, triones, wrinkle **08** the Wagon **09** Big Dipper, cultivate, Great Bear, subsoiler, Ursa Major **10** Seven Stars **11** agriculture, drill-plough, swing-plough, wheel plough **12** Charles's Wain, septentrions **13** septentrions
• **plough into**
03 hit **06** go into **07** collide, run into **08** bump into **09** crash into, drive into, smash into
• **plough through**
11 plod through, wade through **13** trudge through

ploughshare
04 sock **05** share

plover
04 dupe **06** godwit **07** dottrel, killdee, lapwing **08** dotterel, killdeer, wire bird **09** thick knee **10** Charadrius, prostitute, stone snipe
• **flock of plovers**
04 wing

ploy
04 game, move, ruse, wile **05** dodge, trick **06** device, scheme, tactic **08** artifice **09** manoeuvre, stratagem **10** subterfuge **11** contrivance

pluck
03 pip, rob, tug **04** draw, fail, grit, guts, pick, plot, pook, pouk, pull, race, rase, yank **05** heart, nerve, ploat, plunk, spunk, strip, strum, thrum, twang **06** avulse, daring, evulse, finger, fleece, gather, humble, mettle, remove, rescue, snatch, spirit, take in, tweeze, twitch, valour **07** bravery, collect, courage, despoil, extract, harvest, pull off, swindle **08** audacity, backbone, boldness **09** fortitude **10** resolution **11** divellicate, intrepidity **12** fearlessness **13** determination

pluckily
06 boldly **07** bravely **08** daringly **09** valiantly **10** fearlessly, heroically,

intrepidly **11** audaciously, confidently **12** courageously **13** adventurously

plucky
04 bold, game, gamy **05** brave, gamey, gutsy, gutty **06** daring, feisty, gallus, gritty, heroic, spunky **07** gallows, valiant **08** fearless, intrepid, spirited **09** audacious **10** courageous, determined

plug
02 ad **03** DIN, wad **04** blow, bung, cake, chew, cork, dook, fill, hype, neck, pack, puff, push, seal, stem, stop, tent, tout **05** block, blurb, choke, close, promo, punch, SCART, shoot, spile, stuff, twist **06** dossil, dottle, fipple, market, spigot, stop up, tampon **07** go-devil, mention, pessary, promote, stopper, stopple, tampion, tompion **08** good word **09** access eye, advertise, promotion, publicity, publicize **10** commercial **11** suppository **13** advertisement **14** recommendation
* **plug away**
04 toil **06** plod on **07** peg away **08** preserve, slog away, toil away **09** persevere, soldier on **10** keep trying

plum
04 best, kaki **05** cushy, prize, prune **06** choice, damson, mussel **07** bullace, quetsch **08** damaskin, prunello, victoria **09** damascene, damaskeen, damasquin, excellent, greengage, mirabelle, myrobalan, naseberry, persimmon, sapodilla **10** damasceene, first-class

plumb
04 bang, dead, slap, true **05** gauge, level, probe, right, sheer, sound **06** bullet, fathom, search, spot-on **07** exactly, examine, explore, measure, plummet, utterly **08** sound out, vertical **09** delve into, out-and-out, penetrate, precisely, search out, up and down **10** straight up, vertically **11** investigate, verticality **12** straight down **13** thorough-going **15** perpendicularly
* **plumb in**
03 fit, fix, put **05** place, put in, set up **07** install **08** position
* **plumb the depths of**
13 reach the nadir **15** experience fully, reach rock bottom

plumbing
Plumbing fittings and equipment include:
02 WC
03 pan, tap, tee
04 bath, bend, bowl, flux, hose, pipe, plug, pump, sink, tank, trap
05 auger, basin, bidet, float, joint, P-trap, U-bend, union, valve
06 boiler, faucet, gasket, geyser, hopper, nipple, shower, solder, toilet, urinal, washer
07 cistern, coupler, plunger, reducer, stop end, Y-branch

08 ballcock, cylinder, drain rod, lavatory, lever tap, mixer tap, pedestal, pipe clip, radiator, soil vent, stopcock, sump pump, valve key
09 ball valve, blowtorch, draincock, gate valve, mains pipe, nipple key, waste pipe
10 back boiler, bottle trap, check valve, copper pipe, copper tube, elbow joint, flare joint, header tank, pipe bender, pipe cutter, pipe wrench, programmer, septic tank, shower head, Teflon® tape, thermostat, tube cutter
11 water closet
12 basin spanner, ceiling joint, monkey wrench, overflow bend, pipe coupling, siphon washer
13 deburring tool, expansion tank, lavatory chain
14 gas water heater, Stillson® wrench
15 immersion heater

plume
04 tuft **05** crest, preen, quill **06** osprey, pappus, pinion **07** feather, marabou, panache, plumule **08** aigrette, marabout, streamer
* **plume yourself on**
07 exult in **10** boast about **13** preen yourself, pride yourself

plummet
04 dive, drop, fall, lead **05** plumb, sound **06** fathom, hurtle, plunge, tumble **07** descend **08** nose-dive **09** plumb line **11** drop rapidly, fall rapidly **15** decrease quickly

plummy
01 U **04** posh **07** refined **08** affected **09** desirable, high-class **10** profitable, upper-class **12** aristocratic

plump
03 fat **04** blow, bold, drop, dump, fall, flop, full, plop, sink, soss, swap, swop, tidy **05** ample, beefy, blurt, bonny, buxom, clump, dumpy, gross, jolly, large, obese, plunk, podgy, round, shoot, slump, sonsy, souse, squab, stout, swell, tubby **06** bonnie, chubby, cuddly, flabby, fleshy, plunge, portly, rotund, sonsie, strike **07** cluster, deposit, descend, put down, set down, well-fed **08** chopping, collapse, generous, matronly **09** corpulent, downright **10** cuddlesome, embonpoint, roundabout, well-liking, well-padded **11** well-covered, well-rounded **15** well-upholstered
* **plump for**
04 back **06** choose, favour, opt for, prefer, select **07** support **08** side with

plumpness
03 fat **07** fatness, obesity **09** podginess, pudginess, rotundity, stoutness, tubbiness **10** chubbiness, corpulence, fleshiness, portliness

plunder
03 rob **04** loot, peel, pill, prey, raid, rape, reif, sack, swag **05** berob, booty,

harry, prize, reave, reive, rifle, scoff, shave, skoff, spoil, steal, strip **06** fleece, forage, maraud, ravage, spoils, spulye **07** despoil, escheat, hership, pillage, ransack, spulyie, spulzie, stick up **08** lay waste, pickings, spoliate, spuilzie **09** depredate, devastate, herriment, herryment, sprechery **10** spreaghery **14** ill-gotten gains

plunge
03 dip, jab, ram **04** bull, dash, dive, drop, duck, enew, fall, jump, mire, push, rush, sink, stab, tank, tear **05** crash, douse, dowse, drive, lunge, merge, pitch, plump, raker, shove, souse, stick, swoop, throw, whelm **06** beduck, career, charge, go down, hurtle, launch, thrust, tumble **07** demerge, demerse, descend, descent, immerge, immerse, plummet **08** bull into, dive-bomb, emplonge, implunge, nose-dive, submerge **09** immersion **10** submersion **11** drop rapidly, fall rapidly **12** enew yourself **15** decrease quickly
* **take the plunge**
07 go for it **13** bite the bullet **14** commit yourself

plurality
04 bulk, mass, most **06** galaxy, number **07** variety **08** majority **09** diversity, profusion **12** multiplicity, numerousness **13** preponderance

plus
03 and **04** gain, perk, with **05** asset, bonus, extra **06** credit **07** added to, benefit, surplus **08** addition, as well as, increase, positive **09** advantage, good point **10** additional **12** advantageous, in addition to, not to mention, over and above, together with

plush
04 posh, rich **05** ritzy **06** costly, de luxe, glitzy, lavish, luxury, swanky **07** opulent, stylish **08** affluent, palatial **09** luxurious, sumptuous

Pluto
03 Dis **05** Hades

plutocrat
05 Dives **06** fat cat, tycoon **07** Croesus, gold-bug, magnate, rich man **09** moneybags **10** capitalist **11** billionaire, millionaire

plutonium
02 Pu

ply
◇ *anagram indicator*
02 go **03** ren, rin, run, set, use **04** bend, birl, feed, fold, leaf, lush, play **05** apply, beset, birle, ferry, layer, sheet, trade, wield **06** assail, employ, follow, handle, harass, lavish, pursue, strand, supply, travel, work at **07** bombard, carry on, furnish, provide, utilize **08** engage in, exercise, practise **09** condition, importune, thickness **10** manipulate **13** keep supplying

PM *see* prime minister

oach

copy, lift, nick, poke, take **05** potch, eal **06** borrow, pilfer, potche, thrust intrude, trample **08** encroach, fringe, trespass **11** appropriate hunt illegally **14** catch illegally

ocket

containment indicator

bag, bin, fob, pot **04** gain, lift, mini, ck, poke, take, whip **05** filch, funds, eans, money, patch, pinch, pouch, urse, small, steal, touch **06** assets, udget, cavity, hollow, little, pilfer, otted **07** capital, compact, concise, acket, purloin, trouser **08** abridged, nvelope, finances, fob-watch, pint-ze, portable, souvenir **09** miniature, aid-neuk, resources, small area receptacle, small group appropriate, compartment, herewithal, win unfairly **12** isolated rea **14** help yourself to
ee also **steal**

ockmark

pit **04** pock, scar **07** blemish, ockpit

od

cod **04** case, hull, husk, pipi chile, chili, shell, shuck **06** chilli, gume, loment, paunch, peacod, hool **07** musk-bag, peascod, silicle, liqua, silique **08** lomentum, easecod, silicula, silicule, strombus, ugar pea, tamarind **09** green bean, angetout **10** cotton boll **11** pudding-ipe **12** mangetout pea

odgy

fat **05** dumpy, plump, squat, stout, ubby **06** chubby, chunky, fleshy, otund, spuddy, stubby, stumpy paunchy **08** roly-poly corpulent, roll-about

odium

dais, foot, hand **05** stage, stand rostrum **08** platform **09** stylobate

oem

Poem types include:

dit, lay, ode
awdl, ditt, epic, epos, idyl, song, waka
ditty, elegy, epode, haiku, idyll, lyric, rhyme, tanka, verse
ballad, epopee, monody, sonnet
bucolic, couplet, eclogue, epigram, georgic, pantoum, rondeau, sestina, triolet, virelay
cinquain, clerihew, limerick, lipogram, madrigal, palinode, pastoral, thin poem, verselet, versicle
roundelay, shape poem
villanelle
concrete poem, epithalamium, nursery rhyme, prothalamion

Poems and poetry collections include:

If
A Red, Crow, Days, Edda, Hope, Howl, Maud, Odes

---

05 Comus, Lamia
06 Façade, Heaven, Hellas, Marina, The Fly, Villon
07 A Vision, Beowulf, Don Juan, Lycidas, Mariana, Marmion, Red Rose, Requiem, Rondeau, The Quip, Ulysses
08 Bermudas, Endymion, Georgics, Gunga Din, Hiawatha, Hudibras, Hysteria, Insomnia, Kalevala, Lupercal, Queen Mab, Ramayana, The Iliad, The Night, The Pearl, The Tyger, Tithonus, To Autumn
09 Decameron, Human Life, Jerusalem, Kubla Khan, The Aeneid, The Cantos
10 Cherry Ripe, Christabel, Dream Songs, In Memoriam, Lalla Rookh, On an Island, The Dunciad, The Odyssey, The Poetics, The Prelude, The Village, Up in the Air, Very Old Man, View of a Pig
11 Ars Amatoria, Empty Vessel, High Windows, Holy Sonnets, Humming-Bird, Jabberwocky, Mahabharata, Memorabilia, Remembrance, Song of my Cid, Sudden Light, Tall Nettles, Tam O'Shanter, The Eclogues, The Exstasie, The Peasants, The Retreate, The Sick Rose, The Sluggard, The Woodlark
12 A Glass of Beer, Ash Wednesday, A Song to Celia, A Song to David, Auld Lang Syne, Bhagavad Gita, Eugene Onegin, Faith Healing, Four Quartets, Goblin Market, Hawk Roosting, Homage to Clio, Jubilate Agno, Mercian Hymns, Morte d'Arthur, Ode to Evening, Paradise Lost, Piers Plowman, The Hill-Shade, The Lucy Poems, The Troop Ship, The Visionary, The Waste Land, The Windhover
13 Arms and the Boy, Behind the Line, Gilgamesh Epic, Leaves of Grass, Metamorphoses, Missing the Sea, Naming of Parts, Roman de la Rose, September Song, Song by Isbrand, The Book of Thel
14 A Shropshire Lad, Divina Commedia, Leda and the Swan, Les Fleurs du Mal, Love Songs in Age, Lyrical Ballads, Orlando Furioso, Song of Hiawatha, Strange Meeting, The Divine Image, The Feel of Hands, The Garden Party, The Lotus-Eaters, The Ship of Death, Venus and Adonis
15 Canterbury Tales, Cautionary Tales, Love without Hope, Magna est Veritas, Ode on Melancholy, Summoned by Bells, The Age of Anxiety, The Divine Comedy, The Eve of St Agnes, The Faerie Queene, The Garden of Love, The Grauballe Man, The Second Coming, The Sorrow of Love

See also **poetry**; **song**

---

poet

04 bard, scop **06** rhymer **07** elegist,

---

rhymist **08** beat poet, idyllist, lyricist, minstrel **09** balladeer, poetaster, poeticule, rhymester, sonneteer, versifier **10** verse-maker
15 performance poet

Poets include:

03 Gay (John), Lee (Laurie), Paz (Octavio), Poe (Edgar Allan)
04 Amis (Kingsley), Blok (Alexander), Cope (Wendy), Dunn (Douglas), Dyer (Sir Edward), Gray (Thomas), Gunn (Thom), Hill (Geoffrey), Hogg (James), Hood (Thomas), Hunt (Leigh), Lear (Edward), Maro (Publius Vergilius), Muir (Edwin), Nash (Ogden), Ovid, Owen (Wilfred), Pope (Alexander), Rich (Adrienne), Seth (Vikram), Vega (Lope de)
05 Auden (W H), Basho (Matsuo), Benét (Stephen Vincent), Blake (William), Burns (Robert), Byron (George, Lord), Clare (John), Crane (Hart), Dante, Donne (John), Duffy (Carol Ann), Eliot (T S), Frost (Robert), Hardy (Thomas), Harte (Brett), Heine (Heinrich), Henri (Adrian), Hesse (Hermann), Homer, Ibsen (Henrik), Iqbal (Sir Muhammad), Keats (John), Keble (John), Lodge (Thomas), Lorca (Federico García), Marot (Clément), Meung (Jean de), Moore (Thomas), Myers (Frederic William Henry), O'Hara (Frank), Opitz (Martin), Plath (Sylvia), Pound (Ezra), Prior (Matthew), Pulci (Luigi), Raine (Craig), Rilke (Rainer Maria), Sachs (Hans), Sachs (Nelly), Scott (Sir Walter), Smart (Christopher), Smith (Stevie), Spark (Dame Muriel), Tasso (Torquato), Wyatt (Sir Thomas), Yeats (W B)
06 Adcock (Fleur), Aragon (Louis), Arnold (Matthew), Artaud (Antonin), Atwood (Margaret), Barnes (William), Bellay (Joachim du), Belloc (Hilaire), Benoît (Laurence), Bishop (Elizabeth), Brecht (Bertolt), Brontë (Anne), Brontë (Emily), Brooke (Rupert), Camäes (Luís de), Carver (Raymond), Cowper (William), Crabbe (George), Dunbar (William), Eluard (Paul), Empson (Sir William), Ennius (Quintus), Fuller (Roy), Goethe (Johann Wolfgang von), Graves (Robert), Gurney (Ivor), Haller (Albrecht von), Heaney (Seamus), Herder (Johann Gottfried von), Hesiod, Horace, Hughes (Langston), Jensen (Johannes Vilhelm), Larkin (Philip), Lorris (Guillaume de), Lowell (Amy), Lowell (Robert), Millay (Edna St Vincent), Milosz (Czeslaw), Milton (John), Morris (William), Musset (Alfred de), Neruda (Pablo), Ossian, Patten (Brian), Pindar, Porter (Peter), Racine (Jean), Ramsay (Allan), Riding (Laura), Sappho, Sidney (Sir Philip), Surrey

(Henry Howard, Earl of),**Tagore** (Rabindranath),**Thomas** (Dylan), **Thomas** (Edward),**Thomas** (R S), **Valéry** (Paul),**Villon** (François), **Virgil**,**Waller** (Edmund)

07 **Addison** (Joseph), **Akahito** (Yamabe no), **Alberti** (Leon Battista), **Aneurin**, **Angelou** (Maya), **Aretino** (Pietro), **Ariosto** (Ludovico), **Ashbery** (John), **Barbour** (John), **Beckett** (Samuel), **Beddoes** (Thomas Lovell), **Blunden** (Edmund Charles), **Boiardo** (Matteo Maria), **Brodsky** (Joseph), **Büchner** (Georg), **Caedmon**, **Campion** (Thomas), **Causley** (Charles), **Chapman** (George), **Chaucer** (Geoffrey), **Cocteau** (Jean), **Da Ponte** (Lorenzo), **Douglas** (Gawain), **Durrell** (Lawrence), **Emerson** (Ralph Waldo), **Flecker** (James Elroy), **Fröding** (Gustaf), **Gautier** (Théophile), **Herbert** (George), **Herrick** (Robert), **Holberg** (Ludvig, Baron), **Hopkins** (Gerard Manley), **Housman** (A E), **Jiménez** (Juan Ramón), **Johnson** (Samuel), **Kipling** (Rudyard), **Layamon**, **Lydgate** (John), **Macbeth** (George), **MacCaig** (Norman), **MacLean** (Sorley), **Manzoni** (Alessandro), **Martial**, **Marvell** (Andrew), **McGough** (Roger), **Mishima** (Yukio), **Mistral** (Frédéric), **Mistral** (Gabriela), **Montale** (Eugenio), **Novalis**, **Orléans** (Charles Duc d'), **Patmore** (Coventry), **Pushkin** (Alexander), **Quarles** (Francis), **Rimbaud** (Arthur), **Roethke** (Theodore), **Ronsard** (Pierre de), **Rostand** (Edmond), **Sassoon** (Siegfried), **Seferis**, **Seifert** (Jaroslav), **Shelley** (Percy Bysshe), **Sitwell** (Dame Edith), **Sitwell** (Sir Sacheverell), **Skelton** (John), **Spender** (Sir Stephen), **Spenser** (Edmund), **Stevens** (Wallace),**Terence**, **Thomson** (James),**Thoreau** (Henry David),**Vaughan** (Henry),**Vicente** (Gil),**Walcott** (Derek),**Whitman** (Walt),**Wieland** (Christoph Martin)

08 **Anacreon**, **Andersen** (Hans Christian), **Ausonius** (Decimus Magnus), **Banville** (Théodore de), **Berryman** (John), **Brentano** (Clemens), **Brittain** (Vera), **Browning** (Elizabeth Barrett), **Browning** (Robert), **Campbell** (Roy), **Carducci** (Giosuè), **Catullus** (Gaius Valerius), **Claudian**, **Congreve** (William), **cummings** (e e), **Cynewulf**, **Davenant** (Sir William), **De La Mare** (Walter), **Drummond** (William, of Hawthornden), **Firdausi**, **Ginsberg** (Allen), **Henryson** (Robert), **Laforgue** (Jules), **Langland** (William), **Lawrence** (D H), **Leopardi** (Giacomo), **Lovelace** (Richard), **Macaulay** (Dame Rose), **Macaulay** (Thomas), **MacLeish** (Archibald), **MacNeice** (Louis), **Malherbe**

(François de), **Mallarmé** (Stéphane), **Menander**, **Milligan** (Spike), **Palgrave** (Francis Turner), **Paterson** (Andrew Barton), **Petrarch**, **Robinson** (Edwin Arlington), **Rossetti** (Christina), **Rossetti** (Dante Gabriel), **Sandburg** (Carl), **Schiller** (Friedrich), **Schlegel** (August Wilhelm von), **Suckling** (Sir John),**Taliesin**,**Tibullus**,**Traherne** (Thomas),**Verlaine** (Paul),**Whittier** (John Greenleaf)

09 **Aeschylus**, **Akhmatova** (Anna), **Bronowski** (Jacob), **Coleridge** (Samuel Taylor), **D'Annunzio** (Gabriele), **Dickinson** (Emily), **Froissart** (Jean), **Goldsmith** (Oliver), **Hölderlin** (Friedrich), **Lamartine** (Alphonse de), **Lucretius**, **Marinetti** (Filippo Tommaso), **Pasternak** (Boris), **Rochester** (John Wilmot, Earl of), **Rosenberg** (Isaac), **Santayana** (George), **Southwell** (Robert), **Swinburne** (Algernon Charles), **Ungaretti** (Giuseppe), **Zephaniah** (Benjamin)

10 **Baudelaire** (Charles), **Bradstreet** (Anne), **Chatterton** (Thomas), **Chesterton** (G K), **Empedocles**, **FitzGerald** (Edward), **La Fontaine** (Jean de), **Lagerkvist** (Pär), **Longfellow** (Henry Wadsworth), **MacDiarmid** (Hugh), **Mayakovsky** (Vladimir), **McGonagall** (William), **Propertius** (Sextus),**Theocritus**

11 **Apollinaire** (Guillaume), **Callimachus**, **Omar Khayyám**, **Shakespeare** (William), **Yevtushenko** (Yevegeny)

12 **Ferlinghetti** (Lawrence)

13 **Sackville-West** (Vita)

14 **Dante Alighieri**, **Saint-John Perse**

15 **Thomas the Rhymer**

• **poet laureate**
02 PL

Poets laureate:

03 **Pye** (Henry)

04 **Rowe** (Nicholas),**Tate** (Nahum)

06 **Austin** (Alfred), **Cibber** (Colley), **Dryden** (John), **Eusden** (Laurence), **Hughes** (Ted), **Jonson** (Ben), **Motion** (Andrew),**Warton** (Thomas)

07 **Bridges** (Robert), **Southey** (Robert)

08 **Betjeman** (Sir John), **Davenant** (Sir William), **Day-Lewis** (Cecil), **Shadwell** (Thomas),**Tennyson** (Alfred, Lord)

09 **Masefield** (John),**Whitehead** (William)

10 **Wordsworth** (William)

poetic
06 moving **07** flowing, lyrical, rhyming **08** artistic, creative, graceful, metrical, poetical, symbolic **09** beautiful, sensitive **10** expressive, figurative, rhythmical **11** imaginative

poetry
04 muse **05** poems, poesy, rhyme, verse **06** epopee, lyrics **07** doggrel,

iambics, pennill, rhyming, versing **08** doggerel, epopoeia **09** free verse, macaronic, Parnassus, vers libre **10** macaronics **13** versification

Poetry movements include:

04 Beat
05 found, sound
07 Acmeism, digital, epitaph, erasure imagism
08 concrete, medieval, pastoral, Trouvère
09 automatic, modernism, symbolism Troubador, Victorian
10 Parnassian
11 Minnesinger, objectivist, performance, Romanticism,The Movement, traditional
12 metaphysical
13 Black Mountain, New York School non-conformism, post-modernism
14 chanson de geste

See also **poem**

pogrom
06 murder **07** carnage, killing **08** butchery, genocide, homicide, massacre **09** bloodbath, holocaust, slaughter **10** decimation **11** liquidation **12** annihilation **13** extermination **15** ethnic cleansing

poignancy
04 pain **06** misery, pathos **07** emotion feeling, sadness, tragedy **08** distress, keenness, piquancy, pungency **09** intensity, sentiment, sharpness **10** bitterness, tenderness **11** painfulness, piteousness **12** wretchedness **13** evocativeness

poignant
03 sad **05** sharp **06** moving, tender, tragic **07** painful, piquant, piteous, poynant, pungent, tearful **08** haunting pathetic, pricking, stinging, touching, wretched **09** affecting, agonizing, emotional, heartfelt, miserable, sorrowful, upsetting **11** distressing, penetrating **12** heart-rending **13** heartbreaking

poignantly
05 sadly **08** movingly, tenderly **09** miserably, painfully, tearfully **10** tragically, wretchedly **11** emotionally, sorrowfully **12** pathetically

point
01 E, N, S,W **02** pt **03** ace, aim, dot, end, hit, neb, nib, nub, ord, tip, top, use **04** apex, area, cape, case, core, crag, crux, cusp, fang, feat, gist, goal, head, hint, item, lace, mark, meat, ness, node, peak, pike, pith, show, site, spot stop, time, tine, vein, whit **05** drift, facet, heart, issue, level, place, score, sense, speck, spike, stage, state, sting, taper, tenor, theme, topic, total, train, trait, value, verge **06** aspect, burden, clause, denote, detail, direct, marrow, matter, moment, motive, object, period, plight, reason, signal, thrust **07** essence, feature, heading, instant,

keynote, meaning, purpose, quality, sharpen, signify, subject, suggest **08** evidence, foreland, full stop, headland, indicate, juncture, locality, location, position, property, pungency, question, sharp end **09** attribute, condition, designate, extremity, full point, gesture at, intention, main point, north pole, objective, situation, south pole **10** conclusion, importance, particular, promontory, resolution **11** culmination **12** central point, decimal point, significance **14** characteristic, gesture towards

See also **compass**; **horse**

• **beside the point**
09 unrelated **10** immaterial, irrelevant, out of place, red herring **11** unconnected

• **chief points**
03 sum

• **in point of fact**
03 nay **06** indeed, in fact, really **08** actually **09** in reality **15** as a matter of fact

• **lowest point**
04 zero

• **main point**
04 clou, gist

• **on the point of**
07 about to, going to, ready to **10** in danger of **11** just about to, preparing to **12** on the brink of, on the verge of

• **point of view**
03 POV **04** view **05** angle, slant **06** aspect, belief, stance **07** feeling, opinion, outlook **08** approach, attitude, position **09** judgement, sentiment, viewpoint **10** Anschauung, standpoint **11** perspective

• **point out**
04 shew, show **05** judge **06** remind, reveal **07** bring up, mention, point to, presage, specify **08** allude to, identify, indicate **09** highlight **15** call attention to, draw attention to

• **point up**
06 stress **09** emphasize, highlight, underline **15** call attention to

• **to the point**
05 ad rem **07** germane, related **08** apposite, pregnant, relevant **09** connected, pertinent **10** applicable **11** appropriate

• **up to a point**
06 partly **08** slightly, somewhat **12** to some degree, to some extent

point-blank
04 flat, near, open **05** blunt, frank, level, plain, reach **06** candid, direct, openly, rudely **07** bluntly, closely, close to, frankly, plainly **08** abruptly, candidly, directly, explicit, outright, straight, touching **10** explicitly, forthright, unreserved **12** at close range, forthrightly **13** unequivocally **15** straightforward

pointed
04 keen, urdé, urdy **05** clear, edged, sharp, spicy, urdée **06** barbed, biting, Gothic, lancet **07** cutting, mordant,

obvious, precise, telling **08** acicular, aculeate, explicit, forceful, incisive, striking, tapering **09** aculeated, cuspidate, mucronate, trenchant **10** cuspidated, fastigiate, lanceolate, mucronated **11** lanceolated, near the bone, penetrating **12** epigrammatic **14** epigrammatical

pointedly
07 bluntly, plainly **09** defiantly, on purpose **10** explicitly **13** intentionally, provocatively

pointer
03 rod, tip **04** cane, clue, hand, hint, pole, sign **05** arrow, guide, index, stick, style **06** advice, fescue, needle, tongue **07** caution, warning **09** guideline, hyperlink, indicator **10** indication, suggestion **11** trafficator **13** piece of advice **14** recommendation

pointless
◇ *tail deletion indicator*
04 vain **05** inane **06** absurd, futile **07** aimless, foolish, useless **08** muticous **09** a mug's game, fruitless, senseless, to no avail, valueless, worthless **10** ridiculous, unavailing **11** meaningless, nonsensical **12** a waste of time, unproductive, unprofitable **13** insignificant **14** a waste of effort

pointlessly
06 in vain **09** aimlessly **11** senselessly **12** unprofitably **13** meaninglessly **14** unproductively

poise
04 bias, cool, hang **05** grace, hover, pease, peaze, peise, peize, peyse, weigh **06** aplomb, impact, ponder, steady, weight **07** balance, dignity, librate, support, suspend **08** calmness, coolness, elegance, momentum, position, serenity, suspense **09** assurance, composure **10** equanimity **11** equilibrium, self-control **13** self-assurance **14** presence of mind, self-confidence, self-possession

poised
03 set **04** calm, cool **05** paysd, ready, suave **06** all set, serene, urbane **07** assured, waiting **08** balanced, composed, graceful, prepared **09** collected, dignified, expectant, unruffled **11** unflappable **13** self-confident, self-possessed **14** self-controlled

poison
03 mar **04** warp **05** spoil, taint **06** blight, cancer, canker, defile, infect, rankle **07** corrupt, deprave, envenom, pervert, pollute **08** embitter **09** contagion, pollution **10** adulterate, corruption, envenomate, malignancy **11** contaminate **13** contamination

Poisonous creatures include:

03 asp
04 fugu, gila, seps, weta

05 adder, cobra, viper
06 dugite, katipo, taipan
07 redback, sea wasp
08 blowfish, cerastes, jararaca, jararaka, mocassin, moccasin, ringhals, rinkhals, scorpion, sea snake
09 berg-adder, boomslang, funnel-web, globe fish, hamadryad, king cobra, puff adder, stonefish, tarantula
10 bandy-bandy, black snake, black widow, bushmaster, copperhead, coral snake, death adder, puffer fish
11 cottonmouth, gaboon viper, gila monster, rattlesnake
12 box jellyfish, scorpion fish, sea porcupine, violin spider
13 water moccasin
15 funnel-web spider

Poisonous plants include:

04 upas
05 dwale
06 antiar
07 aconite, amanita, anemone, cowbane, hemlock, lantana
08 banewort, foxglove, laburnum, mandrake, oleander, wild arum
09 digitalis, monkshood, naked boys, naked lady, poison ivy, stinkweed, wake-robin, wolfsbane
10 belladonna, cuckoo pint, jimson weed, stramonium, thorn apple, windflower
12 helmet flower
13 giant hockweed, meadow saffron
14 castor oil plant, lords-and-ladies
15 black nightshade

Poisons and toxic substances include:

03 BHC
04 bane, lead
05 abrin, conin, lysol, ozone, ricin, sarin, toxin, venin, venom, VX gas
06 arsine, curare, dioxin, G-agent, iodine, ketene, V-agent, wabain, war gas
07 arsenic, bromine, cacodyl, coniine, cyanide, digoxin, dioxane, mercury, mineral, neurine, ouabain, stibine, tanghin
08 antimony, atropine, chlordan, chlorine, cyanogen, cytisine, fluorine, gossypol, lobeline, melittin, nerve gas, Paraquat®, phosgene, ptomaine, ratsbane, rotenone, thebaine, urushiol
09 aflatoxin, amygdalin, chaconine, chlordane, muscarine, mycotoxin, nux vomica, saxitoxin, white damp
10 acrylamide, aqua Tofana, bufotenine, domoic acid, heptachlor, mustard gas, neurotoxin, oxalic acid, phosphorus, phytotoxin, picrotoxin, strychnine, tetrotoxin
11 enterotoxin, hyoscyamine, nitric oxide, prussic acid, sugar of lead
12 strophanthin, tetrodotoxin
13 Scheele's green, silver nitrate

14 carbon monoxide
15 hydrogen cyanide, nitrogen dioxide

poisoning
03 obi **04** obia **05** obeah

Poisoning types include:

04 food, lead
05 algae, blood
06 iodism
07 bromism, gassing, pyaemia, sausage, toxemia
08 botulism, ergotism, plumbism, ptomaine, toxaemia
09 brominism, crotalism, fluorosis, lead colic, mephitism, sapraemia, saturnism, zinc colic
10 alcoholism, molybdosis, salicylism, salmonella, stibialism, strychnism
11 phosphorism, septicaemia
12 hydrargyrism, intoxication, strychninism
13 mycotoxicosis

poisonous
05 fatal, toxic, venom **06** deadly, lethal, mortal, virose **07** baneful, harmful, noxious, vicious **08** spiteful, toxicant, venomous, virulent **09** cancerous, cankerous, malicious, malignant, offensive **10** corrupting, pernicious **11** deleterious **13** contaminating

See also **poison**

poke
03 bag, dig, hit, jab, peg **04** butt, pick, pock, pote, prod, prog, push, root, rout, stab **05** elbow, goose, grope, nudge, poach, prick, proke, punch, shove, stick, stoop, wroot **06** incite, nuzzle, pocket, potter, powter, stir up, thrust **07** scuffle, snuzzle **08** itchweed, protrude

• poke around
04 root, rout **07** look for **09** search for **11** grope around, rake through **13** rummage around **14** look all over for

• poke fun at
03 cod, rag, rib **04** jeer, joke, mock, quiz **05** get at, spoof, taunt, tease **06** parody, send up **08** ridicule **09** make fun of **11** poke borak at **13** poke mullock at, take the mickey

• poke out
06 beetle, extend, jut out **07** extrude, project **08** overhang, protrude, stick out

poker

Poker-related terms include:

03 pat, shy
04 ante, call, flop, pair, stay, stud
05 blind, bluff, check, flush
06 kicker, suited
08 hole card, showdown, stand pat, straight
09 four-flush, full house
10 royal flush
11 busted flush, pass the buck
13 community card, straight flush

poker-faced
05 blank, empty **06** glazed, vacant **07** deadpan, vacuous **08** lifeless **09** apathetic, impassive **11** emotionless, indifferent, inscrutable **14** expressionless, without feeling **15** uncomprehending

poky
04 slow, tiny **05** small, tight **06** narrow, poking **07** cramped, crowded **08** confined, powerful **10** restricted **12** incommodious

See also **prison**

Poland
02 PL **03** POL

polar
03 icy **04** cold **05** axial **06** arctic, frozen **07** glacial **08** freezing, opposite, Siberian **09** Antarctic **10** ambivalent **11** conflicting, dichotomous **12** antithetical **13** contradictory

polarity
07 duality, paradox **09** dichotomy **10** antithesis, difference, opposition, separation **11** ambivalence, contrariety **12** oppositeness **13** contradiction

polarize
05 split **06** divide **07** break up, split up **08** alienate, disunite, estrange, separate **09** segregate **10** drive apart **11** come between

pole
01 N, S **02** po **03** bar, lug, nib, oar, rod **04** bail, boom, kent, mast, post, rood, spar **05** caber, limit, perch, quant, shaft, staff, stake, stang, stick, sting **06** janker, pillar, Polack, ripeck, rypeck **07** extreme, heavens, ryepeck, support, upright **08** Polander **09** cowl-staff, extremity, stanchion **10** river horse **11** clothes-prop **12** Venetian mast

• poles apart
11 worlds apart **12** incompatible **14** irreconcilable

polecat
05 fitch, skunk **06** ferret **07** fitchet, fitchew, foumart **08** foulmart **10** prostitute

polemic
06 debate **07** dispute, eristic **08** argument, diatribe **09** eristical, invective, polemical **11** contentious, controversy **12** disputatious **13** argumentative, controversial

polemicist
06 arguer **07** debater **08** disputer, polemist **09** contender, disputant **11** logomachist

polemics
06 debate **07** dispute **08** argument **09** logomachy **10** contention **11** controversy, disputation **13** argumentation

police
◇ *anagram indicator*
04 cops, fuzz, heat, pigs, plod **05** check, filth, guard, polis, watch **06** defend, patrol, the law **07** bizzies, control, coppers, monitor, observe, Old Bill, oversee, peelers, protect, rozzers, the Bill, the fuzz **08** regulate, the force **09** keep watch, supervise **10** boys in blue **11** police force **12** constabulary, keep the peace **13** the boys in blue **14** police officers

Police forces and branches include:

02 AP, KP, MP, PD, SS
03 CIB, CID, KGB, Met, MGB, RMP
04 Ogpu, PSNI, RCMP, SWAT
05 cheka, Garda, Stasi
07 Europol, Gestapo, sweeney, the Yard
08 Interpol
09 Air Police, bomb squad, drug squad, porn squad, riot squad, task force, vice squad
10 riot police, Securitate, water guard
11 flying squad, gendarmerie, strike force, sweeney todd, Yardie squad
12 mobile police, Scotland Yard, secret police, Texas Rangers
13 Garda Siochana, mounted police, Schutzstaffel, Special Branch, traffic police
14 military police
15 New Scotland Yard

Police-related terms include:

04 ACPO, beat, book, bust, cell, nick, raid, rank, shop, tana, tank
05 ACPOS, baton, cuffs, fit-up, force, frame, go off, grass, manor, plant, pound, set-up, snout, sting, tanna, thana, tunic
06 arrest, batoon, charge, cordon, curfew, fisgig, fizgig, helmet, line-up, rumble, search, tannah, thanah, thanna, wanted
07 caution, copshop, custody, dragnet, epaulet, jemadar, manhunt, mugshot, pentito, round-up, station, stinger, stoolie, thannah, uniform, warrant
08 evidence, mouchard, panda car, precinct, prowl car, speed gun, squad car
09 blue light, centenier, handcuffs, identikit, meat wagon, on the beat, police dog, radar trap, shakedown, speed trap, truncheon
10 body armour, police cell, police trap, supergrass, tenderloin, tracker dog, watch house
11 fingerprint, flying squad, jam sandwich, Judges' Rules, stool pigeon, utility belt, warrant card
12 bertillonage, incident room, police escort, police-manure, surveillance, walkie-talkie
13 police station, rogues' gallery, search warrant, stop-and-search
14 catch red-handed, criminal record, identity parade
15 bullet-proof vest, long arm of the law, scene of the crime

police officer

2 DI, PC, PS, PW, SC **03** cop, pig, 'tec, WPC **04** bogy, bull, flic, gill, nark, peon, plod, slop, SOCO, trap **05** beast, bizzy, bobby, bogey, Dixon, garda, jawan, polis, sepoy, sowar, traps, wolly **6** askari, copper, escort, lawman, Mounty, peeler, redcap, rozzer, sbirro, the law **07** captain, crusher, gumshoe, John Hop, marshal, Mountie, officer, trooper, zabtieh, zaptiah, zaptieh **8** flat-foot, gendarme, sergeant, serjeant, speed-cop, walloper **9** centenier, commander, constable, detective, inspector, patrolman, policeman, woodentop **10** bluebottle, carabinero, gangbuster, lieutenant, traffic cop **11** Black and Tan, carabiniere, patrolwoman, policewoman **12** master-at-arms, peace officer, state trooper **13** beetle-crusher, branch officer **14** police sergeant, superintendent, warrant officer

Police ranks in the UK:

8 Sergeant
9 Commander, Constable, Inspector
2 Commissioner
4 Chief Constable, Chief Inspector, Superintendent
8 Deputy Commissioner
9 Chief Superintendent
0 Deputy Chief Constable
1 Assistant Commissioner
3 Assistant Chief Constable
7 Deputy Assistant Commissioner

police search

4 heat **07** dragnet, manhunt **9** shakedown

police station

4 nick, tana **05** tanna, thana **6** tannah, thanah, thanna **07** copshop, thannah **08** precinct **10** watch house **1** gendarmerie

policy

4 line, plan **05** rules **06** course, custom, method, scheme, stance, system **07** cunning **08** approach, position, practice, protocol, prudence, schedule, strategy **09** guideline, insurance, procedure, programme **0** guidelines, statecraft **12** constitution **4** code of practice, course of action
the best policy
7 honesty

polish

3 lap, rub, wax **04** buff, bull, file, posh, sand **05** class, clean, glass, glaze, gloss, grace, poise, rub up, scour, sheen, shine, slick, style **06** finish, lustre, Polack, Poland, posh up, refine, smooth, veneer **07** beeswax, brush up, burnish, enhance, finesse, furbish, improve, perfect, planish, slicken, sparkle, touch up, varnish **08** breeding, brighten, elegance, glaciate **9** brilliant, cultivate **10** brightness, brilliance, refinement, smoothness **11** cultivation, rottenstone, satin finish **3** supercalender **14** sophistication

polish off

03 zap **04** bolt, do in, down, kill, wolf **05** eat up, stuff, waste **06** devour, finish, gobble, murder, rub out **07** bump off, consume, destroy, put away, take out, wipe out **08** blow away, complete, dispatch, knock off **09** dispose of, eliminate, liquidate

polished

05 adept, filed, shiny, suave, waxed **06** expert, glassy, glossy, polite, sanded, smooth, snappy, urbane **07** elegant, genteel, perfect, refined, shining, skilful **08** cultured, flawless, gleaming, graceful, lapidary, lustrous, masterly, slippery, well-bred **09** burnished, civilized, excellent, faultless, perfected **10** consummate, cultivated, impeccable, proficient, remarkable **11** outstanding, superlative **12** accomplished, professional, well-mannered **13** sophisticated

polite

05 bland, civil, suave **06** glossy, humane, urbane **07** elegant, gallant, genteel, refined, tactful **08** cultured, delicate, gracious, ladylike, obliging, polished, well-bred **09** civilized, courteous, courtlike **10** chivalrous, cultivated, diplomatic, respectful, thoughtful **11** considerate, deferential, gentlemanly, well-behaved **12** Grandisonian, well-mannered **13** sophisticated

politely

09 gallantly, tactfully **10** graciously, obligingly **11** courteously **12** chivalrously, respectfully, thoughtfully **13** considerately **14** diplomatically

politeness

04 tact **05** grace **06** polish **07** culture, manners, respect **08** civility, courtesy, elegance **09** attention, deference, diplomacy, gentility, politesse **10** cordiality, discretion, refinement **11** courtliness, cultivation, good manners, savoir-vivre **12** complaisance, good breeding, graciousness, mannerliness **14** respectfulness, thoughtfulness **15** considerateness, gentlemanliness

politic

04 sage, wise **06** shrewd **07** prudent, tactful **08** discreet, sensible **09** advisable, expedient, judicious, opportune, political, sagacious **10** diplomatic **12** advantageous **14** constitutional

political

05 civil **06** public **08** judicial **09** executive **11** ministerial **12** bureaucratic, governmental **13** parliamentary **14** administrative, constitutional, party political
See also **parliament**; **party**

Political ideologies include:

06 holism, Maoism, Nazism
07 fascism, Marxism

08 third way, Whiggism
09 anarchism, communism, democracy, neo-nazism, pluralism, socialism, theocracy
10 absolutism, Bolshevism, federalism, liberalism, neo-fascism, Trotskyism
11 imperialism, nationalism, syndicalism, Thatcherism
12 collectivism, conservatism
13 individualism, republicanism, unilateralism
14 egalitarianism, neocolonialism
15 social democracy, totalitarianism

politician

02 MP **07** senator **08** minister **09** president **13** vice president
See also **president**; **prime minister**

Politicians include:

03 Coe (Sebastian, Lord), Fox (Charles James), Fox (Liam), Fox (Sir Marcus), Jay (Margaret, Lady), Lee (Jennie, Lady), Lie (Trygve), May (Theresa), Pym (John), Wet (Christian de), Yeo (Timothy)
04 Amos (Valerie, Baroness), Aziz (Tariq), Bell (Martin), Benn (Anthony Wedgwood 'Tony'), Benn (Hilary), Cato (Marcus Porcius), Cook (Robin), Debs (Eugene Victor), Dole (Robert), Foot (Michael), Gore (Albert), Haig (Alexander), Hain (Peter), Hess (Rudolf), Hoon (Geoff), Howe (Geoffrey, Lord), Hume (John), Hurd (Douglas, Lord), Koch (Ed), Kohl (Helmut), More (Sir Thomas), Nagy (Imre), Opik (Lembit), Owen (David, Lord), Pitt (William, the elder), Reid (John), Reno (Janet), Rice (Condoleezza), Röhm (Ernst), Rusk (Dean), Vane (Sir Henry)
05 Adams (Gerry), Agnew (Spiro), Astor (Nancy, Viscountess), Bacon (Francis), Baker (James Addison), Baker (Kenneth, Lord), Bevan (Aneurin), Bevin (Ernest), Brown (George), Brown (Gordon), Burke (Edmund), Cecil (William), Cimon, Clark (Alan), Cleon, Davis (David), Dayan (Moshe), Dewar (Donald), Field (Frank), Freud (Sir Clement), Hague (William), Huhne (Chris), Kelly (Ruth), Kirov (Sergey), Krenz (Egon), Lenin (Vladimir Ilyich), Marat (Jean Paul), Maude (Francis), Nkomo (Joshua), Perón (Eva), Perón (Isabelita), Scott (Sir Nicholas), Scott (Sir Richard), Short (Clare), Smith (Chris), Smith (Jacqui), Smith (John), Solon, Steel (David, Lord), Straw (Jack), Sulla (Lucius Cornelius), Sully (Maximilien de Béthune, Duc de), Tambo (Oliver), Timms (Stephen), Vance (Cyrus Roberts)
06 Abacha (Sanni), Abbott (Diane), Antony (Mark), Archer (Jeffrey), Benton (Thomas Hart), Blears (Hazel), Boyson (Sir Rhodes), Brandt (Willy), Bright (John), Browne (Des), Butler (Richard,

Lord), **Caesar** (Julius), **Castle** (Barbara, Lady), **Cicero** (Marcus Tullius), **Clarke** (Charles), **Clarke** (Kenneth), **Cobden** (Richard), **Cripps** (Sir Stafford), **Curzon** (George, Marquis), **Danton** (Georges), **Davies** (Denzil), **Djilas** (Milovan), **Dobson** (Frank), **Dubcek** (Alexander), **Dulles** (John Foster), **Erhard** (Ludwig), **Fowler** (Sir Norman), **Gummer** (John), **Hardie** (Keir), **Harman** (Harriet), **Healey** (Denis, Lord), **Hewitt** (Patricia), **Hitler** (Adolf), **Horthy** (Miklós), **Howard** (Michael), **Hughes** (Simon), **Hutton** (John), **Irvine** (Alexander, Lord), **Jinnah** (Muhammad Ali), **Joseph** (Keith, Lord), **Jowell** (Tessa), **Kaunda** (Kenneth), **Lamont** (Norman), **Lawson** (Nigel, Lord), **Letwin** (Oliver), **Lilley** (Peter), **Mallon** (Seamus), **Marius** (Gaius), **Mellon** (Andrew William), **Mellor** (David), **Merkel** (Angela), **Mornay** (Philippe de), **Morton** (John), **Mosley** (Sir Oswald), **Mowlam** (Doctor Marjorie 'Mo'), **Nansen** (Fridtjof), **Necker** (Jacques), **Norris** (Steven), **Pandit** (Vijaya Lakshmi), **Pompey**, **Powell** (Enoch), **Prasad** (Rajendra), **Quayle** (Dan), **Roland** (Jean Mari), **Sidney** (Algernon), **Somers** (John, Lord), **Steele** (Sir Richard), **Suslov** (Mikhail), **Tebbit** (Norman, Lord), **Thorpe** (Jeremy), **Waller** (Edmund), **Walter** (Hubert), **Warren** (Earl), **Wilkes** (John), **Wolsey** (Thomas)

07 **Acheson** (Dean), **Allende** (Salvador), **Arundel** (Thomas), **Ashdown** (Paddy), **Beckett** (Margaret), **Bedford** (John of Lancaster, Duke of), **Boateng** (Paul), **Bormann** (Martin), **Brittan** (Sir Leon), **Cameron** (David), **Canning** (George), **Cassius**, **Colbert** (Jean Baptiste), **Collins** (Michael), **Comines** (Philippe de), **Crassus** (Marcus Licinius), **Dalyell** (Tam), **Dandolo** (Enrico), **Darling** (Alistair), **De Klerk** (Frederik William), **Dorrell** (Stephen), **Fischer** (Joschka), **Fouquet** (Nicolas), **Gemayel** (Amin), **Gemayel** (Bashir), **Gemayel** (Sheikh Pierre), **Grattan** (Henry), **Grimond** (Jo, Lord), **Haldane** (Richard, Viscount), **Halifax** (Edward Frederick Lindley Wood, Earl of), **Halifax** (George Savile, Marquis of), **Harlech** (William David Ormsby Gore, Lord), **Hunyady** (János Corvinus), **Hussein** (Saddam), **Jackson** (Glenda), **Jackson** (Jesse), **Jameson** (Sir Leander Starr), **Jenkins** (Roy, Lord), **Johnson** (Alan), **Kalinin** (Mikhail), **Kaufman** (Gerald), **Kaunitz** (Wenzel Anton Fürst von), **Kennedy** (Charles), **Kennedy** (Edward M), **Kennedy** (Robert F), **Kinnock** (Neil), **Kossuth** (Lajos), **Lepidus** (Marcus Aemilius), **MacLeod** (Iain),

Malraux (André), **Maxwell** (Robert), **Mazarin** (Jules, Cardinal), **Meacher** (Michael), **Mikoyan** (Anastas), **Milburn** (Alan), **Mondale** (Walter Frederick), **Osborne** (George), **Paisley** (Reverend Ian), **Profumo** (John), **Redmond** (John), **Redwood** (John), **Rifkind** (Sir Malcolm), **Russell** (William, Lord), **Salmond** (Alexander), **Schmidt** (Helmut), **Sithole** (Reverend Ndabaningi), **Skinner** (Dennis), **Tallien** (Jean Lambert), **Trimble** (David), **Warwick** (Richard Neville, Earl of), **William** (of Wykeham)

08 **Adenauer** (Konrad), **Albright** (Madeleine), **Antonius** (Marcus), **Blunkett** (David), **Campbell** (Sir Menzies), **Catiline, Constant** (Benjamin), **Cromwell** (Oliver), **Cromwell** (Thomas), **Crossman** (Richard), **Daladier** (Edouard), **Dimitrov** (Georgi), **Dollfuss** (Engelbert), **Falconer** (Charles, Lord), **Franklin** (Benjamin), **Genscher** (Hans-Dietrich), **Goebbels** (Joseph), **Hailsham** (Quintin McGarel Hogg, Viscount), **Hamilton** (Alexander), **Harriman** (William Averell), **Honecker** (Erich), **Humphrey** (Hubert Horatio), **Ibárruri** (Dolores), **Jumblatt** (Kemal), **Karadzic** (Radovan), **Khomeini** (Ayatollah Ruhollah), **Lansbury** (George), **Lucullus** (Lucius Licinius), **Malenkov** (Giorgiy), **Marshall** (George Catlett), **Maudling** (Reginald), **McCarthy** (Eugene Joseph), **McCarthy** (Joseph Raymond), **McGovern** (George Stanley), **McNamara** (Robert Strange), **Miliband** (David), **Mirabeau** (Honoré Gabriel Riqueti, Comte de), **Montfort** (Simon de), **Morrison** (Herbert, Lord), **Pericles, Polignac** (Auguste Jules Armand Marie, Prince de), **Portillo** (Michael), **Prescott** (John), **Rathenau** (Walther), **Sandwich** (John Montagu, Earl of), **Schröder** (Gerhard), **Schüssel** (Wolfgang), **Shephard** (Gillian), **Shinwell** (Manny, Lord), **Stanhope** (James, Earl), **Ulbricht** (Walter), **Whitelaw** (William 'Willie', Viscount), **Williams** (Shirley, Lady), **Zinoviev** (Grigoriy)

09 **Alexander** (Douglas), **Armstrong** (Hilary), **Boothroyd** (Betty), **Bottomley** (Virginia), **Buthelezi** (Chief Mangosuthu), **Ceausescu** (Nicolae), **Churchill** (Randolph, Lord), **Gaitskell** (Hugh), **Godolphin** (Sidney, Earl of), **Goldwater** (Barry Morris), **Heseltine** (Michael), **Kissinger** (Henry), **Kitchener** (Herbert, Earl), **Lafayette** (Marie Joseph, Marquis de), **La Guardia** (Fiorello Henry), **Luxemburg** (Rosa), **Mandelson** (Peter), **Miltiades, Parkinson** (Cecil, Lord),

Podgorniy (Nikolay), **Ramaphosa** (Cyril), **Richelieu** (Armand Jean du Plessis, Cardinal and Duc de), **Robertson** (George, Lord), **Stevenson** (Adlai), **Strafford** (Thomas Wentworth, Earl of), **Streicher** (Julius), **Vyshinsky** (Andrei)

10 **Alcibiades, Carrington** (Peter, Lord), **Cunningham** (Doctor Jack), **Enver Pasha, Hattersley** (Roy, Lord), **McGuinness** (Martin), **Metternich** (Klemens Fürst von), **Ribbentrop** (Joachim von), **Stresemann** (Gustav), **Talleyrand** (Charles Maurice de), **Waldegrave** (William), **Walsingham** (Sir Francis), **Weinberger** (Caspar), **Widdecombe** (Ann)

11 **Beaverbrook** (Max Aitken, Lord), **Bolingbroke** (Henry St John, Viscount), **Castlereagh** (Robert Stewart, Viscount), **Chamberlain** (Joseph), **Chamberlain** (Sir Austen), **Cincinnatus** (Lucius Quinctius), **Demosthenes, George-Brown** (Lord), **Hore-Belisha** (Leslie, Lord), **Livingstone** (Ken), **Machiavelli** (Niccolò), **Mountbatten** (Louis, Earl), **Shaftesbury** (Anthony Ashley Cooper, Earl of), **Wilberforce** (William)

12 **Boutros-Ghali** (Boutros), **Hammarskjöld** (Dag), **Themistocles**

13 **Chateaubriand** (François Auguste René, Viscount of), **Fabius Maximus** (Quintus)

14 **Heathcoat-Amory** (David)

politics
05 state **06** civics **09** diplomacy, power game **10** government, statecraft **11** machination, manoeuvring, Weltpolitik **12** machinations, Machtpolitik, manipulation **13** party politics, power politics, power struggle, public affairs, statesmanship **14** affairs of state, haute politique, political views, wheeler-dealing **15** local government

poll
03 cut, dod, get, net, pow, win **04** clip, gain, head, trim, vote **05** count, shear, tally **06** ballot, census, obtain, parrot, return, sample, survey, voting **07** canvass, dishorn, pollard, receive, returns, solicit, sondage **08** campaign, question, register, sampling **09** ballot-box, head count, interview, straw poll, straw vote **10** Gallup poll, individual, plebiscite, referendum **11** electioneer, opinion poll, show of hands **14** market research

pollack
03 lob **05** coley, lythe **06** saithe **08** coalfish **09** sea salmon

polled
03 not **04** nott

pollen
06 farina **08** bee-bread **09** witchmeal

ollute

anagram indicator

3 mar 04 file, foul, soil, warp
5 blend, dirty, spoil, stain, sully, taint
6 befoul, canker, debase, defile, afect, poison 07 besmear, blacken, orrupt, defiled, deprave, profane, arnish, vitiate 09 make dirty
0 adulterate 11 contaminate

ollution

anagram indicator

3 fug 04 smog 05 stain, taint
7 fouling, soilure 08 foulness, npurity, staining, sullying
9 depravity, dirtiness, infection, nuckiness 10 blackening, corruption, lebasement, defilement, filthiness, arnishing 12 adulteration
3 contamination

olonium

02 Po

olychromatic

6 motley 07 mottled, rainbow
8 many-hued 10 polychrome, ariegated 12 many-coloured, aricoloured 13 kaleidoscopic, nulticoloured, parti-coloured

olyglot

8 linguist 11 multiracial, polyglottal, olyglottic 12 cosmopolitan, nultilingual 13 international, nultilinguist

olymath

6 oracle 07 know-all 10 all-rounder, ansophist, polyhistor

omp

4 show 05 glory, state 06 parade, itual, vanity 07 display, glitter, majesty, riumph 08 ceremony, flourish, grandeur 09 formality, pageantry, olemnity, spectacle, splendour
0 brilliance, ceremonial, procession
1 ostentation 12 magnificence 14 self-importance 15 ceremoniousness

omposity

4 airs 05 pride 06 vanity 07 bombast, ustian 08 euphuism, rhetoric
9 arrogance, loftiness, turgidity
0 pretension, stuffiness 11 affectation, naughtiness, preachiness, presumption
3 condescension, imperiousness, nagniloquence 14 grandiloquence, self-importance 15 pretentiousness

ompous

3 big 04 vain 05 budge, grant, heavy, ofty, proud, state, windy 06 la-di-da, nooty, solemn, stuffy, turgid
7 flowery, fustian, haughty, orotund, oreachy, stately, stilted 08 affected, arrogant, inflated, magnific
9 bombastic, conceited, elaborate, grandiose, high-flown, imperious, mportant, ororotund, overblown
0 aldermanly, euphuistic, magnifical, oortentous 11 highfalutin, magisterial, nagnificent, overbearing, patronizing, oretentious 12 aldermanlike, nighfaluting, high-sounding, nagniloquent, ostentatious,

presumptuous, supercilious
13 condescending, self-important

pond

04 lake, mere, pool, rink, stew, tank, tarn 05 flash, pound, viver 06 puddle
07 piscary, piscina, piscine 08 Atlantic, fish-stew, turlough 09 waterhole
10 oceanarium, seaquarium
12 watering-hole

ponder

04 mull, muse, pore 05 brood, poise, study, think, volve, weigh 06 muse on, reason 07 analyse, examine, reflect, revolve 08 cogitate, consider, incubate, meditate, mull over, pore over, turn over 09 cerebrate, ponderate 10 deliberate, excogitate, puzzle over 11 contemplate, ratiocinate 12 ruminate over 13 give thought to

ponderous

04 dull, huge 05 bulky, heavy, hefty
06 clumsy, dreary, prolix, stodgy, stolid
07 awkward, massive, serious, stilted, tedious, verbose, weighty
08 laboured, lifeless, pedantic, plodding, unwieldy 09 graceless, laborious, lumbering 10 cumbersome, flat-footed, humourless, long-winded, pedestrian, slow-moving
11 elephantine, heavy-footed, heavy-handed

ponderously

06 slowly 07 heavily 08 clumsily, stodgily 09 awkwardly, seriously, tediously, verbosely 11 gracelessly, laboriously 12 cumbersomely, pedantically

ponderousness

06 tedium 08 gravitas 09 heaviness, stolidity 10 stodginess 11 seriousness, weightiness 13 laboriousness
14 humourlessness

pong *see* **smell**

pontifical

05 papal 06 snooty 07 Aaronic, pompous, preachy 08 didactic, dogmatic, prelatic, splendid
09 Aaronical, apostolic, imperious
10 portentous 11 magisterial, overbearing, pretentious, sermonizing
13 condescending, self-important
14 ecclesiastical

pontificate

05 spiel 06 preach 07 declaim, expound, lecture 08 harangue, moralize, perorate, sound off
09 dogmatize, hold forth, pronounce, sermonize 13 lay down the law

pontoon

05 float 07 caisson, vingt-un
09 blackjack, twenty-one, vingt-et-un

pony *see* **horse**

pooh-pooh

04 pish 05 scoff, scorn, sneer, spurn
06 deride, reject, slight 07 disdain, dismiss, sniff at 08 belittle, minimize,

play down, ridicule 09 disparage, disregard 10 brush aside 12 make little of 15 laugh out of court

pool

03 dub, hag, lin, pot, spa 04 ante, bank, bath, dump, flow, fund, hagg, lake, lido, linn, meer, mere, pond, ring, sump, tank, tarn, team 05 flash, group, kitty, merge, plash, plesh, purse, share, stank
06 cartel, chip in, lasher, muck in, puddle, supply 07 combine, jackpot, Jacuzzi®, piscina, piscine, reserve
08 Bethesda 09 backwater, composite, syndicate, waterhole
10 accumulate, amalgamate, collective, consortium, contribute, natatorium 11 put together
12 accumulation, paddling-pool, swimming-bath, swimming-pool, watering-hole 13 swimming-baths

poor

◇ *anagram indicator*

03 bad, low, sad 04 bare, duff, mean, mere, naff, puir, ropy, thin, weak
05 broke, cronk, crook, jerry, lowly, needy, pants, ropey, skint, sober, sorry, stony 06 barren, cruddy, crummy, faulty, feeble, hard-up, humble, hungry, ill off, in need, meagre, measly, ornery, paltry, rotten, scanty, shoddy, skimpy, sparse 07 hapless, lacking, low-rent, obolary, pitiful, reduced, rubbish, unhappy, unlucky, useless, wanting
08 badly off, bankrupt, beggared, beggarly, below par, depleted, deprived, dirt-poor, exiguous, ill-fated, indigent, inferior, low-grade, luckless, mediocre, one-horse, pathetic, pitiable, shameful, strapped, waterish, wretched 09 defective, deficient, destitute, exhausted, flat broke, fruitless, imperfect, miserable, penniless, penurious, third-rate, worthless 10 cleaned-out, distressed, ill-starred, inadequate, low-quality, second-rate, spiritless, stony-broke, straitened, threadbare
11 impecunious, near the bone, necessitous, substandard, unfortunate
12 impoverished, insufficient, on your uppers, unproductive, without means
13 below standard, disadvantaged, in Queer Street 14 on the breadline, on your beam ends, unsatisfactory
15 poverty-stricken, strapped for cash, underprivileged

poorly

◇ *anagram indicator*

03 ill 04 sick 05 badly, seedy 06 ailing, feebly, groggy, meanly, rotten, sickly, unwell 08 below par, faultily, rottenly, shabbily, shoddily 09 off colour
10 indisposed, inexpertly, inferiorly, out of sorts 12 inadequately
13 incompetently 14 insufficiently, unsuccessfully 15 under the weather

pop

◇ *anagram indicator*

03 nip, put 04 bang, boom, cola, dash, drop, papa, pawn, push, rush, shot, slip, snap, soda 05 burst, crack, go off,

pope

hurry, poppa, shoot, shove, slide **06** insert, pistol, poppet, report, thrust **07** darling, explode, popular, propose **08** protrude, suddenly **09** explosion, go quickly **10** fizzy drink **12** leave quickly **13** fizzy lemonade **15** go for a short time

See also **father; pawn; singer; song**

• **pop off**
03 die **06** pass on, peg out **07** snuff it **08** flatline, pass away **09** have had it **13** kick the bucket

• **pop up**
05 occur **06** appear, crop up, show up, turn up **09** come along **11** materialize

pope
03 SSD **04** ruff **05** ruffe **06** Il Papa **07** pontiff **10** Holy Father **11** His Holiness **12** Bishop of Rome **13** Vicar of Christ

Popes:

03 Leo
04 Cono, Joan, John, Mark, Paul, Pius
05 Caius, Donus, Felix, Lando, Linus, Peter, Soter, Urban
06 Adrian, Agatho, Albert, Fabian, Julius, Lucius, Martin, Philip, Sixtus, Victor
07 Anterus, Clement, Damasus, Gregory, Hadrian, Hilarus, Hyginus, Marinus, Paschal, Pontian, Romanus, Sergius, Stephen, Ursinus, Zosimus
08 Agapetus, Anicetus, Benedict, Boniface, Calixtus, Eugenius, Eulalius, Eusebius, Formosus, Gelasius, Honorius, Innocent, John Paul, Liberius, Nicholas, Novatian, Pelagius, Siricius, Theodore, Vigilius, Vitalian
09 Adeodatus, Alexander, Anacletus, Callistus, Celestine, Cornelius, Deusdedit, Dionysius, Dioscorus, Evaristus, Hormisdas, Marcellus, Miltiades, Severinus, Silverius, Sisinnius, Sylvester, Symmachus, Theodoric, Valentine, Zacharias
10 Anastasius, Hippolytus, Laurentius, Sabinianus, Simplicius, Zephyrinus
11 Christopher, Constantine, Eleutherius, Eutychianus, Marcellinus, Telesphorus

popinjay
03 fop **04** beau, dude, toff **05** dandy, pansy, swell **06** parrot **07** coxcomb, peacock

poplar
03 asp **05** abele, aspen **06** aspine **09** tacamahac, tacmahack, tulip tree **10** cottonwood

poppy
07 Papaver, ponceau **08** argemone **09** bloodroot **10** coquelicot **12** eschscholzia **13** eschscholtzia

poppycock
03 rot **04** blah, bosh, bull, bunk, crap, guff, tosh **05** balls, bilge, folly, hooey, trash, tripe **06** drivel, humbug, piffle, waffle **07** baloney, blether, flannel,

hogwash, rhubarb, rubbish, twaddle **08** blathers, claptrap, cobblers, nonsense, tommyrot **09** gibberish, silliness, stupidity **10** balderdash, codswallop **11** foolishness **12** gobbledygook

populace
03 mob **04** folk, herd **05** crowd, plebs **06** masses, people, proles, public, rabble **07** natives, punters, society **08** canaille, citizens, riff-raff **09** community, hoi polloi, multitude, occupants, residents **10** common herd, multitudes **11** inhabitants, proletariat, rank and file, third estate **12** common people **13** general public, great unwashed

popular
02 in **03** big, hip, lay, now, pop **04** cool, laic **05** famed, liked, noted, stock, usual **06** common, famous, modish, simple, trendy, vulgar, wanted **07** admired, amateur, current, demotic, desired, general, massive **08** accepted, approved, exoteric, favoured, idolized, in demand, in favour, ordinary, plebeian, renowned, standard **09** acclaimed, customary, favourite, household, prevalent, universal, well-known, well-liked **10** accessible, all the rage, celebrated, democratic, mass-market, prevailing, simplified, well-graced, widespread **11** fashionable, sought-after **12** conventional, non-technical **13** non-specialist **14** understandable

popularity
04 fame **05** glory, kudos, vogue **06** esteem, favour, regard, renown, repute **07** acclaim, worship **08** approval, currency **09** adoration, adulation **10** acceptance, mass appeal, reputation **11** approbation, idolization, lionization, recognition

popularize
06 spread **08** simplify **09** propagate, vulgarize **10** generalize **11** democratize, familiarize **12** universalize **14** give currency to, make accessible

popularly
03 pop **05** vulgo **06** widely **07** usually **08** commonly **09** generally, regularly **10** ordinarily **11** customarily, universally **13** traditionally **14** conventionally, non-technically

populate
05 dwell **06** live in, occupy, people, settle **07** inhabit, overrun, peopled **08** colonize **09** devastate, inhabited

population
03 pop **04** folk **06** people **07** natives, society **08** citizens, populace **09** community, occupants, residents, stabilate **11** inhabitants

populous
06 packed **07** crowded, teeming **08** crawling, numerous, swarming **11** overpeopled **13** overpopulated

porcelain

Porcelain makes include:

03 Bow
04 Ming, Noke, Wade
05 Arita, Delft, Derby, Spode
06 Minton, Sèvres, Vienna
07 Belleek, Bristol, Chelsea, Dresden, Limoges, Meissen, Nanking, Satsuma
08 Caughley, Coalport, Copeland, Wedgwood
09 Chantilly, Davenport, Worcester
10 Cookworthy, Crown Derby, Rockingham
12 Royal Doulton
14 Royal Worcester

Porcelain types include:

04 bisk, frit
05 Hizen, Imari, ivory, Kraak
06 bamboo, bisque, Canton, jasper, Parian, tender
07 biscuit, crackle, faience, nankeen
08 eggshell, Kakiemon, Yingqing
09 bone china, copper red, hard-paste, soft-paste
10 jasperware, saltglazed
11 Capodimonte, chinoiserie, clair de lune, famille rose
12 blanc-de-Chine, blue and white, famille jaune, famille verte
14 soapstone paste

See also **pottery**

porch
04 hall, stoa **05** foyer, lobby, stoep, stoop **07** galilee, hallway, portico, veranda **09** colonnade, vestibule **12** entrance-hall

porcupine
05 urson **10** porpentine

pore
04 hole, vent **05** stoma **06** outlet, stigma **07** foramen, opening, orifice **08** aperture, lenticel **09** micropore **11** perforation

• **pore over**
03 con, kon **04** read, scan **05** brood, conne, study **06** go over, peruse, ponder **07** dwell on, examine **10** scrutinize **11** contemplate **14** examine closely, study intensely

porgy
04 scup **06** braise, braize **08** scuppaug

porker *see* **pig**

pornographic
04 blue, lewd, pink, porn **05** adult, bawdy, dirty, gross, nasty, porno **06** coarse, erotic, filthy, risqué, X-rated **07** obscene **08** indecent, prurient **09** off-colour, salacious **11** titillating

pornography
04 dirt, porn, smut **05** filth, nasty, porno **07** curiosa, erotica **08** facetiae, peep-show **09** bawdiness, grossness, indecency, obscenity, skinflick, snuff film **10** snuff movie, snuff video, video nasty **13** sexploitation **15** girlie magazines

rous

airy, open **05** holey **06** spongy
foveate **08** cellular, pervious
absorbent, permeable
cancellate, cancellous, foraminous,
netrable, spongelike **11** cancellated,
vernulous, foraminated,
neycombed

rpoise

seahog, sea-pig **07** dolphin,
llach, pellack, pellock, porpess
Phocaena, porpesse, sea swine
mere swine, porcpisce

rridge

gaol, jail, samp, stir **05** kasha, sadza
hominy, supawn **07** brochan,
lenta, pottage, suppawn
parritch, sentence **09** mealie pap,
aiseach, stirabout **12** hasty pudding

rt

L **02** pt **03** bag **04** dock, gate, left,
by **05** carry, haven, hithe, jetty, roads
convey **07** bearing, borough,
rbour, retinue, seaport **08** dockland,
board, porthole, suitcase
anchorage, demeanour, docklands,
adstead **10** deportment, harbourage

rts include:

Gao, Lae, Rio, Vac
Aden, Apia, Baku, Bari, Caen, Cebu,
Ciba, Cork, Deal, Doha, Elat, Faro,
Hull, Kiel, Kobe, Linz, Lomé, Lüda,
Nice, Oban, Omsk, Oran, Oslo,
Oulu, Pula, Riga, Safi, Sfax, Suez,
Suva, Tyre, Vigo, Wick
Accra, Agana, Aqaba, Arica, Basle,
Basra, Beira, Belém, Blyth, Brest,
Busan, Colón, Dakar, Davao, Dover,
Dubai, Emden, Galle, Gavle, Genoa,
Ghent, Gijon, Haifa, Ibiza, Izmir,
Kayes, Kazan, Koper, Lagos, Larne,
Leith, Liège, Macao, Malmo, Masan,
Miami, Nampo, Natal, Omaha,
Osaka, Ostia, Palma, Paris, Poole,
Praia, Pusan, Rouen, Sakai, Salem,
Ségou, Sitra, Skien, Split, Surat,
Tampa, Tanga, Tokyo, Tomsk, Torun,
Tulsa, Tunis, Turku, Ulsan, Vaasa,
Varna, Worms, Wuhan
Aarhus, Abadan, Agadir, Ancona,
Annaba, Ashdod, Avarua, Aveira,
Aviles, Balboa, Bamako, Banjul,
Bastia, Batumi, Beirut, Bergen,
Bissau, Bombay, Boston, Bremen,
Bruges, Calais, Callao, Camden,
Cannes, Cochin, Dalian, Dammam,
Darwin, Denver, Dieppe, Douala,
Dublin, Duluth, Dundee, Durban,
Durres, El Paso, Galway, Gdansk,
Gdynia, Grodno, Hamina, Havana,
Hobart, Huelva, Inchon, Jarrow,
Jeddah, Juneau, Kalgar, Kandla,
Kaunas, Khulna, Lisbon, Lobito,
London, Luanda, Lübeck, Madras,
Malabo, Malaga, Manama,
Manaus, Manila, Maputo, Matrah,
Mersin, Mobile, Muscat, Nacala,
Nagoya, Nantes, Napier, Naples,
Narvik, Nassau, Nelson, Newark,
Niamey, Ningbo, Nouméa, Nyborg,

Odense, Odessa, Oporto, Ostend,
Penang, Phuket, Quebec, Recife,
Rijeka, Rimini, Samara, Samsun,
Santos, Sasebo, Sittwe, Sousse, St
John, St-Malo, St Paul, Sydney,
Szeged, Tacoma, Thurso, Timaru,
Toledo, Toulon, Toyama, Treves,
Vannes, Velsen, Venice, Warsaw,
Whitby, Xiamen, Yangon

07 Aalborg, Abidjan, Ajaccio, Alcudia,
Algiers, Almeria, Antibes, Antwerp,
Bangkok, Belfast, Berbera, Bizerta,
Bourgas, Bristol, Buffalo, Cabinda,
Calabar, Caldera, Calicut, Cardiff,
Catania, Cayenne, Chicago,
Cologne, Colombo, Conakry,
Corinth, Corinto, Cotonou,
Dampier, Detroit, Douglas,
Dunedin, Dunkirk, Esbjerg,
Fukuoka, Funchal, Geelong,
Glasgow, Grimsby, Halifax,
Hamburg, Harstad, Harwich,
Hodeida, Honiara, Honiari,
Houston, Ipswich, Iquique, Jakarta,
Karachi, Kowloon, Kuching,
Kushiro, La Plata, Larnaca, La Union,
Le Havre, Livorno, Marsala, Melilla,
Memphis, Messina, Mindelo,
Mombasa, Newport, New Ross,
Niigata, Niterói, Oakland,
Okayama, Palermo, Papeete,
Paradip, Pasajes, Piraeus, Portree,
Rangoon, Ravenna, Rosaria,
Rosario, Rostock, Salerno, San José,
San Juan, San Remo, Santa Fe, Sao
Tomé, Saratov, Seattle, Seville,
Shimizu, Stanley, St John's, St Louis,
Swansea, Tallinn, Tampico, Tangier,
Taranto, Tel Aviv, Tianjin, Tilbury,
Toronto, Trieste, Tripoli, Vitebsk,
Vitoria, Wroclaw, Xingang, Zhdanov

08 Aberdeen, Abu Dhabi, Acajutla,
Acapulco, Adelaide, Alicante,
Arbroath, Asunción, Auckland,
Benghazi, Bordeaux, Boulogne,
Brindisi, Brisbane, Cagliari, Calcutta,
Cape Town, Castries, Changsha,
Chimbote, Djibouti, Dortmund,
Duisburg, Dunleary, Falmouth,
Flushing, Freeport, Freetown,
Gisborne, Godthaab, Greenock,
Guyaquil, Hakodate, Halmstad,
Hamilton, Hay Point, Helsinki,
Holyhead, Honolulu, Istanbul,
Kawasaki, Keflavik, Kingston,
Kinshasa, Kirkaldy, Kirkwall,
Kismaayo, Klaipeda, La Coruna, La
Guaira, La Spezia, Lattakia,
Limassol, Limerick, Mandalay,
Mannheim, Marbella, Matanzas,
Mazatlan, Monrovia, Montreal,
Montrose, Mormugao, Moulmein,
Mulhouse, Murmansk, Nagasaki,
New Haven, Newhaven, Pago Pago,
Plymouth, Portland, Port Said, Port-
Vila, Ramsgate, Richmond,
Roskilde, Rosslare, Salonica,
Salvador, San Diego, San Pedro,
Santarém, Savannah, Semarang,
Shanghai, Simbirsk, Smolensk, St
Helier, Stockton, St-Tropez,
Surabaya, Syracuse, Szczecin,

Takoradi, Tauranga, Torshavn,
Ullapool, Valencia, Valletta,
Veracruz, Voronezh, Weymouth,
Yokohama, Zanzibar

09 Algeciras, Amsterdam, Anchorage,
Archangel, Astrakhan, Baltimore,
Barcelona, Bujumbura, Cartagena,
Cherbourg, Cleveland, Constance,
Constanta, Dordrecht, Dubrovnik,
Esztergom, Europoort, Famagusta,
Fleetwood, Flensburg, Fortaleza,
Frankfurt, Fremantle, Galveston,
Gateshead, Gibraltar, Gravesend,
Heraklion, Hiroshima, Immingham,
Kagoshima, Kaohsiung, Karlsruhe,
King's Lynn, Kingstown, Kozhikode,
Langesund, Las Palmas, Launceton,
Liverpool, Long Beach, Lowestoft,
Magdeburg, Mahajanga,
Maracaibo, Mariehamn,
Melbourne, Milwaukee,
Mizushima, Mogadishu, Nashville,
Newcastle, Nuku'alofa, Palembang,
Palm Beach, Paranagua, Peterhead,
Phnom Penh, Port Limon, Port
Louis, Port Natal, Port Sudan,
Reykjavík, Rio Grande, Rochester,
Rotterdam, Santander, Sassandra,
Sheerness, Singapore, Stavanger,
St-Nazaire, Stockholm, Stornoway,
Stralsund, Stranraer, Sundsvall,
Takamatsu, Tarragona, Toamasina,
Trebizond, Trondheim, Tuticorin,
Vancouver, Vicksburg, Vientiane,
Volgograd, Walvis Bay, Yaroslavl,
Zeebrugge, Zhenjiang, Zrenjanin

10 Alexandria, Basseterre, Baton
Rouge, Belize City, Bratislava,
Bridgeport, Bridgetown, Cap
Haitian, Casablanca, Charleston,
Chittagong, Cienfuegos,
Copenhagen, East London,
Felixstowe, Folkestone, Fray Bentos,
Fredericia, George Town,
Georgetown, Gothenburg,
Hartlepool, Hildesheim,
Iskenderun, Kansas City,
Kitakyushu, Kompong Som, Kuwait
City, Leeuwarden, Libreville, Little
Rock, Los Angeles, Louisville,
Manchester, Manzanillo,
Marseilles, Mina Qaboos, Mina
Sulman, Montego Bay, Montevideo,
Mostaganem, New Orleans,
Nouadhibou, Nouakchott,
Oranjestad, Paramaribo, Pittsburgh,
Port Gentil, Portishead,
Portsmouth, Port Talbot,
Providence, Sacramento, Salina
Cruz, San Lorenzo, Santa Marta,
Sebastopol, Sevastopol,
Strasbourg, Sunderland,
Talcahuano, Thunder Bay,
Townsville, Valparaiso, Wellington,
Willemstad, Wilmington,
Workington, Zaporozhye

11 Antofagasta, Bahia Blanca, Bandar
Abbas, Brazzaville, Bremerhaven,
Bridlington, Brownsville, Buenos
Aires, Charlestown, Chattanooga,
Dar es Salaam, Fraserburgh,
Grangemouth, Helsingborg,

Krasnoyarsk, Livingstone,
Lossiemouth, Mar del Plata,
Minneapolis, Narayanganj, New
Plymouth, New York City,
Novosibirsk, Panama Canal, Pasir
Gudang, Point-a-Pitre, Pointe-
Noire, Pondicherry, Port Cartier,
Port Moresby, Porto Alegre, Port of
Spain, Punta Arenas, Qinhuangdao,
Richards Bay, Rostov-on-Don,
Southampton, Three Rivers,
Vladivostok

12 Barranquilla, Buenaventura, Fort de
France, Frederikstad, Jacksonville,
Kota Kinabalu, Kristiansand,
Ludwigshafen, New Amsterdam,
New Mangalore, Novorossiysk,
Philadelphia, Ponta Delgada, Port
Adelaide, Port-au-Prince, Port
Harcourt, Port Victoria, Puerto
Cortes, Rio de Janeiro, Saint
George's, San Francisco, San
Sebastian, Santo Domingo, St
Petersburg, Tel Aviv-Jaffa, Ujung
Pandang, Villahermosa

13 Ellesmere Port, Frederikshavn,
Great Yarmouth, Ho Chi Minh City,
Hook of Holland, Middlesbrough,
Port Elizabeth, Semipalatinsk,
Sihanoukville

14 Dnepropetrovsk, Port
Georgetown, Santiago de Cuba

15 Barrow-in-Furness, Charlotte
Amalie, Frankfurt am Main, Nizhniy
Novgorod

• **port authority**
03 PLA

portability
09 handiness **10** movability
11 compactness, convenience
13 manageability

portable
05 handy **07** compact, movable
08 luggable **09** endurable, portatile
10 convenient, conveyable,
manageable **11** lightweight
13 transportable

portal
04 door, gate **05** way in **06** access
07 doorway, gateway, opening
08 entrance

portend
04 bode, omen **05** augur **06** herald,
import, warn of **07** bespeak, betoken,
point to, predict, presage, promise,
purport, signify **08** announce,
forebode, forecast, foreshow, foretell,
forewarn, indicate, threaten
09 adumbrate, be a sign of, foretoken,
harbinger **10** foreshadow
13 prognosticate

portent
04 omen, sign **05** augur, token
06 augury, boding, marvel, ostent,
threat **07** presage, prodigy, warning
08 forecast, prodrome **09** harbinger,
precursor **10** foreboding, forerunner,
indication, prognostic **11** forewarning,
ominousness, premonition
12 presentiment **13** foreshadowing,

prefiguration, signification
15 prognostication

portentous
04 dire, vain **05** proud **06** snooty,
solemn **07** amazing, crucial, fateful,
haughty, ominous, pompous
08 affected, arrogant, menacing,
sinister **09** conceited, grandiose,
imperious, important, momentous
10 astounding, foreboding, impressive,
miraculous, prodigious, remarkable
11 epoch-making, magisterial,
overbearing, patronizing, pretentious,
significant, threatening **12** awe-
inspiring, earth-shaking, ostentatious,
presumptuous, supercilious
13 condescending, extraordinary, self-
important

portentously
08 snootily **09** haughtily, pompously
10 arrogantly **11** conceitedly
13 patronizingly **14** superciliously
15 condescendingly, self-importantly

porter
04 page **05** caddy, cadee, cadie, hamal
06 bearer, caddie, entire, hammal,
humper, redcap **07** bell-boy, bellhop,
carrier, doorman, dvornik, janitor
08 bummaree, doorsman
09 caretaker, concierge, out-porter
10 door-keeper, gatekeeper
11 double-stout, night-porter **12** ticket-
porter **13** door attendant **14** baggage-
carrier, baggage-handler,
commissionaire

portico
04 stoa **05** porch **06** exedra, parvis,
xystus **07** distyle, exhedra, narthex,
parvise, veranda **08** prostyle, verandah
09 colonnade, decastyle, hexastyle,
octastyle, octostyle **10** pentastyle,
tetrastyle **11** dodecastyle

portion
02 go **03** bit, cut, dot, lot, rag **04** deal,
dole, dose, fate, luck, meed, mite, part,
tait, tate, what **05** allot, dowry, grist,
order, piece, quota, ratio, share, slice,
small, space, taste, wedge, whack,
wodge **06** assign, chance, divide,
kismet, morsel, parcel, ration, region
07 carve up, destiny, dole out, fortune,
helping, kenning, measure, rake-off,
scantle, section, segment, serving,
slice up, tranche **08** allocate, division,
fraction, fragment, particle, pittance,
quantity, share out **09** allotment,
allowance, apportion, partition,
scantling, something **10** allocation,
distribute, percentage, proportion

portliness
07 fatness, obesity **08** fullness
09 ampleness, beefiness, dumpiness,
heaviness, plumpness, rotundity,
roundness, stoutness, tubbiness
10 chubbiness, corpulence, fleshiness
11 paunchiness

portly
03 fat **05** ample, gaucy, gawcy, gawsy,
heavy, large, obese, plump, round,

stout **06** gaucie, rotund, stocky
08 matronly **09** corpulent
10 aldermanly, overweight
12 aldermanlike

portrait
04 icon **05** image, pin-up, story, stud
06 Kit-Cat, sketch **07** account,
drawing, picture, profile, retrate
08 likeness, painting, pourtray, retrait
vignette **09** composite, depiction,
miniature, portrayal **10** caricature, fu
length, half-length, photograph,
pourtraict **11** description, whole-
length **12** carte-de-viste, self-portrai
14 representation **15** thumbnail sketc

portray
03 act **04** draw, play, take **05** evoke,
image, paint **06** depict, sketch
07 perform, picture, present
08 describe, portrait, pourtray
09 pantomime, personify, represent
10 illustrate **11** impersonate **12** act th
part of, characterize **13** play the part

portrayal
05 study **06** acting, sketch **07** drawin
picture **08** painting **09** depiction,
evocation, rendering **11** delineation,
description, performance
12 presentation **14** interpretation,
representation

Portugal
01 P **02** Pg **03** PRT

Portuguese
02 Pg

pose
03 act, air, ask, put, set, sit **04** airs, ro
sham **05** cause, claim, feign, front,
model, posit **06** affect, assert, create
façade, lead to, puzzle, stance, subm
07 advance, arrange, bearing, posture
present, pretend, produce, propose,
suggest **08** attitude, carriage, positio
pretence, propound, result in
09 postulate, put on airs **10** constitute
deportment, give rise to, masquerade
put forward, put on an act
11 affectation, impersonate
12 attitudinize, contrapposto **15** pass
yourself off

Poseidon
07 Neptune

poser
04 sham **05** pseud **06** enigma, phone
poseur, puzzle, riddle, sitter
07 dilemma, mystery, poseuse,
problem, show-off, sticker
08 impostor, posturer **09** charlatan,
conundrum, play-actor **10** mind-
bender **11** brainteaser **12** brain-twist
13 attitudinizer, exhibitionist, vexed
question

poseur
04 sham **05** poser, pseud **06** phoney
07 poseuse, show-off **08** impostor,
posturer **09** charlatan, play-actor
13 attitudinizer, exhibitionist

posh
01 U **04** rich, swag **05** dandy, fancy,

grand, money, plush, pluty, smart, swish **06** classy, de-luxe, la-di-da, lavish, luxury, select, snazzy, superb, swanky **07** elegant, opulent, stylish **08** top-class, up-market **09** exclusive, expensive, halfpenny, high-class, luxurious, sumptuous **10** upper-class **11** fashionable

posit
03 set **04** pose **05** state **06** assert, assume, submit **07** advance, dispose, presume **08** propound **09** postulate, predicate **10** put forward

position
03 fix, job, lie, pos, put, set **04** area, case, duty, pose, post, rank, role, site, spot, view **05** array, grade, level, place, point, pozzy, scene, stand, state **06** belief, deploy, factor, lay out, locate, office, orient, plight, possie, settle, stance, status **07** arrange, bearing, dispose, factors, install, opinion, outlook, posture, ranking, setting, situate, station **08** attitude, capacity, function, locality, location, prestige, standing **09** condition, establish, influence, postulate, situation, viewpoint **10** background, employment, occupation, standpoint **11** appointment, arrangement, disposition, point of view, predicament, whereabouts **13** circumstances **14** state of affairs
• **in fixed position**
02 to

positive
01 p **03** pos **04** firm, good, plus, rank, real, sure **05** basic, clear, sheer, utter **06** actual, direct, upbeat, useful **07** assured, certain, express, helpful, hopeful, perfect, positif, precise, reality **08** absolute, cheerful, clear-cut, complete, concrete, decisive, definite, emphatic, explicit, material, outright, thorough **09** assertive, categoric, confident, convinced, downright, out-and-out, practical, promising, veritable **10** conclusive, consummate, convincing, definitive, encouraged, favourable, optimistic, productive, undeniable **11** affirmative, categorical, encouraging, irrefutable, unequivocal, unmitigated **12** constructive, indisputable, matter-of-fact, unmistakable **13** incontestable **14** dextrorotatory

positively
06 firmly, surely **07** finally **09** assuredly, certainly, expressly **10** absolutely, decisively, definitely, undeniably **12** conclusively, emphatically, indisputably, unmistakably **13** categorically, incontestably, unequivocally **14** unquestionably

possess
◊ *containment indicator*
03 get, own **04** gain, have, hold, take **05** boast, enjoy, haunt, imbue, seize, wield **06** attain, inform, obsess, obtain, occupy **07** acquire, bedevil, bewitch, control, enchant, inhabit, inherit,

overget **08** acquaint, demonize, dominate, maintain, take over **09** infatuate, influence **12** be gifted with **13** be blessed with, be endowed with, take control of

possessed
03 mad **06** crazed, cursed, raving **07** berserk, haunted **08** besotted, consumed, demented, frenzied, maddened, obsessed, spirited **09** bewitched, demonized, dominated, enchanted, hag-ridden **10** bedevilled, controlled, infatuated, mesmerized

possession
03 fee **04** grip, hand, hold **05** craze, thing, title **06** having, tenure **07** control, custody, holding, tenancy **08** haunting **09** obsession, occupance, occupancy, ownership **10** domination, occupation **11** infatuation **14** proprietorship
• **in possession**
◊ *containment indicator*

possessions
03 all, ana **04** aver, gear, good **05** goods, stuff, worth **06** assets, estate, riches, things, wealth **07** baggage, clobber, effects, luggage **08** chattels, movables, outsight, property **09** sprechery, territory **10** belongings, spreaghery **12** temporalties **13** accoutrements, paraphernalia, temporalities, worldly wealth **15** personal effects

possessive
06 greedy **07** jealous, selfish **08** clinging, covetous, genitive, grasping **10** dominating **11** acquisitive, controlling, domineering **14** overprotective

possessiveness
05 greed **08** jealousy **11** selfishness **12** covetousness **13** exclusiveness **15** acquisitiveness

possibility
04 fear, hope, odds, risk **05** maybe, posse **06** chance, choice, danger, hazard, option, talent **07** promise **08** prospect, recourse **09** off-chance, potential, prospects **10** advantages, likelihood, preference **11** alternative, contingency, feasibility, probability, proposition **12** capabilities, expectations, potentiality **13** attainability **14** conceivability, practicability

possible
◊ *anagram indicator*
06 doable, likely, odds-on, viable **07** tenable **08** credible, feasible, probable, workable **09** potential, promising **10** achievable, attainable, imaginable, on the cards, realizable **11** conceivable, practicable **13** that can be done **14** accomplishable

possibly
◊ *anagram indicator*
03 e'er **04** ever, well **05** at all, maybe

07 in posse, perhaps **09** hopefully **10** by any means **11** by any chance, conceivably **12** peradventure

possum
04 tait **07** opossum **08** Tarsipes **09** phalanger **10** honey-mouse **11** sugar glider

post
03 dak, job, leg, pin, put **04** beat, bitt, jamb, mail, move, pale, pole, prop, send **05** affix, e-mail, haste, newel, pin up, place, put up, shaft, stake, strut **06** assign, attach, column, locate, office, picket, pillar, report, second **07** airmail, appoint, display, forward, letters, packets, parcels, publish, situate, station, stick up, support, upright, vacancy **08** announce, baluster, banister, delivery, dispatch, junk mail, packages, palisade, position, standard, transfer, transmit **09** advertise, broadcast, circulate, mail-coach, make known, publicize, put on duty, situation, snail mail, stanchion **10** assignment, direct mail, employment, packet-boat, Post Office **11** appointment, surface mail **12** all-up service, postal system, recorded mail **13** postal service **14** communications, correspondence, electronic mail, first-class mail, registered mail **15** second-class mail, special delivery
• **keep someone posted**
06 fill in, inform **12** keep informed, keep up to date **13** keep in the loop

postal order
02 PO

postcard
02 pc

poster
02 ad **04** bill, sign **05** solus **06** advert, notice **07** placard, sticker **08** bulletin, play bill, show bill **12** announcement **13** advertisement

posterior
03 ass, bum **04** back, butt, hind, rear, rump, seat, tail **05** after, later **06** behind, bottom, dorsal, hinder, jacksy, latter **07** ensuing, jacksie **08** backside, buttocks, haunches, rearward **09** following, hinder end, posterity, posticous **10** subsequent, succeeding **12** hindquarters

posterity
04 seed **05** heirs, issue **07** progeny **08** children, mokopuna **09** offspring, posterior **10** succession, successors **11** descendants

posthaste
06 at once, pronto, speedy **07** hastily, quickly, swiftly **08** directly, full tilt, promptly, speedily **09** immediate **11** double-quick, immediately **12** straightaway, with all speed

postman, postwoman
04 post **06** postie **07** courier, mailman **11** mail-carrier, mail handler **12** postal

worker **13** letter-carrier **15** delivery officer

post-mortem
02 PM **06** review **07** autopsy
08 analysis, autopsia, necropsy
10 dissection, necroscopy
11 examination

Post Office
02 PO **03** GPO **04** BFPO

postpone
04 stay, wait **05** defer, delay, frist, refer, table, waive **06** freeze, put off, retard, shelve **07** adjourn, do later, prolong, put back, rejourn, sleep on, suspend **08** hold over, mothball, postpose, prorogue, protract, put on ice, withhold **09** carry over, sleep on it, stand over **10** pigeonhole, reschedule **11** subordinate **13** procrastinate

postponed
05 on ice **06** frozen, put off **07** shelved **08** deferred, held over **09** adjourned, suspended **10** in abeyance, protracted **11** carried over, pigeonholed **15** on the back burner

postponement
04 stay **05** delay **06** freeze, put-off **07** respite **08** deferral **09** deferment **10** moratorium, suspension **11** adjournment, prorogation **13** backwardation

postscript
02 PS **03** PPS **07** codicil **08** addendum, addition, appendix, epilogue **09** afterword **10** supplement **12** afterthought

postulate
05 axiom, claim, posit **06** assume **07** advance, lay down, presume, propose, suppose **08** nominate, petition, theorize **09** stipulate **10** assumption, postulatum, presuppose, put forward **11** hypothesize, stipulation

posture
03 set **04** pike, pose, site, view **05** guard, mudra, stand, strut **06** affect, belief, motion, sprawl, stance **07** bearing, gesture, opinion, outlook, show off **08** attitude, carriage, position **09** arabesque, decubitus, defensive, offensive, put on airs, viewpoint **10** decumbence, decumbency, deportment, standpoint **11** counter-view, disposition, point of view **12** attitudinize **15** strike attitudes

postwoman *see* postman, postwoman

posy
05 motto, poesy, spray **07** bouquet, corsage, nosegay **08** affected **09** sentiment **10** buttonhole **12** tussie mussie

pot
02 po **03** box, can, cup, jar, pan, pat, tea, urn **04** bank, bowl, fund, lota, olla, pool, stew, test, vase **05** basin, crewe, crock, cruse, kitty, lotah, purse **06** aludel, bowpot, caster, chatti, chatty, pipkin, pocket, pottle, tajine, teapot, tipple, trivet, trophy, vessel **07** marmite, pitcher, planter, pothole, reserve **08** boughpot, cauldron, crucible, gallipot, plantpot, pot-au-feu **09** casserole, coffee pot, flowerpot **10** chamberpot, receptacle **11** earthenware, manufacture **13** potentiometer
See also **cannabis**

potable
04 safe **05** clean **08** beverage **09** drinkable **10** fit to drink

potassium
01 K

potato
03 alu, yam **04** aloo, chat, spud **05** boxty, early, tater, tatie **06** batata, camote, murphy, pratie, tattie **07** scallop, scollop

Potatoes include:

04 Cara, chat, seed, ware
05 praty, Sante, Saxon, sweet
06 camote, Estima, kidney, kumara
07 Desiree
09 Charlotte, Kerr's Pink, Maris Peer
10 Duke of York, King Edward, Maris Piper
12 Golden Wonder
15 Pentland Javelin

pot-bellied
03 fat **05** kedge, kedgy, kidge, obese, tubby **06** portly **07** bloated, paunchy **09** corpulent, distended **10** abdominous, gor-bellied, overweight

pot-belly
03 gut, pot **05** belly **06** paunch **08** tunbelly **09** beer belly, bow window, spare tyre **11** corporation

potency
04 kick, sway **05** force, might, power, punch **06** energy, muscle, vigour **07** cogency, control **08** capacity, efficacy, strength **09** authority, headiness, influence, potentate, potential, puissance **12** potentiality, powerfulness **13** effectiveness **14** persuasiveness **15** efficaciousness

potent
06 active, cogent, mighty, prince, strong, virile **07** dynamic, pungent **08** dominant, eloquent, forceful, powerful, puissant, vigorous **09** effective, energetic, potentate **10** commanding, compelling, convincing, impressive, persuasive **11** efficacious, influential **12** intoxicating, overpowering **13** authoritative

potentate
04 czar, king, tsar, tzar **05** chief, mogul, queen, ruler **06** despot, dynast, huzoor, leader, prince, tyrant **07** emperor, empress, monarch **08** autocrat, dictator, overlord **09** chieftain, sovereign **10** panjandrum **11** head of state

potential
◇ *anagram indicator*
04 gift **05** flair **06** future, hidden, latent, likely, powers, talent **07** ability, budding, dormant, promise, virtual, would-be **08** aptitude, aspiring, capacity, implicit, inherent, possible, powerful, probable **09** concealed, embryonic, promising, resources **10** capability, developing, unrealized **11** efficacious, possibility, prospective, undeveloped

potentiality
05 power **07** ability, potence, potency, promise **08** aptitude, capacity, prospect **09** potential **10** capability, likelihood, virtuality **13** possibilities

potentially
◇ *anagram indicator*
07 in posse **08** latently, possibly, probably **09** dormantly, virtually **10** implicitly, inherently, in potentia **15** in all likelihood

potion
04 brew, dose **05** drink, tonic **06** elixir **07** draught, mixture, philtre **08** beverage, medicine, potation **10** concoction

potpourri
04 olio **06** jumble, medley **07** melange, mixture **08** mishmash, pastiche **09** confusion, patchwork, selection **10** assortment, collection, hodgepodge, hotchpotch, miscellany **11** gallimaufry, olla-podrida, smorgasbord

potter
04 muck, poke **05** amble, daker **06** dacker, daidle, daiker, dawdle, dodder, fettle, footle, loiter, niggle, pootle, putter, tiddle, tinker, toddle **07** plotter, plouter, plowter **09** mess about **10** dilly-dally
● **potter about**
05 truck **06** humbug, muddle **09** fart about, fool about, mess about, muck about, play about **10** fart around, fool around, mess around, muck around, play around **11** fiddle about, tinker about **12** fiddle around, tinker around **13** do nothing much

pottery
04 bank

Pottery includes:

04 Ming, Tang, Wade
05 Bizen, china, Crown, Delft, Poole
06 basalt, bisque, Dunoon, flambé, Hummel, Jasper, Parian, Sèvres
07 biscuit, ceramic, Dresden, faience, Meissen, redware
08 ceramics, Coalport, crockery, maiolica, majolica, rakuware, Rookwood, slipware
09 agateware, bone china, creamware, Davenport, delftware, hard-paste, ironstone, Jackfield, pearlware,

porcelain, red figure, saltglaze, soft-paste, stoneware, tin-glazed, Worcester

1 Jasper ware, lead-glazed, lustre ware, Parian ware, Queen's ware, terra cotta, Wemyss ware

1 black figure, earthenware, Florian ware, pâte-sur-pâte, Portmeirion, soufflé ware, spatter ware

2 Royal Doulton, transfer ware, Wedgwood ware

3 Claremont ware, Hazledene ware, Staffordshire, tortoiseshell, willow pattern

4 ironstone china

5 cauliflower ware, Royal Crown Derby, Wedgwood pottery

Pottery makers include:

3 Fry (Laura), Rie (Dame Lucie)

4 Boyd (Arthur), Boyd (Merric), Vyse (Charles), Wood (Aaron), Wood (Enoch), Wood (John), Wood (Ralph), Wood (Ralph, Jnr), Wyse (Henry Taylor)

5 Adams (Truda), Adams (William), Amour (Elizabeth), Cliff (Clarice), Coper (Hans), Finch (Alfred William), Korin (Ogata), Leach (Bernard), Mason (Miles), Moore (Bernard), Perry (Grayson)

6 Cardew (Michael), Carter (Truda), Dwight (John), Hamada (Shoji), Kenzan (Ogata), Murray (William Staite), Taylor (William Howson)

7 Astbury (John), Britton (Alison), Doulton (Sir Henry), Execias, Exekias, Forsyth (Gordon), Fritsch (Elizabeth), Gardner (Peter), Grotell (Maija), Palissy (Bernard), Twyford (Joshua)

8 Fujiwara (Kei), Robineau (Adelaide), Wedgwood (Josiah), Whieldon (Thomas), Yamamoto (Toshu)

9 Kaneshige (Toyo), Moorcroft (William)

10 Euphronios

Pottery terms include:

4 kiln, raku, slip

5 delft, glaze, model

6 basalt, enamel, figure, firing, flambé, ground, jasper, lustre, sagger

7 celadon, ceramic, crazing, faience, fairing

8 armorial, bronzing, flatback, maiolica, majolica, monogram, slip-cast

9 china clay, cloisonné, creamware, grotesque, ironstone, overglaze, porcelain, sgraffito, stoneware

10 art pottery, maker's mark, spongeware, terracotta, underglaze

11 crackleware, earthenware, scratch blue

12 blanc-de-chine

13 Staffordshire, Willow pattern

15 mandarin palette

See also **porcelain**

potty
◊ *anagram indicator*
03 ape, fey, mad 04 avid, bats, daft, fond, gyte, keen, loco, nuts, wild 05 barmy, batty, buggy, crazy, daffy, dippy, dotty, flaky, gonzo, loony, loopy, manic, nutty, petty, queer, silly, wacko, wacky, wiggy 06 ardent, crazed, cuckoo, fruity, insane, maniac, mental, raving, red-mad, screwy 07 bananas, barking, berserk, bonkers, cracked, devoted, frantic, lunatic, meshuga, zealous 08 crackers, demented, deranged, dingbats, doolally, frenetic, frenzied, gazunder, maniacal, trifling, unhinged, unstable 09 disturbed, fanatical, lymphatic, psychotic, up the wall 10 bestraught, chamberpot, distracted, distraught, frantic-mad, infatuated, off the wall, off your nut, out to lunch, passionate, stone-crazy, unbalanced 11 not all there, off the rails, off your head 12 enthusiastic, mad as a hatter, off your chump, round the bend 13 off your rocker, of unsound mind, out of your head, out of your mind, out of your tree, round the twist 14 off your trolley, wrong in the head 15 non compos mentis, out of your senses

pouch
03 bag, sac, tip 04 poke, sack, spur 05 bursa, cecum, purse, scrip 06 caecum, ovisac, pocket, wallet 07 papoose, sporran 08 codpiece, pappoose, reticule 09 container, marsupium, spleuchan 10 receptacle 11 gaberlunzie 12 diverticulum

poultry

Poultry and game birds include:

03 hen
04 duck, teal
05 goose, quail, snipe
06 grouse, pigeon, turkey, wigeon
07 chicken, ostrich, pochard
08 pheasant, woodcock
09 partridge, ptarmigan
10 guinea fowl, woodpigeon

See also **chicken**; **duck**; **game**

pounce
04 dart, dive, drop, fall, grab, jump, leap, pink 05 bound, lunge, punch, swoop 06 ambush, attack, dive on, fall on, jump on, powder, snatch, spring, strike, thrust 07 assault, descend, swoop on 08 puncture, sandarac, sprinkle 09 descend on, sandarach 10 cuttle-bone 12 take unawares 13 catch off guard, catch unawares 14 take by surprise

pound
01 L 02 as, lb 03 bar, pen, pun, sov 04 bang, bash, beat, bray, drum, fold, mash, pace, pelt, plod, pond, punt, quid, thud, walk, yard 05 crush, grind, lay on, libra, nevel, oncer, pownd, smash, squid, stamp, stomp, throb, thump, tramp, tread 06 batter, bruise, corral, hammer, nicker, pestle, powder, pummel, shower, strike, trudge

07 balance, confine, contund, contuse, enclose, iron man, penfold, pinfold, pulsate, smacker 08 compound, levigate 09 comminute, enclosure, granulate, palpitate, pound coin, pulverize, smackeroo, sovereign, triturate 12 jimmy-o'goblin 13 pound sterling

pour
03 jet, ren, rin, run, tip 04 emit, flow, gush, hush, leak, ooze, rain, rush, spew, teem 05 crowd, drain, flood, issue, serve, spill, spout, spurt, swarm 06 course, decant, stream, throng 07 cascade, come out, let flow, pour out 08 disgorge, make flow, pelt down, sprinkle, teem down 09 discharge 10 bucket down, disembogue 15 rain cats and dogs
• **pour forth**
04 gush, vent, well
• **pour out**
04 lave

pout
03 bib 04 lour, mope, moue, poot, sulk, tout, towt 05 blain, boody, poult, scowl 06 brassy, glower 07 grimace 08 long face, make a lip 09 make a moue, pull a face

poverty
04 lack, need, want 06 dearth, penury 07 beggary, paucity 08 distress, hardship, poorness, poortith, scarcity, shortage 09 depletion, indigence, necessity, privation 10 bankruptcy, deficiency, inadequacy, insolvency, meagreness, shabbiness 11 deprivation, destitution, locust-years 13 impecuniosity, insufficiency, pennilessness 14 impoverishment

poverty-stricken
04 poor 05 broke, needy, skint, stony 07 obolary, squalid 08 bankrupt, beggared, dirt-poor, indigent, strapped 09 destitute, flat broke, penniless, penurious 10 cleaned-out, distressed, stony-broke 11 impecunious 12 impoverished, on your uppers 13 in Queer Street 14 on your beam-ends

powder
04 beat, blue, bran, bray, dust, kohl, mash, must, pulv, salt, seed, talc 05 cover, crush, grind, moust, muist, smalt, smash, strew 06 farina, grains, pestle, pounce, pulvil, saline 07 alcohol, araroba, scatter, smeddum 08 amberite, coal dust, levigate, magnesia, pemoline, pulvilio, pulville, sprinkle, woodmeal 09 comminute, granulate, pulverize, pulvillio, triturate, wood flour 10 icing sugar, ivory-black, thimerosal 11 mould-facing, washing-blue 13 efflorescence, platinum black

powdered
04 semé 05 semée 06 seméed

powdery
03 dry 04 ashy, fine 05 dusty, loose, mealy, sandy 06 chalky, floury, grainy,

power

ground, mealie **07** crumbly, friable
08 granular, levigate, powdered
09 pulverous **10** granulated, pulverized
11 pulverulent **12** efflorescent

power
01 P **03** arm, eon, say, vis **04** aeon,
mana, pull, rule, sway, watt **05** clout,
force, index, juice, might, oomph,
right, state, teeth **06** energy, muscle,
nation, people, vigour **07** ability,
command, control, country, faculty,
licence, mastery, potency, warrant
08 capacity, clutches, dominion,
exponent, strength **09** authority,
influence, intensity, potential, privilege,
supremacy **10** ascendancy, capability,
competence, domination, superpower
11 prerogative, sovereignty
12 forcefulness, potentiality,
powerfulness **13** authorization,
effectiveness

Power stations include:

06 Huntly
07 Benmore
08 Bankside, Dounreay, Sizewell,
Yallourn
09 Battersea, Chernobyl, Dungeness,
Manapouri, Windscale
10 Sellafield
11 Wallerawang
12 Marsden Point
14 Snowy Mountains
15 Three Mile Island

• **have sufficient power**
03 can
• **having enough power**
04 able
• **the powers that be**
04 them **09** the system **14** the
authorities

powerful
03 hot **04** high **05** burly, gutty, hardy,
tough **06** brawny, cogent, mighty,
potent, punchy, robust, strong, studly
07 intense, leading, telling, winning
08 dominant, forceful, forcible,
mightful, muscular, puissant
09 effective, energetic, knock-down,
prevalent, strapping **10** commanding,
compelling, convincing, impressive,
noticeable, persuasive, prevailing
11 all-powerful, efficacious,
exceedingly, high-powered, influential
12 overwhelming **13** authoritative

powerfully
04 hard, high **06** highly, strong
08 cogently, forcibly, mightily, potently,
strongly **09** tellingly **10** forcefully,
vigorously **12** convincingly,
impressively, persuasively

powerless
04 numb, weak **05** frail, unfit
06 feeble, infirm, unable **07** unarmed
08 benumbed, disabled, helpless,
impotent **09** castrated, hamstrung,
incapable, paralysed, toothless
10 impuissant, vulnerable, weak-handed
11 debilitated, defenceless, ineffective,
ineffectual **13** incapacitated

practicability
03 use **05** value **07** utility **09** handiness,
viability **10** usefulness **11** feasibility,
operability, possibility, workability
12 practicality, workableness

practicable
02 on **06** doable, viable **08** feasible,
operable, passable, possible, workable
09 practical, realistic **10** achievable,
attainable **11** functioning, performable

practical
04 real **05** handy **06** active, actual,
strong, useful **07** applied, hands on,
skilled, trained, virtual, working
08 everyday, feasible, in effect,
ordinary, sensible, suitable, workable,
workaday **09** effective, efficient,
essential, hard-nosed, pragmatic,
qualified, realistic **10** functional, hard-
boiled, hard-headed, proficient
11 applicative, commonsense, down-
to-earth, experienced, practicable,
pragmatical, serviceable, utilitarian
12 accomplished, businesslike, matter-
of-fact **14** bread-and-butter
• **practical joke**
03 gag **04** feat, hoax, jape, joke, scam
05 antic, caper, prank, stunt, trick
06 frolic **07** fast one, frame-up, leg-pull
09 booby trap **11** apple-pie bed

practicality
05 sense **06** basics **07** realism, utility
08 practice **09** soundness
10 experience, pragmatism, usefulness
11 common sense, feasibility, nitty-
gritty, workability **12** nuts and bolts
13 practicalness **14** practicability,
serviceability

practically
06 all but, almost, nearly **07** morally
08 in effect, sensibly, well-nigh **09** just
about, virtually **10** pretty much, pretty
well, rationally, reasonably
11 essentially, in principle
13 fundamentally, pragmatically,
realistically **14** matter-of-factly

practice
03 ism, job, net, ure, use, way **04** firm,
wont, work **05** drill, habit, study, trade,
usage **06** action, career, custom, dry
run, effect, method, policy, system, try-
out, warm-up **07** company, pursuit,
reality, routine, work-out **08** business,
dummy run, exercise, plotting,
scheming, training, trickery
09 actuality, following, operation,
procedure, rehearsal, tradition
10 convention, employment,
experience, occupation, profession,
run-through **11** application,
partnership, performance, preparation
13 establishment
• **out of practice**
05 rusty **07** disused **10** out of habit
11 unpractised **13** disaccustomed, out
of the habit
• **put into practice**
03 use **05** apply **07** perform
08 exercise, put to use **09** make use of
13 put into action, put into effect

practise
02 do **03** use **04** plot **05** apply, drill,
study, train **06** effect, follow, go over,
polish, pursue, refine, repeat, tamper,
work at, work on **07** execute, observe,
perfect, perform, prepare **08** carry
out, engage in, exercise, frequent,
maintain, rehearse **09** go through,
implement, prosecute, undertake
10 run through **15** put into practice

practised
03 old **04** able **05** adept **06** expert,
traded, versed **07** knowing, skilful,
skilled, trained, veteran **08** finished,
masterly, seasoned **09** prevalent,
qualified **10** consummate, proficient
11 experienced **12** accomplished,
experimented **13** knowledgeable

practitioner
03 ace, pro **04** buff, doer **05** crack
06 expert, master, pundit **07** dab hand,
maestro, old hand **08** virtuoso
09 authority **10** practician, proficient,
specialist **12** professional

pragmatic
05 edict **08** busybody, sensible
09 efficient, hard-nosed, practical,
realistic **10** hard-headed, meddlesome
11 opinionated, utilitarian
12 businesslike, matter-of-fact
13 unsentimental

pragmatism
07 realism **08** ad hocery, humanism
10 unidealism **11** opportunism
12 practicalism, practicality **14** hard-
headedness, utilitarianism
15 instrumentalism

pragmatist
07 realist **08** humanist **11** opportunist,
utilitarian **12** practicalist

praise
03 los, rap **04** hail, hery, laud, loos, puff,
rave, sell, tout, wrap **05** adore, bless,
blurb, carol, cheer, cry up, exalt, extol,
glory, herry, herye, roose **06** admire,
eulogy, homage, honour, talk up,
thanks **07** acclaim, applaud, bouquet,
build up, commend, crack up, flatter,
glorify, hosanna, magnify, ovation,
promote, tribute, worship
08 accolade, applause, appraise,
approval, bouquets, cheering,
devotion, emblazon, encomium,
eulogium, eulogize, flattery, plaudits,
rave over, set forth **09** adoration,
adulation, laudation, panegyric,
recognize **10** admiration, compliment,
hallelujah, wax lyrical **11** acknowledge,
approbation, recognition, speak well
of, testimonial **12** commendation,
congratulate, pay tribute to,
thanksgiving **13** glorification, speak
highly of **14** congratulation
• **expression of praise**
07 hosanna **08** alleluia **10** halleluiah,
hallelujah

praiseworthy
04 fine **06** worthy **08** laudable, sterling
09 admirable, deserving, estimable,

excellent, exemplary, reputable
10 creditable, honourable
11 commendable

praising
09 adulatory, approving, laudative,
laudatory, panegyric **10** eulogistic,
favourable, flattering, plauditory,
worshipful **11** approbatory,
encomiastic, promotional
12 commendatory **13** complimentary
14 congratulatory, recommendatory

pram
05 buggy, praam **08** bassinet, stroller
09 Baby Buggy®, pushchair **12** baby
carriage, perambulator

prance
◇ *anagram indicator*
04 jump, leap, romp, skip **05** bound,
brank, caper, dance, frisk, prank, stalk,
strut, swank, titup, vault **06** canary,
cavort, curvet, frolic, gambol, jaunce,
jaunse, parade, spring, tittup
07 caracol, prankle, show off, swagger,
trounce **08** caracole

prank
03 jig, rig **04** fold, gaud, joke, lark, reak,
reik **05** antic, caper, pleat, stunt, trick
06 escape, frolic, prance, pranck,
vagary, wedgie **07** prancke **08** capering,
escapade, fredaine, prancing
11 monkey shine **13** practical joke

prankster
05 joker, rogue **06** hoaxer, jester
07 funster **08** quipster **09** trickster
14 practical joker

praseodymium
02 Pr

prat
03 ass, mug, nit, oaf **04** berk, clot,
dope, dork, fool, geek, jerk, nerd, twit
05 chump, clown, dumbo, dunce,
idiot, ninny, pratt, prick, twerp, wally
06 cretin, dimwit, dum-dum, muppet,
nitwit, sucker **07** fat-head, halfwit,
pillock, plonker **08** buttocks, imbecile,
innocent, numskull **09** birdbrain,
ignoramus, lamebrain, simpleton,
thickhead **10** nincompoop **11** knuckle-
head
See also **bottom**

prattle
03 gab, gup, jaw, yap **04** chat, talk
06 babble, drivel, gabble, gossip, hot
air, jabber, patter, rattle, tattle, witter
07 blabber, blather, blether, chatter,
gabnash, nashgab, prating, twaddle,
twattle, twitter **08** chitchat, nonsense
09 bavardage, gibberish **11** foolishness

prattler
06 gossip, magpie, rattle, talker, tatler
07 babbler, blether, gabbler, tattler,
windbag **09** chatterer, loudmouth
10 chatterbox **12** blabbermouth

pray
03 ask, beg, bid, say **05** adore, crave,
daven, plead, thank **06** call on, invoke,
praise, talk to **07** beseech, beseeke,
confess, entreat, implore, prithee,

prythee, request, solicit, speak to,
worship **08** petition **09** imprecate
10 be at prayer, say a prayer, supplicate
11 commune with **14** say your prayers,
wrestle with God

prayer
03 act, ave, cry **04** bead, bede, bene,
plea **06** appeal, litany, mantra, novena,
orison, praise **07** collect, request,
worship **08** devotion, doxology,
entreaty, petition, suffrage
09 adoration, communion
10 confession, fellowship, invocation
11 imprecation **12** intercession,
supplication, thanksgiving

Prayers include:

02 Om
03 act
05 adhan, Ardas, grace, salat, Shema
06 Amidah, Gloria, Rosary, Yizkor
07 Angelus, khotbah, khutbah
08 Agnus Dei, Ave Maria, Habdalah,
Hail Mary, Havdalah, Kaddish, Kol
Nidre, shahadah
09 Confiteor, Our Father
10 Benedictus, Lychnapsia,
Magnificat, requiescat
11 Lord's Prayer, Paternoster, Sursum
Corda
12 Divine Office, Kyrie eleison, Nunc
Dimittis
15 act of contrition

• **call to prayer**
04 azan

prayer-book
06 mahzor, missal, primer, siddur
07 liturgy, machzor, ordinal, primmer
08 breviary, Triodion **09** euchology,
formulary **11** euchologion, servicebook

preach
04 urge **05** teach **06** advise, exhort,
sermon **07** address, deliver, lecture
08 admonish, advocate, harangue,
moralize, proclaim, prophesy
09 inculcate, preachify, predicate,
recommend, sermonize **10** apostolize,
evangelize **11** give a sermon,
pontificate **15** spread the gospel

preacher
05 molla **06** mollah, moolah, mullah,
parson, ranter **07** apostle, holy Joe,
martext, prophet **08** homilist, minister,
pulpiter, sermoner, spintext
09 Boanerges, clergyman, gospeller,
itinerant, moralizer, predicant,
predikant, pulpiteer, sermoneer
10 ecclesiast, evangelist, Holy Roller,
licentiate, missionary, revivalist,
sermonizer, tub-thumper **11** Bible-
basher, devil-dodger, lay preacher,
probationer **12** Bible-pounder, Bible-
thumper, circuit rider, pontificater, tent
preacher **13** field preacher, local
preacher, televangelist **15** open-air
preacher

preaching
05 dogma **06** gospel, pulpit
07 evangel, kerygma, message,

sermons **08** doctrine, homilies,
precepts, prophecy, teaching
09 predicant **10** evangelism,
homiletics **11** exhortation, instruction,
sermonizing, tub-thumping **12** Bible-
bashing **13** pontificating, tent
preaching

preachy
02 pi **05** pious **08** didactic, dogmatic,
edifying **09** homiletic, hortatory,
pharisaic, pietistic, religiose
10 moralistic, moralizing, pontifical
11 exhortatory, sermonizing
13 pontificating, sanctimonious, self-
righteous **14** holier-than-thou

preamble
05 proem **06** lead-in **07** preface,
prelude **08** exordium, foreword,
overture, prologue **11** preparation
12 introduction, prolegomenon
13 preliminaries

prearrange
07 diarize, prepare, pre-plan
08 organize, schedule **09** plan ahead
12 predetermine

prearranged
03 set

precarious
◇ *anagram indicator*
04 iffy **05** dicey, dicky, dodgy, hairy,
risky, shaky **06** chancy, unsafe, unsure,
wobbly **07** dubious, trickle
08 doubtful, insecure, ticklish,
unstable, unsteady **09** dangerous,
hazardous, uncertain, unsettled
10 touch and go, unreliable, vulnerable
11 treacherous **12** supplicating,
undependable **13** unpredictable

precariously
◇ *anagram indicator*
07 riskily, shakily **08** unsafely, unstably
10 insecurely, unreliably, unsteadily
11 dangerously, hazardously
13 unpredictably

precaution
04 care **07** caution **08** forewarn,
prudence, security **09** foresight,
insurance, provision, safeguard
10 protection, providence, safety belt
11 forethought, preparation
12 anticipation **13** attentiveness
14 circumspection, farsightedness

precautionary
06 safety **07** prudent **08** cautious
09 judicious, provident **10** far-sighted,
preventive, protective **11** preliminary,
preparatory **12** preventative

precede
04 head, lead **06** forego, herald
07 forerun, preface, prelude, prevene,
prevent, usher in **08** antecede,
antedate, go before **09** come first, go
ahead of, harbinger, introduce
10 anticipate, come before **14** take
precedence

precedence
03 pas **04** lead, rank **05** place
08 eminence, priority **09** seniority,

supremacy **10** ascendancy, first place, preference, right of way **11** preaudience, pre-eminence, superiority **12** pride of place

• **take precedence over**
09 take place **10** come before, take rank of

precedent
04 case, lead **05** model, token **07** example, pattern **08** exemplar, instance, paradigm, parallel, standard **09** criterion, yardstick

preceding
04 past **05** above, prior, supra **06** former **07** earlier, leading **08** anterior, previous **09** aforesaid, foregoing, precedent **10** antecedent, precursive, prevenient **11** preliminary **14** aforementioned

precept
03 law **04** rule **05** axiom, canon, maxim, motto, order **06** charge, decree, dictum, rubric, saying **07** command, mandate, statute **08** doctrine, sentence **09** direction, directive, guideline, institute, ordinance, principle **10** convention, injunction, regulation **11** commandment, instruction

precinct
04 area, land, mall, zone **05** bound, close, court, lands, limit, verge **06** milieu, sector, vihara **07** confine, quarter, section, temenos **08** boundary, building, district, division, environs, galleria, locality, purlieus, vicinity **09** buildings, enclosure, food court, peribolos, peribolus, surrounds **13** neighbourhood **14** shopping centre

preciosity
06 chichi **08** tweeness **11** affectation, floweriness, marivaudage **13** artificiality **14** over-refinement **15** pretentiousness

precious
04 dear, fine, nice, rare, twee **05** ditsy, ditzy, grand, loved, tatty **06** adored, chichi, choice, costly, dainty, prized, valued **07** beloved, darling, dearest, flowery, revered **08** affected, idolized, mannered, valuable **09** cherished, contrived, egregious, expensive, extremely, favourite, priceless, simulated, treasured **10** artificial, dearbought, fastidious, high-priced **11** inestimable, overrefined, pretentious **12** confoundedly

• **precious stone** see **gem**

precipice
04 crag, drop **05** bluff, brink, cliff, krans, kranz, scarp, steep **06** escarp, height, krantz **08** precepit **09** cliff face, sheer drop **10** escarpment

precipitate
04 hurl, rash **05** brief, cause, fling, flock, hasty, heave, hurry, quick, rapid, shoot, speed, swift, throw **06** abrupt, flocks, hasten, induce, plunge, sludge,

speedy, sudden, thrust **07** advance, bring on, frantic, further, hurried, quicken, speed up, trigger, violent **08** expedite, headlong, heedless, occasion, reckless **09** breakneck, hotheaded, impatient, impetuous, impulsive, magistery **10** accelerate, bring about, indiscreet, unexpected **11** precipitant, precipitous

precipitately
06 rashly **07** hastily, quickly, rapidly **08** abruptly, headlong, suddenly **09** violently **10** recklessly **11** frantically, impetuously, impulsively **12** unexpectedly

precipitation

Precipitation includes:

03 dew, fog
04 hail, mist, rain, snow
05 sleet
06 shower
07 drizzle
08 downpour, rainfall, snowfall
09 rainstorm, snowflake

See also **ice**; **snow**; **weather**

precipitous
04 high **05** sharp, sheer, steep **06** abrupt, sudden **07** steepup **08** headlong, steepup, vertical **10** steepdowne **11** steepedowne **13** perpendicular

précis
05 sum up, table **06** digest, résumé, sketch **07** abridge, epitome, outline, run-down, shorten, summary **08** abstract, compress, condense, contract, synopsis **09** epitomize, summarize, synopsize **10** abbreviate, compendium, conspectus **11** abridgement, contraction, encapsulate **12** abbreviation, condensation **13** encapsulation

precise
03 dry **04** nice, prim, very **05** exact, fixed, razor, right, rigid, tight **06** actual, formal, minute, narrow, strict **07** buckram, careful, correct, express, factual, finical, literal, pointed, starchy **08** accurate, clear-cut, definite, detailed, distinct, explicit, faithful, preceese, priggish, punctual, rigorous, specific, succinct, surgical **09** authentic, identical **10** blow-by-blow, fastidious, meticulous, particular, scrupulous **11** ceremonious, punctilious, puritanical, unambiguous, unequivocal, word-for-word **13** conscientious

precisely
03 yes **04** just, slap, to a T, true **05** plumb, quite, right, sharp, smack **06** agreed, bang on, dead on, indeed, just so, spot-on **07** clearly, exactly **08** minutely, of course, on the dot, strictly, verbatim, you got it **09** certainly, correctly, literally **10** absolutely, accurately, distinctly, that's right **11** by the squire, on the button, word for word

precision
04 care **06** detail, rigour **08** accuracy, neatness **09** exactness **10** exactitude **11** correctness, preciseness, reliability **12** distinctness, explicitness, faithfulness **13** particularity **14** fastidiousness, meticulousness, scrupulousness **15** punctiliousness

preclude
03 bar **04** stop **05** avoid, check, debar, estop **06** hinder **07** exclude, inhibit, obviate, prevent, rule out **08** prohibit, restrain **09** eliminate, foreclose, forestall

precocious
04 fast **05** ahead, early, quick, smart **06** bright, clever, farand, gifted, mature **07** farrand, farrant, forward **08** advanced, far ahead, talented **09** brilliant, developed, premature **11** auld-farrant **13** old for your age

preconceive
06 assume, expect, ideate **07** imagine, picture, presume, project **08** conceive, envisage **09** visualize **10** anticipate, presuppose **12** predetermine

preconception
04 bias, idea **06** notion **09** prejudice, prenotion **10** assumption, conjecture **11** expectation, presumption **12** anticipation, prejudgement **14** predisposition, presupposition

precondition
04 must **09** condition, essential, necessity **10** sine qua non **11** requirement, stipulation **12** prerequisite

precursor
04 sign **05** usher **06** herald **07** pioneer, prelude **08** ancestor, forebear, way-maker **09** harbinger, messenger **10** antecedent, forerunner, indication, progenitor **11** morning star, predecessor, trailblazer **13** curtain-raiser

precursory
05 prior **07** warning **08** anterior, previous **09** preceding, prefatory, preludial, prelusive, prodromal **10** antecedent, precursive, prevenient **11** preliminary, preparatory **12** introductory **13** preambulatory

predator see **bird**; **cat**; **spider**

predatory
06 greedy, lupine **07** hunting, preying, wolfish **08** covetous, ravaging, thieving **09** marauding, pillaging, predative, rapacious, raptorial, voracious, vulturine, vulturous **10** avaricious, despoiling, plundering, predaceous, predacious **11** acquisitive, carnivorous, deleterious, destructive, raptatorial

predecessor
08 ancestor, forebear **09** precursor **10** antecedent, antecessor, forefather, forerunner, progenitor

predestination
3 lot 04 doom, fate 07 destiny
1 reprobation 14 foreordination

predestine
4 doom, fate, mean 06 intend
7 destine 08 foredoom, pre-elect
9 preordain 10 foreordain
2 predestinate, predetermine

predetermined
3 set 05 fated, fixed 06 agreed,
loomed 07 settled 08 arranged,
destined, ordained 11 prearranged,
predestined 12 foreordained

predicament
3 box, fix, jam 04 cart, hole, mess,
pass, spot, stew 06 crisis, hiccup,
pickle, plight, scrape, taking
07 dilemma, impasse, trouble
08 chancery, hot water, how-d'ye-do,
quandary 09 deep water, emergency,
situation, tight spot 10 praemunire
2 kettle of fish

predicate
4 aver, avow, base, rest 05 build,
found, imply, posit, state 06 affirm,
assert, avouch, ground, preach
07 contend, declare, premise
08 maintain, proclaim 09 establish,
postulate 11 be dependent

predict
3 bet 04 cast 05 augur 06 divine
07 foresay, foresee, portend, presage,
project, warrant 08 forecast, foreshew,
foreshow, foretell, prophesy
09 auspicate, forespeak 10 vaticinate
1 second-guess 13 prognosticate

predictable
4 sure 05 trite, usual 06 likely, odds-
on 07 certain 08 expected, foregone,
foreseen, knee-jerk, probable, reliable
09 customary 10 dependable,
imaginable, on the cards, unoriginal
1 anticipated, foreseeable
2 unsurprising

prediction
3 bet 06 augury 07 fortune
08 forecast, prophecy, soothsay
09 horoscope, prognosis
10 divination, prognostic
1 auspication, soothsaying
14 fortune-telling 15 prognostication

predictive
07 augural 09 prophetic 10 diagnostic,
divinatory, prognostic 11 foretelling
12 anticipating

predilection
4 bent, bias, love 05 fancy, taste
06 liking 07 leaning 08 affinity,
fondness, penchant, soft spot,
tendency, weakness 09 affection
10 enthusiasm, partiality, preference,
proclivity, propensity 11 inclination
14 predisposition

predispose
4 bias, make, move, sway 06 affect,
induce, prompt 07 dispose, incline
08 persuade 09 influence, prejudice
10 make liable

predisposed
05 prone, ready 06 biased, liable,
minded 07 subject, willing
08 amenable, disposed, inclined,
prepared 09 agreeable 10 favourable,
prejudiced 11 susceptible 12 not
unwilling, well-disposed

predisposition
04 bent, bias 07 leaning 08 penchant,
tendency 09 liability, prejudice,
proneness 10 likelihood, preference,
proclivity, propensity 11 disposition,
inclination, willingness 12 potentiality,
predilection 13 vulnerability
14 susceptibility

predominance
04 edge, hold, rain, sway 05 power,
raine, reign 06 weight 07 control,
mastery, numbers 08 dominion,
hegemony 09 dominance, influence,
supremacy, upper hand
10 ascendancy, leadership,
prepotence, prepotency, prevalence
11 paramountcy, prepollence,
prepollency, superiority
13 preponderance

predominant
04 main 05 chief, prime 06 master,
potent, ruling, strong 07 capital,
leading, primary, supreme
08 dominant, forceful, powerful
09 ascendant, ascendent, important,
in control, paramount, principal,
sovereign 10 prevailing 11 controlling,
influential, most obvious
12 preponderant 13 most important
14 most noticeable, preponderating
15 in the ascendancy

predominantly
06 mainly, mostly 07 as a rule, chiefly,
largely, overall, usually 08 above all,
commonly 09 generally, in general, in
the main, primarily 10 by and large,
especially, on the whole 11 principally
14 for the most part

predominate
04 rule, tell 05 reign 06 obtain
07 prevail 08 dominate, outweigh,
override, overrule 09 outnumber,
transcend 10 overshadow
12 preponderate, rule the roast 15 be in
the majority

pre-eminence
04 fame, palm 06 renown, repute
08 majority, prestige 09 supremacy
10 excellence, prominence
11 distinction, paramountcy, sovereignty,
superiority 12 peerlessness,
predominance 13 matchlessness,
transcendence 15 incomparability

pre-eminent
03 gun 04 arch, star 05 chief, first,
grand, great 06 famous, unique
07 eminent, extreme, leading, palmary,
supreme, topping 08 foremost,
renowned, singular, superior
09 excellent, first-rate, matchless,
palmarian, prominent, unmatched
10 inimitable, unequalled, unrivalled

11 exceptional, outstanding,
superlative, unsurpassed
12 incomparable, transcendent
13 distinguished, most important

pre-eminently
04 only 07 notably 08 paravant,
signally 09 eminently, paravaunt,
primarily, supremely 10 especially,
inimitably, peerlessly, singularly,
strikingly 11 exclusively, matchlessly,
principally 12 emphatically,
incomparably, particularly,
surpassingly 13 conspicuously,
exceptionally, par excellence,
superlatively

pre-empt
05 seize, usurp 06 assume, secure,
thwart 07 acquire, prevent, replace
08 arrogate, supplant 09 forestall
10 anticipate 11 appropriate

preen
03 pin 04 bask, deck, do up, trim, whet
05 adorn, array, clean, exult, gloat,
groom, pique, plume, pride, primp,
prink, proin, proyn, prune, slick 06 doll
up, proign, proine, proyne, smooth, tart
up 07 dress up, trick up 08 beautify,
prettify, spruce up, trick out
12 congratulate

preface
04 open 05 begin, index, proem, start
06 launch, prefix, prolog 07 epistle,
precede, prelims, prelude
08 exordium, foreword, lead up to,
preamble, prologue 09 introduce
11 avant-propos, frontmatter
12 introduction, prolegomenon
13 preliminaries

prefatory
07 opening 08 exordial, proemial
09 preludial, prelusive, prelusory
10 antecedent, precursory
11 explanatory, prefatorial, preliminary,
preparatory 12 introductory,
prolegomenal 13 preambulatory

prefect
05 grave 07 monitor 08 praefect
09 commander, prepostor
10 magistrate, praepostor, prepositor,
supervisor 13 administrator

prefer
03 opt 04 back, file, pick, want, wish
05 adopt, bring, elect, exalt, fancy, go
for, lodge, place, press, raise
06 choose, desire, favour, honour,
move up, opt for, select 07 advance,
elevate, pick out, present, promote,
support 08 advocate, plump for
09 recommend, single out
10 aggrandize, like better 11 be partial
to, would rather, would sooner

preferable
05 nicer 06 better, chosen
08 favoured, superior 09 advisable,
desirable, preferred 11 more desired,
recommended 12 advantageous

preferably
05 first 06 rather, sooner 07 ideally

09 for choice **10** from choice, if possible, much rather, much sooner **12** by preference **13** for preference

preference
03 fad **04** bent, bias, kink, mark, pick, will, wish **05** fancy **06** choice, desire, liking, option **07** leaning **08** cup of tea, druthers, forehand, priority **09** favourite, selection **10** partiality, precedence **11** favouritism, first choice, inclination, pre-election **12** predilection **14** discrimination
• **in preference to**
06 before **08** by choice **09** for choice, in place of, instead of **10** from choice, rather than

preferential
06 better, biased **07** partial, special **08** favoured, partisan, superior **10** favourable, privileged **12** advantageous

preferment
04 rise **06** step up **07** dignity **09** elevation, prelation, promotion, upgrading **10** betterment, exaltation **11** advancement, furtherance, improvement **14** aggrandizement

preferred
03 pet **06** choice, chosen **07** desired **08** approved, favorite, favoured, selected **09** favourite, predilect **10** authorized, sanctioned **11** recommended

prefigure
04 bode, mean, type **05** augur **06** signal **07** portend, predict, presage, promise, signify, suggest **08** indicate, prophesy **10** foreshadow **13** prognosticate

pregnancy
06 cyesis **09** family way, gestation, gravidity **10** conception **11** parturition **12** child-bearing, impregnation **13** fertilization **14** being with child

pregnant
04 full, gone, rich **05** clear, great, heavy, in pig, in pup, pithy, quick, witty **06** cogent, filled, gravid, in calf, in foal, loaded **07** charged, fertile, fraught, obvious, pointed, replete, teeming, telling, weighty **08** eloquent, enceinte, fruitful, preggers, swelling, with calf, with foal **09** expectant, expecting, in the club, in trouble, inventive, momentous, up the duff, up the pole, with child, with young **10** big-bellied, convincing, expressive, fertilized, meaningful, parturient, productive, suggestive, up the spout, up the stick **11** impregnated, significant **12** great-bellied **14** in the family way

prehistoric
03 old **05** early **06** Minoan **07** ancient, archaic, Ogygian **08** earliest, obsolete, outmoded, Pelasgic, primeval **09** out-of-date, primaeval, primitive **10** antiquated, primordial **11** out of the ark **12** antediluvian **14** before the flood

prejudge
06 assume **07** presume **09** forejudge, prejudice **10** anticipate, presuppose **11** prejudicate **12** predetermine

prejudice
03 mar **04** bias, harm, hurt, load, loss, ruin, sway **05** slant, spoil, wreck **06** ageism, colour, damage, hinder, impair, injure, injury, racism, sexism, weight **07** bigotry, distort, incline **08** classism, endanger, jaundice, misogyny **09** condition, detriment, influence, injustice, preoccupy, undermine **10** chauvinism, impairment, partiality, predispose, preference, prepossess, unfairness, xenophobia **11** intolerance, misanthropy, prejudicate **12** anticipation, anti-Semitism, disadvantage, one-sidedness, partisanship, prejudgement **13** preoccupation **14** discrimination **15** be detrimental to

prejudiced
06 ageist, biased, loaded, racist, sexist, unfair, unjust, warped **07** bigoted, ex parte, insular, partial, slanted **08** one-sided, partisan, weighted **09** blinkered, distorted, illiberal, jaundiced, parochial **10** chauvinist, influenced, intolerant, subjective, xenophobic **11** anti-Semitic, conditioned, predisposed, prejudicial **12** chauvinistic, narrow-minded, prepossessed **14** discriminatory

prejudicial
07 harmful, hurtful, noxious **08** damaging, inimical **09** injurious **11** deleterious, detrimental **12** unfavourable **15** disadvantageous

preliminary
04 test **05** early, first, pilot, prior, proem, start, trial **06** basics **07** advance, initial, opening, preface, prelude, primary **08** earliest, exordial, exordium, foreword, preamble, prodrome **09** beginning, inaugural, prefatory, rudiments **10** groundwork, precursory, qualifying **11** exploratory, formalities, foundations, preparation, preparative, preparatory **12** experimental, introduction, introductory, prolegomenon

prelude
05 proem, start **06** entrée, herald, opener, verset **07** intrada, opening, preface **08** exordium, foreword, overture, preamble, prodrome, prologue **09** beginning, harbinger, induction, praeamble, precursor **10** forerunner, praeludium **11** preliminary, preparation **12** commencement, introduction, prolegomenon **13** curtain-raiser

premature
04 prem, rash, soon **05** early, hasty **07** preemie, too soon **08** ill-timed, previous, timeless, too early, untimely **09** impetuous, impulsive, precocial **10** praecocial **11** inopportune,

precipitate **13** ill-considered, jumping the gun

prematurely
05 early **06** rashly **07** hastily, too soon **08** too early, untimely **11** impetuously, impulsively **12** incompletely

premeditated
06 wilful **07** planned **08** intended, prepense, propense **09** conscious, contrived **10** calculated, considered, deliberate, preplanned **11** cold-blooded, intentional, prearranged **12** aforethought **13** predetermined

premeditation
06 design **07** purpose **08** planning, plotting, scheming **09** intention **11** forethought **12** aforethought, deliberation **13** determination **14** deliberateness, prearrangement

premier
03 top **04** head, main **05** chief, first, prime **07** highest, initial, leading, primary, supreme **08** cardinal, earliest, foremost, original **09** paramount, principal **10** chancellor, pre-eminent **13** chief minister, first minister, prime minister

Premiers of New Zealand:

03 Fox (William)
04 Grey (Sir George), Hall (John), Wel◄ (Frederick Aloysius)
05 Stout (Sir Robert), Vogel (Sir Julius)
06 Domett (Alfred), Pollen (Daniel), Seddon (Richard John), Sewell (Henry)
08 Atkinson (Sir Harry Albert), Ballance (John), Stafford (Edward William), Whitaker (Frederick)
10 Waterhouse (George Marsden)

See also **prime minister**

première
05 debut **07** opening **10** first night **12** first showing, opening night

premise
05 basis, lemma, posit, state **06** assert, assume, prefix, reason, thesis **07** lay down **08** argument **09** assertion, postulate, predicate, statement, stipulate **10** assumption, hypothesis, presuppose, take as true **11** hypothesize, proposition, supposition **14** presupposition

premises
04 site **05** place **06** estate, office **07** grounds **08** building, property **13** establishment

premium
02 ap, pm **05** bonus, prize **06** bounty, reward **07** grassum **08** extra sum, interest, key money **09** insurance, surcharge **10** instalment **11** extra charge **12** an arm and a leg, overcharging **14** regular payment **15** daylight robbery
• **at a premium**
04 rare **06** scarce **08** above par **12** hard to come by, like gold dust **13** in great demand, in short supply

• put a premium on
06 favour **08** hold dear, treasure
10 appreciate **12** regard highly, value
greatly **15** set great store by

premonition
04 fear, idea, omen, sign **05** hunch,
worry **07** anxiety, feeling, portent,
presage, specter, spectre, warning
09 intuition, misgiving, suspicion
10 foreboding, gut feeling, prevention,
sixth sense **11** forewarning
12 apprehension, funny feeling,
presentiment

preoccupation
05 thing **06** hang-up **07** concern,
reverie **08** fixation, interest, oblivion
09 obsession, prejudice **10** absorption,
enthusiasm, hobby-horse
11 abstraction, daydreaming,
distraction, engrossment, pensiveness
12 heedlessness, one-track mind
13 obliviousness, prepossession, wool-
gathering **15** bee in your bonnet,
inattentiveness

preoccupied
06 intent **07** engaged, faraway, fixated,
pensive, taken up **08** absorbed,
distrait, heedless, immersed, involved,
obsessed **09** engrossed, oblivious,
wrapped up **10** abstracted, distracted
11 daydreaming **12** absent-minded
13 deep in thought

preoccupy
03 eat **04** bias **05** eat up **06** absorb,
engage, fixate, obsess, occupy, take up
07 involve **09** prejudice **10** prepossess

preordain
04 doom, fate **07** destine
10 foreordain, prearrange, predestine
12 predestinate, predetermine

preparation
◇ *anagram indicator*
04 plan, prep **05** study **06** basics,
lotion, potion, supply **07** address,
mixture **08** assembly, coaching,
compound, cosmetic, homework,
medicine, planning, practice, revision,
training **09** equipping, provision,
readiness, rudiments, spadework
10 concoction, foundation,
groundwork, production
11 application, arrangement,
composition, development, mise en
place **12** construction, organization
13 preliminaries

preparatory
05 basic **07** initial, opening, primary
09 prefatory **10** antecedent,
elementary, precursory
11 fundamental, preliminary,
rudimentary **12** introductory

• preparatory to
06 before **07** prior to **10** previous to
11 in advance of **15** in expectation of

prepare
◇ *anagram indicator*
02 do **03** fix, mix **04** boun, busk, cock,
edit, make, plan **05** bowne, coach,
draft, dress, equip, prime, set up, study,
teach, tee up, train **06** adjust, attire,
cooper, devise, digest, draw up, fit out,
gear up, rig out, supply, warm up
07 arrange, compose, concoct,
fashion, produce, provide, psych up
08 assemble, contrive, exercise, get
ready, instruct, organize, practise
09 construct, make ready **10** pave the
way **11** put together **12** get into shape
13 throw together **14** set the scene for

• prepare yourself
12 gird yourself **13** brace yourself, steel
yourself **15** fortify yourself, gird up
your loins

prepared
◇ *anagram indicator*
03 fit, set **04** yare **05** fixed, ready **07** in
order, planned, waiting, willing
08 arranged, disposed, inclined
09 organized **11** predisposed

• prepared with
03 à la

preparedness
05 order **07** fitness **08** procinct
09 alertness, readiness **10** expectancy
11 preparation **12** anticipation

preponderance
04 bulk, mass, sway **05** force, power
06 weight **08** dominion, majority
09 dominance, supremacy
10 ascendancy, domination, lion's
share, overweight, prevalence
11 superiority **12** predominance
13 extensiveness, greater number

preponderant
06 larger **07** greater **08** dominant,
foremost, superior **09** important
10 overriding, overruling, prevailing
11 controlling, predominant,
significant

preponderate
04 rule, tell **07** prevail **08** dominate,
outweigh, override, overrule
09 outnumber, weigh with
11 predominate **13** turn the scales
14 turn the balance **15** be in the
majority

prepossessing
04 fair **06** taking **07** amiable, lovable,
winning, winsome **08** alluring,
charming, engaging, fetching,
handsome, inviting, likeable, loveable,
magnetic, pleasing, striking
09 appealing, beautiful **10** attractive,
bewitching, delightful, enchanting
11 captivating, fascinating, good-
looking

preposterous
◇ *anagram indicator*
◇ *reversal indicator*
05 crazy **06** absurd **07** asinine, foolish
08 farcical, shocking **09** ludicrous,
monstrous, senseless **10** impossible,
incredible, irrational, monstrous,
outrageous, ridiculous **11** intolerable,
nonsensical, unthinkable
12 unbelievable, unreasonable

preposterously
08 absurdly **10** incredibly, shockingly
11 intolerably, ludicrously
12 outrageously, ridiculously,
unbelievably, unreasonably

prerequisite
04 must **05** basic, vital **06** needed
07 needful, proviso **08** required
09 condition, essential, mandatory,
necessary, necessity, requisite
10 imperative, obligatory, sine qua non
11 fundamental, requirement
12 precondition **13** indispensable,
qualification

prerogative
03 due **05** claim, droit, right **06** choice,
purvey **07** liberty, licence, royalty
08 immunity, sanction **09** advantage,
authority, exemption, privilege
10 birthright **11** entitlement **12** carte
blanche

presage
04 bode, omen, sign **05** abode, augur
06 augury, herald, reveal, threat, warn
of **07** bespeak, betoken, point to,
portend, portent, predict, promise,
signify, warning, warrant **08** announce,
forebode, forecast, foretell, forewarn,
indicate, threaten **09** adumbrate, be a
sign of, foretoken, harbinger, precursor
10 foreboding, forerunner,
foreshadow, indication, prognostic
11 forewarning, premonition
12 presentiment **13** foreshadowing,
prefiguration, prognosticate,
signification **15** prognostication

Presbyterian
04 Whig

prescience
08 prophecy **09** foresight, prevision
11 second sight **12** clairvoyance,
precognition **13** foreknowledge,
propheticness **14** far-sightedness

prescient
06 divine **07** psychic **08** divining
09 far-seeing, prescious, prophetic
10 discerning, divinatory, far-sighted,
perceptive **11** clairvoyant,
foreknowing, foresighted, previsional

prescribe
03 act, fix, set **04** rule **05** lapse, limit,
order **06** advise, decree, define, direct,
enjoin, impose, ordain **07** appoint,
command, confine, dictate, lay down,
require, specify **09** stipulate

prescribed
03 set **07** decreed **08** assigned, laid
down, ordained **09** formulary,
prescript, specified, statutory
10 regulation, statutable, stipulated

prescription
04 drug **05** scrip **06** advice, recipe,
remedy, script **07** formula, mixture
08 leechdom, medicine **09** direction,
guideline, optometry, treatment
10 concoction, guidelines
11 instruction, preparation
14 recommendation

prescriptive
05 rigid **08** didactic, dogmatic

09 customary, normative
10 preceptive **11** dictatorial, legislating, prescribing **13** authoritarian

presence
03 air **04** aura, face **05** being, ghost, poise **06** appeal, person, shadow, spirit **07** bearing, company, dignity, phantom, spectre **08** assembly, carriage, charisma, nearness, Shekinah, vicinity, visitant **09** closeness, demeanour, existence, magnetism, occupancy, proximity, residence, Shechinah **10** apparition, appearance, attendance, attraction **11** personality, propinquity **13** companionship, neighbourhood, self-assurance **14** self-confidence
• **in the presence of**
02 by
• **presence of mind**
04 cool **05** poise **06** aplomb **08** calmness, coolness **09** alertness, composure, sangfroid **10** equanimity **11** self-command **13** self-assurance **14** self-possession, unflappability **15** level-headedness

present
02 pr **03** box, gie, now, tip **04** gift, give, here, host, near, perk, pres, show **05** apply, award, being, endow, grant, mount, offer, put on, ready, stage, there **06** at hand, bestow, bounty, cadeau, confer, convey, depict, donate, extend, favour, moment, nearby, prefer, submit, tender, to hand **07** compère, current, deliver, display, douceur, entrust, exhibit, freebie, handout, hold out, instant, perform, picture, porrect, portray, pressie, prezzie, proffer, propine **08** announce, describe, donation, existent, existing, gratuity, hand over, largesse, offering, organize **09** attending, available, delineate, endowment, immediate, introduce, make known, represent, sweetener **10** present-day, put forward **11** benefaction, close at hand, demonstrate **12** bring forward, characterize, contemporary, contribution, in attendance, put on display
• **at present**
03 now **05** today **06** the now **07** just now **09** currently **10** at this time **11** at the moment
• **for the present**
03 now **06** for now, pro tem **12** for the moment **13** in the meantime **15** for the time being
• **present yourself**
05 arise, occur, pop up **06** appear, arrive, attend, crop up, emerge, happen, show up, turn up **11** come to light, materialize
• **the present day**
03 now **05** today **08** nowadays **09** currently **10** at this time, here and now

presentable
04 neat, tidy **05** clean, smart **06** decent, spruce **08** passable

09 quite good, tolerable **10** acceptable **11** respectable **12** satisfactory **14** smartly dressed

presentation
04 form, show, talk **05** award **06** format, launch, layout, object, speech, system **07** address, display, lecture, program, recital, seminar, showing, staging **08** awarding, bestowal, donating, exterior, granting, mounting **09** collation, conferral, packaging, programme, rendition, structure, unveiling **10** appearance, exhibition, presenting, production **11** arrangement, investiture, making known, performance **12** disquisition, introduction, organization **13** demonstration, poster session **14** representation

present-day
02 AD **06** latest, living, modern **07** current, present **08** existing, up-to-date **11** fashionable **12** contemporary

presenter
02 MC **04** host **05** emcee **06** anchor **07** compère **08** frontman **09** anchorman, announcer **10** postulator **11** anchorwoman, sportcaster **12** sportscaster
See also **radio**; **television**

presentiment
04 fear **05** hunch **07** feeling, presage **08** bad vibes, bodement, forecast **09** intuition, misgiving **10** foreboding, presension **11** expectation, forethought, premonition **12** anticipation, apprehension, forebodement

presently
03 now **04** enow, soon **05** in a mo **06** pronto, the now **07** by and by, in a tick, shortly **08** directly, in a jiffy **09** at present, currently, in a minute, in a moment, in a second, ipso facto, these days **10** before long, inevitably **11** at the moment, immediately, necessarily **12** in a short time **13** in a short while

preservation
06 repair, safety, upkeep **07** defence, keeping, storage, support **08** guarding, security **09** retention, upholding **10** protection **11** cold storage, maintenance, reservation, safekeeping **12** conservation, continuation, freeze-drying, perpetuation, safeguarding **13** refrigeration

preserve
03 can, dry, jam, tin **04** area, corn, cure, hain, keep, salt, save **05** candy, chase, chill, field, guard, jelly, lay up, realm, salve, smoke, store **06** bottle, cocoon, defend, domain, embalm, forest, freeze, keep up, kipper, konfyt, pickle, retain, season, secure, shield, sphere, uphold **07** care for, confect, kyanize, protect, put down, reserve, shelter, sustain **08** chow-chow, conserve, continue, creosote, maintain

09 desiccate, freeze-dry, look after, marmalade, powellize, safeguard, sanctuary **10** perpetuate, safari park, speciality, take care of **11** commemorate, game reserve, quick-freeze, reservation **13** nature reserve

preside
03 run **04** head, lead, rule **05** chair **06** direct, govern, head up, manage **07** conduct, control **08** moderate **09** hold court, officiate **10** administer **12** be in charge of, be in the chair, be the chair of, call the shots, take the chair **15** be the chairman of

president
01 P **04** boss, dean, head, Pres, prex **05** chief, prexy, ruler **06** leader, preses **07** manager, praeses, speaker **08** director, governor **09** commodore, moderator, principal **10** chancellor, chief-baron, controller **11** chief barker, Earl Marshal, head of state **13** Dean of Faculty, Earl Marischal **15** Grand Pensionary

Presidents include:
03 Moi (Daniel arap), Rau (Johannes), Zia (Muhammad)
04 Amin (Idi), Díaz (Porfirio), Khan (Ayub), Ozal (Turgut), René (France-Albert), Rhee (Syngman),Tito (Josip Broz)
05 Ahmed (Shehabuddin), Assad (Hafez al-), Banda (Hastings), Botha (P W), Havel (Vaclav), Heuss (Theodor), Klerk (F W de), Mbeki (Thabo), Menem (Carlos), Obote (Milton), Perón (Juan), Perón (Martínez de), Putin (Vladimir), Ramos (Fidel), Sadat (Anwar el-)
06 Aideed (Mohammed), Aquino (Corazon), Banana (Canaan), Bao Dai, Bhutto (Zulfikar Ali), Biswas (Abdur Rahman), Calles (Plutarco Elías), Castro (Fidel), Chirac (Jacques), Ciampi (Carlo Azeglio), Gaulle (Charles de), Geisel (Ernesto), Herzog (Chaim), Juárez (Benito), Kruger (Paul), Kuchma (Leonid), Lahoud (Émile), Marcos (Ferdinand), Mobutu, Mugabe (Robert), Nasser (Gamal Abdel), Nathan (Sellapan Ramanathan), Ortega (Daniel), Pierce (Franklin), Préval (René), Rahman (Ziaur), Renner (Karl), Santos (José Eduardo dos), Somoza (Anastasio), Somoza (Luis),Valera (Éamon de), Vargas (Getúlio),Walesa (Lech)
07 Atatürk (Mustapha Kemal), Batista (Fulgencio), Bolívar (Simón), Cardoso (Fernando Henrique), Demirel (Süleyman), Estrada (Joseph Ejercito), Gaddafi (Muammar), Gemayel (Amin), Gromyko (Andrei), Habibie (Jusuf), Hussein (Saddam), Iliescu (Ion), Khatami (Sayed Ayatollah Mohammad), Mancham (James), Mandela (Nelson), Masaryk (Thomás), Mubarak (Hosni),

Nkrumah (Kwame), **Parnell** (Charles Stewart), **Sampaio** (Jorge), **Suharto** (Thojib N J), **Sukarno** (Ahmed),**Tudjman** (Franjo), **Weizman** (Ezer),**Yanayev** (Gennady),**Yeltsin** (Boris), **Zhivkov** (Todor)

08 Andropov (Yuri), **Aristide** (Jean-Bertrand), **Bani-Sadr** (Abolhassan), **Brezhnev** (Leonid), **Chamorro** (Violeta), **Childers** (Erskine), **Cosgrave** (William Thomas), **Duvalier** (François 'Papa Doc'), **Duvalier** (Jean-Claude 'Baby Doc'), **Fujimori** (Alberto), **Galtieri** (Leopoldo), **Griffith** (Arthur), **Karadzic** (Radovan), **Kenyatta** (Jomo), **Khamenei** (Sayed Ali), **Kravchuk** (Leonid), **MacMahon** (Patrice de), **Makarios** (Cyprus Enosis), **McAleese** (Mary), **Mengistu** (Haile Mariam), **Museveni** (Yoweri), **Napoleon**, **Pinochet** (Augusto), **Poincaré** (Raymond), **Pompidou** (Georges), **Rawlings** (Jerry), **Robinson** (Mary), **Waldheim** (Kurt),**Weizmann** (Chaim), **Zia Ul-Haq** (Muhammad)

09 Ceausescu (Nicolae), **Chernenko** (Konstantin), **Gorbachev** (Mikhail), **Ho Chi Minh**, **Kim Il-sung**, **Kim Jong Il**, **Mao Zedong**, **Milosevic** (Slobodan), **Narayanan** (Kocheril Raman), **Pilsudski** (Józef), **Sun Yat-Sen**

10 Alessandri (Arturo), **Betancourt** (Rómulo), **Hindenburg** (Paul von), **Jaruzelski** (Wojciech), **Jiang Zemin**, **Khrushchev** (Nikita), **Kubitschek** (Juscelino), **Mannerheim** (Carl Gustav, Baron von), **Mitterrand** (François), **Najibullah** (Mohammad), **Rafsanjani** (Ali Akbar Hashemi), **Stroessner** (Alfredo),**Voroshilov** (Kliment)

13 Paz Estenssoro (Víctor)

14 Mobutu Seze Seko

15 Giscard d'Estaing (Valéry)

Presidents of the United States of America:

03 Abe, **Ike**, **Ron**

04 Bill, **Bush** (George), **Bush** (George W), **Ford** (Gerald R), **Polk** (James K), **Taft** (William H)

05 Adams (John), **Adams** (John Quincy), **Buren** (Martin van), **Grant** (Ulysses S), **Hayes** (Rutherford B), **Nixon** (Richard M),**Tyler** (John)

06 Arthur (Chester A), **Carter** (Jimmy), **Hoover** (Herbert), **Monroe** (James), **Pierce** (Franklin), **Reagan** (Ronald), **Taylor** (Zachary),**Truman** (Harry S), **Wilson** (Woodrow)

07 Clinton (Bill), **Harding** (Warren G), **Jackson** (Andrew), **Johnson** (Andrew), **Johnson** (Lyndon B), **Kennedy** (John F), **Lincoln** (Abraham), **Madison** (James)

08 Buchanan (James), **Coolidge** (Calvin), **Fillmore** (Millard), **Garfield** (James A), **Harrison** (Benjamin),

Harrison (William Henry), **McKinley** (William)

09 Cleveland (Grover), **Jefferson** (Thomas), **Roosevelt** (Franklin D), **Roosevelt** (Theodore)

10 Eisenhower (Dwight D), **Washington** (George)

---

press

02 AP, UP **03** AAP, CUP, hug, jam, lie, mob, OUP, sit, vex **04** airn, bear, cram, iron, mash, pack, push, roll, urge **05** beset, clasp, crowd, crush, flock, force, grasp, hacks, horde, hurry, knead, pinch, plead, print, stamp, stuff, surge, swarm, troop, worry, wring **06** caress, closet, coerce, compel, cuddle, demand, enfold, exhort, harass, lean on, nuzzle, papers, praise, smooth, squash, strain, stress, strive, throng, thrust **07** afflict, besiege, call for, depress, embrace, entreat, express, flatten, implore, imprint, oppress, push for, reports, reviews, squeeze, swing it, thrutch, trample, trouble, urgency **08** articles, bookcase, campaign, compress, coverage, expedite, fast-talk, insist on, petition, pressmen, pressure, push down, soft-soap, the media **09** constrain, criticism, hold close, importune, multitude, news media, paparazzi, reporters, smooth out, sweet-talk, treatment **10** journalism, newspapers, pressurize, presswomen, supplicate **11** Fleet Street, journalists, pull strings, push forward, rotary press **12** fourth estate, newspapermen **13** photographers, printing press, put pressure on **14** correspondents, newspaperwomen, put the screws on **15** printing-machine, the fourth estate, turn the screws on

See also **news**

• **press close**
04 serr **05** serre
• **press forward**
04 push, spur, urge **05** drive
• **member of the press** *see* **journalist**
• **press on**
04 go on, toil **05** crowd **06** plod on **07** carry on, go ahead, peg away, proceed **08** continue, plug away, slog away, toil away **09** keep going, persevere, soldier on, stick at it **10** keep trying, press ahead

pressed

04 laid, lain **06** forced, pushed, rushed **07** bullied, coerced, hard-run, hurried, lacking, short of **08** harassed **09** pressured **10** bludgeoned, browbeaten, railroaded **11** constrained, deficient in, pressurized **15** having too little, not having enough

pressing

03 key **05** acute, vital **06** urgent **07** burning, crucial, exigent, serious **08** critical, crowding **09** demanding, essential, important **10** imperative **11** importunate **12** high-priority

pressman *see* **journalist**

pressure

01 P **04** heat, load, push **05** aggro, bully, drive, force, power, press, stamp **06** burden, coerce, compel, demand, duress, hassle, lean on, oblige, strain, stress, weight **07** dragoon, problem, swing it, tension, trouble, urgency **08** bludgeon, browbeat, bulldoze, bullying, coercion, crushing, fast-talk, railroad, soft-soap **09** adversity, constrain, heaviness, squeezing, sweet-talk **10** compulsion, constraint, difficulty, harassment, impression, obligation, pressurize **11** compression, constraints, pull strings **13** put pressure on **14** put the screws on
• **blood pressure**
02 BP **03** ABP
• **extreme/high/low pressure**
02 EP, HP, LP
• **measurement of pressure**
02 mb, Pa **03** atm, bar, psi **04** torr **05** barye **06** pascal **07** megabar **08** microbar, millibar **10** atmosphere

pressurize

05 bully, drive, force, press **06** coerce, compel, lean on, oblige **07** dragoon, swing it **08** bludgeon, browbeat, bulldoze, fast-talk, pressure, railroad, soft-soap **09** constrain, sweet-talk **11** pull strings **12** put the acid on **13** put pressure on **14** put the screws on

prestige

04 fame, mana **05** charm, izzat, kudos, magic **06** credit, esteem, honour, regard, renown, status **07** glamour, stature **08** eminence, standing **09** authority, influence **10** ascendancy, importance, reputation **11** distinction

prestigious

05 great **06** famous **07** eminent, exalted **08** blue-chip, esteemed, imposing, juggling, renowned, up-market **09** deceitful, important, prominent, reputable, respected, well-known **10** celebrated, impressive **11** high-ranking, illustrious, influential **13** distinguished

presumably

06 I guess **07** no doubt **08** I presume, probably **09** doubtless, seemingly **10** apparently, most likely, very likely **11** doubtlessly **15** in all likelihood

presume

04 dare **05** infer, think **06** assume, deduce, take it **07** believe, go so far, imagine, suppose, surmise, venture **09** undertake **10** make so bold, presuppose, take as read **11** hypothesize **14** take for granted, take the liberty **15** have the audacity
• **presume on**
05 trust **06** bank on, rely on **07** count on, exploit **08** depend on **15** take advantage of

presumption

03 lip **04** gall, neck **05** cheek, guess, mouth, nerve, sauce **06** belief

07 opinion, surmise **08** assuming, audacity, boldness, chutzpah, temerity **09** arrogance, assurance, brass neck, deduction, impudence, inference, insolence, upsetting **10** assumption, conjecture, effrontery, hypothesis, likelihood **11** forwardness, probability, supposition **12** impertinence **13** outrecuidance **14** presupposition

presumptive
06 likely **07** assumed **08** believed, credible, expected, inferred, possible, probable, supposed **09** designate, plausible **10** believable, reasonable, understood **11** conceivable, conjectural, prospective **12** hypothetical

presumptuous
04 bold **05** cocky, fresh, lippy, pushy, saucy **06** cheeky, mouthy **07** forward **08** arrogant, cocksure, impudent, insolent **09** audacious, bigheaded, conceited **11** impertinent **12** over-familiar **13** over-confident

presuppose
05 imply, posit **06** accept, assume **07** premise, presume, suppose **08** consider **09** postulate **11** necessitate **14** take for granted

presupposition
06 belief, theory **07** premise, premiss **10** assumption, hypothesis **11** presumption, supposition **13** preconception

pretence
03 act, lie **04** mask, ruse, sham, show, veil, wile **05** bluff, cloak, cover, feint, front, guise **06** acting, deceit, excuse, façade, faking, humbug, posing, veneer **07** charade, daubery, display, pretext **08** feigning, trickery **09** deception, falsehood, false show, hypocrisy, invention, posturing, semblance, showiness **10** appearance, masquerade, play-acting, pretension, profession, simulation **11** affectation, dissembling, fabrication, make-believe, ostentation **12** false colours **13** dissimulation **15** pretentiousness

pretend
03 act, kid **04** fake, mime, play, sham **05** bluff, claim, feign, frame, kiddy, let on, offer, put on **06** affect, allege, assume, semble **07** imagine, play-act, profess, purport, purpose, put it on, suppose **08** indicate, simulate **09** dissemble, fabricate, imaginary **10** put on an act **11** counterfeit, impersonate, make believe **15** pass yourself off

pretended
04 fake, sham **05** bogus, false, moody, put on **06** avowed, phoney, pseudo **07** alleged, assumed, feigned, pretend **08** affected, so-called, specious, spurious, supposed, vizarded **09** imaginary, professed, purported, soi-disant **10** artificial, fictitious, ostensible, self-styled

11 counterfect, counterfeit **14** supposititious

pretender
06 suitor **07** claimer, would-be **08** aspirant, claimant **09** candidate

pretension
04 airs, show **05** claim **06** demand, vanity **07** conceit, pretext **08** ambition, pretence **09** hypocrisy, pomposity, showiness **10** aspiration, profession, purporting **11** affectation, floweriness, ostentation **12** snobbishness **13** dissimulation, magniloquence **14** self-importance **15** pretentiousness

pretentious
03 big, OTT **04** fine, twee **05** false, large, pseud, showy **06** chichi, phoney, pseudo, shoddy, uppish **07** kitschy, pompous, tinhorn **08** affected, fantoosh, immodest, inflated, mannered, pseudish, snobbish **09** ambitious, bombastic, conceited, elaborate, flaunting, grandiose **10** artificial, flamboyant, over-the-top **11** exaggerated, extravagant **12** high-sounding, magniloquent, ostentatious, vainglorious **13** overambitious, self-important

pretentiously
07 showily **08** uppishly **09** pompously **10** snobbishly **12** artificially, flamboyantly **14** ostentatiously **15** self-importantly

pretentiousness
04 show, side **05** swank **06** chichi, kitsch, posing **08** flummery, grandeur, paraffle, pretence, pretense, pseudery **09** posturing **10** flatulence, flatulency, floridness, pretension, uppishness **11** flamboyance, floweriness, ostentation **13** ambitiousness, theatricality **14** attitudinizing

preternatural
07 no'canny, unusual **08** abnormal **11** exceptional **12** supernatural **13** extraordinary

pretext
04 hook, mask, plea, ploy, ruse, sham, show, veil **05** cloak, cloke, color, cover, guise, salvo, stale **06** colour, excuse **07** off-come, umbrage **08** occasion, pretence, pretense **09** semblance **10** appearance, pretension, red herring **13** alleged reason

prettify
04 deck, do up, gild, trim **05** adorn **06** bedeck, doll up, tart up **07** deck out, garnish, trick up **08** beautify, decorate, ornament, trick out **09** embellish, smarten up

prettily
06 neatly, nicely **08** daintily **09** elegantly, winsomely **10** charmingly, engagingly, gracefully, pleasantly, pleasingly **11** beautifully **12** attractively, delightfully

pretty
04 cute, fair, fine, neat, nice, twee, very

05 bonny, grand, purty, quite **06** bonnie, clever, comely, dainty, fairly, incony, lovely, rather, tricky **07** elegant, fairway, inconie, not half, winsome **08** charming, delicate, engaging, graceful, handsome, keepsake, keepsaky, pleasant, pleasing, somewhat, stalwart **09** appealing, beautiful, extremely, ingenious, tolerably **10** attractive, decorative, delightful, knick-knack, moderately, personable, reasonably **11** commendable, good-looking, substantial **12** chocolate-box, considerable **13** prepossessing

prevail
03 win **04** ring, rule **05** avail, occur, reign **06** abound, have it, obtain, win out **07** conquer, succeed, triumph **08** be common, be normal, hold sway, overcome, override, overrule, persuade, perswade **09** be current, be present **10** be accepted, win through **11** be customary, carry the day, gain mastery, predominate **12** be victorious, preponderate **14** gain ascendancy

● **prevail upon**
03 win **04** rule, sway, urge **06** induce, lean on, prompt **07** incline, win over **08** convince, persuade, pressure, soft-soap, talk into **09** influence, sweet-talk **10** bring round, pressurize **11** pull strings

prevailing
03 set **04** main **05** chief, usual **06** common, ruling **07** average, current, general, in style, in vogue, popular, supreme **08** accepted, dominant, powerful, reigning **09** ascendant, customary, effective, in fashion, most usual, prepotent, prevalent, principal **10** compelling, mainstream, most common, widespread **11** controlling, established, fashionable, influential, predominant **12** preponderant

prevalence
03 ren, rin, run **04** hold, rule, sway **07** mastery, primacy **08** currency, ubiquity **09** frequency, profusion **10** acceptance, ascendancy, commonness, popularity, regularity **11** commonality **12** omnipresence, predominance, universality **13** order of the day, pervasiveness, preponderance

prevalent
03 set **04** rife **05** usual **06** common, vulgar **07** current, endemic, general, popular, rampant, regnant **08** accepted, dominant, enzootic, epidemic, everyday, frequent, powerful **09** customary, extensive, pervasive, universal **10** prevailing, ubiquitous, victorious, widespread **11** established

prevaricate
03 lie **05** cavil, dodge, evade, hedge, mudge, shift **06** waffle **07** deceive, deviate, pervert, quibble, shuffle, whiffle **09** be evasive, pussyfoot, stonewall **10** equivocate, transgress

12 shilly-shally, tergiversate 13 sit on the fence

prevarication
03 fib, lie 04 fibs 06 deceit 07 evasion, fibbing, untruth 08 pretence 09 cavilling, deception, falsehood, half-truth, quibbling 12 equivocation, pussyfooting 13 falsification 14 tergiversation 15 shilly-shallying

prevaricator
04 liar 06 dodger, evader, fibber, Jesuit 07 casuist, sophist 08 caviller, deceiver, quibbler 09 hypocrite 10 dissembler 11 equivocator, pettifogger

prevent
02 sa' 03 bar, let 04 balk, foil, halt, help, keep, save, stop 05 avert, avoid, block, check, debar, deter, stimy 06 arrest, hamper, hinder, impede, stimie, stymie, thwart 07 fend off, head off, inhibit, obviate, precede, ward off 08 hold back, keep from, obstruct, preclude, prohibit, restrain, stave off 09 foreclose, forestall, frustrate, intercept 10 anticipate 11 hold in check

prevention
03 bar 05 check 07 balking, empeach, foiling, halting, impeach 08 obstacle 09 arresting, avoidance, exclusion, hampering, hindrance, obviation, safeguard 10 deterrence, fending off, heading off, hindrance, impediment, precaution, preclusion, staving off, warding off 11 elimination, frustration, obstruction, premonition, prophylaxis 12 anticipation 13 contraception

preventive
05 block 06 remedy, shield 08 obstacle 09 deterrent, hindrance, safeguard 10 impediment, inhibitory, pre-emptive, prevenient, prevention, protection, protective 11 neutralizer, obstruction, obstructive 12 anticipatory, preventative, prophylactic 13 counteractive, precautionary

previous
02 ex- 04 past 05 prior 06 before, former 07 earlier, one-time, quondam 08 sometime 09 erstwhile, foregoing, preceding, premature 10 antecedent

previously
04 erst, fore, once 05 afore 06 before 07 already, earlier 08 formerly, hitherto, until now 09 at one time, earlier on, erstwhile, in the past 10 beforehand, heretofore

prey
03 mug 04 game, kill 05 booty, ravin, soyle 06 quarry, rapine, target, victim 07 afflict, fall guy, plunder, spreagh 08 distress 11 depredation
• **prey on**
03 con, eat 04 hunt, kill 05 bleed, catch, haunt, prowl, seize, worry 06 burden, devour, feed on, fleece,

plague 07 exploit, live off, moth-eat, oppress, predate, raven on, torment, trouble, vampire 08 distress, hang over, pounce on 09 depredate, weigh down 15 take advantage of

price
02 pr 03 fee, sum 04 bill, cost, fare, levy, rate, toll 05 prise, prize, value, worth 06 amount, assess, charge, figure, outlay, result, reward 07 expense, forfeit, payment, penalty 08 appraise, estimate, evaluate, expenses, valorize 09 quotation, sacrifice, valuation 10 assessment 11 consequence, expenditure 12 consequences, preciousness 13 fix the price at, set the price at
• **at any price**
09 at any cost, à tout prix 15 whatever it takes, whatever the cost
• **at a price**
04 dear 09 expensive 11 at a high cost 12 at a high price
• **fix price**
03 peg

priceless
04 dear, rare, rich 05 comic, funny 06 costly, prized 07 amusing, a scream, killing, riotous 08 precious, unvalued, valuable 09 cherished, expensive, hilarious, treasured 10 invaluable 11 inestimable 12 incalculable, incomparable 13 inappreciable, irreplaceable, side-splitting

pricey
04 dear 05 steep 06 costly 07 sky-high 09 excessive, expensive 10 exorbitant, high-priced 11 over the odds 12 costing a bomb, extortionate 15 costing the earth, daylight robbery

prick
03 dot, jab, jag, pin 04 acme, bite, bore, brod, brog, cloy, gash, hole, itch, mark, nick, pain, pang, peak, prod, prog, slit, stab 05 harry, point, punch, rowel, smart, spike, sting, thorn, worry, wound 06 accloy, gnaw at, harass, incite, pierce, plague, prey on, target, tingle, twinge 07 pinhole, prickle, torment, trouble 08 distress, puncture, smarting 09 perforate 11 perforation
• **prick up your ears**
06 attend 09 lend an ear 10 take note of 12 pay attention, take notice of 13 listen eagerly 15 listen carefully, pin back your ears

prickle
03 nip 04 barb, itch, pang, spur, tine 05 point, prick, prong, smart, spike, spine, sting, thorn 06 needle, tingle, twinge 07 acantha, aculeus, itching, spicula 08 smarting, stinging 09 sensation 11 formication 12 paraesthesia 14 pins and needles

prickly
04 edgy, hard 05 armed, jaggy, ratty, rough, spiky, spiny, tough 06 barbed, crabby, grumpy, on edge, shirty, spiked, thorny, touchy, tricky 07 bearded, brambly, bristly, grouchy, pronged,

stroppy 08 aculeate, delicate, echinate, scratchy 09 aculeated, crotchety, difficult, echinated, irritable, sensitive 10 acanaceous 11 bad-tempered, complicated, problematic, thin-skinned, troublesome 12 acanthaceous 13 problematical, short-tempered

prickly pear
04 tuna 05 nopal 07 opuntia 09 Indian fig

pride
03 ego, joy 05 prime 06 flower, honour, mettle, vanity 07 conceit, delight, dignity, disdain, egotism, elation, stomach 08 pleasure, smugness, snobbery 09 arrogance, proudness, self-image, self-worth, splendour 10 exuberance, self-esteem 11 haughtiness, ostentation, presumption, self-conceit, self-respect 12 boastfulness, magnificence, satisfaction, triumphalism 13 bigheadedness, gratification 14 self-importance 15 pretentiousness
• **pride and joy**
03 joy 04 best, pick 05 élite, glory 06 finest, flower 07 darling, delight 10 choice part, select part 14 apple of your eye, crème de la crème, pick of the bunch
• **pride yourself on**
05 vaunt 07 exult in, glory in, revel in 09 brag about, crow about 10 boast about 11 take pride in 13 plume yourself, preen yourself 15 flatter yourself

priest
01 P 02 Pr 03 Eli 05 Aaron, clerk, Zadok 06 cleric, Elijah, Elisha, father, orator 07 prelate, secular 08 man of God 09 churchman, clergyman 10 hierophant, woman of God 11 churchwoman, clergywoman 12 ecclesiastic 13 man of the cloth 15 woman of the cloth

Priests include:

02 HP, PP
04 abbé, arch, curé, high, lama, papa, pope
05 bonze, druid, magus, mambo, padre, rabbi, vicar
06 deacon, flamen, Levite, lucumo, parish, parson, pastor, shaman, zymite
07 Brahman, patrico, pontiff, Pythian, tohunga
08 bacchant, corybant, hierarch, minister, neophyte, seminary, Syriarch
09 bacchanal, confessor, deaconess, lack-Latin, oratorian, patercove, presbyter
10 arch-flamen, masspriest, seminarian, seminarist
11 hedge-parson, hedge-priest
12 concelebrant, Redemptorist

priestess
03 nun 05 mambo 06 abbess, Pythia, sister, vestal 07 beguine, Pythian

08 canoness, prioress **09** bacchante, deaconess, Pythoness, religious **11** clergywoman

priesthood
08 the cloth **09** the church **10** full orders, hierocracy, holy orders, priestship **11** the ministry **12** the pastorate **13** sacerdotalism

priestly
07 Aaronic **08** clerical, hieratic, pastoral **09** Aaronical, canonical **10** priestlike, sacerdotal **14** ecclesiastical

prig
05 filch, prude, thief **06** haggle, tinker **07** coxcomb, entreat, holy Joe, killjoy, old maid, puritan **09** importune, Mrs Grundy, precisian **10** goody-goody, holy Willie

priggish
04 prim, smug **05** prude **06** stuffy **07** prudish, starchy **10** goody-goody **11** puritanical, strait-laced **12** narrow-minded **13** sanctimonious, self-righteous **14** holier-than-thou

prim
03 mim **04** smug **05** fussy, mimsy **06** demure, formal, mimsey, neaten, prissy, proper, quaint, stuffy **07** perjink, precise, primsie, prudish, starchy **08** priggish **10** fastidious, fuddy-duddy, governessy, old-maidish, particular **11** puritanical, strait-laced **12** primigravida **13** schoolmarmish

primacy
07 command **08** dominion **09** dominance, seniority, supremacy **10** ascendancy, leadership, paramouncy **11** pre-eminence, sovereignty, superiority

prima donna
04 diva **10** female lead **11** leading lady, moody person **14** leading soprano

primaeval *see* **primeval, primaeval**

primal
04 main **05** basic, chief, first, major, prime **07** central, highest, initial, primary **08** earliest, greatest, original, primeval **09** paramount, primaeval, primitive, principal **10** primordial **11** fundamental, primigenial, primogenial

primarily
◇ *head selection indicator*
05 first **06** mainly, mostly **07** chiefly, firstly **09** basically, in essence, in the main **10** especially **11** essentially, principally **12** nothing if not, particularly **13** fundamentally, predominantly **15** in the first place

primary
04 main **05** basic, chief, first, prime **06** direct, simple **07** capital, highest, initial, leading, opening, radical, supreme **08** cardinal, dominant, earliest, foremost, greatest, original, primeval, ultimate **09** beginning,

elemental, essential, first-hand, paramount, primaeval, primitive, principal **10** elementary, idiopathic, primordial **11** fundamental, predominant, rudimentary **12** introductory

primate
06 bishop **07** Bigfoot **10** archbishop

03 ape
04 mico
05 chimp, drill, human, indri, jocko, lemur, loris, orang, pigmy, pongo, pygmy, satyr
06 aye-aye, baboon, bonobo, chacma, colugo, dog-ape, galago, gelada, gibbon, indris, macaco, malmag, monkey, sifaka, wou-wou, wow-wow
07 gorilla, hoolock, jacchus, macaque, meercat, meerkat, nagapie, siamang, tarsier, wistiti
08 bushbaby, great ape, hylobate, mandrill, marmoset, mongoose, night-ape
09 babacoote, catarhine, hamadryad, orang-utan, prosimian
10 angwantibo, catarrhine, chimpanzee, protohuman, silverback
11 homo sapiens, orang-outang
12 Cynocephalus, ourang-outang, paranthropus
13 Galeopithecus, Kenyapithecus
15 pygmy chimpanzee

See also **ape; monkey**

prime
03 top **04** acme, best, fang, fill, main, peak **05** bloom, brief, chief, coach, equip, gen up, phang, pride, train **06** charge, choice, clue up, fill in, flower, gear up, height, heyday, inform, notify, select, zenith **07** blossom, classic, highest, leading, premier, prepare, primary, quality, supreme, typical **08** best part, foremost, get ready, maturity, original, pinnacle, standard, top-grade **09** excellent, first-rate, make ready, principal **10** first-class, perfection, pre-eminent **11** culmination, predominant **12** paradigmatic, prototypical **14** characteristic, quintessential

prime minister
02 PM **05** dewan, diwan **07** premier **08** quisling **09** Taoiseach **10** chancellor **11** Grand Vizier **13** chief minister, first minister

04 Cook (Joseph), Holt (Harold), Page (Earle), Reid (George)
05 Bruce (Stanley), Forde (Francis Michael), Hawke (Bob), Lyons (Joseph)
06 Barton (Edmund), Curtin (John), Deakin (Alfred), Fadden (Arthur), Fisher (Andrew), Fraser (Malcolm), Gorton (John), Howard (John), Hughes (Billy), McEwen (John), Watson (Chris)

07 Chifley (Ben), Keating (Paul), McMahon (William), Menzies (Robert), Scullin (James), Whitlam (Gough)

04 King (William Lyon Mackenzie)
05 Abbot (John J C), Clark (Joseph)
06 Borden (Robert), Bowell (Mackenzie), Tupper (Charles), Turner (John)
07 Bennett (R B), Laurier (Wilfrid), Meighen (Arthur), Pearson (Lester B), Trudeau (Pierre)
08 Campbell (Kim), Chrétien (Jean), Mulroney (Brian), Thompson (John S D)
09 Macdonald (John A), Mackenzie (Alexander), St Laurent (Louis)
11 Diefenbaker (John G)

04 Bell (Francis), Kirk (Norman Eric), Nash (Walter), Ward (Joseph)
05 Clark (Helen), Lange (David), Moore (Mike)
06 Bolger (James), Coates (Gordon), Forbes (George William), Fraser (Peter), Massey (William), Palmer (Geoffrey), Savage (Michael Joseph), Seddon (Richard)
07 Holland (Sidney), Muldoon (Robert), Rowling (Wallace), Shipley (Jenny)
08 Holyoake (Keith), Marshall (John Ross)
09 Hall-Jones (William), Mackenzie (Thomas)

See also **premier**

04 Bute (John Stuart, Earl), Eden (Sir Anthony), Grey (Charles Grey, Earl), Home (Alec Douglas-Home, Earl), Peel (Robert), Pitt (William)
05 Blair (Tony), Cecil (Robert), Derby (Edward Stanley, Earl), Heath (Ted), Major (John), North (Frederick North, Lord)
06 Attlee (Clement), Pelham (Henry), Wilson (Harold)
07 Asquith (Herbert), Baldwin (Stanley), Balfour (Arthur), Canning (George), Grafton (Augustus Henry Fitzroy, Duke), Russell (John, Lord), Walpole (Robert)
08 Aberdeen (George Hamilton-Gordon, Lord), Bonar Law (Andrew), Disraeli (Benjamin), Goderich (Frederick John Robinson, Viscount), Perceval (Spencer), Portland (William Henry Cavendish Bentinck, Duke), Rosebery (Archibald Philip Primrose, Earl), Thatcher (Margaret, Lady)
09 Addington (Henry), Callaghan (James, Lord), Churchill (Sir Winston), Gladstone (William), Grenville (George), Grenville (William Wyndham, Lord),

Liverpool (Robert Jenkinson, Earl), MacDonald (Ramsay), Macmillan (Harold), Melbourne (William Lamb, Viscount), Newcastle (Thomas Pelham-Holles, Duke), Salisbury (Robert Gascoyne-Cecil, Marquess), Shelburne (William Petty-Fitzmaurice, Earl)

0 Devonshire (William Cavendish, Duke), Palmerston (Henry John Temple, Viscount), Rockingham (Charles Watson Wentworth, Marquess), Wellington (Arthur Wellesley, Duke), Wilmington (Spencer Compton, Earl)

1 Chamberlain (Neville), Douglas-Home (Alec), Lloyd George (David)

7 Campbell-Bannerman (Henry)

Prime Ministers of other countries include:

2 Nu (U)
3 Ito (Hirobumi)
4 Meir (Golda), Moro (Aldo), Tojo (Hideki)
5 Ahern (Bertie), Assad (Hafez al-), Azaña (Manuel), Aznar (José María), Banda (Hastings Kamuzu), Barak (Ehud), Barre (Raymond), Begin (Menachem), Botha (Louis), Botha (P W), Craxi (Bettino), Desai (Morarji), Faure (Edgar), Hoxha (Enver), Juppé (Alain), Khama (Sir Seretse), Laval (Pierre), Lynch (Jack), Malan (Daniel), Nehru (Jawaharlal), Obote (Milton), Pasic (Nikola), Peres (Shimon), Prodi (Romano), Putin (Vladimir), Rabin (Yitzhak), Sadat (Anwar el-), Singh (Manmohan), Smith (Ian), Smuts (Jan), Spaak (Paul Henri)
6 Bhutto (Benazir), Bhutto (Zulfikar Ali), Briand (Aristide), Bruton (John), Castro (Fidel), Chirac (Jacques), Fabius (Laurent), Gandhi (Indira), Gandhi (Rajiv), Gaulle (Charles de), Hun Sen, Jospin (Lionel), Li Peng, Manley (Michael), Mugabe (Robert), Neguib (Mohammed), O'Neill (Terence, Lord), Pétain (Philippe), Pol Pot, Pombal (Sebastião de Carvalho, Marquês de), Rahman (Sheikh Mujibur), Rhodes (Cecil), Shamir (Yitzhak), Sharif (Nawaz), Sharon (Ariel), Thiers (Adolphe)
7 Berisha (Sali), Cresson (Édith), Gasperi (Alcide de), Halifax (Charles Montagu, Earl of), Haughey (Charles), Hertzog (J B M), Kosygin (Alexei), Lubbers (Ruud), Molotov (Vyacheslav), Nkrumah (Kwame), Nyerere (Julius), Vorster (John), Yeltsin (Boris)
8 Ben Bella (Ahmed), Bismarck (Otto, Fürst von), Bulganin (Nikolai), Daladier (Édouard), de Valera (Éamon), González (Felipe), Kenyatta (Jomo), Mahathir (bin Mohamad), Nakasone (Yasuhiro), Poincaré (Raymond), Pompidou (Georges), Quisling (Vidkun),

Reynolds (Albert), Vajpayee (Atal Bihari), Verwoerd (Hendrik), Zapatero (José Luis Rodríguez)
9 Andreotti (Giulio), Ben-Gurion (David), Hashimoto (Ryutaro), Kim Il-sung, Kim Jong Il, Mussolini (Benito), Netanyahu (Binyamin), Stanishev (Sergei)
10 Balkenende (Jan Peter), Berlusconi (Silvio), Clemenceau (Georges), Fitzgerald (Garrett), Jaruzelski (Wojciech), Lee Kuan Yew
11 Verhofstadt (Guy)
12 Bandaranaike (S W R D), Chernomyrdin (Viktor)
13 Brookeborough (Basil Brooke, Viscount)

primer
05 Donat, Donet 06 manual 08 prodrome, textbook 09 absey-book, detonator, prodromus 12 introduction

primeval, primaeval
03 old 05 basic, early, first 06 inborn, innate, primal 07 ancient, natural, Ogygian 08 earliest, inherent, original 09 intuitive, primitial, primitive 10 primordial 11 instinctive, prehistoric 12 autochthonal

primitive
02 ur- 03 pro- 04 wild 05 crude, early, first, naive, rough 06 primal, savage, simple 07 ancient, natural, primary, radical 08 backveld, earliest, original, primeval 09 barbarian, primaeval 10 aboriginal, antiquated, elementary, primordial, uncultured 11 fundamental, rudimentary, uncivilized, undeveloped 12 antediluvian, old-fashioned, protomorphic 15 unsophisticated

primly
07 fussily 08 prissily, stuffily 09 prudishly

primordial
03 old 05 early, first 07 ancient 08 earliest, original, primeval 09 primaeval, primitive 11 instinctive, prehistoric, rudimentary 12 autochthonal, protomorphic

primp
04 tidy 05 groom, preen 06 doll up, tart up 07 brush up, dress up, smarten 08 beautify, spruce up, titivate

prince
01 P 02 Pr 03 mir, ras 04 amir, duke, khan, king, lord, raja, rana 05 ameer, chief, Mirza, nawab, nizam, queen, rajah, ruler, Tunku 06 leader, lucumo, potent, sharif, sherif, Tengku 07 infante, monarch, shereef 08 archduke, atheling, gospodar, hospodar, maharaja, tetrarch 09 Beelzebub, maharajah, potentate, princekin, princelet, royal duke, sovereign 10 princeling, Upper Roger 13 prince consort 14 porphyrogenite

Princes include:

03 Hal
04 Igor, Ivan, John (of Gaunt)

05 Edgar (the Atheling), Harry, Henry (the Navigator), James
06 Albert, Andrew, Arthur, Edward, Edward (the Black Prince), Philip
07 Charles, Michael (of Kent), Rainier, Richard, William
08 Llywelyn, Vladimir
09 Ferdinand
11 James Stuart
15 Alexander Nevski, Bernhard Leopold

Prince Edward Island
02 PE

princely
04 huge, vast 05 grand, noble, regal, royal 06 lavish, superb 07 immense, liberal, mammoth, massive, prenzie, stately 08 colossal, enormous, en prince, generous, glorious, handsome, imperial, imposing, majestic, splendid 09 bounteous, sovereign, sumptuous 10 impressive, large-scale, stupendous, tremendous 11 magnanimous, magnificent 12 considerable

princess
04 lady, rani 05 begum, ruler 07 infanta, monarch 09 potentate, sovereign 11 archduchess 13 crown princess

Princesses include:

02 Di
03 Ida
04 Anne
05 Alice, Diana, Fiona, Grace, Regan
06 Salome
07 Eudocia, Eugenie, Goneril, Jezebel, Matilda
08 Beatrice, Caroline, Cordelia, Margaret
09 Alexandra, Charlotte, Elizabeth, Stephanie
10 Pocahontas
11 Anna Comnena

principal
03 key 04 arch, boss, head, main 05 chief, first, major, money, prime, ruler 06 assets, leader, rector 07 capital, central, decuman, highest, leading, manager, primary, supreme, truncal 08 cardinal, director, dominant, especial, foremost, in charge, mistress 09 essential, paramount 10 capital sum, controller, headmaster, pre-eminent 11 controlling, head teacher 12 capital funds, headmistress 13 most important 14 superintendent

principality
05 duchy, realm, Wales 06 empire, Monaco, Orange 07 Andorra, dukedom, earldom, kingdom, Muscovy 08 dominion, Walachia 09 archduchy, princedom, sultanate, Wallachia 10 dependency, federation, grand duchy, palatinate, principate 11 archdukedom 12 protectorate 13 confederation, Liechtenstein

principally

06 mainly, mostly **07** chiefly **08** above all **09** capitally, in the main, primarily **10** especially **12** particularly **13** predominantly **14** for the most part

principle

03 key, law **04** code, germ, idea, root, rule, seed, soul **05** axiom, basis, canon, creed, dogma, geist, maxim, Sakti, tenet, truth **06** dictum, ethics, honour, morals, origin, reason, Shakti, source, spirit, theory, virtue **07** brocard, decency, element, formula, precept, probity, theorem **08** doctrine, morality, rudiment, scruples, standard **09** beginning, component, criterion, essential, headstone, institute, integrity, postulate, rationale, rectitude, standards **10** classicism, conscience, golden rule, groundwork, primordial, principium, seminality **11** fundamental, proposition, uprightness **12** classicism

• in principle

07 ideally **08** in theory **09** in essence **10** en principe **13** theoretically

principled

04 just **05** moral **06** decent **07** ethical, upright **08** virtuous **09** righteous **10** high-minded, honourable, scrupulous **11** respectable, right-minded **13** conscientious

print

04 copy, etch, font, lith, mark, oleo, snap, type **05** fount, issue, mould, photo, stamp **06** design, record, run off, strike **07** bromide, edition, engrave, impress, imprint, letters, picture, publish, replica **08** aquatint, put to bed, register, snapshot, typeface **09** aquatinta, engraving, facsimile, footprint, lettering, newspaper, oleograph, reproduce, strike off **10** characters, exactitude, impression, lithograph, photograph, typescript **11** fingerprint **12** reproduction

See also **painter**

• in print

07 in stock **09** available, published **10** obtainable **13** in circulation

• out of print

02 op **07** sold out **10** out of stock **11** unavailable **12** off the market, unobtainable

printer

• instruction to printer

04 dele, hash, stet **05** caret

printing

Printing methods include:

03 CTP
05 laser, litho
06 ink-jet, offset, screen
07 etching, gravure
08 intaglio
09 bubble-jet, collotype, engraving
10 silk-screen, xerography
11 die-stamping, duplicating, flexography, letterpress, lithography, rotary press, stencilling, twin-etching
12 lino blocking, thermography
13 colour-process, electrostatic
14 photoengraving
15 computer-to-plate, copper engraving

Printing and publishing terms include:

02 em, en
03 CTP, TLS, TPS
04 bulk, case, CMYK, copy, demi, font, kern, laid, logo, sewn, stet, text, tint, trim, type, typo
05 bleed, caret, chase, cloth, cover, flong, forme, litho, moiré, press, proof, quoin, roman, widow, zinco
06 galley, gutter, indent, italic, jacket, mackle, margin, matrix, octavo, orphan, Ozalid®, quarto, take in, unsewn, web-fed
07 bromide, carding, cast-off, compose, dot gain, end even, foiling, leaders, leading, literal, opacity, Pantone®, reprint, strip in, woodcut
08 bad break, bold face, Linotype®, logotype, misprint, Monotype®, mottling, offprint, spoilage, strike-on, take over, typeface, type spec
09 backing-up, catchword, condensed, duodecimo, finishing, Intertype®, letterset, lower-case, makeready, newsprint, overprint, run-around, sans serif, signature, trim marks, type scale, upper-case, web offset
10 back margin, collograph, column inch, compositor, dot-etching, dustjacket, feathering, first proof, hard hyphen, imposition, impression, large print, manuscript, perfecting, ragged left, see-through, soft hyphen, stereotype, typescript
11 drum printer, electrotype, initial caps, line printer, ragged right, running head, running text, typesetting, typographer
12 author's proof, character set, expanded type, flat-bed press, inking roller, machine proof, registration, specimen page
13 composing room, cylinder press, image printing, justification, printing press, small capitals, wood engraving
14 relief printing, thermal printer
15 camera-ready copy

See also **typeface**

printmaker *see* **painter**

prior

05 elder **06** former **07** earlier **08** previous **09** foregoing, preceding **10** antecedent, magistrate

• prior to

03 pre **04** till, up to **05** until **06** before **09** preceding **11** earlier than, in advance of

priority

04 rank **07** the lead **09** essential, main thing, seniority, supremacy **10** first place, paramouncy, precedence, preference, right of way **11** pre-eminence, requirement, superiority **12** first concern, highest place, pole position, primary issue, top of the tree **13** supreme matter

priory

05 abbey **06** friary **07** convent, nunnery **08** cloister, priorate **09** béguinage, monastery **14** religious house

prise

03 pry **04** lift, move **05** force, hoist, jemmy, lever, raise, shift **06** winkle **08** dislodge, leverage, purchase

prison

03 bin, can, HMP, jug, pen, pit **04** bird, brig, cage, cell, coop, gaol, jail, nick, quad, quod, stir, tank **05** choky, clink, gulag, kitty, limbo **06** bagnio, chokey, cooler, inside, lock-up, lumber **07** bull pen, confine, custody, dungeon, enclose, hoosgow, slammer **08** bastille, big house, hoosegow, porridge, restrain, the hulks, the joint **09** bridewell, calaboose, detention, jailhouse, Lob's pound, massymore **10** guardhouse **11** confinement **12** imprisonment, penitentiary **15** detention centre

Prisons include:

04 Maze
05 Fleet, Pozzi
06 Albany, Attica, Folsom
07 Brixton, Feltham, Newgate
08 Alcatraz, Bastille, Belmarsh, Dartmoor, Holloway, Long Kesh, Lubyanka, Sing Sing
09 Fremantle, Parkhurst, the Scrubs
10 San Quentin, Wandsworth
11 Hanoi Hilton, Pentonville, Strangeways
12 Devil's Island, Rikers Island, Robben Island
13 Tower of London
14 Wormwood scrubs

prisoner

03 con, lag, POW **05** lifer, trust **06** détenu, inmate, old lag, trusty **07** captive, convict, culprit, détenue, hostage, passman **08** detainee, internee, jailbird, yardbird **10** recidivist **13** prisoner of war, state prisoner

prissily

06 primly **07** fussily **08** stuffily **09** prudishly

prissy

04 prim **05** fussy **06** demure, formal, proper, stuffy **07** finicky, po-faced, precise, prudish, starchy **08** priggish **09** squeamish **10** effeminate, fastidious, old-maidish, particular **11** puritanical, strait-laced **13** schoolmarmish

pristine

04 pure **05** clean, first, fresh **06** former, primal, unused, virgin **07** initial,

primary 08 earliest, original, primeval, unspoilt **09** primaeval, primitive, unchanged, undefiled, unspoiled, unsullied, untouched **10** immaculate, primordial **11** primigenial, uncorrupted

privacy
07 private, privity, retreat, secrecy **08** solitude **09** isolation, quietness, seclusion **10** retirement **11** concealment, privateness **12** independence **13** sequestration **15** confidentiality

private
03 own, Pte, Pvt **04** swad **05** alone, aside, close, privy, quiet, Tommy **06** closed, closet, gunner, hidden, remote, secret, swaddy **07** postern, privacy, soldier, special, squaddy **08** domestic, familiar, homefelt, hush-hush, intimate, isolated, personal, reserved, retiring, secluded, separate, singular, solitary, squaddie **09** concealed, exclusive, innermost, top secret, withdrawn **10** classified, commercial, free-market, individual, particular, privatized, privileged, unofficial **11** clandestine, enlisted man, independent, introverted, out-of-the-way, sequestered, Tommy Atkins, undisturbed **12** confidential, off the record **13** intraparietal, self-contained, self-governing, single soldier **14** denationalized, free-enterprise, private soldier **15** non-governmental, self-determining
• **in private**
07 sub rosa **08** in camera, in secret, secretly **09** privately **12** in confidence **14** confidentially **15** behind the scenes
• **private detective** see **detective**

privateer
06 marque, pirate **07** brigand, corsair, cruiser, sea wolf **09** buccaneer, sea robber **10** filibuster, freebooter

private eye see **detective**

privately
05 aside **06** inside, within **07** at heart, privily, sub rosa **08** deep down, in camera, in secret, inwardly, secretly **09** in private **10** personally, to yourself **12** in confidence, under the rose **13** deep inside you **14** confidentially

privation
04 lack, loss, need, want **06** misery, penury **07** poverty **08** distress, hardship **09** austerity, indigence, neediness, suffering **10** affliction **11** deprivation, destitution

privilege
03 due **05** honor, prise, right, title **06** honour, octroi, patent **07** benefit, faculty, freedom, liberty, licence **08** immunity, priority, sanction **09** advantage, authority, commodity, exemption, franchise **10** birthright, concession, seignorage **11** entitlement, prerogative, seigniorage **12** dispensation, status symbol

privileged
04 rich **05** élite **06** exempt, immune, ruling, secret **07** private, special, wealthy **08** excepted, favoured, honoured, hush-hush, powerful **09** chartered, indulgent, top secret **10** advantaged, authorized, classified, sanctioned, unofficial **12** confidential, off the record

privy
02 WC **03** bog, can, lav, loo **04** Ajax, kazi **05** dunny, gents', heads, jakes, siege **06** cloaca, closet, ladies', secret, toilet, urinal **07** cottage, crapper, draught, latrine, private **08** familiar, intimate, lavatory, rest room, washroom **09** cloakroom, garderobe **10** powder room, thunderbox **11** water closet **12** draught-house, smallest room **14** comfort station
• **privy to**
04 in on **06** wise to **07** aware of **09** clued up on **10** apprised of, genned up on **11** cognizant of **13** informed about **14** in the know about

prize
03 aim, cup, lot, pie, top **04** best, gain, goal, gree, hope, loot, love, palm, plum, tern **05** award, booty, great, honor, match, medal, plate, price, purse, stake, value **06** desire, esteem, honour, revere, reward, spoils, stakes, trophy **07** capture, cherish, jackpot, laurels, pennant, perfect, pillage, plunder, premium, seizure, winning **08** accolade, champion, hold dear, leverage, pickings, purchase, smashing, terrific, top-notch, treasure, winnings **09** excellent, first-rate, treasured **10** appreciate **11** outstanding, wooden spoon **12** award-winning, prize-winning **13** think highly of **14** out of this world **15** set great store by
See also **award**

prize-winner
03 dux **05** champ **06** winner **08** champion, prizeman **09** cup-winner, medallist **10** prizewoman
See also **Nobel Prize**

pro
03 ace, aye, for **06** expert, master, wizard **07** backing, dab hand, old hand **08** virtuoso **09** authority **10** consultant, in favour of, past master, prostitute, specialist, supporting **12** practitioner, probationary, professional
See also **prostitute**

probability
04 odds **05** chance **07** chances **08** prospect **10** likelihood, likeliness **11** expectation, possibility

probable
06 likely, odds-on **07** seeming **08** a fair bet, apparent, credible, expected, feasible, possible **09** plausible **10** believable, forseeable, on the cards

11 anticipated, predictable **12** to be expected

probably
04 like **05** maybe **06** belike, likely **07** perhaps **08** a fair bet, arguably, possibly **09** doubtless, like as not **10** most likely, presumably **11** as like as not, it looks like **13** as likely as not, the chances are **15** in all likelihood

probation
04 test **05** proof, trial **07** testing **09** noviciate **10** test period **11** supervision, trial period **14** apprenticeship

probationer
04 tiro **05** pupil **06** novice, rookie **07** amateur, learner, recruit, student, trainee **08** beginner, neophyte, newcomer, stibbler **09** greenhorn, noviciate **10** apprentice, raw recruit

probe
04 bore, feel, poke, prod, sift, tent, test **05** check, drill, plumb, sound, study, style **06** device, go into, pierce, search, stilet, stylet, tracer **07** analyse, examine, explore, inquest, inquire, inquiry **08** analysis, look into, research, scrutiny, searcher **09** penetrate **10** instrument, scrutinize **11** examination, exploration, investigate **13** investigation **14** scrutinization

Space probes include:
04 Luna
06 Viking
07 Galileo, Mariner, Pioneer, Voyager
09 Messenger
10 Deep Impact
14 Cassini–Huygens

probity
05 worth **06** equity, honour, virtue **07** honesty, justice **08** fairness, fidelity, goodness, morality **09** integrity, rectitude, sincerity **11** uprightness **12** truthfulness **13** righteousness **14** honourableness **15** trustworthiness

problem
◊ *anagram indicator*
02 BO **03** fix, sum **04** bore, boyg, drag, hole, knot, mess, pain, pest, prob, snag **05** facer, issue, poser, thing, worry **06** bother, enigma, hassle, indaba, matter, pickle, plight, puzzle, riddle, unruly **07** dilemma, toughie, trouble, wrinkle **08** irritant, nuisance, quandary, question, vexation **09** annoyance, conundrum, dichotomy, difficult, tight spot **10** conclusion, delinquent, difficulty, irritation, mind-bender **11** brainteaser, dire straits, disobedient, predicament, troublesome **12** brain-twister, complication, intransigent, recalcitrant, unmanageable **13** Chinese puzzle, inconvenience, pain in the neck **14** no-win situation, uncontrollable **15** thorn in your side
See also **economics; environment**

problematic

◇ *anagram indicator*
04 hard, moot 06 thorny, tricky
07 awkward, dubious 08 doubtful,
involved, puzzling 09 debatable,
difficult, enigmatic, intricate, uncertain
10 a minefield, perplexing 11 a can of
worms, troublesome 12 questionable
13 problematical

procedure

02 op 03 way 04 move, play, step
05 drill, means 06 action, course,
custom, fetich, fetish, method, policy,
scheme, system 07 conduct, fetiche,
formula, measure, process, routine,
tactics 08 practice, strategy, technics
09 mechanics, operation, technique
11 advisedness, methodology,
performance 12 plan of action
13 modus operandi 14 course of
action

proceed

02 go, on 03 put 04 come, fand, flow,
fond, go on, make, pass, rake, stem,
sway, yead, yede, yeed 05 arise, begin,
ensue, get on, issue, start, trace
06 come on, derive, follow, happen,
move on, pass on, result, spring
07 advance, carry on, emanate, go
ahead, press on, prosper 08 continue,
progress 09 go forward, originate,
prosecute, take steps 10 make a start
11 get under way, make your way, set in
motion
• **proceed with difficulty**
04 limp

proceedings

04 acta, case, diet 05 deeds, moves,
steps, trial 06 action, annals, doings,
events, report 07 account, affairs,
lawsuit, matters, minutes, process,
records, reports 08 archives,
business, dealings, measures,
ongoings 10 activities, happenings,
litigation, manoeuvres, operations,
procedures 12 transactions 14 course
of action

proceeds

04 gain 05 motza, yield 06 avails,
income, motser, profit, return
07 produce, profits, returns, revenue,
takings 08 earnings, receipts
12 intromission

process

◇ *anagram indicator*
03 way 04 mode, sort, step 05 alter,
edict, means, stage, train, treat
06 action, change, course, growth,
handle, manner, method, refine,
system 07 advance, changes, convert,
prepare 08 attend to, deal with,
movement, practice, progress
09 evolution, formation, narrative,
operation, procedure, technique,
transform 10 proceeding
11 development, progression
• **in the process of**
05 being 11 in the making 13 in
preparation, in the course of, in the
middle of

procession

03 run 04 demo, file, pomp, walk
05 corso, march, train 06 column,
course, exequy, parade, series, stream
07 cortège, funeral, pageant, triumph
08 Moharram, Muharram, Muharrem,
progress, sequence 09 cavalcade,
motorcade 10 succession 11 hunger
march 13 demonstration,
manifestation

proclaim

03 ask, bid, cry 04 ring, show, sing
05 knell, sound 06 affirm, blazon,
herald, notify, out-ask, preach,
summon 07 declare, enounce, give
out, profess, protest, publish, testify,
trumpet 08 announce, denounce,
indicate 09 advertise, broadcast,
circulate, make known, preconize,
pronounce, show forth 10 annunciate,
annuntiate, apostolize, promulgate
11 blaze abroad

proclamation

03 ban 04 oyes, oyez, rule 05 banns,
edict, order 06 decree, notice
07 command, kerygma, placard
08 proclaim 09 broadcast, hue and cry,
indiction, manifesto, preaching
11 affirmation, circulation, declaration,
publication 12 announcement,
annunciation, notification,
promulgation, proscription
13 advertisement, order of the day,
pronouncement 14 pronunciamento

proclivity

04 bent, bias 07 leaning 08 penchant,
tendency, weakness 09 liability,
proneness 10 liableness, propensity
11 disposition, inclination
12 predilection 14 predisposition

procrastinate

05 dally, defer, delay, stall 06 put off,
retard 07 prolong 08 postpone,
protract 09 temporize 10 dilly-dally
11 play for time 12 drag your feet

procrastination

08 deferral, delaying, stalling
10 cunctation 11 temporizing
12 dilatoriness 13 dilly-dallying
15 delaying tactics

procreate

04 sire 05 beget, breed, spawn
06 father, mother 07 produce
08 conceive, engender, generate,
multiply 09 propagate, reproduce

proctor

04 prog 08 proggins

procure

03 buy, get, win 04 earn, find, gain,
hire, hook, pimp, sort 05 ponce
06 come by, hustle, induce, obtain,
pander, pick up, secure 07 acquire,
provide, solicit 08 purchase 09 get
hold of, importune 10 lay hands on
11 appropriate, requisition

procurer

04 bawd, hoon, mack, pimp
05 madam, ponce 06 broker, pander

07 hustler 08 fancy man, mackerel,
panderer 09 procuress, solicitor
11 fleshmonger, whoremonger

prod

03 awl, dig, jab, job 04 brod, butt,
goad, move, poke, push, spur, stir, urge
05 egg on, elbow, goose, nudge, prick,
probe, punch, shove 06 incite, prompt,
skewer, thrust 08 motivate, reminder,
stimulus 09 encourage, prompting,
stimulate 10 motivation
13 encouragement

prodigal

06 lavish, wanton, waster 07 copious,
profuse, wastrel 08 profuser, reckless,
spendall, unthrift, wasteful
09 bounteous, bountiful, excessive,
exuberant, luxuriant, sumptuous,
unsparing, unthrifty 10 big spender,
immoderate, profligate, squanderer
11 extravagant, improvident,
intemperate, spendthrift, squandering

prodigality

05 waste 06 excess, plenty, wastry
07 abandon, wastery 08 richness
09 abundance, amplitude, profusion
10 exuberance, lavishness, luxuriance,
profligacy, wantonness
11 copiousness, dissipation,
squandering 12 extravagance,
immoderation, intemperance,
recklessness, wastefulness
13 bounteousness, plenteousness,
sumptuousness, unthriftiness

prodigious

04 huge, vast 05 giant 07 amazing,
immense, mammoth, massive, unusual
08 abnormal, colossal, enormous,
fabulous, gigantic, striking, terrific
09 fantastic, monstrous, startling,
wonderful 10 astounding, gargantuan,
impressive, inordinate, marvellous,
miraculous, monumental,
phenomenal, portentous, remarkable,
staggering, stupendous, tremendous
11 exceptional, spectacular
12 immeasurable 13 extraordinary
14 flabbergasting

prodigiously

06 vastly 09 amazingly, immensely,
massively, unusually 10 remarkably
11 wonderfully 12 astoundingly,
impressively, phenomenally,
staggeringly 13 exceptionally,
fantastically, spectacularly

prodigy

05 freak 06 genius, marvel, phenom,
rarity, wonder 07 miracle, monster,
portent 08 moniment, monument,
virtuoso, whizz kid 09 curiosity,
sensation 10 mastermind,
phenomenon, wonderwork,
wunderkind 11 child genius, gifted
child, phaenomenon, wonder child

produce

◇ *anagram indicator*
04 bear, crop, eggs, food, give, grow,
kind, make, show 05 beget, breed,
build, cause, crops, dig up, evoke, fruit,

ssue, mount, offer, put on, raise, stage, stuff, throw, wheel, yield **06** create, direct, effect, extend, get out, invent, manage, output, put out, supply, upcome **07** advance, arrange, compose, deliver, develop, execute, exhibit, fashion, furnish, harvest, perform, prepare, present, product, proffer, provide, provoke **08** assemble, bring out, engender, generate, increase, knock out, occasion, organize, proceeds, products, put forth, result in **09** construct, fabricate, originate **10** bring about, bring forth, come up with, foodstuffs, give rise to, put forward, vegetables **11** commodities, demonstrate, give birth to, manufacture, put together **12** bring forward **13** dairy products

producer
04 hand **05** maker **06** farmer, grower **07** manager **08** director, generant **09** generator, presenter, régisseur **10** impresario, undertaker **12** manufacturer

See also **director**

product
04 item, work **05** fruit, goods, issue, wares, yield **06** effect, legacy, output, result, return, upshot **07** article, outcome, produce, spin-off **08** artefact, creation, offshoot **09** by-product, commodity, invention, offspring, outgrowth **10** end-product, production **11** consequence, merchandise, producement

production
◇ *anagram indicator*
04 film, play, show, work **05** drama, fruit, opera, revue, yield **06** fruits, making, output, return **07** concert, harvest, musical, returns, staging **08** assembly, building, creation, mounting **09** direction, extension, formation, producing **10** management **11** achievement, composition, development, fabrication, manufacture, origination, performance, preparation **12** construction, organization, presentation, productivity **13** manufacturing

productive
04 busy, rich **06** fecund, useful **07** fertile, gainful, teeming **08** creative, fructive, fruitful, pregnant, prolific, valuable, vigorous **09** effective, efficient, energetic, inventive, rewarding **10** beneficial, generative, profitable, worthwhile **11** increaseful, procreative **12** constructive, fructiferous, high-yielding

productivity
05 yield **06** output **08** capacity, work rate **10** efficiency, production **12** fruitfulness **14** productiveness

profanation
05 abuse **06** misuse **08** violence **09** blasphemy, sacrilege, violation

10 debasement, defilement, perversion **11** desecration **12** dishonouring

profane
03 lay **04** foul **05** abuse, crude **06** coarse, debase, defile, filthy, misuse, unholy, vulgar **07** abusive, godless, impious, pervert, pollute, secular, unclean, ungodly, violate, worldly **08** temporal **09** desecrate, misemploy **10** foul-spoken, idolatrous, irreverent, unhallowed **11** blasphemous, contaminate, foul-mouthed, irreligious **12** sacrilegious, unsanctified **13** disrespectful, unconsecrated

profanity
04 oath **05** abuse, curse **07** cursing, impiety **08** swearing **09** blasphemy, expletive, obscenity, sacrilege, swear-word **10** execration **11** imprecation, irreverence, malediction, profaneness **14** four-letter word

profess
03 own **04** aver, avow **05** admit, claim, state **06** affirm, allege, assert **07** certify, confess, confirm, declare, make out, pretend, purport **08** announce, maintain, proclaim **09** dissemble **10** lay claim to **11** acknowledge

professed
06 avowed **07** alleged, would-be **08** apparent, declared, so-called, supposed **09** certified, confirmed, pretended, purported, soi-disant **10** ostensible, proclaimed, self-styled **12** acknowledged **13** self-confessed

profession
03 job **04** line, post **05** claim, craft, trade **06** avowal, career, métier, office **07** calling **08** averment, business, position, pretence, vocation **09** admission, assertion, situation, statement, testimony **10** confession, employment, line of work, occupation, walk of life **11** affirmation, appointment, declaration **12** announcement **15** acknowledgement

professional
03 ace, pro **04** able **05** adept, buppy, maven, mavin, whizz, yuppy **06** expert, master, wizard, yuppie **07** dab hand, maestro, old hand, regular, skilful, skilled, trained **08** educated, licensed, masterly, virtuoso **09** authority, competent, dexterous, efficient, practised, qualified **10** consultant, past master, proficient, specialist **11** experienced **12** accomplished, businesslike, practitioner **13** knowledgeable

professor
02 RP **03** don, STP **04** dean, prof **05** chair, hodja, khoja **06** fellow, khodja, reader, regent **07** adjoint, provost **08** academic, emeritus, lecturer **09** principal **12** intellectual **13** head of faculty **14** vice chancellor

proffer
04 hand **05** offer **06** extend, submit, tender **07** advance, hold out, present, propose, suggest **09** volunteer

proficiency
05 knack, skill **06** talent **07** ability, aptness, finesse, mastery **08** aptitude **09** adeptness, dexterity, expertise, technique **10** capability, competence, experience **11** skilfulness **14** accomplishment
• **level of proficiency**
03 dan **05** grade

proficient
03 apt **04** able, wise **05** adept **06** clever, expert, gifted, useful **07** capable, skilful, skilled, trained **08** masterly, talented **09** competent, effective, efficient, qualified **10** past master **11** experienced **12** accomplished, passed master

profile
02 CV **04** biog, form, line, vita **05** cameo, chart, graph, lines, shape, study **06** figure, purfle, résumé, review, sketch, survey, talweg **07** contour, diagram, drawing, outline, thalweg **08** analysis, half-face, portrait, side view, template, vignette **09** biography, half-cheek **10** silhouette **11** description, examination **15** curriculum vitae, thumbnail sketch
• **high profile**
08 exposure **10** prominence, visibility **12** the limelight, the spotlight **15** public attention
• **keep a low profile**
06 lie low **12** escape notice, hide yourself **14** avoid publicity

profit
03 pay, use **04** boot, gain, gelt, perk, vail **05** avail, bonus, bunce, gravy, gross, serve, value, worth, yield **06** excess, income, margin, return **07** benefit, bestead, improve, killing, rake-off, revenue, surplus, takings, vantage **08** dividend, earnings, fast buck, increase, interest, proceeds, receipts, winnings **09** advantage, commodity, make money **10** bottom line, percentage, perquisite, usefulness **11** improvement **13** make megabucks **15** line your pockets, make loadsamoney
• **profit by, profit from**
03 use **04** milk **07** exploit, utilize **08** cash in on **12** capitalize on, put to good use **15** take advantage of, turn to advantage
• **share of profit**
03 lay

profitable
03 fat **05** juicy, utile **06** paying, plummy, useful **07** gainful, helpful, payable **08** behovely, economic, fruitful, valuable **09** available, expedient, lucrative, rewarding **10** beneficial, commercial, in the black, productive, successful, worthwhile **11** moneymaking **12** advantageous,

remunerative **13** advantageable, cost-effective

profitably
08 usefully, valuably **10** fruitfully **12** beneficially, commercially, economically, productively, successfully

profiteer
06 extort, fleece **07** exploit **09** exploiter, racketeer **10** overcharge **11** extortioner **12** extortionist **13** make a fast buck **14** make a quick buck

profiteering
09 extortion **10** Rachmanism **12** exploitation, racketeering

profitless
04 idle, vain **06** futile **07** useless **08** gainless, wasteful **09** fruitless, pointless, thankless, to no avail, worthless **10** unavailing **11** ineffective, ineffectual, to no purpose **12** unproductive, unprofitable **14** unremunerative

profligacy
05 waste **06** excess **09** abundance, depravity, profusion **10** corruption, debauchery, degeneracy, immorality, lavishness, wantonness **11** dissipation, libertinism, prodigality, promiscuity, squandering, unrestraint **12** extravagance, improvidence, recklessness, wastefulness **13** dissoluteness, unthriftiness **14** licentiousness

profligate
04 rake, roué **05** loose **06** wanton, waster, wicked **07** corrupt, Don Juan, immoral, wastrel **08** defeated, depraved, prodigal, reckless, wasteful **09** abandoned, debauched, debauchee, dissolute, excessive, libertine, reprobate **10** Corinthian, degenerate, dissipated, immoderate, iniquitous, licentious, overthrown, squanderer **11** extravagant, improvident, promiscuous, spendthrift, squandering **12** unprincipled

profound
03 sea **04** deep, wise **05** abyss, great, ocean **06** marked **07** erudite, extreme, intense, learned, radical, serious, sincere, weighty **08** absolute, abstruse, complete, esoteric, thorough **09** extensive, heartfelt, recondite, sagacious **10** deep-seated, discerning, exhaustive, thoughtful **11** far-reaching, penetrating **12** impenetrable **13** philosophical, thoroughgoing

profoundly
04 deep **06** deeply, keenly **07** acutely, greatly **08** heartily **09** extremely, intensely, seriously, sincerely **10** thoroughly

profundity
05 depth **06** acumen, wisdom **07** insight **08** learning, sagacity, severity, strength **09** erudition,

extremity, intensity **11** penetration, perspicuity, seriousness **12** abstruseness, intelligence, perspicacity, profoundness **14** perceptiveness

profuse
04 rich **05** ample **06** lavish **07** copious, fulsome, liberal **08** abundant, generous **09** excessive, luxuriant, plentiful, unsparing **10** immoderate, inordinate, over the top, unstinting **11** extravagant, large-handed, overflowing **12** colliquative, overabundant **13** superabundant

profusely
08 lavishly **09** copiously, liberally **10** abundantly **11** unsparingly **12** immoderately, unstintingly **13** extravagantly

profusion
04 glut, lots, riot, tons **05** heaps, loads, waste **06** excess, lavish, plenty, wealth **07** surplus **08** plethora **09** abundance, multitude, plenitude **10** profligacy **11** copiousness, prodigality, superfluity **12** extravagance **13** unsparingness **14** superabundance

progenitor
05 stock **06** father, mother, parent, source, tupuna **07** founder **08** ancestor, begetter, forebear **09** precursor **10** antecedent, forefather, forerunner, instigator, originator, procreator **11** predecessor **12** primogenitor

progeny
04 burd, race, seed **05** breed, issue, stock, young **06** family, scions **07** lineage **08** children, increase, mokopuna **09** offspring, posterity, quiverful **10** generation **11** descendants

prognosis
07 outlook, surmise **08** forecast, prospect **09** diagnosis **10** assessment, evaluation, prediction, projection **11** expectation, forecasting, speculation **15** prognostication

prognosticate
05 augur **06** divine, herald **07** betoken, portend, predict, presage **08** forebode, forecast, foretell, indicate, prophesy, soothsay **09** harbinger **10** foreshadow

prognostication
04 omen **07** surmise **08** forecast, precurse, prophecy **09** horoscope, prejudice, prejudize, prognosis **10** prediction, projection **11** expectation, speculation

programme
04 book, list, plan, show **05** lay on **06** agenda, course, design, line up, line-up, map out, scheme **07** arrange, episode, itemize, listing, project, work out **08** calendar, schedule, syllabus **09** broadcast, formulate, simulcast, timetable **10** curriculum, prearrange,

production, prospectus **11** performance **12** plan of action, presentation, transmission **13** order of events

See also **radio**; **television**

programming *see* **language**

progress
02 go **03** ren, rin, run, way **04** gain, go on, grow, sail **05** bloom, going **06** better, career, come on, course, growth, mature, thrive **07** advance, blossom, circuit, develop, headway, improve, journey, onwards, passage, proceed, prosper, recover, shape up, success **08** continue, distance, flourish, increase, movement, traverse **09** come along, evolution, go forward, promotion, upgrading **10** betterment, forge ahead, periegesis, proceeding, procession **11** advancement, development, improvement, make headway, make strides, make your way, move forward, progression, step forward **12** breakthrough, continuation, make progress, steps forward **14** be getting there **15** forward movement
• **in progress**
02 on **06** on foot **07** en train, going on, in train, on-going **08** on the way, under way **09** happening, occurring **10** continuing, proceeding **11** not finished, on the stocks **12** not completed **13** in preparation, in the pipeline
• **make progress**
04 roll

progression
05 chain, cycle, order, train **06** course, motion, series, stream, string **07** advance, headway, passage, process **08** movement, progress, pub-crawl, sequence **10** paraphonia, precession, resolution, succession **11** advancement, development **12** direct motion **15** forward movement

progressive
04 left, prog **06** modern **07** creator, deviser, dynamic, go-ahead, gradual, growing, liberal, pioneer, radical **08** advanced, left-wing, reformer **09** advancing, developer, innovator, reformist **10** avant-garde, continuing, developing, escalating, increasing, innovative, modernizer, originator **11** enlightened, trailblazer, up-and-coming **12** accelerating, enterprising, fresh thinker, intensifying **13** revolutionary **14** forward-looking **15** forward-thinking

progressively
07 forward **08** bit by bit, by stages, forwards, in stages **09** by degrees, gradually, piecemeal **10** step by step **12** hand over hand, increasingly **14** little by little

prohibit
03 ban, bar **04** stop, veto **06** defend,

enjoin, forbid, hamper, hinder, impede, outlaw **07** exclude, injunct, prevent, rule out **08** obstruct, preclude, restrict **09** interdict, proscribe

prohibited
05 taboo **06** banned, barred, vetoed **07** illegal **08** verboten **09** embargoed, forbidden, off-limits **10** contraband, disallowed, proscribed **11** interdicted

prohibition
03 ban, bar **04** tabu, veto **07** embargo, forbode **08** negation **09** exclusion, forbiddal, interdict **10** constraint, forbidding, injunction, prevention **11** forbiddance, obstruction, restriction **12** disallowance, interdiction, proscription

prohibitionist
03 dry **09** pussyfoot **11** teetotaller **12** abolitionist

prohibitive
05 steep **07** sky-high **09** excessive **10** exorbitant, forbidding, impossible, repressive **11** prohibiting, prohibitory, restraining, restrictive, suppressive **12** extortionate, preposterous, proscriptive

project
03 job, jut **04** cast, hurl, idea, kick, plan, sail, task, work **05** bulge, chuck, fling, gauge, jetty, throw **06** beetle, design, devise, expect, extend, intend, jut out, launch, map out, notion, propel, reckon, reflex, scheme, screen **07** obtrude, predict, propose, venture **08** activity, campaign, contract, estimate, exercise, forecast, outstand, overhang, proposal, protrude, stand out, stick out, workshop **09** calculate, discharge, programme **10** assignment, conception, enterprise, occupation **11** externalize, extrapolate, undertaking **12** predetermine

projectile
04 ball, bomb, shot **05** shell **06** bullet, mortar, rocket, tracer **07** grenade, missile **08** case-shot, fireball **09** ballistic, impelling **13** guided missile

projecting
05 proud **08** beetling, exserted **09** exsertile, extrusive, extrusory, obtrusive, prominent **10** protrudent, protruding, protrusive **11** overhanging, sticking out
• **projecting part**
03 arm, ear, fin **04** nose, tang

projection
03 cam, cog, jut, lug, nab, out, rag **04** beak, nose, peak, plan, sail, sill, spur, tusk **05** bulge, ledge, prong, ridge, sally, scrag, shelf, snout, spike, strap, tooth **06** calcar, corner, design, nozzle, outjet, outjut, relief, tongue **07** jutting, process **08** estimate, forecast, overhang, oversail, planning **09** dentation, reckoning **10** estimation, prediction, prominence, promontory **11** calculation, computation,

excrescence, expectation, orthography **12** protuberance **13** extrapolation

proletarian
06 common **08** ordinary, plebeian **12** working-class

proletariat
03 mob **04** herd **05** plebs **06** lumpen, masses, proles, rabble **08** canaille, riff-raff **09** commoners, hoi polloi **10** commonalty **11** rank and file, third estate **12** common people, lower classes, working class **13** great unwashed

proliferate
05 breed **06** expand, extend, rocket, spread, thrive **07** build up, burgeon **08** escalate, flourish, increase, multiply, mushroom, snowball **09** intensify, reproduce **11** grow quickly **15** increase rapidly

proliferation
06 spread **07** build-up **08** increase **09** expansion, extension, rocketing **10** escalation **11** duplication, ecblastesis, mushrooming, snowballing **13** concentration, rapid increase **14** multiplication **15** intensification

prolific
04 rank **06** broody, fecund **07** copious, fertile, profuse **08** abundant, fruitful **09** luxuriant, plentiful **10** productive **11** fertilizing **12** reproductive

prolix
04 long **05** prosy, wordy **07** diffuse, lengthy, tedious, verbose **08** rambling, tiresome **09** prolonged, rigmarole **10** digressive, discursive, long-winded, pleonastic, protracted

prolixity
06 length **08** longueur, pleonasm, rambling, verbiage **09** prosiness, verbosity, wandering, wordiness **10** boringness **11** diffuseness, tediousness, verboseness **13** copia verborum **14** discursiveness, long-windedness

prologue
05 index, proem **07** preface, prelude **08** exordium, foreword, preamble **09** introduce, prooemion, prooemium **11** preliminary, prolegomena **12** introduction

prolong
05 delay **06** extend, linger **07** drag out, draw out, respite, spin out, stretch, sustain **08** continue, elongate, lengthen, postpone, prorogue, protract **10** perpetuate, stretch out

prolongation
04 tail **08** appendix, urostyle **09** extension, gonophore **10** androphore, carpophore, stretching, trichogyne **11** lengthening, protraction **12** continuation, perpetuation

promenade
04 pier, prom, turn, walk **05** front, mosey, paseo, strut **06** airing, parade, stroll **07** saunter, swagger, terrace, walkway **08** breather, seafront **09** boulevard, esplanade, polonaise, walkabout **10** sally forth **11** perambulate **14** constitutional

promethium
02 Pm

prominence
03 rib **04** boss, bump, crag, cusp, fame, hump, lump, name, note, rank, rise **05** bulge, cliff, crest, mound, torus **06** height, renown, rising, tragus, weight **07** jutting, mastoid, process, stature **08** eminence, emphasis, headland, pinnacle, prestige, standing, swelling **09** celebrity, elevation, greatness **10** antitragus, colliculus, embossment, importance, projection, prominency, promontory, protruding, reputation, top billing **11** distinction, pre-eminence **12** pride of place, protuberance **15** conspicuousness, illustriousness
• **into prominence**
02 up

prominent
03 top **04** main **05** A-list, chief, noted **06** famous, goggle, marked **07** bulging, eminent, jutting, leading, notable, obvious, popular, salient **08** beetling, foremost, renowned, striking **09** acclaimed, egregious, important, obtrusive, respected, to the fore, well-known **10** celebrated, jutting out, noticeable, pre-eminent, projecting, protrudent, protruding, protrusive **11** conspicuous, eye-catching, high-profile, illustrious, outstanding, protuberant, standing out, sticking out **12** unmistakable **13** distinguished, unmistakeable

promiscuity
06 laxity **09** depravity, looseness **10** debauchery, immorality, profligacy, protervity, wantonness **11** dissipation **13** dissoluteness **14** licentiousness, permissiveness, sleeping around

promiscuous
◊ *anagram indicator*
04 fast **05** loose, mixed, slack **06** casual, random, wanton **07** immoral **08** sluttish, swinging **09** abandoned, debauched, dissolute, haphazard **10** accidental, dissipated, licentious, profligate **12** of easy virtue **14** indiscriminate, sleeping around

promise
03 vow **04** avow, bond, hand, hete, hint, oath, sign, word **05** augur, flair, hecht, hight, swear, vouch **06** assure, behote, commit, denote, engage, hint at, pledge, plight, talent **07** ability, behight, betoken, betroth, compact, presage, signify, suggest, warrant **08** aptitude, contract, covenant, evidence, indicate, look like **09** assurance, be a sign of, committal,

guarantee, potential, undertake
10 capability, commitment,
engagement, indication, suggestion,
take an oath **11** expectation,
undertaking **12** give your word, word
of honour **13** pollicitation **15** give an
assurance
• **promised land**
04 Zion **06** Canaan, heaven, Utopia
07 Elysium **08** El Dorado, paradise
09 Shangri-la **13** Elysian fields
See also **heaven**

promising
04 able, rosy **06** bright, gifted, likely
07 budding, hopeful **08** talented,
towardly **09** favorable **10** auspicious,
favourable, optimistic, propitious
11 encouraging, up-and-coming

promissory note
02 pn **03** IOU

promontory
03 hoe, nab **04** bill, cape, head, mull,
naze, ness, spur **05** bluff, cliff, point,
ridge **08** eminence, foreland, headland
09 peninsula, precipice **10** projection,
prominence

promote
03 aid, ren, rin, run **04** back, help, hype,
make, plug, push, sell, urge **05** boost,
exalt, raise **06** assist, foster, honour,
market, move up, peddle, prefer, puff
up **07** advance, elevate, endorse,
espouse, forward, further, nurture,
sponsor, support, upgrade
08 advocate, champion **09** advertise,
encourage, publicize, recommend,
stimulate **10** aggrandize, popularize
11 merchandize **12** contribute to, kick
upstairs

promoter
07 pleader, speaker, sponsor
08 advocate, champion, exponent,
upholder **09** furtherer, projector,
proponent, spokesman, supporter
10 campaigner, evangelist, vindicator
11 spokeswoman **12** spokesperson

promotion
02 ad **04** hype, puff, rise **05** promo
06 advert, move-up, payola, remove,
urging **07** backing, puffery, pushing,
support, venture **08** advocacy,
boosting, campaign, espousal,
plugging, speeding **09** elevation,
fostering, marketing, prelation,
publicity, upgrading **10** exaltation,
preferment, propaganda
11 advancement, advertising,
development, furtherance
12 contribution **13** advertisement,
encouragement **14** aggrandizement,
recommendation

prompt
02 OP **03** cue **04** help, hint, jolt, lead,
make, move, prod, spur, urge **05** alert,
cause, eager, early, frack, impel, quick,
rapid, ready, sharp, swift **06** bang on,
dead on, direct, elicit, incite, induce, on
time, remind, speedy, spot-on, sudden,
timely **07** exactly, inspire, instant,

premove, produce, provoke, willing
08 expedite, motivate, occasion, on
the dot, promptly, punctual, reminder,
result in, stimulus **09** call forth,
encourage, immediate, instigate,
refresher, stimulate **10** give rise to,
pernicious, punctually, responsive
11 expeditious, to the minute
12 unhesitating **13** encouragement,
instantaneous

prompting
04 hint, urge **06** advice, motion, urging
07 jogging, pushing **08** pressing,
pressure, prodding, reminder
09 influence, reminding
10 admonition, assistance, incitement,
persuasion, protreptic, suggestion
13 encouragement

promptly
03 pdq, tit **04** asap, tite, tyte **05** sharp,
tight **06** bang on, dead on, on time,
pronto, spot-on, titely, yarely
07 exactly, lightly, quickly, smartly,
swiftly **08** chop-chop, directly, on
target, on the dot, speedily
09 forthwith, instantly, like a shot,
posthaste, yesterday **10** punctually
11 immediately, to the minute **12** in
short order **14** unhesitatingly, without
more ado **15** before you know it, pretty
damn quick

promptness
05 haste, speed **08** alacrity, dispatch
09 alertness, briskness, eagerness,
quickness, readiness, swiftness
10 expedition **11** promptitude,
punctuality, willingness

promulgate
05 issue **06** decree, notify, spread
07 declare, promote, publish
08 announce, proclaim **09** advertise,
broadcast, circulate, make known,
publicize **10** make public
11 communicate, disseminate

promulgation
08 issuance **11** declaration,
publication, publicizing
12 announcement, proclamation,
promulgating **13** communication,
dissemination

prone
03 apt **04** bent, flat **05** eager, given,
ready **06** homily, liable, likely
07 subject, tending, willing
08 disposed, face down, inclined,
proclive **09** prostrate, recumbent,
stretched **10** full-length, horizontal,
procumbent, vulnerable
11 predisposed, susceptible

proneness
04 bent, bias **07** aptness, leaning
08 penchant, tendency, weakness
09 liability **10** proclivity, propensity
11 disposition, inclination
14 susceptibility

prong
03 tip **04** fang, fork, spur, tang, tine
05 grain, point, spike, tooth
10 projection

pronounce
◇ *homophone indicator*
03 say **04** give, pass, vote **05** judge,
mouth, sound, speak, utter, voice
06 affirm, assert, decree, stress, tongue
07 bring in, declare, deliver, express
08 announce, proclaim, vocalize
09 enunciate **10** adjudicate, articulate

pronounceable
07 sayable, vocable **09** speakable,
utterable **10** enunciable **11** articulable,
expressible

pronounced
◇ *homophone indicator*
05 broad, clear, thick **06** marked,
strong **07** decided, evident, obvious
08 definite, distinct, positive, striking,
terrible **10** noticeable **11** conspicuous
12 unmistakable **13** unmistakeable

pronouncement
05 edict **06** decree, dictum
09 assertion, ipse dixit, judgement,
manifesto, statement **11** declaration
12 announcement, notification,
proclamation, promulgation
14 pronunciamento

pronunciation
06 accent, saying, speech, stress
07 diction, voicing **08** delivery,
orthoepy, uttering **09** elocution,
phonetics **10** inflection, intonation,
modulation **11** enunciation
12 articulation, vocalization

proof
02 ap **04** pull, slip, test **05** assay, issue,
prief, repro, tight **06** galley, priefe,
strong, upshot **07** outcome, proofed,
testing, treated, warrant, witness
08 argument, evidence
09 bombproof, fireproof, foolproof,
leakproof, probation, rainproof,
repellent, resistant, testimony,
windproof **10** argumentum,
childproof, experience, impervious,
smoking gun, soundproof, validation,
waterproof **11** attestation, bulletproof,
tamperproof **12** confirmation,
impenetrable, invulnerable,
verification, weatherproof
13 certification, corroboration,
demonstration, documentation
14 authentication, substantiation
15 impenetrability, invulnerability
• **adduce as proof**
04 cite

prop
03 leg, set **04** lean, post, rest, stay
05 brace, punch, rance, shaft, shore,
sprag, staff, stand, stick, stilt, stoop,
stoup, strut, stull, truss **06** anchor,
brooch, column, crutch, hold up, pillar,
steady, tiepin, uphold **07** balance,
bolster, bunting, fulcrum, shore up,
studdle, support, sustain, upright
08 buttress, mainstay, maintain,
property, underpin, underset,
upholder **09** bolster up, crippling,
propeller, stanchion, supporter
10 underwrite **11** clothes-pole, point
d'appui, proposition **14** flying buttress

propaganda
4 hype 08 Agitprop, ballyhoo
9 promotion, publicity 11 advertising,
information 12 brainwashing
4 disinformation, indoctrination

propagandist
7 plugger 08 advocate, promoter
9 canvasser, proponent, publicist
10 evangelist 11 pamphleteer 12 hot
gospeller, proselytizer 13 indoctrinator

propagandize
6 preach, uphold 07 promote, win
over 08 advocate, argue for,
champion, persuade, press for, talk into
9 brainwash, re-educate 10 pressurize
11 campaign for 12 indoctrinate

propagate
4 grow, pipe 05 beget, breed, layer,
pawn 06 spread 07 diffuse, produce,
promote, propage, provine, publish,
raduce 08 generate, increase,
multiply, proclaim, seminate, transmit
9 broadcast, circulate, procreate,
publicize, reproduce 10 distribute,
promulgate 11 communicate,
disseminate, proliferate

propagation
6 spread 08 breeding, increase,
pawning 09 diffusion, promotion,
preading 10 generation 11 circulation,
procreation 12 distribution,
promulgation, reproduction,
transmission 13 communication,
dissemination, proliferation
4 multiplication

propel
2 ca' 03 caa', leg, oar, row 04 loft,
move, pole, pump, punt, push, sail,
end, swim, waft 05 drive, force, impel,
power, scull, shoot, shove, wheel
6 launch, paddle, thrust 07 project
9 frogmarch 11 push forward

propeller
3 fan 04 prop, vane 05 helix, rotor,
crew 06 pusher 07 tractor
8 airscrew, thruster 09 tail rotor, tilt-
otor

propensity
4 bent, bias 06 foible 07 aptness,
leaning 08 penchant, tendency,
weakness 09 liability, proneness,
readiness 10 proclivity 11 disposition,
inclination 14 predisposition,
susceptibility

proper
1 U 03 ain, due, own 04 prim, real,
true, very 05 exact, right 06 actual,
comely, decent, dueful, formal, goodly,
kosher, polite, seemly, strict 07 correct,
dewfull, fitting, genteel, genuine,
gradely, precise, prudish, refined
8 accepted, accurate, decorous,
graithly, ladylike, orthodox, peculiar,
singular, suitable, thorough
9 befitting, out-and-out, shipshape
10 acceptable 11 appropriate, comme
l faut, established, exceedingly,
gentlemanly, respectable
12 conventional, well-becoming

properly
04 duly 05 right 07 exactly, gradely,
rightly 08 actually, entirely, graithly,
strictly, suitably 09 correctly,
extremely, fittingly, precisely
10 acceptably, accurately, flawlessly,
unerringly 11 faultlessly, respectably
13 appropriately 14 conventionally
• **properly so called**
04 true

property
03 fee 04 gear, land, mark, prop
05 acres, fonds, goods, house, means,
quirk, trait 06 assets, estate, houses,
living, riches, things, wealth 07 capital,
clobber, effects, feature, fitness,
holding, quality 08 chattels, holdings,
premises 09 affection, attribute,
buildings, ownership, propriety,
resources, substance 10 belongings,
real estate 11 appropriate, peculiarity,
possessions 12 idiosyncrasy
13 individuality, paraphernalia
14 characteristic

prophecy
06 augury 07 message 08 forecast
09 preaching, prognosis 10 divination,
prediction 11 second sight,
soothsaying 12 vaticination
14 fortune-telling 15 prognostication

prophesy
05 augur 06 preach 07 foresee,
predict 08 forecast, foretell, forewarn
10 vaticinate 13 prognosticate

prophet, prophetess
04 seer 05 sibyl 06 oracle 07 tipster,
völuspa 10 forecaster, foreteller,
soothsayer 11 clairvoyant, vaticinator
13 fortune-teller 14 prognosticator

*Prophets and prophetesses
include:*

02 Is
03 Dan, Hag, Hos, Isa, Jer, Jon, Mic,
   Nah, Sam
04 Amos, Ezek, Joel, Obad, Zeph
05 Hosea, Jonah, Micah, Moses,
   Nahum
06 Barton (Elizabeth), Daniel, Elijah,
   Elisha, Haggai, Isaiah, Nathan,
   Samuel, St John
07 Ezekiel, Malachi, Obadiah
08 Jeremiah, Mohammed,
   Muhammad, Nehemiah
09 al-Mokanna, Zephaniah, Zoroaster
11 Zarathustra
12 the Nun of Kent
13 the Maid of Kent
14 John the Baptist

• **prophet of doom**
08 doomster, Jeremiah 09 Cassandra,
doomsayer, pessimist 11 doomwatcher
12 doom merchant

prophetic
03 fey 05 vatic 06 mantic 07 augural,
fateful 08 oracular 09 fatidical,
oraculous, presaging, prescient,
sibylline, vaticidal 10 divinatory,
predictive, prognostic 11 apocalyptic,
forecasting 13 foreshadowing

prophylactic
04 safe 06 condom, rubber, sheath
07 Femidom®, johnnie, scumbag,
treacle 09 deterrent 10 inhibitory,
precaution, pre-emptive, preventive,
protective 11 obstructive
12 anticipatory, female condom,
French letter, immunization,
preservative, preventative
13 contraceptive, counteractive,
precautionary, viper's bugloss

propinquity
03 tie 05 blood 07 kinship 08 affinity,
nearness, relation, vicinity
09 adjacency, closeness, proximity
10 connection, contiguity 11 affiliation,
kindredness, kindredship
12 relationship 13 consanguinity,
neighbourhood

propitiate
06 pacify, soothe 07 appease, mollify,
placate, satisfy 09 reconcile
10 conciliate

propitiation
09 atonement, pacifying, placation
11 appeasement, peacemaking
12 conciliation, pacification
13 mollification 14 reconciliation

propitiatory
08 soothing 09 appeasing, assuaging,
expiatory, pacifying, placative, placatory
10 mollifying 11 peacemaking
12 conciliatory, pacificatory,
propitiative 14 reconciliatory

propitious
04 rosy 05 happy, lucky 06 benign,
bright, kindly, timely 08 friendly,
gracious 09 favorable, fortunate,
opportune, promising, wholesome
10 auspicious, beneficial, benevolent,
favourable, prosperous, reassuring
11 encouraging 12 advantageous, well-
disposed

proponent
06 backer, friend, patron 08 advocate,
champion, defender, exponent,
favourer, partisan, proposer, upholder
09 apologist, proposing, supporter
10 enthusiast, propounder, subscriber,
vindicator

proportion
03 cut 04 bulk, mass, part, size
05 depth, quota, ratio, scale, share,
split, whack, width 06 amount, extent,
height, length, volume 07 analogy,
balance, breadth, measure, portion,
segment 08 capacity, division,
fraction, graduate, quotient, symmetry
09 magnitude 10 dimensions,
percentage 11 temperature
12 distribution, measurements,
relationship 14 correspondence, slice
of the cake

proportional
04 even 08 logistic, relative, relevant
09 analogous, equitable
10 comparable, consistent, equivalent,
logistical 12 commensurate
13 corresponding, proportionate

proportionally
06 evenly **07** pro rata **10** comparably, relatively **14** commensurately **15** correspondingly, proportionately

proposal
03 bid **04** plan **05** offer, terms **06** design, motion, scheme, tender **07** project **08** overture, supposal **09** manifesto, programme **10** resolution, suggestion **11** proposition **12** presentation **14** recommendation

propose
03 aim, bid, pop **04** face, mean, moot, move, name, plan, talk, vote **05** offer, place, put up, slate, table **06** design, intend, motion, submit, tender **07** advance, bethink, bring up, imagine, present, proffer, propone, purpose, suggest, suppose **08** advocate, converse, nominate, propound, put forth **09** discourse, enunciate, introduce, recommend **10** ask to marry, have in mind, put forward **14** pop the question **15** plight your troth

proposition
03 job **04** pass, plan, prop, task **05** offer **06** accost, come-on, motion, scheme, tender, theory **07** advance, premise, project, solicit, theorem, venture **08** activity, approach, disjunct, overture, proposal **09** alternant, manifesto, programme, universal **10** hypothesis, suggestion **11** make a pass at, subcontrary, undertaking **14** recommendation

propound
03 put, set **04** move, pose **06** submit **07** advance, contend, lay down, present, propone, propose, purpose, suggest **08** advocate, set forth **09** postulate **10** put forward

proprietary
03 pty

proprietor, proprietress
04 lord **05** owner **06** patron **07** esquire **08** landlady, landlord, zemindar **09** landowner, possessor, publisher **10** deed holder, freeholder, landholder **11** leaseholder, proprietrix, title-holder **12** entrepreneur
See also **newspaper**

propriety
05 mense **07** aptness, decency, decorum, fitness, manners, modesty, p's and q's, quality **08** breeding, civility, courtesy, delicacy, elegance, elegancy, property, protocol, standard **09** character, etiquette, ownership, punctilio, rectitude, rightness **10** bienséance, convention, politeness, refinement, seemliness **11** correctness, good manners **12** becomingness, ladylikeness, social graces, suitableness, the done thing **14** respectability, social niceties **15** appropriateness, gentlemanliness

propulsion
04 push **05** drive, power **06** thrust

07 impetus, impulse **08** momentum, pressure, traction **09** impulsion **10** propelment **11** motive force **12** driving force

pro rata
06 evenly **10** comparably, relatively **14** commensurately, proportionally **15** correspondingly, proportionately

prosaic
03 dry **04** dull, flat, tame **05** banal, bland, stale, trite, vapid **06** boring **07** humdrum, mundane, routine, vacuous **08** everyday, ordinary, workaday **09** hackneyed **10** monotonous, pedestrian, uninspired, unpoetical **11** commonplace, uninspiring **12** matter-of-fact **13** unimaginative

prosaically
05 dully **07** blandly **09** mundanely **10** ordinarily **12** monotonously **13** uninspiringly **15** unimaginatively

proscribe
03 ban, bar **04** damn, doom **05** black, exile, expel **06** banish, deport, forbid, outlaw, reject **07** boycott, censure, condemn, embargo, exclude **08** denounce, disallow, prohibit **09** blackball, interdict, ostracize **10** expatriate **13** excommunicate

proscription
03 ban, bar **05** exile **07** barring, boycott, censure, damning, embargo **08** ejection, eviction, outlawry **09** exclusion, expulsion, interdict, ostracism, rejection **10** banishment **11** deportation, prohibition **12** condemnation, denunciation, expatriation, proclamation **15** excommunication

prosecute
02 do **03** sue, try **05** chase **06** accuse, charge, indict, pursue, summon **07** arraign, proceed, process **08** litigate **10** put on trial **11** take to court **12** bring charges **13** prefer charges

prosecution
05 trial **08** charging **10** accusation, indictment, litigation **11** impeachment **13** taking to court **15** bringing charges

prosecutor
02 DA, PF **06** fiscal **08** quaestor **10** avvogadore **11** prosecutrix **12** Lord Advocate **13** judge advocate **14** advocate-depute

proselyte
07 convert, recruit **08** neophyte **09** new person **10** catechumen **11** new believer **13** changed person

proselytize
07 convert, win over **08** persuade **10** bring to God, evangelize **12** make converts, propagandize **15** spread the gospel

Proserpina
10 Persephone

prosody
Prosody terms include:

04 foot, iamb
05 canto, envoy, epode, ictus, Ionic, metre, paeon
06 choree, dactyl, dipody, dizain, laisse, miurus, rondel, sonnet
07 ballade, caesura, couplet, distich, elision, pantoum, pyrrhic, rondeau, Sapphic, spondee, strophe, triolet, tripody, triseme, trochee, virelay
08 anapaest, choriamb, cinquain, eye rhyme, Pindaric, quatrain, tribrach, trimeter
09 anacrusis, assonance, catalexis, dispondee, ditrochee, free verse, half-rhyme, hexameter, macaronic, monometer, monorhyme, rime riche, tetrapody
10 amphibrach, amphimacer, blank verse, consonance, enjambment, galliambic, heptameter, pentameter, rhyme royal, tetrameter, villanelle
11 Alcaic verse, alexandrine, broken rhyme, linked verse, long-measure, septenarius
12 alliteration, antibacchius, Leonine rhyme, Pythian verse, sprung rhythm
13 abstract verse, feminine rhyme, heroic couplet, hypermetrical, internal rhyme
14 feminine ending, masculine rhyme, rime suffisante
15 feminine caesura, masculine ending, poulters' measure

prospect
04 face, hope, nose, odds, seek, view **05** quest, scene, sight, vista, visto **06** aspect, chance, future, search, survey **07** chances, examine, explore, fossick, inspect, look for, lookout, opening, outlook, promise **08** belle vue, likeness, panorama **09** landscape, spectacle, viewpoint **10** likelihood **11** expectation, opportunity, perspective, possibility, probability **12** anticipation

prospective
04 -to-be **06** coming, future, likely **07** awaited, would-be **08** aspiring, destined, expected, hoped-for, imminent, intended, possible, probable **09** designate, potential **11** anticipated, approaching, forthcoming

prospectus
04 list, plan **06** scheme **07** leaflet, outline **08** brochure, pamphlet, syllabus, synopsis **09** catalogue, manifesto, programme **10** conspectus, literature **11** description **12** announcement

prosper
04 boom, thee **05** bloom, get on **06** do well, flower, thrive **07** advance, blossom, burgeon, proceed, succeed **08** flourish, get ahead, grow rich, progress **09** get on well **11** turn out well

12 be successful, make progress, make your pile **13** hit the big time, hit the jackpot **14** go up in the world **15** get on in the world

prosperity
04 boom, good **06** clover, luxury, plenty, riches, thrift, wealth **07** fortune, success, welfare **08** sunshine **09** affluence, wellbeing **10** bed of roses, easy street **11** good fortune, lap of luxury, the good life **14** the life of Riley
• **spell of prosperity**
02 up **04** boom

prosperous
04 fair, rich **05** blest, lucky, sleek **06** well in **07** blessed, bonanza, booming, opulent, thrifty, wealthy, well-off **08** affluent, blooming, thriving, well-to-do **09** fortunate **10** burgeoning, felicitous, successful, well-heeled, well-to-live **11** flourishing, rolling in it

prostitute
03 pro, pug, tom **04** bawd, dell, drab, moll, punk, road, stew, tart **05** brass, broad, poule, quail, quiff, stale, tramp, trull, wench, whore **06** betray, bulker, callet, debase, demean, floosy, floozy, geisha, harlot, hooker, misuse, mutton, plover **07** cheapen, cocotte, degrade, devalue, floosie, floozie, hetaera, hetaira, hostess, hustler, lorette, pervert, polecat, profane, rent-boy, trollop, venture **08** bona-roba, call-girl, dolly-mop, magdalen, misapply, strumpet **09** courtesan, courtezan, hackneyed, hierodule, loose fish, mercenary, sacrifice, sex worker **10** cockatrice, convertite, fancy woman, loose woman, rough trade, vizard-mask **11** fallen woman, fille de joie, laced mutton, night-walker, poule de luxe, public woman, working girl **12** fille des rues, scarlet woman, street-walker **13** grande cocotte **14** lady of the night, woman of the town

prostitution
04 vice **07** the game, whoring **08** harlotry, whoredom **10** social evil **13** street-walking

prostrate
03 sap **04** fell, flat, laid, ruin, tire **05** all-in, crush, drain, level, prone **06** bushed, fallen, lay low, pooped **07** crushed, exhaust, fatigue, flatten, laid low, wear out, whacked, worn out **08** dead beat, flatling, flatlong, helpless, overcome, tired out, trailing **09** exhausted, flatlings, knock down, lying down, lying flat, overthrow, overwhelm, paralysed, pooped out, powerless **10** devastated, horizontal, procumbent **11** defenceless, overwhelmed, tuckered out
• **prostrate yourself**
05 kneel **06** cringe, grovel, kowtow, submit **07** bow down **13** abase yourself

prostration
03 bow **05** grief **06** kowtow **07** despair **08** collapse, kneeling, weakness **09** abasement, dejection, obeisance, paralysis, weariness **10** depression, desolation, exhaustion, submission **11** despondency **12** genuflection, helplessness **15** slough of despond

protactinium
02 Pa

protagonist
04 hero, lead **06** banker, leader **07** heroine **08** adherent, advocate, champion, exponent, mainstay **09** principal, proponent, supporter, title role **10** prime mover **12** moving spirit **13** leading figure, leading player, main character **14** chief character, standard-bearer

protean
◊ *anagram indicator*
07 amoebic, mutable **08** variable, volatile **09** many-sided, mercurial, multiform, versatile **10** changeable, inconstant **11** polymorphic **12** ever-changing, polymorphous

protect
◊ *containment indicator*
04 keep, save **05** cover, guard **06** defend, escort, screen, secure, shield **07** buckler, care for, harbour, shelter, support, warrant **08** bestride, conserve, enshield, keep safe, preserve, savegard **09** look after, ring-fence, safeguard, watch over **10** overshadow, strengthen, take care of

protected
06 immune

protection
03 lee **04** care, egis, ward, wing **05** aegis, bield, cover, guard **06** armour, asylum, buffer, charge, refuge, safety, screen, shield **07** barrier, buckler, bulwark, custody, defence, defense, shelter **08** security, umbrella, wardship **09** insurance, patronage, safeguard **11** concubinage, defensive, maintenance, safekeeping **12** conservation, entrenchment, guardianship, intrenchment, preservation
• **in protection from**
04 agin **07** against

protective
04 wary **06** condom **07** careful **08** armoured, covering, fatherly, maternal, motherly, paternal, vigilant, watchful **09** defensive, fireproof, shielding, windproof **10** insulating, possessive, sheltering, waterproof **14** over-protective

protector
03 pad **04** faun **05** guard **06** buffer, father, keeper, minder, patron, regent, screen, shield **07** bolster, buckler, counsel, cushion, gardant **08** advocate, champion, Cromwell,

defender, guardant, guardian, pectoral **09** bodyguard, safeguard **10** benefactor, protectrix **11** patron saint, protectress **12** father-figure

protégé, protégée
04 ward **05** pupil **06** charge **07** student **08** disciple, follower **09** dependant, discovery **11** blue-eyed boy **14** white-headed boy

protein

Proteins include:

03 TSP, TVP
04 zein
05 abrin, actin, opsin, prion, renin
06 avidin, casein, cyclin, enzyme, fibrin, globin, gluten, kinase, lectin, leptin, myosin, papain, pepsin, rennin
07 albumen, albumin, elastin, gliadin, histone, hordein, insulin, plasmin, sericin, trypsin, tubulin
08 aleurone, amandine, collagen, cytokine, ferritin, gliadine, globulin, glutelin, integrin, lysozyme, protease, thrombin
09 apoenzyme, fibrillin, invertase, isomerase, luciferin, myoglobin, phaseolin, prolamine, protamine, sclerotin
10 calmodulin, complement, conchiolin, dystrophin, factor VIII, fibronogen, interferon
11 angiostatin, angiotensin, haemoglobin, interleukin, lipoprotein, plasminogen, transferrin, tropomyosin
12 immunoglobin, neurotrophin, proteoglycan
13 ceruloplasmin, lactoglobulin

protest
03 vow **04** avow, demo, fuss, riot **05** abhor, argue, demur, gripe, hikoi, march, sit in, sit-in **06** affirm, appeal, assert, attest, avowal, insist, object, obtest, oppose, outcry, picket, reject, squawk, strike, whinge, work-in **07** boycott, contend, declare, dissent, profess, reclaim, scruple, testify **08** announce, complain, demurral, disagree, insist on, maintain, proclaim, speak out **09** assertion, complaint, deprecate, down tools, exception, objection, take issue **10** contention, disapprove, go on strike, opposition, work to rule, work-to-rule **11** affirmation, attestation, declaration, demonstrate, disapproval, kick up a fuss, mass meeting, remonstrate **12** announcement, disagreement, hunger strike, proclamation, protestation, remonstrance **13** demonstration, remonstration, take exception
• **expression of protest**
01 O **02** oh **03** say, why **04** come, I say!, what **07** come now **08** come come

protestation
03 vow **04** oath **06** avowal, outcry, pledge **07** dissent, protest

09 assurance, complaint, objection, statement, testimony **10** profession **11** affirmation, declaration **12** asseveration, disagreement, remonstrance **13** expostulation, remonstration

protester
05 rebel **06** picket **07** opposer, striker **08** agitator, mutineer, objector, opponent **09** dissenter, dissident **10** complainer **11** Remonstrant **12** demonstrator

protocol
02 IP **03** FTP, TCP, WAP **04** HTTP, IMAP, kawa, MIDI **05** TCP/IP **06** custom **07** decorum, manners, p's and q's **08** good form **09** etiquette, procedure, propriety **10** civilities, convention **11** formalities **15** code of behaviour

prototype
04 type **05** model **06** mock-up **07** example, pattern **08** exemplar, original, paradigm, standard **09** archetype, precedent

protract
06 extend, linger **07** drag out, draw out, prolong, spin out, sustain **08** continue, lengthen, postpone, protrude **09** keep going **10** make longer, stretch out

protracted
04 long **07** endless, lengthy, spun out **08** drawn-out, extended, livelong, overlong **09** postponed, prolonged **12** interminable, long-drawn-out, stretched out

protrude
03 jut, pop **04** peer, poke, pout **05** bulge, stick, strut **06** beetle, exsert, extend, goggle, jut out, strout **07** extrude, obtrude, poke out, project **08** protract, stand out, stick out **11** come through

protruding
05 goofy, proud **06** astrut **07** jutting **09** exsertive, extrusive, extrusory, obtrusive, prominent, underhung **10** jutting out, protrudent, protrusive **11** protuberant, sticking out

protrusion
03 jag, jut **04** bump, knob, lump **05** bulge **06** hernia **07** pedicle, process **08** shoulder, swelling **09** obtrusion, outgrowth **10** projection, staphyloma **11** cephalocele, eventration, meningocele **12** exophthalmia, exophthalmos, exophthalmus, protuberance **13** encephalocele

protuberance
03 bud, nub **04** ball, boss, bulb, bump, hump, knap, knob, lump, nurl, teat, wame, wart, welt **05** bulge, caput, ergot, gemma, inion, knurl, mount, nodus, tuber, whelk **06** casque, nipple, paunch, pimple, tumour, venter, wallet **07** condyle, crankle, mamelon, mamilla, papilla, process **08** mammilla, pot-belly, swelling,

tubercle **09** apophysis, beer belly, outgrowth **10** bulging-out, projection, prominence, protrusion **11** excrescence

protuberant
04 full **05** proud **06** astrut, rotund **07** bottled, bulbous, bulging, bunched, gibbous, jutting, popping, swollen **08** beetling, swelling **09** exsertive, extrusive, extrusory, prominent **10** protrudent, protruding, protrusive

proud
04 brag, glad, smug, vain **05** cocky, dicty, grand, happy, noble, stout **06** dickty, lordly, snooty, superb, worthy **07** content, haughty, jutting, notable, pleased, pompous, stately, stuck-up, sublime **08** arrogant, boastful, fearless, glorious, honoured, imposing, jumped-up, misproud, pleasing, proudful, puffed up, scornful, snobbish, splendid, swelling, thrilled, top-proud **09** bigheaded, cockhorse, conceited, contented, delighted, dignified, gratified, hubristic, imperious, memorable, prominent, red-letter, satisfied, untamable, wonderful **10** complacent, gratifying, high-handed, honourable, jutting out, marvellous, projecting, satisfying **11** egotistical, magnificent, outstanding, overbearing, overweening, protuberant, sticking out, toffee-nosed, walking tall **12** high-spirited, presumptuous, supercilious **13** high and mighty, self-important, self-satisfied **14** full of yourself, self-respecting

proudly
04 brag **06** smugly, vainly **08** snootily **09** haughtily **10** arrogantly, boastfully **11** bigheadedly, conceitedly, contentedly, delightedly, with delight **14** appreciatively

provable
08 testable **09** evincible **10** attestable, verifiable **11** confirmable **12** corroborable, demonstrable **13** establishable

prove
03 try **04** shew, show, test, trie **05** argue, check **06** attest, pan out, prieve, suffer, try out, verify **07** analyse, bear out, certify, confirm, darrain, darrayn, deraign, examine, justify, make out, qualify, stand up, turn out **08** darraign, darraine, document, evidence, validate **09** ascertain, be the case, bring home, come about, darraigne, determine, establish, eventuate, transpire **10** experience **11** corroborate, demonstrate **12** authenticate, substantiate **13** bear witness to

proven
05 tried, valid **06** proved, tested **07** checked **08** accepted, attested, definite, reliable, verified **09** authentic, certified, confirmed, undoubted

10 dependable **11** established, trustworthy **12** corroborated

provenance
06 origin, source, spring **10** birthplace, derivation **11** provenience

provender
03 kai **04** chow, eats, fare, feed, food, grub, nosh, tuck **05** scoff **06** fodder, forage, stores, tucker, viands **07** aliment, edibles, pabulum, pasture, provand, provend, rations **08** eatables, proviant, supplies, victuals **09** groceries, repasture **10** foodstuffs, provisions, sustenance **11** comestibles

proverb
03 saw **05** adage, axiom, gnome, maxim, motto **06** byword, dictum, saying **07** parable, precept **08** aphorism, paroemia **10** apophthegm, whakatauki

proverbial
05 famed **06** famous **07** typical **08** accepted, infamous, renowned **09** axiomatic, customary, legendary, notorious, well-known **10** archetypal **11** traditional **12** acknowledged, conventional, time-honoured

provide
◇ *anagram indicator*
02 do **03** add **04** give, lend, suit **05** allow, besee, bring, cater, equip, lay on, offer, put on, serve, state, stock, yield **06** afford, fit out, impart, kit out, outfit, purvey, supply **07** compare, furnish, lay down, plan for, prepare, present, require, specify **09** stipulate, take steps **10** anticipate, arrange for, contribute, prepare for **11** accommodate **12** make plans for, take measures **13** make provision **15** take precautions
● **provide for**
04 fend, keep **05** besee, cover, do for, endow **07** support, sustain **08** maintain **09** look after **10** take care of

provided
02 so **05** given **06** sobeit **08** as long as, assuming, so long as **09** presuming **10** in the event **11** on condition **14** with the proviso

providence
04 care, fate, luck **06** thrift, wisdom **07** caution, destiny, economy, fortune **08** disaster, God's will, prudence, sagacity **09** foresight, judgement **11** forethought **13** judiciousness **14** circumspection, far-sightedness

provident
06 frugal **07** careful, prudent, thrifty **08** cautious **09** judicious, sagacious **10** economical, far-sighted **11** circumspect

providential
05 happy, lucky **06** timely **07** welcome **09** fortunate, opportune **10** convenient, fortuitous, heaven-sent

providentially
07 happily, luckily **11** coveniently, fortunately, opportunely
12 fortuitously

provider
05 angel, donor, giver **06** earner, funder, patron, source **07** sponsor
08 mainstay, supplier **09** supporter
10 benefactor, wage-earner
11 breadwinner

providing
02 if **05** given **08** as long as, assuming, provided **09** presuming **10** in the event
11 on condition **14** with the proviso

province
04 area, dorp, duty, line, nome, role, zone **05** field, realm, reame, shire, state
06 charge, circar, colony, county, domain, office, pigeon, region, sircar, sirkar, sphere **07** concern, eparchy, nudiria, rectory, satrapy, vilayet
08 business, district, function, nudirieh **09** backwater, backwoods, eparchate, territory, the sticks
10 department, dependency, the boonies **12** patriarchate, the boondocks **14** responsibility
15 middle of nowhere

Canadian provinces and territories:
05 Yukon
06 Quebec
07 Alberta, Nunavut, Ontario
08 Labrador, Manitoba
10 Nova Scotia
12 New Brunswick, Newfoundland, Saskatchewan
14 Yukon Territory
15 British Columbia
18 Prince Edward Island
20 Northwest Territories
23 Newfoundland and Labrador

Ireland's ancient provinces:
06 Ulster
07 Munster
08 Connacht, Leinster

New Zealand provinces:
05 Otago
06 Nelson
08 Auckland, Taranaki, Westland
09 Fiordland, Hawke's Bay, Northland, Southland
10 Canterbury, Wellington
11 Marlborough

South African provinces:
07 Gauteng, Limpopo
09 Free State, North West
10 Mpumalanga
11 Eastern Cape, Western Cape
12 KwaZulu-Natal, Northern Cape

provincial
04 hick **05** local, naive, rural, yokel
06 narrow, rustic **07** country, hayseed, insular, limited, peasant **08** mofussil, outlying, regional, suburban
09 hillbilly, home-grown, parochial, presidial, small-town **10** intolerant,

parish-pump, unpolished **11** small-minded **12** narrow-minded **13** inward-looking **14** country bumpkin
15 unsophisticated

provincialism
08 localism **10** insularity, Patavinity
11 regionalism **12** parochialism, sectionalism **13** provinciality

provision
04 food, plan, step, term **05** rider, stock, store, stuff **06** clause, giving, stocks, stores, supply, viands
07 measure, proviso, rations, service
08 eatables, services, supplies, victuals
09 allowance, amenities, condition, equipping, foodstuff, groceries, resources, stouthrie **10** concession, facilities, furnishing, outfitting, precaution, stoutherie, sustenance
11 arrangement, contingency, preparation, requirement, stipulation
12 contribution **13** qualification, specification

provisional
05 Provo **06** pro tem **07** interim, stopgap **09** makeshift, temporary, tentative **11** conditional, pencilled in
12 transitional

provisionally
06 pro tem **07** interim **09** meanwhile
11 temporarily, tentatively **15** for the time being

proviso
04 term **05** rider **06** clause **07** strings
09 condition, provision **10** limitation
11 requirement, reservation, restriction, stipulation **13** qualification

provocation
04 dare **05** cause, taunt **06** injury, insult, motive, reason **07** affront, grounds, offence **08** angering, enraging, stimulus, vexation
09 annoyance, challenge, eliciting, grievance **10** generation, incitement, inducement, irritation, motivation, production **11** aggravation, inspiration, instigation, stimulation
12 exasperation **13** justification

provocative
04 sexy **05** tarty **06** erotic **07** abusive, galling, piquant, teasing **08** alluring, annoying, arousing, exciting, inviting, tempting **09** insulting, in-yer-face, offensive, seductive **10** in-your-face, irritating, outrageous, suggestive
11 aggravating, challenging, infuriating, stimulating, tantalizing, titillating
12 exasperating

provocatively
06 sexily **08** sexually **10** alluringly, annoyingly, erotically, invitingly, temptingly **11** offensively, seductively
12 outrageously, suggestively
13 infuriatingly **14** exasperatingly

provoke
03 bug, vex **04** goad, miff, move, nark, prod, rile, spur, stir **05** anger, annoy, cause, egg on, evoke, get at, pique,

rouse, sound, taunt, tease **06** appeal, elicit, enrage, entice, excite, harass, hassle, incite, induce, insult, kindle, madden, needle, nettle, offend, prompt, summon, wind up **07** incense, inflame, inspire, produce, promote
08 drive mad, engender, generate, irritate, motivate, occasion
09 aggravate, call forth, challenge, infuriate, instigate, stimulate, tantalize
10 drive crazy, exacerbate, exasperate, give rise to **12** drive bananas **13** make sparks fly **14** drive up the wall

provoking
06 irking, vexing **07** agaçant, galling, irksome **08** agaçante, annoying, tiresome **09** maddening, offensive, vexatious **10** irritating **11** aggravating, infuriating, obstructive, stimulating
12 exasperating

prow
03 bow **04** bows, fore, head, nose, ship, stem **05** front, prore **07** valiant
08 cut-water, forepart

prowess
04 grit, guts **05** nerve, pluck, skill, spunk **06** bottle, daring, genius, talent, valour **07** ability, bravery, command, courage, heroism, mastery
08 aptitude, audacity, facility
09 adeptness, dexterity, expertise, gallantry, vassalage **10** adroitness, attainment, capability **11** intrepidity, proficiency, skilfulness **12** fearlessness
13 dauntlessness **14** accomplishment

prowl
04 hunt, lurk, nose, roam, rove
05 creep, lurch, mouse, prole, proll, proul, range, ratch, skulk, slink, sneak, snoke, snook, snoop, snowk, stalk, steal **06** cruise, patrol, search
08 scavenge **14** move stealthily

prowler
06 patrol, proler, roamer **07** proller, prouler, stalker **08** tenebrio
09 nighthawk, scavenger

proximity
08 nearness, vicinity **09** adjacency, closeness **10** contiguity **11** propinquity
13 juxtaposition, neighbourhood

proxy
05 agent **06** deputy, factor **07** stand-in
08 attorney, delegate **09** surrogate
10 substitute **14** representative
• **by proxy**
02 pp

prude
04 prig **07** old maid, puritan **09** Mrs Grundy **10** goody-goody, schoolmarm

prudence
04 care **05** Metis **06** policy, saving, thrift, wisdom **07** caution, economy
08 planning, sagacity, wariness
09 canniness, foresight, frugality, good sense, husbandry, judgement, vigilance **10** discretion, precaution, providence **11** advisedness, common sense, forethought, happy medium,

heedfulness, penny-wisdom
12 cautiousness, preparedness
13 judiciousness **14** circumspection,
far-sightedness **15** circumspectness

prudent
04 ware, wary, wise **06** frugal, shrewd
07 careful, politic, thrifty **08** cautious,
discreet, sensible, vigilant **09** judicious,
provident, sagacious **10** discerning,
economical, far-sighted
11 circumspect, ware and wise, well-
advised, wise-hearted
13 considerative

prudently
06 warily, wisely **08** sensibly, shrewdly
09 advisedly, carefully **10** discreetly,
vigilantly **11** providently
12 economically, far-sightedly

prudery
08 primness **09** Grundyism
10 prissiness, puritanism, strictness,
stuffiness **11** overmodesty, starchiness
12 priggishness **13** squeamishness
14 old-maidishness

prudish
04 prim **05** mimsy **06** demure,
mimsey, prissy, proper, stuffy **07** po-
faced, starchy **08** overnice, priggish,
pudibund **09** squeamish, Victorian
10 goody-goody, old-maidish
overmodest **11** puritanical, strait-laced
12 narrow-minded **13** schoolmarmish,
ultra-virtuous

prune
03 cut, lop **04** clip, dock, pare, plum,
sned, snip, spur, trim **05** preen, proin,
proyn, shape, shred **06** cut off, dehorn,
prewyn, proign, proine, proyne, pruine,
reduce, reform, switch **07** cut back,
shorten **08** prunello **10** French plum

prurient
04 blue, lewd **05** dirty **06** erotic,
smutty **07** itching, lustful, obscene
08 desirous, indecent **09** lecherous,
salacious **10** cupidinous, lascivious,
libidinous **11** voyeuristic
12 concupiscent, pornographic

pry
03 dig **04** nose, peep, peer, poke, toot
05 delve, prise, snoop **06** ferret,
meddle **07** gumshoe, intrude
08 prodnose **09** interfere
10 stickybeak **12** put your oar in
14 poke your nose in **15** stick your nose
in

prying
04 nosy **05** nosey, peery **06** snoopy,
spying **07** curious, peering
08 meddling, snooping **09** intrusive
10 meddlesome **11** inquisitive,
interfering

psalm
02 Ps **03** Psa **04** hymn, poem, song
05 chant, paean, tract **06** choral,
prayer, proper, venite **07** cantate,
chorale, introit, tractus **08** canticle,
Jubilate, Miserere **09** neckverse
10 paraphrase

psalm tune
04 tone

pseud
04 sham **05** false, fraud, poser
06 humbug, phoney, poseur, trendy
11 pretentious

pseudo
04 fake, mock, sham **05** bogus, false,
pseud, quasi- **06** ersatz, phoney
08 spurious **09** imitation, pretended,
ungenuine **10** artificial **11** counterfeit,
pretentious

pseudonym
05 alias **06** anonym **07** allonym, pen-
name **09** false name, incognito, stage
name **10** nom de plume **11** assumed
name, nom de guerre

> Pseudonyms include:

03 Day (Doris), Pop (Iggy), Tey
(Josephine)
04 Alda (Alan), Bell (Acton), Bell
(Currer), Bell (Ellis), Cage (Nicolas),
Dors (Diana), Ford (Ford Madox),
Gish (Lillian Diana), Hite (Shere),
Holm (Sir Ian), John (Sir Elton), Lulu,
Lynn (Dame Vera), Piaf (Edith),
Reed (Lou), Rhys (Jean), Ross
(Diana), Saki, Sand (George), West
(Dame Rebecca), West
(Nathanael), Wood (Natalie), York
(Susannah)
05 Allen (Woody), Bizet (Georges),
Black (Cilla), Bowie (David), Caine
(Sir Michael), Clark (Petula), Cline
(Patsy), Dylan (Bob), Eliot (George),
Flynn (Errol), Garbo (Greta), Gorky
(Maxim), Grant (Cary), Grant
(Richard E), Hardy (Oliver), Henry
(O), Holly (Buddy), Jason (David),
Keith (Penelope), Lanza (Mario),
Leigh (Vivien), Loren (Sophia),
Moore (Demi), Moore (Julianne),
Niven (David), Queen (Ellery),
Ryder (Winona), Scott (Ronnie),
Seuss (Dr), Smith (Stevie), Solti (Sir
Georg), Stern (Daniel), Sting, Twain
(Mark), Wayne (John), Welch
(Raquel)
06 Bacall (Lauren), Bardot (Brigitte),
Berlin (Irving), Brooks (Mel),
Burton (Richard), Conrad (Joseph),
Crosby (Bing), Curtis (Tony), Fields
(Dame Gracie), Foster (Jodie),
France (Anatole), Gibbon (Lewis
Grassic), Harlow (Jean), Heston
(Charlton), Irving (Sir Henry),
Jolson (Al), Keaton (Diane), Laurel
(Stan), London (Jack), Lugosi (Bela),
McBain (Ed), Mirren (Helen),
Monroe (Marilyn), Morton (Jelly
Roll), Neeson (Liam), Orwell
(George), Peters (Ellis), Rogers
(Ginger), Salten (Felix), Sapper,
Scales (Prunella), Simone (Nina),
Spacey (Kevin), Steele (Tommy),
Turner (Lana), Turner (Tina), Waters
(Muddy), Weldon (Fay), Wesley
(Mary), Wonder (Stevie)
07 Andrews (Dame Julie), Bachman
(Richard), Bennett (Tony), Bogarde

(Sir Dirk), Bronson (Charles), Carroll
(Lewis), Deneuve (Catherine),
Dinesen (Isak), Douglas (Kirk),
Gardner (Ava), Garland (Judy),
Hepburn (Audrey), Higgins (Jack),
Holiday (Billie), Jacques (Hattie),
Karloff (Boris), Kincaid (Jamaica),
Le Carré (John), Lindsay (Robert),
Lombard (Carole), Matthau
(Walter), Mercury (Freddie),
Michael (George), Miranda
(Carmen), Molière, Montand
(Yves), Novello (Ivor), Richard (Sir
Cliff), Robbins (Harold), Russell
(Lillian), Shepard (Sam), Swanson
(Gloria), Wyndham (John), Wynette
(Tammy)
08 Bancroft (Anne), Coltrane
(Robbie), Coolidge (Susan),
Costello (Elvis), Crawford (Joan),
Dietrich (Marlene), Gershwin
(George), Gershwin (Ira), Goldberg
(Whoopi), Hayworth (Rita),
Kingsley (Ben), MacLaine (Shirley),
Ma Rainey, Pickford (Mary),
Robinson (Edward G), Sly Stone,
Stanwyck (Barbara), Stoppard
(Tom), Voltaire, Williams
(Tennessee)
09 Bernhardt (Sarah), Bo Diddley,
Charteris (Leslie), Fairbanks
(Douglas), Lancaster (Burt),
Leadbelly, Offenbach (Jacques),
Streisand (Barbra), Valentino
(Rudolph)
10 Howlin' Wolf, Washington (Dinah),
Westmacott (Mary)
11 Springfield (Dusty)

pshaw
03 och

psych
● **psych out**
03 cow **05** alarm, appal, bully, daunt,
get to, scare, throw, upset **06** coerce,
compel, dismay, lean on, menace, rattle
07 overawe, terrify, warn off
08 browbeat, bulldoze, domineer,
frighten, pressure, unsettle
09 terrorize, tyrannize **10** intimidate,
pressurize **13** put off balance, turn the
heat on **14** put the screws on
● **psych yourself up**
13 brace yourself, nerve yourself, steel
yourself **14** gear yourself up, pluck up
courage, work yourself up

psyche
04 mind, self, soul **05** anima
06 pneuma, spirit **09** awareness, inner
self, intellect **10** inmost self
11 personality **12** intelligence,
subconscious **13** consciousness, heart
of hearts, individuality, innermost self,
understanding **15** deepest feelings

psychiatrist
06 shrink **07** analyst **08** alienist
09 therapist **10** head doctor, psychiater
12 headshrinker, psychologist, trick
cyclist **13** psychoanalyst
14 psychoanalyser **15** man in a white
coat, psychotherapist

psychic
04 seer **05** augur **06** medium, mental, mystic, occult, oracle **07** diviner, prophet **08** mystical, telepath **09** cognitive, emotional, spiritual, visionary **10** mind-reader, prophetess, soothsayer, telepathic **11** clairvoyant, telekinetic **12** extrasensory, intellectual, supernatural **13** fortune-teller, psychological **14** spiritualistic

psychoanalyst *see* **psychiatrist**

psychological
06 mental, unreal **08** cerebral **09** cognitive, emotional, imaginary **10** conceptual, irrational, subjective **11** theoretical, unconscious **12** all in the mind, intellectual, subconscious **13** psychosomatic

psychologically
08 mentally **11** cognitively, emotionally **12** conceptually, subjectively **13** theoretically, unconsciously **14** intellectually

psychology
04 mind **06** habits, make-up **07** mindset, motives **08** conation, hedonics, psychics **09** attitudes **10** child-study, gestaltism **12** pneumatology **14** metapsychology, study of the mind **15** mental chemistry

psychopath
06 madman, maniac, psycho **07** lunatic **08** madwoman **09** mad person, psychotic, sociopath

psychopathic
03 mad **06** insane, psycho **07** lunatic **08** demented, deranged, maniacal **09** psychotic **10** unbalanced

psychosomatic
06 unreal **09** imaginary **10** irrational, subjective **12** all in the mind **13** psychological

psychotic
03 fey **04** bats, gyte, loco, nuts, wild **05** barmy, batty, buggy, crazy, daffy, dippy, dotty, flaky, gonzo, loony, loopy, manic, nutty, potty, queer, wacko, wacky, wiggy **06** crazed, cuckoo, fruity, insane, maniac, mental, raving, red-mad, screwy **07** bananas, barking, berserk, bonkers, cracked, frantic, lunatic, meshuga **08** crackers, demented, deranged, dingbats, doolally, frenetic, frenzied, maniacal, unhinged, unstable **09** disturbed, lymphatic, up the wall **10** bestraught, distracted, distraught, frantic-mad, off the wall, off your nut, out to lunch, stone-crazy, unbalanced **11** not all there, off the rails, off your head **12** mad as a hatter, off your chump, round the bend **13** off your rocker, of unsound mind, out of your head, out of your mind, out of your tree, round the twist **14** off your trolley, wrong in the head **15** non compos mentis, out of your senses

ptarmigan
04 rype

pub *see* **public house**

puberty
05 teens, youth **08** maturity **09** growing up **10** pubescence **11** adolescence **12** teenage years **14** young adulthood

public
03 out **04** fans, open **05** civic, civil, crowd, known, overt, plain, state **06** buyers, common, famous, masses, nation, people, social, tavern, voters **07** country, eminent, exposed, federal, general, obvious, patrons, popular, society **08** audience, citizens, communal, everyone, national, official, populace **09** available, clientèle, community, consumers, customers, followers, important, multitude, prominent, published, respected, universal, well-known **10** accessible, celebrated, collective, electorate, government, population, recognized, spectators, supporters, widespread **11** illustrious, influential, unconcealed **12** acknowledged, nationalized, unrestricted **13** international
• **in public**
06 openly **08** publicly **09** in the open **10** in full view **11** for all to see

public house
02 PH **03** bar, inn, pub **04** houf, howf **05** grill, hotel, houff, house, howff, local, table **06** boozer, lounge, saloon, shanty, tavern **07** brewpub, canteen, counter, potshop, shebeen, taproom, wine bar **08** ale house, bona fide, groggery, hostelry **09** brasserie, free house, gin palace, jerry-shop, lounge bar, lush-house **12** watering-hole

06 Anchor, Castle, George, New Inn, Plough
07 Railway, Red Lion
08 Green Man, Nags Head, Royal Oak, Victoria
09 Black Bull, Cross Keys, King's Arms, King's Head, White Hart, White Lion, White Swan
10 Black Horse, Golden Lion, Queen's Head, Wheatsheaf, White Horse
12 Fox and Hounds, Rose and Crown
13 Hare and Hounds, Prince of Wales
14 Coach and Horses
15 George and Dragon

publican
04 host **06** barman **07** barmaid, tapster **08** hotelier, landlady, landlord, mine host, taverner **09** barperson, bartender, innkeeper, tax farmer **11** hotel-keeper **12** saloon-keeper, tax collector

publication
04 book, buik, buke **05** daily, forum, issue, title **06** serial, volume, weekly **07** booklet, fanzine, journal, leaflet, monthly, release **08** brochure, handbill, hardback, magazine, pamphlet, printing **09** newspaper, paperback, quarterly, reporting **10** disclosure, half-yearly, newsletter, periodical, production, publishing **11** circulation, declaration, festschrift **12** announcement, broadcasting, distribution, notification, proclamation
• **prepare for publication**
04 edit

publicity
03 air **04** hype, plug, puff **05** boost **06** splash **07** acclaim, build-up, réclame **08** ballyhoo **09** attention, limelight, marketing, notoriety, promotion **10** propaganda **11** advertising
• **publicity agent**
02 PA

publicize
04 hype, plug, push **05** blaze **06** market **07** promote **08** announce, headline **09** advertise, broadcast, make known, spotlight **10** make public, promulgate **11** disseminate

public-spirited
08 generous **09** unselfish **10** altruistic, charitable **12** humanitarian **13** conscientious, philanthropic **15** community-minded

public transport *see* **transport**

publish
03 run **04** vent **05** carry, issue, print, sound **06** delate, import, notice, notify, pirate, poster, put out, report, reveal, spread **07** declare, diffuse, divulge, gazette, placard, produce, release **08** announce, bring out, disclose, evulgate, proclaim, put about, put forth, set forth **09** advertise, broadcast, celebrate, circulate, divulgate, fulminate, give forth, make known, paperback, paragraph,

publicize, serialize, syndicate **10** distribute, make public, promulgate **11** communicate, disseminate
See also **printing**

02 DK
03 CUP, OUP, Pan
04 Reed
05 Corgi, Letts, Orion
06 Europa, Puffin, Viking, Virago
07 A&C Black, Berlitz, Cassell, Collins, Longman, Merriam, Methuen, Pearson, Picador, Pimlico, Usborne
08 BBC Books, Chambers, Everyman, Flamingo, Gollancz, Ladybird, Larousse, Michelin, Palgrave
09 Allen Lane, Black Swan, Blackwell, Doubleday, Harlequin, Heinemann, Macmillan, Routledge
10 Allen & Unwin, Bloomsbury, Bodley Head, Faber & Faber, Hutchinson, McGraw-Hill, Paul Hamlyn, Scholastic, Times Books, Transworld
11 Bantam Press, Bertelsmann, Fodor Guides, Rand McNally, Random House, Rough Guides
12 André Deutsch, Butterworths, Chatto & Windus, Edward Arnold, Fourth Estate, Jonathan Cape, Lonely Planet, Mills and Boon, Penguin Books, Reed Elsevier, Sweet & Maxwell, Thames & Hudson
13 AOL/Time Warner, Atlantic Books, Hachette Livre, HarperCollins, Reader's Digest, Little, Brown & Co, Secker & Warburg, Simon & Schuster
14 Canongate Books, Chambers Harrap, Chrysalis Books, Hodder Headline, Springer-Verlag
15 Houghton Mifflin, Mitchell Beazley

pucker
04 fold, ruck, shir **05** pleat, purse, shirr **06** cockle, crease, furrow, gather, ruckle, ruffle **07** crinkle, crumple, screw up, shrivel, wrinkle **08** compress, contract **09** agitation, confusion **11** corrugation

puckered
05 pursy **06** plissé, rucked **07** bullate, creased, ruckled **08** gathered, wrinkled

puckering
04 shir **05** shirr

puckish
03 sly **06** impish **07** naughty, playful, roguish, teasing, waggish **08** sportive **09** whimsical **10** frolicsome **11** mischievous

pudding
03 pie, pud **04** tart **05** sweet **06** afters, pastry **07** dessert
See also **cake**; **dessert**

puddle
03 dub, sop **04** pant, pool, slop, soss, sump **05** flush, plash, plesh **06** muddle **07** muddler, plashet

puddock
04 frog, toad

puerile
05 inane, silly **07** babyish, foolish, trivial **08** childish, immature, juvenile, trifling **09** infantile **10** adolescent **13** irresponsible

Puerto Rico
03 PRI

puff
02 ad **04** blow, drag, draw, fuff, gasp, gulp, gust, huff, pant, plug, pull, push, suck, toke, waff, waft, waif **05** blast, extol, flaff, pluff, skiff, smoke, swell, whiff, whift **06** breath, expand, flatus, flurry, market, praise, wheeze **07** breathe, commend, draught, inflate, promote **09** advertise, marketing, promotion, publicity, publicize **10** homosexual **11** ostentation **12** commendation **13** advertisement
• **puff out**
03 bag, sag **04** bulb, hump **05** belly, bloat, bulge, heave, swell **06** bepuff, billow, blouse, dilate, expand **07** balloon, distend, enlarge, project **08** protrude

puffed
06 done in, winded **07** gasping, panting **08** inflated **09** distended, exhausted **10** breathless **11** out of breath
• **puffed up**
05 bloat, elate, proud **06** pluffy **07** swollen, ventose **08** arrogant, prideful **09** bigheaded **13** high and mighty, self-important, swollen-headed **14** full of yourself

puffin
08 rock-bird, Tom-noddy **09** sea parrot **10** Fratercula **11** Tammie Norie

puffy
05 pursy **07** bloated, dilated, swollen **08** engorged, enlarged, inflated, puffed up **09** bombastic, distended **10** oedematous

pugilism
04 ring **06** boxing **07** the ring **08** fighting, fistiana, the fancy **11** the noble art **12** the prize-ring **13** prize-fighting **15** the noble science

pugilist
03 ham, pug **05** boxer **07** bruiser, fighter **12** prize-fighter

pugnacious
07 hostile **09** bellicose, combative **10** aggressive **11** bad-tempered, belligerent, contentious, hot-tempered, quarrelsome **12** antagonistic, disputatious **13** argumentative

puke
03 cat **04** barf, boke, honk, sick, spew **05** heave, retch, vomit **06** emesis, emetic, sick up **07** bring up, chuck up, chunder, fetch up, throw up, upchuck **08** disgorge, parbreak, retching **10** egurgitate **11** regurgitate

pull
3 lug, rip, row, tow, tug **04** drag, draw, ire, haul, jerk, lure, raid, sole, sowl, suck, sway, tear, turn, yank **05** charm, clout, heave, pluck, power, proof, poole, sowle, steal, tempt, trail, tweak **6** allure, arrest, damage, entice, muscle, pull in, pull up, remove, snatch, sprain, strain, twitch, uproot, weight, wrench **07** attract, bring in, draught, draw out, extract, pull out, root out, stretch, take out **08** exertion, withdraw **9** advantage, dislocate, influence, magnetism, magnetize **10** allurement, attraction, resistance **12** drawing power, forcefulness

• pull apart
3 pan **04** part, pick, slam **05** slate **6** attack **07** run down **08** demolish, distrain, separate **09** criticize, dismantle, dismember, take apart, tear apart **11** pick holes in **12** pick to pieces, pull to pieces, take to pieces, tear to shreds **15** do a hatchet job on

• pull back
4 draw **06** retire **07** back out, retreat **8** draw back, fall back, withdraw **9** disengage

• pull down
7 destroy, unbuild **08** bulldoze, demolish, take down **09** dismantle, knock down **10** dilapidate **15** raze to the ground

• pull in
3 nab **04** book, bust, draw, earn, halt, lure, make, nick, park, stop **05** clear, run in, seize **06** allure, arrest, arrive, be paid, collar, detain, draw in, entice, pull up, rake in **07** attract, bring in, capture, collect, receive **08** take home **09** apprehend **15** take into custody

• pull off
05 pluck **06** detach, fulfil, manage, remove, rip off **07** achieve, succeed, take off, tear off **08** bring off, carry off, carry out, separate **10** accomplish

• pull out
04 quit **05** leave **06** depart, desert **07** abandon, back out, draw out, move out, pluck up, retreat **08** evacuate, withdraw

• pull through
05 rally **07** improve, recover, survive, weather **09** get better **10** recuperate **11** come through **12** get well again

• pull together
04 draw **05** rally **06** team up **09** co-operate **11** collaborate **12** work together

• pull up
04 balk, halt, park, stop **05** baulk, blame, brake, chide, scold **06** arrest, berate, carpet, draw up, pull in, rebuke, uproot, uptear **07** censure, lecture, reprove, tell off, tick off **08** admonish, draw rein, pull over **09** castigate, criticize, eradicate, reprimand **10** take to task **11** come to a halt **14** read the riot act

• pull yourself together
11 snap out of it **15** buck up your ideas, control yourself

pulled up
02 pu

pulley
04 swig

pullover
03 top **06** jersey, jumper, woolly **07** sweater, tank top **10** sweatshirt **11** windcheater

pulp
03 pap **04** beat, gush, mash, mush, must, pith **05** chyme, cream, crush, flesh, gloop, paste, pound, purée, shred, slush **06** bathos, marrow, pomace, squash **07** furnish **08** nonsense, schmaltz **09** corniness, liquidize, nostalgia, pulverize, triturate **10** sloppiness, tenderness **11** mawkishness, romanticism **12** chemical wood, emotionalism **14** sentimentalism, sentimentality

pulpit
03 tub **04** ambo, dais, desk, tent, wood **05** stand **06** mimbar, minbar, podium **07** lectern, rostrum, soapbox **08** platform **11** three-decker

pulpy
04 soft **05** mushy, pappy **06** fleshy, sloppy **07** baccate, crushed, squashy **09** succulent

pulsate
04 beat, drum, thud **05** pound, pulse, throb, thump **06** hammer, quiver **07** vibrate **09** oscillate, palpitate

pulsating
07 pulsing **09** pulsatile, pulsative, pulsatory, vibratile, vibrating, vibrative **11** oscillating, palpitating

pulsation
04 beat **05** ictus, throb **07** beating **09** heartbeat, throbbing, vibration **11** oscillation, palpitation **12** vibratiuncle

pulse
03 dal, pea **04** bean, beat, daal, dahl, dhal, drum, gram, thud, tick **05** pound, throb, thump **06** legume, rhythm, stroke, thrill **07** beating, flutter, pulsate, vibrate **08** drumming, pounding, sphygmus, thudding, thumping **09** calavance, caravance, pulsation, throbbing, vibration **11** oscillation
See also **bean**

pulverize
◊ *anagram indicator*
04 mill, pulp **05** crush, grind, pound, smash **06** bruise, defeat, hammer, powder, squash, thrash **07** crumble, destroy **08** demolish, vanquish **09** comminute, triturate **10** annihilate **12** contriturate

puma
05 tiger **06** cougar **07** couguar, panther **09** catamount **12** mountain lion

pummel
◊ *anagram indicator*
03 fib, hit **04** bang, beat, soak **05** knock, pound, punch, thump **06** batter, hammer, pommel, strike

pump
03 jet **04** draw, gush, push, quiz, send **05** drain, drive, force, grill, spout, spurt, surge **06** bowser, inject, siphon **08** inflater, inflator **09** grease gun, hydropult **11** interrogate **12** cross-examine **13** cross-question **14** put the screws on
See also **footwear**

• pump out
05 drain, empty **06** siphon **07** bail out, draw off **08** force out

• pump up
04 fill **06** blow up, puff up **07** inflate **08** increase

pumpkin
06 cashaw, cushaw **07** pompion, pumpion **12** Jack-o'-lantern **14** Queensland blue **15** vegetable marrow

pun
03 ram **04** quip **05** pound **06** clinch **07** quibble **08** equivoke **09** calembour, equivoque, jeu de mots, witticism **10** pundigrion **11** paronomasia, play on words **13** double meaning, play upon words **14** double entendre

punch
03 bop, box, cut, die, fib, hit, jab, job, mat, zap **04** bash, biff, bite, blow, boff, bore, bust, clip, cuff, dong, hole, kick, plug, poke, prod, slug, sock, wind **05** black, check, clout, drill, drive, force, knock, power, prick, rumbo, stamp, thump, verve **06** energy, impact, pierce, pounce, pummel, stingo, strike, thwack, vigour, wallop, whammy **07** king hit, panache, pizzazz **08** keypunch, puncture, strength **09** bolo punch, perforate **10** roundhouse **11** coup de poing, make a hole in, sucker-punch **12** bunch of fives, counter-punch, forcefulness, fourpenny one **13** effectiveness **15** knuckle sandwich

punch-drunk
05 dazed, dizzy, woozy **06** groggy **07** reeling **08** confused, unsteady **09** befuddled, slap-happy, stupefied **10** staggering

punch-up
03 row **05** brawl, fight, scrap, set-to **06** dust-up, fracas, ruckus, shindy **07** scuffle **08** argument, ding-dong **10** free-for-all **12** stand-up fight

punchy
05 dazed, zappy **06** lively, strong **07** dynamic **08** forceful, incisive, powerful, spirited, vigorous **09** effective **10** aggressive

punctilio
05 pique, punto **06** detail, nicety, puncto **08** ceremony, delicacy **09** exactness, fine point, formality, precision **10** convention, exactitude,

punctilious

particular, refinement, strictness
11 distinction, finickiness, preciseness
13 particularity **14** meticulousness, scrupulousness **15** punctiliousness

punctilious
04 prim **05** exact, fussy, picky
06 choosy, formal, picked, proper,
strict **07** careful, finicky, precise
08 punctual **10** meticulous, nit-
picking, particular, pernickety,
scrupulous **11** ceremonious,
persnickety **13** conscientious

punctiliously
07 exactly **09** carefully, precisely
12 meticulously, scrupulously
15 conscientiously

punctual
05 early, exact, on cue **06** on time,
prompt **07** precise **08** on the dot, up to
time **09** well-timed **10** bang on time,
dead on time, in good time
11 punctilious

punctuality
09 readiness **10** promptness,
regularity, strictness **11** promptitude

punctually
05 sharp **06** bang on, dead on, on
time, prompt, spot-on **07** exactly
08 on the dot, promptly, up to time
09 precisely **11** on the button, on the
stroke, to the minute **13** on the stroke
of

punctuate
04 stop **05** break, point **06** pepper
07 break up **08** sprinkle **09** emphasize,
interject, interrupt **10** accentuate
11 intersperse

punctuation

Punctuation marks include:

04 dash, star
05 colon, comma
06 hyphen, period, quotes
07 solidus
08 asterisk, brackets, ellipsis, full stop
09 backslash, semicolon
10 apostrophe
11 parentheses, speech marks
12 question mark
13 oblique stroke
14 inverted commas, quotation marks, square brackets
15 exclamation mark

puncture
◇ *insertion indicator*
03 cut **04** bite, bore, flat, hole, leak,
nick, slit **05** burst, prick, spike
06 holing, pierce, pounce **07** blow-
out, deflate, flatten, let down, put
down, rupture **08** centesis, flat tyre,
piercing **09** humiliate, penetrate,
perforate, spinal tap **11** make a hole in,
perforation

pundit
04 buff, guru, sage **05** maven, mavin
06 expert, gooroo, master, savant
07 adviser, maestro, teacher
09 authority

pungency
03 nip **04** bite, kick, tang **05** oomph,
point, power, sting **07** pizzazz,
sarcasm **08** mordancy, strength
09 sharpness, spiciness **10** causticity,
trenchancy **11** pepperiness
12 incisiveness **13** strong flavour

pungent
03 hot **04** acid, fell, keen, racy, salt,
sour, tart **05** acrid, acute, fiery, nippy,
sharp, spicy, tangy **06** biting, bitter,
strong **07** burning, caustic, cutting,
mordant, painful, peppery, piquant,
pointed **08** aromatic, incisive, piercing,
poignant, powerful, scathing, stinging
09 sarcastic, trenchant **11** penetrating

punish
◇ *anagram indicator*
03 log **04** beat, cane, fine, flog, gate,
hang, harm, lash, slap, sort, whip
05 abuse, scold, scour, shend, smack,
spank, visit, wreak **06** amerce, batter,
damage, defeat, ground, hammer,
misuse, pay out, strafe, strif, thrash
07 chasten, correct, crucify, justify,
knee-cap, rough up, scourge, sort out,
trounce **08** chastise, decimate,
imprison, keelhaul, maltreat,
masthead, penalize, serve out
09 castigate, strappado **10** come down
on, discipline **11** bring to book
12 come down upon, give it laldie
14 bring to justice, make someone pay,
throw the book at **15** give someone
hell, make an example of
• **be punished**
03 pay

punishable
07 illegal **08** criminal, culpable,
unlawful **10** chargeable, indictable
11 blameworthy, convictable

punishing
04 hard **05** cruel, harsh **06** severe,
taxing, tiring **07** arduous, testing
08 crushing, grinding, grueling,
wearying **09** crippling, demanding,
fatiguing, gruelling, strenuous
10 burdensome, exhausting
12 backbreaking

punishment
04 harm, pine, toco, toko **05** force,
impot **06** damage, ill-use, injury
07 deserts, penalty, revenge
08 ferocity, sentence **10** correction,
discipline, imposition, storminess,
turbulence **11** retribution
12 chastisement, maltreatment
13 rough handling **15** short sharp
shock

Punishments include:

04 cane, fine, gaol, jail, rope
05 exile, lines, strap
06 gating, hiding, prison
07 beating, belting, borstal, capital,
flaying, hitting, jankers, lashing, the
cane, the rack, the rope
08 corporal, demotion, flogging,
slapping, smacking, solitary,
spanking, the birch, whipping

09 chain gang, detention, exclusion,
execution, expulsion, grounding,
larruping, probation, scourging,
strappado, the stocks, thrashing,
torturing
10 banishment, cashiering,
decimation, defrocking,
internment, leathering, suspension,
the slipper, unfrocking
11 confinement, deportation, house
arrest, keelhauling, knee-capping,
mastheading, penal colony
12 confiscation, dressing-down,
imprisonment
13 horsewhipping, incarceration,
sequestration
14 transportation
15 excommunication, walking the
plank

• **place of punishment**
04 cang, gaol, Hell, jail, tron **05** Hade
trone **06** cangue, prison, sin bin
07 borstal, dungeon, gallows, pillory,
tumbrel, tumbril **08** scaffold, solitary,
Tartarus **09** black hole, cart's-tail, the
stocks **10** little-ease **11** penal colony
12 cucking stool, whipping-post
See also **prison**

punitive
04 hard **05** cruel, harsh, penal, stiff
06 severe **08** crushing **09** crippling,
demanding, gruelling, punishing
10 burdensome, chastising, corrective,
vindictive **11** castigatory, retaliatory,
retributive, vindicatory **12** disciplinary

punter
03 guy **04** chap **05** bloke **06** backer,
better, client, fellow, person
07 gambler, wagerer **08** consumer,
customer **10** individual **11** handicappe

puny
04 tiny, weak **05** frail, minor, petty,
scram, small, weary **06** feeble, little,
measly, puisne, puisny, sickly
07 pimping, shilpit, stunted, trivial
08 piddling, reckling, trifling
10 diminutive, undersized
11 undeveloped **13** inexperienced,
insignificant **14** underdeveloped
15 inconsequential

pupil
01 L **04** coed, prep, ward **05** cadet
06 alumna, bursar, day-boy, grader,
junior, novice, old boy, preppy, senior
07 alumnus, ashrama, boarder, day-
girl, learner, monitor, old girl, prefect,
protégé, scholar, student **08** beginner,
bluecoat, disciple, grey-coat, praefect,
protégée, schoolie **09** classmate,
schoolboy, St Trinian **10** abiturient,
academical, apprentice, charity-boy,
day-boarder, day-scholar, gymnasiast,
schoolgirl, Wykehamist **11** charity-girl,
class-fellow, Westminster **12** pupil
teacher **13** apple of the eye,
kindergärtner **14** kindergartener,
parlour-boarder
• **former pupil**
02 OB **06** alumna, old boy
07 alumnus, old girl

puppet
04 doll, dupe, gull, Judy, pawn, tool
05 Punch, puppy 06 mammet,
maumet, mawmet, mommet, motion,
poppet, stooge 07 cat's-paw, Guignol
08 creature, quisling 09 dependant,
fantoccio, rod puppet 10 fantoccino,
figurehead, hand puppet, instrument,
Jack of Lent, marionette, mouthpiece
11 glove puppet, Punchinello 12 finger
puppet

puppy
03 pup 05 whelp 06 lapdog 08 young
dog

purchase
03 buy, get, win 04 deal, earn, gain,
grip, hold 05 asset, booty, goods,
grasp, price, prise, prize 06 assets,
obtain, pay for, pick up, secure, snap
up, strive 07 acquire, bargain, emption,
procure, seizure, shop for 08 foothold,
holdings, invest in, leverage, property
09 advantage 10 go shopping,
investment, possession 11 acquisition,
possessions, splash out on

purchaser
05 buyer, hirer 06 client, emptor,
patron, vendee 07 shopper
08 consumer, customer 11 perquisitor

pure
03 net, pur 04 fair, fine, free, good,
holy, meer, mere, neat, nett, puer, real,
true 05 clean, clear, fresh, moral,
noble, sheer, snowy, solid, total, utter,
white 06 chaste, decent, honest,
kosher, modest, purity, refine, simple,
virgin, worthy 07 aseptic, cleanly,
cleanse, genuine, natural, perfect,
sincere, sterile, unmixed, upright,
utterly 08 absolute, abstract,
academic, complete, flawless, germ-
free, heavenly, hygienic, innocent,
pristine, sanitary, spotless, straight,
thorough, undrossy, unsoiled, virginal,
virginly, virtuous 09 authentic,
blameless, downright, essential,
excellent, incorrupt, righteous,
Saturnian, snow-white, spiritous,
stainless, unalloyed, undefiled,
undiluted, unsullied 10 antiseptic,
completely, homozygous, honourable,
immaculate, intemerate, sterilized,
uninfected, unpolluted 11 conjectural,
disinfected, speculative, theoretical,
unblemished, unmitigated, unqualified
12 unadulterate 13 unadulterated
14 heavenly-minded, uncontaminated

pure-bred
07 blooded 08 pedigree, true-born,
true-bred 09 pedigreed, pure-blood
11 full-blooded, pure-blooded
12 thoroughbred

purée
03 dal 04 fool 06 coulis, hummus,
kissel, humous 07 houmous
08 hoummous 10 baba ganouj 11 baba
ganoush 12 baba ghanouzh

purely
04 just, only 06 merely, simply, solely,

wholly 07 totally, utterly 08 chastely,
entirely 09 unmixedly 10 absolutely,
completely, thoroughly 11 exclusively,
wonderfully 15 unconditionally

purgative
05 aloes, enema, jalap, purge, salts,
yapon, yupon 06 cacoon, emetic,
ipecac, yaupon 07 calomel, drastic,
jalapin, purging, rhubarb 08 aperient,
elaterin, evacuant, laxative, lenitive
09 cathartic, cleansing, colocynth,
croton oil, physic nut 10 abstersive,
cholagogue, depurative, eccoprotic,
Epsom salts, hiera-picra, higry-pigry,
number nine 11 bitter aloes,
cathartical, chrysarobin, ipecacuanha
12 black draught 13 diacatholicon
14 hickery-pickery

purgatory
04 hell 05 agony, swamp 06 misery,
ordeal, ravine 07 anguish, purging,
torment, torture 09 cleansing, expiatory
12 hopelessness, wretchedness

purge
03 rid 04 kill, oust, soil, work 05 clear,
eject, expel, scour 06 depose, purify,
remove 07 absolve, clarify, cleanse,
dismiss, expiate, ousting, removal, root
out, wipe out 08 absterge, clean out,
clear out, disposal, ejection, get rid of
09 catharize, cleansing, eradicate,
expulsion, expurgate, purgative, witch
hunt 10 rooting-out 11 eradication,
exterminate 13 extermination

purification
05 purge 06 lustre 07 elution, lustrum
08 cleaning 09 catharsis, cleansing,
epuration, purgation 10 absolution,
depuration, filtration, fumigation,
lustration, redemption, refinement
11 sublimation 12 desalination,
disinfection, sanitization, zone refining
13 deodorization 14 reverse osmosis,
sanctification 15 decontamination

purify
03 try 04 clay, fine 05 clean, purge,
scrub 06 distil, filter, redeem, refine,
retort, shrive 07 absolve, chasten,
clarify, cleanse, epurate, expurge,
freshen, furbish, mundify, rectify,
sublime 08 chastise, defecate,
depurate, filtrate, fumigate, lustrate,
sanctify, sanitize 09 catharize,
deodorize, disinfect, expurgate,
sterilize, sublimate, sublimize
10 circumcise 13 decontaminate

purifying
06 fining 07 lustral, purging 08 refining
09 cathartic, cleansing, purgative
10 depurative, lustration 11 cathartical,
expurgation 12 purificatory
13 mundificative

purism
08 Atticism, pedantry 09 austerity,
formalism, fussiness, orthodoxy,
restraint 10 classicism, strictness
13 over-precision 14 fastidiousness

purist
05 fussy 06 pedant, strict 07 finicky

08 captious, pedantic, puristic,
quibbler, stickler 09 dogmatist,
formalist, nit-picker, over-exact,
quibbling 10 fastidious, literalist, nit-
picking 11 over-precise 12 precisionist
13 hypercritical 14 over-fastidious,
over-meticulous, over-particular,
uncompromising

puritan
04 prig 05 prude 06 zealot 07 fanatic,
killjoy, pietist 08 Cromwell, Ironside,
moralist, rigorist 09 Ironsides,
precisian, Roundhead 10 goody-
goody, spoilsport 14 disciplinarian

puritanical
04 prim 05 rigid, stern, stiff 06 proper,
severe, strict, stuffy 07 ascetic, austere,
bigoted, precise, prudish, puritan,
zealous 09 fanatical 10 abstemious,
goody-goody, moralistic 11 round-
headed, strait-laced 12 disapproving,
narrow-minded 14 disciplinarian

puritanism
07 bigotry 08 primness, rigidity,
severity, zealotry 09 austerity,
propriety, sternness, stiffness
10 abstinence, asceticism, fanaticism,
narrowness, self-denial, strictness
11 prudishness 12 priggishness,
rigorousness 14 abstemiousness, self-
discipline

purity
04 pure 05 truth 06 candor, honour,
orient, virtue 07 candour, clarity,
decency, honesty 08 chastity, goodness,
morality, nobility, pureness, sanctity
09 chiarezza, cleanness, clearness,
freshness, innocence, integrity,
rectitude, sincerity, virginity
10 perfection, simplicity, worthiness
11 cleanliness, genuineness, uprightness
12 authenticity, flawlessness,
virtuousness 13 blamelessness,
untaintedness, wholesomeness
• **person of purity**
04 lily

purlieus
06 bounds, limits 07 borders, fringes,
suburbs 08 confines, environs, vicinity
09 outskirts, perimeter, periphery,
precincts 12 surroundings
13 neighbourhood

purloin
03 bag, rob 04 lift, nick, take, whip
05 annex, filch, pinch, steal, swipe
06 finger, nobble, pilfer, pocket,
remove, rip off, snitch, thieve
07 cabbage, snaffle 08 abstract,
scrounge, souvenir 10 run off with
11 appropriate 12 make away with

purple

Purples include:

04 anil, plum, puce, puke
05 lilac, mauve, pansy, prune
06 cerise, damson, indigo, maroon,
violet
07 fuchsia, fuschia, heather, magenta,
purpure

08 amethyst, burgundy, hyacinth, lavender, mulberry
09 aubergine
11 royal purple

purport
04 bear, gist, idea, mean, seem, show
05 claim, drift, imply, point, sense, tenor, theme **06** allege, assert, convey, denote, import, intend, pose as, spirit, thrust **07** bearing, betoken, declare, express, meaning, portend, pretend, profess, purpose, signify, suggest
08 indicate, maintain, proclaim, tendency **09** direction, substance
11 implication **12** significance

purportedly
09 allegedly, dubiously **10** apparently, doubtfully, ostensibly, putatively, reportedly, supposedly **13** by all accounts

purpose
03 aim, end, use **04** gain, goal, good, hope, idea, mean, plan, talk, wish, zeal
05 basis, drive, point, teleo-, telos, value **06** aspire, decide, design, desire, effect, intend, motive, object, reason, result, settle, target, vision **07** benefit, outcome, propose, purport, resolve
08 ambition, backbone, converse, devotion, firmness, function, meditate, tenacity **09** advantage, constancy, determine, intention, objective, principle, rationale **10** aspiration, dedication, doggedness, motivation, resolution, usefulness **11** application, contemplate, persistence
12 conversation, perseverance
13 determination, justification, steadfastness
• **on purpose**
08 à dessein, by design, wilfully
09 knowingly, purposely, wittingly
11 consciously **12** deliberately
13 intentionally **14** premeditatedly

purposeful
04 firm **06** dogged **07** decided
08 constant, positive, purposed, resolute, resolved **09** steadfast, tenacious **10** deliberate, determined, persistent, unwavering **11** persevering, unfaltering **12** single-minded, strong-willed

purposefully
10 resolutely **11** steadfastly, tenaciously
12 persistently, unwaveringly
13 perseveringly, unfalteringly
14 single-mindedly

purposeless
04 vain **05** empty **06** wanton
07 aimless, useless, vacuous
08 goalless, needless **09** pointless, senseless, shapeless, unmeaning
10 gratuitous, motiveless, objectless, unasked-for **11** nonsensical, thoughtless, uncalled-for, unnecessary

purposely
08 by design, wilfully **09** expressly, knowingly, on purpose **10** designedly
11 consciously **12** calculatedly,

deliberately, specifically
13 intentionally **14** premeditatedly

purse
◊ *containment indicator*
04 bung, fisc, fisk, gift, prim **05** award, burse, close, funds, means, money, pouch, prize **06** pocket, pucker, reward, wallet **07** coffers, present, tighten, wrinkle **08** compress, contract, crumenal, finances, money-bag, treasury **09** exchequer, resources, spleuchan **10** pocketbook **12** draw together, porte-monnaie **13** press together

pursuance
07 pursuit **08** pursuing **09** discharge, effecting, execution, following
10 completion, fulfilment
11 achievement, performance, prosecution **12** effectuation
14 accomplishment

pursue
03 dog, sew, sue **04** hunt, seek, tail
05 chace, chase, harry, hound, stalk, track, trail **06** aim for, follow, harass, hold to, keep on, keep up, persue, pursew, shadow, try for **07** carry on, conduct, go after, perform, poursew, poursue, run down **08** aspire to, continue, engage in, follow up, hunt down, maintain, practise, run after
09 give chase, make after, persecute, persist in, prosecute, search for, strive for **10** whore after **11** inquire into, investigate, persevere in, work towards **12** have your goal **15** apply yourself to

pursuit
03 aim **04** goal, hunt, line, suit
05 caper, chase, chevy, chivy, craft, hobby, quest, trade, trail **06** attain, chivvy, search **07** hot trod, hunting, pastime, pursual, tailing **08** activity, interest, poursuit, pursuing, stalking, tracking, vocation **09** endeavour, following, hue and cry, poursuitt, pursuance, shadowing, specialty
10 aspiration, employment, occupation, speciality **11** continuance, persistence, wildfowling
12 perseverance **13** investigation

purvey
04 sell **05** cater, stock **06** deal in, pass on, retail, spread, supply **07** furnish, provide, publish, trade in, victual
08 put about, transmit **09** propagate, provision, publicize **11** communicate, disseminate

purveyor
06 dealer, seller, trader, vendor
08 manciple, provedor, provider, providor, provisor, retailer, stockist, supplier **09** provedore **10** propagator, proveditor, victualler **11** proveditore, transmitter **12** communicator, disseminator

pus
06 matter **07** quitter, quittor, seropus
09 diapyesis, discharge **11** suppuration

push
02 go **03** jog, put, ram **04** birr, bunt, butt, cram, goad, horn, hype, jolt, plug, poke, pole, prod, raid, spur, urge
05 boost, bully, drive, dunch, dunsh, egg on, elbow, foray, force, impel, knock, nudge, onset, press, shove
06 charge, coerce, effort, energy, firing, hustle, incite, jostle, market, notice, papers, peddle, plunge, propel, ramrod, squash, the axe, thrust, vigour
07 advance, assault, company, depress, impulse, promote, sacking, squeeze, the boot, the chop **08** ambition, dynamism, invasion, persuade, press for, pressure, the elbow, vitality **09** advertise, constrain, discharge, dismissal, encourage, incursion, influence, manhandle, offensive, onslaught, publicize, your cards **10** enterprise, get-up-and-go, initiative, pressurize
12 forcefulness **13** determination
14 marching orders, put the screws on
• **push around**
05 bully **06** pick on **07** torment
09 terrorize, victimize **10** intimidate
• **push off**
04 move, scat **05** leave, scram **06** beat it, depart, go away **07** buzz off, scarper
08 clear off, clear out, run along, shove off **09** make a move, push along
10 make tracks
• **push on**
04 go on, toil, urge **06** plod on
07 advance, carry on, go ahead, peg away, press on, proceed **08** continue, plug away, slog away, toil away **09** keep going, persevere, soldier on, stick at it
10 keep trying

pushed
06 hard-up, rushed **07** harried, hurried, pinched, pressed, short of
08 harassed, strapped **09** stretched
11 hard-pressed **13** under pressure
14 in difficulties

pushover
03 mug **04** dupe, gull **05** cinch
06 doddle, picnic, stooge, sucker
07 fall guy **08** duck soup, walkover, weakling **09** easy touch, soft touch
10 child's play **11** piece of cake, sitting duck **13** sitting target

pushy
04 bold **05** bossy, brash **07** forward
08 arrogant, assuming, forceful
09 ambitious, assertive **10** aggressive
11 impertinent **12** presumptuous
13 over-confident, self-assertive

pusillanimity
08 timidity, weakness **10** cravenness, feebleness **11** fearfulness, gutlessness, poltroonery **12** cowardliness, timorousness **13** spinelessness

pusillanimous
04 weak **05** timid **06** craven, feeble, scared, yellow **07** chicken, fearful, gutless, wimpish **08** cowardly, timorous **09** spineless, weak-kneed
11 lily-livered **12** faint-hearted, mean-spirited **14** chicken-hearted

pussyfoot
03 pad **05** creep, hedge, prowl, slink, steal **06** tiptoe **09** mess about **10** equivocate **11** prevaricate **12** tergiversate **14** prohibitionist

pustule
04 boil, pock **05** ulcer **06** blotch, fester, papule, pimple **07** abscess, blister, whitlow **08** eruption **09** carbuncle, whitehead **10** uredosorus

put
02 do **03** add, bet, fix, lay, pin, pit, say, set **04** cast, dump, flow, give, have, hurl, levy, park, post, push, rank, rest, risk, sink, sort, turn, word **05** affix, apply, class, couch, drive, exact, force, frame, gauge, grade, group, guess, impel, offer, place, plonk, speak, spend, stake, stand, state, throw, utter, voice **06** append, assert, assign, attach, call on, chance, charge, commit, convey, demand, devote, gamble, impose, impute, incite, invest, locate, oblige, phrase, reckon, reduce, render, repose, set out, settle, submit, tender, thrust **07** arrange, ascribe, bumpkin, connect, convert, deposit, dispose, express, inflict, lay down, present, proceed, proffer, propose, require, set down, situate, station, subject, suggest, venture, work out **08** classify, dedicate, estimate, position, propound, set forth **09** attribute, constrain, establish, formulate, greenhorn, lay before, pronounce, set before, translate, transport **10** categorize, contribute, transcribe **11** guesstimate **12** bring forward

• **put about**
04 tell **06** spread **07** publish **08** announce, distress **09** circulate, make known **11** disseminate

• **put across**
06 convey **07** clarify, explain, express, get over, put over **08** bring off, spell out **09** get across, make clear **11** bring home to, communicate **12** get through to **14** make understood

• **put aside**
04 keep, save, stow **05** hoard, lay by, put by, set by, stash, store **06** retain, shelve **07** reserve **08** lay aside, salt away, set apart, set aside **09** stockpile **12** put to one side **13** keep in reserve

• **put away**
03 eat **04** down, jail, keep, kill, save, stow, wolf **05** drink, eat up, lay by, put by, scoff, snarf, store, waive **06** bang up, commit, devour, guzzle, lock up, pack up, retain, tuck in **07** cashier, certify, confine, consume, divorce, reserve, swallow **08** imprison, lay aside, put aside, renounce, send down, set aside **09** polish off, stockpile **11** incarcerate **13** keep in reserve

• **put back**
05 defer, delay, remit **06** freeze, return, shelve, tidy up **07** adjourn, clear up, replace, repulse, restore, suspend **08** postpone, put on ice, tidy away **09** clear away, reinstate **10** reschedule **13** procrastinate **14** take a raincheck

• **put down**
03 fix, lay, log **04** alay, drop, kill, laid, list, snub, stop **05** abase, aleye, allay, blame, crush, enter, lower, plonk, quash, quell, shame, sneap **06** attach, charge, defeat, humble, reckon, record, slight, squash **07** ascribe, confute, deflate, degrade, destroy, jot down, mortify, repress, set down, silence, squelch, surpass **08** belittle, note down, outshine, register, stamp out, suppress, underlay **09** attribute, deprecate, disparage, humiliate, write down **10** put to sleep, transcribe **12** take down a peg

• **put forward**
03 lay, run **04** move, pose, urge **05** offer, table **06** assign, obtend, prefer, submit, tender **07** advance, present, proffer, propone, propose, suggest **08** nominate **09** hold forth, introduce, recommend

• **put in**
◇ insertion indicator
03 fit **05** enter, input **06** insert, submit **07** install, present **09** introduce

• **put in for**
05 order **06** ask for **07** request **08** apply for **11** requisition, write off for **14** fill in a form for

• **put off**
03 fob, fub **04** daff, doff **05** daunt, defer, delay, deter, lay by, shift **06** dismay, divert, shelve, sicken **07** adjourn, confuse, deflect, dismiss, respite, suspend **08** dissuade, distract, nauseate, postpone, put on ice, turn away **09** sidetrack, talk out of, turn aside **10** demoralize, disconcert, discourage, dishearten, intimidate, reschedule **13** procrastinate **14** take a raincheck

• **put on**
02 do **03** add, don **04** fake, give, robe, sham, wear **05** affix, apply, feign, lay on, mount, place, stage, try on **06** affect, assume, attach, impose, plug in, supply, turn on **07** connect, dress in, get into, perform, present, pretend, produce, provide, start up, throw on **08** activate, organize, simulate, slip into, switch on **10** change into **11** make believe **12** get dressed in **13** get dolled up in

• **put out**
03 irk **04** dout, faze, hurt **05** anger, annoy, douse, dowse, issue, snuff, upset, utter **06** bother, offend, quench **07** dismiss, disturb, extinct, perturb, provoke, publish, smother, trouble **08** announce, bring out, disclose, impose on, irritate, stamp out, unsettle **09** broadcast, circulate, infuriate, make known **10** discommode, disconcert, exasperate, extinguish, mistrysted **13** inconvenience

• **put through**
06 manage **07** achieve, execute, process **08** bring off, complete, conclude, finalize **10** accomplish

• **put together**
04 join **05** build, frame, marry **06** cobble, made up, make up **07** compile, concoct **08** assemble **09** carpenter, construct **11** fit together **13** piece together

• **put up**
◇ reversal down indicator
03 inn, pay **04** give **05** build, erect, float, house, lodge, offer, raise, sling, stake **06** bump up, choose, hike up, invest, jack up, pledge, supply **07** advance, propose, provide, sheathe, shelter, suggest **08** assemble, compound, escalate, increase, nominate **09** construct, recommend **10** put forward **11** accommodate, give a room to

• **put upon**
07 exploit **08** impose on **13** inconvenience, take liberties **14** take for granted **15** take advantage of

• **put up to**
04 goad, urge **05** egg on **06** incite, prompt **08** persuade **09** encourage

• **put up with**
04 bear, lump, take, wear **05** abide, allow, brook, stand **06** accept, endure, suffer **07** stomach, swallow **08** stand for, tolerate **13** take lying down

putative
07 alleged, assumed, reputed **08** presumed, reported, supposed **10** reputative **11** conjectural, theoretical **12** hypothetical, suppositious **13** suppositional

put-down
03 dig **04** gibe, snub **05** sneer **06** insult, rebuff, slight **07** affront, sarcasm **11** humiliation **13** disparagement, slap in the face

put-off
04 curb **06** damper, excuse **07** evasion **08** obstacle **09** deterrent, hindrance, restraint **10** constraint **12** disincentive, postponement **14** discouragement

putrefaction
03 rot **05** decay, mould **06** fungus, mildew, sepsis **07** rotting **08** going bad **09** perishing, putridity **11** putrescence **13** decomposition

putrefy
03 rot **05** addle, decay, go bad, mould, spoil, stink, taint **06** fester, perish **07** corrupt **08** gangrene **09** decompose **11** deteriorate

putrescent
07 rotting **08** decaying, mephitic, stinking **09** festering, perishing **10** putrefying **11** decomposing

putrid
03 bad, off **04** foul, rank **05** addle, fetid **06** addled, foetid, mouldy, rancid, rotten, turned **07** corrupt, decayed, tainted **08** decaying, polluted, stinking **10** decomposed, disgusting **11** decomposing **12** contaminated

put-upon
04 used **06** abused **09** exploited, imposed on **10** maltreated, persecuted **14** inconvenienced

puzzle
◇ *anagram indicator*
04 beat, crux, pose **05** brood, floor, poser, stump, think **06** baffle, bemuse, enigma, fickle, figure, gravel, kittle, ponder **07** bumbaze, confuse, dilemma, flummox, mystery, mystify, nonplus, paradox, perplex, problem, stagger, tickler **08** bewilder, confound, consider, entangle, intrigue, meditate, mull over, muse over, question **09** bamboozle, fascinate **10** complicate, deliberate, mind-bender, perplexity **11** brainteaser **12** bewilderment, brain-twister **13** metagrobolize **14** beat your brains, rack your brains, think hard about

Puzzles include:
04 maze, quiz
05 logic, rebus
06 hanjie, jigsaw, kakuro, riddle, sudoku
07 anagram, hangman, sorites, tangram
08 acrostic, wordgame
09 crossword, conundrum
10 alphametic, cryptogram, Rubik's Cube®, wordsearch
12 magic pyramid

• puzzle out
03 get **04** suss **05** crack, solve **06** decode **07** clear up, resolve, sort out, suss out, unravel, work out **08** decipher, think out, untangle **09** figure out **13** metagrabolize, metagrobolize, piece together **15** find the answer to

puzzled
04 lost **05** at sea **06** beaten **07** at a loss, baffled, floored, in a haze, stumped **08** confused **09** flummoxed, mystified, perplexed **10** bamboozled, bewildered, confounded, nonplussed

puzzlement
05 doubt **06** wonder **08** surprise **09** confusion **10** bafflement, perplexity **11** incertitude, uncertainty **12** astonishment, bewilderment, doubtfulness **13** bamboozlement, mystification **14** disorientation

• expression of puzzlement
02 ha **03** hah, hey, huh **04** anan, anon **05** heigh **06** indeed

puzzling
05 queer, trick **06** arcane, knotty, posing **07** bizarre, cryptic, curious, strange, unclear **08** abstruse, baffling, involved, mystical, peculiar, riddling, tortuous **09** ambiguous, confusing, damnedest, enigmatic, equivocal, intricate **10** misleading, mysterious, mystifying, perplexing, Sphynx-like **11** bewildering, enigmatical, mind-bending **12** impenetrable, inexplicable, labyrinthine, mind-boggling, unfathomable **13** unaccountable

pygmy
03 elf, toy, wee **04** baby, tiny **05** atomy, dwarf, elfin, small **06** midget, minute, pocket **07** manikin, Negrito, stunted **08** dwarfish, half-pint, Tom Thumb **09** miniature, minuscule, pint-sized, thumbling **10** diminutive, fingerling, homunculus, undersized **11** hop-o'-my-thumb, Lilliputian

pyramid
05 stack **08** teocalli, ziggurat, zikkurat

pyromaniac
04 pyro **07** firebug **08** arsonist **10** fire-raiser, incendiary

Q

Q
3 cue 06 Quebec 13 trichosanthin

Qatar
01 Q 02 QA 03 QAT

quack
04 fake, sham 05 bogus, false, fraud,
pseud 06 cowboy, crocus, doctor,
humbug, phoney 07 empiric
08 impostor, so-called, spurious,
supposed, swindler 09 charlatan,
pretended, pretender, trickster
10 fraudulent, medicaster, mountebank
11 counterfeit, masquerader,
quacksalver, saltimbanco, unqualified

quackery
04 sham 05 fraud 06 humbug
09 imposture, phoniness
10 empiricism 11 fraudulence
12 charlatanism 13 mountebankery,
mountebankism

quadrangle
04 quad 05 court, plaza 06 piazza,
square 08 cloister 09 courtyard,
enclosure, esplanade

quaff
04 down, gulp, swig 05 booze, drain,
drink, swill 06 guzzle, imbibe, quaich,
tipple 07 carouse, draught, swallow,
toss off 08 drink off 09 crush a cup,
knock back

quagmire
03 bog, fen, fix 04 hole, mess, mire,
quag 05 marsh, swamp 06 morass,
pickle, slough 07 dilemma, problem
08 entangle, hot water, quandary,
vagmoire 09 deep water, quicksand,
tight spot 10 perplexity

quail
05 colin, cower, daunt, quake, shake,
whore 06 blench, caille, cringe, falter,
flinch, recoil, shiver, shrink, subdue
07 decline, shudder, shy away, slacken,
tremble 08 back away, bobwhite, draw
back, hemipode, languish, percolin,
pull back 09 partridge

quaint
◊ anagram indicator
03 odd 04 fine, twee 05 droll, funky,
queer, sweet 06 queint, whimsy
07 bizarre, cunning, curious, skilful,
strange, unusual, whimsy
08 charming, fanciful, old-world
09 ingenious, whimsical 10 antiquated,
attractive, auld-farand, olde-worlde
11 picturesque 12 old-fashioned

quaintly
05 oddly 09 curiously, strangely,

unusually 10 charmingly
11 whimsically 12 attractively
13 picturesquely

quaintness
05 charm 11 unusualness
13 whimsicalness 14 attractiveness
15 picturesqueness

quake
◊ anagram indicator
04 move, rock, sway 05 heave, quail,
shake, throb 06 didder, dither, quiver,
shiver, tremor, wamble, wobble
07 pulsate, shudder, tremble, vibrate
08 convulse

qualification
05 rider, skill 06 caveat, degree
07 ability, diploma, fitness, proviso
08 aptitude, capacity, training
09 allowance, condition, exception,
exemption, provision 10 adaptation,
adjustment, capability, competence,
limitation 11 certificate, eligibility,
proficiency, reservation, restriction,
stipulation, suitability 12 modification
13 certification 14 accomplishment

Qualifications include:

02 AB, AM, AS, BA, BD, BE, BL, BM, BS,
   DC, DD, DS, IB, MA, MB, MD, MS
03 BAI, BAS, BCh, BCL, BDS, BEd, BRE,
   BSc, ChB, ChM, CSE, DCh, DCL,
   DDS, DEd, DPh, DSc, DTh, EdB, EdD,
   FPC, LHD, LLB, LLD, LLM, MBA,
   MCh, MDS, MEd, MSc, NVQ, ONC,
   OND, PhD, ScB, ScD, SCE, SVQ,
   ThD, VMD
04 BAgr, BCom, BEng, B ès L, B ès S,
   BLit, BMus, BTEC, BVM&S, DEng,
   DIng, DLit, DMus, GCSE, GNVQ,
   LitB, LitD, MBSc, MCom, MDSc,
   MMus, MusB, MusD
05 BArch, BComm, BLitt, BPhil, DLitt,
   DPhil, LittB, LittD, Lower, MEcon,
   MLitt, MPhil, MTech
06 A level, BAgric, BPharm, degree,
   DTheol, Higher, MPharm, O grade,
   O level
07 AS level
10 eleven-plus, Lower grade, School
   Cert
11 Higher grade, Legum doctor
12 Doctor of Laws, Master of Arts,
   Master of Laws
13 Advanced level, Bachelor of Law,
   Doctor of Music, Legum magister,
   Master of Music, Ordinary grade,
   Ordinary level, Standard grade
14 Advanced Higher, Artium Magister,
   Bachelor of Arts, Bachelor of Laws,
   Magister Artium

15 Bachelor of Music, Doctor of
   Letters, Doctor of Science, Doctor
   of Surgery, Master of Letters, Master
   of Science, Master of Surgery,
   Medicinae Doctor

qualified
03 fit 04 able, meet 05 adept
06 expert, fitted 07 bounded,
capable, guarded, limited, skilful,
skilled, trained 08 cautious, eligible,
equipped, licensed, modified,
prepared, reserved, talented
09 certified, chartered, competent,
efficient, equivocal, practised
10 contingent, proficient, restricted
11 conditional, experienced,
provisional 12 accomplished,
professional 13 circumscribed,
knowledgeable

qualify
03 fit 04 ease, pass, vary 05 abate,
allow, alloy, coach, equip, limit,
prove, teach, train 06 adjust, define,
ground, lessen, modify, permit, reduce,
soften, temper, weaken 07 appease,
certify, confirm, delimit, empower,
entitle, license, prepare, warrant
08 classify, diminish, graduate,
instruct, mitigate, moderate, restrain,
restrict, sanction 09 alleviate,
authorize, be allowed, contemper,
make ready 10 be eligible, capacitate,
habilitate 12 characterize 15 make
conditional

quality
01 Q 02 it 04 cast, kind, make, mark,
rank, sort, type 05 class, grade, level,
merit, skill, trait, value 06 aspect,
make-up, manner, nature,
status, timbre 07 calibre, feature,
variety 08 eminence, property,
standard 09 attribute, character,
condition 10 excellence, profession,
refinement 11 distinction, peculiarity,
pre-eminence, superiority
14 accomplishment, characteristic
• **quality assurance**
02 QA

qualm
04 fear 05 doubt, worry 07 anxiety,
concern, scruple 08 disquiet
09 hesitancy, misgiving 10 hesitation,
reluctance, uneasiness
11 compunction, uncertainty
12 apprehension 14 disinclination

quandary
03 fix, jam 04 hole, mess 06 muddle,
pickle 07 dilemma, impasse, problem

09 confusion, tight spot **10** difficulty, perplexity **11** predicament
12 bewilderment

quantify
05 count, weigh **06** number
07 measure, specify **08** evaluate
09 calculate, calibrate, determine, enumerate

quantity
02 qt **03** lot, qty, sum **04** area, bulk, deal, dose, lots, many, mass, much, part, size, tons **05** heaps, loads, quota, reams, scrap, share, total **06** amount, extent, length, masses, number, oodles, stacks, volume, weight
07 breadth, content, expanse, measure, portion **08** capacity, fragment **09** aggregate, allotment, extension, magnitude **10** proportion

See also **measurement**

- **in equal quantities**
01 ā **02** āā **03** ana
- **small quantity**
04 curn, drib, lock
- **unknown quantity**
01 X, Y, Z

quarantine
09 detention, isolation, lazaretto, quarenden, quarender **10** quarrender
11 quarrington, segregation

quarrel
03 jar, row, wap **04** beef, feud, miff, slam, spat, tiff, tift, whid **05** argue, brawl, broil, cavil, chide, clash, fault, fight, flite, flyte, knock, run-in, scrap, set-to, slate **06** barney, bicker, breach, breeze, bust-up, charge, differ, dust-up, fracas, fratch, jangle, quar'le, quarry, ruffle, rumble, schism, square, strife
07 brattle, cast out, censure, contend, dispute, dissent, fall out, outcast, outfall, punch-up, wrangle
08 argument, conflict, disagree, squabble, vendetta **09** caterwaul, complaint, criticize, have words, objection **10** contention, difference, differency, difficulty, dissension, falling-out **11** altercation, controversy, disputation, pick holes in **12** be at variance, disagreement, pull to pieces **13** exchange blows, exchange words, find fault with, part brass rags, shouting match, slanging match **15** be at loggerheads

quarrelling
06 at odds, rowing, strife **07** discord, feuding, warring **08** fighting, variance
09 bickering, scrapping, wrangling
10 at variance, contending, contention, discordant, disharmony, dissension, squabbling **11** altercation, disputation, dissentient **12** argy-bargying
13 argumentation, at loggerheads
14 vitilitigation

quarrelsome
06 chippy **07** scrappy, stroppy
09 bellicose, camstairy, camsteary, debateful, irascible, irritable
10 camsteerie, pugnacious

11 belligerent, contentious, hot-tempered, ill-tempered
12 cantankerous, disputatious
13 argumentative **14** ready for a fight

quarry
04 game, goal, kill, mark, prey
05 chase, curry, prize, spoil **06** currie, object, target, victim **07** quarrel
08 stone pit **09** glory hole, slaughter

quarter
01 E, N, q, S,W **02** qr, qu **03** pad **04** airt, area, digs, east, hand, part, pity, post, side, spot, west, zone **05** board, grace, house, lodge, mercy, north, place, point, put up, quart, rooms, south
06 billet, favour, fourth, ghetto, medina, pardon, region, sector
07 Moorery, section, shelter, station, two bits **08** barracks, clemency, district, division, domicile, dwelling, leniency, locality, lodgings, province, quartern, vicinity **09** direction, residence, territory **10** compassion, habitation, indulgence
11 accommodate, forgiveness
13 accommodation, neighbourhood

See also **compass**

quarterly
02 qu **04** quar **12** three-monthly

quarters
04 camp **05** house **06** ghetto
07 lodging

See also **accommodation**

quartz
04 jasp **05** flint, prase **06** jasper, morion **07** crystal **08** amethyst, tiger eye **09** buhrstone, burrstone, cacholong, cairngorm, carnelian, cornelian, goldstone, tiger's eye
10 avanturine, aventurine, chalcedony
11 rock crystal **12** Bohemian ruby, Spanish topaz **14** Bristol-diamond, cairngorm-stone **15** occidental topaz

quash
04 void **05** annul, crush, quell
06 cancel, defeat, repeal, revoke, scotch, squash, subdue **07** nullify, rescind, reverse **08** abrogate, override, overrule, overturn, set aside, suppress
09 overthrow **10** invalidate, put an end to **11** countermand

quaver
03 sob **05** break, quake, shake, throb, trill, waver **06** quiver, tremor, warble, wobble **07** flicker, flutter, pulsate, shudder, tremble, tremolo, vibrate, vibrato **09** oscillate, trembling, vibration **10** eighth note **11** quaveriness

quay
03 kay, key **04** dock, pier **05** jetty, levee, wharf **07** harbour

queasiness
06 nausea **07** gagging **08** retching, sickness, vomiting **11** airsickness, biliousness, carsickness, seasickness
12 sick headache **14** motion sickness, travel sickness **15** morning sickness

queasy
03 ill **04** sick **05** dizzy, faint, giddy, green, queer, rough **06** groggy, uneasy, unwell **07** bilious **08** nauseous, sickened **09** hazardous, nauseated, squeamish, unsettled **10** fastidious, out of sorts, scrupulous **15** under the weather

Quebec
01 Q **02** QC

queen
01 Q, R **02** ER, FD, HM, Qu, VR **03** VIR
04 idol, rani **05** belle, charm, ranee, ruler, Venus **06** beauty, prince, Brenda regina **07** consort, empress, majesty, monarch **08** princess **09** sovereign
11 head of state

> *Queens include:*
>
> **03** Mab
> **04** Anne, Anne (of Cleves), Emma, Grey (Jane, Lady), Joan (of Navarre), Mary, Mary (Queen of Scots), Mary (of Teck), Parr (Catherine)
> **05** Maeve, Maria, Marie (de Médici), Sheba
> **06** Boleyn (Anne), Esther, Hearts, Himiko, Howard (Catherine), Louisa, Nzinga, Salote, Silvia, Soraya
> **07** Beatrix, Eleanor (of Aquitaine), Eleanor (of Castile), Juliana, Macbeth (Lady), Seymour (Jane), Titania, Zenobia
> **08** Adelaide, Berenice, Boadicea, Boudicca, Caroline (of Ansbach), Caroline (of Brunswick), Clotilda (St), Gloriana, Isabella (of Castile), Kristina, Margaret (St), Margaret (of Anjou), Philippa (of Hainault), Victoria
> **09** Alexandra, Artemisia, Brunhilde, Catherine (de Médici), Catherine (of Aragon), Catherine (of Braganza), Christina, Cleopatra, Elizabeth, Fredegond, Margrethe, Mary Tudor, Nefertiti, Semiramis, Woodville (Elizabeth)
> **10** Hatshepsut, Lakshmi Bai, Wilhelmina
> **13** Margaret Tudor
> **14** Henrietta Maria
> **15** Charlotte Sophia, Marie Antoinette

queenly
05 grand, noble, regal, royal **06** august
07 reginal, stately, sublime **08** gracious imperial, majestic, splendid
09 dignified, imperious, sovereign
11 monarchical

queer
◇ *anagram indicator*
03 gay, ill, mar, odd, rum **04** camp, foil, harm, iffy, ruin, sick **05** botch, butch, cheat, dizzy, faint, fishy, funny, giddy, quare, rough, shady, spoil, upset, weird, wreck **06** Fifish, impair, quaint, queasy, shifty, stymie, thwart, unwell
07 bizarre, curious, deviant, dubious, lesbian, strange, suspect, unusual
08 abnormal, bisexual, doubtful,

ndanger, peculiar, puzzling, ridicule,
ngular, uncommon **09** eccentric,
ustrate, irregular, unnatural
0 homosexual, jeopardize,
ysterious, outlandish, out of sorts,
emarkable, suspicious, unorthodox
1 counterfeit, light-headed
3 extraordinary, funny peculiar
4 unconventional **15** under the weather

queerness
6 oddity **11** abnormality, bizarreness,
uriousness, peculiarity, singularity,
trangeness, unorthodoxy,
nusualness **12** eccentricity,
regularity, uncommonness
3 anomalousness, unnaturalness

quell
3 die **04** alay, calm, hush, kill, rout,
tay **05** abash, abate, aleye, allay, crush,
quash, quiet **06** defeat, pacify, perish,
oothe, squash, stifle, subdue
7 appease, conquer, put down,
ilence, slaying, subside **08** mitigate,
noderate, overcome, suppress,
anquish **09** alleviate, overpower
0 disconcert, extinguish, put an end
o, spifflicate **11** spifflicate

quench
4 cool, sate, stop **05** douse, slake
6 put out, sloken, stanch, stifle
7 destroy, satiate, satisfy, slocken,
mother, staunch **08** snuff out, stamp
ut **10** extinguish

querulous
4 sour **05** cross, fussy, ratty, testy
6 shirty **07** carping, fretful, grouchy,
eevish **08** captious, critical, petulant
9 fractious, grumbling, irascible,
rritable, plaintive **11** complaining
2 cantankerous, discontented,
dissatisfied, fault-finding

query
1 Q **02** qy **03** ask **05** doubt, qualm
6 quaere, qualms **07** dispute, inquire,
nquiry, problem, quibble, suspect
8 distrust, mistrust, question
9 challenge, suspicion **10** disbelieve,
nesitation, scepticism, uneasiness
1 quarrel with, reservation,
ncertainty **12** question mark **13** be
ceptical of, throw doubts on

quest
3 aim **04** bark, goal, hunt, yelp
6 search, voyage **07** crusade, inquiry,
ourney, mission, purpose, pursuit,
eeking, venture **08** ringdove
9 adventure **10** enterprise,
xpedition, pilgrimage, wood pigeon
1 exploration, undertaking
3 investigation
• in quest of
3 for, out **06** out for **08** questing
0 hunting for **11** in pursuit of
2 harking after, searching for, seeking
after, trying to find **14** trying to obtain

question
1 Q **02** Qu **03** ask **04** chin, poll, pose,
ump, quiz **05** demur, doubt, grill,
ssue, point, poser, probe, query,

theme, topic **06** debate, matter,
motion, quaere, riddle, teaser
07 debrief, discuss, dispute, enquiry,
erotema, eroteme, examine, inquire,
inquiry, problem, scruple, subject
08 argument, converse, erotesis,
proposal **09** backspeer, backspeir,
catechize, challenge, conundrum,
interview, objection **10** difficulty,
disbelieve, discussion **11** controversy,
interrogate, investigate, proposition,
uncertainty **12** conversation, cross-
examine, peradventure, point at issue
13 cross-question, interrogation,
interrogatory **15** have doubts about,
have qualms about
• in question
07 at issue **09** concerned **14** being
discussed **15** under discussion
• out of the question
06 absurd **10** impossible, ridiculous
11 unthinkable **12** unacceptable,
unbelievable
• without question
07 on trust **11** immediately
14 unhesitatingly, unquestionably,
without arguing

questionable
◇ *anagram indicator*
04 iffy **05** fishy, shady, vexed
07 dubious, immoral, suspect
08 arguable, doubtful, improper,
unproven **09** debatable, equivocal,
uncertain, unsettled **10** at question,
disputable, suspicious **11** problematic
12 undetermined **13** controversial,
problematical

questioner
07 doubter, sceptic **08** agnostic,
examiner, inquirer **09** catechist
10 catechizer, inquisitor, quizmaster
11 disbeliever, interrogant, interviewer
12 interlocutor, interrogator,
investigator **14** question-master

questionnaire
04 form, quiz, test **06** survey
11 opinion poll **14** market research

queue
03 row **04** file, line, tail **05** chain, order,
train **06** back up, column, fall in, in line,
line up, series, string **07** pigtail
08 sequence, tailback **09** breadline,
crocodile, form a line **10** form a queue,
procession, succession, wait in line
11 stand in line **13** concatenation

quibble
03 pun **04** carp, quip **05** cavil, dodge,
query, quirk **06** haggle, niggle, peck at,
snatch **07** brabble, nit-pick, protest,
quiblin, quiddit, quillet **08** equivoke,
pettifog, quiddity **09** complaint,
criticism, equivoque, objection
10 equivocate, nit-picking, split hairs
11 prevaricate **12** carriwitchet,
equivocation, pettifogging **13** avoid
the issue, find fault with, prevarication

quibbler
07 casuist, niggler, sophist **08** caviller,
chicaner **09** nit-picker **11** equivocator,
pettifogger **12** hair-splitter

quibbling
07 carping, evasive **08** captious,
critical, niggling, overnice
09 ambiguous, casuistic, cavilling,
chicanery, chicaning **10** nit-picking
12 equivocating, pettifogging **13** hair-
splitting, logic-chopping, word-
splitting

quick
03 hot, pdq **04** fast, keen, rath, soon,
yare **05** agile, alive, brief, brisk, flash,
hasty, nifty, nippy, rapid, rathe, ready,
sharp, smart, swift, zippy **06** astute,
clever, dapper, living, mobile, nimble,
presto, prompt, shrewd, speedy,
sudden **07** cursory, express, flutter,
hurried, instant, rapidly, schnell
08 expedite, fleeting, pregnant,
shifting **09** immediate, receptive,
sensitive, sprightly **10** discerning,
perceptive, responsive **11** expeditious,
intelligent, perfunctory, quick-witted,
sharp-witted **12** without delay
13 instantaneous **15** pretty damn
quick, quick off the mark

quicken
04 stir, whet **05** couch, hurry, rouse,
speed **06** arouse, excite, hasten, incite,
kindle, revive, stir up **07** advance,
animate, enliven, hurry up, inspire,
refresh, speed up **08** activate, dispatch,
energize, expedite, revivify
09 galvanize, instigate, stimulate
10 accelerate, couch grass, invigorate,
reactivate, revitalize, strengthen
11 precipitate **12** reinvigorate

quickly
04 cito, fast, soon, vite **05** apace,
quick, slick, swith **06** presto, pronto
07 briskly, express, hastily, rapidly,
readily, smartly, swiftly **08** abruptly,
promptly, smartish, speedily
09 cursorily, hurriedly, instantly, like a
shot, like smoke, overnight, posthaste
11 at the double, immediately,
prestissimo **12** a mile a minute,
lickety-split, with dispatch
13 expeditiously, perfunctorily **14** at a
rate of knots, hell for leather,
unhesitatingly **15** instantaneously, like
the clappers

quickness
05 speed **06** acumen **07** agility
08 celerity, keenness, rapidity
09 acuteness, alertness, briskness,
hastiness, immediacy, nimblesse,
readiness, sharpness, swiftness
10 astuteness, expedition, nimbleness,
promptness, shrewdness, speediness,
suddenness **11** penetration,
promptitude **12** intelligence
13 precipitation **15** quick-wittedness

quick-tempered
05 fiery, testy **06** snappy, touchy
07 waspish **08** choleric, petulant,
shrewish, volcanic **09** excitable,
explosive, impatient, impulsive,
irascible, irritable, splenetic **11** hot-
tempered, quarrelsome
13 temperamental

quick-witted

04 keen **05** acute, alert, sharp, smart, witty **06** astute, bright, clever, crafty, shrewd **09** ingenious, wide-awake **10** perceptive **11** intelligent, penetrating, ready-witted, resourceful **12** nimble-witted **15** quick off the mark

quid

01 L **03** sov **04** chew, oner **05** libra, pound, squid **06** guinea, nicker **07** smacker **09** sovereign, substance **12** jimmy-o'goblin **13** pound sterling

See also **pound**

quid pro quo

04 swap **07** damages **08** exchange, trade-off **09** mutuality, tit for tat **10** equivalent **11** co-operation, equivalence, give-and-take, reciprocity **12** compensation, remuneration **13** reciprocation

quiescent

04 calm **05** inert, quiet, still **06** asleep, at rest, latent, placid, serene, silent **07** dormant, passive, resting **08** inactive, peaceful, sleeping, tranquil **09** reposeful **10** in abeyance, motionless, untroubled **11** undisturbed

quiet

01 p **02** QT, sh **03** dry, low, shy **04** calm, ease, hush, loun, lown, lull, meek, mild, pale, rest, soft **05** doggo, faint, lound, lownd, muted, peace, shtum, sober, still, stoic, stumm **06** gentle, hushed, lonely, low-key, pastel, placid, repose, secret, serene, settle, shtoom, shtumm, silent, sleepy, stilly, subtle **07** appease, easeful, muffled, orderly, private, schtoom, silence, subdued **08** composed, discreet, isolated, man-to-man, peaceful, personal, reserved, reticent, retiring, secluded, serenity, taciturn, tranquil **09** inaudible, introvert, noiseless, quietness, soundless, stillness, withdrawn **10** indistinct, phlegmatic, restrained, thoughtful, untroubled **11** inoffensive, sequestered, undisturbed, unexcitable, unflappable **12** confidential, off-the-record, peacefulness, tranquillity, unfrequented, woman-to-woman **13** imperturbable, noiselessness, soundlessness, unforthcoming, without a sound **15** uncommunicative, undemonstrative

See also **silence**

quieten

04 calm, dull, hush, mute **05** lower, quell, quiet, shush, sober, still **06** deaden, muffle, pacify, reduce, shut up, smooth, soften, soothe, stifle, subdew, subdue **07** compose, silence **08** calm down, diminish **12** tranquillize

quietly

01 p **04** loun, lown, soft **05** lound, lownd, still **06** calmly, gently, meekly, mildly, mutely, softly **08** modestly, placidly, secretly, silently **09** inaudibly, privately **10** peacefully, tranquilly **11** noiselessly, soundlessly **12** deliberately **13** unobtrusively **15** surreptitiously

quietness

04 calm, hush, lull **05** peace, quiet, still **06** repose **07** inertia, silence **08** calmness, dullness, quietude, serenity **09** composure, placidity, stillness **10** inactivity, quiescence **12** peacefulness, tranquillity **14** uneventfulness

quietude

04 calm, hush, rest **05** peace, quiet **06** repose **07** ataraxy, silence **08** ataraxia, calmness, coolness, serenity **09** composure, placidity, quietness, stillness **10** equanimity, sedateness **11** restfulness **12** peacefulness, tranquillity

quietus

03 end **05** death **06** demise **07** decease, release **08** dispatch, quashing **09** death-blow, discharge, silencing **10** extinction **11** acquittance, coup de grâce, death-stroke, elimination **15** finishing stroke

quilt

05 doona, duvet, twilt **06** downie, kantha, thrash **07** comfort **08** bedcover, coverlet **09** bedspread, comforter, eiderdown **11** counterpane **12** counterpoint **14** patchwork quilt

quince

03 bel **04** bael, bhel **06** feijoa **08** japonica **11** chaenomeles, queene-apple

quinine

04 kina **05** china, quina **08** cinchona, kinakina **09** quinquina **10** chinachina, quinaquina

quinsy

06 angina **08** cynanche, prunella **09** squinancy **11** tonsillitis

quintessence

04 core, gist, pith, soul **05** heart **06** elixir, kernel, marrow, spirit **07** essence, extract, pattern **08** exemplar, quiddity **10** embodiment **12** distillation **15** personification, sum and substance

quintessential

05 ideal **06** entire **07** perfect, typical **08** complete, ultimate **09** essential **10** consummate, definitive **12** archetypical, prototypical

quip

03 gag **04** gibe, jest, joke **05** crack, quirk **06** retort, zinger **07** epigram, quibble, riposte **08** one-liner **09** wisecrack, witticism **10** knick-knack, pleasantry **12** carriwitchet

quirk

03 way **04** kink, quip, turn, whim **05** fluke, freak, habit, knack, thing, trait, trick, twist **06** foible, hang-up, oddity, vagary **07** caprice, feature, quibble **09** curiosity, mannerism, obsession **11** peculiarity **12** eccentricity, idiosyncrasy **14** characteristic

quirkiness

06 oddity **07** anomaly **08** zaniness **09** wackiness, weirdness **10** aberration, freakiness **11** abnormality, bizarreness, peculiarity, singularity, strangeness, unorthodoxy **12** eccentricity, freakishness, idiosyncrasy **13** nonconformity **14** capriciousness

quirky

◇ *anagram indicator*

03 odd **04** wild, zany **05** barmy, drôle, droll, funky, funny, kinky, queer, wacky, weird **06** far-out, freaky, way-out, whimsy **07** bizarre, curious, deviant, oddball, strange, uncanny, unusual **08** aberrant, abnormal, atypical, crackers, freakish, original, peculiar, singular, uncommon **09** different, eccentric, irregular, whimsical **10** capricious, off the wall, outlandish, remarkable **11** exceptional **13** extraordinary, idiosyncratic **14** unconventional

quisling

05 Judas **06** puppet **07** traitor **08** betrayer, renegade, turncoat **12** collaborator **14** fifth columnist

quit

02 go **03** end, rid **04** drop, exit, free, part, stop, void **05** avoid, cease, clear, leave, quite, quyte, repay, shift, stash **06** acquit, decamp, depart, desert, desist, give up, go away, pack in, quight, resign, retire, vacate **07** abandon, abstain, forsake, requite **08** leave off, renounce, withdraw **09** surrender **10** chicken out, relinquish **11** discontinue

quite

03 all, yes **04** full, just, real, tout, very **05** clean, clear, fully, right, sheer **06** depart, enough, fairly, indeed, quight, rather, really, resign, wholly **07** absolve, exactly, totally, utterly **08** actually, entirely, every bit, somewhat **09** every whit, perfectly, precisely **10** absolutely, completely, moderately, reasonably, relatively **12** to some degree, to some extent **13** comparatively

● **not quite**

◇ *tail deletion indicator*

06 almost, nearly

quits

04 even, meet **05** equal, evens, level **06** square

● **call it quits**

04 stop **05** cease **08** break off **09** make peace **10** call it a day **11** discontinue **12** stop fighting **14** bury the hatchet **15** lay down your arms

quitter

03 pus, rat **06** skiver **07** shirker **08** apostate, defector, deserter, recreant, renegade **10** delinquent

quiver

◊ anagram indicator
05 quake, shake, throb **06** active, bicker, nimble, quaver, shiver, thrill, tingle, tremor, wobble **07** feather, flicker, flutter, pulsate, shudder, tremble, twinkle, vibrate **08** flichter **09** oscillate, palpitate, pulsation, vibration **11** oscillation, palpitation

quixotic

06 errant **07** Utopian **08** fanciful, romantic **09** impetuous, impulsive, unworldly, visionary **10** chivalrous, idealistic, starry-eyed **11** extravagant, fantastical, unrealistic **13** impracticable

quiz

03 eye **04** hoax, pump, test, yo-yo **05** grill, smoke, trail **07** examine, monocle **08** question **09** bandalore **11** competition, examination, interrogate, questioning **12** cross-examine **13** cross-question, interrogation, questionnaire

Radio and television quiz shows include:
02 QI
03 3–2–1
05 15 to 1
08 Bullseye, Eggheads
09 Countdown, Odd One Out, Small Talk
10 Mastermind, Masterteam, Screen Test
11 Call My Bluff, Catchphrase, Give Us a Clue, Just a Minute, Spot the Tune, The Food Quiz, The News Quiz, What's My Line?
12 Ask the Family, Blockbusters, Bognor or Bust, Face the Music, Fifteen to One, Going for Gold, Lucky Numbers, Name That Tune, Strike It Rich, Take Your Pick, Telly Addicts, Winning Lines
13 Blankety Blank, Bob's Full House, Going for a Song, Strike It Lucky
14 Brain of Britain, Family Fortunes, The Weakest Link, Wheel of Fortune, Winner Takes All
15 Double Your Money, The Price Is Right

quizzical

06 amused **07** amusing, baffled, comical, curious, mocking, puzzled, teasing **08** humorous, sardonic **09** inquiring, mystified, perplexed, satirical, sceptical **11** questioning

quizzically

06 askant **07** askance **09** curiously, mockingly **11** inquiringly, sceptically **13** questioningly

quoit

04 coit, disc, disk, ring
See also **buttocks**

• **target in quoits**
03 hub, pin, tee

quota

03 cut **04** part **05** share, slice, whack **06** quotum, ration **07** portion **09** allowance **10** allocation, assignment, contingent, percentage, proportion **11** slice of cake **14** numerus clausus

quotation

03 bid, tag **04** cost, line, rate **05** piece, price, quote **06** charge, figure, tender **07** cutting, excerpt, extract, listing, passage, remnant **08** allusion, citation, estimate **09** reference, selection **14** locus classicus

quote

04 cite, coat, cote, echo, name **05** coate **06** adduce, allege, drag up, recall, recite, repeat **07** examine, mention, refer to **08** allude to **09** recollect, reproduce **10** scrutinize

quoted

05 cited **06** stated **08** reported **09** instanced **10** referred to, reproduced **13** forementioned **14** above-mentioned

quotidian

05 daily **06** common, normal **07** diurnal, regular, routine **08** day-to-day, everyday, habitual, ordinary, repeated, workaday **09** customary, recurrent **11** bog-standard, commonplace **12** run-of-the-mill

R

R
02 ar **05** Romeo

rabbi

rabbit
03 bun, doe **04** buck, cony, go on, talk
05 bunny, coney, daman, drone, hyrax
06 dassie, dodder, wander, wibble
07 go-devil, maunder **08** confound
09 give forth **11** bunny rabbit

• rabbit on
03 gab, yap **04** go on **06** babble, natter, waffle, witter **07** blather, blether, chatter, maunder **08** witter on **09** go on and on, maunder on

rabble
03 mob, tag **04** herd, rout **05** crowd, horde, meiny, plebs **06** gabble, masses, meiney, meinie, menyie, proles, raffle, ragtag, rascal, tagrag, throng
07 doggery **08** canaille, populace, riff-raff, varletry **09** colluvies, hoi polloi, rascaille, rascality **10** clamjamfry
11 clanjamfray, proletariat, rank and file
12 clamjamphrie, common people, raggle-taggle **13** great unwashed

rabble-rouser
08 agitator **09** demagogue, firebrand
10 incendiary, ringleader, tub-thumper
12 troublemaker

rabble-rousing
10 stirring up **11** tub-thumping
13 troublemaking

Rabelaisian
04 lewd, racy **05** bawdy, gross

06 coarse, earthy, ribald, risqué, vulgar
08 indecent **09** exuberant, satirical
11 extravagant, uninhibited
12 unrestrained

rabid
03 mad **04** wild **06** ardent, crazed, raging **07** berserk, bigoted, burning, extreme, fervent, frantic, furious, violent, zealous **08** frenzied, maniacal
09 fanatical, ferocious, obsessive
10 hysterical, intolerant, irrational
11 hydrophobic, overzealous, unreasoning **12** narrow-minded

rabies
05 lyssa **08** rabidity **09** rabidness
11 hydrophobia

race
03 cut, fly, ren, rin, run, sex, zap, zip
04 bolt, clan, dart, kind, line, rach, rase, raze, rush, seed, slit, tear, zoom
05 blood, breed, chase, erase, genus, house, hurry, pluck, quest, ratch, scoot, slash, speed, stock, trial, tribe
06 career, colour, family, gallop, ginger, hasten, nation, people, snatch, stirps, strain **07** contest, dynasty, kindred, lineage, rivalry, scratch, species
08 ancestry, go all out, piquancy
09 parentage **10** accelerate, contention, extraction, get a move on
11 competition, ethnic group, get cracking, racial group, run like hell
15 take part in a race

08 downhill, marathon, scramble, speedway, stock car, swimming, trotting
09 Grand Prix, greyhound, motocross, motor-race, time trial, walkathon
10 cyclo-cross, Formula One, motorcycle, track event
11 donkey derby, egg-and-spoon, three-legged, wheelbarrow
12 cross-country, steeplechase

racecourse
03 lap **04** turf **05** track **06** course, dromos **07** circuit **08** speedway
09 racetrack **10** hippodrome

racehorse
05 neddy, stiff **06** mudder, novice
07 no-hoper **08** cocktail, outsider, yearling **12** morning glory, thoroughbred
See also **horse**

racial
04 folk **06** ethnic, tribal **07** genetic
08 national **09** ancestral, inherited
12 ethnological, genealogical

raciness
03 pep **04** zest **06** energy **07** pizzazz
08 dynamism, lewdness, ribaldry
09 animation, bawdiness, crudeness, freshness, indecency, vulgarity
10 coarseness, ebullience, indelicacy, liveliness, smuttiness **11** naughtiness, zestfulness **12** exhilaration
14 suggestiveness

racing

05 evens, fence, field, filly, going, heavy, owner, place, silks, stake
06 chaser, faller, jockey, length, maiden, novice, odds-on, pull up, sprint, stable, stayer, tic-tac, weight
07 classic, furlong, gelding, meeting, tipster, trainer
08 blinkers, handicap, hurdling, juvenile, outsider, racecard, stallion, standard, stewards, yearling, yielding
09 ante-poste, bookmaker, favourite, group race, non-runner, pacemaker, short head
10 all-weather, bumper race, flat racing, listed race, parade ring, stakes race
11 accumulator, connections, handicapper, hunter chase, pattern race, photo finish, Triple Crown, winning post
12 handicap race, National Hunt, starting gate, steeplechase, thoroughbred, weighing room
14 conditions race
15 stewards' enquiry

Formula One Grand Prix circuits include:
05 Imola, Monza
06 Sakhir, Sepang, Suzuka
07 Bahrain
08 Istanbul, Shanghai
10 Albert Park, Hockenheim, Interlagos, Magny-Cours, Monte Carlo
11 Hungaroring, Nurburgring, Silverstone
12 Indianapolis
13 Francorchamps

Formula One motor racing teams include:
05 Honda
06 Toyota
07 Ferrari, McLaren, Midland, Red Bull, Renault
08 Williams
09 BMW Sauber, Toro Rosso
10 Super Aguri
13 Red Bull Racing

Motor racing drivers, motorcyclists and associated figures include:
04 Foyt (A J), Hill (Damon), Hill (Graham), Hunt (James), Ickx (Jacky), Moss (Stirling)
05 Alesi (Jean), Clark (Jim), Clark (Roger), Hulme (Denny), Lauda (Niki), McRae (Colin), Olsen (Ole), Petty (Richard), Prost (Alain), Rossi (Valentino), Sainz (Carlos), Senna (Ayrton), Unser (Al), Unser (Bobby)
06 Ascari (Alberto), Berger (Gerhard), Briggs (Barry), Button (Jensen), Doohan (Michael), Dunlop (Joey), Fangio (Juan), Irvine (Eddie), Lawson (Eddie), Mauger (Ivan), Piquet (Nelson), Sheene (Barry), Walker (Murray)
07 Brabham (Sir Jack), Brundle (Martin), Ferrari (Enzo), Fogarty

(Carl), Guthrie (Janet), Mäkinen (Tommi), Mansell (Nigel), McLaren (Bruce), Mikkola (Hannu), Roberts (Kenny), Rosberg (Keke), Rosberg (Nico), Segrave (Sir Henry), Stewart (Sir Jackie), Surtees (John)
08 Agostini (Giacomo), Andretti (Mario), Campbell (Donald), Campbell (Sir Malcolm), Hailwood (Mike), Häkkinen (Mika), Hawthorn (Mike), Oldfield (Barney), Williams (Sir Frank)
09 Blomqvist (Stig), Chevrolet (Louis), Coulthard (David), Earnhardt (Dale), Kankkunen (Juha)
10 Fittipaldi (Emerson), Schumacher (Michael), Schumacher (Ralf), Villeneuve (Jacques)
12 Rickenbacker (Eddie)

Motor racing-related terms include:
03 lap, pit
04 apex, grid, oval, pits, pole, T-car
05 apron, shunt
06 out lap, slicks
07 chicane, cockpit, hairpin, marshal, pace car, paddock, pit lane, pit stop, stagger, steward
08 dirty air, drafting, fishtail, lollipop, outbrake, pit board, straight
09 Brickyard, parade lap, parc fermé, safety car, telemetry
10 back marker, gravel trap, qualifying, racing line, run-off area, slipstream, team orders
11 braking zone, pit straight, victory lane
12 formation lap, pole position
13 launch control, scrutineering, start straight, stop-go penalty, superspeedway
14 finish straight

racism
04 bias **08** jingoism **09** apartheid, prejudice, racialism **10** chauvinism, xenophobia **14** discrimination **15** racial prejudice

racist
04 Nazi **05** bigot **07** bigoted **09** racialist **10** chauvinist, intolerant **13** discriminator **14** discriminatory

rack
04 bink, hack, haik, hake, heck, pain, tear **05** agony, crash, creel, drift, drive, flake, frame, pangs, shake, shelf, stand, touse, touze, towse, towze, track, wrack, wrest, wring **06** extort, harass, harrow, holder, misery, strain, stress, wrench **07** afflict, agonize, anguish, crucify, distort, oppress, remnant, stretch, support, torment, torture, trestle **08** convulse, distress, lacerate, vertebra **09** framework, structure, suffering, vengeance **10** affliction, excruciate, overstrain, punishment **11** destruction, devastation, persecution, portmanteau **13** umbrella stand
• **on the rack**
06 in pain **07** in agony **09** in trouble,

suffering **10** in distress **11** under stress **13** under pressure **14** in difficulties
• **rack your brains**
05 study **09** think hard **11** concentrate, think deeply **13** put your mind to

racket
03 bat, con, din, job, row **04** fuss, game, rort, scam **05** dodge, fraud, noise, trick **06** fiddle, hubbub, outcry, rattle, scheme, tumult, uproar **07** clamour, swindle, yelling **08** business, shouting, snowshoe **09** commotion, deception, gold brick **10** hullabaloo, hurly-burly, occupation **11** dissipation, disturbance, pandemonium **14** responsibility

racketeering
05 fraud **08** cheating, fiddling, fleecing, stealing, stinging **09** extortion, swindling **10** chiselling, defrauding, ripping off **12** overcharging **14** taking for a ride **15** cooking the books

raconteur
07 relater **08** narrator, reporter **09** describer **10** anecdotist, chronicler **11** commentator, storyteller

racquet *see* **racket**

racy
04 blue, rude **05** bawdy, crude, dirty, peppy, salty, spicy, witty, zippy **06** coarse, lively, ribald, risqué, smutty, vulgar **07** buoyant, dynamic, naughty, piquant, pungent, zestful **08** animated, indecent, spirited, vigorous **09** ebullient, energetic, off-colour, sparkling, vivacious **10** boisterous, fast-moving, indelicate, suggestive **12** enthusiastic

radar
• **radar image**
04 blip
• **radar signal**
04 echo **05** angel

raddled
◊ *anagram indicator*
05 drawn, gaunt **06** wasted **07** haggard, in a mess, unkempt, worn out **11** dishevelled **15** the worse for wear

radiance
03 joy **04** glow **05** bliss, gleam, light, sheen, shine **06** lustre **07** delight, ecstasy, elation, glitter, rapture **08** pleasure **09** beaminess, happiness, radiation, splendour **10** brightness, brilliance, effulgence, luminosity, refulgence **12** resplendence **13** incandescence

radiant
05 beamy, happy, lit up **06** bright, elated, joyful **07** beaming, beamish, glowing, lambent, pleased, shining **08** blissful, ecstatic, gleaming, glorious, luminous, splendid **09** brilliant, delighted, effulgent, refulgent, sparkling **10** glittering, in raptures, profulgent **11** illuminated, magnificent,

on cloud nine, over the moon, resplendent **12** incandescent **15** in seventh heaven, on top of the world

radiate

03 ray **04** beam, emit, glow, pour, shed **05** gleam, issue, shine **06** branch, spread **07** diffuse, diverge, emanate, give off, scatter, send out **08** disperse **09** oscillate, send forth, spread out **10** divaricate **11** disseminate

radiation

04 rays **05** waves **08** emission **09** emanation **12** transmission

Radiation includes:

02 ir, UV
03 UVA, UVB, UVC, UVR
04 beta, hard, heat, soft
05 alpha, gamma, light, X-rays
06 cosmic
07 Hawking, visible
08 Cerenkov, gamma ray, infrared, ionizing
09 black body
10 background, black light, insolation, microwaves, radio waves, synchroton
11 ultraviolet
12 beta particle
13 alpha particle
14 bremsstrahlung
15 electromagnetic

• radiation unit

03 rad, rem, rep

radical

03 rad, red **04** amyl, aryl, dyad, root **05** allyl, basic, butyl, cetyl, group, hexad, hexyl, monad, rebel, total, triad, utter, vinyl, yippy **06** acetyl, benzal, benzil, benzyl, entire, heptad, innate, ligand, methyl, native, pentad, phenyl, propyl, tetrad, yippie **07** benzoyl, carbene, drastic, extreme, fanatic, Jacobin, natural, oxonium, primary, radicle **08** absolute, ammonium, carbonyl, carboxyl, complete, glyceryl, glycosyl, hydroxyl, inherent, left-wing, militant, original, profound, reformer, sweeping, thorough **09** elemental, essential, extremist, fanatical, intrinsic, isopropyl, primitive, reformist **10** deep-seated, elementary, exhaustive, nitro-group, rebellious, vinylidene **11** benzylidine, far-reaching, fundamental, methyl group, phosphonium, rudimentary **13** comprehensive, ferricyanogen, ferrocyanogen, revolutionary, thoroughgoing **14** fundamentalist

radio

08 wireless

Radio stations include:

03 LBC, XFM
04 Kiss
06 Jazz FM, Kiss FM, Radio 1, Radio 2, Radio 3, Radio 4
09 Five Live
09 BBC London, Capital FM, Classic FM, Radio Five, Talksport
11 Virgin Radio

12 World Service
13 Radio Caroline, Radio Scotland
15 Radio Luxembourg

Radio programmes include:

02 PM
04 ITMA
05 Today
10 HomeTruths, The Archers, Woman's Hour
11 Just a Minute, You and Yours
12 Any Questions?, Poetry Please, Start the Week
13 Book at Bedtime, Pick of the Week, Round the Horne, The World at One
14 Brain of Britain
15 It's That Man Again

See also **quiz**

• on the radio

◇ *homophone indicator*
02 DJ **10** disc jockey
• radio presenter
02 DJ **10** disc jockey

Radio presenters include:

04 Mayo (Simon), Peel (John), Ross (Jonathan), Tong (Pete)
05 Cooke (Alistair), Evans (Chris), Stern (Howard), Vance (Tommy), Wogan (Terry), Young (Sir Jimmy)
06 Harris (Bob), Jensen (Kid), Lamacq (Steve), Lamarr (Mark), Lawley (Sue), Moyles (Chris), Murray (Jenni), Savile (Sir Jimmy), Travis (Dave Lee), Walker (Johnnie), Whiley (Jo), Wright (Steve)
07 Edmonds (Noel), Everett (Kenny), Freeman (Alan 'Fluff'), Keillor (Garrison), Kershaw (Andy), Pickles (Wilfred), Plomley (Roy), Redhead (Brian), Tarrant (Chris)
08 Anderson (Marjorie), Campbell (Nicky), Humphrys (John), Metcalfe (Jean), Westwood (Tim)
09 Blackburn (Tony), MacGregor (Sue), Radcliffe (Mark)
10 Gambaccini (Paul), Hardcastle (William)
11 Nightingale (Annie)

radioactive

03 hot

radish

05 mooli, runch **06** daikon **08** Raphanus

radium

02 Ra

radon

02 Rn

raffish

04 loud **05** cheap, gaudy, gross, showy **06** casual, coarse, flashy, garish, jaunty, rakish, sporty, tawdry, trashy, vulgar **07** dashing, uncouth **08** bohemian, careless, improper **09** dissolute, tasteless **10** dissipated, flamboyant **12** devil-may-care, disreputable, meretricious

raffle

04 draw **05** notch, sweep **06** jumble,

lumber, rabble, tangle **07** crumple, lottery, rubbish, tombola **08** riff-raff **10** sweepstake

raft

04 heap **05** balsa, crowd, float **09** catamaran **11** Carley float

rag

◇ *anagram indicator*
03 kid, lap, rib, row, tat **04** bait, duds, flag, fray, goof, haze, jeer, mock, sail, slut, tatt **05** argue, cloth, clout, lapje, scold, scrap, shred, taunt, tease, towel **06** badger, banter, duster, lappie, tagrag, tatter, wallop **07** duddery, flannel, garment, remnant, torment, wrangle **08** farthing, ridicule **09** newspaper, schmutter **10** floorcloth, paper money, raggedness **12** handkerchief

See also **newspaper**

• bunch of rags

03 mop

ragamuffin

04 waif **05** gamin, ragga **06** urchin **11** guttersnipe **14** tatterdemalion **15** tatterdemallion

ragbag

03 mix **04** olio **05** salad **06** jumble, medley **07** mixture **08** mishmash, pastiche, slattern **09** confusion, potpourri **10** assemblage, assortment, hodgepodge, hotchpotch, miscellany **11** olla-podrida **14** omnium-gatherum

rage

◇ *anagram indicator*
03 ire **04** bait, bate, bayt, fume, fury, ramp, rant, rave, tear **05** anger, craze, flame, flood, go mad, mania, paddy, party, radge, storm, vogue, wrath **06** ardour, frenzy, raving, see red, seethe, temper, tumult **07** bluster, explode, madness, passion, rampage, tantrum, thunder, violent **08** boil over, paroxysm, violence **09** blow a fuse, do your nut, raise hell, spit blood **10** hit the roof, paddy-whack **11** blow a gasket, blow your top, flip your lid, go up the wall, lose your rag **12** blow your cool, lose your cool, spit feathers **14** foam at the mouth **15** fly off the handle, go off the deep end

• all the rage

02 in **03** now **04** cool **06** trendy **07** in vogue, popular, stylish **08** the craze **10** the in thing **11** fashionable

ragged

◇ *anagram indicator*
04 poor, rag'd, rent, torn **05** duddy, holey, ragde, rough, tatty **06** duddie, frayed, jagged, raguly, ripped, rugged, shabby, shaggy, tagrag, uneven, untidy **07** erratic, in holes, notched, scruffy, tattery, unkempt, worn-out **08** indented, indigent, serrated, tattered **09** destitute, in tatters, irregular **10** down and out, down-at-heel, fragmented, straggling, threadbare **12** disorganized

14 tatterdemalion **15** falling to pieces, tatterdemallion

raging
03 mad **04** amok, wild **05** amuck, angry, irate, rabid **06** fuming, ireful, raving, stormy **07** enraged, furious, violent **08** flagrant, frenzied, furibund, incensed, seething, wrathful **09** turbulent **10** infuriated, tumultuous **11** fulminating

raid
02 do **04** bust, loot, pull, road, rode, rush, sack **05** blitz, foray, onset, rifle, sally, storm, swoop **06** assail, attack, podrag, charge, forage, hold-up, inroad, invade, maraud, sortie, strike **07** air raid, assault, break-in, descent, pillage, plunder, ram-raid, ransack, robbery, set upon, spreagh **08** dawn raid, invasion **09** break into, descend on, excursion, incursion, onslaught, sneak-raid **12** Baedeker raid

raider
05 crook, shark, thief **06** looter, pirate, robber, viking **07** brigand, invader, villain **08** attacker, criminal, marauder, pillager **09** plunderer, ransacker

rail
03 bar **04** flow, gush, jeer, mock, rung, sora, spar **05** abuse, cloak, decry, raile, rayle, scoff **06** attack, banter, Rallus, revile **07** arraign, censure, garment, inveigh, protest, upbraid **08** denounce, reviling, ridicule **09** castigate, criticize, fulminate **10** slang-whang, vituperate, vociferate **11** neckerchief

railing
04 rail **05** fence, rails **06** paling, pulpit **07** barrier, fencing, manrope, parapet, pushpit **08** parclose, raillery **09** fireguard **10** balustrade

raillery
04 joke **05** chaff, irony, sport **06** banter, joking, satire **07** jeering, jesting, kidding, mockery, ragging, railing, ribbing, teasing **08** badinage, diatribe, dicacity, repartee, ridicule **09** chiacking, invective **10** persiflage, pleasantry

railway
02 Ry **03** rly, Rwy **04** line, rail **05** rails, track **08** railroad

See also **train**

• **railway station**

See also **London**

rain
03 wet **04** pelt, pour, roke, sile, smir, smur, spet, spit, teem, weep **05** blash, brash, raine, reign, smirr, storm, water **06** bucket, deluge, mizzle, shower, squall, volley **07** drizzle, skiffle, torrent **08** down-come, downfall, downpour, pour down, rainfall, sprinkle **09** raindrops, rainstorm, sunshower **10** bucket down, cloudburst, Scotch mist, tipple down **12** thunderstorm **13** precipitation, the clouds open **15** rain cats and dogs

rainbow
03 arc, bow **04** arch, iris **05** prism **06** bruise, dew-bow, fog-bow, irised, sunbow **07** moon-bow **08** irisated, spectral, spectrum **09** arc-en-ciel, prismatic, steelhead, water gall **10** iridescent, opalescent, variegated, weather gaw **11** rainbow-like, weather gall **13** kaleidoscopic

raincoat
03 mac **04** mack, mino **08** Burberry® **09** macintosh **10** mackintosh

rainy
03 wet **04** damp, soft **05** moist

06 hyetal, watery **07** drizzly, pluvial, showery **08** pluviose, pluvious **09** inclement

raise
◊ *reversal indicator*
02 up **03** get **04** buoy, grow, jack, levy, lift, moot, rear, rise, stir **05** amass, boost, breed, build, cairn, cause, elate, erect, evoke, exalt, extol, hoist, leave, mount, put up, rally, rouse, set up, utter, weigh **06** araise, arayse, arouse, broach, bump up, create, excite, gather, hike up, hold up, jack up, lift up, muster, obtain, push up, step up, stir up, take up, uplift **07** advance, amplify, augment, bring up, collect, develop, educate, elevate, enhance, heave up, magnify, nurture, present, produce, provoke, recruit, suggest, upgrade **08** activate, assemble, escalate, heighten, increase, purchase **09** construct, cultivate, establish, institute, intensify, introduce, propagate **10** accumulate, give rise to, put forward, strengthen **11** get together

raised
◊ *reversal down indicator*
05 cameo **06** relief **07** applied, relievo **08** appliqué, elevated, embossed

rake
03 hoe **04** comb, hunt, roam, roué **05** amass, graze, level, rifle, scour, slope, track **06** gather, gay dog, harrow, lecher, scrape, search, smooth, strafe, straff, string, wanton **07** collect, incline, journey, pasture, playboy, ransack, rummage, scratch, swinger **08** buckrake, hedonist, Lothario, muck-rake, prodigal, rakehell **09** debauchee, dissolute, horse rake, libertine **10** accumulate, degenerate, profligate, sensualist **11** spendthrift, stubble rake **14** pleasure-seeker
• **rake in**
03 net **04** earn, make, reap **05** fetch, gross **06** haul in, pull in **07** bring in, get paid, receive
• **rake up**
05 dig up, raise **06** drag up, remind, revive **07** bring up, mention **08** dredge up **09** introduce

rake-off
03 cut **04** part **05** share, slice **07** portion **10** percentage, proportion

rakish
05 loose, natty, sharp, smart **06** breezy, casual, dapper, flashy, jaunty, sinful, snazzy, sporty **07** dashing, immoral, raffish, stylish **08** debonair, depraved, prodigal **09** abandoned, debauched, dissolute, lecherous, libertine **10** degenerate, dissipated, flamboyant, licentious, nonchalant, profligate **11** adventurous **12** devil-may-care

rally
04 demo, rely **05** group, march, unite **06** banter, gather, morcha, muster, perk up, pick up, really, reform, revive, summon **07** collect, convene, get well, improve, marshal, meeting, recover,

regroup, renewal, reunion, revival, round up **08** assemble, assembly, comeback, jamboree, mobilize, organize, recovery **09** gathering, get better, re-enforce **10** assemblage, bounce back, conference, congregate, convention, reassemble, recuperate, reorganize, resurgence **11** be on the mend, convocation, get together, improvement, mass meeting, pull through **12** band together, come together, gain strength, recuperation **13** bring together, demonstration

ram
03 hit, jam, pun, tup **04** beat, bump, butt, cram, dash, drum, pack, slam, stem, tamp **05** Aries, crash, crowd, drive, force, pound, smash, stuff, wedge **06** corvus, hammer, punner, strike, thrust, wether **07** block up, squeeze **08** compress

ramble
◊ *anagram indicator*
03 gas, jaw **04** hike, roam, rove, tour, trek, trip, walk, wind **05** amble, drift, jaunt, range, stray, tramp, troll **06** babble, dodder, natter, rabbit, stroll, waffle, wander, wanton, witter, zigzag **07** blather, blether, chatter, digress, diverge, meander, saunter, traipse **08** bushwalk, rabbit on, straggle, witter on **09** excursion, expatiate **15** go off at a tangent

rambler
05 hiker, rover **06** roamer, walker **07** drifter **08** stroller, wanderer, wayfarer **09** saunterer, traveller **10** bushwalker

rambling
◊ *anagram indicator*
05 wordy **06** errant, vagary **07** verbose **08** errantry, trailing **09** desultory, excursive, sprawling, spreading, wandering **10** circuitous, digressive, disjointed, incoherent, long-winded, roundabout, straggling **12** disconnected, long-drawn-out, periphrastic **14** skimble-skamble

rami
04 rhea **10** China grass, grass cloth

ramification
04 limb **06** branch, effect, result, sequel, upshot **07** outcome **08** offshoot **09** branching, outgrowth **11** consequence, development, implication **12** complication, divarication

ramp
03 rob **04** rage, rise, romp **05** climb, grade, slope **06** ramson, snatch, tomboy **07** incline, swindle **08** gradient **09** acclivity, declivity

rampage
◊ *anagram indicator*
04 fury, rage, rant, rave, rush, tear **05** storm **06** charge, frenzy, furore, mayhem, uproar **07** run amok, run riot, run wild, turmoil **08** violence **09** go berserk **10** rush wildly **11** destruction **13** rush violently

• **on the rampage**
◊ *anagram indicator*
04 amok, wild **06** wildly **07** berserk, violent **08** frenzied **09** in a frenzy, violently **12** out of control

rampant
◊ *anagram indicator*
◊ *reversal indicator*
04 rank, rife, wild **06** fierce, raging, wanton **07** profuse, rearing, riotous, violent **08** epidemic, pandemic **09** excessive, out of hand, prevalent, unbridled, unchecked **10** widespread **12** high-spirited, out of control, uncontrolled, unrestrained

rampart
04 bank, fort, ring, wall **05** fence, guard **06** abatis, vallum **07** abattis, bastion, bulwark, defence, parapet, rampire **08** security **09** barricade, earthwork **10** breastwork, embankment, stronghold **13** fortification

ramshackle
◊ *anagram indicator*
05 shaky **06** flimsy, ruined, unsafe **07** rickety, run-down **08** decrepit, derelict, unsteady **09** crumbling, neglected, tottering **10** broken-down, jerry-built, tumbledown **11** dilapidated

ranch
04 farm, tear **05** range **06** estate, spread **07** fazenda, station **08** estancia, hacienda, property **09** dude ranch **10** plantation **12** sheep station **13** cattle station

rancid
03 bad, off **04** foul, high, rank, sour **05** fetid, frowy, musty, stale **06** foetid, frowie, putrid, rotten, turned **07** froughy, noisome, noxious **08** overripe **10** malodorous, unpleasant

rancorous
06 bitter **07** acerbic, hostile **08** spiteful, vengeful, venomous, virulent **09** malignant, resentful, splenetic **10** implacable, malevolent, vindictive **11** acrimonious

rancour
04 hate **05** spite, venom **06** animus, enmity, grudge, hatred, malice, spleen **07** ill-will **08** acrimony, sourness **09** animosity, antipathy, hostility, malignity, virulence **10** bitterness, ill-feeling, resentment **11** malevolence **13** resentfulness **14** vindictiveness

rand
01 R

random
◊ *anagram indicator*
04 spot, wild **05** stray **06** casual, chance **07** aimless, freedom **08** sporadic **09** arbitrary, desultory, haphazard, hit-or-miss, irregular, unplanned **10** accidental, at a venture, fortuitous, hit-and-miss, hitty-missy, incidental, stochastic, unarranged **11** purposeless, scattershot

12 uncontrolled, unmethodical, unsystematic **13** serendipitous **14** indiscriminate
● **at random**
◇ *anagram indicator*
06 hobnob **07** at large **08** at rovers, randomly **09** aimlessly, haphazard **11** arbitrarily, haphazardly, irregularly **12** fortuitously, incidentally, sporadically **13** purposelessly **14** unmethodically **15** à tort et à travers

randomly
◇ *anagram indicator*
08 at random **09** aimlessly **11** arbitrarily, haphazardly, irregularly **12** incidentally, sporadically **13** purposelessly **14** unmethodically

randy
03 hot **04** sexy **05** horny, rudas **06** virago **07** amorous, aroused, goatish, lustful, raunchy, satyric **08** turned-on **09** lecherous **10** boisterous, lascivious **12** concupiscent

range
02 go **03** ren, rin, row, run **04** area, file, kind, line, oven, raik, rank, roam, rove, sort, span, type, vary **05** align, amble, array, carry, chain, class, cover, drift, field, gamut, genus, grade, grass, group, level, orbit, order, reach, ridge, scale, scope, stove, stray, sweep **06** bounds, cooker, domain, draw up, extend, extent, limits, line up, meadow, radius, ramble, series, sierra, sphere, spread, string, stroll, wander **07** arrange, compass, dispose, earshot, grazing, paddock, pasture, purview, species, stretch, variety **08** classify, confines, distance, latitude, province, spectrum **09** amplitude, catalogue, diversity, fluctuate, grassland, pasturage, selection **10** assortment, categorize, cordillera, parameters, pigeonhole, straighten **11** grazing land **12** distribution
See also **mountain**
● **range over**
04 scur, sker **05** skirr **06** squirr

rangy
05 lanky, leggy, roomy, weedy **06** skinny **08** gangling, rawboned **10** long-legged, long-limbed **11** mountainous

rank
03 row **04** état, file, foul, gree, line, lush, mark, nobs, rate, sort, tier, type, vile **05** acrid, align, caste, class, dense, élite, fetid, grade, gross, group, level, lords, lusty, order, peers, place, range, sheer, stale, toffs, total, utter **06** arrant, coarse, column, degree, draw up, estate, family, foetid, gentry, line up, nobles, putrid, rancid, series, status, string, strong **07** arrange, blatant, dispose, echelon, glaring, peerage, profuse, pungent, station, stratum, swollen, utterly, violent **08** absolute, abundant, classify, complete, division,

flagrant, mephitic, nobility, organize, position, shocking, standing, stinking, thorough, vigorous **09** condition, downright, formation, luxuriant, offensive, out-and-out, overgrown, repulsive, revolting, violently **10** categorize, disgusting, graveolent, malodorous, outrageous, unpleasant **11** aristocracy, high society, unmitigated, unqualified **12** disagreeable, evil-smelling **14** classification

Air force ranks:
05 major
07 captain, colonel, general
08 corporal, sergeant
10 air marshal
11 aircraftman
12 air commodore, aircraftsman, group captain, major general, pilot officer
13 aircraftwoman, flying officer, wing commander
14 aircraftswoman, air vice-marshal, flight sergeant, squadron leader, warrant officer
15 air chief marshal, first lieutenant
16 brigadier general, flight lieutenant, second lieutenant
17 lieutenant colonel, lieutenant general
19 leading aircraftsman
20 general of the air force
21 leading aircraftswoman
25 marshal of the Royal Air Force

Army ranks:
05 major
07 captain, colonel, general, marshal, private
08 corporal, sergeant
09 brigadier
10 bombardier, lieutenant
12 field marshal, major general
13 lance-corporal, staff sergeant
14 warrant officer
15 first-lieutenant, lance-bombardier
16 brigadier-general, general of the army, second-lieutenant
17 lieutenant colonel, lieutenant-general

Naval ranks:
06 ensign, rating, seaman
07 admiral, captain
09 captain RN, commander, commodore
10 able seaman, lieutenant, midshipman
11 rear admiral, vice-admiral
12 fleet admiral, petty officer
13 leading seaman, sublieutenant
14 warrant officer
16 commodore admiral
17 admiral of the fleet, chief petty officer
19 lieutenant-commander
21 lieutenant junior grade

See also **nobility**; **police**
● **other ranks**
02 OR

● **rank and file**
03 mob **04** herd **05** crowd, plebs **06** masses, proles, rabble **08** populace, riff-raff, soldiers **09** hoi polloi **10** grassroots **11** ordinary men, proletariat **12** common people **15** private soldiers

rankle
03 bug, irk, vex **04** gall, rile **05** anger, annoy, peeve **06** fester, nettle, poison **08** embitter, irritate **11** get your goat **13** get on your wick, get up your nose, get your back up **14** get your blood up **15** get on your nerves

rank-smelling
04 olid

ransack
04 comb, fish, hunt, loot, raid, rake, ripe, sack **05** harry, rifle, scour, strip **06** maraud, ravage, search **07** despoil, pillage, plunder, rummage **09** depredate, devastate, go through, ranshakle **10** ranshackle **13** turn inside out **14** rummage through, turn upside down

ransom
04 free **05** atone, money, price **06** buy off, pay-off, redeem, rescue **07** deliver, freedom, payment, release, set free **08** liberate **09** atonement **10** liberation, redemption **11** deliverance, restoration, setting free **15** buy the freedom of

rant
03 cry **04** rand, rave, roar, yell **05** mouth, shout, storm **06** bellow, crying, tirade **07** bluster, bombast, declaim, oration, roaring, yelling **08** diatribe, harangue, rhetoric, shouting, tear a cat, tub-thump **09** hold forth, philippic **10** slangwhang, tear the cat, vociferate **11** declamation, rant and rave **12** vociferation

rap
03 hit, pan, tap **04** bang, blow, clip, cuff, flak, grab, knap, rail, slam, whit, wrap **05** blame, boost, clout, crime, flick, flirt, knock, ragga, scold, slate, stick, swear, thump, whack **06** batter, hammer, hip-hop, patter, punish, rattle, rebuke, snatch, strike, yanker **07** censure, commend, gangsta, reprove, run down, slating, testify **08** knocking, slamming **09** castigate, criticize, reprimand **10** come down on, punishment **11** acclamation, castigation, pick holes in **12** pull to pieces, tear to pieces, tear to shreds
● **take the rap**
08 pay for it **10** be punished **12** face the music, take the blame **14** get it in the neck

rapacious
06 greedy **07** preying, wolfish, wolvish **08** esurient, grasping, ravening, ravenous, uncaring, usurious **09** marauding, predatory, voracious, vulturine, vulturish, vulturous

10 avaricious, insatiable, plundering **12** extortionate
• **rapacious person**
04 kite

rapacity
05 greed, usury **07** avarice, avidity **08** voracity **09** esurience, esuriency, vulturism **10** greediness **11** wolfishness **12** graspingness, ravenousness **13** predatoriness, rapaciousness, shark's manners, voraciousness **14** insatiableness

rape
03 rob **04** loot, raid, sack **05** abuse, navew, strip **06** defile, rapine, ravage, ravish **07** assault, despoil, looting, outrage, pillage, plunder, ransack, sacking, seizure, violate, vitiate **08** coleseed, date rape, deflower, gang rape, gang-rape, maltreat, ravaging, spoliate, violence **09** depredate, devastate, stripping, transport, violation **10** defilement, plundering, ransacking, ravishment, spoliation **11** depredation, devastation **12** despoliation, maltreatment **13** sexual assault, statutory rape **15** assault sexually

rapid
03 pdq **04** fast **05** brisk, chute, hasty, nifty, quick, shoot, shute, swift, zippy **06** lively, prompt, speedy **07** express, hurried, stickle **08** headlong **09** splitting **11** expeditious, precipitate **13** like lightning **15** pretty damn quick

rapidity
04 rush **05** haste, hurry, speed **08** alacrity, celerity, dispatch, velocity **09** briskness, fleetness, quickness, swiftness **10** expedition, promptness, speediness **11** promptitude **15** expeditiousness, precipitateness

rapidly
04 fast **05** quick **06** pronto **07** briskly, hastily, like fun, quickly, swiftly **08** promptly, speedily **09** hurriedly **11** at the double, like winking **12** a mile a minute, lickety-split **13** expeditiously, precipitately **14** at a rate of knots, hell for leather **15** like the clappers

rapine
04 prey, rage, raid, rape **05** raven, ravin **06** ravine **07** looting, sacking, seizure **08** ravaging **09** stripping, transport, violation **10** defilement, plundering, ransacking, ravishment, spoliation **11** depredation, devastation **12** despoliation

rapport
04 bond, link **07** empathy, harmony **08** affinity, relation, sympathy **10** connection **12** relationship **13** understanding

rapprochement
07 détente, reunion **09** agreement, softening **13** harmonization, reconcilement **14** reconciliation

rapt
06 intent, way-out **07** charmed,

gripped **08** abducted, absorbed, ecstatic, ravished, snatched, thrilled **09** bewitched, delighted, enchanted, engrossed, entranced **10** captivated, enraptured, enthralled, fascinated, spellbound **11** preoccupied, rhapsodical, transported **12** concentrated

rapture
03 joy **05** bliss **07** delight, ecstasy, elation **08** euphoria, felicity, paroxysm **09** cloud nine, happiness, transport **10** enragement, exaltation **11** delectation, enchantment **12** exhilaration **13** seventh heaven, top of the world
• **go into raptures**
04 fire, gush, rave **05** drool **06** excite, praise **07** enthuse, inspire **08** motivate **10** bubble over, effervesce, wax lyrical

rapturous
05 happy **06** joyful, joyous **07** exalted **08** blissful, ecstatic, euphoric, ravished **09** delighted, entranced, overjoyed, rhapsodic **11** dithyrambic, on cloud nine, over the moon, tickled pink, transported **12** enthusiastic **15** in seventh heaven, on top of the world

rare
◇ *anagram indicator*
04 seld, thin **05** early **06** choice, geason, scarce, sparse, superb **07** curious, unusual **08** precious, sporadic, superior, uncommon **09** excellent, exquisite, matchless, recherché, underdone **10** far between, infrequent, remarkable **11** exceptional, outstanding, superlative **12** incomparable, like gold dust, unparalleled **13** extraordinary, one in a million **15** thin on the ground

rarefied
04 high, thin **05** noble **06** select, subtle **07** private, refined, special, sublime, tenuous **08** esoteric, tenuious **09** exclusive **10** attenuated

rarely
04 seld **06** hardly, little, seldom **08** choicely, scarcely **10** hardly ever, once in a way **12** infrequently, occasionally, once in a while, scarcely ever, sporadically **13** spasmodically **14** intermittently **15** once in a blue moon

raring
04 keen **05** eager, ready **07** itching, longing, willing **09** desperate, impatient **12** enthusiastic

rarity
03 gem **04** find **05** curio, pearl **06** marvel, wonder **08** scarcity, shortage, thinness, treasure **09** curiosity, nonpareil **10** sparseness **11** infrequency, strangeness, unusualness **12** uncommonness **14** collector's item

rascal
03 imp **04** loon, lown **05** devil, lorel, losel, lowne, rogue, scamp, skelm,

smaik **06** lozell, rabble, schelm, skelum, tinker, toerag, varlet **07** a bad hat, cullion, hallian, hallion, hallyon, knavish, lorrell, skellum, villain, wastrel **08** scalawag, schellum, spalpeen, vagabond, wretched **09** rascaille, scallawag, scallywag, scoundrel, skeesicks, son of a gun **10** ne'er-do-well, rascallion, scapegrace **11** rapscallion **13** mischief-maker **14** good-for-nothing, two-for-his-heels

rascally
03 bad, low **04** base, evil, mean **06** arrant, wicked **07** crooked, hangman, knavish, roguish, vicious **09** dishonest, reprobate **10** villainous **11** furciferous, mischievous, scoundrelly **12** disreputable, unscrupulous **14** good-for-nothing

rash
◇ *anagram indicator*
03 run **04** dash, drag, fast, itch, rush, tear, wave **05** flood, hasty, heady, hives, slash, spate, stick **06** deluge, madcap, plague, series, unwary **07** rosacea, roseola, torrent **08** careless, epidemic, eruption, headlong, heat rash, heedless, madbrain, outbreak, reckless, temerous **09** audacious, dare-devil, foolhardy, hot-headed, impetuous, imprudent, impulsive, over-hasty, pompholyx, premature, unguarded, urticaria **10** headstrong, ill advised, indiscreet, irritation, madbrained, nettlerash, unthinking **11** adventurous, furthersome, hare-brained, harum-scarum, hasty-witted, precipitate, temerarious **13** ill-considered, inconsiderate

rashly
07 hastily **08** headlong, unwarily **09** on impulse **10** carelessly, heedlessly, recklessly **11** audaciously, impetuously, imprudently, impulsively, over-hastily **12** indiscreetly **15** without thinking

rashness
08 audacity, hazardry, temerity **09** brashness, hastiness, incaution **10** imprudence **12** carelessness, heedlessness, indiscretion, precipitance, precipitancy, recklessness **13** foolhardiness, impulsiveness, precipitation **14** incautiousness **15** adventurousness, thoughtlessness

rasp
03 bug, jar, rub **04** file, risp, sand **05** croak, grate, grind, peeve, scour **06** abrade, cackle, scrape, squawk **07** grating, scratch, screech **08** grinding, irritate **09** excoriate, harshness, raspberry **10** hoarseness **15** get on your nerves

rasping
05 gruff, harsh, husky, raspy, rough **06** croaky, filing, hoarse **07** grating, jarring, raucous **08** creaking, croaking, gravelly, scratchy **10** stridulant

rat

03 rot, spy **04** blab, blow, fink, mole, nark, nose, shop, sing, stag, vole **05** dob on, grass, hutia, Judas, peach, puppy, sneak, snout, split **06** agouta, betray, canary, finger, fizgig, gopher, inform, ratton, rumble, snitch, squeal, tell on **07** peacher, stoolie, traitor **08** approver, Arvicola, betrayer, denounce, informer, musk-cavy, promoter, renegade, sand mole, snitcher, squeaker, squealer, tell-tale, turncoat **09** bandicoot, informant, sycophant, water vole, whisperer **10** discoverer, supergrass **11** incriminate, stool pigeon **12** cutting grass **13** strike-breaker, whistle-blower

rate

03 fee, MPH, pay, ret, sum, tax **04** cess, cost, deem, duty, hire, mode, pace, rank, time, toll **05** allot, basis, chide, class, count, grade, judge, merit, price, prize, ratio, scale, scold, speed, sum up, tempo, value, weigh, worth **06** admire, amount, assess, charge, degree, esteem, extent, figure, manner, rating, reckon, regard, tariff **07** adjudge, deserve, justify, measure, payment, reprove, respect, tallage, warrant, weigh up **08** appraise, classify, consider, estimate, evaluate, relation, standard, velocity **09** calculate **10** worthy of, categorize, estimation, percentage, proportion **12** be entitled to, have a right to

See also **scold**

• **at any rate**

05 at all **06** anyhow, anyway **07** at least **09** in any case **10** at the least, in any event, regardless **12** nevertheless

rather

03 gay, gey, yes **04** a bit, more, some, very **05** quite **06** a bit of, fairly, indeed, pretty, sooner, sort of **07** a little, instead **08** by choice, slightly, somewhat **09** for choice **10** from choice, moderately, much rather, much sooner, noticeably, preferably, relatively **12** by preference, to some degree, to some extent **13** for preference, significantly

ratification

08 approval **10** validation **11** affirmation, endorsement **12** confirmation **13** authorization, certification, corroboration **14** authentication, seal of approval **15** stamp of approval

ratify

02 OK **04** amen, seal, sign **06** affirm, strike, uphold **07** agree to, approve, certify, confirm, endorse, warrant **08** legalize, sanction, validate **09** authorize, establish, preconize **10** homologate **11** corroborate, countersign **12** authenticate

rating

02 AB **04** mark, rank **05** class, grade, order, score **06** degree, status **07** grading, placing, ranking, set-down **08** category, position, standing **09** adjudging, appraisal **10** assessment, evaluation **14** classification

ratio

04 rate **05** index **07** balance, portion **08** fraction, quotient, relation, symmetry **09** allowance **10** percentage, proportion **11** correlation **12** relationship **14** correspondence

ration

03 lot **04** food, part, save **05** allot, issue, limit, point, quota, share **06** amount, budget, stores, supply, viands **07** control, deal out, dole out, hand out, helping, measure, mete out, portion **08** allocate, conserve, dispense, restrict, supplies, victuals **09** allotment, allowance, apportion, divide out **10** allocation, distribute, foodstuffs, iron ration, measure out, percentage, proportion, provisions **11** compo ration

rational

04 sane, wice, wise **05** lucid, sober, sound **06** normal **07** logical, prudent **08** balanced, cerebral, grounded, sensible, thinking **09** cognitive, judicious, realistic, reasoning, sagacious **10** Apollonian, discursive, reasonable **11** circumspect, clear-headed, enlightened, intelligent, well-founded **12** intellectual **13** philosophical, ratiocinative **15** in your right mind

rationale

05 basis, logic **06** motive, reason, theory, thesis **07** grounds, purpose, reasons **09** principle, reasoning **10** hypothesis, motivation, philosophy **11** explanation, raison d'être

rationalization

06 excuse **08** excusing, updating **11** explanation, vindication **12** streamlining **13** justification, modernization **14** reorganization

rationalize

04 trim **06** excuse, update **07** explain, justify **09** cut back on, modernize, vindicate **10** account for, pragmatize, reorganize, streamline **11** cut out waste, explain away

rationally

06 sanely **07** lucidly **08** sensibly **09** logically, prudently **10** reasonably, thinkingly **11** judiciously, sagaciously, without bias **13** intelligently **15** philosophically

rattle

◇ *anagram indicator*

03 jar, rap **04** bang, bump, faze, jolt, reel, tirl **05** alarm, clang, clank, clink, knock, shake, upset **06** bounce, hurtle, jangle, jingle, put off, put out, racket, ruckle **07** clapper, clatter, confuse, disturb, fluster, jarring, jolting, shaking, sistrum, unnerve, vibrate **08** clanking, clinking, irritate, unsettle **09** crepitate,

vibration **10** disconcert **13** tintinnabulum **15** throw off balance

• **rattle off**

04 list **06** recite, repeat **07** reel off **10** run through **11** list quickly

• **rattle on**

03 gab **04** yack **05** prate **06** cackle, gabble, jabber, natter, witter **07** blether, chatter, chunter, prattle **08** rabbit on

ratty

05 angry, cross, short, testy **06** peeved, snappy, touchy, untidy **07** annoyed, crabbed, grouchy, unkempt **08** wretched **09** impatient, irritable **13** short-tempered

raucous

04 loud **05** harsh, husky, noisy, rough, rusty, sharp **06** hoarse, raucid, shrill **07** grating, jarring, rasping **08** piercing, strident **10** discordant, scratching, screeching **11** ear-piercing

raunchy

04 lewd, sexy **05** bawdy **06** earthy, erotic, nubile, shabby, slinky **07** sensual **08** alluring, arousing, inviting **09** desirable, provoking, salacious, seductive **10** attractive, suggestive, voluptuous **11** flirtatious, provocative, stimulating, titillating **12** pornographic

ravage

◇ *anagram indicator*

04 loot, raze, ruin, sack **05** harry, havoc, level, spoil, wreck **06** damage, maraud **07** despoil, destroy, looting, pillage, plunder **08** demolish, lay waste, wreckage **09** depredate, devastate, ruination **10** desolation, ransacking, spoliation **11** depredation, destruction, devastation **12** despoliation, leave in ruins

ravaged

◇ *anagram indicator*

06 spoilt **07** war-torn, war-worn, wrecked **08** desolate **09** destroyed, ransacked, shattered, war-wasted **10** battle-torn, devastated

rave

◇ *anagram indicator*

02 do **03** cry **04** bash, fume, hail, orgy, rage, rant, roar, yell **05** crazy, disco, extol, go ape, go mad, party, shout, storm, taver **06** babble, bellow, blow up, jabber, ramble, rave-up, see red, seethe, sizzle, taiver **07** acclaim, blow-out, enthuse, explode, knees-up, thunder **08** boil over, carousal, ecstatic, freak out, praising **09** blow a fuse, do your nut, excellent, go bananas, go berserk, laudatory, raise hell, rapturous, wonderful **10** be mad about, favourable, hit the roof, talk wildly, wax lyrical **11** blow a gasket, blow your top, celebration, flip your lid, go up the wall, have kittens, infatuation, lose your rag, rant and rave **12** blow your cool, enthusiastic, fly into a rage, lose your cool, throw a wobbly **13** throw a tantrum **14** acid-house party, foam at the mouth, go into raptures, lose your temper **15** fly off the handle, get all steamed up, go off the deep end

raven
03 jet **04** Grip, inky, prey **05** black, crake, dusky, ebony, ravin, sable **06** corbie, rapine **07** preying **08** jet-black **09** coal-black

ravenous
06 greedy, hungry **07** starved, wolfish, wolvish **08** famished, starving **09** rapacious, voracious **10** insatiable, plundering, very hungry

rave-up
02 do **04** bash, orgy **05** party **06** thrash **07** blow-out, debauch, shindig **08** carousal **11** celebration

ravine
03 gap, lin **04** gill, khor, khud, linn, nala, pass, prey **05** abyss, cañon, chine, flume, ghyll, gorge, goyle, grike, gryke, gulch, gully, heuch, heugh, kloof, nalla, nulla **06** arroyo, canyon, clough, coulée, gullet, gulley, nallah, nullah, rapine **07** preying **09** purgatory

See also **gorge**

raving
◊ *anagram indicator*
03 mad **04** wild **05** barmy, batty, crazy, loony, loopy **06** insane, maniac, mental **07** berserk, furious **08** demented, deranged, frenzied **09** delirious **10** barking mad, frantic-mad, hysterical, irrational, unbalanced **12** round the bend **13** out of your mind, round the twist

ravings
06 drivel, yammer **07** prattle, rubbish, twaddle **08** nonsense **09** gibberish **10** balderdash, mumbo-jumbo **12** gobbledygook

ravish
04 rape **05** abuse, charm, force **06** abduct, defile **07** assault, bewitch, delight, enchant, enthral, oppress, outrage, overjoy, violate **08** entrance, maltreat, stuprate, suppress **09** captivate, enrapture, fascinate, spellbind **11** constuprate **15** assault sexually, force yourself on

ravishing
06 lovely, raping **07** radiant **08** alluring, charming, dazzling, gorgeous, stunning **09** beautiful, seductive **10** bewitching, delightful, enchanting **11** enthralling **12** transporting

raw
03 new, red, wet **04** bare, cold, damp, hard, open, sore **05** basic, bleak, blunt, chill, crude, crudy, cruel, frank, fresh, green, harsh, naive, naked, nippy, plain, rough, wersh **06** biting, bitter, bloody, brutal, callow, candid, chafed, chilly, grazed, strong, tender **07** abraded, exposed, intense, natural, scraped, tartare **08** freezing, ignorant, immature, piercing, uncooked,

ungenial **09** outspoken, realistic, scratched, sensitive, unrefined, unskilled, untrained, untreated, untutored, unwrought **10** excoriated, forthright, true-to-life, unfinished, unprepared **11** unpractised, unprocessed **13** inexperienced

ray
02 re **04** beam, hint, look **05** array, dirty, dress, flash, gleam, glint, manta, roker, shaft, skate, spark, trace **06** defile, glance, streak, stream **07** flicker, glimmer, homelyn, radiate, torpedo, twinkle **09** cramp-fish, thornback **10** indication, sea vampire, suggestion

raze
04 fell, race, rase, ruin **05** erase, graze, level, wreck **06** scrape, slight **07** destroy, flatten **08** bulldoze, demolish, pull down, tear down **09** dismantle, knock down

razor
04 keen **05** sharp **06** shaver **07** precise **09** cut-throat **11** cutting edge

re
03 are, ray **05** about **09** regarding **10** concerning **12** with regard to **14** on the subject of **15** with reference to

reach
03 bay, fax, hit, rax, win **04** call, come, deal, gain, hand, hent, hold, make, pass, ring, shot, span, take **05** ambit, get at, get to, grasp, phone, power, range, retch, scope, seize, touch **06** amount, arrive, attain, come at, come to, extend, extent, go up to, snatch, spread, strike **07** achieve, command, compass, contact, control, get onto, project, speak to, stretch, write to **08** amount to, arrive at, artifice, come up to, continue, distance, go down to, latitude, make it to **09** authority, extension, get hold of, go as far as, influence, telephone **10** come down to, stretch out **12** get through to, jurisdiction **14** get in touch with **15** communicate with

See also **retch**

• reach down
03 dip

• reach out
04 push

react
◊ *anagram indicator*
03 act **04** defy **05** rebel, reply **06** answer, behave, oppose, resist, rise up **07** dissent, respond **08** kick back, retroact **09** retaliate **11** acknowledge, reciprocate

reaction
05 reply, stink **06** answer, recoil, reflex **08** backlash, backwash, feedback, kickback, response, reversal **09** reversion, swing-back **11** retaliation **12** repercussion **13** counteraction, reciprocation **14** antiperistasis, counterbalance **15** acknowledgement

reactionary
◊ *anagram indicator*
◊ *reversal indicator*
06 Junker **07** Bourbon, diehard, redneck **08** mandarin, rightist, Sadducee **09** right-wing, young fogy **10** Neandertal, young fogey **11** Neanderthal, right-winger, traditional **12** conservative, Neandertaler **13** Neanderthaler **14** Neanderthal man, traditionalist **15** backward-looking

read
03 maw, rad **04** look, name, scan, show, skim **05** solve, speak, study, teach, utter **06** advise, browse, decode, glance, look at, peruse, recite, record, saying **07** counsel, declaim, declare, deliver, dip into, display, examine, expound, learned, measure, perusal **08** abomasum, browsing, construe, decipher, indicate, pore over, register, scanning, scrutiny, skimming **09** interpret **10** comprehend, scrutinize, understand **11** leaf through **12** flick through, thumb through **13** browse through **14** interpretation

• read aloud
◊ *homophone indicator*

• read into
05 infer **06** deduce, reason **08** construe **09** interpret **12** misinterpret

readable
05 clear **07** legible **08** gripping **09** enjoyable **10** easy to read **11** captivating, enthralling, interesting, stimulating **12** decipherable, entertaining, intelligible, worth reading **13** unputdownable **14** comprehensible, understandable

reader
06 hearer, lector, taster **08** audience, bookworm, epistler, lectress, lecturer, listener **09** addressee, epistoler, prelector **10** pocketbook **13** bibliophagist

readership
08 audience, regulars **09** following **11** subscribers

readily
04 soon **06** easily, freely, gladly **07** eagerly, happily, lightly, quickly, rapidly, swiftly **08** promptly, smoothly, speedily, with ease **09** willingly **12** effortlessly **14** unhesitatingly

readiness
04 ease **05** alert, skill **07** fitness **08** alacrity, aptitude, facility, gameness, keenness, rapidity **09** eagerness, handiness, quickness **10** promptness **11** inclination, preparation, promptitude, willingness **12** availability, preparedness

• in readiness
05 ready **06** on call **07** at point **08** at a point, at points, prepared **09** available, on standby **10** standing by **11** at all points, on full alert **13** in preparation

reading
04 scan, text **05** piece, study **06** figure, lesson, record **07** display, edition, lection, passage, perusal, recital, section, version **08** browsing, decoding, register, scrutiny **09** rendering, rendition **10** indication, inspection, recitation **11** deciphering, examination, measurement **13** understanding **14** interpretation
• **variant reading**
02 vl

reading-desk
04 ambo **07** lectern

ready
02 go **03** apt, fit, set **04** boun, cash, easy, free, game, keen, near, ripe, yare **05** alert, bound, bowne, close, eager, equip, handy, happy, order, prest, prime, prone, quick, rapid, sharp, swift **06** all set, astute, at hand, clever, direct, on hand, prompt, speedy, to hand **07** about to, address, ad manum, arrange, attired, dressed, forward, pleased, prepare, present, scratch, waiting, willing **08** arranged, disposed, equipped, finished, geared up, hard cash, inclined, liable to, likely to, organize, pregnant, prepared **09** addressed, available, completed, dexterous, fitted out, immediate, organized, psyched up, rigged out **10** accessible, convenient, discerning, perceptive, pernicious, ready money, the needful **11** predisposed, resourceful, within reach **12** enthusiastic, on the point of, on the verge of, unhesitating **14** argent comptant
• **at the ready**
03 set **06** all set, poised **08** prepared **09** mobilized

real
04 rial, ryal, sure, trew, true **05** quite, right, royal, truly, utter, valid **06** actual, dinkum, honest, proper, really, thingy **07** certain, dinki-di, dinky-di, factual, fervent, genuine, sincere **08** absolute, bona fide, complete, concrete, dinky-die, existing, material, official, physical, positive, rightful, tangible, thorough, truthful, unfabled **09** authentic, heartfelt, immovable, occurring, simon-pure, unfeigned, veritable **10** fair dinkum, legitimate, sure-enough, unaffected **11** substantial, substantive **12** from the heart

realign
◇ *anagram indicator*
09 reshuffle **10** straighten

realism
06 sanity **08** saneness **09** actuality **10** naturalism, pragmatism, televérité **11** genuineness, naturalness, rationality **12** authenticity, cinéma vérité, faithfulness, lifelikeness, practicality, sensibleness, truthfulness

realistic
04 real, true **05** close, vivid **07** genuine, graphic, logical, natural

08 detached, faithful, lifelike, rational, real-life, sensible, truthful **09** authentic, hard-nosed, objective, practical, pragmatic **10** figurative, hard-boiled, hard-headed, true-to-life, unromantic, commonsense, down-to-earth, level-headed **12** businesslike, clear-sighted, matter-of-fact **13** unsentimental

realistically
05 truly **07** vividly **08** sensibly **09** genuinely, logically **10** faithfully, rationally, truthfully **11** graphically, objectively, practically **12** figuratively **13** authentically, pragmatically **14** unromantically **15** unsentimentally

reality
04 fact **05** truth **06** effect, verity **07** realism **08** positive, real life, validity **09** actuality, certainty, existence, real world, thingness **10** thinginess **11** genuineness, materiality, tangibility, thingliness **12** authenticity, corporeality **14** substantiality
• **in reality**
05 truly **06** indeed, in fact, really **07** for real, in truth **08** actually **09** in earnest **10** in practice **12** in actual fact, in all but name **13** in point of fact **15** as a matter of fact

realization
04 gain **05** grasp **06** making **07** earning, selling **08** clearing, fetching **09** awareness **10** acceptance, cognizance, completion, fulfilment, perception **11** achievement, discernment, performance, recognition **12** appreciation, apprehension, consummation **13** actualization, comprehension, consciousness, understanding **14** accomplishment, implementation
• **expression of realization**
03 why

realize
03 get, net, see **04** earn, gain, make, twig **05** clear, fetch, glean, grasp, learn **06** accept, effect, encash, fulfil, obtain, take in **07** achieve, bring in, catch on, discern, perform, produce, sell for **08** complete, cotton on, discover, perceive, register, tumble to **09** actualize, apprehend, ascertain, implement, recognize **10** accomplish, appreciate, articulate, bring about, comprehend, concretize, consummate, effectuate, understand **11** see the light **13** become aware of

really
03 way **04** very **05** quite, rally, truly **06** highly, indeed, in fact, quight, simply, surely, verily **08** actually, honestly, in effect, severely **09** certainly, extremely, genuinely, intensely, sincerely **10** absolutely, positively, remarkably, straight up, thoroughly **11** undoubtedly **13** as large as life, categorically, exceptionally

realm
04 area, land **05** field, orbit, reame,

reign, state, world **06** domain, empire, region, sphere **07** country, kingdom, royalty **08** monarchy, province, queendom **09** territory **10** department **12** principality

reap
03 cut, get, mow, win **04** crop, gain, swap, swop **05** shear **06** derive, garner, gather, obtain, secure **07** acquire, collect, harvest, realize, receive

rear
◇ *reversal indicator*
◇ *tail selection indicator*
03 end **04** back, grow, hind, last, lift, loom, rise, rump, soar, tail **05** breed, erect, hoist, nurse, raise, rouse, set up, stern, tower, train **06** behind, bottom, foster, hinder, hold up, lift up, parent, rise up, stir up, take up **07** bring up, build up, care for, educate, elevate, nurture, tail-end **08** backside, buttocks, hindmost, instruct, lavatory, rearmost **09** cultivate, look after, originate, posterior
See also **toilet**

rearrange
◇ *anagram indicator*
04 vary **05** alter, rejig, shift **06** adjust, change **07** reorder **08** rejigger **09** reshuffle **10** reposition, reschedule **11** consolidate

reason
03 aim, end, wit **04** case, goal, mind, nous **05** argue, basis, brain, cause, color, infer, logic, sense, solve, think **06** colour, debate, deduce, excuse, ground, induce, motive, object, reckon, remark, sanity, wisdom **07** defence, discuss, examine, grounds, impetus, premise, pretext, purpose, resolve, thought, warrant, work out **08** argument, cogitate, conclude, converse, gumption, occasion, think out **09** cerebrate, discourse, encheason, incentive, intellect, intention, judgement, rationale, reasoning, syllogize **10** inducement, moderation, motivation, proportion **11** common sense, explanation, raison d'être, ratiocinate, rationality **12** intelligence, use your brain **13** comprehension, consideration, justification, ratiocination, understanding **15** intellectuality
• **reason with**
04 coax, move, urge **08** persuade **09** argue with, plead with **10** debate with **11** discuss with, expostulate **15** remonstrate with
• **within reason**
10 moderately **12** in moderation, within bounds, within limits **15** with self-control

reasonable
02 OK **03** low **04** fair, just, okay, sane, wise **05** sound **06** modest, viable **07** average, logical **08** credible, moderate, possible, rational, reasoned, sensible **09** judicious, plausible, practical, sagacious, tolerable,

wholesome **10** acceptable
11 competitive, inexpensive,
intelligent, justifiable, well-advised
12 satisfactory **13** no great shakes
14 understandable, well-thought-out

reasonably

02 OK **04** okay **05** quite **06** fairly,
rather, wisely **08** passably, sensibly,
somewhat **09** plausibly, tolerably
10 adequately, moderately, rationally
13 intelligently

reasoned

05 clear, sound **07** logical **08** rational,
sensible **09** judicious, organized
10 methodical, systematic **14** well-
thought-out

reasoning

04 case **05** logic, proof **07** ijtihad,
thought **08** analysis, argument,
thinking **09** casuistry, deduction,
induction, rationale, syllogism,
synthesis **10** hypothesis, philosophy
11 cerebration, supposition
13 argumentation, ratiocination
14 interpretation **15** rationalization

reassemble

◇ *anagram indicator*
05 rally **07** rebuild **09** re-enforce
11 reconstruct

reassurance

05 cheer **06** urging **07** coaxing,
comfort, succour **08** cheering
10 heartening, incitement, motivation,
persuasion **11** consolation,
exhortation, inspiration, stimulation
13 encouragement
See also **encouragement**

reassure

05 brace, cheer, nerve, rally **06** buoy
up, stroke **07** bolster, cheer up,
comfort, confirm, hearten, inspire
08 inspirit, reinsure **09** cosy along,
encourage

rebate

04 dull **05** abate, blunt **06** rabbet,
reduce, refund **08** decrease, discount
09 allowance, deduction, reduction,
repayment

rebel

◇ *anagram indicator*
04 defy, riot **06** flinch, mutine, mutiny,
oppose, recoil, resist, revolt, rise up,
shrink **07** aginner, beatnik, defiant,
disobey, dissent, heretic, run riot, shy
away **08** agitator, apostate, mutineer,
mutinous, pull back, recusant, revolter
09 dissenter, guerrilla, insurgent
10 malcontent, rebellious, schismatic
11 disobedient, turn against
12 malcontented, paramilitary
13 insubordinate, nonconformist,
revolutionary **14** freedom fighter
15 insurrectionary

Rebels include:

04 Aske (Robert), Ball (John), Cade
(Jack), Kett (Robert)
05 Lalor (Peter)
06 Fawkes (Guy)

09 Glendower (Owen)
10 Engelbrekt

See also **revolutionary**

rebellion

04 coup, riot **06** heresy, mutine, mutiny,
revolt, rising **07** dissent, treason
08 defiance, uprising **09** coup d'état
10 insurgence, insurgency, opposition,
resistance, revolution **12** disobedience,
insurrection **15** insubordination

Rebellions include:

03 Rum
07 Fifteen, Whiskey
08 Jacobite
09 Forty-Five
10 the Fifteen
12 Easter Rising, the Forty-Five
14 Eureka Stockade

rebellious

◇ *anagram indicator*
◇ *reversal indicator*
06 unruly **07** defiant, rioting
08 mutinous **09** insurgent, malignant,
obstinate, rebelling, resistant, seditious
10 disorderly, refractory
11 disobedient, intractable
12 contumacious, recalcitrant,
ungovernable, unmanageable
13 insubordinate, revolutionary
15 insurrectionary

rebirth

07 renewal, revival **11** reawakening,
renaissance, restoration
12 regeneration, rejuvenation,
resurrection, risorgimento
13 reincarnation **14** revitalization

rebound

04 fail **05** carom **06** bounce, double,
recoil, re-echo, resile, result, return,
spring **07** bricole, redound
08 backfire, ricochet **09** boomerang,
carambole, reflexion, throw back
10 backfiring, bounce back, reflection,
spring back **11** reverberate **12** defeat
itself, repercussion **13** reverberation
14 score an own goal **15** be self-
defeating, come home to roost

rebuff

03 cut **04** snub **05** check, noser, spurn
06 refuse, reject, rubber, slight
07 decline, put down, put-down,
refusal, repulse, set-down, squelch
08 brush-off, spurning, turn down
09 knock back, rejection, repudiate
10 discourage **11** counterbuff, one in
the eye, repudiation **12** cold shoulder,
cold-shoulder **13** slap in the face **14** a
flea in your ear, discouragement, kick in
the teeth

rebuild

◇ *anagram indicator*
06 reform, remake **07** re-edify,
remodel, restore **08** renovate
09 reaedifye, refashion **10** reassemble
11 reconstruct **12** haussmannize,
rehabilitate

rebuke

04 rate, slap, snub, trim **05** blame,

check, chide, sauce, scold, score, stick
06 carpet, earful, lesson, talk to, threap
threep **07** censure, lecture, reproof,
reprove, rollick, speak to, tell off, tick
off, trounce, upbraid **08** admonish, cal
down, keelhaul, reproach, restrain,
scolding, trimming **09** carpeting,
castigate, dress down, go crook at, go
crook on, objurgate, pitch into,
raspberry, reprimand **10** admonition,
go to town on, rollicking, telling-off,
ticking-off **11** castigation, comeuppance
remonstrate **12** countercheck, dressing-
down, give an earful **13** remonstration,
tear off a strip **14** throw the book at
15 give someone hell

rebut

05 elide, quash, repel **06** defeat,
negate, recoil, refute **07** confute,
explode **08** disprove, overturn
09 discredit **10** invalidate **12** give the
lie to

rebuttal

06 defeat **08** disproof, negation
09 overthrow **10** refutation
11 confutation **12** invalidation

recalcitrance

08 defiance **09** obstinacy
10 wilfulness **11** waywardness
12 disobedience, stubbornness
13 unwillingness **14** refractoriness
15 insubordination

recalcitrant

06 unruly, wilful **07** defiant, wayward
08 contrary, renitent, stubborn
09 obstinate, unwilling **10** refractory
11 disobedient, intractable
12 contumacious, ungovernable,
unmanageable, unsubmissive
13 insubordinate, unco-operative
14 uncontrollable

recall

◇ *reversal indicator*
05 annul, evoke **06** call up, cancel, go
over, memory, repeal, revoke, summon
07 nullify, reclaim, rescind, retract,
retreat, think of, unswear **08** abrogate,
call back, dredge up, recision,
remember, summon up, withdraw
09 annulment, bring back, order back,
recollect, reminisce **10** abrogation, call
to mind, retraction, revocation,
summon back, withdrawal
11 countermand, remembrance, think
back to **12** cancellation, recollection
13 nullification, order to return
14 countermanding

recant

04 deny **05** unsay **06** abjure, disown,
recall, revoke **07** disavow, rescind,
retract **08** abrogate, disclaim, forswear,
renounce, unpreach, withdraw
09 repudiate **10** apostatize

recantation

06 denial, revoke **08** apostasy,
palinode, palinody **09** disavowal
10 abjuration, disclaimer, disownment,
revocation, withdrawal **11** repudiation
12 renunciation, retractation

recapitulate

5 recap, sum up **06** go over, repeat, review **07** recount, restate, run over **09** reiterate, summarize

recapitulation

06 review **07** summary **08** epanodos **09** summing-up **10** repetition **11** reiteration, restatement, summarizing

recast

◇ *anagram indicator*
5 alter **06** modify, revamp, revise, rework **07** rewrite **08** rephrase, revision

recce

04 case, scan **05** probe **06** patrol, search, spy out, survey **07** examine, explore, inspect, observe **08** check out, scouting, scrutiny **10** expedition, inspection, scrutinize **11** examination, exploration, investigate, observation, reconnoitre **13** investigation, reconnoitring **14** reconnaissance

recede

◇ *reversal indicator*
03 ebb **04** drop, fade, sink, wane **05** abate **06** go back, lessen, retire, return, shrink **07** decline, dwindle, fall off, regress, retreat, slacken, subside **08** decrease, diminish, move away, withdraw **10** retrograde

receipt

03 pay, rec **04** chit, note, rept, slip, stub **05** gains, paper, recpt, tally **06** chitty, docket, income, recipe, return, ticket **07** gaining, getting, profits, returns, takings, voucher, warrant **08** capacity, delivery, deriving, earnings, proceeds, turnover **09** obtaining, quittance, receiving, reception **10** acceptance **11** acquittance, counterfoil, dock-warrant **13** money received **14** deposit-receipt **15** acknowledgement, proof of purchase

receive

◇ *containment indicator*
03 get **04** bear, draw, gain, hear, hold, take **05** admit, fence, greet, latch, let in **06** accept, come by, derive, gather, obtain, pick up, suffer, take up **07** acquire, be given, collect, contain, embrace, harbour, inherit, react to, sustain, undergo, welcome **08** meet with, perceive **09** apprehend, encounter, entertain, entertake, go through, respond to **10** experience, learn about **11** accommodate, take on board **12** be informed of, find out about

receiver

03 tap **05** donee, fence, radio, tuner **07** catcher, grantee, handset, legatee **08** assignee, receptor, wireless **09** apparatus, recipient, televisor **10** radiopager **11** beneficiary **13** satellite dish **14** stamp collector **15** direction-finder, superheterodyne

recent

03 low, new **04** late **05** fresh, novel, young **06** latest, latter, modern **07** current **08** ci devant, neoteric, up-to-date **09** latter-day **10** neoterical, present-day **11** Post-Glacial **12** contemporary **13** up-to-the-minute

recently

04 late **05** newly **06** lately, of late **07** freshly **09** yesterday **10** not long ago **13** a short time ago

receptacle

04 bath, sink **05** bosom, purse **06** holder, vessel **09** container, reservoir **10** repository **11** conceptacle, reservatory **12** receptaculum

reception

02 do **04** bash **05** beano, levee, party **06** accoil, at-home, durbar, pick-up, rave-up, ruelle, social **07** ovation, receipt, reunion, shindig, welcome **08** assembly, function, greeting, occasion, reaction, response **09** admission, gathering, treatment **10** acceptance, assumption, bel-accoyle, bon accueil, recipience, recipiency **11** get-together, recognition **12** entertaining **13** entertainment **15** acknowledgement

receptive

04 open **05** quick **07** willing **08** amenable, flexible, friendly, pregnant **09** recipient, sensitive, welcoming **10** accessible, favourable, hospitable, interested, open-minded, responsive **11** suggestible, susceptible, sympathetic **12** approachable, open to reason **13** accommodating

recess

◇ *reversal indicator*
03 bay, cwm **04** apse, bole, bunk, cove, ingo, nook, rest **05** ambry, awmry, bower, break, heart, hitch, niche, oriel, press, sinus **06** alcove, almery, aumbry, awmrie, bowels, bunker, cavity, cirque, closet, corner, corrie, depths, exedra, hollow, indent, locule **07** adjourn, exhedra, holiday, innards, loculus, mortice, mortise, outshot, reaches, respite, time off, time out **08** cupboard, interior, interval, playtime, vacation **09** blank door, breaktime, embrasure, embrazure, seclusion, sepulcher, sepulchre **10** depression, penetralia, retirement **11** blank window, columbarium, indentation **12** confessional, intermission

recession

05 crash, slide, slump **06** trough **07** decline, failure **08** collapse, downturn, shake-out **10** depression, withdrawal **15** economic decline

recherché

04 rare **06** arcane, choice, exotic, select **07** obscure, refined, tenuous **08** abstruse, esoteric **10** far-fetched

recipe

01 r **03** rec, way **04** dish, take **05** guide, means **06** method, system **07** formula, process, receipt **09** procedure, technique **10** directions **11** ingredients **12** instructions, prescription

recipient

05 donee **06** vessel **07** grantee, legatee **08** assignee, donatory, receiver **09** receiving, receptive **10** suscipient **11** beneficiary

reciprocal

05 joint **06** mutual, reflex, shared **07** inverse **08** requited, returned **09** commutual, exchanged, reflexive **10** equivalent, quid pro quo **11** alternating, correlative, give-and-take **13** complementary, corresponding **14** interdependent **15** interchangeable

reciprocate

04 swap **05** equal, match, repay, reply, trade **06** return **07** requite, respond **08** exchange **09** alternate, do the same **10** correspond **11** interchange **12** give in return

reciprocity

08 exchange **09** isopolity, mutuality **11** alternation, equivalence, give-and-take **14** correspondence **15** interdependence

recital

04 show **06** report **07** account, concert, reading, telling **08** relation **09** narration, rendering, rendition **10** recitation, repetition **11** commination, declamation, description, enumeration, performance, solmization **14** interpretation

recitation

03 ave **04** poem, tale **05** piece, story, verse **07** passage, reading, recital, telling **09** monologue, narration, rendering **10** party piece **11** incantation, performance

recite

04 scan, tell **05** chant, chime, daven, speak **06** chaunt, relate, repeat **07** declaim, deliver, itemize, narrate, perform, recount, reel off **08** say aloud **09** enumerate, improvise, rattle off **10** articulate, rhapsodize **11** improvisate

reckless

◇ *anagram indicator*
04 rash, wild **05** brash, hasty, perdu, ton-up **06** madcap, perdue **07** wildcat **08** careless, heedless, kamikaze, mindless, tearaway **09** blindfold, daredevil, desperate, foolhardy, imprudent, negligent, rantipole, rechlesse, retchless **10** ill-advised, incautious, indiscreet **11** harum-scarum, inattentive, precipitate, temerarious, thoughtless **12** devil-may-care **13** irresponsible

recklessly

◇ *anagram indicator*
06 rashly **07** hastily **09** full fling, like water **10** carelessly, mindlessly

11 desperately, negligently
13 irresponsibly, thoughtlessly

recklessness
06 Bayard **07** madness **08** rashness
09 incaution **10** imprudence,
negligence **11** desperation,
gallowsness, inattention
12 carelessness, heedlessness,
mindlessness **13** foolhardiness
15 thoughtlessness

reckon
03 sum **04** call, deem, make, rate
05 add up, class, count, fancy, gauge,
guess, judge, place, sum up, tally, think,
total, value, vogue **06** assess, assume,
esteem, expect, figure, impute,
number, regard **07** account, believe,
compute, imagine, put down, suppose,
surmise, think of, work out **08** appraise,
consider, estimate, evaluate, look upon
09 calculate, designate, enumerate,
figure out **10** conjecture
• **reckon on**
04 face **06** bank on, expect, rely on
07 count on, foresee, hope for, plan for,
trade on, trust in **08** depend on, figure
on **10** anticipate, bargain for **14** take for
granted **15** take into account
• **reckon with**
04 cope, deal, face **05** treat **06** expect,
handle **07** foresee, plan for
08 consider **10** anticipate, bargain for
15 take into account
• **reckon without**
06 ignore **08** overlook **09** disregard,
not expect, not notice **13** fail to think of
• **to be reckoned with**
05 great **06** mighty, strong **07** weighty
08 forceful, powerful **09** important
10 formidable **11** influential, significant
12 considerable

reckoning
03 due, tab **04** bill, doom, tale, time
05 count, datal, lawin, score, tally, total
06 charge, lawing, number, paying
07 account, daytale, opinion, payment
08 addition, counting, estimate
09 appraisal, damnation, judgement
10 assessment, estimation, evaluation,
fellowship, imputation, punishment,
settlement, working-out
11 calculation, computation,
enumeration, retribution

reclaim
04 tame **05** waste **06** appeal, assart,
polder, recall, redeem, regain, rescue
07 get back, recover, restore, salvage
08 civilize, retrieve, take back,
wildness **09** claim back, recapture,
reinstate **10** regenerate, submersion

reclamation
06 rescue **07** salvage **08** recovery
09 regaining, retrieval **11** restoration
12 regeneration **13** reinstatement

recline
03 lie **04** bend, loll, rest **06** lounge,
repose, sprawl **07** incline, lie down
08 lean back **09** recumbent **10** stretch
out

recluse
04 monk **05** loner **06** anchor, hermit
07 ascetic, eremite, stylite
08 anchoret, enclosed, monastic,
retiring, secluded, solitary
09 anchoress, anchorite, solitaire
10 monastical, solitarian
11 monasterial

reclusive
07 ascetic, recluse **08** eremitic,
isolated, monastic, retiring, secluded,
solitary **09** withdrawn **10** anchoritic,
cloistered, hermitical **11** sequestered

recognition
06 honour, recall, reward, salute,
thanks **07** grating, knowing, placing,
respect **08** allowing, approval,
sanction, spotting **09** admission,
awareness, detection, discovery,
gratitude, knowledge **10** acceptance,
admittance, cognizance, confession,
perception, validation
11 endorsement, realization,
remembrance **12** appreciation,
recognizance, recollection,
thankfulness **13** consciousness,
understanding **14** identification
15 acknowledgement

recognize
03 ken, own, see, wit **04** know, nose,
spot, tell **05** admit, adopt, allow, grant,
place **06** accept, acknow, honour,
notice, recall, reward, salute
07 approve, concede, confess, discern,
endorse, not miss, pick out, realize,
respect **08** identify, perceive,
remember, sanction, validate
09 apprehend, be aware of, recollect
10 appreciate, call to mind, legitimate,
not mistake, understand
11 acknowledge, know by sight **13** be
conscious of, be thankful for

recoil
◇ *reversal indicator*
03 shy **04** kick **05** quail, react, rebut
06 falter, flinch, recule, resile, revert,
shrink, spring **07** misfire, rebound,
recoyle, recuile, redound, retreat, shy
away **08** backfire, backlash, draw
back, jump back, kickback, move
back, reaction, requoyle, undertow,
withdraw **09** boomerang
10 degenerate, resilience, resiliency,
spring back **11** reverberate
12 repercussion **15** come home to roost

recollect
◇ *anagram indicator*
◇ *reversal indicator*
05 think **06** recall **07** bethink
08 récollet, remember, summon up
09 reminisce **10** call to mind

recollection
◇ *anagram indicator*
06 memory, recall **08** souvenir
09 anamnesis **10** impression
11 remembrance **12** reminiscence

recommend
04 move, plug, tout, urge, wish
05 guide **06** advise, commit, exhort,

inform, praise, preach **07** advance,
approve, commend, consign, counsel,
endorse, propose, suggest
08 advocate, set forth, vouch for **10** put
forward

recommendation
03 tip **04** plug **06** advice, coupon,
praise, urging **07** counsel **08** advocacy
approval, blessing, good word,
guidance, proposal, sanction
09 reference **10** suggestion
11 endorsement, testimonial
12 commendation, exhortations
14 special mention

recompense
03 fee, pay **05** repay, wages
06 amends, answer, return, reward
07 damages, guerdon, payment,
redress, requite, satisfy **08** requital
09 indemnify, make up for, reimburse,
repayment **10** compensate,
remunerate, reparation **11** restitution
12 compensation, remuneration,
remuneratory, satisfaction
13 consideration, gratification
15 indemnification

reconcile
04 mend, wean **05** agree, atone
06 accept, accord, adjust, attone, make
up, pacify, regain, remedy, settle,
square, submit, upknit **07** appease,
compose, mollify, patch up, placate,
rectify, resolve, reunite **08** face up to,
put right **09** harmonize, make peace
10 conciliate, propitiate, shake hands
11 accommodate **12** come to accept,
reconsecrate **13** bring together, make
your peace **14** bury the hatchet

reconciliation
05 peace **06** accord **07** détente,
harmony, reunion **08** squaring
09 agreement, atonement
10 adjustment, compromise,
resolution, settlement, syncretism
11 appeasement, explanation,
harmonizing **12** conciliation,
pacification, propitiation
13 accommodation, mollification,
rapprochement

recondite
04 dark, deep **06** arcane, hidden,
secret **07** obscure, retired **08** abstruse,
esoteric, involved, mystical, profound
09 concealed, difficult, intricate
10 mysterious **11** complicated

recondition
◇ *anagram indicator*
03 fix **05** refit, renew **06** repair, revamp
07 remodel, restore **08** overhaul,
renovate **09** refurbish

reconfigure
◇ *anagram indicator*

reconnaissance
04 scan **05** probe, recce, recco, reccy
06 patrol, search, survey **08** scouting,
scrutiny **09** discovery **10** expedition,
inspection **11** examination,
exploration, observation
13 investigation, reconnoitring

reconnoitre
4 case, scan 05 probe, recce, scout 6 patrol, spy out, survey 07 examine, xplore, inspect, observe 08 check ut, remember 10 scrutinize 1 investigate

reconsider
6 modify, review, revise 07 rethink 8 reassess 09 re-examine, think over 0 think twice 13 think better of

reconsideration
5 review 07 rethink 09 fresh look 2 reassessment 13 re-examination 4 second thoughts

reconstitute
anagram indicator

reconstruct
anagram indicator
4 redo 06 recast, reform, remake, evamp 07 rebuild, remodel, restore 8 make over, recreate, renovate 9 refashion, reproduce 0 reassemble, regenerate, reorganize 1 recondition, re-establish

record
2 CD, EP, LP 03 can, cut, log, rec 4 best, burn, case, data, disc, disk, dit, file, -gram, keep, list, make, mark, nono, note, read, show, tape 5 album, chart, diary, elpee, enrol, nter, entry, notes, score, trace, video, inyl 06 annals, career, enroll, manage, nemoir, memory, minute, obtain, eport, single 07 account, achieve, halk up, display, dossier, express, astest, history, journal, lay down, ogbook, minutes, myogram, narrate, otch up, produce, put down, release, et down, supreme, swinger, tracing, vitness 08 aerogram, annalize, rchives, best ever, calendar, cassette, omplete, document, evidence, ndicate, inscribe, kymogram, nemorial, MiniDisc®, preserve, rotocol, rap sheet, register, reminder, ake down 09 anemogram, catalogue, elebrate, chronicle, documents, ecording, testimony, videotape, write own 10 accomplish, background, nnregister, instrument, memorandum, eismogram, tape-record, top-anking, transcribe, unequalled 1 compact disc, fastest time, neteorogram, photography, put on ecord, remembrance, sphygmogram, uperlative, track record, unsurpassed, vorld record 12 personal best, nparalleled, without equal, world-eating 13 documentation 4 autoradiograph, record-breaking 5 best performance, curriculum vitae ee also **recording**

• **off the record**
7 private, sub rosa 09 privately 0 unofficial 12 confidential, nofficially 14 confidentially
• **on record**
4 ever 05 noted 06 on file 0 documented 11 written down 3 publicly known

recorder
03 VCR, VTR 05 clerk, video 06 marker, scorer, scribe 07 diarist, Walkman® 08 annalist, black box, CD burner 09 archivist, DVD burner, flûte-à-bec, historian, registrar, secretary 10 chronicler, Dictaphone® 11 chronologer, fipple flute, score-keeper, tape machine 12 English flute, remembrancer, stenographer, tape recorder 13 video recorder 14 cassette-player

recording

Recordings include:

02 45, 78, CD, EP, LP
03 DAT, DVD, MP3, vid
04 disc, mono, tape, tele
05 album, video, vinyl
06 record, single, stereo
08 cassette, MiniDisc®
09 audiotape, phonogram, video disc, videotape
11 compact disc, compact disk, long-playing
12 extended play, magnetic tape
13 microcassette, video cassette

recount
04 tell 05 refer 06 depict, detail, impart, recite, relate, repeat, report, run off, unfold 07 account, narrate, portray 08 describe, rehearse 09 reminisce 11 communicate

recoup
05 repay 06 refund, regain 07 get back, recover, recruit, win back 08 claw back, make good, retrieve 09 indemnify, reimburse, repossess 10 compensate, recompense

recourse
04 flow 06 access, appeal, choice, option, refuge, remedy, resort, return, way out 09 turning to 10 recurrence, withdrawal 11 alternative, possibility
• **have recourse to**
03 use 04 take 06 betake, employ, turn to 07 utilize 08 exercise, resort to 09 make use of 10 fall back on 15 avail yourself of

recover
◇ *anagram indicator*
04 cure, heal, mend 05 amend, rally 06 attain, pick up, recoup, recure, redeem, regain, rescue, retake, revive 07 fetch up, get back, get over, get well, improve, reclaim, recoure, recower, recruit, recycle, replevy, restore, salvage, win back 08 overcast, replevin, retrieve 09 come round, get better, recapture, repossess 10 ameliorate, bounce back, convalesce, feel better, recuperate 11 be on the mend, get stronger, pull through, revendicate 12 gain strength 13 turn the corner

recovered
04 over

recovery
05 rally 06 pick-up, recure, regain,

rescue, upturn 07 healing, mending, recover, revival, salvage, upswing 08 comeback, rallying 09 recapture, recouping, recycling, regaining, retrieval 10 second wind 11 improvement, reclamation, restoration 12 amelioration, recuperation, regeneration, repossession 13 convalescence, convalescency, dead-cat bounce 14 electrowinning, rehabilitation 15 reconvalescence

recreate
◇ *anagram indicator*
05 amuse, renew 07 refresh 09 replicate, reproduce 11 reconstruct 12 reinvigorate

recreation
03 fun, rec 04 game, play 05 hobby, sport 07 leisure, pastime 08 pleasure 09 amusement, diversion, enjoyment 10 relaxation 11 distraction, refreshment 12 intermission 13 entertainment 14 leisure pursuit 15 leisure activity

recrimination
06 retort 07 quarrel 08 comeback, reprisal 09 bickering 10 accusation 11 retaliation 13 counter-attack, countercharge

recruit
02 AR 03 yob 04 levy, tiro 05 draft, enrol, raise, rooky, sprog 06 engage, enlist, gather, muster, nig-nog, novice, nozzer, obtain, rookie, sign up, swabby, take on 07 acquire, convert, draftee, learner, procure, renewal, restore, trainee 08 assemble, beginner, headhunt, initiate, mobilize, newcomer, unionize, yardbird 09 conscript, greenhorn, reinforce, replenish 10 apprentice, new entrant, talent-spot 11 put together, restoration 12 reinvigorate 13 reinforcement

recruitment
05 press 08 drafting, engaging 09 enlisting, enrolment, signing-up 10 engagement 12 conscription, mobilization

rectification
09 amendment 10 adjustment, correction, making good 11 improvement, reformation 12 putting right, setting right

rectify
03 fix 04 cure, mend 05 amend, emend, right 06 adjust, better, reform, remedy, repair 07 correct, improve, redress 08 make good, put right, set right 10 ameliorate 11 dephlegmate

rectitude
06 honour, virtue 07 decency, honesty, justice, probity 08 goodness, morality 09 exactness, integrity, rightness 11 correctness, uprightness 12 straightness 13 righteousness 14 scrupulousness

recto
02 ro

rector
01 R **04** Rect **06** parson

recumbent
04 flat **05** lying, prone **06** supine
07 leaning, recline, resting
08 lounging, reclined **09** lying down,
prostrate, reclining, sprawling
10 horizontal

recuperate
04 mend **05** rally **06** pick up, revive
07 get well, improve, recover **09** get
better **10** bounce back, convalesce
11 be on the mend, get stronger, pull
through **13** turn the corner

recuperation
05 rally **06** recure, upturn **07** healing,
mending, revival **08** rallying, recovery
11 improvement, restoration
12 amelioration **13** convalescence,
convalescency **14** rehabilitation
15 reconvalescence

recur
03 ren, rin, run **05** prime **06** repeat,
return, revert **07** persist **08** reappear
09 come round **11** happen again,
perseverate **12** repeat itself **14** come
round again

recurrence
06 return, rhythm **08** paroxysm,
recourse **09** flashback, reversion
10 appearance, regularity, repetition,
restenosis, revolution **11** persistence
12 alliteration, continuation,
reminiscence **14** redintegration

recurrent
◇ *reversal indicator*
07 chronic, regular **08** cyclical,
frequent, habitual, periodic, repeated
09 continual, recurring **10** persistent,
repetitive **12** intermittent

recycle
◇ *anagram indicator*
04 save **05** re-use **07** reclaim, recover,
salvage **09** reprocess

red
◇ *anagram indicator*
01 c **04** cent, comb, redd, rede, rosy
06 florid, refuse, rubric **07** clear up,
flaming, flushed, glowing, leftist,
reddish, rubbish, vacated **08** blushing,
inflamed, rubicund **09** bloodshot,
Bolshevik, communist, rubescent,
rufescent, socialist **10** erubescent,
shamefaced, testaceous
11 carbuncular, disentangle,
embarrassed, incarnadine, lateritious,
sanguineous **12** Cain-coloured
13 revolutionary

Reds include:

04 guly, pink, rose, ruby, rust, wine
05 brick, gules, henna, ruddy
06 auburn, cerise, cherry, claret,
damask, ginger, maroon, minium,
modena, murrey, rufous, russet,
Titian, tomato, Tyrian

07 carmine, carroty, cramesy, crimson,
fuschia, lobster, nacarat, scarlet,
stammel, vermeil
08 beetroot, blood-red, brick-red,
burgundy, cardinal, chestnut,
cinnabar, cramoisy, sanguine
09 carnation, solferino, vermilion
10 Chinese red, coccineous,
coquelicot, terracotta
11 burnt sienna, incarnadine, sang-de-
boeuf

• in the red
04 bust **05** broke **06** in debt
08 bankrupt **09** in arrears, insolvent,
overdrawn, penniless **10** on the rocks,
owing money **12** impoverished, on
your uppers **13** gone to the wall **14** on
your beam ends
• red and inflamed
03 raw
• see red
05 go mad **07** explode **08** boil over
09 do your nut **10** hit the roof
11 become angry, blow your top, lose
your rag **12** blow your cool, fly into a
rage, lose your cool **14** lose your
temper **15** fly off the handle

red-blooded
05 lusty, manly **06** hearty, lively, robust,
strong, virile **08** vigorous
09 masculine

redcap
02 MP

redden
03 rud **04** gild, rosy, ruby **05** blush,
flush, go red **06** colour, rubefy
07 crimson, scarlet, suffuse

reddish
03 red **04** pink, rosy **05** ruddy, sandy
06 flushy, ginger, rufous, russet
08 pyrrhous, rubicund **09** bloodshot,
gingerous, rufescent
• reddish brown
03 bay **04** rust, sore **06** russet

redecorate
04 do up, redo **09** refurbish

redeem
03 buy **04** cash, free, save **05** lowse,
trade **06** acquit, cash in, change, offset,
ransom, recoup, regain, rescue
07 absolve, buy back, convert, deliver,
expiate, get back, reclaim, recover,
release, reprive, repryve, salvage, set
free, trade in **08** atone for, exchange,
liberate, outweigh, repreeve, reprieve,
retrieve **09** discharge, make up for,
repossess **10** emancipate, recuperate,
repurchase **13** compensate for **14** give
in exchange **15** remove guilt from

redemption
06 ransom, rescue **07** freedom,
release, trade-in **08** exchange,
recovery **09** atonement, expiation,
retrieval, salvation **10** fulfilment,
liberation, reparation, repurchase
11 deliverance, reclamation
12 compensation, emancipation,
repossession **13** reinstatement

redeploy
◇ *anagram indicator*

redevelop
◇ *anagram indicator*

redevelopment
◇ *anagram indicator*

red-handed
07 napping **08** in the act, off-guard, on
the hop, unawares **10** by surprise **12** in
the very act

redistribute
◇ *anagram indicator*

redistribution
◇ *anagram indicator*

redness
03 rud **04** glow, heat **05** flush

redolent
07 odorous, scented **08** aromatic,
fragrant, perfumed **09** evocative,
remindful **10** suggestive **11** reminiscent
13 sweet-smelling

redoubtable
05 awful **06** mighty, strong **07** fearful,
valiant **08** dreadful, fearsome,
powerful, resolute, terrible
10 formidable

redound
04 cast, tend **05** ensue, surge
06 effect, result, return **07** conduce,
rebound, reflect **08** overflow
10 contribute

redraft
◇ *anagram indicator*
06 revise, rework **07** rewrite

redress
03 aid **04** help **05** amend, right
06 adjust, avenge, reform, relief,
remead, remede, remedy, remeid
07 balance, correct, justice, payment,
rectify, requite, restore **08** put right,
readjust, regulate, requital
09 atonement **10** assistance,
compensation, correction, recompense,
reparation **11** restitution
12 compensation, satisfaction
15 indemnification

reduce
◇ *tail deletion indicator*
02 ax **03** axe, cut, put **04** alay, clip, diet,
dock, ruin, slim, trim **05** abate, adapt,
aleye, allay, annul, drive, force, halve,
lower, scant, slake, slash **06** absorb,
adjust, deduct, demote, dilute, draw in,
humble, impair, lessen, master, rebate,
shrink, subdue, weaken **07** conquer,
curtail, cut back, cut down, deflate,
degrade, deplete, devalue, disband,
shorten, thicken **08** beat down, come
down, condense, contract, decrease,
diminish, discount, downsize, make
less, minimize, mitigate, moderate,
overcome, restrict, separate, step
down, take down, vanquish, wear
down, wind down **09** bring down,
comminute, deoxidate, deoxidize,
downgrade, go on a diet, humiliate,
knock down, overpower, translate,

water down **10** abbreviate, de-escalate, impoverish, lose weight **11** make smaller, weight-watch **12** disintegrate **13** whittle away at **14** take the edge off

reduction
◇ *tail deletion indicator*
03 cut **04** drop, fall, loss, wear **06** rebate **07** cutback, decline **08** batement, clipping, decrease, discount, drawdown **09** allowance, deduction, lessening, narrowing, shrinkage, weakening **10** concession, correction, diminution, downsizing, hatchet job, limitation, moderation, rebatement, shortening **11** compression, contraction, curtailment, devaluation, discounting, restriction, subjugation, subtraction **12** abbreviation, condensation, depreciation, minimization

redundancy
04 boot, push, sack **05** cards, elbow **06** excess, firing, notice, papers **07** jotters, removal, sacking, surplus **08** cheville, pleonasm **09** discharge, dismissal, expulsion, laying-off, prolixity, tautology, verbosity, wordiness **10** downsizing, exuberance, exuberancy, repetition **11** superfluity, uselessness **12** outplacement **14** marching-orders

redundant
05 extra, fired, wordy **06** excess, otiose, padded, sacked **07** copious, jobless, laid off, surging, surplus, verbose **08** unneeded, unwanted **09** dismissed, excessive, out of work **10** pleonastic, unemployed **11** inessential, overflowing, repetitious, superfluous, unnecessary **12** periphrastic, tautological **13** supernumerary

redwood
07 big tree, sequoia

re-edit
◇ *anagram indicator*

reef
03 cay, key **04** bank, motu, scar **05** ridge, scaur, shoal **06** skerry **07** bombora, sandbar **08** sandbank **10** square knot
• **reefer**
05 coral
See also **cannabis**

reek
03 hum **04** fume, honk, ming, niff, pong **05** fetor, fumes, odour, reech, smell, smoke, stink, whiff **06** exhale, stench, vapour **08** malodour, mephitis **09** effluvium **10** exhalation

reel
◇ *anagram indicator*
03 din **04** pirn, rock, roll, spin, sway, swim **05** fling, lurch, pitch, spool, swift, swirl, twirl, waver, wheel, whirl, wince, winch **06** bobbin, falter, gyrate, rattle, totter, wobble **07** revolve, stagger,

stumble **08** hoolican **09** eightsome, hoolachan **10** multiplier
• **reel off**
04 list **06** recite, repeat **09** rattle off **10** run through **11** list quickly

refashion
◇ *anagram indicator*
06 adjust, reform, rehash **07** convert, rebuild **11** reconstruct

refer
04 cite, mean, send **05** apply, guide, point, quote, remit **06** advert, allude, appeal, assign, belong, commit, direct, hand on, hint at, look at, look up, pass on, permit, relate, turn to **07** bring up, concern, consult, deliver, mention, pertain, put over, speak of, touch on **08** describe, indicate, relegate, resort to, transfer **09** recommend, represent, reproduce **10** be relevant
• **refer to**
03 see

referee
03 ref, ump **05** judge, zebra **06** umpire **07** arbiter, mediate **08** linesman, mediator **09** arbitrate, intercede **10** adjudicate, arbitrator **11** adjudicator, commissaire, referendary

reference
03 ref **04** hint, note **05** mensh **06** regard, remark, source, squint **07** bearing, mention, respect **08** allusion, citation, footnote, innuendo, instance, relation **09** authority, character, quotation **10** connection, pertinence, retrospect **11** credentials, endorsement, testimonial **12** illustration **13** applicability **14** recommendation
• **with reference to**
02 re **05** about **07** apropos **09** as regards, regarding **10** concerning, relating to, relevant to, respecting **11** referring to **12** with regard to **13** in the matter of, with respect to **14** on the subject of

referendum
04 poll, vote **06** survey, voting **10** plebiscite

referral
07 sending **08** handover, pointing, transfer **09** direction, handing on, passing on

refine
◇ *anagram indicator*
03 try **04** fine, hone, pure, sift, test **05** clear, exalt, treat **06** distil, filter, polish, purify, rarefy, repure, strain **07** chasten, clarify, cleanse, elevate, improve, perfect, process **08** chastise, civilize, freebase, repurify **09** cultivate, elaborate, sublimize, subtilize **11** cut and carve **12** spiritualize

Products and byproducts of refining include:

03 tar
05 sugar
07 asphalt, bitumen, treacle

08 molasses
11 golden syrup

See also **fuel**; **hydrocarbon**; **sugar**

refined
04 fine, pure **05** Attic, civil, clear, couth, exact, horsy **06** gentle, horsey, inland, picked, polite, subtle, urbane **07** classic, courtly, elegant, foppish, genteel, precise, stylish, treated **08** Augustan, cultured, cutglass, delicate, educated, filtered, gracious, ladylike, polished, precious, purified, rarefied, well-bred **09** civilized, distilled, processed, sensitive, spiritual **10** cultivated **11** gentlemanly **12** well-mannered **13** gentlewomanly, sophisticated **14** discriminating

refinement
05 grace, style, taste **06** nicety, polish **07** culture, exility, finesse **08** addition, breeding, chastity, civility, delicacy, elegance, elegancy, subtlety, urbanity **09** amendment, gentility, technique **10** alteration, subtleness **11** cultivation, elaboration, good manners, improvement **12** amelioration, modification **14** discrimination, sophistication

refit
◇ *anagram indicator*
04 mend **05** renew **06** repair, revamp **07** furbish **08** facelift, renovate **09** refurbish **10** renovation

reflect
◇ *reversal indicator*
04 cast, chew, echo, mull, muse, shed, show **05** brood, dwell, glass, glint, image, shine, study, think **06** advise, depict, mirror, ponder, reveal **07** bespeak, display, exhibit, express, imitate, portray, redound, scatter, tarnish **08** cogitate, consider, disgrace, indicate, manifest, meditate, mull over, ruminate, send back **09** bounce off, cerebrate, discredit, repercuss, reproduce, speculate, throw back **10** chew the cud, deliberate **11** communicate, contemplate, demonstrate, reverberate **14** give a bad name to, put in a bad light

reflection
◇ *reversal indicator*
04 baby, echo, idea, life, slur, view **05** blame, image, shame, study **06** belief, musing, reflex **07** censure, display, eidolon, feeling, opinion, rebound, thought **08** disgrace, feelings, likeness, reproach, thinking **09** aspersion, criticism, discredit, disrepute, portrayal, snowblink, viewpoint **10** cogitation, epiphonema, expression, impression, indication, meditation, rumination **11** cerebration, mirror image, observation **12** deliberation, repercussion **13** consideration, contemplation, demonstration, manifestation

reflective
06 dreamy **07** pensive **08** absorbed

09 pondering, reasoning
10 cogitating, meditative, ruminative, thoughtful **12** deliberative
13 contemplative

reflex
06 direct **07** natural, project
08 autotomy, knee-jerk, unwilled
09 automatic, re-entrant
10 expression, mechanical, reciprocal, re-entering **11** instinctive, involuntary, spontaneous **13** manifestation
14 Babinski effect, uncontrollable
15 without thinking

reform
◊ *anagram indicator*
04 mend **05** amend, prune, purge
06 anneal, better, change, repair, revamp, revise **07** correct, disband, dismiss, improve, rebuild, rectify, redress, remodel, restore, shake up, shake-up **08** chastise, renovate, revision **09** amendment, refashion, transform **10** ameliorate, betterment, correction, rebuilding, regenerate, renovation, reorganize
11 improvement, reconstruct, remodelling, restoration
12 reconstitute, rehabilitate
13 rectification, revolutionize
14 reconstruction, rehabilitation, reorganization

reformat
◊ *anagram indicator*

reformation
◊ *anagram indicator*
08 progress, revision **09** amendment
10 renovation **11** improvement, restoration **12** amelioration, palingenesis, regeneration
13 rectification **14** rehabilitation

reformer
03 rad **06** mucker **07** Hussite, liberal, Lollard, Owenite, radical **08** do-gooder, Lutheran **09** Calvinist, reformado, Wyclifite, Zwinglian
10 Wycliffite **11** progressive
12 Pestalozzian **13** bleeding heart, revolutionary, whistle-blower

Reformers include:

03 Hus (Jan)
04 Huss (John), Knox (John), Mill (John Stuart), Owen (Robert)
05 Perón (Evita)
06 Calvin (John), Luther (Martin), Wiclif (John), Wyclif (John)
07 Stanton (Elizabeth Cady), Wycliff (John), Zwingli (Huldreich), Zwingli (Ulrich)
08 Wicliffe (John), Wycliffe (John)
10 Pestalozzi (Johann)
11 Wilberforce (William)

refractory
05 balky, surly, tough **06** mulish, sturdy, unruly, wilful **07** defiant, naughty, restive **08** perverse, stubborn
09 difficult, obstinate, resistant
10 headstrong, rebellious
11 contentious, disobedient, intractable **12** cantankerous,

contumacious, disputatious, recalcitrant, unmanageable **13** fire-resistant, unco-operative
14 uncontrollable

refrain
03 bob, tag **04** curb, fa la, juba, keep, quit, song, stop, tune **05** avoid, cease, forgo, spare, wheel **06** burden, chorus, desist, eschew, fading, fa la la, forego, give up, melody, strain **07** abstain, burthen, ducdame, forbear, hold off
08 faburden, falderal, leave off, overcome, overture, renounce, repetend, response, restrain, rum-ti-tum, surcease, withhold **09** do without, hemistich, supersede, tirra-lyra, turnagain, undersong
10 epistrophe, ritornello, tirra-lirra
11 rumti-iddity **12** rumpti-iddity

refresh
03 jog **04** cool, prod, stir **05** brace, renew, slake **06** arouse, prompt, refect, remind, repair, repose, revive
07 enliven, fortify, freshen, restore
08 activate, energize, recreate, revivify
09 reanimate, recomfort, stimulate
10 exhilarate, invigorate, rejuvenate, revitalize **11** refocillate **12** reinvigorate

refreshing
03 new **04** cool **05** fresh, novel
06 caller **07** bracing, welcome
08 original, reviving **09** different, inspiring **10** energizing, freshening, not another, unexpected **11** inspiriting, refrigerant, stimulating **12** exhilarating, invigorating **15** thirst-quenching

refreshment
03 tea **04** bait, food **05** drink, snack
06 drinks, repast **07** elevens, renewal, revival **09** elevenses, four-hours, refection, twalhours **10** freshening, recreation, sustenance **11** reanimation, restoration, stimulation, water of life
12 food and drink, invigoration
14 reinvigoration, revitalization

refreshments
04 eats, food, grub, nosh **06** drinks, snacks, tucker **07** aliment, titbits
08 eatables **09** elevenses **10** provisions, sustenance **12** food and drink

refrigerate
03 ice **04** cool **05** chill **06** freeze
08 keep cold

refuge
04 dive, hole, holt, home **05** haven
06 asylum, burrow, harbor, island, resort **07** harbour, hideout, hospice, retreat, shelter **08** bolthole, funkhole, hideaway, security **09** sanctuary
10 protection, stronghold, subterfuge
11 sheet anchor **13** place of safety

refugee
05 exile, reffo **06** émigré **07** escapee, runaway **08** fugitive **10** contraband
12 asylum seeker **15** displaced person, stateless person

refulgent
06 bright **07** beaming, lambent,

radiant, shining **08** gleaming, lustrous
09 brilliant, irradiant **10** glistening, glittering **11** resplendent

refund
05 repay **06** rebate, return **07** imburse, pay back, restore **08** give back
09 reimburse, repayment
10 redisburse **13** reimbursement

refurbish
◊ *anagram indicator*
04 do up, mend **05** refit **06** repair, revamp **07** re-equip, remodel, restore
08 overhaul, renovate **10** redecorate
11 recondition

refurbishment
◊ *anagram indicator*
07 doing-up **09** refitting, repairing, revamping **10** renovation
11 recondition, restoration
12 redecoration

refusal
02 no **04** veto **06** denial, nay-say, rebuff **07** repulse **08** negation, spurning **09** knock-back, raspberry, rejection **11** repudiation, turning-down, withholding **12** incompliance, non-admission, nothing doing **13** non-acceptance **14** nolo episcopari
• **first refusal**
06 choice, option **11** opportunity
13 consideration **15** right of purchase

refuse
◊ *anagram indicator*
03 jib, red **04** bran, deny, junk, marc, nill, rape, redd, scum **05** draff, dregs, dross, flock, husks, offal, repel, say no, spurn, trash, waste **06** debris, litter, naysay, pass up, rebuff, reject, resist, scoria, sewage **07** decline, garbage, offscum, rubbish, sullage **08** leavings, renounce, tailings, turn down, withhold **09** knock back, repudiate, riddlings, throw back **11** offscouring
12 kitchen-stuff, offscourings, rejectamenta **13** draw the line at, shake your head **14** dig your heels in

refutation
08 disproof, elenchus, negation, rebuttal **09** overthrow **11** confutation

refute
04 deny, meet **05** rebut, refel
06 negate **07** confute, counter, reprove, silence **08** disprove, redargue
09 discredit, overthrow **12** deny strongly, give the lie to

regain
04 find **06** recoup, retake **07** get back, reclaim, recover, win back **08** recovery, retrieve, return to, take back
09 recapture, reconcile, repossess

regal
05 noble, royal **06** kingly, lordly
07 queenly, stately **08** imperial, majestic, princely, sceptred
09 sceptered, sovereign **11** magnificent

regale
03 ply **05** amuse, feast, serve
06 divert, junket **07** delight, gratify,

itchen, refresh **09** captivate, entertain,
ascinate

egard
3 eye, see **04** care, deem, gaum,
orm, heed, look, love, mark, note,
ate, view **05** gauge, judge, point,
hink, value, watch **06** aspect, behold,
etail, esteem, follow, gaze at, hold of,
onour, look at, look on, matter, notice,
epute, tender **07** believe, concern,
magine, observe, respect, set down,
ubject, suppose, weigh up
8 appraise, approval, consider,
stimate, listen to, look upon, relation,
espects, sympathy **09** affection,
ttention, deference, greetings,
ntention, reference **10** admiration,
dvertence, advertency, bear in mind,
est wishes, estimation, good wishes,
articular, retrospect, scrutinize
1 approbation, compliments,
ontemplate, observation, salutations
2 take notice of **13** consideration
4 loving kindness, pay attention to
5 give the once-over, take into account
   with regard to, in regard to
2 re **04** as to **05** about, anent
7 apropos, vis-à-vis **09** as regards, in
erms of **10** as concerns, concerning
2 in relation to **13** with respect to
4 on the subject of **15** with reference
o

egardful
5 aware **07** careful, dutiful, heedful,
nindful **08** noticing, watchful
9 attentive, observant **10** respectful,
espective, thoughtful **11** circumspect,
onsiderate

egarding
2 re **04** as to **05** about **07** apropos,
is-à-vis **09** as regards **10** concerning,
n regard to **12** in relation to, with
egard to **13** when it comes to, with
espect to **14** on the subject of **15** with
eference to

egardless
 deletion indicator
6 anyhow, anyway **08** careless,
eedless **09** at any cost, negligent,
nmindful **10** at any price, neglectful
1 come what may, inattentive,
ndifferent, nonetheless, respectless,
nconcerned **12** disregarding,
rregardless, nevertheless, no matter
vhat **13** inconsiderate

egenerate
 anagram indicator
5 renew **06** change, revive, uplift
7 refresh, renewed, restore
8 inspirit, reawaken, rekindle,
enovate, revivify **09** reproduce,
wice-born **10** invigorate, rejuvenate,
evitalize **11** reconstruct, re-establish
2 reconstitute, reinvigorate

egenerated
 anagram indicator
3 new

egeneration
7 renewal **10** neogenesis, renovation

11 reformation, restoration
12 morphallaxis, palingenesis,
rejuvenation, reproduction
13 homomorphosis **14** reconstitution,
reconstruction, reinvigoration **15** re-
establishment

regime
03 way **04** diet, fast, rule **05** order,
reign **06** method, system
07 command, control, formula,
pattern, regimen, routine **08** practice,
schedule, tyrannis **09** direction,
procedure, programme **10** abstinence,
government, leadership, management
11 kleptocracy **13** establishment
14 administration **15** short sharp shock

regiment
04 army, band, body, crew, gang
05 group **06** cohort, pultun, tercio
07 battery, brigade, company, platoon
08 squadron

Army regiments include:
02 RA, RE, TA
03 SAS
04 REME
05 Kings, Paras
06 London
07 Gurkhas, Lowland
08 Cheshire
09 Fusiliers, Parachute, Royal Tank
10 Black Watch, Life Guards, Royal
  Irish, Royal Scots, Royal Welsh
11 Highlanders, Horse Guards, Irish
  Guards, Scots Guards, Welsh
  Guards
12 Army Air Corps, Close Support,
  Green Howards, Green Jackets,
  Gurkha Rifles, Rifle Brigade, Royal
  Anglian, Royal Hussars, Royal
  Lancers, Royal of Wales
13 Artists' Rifles, Light Dragoons, Light
  Infantry, Staffordshire
14 General Support, Royal Artillery,
  Royal Engineers
15 Grenadier Guards, Rifle Volunteers,
  Territorial Army

regimented
06 strict **07** ordered **09** organized,
regulated **10** controlled, methodical,
systematic **11** disciplined
12 standardized, systematized

region
01 E **03** end **04** area, belt, high, land,
part, wild, zona, zone **05** ambit,
bundu, burgh, duchy, field, manor,
orbit, place, range, realm, reame,
scope, shire, state, tract, waste, wilds,
world **06** county, domain, empire,
estate, garden, ghetto, parish, riding,
sector, sphere **07** borough, climate,
country, diocese, emirate, expanse,
granary, heavens, hundred, kingdom,
mission, quarter, section, suburbs,
terrain **08** autonomy, badlands,
district, division, dominion, foreland,
interior, province, time zone
09 backwoods, bailiwick, climature,
continent, goldfield, heartland, inner
city, outskirts, periphery, territory
10 borderland, hemisphere,

playground, wilderness
11 breadbasket, God's country,
reservation, terra ignota
12 municipality, principality,
subcontinent **13** catchment area,
neighbourhood **14** God's own
country, postal district, terra incognita

Regions include:
03 Zug
04 Jura, León, Midi, Ruhr, Vaud
05 Angus, Dixie, Gower, Lazio, Liège,
  Loire, Marne, Namur, Norte, Otago,
  Rhine, Rhône, Rioja, Somme,
  Taupo, Tyrol, Urals
06 Acadia, Alsace, Apulia, Aragón,
  Argyll, Azores, Bayern, Beiras,
  Burgos, Centro, Crimea, Hessen,
  Iberia, Latium, Lisboa, Molise, Mt
  Cook, Murcia, Nelson, Ozarks,
  Puglia, Savoie, Saxony, Sicily, Top
  End, Umbria, Valais, Veneto, Vosges,
  Wanaka
07 Abruzzo, Algarve, Almería,
  Ardenne, Bavaria, Bohemia,
  Borders, Brabant, Castile, Corsica,
  Drenthe, Galicia, Hainaut, Jutland,
  La Loire, La Rioja, Liguria, Limburg,
  Lucerne, Madeira, Marches,
  Midwest, Moselle, Navarra,
  Navarre, Picardy, Riviera, Rotorua,
  Ruapehu, Shannon, Siberia, Silesia,
  Thurgau, Tuscany, Utrecht, Venetia,
  Waikato, Zeeland
08 Alentejo, Alicante, Ardennes,
  Asturias, Auvergne, Bretagne,
  Brittany, Burgundy, Calabria,
  Calvados, Campania, Canaries,
  Cataluña, Caucasus, Charente,
  Chechnya, Dalmatia, Dordogne,
  Eastland, Flanders, Grampian,
  Hebrides, Holstein, Lappland,
  Limousin, Lombardy, Lorraine,
  Manawatu, Normandy, Picardie,
  Piedmont, Provence, Pyrenees,
  Rust Belt, Saarland, Sardinia,
  Taranaki, Trentino, Val d'Oise,
  Valencia, Wallonia, Wanganui
09 Andalucía, Andalusia, Aquitaine,
  Bible Belt, Bourgogne, Cantabria,
  Carinthia, Castellón, Catalonia,
  Champagne, Charentes, Côte
  d'Azur, Deep South, Fiordland,
  Flevoland, Friesland, Groningen,
  Gulf Coast, Hawkes Bay, Highlands,
  Languedoc, Maritimes, Neuchâtel,
  Northland, Pomerania, Red Centre,
  Rhineland, Schleswig, Snowdonia,
  Southland, Southwest, The Burren,
  Thuringia, Trossachs, Wairarapa,
  West Coast
10 Appalachia, Basilicata, Canterbury,
  Coromandel, Costa Brava,
  Gelderland, Graubünden, Great
  Lakes, Horowhenua, New England,
  Overijssel, Palatinate, Westphalia
11 Bay of Plenty, Black Forest,
  Brandenburg, Central Belt, Costa
  Blanca, Costa del Sol, Costa
  Dorada, Extremadura, Great Plains,
  Île-de-France, Marlborough, Mid-
  Atlantic, Zuid-Holland
12 American West, Bay of Islands,

Noord-Brabant, Noord-Holland, The Kimberley
13 Barossa Valley, Basque Country, Brecon Beacons, Canary Islands, Emilia-Romagna, Middle America, Pays-de-la-Loire
14 Castile and Leon, Channel Islands, Snowy Mountains
15 Balearic Islands, Bernese Oberland, Eastern Seaboard

See also **council**; **county**; **department**; **district**; **electorate**; **geography**; **province**; **state**

• **in the region of**
03 odd **04** near, some **05** about, circa **06** around, nearly **07** close to, loosely, roughly **09** just about, not far off, rounded up **10** give or take, more or less, round about **11** approaching, rounded down **13** approximately, or thereabouts, something like **14** in round numbers **15** in the vicinity of

regional
05 local, zonal **08** district **09** localized, parochial, sectional **10** provincial

register
03 log, say, tax **04** cast, file, list, mark, note, poll, read, roll, show, tone **05** album, clock, diary, enrol, enter, files, index, notes, range, voice **06** annals, betray, book in, docket, enlist, enroll, ledger, lidger, muster, record, regest, reveal, roster, sign on, turn in **07** almanac, check in, diptych, display, exhibit, express, journal, listing, notitia, put down, set down, terrier **08** archives, cadastre, indicate, inscribe, manifest, menology, obituary, schedule, take down **09** cartulary, catalogue, chronicle, directory, enrolment, matricula, registrar **10** enregister, enrollment **11** demonstrate, matriculate, patent-rolls **12** put in writing, transfer book

registrar
05 clerk **07** actuary **08** annalist, greffier, official, recorder, register **09** archivist, secretary **10** cataloguer, chronicler **11** protocolist, protonotary **12** prothonotary, sheriff clerk **13** administrator

registration
04 list, rego **05** reggo **06** noting, record **07** logging **08** entering, register **09** enrolment, recording, signing-on **10** checking-in **11** inscription

regress
◇ *reversal indicator*
03 ebb **04** wane **05** lapse **06** recede, return, revert **07** re-entry, relapse, retreat **09** backslide, retrocede, reversion **10** degenerate, retrogress **11** deteriorate

regret
03 rew, rue **04** weep **05** grief, mourn, shame **06** bemoan, desire, grieve, lament, relent, repent, sorrow **07** be sorry, deplore, remorse **08** had-I-wist **09** deprecate, feel sorry, penitence

10 bitterness, contrition, repentance **11** compunction **12** be distressed, feel bad about, self-reproach **14** be disappointed, disappointment

• **expression of regret**
02 ay **03** ach, och **04** alas **05** alack, ewhow **06** if only **07** out upon **09** alack-a-day

regretful
03 sad **05** sorry **06** rueful **07** ashamed **08** contrite, penitent **09** repentant, sorrowful **10** apologetic, remorseful **12** disappointed

regrettable
03 sad **05** sorry, wrong **06** too bad **07** unhappy, unlucky **08** shameful **09** upsetting **10** deplorable, ill-advised, lamentable **11** disgraceful, distressing, unfortunate **13** disappointing, reprehensible

regrettably
04 alas **05** sadly **08** sad to say **09** unhappily, unluckily, worse luck **11** sad to relate **13** unfortunately

regular
03 set **04** even, flat **05** daily, fixed, level, loyal, swell, usual **06** common, giusto, hourly, normal, proper, smooth, stated, steady, strict, weekly, yearly **07** average, canonic, certain, classic, correct, monthly, orderly, private, routine, typical, uniform **08** approved, balanced, constant, everyday, frequent, habitual, official, ordinary, orthodox, periodic, rhythmic, standard, standing, thorough **09** canonical, customary, out-and-out, permanent, recurring, unvarying, veritable **10** consistent, methodical, periodical, systematic, unchanging **11** commonplace, established, symmetrical **12** conventional, evenly spread, professional, time-honoured **13** well-organized

regularly
◇ *hidden alternately indicator*
05 often **10** frequently **13** like clockwork

regulate
◇ *anagram indicator*
03 run, set **04** rule, tune **05** align, aline, guide, order **06** adjust, baffle, direct, govern, handle, manage, settle, square **07** arrange, balance, conduct, control, monitor, oversee **08** moderate, modulate, organize **09** supervise **10** administer **11** superintend, synchronize

regulation
02 AR **03** act, law, set **04** code, rule **05** by-law, edict, fixed, order, usual **06** bye-law, curfew, decree, dictum, dosage, normal, pusser, ruling **07** command, control, dictate, precept, statute **08** accepted, guidance, official, orthodox, required, standard **09** customary, direction, directive, mandatory, ordinance, principle, procedure, statutory **10** management,

obligatory, prescribed **11** commandment, requirement, supervision **12** dispensation **13** pronouncement **14** administration **15** superintendence

regurgitate
04 puke, spew **05** heave, retch, vomit **06** posset, repeat, sick up, spit up **07** bring up, fetch up, regorge, restate, throw up **08** disgorge, ruminate, say again **09** reiterate, tell again **12** recapitulate

rehabilitate
04 mend, save **05** clear, rehab, renew **06** adjust, redeem, reform **07** convert, rebuild, restore **08** renovate **09** normalize, reinstate **11** recondition, reconstruct, re-establish, reintegrate **12** reconstitute, reinvigorate

rehash
◇ *anagram indicator*
05 alter, rejig **06** change, rework **07** restate, rewrite **08** rejigger **09** rearrange, refashion, rejigging, reshuffle, reworking **11** restatement **13** rearrangement

rehearsal
05 drill **06** dry run **07** hersall, reading, recital **08** band-call, dummy run, exercise, practice, trial run, woodshed **09** narration **10** repetition, run-through **11** enumeration, preparation, read-through, walk-through

rehearse
05 block, drill, train **06** go over, recite, relate, repeat, try out **07** narrate, pour out, prepare, recount **08** block out, practise **09** enumerate, pour forth **10** run through

reign
04 rain, ring, rule, sway **05** exist, occur, power, raine, rayne, realm **06** be king, domain, empire, govern, obtain **07** queen, command, control, kingdom, prevail **08** dominion, hold sway, monarchy **09** be in power, be present, influence, Silver Age, supremacy **10** ascendancy, be in charge, government **11** be in command, be in control, pontificate, predominate, sovereignty **12** predominance **14** be in government, sit on the throne

reigning
05 world **06** ruling **07** current, in power, present, regnant **09** governing, in command, in control, incumbent, presiding **10** victorious

reimburse
05 repay **06** refund, return **07** pay back, restore **08** give back **09** indemnify **10** compensate, recompense, remunerate

reimbursement
06 refund **09** indemnity, repayment **10** recompense **12** compensation

rein
04 curb, halt, hold, stop **05** brake, check, limit **06** answer, arrest, bridle

control, harness **08** hold back,
hinder, restrain, restrict
9 overcheck, restraint **11** restriction
free rein
7 freedom, liberty **08** free hand
9 free-for-all **11** blank cheque, open
rather **12** carte blanche, laissez-faire

reincarnation
7 rebirth, samsara **12** palingenesis
14 metempsychosis

reindeer
4 deer, rein **06** tarand **07** caribou

Father Christmas's reindeer:

5 Comet, Cupid, Vixen
6 Dancer, Dasher, Donner
7 Blitzen, Prancer, Rudolph

reinforce
containment indicator
4 line, prop, stay **05** brace, shore, steel
6 beef up, harden, stress, supply
7 augment, enforce, fortify, recruit,
stiffen, support, toughen **08** buttress,
increase, renforce **09** emphasize, reinforce, underline **10** strengthen,
supplement **11** consolidate

reinforcement
4 help, prop, stay **05** brace, shore
6 back-up **07** recruit, support
8 addition, buttress, emphasis,
increase, reserves **09** hardening
10 supplement **11** auxiliaries,
enlargement **12** augmentation
13 amplification, fortification, reinforcement, strengthening
15 supplementaries

reinstate
6 recall, return **07** replace, reseize,
restore **08** give back **09** reappoint,
reinstall **11** re-establish **12** rehabilitate

reinstatement
6 recall, return **10** giving-back,
reposition **11** replacement, restoration
15 re-establishment

reiterate
4 ding **05** recap, resay **06** repeat,
retell, stress **07** iterate, restate
8 rehearse **09** emphasize
10 ingeminate **12** recapitulate

reject
reversal indicator
3 bin, nix, pip **04** cast, deny, dice, jilt,
kill, spin, veto **05** repel, scrap, spurn,
trash **06** rebuff, recuse, refuse, second
7 cast off, cast-off, condemn, decline,
despise, discard, dismiss, exclude,
jailbar, forsake, outcast, repulse, say no
to **08** athetize, brush off, disallow,
disclaim, jettison, renounce, set aside,
throw out, turn away, turn down
9 eliminate, knock back, reprobate,
repudiate, throw away **10** disapprove
11 give the push **13** kick into touch
14 throw overboard, turn your back on
15 wash your hands of

rejection
4 push, veto **05** spurn **06** denial, rebuff
7 heave-ho, refusal **08** brush-off,

turn-down **09** athetesis, declining,
dismissal, exclusion, knock-back
10 discarding **11** elimination,
jettisoning, reprobation, repudiation,
turning-down **12** cold shoulder,
renunciation **14** Dear John letter

rejig
◇ *anagram indicator*
07 re-equip, shake up **09** modernize,
rearrange **10** reorganize, streamline
11 rationalize, restructure

rejoice
03 joy **05** exult, glory, revel **07** be
happy, delight, gladden, triumph **08** be
joyful, jubilate **09** be pleased,
celebrate, make merry, whoop it up
10 jump for joy **11** be delighted **12** take
pleasure

rejoicing
03 joy **05** glory **07** delight, elation,
ovation, revelry, triumph **08** euphoria,
gladness, jubilant, pleasure **09** festivity,
happiness **10** exaltation, exultation,
jubilation **11** celebration, merrymaking

rejoin
◇ *anagram indicator*
04 quip **05** reply **06** answer, retort
07 respond, riposte **08** repartee

rejoinder
04 quip **05** reply **06** answer, retort
07 riposte **08** comeback, repartee,
response

rejuvenate
05 renew **06** revive **07** refresh, restore
08 recharge, rekindle, revivify
09 freshen up, reanimate
10 regenerate, revitalize
12 reinvigorate

rejuvenation
07 renewal, revival **11** restoration,
shunamitism **12** regeneration
14 reinvigoration, revitalization

relapse
04 fail, sink, weed, weid **05** lapse
06 revert, weaken, worsen **07** decline,
regress, setback **08** fall away
09 backslide, reversion, weakening,
worsening **10** degenerate, recurrence,
regression, retrogress **11** backsliding,
deteriorate, hypostrophe
13 deterioration, retrogression

relate
04 ally, join, link, rede, tell **05** apply,
fable, refer, story **06** couple, detail,
empart, impart, recite, report
07 compare, concern, connect, feel
for, narrate, pertain, present, recount,
respect **08** describe, hit it off, identify
09 appertain, associate, bring back,
correlate, delineate, discourse,
empathize, get on with, make known
10 be relevant, sympathize,
understand **11** communicate **12** have a
rapport **13** get on well with **14** have a
bearing on

related
03 kin, rel **04** akin **05** joint, of kin
06 affine, agnate, allied, kinred, linked,

mutual **07** affined, cognate, kindred
08 narrated, referred, relevant
09 connected, pertinent **10** affiliated,
associated, correlated **11** concomitant
12 accompanying, interrelated
14 consanguineous, interconnected
15 of the same family

relation
03 kin, rel, sib **04** bond, link, term
05 ratio **06** affine, family, regard, rellie
07 bearing, kindred, kinsman, linking,
rapport, recital, respect **08** alliance,
kinsfolk, relative **09** connexion,
kinswoman, narrative, reference,
relevance, statement **10** collateral,
comparison, connection, pertinence,
similarity **11** affiliation, application,
correlation, information
12 relationship **13** interrelation
14 correspondence, correspondency
15 interconnection, interdependence
See also **narrative; relative**

relations
03 kin, sex **05** folks, terms, union
06 coitus, family **07** affairs, coition,
contact, kindred, kinsman, liaison,
quarter, rapport, rellies **08** contacts,
dealings, intimacy, kinsfolk
09 kinswoman, relatives **10** copulation,
love-making **11** connections,
interaction, intercourse
12 associations, consummation,
relationship **14** communications
15 carnal knowledge

relationship
03 kin, tie **04** bond, link, ties **05** blood,
fling, ratio, thing, tie-up **06** affair
07 account, kinship, liaison, rapport,
romance, sibship **08** affinity, alliance,
intimacy, parallel **09** chemistry,
closeness **10** connection, flirtation,
friendship, love affair, proportion,
similarity **11** association, correlation
• **end relationship**
04 dump, jilt **07** break up, divorce, split
up

relative
03 kin, rel **06** family, rellie **07** germane,
kindred, kinsman, related **08** apposite,
kinsfolk, moderate, parallel, relation,
relevant **09** connected, connexion,
dependant, dependent, kinswoman,
pertinent **10** applicable, comparable,
connection, reciprocal, respective
11 appropriate, comparative,
correlative **12** commensurate,
interrelated, proportional
13 corresponding, proportionate

Relatives include:

02 ex
03 bro, dad, mom, mum, sis, son
04 aunt, gran, heir, nana, twin, wife
05 aunty, daddy, mummy, nanna,
nanny, niece, uncle
06 auntie, cousin, ex-wife, father,
german, godson, grampa, granny,
mother, nephew, parent, sister,
spouse
07 brother, grandad, husband, partner,
sibling, stepdad, stepmum, stepson

08 daughter, godchild, grandson
09 ex-husband, godfather, godmother, stepchild
10 grandchild, half-sister, stepfather, stepmother, step-parent, stepsister, twin-sister
11 first cousin, foster-child, god-daughter, grandfather, grandmother, grandparent, half-brother, stepbrother, twin-brother
12 foster-parent, second cousin, stepdaughter
13 grand-daughter

relatively
05 quite **06** fairly, rather **08** somewhat
12 by comparison, in comparison
13 comparatively

relax
◊ *anagram indicator*
03 veg **04** calm, ease, fall, rest
05 abate, chill, loose, lower, remit, slump **06** cool it, lessen, loosen, reduce, relent, sedate, soften, unbend, unknit, unrein, unwind, veg out, weaken **07** ease off, mollify, resolve, slacken, unbrace, unclasp, unpurse
08 calm down, chill out, de-stress, diminish, kick back, loosen up, moderate, wind down **09** hang loose, lighten up **10** liberalize, take it easy
12 tranquillize **13** let yourself go, put your feet up **14** take things easy **15** let your hair down

relaxation
03 fun **04** rest **05** let-up **06** easing, repose **07** détente, leisure, relâche
08 chill-out, pleasure **09** abatement, amusement, enjoyment, lessening, loosening, reduction, softening, unwinding, weakening **10** autogenics, meditation, misericord, moderation, recreation, slackening **11** délassement, distraction, loosening up, misericorde, refreshment **13** entertainment

relaxed
◊ *anagram indicator*
04 calm, cool, easy **05** loose **06** at ease, atonic, casual, comodo, unbent
07 commodo, languid, restful
08 carefree, composed, downbeat, informal, laid-back, toneless, unbraced, unstrung **09** collected, easy-going, graspless, leisurely, unhurried **11** comfortable, uninhibited
12 happy-go-lucky

relay
◊ *anagram indicator*
04 send, time, turn **05** carry, shift, spell, stint **06** hand on, pass on, period, spread, supply **07** message
08 dispatch, transmit **09** broadcast, circulate, programme **11** communicate
12 transmission **13** communication

release
04 free, undo **05** exeem, exeme, issue, let go, loose, remit, untie **06** acquit, convey, excuse, exempt, launch, let off, let-off, loosen, reveal, unbind, unlock, unveil **07** absolve, acquite, deliver,

divulge, freedom, liberty, present, publish, relieve, set free, slacken, unchain, unclasp, unleash, unloose
08 acquight, announce, bulletin, disclose, liberate, uncouple, unfasten
09 acquittal, circulate, discharge, disengage, exemption, exonerate, make known, quitclaim, quittance, remission, surrender, unshackle
10 absolution, disclosure, distribute, emancipate, liberation, make public, publishing, relinquish, revelation
11 acquittance, declaration, deliverance, enlargement, exoneration, manumission, publication
12 announcement, emancipation, proclamation **13** make available

relegate
05 eject, exile, expel, refer **06** assign, banish, demote, deport, reduce
07 consign, degrade, entrust
08 delegate, dispatch, sideline, transfer
09 downgrade **10** expatriate
12 Stellenbosch

relent
04 ease, melt **05** abate, allow, let up, relax, yield **06** give in, regret, repent, soften, unbend, weaken **07** die down, ease off, give way, melting, slacken, slowing **08** moderate **09** come round
10 capitulate **14** change your mind

relentless
04 grim, hard **05** cruel, harsh, stern
06 fierce **08** pitiless, ruthless **09** cut-throat, incessant, merciless, punishing, unceasing **10** implacable, inexorable, inflexible, persistent, unflagging, unyielding **11** cold-hearted, hard-hearted, remorseless, unforgiving, unrelenting, unremitting
14 uncompromising

relevance
07 aptness, bearing **10** pertinence
11 suitability **12** appositeness, significance **13** applicability
15 appropriateness

relevant
03 apt **04** live **06** german, proper
07 apropos, fitting, germane, related
08 apposite, material, relative, suitable
09 congruous, pertinent **10** admissible, applicable, to the point **11** appropriate, significant **12** proportional, to the purpose

reliability
07 honesty **09** certainty, constancy, integrity, precision **10** steadiness
12 faithfulness **13** dependability
14 responsibility **15** trustworthiness

reliable
04 safe, sure, true **05** solid, sound, white **06** honest, stable, tested, trusty
07 certain, devoted, dutiful, regular, staunch **08** bankable, constant, credible, faithful **09** unfailing
10 dependable **11** predictable, responsible, trustworthy, well-founded
12 well-grounded **13** authoritative, conscientious **14** copper-bottomed

reliance
05 faith, trust **06** belief, credit
09 assurance **10** confidence, conviction, dependance, dependence

relic
05 scrap, shell, token, trace **06** corpse, fossil, relict **07** antique, memento, relique, remains, remanié, remnant, vestige **08** artefact, fragment, heirloom, holdover, keepsake, moniment, monument, reminder, souvenir, survival **09** antiquity
11 remembrance

relief
03 aid **04** alms, cure, help, rest
05 break, let-up, locum, proxy
06 back-up, easing, remedy, repose, rescue, saving, succor, supply
07 comfort, redress, release, relievo, reserve, respite, rilievo, stand-by, stand-in, succour, support **08** allaying, breather, calmness, easement, soothing **09** abatement, assuaging, diversion, happiness, lessening, reduction, remission, surrogate
10 assistance, mitigation, palliation, relaxation, substitute, sustenance, understudy **11** alleviation, consolation, deliverance, reassurance, refreshment, replacement **12** interruption
• **expression of relief**
04 phew, whew **06** wheugh **08** thank God **12** thank heavens **13** thank goodness

relieve
03 aid **04** beet, bete, cure, ease, feed, free, heal, help, save, stop **05** abate, allay, break, expel, pause, spare, spell
06 assist, excuse, exempt, lessen, reduce, remove, rescue, soften, soothe, succor **07** assuage, bestead, break up, comfort, console, deliver, dismiss, release, replace, set free, slacken, succour, support, sustain
08 liberate, mitigate, palliate, reassure, unburden **09** alleviate, discharge, interrupt, punctuate **10** stand in for, substitute **11** discontinue **12** bring to an end, take over from **14** take the place of

relieved
04 glad **05** eased, happy **07** cheered, pleased **08** thankful **09** refreshed
10 encouraged

religion
04 code **05** creed, dogma, faith
07 beliefs **08** doctrine **12** belief system

Religions include:

03 Bon, Zen
04 Shi'a
05 Amish, Baha'i, Druze, Islam, Sunni
06 Sufism, Taoism, voodoo
07 animism, Baha'ism, Essenes, Jainism, Jesuits, Judaism, Lamaism, Moonies, Opus Dei, Orphism, Quakers, Saivism, Saktism, Sikhism
08 Baptists, Buddhism, Druidism, Hasidism, Hinduism, paganism, Tantrism, Wahhabis
09 Ahmadiyya, Cabbalism, Calvinism,

Methodism, Mithraism,
Mormonism, occultism, Parseeism,
shamanism, Shintoism, Vedantism,
Waldenses
) Adventists, Brahmanism,
Evangelism, Gnosticism,
Iconoclasm, Puritanism, Soka
Gakkai
Anabaptists, Anglicanism,
Catholicism, Creationism,
Freemasonry, Hare Krishna,
Lutheranism, Manichaeism,
Scientology, Zen Buddhism
Albigensians, Christianity,
Confucianism, Nestorianism,
Unitarianism
Church in Wales, Protestantism,
Reform Judaism, Salvation Army
Fundamentalism, Oxford
Movement, Pentecostalism,
Rastafarianism, Rosicrucianism,
Society of Jesus, Ultramontanism,
Zoroastrianism
ancestor-worship, Church of
England, Presbyterianism

eligious
2 pi 03 pia 04 holy 05 godly, pious
6 devout, divine, sacred, strict
7 serious 08 reverent, rigorous
9 believing, committed, doctrinal,
ghteous, spiritual 10 devotional,
iod-fearing, meticulous, practising,
criptural, scrupulous 11 church-
oing, theological 13 conscientious
ee also **Bible; festival; scripture;
ervice; symbol**

Religious buildings include:

4 Kaba
5 Ka'aba
6 Kasbah
7 Abu Mena, al-Azhar
8 Pantheon
9 Abu Simbel, Acropolis, Borobudur,
Eye Temple, Kinkakuji, Parthenon,
Propylaea, Sacred Way, Sun Temple,
Temple Bar
0 Blue Mosque, Erechtheum,
Harimandir, Sacré Coeur
Ajanta caves, Ellora caves,
Erechtheion, Great Sphinx, Hagia
Sophia, Temple Mount, Wailing
Wall, Western Wall, York Minster
2 Boyana Church, Ely Cathedral,
Golden Temple, Great Pyramid,
Monte Cassino, Norton Priory,
Pagan temples, Temple of Hera,
Temple of Isis, Watton Priory
3 Cordoba Mosque, Dome of the
Rock, Horyuji Temple, Kailasa
Temple, Muhammad's Tomb, Rila
Monastery, Vézelay Church
4 Belém Monastery, Dilwara temples,
Golden Pavilion, Kazan Cathedral,
Mahamuni Pagoda, My Son
Sanctuary, Reims Cathedral, Ripon
Cathedral, Sagrada Familia,
Suleiman Mosque, Temple of
Amon-Ra, Temple of Apollo, Temple
of Athena, Temple of Heaven,
Ummayyad Mosque, Wells
Cathedral

15 Aachen Cathedral, Amiens
Cathedral, Chavín de Huantar,
Durham Cathedral, Exeter
Cathedral, Ggantija temples,
Pyramid of Cheops, Pyramid of the
Sun, Shwe Dagon Pagoda,
Shwezigon Pagoda, Speyer
Cathedral, Temple of Artemis,
Temple of Hathoor, Temple of
Solomon, Temple of Somnath

See also **abbey; cathedral; worship**

Religious figures include:

03 Fry (Elizabeth), Hus (Jan), Roy (Ram
Mohan)
04 Bede (St, 'the Venerable'), Eddy
(Mary), Huss (John), John (of
Leyden), King (Martin Luther),
Knox (John), Penn (William), Pire
(Dominique), Shaw (Anna
Howard), Tutu (Desmond), Weil
(Simone)
05 Amman (Jacob), Booth (William),
Condé (Louis Prince de), Farel
(Guillaume), Grove (Sir George),
Jesus, Keble (John), Lao Zi, Lewis
(Clive Staples), Mahdi (El), Paley
(William), Paris (Matthew), Smith
(Joseph), Soper (Donald, Lord),
Waite (Terry), Young (Brigham)
06 Arnold (of Brescia), Baxter
(Richard), Becket (St Thomas à),
Besant (Annie), Boehme (Jakob),
Borgia, Browne (Robert), Browne
(Sir Thomas), Buddha, Bunyan
(John), Calvin (John), Christ,
Gandhi (Mohandas), Garvey
(Marcus), Graham (Billy), Hillel,
Hutter (Leonhard), Jowett
(Benjamin), Julian (of Norwich),
Kempis (Thomas à), Lao-tzu,
Luther (Martin), Mather (Cotton),
Mesmer (Franz Anton), Olcott
(Colonel Henry Steel), Pilate
(Pontius), Raikes (Robert), Ridley
(Nicholas), Rogers (John), Sieyès
(Emmanuel Joseph Comte), Tetzel
(Johann), Wesley (John)
07 Aga Khan, al-Banna (Hassan),
Ayeshah, Buchman (Frank), Coligny
(Gaspard de), Cranmer (Thomas),
Crowley (Aleister), Erasmus
(Desiderius), Falwell (Jerry),
Fénelon (François), Hubbard
(L Ron), Jackson (Jesse), Latimer
(Hugh), Mahatma, Müntzer
(Thomas), Paisley (Reverend Ian),
Photius, Russell (Charles Taze),
Russell (Jack), Sithole (Reverend
Ndabaningi), Spooner (William
Archibald), Steiner (Rudolf),
Tyndale (William), William (of
Malmesbury), William (of
Ockham), William (of Tyre), Wishart
(George), Zwingli (Huldreich)
08 Agricola (Johann), Andrewes
(Lancelot), Barabbas, Buchanan
(George), Caiaphas, Khomeini
(Ayatollah Ruhollah), Mahavira
(Vardhamana), Mohammed,
Muhammad, Pelagius, Rasputin
(Grigoriy), Selassie (Emperor Haile),

Williams (Roger), Wycliffe (John)
09 Akhenaten, Bar Kokhba (Simon),
Blavatsky (Madame Helena),
Confucius, Dalai Lama, Guru
Nanak, Joan of Arc (St), McPherson
(Aimee Semple), Niemöller
(Martin), Zoroaster
10 Belshazzar, Fateh Singh (Sant),
Huntingdon (Selina Hastings,
Countess of), Manichaeus,
Savonarola (Girolamo),
Swedenborg (Emmanuel),
Torquemada (Tomás de),
Whitefield (George)
11 Bodhidharma, Jesus Christ, Prester
John, Ramakrishna, Wilberforce
(William)
12 Krishnamurti (Jiddu)
13 Judas Iscariot
15 Francis of Assisi (St)

Religious officers include:

03 nun
04 dean, guru, imam, monk, pope
05 abbot, canon, elder, friar, imaum,
kohen, padre, prior, rabbi, rebbe,
swami, vicar
06 abbess, bishop, clergy, curate,
deacon, father, mullah, parson,
pastor, priest, rector
07 muezzin, prelate, proctor
08 cardinal, chaplain, minister,
preacher
09 ayatollah, clergyman, Dalai Lama,
deaconess, Monsignor, Tashi Lama
10 archbishop, archdeacon, arch-
priest, chancellor
11 clergywoman, Panchen Lama
14 mother superior

See also **archbishop; cardinal;
missionary; pope; theologian**

Religious orders include:

04 IBVM, Sufi
05 Taizé
06 Culdee, Essene, Jesuit, Loreto,
Marist
07 Jesuits, Marists, Rifaite
08 Buddhist, Capuchin, Grey nuns,
Minorite, Trappist, Ursuline
09 Barnabite, Capuchins, Carmelite,
Dominican, Marianist, Mawlawite,
mendicant, Salesians, Trappists,
Ursulines
10 Bernardine, Carmelites, Carthusian,
Celestines, Cistercian, Conventual,
Dominicans, Franciscan, Gilbertine,
Grey friars, Norbertine, Oratorians,
Poor Clares
11 Augustinian, Benedictine, Black
friars, Camaldolite, Carthusians,
Cistercians, Franciscans,
Ignorantine, Sylvestrine, White friars
12 Augustinians, Austin friars,
Benedictines
13 Society of Mary
14 Knights Templar, Sisters of Mercy,
Society of Jesus

See also **monastery; sect**

• **religious education**
02 RE, RI

religiously
08 strictly **10** rigorously **11** doctrinally, spiritually **12** meticulously, scrupulously **13** theologically **15** conscientiously

relinquish
04 cede, drop, part, quit **05** cease, demit, forgo, let go, waive, yield **06** desert, desist, forego, give up, resign **07** abandon, abstain, discard, forsake, give out, release, retreat **08** abdicate, hand over, part with, renounce **09** repudiate, surrender **11** discontinue

reliquary
04 chef, tope **09** encolpion **10** tabernacle

relish
03 sar **04** gout, gust, like, love, lust, tang, zest **05** adore, charm, enjoy, gusto, sauce, savor, smack, spice, taste, tooth **06** bumalo, degust, flavor, palate, pickle, savour, vigour **07** botargo, bummalo, chutney, delight, flavour, garnish, kitchen, rellish, revel in, stomach **08** appetite, bumaloti, caponata, opsonium, piquancy, pleasure, vivacity **09** appetizer, bummaloti, condiment, delight in, enjoyment, seasoning **10** appreciate, Bombay duck, experience, flavouring, liveliness **12** appreciation, satisfaction
• **lose relish**
04 pall

relocate
02 go **04** move **05** leave **06** go away, remove **08** move away, transfer, up sticks **09** move house **13** change address

reluctance
07 dislike **08** aversion, distaste, loathing **09** hesitancy, renitency **10** hesitation, opposition, repugnance, resistance **12** backwardness **13** indisposition, recalcitrance, unwillingness **14** disinclination

reluctant
03 shy **04** loth, slow **05** loath **06** averse **08** backward, grudging, hesitant, loathful, renitent **09** resisting, squeamish, unwilling **10** indisposed, struggling **11** disinclined **14** unenthusiastic

rely
04 bank, lean, rest **05** count, trust **06** be sure, depend, reckon **07** swear by

remain
02 be **03** lie **04** bide, keep, last, rest, stay, wait **05** abide, abode, await, dwell, leave, stand, stick, tarry **06** endure, linger, stay on **07** climate, persist, prevail, subsist, survive **08** continue, outstand **09** hang about, stand good **10** be left over, hang around, stay behind **11** stick around

remainder
04 lave, rest **06** excess **07** balance, remains, remanet, remnant, residue,

surplus **08** remanent, residuum, vestiges **09** carry-over, leftovers **11** superfluity

remaining
03 odd **04** last, left, over **05** other, spare **06** unused **07** abiding, lasting, remnant, unspent **08** left over, remanent, residual **09** lingering, surviving **10** persisting, unfinished **11** outstanding

remains
03 ash **04** body, dust, rest, ruin **05** ashes, bones, dregs, ruins **06** corpse, crumbs, debris, relics, scraps, traces **07** cadaver, carcase, residue **08** dead body, detritus, leavings, oddments, remnants, vestiges **09** fragments, leftovers, reliquiae, remainder, reversion **11** odds and ends

remake
◇ *anagram indicator*
06 mutate **07** rebuild **09** modernize, reproduce, transmute **11** reconstruct **12** metamorphose

remark
03 hit, say **04** barb, jeer, note, quip, shot **05** ad-lib, sally, state **06** assert, insult, notice, reason **07** clanger, comment, declare, mention, observe, opinion **08** brickbat, cynicism, intimacy, one-liner, remarque **09** assertion, gallantry, pronounce, reference, statement, stricture, utterance, witticism **10** commentary, reflection, trivialism **11** commonplace, declaration, discourtesy, non sequitur, observation **12** obiter dictum **13** pronouncement **14** noteworthiness **15** acknowledgement

remarkable
◇ *anagram indicator*
03 odd **04** fine, rare, some, tall, unco **06** signal **07** amazing, notable, strange, unusual **08** singular, striking, uncommon **09** damnedest, important, memorable, momentous, prominent **10** hellacious, impressive, inimitable, miraculous, noteworthy, phenomenal, pre-eminent, surpassing, surprising **11** conspicuous, exceptional, outstanding, significant **12** considerable, unbelievable **13** distinguished, extraordinary
• **remarkable thing**
04 lulu

remarkably
04 unco **08** signally, uncommon **09** unusually **10** uncommonly **12** considerably, surprisingly **13** exceptionally, outstandingly, significantly **15** extraordinarily

remedy
◇ *anagram indicator*
03 fix **04** cure, ease, heal, help, mend, sort **05** azoth, dinic, salve, solve, tonga, treat **06** answer, bicarb, nosode, physic, posset, recure, relief, remead, remede, remeid, repair, soothe **07** arcanum, control, correct, nostrum,

panacea, plaster, rectify, redress, relieve, restore, sort out, therapy **08** antidote, cephalic, corn-cure, leechdom, lungwort, medicine, mitigate, pilewort, put right, solution, specific **09** echinacea, eyebright, Galenical, hoarhound, horehound, magistery, prescript, salvarsan, treatment **10** catholicon, corrective, counteract, medicament, medication, reparation, simillimum, tarantella **11** oil of cloves, restorative **12** panpharmacon **13** antiscorbutic, antispasmodic, viper's bugloss **14** countermeasure, white horehound

remember
03 mem **04** keep, mark, mind **05** evoke, learn, place, think **06** honour, recall, record, remind, retain **07** mention, think of **08** hark back, look back, memorize, summon up **09** celebrate, recognize, recollect, reminisce, think back **10** bear in mind, call to mind **11** commemorate, hold against, reconnoitre **12** learn by heart, pay tribute to **13** send greetings **14** commit to memory, send best wishes, send good wishes **15** send your regards

remembrance
04 mind **05** relic, token **06** memory, recall, record **07** memento, thought **08** keepsake, memorial, monument, reminder, souvenir **09** nostalgia, sovenance **10** memorandum, retrospect **11** recognition, recordation, testimonial **12** recollection, reminiscence **13** commemoration

remind
04 hint **05** evoke, nudge **06** call up, prompt **08** remember, take back **10** call to mind **11** bring to mind **13** jog your memory **14** make you think of, put you in mind of

reminder
04 hint, memo, note, prod **05** nudge, token **06** prompt **07** memento **08** keepsake, souvenir **09** red letter **10** memorandum, phylactery, prompt-note, suggestion, verbal note **11** aide-mémoire, remembrance **12** reality check

reminisce
06 recall, review **08** hark back, look back, remember **09** recollect, think back **10** retrospect

reminiscence
06 memoir, memory, recall, review **08** anecdote **10** reflection **11** remembrance **12** recollection **13** retrospection
• **collection of reminiscences**
03 ana

reminiscent
08 redolent **09** evocative, nostalgic, remindful **10** suggestive

remiss
03 lax **04** slow **05** slack, tardy **06** casual, sloppy **07** wayward

8 careless, culpable, dilatory,
needless, slipshod **09** forgetful,
negligent, unmindful **10** neglectful
11 inattentive, indifferent, slack-
handed, thoughtless **13** lackadaisical

remission
3 ebb **04** lull **05** let-up **06** excuse,
pardon, repeal **07** amnesty, release,
respite **08** decrease, remittal, reprieve
9 abatement, acquittal, annulment,
discharge, exemption, lessening,
reduction, remitment, weakening
0 abrogation, absolution, diminution,
indulgence, indulgency, moderation,
relaxation, rescinding, revocation,
slackening, suspension **11** alleviation,
exoneration, forgiveness
2 cancellation **13** acceptilation

remit
3 pay **04** mail, post, send **05** abate,
brief, refer, relax, scope, untax
6 cancel, desist, direct, give up,
orders, pardon, pass on, repeal, revoke,
settle **07** forward, release, rescind,
suspend **08** abrogate, dispatch, hold
over, set aside, transfer, transmit
0 guidelines, overslaugh
2 instructions **13** authorization
4 responsibility

remittance
3 fee **07** payment, sending
8 dispatch **09** allowance, remitment
3 consideration

remnant
3 bit, end, tag **04** butt, fent, rump
5 piece, scrap, shred, trace, wrack
6 offcut **07** balance, oddment, outlier,
remains, residue, vestige, witness
8 fragment, leftover, remanent
9 quotation, remainder, remaining
2 odd-come-short

remodel
◇ anagram indicator
4 turn **05** adapt, alter, renew, shape
6 adjust, change, mutate, reform
7 convert, furbish, rebuild
8 renovate **09** modernize, refurbish,
transform **11** recondition, reconstruct
2 metamorphose

remonstrance
7 protest, reproof **08** petition
9 complaint, exception, grievance,
objection, reprimand **10** opposition
2 protestation **13** expostulation
4 representation

remonstrate
5 argue, gripe **06** object, oppose
7 dispute, dissent, protest
8 complain **09** challenge
11 demonstrate, expostulate **13** take
issue with **15** take exception to

remorse
3 rew, rue **04** bite, pity, ruth, worm
5 grief, guilt, shame **06** regret, sorrow
8 ayenbite, had-I-wist **09** penitence
10 contrition, mitigation, repentance,
ruefulness **11** compunction
2 contriteness, self-reproach **13** bad
conscience

remorseful
03 sad **05** sorry **06** guilty, rueful
07 ashamed **08** contrite, penitent
09 chastened, regretful, repentant,
sorrowful **10** apologetic **11** guilt-
ridden **12** compunctious, on a guilt trip
13 compassionate

remorseless
04 hard **05** cruel, harsh, stern
06 savage **07** callous **08** inhumane,
pitiless, ruthless **09** merciless
10 implacable, inexorable, relentless,
unmerciful **11** hard-hearted,
undeviating, unforgiving, unrelenting,
unremitting, unstoppable
12 unremorseful

remorselessly
07 cruelly, harshly **08** savagely
09 callously **10** implacably, inexorably,
ruthlessly **11** mercilessly **12** relentlessly
13 unremittingly

remote
03 far, out **04** back, long, poor, slim
05 aloof, faint, inapt, small **06** far-off,
lonely, meagre, slight, upland
07 devious, distant, dubious, faraway,
outback, outside, removed, slender
08 backveld, detached, doubtful,
isolated, outlying, reserved, secluded,
unlikely **09** not matter, ungermane,
unrelated, up the bush, withdrawn
10 extraneous, immaterial,
improbable, inapposite, in the mulga,
irrelative, irrelevant, negligible, out of
place, peripheral, tangential,
uninvolved, up the mulga **11** back-
country, god-forsaken, in the sticks, off
the point, out-of-the-way, standoffish,
unconcerned, unconnected,
unimportant, up the Boohai
12 inaccessible, inapplicable,
inconsequent, long-distance
13 beside the mark, inappropriate,
insignificant **14** beside the point,
inconsiderable, unapproachable
15 having no bearing, not coming into
it, uncommunicative

removable
07 movable **09** separable
10 detachable, eradicable
12 transferable

removal
04 boot, move, push, sack **05** elbow,
shift **06** firing, murder **07** ousting,
purging, sacking **08** ablation, deletion,
disposal, ejection, eviction, riddance,
shifting **09** abolition, clearance,
departure, discharge, dismissal,
expulsion, taking-off, uprooting
10 conveyance, deposition,
detachment, displacing, evacuation,
extraction, relegation, relocation,
taking away, withdrawal **11** subtraction,
transferral **12** dislodgement,
obliteration, transference, transporting
14 transportation

remove
03 nip, rid **04** dele, doff, fire, flit, lift,
move, oust, pick, sack, shed, take, void,
weed **05** amove, carry, eject, eloin,

erase, evict, expel, purge, raise, shift,
strip **06** ablate, convey, cut off, cut out,
delete, depose, detach, efface, eloign,
excise, extort, get out, go away, lop off,
remble, rub out, unseat **07** abolish,
absence, boot out, cart off, cashier,
cast out, collect, destroy, dismiss, edge
out, expurge, extract, pull off, pull out,
put away, removal, take off, take out,
tear off **08** amputate, cross out,
dislodge, disloign, displace, estrange,
get rid of, relegate, relocate, separate,
subtract, take away, throw out, transfer,
withdraw **09** discharge, eliminate, go
off with, strike out, translate, transport
10 blue-pencil, obliterate
11 deaccession

remunerate
03 pay **05** repay **06** reward **07** redress
09 indemnify, reimburse
10 compensate, recompense

remuneration
03 fee, pay **04** sold **05** solde, wages
06 income, profit, reward, salary
07 payment, stipend **08** earnings,
retainer **09** emolument, indemnity,
repayment **10** honorarium,
recompense, remittance
12 compensation **13** reimbursement

remunerative
04 rich **06** paying **07** gainful **08** fruitful
09 lucrative, rewarding **10** profitable,
worthwhile **11** moneymaking

renaissance
07 new dawn, rebirth, renewal, revival
08 new birth **09** awakening
10 renascence, resurgence
11 reawakening, re-emergence,
restoration **12** reappearance,
regeneration, rejuvenation,
resurrection, Risorgimento
13 recrudescence

renascent
06 reborn **07** renewed, revived
09 born again, redivivus, resurgent
10 reanimated, reawakened, re-
emergent **11** resurrected

rend
03 rip **04** rent, rive, stab, tear **05** break,
burst, sever, smash, split, wring
06 cleave, divide, pierce, to-rend
07 rupture, shatter **08** fracture,
lacerate, separate, splinter **09** tear
apart **10** dilacerate

render
◇ anagram indicator
02 do **03** gie, pay, put, try **04** give,
make, melt, play, show, sing, turn
05 leave, yield **06** change, depict, give
up, make up, return, submit, supply,
tender **07** clarify, deliver, display,
exhibit, explain, furnish, perform,
present, proffer, provide **08** describe,
give back, hand over, manifest
09 cause to be, interpret, represent,
reproduce, surrender, translate
10 contribute, transcribe

rendering
04 crib, show **05** gloss **06** acting

07 reading, version **09** portrayal, rendition, rewording **10** appearance, paraphrase, production, rephrasing **11** explanation, metaphrasis, performance, translation **12** presentation **13** transcription **14** interpretation, representation, simplification **15** transliteration

rendezvous
02 RV **04** date, meet **05** haunt, rally, tryst, venue **06** gather, muster, resort **07** collect, convene, meeting **08** assemble, converge **10** engagement **11** appointment, assignation **12** come together, meeting-place **13** trysting-place

rendition
05 gloss **07** reading, version **08** delivery **09** depiction, execution, portrayal, rendering, rewording, surrender **10** paraphrase, rephrasing **11** arrangement, explanation, performance, translation **12** construction, presentation **13** transcription **14** interpretation, simplification **15** transliteration

renegade
◇ *anagram indicator*
03 rat **05** rebel **06** outlaw **07** runaway, traitor **08** apostate, betrayer, defector, deserter, disloyal, mutineer, mutinous, recreant, runagate, turncoat **09** dissident **10** backslider, perfidious, rebellious, traitorous, unfaithful **11** backsliding, treacherous **13** tergiversator

renege
04 deny, pike **05** renig, welsh **06** refuse **07** default, renague, renegue **08** renounce **09** backslide, repudiate **10** apostatize **13** cross the floor

renegotiate
◇ *anagram indicator*

renew
◇ *anagram indicator*
03 new **04** mend, stum **05** boost, refit **06** extend, reform, reline, repair, repeat, reseat, resume, revive **07** brush up, prolong, refresh, remodel, replace, reprise, reprize, restart, restate, restock, restore, retrace **08** continue, innovate, overhaul, reaffirm, recreate, renforce, renovate **09** modernize, refurbish, reiterate, replenish, transform **10** invigorate, recommence, regenerate, rejuvenate, revitalize **11** recondition, re-establish, resuscitate **12** reconstitute, reinvigorate

renewal
05 flush **06** repair **07** rebirth, recruit, revival **08** new birth, nidation **09** recruital **10** kiss of life, re-creation, renovation, repetition, resumption **11** continuance, reiteration, restatement **12** instauration, regeneration, rejuvenation, resurrection **13** reaffirmation, refurbishment, replenishment, resuscitation **14** recommencement,

reconditioning, reconstitution, reconstruction, reinvigoration, revitalization, revivification

renounce
03 cut **04** deny, reny, shun **05** forgo, renay, reney, renig, spurn, waive **06** abjure, desist, disown, eschew, forego, forsay, give up, pass up, recant, recede, refuse, reject, renege, resign, revolt **07** abandon, abstain, discard, disgown, foresay, forsake, put away, renague, renegue **08** abdicate, abnegate, disclaim, forswear, sign away, swear off **09** repudiate, surrender **10** declare off, disinherit, disprofess, relinquish **14** forisfamiliate **15** wash your hands of

renovate
◇ *anagram indicator*
04 do up **05** refit, renew **06** reform, repair, revamp **07** furbish, improve, remodel, restore **08** overhaul **09** modernize, refurbish, translate **10** redecorate, regenerate **11** recondition **12** rehabilitate **13** give a facelift

renovation
05 refit **06** repair **07** renewal **08** facelift **11** improvement, restoration **13** modernization, refurbishment **14** reconditioning

renown
04 bays, fame, , mana, mark, note **05** glory, kudos, rumor **06** esteem, honour, luster, lustre, repute, rumour **07** acclaim, stardom **08** eminence, prestige **09** celebrate, celebrity **10** prominence, reputation **11** distinction, pre-eminence **15** illustriousness

renowned
05 famed, noted **06** fabled, famous **07** eminent, notable **08** of repute **09** acclaimed, prominent, splendent, well-known **10** celebrated, illustrate, pre-eminent **11** illustrious, prestigious **13** distinguished

rent
◇ *anagram indicator*
03 fee, let, rip **04** cost, farm, gale, hire, mail, rate, ript, take, tare, tear, tore, torn **05** cuddy, gavel, lease, riven, split **06** let out, rental, ripped, screed, sublet **07** charter, divided, fissure, hire out, payment, rent out, revenue, severed **08** lacerate, purchase, ruptured **09** lacerated, torn apart **11** ripped apart

renunciation
06 denial **07** kenosis, waiving **08** giving up, shunning, spurning **09** disowning, forsaking, rejection, surrender **10** abdication, abnegation, abstinence, desistance, discarding, disclaimer **11** abandonment, disclaiming, recantation, repudiation **13** disinheriting **14** relinquishment, self-abnegation

reorder
◇ *anagram indicator*
04 edit **09** rearrange, transpose

reorganize
◇ *anagram indicator*
05 rejig **07** shake up **09** modernize, rearrange **10** streamline **11** rationalize, restructure **12** reconstitute

repackage
◇ *anagram indicator*

repair
◇ *anagram indicator*
02 go **03** fix, sew **04** darn, form, heal, mend, move, nick, turn **05** order, patch, refit, renew, shape, state **06** adjust, doctor, fettle, kilter, make up, remead, remede, remedy, remeid, remove, resort, retire, return, tinker **07** mending, patch up, rectify, redress, refresh, restore, service **08** maintain, make good, overhaul, put right, renovate, revivify, stitch up, withdraw **09** concourse, condition **10** adjustment, reparation **11** improvement, maintenance, restoration, wend your way **12** preservation, working order

reparable
07 curable, savable **10** corrigible, remediable, restorable **11** recoverable, rectifiable, retrievable, salvageable

reparation
04 boot **06** amends, remead, remede, remedy, remeid, repair **07** damages, redress, renewal **08** requital, solatium **09** atonement, indemnity **10** assythment, recompense **11** restitution **12** compensation, propitiation, satisfaction

repartee
03 wit **06** banter, retort **07** jesting, riposte **08** backchat, badinage, wordplay **09** bantering, cross-talk, witticism **11** give and take

repast
04 feed, food, meal **05** board, lunch, snack, table **06** spread **08** victuals **09** collation, refection **11** nourishment
See also **meal**

repatriate
04 oust **05** exile, expel **06** banish, deport **09** extradite, ostracize, transport

repay
03 pay **04** apay, quit **05** appay, quite, quyte, yield **06** avenge, quight, rebate, refund, return, reward, settle, square **07** pay back, requite, revenge **09** get back at, quittance, reimburse, retaliate **10** compensate, recompense, remunerate **11** get even with, reciprocate **12** settle up with **14** settle the score

repayment
06 amends, rebate, refund, reward **07** payment, redress, revenge **08** requital **09** tit for tat, vengeance **10** recompense, reparation **11** eye for an eye, restitution, retaliation, retribution **12** compensation, remuneration **13** reciprocation, reimbursement

repeal
04 lift, void 05 annul, quash, unlaw
06 abjure, cancel, recall, recant, revoke
07 abolish, nullify, repress, rescind,
retract, reverse 08 abrogate, quashing,
reversal, set aside, withdraw
09 abolition, annulment
10 abrogation, invalidate, rescinding,
rescission, revocation, withdrawal
11 countermand, rescindment
12 cancellation, invalidation
13 nullification

repeat
◇ repetition indicator
03 rep, rpt 04 copy, echo, redo
05 ditto, labor, quote, recap, recur,
renew, rerun, thrum 06 do over, go
over, labour, parrot, patter, recite,
record, re-echo, relate, replay, reshow,
retail, retell, reword, run off, screed
07 confirm, divulge, iterate, persist,
recount, replica, reprise, reprize,
restate 08 redouble, rehearse,
remurmur, say again 09 celebrate,
circulate, do to death, duplicate,
reiterate, replicate, reproduce,
reshowing 10 repetition
11 duplication, perseverate,
rebroadcast, reduplicate, restatement
12 recapitulate, reproduction
14 recapitulation

repeated
◇ repetition indicator
07 regular 08 constant, frequent,
multiple, periodic 09 continual,
recurrent, recurring 10 persistent,
reiterated, rhythmical 12 repercussive

repeatedly
◇ repetition indicator
05 often 10 frequently 11 over and over
12 time and again 13 again and again,
time after time

repel
◇ reversal indicator
05 check, fight, parry, rebut, spurn
06 offend, oppose, rebuff, refuse,
reject, resist, revolt, sicken 07 beat off,
decline, disgust, hold off, repulse, turn
off, ward off 08 beat back, drive off,
fight off, nauseate, push back 09 drive
back, force back, keep at bay,
repudiate 11 make you sick 13 be
repugnant to 15 turn your stomach

repellent
04 foul, grim, vile 05 nasty 06 horrid
07 hateful, obscene 08 shocking
09 abhorrent, loathsome, obnoxious,
offensive, repugnant, repulsive,
revolting, sickening 10 abominable,
despicable, disgusting, nauseating, off-
putting, unpleasant 11 distasteful,
rebarbative 12 contemptible,
disagreeable 13 objectionable
• insect repellent
04 deet 07 camphor

repent
03 rue 04 turn 06 lament, recant,
regret, relent, sorrow 07 be sorry,
confess, deplore, reptant 08 do a U-
turn 09 be ashamed 10 be contrite

11 be converted, feel remorse, see the
light 14 beat your breast

repentance
03 rue 05 grief, guilt, ruing, shame, U-
turn 06 regret, rueing, sorrow
07 penance, remorse 08 metanoia
09 penitence 10 confession, contrition,
conversion 11 compunction,
recantation

repentant
05 sorry 06 guilty, rueful 07 ashamed,
attrite 08 contrite, penitent
09 chastened, regretful, sorrowful
10 apologetic, remorseful

repercussion
04 echo 06 effect, recoil, result, ripple
07 rebound, spin-off 08 backlash,
backwash 09 shock wave
10 reflection, side-effect
11 consequence 13 reverberation

repertoire
04 list 05 range, stock, store 06 supply
07 reserve 09 repertory, reservoir
10 collection, repository

repetition
◇ repetition indicator
04 echo, rote 05 troll 06 answer,
repeat, return 07 copying, echoing,
quoting, reprise 08 iterance
09 echolalia, iteration, rehearsal,
replicate, tautology 10 recurrence,
redundancy 11 duplication,
epanalepsis, reiteration, restatement,
superfluity 12 reappearance
14 recapitulation

repetitious
04 dull 05 windy, wordy 06 boring,
prolix 07 tedious, verbose 08 unvaried
09 redundant 10 long-winded,
monotonous, pleonastic, unchanging
12 pleonastical, tautological

repetitive
04 dull 05 samey 06 boring 07 tedious
08 unvaried 09 automatic, iterative,
recurrent 10 mechanical,
monotonous, unchanging 14 soul-
destroying

rephrase
06 recast, reword 07 rewrite
10 paraphrase 13 put another way
14 ask differently, say differently 15 put
in other words

repine
04 beef, fret, moan, mope, pine, sulk
05 brood 06 grieve, grouch, grouse,
grudge, lament, murmur 07 grumble
08 complain, languish

replace
◇ anagram indicator
04 oust 06 act for, change, follow, hang
up, refund, return 07 pre-empt, put
back, relieve, replant, restore, succeed
08 deputize, displace, exchange, make
good, supplant 09 come after, fill in for,
reinstate, supersede 10 stand in for,
substitute 11 re-establish 14 take the
place of

replaceable
09 throwaway 10 disposable,
expendable 12 exchangeable
13 biodegradable, non-returnable,
substitutable 15 interchangeable

replacement
05 proxy 06 fill-in, supply 07 bionics,
reserve, stand-in 09 spare part,
successor, surrogate 10 jury-rudder,
substitute, understudy 12 arthroplasty,
substitution

replenish
04 fill 05 renew, stock, top up 06 fill up,
make up, people, refill, reload, supply
07 furnish, provide, recruit, refresh,
replace, restock, restore 08 recharge

replenishment
06 supply 07 filling, renewal
09 provision, refilling 10 recharging,
restocking, supplyment
11 replacement, restoration

replete
04 full 05 sated 06 filled, full up,
gorged, jammed 07 brimful, charged,
chocker, crammed, glutted, implete,
stuffed, teeming, well-fed
08 brimming, satiated 09 abounding,
chock-full, jam-packed 11 chock-a-
block, well-stocked 12 well-provided

repletion
04 glut 07 satiety 08 fullness, plethora
09 plenitude, satiation 11 superfluity
12 completeness, overfullness
14 superabundance

replica
04 copy, spit 05 clone, dummy, model
06 repeat 08 gold disc, gold disk
09 duplicate, facsimile, imitation
10 immortelle 12 reproduction

replicate
03 ape 04 copy 05 clone, mimic, reply
06 follow, repeat 08 recreate
09 duplicate, reproduce 10 repetition
11 reduplicate

reply
04 echo 05 duply, react 06 answer,
come in, rejoin, retort, return, triply
07 counter, respond, riposte 08 come
back, comeback, reaction, rebutter,
repartee, response, surrebut, talk back
09 drink-hail, quadruply, rejoinder,
replicate, retaliate, surrejoin, write back
11 acknowledge, reciprocate,
replication, retaliation, surrebutter
12 surrejoinder, triplication 13 counter-
signal 15 acknowledgement

report
◇ homophone indicator
03 air, cry, rat, rpt 04 bang, boom,
buzz, fame, file, item, name, news,
note, rept, shop, shot, tale, talk, tell,
word 05 blast, brief, bruit, cover, crack,
crash, grass, noise, piece, relay, split,
state, story, voice 06 cahier, convey,
credit, detail, esteem, furphy, gossip,
honour, notify, pass on, record, relate,
renown, repute, return, rumour, squeal,
tell on, update 07 account, article,

declare, divulge, dossier, give out, hearsay, message, minutes, narrate, opinion, publish, recount, stature, stool on, whisper, write-up **08** announce, blue book, bulletin, complain, describe, disclose, document, inform on, proclaim, register, relation, set forth, standing **09** appraisal, broadcast, celebrity, character, chronicle, circulate, delineate, explosion, judgement, narrative, statement, testimony **10** assessment, communiqué, evaluation, inspection, reputation, stenograph **11** communicate, compte rendu, declaration, delineation, description, distinction, examination, information **12** announcement, press release, procès-verbal **13** communication, reverberation

reportedly
◇ *homophone indicator*
09 allegedly **10** apparently, ostensibly, putatively, supposedly **13** by all accounts

reporter
03 cub **04** hack **05** press **06** leg-man **07** fireman, Jenkins **08** leg-woman, newshawk, pressman **09** announcer, columnist, newshound, roundsman **10** journalist, newscaster, news-writer, presswoman, tripehound **11** commentator **12** newspaperman **13** correspondent **14** newspaperwoman

repose
03 kef, kif, lay, lie, put, set **04** affy, calm, ease, kaif, laze, lean, rest **05** lodge, peace, place, poise, quiet, relax, sleep, store **06** aplomb, invest **07** confide, deposit, dignity, entrust, recline, respite, slumber **08** calmness, quietude, serenity **09** composure, night-rest, quietness, stillness **10** equanimity, inactivity, relaxation **11** restfulness **12** tranquillity **14** self-possession

reposition
◇ *anagram indicator*
05 shift **09** rearrange

repository
03 urn **04** bank, mart, safe, tomb **05** depot, store, vault **06** museum **07** archive, dustbin, spicery **08** magazine, treasury **09** confidant, container, repertory, salvatory, sepulchre, warehouse **10** collection, depository, promptuary, receptacle, storehouse

reprehensible
03 bad, ill **04** base **06** errant, erring, remiss **07** ignoble **08** blamable, culpable, shameful, unworthy **10** censurable, delinquent, deplorable **11** blameworthy, condemnable, disgraceful, opprobrious **13** discreditable, objectionable

represent
◇ *anagram indicator*
02 be **03** act, set **04** draw, mark, mean,

show **05** act as, enact, evoke, refer **06** act for, allege, denote, depict, embody, figure, render, sketch, typify **07** display, exhibit, express, perform, picture, portray, present **08** amount to, appear as, describe, speak for, stand for **09** appear for, character, depicture, designate, epitomize, exemplify, personify, sculpture, symbolize **10** constitute, illustrate **11** deputize for **12** characterize, correspond to **13** act on behalf of **14** act in the name of, be equivalent to **15** speak on behalf of

representation
◇ *anagram indicator*
02 MP **04** bust, icon, ikon, play, show **05** envoy, image, model, proxy, stage **06** deputy, reflex, report, shadow, sketch, statue **07** account, drawing, picture, protest, request, showing, stand-in **08** delegate, likeness, petition, portrait, prospect **09** complaint, depiction, depicture, pictogram, portrayal, spectacle, spokesman, statement, tablature **10** allegation, ambassador, councillor, delegation, deputation, mouthpiece, production, thermoform **11** Congressman, delineation, description, explanation, performance, presentment, restoration, spokeswoman **12** cross-section, illustration, presentation, remonstrance, reproduction, spokesperson **13** Congresswoman, expostulation, tableau vivant **14** reconstruction, representative

representative
02 MP **03** rep **05** agent, envoy, proxy, rider, usual, vakil **06** bagman, chosen, deputy, exarch, normal, sample, vakeel **07** drummer, elected, stand-in, typical **08** delegate, devolved, elective, salesman, specimen, symbolic **09** appointed, delegated, exemplary, nominated, spokesman, traveller **10** ambassador, archetypal, authorized, councillor, delegation, deputation, emblematic, exhibitive, indicative, mouthpiece, saleswoman **11** congressman, salesperson, spokeswoman **12** ambassadress, commissioned, commissioner, illustrative, representant, spokesperson **13** decentralized, heir-portioner **14** characteristic **15** knight of the road

repress
◇ *containment indicator*
04 cork, curb **05** check, crush, quash, quell, sit on, sneap **06** cork up, master, muffle, repeal, stifle, subdue **07** control, inhibit, oppress, put down, reprime, silence, sit upon, smother, swallow **08** bottle up, dominate, domineer, hold back, keep back, keep down, overcome, restrain, suppress, vanquish **09** overpower, subjugate **11** bite your lip

repressed
06 hung-up, pent-up **07** uptight

09 inhibited, withdrawn **10** frustrated **11** introverted **14** self-restrained

repression
07 control, gagging, tyranny **08** coercion, crushing, muffling, quashing, quelling, stifling **09** despotism, restraint **10** censorship, constraint, domination, inhibition, oppression, smothering **11** holding-back, subjugation, suffocation, suppression **12** dictatorship

repressive
05 cruel, harsh, tough **06** severe, strict **08** absolute, coercive, despotic **10** autocratic, dominating, oppressive, tyrannical **11** dictatorial **12** totalitarian **13** authoritarian

reprieve
05 let-up, spare **06** acquit, let off, pardon, redeem, relief, rescue **07** amnesty, forgive, relieve, reprive, reprove, respite **08** abeyance, repreeve, show pity **09** abatement, deferment, remission, show mercy **10** suspension **12** postponement **13** let off the hook **15** stay of execution

reprimand
04 jobe, lace **05** blame, check, chide, scold, slate, targe **06** berate, bounce, carpet, earful, rebuke, rocket, see off **07** bawl out, catch it, censure, chew out, go off at, lambast, lecture, reproof, reprove, rouse on, tell off, tick off, wigging **08** admonish, lace into, lambaste, reproach **09** carpeting, castigate, criticize, dress down, pull apart, schooling, take apart, talking-to **10** admonition, telling-off, ticking-off, upbraiding **11** castigation **12** dressing-down **13** call to account, tongue-lashing **14** bring to account, slap on the wrist **15** smack on the wrist

reprisal
05 prize **06** ultion **07** redress, reprise, reprize, revenge **08** requital **09** recaption, recapture, tit for tat, vengeance **11** eye for an eye, retaliation, retribution **12** compensation **13** counter-attack, recrimination

reprise
03 act **04** play, sing **05** prize, put on, renew **06** relate, repeat **07** copying, echoing, narrate, perform, quoting, reissue **08** iterance, reprisal **09** iteration, recapture, rehearsal **10** repetition **11** reiteration, restatement **12** compensation **14** recapitulation

reproach
04 blot, slur, twit, wite, wyte **05** blame, braid, chide, scold, scorn, shame, shend, slate, smear, stain, taunt, touch, wight **06** bounce, carpet, defame, earful, rebuke, rocket, see off, stigma, upcast **07** bawl out, blemish, catch it, censure, chew out, condemn, nayword, obloquy, reproof, reprove,

tell off, tick off, upbraid, wigging
08 admonish, contempt, disgrace,
dishonor, ignominy, repriefe, scolding
09 carpeting, criticism, criticize,
discredit, dishonour, disparage,
dispraise, disrepute, dress down,
mispraise, pull apart, reprehend,
reprimand, take apart, talking-to
10 admonition, cri de coeur,
disrespect, imputation, opprobrium,
reflection, telling-off, ticking-off
11 degradation, disapproval
12 condemnation, dressing-down
13 find fault with **14** slap on the wrist
15 smack on the wrist
• **term of reproach**
03 gib **04** runt **05** besom, bisom,
madam **06** ronyon, truant **07** Cataian,
Catayan, runnion **09** rigwiddie,
rigwoodie

reproachful
08 critical, scolding, scornful
09 reproving **10** censorious,
upbraiding **11** castigating, disgraceful,
disparaging, opprobrious
12 disappointed, disapproving, fault-
finding

reprobate
03 bad, rep **04** base, rake, roué, vile
05 knave, rogue, scamp **06** damned,
disown, rascal, reject, sinful, sinner,
wicked, wretch **07** censure, corrupt,
dastard, immoral, villain **08** criminal,
depraved, evildoer, hardened,
vagabond **09** abandoned, dissolute,
miscreant, scallywag, scoundrel,
shameless, wrongdoer **10** degenerate,
ne'er-do-well, profligate
11 reprobative, reprobatory
12 condemnatory, incorrigible,
troublemaker, unprincipled
13 mischief-maker

reprocess
◇ *anagram indicator*
07 recycle

reproduce
◇ *anagram indicator*
03 ape **04** copy, echo, redo **05** breed,
cline, clone, match, mimic, print, refer,
spawn, Xerox® **06** follow, mirror,
pirate, remake, render, repeat
07 emulate, enlarge, express,
gemmate, imitate, reflect **08** autotype,
generate, multiply, recreate, refigure,
simulate **09** bear young, duplicate,
facsimile, give birth, photocopy,
Photostat®, phototype, procreate,
propagate, replicate **10** hectograph,
regenerate, transcribe **11** proliferate,
reconstruct

reproduction
04 copy, hi-fi, mono **05** clone, print,
repro, Xerox® **06** ectype, piracy
07 edition, picture, replica
08 breeding, monogeny, monogony
09 duplicate, facsimile, imitation,
photocopy, Photostat®
10 amphimixis, generation, viviparism
11 gamogenesis, monogenesis,
procreation, propagation, replication

12 regeneration **14** multiplication,
representation

reproductive
03 sex **06** sexual **07** genital **08** prolific
10 generative **11** procreative,
progenitive, propagative

reproof
04 rate **05** shame, sloan **06** earful,
lesson, rebuke, rocket, sermon
07 censure, jarring, lecture, upbraid,
wigging **08** berating, disgrace,
disproof, repriefe, reproach, reproval,
scolding **09** carpeting, criticism,
reprimand, reproving, schooling,
talking-to **10** admonition, correption,
telling-off, ticking-off, upbraiding
11 castigation **12** condemnation,
dressing-down, reprehension
14 curtain lecture, disapprobation, slap
on the wrist **15** smack on the wrist
• **expression of reproof**
03 now, tut **04** come, toot, tuts
05 toots **06** tut-tut **07** come now, now
then **08** come come

reprove
03 rap **04** rate **05** chide, scold, slate
06 berate, bounce, carpet, rebuke,
refute, see off, take up **07** bawl out,
catch it, censure, chew out, condemn,
lecture, rouse on, tell off, tick off,
upbraid **08** admonish, call down,
disprove, reprieve, reproach
09 castigate, criticize, dress down, pull
apart, reprehend, reprimand, take
apart **10** take to task

reptile

04 croc, tegu
05 gator
06 caiman, cayman, garial, gavial,
    mugger, turtle
07 gharial, hicatee, snapper, tuatara
08 aligarta, galapago, hiccatee,
    matamata, stinkpot, teguexin,
    terrapin, tortoise
09 alligarta, alligator, crocodile,
    hawksbill, mud turtle, sea turtle
10 loggerhead, musk turtle
11 green turtle, leatherback
13 giant tortoise, water tortoise
14 leathery turtle, snapping turtle
15 hawksbill turtle

See also **animal; dinosaur; lizard; snake**

republic

03 USA
04 Chad, Cuba, Fiji, Iran, Iraq, Laos,
    Mali, Peru, Togo
05 Benin, Burma, Chile, China, Congo,
    Egypt, Gabon, Ghana, Haiti, India,
    Italy, Kenya, Malta, Nauru, Niger,
    Palau, Sudan, Syria, Yemen
06 Angola, Brazil, Cyprus, France,
    Greece, Guinea, Guyana, Israel,
    Latvia, Malawi, Mexico, Panama,
    Poland, Russia, Rwanda, Taiwan,
    Turkey, Uganda, Zambia
07 Albania, Algeria, Armenia, Austria,

Belarus, Bolivia, Burundi, Croatia,
    Ecuador, Estonia, Finland, Georgia,
    Germany, Hungary, Iceland, Ireland,
    Lebanon, Liberia, Moldova,
    Myanmar, Namibia, Nigeria,
    Romania, Senegal, Somalia, Tunisia,
    Ukraine, Uruguay, Vanuatu, Vietnam
08 Botswana, Bulgaria, Cameroon,
    Colombia, Djibouti, Ethiopia,
    Honduras, Kiribati, Maldives,
    Mongolia, Pakistan, Paraguay,
    Portugal, Slovakia, Slovenia, Sri
    Lanka, Suriname, Tanzania,
    Zimbabwe
09 Argentina, Cape Verde, Costa Rica,
    East Timor, Guatemala, Indonesia,
    Lithuania, Macedonia, Mauritius,
    Nicaragua, San Marino, Singapore,
    The Gambia, Venezuela
10 Azerbaijan, Bangladesh, El Salvador,
    Kazakhstan, Kyrgyzstan,
    Madagascar, Mauritania,
    Mozambique, North Korea,
    Seychelles, South Korea, Tajikistan,
    Uzbekistan
11 Burkina Faso, Côte d'Ivoire,
    Philippines, Sierra Leone, South
    Africa, Switzerland
12 Guinea-Bissau, Turkmenistan
13 Czech Republic, Western Sahara
15 Marshall Islands

See also **country**

repudiate
04 deny **05** repel **06** abjure, desert,
disown, nochel, reject, revoke
07 abandon, cast off, disavow, discard,
divorce, forsake, notchel, rescind,
retract, reverse **08** denounce,
disclaim, renounce **09** disaffirm
10 disprofess **14** turn your back on

repudiation
06 denial **09** disavowal, disowning,
rejection **10** abjuration, disclaimer,
retraction **11** recantation
12 renunciation **13** disaffirmance
14 disaffirmation

repugnance
05 odium **06** hatred, horror, nausea,
revolt **07** allergy, disgust, dislike
08 aversion, distaste, loathing
09 abhorring, antipathy, repulsion,
revulsion **10** abhorrence, reluctance,
repugnancy **11** reluctation
13 inconsistency

See also **disgust; distaste**

repugnant
04 foul, vile **05** alien **06** averse, horrid,
odious **07** adverse, hateful, hostile,
noisome, opposed **08** inimical
09 abhorrent, loathsome, obnoxious,
offensive, repellent, resisting,
revolting, sickening, unwilling
10 abominable, disgusting, nauseating
11 distasteful **12** antagonistic,
antipathetic, incompatible,
inconsistent, unacceptable
13 contradictory, objectionable

repulse
04 foil, snub **05** check, refel, repel,

spurn **06** defeat, rebuff, refuse, reject
07 beat off, disdain, failure, put back,
refusal, reverse **08** spurning
09 disregard, drive back, rejection
11 repudiation **14** disappointment

repulsion

06 action, effect, hatred **07** disgust
08 aversion, distaste, loathing
09 disrelish, revulsion **10** abhorrence,
repellence, repellency, repugnance
11 detestation, raison d'être

repulsive

04 cold, foul, icky, loth, ugly, vile
05 gross, loath, nasty **06** horrid, odious
07 hateful, heinous, hideous, squalid
08 reserved, shocking **09** abhorrent,
loathsome, obnoxious, offensive,
repellent, repelling, repugnant,
revolting, sickening **10** abominable,
despicable, disgusting, forbidding,
nauseating, off-putting, unpleasant
11 distasteful **12** contemptible,
disagreeable, evil-favoured,
unattractive **13** objectionable,
reprehensible

repulsively

10 abominably, despicably, shockingly
11 obnoxiously **12** disagreeably,
disgustingly, nauseatingly, unpleasantly
13 objectionably

reputable

04 good, gude, guid **06** honest,
worthy **07** upright **08** esteemed,
reliable, virtuous **09** admirable,
estimable, excellent, respected
10 creditable, dependable, honourable
11 respectable, trustworthy **12** of good
repute, of high repute **13** well-thought-
of **14** irreproachable

reputation

03 los, rep **04** fame, loos, name, note,
pass, rank **05** image, izzat, voice
06 credit, esteem, honour, infamy,
renown, repute, status **07** opinion,
respect, stature **08** estimate, good
name, position, prestige, standing
09 celebrity, character, notoriety
10 estimation **11** distinction **12** good
standing **14** respectability

repute

04 fame, name, odor **05** odour, rumor,
savor, stock **06** esteem, regard,
renown, report, rumour, savour
07 stature **08** good name, standing
09 celebrity **10** estimation, reputation
11 distinction
• **of doubtful repute**
03 shy

reputed

03 dit **04** held, said **06** judged
07 alleged, assumed, seeming, thought
08 apparent, believed, presumed,
putative, reckoned, regarded,
rumoured, supposed **09** estimated
10 considered, ostensible, reputative

reputedly

09 allegedly, seemingly **10** apparently,
ostensibly, supposedly **12** reputatively
13 by all accounts

request

03 ask, beg, hit **04** boon, call, plea,
seek, suit, wish **05** apply, order
06 adjure, appeal, ask for, behest,
demand, desire, invite, prayer
07 beseech, bespeak, call for, call out,
entreat, require, send for, solicit
08 apply for, entreaty, petition,
pleading, put in for **09** impetrate
10 invitation, supplicate, write in for
11 application, imploration,
petitioning, requisition, write off for
12 solicitation, supplication

require

03 ask **04** draw, lack, make, miss, need,
take, want, will, wish **05** crave, exact,
force, order **06** call on, compel,
demand, desire, direct, enjoin, entail,
govern, oblige **07** call for, command,
involve, requere, request, solicit
08 insist on, instruct **09** be short of,
constrain, stipulate **11** necessitate
13 be deficient in

required

03 set **05** vital **06** needed **07** advised
08 demanded **09** essential, mandatory,
necessary, requisite **10** compulsory,
obligatory, prescribed, stipulated
11 recommended, unavoidable

requirement

04 fike, lack, must, need, term, want
06 demand **07** proviso **08** occasion
09 condition, essential, necessity,
provision, requisite **10** obligation, sine
qua non **11** desideratum, stipulation
12 precondition, prerequisite
13 qualification, specification

requisite

03 due, set **04** must, need **05** vital
06 needed **07** needful **08** required
09 condition, essential, implement,
mandatory, necessary, necessity
10 compulsory, obligatory, prescribed,
sine qua non **11** desideratum,
requirement, stipulation
12 desiderative, precondition,
prerequisite **13** indispensable,
qualification, specification

requisition

03 use **04** call, take **05** order, press,
seize **06** demand, indent, occupy
07 request, seizure, summons **08** put
in for, take over, takeover
10 commandeer, confiscate,
occupation **11** application, appropriate
12 confiscation **13** appropriation,
commandeering

requital

06 amends, pay-off, return
07 payment, quittal, redress
09 indemnity, quittance, repayment
10 recompence, recompense,
reparation **11** restitution, retribution
12 compensation, satisfaction
15 indemnification

requite

03 pay **04** apay, quit **05** repay
06 avenge, pay off, return, reward
07 redress, respond, satisfy **08** even up

on, requight **09** reimburse, retaliate
10 compensate, recompense,
remunerate **11** reciprocate
14 counterbalance

rescind

04 void **05** annul, quash **06** cancel,
negate, recall, repeal, revoke **07** cut
away, nullify, retract, reverse
08 abrogate, overturn, set aside
10 invalidate **11** countermand

rescission

06 recall, repeal **08** negation, reversal,
voidance **09** annulment
10 abrogation, retraction, revocation
11 rescindment **12** cancellation,
invalidation **13** nullification

rescue

04 free, save **05** pluck **06** ransom,
redeem, relief, reskew, reskue, saving
07 deliver, freeing, recover, release,
relieve, reprive, repryve, salvage, set
free **08** bring off, liberate, recovery,
repreeve, reprieve, retrieve
09 extricate, salvation **10** emancipate,
liberation, redemption **11** deliverance
12 emancipation

research

03 res **04** test **05** probe, study, tests
06 assess, review, search **07** analyse,
examine, explore, inquiry, inspect,
postdoc, testing **08** analysis, look into,
scrutiny **10** assessment, experiment,
groundwork, inspection, scrutinize
11 examination, exploration, fact-
finding, investigate **13** investigation
15 experimentation

researcher

06 boffin **07** analyst, student
08 inquirer **09** inspector **11** field
worker **12** investigator

resemblance

04 like **05** image, match **06** parity
07 analogy **08** affinity, likeness,
nearness, parallel, sameness
09 agreement, assonance, closeness,
congruity, facsimile, homophyly
10 appearance, comparison,
conformity, likelihood, similarity,
similitude, uniformity **11** parallelism
13 comparability **14** correspondence

resemble

04 echo **05** favor, mimic **06** be like,
depict, favour, mirror **07** compare
08 approach, look like, parallel
09 duplicate, take after **11** be similar to

resent

04 envy **06** grudge **07** dislike, stomach
08 begrudge, object to **09** be angry at,
grumble at, take amiss **12** have a derry
on **13** take offence at, take umbrage at
15 feel aggrieved at, feel bitter about,
take exception to

resentful

04 hurt **05** angry, irked **06** bitter, ireful,
miffed, peeved, piqued, put out
07 envious, jealous, wounded
08 grudging, incensed, offended,
spiteful **09** aggrieved, indignant,

ritated, malicious **10** embittered,
tomachful, stomachous, vindictive
13 in high dudgeon

resentment
3 ire **04** envy, hurt, miff **05** anger,
erry, pique, snuff, spite **06** grudge,
nalice **07** dudgeon, ill-will, offence,
mbrage **08** bad blood, ill blood,
ealousy, vexation **09** animosity,
nnoyance, hostility **10** bad feeling,
itterness, ill-feeling, irritation
11 displeasure, high dudgeon,
ndignation **12** hard feelings
14 vindictiveness

eservation
3 res, rez **04** park **05** demur, doubt,
rder, qualm, salvo, tract **06** doubts,
ualms, safety, saving, upkeep
07 booking, defence, enclave,
eeping, proviso, reserve, scruple,
torage, support **08** guarding,
omeland, preserve, scruples, security
09 condition, hesitancy, misgiving,
etention, sanctuary, upholding
10 engagement, hesitation, limitation,
nisgivings, protection, scepticism
11 appointment, arrangement,
naintenance, safekeeping, stipulation
12 conservation, continuation,
erpetuation, preservation,
afeguarding **13** arrière-pensée,
ualification **14** advance booking,
rearrangement, second thoughts
• **without reservation**
07 utterly **08** entirely, outright
09 gloves-off **10** completely **11** boots
nd all **12** unreservedly
14 unhesitatingly, wholeheartedly

eserve
02 TA **03** AVR, ice, MNR, res, RNR
04 area, bank, book, fund, help, hold,
eep, park, pool, RNVR, save
05 cache, defer, delay, extra, hoard,
rder, proxy, spare, stock, store, tract
06 backup, engage, fill-in, put off,
etain, secure, shelve, supply
07 adjourn, backlog, earmark, enclave,
nodesty, savings, shyness, stand-in,
upport, suspend **08** coldness,
oolness, distance, hold back, hold
ver, keep back, Landwehr, lay aside,
ostpone, preserve, set apart, set
side, Wavy Navy **09** aloofness,
uxiliary, reservoir, restraint, reticence,
ing-fence, sanctuary, secondary,
tockpile, successor, surrogate
10 accumulate, additional, arrange for,
rrière-ban, detachment, limitation,
rearrange, remoteness, substitute,
nderstudy **11** alternative, auxiliaries,
eplacement, reservation, restriction
12 accumulation, put on one side, put
o one side **13** secretiveness, self-
estraint **14** reinforcements
15 supplementaries
• **in reserve**
02 by **05** spare **06** in hand, stored, to
hand, unused **07** in petto, in store
08 set aside **09** available, in pectore

eserved
03 shy **04** cold, cool, held, kept

05 aloof, close, meant, saved, taken
06 booked, modest, remote, silent
07 distant, engaged, on appro,
ordered, private, retired, strange
08 arranged, backward, cautious,
destined, intended, retained, reticent,
retiring, set aside, taciturn **09** diffident,
earmarked, repulsive, secretive,
spoken for, withdrawn **10** designated,
restrained, unsociable **11** introverted,
prearranged, standoffish
12 unresponsive **13** self-contained,
unforthcoming **14** unapproachable
15 uncommunicative

reservoir
03 vat **04** bank, fund, lake, loch, pond,
pool, sump, tank, well **05** basin, stock,
store **06** gilgai, header, holder, source,
supply **07** cistern, gas tank, ghilgai, hot
well, urinary **08** fountain, reserves
09 container, inkholder, stockpile,
wind chest **10** header tank, receptacle,
repository, steam chest **11** reservatory
12 accumulation

resettle
◇ *anagram indicator*
07 migrate **08** emigrate **09** immigrate
10 transplant

reshape
◇ *anagram indicator*
05 alter **06** adjust, modify, mutate
07 convert **12** metamorphose

reshuffle
◇ *anagram indicator*
05 shift **06** change, revise **07** realign,
regroup, shake up, shake-up, shuffle
08 revision, upheaval **09** rearrange
10 regrouping, reorganize
11 interchange, realignment,
restructure **12** redistribute
13 rearrangement, restructuring
14 redistribution, reorganization

reside
03 lie, sit **04** hive, keep, live, rest, stay
05 abide, board, dwell, exist, house,
lodge **06** inhere, occupy, remain,
settle **07** hang out, inhabit, sojourn
09 be present **10** be inherent **11** be
contained

residence
03 pad, res **04** digs, flat, hall, home,
nest, seat, stay **05** abode, house,
lodge, manor, place, villa **06** des res,
palace **07** cottage, domicil, lodging,
mansion, sojourn **08** domicile,
dwelling, lodgings, mansonry, quarters
09 apartment, residency **10** habitation,
mansionary, praetorium, presidency,
second home **11** country seat,
inhabitance, inhabitancy, squarsonage,
summerhouse **12** country house
13 dwelling-place **14** winter quarters

resident
05 guest, local **06** client, inmate,
ledger, leiger, lieger, live-in, lodger,
tenant **07** citizen, dweller, en poste,
gremial, leidger, patient, resiant,
resider, settled **08** dwelling, inherent,
living-in, occupant, occupier

09 commorant, permanent, sojourner,
transient **10** inhabitant, inhabiting,
stationary **11** householder
13 neighbourhood

residential
07 exurban **08** commuter, suburban
09 dormitory

residual
03 net **06** excess, unused **07** surplus
08 left-over **09** reliquary, remaining
10 unconsumed

residue
04 coke, gunk, lees, rest **05** dregs,
extra, mazut, pitch, scrap, snuff
06 excess, mazout, pomace, slurry
07 asphalt, astatki, balance, clinker,
remains, remnant, surplus, tankage,
vinasse **08** charcoal, mine dump,
overflow, residuum **09** asphaltum,
carry-over, leftovers, remainder
10 difference, racemation, terra rossa
11 apiezon oils **12** caput mortuum

resign
04 quit **05** demit, forgo, leave, waive,
yield **06** forego, give up, retire, submit,
vacate **07** abandon, entrust, forsake,
throw up **08** abdicate, forelend,
renounce, step down **09** stand down,
surrender **10** relinquish
• **resign yourself**
03 bow **05** yield **06** accept, comply,
submit **09** acquiesce **11** come to terms

resignation
06 notice **07** waiving **08** giving-up,
patience, stoicism, yielding
09 defeatism, demission, departure,
passivity, surrender **10** abdication,
acceptance, compliance, retirement,
submission **12** acquiescence,
renunciation, standing-down,
stepping-down **13** non-resistance
14 reconciliation, relinquishment
• **expression of resignation**
04 well **05** ho-hum **07** heigh-ho

resigned
07 passive, patient, stoical **08** yielding
09 defeatist **10** reconciled, submissive
11 acquiescent, unresisting
12 unprotesting **13** long-suffering,
philosophical, uncomplaining

resignedly
09 patiently, stoically **12** submissively
15 philosophically, uncomplainingly

resilience
04 give, kick **06** bounce, recoil, spring
07 granite **08** buoyance, buoyancy,
strength **09** hardiness, toughness
10 bounciness, elasticity, plasticity,
pliability, suppleness **11** flexibility,
springiness **12** adaptability
14 unshockability

resilient
05 hardy, tough **06** bouncy, strong,
supple **07** buoyant, elastic, plastic,
pliable, rubbery, springy **08** flexible
09 adaptable, recoiling, springing
10 rebounding **11** unshockable
13 irrepressible

resin

03 lac **04** aloe, hing, kino **05** alkyd, aloes, amber, animé, copal, damar, elemi, epoxy, pitch, rosin, Saran®, vinyl **06** balsam, conima, dammar, dammer, guaiac, mastic, storax **07** acrylic, caranna, carauna, copaiba, copaiva, gamboge, hashish, jalapin, ladanum, mastich, Perspex®, shellac, xylenol **08** Araldite®, Bakelite®, cannabin, galbanum, guaiacum, hasheesh, kauri gum, olibanum, opopanax, propolis, retinite, sandarac, scammony, sweet gum **09** asafetida, courbaril, elaterite, sagapenum, sandarach, tacamahac, tacmahack **10** asafoetida, assafetida, euphorbium, turpentine **11** assafoetida, gum ammoniac, podophyllin **12** Canada balsam, frankincense, gum sandarach **13** Burgundy pitch, spirit varnish, thermoplastic

resist

04 buck, curb, defy, face, fend, halt, stem, stop, wear **05** avoid, check, fight, repel **06** battle, combat, defend, hinder, impede, jack up, oppose, refuse, thwart **07** contend, counter, deforce, prevent, weather **08** confront, fight off, obstruct, restrain, stick out, struggle **09** stand up to, withstand **10** counteract, gainstrive **12** stand against **14** hold out against

resistance

01 R **04** drag, kick, pull **05** fight, stand **06** battle, combat **07** refusal **08** defiance, fighting, struggle **09** avoidance, contumacy, hindrance, impedance, repulsion, restraint, thwarting **10** contention, impediment, opposition, prevention **11** contumacity, counter-time, obstruction **12** counter-stand, withstanding **13** confrontation, counteraction, intransigence **14** antiperistasis
• **passive resistance**
09 passivism **10** satyagraha **11** vis inertiae

resistant

04 anti- **05** proof, stiff, tough **06** immune, strong **07** defiant, opposed, viscous **08** renitent **09** unwilling, windproof **10** impervious, shellproof, shockproof, unaffected, unyielding, waterproof **12** antagonistic, intransigent, invulnerable **13** unsusceptible

resolute

03 set **04** bold, firm **05** fixed, hardy, stout, tough **06** dogged, intent, steady, strong, sturdy **07** adamant, decided, diehard, earnest, granite, serious, staunch **08** constant, obdurate, resolved, stalwart, stubborn **09** dauntless, dedicated, obstinate, steadfast, tenacious, unbending, undaunted **10** determined, flat-footed, inflexible, relentless, unswerving, unwavering, unyielding **11** persevering, unflinching **12** single-minded, strong-willed

resolutely

06 firmly **08** steadily, strongly **09** adamantly, earnestly, seriously, staunchly **10** inflexibly, resolvedly, stubbornly **11** dauntlessly, obstinately, steadfastly **12** relentlessly, unswervingly, unwaveringly **13** unflinchingly **14** single-mindedly

resolution

◇ *anagram indicator*
03 res **04** rede, zeal **05** point **06** answer, decree, motion, result **07** courage, finding, granite, melting, resolve, solving, thought, verdict **08** analysis, boldness, decision, devotion, firmness, solution, tenacity **09** constancy, judgement, willpower **10** abreaction, commitment, dedication, doggedness, intentness, sorting out, working out **11** declaration, earnestness, persistence, proposition, seriousness, unravelling **12** perseverance **13** determination, disentangling, inflexibility, steadfastness

resolve

◇ *anagram indicator*
03 fix, vow **04** melt, zeal **05** lapse, patch, relax, solve, untie **06** answer, assure, bottle, decide, detail, divide, inform, pecker, reduce, settle **07** analyse, analyze, break up, convert, courage, itemize, sort out, sublate, talk out, unravel, work out **08** boldness, conclude, devotion, dissolve, firmness, separate, settle on, tenacity **09** anatomize, break down, constancy, decompose, determine, dissipate, factorize, transform, willpower **10** commitment, dedication, doggedness, intentness **11** disentangle, earnestness, persistence, seriousness **12** disintegrate, perseverance **13** determination, inflexibility, steadfastness, straighten out **14** make up your mind, sense of purpose

resonance

05 depth **08** fullness, richness, sonority, strength, vibrancy **09** plangency **10** mesomerism, resounding **12** canorousness **13** reverberation

resonant

04 deep, full, rich **06** fruity, plummy, strong **07** booming, echoing, ringing, vibrant **08** canorous, plangent, sonorous **10** pear-shaped, resounding **11** reverberant **13** reverberating

resonate

04 boom, echo, ring **05** sound **06** re-echo **07** resound, thunder **11** reverberate

resort

◇ *anagram indicator*
02 go **03** spa, use **04** dive, draw, seek, spot, step **05** apply, frame, haunt, trade, visit **06** appeal, center, centre, chance, course, lounge, museum, option, refuge, repair, revert **07** doggery, measure **08** frequent,

recourse **09** concourse, dude ranch, frequency, patronize, thronging **10** rendezvous, sanatorium, sanitarium **11** alternative, night-cellar, possibility **12** health resort **13** holiday centre **14** course of action, stamping-ground

Resorts include:

04 Nice, Rhyl
05 Aspen, Davos
06 Cairns, Cannes, St Ives, St-Malo, Whitby
07 Funchal, Margate, Newquay, Torquay, Ventnor, Zermatt
08 Alicante, Aviemore, Benidorm, Biarritz, Chamonix, Honolulu, Klosters, Marbella, Montreux, Penzance, Skegness, St Helier, St Moritz, St-Tropez, Weymouth
09 Albufeira, Blackpool, Galveston, Gold Coast, Kitzbühel, Lanzarote, Morecambe, Nantucket
10 Baden Baden, Bondi Beach, Costa Brava, Eastbourne, Lake Placid, Long Island, Miami Beach, Monte Carlo, Windermere
11 Bognor Regis, Bournemouth, Bridlington, Cleethorpes, Coney Island, Costa Blanca, Costa del Sol, Costa Dorada, Gran Canaria, Grand Bahama, Palm Springs, Scarborough
12 San Sebastian, Santa Barbara, Waikiki Beach
13 Great Yarmouth, Southend-on-Sea
15 Martha's Vineyard, Weston-super-Mare

See also **spa**
• **in the last resort**
06 at last **07** finally **08** after all, in the end **10** eventually, ultimately **13** fundamentally, sooner or later
• **resort to**
03 use **04** seek **06** employ, invoke, turn to **07** utilize **08** exercise, frequent **09** make use of **10** fall back on **14** have recourse to **15** avail yourself of

resound

04 boom, echo, ring **05** sound **06** re-echo **07** thunder, vibrate **08** resonate **11** reverberate

resounding

04 full, loud, rich **05** great, vocal **07** booming, echoing, notable, reboant, ringing, roaring, vibrant **08** decisive, emphatic, plangent, resonant, rumorous, sonorous, striking, thorough **09** memorable, resonance **10** conclusive, impressive, remarkable, resonating, thunderous **11** outstanding **13** reverberating

resource

03 wit **04** fund, pool **05** funds, means, money, power, store **06** assets, course, device, fodder, resort, riches, source, supply, talent, wealth **07** ability, capital, reserve **08** artifice, holdings, property, reserves, supplies **09** expedient, ingenuity, materials, stockpile **10** capability, chevisance, enterprise, initiative **11** contrivance, imagination,

wherewithal **12** accumulation
13 inventiveness **15** resourcefulness

resourceful
04 able **05** fendy, sharp, witty
06 adroit, bright, clever **07** capable
08 creative, original, talented
09 ingenious, inventive, versatile
10 innovative **11** imaginative, quick-witted **12** enterprising

resourceless
06 feeble **07** useless **08** feckless,
helpless, hopeless **09** shiftless
10 inadequate

respect
03 way **04** duty, face, heed, obey
05 facet, honor, point, sense, value
06 admire, aspect, detail, esteem,
follow, fulfil, homage, honour, matter,
notice, praise, regard, revere
07 bearing, devoirs, feature, observe,
regards, worship **08** adhere to,
consider, courtesy, relation, venerate
09 approve of, attention, deference,
greetings, obeisance, reference,
reverence **10** admiration, appreciate,
best wishes, cognizance, comply with,
connection, good wishes, high regard,
particular, politeness, veneration
11 approbation, compliments, high
opinion, recognition, salutations
12 appreciation **13** attentiveness,
consideration, show regard for, think
highly of **14** characteristic, pay
attention to, thoughtfulness **15** set
great store by, take into account
• **title of respect, word of
respect**
01 U **03** Esq, oom, sir **04** Esqr, tuan
05 hodja, honor, khoja, molla
06 father, gaffer, honour, khodja,
kumari, mollah, moolah, mullah
07 Bahadur, effendi, esquire **08** holiness,
talapoin **10** burra sahib, worshipful
• **with respect to**
02 of, on, re **03** for, wrt **04** as to
05 about **07** apropos **09** as regards
10 concerning, in regard to **12** in
relation to, with regard to **14** on the
subject of **15** with reference to

respectability
07 decency, honesty **09** gentility,
integrity **10** worthiness **11** uprightness
15 trustworthiness

respectable
02 OK **04** fair, good, neat, nice, tidy
05 clean **06** decent, honest, not bad,
seemly, worthy **07** savoury, upright
08 adequate, all right, clean-cut,
decorous, mediocre, menseful,
passable, superior **09** dignified,
reputable, respected, sponsible,
tolerable **10** above-board, acceptable,
fairly good, honourable, reasonable,
salubrious **11** appreciable, clean-living,
presentable, trustworthy
12 considerable

respected
06 valued **07** admired **08** esteemed
12 highly valued **14** highly esteemed,
highly regarded **15** thought highly of

respectful
05 civil **06** humble, polite **07** courtly,
dutiful **08** reverent **09** courteous,
regardful **11** deferential, reverential,
subservient **12** well-mannered

respectfully
07 civilly **08** mannerly, politely
10 reverently **11** courteously
13 deferentially, reverentially

respecting
05 about **07** vis-à-vis **09** regarding
10 concerning **11** considering, in respect
of **12** with regard to **13** with respect to

respective
03 own **07** heedful, several, special,
various **08** personal, relative, relevant,
separate, specific **09** regardful
10 individual, particular **11** considerate
13 corresponding **14** discriminating

respectively
06 in turn **08** one by one **09** severally,
specially **12** individually, particularly,
specifically **15** correspondingly, in the
order given

respite
03 gap **04** halt, lull, rest, stay **05** break,
delay, frist, let-up, pause, truce **06** give
up, hiatus, put off, recess, relief
07 leisure, prolong **08** breather,
interval, reprieve **09** abatement,
breathing, cessation, deferment,
remission **10** moratorium, relaxation,
suspension **11** adjournment
12 intermission, interruption,
postponement **14** breathing space

resplendent
06 bright **07** beaming, fulgent, radiant,
shining **08** dazzling, gleaming,
glorious, luminous, lustrous, splendid
09 brilliant, effulgent, irradiant,
refulgent **10** glittering **11** magnificent
13 splendiferous

respond
04 rise **05** react, reply **06** answer,
behave, rejoin, retort, return
07 counter **10** answer back
11 acknowledge, reciprocate

response
03 tic **04** echo, rise **05** reply, touch
06 answer, retort, return **07** riposte
08 comeback, feedback, reaction
09 rejoinder **10** phototaxis
11 respondence **15** acknowledgement

responsibility
04 baby, care, duty, onus, role, task
05 blame, fault, guilt, power, trust
06 affair, burden, charge, pidgin, racket
07 concern, honesty **08** business,
maturity **09** adulthood, authority,
soundness, stability **10** obligation
11 culpability, reliability
13 answerability, dependability
14 accountability **15** trustworthiness

responsible
04 sane **05** adult, sober, sound
06 guilty, honest, liable, mature, stable,
steady **07** at fault, leading, to blame
08 culpable, managing, powerful,

rational, reliable, sensible, solidary
09 executive, high-level, important
10 answerable, dependable, in charge
of, reasonable **11** accountable,
blameworthy, controlling, in control of,
level-headed, trustworthy
13 authoritative, conscientious,
correspondent **14** decision-making

responsibly
08 honestly, reliably, sensibly, steadily
10 dependably, rationally, reasonably
15 conscientiously

responsive
04 open **05** alert, alive, awake, aware,
quick, sharp **06** with it **08** amenable,
reactive, sentient, swinging
09 answering, excitable, on the ball,
receptive, sensitive, teachable
10 perceptive, respondent, stimulable,
switched on **11** forthcoming,
susceptible, sympathetic
12 responsorial **13** correspondent
14 impressionable

responsiveness
05 mouth **08** openness **09** alertness,
awareness **11** sensitivity
13 receptiveness **14** susceptibility

rest
03 alt, lie, nap, sit, veg **04** base, calm,
doze, ease, halt, hang, last, laze, lean,
lull, noon, prop, rely, stay, stop
05 break, cease, hinge, light, pause,
quiet, relax, sleep, smoko, spell, stand
06 alight, anchor, bottom, cradle,
depend, endure, excess, feutre, fewter,
holder, lounge, others, recess, remain,
repose, settle, siesta, snooze, steady,
veg out **07** balance, be based, breathe,
holiday, leisure, lie down, lie-down,
persist, recline, relâche, remains,
remnant, residue, respite, sit down,
slumber, support, surplus, time off
08 breather, continue, idleness,
interval, quietude, remnants, residuum,
vacation **09** anchorage, cessation,
interlude, leftovers, remainder,
sabbatism, stillness **10** inactivity,
quiescence, quiescency, relaxation,
standstill, take breath, take it easy
12 intermission, tranquillity **13** put your
feet up **14** breathing space,
motionlessness
• **and the rest**
07 and so on **08** et cetera, et ceteri
10 and so forth
• **lay to rest**
04 bury **05** inter
• **rest upon**
04 ride

restaurant

04 café, caff
05 diner, grill, NAAFI
06 bistro, buffet, chippy, pull-in
07 canteen, carvery, chipper, milk bar,
taverna, tea room, tea shop
08 creperie, mess room, pizzeria,
snack-bar, sushi bar, taqueria,
teahouse

09 brasserie, burger bar, cafeteria, coffee bar, dining-car, grill room, refectory, trattoria
10 dining room, health food, rotisserie, steakhouse
11 eating-house, greasy spoon, sandwich bar, self-service
12 drivethrough, Internet café, luncheonette, motorway café
13 transport café
15 fish-and-chip shop, ice-cream parlour

Restaurants include:

06 The Ivy
07 El Bulli
09 L'Escargot
10 Paul Bocuse, Savoy Grill, The Fat Duck
11 The Wolseley
12 Gordon Ramsay, Heinz Winkler, The River Café, Waterside Inn
15 Les Pres d'Eugenie, Patrick Guilbaud

Fast food restaurant chains include:

03 KFC
06 Wendy's
08 Pizza Hut, Taco Bell
09 Harvester, McDonald's
10 Burger King, Dairy Queen, Little Chef
12 Domino's Pizza, Dunkin' Donuts, Hard Rock Café, Pizza Express
13 Baskin-Robbins, Harry Ramsden's
14 Subway Sandwich

restaurateur *see* **chef**

restful
04 calm **05** quiet, still **06** placid, serene **07** calming, languid, relaxed **08** peaceful, relaxing, soothing, tranquil **09** leisurely, unhurried **11** comfortable, undisturbed

restitution
06 amends, refund, return **07** damages, redress, restore **08** requital **09** indemnity, repayment, restoring **10** recompense, reparation **11** restoration **12** compensation, remuneration, satisfaction **13** reimbursement **15** indemnification

restive
04 edgy **05** inert, jumpy, resty, tense **06** on edge, uneasy, unruly, wilful **07** anxious, fidgety, fretful, nervous, restiff, uptight, wayward **08** agitated, restless **09** fidgeting, impatient, obstinate, turbulent, unsettled **10** hot-mouthed, refractory **12** recalcitrant, unmanageable **13** undisciplined **14** uncontrollable

restiveness
10 turbulence, unruliness, wilfulness **11** waywardness **12** restlessness

restless
◇ *anagram indicator*
04 edgy, toey **05** jumpy **06** broken, on edge, uneasy, unruly **07** agitato,

anxious, fidgety, fretful, jittery, nervous, restive, unquiet, uptight, worried
08 agitated, disquiet, troubled **09** disturbed, fidgeting, impatient, sleepless, turbulent, unsettled **10** changeable, wanrestful **13** uncomfortable

restlessly
09 anxiously, fretfully, nervously **11** impatiently, turbulently

restlessness
04 fike **05** hurry **06** bustle, fidget, unrest **07** anxiety, jitters, turmoil **08** activity, disquiet, dynamism, edginess, insomnia, movement **09** agitation, dysphoria, gate fever, jumpiness **10** fitfulness, inquietude, transience, turbulence, uneasiness **11** disturbance, fretfulness, inconstancy, instability, jactitation, nervousness, restiveness, spring fever, worriedness **12** fermentation **13** heebie-jeebies, unsettledness

restoration
◇ *anagram indicator*
06 repair, return **07** recruit, renewal, revival **08** recovery **09** recruital **10** kiss of life, rebuilding, renovation **11** refreshment, replacement, restitution **12** instauration, refurbishing, rejuvenation **13** reinstatement **14** reconstitution, reconstruction, rehabilitation, reinstallation, revitalization **15** re-establishment

restore
◇ *anagram indicator*
03 fix **04** do up, heal, mend, stet **05** renew **06** reform, repair, return, revamp, revive **07** build up, rebuild, recover, recruit, redress, refresh, replace, retouch **08** give back, hand back, refigure, re-impose, renovate, retrieve, revivify, undelete **09** reanimate, redeliver, re-enforce, refurbish, reinstate, restitute **10** bring round, redecorate, rejuvenate, revitalize, strengthen **11** recondition, reconstruct, re-establish, reintegrate, reintroduce, restitution **12** reconstitute, redintegrate, rehabilitate, reinvigorate

restrain
◇ *containment indicator*
03 bit, dam, tie **04** bank, bind, curb, heft, hold, jail, keep, rein, stay, stop **05** bound, chain, check, still, stint, trash **06** arrest, behold, bridle, coerce, detain, fetter, forbid, govern, hinder, hold in, hopple, impede, keep in, prison, rebuke, strain, subdue, tether **07** abstain, chasten, cohibit, confine, contain, control, impound, inhibit, injunct, manacle, prevent, refrain, repress, tighten **08** bottle up, chastise, compesce, conclude, hold back, hold down, imprison, keep back, keep down, obstruct, regulate, restrict, suppress, withhold **09** immanacle, temperate **10** hamshackle **11** hold captive, hold in check, keep in check

restrained
03 dry **04** calm, cold, cool, mild, soft **05** aloof, muted, quiet, sober **06** chaste, formal, low-key, modest, severe, steady, subtle **07** captive, classic, ordered, refined, relaxed, subdued **08** discreet, measured, moderate, reserved, ritenuto, tasteful **09** forbidden, temperate **10** abstemious, controlled **11** unemotional, unobtrusive **14** self-controlled, self-restrained **15** uncommunicative

restraint
03 dam, lid, tie **04** curb, grip, hold, rein, stay **05** block, bonds, check, cramp, limit, stint, trash **06** bridle, chains, duress, limits **07** barrier, bondage, control, fetters, measure, reserve **08** coercion, prudence **09** captivity, hindrance **10** constraint, inhibition, limitation, moderation, prevention **11** confinement, restriction, self-control, suppression **12** countercheck, imprisonment, restrictions, straitjacket **13** judiciousness **14** self-discipline

restrict
◇ *containment indicator*
03 tie **04** bind, curb, fast, hold **05** bound, cramp, hem in, limit, pinch, scant, stint, thirl **06** go slow, hamper, hinder, impede, ration **07** astrict, combine, confine, contain, control, curtail, inhibit, keep, peg down, tighten **08** handicap, localize, regulate, restrain, straiten, strangle **09** condition, constrain, constrict, demarcate **15** draw in your horns, pull in your horns

restricted
05 close, small, tight **06** closed, narrow, secret, strict **07** bounded, cramped, limited, private **08** confined **09** exclusive, parochial, regulated **10** controlled **11** constricted

restriction
03 ban **04** curb, rule **05** bound, check, limit, stint **06** burden, chains, ration **07** confine, control, embargo, proviso, reserve **08** handicap **09** condition, restraint, stricture **10** constraint, limitation, regulation **11** stipulation **13** qualification

restructure
05 rejig **07** shake up **09** modernize, rearrange **10** reorganize, streamline **11** rationalize

result
03 end, sum, win **04** flow, make, mark, stem, turn **05** arise, ensue, event, fruit, grade, issue, occur, score **06** answer, derive, effect, emerge, evolve, finish, follow, fruits, happen, pan out, pay-off, revert, sequel, spring, upshot **07** develop, emanate, outcome, proceed, product, rebound, spin-off, verdict **08** decision, reaction **09** by-product, come out of, corollary, culminate, eventuate, judgement,

terminate **10** conclusion, end-product, resolution, side effect **11** consequence, implication, termination **12** repercussion

resultant
07 ensuing **09** following, resulting **10** consequent, subsequent

resume
04 go on **06** reopen, take up **07** carry on, proceed, restart **08** continue, re-occupy, take back **09** reconvene, summarize **10** begin again, recommence, start again **11** rejuvenesce, take up again

résumé
02 CV **05** recap **06** digest, précis, review, sketch, wrap-up **07** epitome, outline, run-down, summary **08** abstract, overview, pirlicue, purlicue, synopsis **09** breakdown **14** recapitulation **15** curriculum vitae

resumption
06 sequel **07** re-entry, renewal, reprise, restart **09** reopening **10** proceeding, resurgence **11** epanalepsis **12** continuation **14** recommencement **15** re-establishment

resurgence
06 return **07** rebirth, revival **10** renascence, resumption **11** re-emergence, renaissance **12** re-appearance, resurrection, risorgimento **13** recrudescence **14** revivification

resurrect
05 renew **06** revive **07** restore **08** disinter **09** bring back, re-install **10** reactivate, revitalize **11** re-establish, reintroduce, resuscitate **13** restore to life **15** bring back to life

resurrection
06 return **07** rebirth, renewal, revival **08** comeback **09** anastasis **10** resurgence **11** renaissance, restoration **12** reappearance **13** resuscitation **14** revitalization **15** re-establishment

resuscitate
04 save **05** renew **06** rescue, revive **07** quicken, restore **08** revivify **09** reanimate, resurrect **10** bring round, revitalize **12** reinvigorate

resuscitated
07 revived **08** restored **09** redivivus **11** resurrected **12** redintegrate **13** redintegrated

resuscitation
03 CPR **07** renewal, revival **10** quickening **11** restoration **12** resurrection, revitalizing **14** reinvigoration, revivification

retain
◇ *containment indicator*
03 pay, ret **04** grip, heft, hire, hold, keep, save **05** brief, grasp **06** employ,

engage, keep on, keep up, recall **07** contain, occlude, reserve **08** conserve, continue, contract, hang on to, hold back, maintain, memorize, preserve, remember **09** recollect **10** bear in mind, call to mind, commission, hold fast to, keep hold of, keep in mind

retainer
03 fee **05** valet **06** lackey, menial, vassal **07** advance, deposit, footman, jackman, samurai, servant **08** domestic, follower **09** attendant, dependant, supporter **10** galloglass **11** gallowglass **12** retaining fee

retaliate
06 avenge **07** hit back, pay home **09** fight back, get back at **10** strike back **11** get even with, reciprocate, take revenge **13** counter-attack **14** get your own back, pay someone back

retaliation
06 retort, talion, ultion **07** revenge **08** reprisal **09** retorsion, retortion, tit for tat, vengeance **10** quid pro quo **11** eye for an eye, lex talionis, like for like, retribution **13** an eye for an eye, counter-attack, reciprocation

retard
03 lag **04** curb, slow **05** brake, check, delay, tardy **06** belate, hinder, hold up, impede **07** slacken **08** handicap, obstruct, postpone, restrict, slow down **10** decelerate **11** put a brake on **12** incapacitate **13** put the brake on

retardation
03 lag **05** delay **07** slowing **08** dullness, impeding, slowness **09** hindering, hindrance **10** deficiency, hysteresis, incapacity, inhibition, retardment **11** obstruction **12** incapability **14** mental handicap

retch
03 gag **04** barf, boak, bock, boke, keck, puke, reck, spew **05** heave, reach, vomit **06** sick up, strain **07** chuck up, fetch up, throw up **08** disgorge **11** regurgitate **13** heave the gorge

retching
04 heft, keck **06** nausea, puking **07** gagging, spewing **08** reaching, vomiting **12** vomiturition

retention
05 gripe **06** saving **07** custody, holding, keeping **09** hanging-on, holding on **11** continuance, keeping hold, maintenance **12** preservation

rethink
06 modify, review, revise **08** forthink, reassess **09** re-examine, think over **10** reconsider, think twice **13** think better of

reticence
07 reserve, silence **08** muteness **09** quietness, restraint **10** diffidence **11** taciturnity **13** secretiveness

reticent
03 shy **05** quiet **06** silent **08** boutonné, reserved, taciturn **09** boutonnée, diffident, inhibited, secretive **10** restrained **11** close-lipped, tight-lipped **12** close-mouthed, close-tongued **13** unforthcoming **15** uncommunicative

reticule *see* bag

retinue
04 many, port, tail **05** aides, meiny, staff, suite, train **06** escort, meiney, meinie, menyie **07** cortège, sowarry **08** equipage, servants, sowarree **09** comitatus, entourage, followers, following, personnel **10** attendancy, attendants

retire
◇ *reversal indicator*
02 go **03** den **04** move, step **05** leave **06** bow out, decamp, depart, go away, recede, resign, return **07** go aside, retreat, scratch **08** draw back, step down, stop work, withdraw **09** leave work **10** give up work, retirement **11** stop working **14** lick your wounds

retired
◇ *reversal indicator*
02 ex- **03** ret, rtd **04** past, retd **06** former **07** private **08** emeritus, secluded, solitary **09** recondite, withdrawn **11** sequestered

retirement
04 exit **06** recess **07** bedtime, privacy, retreat **08** solitude **09** departure, obscurity, seclusion **10** loneliness, withdrawal **11** recluseness, resignation

retiring
◇ *reversal indicator*
03 coy, shy **05** quiet, timid **06** humble, modest **07** bashful, recluse **08** reserved, reticent **09** diffident, shrinking **10** retreating, unassuming **11** unassertive, unobtrusive **12** self-effacing

retort
04 quip **05** reply, sally **06** answer, clinch, rejoin, return, zinger **07** counter, floorer, respond, riposte, squelch **08** backword, comeback, outfling, repartee, response, turn upon **09** rejoinder, retaliate, squelcher, throw back, wisecrack **11** retaliation

retract
◇ *reversal indicator*
04 deny **05** unsay **06** abjure, cancel, disown, draw in, move in, recant, renege, repeal, revoke **07** disavow, rescind, reverse, unspeak, unswear **08** abrogate, disclaim, draw back, move back, pull back, renounce, take back, withdraw **09** repudiate

retreat
◇ *reversal indicator*
03 den, mew **04** flee, lair, nest, neuk, nook, quit, rout **05** arbor, haven, leave, lodge, tower **06** alcove, arbour, ashram, asylum, bug out, decamp,

depart, flight, recede, recoil, recule, reduit, refuge, retire, shrink 07 back off, give way, harbour, hideout, privacy, recoyle, recuile, redoubt, retrait, retrate, shelter 08 crawfish, draw back, fall back, funkhole, growlery, hideaway, pull back, pull-back, retraict, retraite, solitude, turn back, turn tail, withdraw 09 back-pedal, climb down, climb-down, departure, hermitage, katabasis, sanctuary, seclusion 10 disadvance, evacuation, give ground, ivory tower, retirement, withdrawal 11 drawing-back, falling-back, pulling-back 12 beat a retreat, hibernaculum, interglacial, interstadial

retrench
03 cut 04 pare, save, trim 05 limit, prune 06 lessen, reduce 07 curtail, cut back, husband 08 decrease, diminish, slim down 09 economize 15 tighten your belt

retrenchment
03 cut 07 cutback, economy, pruning, run-down 09 reduction, shrinkage 11 contraction, cost-cutting, curtailment, cutting back

retribution
03 utu 05 karma 06 reward, talion 07 justice, Nemesis, payment, redress, revenge 08 reprisal, requital 09 reckoning, repayment, vengeance, vengement 10 punishment, recompense 11 just deserts, retaliation 12 compensation, satisfaction

retrieve
04 mend, read, save 05 fetch 06 access, recoup, redeem, regain, remedy, repair, rescue, return 07 get back, read out, reclaim, recover, restore, salvage 08 make good 09 bring back, recapture, repossess 11 put to rights

retro
03 old 04 past 05 passé 06 bygone, former, period 07 antique, old-time 10 olde-worlde 12 old-fashioned 13 in period style

retrograde
◇ *reversal indicator*
06 recede 07 inverse, regrede, reverse 08 backward, contrary, downward, negative 09 declining, reverting, worsening 10 retrogress 11 deteriorate 12 degenerating 13 deteriorating, retrogressive

retrogress
◇ *reversal indicator*
03 ebb 04 drop, fall, sink, wane 06 recede, retire, return, revert, worsen 07 decline, regress, relapse, retreat 08 withdraw 09 backslide 10 degenerate, retrograde 11 deteriorate 12 degeneration

retrogression
03 ebb 04 drop, fall 06 return 07 decline, regress, relapse 09 worsening 10 recidivism, regression 13 deterioration 14 retrogradation

retrospect
06 regard, review, survey 08 look back 09 hindsight 10 reflection 11 remembrance 12 afterthought, recollection, thinking back 13 re-examination
• **in retrospect**
◇ *reversal indicator*
11 looking back 12 on reflection, thinking back 13 retroactively, with hindsight 15 retrospectively

retrospective
◇ *reversal indicator*
11 ex post facto, retro-active 14 retro-operative 15 backward-looking

retrospectively
11 ex post facto, looking back 12 in retrospect, on reflection, thinking back 13 retroactively, with hindsight

return
◇ *reversal indicator*
03 ret 04 data, form, gain, turn 05 equal, match, recur, remit, repay, reply, yield 06 answer, go back, income, profit, record, refund, rejoin, render, report, retort, retour, revert, reward 07 account, benefit, bring in, counter, declare, deliver, get back, pay back, put back, redound, regress, replace, requite, respond, restore, revenue, riposte, takings 08 announce, come back, comeback, come home, delivery, document, exchange, give back, hand back, hand down, interest, proceeds, reappear, recourse, requital, send back, take back, turn away, turn back 09 advantage, backtrack, come again, do the same, pronounce, recursion, reimburse, reinstate, repayment, reversion, round-trip, statement 10 correspond, giving-back, home-coming, recompense, recurrence, taking-back 11 handing-back, happen again, reciprocate, replacement, restoration 12 reappearance 13 reciprocation, reinstatement
• **in return**
◇ *reversal indicator*
08 mutually 10 in exchange, in response 12 equivalently, reciprocally
• **point of no return**
07 Rubicon

Réunion
03 REU

re-use
◇ *anagram indicator*
07 recycle 12 reconstitute

revamp
◇ *anagram indicator*
04 do up 05 refit 06 recast, repair, revise 07 rebuild, restore 08 overhaul, renovate 09 modernize, refurbish 11 recondition, reconstruct 12 rehabilitate

reveal
◇ *anagram indicator*
04 ingo, leak, show, tell 05 let on 06 betray, bewray, descry, expose,

impart, let out, unfold, unmask, unveil 07 confess, display, divulge, exhibit, express, ingoing, lay bare, let slip, presage, publish, throw up, unbosom, uncover, unearth, unshale 08 announce, decipher, disbosom, disclose, discover, give away, manifest, proclaim, unshadow 09 broadcast, make aware, make known, publicize, undeceive 10 make public 11 communicate 12 blow the lid on, bring to light, expose to view, lift the lid on 15 take the wraps off

revealing
05 sheer 06 daring, low-cut 08 giveaway, telltale 10 diaphanous, indicative, revelatory, see-through 11 significant

revel
◇ *anagram indicator*
02 do 03 fug, joy 04 bask, crow, gala, orgy, rave, riot, wake 05 comus, enjoy, gloat, glory, lap up, party, roist, spree 06 rave-up, relish, savour, shivoo, thrive, wallow 07 carouse, debauch, delight, indulge, knees-up, large it, rejoice, roister, royster 08 carousal, live it up 09 bacchanal, celebrate, festivity, luxuriate, make merry, night-rule, whoop it up 10 have a party, saturnalia 11 celebration, have it large, merrymaking, take delight 12 raise the roof, take pleasure 13 jollification 14 push the boat out 15 paint the town red

revelation
04 fact, leak, news, show 06 detail, vision 07 display 08 betrayal, epiphany, exposure, giveaway 09 admission, eye-opener, unmasking, unveiling 10 apocalypse, confession, disclosure, divulgence, exhibition, expression, revealment, uncovering, unearthing 11 information, publication 12 announcement, broadcasting, proclamation 13 communication, manifestation

reveller
05 raver 07 roister, royster 08 bacchant, carouser, corybant 09 bacchanal, party-goer, roisterer, wassailer 10 celebrator, goodfellow, merrymaker, roaring boy 12 bacchanalian 14 pleasure-seeker

revelry
03 fun 04 riot 05 party, reels 07 jollity, wassail 08 carousal 09 festivity 10 debauchery 11 celebration, festivities, merrymaking 12 celebrations 13 jollification

revenge
03 get, utu 05 repay 06 avenge, pay off, ultion 07 hit back, redress, wreak of 08 avenging, reprisal, requital, revanche, serve out, vendetta 09 fight back, get back at, retaliate, tit for tat, vengeance 10 avengement, punishment 11 eye for an eye, get even with, retaliation, retribution 12 satisfaction, settle a score 14 get

your own back, pay someone back
15 take vengeance on

revengeful
06 bitter **08** pitiless, spiteful, vengeful,
wreakful **09** malicious, malignant,
merciless, resentful, vengeable
10 implacable, malevolent, unmerciful,
vindictive **11** unforgiving, vindicative

revenue
04 fisc, fisk, gain, rent **05** yield
06 income, profit, return **07** profits,
rewards, takings **08** incoming, interest,
proceeds, receipts **09** patrimony,
primitiae

reverberate
04 boom, echo, ring **06** recoil, re-echo
07 rebound, reflect, resound, vibrate
08 resonate **09** repercuss

reverberation
04 echo, wave **06** effect, recoil, result,
ripple **07** rebound, ringing **09** re-
echoing, resonance, shock wave,
vibration **10** reflection, resounding
11 consequence, replication
12 repercussion

revere
04 fear **05** adore, exalt **06** admire,
esteem, honour **07** idolize, respect,
worship **08** look up to, venerate
09 reverence **11** pay homage to
13 think highly of

reverence
03 awe **04** fear **05** adore, dread
06 admire, esteem, hallow, homage,
honour, revere **07** idolism, overawe,
respect, worship **08** devotion,
venerate **09** adoration, deference,
obeisance **10** admiration, exaltation,
high esteem, necrolatry, veneration
11 acknowledge, bibliolatry
13 ecclesiolatry

reverent
04 awed **05** pious **06** devout, humble,
loving, solemn **07** adoring, devoted,
dutiful **08** admiring, obeisant
10 respectful **11** deferential,
reverential, worshipping

reverie
05 study **06** musing, trance
08 daydream **10** brown study
11 abstraction, daydreaming,
inattention **13** preoccupation,
woolgathering

reversal
◇ *reversal indicator*
02 un- **04** blow, swap **05** check, delay,
knock, trial, upset, U-turn **06** defeat,
mishap, repeal **07** failure, problem,
reverse, setback, turning, undoing
08 exchange, hardship, negation
09 about face, adversity, annulment,
inversion, revulsion, turnabout,
turnround, volte-face **10** affliction,
difficulty, misfortune, rescinding,
revocation, turnaround
12 cancellation, misadventure
13 nullification **14** countermanding,
disappointment

reverse
◇ *reversal indicator*
04 back, blow, pile, rear, swap, turn,
undo **05** alter, annul, check, delay,
quash, tails, trial, up-end, upset, verso,
woman **06** cancel, change, defeat,
invert, mishap, negate, repeal, return,
revert, revoke, stroke **07** backset,
counter, failure, inverse, problem,
regress, rescind, retract, retreat,
setback, transit **08** backward, contrary,
converse, exchange, flip-flop, flipside,
hardship, inverted, opposite, overrule,
overturn, renverse, reversal, set aside,
withdraw **09** adversity, back-pedal,
backtrack, disaffirm, other side,
overthrow, transpose, turn round,
underside **10** affliction, antithesis,
backhanded, difficulty, invalidate,
misfortune, transverse, turn around
11 change round, countermand,
vicissitude **12** misadventure **13** move
backwards **14** disappointment, drive
backwards, put back to front, turn
upside-down

reversion
◇ *reversal indicator*
06 return **07** atavism, escheat, regress
09 puerilism, throwback **10** giving-
back, regression, taking-back
11 handing-back, hypostrophe,
restoration **13** reinstatement,
retrogression

revert
◇ *reversal indicator*
04 fall **05** lapse, recur **06** a tempo, fall
in, go back, recoil, resort, result,
resume, return **07** cut back, regress,
relapse, reverse, run wild, try back
08 fail safe **09** throw back, turn again
10 retrogress

review
◇ *anagram indicator*
◇ *reversal indicator*
03 pan **04** crit, view **05** judge, slate,
study, weigh **06** appeal, assess, go
over, notice, rating, report, revise, size
up, survey **07** analyse, discuss,
examine, inspect, journal, rethink,
weigh up, write up, write-up
08 analysis, appraise, critique,
evaluate, magazine, reassess, reviewal,
revision, scrutiny **09** appraisal,
comment on, criticism, criticize,
judgement, recension, re-examine,
summing-up **10** assessment,
commentary, evaluation, periodical,
reconsider, re-evaluate, retrospect,
scrutinize **11** examination, take stock of
12 reassessment, recapitulate, re-
evaluation, tour d'horizon **13** re-
examination **14** recapitulation
15 reconsideration

reviewer
05 judge **06** critic **07** arbiter
08 essayist, observer **11** commentator,
connoisseur

revile
04 hate, rail **05** abuse, libel, scorn,
smear **06** defame, malign, missay, vilify

07 despise, inveigh, miscall, slander,
traduce **08** reproach **09** denigrate
10 blackguard, calumniate, vituperate

revise
◇ *anagram indicator*
03 Rev **04** cram, edit **05** alter, amend,
emend, learn, mug up, study
06 change, go over, modify, peruse,
recast, revamp, review, reword,
rework, swot up, update **07** correct,
recense, redraft, rewrite **08** bone up
on, memorize, optimize **09** expurgate,
re-examine **10** reconsider **13** think
better of

revision
03 Rev **06** change, recast, review
07 editing **08** homework, learning,
studying, swotting, updating
09 amendment, recasting, recension,
rereading, reworking, rewriting
10 alteration, correction, diorthosis,
emendation, memorizing
12 modification **13** re-examination
14 reconstruction

revitalize
05 renew **06** revive **07** refresh, restore
08 revivify **09** reanimate, resurrect
10 reactivate, rejuvenate
12 reinvigorate

revival
04 Romo **06** upturn **07** Odinism,
rebirth, renewal, upsurge
08 comeback, wakening
09 awakening, lightning
10 quickening, resurgence
11 neopaganism, reawakening,
renaissance, restoration
12 resurrection, risorgimento
13 resuscitation, the kiss of life
14 reintroduction, revitalization **15** re-
establishment

revive
04 wake **05** rally, renew, rouse
06 awaken, rake up, relive **07** animate,
cheer up, comfort, quicken, recover,
refresh, restore **08** reawaken, rekindle,
revivify **09** reanimate, resurrect
10 bring round, invigorate, reactivate,
revitalize **11** re-establish, reintroduce,
resuscitate **12** reinvigorate

• **revivers**
10 Epsom salts

revivify
05 renew **06** repair, revive **07** refresh,
restore **08** inspirit **09** reanimate
10 invigorate, reactivate, revitalize
11 resuscitate

reviving
05 tonic **07** bracing, cordial
11 reanimating, revivescent,
revivifying, reviviscent, stimulating
12 enheartening, exhilarating,
invigorating, refreshening,
regenerating **13** resuscitative
14 reinvigorating

revocation
06 repeal, revoke **08** negation,
quashing, reversal, revoking
09 abolition, annulment, repealing

10 rescinding, rescission, retraction, revokement, withdrawal **11** countermand, repudiation **12** cancellation, invalidation, retractation **13** nullification **14** countermanding

revoke
04 lift **05** annul, check, quash, recal, renig **06** cancel, negate, recall, recant, renege, repeal, unpray **07** abolish, nullify, renague, renegue, rescind, retract, reverse, unshoot, unshout **08** abrogate, withdraw **09** unpredict **10** invalidate, revocation **11** countermand

revolt
◇ anagram indicator
04 coup, riot, rise **05** rebel, repel, shock **06** defect, mutiny, offend, putsch, resist, rise up, rising, sicken **07** disgust, dissent, fall off, outrage **08** apostasy, fall away, futurism, nauseate, uprising **09** breakaway, coup d'état, defection, Jacquerie, rebellion, revulsion, secession **10** revolution, scandalize, take up arms **12** insurrection **13** expressionism **15** Romantic Revival, the Paris Commune, turn your stomach

revolting
◇ anagram indicator
02 up **04** foul, vile **05** grody, nasty **07** hateful, heinous **08** horrible, shocking **09** abhorrent, appalling, insurgent, loathsome, obnoxious, offensive, repellent, repugnant, repulsive, sickening **10** abominable, disgusting, nauseating, off-putting **11** distasteful **13** reprehensible

revolution
◇ anagram indicator
◇ reversal indicator
04 coup, roll, spin, turn **05** cycle, orbit, round, wheel, whirl **06** change, circle, mutiny, putsch, revolt, rising **07** circuit, inqilab, revolve **08** gyration, mutation, rotation, upheaval, uprising **09** cataclysm, coup d'état, rebellion, sex change **10** innovation, insurgence, revolvency **11** reformation **12** insurrection **13** metamorphosis **14** transformation

revolutionary
◇ anagram indicator
◇ reversal indicator
03 new, red **04** trot **05** novel, rebel **07** drastic, radical **08** complete, Leninist, mutineer, mutinous **09** anarchist, Bolshevik, different, extremist, insurgent, Menshevik, seditious **10** avant-garde, filibuster,

innovative, rebellious, Sandinista, subversive, Trotskyist, Trotskyite **11** anarchistic, progressive, sansculotte **12** experimental **13** revolutionist, thoroughgoing **14** ground-breaking **15** insurrectionary, insurrectionist

revolutionize
06 reform **09** transform **10** reorganize **11** restructure, transfigure **14** turn upside-down

revolve
02 go **03** ren, rev, rin, run **04** move, spin, turn **05** orbit, pivot, think, twist, wheel, whirl **06** circle, gyrate, hang on, ponder, return, rotate, swivel, turn on **07** focus on, hinge on, turning **08** centre on, roll back **10** circumduct, revolution **11** circumvolve **13** concentrate on

revolver
03 gat, gun, rod **04** Colt®, iron **05** rifle **06** airgun, pistol **07** bulldog, firearm, handgun, shooter, shotgun **10** peacemaker, six-shooter **12** shooting iron

revolving
07 turning **08** gyrating, gyratory, rotating, spinning, whirling **12** peristrephic

revulsion
04 hate **06** hatred, nausea, recoil, revolt **07** disgust, dislike **08** aversion, distaste, loathing **09** repulsion **10** abhorrence, repugnance, withdrawal **11** abomination, detestation
See also **disgust**; **distaste**

reward
03 pay **04** gain, meed, wage **05** bonus, medal, merit, prise, prize, repay, wages, yield **06** bounty, desert, honour, pay-off, profit, quarry, return **07** benefit, guerdon, payment, premium, present, requite, salvage, testern, warison **08** consider, decorate, requital, sanction, warrison **09** head money, recognize, reguerdon, repayment **10** compensate, decoration, punishment, recompense, remunerate **11** just deserts, retribution **12** compensation, remuneration

rewarding
08 edifying, fruitful, pleasing, valuable **09** enriching, lucrative **10** beneficial, fulfilling, gratifying, productive, profitable, satisfying, worthwhile **11** retributive **12** advantageous, remunerative

rewording
04 edit **08** revision **09** rewriting **10** metaphrase, paraphrase, rephrasing **11** metaphrasis

rework
◇ anagram indicator
04 edit **05** alter, amend, emend **06** change, go over, modify, peruse, recast, revamp, review, revise, reword, update **07** correct, recense, redraft, rewrite **09** expurgate, re-examine, refashion **10** reconsider **13** think better of

rewrite
◇ anagram indicator
04 edit **05** emend, tweak **06** recast, revise, reword, rework **07** correct, redraft, rescore **08** inscribe, rescript

Rex
01 R

rhea
03 Ops **04** rami **05** nandu, ramee, ramie **06** nandoo, nhandu

rhenium
02 Re

rhesus
02 Rh

rhetoric
07 bombast, fustian, oratory, periods

09 eloquence, hyperbole, pomposity, prolixity, verbosity, wordiness
10 oratorical **11** speechcraft
13 magniloquence **14** grandiloquence, long-windedness

rhetorical
05 grand, showy, wordy **06** florid, prolix **07** aureate, flowery, pompous, verbose **09** bombastic, high-flown, insincere, stylistic **10** artificial, flamboyant, long-winded, oratorical
11 declamatory, pretentious
12 Churchillian, high-sounding, magniloquent **13** grandiloquent

Rhetorical devices include:

03 pun
05 irony, trope
06 aporia, bathos, climax, simile, zeugma
07 auxesis, epigram, erotema, litotes, meiosis, paradox
08 anaphora, chiasmus, diallage, diegesis, ellipsis, epanodos, erotetic, innuendo, metaphor, metonymy, oxymoron, parabole, symploce
09 asyndeton, cataphora, dissimile, epizeuxis, euphemism, hendiadys, hypallage, hyperbole, increment, prolepsis, syllepsis, tautology
10 abscission, anastrophe, anticlimax, antithesis, apostrophe, dysphemism, enantiosis, epanaphora, epiphonema, epistrophe, metalepsis, synchrysis, synecdoche
11 anacoluthon, anadiplosis, antiphrasis, antonomasia, catachresis, enumeration, epanalepsis, hypostrophe, hypotyposis, paraleipsis, parenthesis
12 alliteration, antimetabole, epanorthosis, onomatopoeia
13 amplification, dramatic irony, epanadiplosis, mixed metaphor, vicious circle
14 antimetathesis, double entendre, figure of speech
15 pathetic fallacy, personification

rheumatoid arthritis
02 RA

rhino *see* **money**

Rhode Island
02 RI

rhodium
02 Rh

rhubarb
03 rot, row **05** Rheum **06** rumpus
08 nonsense, pie-plant, squabble
09 rhapontic

rhyme
03 ode **04** poem, rime, song, tink
05 chime, ditty, rhime, verse
06 crambo, jingle, poetry, rhythm, verses **07** couplet **08** limerick
09 harmonize **13** versification

Rhymes include:

03 end, eye
04 half, head, male, near, rich, tail

05 slant, vowel
06 female, riding, tailed
08 feminine, internal
09 assonance, identical, masculine, pararhyme, rime riche
10 apocopated, cynghanedd, rhyme royal
13 rime suffisant

rhythm
04 beat, flow, lilt, stot, time **05** metre, pulse, rhyme, swing, tempo, throb
06 accent **07** cadence, cadency, harmony, measure, numbers, pattern
08 movement **09** voltinism

rhythmic
04 go-go **06** metric, steady
07 flowing, lilting, pulsing, regular
08 metrical, periodic, repeated
09 pulsating, throbbing **10** rhythmical
• rhythmic pattern
04 raga, tala **05** talea

rib
03 bar **04** band, bone, cord, gill, vein, wale, welt, wife **05** costa, groin, nerve, ogive, ridge, shaft, tease **06** cutlet, lierne, purlin **07** feather, futtock, nervure, ribbing, support
08 moulding, pork-chop, ridicule
09 tierceron **10** mutton chop **13** cross-springer **14** pleurapophysis

ribald
03 low **04** base, blue, lewd, mean, racy, rude **05** bawdy, gross **06** coarse, earthy, filthy, ribaud, risqué, smutty, vulgar **07** jeering, mocking, naughty, obscene, rybauld **08** derisive, indecent **09** off-colour, satirical
10 irreverent, licentious, scurrilous
11 foul-mouthed, Rabelaisian
13 disrespectful

ribaldry
04 smut **05** filth **07** jeering, lowness, mockery **08** baseness, derision, raciness, ribaudry, rudeness
09 bawdiness, grossness, indecency, obscenity, rybaudrye, vulgarity
10 coarseness, earthiness, scurrility, smuttiness **11** naughtiness
14 licentiousness

ribbing
06 banter **07** baiting, goading, kidding, mocking, ragging, teasing
08 annoying, ridicule, taunting
09 badgering **11** provocation

ribbon
03 jag, pad, tie **04** band, cord, line, pads, sash, tape **05** braid, cloth, flash, shred, strip, tenia **06** caddis, cordon, ferret, fillet, radula, riband, streak, stripe, taenia, tassel, tatter **07** caddice, caddyss, elastic, hatband, ribband, tieback **08** hair-band, headband, quilling, streamer **09** petersham, sword knot **10** cordon bleu, ticker tape
11 multistrike, watchspring

rice
04 reis, twig **05** paddy **07** arborio, zizania **09** brushwood

rich
03 fat **04** busy, deep, fine, full, high, lush, oily, oofy, warm **05** ample, fatty, flush, grand, heavy, juicy, ritzy, spicy, sweet, tasty, vivid **06** absurd, active, bright, costly, creamy, fecund, fruity, ironic, lavish, lively, loaded, mellow, monied, ornate, packed, strong
07 copious, fertile, intense, moneyed, opulent, profuse, replete, rolling, savoury, steeped, vibrant, wealthy, well-off **08** abundant, affluent, eventful, exciting, fruitful, gorgeous, luscious, palatial, precious, prolific, resonant, sonorous, splendid, valuable, well-to-do **09** abounding, brilliant, delicious, elaborate, expensive, laughable, luxurious, pecunious, plenteous, plentiful, priceless, sumptuous **10** filthy rich, full-bodied, in the money, outrageous, productive, prosperous, ridiculous, well-heeled
11 made of money, magnificent, mellifluous, overflowing, rolling in it
12 preposterous, rhinocerical, stinking rich, unreasonable, well-provided, well-supplied **13** full-flavoured **15** with money to burn

riches
04 dosh, gold, loot, pelf **05** brass, bread, dough, gravy, lolly, lucre, means, money, ready, smash **06** assets, greens, mammon, moolah, stumpy, wealth
07 fortune, readies, scratch, shekels
08 greenies, opulence, property, treasure **09** affluence, megabucks, resources, substance **10** prosperity
11 filthy lucre, spondulicks **12** the necessary

richly
04 well **05** fully **08** floridly, lavishly, properly, strongly, suitably
09 elegantly, opulently **10** completely, gorgeously, palatially, splendidly, thoroughly **11** elaborately, expensively, exquisitely, luxuriously, sumptuously
13 appropriately

richness
05 depth, taste **07** fatness **08** business, elegance, fullness, loudness, oiliness
09 abundance, fattiness, fertility, heaviness, intensity, juiciness, provision, resonance, splendour
10 creaminess, excitement, lavishness, liveliness, luxuriance, mellowness
12 eventfulness, magnificence
13 exquisiteness, luxuriousness, plentifulness, sumptuousness

rickety
◇ *anagram indicator*
05 crazy, shaky **06** feeble, flimsy, wobbly **07** tottery **08** decrepit, derelict, insecure, unstable, unsteady
10 broken-down, jerry-built, ramshackle **11** dilapidated

ricochet
03 bob, dap **04** jump, leap, stot
05 bound, carom, stoit, throw
06 bounce, recoil, spring **07** rebound
10 bounce back, spring back

rid

04 free, quit **05** clear, expel, purge, shift **06** purify, remove **07** cleanse, deliver, relieve **08** unburden **11** disencumber

• **get rid of**
04 cast, dump, junk **05** chuck, ditch, eject, expel, scrap, shake, shunt **06** remove, see off, unload **07** abolish, deep-six, discard **08** choke off, chuck out, clear off, clear out, down with, jettison, railroad, shake off, shrug off, throw out **09** dispose of, eliminate, eradicate, get shot of, throw away **10** do away with, put an end to **12** dispense with, make away with

riddance

06 relief **07** freedom, release, removal **08** disposal, ejection **09** clearance, expulsion, purgation **11** deliverance, elimination **13** extermination

riddle

03 mar **04** fill, koan, sift **05** guess, poser, sieve, solve **06** enigma, filter, infest, pepper, pierce, puzzle, strain, teaser, winnow **07** charade, cribble, mystery, pervade, problem **08** permeate, puncture **09** conundrum, logograph, perforate **10** conclusion, mind-bender **11** brainteaser **12** brain-twister

ride

02 go **03** sit **04** burn, lift, move, road, rode, spin, surf, trip, trot **05** cycle, drive, jaunt, pedal, steer **06** gallop, handle, manage, outing, saddle, travel **07** bobsled, control, journey, overlap **08** bestride, dominate, progress **09** bobsleigh, promenade **12** steeplechase

rider

02 PS **05** biker, bikie **06** hussar, jockey, knight **07** dragoon, eventer **08** horseman, reinsman **09** corollary **10** cavalryman, equestrian, horsewoman, showjumper **11** mosstrooper **12** equestrienne, horse soldier

ridge

02 ås **03** bur, hoe, rib, rig **04** balk, band, bank, burr, drum, edge, hill, kame, keel, list, lump, nurl, rand, reef, wale, welt **05** arête, baulk, costa, crest, esker, halse, hause, hawse, knurl, ledge, linch, raphe, torus **06** crista, ripple, saddle **07** corn rig, crinkle, drumlin, hogback, hummock, linchet, lynchet, wrinkle, yardang **08** eminence, hog's back, sastruga **09** knife-edge, razorback **10** escarpment, promontory **12** superciliary, thank-you-ma'am

ridicule

03 guy, kid, rag, rib **04** gibe, goof, jeer, jest, josh, mock **05** chaff, irony, mimic, queer, scoff, scorn, smoke, sneer, taunt, tease **06** banter, deride, parody, poo-poo, satire, send up **07** crucify, jeering, lampoon, laugh at, mockery, pillory, reticle, sarcasm, teasing **08** badinage,

derision, laughter, pooh-pooh, reticule, satirize, taunting **09** absurdity, burlesque, humiliate, make fun of, poke fun at **10** caricature, make game of **11** make a game of **12** depreciation **13** have a game with, poke mullock at

ridiculous

◇ anagram indicator
04 rich **05** crazy, droll, funny, silly **06** absurd, mental, stupid **07** comical, damfool, foolish, risible **08** derisory, farcical, humorous, shocking **09** facetious, hilarious, laughable, ludicrous **10** cockamamie, incredible, outrageous **11** nonsensical **12** contemptible, preposterous, unbelievable

ridiculously

◇ anagram indicator
08 absurdly **09** laughably **10** incredibly, shockingly **11** ludicrously **12** outrageously, surprisingly, unbelievably, unreasonably **14** preposterously

rife

06 common, raging **07** current, general, rampant, teeming **08** abundant, epidemic, frequent, swarming **09** abounding, extensive, prevalent **10** ubiquitous, widespread **11** overflowing, predominant

riff-raff

03 mob **04** raff, scum **05** dregs, scaff **06** rabble, raffle **07** rubbish **08** canaille, rent-a-mob **09** hoi polloi, scaff-raff **12** undesirables

rifle

◇ anagram indicator
02 M1 **03** gun, gut, rob, SLR **04** loot, pick, sack **05** fusil, strip **06** burgle, injure, maraud, Mauser, musket, search, weapon **07** bandook, bundook, carabin, carbine, despoil, express, firearm, Martini, pillage, plunder, ransack, rummage, shotgun **08** Armalite®, carabine, disarray, firelock, petronel **09** chassepot, flintlock **10** Lee Enfield, Winchester® **11** elephant gun **12** Martini-Henry

rift

03 gap, row **04** feud, hole, slit **05** belch, break, chink, cleft, crack, fault, fight, space, split **06** breach, cavity, cleave, cranny, schism **07** crevice, fissure, opening **08** argument, conflict, division, fracture **10** alienation, difference, separation **11** altercation **12** disagreement, estrangement

rig

◇ anagram indicator
03 kit **04** cook, fake, garb, gear **05** dress, equip, fit up, forge, prank, ridge, set up, trick, twist **06** clothe, doctor, fiddle, fit out, frolic, gunter, jack-up, outfit, tackle **07** distort, falsify, massage, pervert, swindle **08** fittings, fixtures **09** apparatus, equipment, machinery, structure **10** manipulate,

tamper with **12** misrepresent **13** accoutrements

• **rig out**
03 fit **04** garb, robe, trim, wear **05** array, dress, equip, get up, put on **08** attire, clothe, fit out, kit out, outfit, supply **07** dress up, furnish, get into, provide, trick up, turn out **08** accoutre, trick out **09** make ready

• **rig up**
05 build, dress, equip, erect, fit up, fix up **07** arrange, knock up **08** assemble **09** construct, improvise **11** put together **13** throw together **14** cobble together

right

01 r **02** OK, rt **03** due, fit, fix, oke **04** fair, good, just, lien, okay, real, Tory, true, user, well **05** claim, droit, exact, legal, moral, power, quite, sound, truth, utter, valid **06** actual, avenge, bang-on, direct, equity, ethics, fairly, honest, honour, justly, lawful, pronto, proper, repair, seemly, settle, spot on, virtue, wholly **07** charter, correct, ethical, exactly, factual, fitting, freedom, genuine, honesty, justice, licence, precise, rectify, redress, stand up, totally, upright, utterly, warrant **08** absolute, accepted, accurate, approved, becoming, business, complete, directly, entirely, fairness, goodness, legality, morality, properly, put right, sanction, slap bang, straight, suitable, thorough, true-blue, virtuous **09** all the way, authentic, authority, by the book, correctly, desirable, equitable, factually, impartial, integrity, like a shot, opportune, precisely, privilege, propriety, rectitude, righteous, rightness, right-wing, territory, title deed, veritable, vindicate, yesterday **10** absolutely, acceptable, accurately, admissible, auspicious, birthright, completely, convenient, favourable, favourably, honourable, lawfulness, permission, preferable, principled, propitious, put in order, reasonable, straighten **11** appropriate, entitlement, immediately, opportunity, prerogative, reactionary, straightway, uprightness **12** advantageous, conservative, impartiality, satisfactory, the done thing, truthfulness, without delay **13** perpendicular, righteousness, straighten out **14** as the crow flies, characteristic, satisfactorily **15** before you know it, in a straight line

• **by rights**
06 de jure, justly **07** legally, rightly **08** lawfully, properly **09** correctly **10** in fairness, rightfully **11** justifiably **12** legitimately

• **in the right**
09 justified, warranted **10** vindicated

• **put to rights, set to rights**
03 fix **04** sort **05** fix up **06** remedy, settle **07** correct, rectify **10** put in order, straighten **13** straighten out

• **right away**
03 now **04** ASAP **06** at once, pronto **08** directly, in a jiffy, promptly

09 forthwith, instantly, like a shot, yesterday **11** immediately **12** straight away, without delay **13** from the word go **15** before you know it
• **right-hand man, right-hand woman**
02 PA **04** aide **06** deputy, helper **08** henchman **09** assistant, man Friday, number two, secretary **10** girl Friday, henchwoman, lieutenant, understudy **11** backroom boy, helping hand, henchperson, subordinate **12** backroom girl **15** second-in-command
• **right of way**
04 lead, rank **08** eminence, priority **09** seniority, supremacy **10** first place, precedence, preference **11** pre-eminence, superiority
• **within your rights**
07 allowed **08** entitled **09** justified, permitted **10** reasonable

righteous
04 fair, good, just, pure **05** legal, moral, valid **06** honest, lawful, proper, worthy **07** ethical, saintly, sinless, upright **08** virtuous **09** blameless, equitable, excellent, excusable, guiltless, incorrupt, justified, warranted **10** acceptable, defensible, God-fearing, honourable, law-abiding, legitimate, reasonable **11** explainable, justifiable, supportable, well-founded **14** irreproachable

righteousness
06 dharma, equity, honour, purity, virtue **07** honesty, justice, probity **08** goodness, holiness, morality **09** integrity, rectitude **11** ethicalness, uprightness **12** faithfulness **13** blamelessness **14** sanctification

rightful
03 due **04** just, real, true **05** legal, valid **06** de jure, lawful, proper **07** correct, genuine **08** bona fide, suitable **10** authorized, legitimate

rightfully
06 de jure, justly **07** legally, rightly **08** by rights, lawfully, properly **09** correctly **11** justifiably **12** legitimately

rightly
04 well **06** fairly, justly **07** legally, morally **08** by rights, lawfully, properly **09** correctly, equitably, fittingly **10** reasonably **11** justifiably **12** legitimately **13** appropriately

rigid
03 set **04** firm, hard **05** fixed, harsh, stern, stiff, stony, tense **06** ramrod, severe, starch, strict **07** austere, hard-set, spartan **08** cast-iron, rigorous, stubborn **09** inelastic, stringent, tramlined, unbending **10** inflexible, invariable, unyielding **11** unalterable, unrelenting **12** intransigent **14** uncompromising

rigidity
06 fixity **08** hardness, obduracy **09** obstinacy, stiffness **10** stringency

12 immovability, immutability, inelasticity, stubbornness, unsuppleness **13** immutableness, inflexibility, intransigence **14** intractability

rigmarole
04 fuss, to-do **06** bother, hassle, jargon, ragman **07** carry-on, palaver, process, ragment, twaddle **08** nonsense **09** gibberish **11** performance, riddle-me-ree

rigorous
04 firm, hard **05** close, exact, harsh, rigid, stern, tough **06** severe, strait, strict **07** ascetic, austere, precise, spartan, violent **08** accurate, exacting, straight, streight, thorough **09** laborious, stringent, unsparing **10** meticulous, scrupulous **11** painstaking, punctilious **12** intransigent **13** barrack square, conscientious **14** uncompromising

rigorously
06 strait **07** exactly **08** straight, streight **09** precisely **10** accurately, thoroughly **12** meticulously, scrupulously **13** painstakingly, punctiliously

rigour
05 trial **06** ordeal **08** accuracy, firmness, hardness, hardship, rigidity, severity **09** austerity, exactness, harshness, precision, privation, sternness, stiffness, suffering, toughness **10** strictness, stringency **11** preciseness **12** thoroughness **13** inflexibility, intransigence **14** meticulousness **15** punctiliousness

rig-out
03 kit **04** garb, gear, togs **05** dress, get-up, habit **06** livery, outfit, things **07** apparel, clobber, clothes, costume, raiment, uniform **08** clothing, garments

rile
◇ *anagram indicator*
03 bug, irk, vex **04** roil **05** anger, annoy, peeve, pique, upset **06** hassle, nettle, put out, wind up **07** agitate, hack off, tick off **08** brass off, irritate **09** aggravate, cheese off, drive nuts **10** drive crazy, exasperate **11** get your goat **12** drive bananas **13** get on your wick, get up your nose, get your back up, make sparks fly **14** drive up the wall, get your blood up, give you the hump **15** get on your nerves, get your dander up

rill *see* **brook**

rim
03 lip **04** brim, edge, ring, shoe, wood **05** apron, bezel, brink, chimb, chime, chine, felly, helix, rymme, skirt, velum, verge **06** border, felloe, fiddle, girdle, margin, strake **08** membrane **10** peritoneum **13** circumference

rind
04 bark, husk, peel, rine, rynd, skin, zest **05** crust, gourd, shell **06** citron

07 epicarp, outside **09** crackling **10** integument, orange peel

ring
01 O **03** mob, rim **04** area, band, bell, belt, buzz, call, cell, club, crew, dial, ding, disc, disk, echo, gang, gird, halo, hoop, link, loop, peal, sing, tang, ting, toll, tore **05** arena, atoll, chime, clang, clink, group, hem in, knell, phone, reach, reign, round, sound, torus **06** cage in, call up, cartel, circle, clique, collar, girdle, jingle, keeper, league, re-echo, ring up, signet, terret, territ, tingle, tinkle, torret, turret **07** annulet, annulus, circlet, circuit, combine, coterie, enclose, resound, society, vibrate **08** alliance, ding-dong, encircle, proclaim, pugilism, resonate, sorority, surround **09** enclosure, encompass, gathering, give a bell, give a buzz, phone call, syndicate, telephone **10** fraternity **11** association, give a tinkle, reverberate, wedding band **12** circumscribe, organization **14** tintinnabulate
• **prize ring**
02 PR
• **ring of wagons**
04 laer **06** corral, laager

ringleader
05 chief **06** brains, leader **08** fugleman **09** spokesman **10** bell-wether, mouthpiece **11** spokeswoman **12** spokesperson

ringlet
04 curl, lock

rinse
03 dip, wet **04** sind, synd, wash **05** bathe, clean, flush, swill **06** sloosh **07** cleanse, wash out **09** flush away, wash clean

riot
◇ *anagram indicator*
03 row **04** fray, hoot, orgy, rage, rant, rave, rout, show, tear **05** brawl, fight, laugh, mêlée, rebel, revel, storm **06** affray, charge, fracas, hubbub, mutiny, rave-up, revolt, rise up, rising, scream, strife, tumult, uproar **07** anarchy, display, quarrel, rampage, revelry, run amok, run riot, run wild, turmoil, whoobub **08** disorder, feasting, flourish, hubbuboo, partying, race riot, uprising **09** commotion, confusion, go berserk, rebellion **10** debauchery, exhibition, indulgence, insurgence, rush wildly, turbulence **11** disturbance, lawlessness, merrymaking **12** extravaganza, insurrection **14** go on the rampage
• **run riot**
◇ *anagram indicator*
04 rage, rant, rave, tear **05** storm **06** charge **07** rampage, run amok, run wild **09** go berserk **10** rush wildly **14** go on the rampage

riotous
◇ *anagram indicator*
04 loud, wild **05** noisy, rowdy **06** unruly, wanton **07** lawless, roaring,

violent **08** mutinous **10** boisterous, disorderly, ragmatical, rebellious, tumultuous, uproarious **12** ungovernable, unrestrained **13** insubordinate **14** uncontrollable **15** insurrectionary

riotously
◇ *anagram indicator*
05 ariot **06** loudly, wildly **07** noisily **12** tumultuously **14** uncontrollably

rip
◇ *anagram indicator*
03 cut **04** coop, gash, hack, hole, rend, rent, ripp, slit, tear **05** burst, shred, slash, split **06** ladder **07** handful, rupture **08** cleavage, lacerate, separate
• **rip off**
02 do **03** con, rob **04** dupe **05** cheat, steal, sting, trick **06** diddle, fleece **07** defraud, exploit, swindle **09** gold-brick **10** overcharge

ripe
03 fit **05** grope, grown, ready, right **06** mature, mellow, search, timely **07** forward, perfect, ransack, ripened **08** complete, drop-ripe, finished, in season, rare-ripe, seasoned, spoiling, suitable, thorough **09** developed, excellent, excessive, opportune, premature, ratheripe, under-ripe **10** auspicious, favourable, fully grown, propitious **11** spoiling for **12** advantageous **14** fully developed

ripen
03 age **06** mature, mellow, season **07** develop **13** gather to a head **14** come to maturity **15** bring to maturity

rip-off
03 con **04** scam, swiz **05** cheat, fraud, sting, theft **06** diddle **07** robbery, swindle **08** cheating, con trick, stealing **09** gold brick **12** exploitation **15** daylight robbery

riposte
04 quip **05** reply, sally **06** answer, rejoin, retort, return **07** respond **08** comeback, repartee, response **09** rejoinder **11** reciprocate

ripple
◇ *anagram indicator*
04 curl, eddy, flow, fret, pirl, purl, ring, wave **06** babble, burble, crease, effect, gurgle, jabble, pucker, result, riffle, ruffle, wimple **07** crumple, lapping, ripplet, wavelet, whimple, wrinkle **08** undulate **09** shock wave **10** crispation, undulation **11** consequence, disturbance **12** repercussion **13** reverberation

rise
◇ *reversal down indicator*
02 up **03** sty, try **04** buoy, flow, go up, grow, head, hill, leap, lift, loom, riot, soar, stie, stye **05** arise, begin, climb, get up, issue, mount, pluff, prove, raise, rebel, slope, start, swell, tower **06** appear, ascend, ascent, come in, defect, emerge, growth, harden, jump up, leap up, mutiny, origin, resist, revolt, rising, rocket, source, spring, upturn, volume **07** advance, attempt, climb up, dissent, emanate, improve, incline, prosper, react to, respond, slope up, soaring, stand up, upsurge **08** approach, commence, escalate, increase, occasion, overgrow, progress, response, spring up, surmount, towering **09** acclivity, ascendant, ascendent, elevation, get higher, increment, intensify, originate, promotion **10** be promoted, do your best, escalation, take up arms **11** advancement, get out of bed, improvement, move upwards, upward slope **12** amelioration, make progress **13** exert yourself, get to your feet **14** aggrandizement
• **give rise to**
◇ *reversal down indicator*
04 make **05** cause, evoke, raise, spawn **06** create, effect, elicit, induce, lead to, prompt **07** bring on, inspire, produce, provoke **08** engender, generate, persuade **09** influence, originate **10** bring about

risible
05 comic, droll, funny **06** absurd **07** amusing, comical **08** farcical, humorous **09** hilarious, laughable, ludicrous **10** ridiculous **11** rib-tickling **13** side-splitting

rising
◇ *reversal down indicator*
04 bull, hill, riot, rise **06** émeute, origin, revolt, uprest, uprise, uprist **07** growing, soaring **08** emerging, mounting, naissant, swelling, uprising **09** advancing, ascendant, ascendent, ascending, assurgent, insurgent **10** increasing, prominence, revolution **11** approaching **12** insurrection, intensifying

risk
04 dare, dice, fear **05** flier, peril, stake, throw **06** chance, danger, gamble, hazard, impawn, threat **07** imperil, venture **08** chance it, endanger, jeopardy **09** adventure **10** go for broke, jeopardize, self-danger **11** possibility, speculation, take a chance, uncertainty **12** lay on the line, play with fire, put on the line **13** put in jeopardy
• **against all risks**
03 aar
• **at the risk of**
02 on

risky
04 iffy **05** dicey, dodgy, hairy **06** chancy, risqué, touchy, tricky, unsafe **07** chancey **08** high-risk, perilous **09** dangerous, hazardous, uncertain **10** precarious, touch-and-go **11** venturesome

risqué
04 blue, racy, rude **05** adult, bawdy, crude, dirty, risky, saucy, spicy **06** coarse, earthy, fruity, ribald, smutty **07** naughty **08** immodest, improper, indecent **09** off-colour **10** indelicate, suggestive **14** near the knuckle

rite
03 act **04** bora, form, orgy **05** pawaw, right, usage **06** custom, office, powwow, ritual, symbol **07** dry Mass, liturgy, service, worship **08** ceremony, practice **09** formality, ordinance, procedure, sacrament **10** ceremonial, commixtion, commixture, dry service, initiatory, observance **11** subincision **12** confirmation, superstition

ritual
03 act, set **04** form, rite, wont **05** habit, usage **06** Agadah, cultus, custom, fetich, fetish, formal, lavabo **07** fetiche, Haggada, liturgy, routine, sacring, service **08** ceremony, habitual, Haggadah, lavatory, practice, trumpery **09** customary, custumary, formality, formulary, ordinance, procedure, sacrament, solemnity, tradition **10** ceremonial, consuetude, convention, mumbo-jumbo, observance, prescribed, procedural **11** apotropaism, celebration, traditional **12** conventional, prescription **14** consuetudinary

ritualistic
06 formal, ritual, solemn **07** festive, stately **08** official **09** customary, dignified, formulaic, formulary **10** ceremonial **11** traditional

ritzy
04 posh, rich **05** cushy, grand, plush **06** costly, de luxe, glitzy, lavish, swanky **07** elegant, opulent, stylish **08** affluent, pampered, splendid **09** expensive, luxurious, sumptuous **11** comfortable, magnificent **13** self-indulgent, well-appointed

rival
03 vie **04** mate, peer, vier **05** equal, match, touch **06** fellow, oppose **07** emulate, nemesis, opposed, paragon, partner, vie with **08** corrival, opponent, opposing, parallel **09** adversary, competing, contender **10** antagonist, challenger, collateral, competitor, contestant, in conflict, opposition **11** compare with, compete with, competitive, conflicting, contend with, measure up to **12** in opposition **13** in competition

rivalry
05 vying **06** strife **07** contest **08** conflict, rivality, struggle **09** emulation **10** antagonism, contention, corrivalry, in-fighting, opposition **11** competition **12** corrivalship **15** competitiveness

riven
04 rent **05** split **07** divided, severed **08** ruptured **09** torn apart **11** ripped apart

river
01 R **03** lee, rio **05** flood **11** watercourse

River and watercourse types include:

02 ea
03 cut, pow, sny
04 beck, burn, flow, khor, kill, lake, lane, nala, rill, snye, wadi, wady
05 bourn, brook, canal, creek, delta, ditch, drain, firth, flume, fresh, frith, inlet, mouth, nalla, nulla, rhine, shott, whelm
06 arroyo, broads, influx, nallah, nullah, rapids, rillet, runnel, source, spruit, stream
07 channel, estuary, freshet, riveret, rivulet, torrent
08 affluent, brooklet, effluent, influent, waterway
09 anabranch, backwater, billabong, confluent, headwater, streamlet, tributary
10 confluence, head-stream, millstream, streamling
11 trout stream, water splash
12 distributary, embranchment, water-channel
14 mountain stream

Rivers include:

02 Ob, Po
03 Ain, Axe, Bug, Cam, Dee, Don, Ems, Esk, Exe, Fal, Fly, Han, Ill, Inn, Lea, Lee, Lim, Lot, Mun, Nid, Our, Red, San, Tay, Taz, Ure, Usk, Váh, Wye
04 Aare, Adur, Aire, Amur, Arno, Avon, Bann, Cher, Coco, Dart, East, Ebro, Eden, Elbe, Gail, Hong, Isis, Kemi, Lena, Nene, Neva, Nile, Oder, Ohio, Ouse, Oxus, Ping, Ravi, Ruhr, Saar, Spey, Swan, Taff, Tees, Test, Towy, Tyne, Ural, Vaal, Wear, Yalu, Yare
05 Adige, Argun, Benue, Boyne, Cauca, Chari, Clyde, Congo, Donau, Douro, Fleet, Forth, Glåma, Indus, Jumna, Loire, Marne, Meuse, Mosel, Neath, Negro, Neman, Niger, Peace, Pearl, Pecos, Plata, Plate, Rhine, Rhône, Saône, Seine, Snake, Somme, Tagus, Tamar, Teifi, Tiber, Tisza, Trent, Tweed, Volga, Volta, Weser, Yukon, Zaire
06 Amazon, Angara, Brazos, Chenab, Clutha, Danube, Dnestr, Escaut, Fraser, Gambia, Ganges, Grande, Hudson, Humber, Irtysh, Jhelum, Jordan, Kagera, Kistna, Kolyma, Liffey, Mekong, Mersey, Murray, Orange, Ottawa, Pahang, Paraná, Ribble, Salado, Severn, Seyhan, Sutlej, Thames, Tigris, Tornio, Ubangi, Vltava, Wabash, Yamuna, Yellow
07 Alpheus, Darling, Dnieper, Garonne, Glommen, Helmand, Huang He, Huang Ho, Lachlan, Limpopo, Lualaba, Madeira, Marañón, Maritsa, Narmada, Orinoco, Pechora, Potomac, Salween, Schelde, Selenga, Sénégal, Shannon, Tarim He, Ucayali, Uruguay, Vistula, Waikato, Yangtze, Yenisei, Zambezi
08 Arkansas, Blue Nile, Canadian, Colorado, Columbia, Delaware, Dniester, Dordogne, Missouri, Okavango, Paraguay, Tunguska, Wanganui, Zhu Jiang
09 Churchill, Crocodile, Euphrates, Great Ouse, Irrawaddy, Mackenzie, Rio Grande, Tennessee, White Nile
10 Albert Nile, Bass Strait, Des Plaines, Sacramento, San Joaquin, Shenandoah, St Lawrence, Walla Walla
11 Mississippi, Shatt al-Arab
12 Murrumbidgee, Saskatchewan, Victoria Nile

Mythical rivers include:

04 Alph, Styx
05 Lethe
07 Acheron, Alpheus, Cocytus, Oceanus
08 Achelous, Eridanos
10 Phlegethon

• river valley

04 wadi, wady **05** water **07** wind gap

rivet

04 grip **05** clink **06** absorb, arrest, clinch, excite **07** engross, enthral **08** intrigue **09** captivate, fascinate

• fix rivet

04 pane, pean, peen, pein, pene

riveting

08 exciting, gripping, hypnotic, magnetic **09** absorbing, arresting **10** engrossing **11** captivating, enthralling, fascinating, interesting **12** spellbinding

road

03 via **04** raid, ride, rode, tour **06** course **07** railway, roadway **09** dismissal, incursion **10** journeying, prostitute, travelling

Road types include:

01 A, B, C, E
02 Rd, St
03 Ave, way
04 drag, high, lane, mews, pass, ring, side, slip, toll
05 alley, byway, close, gated, Roman, route, strip, track, trunk
06 avenue, bypass, parade, rat run, relief, strand, street, subway
07 beltway, dead end, flyover, freeway, highway, off ramp, parkway, private, through
08 alleyway, autobahn, causeway, clearway, crescent, cul-de-sac, metalled, motorway, overpass, red route, short cut, speedway, trackway, turnpike
09 autoroute, boulevard, bridleway, cart track, dirt track, esplanade, green lane, promenade, underpass
10 autostrada, bridlepath, cloverleaf, expressway, interstate, unmetalled
11 gravel track, scenic route, single track
12 mountain pass, superhighway, thoroughfare, unclassified
14 gyratory system
15 dual-carriageway

Roads include:

02 A1, M1, M2, M3, M4, M5, M6, M8, M9
03 M25, M40, M62
07 Route 66, Westway
08 Fosse Way, Highway 1, Silk Road
09 Appian Way, Burma Road, Highway 61
10 Cassian Way, Dere Street, Khyber Pass
12 El Camino Real, King's Highway, Périphérique, Sturt Highway
13 North Circular, South Circular, Stuart Highway, Watling Street
14 Great Ocean Road, Great River Road, Le Périphérique, Pacific Highway

roadhouse *see* **public house**

roam

04 rake, rove, trek, walk **05** amble, drift, prowl, range, raven, stray, tramp, wheel **06** ramble, stroam, stroll, travel, wander **07** meander **08** ambulate, squander, traverse **09** wandering **11** perambulate, peregrinate

roar

03 cry **04** bawl, bell, boom, hoot, howl, roin, rore, rote, rout, yell **05** blare, crash, laugh, royne, shout **06** bellow, guffaw, holler, rumble, scream, shriek **07** break up, thunder **08** crease up **09** fall about **14** split your sides **15** laugh like a drain

roaring

04 full, loud, rich **05** great **07** bluster, booming, echoing, notable, ringing, riotous, vibrant **08** decisive, emphatic, resonant, sonorous, striking, thorough **09** memorable **10** conclusive, impressive, remarkable, resonating, resounding, thunderous **11** outstanding **13** reverberating

roast

04 bake, rost **05** brown, parch, swale, swayl, sweal, sweel **06** banter **07** torrefy **08** barbecue **11** decrepitate

rob

02 do **03** mug, pad, rub **04** blag, fake, loot, mill, nick, raid, ramp, roll, sack **05** berob, bunco, bunko, cheat, flimp, heist, pluck, reave, reive, rifle, screw, stiff, sting **06** burgle, do over, hijack, hold up, pirate, rip off **07** bereave, defraud, deprive, despoil, pillage, plunder, ransack, stick up, swindle **08** highjack, knock off, turn over **09** depredate, steal from

robber

04 Tory **05** cheat, fraud, rover, thief **06** bandit, con man, dacoit, dakoit, latron, looter, mugger, pirate, raider **07** brigand, burglar, cateran, ladrone, pandoor, pandour, stealer **08** hijacker, swindler **09** embezzler, plunderer **10** highjacker, highwayman, land-pirate, roberdsman, robertsman **11** motor-bandit

See also **thief**

robbery

04 blag, raid, toby **05** fraud, heist, theft
06 hold-up, piracy, rip-off, snatch
07 break-in, dacoity, dakoiti, larceny,
low toby, mugging, pillage, plunder,
stick-up, swindle **08** burglary, high
toby, stealing **09** dacoitage, latrociny,
pilferage **10** plundering **11** latrocinium
12 embezzlement, smash-and-grab
13 housebreaking

robe

04 garb, gown, vest, wrap **05** camis,
camus, drape, dress, habit, talar
06 attire, chimer, clothe, dolman,
khalat, khilat, killut, kimono, peplos,
peplus, purple **07** apparel, cassock,
chimere, chrisom, costume, kellaut,
wrapper **08** bathrobe, christom,
parament, peignoir, vestment,
wardrobe **09** housecoat, nightgown
10 palliament **12** chrisom-cloth,
dressing-gown

Robert

03 Bob, Rob **05** Bobby **06** Bobbie,
Rabbie, Robbie

Robin Hood *see* legend

robot

05 golem **06** cyborg, zombie
07 android, machine, nanobot
08 telechir **09** automaton

robust

03 fit, raw **04** hale, iron, rude, well
05 crude, hardy, sonsy, stout, tough
06 coarse, direct, earthy, hearty, ribald,
risqué, rugged, sonsie, strong, sturdy
07 healthy, sthenic **08** athletic, forceful,
muscular, powerful, stalwart, thickset,
vigorous **09** energetic, strapping, well-
built **10** able-bodied, no-nonsense
11 down-to-earth **15** straightforward,
tough as old boots

rock

◇ *anagram indicator*
03 AOR, jow, tip **04** cill, coin, crag,
daze, reef, reel, roll, sill, stun, sway, tilt,
toss, trap, tuff, whin **05** crack, lurch,
pitch, shake, shock, stone, swing
06 danger, pebble, totter, wobble
07 astound, boulder, diamond, distaff,
outcrop, shoggle, stagger, startle
08 astonish, bewilder, hard core,
obstacle, surprise, take back, undulate
09 dumbfound, oscillate **12** move to
and fro

See also **singer**

Rocks include:

02 aa
03 ore
04 coal, lava, marl
05 chalk, chert, flint, shale, slate
06 basalt, gabbro, gneiss, gravel,
marble, schist
07 breccia, granite
08 dolerite, hornfels, obsidian, porphyry
09 argillite, greywacke, limestone,
sandstone, soapstone
10 greenstone, serpentine
11 pumice stone
12 conglomerate

• on the rocks

06 doomed, failed, in a fix, in a jam
07 failing, in a hole, in a mess
08 hopeless, in pieces, in shreds,
slipping, unstable **09** in a bad way, in a
scrape, penniless **11** at an impasse **12** in
difficulty **14** in difficulties

rocket

02 V-1, V-2 **04** soar, wald, weld
05 onion, retro, tower **06** rucola
07 arugula, missile, shoot up
08 Congreve, escalate, roquette,
thruster **09** reprimand **10** flying bomb,
projectile **13** guided missile, launch
vehicle **15** increase quickly, St Barbara's
cress

rocky

◇ *anagram indicator*
04 hard, weak **05** rough, shaky, stony,
tipsy **06** craggy, flinty, pebbly, rugged,
wobbly **08** unstable, unsteady,
wobbling **09** difficult, tottering,
uncertain **10** staggering, unpleasant,
unreliable **14** unsatisfactory

rococo

04 bold **05** showy **06** florid, ornate
07 baroque, flowery **08** fanciful,
rocaille, vigorous **09** decorated,
elaborate, exuberant, fantastic,
grotesque, whimsical **10** convoluted,
flamboyant **11** embellished,
extravagant, overwrought
13 overdecorated, overelaborate
15 churrigueresque

rod

03 bar, cue, lug **04** calm, came, cane,
mace, pole, reed, rood, spit, twig, vare,
wand **05** baton, shaft, staff, stave, stick,
strut, swits **06** pistol, switch
07 ellwand, probang, sceptre, scollop,
tringle **08** caduceus, metewand,
meteyard, revolver, stanchel, stancher
09 metestick, stanchion

See also **gun**

rodent

Rodents include:

03 rat
04 cavy, cony, hare, paca, pika, vole
05 aguti, coypu, mouse
06 agouti, beaver, ferret, gerbil,
gopher, hog-rat, jerboa, marmot,
rabbit
07 cane rat, hamster, lemming,
meerkat, muskrat, ondatra,
potoroo
08 black rat, brown rat, capybara,
chipmunk, dormouse, hampster,
hedgehog, musquash, sewer rat,
squirrel, tucutuco, viscacha, water
rat
09 bandicoot, groundhog, guinea
pig, porcupine, water vole,
woodchuck
10 chinchilla, fieldmouse, prairie dog,
springhaas, springhase
11 kangaroo rat, red squirrel,
spermophile
12 grey squirrel, harvest mouse

roe

04 melt, milt, raun, rawn **06** caviar,
cavier **07** caviare **08** caviarie

roentgenium

02 Rg

rogue

◇ *anagram indicator*
05 cheat, crook, drôle, fraud, gipsy,
Greek, gypsy, hempy, knave, scamp
06 con man, donder, limmer, rascal,
scally, terror, varlet **07** skellum, vagrant,
villain, wastrel, wrong 'un **08** deceiver,
dummerer, palliard, swindler
09 fraudster, miscreant, prankster,
reprobate, scallywag, scoundrel, son
of a gun **10** disruptive, ne'er-do-well,
rascallion, slip-string **11** mischievous,
rapscallion **12** hedge-creeper
14 good-for-nothing

roguish

04 arch **05** hempy, shady **06** cheeky,
impish, wicked **07** crooked, knavish,
playful, waggish **08** criminal, espiègle,
rascally **09** deceitful, deceiving,
dishonest, swindling **10** confounded,
coquettish, fraudulent, frolicsome,
rascal-like, slip-string, villainous
11 mischievous **12** unprincipled,
unscrupulous

roister

04 brag, romp **05** boast, revel, strut
06 frolic **07** bluster, carouse, large it,
rollick, swagger **09** blusterer,
celebrate, make merry, whoop it up
11 have it large **15** paint the town red

roisterer

06 buster, ranter **07** boaster, roister
08 braggart, carouser, reveller
09 blusterer, swaggerer

roisterous

04 loud, wild **05** noisy, rowdy
09 clamorous, exuberant
10 boisterous, disorderly, uproarious
12 obstreperous

role

03 bit, fat, job **04** duty, lead, part, post,
task **05** cameo, place, stead
08 capacity, function, name part,
position **09** cameo-part, character,
portrayal, situation **11** comprimario
12 principal boy, spear carrier
13 character part, impersonation
14 representation

roll

◇ *anagram indicator*
02 go **03** bap, bun, ren, rin, rob, run,
wad **04** bind, boom, bowl, coil, curl,
drum, echo, file, flow, fold, furl, list,
move, pass, peal, reel, roar, rock, spin,
sway, toss, turn, waul, wawl, wind, wrap
05 crush, cycle, dandy, index, level,
lurch, pitch, press, spool, start, swell,
swing, trill, twirl, twist, wheel, whirl
06 annals, billow, bobbin, census,
elapse, enfold, enwrap, gyrate, rafale,
record, rental, roller, roster, rotate,
rumble, scroll, smooth, tumble, volley,
volume, volute, wallow, wander, welter
07 envelop, flatten, go round, grumble,

notitia, reeling, resound, revolve, rocking, rouleau, stagger, swagger, terrier, thunder, tossing, trindle, trundle **08** crescent, cylinder, gyration, pitching, register, rotation, schedule, undulate **09** billowing, catalogue, chronicle, directory, inventory, press down, resonance, turn round **10** muster-file, revolution, undulation **11** reverberate **13** reverberation

See also **bread**

• roll in
04 come **06** appear, arrive, blow in, come in, flow in, pour in, rush in, show up, turn up **07** flood in **09** be present **10** be received

• rolling in it
04 rich **05** flush **06** loaded **07** moneyed, wealthy, well-off **08** affluent, well-to-do **10** filthy rich, in the money, prosperous, well-heeled **11** made of money **12** stinking rich **15** with money to burn

• roll up
04 furl **06** arrive, gather **07** convene **08** assemble **10** congregate, intervolve

roller
02 RR **07** trundle **10** Rolls-Royce®

rollicking
◊ *anagram indicator*
05 merry, noisy **06** banzai, frisky, hearty, jaunty, jovial, joyous, lively, rebuke, rocket **07** censure, chiding, lecture, playful, reproof, romping **08** berating, carefree, harangue, reproach, roisting, scolding, spirited, sportive **09** cavorting, exuberant, reprimand, sprightly, talking-to **10** boisterous, frolicsome, rip-roaring, roisterous, telling-off, upbraiding **12** devil-may-care, dressing-down, light-hearted **13** swashbuckling

rolling
◊ *anagram indicator*
06 goggle, waving **07** heaving, surging **08** rippling, undulant **10** undulating, volutation

roll-on roll-off
04 ro-ro

roly-poly
03 fat **05** buxom, plump, podgy, pudgy, round, tubby **06** barrel, chubby, rotund **07** rounded **10** butterball, overweight

Roman

See also **god, goddess; mythology; numeral**

romance
03 lie, see, woo **04** date, gest, tale **05** amour, charm, chase, court, fling, geste, idyll, novel, story, thing **06** affair, colour, legend, whimsy **07** crusade, fantasy, fiction, glamour, liaison, mystery, passion, Romanic, romaunt **08** intrigue **09** adventure, fairytale, fantasize, go out with, love story, melodrama, overstate, sentiment **10** attachment, exaggerate, excitement, fairy story, love affair **11** fascination **12** bodice-ripper, go steady with, relationship **15** romantic fiction

Romania
02 RO **03** ROU

romantic
04 fond, wild **05** soppy **06** dreamy, Gothic, loving, sloppy, tender **07** amorous, dreamer, idyllic, utopian **08** exciting, fanciful, idealist, quixotic, stardust, unlikely **09** fairytale, fantastic, imaginary, legendary, visionary **10** fictitious, idealistic, improbable,
lovey-dovey, mysterious, optimistic, passionate, starry-eyed **11** extravagant, fascinating, impractical, sentimental, unrealistic **14** sentimentalist

romantically
06 fondly **08** lovingly, tenderly **09** amorously **10** excitingly, fancifully **12** mysteriously, passionately **13** extravagantly, impractically, sentimentally **14** idealistically, optimistically **15** unrealistically

Rome *see* **hill**

Romeo
01 R **05** lover **06** gigolo **07** Don Juan **08** Casanova, Lothario **09** ladies' man **10** lady-killer

romp
03 rig **04** lark, play, ramp, skip **05** caper, frisk, hempy, revel, sport, spree **06** cavort, frolic, gambol, hoiden, hoyden, tomboy **07** roister, rollick

rondo
04 rota

roof
05 vault **06** canopy **07** ceiling, rigging, shelter **08** covering, dwelling **11** culmination

• hit the roof
05 go mad **06** blow up, see red **07** explode **08** boil over, freak out **09** do your nut **11** blow your top, flip your lid, go up the wall, lose your rag **12** blow your cool, lose your cool **15** fly off the handle, go off the deep end

roof-gutter
04 roan, rone **05** rhone **08** roanpipe, ronepipe

rook
01 R **02** do **03** con **04** bilk, crow **05** cheat, squab, sting **06** castle, diddle, fleece, rip off **07** defraud, swindle **09** card-sharp, gold-brick, simpleton **10** overcharge **12** take for a ride

room
02 rm **03** ben, but, end, oda **04** area, seat **05** range, scope, space, stead **06** chance, extent, leeway, margin, volume **07** expanse, legroom **08** capacity, headroom, latitude, occasion **09** allowance, elbow-room **10** Lebensraum **11** appointment, compartment, opportunity

Rooms include:

02 WC
03 bed, box, day, den, loo
04 ante, bath, cell, dark, hall, loft, play, rest, sick, tack, wash, work
05 attic, board, cabin, class, cloak, court, foyer, front, games, green, guard, guest, lobby, music, porch, salon, spare, staff, state, stock, store, study
06 cellar, common, dining, engine, family, larder, living, locker, lounge, lumber, office, pantry, rumpus, saddle, strong, studio, toilet
07 boudoir, buttery, chamber, control, cubicle, drawing, fitting, kitchen, landing, laundry, lecture, library, meeting, morning, nursery, parlour, reading, seminar, sitting, smoking, utility, waiting
08 assembly, basement, chambers, changing, dressing, lavatory, scullery, workshop
09 breakfast, dormitory, mezzanine, reception, sun lounge
10 consulting, laboratory, recreation
11 kitchenette, lounge-diner
12 conservatory, kitchen-diner
15 en suite bathroom

• have room for
04 stow

roomy
04 wide **05** ample, broad, large, rangy
07 sizable **08** generous, sizeable, spacious **09** capacious, extensive
10 commodious, voluminous

root
03 fix, nub, rad, set, tap, yam **04** axis, base, core, germ, grub, hail, home, moor, more, pull, seat, seed, spur, stem
05 basis, cause, cheer, embed, fount, heart, radix, shout, stick, tuber
06 anchor, bottom, etymon, family, fasten, ground, kernel, nuzzle, origin, radish, reason, sinker, source
07 applaud, calamus, cheer on, essence, ginseng, implant, nucleus, origins, parsnep, parsnip, radical, radicle, rhizome, rummage, snuzzle, support, turbith, turpeth, vetiver
08 entrench, heritage, radicate, scammony **09** beginning, encourage, establish, principle **10** background, beginnings, birthplace, derivation, foundation **11** fundamental
12 fountainhead, sarsaparilla
13 starting point

• put down roots
09 set up home **10** settle down
12 make your home

• root and branch
06 wholly **07** finally, totally, utterly
08 complete, entirely, thorough
09 radically **10** completely, thoroughly

• root around
03 dig, pry **04** hunt, nose, poke
05 delve **06** burrow, ferret, forage
07 rummage

• root out
06 dig out, remove, uproot **07** abolish, destroy, outweed, uncover, unearth
08 discover, get rid of **09** clear away, eliminate, eradicate, extirpate **10** put an end to **11** exterminate

• take root
08 take hold **11** become fixed
15 establish itself

rooted
04 deep, felt, firm **05** fixed, rigid
06 deeply **07** radical **08** radicate
09 confirmed, ingrained, radicated
10 deep-seated, entrenched
11 established

rootless
04 free **06** moving **07** nomadic
08 carefree, drifting, floating, homeless
09 itinerant, transient, unsettled, wandering **14** of no fixed abode

rootstock
04 race **05** orris

rope
03 tie **04** bind, jeff, lash, moor, stay
05 hitch, lasso **06** fasten

Rope types include:

03 guy, tow
04 cord, drag, fall, head, line, seal, stay, tack, vang, warp
05 brace, cable, lasso, noose, widdy
06 bridle, halter, hawser, hobble, lariat, runner, strand, string, tackle, tether
07 bobstay, bowline, cordage, cringle, halyard, lanyard, lashing, marline, mooring, outhaul, painter, ratline
08 buntline, clew-line, dockline, downhaul, dragline, gantline
09 hackamore

• know the ropes
05 learn **06** master **12** know the drill, know the score **13** know what's what

• rope in
06 engage, enlist **07** involve
08 inveigle, persuade, talk into

ropy, ropey
04 duff, poor **05** rough **06** unwell
07 stringy **08** below par, inferior
09 deficient, glutinous, off colour
10 inadequate **11** substandard **14** not up to scratch, unsatisfactory

rose
03 riz **04** geum, Jack, moss **05** avens, brere, briar, brier **07** Bourbon, monthly, paragon, rosette **08** noisette, primrose
09 crampbark, eglantine, perpetual, remontant **10** erysipelas, floribunda, water elder **12** snowball tree
13 cranberry bush, cranberry tree

• rose fruit
03 hep, hip

rosette
04 chou, rose **06** rosace, rosula
07 cockade **13** wedding favour
14 provincial rose

rosin
05 resin, roset, rosit, rozet, rozit
09 colophony

roster
04 list, roll, rota **05** index **07** listing
08 register, schedule **09** directory

rostrum
04 beak, bema, dais **05** stage
06 podium **08** platform

rosy
03 red **04** pink, rose **05** fresh, ruddy, sunny **06** bright, florid **07** auroral, flushed, glowing, hopeful, reddish, roseate, rose-red **08** aurorean, blooming, blushing, cheerful, inflamed, rose-hued, roselike, rose-pink, rubicund **09** bloodshot, promising **10** auspicious, favourable, optimistic, reassuring **11** encouraging, rose-scented **12** rose-coloured
14 healthy-looking

rot
◇ *anagram indicator*
03 rat, ret **04** blah, bosh, bunk, halt, joke, rait, rate, rust, tosh **05** decay, go bad, go off, hooey, mould, spoil, taint, tease **06** bluing, bunkum, drivel, fester, go sour, humbug, kibosh, kybosh, perish, piffle **07** baloney, blueing, corrode, corrupt, crumble, garbage, hogwash, putrefy, rhubarb, rubbish
08 claptrap, cobblers, collapse, malarkey, Merulius, nonsense
09 corrosion, decompose, moonshine, poppycock **10** codswallop, corruption, degenerate **11** deteriorate
12 disintegrate, putrefaction
13 decomposition, deterioration
14 disintegration

rota
04 list, roll **05** canon, index, rondo, round **06** course, roster **07** listing, routine **08** register, schedule
09 directory

rotary
07 turning **08** gyrating, gyratory, rotating, spinning, whirling
09 revolving **10** roundabout

rotate
◇ *reversal indicator*
04 reel, roll, spin, turn **05** pivot, rabat, whirl **06** gyrate, swivel **07** go round, rabatte, revolve, twiddle **09** alternate, move round, spin round, turn about, turn round **10** change face
11 interchange, reciprocate, take in turns **13** take it in turns

rotation
04 spin, turn **05** cycle, orbit, round, whirl **06** swivel **07** turning **08** gyration, sequence, spinning, whirling
10 revolution, succession, swivelling
11 alternation

rote
• learn by rote
08 memorize **11** learn off pat
14 commit to memory **15** learn from memory, learn off by heart

rotten
◇ *anagram indicator*
03 bad, ill, off, rat **04** evil, foul, mean, poor, poxy, punk, rank, ropy, sick, sour
05 awful, dirty, fetid, lousy, manky, nasty, putid, ropey, rough **06** addled, bloody, crummy, damned, darned,

ashed, foetid, grotty, guilty, mouldy,
oorly, putrid, spoilt, unwell, wicked
7 beastly, blasted, corrupt, decayed,
aming, gone off, immoral, rotting,
ainted, unsound **08** blinking,
'ooming, decaying, dratting,
readful, flipping, horrible, inferior,
afernal, low-grade, stinking, terrible,
vretched **09** dishonest, off colour,
utrefied **10** confounded,
ecomposed, despicable, inadequate,
aouldering, putrescent, unpleasant
2 contemptible, unprincipled
3 dishonourable **14** disintegrating

otter

3 cad, cur, pig, rat **04** fink, heel
5 beast, louse, rogue, swine
7 bounder, dastard, stinker
8 blighter **09** scoundrel
0 blackguard

otund

3 fat **04** full, rich **05** heavy, obese,
lump, podgy, round, stout, tubby
6 chubby, fleshy, portly **07** bulbous,
rotund, rounded, spheral, spheric
8 globular, resonant, roly-poly,
onorous **09** corpulent, orbicular,
otundate, spherical, spherular
0 impressive **12** magniloquent
3 grandiloquent

oué

4 rake **06** lecher, wanton **08** rakehell
9 debauchee, libertine **10** profligate,
ensualist

ough

◇ anagram indicator
3 ill, ned, row, yob **04** curt, hard, hazy,
ude, sick, thug, wild **05** asper, basic,
lunt, bully, bumpy, crude, cruel, dirty,
Iraft, gruff, gurly, hairy, harsh, hasty,
ausky, lousy, lumpy, model, nasty, noisy,
lain, quick, raggy, raspy, rocky, rowdy,
uggy, rusty, scaly, sharp, stern, stony,
ough, tousy, touzy, towsy, towzy,
ague, yobbo **06** brutal, choppy,
coarse, craggy, grotty, hoarse, jagged,
ively, mock-up, poorly, raucle, rotten,
uffle, rugged, severe, shaggy, sketch,
tormy, uneven, unkind, unwell, vulgar
7 bristly, bruiser, brusque, brutish,
cursory, drastic, extreme, general,
gnarled, grained, hirsute, inexact, of a
ort, of sorts, outline, prickly, rasping,
aucous, ruffian, sketchy, throaty,
ankempt, unshorn, violent **08** agitated,
aspirate, below par, croaking, forceful,
gravelly, guttural, hooligan, impolite,
nuricate, scabrous, scratchy, strident,
anbroken, ungentle, unshaven
9 difficult, energetic, estimated,
aarrowing, imprecise, iron-sided,
rregular, merciless, muricated, off
colour, primitive, roughneck,
turbulent, unfeeling, unhealthy,
anrefined **10** aggressive, astringent,
oisterous, broadbrush, discordant,
disorderly, hard-handed, incomplete,
anfinished, unpleasant, unpolished
11 approximate, belligerent,
nsensitive, ramgunshoch,
udimentary, tempestuous, uncivilized

12 tiger country, unelaborated
15 under the weather
• **rough out**
05 draft **06** mock up, sketch **07** outline
11 draw in rough **14** give a summary of
• **rough up**
03 mug **04** bash, do in **06** beat up
08 maltreat, mistreat **09** manhandle
10 knock about

rough-and-ready

05 basic, crude, plain **06** bodgie,
make-do, simple **07** hurried, sketchy,
stop-gap **09** makeshift, unrefined
10 unpolished **11** approximate,
provisional

rough-and-tumble

05 brawl, fight, mêlée, scrap **06** affray,
dust-up, fracas, rumpus **07** punch-up,
scuffle **08** struggle

roughen

◇ anagram indicator
04 chap, hack, rasp, stab **05** chafe,
graze, rough, scuff, spray **06** abrade,
ruffle **07** coarsen, harshen, spreaze,
spreeze **08** asperate, spreathe,
spreethe, unsmooth **09** granulate

roughly

◇ anagram indicator
01 c **02** ca **03** cir **04** circ **05** about,
circa **06** around, nearly, wildly **07** close
to, cruelly, harshly, loosely, noisily,
rowdily, toughly **08** brutally, unkindly
09 just about, not far off, rounded up,
violently **10** forcefully, give or take,
more or less, round about
11 approaching, mercilessly, rounded
down **12** boisterously
13 approximately, energetically,
insensitively, in the region of, or
thereabouts, something like **14** in
round figures, in round numbers **15** in
the vicinity of

roughneck

04 lout, thug **05** rough, rowdy, tough,
yobbo **06** keelie **07** bruiser, ruffian
08 bully boy, hooligan, larrikin

roulade

03 run **05** trill

round

◇ anagram indicator
◇ containment indicator
◇ reversal indicator
01 O **03** fat, lap, orb **04** ball, band,
beat, bend, bout, coil, disc, disk, full,
game, heat, hoop, past, path, ring, rota,
tour, walk **05** about, ample, cycle,
flank, globe, globy, level, plump, rough,
route, scope, skirt, stage, stout
06 around, beyond, bypass, candid,
chubby, circle, course, curved, honest,
patrol, period, portly, rotund, series,
sphere, sphery **07** all over, circlet,
circuit, discoid, globate, go round,
rounded, routine, session, whisper
08 circular, cylinder, dislike, framed
by, globular, hooplike, milk-walk, move
past, sequence, sonorous, spheroid, to
and fro, vigorous **09** corpulent,
discoidal, enclosing, estimated, finish

off, full-orbed, globelike, imprecise,
orbicular, spherical, unsparing **10** ball-
shaped, disc-shaped, encircling,
enveloping, everywhere, indirectly, on
all sides, ring-shaped, succession,
throughout, to all parts
11 approximate, cylindrical, on every
side, plain-spoken, surrounding, travel
round, unqualified **12** circuitously,
encompassing, everywhere in, here
and there, on all sides of, to all parts of
13 on every side of **15** in all directions
• **round about**
01 c **02** ca **03** cir **04** circ **05** about,
circa **06** around, nearly **07** close to,
loosely, roughly **09** just about, not far
off, rounded up **10** give or take, more
or less **11** approaching, rounded down
13 approximately, in the region of, or
thereabouts, something like **14** in
round numbers **15** in the vicinity of
• **round off**
03 cap, end **04** turn **05** close, crown
06 finish, parcel, top off **08** complete,
conclude **09** finish off
• **round on**
05 abuse **06** attack, turn on **07** lay into,
set upon
• **round up**
04 herd **05** group, rally **06** gather,
muster **07** collect, marshal
08 assemble **13** bring together

roundabout

05 plump **06** rotary **07** devious,
evasive, oblique, waltzer, winding
08 indirect, tortuous, twisting
10 circuitous, meandering **12** merry-
go-round, periphrastic **13** traffic circle
14 circumlocutory
15 circumambagious

roundly

06 openly **07** bluntly, frankly, sharply
08 fiercely, severely **09** intensely,
violently **10** completely, forcefully,
rigorously, thoroughly, vehemently
11 outspokenly

round-up

05 rally, rodeo **06** muster, précis,
survey **07** herding, summary
08 assembly, overview **09** collation,
gathering **10** collection **11** marshalling
14 bang-tail muster

rouse

◇ anagram indicator
04 call, fire, firk, move, rear, send, stir,
wake, yerk **05** abray, amove, anger,
awake, evoke, flush, get up, impel,
raise, roust, set up, shake, start, steer,
stire, styre, unbed, waken **06** abrade,
abraid, arouse, awaken, bumper, call
up, excite, incite, induce, kindle, ruffle,
stir up, summon, turn on, wake up,
whip up, work up **07** agitate, disturb,
inflame, knock up, provoke, shake up
08 carousal, enkindle, irritate, reveille
09 galvanize, instigate, look alive,
stimulate, suscitate

rousing

05 brisk, great **06** lively, moving
07 beating, violent, wakeful

08 exciting, spirited, stirring, vigorous **09** awakening, inspiring **10** incitation **11** stimulating **12** electrifying, exhilarating **13** heart-stirring **14** spirit-stirring

rout
04 beat, fuss, grub, herd, lick, pack, riot, roar, rowt **05** brawl, chase, crush, flock, snore **06** bellow, defeat, dispel, flight, grub up, hammer, rabble, thrash, turn up **07** beating, clamour, clobber, conquer, retreat, scatter, trounce, turn out **08** conquest, drubbing, stampede, vanquish **09** discomfit, hurricane, overthrow, shoot down, slaughter, subjugate, thrashing, trouncing **11** disturbance, put to flight, subjugation, walk all over

route
03 run, way **04** beat, line, path, road, send, tail, walk **05** round, trail **06** avenue, bypass, convey, course, direct **07** airline, circuit, forward, journey, passage, transit **08** delivery, despatch, dispatch, main line, sideline **09** direction, itinerary, milk round **10** flight path, navigation **11** long paddock **12** wallaby track

routine
03 act, run, rut, way, yak **04** dull, rota, wont **05** banal, chain, chore, drill, habit, heigh, ho-hum, lines, order, piece, round, spiel, usage, usual **06** boring, common, custom, groove, method, normal, patter, regime, schtik, shtick, system, wonted **07** formula, heigh-ho, humdrum, jogtrot, milk run, mundane, pattern, schtick, tedious, typical **08** day-to-day, everyday, familiar, habitual, heich-how, ordinary, practice, schedule, standard, tiresome, workaday **09** customary, hackneyed, mechanics, procedure, programme, treadmill, unvarying **10** monotonous, unoriginal **11** journey-work, performance, perfunctory, predictable **12** conventional, run-of-the-mill **13** institutional **14** bread-and-butter

routinely
07 usually **08** commonly, normally **09** regularly, typically **10** habitually **11** customarily **14** conventionally

rove
◇ *anagram indicator*
04 roam **05** drift, range, stray **06** cruise, ramble, stroll, wander **07** meander, traipse **08** stravaig **09** gallivant, wandering **11** go walkabout

rover
05 Gypsy, nomad **06** nomade, pirate, ranger, robber **07** drifter, rambler, seacock, vagrant **08** gadabout, wanderer **09** itinerant, transient, traveller **10** stravaiger

row
03 din, oar, rag **04** bank, deen, file, line, pull, rank, roll, tier, tiff **05** argue, brawl, chain, fight, noise, queue, rammy, range, rough, scold, scrap, set-to

06 assail, bicker, column, dust-up, fracas, hubbub, racket, rumpus, series, shindy, splore, string, stroke, tumult, uproar **07** bobbery, clamour, dispute, quarrel, ruction, shindig, wrangle **08** argument, conflict, rebuking, remigate, scolding, sequence, squabble **09** commotion **10** falling-out **11** altercation, arrangement, controversy, disturbance **12** disagreement **13** slanging match

• **in a row**
04 arew, arow **06** in turn, serial **09** on the trot **10** back to back **12** continuously, sequentially, successively **13** consecutively **15** uninterruptedly

rowan
04 sorb

rowdy
03 yob **04** loud, lout, wild **05** money, noisy, rorty, rough, tough, yahoo, yobbo **06** apache, blowsy, blowzy, keelie, unruly **07** brawler, hoodlum, lawless, riotous, ruffian, stroppy **08** hooligan, larrikin, tearaway **09** bovver boy **10** boisterous, brat packer, disorderly **12** obstreperous, unrestrained

rower
03 oar **06** stroke **07** oarsman, sculler **09** oarswoman, stroke oar

rowing

Rowing-related terms include:

03 bow, cox, rig
04 crew, easy, four, gate, keel, loom, pair, quad, rate, skeg, span, wash
05 blade, catch, coxed, drive, eight, pitch, scull, shell, stern
06 boatie, button, collar, gunnel, length, puddle, rating, rigger, skying, stroke
07 bowside, coxless, gunwale, regatta, row over, sculler
08 coxswain, paddling, rowlocks
09 ergometer, head races, outrigger, slide seat, stretcher
10 catch a crab, feathering, pivot point, strokeside
11 double scull, single scull, the Boat Race
13 getting spoons
15 jumping the slide

• **rowing boat**
04 four, pair **05** eight

royal
04 king, real, rial, ryal **05** grand, queen, regal **06** august, kingly, prince, regius, superb **07** queenly, stately **08** imperial, imposing, kinglike, majestic, princely, princess, splendid **09** basilical, queenlike, sovereign **10** impressive **11** magnificent, monarchical

royally
07 grandly, greatly **08** superbly **10** splendidly **11** wonderfully **12** impressively, tremendously **13** magnificently

royalty
08 residual

rub
◇ *anagram indicator*
03 dub, pat, rob, wax **04** buff, faze, fret, snag, soap, wipe **05** apply, catch, chafe, clean, curry, emery, grate, grind, hitch, knead, pinch, put on, rosin, scour, scrub, shine, smear, stone, towel **06** abrade, buff up, caress, fondle, fridge, impede, liquor, nuzzle, polish, rubber, scrape, smooth, spread, stroke, work in **07** burnish, flannel, furbish, massage, problem, rub-down, scratch, snuzzle, trouble **08** drawback, irritate, kneading, obstacle, soft-soap **09** embrocate, hindrance, triturate **10** difficulty, impediment

• **rub along**
04 cope **05** get by, get on **06** manage **08** get along

• **rub down**
03 dry **04** wash, wisp **05** clean, curry **06** smooth, sponge **07** massage **08** wash down

• **rub in**
06 harp on, stress **08** insist on **09** emphasize, highlight, underline **10** make much of

• **rub off on**
05 alter **06** affect, change **09** influence, transform **14** have an effect on

• **rub out**
04 do in, kill **05** erase **06** cancel, delete, efface, murder **07** bump off **09** eliminate, finish off, liquidate **10** do away with, obliterate, put to death **11** assassinate

• **rub up the wrong way**
03 bug, get, irk, vex **05** anger, annoy, get to, peeve **06** needle, niggle, wind up **08** irritate **11** get your goat **13** get up your nose

rubber

Rubber types and trees include:

03 ule
04 buna, cold, foam, hard, hule, pará, root
05 butyl, crêpe, hevea, India, Lagos, sorbo
06 sponge
07 ebonite, guayule, seringa
08 Funtumia, neoprene, Silastic®
09 camelback, vulcanite
10 caoutchouc, gum elastic, mangabeira
14 high-hysteresis

rubberneck
04 gape, gawk, gawp, view **05** stare, watch **06** goggle, look at **07** tourist

rubbish
◇ *anagram indicator*
03 red, rot, tat **04** blah, bosh, bull, bunk, cack, crap, dirt, gash, grot, guff, junk, kack, mush, redd, tosh **05** balls, bilge, brock, chaff, culch, dreck, dross, garbo, hokum, hooey, pants, scrap, stuff, trade, trash, tripe, truck, waste **06** bunkum, cultch, debris, drivel, litter,

piffle, raffle, refuse, rubble **07** baloney, eyewash, garbage, gubbins, hogwash, mullock, rhubarb, twaddle **08** bulldust, claptrap, cobblers, detritus, malarkey, nonsense, riff-raff, tommyrot, trashery, trumpery **09** bull's wool, gibberish, moonshine, mouthwash, poppycock, sweepings **10** balderdash, clamjamfry, codswallop, excrementa, tomfoolery **11** clanjamfray **12** clamjamphrie, gobbledegook, gobbledygook

rubbish heap
03 tip **04** coup, cowp, dump, toom **06** midden **08** laystall **09** scrapheap **13** kitchen midden

rubbishy
05 cheap, junky, petty, tatty, tripy **06** cruddy, crummy, grotty, paltry, shoddy, tawdry, tinpot, trashy, tripey **08** gimcrack, inferior, riff-raff **09** third-rate, throw-away, valueless, worthless **10** low-quality, second-rate **14** unsatisfactory

rubble
04 muck **05** ruins, waste, wreck **06** debris **07** moellon, remains, rubbish **08** hard core, wreckage **09** fragments

rubidium
02 Rb

ruby
05 agate, balas, blood **06** redden **09** starstone **12** pigeon's-blood

ruction
03 din, row **04** fuss, rout, to-do **05** brawl, noise, scrap, storm **06** fracas, racket, ruffle, rumpus, uproar **07** carry-on, dispute, protest, quarrel, rookery, trouble **09** commotion, hue and cry, kerfuffle **11** altercation, disturbance

ruddy
03 red **04** rosy **05** fresh **06** bloody, blowsy, blowzy, bright, cherry, darned, dashed, florid, rubric **07** blasted, crimson, flushed, glowing, healthy, reddish, rubious, scarlet **08** annoying, blooming, blushing, flipping, infernal, rubicund, sanguine, sunburnt **10** confounded **11** carnationed, flammulated **12** apple-cheeked, high-coloured

rude
◇ *anagram indicator*
04 blue, curt, lewd **05** basic, bawdy, crude, dirty, gross, harsh, nasty, rough, sharp, short **06** abrupt, cheeky, coarse, filthy, ribald, risqué, robust, rugged, simple, smutty, sudden, vulgar **07** abusive, bestial, boorish, brusque, ill-bred, naughty, obscene, peasant, uncivil, uncouth, violent **08** barbaric, churlish, ignorant, impolite, improper, impudent, indecent, insolent **09** barbarian, giant rude, goustrous, insulting, makeshift, offensive, primitive, salacious, startling, unrefined, unskilled, untutored, unwrought **10** heathenish, illiterate,

indelicate, uncultured, uneducated, unexpected, unpleasant, unpolished **11** bad-mannered, bad-tempered, ill-mannered, impertinent, near the bone, rudimentary, uncivilized, undeveloped **12** disagreeable, discourteous **13** disrespectful, rough-and-ready **14** near the knuckle

rudely
06 curtly **07** harshly **08** abruptly, suddenly **09** abusively, brusquely **10** impolitely, impudently, insolently **12** disagreeably, unexpectedly, unpleasantly **14** discourteously **15** disrespectfully

rudeness
05 abuse **09** barbarism, Gothicism, impudence, insolence, rusticity **10** bad manners, disrespect, ill manners, incivility **11** discourtesy, grossièreté, uncouthness **12** impertinence, impoliteness **14** unpleasantness

rudimentary
03 pro- **05** basic, crude, rough **06** simple **07** initial, primary, reduced, seminal **08** inchoate **09** embryonic, embryotic, essential, imperfect, makeshift, primitive, remaining, surviving, vestigial **10** elementary, incomplete, primordial **11** abecedarian, fundamental, undeveloped **12** functionless, introductory **13** rough-and-ready **15** unsophisticated

rudiments
03 ABC **05** abcee, absey **06** basics **08** elements **10** beginnings, essentials, principles **11** foundations **12** fundamentals **15** first principles

rue
03 rew **04** pity, Ruta **05** mourn **06** bemoan, bewail, grieve, lament, regret, repent, sorrow **07** be sorry, deplore, harmala **09** herb-grace **10** repentance, thalictrum **11** be regretful, herb-of-grace **14** feel remorse for

rueful
03 sad **05** sorry **06** dismal, woeful **07** doleful, piteous, pitiful **08** contrite, grievous, mournful, penitent, pitiable **09** plaintive, regretful, repentant, sorrowful, woebegone **10** apologetic, deplorable, lugubrious, melancholy, remorseful **15** self-reproachful

ruff
03 ree **04** band, pope, slam **05** frill, reeve, rough, trump **06** fraise, ruffle, tippet **07** applaud, elation, partlet **08** applause **09** blackfish **10** excitement

ruffian
03 ned, yob **04** hoon, lout, thug **05** brute, bully, rogue, rough, rowdy, tough, yobbo **06** Apache, brutal, rascal, thuggo, toerag **07** bruiser, hoodlum, sweater, villain, violent **08** bully-boy, hooligan, larrikin, plug-ugly **09** bovver boy, bully-rook,

cut-throat, desperado, lager lout, miscreant, roughneck, ruffianly, scoundrel **10** highbinder **11** trailbaston

ruffle
◇ *anagram indicator*
03 bug, irk, vex **04** fold, line, rile, ruff, tuck **05** anger, annoy, frill, pleat, rough, rouse, upset **06** bustle, crease, fringe, furrow, gather, hassle, nettle, pucker, put out, rattle, ripple, rumple, snatch, tangle, tousle, tumult, wind up **07** agitate, bluster, confuse, crinkle, crumple, falbala, flounce, fluster, flutter, perturb, quarrel, swagger, trouble, valance, wrinkle **08** brass off, dishevel, disorder, irritate, struggle, trimming **09** aggravate, agitation, annoyance, cheese off, drive nuts, encounter, pantalets **10** disarrange, discompose, drive crazy, exasperate **11** pantalettes **12** drive bananas **13** make sparks fly **14** drive up the wall

rug
03 mat, rya, tug, wig **04** felt, haul, kali, snug **05** kelim, kilim, pilch, share, throw **06** carpet, khilim, Kirman, numdah, secure, toupee, toupet **07** bergama, doormat, flokati, matting **08** bergamot, covering, underlay **09** hairpiece, prayer mat, underfelt **11** buffalo robe **13** floor-covering, Persian carpet

See also **carpet**

rugby
02 RL, RU

Rugby League teams and nicknames include:

04 Eels, Reds
05 Bears, Bulls, Kiwis, Lions, Storm
06 Eagles, Giants, Hull FC, Kumuls, Rhinos, Sharks, Tigers, Wolves
07 Blue Sox, Broncos, Cowboys, Dragons, Knights, Raiders
08 Bulldogs, Panthers, Roosters, Warriors, Wildcats
09 Kangaroos, Rabbitohs, Tomahawks
10 Lionhearts
11 Bravehearts, Leeds Rhinos, St Helens RFC
13 Bradford Bulls, London Broncos, Widnes Vikings, Wigan Warriors
15 Irish Wolfhounds, Leigh Centurions, Les Chanticleers, Salford City Reds

Rugby League-related terms include:

02 RL
03 try
04 back, feed, lock, pack, prop, punt
05 dummy, put-in, scrum
06 centre, hooker, in-goal, tackle, winger
07 dropout, forward, hand-off, knock on, offload, offside, penalty, try line
08 blood bin, drop goal, free-kick, front row, full-back, gain line, goal line, half-back, handover, open side, scissors, sidestep, stand-off, turnover
09 blind side, dummy half, field goal,

place kick, scrum-half
10 charge down, conversion, five-eighth, penalty try, up and under, zero tackle
11 forward pass, grubber kick, play-the-ball, sixth tackle, touch-in-goal
12 dead-ball line, loose forward, three-quarter
13 loose-head prop
14 acting half-back
15 twenty-metre line

maul, pack, ping, prop, ruck
05 clear, drive, dummy, phase, put-in, scrum, touch, wheel
06 centre, hooker, in-goal, jumper, sevens, tackle, uglies, winger
07 back row, binding, box kick, dropout, flanker, fly hack, fly-half, forward, hand-off, knock on, lifting, line-out, offload, offside, recycle, restart, try line
08 blood bin, crossing, drop goal, free-kick, front row, full back, gain line, goal line, half-back, miss move, open side, scissors, scrum cap, set piece, sidestep, standoff, turnover
09 back three, blind side, breakdown, crash ball, front five, grand slam, place kick, scrum-half, second row, tap tackle, third half, tight five, touchline, twenty-two
10 charge down, conversion, pack leader, penalty try, tap penalty, touch judge, up and under
11 cover tackle, forward pass, grubber kick, number eight, outside half, pushover try, ten-man rugby, triple crown, up the jumper, wing forward
12 dead-ball line, inside centre, loose forward, three-quarter
13 dummy scissors, loose-head prop, outside centre, tight-head prop
14 against the head
15 truck and trailer

rugged
04 firm, rude, wild **05** bumpy, burly, hardy, rocky, rough, stark, stony, tough **06** craggy, jagged, knaggy, knotty, robust, shaggy, sinewy, stormy, strong, sturdy, uneven **07** gnarled, uncouth **08** furrowed, muscular, resolute, stalwart, vigorous **09** iron-bound, irregular, tenacious, well-built **10** determined, unwavering **11** unflinching **13** weather-beaten

ruggedly
07 rockily, roughly, starkly, toughly **08** strongly, unevenly **10** muscularly, vigorously **11** irregularly

ruin
◇ *anagram indicator*
03 mar **04** cook, dish, do in, doom, fall, harm, heap, Hell, loss, raze, sink **05** botch, break, chaos, crash, crush, decay, do for, folly, fordo, havoc, smash, spoil, whelm, wreck **06** banjax, damage, debris, defeat, injure, jigger, mess up, penury, perish, ravage, relics, rubble, traces, unmake **07** carcase, carcass, cripple, destroy, failure, remains, screw up, scupper, scuttle, shatter, subvert, undoing **08** bankrupt, collapse, demolish, detritus, disaster, down-come, downfall, lay waste, remnants, shambles, vestiges, wreckage **09** breakdown, devastate, disrepair, fragments, indigence, overthrow, overwhelm, perdition, ruination, seduction, shipwreck **10** bankruptcy, demolition, impoverish, insolvency, subversion, wreak havoc **11** destruction,

devastation **12** do violence to, make bankrupt **13** make insolvent **14** bouleversement, disintegration
• **in ruins**
04 sunk **06** ruined **07** damaged, ruinate, wrecked **08** decrepit **09** destroyed **10** broken-down, devastated, ramshackle, tumbledown **11** dilapidated **12** falling apart

ruination
04 fall **05** decay, havoc **06** damage, defeat **07** failure, undoing **08** collapse, downfall, wreckage **09** breakdown, disrepair, overthrow **11** destruction, devastation **14** disintegration

ruined
◇ *anagram indicator*
See **bankrupt**

ruinous
05 waste **06** ruined **07** damaged, decayed, in ruins, wrecked **08** decrepit, tottered **09** crippling, destroyed, excessive, shattered **10** broken-down, calamitous, devastated, disastrous, exorbitant, immoderate, ramshackle **11** cataclysmic, devastating, dilapidated **12** catastrophic, extortionate, unreasonable

ruinously
11 excessively **12** exorbitantly, immoderately, unreasonably **14** extortionately

rule
01 r **03** law, raj **04** dash, find, form, lead, line, norm, rain, ring, sway, wont **05** axiom, canon, guide, habit, judge, maxim, norma, order, power, raine, reign, sutra, tenet, truth **06** custom, decide, decree, direct, govern, manage, method, regime, rubric, ruling, settle, squier, squire, truism **07** command, conduct, control, dictate, formula, lay down, mastery, ordinar, plummet, precept, prevail, resolve, routine, royalty, statute **08** dominate, dominion, kingship, ordinary, practice, protocol, regulate, standard, thearchy **09** authority, criterion, determine, direction, establish, guideline, gynocracy, hagiarchy, influence, mobocracy, officiate, ordinance, prescript, principle, procedure, pronounce, queenship, supremacy **10** adjudicate, administer, convention, corrective, government, leadership, mastership, ochlocracy, prevalence, regulation **11** be in control, commandment, gubernation, instruction, preside over, restriction, sovereignty, stratocracy, tridominium **12** call the shots, jurisdiction **14** administration
• **as a rule**
06 mainly **07** usually **08** normally **09** generally, in general, in the main **10** by and large, on the whole, ordinarily **14** for the most part
• **collection of rules**
03 pie, pye **04** code

• rule out
3 ban **06** forbid, reject **07** dismiss, exclude, prevent **08** disallow, preclude, prohibit **09** eliminate

uler

3 aga, mir, oba
4 amir, czar, duce, emir, head, jarl, kaid, khan, king, ksar, lord, meer, naik, raja, rana, rani, ratu, shah, tsar, tzar
5 begum, mpret, nawab, nizam, queen, rajah, ratoo
6 atabeg, atabek, caesar, caliph, consul, Führer, gerent, kaiser, leader, mikado, prince, regent, satrap, sheikh, shogun, sultan
7 czarina, emperor, empress, monarch, pharaoh, sultana, toparch, tsarina, viceroy
8 governor, maharani, overlord, padishah, princess, suzerain
9 commander, maharajah, potentate, president, sovereign
10 controller
11 gouvernante, head of state
15 governor-general

See also **emperor; empress; king; monarch; president; prime minister; queen**

uling
4 main **05** chief **06** decree
7 finding, leading, supreme, verdict
8 decision, dominant, in charge, judgment, reigning **09** governing, in control, judgement, principal, sovereign **10** commanding, resolution
11 controlling, on the throne, predominant **12** adjudication
13 pronouncement **15** most influential

rum
◇ *anagram indicator*
3 odd **04** good **05** droll, funny, queer, rafia, weird **06** taffia **07** Bacardi®, bizarre, cachaça, curious, strange, suspect, unusual **08** abnormal, demerara, freakish, peculiar, singular **10** suspicious **13** funny-peculiar

rumble
04 boom, roar, roll **05** grasp, groan **06** lumber, mutter **07** grumble, quarrel, thunder **11** disturbance, reverberate **13** reverberation

rumbustious
04 loud, wild **05** noisy, rough, rowdy **06** robust, unruly, wilful **07** wayward **08** roisting **09** clamorous, exuberant **10** boisterous, disorderly, refractory, roisterous, uproarious **12** obstreperous, unmanageable

ruminant
10 meditative

02 ox
03 cow
04 goat
05 camel, sheep
06 musk ox

07 giraffe
08 antelope, cavicorn
09 pronghorn

See also **cattle; antelope**

05 bible, rumen
06 bonnet, fardel, paunch
09 king's-hood, manyplies, rennet-bag, reticulum

ruminate
04 muse **05** brood, think **06** ponder **07** reflect **08** chew over, cogitate, consider, meditate, mull over **10** chew the cud, deliberate **11** contemplate

rummage
03 tat **04** fish, hunt, junk, root, stir **05** delve, rifle, touse, touze, towse, towze, wroot **06** ferret, forage, jumble, powter, search **07** examine, explore, fossick, ransack **08** overhaul, turn over, upheaval **09** bric-à-brac, commotion **10** poke around, root around **11** odds and ends **13** search through

rumour
03 cry, say **04** buzz, fame, goss, hint, kite, news, talk, tell, word **05** bruit, noise, on-dit, say-so, sough, story, voice **06** breeze, canard, furphy, gossip, murmur, outcry, renown, report, repute, speech **07** clamour, hearsay, publish, scandal, tidings, whisper **08** put about **09** circulate, grapevine **10** bruit about **11** bruit abroad, fama clamosa, information, noise abroad, scuttlebutt, speculation, underbreath **12** tittle-tattle **13** bush telegraph

rump
03 ass, bum, can **04** butt, coit, dock, duff, prat, rear, seat, tail, tush **05** booty, croup, fanny, nache, natch, podex, quoit, stern, trace **06** behind, bottom, breech, croupe, haunch, heinie **07** keister, remains, remnant, residue, vestige **08** backside, buttocks, derrière, haunches **09** fundament, leftovers, posterior, remainder, uropygium **12** hindquarters

rumple
04 fold **05** crush, touse, touze, towse, towze **06** crease, pucker, ruffle, tousle, tumble **07** crinkle, crumple, derange, scrunch, wrinkle **08** dishevel, disorder

rumpus
03 row **04** fuss, rout **05** brawl, noise **06** fracas, furore, ruckus, shindy, tumult, uproar **07** bagarre, rhubarb, ruction **08** brouhaha **09** commotion, confusion, kerfuffle, shemozzle, shimozzle **10** disruption, schemozzle, shlemozzle **11** disturbance

run
◇ *anagram indicator*
01 r **02** do, go **03** cut, hit, jet, jog, own, pen, ply, ren, rin, rip, set, sty, use, way **04** bolt, call, coop, dart, dash, drip, emit, flee, flow, fold, fuse, gash, goal, go on, gush, hare, have, head, hole,

hunt, keep, kind, last, lauf, lead, leak, line, lope, mark, melt, move, need, pass, pour, race, ride, road, roll, romp, rush, show, slip, slit, snag, sort, spew, spin, take, tear, tend, trip, trot, type, work, yard **05** bleed, brush, carry, chain, chase, class, corso, cross, cycle, drive, enter, glide, hurry, incur, issue, jaunt, point, pound, print, range, reach, round, route, scoot, score, shoal, slash, slide, speed, spell, split, spurt, stand, track, trill **06** become, career, chance, charge, convey, course, curdle, demand, direct, elapse, extend, follow, fulfil, gallop, hasten, ladder, manage, outing, period, pierce, schuss, scurry, series, spread, sprint, stream, string, thrust, travel **07** average, be valid, carry on, cascade, clamour, compete, conduct, contend, control, execute, feature, include, journey, operate, oversee, paddock, passage, perform, possess, proceed, promote, publish, revolve, roulade, run away, scamper, scarper, scutter, scuttle, shuttle, smuggle, stretch, trickle, variety **08** be played, be staged, carry out, category, continue, distance, function, maintain, organize, overflow, pressure, progress, regulate, sequence, step on it, traverse **09** be mounted, broadcast, challenge, coagulate, discharge, enclosure, excursion, free use of, give a lift, give a ride, implement, supervise, transport, undertake **10** administer, be in effect, be produced, co-ordinate, flight path, prevalence, succession, take part in **11** be performed, be presented, communicate, opportunity, superintend **12** be in charge of **13** be in control of, be in operation **15** travel regularly

• in the long run
06 at last **08** in the end **10** eventually, ultimately

• on the run
04 free **07** at large, escaped, pursued **08** on the lam **09** at liberty **10** on the loose, unconfined **11** running away **14** trying to escape

• run across
04 meet **07** run into **08** bump into **09** encounter **10** chance upon, come across **12** meet by chance

• run after
04 tail **05** chase **06** follow, pursue

• run along
04 scat **05** be off, leave **06** go away **07** buzz off, scarper **08** clear off, off you go **09** on your way **10** off with you **11** away with you

• run along the ground
04 taxi

• run away
03 cut **04** bolt, bunk, flee, lift, nick **05** avoid, dodge, elope, evade, filch, leave, pinch, scapa, steal **06** beat it, decamp, desert, escape, ignore, pocket, run off, scarpa **07** abscond, make off, neglect, nick off, purloin, scarper, vamoose **08** cheese it, clear off, overlook **09** coast home,

disregard, do a runner, skedaddle, win easily **10** brush aside **11** appropriate, make off with, walk off with **12** win hands down **13** make a run for it **14** shut your eyes to, take no notice of, turn your back on

• **run down**
03 cut, hit, pan **04** bust, drop, slag, slam, tire, trim **05** knock, slate, weary **06** attack, defame, pooped, reduce, strike, weaken **07** curtail, exhaust, rubbish, run over, slag off, whacked **08** belittle, decrease, denounce, lose time **09** criticize, cut back on, denigrate, disparage, knackered, knock down, knock over **12** pull to pieces, tear to pieces

• **run for it**
03 fly **04** bolt, flee **05** scram **06** escape **07** do a bunk, make off, retreat, scarper, vamoose **09** skedaddle **11** give leg bail

• **run in**
03 nab **04** bust, jail, lift, nail, nick **05** pinch **06** arrest, collar, pick up **09** apprehend

• **run into**
03 hit, ram **04** face, meet **05** crash, equal **06** come to, strike **07** add up to **08** amount to, bump into **09** encounter, run across **10** chance upon, come across, experience **11** collide with **12** meet by chance **13** come up against

• **run off**
04 bolt, copy **05** elope, print, Xerox® **06** decamp, escape, repeat **07** abscond, make off, produce, recount, run away, scarper **09** duplicate, photocopy, Photostat®, skedaddle

• **run off with**
04 lift, nick **05** filch, pinch, steal **06** pocket **07** purloin **08** take away **09** elope with **11** appropriate, make off with, run away with, walk off with **12** make away with

• **run on**
04 go on, last **05** reach **06** extend **07** carry on **08** continue

• **run out**
02 ro **03** end **04** fail, leak **05** cease, close, dry up **06** elapse, expire, finish **07** exhaust, give out **08** be used up **09** terminate **10** be finished **11** be exhausted

• **run out on**
04 dump, jilt **05** chuck, ditch, leave **06** desert, maroon, strand **07** abandon, forsake **09** walk out on **15** leave in the lurch

• **run over**
03 hit **04** flow, heat **05** recap **06** go over, repeat, review, strike, survey **07** run down **08** overflow, practise, rehearse **09** knock down, overthrow, reiterate **10** run through **12** recapitulate

• **run through**
04 read **05** spend, waste **06** review, survey **07** examine, exhaust, run over **08** practise, rehearse, squander

09 dissipate, go through **11** fritter away, read through

• **run to**
05 equal, total **06** afford, come to **07** add up to **08** amount to **12** have enough of

• **run together**
03 mix **04** fuse, join **05** blend, merge, unite **06** concur, mingle **07** combine **08** coalesce **09** commingle **10** amalgamate

runaway
04 wild **05** fugie, loose **06** flight, truant **07** escaped, escapee, escaper, refugee **08** deserter, fugitive **09** absconder **11** loup-the-dyke **12** out of control, uncontrolled

run-down
03 cut, ill **04** drop, weak **05** dingy, peaky, recap, seedy, tired, weary **06** grotty, résumé, review, shabby, sketch, unwell **07** cutback, decline, drained, outline, summary, worn-out **08** analysis, briefing, decrease, decrepit, fatigued, synopsis **09** enervated, exhausted, neglected, reduction, unhealthy **10** broken-down, ramshackle, run-through, tumble-down, uncared-for **11** curtailment, debilitated, dilapidated

rune
03 ash, wen, wyn **04** aesc, wynn

run-in
05 brush, fight, set-to **06** dust-up, tussle **07** dispute, quarrel, wrangle **08** approach, argument, skirmish **11** altercation, contretemps **13** confrontation

runnel *see* **brook**

runner
03 ski **04** scud, skid, slip, stem, tout **05** agent, blade, miler, racer, shoot, slide, slipe, sprig **06** bearer, jogger, sprout, stolon **07** athlete, courier, courser, harrier, slipper, tendril **08** fugitive, offshoot, smuggler, sprinter **09** flagellum, lampadist, messenger, racehorse, sarmentum **10** competitor **11** participant **13** dispatch rider

• **do a runner**
02 go **04** exit, quit **05** scoot **06** decamp, depart, go away, hook it, set out **07** do a bunk, pull out, push off, take off, vamoose **08** clear off, shove off, up sticks **09** disappear, push along **10** make tracks **13** sling your hook, take your leave **15** take French leave

• **runners**
05 field

running
◊ *anagram indicator*
04 easy **05** hasty **06** charge, in a row, moving, racing **07** conduct, contest, control, current, cursive, flowing, jogging, ongoing, rushing, working **08** constant, unbroken **09** candidacy, ceaseless, direction, incessant, itinerant, on the trot, operation, perpetual, shortlist, sprinting,

stampede, unceasing **10** contention, continuous, leadership, management, regulation, successive **11** competition, consecutive, controlling, discharging, functioning, performance, supervision **12** co-ordination, in succession, organization **13** uninterrupted **14** administration **15** superintendency

runny
◊ *anagram indicator*
05 fluid **06** liquid, melted, molten, watery **07** diluted, flowing **09** liquefied

run-of-the-mill
02 OK **04** fair, so-so **06** common, normal **07** average **08** everyday, mediocre, middling, ordinary **09** tolerable **11** bog standard, not up to much **12** unimpressive, unremarkable **13** no great shakes, unexceptional **14** common-or-garden **15** undistinguished

rupture
◊ *anagram indicator*
04 rend, rent, rift, tear **05** break, burst, crack, sever, split **06** breach, bust-up, cut off, divide, hernia, rhexis, schism **07** quarrel **08** breaking, bursting, division, fracture, puncture, scissure, separate **09** amniotomy **10** falling-out, separation **12** disagreement, estrangement

rural
04 hick **06** forane, rustic, sylvan, upland **07** bucolic, country, peasant, predial **08** agrarian, agrestic, mofussil, pastoral, praedial **09** bucolical, uplandish **11** countryside **12** agricultural **13** cracker-barrel

ruse
04 hoax, plan, plot, ploy, sham, wile **05** blind, dodge, stall, trick **06** device, scheme, tactic **08** artifice **09** deception, imposture, manoeuvre, stratagem **10** subterfuge

rush
03 fly, ren, rin, rip, run **04** belt, bolt, bomb, call, dart, dash, fall, flaw, flow, gush, lash, leap, need, pelt, push, race, raid, rash, star, stir, tear **05** fling, flood, haste, hurry, onset, press, run at, scour, shoot, spate, speat, speed, starr, storm, surge **06** attack, bustle, career, charge, demand, flurry, gallop, hasten, random, sprint, streak, stream, strike **07** assault, cariere, clamour, defraud, quicken, speed up, tantivy, urgency, viretot **08** activity, despatch, dispatch, pressure, rapidity, scramble, stampede **09** commotion, make haste, onslaught, star grass, swiftness **10** accelerate, excitement, get a move on, hurly-burly, overcharge, shave-grass, spring tide, starr grass **11** run like hell **13** precipitation **14** hive of activity **15** hustle and bustle

rushed
04 busy, fast **05** brisk, hasty, quick, rapid, swift **06** hectic, prompt, urgent

07 cursory, hurried 08 careless
09 emergency 11 expeditious,
superficial

Russia
03 RUS

*Russian cities and notable towns
include:*

04 Omsk
05 Kazan
06 Moscow, Moskva, Samara
07 Irkutsk
08 Novgorod
09 Archangel, Volgograd
11 Archangelsk, Chelyabinsk,
Novosibirsk, Rostov-on-Don,
Vladivostok
12 Ekaterinburg, St Petersburg
13 Yekaterinburg
15 Nizhniy Novgorod

Russian
04 czar, tsar, tzar 05 Lenin, Putin, Raisa
07 czarina, Trotsky, tsarina, Yeltsin
08 czaritsa, Rasputin, tsaritsa
09 Gorbachev

Russians include:

05 Khant
06 Buryat, Ostyak
07 Bashkir, Cossack
08 Siberian
09 Muscovite
10 Volga Tatar

rust
03 rot 05 decay, dross, stain, uredo
07 corrode, decline, ferrugo, oxidize,
tarnish 09 corrosion, oxidation,
verdigris 11 deteriorate

rust-coloured
03 red 05 brown, rusty, sandy, tawny
06 auburn, copper, ginger, russet, titian
07 coppery, gingery, reddish

08 chestnut 10 rubiginose, rubiginous
11 ferruginous 12 ferrugineous,
reddish-brown

rustic
◊ *anagram indicator*
03 hob, oaf 04 boor, carl, clod, hick,
hind, rude 05 bacon, borel, churl,
clown, crude, Hodge, plain, rough,
rural, swain, yokel 06 borrel, clumsy,
coarse, forest, hodden, oafish, russet,
simple, sylvan 07 artless, awkward,
boorish, borrell, bucolic, bumpkin,
Corydon, country, culchie, hayseed,
peasant, uncouth, woollen
08 backveld, clownish, homespun,
pastoral, Strephon 09 bucolical,
chawbacon, graceless, hillbilly,
Hobbinoll, ingenuous, maladroit,
unrefined, uplandish 10 bogtrotter,
clodhopper, countryman, indelicate,
provincial, uncultured 11 clodhopping,
countrified, countryside
12 countrywoman 13 country cousin,
cracker-barrel 15 unsophisticated

rustle
◊ *anagram indicator*
04 raid, sigh 05 steal, swish 06 bustle,
fissle, hustle, whoosh 07 crackle,
whisper 08 crepitus, rustling, susurrus
09 crinkling, susurrate 10 whispering
11 crepitation, susurration
• **rustle up**
04 make 07 scare up 10 get quickly
11 get together, put together
14 prepare quickly, provide quickly

rusty
03 red 04 dull, poor, weak 05 brown,
dated, rough, sandy, stale, stiff, tawny
06 auburn, copper, ginger, russet,
rusted, titian 07 coppery, gingery,
raucous, reddish 08 chestnut,
corroded, creaking, impaired,

outmoded, oxidized, time-worn
09 deficient, obstinate, tarnished
10 aeruginous, antiquated, rubiginose,
rubiginous 11 discoloured, ferruginous,
rust-covered, unpractised
12 ferrugineous, old-fashioned,
reddish-brown, rust-coloured 13 out
of practice

rut
05 ditch, gouge, grind, habit, track
06 furrow, groove, gutter, system,
trough 07 channel, humdrum, pattern,
pothole, routine 09 treadmill,
wheelmark 10 daily grind, wheel track
11 indentation 12 same old place, same
old round

ruthenium
02 Ru

rutherfordium
02 Rf

ruthless
04 fell, grim, hard 05 cruel, harsh, stern
06 brutal, fierce, savage, severe
07 callous, inhuman, vicious
08 felonous, pitiless 09 barbarous, cut-
throat, dog-eat-dog, Draconian,
ferocious, heartless, merciless,
unfeeling, unsparing 10 hard-bitten,
implacable, inexorable, relentless,
unmerciful 11 hard-hearted,
remorseless, third-degree,
unforgiving, unrelenting

ruthlessly
06 grimly 07 cruelly, harshly
08 brutally, fiercely, savagely, severely
09 callously 10 inexorably, pitilessly
11 mercilessly, unfeelingly
12 unmercifully 13 hard-heartedly,
remorselessly

Rwanda
03 RWA

S

S
02 es **03** ess **06** sierra
• **S-shape**
04 ogee **08** swan neck

Sabbath
01 S **03** Sat, Sun **06** Sunday **07** Shabbat
08 Saturday

sable
03 jet **04** dark, inky **05** black, dusky,
ebony, raven **06** darken, pitchy, sombre
08 midnight, zibeline **09** coal-black,
pitch-dark, zibelline **10** pitch-black

sabotage
◇ anagram indicator
03 mar **04** ruin **05** spoil, wreck
06 damage, impair, ratten, thwart,
weaken **07** cripple, destroy, disable,
disrupt, scupper **08** spoiling,
wrecking **09** crippling, disabling,
rattening, undermine, vandalism,
vandalize, weakening **10** disruption,
impairment **11** destruction
12 incapacitate

sac
03 bag, pod **04** cyst **05** bursa, pouch,
theca **06** ink-bag, pocket, vesica
07 bladder, capsule, saccule, vesicle
08 aerostat, cisterna, follicle,
tympanum, vesicula **09** lithocyst,
spore case **10** air-bladder, nematocyst,
sporangium, vitellicle **11** gall bladder,
pericardium **12** diverticulum

saccharine
05 gushy, mushy, soppy, sweet
06 sickly, sloppy, sugary, syrupy
07 cloying, dulcite, dulcose, honeyed,
maudlin, mawkish **08** dulcitol
09 oversweet, schmaltzy
10 nauseating **11** sentimental, sickly-
sweet

sachet
03 bag **04** pack **06** packet **07** musk-
bag, package **08** envelope, musk-ball,
scent bag, wrapping **09** container
12 bouquet garni

sack
◇ anagram indicator
◇ deletion indicator
03 axe, bag, bed, can, mat, rob **04** fire,
loot, muid, pack, raid, rape, raze, ruin
05 cards, gunny, level, pouch, rifle,
spoil, strip, waste **06** budget, firing, lay
off, maraud, notice, papers, pocket,
rapine, ravage, razing, remove, the axe
07 boot out, despoil, destroy, dismiss,
dust bag, jotters, looting, pillage,
plunder, sacking, satchel, the boot,
the chop, the push **08** demolish,

earth-bag, lay waste, the elbow
09 depredate, desecrate, devastate,
discharge, dismissal, hop-pocket,
levelling, marauding, select out **10** give
notice, plundering, the heave-ho
11 depredation, desecration,
destruction, devastation, send packing
12 despoliation **13** make redundant
14 marching orders

sacrament
04 rite **05** order **06** ritual **07** mystery,
nagmaal, penance **08** ceremony,
practice **09** communion, Eucharist,
ordinance **10** holy orders, observance
11 institution **13** Holy Communion
14 extreme unction

sacred
04 holy **05** godly **06** divine, secure
07 blessed, devoted, revered, sainted,
saintly **08** accursed, defended,
hallowed, heavenly, priestly
09 dedicated, protected, religious,
respected, spiritual, venerable
10 devotional, inviolable, sacrosanct,
sanctified **11** consecrated,
impregnable, untouchable
14 ecclesiastical

sacredness
08 divinity, holiness, sanctity
09 godliness, solemnity **11** saintliness
13 inviolability, sacrosanctity
15 invulnerability

sacrifice
◇ deletion indicator
04 loss **05** forgo, let go, offer **06** forego,
gambit, give up, victim **07** abandon,
forfeit, offer up, sacrify **08** giving-up,
hecatomb, immolate, lustrate, oblation,
offering, renounce **09** holocaust,
martyrize, molochize, sacrifide,
slaughter, surrender **10** immolation,
juggernaut, lustration, relinquish
11 abandonment, destruction, sin-
offering, taurobolium **12** propitiation,
renunciation **13** acceptilation, burnt-
offering, heave-offering, heave-
shoulder, suovetaurilia **14** blood-
sacrifice

sacrificial
06 votive **07** atoning **08** oblatory,
piacular **09** expiatory **10** reparative
12 propitiatory

sacrilege
06 heresy **07** impiety, mockery,
outrage **09** blasphemy, profanity,
violation **10** disrespect, irreligion
11 desecration, irreverence,
profanation

sacrilegious
06 unholy **07** godless, impious,
profane, ungodly **09** heretical
10 irreverent **11** blasphemous,
desecrating, irreligious, profanatory
13 disrespectful

sacrosanct
06 sacred, secure **08** hallowed
09 protected, respected **10** inviolable
11 impregnable, untouchable

sad
◇ anagram indicator
02 wo **03** low, woe **04** blue, down,
dull, glum **05** dowie, dusky, fed up,
grave, heavy, mesto, sated, sober,
sorry, staid, stiff, upset **06** dismal,
doughy, gloomy, sedate, tragic
07 doleful, earnest, joyless, painful,
pitiful, serious, tearful, unhappy, wistful
08 constant, dejected, downcast,
grievous, lovesick, mournful, pathetic,
pitiable, poignant, shameful, subtrist,
touching, tragical, wretched
09 depressed, heart-sore, long-faced,
miserable, sorrowful, sportless,
steadfast, upsetting, woebegone
10 calamitous, deplorable, depressing,
despondent, disastrous, distressed,
lamentable, melancholy, rock bottom
11 crestfallen, disgraceful, distressing,
downhearted, low-spirited,
regrettable, unfortunate **12** at rock
bottom, disconsolate, heart-rending,
heavy-hearted, in low spirits **13** grief-
stricken, heartbreaking **14** down in the
dumps

Sadat
05 Anwar

sadden
05 upset **06** deject, dismay, grieve
07 attrist, depress **08** cast down,
contrist, dispirit, distress **09** bring
down **10** discourage, dishearten
14 break your heart, drive to despair,
get someone down

saddle
03 col, pad, tax **04** land, load, seat, sell
05 panel, pilch, selle **06** burden,
charge, impose, lumber **07** kajawah,
pigskin, pillion **08** encumber

sadism
05 spite **07** cruelty **08** savagery
09 barbarity, brutality **10** bestiality,
inhumanity **11** callousness,
malevolence, viciousness
12 ruthlessness **13** heartlessness, sado-
masochism, schadenfreude,
unnaturalness

sadist
5 brute **06** abuser, savage, terror
7 monster **08** molester, torturer
9 barbarian

sadistic
5 cruel **06** brutal, savage **07** bestial,
inhuman, vicious **08** pitiless
9 barbarous, merciless, perverted,
unnatural

sadly
anagram indicator
4 alas **08** dismally, gloomily, sad
to say **09** miserably, tearfully,
unhappily, unluckily, weepingly, worse
luck **10** dejectedly **11** regrettably,
sad to relate, sorrowfully
2 despondently **13** unfortunately
4 heavy heartedly

sadness
3 woe **04** pain **05** grief **06** dismay,
misery, pathos, regret, sorrow
7 tragedy, waeness **08** distress,
glumness **09** bleakness, dejection,
heartache, poignancy **10** depression,
desolation, dismalness, gloominess,
low spirits, melancholy, misfortune,
sombreness **11** despondency,
dolefulness, joylessness, tearfulness,
unhappiness, Weltschmerz
2 mournfulness, wretchedness
3 cheerlessness, contristation,
sorrowfulness **14** lugubriousness

safe
4 fine, good, hunk, sure **05** ambry,
awmry, chest, peter, sound, timid, tried,
vault **06** almery, aumbry, awmrie,
coffer, condom, honest, immune,
intact, proven, secure, tested, unhurt
7 cash box, certain, guarded, keister,
prudent, upright **08** all right, cautious,
defended, harmless, non-toxic,
reliable, unharmed **09** innocuous,
protected, sheltered, strongbox,
undamaged, uninjured, unscathed
10 dependable, deposit box,
depository, home and dry, honourable,
repository **11** circumspect,
impregnable, in good hands, out of
danger, responsible, trustworthy
12 conservative, invulnerable, non-
poisonous, safe and sound, safe as
houses, unassailable **13** out of harm's
way, unadventurous, with whole skin
14 copper-bottomed,
uncontaminated, unenterprising

safe-conduct
04 jark, pass **06** convoy, permit
07 licence, warrant **08** passport
09 safeguard **13** authorization, laissez-
passer

safeguard
05 cover, guard **06** defend, screen,
secure, shield, surety **07** defence,
protect, shelter **08** preserve, security
09 assurance, guarantee, insurance,
look after, palladium **10** precaution,
preventive, protection, take care of
11 safe-conduct **12** preservative,
preventative

safekeeping
04 care, ward **05** trust **06** charge
07 custody, keeping **08** wardship
10 protection **11** supervision
12 guardianship, surveillance

safely
06 surely **08** securely **11** impregnably,
out of danger, without harm, without
risk **13** out of harm's way, without
injury

safety
05 cover **06** refuge **07** shelter, welfare
08 fail-safe, immunity, safeness,
security **09** safeguard, sanctuary,
soundness **10** preventive, protection,
protective **11** reliability
12 harmlessness, preventative
13 dependability, precautionary
14 impregnability **15** trustworthiness

sag
03 bag, dip, low **04** bend, drop, fail, fall,
flag, flop, give, hang, sink, slip, swag,
wilt **05** droop, slide, slump **06** falter,
weaken **07** decline, spinach, subside
08 downturn, low point **09** dwindling,
reduction **10** depression **11** hang
loosely

saga
04 Edda, epic, epos, tale, yarn **05** story
06 epopee **07** history, romance
08 epopoeia **09** adventure, chronicle,
narrative, soap opera **11** roman fleuve

sagacious
03 fly **04** able, sage, wary, wily, wise
05 acute, canny, quick, sharp, smart
06 astute, shrewd **07** knowing,
prudent, sapient **09** judicious, wide-
awake **10** discerning, far-sighted,
insightful, long-headed, perceptive,
percipient **11** intelligent, long-sighted,
penetrating **13** perspicacious

sagacity
05 sense **06** acumen, wisdom
07 insight **08** judgment, prudence,
sapience, wariness, wiliness
09 acuteness, canniness, foresight,
judgement, sharpness **10** astuteness,
shrewdness **11** discernment,
knowingness, penetration,
percipience **12** perspicacity
13 judiciousness, understanding

sage
04 guru, wise **05** canny, clary, elder,
hakam, orval, rishi **06** astute, expert,
master, Nestor, oracle, pundit, salvia,
saulge, savant, tohunga **07** knowing,
learned, mahatma, politic, prudent,
sapient, Solomon, teacher, wise man
08 sensible, wiseacre **09** authority,
judicious, maharishi, sagacious, wise
woman **10** discerning, wise person
11 intelligent, philosopher
13 knowledgeable, perspicacious

The Seven Sages:
04 Bias (of Priene in Caria)
05 Solon (of Athens)
06 Chilon (of Sparta), Thales (of
Miletus)

08 Pittacus (of Mitylene)
09 Cleobulus (tyrant of Lindus in
Rhodes), Periander (tyrant of
Corinth)

sagely
04 ably **06** wisely **07** acutely, quickly,
sharply **08** astutely, shrewdly
09 knowingly, prudently **11** judiciously
12 discerningly, perceptively
13 intelligently **15** perspicaciously

saggy
03 lax **04** limp, weak **05** loose, slack
06 droopy, feeble, floppy **07** falling,
sagging **08** drooping, dropping

said
◇ *homophone indicator*
03 quo', sed **04** quod **05** quoth

sail
03 fan, fly, ply, rag, van **04** boat, scud,
ship, skim, soar, Vela, waft, wing
05 coast, float, glide, pilot, plane, steer,
sweep, yacht **06** cruise, embark, put
off, voyage **07** captain, go by sea, sea
wing, set sail, skipper **08** navigate, put
to sea **09** leave port **11** travel by sea,
weigh anchor

Sails include:
03 jib, lug, rig, sky, top, try
04 fore, gaff, head, kite, main, moon,
stay, stun
05 drift, genoa, royal, smoke, sprit,
storm
06 bonnet, canvas, course, jigger,
lateen, mizzen, square, stuns'l
07 foretop, gaff-top, jury rig, maintop,
spanker, spencer
08 forestay, gennaker, storm try,
studding
09 crossjack, foreroyal, moonraker,
spinnaker, stargazer
10 Bermuda rig, fore-and-aft, main
course, skyscraper, topgallant
13 fore-and-aft rig
14 fore-topgallant

• **part of a sail**
04 bunt, luff, nock, reef **05** belly
06 bonnet

• **sail into**
05 shoal **06** attack, let fly, turn on
07 assault, lay into **08** set about, tear
into

• **sail through**
10 pass easily **11** romp through
15 succeed in easily

sailing
07 boating **08** yachting

Sailing-related terms include:
04 beat, gybe, helm, jibe, port
05 abaft, fetch, lay up
06 astern, course, leeway, upwind,
yawing
07 backing, bearing, beating, heeling,
lee helm, running, tacking
08 downwind, port tack, reaching,
under way, windward
09 alongside, laying off, letting go,
starboard
10 broad reach, casting off, close

reach, going about, ready about!
11 close-hauled, coming about, goose-winged, steerage way
12 sail trimming, spilling wind
13 across the wind, hard on the wind, starboard tack
15 fixing a position, stepping the mast, taking soundings

sailor

Sailor types include:

02 AB, OS, PO
03 cox, gob, mid, tar
04 hand, jack, mate, salt, tarp, Wren
05 bosun, janty, limey, matlo, middy, pilot, rower
06 bargee, hearty, jaunty, lascar, marine, master, matlow, pirate, purser, rating, sea boy, seadog, seaman, swabby, topman, Triton
07 boatman, captain, crewman, Jack tar, jauntie, mariner, matelot, oarsman, old salt, sculler, shipman, skipper, waister
08 Argonaut, cabin boy, coxswain, deck hand, helmsman, leadsman, seafarer, shipmate, water dog, water rat
09 boatswain, buccaneer, fisherman, galiongee, greenhand, navigator, sailor-man, sea lawyer, shellback, steersman, tarpaulin, yachtsman
10 able rating, able seaman, bluejacket, liberty-man, midshipman, tarpauling
11 foremastman, leatherneck, tarry-breeks, yachtswoman
12 able seawoman
13 canvas-climber

Sailors include:

04 Ahab (Captain), Byng (George), Byng (John), Cook (James), Diaz (Bartolomeu), Gama (Vasco da), Hood (Samuel, Viscount), Howe (Richard, Earl), Kidd (William), Ross (Horatio), Ross (Sir James Clark), Ross (Sir John), Spee (Count Maximilian von)
05 Adams (Will), Blake (Robert), Bligh (William), Cabot (John), Cabot (Sebastian), Doria (Andrea), Drake (Sir Francis), Hawke (Edward, Lord), Henry (the Navigator), Jones (Paul), Peary (Robert Edwin), Tromp (Maarten)
06 Baffin (William), Beatty (David, Earl), Benbow (John), Bering (Vitus), Dönitz (Karl), Fisher (John, Lord), Hudson (Henry), Nelson (Horatio, Viscount), Nimitz (Chester), Ruyter (Michiel Adriaanzoon de), Tasman (Abel Janszoon), Vernon (Edward)
07 Barentz (William), Decatur (Stephen), Fitzroy (Robert), Hawkins (Sir John), Hawkyns (Sir John), Kolchak (Alexander), Lord Jim, Marryat (Captain Frederick), Pytheas, Raleigh (Sir Walter), Selkirk (Alexander), Tirpitz (Alfred von), Weddell (James)

08 Beaufort (Sir Francis), Columbus (Christopher), Cousteau (Jacques Yves), Elvström (Paul), Jellicoe (John Rushworth, Earl), Magellan (Ferdinand), Pitcairn (Robert), Sandwich (Edward Montagu, Earl of), Vespucci (Amerigo)
09 Christian (Fletcher), Frobisher (Sir Martin), Grenville (Sir Richard), MacArthur (Dame Ellen), St Vincent (John Jervis, Earl of), Vancouver (George)
10 Chichester (Sir Francis), Erik the Red, Villeneuve (Pierre de)
11 Collingwood (Cuthbert, Lord), Elphinstone (George Keith, Viscount Keith), Mountbatten (Louis, Earl)
12 Bougainville (Louis Antoine, Comte de), Knox-Johnston (Sir Robin), Themistocles

See also **admiral; pirate; ship**

• sailors

02 MN, RM, RN **03** RAN, RFA, RYA, RYS
04 navy

saint

01 S **02** St **03** Ste **04** hagi-, holy, sant
05 angel, hagio-, saunt **06** hallow, patron, santon **07** tutelar **08** tutelary
11 patron saint **13** guardian saint

Saints include:

03 Ivo, Leo
04 Adam, Anne, Bede, Gall, Joan (of Arc), John, John (Chrysostom), John (of the Cross), John (the Baptist), Jude, Lucy, Luke, Mark, Mary, Mary (Magdalene), Paul, Zita
05 Agnes, Aidan, Alban, Amand, Basil (the Great), Bruno (of Cologne), Clare, Cyril, Cyril (of Alexandria), David, Denis, Edwin, Giles, James, Louis, Paula, Peter, Titus, Vitus
06 Albert (the Great), Andrew, Anselm, Antony, Antony (of Padua), Aquila, Cosmas, Damian, Dismas, Edmund, Edmund (Campion), Edward (the Martyr), Fiacre, George, Helena, Hilary (of Poitiers), Jerome, Joseph, Joseph (of Arimathea), Justin, Martha, Martin, Monica, Oliver, Oliver (Plunket), Oswald, Philip, Prisca, Robert, Simeon, Teresa (of Avila), Thomas, Thomas (Aquinas), Thomas (Becket), Thomas (More), Thomas (à Becket), Ursula
07 Adamnan, Ambrose, Anthony, Anthony (of Padua), Barbara, Bernard (of Clairvaux), Bernard (of Menthon), Bridget, Cecilia, Clement, Columba, Crispin, Cyprian, Dominic, Dorothy, Dunstan, Erasmus, Francis (Romulus), Francis (Xavier), Francis (of Assisi), Francis (of Sales), Gabriel, Gregory (of Nazianzus), Gregory (of Tours), Gregory (the Great), Isidore (of Seville), Leonard, Matthew, Michael, Pancras, Patrick, Stephen, Swithin, Theresa (of

Lisieux), Timothy, Vincent (de Paul), Wilfrid
08 Albertus (Magnus), Angelico, Barnabas, Benedict (of Nursia), Boniface, Cuthbert, Genesius, Ignatius (of Loyola), Irenaeus, Lawrence, Margaret, Matthias, Nicholas, Polycarp, Veronica, Vladimir, Walpurga
09 Alexander, Alexander (Nevsky), Augustine (of Canterbury), Augustine (of Hippo), Catherine, Genevieve, Homobonus, Honoratus, John Bosco, John of God, Kentigern, Ladislaus, Methodius, Sebastian, Valentine, Wenceslas
10 Appollonia, Athanasius, Bernadette, Crispinian, John Fishe Stanislaus, Thomas More, Wenceslaus
11 Bonaventure, Christopher
12 Justin Martyr
13 Martin of Tours, Thomas Apostle, Thomas Aquinas
14 Albert the Great, Francis de Sales, Francis of Paola
15 Aquila and Prisca, Cosmas and Damian, Francis of Assisi, Gregory the Great, Our Lady of Loreto, Raymond Nonnatus

St Helena
03 SHN

St Kitts and Nevis
03 KNA, SCN

saintliness
05 faith, piety **06** purity, virtue
08 chastity, goodness, holiness, morality, sanctity **09** godliness, innocence **10** asceticism, devoutness, sanctitude, self-denial **11** blessedness, sinlessness, uprightness
12 selflessness, spirituality, spotlessness **13** blamelessness, righteousness, self-sacrifice, unselfishness

St Lucia
02 WL **03** LCA

saintly
04 good, holy, pure **05** godly, moral, pious **06** devout, worthy **07** angelic, blessed, ethical, sinless, upright
08 innocent, spotless, virtuous
09 believing, blameless, religious, righteous, saintlike, spiritual **10** God-fearing

St Vincent and the Grenadines
02 WV **03** VCT

sake
03 aim **04** gain, goal, good, saki
05 cause **06** behalf, object, profit, reason, regard **07** account, benefit, purpose, respect, welfare **08** interest
09 advantage, objective, wellbeing
13 consideration

salacious
04 blue, lewd, salt **05** bawdy, horny, randy **06** carnal, coarse, erotic, fruity,

ribald, smutty, steamy, wanton
07 lustful, obscene, raunchy, ruttish
08 improper, indecent, prurient
09 lecherous **10** lascivious, libidinous, lubricious, scurrilous **12** concupiscent, pornographic

salaciousness

08 lewdness **09** bawdiness, indecency, obscenity, prurience **10** smuttiness, steaminess **11** lustfulness, pornography
13 concupiscence, lecherousness
14 lasciviousness

salad

◇ *anagram indicator*

Salads include:

04 herb, rice, slaw
05 fruit, Greek, green, pasta
06 Caesar, potato, tomato
07 mesclum, mesclun, niçoise, Russian, seafood, tabouli, Waldorf
08 coleslaw, couscous
09 mixed leaf, tabbouleh, three bean
11 bulgar wheat
15 mustard and cress

Salad ingredients include:

03 egg, ham, nut
04 meat, tuna
05 bacon, chard, cress, olive
06 borage, carrot, celery, endive, lovage, potato, rocket, tomato
07 anchovy, arugula, chicken, chicory, crouton
08 bacon bit, beetroot, cold meat, coleslaw, cucumber
09 boiled egg, corn-salad, green bean, new potato, radicchio, sweetcorn
10 cos lettuce, lollo rosso, mayonnaise, salad cream, watercress
11 salad burnet, spring onion
12 cherry tomato, lamb's lettuce, round lettuce
13 hard-boiled egg, roasted pepper, salad dressing
14 iceberg lettuce, sundried tomato

See also **lettuce**

Salad dressings include:

06 Caesar, French
07 Italian, Russian
10 blue cheese, mayonnaise, salad cream
11 vinaigrette
14 Thousand Island

salamander

03 olm **07** axolotl **08** mudpuppy
10 hellbender **12** springkeeper

salaried

04 paid **05** waged **11** emolumental, remunerated, stipendiary
12 emolumentary

salary

03 fee, pay **05** screw, wages
06 income **07** stipend **08** earnings
09 allowance, emolument
10 honorarium **12** remuneration

sale

04 deal, seal, vend, vent **05** trade

06 wicker, willow **07** selling, traffic, vending **08** disposal **09** marketing
10 bargaining **11** transaction

Sales include:

04 boot, fair, work
06 autumn, bazaar, forced, garage, jumble, market, online, public, spring, summer, winter
07 auction, car-boot, charity, January, private, rummage, warrant
08 bazumble, clearing, cold call, e-auction, tabletop
09 clearance, end-of-line, mail order, mid-season, pre-season, remainder, telesales, trade show
10 exhibition, exposition, fleamarket, open market, second-hand
11 bring-and-buy, closing-down, end-of-season, on-promotion, stocktaking
12 bargain offer, church bazaar, grand opening, of the century, special offer
13 online auction
14 pyramid selling
15 of bankrupt stock

• for sale

06 on sale, to sell **07** in stock
09 available, up for sale **10** in the shops, obtainable, up for grabs **11** for purchase, on the market **12** wanted to sell

• sale or return

03 SOR

saleable

08 vendible **09** desirable
10 marketable **11** sought-after
12 merchantable

salesperson

03 rep **05** clerk **07** shop-boy
08 salesman, shop-girl **09** salesgirl, saleslady **10** salesclerk, saleswoman, shopkeeper **13** sales engineer, shop assistant **14** representative, sales assistant

salient

04 main **05** bulge, chief **06** signal
07 leaping, obvious, saltant **08** striking
09 arresting, important, principal, prominent, springing **10** noticeable, pronounced, remarkable
11 conspicuous, outstanding, significant

saliva

04 foam, spit **05** drool, spawl, water
06 phlegm, slaver, sputum **07** dribble, spittle **13** expectoration

sallow

03 wan **04** pale, sale, seal **05** adust, ashen, pasty, sally, sauch, saugh, waxen
06 pallid, sickly, willow, yellow
07 anaemic **09** jaundiced, unhealthy, yellowish **10** colourless, goat-willow

sally

04 dash, jest, joke, quip, raid, rock, rush, sway, trip **05** amble, bound, crack, drive, erupt, foray, issue, jaunt, mosey, surge **06** attack, bon mot,

breeze, charge, escape, frolic, outing, retort, sallee, sallow, sortie, stroll, thrust, wander **07** assault, outrush, riposte, saunter, venture **08** escapade
09 excursion, incursion, offensive, promenade, wisecrack, witticism
10 jeu d'esprit, projection **11** snatch squad

salmon

03 fry, lax, lox **04** chum, cock, coho, kelt, keta, masu, mort, parr **05** cohoe, nerka, smolt, sprod **06** baggit, dorado, grilse, kipper, ligger, samlet
07 bluecap, gravlax, kokanee, quinnat, redfish, salamon, shedder, skegger, sockeye **08** blueback, humpback, rockfish, springer **09** blackfish, brandling, bull trout, gravadlax
10 fingerling, ouananiche
12 Oncorhynchus

salt

02 AB **03** sal, tar, wit, zip **04** corn, cure, dear, leap, saut, zest **05** briny, punch, rapid, salty, sault, smack, taste
06 marine, rating, relish, sailor, saline, salted, savour, seaman, vigour
07 flavour, mariner, pungent, saltish, sea-salt **08** brackish, interest, merum sal, mordancy, piquancy, pungency, seafarer **09** expensive, salacious, seasoning, waterfall **10** liveliness, trenchancy **11** acclimatize **14** sodium chloride

Salts include:

05 azide
06 aurate, borate, folate, halite, iodate, iodide, malate, oleate
07 bay salt, caprate, citrate, cyanate, ferrate, formate, lactate, maleate, nitrate, nitrite, oxalate, sorbate, tannate, toluate, viscose
08 arsenite, benzoate, butyrate, caproate, chlorate, chloride, chromate, plumbate, pyruvate, rock salt, silicate, stearate, sulphate, sulphide, sulphite, tartrate, vanadate, xanthate
09 ascorbate, bath salts, carbamate, carbonate, glutamate, manganate, molybdate, periodate, phosphate, phthalate, solar salt, succinate, table salt
10 antimonite, bichromate, dichromate, Epsom salts, liver salts, salicylate
11 bicarbonate, health salts, persulphate, sal volatile
12 borosilicate, permanganate, Rochelle-salt
13 smelling salts

• salt away

04 bank, hide, save **05** amass, cache, hoard, stash **07** collect, put away, store up **08** put aside, set aside **09** stockpile
10 accumulate

• take with a pinch of salt, take with a grain of salt

08 hesitate, question **10** disbelieve
14 have misgivings **15** have hesitations, not fully believe

salty

04 racy, salt **05** briny, spicy, tangy, witty
06 lively, saline, salted **07** mordant,
piquant, savoury **08** animated,
brackish, exciting, vigorous
09 trenchant **11** salsuginous,
stimulating

salubrious

06 benign, decent **07** healthy
08 hygienic, pleasant, salutary, sanitary
09 healthful, wholesome
10 beneficial, refreshing **11** respectable
12 health-giving, invigorating

salutary

04 good **06** timely, useful **07** healthy,
helpful **08** hygienic, sanitary, valuable
09 practical, wholesome **10** beneficial,
profitable, refreshing **12** advantageous,
health-giving, invigorating

salutation

03 ave, hat **04** g'day, hail, skol
05 jambo, skoal **06** homage, prosit,
salaam, salute **07** address, all-hail, ave
Mary, good-day, good-den, good-
e'en, wassail, welcome **08** ave Maria,
good-even, greeting, Hail Mary,
regreets, respects **09** goodnight,
obeisance, reverence, time of day
10 excitement, good-morrow
11 good-evening, good-morning
13 good afternoon
See also **greeting**

salute

03 bow, cap, nod **04** hail, mark, move,
wave **05** coupé, greet, halse, salue,
salvo **06** banzai, coupee, homage,
honour **07** address, gesture, half-cap,
present, tribute, welcome **08** greeting,
Sieg Heil **09** celebrate, handshake,
recognize, reverence **11** acknowledge,
celebration, present arms, recognition
12 pay tribute to **15** acknowledgement,
make your manners

salvage

04 save **05** salve **06** redeem, repair,
rescue, retain, savage, saving **07** get
back, raising, reclaim, recover, restore
08 conserve, preserve, recovery,
retrieve **09** regaining, retrieval
10 recuperate **11** reclamation,
restoration **12** regeneration
13 reinstatement

salvation

06 rescue, saving **08** lifeline
10 liberation, redemption
11 deliverance, reclamation,
soteriology **12** preservation

salve

03 saw **04** balm, calm, ease, hail, heal
05 cream, smear **06** anoint, lotion,
remedy, soothe **07** clear up, comfort,
explain, lighten, relieve, salvage
08 greeting, liniment, ointment
09 harmonize, vindicate
10 medication **11** application,
embrocation, preparation

salver

04 dish, tray **05** plate **06** server, waiter
07 charger, platter **08** trencher

samarium

02 Sm

same

02 ae, do, id **03** ilk, one **04** idem, like,
self, twin, very, ylke **05** alike, ditto,
equal, samey, thick, thilk **06** all one, as
much, mutual, thicky **07** similar,
uniform **08** matching, selfsame,
unvaried **09** duplicate, identical,
unchanged, unvarying **10** carbon copy,
changeless, comparable, consistent,
equiparate, equivalent, reciprocal,
synonymous, unchanging, unvariable
11 the very same **12** the aforesaid
13 corresponding, one and the same,
substitutable, the above-named
15 interchangeable

• **all the same**
03 but, yet **05** still **06** anyhow, anyway,
even so **07** however **09** in any case
10 by any means, for all that, in any
event, not but what, regardless, tout de
même **11** by some means, nonetheless
12 nevertheless **15** birds of a feather,
notwithstanding

• **the same as**
02 iq **08** idem quod

sameness

06 déjà vu, tedium **07** oneness
08 ding-dong, equality, identity,
likeness, monotone, monotony
09 dead-level, mannerism
10 repetition, similarity, uniformity
11 consistency, duplication,
resemblance **13** identicalness,
indistinction, invariability
14 changelessness, predictability
15 standardization

samey

04 same **05** alike **07** similar, tedious,
uniform **09** identical **10** monotonous,
unchanging **11** predictable **12** cookie-
cutter

Samoa

02 WS **03** WSM

sample

◇ *hidden indicator*
03 sip, try **04** blad, cast, core, sign, test,
type **05** dummy, match, model, piece,
pilot, taste, toile, trial **06** muster,
swatch, taster, try out **07** examine,
example, inspect, pattern, typical
08 instance, prospect, sampling,
specimen, transect **09** breakbeat,
foretaste, scantling **10** assay-piece,
experience, indication **12** cross-
section, illustration, illustrative
13 demonstration, demonstrative
14 representative **15** depleted uranium

sanatorium

03 san **06** clinic **07** sick bay
08 hospital **09** infirmary **10** health
farm, sanitarium **12** health centre,
health resort **13** medical centre

sanctification

05 piety **06** purity **08** devotion,
holiness **09** godliness **10** sacredness
11 blessedness **12** spirituality
13 righteousness

sanctify

04 back, wash **05** allow, bless, exalt
06 anoint, hallow, permit, purify, ratify
07 absolve, approve, cleanse, confirm,
endorse, license, support, warrant
08 accredit, canonize, dedicate, make
holy, sanction, set apart **09** authorize
10 consecrate, legitimize, make sacred,
underwrite

sanctimonious

02 pi **04** holy, smug **05** pious
08 priggish, superior, unctuous
09 pietistic **10** goody-goody, moralizing
11 pharisaical **12** hypocritical **13** self-
righteous **14** holier-than-thou

sanctimoniousness

04 cant **06** humbug **07** pietism
08 saintism, smugness **09** hypocrisy
10 moralizing, pharisaism
11 complacency, preachiness
12 priggishness, unctuousness
13 righteousness

sanction

02 OK **03** ban, oke **04** back, fiat, okay
05 allow **06** permit, ratify **07** approof,
approve, backing, boycott, confirm,
embargo, endorse, go-ahead, licence,
license, penalty, support, sustain,
warrant **08** accredit, approval, royalize,
sanctify, sentence, suffrage, thumbs-
up **09** agreement, authority, authorize,
deterrent **10** green light, legitimize,
permission, punishment, underwrite
11 approbation, countenance,
endorsement, prohibition, restriction
12 confirmation, ratification,
subscription **13** accreditation,
authorization

sanctity

05 grace, piety **06** purity, virtue
08 devotion, goodness, holiness
09 godliness, saintship **10** sacredness
11 blessedness, saintliness
12 spirituality **13** inviolability,
religiousness, righteousness,
sacrosanctity **14** sanctification

sanctuary

04 area, park **05** altar, frith, girth, grith,
haven, tract **06** asylum, church, oracle,
refuge, safety, shrine, temple
07 Alsatia, chancel, enclave, hideout,
reserve, retreat, sanctum, shelter
08 delubrum, hideaway, immunity,
preserve, security **09** holy place,
nymphaeum, privilege, sacrarium,
safeguard **10** frithsoken, protection,
tabernacle **11** reservation **12** holy of
holies **14** place of worship

sanctum

03 den **05** study **06** refuge, shrine
07 hideout, retreat **08** hideaway
09 cubbyhole, holy place, sanctuary
12 holy of holies

sand

04 grit, rock **05** beach, sands, shore
06 desert, strand **08** seashore
10 wilderness

• **sand dune, sand dunes**
03 erg **04** areg, dene, down, seif

06 barkan **07** barchan, barkhan
08 barchane

sandal
04 geta, zori **05** jelly, thong **06** galosh,
golosh, Jandal® **07** chappal, galoche,
talaria **08** flip-flap, flip-flop, huarache,
slipslop **09** alpargata **12** calceamentum

sandalwood
05 algum, almug **06** santal **07** sanders
08 quandang, quandong, quantong
10 buffalo-nut **11** sanderswood
13 Barbados pride

sandarac
04 arar

sandbank
02 ås **03** bar, key **04** dune, kaim, kame,
reef **05** esker, hurst, shelf, shoal
07 sand bar, yardang **08** sandhill
10 harbour-bar
• **opening between sandbanks**
03 gat

sand-eel
04 grig, lant **05** lance **06** launce

Sandhurst
03 RMA **04** RMAS

sandpiper
03 ree **04** knot, ruff **05** reeve, terek
06 dunlin, ox-bird, willet **07** sea lark
08 peetweet, redshank, sand-lark,
sand-peep, sea snipe **10** greenshank,
sanderling, yellowlegs

sandstone
04 grit **05** fakes **06** arkose, dogger,
faikes, Flysch, kingle **07** hassock
08 sand-flag **09** bluestone, firestone,
greensand, gritstone, holystone,
quartzite, tile stone **10** brownstone
13 millstone grit

sandwich
◇ *containment indicator*
03 bap, BLT, wad **04** roti, wrap **05** butty,
piece, round **06** burger, hoagie, sarney,
sarnie **07** toastie **09** submarine
10 jeely piece **11** intercalate, three-
decker **12** double-decker **14** croque-
monsieur

sandy
◇ *dialect indicator*
03 red **04** Scot **05** light, rusty, tawny
06 auburn, ginger, gritty, Titian, yellow
07 coppery, gingery, reddish, yellowy
08 sabulose, sabulous **09** gingerous,
psammitic, yellowish **10** arenaceous
13 reddish-yellow

sane
04 wice, wise **05** lucid, sober, sound
06 formal, normal, stable **07** herself,
himself **08** all there, balanced,
moderate, rational, sensible, yourself
09 judicious **10** reasonable **11** level-
headed, of sound mind, responsible,
right-minded **12** compos mentis, well-
balanced **15** in your right mind

sangfroid
04 cool **05** nerve, poise **06** aplomb,
phlegm **08** calmness, coolness
09 assurance, composure

10 dispassion, equanimity
11 nonchalance, self-control
12 indifference **14** cool-headedness,
self-possession, unflappability

sanguinary
04 gory, grim **05** cruel **06** bloody,
brutal, savage **08** bloodied, pitiless,
ruthless **09** merciless, murderous
12 bloodthirsty

sanguine
03 red **04** gory, pink, rosy **05** fresh,
ruddy **06** ardent, bloody, florid, lively
07 assured, buoyant, flushed, hopeful,
roseate, unbowed **08** animated,
blood-red, cheerful, rubicund, spirited
09 confident, expectant, unabashed
10 optimistic **13** over-confident
14 over-optimistic

sanitary
04 pure **05** clean **07** aseptic, healthy,
sterile **08** germ-free, hygienic
09 wholesome **10** antiseptic,
salubrious, unpolluted **11** disinfected
14 uncontaminated

sanitize
05 clean **06** filter, purify, refine
07 cleanse, clean up, freshen
08 fumigate **09** deodorize, disinfect,
expurgate, sterilize **13** decontaminate,
make palatable **14** make acceptable
15 make presentable

sanity
04 mind **05** sense **06** health, reason,
wisdom **08** lucidity, prudence
09 good sense, normality, soundness,
stability **11** common sense, rationality
13 balance of mind, judiciousness
14 responsibility **15** level-headedness,
right-mindedness, soundness of mind

San Marino
03 RSM, SMR

Santa Claus
06 St Nick **10** St Nicholas **11** Kris
Kringle **12** Kriss Kringle **15** Father
Christmas

São Tomé and Príncipe
02 ST **03** STP

sap
03 box, git, mug, nit **04** clot, fink, fool,
jerk, ooze, prat, sura, twit **05** bleed,
drain, erode, idiot, juice, moron, toddy
06 energy, impair, nitwit, reduce,
trench, vigour, weaken **07** deplete,
essence, exhaust **08** diminish,
enervate, enfeeble, imbecile, palm
wine, vitality, wear away, wear down
09 lifeblood, palm-honey, undermine
10 debilitate, karyolymph, plant fluid,
vital fluid

sapi-utan
04 anoa

sapling
05 plant **06** tellar, teller, tiller **08** ash-
plant, flittern **09** ground-ash, ground
oak

sapper
02 RE

sarcasm
04 jibe, wipe **05** irony, scorn **06** gibing,
satire **07** acidity, mockery
08 acrimony, contempt, cynicism,
derision, mordancy, ridicule, scoffing,
sneering **09** invective **10** bitterness,
resentment, trenchancy
12 spitefulness
• **expression of sarcasm**
03 gee

sarcastic
04 acid **05** sarky, sharp, snide, witty
06 biting **07** acerbic, caustic, cutting,
cynical, jeering, mocking, mordant,
pungent, satiric **08** derisive, derisory,
incisive, ironical, sardonic, scathing,
scoffing, scornful, sneering, taunting
09 invective, satirical **10** back-handed,
Juvenalian, Voltairian **11** disparaging
12 sharp-tongued

sarcastically
09 cynically, jeeringly **10** ironically,
scathingly, scornfully, tauntingly
11 satirically

sardonic
03 dry, wry **05** cruel **06** biting, bitter
07 acerbic, cynical, jeering, mocking,
mordant **08** derisive, scornful,
sneering **09** heartless, malicious,
sarcastic **11** acrimonious
12 contemptuous

sash
03 obi **04** belt **05** lungi, scarf, shash
06 girdle **07** baldric, burdash, chassis
08 baldrick, cincture **09** waistband
10 cummerbund

Saskatchewan
02 SK

sassy
04 pert **05** fresh, lippy, saucy
06 brazen, cheeky, mouthy **07** forward
08 impudent, insolent **09** audacious
11 impertinent **12** overfamiliar
13 disrespectful

Satan
05 devil **06** Belial **07** Abaddon, arch-
foe, Lucifer, Old Nick, Shaitan
08 Apollyon, the Devil, the Enemy
09 arch-enemy, arch-felon, arch-fiend,
Beelzebub, leviathan **10** the Evil One,
the serpent, the Tempter **12** the
Adversary **13** the old serpent
14 Mephistopheles

satanic
04 dark, evil **05** black **06** damned,
sinful, wicked **07** demonic, hellish
inhuman **08** accursed, devilish,
diabolic, fiendish, infernal **09** satanical
10 abominable, diabolical, iniquitous,
malevolent, sulphurous

sate
04 cloy, fill, glut **05** gorge, satay, slake
06 accloy, sicken, stodge **07** gratify,
satiate, satisfy, surfeit **08** overfill,
saturate

sated
03 sad

satellite

04 aide, moon **06** colony, lackey, minion, planet, puppet, vassal **07** moonlet **08** adherent, disciple, dominion, follower, hanger-on, parasite, province, retainer, sidekick, smallsat **09** attendant, dependant, spaceship, sycophant **10** dependency, spacecraft **11** subordinate **12** orbiting body, protectorate, space station

Satellites include:

03 CAT
04 ECHO
05 Astra, TIROS
06 Oshumi, Rohini
07 Asterix, Horizon, Sputnik, Transit
08 Explorer, INMARSAT, Intelsat, Prospero
09 Early Bird, Long March
11 Black Knight

See also **moon**

satiate

04 cloy, fill, glut, jade, sate **05** gorge, slake, stuff **07** engorge, glutted, satisfy, surfeit **08** nauseate, overfeed, overfill

satiety

07 surfeit **08** cloyment, fullness **09** repletion, satiation **10** saturation **11** repleteness **12** over-fullness, satisfaction **13** gratification **14** overindulgence

satire

03 wit **04** jeer, skit **05** irony, satyr, spoof, squib **06** glance, parody, send-up, taxing **07** lampoon, Pasquil, Pasquin, sarcasm, Sotadic, take-off **08** raillery, ridicule, Sotadean, travesty **09** burlesque, invective **10** caricature, mazarinade **12** mickey-taking **15** comedy of manners

satirical

06 biting, bitter **07** abusive, acerbic, caustic, cutting, cynical, mocking, mordant **08** derisive, incisive, ironical, sardonic, Swiftian, taunting **09** invective, sarcastic, trenchant **10** irreverent, ridiculing **12** Archilochian

satirist

05 satyr **06** mocker, satire **07** Pasquil, Pasquin **08** parodist **09** lampooner, pasquiler, ridiculer **10** cartoonist, lampoonist, pasquilant **11** pasquinader **12** caricaturist

Satirists include:

03 Loy (Myrna)
04 Cech (Svatopluk), Isla (José Francisco de), Pope (Alexander)
05 Börne (Ludwig), Brown (Thomas), Cooke (Ebenezer), Ellis (George), Larra (Mariano José de), Meung (Jean de), Nashe (Thomas), Nesin (Aziz), Swift (Jonathan)
06 Butler (Samuel), Giusti (Giuseppe), Horace, Lucian, Murner (Thomas), Pindar (Peter), Wolcot (John)
07 Barclay (John), Juvenal, Marston (John), Mencken (Henry Louis),

Persius, Régnier (Mathurin), Thurber (James)
08 Apuleius (Lucius), Beerbohm (Max), Fischart (Johann), Lucilius (Gaius), Rabelais (François)
09 Churchill (Charles), Delavigne (Casimir), Junqueiro (Ablio Manuel Guerra), Petronius (Arbiter), Whitehead (Paul)
10 Mandeville (Bernard)
12 Konstantinov (Aleko)

See also **comedian**

satirize

04 mock **06** deride, parody, send up **07** lampoon, Pasquil, Pasquin, take off **08** ridicule **09** burlesque, criticize, make fun of, poke fun at **10** caricature

satisfaction

03 pay **04** ease **05** pride **06** amends, change, liking **07** comfort, content, damages, delight, payment, redress **08** pleasure, requital **09** atonement, enjoyment, happiness, indemnity, quittance, wellbeing **10** conviction, fulfilment, recompense, reparation, settlement, suffisance **11** complacence, complacency, contentment, restitution, vindication **12** compensation **13** gratification, reimbursement **15** indemnification

satisfactorily

06 nicely **08** passably **10** acceptably, adequately, favourably **11** competently **12** sufficiently

satisfactory

02 OK **03** A-OK, oke **04** fair, fine, nice, okay, well **05** sweet **06** cushty, proper **07** atoning, average **08** adequate, all right, passable, suitable **09** competent, copacetic, copasetic, favorable, kopasetic **10** acceptable, convincing, favourable, sufficient, tickety-boo **11** tickettyboo, up to scratch, up to the mark

satisfied

04 full, paid, smug, sure **05** happy, sated **07** certain, content, pleased, replete **08** pacified, positive, satiated **09** contented, convinced, persuaded, reassured **13** self-satisfied

satisfy

03 pay **04** apay, fill, meet, sate, stay **05** agree, appay, serve, slake **06** answer, assure, defray, fulfil, please, quench, settle, supply **07** appease, assuage, content, delight, gratify, indulge, placate, qualify, requite, satiate, suffice, surfeit **08** convince, live up to, persuade, reassure **09** discharge, indemnify **10** comply with **13** be adequate for, compensate for **15** be sufficient for

satisfying

04 cool **06** enough, far-out, square, way-out **07** filling **08** cheering, pleasing **10** convincing, fulfilling, gratifying, harmonious, persuasive, refreshing **11** pleasurable **12** satisfactory

saturate

03 wet **04** fill, glut, sate, soak **05** flood, imbue, souse, steep **06** drench **07** pervade, suffuse, surfeit **08** overfill, permeate, waterlog **09** surcharge **10** impregnate **14** make wet through

saturated

05 drunk **06** imbued, soaked, sodden, soused **07** flooded, soaking, sopping, steeped **08** drenched, dripping, suffused, wringing **09** permeated **11** impregnated, waterlogged

saturation

06 sating **07** filling, soaking **08** flooding, glutting **09** pervading, satiation, suffusion **10** permeation

Saturday

03 Sat

Saturn

06 Cronus

saturnine

04 dour, dull, glum **05** grave, heavy, moody, stern **06** dismal, gloomy, morose, severe, sombre **07** austere **08** taciturn **09** withdrawn **10** melancholy, phlegmatic, unfriendly **15** uncommunicative

satyr

05 silen **06** satire **07** silenus **08** satirist, woodwose **09** orang-utan, woodhouse

sauce

03 dip, lip **04** sass **05** brass, cheek, mouth, nerve **06** rebuke, relish **08** audacity, backchat, belabour, dressing, pertness, rudeness **09** condiment, flippancy, freshness, impudence, insolence, sauciness **10** brazenness, cheekiness, disrespect, flavouring **11** irreverence, presumption **12** impertinence, malapertness

Sauces include:

02 HP®
03 jus, red, soy
04 fish, hard, mint, mole, soja, soya, wine
05 apple, bread, brown, caper, cream, curry, fudge, garum, gravy, melba, pesto, salsa, satay, shoyu, white
06 catsup, cheese, chilli, coulis, fondue, fu yung, hoisin, mornay, nam pla, oxymel, oyster, panada, reform, tamari, tartar, tomato, tommy K
07 catchup, custard, Daddies®, harissa, ketchup, nuoc mam, passata, rouille, sabayon, soubise, supreme, Tabasco®, tartare, velouté
08 barbecue, béchamel, bigarade, chasseur, marinara, piri-piri, salpicon, yakitori
09 béarnaise, black bean, bolognese, carbonara, chocolate, cranberry, demi-glace, espagnole, Marie Rose, remoulade, Worcester
10 avgolemono, chaudfroid,

Cumberland, mayonnaise, mousseline, napoletana, puttanesca, salad cream, salsa verde, stroganoff
11 bourguignon, beurre blanc, hollandaise, horseradish, vinaigrette
12 brandy butter, sweet-and-sour
13 crème anglaise, salad dressing
14 Worcestershire

saucepan
03 pan, pot, wok **05** fryer **06** chafer, goblet, vessel **07** milk pan, skillet **08** pancheon **09** casserole, container, frying-pan **12** double boiler

saucy
04 pert, rude **05** fresh, lippy, peart, piert, sassy **06** brazen, cheeky, fruity, gallus **07** forward, gallows **08** flippant, impudent, insolent, malapert **10** disdainful, irreverent, lascivious **11** impertinent **12** presumptuous **13** disrespectful

Saudi Arabia
02 SA **03** SAU

saunter
04 walk **05** amble, daker, mooch, mosey, shool, shule **06** dacker, daiker, dander, dauner, dawdle, dawner, ramble, shoole, stroll, toddle, wander **07** daunder, meander **09** promenade **10** knock about **11** knock around **14** constitutional

sausage

Sausages include:

04 beef, lamb, lola, pork
05 blood, liver, Lorne, Lyons, snags, weeny, wurst
06 banger, bumbar, garlic, hot dog, kishke, lolita, mumbar, polony, salami, summer, weenie, Wiener, wienie
07 abruzzo, baloney, Bologna, boloney, cabanos, chorizo, corn dog, kabanos, klobasa, merguez, saveloy, zampone
08 cervelat, chaurice, chourico, cocktail, drisheen, kielbasa, linguica, peperoni, Toulouse
09 andouille, bierwurst, blutwurst, boerewors, bratwurst, chipolata, cotechino, lap cheong, loukanika, pepperoni, saucisson
10 bauerwurst, boudin noir, cervellata, Cumberland, knackwurst, knockwurst, liverwurst, mortadella
11 boudin blanc, boudin rouge, frankfurter, Wienerwurst
12 andouillette, black pudding, Lincolnshire

savage
04 bite, boor, claw, fell, grim, maul, slam, tear, wild **05** beast, brute, churl, cruel, feral, harsh, slate **06** attack, bloody, brutal, fierce, immane, mangle **07** beastly, furious, inhuman, monster, rubbish, run down, salvage, untamed, vicious, wild man **08** barbaric,

denounce, lacerate, pitiless, ruthless, sadistic, terrible, warrigal **09** barbarian, barbarous, cut-throat, dog-eat-dog, ferocious, merciless, murderous, primitive, wild woman **10** go to town on, wild person **11** pick holes in, uncivilized **12** bloodthirsty, catamountain, cat o' mountain, pull to pieces, pull to shreds, tear to pieces, tear to shreds **14** undomesticated **15** do a hatchet job on

savagely
07 cruelly, harshly **08** brutally, fiercely **09** viciously **10** pitilessly, ruthlessly **11** barbarously, ferociously, mercilessly **12** barbarically

savagery
06 ferity, sadism **07** cruelty **08** ferocity, wildness **09** barbarism, barbarity, brutality, roughness **10** bestiality, fierceness, inhumanity **11** brutishness, viciousness **12** pitilessness, ruthlessness **13** mercilessness, murderousness, primitiveness

savant
04 guru, sage **06** master, pundit **07** learned, scholar **09** authority **10** mastermind **11** philosopher **12** accomplished, intellectual, man of letters **14** woman of letters

save
02 sa' **04** free, hain, hold, keep, safe **05** guard, hoard, lay up, put by, spare, stash, store **06** budget, but for, except, export, gather, hinder, redeem, rescue, retain, screen, shield, snudge, unless **07** bail out, collect, cut back, deliver, obviate, prevent, protect, reclaim, recover, release, reserve, salvage, set free, use less **08** conserve, cut costs, excepted, keep safe, liberate, preserve, put aside, retrieve, set aside, sock away **09** apart from, aside from, be thrifty, economize, except for, excluding, safeguard, stockpile **10** buy cheaply **11** not counting **13** scrimp and save **14** live on the cheap **15** get someone out of, tighten your belt

saving
03 cut **04** fund **05** store **06** frugal, thrift **07** bargain, capital, careful, economy, nest egg, sparing, thrifty **08** discount, reserves **09** excepting, redeeming, reduction, resources, salvatory **10** economical, mitigating, preserving, protecting, qualifying **11** extenuating, investments, reservation **12** compensating, compensatory, conservation, preservation

saviour
04 Jesu **05** Jesus **06** Christ **07** Messiah, rescuer **08** champion, defender, Emmanuel, guardian, Mediator, redeemer **09** deliverer, Lamb of God, liberator, protector **11** emancipator

savoir-faire
04 tact **05** poise **07** ability, finesse, knowhow **08** urbanity **09** assurance, diplomacy, expertise **10** capability,

confidence, discretion **11** social grace **12** social graces **14** accomplishment

savour
03 sar **04** hint, like, odor, sair, salt, tang, zest **05** aroma, enjoy, odour, scent, smack, smell, speak, spice, taste, touch, trace **06** relish, repute, resent, season **07** bouquet, flavour, perfume, revel in, suggest **08** piquancy, seem like **09** delight in, fragrance **10** appreciate, smattering, suggestion **14** enjoy to the full, take pleasure in, taste to the full

savoury
04 tapa **05** gusty, salty, sapid, snack, spicy, tangy, tapas, tasty, yummy **06** canapé, gustie, nibble, samosa, spiced **07** gustful, piquant, scrummy **08** aigrette, aromatic, fragrant, luscious **09** appetizer, delicious, palatable **10** appetizing **11** amuse-bouche, amuse-gueule, bonne-bouche, flavoursome, hors d'oeuvre, respectable, scrumptious **13** mouthwatering

savvy
03 sly **04** keen, know, wily **05** acute, alert, canny, sharp, skill, smart **06** artful, astute, callid, clever, crafty, shrewd **07** cunning, know-how, knowing **09** judicious, observant, sagacious **10** calculated, discerning, far-sighted, perceptive, understand **11** calculating, intelligent, well-advised **13** knowledgeable, perspicacious **14** discriminating

saw
03 mot, say, sow **05** adage, axiom, gnome, maxim, salve **06** byword, decree, dictum, saying **07** epigram, proverb **08** aphorism **10** apophthegm **11** commonplace

Saws include:

03 jig, rip
04 band, fret, hack, hand
05 bench, chain, panel, tenon
06 coping, rabbet, scroll
07 compass, pruning
08 circular, crosscut
09 radial-arm
11 power-driven

say
◇ *homophone indicator*
02 eg **03** add, put, saw **04** read, sway, tell, vote, word **05** assay, claim, clout, drawl, grunt, guess, imply, judge, orate, order, power, reply, speak, state, utter, voice **06** affirm, allege, answer, assert, assume, convey, mutter, phrase, recite, reckon, rejoin, remark, render, repeat, report, retort, reveal, rumour, speech, weight **07** comment, declare, deliver, divulge, exclaim, express, imagine, mention, observe, opinion, perform, presume, respond, signify, suggest, suppose, surmise **08** announce, disclose, estimate, indicate, instruct, intimate, maintain, rehearse **09** authority, ejaculate, enunciate, influence, pronounce **10** articulate, for

example **11** come out with, communicate, turn to speak **12** put into words **13** approximately, chance to speak

• **that is to say**
02 ie, sc **03** viz **05** id est, to wit **06** namely, that is **09** c'est-à-dire, videlicet **12** in other words

saying
◇ *homophone indicator*
03 mot, saw **04** cant, dict, read, rede, reed, word **05** adage, axiom, gnome, maxim, motto, reede **06** bon mot, byword, cliché, dictum, phrase, remark, slogan, wisdom **07** diction, epigram, fadaise, precept, proverb **08** aphorism, apothegm, overword **09** platitude, quotation, rusticism, statement **10** apophthegm, expression **11** catch phrase **12** word of wisdom **13** household word, pearl of wisdom

say-so
02 OK **04** word **06** dictum, rumour **07** backing, consent, go-ahead, hearsay **08** approval, sanction, thumbs-up **09** agreement, assertion, assurance, authority, guarantee **10** green light, permission **11** affirmation **12** asseveration, ratification **13** authorization

scab
03 rat **08** blackleg **13** strike-breaker

scabies
04 itch **05** psora

scaffold
05 stage, tower **06** gantry, gibbet **07** catasta, gallows, hanging, sustain, the rope **08** platform **09** framework **11** scaffolding

scald
04 burn, leep, plot, poet, sear **05** brand, ploat, scaud, skald **06** paltry, scabby, scorch, scurfy **07** blister **09** cauterize

scalding
07 boiling, burning **08** steaming **09** piping hot **10** blistering **12** extremely hot

scale
04 coat, film, go up, leaf, scan **05** climb, crust, flake, gamme, gamut, layer, level, Libra, mount, order, palea, plate, range, ratio, reach, scope, scurf, shell, skail, weigh **06** ascend, degree, extent, furfur, gunter, ladder, lamina, plaque, series, shin up, spread, squama, tartar **07** clamber, coating, compass, conquer, deposit, measure, ranking **08** escalade, register, scramble, sequence, spectrum, surmount **09** hierarchy, limescale **10** graduation, proportion **11** calibration, progression **12** encrustation, pecking order, relative size **15** measuring system

• **scale down**
04 drop **06** lessen, reduce, shrink **07** cut back, cut down **08** contract, decrease, make less

• **scale up**
05 boost, raise **06** bump up, expand,

hike up, step up **07** augment, build up, develop, enhance, further, improve **08** increase **09** intensify **10** accumulate, strengthen

scaliness
06 furfur **08** dandruff **09** flakiness, leprosity **10** scurfiness, squamation, squamosity **12** scabrousness

scallop
03 dag **04** clam, gimp, mush **05** grill **06** pecten **07** queenie **08** coquille

scaly
05 flaky, rough **06** branny, scabby, scurfy, shabby **07** leprose, leprous **08** lepidote, scabrous, scarious, squamate, squamose, squamous **09** furfurous **10** squamulose **12** desquamative, desquamatory, furfuraceous

scam
03 con **04** game **05** dodge, fraud, trick **06** fiddle, racket, rip-off, scheme **07** swindle **08** business **09** deception, gold brick

scamp
03 imp **05** devil, losel, rogue **06** fripon, monkey, rascal, skelum, wretch **07** skellum **08** blighter, scalawag, schellum, spalpeen, vagabond **09** reprobate, scallawag, scallywag **10** highwayman **12** troublemaker **13** mischief-maker **14** good-for-nothing, whippersnapper

scamper
03 fly, ren, rin, run **04** dart, dash, lamp, race, romp, rush **05** hurry, scoot, scoup, scowp **06** decamp, frolic, gambol, hasten, scurry, sprint **07** scuttle, skitter **08** scramble

scan
03 con, kon **04** read, skim, test **05** check, climb, conne, judge, probe, scale, spell, study, sweep **06** go over, review, search, survey **07** CAT scan, examine, inspect, run over **08** glance at, scrutiny **09** interpret, screening **10** inspection, run through, scrutinize, sector scan **11** examination, flip through, investigate, leaf through **12** flick through, thumb through **13** browse through, investigation, scintilliscan **14** run your eye over

scandal
04 blot, dirt, -gate, pity, slur **05** libel, shame, shock, smear, stain **06** defame, furore, gossip, outcry, uproar **07** calumny, obloquy, offence, outrage, rumours, slander **08** disgrace, ignominy, reproach **09** black mark, discredit, dishonour **10** defamation, dirty linen, opprobrium **11** crying shame **12** dirty laundry, dirty washing **13** embarrassment

scandalize
05 appal, repel, shock **06** dismay, insult, offend, revolt **07** affront, disgust, horrify, outrage, slander **08** disgrace

scandalmonger
06 gossip, tattle **07** defamer, tattler

08 busybody, quidnunc, traducer **09** muck-raker **10** talebearer **11** calumniator, Nosey Parker, sweetie-wife **12** gossip-monger

scandalous
05 gamey, juicy **06** untrue **07** blatant **08** flagrant, improper, infamous, shameful, shocking, unseemly **09** appalling, atrocious, libellous, malicious, monstrous **10** abominable, defamatory, outrageous, scurrilous, slanderous **11** disgraceful, opprobrious, sensational, unspeakable **12** disreputable **13** dishonourable

Scandinavian
05 Norse

Scandinavians include:

04 Dane, Finn
05 Swede
06 Norman, viking
08 Norseman
09 Icelander, Norwegian, Varangian

scandium
02 Sc

scanner

Scanners include:

02 CT
03 CAT, PET
04 body, SPET
07 barcode, flatbed
10 Emi-Scanner®

scant
04 bare, jimp **05** short, stint **06** barely, jimply, little, measly, reduce, slight, sparse **07** limited, minimal, sparing **08** exiguous, restrict, scantily, scarcity **09** deficient, hardly any **10** inadequate, little or no **12** insufficient

scantily
06 barely, poorly **08** meagrely, scarcely, skimpily, sparsely **11** deficiently **12** inadequately **14** insufficiently

scanty
03 low, shy **04** bare, hard, poor, thin **05** brief, light, scant, short, skimp, spare **06** little, meagre, narrow, scrimp, skimpy, sparse **07** limited, scrimpy **08** exiguous **09** deficient, penurious **10** inadequate, restricted **12** insufficient **13** insubstantial

scapegoat
05 bunny, patsy **06** stooge, sucker, victim **07** fall guy **11** whipping-boy

scar
04 mark, wipe **05** brand, cliff, hilum, scare, scaur, shock, spoil, wound **06** blotch, damage, deface, injure, injury, keloid, lesion, stigma, trauma, ulosis **07** blemish, desmoid, pockpit **08** cicatrix, pockmark, sword-cut **09** cicatrice, cicatrize, discolour, disfigure **10** cicatricle, defacement, stigmatize, traumatize **11** cicatricula, leaf-cushion **12** cicatrichule, parrot-wrasse **13** disfigurement **14** discolouration

carce

3 few 04 dear, rare 05 scant, tight
5 meagre, scanty, sparse 07 lacking,
paring, unusual 08 uncommon
9 deficient, not enough, too little
4 inadequate, infrequent
2 insufficient, like gold dust 13 in short
apply

make yourself scarce
5 scoot 06 go fast 07 dash off 08 run
or it, rush away 10 make tracks
2 leave quickly 15 take to your heels

carcely

3 not 05 uneth 06 barely, hardly,
neath 08 no sooner, not at all, only
ust, scantily, scrimply, uneathes,
nnethes 12 certainly not 13 definitely
ot

carcity

4 lack, want 05 scant 06 dearth,
amine, rarity 07 paucity 08 exiguity,
areness, shortage 09 scantness
0 deficiency, scantiness, sparseness
4 infrequency 12 uncommonness
3 insufficiency, niggardliness

care

4 scar, scat, shoo 05 alarm, appal,
aunt, gally, gliff, glift, panic, scaur,
hock, skear, skeer, start 06 affray,
ismay, fright, horror, menace, rattle,
carre, terror 07 perturb, petrify,
tartle, terrify, unnerve 08 frighten,
ysteria, threaten 09 terrorize
0 intimidate, make afraid, scare silly
1 fearfulness 12 put the wind up
4 make frightened

carecrow

4 bogy 05 bogle, sewel 06 boggle,
nalkin, mawkin, shewel 07 boggard,
oggart 09 galli-crow, gally-crow
0 crow-keeper 11 galli-bagger, galli-
eggar, gally-bagger, gally-beggar,
ootato bogle, tattiebogle

cared

3 rad 05 cowed 06 afraid, shaken
7 alarmed, anxious, chicken, fearful,
ttery, nervous, panicky, quivery,
vorried 08 startled, unnerved
9 petrified, terrified 10 frightened,
errorized 11 in a blue funk 13 having
ittens, panic-stricken, scared to death
4 terror-stricken

caremonger

8 alarmist 09 Cassandra, jitterbug,
pessimist 11 doomwatcher 13 prophet
of doom

carf

0 chaplaincy

*Scarfs, veils and other head cloths
include:*

4 caul, doek, haik, hyke, rail, sash, veil
5 curch, fichu, haick, hejab, hijab,
pagri, shawl, stole, volet, whisk
6 chadar, chador, cravat, haique, kiss-
me, madras, rebozo, screen, tippet,
turban, weeper, wimple
7 belcher, chaddar, chaddor,
chuddah, chuddar, dopatta,

dupatta, foulard, kufiyah, modesty,
muffler, necktie, orarium, puggery,
puggree, whimple, yashmak
08 babushka, chrismal, kaffiyeh,
kalyptra, keffiyeh, kerchief,
mantilla, neckatee, puggaree,
vexillum
09 comforter, headcloth, headscarf,
muffettee
10 fascinator, headsquare, lambrequin
11 kiss-me-quick, neckerchief,
nightingale

scarlet
03 red 06 redden, vermil 07 vermeil,
vermell, vermily 08 cardinal
09 vermeille, vermilion

scarper
02 go 04 bolt, flee, flit 05 leave, scram
06 beat it, decamp, depart, escape,
vanish 07 abscond, bunk off, do a
bunk, run away, vamoose 08 clear off,
run for it 09 disappear, skedaddle
10 hightail it 13 make a run for it

scary
05 eerie, hairy 06 creepy, skeary,
skeery, spooky 08 alarming, chilling,
daunting, fearsome, shocking,
timorous 10 disturbing, forbidding,
formidable, horrifying, petrifying,
terrifying 11 frightening, hair-raising
12 intimidating, white-knuckle
13 bloodcurdling, spine-chilling

scathing
04 acid 05 harsh 06 biting, bitter,
brutal, fierce, savage, severe
07 caustic, cutting, mordant 08 critical,
scornful, stinging 09 ferocious,
sarcastic, trenchant, unsparing,
vitriolic, withering 11 detrimental,
devastating

scatter
◊ anagram indicator
03 dot, sow 05 blind, fling, flurr, scail,
scale, shake, skail, strew 06 berley,
burley, dispel, divide, litter, shower,
spread 07 break up, diffuse, disband,
disject, scamble, shatter, spatter
08 disperse, disunite, separate,
splutter, sprinkle, squander
09 bescatter, broadcast, dissipate
10 dispersion, scattering, sprinkling
11 backscatter, disseminate,
intersperse 12 disintegrate 14 cast to
the winds 15 fling to the winds, throw
to the winds

scatterbrained
05 ditsy, ditzy, dizzy 06 scatty
08 carefree, careless 09 airheaded,
forgetful, frivolous, impulsive,
slaphappy 10 unreliable 11 empty-
headed, hare-brained, inattentive,
thoughtless 12 absent-minded
13 irresponsible, wool-gathering
14 feather-brained

scattering
03 few 07 break-up, handful, poor-
oot, pour-out 10 dispersion,
smattering, sprinkling 12 disgregation

scatty
◊ anagram indicator
10 abstracted 11 empty-headed, hare-
brained, harum-scarum 12 absent-
minded 14 scatterbrained

scavenge
04 hunt, rake 06 forage, search
07 cleanse, look for, rummage
08 scrounge

scavenger
04 dieb, hyen 05 hyena, raker
06 hyaena, jackal 07 forager, gorcrow,
scaffie, vulture 08 caracara, night-man,
rummager, scavager 09 scrounger
13 lion's provider

scenario
04 plan, plot 05 scene, state
06 résumé, scheme, script 07 outline,
summary 08 sequence, synopsis
09 programme, situation, storyline
10 continuity, projection, screenplay
13 circumstances 14 state of affairs

scene
03 act, set 04 area, clip, fuss, part,
show, site, spot, to-do, veil, view
05 arena, drama, field, place, scena,
sight, stage, vista 06 circus, furore,
locale, milieu, screen 07 context,
curtain, display, episode, outlook,
pageant, picture, scenery, setting,
tableau, tantrum 08 backdrop,
division, incident, locality, location,
outburst, panorama, position,
prospect 09 commotion, induction,
kerfuffle, landscape, situation,
spectacle 10 background, exhibition,
proceeding, speciality
11 environment, performance,
streetscape, whereabouts 13 tableau
vivant 14 area of activity, area of
interest 15 three-ring circus

• behind the scenes
06 within 08 secretly 09 backstage, in
private, privately 10 on the quiet, out of
sight 11 not in public 15 surreptitiously
• scenes
04 play

scenery
03 set 04 view 05 décor, scene,
vista 07 film set, outlook, scenary,
setting, terrain 08 backdrop,
panorama, prospect 09 landscape
10 background 11 mise-en-scène
12 surroundings

scenic
05 grand 06 pretty 08 striking
09 beautiful, panoramic 10 attractive,
impressive 11 picturesque, spectacular
12 awe-inspiring, breathtaking

scent
04 nose, odor, sent, vent, waft
05 aroma, fumet, odour, sense, smell,
sniff, spoor, trace, track, trail 06 detect
07 bouquet, cologne, discern, essence,
fumette, nose out, perfume
08 perceive, sniff out 09 fragrance,
recognize, redolence 11 toilet water
12 eau-de-cologne 13 become aware
of, eau-de-toilette

scented
04 rank 07 roseate 08 aromatic, fragrant, perfumed 13 sweet-smelling

sceptic
05 cynic 07 atheist, doubter, scoffer 08 agnostic 10 questioner, unbeliever 11 disbeliever, rationalist 14 doubting Thomas

sceptical
07 cynical, dubious, infidel 08 academic, doubtful, doubting, hesitant, scoffing 10 hesitating, suspicious, Voltairian 11 distrustful, incredulous, mistrustful, pessimistic, questioning, unbelieving, unconvinced 12 disbelieving

scepticism
05 doubt 07 atheism, dubiety 08 cynicism, distrust, nihilism, unbelief 09 disbelief, hesitancy, pessimism, Sadducism, suspicion 10 Pyrrhonism 11 agnosticism, incredulity, rationalism, Sadduceeism 12 doubtfulness
• **expression of scepticism**
02 ha 04 umph 09 away you go! 11 away with you! 12 pigs might fly

sceptre
03 rod 05 baton, staff 06 bauble

schedule
04 book, form, list, plan, time 05 diary, slate, table 06 agenda, assign, scheme 07 appoint, arrange 08 calendar, organize, syllabus 09 catalogue, inventory, itinerary, programme, timetable 10 enschedule
• **behind schedule**
04 late 07 overdue 10 behindhand, behind time 11 running late
• **on schedule**
05 on tap 06 on time 07 on track 08 on course, on target 15 according to plan
• **place in schedule**
04 slot 06 window

schema
03 map 04 form, plan 05 chart, shape 06 design, figure, layout, scheme, sketch 07 diagram, outline, profile, tracing 09 lineament 11 delineation 13 configuration

schematic
07 graphic 08 symbolic 10 simplified 12 diagrammatic, illustrative

scheme
◇ *anagram indicator*
03 gin, key, map 04 dart, game, idea, plan, plat, plot, ploy, ruse 05 angle, chart, draft, frame, shape, shift, table 06 bubble, design, device, devise, layout, method, schema, sketch, system, tactic 07 collude, connive, diagram, nostrum, outline, pattern, project, tactics, work out 08 conspire, contrive, escapade, intrigue, pedigree, platform, practice, practise, proposal, schedule, strategy 09 blueprint, machinate, manoeuvre, procedure, programme, stratagem, underplot 10 conspiracy, manipulate, mastermind, suggestion

11 arrangement, delineation, disposition, proposition, pull strings 12 machinations 13 configuration 14 course of action

schemer
03 fox 07 plotter, wangler 08 conniver, deceiver 09 contriver, intrigant, intriguer 10 intrigante, intriguant, machinator, mastermind, politician, wire-puller 11 intriguante, Machiavelli 13 éminence grise, Machiavellian, wheeler-dealer

scheming
03 sly 04 foxy, wily 06 artful, crafty, tricky 07 cunning, devious 08 practice, slippery 09 conniving, deceitful, designing, insidious, underhand 11 calculating, duplicitous 12 manipulative, unscrupulous 13 Machiavellian

schism
04 rift, sect 05 break, group, split 06 breach 07 discord, faction, rupture 08 disunion, division, scission, splinter 09 severance 10 detachment, separation 12 estrangement

schismatic
05 rebel 08 apostate, renegade, seceding 09 breakaway, heretical 10 dissenting, separatist 12 secessionist

schmaltz
04 glop, gush, mush, pulp 05 slush 09 soppiness 10 sloppiness 11 mawkishness, romanticism 12 emotionalism 14 sentimentality

scholar
01 L 02 BA, MA 05 clerk, pupil 06 day-boy, expert, pundit, savant 07 artsman, bookman, Dantist, day-girl, egghead, Grecian, learner, Maulana, Pauline, savante, student 08 academic, bookworm, boursier, disciple, Saxonist, schoolie, Semitist, taberdar 09 authority, Gothicist, schoolboy, schoolman, Talmudist 10 Carthusian, day-scholar, mastermind, postmaster, scholastic, schoolgirl 11 philosopher, schoolchild 12 intellectual, man of letters 14 woman of letters 15 person of letters

scholarly
06 school 07 bookish, clerkly, erudite, learned 08 academic, highbrow, lettered, literate, studious, well-read 09 clerklike 10 analytical, scholastic, scientific 12 intellectual 13 conscientious, knowledgeable

scholarship
05 award, burse, grant 06 wisdom 07 bursary 08 learning 09 education, endowment, erudition, knowledge, schooling 10 exhibition, fellowship 11 learnedness, Orientalism

scholastic
06 subtle 07 bookish, learned, precise, teacher 08 academic, lettered, literary, pedantic 09 pedagogic, scholarly,

schoolman 10 analytical 11 educational

school
02 GS 03 gam, pod, Sch, set 04 club, coed, high, prep, scul, sect 05 class, coach, drill, flock, group, guild, prime scull, shoal, teach, train, troop, tutor, verse 06 circle, clique, infant, junior, league, pupils, sculle 07 academy, college, company, coterie, educate, faction, faculty, madrasa, prepare, primary, society, yeshiva 08 admonish division, instruct, madrasah, madrassa seminary, students, yeshivah 09 institute, madrassah, medresseh, palaestra, secondary 10 assemblage, department, discipline, foundation, kohanga reo, university 11 association institution, pedagoguery 12 indoctrinate

See also art; educational

schoolboy, schoolgirl *see* pupil

schooling
05 drill 07 reproof, tuition 08 coaching, guidance, learning, teaching, training 09 education, grounding, reprimand 10 discipline 11 instruction, preparation 12 book-learning 14 indoctrination

schoolteacher
06 master 07 dominie, teacher 08 educator, mistress, schoolie 09 pedagogue 10 instructor, schoolmarm 12 schoolmaster 14 schoolmistress

schooner
04 tern 12 fore-and-after

science
03 art, sci 05 skill 09 dexterity, expertise, knowledge, technique 10 discipline, technology 11 proficiency 14 specialization

07 anatomy, biology, ecology, geology, medical, natural, physics, zoology
08 chemurgy, computer, domestic, dynamics, genetics, robotics
09 acoustics, astronomy, chemistry, dietetics, economics, materials, mechanics, pathology, political, sociology
10 biophysics, entomology, geophysics, graphology, hydraulics, metallurgy, mineralogy, morphology, physiology, psychology, toxicology, veterinary
11 aeronautics, archaeology, behavioural, climatology, cybernetics, diagnostics, electronics, engineering, linguistics, mathematics, meteorology, ornithology, ultrasonics
12 aerodynamics, agricultural, anthropology, astrophysics, biochemistry, geochemistry, geographical, macrobiotics, microbiology, pharmacology
13 environmental
14 geoarchaeology, nuclear physics, radiochemistry, thermodynamics
15 electrodynamics, space technology

See also **science fiction** *under* **fiction**

scientific
05 exact **07** orderly, precise
08 accurate, thorough **09** regulated, scholarly **10** analytical, controlled, methodical, systematic
12 mathematical **13** demonstrative
See also **law**

Scientific concepts include:
04 area, heat, mass, time, work
05 force, power
06 energy, length, stress, torque, volume
07 density
08 enthalpy, momentum, pressure, velocity
09 frequency, impedance, reactance, viscosity
10 admittance, plane angle, solid angle
11 capacitance, conductance, power factor, susceptance, temperature
12 acceleration, electric flux, illumination, luminous flux, magnetic flux, permeability, permittivity
13 electric force, kinetic energy, moment of force
14 electric charge, mass rate of flow, self inductance, surface tension
15 angular momentum, electric current, moment of inertia, potential energy, velocity of light

Scientific instruments include:
06 strobe
07 coherer, vernier
08 barostat, cryostat, rheocord, rheostat
09 decoherer, heliostat, hodoscope, hydrostat, hygrostat, image tube, microtome, slide rule, telemeter,

tesla coil, thyratron, zymoscope
10 centrifuge, collimator, eudiometer, heliograph, humidistat, hydrophone, hydroscope, hygrograph, iconoscope, microscope, nephograph, pantograph, radarscope, radiosonde, tachograph, teinoscope, thermostat
11 chronograph, fluoroscope, stactometer, stauroscope, stroboscope, transformer, transponder, tunnel diode
12 dephlegmator, electrosonde, oscillograph, oscilloscope, spectroscope
13 Geiger counter, phonendoscope, tachistoscope
14 absorptiometer, image converter, interferometer, torsion balance
15 electromyograph, telethermoscope

scientist
05 brain **06** boffin, doctor, expert, genius **07** analyst, ologist, planner, thinker **08** designer, engineer, inventor **09** intellect, magnetist **10** alchemist, mastermind, researcher **11** backroom-boy **12** entomologist, experimenter, intellectual, investigator, technologist **14** explorationist, research worker

See also **anatomy; anthropology; archaeology; astronomer; bacteriology; biochemistry; biology; botany; chemist; computer; economist; engineer; genetics; geography; inventor; mathematics; palaeontologist; physics; physiology; psychology; zoology**

scintilla
03 bit, jot **04** atom, hint, iota, mite, spot, whit **05** grain, piece, scrap, shred, spark, speck, trace **07** modicum, remnant, snippet **08** fragment, particle, skerrick

scintillate
04 wink **05** blaze, flash, gleam, glint, shine, spark **07** glisten, glitter, sparkle, twinkle **09** coruscate

scintillating
05 witty **06** bright, lively **07** shining **08** animated, dazzling, exciting, flashing **09** brilliant, ebullient, sparkling, twinkling, vivacious **10** glittering **11** stimulating **12** exhilarating, invigorating

scion
03 imp **04** cion, heir, sien, syen, twig **05** child, graft, plant, seyen, shoot, sient, sprig **06** branch, sprout **08** offshoot **09** offspring, successor **10** descendant **11** engraftment

scissors
06 cizers, forfex, shears **13** pinking shears

scoff
03 dor, eat, rib **04** bolt, chow, eats, food, gall, geck, gibe, grub, gulp, jeer, jibe, meal, mock, nosh, rail, tuck, wolf

05 binge, knock, scaff, scorn, scran, snarf, sneer, taunt, tease **06** deride, devour, gall at, geck at, gobble, guzzle, nosh-up, revile **07** consume, despise, laugh at, mockery, plunder, poke fun, put away **08** belittle, eatables, pooh-pooh, ridicule **09** disparage, finish off, nutriment, nutrition **10** foodstuffs, provisions, sustenance **11** comestibles, nourishment, subsistence
12 refreshments

scoffing
07 cynical, mocking **08** derisive, derisory, fiendish, scathing, sneering, taunting **09** sarcastic **11** disparaging **14** Mephistophelic
15 Mephistophelean, Mephistophelian

scold
03 jaw, nag, rag, row, wig, yap **04** Fury, rage, rant, rate, yaff **05** blame, brawl, chide, flite, flyte, go off, shrew, slang, vixen **06** berate, blow up, callet, dragon, rattle, rebuke, virago, yankie **07** censure, earbash, go off at, jawbone, lambast, lecture, reprove, rouse on, speak to, start on, tell off, tick off, trimmer, upbraid **08** admonish, harridan, reproach, spitfire, tear into, Xantippe **09** brimstone, castigate, go crook at, henpecker, objurgate, reprimand, start in on, take apart, termagant **10** take to task
11 clapperclaw **15** give it to someone

scolding
03 row **05** doing **06** dirdam, dirdum, earful, rating, rebuke **07** chiding, hearing, lecture, reproof, rollick, wigging **08** jobation, sasarara, siserary, slanging **09** carpeting, jawbation, reprimand, sassarara, sisserary, talking-to, termagant **10** earbashing, earwigging, telling-off, ticking-off, upbraiding **11** castigation, throughgaun **12** dressing-down, through-going

scombroid fish
04 seer, seir

scoop
03 dig, dip, lap **04** bail, coup, grab, lade, pale **05** empty, gouge, ladle, spoon **06** bailer, bucket, dipper, exposé, hollow, latest, remove, scrape, shovel **07** helping, portion **08** excavate, ladleful, spoonful **09** exclusive, sensation **10** revelation **11** inside story

scoot
03 run, zip **04** belt, bolt, dart, dash, rush, scud, tear **05** hurry, scout, shoot **06** beat it, career, scurry, sprint, squirt, tootle **07** scarper, scuttle, vamoose **09** skedaddle

scope
03 aim, VDU, way **04** area, play, room, span, wale **05** ambit, field, orbit, range, reach, realm, remit, round, space, sweep, swing, verge **06** cinema, domain, extent, leeway, limits, scouth, scowth, sphere **07** breadth, compass,

display, freedom, liberty, monitor, purpose, purview **08** capacity, confines, coverage, latitude **09** dimension, elbow-room **11** opportunity **12** spaciousness

scorch

03 fry **04** burn, char, plot, sear **05** adust, blast, dry up, parch, ploat, roast, scald, scath, singe, slash, swale, swayl, sweal, sweel **06** birsle, scaith, scathe, sizzle, skaith, wither **07** blacken, frizzle, scowder, shrivel, torrefy **08** scouther, scowther **09** discolour

scorching

05 blast **06** baking, red-hot, torrid **07** boiling, burning, searing **08** roasting, sizzling, tropical **09** withering **10** blistering, scowdering, sweltering **11** scouthering **12** extremely hot

score

02 XX **03** cut, get, law, net, rit, run, set, sum, win **04** case, earn, gain, gash, hail, hits, line, lots, make, mark, nick, ritt, runs, slit **05** adapt, basis, count, facts, goals, gouge, graze, hosts, issue, marks, notch, put on, slash, tally, total, truth, write **06** aspect, attain, crowds, droves, groove, grudge, incise, indent, masses, matter, points, reason, record, result, scotch, scrape, shoals, swarms, target, the gen, twenty **07** account, achieve, arrange, be one up, chalk up, concern, dispute, engrave, grounds, legions, motives, myriads, notch up, outcome, quarrel, scratch, subject **08** argument, hundreds, incision, millions, question, register **09** complaint, enumerate, grievance, reckoning, situation, thousands, what's what **10** instrument, keep a tally, multitudes, the picture **11** explanation, have the edge, orchestrate **12** be successful **13** hit the jackpot **14** state of affairs **15** the whole picture

• **even the score**
06 avenge **07** get back **09** retaliate **14** settle the score

• **score off**
09 humiliate **11** have the edge **12** get one over on

• **score out**
05 erase **06** cancel, delete, efface, remove **07** expunge **08** cross out **09** strike out **10** obliterate

scorn

04 geck, mock, shun, spit, zing **05** blurt, spurn **06** deride, rebuff, refuse, reject, scorch, slight **07** crucify, despise, disdain, disgust, dismiss, laugh at, mockery, sarcasm, scoff at, sneer at, sniff at **08** contempt, derision, mesprize, mesprize, misprise, misprize, ridicule, sneering **09** contumely, disparage **10** look down on **11** haughtiness **12** scornfulness **13** disparagement

scornful

07 haughty, jeering, mocking

08 arrogant, derisive, sardonic, scathing, scoffing, sneering **09** insulting, sarcastic, slighting **10** disdainful, dismissive **11** disparaging **12** contemptuous, supercilious

scornfully

09 haughtily **10** arrogantly, derisively, scathingly, sneeringly **11** slightingly, witheringly **12** disdainfully, dismissively **13** disparagingly **14** contemptuously, superciliously

scorpion

07 Scorpio **08** ballista, pedipalp **11** Eurypterida

Scot

◊ *dialect indicator*
03 Mac **04** Gael
See also **Scottish**

scotch

04 gash, halt, maim, ruin, stop **05** block, quash, score, strut, wedge, wreck **07** scupper, scuttle **09** frustrate **10** put an end to, put a stop to **11** put the lid on **12** bring to an end **13** pull the plug on

scot-free

04 safe **05** clear **06** unhurt **07** untaxed **08** shot-free, unharmed **09** undamaged, uninjured, unrebuked, unscathed **10** unpunished **12** unreproached **13** unreprimanded **15** without a scratch

Scotland *see* **council; town**

Scotsman *see* **Scot; Scottish**

Scottish

◊ *dialect word indicator*
See also **monarch**

Scottish first names include:

03 Ian, Rab, Rae
04 Doug, Euan, Ewan, Ewen, Greg, Iain, Iona, Isla, Jess, Jock
05 Ailsa, Angus, Arran, Blair, Calum, Clyde, Colin, Craig, Isbel, Logan, Lorna, Lorne, Sandy
06 Aileen, Callum, Dougie, Elspet, Gordon, Gregor, Hamish, Kelvin, Lilias, Mhàiri, Rabbie, Ranald, Vanora
07 Cameron, Douglas, Elspeth, Malcolm
08 Campbell, Catriona

Scottish clans include:

04 Ross
05 Baird, Bruce, Grant, Innes, Munro, Scott
06 Brodie, Buchan, Dunbar, Duncan, Dundas, Eliott, Elliot, Forbes, Fraser, Gordon, Graeme, Graham, Irvine, Irving, Lennox, Mackay, Macnab, Macrae, Moffat, Monroe, Murray, Napier, Ogilvy, Ramsay, Stuart
07 Balfour, Cameron, Douglas, Macduff, Maclean, Macleod, Macneil, Malcolm, Ogilvie, Stewart, Wallace
08 Anderson, Campbell, Drummond, Ferguson, Hamilton, Macaulay,

MacInnes, Macneill, Oliphant, Sinclair, Stirling, Urquhart
09 Armstrong, Colquhoun, Fergusson, Henderson, Johnstone, MacAlpine, MacAndrew, MacArthur, MacCallum, Macdonald, Macgregor, Macintosh, Macintyre, Mackenzie, Mackinnon, Macmillan, Nicholson, Robertson
10 Macdonnell, Macdougall, Mackintosh, Macpherson, Sutherland
11 MacAllister, MacLauchlan, MacLaughlan, Macnaughton

scoundrel

03 cur, dog, rat **04** scab **05** cheat, hound, louse, rogue, scamp, swine **06** donder, louser, rascal, rotter, scally **07** bounder, dastard, ruffian, stinker, villain **08** blighter, spalpeen, vagabond **09** miscreant, reprobate, scallywag **10** blackguard, hounds-foot, ne'er-do-well **14** good-for-nothing

scour

◊ *anagram indicator*
03 rub **04** comb, drag, full, hunt, rake, scur, sker, wash, wipe **05** clean, flush, purge, scout, scrub, skirr, skirt **06** abrade, forage, polish, punish, scrape, search, squirr **07** burnish, cleanse, ransack, rummage **08** clear out **14** turn upside-down

scourge

04 bane, beat, cane, evil, flog, lash, whip **05** birch, curse, flail, strap, trial **06** burden, menace, plague, punish, switch, terror, thrash **07** afflict, penalty, torment, torture **08** chastise, nuisance, scorpion **09** devastate, flagellum **10** affliction, discipline, misfortune, punishment **13** cat-o'-nine-tails **14** disciplinarium **15** thorn in your side

scout

03 cub, spy **04** case, hunt, look, mock, seek **05** flout, probe, recce, rover, scoot, sixer, snoop, spial, watch **06** beaver, escort, person, search, spying, spy out, survey **07** explore, inspect, look for, lookout, observe, pickeer, scourer, spotter, wolf cub **08** check out, outrider, scurrier, vanguard **09** recruiter, scurriour **10** discoverer, tenderfoot **11** investigate, reconnoitre, voortrekker **12** advance guard **13** talent spotter

scowl

04 lour, pout **05** frown, glare, gloom, lower **06** glower **07** grimace **09** black look, dirty look, overgloom **13** look daggers at

scrabble

◊ *anagram indicator*
03 dig, paw **04** claw, grub, root **05** grope **06** scrape, scrawl **07** clamber, scratch **08** scramble

scraggy

◊ *anagram indicator*
04 bony, lean, thin **05** gaunt, lanky **06** skinny, wasted **07** angular, scrawny,

unkempt **08** raw-boned
09 emaciated, irregular **10** straggling
14 undernourished

scram
04 bolt, flee, puny, quit, scat **05** leave,
scoot **06** beat it, depart, get out, go
away **07** buzz off, do a bunk, scarper,
vamoose **08** clear off, clear out, shove
off, withered **09** disappear, skedaddle
15 take to your heels

scramble
◇ anagram indicator
03 mix, ren, rin, run, vie **04** dash, muss,
push, race, rush **05** climb, crawl, grope,
hurry, mêlée, mix up, musse, scale,
vying **06** battle, bustle, hasten, hustle,
infuse, jockey, jostle, jumble, muddle,
scurry, strive, swerve, tussle
07 clamber, compete, contend, disturb,
grabble, rat race, scaling, scamble,
shuffle **08** scrabble, sprattle,
stampede, struggle **09** commotion,
confusion **10** free-for-all
11 competition, disorganize

scrap
03 axe, bit, ort, rag, row **04** atom, bite,
bits, drop, dump, glim, iota, junk, mite,
part, shed, snap, tiff **05** argue, brawl,
crumb, crust, ditch, fight, grain, patch,
piece, scrip, set-to, shard, sherd, shred,
trace, waste **06** battle, bicker, bundle,
cancel, dust-up, fracas, morsel, sliver,
splore, stitch, tatter, verset **07** abandon,
break up, discard, dispute, fall out,
punch-up, quarrel, remains, remnant,
residue, scissel, scissil, scuffle, snippet,
vestige, wrangle **08** argument, chuck
out, demolish, disagree, fraction,
fragment, get rid of, jettison, leavings,
leftover, mouthful, particle, quantity,
skerrick, squabble, write off
09 leftovers, scrapings, throw away
11 odds and ends, odds and sods
12 disagreement **13** bits and pieces
• **on the scrap heap**
06 dumped **07** ditched **08** rejected
09 discarded, forgotten, redundant
10 jettisoned, written off

scrape
03 cut, fix, hoe, paw, rub **04** bark, clat,
claw, file, hole, mess, rake, rase, rasp,
raze, skin **05** claut, clean, curet, erase,
flesh, grate, graze, grind, scalp, scart,
scour, scrab, scuff, shave, shred
06 abrade, hobble, pickle, plight,
remove, splore **07** curette, descale,
dilemma, scratch, snapper, trouble
08 abrasion, distress, scrabble, wrong
box **09** curettage, shemozzle,
shimozzle, tight spot **10** difficulty,
praemunire, schemozzle, shlemozzle
11 predicament
• **scrape by**
05 get by, skimp **06** eke out, scrimp
13 muddle through
• **scrape through**
08 just pass **09** barely win **11** only just
win **13** just succeed in
• **scrape together**
07 round up, scuffle **11** get together
12 pool together **15** just manage to get

scrappy
◇ anagram indicator
05 bitty **06** untidy **07** sketchy
08 slapdash, slipshod **09** piecemeal
10 disjointed, incomplete
11 belligerent, fragmentary,
quarrelsome, superficial
12 disconnected, disorganized

scraps
04 odds **05** brock, trash **08** dog's-
meat

scratch
◇ anagram indicator
◇ deletion indicator
03 cut, rit, rub **04** cash, clat, claw, etch,
gash, line, mark, nick, race, rase, ritt,
skin, tear **05** claut, curry, Devil, fluke,
gouge, graze, rough, scart, score,
scrab, scram, scrat, scuff, tease, wound
06 abrade, casual, incise, scramb,
scrape, scrawm, streak **07** engrave
08 abrasion, lacerate, scrabble
09 haphazard, impromptu
10 improvised, laceration, ready
money **11** clapperclaw, unrehearsed
13 rough-and-ready
• **up to scratch**
02 OK **08** adequate **09** competent,
tolerable, up to snuff **10** acceptable,
good enough, reasonable **11** up to the
mark **12** satisfactory

scrawl
03 jot, pen **06** doodle **07** dash off, jot
down, scratch, writing **08** scrabble,
scribble, squiggle **10** cacography
11 handwriting **12** write quickly **14** bad
handwriting

scrawny
04 bony, lean, thin **05** lanky
06 meagre, skinny, sparse **07** angular,
scraggy, scranny **08** raw-boned,
underfed **09** emaciated
14 undernourished

scream
03 cry, eek, wit **04** bawl, hoot, howl,
riot, roar, wail, yawp, yell, yelp
05 comic, joker, laugh, shout **06** holler,
shriek, squawk, squeal **07** screech
08 comedian **09** character **13** cry blue
murder **15** shout blue murder

screech
03 cry **04** howl, yell, yelp **06** screak,
scream, shriek, squawk, squeal
07 scraich, scraigh, screich, screigh,
scriech, scritch, shriech, shritch,
skreigh, skriech, skriegh, ululate

screen
03 net, VDU, vet **04** grid, hide, mask,
mesh, scan, show, sift, sort, test, veil
05 blind, check, chick, cloak, cover,
front, gauge, grade, grill, guard, scope,
shade, sieve **06** awning, canopy,
defend, façade, filter, grille, purdah,
riddle, sconce, shield, shroud
07 conceal, cribble, curtain, divider,
examine, monitor, netting, picture,
present, process, protect, reredos,
shelter **08** abat-jour, disguise, evaluate,
parclose, traverse **09** broadcast,

dashboard, faceplate, partition,
reredorse, reredosse, safeguard
10 camouflage, protection
11 concealment, investigate, room-
divider **12** clothes-horse
• **screen off**
04 hide **06** divide **07** conceal, protect
08 fence off, separate **09** divide off,
partition **11** separate off **12** partition off

screenwriter see playwright

screw
◇ anagram indicator
03 fix, pay, pin, rob **04** bolt, brad, milk,
nail, tack, turn, wind **05** bleed, cheat,
clamp, force, rivet, twist, wages, wrest,
wring **06** adjust, burgle, extort, fasten,
pucker, salary **07** defraud, distort,
extract, squeeze, tighten, wrinkle
08 compress, contract, fastener,
pressure **09** constrain, skinflint
10 pressurize **12** extortionist
• **put the screws on**
05 force **06** coerce, compel, lean on
07 dragoon **09** constrain, strongarm
10 pressurize
• **screwed up**
05 upset **06** hung up **07** mixed up,
muddled, puzzled **08** confused,
messed up **09** disturbed, perplexed
10 bewildered, disordered, distracted,
distraught **11** disoriented, maladjusted
• **screw up**
04 knot, ruin **05** botch, spoil, twist
06 bungle, cock up, mess up, pucker
07 contort, crumple, disrupt, distort,
louse up, squinch, stuff up, tighten,
wrinkle **08** contract, summon up
09 mishandle, mismanage **11** make a
hash of

screwy
◇ anagram indicator
03 mad, odd **04** daft **05** batty, crazy,
dotty, nutty, queer, tipsy, weird
08 crackers **09** eccentric **12** round the
bend **13** round the twist

scribble
03 jot, pen **05** write **06** doodle, scrawl
07 dash off, jot down, scratch, writing
08 bescrawl, scrabble, squiggle
10 bescribble, cacography
11 handwriting **14** bad handwriting

scribbler
04 hack **06** writer **09** ink-jerker, pen-
pusher, pot-boiler **10** ink-slinger
11 inkhorn-mate, verse-monger
12 paper-stainer

scribe
04 hack **05** clerk, write **06** author,
incise, mallam, penman, writer
07 copyist **08** recorder, reporter
09 pen-pusher, scrivener, secretary
10 amanuensis **11** transcriber
12 calligrapher, hierographer

scrimmage
03 row **04** fray, riot **05** brawl, bully,
fight, mêlée, rouge, scrap, scrum, set-
to **06** affray, bovver, dust-up, shindy
07 scuffle **08** skirmish, squabble,
struggle **10** free-for-all **11** disturbance

scrimp

04 save **05** limit, pinch, skimp, stint
06 barely, reduce, scanty, scrape
07 curtail, shorten, stinted **08** restrict
09 cut back on, economize **15** tighten
your belt

script

02 MS **04** book, copy, hand, Jawi, text
05 Cufic, Kufic, lines, ronde, words
06 Arabic, nagari **07** letters, linear A,
linear B, writing **08** dialogue,
Gurmukhi, libretto, longhand, nastalik,
nasta'liq, Sumerian **09** minuscule
10 devanagari, manuscript, screenplay
11 calligraphy, Cypro-Minoan,
handwriting, running-hand **14** rustic
capitals, shooting script
• **insert into script**
03 cue

scripture

02 RE, RI

Religious writings include:

02 NT, OT
05 Bayan, Bible, Koran, Qur'an, sutra,
Torah, Vedas, Zohar
06 Gemara, gospel, Granth, Hadith, I
Ching, Kojiki, Mishna, Talmud, Tantra
07 epistle, Li Ching, Puranas, Shari'ah
08 Haft Wadi, Halakhah, Ramayana,
Shu Ching
09 Adi Granth, Apocrypha, Chuang-
tzu, Chu'un Ch'iu, Decalogue,
Digambara, Hexateuch, scripture,
Shih Ching, Tripitaka
10 Heptateuch, Lotus Sutra, Nohon
Shoki, Pentateuch, Svetambara, Tao-
te-ching, Upanishads, Zend-Avesta
11 Bardo Thodol, Mahabharata
12 Bhagavad Gita, Kitab al-Aqdas,
Milindapanha, New Testament, Old
Testament
14 Dead Sea Scrolls, Mahayana Sutras,
Revised Version
15 Ten Commandments

See also **Bible**

scroll

04 curl, list, roll **05** draft, paper, scrow,
Sefer, Torah **06** mezuza, scrowl,
stemma, Thorah, volume, volute
07 mezuzah, scrowle **08** cartouch,
makimono, megillah, rocaille,
schedule **09** cartouche, inventory,
parchment **10** monkey tail, phylactery,
Sefer Torah

Scrooge

05 crowd, miser **06** meanie
07 niggard, squeeze **08** tightwad
09 skinflint **10** cheapskate **12** money-
grubber, penny-pincher

scrounge

03 beg, bum **04** blag **05** cadge
06 bludge, borrow, scunge, sponge
07 purloin

scrounger

03 bum **05** mooch, mouch **06** beggar,
cadger, scunge **07** bludger, moocher,
sponger **08** borrower, parasite
10 freeloader

scrub

◇ *deletion indicator*
03 axe, rub **04** bush, drop, wash, wipe
05 brush, clean, scour, shrub
06 cancel, delete, drudge, forget, give
up, purify **07** abandon, abolish,
cleanse, garigue, thicket **08** garrigue
09 backwoods, brushwood, exfoliate,
holystone, scrubland **10** improvised,
undersized **11** discontinue,
undergrowth **13** insignificant

scruff

04 nape **05** scuff, scuft

scruffy

◇ *anagram indicator*
05 daggy, dirty, messy, seedy **06** grotty,
ragged, scurvy, shabby, sloppy, untidy
07 run-down, squalid, unkempt, worn-
out **08** dog-eared, slovenly, sluttish,
tattered **09** ungroomed
10 bedraggled, down-at-heel,
slatternly **11** dishevelled
12 disreputable
• **scruffy person**
03 dag **04** slob **06** scruff

scrum

04 ruck

scrumptious

05 tasty, yummy **06** morish
07 moreish, scrummy **08** gorgeous,
luscious **09** delicious, exquisite,
succulent **10** appetizing, delectable,
delightful **11** magnificent
13 mouthwatering

scrunch

04 chew, mash **05** champ, crush, grate,
grind, screw, twist **06** crunch, squash
07 crumple, screw up **09** crumple up

scruple

03 scr **04** balk **05** demur, doubt,
qualm, stick **06** boggle, ethics, morals,
shrink **07** protest, stickle **08** hesitate,
hold back, question **09** disbelief,
misgiving, objection, standards,
vacillate **10** difficulty, hesitation,
perplexity, principles, reluctance, think
twice, uneasiness **11** be reluctant,
compunction, reservation, vacillation
13 point of honour **14** second thoughts

scrupulous

04 nice **05** exact, moral **06** honest,
minute, queasy, queazy, spiced, strict,
tender **07** careful, ethical, precise,
upright **08** captious, rigorous,
thorough **09** religious **10** fastidious,
honourable, meticulous, principled
11 painstaking, punctilious
13 conscientious **14** high-principled

scrutinize

04 coat, cote, scan, sift **05** coate,
probe, quote, study **06** go over,
peruse, search **07** analyse, canvass,
examine, explore, inspect, run over
08 look over **09** go through **10** run
through **11** investigate, look through

scrutiny

05 probe, study **06** search **07** canvass,
check-up, close-up, inquiry, perusal

08 analysis, docimasy **10** inspection
11 examination, exploration
13 investigation

scud

03 fly **04** blow, dart, East, gust, race,
sail, skim, slap **05** shoot, speed,
spoom, spoon

scuff

03 rub **04** cuff, drag **05** brush, graze,
scuft **06** abrade, scrape, scruff
07 scratch

scuffle

◇ *anagram indicator*
03 hoe, row **04** fray **05** brawl, clash,
fight, scrap, set-to **06** affray, cuffle,
dust-up, rumpus, tussle **07** bagarre,
contend, grapple, punch-up, quarrel,
scarify, shuffle **08** pull caps, struggle
09 commotion **11** come to blows,
disturbance **14** rough-and-tumble

sculpt

◇ *anagram indicator*
03 cut, hew **04** cast, form **05** carve,
model, mould, shape **06** chisel
07 fashion **09** represent, sculpture
• **he/she sculpted**
02 sc **08** sculpsit

sculptor

05 hewer, mason **06** artist, carver,
caster **07** moulder, plastic **08** figurist,
modeller **09** chiseller, craftsman
10 sculptress **11** craftswoman, stone-
carver

Sculptors include:

03 Arp (Hans), Ray (Man)
04 Bell (John), Bone (Phyllis), Caro (Sir
Anthony), Gabo (Naum), Gill (Eric),
King (Philip), Mach (David), Rude
(François)
05 Andre (Carl), Bacon (John), Beuys
(Joseph), Cragg (Tony), Davey
(Grenville), Frink (Dame Elisabeth),
Johns (Jasper), Koons (Jeff), Manzú
(Giacomo), Moore (Henry), Myron,
Rodin (Auguste), Smith (David
Roland), Story (William)
06 Calder (Alexander), Canova
(Antonio), Cousin (Jean), Deacon
(Richard), Hatoum (Mona), Kapoor
(Anish), Marini (Marino), Pisano
(Andrea), Pisano (Giovanni),
Robbia (Luca della), Scopas, Walker
(Dame Ethel)
07 Bernini (Gianlorenzo), Cellini
(Benvenuto), Christo, Duchamp
(Marcel), Epstein (Sir Jacob),
Gormley (Antony), Klinger (Max),
Longman (Evelyn), Millett (Kate),
Phidias, Samaras (Lucas)
08 Boccioni (Umberto), Brancusi
(Constantin), Chadwick (Lynn),
Ghiberti (Lorenzo), Hepworth
(Dame Barbara), Landseer (Sir
Edwin), Paolozzi (Eduardo Luigi),
Pheidias, Tinguely (Jean)
09 Borromini (Francesco), Bourgeois
(Louise), Donatello, Oldenburg
(Claes), Roubiliac (Louis François),
Whiteread (Rachel)

10 Giacometti (Alberto), **Polyclitus, Praxiteles, Schwitters** (Kurt), Verrocchio (Andrea del)
11 Della Robbia (Luca), **Goldsworthy** (Andy)
12 Jeanne-Claude, Michelangelo
14 Gaudier-Brzeska (Henri)
15 Leonardo da Vinci

sculpture
◇ *anagram indicator*

Sculpture types include:

04 bust, cast, head, herm, kore
05 group
06 bronze, effigy, figure, kouros, marble, relief, statue
07 carving, kinetic, telamon, waxwork
08 caryatid, Daibutsu, figurine, maquette, moulding
09 bas-relief, statuette
10 high-relief
11 plaster cast

Sculptures and statues include:

04 Adam, Kore, Zeus
05 Angel, Cupid, David, House, Medea, Moses, Pietà, Torso
06 Balzac
07 Bacchus, Genesis, Liberty, Lincoln, Mercury, Merzbau, Spiders, The Kiss, The Wall
08 Cantoria, Ecce Homo, Eggboard, Have Pity!, Mahamuni, Piscator
09 A Universe, Seated Man, Slate Cone
10 Discobolus, Doryphorus, Double Talk, Ledge Piece, Orange Bath, Running Man, Single Form, The Thinker
11 Gomateswara, Kiss and Tell, Pierced Form, Spear Bearer, Venus de Milo
12 Cactus People, Elgin Marbles, Feast of Herod
13 Discus Thrower, Fallen Warrior, People in a Wind, Veduggio Sound
14 Cosimo de' Medici, Fontana Magiore, Horse Lying Down, Japanese War God, Sailing Tonight, The Age of Bronze, The Gates of Hell, The Three Graces
15 Angel of the North, Athena Promachos, Buddhas of Bamian, Christ in Majesty, Figure and Clouds, Giant Clothespin, Madonna and Child, Recumbent Figure

scum
04 dirt, film, foam, slag **05** dregs, dross, froth, layer, plebs, spume, trash **06** mantle, mother, rabble **07** rubbish, sullage **08** covering, pellicle, riff-raff, sandiver **09** epistasis, glass-gall **10** impurities **12** undesirables **13** great unwashed **14** dregs of society, lowest of the low

scupper
03 axe **04** foil, kill, ruin, sink **05** do for, wreck **06** cock up, defeat, mess up **07** destroy, disable, louse up, screw up, scuttle, torpedo **08** demolish, submerge **09** overthrow, overwhelm

scurf
05 scald, scale **06** furfur, scruff **07** furfair **08** dandriff, dandruff **09** flakiness, scaliness **12** scabrousness

scurfy
05 flaky, lepra, scald, scaly **06** scabby, scurvy **07** leprose, leprous, scabrid **08** lepidote, scabrous, scarious **09** furfurous **11** scaberulous **12** furfuraceous

scurrility
05 abuse **07** obloquy **08** foulness, rudeness **09** grossness, indecency, invective, nastiness, obscenity, vulgarity **10** coarseness **11** abusiveness **12** vituperation **13** offensiveness **14** scurrilousness

scurrilous
04 foul, rude **06** coarse, vulgar **07** abusive, obscene, Sotadic **08** indecent, Sotadean **09** insulting, libellous, offensive, salacious **10** defamatory, Fescennine, scandalous, slanderous **11** disparaging **12** vituperative

scurry
03 fly, ren, rin, run **04** dart, dash, race, rush, scud, scur, sker, skim, trot **05** hurry, scoot, scour, skirr, whirl **06** beetle, bustle, flurry, hasten, skurry, sprint, squirr **07** scamper, scutter, scuttle, skelter **08** bustling, scramble **09** beetle off **10** scampering **15** hustle and bustle

scurvy
03 bad, low **04** base, mean, vile, yaws **05** dirty, scall, sorry **06** abject, rotten, scurfy, shabby **07** ignoble, low-down, pitiful, roynish, scruffy **08** whoreson **09** worthless **10** despicable **12** contemptible **13** dishonourable

scuttle
◇ *anagram indicator*
03 hod, ren, rin, run **04** rush, scud **05** hurry **06** bustle, hasten, scurry **07** scamper, scuddle, scutter, skuttle **08** scramble, scrattle **09** purdonium

scythe
03 mow **11** bushwhacker
● **part of scythe**
04 sned **05** snath, snead **06** snathe, sneath

sea
03 mer **04** deep, host, main, mass, salt, tide **05** briny, ocean, swell, waves **06** afloat, marine **07** aquatic, expanse, oceanic **08** maritime **09** abundance, multitude, profusion, roughness, saltwater, seafaring **11** large number

Seas include:

03 Med, Red
04 Aral, Azov, Dead, East, Java, Kara, Ross, Sulu
05 Banda, Black, Coral, Crete, Irish, Japan, North, Timor, White
06 Aegean, Baltic, Bering, Celtic, Flores, Inland, Ionian, Laptev, Nan Hai, Scotia, Tasman, Yellow

07 Andaman, Arabian, Arafura, Barents, Caspian, Celebes, Dong Hai, Galilee, Marmara, Okhotsk, Solomon, Weddell
08 Adriatic, Amundsen, Beaufort, Bismarck, Hebrides, Huang Hai, Labrador, Ligurian, McKinley, Sargasso
09 Caribbean, East China, Greenland, Norwegian
10 Philippine, Setonaikai, South China, Tyrrhenian
11 Yam Kinneret
12 East Siberian
13 Mediterranean
14 Bellingshausen

See also **moon; ocean**
● **at sea**
◇ *anagram indicator*
04 lost **06** adrift, afloat **07** baffled, puzzled **08** confused **09** mystified, perplexed **10** bewildered **11** disoriented **12** disorganized **13** disorientated

seabird *see* bird

seaborgium
02 Sg

sea bream
03 sar, tai **05** porgy, sargo **06** braise, braize, porgie, sargos, sargus **07** old wife **08** tarwhine

seafaring
05 naval **06** marine **07** oceanic, sailing **08** maritime, nautical, sea-going **10** ocean-going

seafood

Seafood and seafood dishes include:

04 bisk, clam, crab
05 prawn, squid, sushi, whelk
06 bisque, cockle, mussel, oyster, paella, scampi, shrimp, winkle
07 abalone, lobster, octopus, risotto, scallop, tempura, toheroa
08 calamari, coquille, crawfish, crevette, marinara, zarzuela
09 jambalaya, king prawn, surf'n'turf
10 tiger prawn
11 clam-chowder, Dublin prawn, fritto misto, fruits de mer, langoustine, tiger shrimp
13 bouillabaisse, Norway lobster, prawn cocktail
14 Dublin Bay prawn

See also **crustacean; fish; mollusc**

seahorse
06 tangie, walrus **08** pipefish **09** hippodame, sea dragon **11** hippocampus, lophobranch

seal
04 chop, cork, jark, lute, plug, seel, shut, stop **05** bulla, close, O-ring, plumb, puppy, sigil, stamp, tie up **06** cachet, clinch, enseal, fasten, obsign, ratify, secure, settle, signet, stop up, wicker, willow **07** close up, confirm, consign, enclose, stopper, tar-seal, tighten, ziplock **08** bachelor,

conclude, finalize, insignia, set apart **09** assurance, footprint, obsignate **10** impression, imprimatur, shake hands, waterproof **11** attestation, counterseal **12** confirmation, make airtight, ratification **14** authentication, make watertight

Seals include:

03 fur
04 grey, hair, harp, monk
05 otary, phoca, silky
06 common, hooded, ribbon, sea dog, sealch, sealgh, selkie, silkie
07 harbour, sea bear, sea calf, sea lion, Weddell
08 Atlantic, elephant, seecatch
09 crab-eater, Greenland, whitecoat
10 saddleback, sea leopard
11 sea elephant

• **in the place of the seal**
02 LS **11** loco sigilli
• **seal off**
03 cap **06** cut off, fasten **07** block up, isolate, shut off **08** close off, fence off **09** cordon off, segregate **10** quarantine

sealed
04 shut **06** closed, corked **07** plugged **08** hermetic **09** sigillate **10** hermetical, watertight **12** draught-proof

seam
04 fell, join, line, lode, saim, vein, weld **05** joint, layer, quilt, raphe, seame **06** grease, suture, thread **07** closure, joining, stratum, wrinkle **08** cartload, edge coal, junction, wayboard **09** stitching **10** weighboard **12** dorsal suture **15** middle-stitching

seaman
02 AB **03** Kru, tar **04** Kroo **06** merman, sailor **07** killick, killock
See also **sailor**

sea-mist
04 haar

sea-monster
03 orc **04** cete **05** Phoca **06** kraken **07** ziffius **08** seahorse **09** leviathan, rosmarine, sea satyre, wasserman, whirlpool **11** hippocampus
See also **monster**

seamy
03 low **04** dark **05** nasty, rough **06** sleazy, sordid **07** squalid **09** unsavoury **10** unpleasant **12** disreputable

sear
03 dry, fry **04** burn, char, seal, sere, wilt **05** brand, brown, dry up, parch, seare, singe **06** scorch, sizzle, wither **07** burning, shrivel **08** withered **09** cauterize

search
03 pry **04** comb, fish, hunt, rake, ripe, scur, seek, sift, sker **05** check, frisk, grope, probe, quest, rifle, scour, sieve, skirr, sweep **06** ferret, forage, squirr, survey **07** enquire, enquiry, examine, explore, fossick, inquire, inquiry,

inspect, look for, pursuit, ransack, rifling, rummage **08** prospect, research, scrutiny **09** cast about, go through, ranshakle **10** inspection, ransacking, ranshackle, scrutinize **11** examination, exploration, investigate, look through **12** perquisition **13** investigation, perscrutation, turn inside-out **14** turn upside-down
• **in search of**
07 seeking **09** in quest of **10** looking for **11** in pursuit of **12** searching for **15** on the lookout for
• **search me**
05 dunno **09** I don't know, it beats me, I've no idea **12** ask me another **15** I haven't got a clue, you've got me there
• **search out**
04 scan **06** ferret **07** explore **08** indigate **10** run to earth **11** run to ground

searching
04 home, keen **05** alert, close, quest, sharp **06** intent, minute, trying **07** probing **08** piercing, thorough **09** observant **10** discerning **11** penetrating, prospecting **13** inquisitional **14** strand-scouring

searing
05 cruel **06** brutal, fierce, savage, severe **07** blazing, burning, extreme, intense, mordant **08** scathing **09** ferocious, scorching, trenchant, vitriolic **10** unbearable **11** devastating **12** insufferable

seaside
05 beach, coast, sands, shore **06** strand **08** seashore

season
03 age **04** fall, salt, seal, seel, seil, sele, span, term, tide, time **05** inure, pep up, phase, prime, ripen, savor, spell, spice, train, treat **06** harden, haysel, master, mature, mellow, period, savour, temper **07** flavour, prepare, toughen **08** festival, interval, moderate, tone down **09** condiment, condition **10** add herbs to, add sauce to, fence month, summertide, summertime **11** add pepper to, add relish to **13** add flavouring

Seasons include:

03 dry, wet
04 high, open
05 close, rainy, silly
06 autumn, closed, spring, summer, winter
07 festive, holiday, monsoon
08 breeding, shooting
12 Indian summer

• **in season**
02 in **07** growing **09** available **10** obtainable **11** on the market

seasonable
04 tidy **06** timely, timous **07** fitting, timeous, welcome **08** suitable **09** opportune, well-timed **10** convenient, forehanded,

tempestive **11** appropriate **12** providential

seasoned
03 old **04** salt **06** mature, spiced **07** veteran **08** cayenned, hardened **09** practised, toughened, weathered **10** habituated, well-versed **11** conditioned, established, experienced, long-serving **12** acclimatized **13** battle-scarred, weather-beaten

seasoning
04 salt **05** herbs, salad, sauce, spice **06** pepper, relish, spices **07** salting **08** dressing, duxelles **09** condiment **10** celery salt, flavouring, weathering **11** fines herbes
See also **herb**

seat
03 fit, fix, hub, pew, put, see, set, sit **04** axis, base, form, hold, home, pouf, sell, site, sofa, sunk, take **05** abode, bench, cause, chair, heart, house, perch, place, sedes, selle, siege, slide, stall, stool, swing, villa **06** bottom, centre, dukery, ground, humpty, locate, origin, pouffe, reason, saddle, settle, source, throne **07** capital, contain, deposit, footing, install, mansion, pillion, sitting, station **08** location, position, sociable, tribunal **09** faldstool, residence, situation **10** foundation, metropolis, strapontin **11** accommodate, have room for, reservation, stately home **12** confessional, headquarters, rumble-tumble
See also **chair**

seating
04 room **05** seats **06** chairs, places **13** accommodation

sea trout
04 peal, peel **05** sewen, sewin **06** finnac **07** finnack, finnock, herling, hirling

seaweed

Seaweeds include:

03 ore, red
04 agar, alga, kelp, kilp, nori, tang, ulva, ware
05 arame, domoi, dulse, fucus, kombu, laver, varec, vraic, wrack
06 fucoid, tangle, varech, wakame
07 oarweed, oreweed, redware, sea lace, sea moss, seaware
08 agar-agar, bull kelp, gulfweed, porphyra, rockweed, sargasso, seawrack, whipcord
09 carrageen, coralline, coral weed, driftweed, Irish moss, Laminaria, nullipore, sargassum, seabottle, sea girdle, sea tangle, thongweed
10 badderlock, carragheen, Ceylon moss, green laver, sea lettuce, see whistle, tangleweed
11 purple laver, sea furbelow
12 bladderwrack, peacock's tail, phaeophyceae, Rhodophyceae

See also **alga, algae**

secede
04 quit **05** break, leave **06** resign, retire **08** separate, split off, withdraw **09** break away **10** apostatize **12** disaffiliate **14** turn your back on

seceders
04 cave

secession
05 break, split **06** revolt, schism **08** apostasy, seceding **09** breakaway, defection **10** withdrawal **14** disaffiliation

secluded
03 shy **05** close **06** cut off, hidden, lonely, remote, secret **07** private, recluse, retired, shadowy **08** in purdah, isolated, purdahed, shut away, solitary, umbratic **09** claustral, cloistral, concealed, sheltered, withdrawn **10** cloistered **11** out-of-the-way, sequestered, umbratilous **12** unfrequented

seclusion
04 nook **06** bypath, hiding, purdah, recess **07** byplace, privacy, retreat, secrecy, shelter **08** bolt hole, retiracy, solitude **09** hermitage, isolation, reclusion, sequester **10** remoteness, retirement, withdrawal **11** concealment, recluseness **13** sequestration

second
01 s **02** mo **03** aid, sec **04** back, beta, help, jiff, move, next, send, tick, twin **05** extra, flash, jiffy, lower, other, shift, spare, trice, vouch **06** assign, assist, backer, back up, back-up, change, deputy, double, helper, lesser, minute, moment **07** advance, another, approve, endorse, forward, further, helpful, instant, promote, support **08** inferior, relocate, repeated, transfer **09** agree with, alternate, assistant, attendant, duplicate, encourage, favouring, following, secondary, supporter, twinkling **10** additional, subsequent, succeeding, supporting **11** alternative, split second, subordinate **12** right-hand man **13** supplementary **14** right-hand woman **15** second-in-command

• **second to none**
04 best **06** superb **07** supreme **08** peerless **09** brilliant, matchless, nonpareil, paramount **10** inimitable, unrivalled **11** superlative, unsurpassed **12** incomparable, without equal **13** beyond compare, nulli secundus **15** without parallel

secondary
05 extra, lower, minor, spare **06** back-up, deputy, feeder, lesser, relief, second **07** derived, reserve **08** delegate, indirect, inferior, Mesozoic **09** ancillary, auxiliary, resulting **10** derivative, subsidiary, supporting **11** alternative, subordinate, unimportant **12** non-essential

second-class
01 B **08** inferior, mediocre **10** second-best, second-rate, uninspired

11 indifferent, unimportant, uninspiring **15** undistinguished

second-hand
03 old **04** used, worn **08** borrowed, indirect, pre-owned **09** nearly-new, obliquely, secondary, vicarious **10** derivative, hand-me-down, indirectly **11** reach-me-down **12** incidentally, tralaticious, tralatitious **13** formerly owned **14** on the grapevine

second-in-command
06 backer, deputy, helper **09** assistant, attendant, number two, supporter **12** right-hand man **14** right-hand woman

secondly
03 too **04** also, next **06** as well **07** besides, further **08** moreover **09** what's more **10** in addition **11** furthermore **12** additionally **14** into the bargain

second-rate
04 poor, ropy **05** cheap, crook, lousy, ropey, tacky **06** grotty, lesser, shoddy, tawdry, tinpot **08** inferior, low-grade, mediocre **10** second-best, uninspired **11** second-class, substandard, unimportant, uninspiring **15** undistinguished

secrecy
04 dern **05** dearn, wraps **07** hidling, hidlins, mystery, privacy, privity, silence, stealth **08** disguise, hidlings **09** seclusion **10** camouflage, confidence, covertness **11** concealment, furtiveness **12** hugger-mugger, stealthiness **15** confidentiality

secret
03 key, sly **04** code, dark, deep, dern, rune **05** close, dearn, hushy, privy **06** answer, arcane, closet, covert, cut off, enigma, hidden, inward, lonely, mystic, occult, recipe, remote, unseen **07** arcanum, covered, cryptic, formula, furtive, hidling, hidlins, mystery, nostrum, private, retired, unknown **08** abstruse, back-door, discreet, esoteric, hidlings, hush-hush, isolated, secluded, shrouded, shut away, sneaking, solitary, solution, stealthy **09** concealed, disguised, recondite, sensitive, sheltered, tête-à-tête, top secret, underhand **10** backstairs, classified, cloistered, confidence, mysterious, restricted, undercover, unrevealed **11** camouflaged, clandestine, inside story, know-nothing, out-of-the-way, sequestered, underground, undisclosed, unpublished **12** confidential, hugger-mugger, Naples yellow, unfrequented, unidentified **13** hole-and-corner, private matter, surreptitious **14** cloak-and-dagger **15** between you and me, under-the-counter

• **in secret**
07 in petto, on the qt, privily, quietly **08** covertly, in camera, on the sly,

secretly **09** furtively, in pectore, in private, privately **10** on the quiet, stealthily, under cover, unobserved **12** hugger-mugger, in confidence, subterranean **13** clandestinely **14** confidentially **15** surreptitiously

• **secret agent**
03 spy **04** Bond, mole **05** scout **07** snooper **10** enemy agent **11** double agent **12** foreign agent **14** fifth columnist **15** undercover agent

secretary
02 PA **03** Sec **04** Secy, temp **05** clerk **06** munshi, scribe, typist **07** famulus **08** moonshee **09** assistant, man Friday, town clerk **10** amanuensis, chancellor, girl Friday, secretaire **11** protonotary **12** person Friday, prothonotary, stenographer

secrete
04 bury, emit, hide, leak, ooze, take, veil **05** cache, cover, exude, leach, water **06** screen, secern, shroud **07** conceal, cover up, emanate, excrete, give off, lactate, produce, release, send out **08** disguise, salivate **09** discharge, sequester, stash away **11** appropriate

secretion
04 lerp **05** sebum, slime **06** liquor, oozing, pruina, smegma, succus **07** cerumen, hormone, leakage, osmosis, release **08** autacoid, emission, honeydew **09** discharge, emanation, exudation, incretion, lactation, recrement **10** osmidrosis, production, royal jelly, secernment **12** lachrymation

secretive
03 sly **04** cagy, deep **05** cagey, close, quiet **06** intent **07** cryptic **08** reserved, reticent, taciturn **09** enigmatic, withdrawn **11** tight-lipped **13** unforthcoming **15** uncommunicative

secretively
07 quietly **08** silently **10** reticently, taciturnly **13** enigmatically

secretly
05 close **06** dernly **07** dearnly, on the qt, privily, quietly **08** covertly, in camera, in secret, on the sly **09** furtively, in private, privately **10** on the quiet, stealthily, under-board, under cover, unobserved **11** underground **12** in confidence **13** clandestinely **14** confidentially **15** surreptitiously

sect
03 sex **04** camp, clan, cult, wing **05** group, order, party **06** church, school **07** cutting, faction **08** division **09** tradition **11** subdivision **12** denomination **13** splinter group

Religious sects include:
05 Amish
07 Ahmadis, Cathars, Moonies, Shakers, Zealots

09 Ahmadiyya, Lubavitch
10 Mennonites
11 Hare Krishna, Therapeutae

See also **sectarian**

sectarian
04 Babi **05** Amish, Babee, bigot, Cynic, hodja, khoja, rigid, Saiva, Yezdi **06** Berean, Cathar, Dunker, khodja, Marist, Moonie, Mormon, Mucker, narrow, Ophite, ranter, Sabian, Seeker, Senusi, Shaiva, Shiite, Tunker, Wahabi, Yezidi, Zabian, zealot **07** Adamite, Alawite, Baptist, bigoted, Cainite, Dunkard, extreme, fanatic, hillmen, insular, Ismaili, Karaite, limited, Senussi, Tsabian, Wahabee, Wahhabi, Yezidee, Zezidee **08** Calixtin, cliquish, Darbyite, dogmatic, Donatist, Dukhobor, Familist, hillfolk, Mandaean, Maronite, Mendaite, partisan, Pharisee, Senoussi, Stundist **09** Calixtine, dogmatist, Doukhobor, Encratite, exclusive, extremist, factional, fanatical, Harmonist, Harmonite, Hesychast, hidebound, Israelite, Mennonite, Nasoraean, parochial, Paulician **10** anabaptist, Holy Roller, Karmathian, prejudiced, separatist **11** abecedarian, Albigensian, Black Muslim, Campbellite, doctrinaire, Hare Krishna, Lubavitcher, Plymouthist, Plymouthite, Sandemanian **12** denomination, Muggletonian, narrow-minded **13** convulsionary, fractionalist, Hemerobaptist, Perfectionist, Philadelphian, Schwenkfelder **14** denominational, Schwenkfeldian **15** Christadelphian, Plymouth Brother

section
01 s **03** bit **04** area, part, sect, unit, wing, zone **05** conic, piece, share, slice **06** branch, region, sector **07** article, chapter, passage, portion, segment **08** campfire, district, division, fraction, fragment **09** Caesarean, Caesarian, component, induction, paragraph **10** department, instalment **11** subdivision
• **all sections**
02 AS

sectional
05 class, local **06** racial **07** divided, partial **08** regional, separate **09** exclusive, factional, localized, sectarian **10** individual, separatist

sector
04 area, gore, part, zone **05** field **06** branch, octant, region **07** quarter, section, sextant **08** category, district, division, precinct, quadrant **11** subdivision

secular
03 lay **05** civil, state **06** age-old, layman **07** agelong, earthly, profane, worldly **08** temporal **12** non-religious, non-spiritual

secure
◇ *containment indicator*
03 bag, bar, fix, get, pin, pot, rug, tie,

win **04** bolt, bond, fast, firm, gain, hunk, land, lash, lock, moor, nail, safe, shut, sure, take, vest **05** chain, close, cover, fixed, guard, happy, quoin, rivet, solid, tie up, tight **06** anchor, assure, attach, closed, come by, defend, ensure, fasten, immune, line up, locked, lock up, obtain, screen, sealed, shield, stable, steady, sturdy, take up **07** acquire, assured, certain, confirm, endorse, padlock, procure, protect, relaxed, settled, sponsor, warrant **08** careless, definite, fastened, make fast, make safe, reliable, shielded, unharmed **09** confident, contented, establish, fortified, get hold of, guarantee, immovable, protected, reassured, safeguard, sheltered, steadfast, undamaged **10** batten down, conclusive, dependable, home and dry, strengthen, underwrite **11** comfortable, established, impregnable, make certain, self-assured, well-founded **13** make certain of, out of harm's way, self-confident

securely
06 firmly, safely, stably **07** tightly **08** robustly, steadily, strongly, sturdily **09** immovably **11** impregnably, out of danger, steadfastly

security
03 wad, wed **04** care, ease, gage, gilt, lock **05** cover **06** anchor, asylum, pledge, refuge, safety, surety **07** caution, custody, defence **08** guaranty, immunity, warranty **09** assurance, certainty, guarantee, insurance, safeguard, sanctuary **10** collateral, confidence, conviction, precaution, protection, safeguards **11** peace of mind, precautions, safe-keeping **12** carelessness, positiveness, preservation, surveillance **14** over-confidence **15** invulnerability

sedan
05 chair **06** jampan, litter **09** palanquin

sedate
03 sad **04** calm, cool, dull **05** douce, grave, noble, quiet, relax, sober, staid, stiff **06** demure, pacify, proper, seemly, serene, solemn, soothe, worthy **07** earnest, serious **08** calm down, composed, decorous, tranquil **09** collected, dignified, unruffled **10** deliberate, slow-moving, unexciting **11** quieten down, unflappable **12** tranquillize **13** imperturbable

sedately
05 nobly **06** calmly **07** quietly, soberly **08** demurely, serenely, worthily **09** earnestly, seriously **10** decorously **11** with dignity **12** deliberately **13** imperturbably

sedative
06 downer, opiate **07** anodyne, calming **08** lenitive, narcotic, quietive, relaxing, soothing **09** calmative, composing, soporific **10** depressant **11** barbiturate **12** sleeping-pill **13** tranquillizer **14** tranquillizing

06 Amytal®, Ativan®, Valium® **07** codeine, Librium®, lupulin **08** diazepam, Nembutal®, Rohypnol®, tetronal, thridace **09** barbitone, clozapine, lorazepam, Temazepam **10** clonazepam **11** amobarbital, deserpidine, laurel-water, scopalamine, thalidomide **12** meprobramate, methaqualone, promethazine **14** chloral hydrate, cyclobarbitone, pentobarbitone, phenobarbitone

sedentary
05 still **06** seated **07** sessile, sitting **08** immobile, inactive, unmoving **09** desk-bound **10** stationary

sedge

Sedges include:
04 star **05** Carex, chufa, starr **07** bulrush, papyrus **08** clubrush, sawgrass, tiger nut **09** deergrass **13** umbrella plant, water chestnut

sediment
03 lee **04** lees, silt, warp **05** crust, dregs, feces, grout, varve **06** bottom, faeces, fecula **07** bottoms, deposit, grounds, residue **08** residuum **09** turbidite **10** deposition, hypostasis **11** precipitate **13** coffee grounds

sedition
06 mutiny, revolt **07** treason **09** agitation, rebellion, treachery **10** disloyalty, subversion **11** fomentation **12** insurrection **13** rabble-rousing **15** insubordination

seditious
08 disloyal, factious, inciting, mutinous **09** agitating, dissident, fomenting **10** rebellious, refractory, subversive, traitorous **13** insubordinate, rabble-rousing, revolutionary **15** insurrectionist

seduce
◇ *insertion indicator*
04 jape, lure, pull, ruin, undo, vamp **05** charm, tempt, wrong **06** allure, betray, chat up, entice **07** attract, beguile, corrupt, debauch, deceive, deprave, ensnare, mislead **08** bejesuit, dishonor, inveigle **09** dishonour **10** get into bed, lead astray **12** make a play for **15** take advantage of

seducer
04 goat, rake, wolf **05** flirt, Romeo **06** undoer **07** charmer, Don Juan **08** betrayer, Casanova, deceiver, lady's man, Lothario **09** ladies' man, libertine, womanizer **11** philanderer

seduction
04 lure, ruin **05** charm **06** allure, appeal, come-on **09** deception **10** allurement, attraction, corruption,

enticement, misleading, temptation
11 beguilement

seductive
04 sexy **06** honied, luring, sultry
07 honeyed **08** alluring, arousing,
charming, enticing, inviting, tempting
09 appealing, beguiling, deceiving
10 attractive, bewitching, come-
hither, misleading **11** captivating,
flirtatious, provocative, tantalizing,
temptatious **12** honey-tongued,
irresistible

seductress
04 vamp **05** Circe, siren **07** Delilah,
Lorelei **09** temptress **11** femme fatale

sedulous
04 busy **08** constant, diligent,
resolved, tireless, untiring
09 assiduous, laborious
10 determined, persistent, unflagging
11 industrious, painstaking,
persevering, unremitting
13 conscientious

see
01 C, v **02** la, lo **03** ask, Ely, get **04** date,
deek, deem, ecce, espy, know, lead,
look, mark, meet, note, seat, show,
spot, take, vide, view **05** court, get it,
grasp, judge, learn, sight, think, usher,
visit, voilà, watch **06** behold, decide,
escort, fathom, follow, go with, look at,
notice, regard, take in **07** consult,
diocese, discern, find out, foresee,
glimpse, imagine, inquire, make out,
observe, picture, predict, realize,
reflect, run into, speak to, take out,
witness **08** bump into, consider,
discover, envisage, forecast, identify,
perceive **09** accompany, apprehend,
ascertain, determine, encounter, go
out with, interview, latch onto, lay eyes
on, recognize, set eyes on, visualize
10 anticipate, appreciate, chance
upon, clap eyes on, come across,
comprehend, confer with, cotton onto,
experience, get a look at, understand
11 distinguish **12** investigate **13** catch
sight of **15** keep company with
See also **diocese**
• **see about**
02 do **03** fix **06** manage, repair
07 arrange, sort out **08** attend to,
consider, deal with, organize **09** look
after **10** take care of
• **see around**
◇ *containment indicator*
• **see through**
06 fathom, hang in, rumble **07** persist,
realize, support, sustain **08** continue,
stick out **09** encourage, get wise to,
keep going, not give up, penetrate,
persevere **10** get through, understand
14 not be taken in by **15** not be
deceived by
• **see to**
02 do **03** fix **04** mind **06** ensure,
manage, repair **07** arrange, sort out
08 attend to, deal with, make sure,
organize **09** look after **10** take care of
11 make certain

seed
03 egg, nut, pea, pip, pit, sow, urd
04 bean, corn, dust, germ, moit, mote,
ovum, race, root **05** argan, carvy,
cause, child, grain, heirs, lupin, ovule,
piñon, semen, spawn, sperm, start,
stone, young **06** bonduc, embryo,
family, kernel, lentil, lupine, origin,
powder, reason, source **07** genesis,
nucleus, reasons **08** chickpea,
children, peaberry, sprinkle, young one
09 beginning, fruit body, jequirity,
offspring, sword-bean, young ones
10 successors **11** descendants
12 fruiting body, spermatozoon
13 jequirity bean, water chestnut
• **go to seed, run to seed**
04 bolt **05** decay **07** decline, go to pot
08 get worse, go to hell **10** degenerate,
go downhill **11** deteriorate, go to the
dogs **14** go down the tubes
• **seed covering**
03 bur, ear **04** aril, burr, husk

seediness
05 decay, scuzz **09** dirtiness
10 shabbiness, untidiness
11 squalidness **12** dilapidation

seedy
◇ *anagram indicator*
03 ill **04** sick **05** dirty, mangy, ribby,
rough, tatty **06** ailing, chippy, crummy,
groggy, grotty, mangey, maungy,
poorly, shabby, sleazy, untidy, unwell
07 run-down, scruffy, squalid
08 decaying **09** off-colour **10** out of
sorts **11** dilapidated **15** under the
weather

seek
03 aim, ask, beg, try **04** cast, hunt,
want **05** chase, court **06** aspire, desire,
follow, gun for, invite, lay out, pursue,
resort, search, strive **07** attempt,
enquire, entreat, examine, hunt for,
inquire, look for, mole out, request,
solicit **08** petition, prospect
09 endeavour, look after, search for, try
to find

seeker
05 chela, hound **06** novice **07** student,
zetetic **08** disciple, enquirer, inquirer,
searcher

seem
04 feel, look **05** befit, sound
06 appear, semble **08** look like
11 pretend to be, show signs of, strike
you as **12** come across as **13** have the
look of

seeming
05 quasi- **06** pseudo **07** assumed,
outward, surface **08** apparent,
external, semblant, specious,
supposed **09** pretended **10** ostensible,
semblative **11** superficial

seemingly
09 allegedly, outwardly **10** apparently,
ostensibly **12** on the surface **13** on the
face of it, superficially

seemly
03 fit **04** meet, nice **06** comely,

decent, honest, proper, suited
07 fitting **08** becoming, decorous,
handsome, maidenly, suitable
09 befitting **10** attractive
11 appropriate, comme il faut,
respectable

seep
04 drip, leak, oose, ooze, sipe, soak,
sype, well **05** drain, exude **07** dribble,
trickle **08** permeate **09** percolate

seepage
04 leak **06** oozing **07** leakage, osmosis
08 dripping **09** exudation
11 percolation

seer
04 seir **05** augur, sibyl **07** prophet,
seeress, spaeman, wise man
08 spaewife **10** prophetess,
soothsayer

seesaw
04 yo-yo **05** pitch, swing **06** teeter
08 wild mare **09** alternate, fluctuate,
oscillate

seethe
◇ *anagram indicator*
04 boil, fizz, foam, fume, rage, rise,
teem **05** froth, go ape, storm, surge,
swarm, swell **06** blow up, bubble,
buller, see red, simmer **07** be angry, be
livid, explode, ferment **08** boil over,
smoulder **09** be furious, blow a fuse
10 be incensed, be outraged,
effervesce **11** blow a gasket, go ballistic
12 blow your cool, lose your cool
14 foam at the mouth **15** fly off the
handle, go off the deep end

see-through
05 filmy, gauzy, sheer **06** flimsy
08 gossamer **09** gossamery
11 translucent, transparent

segment
03 bit, pig **04** exon, link, lith, part, ring
05 cut up, femur, halve, joint, piece,
slice, split, urite, wedge **06** divide,
scliff, skliff, somite, telson **07** article,
isomere, overlay, portion, section,
uromere **08** division, metamere,
separate **09** anatomize, propodeon,
prothorax, sternebra **10** arthromere,
metathorax, proglottid, proglottis,
trochanter **11** compartment
12 articulation

segregate
06 cut off **07** exclude, isolate, seclude
08 separate, set apart **09** keep apart,
ostracize, sequester **10** dissociate,
quarantine

segregation
09 apartheid, isolation **10** quarantine,
separation **12** dissociation, setting
apart **13** sequestration
14 discrimination

seize
◇ *containment indicator*
03 bag, cly, nab, nap **04** bone, grab,
grip, hend, hold, nail, snap, take
05 annex, catch, ceaze, cleek, grasp,
latch, reach, sease, seaze, seise, usurp

06 abduct, areach, arrest, attach, attain, clutch, collar, graple, hijack, kidnap, nobble, ravish, snatch, tackle **07** capture, forhent, grapple, impound, possess, prehend **08** forehent **09** apprehend, deprehend, get hold of, lay hold of, lay hold on, penetrate **10** commandeer, confiscate, grab hold of, lay hands on, take hold of **11** appropriate, catch hold of, requisition, sequestrate
• **seize on**
04 grab **07** exploit **08** fasten on **12** grasp eagerly
• **seize up**
03 jam **04** stop **06** go phut, pack up **07** conk out **09** break down **11** malfunction, stop working

seizure
03 fit **04** grab, rape **05** catch, prise, prize, spasm **06** arrest, attack, extent, hijack, rapine, taking **07** capture, seysure **08** paroxysm, purchase, reprisal, wingding **09** abduction, distraint, snatching **10** annexation, attachment, convulsion, pre-emption **12** apprehension, confiscation **13** appropriation, commandeering, sequestration

seldom
04 rare **06** rarely **07** unoften **10** hardly ever, infrequent **12** infrequently, occasionally, scarcely ever **15** once in a blue moon

select
03 top **04** best, cull, pick, posh, sort **05** elect, élite, prime **06** choice, choose, favour, finest, invite, opt for, prefer **07** appoint, extract, limited, special, supreme **08** decide on, selected, settle on, superior **09** excellent, exclusive, first-rate, single out **10** cherry-pick, first-class, hand-picked, privileged **11** high-quality **12** make choice of

selection
04 blad, pick **05** blaud, range **06** choice, dim sum, line-up, medley, option **07** Auslese, palette, variety **09** anthology, cold table, potpourri **10** assortment, collection, miscellany, preference **11** smörgåsbord

selective
05 fussy, picky **06** choosy **07** careful, finicky **10** discerning, fastidious, particular, pernickety **11** persnickety **14** discriminating

selectively
08 by choice **09** carefully **12** discerningly, particularly **14** differentially, preferentially

Selene
04 Luna

selenium
02 Se

self
01 I **03** ego, own, sel **04** same, sell, soul, very **05** atman, seity **06** person

08 identity **09** identical, number one, the real me **10** inner being, yours truly **11** body and soul, personality **13** heart of hearts

self-assembly
03 DIY **07** kit-form **08** flat-pack **13** prefabricated

self-assertive
05 bossy, perky, pushy **07** pushing **08** forceful, immodest **10** aggressive, commanding, high-handed, peremptory **11** dictatorial, domineering, heavy-handed, overbearing, overweening **13** authoritarian

self-assurance
06 aplomb **09** assurance, cockiness **10** confidence **11** assuredness **12** cocksureness, positiveness **14** overconfidence, self-confidence, self-possession

self-assured
05 cocky **07** assured **08** cocksure **09** confident **13** overconfident, self-collected, self-confident, self-possessed **14** sure of yourself

self-centred
07 selfish **09** egotistic **10** egocentric **11** egotistical, self-seeking, self-serving **12** narcissistic, self-absorbed **14** self-interested

self-confidence
03 ego **05** poise **06** aplomb **07** opinion **09** assurance, composure **10** confidence **12** positiveness, self-reliance **13** self-assurance

self-confident
04 bold, cool **07** assured **08** cocksure, composed, fearless, positive **09** confident, unabashed **11** self-assured, self-reliant **13** self-possessed

self-conscious
03 coy, shy **05** timid **07** awkward, bashful, nervous **08** blushing, insecure, retiring, sheepish, timorous **09** diffident, ill at ease, shrinking **10** shamefaced **11** embarrassed **12** self-effacing **13** uncomfortable

self-contained
02 s/c **05** quiet **07** private **08** discrete, reserved, separate **09** secretive **11** independent, self-reliant **12** free-standing **14** self-sufficient

self-control
04 cool **06** temper **07** dignity, encraty **08** calmness, patience **09** composure, restraint, willpower **10** self-denial, temperance **11** self-mastery **13** self-restraint **14** self-discipline
• **lose self-control**
04 flip, snap **05** break

self-defence *see* **martial art**

self-denial
10 asceticism, moderation, temperance **12** selflessness **13** self-sacrifice, unselfishness **14** abstemiousness, self-abnegation

self-discipline
07 resolve **09** willpower **11** persistence, self-control, self-mastery **13** determination

self-employed
06 casual **08** part-time **09** freelance, temporary **10** consultant, out-of-house **11** independent

self-esteem
03 ego **05** pride **07** conceit, dignity **09** self-image, self-pride **10** self-regard **11** amour-propre, self-respect **13** self-assurance **14** self-confidence

self-evident
05 clear, plain **07** obvious **08** manifest **09** axiomatic **10** undeniable **11** inescapable **14** unquestionable

self-explanatory
05 clear, plain **07** obvious **10** accessible, easy-to-read **11** self-evident **12** approachable, easy-to-follow, intelligible **14** comprehensible, understandable

self-glorification
07 egotism **09** egotheism **14** self-admiration, self-exaltation

self-governing
04 free **09** autonomic, sovereign **10** autonomous **11** independent **15** self-determining

self-government
06 swaraj **08** autarchy, autonomy, home rule **09** democracy **11** sovereignty **12** independence **15** self-sovereignty

self-importance
04 pomp **06** vanity **07** conceit, donnism **09** arrogance, cockiness, pomposity, pushiness **10** pretension **11** pompousness, self-opinion **13** bigheadedness, bumptiousness, conceitedness **15** self-consequence

self-important
04 coxy, vain **05** cocky, proud, pushy **06** chesty, cocksy **07** pompous **08** arrogant, egoistic **09** bigheaded, bumptious, conceited, egotistic, strutting **10** portentous, swaggering **11** egotistical, overbearing, pragmatical, pretentious, swell-headed **13** consequential, swollen-headed **14** self-consequent

self-indulgence
06 excess **08** hedonism **10** high living, profligacy, sensualism **11** dissipation **12** extravagance, intemperance **13** dissoluteness

self-indulgent
06 wanton **09** dissolute **10** dissipated, hedonistic, immoderate, profligate **11** extravagant, intemperate **15** pleasure-seeking

self-interest
04 self **08** self-love **10** expediency, self-regard **11** selfishness, self-serving

selfish
04 mean 06 greedy 07 miserly
08 covetous 09 egotistic, mercenary
10 egocentric 11 calculating, egotistical,
self-centred, self-seeking, self-serving
13 inconsiderate 14 self-interested

selfishly
08 greedily 12 ungenerously
13 egotistically 14 egocentrically
15 inconsiderately, only for yourself

selfishness
05 greed 06 egoism 07 egotism
08 meanness, self-love 10 self-regard
11 self-seeking, self-serving 12 self-
interest 15 self-centredness

selfless
08 generous 09 unselfish 10 altruistic
11 magnanimous, self-denying
13 philanthropic 15 self-sacrificing

selflessness
08 altruism 10 generosity, self-denial
11 magnanimity 12 philanthropy
13 self-sacrifice, unselfishness

self-possessed
04 calm, cool 06 poised 07 assured
08 composed, together 09 collected,
confident, unruffled 11 self-assured,
unflappable 13 self-collected

self-possession
04 cool, head 05 nerve, poise
06 aplomb 08 calmness, coolness
09 assurance, composure, sangfroid
10 confidence 11 self-command
13 collectedness, self-assurance
14 self-confidence, unflappability

self-reliance
07 autarky 11 self-support
12 independence 14 self-sustenance
15 self-sufficiency, self-sustainment

self-reliant
08 autarkic 10 autarkical
11 independent 14 self-sufficient, self-
supporting, self-sustaining

self-respect
05 pride 07 dignity 10 self-esteem,
self-regard 11 amour-propre 13 self-
assurance 14 self-confidence

self-restraint
07 encraty 08 patience 09 willpower
10 continence, continency,
moderation, self-denial, temperance
11 forbearance, self-command, self-
control 14 abstemiousness, self-
discipline, self-government

self-righteous
02 pi 04 smug 05 pious 08 priggish,
superior 09 pietistic 10 complacent,
goody-goody, moralistic 11 pharisaical
12 hypocritical 13 sanctimonious
14 holier-than-thou

self-righteousness
09 goodiness, piousness 10 pharisaism
12 priggishness 14 goody-goodiness
15 pharisaicalness

self-sacrifice
08 altruism 10 generosity, self-denial

12 selflessness 13 unselfishness
14 self-abnegation

self-satisfaction
05 pride 08 smugness
11 complacency, contentment 12 self-
approval 15 self-approbation

self-satisfied
04 smug 05 proud 08 puffed up
10 complacent 13 self-righteous

self-seeking
07 selfish 09 careerist, mercenary, on
the make 10 self-loving 11 acquisitive,
calculating, gold-digging, self-serving
12 self-endeared 13 opportunistic
14 fortune-hunting, self-interested

self-styled
07 would-be 08 so-called
09 pretended, professed, soi-disant
10 self-titled 13 self-appointed

self-sufficient
11 independent, self-reliant 13 self-
contained 14 self-supporting, self-
sustaining

self-supporting
11 independent, self-reliant 13 self-
financing 14 self-sufficient, self-
sustaining

self-willed
05 elvan, elven 06 cussed, elfish,
elvish, wilful 07 froward, willful
08 perverse, stubborn 09 obstinate,
pig-headed 10 headstrong, refractory
11 intractable, opinionated, stiff-
necked 12 bloody-minded,
ungovernable 15 self-opinionated

sell
04 flog, hawk, hype, mart, push, seat,
self, tout, vend, vent 05 carry, cry up,
go for, selle, shift, stock, trade, trick
06 barter, betray, deal in, export,
handle, import, market, peddle, praise,
retail, saddle, smouch 07 auction,
chaffer, let-down, promote, trade in,
win over 08 exchange, persuade,
retail at 09 advertise, deception,
dispose of, traffic in 10 be priced at,
bring round 11 merchandize 13 get
support for 14 disappointment, get
approval for
• **sell out**
04 fail 05 rat on 06 betray, fink on
07 stool on 08 run out of 11 be
exhausted, double-cross 12 be out of
stock, have none left 13 stab in the
back

seller
06 trader, vendor 08 huckster,
merchant, stockist, supplier
• **seller's opinion**
02 so

selling
07 dealing, trading, traffic, vending
09 marketing, promotion, vendition
11 trafficking 12 salesmanship,
transactions 13 merchandizing

selvage
04 list, roon, rund 05 royne

semblance
03 air 04 copy, garb, idol, life, look,
mask, show, sign 05 front, ghost, guise,
image 06 aspect, façade, veneer
07 seeming 08 likeness, pretence,
pretense 10 apparition, appearance,
likelihood, similarity, similitude,
simulacrum 11 resemblance

semen
03 cum 04 come, gism, jism, jizz, seed
05 sperm, spoof, spunk 06 jissom
09 ejaculate 12 seminal fluid

semi-liquid
04 slab 05 slimy 06 blashy, globby

seminal
05 major 08 creative, germinal,
original, seminary 09 formative,
important 10 generative, innovative,
productive 11 imaginative, influential,
rudimentary

seminar
05 class, forum 07 lecture, meeting,
session 08 colloquy, tutorial,
workshop 09 symposium
10 colloquium, conference,
convention, discussion, study group

seminary
03 Sem 06 school 07 academy,
college, nursery, yeshiva 08 yeshivah
09 institute 10 theologate 11 institution
15 training college

send
04 beam, cast, emit, fire, hurl, mail,
make, move, post, turn 05 drive, fling,
grant, radio, relay, remit, shoot, swash,
throw 06 arouse, commit, convey,
direct, excite, get off, launch, propel,
thrill, turn on 07 address, consign,
deliver, forward, project 08 despatch,
dispatch, redirect, televise, transmit
09 broadcast, cause to be, discharge,
give a buzz, give a kick, messenger,
stimulate 11 communicate 12 put in the
mail, put in the post 14 give pleasure to
• **send away**
04 hunt, pack, void 05 drive
07 dismiss, pack off 08 despatch,
dispatch
• **send for**
05 get in, order 06 summon 07 call for,
command, request
• **send forth**
04 beam, pour 05 fling, shoot, speed
08 expedite 09 discharge
• **send off**
04 ship 06 let fly, set off 08 despatch,
dispatch, order off 12 order to leave
• **send up**
◇ *reversal down indicator*
04 mock 05 mimic 06 parody
07 imitate, take off 08 ridicule, satirize

send-off
05 start 07 goodbye, push-off
08 farewell 09 departure 11 leave-
taking

send-up
04 skit 05 spoof 06 parody, satire
07 mockery, take-off 09 burlesque,
imitation 10 mickey-take

Senegal
02 SN **03** SEN

senile
03 old **04** aged, gaga **06** doited, doitit
07 failing **08** confused, decrepit
09 doddering, senescent

senility
03 eld **04** eild **06** dotage, old age
07 anility, paracme **08** caducity
09 infirmity **10** senescence
11 decrepitude **14** senile dementia
15 second childhood

senior
02 Sr **03** Sen, Snr **04** âiné, sire
05 âinée, chief, doyen, elder, first,
major, older **06** higher **07** ancient,
doyenne **08** superior **11** high-ranking
• **senior citizen**
03 OAP **09** pensioner **10** golden ager
12 coffin-dodger **13** retired person
15 old-age pensioner

seniority
03 age **04** rank **06** status **08** priority,
standing **09** ancientry, antiquity,
signeurie **10** importance, precedence
11 superiority

sensation
03 hit, wow **04** aura, itch, stir **05** sense,
vibes **06** furore, pit-pat, splash, thrill,
tingle, winner **07** emotion, feeling,
outrage, pitapat, prickle, scandal,
success, symptom, triumph
08 goneness, pitty-pat **09** agitation,
awareness, commotion
10 Empfindung, excitement,
impression, perception
13 consciousness

sensational
04 gamy, pulp **05** gamey, juicy, lurid,
shock **06** superb, yellow **07** amazing
08 dramatic, drop-dead, exciting,
fabulous, galvanic, gorgeous,
shocking, smashing, stirring, terrific
09 excellent, fantastic, revealing,
startling, thrilling, wonderful
10 astounding, horrifying, impressive,
incredible, marvellous, scandalous,
staggering **11** exceptional, spectacular
12 breathtaking, electrifying,
melodramatic **15** blood-and-thunder

sense
03 wit **04** feel, gist, mind, nous, wits
05 brain, drift, grasp, logic, point,
savvy, tenor **06** brains, detect, divine,
import, intuit, notice, nuance, pick up,
reason, wisdom **07** ability, discern,
faculty, feeling, meaning, observe,
opinion, purport, purpose, realize,
suspect **08** gumption, judgment,
perceive, prudence **09** awareness, be
aware of, direction, intuition,
judgement, recognize, sensation,
substance **10** appreciate, cleverness,
comprehend, definition, denotation,
experience, impression, perception,
understand **11** common sense,
discernment, implication, sensibility
12 appreciation, apprehension,
intelligence, significance **13** be

conscious of, comprehension,
consciousness, judiciousness,
understanding **14** interpretation,
reasonableness
• **in this sense**
02 hs **08** hoc sensu
• **make sense of**
05 grasp **06** fathom **07** make out
09 figure out **10** comprehend, make
much of, understand

senseless
03 mad, out **04** daft, numb, surd
05 batty, crazy, dotty, inane, silly
06 absurd, futile, insane, stupid, unwise
07 fatuous, foolish, idiotic, moronic,
out cold, stunned **08** deadened,
mindless **09** illogical, insensate,
ludicrous, pointless, unfeeling
10 insensible, irrational, ridiculous
11 meaningless, nonsensical,
purposeless, unconscious
12 unreasonable **13** anaesthetized,
load of rubbish **14** load of nonsense

sense-organ
03 ear, eye **04** nose, palp **06** tongue
09 sensillum **15** mechanoreceptor

sensibility
05 taste **07** feeling, insight **08** delicacy,
emotions, feelings **09** awareness,
intuition, sentiment **10** sentiments
11 discernment, sensitivity
12 appreciation **13** sensitiveness,
sensitivities **14** perceptiveness,
responsiveness, sentimentality,
susceptibility

sensible
04 sane, wise **05** aware, sharp, sober,
solid, sound, tough, witty **06** clever,
mature, shrewd, strong **07** evident,
logical, prudent, working **08** everyday,
ordinary, rational, wise-like
09 judicious, practical, realistic,
sagacious, sensitive, wholesome
10 discerning, far-sighted, functional,
no-nonsense, perceptive, reasonable,
responsive, vulnerable **11** appreciable,
clear-headed, commonsense, down-
to-earth, hard-wearing, intelligent,
level-headed, perceptible,
serviceable, susceptible, well-advised
14 commonsensical
• **sensible of**
07 alive to, aware of **09** mindful of
11 cognizant of, conscious of,
convinced of, observant of, sensitive to
13 understanding **14** acquainted with

sensibly
06 wisely **07** handily **08** cleverly,
shrewdly, strongly, suitably, usefully
09 logically, prudently **10** rationally,
reasonably **11** judiciously, practically,
sagaciously, serviceably
12 functionally **13** realistically

sensitive
04 fine, soft **05** aware, exact, quick
06 kittly, tender, touchy, tricky
07 awkward, brittle, careful, fragile,
precise, tactful **08** delicate, discreet,
reactive, sentient **09** cold-short,
difficult, emotional, irritable

10 diplomatic, discerning, perceptive,
responsive, sensitized, vulnerable
11 considerate, problematic,
susceptible, sympathetic, thin-skinned
12 appreciative, highly strung
13 controversial, hyperesthetic,
temperamental **14** hyperaesthesic,
hyperaesthetic, impressionable, well-
thought-out

sensitivity
07 algesia **08** delicacy, esthesia,
fineness, softness, sympathy
09 aesthesia, aesthesis, awareness,
fragility **11** discernment
12 appreciation, radiesthesia,
reactiveness **13** receptiveness,
vulnerability **14** perceptiveness,
responsiveness, susceptibility

sensual
04 lewd, sexy **05** brute, gross, horny,
randy **06** animal, bodily, brutal, carnal,
erotic, sexual, sultry **07** fleshly, lustful,
swinish, worldly **08** embodied,
physical **09** lecherous, pandemian
10 licentious, voluptary, voluptuous
12 encarnalized **13** self-indulgent

sensuality
08 lewdness, pleasure, sexiness
09 animalism, carnality, eroticism,
prurience **10** debauchery, profligacy
11 gourmandize, libertinism,
lustfulness **13** lecherousness,
salaciousness **14** lasciviousness,
licentiousness, voluptuousness

sensuous
04 lush, rich **08** pleasant, pleasing
09 aesthetic, luxurious, sumptuous
10 gratifying, voluptuous
11 pleasurable

sensuously
06 lushly, richly **11** luxuriously,
pleasurably, sumptuously
12 gratifyingly, voluptuously

sentence
03 swy **04** bird, doom, time **05** curse,
judge, lifer, maxim, order **06** decree,
period, punish, ruling **07** condemn,
opinion, verdict **08** aphorism,
decision, judgment, penalize, porridge
09 judgement **10** adjudgment,
punishment **11** adjudgement
12 condemnation **13** pronouncement
15 condemnation on

sententious
05 brief, pithy, short, terse **06** gnomic
07 canting, compact, concise, laconic,
pointed, pompous, preachy
08 succinct **09** axiomatic
10 aphoristic, moralistic, moralizing
11 judgemental **12** epigrammatic
13 sanctimonious

sentient
04 live **05** aware **06** living **07** feeling,
sensile **08** reactive **09** conscious,
sensitive **10** responsive

sentiment
04 idea, posy, view **05** maxim, slops
06 belief, hobnob, pledge **07** emotion,

feeling, opinion, romance, thought
08 attitude, judgment, softness
09 judgement **10** persuasion,
tenderness **11** mawkishness, point of
view, romanticism, sensibility
14 sentimentality **15** soft-heartedness

sentimental
05 corny, gooey, gucky, gushy, hokey,
mushy, soppy, weepy, yucky, yukky
06 gloopy, loving, sickly, sloppy, slushy,
sugary, tender, too-too **07** boy-girl,
gushing, maudlin, mawkish, missish,
treacly **08** cornball, pathetic, romantic,
rose-pink, shmaltzy, touching
09 emotional, nostalgic, rosewater,
schmaltzy **10** lovey-dovey, Wertherian
11 soft-hearted, tear-jerking
12 affectionate, chocolate-box
13 lackadaisical

sentimentality
03 goo, yuk **04** gush, mush, pulp, yuck
05 gloop, slush **06** bathos **07** feeling,
shmaltz, treacle **08** schmaltz
09 corniness, nostalgia, sentiment
10 sloppiness, tenderness
11 mawkishness, romanticism,
sensibility **12** emotionalism
14 sentimentalism

sentry
05 guard, watch **06** centry, picket
07 lookout, vedette **08** sentinel,
watchman **09** out-sentry

separable
08 distinct, dividant, dividual, partible
09 different, divisible, removable
10 detachable, particular
11 independent **15** distinguishable

separate
03 red, sep, try **04** comb, part, redd,
shed, sort, twin **05** alone, apart, break,
sever, shear, split, twine **06** cut off,
demark, depart, detach, divide,
reduce, remove, secede, single,
sunder, sundry, winnow **07** break up,
discerp, disjoin, dislink, dispart,
diverge, divided, divorce, isolate,
seclude, several, sort out, split up
08 abstract, break off, detached,
discreet, discrete, disperse, dissever,
distinct, distract, disunite, divorced,
isolated, offprint, prescind, set apart,
solitary, uncouple, withdraw **09** come
apart, demarcate, different, disengage,
dismantle, disparate, disunited,
intervene, keep apart, partition,
segregate, single out, take apart,
uncombine, unrelated
10 autonomous, disconnect,
disjointed, dissociate, individual,
particular, segregated, unattached
11 disentangle, independent, part
company, unconnected **12** disaffiliate,
disconnected **15** become estranged

separated
05 apart **06** parted, remote
07 divided, split up **08** isolated,
separate, sundered **09** disunited
10 dissociate, poles apart, segregated
12 disconnected, poles asunder
13 disassociated, discontinuous

separately
05 alone, apart **06** singly **07** asunder,
divisim **08** one by one **09** in several,
severally **10** absolutely, discretely,
personally **12** individually
13 independently **14** discriminately

separating
07 parting, sifting **08** abducent,
dividing, divisive **09** isolating,
precisive **10** discretive **11** intervening,
segregating **12** partitioning
13 disengagement

separation
03 gap **04** gulf, rift **05** split **06** schism,
wrench **07** break-up, divorce,
freedom, parting, split-up **08** avulsion,
dialysis, disunion, dividing, division,
farewell, interval, solution
09 apartheid, isolation, severance
10 detachment, divergence,
uncoupling **11** demarcation,
demarkation, disjunction, distinction,
leave-taking, segregation
12 disgregation, disseverment,
dissociation, estrangement
13 disconnection, disengagement
14 centrifugation

separatist
05 rebel **08** apostate, renegade,
seceding **09** breakaway, dissenter,
heretical **10** dissenting, schismatic
11 Independent **12** secessionist

separatists
03 ETA

September
03 Sep **04** Sept

septic
06 putrid **08** infected, poisoned
09 festering **10** putrefying
11 suppurating **12** putrefactive

sepulchral
03 sad **04** deep **05** grave **06** dismal,
gloomy, hollow, morbid, solemn,
sombre, woeful **07** charnel
08 funereal, mournful **09** cheerless
10 lugubrious, melancholy
11 sepulchrous

sepulchre
04 tomb **05** grave, vault **06** burial,
entomb **09** mausoleum **10** repository
11 burial place

sequel
03 end **05** issue, suite **06** pay-off,
result, upshot **07** outcome **08** follow-
up, sequence **09** after-clap, followers
10 conclusion, successors
11 consequence, development
12 consequences, continuation

sequence
03 run, set **04** line, suit **05** chain, cycle,
order, track, train **06** course, series,
string **10** procession, succession
11 arrangement, consequence,
progression

sequester
04 take **05** seize **06** detach, remove
07 impound, isolate, seclude, shut off

08 alienate, insulate, set apart, set
aside, shut away **09** seclusion
10 commandeer, confiscate
11 appropriate, sequestrate

sequestered
05 quiet **06** lonely, remote **07** outback,
private, retired **08** isolated, secluded
10 cloistered **11** out-of-the-way
12 unfrequented

sequestrate
04 take **05** seize **07** impound
09 sequester **10** commandeer,
confiscate **11** appropriate

seraphic
04 holy, pure **06** divine, serene
07 angelic, saintly, sublime **08** beatific,
blissful, heavenly, innocent **09** celestial
10 seraphical

Serbia and Montenegro
03 SCG, YUG

serenade
04 wake **07** horning **08** chivaree,
shivaree **09** charivari

serendipitous
05 happy, lucky **06** chance
09 fortunate **10** accidental, fortuitous,
unexpected

serendipity
04 luck **06** chance **07** fortune
08 accident, fortuity **11** coincidence,
good fortune

serene
04 calm, cool **05** clear, quiet, still
06 placid, serein **07** halcyon
08 composed, peaceful, seraphic,
tranquil **09** unclouded, unruffled
10 seraphical, untroubled
11 undisturbed, unflappable
12 tranquillize **13** imperturbable

serenely
06 calmly **07** quietly **08** placidly
10 peacefully, tranquilly
13 imperturbably

serenity
04 calm, cool **05** peace **06** repose
08 calmness, quietude **09** composure,
placidity, quietness, stillness
12 peacefulness, tranquillity
14 unflappability

serf
05 helot, slave, thete, thirl **06** thrall
07 bondman, servant, villein
08 adscript, bondmaid, bondsman
09 bond-slave, bondwoman
10 bondswoman **11** bondservant

sergeant
02 PS **03** NCO, Sgt **04** Cuff, Serg, Troy
05 Bilko, chips, sarge, Sergt **06** Buzfuz
08 havildar

series
03 row, run, ser, set **04** line **05** chain,
cycle, early, order, train **06** catena,
course, stream, string **07** library
08 bead-roll, pedigree, sequence
10 succession **11** arrangement,
progression **13** concatenation

- **new series**
02 NS

serious
03 bad, big, sad 04 deep, dour, grim, tidy 05 acute, ample, grave, great, heavy, large, quiet, sober, staid, stern 06 honest, lavish, no joke, severe, solemn, somber, sombre, urgent 07 crucial, earnest, genuine, pensive, sincere, sizable, weighty 08 abundant, critical, generous, grievous, perilous, pressing, sizeable, worrying 09 dangerous, difficult, important, long-faced, momentous, plentiful, unsmiling 10 humourless, precarious, thoughtful, unlaughing 11 far-reaching, preoccupied, significant, substantial 12 considerable, life-and-death 13 consequential, of consequence

seriously
04 very 05 badly, jolly 06 highly, really, sorely 07 acutely, awfully, for real, gravely, greatly, utterly 08 severely, solemnly, terribly 09 au sérieux, decidedly, earnestly, extremely, intensely, sincerely, unusually 10 critically, dreadfully, grievously, remarkably, thoroughly, uncommonly 11 dangerously, exceedingly, excessively, frightfully, joking apart, joking aside 12 immoderately, inordinately, terrifically, thoughtfully, unreasonably 13 distressingly, exceptionally 15 extraordinarily

seriousness
06 moment, weight 07 gravity, urgency 08 gravitas, sobriety 09 solemnity, staidness, sternness 10 importance, sedateness 11 earnestness 12 significance 14 humourlessness

sermon
03 ser 04 talk 06 homily, preach 07 address, karakia, khotbah, khotbeh, khutbah, lecture, message, oration, reproof 08 harangue 09 discourse, talking-to 10 preachment 11 declamation, exhortation

serow
04 thar

serpent
05 lamia, snake 06 ellops 08 basilisk, sea snake 09 ouroboros 10 cockatrice
See also **snake**

serpentine
05 snaky 06 ophite 07 coiling, crooked, sinuous, snaking, winding 08 asbestos, tortuous, twisting 09 ophiolite, snakelike 10 chrysotile, meandering, retinalite 12 serpentiform

serrated
06 jagged, pinked 07 notched, sawlike, toothed 08 indented, saw-edged 09 crenulate 10 crenulated, saw-toothed, serrulated 11 serratulate 12 diprionidian 14 monoprionidian

serried
05 close, dense 06 massed

07 compact, crowded 08 close-set 13 close together

servant
03 boy, man 04 drug, help, jack 06 drudge, helper 07 subject 08 hireling 09 ancillary, assistant, attendant 10 ministrant

Servants include:
03 fag, gip, gyp
04 char, chef, cook, hind, maid, page
05 boots, carer, daily, groom, nanny, slave, valet, wench
06 au pair, barman, batman, butler, chokra, garçon, haiduk, lackey, menial, ostler, skivvy, tweeny, waiter
07 barmaid, bellboy, bellhop, cleaner, equerry, flunkey, footman, gossoon, pageboy, steward, tapsman
08 charlady, coachman, dogsbody, domestic, factotum, handmaid, henchman, home help, house boy, retainer, scullion, servitor, turnspit, waitress, wet nurse
09 chauffeur, errand boy, governess, housemaid, lady's maid, seneschal
10 chauffeuse, handmaiden, henchwoman, manservant, stewardess
11 body servant, boot-catcher, chambermaid, henchperson, housekeeper, kitchen-maid, parlour-maid
12 domestic help, scullery maid
13 care assistant, lady-in-waiting, livery-servant
14 commissionaire

serve
◇ *anagram indicator*
02 do, ka 03 ace, act, aid, kae, let 04 deal, help, sair, wait 05 avail, valet 06 answer, assist, attend, dish up, fulfil, lackey, supply, wait on 07 benefit, deliver, dish out, dole out, further, give out, lacquey, perform, present, provide, satisfy, succour, suffice, support, undergo, work for, work out, worship 08 carry out, complete, function, wait upon 09 be of use to, discharge, go through 10 distribute, minister to, take care of 11 do the work of 12 be employed by 13 be of benefit to, be of service to, do a good turn to

- **serve up**
◇ *reversal down indicator*

service
02 RN 03 ace, fee, job, let, RAF, use 04 army, duty, help, navy, rite, sorb, tune, turn, work 05 check, usage 06 course, duties, forces, go over, labour, repair, ritual 07 amenity, benefit, repairs, utility, worship 08 activity, air force, business, ceremony, disposal, facility, function, maintain, military, overhaul, resource 09 advantage, ordinance, sacrament, servicing 10 assistance, employment, expediting, observance, usefulness 11 maintenance, performance, recondition 12 availability

Religious services include:
04 Mass
06 matins
07 baptism, evening, funeral, morning wedding
08 compline, evensong, High Mass, marriage, memorial
09 communion, Eucharist
10 bar mitzvah, bat mitzvah, dedication
11 christening, Christingle, Lord's Supper, nuptial Mass, remembrance, Requiem Mass
12 confirmation, Midnight Mass, thanksgiving
13 Holy Communion, Holy Matrimony
14 First Communion, morning prayers
15 harvest festival

- **in service**
05 in use 07 working 09 operative 10 functional 11 in operation 12 in regular use 14 in working order
- **of service**
06 useful 07 helpful 09 of benefit 10 beneficial, profitable 12 advantageous
- **on active service**
03 oas
- **out of service**
04 phut 05 kaput 06 broken, faulty, kaputt 08 out of use, packed up 09 conked out, defective 10 not working, on the blink, on the fritz, out of order

serviceable
04 good 05 plain, tough 06 simple, strong, usable, useful 07 durable, helpful 08 availful, sensible 09 effective, efficient, practical, unadorned 10 beneficial, commodious, convenient, dependable, functional, profitable 11 hard-wearing, utilitarian 12 advantageous

serviceman *see* **aircraftsman; sailor; soldier**

servicemen *see* **air force; army; navy**

servile
03 low 04 base, mean 05 lowly, slimy 06 abject, humble, menial, vassal 07 fawning, slavish, subject 08 cringing, toadying, unctuous 09 groveling, controlled, grovelling, obsequious, submissive 11 bootlicking, subservient, sycophantic

servility
05 slime 07 fawning 08 baseness, meanness, toadyism 09 abjection 10 abjectness, grovelling, sycophancy 11 bootlicking, slavishness 12 subservience, unctuousness 13 self-abasement 14 obsequiousness, submissiveness

serving
05 share 06 amount, ration 07 bowlful, helping, portion 08 plateful, spoonful 11 ministering

ervitude
5 bonds 06 chains, thrall 07 bondage,
eonage, peonism, serfdom, slavery
8 thirlage, thraldom 09 obedience,
assalage 10 stillicide, subjection,
illeinage 11 enslavement, subjugation

esame
3 til 04 beni, teel 05 benne, benni
6 semsem 07 gingili, jinjili 08 gingelly

ession
4 bevy, sesh, Sess, term, time, year
5 bevvy, drill, shoot, spell 06 clinic,
rog-on, grog-up, period, séance
7 hearing, meeting, sitting, stretch
8 assembly, semester 09 scrimmage,
alkathon 10 conference, discussion
1 church court, down-sitting
ee also **term**
• **be in session**
3 set, sit
• **close a session**
4 rise

et
◇ anagram indicator
2 TV 03 dip, dot, fix, gel, kit, lay, lot,
it, ply, put 04 band, bulb, cake, club,
lump, firm, gang, give, jell, knit, look,
ame, park, plan, rate, rest, sink, stud,
urn 05 adapt, apply, array, batch, befit,
egin, cause, class, crowd, embed,
ixed, frame, grant, group, jelly, lodge,
nount, pitch, place, plant, plonk, posit,
adio, ready, rigid, scene, score, set up,
tage, stake, start, stick, stock, telly,
isual, value, wings, write 06 adjust,
greed, all set, assign, become,
:hoose, circle, clique, create, decide,
levise, direct, formal, go down,
harden, impose, incite, insert, lead to,
ocate, ordain, outfit, prompt, select,
;eries, set off, set out, settle, strict,
-anish 07 agree on, appoint, arrange,
Dearing, compose, confirm, congeal,
:onsign, coterie, decided, decline,
leposit, dispose, faction, install, lay
Jown, posture, prepare, produce,
Drovide, regular, resolve, routine,
;cenery, setting, settled, sharpen,
;ituate, specify, station, stiffen, subside,
hicken, trigger 08 allocate, arranged,
Dackdrop, category, conclude,
Jelegate, equipped, everyday,
finished, get ready, habitual, occasion,
Drdained, organize, position, prepared,
Dropound, put right, regulate, result in,
;chedule, sequence, solidify, sprinkle,
;tandard 09 appointed, coagulate,
:ompleted, customary, designate,
Jetermine, direction, disappear,
:stablish, harmonize, ingrained, make
ready, organized, prescribe,
;cheduled, specified, stipulate,
-ariegate 10 assemblage, assortment,
Dackground, become firm, become
hard, bring about, collection,
:ompendium, complement, co-
ordinate, deliberate, determined,
:ntrenched, expression, give rise to,
inaugurate, inflexible, prescribed,
television, trigger off 11 crystallize,
:stablished, inclination, intentional,

mise-en-scène, orchestrate,
prearranged, stereotyped,
synchronize, traditional
12 conventional 13 predetermined
14 bring into being
• **set about**
05 begin, frame, start 06 attack, tackle
08 commence, embark on 09 get
down to, undertake
• **set against**
05 weigh 06 assail, divide, oppose
07 balance, compare 08 alienate,
contrast, disunite, estrange
09 juxtapose
• **set apart**
04 seal 06 divide, ordain 07 mark off,
reserve 08 put aside, separate
09 segregate, sequester 11 distinguish,
peculiarize 12 put on one side, put to
one side 13 differentiate, make
different
• **set aside**
04 keep, save 05 allot, annul, break, lay
by, put by 06 cancel, ignore, reject,
repeal, revoke, select 07 discard,
earmark, put away, reserve, reverse
08 abrogate, discount, keep back, lay
aside, mothball, overrule, overturn, put
aside, separate, set apart 09 sequester,
slight off, stash away, supersede 10 give
over to 13 keep in reserve
• **set back**
◇ reversal indicator
04 cost, slow 05 check, delay
06 hinder, hold up, impede, retard,
thwart 07 reverse 08 surprise
• **set down**
03 lay 04 drop, land, note, snub, take
05 judge, pitch, state 06 affirm, assert,
depose, encamp, esteem, record,
regard 07 ascribe, deposit, lay down
08 note down 09 attribute, discharge,
establish, formulate, prescribe, stipulate,
subscribe, write down 12 put in writing
• **set forth**
03 say 04 shew, show 05 leave, state
06 depart, praise, record, set off, set out
07 clarify, declare, display, exhibit,
explain, expound, present, publish
08 describe, start out 09 delineate,
elucidate, explicate, recommend
• **set in**
◇ insertion indicator
04 come 05 begin, inset, start
06 arrive 08 commence
• **set off**
05 begin, leave, light, start 06 blow up,
depart, ignite, prompt, set out
07 commend, display, enhance,
explode, show off, trigger 08 activate,
contrast, detonate, heighten, initiate,
set forth, start out, touch off
09 encourage, intensify 10 trigger off
11 set in motion, take the road
14 counterbalance 15 throw into relief
• **set on**
03 mug, out, sic, tar 04 bent, firm, sick,
sool 05 fixed, go for, tarre 06 attack,
beat up, dogged, intent, strong, turn on
07 assault, dead set, decided, lay into,
set upon 08 fall upon, hell-bent,
resolute, resolved, stubborn

09 insistent, steadfast, tenacious
10 determined, persistent, purposeful,
unwavering 11 persevering,
unflinching 12 single-minded, strong-
minded, strong-willed
14 uncompromising
• **set out**
◇ anagram indicator
03 put 04 boun, laid 05 adorn, begin,
bowne, leave, start 06 depart, lay out,
set off, strike 07 arrange, display,
exhibit, explain, expound, present,
take off 08 describe, start out
• **set up**
◇ reversal down indicator
02 up 03 rig 04 form, rear, trap
05 array, begin, build, erect, fit up,
found, frame, pitch, raise, sport, start
06 create, settle 07 arrange, compose,
dispose, elevate, mounted, prepare
08 assemble, initiate, organize
09 construct, establish, institute,
introduce 10 constitute, inaugurate
11 incriminate 13 accuse falsely
14 bring into being

setback
◇ reversal indicator
04 blip, blow, snag 05 check, delay,
hitch, knock, upset 06 blight, defeat,
hiccup, hold-up, rebuff, whammy
07 problem, relapse, reverse 08 body
blow, hiccough, reversal 09 hindrance,
throwback 10 difficulty, impediment,
misfortune 11 obstruction
14 disappointment, stumbling-block

settee
04 sofa 05 couch, futon, squab
06 canapé, day-bed, lounge
07 bergère, dos-à-dos, sofa bed
09 bed-settee, davenport, tête-à-tête
12 chesterfield

setter
01 I 02 me 03 spy 07 dropper
• **setter's**
04 mine
See also **crossword**

setting
04 site, vail 05 frame, scene 06 chaton,
locale, milieu, period 07 context,
framing, monture, scenery 08 fixation,
location, mounting, position
09 placement 10 background
11 environment, mise-en-scène,
perspective 12 surroundings

setting-up
05 start 08 creation, founding
09 inception 10 foundation, initiation
11 institution 12 inauguration,
introduction 13 establishment

settle
03 fix, pay 04 drop, fall, foot, kill, land,
lite, live, nest, perk, rest, sink, stun
05 agree, bench, clear, fix up, ledge,
light, lodge, lower, order, perch, pitch,
plant, quiet, solve, state 06 accept,
adjust, alight, ante up, choose, clinch,
decide, defray, go down, occupy,
people, repose, reside, square
07 agree on, appoint, arrange,

settlement

compact, compose, confirm, cough up, descend, discuss, dispose, fork out, inhabit, install, patch up, resolve, subside **08** colonize, come down, complete, conclude, decide on, organize, populate, regulate, settle up, square up **09** determine, discharge, establish, light upon, reconcile **10** compromise, put in order **12** make your home, put down roots **13** do the business

• **settle down**
05 still **06** shut in, soothe **07** compose, quieten **08** calm down **09** buy a house, get down to, gravitate **10** get married **12** buckle down to, put down roots, start a family **13** concentrate on, knuckle down to **15** apply yourself to, make comfortable

settlement
◊ *anagram indicator*
02 pa **03** pah, utu **04** camp, fine, post **05** truce **06** bustee, colony, hamlet **07** kibbutz, manyata, outpost, payment, sinking, village **08** clearing, contract, decision, defrayal, manyatta, ordering, presidio **09** agreement, Ausgleich, bandobast, Botany Bay, bundobust, clearance, community, discharge, rancherie **10** completion, conclusion, encampment, occupation, patching up, plantation, population, resolution, subsidence **11** arrangement, down-sitting, liquidation, termination **12** colonization, lake dwelling, organization, satisfaction **13** accommodation, establishment **14** reconciliation

settler
07 bushman, incomer, new chum, pilgrim, pioneer, planter **08** colonist, newcomer, shagroon, squatter **09** colonizer, immigrant, inhabiter, Varangian **10** pure Merino **11** beachcomber, Cromwellian **12** frontiersman **14** frontierswoman

set-to
03 row **04** bout, spat **05** brush, fight, scrap **06** barney, bust-up, dust-up, fracas **07** contest, quarrel, wrangle **08** argument, conflict, exchange, squabble **09** argy-bargy **11** altercation **12** disagreement **13** slanging-match

set-up
◊ *reversal down indicator*
06 format, system **08** business **09** framework, structure **10** conditions **11** arrangement, composition, disposition **12** organization **13** circumstances

seven
01 S **03** VII **06** heptad, Pleiad **08** hebdomad **09** septenary

Seven Against Thebes

The Seven Greek champions who attacked Thebes:

06 Tydeus
08 Adrastus, Capaneus

09 Polynices
10 Amphiaraus, Hippomedon
13 Parthenopaeus

Seven Deadly Sins *see* sin

seven hills of Rome *see* hill

Seven Sisters colleges *see* university

seventeen
04 XVII

seventy
03 LXX

Seven Wonders of the World *see* wonder

sever
03 cut, end, hew, nip **04** chop, hack, part, pith, rend **05** break, cease, split **06** cleave, cut off, detach, divide, lop off, nip off **07** chop off, disjoin, divorce, tear off **08** alienate, amputate, break off, dissever, dissolve, disunite, estrange, separate **09** disbranch, terminate **10** disconnect, dissociate **13** cut the painter

several
04 a few, many, some **06** divers, sundry **07** diverse, various **08** assorted, distinct, separate **09** a number of, different, disparate, quite a few **10** individual, particular

severally
06 apiece, singly **08** seriatim **10** discretely, separately **12** individually, in particular, particularly, respectively, specifically

severe
03 bad, ill **04** cold, dour, grim, hard **05** acute, cruel, eager, grave, harsh, penal, plain, rigid, sharp, snell, sober, stark, stern, tough **06** fierce, modest, morose, shrewd, simple, strict, strong, taxing, trying **07** arduous, ascetic, austere, caustic, drastic, extreme, intense, serious, spartan, violent **08** Catonian, critical, Draconic, exacting, forceful, grievous, grinding, perilous, pitiless, powerful, rigorous, ruthless **09** agonizing, dangerous, demanding, difficult, Draconian, Dracontic, inclement, merciless, punishing, splitting, stringent, swingeing, unadorned, unbending, unsmiling, unsparing **10** astringent, burdensome, forbidding, functional, hard-handed, inexorable, iron-fisted, iron-handed, relentless, tyrannical, unbearable **11** strait-laced, undecorated **12** businesslike, disapproving, excruciating **13** Rhadamanthine, unembellished, unsympathetic

severely
04 hard, sore **05** badly **06** coldly, dourly, grimly, hardly, sorely **07** acutely, gravely, harshly, sharply, sternly **08** bitterly, strictly **09** extremely, intensely **10** critically, rigorously **11** dangerously **14** disapprovingly

severity
05 wrath **06** rigour **07** gravity **08** bareness, coldness, grimness, hardness, strength **09** acuteness, austerity, extremity, harshness, intensity, plainness, sharpness, sternness, toughness **10** asceticism, fierceness, severeness, simplicity, spartanism, strictness, stringency **11** seriousness **12** forcefulness, pitilessness, ruthlessness, ungentleness **13** mercilessness

sew
03 hem, run, sue **04** bind, darn, mend, ooze, seam, tack, whip, work **05** baste, drain **06** needle, stitch **08** overcast, overhand **09** embroider **10** buttonhole, whipstitch **12** saddle-stitch

sewage
04 soil **07** sullage

sewer
04 sure **05** drain, shore, sough **06** cloaca, needle, tailor

sex
01 f, m **04** male **05** union **06** allure, coitus, female, gender, libido **07** coition, glamour **08** congress, embraces, intimacy, sexiness **09** magnetism, sex appeal, sexuality **10** commixtion, copulation, lovemaking, sensuality **11** fornication, intercourse **12** consummation, desirability, reproduction, **13** seductiveness **14** voluptuousness **15** carnal knowledge, sexual relations

sex appeal
02 it, SA **05** oomph

sexless
01 n **06** neuter **07** asexual, unsexed **08** unsexual **10** undersexed, unfeminine **11** unmasculine **15** parthenogenetic

sexton
06 fossor, verger **09** caretaker, sacristan **10** grave-maker **11** grave-digger

sexual
03 sex **05** gamic **06** carnal, coital, erotic **07** genital, raunchy, sensual **08** venereal **11** procreative **12** reproductive

sexuality
04 lust **06** desire **08** sexiness, virility **09** carnality, eroticism **10** sensuality, sexual urge **12** sexual desire **14** voluptuousness **15** sexual instincts

sexy
04 phat **06** erotic, nubile, slinky, steamy **07** raunchy, sensual **08** alluring, arousing, beddable, exciting, inviting, tempting **09** desirable, provoking, salacious, seductive **10** attractive, suggestive, voluptuous **11** fascinating, flirtatious, provocative, stimulating, titillating **12** pornographic

Seychelles
02 SY **03** SYC

shabbily
08 rottenly, unfairly **09** scruffily
10 despicably, shamefully
11 inelegantly **12** contemptibly,
disreputably, unacceptably
13 dishonourably, unfashionably

shabby
03 low **04** mean, poky, worn **05** cheap,
dingy, dirty, dowdy, faded, mangy,
oorie, ourie, owrie, pokey, scaly, seedy,
tacky, tatty **06** frayed, mangey, maungy,
paltry, poking, ragged, rotten, scurvy,
shoddy, unfair **07** raunchy, run-down,
scruffy, squalid, worn-out **08** dog-
eared, low-lived, shameful, tattered,
unworthy **09** moth-eaten, out at heel
10 broken-down, despicable, down-
at-heel, flea-bitten, ramshackle,
threadbare, tumbledown
11 dilapidated, in disrepair
12 contemptible, disreputable,
unacceptable **13** discreditable,
dishonourable

shack
03 hut **04** dump, hole, shed **05** cabin,
hovel, hutch **06** lean-to, shanty

shackle
03 tie **04** bind, bond, gyve, iron, rope
05 chain, limit **06** couple, fetter,
hamper, hobble, impede, secure,
tether, thwart **07** darbies, inhibit,
manacle, trammel **08** encumber,
handcuff, handicap, obstruct, restrain,
restrict **09** bracelets, constrain,
hamstring, hindrance, restraint
10 constraint, fetterlock, hamshackle
11 encumbrance, obstruction,
restriction

shad
05 allis **06** allice, twaite

shade
03 dim, hue, tad **04** cast, dash, dusk,
hide, hint, part, tint, tone, ugly, veil
05 blind, cloud, color, cover, ghost,
gloom, swale, tinge, touch, trace,
umbra, visor, vizor **06** amount,
awning, canopy, colour, darken,
degree, memory, nuance, screen,
shadow, shield, shroud, spirit
07 conceal, curtain, dimness, obscure,
parasol, phantom, protect, shadows,
shelter, spectre, umbrage, variety
08 bongrace, covering, darkness,
gloaming, overcast, reminder,
sunblind, sunshade, tincture, twilight,
umbrella **09** gradation, inumbrate,
murkiness, obscurity, represent,
semblance, shadiness, suspicion
10 apparition, difference, gloominess,
overshadow, protection, suggestion
12 semi-darkness **14** block light from

See also **black**; **blue**; **colour**; **dye**; **green**;
grey; **orange**; **pigment**; **pink**; **purple**;
rainbow; **red**; **white**; **yellow**

- **a shade**
04 a bit **06** a touch, a trace, rather **07** a
little, a trifle **08** slightly

- **put in the shade**
03 top **04** beat **05** dwarf, excel
07 eclipse, outrank, surpass
08 outclass, outshine
- **shade off**
04 melt, pass **05** blend **07** gradate
10 intergrade

shadow
03 dog, pal **04** dusk, hide, hint, pall,
scog, scug, skug, stag, tail **05** cloud,
cover, ghost, gloom, image, scoog,
scoug, shade, shape, stalk, trace, trail,
umbra, watch **06** blight, darken, follow,
screen, shield, sleuth, spirit, typify,
unreal **07** dimness, feigned, obscure,
outline, remnant, sadness, shelter,
trouble, umbrage, vestige **08** darkness,
follower, gloaming, overhang,
penumbra, sidekick, twilight
09 companion, detective, obscurity,
remainder, suspicion **10** foreboding,
overshadow, protection, silhouette,
suggestion **11** tenebrosity **12** semi-
darkness **14** Brocken spectre,
representation

- **a shadow of your former self**
07 apology, remnant, vestige **13** poor
imitation, weaker version
- **without a shadow of a doubt**
05 truly **06** surely **07** clearly, no doubt
08 of course **09** assuredly, certainly,
doubtless **10** most likely **11** indubitably,
undoubtedly **12** indisputably, without
doubt **14** unquestionably

shadowy
03 dim **04** dark, hazy **05** faint, murky,
shady, vague **06** gloomy, unreal
07 ghostly, obscure, phantom, unclear
08 ethereal, illusory, nebulous,
secluded, spectral, symbolic
09 dreamlike, imaginary, tenebrose,
tenebrous **10** ill-defined, indistinct,
intangible, mysterious, tenebrious
11 crepuscular, umbratilous
13 indeterminate, unsubstantial

shady
03 dim **04** cool, dark, iffy **05** bosky,
fishy, leafy **06** bowery, louche, opaque,
shaded, shifty, veiled **07** clouded,
covered, crooked, dubious, obscure,
shadowy, suspect, umbrose, umbrous
08 screened, shielded, shrouded,
sinister, slippery **09** dishonest,
protected, tenebrose, tenebrous,
umbratile, underhand, unethical
10 caliginous, mysterious, suspicious,
tenebrious, umbrageous, unreliable
11 umbratilous, umbriferous
12 disreputable, questionable,
unscrupulous **13** untrustworthy

shaft
03 ash, bar, fil, pit, ray, rod **04** beam,
butt, dart, duct, dupe, fill, flue, fust, hilt,
pole, sink, stem, tige, well **05** arbor,
arrow, scape, shank, stale, stalk, stave,
steal, steel, steil, stele, stick, stock,
stulm, winze **06** handle, pencil, pillar,
rachis, scapus, steale, tunnel
07 missile, passage, swindle, upright,
winning **08** hoistway **09** truncheon

shaggy
04 rag'd **05** bushy, hairy, nappy, ragde,
tousy, touzy, towsy, towzy **06** horrid,
ragged, woolly **07** crinose, hirsute,
unkempt, unshorn **09** mop-headed
10 long-haired **11** dishevelled

shake
◇ *anagram indicator*
03 jog, wag, wap **04** bump, faze, jerk,
jolt, pump, rock, roll, shog, stir, sway,
wave **05** alarm, alert, crack, heave,
lower, quake, rouse, shock, split,
swing, throb, trill, upset, waver, wield,
wring **06** bounce, didder, dindle,
dinnle, dismay, dodder, happen, hustle,
jigger, jiggle, joggle, jostle, judder,
justle, lessen, moment, quiver, rattle,
reduce, shiver, summon, totter, trillo,
twitch, weaken, wobble **07** agitate,
concuss, disturb, fissure, perturb,
quaking, rocking, shake up, shoggle,
shoogle, shudder, tremble, unnerve,
vibrate **08** brandish, convulse,
diminish, distress, flourish, frighten,
unsettle **09** oscillate, shivering,
throbbing, trembling, undermine,
vibration **10** convulsion, discompose,
intimidate, shuddering, unsettling
11 disturbance, oscillation

- **shake a leg**
05 hurry **07** hurry up **08** step on it
10 get a move on, look lively **11** get
cracking **15** get your skates on
- **shake off**
04 heal, lose, mend **05** elude, rally
06 escape, pick up, revive **07** get away,
get over, get well, improve **08** dislodge,
get rid of, outstrip, shrug off **09** get
better **10** bounce back, convalesce,
feel better, recuperate **11** be on the
mend, get away from, give the slip,
leave behind, outdistance, pull
through, recover from **12** gain strength
13 turn the corner
- **shake up**
03 mix **05** alarm, rouse, shock, upset
06 jumble, rattle **07** disturb, succuss,
unnerve, upbraid **08** distress, unsettle
09 rearrange, reshuffle **10** reorganize
11 restructure

Shakespeare
02 WS **07** the Bard **13** The Swan of
Avon

Shakespeare's characters include:
03 Hal (Prince), Nym, Sly (Christopher)
04 Ajax, Anne (Lady), Dull, Fool (The),
Ford (Mistress), Hero, Iago, John
(Don), John (King), Kate, Kent (Earl
of), Lear (King), Moth, Page
(Mistress), Puck, Snug
05 Ariel, Bagot, Belch (Sir Toby), Bushy,
Celia, Diana, Edgar, Feste, Flute,
Gobbo (Launcelot), Green, Julia,
Maria, Nurse, Paris (Count), Pedro
(Don), Regan, Romeo, Snout,
Speed, Timon, Titus, Viola
06 Alonso, Angelo, Antony (Mark),
Armado (Don Adriano de), Audrey,
Banquo, Bianca, Bottom (Nick),
Brutus, Cassio, Cloten, Cobweb,
Dromio, Duncan (King), Edmund,

Emilia, Fabian, Hamlet, Hecate, Hector, Helena, Henry V (King), Hermia, Imogen, Jaques, Juliet, Launce, Marina, Oberon, Oliver (de Bois), Olivia, Orsino, Oswald, Pistol, Pompey, Porter, Portia, Quince, Silvia, Thisbe, Ursula, Verges, Yorick

07 Adriana, Antonio, Berowne, Bertram (Count of Rousillon), Caliban, Capulet, Cesario, Claudio, Costard, Fleance, Goneril, Gonzalo, Henry IV (King), Henry VI (King), Horatio, Hotspur, Iachimo, Jessica, Laertes, Lavinia, Leontes, Lepidus, Lorenzo, Luciana, Macbeth, Macbeth (Lady), Macduff, Malcolm, Mariana, Martext (Sir Oliver), Miranda, Nerissa, Octavia, Ophelia, Orlando, Othello, Paulina, Perdita, Proteus, Pyramus, Quickly (Mistress), Shallow, Shylock, Sycorax, Theseus, Titania, Troilus

08 Bardolph, Bassanio, Beatrice, Benedick, Benvolio, Charmian, Claudius, Cordelia, Cressida, Dogberry, Falstaff (Sir John), Florizel, Fluellen, Ganymede, Gertrude, Hermione, Isabella, Laurence (Friar), Lucretia, Lysander, Malvolio, Mercutio, Montague, Pandarus, Parolles, Pericles, Polonius, Prospero, Rosalind, Rosaline, Stephano, Trinculo

09 Aguecheek (Sir Andrew), Antigonus, Cleopatra, Collatine, Cornelius, Cymbeline, Demetrius, Desdemona, Enobarbus, Ferdinand, Ferdinand (King of Navarre), Frederick (Duke), Henry VIII (King), Hippolyta, Hortensio, Katharina, Katharine (Princess of France), Nathaniel (Sir), Petruchio, Polixenes, Richard II, Sebastian, Valentine, Vincentio (Duke)

10 Antipholus (of Ephesus), Antipholus (of Syracuse), Collatinus, Coriolanus, Fortinbras, Gloucester (Earl of), Holofernes, Jaquenetta, Richard III, Starveling, Tarquinius, Touchstone

11 Mustard-seed, Peasblossom, Rosencrantz

12 Guildenstern, Julius Caesar, Three Witches

15 Robin Goodfellow, Titus Andronicus

Shakespeare's plays:

06 Hamlet, Henry V
07 Macbeth, Othello
08 King John, King Lear, Pericles
09 Cymbeline, Henry VIII, Richard II
10 Coriolanus, Richard III, The Tempest
11 As You Like It
12 Julius Caesar, Twelfth Night
13 Timon of Athens
14 Henry IV Part One, Henry IV Part Two, Henry VI Part One, Henry VI Part Two, Romeo and Juliet, The Winter's Tale
15 Titus Andronicus

16 Henry VI Part Three, Love's Labours Lost
17 Measure for Measure, The Comedy of Errors
18 Antony and Cleopatra, Troilus and Cressida
19 Much Ado About Nothing, The Merchant of Venice, The Taming of the Shrew
20 All's Well That Ends Well
21 A Midsummer Night's Dream, Hamlet, Prince of Denmark
22 The Merry Wives of Windsor
23 The Two Gentlemen of Verona

shake-up
08 upheaval **09** reshuffle **11** disturbance **13** rearrangement, restructuring **14** reorganization

shaky
◇ anagram indicator
04 weak **05** dicky, loose, quaky, rocky, wonky **06** coggly, cranky, dickey, flimsy, wobbly **07** dubious, quavery, rickety, suspect, tottery, unsound **08** insecure, unstable, unsteady, wavering **09** doddering, faltering, quivering, tentative, tottering, trembling, tremulous, uncertain, unfounded **10** precarious, staggering, ungrounded, unreliable **11** unsupported **12** questionable **13** untrustworthy

shale
04 husk, till **05** blaes, fakes, shell **06** blaise, blaize, faikes **09** torbanite **12** porcellanite **14** Kupferschiefer

shall
02 'll

shallow
03 ebb **04** bank, flat, flew, flue, idle **05** empty, fleet, petty, shoal **06** flimsy, shoaly, simple, slight, spread **07** foolish, surface, trivial **08** ignorant, skin-deep, trifling **09** frivolous, insincere **11** meaningless, superficial, unscholarly **13** rattle-brained **14** one-dimensional

sham
◇ anagram indicator
03 cod **04** copy, fake, hoax, idol, mock **05** bogus, cheat, dummy, false, feign, fraud, mimic, pseud, put on, put-on, snide **06** affect, con man, humbug, phoney, pseudo, shoddy, stumer **07** feigned, forgery, imitate, pretend **08** deceiver, fakement, feigning, imposter, impostor, pretence, pretense, simulate, spurious, swindler **09** brummagem, charlatan, dissemble, gold brick, imitation, imposture, pinchbeck, pretended, pretender, simulated, synthetic **10** artificial, pasteboard, simulation **11** counterfeit, make believe, make-believe, mock-modesty, synthetical **12** impersonator

shaman
05 pawaw **06** healer, powwow **07** angekok, tohunga **08** angekkok, magician, sorcerer **11** medicine man, witch doctor **13** medicine woman

shamble
04 drag, limp **06** doddle, falter, hobble, scrape, toddle **07** bauchle, scamble, shuffle

shambles
04 mess **05** chaos, havoc, wreck **06** bedlam, muddle, pigsty **07** anarchy **08** abattoir, butchery, disarray, disorder, madhouse **09** confusion **10** slaughtery **14** slaughterhouse **15** disorganization

shambling
05 loose **06** clumsy **07** awkward **08** lurching, ungainly, unsteady **09** lumbering, shuffling **10** disjointed **13** unco-ordinated

shambolic
05 messy **07** chaotic, muddled **08** confused **10** in disarray **12** disorganized **14** all over the shop

shame
03 fie, fye, out, sin **04** alas, pity **05** abash, aidos, guilt, pudor, shend, stain, sully, taint **06** ashame, debase, humble, infamy, rebuke, show up, stigma, too bad **07** bad luck, beshame, degrade, modesty, mortify, remorse, reproof, scandal **08** confound, disgrace, dishonor, ignominy, repriefe, reproach, ridicule **09** confusion, discredit, dishonour, disrepute, embarrass, humiliate **10** misfortune, opprobrium, put to shame **11** bashfulness, compunction, degradation, humiliation **13** embarrassment, mortification **14** disappointment, shamefacedness

• **put to shame**
05 shend **06** humble, rebuke, show up **07** eclipse, mortify, surpass, upstage **08** disgrace, outclass, outshine, outstrip **09** embarrass, humiliate

shamefaced
05 sorry **06** guilty **07** abashed, ashamed **08** blushing, contrite, penitent, pudibund, red-faced, sheepish **09** mortified, regretful **10** apologetic, humiliated, remorseful **11** embarrassed **13** uncomfortable

shameful
03 low **04** base, foul, mean, poor, vile **06** wicked **07** heinous, ignoble, shaming **08** indecent, shocking, unworthy **09** atrocious, pudendous **10** abominable, inglorious, mortifying, outrageous, scandalous **11** disgraceful, humiliating, ignominious **12** contemptible, embarrassing **13** discreditable, dishonourable, reprehensible

shamefully
10 shockingly **11** atrociously **12** confoundedly, outrageously, scandalously **13** disgracefully, ignominiously, reprehensibly **14** embarrassingly

shameless
05 brash **06** brazen, wanton **07** blatant, corrupt, defiant **08** blattant, browless, depraved, flagrant,

ardened, immodest, improper,
impudent, indecent, insolent,
unseemly, unshamed **09** abashless,
audacious, bald-faced, barefaced,
dissolute, frontless, unabashed,
unashamed, unbashful **10** brass-faced,
impenitent, indecorous, unbecoming,
unblushing **11** ithyphallic, unregretful,
unrepentant **12** incorrigible,
unprincipled

hamelessly
09 blatantly, defiantly **10** immodestly,
improperly, indecently
11 unashamedly **12** incorrigibly

hanty
03 hut **04** shed **05** bothy, cabin, hovel,
hutch, shack **06** chanty, lean-to
07 chantey, chantie, shantey

• shanty town
06 favela **10** bidonville

shape
◊ anagram indicator
03 air, cut, hew **04** cast, form, look,
make, plan, trim, turn **05** adapt, alter,
block, build, carve, forge, frame, guide,
guise, image, lines, model, mould, state
06 adjust, aspect, create, define,
design, devise, direct, embody, fettle,
figure, format, health, kilter, modify,
sculpt **07** conduce, develop, fashion,
outline, pattern, prepare, produce,
profile, purpose, remodel, whittle
08 contours, likeness, organize,
physique, regulate **09** character,
condition, construct, determine,
influence, sculpture, semblance,
structure **10** apparition, appearance,
silhouette **11** accommodate
13 configuration

See also **circle**; **figure**; **triangle**

• shape up
06 come on **07** develop, improve
08 flourish, progress **09** take shape
11 make headway, move forward
12 make progress

• take shape
03 gel **04** form **06** inform **11** become
clear, materialize **12** come together
14 become definite

shapeless
◊ anagram indicator
05 dumpy **07** chaotic **08** deformed,
formless, indigest, nebulous,
unformed, unframed **09** amorphous,
irregular, misshapen **11** purposeless,
undeveloped, unfashioned
12 unstructured **13** unfashionable
15 ill-proportioned

shapely
04 neat, tidy, trig, trim **06** comely,
gainly, pretty **07** elegant, featous
08 feateous, featuous, graceful **09** well-
set-up **10** attractive, curvaceous,
forehanded, voluptuous, well-formed,
well-turned **11** clean-limbed

shard
03 bit, gap **04** chip, part **05** piece,
scrap, sherd **06** shiver, sliver
08 fragment, particle, splinter

share
03 cut, due, lot, rug **04** divi, part, snap,
snip, sock **05** allot, divvy, halve, quota,
snack, split, whack **06** assign,
common, divide, finger, ration
07 carve up, deal out, dole out, give
out, go Dutch, hand out, partake,
portion, rake-off, section **08** allocate,
dividend, division, go halves, interest,
ordinary, share out **09** allotment,
allottery, allowance, apportion, bank-
stock, co-portion **10** allocation,
contingent, distribute, percentage,
plough-iron, proportion **11** go
halvesies, participate **12** compare
notes, contribution, go fifty-fifty, have a
share in **14** slice of the cake

• share out
05 allot, split **06** assign **07** divvy up,
give out, hand out, mete out **08** divide
up **09** apportion, parcel out
10 distribute

• shareholder
09 ploughman

shark
05 crook **07** fleecer, sharper, slicker,
sponger **08** man-eater, operator,
parasite, swindler **11** extortioner
12 extortionist **13** wheeler-dealer

> Sharks include:

03 cat, fox, saw
04 blue, bull, mako
05 blind, dusky, ghost, lemon, night,
nurse, sagre, swell, tiger, whale,
zebra
06 beagle, carpet, goblin, salmon,
school, sea cat
07 basking, bramble, dogfish, leopard,
requiem, sleeper, soupfin
08 blacktip, grey reef, mackerel,
thresher, whitetip
09 angelfish, epaulette, Greenland,
man-eating, porbeagle, sand tiger,
sevengill, sharpnose, wobbegong
10 Colclough's, great white,
hammerhead, Portuguese,
shovelhead
11 ragged-tooth, smooth-hound

sharp
03 fit, sly **04** able, acid, cold, curt, edgy,
fine, gleg, keen, neat, sour, tart, tidy,
wily **05** acidy, acrid, acute, alert, brisk,
clear, crisp, cruel, eager, edged, harsh,
natty, nifty, quick, rapid, razor, smart,
snell, spiky, stark, tangy, tight
06 abrupt, acidic, artful, astute,
barbed, biting, bitter, bright, clever,
crafty, fierce, hungry, jagged, marked,
severe, shrewd, snappy, strong, sudden
07 acerbic, brusque, burning, caustic,
cunning, cutting, elegant, exactly,
extreme, hairpin, hurtful, intense,
nipping, piquant, pointed, pungent,
stylish, varment, varmint, violent
08 abruptly, all there, clear-cut,
definite, distinct, freezing, incisive, on
the dot, peracute, piercing, poignant,
promptly, sardonic, scathing, serrated,
shooting, stabbing, stinging, suddenly,
venomous, vinegary **09** deceptive,

dishonest, malicious, observant, on
the ball, precisely, sarcastic, trenchant,
vitriolic, voiceless **10** astringent,
discerning, knife-edged, needle-like,
perceptive, punctually, razor-edged,
razor-sharp, unexpected
11 acrimonious, fashionable,
intelligent, penetrating, quick-witted,
well-defined **12** twenty-twenty,
unexpectedly

sharpen
03 set **04** edge, file, hone, keen, whet
05 frost, grind, point, stone, strop
09 acuminate

sharp-eyed
08 hawk-eyed, noticing **09** eagle-
eyed, observant **10** perceptive
11 keen-sighted **12** eagle-sighted

sharply
05 smack **06** curtly **07** acutely, clearly,
harshly, quickly, rapidly, starkly, tightly
08 abruptly, bitterly, fiercely, markedly,
suddenly **09** brusquely **10** definitely,
distinctly, venomously
12 unexpectedly **13** acrimoniously,
sarcastically, vitriolically

sharpness
04 edge, whet **05** venom **06** acuity,
acumen **07** clarity, cruelty, sarcasm,
vitriol **08** keenness, severity
09 acuteness, crispness, eagerness,
harshness, intensity, precision
10 astuteness, definition, fierceness,
shrewdness **11** brusqueness,
discernment, observation, penetration
12 incisiveness **14** perceptiveness

shatter
◊ anagram indicator
04 bust, dash, ruin, star **05** blast, break,
burst, crack, craze, crush, smash, split,
upset, wreck **06** shiver **07** destroy,
explode, scatter **08** demolish,
fragment, overturn, splinter
09 devastate, overwhelm, pulverize
10 disappoint, smithereen **14** break
your heart

shattered
◊ anagram indicator
05 all in, weary **06** broken, done in,
pooped, zonked **07** crushed, worn out
08 dead beat, dog-tired, tired out
09 exhausted, fagged out, knackered,
plastered, pooped out **10** devastated
11 overwhelmed, ready to drop,
tuckered out

shattering
06 severe **08** crushing, damaging,
smashing **10** paralysing **11** devastating
12 overwhelming

shave
03 cut **04** barb, crop, pare, trim
05 brush, graze, plane, shear, touch
06 barber, fleece, paring, scrape
07 plunder

• close shave
09 close call, near touch **10** close
thing, narrow miss **11** lucky escape
12 narrow escape

Shaw
03 GBS

shawl
04 wrap 05 scarf, stole, tozie
06 afghan, tonnag, zephyr 07 blanket, dopatta, dupatta, tallith, whittle
08 pashmina, shatoosh, turnover
09 shahtoosh 10 India shawl 11 prayer shawl 12 Kashmir shawl, Paisley shawl

she
01 a 03 her 04 elle
See also **girl**

sheaf
04 gait, garb 05 bunch, garbe, gerbe, truss 06 armful, bundle 07 dorlach

shear
03 cut 04 clip, crop, trim 05 shave, strip
06 barber, fleece 07 scissor, tonsure
08 clipping, separate 09 penetrate

sheath
04 case 05 ocrea, shard, shell, theca, volva 06 casing, cocoon, condom, ochrea, rubber, sleeve, vagina
07 johnnie, root cap, velamen
08 covering, envelope, scabbard, urceolus, vaginula, vaginule, wrapping
09 epidermis 10 caddis-case, coleoptile, endodermis, neurilemma, neurolemma, rhinotheca, thumbstall, zoothecium 11 perineurium 12 French letter, perichaetium, prophylactic, rhamphotheca

shed
◇ *deletion indicator*
03 hut, mew, sow 04 cast, drop, emit, give, molt, part, pour, skeo, skio
05 hovel, linny, moult, shack, shine, spend, spill, spilt, throw 06 impart, lean-to, linhay, linney, remove, shower, slough 07 cast off, diffuse, discard, emitted, fall off, let fall, parting, radiate, scatter, send out, shippen, shippon
08 building, disperse, get rid of, give away, outhouse, separate, skillion
10 besprinkle
• **shed tears**
03 sob 04 bawl, howl, wail, weep
05 whine 06 snivel 07 blubber, whimper 09 be in tears 14 burst into tears, cry your eyes out

sheen
05 gleam, gloss, shine, water 06 bright, luster, lustre, patina, polish 07 burnish, shimmer, shining, sparkle, varnish
08 radiance 09 beautiful, shininess
10 brightness, brilliance

sheep
03 ewe, hog, joe, keb, mug, ram, teg, tup, yeo, yow 04 fold, hogg, lamb, tegg, yowe 05 crone, flock, yowie
06 bident, gimmer, hidder, hirsel, hogget, lamber, theave, wether, woolly
07 jumbuck, twinter 08 hoggerel
09 shearling 10 bell-wether, woollyback

Sheep include:
03 Rya
04 Dala, Gute, Soay
05 ammon, ancon, aodad, Jacob, Lleyn, Lonck, Masai, Rygja, Texel, Tunis, urial
06 aoudad, Arcott, argali, Awassi, Balwen, Beltex, bharal, burhel, burrel, Dorper, Galway, Masham, merino, muflon, Romney
07 Barbary, bighorn, burrell, burrhel, caracul, Cheviot, Colbred, Gotland, karakul, Karaman, Lincoln, Loghtan, Loghtyn, mouflon, Romanov, Roussin, Ryeland, St Croix, Steigar, Suffolk, Tibetan, Vendeen
08 Columbia, Cotswold, herdwick, Katahdin, Loaghtan, Meatlinc, moufflon, Ouessant, Peliquey, Portland, Shetland, thinhorn, troender
09 blackface, Charolais, Costentin, Leicester, Marco Polo, Southdown, Teeswater
10 Charollais
11 Wensleydale
15 Border Leicester

• **flock of sheep**
04 fold, trip

sheepish
05 silly 07 abashed, ashamed, foolish
09 chastened, mortified
10 shamefaced 11 embarrassed
13 self-conscious, uncomfortable

sheepskin
04 napa, roan 05 basan, Mocha, nappa
06 mouton, shammy, skiver
07 chamois, morocco 11 wash leather
13 shammy leather
• **sheepskin coat**
07 posteen, zamarra, zamarro
08 poshteen 10 Afghan coat

sheer
04 bend, fine, flat, full, main, mere, pure, rank, thin, turn, veer 05 blank, clear, drift, gauzy, light, plumb, quite, sharp, shift, stark, steep, swing, total, utter 06 abrupt, bright, flimsy, simple, swerve 07 deflect, deviate, diverge, perfect 08 absolute, complete, delicate, gossamer, thorough, unbroken, vertical 09 deviation, downright, out-and-out, unmingled, veritable 10 diaphanous, see-through, vertically 11 precipitous, translucent, transparent, unmitigated, unqualified
12 unadulterate 13 perpendicular, thoroughgoing, unadulterated, unconditional

sheet
03 cel, sht, web 04 cell, coat, film, leaf, page, pane, sail, sill, skin, slab 05 cover, folio, layer, panel, piece, plate, reach, sweep 06 lamina, shroud, veneer
07 blanket, blotter, coating, expanse, overlay, stratum, stretch, surface
08 bed linen, covering, membrane, pamphlet 09 Celluloid®, newspaper
10 broadsheet

shelf
03 bar 04 bank, bink, rack, reef, sill, step 05 bench, ledge, shoal, stage
06 shelve, shrine 07 bracket, counter, retable, sand bar, terrace 08 credence, credenza, informer, sandbank, shelving 11 mantelpiece, mantelshelf
12 chimney piece
• **on the shelf**
06 single 09 on your own, unmarried
10 spouseless, unattached 15 without a partner

shell
◇ *anagram indicator*
◇ *ends deletion indicator*
03 pod 04 body, bomb, case, clam, hull, husk, mail, rind, shot 05 blitz, chank, conch, cowry, crust, frame, ormer, shale, shard, sheal, sheel, shiel, shill, shuck, testa 06 attack, bullet, casing, cockle, cowrie, fire on, mussel, pellet, sea pen 07 admiral, barrage, bombard, carcase, carcass, chassis, cochlea, grenade, limacel, missile, scallop, scollop 08 carapace, covering, sea acorn, skeleton, univalve
09 explosive, framework, Midas's ear, structure, turbinate 10 integument, projectile 11 globigerina 12 pelican's-foot
• **shell money**
04 peag, peak 06 wakiki, wampum
10 wampumpeag
• **shell out**
04 ante, give 05 pay up, spend 06 ante up, donate, expend, lay out, pay out
07 cough up, fork out 08 disburse
10 contribute

shellfish
• **young shellfish**
04 spat
See also **fish; mollusc; seafood**

shelter
◇ *containment indicator*
03 cot, lee 04 cote, hide, loun, lown, roof, scog, scug, skug, tent 05 bield, bivvy, bothy, cover, guard, haven, house, hovel, lound, lownd, put up, scoog, scoug, shade 06 asylum, bunker, covert, defend, dugout, harbor, maimai, refuge, safety, sconce, screen, shadow, shield, shroud, wiltja
07 conceal, defence, embower, harbour, imbower, lodging, protect, retreat, roofing 08 security, snow-hole
09 coverture, safeguard, sanctuary, screening 10 overshadow, protection
11 accommodate, cold harbour, weather-fend 13 accommodation

sheltered
03 lee 04 cosy, loun, lown, snug, warm
05 lound, lownd, quiet, shady
06 shaded 07 covered, retired, sharded 08 isolated, screened, secluded, shielded 09 protected, reclusive, unworldly, withdrawn
10 cloistered, in the shade

shelve
04 halt 05 defer, ledge, shelf, shunt, slope 06 put off 07 incline, suspend
08 lay aside, mothball, postpone, put aside, put on ice 09 sidetrack
10 pigeonhole

epherd
Acis, herd, lead **05** guide, steer,
vain, usher **06** convoy, escort, feeder,
astor, tar-box **07** conduct, herdboy,
erdess, marshal **08** guardian,
erdsman **09** herd-groom, protector
flockmaster, shepherd boy,
epherdess **12** shepherdling

eriff
grieve, lawman, shirra **07** bailiff
landdros, shireman, viscount
landdrost **10** shire-reeve

erry
fino **05** Xeres **06** doctor
amoroso, oloroso, sherris
Montilla **10** manzanilla
amontillado, Bristol-milk
sherry glass
copita **08** schooner

ield
cover, fence, guard, pelta, shade,
rge **06** buckle, defend, screen,
adow **07** buckler, bulwark, defence,
rfend, mantlet, protect, rampart,
elter, support, ward off **08** keep safe,
antelet, plastron **09** protector,
feguard **10** escutcheon, protection

ift
anagram indicator
rid **04** core, move, post, quit, sell,
p, span, tack, time, tour, turn, vary,
er, warp, work **05** alter, budge, carry,
mar, cymar, evade, relay, smock,
ell, stint, swing, U-turn **06** adjust,
ange, fidget, go away, hirsle, manage,
odify, period, put off, remove,
erve, switch, wrench **07** chemise,
nsume, removal, stretch, swallow
artifice, dislodge, displace, get rid
movement, pis aller, relocate,
ansfer **09** cutty-sark, expedient,
uctuate, rearrange, transpose,
ariation **10** alteration, relocation,
eposition **11** contrivance, fluctuation,
dging turn, prevaricate
displacement, modification,
ergiversate **13** rearrangement,
ansposition

iftless
idle, lazy **05** inept **07** aimless
feckless, goalless, indolent, slothful
incompetent, ineffectual, inefficient,
nambitious **12** resourceless
directionless, irresponsible,
ckadaisical **14** good-for-nothing,
nenterprising

ifty
anagram indicator
iffy, wily **05** shady **06** crafty, louche,
icky **07** cunning, devious, dubious,
vasive, furtive **08** scheming, slippery
deceitful, dishonest, underhand
contriving **11** duplicitous
untrustworthy

illing
s **03** bob, hog **06** deaner, teston
twalpenny **11** shovelboard,
walpennies, twelve-penny
shuffleboard

shilly-shally
05 waver **06** dither, falter, seesaw,
teeter **08** hesitate, hum and ha
09 fluctuate, hem and haw, mess
about, vacillate **10** dilly-dally
11 prevaricate, vacillation **12** be
indecisive, indecisively **13** sit on the
fence **14** whittie-whattie

shimmer
◇ *anagram indicator*
04 glow, haze, play **05** gleam, glint
06 lustre **07** flicker, glimmer, glisten,
glitter, sparkle, twinkle **10** glistening
11 iridescence, scintillate

shimmering
◇ *anagram indicator*
05 shiny **07** glowing, shining
08 gleaming, luminous, lustrous
09 chatoyant **10** avanturine,
aventurine, glistening, glittering,
iridescent **12** incandescent

shin
03 sin **04** soar **05** climb, mount, scale,
shoot, skink, swarm **06** ascend, shinny
07 clamber **08** scrabble, scramble

shine
03 rub, wax **04** beam, buff, dash, emit,
glow, lamp, leam, leme, star **05** brush,
excel, flash, glare, glaze, gleam, glint,
gloss, light, party, rub up, sheen, skyre
06 beacon, come up, dazzle, lustre,
patina, polish, shindy **07** burnish,
effulge, flicker, give off, glimmer,
glisten, glitter, radiate, shimmer,
sparkle, twinkle **08** lambency,
radiance, resplend, stand out
09 irradiate **10** brightness, effulgence,
incandesce **11** be brilliant, be excellent
12 be pre-eminent, luminescence,
phosphoresce **13** be outstanding,
incandescence

shingle
06 chesel, chisel

shingles
04 zona **06** zoster **12** herpes zoster

shininess
05 gleam, sheen, shine **06** lustre,
polish **07** burnish, glitter **10** brightness,
effulgence, glossiness

shining
04 glow, neat **05** beamy, glary, light,
lucid, moony, nitid, sheen **06** bright,
candid, glossy, golden, lucent, marble,
starry **07** aeneous, beaming, eminent,
fulgent, glowing, lamping, leading,
perfect, radiant **08** flashing, gleaming,
glinting, glooming, glorious, luminous,
lustrous, relucent, rutilant, splendid
09 brilliant, effulgent, excellent,
sparkling, splendent, twinkling
10 celebrated, flickering, glistening,
glittering, pre-eminent, profulgent,
shimmering **11** conspicuous, illustrious,
magnificent, outstanding, resplendent
12 incandescent **13** distinguished
14 phosphorescent

shiny
05 raven, silky, sleek **06** bright, glossy,

sheeny **07** shining **08** gleaming,
lustrous, polished **09** burnished
10 glistening, shimmering

ship
04 boat, post, send **05** craft
06 embark, vessel **07** send off
08 aircraft

Ship and boat types include:

01 E, Q, U
02 el, mv, NS, SS, TB
03 air, ark, bum, cat, cog, cot, day, dow,
fly, gig, gun, HMS, hoy, ice, jet, kit,
man, MTB, mud, pig, RMS, row, sub,
tow, tub, tug, USS, war
04 bark, brig, buss, cock, cott, dhow,
dory, falt, fire, flag, flat, fold, four,
grab, HMAS, HMCS, hulk, hush,
junk, keel, koff, life, long, mail, maxi,
pair, pink, pont, post, pram, prau,
proa, prow, punt, ro-ro, saic, scow,
show, snow, surf, tall, tern, tilt, Turk,
waka, well, wind, yawl, zulu
05 aviso, barca, barge, botel, butty,
cabin, canal, canoe, casco, coble,
coper, crare, dandy, dingy, drake,
ferry, funny, guard, gulet, hatch,
horse, house, jolly, kayak, ketch,
laker, light, liner, motor, oiler, peter,
pilot, plate, power, praam, prahu,
prore, razee, river, rotor, saick,
scout, scull, seine, shell, shore, skiff,
slave, sloop, smack, speed, stake,
steam, store, swamp, tanka, track,
tramp, troop, umiak, wager, waist,
whale, whiff, xebec, yacht, zabra
06 advice, argosy, banker, barque,
bateau, battle, bethel, bireme,
caique, carvel, castle, coaler,
cobble, cockle, codder, coffin,
convoy, cooper, crayer, cutter,
dingey, dinghy, dogger, dragon,
droger, dromon, drover, dugout,
flying, galiot, galley, gay-you,
hooker, hopper, jigger, lateen,
launch, lorcha, lugger, masula,
monkey, mother, narrow, nuggar,
oomiac, oomiak, packet, paddle,
pedalo, pirate, prison, puffer,
pulwar, puteli, randan, reefer,
rowing, runner, sailer, saique,
sampan, sandal, sanpan, school,
schuit, schuyt, settee, slaver, tanker,
tartan, torpid, trader, turret,
wangan, wangun, wherry
07 assault, Berthon, birlinn, budgero,
capital, caravel, clipper, coaster,
collier, consort, coracle, corsair,
cruiser, currach, curragh, dredger,
drifter, drogher, dromond, factory,
felucca, four-oar, frigate, gabbard,
gabbart, galleon, galliot, Geordie,
gondola, landing, liberty, lighter,
lymphad, man-o'-war, mistico,
mudscow, mystery, nacelle,
oomiack, pair-oar, passage,
patamar, pearler, pinnace, piragua,
pirogue, polacca, pontoon, sailing,
scooter, shallop, sharpie, sponger,
steamer, tartane, torpedo, trawler,
trireme, vedette, victory, wanigan,
warship, weather

08 bilander, billyboy, budgerow, car ferry, corocore, corocoro, corvette, dahabieh, dispatch, eight-oar, galleass, galliass, gallivat, hospital, hoveller, Indiaman, ironclad, log-canoe, longship, mackinaw, man-of-war, masoolah, massoola, merchant, monohull, montaria, periagua, pleasure, repeater, row barge, runabout, sally-man, schooner, skipjack, smuggler, Spaniard, training, trimaran, water bus, woodskin

09 bomb-ketch, Bucentaur, catamaran, commodore, container, dahabeeah, dahabiyah, dahabiyeh, daysailer, daysailor, destroyer, firefloat, flying jib, freighter, herringer, Hollander, hydrofoil, klondiker, klondyker, lapstrake, lapstreak, leviathan, long-liner, minelayer, monoxylon, motoscafo, multihull, Norwegian, oil-burner, oil tanker, outrigger, privateer, randan gig, receiving, sallee-man, speedster, steamship, store ship, submarine, surf canoe, transport, two-decker, two-master, vaporetto, well smack

10 armour-clad, bomb-vessel, brigantine, free-trader, hovercraft, icebreaker, minehunter, quadrireme, seal-fisher, tea clipper, trekschuit, triaconter, victualler, windjammer

11 bulk carrier, cockleshell, dreadnought, galley-foist, merchantman, minesweeper, motor launch, penteconter, purse-seiner, quinquereme, sallee-rover, salmon coble, side-wheeler, steam launch, steam packet, steam vessel, submersible, three-decker, three-master, victualling, wooden horse

12 cabin cruiser, deepwaterman, double-decker, East-Indiaman, line-of-battle, screw steamer, single-decker, square-rigger, stern-wheeler, tangle-netter, tramp steamer, troop carrier

13 Canadian canoe, paddle steamer, revenue cutter, roll-on roll-off

14 Flying Dutchman, ocean-greyhound, turbine steamer

15 aircraft-carrier, floating battery, logistics vessel

03 QE2
04 Ajax, Argo, Hood, Nina
05 Argus, Maine, Pinta
06 Beagle, Bounty, Cathay, Oriana, Pequod, Renown
07 Alabama, Amistad, Belfast, Blücher, Olympic, Pelican, Potomac, Repulse, Tirpitz, Titanic, Victory
08 Ark Royal, Bismarck, Canberra, Fearless, Graf Spee, Intrepid, Iron Duke, Mary Rose, Royal Oak
09 Adventure, Aquitania, Britannia, Britannic, Carinthia, Cutty Sark, Discovery, Endeavour, Gipsy Moth,

Gneisenau, Lexington, Lusitania, Mayflower, Normandie, Queen Mary, Sheffield, Téméraire, Terranova
10 Golden Hind, Hispaniola, Invincible, Mauretania, Prinz Eugen, Resolution, Santa Maria, Washington
11 Dawn Treader, Dreadnought, Illustrious, Scharnhorst
12 African Queen, Great Britain, Great Eastern, Great Western, Marie Celeste
13 Prince of Wales
14 Flying Dutchman, Queen Elizabeth
15 Admiral Graf Spee, General Belgrano, Queen Elizabeth 2

03 bow, box, oar, rig
04 beam, brig, brow, bunk, cant, deck, head, hold, hull, keel, mast, poop, port, prow, sail
05 berth, bilge, cabin, cable, cleat, davit, hatch, hawse, stern, wheel, winch
06 anchor, bridge, fender, fo'c'sle, funnel, galley, gunnel, hawser, rigger, rudder, tiller
07 bollard, bulwark, caboose, capstan, counter, gangway, gun deck, gunwale, hammock, landing, quarter, rowlock, top deck, transom
08 binnacle, boat deck, bulkhead, hatchway, main deck, poop deck, porthole, wardroom
09 afterdeck, chart room, crosstree, crow's nest, forecabin, gangplank, lower deck, radio room, stanchion, starboard, stateroom, waterline
10 boiler room, engine room, figurehead, flight deck, forecastle, pilot house, stabilizer
11 chain locker, paddle wheel, quarter deck
12 companion way, Plimsoll line
13 promenade deck
14 superstructure
15 companion ladder

02 AB
04 mate
06 master, purser
07 captain, steward
08 cabin-boy, ship's boy
09 first mate
10 able rating, able seaman

See also **sailor**

shipping

04 Sole, Tyne
05 Dover, Forth, Lundy, Malin, Wight
06 Bailey, Biscay, Dogger, Faroes, Fisher, Humber, Thames, Viking
07 Fastnet, FitzRoy, Forties, Rockall, Shannon
08 Cromarty, Fair Isle, Hebrides, Irish Sea, Plymouth, Portland

09 Trafalgar
10 Finisterre
11 German Bight, North Utsire, South Utsire
16 South-East Iceland

• **shipping order**
02 so

shipshape
04 neat, tidy, trig, trim **06** proper, spruce **07** orderly **11** well-planned **12** businesslike, spick and span **13** well organized, well-regulated

shirk
04 balk, duck, funk, shun **05** avoid, baulk, dodge, evade, skive, slack **06** bludge **07** goof off, soldier **08** get out of **09** duck out of, duckshove, gold-brick **10** play truant, shrink from **12** wriggle out of

shirker
05 idler, piker, poler, shirk **06** dodger, loafer, skiver, truant **07** bludger, goof-off, quitter, slacker, sneak-up, soldier **08** absentee, embusqué, layabout **09** gold brick **10** duckshover, malingerer **12** carpet-knight

shirt
01 T **04** sark, serk **05** kurta, parka **06** caftan, camese, camise, kaftan, khurta **07** dasheki, dashiki, partlet **08** guernsey, subucula

shiver
◇ *anagram indicator*
03 bit **04** chip, grew, grue **05** break, crack, flake, piece, quake, shake, shard, shred, shrug, smash, split, start **06** didder, dither, quiver, sliver, tremor, twitch **07** chitter, flutter, frisson, shatter, shaving, shudder, tremble, vibrate **08** cold sore, fragment, splinter **09** disshiver, palpitate, vibration **10** smithereen **11** smithereens

shivery
04 cold **05** ourie **06** chilly **07** brittle, chilled, nervous, quaking, quivery, shaking, trembly **08** fluttery, shuddery **09** trembling

shoal
03 bar, mob, ren, rin, run **04** bank, mass, reef **05** flock, group, horde, shelf, swarm **06** school, throng **07** schoole, shallow **08** sandbank **09** multitude **10** assemblage

shock
◇ *anagram indicator*
03 jar, mat, mop **04** blow, daze, head, jerk, jolt, mane, mass, numb, shog, stun, turn **05** amaze, appal, crash, knock, repel, shake, shook, sixty, start, stook, upset **06** dismay, fright, horror, impact, offend, poodle, revolt, sicken, stound, stownd, tangle, thatch, trauma, whammy **07** agitate, astound, disgust, horrify, jarring, outrage, perturb, scandal, stagger, startle, stupefy, unnerve **08** astonish, bewilder, bowl over, confound, disquiet, distress, gross out, nauseate, paralyse, surprise,

unsettle **09** bombshell, collision, dumbfound, knock back, take aback **10** scandalize, traumatize **11** thunderbolt **12** perturbation **13** consternation, rude awakening **15** bolt from the blue

• **shock absorber**
04 oleo **07** oleo leg, snubber

• **shock treatment**
03 ECT, EST

• **shocked**
06 aghast

shocking
04 foul, vile **05** awful **06** daring **07** épatant, ghastly, hideous **08** dreadful, horrible, horrific, terrible **09** abhorrent, appalling, atrocious, execrable, frightful, loathsome, monstrous, offensive, repugnant, repulsive, revolting, sickening **10** abominable, deplorable, detestable, diabolical, disgusting, horrifying, nauseating, outrageous, perturbing, scandalous, unbearable, unsettling **11** disgraceful, disquieting, distressing, intolerable, unspeakable

shockingly
08 terribly **10** abominably, deplorably, dreadfully, unbearably **11** appallingly, atrociously, frightfully, repulsively, revoltingly, sickeningly **12** disgustingly, outrageously, scandalously **13** disgracefully

shoddy
▷ *anagram indicator*
04 poor, ropy, sham **05** cheap, crook, dopey, tacky, tatty **06** tawdry, trashy **07** rag-wool, rubbish **08** careless, gimcrack, inferior, jimcrack, rubbishy, slapdash, slipshod **09** cheapjack, third-rate **10** devil's dust, second-rate **11** poor-quality

shoe *see* **footwear**

shoemaker
04 snab, snob **05** sutor **06** cosier, cozier, soutar, souter, sowter **07** cobbler, crispin **08** cordiner **09** bootmaker **10** cordwainer

shoemaking
08 cobblery, cobbling **10** bootmaking **14** the gentle craft

shoot
03 aim, bud, fly, gun, hit, imp, lob, pop, pot, rod, tip, zap, zip **04** belt, cast, chit, cyme, dart, dash, dump, film, fire, germ, grow, hurl, kick, kill, plug, poot, pout, race, rush, slip, snap, tear, twig, wand, whip, whiz **05** blast, chute, fling, graft, hurry, loose, pluff, rapid, scion, scoot, shell, slide, spear, speed, spire, spray, sprig, start, throw, tower, video, whisk, wound **06** branch, charge, direct, hurtle, injure, launch, let fly, let off, propel, sprint, sprout, streak, strike, sucker **07** bombard, burgeon, cutting, gun down, mow down, pick off, project, shoot up, snipe at, stretch, tendron **08** detonate, go all out, offshoot, open fire **09** bring down,

discharge, germinate, spindling **10** get a move on, photograph **11** crystallize, precipitate

shooter *see* **gun; gunman**

shop
03 buy, get, rat **05** grass, split, store **06** betray, pick up, prison, squeal, tell on **07** stool on **08** emporium, imprison, inform on, purchase **09** buy things, stock up on **10** go shopping **11** tell tales on **12** retail outlet **13** do the shopping

Shop types include:

01 e
02 op, PX
03 toy
04 book, chip, deli, farm, grog, shoe, tuck
05 baker, dairy, dress, offie, phone, stall, sweet, video
06 barber, bazaar, bookie, bottle, chippy, corner, draper, grocer, market, online, record, tailor
07 betting, butcher, charity, chemist, chipper, clothes, florist, saddler
08 boutique, hardware, jeweller, milliner, pharmacy, takeaway
09 bookmaker, drugstore, newsagent, outfitter, stationer, superette
10 candy store, chain store, electrical, fishmonger, health-food, ironmonger, mini-market, off-licence, pawnbroker, post office, radio and TV, second-hand, superstore
11 bottle store, fish and chip, five-and-dime, greengrocer, haberdasher, hairdresser, hypermarket, launderette, online store, opportunity, supermarket, tobacconist
12 cash-and-carry, confectioner, delicatessen, general store, indoor market
13 computer store, farmers' market
15 department store

French shops include:

05 tabac
08 boutique, épicerie
09 boucherie, librairie
10 bijouterie, confiserie, fromagerie, parfumerie, pâtisserie, rôtisserie
11 boulangerie, charcuterie
12 chocolaterie, grand magasin, poissonnerie

Shops include:

03 BHV
04 Tati
05 Macy's
07 Hamleys, Harrods, Jenners, Liberty
08 Tiffany's
09 Century 21, Printemps
10 FAO Schwarz, Selfridge's
11 Le Bon Marché
13 Bloomingdale's, Harvey Nichols, La Samaritaine
15 Bergdorf Goodman, Fortnum and Mason, Saks Fifth Avenue

shopkeeper
05 owner **06** dealer, trader **07** manager **08** merchant, retailer, salesman, stockist **09** bourgeois, boxwallah, tradesman **10** proprietor, saleswoman **11** storekeeper, tradeswoman **13** counter-jumper **14** counter-skipper

shopper
05 buyer **06** client **08** consumer, customer **09** purchaser

shore
04 bank, hold, prop, sand, stay, warn **05** beach, brace, coast, drain, front, offer, rance, sands, sewer **06** hold up, menace, prop up, rivage, strand **07** seaside, shingle, support **08** buttress, lakeside, littoral, seaboard, seashore, threaten, underpin **09** foreshore, promenade, reinforce, waterside **10** strengthen, waterfront **11** threatening

shorebird
04 knot **06** dunlin, ox-bird **07** sea lark **08** sand-lark, surfbird
See also **bird**

shorn
03 cut **04** bald **06** polled, shaved, shaven **07** crew-cut, cropped **08** deprived, stripped **09** beardless

short
◇ *tail deletion indicator*
03 low, shy, wee **04** curt, neat, poor, rude **05** blunt, brief, crisp, dumpy, gruff, hasty, pithy, quick, scant, sharp, small, squat, swift, teeny, terse, tight **06** abrupt, curtly, direct, little, meagre, petite, scanty, scarce, slight, snappy, sparse, stubby, teensy **07** briefly, brittle, brusque, compact, concise, cursory, lacking, limited, passing, summary, uncivil, wanting **08** abridged, abruptly, fleeting, impolite, pint-size, snappish, succinct, suddenly **09** condensed, curtailed, deficient, ephemeral, fugacious, minuscule, momentary, pint-sized, shortened, temporary, transient, truncated **10** aphoristic, compressed, diminutive, evanescent, inadequate, short-lived, summarized, to the point, transitory **11** abbreviated, Lilliputian **12** abbreviation, discourteous, insufficient, unexpectedly

• **fall short**
05 fault, under **09** be lacking **12** be inadequate **14** be insufficient

• **in short**
04 once **05** in sum **06** in fine **07** at a word, briefly, in a word, in brief, to sum up **09** concisely, in one word **11** in a few words, in a nutshell, summarizing **12** in conclusion

• **little short of**
02 on **07** towards

• **short of**
03 bar, but **04** save **05** low on, under **06** but for **07** barring, besides, lacking, missing, short on, wanting **08** less than, omitting **09** apart from, aside from,

except for, excepting, excluding, other than, pushed for **10** leaving out, this side of **11** deficient in, not counting

shortage
04 lack, need, shtg, want **06** dearth, drouth **07** absence, deficit, drought, paucity, poverty, wantage **08** scarcity **09** shortfall, skills gap **10** deficience, deficiency, inadequacy **13** insufficiency

shortcoming
03 sin **04** flaw **05** fault **06** defect, foible **07** failing, frailty **08** drawback, weakness **09** weak point **12** imperfection

shorten
◇ *tail deletion indicator*
03 cut **04** clip, crop, dock, pare, trim **05** check, prune, sum up **06** lessen, reduce, take up **07** abridge, curtail, cut down, scantle **08** compress, condense, contract, decrease, diminish, pare down, truncate **09** epitomize, telescope **10** abbreviate **11** make shorter **13** become shorter

shortened
◇ *tail deletion indicator*
03 cut **06** curtal **07** curtate **08** abridged **09** condensed **10** abbreviate, abstracted, contracted, summarized **11** abbreviated **12** abbreviatory

shortfall
04 lack, loss **07** arrears, default, deficit **08** shortage **10** deficiency

shorthand
02 s/h **11** phonography, stenography, tachygraphy **12** Speedwriting®

short-lived
05 brief, short **07** passing **08** caducous, fleeting, volatile **09** ephemeral, fugacious, momentary, temporary, transient **10** evanescent, transitory **11** impermanent

shortly
◇ *tail deletion indicator*
04 soon **06** curtly, rudely **07** bluntly, briefly, by and by, gruffly, sharply, tersely **08** abruptly, directly, in a while **09** brusquely, presently, uncivilly **10** before long, impolitely **14** discourteously, in a little while

shorts
07 baggies, cut-offs **08** Bermudas, hot pants

short-sighted
04 rash **05** hasty **06** myopic, unwise **08** careless, heedless **09** impolitic, imprudent **10** ill-advised, unthinking **11** improvident, injudicious, near-sighted, thoughtless **13** ill-considered, uncircumspect

short-staffed
11 shorthanded **12** understaffed **13** below strength

short-tempered
05 fiery, ratty, testy **06** crusty, touchy

07 grouchy **08** choleric **09** crotchety, impatient, irascible, irritable **10** crotcheted **11** bad-tempered, hot-tempered **13** quick-tempered

short-winded
05 puffy, pursy **07** gasping, panting, puffing, purfled **10** breathless

shot
◇ *anagram indicator*
02 go **03** ace, aim, fix, get, hit, jab, lob, peg, pop, pot, shy, try **04** ball, bang, bash, burl, dink, dose, dram, kick, putt, scot, slug, snap, stab, turn **05** blast, crack, fling, guess, image, moiré, photo, pluff, print, range, reach, set-up, shoat, shote, slide, snipe, spell, throw, whack **06** bullet, corner, effort, gunner, header, hunter, jumper, pellet, ruined, shotte, sitter, sniper, strike, stroke **07** attempt, gunfire, missile, mottled, payment, pelican, penalty, picture, shooter, watered **08** advanced, marksman, moon-ball, snapshot **09** discharge, endeavour, explosion, injection, mitraille **10** ammunition, cannonball, iridescent, markswoman, photograph, point-blank, projectile, variegated **11** inoculation, vaccination **12** contribution, immunization, transparency

• call the shots
04 head, lead **06** direct, head up, manage **07** command **09** give a lead, supervise **10** be in charge **15** wear the trousers

• good shot
07 deadeye

• like a shot
06 at once **07** eagerly, quickly **09** instantly, willingly **11** immediately **12** without delay **14** unhesitatingly

• not by a long shot
04 ne'er **05** never, no way **07** in no way **08** not at all **09** by no means **12** certainly not **13** not in the least

• shot in the arm
04 lift **05** boost **06** fillip, uplift **07** impetus **08** stimulus **11** fresh talent **13** encouragement

• shot in the dark
05 guess **09** guesswork, wild guess **10** blind guess, conjecture **11** speculation

shoulder
04 bear, hump, push **05** carry, elbow, force, press, shove, spald, spall, spaul **06** accept, assume, jostle, spalle, spauld, take on, thrust **07** support, sustain **09** undertake **10** coathanger **13** heave-offering

• give someone the cold shoulder
03 cut **04** shun, snub **05** blank, shame, spurn **06** humble, ignore, insult, rebuff, rebuke, slight, squash **07** mortify, put down **08** brush off **09** disregard, humiliate **13** slap in the face **14** kick in the teeth

• rub shoulders with
07 mix with **08** meet with **10** hobnob with **13** associate with, hang about

with, socialize with **14** fraternize with, hang around with, knock about with **15** knock around with

• shoulder to shoulder
06 united **07** closely **08** together **10** hand in hand, in alliance, side by sid **13** co-operatively **15** working togethe

shout
03 bay, cry **04** bawl, call, howl, roar, rort, yawp, yell **05** cheer, claim, clame jodel, round, stand, treat, yodel, yodle **06** bellow, cry out, heckle, holler, scream, shriek, squawk **07** barrack, call out, exclaim, glory be, sing out **11** acclamation, rant and rave, stand a round **12** buy drinks for, conclamatior **14** raise your voice

Shouts and cries include:
02 io
03 hup, nix
04 euoi, evoe, fall, fore, haro, I-spy, riv
shoo, sola
05 chevy, chivy, evhoe, evohe, havoc,
heigh, holla, hollo, hooch, huzza
06 banzai, chivvy, eureka, halloa,
halloo, harrow, hoicks, yoicks
07 glory be, heureka, kamerad, tally-
ho, tantivy
08 alleluia, gardyloo, Geronimo,
harambee
09 scaldings, stop thief!
10 halleluiah, hallelujah, view-halloo,
westward ho!

See also **war cry** *under* **war**

shouting
03 hue

shove
04 bump, bung, jolt, push **05** barge, crowd, drive, elbow, force, press **06** jostle, propel, thrust **07** thrutch **08** shoulder

• shove off
04 scat **05** hop it, leave, scoot, scram **06** beat it, depart, go away **07** buzz off do a bunk, get lost, push off, rack off, scarper, vamoose **08** choof off, clear off, clear out, run for it **09** skedaddle

shovel
03 dig, van **04** heap, main, move, peel **05** clear, scoop, shift, shool, spade **06** bucket, dredge **07** backhoe, dust-pan **08** excavate **09** excavator **13** backhoe loader

show
◇ *hidden indicator*
03 air, con **04** come, expo, fair, give, lead, mean, pose, shew, sign, take, wear **05** array, front, guide, guise, offer, prove, sight, steer, teach, usher **06** affair, appear, arrive, attend, chance, depict, direct, escort, expose, façade, parade, record, reveal, set out, turn up **07** clarify, conduct, display, divulge, exhibit, explain, expound, express, panache, pizzazz, portray, present, produce, showing, signify, staging, suggest, uncover **08** disclose, evidence, illusion, indicate, instruct, manifest, point out, pretence, register

09 accompany, elucidate, exemplify, make clear, make known, make plain, operation, programme, semblance, showiness, spectacle **10** appearance, be evidence, exhibition, exposition, illustrate, impression, indication, play-acting, production, profession **11** affectation, arrangement, demonstrate, flamboyance, make it clear, make visible, materialize, opportunity, ostentation, performance, proceedings, undertaking **12** extravaganza, organization, plausibility, presentation **13** bear witness to, demonstration, entertainment, exhibitionism, manifestation **14** representation, window dressing

● **show off**
◇ *anagram indicator*
04 brag **05** boast, pronk, strut, swank, vapor **06** flaunt, hot-dog, parade, set off, vapour **07** display, enhance, exhibit, swagger **08** brandish, flourish **09** advertise **10** grandstand, put on an act **11** demonstrate **15** show to advantage

● **show up**
04 come **05** lodge, shame **06** appear, arrive, bewray, expose, hand in, reveal, turn up, unmask **07** lay bare, let down, mortify, uncloak **08** disgrace, pinpoint **09** embarrass, highlight, humiliate **10** put to shame **11** make visible, materialize

showdown
05 clash **06** climax, crisis **07** face-off **10** dénouement **11** culmination **13** confrontation, moment of truth

shower
◇ *anagram indicator*
04 fall, hail, heap, load, pang, pelt, play, pour, rain, scat, scud, skit **05** drift, pound, skatt, spray, water **06** attack, deluge, lavish, pelter, pepper, stream, volley **07** barrage, scowder, torrent **08** inundate, rainfall, scouther, scowther, sprinkle **09** aspersion, avalanche, drizzling, overwhelm **10** kitchen tea, sprinkling **13** thunder-shower
See also **meteor**

showiness
05 glitz, swank **07** glitter, pizzazz, varnish **09** ritziness **10** flashiness, razzmatazz **11** flamboyance, ostentation **12** razzle-dazzle **15** pretentiousness

showing
04 expo, show **06** record **07** account, display, staging **08** evidence, symbolic **09** endeictic, ostensive, statement **10** appearance, exhibition, impression, indicative, revelatory **11** descriptive, elucidative, explanatory, explicatory, performance, significant, track record **12** illustrative, presentation **13** demonstrative **14** representation, representative **15** past performance

showing-off
05 swank **07** egotism, swagger

08 boasting, bragging **09** vainglory **10** peacockery **11** braggadocio **13** exhibitionism

showjumper *see* **equestrian**

showman
07 show-off **09** performer, publicist **10** impresario, ring-master **11** entertainer **14** self-advertiser

show-off
05 poser **06** poseur **07** boaster, egotist, know-all, peacock, swanker **08** braggart **09** swaggerer **13** exhibitionist

showy
03 gay **04** fine, loud **05** brave, fancy, flash, flory, gaudy, ritzy, spicy, viewy **06** branky, brassy, dressy, flashy, flossy, garish, glitzy, ornate, swanky, tawdry **07** buckeye, dashing, pompous, splashy, stylish **08** fantoosh, gorgeous, sparkish, specious, tinselly **10** bling-bling, flamboyant, glittering **11** conspicuous, pretentious **12** ostentatious

shred
03 bit, cut, jot, rag, rip, tag **04** atom, chop, iota, mite, snip, spot, tear, whit, wisp **05** cut up, grain, grate, piece, prune, rip up, scrap, slice, speck, taver, trace **06** agnail, cut off, paring, ribbon, screed, sliver, taiver, tatter, tear up **07** frazzle, mammock, modicum, mummock, peeling, remnant, snippet, vestige **08** clipping, fragment, hangnail, julienne, particle

shrew
03 nag **04** Fury, Kate, tana **05** bitch, curse, scold, shrow, sorex, vixen **06** dragon, Tupaia, virago **07** muskrat, sondeli **08** banxring, harridan, spitfire **09** bangsring, henpecker, Katharina, termagant, Xanthippe **10** petrodrome

shrewd
03 sly **04** arch, evil, hard, keen, wily, wise **05** acute, alert, canny, savey, savvy, sharp, smart **06** argute, artful, astute, biting, callid, clever, crafty, keenly, savvey, severe, shrowd **07** cunning, gnostic, hurtful, knowing, prudent **08** piercing, shrewish, spiteful, vixenish **09** judicious, observant, sagacious **10** calculated, discerning, far-sighted, formidable, hard-headed, ill-natured, long-headed, perceptive **11** calculating, intelligent, mischievous, well-advised **12** cut-and-thrust, sharp-sighted **13** perspicacious **14** discriminating, ill-conditioned

shrewdly
05 slyly **06** wisely **07** cannily **08** argutely, artfully, astutely, cleverly, craftily **09** knowingly, unhappily **11** judiciously, sagaciously **12** far-sightedly, perceptively **15** perspicaciously

shrewdness
05 grasp **06** acumen, wisdom **08** astucity, gumption, prudence,

sagacity **09** acuteness, callidity, canniness, judgement, sharpness, smartness **10** astuteness **11** discernment, knowingness, penetration **12** intelligence, perspicacity **14** perceptiveness

shrewish
06 shrewd **07** nagging, peevish **08** captious, petulant, scolding, vixenish **09** querulous, termagant **10** henpecking, ill-natured, wasp-tongu'd **11** bad-tempered, complaining, ill-humoured, ill-tempered, quarrelsome **12** discontented, fault-finding, sharp-tongued

shriek
03 cry **04** howl, wail, yell, yelp **05** pling, shout, skirl **06** cry out, scream, scrike, shreek, shreik, shrike, squawk, squeal **07** screech, screich, screigh, scriech, shright, shritch, skreigh, skriech, skriegh **08** screamer **09** caterwaul **11** exclamation **15** exclamation mark

shrill
04 high, keen **05** acute, sharp **06** argute, treble **08** piercing, screechy, strident **09** screaming **10** screeching **11** ear-piercing, high-pitched, penetrating **12** ear-splitting

shrimp
05 krill, prawn **06** squill **07** squilla **08** crevette **09** Euphausia, schizopod **10** stomatopod

shrine
04 dome, fane, tope **05** chest, darga, image, stupa **06** chapel, church, dagaba, dagoba, pagoda, scrine, scryne, temple, vimana **07** cabinet, martyry **08** delubrum, feretory, marabout **09** holy place, sanctuary **10** tabernacle **11** sacred place

shrink
04 balk, dare, nirl, shun **05** cling, cower, crine, quail, shrug, wince **06** blench, cringe, flinch, gizzen, lessen, narrow, recoil, reduce, retire, shy off, swerve, wither **07** atrophy, drop off, dwindle, fall off, give way, retreat, shorten, shrivel, shy away, wrinkle **08** back away, contract, decrease, diminish, draw back, withdraw **09** cower away, start back **10** constringe, withdrawal **11** contraction, grow smaller **12** psychiatrist **13** become smaller **15** have qualms about

shrivel
03 dry **04** burn, nirl, sear, welk, wilt **05** cling, crine, dry up, parch **06** blight, gizzen, pucker, scorch, shrink, wither **07** dwindle, frizzle, wrinkle **08** pucker up **09** dehydrate, desiccate

shrivelled
03 dry **04** sere **06** gizzen, shrunk **07** dried up, wizened **08** puckered, shrunken, withered, wrinkled, writhled **09** emaciated **10** desiccated

shroud
03 fog, lop **04** hide, pall, veil, wrap
05 cloak, cloth, cloud, cover, shade
06 branch, mantle, screen, sindon,
swathe **07** blanket, clothes, conceal,
envelop, garment, shelter
08 cerement, covering, enshroud,
loppings **09** cerecloth
12 graveclothes, winding-sheet

shrouded
06 hidden, veiled **07** cloaked, clouded,
covered, swathed, wrapped
09 blanketed, concealed, enveloped
10 enshrouded

shrub
04 bush **07** arboret

Shrubs include:

03 box, ivy, til
04 coca, hebe, nabk, Rosa, rose
05 brere, briar, brier, broom, buaze,
buchu, bucku, bwazi, holly, lilac,
nebek, peony, yucca
06 azalea, daphne, laurel, mallow,
mimosa, nebbuk, nebeck, privet,
sesame
07 arbutus, Banksia, boronia, bramble,
dogwood, fuchsia, heather,
jasmine, phlomis, rhatany, spiraea,
weigela
08 barberry, berberis, bilberry,
buddleia, camellia, clematis,
euonymus, gardenia, japonica,
krameria, laburnum, lavender,
magnolia, musk rose, viburnum,
wistaria, wisteria
09 beach plum, bean caper,
eucryphia, firethorn, forsythia,
hydrangea
10 bitter-king, buffalo-nut,
buttonbush, mock orange, witch
hazel
11 calycanthus, cotoneaster,
honeysuckle
12 blackcurrant, buffalo-berry,
rhododendron
13 Barbados pride, butcher's broom,
mountain avens

See also **plant**

shrug
• **shrug off**
06 ignore **07** dismiss, neglect **08** brush
off **09** disregard **14** take no notice of

shrunken
05 gaunt **06** shrunk, wasted
07 reduced **09** emaciated
10 cadaverous, contracted, shrivelled,
sphacelate **11** sphacelated

shudder
04 grew, grue **05** creep, grise, heave,
quake, shake, shrug, spasm **06** judder,
quiver, shiver, tremor **07** frisson,
tremble, vibrate **08** convulse
10 convulsion

shuffle
◇ *anagram indicator*
03 mix **04** drag, limp, make, pack
05 dodge, hedge, mix up, scuff, stack
06 doddle, falter, hobble, jumble, riffle,

scrape, switch, toddle **07** confuse,
evasion, patch up, scuffle, shamble
08 artifice, disorder, intermix, jumble
up, scramble, shauchle **09** rearrange,
reshuffle **10** move around, reorganize
11 shift around **12** tergiversate

shun
◇ *deletion indicator*
03 shy **04** snub **05** avoid, elude, evade,
evite, spurn **06** eschew, ignore
09 attention, ostracize **11** shy away
from **12** cold-shoulder, keep away
from, steer clear of

shunt
04 move, take **05** bring, budge, carry,
crash, fetch, shift, swing **06** bypass,
mishap, shelve, switch **08** relocate,
transfer **09** sidetrack, transport,
transpose

shut
02 to **03** bar **04** bolt, jail, lock, seal,
slam, spar, tine **05** close, latch, put to,
shoot, steek **06** cage in, closed, coop
up, fasten, immure, intern, lock up,
secure **07** confine **08** imprison
11 incarcerate, put the lid on
• **shut down**
04 halt, stop **05** cease, close, scram
07 suspend **09** close down, switch off,
terminate **10** inactivate **11** discontinue
• **shut in**
04 cage **05** box in, embar, hem in,
imbar **06** cage in, empale, immure,
impale, keep in **07** confine, enclose,
fence in, inclose, occlude **08** imprison,
restrain **10** encloister
• **shut off**
06 cut off **07** exclude, isolate, occlude,
seclude **08** obstruct, separate
09 segregate, switch off
• **shut out**
03 bar **04** fend, hide, mask, veil
05 cover, debar, exile **06** banish,
outlaw, screen **07** conceal, cover up,
exclude, lock out **08** block out
09 ostracize
• **shut up**
03 gag, pen **04** hush, jail, lock, pent
05 cabin, close, frank, quiet **06** bang
up, cage in, clam up, closet, coop up,
encage, hush up, immure, incage,
intern, lock up **07** confine, keep mum,
quieten, silence **08** imprison, pipe
down **09** endungeon **11** incarcerate
14 hold your tongue

shutter
05 blind, shade **06** douser, louver,
louvre, screen **07** scuttle **08** abat-jour,
jalousie

shuttle
03 ply, run **05** flute, shunt **06** seesaw,
travel **07** commute, shottle
09 alternate **10** go to and fro
11 shuttlecock **13** netting-needle

shy
03 coy, jib **04** cagy, gibe, shot, shun,
toss, wild **05** chary, fling, mousy,
squab, throw, timid **06** demure,
modest, mousey, scanty, skeigh
07 attempt, bashful, indrawn, nervous,

startle, strange **08** backward, cautious,
farouche, hesitant, reserved, reticent,
retiring, secluded, timorous, willyard,
willyart **09** diffident, inhibited,
shrinking, withdrawn **10** suspicious
11 embarrassed, introverted **12** self-
effacing, unproductive **13** self-
conscious
• **fight shy of**
04 shun **05** avoid, spurn **06** eschew
12 steer clear of
• **shy away**
03 jib **04** balk, buck, rear **05** avoid,
quail, spook, start, wince **06** flinch,
recoil, shrink, swerve **07** startle
08 back away

shyly
05 coyly **06** cagily **07** charily, timidly
09 bashfully **10** cautiously, hesitantly,
reticently **11** diffidently **15** self-
consciously

shyness
07 coyness, modesty **08** caginess,
timidity **09** chariness, hesitancy,
mousiness, reticence, timidness
10 constraint, diffidence, inhibition
11 bashfulness, nervousness
12 timorousness **13** embarrassment

SI

SI prefixes include:

03 exa
04 atto, deca, deci, giga, kilo, mega,
nano, peta, pico, tera
05 centi, femto, hecto, micro, milli,
yocto, yotta, zepto, zetta

sibling
04 twin **06** german, sister **07** brother

sibyl
04 seer **06** oracle, Pythia **07** seeress,
völuspa **09** pythoness, sorceress, wise
woman **10** prophetess

sick
◇ *anagram indicator*
03 ill **04** weak **05** angry, black, bored,
chase, crook, cruel, fed up, gross,
rough, seedy, tired, weary **06** ailing,
feeble, groggy, laid up, pining, poorly,
puking, queasy, sickly, unwell, vulgar
07 airsick, annoyed, bilious, carsick,
enraged, heaving, macabre, seasick,
set upon **08** diseased, gruesome,
nauseous, retching, vomiting
09 disgusted, hacked off, mortified,
nauseated, off colour, spewing up,
tasteless, uncle Dick **10** browned off,
cheesed off, in bad taste, indisposed,
out of sorts, throwing up, travel-sick
11 disgruntled **12** disappointed, sick
and tired **15** under the weather
• **be sick**
03 ail, gag **04** barf, puke, spew, spue
05 heave, retch, vomit **07** fetch up,
throw up **10** feel queasy **12** feel
nauseous

sicken
03 ail, get **05** appal, catch, repel
06 pick up, put off, revolt **07** develop,
disgust, turn off **08** contract, nauseate

09 become ill, succumb to **10** go down with **12** come down with **13** become ill with **15** turn your stomach

sickening
04 foul, vile **08** nauseous, shocking **09** appalling, loathsome, offensive, repellent, repulsive, revolting **10** chunderous, disgusting, nauseating, off-putting **11** distasteful **12** cringe-making, cringeworthy **14** stomach-turning

sickly
03 wan **04** pale, puly, sick, weak **05** faint, frail, gushy, mushy, soppy, sweet, wersh **06** ailing, donsie, feeble, infirm, morbid, pallid, slushy, sugary, syrupy, weakly **07** anaemic, bilious, cloying, insipid, languid, mawkish, pimping, queachy, queechy **08** delicate **09** revolting, schmaltzy, unhealthy, washed out **10** indisposed, nauseating **14** valetudinarian

sickness
03 bug, mal **04** dwam, puna **05** dwalm, dwaum, qualm, virus **06** malady, nausea, puking **07** ailment, disease, heaving, illness, soroche, surfeit **08** disorder, retching, vomiting **09** complaint, ill-health, infirmity, spewing up **10** affliction, queasiness, throwing up **11** airsickness, biliousness, carsickness, seasickness **13** indisposition **14** motion sickness, travel sickness **15** morning sickness

side
◇ *ends selection indicator*
01 L, R **02** 11, XI, XV **03** end, rim **04** area, bank, camp, edge, face, hand, jamb, left, long, page, sect, team, teme, view, wing, zone **05** angle, brink, cause, facet, flank, limit, minor, party, right, shore, slant, verge **06** aspect, border, eleven, fringe, lesser, margin, region, sector **07** faction, fifteen, lateral, oblique, profile, quarter, section, surface **08** boundary, district, division, flanking, interest, marginal, sidelong, sideward, sideways **09** arrogance, direction, periphery, secondary, viewpoint **10** department, incidental, standpoint, subsidiary **11** point of view, subordinate **13** neighbourhood, splinter group

See also **football**

• **at the side of**
02 by
• **both sides**
◇ *ends selection indicator*
• **change sides**
06 defect **08** come over
• **from side to side**
04 over **06** across
• **side by side**
06 jugate **07** abreast **10** collateral **11** cheek by jowl, neck and neck **14** heads and thraws **15** next to each other
• **side-effect**
04 echo **06** effect, recoil, result, ripple **07** outcome, rebound, spin-off

08 backwash **09** aftermath, by-product **11** consequence **12** repercussion **13** reverberation
• **side with**
04 back **06** favour, prefer **07** support, vote for **08** join with **09** agree with **10** team up with **13** be on the side of **15** give your backing, give your support
• **take someone's side**
04 back, help **06** favour, prefer **07** support, vote for **08** join with, motivate **09** encourage **13** be on the side of **14** sympathize with

sideline
04 game, omit **05** eject, exile, expel, hobby, sport **06** banish, demote, deport **07** degrade, exclude, pastime, pursuit **08** interest, relegate, transfer **09** amusement, diversion, downgrade, second job **10** expatriate, recreation, relaxation **13** entertainment **14** divertissement, leisure pursuit **15** leisure activity

sidelong
06 covert, secret, tilted **07** oblique, sloping **08** indirect, sideward, sideways **13** surreptitious

side-splitting
05 funny **07** amusing, a scream, comical, killing, riotous **08** farcical, humorous **09** hilarious, laughable **10** hysterical, uproarious

sidestep
04 duck **05** avoid, dodge, elude, evade, shirk, skirt **06** bypass **09** give a miss **10** circumvent **14** find a way around

sidetrack
05 shunt **06** divert **07** deflect, head off **08** distract **12** lead away from

sideways
04 side **07** askance, athwart, lateral, oblique, slanted **08** crabwise, edgeways, edgewise, indirect, sidelong, sideward **09** laterally, obliquely, sidewards, to the side **14** from side to side

siding
03 lie, lye **04** spur **07** turnout **09** sidetrack

sidle
04 edge, inch **05** creep, slink, sneak

siege
04 dung, rank, seat **05** class, privy, sedge **06** throne **07** leaguer **08** blockade **09** obsession, offensive **11** besiegement, distinction **12** encirclement **13** beleaguerment

Sieges include:

04 Acre, Metz, Troy, Waco
05 Alamo, Derry, Kuito, Paris, Rouen
06 Janina, London, Quebec, Toulon, Vienna
07 Antioch, Bristol, Granada, Lucknow, Orléans
08 Damascus, Drogheda, Limerick,

Mafeking, Roxburgh, Sarajevo, Syracuse, The Alamo
09 Barcelona, Jerusalem, Kimberley, Ladysmith, Leningrad, Silistria, Singapore, Vicksburg
10 Charleston, Kut al-amara, Montevideo, Sevastopol
12 Tenochtitlán
14 Balcombe Street, Constantinople, Entebbe Airport, Iranian Embassy, Munich Olympics, Spaghetti House

sierra
01 S

Sierra Leone
03 SLE, WAL

siesta
03 nap **04** doze, rest **05** sleep **06** catnap, repose, snooze **10** forty winks, relaxation **12** afternoon nap

sieve
03 sye **04** sift, sort, tems **05** temse **06** bolter, filter, girdle, remove, riddle, screen, searce, search, sifter, strain, winnow **07** boulter, cribble, griddle, trommel **08** colander, separate, strainer

sift
03 try **04** bolt, sort, tems **05** boult, probe, sieve, study, temse **06** filter, garble, review, riddle, screen, searce, search, strain, winnow **07** analyse, cribble, discuss, examine **08** pore over, separate **10** scrutinize **11** investigate

sigh
04 moan **05** heave, sithe, sough, swish **06** besigh, exhale, grieve, lament, rustle **07** breathe, crackle, suspire, whisper **08** complain **09** susurrate
• **sigh for**
03 cry **04** long, pine, weep **05** mourn, yearn **06** grieve, lament **08** languish **13** cry for the moon

sight
03 eye, see **04** bead, espy, look, show, spot, vane, view **05** range, scene, skill, visor **06** beauty, behold, fright, glance, marvel, seeing, vision, wonder **07** amenity, discern, display, eyesore, feature, glimpse, insight, make out, observe, perusal **08** eyesight, judgment, landmark, perceive, prospect **09** beholding, curiosity, judgement, spectacle, splendour **10** appearance, estimation, exhibition, perception, visibility **11** distinguish, monstrosity, observation **12** ability to see, conspectuity, sense of sight **13** field of vision, range of vision **14** faculty of sight **15** place of interest

Ways of describing sight impairment include:

06 myopic
08 purblind
09 amaurotic, cataracts, half-blind, sand-blind, snow-blind
10 astigmatic, far-sighted, night-blind, nyctalopic, presbyopic, stone-blind

11 blind as a bat, colour-blind, hemeralopic, long-sighted, near-sighted
12 glaucomatous, short-sighted, trachomatous
13 hypermetropic

• **catch sight of**
03 see, spy **04** espy, mark, note, spot, view **05** watch **06** look at, notice **07** discern, glimpse, make out **08** identify, perceive **09** recognize, set eyes on **10** clap eyes on
• **lose sight of**
04 omit **06** forget, ignore **07** neglect **08** overlook, put aside **09** disregard **12** slip your mind **14** fail to remember
• **set your sights on**
05 aim at **06** seek to **07** plan for **08** intend to **09** strive for **11** work towards **13** aspire towards

sightless
05 blind **07** eyeless **08** unseeing **09** invisible, unsighted, unsightly **10** visionless

sightseer
07 tourist, tripper, visitor **10** rubberneck **12** excursionist, holidaymaker

sign
01 V **03** act, nod, tag **04** bode, clue, code, hint, levy, logo, mark, omen, shew, show, wave, wink, word **05** badge, board, draft, enrol, frank, proof, raise, sigil, stamp, token, trace, write **06** action, attest, augury, banner, beckon, caract, cipher, effigy, emblem, engage, enlist, ensign, figure, gather, marker, motion, muster, notice, obelus, obtain, poster, ratify, signal, sign up, symbol, take on **07** acquire, ale-bush, ale-pole, betoken, bus stop, earnest, endorse, express, gesture, glimmer, initial, insigne, placard, pointer, portent, presage, promise, recruit, symptom, witness **08** ale-stake, assemble, evidence, headhunt, ideogram, indicate, inscribe, insignia, mobilize, movement, signpost **09** autograph, character, conscript, harbinger, ideograph, indicator, sacrament, subscribe **10** death-token, denotement, foreboding, indication, suggestion, talent-spot, three balls **11** barber's pole, communicate, countersign, forewarning, gesticulate, phraseogram, put together, recognition, significant **12** shilling mark **13** gesticulation, manifestation **14** representation **15** prognostication

See also **zodiac**

• **from the sign**
02 DS **08** dal segno
• **sign over**
06 convey **07** consign, deliver, entrust **08** make over, transfer, turn over **09** surrender
• **sign up**
04 hire, join **05** enrol **06** employ, engage, enlist, join up, sign on, take on **07** recruit **08** register **09** volunteer **15** join the services

signal
◇ *anagram indicator*
04 clue, hint, mark, show, sign, toll, waff, waft **05** alert, recal, token **06** beckon, convey, famous, gryfon, maroon, motion, recall, target, tip-off **07** eminent, express, gesture, griffin, griffon, gryphon, message, notable, pointer, signify, symptom, warning **08** evidence, glorious, indicate, intimate, striking **09** important, memorable, momentous, telegraph **10** impressive, indication, intimation, noteworthy, remarkable **11** communicate, conspicuous, exceptional, gesticulate, outstanding, significant **13** distinguished, extraordinary

> **Signals and warnings include:**

03 cue, gun, nod, pip, SOS
04 bell, buoy, fire, flag, gong, home, honk, horn, pips, taps, toot, wave, wink
05 alarm, bugle, flare, knell, larum, light, pager, robot, shout, siren, vigia
06 beacon, buzzer, hooter, klaxon, mayday, rocket, tattoo, tocsin, war cry, winker
07 bleeper, car horn, foghorn, go-ahead, red card, red flag, torpedo, whistle
08 car alarm, diaphone, drumbeat, high sign, password, red alert, red light, reveille
09 alarm-bell, detonator, fire alarm, indicator, larum-bell, Morse code, signal box, storm cone, Very light, watch fire, watchword, white flag
10 alarm clock, amber light, Bengal fire, curfew bell, green light, hand signal, heliograph, lighthouse, Lutine bell, smoke alarm, time signal, yellow card, yellow flag
11 Bengal light, bicycle bell, gale warning, smoke signal, starter's gun, storm signal, trafficator, trumpet call, warning shot
12 burglar alarm, final warning, storm warning, warning light
13 Belisha beacon, flashing light, personal alarm, police whistle, security alarm, signal letters, traffic lights
14 distress signal
15 semaphore signal

signature
01 X **03** sig, tag **04** hand, mark, name **05** cross, frank, sheet **08** initials **09** autograph, theme song, theme tune **10** criss-cross, sign-manual **11** endorsement, inscription, John Hancock **12** subscription

significance
04 gist, pith **05** ethos, force, point, sense **06** import, matter, slight, weight **07** essence, meaning, message, purport **08** interest **09** magnitude, relevance, solemnity **10** importance, inwardness **11** consequence, implication, seriousness **12** implications **13** consideration

significant
03 big, key **04** sign **05** vital **06** cosmic, marked, of note **07** crucial, fateful, meaning, ominous, serious, telling, weighty **08** critical, eloquent, material, pregnant, relevant, senseful, symbolic **09** important, memorable, momentous **10** expressive, indicative, meaningful, noteworthy, suggestive **11** appreciable, symptomatic **12** considerable **13** consequential

significantly
07 notably, vitally **09** crucially, knowingly, meaningly **10** critically, eloquently, materially, noticeably, remarkably **11** appreciably, perceptibly **12** considerably, expressively, meaningfully, suggestively

signify
04 mark, mean, show **05** count, imply, skill, spell **06** bemean, convey, denote, import, matter, signal **07** betoken, connote, declare, exhibit, express, magnify, portend, suggest **08** indicate, intimate, proclaim, stand for, transmit **09** be a sign of, importune, make waves, represent, symbolize **10** be relevant **11** be important, carry weight, communicate **13** have influence **14** be of importance **15** be of consequence

signpost
04 clue, sign **06** marker **07** placard, pointer, waypost **08** handpost **09** guidepost, indicator **10** fingerpost, indication

silence
03 gag **04** calm, hush, lull, mute **05** abate, burke, peace, quell, quiet, still **06** deaden, muffle, muzzle, stifle, subdue **07** clamour, infancy, put down, quieten, reserve, secrecy **08** calmness, cut short, dumbness, muteness, oblivion, suppress **09** cough down, dumbfound, quietness, reticence, stillness **10** quiescence, strike dumb **11** taciturnity **12** peacefulness, tranquillity, wordlessness **13** noiselessness, secretiveness, soundlessness, voicelessness **14** altum silentium, speechlessness
• **expressions invoking silence**
02 sh, st **03** mum, shh **04** hist, hush, tace **05** dry up, peace, quiet, shush, whish, whist **06** belt up, shut up, wheesh, whisht, wrap up **07** wheesht **08** button it, give over, pack it in, pipe down **09** say no more **10** enough said, keep shtoom, stay shtoom **11** give it a rest **12** cut the cackle, put a sock in it, shut your face **13** hold your peace, shut your mouth **14** hold your tongue, not another word

See also **quiet**

silent
03 mum **04** calm, dumb, hush, mute **05** dummy, muted, quiet, shtum, still, stumm, tacit, whist **06** hushed,

shtoom, shtumm, sullen, whisht
07 implied, schtoom, sulking, wheesht
08 implicit, peaceful, reserved,
reticent, taciturn, tuneless, unspoken,
unvoiced, wordless **09** conticent,
inaudible, mumchance, noiseless,
quiescent, secretive, soundless,
voiceless **10** creepmouse,
dumbstruck, speechless, tongue-tied,
understood **11** inoperative,
obmutescent, tight-lipped,
unexpressed **12** languageless

silently
06 calmly, dumbly, mutely, stilly
07 quietly, tacitly, unheard **08** ex tacito
09 inaudibly **10** wordlessly
11 noiselessly, quiescently, soundlessly
12 speechlessly, without a word

silhouette
04 form **05** shape **06** shadow
07 contour, outline, profile, skyline
08 stand out **09** configure, delineate
11 configurate, delineation **12** shadow
figure **13** configuration

silicon
02 Si

silk
02 KC, QC **03** bur **04** burr **05** crape,
moire, satin, surah, tulle **06** crepon,
faille, pongee, sendal **07** alamode,
challie, challis, marabou, organza,
ottoman, taffeta **08** boulting,
marabout, prunella, prunelle, prunello,
taffetas **09** barrister, filoselle,
grenadine **10** peau de soie **11** Canton
crepe **12** bolting cloth, King's
Counsel, moire antique **13** Queen's
Counsel
• **silk yarn**
04 tram **08** chenille **09** organzine

silky
04 fine, seal, soft **05** sleek **06** glossy,
satiny, selkie, silken, silkie, smooth
07 velvety **08** lustrous **09** sericeous
10 diaphanous

silliness
◇ *anagram indicator*
05 folly **06** idiocy **08** daftness,
rashness **09** absurdity, barminess,
frivolity, inaneness, looniness,
loopiness, pottiness, stupidity
10 immaturity **11** fatuousness,
foolishness **12** childishness,
recklessness **13** foolhardiness,
frivolousness, irrationality,
ludicrousness, pointlessness,
senselessness **14** ridiculousness
15 meaninglessness

silly
◇ *anagram indicator*
03 nit **04** berk, clot, daft, dope, dumb,
fool, rash, soft, twit **05** apish, barmy,
bunny, dazed, dilly, dizzy, dotty,
dumbo, goose, idiot, inane, inept,
loopy, ninny, nutty, potty, seely, wally
06 absurd, cuckoo, dotish, drippy,
duffer, feeble, humble, nitwit, simple,
spoony, stupid, unwise **07** fatuous,
foolish, halfwit, idiotic, missish, puerile,

spooney, strange, stunned **08** childish,
harmless, immature, pitiable, reckless
09 airheaded, brainless, foolhardy,
frivolous, hen-witted, ignoramus,
illogical, imprudent, ludicrous,
pointless, senseless, simpleton
10 irrational, nincompoop, ridiculous,
silly-billy **11** defenceless, hair-brained,
hare-brained, injudicious,
meaningless, nonsensical, thoughtless
12 feeble-minded, preposterous,
unreasonable **13** irresponsible,
unintelligent **14** feather-brained,
scatterbrained

silt
03 mud **04** ooze **06** sludge **07** deposit,
residue, sullage **08** alluvium, illuvium,
sediment **10** brick-earth
• **silt up**
03 dam **04** clog **05** block, choke
06 clog up **07** block up, congest

silvan
05 leafy **06** forest, wooded
08 arcadian, forestal, forested,
woodland **09** arboreous, forestine
11 tree-covered

silver
02 Ag **05** plate, snowy **06** albata,
argent, siller **07** bonanza, cutlery
08 pale grey **11** whitish-grey **12** British
plate, greyish-white

similar
04 akin, like **05** alike, close, samey
07 related, uniform **08** such like
09 analogous, semblable
10 coincident, comparable,
equivalent, homologous, resembling
11 homogeneous, much the same
13 corresponding

similarity
06 kinred **07** analogy, kindred, kinship
08 affinity, homogeny, likeness,
relation, sameness **09** agreement,
closeness **10** conformity,
congruence, similitude, uniformity
11 concordance, equivalence,
homogeneity, isomorphism,
parallelism, resemblance
13 comparability, compatibility
14 correspondence

similarly
08 likewise **09** by analogy, uniformly
12 in the same way **14** by the same
token **15** correspondingly

similitude
07 analogy, parable **08** affinity,
likeness, relation, sameness
09 agreement, closeness, semblance
10 comparison, congruence,
likelihood, similarity, uniformity
11 equivalence, parallelism,
resemblance **13** comparability,
compatibility **14** correspondence

simmer
04 boil, burn, fume, rage, stew
06 bubble, seethe **08** smoulder **10** boil
gently, cook gently
• **simmer down**
06 lessen **07** subside **08** calm down,

cool down **15** become less angry,
collect yourself, control yourself

simpering
03 coy **05** silly **06** smirky **07** missish
08 affected, giggling **13** schoolgirlish,
self-conscious

simple
04 bald, easy, mean, mere, open, slow
05 afald, basic, blunt, clear, crude,
cushy, green, lucid, naive, naked, plain,
seely, sheer, silly, sorry, stark **06** a cinch,
aefald, afawld, candid, direct, honest,
semple, soigné, stupid **07** a doddle,
aefauld, artless, austere, classic,
foolish, gullish, idiotic, low-tech,
natural, onefold, sincere, soignée,
spartan, unfussy **08** Arcadian,
backward, homespun, innocent,
inornate, no-frills, ordinary, retarded,
semplice **09** a cakewalk, a pushover, a
walkover, boastless, credulous, easy as
pie, easy-peasy, Galenical, guileless,
ingenuous, primitive, Saturnian,
unadorned, unlearned, unskilled
10 effortless, elementary, half-witted,
unaffected, uninvolved
11 incomposite, inelaborate, Mickey
Mouse, open-and-shut, rudimentary,
unambiguous, undecorated **12** a piece
of cake, feeble-minded, inartificial,
simple-minded, unsuspecting **13** low
technology, rough and ready,
uncomplicated, unembellished,
unpretentious **14** comprehensible,
understandable, unsophisticate
15 straightforward, unsophisticated

simple-minded
03 twp **05** dopey, goofy, idiot
06 simple, stupid **07** artless, foolish,
idiotic, moronic, natural **08** backward,
imbecile, innocent, retarded
09 brainless, cretinous, dim-witted
12 addle-brained, feeble-minded
14 not the full quid **15** unsophisticated

simpleton
03 daw, mug **04** clot, dolt, dope, dupe,
flat, fool, gaby, loon, poop, rook, simp,
tony, twit, zany **05** booby, bunny,
cokes, dunce, goose, idiot, moron,
ninny, noddy, patsy, spoon, sumph,
twerp **06** gander, Johnny, nincom,
nincum, nitwit, noodle, simple, stupid
07 dawcock, dullard, gomeral, gomeril,
jackass, Johnnie, juggins, mafflin
08 Abderite, flathead, imbecile,
maffling, numskull, shot-clog,
softhead, wiseacre, woodcock
09 blockhead, Gothamist, Gothamite,
greenhorn, nicompoop **10** green
goose, hoddy-doddy, nickumpoop,
nincompoop **11** ninny-hammer
See also **fool**

simplicity
04 ease **06** purity **07** candour, clarity,
honesty, naiveté, naivety **08** easiness,
facility, lucidity, openness, simplism
09 frankness, gracility, innocence,
niaiserie, plainness, restraint, rusticity,
simplesse, sincerity, starkness **10** clean
lines, directness, simpleness

11 artlessness, naturalness
13 guilelessness **14** elementariness
15 intelligibility

simplification
09 reduction **10** paraphrase
11 abridgement, explanation
13 clarification **14** interpretation,
popularization

simplify
06 reduce **07** abridge, clarify, explain,
sort out, unravel **08** decipher, make
easy, untangle **09** interpret **10** make
easier, paraphrase, popularize,
streamline **11** disentangle **14** make
accessible

simplistic
03 pat **04** naif **05** naive **06** facile,
simple **07** shallow **08** sweeping
10 oversimple **11** superficial
14 oversimplified

simplistically
06 simply **07** naively **08** facilely
09 shallowly **13** superficially

simply
04 just, only **05** quite, truly **06** easily,
merely, purely, really, solely, wholly
07 clearly, lucidly, plainly, totally, utterly
08 directly, semplice **09** naturally,
obviously, shallowly, tout court
10 absolutely, altogether, completely,
positively, undeniably **11** simpliciter
12 intelligibly, unreservedly, without
doubt **14** unquestionably
15 unconditionally

Simpson
02 OJ **04** Bart, Lisa **05** Homer, Marge
06 Maggie, Wallis

simulate
03 act **04** copy, echo, fain, fake, mock,
sham **05** faine, fayne, feign, mimic, put
on **06** affect, assume, parrot
07 feigned, imitate, pretend, reflect
08 parallel **09** duplicate, reproduce
11 counterfeit, make believe

simulated
04 fake, faux, mock, sham **05** bogus,
put-on **06** phoney, pseudo
07 assumed, feigned, man-made
08 spurious **09** imitation, insincere,
pretended, synthetic **10** artificial,
substitute **11** inauthentic, make-
believe

simultaneous
05 simul **08** parallel **10** coexistent,
coinciding, concurrent, synchronic
11 concomitant, synchronous
15 coinstantaneous,
contemporaneous

simultaneously
06 at once **07** at one go **08** in unison,
together **09** all at once, at one time
10 in parallel **11** all together **13** at the
same time, synchronously
14 synchronically

sin
03 err **04** debt, evil, fall, pity, shin, sine
05 crime, error, fault, folly, guilt, lapse,

shame, since, stray, wrong **06** offend
07 badness, do wrong, go wrong,
impiety, misdeed, offence, offense
08 go astray, iniquity, trespass
09 misbehave **10** commit a sin,
immorality, sinfulness, transgress,
wickedness, wrongdoing
11 ungodliness **12** misdemeanour
13 fall from grace, transgression
15 irreligiousness, unrighteousness

The Seven Deadly Sins:
04 envy, lust
05 anger, greed, pride, sloth, wrath
06 acedia
07 accidie, avarice
08 gluttony
12 covetousness

since
02 as **03** ago, sin **04** past, sens, sine,
sith, syne, ygoe **05** after, agone, being,
until **06** seeing, sithen **07** because,
owing to, sithens, through **08** sithence,
until now **09** following **10** inasmuch
as, seeing that **11** as a result of, on
account of **12** from that time,
subsequent to **13** from the time of
15 considering that, from the time
that

sincere
04 open, pure, real, true **05** afald, frank
06 aefald, afawld, candid, dinkum,
direct, hearty, honest, simple, single
07 aefauld, artless, cordial, dinki-di,
earnest, fervent, genuine, natural,
serious, unmixed, up front **08** bona
fide, truthful **09** guileless, heartfelt,
ingenuous, unfeigned **10** above board,
fair dinkum, heart-whole, no-
nonsense, unaffected **11** plain-spoken,
true-hearted, trustworthy, undesigning
12 plain-hearted, wholehearted
13 simple-hearted, single-hearted,
unadulterated **15** straightforward

sincerely
05 truly **06** entire, really, simply
08 honestly **09** earnestly, genuinely, in
earnest, seriously **10** truthfully
11 unfeignedly **12** unaffectedly
14 wholeheartedly

sincerity
05 truth **06** candor, honour, purity
07 candour, honesty, probity, realtie
08 openness **09** frankness, integrity
10 directness **11** artlessness,
earnestness, genuineness, seriousness,
uprightness **12** truthfulness
13 guilelessness, ingenuousness
15 trustworthiness

sinecure
05 cinch **06** doddle, picnic **07** plum
job **08** cushy job **10** gravy train, soft
option **11** money for jam **15** money for
old rope

sinewy
04 wiry **05** burly **06** brawny, robust,
strong, sturdy **07** nervous, stringy
08 athletic, muscular, stalwart,
vigorous **09** strapping

sinful
03 bad **04** evil **05** wrong **06** erring,
fallen, guilty, unholy, wicked
07 corrupt, immoral, impious, ungodly
08 criminal, depraved, wrongful
10 iniquitous **11** irreligious,
unrighteous

sinfulness
03 sin **05** guilt **07** impiety **08** iniquity,
peccancy **09** depravity **10** corruption,
immorality, wickedness **11** peccability,
ungodliness **13** transgression
15 unrighteousness

sing
03 hum **04** lilt, pipe, rant, ring, scat,
slur **05** carol, chant, chirp, croon, jodel,
trill, yodel, yodle **06** chaunt, chorus,
intone, quaver, record, second, squall,
squeal, strain, warble **07** confess,
measure, perform, whistle
08 serenade, vocalize **09** celebrate
13 burst into song
• **sing out**
03 cry **04** bawl, call, yell **05** cooee,
peach, shout **06** bellow, cry out, holler,
inform

Singapore
03 SGP

singe
04 burn, char, sear **05** swale, swayl,
sweal, sweel **06** scorch, swinge
07 blacken, scowder **08** scouther,
scowther

singer

Singer types include:
03 pop
04 alto, bard, bass, diva, folk, wait
05 carol, mezzo, opera, tenor
06 chorus, treble
07 crooner, pop star, soloist, soprano,
warbler
08 baritone, barytone, castrato,
choirboy, falsetto, minstrel,
songster, vocalist
09 balladeer, chanteuse, choirgirl,
chorister, contralto, precentor,
sopranist
10 prima donna, songstress,
troubadour
11 Heldentenor
12 counter-tenor, mezzo-soprano
13 basso profondo, basso profundo

See also **bird**

Singers include:
03 Day (Doris)
04 Cole (Nat 'King'), Lynn (Dame
Vera), Piaf (Edith)
05 Lloyd (Marie), Paige (Elaine)
06 Atwell (Winifred), Bassey (Dame
Shirley), Church (Charlotte), Crosby
(Bing), Fields (Dame Gracie),
Jolson (Al), Lauder (Sir Harry),
Lillie (Beatrice), Steele
(Tommy)
07 Andrews (Dame Julie), Garland
(Judy), Miranda (Carmen),
Robeson (Paul), Secombe (Sir
Harry), Sinatra (Frank)

08 Bygraves (Max), Liberace
09 Belafonte (Harry), Chevalier (Albert)

Classical singers include:

4 Butt (Dame Clara), Lind (Jenny), Popp (Lucia), Tear (Robert)
5 Baker (Dame Janet), Craig (Charles), Evans (Sir Geraint), Ewing (Maria), Field (Helen), Gigli (Beniamino), Lanza (Mario), Lenya (Lotte), Melba (Dame Nellie), Patti (Adelina), Pears (Sir Peter)
6 Bowman (James), Callas (Maria), Caruso (Enrico), Davies (Ryland), Deller (Alfred), Kirkby (Emma), Norman (Jessye), Terfel (Bryn), Turner (Dame Eva), Van Dam (José)
7 Baillie (Dame Isobel), Bartoli (Cecilia), Caballé (Montserrat), Domingo (Plácido), Ferrier (Kathleen), Garrett (Lesley), Hammond (Dame Joan), Lehmann (Lotte), Nilsson (Birgit), Vickers (Jon)
8 Carreras (José), Flagstad (Kirsten), Te Kanawa (Dame Kiri)
9 Chaliapin (Fyodor), Forrester (Maureen), McCormack (John), Pavarotti (Luciano)
10 Söderström (Elisabeth), Sutherland (Dame Joan)
11 Schwarzkopf (Dame Elisabeth)
12 De Los Angeles (Victoria)

Folk singers, musicians and bands include:

03 Gow (Niel)
04 Baez (Joan), Bain (Aly), Reid (Robert)
05 Sharp (Cecil James), Simon (Paul)
06 Browne (Ronnie), Fisher (Archie), Foster (Stephen Collins), Fraser (Marjory Kennedy), Mackay (Charles), Martyn (John), Nairne (Carolina), Pogues, Runrig, Seeger (Pete)
07 Burgess (John Davey), Cassidy (Eva), Clannad, Donegan (Lonnie), Donovan, Gaughan (Dick), Guthrie (Woody), MacColl (Ewan), Robeson (Paul), Skinner (James Scott), Thomson (George)
08 Marshall (William), Morrison (Van), O'Donnell (Daniel), Rafferty (Gerry)
09 Dubliners, Henderson (Hamish), Leadbelly, Robertson (Jeannie), The Pogues
10 Williamson (Roy)

Jazz singers and musicians include:

03 Guy (Buddy), Ory (Kid)
04 Cole (Nat 'King'), Getz (Stan), Kidd (Carole), King (B B), Monk (Thelonius), Pine (Courtney), Shaw (Artie)
05 Baker (Chet), Basie (Count), Corea (Chick), Davis (Miles), Evans (Gil), Hines (Earl), Jones (Quincy), Krupa (Gene), Laine (Dame Cleo), Roach (Max), Scott (Ronnie), Smith (Bessie), Smith (Tommy), Sun Ra, Tatum (Art), Young (Lester)
06 Barber (Chris), Bechet (Sidney), Blakey (Art), Domino (Fats), Dorsey (Tommy), Garner (Errol), Gordon (Dexter), Herman (Woody), Hodges (Johnny), Hooker (John Lee), Joplin (Scott), Kenton (Stan), Miller (Glenn), Mingus (Charles), Morton (Jelly Roll), Oliver (King), Parker (Charlie), Powell (Bud), Simone (Nina), Tracey (Stan), Walker (T-Bone), Waller (Thomas 'Fats'), Waters (Muddy)
07 Bennett (Tony), Broonzy (Big Bill), Brubeck (Dave), Charles (Ray), Coleman (Ornette), Goodman (Benny), Hampton (Lionel 'Hamp'), Hancock (Herbie), Hawkins (Coleman), Holiday (Billie 'Lady Day'), Hot Five, Ibrahim (Abdullah), Jackson (Milt), Jarrett (Keith), Johnson (James Price), Metheny (Pat), Mezzrow (Mezz), Rollins (Sonny), Shorter (Wayne), Vaughan (Sarah)
08 Adderley (Cannonball), All Stars, Calloway (Cab), Coltrane (John), Eldridge (Roy), Franklin (Aretha), Gershwin (George), Hot Seven, Marsalis (Wynton), Mulligan (Gerry), Peterson (Oscar)
09 Armstrong (Louis 'Satchmo'), Christian (Charlie), Dankworth (Sir John), Ellington (Duke), Gillespie (Dizzy), Grappelli (Stephane), Henderson (Fletcher), Leadbelly, Lunceford (Jimmie), Lyttelton (Humphrey), Reinhardt (Django), Teagarden (Jack)
10 Fitzgerald (Ella), McLaughlin (John), Thielemans (Toots), Washington (Dinah)
11 Beiderbecke (Bix), Howling Wolf
12 Jazz Warriors

Opera singers include:

03 Mei (Lanfang)
04 Lind (Jenny), Pons (Lily), Popp (Lucia), Tear (Robert), Ward (David)
05 Allen (Sir Thomas), Baker (Dame Janet), Evans (Sir Geraint), Ewing (Maria), Freni (Mirella), Gedda (Nicolai), Gigli (Beniamino), Gobbi (Tito), Horne (Marilyn), Jones (Dame Gwyneth), Kollo (René), Kraus (Alfredo), Lanza (Mario), Luxon (Benjamin), Melba (Dame Nellie), Patti (Adelina), Pears (Sir Peter), Pinza (Ezio), Price (Leontyne), Siepi (Cesare), Sills (Beverly), Teyte (Dame Maggie)
06 Bowman (James), Callas (Maria), Caruso (Enrico), Davies (Ryland), Dawson (Peter), Deller (Alfred), de Luca (Giuseppe), Farrar (Geraldine), García (Manuel), Garden (Mary), Harper (Heather), Hotter (Hans), Ludwig (Christa), Minton (Yvonne), Norman (Jessye), Reszke (Jean de), Scotto (Renata), Studer (Cheryl), Tauber (Richard), Terfel (Bryn), Turner (Dame Eva), Van Dam (José)
07 Barstow (Dame Josephine), Bartoli (Cecilia), Caballé (Montserrat), Domingo (Placido), Farrell (Eileen), Ferrier (Kathleen), Garrett (Lesley), Jurinac (Sena), Lehmann (Lilli), Lehmann (Lotte), Migenes (Julia), Milanov (Zinka), Nilsson (Birgit), Stratas (Teresa), Tebaldi (Renata), Tibbett (Lawrence), Traubel (Helen), Vickers (Jon)
08 Anderson (Marian), Berganza (Teresa), Bergonzi (Carlo), Björling (Jussi), Carreras (José), Dernesch (Helga), Flagstad (Kirsten), Lawrence (Marjorie), Melchior (Lauritz), Piccaver (Alfred), Ponselle (Rosa), Schumann (Elisabeth), Seefried (Irmgard), Te Kanawa (Dame Kiri)
09 Berberian (Cathy), Brannigan (Owen), Chaliapin (Feodor), Christoff (Boris), Della Casa (Lisa), Del Monaco (Mario), Forrester (Maureen), Hendricks (Barbara), McCormack (John), McCracken (James), Pavarotti (Luciano)
10 Galli-Curci (Amelita), Los Angeles (Victoria de), Martinelli (Giovanni), Söderström (Elisabeth), Sutherland (Dame Joan), Tetrazzini (Luisa)
11 Schwarzkopf (Dame Elisabeth)
12 de los Angeles (Victoria), Shirley-Quirk (John)
14 Fischer-Dieskau (Dietrich)

Pop and rock singers, musicians and bands include:

02 U2
03 ELO, Eno (Brian), Jam, Lee (Peggy), Pop (Iggy), REM, Yes
04 Abba, AC/DC, B52s, Baez (Joan), Blur, Bush (Kate), Cash (Johnny), Cher, Cray (Robert), Crow (Sheryl), Cure, Devo, Dion (Celine), Dury (Ian), Gaye (Marvin), Joel (Billy), John (Sir Elton), Khan (Chaka), King (Carole), Kiss, Lulu, Piaf (Edith), Pulp, Reed (Lou), Ross (Diana), Rush, Sade, Shaw (Sandie), UB40, Vega (Suzanne), Wham!
05 Adams (Bryan), Berry (Chuck), Black (Cilla), Bolan (Marc), Bowie (David), Brown (James), Byrds, Byrne (David), Carey (Mariah), Clash, Cohen (Leonard), Davis (Sammy, Junior), Doors, Dylan (Bob), Ferry (Bryan), Flack (Roberta), Haley (Bill, and the Comets), Jarre (Jean-Michel), Jones (Grace), Jones (Tom), Kinks, Lewis (Jerry Lee), Melua (Katie), Moyet (Alison), Oasis, Queen, Simon (Carly), Simon (Paul), Smith (Patti), Starr (Ringo), Twain (Shaniah), Verve, Waits (Tom), White (Barry), Wings, Young (Neil), Zappa (Frank), ZZ Top
06 Atwell (Winifred), Bassey (Shirley), Cocker (Joe), Cooper (Alice), Crosby (Bing), Damned, Denver (John), Domino (Fats), Eagles,

Easton (Sheena), **Fields** (Dame Gracie), **Jolson** (Al), **Joplin** (Janis), **Knight** (Gladys, and the Pips), **Lauper** (Cyndi), **Lennon** (John), **Lennox** (Annie), **Marley** (Bob), **Midler** (Bette), **Newman** (Randy), **Palmer** (Robert), **Pitney** (Gene), **Pogues, Police, Prince, Richie** (Lionel), **Sedaka** (Neil), **Simone** (Nina), **Smiths, Summer** (Donna), **Taylor** (James),**The Who,Turner** (Tina),**Wonder** (Stevie)

07 **Animals, Beatles, Bee Gees, Blondie, Bon Jovi, Charles** (Ray), **Clapton** (Eric), **Cochran** (Eddie), **Collins** (Phil), **Diamond** (Neil), **Diddley** (Bo), **Donovan, Gabriel** (Peter), **Garland** (Judy), **Genesis, Hendrix** (Jimi), **Hollies, Houston** (Whitney), **Jackson** (Janet), **Jackson** (Michael), **Madonna, Mercury** (Freddie), **Michael** (George), **Minogue** (Kylie), **Monkees, Orbison** (Roy), **Osmonds, Pickett** (Wilson), **Presley** (Elvis), **Redding** (Otis), **Richard** (Sir Cliff), **Santana** (Carlos), **Shadows, Sinatra** (Frank), **Squeeze, Stevens** (Cat), **Stewart** (Rod), **Vincent** (Gene),**Warwick** (Dionne)

08 **Coldplay, Costello** (Elvis), **Franklin** (Aretha), **Green Day, Harrison** (George), **Liberace, Mitchell** (Joni), **Morrison** (Van), **New Order, Oldfield** (Mike), **Robinson** (Smokey),**Vandross** (Luther),**Van Halen,Williams** (Robbie)

09 **Aerosmith, Beach Boys, Chevalier** (Albert), **Garfunkel** (Art), **Kraftwerk, McCartney** (Paul), **Motorhead, Pink Floyd, Radiohead, Roxy Music, Simply Red, Status Quo, Steely Dan, Streisand** (Barbra),**The Pogues,Thin Lizzy**

10 **Carpenters, Deep Purple, Def Leppard, Duran Duran, Eurythmics, Guns 'n' Roses, Iron Maiden, Moody Blues, Portishead, Pretenders, Sex Pistols, Shangri-las, Spice Girls, Stranglers**

11 **Armatrading** (Joan), **Culture Club, Cypress Hill, Dire Straits, Human League, Joy Division, Judas Priest, Led Zeppelin, Public Enemy, Simple Minds, Springfield** (Dusty), **Springsteen** (Bruce),**Temptations**

12 **Black Sabbath, Dead Kennedys, Fleetwood Mac, Grateful Dead, Talking Heads**

13 **Little Richard, Rolling Stones, Spandau Ballet**

14 **Everly Brothers, Pointer Sisters, Public Image Ltd**

15 **Neville Brothers**

---

single
03 ane, one 04 free, lone, only, poor, sole, solo, thin, unit, weak 05 afald, alone, small, unwed 06 aefald, afawld, honest, one run, simple, slight, unique, versal 07 aefauld, one-fold, simplex, sincere 08 by itself, celibate, distinct, isolated, man-to-man, one-to-one, separate, singular, solitary, unbroken,

unshared 09 available, exclusive, on your own, undivided, unmarried 10 by yourself, determined, individual, one and only, particular, unattached, uncombined 12 woman-to-woman 14 person-to-person

• **single out**
04 pick 05 hit on 06 choose, pick on, select 07 hit upon, isolate 08 decide on, hand-pick, identify, pinpoint, separate, set apart 09 highlight, victimize 11 distinguish, separate out

single-handed
04 solo 05 alone 07 unaided 09 on your own 10 by yourself, unassisted 11 independent, without help 13 independently, unaccompanied

single-minded
03 set 05 afald, fixed 06 aefald, afawld, dogged 07 aefauld, devoted, onefold 08 resolute, tireless 09 committed, dedicated, ingenuous, obsessive, steadfast 10 determined, unswerving, unwavering 11 persevering, undeviating 12 monomaniacal

singly
04 only 05 alone 06 solely 08 one by one 10 distinctly, one at a time, on their own, separately, singularly 12 individually 13 independently

singular
01 s 03 odd 04 sing 05 queer 06 proper, single, unique 07 curious, eminent, private, strange, unusual 08 atypical, peculiar, uncommon 09 eccentric 10 noteworthy, pre-eminent, remarkable 11 conspicuous, exceptional, out-of-the-way, outstanding 12 unparalleled 13 extraordinary

singularity
05 quirk, twist 06 oddity 07 oddness, oneness 09 queerness 10 uniqueness 11 abnormality, curiousness, peculiarity, strangeness 12 eccentricity, idiosyncrasy, irregularity 13 individuality, particularity

singularly
06 singly 07 notably 08 signally 09 bizarrely, strangely, unusually 10 especially, peculiarly, remarkably, uncommonly 12 particularly, pre-eminently, prodigiously, surprisingly 13 conspicuously, exceptionally, outstandingly 15 extraordinarily

sinister
01 L 02 lh 04 dark, evil, left 05 cruel, shady 06 Gothic, louche, malign, wicked 07 harmful, ominous, unlucky, vicious 08 menacing 09 underhand 10 disturbing, forbidding, malevolent, misleading, portentous, terrifying 11 disquieting, frightening, threatening 12 inauspicious

sink
◇ *anagram indicator*
03 bog, dig, dip, ebb, lay, pay, pot, sag, set 04 bore, damn, dive, drop, fade,

fail, fall, flag, foil, fund, mire, risk, ruin, slip 05 abate, basin, bason, decay, drill, drive, droop, drown, embed, lapse, let in, lower, merge, put in, shaft, slump, stoop, wreck 06 cloaca, devall, engulf, fall in, go down, insert, invest, jawbox, lay out, lessen, plough, plunge, settle, vanish, weaken, worsen 07 abandon, abolish, capsize, conceal, decline, degrade, descend, destroy, dwindle, founder, go lower, go to pot, go under, immerse, plummet, put down, scupper, scuttle, subside, succumb, venture 08 cesspool, collapse, decrease, demolish, diminish, excavate, submerge, suppress 09 devastate, disappear, gravitate, penetrate 10 degenerate, go downhill 12 draught-house

sinless
04 pure 08 innocent, virtuous 09 faultless, guiltless, undefiled, unspotted, unsullied 10 immaculate, impeccable 11 unblemished, uncorrupted

sinner
08 criminal, evil-doer, offender 09 miscreant, reprobate, wrongdoer 10 backslider, impenitent, malefactor, trespasser 12 transgressor

sinuous
04 ogee, wavy 05 lithe 06 curved, slinky 07 bending, coiling, curling, curving, sinuate, turning, weaving, winding, wriggly 08 tortuous, twisting 10 meandering, serpentine, undulating

sip
03 sup 04 drop, sowp, tiff, tift 05 drink, taste 06 sample, sipple 08 delibate, mouthful, spoonful 11 drink slowly

sir
02 Sr 03 Dan, Don 04 baas, Herr, stir, tuan 05 bwana, sahib, Señor 06 Mister, Signor, sirrah, stirra 07 lording, mynheer, Signior, Signore, stirrah 08 Monsieur

siren
04 vamp 05 alarm, Circe, syren 06 hooter, tocsin 07 charmer, Delilah, foghorn, Lorelei, mermaid 08 car alarm 09 fire alarm, temptress 10 seductress 11 femme fatale 12 burglar alarm 13 moaning minnie, personal alarm, security alarm

sissy *see* **cissy**

sister
02 Sr 03 nun, sib, sis 04 siss 05 titty 06 abbess, fellow, friend, german, vowess 07 comrade, partner, sibling 08 prioress, relation, relative 09 associate, colleague, companion 10 full sister, half-sister, twin-sister 11 blood-sister

sit
02 do 03 fit, lie, put 04 bear, hang, hold, meet, pass, pose, rest, seat, take 05 befit, brood, clock, model, perch, place, press, roost, serve, squat, stand,

site

weigh **06** gather, locate, reside, settle
07 consult, contain, convene, deposit,
sit down, situate **08** assemble, be
seated, position, study for, take part
09 be a member, squat down
10 deliberate, take part in
11 accommodate, be a member of, be
in session, have room for **12** have space
for, take your seat
• **sit back**
05 relax **09** do nothing **15** not be
involved in
• **sit in on**
04 join **05** watch **06** attend **07** observe
11 be present at
• **sit on**
04 ride **05** brood, cover
• **sit upright**
04 perk

site
03 lot, put, set **04** area, plot, seat, spot
05 place, scene, venue **06** ground,
locate **07** install, posture, setting,
situate, station, website **08** locality,
location, platform, position **09** situation

sitting
04 seat **05** spell **06** assize, clutch,
period, seated, sejant **07** hearing,
meeting, sejeant, session **08** assembly,
brooding, sederunt **12** consultation

sitting room
06 lounge, parlor, sitter **07** day room,
parlour **08** anteroom **09** front room
10 living room **11** drawing room
13 reception room

situate
03 put, set **04** site **05** place **06** locate
07 install, station **08** position
12 circumstance

situation
03 job, lie **04** case, post, rank, seat, site,
spot **05** place, score, set-up, state
06 locale, milieu, office, status
07 affairs, climate, picture, setting,
station **08** juncture, locality, location,
position, scenario **09** condition
10 conditions, employment
11 appointment, environment,
predicament, state of play **12** lie of the
land, what's going on **13** circumstances
14 state of affairs

six
02 VI **04** sice, size **05** hexad **06** senary,
sestet **07** sestett **08** sestette **09** half-
dozen **10** half-a-dozen

six-footer *see* **insect**

sixpence
04 kick, zack **05** tizzy **06** bender,
tanner, tester, teston **07** testern, testril
08 testrill

sixteen
03 XVI

sixty
02 LX

sizable, sizeable
05 hefty **06** decent, goodly
07 biggish, largish **08** generous **11** fairly

large, respectable, substantial
12 considerable

size
04 area, bulk, mass **05** range, scale
06 amount, assize, extent, height,
length, volume **07** bigness, expanse,
measure **08** quantity, vastness
09 allowance, dimension, greatness,
immensity, largeness, magnitude
10 dimensions **11** measurement,
proportions **12** measurements
• **size up**
04 rate **05** gauge, judge **06** assess
07 measure, suss out, weigh up
08 appraise, estimate, evaluate

sizeable *see* **sizable, sizeable**

sizzle
03 fry **04** hiss, sear, spit **06** scorch
07 crackle, frizzle, sputter

skate
03 ray **04** rink **06** rocker
See also **ice skating**

skeletal
05 drawn, gaunt **06** wasted
07 haggard **08** shrunken
09 emaciated, fleshless, unfleshed
10 cadaverous **11** skin-and-bone
13 hollow-cheeked

skeleton
04 plan **05** atomy, basic, bones, draft,
frame **06** lowest, sketch **07** anatomy,
minimum, outline, reduced, support
08 corallum, smallest **09** bare bones,
blueprint, framework, polyzoary,
structure, tentorium **10** coenosteum
11 polyzoarium **12** endoskeleton

sketch
03 act **04** draw, line, plan, skit, turn
05 draft, paint, rough, scene, skiff,
spoof, trick **06** aperçu, depict, design,
memoir, parody, pencil, précis, résumé,
satire, send-up, visual **07** cartoon,
croquis, diagram, draught, drawing,
ébauche, modello, outline, portray,
profile, summary, take-off **08** abstract,
block out, bozzetto, esquisse, platform,
rough out, scenario, skeleton, synopsis,
vignette **09** bare bones, bare facts,
burlesque, delineate, framework,
programme, represent, rough idea,
thumbnail **10** caricature, designment,
main points, pencilling, prospectus
11 delineation, description **12** mickey-
taking **13** prosopography
14 representation **15** thumbnail sketch

sketchily
07 hastily, roughly, vaguely **08** patchily
09 cursorily **11** imperfectly
12 inadequately, incompletely
13 perfunctorily

sketchy
◇ *anagram indicator*
05 bitty, crude, hasty, rough, vague
06 meagre, patchy, slight **07** cursory,
scrappy **09** defective, deficient,
imperfect **10** inadequate, incomplete,
unfinished, unpolished **11** perfunctory,
provisional, superficial **12** insufficient

skew
04 awry, bias **05** slant, twist, weigh
06 biased, colour **07** distort, falsify,
oblique **09** obliquity **12** asymmetrical,
misrepresent

skewer
04 prod **05** kebab **06** skiver
09 brochette

skier

skiing

skilful
03 hot, sly **04** able, deft, good, hend,
mean, wise **05** adept, canny, handy,
smart **06** adroit, artful, clever, expert,
gifted, quaint, skeely, versed
07 capable, cunning, knowing,
learned, skilled, trained **08** dextrous,
masterly, tactical, talented, well-seen
09 competent, dexterous, efficient,
ingenious, practised **10** diplomatic,
proficient, well-versed
11 experienced, industrious,
workmanlike **12** accomplished,

diplomatical, professional **14** nimble-fingered

skilfully
04 ably, well **06** deftly, yarely
07 capably, handily **08** cleverly,
expertly **11** competently
12 proficiently

skill
03 art **04** chic, feat, hand **05** craft,
knack, power, savey, savvy, sight, touch
06 matter, reason, savvey, talent
07 ability, cunning, finesse, know-how,
mastery, quality, science, signify
08 aptitude, artifice, deftness, facility,
training **09** adeptness, expertise,
handiness, knowledge, smartness,
technique **10** adroitness, cleverness,
competence, efficiency, experience,
expertness **11** proficiency, skilfulness
12 intelligence **14** accomplishment,
discrimination **15** professionalism

skilled
04 able, good **05** adept **06** expert,
gifted **07** capable, skilful, trained
08 complete, masterly, schooled,
talented **09** competent, efficient,
practised, qualified **10** consummate,
proficient **11** experienced
12 accomplished, professional

skim
03 fly **04** ream, sail, scan, skip
05 brush, cream, float, glide, graze,
plane, skate, skiff, touch **06** bounce
07 run over, skitter, take off **08** glance
at, separate **09** despumate
10 hydroplane, run through **11** flip
through, leaf through, look through,
read quickly **12** flick through, thumb
through **13** browse through

skimp
05 pinch, spare, stint **06** scanty, scrimp
08 withhold **09** cut back on,
economize **10** be mean with, cut
corners **12** be economical **15** tighten
your belt

skimpy
04 mean, thin **05** brief, short, small,
tight **06** meagre, measly, scanty,
sparse, stingy **07** miserly, sketchy
08 beggarly, exiguous **09** niggardly
10 inadequate **12** insufficient
13 insubstantial

skin
03 pod **04** drum, fell, film, flay, hide,
hull, husk, peel, pelt, rind, rine
05 cover, crust, graze, layer, strip
06 casing, fleece, scrape **07** coating,
outside, surface, swindle **08** covering,
membrane, tegument **10** complexion,
integument

Skin parts include:
04 derm, hair, hide, pore
05 cutis, derma
06 corium, dermis
07 cuticle, papilla
09 epidermis
10 sweat gland
11 lower dermis
12 hair follicle
14 sebaceous gland

Skin diseases and conditions include:
02 EB, XP
04 acne, boba, buba, rash, yaws
05 favus, tinea, warts
06 eczema, herpes, ulcers
07 anthrax, gum rash, leprosy, scabies
08 dandruff, melanoma, ringworm
09 keratosis, psoriasis
10 dermatitis, dermatosis, framboesia
11 prickly heat
12 athlete's foot, button scurvy

• by the skin of your teeth
06 barely **08** narrowly, only just **10** a
near thing, by a whisker **11** a close thing

skin-deep
05 empty **07** outward, shallow, surface
08 external **10** artificial
11 meaningless, superficial
13 superficially

skinflint
05 miser, screw **06** meanie **07** niggard,
Scrooge **08** tightwad **09** flay-flint
11 cheeseparer **12** penny-pincher

skinny
04 lean, thin **07** scraggy, scrawny
08 skeletal, underfed **09** emaciated
11 skin-and-bone **12** tight-fitting
14 undernourished

skip
◇ *anagram indicator*
◇ *deletion indicator*
03 bob, cut, hop **04** dart, jump, leap,
miss, omit, pass, race, rush, tear
05 bound, caper, dance, dodge, flisk,
frisk, slipe **06** bounce, cavort, gambol,
prance, spring, tittup **07** captain, miss
out, scamper, skipper, trounce
08 dumpster, leave out, overleap,
overskip, ricochet **10** bottle bank
11 move quickly

skirmish
05 argue, brawl, brush, clash, fight,
mêlée, scrap, set-to **06** affray, battle,
combat, dust-up, fracas, tussle
07 contend, dispute, fall out, pickeer,
punch-up, quarrel, scuffle, wrangle
08 argument, conflict, scarmoge
09 encounter **10** engagement,
velitation **11** altercation, escarmouche
13 confrontation, running battle

skirt
03 hug, rim **04** coat, edge, gore, kilt,
maxi, mini, tutu **05** avoid, evade, flank,
woman, women **06** border, bypass,
circle, margin, piupiu **07** go round,
midriff **08** lava-lava, wrapover
09 move round, petticoat
10 circumvent, wraparound **13** find a
way round **14** circumnavigate

skit
03 act **04** hoax, turn **05** scene, spoof
06 parody, satire, send-up, sketch
07 take-off **09** burlesque **10** caricature
12 mickey-taking

skittish
03 coy **05** jumpy **06** fickle, frisky, lively,
skeigh, wanton **07** fidgety, kitteny,
nervous, playful, restive **08** startish,
unsteady, volatile **09** excitable,
frivolous, kittenish **10** changeable
11 light-headed **12** highly-strung

skittles
04 pins **05** bowls, kails **07** tenpins
08 ninepins **10** kettle-pins, kittle-pins
11 skittle-pins **13** tenpin bowling

skive
04 idle, laze **05** dodge, evade, shirk,
skulk, slack **07** bunk off, goof off
08 malinger **09** avoid work **12** swing
the lead

skiver
05 idler **06** dodger, loafer, skewer
07 goof-off, shirker, slacker **09** do-
nothing **10** malingerer

skivvy *see* servant

skulduggery
08 trickery **09** chicanery, duplicity,
swindling **10** hanky-panky
11 fraudulence, shenanigans
12 machinations **13** double-dealing,
jiggery-pokery **15** underhandedness

skulk
03 pad **04** hide, lurk, lusk **05** creep,
miche, mooch, mouch, prowl, shool,
shule, slide, slink, sneak, steal **06** loiter,
shoole **08** malinger **09** lie in wait,
pussyfoot

skunk
04 atoc, atok **05** zoril **06** zorino
07 polecat, zorilla, zorille, zorillo

sky
03 air **04** blue, lift **05** azure, carry,
space **06** welkin **07** ambient, heavens,
the blue, weather **08** empyrean
09 firmament **10** atmosphere **12** upper
regions **13** vault of heaven

skyscraper
10 tower block **14** sliver building

slab
03 mud, tab **04** blad, hawk, hunk,
lump, pane, slat, tile, turf **05** blaud,
block, board, brick, chunk, dalle,
piece, plate, slate, slice, stela, stele,
table, wedge, wodge **06** bunker, ice
pan, ledger, lidger, marble, marver,
metope, mihrab, peever, planch,
plaque, quarry, sheave, tablet
07 briquet, portion, viscous
08 capstone **09** briquette **10** altar-
stone, superaltar **11** paving-stone
12 drawing board, Moabite stone,
plasterboard

slack
◇ *anagram indicator*
03 lax **04** ease, give, idle, lash, lazy,
limp, play, room, slow, veer **05** baggy,
dodge, loose, quiet, shirk, skive, surge,
tardy **06** excess, flabby, leeway, lessen,
reduce, remiss, sloppy, softly
07 flaccid, get less, hanging, languid,
neglect, relaxed, sagging, slacken

08 careless, decrease, diminish, flapping, flexible, inactive, malinger, moderate, slapdash, slow down, sluggish **09** easy-going, looseness, negligent, nerveless, partially **10** neglectful, permissive **11** inattentive, promiscuous **12** become slower **13** spare capacity **14** insufficiently

slacken
- **slacken off**

04 ease, slow **05** abate, relax **06** lessen, loosen, reduce **07** ease off, get less, release **08** decrease, diminish, forslack, moderate, slow down **10** take it easy **12** become slower

slacker
05 idler **06** loafer, skiver **07** dawdler, shirker **08** embusqué, layabout **10** malingerer **12** clock-watcher **14** good-for-nothing

slag
- **slag off**

04 mock, slam **05** abuse, knock, slate **06** berate, deride, insult, malign **07** lambast, run down **08** lambaste **09** criticize

slake
03 mud **04** daub, lick, sate **05** abate, allay, slime, smear **06** deaden, quench, reduce, sloken **07** assuage, gratify, hydrate, moisten, mudflat, satiate, satisfy, slacken, slocken, subside **08** mitigate, moderate **10** extinguish

slam
03 pan **04** bang, clap, dash, hurl, ruff, slag, slap, swap, swop **05** clash, crash, fling, slate, smash, throw, thump, trump **06** attack **07** censure, rubbish, run down, slag off **08** denounce **09** criticize **12** pull to pieces, tear to pieces, tear to shreds **13** find fault with **15** do a hatchet job on

slander
03 mud **04** slur **05** libel, smear **06** defame, malign, missay, vilify **07** asperse, calumny, obloquy, scandal, traduce **08** backbite, badmouth, vilipend **09** aspersion, denigrate, disparage, sclaunder **10** backbiting, calumniate, defamation, detraction, fling mud at, muck-raking, scandalize, sling mud at, throw mud at **11** denigration, mudslinging, speak evil of, traducement **12** evil-speaking, vilification **13** disparagement, smear campaign **14** cast aspersions

slanderous
05 false **06** untrue **07** abusive **08** damaging **09** aspersive, aspersory, insulting, libellous, malicious **10** backbiting, calumnious, defamatory **12** calumniatory, venom'd-mouth'd

slang
04 cant **05** argot, chain, lingo, scold **06** jargon, patois, patter **07** cockney **09** vulgarism **10** mumbo-jumbo, vituperate, watch chain **11** criminalese,

doublespeak **12** gobbledygook **13** colloquialism

slanging match
03 row **04** spat **05** set-to **06** barney **07** dispute, quarrel **08** argument **09** argy-bargy **11** altercation **13** shouting match

slant
03 dip **04** bend, bias, jibe, lean, list, ramp, skew, spin, tilt, view, warp **05** angle, bevel, pitch, slash, slope, splay, twist **06** camber, chance, colour, glance, shelve, sklent, weight **07** be askew, distort, incline, leaning, oblique, opinion, sloping **08** attitude, diagonal, emphasis, gradient **09** embrasure, embrazure, obliquity, prejudice, viewpoint **10** distortion **11** inclination, point of view **12** forward slash, one-sidedness

slanting
05 askew, bevel, slope **06** aslant, tilted **07** asklent, dipping, leaning, listing, oblique, sloping, tilting **08** at a slant, diagonal **09** inclining **11** on an incline

slap
03 hit, set **04** bang, biff, blow, clap, cuff, daub, dead, scud, slam, snub, sock, spat, swap, yank **05** apply, clout, pandy, plonk, plumb, plump, punch, right, skelp, smack, spank, stick, thump, twank, whack **06** breach, buffet, clatch, make-up, pierce, rebuke, sclaff, spread, strike, wallop **07** clobber, exactly, plaster, put down, set down **08** directly, slap-bang, straight, suddenly **09** precisely, violently **10** paddy-whack **11** strike hands
- **slap in the face**

04 blow, snub **06** insult, rebuff, rebuke **07** affront, put-down, repulse **09** indignity, rejection **11** humiliation
- **slap on the wrist**

04 flak **05** blame, stick **06** earful, rebuke **07** censure, slating **08** knocking, slamming **09** carpeting, reprimand **10** punishment, rollicking, telling-off, ticking-off **11** castigation, comeuppance **12** dressing-down

slapdash
◊ *anagram indicator*

04 rash **05** hasty, messy **06** clumsy, sloppy, untidy **07** hurried, offhand **08** careless, slipshod, slovenly **09** haphazard, negligent, roughcast **10** disorderly, last-minute **11** perfunctory, thoughtless **14** thrown-together

slap-happy
05 dazed, giddy, woozy **06** casual **07** reeling **08** reckless, slapdash **09** haphazard, hit-or-miss **10** boisterous, nonchalant, punch-drunk **12** happy-go-lucky **13** irresponsible

slapstick
05 farce **06** comedy **09** horseplay, low comedy **10** buffoonery, custard pie, knockabout, tomfoolery

slap-up
06 lavish, superb **08** princely, splendid **09** elaborate, excellent, first-rate, luxurious, sumptuous **10** first-class **11** magnificent, superlative

slash
03 axe, cut, jag, rip **04** curb, gash, hack, race, rase, rash, raze, rend, rent, slit, snip, tear **05** knife, prune, score, slant, slice **06** reduce, scorch, stroke **07** curtail, oblique, solidus, urinate, virgule **08** decrease, diagonal, incision, lacerate **09** carbonado **10** laceration, separatrix **12** forward slash

See also **urinate**

slate
03 cam, pan, rag **04** calm, caum, ragg, slag, slam, slat **05** abuse, blame, knock, scold, set on **06** berate, killas, rebuke, sklate **07** censure, propose, rubbish, run down, slag off **08** schedule, tomahawk **09** alum-shale, criticize, pull apart, reprimand, spilosite **10** black chalk, tabula rasa **11** sclate-stane **12** pull to pieces, tear to pieces, tear to shreds **14** Knotenschiefer **15** do a hatchet job on
- **size of roofing slate**

04 lady **05** peggy, queen, small **06** double **07** duchess **08** countess, princess **09** small lady **11** marchioness, viscountess

slatternly
05 dirty, dowdy **06** frowzy, frumpy, sleazy, sloppy, untidy **07** unclean, unkempt **08** frumpish, slipshod, slovenly, sluttish **10** bedraggled

slaughter
04 beat, best, drub, kill, lick, rout, slay **05** halal, worst **06** battue, defeat, hallal, hammer, murder, outwit, subdue, thrash **07** butcher, carnage, clobber, conquer, killing, murther, outplay, trounce **08** butchery, massacre, outsmart, overcome, vanquish **09** bloodbath, bloodshed, holocaust, liquidate, mactation, overpower, overwhelm, sacrifice, subjugate **10** annihilate, put to death **11** exterminate, liquidation, meat packing **12** annihilation **13** extermination, have the edge on **14** get the better of, putting to death

slaughtered
◊ *anagram indicator*

See **drunk**

slaughterhouse
08 abattoir, butchery, shambles

Slav
04 Serb, Sorb, Wend **05** Sclav **06** bohunk

See also **European**

slave
03 boy **04** esne, serf, slog, toil **05** grind, sweat, theow **06** abject, addict, drudge, labour, lackey, maroon, menial, sclave, skivvy, thrall, vassal **07** bondman, captive, odalisk, predial,

slave (continued)
servant, villein **08** bondmaid, bondsman, Mameluke, odalique, praedial **09** bond-slave, bondwoman, Gibeonite, odalisque **10** bondswoman, contraband **11** bondservant, galley slave **15** work your guts out

slave-driver
05 bully **06** despot, tyrant **08** autocrat, dictator, martinet **09** oppressor **10** taskmaster

slaver
05 drool, spawl **06** drivel **07** dribble, slobber, spittle **08** salivate **09** beslobber

slavery
04 yoke **06** thrall **07** bondage, serfdom **08** drudgery, nativity, slabbery, thraldom **09** captivity, servitude, thralldom, vassalage **11** bond-service, enslavement, enthralment, subjugation **12** enthrallment

slavish
03 low **04** mean, meek **06** abject, menial, strict **07** fawning, literal, servile **08** cringing **09** imitative, laborious **10** grovelling, obsequious, submissive, uninspired, unoriginal **11** deferential, subservient, sycophantic **13** unimaginative

slavishly
06 meekly **08** strictly **12** submissively, unoriginally **13** unresistingly **15** unimaginatively

slay
04 kill **06** murder, rub out **07** butcher, destroy, execute **08** despatch, dispatch, massacre **09** eliminate, slaughter **10** annihilate **11** assassinate, exterminate

slaying
05 quell **06** murder **07** killing **08** butchery, despatch, dispatch, massacre **09** mactation, slaughter **11** destruction, elimination **12** annihilation **13** assassination, extermination

sleazy
03 low **05** grody, seedy, tacky **06** crummy, sleezy, sordid **07** corrupt, squalid **10** slatternly **12** disreputable

sledge
03 bob **04** dray, luge, pulk, sled **05** pulka, slide, slipe, train **06** hurdle, pulkha, Ski-doo®, sleigh **07** bobsled, dogsled, kibitka, travois **08** toboggan **09** bobsleigh **10** fore-hammer **11** hurly-hacket, skeleton bob **12** sledgehammer

sleek
04 calm, smug, soft **05** glide, shiny, silky, slick, smalm, smarm **06** glossy, oilily, silken, smooth, soothe **07** stylish **08** lustrous, smoothly, thriving **10** prosperous **11** insinuating, well-groomed

sleep
03 kip, nap, ziz **04** bunk, doss, doze, rest, zizz **05** death, dover, go off **06** catnap, drowse, nod off, repose, siesta, snooze **07** bye-byes, drop off, shut-eye, slumber **08** be asleep, crash out, dormancy, doss down, drift off, flake out, REM sleep **09** hibernate **10** fall asleep, forty winks **11** have a snooze, hibernation **12** get some sleep **13** sleep like a log **14** have forty winks **15** go out like a light
• **go to sleep**
03 kip **04** dove, doze **05** go off **06** catnap, nod off, snooze **07** doze off, drop off **08** crash out, drift off, fall over **10** fall asleep **14** have forty winks
• **put to sleep**
06 sopite **07** destroy, put down

sleepily
06 slowly **07** heavily, quietly, wearily **08** drowsily, torpidly **09** languidly **10** inactively, sluggishly **13** lethargically

sleepiness
06 torpor **07** languor **08** doziness, lethargy **09** drowsihed, heaviness, oscitancy **10** drowsihead, drowsiness, oscitation, somnolence, somnolency

sleeping
04 idle **06** asleep **07** dormant, passive, unaware **08** abeyance, becalmed, dormient, inactive, off guard **10** slumbering **11** daydreaming, hibernating, inattentive **12** spine-bashing

sleepless
05 alert, awake **07** wakeful **08** restless, vigilant, watchful **09** disturbed, insomniac, wide-awake **10** unsleeping

sleeplessness
08 insomnia **11** wakefulness **12** insomnolence

sleepwalker
10 somnambule **11** night-walker **12** noctambulist, somnambulist

sleepwalking
12 noctambulism, somnambulism **13** somnambulance **14** noctambulation, somnambulation

sleepy
04 dull, slow **05** heavy, quiet, still, tired, weary **06** drowsy, lonely, torpid **07** languid, slumbry **08** comatose, hypnotic, inactive, isolated, peaceful, sleepery, sluggish, slumbery, soporose, soporous, tranquil **09** lethargic, slumbrous, somnolent, soporific **10** languorous, slumberous **11** lethargical, sequestered, undisturbed **12** unfrequented

sleeve
03 arm **04** bush **05** brass, gigot, gland, liner **06** drogue, manche **08** wind cone

sleigh
04 dray, luge **05** pulka, slide, slipe, train **06** Ski-doo®, sledge **07** bobsled, dogsled, kibitka, travois **08** toboggan **09** bobsleigh **10** snowmobile **11** hurly-hacket, skeleton bob

sleight of hand
05 magic, skill **08** artifice, trickery **09** deception, dexterity **10** adroitness **11** legerdemain **12** manipulation

slender
04 fine, jimp, lean, slim, thin, trim **05** faint, scant, small, swank **06** feeble, flimsy, little, meagre, narrow, remote, scanty, slight, svelte **07** gracile, tenuous, thready, willowy **08** exiguous, graceful, tenuious **09** deficient, sylphlike, willowish **10** inadequate **12** insufficient **14** inconsiderable

sleuth
04 dick, tail **05** track, trail **06** shadow **07** gumshoe, tracker **09** detective, Pinkerton **10** bloodhound, private eye
See also **detective**

slice
◇ *hidden indicator*
03 cut **04** chip, chop, fade, hunk, part, slab **05** carve, chunk, crisp, cut up, lunch, piece, round, sever, share, shive, slash, swipe, wafer, wedge, whack, whang **06** cantle, collop, croûte, divide, rasher, runner, sheave, sliver **07** frustum, helping, portion, scallop, scollop, section, segment, shaving, tranche **08** doorstep, separate **09** allotment **10** allocation **14** slice of the cake

slick
04 deft, easy, glib, trim **05** quick, sharp, sheen, shiny, sleek, smart, suave **06** adroit, deftly, glibly, glossy, polish, smarmy, smooth, tidy up, urbane **07** quickly, skilful **08** masterly, polished, smoothly, unctuous **09** dexterous, efficient, insincere, plausible, well-oiled **10** altogether, persuasive, simplistic **11** streamlined **12** professional **13** smooth-talking, smooth-tongued, sophisticated, well-organized **14** smooth-speaking

slide
◇ *anagram indicator*
03 ski **04** drop, fall, skid, skim, slip **05** chute, coast, glide, lapse, mount, plane, shoot, skate **06** decamp, hirsle, ice run, lessen, plunge, runner, sledge, worsen **07** decline, descend, descent, falling, plummet, relapse, slidder, slither **08** decrease, get worse, glissade, landslip, toboggan **10** depreciate, go smoothly **11** deteriorate, diapositive **12** depreciation, move smoothly, transparency **13** helter-skelter

slight
03 cut, pet **04** raze, slim, slur, snub, thin **05** elfin, frail, light, minor, petty, scant, scorn, small, spurn, wispy **06** dainty, flimsy, ignore, insult, little, meanly, minute, modest, offend, paltry, petite, rebuff, single, smooth, subtle **07** affront, despise, disdain, fragile,

neglect, sketchy, sleight, slender,
tenuous, trivial **08** brush-off,
contempt, delicate, misprise, misprize,
overlook, rudeness, tenuious, trifling
09 disparage, disregard **10** diminutive,
disrespect, negligence, negligible
11 discourtesy, unimportant **12** cold
shoulder, cold-shoulder, indifference
13 imperceptible, inappreciable,
insignificant, insubstantial, slap in the
face **14** inconsiderable, kick in the
teeth **15** inconsequential

slighting
07 abusive **08** mesprise, mesprize,
misprise, misprize, scornful
09 insulting, offensive **10** belittling,
defamatory, derogatory, disdainful,
neglectful, slanderous **11** disparaging
12 supercilious **13** disrespectful
15 uncomplimentary

slightly
04 a bit **05** quite **06** rather **07** a little, a
trifle, halfway, lightly **08** somewhat
12 to some degree, to some extent

slim
03 axe **04** diet, lean, poor, thin, trim
05 faint, leggy, lower, scant, small
06 crafty, flimsy, lessen, little, meagre,
reduce, remote, scanty, shrink, slight,
svelte, weaken **07** curtail, cut back, cut
down, slender, tenuous, willowy
08 contract, decrease, downsize,
graceful, make less, minimize,
moderate, restrict, sylphine, sylphish,
wind down **09** bring down, go on a
diet, sylphlike, willowish
10 inadequate, lose weight **11** make
smaller **12** insufficient
14 inconsiderable

slime
03 goo, mud **04** gunk, mess, muck,
ooze, yuck **05** slake **06** matter, sludge
07 bitumen

slimy
04 miry, oily, oozy **05** gucky, muddy
06 glairy, greasy, limous, mucous,
sludgy, smarmy, sticky **07** servile,
viscous **08** creeping, glareous,
slippery, toadying, unctuous
09 glaireous, uliginose, uliginous
10 disgusting, grovelling, obsequious
11 sycophantic **12** ingratiating

sling
03 lob, shy **04** band, give, hang, hurl,
loop, pass, toss **05** bribe, chuck, fling,
heave, pitch, put up, scarf, strap,
sweep, swing, throw **06** dangle, prusik
07 bandage, support, suspend
08 ballista, catapult, selvagee
09 parbuckle

slink
04 lean, lurk, mean, slip **05** creep,
droop, miche, prowl, sidle, skulk,
sneak, steal **07** starved

slinky
04 lean **05** sleek, tight **07** sinuous
08 clinging **09** skin-tight **12** close-
fitting, tight-fitting **13** figure-hugging

slip
◇ *anagram indicator*
03 don, err, ren, rin, run **04** boob, cast,
chit, drop, fall, flub, goof, note, shim,
sink, skid, skip, trip, wear **05** creep,
error, fault, glide, jupon, lapse, leash,
paper, piece, plant, put on, scape,
scrap, skate, slide, slink, slive, slump,
sneak, steal, strip **06** booboo, cave in,
cock-up, coupon, escape, howler,
kirtle, lapsus, piping, plunge, pull on,
runner, sledge, slip-up, worsen
07 bloomer, blunder, clanger, cutting,
decline, failure, get into, go to pot,
incline, mistake, plummet, scedule,
slidder, slither, stumble, take off,
voucher **08** decrease, get worse,
omission, quickset, schedule
09 disengage, landslide, oversight,
petticoat **10** change into, descendant,
underskirt **11** certificate, change out of,
deteriorate, galley proof, go to the dogs
12 get dressed in, indiscretion, lapsus
calami **13** lapsus linguae **14** go down
the tubes, lapsus memoriae **15** lose
your balance, lose your footing
• a slip of a
04 slim, thin **05** small, young **06** slight
07 fragile, slender **08** delicate
• give someone the slip
04 duck **05** dodge **08** flee from, shake
off **10** escape from **11** get away from,
run away from **14** break loose from
• let slip
04 balk, blab, leak, miss, tell **05** baulk
06 betray, let out, reveal, squeal
07 divulge **08** disclose, give away,
overslip **13** spill the beans **15** give the
game away
• slip away
05 evade **06** elapse
• slip up
03 err **04** boob, fail, goof **05** botch, fluff
06 bungle, cock up, goof up **07** blunder,
deceive, go wrong, screw up, stumble
08 get wrong **10** disappoint **12** make a
mistake, miscalculate

slipper
04 muil, mule, pump **06** loafer, panton,
sandal **07** baboosh, babuche
08 babouche, flip-flop, mocassin,
moccasin, pabouche, pantable,
pantofle, slip-shoe **09** houseshoe,
pantoffle, pantoufle **13** carpet-slipper

slippery
◇ *anagram indicator*
03 icy, wet **04** foxy, glib, glid, oily
05 false, slime, slimy **06** clever, crafty,
glassy, greasy, shifty, skiddy, slippy,
smarmy, smooth **07** cunning, devious,
elusive, evasive, glidder, slither
08 glibbery, gliddery, perilous, sliddery,
slithery, two-faced, unstable
09 dangerous, deceitful, dishonest,
lubricous, uncertain **10** lubricious,
perfidious, unreliable **11** duplicitous,
treacherous **13** unpredictable,
untrustworthy

slipshod
◇ *anagram indicator*
03 lax **06** casual, sloppy, untidy

08 careless, slapdash, slovenly
09 negligent **12** disorganized

slip-up
04 boob, flub, goof, slip **05** error, fault
06 booboo, cock-up, howler
07 bloomer, blunder, clanger, failure,
mistake **08** omission **09** oversight
12 indiscretion

slit
03 cut, rip, rit **04** fent, gash, loop, loup,
peep, race, rend, rent, ritt, sipe, slot,
snip, tear, vent **05** knife, lance, slash,
slice, spare, speld, split **06** pierce
07 fissure, opening, pertuse
08 aperture, incision, loophole,
pertused **09** pertusate, pertusion
10 buttonhole **11** placket-hole

slither
04 skid, slip, worm **05** creep, glide,
slide, slink, snake **08** slippery

sliver
03 bit **04** chip, rove **05** flake, piece,
scrap, shard, shred, slice, wafer
06 paring, shiver **07** shaving
08 fragment, splinter

slob
03 mud, oaf, yob **04** boor, lout, ooze
05 churl **06** sloven, sludge **07** mud-flat
08 layabout **10** philistine **14** good-for-
nothing

slobber
04 slop **05** drool **06** drivel, slaver
07 dribble **08** salivate **14** foam at the
mouth

slog
03 hit **04** bash, belt, hike, plod, slug,
sock, toil, trek, work **05** clout, graft,
grind, slave, slosh, smite, sweat, thump,
tramp **06** effort, labour, strike, trudge,
wallop **08** exertion, struggle, work
hard **09** peg away at, persevere **10** plug
away at, sweat blood **13** plough
through **15** work till you drop

slogan
03 cry **04** logo **05** chant, motto
06 jingle, splash, war cry **07** tag line
08 slughorn **09** battle-cry, catchword,
slughorne, watchword **10** shibboleth
11 catch phrase, rallying cry **12** back to
basics

sloop
03 hoy **05** dandy, smack **06** cutter

slop
05 slosh, slush, spill **06** puddle, splash
07 slather, slobber, spatter
08 overflow, slattern, splatter, wash
away **09** policeman

slope
03 bow, dip, lie, tip **04** bank, brae, cant,
drop, fall, heel, kant, lean, rake, ramp,
rise, tilt **05** pitch, slant, splay, verge
06 ascent, aslant, breast, decamp,
escarp, glacis, shelve **07** decline,
descent, incline, upgrade **08** fall away,
shelving, slanting **09** acclivity,
disappear, downgrade, watershed
11 inclination

slope off
06 decamp, go away **08** slip away, sneak off **09** steal away **12** leave quietly

sloping
03 dip **05** askew, slant **06** angled, canted, supine **07** canting, leaning, oblique, tilting **08** at a slant, bevelled, inclined, shelving, sidelong, slanting **09** acclivous, declivous, inclining **11** acclivitous, declivitous

sloppily
07 hastily, messily **08** untidily **09** hurriedly **10** carelessly **11** haphazardly **15** lackadaisically

sloppy
◇ *anagram indicator*
03 wet **05** baggy, corny, gooey, gucky, gushy, hasty, messy, muddy, mushy, runny, slack, soggy, soppy **06** clumsy, liquid, sickly, slushy, sozzly, untidy, watery **07** gushing, hurried, maudlin, mawkish, splashy **08** careless, romantic, slapdash, slattery, slipshod, slovenly **09** haphazard, hit-or-miss, schmaltzy **10** amateurish, wishy-washy **11** sentimental **12** disorganized **13** lackadaisical

slosh
◇ *anagram indicator*
03 hit **04** bash, beat, biff, pour, slap, slog, slop, slug, sock, wade **05** clout, punch, spray, swash, swipe, thump **06** shower, splash, strike, thwack, wallop **08** flounder

slot
03 bar, fit, gap, put **04** bolt, hole, slit, spot, time, vent **05** crack, niche, notch, place, space, track **06** assign, groove, insert, tracks, window **07** channel, install, opening, vacancy **08** aperture, position **10** pigeonhole

sloth
02 ai **04** unau **06** acedia, torpor **07** accidie, inertia, mylodon **08** idleness, laziness, mylodont **09** fainéance, indolence, slackness **10** inactivity **12** listlessness, slothfulness, sluggishness

slothful
04 idle, lazy **05** inert, slack, sweer, sweir **06** sweert, sweirt, torpid **07** skiving, sweered, workshy **08** fainéant, inactive, indolent, listless, sluggish **09** do-nothing

slouch
04 bend, loll **05** droop, hunch, mooch, slump, stoop **06** lounge **07** shamble, shuffle **08** drooping

Slovakia
02 SK **03** SVK

Slovenia
03 SLO, SVN

slovenly
◇ *anagram indicator*
05 dirty, messy **06** sloppy, untidy **07** scruffy, unclean, unkempt **08** careless, slattery, slipshod, sluttish

09 slammakin **10** slammerkin, slatternly **12** disorganized

slow
03 dim, twp **04** daft, dead, dull, dumb, lash, late, lazy, poky **05** delay, dense, dopey, gross, largo, lento, loath, pokey, quiet, slack, tardy, thick, unapt **06** adagio, averse, boring, obtuse, retard, sleepy, stupid **07** andante, delayed, glacial, gradual, lagging, slacken, slack up, tedious **08** creeping, dawdling, dilatory, hesitant, measured, plodding, retarded, sluggish, stagnant, tiresome **09** larghetto, leisurely, lingering, loitering, ponderous, prolonged, reluctant, slacken up, unhurried, unwilling, wearisome **10** deliberate, dull-witted, indisposed, lentissimo, protracted, slow-motion, slow-moving, slow-witted, uneventful **11** disinclined **12** long-drawn-out **13** at a snail's pace, time-consuming, unintelligent, uninteresting **14** slow off the mark **15** slow on the uptake

• slow down
04 curb, stem **05** brake, check, delay, relax **06** detain, do less, ease up, hold up, relent, retard, wait up **08** calm down, chill out, handicap, hold back, keep back, restrict **09** hang loose **10** decelerate, take it easy **11** reduce speed **12** throttle back, throttle down **14** put the brakes on

• slowing down
03 rit **04** rall **08** ritenuto **10** ritardando **11** rallentando

• slow up
04 rein

slowly
05 largo, lento **06** adagio, lazily **08** steadily **09** by degrees, gradually, larghetto, leisurely **10** lentissimo, ploddingly, sluggishly **11** ponderously, unhurriedly **13** at a snail's pace **14** little by little **15** slowly but surely

sludge
03 mud **04** gunk, mire, muck, ooze, silt, slag, slob, slop **05** dregs, gunge, mudge, slime, slush, swill **07** residue **08** sediment

slug
04 bash, boff, gulp, oner, swat **05** douse, dowse, limax, one-er, slosh, souse, swash **06** bullet, lander, wallop, wunner **07** lounder, swallow **08** Linotype®, sea lemon **10** bêche-de-mer

sluggish
04 dull, idle, lazy, slow **05** heavy, inert, resty, tardy **06** jacent, torpid **07** languid **08** inactive, indolent, lifeless, listless, slothful **09** apathetic, lethargic, somnolent **10** languorous, phlegmatic, slow-moving **12** unresponsive

sluggishness
05 sloth **06** apathy, lentor, phlegm, torpor **07** inertia, languor **08** dullness, lethargy, slowness **09** fainéance, heaviness, indolence, lassitude

10 drowsiness, somnolence, stagnation **12** listlessness, slothfulness

sluice
04 wash **05** drain, flush, inlet, koker, sasse, slosh, sluse, slush, swill **06** drench, outlet **07** channel, cleanse, conduit, passage **08** irrigate, lock gate, penstock **09** floodgate, water gate

slum
05 hovel **06** favela, ghetto **07** rookery **10** shanty town **11** cabbagetown **15** across the tracks

slumber
03 kip, nap **04** doze, rest **05** sleep, sloom **06** drowse, repose, snooze **07** shut-eye **08** lethargy **10** forty winks

slummy
05 dirty, seedy **06** sleazy, sordid **07** decayed, run-down, squalid **08** wretched **10** ramshackle **11** overcrowded

slump
03 low, sag **04** bend, drop, fail, fall, flop, loll, sink **05** crash, droop, flump, plump, slide, stoop **06** go down, lounge, plunge, slouch, trough, worsen **07** decline, failure, plummet, subside **08** collapse, decrease, downturn, lowering, nosedive **09** downswing, recession, worsening **10** depression, go downhill, stagnation **11** deteriorate, devaluation **13** deterioration

slur
04 blot, blur **05** cheat, libel, smear, stain **06** insult, mumble, slight, stigma **07** affront, calumny, slander, stumble **08** besmirch, disgrace, innuendo, ligature, reproach, splutter **09** aspersion, discredit, disparage **11** insinuation **13** disparagement **14** speak unclearly

slush
04 gush, mush, pulp, slop, snow **05** slosh, sposh, swash **06** lapper, lopper **07** wet snow **08** schmaltz **09** soppiness **10** sloppiness **11** mawkishness, melting snow, romanticism **12** emotionalism **14** sentimentality

slut
04 drab, slag, tart **05** bitch, hussy **06** clatch, drazel, hooker, pussel, puzzle, sloven **07** floozie, pucelle, trollop **08** dolly-mop, scrubber, slattern, slummock **09** dratchell **10** loose woman, prostitute **11** draggle-tail
See also **prostitute**

sly
03 fly **04** foxy, leer, slee, wily **05** canny, carny, peery, smart **06** artful, astute, carney, clever, covert, crafty, expert, impish, secret, shifty, shrewd, sleeky, sneaky, subtle, tricky **07** cunning, devious, furtive, illicit, knowing, roguish, sleekit **08** guileful, scheming, stealthy, weaselly **09** conniving, insidious, secretive, underhand

11 clandestine, mischievous
13 surreptitious

• **on the sly**
07 on the qt 08 covertly, in secret,
secretly 09 furtively, in private,
privately 10 stealthily, under cover
13 clandestinely, underhandedly
15 surreptitiously

• **sly person**
03 tod 04 coon 06 weasel

slyly
◇ anagram indicator
07 cannily 08 artfully, covertly,
shrewdly 09 cunningly, deviously,
furtively 10 stealthily
13 underhandedly 15 surreptitiously

smack
03 box, hit, pat, tap 04 bang, belt, biff,
blow, clap, cuff, dash, hint, kiss, like,
slap, sock, tack, tang, thud, zest
05 clout, crack, crash, enjoy, evoke,
plumb, punch, right, smell, spank,
speck, spice, taste, thump, tinge,
touch, trace, twang, whack, whiff
06 bawley, flavor, heroin, hint at,
hooker, nuance, relish, savour, smatch,
smouch, strike, thwack, wallop
07 clobber, coaster, exactly, flavour,
revel in, sharply, smacker, suggest
08 directly, intimate, piquancy, savour
of, slap-bang, straight 09 delight in,
precisely 10 absolutely, appreciate,
impression, intimation, paddy-whack,
suggestion 11 bring to mind, remind
you of 13 give a hiding to 14 take
pleasure in 15 put over your knee

See also hit; kiss

• **smack your lips**
05 enjoy 06 relish, savour 09 delight
in, drool over 10 anticipate

smacker *see* kiss

small
◇ deletion indicator
01 S 03 low, sma, wee 04 mean, mini,
pink, poky, puny, tiny 05 bitsy, diddy,
dwarf, minor, petty, pinky, short, teeny,
tiddy, totty, young 06 broken, dilute,
humble, little, meagre, minute, narrow,
paltry, peerie, peewee, petite, pinkie,
pocket, scanty, single, slight, stupid,
teensy, tottie 07 ashamed, compact,
cramped, crushed, foolish, ignoble,
limited, slender, trivial 08 confined,
deflated, degraded, delicate, dwarfish,
pint-size, trifling 09 disgraced,
miniature, minuscule, pint-sized
10 diminutive, humiliated, inadequate,
negligible, ungenerous, unimposing
11 embarrassed, microscopic, pocket-
sized, unimportant 12 insufficient,
teensy-weensy 13 inappreciable,
infinitesimal, insignificant
14 inconsiderable

small-minded
04 mean 05 petty, rigid 06 biased, little
07 bigoted, insular 09 cat-witted,
hidebound, illiberal, parochial
10 intolerant, prejudiced, ungenerous
12 narrow-minded

smallness
07 exility, fewness, paucity 08 tininess
09 small size 10 littleness, minuteness,
slightness 11 compactness,
parvanimity 12 microcephaly
14 diminutiveness

small-time
05 minor, petty 08 piddling 09 no-
account 10 small-scale 11 unimportant
13 insignificant 15 inconsequential

smarminess
07 suavity 08 oiliness, toadying
09 servility 10 sycophancy, unctuosity
12 unctuousness 14 obsequiousness

smarmy
04 oily 05 suave 06 smooth
07 fawning, servile 08 crawling,
toadying, unctuous 10 obsequious
11 bootlicking, sycophantic
12 ingratiating

smart
01 U 03 nip 04 ache, bite, burn, chic,
cool, fine, flip, hurt, neat, pacy, pert,
posh, smug, tidy, trim 05 acute, brisk,
dandy, gemmy, janty, jemmy, kooky,
natty, nifty, nobby, pacey, prick, ritzy,
saucy, sharp, slick, smoke, spiff, sting,
swank, sweat, swish, throb, tippy, witty
06 astute, brainy, bright, clever, dapper,
glitzy, jaunty, kookie, larney, modish,
pusser, shrewd, snappy, snazzy, spiffy,
spruce, swanky, tiddly, tingle, twinge
07 crabbit, elegant, stylish, swagger,
tiddley 08 all there, rattling, sprauncy
09 expensive, on the ball, vivacious
11 fashionable, intelligent, presentable,
well-dressed, well-groomed 13 well-
turned-out

• **smart alec**
07 know-all, wise guy 08 wiseacre
09 smartarse 10 clever dick 11 clever
clogs, smartyboots, smartypants

smarten
04 tidy 05 clean, groom, primp, prink
06 neaten, polish, spruce, tidy up
08 beautify, make neat, make tidy,
spruce up

smartly
06 neatly, tidily 07 briskly, hastily,
nattily, quickly, rapidly, readily,
swiftly 08 abruptly, directly, promptly,
snazzily, speedily 09 elegantly,
hurriedly, instantly, stylishly
11 fashionably, immediately,
presentably 14 unhesitatingly
15 instantaneously

smash
◇ anagram indicator
02 go 03 hit, run, wow 04 bang, bash,
bump, cash, dash, ruin 05 break, crack,
crash, crush, drive, knock, prang,
thump, wreck 06 bingle, defeat, pile-
up, plough, shiver, strike, winner
07 collide, destroy, shatter, smash-up,
success, triumph 08 accident,
demolish, knockout, smash hit,
splinter, squabash, stramash
09 collision, pulverize, sensation
12 disintegrate

smashing
05 great, super 06 superb 07 dashing
08 crushing, fabulous, terrific
09 excellent, fantastic, first-rate,
wonderful 10 first-class, marvellous,
shattering, stupendous, tremendous
11 magnificent, sensational, superlative
12 exhilarating

smattering
03 bit 04 dash 06 basics, smatch
07 modicum 08 elements
09 rudiments 10 sprinkling

smear
03 dab, gum, oil, pay, rub, tar, wax
04 blot, blur, coat, daub, gaum, gild,
gorm, lard, lick, mark, slap, slur, soot,
spot 05 blood, cover, libel, patch,
pitch, salve, slake, slime, smalm,
smarm, stain, sully, taint 06 anoint,
bedaub, blotch, defame, grease,
malign, slairg, smudge, spread, streak,
vilify 07 blacken, obloquy, plaster,
slander, slather, slubber, splodge,
splotch, tarnish, treacle 08 badmouth
09 aspersion 10 calumniate,
defamation, muck-raking, turpentine
11 false report, mudslinging
12 vilification

smell
03 fug, hum 04 funk, fust, gale, guff,
ming, must, niff, nose, odor, pong,
ponk, reek 05 aroma, fetor, odour,
scent, sniff, snuff, stink, trace, whiff
06 miasma, savour, stench 07 bouquet
08 malodour, mephitis, pungency
09 fragrance, redolence

Particular smells include:
02 BO
04 feet, musk, rose
05 basil, booze, ozone, smoke, spice
06 cheese, coffee, garlic, nutmeg,
pepper
07 alcohol, camphor, incense,
menthol, perfume, vanilla
08 bergamot, lavender
09 body odour, patchouli, pot pourri,
woodsmoke
10 eucalyptus, peppermint
11 wintergreen

smelly
03 bad, off 04 foul, high, nosy, olid,
rank, ripe 05 fetid, nosey, olent, pongy
06 foetid, mingin, putrid 07 honking,
humming, noisome, reeking
08 mephitic, stinking 10 malodorous
12 foul-smelling 14 strong-smelling

smile
04 beam, grin, leer 05 drink, laugh,
smirk, sneer, treat 06 favour, giggle,
simper, smoile, smoyle, titter
07 chuckle, snigger 11 be all smiles

smirk
04 grin, leer, trim 05 sneer 06 simper,
spruce 07 grimace, snigger

smitten
05 beset, épris 06 éprise, in love,
struck 07 charmed, hard-hit, plagued
08 beguiled, burdened, obsessed,

troubled **09** afflicted, attracted, bewitched, enamoured **10** bowled over, captivated, infatuated **12** enthusiastic

smock
04 slop **05** frock, shift **07** chemise, smicket
- **lady's smock**

05 spink **09** cardamine **12** cuckoo flower

smog
03 fog **04** haze, mist **05** fumes, smoke **06** vapour **07** exhaust **09** pea-souper, pollution

smoke
03 dry, fog, gas **04** cure, draw, fume, lunt, mist, puff, quiz, reek, roke, smog **05** fumes, reast, reest, reist, smart, smoor **06** draw on, puff on, smudge, suffer, thrash, vapour **07** exhaust, light up, smother, tear gas **08** preserve, ridicule, smoulder **09** London ivy

See also **cigarette**; **tobacco**

smoky
04 dark, grey, hazy **05** black, foggy, fuggy, grimy, murky, peaty, reeky, sooty **06** cloudy, rechie, reechy, reekie, smoggy, smudgy **07** reechie **10** suspicious

smooch
03 hug, pet **04** hold, kiss, neck, snog **05** clasp, nurse **06** caress, cuddle, enfold, fondle, nestle **07** embrace, snuggle **08** canoodle

smooth
03 aid, dub **04** calm, ease, easy, even, file, flat, glib, help, iron, mild, rich, roll, sand, smug, snod, soft, trim **05** allay, bland, brent, dress, filed, float, flush, grind, level, plane, press, shiny, silky, sleek, slick, sooth, still, suave, sweet, terse, thick **06** assist, classy, creamy, fluent, glassy, glossy, legato, mature, mellow, pacify, polish, serene, silken, simple, sleeky, smarmy, soothe, steady, urbane **07** appease, assuage, elegant, equable, even out, fawning, flatten, flatter, flowing, mollify, plaster, regular, rub down, sleekit, slicken, uniform, velvety, worsted **08** blandish, calm down, charming, crawling, glabrate, glabrous, hairless, levigate, mitigate, palliate, peaceful, polished, rhythmic, slippery, tranquil, unbroken, unctuous **09** agreeable, alleviate, burnished, encourage, oppress, overlie, repress, unruffled **10** continuous, effortless, facilitate, horizontal, make easier, persuasive, unwrinkled **11** legatissimo, like a mirror, mellifluent, mellifluous, plaster down, problem-free, trouble-free, undisturbed **12** ingratiating, plain sailing **13** full-flavoured, over-confident, smooth-talking, sophisticated, uninterrupted **14** clear the way for **15** straightforward

smoothly
06 calmly, easily, evenly, legato, mildly **07** cleanly, equably, sleekly, slickly,

voluble **08** fluently, serenely, steadily **10** peacefully, pleasantly, soothingly, swimmingly, tranquilly **11** legatissimo **12** effortlessly

smoothness
04 ease, flow **05** shine **06** finish, polish, rhythm **07** fluency **08** calmness, evenness, facility, flatness, serenity, softness **09** levelness, lubricity, silkiness, sleekness, stillness **10** efficiency, glassiness, regularity, steadiness **11** velvetiness **12** unbrokenness **14** effortlessness

smooth-talking
04 glib **05** bland, slick, suave **06** facile, smooth **09** plausible **10** flattering, persuasive **12** conciliatory **13** silver-tongued

smother
04 damp, hide, wrap **05** choke, cover, smoke, smoor, smore, snuff **06** cocoon, dampen, muffle, put out, shroud, stifle, welter **07** conceal, envelop, oppress, overlie, repress **08** damp down, inundate, keep back, smoulder, strangle, suppress, surround, throttle **09** overwhelm, suffocate **10** asphyxiate, extinguish **11** suffocation

smoulder
04 boil, burn, foam, fume, rage **05** smoke **06** fester, seethe, simmer **07** smother

smudge
04 blot, blur, daub, mark, soil, spot **05** dirty, smear, stain **06** blotch, offset, smouch, smutch, streak **07** blacken, blemish **08** besmirch **09** dirty mark, make dirty

smug
04 neat, prim **05** sleek, steal **06** hush up, smooth, spruce **08** priggish, smirking, superior, unctuous **09** conceited **10** complacent **13** self-righteous, self-satisfied **14** holier-than-thou

smuggle
03 owl, ren, rin, run **05** steal **07** bootleg

smuggler
04 mule **05** owler **06** runner **07** courier **10** bootlegger, drug-runner, free-trader, moonshiner **13** contrabandist

smutty
04 blue, lewd, racy, rude **05** bawdy, crude, dirty, gross **06** coarse, filthy, fruity, ribald, risqué, sleazy, vulgar **07** obscene, raunchy **08** improper, indecent, prurient **09** off colour, salacious **10** indelicate, suggestive **12** pornographic

snack
04 bite, gorp, meze, snap, tapa, wrap **05** bever, butty, chack, fours, lunch, share, tapas, taste **06** buffet, crisps, nacket, nibble, nocket, snatch, supper, tidbit, titbit **07** bar meal, elevens,

fourses, nibbles, zakuska **08** bar lunch, pick-me-up, sandwich, scroggin, trail mix **09** appetizer, bite to eat, Bombay mix, elevenses, light meal **11** amuse-bouche, hors d'oeuvre, refreshment **12** potato crisps, refreshments **15** pork scratchings

snaffle
03 bag, nab, win **04** gain, grab, grip, nail, pull, take **05** grasp, pluck, seize, steal, swipe, wrest **06** arrest, clutch, collar, secure, wrench **07** bridoon, capture, purloin, snabble **08** pounce on **09** get hold of **10** take hold of **11** make off with

snag
03 bug, jag, nog, rip **04** hole, sneb, snub, tear **05** catch, hitch, stump **06** banger, ladder, obtain, secure, snubbe **07** problem, sausage, setback **08** drawback, obstacle **10** difficulty **12** complication, disadvantage **13** inconvenience **14** stumbling-block

snail
05 crawl, helix **06** dodman, nerite **08** escargot, wallfish **09** hodmandod, wing shell

snake
04 bend, drag, loop, naga, wind, worm **05** creep, curve, twine **06** drudge, ramble, spiral, wretch, zigzag **07** deviate, meander, serpent **08** Joe Blake, ophidian

Snakes include:

03 asp, boa, rat, sea
04 boma, bull, corn, file, hoop, king, milk, naga, Naia, Naja, pine, pipe, ring, rock, sand, seps, tree, whip, worm
05 adder, black, blind, brown, cobra, coral, Elaps, grass, green, krait, mamba, racer, tiger, viper, water
06 carpet, dipsas, dugite, ellops, flying, gaboon, garter, gopher, indigo, karait, python, ribbon, smooth, taipan
08 anaconda, cerastes, colubrid, cylinder, jararaca, jararaka, mocassin, moccasin, pit viper, ringhals, rinkhals, sucurujú
09 berg-adder, boomslang, coachwhip, hamadryad, hamadryas, king cobra, puff adder, river-jack
10 bandy-bandy, bushmaster, copperhead, death adder, dendrophis, fer-de-lance, Gabon viper, massasauga, sidewinder
11 constrictor, cottonmouth, diamondback, gaboon viper, horned viper, massasauger, rattlesnake
12 carpet python
13 diamond python, water moccasin
14 boa constrictor, river-jack viper

snap
03 nip, pic **04** bark, bite, chop, film, grip, knap, shot, snip, span, take, tick, time, whit **05** break, catch, cheat, click,

clink, crack, flick, gnash, grasp, growl,
hanch, photo, print, scrap, seize, share,
shoot, snack, snarl, snick, spell, split,
still, stint **06** abrupt, bark at, fillip,
period, record, retort, snatch, sudden
07 crackle, earring, give way, growl at,
instant, offhand, picture, sharper, snarl
at, stretch **08** collapse, fracture,
separate, snapshot, splinter
09 crepitate, immediate, lash out at,
on-the-spot **10** photograph,
unexpected **14** speak angrily to, speak
sharply to
• **snap up**
03 nab **04** grab **05** grasp, pluck, seize
06 pick up, snatch **08** pounce on
10 buy quickly

snappy
04 chic, edgy **05** brisk, cross, hasty,
natty, quick, ratty, smart, testy
06 crabby, crusty, lively, modish,
snazzy, touchy, trendy **07** brusque,
crabbed, elegant, grouchy, stroppy,
stylish **08** polished, up-to-date
09 crotchety, energetic, irascible,
irritable **10** ill-natured **11** bad-
tempered, fashionable, ill-tempered
13 instantaneous, quick-tempered,
short-tempered, up-to-the-minute
• **make it snappy**
05 hurry **06** buck up **07** hurry up **08** go
all out, jump to it, step on it **09** come
along, look sharp, shake a leg **10** look
lively **11** get cracking **15** get your skates
on

snare
◇ *containment indicator*
03 gin, net, web **04** grin, hook, toil,
trap, weel, wire **05** catch, fraud, noose,
seize, toils **06** cobweb, engine, entrap,
spring, trepan **07** capture, ensnare,
pitfall, springe **08** lime-twig **09** spider
web **10** allurement, temptation
12 entanglement

snarl
◇ *anagram indicator*
04 bark, girn, gnar, gurn, howl, knar,
knot, snap, snar, yelp **05** gnarl, gnarr,
growl, ravel, twist **06** enmesh, jumble,
muddle, tangle **07** confuse, embroil,
ensnare, entwine, grumble
08 complain, entangle **09** lash out at
10 complicate **13** show your teeth

snarl-up
04 mess **05** mix-up **06** jumble, muddle,
tangle **08** gridlock **09** confusion
10 traffic jam **12** entanglement

snatch
03 bag, bit, nab, nip, rap, win **04** gain,
glom, grab, grip, nail, part, pull, race,
ramp, rase, snap, snip, take **05** catch,
grasp, piece, pluck, reach, seize, snack,
spell, steal, swipe, whiff, wrest
06 abduct, clutch, collar, gobble,
kidnap, ruffle, secure, twitch, wrench
07 claucht, claught, quibble, robbery,
section, segment, snippet **08** fraction,
fragment, pounce on **09** get hold of
10 kidnapping, smattering, take hold of
11 make off with **13** take as hostage

snazzy
05 jazzy, ritzy, showy, smart **06** flashy,
snappy, sporty, with it **07** dashing,
raffish, stylish **08** swinging
10 attractive, flamboyant
11 fashionable **13** sophisticated

sneak
03 pad, rat **04** lurk, mole, peak, shop,
slip **05** creep, grass, prowl, quick, sidle,
skulk, slide, slink, snoke, snook, snowk,
split, steal **06** covert, cringe, secret,
snitch, spirit, squeal **07** furtive, grass
on, smuggle, stoolie, stool on
08 informer, inform on, squealer,
stealthy, surprise, tell-tale **09** tell tales
11 clandestine, stool pigeon
13 surreptitious, whistle-blower

sneaking
04 mean **06** hidden, secret **07** furtive,
lurking, nagging, private, sleekit
08 grudging, niggling, unvoiced,
worrying **09** crouching, intuitive,
underhand **10** persistent, suppressed
11 sheep-biting, unexpressed
13 surreptitious, uncomfortable

sneaky
03 low, sly **04** base, mean **05** nasty,
shady, snide **06** shifty **07** cunning,
devious, furtive, low-down
08 cowardly, guileful, slippery
09 deceitful, dishonest, malicious,
unethical **10** unreliable
12 contemptible, disingenuous,
unscrupulous **13** double-dealing,
untrustworthy

sneer
04 gibe, grin, jeer, mock **05** laugh,
scoff, scorn, smirk, taunt **06** deride,
insult, slight, twitch **07** disdain,
mockery, snicker, snigger **08** derision,
ridicule **10** look down on **12** curl your
lips

sneeze
05 neese, neeze **07** atishoo

sneezing
12 sternutation

snicker
05 laugh, neigh, sneer **06** giggle,
nicker, titter **07** chortle, chuckle,
snigger, snirtle

snide
04 base, mean, sham **05** nasty
06 biting, unkind **07** caustic, cynical,
hurtful, jeering, mocking **08** derisive,
scathing, scoffing, scornful, sneering,
spiteful, taunting **09** dishonest,
malicious, sarcastic **10** derogatory, ill-
natured **11** counterfeit, disparaging

sniff
04 hint, nose, sent, vent **05** aroma,
scent, shmek, smell, snift, snuff, trace,
whiff **06** inhale, nuzzle, snivel
07 breathe, schmeck, sniffle, snifter,
snuffle **10** impression, intimation,
suggestion **11** get a whiff of
• **sniff at**
04 mock, shun, vent **05** scorn, spurn
06 deride, refuse, reject, slight

07 disdain, dismiss, laugh at, scoff at,
smell at, sneer at **08** overlook
09 disparage, disregard **10** look down
on

sniffy
06 snobby **07** haughty **08** scoffing,
scornful, sneering, snobbish, superior
10 disdainful **12** contemptuous,
supercilious **13** condescending

snifter *see* **dram**

snigger
05 laugh, smirk, sneer **06** giggle,
nicher, nicker, titter **07** chortle,
chuckle, snicker, whicker

snip
03 bit, cut **04** clip, crop, dock, nick, slit,
snap, trim **05** notch, piece, prune,
scrap, share, shred, slash, sneck, snick,
steal **06** incise, snatch, tailor
07 bargain, good buy, snippet
08 clipping, discount, fragment,
giveaway **09** certainty, reduction
12 special offer **13** value for money

snipe
04 fool, walk, wisp **05** scape **06** attack
09 criticism, criticize **12** heather-bleat
14 heather-bleater, heather-bluiter,
heather-blutter

sniper
06 haiduk **08** partisan **09** guerrilla,
irregular, terrorist **11** bushwhacker,
franc-tireur, guerrillero **14** freedom
fighter

snippet
03 bit **04** part, snip **05** piece, scrap,
shred **06** snatch **07** cutting, portion,
section, segment **08** clipping,
fragment, particle

snivel
03 cry, sob **04** bawl, blub, cant, moan,
weep **05** sniff, snift, whine **06** whinge
07 blubber, grizzle, sniffle, snuffle,
whimper

snivelling
06 crying **07** moaning, weeping,
whining **09** grizzling, sniffling,
snuffling, whingeing **10** blubbering,
whimpering

snob
04 scab **05** swank **07** bighead,
cobbler, élitist, high-hat, parvenu
08 blackleg, townsman **09** shoemaker
13 social climber

snobbery
04 airs, side **05** pride **07** disdain
09 arrogance, loftiness **10** pretension,
snootiness, uppishness **11** haughtiness,
superiority **12** snobbishness **13** airs
and graces, condescension
15 pretentiousness

snobbish
05 dicty, lofty, proud **06** dickty, snobby,
snooty, uppish, uppity **07** haughty,
stuck-up **08** affected, arrogant,
jumped-up, superior **10** disdainful,
hoity-toity, toffee-nose **11** patronizing,
pretentious, toffee-nosed

12 supercilious **13** condescending, high and mighty

snog
03 hug, pet **04** hold, kiss, neck **05** clasp, nurse **06** caress, cuddle, enfold, fondle, nestle, smooch **07** embrace, snuggle **08** canoodle

snoop
03 pry, spy **04** nose **05** sneak **06** meddle **07** gumshoe, meddler, Paul Pry, snooper **08** busybody, meddling **09** interfere **11** Nosey Parker **12** interference, put your oar in **14** poke your nose in, stick your oar in **15** stick your nose in

snooper
03 pry, spy **05** snoop **07** meddler, Paul Pry **08** busybody **11** Nosey Parker **12** eavesdropper

snooty
05 lofty, proud **06** snobby, uppity **07** haughty, stuck-up **08** affected, arrogant, jumped-up, snobbish, superior **10** disdainful, hoity-toity **11** patronizing, pretentious, toffee-nosed **12** supercilious **13** condescending, high and mighty

snooze
03 kip, nap **04** calk, doze **05** caulk, dover, sleep **06** catnap, nod off, repose, siesta **07** drop off, shut-eye, slumber **10** forty winks **14** have forty winks

snout
03 neb **04** beak, nose **05** sword, trunk **06** muzzle, nozzle, snitch **07** gruntle, tobacco **08** informer **09** cigarette, proboscis, schnozzle
See also **nose**

snow
03 ice **05** linen **06** heroin, whiten, winter **07** cocaine **08** blizzard, morphine, snowfall **09** snowdrift, snowstorm **10** snowflakes **12** snow flurries

Snow types and formations include:
03 red
04 corn, crud, firn, névé
05 drift, flake, sleet, slush
06 powder, sludge, yellow
07 cornice, flaught
08 sastruga
09 avalanche, spindrift

See also **ice**

snowman
04 yeti **06** frosty

snub
03 cut **04** knob, shun, slap, snag, sneb, snib, stop, stub **05** blank, check, frump, shame, sloan, sneap, snool, spurn **06** humble, ignore, insult, rebuff, rebuke, slight, squash **07** affront, heave-ho, mortify, put down, put-down, set-down, squelch **08** brush off, brush-off **09** disregard, humiliate **11** down-setting, humiliation **12** cold

shoulder, cold-shoulder **13** slap in the face **14** give the heave-ho, kick in the teeth

snuff
04 stop, vent **06** pulvil, rappee, sneesh
• **snuff out**
03 end **04** kill **05** choke, crush, douse, erase **06** put out, quench, remove, stifle **07** abolish, blow out, destroy, smother **08** suppress **09** eliminate, eradicate **10** dampen down

snug
03 rug **04** cosh, cosy, cozy, snod, warm **05** comfy, tight **06** couthy, homely, secure **07** compact, couthie **08** friendly, intimate **09** sheltered, skintight **11** comfortable **12** close-fitting **13** figure-hugging

snuggle
03 hug **04** cose **06** cozy up, cuddle, curl up, nestle, nuzzle **07** croodle, embrace

snugly
06 cosily, warmly **07** tightly **08** securely **11** comfortably

so
02 as **03** sae, sic, soh, sol **04** ergo, thus, well **05** hence **06** soever **08** insomuch, likewise, provided **09** therefore, thereupon **10** thereafter **11** accordingly

soak
03 mop, ret, sog, sop, wet **04** beat, buck, rait, rate, sipe, sype **05** bathe, imbue, souse, steep **06** drench, embrue, guzzle, imbrue, infuse, pummel, seethe, sodden, sponge **07** embrewe, immerse **08** macerate, marinate, permeate, saturate, submerge **09** drenching, penetrate **10** overcharge
See also **drunkard**

soaking
03 sop **05** steep **06** sluicy, soaked, sodden **07** sopping **08** drenched, dripping, wringing **09** saturated, streaming **10** sopping wet, wet through **11** waterlogged **15** soaked to the skin

soap
04 ball, cake, curd **05** money **06** sudser, tablet **07** flannel, flatter **08** flattery, washball **09** soap opera **12** shaving-stick

Soaps include:
03 Lux®
04 Dove®, hard, soft
05 glass, Pears®, sugar
06 liquid, marine, saddle, toilet, yellow
07 Castile, coal-tar, shaving, Spanish, Windsor
08 carbolic, mountain, olive-oil
09 Palmolive®
10 coconut-oil

Soap operas include:
06 Dallas
07 Dynasty, The Bill

08 Casualty
09 Brookside, Emmerdale, Holby City, Hollyoaks, River City
10 EastEnders, Neighbours, The Archers
11 Home and Away

soar
03 fly **04** rise, sore, wing, zoom **05** climb, fly up, glide, mount, plane, soare, tower **06** ascend, rocket, sorrel, spiral **07** take off **08** escalate **09** skyrocket **15** increase quickly

sob
03 cry, sab **04** bawl, blub, howl, weep, yoop **06** boohoo, snivel **07** blubber, singult, snotter **09** shed tears

sober
02 TT **03** dry, sad **04** calm, cool, dark, drab, dull, poor, sane **05** douce, grave, plain, quiet, staid **06** demure, feeble, sedate, serene, severe, solemn, sombre, steady **07** austere, earnest, serious, subdued **08** composed, moderate, rational, teetotal **09** abstinent, dignified, drying out, practical, realistic, temperate, unexcited, unruffled **10** abstemious, on the wagon, reasonable, restrained, thoughtful, unliquored **11** clear-headed, level-headed, unconcerned **12** off the bottle **13** dispassionate, sober as a judge **14** self-controlled, stone-cold sober
• **sober up**
06 dry out **10** sleep it off **13** clear your head

sobriety
07 gravity **08** calmness, coolness **09** composure, restraint, soberness, solemnity, staidness **10** abstinence, moderation, sedateness, steadiness, temperance **11** seriousness, teetotalism **13** self-restraint **14** abstemiousness **15** level-headedness

sobriquet, soubriquet
03 tag **04** name, term **05** label, style, title **06** handle **07** epithet **08** cognomen, monicker, nickname **11** appellation, designation **12** denomination

so-called
07 alleged, nominal, would-be **08** supposed **09** pretended, professed, purported, soi-disant **10** ostensible, self-styled

soccer *see* **football**

sociability
10 affability, chumminess, cordiality **12** congeniality, conviviality, friendliness **14** gregariousness **15** neighbourliness

sociable
04 maty, warm **05** matey **06** chummy, clubby, folksy, genial, social **07** affable, cordial **08** clubable, familiar, friendly, outgoing **09** clubbable, convivial, extrovert **10** accessible, gregarious,

hospitable **11** companiable,
conversable, neighbourly
12 approachable **13** companionable

social
02 do **04** bash **05** civic, dance, group,
party **06** at-home, common, public,
rave-up, thrash **07** blow-out, general,
knees-up, leisure **08** communal,
function, sociable, societal
09 amusement, community, convivial,
gathering, organized **10** collective,
gregarious, neighborly, sociologic
11 get-together, neighbourly,
sympathetic **12** recreational,
sociological **13** entertainment
- **social insect**
03 ant **05** queen
- **social standing**
04 rank **05** class **11** consequence

socialism
07 leftism, Marxism **08** Leninism
09 communism, Stalinism, welfarism
10 Trotskyism **12** collectivism

socialist
03 red, Soc **04** pink, Trot **05** pinko
06 commie, leftie **07** leftist **08** hard-
left, left-wing **09** Bolshevik,
communist, Menshevik, welfarist
10 left-winger, Trotskyist, Trotskyite
11 parlour pink

socialize
03 mix **05** go out **06** hobnob, mingle
08 converse **09** entertain **10** be
sociable, fraternize, meet people
11 get together **12** meet socially

society
01 S **03** Soc **04** band, body, club, nobs,
tong **05** élite, group, guild, toffs, union
06 circle, gentry, league, nation,
people, public, swells **07** company,
culture, mankind **08** alliance,
humanity, nobility, sorority
09 community, humankind, human
race, top drawer **10** federation,
fellowship, fraternity, friendship,
population, sisterhood **11** aristocracy,
association, brotherhood,
camaraderie, corporation, high
society, the smart set **12** civilization,
organization, upper classes
13 companionship, polite society,
Sloane Rangers, the upper crust

sock
04 drub, hose, tabi **06** argyle, Argyll,
thrash **08** half-hose, knee-high
11 ploughshare

socket
03 pod **04** hose, jack, ouch, port
05 hosel, point **06** budget, eye-pit,
keeper **07** eyehole, hot shoe, torulus

08 alveolus **10** lampholder, power
point, tabernacle

sod
04 delf, fail, turf **05** delph, divot, scraw,
sward **06** ground

sodden
03 wet **04** miry **05** boggy, soggy
06 boiled, doughy, marshy, poachy,
soaked **07** drookit, soaking, sopping
08 drenched **09** saturated
11 waterlogged

sodium
02 Na

sofa

soft
01 B, p **02** mp, pp **03** dim, lax, low
04 easy, fool, hold, kind, lash, mild,
pale, waxy, weak **05** bland, cushy,
downy, faint, fuffy, furry, light, milky,
mulch, mulsh, mushy, muted, piano,
pulpy, quiet, rainy, silky, sweet
06 crumby, doughy, dulcet, fleecy,
gentle, gently, hushed, low-key,
mellow, pastel, pliant, shaded, silken,
smooth, sonant, spongy, supple,
tender, voiced **07** cottony, diffuse,
ductile, elastic, flowing, fungous,
lenient, liberal, pillowy, plastic, pliable,
quietly, springy, squashy, squishy,
subdued, unsized, velvety **08** cushiony,
delicate, diffused, flexible, generous,
merciful, pleasant, soothing, squelchy,
tolerant, yielding **09** easy-going,
forgiving, indulgent, luxurious,
malleable, melodious, sensitive,
spineless, whispered **10** bituminous,
effeminate, forbearing, mezzo-piano,
permissive, pianissimo, prosperous,
restrained, successful, unarmoured
11 a bed of roses, comfortable,
mellifluous, soft-hearted, sympathetic,
unprotected **12** affectionate, dough-
kneaded
- **soft in the head**
04 daft **05** barmy, dotty, loopy, nutty,
potty **06** stupid, unwise **07** foolish,
puerile **08** childish, immature
09 senseless **13** irresponsible,
unintelligent
- **soft spot**
06 liking **08** fondness, penchant,
weakness **10** fontanelle, partiality,
proclivity

soften
03 pad, ret **04** blet, calm, cree, ease,
melt, rait, rate, soak **05** abate, lower,
malax, quell, relax, still, water
06 digest, lessen, mellow, muffle,

reduce, relent, soothe, subdue, temper
07 appease, assuage, cushion, lighten,
liquefy, mollify, quicken, unsteel
08 calm down, diminish, dissolve,
humanize, macerate, malaxate,
mitigate, moderate, modulate, palliate,
tone down **09** alleviate, emolliate
10 intenerate
- **soften up**
04 melt **06** disarm, weaken **07** win
over **08** butter up, persuade, soft-soap
10 conciliate

soft-hearted
04 kind **06** gentle, tender **08** generous
10 benevolent, charitable
11 sentimental, sympathetic, warm-
hearted **12** affectionate
13 compassionate, tender-hearted

softly-softly
06 low-key **07** careful, patient
08 cautious, delicate, indirect
09 tentative **10** diplomatic, restrained
11 circumspect

soft-pedal
06 go easy, subdue **08** minimize,
moderate, play down, tone down

soggy
03 wet **04** damp **05** boggy, heavy,
moist, pulpy, soppy **06** marshy, soaked,
sodden, spongy, sultry, swampy
07 soaking, sopping **08** drenched,
dripping **09** saturated **10** sopping wet,
spiritless **11** waterlogged

soil
04 clay, dirt, dung, dust, foul, lair, land,
loam, mire, smut, spot, tash **05** black,
dirty, earth, filth, humus, mould,
muddy, smear, solum, stain, sully
06 befoul, damage, defile, fatten,
ground, region, sewage, smudge
07 begrime, country, pollute, slubber,
tarnish **08** besmirch **09** territory
10 terra firma

soiled
05 dingy, dirty, grimy, manky, tarry
06 grubby **07** spotted, stained, sullied
08 maculate, polluted **09** tarnished

sojourn
04 rest, stay, stop **05** abide, dwell,
lodge, tarry, visit **06** reside **08** stopover
09 tarriance **10** tabernacle
13 peregrination

Sol
06 Helios

solace
05 allay, cheer **06** relief, soften, soothe
07 comfort, console, succour, support
08 mitigate, pleasure **09** alleviate,
amusement **10** condolence
11 alleviation, consolation

soldier
03 ant, Joe, man, vet **04** swad **05** shirk
06 swaddy **07** shirker, veteran **10** red
herring

04 merc, para, peon
05 cadet, poilu, tommy
06 ensign, gunner, hussar, lancer, marine, sapper, sentry, sniper, troops
07 dragoon, fighter, officer, orderly, private, recruit, regular, terrier, trooper, warrior
08 commando, fusilier, partisan, rifleman
09 centurion, conscript, guardsman, guerrilla, irregular, mercenary, minuteman
10 cavalryman, serviceman
11 infantryman, legionnaire, paratrooper, Territorial
12 sharpshooter

Soldiers include:

02 Li (Hongzhang)
03 Cid (El), Lee (Robert E), Ney (Michel), Wet (Christian de), Zia (Muhammad)
04 Alba (Ferdinand Alvarez de Toledo, Duke of), Alva (Ferdinand Alvarez de Toledo, Duke of), Cade (Jack), Foch (Ferdinand), Haig (Alexander), Haig (Douglas, Earl), Jodl (Alfred), John (Don), Khan (Ayub), Röhm (Ernst), Tojo (Hideki)
05 Allen (Ethan), Bader (Sir Douglas), Barak (Ehud), Botha (Louis), Bowie (James), Bruce (Robert), Cimon, Clive (Robert, Lord), Dayan (Moshe), Essex (Robert Devereux, Earl of), Gates (Horatio), Grant (Ulysses S), Inönü (Ismet), Monck (George), Murat (Joachim), Perón (Juan), Pride (Sir Thomas), Rabin (Yitzhak), Smuts (Jan), Sucre (Antonio José de), Sully (Maximilien de Béthune, Duc de), Timur, Zhu De
06 Anders (Wladyslaw), Antony (Mark), Arnold (Benedict), Blamey (Sir Thomas Albert), Brutus (Marcus Junius), Butler (Benjamin Franklin), Caesar (Julius), Cortés (Hernán), Custer (George Armstrong), Dundee (John Graham, Viscount of), Dunois (Jean d'Orléans Comte), Edward (the Black Prince), Egmont (Graaf van Gavre), Ershad (Hossain Muhammad), Eugene (of Savoy), Franco (Francisco), Gaulle (Charles de), Gordon (Charles George), Granby (John Manners, Marquis of), Greene (Nathanael), Ireton (Henry), Keitel (Wilhelm), Marius (Gaius), Moltke (Helmuth, Graf von), Napier (Robert, Lord), Nasser (Gamal Abd al-), Neguib (Mohammed), Patton (George), Pétain (Philippe), Pompey, Prokop (the Bald), Raglan (Fitzroy James Henry Somerset, Lord), Rahman (Ziaur), Revere (Paul), Rommel (Erwin), Rupert (Prince), Scipio (Publius Cornelius), Vauban (Sebastien le Prestre de), Wavell (Archibald, Earl), Zhukov (Giorgiy)
07 Agrippa (Marcus Vipsanius), Allenby (Edmund, Viscount),

Almagro (Diego de), Artigas (José Gervasio), Atatürk (Mustapha Kemal), Baldwin, Bazaine (Achille), Bedford (John of Lancaster, Duke of), Blücher (Gebbard Leberecht von Fürst von), Bourbon (Charles), Boycott (Charles Cunningham), Bradley (Omar Nelson), Cadogan (William, Earl), Cassius, Coligny (Gaspard de), Dreyfus (Alfred), Fairfax (Thomas, Lord), Farnese (Alessandro), Gaddafi (Muammar), Gemayel (Bashir), Hunyady (János Corvinus), Jackson (Thomas Jonathan), Kolchak (Alexander), Kutuzov (Mikhail, Knyaz), Lambert (John), Masséna (André), Maurice (Prince), Metaxas (Ioannis), Mortier (Edouard Adolphe Casimir Joseph), Pizarro (Francisco), Ptolemy, Roberts (Frederick, Earl), Sherman (William Tecumseh), St Leger (Barry), Tancred, Turenne (Henri de la Tour d'Auvergne, Vicomte de), Vendôme (Louis Joseph Duc de), Warwick (Richard Neville, Earl of), William (Prince of Orange), Wrangel (Pyotr, Lord)
08 Agricola (Gnaeus Julius), Alvarado (Pedro de), Anglesey (Henry William Paget, Marquis of), Antonius (Marcus), Arminius, Badoglio (Pietro), Bentinck (William, Lord), Boadicea, Burgoyne (John), Burnside (Ambrose Everett), Campbell (Sir Colin), Cardigan (James Thomas Brudenell, Earl of), Cromwell (Oliver), Eichmann (Adolf), Ginckell (Godert de), Guiscard (Robert), Hamilton (James, Duke of), Harrison (William Henry), Hereward (the Wake), Horrocks (Sir Brian), Ironside (William, Lord), Itúrbide (Agustín de), Lawrence (Thomas Edward), Lucullus (Lucius Licinius), MacMahon (Marie Edme Patrice Maurice de), Marshall (George Catlett), Mengistu (Haile Mariam), Montfort (Simon de), Montrose (James Graham, Marquis of), Napoleon, Nobunaga (Oda), Pershing (John Joseph), Potemkin (Grigoriy), Pugachev (Emelyan), Seleucus, Sheridan (Philip Henry), Sikorski (Wladyslaw), Skorzeny (Otto), Stanhope (James, Earl), Tokugawa (Ieyasu), Valdivia (Pedro de), Wolseley (Garnet, Viscount), Xenophon, Yamagata (Prince Aritomo), Zia Ul-Haq (Muhammad)
09 Alexander (Harold, Earl), Antonescu (Ion), Bonaparte (Jérôme), Carausius (Marcus Aurelius Mausaeus), Cavendish (William), Garibaldi (Giuseppe), Gneisenau (August, Graf Neithardt von), Hasdrubal, Hideyoshi (Toyotomi), Kim Il-sung, Kitchener (Herbert, Earl), Lafayette (Marie Joseph, Marquis de), MacArthur (Douglas), Miltiades, Spartacus

10 Abercromby (Sir Ralph), Alanbrooke (Alan Francis Brooke, Viscount), Alcibiades, Auchinleck (Sir Claude), Belisarius, Clausewitz (Karl von), Cornwallis (Charles, Marquis), Cumberland (William, Duke of), Eisenhower (Dwight D), Germanicus, Hindenburg (Paul von), Karageorge, Montgomery (Bernard, Viscount), Schlieffen (Alfred, Graf von), Stroessner (Alfredo), Voroshilov (Kliment), Washington (George), Wellington (Arthur Wellesley, Duke of)
11 Baden-Powell (Robert, Lord), Black Prince, Genghis Khan, Marlborough (John Churchill, Duke of), Mohammed Ali, Münchhausen (Baron von)
12 Ptolemy Soter, Stauffenburg (Claus, Graf von)
13 Fabius Maximus (Quintus), Rouget de Lisle (Claude Joseph)
14 Pinochet Ugarte (Augusto)
15 Scipio Africanus (Publius Cornelius), Seleucus Nicator

● **soldier on**
06 hang on, hold on, keep on, remain
08 continue, keep at it, plug away
09 keep going, persevere, stick at it
11 hang in there
● **soldiers**
02 OR, RE, TA **03** GIs **04** army
06 legion **08** garrison

sole
03 one **04** lone, only, palm, pull, sill, slip, sowl **05** alone, capon, clump, mered, soole, sowle **06** meered, single, thenar, unique **07** uniform
08 singular, solitary **09** exclusive, scaldfish **10** individual

solecism
04 boob **05** error, gaffe, lapse
06 booboo, howler **07** blunder, faux pas, mistake **08** cacology **09** absurdity, gaucherie, indecorum **11** anacoluthon, impropriety, incongruity

solely
04 just, only **05** alone **06** merely, simply, singly **08** entirely, uniquely
09 allenarly **10** completely
11 exclusively **14** single-handedly

solemn
02 po **04** awed, glum **05** grand, grave, pious, sober, state **06** august, devout, formal, honest, owlish, ritual, sedate, sombre **07** earnest, genuine, po-faced, pompous, serious, sincere, stately **08** imposing, majestic
09 committed, dignified, momentous, venerable **10** ceremonial, impressive, portentous, thoughtful
11 ceremonious, reverential **12** awe-inspiring, wholehearted

solemnity
04 rite **06** ritual **07** dignity, gravity
08 ceremony, grandeur, sanctity
09 formality **10** ceremonial, observance, sacredness
11 celebration, earnestness,

solemnize *(continued)*
proceedings, seriousness, stateliness
13 momentousness **14** impressiveness,
portentousness

solemnize
04 keep **06** honour **07** dignify,
observe, perform **09** celebrate
11 commemorate

solemnly
07 gravely, soberly **08** formally
09 earnestly, seriously **10** faithfully

sol-fa see note

solicit
03 ask, beg, sue, woo **04** bash, drum,
pray, seek, tout **05** apply, court, crave,
plead **06** accost, ask for, hustle, incite,
manage **07** accoast, beseech, canvass,
conduct, entreat, implore, request,
require **08** apply for, petition
09 importune **10** supplicate
11 proposition

solicitor
02 QC, SL,WS **03** Att, Sol, SSC **04** Atty,
Solr, tout **06** lawyer **08** advocate,
attorney, law agent, recorder
09 barrister, canvasser **10** crown agent

solicitous
05 eager **06** caring, uneasy
07 anxious, careful, earnest, jealous,
worried, zealous **08** troubled
09 attentive, concerned **11** considerate
12 apprehensive

solicitude
04 care, cark, fear **05** worry **06** regard
07 anxiety, concern, trouble
08 disquiet **10** uneasiness
13 attentiveness, consideration
15 considerateness

solid
04 firm, hard, pure, real **05** cubic,
dense, gross, sober, sound, thick, valid
06 cogent, decent, square, stable,
strong, sturdy, trusty, worthy
07 compact, cubical, durable, genuine,
serious, unmixed, upright, wealthy,
weighty **08** concrete, reliable,
sensible, tangible, unbroken, unvaried
09 steadfast, unalloyed, unanimous,
undivided, well-built **10** compressed,
continuous, dependable, holosteric,
unshakable, upstanding **11** level-
headed, long-lasting, respectable,
substantial, trustworthy, unshakeable,
well-founded **12** well-grounded
13 authoritative, unadulterated,
uninterrupted

solidarity
05 unity **06** accord **07** concord,
harmony **08** cohesion **09** agreement,
consensus, soundness, stability,
unanimity **10** team spirit
11 camaraderie **13** esprit de corps
14 like-mindedness

solidify
03 gel, set **04** cake, clot, jell **06** go
hard, harden **07** congeal **09** coagulate,
corporify **10** become hard
11 crystallize

soliloquy
06 homily, sermon, speech **07** address,
lecture, monolog, oration
09 monologue

solitary
03 one **04** lone, monk, sole **05** alone,
loner **06** hermit, lonely, remote, single
07 ancress, ascetic, dernful, eremite,
recluse, retired, stylite **08** dearnful,
desolate, isolated, lonesome, lone
wolf, monastic, secluded, separate
09 anchoress, anchorite, reclusive,
untrodden, unvisited, withdrawn **10** by
yourself, cloistered, friendless,
hermitical, monastical, unsociable
11 introverted, monasterial, out-of-the-
way, sequestered **12** inaccessible,
Jimmy Woodser, unfrequented
13 companionless, individualist

solitude
07 privacy **09** aloneness, isolation,
seclusion **10** desolation, loneliness,
remoteness, retirement, singleness
12 introversion, lonesomeness
13 reclusiveness, unsociability
14 friendlessness

solo
04 aria, ayre, lone **05** alone, break, récit
06 single **07** cadenza **09** on your own
10 by yourself, unattended, unescorted
12 single-handed **13** unaccompanied

Solomon Islands
03 SLB

solution
◇ *anagram indicator*
02 aq **03** fix, gel, key, lye, mix, sol
05 blend, brine **06** answer, liquid,
liquor, remedy, result, saline, way out
07 cure-all, formula, mixture, panacea,
solvent **08** compound, emulsion,
quick fix **09** rationale, unfolding
10 resolution, suspension
11 elucidation, explanation, unravelling
12 decipherment **13** clarification
15 disentanglement

solve
◇ *anagram indicator*
04 read, undo, work **05** crack, guess,
loose, untie **06** answer, assoil, fathom,
puzzle, remedy, riddle, settle, unbind,
unfold **07** clarify, clear up, explain,
expound, rectify, resolve, unravel, work
out **08** decipher, put right, solution,
think out, unriddle **09** figure out,
interpret, puzzle out **11** disentangle
12 think through

solvent
04 DMSO **05** ether, sound **06** dioxan,
toluol **07** benzine, dioxane, toluene
08 alcahest, alkahest, methanol,
terebene **09** able to pay, banana oil,
detergent, financial, menstruum, out of
debt **10** chloroform, extractant, in the
black, in the clear, unindebted
11 cyclohexane **12** banana liquid,
creditworthy, ethyl acetate,
nitromethane, salt of sorrel **14** banana
solution, petroleum ether
15 propylene glycol, trichloroethane

solver
11 solutionist
• **solvers**
02 ye **03** you

Somalia
02 SO **03** SOM

sombre
03 dim, sad **04** dark, drab, dull
05 dingy, grave, morne, shady, sober
06 dismal, gloomy, morose, solemn
07 doleful, joyless, obscure, serious,
shadowy, subfusc, subfusk
08 funereal, mournful **09** depressed
10 lugubrious, melancholy

some
◇ *hidden indicator*
03 any, few, one **04** they **07** certain,
several **10** remarkable **11** outstanding,
such-and-such **12** considerable

somebody
03 one,VIP **04** name, star **05** mogul,
nabob **06** bigwig, quidam **07** big shot,
magnate, notable, someone **08** big
noise, big wheel, luminary
09 celebrity, dignitary, personage,
superstar **10** panjandrum
11 heavyweight **13** household
name

someday
05 later **06** one day **07** by and by, later
on **08** sometime **10** eventually,
ultimately **11** in due course **13** sooner
or later **14** one of these days

somehow
◇ *anagram indicator*
06 in a way **11** by some means, come
what may **15** by hook or by crook, one
way or another

someone see **somebody**

somersault
◇ *anagram indicator*

sometime
02 ex **04** late, then **06** former, one day
07 earlier, one-time, quondam, retired,
someday **08** emeritus, formerly,
previous **09** erstwhile, in the past
10 occasional, previously **11** another
time

sometimes
07 at times **08** off and on, on and off
09 somewhile **10** now and then, on
occasion, otherwhile, somewhiles
11 now and again, on occasions,
otherwhiles **12** every so often,
occasionally, once in a while **14** from
time to time

somewhat
04 a bit **05** kinda, quite **06** a bit of,
fairly, kind of, pretty, rather, sort of **07** a
little **08** slightly **10** moderately,
relatively **12** to some degree, to some
extent

somnolent
04 dozy **06** drowsy, sleepy, torpid
08 comatose, oscitant **09** half-awake,
heavy-eyed, soporific

Somnus
06 Hypnos

son
01 s 03 boy, lad 04 fils 05 child, lewis
06 epigon, filius, laddie, native
07 epigone 08 disciple 09 offspring
10 descendant, inhabitant

Sons include:

04 Abel, Amis (Martin), Bush (George W), Cain, Esau, Pitt (William)
05 Dumas (Alexandre), Groan (Titus), Harry (Prince), Isaac, Jacob, Milne (Christopher Robin), Morel (Paul), Waugh (Auberon)
06 Andrew (Prince), Edward (Prince), Gandhi (Rajiv), Hamlet, Joseph
07 Absalom, Charles (Prince), Douglas (Michael), Hotspur, Laertes, Oedipus, Simpson (Bart), William (Prince)
08 Benjamin, Dimbleby (David), Dimbleby (Jonathan), Florizel, Pontifex (Ernest)
09 Dumas fils
10 Duke of York
11 Jesus Christ
13 Prince of Wales
14 Pitt the Younger (William)

• **son of**
01 M', O' 02 Mc 03 Mac

song

Songs include:

03 air, art, fit, lay, oat, ode, pop, pub, war
04 aria, bird, duet, folk, glee, hymn, lied, lilt, love, pean, rock, rune, tune
05 blues, carol, catch, chant, dirge, ditty, elegy, lyric, paean, plain, psalm, torch, yodel
06 amoret, anthem, ballad, chorus, gospel, jingle, lieder, lyrics, melody, number, shanty
07 calypso, cantata, canzone, chanson, descant, lullaby, refrain, requiem, wassail
08 bird call, canticle, canzonet, madrigal, serenade, threnody
09 barcarole, cantilena, dithyramb, epinikion, roundelay, spiritual
10 plainchant, recitative
11 bothy ballad, chansonette, rock and roll
12 epithalamium, nursery rhyme

See also **poem**

Pop songs include:

03 Bad
04 1999, Gold, Help!, True
05 Clair, Diana, Faith, Layla, My Way, Relax, Shout
06 Apache, Atomic, The End, Vienna, Volare
07 Delilah, D.I.V.O.R.C.E., Hey Jude, Holiday, Imagine, Jamming, Let It Be, Rat Trap, Respect, Sailing, Starman
08 Answer Me, Antmusic, At the Hop, Baby Love, Downtown, Love Me Do, Mamma Mia, Our House, Parklife, Peggy Sue, The Boxer, The Model, Thriller, Wannabee, Waterloo
09 Albatross, Dance Away, I Feel Love, Maggie May, Metal Guru, Penny Lane, Praise You, Release Me, Something, Stand By Me, Wild Thing, Yesterday
10 All Shook Up, Annie's Song, Band of Gold, Billie Jean, Blue Monday, Bye Bye Baby, House of Fun, King Creole, Lazy Sunday, Living Doll, Millennium, Moving On Up, Night Fever, Perfect Day, Purple Haze, Reet Petite, Ring of Fire, Wonderwall
11 All Right Now, American Pie, Back for Good, Baker Street, Cathy's Clown, Firestarter, From Me to You, Glad All Over, Golden Brown, I Got You Babe, I'm Not in Love, Light My Fire, Like a Virgin, Lily the Pink, Mrs Robinson, Oliver's Army, Space Oddity, Tainted Love, Voodoo Chile
12 All or Nothing, Bat Out of Hell, Born in the USA, Born to be Wild, Come on Eileen, Common People, Dancing Queen, Eleanor Rigby, God Only Knows, Material Girl, No Woman No Cry, The Birdy Song, West End Girls
13 Blueberry Hill, Brass in Pocket, Design for Life, Don't You Want Me, Into the Groove, It's Not Unusual, It's Now or Never, Jailhouse Rock, Last Christmas, Long Tall Sally, Mary's Boy Child, Mull of Kintyre, Oh, Pretty Woman, Only the Lonely, Pinball Wizard, Summer Holiday, Tears in Heaven
14 20th Century Boy, A Hard Day's Night, Blue Suede Shoes, Good Vibrations, Karma Chameleon, Stand By Your Man, Sunny Afternoon, That'll Be the Day, The Power of Love, Waterloo Sunset, White Christmas, Wonderful World
15 Baby One More Time, Begin the Beguine, Blowin' in the Wind, Candle in the Wind, Careless Whisper, Congratulations, God Save the Queen, Heartbreak Hotel, Hotel California, I Shot the Sheriff, Jumpin' Jack Flash, Killing me Softly, Love is all Around, Paperback Writer, Puppet on a String, Rivers of Babylon, Unchained Melody, When I Fall In Love, Yellow Submarine

See also **musical**

• **song and dance**
03 ado 04 flap, fuss, stir, to-do 05 hoo-ha, tizzy 06 bother, furore, pother, tumult 09 commotion, kerfuffle
11 performance

songster
06 singer 07 crooner, soloist, warbler
08 minstrel, vocalist 09 balladeer, chanteuse, chorister 10 troubadour

songwriter

Songwriters and lyricists include:

03 Pop (Iggy)
04 Bart (Lionel), Cahn (Sammy), Cash (Johnny), Hart (Lorenz), John (Sir Elton), Kern (Jerome), Reed (Lou), Rice (Sir Tim)
05 Berry (Chuck), Brown (James), Cohan (George Michael), Davis (Miles), Dylan (Bob), Holly (Buddy), Loewe (Frederick), Simon (Paul), Smith (Tommy), Sousa (John Philip), Swann (Donald), Weill (Kurt)
06 Berlin (Irving), Coward (Sir Noël), Fields (Dorothy), Joplin (Scott), Lennon (John), Lerner (Alan Jay), Marley (Bob), Mercer (Johnny H), Morton (Jelly Roll), Oliver (King), Parker (Charlie), Porter (Cole), Seeger (Pete), Waller (Thomas 'Fats'), Warren (Harry)
07 Collins (Phil), Dickson (Barbara), Donovan, Gilbert (Sir Wiliam), Guthrie (Woody), Hendrix (Jimi), Loesser (Frank), MacColl (Ewan), Mancini (Henry), Novello (Ivor), Orbison (Roy), Rodgers (Richard), Romberg (Sigmund)
08 Coltrane (John), Costello (Elvis), Gershwin (George), Mitchell (Joni), Morrison (Van), Sondheim (Stephen)
09 Bernstein (Leonard), Ellington (Duke), Faithfull (Marianne), Gillespie (Dizzy), McCartney (Sir Paul)
10 Carmichael (Hoagy)
11 Armatrading (Joan), Hammerstein (Oscar), Lloyd Webber (Andrew, Lord), Springsteen (Bruce)

sonorous
04 full, loud, rich 05 round 07 orotund ringing, rounded 08 plangent, resonant, sounding 09 high-flown, ororotund 10 full-voiced, resounding
11 full-mouthed 12 full-throated, high-sounding 13 grandiloquent

soon
04 anon 05 early, quick 06 pronto, timely 07 betimes, ere long, in a tick, just now, readily, shortly 08 in a hurry, in a jiffy, in no time 09 any minute, in a minute, in a moment, presently, willingly 10 before long 12 any minute now, in a short time, without delay
13 in no time at all 14 in a little while, in a moment or two, round the corner
15 in the near future

• **as soon as**
04 once, when 07 whene'er
08 directly, eftsoons, whenever
10 right after 11 immediately, in the wake of 13 directly after

sooner
06 before, rather 07 earlier, instead
08 by choice 09 for choice, in advance
10 beforehand, from choice, much rather, preferably 12 by preference
13 for preference

• **no sooner than**
06 barely, hardly 08 only just, scarcely

• **sooner or later**
06 at last 07 finally 08 after all, at length, in the end 10 eventually, ultimately 11 in due course 12 in the long run, subsequently

ot

coom, smut **05** colly **06** smutch
gas black **09** lampblack

othe

balm, calm, coax, ease, hush, lull
accoy, allay, quiet, salve, sleek, still
augury, back up, cajole, pacify,
ttle, smooth, soften, temper
appease, assuage, comfort,
mpose, confirm, flatter, mollify,
ieten, relieve, support **08** blandish,
lm down, mitigate, palliate
alleviate **10** settle down **11** quieten
wn **12** foretokening, tranquillize

othing

soft **05** balmy **06** anetic, gentle
anodyne, calming, easeful, lenient,
stful **08** balsamic, lenitive, relaxing
assuasive, demulcent, emollient,
regoric **10** palliative

othsayer

seer **05** augur, sibyl **07** Chaldee,
viner, prophet **08** Chaldaic, haruspex
foreteller, prophetess
prognosticator

phisticated

cool, gold **05** couth, slick, suave
hi-tech, inland, subtle, urbane
complex, elegant, refined, stylish,
orldly **08** advanced, cultured,
licate, high-tech, joined-up,
lished, seasoned, space-age
civilized, elaborate, executive,
pensive, falsified, intricate
cultivated **11** adulterated,
mplicated, experienced, worldly
ise **12** cosmopolitan **13** state-of-the-
t **15** highly developed

phistication

poise **07** culture, finesse
elegance, urbanity **10** experience
savoir-faire, savoir-vivre, worldliness

phistry

fallacy, quibble, sophism
elenchus **09** casuistry, choplogic
paralogism **14** false reasoning

porific

hypnic, opiate, sleepy **07** poppied,
conal® **08** hypnotic, narcotic,
dative **09** dormitive, somnolent
poppy water **11** anaesthetic
sleeping pill **13** sleep-inducing,
anquillizer **14** benzodiazepine,
eeping tablet, tranquillizing

oppy

wet **04** daft, soft, wild **05** corny,
azy, gooey, mushy, silly, soggy, weepy
cheesy, gloopy, sloppy, slushy
cloying, maudlin, mawkish,
impish **08** drenched **09** schmaltzy
lovey-dovey **11** sentimental
overemotional

oprano

S **03** sop **05** mezzo **06** treble
castrato

orcerer

mage **05** magus, witch **06** magian,
odoo, wizard **07** angekok, warlock

08 angekkok, magician **09** enchanter,
sorceress **10** reim-kennar
11 enchantress, necromancer
13 thaumaturgist

sorcery

05 charm, magic, spell, wicca
06 voodoo **07** pisheog **08** diablery,
malefice, pishogue, witching, wizardry
09 diablerie, warlockry **10** black
magic, necromancy, witchcraft
11 enchantment, incantation,
thaumaturgy

sordid

03 low **04** base, foul, mean, vile
05 dirty, grimy, mucky, seamy, seedy
06 filthy, scungy, shabby, sleazy, soiled,
tawdry **07** corrupt, debased, immoral,
miserly, squalid, stained, unclean
08 degraded, grasping, shameful,
wretched **09** abhorrent, debauched,
dishonest, mercenary, niggardly
10 degenerate, despicable
11 ignominious, self-seeking
12 disreputable **13** dishonourable

sore

03 cut, raw, red **04** bite, boil, gall, hard,
hurt, sair **05** angry, blain, botch, chafe,
felon, graze, grief, nasty, nerve, ulcer,
upset, vexed, wound **06** aching, bitter,
chafed, fester, lesion, miffed, peeved,
scrape, shiver, sorrel, tender, the raw,
touchy **07** abscess, annoyed, anthrax,
bruised, burning, eagerly, hurting,
injured, painful, quittor, wounded
08 abrasion, grievous, inflamed,
offended, reddened, severely,
smarting, stinging, swelling
09 afflicted, aggrieved, irritable,
irritated, painfully, resentful, sensitive
10 affliction, cheesed off, distressed,
grievously, laceration **12** inflammation
13 distressingly

sorely

04 much **06** highly **07** greatly, notably
08 markedly, very much **09** extremely
10 noticeably, powerfully, remarkably
11 exceedingly **13** significantly,
substantially

sorrel

03 oca **04** soar, sore **05** soare, sorel
06 oxalis, sorell **07** bilimbi, sourock
08 shamrock, sourwood
09 carambola, sour-gourd

sorrow

03 rew, rue, woe **04** moan, pain, pine,
pity, ruth, weep **05** be sad, grief,
mourn, night, sorra, trial, worry
06 bemoan, bewail, dolour, grieve,
lament, misery, regret, repent
07 agonize, anguish, feel sad, remorse,
sadness, trouble **08** distress, hardship,
mourning **09** dejection, heartache,
suffering, tristesse **10** affliction,
compassion, contrition, heartbreak,
misfortune **11** be miserable,
lamentation, tribulation, unhappiness,
Weltschmerz **12** wretchedness **13** feel
miserable

See also **grief**

sorrowful

02 wo **03** sad, wae, woe **05** sorry, trist,
woful **06** dismal, rueful, triste, woeful
07 baleful, careful, doleful, painful,
piteous, ruthful, tearful, unhappy,
wailful **08** dejected, grievous,
mournful, wretched **09** afflicted,
depressed, miserable, woebegone
10 lamentable, lugubrious, melancholy
11 distressing, heartbroken
12 disconsolate, heart-rending, heavy-
hearted

sorry

◊ *anagram indicator*
02 wo **03** bad, sad, woe **04** mean,
poor **05** moved, upset **06** dismal,
rueful, simple **07** ashamed, pitiful,
pitying, unhappy **08** contrite, grievous,
pathetic, penitent, shameful, wretched
09 concerned, miserable, regretful,
repentant, worthless **10** apologetic,
distressed, remorseful, shamefaced
11 distressing, guilt-ridden,
sympathetic, unfortunate
12 contemptible, heart-rending
13 compassionate, understanding

• **be sorry for**
03 rew, rue **06** repent **08** forthink

sort

◊ *anagram indicator*
03 fit, ilk, lot, set **04** beat, geld, kind,
make, race, rank, sift, type **05** agree,
allot, befit, brand, breed, class, genre,
genus, grade, group, order, stamp,
style, woman **06** accord, adjust, assign,
divide, family, kidney, manner, nature,
parcel, person, punish, screen, select
07 arrange, company, consort,
dispose, fashion, procure, provide,
quality, species, variety **08** category,
classify, organize, separate
09 catalogue, character, segregate
10 categorize, collection, distribute,
put in order **11** description, systematize
12 denomination

• **out of sorts**
◊ *anagram indicator*
03 ill **04** mean, sick, weak **05** crook,
cross, dicky, frail, narky, nohow, ratty,
rough, seedy **06** ailing, crabby,
crummy, feeble, groggy, grumpy,
infirm, laid up, poorly, queasy, rotten,
shirty, snappy, unwell **07** crabbed,
grouchy, in a huff, in a mood, in a sulk,
run down, run-down, stroppy
08 below par, choleric, diseased,
nohowish **09** bedridden, crotchety,
fractious, impatient, in a bad way,
irritable, off-colour, unhealthy **10** in a
bad mood **11** bad-tempered **13** mops
and brooms, quick-tempered **14** down
in the dumps, down in the mouth
15 under the weather

• **sort of**
◊ *anagram indicator*
04 a bit **05** kinda, quite **06** fairly, kind
of, pretty, rather **07** a little **08** slightly,
somewhat **10** moderately, relatively
12 to some degree, to some extent

• **sort out**
04 rank **05** class, grade, group, order,

solve **06** choose, divide, select
07 arrange, clear up, resolve, work out
08 classify, organize, put right, separate
09 segregate **10** categorize, put in
order

sortie
04 raid, rush **05** foray, sally, swoop
06 attack, charge **07** assault, outfall
08 invasion **09** offensive

so-so
02 OK **04** fair **06** not bad **07** average,
neutral **08** adequate, mediocre,
middling, moderate, ordinary, passable
09 tolerable **11** indifferent, respectable
12 run-of-the-mill **13** no great shakes,
unexceptional **14** comme ci comme
ça, fair to middling **15** undistinguished

soubriquet *see* sobriquet,
soubriquet

sought-after
02 in **03** big, hip, hot, now **04** cool
05 liked **06** modish, trendy, wanted
07 admired, desired, popular
08 approved, favoured, in demand, in
favour **09** favourite, well-liked **10** all
the rage **11** fashionable **13** in great
demand

soul
02 ba, ka **03** âme, ego, man **04** alma,
life, mind **05** anima, model, shade,
woman **06** person, pneuma, psyche,
reason, spirit **07** element, epitome,
essence, example, feeling, passion
08 creature, humanity, inner man,
sympathy **09** character, inner self,
intellect **10** compassion, embodiment,
human being, individual, inner being,
inner woman, tenderness, vital force
11 inspiration, sensitivity
12 appreciation **13** heart of hearts,
understanding **15** personification

soulful
06 moving **08** eloquent, mournful,
profound **09** emotional, heartfelt,
sensitive **10** expressive, meaningful

soulless
04 cold, dead, mean **05** bleak, cruel,
empty **06** unkind **07** callous, ignoble,
inhuman **08** lifeless **09** unfeeling
10 mechanical, spiritless
11 dehumanized **12** mean-spirited
13 characterless, uninteresting,
unsympathetic **14** soul-destroying

sound
◇ *homophone indicator*
03 din, fit, say, voe **04** deep, firm, goad,
good, hale, look, mean, safe, sane,
seem, tend, test, toll, tone, trig, true,
vibe, well **05** firth, fiord, fjord, gauge,
go off, inlet, noise, plumb, probe, radio,
right, sense, solid, swoon, tease, tenor,
utter, valid, voice, whole **06** appear,
cogent, deeply, fathom, intact, notion,
proven, robust, secure, severe, strait,
strong, sturdy, timbre, unhurt
07 channel, declare, earshot, estuary,
examine, express, extreme, feeling,
greatly, healthy, inspect, intense,
logical, measure, passage, perfect,

provoke, publish, resound, serious,
weighty **08** announce, complete,
orthodox, proclaim, profound,
rational, reliable, resonate, severely,
thorough, unbroken, very much,
vigorous **09** enunciate, excellent,
extremely, intensely, judicious,
pronounce, resonance, seriously,
undamaged, uninjured, very great,
wholesome **10** articulate, completely,
dependable, impression, profoundly,
reasonable, thoroughly, unimpaired,
vigorously **11** disease-free, implication,
in good shape, investigate, reverberate,
substantial, trustworthy, well-founded
12 in fine fettle, in good health, sound
as a bell, well-grounded
13 authoritative, reverberation **15** in
good condition

03 cry, hum, pip, pop, sob, tap
04 bang, beep, boom, buzz, chug,
clap, echo, fizz, hiss, honk, hoot,
moan, peal, ping, plop, ring, roar,
sigh, slam, snap, thud, tick, ting,
toot, wail, whiz, yell, yoop
05 blare, blast, bleep, chime, chink,
chirm, clack, clang, clank, clash,
click, clink, clunk, crack, crash,
creak, drone, grate, groan, knock,
plonk, skirl, slurp, smack, sniff,
snore, snort, swish, throb, thump,
twang, vroom, whine, whirr, whish,
whizz, whoop
06 bubble, crunch, gabble, gollar,
goller, gurgle, hiccup, jangle, jingle,
murmur, patter, rattle, report,
rumble, rustle, scrape, scream,
sizzle, splash, squeak, squeal,
tinkle, whoosh
07 brattle, chatter, clatter, crackle,
explode, graunch, grizzle, pitapat,
screech, squelch, thunder,
whimper, whistle
08 splutter
11 taratantara

03 baa, bay, caw, coo, kaw, low, mew,
moo, wee, yap
04 bark, bell, blat, bray, bump, crow,
hiss, honk, hoot, howl, purr, roar,
woof, yawp, yelp, yowl
05 bleat, cheep, chirp, cluck, crake,
croak, groin, growl, grunt, miaow,
neigh, pewit, quack, scape, snarl,
tweet
06 bellow, cackle, gobble, heehaw,
peewit, squawk, squeak, warble,
whinny
07 chirrup, gruntle, looning, screech,
trumpet, twitter, whicker
09 caterwaul

03 Hoy, Rum
04 Bute, Calf, Crow, Deer, Eigg, Holm,
Iona, Jura, King, Mull, Papa, Rock,
Yell
05 Barra, Canna, Cross, Exuma, Gigha,
Inner, Islay, Luing, Puget, Sanda,
Shuna, Sleat

06 Breton, Harris, Norton, Pabbay,
Raasay, Ramsey, Sanday, Shiant,
Turner
07 Arisaig, Bardsey, Caswell, Cuillin,
Gairsay, McMurdo, Milford,
Pamlico, St Mary's
08 Auskerry, Bluemull, Breaksea,
Colgrave, Doubtful, Kotzebue,
Taransay
09 Albemarle, Casiguran, Currituck,
Eynhallow, Lancaster, Shapinsay
10 Chandeleur, Cumberland,
Kilbrannan, King George, Long
Island, New Georgia, Possession
11 Mississippi, Roes Welcome
12 Prince Albert
13 Prince William

• by the sound of it
◇ *homophone indicator*
• sound measure/unit
02 dB **03** bel **04** phon, sone
07 decibel, phoneme, segment
09 kilohertz
• sound out
03 ask **04** pump **05** probe **06** survey
07 canvass, examine, suss out
08 question, research **11** investigate

soundly
04 fast **05** fully, quite, tight **06** deeply
07 greatly, solidly, totally, utterly, validl
08 entirely, securely, severely, very
much **09** downright, extremely,
intensely, logically, perfectly, seriously
10 absolutely, completely, dependably
profoundly, reasonably, thoroughly,
vigorously **15** authoritatively

soundtrack
10 theme music

soup
◇ *anagram indicator*

03 dal, pea, pho
04 cawl, crab, dhal, game, miso
05 adrak, blaff, broth, egusi, gumbo,
locro, misua, rasam, snert, stock
06 ajiaco, asapao, barley, birria, bisque
borsch, cocido, congee, fennel,
guacho, harira, lentil, noodle, oxtail
pazole, posole, potage, potato,
reuben, sambar, tomato, turtle, wo
ton
07 borscht, chicken, chowder, tarator,
turbana
08 borschch, broccoli, callaloo,
chirmole, consommé, ful nabed,
gazpacho, halászlé, julienne,
mondongo, mushroom, okroshka,
sancocho, solianka, split pea
09 asparagus, bird's nest, cacciucco,
Clanallen, escabeche, fasolatha,
pea and ham, pepperpot, picadillo
quimbombo, royal game,
rozsolnyk, shark's fin, tom kha gai,
white foam
10 avgolemono, caldo verde,
minestrone, mock turtle, mole de
olla, sauerkraut, superkanja,
watercress
11 clam chowder, cock-a-leekie,
cullen skink, French onion, gaeng

sour

som kai, gaeng som pla, Scotch broth, tom yam goong, vichyssoise **12** bouneschlupp, brown Windsor, cockieleekie, guriltai shul, mulligatawny **13** bouillabaisse, chicken noodle, cream of tomato, potato and leek, stracciatella **14** lentil and bacon **15** Queen Anne's broth

sour

03 bad, off **04** acid, rank, tart, tiff, tift, turn **05** acerb, acidy, aygre, eager, heavy, nasty, ratty, sharp, spoil, surly, tangy, wersh **06** acetic, bitter, canker, crusty, morose, rancid, shirty, strong, turned **07** acerbic, acetous, austere, crabbed, curdled, envenom, grouchy, peevish, pungent, subacid **08** alienate, churlish, embitter, verjuice, vinegary **09** acidulent, acidulous, resentful **10** disenchant, embittered, exacerbate, exasperate, make bitter, unpleasant **11** acrimonious, bad-tempered, ill-tempered **12** disagreeable, inharmonious, unsuccessful

source

03 urn **04** font, head, mine, rise, root, well, ylem **05** cause, fount, radix, start, stock **06** author, origin, source, spring, supply, whence **07** surging **08** wellhead **09** authority, beginning, generator, good hands, informant, principle, rootstock, water head **10** derivation, originator, primordium, provenance, springhead, wellspring **11** fons et origo **12** commencement, fountainhead

sourpuss

04 crab **05** grump, shrew **06** grouse, kvetch, misery, whiner **07** killjoy, whinger **08** buzzkill, grumbler **10** crosspatch **14** dog in the manger

souse

03 dip, ear, sou **04** dash, duck, dunk, sink, soak, wash **05** douse, plump, smite, souce, sowce, sowse, steep, thump **06** drench, impact, pickle, plunge, sowsse, strike **07** ducking, immerse, impinge **08** drunkard, marinade, marinate, saturate, submerge, suddenly **09** drenching

south

◇ *tail selection down indicator*
01 S **02** So **03** Sth **04** Midi

South Africa

02 SA, ZA **03** RSA, ZAF **04** S Afr

South African

02 SA **04** S Afr

South America *see* America; god, goddess

South Carolina

02 SC

South Dakota

02 SD **04** S Dak

south-east, south-eastern

02 SE

southern

01 S **05** south **07** austral **09** southerly **10** meridional

south-west, south-western

02 SW

souvenir

05 relic, steal, token **06** trophy **07** memento, purloin, relique **08** keepsake, reminder **11** remembrance

sovereign

01 K, L, Q **02** ER, HM **03** bar, sov **04** king, quid, tsar **05** chief, crown, pound, queen, royal, ruler, squid **06** canary, couter, kingly, nicker, prince, ruling, shiner, sovran, utmost **07** emperor, empress, extreme, monarch, queenly, smacker, supreme, thick'un **08** absolute, autocrat, dominant, imperial, majestic, princely **09** paramount, potentate, principal, unlimited **10** autonomous, self-ruling, unequalled, unrivalled **11** independent, outstanding, predominant **12** jimmy-o'goblin **13** pound sterling, self-governing

See also **king**; **queen**

sovereignty

03 raj **04** sway **07** primacy, royalty **08** autonomy, chiefdom, dominion, imperium, kingship, regality, synarchy **09** chiefship, princedom, queenship, supremacy **10** ascendancy, domination, suzerainty **11** condominium, pre-eminence **12** independence **13** thalassocracy, thalattocracy **14** rangatiratanga, self-government

sow

03 elt, saw **04** gilt, seed, yelt **05** drill, lodge, plant, strew **06** spread **07** bestrew, implant, scatter **08** disperse, seminate **09** broadcast **10** distribute, inseminate **11** disseminate

See also **pig**

sozzled

◇ *anagram indicator*
05 happy, merry, tight, tipsy **06** blotto, tiddly **07** drunken, pickled, squiffy, tiddley **09** crapulent, plastered **10** inebriated **11** intoxicated

spa

06 spring **07** Kurhaus

Spas include:

03 Dax
04 Bath
05 Baden, Baños, Epsom, Sochi, Vichy
06 Aachen, Boston, Buxton, Ilkley, Trebon
07 Lourdes, Malvern, Matlock
08 Carlsbad, Shearsby, Woodhall
09 Bad Elster, Droitwich, Harrogate, Marienbad, Velingrad
10 Baden Baden, Cheltenham, Leamington
11 Bad Dürrheim, Scarborough
12 Strathpeffer

13 Aix-la-Chapelle, Knaresborough
14 Tunbridge Wells

space

02 em, en **03** gap **04** area, lung, play, room, seat, span, time, void **05** array, blank, break, chasm, order, place, range, scope, shift, spell, stint, sweep **06** cosmos, extent, galaxy, lacuna, leeway, margin, period, volume **07** arrange, be apart, dispose, expanse, opening, stretch **08** capacity, interval, latitude, omission, set apart, space out, universe **09** amplitude, clearance, deep space, elbow-room, expansion, string out **10** empty space, interstice, Lebensraum, outer space, put in order, stretch out **11** the Milky Way **12** intermission **13** accommodation

Space travel-related terms include:

03 bus, ELV, ESA, ISS, LOX, LRV, MCC
04 NASA
05 abort, flyby, orbit
06 CAPCOM, drogue, G force, hydyne, launch, module, rocket
07 booster, coolant, docking, lift-off, mission, payload, re-entry, shuttle, vidicon
08 attitude, blast-off, free-fall, fuel cell, fuel tank, lunanaut, moonwalk, nose cone, sloshing
09 astronaut, cosmonaut, hydrazine, launch pad, light year, lunarnaut, spaceship, space suit
10 heat shield, pogo effect, propellant, rendezvous, spacecraft, space probe, trajectory
11 lunar module, solar system, zero gravity
12 ascent module, launch window, lunar landing, man on the moon, microgravity, space station
13 command module, descent module, jet propulsion, launch vehicle, space sickness
14 escape velocity, mission control, weightlessness
15 re-entry corridor

Spacecraft include:

02 LM
03 ISS, LEM, Mir
06 Skylab, Tardis
07 Gemini 4, Vostok 1, Vostok 5, Vostok 6
08 Apollo 11, Apollo 13, Apollo 17, Columbia, Freedom 7, Nostromo, Red Dwarf, Sputnik 1, Sputnik 2, Voskhod 1, Voskhod 2
09 Discovery, Endeavour, Liberator, Pioneer 10, Shenzhou V
10 Challenger, USS Voyager
11 Fireball XL5, Heart of Gold
12 SS Discovery 1, Thunderbird 3, Thunderbird 5
13 Moonbase Alpha, USS Enterprise

See also **probe**

spaceman, spacewoman *see* astronaut

spacious
03 big **04** huge, open, vast, wide
05 ample, broad, large, roomy
07 immense, sizable **08** palatial,
sizeable **09** capacious, expansive,
extensive, uncrowded **10** commodious

spade
01 S **03** loy **04** pick, spay, spit **05** graft,
slane, spado, spayd **06** paddle, pattle,
pettle, spayad, tuskar, tusker **07** cas
crom, tushkar, tushker, twiscar
08 caschrom **09** flaughter **11** paddle-
staff **12** breastplough
• **spades**
01 S

spadework
06 labour **08** drudgery, homework
10 donkey-work, foundation,
groundwork **11** preparation
15 preliminary work

Spain
01 E **03** ESP **06** España
• **in Spain**
◇ *foreign word indicator*

span
04 arch, last, link, term, time, yoke
05 cover, cross, fresh, piece, range,
reach, scope, spell, vault **06** bridge,
extend, extent, length, period, spread,
wind up **07** compass, include,
measure, overlay, stretch **08** bestride,
distance, duration, interval, traverse
09 encompass **10** overbridge

spangle
01 O **06** sequin **07** glitter **09** paillette

Spaniard
03 don

spaniel
04 mean **07** fawning

Spaniels include:

03 toy
04 land
05 field, water
06 cocker, Sussex
07 clumber
08 Blenheim, papillon, springer
10 Irish water, Maltese dog
11 King Charles

Spanish *see* **day; month; number**

spank
03 tan **04** cane, slap **05** smack, whack
06 paddle, strike, thrash, thwack,
wallop **07** slipper **15** put over your
knee

spanking
04 fast, fine, very **05** brand, brisk,
quick, scuds, smart, swift **06** lively,
snappy, speedy **07** exactly, totally,
utterly **08** gleaming, spirited, striking,
vigorous **09** energetic **10** absolutely,
completely, paddy-whack, positively,
strikingly **12** invigorating

spanner
03 key **06** wrench **12** monkey wrench

spar
03 bar, box **04** gaff, pole, rail, shut, spat,

tiff **05** argue, scrap, sprit **06** barite,
bicker, fasten, rafter, ricker, steeve
07 barytes, contend, contest, dispute,
fall out, quarrel, wrangle, wrestle
08 bowsprit, cryolite, mainboom,
skirmish, squabble **09** outrigger
10 martingale **11** torpedo boom
12 swinging-boom, wollastonite
13 rhodochrosite

spare
04 bony, free, gash, give, hain, lank,
lean, over, save, slim, thin **05** allow,
avoid, extra, gaunt, grant, guard, hoard,
scant, skimp, stint **06** afford, defend,
frugal, let off, meagre, modest, pardon,
scanty, secure, skimpy, skinny, unused
07 forbear, forgive, leisure, not harm,
protect, provide, refrain, release,
reserve, scraggy, scrawny, slender,
sparing, surplus **08** buckshee, leftover,
part with, reprieve, unwanted,
withhold **09** auxiliary, do without,
emergency, remaining, safeguard,
subsecive **10** additional, subsidiary,
take care of, unoccupied **11** show
mercy to, superfluous **12** dispense
with **13** manage without,
supernumerary, supplementary **15** all
skin and bones
• **to spare**
05 extra **06** unused **07** surplus **08** left
over **09** in reserve, remaining
• **with little to spare**
04 fine **06** narrow

sparing
05 canny, mingy, scant **06** frugal,
meagre, scarce, stingy, strait **07** careful,
miserly, prudent, thrifty **09** penurious
10 economical **11** close-fisted, tight-
fisted

sparingly
06 nighly **08** frugally, meagrely,
scrimply, stingily **09** carefully,
prudently **12** economically

spark
03 bit, jot **04** atom, beau, funk, hint,
iota **05** flake, flame, flare, flash, gleam,
glint, lover, scrap, spunk, touch, trace
06 kindle **07** animate, bluette, flaught,
flicker, glimmer, sparkle, vestige
08 skerrick **09** scintilla **10** suggestion
11 electrician
• **spark off**
04 stir **05** cause, start **06** excite, incite,
kindle, prompt, set off **07** inspire,
provoke, trigger **08** occasion, start off,
touch off **09** stimulate **10** give rise to,
trigger off **11** precipitate

sparkle
03 vim **04** beam, brio, dash, fire, fizz,
glow, life, zest **05** flash, gleam, glint,
shine, spark **06** bubble, dazzle, energy,
spirit **07** be witty, emicate, flicker,
glimmer, glisten, glister, glitter, pizzazz,
shimmer, twinkle **08** be bubbly, be
lively, radiance, vitality, vivacity
09 animation, coruscate, emication
10 be animated, be spirited, brilliance,
ebullience, effervesce, enthusiasm,
get-up-and-go, liveliness **11** be

ebullient, be vivacious, coruscation,
scintillate **13** scintillation **14** be
effervescent, be enthusiastic

sparkling
05 fizzy, witty **06** bubbly, lively
07 emicant **08** aglitter, animated,
flashing, gleaming, spritzig **09** brilliant,
frizzante, pétillant, twinkling
10 carbonated, glistening, glittering
11 coruscating, scintillant
12 effervescent **13** scintillating
• **make sparkling**
09 carbonate

sparrow
04 tody **05** sprug **06** mossie
07 dunnock, pinnock, spadger, titling
08 accentor, prunella, ricebird
09 paddy-bird **11** whitethroat
13 hedge-accentor

sparse
04 rare, thin **06** meagre, scanty, scarce,
slight **07** scrawny **08** scattery, sporadic
09 scattered **10** infrequent

sparsely
08 meagrely, scantily, scarcely, slightly
12 sporadically

spartan
05 bleak, hardy, harsh, plain **06** frugal,
severe, simple, strict **07** ascetic,
austere, harmost, joyless, laconic
08 rigorous **09** stringent, temperate
10 abstemious **11** disciplined, self-
denying **12** militaristic

spasm
03 fit, tic **04** bout, grip, jerk **05** burst,
cramp, crick, gripe, spell, start, thraw,
throe, throw, tonus **06** access, attack,
clonus, frenzy, hippus, throwe, twitch
07 seizure, trismus **08** eruption,
outburst, paroxysm **10** blepharism,
convulsion, tonic spasm **11** clonic
spasm, contraction, laryngismus
12 childcrowing

spasmodic
◇ *anagram indicator*
05 jerky **06** fitful **07** erratic, spastic
08 periodic, sporadic **09** irregular
10 convulsive, occasional
12 intermittent

spasmodically
08 off and on, on and off **11** now and
again **12** occasionally, periodically,
sporadically **14** intermittently

spate
04 flow, rush **05** flood, speat
06 deluge, series **07** torrent
10 outpouring

spatter
◇ *anagram indicator*
03 jap **04** daub, jaup, soil **05** dirty,
spray **06** bedaub, dabble, shower,
splash **07** bestrew, scatter, speckle,
splodge **08** splatter, sprinkle
09 bespatter **10** besprinkle

spawn
03 fry, roe **04** blot, make, redd, seed,
spat, spit, teem **05** brood, cause, culch,

perm **06** create, cultch, lead to bring on, produce **08** engender, enerate **09** offspring, originate bring about, give rise to

pay
fix **04** geld **05** spade, spayd doctor, neuter, spayad **08** castrate sterilize **10** emasculate

peak
homophone indicator
gab, say, yak **04** chat, mang, pipe, lk, tell, word **05** argue, sound, state, tter, voice **06** witter **07** address, atter, declaim, declare, discuss, xpound, express, lecture, mention converse, describe, harangue, atform **09** enunciate, hold forth, ronounce **10** articulate communicate **13** have a word ith

  speak angrily
pelt

  speak for
act for **08** stand for **09** represent speak on behalf of

  speak of
voice **07** discuss, mention, refer to make mention of **15** make reference

  speak out
ope **04** open **06** defend **07** protest, upport **11** say publicly, speak openly

  speak tediously
prose

  speak to
warn **05** scold **06** accost, attest, ounce, carpet, rebuke **07** address, awl out, discuss, lecture, rouse on, tell ff, tick off, upbraid **08** admonish dress down, go crook at, pull apart, eprimand, take apart **10** go to town on bring to book **13** have a word with throw the book at **15** give someone ell

  speak up
defend **07** protest, support **10** talk udly **11** say publicly, speak openly raise your voice, talk more loudly

peaker
mouth **06** orator, talker, woofer tweeter **07** lecturer, top tweet spokesman, subwoofer mouthpiece, prolocutor **11** first erson, spokeswoman spokesperson

pear
ash, gad, gig **04** dart, gade, gaid, ike, pile, reed **05** lance, pilum, spire, tick **06** glaive, gleave, waster assagai, assegai, harpoon, javelin, eister, trident **08** assegaai, gavelock, ancegay **09** boar-spear, demi-lance, sh-spear, handstaff, truncheon burn the water

pearhead
van **04** head, lead **05** front, guide launch, leader **07** pioneer initiate, overseer, vanguard **09** front ine **11** cutting edge, trailblazer leading position

special
◇ *anagram indicator*
01 S **02** sp **05** exact, major **06** choice, select, unique **07** notable, precise, unusual **08** detailed, intimate, peculiar, singular, specific **09** different, dividuous, exclusive, important, memorable, momentous, red-letter **10** individual, noteworthy, particular, remarkable **11** distinctive, exceptional, outstanding, significant **13** distinguished, extraordinary **14** characteristic

specialist
06 brains, expert, master **07** attaché **08** boutique **09** authority **10** consultant **11** connoisseur **12** professional

Specialists include:
03 vet
07 Arabist, biblist, cambist, chemist
08 alienist, apiarist, aquarist, arborist, botanist, canonist
09 archivist, biblicist, biologist, Braillist, campanist, Celticist
10 aerologist, aeronomist, agrologist, agronomist, algebraist, algologist, batologist, biochemist, bryologist
11 carpologist
12 apiculturist, bibliopolist, biophysicist, bioscientist, cerographist, choreologist
13 acupuncturist, agrobiologist, anagrammatist, arachnologist, archaeologist, calligraphist, campanologist, carcinologist, chirographist
14 aerodynamicist, anthropologist, bacteriologist, chalcographist
15 agriculturalist, arboriculturist, biopsychologist, biotechnologist

See also **medical**

speciality
03 bag **04** gift **05** field, forte **06** talent **07** feature **08** strength **09** specialty **11** area of study **12** field of study

specialization
05 focus **12** special study **13** concentration **14** special subject **15** special interest

specialize
05 major, study **06** follow **07** focus on, major in, specify **13** concentrate on, differentiate

specially
◇ *anagram indicator*
07 express **08** uniquely **09** expressly **10** distinctly, explicitly **11** exclusively **12** in particular, particularly, specifically

species
02 sp **03** spp **04** kind, sort, type **05** breed, class, genus, group **07** variety **08** category **10** collection **11** description

specific
03 set **05** exact, fixed **07** express, limited, precise, special, trivial **08** clear-cut, concrete, definite, detailed, explicit **10** determined, particular **11** unambiguous, unequivocal, well-defined

specifically
07 clearly, exactly, plainly **09** expressly, specially **10** definitely, distinctly **11** exclusively **12** in particular, particularly **13** unambiguously

specification
04 item, spec **06** detail, naming **07** listing **09** condition, statement **10** particular **11** delineation, description, designation, instruction, requirement, stipulation **13** qualification

specify
04 cite, list, name **05** limit, state **06** assign, define, detail, set out **07** frutify, itemize, mention **08** describe, indicate, spell out **09** delineate, designate, enumerate, stipulate **10** condescend, specialize **13** particularize **14** condescend upon

specimen
04 copy, sort, swab, type **05** assay, model, piece **06** person, sample **07** example, exhibit, pattern **08** exemplar, instance, paradigm **12** illustration **14** representative

specious
04 fair **05** false, showy **06** untrue **07** pageant, unsound **08** imposing **09** beautiful, casuistic, deceptive, fair-faced, plausible, sophistic **10** fallacious, misleading **11** sophistical

speck
03 bit, dot, fat, jot, pip **04** atom, blot, flaw, iota, mark, mite, mote, peep, spek, spot, whit **05** bacon, fault, fleck, grain, peepe, shred, stain, trace **06** defect, sheave, tittle **07** blemish, floater, spangle, speckle **08** particle

speckled
03 gay **05** mealy **06** dotted, mealie, spotty, ticked **07** brinded, brindle, dappled, flecked, mottled, spotted **08** brindled, freckled, stippled **09** fleckered, sprinkled **11** lentiginous **13** trout-coloured

spectacle
04 shew, show **05** scene, sight **06** marvel, object, parade, wonder **07** display, pageant, picture **09** bullfight, curiosity, pageantry, raree-show **10** exhibition, outspeckle, phenomenon **11** performance **12** extravaganza, son et lumière

spectacles
02 OO **05** specs **06** specks **07** glasses, goggles, lorgnon **08** bifocals, cheaters, gig-lamps, horn-rims **09** barnacles, glass eyes, lorgnette, preserves, trifocals **10** eyeglasses, sunglasses, varifocals **13** granny glasses, pebble-glasses **14** National Health, pinhole glasses

spectacular
04 show 05 grand 06 daring
07 amazing, display, opulent, pageant
08 dazzling, dramatic, glorious,
splendid, striking, stunning
09 colourful, spectacle 10 exhibition,
flamboyant, impressive, remarkable,
staggering 11 astonishing, eye-
catching, magnificent, outstanding,
resplendent, sensational
12 breathtaking, extravaganza,
ostentatious 13 extraordinary

spectacularly
09 amazingly 10 gloriously,
remarkably, strikingly, stunningly
12 impressively, staggeringly
13 astonishingly, magnificently,
outstandingly, sensationally
15 extraordinarily

spectator
06 viewer 07 watcher, witness
08 beholder, looker-on, observer,
onlooker, passer-by 09 bystander,
ringsider 10 eyewitness, groundling,
rubberneck, supervisor, wallflower

spectral
05 eerie, weird 06 spooky 07 ghostly,
phantom, shadowy, uncanny
08 eldritch 09 phantosme, unearthly
11 disembodied, incorporeal
12 supernatural 13 insubstantial

spectre
04 fear 05 bogle, dread, ghost, larva,
shade, spook 06 bodach, Empusa,
menace, shadow, spirit, threat, vision,
wraith 07 phantom 08 phantasm,
presence, revenant, visitant
09 phantosme 10 apparition

spectrum
05 gamme, prism, range 07 rainbow
10 after-image

speculate
04 muse, risk, view 05 guess
06 gamble, hazard, wonder
07 examine, imagine, observe, reflect,
suppose, surmise, venture 08 cogitate,
consider, meditate, theorize
10 conjecture, deliberate
11 contemplate, hypothesize

speculation
04 risk, spec 05 flier, flyer, guess
06 gamble, hazard, theory, vision,
wisdom 07 flutter, surmise, theoric,
venture, viewing 08 gambling,
ideology, observer 09 adventure,
guesswork, theorique 10 conjecture,
hypothesis, theorizing 11 imagination,
supposition 12 deliberation
13 consideration, contemplation, flight
of fancy 14 a shot in the dark

speculative
04 iffy 05 dicey, risky, vague 06 chancy
08 abstract, academic, notional,
unproven 09 hazardous, tentative,
theoretic, uncertain 10 indefinite
11 conjectural, theoretical
12 hypothetical, transcendent
13 suppositional, unpredictable

speculator
04 bear, bull 05 piker 07 gambler,
lookout 08 boursier, watchman
09 pinhooker 10 adventurer, land-
jobber 11 adventuress, speculatist,
speculatrix, stockjobber 12 money-
spinner

speech
◇ *anagram indicator*
◇ *homophone indicator*
03 say 04 rant, talk 05 lingo, spiel,
voice 06 accent, homily, jargon,
korero, parole, patter, rumour, saying,
sermon, tirade, tongue 07 address,
dialect, diction, lecture, mention,
message, oration 08 colloquy, delivery,
dialogue, diatribe, harangue, language,
parlance 09 discourse, elocution,
monologue, philippic, soliloquy,
utterance 11 enunciation
12 articulation, conversation
13 communication, pronunciation

Parts of speech include:
01 a, n, v
02 vb, vi, vt
03 adj, adv, art
04 noun, prep, verb
06 adnoun, adverb, gerund, plural,
   prefix, suffix
07 article, pronoun
08 singular
09 adjective, gerundive
10 common noun, connective,
   copulative, participle, proper noun
11 conjunction, phrasal verb,
   preposition
12 abbreviation, interjection
13 auxiliary verb
14 transitive verb
15 definite article, relative pronoun

● **speech defect**
04 lisp 07 stammer, stutter
10 impediment

speechless
03 mum 04 dumb, mute 06 aghast,
amazed, silent 07 shocked
08 unworded 09 astounded, voiceless
10 dumbstruck, struck dumb, tongue-
tied 11 dumbfounded, obmutescent
12 inarticulate, languageless, lost for
words 13 thunderstruck

speed
01 v 02 AS 03 bat, mph 04 belt, clip,
dash, fare, knot, pace, pelt, race, rate,
rush, tear, zoom 05 haste, hurry,
tempo, whisk 06 career, cruise, gallop,
hasten, hurtle, sprint 07 quicken,
succeed, success 08 alacrity, celerity,
despatch, dispatch, momentum,
rapidity, step on it, velocity 09 bowl
along, quickness, swiftness
10 accelerate, promptness
11 amphetamine 12 acceleration, step
on the gas 14 step on the juice
15 expeditiousness, put your foot
down
● **increase speed**
03 gun 10 accelerate, give the gun
● **speed up**
05 hurry 06 hasten, open up, spur on,

step up 07 advance, forward, further,
promote, quicken 08 expedite, go
faster, step on it 09 stimulate
10 accelerate, facilitate 11 drive faster,
gather speed, pick up speed,
precipitate, put on a spurt 12 gain
momentum, step on the gas 14 step on
the juice 15 put your foot down

speedily
04 fast, post 06 pronto 07 betimes,
hastily, on wings, quickly, rapidly,
swiftly 08 in a hurry, promptly
09 hurriedly, posthaste 11 at the double
12 a mile a minute, lickety-split
13 expeditiously 14 at a rate of knots,
hell for leather 15 like the clappers

speedwell
06 hen-bit 08 bird's-eye, fluellin,
neckweed, veronica 09 brooklime

speedy
03 pdq 04 fast 05 hasty, nippy, quick,
rapid, swift, zappy, zippy 06 nimble,
prompt 07 cursory, express, hurried,
summary 09 immediate, posthaste
11 expeditious, precipitate 15 pretty
damn quick

spell
02 go 03 fit, hex, jag, ren, rin, run
04 bout, mean, mojo, pull, rest, rune,
rung, scan, scat, span, tack, term, time,
turn 05 augur, charm, imply, magic,
patch, shift, skatt, spurt, stint, trick,
weird 06 allure, course, extent, grigri,
herald, lead to, lesson, period, season,
signal, snatch, trance, whammy
07 cantrip, enchant, glamour, innings,
portend, presage, promise, relieve,
session, signify, sorcery, stretch,
suggest 08 amount to, greegree,
grisgris, indicate, interval, splinter,
witchery 09 discourse, influence,
magnetism 10 attraction, open sesame
11 abracadabra, bewitchment,
conjuration, contemplate,
enchantment, fascination, incantation,
paternoster 12 drawing power,
entrancement, supplication
● **cast a spell on**
05 charm 07 attract, bewitch, enchant,
encharm, enthral 09 captivate,
fascinate, mesmerize
● **spell out**
06 detail 07 clarify, explain, specify
09 elucidate, emphasize, make clear,
stipulate

spellbinding
08 gripping, riveting 10 bewitching,
enchanting, entrancing 11 captivating,
enthralling, fascinating, mesmerizing

spellbound
04 rapt 07 charmed, gripped, riveted
09 bewitched, enchanted, entranced
10 captivated, enraptured, enthralled,
fascinated, hypnotized, mesmerized,
transfixed 11 transported

spelling
02 sp 11 orthography

spend
02 do 03 use 04 blow, fill, kill, live,

pass, shed, ware **05** apply, put in, use up, waste **06** devote, employ, expend, finish, invest, lay out, occupy, pay out, take up **07** consume, cough up, exhaust, fork out, fritter, outwear, stump up **08** contrive, disburse, shell out, squander **09** splash out, while away **14** spend like water

spendthrift
06 waster **07** wastrel **08** prodigal, profuser, unthrift, wasteful **10** high-roller, profligate, squanderer **11** extravagant, improvident, scattergood, squandering

spent
04 gone, used **05** all in, weary **06** bushed, done in, effete, fagged, pooped, used up, zonked **07** drained, wearied, whacked, worn out **08** burnt out, consumed, dead beat, dog-tired, expended, finished, jiggered, overworn, tired out, weakened **09** exhausted, fagged out, knackered, pooped out, shattered **11** debilitated, tuckered out

sperm
04 eggs **05** brood, semen, spawn **06** gamete **07** sex cell **08** germ cell **09** offspring **10** spermaceti **11** spermatozoa **12** seminal fluid, spermatozoon

spew
04 barf, emit, gush, puke **05** belch, issue, retch, spurt, vomit **06** sick up **07** bring up, chuck up, chunder, fetch up, spit out, throw up **08** disgorge **11** regurgitate

sphere
03 orb, set **04** area, ball, band, rank **05** class, crowd, field, globe, group, orbit, range, realm, round, scope, world **06** circle, clique, domain, extent, planet **07** compass, globule **08** capacity, function, province, universe **09** territory **10** department, discipline, speciality

spherical
05 round **06** global, rotund **07** globate, globoid, globose **08** globular **09** orbicular **10** ball-shaped **11** globe-shaped

spice
03 pep, zap, zip **04** kick, life, mull, stir, tang, vary, zest **05** gusto, hot up, liven, pep up, rouse, touch **06** buck up, colour, jazz up, perk up, relish, savour, stacte, stir up **07** animate, enliven, liven up **08** brighten, energize, ginger up, piquancy, tincture, vitalize **09** diversify, seasoning **10** excitement, flavouring, invigorate, sweetmeats **11** put life into
See also **herb**

spick and span
04 neat, tidy, trim **05** clean **06** spruce **08** polished, scrubbed, spotless, well-kept **09** shipshape **10** immaculate **11** uncluttered

spicy
03 hot **04** blue, racy, tart **05** adult, juicy, sharp, showy, tangy **06** ribald, risqué **07** peppery, picante, piquant, pointed, pungent, raunchy **08** aromatic, fragrant, improper, indecent, seasoned, unseemly **09** flavoured **10** indecorous, indelicate, scandalous, suggestive **11** flavoursome, near the bone, sensational **12** well-seasoned **14** near the knuckle

spider
07 beastie, spinner

Spiders and arachnids include:

03 red
04 bird, mite, tick, wolf
05 bolas, money, water, zebra
06 diadem, epeira, katipo, mygale, violin
07 araneid, harvest, hunting, jumping, limulus, redback
08 huntsman, scorpion, trapdoor
09 funnel-web, harvester, phalangid, tarantula
10 black widow, cheesemite, harvestman, saltigrade
11 harvest mite, harvest tick
12 book-scorpion, whip scorpion
13 horseshoe crab

spiel
04 line **05** pitch **06** patter, speech **07** oration, recital **11** sales patter

spies *see* spy

spignel
03 meu **09** baldmoney

spike
03 add, ear, gad, nib **04** barb, brod, cloy, drug, lace, nail, spit, tang, tine **05** beard, chape, mix in, point, prick, prong, rowel, spear, spick, spine, spire, stake, stick **06** catkin, impale, reject, skewer, spadix **07** bayonet, pricket **09** dosshouse, frustrate, strobilus **10** filopodium, projection **11** contaminate **13** Anglo-Catholic

spill
03 ren, rin, run, tip **04** drip, fall, flow, kill, leak, pour, shed, slop, well **05** scail, scale, skail, spile, taper, throw, upset, waste **06** escape, oozing, run out, tumble **07** cropper, destroy, fidibus, leakage, leaking, run over, scatter, seepage, seeping, slatter, swatter **08** accident, disgorge, overflow, overturn, spillage, spilling **09** discharge, pipe-light **11** lamplighter, percolation, pipe-lighter **13** candle-lighter
- **spill the beans**
03 rat **04** blab, tell **05** grass, split **06** inform, squeal, tell on **07** tell all **11** blow the gaff **15** give the game away

spin
◊ *anagram indicator*
03 cut, run **04** flap, play, reel, ride, tell, tizz, trip, turn **05** drive, jaunt, panic, spirt, state, swirl, tizzy, twirl, twist, wheel, whirl, whirr **06** circle, dither,

gyrate, hurtle, invent, make up, outing, relate, rotate, swivel **07** draw out, dream up, fluster, go round, journey, narrate, revolve, twizzle **08** gyration, rotation **09** agitation, commotion, fabricate, pirouette, turn about, turn round **10** revolution
- **spin doctor**
03 pro **07** spinner
- **spin out**
06 extend, pad out **07** amplify, prolong **08** lengthen, protract, wiredraw **09** keep going
- **spin round**
04 gyre, purl

spindle
03 pin, rod **04** axis, axle, spit **05** arbor, fusee, fuzee, pivot, staff, verge

spindly
04 long, thin **05** lanky, weedy **06** gangly, skinny **07** spidery **08** fusiform, gangling, skeletal **09** attenuate **10** attenuated **14** spindle-shanked

spine
04 barb, grit, guts **05** chine, pluck, quill, spike, spunk, thorn **06** bottle, dorsum, mettle, needle, rachis, spirit **07** bravery, bristle, courage, prickle, rhachis, spinule **08** backbone, spiculum, strength **09** fortitude, Jew's-stone, ridge bone, vertebrae **10** resolution **12** spinal column **13** determination **15** ichthyodorulite, ichthyodorylite, vertebral column

spine-chilling
05 eerie, scary **06** spooky **10** horrifying, terrifying **11** frightening, hair-raising **13** bloodcurdling

spineless
03 wet **04** soft, weak **05** cissy, milky, timid, wussy **06** feeble, yellow **07** chicken, wimpish **08** boneless, cowardly, muticous, timorous **09** weak-kneed **10** indecisive, irresolute, spiritless, submissive **11** ineffective, lily-livered, vacillating **12** faint-hearted, invertebrate

spin-off
06 effect, result **10** side effect **11** consequence **12** repercussion **13** reverberation

spinster
07 old maid

spiny
05 spiky **06** briery, thorny **07** prickly, spinose, spinous, thistly **08** spicular **09** acanthoid, acanthous, perplexed, spiculate **11** spiniferous, spinigerous, troublesome **12** acanthaceous

spiral
04 coil, dive, go up, gyre, rise, soar, wind **05** climb, helix, screw, spire, twist, whorl **06** circle, coiled, gyrate, plunge, rocket, volute, wreath **07** cochlea, helical, plummet, voluted, whorled, winding, wreathe **08** circular, cochlear, curlicue, dive-bomb,

escalate, gyroidal, increase, nosedive, scrolled, tailspin, twisting, volution **09** cochleate, corkscrew, skyrocket **10** cochleated **11** convolution, drop rapidly, fall rapidly **15** decrease quickly

spire
03 tip, top **04** coil, cone, peak, reed **05** crest, crown, point, shoot, spear, spike, spyre, stalk, tower **06** belfry, broach, flèche, spiral, sprout, summit, turret **07** shoot up, steeple **08** pinnacle

spirit
02 ka **03** air, div, fay, imp, nix, pep, zip **04** atua, brio, deev, deva, fire, gist, grit, guts, jinn, kick, life, mind, mood, nixy, soul, zeal, zest **05** angel, anima, cheer, demon, devil, drift, fairy, fiend, force, genie, ghost, jinni, monad, nixie, pluck, sense, shade, spook, spunk, tenor, verve **06** ardour, bottle, breath, djinni, energy, humour, jinnee, kidnap, make-up, mettle, morale, psyche, shadow, sprite, temper, vigour, wraith **07** bravery, courage, essence, feeling, meaning, mindset, outlook, phantom, pizzazz, purport, quality, sparkle, spectre **08** attitude, backbone, feelings, presence, revenant, tendency, visitant, vivacity **09** animation, breathing, character, élan vital, elemental, encourage, inner self, kidnapper, principle, substance, willpower **10** apparition, atmosphere, complexion, enterprise, enthusiasm, inner being, liveliness, motivation, resolution, vital force **11** disposition, frame of mind, implication, state of mind, temperament **13** dauntlessness, determination **14** characteristic

See also **mythical**

• spirit away
05 carry, seize, steal, whisk **06** abduct, convey, kidnap, remove **07** capture, purloin, snaffle **08** abstract

spirited
04 bold, gamy, racy **05** fiery, gamey, gutty **06** active, ardent, feisty, gallus, lively, plucky, spunky **07** dashing, gallows, valiant, zealous **08** animated, resolute, spanking, stomachy, valorous, vigorous **09** confident, energetic, sparkling, vivacious **10** courageous, determined, mettlesome, passionate, sprightful, stomachful, stomachous **12** high-spirited

spiritless
03 low **04** cold, dead, dowf, dull, poor, tame, weak **05** amort, soggy **06** craven, droopy, jejune, mopish, torpid **07** anaemic, hilding, languid, unmoved **08** dejected, enervate, lifeless, listless **09** apathetic, bloodless, depressed, exanimate, inanimate **10** despondent, dispirited, lacklustre, melancholy, wishy-washy **11** sprightless **12** faint-hearted, muddy-mettled **14** unenthusiastic

spirit-level
04 vial

spirits
04 ginn, jinn, mood **05** djinn, hooch **06** humour, liquor, temper **07** alcohol **08** attitude, emotions, feelings **09** firewater, moonshine **11** strong drink, temperament **12** strong liquor, the hard stuff

Spirits include:

03 gin, kir, rum, rye
04 feni, grog, ouzo, raki, sake
05 fenny, Pimm's®, vodka
06 brandy, cognac, eggnog, geneva, grappa, kirsch, mescal, mezcal, pastis, Pernod®, poteen, Scotch, whisky
07 aquavit, Bacardi®, bitters, bourbon, Campari, dark rum, genever, pink gin, sloe gin, tequila, whiskey
08 Armagnac, Calvados, eau de vie, Hollands, hot toddy, sambucca, schnapps, vermouth, white rum, witblits
09 apple-jack, aqua vitae, framboise, golden rum, mirabelle, slivovitz, spiced rum
10 malt whisky, usquebaugh
11 gold tequila, Hollands gin, peach brandy
12 añejo tequila
13 peach schnapps, silver tequila
15 reposado tequila

See also **cocktail**; **liqueur**

spiritual
04 aery, holy **05** aerie, witty **06** clever, divine, sacred **07** psychic **08** ethereal, heavenly **09** pneumatic, psychical, religious, unfleshly, unworldly **10** devotional, immaterial, intangible **11** incorporeal **12** metaphysical, otherworldly, supernatural, transcendent **14** ecclesiastical

spit
03 dig, gob, yex **04** fuff, hawk, hiss, hook, jack, rasp, slag, spet, yesk **05** drool, eject, issue, spade, spawl, spawn, spume, sword **06** bespit, broach, phlegm, saliva, skewer, slaver, sputum **07** dribble, replica, spittle, sputter **08** broacher, emptysis, spadeful, splutter, turnspit **09** brochette, discharge, smoke-jack **10** rotisserie **11** expectorate **13** expectoration

• spitting image
04 twin **05** clone **06** double, ringer **07** picture, replica **08** dead spit, likeness **09** lookalike **10** dead ringer **13** exact likeness

spite
03 irk, vex **04** evil, gall, hate, hurt **05** annoy, upset, venom, wound **06** grudge, hatred, injure, malice, maugre, offend, put out, rancor, spight, thwart **07** ill-will, maulgre, provoke, rancour **08** irritate **09** animosity, hostility, ill nature, malignity, vengeance **10** bitterness, ill-feeling, resentment **11** malevolence **12** hard feelings, spitefulness **13** maliciousness **14** vindictiveness

• in spite of
03 for **04** with **06** malgré, maugre **07** against, defying, despite, maulgre **08** after all, malgrado **11** in the face of **12** nevertheless, regardless of, undeterred by **13** be that as it may **15** notwithstanding

spiteful
05 catty, cruel, nasty, petty, snide **06** barbed, bitchy, bitter, shrewd, wicked **07** cattish, hostile, vicious, waspish **08** vengeful, venomous, viperish **09** cat-witted, malicious, malignant, rancorous, resentful **10** ill-natured, malevolent, vindictive **11** ill-disposed **12** evil-tempered

spitefully
07 cruelly **08** bitchily, bitterly **10** venomously **11** maliciously, resentfully **12** malevolently, vindictively

spitting image *see* spit

splash
◊ *anagram indicator*
03 jap, lap, wet **04** beat, dash, daub, jaup, plop, show, slop, soss, spat, spot, stir, wade, wash **05** bathe, blash, blaze, break, burst, patch, plash, slosh, slush, smack, spray, stain, surge, swash, touch **06** batter, bedash, blazon, buffet, dabble, effect, flaunt, flouse, floush, impact, jabble, paddle, plunge, shower, sozzle, splish, splosh, spread, squirt, streak, strike, wallow **07** beating, display, exhibit, plaster, scatter, slatter, spatter, splatch, splodge, splotch, splurge, swatter, trumpet **08** splatter, sprinkle, squatter **09** publicity, publicize, sensation **10** excitement, impression **11** ostentation

• splash out
05 spend **07** lash out, splurge **08** invest in **13** be extravagant **14** push the boat out

spleen
03 pip **04** bile, gall, lien, melt, milt **05** anger, miltz, mirth, pique, spite, venom, wrath **06** animus, hatred, malice **07** boredom, caprice, ill-will, impulse, rancour, stomach **08** acrimony **09** animosity, bad temper, hostility, ill-humour, malignity **10** bitterness, melancholy, resentment **11** biliousness, malevolence, peevishness **12** spitefulness **14** vindictiveness

splendid
04 braw, fine, rich **05** bonny, grand, great, jolly, super **06** bonnie, bright, divine, lavish, superb **07** gallant, glowing, opulent, radiant, stately, sublime, supreme **08** dazzling, fabulous, glorious, gorgeous, imposing, lustrous, pontific, renowned, terrific **09** admirable, brilliant, effulgent, excellent, luxurious, refulgent, sumptuous, wonderful **10** celebrated, first-class, glittering, impressive, marvellous, pontifical,

remarkable **11** exceptional, illustrious, magnificent, outstanding, resplendent **13** distinguished

splendidly
07 grandly **08** superbly **09** admirably **10** remarkably **11** brilliantly, wonderfully **12** impressively, marvellously **13** exceptionally, magnificently, outstandingly

splendour
04 glow, pomp, show **05** éclat, gleam, glory, pride **06** dazzle, finery, fulgor, luster, lustre, luxury **07** display, fulgour, majesty, panache **08** ceremony, flourish, grandeur, opulence, radiance, richness **09** solemnity, spectacle **10** brightness, brilliance **12** magnificence, resplendence **13** sumptuousness **15** illustriousness

splenetic
04 acid, sour **05** angry, cross, ratty, testy **06** bitchy, crabby, morose, sullen, touchy **07** bilious, crabbed, fretful, peevish **08** choleric, churlish, petulant, spiteful **09** envenomed, irascible, irritable, irritated, rancorous **10** melancholy **11** atrabilious, bad-tempered

splice
◇ *anagram indicator*
03 tie **04** bind, join, knit, mesh **05** braid, graft, marry, plait, unite **06** fasten **07** connect, entwine **09** interlace **10** intertwine, interweave
• **get spliced**
03 wed **10** get hitched, get married, tie the knot **13** take the plunge **15** plight your troth

splinter
03 bit **04** chip, flaw **05** break, flake, piece, shard, shred, skelf, smash, spale, spall, spalt, speel, spelk, spell, split **06** cleave, paring, shiver, sliver, splint **07** crumble, flinder, shatter, shaving, spicula, spicule **08** flinders, fracture, fragment **11** smithereens **12** disintegrate **15** break into pieces

split
◇ *insertion indicator*
03 cut, gap, rat, rip **04** chop, dual, open, part, rend, rent, rift, rive, shop, slit, tear **05** allot, break, burst, cleft, crack, grass, halve, leave, peach, sever, shake, share, slash, spall, spalt, wreck **06** betray, bisect, breach, broken, cleave, cloven, divide, rumble, schism, shiver, sliver, spring, sprung, squeal, stitch, tell on **07** break up, break-up, carve up, cracked, crevice, disband, discord, disrupt, divided, divorce, divulge, dole out, fissure, hand out, rupture, spalted, stool on, twofold **08** allocate, bisected, cleavage, crevasse, disunion, disunite, division, inform on, ruptured, separate, set apart, share-out, splinter **09** apportion, fractured, parcel out, partition **10** alienation, difference, dissension, distribute, divergence,

separation **11** incriminate, part company **12** estrangement **14** dissociate from **15** become alienated, become estranged
• **split up**
04 part **06** divide **07** break up, disband, divorce **08** separate **11** get divorced, part company

split-up
07 break-up, divorce, parting **10** alienation, separation **12** estrangement

spoil
◇ *anagram indicator*
03 end, gum, mar, mux, pie, ret, rot **04** baby, cook, foul, game, harm, hurt, kill, rait, rate, ruin, sour, turn **05** bitch, blunk, bodge, booty, botch, bribe, decay, go bad, go off, gum up, louse, queer, strip, taint, upset, wreck, wrong **06** boodle, coddle, cosset, curdle, damage, deface, deform, foul up, go sour, impair, injure, mangle, mess up, murder, pamper, poison, prizes, quarry, wash up **07** bauchle, bitch up, blemish, butcher, corrupt, deprive, despoil, destroy, distort, indulge, louse up, pillage, plunder, pollute, screw up, tarnish, viciate, vitiate **08** distaste, go rotten, mutilate **09** decompose, disfigure, spoon-feed, vulgarize **10** impairment, obliterate, spoliation **11** contaminate, deteriorate, mollycoddle, overindulge, prejudice **12** acquisitions, become rotten, put a damper on **15** cast a shadow over, pour cold water on
• **spoil for**
07 long for **08** be keen on, yearn for **10** be eager for, be intent on

spoils
04 gain, haul, loot, swag **05** booty, bribe **06** boodle, damage, prizes, profit, trophy **07** benefit, pillage, plunder, spulzie, the game **08** pickings, winnings **10** impairment, spoliation **11** spolia opima **12** acquisitions, despoliation

spoilsport
04 nark **06** damper, misery, wowser **07** killjoy, meddler **08** buzzkill **10** wet blanket **11** party-pooper **14** dog in the manger

spoke
04 rung **06** radius

spoken
◇ *homophone indicator*
03 sed **04** oral, said, told **06** stated, verbal, voiced **07** uttered **08** declared, phonetic, viva voce **09** expressed, unwritten

spokesman, spokeswoman
05 agent, mouth, voice **06** broker, orator **07** foreman **08** delegate, mediator **09** forewoman, go-between **10** arbitrator, foreperson, mouthpiece, negotiator, prolocutor **12** intermediary, propagandist, spokesperson **14** representative

sponge
03 beg, bum, mop **04** mump, swab, wash, wipe **05** cadge, clean, mooch, mouch, shool, shule **06** bludge, borrow, loofah, shoole, spunge, sucker **07** monaxon, zimocca **08** bedeguar, drunkard, freeload, hanger-on, parasite, quandang, quandong, quantong, scrounge, victoria **09** glass-rope, hyalonema, sea orange **13** mermaid's glove, sulphur sponge
See also **drunkard**
• **sponge cake**
06 coburg, trifle **09** lamington, madeleine, Swiss roll **11** lady's finger **12** lady's fingers **14** charlotte russe
• **sponge spicule**
06 hexact, sclere, tylote **07** monaxon, pentact, rhabdus, tetract, triaxon **08** polyaxon, tetraxon, triaxial **09** polyaxial, spiraster

sponger
03 bum **06** beggar, bummer, cadger **07** bludger, moocher **08** borrower, hanger-on, parasite, scambler **09** scrounger **10** freeloader, smell-feast

spongy
◇ *anagram indicator*
04 fozy, soft **05** light **06** poachy, porous **07** drunken, elastic, fungous, springy, squashy **08** cushiony, yielding **09** absorbent, cushioned, resilient **10** absorptive, cancellate, cancellous **11** cancelled

sponsor
04 back, fund **05** angel, vouch **06** backer, friend, gossip, patron, surety **07** finance, promise, promote, support **08** bankroll, promoter, stand for **09** godfather, godmother, guarantee, guarantor, patronize, subsidize, supporter, susceptor **10** subsidizer, undertaker, underwrite **11** be a patron of, underwriter

sponsorship
03 aid **05** funds, grant **07** backing, finance, subsidy, support **09** patronage, promotion **10** assistance **11** endorsement **12** financial aid

spontaneity
07 impulse **08** instinct **11** naturalness **13** improvisation **15** extemporization, instinctiveness

spontaneous
04 free **06** reflex **07** natural, willing **08** free-will, knee-jerk, unbidden, unforced, untaught **09** automatic, autonomic, extempore, impromptu, impulsive, unplanned, unstudied, voluntary **10** ultroneous, unprompted **11** instinctive, uncompelled, unrehearsed **12** unhesitating **14** unpremeditated **15** spur of the moment

spontaneously
05 ad-lib **06** freely **09** extempore, impromptu, on impulse, unplanned, willingly **10** off the cuff, unprompted

11 impulsively, voluntarily
13 instinctively **15** of your own accord

spoof
03 con **04** fake, game, hoax, joke
05 bluff, prank, trick **06** parody, satire,
send-up **07** lampoon, leg-pull,
mockery, take-off **08** travesty
09 burlesque, deception **10** caricature

spooky
05 eerie, scary, weird **06** creepy
07 ghostly, macabre, uncanny
08 chilling **09** unearthly **10** mysterious
11 frightening, hair-raising
12 supernatural **13** spine-chilling

spool
04 pirn, reel **06** bobbin **07** trundle

spoon
05 court, labis, ladle, scoop **07** spatula
08 cochlear **09** cochleare, courtship,
simpleton

spoon-feed
04 baby **05** spoil **06** cosset, pamper
07 indulge **10** featherbed
11 mollycoddle, overindulge

sporadic
06 random, uneven **07** erratic
08 episodic, isolated **09** irregular,
scattered, spasmodic **10** episodical,
infrequent, occasional **12** intermittent

sporadically
08 off and on, on and off **10** now and
then **11** now and again **12** occasionally,
periodically **13** spasmodically
14 intermittently

sport
◇ *anagram indicator*
03 fun, gig **04** game, jest, joke, laik,
lake, play, wear **05** amuse, mirth, wager
06 banter, frolic, humour, joking, trifle
07 display, exhibit, jesting, kidding,
mockery, pastime, show off, teasing
08 activity, exercise, pleasure, ridicule,
sneering, squander **09** amusement,
dalliance, diversion, plaything
10 recreation **13** entertainment

See also **athletics; American football;
Australian football; baseball; boxing;
competition; cricket; football; golf;
gymnastics; ice hockey; race; rugby;
stadium; tennis**

Sports include:

04 golf, judo, polo, pool
05 bowls, darts, fives, rugby
06 boules, boxing, discus, diving,
futsal, hockey, karate, kung fu,
luging, Nascar®, pelota, quoits,
rowing, shinty, skiing, slalom,
soccer, squash, tennis
07 angling, aquafit, archery, camogie,
cricket, croquet, curling, fencing,
fishing, gliding, hunting, hurling,
jogging, jujitsu, keep-fit, netball,
putting, running, sailing, shot put,
snooker, surfing, walking
08 aerobics, baseball, biathlon,
canoeing, climbing, football,
handball, high-jump, hurdling,
lacrosse, long-jump, pétanque,

ping-pong, rounders, shooting,
swimming, trotting, yachting
09 athletics, badminton, billiards,
bobsleigh, decathlon, go-karting,
ice-hockey, pole vault, pot-holing,
sky-diving, tae kwon do, triathlon,
water polo, wrestling
10 basketball, drag-racing,
gymnastics, ice-skating,
pentathlon, real tennis, skin-diving,
triple-jump, volleyball
11 cycle racing, horse-racing, motor
racing, show-jumping, table-
tennis, tobogganing, water-skiing,
windsurfing
12 aqua aerobics, cross-country,
orienteering, pitch and putt, rock-
climbing, snowboarding, speed
skating, trampolining
13 bungee jumping, coarse fishing,
roller-skating, tenpin bowling,
weightlifting
14 downhill skiing, Gaelic football,
mountaineering, speedway racing,
stock-car racing
15 greyhound-racing

Sports equipment includes:

03 bow, cue, fly, jig, mat, net, oar, ski,
tee
04 bail, bait, beam, bolt, bowl, épée,
foil, gaff, hook, jack, lure, mask,
mitt, nets, pins, puck, rack, reel,
rest, rope, shot, wood
05 arrow, boule, brush, caman, chalk,
float, rings, sabre, stump, table,
trace
06 bridge, discus, fly rod, hammer,
hurley, priest, spider, wicket
07 cue ball, fly reel, javelin, keep-net,
netball, snorkel
08 aqualung, baseball, crossbow,
football, gang-hook, golfball, golf
club, ice-skate, punch-bag, ski
stick, toboggan, water-ski
09 disgorger, face-guard, gum shield,
punch-ball, rugby ball, sailboard,
snow board, surfboard
10 basketball, cricket bat, fishing-rod,
hockey ball, roller boot,
skateboard, speed skate, tennis ball,
trampoline, volleyball
11 balance beam, baseball bat,
bowling ball, boxing glove, cricket
ball, fishing-line, hockey skate,
hockey stick, in-line skate,
paternoster, pommel horse, racket
press, rollerblade, roller-skate,
shuttlecock, snooker ball, spinning
rod, springboard
12 billiard ball, curling stone, golfing
glove, isometric bar, parallel-bars,
tennis racket
13 catcher's glove, horizontal bar,
vaulting horse
14 ice-hockey stick
15 badminton racket

Sports positions include:

04 lock, slip, wing
05 cover, gully, mid-on, point, rover
06 batter, centre, goalie, hooker, libero,

long on, mid-off, setter, winger
07 batsman, catcher, fine leg, flanker,
fly-half, fly slip, forward, leg slip,
long leg, long off, number 8, pitcher
ruckman, sweeper, torpedo
08 attacker, backstop, defender,
fullback, halfback, left back, left
wing, long stop, short leg, split end,
third man, tight end, wing back
09 deep cover, deep point, first base,
first slip, left field, left guard, leg
gulley, mid-wicket, right back, right
wing, ruck rover, scrum-half, short
stop, square leg, third base, third
slip
10 back pocket, cover point,
defenceman, extra cover, goal
attack, goalkeeper, goaltender,
inside left, left tackle, midfielder,
point guard, right field, right guard,
second base, second slip, silly mid-
on, silly point, wing attack
11 centre field, deep fine leg, full-
forward, goal defence, goal shooter,
inside right, left forward, prop
forward, quarterback, right tackle,
silly mid-off, wing defence
12 left half-back, power forward, right
forward, short fine leg, small
forward, stand-off half,
wicketkeeper
13 backward point, centre-forward,
deep mid-wicket, deep square leg,
forward pocket, half-back flank,
loosehead prop, right half-back,
shooting guard, tighthead prop
14 centre half-back, deep extra cover,
left corner-back, short mid-wicket
15 left half-forward, right corner-back,
short extra cover

sporting
◇ *anagram indicator*
04 fair, just **06** decent, modest
08 ladylike **10** honourable, reasonable
11 considerate, gentlemanly,
respectable **13** sportsmanlike

sportive
03 gay **05** ludic, merry **06** frisky, jaunty,
lively, wanton **07** amorous, coltish,
playful, toysome **08** gamesome,
prankish, skittish **09** kittenish,
ludicrous, sprightly, vivacious
10 frolicsome, rollicking

sportsperson
04 blue, jock

Sportspeople include:

04 Bird (Larry), **Dean** (Christopher),
Khan (Jahangir), **Lowe** (John), **Nudd**
(Bob), **Witt** (Katerina)
05 Curry (John), **Davis** (Fred), **Davis**
(Joe), **Davis** (Steve), **Ender**
(Kornelia), **Kelly** (Sean), **O'Neal**
(Shaquille), **Spitz** (Mark), **White**
(Jimmy)
06 Briggs (Karen), **Bryant** (David),
Davies (Sharron), **Fraser** (Dawn),
Hendry (Stephen), **Jordan** (Michael),
LeMond (Greg), **Malone** (Karl),
Merckx (Eddy), **Pulman** (John),
Wilkie (David), **Wilson** (Jocky)

07 Allcock (Tony), Bristow (Eric), Cousins (Robin), Gretzky (Wayne), Harding (Tonya), Higgins (Alex 'Hurricane'), Hinault (Bernard), Johnson (Earvin 'Magic'), O'Reilly (Wilfred), Reardon (Ray), Rodnina (Irina),Torvill (Jayne), Zaitsev (Aleksandr)
08 Boardman (Chris), Indurain (Miguel), Kerrigan (Nancy), Redgrave (Sir Steve),Williams (Rex)
09 Cipollini (Mario), Hazelwood (Mike)
10 Barrington (Jonah)
11 Abdul-Jabbar (Kareem), Chamberlain (Wilt 'the Stilt'), Weissmuller (Johnny)

See also **athlete; Australian football; baseball; boxer; chess; cricket; footballer; golfer; gymnastics; horseman, horsewoman; motor; mountaineering; rugby; skier; tennis**

sporty
03 fit **04** loud **05** natty, showy
06 casual, flashy, jaunty, lively, snazzy, trendy **07** outdoor, stylish **08** athletic, informal **09** energetic

spot
03 bit, dot, eye, fix, jam, pin, pip, see, zit **04** area, bite, blob, blot, blur, boil, daub, drop, espy, flaw, fret, give, hole, lend, mail, mark, meal, mess, moil, mold, mole, peep, plot, pock, show, site, slot, smut, soil, some, sore, time, turn **05** cloud, fleck, freak, hilum, naeve, nerve, nevus, niche, patch, peepe, place, plook, plouk, point, pupil, scene, speck, stain, sully, swale, taint **06** blotch, descry, detect, garden, little, locale, locate, macula, morsel, naevus, notice, papula, papule, pickle, pimple, plight, recess, scrape, smudge, splash, stigma **07** airtime, blemish, discern, flecker, freckle, lentigo, make out, observe, ocellus, opening, pick out, pustule, setting, spangle, speckle, splodge, splotch, tarnish, trouble **08** fenestra, identify, locality, location, maculate, position, quandary **09** birthmark, blackhead, freckling, programme, recognize, reprehend, situation **10** cicatricle, death-token, difficulty, maculation **11** cicatricula, performance, predicament, small amount **12** catch sight of, cicatrichule **13** discoloration
• **on the spot**
02 in **04** down, next **05** alert **06** at once, pronto **07** quickly **08** directly, in a jiffy, promptly, right now, speedily, sur place **09** forthwith, instantly, like a shot, right away **10** this minute **11** immediately, this instant **12** straight away, there and then, without delay **13** straightforth, with a siserary **14** unhesitatingly, without more ado **15** before you know it, instantaneously, without question
• **spot-on**
04 true **05** close, exact, right **06** bang

on, dead-on, strict **07** correct, factual, precise **08** accurate, definite, detailed, explicit, flawless, specific, unerring **09** excellent, faultless, on the nail **10** on the money **11** on the button

spotless
04 pure **05** clean, white **06** chaste, virgin **07** shining **08** gleaming, innocent, unmarked, virginal **09** blameless, faultless, snow-white, unstained, unsullied, untainted, untouched **10** immaculate **11** unblemished **12** spick and span **14** irreproachable

spotlight
04 baby, fame, spot **05** brute **06** stress **07** feature, focus on, point up **08** emphasis, interest **09** attention, emphasize, highlight, limelight, notoriety, public eye, underline **10** accentuate, foreground, illuminate **15** draw attention to, public attention, throw into relief

spotted
03 gay **04** pied **06** dotted, macled, parded, spotty **07** brindle, dappled, flecked, guttate, macular, mottled, piebald **08** brindled, guttated, maculose, polka-dot, speckled

spotty
04 pied, poxy **05** acned, bitty **06** dotted, measly, patchy, pimply, uneven **07** blotchy, dappled, erratic, flecked, mottled, piebald, pimpled, spotted, varying **08** speckled **12** inconsistent

spouse
04 feer, fere, mate, wife **05** feare, fiere, hubby **06** missus, pheere **07** consort, husband, partner **09** companion, other half **10** better half

spout
03 jet **04** blow, emit, flow, go on, gush, pawn, pour, rant, rose, spew **05** chute, erupt, mouth, orate, shoot, spiel, spray, spurt, surge **06** geyser, nozzle, outlet, squirt, stream, stroup, waffle, witter **07** bespout, declaim **08** disgorge, fountain, gargoyle, pawnshop, rabbit on, spout off, witter on **09** discharge, expatiate, hold forth, sermonize **10** spout forth, waterspout **11** pontificate

sprain
03 hip **04** pull, rick, turn **05** crick, stave, twist, wrest, wrick **06** injure, wrench **09** dislocate **12** shoulder slip

sprat
04 brit, Jack **06** garvie **07** garvock **08** brisling

sprawl
04 flop, loll **05** slump, trail **06** lounge, ramble, repose, slouch, spread **07** recline, scamble, stretch **08** sprangle, straggle

spray
◇ *anagram indicator*
03 jet, wet **04** Alar®, foam, gush,

Mace®, mist, posy, scud, twig **05** froth, shoot, spout, sprig, spume, swish **06** branch, drench, mister, shower, spritz, squirt, wreath **07** aerosol, bouquet, corsage, diffuse, drizzle, garland, nosegay, scatter, spatter, sprayer **08** aigrette, atomizer, disperse, moisture, mothball, nebulize, spray gun, sprinkle, vaporize **09** aspersion, nebulizer, spindrift, sprinkler, squirt gun, vaporizer **10** golden rose, propellant, spoondrift, waterspout **11** disseminate **13** water-sprinkle

spread
◇ *anagram indicator*
03 air, lay, ren, rin, run, set, sow, ted **04** coat, grow, laid, open, span, teer, walk **05** apply, cover, feast, flare, layer, order, party, put on, ranch, reach, scale, smear, spray, strew, sweep, swell, treat, widen **06** dilate, dinner, effuse, expand, extend, extent, fan out, lay out, mantle, repast, slairg, smooth, sprawl, unfold, unfurl, unroll **07** advance, arrange, banquet, blow-out, broaden, compass, develop, diffuse, enlarge, expanse, go round, open out, overlay, publish, radiate, scatter, stretch **08** disperse, escalate, extended, get round, increase, mushroom, swelling, transmit **09** advertise, broadcast, circulate, diffusion, displayed, expansion, large meal, make known, percolate, propagate, publicize, spill over **10** dispersion, distribute, escalation, gain ground, grow bigger, make public, promulgate **11** communicate, development, dinner party, disseminate, mushrooming, proliferate, propagation **12** become bigger, broadcasting, distribution, transmission **13** communication, dissemination, proliferation

Spreads include:
03 jam
04 marg, oleo, pâté
05 honey, marge
06 butter
07 Marmite®, Nutella®
08 dripping, Vegemite®
09 butterine, lemon curd, margarine, marmalade
11 lemon cheese
12 peanut butter
13 oleomargarine

spree
03 bat, bum, jag **04** bout, bust, orgy, tear **05** binge, blind, fling, revel, skite, skyte **06** bender, junket, randan, razzle, splore **07** blinder, carouse, debauch, splurge **08** jamboree **12** razzle-dazzle

sprig
04 brad, stem, twig **05** bough, scion, shoot, spray **06** branch

sprightly
04 airy, spry **05** agile, brisk, perky **06** active, blithe, gallus, hearty, jaunty, lively, nimble, sprack **07** gallows, ghostly, playful **08** animated, cheerful,

spirited **09** energetic, mercurial, vivacious **10** frolicsome, spirituous **12** light-hearted

spring
◇ *anagram indicator*
03 eye, gin, hop, lep, spa **04** bend, bolt, come, dawn, give, grow, hair, jump, leap, Lent, open, rise, root, skip, stem, stot, voar, ware, warp, well **05** arise, basis, bound, burst, cause, copse, crack, dance, issue, prime, shoot, spang, split, start, vault, youth **06** appear, bounce, derive, emerge, energy, geyser, origin, pounce, recoil, salina, source, spirit, sprout, strain **07** descend, develop, emanate, explode, proceed, rebound **08** balneary, brine-pan, brine-pit, buoyancy, wellhead **09** animation, beginning, briskness, originate **10** bounciness, elasticity, liveliness, resilience, wellspring **11** black smoker, flexibility, springiness, undergrowth **12** cheerfulness, fountainhead **14** reveal suddenly
• **spring up**
04 grow, rise **05** start **06** upblow **07** develop, shoot up **08** fountain, mushroom, sprout up **11** proliferate **13** come into being **14** appear suddenly

springtime *see* spring

springy
05 crisp, lofty **06** bouncy, spongy **07** buoyant, elastic, rubbery, squidgy, tensile **08** flexible, stretchy, tensible **09** resilient

sprinkle
◇ *anagram indicator*
03 dot, set **04** drop, dust, salt, sand, seed, sift **05** flake, flour, spang, spray, strew, sugar **06** dredge, pepper, pounce, powder, shower, sparge, splash **07** asperge, sawdust, scatter, spairge, spatter, trickle **08** beflower, disponge, dispunge, lavender, strinkle **09** bespatter, diversify **10** scowdering **11** aspersorium, scouthering

sprinkling
03 few **04** dash **05** touch, trace **07** baptism, dusting, handful, scatter, sifting, trickle **08** sprinkle **09** admixture, aspersion **10** scattering, smattering

sprint
03 fly, run, zip **04** belt, dart, dash, race, tear **05** scoot, shoot **06** career, scurry

sprite
03 elf, imp, pug **04** bogy, puck **05** bogle, dryad, fairy, gnome, kelpy, naiad, nymph, pixie, pouke, sylph **06** goblin, kelpie, spirit **07** apsaras, brownie, spright **10** apparition, leprechaun **11** water spirit

sprout
03 bud **04** chit, germ, grow **05** scion, shoot, spire, spirt **06** come up, spring **07** develop, tendron **08** put forth, spring up **09** germinate, pullulate, turnip top **10** descendant

spruce
04 chic, cool, neat, smug, trim **05** brisk, natty, nifty, Picea, sleek, smart, smirk, spiff, Tsuga **06** dapper, snazzy, spiffy, sprush **07** band-box, elegant, finical, hemlock, smarten **11** well-dressed, well-groomed **13** well-turned-out
• **spruce up**
04 tidy **05** groom, preen, primp **06** neaten, tart up, tidy up **08** titivate **09** smarten up

spry
05 agile, alert, brisk, nippy, peppy, quick, ready **06** active, nimble, supple **09** energetic, sprightly

spud *see* potato

spume
04 fizz, foam, head, scum, spit, suds **05** froth, yeast **06** lather **07** bubbles **13** effervescence

spunk
04 grit, guts **05** heart, match, nerve, pluck, spark **06** bottle, fire up, mettle, spirit, tinder **07** courage **08** backbone, chutzpah, gameness **09** touchwood, toughness **10** resolution

spur
04 goad, heel, limb, poke, prod, stud, urge **05** drive, ergot, impel, prick, prong, rowel, spica, spike, strut **06** branch, calcar, fillip, hasten, incite, induce, motive, offset, prompt, propel, Rippon, siding, spurne **07** impetus **08** motivate, stimulus **09** encourage, incentive, star wheel, stimulant, stimulate **10** incitement, inducement, motivation, projection, protrusion **12** embranchment, protuberance **13** encouragement
• **on the spur of the moment**
08 suddenly **09** extempore, impromptu, on impulse, on the spot **10** upon the gad **11** impetuously, impulsively **12** unexpectedly **13** spontaneously, thoughtlessly **15** without planning

spurious
◇ *anagram indicator*
03 bad, dog **04** fake, mock, sham **05** bogus, cronk, false **06** forged, phoney, pseudo **07** bastard, feigned **08** pseudish **09** contrived, deceitful, imitation, pretended, simulated, trumped-up **10** adulterate, adulterine, apocryphal, artificial, fraudulent **11** counterfeit, make-believe **12** illegitimate **14** supposititious

spurn
04 kick, snub, trip **05** scorn, tread **06** ignore, rebuff, reject, slight **07** condemn, despise, disdain, repulse, say no to **08** turn away, turn down **09** disregard, repudiate **10** look down on **12** cold-shoulder

spurt
03 fit, jet **04** boak, bock, boke, gush, kick, pour, pump, rush, spin, well **05** burst, erupt, issue, shoot, spate,

spray, start, surge **06** access, skoosh, squirt, stream **07** welling **08** eruption, increase **10** outpouring

spy
03 eye, see **04** espy, look, mole, nark, spie, spot, tout, wait **05** agent, plant, scout, spial, spook, spyal **06** beagle, descry, notice, setter, shadow, survey **07** discern, glimpse, make out, observe, sleeper, snooper **08** discover, emissary, mouchard **10** enemy agent **11** double agent, secret agent, under-espial **12** catch sight of, foreign agent **13** intelligencer **14** fifth columnist **15** undercover agent

Spies include:
03 Pym (Magnus)
04 Bond (James), Hale (Nathan), Hiss (Alger)
05 André (John), Blake (George), Blunt (Anthony Frederick), Fuchs (Klaus Emil Julius), Karla, Szabo (Violette), Wynne (Greville)
06 Howell (James), Philby (Kim), Smiley (George), Tubman (Harriet), Vidocq (Eugène François), Werner (Ruth)
07 Burgess (Guy Francis de Moncy), Maclean (Donald)
08 Lonsdale (Gordon Arnold), Mata Hari
09 Carstares (William), Rosenberg (Ethel), Rosenberg (Julius)
10 Cairncross (John)

• **spies**
02 MI **03** CIA, KGB, MI5, MI6 **05** Stasi **06** Mossad
• **spy on**
04 tout **05** watch **07** observe **10** keep tabs on **11** keep an eye on **14** observe closely

spymaster
01 M

squabble
03 row **04** spat, tiff, tift **05** argue, brawl, clash, fight, scrap, set to, set-to **06** barney, bicker **07** dispute, quarrel, rhubarb, wrangle **08** argument **09** have words **12** disagreement

squad
03 set **04** band, crew, gang, team, unit **05** force, group, troop **06** outfit **07** brigade, company, platoon

squadron
03 red, RYS, sqn **04** blue **10** escadrille

squalid
03 low **04** foul, mean, vile **05** dingy, dirty, grimy, mucky, nasty, ribby, seedy **06** filthy, grotty, grubby, sleazy, slummy, sordid, untidy **07** obscene, run-down, unclean, unkempt **08** improper, shameful, slovenly, wretched **09** neglected, offensive, repulsive **10** broken-down, Dickensian, disgusting, ramshackle, uncared-for, unpleasant **11** dilapidated, disgraceful

squall
03 cry **04** blow, drow, gale, gust, howl,

squally

moan, wail, wind, yell, yowl **05** groan, storm **06** flurry **07** sumatra, tempest **08** williwaw **09** hurricane, windstorm

squally
04 wild **05** blowy, gusty, rough, windy **06** stormy **07** gustful **08** blustery **09** turbulent **10** blustering **11** tempestuous

squalor
04 dirt, slum **05** decay, filth, grime **07** neglect, skid row **08** dung-heap, dung-hill, foulness, meanness, skid road **09** dinginess, dirtiness, griminess, muckiness **10** filthiness, grubbiness, sleaziness **11** squalidness, uncleanness **12** wretchedness

squander
04 blow, blue, lash, muck, roam **05** spend, sport, waste **06** bezzle, expend, gamble, lavish, misuse, mucker, plunge, wander **07** consume, fritter, scamble, scatter, slather, splurge **08** disperse, fool away, misspend, straggle **09** dissipate, sport away, throw away **10** muddle away **11** fritter away, splash out on

square
01 S,T **02** sq **03** fit, pay **04** even, fair, full, just, quad, rule, suit, true **05** adapt, agree, align, bribe, canon, exact, fogey, level, match, order, plaza, scarf, solid, tally **06** accord, adjust, dinkum, equity, evenly, fairly, honest, settle, tailor **07** balance, conform, diehard, ethical, fitting, genuine, honesty, quarrel, resolve, solidly, swagger, upright **08** complete, directly, fairness, honestly, old fogey, put right, regulate, set right, settle up, standard, straight, suitable, thick-set **09** conformer, criterion, equitable, harmonize, headscarf, make equal, reconcile **10** above-board, conformist, correspond, dissension, fuddy-duddy, honourable, on the level, quadrangle, satisfying, straighten, town square **11** marketplace, rectangular, right-angled, strait-laced, unequivocal **12** buttoned-down, conservative, market square, old-fashioned **13** perpendicular, quadrilateral, stick-in-the-mud **14** traditionalist **15** be congruous with, conventionalist

Squares include:

03 Red
05 Times
06 Sloane
07 Central, Madison, People's
08 Berkeley, Victoria
09 Leicester, Tiananmen, Trafalgar
10 Bloomsbury, Washington
12 Covent Garden

squarely
04 bang, dead, just **05** plumb, right, smack **07** exactly **08** directly, straight **09** precisely **12** unswervingly

squash
03 jam **04** mash, pack, pulp, snub **05** crowd, crush, grind, pound, press, quash, quell, smash, stamp **07** distort, flatten, put down, silence, squeeze, squelch, squidge, trample **08** compress, macerate, suppress **09** dilutable, humiliate, pulverize, squeezing **10** annihilate

squashy
04 soft **05** mushy, pappy, pulpy **06** spongy **07** sopping, springy, squidgy, squishy **08** squelchy, yielding **10** squelching

squat
03 sit **04** bend, ruck **05** croup, dumpy, fubby, fubsy, hunch, kneel, podgy, pudgy, short, stoop **06** chunky, crouch, croupe, hunker, pyknic, stocky, stubby **07** squabby **08** thickset **09** crouching **10** hunker down **12** absquatulate, Humpty-dumpty

squawk
03 cry, nag **04** beef, carp, crow, fuss, hoot, moan, yelp **05** bitch, bleat, croak, gripe, groan, growl, grump, whine **06** cackle, grouch, grouse, object, scream, shriek, squeal, whinge **07** carry on, grumble, protest, scrauch, scraugh, screech **08** complain **09** bellyache, criticize, find fault **11** kick up a fuss, raise a stink **15** have a bone to pick

squeak
03 eek **04** peep, pipe **05** cheep, chirk, creak, whine **06** inform, squeal **07** confess

squeal
03 cry, rat, wee **04** howl, shop, sing, tell, wail, yell, yelp **05** grass, shout, sneak, split, stool **06** betray, inform, scream, shriek, snitch, squawk **07** screech, sell out **08** complain **09** tell tales

squeamish
03 coy **04** sick **06** queasy, queazy **07** finicky, mawkish, missish, prudish **08** delicate, nauseous **09** nauseated **10** fastidious, particular, scrupulous **11** punctilious, strait-laced **12** mealy mouthed

squeeze
◇ *containment indicator*
03 hug, jam, nip, ram **04** cram, grip, hold, mash, milk, pack, pulp, push, shoe, suck **05** bleed, chirt, clasp, crowd, crush, force, grasp, gripe, juice, pinch, press, shove, stuff, sweat, twist, wedge, wrest, wring **06** clutch, cuddle, enfold, extort, fleece, jostle, lean on, mangle, scruze, squash, strain, thrust **07** embrace, extract, rubbing, scrooge, scrouge, squidge, thrutch, tighten **08** compress, pressure, sandwich, scrowdge, shoehorn, wring out **09** boyfriend, hold tight **10** congestion, girlfriend, pressurize **14** put the screws on

squid
01 L **04** quid **05** pound **06** loligo, nicker **07** ink-fish, smacker **08** calamari, calamary **10** sleeve fish

squiffy
◇ *anagram indicator*
05 happy, merry, tight, tipsy **06** blotto, tiddly **07** drunken, pickled, sozzled, tiddley **09** crapulent, plastered **10** inebriated **11** intoxicated

squint
03 aim **04** awry, cast, gaze, glee, gley, hint, peep, peer, pink, scan **05** askew, blink, twire **06** aslant, glance, gledge, gleyed, skelly, squiny **07** crooked, glimpse, oblique, skellie, squinny **08** cockeyed, cross-eye, indirect, strabism, tendency, walleyed **09** obliquely, off-centre, skew-whiff **10** hagioscope, side-glance, strabismic, strabismus **11** look askance **12** sideways look

squire
04 rule **05** canon **06** attend, donzel, escort, Junker, squier **08** scutiger, squarson **12** armour-bearer

squirm
◇ *anagram indicator*
04 move, worm **05** shift, twist **06** fidget, wiggle, writhe **07** agonize, wriggle **08** flounder, squiggle

squirrel
03 bun **04** skug, vair **05** hoard **06** gopher, suslik, taguan **07** meercat, meerkat **08** chipmuck, chipmunk **09** chickaree **10** prairie dog **11** flickertail, spermophile
• **squirrel away**
04 hide, save **05** hoard, lay in, lay up, put by, store **06** save up **07** conceal, put away, stock up **08** salt away, set aside **09** stash away, stockpile
• **squirrel's nest**
04 cage, dray, drey

squirt
03 jet **04** emit, gush, pour, spew, well **05** chirt, eject, expel, issue, scoot, shoot, spirt, spout, spray, spurt, surge **06** scoosh, skoosh, stream **07** spew out **09** discharge, ejaculate
• **sea squirt**
08 ascidian, cunjevoi

Sri Lanka
02 CL **03** LKA

stab
02 go **03** cut, jab, try **04** ache, bash, dirk, fork, gash, gore, kris, pain, pang, pink, push, shot **05** crack, essay, knife, prick, prong, slash, spasm, spear, stick, throb, whirl, wound **06** injure, injury, pierce, skewer, thrust, twinge **07** attempt, bayonet, poniard, venture **08** incision, puncture, stiletto, transfix **09** endeavour
• **stab in the back**
06 betray **07** deceive, let down, sell out, slander **08** inform on **11** double-cross

stabbing
05 acute, sharp **07** knifing, painful **08** piercing, shooting, stinging **09** throbbing

stability

06 fixity, fixure **07** balance
08 firmness, solidity **09** constancy,
soundness **10** durability, regularity,
secureness, steadiness, sturdiness,
uniformity **11** reliability
15 unchangeability

stabilize

03 fix, peg **06** firm up, freeze, secure,
steady **07** balance, support
08 equalize, valorize **09** establish
10 keep steady, make stable **11** make
uniform

stable

04 barn, fast, firm, sure **05** fixed, solid,
sound, stall **06** secure, static, steady,
strong, sturdy **07** abiding, durable,
lasting, regular, uniform **08** balanced,
constant, enduring, reliable, together
09 permanent **10** deep-rooted,
dependable, invariable, unchanging,
unswerving, unwavering
11 established, long-lasting,
substantial, well-founded
12 unchangeable **13** self-balancing
• **stablehand**
06 ostler

stack

03 lot **04** fill, flue, heap, load, many,
mass, pile, rick, ruck, save, tons, vent
05 amass, clamp, heaps, hoard, loads,
mound, piles, shaft, stash, stock, store
06 funnel, gather, granum, masses,
oodles **07** chimney **08** assemble **09** a
good deal, stockpile **10** accumulate, a
great deal, collection **12** accumulation,
a large amount, great numbers

stadium

04 bowl, park, ring **05** arena, field,
pitch, track, venue **06** ground
08 coliseum **09** colosseum,
velodrome **11** sports field
12 amphitheatre, sports ground

Sports stadia and venues include:

04 Oval
05 Ascot, Epsom, Ibrox, Imola, Lords,
Monza, Troon
06 Henley, Le Mans
07 Aintree, Anfield, Daytona, Olympia,
San Siro, The Oval
08 Highbury, Sandwich
09 Cresta Run, Edgbaston, Longchamp,
Muirfield, Newmarket, St Andrews,
The Belfry, Turnberry, Villa Park,
Wimbledon
10 Brooklands, Carnoustie, Celtic Park,
Cheltenham, Elland Road,
Fairyhouse, Headingley,
Hockenheim, Interlagos,
Meadowbank, Millennium, Monte
Carlo, Twickenham
11 Belmont Park, Brands Hatch,
Hampden Park, Murrayfield, Old
Trafford, Royal Lytham, Sandown
Park, Silverstone, The Crucible, The
Rose Bowl, Trent Bridge, Windsor
Park
12 Goodison Park, Texas Stadium,
Wembley Arena
13 Azteca Stadium, Caesar's Palace,
Crystal Palace, Heysel Stadium,
Royal Birkdale, The Albert Hall,
White Hart Lane
14 Anaheim Stadium, Churchill
Downs, Stamford Bridge, Wembley
Stadium
15 Bernabeu Stadium, Cardiff Arms
Park, Flushing Meadows, Maracana
Stadium

staff

03 man, rod **04** cane, crew, mace, pike,
pole, prop, team, wand, work
05 baton, crook, cross, equip, stave,
stick **06** burden, crutch, cudgel,
occupy, stanza, supply, taiaha, warder
07 bourdon, crosier, crozier, operate,
provide, scepter, sceptre, support,
workers **08** arbalest, ash-plant,
manpower, officers, pastoral, teachers
09 employees, personnel, truncheon,
workforce **10** alpenstock **11** secretariat
12 secretariate **13** establishment
14 human resources

stag

03 dog **04** colt, male **05** royal, staig
06 follow, humble, hummel, shadow
07 brocket, knobber **08** imperial,
informer, stallion **10** ten-pointer

stage

02 do **03** lap, leg, pin **04** dais, give,
step, tier, time, trek **05** apron, arena,
field, floor, lay on, level, mount, phase,
point, put on, realm, scene, shelf, stand
06 direct, length, period, podium,
sphere, storey **07** arrange, perform,
present, produce, rostrum, setting,
soapbox **08** backdrop, division,
engineer, juncture, organize, platform,
scaffold **10** background **11** orchestrate,
put together, stage-manage
• **the stage**
03 rep **05** drama **07** theatre, the play
09 dramatics, theatrics, the boards
11 Thespian art **12** show business
13 the footlights

stagecoach

03 fly **05** dilly **09** diligence

stagger

◊ *anagram indicator*
04 reel, rock, roll, step, stot, stun, sway
05 amaze, lurch, pitch, shake, shock,
stoit, waver **06** bumble, daidle, falter,
recoil, recule, teeter, totter, wintle,
wobble **07** astound, blunder, nonplus,
recoyle, recuile, stoiter, stotter, stupefy
08 astonish, bowl over, confound,
hesitate, keel over, surprise, titubate,
wavering **09** dumbfound, overwhelm
11 flabbergast

staggered

◊ *anagram indicator*
05 dazed **06** amazed **07** shocked,
stunned **08** open-eyed, startled
09 astounded, surprised
10 astonished, bewildered, bowled
over, confounded, gobsmacked, taken
aback **11** dumbfounded **12** lost for
words **13** flabbergasted, knocked for
six

staggering

◊ *anagram indicator*
06 groggy **07** amazing, rolling
08 dramatic, shocking, stunning
09 titubancy **10** astounding,
stupefying, surprising, titubation,
unexpected, unforeseen
11 astonishing **12** mind-boggling

stagnant

04 dull, foul, slow **05** dirty, dying, inert,
quiet, stale, still **06** filthy, smelly, torpid
08 brackish, inactive, moribund,
sluggish, standing **09** lethargic,
unflowing, unhealthy **10** motionless

stagnate

03 rot **04** idle, rust **05** decay **06** fester
07 decline, putrefy **08** languish,
vegetate **09** do nothing **10** degenerate
11 deteriorate **14** become stagnant

staid

03 sad **04** calm, prim **05** grave, quiet,
sober, stiff **06** demure, formal, proper,
sedate, solemn, sombre, steady
07 serious, starchy **08** composed,
decorous **09** permanent **12** buttoned-
down **13** serious-minded

stain

03 dye **04** blot, mail, mark, meal, mote,
slur, smit, soil, spot, tint **05** bedye,
black, chica, chico, cloud, color, dirty,
henna, paint, shame, smear, sully, taint,
tinge **06** blotch, chicha, colour,
damage, embrue, imbrue, injure, injury,
marble, smirch, smudge, smutch
07 attaint, blacken, blemish, corrupt,
embrewe, inkspot, soilure, splodge,
splotch, tarnish, varnish **08** besmirch,
Congo red, discolor, disgrace,
maculate, sanguine **09** discolour,
dishonour, osmic acid, pollution,
soiliness **10** ensanguine, trypan blue
11 contaminate **12** methyl violet,
picrocarmine **13** Coomassie Blue®,
discoloration **14** discolouration

stair, stairs

04 ghat, pair, trap, vice **05** ghaut,
grece, scale, sweep **06** perron, stayre
07 caracol **08** caracole, escalier,
turnpike **09** escalator, forestair
10 backstairs, scale stair **11** common
stair **12** companionway, winding stair
13 scale and platt, turnpike stair
14 apples and pears, escalier dérobé,
scale staircase **15** companion ladder,
moving staircase, spiral staircase

stake

02 go **03** bet, peg, pot, put, rod, set,
tie, vie **04** ante, gage, hold, mise, pale,
pawn, pile, play, pole, post, prop, race,
rest, risk, stob **05** brace, claim, prize,
put in, put on, share, spike, spile,
stang, state, stick, tie up, wager
06 assert, chance, demand, fasten,
gamble, hazard, hold up, loggat,
paling, picket, pierce, piquet, pledge,
prop up, secure, tether **07** concern,
contest, declare, picquet, support,
venture **08** interest, standard, winnings
09 establish **10** investment, lay claim to
11 competition, involvement, requisition

• **stake out**
05 watch 06 define, survey 07 delimit, mark off, mark out, outline, reserve 08 stake off 09 demarcate 11 keep an eye on

stakes
03 bet 04 pool
• **row of stakes**
04 wear, weir 05 orgue 06 paling, zareba, zariba, zereba, zeriba 07 zareeba 08 estacade, palisade, stockade 09 worm fence

stale
03 dry, off, old 04 flat, hard, lure, sour 05 banal, blown, corny, fusty, jaded, musty, shaft, stalk, stock, tired, trite, urine 06 handle, mouldy 07 gone off, insipid, pretext, tainted, urinate, worn-out 08 clichéed, hardened, overused 09 hackneyed, tasteless, worthless 10 uninspired, unoriginal 11 commonplace, stereotyped 12 cliché-ridden, overfamiliar, run-of-the-mill 13 platitudinous

stalemate
03 tie 04 draw, halt 07 impasse 08 blockade, deadlock, stand-off, zugzwang 10 standstill 15 Mexican standoff

stalk
03 bun, kex 04 haft, hunt, keck, pace, rush, seta, stem, step, tail, twig, walk 05 chase, haunt, kecks, march, quill, shaft, shoot, spire, stale, stipe, strig, track, trail, trunk 06 bennet, branch, follow, kecksy, keksye, pursue, shadow, stride 07 pedicel, pedicle, petiole 08 peduncle 09 creep up on, give chase, track down 10 sporophore

See also **stem**

stall
03 bay, pen, pew 04 bulk, coop, crib, ruse, slow, staw, trap 05 booth, decoy, defer, delay, dwell, hedge, kiosk, place, stand, table, trick 06 corral, hold up, induct, put off, stable, travis, trevis 07 counter, cowshed, cubicle, install, shamble, surface, surfeit, sutlery, treviss, tribune 08 fauteuil, flypitch, horse box, obstruct, platform, postpone, put on ice, slow down 09 enclosure, news-stand, stasidion, stonewall, temporize 10 equivocate, standstill 11 compartment, play for time 12 drag your feet

stallion
04 stag 05 staig 06 cooser, cusser, entire 07 cuisser, kestrel, staniel, stannel, stanyel 09 courtesan, stud horse 10 stonehorse

stalwart
05 burly, hardy, loyal, stout 06 brawny, daring, pretty, robust, rugged, steady, strong, sturdy, trusty 07 buirdly, devoted, staunch, valiant 08 athletic, faithful, intrepid, muscular, reliable, resolute, vigorous 09 committed, stalworth, steadfast, strapping

10 dependable, determined 11 indomitable

stamina
04 grit, guts 05 fiber, fibre, force, power 06 bottom, energy, vigour 07 stamens 08 strength 09 endurance, fortitude 10 resilience, resistance 12 staying power

stammer
03 hum 04 lisp 06 babble, falter, gibber, mumble 07 stumble, stutter 08 hesitate, splutter 12 speech defect

stamp
03 cut, die, fix, tag 04 beat, cast, coin, form, kind, mark, mash, mint, pulp, seal, sort, type 05 brand, breed, crush, grind, label, mould, pound, press, print, punch, tread 06 cachet, emboss, enface, incuse, preace, prease, signet, squash, stramp, strike 07 engrave, fashion, impress, imprint, mintage, preasse, quality, trample, variety 08 hallmark, identify, inscribe 09 character, designate, signature 10 categorize, definitive, impression, tripudiate 11 attestation, description 12 characterize 13 authorization

Famous and rare stamps include:
08 Bull's eye, Penny Red
09 Basel dove, Penny Blue
10 Mount Athos, Penny Black, Red Mercury, Scinde Dawk, VR official
11 Jenny invert, St Louis bear
12 Inverted swan
13 Black Honduras, Inverted Jenny, Uganda Cowries

• **stamp out**
03 end 04 curb, kill 05 crush, quash, quell 06 quench, scotch 07 destroy, put down 08 suppress 09 eliminate, eradicate, extirpate 10 extinguish, put an end to

stampede
03 fly, ren, rin, run 04 dash, flee, race, rout, rush, tear 05 shoot 06 charge, flight, gallop, onrush, sprint 07 debacle, scatter 09 breakaway 10 scattering 12 sauve qui peut

stance
04 line 05 angle, slant, stand 06 policy, stanza 07 bearing, opinion, posture, stretch 08 attitude, carriage, position 09 viewpoint 10 deportment, standpoint 11 point of view

stanch
03 dam 04 halt, plug, stay, stem, stop 05 allay, block, check, loyal 06 arrest, hearty, quench, trusty 07 styptic, zealous 08 constant 09 floodgate, seaworthy 10 watertight

stand
02 be 03 bin, nef, put, set 04 base, bear, bier, case, dais, desk, hold, line, park, post, rack, rise, wait 05 abide, allow, angle, bipod, booth, brook, erect, exist, frame, get up, place, plant, shelf, slant, stage, stall, stool, table, up-end 06 cradle, endure, locate, obtain,

policy, remain, stance, suffer, tripod 07 be erect, be valid, counter, dumpbin, monopod, opinion, prevail, stand up, station, stomach, support, sustain, swallow, tribune, undergo, weather 08 attitude, cope with, guéridon, live with, monopode, pedestal, platform, position, stillage, stilling, stillion, stoppage, tolerate 09 be in force, be upright, put up with, viewpoint, withstand 10 be in effect, experience, resistance, standpoint 11 point of view 12 be on your feet, straighten up 13 get on your feet, get to your feet 14 rise to your feet

• **stand by**
04 back 06 affirm, defend, hold to, uphold 07 stick by, support 08 adhere to, champion, side with 10 stand up for, stick up for

• **stand down**
04 quit 06 give up, resign, retire 08 abdicate, step down, withdraw

• **stand for**
04 bear, mean 05 allow, brook 06 denote, endure 07 betoken, signify, stomach 08 indicate, tolerate 09 put up with, represent, symbolize

• **stand in for**
07 replace 08 cover for 10 understudy 11 deputize for 13 substitute for 14 hold the fort for, take the place of

• **stand out**
04 show 06 extend, jut out, strout 07 jump out, poke out, project 08 stick out 09 be obvious 11 catch the eye 12 be noticeable 13 be conspicuous, stick out a mile

• **stand up**
04 jilt, rise, wash 05 get up 06 cohere, hold up 07 let down, upstare 09 hold water 10 fail to meet 11 remain valid 12 straighten up 13 get to your feet 14 rise to your feet

• **stand up for**
06 adhere, defend, uphold 07 protect, stand by, support 08 champion, fight for, side with 10 stick up for 13 remain loyal to

• **stand up to**
04 defy, face 05 brave 06 endure, oppose, resist 08 confront, face up to 09 challenge, withstand

standard
03 par, set, std 04 base, code, flag, mark, norm, rate, rule, type 05 basic, color, ethic, fixed, gauge, grade, guide, ideal, level, model, moral, norma, stock, usual 06 banner, colors, colour, ensign, normal, pennon, sample, square, staple 07 average, classic, colours, example, labarum, measure, pattern, pennant, popular, quality, regular, routine, scruple, typical 08 accepted, approved, exemplar, gonfalon, habitual, official, ordinary, orthodox, paradigm, streamer, vexillum 09 archetype, benchmark, criterion, customary, guideline, horsetail, principle, yardstick 10 definitive, prevailing, recognized, touchstone 11 established, Lesbian

rule, requirement **12** conventional **13** authoritative, specification

standard-bearer
06 cornet, ensign **07** alférez, ancient **08** standard **09** vexillary **11** gonfalonier

standardize
08 equalize, regiment **09** normalize **10** homogenize, regularize, stereotype **11** mass-produce, systematize

stand-in
03 sub **04** temp **05** locum, proxy **06** deputy, second **08** delegate, stuntman **09** surrogate **10** stuntwoman, substitute, understudy **11** pinch-hitter **14** representative **15** second-in-command

standing
04 foul, rank **05** dirty, erect, fixed, stale, still **06** filthy, repute, smelly, status **07** footing, lasting, rampant, regular, settled, station, up-ended, upright **08** brackish, duration, eminence, position, repeated, stagnant, vertical **09** existence, permanent, perpetual, seniority, unflowing, unhealthy **10** experience, motionless, on your feet, reputation **11** continuance, established **13** perpendicular

stand-off
03 tie **04** draw, halt **07** impasse **08** blockade, deadlock **10** five-eighth, standstill

standoffish
04 cold, cool **05** aloof **06** remote **07** distant **08** detached, reserved **09** withdrawn **10** unfriendly, unsociable **14** unapproachable **15** uncommunicative

standpoint
05 angle, slant **06** stance **07** station **08** position **09** viewpoint **11** perspective, point of view **12** vantage point

standstill
03 jam, jib **04** halt, lull, rest, stop **05** pause, stall, stand, tie-up **06** hold-up, log jam **07** dead-set, impasse **08** deadlock, dead stop, gridlock, stoppage, unmoving **09** cessation, stalemate **10** dead-finish, stationary, still-stand
• **to a standstill**
02 up **04** down

staple
03 key **04** main **05** basic, chief, major, sadza, vital **06** matoke **07** leading, matooke, primary, stapple, stopple **08** foremost, plantain, standard **09** essential, fastening, important, necessary, principal **11** fundamental, ship biscuit **13** indispensable

star
03 orb, sun **04** idol, lead, moon, nova **05** celeb, major, shine **06** bigwig, famous, planet, shiner, sphere **07** big name, big shot, leading **08** asterisk, asteroid, luminary, talented **09** bespangle, brilliant, celebrity,

paramount, personage, principal, prominent, satellite, superstar, well-known **10** celebrated, leading man, pre-eminent **11** illustrious, leading lady **12** heavenly body, leading light **13** celestial body, household name

03 Dog, sun
04 Mira, nova, Pole, Vega
05 Deneb, Dubhe, Merak, North, Rigel, Spica
06 meteor, Pollux, pulsar, quasar, Sirius
07 Alphard, Antares, Canopus, Capella, falling, neutron, Polaris, Procyon
08 Achernar, Arcturus, Barnard's, red dwarf, red giant, shooting
09 Aldebaran, Alderamin, Fomalhaut, supernova
10 Beta Crucis, Betelgeuse, brown dwarf, supergiant, white dwarf
11 Alpha Boötis, Alpha Crucis, Delta Cephei
12 Alpha Doradus
13 Alpha Centauri
15 Proxima Centauri

See also **constellation**

starboard
01 R **05** right

starchy
04 prim **05** staid, stiff **06** formal, stuffy **07** precise **11** ceremonious, punctilious, strait-laced **12** conventional

stare
04 dare, gape, gawk, gawp, gaze, gorp, look, ogle **05** glare, watch **06** glower, goggle **07** fisheye, outface **08** starling **10** rubberneck
• **be staring you in the face**
09 be blatant **13** be conspicuous, be very obvious, stick out a mile

starfish
07 asterid **08** asteroid **09** stellerid **10** asteridian, bipinnaria, fivefinger **11** fivefingers, stelleridan **13** crown of thorns

stark
04 bald, bare, grim, pure **05** bleak, blunt, clean, clear, empty, harsh, plain, quite, sharp, sheer, stern, stiff, total, utter **06** arrant, barren, dreary, gloomy, severe, simple, wholly **07** austere, obvious, totally, utterly **08** absolute, clear-cut, complete, desolate, distinct, entirely, flagrant, forsaken, starkers, thorough **09** downright, out-and-out, unadorned **10** absolutely, altogether, completely, consummate, depressing, stark-naked, start-naked **11** undecorated, unmitigated, unqualified **13** unembellished

stark-naked
04 nude **05** naked, stark **06** unclad **08** en cuerpo, in the raw, starkers, stripped **09** in the buff, in the nude, undressed **15** in the altogether

start
◇ *head selection indicator*
03 bug, fit, gin, law, off, set **04** dart, dawn, fire, jerk, jump, leap, make, open, roll **05** abray, arise, begin, birth, braid, break, burst, debut, found, get-go, go-off, issue, leave, onset, rouse, set up, shoot, spasm, spurt, wince **06** abrade, abraid, appear, boggle, create, depart, flinch, kick in, launch, origin, outset, recoil, set off, set out, shrink, spring, turn on, twitch **07** combust, getaway, jump-off, kick off, kick-off, opening, pioneer, trigger **08** activate, commence, conceive, embark on, fire away, get going, initiate, outburst **09** beginning, emergence, establish, inception, instigate, institute, introduce, originate, set on foot **10** convulsion, embark upon, foundation, inaugurate, initiation, trigger off **11** get cracking, get under way, institution, origination **12** commencement, inauguration, introduction **13** come into being **14** bring into being **15** get things moving
• **did not start, fail to start**
◇ *head deletion indicator*

starter
◇ *head selection indicator*
04 meze, whet **05** tapas **06** bhajee, canapé, entrée, relish **08** antepast, apéritif, cocktail **09** appetizer **11** first course, hors d'oeuvre **13** prawn cocktail

starting point
03 tee **04** base **06** origin **07** scratch **08** terminus **11** springboard

startle
03 shy **04** rock **05** alarm, amaze, scare, shock, spook, start, upset **06** affray **07** agitate, astound, disturb, perturb **08** astonish, frighten, surprise, unsettle **11** make you jump

startling
06 sudden **07** épatant **08** alarming, dramatic, galvanic, shocking **10** astounding, staggering, surprising, unexpected, unforeseen **11** astonishing **12** electrifying **13** extraordinary

starvation
04 pine **05** death **06** famine, hunger **07** fasting **10** famishment **12** malnutrition **13** extreme hunger

starve
03 die **04** clem, deny, diet, fast, pine **05** faint **06** famish, hunger, perish, sterve **07** atrophy, deprive **11** deteriorate

starving
05 dying, faint **06** hungry **08** famished, ravenous, underfed **10** very hungry **14** undernourished

stash
04 fund, heap, hide, mass, pile, quit, stop, stow **05** cache, hoard, lay up, store **06** closet, desist, save up **07** conceal, reserve, secrete **08** salt

way **09** reservoir, stockpile
) collection **12** accumulation, squirrel
way

tate
homophone indicator
3 put, say **04** aver, case, état, flap,
nd, name, pomp, tell **05** endow,
ory, panic, phase, realm, shape,
age, tizzy, utter, voice **06** affirm,
ssert, bother, canopy, dither, estate,
ormal, nation, plight, public, report,
eveal, set out, settle, status, tizwas
7 council, country, declare, dignity,
splay, divulge, express, fluster, install,
ingdom, majesty, pompous, present,
pecify, stately **08** announce,
eremony, disclose, grandeur, national,
fficial, position, proclaim, property,
epublic **09** condition, establish,
ormulate, make known, situation,
plendour, statement, territory
0 articulate, ceremonial, federation,
overnment, parliament, promulgate
1 authorities, communicate,
nagnificent, predicament
2 governmental **13** circumstances,
stablishment, parliamentary
4 administration

ee also **province**

Australian states and territories:
2 NT, SA, WA
3 ACT, NSW, QLD, TAS, VIC
8 Tasmania (TAS), Victoria (VIC)
0 Queensland (QLD)
3 New South Wales (NSW)
4 South Australia (SA)
6 Western Australia (WA)
7 Northern Territory (NT)
6 Australian Capital Territory (ACT)

Australian state residents' nicknames:
8 Top Ender
9 cornstalk, Croweater, gumsucker, Taswegian
0 sandgroper
1 Territorian, Vandemonian
2 bananabender
3 Apple Islander
4 Cabbage Patcher
5 Cabbage Gardener

Indian states and union territories:
3 Goa
5 Assam, Bihar, Delhi
6 Kerala, Orissa, Punjab, Sikkim
7 Gujarat, Haryana, Manipur, Mizoram, Tripura
8 Nagaland
9 Jharkhand, Karnataka, Meghalaya, Rajasthan, Tamil Nadu
0 Chandigarh, West Bengal
1 Daman and Diu, Lakshadweep, Maharashtra, Pondicherry, Uttaranchal
2 Chhattisgarh, Uttar Pradesh
3 Andhra Pradesh, Madhya Pradesh
5 Himachal Pradesh, Jammu and Kashmir
6 Arunachal Pradesh

17 Andaman and Nicobar
19 Dadra and Nagar Haveli

US states:
04 Iowa, Ohio, Utah
05 Idaho, Maine, Texas
06 Alaska, Hawaii, Kansas, Nevada, Oregon
07 Alabama, Arizona, Florida, Georgia, Indiana, Montana, New York, Vermont, Wyoming
08 Arkansas, Colorado, Delaware, Illinois, Kentucky, Maryland, Michigan, Missouri, Nebraska, Oklahoma, Virginia
09 Louisiana, Minnesota, New Jersey, New Mexico, Tennessee, Wisconsin
10 California, Washington
11 Connecticut, Mississippi, North Dakota, Rhode Island, South Dakota
12 New Hampshire, Pennsylvania, West Virginia
13 Massachusetts, North Carolina, South Carolina
18 District of Columbia

US state abbreviations and zip codes:
02 AK (Alaska), AL (Alabama), AR (Arkansas), AZ (Arizona), CA (California), CO (Colorado), CT (Connecticut), DC (District of Columbia), DE (Delaware), FL (Florida), GA (Georgia), HI (Hawaii), IA (Iowa), ID (Idaho), IL (Illinois), IN (Indiana), KS (Kansas), KY (Kentucky), LA (Louisiana), MA (Massachusetts), MD (Maryland), ME (Maine), MI (Michigan), MN (Minnesota), MO (Missouri), MS (Mississippi), MT (Montana), NC (North Carolina), ND (North Dakota), NE (Nebraska), NH (New Hampshire), NJ (New Jersey), NM (New Mexico), NV (Nevada), NY (New York), OH (Ohio), OK (Oklahoma), OR (Oregon), PA (Pennsylvania), RI (Rhode Island), SC (South Carolina), SD (South Dakota), TN (Tennessee), TX (Texas), UT (Utah), VA (Virginia), VT (Vermont), WA (Washington), WI (Wisconsin), WV (West Virginia), WY (Wyoming)
03 Ala (Alabama), Ark (Arkansas), Del (Delaware), Fla (Florida), Ill (Illinois), Ind (Indiana), Nev (Nevada), Tex (Texas), Wis (Wisconsin), W Va (West Virginia), Wyo (Wyoming)
04 Ariz (Arizona), Colo (Colorado), Conn (Connecticut), Kans (Kansas), Mass (Massachusetts), Mich (Michigan), Minn (Minnesota), Miss (Mississippi), Mont (Montana), N Dak (North Dakota), Nebr (Nebraska), N Mex (New Mexico), Okla (Oklahoma), Oreg (Oregon), S Dak (South Dakota), Tenn (Tennessee), Wash (Washington)
05 Calif (California)

US state nicknames:
08 Bay State (Massachusetts), Gem State (Idaho)
09 Beef State (Nebraska), Corn State (Iowa), Free State (Maryland), Old Colony (Massachusetts)
10 Aloha State (Hawaii), First State (Delaware), Peach State (Georgia), Sioux State (North Dakota)
11 Beaver State (Oregon), Coyote State (South Dakota), Creole State (Louisiana), Empire State (New York), Garden State (New Jersey), Golden State (California), Gopher State (Minnesota), Little Rhody (Rhode Island), Nutmeg State (Connecticut), Show Me State (Missouri), Silver State (Nevada), Sooner State (Oklahoma), Sunset State (Oklahoma)
12 Beehive State (Utah), Buckeye State (Ohio), Bullion State (Missouri), Chinook State (Washington), Diamond State (Delaware), Granite State (New Hampshire), Hawkeye State (Indiana), Heart of Dixie (Alabama), Hoosier State (Indiana), Old Line State (Maryland), Prairie State (Illinois), Tar Heel State (North Carolina)
13 Big Sky Country (Montana), Camellia State (Alabama), Equality State (Wyoming), Keystone State (Pennsylvania), Land of Lincoln (Illinois), Lone Star State (Texas), Magnolia State (Mississippi), Mainland State (Alaska), Mountain State (West Virginia), Old North State (North Carolina), Palmetto State (South Carolina), Pine Tree State (Maine), Sunshine State (Florida, New Mexico, South Carolina), Treasure State (Montana)
14 Bluegrass State (Kentucky), Evergreen State (Washington), Great Lake State (Michigan), Jayhawker State (Kansas), North Star State (Minnesota), Panhandle State (West Virginia), Sagebrush State (Nevada), Volunteer State (Tennessee), Wolverine State (Michigan)
15 Centennial State (Colorado), Plantation State (Rhode Island), The Last Frontier (Alaska)
16 Flickertail State (North Dakota), Grand Canyon State (Arizona), Peace Garden State (North Dakota)
17 America's Dairyland (Wisconsin), Constitution State (Connecticut), Land of Enchantment (New Mexico), Land of Opportunity (Arkansas)
18 Green Mountain State (Vermont), Mother of Presidents (Virginia)

• in a state
05 het up, upset **07** anxious, hassled, in a stew, ruffled, worried **08** agitated, in a

tizzy, troubled, worked up **09** flustered **10** distressed **13** panic-stricken

• **state of affairs**
03 job **04** case **05** scene **06** crisis, plight, status **07** posture **08** juncture, position **09** condition, situation **11** predicament **12** kettle of fish, lie of the land **13** circumstances

stately
05 grand, lofty, noble, proud, regal, royal **06** august, solemn **07** courtly, elegant, pompous **08** glorious, graceful, imperial, imposing, majestic, measured, splendid **09** dignified, mausolean **10** ceremonial, deliberate, impressive, majestical **11** ceremonious, magnificent

statement
04 note **05** state, story, table **06** exposé, report, verbal **07** account, preface **08** averment, bulletin, manifest, relation **09** assertion, testimony, utterance **10** communiqué, disclosure, divulgence, revelation, white paper **11** affirmation, declaration, enunciation, presentment **12** announcement, constatation, presentation, press release, procès-verbal, proclamation, promulgation **13** communication **14** representation

state-of-the-art
02 in **03** hip, new **04** cool **05** fresh, novel **06** hi-tech, latest, modern, modish, recent, trendy, with it **07** complex, go-ahead, in vogue, present **08** advanced, high-tech, space-age, up-to-date **09** inventive, the latest **10** futuristic, innovative, newfangled, present-day **11** complicated, cutting edge, modernistic, progressive **12** contemporary **13** up-to-the-minute **14** forward-looking **15** highly developed

statesman, stateswoman
03 GOM **06** leader **08** diplomat, wealsman **10** homme d'état, politician **11** grand old man **14** elder statesman

See also **politician**

static
05 fixed, inert, still **06** stable, steady **07** resting **08** constant, immobile, unmoving **09** unvarying **10** changeless, motionless, stationary, unchanging **11** undeviating **13** at a standstill, Maginot-minded

station
03 lay, set, Sta **04** base, camp, farm, halt, post, rank, seat, send, site, stop **05** class, depot, grade, level, place, plant, point, rowme, stand **06** assign, centre, locate, office, status **07** appoint, channel, habitat, install, quarter **08** exchange, garrison, location, position, standing, terminus **09** establish, fare-stage **10** wavelength **11** park-and-ride, place of duty,

whistle stop **12** headquarters **13** establishment, stopping-place

See also **London**; **police station**; **power**; **radio**; **railway station** *under* **railway**

stationary
05 fixed, inert, still **06** at rest, ledger, lidger, moored, parked, static **07** resting, sessile, settled **08** constant, immobile, standing, unmoving **09** sedentary **10** motionless, standstill **13** at a standstill

stationery

Stationery items include:

03 ink, pen, pin
04 file
05 diary, label, ruler, toner
06 eraser, folder, marker, pencil, rubber, staple, Tipp-Ex®
07 blotter, Blu-Tack®, divider, file tab, Filofax®, memo pad
08 calendar, cash book, envelope, Jiffy bag®, notebook, scissors, stamp pad
09 card index, clipboard, desk diary, flip chart, index card, notepaper, paper clip, Sellotape®, wall chart
10 calculator, drawing pin, filing tray, floppy disk, graph paper, paper knife, Post-it note®, ring binder, rubber band
11 account book, address book, bulldog clip, carbon paper, elastic band, rubber stamp, treasury tag
12 adhesive tape, computer disk, copying paper, pocket folder, printer label, printer paper, writing paper
13 expanding file, lever arch file, paper fastener, printer ribbon, tape dispenser
14 document folder, document wallet, manila envelope, spiral notebook, suspension file, window envelope
15 cartridge ribbon, correcting paper, correction fluid, headed notepaper, pencil-sharpener

statue
02 ka **04** bust, head, idol, kore, tiki **05** gnome, image, torso **06** bronze, effigy, figure, kouros, xoanon **07** carving, stookie **08** acrolith, colossus, figurine, monument **09** sculpture, statuette **10** polychrome **11** garden gnome, whole-length **14** representation

See also **sculpture**

statuesque
04 tall **05** regal **07** stately **08** handsome, imposing, majestic **09** dignified **10** impressive

stature
04 fame, rank, size **06** height, inches, renown, weight **08** attitude, eminence, prestige, standing, tallness **09** elevation, loftiness **10** importance, prominence, reputation **11** consequence

status
04 rank **05** class, grade, level, state

06 degree, weight **07** quality, station **08** eminence, position, prestige, standing **09** character, condition **10** importance, reputation **11** consequence, distinction **14** territoriality

statute
03 act, law **04** rule **05** edict, ukase **06** assize, decree **07** Riot Act **09** capitular, enactment, ordinance **10** lex scripta, regulation, written law **13** interlocution, Septennial Act **15** act of parliament

staunch
04 firm, halt, plug, stay, stem, stop, sure, true **05** allay, block, check, loyal, sound, stout **06** arrest, hearty, quench, stanch, strong, trusty **07** devoted, styptic, zealous **08** constant, faithful, reliable, resolute, yeomanly **09** committed, floodgate, seaworthy, steadfast **10** dependable, watertight **11** trustworthy

staunchly
06 firmly **08** yeomanly **10** implacably, resolutely **11** steadfastly **12** unswervingly **13** unfalteringly, unflinchingly

stave
03 bar, lag, rod **05** break, shaft, staff **06** sprain, stanza **07** break up

• **stave off**
04 foil **05** avert, avoid, parry, repel **07** deflect, fend off, prevent, repulse, ward off **08** keep back **09** keep at bay, turn aside

stay
04 curb, halt, hold, keep, last, live, prop, rest, sist, stop, wait, wire **05** abide, abode, allay, await, block, board, brace, cease, check, defer, delay, dwell lodge, pause, put up, quell, strut, tarry, visit **06** arrest, desist, detain, endure, hinder, linger, put off, remain, reside, settle **07** adjourn, appease, control, holiday, persist, prevent, satisfy, shoring, sojourn, stay put, support, suspend **08** buttress, continue, obstacle, obstruct, postpone, prorogue, put on ice, reprieve, restrain, stopover, suppress, vacation **09** deferment, endurance, hang about, remission, restraint, stanchion **10** hang around, suspension **11** continuance, discontinue, take a room at **12** postponement **13** reinforcement

staying power
04 grit, guts **05** fibre, force, power, steel **06** bottom, energy, vigour **07** stamina **08** strength **09** endurance, fortitude **10** resilience, resistance

steadfast
03 sad **04** fast, firm **05** fixed, loyal **06** intent, manful, stable, steady, strong, sturdy **07** staunch **08** constant, faithful, reliable, resolute **09** dedicated, immovable **10** dependable, implacable,

unswerving, unwavering
11 established, perseverant, persevering, unfaltering, unflinching
12 single-minded, stout-hearted

steadily
06 calmly, evenly **07** soberly
08 sensibly **09** regularly, seriously
10 constantly, rationally **12** all year round, on an even keel **13** round the clock **15** uninterruptedly

steady
03 fix **04** calm, even, firm, rest
05 brace, check, fixed, relax, sober, staid, still, usual **06** poised, secure, soothe, stable, subdue **07** balance, compose, control, regular, serious, settled, support, uniform **08** balanced, constant, habitual, reliable, resolute, restrain, sensible, unbroken, unmoving
09 boyfriend, ceaseless, customary, immovable, incessant, perpetual, rock-solid, stabilize, steadfast, unexcited, unvarying **10** consistent, controlled, dependable, girlfriend, motionless, persistent, unchanging, unvariable, unwavering **11** consistence, consistency, established, industrious, unexcitable, unfaltering, unflappable, unremitting **12** on an even keel, tranquillize, well-balanced
13 imperturbable, uninterrupted
14 self-controlled

steak
05 T-bone **08** pope's eye **09** entrecôte
11 porterhouse **13** Chateaubriand

steal
03 bag, cly, dip, lag, mag, nap, nim, nip, rob **04** blag, bone, crib, duff, glom, knap, lift, magg, mill, nick, pick, pull, slip, smug, snip, take, whip **05** annex, boost, bribe, creep, filch, heist, hoist, miche, mooch, mouch, pinch, poach, purse, shaft, shank, slide, slink, sneak, steel, steil, stele, swipe, theft
06 abduct, burgle, convey, finger, handle, hijack, kidnap, nobble, pickle, pilfer, pocket, rip off, rustle, scrump, skrimp, skrump, snatch, snitch, steale, thieve, tiptoe, twitch **07** bargain, break in, cabbage, good buy, knock up, purloin, slither, smuggle, snaffle
08 abstract, discount, embezzle, giveaway, half-inch, high-jack, knock off, liberate, peculate, scrounge, shoplift, souvenir **09** condiddle, duckshove, go off with, reduction, relieve of **10** burglarize, plagiarize, run off with **11** appropriate, make off with, pick a pocket, walk off with **12** make away with, special offer **13** value for money **14** help yourself to, misappropriate

stealing
05 swipe, theft **06** piracy, snatch
07 break-in, larceny, mugging, nicking, robbery, stick-up **08** burglary, filching, pinching, poaching, thievery, thieving
09 pilferage, pilfering, sprechery
10 peculation, plagiarism, purloining, spreaghery **11** shoplifting

12 embezzlement, smash-and-grab
13 appropriation

stealth
05 theft **07** secrecy, slyness
10 covertness, sneakiness
11 furtiveness **12** stealthiness
15 unobtrusiveness
• **by stealth**
08 stowlins **09** stownlins **10** à la dérobée, stolenwise

stealthily
05 slyly **08** covertly, secretly **09** by stealth, cunningly, furtively, stownlins
10 à la dérobée, stolenwise
15 surreptitiously

stealthy
03 sly **05** mousy, quiet **06** covert, mousey, secret, sneaky **07** catlike, cunning, furtive **09** secretive, underhand **11** clandestine, unobtrusive
13 surreptitious

steam
04 haze, mist, roke **05** force **06** energy, exhale, spirit, vapour, vigour
07 stamina **08** activity, dampness, moisture, momentum, outdated
09 eagerness **10** enthusiasm, exhalation, liveliness **11** water vapour
12 condensation, old-fashioned
• **get steamed up**
07 explode **08** boil over, get angry, get het up **09** blow a fuse, do your nut
10 get annoyed, get excited, hit the roof
11 have kittens, lose your rag **12** blow your cool, fly into a rage, get flustered, lose your cool **15** fly off the handle
• **let off steam**
08 sound off **13** let yourself go **15** air your feelings
• **steam up**
05 fog up **06** mist up
• **under your own steam**
05 alone **07** unaided **10** by yourself
11 without help **13** independently

steamer
02 SS **03** str, USS **06** packet, puffer
09 propeller, steamboat, steamship, vaporetto, whaleback **10** packet-boat, packet-ship, paddle-boat **11** side-wheeler, steam-packet, steam vessel
12 screw steamer **13** paddle steamer
14 ocean-greyhound

steaming
◊ *anagram indicator*
See **drunk**

steamy
03 hot **04** blue, damp, hazy, sexy
05 close, humid, misty, muggy, stewy
06 erotic, sticky, sultry, sweaty
07 amorous, gaseous, lustful, raunchy, sensual, vapoury **08** steaming, vaporous **09** seductive, vapourish
10 lubricious, passionate, sweltering, vaporiform

steed
03 nag **04** hack, jade, sted **05** horse, mount, stedd, stede **06** stedde
07 charger **09** Rosinante

steel
05 brace, nerve, psych, shaft, shank, steal, steil, stele, sword **06** handle, harden, steale **07** fortify, prepare, toughen **15** trustworthiness

steely
04 firm, grey, hard **05** harsh **06** strong
08 blue-grey, pitiless, resolute
09 merciless, steel-blue
10 determined, inflexible, unyielding
13 steel-coloured

steep
03 sop **04** bold, buck, damp, dear, fill, high, mask, plot, soak, stey **05** bathe, bluff, brent, brine, embay, imbue, lofty, sharp, sheer, souse, stiff **06** abrupt, costly, drench, imbrue, infuse, pickle, rennet, seethe, steepy, sudden
07 arduous, cragged, ensteep, extreme, immerse, moisten, pervade, stickle, suffuse **08** headlong, macerate, marinate, permeate, saturate, submerge, vertical
09 difficult, excessive, expensive
10 exorbitant, incredible, inordinate, overpriced, over the top, precipiced
11 acclivitous, declivitous, exaggerated, exponential, high-pitched, precipitous, uncalled-for
12 extortionate, unreasonable
13 perpendicular

steeple
05 spire, tower **06** belfry, turret
11 rood-steeple **12** spire-steeple

steeply
07 rapidly, sharply **08** abruptly, suddenly

steer
03 con, cox **04** beef, cann, conn, helm, lead, stir, stot, tack **05** drive, guide, pilot, usher **06** direct, govern, steare
07 conduct, control **08** navigate
• **steer clear of**
04 shun **05** avoid, dodge, evade, skirt
06 bypass, escape, eschew
10 circumvent **12** keep away from

stem
03 dam, pin, ram **04** axis, beam, bine, cane, come, corm, culm, curb, flow, halm, halt, plug, race, runt, stop, tail, tamp **05** arise, block, check, haulm, issue, shaft, shank, shoot, stalk, stock, trunk **06** arrest, bamboo, branch, breast, derive, family, oppose, resist, spring, stanch **07** contain, develop, emanate, hop-vine, staunch **08** kail-runt, peduncle, restrain **09** originate
11 pipe-stapple, pipe-stopple **14** have its origins

stench
04 niff, pong, reek **05** odour, smell, stink, whiff **06** miasma **08** mephitis

stentorian
04 full, loud **06** strong **07** booming, ringing, vibrant **08** carrying, powerful, resonant, sonorous, strident
10 thundering, thunderous
13 reverberating

step

03 act, fix, pas, peg **04** deed, gait, gree, gris, move, pace, rank, rung, trip, walk **05** glide, grade, grece, grees, grese, grice, grise, grize, level, notch, phase, point, print, stage, stair, stamp, stile, titup, trace, track, tramp, tread **06** action, degree, effort, gradin, greece, greese, griece, pit-pat, remove, stride, tittup **07** advance, gradine, grecian, measure, pitapat, process, shuffle, stempel, stemple, twinkle **08** démarche, footfall, footstep, greesing, gressing, halfpace, movement, pitty-pat, progress **09** expedient, footprint, gradation, manoeuvre, procedure **10** impression, proceeding **11** development, pas de basque, progression **14** course of action

See also **dance**

• **in step**
08 in accord, in unison, together **09** in harmony **11** in agreement

• **out of step**
06 at odds **09** not in step **13** at loggerheads **14** in disagreement

• **step by step**
06 slowly **08** bit by bit, gradatim **09** gradually **13** progressively **14** little by little, one step at a time

• **step down**
04 quit **05** leave **06** resign, retire **08** abdicate, withdraw **09** stand down **14** give up your post

• **step in**
07 intrude, mediate **09** arbitrate, intercede, interfere, interrupt, intervene

• **step up**
05 boost, raise **07** augment, build up, speed up **08** escalate, increase **09** intensify **10** accelerate

• **watch your step**
07 look out **08** take care, watch out **09** be careful **11** be attentive **12** mind how you go

stereotype

03 tag **04** cast **05** label, model, mould **06** cliché, stereo **07** formula, pattern **08** typecast **09** formalize **10** categorize, convention, pigeonhole **11** mass-produce, standardize **15** conventionalize, fixed set of ideas

stereotyped

05 banal, corny, fixed, stale, stock, tired, trite **07** cliché'd **08** clichéed, overused, standard **09** hackneyed **10** threadbare, unoriginal **12** cliché-ridden, conventional, mass-produced, standardized, unchangeable **13** platitudinous, stereotypical

sterile

03 dry **04** arid, bare, pure, vain **05** clean, moory, stale **06** barren, futile **07** aseptic, moorish, useless **08** abortive, acarpous, germ-free, germless, infecund, lifeless **09** fruitless, infertile, pointless **10** antiseptic, sterilized, unfruitful, uninfected,

uninspired, unyielding **11** disinfected, ineffectual **12** unproductive, unprofitable **13** unimaginative **14** uncontaminated

sterility

06 atocia, purity **07** asepsis **08** futility **09** cleanness, impotence **10** barrenness, inefficacy **11** infertility, unfecundity, uselessness **12** disinfection **13** fruitlessness, pointlessness **14** unfruitfulness **15** ineffectiveness

sterilize

04 geld, spay **05** clean **06** doctor, neuter, purify, retort **07** cleanse **08** castrate, fumigate **09** autoclave, disinfect **13** make infertile

sterling

03 ace, stg **04** mean, neat, pure, real, ster, true **05** brill, great, sound **06** worthy **07** genuine **08** smashing, standard, starling, terrific, top-notch **09** authentic, excellent **10** first-class **11** superlative **12** second to none **14** out of this world

stern

04 back, grim, hard, helm, iron, poop, rear, rump, star, tail **05** cruel, harsh, rigid, stark, starn, tough **06** ramrod, severe, sombre, strict **07** austere, tail end **08** exacting, rigorous **09** demanding, Draconian, stringent, unsmiling, unsparing **10** forbidding, inflexible, relentless, tyrannical, unyielding **11** unrelenting **13** authoritarian

sternly

06 grimly **07** cruelly, harshly **08** severely, sombrely, strictly **10** inflexibly **12** forbiddingly, relentlessly

Stevenson

03 RLS

stew

◇ *anagram indicator*
03 fix, jug **04** boil, cook, fret, fuss, hash, hole **05** daube, salmi, stove, sweat, tizzy, worry **06** bother, braise, burgoo, paella, pother, ragout, salmis, scouse, simmer, tajine, tizwas **07** agonize, cholent, chowder, fluster, goulash, haricot, navarin, stovies, swelter, tzimmes **08** matelote, mulligan, pot-au-feu, zarzuela **09** agitation, carbonade, carbonado, casserole, cassoulet, Irish stew, lobscouse, potpourri, succotash **10** carbonnade, lob's course, maconochie, prostitute **11** olla-podrida, ratatouille, slumgullion **13** bouillabaisse

steward

05 dewan, diwan, reeve **06** bailie, butler, commis, factor, waiter **07** bailiff, baillie, foreman, maître d', marshal, mormaor **08** khansama, manciple, official, overseer, waitress **09** attendant, caretaker, custodian, khansamah, major-domo, seneschal, sommelier **10** air hostess, stewardess,

supervisor **11** chamberlain **12** maître d'hôtel **14** homme d'affaires **15** flight attendant

stick

03 fix, gad, gum, jab, jam, jut, lay, pin, put, set **04** bear, bind, bond, clog, drop, flak, fuse, glue, grip, hang, hold, join, last, poke, push, rest, site, stab, stay, stop, tack, tape, trap, twig, weld, yard **05** abide, abuse, affix, blame, cling, dwell, paste, place, prick, spear, stand, tally **06** adhere, attach, branch, cement, clog up, endure, fasten, impale, insert, linger, locate, pierce, remain, rocket, secure, solder, switch, thrust **07** carry on, confine, deposit, install, persist, reproof, scruple, set down, stomach, swallow **08** continue, position, protrude, puncture, tolerate, transfix **09** criticism, hostility, penetrate, put up with **10** punishment **11** come to a halt **12** dressing-down **13** get bogged down

02 ko
03 bat, lug, rod
04 cane, club, cosh, pike, pole, post, wand, whip
05 baton, billy, birch, crook, lathi, staff, stake, waddy
06 alpeen, crutch, cudgel, hockey, kierie, tripod
07 sceptre, walking, woomera
08 bludgeon, cocktail
09 truncheon
10 alpenstock, knobkerrie, shillelagh

• **stick at**
04 balk **05** demur, doubt, pause **06** keep at, recoil, stop at **07** persist, scruple **08** continue, hesitate, plug away **09** persevere **10** shrink from **13** draw the line at

• **stick by**
04 back **06** defend, hold to, uphold **07** stand by, support **08** adhere to, champion, side with **10** stand up for, stick up for

• **stick it out**
07 persist **08** continue, keep at it, plug away **09** persevere **11** hang in there **13** grin and bear it

• **stick out**
04 perk **05** bulge **06** extend, jut out, tongue **07** poke out, project **08** protrude **09** be obvious **12** be noticeable **13** be conspicuous

• **stick to**
04 obey **06** accept, follow, fulfil, hold to, keep to, uphold **07** abide by, agree to, observe, respect, stand by **08** adhere to, carry out, submit to **09** conform to, discharge **10** comply with, toe the line **11** go along with, go by the book

• **stick up for**
06 defend, uphold **07** protect, stand by, support **08** champion, fight for **10** speak up for, stand up for **13** take the part of, take the side of

• **the sticks**
04 bush, wops **05** scrub **07** boonies,

nickdom, outback, wop-wops
8 backveld, yokeldom
09 backwoods, boondocks **10** back-
blocks **11** remote areas, up the Boohai
13 end of the earth **15** middle of
nowhere

sticker
03 bur **04** tine

stickiness
03 goo **04** gaum, gorm, tack
09 glueyness, gooeyness, gumminess,
tackiness, viscidity **10** syrupiness
12 adhesiveness **13** glutinousness

stick-in-the-mud
05 fogey **06** fossil, square **08** fogeyish,
old fogey, outmoded **09** Victorian
10 antiquated, back number, fossilized,
fuddy-duddy **12** antediluvian,
buttoned-down, conservative
13 unadventurous

stickler
03 nut **06** backer, maniac, pedant,
purist, second, umpire **07** fanatic,
fusspot **08** mediator **09** regulator
10 fussbudget **12** precisianist
13 perfectionist, quarterdecker

sticky
04 limy **05** chewy, close, dauby, gluey,
gooey, goopy, gummy, humid, jammy,
muggy, tacky, tough **06** claggy,
clammy, clarty, clingy, cloggy,
gummed, smeary, stodgy, sultry,
sweaty, thorny, tricky, viscid
07 awkward, viscous **08** adhesive,
delicate, ticklish **09** difficult, glutinous,
sensitive, tenacious **10** oppressive,
sweltering, unpleasant
12 embarrassing
• **sticky substance**
03 goo, gum **04** glit, goop, gunk, lime
05 gunge **06** viscin **08** mucilage,
propolis

stiff
03 rob **04** cold, dead, firm, hard, prim,
taut, very **05** brisk, cheat, dense, fresh,
harsh, large, rigid, solid, stark, stoor,
stour, sture, tense, thick, tight, tough,
windy **06** aching, chilly, corpse, formal,
murder, potent, severe, stowre, strict,
strong, tiring **07** arduous, austere,
awkward, certain, drastic, extreme,
pompous, stilted, unlucky, viscous
08 decorous, exacting, forceful,
hardened, priggish, reserved, rigorous,
stubborn, vigorous **09** alcoholic,
arthritic, demanding, difficult,
Draconian, excessive, extremely,
inelastic, laborious, resistant,
rheumatic, stringent, unbending
10 ceremonial, formidable, inflexible,
solidified, unyielding **11** ceremonious,
challenging, constrained, rheumaticky,
standoffish **12** intoxicating,
pertinacious

stiffen
03 gel, set **04** jell **05** brace, stark, steel,
tense **06** harden, starch **07** congeal,
fortify, tense up, thicken, tighten
08 ankylose, solidify **09** anchylose,

bandoline, coagulate, reinforce,
Trubenise, Trubenize® **10** strengthen

stiff-necked
05 proud **06** formal **07** haughty
08 arrogant, stubborn **09** obstinate,
pig-headed, unnatural **11** opinionated
12 contumacious **14** uncompromising

stifle
04 curb, funk, hush **05** check, choke,
crush, quash, quell, stive **06** dampen,
deaden, hush up, keep in, muffle,
subdue **07** repress, silence, smother,
swallow **08** gulp back, gulp down,
hold back, restrain, scomfish, strangle,
suppress **09** constrain, suffocate
10 asphyxiate, extinguish

stigma
04 blot, mark, note, pore, scar, slur,
spot **05** brand, shame, stain, taint
07 blemish **08** disgrace, spiracle
09 dishonour

stigmatize
04 mark, note **05** brand, label, shame,
stain **06** vilify **07** blemish, condemn
08 demonize, denounce, disgrace,
vilipend **09** discredit

still
03 but, e'en, ene, yet **04** calm, deep,
even, hush, kill, mild **05** abate, accoy,
allay, inert, peace, quiet **06** always,
distil, even so, hushed, pacify, serene,
settle, silent, smooth, soothe, static,
subdue, though **07** appease, assuage,
however, quieten, quietly, restful,
silence **08** although, constant,
immobile, inactive, lifeless, moderate,
peaceful, restrain, serenity, stagnant,
tranquil, unmoving, until now
09 continual, noiseless, quiescent,
quietness, sedentary, stillness,
unruffled **10** constantly, for all that,
inactively, motionless, stationary, stock-
still, unstirring **11** nonetheless,
undisturbed **12** nevertheless,
peacefulness, tranquillity, tranquillize,
up to this time **13** in spite of that, in
spite of this, noiselessness
15 notwithstanding
• **be still**
03 lie **04** hush, rest **06** remain, repose

stillness
04 calm, hush, rest **05** peace, quiet
06 repose **07** silence **08** calmness,
coolness, quietude, serenity
09 composure, placidity, quietness
10 equanimity, sedateness
11 restfulness **12** peacefulness,
tranquillity

stilted
05 stiff **06** forced, wooden
08 laboured, mannered **09** unnatural
10 artificial **11** constrained

stimulant
01 E **03** kat, qat **04** khat **05** betel, chile,
chili, tonic, upper **06** chilli, cinder
07 caffein, cardiac, digoxin, ecstasy,
guaraná, pep pill, reviver **08** caffeine,
coramine, doxapram, excitant, incitant,
lobeline, pemoline, pick-me-up

09 analeptic, cantharis, dance drug,
digitalin, nux vomica, sassafras,
whetstone **11** nikethamide, purple
heart, restorative, winter's bark
13 dexamfetamine, smelling salts
14 dexamphetamine
15 methamphetamine

stimulate
03 fan, jog **04** fire, goad, hype, spur,
urge **05** gee up, hop up, impel, rouse
06 arouse, buck up, excite, fillip, hype
up, incite, induce, kindle, prompt, whip
up **07** animate, hearten, inflame,
inspire, provoke, quicken, trigger
08 activate, irritate, motivate
09 challenge, encourage, instigate
10 potentiate, trigger off

stimulating
07 bracing, piquant, rousing
08 excitant, exciting, galvanic, stirring
09 inspiring, provoking, stimulant
10 intriguing, suggestive **11** interesting,
provocative **12** exhilarating

stimulation
06 ginger **07** arousal **08** kindling
09 animation, prompting
10 excitement, incitement, irritation,
motivation, quickening **11** inspiration,
instigation, provocation
13 encouragement

stimulus
03 jog **04** goad, jolt, kick, prod, push,
spur, whet **05** drive, sting **06** fillip
07 impetus **09** incentive
10 incitement, inducement
11 provocation **12** shot in the arm
13 encouragement

sting
02 do **03** con, nip, rob **04** barb, bite,
burn, edge, goad, hurt, lurk, pain, pole,
scam, tang **05** annoy, cheat, fraud,
point, prick, smart, spite, stang, trick,
upset, wound **06** diddle, fiddle, fleece,
grieve, injure, injury, malice, needle,
nettle, offend, racket, rip off, rip-off,
tingle **07** aculeus, deceive, defraud,
incense, piercer, provoke, sarcasm,
swindle, torment **08** distress, irritate,
pungency, stimulus, trickery, urticate
09 deception, gold brick, gold-brick,
heartache, sharpness **10** causticity,
exasperate, incitement, irritation
11 causticness, viciousness
12 incisiveness, take for a ride
13 double-dealing, sharp practice

stinging
05 smart, urent **07** burning, hurtful,
piquant **08** aculeate, poignant,
smarting, tingling, urticant, wounding
09 aculeated, injurious, offensive
10 irritating **11** distressing

stingy
04 hard, mean, near **05** close, mingy,
tight **06** hungry, skimpy, snippy
07 costive, miserly, niggard, save-all
09 niggardly, penurious **11** bad-
tempered, tight-fisted **12** candle-
paring, cheeseparing, parsimonious
13 penny-pinching

stink

03 hum, row 04 flap, fuss, guff, honk, ming, niff, pong, reek, stir, suck 05 be bad, hoo-ha, odour, smell 06 bother, furore, hassle, stench 07 be awful, be nasty, fluster, trouble 08 bad smell, malodour, mephitis 09 commotion, foul smell 12 be despicable, be unpleasant, song and dance

stinker

03 cur, dog, rat 04 scab 05 cheat, hound, louse, rogue, scamp, swine 06 fulmar, horror, louser, petrel, plight, rascal, rotter 07 bounder, dastard, problem, ruffian, shocker, villain 08 blighter, stinkard, vagabond 09 miscreant, reprobate, scallywag, scoundrel 10 blackguard, difficulty, impediment, ne'er-do-well 11 predicament 14 good-for-nothing

stinking

03 bad 04 foul, vile 05 awful, fetid, nasty, niffy, pongy 06 foetid, mingin', rotten 07 humming, minging, stenchy 08 terrible 10 disgusting, unpleasant 12 contemptible

stint

03 bit 04 bout, save, stop, time, turn 05 allot, cease, check, limit, pinch, quota, scant, share, shift, skimp, spare, spell, stent 06 period, scrimp 07 scantle, skimp on, stretch 08 begrudge, restrain, restrict, withhold 09 allowance, apportion, economize, restraint 11 restriction

stipend

03 ann 05 annat, grant 06 income, salary 07 alimony, annuity, benefit, payment, pension 08 expenses 09 allowance 10 assistance 11 maintenance 12 contribution

stipulate

06 demand 07 article, lay down, provide, require, set down, specify 08 covenant, insist on 09 guarantee

stipulation

05 point, rider 06 clause, demand 07 proviso 08 contract 09 condition, postulate, provision 11 requirement 12 precondition, prerequisite 13 specification

stir

◊ *anagram indicator*
03 ado, jee, jog, mix, wag 04 beat, flap, fuss, moot, move, to-do, turn, whip 05 blend, budge, churn, hoo-ha, pique, quich, raise, rouse, shake, shift, steer, stire, tizzy, touch 06 affect, bustle, excite, flurry, muddle, prison, puddle, quatch, quetch, quitch, quiver, racket, riffle, rustle, thrill, tumult, twitch, uproar 07 agitate, clutter, disturb, ferment, flutter, inspire, provoke, quinche, rummage, tempest, torment, tremble 08 activity, disorder, movement 09 agitation, commotion, kerfuffle, sensation 10 excitement 11 disturbance 12 song and dance

See also **prison**

• stir up

03 jog 04 fire, poke, rear, spur, wake 05 amove, awake, drive, impel, poach, raise, rouse, roust, waken 06 arouse, awaken, excite, incite, kindle, prompt, racket, rustle 07 agitate, animate, disturb, inflame, inspire, provoke, quicken, rummage 08 motivate 09 electrify, encourage, galvanize, instigate, stimulate

stirring

◊ *anagram indicator*
04 live 05 heady 06 lively, moving 07 emotive, rousing, working 08 dramatic, exciting, spirited 09 animating, inspiring, thrilling 11 impassioned, stimulating 12 exhilarating, intoxicating

stitch

03 hem, sew 04 darn, mend, seam, tack 06 repair 09 embroider

See also **embroidery**

• stitch up

03 con 04 shop, trap 05 fit up, grass, plant, set up 06 rumble, suture 07 swindle 11 double-cross, incriminate 13 stab in the back

stock

03 box, log, set 04 cows, fund, heap, keep, line, name, pack, pigs, pile, post, race, sell, team 05 banal, basic, block, blood, bonds, breed, cache, carry, equip, fumet, funds, goods, herds, hoard, money, plant, range, sheep, store, stump, talon, tired, trite, trunk, usual, wares 06 assets, cattle, common, credit, deal in, family, flocks, handle, horses, kit out, market, repute, shares, source, strain, supply, trough 07 animals, average, capital, descent, fumette, furnish, holding, kindred, lineage, opinion, plenish, provide, regular, reserve, routine, species, stretch, trade in, variety, worn-out 08 accoutre, ancestry, clichéd, equities, good name, ordinary, overused, pedigree, pressure, quantity, standard, standing, stoccado 09 amassment, customary, equipment, essential, genealogy, hackneyed, inventory, livestock, parentage, portfolio, provision, relatives, reservoir, selection, stockpile, traffic in 10 assortment, background, collection, estimation, extraction, investment, repertoire, reputation, securities 11 commodities, farm animals, merchandise, merchandize, stereotyped, traditional 12 accumulation, conventional, run-of-the-mill

• in stock

06 on sale 07 for sale 09 available 11 on the market 12 on the shelves

• stock up

03 buy 04 fill, heap, load, save 05 amass, buy up, hoard, lay in, store 06 fill up, gather, heap up, pile up 07 put away, stack up, store up 08 put aside, salt away 09 provision, replenish, stash away, stockpile 10 accumulate

• take stock

06 assess, review, size up, survey 07 weigh up 08 appraise, estimate, evaluate, reassess 09 re-examine 10 re-evaluate

stockade

06 zareba, zariba, zereba, zeriba 07 zareeba

stocking

05 nylon, stock 06 hogger, moggan 07 popsock, spattee 08 boothose, knee-high 10 understock 11 netherstock

See also **sock**

stockings

04 hose 07 hold-ups, legwear 11 netherlings

stockpile

04 fund, heap, keep, pile, save 05 amass, cache, hoard, stock, store 06 gather, heap up, pile up 07 put away, reserve, store up 08 put aside 09 amassment, reservoir 10 accumulate 12 accumulation

stock-still

05 inert, still 06 static 08 immobile, inactive, unmoving 10 motionless, stationary, unstirring

stocky

05 broad, dumpy, short, solid, squat 06 blocky, chunky, stubby, stumpy, sturdy 07 nuggety 08 thickset 11 mesomorphic

stodgy

04 dull 05 heavy, solid, staid 06 boring, formal, leaden, solemn, stuffy, turgid 07 filling, starchy, tedious 08 laboured 10 fuddy-duddy, spiritless, unexciting, uninspired 11 substantial 12 indigestible 13 unimaginative 14 unenterprising

stoical

04 calm, cool 07 patient 08 resigned 09 accepting, impassive 10 forbearing, phlegmatic 11 indifferent, unemotional, unexcitable 13 dispassionate, imperturbable, long-suffering, philosophical, uncomplaining 14 self-controlled 15 self-disciplined

stoicism

07 ataraxy 08 ataraxia, calmness, fatalism, patience 09 fortitude, stolidity 10 acceptance, dispassion, philosophy 11 forbearance, impassivity, resignation 12 indifference 13 long-suffering 14 unexcitability

stoke

04 tend 09 add coal to, add fuel to, add wood to 11 keep burning 12 feed with fuel

stokes

01 S

stolen

03 hot 04 bent 05 taken 06 nicked, swiped 07 nobbled, punched

08 pilfered **09** ill-gotten, purloined, ripped off **10** knocked off

• **stolen goods**
03 tom **04** crib, loot, soup, waif **05** cheat, theft **07** stealth **08** tweedler **09** stouthrie **10** stoutherie, tomfoolery

stolid
02 po **04** dull, slow **05** beefy, heavy **06** bovine, solemn, wooden **07** lumpish, po-faced **08** blockish **09** apathetic, impassive **10** phlegmatic **11** indifferent, unemotional, uninspiring **13** unimaginative

stomach
03 gut, maw, tum **04** bear, craw, guts, puku, read, take, vell, zest **05** abide, belly, bible, bingy, brook, gorge, pride, rumen, stand, taste, tummy **06** bonnet, desire, digest, endure, fardel, hunger, inside, liking, omasum, paunch, relish, rennet, resent, spirit, spleen, suffer, tum-tum, venter **07** abdomen, courage, gizzard, insides, passion **08** abomasum, appetite, pot-belly, submit to, tolerate **09** approve of, king's-hood, manyplies, put up with, rennet-bag, reticulum **10** little Mary, psalterium **11** bread basket, corporation, disposition, inclination **13** determination
See also **ruminant**

• **without stomach**
◇ *middle deletion indicator*

stomach ache
05 colic **06** gripes, gut rot **09** bellyache, dyspepsia, tummy ache **12** hypochondria **13** grass staggers **15** stomach staggers

stone
02 st **03** gem, pip, pit, rag, set **04** flag, hone, plum, rock, seed, sett, slab **05** jewel, lapis **06** cobble, gibber, gonnie, goolie, kernel, mirror, pebble, yonnie **07** boondie, boulder, brinnie **08** endocarp, gemstone, sardonyx, testicle **09** flagstone, headstone, tombstone **10** concretion, gravestone
See also **birth**; **gem**; **rock**

stoned *see* **drunk**

stonewall
03 lie **05** dodge, evade, hedge, shift **06** waffle **07** deceive, quibble, shuffle **09** be evasive, pussy-foot **10** equivocate **11** prevaricate **12** shilly-shally **13** sit on the fence

stony
03 icy **04** cold, hard **05** blank, rigid, rocky, stern **06** chilly, frigid, frosty, gritty, pebbly, severe, steely **07** adamant, callous, deadpan, hostile, petrous, shingly **08** gravelly, obdurate, pitiless **09** heartless, lapideous, merciless, unfeeling **10** inexorable, petrifying, poker-faced, unfriendly **11** indifferent, unforgiving **12** unresponsive **14** expressionless

stooge
04 butt, dupe, feed, foil, pawn

06 drudge, lackey, puppet **07** cat's paw, fall guy **08** henchman **09** scapegoat **11** subordinate

stool
05 coppy, stand **06** buffet, sunkie, tripod **07** creepie, cricket, taboret, tumbrel, tumbril **08** stillage, tabouret

stoop
03 bow, sag **04** bend, curb, duck, lean, lout, lowt, poke, post, prop, sink **05** courb, deign, droop, hunch, kneel, lower, porch, slump, squat, steep, stoep, stope, stoup, swoop **06** bucket, cringe, crouch, patron, resort, slouch, stoope, submit **07** bending, decline, descend, descent, ducking, incline **08** hunching, lowering, verandah **09** go so far as, go so low as, supporter, vouchsafe **10** condescend **11** inclination **13** condescension, lower yourself

stop
03 bar, can, dit, end **04** bung, cork, halt, hold, kick, kill, live, plug, poop, quit, rein, rest, seal, sist, snub, stap, stay, stem **05** block, board, break, cease, check, choke, close, cover, dwell, embar, imbar, lodge, media, pause, put up, snuff, sprag, stage, stall, stash, stimy, tarry, visit **06** anchor, arrest, cut off, desist, detain, devall, draw up, finish, hinder, impede, keep up, pack in, pack up, rein in, reside, scotch, settle, stanch, stimie, stop up, stymie, thwart, wind up **07** abandon, bus stop, chuck it, close up, occlude, prevent, refrain, sojourn, station, staunch, suspend **08** conclude, draw rein, give over, hold hard, knock off, leave off, obstacle, obstruct, pack it in, pack it up, restrain, stopover, stoppage, suppress, terminus, withhold **09** cessation, diaphragm, fare stage, foreclose, frustrate, hindrance, intercept, interrupt, obstruent, punctuate, terminate **10** conclusion, standstill **11** come to an end, come to a rest, destination, discontinue, termination **12** bring to an end, bring to a rest, interruption **13** stopping-place **14** discontinuance **15** discontinuation
See also **organ**

• **expressions ordering a stop**
02 ha, ho, wo **03** hoa, hoh **04** easy, proo, pruh, toho, whoa **05** avast

stopgap
05 shift **06** resort **09** emergency, expedient, impromptu, makeshift, temporary **10** improvised, substitute **11** provisional **12** expediential **13** improvisation, rough-and-ready

stopover
04 rest, stop **05** break, visit **07** layover, sojourn, stop-off **13** overnight stay

stoppage
03 cut, jam **04** blin, halt, stop **05** check, choke, hitch, sit-in, stand, stick **06** arrest, freeze, hartal, hold-up, outage, pull-up, strike **07** closure,

embargo, removal, shut-off, walk-out **08** asphyxia, blackout, blockage, decrease, discount, obstacle, shutdown, stayaway **09** allowance, breakdown, cessation, deduction, hindrance, occlusion, reduction, taking off **10** inhibition, standstill, taking away, withdrawal **11** haemostasis, obstruction, subtraction, suppression, termination **12** heart failure, interruption **14** discontinuance **15** discontinuation

stopper
03 tap **04** bung, cork, plug, seal **06** spigot **07** stopple **08** screwtop

storage
• **computer storage**
03 RAM, ROM

store
03 lot **04** bank, barn, fund, heap, keep, load, mine, pack, save, shop, stow **05** cache, hoard, house, lay by, lay in, lay up, stash, stock, stuff, value **06** coffer, esteem, garner, gather, larder, panary, plenty, supply, vintry **07** buttery, collect, deposit, furnish, keeping, lay down, put down, reserve **08** cupboard, minimart, multiple, put aside, quantity, salt away, treasury **09** abundance, amassment, livestock, provision, reservoir, stockpile, storeroom, warehouse **10** accumulate, chain store, corner shop, depository, groceteria, repository, storehouse **11** hypermarket, stock up with, sufficiency, supermarket **12** accumulation, retail outlet, squirrel away **15** department store

• **set store by, lay store by**
05 value **06** admire, esteem **13** think highly of **14** consider highly

storehouse
04 barn, fund, hold, silo **05** depot, étape, vault **06** cellar, garner, larder, pantry, pataka, wealth **07** armoury, arsenal, buttery, granary **08** dene-hole, elevator, entrepot, magazine, treasury **09** repertory, thesaurus, warehouse **10** depository, repository **12** conservatory

storey
04 deck, flat, tier **05** attic, étage, floor, level, stage **06** flight **07** stratum **08** basement, bel étage, entresol **09** triforium **10** clearstory, clerestory, downstairs, first floor **11** ground floor

stork
06 argala, jabiru **08** adjutant, shoebill **09** whale-head **10** saddlebill

storm
◇ *anagram indicator*
03 row **04** fume, rage, rand, rant, rave, roar, rush, stir, tear, to-do **05** shout, stamp **06** assail, attack, charge, furore, outcry, rumpus, seethe, tumult, uproar **07** assault, clamour, explode, flounce, turmoil **08** brouhaha, outbreak, outburst, paroxysm **09** agitation, commotion, kerfuffle, offensive,

onslaught **10** hit the roof
11 disturbance **12** lose your cool
14 foam at the mouth

03 ice, sea, sun
04 dust, gale, hail, line, rain, sand, snow
05 buran, devil
06 baguio, calima, haboob, meteor, pelter, squall
07 cyclone, monsoon, Shaitan, tempest, thunder, tornado, typhoon, violent
08 blizzard, downpour, magnetic
09 bourasque, dust devil, hurricane, whirlwind
10 cloudburst, electrical

stormy
◇ *anagram indicator*
04 foul, wild **05** dirty, gusty, rainy, rough, windy, wroth **06** choppy, raging, rugged, unruly, wintry
07 gustful, squally, wintery **08** blustery, oragious, stormful **09** inclement, turbulent **10** boisterous, passionate
11 tempestuous

story
03 bar, fib, gag, lie, rib **04** baur, bawr, epic, idyl, item, joke, myth, plot, saga, tale, tier, yarn **05** fable, floor, idyll, novel, rumor, theme **06** legend, record, relate, report, rumour, serial, storey **07** account, article, episode, fantasy, feature, fiction, history, recital, romance, shocker, untruth
08 anecdote, jeremiad, nouvelle, oratorio, phantasy, relation, thriller
09 chronicle, falsehood, narrative, statement, storyline **10** allegation, Munchausen, rib-tickler **11** fabrication, historiette, Munchhausen **12** old wives' tale, spine-chiller
See also **novel**; **tale**

storyteller
04 bard, liar **06** author, writer
08 narrator, novelist, romancer, tell-tale
09 raconteur **10** anecdotist, chronicler, raconteuse

stout
03 big, fat **04** bold, tall **05** beefy, brave, bulky, burly, cobby, gutsy, hardy, heavy, lusty, obese, plump, proud, solid, thick, tough, tubby **06** brawny, entire, fierce, fleshy, gritty, heroic, manful, plucky, portly, robust, spunky, stanch, stocky, strong, stuffy, stuggy, sturdy
07 durable, gallant, hulking, staunch, valiant **08** arrogant, athletic, chopping, enduring, fearless, forceful, intrepid, muscular, resolute, stalwart, stubborn, thickset, valorous, vigorous
09 corpulent, dauntless
10 courageous, determined, embonpoint, overweight, unyielding
11 substantial

stoutly
06 boldly **07** toughly **08** fiercely, strongly **09** staunchly **10** fearlessly, resolutely

stove
03 Aga **04** kiln, oven, stew **05** grill, range **06** cockle, cooker, heater, Primus® **07** caboose, chaufer, furnace
08 chauffer, hothouse, pot-belly
09 gas cooker, kitchener **10** base-burner, calefactor, salamander
12 cooking-range

stow
◇ *containment indicator*
04 cram, crop, load, pack **05** place, stash, store, stuff **06** bundle
07 deposit, put away **11** flemish down
• **stow away**
04 hide, snug, tuck **05** put up **07** put away **14** travel secretly **15** conceal yourself

straggle
03 gad, lag **04** roam, rove, tail
05 amble, drift, range, stray, trail
06 loiter, ramble, sprawl, spread, wander **07** scatter, vagrant
08 sprangle, squander **09** string out
10 dilly-dally

straggly
05 loose **06** random, untidy **07** aimless
08 drifting, rambling, straying
09 irregular, spreading, strung out
10 straggling **12** disorganized

straight
03 het, str **04** even, fair, flat, gain, just, neat, pure, slap, tidy, true **05** blunt, frank, level, right, smack, spang **06** at once, candid, decent, direct, honest, normal, pronto, square, unbent
07 aligned, bluntly, clearly, frankly, in order, orderly, plainly, settled, sincere, unmixed, upright **08** accurate, arranged, balanced, candidly, directly, faithful, honestly, promptly, reliable, slap-bang, unbroken, uncurved, vertical **09** downright, instantly, on the trot, organized, outspoken, right away, shipshape, tramlined, unbending, uncurving, undiluted **10** consistent, continuous, forthright, honourable, horizontal, law-abiding, point-blank, successive, unswerving, upstanding
11 consecutive, immediately, outspokenly, rectilineal, rectilinear, respectable, trustworthy, undeviating
12 continuously, conventional, forthrightly, heterosexual, orthotropous, successively, without delay **13** consecutively, unadulterated, uninterrupted **14** as the crow flies
15 straightforward, uninterruptedly
• **off the straight**
04 agee, ajee **08** cockeyed
• **straight away**
03 now **06** at once, pronto **08** directly, like that **09** instantly, right away
11 immediately, incontinent **12** just like that, there and then, without delay
13 incontinently

straighten
◇ *anagram indicator*
04 tidy, yelm **05** align, dress, order, range, yealm **06** adjust, neaten, tidy up, unbend **07** arrange, stretch **08** put

right **10** put in order **12** make straight
14 become straight
• **straighten out**
06 extend, settle, tidy up **07** clear up, correct, realign, rectify, resolve, sort out, untwist **08** put right **10** put in order, regularize **11** disentangle
• **straighten up**
05 stand **07** stand up **10** stand erect
12 stand upright

straightforward
04 easy, even, open **05** clear, frank, pakka, plain, pucka, pukka **06** candid, direct, honest, simple **07** genuine, jannock, sincere, up-front **08** no frills, truthful **09** outspoken **10** child's play, elementary, forthright, on the level, penny-plain, point-blank, unexacting
11 undemanding, undesigning **12** a piece of cake **13** plain-speaking, uncomplicated, without frills

strain
03 air, fit, rax, sye, tax, try, tug, way
04 aria, fitt, hurt, kind, play, pull, race, rack, rick, seil, sift, sile, sing, song, sort, tear, tire, tune, type, vein, work
05 blood, breed, drain, drive, exert, fitte, force, fytte, heave, labor, music, point, press, retch, shear, sieve, sound, stock, theme, trace, trait, twist, worry, wrick, wring **06** burden, demand, duress, effort, extend, family, filter, goggle, injure, injury, labour, melody, purify, riddle, screen, sprain, spring, streak, stress, stripe, strive, tauten, weaken, wrench **07** anxiety, descent, distend, element, embrace, express, fatigue, lineage, measure, overtax, quality, squeeze, stretch, tension, tighten, variety **08** ancestry, compress, elongate, exertion, go all out, overwork, pedigree, pressure, restrain, separate, struggle, tendency
09 endeavour, offspring, percolate, suspicion, tiredness, weariness
10 exhaustion, extraction, proclivity, suggestion **11** disposition **12** do your utmost **14** beyond the limit, characteristic, push to the limit
15 make every effort

strained
05 drawn, false, heavy, stiff, tense
06 forced, sprung, uneasy, wooden
07 awkward, intense **08** laboured
09 intensive, unnatural, unrelaxed
10 artificial, non-natural
11 constrained, embarrassed **13** self-conscious, uncomfortable

strainer
03 sye **04** seil, sile, tems **05** sieve, siler, tammy, temse **06** filter, milsey, riddle, screen, sifter **08** colander **09** cullender

strait
02 St **03** fix, gat, gut, jam **04** belt, hole, kyle, mess **05** close, inlet, needy, sound, tight **06** crisis, narrow, pickle, plight, strict **07** channel, closely, dilemma, narrows, poverty, tighten, tightly **08** distress, hardship, narrowly, rigorous, straight, streight, strictly

09 emergency, extremity **10** difficulty, perplexity, rigorously **11** hard-pressed, predicament **13** embarrassment

Straits include:

03 Rae
04 Adak, Bass, Cook, Haro, Irbe, Kara, Palk, Pitt, Soya
05 Banks, Bohai, Cabot, Canso, Davis, Dease, Dover, Kerch, Korea, Luzon, Menai, Osumi, Sunda, Tatar
06 Bering, Dundas, Etolin, Fisher, Hecate, Hormuz, Hudson, Lombok, Solent, Sunday, Tablas, Taiwan, Tokara, Torres, Vitiaz
07 Balabac, Chatham, Dampier, Denmark, Florida, Formosa, Foveaux, Georgia, Le Maire, Makasar, Malacca, McClure, Messina, Mindoro, Otranto, Polillo, Rosario, Tsugaru
08 Bosporus, Clarence, Karimata, Kattegat, Mackinac, Magellan, Makassar, Shelikof, Tsushima, Victoria
09 Belle Isle, Bonifacio, Bosphorus, Gibraltar, Great Belt, La Pérouse, Linapacan, Van Diemen
10 Juan de Fuca, Little Belt
11 Dardanelles
12 Bougainville, Investigator
13 San Bernardino
14 Northumberland, Queen Charlotte
15 Dolphin and Union

straitened
04 poor **07** limited, reduced **09** difficult **10** distressed, restricted **11** embarrassed **12** impoverished

strait-laced
04 prim **06** narrow, proper, strict, stuffy **07** prudish, starchy, uptight **08** priggish, unstuffy **09** tight-lace **10** moralistic, tight-laced **11** puritanical **12** narrow-minded **13** prim and proper

strand
03 ply **04** kemp, lock, sand, wire, wisp **05** beach, fibre, front, piece, sands, shore, tress, twist **06** bundle, factor, gutter, length, maroon, sliver, string, strond, thread **07** element, feature, monofil, rivulet **08** filament, multifil, seashore **09** component, foreshore **10** ingredient, waterfront **11** homopolymer **12** optical fibre **13** multifilament **14** vascular bundle

stranded
07 aground, beached, wrecked **08** forsaken, grounded, helpless, marooned **09** abandoned, penniless **10** high and dry, in the lurch **11** shipwrecked **14** left in the lurch

strange
◇ *anagram indicator*
03 new, odd, rum, shy **04** unco **05** alien, crazy, fraim, fremd, funny, kinky, novel, queer, silly, unked, unket, unkid, wacky, weird **06** exotic, freaky, fremit, stupid, unreal **07** bizarre, curious, foreign, oddball, offbeat, surreal, uncanny, uncouth, unknown,

untried, unusual **08** abnormal, peculiar, selcouth, singular, straunge, uncommon, unversed, wondrous **09** eccentric, estranged, fantastic, irregular, unheard-of, wonderful, wonderous **10** mysterious, mystifying, off the wall, outlandish, perplexing, remarkable, surprising, unexpected, unfamiliar **11** exceptional, unexplained **12** inexplicable, unaccustomed, unacquainted **13** extraordinary

strangely
◇ *anagram indicator*
05 oddly **07** weirdly **08** wondrous **09** bizarrely, curiously, unusually, wonderous **10** abnormally, peculiarly, remarkably, singularly, uncommonly **12** inexplicably, unexpectedly **13** exceptionally

strangeness
01 S **06** oddity **07** oddness **08** eeriness **09** queerness **10** exoticness **11** abnormality, bizarreness, peculiarity, singularity, uncanniness **12** eccentricity, irregularity

stranger
04 unco **05** alien, fraim, fremd, guest **06** fremit, frenne **07** incomer, pilgrim, visitor **08** newcomer, outsider **09** foreigner, non-member **10** new arrival

• **a stranger to**
10 unversed in **14** unaccustomed to, unfamiliar with **15** inexperienced in

strangle
03 gag **04** kill **05** check, choke **06** impede, keep in, stifle **07** garotte, garrote, inhibit, repress, smother **08** garrotte, hold back, restrain, suppress, thrapple, thropple, throttle **09** bowstring, constrict, suffocate **10** asphyxiate **11** strangulate

strap
03 tab, tie **04** band, beat, belt, bind, cord, flog, hang, jess, lash, rein, taws, whip **05** leash, sling, strop, tawse, thong, truss **06** barber, credit, fasten, muzzle, secure **07** bandage, leather, scourge **08** backband, selvagee **10** watchguard

strapping
03 big **05** beefy, burly, hefty, hunky, husky **06** brawny, robust, strong, sturdy **07** hulking **08** chopping, swanking **09** thrashing, two-handed, well-built

stratagem
04 coup, plan, plot, ploy, ruse, wile **05** dodge, fetch, guile, guyle, trick **06** device, feeler, scheme, tactic **08** artifice, intrigue, maneuver, trickery **09** deception, malengine, manoeuvre **10** subterfuge **11** counter-plot, machination **12** ruse de guerre

strategic
03 key **05** vital **07** crucial, planned, politic **08** critical, decisive, tactical **09** essential, important **10** calculated,

commanding, deliberate, diplomatic **11** strategical

strategy
03 ESS **04** plan **06** design, policy, scheme **07** maximin, minimax, tactics **08** approach, game plan, planning, schedule **09** blueprint, procedure, programme **11** generalship, geostrategy **12** plan of action **14** shark repellent

stratification
07 bedding, ranking, sorting **08** division, layering **09** gradation, hierarchy **10** graduation **14** categorization, classification

stratum
03 bed **04** lode, post, rank, seam, tier, vein **05** caste, class, grade, group, layer, level, table **06** region **07** bracket, cap rock, coal-bed, day-coal, station **08** category, wayboard **09** Corallian **10** weighboard **14** stratification

straw
04 halm, wase **05** chaff, haulm, strae **06** buntal, litter, thatch **07** stubble **08** strammel, strummel

• **bundle of straw, bundles of straw**
04 wisp, yelm **05** truss, yealm **06** kemple

• **straw hat**
04 hive **06** basher, boater **07** leghorn **09** coolie hat, Dunstable **10** balibuntal

stray
◇ *anagram indicator*
03 err, odd, tag **04** lost, roam, rove, waff, waif **05** amble, drift, freak, range, traik **06** casual, chance, common, estray, ramble, random, wander, wilder **07** deviate, digress, diverge, erratic, get lost, go wrong, meander, roaming, saunter **08** alleycat, drifting, go astray, homeless, isolated, maverick, straggle, stravaig, stray cat, stray dog **09** abandoned, forwander, scattered, straggler, wandering, wander off **10** accidental, exorbitate, occasional **15** go off at a tangent, go off the subject

streak
03 fly **04** band, belt, dart, dash, daub, lace, line, mark, race, rach, roll, rush, tear, time, vein, waif, wake, wale, wave, weal, zoom **05** flash, fleck, freak, layer, ratch, smear, speed, spell, stint, stria, strip, sweep, touch, trace, vibex, whizz **06** beat it, gallop, hurtle, period, ribbon, scurry, smudge, sprint, strain, strake, stripe, stroke **07** element, scarper, scratch, stretch, striate, vamoose, whistle **09** skedaddle

streaked
05 lined **06** banded, barred, hawked, hawkit, veined **07** brinded, brindle, flecked, streaky, striate, striped **08** brindled **09** fleckered **11** tear-stained

stream
03 fly, jet, pow, ren, rin, run **04** beck, burn, flap, flow, gush, kill, lake, lane,

nala, pour, rill, rush, shed, tide, well
05 brook, burst, creek, crowd, drift, float, flood, issue, nalla, nulla, river, spill, spout, surge, trail **06** course, deluge, efflux, gutter, nallah, nullah, rillet, streel, volley **07** cascade, current, flutter, rivulet, torrent **08** affluent, influent, tendency **09** tributary **10** outpouring, succession **11** watercourse

streamer
04 flag, vane **05** plume **06** banner, ensign, fallal, pennon, pinnet, ribbon **07** bandrol, pennant **08** banderol, bannerol, gonfalon, standard, vexillum **09** banderole, bannerall

streamlined
05 sleek, slick **06** smooth **07** well-run **08** graceful **09** efficient, organized **10** modernized, time-saving **11** aerodynamic **12** rationalized **13** smooth-running, up-to-the-minute

street
02 St **03** rue, way **04** gate, lane, road **06** avenue **12** thoroughfare

See also **London**; **New York**; **Paris**; **road**

- **man in the street, woman in the street**
07 Joe Blow **09** Joe Bloggs, Joe Public, Mr Average **10** Joe Sixpack, Mrs Average **13** average person, average punter **14** ordinary person **15** ordinary citizen

streetwalker *see* **prostitute**

strength
04 bant, bent, gift, grit, guts, iron, main, thew **05** asset, brawn, clout, depth, force, forte, might, nerve, point, power, sinew, thing, truth, vigor **06** ardour, energy, fizzen, foison, fusion, health, métier, muscle, spirit, talent, vigour, weight **07** ability, bravery, cogency, courage, fitness, fushion, passion, potence, potency, stamina, urgency **08** aptitude, fervency, firmness, keenness, pungency, solidity, validity **09** advantage, fortitude, hardiness, influence, intensity, sharpness, solidness, soundness, specialty, stoutness, toughness, vehemence, vividness **10** brute force, complement, durability, resilience, resistance, resolution, robustness, speciality, sturdiness **11** athleticism, graphicness, persistence, strong point **12** forcefulness, might and main **13** assertiveness, determination, effectiveness **14** impregnability, persuasiveness

- **lose strength**
04 fade, pall **05** faint, waste **08** wind down

- **on the strength of**
07 based on **09** because of **10** by virtue of **11** on account of **12** on the basis of

strengthen
03 arm, man **04** fish, line, stay

05 brace, cleat, edify, force, rally, serve, sinew, steel, wharf **06** anneal, back up, beef up, harden, munite, picket, piquet, prop up, turn up **07** afforce, bolster, build up, confirm, fortify, hearten, nourish, picquet, protect, refresh, restore, shore up, stiffen, support, toughen **08** buttress, heighten, increase **09** encourage, intensify, reinforce **10** invigorate, work-harden **11** consolidate, corroborate **12** substantiate

strenuous
04 bold, hard, keen, warm **05** eager, heavy, tough **06** active, taxing, tiring, uphill, urgent **07** arduous, earnest, weighty, zealous **08** forceful, resolute, spirited, tireless, vigorous **09** demanding, difficult, energetic, gruelling, laborious, tenacious **10** blistering, determined, exhausting **13** indefatigable

strenuously
06 boldly **08** actively **10** forcefully, resolutely, tirelessly, vigorously **11** tenaciously

stress
◇ *anagram indicator*
04 beat, birr, rack **05** brunt, force, ictus, shear, value, worry **06** accent, burden, hassle, repeat, strain, trauma, weight **07** anxiety, point up, straits, tension, trouble **08** distress, emphasis, hardship, pressure, priority **09** distraint, emphasize, highlight, spotlight, underline **10** accentuate, difficulty, exaggerate, importance, underscore, uneasiness **12** accentuation, apprehension, significance, thermal shock

stressed
04 edgy **05** jumpy, tense **06** on edge, strong, uneasy **07** anxious, fidgety, jittery, keyed up, nervous, uptight, worried **08** emphatic, restless, strained **09** screwed up **10** distraught, emphatical **11** overwrought, stressed out **12** apprehensive **13** under pressure

stressful
05 tense **06** uneasy **07** charged, fraught **08** strained, worrying **10** nail-biting **12** high-pressure, nerve-racking

stretch
03 rax, ren, rin, run, tax, try **04** area, last, line, pull, push, rack, span, term, test, time **05** offer, perch, range, reach, space, spell, stint, sweep, tract, widen **06** bouncy, expand, extend, extent, go up to, lay out, length, period, pliant, return, spread, strain, streek, supple, tauten, unfold, unroll **07** broaden, buoyant, draw out, elastic, expanse, hold out, plastic, pliable, present, proffer, project, prolong, rubbery, springy, tighten **08** come up to, continue, distance, elongate, flexible, go down to, lengthen, protract, reach out, straucht, straught, stretchy, yielding **09** challenge, extension, go as far as, make wider, resilient, spread out,

stimulate **10** come down to, exaggerate, make longer, straighten **11** become wider, elasticated, stretchable **12** become longer, exaggeration, put demands on **13** extensibility

- **stretch out**
05 crane, reach, relax **06** extend, intend, put out, sprawl, string **07** hold out, lie down, recline

- **stretch your legs**
06 stroll **08** exercise **09** move about, promenade, take a walk **10** go for a walk, take the air **13** take a breather

stretcher
04 rack **06** gurney, litter

strew
03 sow **04** lard, rush, snow, toss **05** level, straw, strow **06** litter, spread **07** bestrew, scatter **08** bespread, disperse, sprinkle **10** besprinkle

stricken
03 hit **06** struck **07** injured, smitten, wounded **08** affected **09** afflicted

strict
04 firm, hard, true **05** clear, close, exact, harsh, rigid, stern, tight, total, tough, utter **06** giusto, narrow, proper, severe, strait **07** austere, literal, precise, regular **08** absolute, accurate, clear-cut, complete, faithful, intimate, orthodox, rigorous, straight, streight **09** Draconian, religious, stringent **10** inflexible, iron-fisted, iron-handed, meticulous, no-nonsense, particular, restricted, scrupulous **11** hard and fast **13** authoritarian, barrack square, conscientious, thoroughgoing **14** disciplinarian, uncompromising

strictly
04 only **06** firmly, purely, strait, wholly **07** sternly, totally **08** narrowly, properly, severely, straight, straitly, streight, uniquely **10** absolutely, completely, definitely, in every way, inflexibly, positively, rigorously **11** exclusively **13** categorically, unambiguously, unequivocally **14** in every respect, unquestionably

- **strictly speaking**
07 exactly **09** literally, precisely **11** to the letter

strictness
06 rigour **08** accuracy, firmness, rigidity, rigorism, severity **09** austerity, exactness, harshness, precision, rigidness, sternness **10** stringency **12** rigorousness **13** barrack square, stringentness **14** meticulousness, scrupulousness

stricture
04 flak **05** blame, bound, limit **06** rebuke **07** binding, censure, closure, confine, control, reproof **09** criticism, restraint, tightness **10** constraint, strictness **11** restriction **13** animadversion

stride
04 lamp, lope, pace, sten, step, walk

05 stalk, stend, tread 06 stroam
07 advance, galumph 08 bestride,
gallumph, movement, progress,
straddle 10 overstride 11 progression
• **take something in your stride**
11 do blindfold, make light of 14 cope
with easily, deal with easily, think
nothing of

strident

04 loud 05 harsh, rough 06 shrill,
urgent 07 booming, grating, jarring,
rasping, raucous, roaring 08 clashing,
jangling 09 clamorous, unmusical
10 discordant, screeching, stentorian,
stridulant, thundering, vociferous

strife

03 row 04 bate, feud 05 sturt
06 barrat, battle, brigue, combat,
debate, hassle, mutiny 07 bargain,
conteck, contest, discord, dispute, ill-
will, quarrel, rivalry, trouble, warfare
08 argument, conflict, fighting,
friction, striving, struggle, variance
09 animosity, bickering, hostility,
wrangling 10 contention, dissension,
ill-feeling 11 controversy, quarrelling
12 colluctation, contestation,
disagreement

strike

03 bop, box, cob, fix, hit, lam, pat, ram,
rap, tip, wap, zap 04 bang, beat, belt,
biff, blad, blow, buff, chap, chip, clap,
coin, cuff, dart, deal, draw, feel, find,
fist, flog, gowf, hook, knee, look, neck,
pane, pash, pean, peck, peen, pein,
pene, pole, raid, rush, seem, slam, slap,
slat, sock, swap, swop, take, toll, tonk,
trap, yerk 05 adopt, bandh, blast,
blaud, catch, chime, clout, crash,
douse, dowse, fight, impel, knock,
lower, plump, pound, prang, print,
punch, reach, shoot, sit-in, slant,
smack, smite, sound, souse, spank,
stamp, storm, swipe, thump, touch,
whack 06 affect, affrap, alight,
ambush, appear, assail, assume, attack,
batter, blight, broach, buffet, cancel,
charge, clinch, come to, dawn on,
delete, go-slow, hammer, hit out,
mutiny, paddle, poleax, ratify, revolt,
sclaff, set out, settle, smooth, stroke,
take on, thrash, thwack, wallop
07 achieve, afflict, agree on, assault,
bewitch, clobber, come out, compute,
deliver, embrace, impinge, impress,
inflict, occur to, percuss, poleaxe,
protest, torpedo, uncover, unearth,
walk out, walk-out 08 arrive at, come
upon, describe, discover, estimate,
look like, pounce on, register, set
about, settle on, siderate, stayaway,
stoppage, stop work, storming, strickle
09 dismantle, down tools, encounter,
événement, interpose, penetrate,
surrender 10 bird impact, chance
upon, come to mind, constitute,
happen upon, work to rule, work-to-
rule 11 collide with 13 have the look
of
• **on strike**
03 out

• **strike back**
07 hit back 09 fight back, get back at,
retaliate 11 get even with, reciprocate
14 get your own back, pay someone
back
• **strike down**
04 fell, kill, ruin, slay 05 smite
06 murder 07 afflict, destroy
11 assassinate
• **strike out**
03 paw 05 erase 06 cancel, delete,
efface, remove, rub out 08 cross out
09 strike off 10 obliterate 13 strike
through
• **strike up**
05 begin, start 07 kick off
08 commence, initiate 09 establish,
instigate, introduce

strike-breaker *see* scab

striking

04 bold, dash, fine 06 pretty, strike
07 beating, evident, obvious, salient,
visible 08 dazzling, distinct, frappant,
gorgeous, sizzling, spanking, stunning
09 arresting, beautiful, distingué,
glamorous, memorable 10 attractive,
distinguée, impressive, incidental,
noticeable, percussion, percutient,
photogenic, remarkable
11 astonishing, conspicuous, eye-
catching, good-looking, outstanding
13 extraordinary

string

01 G 03 row, tie 04 cord, file, hang,
hoax, lace, line, link, loop, nete, rake,
rope, yarn 05 cable, chain, chord,
drove, fibre, leash, queue, quint, sling,
strap, tie up, train, twine 06 column,
fasten, humbug, number, series, strand,
stream, thairm, thread 07 connect,
elastic, festoon, suspend 08 lichanos,
nicky-tam, paramese, paranete,
sequence, shoelace 10 procession,
succession
• **string along**
04 dupe, fool, hoax 05 bluff
06 humbug 07 deceive, mislead
09 co-operate, play false 12 put one
over on, take for a ride
• **string out**
06 extend, fan out, wander
08 disperse, lengthen, protract, space
out, straggle 09 spread out 10 stretch
out
• **strings of a lyre**
04 mese, nete 05 trite 06 hypate
08 lichanos, paramese, paranete
09 parhypate
• **string up**
03 top 04 hang, kill, kilt 05 lynch, run
up, truss 15 send to the gibbet
• **with no strings attached**
13 unconditional

stringency

06 rigour 07 demands 08 firmness
09 exactness, toughness 10 strictness
12 rigorousness 13 inflexibility

stringent

04 firm, hard 05 harsh, rigid, tight,
tough 06 severe, strict 07 binding,

extreme 08 exacting, rigorous
09 demanding 10 inflexible
14 uncompromising

stringy

04 ropy, wiry 05 chewy, ropey, tough
06 sinewy 07 fibrous, gristly
08 leathery

strip

03 bar, bit, gut, jib, rig 04 area, band,
bare, bark, belt, bend, doff, flay, gear,
husk, lath, list, loot, peel, pull, rand,
roon, rund, sash, skin, slat, slip, tack,
tirl, tirr, togs, welt, zona, zone 05 clear,
empty, get-up, ledge, linch, piece,
pluck, press, royne, ruler, shear, shred,
shuck, spoil, strap, thong, tract, unrip
06 denude, devest, divest, expose,
extent, lardon, outfit, peeler, ribbon,
rig-out, screed, splent, spline, splint,
straik, strake, stripe, stroke, swathe,
things, uncase, unload 07 clobber,
clothes, colours, deprive, despoil,
disrobe, expanse, feather, flaught,
flitter, fumetto, lardoon, lay bare,
parking, peeling, pillage, plunder,
ransack, stretch, tear off, uncover,
undress 08 airstrip, clean out, clothing,
degrease, flake off, separate, unclothe
09 dismantle, excoriate, pull apart, take
apart 10 disfurnish, dispossess,
striptease 11 disassemble
12 straightedge, take to pieces
13 swaddling-band

stripe

03 bar 04 band, belt, blow, lash, line,
list, pale, snip, zone 05 flash, fleck,
guard, slash, strip, vitta, whelk
06 ribbon, straik, strain, strake, streak
07 chevron, endorse 09 laticlave, pinstripe

striped

06 banded, barred, pirnie, pirnit, stripy
07 bausond, guarded, streaky, vittate
08 endorsed, streaked, striated
10 variegated 11 finch-backed

stripling

03 boy, lad 05 youth 07 young 'un
08 teenager 09 fledgling, youngster
10 adolescent 11 hobbledehoy

strive

03 try, tug, vie 04 toil, work 05 bandy,
fight, force, heave, press 06 aspire,
battle, combat, engage, follow, labour,
pingle, preace, prease, resist, strain
07 attempt, bargain, compete,
contend, contest, enforce, preasse, try
hard, wrestle 08 campaign, do battle,
endeavor, purchase, struggle
09 endeavour, persevere 10 do your
best 11 give your all 12 do your utmost
13 exert yourself

stroke

03 cut, hit, pat, pet, rub 04 beat, bell,
belt, biff, blow, coup, dash, dint, hand,
jole, joll, jowl, line, milk, move, push,
shot, slap, touk, tuck, whet 06 boast,
chuck, cross, ictus, joule, knock, pulse,
scoop, shock, smack, spasm, strip,
sweep, swipe, thump, touch, trait,

whack **06** action, attack, buffet, caress, fondle, glance, motion, stound, stownd, strike, struck, thwack, tittle, wallop **07** clobber, flatter, massage, nobbler, outlash, reverse, reverso, seizure, solidus, strooke, upright, whample **08** collapse, flourish, movement **09** encourage, grand coup **10** back-hander, coup d'éclat, pile-driver, sideration, thrombosis **11** achievement **12** punto reverso, punto riverso, repercussion **14** accomplishment

See also **swimming**

stroll
04 turn, walk **05** amble, troll **06** bummel, dander, dauner, dawdle, dawner, lounge, ramble, toddle, wander **07** daunder, meander, saunter **08** ambulate **10** go for a walk **14** constitutional **15** stretch your legs

stroller
06 walker **07** dawdler, flâneur, rambler, vagrant **08** wanderer **09** itinerant, pushchair, saunterer

strong
01 f **03** fit, hot, str **04** able, bull, deep, firm, full, hale, keen, rank, sour, very, well, yald **05** beefy, brave, burly, clear, eager, great, gross, gutsy, hardy, heady, heavy, lusty, nappy, pithy, sharp, solid, sound, spicy, stiff, stout, thewy, tough, valid, vivid, wight, yauld **06** active, ardent, biting, brawny, cogent, fierce, marked, mighty, potent, robust, rugged, secure, severe, sinewy, sturdy, trusty, urgent **07** devoted, doughty, durable, evident, fervent, graphic, healthy, intense, marrowy, obvious, piquant, pollent, pungent, telling, violent, weighty **08** athletic, cast-iron, clear-cut, decisive, definite, forceful, forcible, grievous, muscular, numerous, positive, powerful, profound, resolute, stalwart, stressed, vehement, vigorous **09** assertive, committed, competent, confident, effective, efficient, excelling, heavy-duty, plausible, resilient, resistant, steadfast, strapping, undiluted, well-built **10** aggressive, compelling, convincing, courageous, determined, emphasized, fast-moving, formidable, hogen-mogen, passionate, persistent, persuasive, pronounced, reinforced, remarkable **11** efficacious, hard-wearing, long-lasting, substantial **12** concentrated, enthusiastic, single-minded, strong-minded, strong-willed **13** well-protected **14** highly seasoned **15** highly flavoured

• **strong point**
04 bent, gift **05** asset, forte, thing **06** métier, talent **08** aptitude, strength **09** advantage, specialty **10** speciality

strongarm
06 terror **07** violent **08** bully-boy, bullying, coercive, forceful, physical, thuggish **10** aggressive, oppressive **11** threatening **12** intimidatory

strongbox
04 safe **05** chest, vault **06** coffer **07** cash box **10** deposit box, depository, repository

stronghold
04 aery, eyry, fort, hold, holt, keep **05** aerie, ayrie, eyrie, tower **06** castle, center, centre, refuge **07** bastion, citadel, outpost **08** fastness, fortress, hill-fort

strongly
06 deeply, firmly **07** durably, solidly, toughly **08** markedly **09** intensely **10** definitely, forcefully, muscularly, positively, powerfully, resolutely **11** resiliently **12** athletically **13** substantially

strong-minded
04 firm **08** resolute **09** steadfast, tenacious, unbending **10** determined, iron-willed, unwavering **11** independent **12** strong-willed **14** uncompromising

strong-willed
06 wilful **07** wayward **08** obdurate, stubborn **09** obstinate **10** inflexible, refractory, self-willed **11** intractable **12** intransigent, recalcitrant

strontium
02 Sr

stroppy
05 ratty, rowdy **06** shirty **07** awkward, bolshie **08** perverse **09** difficult, unhelpful **10** refractory **11** bad-tempered, quarrelsome **12** bloody minded, cantankerous, obstreperous **13** unco-operative

structural
06 design **07** organic **08** tectonic **09** edificial **11** formational **14** constructional, organizational **15** configurational

structure
◇ *anagram indicator*
04 form, make **05** build, frame, set-up, shape **06** design, fabric, make-up, system **07** arrange, build up, chassis, edifice **08** assemble, building, erection, organize **09** construct, formation, framework **10** contexture **11** arrangement, composition **12** architecture, conformation, constitution, construction, organization **13** configuration

struggle
◇ *anagram indicator*
03 tug, vie, war **04** agon, camp, toil, work **05** agony, brawl, clash, fight, pains, scrum **06** battle, combat, effort, engage, hassle, labour, ruffle, strain, strife, strift, strive, tussle **07** agonize, compete, contend, contest, grapple, problem, scuffle, trouble, try hard, tuilyie, tuilzie, warfare, wrestle **08** conflict, exertion, flounder, skirmish, slugfest, sprangle **09** encounter, handgrips, luctation, scrimmage, scrummage **10** difficulty,

do your best **11** competition, give your all, hostilities **12** do your utmost **13** exert yourself, passage of arms

strumpet *see* **prostitute**

strut
03 jet **04** cock, prop, spur **05** brank, bulge, dwang, glory, major, pronk, raker, stalk, swank **06** flaunt, parade, prance, scotch, strout, strunt **07** nervure, peacock, swagger **08** protrude, stanchel, stancher, tail boom **09** stanchion

stub
03 end **04** butt, grub, snub, stob **05** stump **06** dog-end, fag end, snubbe **07** remnant **11** counterfoil

stubborn
05 rigid, stiff, stoor, stour, stout, sture **06** dogged, mulish, ornery, stowre, thrawn, wilful **07** adamant **08** obdurate, obstacle, perverse **09** difficult, hidebound, obstinate, opinioned, pig-headed, rigwiddie, rigwoodie, tenacious, unbending **10** headstrong, inflexible, inveterate, persistent, refractory, self-willed, unyielding **11** intractable, opinionated, stiff-necked **12** cantankerous, contumacious, intransigent, opinionative, pertinacious, recalcitrant, stiff-hearted, strong-willed, unmanageable **14** overdetermined, uncompromising **15** not open to reason, stubborn as a mule

See also **obstinate**

stubbornly
08 doggedly, wilfully **10** inflexibly, perversely **11** obstinately, pig-headedly, tenaciously **12** persistently **14** intransigently

stubby
05 dumpy, short, squat **06** chunky, stumpy **08** thickset

stuck
04 fast, firm **05** fixed, glued **06** beaten, jammed, joined, rooted **07** at a loss, baffled, stalled, stumped **08** cemented, embedded, fastened, immobile **09** perplexed, unmovable **10** bogged down, nonplussed **13** at your wits' end

• **get stuck into**
05 begin, start **06** tackle **08** embark on, set about **09** get down to

• **stuck on**
05 mad on **06** fond of, keen on, nuts on **07** sweet on **09** wild about **10** crazy about, dotty about **12** obsessed with **14** infatuated with

stuck-up
05 proud **06** snooty, uppish **07** haughty **08** arrogant, snobbish, toplofty **09** bigheaded, conceited **10** hoity-toity **11** patronizing, toffee-nosed, toploftical **12** supercilious **13** condescending, high and mighty

stud
03 seg, set **04** boss, knob, nail, race, spur, stop, tack **05** pitch, prick, rivet, stump **06** popper **07** clinker **08** doornail **11** pop-fastener **12** clip-fastener, snap-fastener **13** press fastener

studded
03 set **06** dotted **07** flecked, spotted, starred **08** mamillar, spangled, speckled **09** mamillary, scattered, sprinkled **10** bejewelled, bespangled, icy-pearled, ornamented **12** star-spangled

student
01 L **04** semi, soph **05** bejan, pupil, semie, softa, welly **06** bejant, bursar, medico, premed, tosher, wellie **07** alumnus, bookman, fresher, grinder, learner, scarfie, scholar, Templar, trainee **08** disciple, freshman, premedic **09** collegian, schoolboy, semi-bajan, sophomore **10** apprentice, green welly, schoolgirl **11** collegianer, probationer **12** extensionist, postgraduate **13** undergraduate

• **student group**
03 NUS

studied
05 voulu **06** forced, versed, wilful **07** planned **08** affected, designed, well-read **09** conscious, contrived, unnatural **10** artificial, calculated, deliberate, purposeful **11** intentional **12** premeditated **13** over-elaborate

studio
06 school **07** atelier, bottega, gallery **08** workroom, workshop

studious
05 eager **07** bookish, careful, earnest, serious **08** academic, diligent, sedulous, thorough **09** assiduous, attentive, scholarly **10** deliberate, meticulous, reflective, thoughtful **11** hard-working, industrious **12** intellectual

study
03 con, den, dig, kon **04** cram, muse, plod, read, scan, swot, work, zeal **05** conne, essay, learn, mug up, paper, train **06** bone up, devise, digest, office, peruse, ponder, read up, report, review, revise, studio, survey, thesis **07** analyse, article, examine, inquiry, library, major in, perusal, reading, reflect, reverie, subject, thought **08** analysis, bone up on, consider, cramming, critique, homework, instruct, interest, learning, meditate, pore over, research, revision, scrutiny, swotting, workroom **09** attention, monograph, workplace **10** deliberate, inspection, scrutinize **11** contemplate, examination, inclination, investigate, lucubration, preparation, prolegomena, scholarship **12** propaedeutic **13** consideration, contemplation, investigation

Subjects of study include:
02 D&T, IT
03 art, ICT, law, PSE
04 PHSE
05 craft, dance, drama, music, sport
06 botany, design
07 anatomy, biology, driving, ecology, fashion, fitness, geology, history, physics, pottery, science, zoology
08 commerce, eugenics, genetics, heraldry, medicine, penology, politics, theology
09 astrology, astronomy, chemistry, cosmology, economics, education, erotology, ethnology, forensics, geography, languages, logistics, marketing, mechanics, mythology, pathology, shorthand, sociology, surveying, web design
10 humanities, journalism, literature, metallurgy, philosophy, physiology, psychology, publishing, statistics, technology, visual arts
11 accountancy, agriculture, archaeology, calligraphy, citizenship, dressmaking, electronics, engineering, linguistics, mathematics, metaphysics, meteorology, ornithology, photography, the Classics, typewriting
12 anthropology, architecture, horticulture, lexicography, media studies, oceanography, pharmacology
13 gender studies, home economics, librarianship, marine studies, women's studies
14 food technology, leisure studies, natural history, social sciences, word processing
15 building studies, business studies, computer studies, creative writing, hotel management

stuff
03 jam, kit, pad, ram, wad **04** clog, cram, crap, fill, gear, hoax, lard, line, load, pack, pang, push, sate, stap, stow, trig, tuck **05** binge, blash, block, cloth, crowd, farce, force, fudge, goods, gorge, items, money, press, shove, squab, store, wedge **06** bung up, fabric, gobble, guzzle, liquor, matter, pig out, steeve, stodge, tackle, things, thrust **07** bombast, clobber, essence, filling, furnish, luggage, objects, rubbish, satiate, squeeze, woollen **08** articles, compress, garrison, gross out, material, nonsense, obstruct, stuffing **09** equipment, furniture, materials, provision, substance **10** belongings, gormandize **11** overindulge, possessions **13** paraphernalia

stuffing
◊ *containment indicator*
◊ *hidden indicator*
05 farce, kapok **07** bombast, farcing, filling, packing, padding, pudding, wadding **08** dressing, quilting, stopping **09** deafening, forcemeat, taxidermy

stuffy
04 dull, prim **05** close, fuggy, fusty, heavy, muggy, musty, staid, stale, stiff, stivy, stout, sulky **06** dreary, frowsy, frowzy, poking, stodgy, sturdy, sultry **07** airless, pompous, starchy **08** stifling **10** fuddy-duddy, oppressive **11** strait-laced, suffocating **12** buttoned-down, conventional, old-fashioned, unventilated **13** uninteresting

stultify
04 dull, numb **05** blunt **06** negate, stifle, thwart **07** nullify, smother, stupefy **08** hebetate, suppress **10** invalidate

stumble
◊ *anagram indicator*
03 err **04** fall, peck, reel, slip, trip **05** lapse, lurch, stoit **06** falter, hamble **07** blunder, founder, snapper, stagger, stammer, stotter, stutter **08** flounder, hesitate, titubate **09** false step **10** disconcert **15** lose your balance

• **stumble across, stumble on**
04 find **08** discover **09** encounter **10** chance upon, come across, happen upon

stumbling-block
03 bar **04** snag **06** hurdle **07** barrier, scandal **08** obstacle **09** hindrance **10** difficulty, impediment **11** obstruction **12** Becher's Brook

stump
03 end, leg, nog, peg **04** butt, dare, foil, more, runt, snag, stob, stub, stud **05** floor, scrag, stock, stool, trunk **06** baffle, defeat, dog-end, fag end, outwit, puzzle, wicket **07** confuse, flummox, mystify, nonplus, perplex, remains, remnant, staddle, stubble **08** bewilder, confound **09** bamboozle, challenge, dumbfound, tortillon

• **stump up**
03 pay **05** pay up **06** ante up, chip in, donate, pay out **07** cough up, fork out **08** hand over, shell out **10** contribute

stumped
02 st **05** stuck **07** baffled, floored, stymied **09** flummoxed, perplexed **10** bamboozled, nonplussed

stumpy
04 cash **05** dumpy, heavy, nirly, short, squat, thick **06** chunky, nirlie, stocky, stubby **07** stubbed **08** thickset

stun
02 KO **04** daze, kayo **05** amaze, devel, dover, knock, shock, stonn, stoun, Taser® **06** abrade, bruise, deafen, devvel, settle, stonne, stound **07** astound, confuse, stagger, stupefy **08** astonish, bedeafen, bewilder, bowl over, confound, knock out, overcome **09** dumbfound, overpower **11** flabbergast, knock for six

stunned
04 numb **05** dazed, silly **06** aghast, amazed, stupid **07** floored, in a daze, shocked **09** astounded, staggered, stupefied **10** astonished, devastated,

gobsmacked **11** dumbfounded
13 flabbergasted

stunner

02 KO **03** wow **05** peach, siren
06 beauty, looker, lovely **07** charmer,
cracker, dazzler, smasher **08** knockout
09 sensation **10** eye-catcher, good-
looker, heart-throb **11** femme fatale

stunning

05 great **06** dazing, lovely **07** amazing
08 dazzling, drop-dead, fabulous,
gorgeous, smashing, striking
09 beautiful, brilliant, ravishing,
wonderful **10** impressive, incredible,
marvellous, remarkable, staggering,
stupefying **11** sensational, spectacular
12 stupefaction **13** extraordinary

stunningly

09 amazingly **10** fabulously,
gorgeously, remarkably, strikingly
11 beautifully, brilliantly, wonderfully
12 impressively, marvellously,
staggeringly **13** spectacularly
15 extraordinarily

stunt

03 act **04** curb, deed, feat, hype, nirl,
ramp, slow, stop, turn **05** check, dwarf,
stock, trick **06** action, arrest, hamper,
hinder, impede, retard, wheeze
07 exploit, inhibit **08** restrict
10 enterprise **11** performance

stunted

04 puny, tiny **05** nirly, small **06** little,
nirlie **07** dwarfed, scroggy, scrubby
08 dwarfish, scroggie, scrubbed,
withered **10** diminutive, undersized,
wanthriven

stupefaction

04 daze **06** wonder **08** blackout,
numbness, stunning **09** amazement
10 amazedness, bafflement
12 astonishment, bewilderment, state
of shock **13** senselessness

stupefy

04 daze, drug, dull, mull, numb, stun
05 amaze, dozen, hocus, shock
06 bemuse, benumb, drowse, fuddle,
mither, moider **07** astound, mother,
stagger **08** bowl over, etherize, knock
out, somniate **09** devastate,
dumbfound **11** knock for six

stupendous

04 huge, vast **06** killer, superb
07 amazing, immense **08** colossal,
enormous, fabulous, gigantic, stunning
09 fantastic, wonderful **10** astounding,
marvellous, phenomenal, prodigious,
staggering, tremendous
12 breathtaking, overwhelming
13 extraordinary

stupid

◇ *anagram indicator*
03 dim, jay, mad, twp **04** dopy, dull,
dumb, rash, slow **05** barmy, brute,
crass, crazy, dazed, dense, divvy,
dopey, doted, dovie, dunny, flaky,
foggy, goofy, gross, inane, looby, loony,
loopy, muddy, potty, silly, stupe, thick

06 absurd, boring, bovine, donsie,
facile, futile, groggy, lumpen, owlish,
tavert, wooden **07** damfool, doltish,
donnard, donnart, donnerd, donnert,
fatuous, foolish, glaiket, glaikit, idiotic,
insulse, lunatic, moronic, puerile,
stunned, taivert, witless **08** anserine,
backward, besotted, blockish,
Boeotian, boobyish, clueless,
donnered, gaumless, gormless,
mindless, sluggish **09** brainless, fat-
witted, foolhardy, half-assed, imbecilic,
laughable, ludicrous, pointless,
senseless, stupefied **10** beef-witted,
dull-witted, fatbrained, half-witted, ill-
advised, indiscreet, insensible **11** beef-
brained, blunt-witted, clay-brained,
conceitless, hair-brained, hare-
brained, heavy-headed, injudicious,
meaningless, nonsensical, not all there,
thickheaded, unconscious **12** feeble-
minded, hammer-headed,
muttonheaded, simple-minded,
sodden-witted, thick-skulled,
woodenheaded **13** chuckle-headed,
irresponsible, pudding-headed,
semiconscious, thick as a plank
15 slow on the uptake

stupidity

05 folly **06** bêtise, idiocy, lunacy,
torpor **07** dimness, duncery, fatuity,
goosery, inanity, madness, naivety
08 dopiness, doziness, dullness,
dumbness, futility, insanity, rashness,
slowness **09** absurdity, asininity,
bruteness, crassness, denseness,
insulsity, oscitancy, puerility, silliness,
thickness **10** crassitude, imbecility,
ineptitude, obtuseness **11** fatuousness,
foolishness, glaikitness **12** indiscretion
13 brainlessness, foolhardiness,
ludicrousness, pointlessness,
senselessness **14** impracticality

• **expression of stupidity**
03 doh, duh

stupidly

◇ *anagram indicator*
07 inanely, sillily **08** absurdly
09 fatuously, foolishly **10** mindlessly
12 unthinkingly **13** irresponsibly

stupor

04 coma, daze **06** torpor, trance
07 inertia **08** blackout, lethargy,
numbness, oblivion **12** state of shock,
stupefaction **13** insensibility
15 unconsciousness

sturdy

03 gid **04** dunt, firm **05** burly, giddy,
hardy, husky, rough, solid, stout
06 hearty, mighty, robust, rugged,
steeve, stieve, stocky, strong, stuffy
07 durable, staunch, violent
08 athletic, lubberly, muscular,
powerful, resolute, stalwart, turnsick,
vigorous, well-made **09** impetuous,
obstinate, steadfast, tenacious, well-
built **10** determined, refractory
11 flourishing, substantial

sturgeon

04 huso **05** elops **06** beluga, ellops

07 osseter, sevruga, sterlet
10 shovelnose

stutter

04 lisp **06** falter, mumble **07** sputter,
stammer, stumble **08** hesitate, splutter
12 speech defect

style

◇ *anagram indicator*
03 cut, dub, pen, tag, way **04** call, chic,
dash, form, hand, kind, make, mode,
name, sort, term, tone, type, vein
05 adapt, flair, genre, index, label,
shape, taste, tenor, title, trend, vogue
06 custom, design, gnomon, luxury,
manner, method, phrase, polish, tailor,
wealth **07** address, comfort, diction,
entitle, fashion, panache, pattern,
pointel, pointer, produce, variety,
wording **08** approach, category,
elegance, grandeur, language,
phrasing, urbanity **09** affluence,
designate, smartness, suaveness,
technique **10** appearance,
denominate, dressiness, expression,
refinement **11** flamboyance,
methodology, stylishness
14 sophistication

• **in the style of**
03 à la **05** after, -esque

stylish

03 fly **04** chic, posh **05** janty, natty,
nifty, ritzy, sharp, showy, smart, swish
06 chichi, classy, dressy, jaunty, modish,
snappy, snazzy, sporty, trendy, urbane
07 à la mode, dashing, elegant, in
vogue, refined, voguish **08** polished
11 fashionable **13** sophisticated

stylus

03 gad, pen **04** hand **05** index, probe,
style **06** needle **07** pointer
08 graphium

stymie

04 balk, foil **05** stump **06** baffle,
defeat, hamper, hinder, hogtie,
impede, puzzle, thwart **07** flummox,
mystify, nonplus, snooker **08** confound
09 bamboozle, frustrate, interfere

styptic

06 amadou, matico, stanch **07** staunch
10 astringent **11** haemostatic

suave

04 glib **05** bland, civil **06** polite,
smooth, urbane **07** affable, refined,
worldly **08** charming, debonair,
polished, unctuous **09** agreeable,
civilized, courteous **10** soft-spoken
13 sophisticated

suavity

05 charm **08** civility, courtesy, urbanity
09 blandness **10** politeness,
refinement, smoothness
11 worldliness **12** agreeability,
unctuousness **14** sophistication

sub

04 dues, gift, lend, temp **05** agent,
locum, proxy, U-boat **06** deputy, fill-in,
relief, supply **07** advance, payment,
reserve, stand-by, stand-in, stopgap

08 donation, offering **09** makeshift, surrogate **10** substitute, understudy **11** locum tenens, pinch-hitter, replacement **12** contribution, subscription **13** membership fee

subaquatic
07 subaqua **08** demersal, undersea **09** submarine, submersed **10** subaqueous, underwater

subatomic particle *see* **particle**

subconscious
02 id **03** ego **04** deep, mind **05** inner **06** hidden, latent, psyche **08** super-ego **09** innermost, inner self, intuitive, repressed **10** inner being, subliminal, suppressed, underlying **11** instinctive, unconscious **15** unconscious self

subcontract
07 farm out **08** delegate **09** outsource **11** contract out **12** give to others, pass to others

subdue
03 cow **04** adaw, damp, mate, tame **05** accoy, allay, break, charm, check, crush, daunt, quail, quash, quell **06** defeat, do down, humble, master, mellow, pacify, reduce, soften, starve, step on, stifle, subact, subdew, take in **07** achieve, chasten, conquer, control, crucify, daunton, mortify, overrun, quieten, repress, subject **08** chastise, moderate, overcome, restrain, suppress, vanquish **09** overpower, soft-pedal, subjugate **10** bring under, discipline **12** put a damper on **14** get the better of **15** gain mastery over

subdued
03 dim, sad **04** soft **05** grave, muted, quiet, sober, still **06** abated, hushed, low-key, pastel, shaded, silent, solemn, sombre, subtle **07** captive, passive, serious, submiss **08** dejected, delicate, downcast, lifeless, softened **09** depressed, noiseless, toned-down, unexcited **10** restrained **11** crestfallen, unobtrusive **13** irrepressible **14** down in the dumps

subject
03 apt, put, sub **04** case, open, subj **05** bound, field, issue, liege, motif, point, prone, theme, thirl, topic **06** affair, aspect, client, expose, ground, liable, likely, matter, native, subdew, subdue, submit, vassal, victim **07** caitive, captive, citizen, exposed, hanging, lay open, patient, resting, servant, servile **08** amenable, business, disposed, inferior, liegeman, national, obedient, question, resident **09** dependant, dependent, depending, guinea pig, subjugate, substance, underling **10** answerable, cognizable, contingent, discipline, inhabitant, subjugated, submissive, underlying, vulnerable **11** accountable, area of study, conditional, constrained, participant, subordinate, subservient, susceptible **12** field of study

See also **study**

subjection
06 chains, defeat **07** bondage, mastery, slavery **08** exposure, question, shackles **09** captivity, servitude, vassalage **10** discipline, domination, oppression **11** enslavement, subjugation

subjective
06 biased **07** bigoted **08** personal **09** emotional, intuitive **10** individual, nominative, prejudiced **11** instinctive **13** idiosyncratic, introspective

subjugate
04 tame **05** crush, quell **06** defeat, master, reduce, subdue, thrall **07** conquer, enslave, oppress **08** overcome, suppress, vanquish **09** overpower, overthrow **14** get the better of **15** gain mastery over

sublimate
04 turn **05** exalt **06** divert, purify, refine **07** alcohol, channel, elevate, flowers **08** heighten, redirect, transfer **09** transmute

sublime
04 high **05** exalt, grand, great, lofty, noble, utter **06** august, winged **07** Dantean, exalted, extreme, intense, supreme **08** complete, elevated, empyreal, glorious, heavenly, imposing, majestic **09** celestial, Dantesque, spiritual **10** majestical **11** magnificent **12** transcendent

subliminal
06 hidden **09** concealed **11** unconscious **12** subconscious, subthreshold

submarine
03 sub **05** U-boat **06** hoagie, X-craft **07** pigboat

submerge
03 dip **04** bury, dive, duck, dunk, sink, take **05** drown, flood, swamp, whelm **06** deluge, engulf, go down, plunge **07** conceal, immerse, plummet **08** implunge, indrench, inundate, overflow, submerse, suppress **09** overwhelm **12** go under water **13** put under water

submerged
04 sunk **06** hidden, sunken, unseen, veiled **07** cloaked, drowned, swamped **08** immersed, obscured **09** concealed, inundated, submersed **10** underwater

submission
05 entry **06** assent, tender **07** tabling **08** averment, giving in, meekness, offering, proposal **09** agreement, assertion, deference, obedience, passivity, statement, surrender, tendering **10** compliance, confession, suggestion **11** resignation **12** acquiescence, capitulation, contribution, introduction, presentation, resignedness, subscription **13** subordination **14** submissiveness

submissive
04 meek, weak **06** docile, humble, supine **07** passive, patient, servile, subdued **08** biddable, obedient, resigned, yielding **09** compliant, malleable **10** weak-willed **11** acquiescent, deferential, downtrodden, reverential, subordinate, subservient, unresisting **12** ingratiating, self-effacing **13** accommodating, uncomplaining

submissively
06 humbly, meekly, weakly **09** cap in hand, passively, patiently **10** obediently **13** deferentially, subserviently **15** uncomplainingly

submit
03 bow, put **04** aver, bend, move **05** agree, argue, claim, defer, lower, offer, posit, refer, state, stoop, table, yield **06** accede, assert, comply, expose, give in, permit, prefer, render, resign, send in, tender **07** consent, give way, lay down, passage, present, proffer, propose, subject, succumb, suggest, violate **08** propound **09** acquiesce, introduce, lay before, subscribe, surrender **10** bow the knee, capitulate, come to heel, kiss the rod, put forward **11** bend the knee, come to terms, subordinate **12** knuckle under **13** bite the bullet **15** lay down your arms

subnormal
03 low **04** slow **08** backward, inferior, retarded **11** below normal **12** below average, feeble-minded

subordinate
◇ *juxtaposition down indicator* **04** aide **05** lower, lowly, minor, under **06** deputy, junior, lesser, menial, second, skivvy, stooge, submit, vassal **07** subject **08** dogsbody, inferior, marginal, offsider, servient, sidekick **09** ancillary, assistant, attendant, auxiliary, dependant, dependent, secondary, subaltern, underling **10** submissive, subsidiary, underlying **11** lower in rank, subservient **12** lower-ranking, second fiddle **14** understrapping

subordination
09 servitude **10** dependence, subjection, submission **11** inferiority **12** subservience

subscribe
04 back, give, sign, take **05** agree **06** answer, assent, chip in, donate, pledge, submit **07** approve, endorse, fork out, support **08** advocate, shell out, sign up to **10** contribute, underwrite **12** buy regularly **13** take regularly **15** pay for regularly

subscriber
06 member **08** customer **13** regular reader

subscription
04 dues, gift **06** assent **07** payment **08** donation, offering, sanction

09 signature **10** abonnement, submission **11** endorsement **12** contribution **13** membership fee

subsequent
04 next **05** later **06** future **07** ensuing **09** following, resulting **10** consequent, succeeding **12** postliminary

subsequently
05 after, later **09** afterward **10** afterwards **12** consequently

subservience
08 humility **09** deference, obedience, servility, servitude **10** subjection **11** dutifulness **12** acquiescence **13** subordination **14** submissiveness

subservient
05 lower, minor **06** junior, lesser **07** fawning, servile, slavish, subject **08** inferior, toadying, unctuous **09** ancillary, auxiliary, dependent, secondary **10** obsequious, submissive, subserving, subsidiary **11** bootlicking, deferential, subordinate, sycophantic **12** ingratiating, instrumental, subalternate **13** less important

subside
03 ebb **04** adaw, drop, ease, fall, lull, sink, wane **05** abate, let up, lower, quell, slake, sound, swoon, swoun **06** cave in, lessen, quench, recede, settle, swound **07** assuage, decline, descend, die down, dwindle, founder, quieten, slacken **08** collapse, decrease, diminish, dissolve, get lower, moderate, peter out, pipe down

subsidence
03 ebb, sag **04** swag **07** decline, descent, sinking **08** collapse, decrease, settling **09** abatement, lessening **10** diminution, settlement, slackening **12** de-escalation, detumescence

subsidiary
02 by **03** bye **04** part, side, wing **05** minor **06** aiding, branch, feeder, lesser **07** section **08** division, offshoot **09** accessory, adjective, affiliate, ancillary, assistant, auxiliary, secondary, succursal **10** additional, collateral, supporting **11** subordinate, subservient **12** contributory **13** supplementary

subsidize
03 aid **04** back, fund **07** endorse, finance, promote, sponsor, support **08** invest in **10** underwrite **12** contribute to **14** give a subsidy to

subsidy
03 aid **04** help **05** grant **07** backing, finance, funding, headage, support **09** allowance **10** assistance, investment, subvention **11** endorsement, sponsorship **12** contribution, underwriting

subsist
04 last, live **05** exist **06** endure, remain **07** consist, hold out, survive **08** continue

subsistence
04 food, keep **06** living **07** aliment, rations, support **08** survival **09** existence **10** livelihood, provisions, sustenance **11** continuance, maintenance, nourishment

substance
03 sum **04** body, gist, mass, meat, pith, quid, text **05** basis, being, force, means, money, power, stuff, theme, topic, truth **06** amount, assets, burden, entity, fabric, ground, import, matter, medium, riches, wealth, weight **07** essence, fortune, meaning, reality, subject **08** material, property, solidity, validity **09** actuality, affluence, influence, marijuana, resources **10** foundation, prosperity **11** consistence, consistency, materiality, tangibility **12** concreteness, corporeality, significance **13** subject matter **14** meaningfulness

substandard
04 poor **05** crook **06** shoddy **07** damaged **08** below par, inferior **09** imperfect **10** inadequate, second-rate **12** unacceptable **14** not up to scratch

substantial
03 big **04** firm, hard, main, real, rich, tidy, true **05** ample, basic, bulky, great, large, solid, sound, stout, tough **06** actual, hearty, pretty, stable, strong, sturdy **07** central, durable, filling, notable, primary, sizable, wealthy, weighty **08** affluent, cast-iron, concrete, enduring, existing, generous, inherent, material, powerful, sizeable, tangible, valuable, well-to-do **09** corporeal, essential, heavy-duty, important, intrinsic, principal, well-built **10** meaningful, measurable, prosperous, remarkable, successful, worthwhile **11** fundamental, influential, significant **12** considerable

substantially
06 mainly **07** at heart, largely **08** in effect **09** in the main **10** materially **11** essentially **12** considerably **13** fundamentally, significantly **14** to a great extent

substantiate
05 prove **06** back up, embody, uphold, verify **07** bear out, confirm, support **08** validate **11** corroborate **12** authenticate

substantive
02 sb **04** noun, real **05** solid, subst, valid **07** factual **08** concrete, material **09** intrinsic **11** fundamental, substantial

substitute
03 sub **04** -ette, heir, lieu, swap, temp **05** agent, cover, locum, proxy, vicar **06** acting, change, deputy, double, ersatz, fill in, fill-in, relief, supply, switch **07** commute, fig leaf, relieve, replace, reserve, stand-by, stand in, stand-in, stopgap **08** deputize, exchange, replacer, take over **09** alternate,

makeshift, prorector, subrogate, surrogate, temporary **10** changeling, proproctor, understudy, use instead **11** alternative, interchange, locum tenens, pinch-hitter, replacement **12** act instead of **14** take the place of

substitution
04 swap **06** change, switch **08** exchange, novation, swapping **09** switching **10** delegation, innovation, resolution **11** interchange, replacement

subsume
03 add **04** hold **05** add in, admit, cover, enter, put in **06** embody, insert, take in **07** contain, count in, embrace, enclose, include, swallow **08** comprise, take over **09** encompass, introduce **10** comprehend **11** incorporate

subterfuge
04 hole, ploy, ruse, wile **05** dodge, trick **06** excuse, refuge, scheme **07** evasion, off-come, pretext **08** artifice, intrigue, pretence **09** creep-hole, deception, duplicity, expedient, manoeuvre, stratagem **11** deviousness, machination

subtle
◊ *anagram indicator*
03 sly **04** deep, fine, mild, nice, wily **05** faint **06** artful, astute, clever, crafty, low-key, minute, shrewd, slight, subtil, suttle, tricky **07** complex, cunning, devious, elusive, implied, refined, tactful, tenuous **08** abstruse, delicate, dextrous, discreet, indirect, profound, rarefied, ticklish **09** dexterous, insidious, intricate, sophistic, strategic, toned-down **10** impalpable, indefinite, indistinct, scholastic **11** overrefined, sophistical, understated **13** sophisticated **14** discriminating

subtlety
05 guile, skill **06** acumen, nicety, nuance **07** cunning, finesse, quillet, slyness **08** delicacy, sagacity, wiliness **09** acuteness, faintness, intricacy, mutedness, suttletie **10** artfulness, astuteness, cleverness, craftiness, refinement **11** deviousness, discernment **14** discrimination, indefiniteness, indistinctness, sophistication

subtly
◊ *anagram indicator*
05 slyly **06** mildly, suttly **07** faintly **08** artfully, astutely, cleverly **09** cunningly, deviously, tenuously **10** indirectly **11** deceitfully **12** indefinitely, indistinctly

subtract
04 dock, take **05** debit **06** deduct, remove **07** detract **08** diminish, take away, withdraw, withhold

suburb
04 burb **08** banlieue, faubourg, purlieus, suburbia **09** dormitory, outskirts **12** commuter belt

13 bedroom suburb, dormitory town **15** dormitory suburb, residential area

suburban
04 dull **06** narrow **07** insular **08** commuter **09** bourgeois, parochial **10** provincial **11** middle-class, residential **12** conventional, narrow-minded **13** unimaginative **14** common-or-garden

subversive
07 riotous, traitor **08** quisling **09** dissident, seditious, terrorist, weakening **10** disruptive, incendiary, traitorous, treasonous **11** destructive, seditionist, treacherous, undermining **12** discrediting, inflammatory, troublemaker **13** revolutionary, troublemaking **14** fifth columnist, freedom fighter

subvert
04 raze, ruin **05** upset, wreck **06** debase, poison **07** corrupt, deprave, destroy, disrupt, pervert, vitiate **08** confound, demolish, overthrow, sabotage **09** overthrow, undermine **10** demoralize, invalidate **11** contaminate

subway
04 dive, tube **05** metro **06** tunnel **09** underpass **11** underground

succeed
04 fare, work **05** cut it, ensue, fadge, get on, reach, speed **06** answer, attain, come on, do well, follow, fulfil, make it, manage, result, thrive, walk it, win out **07** achieve, crack it, devolve, inherit, make out, prevail, prosper, pull off, realize, replace, triumph, turn out, work out **08** approach, bring off, carry out, complete, flourish, get there, go places, make good, take over **09** come after, win the day **10** accomplish, get results, strike gold, take effect, win through **11** come through, squeeze home **12** be successful, make the grade, steal the show, turn up trumps **13** hit the jackpot **14** fall on your feet, land on your feet, take the place of
• **succeed to**
06 accede, assume **07** inherit, replace **08** come into, take over **09** enter upon, supersede

succeeding
04 next **05** later **06** coming, to come **07** ensuing **09** following **10** hereditary, subsequent, successive

success
02 go, up **03** hit, VIP, win, wow **04** fame, luck, riot, star **05** celeb, fluke, smash **06** bigwig, upshot, winner **07** big name, big shot, fortune, sell-out, triumph, victory **08** eminence, sequence, smash hit, somebody, speeding **09** celebrity, happiness, sensation **10** attainment, bestseller, completion, fulfilment, prosperity, succession **11** achievement, realization **12** box-office hit **13** coup de théâtre, flash in the pan, flying colours

14 accomplishment, positive result
• **expression of success**
03 Jai **05** bingo **06** eureka, hurrah **07** heureka, hey pass **09** hey presto

successful
03 top **05** boffo, lucky, socko **06** famous **07** booming, leading, popular, thriven, wealthy, winning **08** affluent, fruitful, thriving, unbeaten **09** fortunate, lucrative, rewarding, well-known **10** home and dry, productive, profitable, prosperous, riding high, satisfying, triumphant, victorious **11** bestselling, flourishing, moneymaking **12** chart-busting

successfully
04 fine, well **05** great **08** famously **09** feliciter **10** swimmingly **11** beautifully **12** victoriously

succession
03 run **04** flow, line **05** chain, cycle, order, train **06** course, series, string **08** pedigree, sequence **09** accession, attaining, elevation, posterity **10** assumption, procession, survivance **11** continuance, inheritance, progression **12** continuation
• **in succession**
06 in a row, in turn **07** by-and-by, en suite, running **08** seriatim, straight **09** on the trot **12** sequentially, successively **13** consecutively **15** uninterruptedly

successive
06 serial **07** running, sequent **09** following **10** hereditary, sequential, succeeding **11** consecutive

successively
07 running **09** on the trot **12** in succession, sequentially **13** consecutively **15** uninterruptedly

successor
04 heir **05** coarb **06** co-heir, comarb, epigon, relief **07** epigone, khalifa **08** khalifah **09** inheritor, succeeder **10** descendant, next in line, substitute **11** beneficiary, replacement

succinct
05 brief, crisp, pithy, short, terse **07** compact, concise, in a word, summary **08** Laconian **09** condensed **10** to the point **12** close-fitting

succinctly
07 briefly, crisply, in a word, in brief, pithily, tersely **09** compactly, concisely **10** to the point

succour
03 aid **04** help **05** nurse **06** assist, foster, relief **07** comfort, help out, relieve, support **08** befriend **09** encourage **10** assistance, minister to **11** helping hand **13** ministrations

succulent
04 lush, rich **05** juicy, moist, sappy, tasty **06** cactus, fleshy, mellow **08** ice plant, luscious, spekboom, stapelia **09** echeveria, kalanchoe **11** sempervivum **13** mouthwatering

succumb
03 die **04** fall **05** catch, die of, yield **06** give in, pick up, submit **07** die from, give way **08** collapse, contract **09** surrender **10** capitulate, go down with **12** knuckle under

suck
04 draw, pull **05** drain **06** absorb, blot up, draw in, hoover, imbibe, soak up, sponge, suckle **07** exhaust, extract, suction
• **suck up to**
04 fawn **05** creep, toady **06** grovel **07** flatter, truckle **10** ingratiate **11** curry favour

sucker
03 mug, sap **04** butt, dupe, fool **05** graft, leech, patsy, sweet, toady **06** sponge, stooge, tellar, teller, tiller, victim **07** cat's-paw, muggins, osculum **08** lollipop, parasite, pushover, surculus **10** acetabulum

suckle
04 feed **05** nurse **07** nourish **08** wet-nurse **10** breastfeed

suction
07 sucking **08** draining **09** absorbing, drawing-in **10** extraction

Sudan
03 SDN, SUD

sudden
04 fast, rash, snap **05** ferly, flash, hasty, quick, rapid, sharp, swift **06** abrupt, prompt, speedy **07** hurried, quantum **08** dramatic, meteoric **09** extempore, immediate, impetuous, impulsive, overnight, startling **10** improvised, surprising, unexpected, unforeseen **11** subitaneous **13** instantaneous, unanticipated **15** spur-of-the-moment

suddenly
03 pop **04** slap, swap, swop **05** souse **06** astart, subito **07** asudden, at a blow, quickly, sharply **08** abruptly, unwarely **09** all at once, extempore **11** immediately **12** à l'improviste, all of a sudden, out of the blue, unexpectedly **13** with a siserary **14** at one fell swoop, in one fell swoop, without warning **15** instantaneously

suddenness
05 haste **09** hastiness **10** abruptness **11** hurriedness **13** impulsiveness **14** unexpectedness

suds
04 beer, foam **05** froth **06** lather **07** bubbles **09** soapiness

sue
03 beg **05** court, plead **06** appeal, charge, follow, indict, pursue, summon **07** beseech, entreat, implead, process, solicit **08** petition **09** prosecute **11** beg for a fool, take to court **12** bring to trial

suffer
◊ *anagram indicator*
03 die, let, pay **04** ache, bear, feel,

have, hurt **05** abide, allow, gripe, incur, prove, stand, thole **06** endure, grieve, permit, sorrow **07** agonize, support, sustain, undergo **08** be in pain, meet with, tolerate **09** go through, put up with **10** experience **11** be afflicted

suffering
◇ *anagram indicator*
04 hurt, pain, pine **05** agony, trial **06** misery, ordeal, plight **07** anguish, hurting, passion, torment, torture **08** distress, hardship **09** adversity, afflicted, endurance **10** affliction, discomfort **12** wretchedness

suffice
02 do **05** serve **06** answer **07** content, satisfy **08** be enough **09** measure up **10** be adequate, fit the bill **11** fill the bill **12** be sufficient

sufficiency
05 store **06** enough, plenty **07** satiety **08** adequacy, bellyful **09** abundance **10** competence, competency **11** sufficience **12** adequateness

sufficient
04 enow, good **05** ample **06** decent, enough, plenty **08** adequate **09** competent, effective **12** satisfactory
• **a sufficient quantity**
02 qs **15** quantum sufficit

suffocate
05 choke, smoke, smoor, smore, stive **06** stifle **07** oppress, smother **08** strangle, throttle **10** asphyxiate **12** be breathless **14** make breathless

suffrage
04 vote **06** prayer **08** sanction **09** franchise **11** right to vote **15** enfranchisement

suffuse
03 dip **04** gild **05** bathe, cover, flood, imbue, steep, tinge **06** colour, infuse, mantle, redden, spread **07** pervade **08** permeate **09** transfuse

sugar
03 LSD **05** money, sweet **06** heroin **08** flattery

sugary
05 corny, gushy, mushy, soppy, sweet **06** sickly, sloppy, slushy, syrupy **07** gushing, maudlin, mawkish, sugared **08** touching **09** emotional, schmaltzy, sweetened **10** lovey-dovey, saccharine **11** sentimental

suggest
04 hint, move, vote **05** evoke, float, imply, smack, smell, table, tempt **06** advise, allude, hint at, prompt, savour, submit **07** connote, counsel, present, propose, smack of, smell of **08** advocate, envisage, indicate, intimate, nominate **09** insinuate, recommend **10** come up with, put forward **11** bring to mind **12** bring forward

suggestion
04 hint, idea, kite, note, plan, ring, wind **05** smack, touch, trace, twang, whiff **06** motion **07** pointer, wrinkle **08** allusion, innuendo, proposal **09** prompting, prompture, suspicion **10** incitement, indication, intimation, submission, temptation **11** implication, insinuation, proposition **12** aesthesiogen **13** piece of advice **14** recommendation

suggestive
04 blue, lewd **05** bawdy, dirty **06** ribald, risqué, sexual, smutty **07** meaning **08** immodest, improper, indecent, redolent **09** evocative, off-colour **10** expressive, indelicate, indicative **11** provocative, reminiscent, stimulating, titillating

suicide
06 suttee **07** seppuku **08** felo de se, hara-kiri, hari-kari **10** self-murder **11** ending it all, parasuicide **12** self-violence **13** happy dispatch, self-slaughter **14** self-immolation **15** killing yourself, self-destruction, topping yourself
• **commit suicide**
08 end it all **11** top yourself **12** do yourself in, kill yourself, take your life **14** commit hari-kari **15** take your own life

suit
03 fit, gee, hit, set **04** case, meet **05** agree, apply, befit, besit, cause, clubs, do for, match, queme, suite, trial **06** action, answer, attire, become, drapes, effeir, effere, hearts, outfit, please, series, spades, square **07** contest, costume, crawler, dispute, fashion, flatter, furnish, gratify, lawsuit, overall, process, provide, pursuit, satisfy, suffice **08** argument, clothing, diamonds, ensemble, petition, sequence, tailleur **09** agree with, courtship, plus fours, tally with **10** complement, fit the bill, go well with, litigation, look good on, qualify for **11** fill the bill, proceedings, prosecution **12** set of clothes **13** be suitable for, harmonize with **14** be acceptable to, be applicable to **15** be convenient for

suitability
07 aptness, fitness **09** congruity, rightness **10** competence, competency, congruence, congruency, timeliness **11** convenience, fittingness **12** appositeness **13** opportuneness **14** correspondence, correspondency **15** appropriateness

suitable
03 apt, due, fit **04** able, good **05** right **06** giusto, liable, proper, seemly, suited **07** fitting **08** adequate, agreeing, all right, apposite, becoming, decorous, relevant **09** agreeable, befitting, competent, congruent, consonant, in keeping, opportune, pertinent **10** acceptable, applicable, compatible, convenient, well-suited **11** appropriate, well-matched **12** satisfactory

suitably
05 fitly, quite **06** as well **08** properly **09** fittingly **10** acceptably **11** accordingly **13** appropriately

suitcase
03 bag **04** case, port **05** trunk **06** valise **07** holdall **09** flight bag, portfolio, travel bag **10** vanity-case **11** attaché case, hand-luggage, portmanteau **12** overnight-bag

suite
03 set **04** flat, tail **05** court, rooms, train **06** ballet, escort, sequel, series **07** partita, retinue **08** chambers, sequence, servants **09** apartment, cassation, entourage, followers, furniture, household, retainers **10** attendants, collection, set of rooms **11** hospitality **12** divertimento

suitor
04 beau **05** lover, swain, wooer **07** admirer **08** follower, young man **09** boyfriend, pretender **10** petitioner, pretendant, pretender **11** detrimental

sulk
03 dod, pet **04** dort, huff, miff, mood, mope, mump, pout **05** boody, brood, grump, pique **06** grouse, temper **07** bad mood **08** be miffed **09** bad temper, be in a huff **13** pull a long face
• **the sulks**
03 pet **04** dods, hump, tout, towt **05** glout, grump **06** glumps, strunt **07** strunts

sulkily
07 crossly, moodily **08** morosely, sullenly **10** grudgingly **11** resentfully

sulky

05 aloof, cross, huffy, humpy, moody, pouty, ratty **06** glumpy, grouty, grumpy, jinker, miffed, moping, morose, put out, stuffy, sullen **07** pettish **08** brooding, grudging, stunkard **09** resentful **10** out of sorts, unsociable **11** bad-tempered, disgruntled **13** gumple-foisted

sullen

04 dark, dour, dull, glum, grim, sour **05** black, cross, heavy, moody, sulky, surly **06** broody, dismal, dogged, gloomy, leaden, morose, silent, solein, sombre **07** lumpish, mumpish **08** churlish, farouche, perverse, stubborn, stunkard **09** cheerless, obstinate, resentful, simpleton **11** black-browed **15** uncommunicative

sullenly

06 glumly, sourly **07** crossly, moodily, sulkily **08** gloomily, morosely **10** churlishly, stubbornly **11** obstinately, resentfully

sullenness

05 gloom **08** brooding, glumness, sourness **09** glowering, heaviness, moodiness, sulkiness, surliness **10** moroseness

sully

03 mar **04** soil, spot **05** dirty, spoil, stain, taint **06** assoil, befoul, damage, darken, defile, smirch, smutch **07** blemish, distain, pollute, tarnish **08** besmirch, disgrace **09** dishonour **11** contaminate

sulphur

01 S **09** brimstone

sultan, sultana

06 despot, fiddle, raisin, sharif, sherif, soldan **07** shereef **08** padishah **09** Grand Turk **12** Grand Signior **13** Grand Seignior

sultanate

04 Oman **06** Brunei

sultry

03 hot **04** sexy **05** close, humid, lurid, muggy, soggy **06** sticky, stuffy **07** airless, sensual, sweltry **08** alluring, stifling, tempting **09** seductive **10** attractive, indelicate, oppressive, passionate, sweltering, voluptuous **11** provocative, suffocating

sum

03 add **05** penny, score, tally, total, whole **06** amount, answer, height, number, result **07** summary **08** entirety, quantity, sum total **09** abatement, aggregate, carry-over, exemplify, reckoning, summarize, summation **10** completion, remittance **11** culmination

- **large sum**
04 pots **11** golden hello **12** a king's ransom, a pretty penny **15** golden handshake
- **small sum**
04 dime **05** groat, penny **08** pittance

- **sum up**
03 add **04** foot, wind **05** close, compt, count, gauge, recap **06** assess, embody, review, size up, upknit **08** conclude, consider, evaluate **09** epitomize, exemplify, inventory, summarize **11** encapsulate **12** recapitulate **14** put in a nutshell

summarily

07 hastily, swiftly **08** abruptly, promptly, speedily **09** forthwith **11** arbitrarily, immediately **12** peremptorily, without delay **13** expeditiously

summarize

03 pot, sum **05** recap, sum up **06** docket, minute, précis, resume, review, sketch **07** abridge, outline, shorten **08** abstract, condense, pirlicue, purlicue **09** epitomize, synopsize **10** abbreviate **11** encapsulate

summary

02 CV **04** curt, plan **05** brief, creed, hasty, recap, short, summa, swift **06** aperçu, digest, direct, docket, précis, prompt, résumé, review, speedy, summar, wrap-up **07** cursory, docquet, epitome, instant, minutes, offhand, outline, rundown, sylloge, tabloid **08** abstract, argument, overview, succinct, synopsis **09** arbitrary, condensed, immediate, summation, summing-up **10** compendium, conspectus, Hitopadesa, main points, memorandum, peremptory **11** abridgement, aide-mémoire, compendious **12** balance-sheet, condensation, without delay **13** bank statement, instantaneous, unceremonious **14** recapitulation **15** abstract of title, curriculum vitae

summerhouse

06 gazebo **08** pavilion **09** belvedere, root house **11** garden-house

summit

◇ *head selection indicator*
03 top **04** acme, acro-, apex, head, peak, pike **05** crest, crown, glory, point, spire, talks **06** apogee, climax, height, vertex, zenith **07** hilltop, meeting **08** pinnacle **09** sublimity **10** conference, discussion **11** culmination, negotiation **12** altaltissimo, consultation

summon

03 bid **04** buzz, call, cite, gong, hail, hist, hoop, page, ring, sist, toll, warn **05** knell, order, rally, rouse, shake, whoop **06** accite, arouse, beckon, call up, demand, drum up, gather, invite, muster, ring up, work up **07** call out, conjure, convene, convent, convoke, history, pluck up, provoke, screw up, send for, trumpet, muster up **08** assemble, mobilize, muster up **09** challenge, preconize, recollect

- **summon up**
05 evoke, rally, rouse **06** arouse,

gather, muster, revive, work up **07** convene, pluck up, screw up **08** assemble, mobilize **09** recollect **10** call to mind

summons

04 call, writ **05** bluey, cital, order, rouse **06** gather, what ho, wo ha ho **07** warning, war note, whistle **08** citation, monition, reveille, subpoena **09** challenge **10** arrière-ban, injunction, invocation **11** clarion call, curtain call **12** gathering-cry **13** parking ticket **14** interpellation

sumptuous

04 dear, rich **05** grand, plush **06** costly, de luxe, lavish, slap-up, superb **07** opulent **08** gorgeous, palatial, princely, splendid **09** expensive, luxurious **11** extravagant, magnificent

sun

01 S **03** day, tan **04** bake, bask, star, year **05** brown, light **07** daystar **08** daylight, eye of day, insolate, sunbathe, sunlight, sunshine

- **sun god**
02 Ra, Re **03** Sol **05** Horus, Surya **06** Apollo, Helios, Tammuz **07** Phoebus

sunbathe

03 sun, tan **04** bake, bask **05** brown **07** sunbake **08** insolate

sunburnt

03 red **05** brown, burnt **07** peeling **08** inflamed **09** blistered **10** blistering **13** weather-beaten

Sunday

01 S **03** Sun

sunder

03 cut **04** chop, part **05** sever, split **06** cleave, divide, sundra, sundri **07** disally, sundari **08** dissever, disunite, separate **09** dissunder

sundry

04 a few, some **06** divers, varied **07** diverse, several, various **08** assorted, separate **09** different **13** miscellaneous

sunk

◇ *anagram indicator*
03 pad **04** bank, deep, lost **06** doomed, failed, in a fix, in a jam, ruined **07** done for **08** finished, knee-deep **09** submerged **10** up the creek, up the spout

sunken

05 drawn, laigh, lower **06** buried, hollow **07** concave, haggard, lowered **08** hollowed, recessed **09** cellarous, depressed, submerged

sunless

04 dark, grey, hazy **05** bleak **06** cloudy, dismal, dreary, gloomy, sombre **08** overcast **09** cheerless **10** depressing

sunlight

03 sun **05** light **08** daylight, sun's rays **12** natural light

sunny

04 fine, glad **05** clear, happy, merry **06** blithe, bouncy, bright, bubbly, cheery, genial, joyful, sunlit **07** beaming, buoyant, hopeful, radiant, smiling, summery **08** cheerful, pleasant, sunshiny **09** brilliant, cloudless, unclouded **10** optimistic **12** light-hearted

sunrise

04 dawn **05** sun-up **06** aurora, orient **07** morning **08** cock-crow, daybreak, daylight **10** break of day, first light **11** crack of dawn

sunset

04 dusk **07** evening, sundown **08** gloaming, twilight **09** nightfall **10** close of day

sup *see* eat; dine

super

03 ace **04** cool, good!, mega, neat **05** brill, great **06** lovely!, superb, wicked **08** glorious, peerless, smashing, terrific, top-notch **09** excellent, matchless, wonderful **10** delightful, marvellous **11** magnificent, outstanding, sensational **12** incomparable

superannuated

03 old **04** aged **06** past it, senile **07** elderly, retired **08** decrepit, moribund, obsolete **10** antiquated **12** pensioned off **13** put out to grass

superb

03 ace **04** fine, neat, posh **05** brill, grand, great, proud **06** choice, lavish **07** haughty **08** clipping, dazzling, fabulous, gorgeous, jim-dandy, smashing, splendid, superior, terrific **09** admirable, brilliant, excellent, exquisite, first-rate, wonderful **10** first-class, impressive, marvellous, remarkable, unrivalled **11** fantabulous, magnificent, outstanding, superlative, unsurpassed **12** breathtaking

supercilious

05 lofty, proud **06** lordly, overly, snooty, snotty, snouty, uppish, uppity **07** haughty, stuck-up **08** arrogant, cavalier, insolent, jumped-up, scornful, superior **09** imperious **10** disdainful, hoity-toity, toffee-nose **11** high-sighted, overbearing, patronizing, toffee-nosed **12** contemptuous, vainglorious **13** condescending

superficial

◊ *containment indicator*

05 hasty, outer **06** casual, facile, slight **07** alleged, cursory, hurried, outside, outward, passing, seeming, shallow, sketchy, surface, trivial **08** apparent, careless, cosmetic, exterior, external, skin-deep, slapdash **09** frivolous, surficial **10** ostensible, peripheral **11** lightweight, perfunctory **13** insignificant **14** one-dimensional

superficiality

09 lightness **10** simplicity, slightness, triviality **11** externality, shallowness **13** frivolousness, worthlessness

superficially

07 outward **08** casually, skin-deep **09** hurriedly, outwardly, seemingly **10** apparently, carelessly, externally, ostensibly **12** on the surface

superfine

03 sup **04** supe **05** super **09** rosewater

superfluity

04 glut **05** extra **06** excess **07** surfeit, surplus **08** pleonasm, plethora **09** overflush, superflux **10** exuberance, overgrowth, redundancy, surplusage **13** excessiveness **14** superabundance

superfluous

05 extra, spare, waste **06** de trop, excess, frilly, otiose **07** surplus, to spare **08** needless, unneeded, unwanted **09** excessive, redundant, remaining **10** excrescent, fifth-wheel, gratuitous, prolixious **11** at a discount, uncalled-for, unnecessary, unwarranted **13** supernumerary

superhuman

03 god **04** hero **05** great **06** bionic, divine, heroic **07** goddess, immense **09** herculean **10** paranormal, phenomenal, prodigious, stupendous **12** supernatural **13** extraordinary, preternatural

superimpose

03 add **05** lay on, put on **07** lay over, overlay **08** transfer **10** overstrike

superintend

03 run **05** steer **06** direct, handle, manage **07** control, inspect, oversee **08** overlook **09** supervise **10** administer **12** be in charge of **13** be in control of

superintendence

04 care **06** charge, survey **07** control, running **08** episcopy, guidance **09** direction, oversight **10** government, inspection, management **11** supervision **12** surveillance **14** administration

superintendent

04 boss, Supt **05** chief, super **06** gaffer, viewer, warden **07** curator, manager **08** curatrix, director, governor, overseer **09** conductor, inspector, intendant **10** controller, provincial, supervisor **13** administrator

superior

03 sup **04** boss, fine, over **05** chief, elder, fancy, lofty, prime, prize, upper **06** better, choice, de luxe, higher, la-di-da, lordly, select, senior, snooty, uppish, uppity **07** foreman, generic, greater, haughty, manager, premium, quality, stuck-up, upstage **08** director, jumped-up, lah-di-dah, overlord, snobbish, top-notch **09** admirable, excellent, exclusive, first-rate, high-class, high-grade, high-toned, paramount, preferred, principal, top-drawer, top-flight, top-sawyer **10** disdainful, first-class, supervisor, unrivalled **11** exceptional, good-quality, high-quality, outstanding, patronizing, pretentious, toffee-nosed **12** higher in rank, supercilious, transcendent **13** condescending, distinguished, par excellence

• **without superior**

04 odal, udal **07** alodial, topless **08** allodial

superiority

04 edge, gree, lead **07** numbers **08** eminence **09** advantage, dominance, supremacy **10** ascendancy, mastership **11** pre-eminence **12** predominance

superlative

03 ace, -est, sup **04** best **05** brill **06** superl **07** highest, supreme **08** greatest, peerless, unbeaten **09** brilliant, excellent, first-rate, matchless **10** consummate, first-class, unbeatable, unrivalled **11** magnificent, outstanding, unsurpassed **12** transcendent, unparalleled

supermarket

08 minimart **09** superette **10** superstore **11** hypermarket **12** cash-and-carry

supernatural

03 fay, fey, fie **05** eerie, magic, weird **06** hidden, mystic, occult **07** ghostly, magical, phantom, psychic, uncanny **08** abnormal, daemonic, daimonic, eldritch, mystical **09** spiritual, unnatural, witchlike **10** miraculous, mysterious, paranormal **12** metaphysical, otherworldly **13** hyperphysical, preternatural **14** transcendental

See also occult

supernumerary

04 orra **05** extra, spare **06** excess **07** surplus **09** excessive, redundant **11** superfluous **13** extraordinary

supersede

04 oust **05** usurp **06** desist, remove **07** discard, refrain, replace, succeed **08** displace, override, set aside, supplant **12** Stellenbosch, take over from **14** take the place of

supersonic transport

03 AST, SST

superstition

04 myth **05** magic **07** fallacy **08** delusion, illusion **10** Aberglaube **11** apotropaism **12** old wives' tale

superstitious

05 false **06** freety, freity **08** delusive, illusory, mythical **10** fallacious, groundless, irrational

supervise

03 run **04** edit **05** guide, nanny, targe, watch **06** direct, handle, manage, umpire **07** conduct, control, inspect, monitor, oversee **08** bear-lead **09** look after, watch over **10** administer, nvigilate **11** keep an eye on, preside over, superintend **12** be in charge of **13** be in control of

supervision
04 care, duty **06** charge **07** control, running **08** guidance **09** direction, oversight **10** inspection, management **11** instruction **12** surveillance **14** administration **15** superintendence

supervisor
04 boss **05** chief **06** umpire, warden **07** foreman, manager, monitor, proctor, steward **08** director, governor, overseer **09** forewoman, inspector, roundsman, spectator **10** brewmaster, foreperson, sheep-biter, toolpusher **11** floorwalker, invigilator **12** floor manager **13** administrator **14** superintendent

supervisory
09 executive **10** managerial, overseeing **11** directorial **14** administrative, superintendent

supine
03 sup **04** flat, idle, lazy, weak **05** bored, inert **06** torpid **07** languid, passive, sloping, upright **08** careless, heedless, inactive, inclined, indolent, listless, resigned, slothful, sluggish **09** apathetic, lethargic, negligent, prostrate, recumbent, spineless **10** horizontal, spiritless **11** indifferent, unresisting **12** uninterested

supper
03 tea **04** mass **05** snack **06** dinner, hawkey, hockey, horkey **07** nagmaal **10** rere-supper **11** aftersupper, evening meal

supplant
04 oust **05** usurp **06** cut out, remove, topple, unseat, uproot **07** pre-empt, replace **08** displace **09** overthrow, supersede **12** take over from **14** take the place of

supple
05 agile, leish, lithe, lofty, wanle **06** limber, pliant, souple, wandle, wannel, whippy **07** bending, elastic, fawning, plastic, pliable, sinuous **08** flexible, graceful, yielding **09** willowish **10** stretching **11** loose-limbed **12** loose-jointed **13** double-jointed

supplement
02 PS **03** eik, eke, SCP, sup, TES, TLS **04** mend, supp **05** add-on, add to, annex, boost, extra, relay, rider, suppl, top up **06** eke out, extend, fill up, insert, make up, sequel, supply **07** augment, codicil, help out, pull-out **08** addendum, addition, additive, appendix, increase, salt lick, schedule **09** Beta fibre, reinforce, sooterkin **10** Beres drops, complement, Incaparina, postscript, suppletion

supplementary
05 added, extra **06** bolt-on, second **07** ripieno **08** attached **09** ancillary,

auxiliary, corollary, expletory, secondary, suppliant **10** additional **12** accompanying **13** complementary

suppliant
07 begging, craving **09** imploring **10** beseeching, entreating **11** importunate, reinforcing **12** supplicating **13** supplementary

supplicant
06 suitor **07** pleader **09** applicant, postulant, suppliant **10** petitioner

supplicate
04 pray **05** plead **06** appeal, invoke **07** beseech, entreat, request, solicit **08** petition

supplication
04 plea, suit **06** appeal, orison, prayer **07** request **08** entreaty, petition, pleading, rogation **10** invocation **11** conjuration, imploration, obsecration **12** solicitation

supplicatory
06 humble **07** begging **09** imploring, precative, precatory **10** beseeching **11** imprecatory, petitioning, postulatory **12** supplicating

supplier
05 donor **06** dealer, seller, vendor **08** provider, retailer **09** connexion, outfitter **10** connection, wholesaler **11** contributor

supply
◇ *anagram indicator*
03 due, fit, gas **04** bank, crop, feed, fill, find, food, fund, give, heap, help, lend, load, mass, pile, sell, temp, wood **05** cache, endew, endow, endue, equip, grant, grist, hoard, indew, indue, labor, plumb, serve, stake, stock, store, yield **06** amount, donate, fit out, labour, occupy, outfit, output, plenty, purvey, source, stores **07** furnish, plenish, produce, proffer, provide, rations, reserve, satisfy, service, victual **08** minister, quantity **09** equipment, materials, reinforce, replenish, reservoir, stockpile **10** contribute, cornucopia, provisions, substitute, supplement **11** necessities **15** cut and come again

support
◇ *juxtaposition down indicator*
03 aid, arm, bra, cup, leg, tee **04** abet, axle, back, base, bear, care, feed, food, fund, help, keep, pier, pole, post, prop, raft, rest, root, skid, stay **05** brace, carry, grant, truss **06** assist, back up, be with, corset, crutch, defend, endure, foster, hold up, pillar, prop up, ratify, relief, second, uphold, verify **07** backing, bear out, bolster, capital, care for, comfort, confirm, defence, endorse, espouse, finance, funding, further, loyalty, nourish, promote, run with, shore up, sponsor, subsidy, sustain, trestle **08** advocate, approval, be behind, befriend, be kind to, buttress, champion, document, donation, espousal, evidence,

maintain, motivate, skeleton, strength, sympathy, underpin, validate **09** bolster up, encourage, look after, patronage, provision, reinforce, subsidize **10** allegiance, assistance, foundation, friendship, motivation, protection, provide for, rally round, strengthen, sustenance, take care of, underwrite, validation **11** corroborate, foundations, maintenance, sponsorship, subsistence **12** authenticate, be in favour of, confirmation, contribute to, contribution, moral support, ratification, substantiate, substructure, underpinning, verification **13** encouragement **14** authentication, be supportive to, give strength to, substantiation, sympathize with **15** give a donation to, take the weight of, tower of strength
• **be supported**
04 live, rest **05** float
• **expression of support**
03 olé

supporter
◇ *juxtaposition down indicator*
03 bra, fan, leg **04** ally, beam, belt, foot, prop **05** angel, donor, stoop, voter **06** braces, friend, helper, patron, pillar, second **07** apostle, booster, partner, sponsor **08** adherent, advocate, champion, co-worker, defender, follower, henchman, janizary, militant, promoter, seconder, upholder **09** apologist, crossbeam **10** ideologist, well-wisher **11** contributor, sympathizer **12** bottle-holder, understander

supporting
03 pro- **06** behind

supportive
06 caring **07** helpful **08** positive **09** attentive, sensitive **10** comforting, reassuring **11** affirmative, encouraging, sympathetic **13** understanding **14** on someone's side

suppose
02 if **03** say **04** take **05** fancy, guess, imply, infer, judge, opine, posit, sepad, think **06** assume, devise, expect, reckon, uphold **07** believe, dare say, imagine, presume, propose, put case, require, surmise, warrant **08** conceive, conclude, consider, perceive **09** calculate, postulate **10** conjecture, presuppose, put the case **11** expectation, hypothesize **14** take for granted

supposed
07 alleged, assumed, feigned, reputed **08** believed, imagined, presumed, putative, reported, rumoured, so-called **11** conjectured **12** hypothetical **14** supposititious
• **supposed to**
07 meant to **09** obliged to **10** expected to, intended to, required to

supposedly
09 allegedly **10** apparently, ostensibly,

putatively, reportedly **13** by all accounts

supposing that
02 if

supposition
02 if **04** idea **05** guess **06** notion, theory **07** fiction, opinion, surmise **10** assumption, conjecture, hypothesis **11** postulation, presumption, speculation **14** presupposition

suppress
04 kill, sink, stay, stop **05** burke, check, choke, crush, elide, mince, quash, quell, sit on **06** cancel, censor, hold in, hush up, ravish, squash, stifle, subdue **07** conceal, contain, control, cushion, inhibit, put down, repress, silence, sit upon, smother, squelch **08** black out, blank out, block out, gulp back, gulp down, hold back, moderate, restrain, stamp out, strangle, submerge, throttle, vanquish, vote down, withhold **09** choke back, choke down **10** put an end to **11** clamp down on, crack down on, keep in check, strangulate **14** knock on the head, put the tin hat on, put the tin lid on

suppression
05 check **07** cover-up, elision **08** blackout, crushing, ischuria, quashing, quelling, stoppage **09** clampdown, crackdown, epistasis **10** censorship, ecthlipsis, extinction, inhibition, smothering **11** comstockery, concealment, dissolution, elimination, prohibition, termination

suppurate
04 ooze, weep **06** fester, gather **08** maturate **09** discharge

suppuration
03 pus **09** diapyesis, festering, mattering, pyorrhoea

supremacy
04 rule, sway **05** power **07** control, mastery, primacy **08** dominion, hegemony, lordship, regalism **09** dominance **10** ascendancy, domination **11** paramountcy, pre-eminence, sovereignty **12** predominance

supreme
03 sup, top **04** best, head, last, Supr **05** chief, final, first, grand, prime **06** sudder, utmost **07** extreme, highest, leading, sublime **08** crowning, foremost, greatest, imperial, peerless, ultimate **09** excellent, first-rate, matchless, paramount, principal, sovereign **10** consummate, first-class, pre-eminent, prevailing **11** culminating, predominant, superlative, unsurpassed **12** incomparable, second-to-none, transcendent, world-beating

supremely
04 very **06** highly, really **07** acutely, greatly, utterly **08** severely **09** decidedly, extremely, intensely,

unusually **10** remarkably, thoroughly, uncommonly **11** exceedingly, excessively, sovereignly **12** inordinately, terrifically **13** exceptionally **15** extraordinarily

sure
02 OK **03** yes **04** fast, fine, firm, okay, safe **05** bound, clear, loyal, pakka, pucka, pukka, right, sewer, solid **06** agreed, indeed, secure, siccar, sicker, stable, steady, tested **07** assured, certain, decided, precise **08** accurate, all right, definite, faithful, of course, positive, reliable, sure-fire, unerring, very well **09** certainly, confident, convinced, effective, foolproof, steadfast, undoubted, unfailing **10** dependable, guaranteed, home and dry, inevitable, infallible, sure-footed, undeniable, unwavering **11** efficacious, irrevocable, trustworthy, undoubtedly, unfaltering **12** indisputable, never-failing, safe as houses, unmistakable **14** unquestionable

• for sure
06 indeed **07** clearly, plainly **09** certainly, obviously **10** absolutely, definitely, for certain, positively, undeniably **11** indubitably, undoubtedly **12** unmistakably, without doubt **13** categorically **14** unquestionably **15** without question

• make sure
04 look **05** check **06** assure, ensure, insure, secure, verify **07** betroth, confirm **09** ascertain, guarantee **11** make certain

• make sure of having
03 see

surely
05 syker **06** firmly, safely, siccar, sicker **07** no doubt **09** assuredly, certainly **10** definitely, inevitably, inexorably **11** confidently, doubtlessly, indubitably, undoubtedly **12** without doubt **14** unquestionably

surety
04 bail, bond **06** borrow, pledge, safety **07** caution, deposit, hostage, sponsor, warrant **08** bondsman, security, warranty **09** assurance, cautioner, certainty, frithborh, guarantee, guarantor, indemnity, insurance, mortgagor, safeguard **10** undertaker

surface
03 top **04** area, face, rise, side, skin **05** arise, outer, plane **06** appear, come up, emerge, façade, veneer **07** outside, outward **08** aerofoil, apparent, covering, exterior, external, reappear **11** come to light, materialize, superficial

• on the surface
04 upon **09** seemingly **10** apparently, externally, ostensibly **13** at first glance, superficially

surfeit
04 cram, fill, glut, staw **05** gorge, stall,

stuff **06** excess, gutful **07** gorging, satiate, satiety, surplus **08** bellyful, cloyment, gluttony, overcloy, overfeed, overfill, plethora **09** repletion, satiation **11** overfulness, repleteness, superfluity **14** overindulgence, superabundance

surge
03 jaw **04** eddy, flow, gush, jerk, pour, rise, roll, rush, wave **05** break, heave, spike, sweep, swell, swirl, waves, whelm **06** billow, efflux, roller, seethe, stream, upgush, uprush, wallow, welter **07** breaker, pouring, redound, upsurge, upswing **08** escalate, increase **09** transient **10** escalation **15** intensification

surgeon
02 BS, ch, CM, DS, MS **03** BCh, ChB, ChM, DCh, LCh, MCh, vet **04** surg **05** LChir **06** doctor, extern, intern **07** externe, interne **08** orthopod, sawbones **09** trephiner **10** chirurgeon **11** lithotomist **12** lithotritist **13** lithotriptist **14** lithontriptist

See also **doctor**; **medical**

• sea surgeon
04 tang **06** doctor **10** doctor-fish

surgery
03 ops

thyroidectomy, tonsillectomy
14 appendicectomy, coronary bypass, pancreatectomy, reconstructive
15 cholecystectomy, thoracocentesis

Surgery-related terms include:

02 op
04 CABG, seam
05 couch, curet, donor, graft, stoma, taxis, truss
06 canula, domino, dossil, garrot, hobday, lancet, post-op, reduce, stitch, trepan, trocar
07 cannula, catling, curette, forceps, garotte, myotome, operate, scalpel, section, theatre, torsion
08 ablation, adhesion, bistoury, cannular, capeline, centesis, clinical, compress, cosmesis, crow-bill, curarine, écraseur, garrotte, incision, incisure, invasive, trephine
09 abduction, autograft, cannulate, capelline, collodion, crow's-bill, curettage, depressor, dermatome, diastasis, enucleate, operation, osteotome, piggyback, resection, retractor, tamponade, tamponage, tenaculum
10 deligation, diorthosis, discussion, guillotine, lithotrite, lithotrity, osteoclast
11 anaesthetic, arthrodesis, autoplastic, cannulation, curettement, decapsulate, exteriorize, incarnation, laparoscope, lithotripsy, lithotritor, prosthetics
12 fenestration, lithotripter, lithotriptor, lunar caustic, paracentesis, scarificator, short circuit, tissue-typing
13 cyclodialysis, decompression, herniorrhaphy, operating room, post-operative, premedication, under the knife
14 embryo transfer, operating table

surgical *see* **medical**

Suriname
03 SME, SUR

surly
04 grum **05** bluff, cross, cynic, gruff, gurly, stoor, stour, sture, sulky, testy **06** crusty, grumpy, morose, stowre, sullen **07** brusque, crabbed, cynical, grouchy, haughty, uncivil **08** churlish **09** crotchety, irascible **10** ill-natured, refractory, ungracious **11** bad-tempered **12** cantankerous

surmise
04 idea **05** fancy, guess, infer, opine **06** assume, deduce, notion **07** imagine, opinion, presume, suppose, suspect, thought **08** conclude, consider **09** deduction, inference, speculate, suspicion **10** allegation, assumption, conclusion, conjecture, hypothesis **11** possibility, presumption, speculation, supposition

surmount
03 top **04** rise, rush **05** crest **06** breast,

exceed, master **07** conquer, get over, surpass **08** overcome, superate, vanquish **09** transcend **11** prevail over, triumph over

surpass
03 cap, top **04** bang, beat, ding, pass, whap, whop **05** excel, outdo, outgo **06** better, exceed, overgo **07** eclipse, outbrag, outpeer, overtop, paragon, put down **08** go beyond, outclass, outrival, outshine, outstrip, surmount, underlay **09** transcend **10** overshadow, tower above **12** beat to sticks, leave for dead **13** knock spots off

surpassing
04 rare **07** corking, supreme, topping **08** frabjous **09** bettering, exceeding, matchless **10** inimitable, phenomenal, unrivalled **11** exceptional, outstanding, unsurpassed **12** incomparable, transcendent **13** extraordinary

surplice
04 sark **05** cotta, ephod, stole **06** rochet

surplus
04 glut, over, plus **05** extra, spare **06** excess, unused **07** balance, o'ercome, overage, residue, surfeit **08** left over, overcome, overplus, owrecome, wine lake **09** carry-over, leftovers, redundant, remainder, remaining **11** superfluity, superfluous

surprise
03 wow **04** drop, find, stun **05** alert, amaze, seize, shock, start **06** dismay, expose, unmask, wonder **07** astound, confuse, find out, nonplus, stagger, startle **08** astonish, bewilder, blow away, bowl over **09** amazement, bombshell, burst in on, curveball, surprisal, take aback **10** disconcert, revelation, wonderment **11** flabbergast, incredulity, knock for six, thunderbolt **12** astonishment, bewilderment **13** catch in the act, catch unawares **14** catch red-handed **15** bolt from the blue

• **expression of surprise**
01 O **02** ah, eh, ha, ho, my, oh **03** aha, coo, cor, gee, god, hah, hoa, hoh, law, lor, man, oho, ooh, ook, say, wow **04** dear, egad, gosh, hech, igad, I say, Jeez, lawk, lord, losh, odso, phew, well, what, whew, yike **05** arrah, blimy, fancy, gadso, glory, godso, golly, hallo, hello, hullo, Jeeze, Jesus, lawks, lordy, lumme, lummy, ma foi, mercy, musha, my God, my hat, never, wowee, yikes, zowie **06** blimey, by Jove, Christ, cricky, crikey, cripes, crumbs, dear me, gemini, geminy, gemony, heaven, indeed, jiminy, my word, oh dear, wheugh, whoops, zounds **07** bless me, brother, caramba, cravens, crickey, crimine, crimini, crivens, deary me, gee whiz, glory be, good-now, heavens, jeepers, stone me, too much **08** crivvens, dearie me, good-lack, goodness, gorblimy, gracious, I declare, man alive, stroll on, well well **09** blood

oath, cor blimey, fancy that, good grief, gorblimey, I never did, Jesus wept, mercy on us, son of a gun **10** conscience, gracious me, Great Scott, hell's bells, hell's teeth, hoity-toity, upon my soul, upon my word, well I never **11** bless my soul, good heavens, to think of it **12** good gracious, heavens above, my conscience, strike a light, well I declare **13** Gordon Bennett, just think of it, stone the crows **14** it's a small world **15** jeepers creepers

surprised
05 agape **06** amazed **07** shocked, stunned **08** jiggered, startled **09** astounded, staggered **10** astonished, gobsmacked, nonplussed, speechless **11** dumbfounded, open-mouthed **12** lost for words **13** flabbergasted, thunderstruck

surprising
◊ *anagram indicator*
05 funny **07** amazing, strange **08** shocking, stunning **09** obreption, startling, wonderful **10** astounding, incredible, remarkable, staggering, unexpected, unforeseen **11** astonishing, jaw-dropping, unlooked-for **13** extraordinary

surprisingly
◊ *anagram indicator*
07 funnily **09** amazingly, strangely **10** incredibly, remarkably, stunningly **11** wonderfully **12** staggeringly, unexpectedly **13** astonishingly **15** extraordinarily

surrender
04 cede, quit **05** forgo, waive, yield **06** bail up, forego, give in, give up, remise, render, resign, strike, submit, turn in **07** abandon, cession, concede, enfeoff, kamerad, let go of, release, succumb, waiving **08** abdicate, renounce, yielding **09** rendition, sacrifice, surrendry **10** abdication, capitulate, relinquish, submission **11** abandonment, leave behind, resignation **12** capitulation, lower the flag, renunciation **13** cessio bonorum, strike the flag **14** relinquishment **15** lay down your arms, throw in the towel, throw in your hand

surreptitious
03 fly, sly **06** covert, hidden, secret, sneaky, veiled **07** furtive **08** stealthy **09** underhand **10** behind-door, subreptive **11** clandestine **12** unauthorized

surrogate
05 proxy **06** deputy **07** stand-in **10** substitute **11** replacement **14** representative

surround
◊ *containment indicator*
03 lap, orb, rim **04** brim, edge, gird, halo, moat, pack, ring, zone **05** beset, bound, brink, hedge, hem in, limit,

round, verge, water **06** begird, border, bounds, edging, empale, encase, enhalo, fringe, garter, girdle, impale, incase, invest, margin, picket, piquet **07** besiege, compass, confine, embosom, enclave, enclose, enround, envelop, environ, fence in, go round, imbosom, inclose, picquet, rampart, setting **08** cincture, confines, encircle, overflow, palisade, stockade **09** encompass, perimeter, periphery **10** circumvent, water about **11** close in upon **13** circumference, circumvallate

surrounding
◇ *containment indicator*
06 gherao, nearby **07** ambient **08** adjacent **09** adjoining, bordering **10** encircling **12** encompassing, neighbouring

surroundings
05 scene **06** milieu **07** context, element, habitat, setting **08** ambience, environs, locality, vicinity **10** background **11** environment, mise en scène **12** circumstance **13** neighbourhood

surveillance
04 care **05** check, watch **06** charge, spying **07** control **08** scrutiny **09** direction, vigilance **10** inspection, monitoring, regulation **11** observation, stewardship, supervision **12** guardianship, suicide watch **15** superintendence

survey
03 map, spy **04** form, plan, plot, poll, quiz, scan, test, view **05** chart, level, probe, recce, study, sweep **06** assess, look at, review, size up **07** examine, inspect, measure, observe, overeye, surview **08** appraise, consider, episcopy, estimate, evaluate, look over, once-over, overview, perceive, prospect, research, scrutiny, traverse **09** appraisal, summing-up, supervise, valuation **10** assessment, conspectus, inspection, plane-table, scrutinize **11** contemplate, examination, measurement, opinion poll, reconnoitre, triangulate **12** Domesday book, Doomsday book, tour d'horizon **13** consideration, perambulation, questionnaire, triangulation **14** market research, reconnaissance **15** superintendence

surveyor
02 CS **08** assessor, examiner, overseer **09** geodesist, inspector

survival
06 coping **08** hangover, leftover, managing **09** endurance, existence **10** will to live **11** continuance, persistence, withholding **12** perseverance, staying power

survive
04 cope, last, live, stay **05** exist, rally **06** endure, live on, make it, manage, remain **07** die hard, hold out, live out,

outlast, outlive, persist, recover, weather **08** be extant, continue **09** withstand **10** get through **11** come through, live through, pull through

susceptibility
07 feeling **08** openness, tendency, weakness **09** liability, proneness **10** proclivity, propensity **11** gullibility, sensitivity **13** sensibilities, vulnerability **14** predisposition, responsiveness, suggestibility **15** defencelessness

susceptible
04 open, weak **05** given, prone **06** at risk, liable, tender **07** capable, patient, subject **08** disposed, gullible, inclined **09** credulous, easily led, receptive, sensitive **10** responsive, vulnerable **11** defenceless, impressible, predisposed, suggestible **14** impressionable

suspect
◇ *anagram indicator*
03 sus **04** fear, feel, iffy, suss **05** dodgy, doubt, fancy, fishy, guess, infer, smoke, sniff, snuff **07** believe, dubious, jalouse, misdeem, suppose, surmise **08** be wary of, conclude, consider, distrust, doubtful, jealouse, misdoubt, mistrust **09** debatable, mislippen, smell a rat, speculate, suspicion **10** conjecture, have a hunch, inadequate, suspicious, unreliable **11** misconceive **12** insufficient, questionable **13** be uneasy about **15** have doubts about, have qualms about

suspend
04 hang, hold, side, stay **05** cease, debar, defer, delay, expel, swing **06** arrest, dangle, ground, hang up, put off, recess, remove, shelve **07** adjourn, dismiss, entrain, exclude, keep out, shut out, unfrock **08** disperse, postpone, prorogue, put on ice, sideline, stand off **09** interrupt **10** pigeonhole **11** discontinue **13** put in abeyance

suspended
06 put off **07** delayed, hanging, pendent, pending, pensile, shelved **08** dangling, deferred, put on ice **09** postponed **10** underslung

suspense
05 doubt, poise **07** anxiety, tension **09** cessation, deferring **10** excitement, expectancy, indecision, insecurity **11** expectation, nervousness, uncertainty **12** anticipation, apprehension, doubtfulness, intermission

• in suspense
06 on edge **07** eagerly, keyed up **09** anxiously **11** expectantly **13** on tenterhooks **15** with bated breath

suspension
03 sol **04** foam, mist, stay **05** break, delay **07** removal, respite **08** abeyance, abeyancy, deferral **09** cessation, debarment, deferment, dismissal, exclusion, expulsion,

grounding, remission **10** inhibition, moratorium, unfrocking **11** adjournment, standing-off **12** intermission, interruption, postponement **14** pseudosolution

suspicion
03 sus **04** dash, hint, idea, suss **05** doubt, hunch, qualm, shade, sniff, tinge, touch, trace **06** belief, breath, notion, qualms, shadow **07** caution, feeling, glimmer, inkling, opinion, soupçon, surmise, suspect, umbrage **08** distrust, misdoubt, mistrust, paranoea, paranoia, wariness **09** chariness, intuition, misgiving, scintilla **10** conjecture, intimation, misdeeming, misgivings, scepticism, sixth sense, suggestion **12** apprehension, funny feeling

suspicious
◇ *anagram indicator*
03 odd **04** iffy, suss, wary **05** chary, dodgy, fishy, funny, queer, shady, smoky **06** guilty, shifty, uneasy, unsure **07** dubious, strange, suspect **08** doubtful, peculiar **09** dishonest, equivocal, irregular, sceptical **10** misdeeming, suspectful, suspecting **11** distrustful, mistrustful, unbelieving **12** apprehensive, disbelieving, questionable

suspiciously
05 oddly **06** warily **07** shadily **09** dubiously, strangely **10** doubtfully **11** dishonestly, sceptically **12** questionably **13** distrustfully, mistrustfully, unbelievingly **14** apprehensively, disbelievingly

Sussex
• division of Sussex
04 rape

sustain
03 aid **04** bear, buoy, face, feed, help, hold, prop, ride **05** abide, carry, stand **06** assist, buoy up, endure, foster, hold up, keep up, prop up, suffer, upbear, uphold, upstay **07** aliment, carry on, comfort, endorse, nourish, nurture, prolong, receive, relieve, ride out, support, suspend, undergo **08** continue, happen to, maintain, protract, sanction, scaffold **09** encourage, go through, keep going, underbear **10** experience, provide for, sustentate **14** give strength to

sustained
06 steady, tenuto **07** ongoing **08** constant **09** perpetual, prolonged, sostenuto **10** continuing, continuous, protracted **11** unremitting **12** long-drawn-out

sustenance
04 fare, food, grub, nosh **05** scoff **06** viands **07** aliment, support **08** victuals **09** autophagy, provender, refection **10** autophagia, livelihood, provisions **11** comestibles, maintenance, nourishment, subsistence, sufficience

svelte
04 slim **05** lithe **06** lissom, urbane
07 elegant, shapely, slender, willowy
08 graceful, polished **09** sylphlike
13 sophisticated

swag
03 sag **04** drum, sway **05** bluey **07** bed
roll, festoon, matilda, plunder
10 depression, subsidence

swagger
04 brag, cock, crow, roll, show
05 boast, brank, pronk, smart, strut,
swank, vapor **06** parade, prance, ruffle,
square, vapour **07** bluster, panache,
roister, royster, show off **08** parading,
prancing, tigerism **09** arrogance
11 ostentation **12** go over the top

swallow
◇ *containment indicator*
03 buy, eat, pop **04** bear, bolt, down,
gulp, slug, swig, take **05** abide, abyss,
ariel, drink, gorge, gulch, quaff, scoff,
shift, stand, thole, trust **06** accept,
devour, endure, englut, gobble, guzzle,
ingest, martin, Progne, stifle, take in,
throat, up with **07** believe, consume,
contain, fall for, martlet, repress,
smother, stomach, subsume, take off
08 down with, gobble up, gulp down,
hold back, martinet, suppress, tolerate
09 knock back, polish off, put up with,
worry down **11** be certain of, house
martin
• **swallow hole**
04 sink **06** dolina, doline **07** swallet
08 sinkhole
• **swallow up**
06 absorb, enfold, engulf **07** engulph,
envelop, ingulph, overrun **08** take over
09 overwhelm **10** assimilate
11 ingurgitate

swamp
03 bog, fen, mud, vly **04** mire, quag,
sink, vlei **05** beset, cowal, flood, Lerna,
Lerne, marsh **06** deluge, Dismal,
drench, engulf, morass, muskeg,
slough **07** besiege, bog down, Dismals,
wash out **08** inundate, loblolly,
overload, quagmire, saturate,
submerge, waterlog **09** overwhelm,
purgatory, quicksand, swampland,
weigh down

swampy
03 wet **04** miry **05** boggy, fenny, soggy
06 marshy, quaggy **07** paludal
08 squelchy **09** uliginose, uliginous
11 waterlogged

swan
03 cob, pen **04** Leda **06** cygnet,
Cygnus

Swans include:
04 mute
05 black
07 Bewick's, whooper
08 whooping
09 trumpeter, whistling

swank
04 brag, show, swot **05** agile, boast,

pronk, smart, strut **06** parade, pliant
07 conceit, display, posture, show off,
slender, swagger **08** bragging
09 vainglory **10** showing-off
11 ostentation **12** attitudinize,
boastfulness **13** conceitedness, preen
yourself **15** pretentiousness

swanky
04 posh, rich **05** fancy, flash, grand,
plush, ritzy, showy, smart, swish **06** de
luxe, flashy, lavish, plushy **07** stylish
09 exclusive, expensive, glamorous,
luxurious, sumptuous **11** fashionable,
pretentious **12** ostentatious

swap, swop
◇ *anagram indicator*
03 hit **04** blow, flop, slam **05** bandy,
plump, smite, trade **06** barter, strike,
stroke, switch **07** traffic **08** exchange,
suddenly, trade-off **09** transpose
10 substitute **11** interchange
12 substitution **13** transposition

sward
03 sod **04** turf

swarm
03 fry, mob **04** army, bike, body, byke,
cast, herd, host, mass, nest, pack, shin,
teem **05** crowd, drove, flock, flood,
horde, shoal, surge, troop **06** abound,
colony, hotter, myriad, stream, swerve,
throng **08** offshoot **09** multitude
10 congregate
• **be swarming with**
08 abound in **13** be crowded with, be
overrun with, be teeming with **14** be
crawling with, be hotching with, be
thronged with **15** be bristling with

swarthy
04 dark **05** black, brown, dusky
06 tanned **08** blackish **11** black-a-
vised, dark-skinned

swashbuckling
04 bold **06** daring, robust **07** dashing,
gallant **08** exciting, spirited **09** daredevil **10** courageous, flamboyant,
swaggering **11** adventurous

swat
03 hit **04** biff **05** lunge, swipe, whack
06 strike, wallop **07** fly-flap, lash out

swathe
03 lap **04** bind, fold, furl, wind, wrap
05 cloak, drape **06** enwrap, shroud
07 bandage, envelop, sheathe,
swaddle **08** enshroud, wrapping

sway
04 bend, lean, reel, rock, roll, rule,
shog, swag, swee, swey, veer, wave
05 clout, hoist, lurch, power, sally,
shake, swale, swing, thraw, wield
06 affect, direct, divert, govern,
induce, swerve, swinge, teeter, titter,
totter, waddle, wobble **07** command,
control, convert, incline, proceed,
reeling, rocking, shoogie, shoogle,
stagger, win over **08** convince,
dominate, dominion, hegemony,
overrule, persuade, rotation
09 authority, dominance, fluctuate,

influence, oscillate, supremacy,
vacillate **10** ascendancy, bring round,
government, leadership **11** fluctuation,
oscillation, prevail upon, sovereignty
12 jurisdiction, predominance
13 preponderance
• **hold sway**
04 rule **05** reign **07** prevail **09** have
power **10** wield power **13** exercise
power, have authority, have influence,
lay down the law

Swaziland
02 SD **03** SWZ

swear
03 eff, rap, vow **04** aver, avow, cuss,
damn, oath **05** abuse, blind, curse
06 abjure, adjure, affirm, assert, attest,
depose, insist, invoke, objure, pledge
07 declare, promise, testify **08** be on
oath, forswear, maledict
09 blaspheme, imprecate, overswear
10 asseverate, take an oath **11** be under
oath, eff and blind, take the oath
12 damn and blast **14** abjure the realm,
pledge yourself, turn the air blue, use
bad language **15** promise solemnly
• **swear by**
06 rely on **07** trust in **08** depend on
09 believe in **11** have faith in **14** put
your faith in

swearing
07 cursing, cussing **08** language
09 blasphemy, profanity **10** coprolalia,
expletives **11** bad language **12** foul
language, imprecations, maledictions
14 strong language

swear-word
04 cuss, oath **05** curse **08** cussword,
swearing **09** blasphemy, expletive,
obscenity, profanity **11** bad language,
imprecation **12** foul language **14** four-
letter word

sweat
04 drip, flap, fuss, toil **05** chore, exude,
panic, smart, sudor, tizzy, worry
06 dither, effort, labour, lather, sudate,
tizwas **07** anxiety, fluster, secrete,
soldier, swelter **08** drudgery, hidrosis,
moisture, perspire, sudation
09 agitation, cold sweat, death-damp,
mucksweat **10** osmidrosis, perspirate,
stickiness **11** bloody-sweat,
diaphoresis **12** perspiration, sweat
buckets **13** sweat like a pig

sweaty
04 damp **05** moist **06** clammy, sticky
08 forswatt, sudorous, sweating
10 perspiring

Sweden
01 S **03** SWE

sweep
03 arc, fly **04** bend, drag, dust, lash,
move, pass, poke, push, race, roll, sail,
scud, skim, soop, span, sway, tear,
wash, whip, wipe **05** besom, broom,
brush, clean, clear, curve, drive, elbow,
force, glide, range, scoop, scope,
shove, sling, surge, swath, swing,
swipe, swoop, vista, whisk **06** action,

extent, glance, hurtle, jostle, onrush, remove, search, stroke, swathe, thrust, vacuum **07** clean up, clear up, compass, ensweep, expanse, gesture, impetus, stretch **08** besom out, movement, overrake, snowball, vastness **09** besom away, clearance, curvature, immensity, sooterkin **10** blackguard, pump-handle **11** move quickly **13** spread quickly

• **sweep under the carpet**
04 hide **06** hush up **07** conceal, cover up **08** suppress **09** gloss over, paper over

sweeper
05 broom **06** libero

sweeping
04 sway, wide **05** broad, swing **06** global **07** blanket, general, radical, rubbish **08** thorough **09** extensive, universal, wholesale **10** simplistic **11** far-reaching, wide-ranging **12** all-embracing, all-inclusive **13** comprehensive, thoroughgoing **14** across-the-board, indiscriminate, oversimplified

sweepstake
04 draw **05** sweep, Tatts **07** lottery **08** gambling **11** sweepstakes, Tattersall's

sweet
03 pud **04** cute, dear, easy, icky, kind, mild, pure, ripe, soft, soot, toot **05** balmy, candy, clean, clear, dolce, fresh, glacé **06** afters, benign, dulcet, gentle, kindly, lovely, mellow, pretty, sickly, sugary, syrupy, tender **07** amiable, beloved, candied, darling, dessert, honeyed, lovable, musical, odorous, pudding, sweetie, tuneful, winning, winsome **08** adorable, all right, aromatic, charming, engaging, fragrant, gracious, likeable, loveable, luscious, perfumed, pleasant, pleasing, precious, redolent **09** agreeable, ambrosial, appealing, beautiful, cherished, delicious, melodious, sweetened, sweetmeat, treasured, wholesome **10** attractive, confection, delightful, euphonious, harmonious, saccharine **11** mellifluous, odoriferous, sickly sweet **12** affectionate, ingratiating, satisfactory, sweet-scented **13** confectionery, sweet-sounding

Sweets include:

03 gum, ice
04 jube, Mars®, mint, rock
05 fudge, halva, jelly
06 bonbon, confit, humbug, jujube, nougat, tablet, toffee
07 alcorza, caramel, fondant, gumdrop, lozenge, pomfret, praline, truffle, wine gum
08 acid drop, bull's eye, confetti, lollipop, marzipan, noisette, pastille, pear drop
09 chocolate, jelly baby, jelly bean, lemon drop, liquorice
10 candyfloss, chewing-gum,

gobstopper, peppermint
11 aniseed ball, barley sugar, marshmallow, toffee apple
12 butterscotch, dolly mixture
13 Edinburgh rock, fruit pastille
14 pineapple chunk, Turkish delight

See also **cake**; **dessert**

• **sweet on**
06 fond of, keen on, liking **08** mad about **09** far gone on **10** crazy about **12** ravished with **14** infatuated with

sweetbread
03 bur **04** burr

sweeten
04 ease **05** honey, sugar **06** mellow, pacify, soften, soothe, temper **07** appease, cushion, mollify, relieve **08** mitigate **09** alleviate **10** add sugar to, edulcorate

sweetheart
02 jo **03** joe **04** beau, dear, dona, duck, girl, lass, love **05** bonny, donah, flame, leman, lover, Romeo, swain, toots **06** amoret, bonnie, steady, suitor, sweety, tootsy **07** admirer, beloved, darling, sweetie **08** Dulcinea, follower, lady-love, truelove, young man **09** betrothed, boyfriend, inamorata, inamorato, valentine, young lady **10** girlfriend

sweetly
04 soot **05** dolce, soote **06** easily, evenly, in tune, kindly, softly **08** lovingly, mellowly, smoothly, steadily, tenderly **09** tunefully, winsomely **10** charmingly, dolcemente, pleasantly **11** melodiously **12** delightfully, effortlessly, euphoniously, harmoniously **14** affectionately

sweetness
04 love **05** aroma, charm, sirup, syrup **07** douceur, euphony, harmony **08** kindness **09** balminess, dulcitude, fragrance, freshness, saccharin **10** amiability, loveliness, mellowness, saccharine, succulence, sugariness, tenderness **11** sweet temper, winsomeness **12** lusciousness, mellifluence, pleasantness

sweet-smelling
05 balmy **07** odorous **08** aromatic, fragrant, perfumed, redolent **09** ambrosial **11** odoriferous **12** sweet-scented

swell
03 bag, don, fop, sea **04** beau, blab, boll, bulb, bulk, dude, grow, hove, huff, lord, plim, posh, puff, rise, toff, wave **05** adept, belly, berry, blast, bloat, bulge, bunch, dandy, elate, farce, grand, great, heave, mount, plump, raise, ritzy, smart, surge **06** bigwig, billow, blow up, de luxe, dilate, expand, extend, fatten, flashy, louden, puff up, step up, strout, swanky, tumefy, volume, wallow **07** augment, balloon, distend, enlarge, ferment, heaving,

incline, inflate, stylish, tumesce **08** belly out, escalate, heighten, increase, mushroom, outswell, snowball **09** backwater, cockscomb, excellent, exclusive, intensify, intumesce, loudening, roughness, skyrocket, wonderful **10** accelerate, distension, grow larger, undulation **11** enlargement, fashionable, proliferate

swelling
03 sty **04** boil, boll, bulb, bump, gall, knob, knot, lump, node, stye **05** bulge, heave, mouse, nodus, proud, tuber, tumor **06** bruise, nodule, pimple, rising, torose, torous, tumour, venter **07** blister, chancre, pillowy, tympany, vesicle **08** nodosity, pulvinus, scirrhus, tubercle **09** chilblain, gathering, puffiness **10** distension, tumescence, turgescent **11** enlargement, tumefaction **12** inflammation, intumescence, protuberance

sweltering
03 hot **05** humid, muggy, stewy **06** baking, clammy, steamy, sticky, sultry, torrid **07** airless, boiling **08** roasting, sizzling, stifling, tropical **09** scorching **10** oppressive **11** suffocating

swerve
03 wry **04** bend, lean, skew, sway, swee, swey, turn, veer, warp **05** faint, sheer, shift, stray, swarm, swing, twist **06** shrink, wander **07** deflect, deviate, diverge, incline, inswing **08** outswing, scramble **09** deviation **10** deflection

swift
04 fast **05** agile, brief, brisk, fleet, hasty, nippy, quick, rapid, ready, short, wight **06** abrupt, flying, lively, nimble, prompt, speedy, sudden, winged **07** express, flighty, hurried **09** feathered, immediate, screecher **10** pernicious **11** dispatchful, expeditious, tiger-footed **13** screech-martin

swiftly
04 fast **05** apace **07** express, hotfoot, quickly, rapidly **08** promptly, speedily **09** hurriedly, instantly, posthaste **10** at full tilt **11** double-quick **13** expeditiously

swiftness
05 speed **08** alacrity, celerity, despatch, dispatch, rapidity, velocity **09** fleetness, immediacy, quickness, readiness **10** expedition, promptness, speediness, suddenness **13** immediateness, instantaneity

swill
◊ *anagram indicator*
04 gulp, swig, wash **05** drain, drink, quaff, rinse, slops, waste **06** gargle, guzzle, imbibe, refuse, sluice **07** consume, hogwash, pigwash, swallow, toss off **08** pig's-wash, pigswill **09** knock back, scourings

- **swill out**
05 clean, flush, rinse 06 drench,
sluice 07 cleanse, wash out 08 wash
down

swim
◇ anagram indicator
03 bob, dip, fin, ren, rin, run 04 soom,
swan, whim 05 bathe, crawl, float
06 paddle 07 snorkel 08 take a dip
09 strike out 10 tread water

swimmer see **fish**

swimming
◇ anagram indicator

Swimming strokes include:

03 fly
05 crawl
07 trudgen
09 back crawl, butterfly, dog-paddle,
freestyle
10 backstroke, front crawl, sidestroke
11 doggy-paddle
12 breaststroke
15 Australian crawl

*Swimming- and diving-related
terms include:*

02 IM
03 fly, rip
04 pike, tuck
05 block, boost, entry, scull, split
06 inward, layout, length, medley
07 forward, reverse
08 armstand, backward, flamingo
09 ballet leg, eggbeater, elevation
10 tumble turn
11 dolphin kick, flutter kick, rocket
split
12 combined spin
13 negative split
14 continuous spin
15 backstroke flags

Swimmers and divers include:

04 Klim (Michael), Otto (Kristin), Rose
(Murray), Webb (Matthew)
05 Crapp (Lorraine), Curry (Lisa),
Ender (Kornelia), Evans (Janet),
Gould (Shane), Gross (Michael),
Lewis (Hayley), Riley (Samantha),
Spitz (Mark)
06 Biondi (Matt), Davies (Sharron),
Durack (Fanny), Ederle (Gertrude),
Fraser (Dawn), Loader (Danyon),
O'Neill (Susie), Phelps (Michael),
Thorpe (Ian), Wilkie (David)
07 Goodhew (Duncan), Hackett
(Grant), Perkins (Kieren), Wickham
(Tracey)
08 Champion (Malcolm), Charlton
(Boy), De Bruijn (Inge), Louganis
(Greg), Streeter (Alison), Van Wisse
(Tammy), Williams (Esther)
09 Armstrong (Duncan), Kellerman
(Annette)
11 Beaurepaire (Sir Frank),
Weissmuller (Johnny)

- **swimming organ**
03 oar 05 ctene

swimming costume see **swimsuit**

swimmingly
06 easily 08 smoothly, very well
12 successfully 13 like clockwork,
without a hitch

swimming-pool
04 lido 05 baths 10 natatorium
11 leisure pool 12 swimming-bath,
swimming-pond 13 swimming-baths

swimsuit
03 tog 04 togs 05 tanga, thong
06 bikini, cossie, trunks 07 bathers,
maillot, tankini 08 monokini, one-
piece 11 bathing suit 12 bathing dress
14 bathing costume 15 swimming
costume

swindle
02 do 03 con, gyp, rig 04 beat, chiz,
dupe, fake, have, lurk, ramp, rook,
scam, skin, take 05 bunco, bunko,
cheat, chizz, fraud, gouge, grift, let in,
mulct, pluck, shaft, sting, trick, twist
06 bucket, chouse, diddle, fiddle,
fleece, hustle, nobble, racket, rip off,
rip-off 07 con game, deceive, defraud,
exploit, skelder, tweedle 08 clean-out,
con trick, fakement, sell a pup, stitch
up, trickery 09 bamboozle, deception,
financier, gold brick, gold-brick, sell
smoke 10 overcharge 12 put one over
on, take for a ride 13 double-dealing,
sharp practice

swindler
03 con, leg 04 hood, rook 05 cheat,
crook, fraud, rogue, shark 06 chouse,
con man, escroc, rascal 07 fiddler,
grifter, hoodlum, hustler, magsman,
slicker, spieler 08 blackleg, con
woman, impostor 09 charlatan,
chiseller, con artist, fraudster, trickster
10 mountebank 12 bunko-steerer

swine
03 hog, pig 04 boar, boor 05 beast,
brute, rogue 06 rascal 09 scoundrel
14 good-for-nothing

- **bit of a swine**
03 ham 05 bacon

swing
◇ anagram indicator
03 fix, get 04 bend, hang, hurl, jive,
lean, make, move, rock, shog, spin,
sway, swee, swey, turn, vary, veer, wave,
wind 05 curve, fix up, pivot, scope, set
up, shift, sling, sweep, twist, wheel,
whirl 06 change, dangle, excite,
motion, rhythm, rotate, stroke, swerve,
waving 07 achieve, arrange, attract,
control, impetus, incline, shoogie,
vibrate 08 brandish, fishtail,
movement, organize, sweeping
09 fluctuate, oscillate, pendulate,
variation, vibration 11 fluctuation,
oscillating, oscillation

swingeing
04 huge 05 great, harsh, heavy
06 severe 07 drastic, extreme, serious
08 thumping 09 Draconian, excessive,
punishing, stringent 10 exorbitant,
oppressive 11 devastating
12 extortionate

swinging
◇ anagram indicator
03 hip 06 lively, modern, trendy, with it
07 dynamic, hanging, stylish, swaying,
turning 08 exciting, up-to-date 10 jet-
setting 11 fashionable, oscillatory
12 contemporary 13 up-to-the-
minute

swipe
03 hit 04 biff, blow, gulp, lift, nick, slap,
sock, swat, whip, wipe 05 clout, filch,
lunge, pinch, slice, smack, steal, swath,
whack 06 pilfer, strike, stroke, wallop
07 lash out, purloin

swirl
◇ anagram indicator
04 curl, eddy, purl, spin, wind 05 churn,
twirl, twist, wheel, whirl 07 agitate,
revolve, swizzle 09 circulate
10 tourbillon 11 tourbillion

swish
04 cane, flog, lash, posh, wave, whip
05 birch, flash, grand, plush, ritzy,
smart, swell, swing, swirl, twirl, whirl,
whisk, whizz 06 de luxe, rustle,
swanky, swoosh, thrash, whoosh
07 elegant, stylish, whistle
08 brandish, flourish 09 exclusive,
sumptuous 11 fashionable

switch
◇ anagram indicator
◇ reversal indicator
03 put, rod 04 beat, cane, jerk, lash,
swap, turn, twig, veer, whip 05 birch,
lever, prune, relay, shift, shoot, shunt,
thong, trade, tress, whisk 06 barter,
beat up, branch, button, change, divert,
gain-up, scutch, toggle, twitch
07 control, convert, deflect, deviate,
replace 08 cryotron, exchange,
reversal 09 about-turn, rearrange,
transpose 10 alteration, changeover,
substitute 11 interchange, on-off
device, replacement 12 substitution
13 chop and change 14 circuit-breaker

- **switch off**
03 cut 07 shut off, turn off, turn out
08 flick off 09 close down 11 stop
working

- **switch on**
05 put on 06 set off, turn on 07 flick on,
operate 08 activate 10 trigger off

Switzerland
02 CH 03 CHE

swivel
04 spin, turn 05 pivot, twirl, wheel
06 gyrate, rotate 07 revolve
09 pirouette

swollen
04 rank 05 bloat, puffy, tumid
06 bolled, bollen, gourdy, turgid
07 blabber, bloated, bulbous, bulging,
dilated, distent, gibbose, gibbous
08 blubbery, engorged, enlarged,
expanded, hydropic, inflamed,
inflated, puffed up 09 blubbered,
distended, tumescent 11 incrassated

swoop
04 dive, drop, fall, rush 05 lunge, souse,

stoop 06 attack, plunge, pounce
07 descend, descent 09 onslaught
• **at one fell swoop**
07 in one go 08 suddenly 09 all at
once, at one time, by one blow 13 on
one occasion 15 by a single action

swop *see* swap, swop

sword
03 war 04 spit

Swords include:

03 fox
04 back, épée, foil, simi
05 bilbo, blade, brand, broad, court,
estoc, kukri, saber, sabre, short,
skean, skene, small, steel
06 espada, glaive, hanger, katana,
kirpan, rapier, sweard, Toledo,
waster
07 curtana, curtaxe, gladius, hunting,
Morglay, shabble, spurtle, whinger,
yatagan
08 claymore, curtalax, damaskin,
falchion, schläger, scimitar,
spadroon, whiniard, whinyard,
white arm, yataghan
09 curtalaxe, damascene, damaskeen,
damasquin, Excalibur
10 damasceene
12 spurtle-blade, toasting fork,
toasting iron

See also **dagger**; **knife**

• **cross swords**
05 argue, fight 06 bicker 07 contend,
contest, dispute, quarrel, wrangle
08 be at odds, disagree 15 be at
loggerheads

sworn
07 devoted, eternal 08 attested
09 confirmed 10 implacable,
inveterate, relentless

swot
03 mug 04 cram, work 05 learn, mug
up, study, swank 06 bone up, revise
08 memorize

sybarite
07 epicure, playboy 08 hedonist,
parasite 09 bon vivant, epicurean,
pleasurer 10 sensualist, voluptuary
14 pleasure-seeker

sybaritic
04 easy 07 sensual 09 epicurean,
luxurious, parasitic 10 hedonistic,
voluptuous 13 self-indulgent
14 pleasure-loving 15 pleasure-
seeking

sycophancy
07 fawning 08 cringing, flattery,
toadyism 09 adulation, kowtowing,
servility, truckling 10 grovelling, toad-
eating 11 bootlicking, slavishness
14 backscratching, obsequiousness,
oleaginousness

sycophant
05 slave, toady 06 fawner, yes-man
07 crawler, cringer, placebo, sponger
08 claqueur, hanger-on, parasite,
truckler 09 flatterer, groveller,

toad-eater 10 bootlicker 12 cookie-
pusher 13 apple polisher,
backscratcher

sycophantic
05 slimy 06 smarmy 07 fawning,
servile, slavish 08 cringing, toadying,
unctuous 09 truckling 10 flattering,
grovelling, obsequious, oleaginous,
toad-eating 11 bootlicking,
parasitical, time-serving 12 ingratiating
13 sycophantical 14 backscratching

syllabus
03 syl 04 plan 05 table 06 course
07 outline 08 schedule 09 programme
10 curriculum

syllogism
08 argument 09 abduction,
deduction, enthymeme
11 epicheirema, proposition

sylph-like
04 slim 05 lithe 06 slight, svelte
07 elegant, slender, willowy
08 graceful 11 streamlined

sylvan *see* silvan

symbiotic
07 epizoan, epizoic 09 commensal,
epizootic 10 endophytic, synergetic
11 co-operative, interactive
14 interdependent

symbol
04 mark, rune, sign, type 05 creed,
image 06 figure 09 character,
ideograph 14 representation

Symbols include:

01 A, Å, @, B, C, ©, D, e, F, g, H, I, J, K, L,
M, N, O, P, Q, R, ®, S, T, U, V, W, X, Y, Z
02 Ac, Ag, Al, Am, Ar, As, At, Au, Ba, BB,
Be, Bh, Bi, Bk, Bq, Br, Ca, Cd, Ce, Cf,
Cl, Cm, Co, CQ, Cr, Cs, Cu, Db, Ds,
Dy, Er, Es, Eu, Fe, ff, Fm, Fr, Ga, Gd, Ge,
Gy, Ha, He, Hf, Hg, HH, Ho, Hs, Hz,
In, Ir, kg, Kr, La, Li, lm, Lr, Lu, Lw, lx,
Md, Mg, Mn, Mo, Mt, MV, Na, Nb,
Nd, Ne, Ni, No, Np, Oe, Os, Pa, Pb,
Pd, Pm, Po, Pr, Pt, Pu, Ra, Rb, Re, Rf,
Rg, Rh, Rn, Ru, Sb, Sc, Se, Sg, Si, Sm,
Sn, Sr, Sv, Ta, Tb, Tc, Te, Th, Ti, Tl, Tm,
Wb, Xe, Yb, Zn, Zr
03 BBB, dBA, kat, LXX, mol, rad
04 icon, ikon, logo
05 badge, brand, crest, motif, token,
totem
06 cipher, emblem, smiley, uraeus
08 caduceus, ideogram, insignia,
logogram, monogram, swastika
09 pentagram, trademark, watermark
10 coat of arms, hieroglyph,
pictograph
12 yellow ribbon

Religious symbols include:

02 Om
03 IHC, IHS
04 ankh, fish, yoni
05 cross, linga
06 chakra, filfot, fylfot, lingam
07 Ik Onkar, mandala, menorah, yin-
yang

08 crescent, swastika
11 Christingle, star of David

See also **element**

symbolic
05 token 07 shadowy, typical
10 emblematic, figurative, meaningful,
symbolical 11 allegorical, significant
12 illustrative, metaphorical
14 representative

symbolically
07 as a sign 09 as a symbol 10 as an
emblem 11 by this token 12 figuratively
14 emblematically

symbolize
04 mean, type 05 agree 06 denote,
emblem, figure, symbol, typify
07 betoken, combine, express,
present, signify 08 stand for
09 epitomize, exemplify, personate,
personify, represent

symmetrical
03 sym 04 even 07 dimeric, regular,
uniform 08 balanced, parallel
10 consistent, harmonious 11 well-
rounded, zygopleural 12 isobilateral,
proportional, right-and-left
13 actinomorphic, corresponding

symmetry
07 balance, harmony 08 evenness
09 agreement, congruity
10 proportion, regularity, uniformity
11 consistency, parallelism, proportions
14 correspondence

sympathetic
04 kind, soft, warm 06 caring, genial,
kindly, social, tender 07 feeling, pitying
08 friendly, likeable, pleasant, sociable,
tolerant 09 agreeable, concerned,
congenial, consoling, simpatico
10 comforting, compatible,
favourable, interested, like-minded,
solicitous, supportive 11 considerate,
encouraging, kind-hearted,
neighbourly, warm-hearted
12 affectionate, appreciative, well-
disposed 13 commiserating,
commiserative, companionable,
compassionate, sympathetical,
understanding

sympathetically
06 kindly, warmly 09 feelingly,
pityingly 11 consolingly, sensitively
12 comfortingly, responsively,
supportively 13 warm-heartedly
14 appreciatively 15 compassionately,
understandingly

sympathize
03 rap 04 pity 07 care for, comfort,
condole, console, feel for 09 empathize,
encourage, respond to 10 appreciate,
correspond, understand 11 commiserate,
show concern 12 be supportive, feel
sorry for, identify with, show interest

sympathizer
03 fan 06 backer 07 admirer
08 adherent, condoler, partisan
09 supporter 10 copperhead, well-
wisher 15 fellow-traveller

sympathy
04 pity **05** aroha **06** accord, solace, warmth **07** comfort, empathy, harmony, rapport, support **08** affinity, approval, kindness **09** agreement, closeness **10** compassion, tenderness **11** approbation, condolences, consolation, correlation, Weltschmerz **12** appreciation **13** commiseration, consideration, encouragement, fellow-feeling, understanding **14** correspondence, thoughtfulness **15** warm-heartedness

• expression of sympathy
02 ah, aw **04** dear **05** shame, sorry, there **06** dear me, oh dear, too bad **07** deary me **08** dearie me, good-lack **09** hard lines, tough luck **10** hard cheese

symptom
03 sym **04** mark, note, sign **05** fever, hives, rigor, token **06** signal **07** anxiety, display, feature, hard pad, warning **08** evidence, merycism, necrosis, prodrome **09** ketonuria, prodromus, rosetting **10** diagnostic, expression, indication, nettle rash, prognostic **11** hydrophobia, proteinuria **13** demonstration, epiphenomenon, malabsorption, manifestation **14** characteristic
See also **disease**

symptomatic
07 typical **10** associated, indicative, suggesting, suggestive **14** characteristic

synagogue
04 shul **06** temple

synchronize
04 sync, tune **05** synch

syndicate
04 bloc, ring **05** group, judge **06** cartel

07 censure, combine, council **08** alliance **11** association, combination

synonymous
07 similar, the same **09** identical **10** comparable, equivalent, tantamount **13** corresponding, substitutable **15** interchangeable

synopsis
05 recap **06** digest, précis, résumé, review, schema, sketch **07** outline, run-down, summary **08** abstract **09** summation **10** abridgment, compendium, conspectus, tabulation **11** abridgement **12** condensation **14** recapitulation

synthesis
05 alloy, blend, union **06** fusion **07** amalgam, welding **08** compound, pastiche **09** anabolism, composite **11** coalescence, combination, integration, pantheology, unification **12** amalgamation, glycogenesis **13** individuation

synthesize
04 fuse, weld **05** alloy, blend, merge, unify, unite **07** combine **08** coalesce, compound **09** integrate **10** amalgamate

synthetic
◇ *anagram indicator*
03 syn **04** fake, faux, mock, sham **05** bogus **06** ersatz, pseudo **07** man-made, plastic **09** imitation, simulated **10** artificial **12** manufactured

Syria
03 SYR

syrup
03 rob **05** sirup **06** orgeat **07** glucose, linctus, treacle **08** quiddany

09 cocky's joy, diacodion, diacodium, grenadine, moskonfyt **10** capillaire, maple syrup

syrupy
05 corny, gushy, mushy, soppy, sweet, weepy **06** loving, sickly, sloppy, slushy, sugary **07** gushing, honeyed, maudlin, mawkish **08** pathetic, romantic **09** emotional, oversweet, schmaltzy, sweetened **10** lovey-dovey, saccharine **11** sentimental, sickly sweet, tear-jerking **12** affectionate

system
03 way **04** mode, plan, rule, them **05** logic, means, order, set-up, usage **06** method, scheme **07** network, process, routine **08** approach, practice **09** apparatus, framework, mechanism, procedure, structure, technique **11** arrangement, methodology, orderliness **12** co-ordination, organization **13** modus operandi, the government **14** classification, the authorities **15** systematization, the powers that be

systematic
07 logical, ordered, orderly, planned **08** habitual, methodic **09** efficient, organized **10** methodical, scientific, structured **11** intentional, well-ordered, well-planned **12** businesslike, standardized, systematized **13** well-organized

systematize
04 plan **05** order **06** codify **07** arrange, dispose **08** classify, organize, regiment, regulate, tabulate **09** methodize, structure **10** schematize **11** make uniform, rationalize, standardize

T

T
03 tee, toc **04** tock **05** tango

TA
10 volunteers **15** Territorial Army

tab
03 fob, tag **04** bill, cost, drug, flap, pill **05** check, label, strap, tally **06** marker, tablet, ticket **07** Ecstasy, sticker, trimmer **08** ring pull, tabulate **09** cigarette, tabulator
• **keep tabs on**
07 observe **11** keep an eye on **12** watch closely

tabby
04 girl, wavy **05** woman **06** banded, stripy **07** brindle, mottled, striped **08** brindled, streaked **10** variegated

table
03 bar **04** chow, diet, dish, fare, food, grub, list, menu, move, nosh, plan, slab, tuck **05** bench, chart, graph, index, layer, panel, stand **06** figure, record, submit **07** diagram, picture, propose, suggest, worktop **08** register, schedule, syllabus, tabulate **09** catalogue, committee, inventory, programme, timetable **10** put forward, speciality, tabulation **12** string-course **13** entertainment

Tables include:

03 bed, loo, tea, top
04 bird, card, desk, draw, drum, high, pier, pool, sand, side, sofa, work
05 altar, board, lunch, night
06 bureau, coffee, dining, dinner, dolmen, gaming, inking, lowboy, picnic, teapoy, toilet, vanity
07 capstan, console, counter, cricket, drawing, draw-top, dresser, gateleg, snooker, trestle, writing
08 billiard, credence, credenza, draw-leaf, dressing, drop-leaf, guéridon, mahogany, pembroke, piecrust
09 breakfast, communion, operating, refectory
10 dissecting, gate-legged, greencloth, occasional
12 council-board
13 bonheur-du-jour

Tableware includes:

03 cup, jug, mug
04 bowl
05 ashet, cruet, plate
06 goblet, saucer, teacup, teapot, tureen
07 creamer, milk jug, platter, tumbler
08 cream jug, flatware, mazarine, rice bowl, salt mill

09 coffee cup, coffee pot, gravy boat, pasta bowl, pasta dish, pepper pot, salad bowl, sauceboat, side plate, soup plate, sugar bowl, toast rack, wineglass
10 bread plate, butter dish, cereal bowl, cruet-stand, pepper mill, salt shaker, soup tureen
11 butter plate, cheese plate, dessert bowl, dessert dish, espresso cup, serving bowl, serving dish
12 dessert plate, mazarine dish, pudding-plate
13 mazarine plate
14 serving platter

• **inner table**
04 home

tableau
05 scene **07** diorama, picture **08** vignette **09** portrayal, spectacle **13** tableau vivant **14** representation

tableland
04 mesa, puna **05** Karoo **06** Karroo **07** plateau

tablet
01 E **03** pad, tab **04** ball, dove, pill, slab **05** album, benny, bolus, panel, plate, stela, stele **06** abacus, caplet, marker, pellet, plaque, Roofie, tabula, troche **07** capsule, diptych, lozenge, sleeper, surface **08** monument, triglyph **09** medallion, tablature, wobbly egg **10** osculatory, tabula rasa **11** purple heart **12** disco biscuit, Rosetta stone

tabletalk
03 ana

tabloid *see* **newspaper**

taboo
03 ban **04** tabu, tapu, veto **05** curse **06** banned, vetoed **08** anathema, ruled out **09** exclusion, forbidden, interdict, ostracism, restraint **10** prohibited, proscribed, sacrosanct **11** prohibition, restriction, unthinkable **12** interdiction, proscription, unacceptable **13** unmentionable

tabulate
03 tab **04** list, sort **05** chart, index, order, range, table **06** codify **07** arrange **08** classify **09** catalogue **10** categorize, tabularize **11** systematize

tabulation
07 listing, sorting, tabling **08** indexing, ordering **11** arrangement, cataloguing **14** categorization, classification

tacit
06 silent **07** implied **08** implicit, inferred, unspoken, unstated, unvoiced, wordless **10** understood **11** unexpressed

taciturn
04 cold, dumb, mute **05** aloof, quiet **06** silent **07** distant **08** detached, reserved, reticent **09** withdrawn **10** of few words **11** tight-lipped, untalkative **12** close-mouthed **13** unforthcoming **15** uncommunicative

tack
03 add, fix, pin, sew, tag, way **04** line, nail, path, plan, take, turn, veer **05** affix, annex, baste, catch, lease, smack, spell **06** append, attach, attack, course, fasten, method, policy, sleaze, staple, stitch, swerve, tactic, tenure, tingle, zigzag **07** bearing, go about, heading, process, tintack **08** approach, club-haul, strategy **09** come about, direction, procedure, technique, thumbtack **10** drawing-pin, stickiness **12** change course, line of action **14** course of action **15** change direction
See also **horse**

tackle
◇ *containment indicator*
03 cat, rig, try **04** chin, foul, gear, grab, halt, sack, stop, take, whip **05** begin, block, catch, grasp, hoist, seize, stuff, tools **06** attack, burton, garnet, handle, jigger, outfit, pulley, take on, things **07** address, attempt, clobber, deflect, go about, harness, have a go, rigging, weapons **08** attend to, confront, deal with, embark on, face up to, obstruct, set about, wade into **09** apparatus, challenge, encounter, equipment, get down to, intercept, trappings, undertake **10** clew-garnet, get to grips, ground-hold, implements, take hold of **11** come to grips, grapple with, topping lift **12** interception, intervention **13** accoutrements, paraphernalia **14** get to grips with **15** apply yourself to, come to grips with

tacky
03 wet **04** naff **05** dingy, gaudy, gluey, gooey, gummy, messy, tatty **06** flashy, grotty, ragged, shabby, shoddy, sleazy, sloppy, sticky, tawdry, untidy, vulgar **07** kitschy, scruffy **08** adhesive, plimsoll, tattered **09** tasteless **10** threadbare

tact
05 skill **07** finesse **08** delicacy,

judgment, prudence, subtlety
09 dexterity, diplomacy, judgement
10 adroitness, discretion, perception
11 discernment, savoir-faire, sensitivity, tactfulness **13** consideration, judiciousness, understanding
14 thoughtfulness

tactful
06 adroit, polite, subtle, tender
07 careful, politic, prudent, skilful
08 delicate, discreet, kid-glove
09 judicious, sensitive **10** diplomatic, discerning, perceptive, thoughtful
11 considerate **12** diplomatical
13 understanding

tactfully
08 politely, tenderly **09** carefully, prudently, skilfully **10** delicately, discreetly **11** judiciously, sensitively
12 thoughtfully **14** diplomatically

tactic
03 way **04** move, plan, ploy, ruse
05 means, moves, shift, trick
06 course, device, method, policy, scheme **07** audible **08** approach, campaign, game plan, hardball, soft sell, strategy **09** expedient, manoeuvre, procedure, stratagem
10 manoeuvres, subterfuge **12** line of attack **14** course of action, full-court press

tactical
05 smart **06** adroit, artful, clever, shrewd **07** cunning, planned, politic, prudent, skilful **09** judicious, strategic
10 calculated

tactician
05 brain **07** planner **08** diplomat, director **10** campaigner, mastermind, politician, strategist **11** co-ordinator
12 orchestrator

tactless
04 rude **05** crass, rough **06** clumsy, gauche, unkind **07** awkward, hurtful
08 careless, impolite, unsubtle
09 impolitic, imprudent, maladroit, unfeeling **10** blundering, indelicate, indiscreet **11** injudicious, insensitive, thoughtless **12** discourteous, undiplomatic **13** inappropriate, inconsiderate

tactlessness
08 rudeness **09** bad timing, gaucherie
10 clumsiness, crassitude, indelicacy, ineptitude, maladdress **11** boorishness, discourtesy **12** impoliteness, indiscretion **13** insensitivity, maladroitness **15** thoughtlessness

tadpole
08 polliwig, polliwog, pollywig, pollywog **09** porwiggle

tag
03 add, dag, dub, tab, tig **04** call, flap, mark, name, note, slip, tack, term
05 affix, aglet, annex, badge, label, maxim, moral, motto, quote, shred, strap, style, tally, title **06** adjoin, aiglet, anklet, append, attach, cliché, dictum,

docket, fasten, phrase, rabble, saying, ticket **07** entitle, epithet, kabaddi, proverb, refrain, remnant, sticker
08 allusion, bracelet, christen, identify, nickname **09** designate, quotation
10 aglet babie, expression, Kimball tag
11 aiguillette, description, stock phrase, treasury tag **12** identity disc
14 identification

• **tag along**
04 tail **05** trail **06** follow, shadow
09 accompany

tail
◇ *tail selection indicator*
03 dog, end, fan, fud, uro- **04** back, flag, herd, rear, rump, scut **05** brush, queue, stalk, stern, suite, track, trail, train **06** behind, bottom, follow, pursue, shadow, shamus, sleuth
07 gumshoe, limited, rear end, retinue
08 backside, buttocks, cynosure, straggle **09** appendage, detective, extremity, posterior **10** conclusion, private eye **11** termination
12 investigator

• **part of tail**
03 fin **04** dock

• **tail back**
03 jam **04** line **05** queue **06** back up

• **tail off**
03 die **04** drop, fade, wane **06** die out
07 decline, drop off, dwindle
08 decrease, fall away, peter out, taper off

• **turn tail**
04 bolt, flee **06** beat it, decamp, escape **07** abscond, run away, scarper
09 skedaddle

tailback
03 row **04** file, line, tail **05** queue, train
06 backup, column **09** crocodile
10 procession

tailor
◇ *anagram indicator*
03 cut, fit **04** dung, snip, suit, trim
05 adapt, alter, darzi, flint, mould, shape, style **06** adjust, cutter, modify, sartor, teller **07** convert, fashion, modiste, whipcat **08** clothier, costumer, seamster **09** costumier, couturier, customize, outfitter
10 dressmaker, prick-louse, seamstress, whipstitch **11** accommodate, personalize **13** prick-the-louse

tailor-made
05 ideal, right **06** fitted, suited
07 bespoke, perfect **08** tailored
11 custom-built **13** made-to-measure

taint
◇ *anagram indicator*
04 blot, flaw, harm, ruin, soil, spot, wilt
05 dirty, fault, muddy, shame, smear, smoke, spoil, stain, sully, tinge
06 befoul, blight, damage, defect, defile, infect, injure, mildew, poison, stigma, weaken, wither **07** blacken, blemish, corrupt, deprave, envenom, pollute, tarnish **08** disgrace
09 attainder, contagion, dishonour, infection, pollution **10** adulterate,

corruption **11** contaminate
12 adulteration **13** contamination

Taiwan
02 RC **03** TWN

Tajikistan
02 TJ **03** TJK

take
◇ *containment indicator*
01 r **02** do **03** bag, buy, eat, fet, get, nim, rec, use, win **04** bear, bite, book, deem, draw, fall, fett, gain, gate, give, grab, grip, haul, have, help, hent, hire, hold, last, lead, lift, need, nick, note, pick, read, rent, seat, show, twig, view, work **05** abide, admit, adopt, angle, begin, bring, carry, catch, charm, cheat, drink, drive, ferry, fetch, filch, grasp, guide, learn, lease, pinch, scoff, seize, slant, stand, steal, study, teach, think, use up, usher, visit, whisk, yield
06 abduct, accept, aspect, assume, attain, become, betake, blight, choose, clutch, come by, convey, decide, deduct, demand, derive, detect, devour, endure, engage, escort, fathom, follow, freeze, gather, guzzle, handle, imbibe, income, ingest, inhale, kidnap, obtain, occupy, pay for, profit, pursue, recipe, reckon, regard, remove, return, secure, select, snatch, strike, suffer, tuck in **07** achieve, acquire, be given, believe, bewitch, call for, capture, conduct, conquer, consume, contain, deceive, deliver, detract, examine, execute, extract, find out, go along, major in, measure, mistake, observe, perform, portray, presume, procure, profits, purloin, react to, receive, require, returns, revenue, set down, stomach, succeed, suppose, swallow, swindle, takings, undergo
08 attitude, be taught, carry off, consider, cope with, cotton on, deal with, discover, look upon, proceeds, purchase, receipts, remember, research, settle on, shepherd, submerge, subtract, surprise, take away, tolerate, vanquish
09 accompany, apprehend, ascertain, captivate, determine, eliminate, establish, fathom out, gate-money, get hold of, lay hold of, put up with, respond to, transport, undertake, viewpoint, withstand **10** bear in mind, comprehend, confiscate, drive along, experience, photograph, standpoint, take effect, understand
11 accommodate, acknowledge, appropriate, be effective, frame of mind, have room for, necessitate, perspective, point of view, subscribe to, travel along **12** have space for, vantage point **13** be efficacious
14 interpretation, produce results
15 have a capacity of

• **let him/her take**
03 cap

• **take after**
04 echo **06** be like, favour, mirror
08 look like, resemble, surprise **11** be similar to

- **take against**
06 oppose 07 despise, dislike
08 object to 12 disapprove of
- **take apart**
03 nag, pan 04 carp, slag, slam
05 blame, knock, slate, snipe 06 attack
07 analyse, censure, condemn, nit-pick, rubbish, run down, slag off
08 badmouth, denounce, separate
09 criticize, dismantle, disparage
10 come down on, go to town on
11 disassemble, pick holes in
12 disapprove of, pull to pieces, put the boot in, take to pieces, tear to shreds
13 find fault with, tear a strip off 15 do a hatchet job on, pass judgement on
- **take back**
04 deny 05 evoke 06 call up, recant, regain, remind, resume, retake, return
07 get back, reclaim, replace, restore, retract 08 disclaim, give back, hand back, renounce, send back, withdraw
09 repossess, repudiate 12 eat your words 14 make you think of, put you in mind of
- **take down**
04 note, raze 05 level, lower
06 record, reduce, remove
07 demount, get down, put down, set down 08 demolish, pull down
09 dismantle, write down 10 put on paper, transcribe 11 disassemble, make a note of
- **take in**
◇ *containment indicator*
03 con, lap 04 dupe, fool 05 admit, cheat, cover, grasp, trick 06 absorb, digest 07 contain, deceive, embrace, include, mislead, realize, receive, shelter, swindle, welcome
08 comprise, hoodwink
09 bamboozle, encompass
10 appreciate, assimilate, comprehend, understand
11 accommodate, incorporate
- **take off**
◇ *deletion indicator*
02 go 03 ape, fly 04 bolt, doff, drop, flee, mock, rise, shed, soar, work
05 climb, leave, mimic, mount, strip
06 ascend, decamp, deduct, depart, detach, divest, do well, make it, parody, remove, send up 07 abscond, bunk off, catch on, discard, imitate, lift off, prosper, pull off, run away, scarper, succeed, tear off, undress 08 discount, flourish, go places, satirize, subtract, take away, throw off 09 disappear, do a runner, skedaddle 10 caricature, strike gold 11 impersonate 12 get undressed
13 become popular, hit the jackpot
14 become airborne
- **take on**
◇ *containment indicator*
◇ *juxtaposition indicator*
04 copy, face, hire, kill 05 enrol, fight
06 accept, assume, defeat, employ, engage, enlist, escort, oppose, retain, tackle 07 acquire, destroy, extract, recruit, vie with 08 get angry, get upset
09 entertain, make a fuss, undertake
11 compete with, contend with

- **take out**
03 fix, see, zap 04 dele, do in, draw, kill
05 set up, shoot, waste 06 be lent, borrow, cut out, defeat, delete, detach, escort, except, excise, get out, go with, murder, remove, rub out 07 arrange, bump off, butcher, destroy, execute, extract, pull out, wipe out, work out
08 blow away, despatch, dispatch, knock off, massacre, organize, settle on
09 accompany, eliminate, finish off, go out with, have a loan, liquidate, polish off 10 do away with, put to death
11 assassinate, exterminate 14 use temporarily
- **take over**
05 adopt 06 buy out 07 subsume
10 run the show 12 take charge of
13 gain control of
- **take to**
04 like 05 begin, start 08 commence, set about 09 undertake 10 appreciate, launch into 12 become keen on, find pleasant 14 find attractive
- **take up**
◇ *insertion indicator*
◇ *reversal down indicator*
03 use 04 fill, lift, rear 05 adopt, begin, raise, start, use up 06 absorb, accept, assume, engage, occupy, pick up, pursue, resume 07 agree to, carry on, consume, engross 08 commence, continue, embark on 10 monopolize
13 hang about with 14 knock about with 15 get involved with

take-off
05 spoof 06 ascent, flight, flying, parody, send-up 07 lift-off, mimicry
08 climbing, drawback, scramble, travesty 09 departure, imitation
10 caricature 13 impersonation

takeover
04 coup 06 buyout, merger
09 coalition 11 combination
12 amalgamation 13 incorporation

taking
04 gain, gate 05 yield 06 income, plight 07 profits, returns, revenue, winning, winsome 08 alluring, catching, charming, earnings, engaging, fetching, pickings, pleasing, proceeds, receipts, winnings
09 agitation, appealing, beguiling, gate-money 10 attractive, compelling, delightful, enchanting, infectious, intriguing, perplexity 11 bewitchment, captivating, fascinating
13 prepossessing

tale
03 bam, fib, lie, toy 04 epic, gest, hoax, myth, rede, reed, saga, talk, yarn
05 blood, fable, geste, novel, porky, reede, roman, spiel, story, total, weird
06 legend, number, report, rumour
07 account, fabliau, Märchen, mystery, novella, odyssey, parable, romance, untruth, whopper 08 allegory, anecdote, jeremiad, sob story
09 discourse, fairytale, falsehood, folk story, narrative, reckoning, storiette, storyette, tall story, tradition 10 fairy

story, hair-raiser 11 fabrication 12 old wives' tale, superstition 14 traveller's tale

talent
04 bent, feel, gift, nous 05 flair, forte, knack, power, skill, talon 06 genius
07 ability, aptness, faculty 08 aptitude, capacity, facility, ingenium, long suit, new blood, strength 09 endowment
11 disposition, showmanship, strong point 12 shot in the arm

talented
04 able, deft 05 adept 06 adroit, clever, gifted 07 capable, skilful 08 artistic
09 brilliant, versatile 10 proficient
11 well-endowed 12 accomplished

talisman
04 idol, ju-ju 05 charm, totem
06 amulet, fetish, mascot, symbol, telesm 07 abraxas, periapt
10 phylactery

talk
03 gab, gas, jaw, rap, say, yak 04 blab, bull, cant, chat, tell, yack 05 grass, haver, lingo, moody, mouth, noise, noyes, orate, parle, slang, speak, spiel, utter, voice, words 06 babble, confab, confer, debate, devise, gossip, haggle, havers, jabber, jargon, jaw-jaw, korero, natter, parley, rabbit, report, rumour, sermon, speech, squeal, yabber
07 address, baloney, bargain, blether, boloney, chatter, chinwag, clatter, confess, dialect, discuss, earbash, express, hearsay, lecture, malarky, meeting, oration, palaver, prattle, seminar, twaddle 08 badinage, chitchat, conclave, converse, dialogue, flimflam, haggling, idiolect, inform on, language, malarkey 09 discourse, gibberish, interview, negotiate, symposium, tell tales, tête-à-tête, utterance 10 articulate, balderdash, bargaining, conference, discursion, discussion, namby-pamby
11 communicate, negotiation
12 consultation, conversation, disquisition, tittle-tattle 13 rabbit and pork, spill the beans, spread rumours
15 give the game away
- **foolish talk**
04 bosh 05 haver 06 havers
- **impudent talk**
03 lip 08 slack jaw
- **talk back**
06 retort 07 riposte 09 retaliate
10 answer back, be cheeky to
12 answer rudely
- **talk big**
04 brag, crow 05 boast, swank, vaunt
07 bluster, show off 10 exaggerate
- **talk down to**
07 despise 09 patronize 10 look down on
- **talk into**
04 coax, sway 07 win over
08 convince, persuade 09 encourage
10 bring round
- **talk nonsense**
03 gum, rot 04 jive 05 bleat, haver
06 havers

• talk out of
04 stop 05 deter 06 put off 07 prevent
08 dissuade 10 discourage

talkative
04 gash 05 gabby, gassy, talky, vocal,
wordy 06 chatty, mouthy 07 gossipy,
verbose, voluble 09 expansive,
garrulous 10 long-winded, loquacious,
unreserved 11 forthcoming, long-
tongued 13 communicative

talker
05 prose 06 orator, tatler 07 speaker,
tattler, twaddle 08 lecturer
09 chatterer 10 chatterbox,
motormouth 11 speechmaker
12 blatherskite, bletherskate,
communicator 14 bletheranskate

talking-to
06 rebuke, rocket 07 lecture, reproof,
wigging 08 reproach, scolding
09 carpeting, criticism, reprimand
10 telling-off, ticking-off 12 dressing-
down

tall
03 big 04 hard, high, long 05 giant,
great, lanky, lofty, stout, taunt
06 absurd, taxing, towery, trying
07 doughty, dubious, sky-high, soaring
08 elevated, exacting, gigantic,
towering, unlikely 09 bombastic,
demanding, difficult, overblown
10 far-fetched, improbable, incredible,
remarkable 11 challenging,
exaggerated, implausible
12 preposterous, unbelievable

tallness
06 height 07 stature 08 altitude
09 loftiness, procerity

tally
03 add, fit, sum, tab, tag 04 list, nick,
roll, stub, suit, tick 05 adapt, add up,
agree, count, label, match, score, stick,
stock, tie in, total 06 accord, concur,
credit, figure, reckon, record, square,
ticket 07 account, conform
08 coincide, register 09 calculate,
duplicate, harmonize, nickstick,
reckoning 10 correspond
11 counterfoil, counterpart,
enumeration

tame
03 pet 04 calm, curb, dull, flat, lame,
mail, meek, weak 05 bland, break,
quell, train, vapid 06 boring, bridle,
docile, entame, feeble, gentle,
humble, master, mellow, pacify, soften,
subdue, temper, wonted 07 amenage,
break in, conquer, humdrum, insipid,
reclaim, repress, subdued, tedious,
trained 08 amenable, biddable,
broken in, domestic, lifeless,
mansuete, obedient, overcome,
suppress 09 kids' stuff, subjugate,
tractable, wearisome 10 accustomed,
cultivated, discipline, house-train,
manageable, spiritless, submissive,
unexciting, uninspired 11 bring to heel,
disciplined, domesticate, uninspiring,
unresisting 12 domesticated

13 unadventurous, uninteresting
14 unenterprising

tamper
03 fix, rig 04 work 05 alter 06 bishop,
damage, doctor, fiddle, juggle,
meddle, monkey, temper, tinker
07 falsify 08 contrive, medicate,
practise 09 interfere, mess about,
muck about, undermine
10 manipulate 11 interpolate 12 put
your oar in 14 poke your nose in, stick
your oar in 15 stick your nose in

tan
04 bark, beat, belt, cane, flay, flog, lash,
whip 05 beige, birch, brown, clout,
spank, strap, tawny, whack 06 bronze,
thrash, wallop 07 go brown, tangent
09 turn brown 10 light brown, make
darker 12 become darker 14 yellowish
brown

tang
03 pep 04 barb, bite, edge, hint, kick,
ring 05 aroma, point, prong, punch,
scent, smack, smell, spice, spike, sting,
taste, tinge, touch, trace, whiff
06 savour 07 flavour 08 overtone,
piquancy, pungency 09 sharpness
10 sea-surgeon, suggestion

tangible
04 hard, real 05 solid 06 actual
07 evident, tactile, visible 08 concrete,
definite, manifest, material, palpable,
physical, positive 09 corporeal,
touchable 11 discernible, perceptible,
substantial, well-defined
12 unmistakable

tangle
◇ *anagram indicator*
03 mat, ore, web 04 coil, fank, knot,
maze, mesh, mess, nest, taut, tawt, trap
05 catch, mix-up, ravel, skein, snarl,
twist 06 burble, enmesh, entrap,
fankle, hamper, icicle, jumble, muddle,
raffle 07 confuse, embroil, ensnare,
involve, perplex, snarl-up
08 argument, conflict, convolve,
entangle, mess with 09 confusion,
drift-weed, embroglio, imbroglio,
implicate, interlace, labyrinth,
Laminaria 10 intertwine, intertwist,
interweave, perplexity, wilderness
11 convolution, embroilment,
intertangle 12 complication,
entanglement

tangled
◇ *anagram indicator*
05 messy 06 knotty, matted
07 complex, haywire, jumbled,
knotted, mixed up, muddled, snarled,
tousled, twisted 08 confused,
involved, tortuous 09 entangled,
intricate 10 convoluted
11 complicated, dishevelled

tango
01 T

tangy
04 acid, tart 05 fresh, sharp, spicy
06 biting, strong 07 piquant, pungent

tank
03 vat 04 pond, pool, stew 05 basin
06 defeat, header, panzer, refuel,
thrash 07 cistern, sponson, whippet
08 aquarium, flush-box, sponsing
09 baptistry, container, gasholder,
gasometer, reservoir, Valentine
10 baptistery, receptacle, septic tank,
shield pond 11 armoured car
12 precipitator 13 shielding pond
15 armoured vehicle

tanning material
04 puer, pure 07 valonea, valonia
08 vallonia

tantalize
04 bait, balk, mock 05 taunt, tease,
tempt 06 allure, entice, lead on, thwart
07 beguile, provoke, torment, torture
09 frustrate, titillate 10 disappoint

tantalum
02 Ta

tantamount
05 equal 08 as good as 09 the same as
10 equivalent, synonymous
12 commensurate

tantrum
03 fit, pet 04 fury, rage 05 paddy,
scene, storm 06 blow-up, temper,
wobbly 07 flare-up 08 hissy fit,
outburst, paroxysm, tirrivee, tirrivie
10 conniption 11 fit of temper

Tanzania
03 EAT, TZA

tap
03 bob, bug, hit, pat, rap, tat, tip, tit,
top, use 04 beat, blip, bung, cock,
drum, milk, mine, plug, tack, tick, touk,
tuck 05 bleed, chuck, drain, knock,
spout, touch, valve 06 broach, draw
on, faucet, pierce, pirate, pit-pat,
quarry, siphon, spigot, strike, stroup
07 bibcock, draw off, exploit, monitor,
percuss, petcock, pitapat, stopper,
utilize, wiretap 08 draw upon, listen to,
pitty-pat, receiver, stopcock 09 light
blow, make use of 10 listen in on
11 eavesdrop on 15 listening device,
take advantage of
• on tap
05 handy, ready 06 at hand, on hand
09 available 10 accessible

tape
03 tie 04 band, bind, seal 05 stick,
strip, video 06 fasten, record, ribbon,
secure, string 07 binding 08 cassette
09 audiotape, recording, Sellotape®,
videotape 10 gaffer tape, Scotch
tape®, sticky tape, tape-record
11 masking tape, video-record
12 adhesive tape, magnetic tape,
passe-partout 13 audio cassette, tape-
recording, video cassette 14 video
recording

taper
04 fade, nose, slim, thin, wane, wick
05 spill 06 acumen, candle, die off,
lessen, narrow, reduce 07 die away,
dwindle, tail off, thin out 08 decrease,

diminish, make thin, peter out, wax light **09** attenuate **10** become thin, make narrow **12** become narrow

tapir
04 anta **07** sladang **08** seladang

tar
05 set on **06** maltha, sailor **11** pissasphalt

See also **sailor**

• **smear with tar**
03 pay

• **tar derivative**
05 furan, indol, pitch **06** cresol, furane, indene, indole, phenol, picene, retene, xylene **07** acridin, aniline, benzene, indulin, naphtha, picamar, skatole, styrene **08** acridine, cerulein, creasote, creosote, heavy oil, induline, nigrosin, pyridine, safranin **09** carbazole, coumarone, nigrosine, primuline, safranine **10** anthracene, benzpyrene **11** creosote oil, naphthalene, phenanthene

tardily
04 late **06** slowly **09** belatedly **10** sluggishly **12** late in the day, unpunctually **13** not before time **15** at the last minute

tardiness
05 delay **08** dawdling, lateness, slowness **11** belatedness **12** dilatoriness, sluggishness **13** unpunctuality **15** procrastination

tardy
03 lag **04** late, slow **05** slack **06** retard **07** belated, delayed, overdue **08** backward, dawdling, dilatory, retarded, sluggish **09** loitering **10** behindhand, last-minute, unpunctual **12** eleventh-hour **15** procrastinating

tare
01 t **04** tine, weed **05** vetch **06** darnel

target
03 aim, end **04** butt, game, goal, mark, prey, seek **05** aim at **06** aim for, object, quarry, try for, victim **07** purpose **08** ambition, bull's eye **09** intention, objective **11** destination **14** have as your goal

• **centre of target**
03 pin **04** bull **06** carton **08** bull's-eye

• **on target**
05 exact **06** bang on, on time, spot-on **07** precise **08** accurate, on course **10** on schedule **15** according to plan

tariff
03 tax **04** duty, levy, menu, rate, toll **06** excise, zabeta **07** charges, customs **08** schedule **09** price list **10** bill of fare **13** list of charges

tarnish
03 dim, mar **04** blot, dull, film, rust, soil, spot **05** spoil, stain, sully, taint **06** befoul, darken, impair, patina **07** blacken, blemish, corrode **08** besmirch **09** discolour **10** blackening **13** discoloration

taro
04 coco, eddo **05** cocco **07** dasheen

tarry
03 lag **04** bide, leng, rest, stay, stop, wait **05** abide, await, dally, delay, pause **06** dawdle, linger, loiter, remain, stay on **07** sojourn

tart
03 pie, pro, tom **04** acid, bawd, drab, flan, moll, slut, sour **05** brass, broad, patty, quiff, sharp, tangy, tramp, wench, whore **06** biting, bitter, geisha, harlot, hooker, pastry, quiche **07** acerbic, caustic, cocotte, cutting, floozie, hetaera, hostess, hustler, lorette, piquant, pungent, rent-boy, strudel, tartlet, trollop **08** call girl, incisive, magdalen, mirliton, sardonic, scathing, scrubber, strumpet, vinegary **09** acidulous, charlotte, courtesan, croquante, hierodule, loose fish, sarcastic, trenchant **10** astringent, fancy woman, loose woman, prostitute, rough trade, vizard-mask **11** fallen woman, fille de joie, night-walker, poule de luxe, working girl **12** fille des rues, scarlet woman, street-walker **13** grande cocotte **14** lady of the night, woman of the town

• **tart up**
06 doll up **07** dress up, smarten **08** decorate, renovate **09** embellish, smarten up **10** redecorate

tartar
05 scale, Tatar **08** beeswing, calculus

task
03 job, tax **04** darg, duty, pain, snap, toil, work **05** chore, grind, stint **06** burden, charge, errand, killer, labour, pensum **07** mission, stretch **08** activity, business, exercise, hard time, trauchle **09** challenge, job of work, soft thing **10** assignment, commission, employment, engagement, enterprise, imposition, occupation **11** piece of work, undertaking

• **take to task**
04 slam **05** blame, knock, scold, slate **06** attask, pull up, rebuke **07** censure, chapter, lecture, reprove, tell off, tick off, upbraid **08** reproach **09** criticize, reprimand

Tasmania
03 Tas **06** Tassie

taste
03 bit, eat, sar, sip, try **04** bent, bite, dash, drop, feel, gout, know, meet, pree, tang, test **05** enjoy, fancy, grace, piece, smack, style **06** choice, desire, hunger, liking, morsel, nibble, polish, relish, sample, savour, thirst, titbit **07** culture, decorum, discern, finesse, flavour, leaning, make out, soupçon, undergo **08** appetite, breeding, elegance, fondness, judgment, mouthful, penchant, perceive **09** encounter, etiquette, hankering, judgement, propriety **10** experience, partiality, perception, preference,

refinement **11** cultivation, discernment, distinguish, inclination, sensitivity, stylishness **12** appreciation, predilection, tastefulness **13** differentiate **14** discrimination

03 hot
04 acid, sour, tart
05 acrid, bland, fishy, meaty, nutty, salty, sapid, sharp, spicy, sweet, tangy
06 acidic, bitter, citrus, creamy, fruity, sugary
07 insipid, peppery, piquant, pungent, savoury
08 vinegary
11 bittersweet

tasteful
05 smart, tasty **06** dainty, pretty **07** correct, elegant, refined, stylish **08** artistic, charming, cultured, delicate, graceful, gracious, pleasing, polished **09** aesthetic, beautiful, exquisite, judicious **10** cultivated, fastidious, harmonious, restrained, well-judged **14** discriminating

tastefully
07 smartly **09** elegantly, stylishly **10** charmingly, delicately, graciously **11** beautifully, exquisitely, judiciously **12** artistically, harmoniously

tasteless
04 dull, flat, loud, mild, naff, rude, thin, weak **05** bland, cheap, crass, crude, gaudy, plain, showy, stale, tacky, vapid, wersh **06** boring, flashy, garish, kitsch, tawdry, vulgar, watery **07** insipid, insulse, uncouth, wearish **08** improper, tactless, unseemly **09** graceless, inelegant, unfitting, unsavoury **10** indiscreet **11** flavourless, watered-down **13** uninteresting

tasting
05 assay, smack, trial **07** testing **08** sampling **09** gustation **10** assessment

tasty
04 nice **05** spicy, sweet, tangy, yummy **06** morish **07** gustful, moreish, piquant, savoury **08** luscious, tasteful **09** delicious, flavorous, palatable, succulent, toothsome **10** appetizing, attractive, delectable **11** flavoursome, interesting, scrumptious **13** mouthwatering

tatter
• **in tatters**
03 rag **06** broken, in bits, in rags, ragged, ruined **07** in ruins, wrecked **08** in pieces, in shreds **09** destroyed, in ribbons, shattered **10** devastated

tattered
◇ *anagram indicator*
04 torn **05** tatty **06** frayed, ragged, ripped, shabby **07** scruffy **10** threadbare **14** tatterdemalion **15** tatterdemallion

tattie *see* **potato**

tattler
04 blab **06** gossip **08** busybody, tell-tale **09** chatterer **10** newsmonger, talebearer, tale-teller **12** rumour-monger **13** scandalmonger

tattoo
03 tat **04** moko, tatu **06** tattow **08** drumming

taunt
03 dig, rib **04** bait, barb, gibe, gird, goad, jeer, jest, jibe, jive, mock, twit **05** fling, sneer, tease **06** deride, insult, revile **07** catcall, censure, mockery, provoke, sarcasm, teasing, torment **08** brickbat, derision, reproach, ridicule, taunting **09** make fun of, poke fun at **11** provocation

taut
03 mat **05** rigid, stiff, tense, tight **06** tangle, tensed **07** anxious, fraught, worried **08** strained **09** stretched, tightened, unrelaxed **10** contracted

tautological
05 wordy **07** verbose **09** redundant **10** pleonastic, repetitive **11** superfluous

tautology
08 pleonasm **09** iteration, verbosity **10** redundancy, repetition **11** duplication, perissology, superfluity **14** repetitiveness

tavern
03 bar, inn, pub **04** bush, dive **05** fonda, joint, local **06** boozer, Kneipe, public **08** alehouse, hostelry, tap-house **09** roadhouse **10** night-house, trust-house **11** night-cellar, public house

taw
03 tew **04** ally, flog, whip **05** alley, thong

tawdry
05 cheap, fancy, gaudy, showy, tacky, tatty **06** cheapo, flashy, garish, vulgar **07** chintzy **08** tinselly, trumpery **09** tasteless **10** glittering **11** gingerbread

tawny
03 tan **04** fawn **05** khaki, sandy **06** fulvid, golden, yellow **07** fulvous **08** xanthous **11** golden brown

tax
03 aid, lot, sap, try **04** cess, duty, levy, load, rate, scot, sess, soak, test, tire **05** drain, exact, stent, weary, weigh **06** assess, burden, charge, demand, impose, impost, strain, stress, tariff, weaken, weight **07** exhaust, stretch, wear out **08** encumber, enervate, overload, pressure **09** agistment, weigh down **10** accusation, assessment, imposition **12** contribution **13** make demands on

Taxes include:
02 PT
03 GST, sur, VAT
04 geld, gelt, PAYE, poll, scat, skat, toll
05 rates, scatt, tithe
06 excise, income
07 airport, council, customs, gabelle
08 property, Rome-scot
09 death duty, head money, insurance
10 capitation, estate duty, value added
11 corporation, inheritance, Peters' pence
12 capital gains, pay as you earn
15 capital transfer, community charge

• tax collectors
02 IR **03** IRS

taxi
03 cab **06** fiacre, samlor **07** Joe Baxi, minicab, taxicab **09** hansom-cab **10** hackney cab **12** hackney coach **15** hackney carriage

taxing
04 hard **05** heavy, tough **06** satire, tiring, trying **07** censure, onerous, testing, wearing **08** draining, exacting, wearying **09** demanding, punishing, stressful, wearisome **10** burdensome, enervating, exhausting

taxman
02 IR **03** IRS

tea
03 cha, tay **04** char **05** cuppa **06** tisane **07** Rosy Lee **08** infusion, Rosie Lee, stroupan **09** stroupach
See also **cannabis**

Teas and herbal teas include:
03 ice, kat, qat
04 beef, bush, chai, herb, iced, khat, mate, mint, sage
05 Assam, black, bohea, brick, caper, China, congo, fruit, green, hyson, lemon, pekoe, senna, yerba
06 Ceylon, congou, herbal, oolong, oulong
07 cambric, instant, jasmine, lapsang, redbush, rooibos, rosehip, Russian, twankay
08 camomile, Earl Grey, Lady Grey, souchong, switchel
09 breakfast, chamomile, gunpowder
10 Darjeeling
11 orange pekoe
13 decaffeinated
15 lapsang souchong

teach
03 con, kon **04** cram, larn, lear, leir, lere, read, show, take **05** coach, conne, din in, drill, edify, guide, leare, learn, train, tutor, verse **06** advise, direct, ground, impart, inform, parrot, preach, school **07** counsel, din into, educate, lecture, perfect **08** accustom, disciple, hammer in, instruct **09** brainwash, condition, enlighten, foreteach, inculcate, pedagogue **10** discipline, hammer into, potty-train **11** demonstrate, give lessons **12** indoctrinate

teacher
03 rav **04** Miss **05** guide **07** dominie, prophet **08** educator, schoolie **09** pedagogue, schoolman **10** instructor, scholastic **12** demonstrator, instructress **13** gerund-grinder

Teacher types include:
03 AST, don
04 dean, form, guru, head
05 barbe, coach, molla, rabbi, rebbe, tutor, usher
06 docent, doctor, duenna, fellow, gooroo, mallam, master, mentor, mollah, moolah, mullah, munshi, pedant, pundit, reader, school, supply
07 acharya, adviser, crammer, starets, staretz, student, trainer
08 lecturer, mistress, moonshee, sol-faist
09 governess, maharishi, mnemonist, pedagogue, preceptor, principal, professor, rebbetzin, reception
10 counsellor, deputy head, headmaster, head of year, instructor, paedotribe, schoolmarm
11 housemaster, preceptress, upper school
12 demonstrator, headmistress, mademoiselle, middle school, pastoral head, posture-maker, private tutor, schoolmaster
13 housemistress, nursery school, posture-master, primary school
14 schoolmistress, senior lecturer
15 college lecturer, secondary school

Teachers include:
04 Beck (Madame), Eyre (Jane), Hart (Sheba), King (Anna), Lamb (Michael), Nunn (Sir Percy), Wilt (Henry)
05 Brill (Miss), Chips (Mr), Crane (Edwina), Crick (Tom), Dixon (Jim), Doyle (Patrick), Handy (Charles Brian), Henri (Frances), Levin (Sam), Odili, Snape (Severus)
06 Alcott (Bronson), Angelo (Albert), Arnold (Thomas), Brodie (Miss Jean), Coppin (Fanny Marion Jackson), Cotton (George Edward Lynch), Covett (Barbara), Graham (Martha), Grimes (Captain), Gyatso (Geshe Kelsang), Hagrid (Rubeus), Harris (Crocker), Hillel, Hornby (A S), Ramsay (Dunstan), Solent (Wolf)
07 Darling (Sir James Ralph), Eckhart (Miss), Enketei (Mira), Fischer (Marcus), Keating (John), Krishna, Lowther (Gordon), Matthay (Tobias), Mr Chips, Mulcahy (Henry), Peecher (Emma), Porpora (Nicola), Saville (Colin), Squeers (Wackford), Vaughan (Barbara), Wackles (Sophy)
08 Bridgman (Laura Dewey), Caldwell (George), Chipping (Mr), Doubloon (Maggie), Lewisham (George), Prodicus, Sullivan (Anne)
09 Batchelor (Barbie), Bellgrove (Professor), Braidwood (Thomas), Hartright (Walter), Headstone (Bradley), Strasberg (Lee)
10 Dumbledore (Albus), Leadbetter

(David), **Madame Beck, Madam Hooch, McGonagall** (Minerva), Protagoras
12 Pennyfeather (Paul), **Stanislavsky**
13 M'Choakumchild (Mr)

- **teachers**
03 ATL, NUT **06** NASUWT

teaching
04 lair, lare, lore, TEFL, TESL **05** dogma, tenet, TESOL **06** loring, wisdom **07** precept, tuition **08** doctrine, pedagogy **09** didactics, education, principle, tradition **10** pedagogism **11** instruction, instructive, pedagoguism

team
02 11, XI, XV **03** set **04** band, crew, gang, pair, side, yoke **05** brood, bunch, chain, group, shift, squad **06** équipe, line-up, litter, outfit, pick-up, stable, troupe **07** company, offence, offense, turn-out **08** equipage

National team nicknames in Australia and New Zealand include:
05 Opals
07 Boomers, Olyroos
08 Matildas
09 All Blacks, All Whites, Kangaroos, Socceroos, Wallabies
10 Hockeyroos
11 Kookaburras, Silver Ferns

See also **Australian football; baseball; basketball; cricket; football; racing; rugby**

- **team up**
04 join, yoke **05** match, unite **06** couple **07** combine **09** co-operate **10** join forces **11** collaborate **12** band together, come together, work together

teamwork
10 fellowship, team spirit **11** co-operation, joint effort **12** co-ordination **13** collaboration, esprit de corps

tear
03 fly, nip, rag, ren, rin, rip, run, zap, zip **04** bead, belt, blob, bolt, bomb, claw, dart, dash, gash, grab, hole, plow, pull, race, rage, rash, rend, rent, rive, rush, slip, slit, snag, tire, yank, zing, zoom **05** hurry, pluck, ranch, scoot, seize, sever, shoot, shred, slash, speed, split, spree, vroom, whizz, wound, wrest **06** career, charge, divide, gallop, injure, injury, ladder, mangle, plough, screed, snatch, sprint, sunder, tatter, unroot **07** eye-drop, mammock, rupture, scratch **08** lacerate, mutilate, step on it **09** pull apart, water drop **10** break apart, laceration, mutilation

- **in tears**
03 sad **05** upset, weepy **06** crying **07** sobbing, tearful, wailing, weeping **09** emotional, sorrowful **10** blubbering, distressed, whimpering

- **tear down**
07 destroy **08** demolish, pull down **09** dismantle, knock down

tearaway
05 rough, rowdy, tough **06** madcap, rascal **07** hoodlum, hothead, ruffian **08** hooligan, reckless **09** daredevil, impetuous, roughneck **10** delinquent **14** good-for-nothing

tearful
03 sad, wet **05** misty, moist, upset, weepy **06** crying **07** doleful, in tears, sobbing, weeping **08** mournful **09** emotional, sorrowful, upsetting **10** blubbering, distressed, lachrymose, whimpering **11** distressing

tease
◊ *anagram indicator*
03 kid, mag, rag, rib, rot, vex **04** bait, chip, gibe, goad, goof, grig, josh, mock, nark, tose, toze **05** annoy, chaff, kiddy, sound, taunt, teaze, toaze, touse, touze, towse, towze, worry **06** badger, banter, bother, chiack, chyack, needle, pester, plague, wind up **07** mamaguy, perplex, provoke, torment **08** back-comb, irritate, ridicule **09** aggravate, have a go at, make fun of, poke fun at, tantalize

technetium
02 Tc

technical
06 expert **07** applied **09** practical **10** artificial, electronic, industrial, mechanical, scientific, specialist **11** specialized **12** computerized, professional **13** technological

technically
11 practically **12** mechanically **14** electronically, professionally, scientifically **15** technologically

technician
06 fitter **08** engineer, mechanic, operator **09** machinist, operative, rocketeer **11** mechanician, vision mixer **12** phlebotomist, radiographer

technique
03 art, way **04** mode **05** craft, ELISA, knack, means, skill, style, touch, trick **06** course, manner, method, system **07** ability, fashion, knowhow, mastery, technic **08** approach, artistry, delivery, facility, technics **09** animation, dexterity, execution, expertise, procedure, serialism **10** capability, holography, millefiori, rag-rolling **11** performance, proficiency, skilfulness **12** oil immersion **13** craftsmanship, modus operandi

technology
- **appropriate technology, alternative technology**
02 AT
- **information technology**
02 IT **08** infotech **11** informatics

tedious
04 drab, dull, flat, long **05** a drag, banal, prosy, samey, weary **06** boring, draggy, dreary, dreich, tiring **07** humdrum, irksome, operose, prosaic, routine **08** lifeless, long-spun, tiresome,

unvaried, wearying **09** laborious, wearisome **10** dragsville, long-winded, monotonous, unexciting, uninspired **11** balls-aching **12** long-drawn-out, run-of-the-mill **13** uninteresting

- **tedious person**
04 bore **06** foozle

tedium
03 rut **05** ennui **07** boredom, routine **08** banality, drabness, dullness, monotony, sameness, vapidity **09** prosiness **10** dreariness **11** irksomeness, tediousness **12** lifelessness **14** monotonousness

tee
01 T

teem
04 bear, brim, pour, rain **05** burst, crawl, empty, spawn, swarm **06** abound, be full **07** bristle, produce **08** increase, multiply, overflow, pelt down **09** pullulate **10** bucket down **11** chuck it down, proliferate **15** rain cats and dogs

teeming
04 full **05** alive, great, thick **06** packed **07** copious, crowded, replete **08** abundant, brimming, bursting, childing, crawling, fruitful, numerous, pregnant, seething, swarming **09** bristling, chock-full, plentiful **11** chock-a-block, overflowing, pullulating

teenage
05 young **08** immature, juvenile, teenaged, youthful **10** adolescent

teenager
03 boy, Mod, yob **04** girl, teen **05** minor, youth **06** rocker **07** sharpie **08** juvenile **09** rangatahi **10** adolescent, bobbysoxer, junior miss, young adult **11** teeny-bopper, young person **13** emerging adult

teeny
03 wee **04** tiny **06** minute, teensy, teenty, titchy **07** teentsy **09** miniature, minuscule **10** diminutive, teeny-weeny **11** microscopic **12** teensy-weensy

teeter
◊ *anagram indicator*
04 reel, rock, roll, sway **05** lurch, pitch, pivot, shake, waver **06** seesaw, totter, wobble **07** balance, stagger, tremble **08** hesitate **09** vacillate

teeth

Teeth include:
03 cap, dog, egg, eye, gag, gam, jaw **04** baby, back, buck, fang, fore, gold, milk, mill, tush, tusk, wang, wolf **05** cheek, colt's, crown, false, first, molar, plate, store, sweet, upper **06** bridge, canine, chisel, corner, cuspid, wisdom **07** denture, grinder, incisor, scissor, snaggle **08** bicuspid, dentures, impacted, premolar

09 milk-molar, permanent, sectorial, serration
10 carnassial, first molar, masticator, molendinar, third molar
11 multicuspid, second molar
12 snaggletooth
13 first premolar
14 central incisor, lateral incisor, second premolar

teetotal
02 TT **05** sober **06** tee-tee **08** complete
09 abstinent, out-and-out, temperate
10 abstemious, on the wagon

teetotaller
02 TT **06** tee-tee, wowser
09 abstainer, nephalist, Rechabite
10 non-drinker **12** water-drinker

telegram
03 fax **04** wire **05** cable, telex
09 cablegram, radiogram, telegraph
11 night letter, Telemessage®

telegraph
04 send, wire **05** cable, telex **06** signal
08 telegram, transmit **10** radiograph
11 teleprinter **12** Telautograph®
14 radiotelegraph
• **telegraph office**
02 TO

telepathy
03 ESP **10** sixth sense **11** mind-reading, second sight **12** clairvoyance

telephone
03 tel **04** buzz, call, dial, ring, tele-
05 phone **06** blower, call up, ring in, ring up **07** contact, handset, hot line
08 receiver **09** give a bell, give a buzz, make a call **10** get in touch **11** give a tinkle
• **on the telephone**
◇ *homophone indicator*

telescope
03 cut **04** trim, tube **05** crush, optic, scope **06** reduce, shrink, squash
07 abridge, compact, curtail, shorten, squeeze **08** compress, condense, contract, spyglass, truncate
09 binocular, optic tube, reflector, refractor **10** abbreviate, binoculars, concertina, equatorial **11** perspective
13 prospect-glass

televise
03 air **04** beam, show **05** cable, put on, relay **06** screen **08** transmit **09** broadcast

television
02 TV **03** box, set **04** tele, tube
05 cable, telly **06** the box **07** the tube
08 boob tube, idiot box, receiver
09 goggle-box **11** cablevision, small screen **13** narrowcasting

Television programme types include:

04 news, soap
05 anime, drama
06 repeat, sitcom
07 cartoon, phone-in, reality
08 bulletin, chat show, docusoap, game show, quiz show
09 panel game, soap opera
11 documentary
12 makeover show

Television channels include:

02 E4
03 ABC, CNN, Fox, HBO, MTV, NBC, QVC, S4C, VH1
04 BBC1, BBC2, BBC3, BBC4, CBBC, CNBC, Five, ITV1, ITV2, ITV3
06 Sky One
07 Fox News, History, Sky News
08 BBC World, Cbeebies, Channel 4, FilmFour, Living TV
09 al-Jazeera, BBC News 24, Bloomberg, Discovery, Eurosport, Sky Movies, Sky Sports
11 Nickelodeon

Television programmes include:

02 ER, QI
03 CSI, QED
04 GMTV, M*A*S*H
05 Arena, Bread, Kojak, LA Law, Shaft
06 Batman, Bottom, Cheers, Dallas, Hi-De-Hi, Lassie, Minder, Mr Bean, Quincy, Sharpe, Tiswas
07 Bagpuss, Blake's 7, Columbo, Dynasty, Frasier, Friends, Holiday, Horizon, Lovejoy, Maigret, Mr Magoo, Omnibus, Poldark, Pop Idol, Rainbow, Rawhide, Spender, Taggart, The Bill, The Word, Tonight, Top Gear
08 'Allo 'Allo, Baywatch, Bergerac, Casualty, Dad's Army, Eldorado, Faking It, NYPD Blue, Panorama, Porridge, Red Dwarf, Roseanne, Seinfeld, Sgt Bilko, Star Trek, Stingray, The Saint, Time Team, Trumpton, Watchdog, Wife Swap
09 Andy Pandy, Blind Date, Blue Peter, Brookside, Countdown, Doctor Who, Dr Kildare, Emmerdale, Father Ted, Happy Days, Heartbeat, Holby City, Hollyoaks, I Love Lucy, Jackanory, Miami Vice, News at Ten, Newsnight, Newsround, Parkinson, South Park, That's Life, The X Files, Twin Peaks, Up Pompeii!
10 Ally McBeal, Big Brother, Blackadder, Crossroads, Deputy Dawg, EastEnders, Gladiators, Grandstand, Grange Hill, Howards' Way, Jim'll Fix It, Kavanagh QC, Masterchef, Mastermind, Miss Marple, Neighbours, On the Buses, Pebble Mill, Perry Mason, Play School, Postman Pat, Quatermass, Rising Damp, The Goodies, The Monkees, The Sweeney, The Waltons, The Wombles, The X-Factor, Wacky Races
11 Animal Magic, Call My Bluff, Catchphrase, Come Dancing, Crackerjack, Fame Academy, Give Us a Clue, Ground Force, Hawaii Five-O, Home and Away, Juke Box Jury, Life on Earth, Teletubbies, The Avengers, The Fast Show, The Fugitive, The Good Life, The Prisoner, The Simpsons, Tom and Jerry, What's My Line?, Yes, Minister
12 As Time Goes By, Blockbusters, Candid Camera, Citizen Smith, Fawlty Towers, Fifteen to One, It's a Knockout, Knots Landing, Melrose Place, Moonlighting, Mork and Mindy, Open All Hours, Peak Practice, Points of View, Question Time, Sesame Street, Terry and June, The Young Ones, Thunderbirds, Top of the Pops
13 A Touch of Frost, Blankety Blank, Bob the Builder, Breakfast Time, Emmerdale Farm, Hamish Macbeth, Ivor the Engine, Little Britain, Match of the Day, May to December, Muffin the Mule, Pinky and Perky, Ready, Steady, Go, Sex and the City, Songs of Praise, Spitting Image, Steptoe and Son, The Likely Lads, The Liver Birds, The Lone Ranger, The Muppet Show, The Sky at Night, The Two Ronnies, The World at War, Whicker's World
14 Animal Hospital, Ballykissangel, Cagney and Lacey, Captain Pugwash, Charlie's Angels, Family Fortunes, Gardener's World, Inspector Morse, Murder, She Wrote, My Friend Flicka, Record Breakers, The Flintstones, The Frost Report, The Weakest Link, This Is Your Life, Tomorrow's World, To the Manor Born, Wheel of Fortune, Worzel Gummidge
15 Birds of a Feather, Camberwick Green, Hill Street Blues, Midsomer Murders, One Man and His Dog, Ready Steady Cook, Remington Steele, Starsky and Hutch, The Addams Family, The Big Breakfast, The Man from UNCLE, The New Statesman, The Price is Right, The Twilight Zone, Watch with Mother, You've Been Framed

See also **quiz**

Television presenters include:

03 Ant (Anthony McPartlin), Dec (Declan Donnelly)
04 Muir (Frank), Ross (Jonathan)
05 Aspel (Michael), Black (Cilla), Bragg (Melvyn, Lord), Evans (Chris), Frost (Sir David), James (Clive), Moore (Sir Patrick), Negus (Arthur), Wogan (Terry)
06 Carson (Johnny), Norden (Denis), Norman (Barry), Paxman (Jeremy), Rayner (Claire), Savile (Sir Jimmy)
07 Andrews (Eamon), Bellamy (David), Edmonds (Noel), Forsyth (Bruce), Kennedy (Sir Ludovic), Madeley (Richard), Rantzen (Esther), Starkey (David), Tarrant (Chris), Wheldon (Sir Huw), Whicker (Alan), Winfrey (Oprah)
08 Bakewell (Joan), Campbell (Nicky), Finnigan (Judy), Stoppard (Miriam), Sullivan (Ed)
09 Ant and Dec (Anthony McPartlin/Declan Donnelly), Magnusson (Magnus), Parkinson (Michael)

10 Titchmarsh (Alan)
12 Attenborough (Sir David)
14 Richard and Judy (Richard Madeley/Judy Finnigan)

- **television system**
03 PAL **10** flat-screen **13** closed circuit

tell
03 bid, rat, say, see **04** blab, shop, show, talk **05** alter, brief, count, drain, grass, order, speak, state, story, utter **06** advise, affect, assure, betray, change, charge, decree, direct, gossip, impart, inform, notify, recite, relate, report, reveal, sketch, squeal, tattle, unfold **07** apprise, command, confess, declare, dictate, discern, divulge, exhaust, explain, let know, make out, mention, narrate, portray, recount, require, versify **08** acquaint, announce, count out, denounce, describe, disclose, discover, identify, inform on, instruct, perceive, proclaim **09** authorize, broadcast, delineate, elucidate, make known, recognize, tell apart, tell tales, transform **10** comprehend, understand **11** blow the gaff, communicate, distinguish **12** discriminate **13** differentiate, spill the beans, take its toll of **14** give the low-down, have an effect on **15** give the game away

- **tell off**
04 slam **05** chide, knock, scold, slate **06** berate, bounce, carpet, rebuke, see off **07** bawl out, catch it, censure, chew out, lecture, reprove, tick off, upbraid **08** reproach **09** dress down, pull apart, reprimand, take apart **14** give a talking-to

teller
05 clerk, griot **06** banker, tailor, tellar, tiller **07** cashier, sapling **09** bank clerk, raconteur, treasurer **10** Munchausen, raconteuse **11** Munchhausen

telling
06 cogent, marked **07** pointed **08** powerful **09** effective, narration, narrative, numbering, revealing **10** convincing, impressive, meaningful, persuasive **11** instruction, significant

telling-off
03 row **06** earful, rebuke, rocket **07** chiding, lecture, reproof, wigging **08** reproach, scolding **09** carpeting, reprimand, talking-to **10** bawling-out, ticking-off, upbraiding **11** castigation **12** dressing-down **14** kick in the pants, slap on the wrist **15** smack on the wrist

tell-tale
03 spy **05** clype, grass, sneak **06** buzzer, snitch **07** stoolie, tattler **08** blabbing, give-away, informer, snitcher, squealer **09** betraying, revealing **10** indicating, meaningful, noticeable, revelatory, suggestive, tale-teller, tattle-tale **11** perceptible, secret agent **12** unmistakable **15** snake in the grass

tellurium
02 Te

telly *see* **television**

temerity
04 gall **05** cheek, nerve **06** daring **08** audacity, boldness, rashness **09** impudence **10** effrontery **11** presumption **12** impertinence, recklessness **13** impulsiveness

temper
03 wax **04** alay, calm, cool, fury, mood, rage, tone, trim, tune **05** aleye, allay, alloy, anger, assay, blood, delay, paddy, radge, scene, storm **06** adjust, anneal, attune, harden, humour, lessen, master, meddle, modify, nature, reduce, season, soften, soothe, tamper, weaken **07** assuage, bad mood, chasten, flare-up, fortify, passion, roughen, tantrum, toughen **08** attitude, calmness, comeddle, mitigate, moderate, palliate, tone down **09** alleviate, annoyance, character, composure, condition, fireworks, ill-humour, petulance **10** resentment, strengthen **11** disposition, fit of temper, frame of mind, self-control, state of mind, temperament **12** constitution, irritability, pyrotechnics, tranquillity

See also **bad-tempered**

- **lose your temper**
05 go mad **06** see red **07** explode **08** boil over, freak out, get angry **09** blow a fuse, do your nut, go bananas, go up a wall, raise hell **10** hit the roof **11** blow a gasket, blow your top, flip your lid, get up in arms, go up the wall, lose your rag **12** blow your cool, fly into a rage, lose your cool, throw a wobbly **13** get aggravated, have a hissy fit, hit the ceiling, throw a tantrum **14** foam at the mouth **15** fly off the handle, get all steamed up, go off the deep end

temperament
04 bent, mood, soul **05** blood, humor **06** humour, kidney, make-up, mettle, nature, phlegm, spirit, temper **07** climate, outlook **08** attitude, tendency **09** character, composure, fieriness, moodiness, tempering **10** complexion, compromise, impatience, touchiness, volatility **11** disposition, frame of mind, personality, sensitivity, state of mind **12** constitution, excitability, idiosyncrasy, irritability **13** explosiveness, hot-headedness, red-headedness

temperamental
05 fiery, moody **06** inborn, innate, touchy **07** natural **08** artistic, inherent, neurotic, petulant, volatile **09** emotional, excitable, explosive, hot-headed, impatient, ingrained, irritable, mercurial, sensitive **10** capricious, congenital, hot-blooded, passionate, unreliable **12** highly strung **13** over-emotional, over-sensitive,

unpredictable **14** constitutional, hypersensitive

temperamentally
08 innately **09** basically, naturally **10** inherently **13** fundamentally

temperance
08 sobriety **09** austerity, restraint **10** abstinence, continence, moderation, self-denial **11** prohibition, self-control, teetotalism **13** self-restraint **14** abstemiousness, self-discipline

temperate
04 calm, fair, mild **05** balmy, sober **06** gentle, stable **07** clement, equable **08** balanced, composed, moderate, pleasant, sensible, teetotal **09** abstinent, agreeable, continent **10** abstemious, controlled, reasonable, restrained **11** self-denying **12** even-tempered **14** self-controlled, self-restrained

temperature
01 t **04** temp **05** fever **07** mixture **10** proportion **12** constitution

tempest
04 gale **05** storm **06** furore, squall, tumult, uproar **07** cyclone, ferment, tornado, turmoil, typhoon **08** upheaval **09** bourasque, commotion, hurricane **11** disturbance

tempestuous
04 high, wild **05** gusty, rough, windy **06** fierce, heated, raging, stormy, wrathy **07** furious, intense, squally, violent **08** blustery, feverish **09** turbulent **10** boisterous, passionate, tumultuous **11** impassioned **12** uncontrolled

template
03 jig **04** form, mold **05** frame, model, mould **06** master, matrix **07** pattern, profile **08** strickle **09** blueprint, prototype **10** master page, stylesheet **12** cookie-cutter

temple
03 wat **04** fane, naos **06** church, haffet, haffit, mandir, mosque, pagoda, shrine **07** mandira **08** teocalli **09** joss house, sanctuary, synagogue **10** tabernacle **14** place of worship

See also **religious; worship**

tempo
04 beat, pace, rate, time **05** agoge, metre, pulse, speed, throb **06** rhythm **07** cadence, measure **08** movement, velocity

temporal
04 good **05** civil **06** carnal, mortal, timely **07** earthly, fleshly, profane, secular, worldly **08** material **11** terrestrial **12** temporaneous

temporarily
06 for now, pro tem **07** briefly **08** for a time **10** fleetingly **11** momentarily, transiently **12** in the interim, transitorily **15** for the time being

temporary

05 brief **06** fill-in, pro tem **07** Band-aid®, interim, passing, stopgap **08** fleeting, temporal **09** ephemeral, fugacious, makeshift, momentary, provisory, short-term, transient **10** evanescent, short-lived, transitory **11** impermanent, provisional **12** temporaneous **14** extemporaneous

temporize

05 delay, pause, stall **08** hang back **09** hum and haw **10** equivocate **11** play for time **12** tergiversate **13** procrastinate

tempt

03 woo **04** bait, bayt, coax, draw, lure, tice **05** assay, educe, egg on **06** allure, cajole, entice, incite, induce, invite **07** attempt, attract, dispose, incline, provoke, suggest **08** inveigle, persuade **09** tantalize

temptation

04 bait, draw, lure, pull **05** snare, trial **06** allure, appeal, urging **07** attempt, coaxing **08** cajolery **09** influence, seduction, tentation **10** allurement, attraction, cloven hoof, enticement, incitement, inducement, invitation, invitement, persuasion, suggestion

tempting

04 sexy **08** alluring, enticing, inviting **09** lickerish, liquorish, seductive **10** appetizing, attractive **11** tantalizing **13** mouthwatering

temptress

04 vamp **05** Circe, flirt, siren **06** Dalila **07** Dalilah, Delilah, Lorelei **08** coquette **09** sorceress **10** seductress **11** enchantress, femme fatale

ten

01 X **02** 10 **05** decad **06** decade, dectet, denary

tenable

05 sound **06** viable **08** arguable, credible, feasible, rational **09** plausible **10** believable, defendable, defensible, reasonable **11** justifiable, supportable **12** maintainable

tenacious

04 fast, firm **05** tight, tough **06** claggy, dogged, grippy, secure, sticky **07** adamant **08** adhesive, clinging, cohesive, obdurate, resolute, stubborn **09** obstinate, retentive, steadfast **10** determined, persistent, purposeful, relentless, unshakable, unswerving, unyielding **11** persevering, unshakeable **12** intransigent, single-minded

tenacity

04 guts, hold **05** force, power **07** resolve **08** fastness, firmness, obduracy, solidity, strength **09** diligence, obstinacy, solidness, toughness **10** doggedness, resolution **11** application, persistence, pertinacity, staunchness **12** forcefulness, perseverance, resoluteness,

stubbornness **13** determination, inflexibility, intransigence, steadfastness **14** indomitability

tenancy

05 lease **06** tenure **07** holding, renting **09** leasehold, occupancy, residence **10** incumbency, occupation, possession

tenant

04 ryot **05** baron, dwell, gebur, thane **06** farmer, lessee, mailer, occupy, raiyat, renter, socman **07** cottier, métayer, socager, sokeman **08** gavelman, occupant, occupier, resident, suckener **09** incumbent, pendicler **10** inhabitant, landholder **11** householder, leaseholder

• **be a tenant**
03 sit

tend

02 go **03** aim, ren, rin, run **04** bear, bend, grow, head, herd, keep, lamb, lead, lean, make, mind, move, wait **05** dress, groom, guard, nurse, offer, point, see to, serve, sound, verge, watch **06** affect, attend, escort, handle, invite, manage, wait on **07** care for, conduce, hearken, incline, nurture, protect **08** attend to, be liable, maintain, wait upon **09** cultivate, gravitate, look after, watch over **10** be inclined, minister to, take care of **11** keep an eye on **13** show a tendency

tendency

03 set **04** bent, bias, turn **05** drift, trend **06** course, genius, levity **07** aptness, bearing, conatus, heading, leaning **08** movement **09** direction, liability, proneness, readiness **10** partiality, proclivity, propensity **11** disposition, inclination **14** predisposition, susceptibility

tendentious

06 biased **07** at issue **08** disputed, doubtful **09** debatable, polemical **10** disputable **11** contentious **12** questionable **13** controversial

tender

03 bid, new, raw, red **04** care, fond, give, kind, nesh, plan, pram, sair, soft, sore, warm, weak **05** chary, coins, early, frail, green, juicy, money, offer, praam, price, value, young **06** aching, callow, caring, dainty, extend, feeble, fleshy, gentle, humane, kindly, loving, regard, render, submit **07** advance, amoroso, amorous, beloved, bruised, cherish, concern, fragile, painful, pinnace, present, proffer, propose, suggest **08** currency, delicate, estimate, fondness, footsore, generous, immature, inflamed, merciful, pathetic, proposal, romantic, smarting, youthful **09** banknotes, easy to cut, emotional, evocative, quotation, sensitive, soft-paste, succulent, throbbing, volunteer **10** affettuoso, benevolent, easy to chew, scrupulous, submission, suggestion, vulnerable **11** considerate,

proposition, sentimental, soft-hearted, sympathetic **12** affectionate **13** compassionate, inexperienced, tender-hearted **14** impressionable

tender-hearted

04 fond, kind, mild, warm **06** benign, caring, gentle, humane, kindly, loving **07** feeling, pitying **08** merciful **09** sensitive **10** benevolent, responsive **11** considerate, kind-hearted, sentimental, soft-hearted, sympathetic, warm-hearted **12** affectionate **13** compassionate

tenderly

06 fondly, gently, warmly **08** lovingly **10** affettuoso, generously **11** emotionally, sensitively **12** benevolently, romantically **13** considerately, sentimentally **14** affectionately **15** compassionately, sympathetically

tenderness

04 ache, care, love, pain, pity **05** mercy, youth **06** aching, liking, warmth **07** feeling, rawness **08** bruising, delicacy, devotion, fondness, humanity, kindness, softness, soreness, sympathy, weakness **09** affection, fragility, frailness, greenness, juiciness, sweetness **10** attachment, callowness, compassion, feebleness, gentleness, humaneness, immaturity, irritation, succulence **11** amorousness, benevolence, painfulness, sensitivity **12** delicateness, inexperience, inflammation, youthfulness **13** consideration, sensitiveness, vulnerability **14** loving-kindness, sentimentality **15** soft-heartedness, warm-heartedness

tendon

05 sinew **06** leader, paxwax **09** hamstring **11** aponeurosis, heart-string

tenet

04 rule, view **05** canon, credo, creed, dogma, maxim **06** belief, thesis **07** opinion, precept **08** doctrine, teaching **09** principle **10** adiaphoron, conviction **11** presumption **14** article of faith

Tennessee

02 TN **04** Tenn

tennis

10 jeu de paume **12** sphairistike

Tennis players include:

04 Ashe (Arthur), Borg (Björn), Cash (Pat), Graf (Steffi), Hoad (Lew), King (Billie Jean), Ryan (Elizabeth), Wade (Virginia)
05 Budge (Don), Bueno (Maria), Court (Margaret), Evert (Chris), Jones (Ann), Laver (Rod), Lendl (Ivan), Lloyd (Chris), Perry (Fred), Roche (Tony), Seles (Monica), Stich (Michael), Vilas (Guillermo), Wills (Helen)

06 Agassi (Andre), Austin (Tracy),
06 Agassi (Andre), Austin (Tracy), Barker (Sue), Becker (Boris), Cawley (Evonne), Drobny (Jaroslav), DuPont (Margaret), Edberg (Stefan), Gibson (Althea), Henman (Tim), Hewitt (Lleyton), Hingis (Martina), Hopman (Harry), Kramer (Jack), Murray (Andy), Rafter (Pat),Tilden (Bill)

07 Borotra (Jean), Brookes (Sir Norman Everard), Connors (Jimmy), Emerson (Roy), Federer (Roger), Godfree (Kitty), Lacoste (Rene), Lenglen (Suzanne), Maskell (Dan), McEnroe (John), Nastase (Ilie), Novotna (Jana), Renshaw (Willie), Sampras (Pete), Sedgman (Frank), Shriver (Pam)

08 Capriati (Jennifer), Connolly (Maureen 'Little Mo'), Gonzales (Pancho), Krajicek (Richard), Newcombe (John), Rosewall (Ken), Rusedski (Greg), Sabatini (Gabriela),Williams (Serena), Williams (Venus)

09 Davenport (Lindsay), Goolagong (Evonne), Sharapova (Maria), Woodforde (Mark)

10 Ivanisevic (Goran), Kafelnikov (Yevgeny), Kournikova (Anna),Wills Moody (Helen),Woodbridge (Todd)

11 Navratilova (Martina)

15 Goolagong Cawley (Evonne)

Tennis-related terms include:

03 ace, ATP, let, lob, LTA, set,WTA
04 love, pass
05 AELTC, break, deuce, drive, fault, rally, serve, slice, smash
06 return, umpire, volley, winner
07 ballboy, net cord, runback
08 backhand, ballgirl, baseline, drop shot, forehand, line call, love game, midcourt, net judge, overhead, overrule, set point, tie-break, wood shot
09 advantage, backcourt, baseliner, break back, foot fault, forecourt, hold serve, line judge, mini-break, sweet spot, tramlines, two-handed
10 break point, cross court, deuce court, match point
11 block volley, double fault, service game, service line
12 approach shot, ground stroke, mixed doubles, service court
13 second service
14 advantage court, serve and volley

tenor
01 T **03** aim, way **04** feck, gist, path **05** drift, point, sense, theme, trend,Trial **06** burden, course, intent, spirit **07** essence, meaning, purport, purpose, texture **08** tendency **09** direction, substance

tense
01 t **04** edgy, taut, work **05** brace, drawn, heavy, jumpy, rigid, stiff, tight **06** narrow, on edge, strain, taught, uneasy **07** anxious, charged, fidgety, fraught, jittery, keyed up, nervous,

stiffen, stretch, tighten, uptight, worried **08** contract, exciting, restless, strained, worrying **09** inflexion, screwed up, stressful, stretched **10** distraught, inflection, nail-biting **11** overwrought, stressed out **12** apprehensive, nerve-racking **13** under pressure

Grammatical tenses include:

02 pt
03 pat
04 past
06 aorist, future
07 perfect, present
08 preterit
09 imperfect, preterite
10 pluperfect
11 conditional, past perfect
12 gnomic aorist, past historic
13 future perfect
14 present perfect
15 paragogic future

tensely
08 in a state, uneasily **09** anxiously, nervously, worriedly **10** restlessly **11** stressed out **14** apprehensively

tension
04 feud **05** clash, worry **06** nerves, strain, stress, strife, unrest, wobbly **07** anxiety, discord, dispute, ill-will, jitters, quarrel, willies **08** conflict, disquiet, distress, edginess, friction, pressure, rigidity, suspense, tautness, variance **09** agitation, antipathy, hostility, stiffness, straining, tightness **10** antagonism, contention, dissension, opposition, stretching, uneasiness **11** butterflies, nervousness **12** apprehension, collywobbles, disagreement, hypertension, restlessness **13** confrontation, heebie-jeebies

• **equal tension**
08 isotonic
• **high tension**
02 HT
• **low tension**
02 LT
• **premenstrual tension**
03 PMT
• **surface tension**
01 T

tent
04 camp, heed **05** probe

Tents include:

03 box, ger, gur, mat
04 bell, dome, kata, tilt, tipi, yurt
05 bivvy, black, frame, lodge, ridge, tepee, tupik, yourt
06 big top, canopy, canvas, teepee, tunnel, wigwam
07 conical, marquee, touring, trailer, yaranga
10 single hoop, tabernacle
11 hooped bivvy
12 sloping ridge, sloping wedge
13 barrel-vaulted, crossover pole

• **tent village**
04 duar **05** douar, dowar

tentacle
03 arm **04** horn **06** feeler **12** hectocotylus

tentative
04 test **05** pilot, timid, trial **06** unsure **08** cautious, doubtful, hesitant, unproven, wavering **09** diffident, faltering, peirastic, uncertain, undecided **10** indefinite **11** conjectural, exploratory, provisional, speculative, unconfirmed **12** experimental **13** to be confirmed

tentatively
06 on spec **07** timidly **08** gingerly **10** cautiously, doubtfully, hesitantly **12** indefinitely **13** peirastically, provisionally, speculatively **14** experimentally

tenterhooks
• **on tenterhooks**
05 eager **07** anxious, excited, keyed up, nervous, waiting **08** watchful **09** expectant, impatient **10** in suspense **15** with bated breath

tenuous
04 fine, hazy, slim, thin, weak **05** shaky, vague **06** flimsy, slight, subtle **07** dubious, fragile, slender **08** delicate, doubtful, rarefied **09** recherché **10** indefinite **12** questionable **13** insubstantial

tenure
03 fee, feu **04** tack, term, time **05** lease, tenor **06** papacy, socage **07** burgage, fee-farm, holding, popedom, soccage, tenancy **08** frank-fee, steelbow, vasavory, venville **09** commendam, gavelkind, leasehold, occupancy, pastorate, priorship, rabbinate, residence, sokemanry, villenage **10** archontate, cottierism, government, habitation, incumbency, occupation, possession, villeinage **12** frankalmoign **13** knight service **14** proprietorship, subinfeudation

tepee
04 tent, tipi

tepid
03 lew **04** cool **07** warmish **08** lukewarm **09** apathetic **11** half-hearted, indifferent **14** unenthusiastic

terbium
02 Tb

term
03 dub, end, tag **04** call, fees, name, span, time, word **05** bound, close, costs, label, limit, point, rates, space, spell, style, title **06** clause, course, detail, finish, period, phrase, prices, season, tariff **07** charges, entitle, epithet, footing, proviso, session, stretch **08** boundary, duration, fruition, interval, locution, position, semester, standing, terminus **09** condition, designate, provision, relations, trimester **10** conclusion, denominate, expression, particular **11** appellation, culmination, designation, restriction,

stipulation **12** denomination, relationship **13** qualification, specification

04 Lent
06 Easter, Hilary
07 Trinity
10 Michaelmas

• **come to terms**
06 accept, submit **08** compound
10 articulate **11** accommodate
12 come to accept **14** resign yourself
• **in terms of**
09 as regards **10** in regard to **12** in relation to, with regard to **13** with respect to
• **on good terms**
02 in

terminal
◊ *tail selection indicator*
03 end, VDU **04** last, pole, POST, RJET
05 acute, depot, dying, fatal, final, limit
06 deadly, ending, garage, lethal, mortal, utmost **07** console, extreme, killing, monitor, station **08** boundary, desinent, keyboard, last stop, limiting, railhead, terminus, ultimate
09 confining, extremity, incurable
10 concluding **11** desinential, termination, untreatable, workstation
12 end of the line
• **terminal part**
03 cap **06** cloaca, rectum **12** sigmoid colon **14** sigmoid flexure

terminally
07 fatally **08** lethally, mortally
09 incurably **11** malignantly

terminate
03 end **04** fall, stop **05** abort, cease, close, issue, lapse **06** cut off, expire, finish, result, run out, wind up
07 dismiss **08** complete, conclude, dissolve, leave off **10** put an end to
11 come to an end, discontinue
12 bring to an end

termination
03 end **05** close, finis, issue **06** demise, effect, ending, expiry, finale, finish, result **07** success **08** abortion, boundary, naricorn **09** cessation
10 completion, conclusion, dénouement **11** consequence
15 discontinuation

terminology
05 terms, words **06** jargon
08 language **10** glossology, vocabulary
11 expressions, phraseology
12 nomenclature

terminus
◊ *tail selection indicator*
03 end **04** goal **05** close, depot, limit
06 garage, target **07** station
08 boundary, terminal **09** extremity
11 air terminal, destination, termination
12 end of the line **13** starting-point

termite
03 ant **07** duck-ant, royalty, wood ant
08 white ant **09** woodlouse

Terra
04 Gaia

terrace
03 Ter **04** Terr **05** beach, bench, linch, shelf **06** offset, perron, tarras
07 balcony, sun deck, veranda
08 barbette, crescent, platform, verandah **09** promenade **10** undercliff

terrain
04 land **06** ground **07** country, terrane, terrene **09** landscape, territory
10 topography **11** countryside

terrapin
04 emys **06** slider **08** redbelly
11 diamondback **13** water tortoise

terrestrial
04 land **06** global, layman **07** earthly, mundane, terrene, worldly
09 subastral, tellurian

terrible
◊ *anagram indicator*
03 bad, big, ill **04** foul, grim, naff, poor, poxy, ropy, sick, vile, weak **05** awful, great, large, lousy, nasty, pants, ropey, sorry **06** aching, crappy, crummy, faulty, gloomy, guilty, horrid, in pain, poorly, severe, unwell **07** ashamed, extreme, fearful, hateful, hideous, intense, notable, painful, serious, tearing, the pits, unhappy, useless **08** contrite, diseased, dreadful, gruesome, hopeless, horrible, horrific, inferior, mediocre, pathetic, pokerish, shocking
09 abhorrent, appalling, defective, deficient, frightful, harrowing, imperfect, monstrous, obnoxious, offensive, repulsive, revolting, third-rate **10** abortional, apologetic, despondent, disgusting, hellacious, inadequate, indisposed, outrageous, pronounced, remorseful, second-rate, shamefaced, unpleasant **11** a load of crap, distressing, exceptional, incompetent, ineffective, substandard, unspeakable **12** unacceptable **14** a load of garbage, a load of rubbish, unsatisfactory **15** under the weather

terribly
◊ *anagram indicator*
04 evil, much, very **06** evilly
07 awfully, greatly **09** decidedly, extremely, seriously **10** thoroughly
11 desperately, exceedingly, frightfully

terrier
04 roll **08** register, rent-roll
09 inventory **11** territorial

03 fox
04 bull, Skye
05 cairn, foxie, Irish, Welsh
06 Border, Boston, Scotch, Scotty, Westie, Yorkie
07 pit bull, Scottie, Tibetan
08 Aberdeen, Airedale, Doberman, Scottish, Sealyham, wire-hair
09 Kerry blue, schnauzer, Yorkshire
10 Australian, Bedlington, Manchester, wire-haired
11 Jack Russell
12 West Highland
13 Dandie Dinmont
15 American pit bull

terriers
02 TA

terrific
03 ace **04** cool, huge, mega, neat, wild
05 brill, crack, great, large, super, triff
06 superb, wicked **07** amazing, awesome, crucial, extreme, hell of a, intense **08** dreadful, enormous, fabulous, gigantic, smashing
09 brilliant, excellent, excessive, fantastic, wonderful **10** marvellous, prodigious, remarkable, stupendous, terrifying, tremendous **11** frightening, magnificent, outstanding, sensational
12 breathtaking **13** extraordinary
14 out of this world

terrifically
04 very **05** jolly **06** highly, really
07 acutely, awfully, greatly, utterly
08 severely, terribly **09** decidedly, extremely, intensely, unusually
10 dreadfully, remarkably, thoroughly, uncommonly **11** exceedingly, excessively, frightfully
12 immoderately, inordinately, unreasonably **13** exceptionally
15 extraordinarily

terrified
04 awed **06** aghast, scared **07** alarmed
08 appalled, dismayed **09** horrified, petrified **10** frightened **11** in a blue funk, intimidated, scared stiff
12 horror-struck **13** having kittens, panic-stricken, scared to death

terrify
04 fear, gast, numb **05** alarm, appal, ghast, grise, panic, scare, shock
06 agrise, agrize, agryze, dismay, rattle
07 horrify, petrify **08** affright, frighten, paralyse **09** terrorize **10** intimidate, scare stiff **12** put the wind up

territorial
04 area **05** zonal **08** district, domainal, regional **09** localized, sectional
11 topographic **12** geographical

territorials
02 TA

territory
03 Ter **04** area, land, mark, Terr, turf, zone **05** field, state, tract **06** county, domain, region, sector **07** abthane, apanage, country, outland, terrain
08 appanage, backyard, district, outlands, preserve, province, sheikdom, toparchy, township
09 khedivate, sheikhdom
10 dependency, home ground, khediviate, possession, Reichsland
11 trusteeship **12** jurisdiction
See also **province; state**

terror
03 bug **04** bogy, fear **05** alarm, bogle, demon, devil, dread, fiend, panic, poker, rogue, shock **06** dismay, fright,

terrorist

horror, rascal **07** bugbear, monster
08 affright, blue funk, tearaway
09 cold sweat, scarecrow, terrorism
10 amazedness **11** trepidation
12 intimidation **13** consternation

terrorist
06 bomber, gunman, player **07** butcher
08 agitator, assassin, attacker, militant
09 aggressor, anarchist, assailant,
guerrilla **11** seditionist **13** revolutionary
14 freedom fighter, fundamentalist,
urban guerrilla
• **terrorist militia**
02 SA

terrorize
04 prey **05** alarm, bully, scare, shock
06 coerce, menace **07** horrify, oppress,
petrify, terrify **08** browbeat, frighten,
threaten **09** strongarm **10** intimidate
12 put the wind up

terse
04 curt **05** blunt, brief, crisp, pithy,
short **06** abrupt, gnomic, smooth,
snappy **07** brusque, compact, concise,
laconic **08** clean-cut, incisive, succinct
09 condensed **10** elliptical, to the point
12 epigrammatic, monosyllabic

test
03 MOT, pix, pyx, sap, SAT, try, van
04 Esda, exam, load, pass, quiz, tire
05 assay, check, drain, exact, probe,
proof, prove, study, testa, touch, trial,
trier, weary **06** assess, burden, dry run,
impose, ordeal, prieve, sample, screen,
strain, try out, try-out, verify, weaken
07 analyse, check-up, examine,
exhaust, inspect, reagent, scratch,
stretch, wear out **08** analysis, appraise,
audition, check out, crucible,
encumber, enervate, evaluate,
overload, prospect, sounding, trial run
09 challenge, criterion, probation,
questions, testimony, time trial
10 assessment, evaluation, experience,
experiment, inspection, pilot study,
scrutinize, shibboleth **11** examination,
exploration, investigate
13 investigation, make demands on,
questionnaire **14** scrutinization
See also **examination**
• **stand the test**
04 wash

testament
02 NT, OT **04** Test, will **05** proof
07 earnest, tribute, witness
08 covenant, evidence **09** testimony
11 attestation **13** demonstration
15 exemplification

testicles
04 nuts **05** balls, groin **07** cojones,
doucets, dowsets, gooleys, goolies
08 cobblers, knackers, lamb's fry
12 family jewels

testify
03 rap **04** avow, show **05** state, swear,
vouch **06** affirm, assert, attest, back up,
depone, verify **07** certify, confirm,
declare, endorse, speak to, support
08 proclaim **09** establish **11** bear

witness, corroborate, demonstrate
12 give evidence, substantiate

testimonial
04 chit **06** chitty **07** tribute
09 character, reference **10** credential
11 certificate, endorsement
12 commendation
14 recommendation

testimony
05 proof **06** attest, report **07** support,
tribute, witness **08** evidence
09 affidavit, assertion, statement
10 deposition, indication, profession,
submission **11** affirmation, attestation,
declaration **12** confirmation,
verification **13** corroboration,
demonstration, manifestation

testy
05 cross, ratty **06** crusty, grumpy, shirty,
snappy, sullen, tetchy, touchy
07 crabbed, fretful, peevish, stroppy,
waspish **08** captious, petulant,
snappish **09** crotchety, impatient,
irascible, irritable, splenetic **11** bad-
tempered, quarrelsome
12 cantankerous **13** quick-tempered,
short-tempered

tetchy
05 ratty **06** crusty, grumpy, shirty,
touchy **07** grouchy, peevish, teachie
08 scratchy, snappish **09** crotchety,
irascible, irritable **11** bad-tempered
13 short-tempered

tête-à-tête
03 jaw **04** chat, talk **06** confab, natter,
secret **07** twasome, twosome
08 chitchat, dialogue **10** face to face
12 a quattr'occhi, confidential,
conversation, heart-to-heart

tether
03 tie **04** bind, bond, cord, lash, lead,
line, rope **05** chain, hitch, leash, tie up
06 fasten, fetter, picket, piquet, secure
07 manacle, picquet, shackle
08 restrain **09** fastening, restraint

Teutonic
03 Ger **04** Teut **05** Dutch **06** German
08 Germanic

Texas
02 TX **03** Tex

text
04 body, book **05** Bible, issue, point,
theme, topic, verse, words **06** matter,
source **07** chapter, content, passage,
reading, set book, subject, wording
08 libretto, sentence, textbook
09 paragraph **10** main matter
11 boilerplate **13** subject matter

texture
03 web **04** feel, wale, woof **05** grain,
touch, weave **06** fabric, finish, tissue
07 quality, surface, weftage
09 character, structure, texturize
10 appearance **11** composition,
consistency **12** constitution

Thailand
01 T **03** THA

thallium
02 Tl

thank
03 owe **06** credit **07** aggrate, remercy
09 recognize **10** appreciate, be
grateful **11** acknowledge **13** say thank
you to

thankful
07 obliged, pleased **08** beholden,
grateful, indebted, relieved
09 contented **12** appreciative

thankfulness
09 gratitude **10** obligation
12 appreciation, indebtedness

thankless
07 useless **09** fruitless **10** ungrateful,
unrequited, unrewarded
11 unrewarding **12** unprofitable,
unrecognized **13** unappreciated
14 unacknowledged

thanks, thank you
02 ta **05** mercy **06** cheers, credit
08 bless you, gramercy, thank you
09 gratitude **10** many thanks **11** much
obliged, recognition **12** appreciation,
gratefulness, thanksgiving **13** thank-
offering **14** acknowledgment
15 acknowledgement
• **thanks to**
05 due to **07** owing to, through
09 because of **11** as a result of, on
account of

that
02 as, so, yt **03** how, yon **04** such
05 which **07** because
• **that French**
03 que, qui
• **that is, that's**
02 dh, ie **05** id est **09** das heisst

thatching
04 atap, reed **05** attap

thaw
04 melt, warm **05** de-ice, fresh, relax
06 heat up, soften **07** defrost, liquefy
08 defreeze, dissolve, loosen up,
unfreeze **09** uncongeal

the
01 t' **02** ye
• **the French**
02 la, le **03** les
• **the German**
03 das, der, die
• **the Italian**
01 i **02** il, la, le
• **the Spanish**
02 el, la **03** las, los

theatre
04 hall, shop **05** drama **06** cinema
08 the stage **09** dramatics, playhouse,
theatrics, the boards **10** opera house
11 Thespian art **12** amphitheatre, show
business **13** the footlights
See also **cinema**

Theatres include:

03 Pit
04 Rose, Swan
05 Abbey, Globe, Lyric, Savoy

06 Albery, Apollo, Donmar, Lyceum, Old Vic, Palace, Queen's
07 Adelphi, Aldwych, Almeida, Garrick, Gielgud, Mermaid, Olivier, Phoenix
08 Barbican, Broadway, Coliseum, Crucible, Dominion, Festival, National, Young Vic, Ziegfeld
09 Cottesloe, Criterion, Drury Lane, Haymarket, Lyttelton, Palladium, Playhouse
10 Royal Court
11 Comedy Store, Duke of York's, Her Majesty's, Moulin Rouge, Royal Lyceum, Shaftesbury
12 Covent Garden, Sadler's Wells, Theatre Royal, Winter Garden
13 Folies Bergère, Prince of Wales, The Other Place, The Roundhouse
14 Barbican Centre
15 Donmar Warehouse, London Palladium

Theatre parts include:

03 box, pit, set
04 area, drop, flat, grid, loge
05 apron, decor, flies, house, logum, spots, stage, wings
06 border, bridge, circle, floats, floods, lights, loggia, scruto, stalls
07 balcony, catwalk, curtain, cut drop, gallery, leg drop, rostrum, the gods, upstage
08 backdrop, coulisse, trapdoor
09 backstage, cyclorama, downstage, forestage, green room, mezzanine, open stage, tormentor
10 auditorium, footlights, fourth wall, ghost light, prompt side, proscenium
11 drop-curtain, house lights, upper circle
12 orchestra pit
13 safety curtain
14 opposite prompt, proscenium arch, revolving stage
15 proscenium doors

Theatre-related terms include:

02 BS, LX, OB, OP, PS
03 act, cue, fée, fly, gel, rep, run, vis, yok
04 call, cast, flat, grid, juve, loge, plot, pong, rake, tabs, wash, yock
05 actor, ad lib, angel, aside, derig, dry up, fit-up, genre, get-in, lines, lodge, props, re-rig, scene, spike, usher
06 baffle, chorus, corpse, critic, double, dry ice, Equity, flyman, fringe, get-out, make-up, miscue, places, prompt, review, script, walk-on
07 actress, costume, curtain, dresser, matinee, pittite, preview, project, rhubarb, rigging, scenery, tableau, upstage, West End
08 audience, audition, blackout, block out, Broadway, business, coulisse, dialogue, director, duologue, entr'acte, interval, libretto, overture, pass door, play-goer, producer, ring down, thespian, wardrobe, white out

09 backlight, backstage, beginners, box office, break a leg, chaperone, curtain up, cyclorama, double act, downstage, footlight, full house, limelight, monologue, periaktos, programme, rehearsal, repertory, soliloquy, soubrette, spotlight, stage crew, stage door, stage hand, stage left, usherette, visual cue
10 book-holder, dénouement, first night, followspot, fourth wall, get the bird, in the wings, prompt book, prompt copy, prompt desk, prompt side, stagecraft, stage right, understudy, walk-around
11 bastard side, centre stage, curtain call, curtain time, die the death, greasepaint, house lights, iron curtain, leading lady, off-Broadway, quick change, read-through, stage fright, top one's part, wind machine
12 breeches part, breeches role, first-nighter, front of house, intermission, jeune premier, juvenile lead, monstre sacré, principal boy, prompt corner, prompt script, stage manager, travesty role
13 bastard prompt, curtain-raiser, curtain speech, grande vedette, jeune première, safety curtain
14 dress rehearsal, opposite prompt, special effects
15 genteel business, opposite bastard

See also **director**

● **theatre award**
04 Tony

theatrical
◇ *anagram indicator*
03 OTT **04** camp **05** showy, stagy **06** forced, scenic, unreal **07** actorly, pompous **08** actorish, actressy, affected, dramatic, mannered, overdone, thespian **09** emotional **10** artificial, histrionic, over the top **11** exaggerated, extravagant **12** histrionical, melodramatic, ostentatious

---

Theatrical forms include:

03 Noh
04 mime, play
05 farce, opera, revue
06 Absurd, ballet, circus, comedy, fringe, kabuki, masque, puppet, street
07 cabaret, Cruelty, mummery, musical, pageant, tableau, tragedy
08 duologue, operetta
09 burlesque, melodrama, monologue, music hall, pantomime
10 in-the-round
11 black comedy, kitchen-sink, miracle play, mystery play
12 Grand Guignol, morality play, Punch and Judy
13 fringe theatre, musical comedy, puppet theatre, street theatre
14 comedy of menace
15 comedy of humours, comedy of manners, legitimate drama

Thebes *see* **Seven Against Thebes**

theft
03 job **04** blag, crib **05** fraud, heist, steal, sting, swipe, touch **06** mainor, rip-off, stouth, walk-in **07** larceny, lifting, mugging, nicking, pilfery, robbery, stealth, stick-up, swiping **08** burglary, filching, nobbling, pinching, plagiary, rustling, stealing, thieving **09** autocrime, pilferage, pilfering, stouthrie, swindling **10** purloining, stoutherie, stouthrief **11** kleptomania, shoplifting **12** embezzlement, smash-and-grab

them
02 'em **03** hem **04** some

thematic
08 notional **09** taxonomic **10** conceptual **14** classificatory

theme
03 peg **04** gist, idea, song, talk, text, tune **05** essay, lemma, motif, paper, story, topic, topos **06** burden, matter, melody, mythos, mythus, thesis, thread **07** burthen, essence, keynote, o'ercome, subject, subtext **08** argument, overcome, owrecome **09** leitmotif, leitmotiv **11** composition **12** dissertation **13** subject matter

then
03 now, tho, too **04** also, next, soon, syne, thus **05** after, and so **06** as well **07** besides, further **08** moreover **09** as a result, therefore, whereupon **10** afterwards, at that time, by that time, in addition **11** accordingly, at that point, furthermore, in those days **12** additionally, at a later date, at that moment, consequently, subsequently

theocracy
04 Zion **08** thearchy

theologian
02 DD **03** ThD **06** divine **09** schoolman

Theologians include:

03 Eck (Johann), Ela (Jean-Marc)
04 Baur (Ferdinand Christian), Bede ('the Venerable', St), John (of Damascus, St), More (Henry), Otto (Rudolf), Paul (St)
05 Arius, Barth (Karl), Buber (Martin), Colet (John), Cyril (of Alexandria, St), Llull (Ramón), Mbiti (John S), Paley (William), Pusey (Edward Bouverie), Young (Thomas)
06 Alcuin, Anselm (St), Butler (Joseph), Calvin (John), Hooker (Richard), Jansen (Cornelius), Jerome (St), Mather (Increase), Newman (John Henry, Cardinal), Ockham (William of), Origen, Pascal (Blaise), Rahner (Karl)
07 Abelard (Peter), Aquinas (St Thomas), Arnauld (Antoine), Bernard (of Clairvaux, St), Clement (of Alexandria), Cyprian (St), Eckhart (Johannes), Edwards (Jonathan), Gregory (of Nazianzus,

St), **Gregory** (of Nyssa), **Grotius** (Hugo), **Lombard** (Peter), **Sankara**, **Spinoza** (Baruch),**Tillich** (Paul Johannes),**William** (of Ockham)

08 **Arminius** (Jacobus), **Berengar** (of Tours) **Bultmann** (Rudolf Karl), **Chalmers** (Thomas), **Cudworth** (Ralph), **Eusebius**, **Ignatius** (of Loyola, St), **Irenaeus** (St), **Sprenger** (Jacob)

09 **Augustine** (St), **Bessarion** (John), **Nagarjuna**, **Söderblom** (Nathan)

10 **Athanasius** (St), **Bellarmine** (St Robert), **Bonhoeffer** (Dietrich), **Duns Scotus** (John), **Macquarrie** (John), **Rosenzweig** (Franz), **Schweitzer** (Albert), **Swedenborg** (Emanuel),**Tertullian**,**Weizsäcker** (Karl Heinrich)

11 **Bonaventure** (St), **Kierkegaard** (Sören Aabye)

12 **Justin Martyr** (St)

14 **Schleiermacher** (Friedrich)

theological
06 divine **09** doctrinal, religious **10** scriptural **12** hierological **14** ecclesiastical

theology
08 divinity **09** dogmatics **14** school-divinity

theorem
04 rule **06** dictum **07** formula **09** deduction, postulate, principle, statement **10** hypothesis **11** proposition

theoretical
04 pure **05** ideal **07** a priori, on paper **08** abstract, academic, armchair, notional **10** conceptual **11** conjectural, doctrinaire, speculative **12** hypothetical **13** suppositional

theoretically
07 a priori, ideally, on paper **08** in theory **09** nominally, seemingly **10** notionally **11** in principle **12** conceptually **14** hypothetically

theorize
05 guess **07** suppose **08** propound **09** formulate, postulate, speculate **10** conjecture **11** hypothesize

theory
03 ism, law **04** idea, plan, view **05** guess **06** notion, scheme, system, thesis **07** opinion, surmise **08** proposal **09** principle, rationale **10** assumption, conjecture, hypothesis, philosophy **11** abstraction, postulation, presumption, speculation, supposition

Theories include:
03 GUT,TOE
04 game
05 chaos
06 atomic, number, string
07 Big Bang, quantum
09 collision, Darwinism, evolution
10 panspermia, relativity
11 catastrophe
12 Grand Unified, Milankovitch

14 plate tectonics
15 butterfly effect

• in theory
07 a priori, ideally, on paper **09** seemingly **10** notionally **11** in principle **12** conceptually **13** in the abstract, theoretically **14** hypothetically

therapeutic
04 good **05** tonic **06** curing **07** healing **08** curative, remedial, salutary, sanative **09** medicinal **10** beneficial, corrective **11** restorative **12** advantageous, ameliorative, health-giving

therapy
04 cure **05** tonic **06** remedy **07** healing **09** treatment **12** therapeutics

Therapies include:
02 OT
03 art, CST, HRT, LDT, ORT, sex
04 drug, play, zone
05 aroma, chemo, drama, group, hydro, hypno, music, photo, radio, reiki
06 beauty, family, physio, primal, psycho, retail, speech
07 electro, Gestalt, Rolfing, shiatsu
08 aversion
09 behaviour, cognitive, herbalism
10 homeopathy, osteopathy, regression, ultrasound
11 acupressure, acupuncture, biofeedback, homoeopathy, irradiation, moxibustion, naturopathy, reflexology
12 chiropractic, craniosacral, electroshock, faith healing, horticulture, occupational, reminiscence
13 confrontation, dream analysis, heat treatment

See also **psychological**

there
04 ecco **06** yonder

thereabouts
05 about **07** roughly **12** near that date **13** approximately **14** near that number

thereafter
02 so **04** next, upon **09** after that **10** afterwards **11** accordingly **12** subsequently **13** after that time

therefore
02 so **04** ergo, then, thus **05** and so, argal **06** forthy, so then **09** as a result **11** accordingly **12** consequently **13** for that reason

thereupon
02 so **06** withal **08** with that, with this **11** immediately

thesaurus
05 Roget **07** lexicon **08** synonymy, treasury, wordbook **10** dictionary, repository, storehouse, vocabulary, wordfinder **12** encyclopedia

these
04 thir

thesis
04 idea, view **05** essay, paper, theme, topic **06** theory **07** opinion, premise, subject **08** argument, position, proposal, treatise **09** monograph, statement **10** contention, hypothesis **11** composition, proposition **12** disquisition, dissertation

thick
03 big, fat, hub **04** daft, deep, dull, dumb, fast, full, slow, this, warm, wide **05** broad, bulky, close, dense, dippy, dopey, focus, foggy, gross, gruff, heart, heavy, husky, lumpy, midst, murky, rough, solid, soupy, stiff, stout **06** centre, chunky, creamy, croaky, filled, grouty, hoarse, marked, middle, opaque, packed, simple, smoggy, strong, stupid, turbid, unfair **07** chocker, closely, clotted, compact, crowded, foolish, muffled, obvious, rasping, teeming, thicket, thickly, throaty, unclear, viscous, woollen **08** abundant, brimming, bursting, close-set, crawling, croaking, definite, frequent, gormless, gravelly, guttural, intimate, numerous, striking, swarming **09** abounding, brainless, bristling, condensed, dim-witted, excessive, semi-solid, squabbish **10** coagulated, frequently, indistinct, noticeable, pronounced **11** chock-a-block, overflowing, substantial **12** concentrated, impenetrable **13** thick as a plank, unintelligent

thicken
03 gel, set **04** cake, clot, curd, jell, meal **05** upset **06** curdle, reduce **07** congeal, stiffen **08** condense, solidify **09** coagulate **10** incrassate, inspissate **13** make more solid **15** become more solid

thickening
04 roux **08** clubbing **09** callosity **14** hyperkeratosis **15** atherosclerosis, middle-age spread, primitive streak

thicket
04 bosk, wood **05** brake, brush, copse, cover, grove, shola **06** bosket, greave, maquis, queach **07** bosquet, coppice, spinney **08** chamisal, fernshaw, reed-rand, reed-rond **09** canebrake, chaparral, salicetum **10** dead-finish **11** bramble-bush

thickhead
03 git, oaf **04** berk, clot, dope, dork, fool, geek, prat, twit **05** chump, dummy, dunce, idiot, moron, ninny, twerp **06** dimwit, nitwit **07** buffoon, fathead, halfwit, pinhead **08** imbecile, numskull **09** blockhead **10** nincompoop

thick-headed
04 dumb, slow **05** barmy, dense, dopey, loony, loopy, potty, thick **06** obtuse, stupid **07** asinine, doltish, foolish, idiotic, moronic **08** gormless **09** brainless, dim-witted, imbecilic **10** dull-witted, slow-witted **11** blockheaded, not all there **13** thick as a plank **15** slow on the uptake

thickness

03 bed, ply **04** band, body, bulk, coat, film, loft, seam, vein **05** layer, sheet, width **06** extent, lamina **07** breadth, density, deposit, stratum **08** diameter **09** bulkiness, closeness, solidness, viscosity **11** consistency, pachydermia **14** third dimension

thickset

05 beefy, bulky, burly, dense, heavy, solid, squat **06** brawny, robust, stocky, strong, sturdy **07** nuggety, squabby **08** muscular, powerful **09** well-built **12** heavily built

thick-skinned

05 tough **06** inured **07** callous **08** hardened **09** hard-nosed, unfeeling **10** hard-boiled, impervious **11** insensitive **12** case-hardened, invulnerable **14** pachydermatous **15** tough as old boots

thief

05 crook **06** magpie, nicker **07** filcher, stealer, tea leaf **08** larcener, pilferer **09** Autolycus, larcenist, plunderer **12** kleptomaniac

Thieves and robbers include:

03 dip, pad
04 bung, coon, file, prig, Tory, wire, yegg
05 diver, fraud, heist, kiddy, rover, sneak
06 bandit, bulker, chummy, con man, dacoit, dakoit, dipper, hotter, ice man, latron, lifter, limmer, looter, mugger, nipper, pirate, raider, robber
07 abactor, blagger, booster, brigand, burglar, cateran, cosh boy, footpad, hoister, ladrone, land-rat, nobbler, nut-hook, pandoor, pandour, poacher, prigger, rustler, twoccer, whizzer, yeggman
08 cly-faker, cutpurse, hijacker, huaquero, rapparee, river-rat, swindler
09 area-sneak, cracksman, embezzler, fraudster, pick-purse, ram-raider, sea robber
10 cat-burglar, gully-raker, highjacker, highwayman, horse-thief, land-pirate, man-stealer, pickpocket, roberdsman, robertsman, shoplifter, sneak thief, water thief
11 motor-bandit, poddy-dodger, safe-breaker, safe-cracker, snatch-purse, snow-dropper, stair-dancer
12 appropriator, baby-snatcher, cattle duffer, cattle-lifter, housebreaker, sheep-stealer, snow-gatherer
13 highway robber
15 resurrectionist, resurrection man

thieve

03 bag, lag, rob **04** blag, lift, nick, pull, whip **05** cheat, filch, heist, hoist, pinch, poach, steal, swipe **06** burgle, nobble, pilfer, rip off **07** plunder, purloin, snaffle, swindle **08** abstract, embezzle, knock off, peculate **10** run off with **11** make off with **14** misappropriate

thieving

05 theft **06** piracy **07** crooked, larceny, lifting, mugging, nicking, pugging, robbery **08** banditry, burglary, filching, stealing, thievery **09** dishonest, furacious, larcenous, pilferage, pilfering, predatory, rapacious **10** fraudulent, peculation, plundering, ripping off **11** crookedness, knocking off, sheep-biting, shoplifting **12** embezzlement **13** light-fingered **14** sticky-fingered

thievish

07 crooked, furtive **08** thieving **09** dishonest, furacious, larcenous, predatory, rapacious, theftuous **10** fraudulent **13** light-fingered, tarry-fingered **14** nimble-fingered, sticky-fingered

thin

04 bony, fine, lame, lank, lean, poor, rare, slim, soft, trim, weak **05** faint, filmy, gaunt, gauzy, lanky, light, quiet, runny, scant, sheer, spare, wispy **06** dilute, feeble, flimsy, lessen, meagre, narrow, paltry, rarefy, reduce, refine, scanty, scarce, single, skimpy, skinny, slight, sparse, svelte, wasted, watery, weaken **07** diluted, dwindle, scraggy, scrawny, slender, spindly, tenuous, weed out **08** anorexic, decrease, delicate, diminish, gossamer, rarefied, scrannel, shrunken, skeletal, straggly, tenuious, tinkling **09** attenuate, defective, deficient, emaciated, paper-thin, scattered, untenable, wafer-thin, water down **10** attenuated, diaphanous, inadequate, see-through, wishy-washy **11** high-pitched, implausible, lightweight, thin as a rake, translucent, transparent, underweight **12** inconclusive, unconvincing **13** insubstantial **14** make more watery, undernourished

- **on thin ice**
06 at risk, unsafe **08** insecure **10** in jeopardy, precarious, vulnerable **12** open to attack

thing

02 it **03** act, aim, bag, job **04** baby, bent, bias, body, deed, fact, fear, feat, gear, idea, item, love, task, togs, tool **05** chore, court, event, fancy, gismo, goods, mania, point, stuff, taste, tools, trait, waldo **06** action, affair, aspect, attire, desire, detail, device, dinges, doodah, entity, factor, fetish, gadget, hang-up, horror, liking, matter, notion, object, phobia, tackle, thingy **07** apparel, article, baggage, clobber, clothes, concept, council, dislike, effects, element, episode, exploit, feature, leaning, luggage, machine, problem, quality, thought, whatsit **08** activity, affinity, assembly, aversion, clothing, creature, cup of tea, fixation, fondness, garments, idée fixe, incident, oddments, penchant, property, soft spot, tendency, thingamy, weakness **09** affection, apparatus, attribute, condition, equipment, happening, implement, mechanism, obsession, proneness, situation, substance, thingummy **10** attraction, belongings, instrument, occurrence, parliament, partiality, particular, phenomenon, possession, preference, proceeding, proclivity, propensity, speciality **11** arrangement, bits and bobs, contrivance, eventuality, inclination, odds and ends, possessions, undertaking, what you like **12** appreciation, circumstance, one-track mind, predilection, thingummybob, thingummyjig, what's-its-name **13** bits and pieces, paraphernalia, preoccupation **14** characteristic, responsibility, what-d'you-call-it, what turns you on

- **the thing**
03 hip **04** cool **06** latest, modish, trendy **07** current, in vogue, popular **09** in fashion, the latest **10** all the rage **11** fashionable

think

04 deem, feel, hold, muse, seem **05** brood, cense, guess, judge, opine **06** design, esteem, expect, figure, intend, look on, ponder, reason, recall, reckon, regard, review **07** believe, conceit, foresee, imagine, presume, purpose, reflect, suppose, surmise, thought, weigh up **08** chew over, cogitate, conceive, conclude, consider, envisage, estimate, meditate, mull over, remember, ruminate **09** calculate, cerebrate, determine, recollect, sleep on it, take stock, visualize **10** anticipate, assessment, cogitation, conjecture, deliberate, evaluation, meditation, reflection **11** concentrate, contemplate **12** deliberation **13** consideration, contemplation

- **think better of**
06 revise **07** rethink **10** reconsider, think again, think twice **11** get cold feet **13** decide not to do

- **think much of**
04 rate **05** prize, value **06** admire, esteem, reckon **07** respect **10** set store by **13** think highly of

- **think nothing of**
13 consider usual **14** consider normal

- **think over**
06 digest, ponder **07** weigh up **08** chew over, consider, meditate, mull over, ruminate **11** contemplate, reflect upon

- **think up**
06 create, design, devise, invent **07** concoct, dream up, imagine **08** conceive, contrive **09** visualize

thinkable

06 likely **08** feasible, possible **09** cogitable **10** imaginable, reasonable, supposable **11** conceivable

thinker

04 sage **05** brain **07** scholar **08** theorist **09** intellect **10** ideologist, mastermind, philosophe **11** philosopher **12** theoretician

thinking
04 idea, view **06** theory **07** logical, opinion, outlook, thought **08** cultured, judgment, position, rational, sensible, thoughts **09** appraisal, judgement, reasoning **10** analytical, assessment, conclusion, evaluation, meditative, philosophy, reflective, thoughtful **11** conclusions, intelligent **12** excogitation, intellectual **13** contemplative, philosophical, sophisticated

thin-skinned
04 soft **06** tender, touchy **07** prickly **08** snappish **09** irritable, sensitive **10** vulnerable **11** easily upset, susceptible **14** hypersensitive

third-rate
03 bad **04** naff, poor, poxy, ropy **05** awful, lousy, pants, ropey **06** crappy, crummy, shoddy **07** botched, the pits, useless **08** inferior, low-grade, mediocre, pathetic, slipshod, terrible **10** low-quality **11** a load of crap, indifferent, poor-quality, substandard **13** cheap and nasty **14** a load of garbage, a load of rubbish, not up to scratch, unsatisfactory

thirst
03 yen **04** long, lust, want **05** crave, yearn **06** desire, drouth, hanker, hunger, thrist, thrust **07** aridity, craving, drought, dryness, longing, passion **08** appetite, keenness, yearning **09** eagerness, hankering **11** drouthiness, have a yen for, parchedness, thirstiness

thirsty
03 dry **04** adry, arid, avid, keen **05** dying, eager **06** greedy, hungry **07** athirst, burning, craving, drouthy, gasping, itching, longing, parched, thristy **08** desirous, droughty, hydropic, yearning **09** hankering, thirsting **10** dehydrated

thirteen
04 XIII

thirty
03 XXX

this
03 hic, hoc

Thomas
03 Tom

thong
03 taw **04** band, belt, cord, lash, lore, riem **05** strap, strip, whang **06** Jandal® **07** latchet **08** flip-flop **11** shoe latchet

thorium
02 Th

thorn
04 barb **05** doorn, point, prick, spike, spine **06** needle **07** acantha, aculeus, bristle, prickle

thorny
05 armed, dicey, sharp, spiky, spiny, tough, vexed **06** barbed, briery, knotty, sticky, tricky, trying **07** awkward, bristly, complex, irksome, pointed, prickly, spinose, spinous **08** delicate, ticklish, worrying **09** acanthous, difficult, harassing, intricate, upsetting **10** convoluted **11** problematic, troublesome

thorough
04 deep, full, good, pure **05** close, pakka, pucka, pukka, sheer, sound, total, utter **06** damned, entire, narrow, proper **07** careful, in-depth, ingoing, perfect, radical, regular, through **08** absolute, complete, rigorous, sweeping **09** downright, efficient, extensive, intensive, out-and-out, searching **10** exhaustive, methodical, meticulous, resounding, scrupulous, widespread **11** down-the-line, painstaking, unmitigated, unqualified **12** all-embracing, all-inclusive **13** comprehensive, conscientious, thoroughgoing

thoroughbred
07 blooded, pur sang **08** pedigree, pure-bred **09** pedigreed, pure-blood **11** full-blooded, pure-blooded **12** high-spirited

thoroughfare
03 way **04** road **05** corso **06** access, avenue, street **07** highway, passage, roadway **08** broadway, motorway, turnpike **09** boulevard, concourse **10** passageway **12** king's highway

thoroughgoing
04 deep, full, pure **05** sheer, total, utter **06** entire, strict **07** careful, in-depth, perfect **08** absolute, complete, deep-dyed, outright, rigorous, sweeping **09** downright, extensive, intensive, out-and-out **10** exhaustive, methodical, meticulous, scrupulous, widespread **11** painstaking, unmitigated, unqualified **12** all-embracing, all-inclusive **13** comprehensive **14** uncompromising

thoroughly
02 up **03** out **04** well **05** à fond, fully, good-o, quite **06** good-oh, mortal **07** soundly, totally, utterly **08** entirely, even-down **09** carefully, downright, every inch, inside out, perfectly, throughly **10** absolutely, completely, sweepingly **11** assiduously, back to front, efficiently, intensively **12** exhaustively, meticulously, scrupulously, well and truly **13** painstakingly, root and branch **15** comprehensively, conscientiously

those
03 tho **04** thae, them, they

though
02 if **03** but, yet **05** still, while **06** even if, even so **07** granted, however **08** allowing, although **09** admitting **10** all the same, for all that **11** nonetheless **12** nevertheless **15** notwithstanding

thought
03 aim **04** care, heed, hint, hope, idea, idée, mind, muse, plan, view **05** dream, fancy, grief, study, think, touch, trace **06** belief, design, musing, notion, pensée, reason, regard, theory **07** anxiety, conceit, concept, concern, feeling, gesture, opinion, purpose **08** judgment, kindness, prospect, scrutiny, sympathy, thinking **09** appraisal, attention, intention, judgement, pondering, reasoning **10** aspiration, assessment, cogitation, compassion, conception, conclusion, conviction, estimation, meditation, reflection, resolution, rumination, solicitude, tenderness **11** cerebration, expectation, point of view **12** anticipation, deliberation **13** consciousness, consideration, contemplation, introspection **14** thoughtfulness **15** considerateness

thoughtful
04 deep, kind, wary **05** quiet **06** caring, dreamy, solemn, tender **07** careful, heedful, helpful, mindful, pensive, prudent, serious, wistful **08** absorbed, cautious, profound, sobering, studious, thinking **09** attentive, unselfish **10** abstracted, cogitative, conceitful, methodical, pensieroso, reflective, solicitous **11** considerate, sympathetic **13** compassionate, considerate, contemplative, in a brown study, introspective, lost in thought

thoughtfully
06 deeply **07** quietly **08** dreamily **09** carefully, helpfully, mindfully, pensively, seriously, wistfully **10** cautiously, profoundly **11** unselfishly **12** methodically, reflectively **13** considerately **15** compassionately, contemplatively, introspectively, sympathetically

thoughtless
04 rash, rude, vain **05** hasty, silly **06** remiss, stupid, unkind, unwise **07** étourdi, foolish, selfish **08** carefree, careless, étourdie, heedless, impolite, mindless, reckless, tactless, uncaring **09** blindfold, frivolous, imprudent, negligent, unfeeling **10** ill-advised, incogitant, indiscreet, unthinking, unweighing **11** giddy-headed, improvident, inattentive, insensitive, light-headed, precipitate **12** absent-minded, undiplomatic **13** ill-considered, inconsiderate

thoughtlessly
06 rashly, rudely **08** stupidly **09** foolishly **10** carelessly, impolitely, recklessly, tactlessly **11** unfeelingly **12** indiscreetly **13** inattentively, insensitively **15** inconsiderately

thousand
01 G, K, M **04** thou **05** grand, mille **07** chiliad **09** millenary

thrall
04 grip, serf **05** hands, power, slave

07 bondage, control, enslave, serfdom, slavery **08** clutches, enslaved, thraldom **09** servitude, vassalage **10** subjection **11** enslavement, subjugation

thrash
02 do **03** hit, lam, pay, tan **04** beat, belt, cane, drub, flog, jerk, lace, lash, lick, rout, rush, sock, tank, toss, trim, whap, whip, whop **05** bless, cream, crush, dress, flail, party, paste, pound, quilt, smoke, spank, swish, targe, towel, whack, whale **06** beat up, defeat, donder, hammer, larrup, lather, punish, raddle, thresh, wallop, writhe **07** clobber, lambast, lay into, leather, scourge, swaddle, trounce **08** beat up on, demolish, lambaste, vanquish, work over **09** dress down, horsewhip, marmelize, overwhelm, pulverize, slaughter, surcingle **11** walk all over **13** have the edge on
• **thrash out**
06 debate, settle **07** discuss, hash out, resolve **09** hammer out, negotiate **11** clear the air

thrashing
04 rout **05** doing, laldy **06** caning, defeat, hiding, laldie, wiping **07** beating, belting, lamming, lashing, licking, pasting, tanking, tanning, whaling **08** crushing, dressing, drubbing, flogging, quilting, strap-oil, whacking, whipping, whopping **09** hammering, strapping, towelling, trouncing, walloping **10** clobbering, leathering, punishment **12** chastisement, dressing-down

thread
03 end **04** ease, inch, line, move, pass, plot, push, silk, wind, yarn **05** braid, drift, fibre, Lurex®, motif, seton, shoot, strip, tenor, theme, thrid, thrum, twine, twist, weave **06** course, lingel, lingle, needle, strand, streak, string, suture **07** meander, subject, worsted **08** filament **09** direction, storyline **14** train of thought

threadbare
03 old **04** bare, poor, worn **05** corny, stale, stock, tatty, tired, trite **06** frayed, meagre, ragged, shabby **07** napless, scruffy, worn-out **08** overused, overworn, tattered, well-worn **09** hackneyed, moth-eaten **11** commonplace, stereotyped **12** cliché-ridden

threat
04 omen, risk **05** peril, stick **06** danger, hazard, menace **07** portent, presage, war drum, warning **08** big stick **09** blackmail, ultimatum **10** foreboding **11** commination **12** brutum fulmen, denunciation **14** enemy at the door

threaten
03 cow, vow **04** burn, loom, mint, warn **05** augur, bully, flank, shore **06** extort, impend, lean on, loom up, menace, scorch **07** imperil, portend, presage, scowder, warn off **08** approach,

browbeat, endanger, forebode, hang over, look like, scouther, scowther **09** blackmail, comminate, terrorize **10** be imminent, foreshadow, intimidate, jeopardize, pressurize, push around **11** lift a hand to **13** be in the offing **14** lift your hand to, put the screws on

threatening
04 grim, ugly **05** lurid, nasty, shore **07** bravado, looming, ominous, warning **08** frowning, imminent, menacing, minatory, sinister **09** impending, minacious **10** broodiness, cautionary, forbidding, foreboding **11** commination, comminative **12** denunciatory, inauspicious, intimidatory
• **threatening character**
04 omen

three
03 III, ter-, tri- **04** tern, tray, trey, trio **05** leash, prial, triad **06** parial **07** pairial, triplet **09** pair-royal
• **Three Wise Men** see **wise man** *under* **wise**

threesome
04 trio **05** triad **06** triple, triune, troika **07** trilogy, trinity, triplet **08** triptych **11** triumvirate

thresh
03 hit **04** flog, jerk, rush, toss **05** flail, swish **06** thrash, writhe

threshold
04 cill, dawn, door, sill **05** brink, entry, limen, start, verge **06** outset **07** doorway, opening **08** door-sill, doorstep, entrance **09** beginning, inception **12** commencement **13** starting-point

thrice see **three**

thrift
04 gain **06** saving **07** economy, savings, sea pink **08** prudence, sea grass **09** frugality, husbandry, parsimony **10** prosperity, providence **11** carefulness **12** conservation **14** sea gillyflower

thriftless
06 lavish **08** prodigal, wasteful **09** imprudent, unthrifty **10** profligate **11** dissipative, extravagant, improvident, spendthrift

thrifty
04 wary **05** fendy **06** frugal, saving **07** careful, prudent, sparing **09** husbandly, provident **10** conserving, economical, prosperous **12** parsimonious

thrill
03 gas, joy **04** bang, buzz, dirl, glow, kick, move, stir **05** flush, pulse, rouse, shake, thirl, throb **06** arouse, charge, dindle, dinnle, excite, pierce, quiver, shiver, tingle, tremor **07** delight, feeling, flutter, frisson, pulsate, shudder, tremble, vibrate **08** pleasure **09** adventure, electrify, galvanize,

sensation, stimulate, vibration **10** excitement, exhilarate, the shivers **11** give a buzz to, give a kick to, stimulation

thrilling
07 quaking, rousing, shaking, vibrant **08** electric, exciting, gripping, riveting, stirring, tinglish **09** shivering, trembling, vibrating **10** rip-roaring, shuddering **11** hair-raising, sensational, stimulating **12** action-packed, electrifying, exhilarating, soul-stirring **13** heart-stirring

thrive
02 do **04** boom, gain, grow, thee **05** bloom **06** come on, do well, profit **07** advance, blossom, burgeon, develop, prosper, succeed **08** flourish, increase **11** make headway **12** make progress

thriving
04 well **07** booming, growing, healthy, wealthy **08** affluent, blooming **10** blossoming, burgeoning, developing, prosperous, successful **11** comfortable, flourishing

throat
04 crag, craw **05** gorge, halse, hause, hawse **06** fauces, gullet **07** pharynx, swallow, trachea, weasand **08** prunella, thrapple, thropple, throttle, windpipe **10** oesophagus, the Red Lane
• **part of throat**
04 gula

throaty
03 low **04** deep **05** gruff, husky, thick **06** hoarse **07** rasping, raucous **08** croaking, guttural **12** full-throated

throb
◇ *anagram indicator*
04 beat, drum, jump, pant, quop **05** pound, pulse, thump **06** stound, stownd, tingle **07** pulsate, vibrate **08** drumming, pounding, thumping **09** heartbeat, palpitate, pulsation, vibration **11** palpitation

throe
03 fit **04** pain, pang, stab **05** agony, spasm, thraw **07** anguish, seizure, torture, travail **08** distress, paroxysm **09** deid-thraw, suffering **10** convulsion
• **in the throes of**
08 busy with **12** in the midst of **13** in the middle of, wrestling with **14** in the process of, struggling with **15** preoccupied with

thrombosis
03 DVT **08** apoplexy, coronary **09** blood clot **11** heart attack

throne
03 see **04** gadi, seat **05** exalt, siege, stool **07** tribune **08** cathedra, enthrone, kingship, lavatory **09** mercy-seat **12** bed of justice
See also **toilet**

throng
03 jam, mob **04** bevy, busy, cram, fill,

herd, host, mass, pack **05** bunch, crowd, crush, flock, horde, press, swarm **06** jostle, preace, prease, thrang **07** besiege, crowded, preasse **08** converge, crowding, intimate **09** multitude **10** assemblage, congregate, mill around **12** congregation, grex venalium

throttle
03 gag, gun **05** check, choke, scrag **06** keep in, stifle **07** inhibit, silence, smother **08** hold back, restrain, strangle, suppress, thrapple, thropple, wiredraw **09** suffocate **10** asphyxiate **11** accelerator, strangulate

through
02 by, in **03** per, tra-, via **04** done, yond, yont **05** among, clear, due to, ended, fully, using **06** across, direct, during **07** between, by way of, clear of, express, non-stop, owing to, totally **08** entirely, finished, thanks to **09** because of, by means of, completed, connected, throughly **10** by virtue of, completely, terminated, thoroughly, throughout, to the end of **11** as a result of, on account of **12** continuously **13** until the end of, with the help of **15** all the way across, uninterruptedly, without a break in
• **through and through**
05 fully **06** wholly **07** totally, utterly **08** entirely, to pieces **09** to the core **10** altogether, completely, thoroughly **11** all to pieces **12** unreservedly **13** to the backbone **14** in every respect **15** from top to bottom

throughout
04 over **05** along **06** during, widely **07** all over **08** all round **09** up and down **10** all through, completely, everywhere, in all parts **11** extensively, in every part **12** in the whole of, ubiquitously **13** in every part of, in the course of

throughput
05 yield **06** fruits, output, return **07** harvest, outturn, product, turnout **10** production **11** manufacture **12** productivity

throw
◊ *anagram indicator*
02 go **03** hip, lob, peg, put, shy, wap **04** blow, bung, cast, dash, emit, faze, fell, flip, give, host, hurl, lose, puck, putt, scat, send, shed, shot, toss, turn, whap, whop, work, yerk **05** chuck, ditch, fling, floor, force, heave, lay on, pitch, put on, skatt, sling, spang, spasm, spill, upset, whang, while **06** baffle, bemuse, direct, launch, propel, purler, put out, rattle, unseat, upcast, wheech, wuther **07** arrange, confuse, disturb, execute, give off, operate, perform, perplex, produce, project, radiate, unhorse, whither **08** astonish, cataput, confound, dislodge, jaculate, occasion, organize, overturn, paroxysm, surprise, switch on,

unsaddle **09** bring down, discomfit, dumbfound, prostrate **10** disconcert **11** cause to fall, move quickly
See also **wrestling**
• **throw away**
04 blow, dump, lose **05** ditch, scrap, waste **06** reject **07** discard **08** chuck out, get rid of, jettison, squander, throw out **09** chuck away, dispose of **11** fritter away **12** dispense with
• **throw headlong**
04 purl
• **throw off**
04 cast, drop, shed **05** elude **06** divest **07** abandon, cast off, discard, discuss **08** get rid of, jettison, shake off **10** escape from
• **throw out**
04 cast, dump, emit **05** ditch, eject, evict, expel, exude, fling, scrap **06** reject, unseat **07** bring up, diffuse, discard, dismiss, emanate, give off, mention, produce, project, radiate, refer to, send out, turf out, turn out **08** distance, distract, jettison, point out, turn down **09** introduce, throw away **10** disconcert, speak about **12** dispense with
• **throw over**
04 drop, jilt, quit **05** chuck, leave **06** desert, reject **07** abandon, discard, forsake **10** finish with
• **throw up**
03 gag **04** barf, jack, puke, quit, spew, toss **05** heave, leave, retch, vomit **06** cast up, give up, jack in, pack in, resign, reveal, sick up **07** abandon, bring up, chuck in, chuck up, chunder, fetch up, upchuck **08** disgorge, renounce **10** relinquish **11** regurgitate

throwaway
05 cheap **06** casual **07** offhand, passing **08** careless **10** disposable, expendable, undramatic, unemphatic **13** biodegradable, non-returnable

throwback
06 return **07** setback **09** reversion **10** taking back **11** restoration **13** reinstatement, retrogression

thrush
04 chat **05** mavis, sprue, veery **06** missel, sylvia, Turdus **07** antbird, redwing, wagtail **08** throstle **09** fieldfare, olive-back, ring ouzel, solitaire, stormcock **10** bush-shrike, missel-bird **12** throstle-cock

thrust
03 dig, jab, jam, pop, put, ram, ren, rin, run **04** bear, butt, chop, dash, foin, gist, poke, pote, prod, prog, push, rash, side, sock, stab, stap, stop, tilt, urge **05** crowd, drift, drive, foist, force, impel, lunge, pitch, poach, point, power, press, shove, stick, stuck, tenor, theme, wedge **06** burden, impose, motive, muscle, muzzle, pierce, plunge, potche, propel, saddle, thirst **07** aventre, essence, impetus, impulse, inflict, intrude, message, thrutch **08** encumber, momentum, pressure,

protrude **09** have-at-him, penetrate, substance **10** imbroccata **11** pertinacity **13** determination

thrustplane
04 sole

thud
04 bang, bash, beat, dump, plod, wham **05** clonk, clump, clunk, crash, flump, knock, smack, thump **06** bounce, wallop **07** thunder

thug
04 goon **05** rough, tough, yobbo **06** bandit, goonda, killer, mugger, robber, thuggo, tsotsi **07** cosh boy, gorilla, hoodlum, ruffian, villain **08** assassin, gangster, hooligan, murderer, plug-ugly **09** cut-throat, phansigar, roughneck

thuggery
05 abuse **06** murder **07** killing **08** atrocity, butchery, foul play, violence **09** brutality, vandalism **10** inhumanity **11** hooliganism, viciousness

thulium
02 Tm

thumb
04 inch **06** pollex
• **thumb through**
04 scan, skim **06** peruse **08** glance at **11** flip through, leaf through **12** flick through **13** browse through

thumbnail
05 brief, pithy, quick, short, small **07** compact, concise **08** succinct **09** miniature

thumbs-down
02 no **06** rebuff **07** refusal **08** negation, turn down **09** rejection **11** disapproval

thumbs-up
02 OK **03** yes **07** go-ahead **08** approval, sanction **10** acceptance, green light **11** affirmation **13** encouragement

thump
03 box, cob, dad, dod, hit, rap **04** bang, beat, blow, bonk, bump, cuff, daud, dawd, ding, dong, dump, dunt, paik, slap, thud, tund, whap, whop **05** clout, clunk, crash, knock, pound, punch, smack, souse, throb, whack **06** batter, hammer, pummel, strike, thrash, thwack, wallop **07** bethump, pulsate, trounce **09** palpitate

thumping
03 big **04** huge, mega, very **05** great **06** highly, really, severe **07** extreme, greatly, immense, intense, mammoth, massive, titanic **08** colossal, enormous, gigantic, severely, terrific, towering, whopping **09** excessive, extremely, intensely, seriously, swingeing, unusually **10** exorbitant, gargantuan, impressive, monumental, remarkably, thundering, tremendous **12** tremendously

thunder
03 cry **04** bang, bawl, boom, clap, howl, peal, roar, roll, yell **05** blast, crack, crash, shout **06** bellow, holler, rumble, scream, shriek **07** clamour, boulder, resound **08** crashing, intonate, outburst **09** explosion, fulminate, upthunder **11** reverberate
13 reverberation **14** raise your voice

thundering
04 very **05** great **06** really, tonant **07** greatly **08** enormous, severely **09** excessive, extremely, intensely, unusually **10** altitonant, foudroyant, monumental, remarkable, tremendous **11** unmitigated

thunderous
04 loud **05** noisy **07** booming, roaring **08** rumbling **09** deafening **10** resounding, tumultuous **12** ear-plitting **13** reverberating

thunderstruck
05 agape, dazed **06** aghast, amazed **07** floored, shocked, stunned **09** astounded, flummoxed, paralysed, petrified, staggered **10** astonished, bowled over, nonplussed **11** dumbfounded, open-mouthed **12** wonder-struck **13** flabbergasted, knocked for six **14** wonder-stricken

Thursday
02 Th **03** Thu **04** Thur **05** Thurs

thus
02 so **04** ergo, then **05** hence **08** like this **09** as follows, in this way, therefore **11** accordingly **12** consequently, frankincense
• **thus far**
05 so far **07** up to now **08** until now **09** up till now **13** up to this point **14** up to the present

thwack
03 hit **04** bash, beat, blow, cuff, flog, slap **05** clout, smack, thump, whack **06** buffet, strike, wallop

thwart
03 pip **04** balk, foil, stop **05** baulk, block, check, crimp, cross, spite, stimy, thraw **06** across, baffle, banjax, defeat, hamper, hinder, hogtie, impede, nobble, oppose, stimie, stymie **07** adverse, athwart, pre-empt, prevent, snooker, stonker **08** conflict, obstruct, perverse, traverse **09** crosswise, forestall, frustrate, hindrance **10** transverse **11** frustration **12** cross-grained **13** put the skids on

tic
04 jerk **05** spasm **06** twitch **13** tic douloureux

tick
02 mo **03** dot, jar, pat, sec, tap **04** beat, line, mark, tock, work, worm **05** check, click, flash, jiffy, tally, trice, trust **06** choose, credit, minute, moment, second, select, stroke, whimsy **07** instant **08** indicate, tick-tock **09** twinkling **10** crib-biting

• **tick off**
04 mark, pick **05** check, chide, prick, scold **06** bounce, carpet, rebuke, see off, select **07** bawl out, catch it, chew out, reprove, rollick, rouse on, tell off, upbraid **08** call down, check off, indicate, reproach **09** dress down, go crook at, go crook on, pull apart, reprimand, take apart **10** go to town on **13** tear off a strip **14** throw the book at **15** give someone hell, put a tick against

ticker
05 clock, heart, watch **08** examiner

ticket
03 tag **04** card, pass, slip, stub **05** carte, check, label, token **06** ballot, coupon, docket, permit, return **07** licence, sticker, voucher, warrant **09** pass-check **11** certificate, counterfoil **12** lunch voucher **13** authorization **15** luncheon voucher
• **ticket seller**
04 tout

tickle
04 beat, nice **05** amuse, touch **06** divert, excite, kittle, please, stroke, thrill, tingle **07** delight, gratify, perplex **08** insecure, interest, ticklish, unstable **09** entertain, stimulate, titillate

ticklish
04 nice **05** dodgy, risky **06** kittly, knotty, subtle, thorny, touchy, tricky **07** awkward, trickle **08** critical, delicate, unchancy, unstable **09** difficult, hazardous, sensitive **10** precarious **11** problematic

tiddly *see* **drunk**

tide
03 ebb, ren, rin, run, sea **04** flow, flux, neap, tied, time **05** drift, flood, tenor, trend, water **06** course, happen, season, spring, stream **07** current **08** festival, movement, sea-water, tendency **09** direction **10** rising tide **11** opportunity
• **sudden rise of tide**
04 bore, eger **05** eagre
• **tide over**
03 aid **04** help **06** assist **07** help out, sustain **09** keep going **10** see through **11** help through

tidily
06 just so, neatly **07** in order, in place, orderly, smartly **12** immaculately, methodically **14** systematically

tidings
03 gen **04** dope, news, word **06** advice, report **07** message **08** bulletin **09** greetings **11** information **12** intelligence **13** communication

tidy
◇ *anagram indicator*
02 do **03** red **04** fair, good, neat, redd, trim **05** ample, clean, groom, kempt, large, order, plump, primp, slick, smart, spick **06** comely, fettle, neaten, redd up, spruce **07** arrange, band-box, brush up, clean up, clear up, in order,

ordered, orderly, shapely, sizable, smarten, tiddley **08** clear out, generous, sizeable, spruce up, well-kept **09** declutter, efficient, organized, shipshape **10** immaculate, methodical, seasonable, square away, straighten, systematic **11** respectable, substantial, uncluttered, well-groomed, well-ordered **12** businesslike, considerable, spick-and-span, straighten up **13** clear the decks, straighten out

tie
03 fix **04** band, bind, bond, clip, curb, draw, duty, join, knot, lace, lash, link, moor, rope, tape **05** chain, cramp, limit, strap, unite **06** attach, be even, copula, couple, fasten, hamper, hinder, impede, oblige, ribbon, secure, tether **07** be equal, confine, confirm, connect, kinship, liaison, necktie, shackle **08** dead heat, deadlock, ligature, restrain, restrict **09** constrain, fastening, hindrance, restraint, stalemate **10** allegiance, commitment, connection, constraint, friendship, limitation, obligation **11** affiliation, be all square, restriction **12** relationship **13** be neck and neck

Ties include:
03 bow
04 bolo, neck
05 ascot, dicky, stock
06 clip-on, cravat, dickey, dickie, kipper, string
07 overlay, owrelay, soubise
08 bootlace, kerchief
09 neckcloth, solitaire, steenkirk, waterfall
10 tawdry lace
11 neckerchief

• **tie down**
03 fix **05** limit **06** hamper, hinder **07** confine **08** restrain, restrict **09** constrain
• **tied up**
04 busy
• **tie in with**
08 relate to **09** agree with, fit in with **13** correlate with **15** be connected with
• **tie together**
04 knit **05** fagot **06** faggot
• **tie up**
04 bind, do up, lash, moor, rope, seal **05** cable, chain, truss **06** attach, bail up, commit, engage, fasten, invest, ligate, occupy, secure, settle, string, tether, wind up, wrap up **07** connect, engross, Gordian, reserve **08** conclude, finalize, keep busy, restrain **09** terminate **11** spread-eagle **15** make unavailable

tie-in
04 link **05** tie-up **06** hook-up **07** liaison **08** relation **10** connection **11** affiliation, association **12** co-ordination, relationship

tier
03 row **04** band, bank, belt, deck, line, rank, tire, zone **05** floor, layer, level, stage, story **06** gradin, storey

07 echelon, gradine, stratum **09** bleachers

tie-up
04 bond, link **05** tie-in **07** analogy, mooring **08** alliance, parallel, relation **09** reference **10** connection, stand-still **11** association, correlation **12** entanglement, relationship **13** interrelation **14** correspondence

tiff
03 pet, row, sip **04** dram, huff, miff, sour, spat, sulk **05** dress, drink, lunch, scrap, set-to, stale, words **06** barney, dust-up, temper **07** dispute, quarrel, tantrum **08** squabble, trick out **09** ill-humour **10** difference, falling-out **12** disagreement

tiger
04 puma **06** jaguar **07** leopard, stripes **08** man-eater **11** Machaerodus, Machairodus

tight
◇ *anagram indicator*
04 even, fast, firm, hard, mean, near, neat, pang, snug, taut, trig, trim **05** close, dodgy, drunk, fixed, harsh, merry, rigid, stiff, tense, tipsy, tough **06** at once, narrow, scanty, scarce, sealed, secure, severe, stingy, stoned, strict, tiddly, tricky **07** awkward, compact, concise, cramped, legless, limited, miserly, precise, sloshed, smashed, soundly, sozzled **08** airtight, clenched, delicate, hermetic, promptly, rigorous, strained, tanked up **09** competent, dangerous, difficult, niggardly, not enough, plastered, skin-tight, stretched, stringent, too little, well-oiled **10** compressed, hard-fought, impervious, inadequate, inflexible, restricted, soundproof, watertight **11** constricted, intoxicated, neck and neck, problematic, tight-fisted, well-matched **12** close-fitting, impenetrable, insufficient, parsimonious **13** evenly matched, figure-hugging, in short supply, penny-pinching

tighten
03 fix **04** swig **05** brace, cinch, close, cramp, crush, screw, swift, tense **06** beef up, fasten, firm up, narrow, pull up, secure, strait, take in, tauten, wind up **07** squeeze, stiffen, stretch **08** heighten, increase, make fast, restrain, rigidify, straiten **09** constrict, pull tight, toughen up **10** constringe, strengthen **12** make stricter

tight-fisted
04 mean **05** mingy, tight **06** stingy **07** miserly, sparing **08** grasping **09** niggardly **10** fast-handed **12** parsimonious **13** penny-pinching

tight-lipped
03 mum **04** mute **05** quiet **06** silent **08** reserved, reticent, taciturn **09** secretive **11** close-lipped **12** close-mouthed **13** unforthcoming **15** uncommunicative

till
02 to **03** dig, ear, ere, set **04** EPOS, farm, up to, work **05** peter, shale, until **06** plough **07** cash box, through, towards **08** checkout, rotavate, rotovate **09** cultivate **10** all through, cash drawer **11** boulder clay **12** cash register **13** up to the time of

tilt
03 hut, tip **04** bank, cant, cock, duel, heel, just, kant, lean, list, peak, ride, rock, rush, spar, tent, toss, trip **05** angle, clash, cover, fight, joust, pitch, slant, slope **06** attack, awning, camber, careen, charge, combat, jostle, justle, thrust **07** contend, contest, dispute, incline **08** attitude, heel over, tilt yard **09** encounter, pas d'armes **10** tournament **11** inclination
• **at full tilt**
06 all out **07** flat out **08** very fast **10** at full pelt, at top speed **11** at full blast, at full speed, very quickly **13** with full force

timber
03 log, rib **04** balk, beam, lath, pole, rung, spar, tree, wale, wood **05** baulk, board, build, karri, maple, plank, trees **06** forest, lumber, wooden **07** bunting, chestnut, templet **08** chestnut, stumpage, template, woodland **09** beechwood, sapodilla, unmusical **10** afrormosia, swing-stock **11** palmyra wood
See also **tree**; **wood**
• **measurement of timber** *see* measurement of wood *under* wood
• **timber carrier**
04 gill, jill

timbre
04 ring, tone **05** clang, color, klang, sound **06** colour, tamber **07** quality **08** tonality **09** resonance **10** klangfarbe, tone colour **12** voice quality

time
01 t **03** fix, set **04** aeon, beat, date, life, mora, peak, sith, span, term, tide **05** clock, count, meter, metre, point, space, spell, stage, tempo, while **06** adjust, heyday, rhythm **07** arrange, control, measure, session, stretch **08** duration, instance, interval, juncture, lifespan, occasion, regulate, schedule **09** calculate, programme, timetable **15** fourth dimension

Times and periods of time include:
02 am, pm **03** age, day, eon, era, min **04** dawn, dusk, fall, hour, morn, noon, week, year **05** epoch, month, night, sun-up, today **06** autumn, decade, midday, minute, moment, morrow, period, season, second, spring, summer, sunset, winter **07** bedtime, century, chiliad, daytime, evening, instant, midweek, morning, quarter, sunrise, teatime, tonight, weekday, weekend

08 eternity, high noon, lifetime, tomorrow, twilight **09** afternoon, decennium, fortnight, light-year, midsummer, nightfall, night-time **10** generation, millennium, nanosecond, yesteryear **11** long-weekend, microsecond, millisecond **12** quinquennium **13** the early hours, wee small hours

Time zones include:
02 AT, CT, ET, MT, PT **03** AST, BST, CET, CST, EET, EST, GMT, HST, MST, PST, WET **04** AKST, CYST, HAST, WAST, WEST **08** zulu time **10** Alaska Time **11** Central Time, Eastern Time, Pacific Time **12** Atlantic Time, Mountain Time **13** Greenwich Time

See also **geology**
• **after expected time**
04 late
• **ahead of time**
05 ahead, early **06** sooner **07** earlier, in front, up front **09** in advance **10** beforehand, previously
• **ahead of your time**
03 new **05** novel **07** radical **10** avant-garde, innovative **11** progressive **12** experimental **13** revolutionary
• **all the time**
05 among **06** always **07** forever, nonstop **08** all along **10** constantly **11** continually, incessantly, perpetually **12** continuously, interminably **15** twenty-four-seven
• **at all times**
03 e'er **04** ever **12** early and late
• **at any time**
03 e'er **04** ever, once, onst **07** anytime
• **at one time**
04 once **07** long ago **08** formerly **10** a one point, previously **11** in times past **14** simultaneously
• **at the proper time**
04 duly
• **at the right time**
03 pat
• **at the same time**
03 but, yet **04** then **05** still **06** anyway, at once, even so **07** however **08** meantime, together **09** meanwhile **10** for all that, in parallel **11** all together, nonetheless **12** concurrently, nevertheless **14** simultaneously **15** in the same breath, notwithstanding
• **at times**
06 whiles **08** off and on, on and off **09** sometimes **10** now and then **11** now and again, on occasions **12** every so often, occasionally **14** from time to time
• **behind the times**
03 old **04** past **05** dated **06** old hat **08** obsolete **09** out of date **10** fuddy-duddy, oldfangled **11** god-forsaken **12** god-forgotten, old-fashioned, out of fashion **13** unfashionable

- **behind time**
04 late 05 tardy 06 behind 07 delayed, overdue 10 unpunctual 14 behind schedule
- **brief space of time**
02 mo 03 bit, sec, wee
- **common time**
01 C
- **fit time**
03 tid
- **former times**
03 eld 04 yore
- **for the time being**
06 for now, pro tem 07 just now 08 meantime, right now 09 at present, meanwhile, presently 10 pro tempore 11 at the moment, temporarily 12 for the moment 13 for the present, in the meantime
- **from time to time**
07 at times 09 sometimes 10 now and then, on occasion 11 ever and anon, now and again, still and end 12 every so often, occasionally, once in a while, periodically, sporadically, still and anon 13 spasmodically 14 intermittently 15 every now and then
- **in good time**
05 early 06 indeed, on time, timely, timous 07 betimes, timeous 08 timously 09 timeously 10 punctually 11 ahead of time 14 bright and early 15 ahead of schedule, with time to spare
- **in time**
06 on time 10 eventually, not too late, punctually 11 early enough
- **on time**
05 sharp 06 bang on, dead on, spot on, spot-on 07 exactly 08 on the dot, promptly, punctual 09 precisely 10 on schedule, punctually
- **opportune time**
04 seal, seel, seil, sele
- **play for time**
05 delay, stall 08 hang fire, hesitate 09 stonewall, temporize 10 filibuster 12 drag your feet 13 procrastinate
- **taking extra time**
04 lean
- **time after time**
05 often 09 many times 10 frequently, repeatedly 11 recurrently 12 time and again 13 again and again 15 on many occasions

time-honoured
03 old 05 fixed, usual 06 age-old 07 ancient 08 historic 09 customary, venerable 10 accustomed 11 established, traditional 12 conventional 15 long-established

timeless
07 abiding, ageless, endless, eternal, lasting 08 enduring, ill-timed, immortal, unending, untimely 09 deathless, immutable, permanent, premature 10 changeless, unchanging 11 everlasting 12 imperishable 14 indestructible

timely
04 soon 05 early 06 prompt

08 punctual, suitable, temporal 09 opportune, well-timed 10 convenient, felicitous, propitious, seasonable, tempestive 11 appropriate 14 at the right time

times
01 X

timetable
03 fix, set 04 list, rota 05 diary, set up 06 agenda, roster 07 arrange, diarize, listing 08 calendar, schedule 09 programme 10 curriculum

time-worn
03 old 04 aged, worn 05 dated, hoary, lined, passé, rusty, stale, stock, tired, trite 06 ragged, ruined, shabby 07 ancient, cliché'd, outworn, run-down, worn out 08 bromidic, clichéed, decrepit, dog-eared, well-worn, wrinkled 09 hackneyed, out of date, weathered 10 broken-down, threadbare

timid
03 shy 05 cissy, pavid, wimpy 06 afraid, modest, mousey, scared, yellow 07 bashful, chicken, fearful, gutless, nervous, wimpish 08 cowardly, retiring, timorous 09 shrinking, spineless 10 frightened, hen-hearted, irresolute, meticulous 11 lily-livered 12 apprehensive, faint-hearted 13 pigeon-hearted, pusillanimous 14 chicken-hearted, chicken-livered

timidity
04 fear 07 shyness 09 cowardice 11 bashfulness, fearfulness 13 pusillanimity

timorous
03 coy, shy 04 eery 05 aspen, eerie, mousy, scary, timid 06 afraid, aspine, modest, mousey, scared, scarey 07 bashful, fearful, meacock, nervous 08 cowardly, retiring 09 diffident, shrinking, tentative, trembling, tremulous 10 frightened, irresolute 12 apprehensive, faint-hearted 13 pusillanimous, unadventurous

tin
02 Sn 03 can 05 money 06 paltry 09 argentine, Dutch oven
See also **money**

tincture
02 or 03 dye, fur, hue, Sol 04 bufo, dash, hint, tint 05 aroma, imbue, metal, scent, shade, smack, spice, stain, tinge, touch, trace 06 arnica, colour, elixir, infuse, season, smatch 07 flavour, sericon, suffuse 08 laudanum, permeate 09 seasoning 10 suggestion 12 friar's balsam

tine
03 bay, bez 04 lose, shut, snag, tare, teen, tiny, tray, trey, trez 05 point, prong, royal, spike, spire 06 kindle, perish 07 bay-tine, enclose 08 brow-tine, surroyal, trey-tine 09 bay-antler 10 affliction, brow-antler, trey-antler 11 crown antler

tinge
03 bit, dye, eye 04 cast, dash, drop, hint, tang, tint, wash 05 imbue, pinch, shade, smack, stain, taint, tinct, touch, trace 06 colour 07 flavour, suffuse 08 encolour, tincture 09 encrimson 10 smattering, sprinkling, suggestion

tingle
04 glow, itch, ring 05 prick, sting, thirl, throb 06 dindle, dinnle, quiver, shiver, thrill, tickle, tinkle, tremor 07 itching, prickle, tremble, vibrate 08 stinging, tickling 09 prickling 10 gooseflesh 12 goosepimples 14 pins and needles

tingling
04 dirl 05 sting 06 dindle, dinnle 07 prickly

tinker
03 toy 04 play, prig, tink 05 caird, fixer, Gypsy 06 dabble, fiddle, hawker, meddle, mender, pedlar, potter, rascal, repair, tamper, trifle 07 botcher, bungler, didakai, didakei, didicoi, didicoy, tinkler 08 diddicoy 09 fool about, itinerant, mess about 10 fool around, mess around

tinkle
04 bell, buzz, call, ding, peal, ring 05 chime, chink, clink 06 jangle, jingle, tingle 07 urinate 09 phone call

tinny
04 thin 05 cheap, harsh, lucky 06 flimsy, jingly 07 jarring 08 jangling, metallic 09 cheapjack 11 high-pitched, poor-quality 13 insubstantial

tinpot
03 bad 04 poor, ropy 05 awful, ropey 06 crummy, paltry, shoddy 07 useless 08 inferior, mediocre, pathetic, rubbishy, slipshod 09 defective, imperfect 10 low-quality, second-rate 11 incompetent, substandard 13 insignificant 14 unsatisfactory

tinsel
04 loss, sham, show 05 cheap, gaudy, showy 06 flashy, tawdry, trashy 07 display, glitter, spangle 08 frippery, gimcrack, specious 09 clinquant, gaudiness 10 garishness, pretension, triviality 11 flamboyance, ostentation, superficial 12 meretricious, ostentatious 13 artificiality, worthlessness 14 insignificance 15 meaninglessness

tint
03 dye, hew, hue 04 cast, tone, wash 05 color, rinse, shade, stain, taint, tinct, tinge, touch, trace 06 affect, colour, streak 08 tincture

tinware
04 tole

tiny
03 wee 04 mini 05 diddy, small, teeny, weeny 06 little, midget, minute, petite, pocket, slight, teensy 08 dwarfish, trifling 09 itsy-bitsy, itty-bitty, miniature, minuscule, pint-sized 10 diminutive, fractional, negligible,

teeny-weeny **11** Lilliputian, microscopic **13** infinitesimal, insignificant **14** circumstantial

tip

◇ *head selection indicator*
03 cap, end, nap, nib, tap, top **04** acme, apex, bung, cant, clue, dump, gift, give, hand, head, hint, horn, lean, list, noop, pass, peak, perk, pour, tell, tilt, toom, toss, vail, warn **05** bonus, crown, dodge, empty, point, pouch, shoot, slant, spill, trick, upset, vales **06** advice, advise, convey, gryfon, inform, midden, reward, summit, tip off, tip-off, topple, unload **07** capsize, caution, cumshaw, douceur, griffin, griffon, gryphon, incline, pointer, pour out, present, propine, slender, staithe, suggest, warning, wrinkle **08** bonamano, forecast, forewarn, gratuity, overturn, pinnacle, slag heap, surmount **09** backshish, bakhshish, baksheesh, buonamano, extremity, pourboire **10** backsheesh, perquisite, refuse-heap, remunerate, suggestion, topple over **11** information, rubbish-heap **13** gratification **14** recommendation

tip-off

◇ *head deletion indicator*
04 clue, hint, wire **07** pointer, warning **10** suggestion **11** information

tipple

03 bib, pot **04** down, dram, swig **05** booze, drink, paint, quaff, usual **06** imbibe, liquor, poison **07** alcohol, indulge **09** knock back **12** regular drink **14** favourite drink

tippler

03 sot **04** lush, soak, wino **05** alkie, dipso, drunk, toper **06** bibber, boozer, sponge **07** drinker, tosspot, winebag **08** drunkard, maltworm **09** inebriate **11** dipsomaniac, hard drinker

tipsy

◇ *anagram indicator*
03 wet **04** awry **05** askew, bosky, drunk, happy, lushy, merry, moony, muzzy, nappy, oiled, rocky, tight, totty, woozy **06** mellow, screwy, slewed, sprung, squiff, tiddly **07** a pip out, screwed, squiffy, tiddled **08** cockeyed, glorious, pleasant, top-heavy **09** a peepe out, well-oiled **10** a peg too low **15** the worse for wear

tirade

04 rant **05** abuse **06** laisse **07** lecture **08** diatribe, harangue, outburst **09** invective, monorhyme, philippic **11** fulmination **12** admonishment, denunciation

tire

03 tax **04** bore, cook, drop, flag, tyre **05** drain, dress, sew up, train, use up, weary **06** attire, bejade, strain, tucker, volley **07** apparel, breathe, exhaust, fatigue, tire out, wear out **08** enervate, outweary, pinafore **09** broadside, equipment, furniture, headdress

tired

03 old **04** beat, jack, sick **05** all in, blown, bored, corny, fed up, jaded, rough, stale, trite, weary **06** bushed, drowsy, pooped, sleepy, wabbit, zonked **07** cliché'd, drained, shagged, wappend, wearied, whacked, worn-out **08** clichéed, dead-beat, dog-tired, dog-weary, fatigate, fatigued, flagging, outspent **09** enervated, exhausted, fagged out, forjaskit, forjeskit, hackneyed, knackered, pooped out, shattered, washed-out **10** clapped-out, shagged out, war-wearied, world-weary **11** ready to drop, tuckered out **12** sick and tired, world-wearied

tireless

08 diligent, resolute, untiring, vigorous **09** energetic, unwearied **10** determined, unflagging **11** industrious **13** indefatigable, inexhaustible

tirelessly

10 diligently, resolutely, untiringly, vigorously **13** energetically, indefatigably

tiresome

04 dull **05** weary **06** boring, gallus, tiring, trying **07** gallows, humdrum, irksome, routine, tedious **08** annoying **09** fatiguing, laborious, vexatious, wearisome **10** irritating, monotonous, prolixious, unexciting **11** troublesome **12** exasperating **13** uninteresting

tiring

04 hard **05** stiff, tough **06** taxing **07** arduous **08** draining, exacting, wearying **09** demanding, difficult, fatiguing, laborious, strenuous, wearisome **10** enervating, exhausting

tiro, tyro

05 pupil **06** novice **07** learner, starter, student, trainee **08** beginner, freshman, initiate, neophyte **09** greenhorn, novitiate **10** apprentice, catechumen, tenderfoot

tissue

03 web **04** mesh, suet, tela **05** gauze, stuff, weave **06** fabric, matter **07** Kleenex®, network, texture **08** gossamer, material **09** structure, substance, variegate **10** aerenchyma, interweave, mesenchyme **11** toilet paper **12** facial tissue, sclerenchyma, toilet tissue

titan

05 Atlas, giant **06** Helios **08** colossus, Hercules, Hyperion, superman **09** leviathan **10** Prometheus

titanic

04 huge, vast **05** giant, jumbo **06** mighty **07** immense, mammoth, massive **08** colossal, enormous, gigantic, towering **09** cyclopean, herculean, monstrous **10** monumental, prodigious, stupendous **11** mountainous

titanium

02 Ti

titbit

05 scrap, snack, treat **06** dainty, morsel **08** delicacy **09** appetizer **11** bonne-bouche

tit for tat

03 hat **06** in kind, titfer **07** revenge **08** reprisal, requital **10** quid pro quo **11** blow for blow, counterblow, counterbuff, lex talionis, like for like, retaliation **13** an eye for an eye, countercharge

tithe

03 pay, tax **04** duty, give, levy, rate, rent, toll **05** disme, teind, tenth **06** assess, charge, impost, take in, tariff **07** tribute **08** decimate, hand over **10** assessment

titillate

05 tease **06** arouse, excite, thrill, tickle, turn on **07** provoke **08** interest, intrigue **09** stimulate, tantalize

titillating

04 lewd, sexy **05** lurid **06** erotic **07** naughty, teasing **08** arousing, exciting **09** seductive, thrilling **10** intriguing, suggestive **11** captivating, interesting, provocative, sensational, stimulating

titivate

05 groom, preen, primp, prink **06** doll up, make up, tart up **07** touch up **09** refurbish, smarten up

title

03 dub, tag **04** book, call, game, head, name, rank, term, work **05** claim, crown, deeds, label, match, prize, right, style **06** credit, eponym, handle, legend, office, stakes, status, trophy **07** caption, contest, credits, dukedom, entitle, epithet, heading, laurels **08** headline, monicker, nickname, position, subtitle **09** designate, honorific, ownership, privilege, pseudonym, sobriquet **10** nom-de-plume, soubriquet **11** appellation, competition, designation, entitlement, inscription, prerogative, publication **12** championship, denomination **13** form of address **14** proprietorship

Titles include:

01 M, U
02 Dr, Mr, Ms
03 bey, Dan, Dom, Don, Mrs, Pir, Rav, Reb, Rex, san, Sir, Sri, Ven
04 amir, Aunt, babu, bhai, Capt, Dame, Devi, Doña, emir, Frau, Herr, Imam, Lady, Lord, Ma'am, Miss, Prof, sama, Sant, Shri, tuan
05 baboo, begum, ghazi, hodja, khoja, Madam, Mirza, molla, padre, pasha, Rebbe, Señor, Swami, Uncle
06 Doctor, Father, khodja, kumari, Madame, Master, Mister, mollah, moolah, Mother, mullah, Regina, Señora, Signor, Sister, Tuanku
07 Bahadur, Brother, Captain, Colonel,

titter

effendi, esquire, Signior, Signora , Signore **08** Fräulein, Highness, memsahib, Mistress, Monsieur, Señorita, Viscount **09** Monsignor, Professor, Signorina, Signorino, Your Grace **10** burra sahib **11** Monseigneur, Your Majesty, Your Worship **12** Mademoiselle **15** Right Honourable

titter

04 mock, sway **05** laugh, te-hee **06** cackle, giggle, tee-hee, totter **07** chortle, chuckle, snicker, snigger, whicker

tittle-tattle

03 jaw, yak **04** chat, idle, yack **06** babble, cackle, gossip, natter, rumour, witter **07** blather, blether, chatter, hearsay, prattle, twaddle **08** chitchat, rabbit on, yack-yack **09** tell tales **10** yackety-yak

titular

05 token **06** formal, puppet **07** nominal **08** honorary, official, putative, so-called **10** in name only, self-styled

to

01 t' **02** at, au, of, on **03** à la, aux, for, tae **04** near, till, unto **05** until **06** before, beside **07** against, as far as, forward, towards

toad

04 bufo, pipa **07** paddock, puddock **10** natterjack

toadstool *see* **mushroom**

toady

04 fawn, sook, zany **05** crawl, creep **06** cringe, fawner, grovel, jackal, kowtow, lackey, minion, sucker, suck up, yes-man **07** crawler, flatter, flunkey, Jenkins, truckle **08** bootlick, butter up, hanger-on, parasite, suck-hole, toadfish, truckler **09** flatterer, groveller, sycophant **10** bootlicker, tuft-hunter **11** curry favour, kiss the feet, lick-platter, lickspittle **12** bow and scrape

to and fro

◇ *palindrome indicator*

toast

04 bake, heat, warm **05** brown, crisp, drink, grill, roast **06** birsle, heat up, honour, pledge, salute, scorch, warm up **07** drink to, tribute **08** barbecue, brindisi, scouther **09** sentiment **10** best wishes, compliment, salutation **11** compliments

See also **cheers**

tobacco

04 burn, chaw, chew, pipe, plug, quid, weed **05** bacco, baccy **07** the weed

Tobacco and tobacco preparations include:

04 capa, shag **05** régie, snout, snuff, snush, twist

06 burley, dottle, rappee, return, sneesh **07** caporal, chewing, Latakia, nail-rod, perique, pigtail **08** bird's-eye, canaster, honeydew, short-cut, Virginia **09** broad-leaf, cavendish, flue-cured, mundungus, strip-leaf

Tobacco pipes include:

03 cob **04** bong, clay **05** briar, brier, cutty, hooka, peace, water **06** dudeen, hookah, kalian **07** calumet, chibouk, chillum, corncob, dudheen, nargile, nargily **08** calabash, narghile, narghily, nargileh, nargilly **09** chibouque, narghilly **10** meerschaum **12** churchwarden, hubble-bubble **13** woodcock's-head

toboggan

04 dray, luge **05** pulka, slide, slipe, train **06** Ski-doo®, sledge, sleigh **07** bobsled, dogsled, kibitka, travois **09** bobsleigh **11** hurly-hacket, skeleton bob

today

03 now **06** the day **07** just now, this day **08** nowadays, right now **09** these days **11** this evening, this morning, this very day **12** at this moment **13** the present day, this afternoon **14** the present time

toddle

04 reel, rock, sway **05** lurch, shake, waver **06** falter, teeter, totter, waddle, wobble **07** saunter, stagger, stumble **14** move unsteadily, walk unsteadily

toddler

04 trot

to-do

03 ado **04** flap, fuss, stew, stir **05** hoo-ha **06** bother, bustle, flurry, furore, rumpus, tumult, unrest, uproar **07** quarrel, ruction, turmoil **08** brouhaha, razmataz **09** agitation, commotion **10** excitement, hullabaloo, razzmatazz **11** disturbance, performance, razzamatazz

toe

04 kick **05** digit **06** hallux, tootsy **07** dewclaw, tootsie **09** prehallux **12** tootsy-wootsy

together

03 cum **04** calm, cool **05** as one, atone, on end **06** attone, in a row, stable, united **07** as a team, jointly **08** composed, in unison, mutually, sensible **09** all at once, at one time, in company, in concert, on the trot, organized, pari passu **10** back to back, hand in hand, side by side **11** down-to-earth, level-headed, unflappable **12** collectively, concurrently, continuously, in succession, successively, well-adjusted, well-balanced **13** at the same time,

consecutively, in conjunction, well-organized, without a break **14** as a partnership, commonsensical, simultaneously **15** in collaboration, working together

• **come together**

03 gel **04** jell, meet **05** close, rally **07** collect, convene **10** amalgamate

Togo

02 TG **03** TGO

toil

03 net, tew, tug **04** grub, moil, slog, trap, work **05** graft, grind, labor, slave, snare, sweat, swink, yakka **06** drudge, effort, labour, murder, strive, yacker, yakker **07** fatigue, murther, slaving, travail, turmoil **10** drudgery, drudgism, exertion, hard work, industry, plug away, struggle **09** persevere **10** contention, donkey-work **11** application, elbow grease **12** push yourself **14** Hercules' choice **15** work like a Trojan

toiler

05 navvy, slave **06** drudge, menial, worker **07** grafter, slogger **08** labourer **09** struggler, workhorse **10** workaholic

toilet

02 WC **03** APC, bog, can, lat, lav, loo **04** dike, head, john, kazi, toot, tout **05** dunny, Elsan®, heads, jacks, lavvy, potty **06** lavabo, throne, urinal **07** cludgie, cottage, crapper, latrine **08** bathroom, lavatory, outhouse, Portaloo®, rest room, superloo, the gents', washroom **09** cloakroom, necessary, the ladies' **10** facilities, powder room, reredorter, throne room, thunderbox **11** convenience, earth-closet, water closet **12** dressing-room, smallest room **14** comfort station, little boys' room, necessary house, necessary place **15** Parliament House

toilsome

04 hard **05** tough **06** severe, taxing, uphill **07** arduous, painful, tedious, toiling, toylsom **08** tiresome **09** difficult, fatiguing, herculean, laborious, strenuous, toylesome, wearisome **10** burdensome **12** backbreaking

token

04 clue, disc, mark, seal, sign, slug **05** check, index, jeton, proof, scrip, staff **06** coupon, emblem, hollow, jetton, pledge, signal, slight, symbol **07** counter, memento, minimal, nominal, portent, tessera, voucher, warning **08** cosmetic, evidence, keepsake, memorial, moniment, monument, reminder, souvenir, symbolic **09** insincere, precedent, sacrament, triumphal **10** abbey-piece, emblematic, expression, indication, plague-spot **11** perfunctory, recognition, remembrance, superficial **12** abbey-counter, recognizance **13** demonstration, manifestation **14** representation

told
◊ *homophone indicator*

tolerable
02 OK **04** fair, so-so **06** not bad
07 average **08** adequate, all right,
bearable, mediocre, middling,
ordinary, passable **09** endurable, tol-
lolish **10** acceptable, fairly good, not
much cop, reasonable, sufferable
11 indifferent **12** run-of-the-mill,
satisfactory **13** no great shakes,
unexceptional

tolerably
06 enough, fairly **08** bearably
10 acceptably, adequately, ordinarily,
reasonably **12** sufficiently
13 indifferently

tolerance
04 give, play **05** swing **06** lenity
07 laxness, stamina **08** leniency,
patience, sympathy **09** allowance,
clearance, endurance, fortitude,
toughness, variation **10** good-humour,
indulgence, liberalism, resilience,
resistance, toleration **11** fluctuation,
forbearance, magnanimity
13 understanding **14** open-
mindedness, permissiveness **15** broad-
mindedness

tolerant
03 lax **04** fair, soft **06** decent
07 lenient, liberal, patient **08** catholic,
enduring, mellowed **09** compliant,
easy-going, forgiving, indulgent
10 charitable, forbearing, open-
minded, permissive **11** broad-minded,
free and easy, kind-hearted,
magnanimous, sympathetic
12 unprejudiced **13** long-suffering,
understanding

tolerate
04 bear, have, take, wear **05** abear,
abide, admit, allow, stand, thole
06 accept, endure, pardon, permit,
suffer **07** condone, indulge, receive,
stomach, swallow, warrant **08** sanction
09 put up with **11** countenance

toleration
06 lenity **07** laxness, stamina
08 leniency, patience, sanction,
sympathy **09** allowance, endurance,
fortitude, toughness **10** acceptance,
indulgence, liberalism, resilience,
resistance, sufferance **11** forbearance,
magnanimity **13** understanding
14 open-mindedness, permissiveness
15 broad-mindedness

toll
03 bar, due, fee, jow, tax **04** call, cost,
duty, harm, jole, joll, jowl, levy, loss,
lure, peal, pike, rate, ring, warn
05 chime, clang, death, decoy, joule,
knell, price, sound **06** charge, damage,
demand, herald, injury, octroi, signal,
strike, tariff **07** payment, penalty,
pierage, pontage, scavage, tallage,
tollage **08** announce, hardship
09 streetage, suffering **13** adverse
effect

tomb
04 bury, cist **05** crypt, death, grave,
speos, vault **06** burial, dolmen,
entomb, heroon, marble, shrine, tholus
07 funeral, mastaba, reposit
08 catacomb, cenotaph, hypogeum,
monument, sacellum **09** hypogaeum,
mausoleum, sepulcher, sepulchre,
sepulture **10** repository **11** burial-
place, sarcophagus **13** Holy Sepulchre

tomboy
04 ramp, romp **05** hempy **06** hoiden,
hoyden

tombstone
05 stone **06** marble **08** memorial,
monument **09** headstone
10 gravestone **12** through-stane,
through-stone **13** memorial stone

tomcat
03 gib

tome
03 tom **04** book, opus, work
06 volume

tomfoolery
03 tom **05** hooey, larks **06** idiocy
07 inanity, rubbish, trifles **08** clowning,
mischief, nonsense **09** horseplay,
jewellery, ornaments, silliness,
stupidity **10** buffoonery, carrying on,
skylarking **11** foolishness, shenanigans
12 childishness, larking about, messing
about

ton
01 t **03** tun **07** fashion

tone
03 air, hue **04** cast, feel, mood, note,
suit, tint, tune, vein **05** blend, drift,
force, match, pitch, shade, sound, style,
tenor, tinge, twang **06** accent, colour,
effect, go with, humour, manner, spirit,
stress, temper, timbre, volume
07 quality **08** attitude, emphasis,
strength, tincture, tonality **09** character,
harmonize **10** co-ordinate, expression,
go well with, inflection, intonation,
modulation **12** accentuation

• high tone
03 alt

• tone down
03 dim **06** dampen, reduce, soften,
subdew, subdue, temper **07** assuage,
lighten **08** mitigate, moderate, play
down, restrain **09** alleviate, soft-pedal

• tone up
04 buck, trim **05** brace **06** buck up,
tune up **07** freshen, shape up, touch up
08 brighten, limber up **09** sharpen up
10 invigorate

toneless
03 dim **04** dull, grey **05** faded
07 neutral, relaxed **08** listless, tuneless
09 soundless, unmusical **10** colourless
11 unmelodious **12** unexpressive
14 expressionless

Tonga
03 TON

tongue
04 cant, doab, lick, rasp, spit, talk, vote

05 argot, clack, idiom, lingo, slang,
utter, voice **06** glossa, jargon, lingua,
patois, radula, red rag, speech
07 clapper, dialect **08** language,
parlance **09** discourse, pronounce,
utterance **10** articulate, vernacular
12 articulation

See also **language**

tongue-tied
04 dumb, mute **06** silent **08** wordless
09 voiceless **10** dumbstruck,
speechless **11** mush-mouthed
12 inarticulate, lost for words, tongue-
tacked

tonic
01 t **05** boost, final **06** bracer, fillip,
saloop **07** cordial, home key, keynote
08 pick-me-up, roborant **09** analeptic,
refresher, stimulant **11** restorative
12 shot in the arm **15** fundamental note

See also **note**

too
03 tae **04** also, over, very **06** as well,
overly, unduly **07** besides **08** likewise,
moreover **09** extremely **10** in addition
11 excessively, furthermore
12 inordinately, ridiculously,
unreasonably

tool
03 cut **04** dupe, over, pawn, work,
yoke **05** agent, chase, gismo, means,
shape, tanto **06** agency, device,
gadget, medium, minion, puppet,
stooge, troppo, weapon **07** cat's-paw,
fashion, flunkey, machine, utensil,
vehicle **08** artefact, decorate, hireling,
ornament **09** apparatus, appliance,
implement **10** instrument, over-the-
top **11** contraption, contrivance
12 intermediary

Tools include:

02 ax
03 awl, axe, gad, hod, hoe, loy, saw,
sax, van
04 adze, burr, card, celt, file, fork, froe,
goad, hawk, jack, mace, mall, maul,
peel, pick, plow, prod, prog, rake,
rasp, risp, rule, snap, spud, vice
05 auger, bevel, clamp, dolly, drill,
level, plane, punch, snips, spade,
steel, tongs
06 bodkin, chaser, chisel, dibber,
dibble, fuller, gimlet, hammer, jigsaw, mallet, mortar, needle, pestle,
pliers, plough, sander, scutch,
scythe, shears, shovel, sickle,
trowel, wrench
07 bolster, bradawl, chopper, cleaver,
crowbar, forceps, fretsaw, hacksaw,
handsaw, hay fork, jointer, mattock,
nail gun, pick-axe, pincers, scalpel,
scriber, stapler, swingle, T-square
08 billhook, chainsaw, dividers,
penknife, scissors, spraygun, tenon-
saw, thresher, tommy bar, tweezers
09 grass-rake, jack-plane, pitchfork,
plumb-line, secateurs, set-square
10 jackhammer, paper-knife,
protractor

11 brace and bit, crochet hook, paper-cutter, pocket-knife, screwdriver, spirit level
12 angle grinder, caulking-iron, digging stick, pruning-knife, sledgehammer, socket-wrench, wirestripper
13 pinking-shears, pruning-shears, soldering-iron

See also **gardening**; **saw**

tooth
03 cog, jag **05** crena, prong, taste **06** dentil, joggle, relish **08** appetite, denticle **09** interlock, serration **10** serrations **13** denticulation

See also **teeth**

toothsome
04 nice **05** sweet, tasty, yummy **06** dainty, morish **07** moreish, savoury, scrummy **08** luscious, pleasant, tempting **09** agreeable, delicious, palatable **10** appetizing, attractive, delectable **11** flavoursome, scrumptious **13** mouthwatering

top
◇ *head selection indicator*
02 up **03** cap, cop, lid, nun, tip **04** acme, apex, beat, best, comb, cork, head, kill, lead, main, peak, roof, rule, tuft **05** chief, cover, crest, crown, excel, first, outdo, prime, ridge, shirt, smock, upper **06** apogee, better, blouse, climax, coppin, exceed, finest, finish, height, jersey, jumper, ruling, summit, T-shirt, upmost, upward, utmost, vertex, zenith **07** cacumen, command, eclipse, garnish, highest, leading, maximum, premier, premium, spinner, stopper, supreme, surpass, sweater, tank top, topmost, topsail, topspin **08** crowning, decorate, dominant, foremost, greatest, outshine, outstrip, pinnacle, pullover, superior, surmount, tee shirt, very good **09** be first in, finish off, paramount, principal, sovereign, transcend, uppermost **10** pre-eminent, sweatshirt **11** culminating, culmination **12** highest point

See also **cut**

• **over the top**
03 OTT **05** undue **06** lavish **07** extreme, too much **08** a bit much **09** excessive **10** exorbitant, immoderate, inordinate **11** extravagant, uncalled-for **12** unreasonable

• **top and tail**
◇ *ends deletion indicator*

• **top off**
◇ *head deletion indicator*

• **top up**
05 add to, boost **06** fill up, refill, reload **07** augment **08** increase, recharge **09** replenish **10** supplement

topi
03 hat **04** sola **05** solah **07** sola hat **10** sola helmet

topic
04 head, text **05** issue, place, point,

theme, topos **06** matter, thesis **07** subject **08** argument, question **09** hot button **10** hobby-horse, touch-me-not **11** commonplace, hardy annual, old chestnut **12** talking point **13** subject matter

topical
05 local **06** recent **07** current, popular **08** familiar, relevant, up-to-date **10** newsworthy **12** contemporary **13** up-to-the-minute

topless
◇ *head deletion indicator*

topmost
03 top **05** first, upper **06** apical **07** highest, leading, maximum, supreme **08** dominant, foremost, loftiest, supernal **09** paramount, principal, uppermost

top-notch
02 A1 **03** ace, top **04** cool, fine, mega **05** crack, prime, super **06** superb, way-out, wicked **07** leading, premier, radical, supreme **08** peerless, splendid, superior **09** admirable, excellent, first-rate, matchless, top-flight **10** first-class **11** exceptional, outstanding, superlative **12** second-to-none **14** out of this world

topping
◇ *juxtaposition down indicator*
05 crust **07** tipping **08** arrogant **09** excellent, wonderful

topple
◇ *anagram indicator*
03 tip **04** fall, oust **05** upset **06** totter, tumble, unseat **07** capsize, dismast, tip over **08** collapse, dethrone, displace, fall over, keel over, overturn **09** bring down, knock down, knock over, overthrow **11** overbalance

top-secret
06 secret **07** private **08** hush-hush, intimate, personal **09** sensitive **10** classified, restricted **12** confidential, off-the-record

topsy-turvy
◇ *anagram indicator*
05 messy **06** untidy **07** chaotic, jumbled, mixed-up **08** confused **09** confusion, inside out **10** disorderly, in disorder, upside down **11** disarranged, in confusion **12** disorganized, looking-glass, tapsalteerie, tapsieteerie

torch
04 burn, link, tead, wisp **05** brand, flare, light, teade **06** ignite, lampad **07** cresset, roughie **08** arsonist, flambeau, splinter **09** firebrand, set alight, set fire to, set on fire **10** flashlight **11** put a match to

torment
◇ *anagram indicator*
03 vex **04** bane, pain, pest, pine **05** agony, annoy, curse, grill, hound, tease, worry, wrack **06** badger, bother, harass, harrow, misery, ordeal, pester,

plague **07** afflict, agitate, anguish, bedevil, crucify, furnace, Gehenna, provoke, scourge, torture, trouble **08** distress, irritate, nuisance, vexation **09** annoyance, martyrdom, persecute, suffering, tantalize **10** affliction, harassment, irritation **11** persecution, provocation **13** pain in the neck **15** thorn in the flesh

torn
◇ *anagram indicator*
03 cut **04** rent, slit **05** split **06** ragged, ribbon, ripped, unsure **07** divided, enriven **08** lacerate, wavering **09** dithering, lacerated, uncertain, undecided **10** in two minds, irresolute **11** vacillating

tornado
04 gale **05** storm **06** squall **07** cyclone, monsoon, tempest, twister, typhoon **09** hurricane, whirlwind **10** waterspout

torpedo
03 ray **05** wreck **07** tin fish **09** cramp-fish **11** electric ray

torpid
04 dead, dull, lazy, numb, slow **05** inert **06** drowsy, sleepy, supine **07** dormant, passive **08** deadened, inactive, indolent, lifeless, listless, sluggish **09** apathetic, lethargic, nerveless, somnolent **10** insensible, languorous **11** lethargical

torpor
05 sloth **06** acedia, apathy, stupor **07** inertia, languor **08** dullness, hebetude, laziness, lethargy, numbness, slowness **09** indolence, inertness, passivity, stupidity, torpidity **10** drowsiness, inactivity, sleepiness, somnolence **12** lifelessness, listlessness, sluggishness

torrent
04 gush, rush **05** flood, spate, storm **06** deluge, stream, volley **07** barrage, blatter, cascade **08** downpour, outburst **10** inundation

torrential
05 heavy **07** driving, pelting, teeming **10** inundating, persistent **11** pouring down **13** bucketing down

torrid
03 hot **04** arid, sexy **06** desert, erotic, red-hot, steamy **07** amorous, blazing, boiling, parched **08** scorched, sizzling, stifling, tropical **09** scorching, waterless **10** blistering, passionate, sweltering

torsk
04 cusk

tortoise
06 gopher **07** hicatee, testudo **08** galapago, hiccatee, terrapin

tortuous
◇ *anagram indicator*
06 zigzag **07** curving, devious,

sinuous, winding **08** indirect, involved, twisting **09** ambagious, Byzantine **10** circuitous, convoluted, meandering, roundabout, serpentine **11** complicated

torture

◇ *anagram indicator*

03 fry, gip, gyp **04** pain, pine **05** abuse, agony, worry, wrack **06** harrow, martyr, misery, murder, plague, punish **07** afflict, agonize, anguish, crucify, murther, trouble **08** distress, ill-treat, mistreat **09** martyrdom, persecute, suffering, tantalize **10** affliction, excruciate, punishment **11** forcipation, persecution **12** excruciation, ill-treatment, mistreatment

Torture forms and instruments include:

03 gin, saw
04 boot, cage, pear, rack
05 brank, gadge, irons, jougs, screw, wheel
06 carcan, engine, harrow, picana, shabeh, spider, stocks, turcas
07 bilboes, boiling, cat's paw, hooding, picquet, pillory, pincers, scourge, stoning, torment
08 bootikin, branding, garrotte, knotting, pendulum, pressing, shin vice, trip-hook
09 bastinado, gauntlets, gridirons, picketing, scarpines, strappado, treadmill
10 brazen bull, cattle prod, impalement, iron collar, iron maiden, Judas scale, pilliwinks, spiked hare, starvation, suspension, thumbscrew, treadwheel
11 cave of roses, forcipation, German chair, head crusher, Judas cradle, keelhauling, knee-capping, squassation, thumbscrews, wooden horse
12 ball and chain, ducking-stool, flesh tearers, scold's bridle, shrew's fiddle, skull crusher, Spanish chair, water torture
13 cat-o'-nine-tails, electric shock, heretic's forks, Spanish mantle
14 Austrian ladder, devil-on-the-neck, disembowelment, drunkard's cloak
15 confession chair

Tory

01 C **03** Con **04** blue **07** tantivy **08** Abhorrer **12** Conservative

toss

◇ *anagram indicator*

03 bum, lob, shy, tip **04** birl, cant, cast, flip, hurl, jerk, jolt, loft, perk, puck, rock, roll, sway **05** bandy, brank, chuck, drink, fling, heave, lurch, pitch, shake, sling, throw **06** bridle, dandle, slight, sprawl, squirm, thrash, tumble, welter, writhe **07** agitate, blanket, canvass, flutter, wriggle **09** commotion, confusion

tot

03 dop, nip, sum **04** baby, dram, mite, shot, slug, swig **05** bairn, child

06 finger, infant **07** measure, swallow, toddler

See also **add**; **baby**; **drink**

• tot up

03 add, sum **05** add up, count, mount, tally, total **06** reckon **07** compute, count up, mount up **09** calculate

total

03 add, all, lot, sum, tot **04** full, make, mass, rank **05** add up, count, gross, reach, sheer, sum up, tot up, utter, whole **06** all-out, amount, come to, entire, reckon **07** count up, full-out, perfect, pur sang **08** absolute, amount to, complete, entirety, integral, outright, subtotal, thorough, totality **09** aggregate, downright, out-and-out **10** consummate, grand total, undisputed **11** unmitigated, unqualified **13** comprehensive, thoroughgoing, unconditional

totalitarian

08 despotic, one-party **09** tyrannous **10** monocratic, monolithic, omnipotent, oppressive **11** dictatorial **12** undemocratic **13** authoritarian

totality

03 all, sum **05** total, whole **06** cosmos **07** pleroma **08** entirety, fullness, universe **09** aggregate, wholeness **10** entireness, everything **12** completeness

totally

05 fully, quite **06** wholly **07** utterly **08** entirely, outright **09** perfectly **10** absolutely, completely, thoroughly **11** boots and all, undividedly **12** consummately, undisputedly **13** unmitigatedly **14** wholeheartedly **15** comprehensively, unconditionally

totter

◇ *anagram indicator*

04 reel, rock, roll, sway **05** lurch, shake, waver **06** daddle, dodder, falter, hotter, quiver, teeter, titter, topple, waddle, wobble **07** be shaky, stagger, stumble, tremble **10** be insecure, be unstable, be unsteady **12** be precarious **14** move unsteadily

touch

03 art, bit, dab, eat, hit, jot, nie, pat, pet, tap, tat, tig, use, way **04** abut, blow, dash, draw, feel, hand, harm, hint, hold, kiss, make, meet, move, nigh, nose, palm, palp, skim, spot, stir, take **05** bribe, brush, cheat, cover, drink, equal, flair, grain, graze, knack, match, pinch, point, reach, rival, skiff, skill, smack, speck, spice, stamp, style, taste, theft, tinge, trace, trait, upset, verge, weave, whiff, wound **06** adjoin, affect, aspect, attain, better, border, broach, caress, come to, detail, devour, finger, finish, fondle, handle, injure, little, manner, method, molest, muzzle, nicety, pierce, pocket, regard, sadden, smatch, strike, stroke, tickle **07** ability, concern, consume, contact, disturb, feature, impinge, impress, inspire,

involve, knuckle, mention, minutia, rapport, receive, refer to, soupçon, speak of, surface, taction, texture, touch up **08** addition, allude to, approach, come near, deal with, fineness, remark on **09** dexterity, direction, influence, suspicion, tactility, technique **10** connection, suggestion, touchstone **11** association **12** lay a finger on, put a finger on **13** communication, craftsmanship, hold a candle to **14** be contiguous to, correspondence, have an effect on, have an impact on **15** come into contact

• touch down

04 land **05** rouge **06** come in **11** come to earth **12** come in to land

• touch off

04 fire **05** begin, cause, light **06** arouse, foment, ignite, set off **07** actuate, inflame, provoke, trigger **08** detonate, initiate, spark off **10** trigger off

• touch up

03 tat **04** tatt **06** revamp **07** brush up, enhance, improve, patch up, perfect, retouch **08** polish up, renovate, round off **09** finish off

touch-and-go

04 dire, near **05** close, dodgy, hairy, risky **06** sticky, tricky **07** offhand, parlous **08** critical, perilous **09** dangerous, hazardous, uncertain **10** precarious **12** nerve-racking

touchdown

07 arrival, landing **08** coming in **14** coming in to land

touched

03 mad **04** daft **05** barmy, batty, crazy, dotty, loopy, moved, nutty, upset **06** insane **07** bonkers, stirred **08** affected, deranged, inspired **09** disturbed, eccentric, impressed **10** influenced, unbalanced

touchiness

09 bad temper, petulance, surliness, testiness **10** grumpiness, tetchiness **11** crabbedness, grouchiness, peevishness, pettishness **12** captiousness, irascibility, irritability

touching

03 sad **05** hongi **06** libant, moving, tender **07** attaint, darshan, piteous, pitiful, tangent **08** handball, pathetic, pitiable, poignant, stirring, tangency **09** affecting, emotional, fingering, upsetting **10** concerning, contiguous, disturbing, impressive **11** cloud-topped **12** cloud-kissing, heart-rending **13** heartbreaking

touchstone

04 norm, test **05** gauge, guide, model, proof **07** measure, pattern **08** standard, template **09** benchmark, criterion, yardstick **11** Lydian stone

touchwood

04 funk, monk, punk **05** spunk **09** matchwood

touchy

04 edgy, sore **05** cross, huffy, miffy, mifty, risky **06** badass, chippy, feisty, grumpy, ornery, snuffy, tricky **07** awkward, crabbed, grouchy, huffish, peevish, prickly **08** badassed, captious, delicate **09** difficult, irascible, irritable, sensitive **11** bad-tempered, problematic, thin-skinned **13** controversial, over-sensitive, quick-tempered

tough

03 fit, nut, yob **04** firm, grim, hard, lout, thug **05** brute, bully, burly, butch, chewy, hardy, harsh, rigid, rough, rowdy, solid, stern, stiff, teuch, teugh, yobbo **06** badass, ballsy, keelie, knotty, robust, rugged, severe, sticky, strict, strong, sturdy, taxing, thorny, uphill **07** adamant, arduous, callous, durable, fibrous, gristly, rubbery, ruffian, unlucky, vicious, violent, viscous **08** badassed, baffling, criminal, exacting, hardened, hooligan, leathery, muscular, plug-ugly, puzzling, resolute, stalwart, vigorous **09** bovver boy, cut-throat, difficult, hardnosed, laborious, lager lout, obstinate, resilient, resistant, roughneck, strenuous, tenacious, violently, well-built **10** determined, disorderly, inflexible, perplexing, refractory, unpleasant, unyielding **11** distressing, intractable, troublesome, unfortunate **12** aggressively **13** uncomfortable **14** tough as leather, uncompromising

toughen

04 neal **05** brace **06** anneal, harden **07** fortify, stiffen **09** reinforce **10** strengthen **12** make stricter, substantiate

toughness

04 grit, guts **08** firmness, obduracy, strength, tenacity **09** hardiness **10** resilience, resistance, ruggedness, sturdiness **13** determination, inflexibility

toupee

03 jiz, rug, wig **04** gizz **05** caxon, jasey, major **06** bagwig, bobwig, Brutus, peruke, tie-wig **07** buzz-wig, periwig, Ramilie, spencer **08** postiche **09** hairpiece **10** scratch-wig **14** transformation

tour

◇ *anagram indicator*
02 do **03** van **04** hike, ride, road, rode, trip **05** drive, jaunt, round, tramp, visit **06** course, outing **07** circuit, explore, go round, journey **08** roadshow, sightsee **09** barnstorm, excursion, walkabout **10** expedition, inspection **11** travel round **12** drive through **13** peregrination **14** journey through

tourist

05 emmet **06** tourer **07** grockle, tripper, visitor, voyager **09** sightseer, sojourner, traveller **10** day-tripper, rubberneck **12** excursionist, globetrotter, holidaymaker

• tourist attraction *see* Africa; America; Asia; Australia; Canada; Europe; London; Middle East; New York; New Zealand; Paris

tournament

04 meet, seed **05** basho, event, jerid, joust, match **06** jereed, series **07** contest, meeting, tourney **08** carousel **09** carrousel **10** round robin **11** bridge-drive, competition **12** championship

tousled

06 untidy **07** ruffled, rumpled, tangled, tumbled, unkempt **08** messed up **10** disordered, in disarray **11** disarranged, dishevelled

tout

03 all, ask, pet **04** hawk, hype, plug, pout, push, seek, sell **05** blast, every, plier, trade, watch, whole **06** appeal, barker, inhale, market, peddle, praise, runner, toilet **07** commend, endorse, promote, solicit **08** petition **09** advertise **11** workwatcher

tow

03 lug, tug **04** drag, draw, haul, pull, rope **05** track, trail **09** transport

• in tow

08 in convoy **10** by your side **12** accompanying

towards

02 to **03** for **04** near **05** about, anent, -wards **06** almost, nearly **07** close to, nearing **09** regarding **10** concerning, on the way to **11** approaching **12** to help pay for, with regard to **13** with respect to

tower

03 cap, top **04** loom, rear, rise, sail, soar **05** excel, mount, shoot **06** ascend, exceed **07** eclipse, surpass **08** dominate, overlook **09** transcend **10** overshadow
See also tug

Tower types include:

04 bell, fort, gate, keep, mill, peel, rood, shot **05** block, broch, clock, ivory, minar, pagod, round, spire, Texas, watch, water **06** belfry, castle, church, column, donjon, gopura, nurhag, pagoda, turret **07** bastion, citadel, conning, control, cooling, lookout, minaret, mirador, nuraghe, steeple **08** barbican, bastille, brattice, fortress, hill-fort, martello, scaffold **09** belvedere, campanile, smock mill, tower mill **10** skyscraper, stronghold **11** demi-bastion **13** fortification

Towers include:

02 CN **03** AMP, Sky **04** Pisa **05** Babel, Clock, Macau, Sears, Seoul, Tokyo **06** Big Ben, Dragon, Eiffel, Kiev TV, London, Riga TV, Tahoto **07** Alma-Ata, Leaning, Olympic, Praha TV, Yueyang **08** Tallin TV, Tashkent, Tengwang **09** Blackpool, Donauturm, Ostankino, Tianjin TV **10** Collserola, Liberation **11** Fernsehturm, The Euromast, Yellow Crane **12** Petronas Twin, Stratosphere **15** Oriental Pearl TV

• tower of strength

04 prop **06** pillar **07** support **08** mainstay **09** supporter **12** friend in need

towering

04 high, tall **05** great, lofty **07** extreme, soaring, sublime, supreme **08** colossal, elevated, gigantic, imposing **10** impressive, inordinate, monumental, surpassing, unrivalled **11** magnificent, outstanding **12** incomparable, overpowering **13** extraordinary

town

04 burg, city, dorp, toun **05** borgo, bourg, burgh, urban **06** favela, Podunk, pueblo **07** borough, new town, suburbs, village **08** township **09** enclosure, outskirts, urban area **10** county town, market town, metropolis, settlement **11** conurbation **12** municipality **13** urban district

County towns include:

03 Ayr **04** Mold, Wick, York **05** Banff, Cupar, Derry, Elgin, Lewes, Nairn, Omagh, Perth, Truro **06** Armagh, Brecon, Durham, Exeter, Forfar, Lanark, London, Oakham, Oxford **07** Appleby, Bedford, Belfast, Bristol, Cardiff, Chester, Denbigh, Dornoch, Ipswich, Kinross, Lerwick, Lincoln, Matlock, Morpeth, Newport, Norwich, Peebles, Preston, Reading, Renfrew, Selkirk, Taunton, Warwick, Wigtown **08** Aberdeen, Barnsley, Beverley, Cardigan, Carlisle, Cromarty, Dingwall, Dumfries, Greenlaw, Hereford, Hertford, Jedburgh, Kingston, Kirkwall, Monmouth, Pembroke, Rothesay, Stafford, Stirling **09** Aylesbury, Beaumaris, Cambridge, Dolgellau, Dumbarton, Newcastle **10** Haddington, Huntingdon, Linlithgow, Manchester, Montgomery, Nottingham, Presteigne, Shrewsbury, Stonehaven, Trowbridge, Winchester **11** Clackmannan, Downpatrick, Enniskillen, Northampton **12** Kircudbright **13** Middlesbrough, Northallerton

See also **city**; **United Kingdom**

• **mushroom town**
04 camp

• **open space in town**
04 lung

town-dweller
03 cit **05** towny **07** burgher, citizen, oppidan **08** townsman, urbanite **10** townswoman

township
02 tp **04** deme, vill **06** parish **07** village **09** community

toxic
06 deadly, lethal **07** baneful, harmful, noxious **08** poisoned **09** dangerous, poisonous, unhealthy

See also **poison**

toy
04 jest, play, whim **05** dally, flirt, knack, model, sport, trick **06** bauble, beaker, fiddle, gewgaw, paddle, tinker, trifle **07** reduced, replica, trinket **08** crotchet **09** automaton, mess about, miniature, plaything **10** knick-knack, mess around, small-scale **12** reproduction

05 coral, Dinky®, slide, swing, teddy, trike
06 cap-gun, garage, go-kart, guitar, paints, pop-gun, puzzle, rattle, rocker, seesaw, tea set
07 balloon, bicycle, box-kite, crayons, Digimon®, dreidel, drum set, Frisbee®, Game Boy®, marbles, Meccano®, ocarina, Play-Doh®, Pokémon®, rag doll, sandpit, scooter, shoofly, soft-toy, tumbler, Turtles®
08 catapult, doll's cot, football, GameCube®, golliwog, hula-hoop, Matchbox®, mirliton, model car, model kit, Nintendo®, Noah's ark, pedal-car, pinwheel, skipjack, squeaker, Subbuteo®, train set, tricycle, windmill
09 Action Man®, aeroplane, bandalore, Care Bears, doll's pram, gyroscope, playhouse, pogo stick, Sindy doll®, swingball, teddy bear, video game, whirligig
10 baby-walker, Barbie doll®, doll's buggy, doll's house, fivestones, hobby-horse, kewpie doll, musical box, pantograph, peashooter, Plasticene®, Rubik's Cube®, Scalextric®, skateboard, Steiff bear, Super Mario®, tin soldier, toy soldier, trampoline, typewriter, weather box, Wendy house
11 baby-bouncer, glove puppet, PlayStation®, shape-sorter, spacehopper, spinning top, stroboscope, Tantalus cup, thaumatrope, tiddly winks, water pistol, wheel of life
12 action figure, boxing-gloves, computer game, executive toy, jack-in-the-box, jigsaw puzzle, kaleidoscope, model railway, mountain bike, My Little Pony, paddling-pool, Power Rangers®, praxinoscope, rocking-horse, skipping-rope, walkie-talkie, weather house
13 Bob the Builder®, building block, climbing-frame, modelling clay, Newton's cradle, sewing machine, Space Invaders®, Tiny-Tears doll®
14 activity centre, bucket and spade, building-blocks, building-bricks, Cartesian devil, Cartesian diver, electronic game, Paddington Bear, Powerpuff Girls®

trace

03 bit, dog, jot, map, way **04** calk, copy, dash, draw, dreg, drop, find, hint, hunt, mark, move, plan, scar, seek, show, sign, spot, walk **05** chart, dig up, draft, pinch, relic, savor, scent, smack, spoor, stalk, tinge, token, touch, track, tract, trail, whiff, write **06** course, depict, derive, detect, engram, follow, fossil, pursue, record, savour, shadow, sketch **07** analyse, mark out, outline, proceed, remains, remnant, run down, soupçon, thought, uncover, unearth, vestige **08** chalk out, describe, discover, engramma, evidence, footmark, generate, moniment, monument, traverse **09** delineate, footprint, scintilla, suspicion, track down **10** hide or hair, impression, indication, suggestion **11** counterdraw, hide nor hair

track

03 dog, pug, ren, rin, run, way **04** beat, hunt, line, loke, mark, path, race, rack, rail, rake, road, sent, sign, slot, tail, tram, trod, wake **05** chase, drift, orbit, piste, route, scent, spoor, stalk, trace, tract, trade, trail, tread, troad, trode **06** course, follow, groove, ground, inside, pursue, riding, runway, shadow, sleuth, troade **07** circuit, footing, monitor, portage, tramway **08** argument, cycleway, footmark, footstep, sequence, sideline, speedway, traverse **09** cyclepath, footprint **10** serpentine, trajectory

See also **athletics**

- **keep track of**
04 plot **05** check, grasp, trace, watch **06** follow, record **07** monitor, observe, oversee **10** keep up with, understand **11** keep an eye on
- **lose track of**
04 miss **06** forget **08** misplace **13** lose touch with **15** lose contact with
- **make tracks**
02 go **04** dash **05** leave, scram **06** beat it, depart **07** dash off, make off **09** disappear **10** hit the road **15** leave footprints
- **off the beaten track**
06 remote **07** private **08** isolated, outlying, secluded **11** god-forsaken, in the sticks, out-of-the-way **12** unfrequented
- **on track**
06 on time **08** on course, on target **10** on schedule
- **track down**
04 find **05** catch, dig up, trace **06** detect, expose, turn up **07** capture, nose out, run down, uncover, unearth **08** discover, hunt down, sniff out **09** ferret out **10** run to earth **11** run to ground
- **tracks**
02 Ry

tract

03 lot **04** area, dene, plot, vast, zone **05** clime, essay, monte, trace, track **06** desert, extent, homily, region, sermon **07** booklet, expanse, leaflet, quarter, stretch, terrain **08** brochure, district, pamphlet, tractate, treatise **09** discourse, monograph, territory **12** disquisition, dissertation

tractable

04 tame **05** tawie **06** docile, pliant **07** pliable, willing **08** amenable, biddable, obedient, towardly, tractile, workable, yielding **09** compliant, malleable, treatable **10** governable, manageable, submissive **11** complaisant, persuadable **12** controllable

traction

04 drag, grip, pull **07** draught, drawing, haulage, pulling **08** adhesion, friction **09** telferage **10** propulsion, telpherage

tractor

03 cat **07** backhoe, pedrail, skidder **09** bulldozer **13** backhoe loader **14** traction engine

trade

02 go **03** art, buy, job, ply, ren, rin, run, way **04** deal, line, mart, sell, swap, work **05** craft, skill, track, trail, tread **06** barter, buying, career, course, custom, market, métier, mister, occupy, peddle, resort, switch **07** bargain, calling, dealing, rubbish, selling, traffic **08** business, commerce, exchange, medicine, merchant, peddling, practice, sideline, transact, treading, vocation **09** carpentry, clientele, customers, marketing **10** contraband, do business, employment, line of work, occupation, profession **11** commodities, merchandize, shopkeeping, trafficking **12** transactions

trademark

04 logo, mark, name, sign **05** badge, brand, crest, label, quirk, stamp **06** emblem, symbol **07** feature **08** hallmark, insignia **09** attribute, brand name, idiograph, tradename **10** brand label, speciality **11** peculiarity **12** idiosyncrasy **14** characteristic, typical quality **15** proprietary name

tradename

02 TN **05** brand, label

trader

05 bania, buyer, plier **06** banian, banyan, broker, dealer, seller, vendor **07** higgler, peddler **08** marketer, merchant, pitchman, retailer, supplier **09** barrow boy, marketeer, tradesman **10** easterling, shopkeeper, trafficker, wholesaler **11** tradeswoman

tradesman, tradeswoman

05 buyer **06** dealer, seller, trader, vendor, worker **07** artisan **08** mechanic, merchant, retailer **09** craftsman **10** journeyman, shopkeeper **11** craftswoman

tradition

03 way **04** rite **05** habit, usage **06** belief, cabala, custom, kabala, legend, praxis, ritual **07** cabbala, kabbala, qabalah, routine **08** ceremony, folklore, kabbalah, practice **10** convention, observance **11** institution

traditional

03 old, set **04** folk, oral **05** fixed, usual **06** age-old **07** old-line, pompier, routine **08** habitual, historic **09** customary, traditive, unwritten **10** accustomed, ceremonial **11** established **12** conservative, conventional, time-honoured, tralaticious, tralatitious **15** long-established

traditionalist
07 diehard **08** old fogey, old guard, old-liner **09** formalist **11** reactionary **12** conservative **13** stick-in-the-mud **15** conventionalist

traduce
04 slag **05** abuse, decry, knock, smear **06** defame, insult, malign, revile, vilify **07** asperse, blacken, detract, run down, slag off, slander **08** transmit **09** denigrate, deprecate, disparage, propagate, translate **10** calumniate, depreciate **12** misrepresent

traducer
06 abuser **07** defamer, knocker, smearer **08** asperser, vilifier **09** detractor, slanderer **10** denigrator, deprecator, disparager, mud-slinger **11** calumniator

traffic
03 buy **04** cars, deal, sell **05** queue, trade, truck **06** barter, hold-up, peddle **07** bargain, contact, dealing, freight, trade in, trading **08** business, commerce, dealings, exchange, gridlock, intrigue, peddling, shipping, tailback, vehicles **09** negotiate, relations, transport **10** congestion, do business, passengers, traffic jam **11** commodities, intercourse, trafficking **13** communication **14** transportation

trafficker
05 agent **06** broker, dealer, monger, seller, trader **07** peddler **08** marketer, merchant, supplier **11** distributor **12** merchandizer

tragedy
04 blow **06** buskin **08** calamity, disaster **09** adversity **10** affliction, misfortune **11** catastrophe, unhappiness

tragic
◇ *anagram indicator*
03 sad **04** dire **05** awful, fatal **06** deadly **07** unhappy, unlucky **08** buskined, dreadful, ill-fated, pathetic, pitiable, shocking, terrible, Thespian, wretched **09** appalling, miserable, sorrowful **10** calamitous, deplorable, disastrous **11** unfortunate **12** catastrophic **13** heartbreaking

tragically
07 awfully **08** terribly **10** dreadfully, shockingly, wretchedly **11** appallingly

trail
◇ *juxtaposition indicator*
03 dog, lag, tow, way **04** drag, draw, fall, hang, haul, hunt, path, pull, road, sign, tail, wake **05** chase, droop, marks, piste, reach, route, scent, spoor, stalk, sweep, trace, track, trade, train **06** dangle, dawdle, extend, follow, linger, loiter, pursue, ramble, runway, shadow, sleuth, stream, streel, trapes **07** abature, draggle, traipse **08** footpath, straggle, tag along, trauchle **09** footmarks **10** footprints

• destroy trail
04 foil

• trail away
04 fade, sink **06** lessen, shrink, weaken **07** die away, dwindle, subside, tail off **08** decrease, diminish, fade away, fall away, melt away, peter out, taper off, trail off **09** disappear

trailblazer
06 leader **07** founder, pioneer **09** developer, innovator **10** discoverer, pathfinder **13** ground-breaker

train
◇ *anagram indicator*
03 aim, set **04** drag, file, line, lure, path, sack, tail, tire **05** breed, chain, coach, court, drill, flier, flyer, focus, groom, learn, level, local, longe, lunge, order, point, staff, study, suite, teach, track, trail, tutor **06** allure, cafila, column, convoy, direct, ground, kafila, lesson, nuzzle, school, series, sledge, stream, string **07** bring up, caffila, caravan, cortège, educate, improve, prepare, process, retinue, work out **08** be taught, choo-choo, exercise, instruct, practise, puff-puff, rehearse, sequence **09** be trained, entourage, followers, following, household, inculcate **10** attendants, be prepared, discipline, procession, succession **11** progression **12** indoctrinate **13** concatenation

Train types include:
01 Q
02 up
03 APT, HST, owl, TGV, way
04 boat, down, loco, mail, milk
05 goods, hover, mixed, paddy, steam
06 bullet, diesel, Maglev
07 baggage, express, freight, through
08 cable-car, corridor, monorail, push-pull
09 aerotrain, excursion, high-speed, Intercity®, manriding
10 locomotive
12 Freightliner®
13 accommodation
14 shuttle service
15 steam locomotive

Trains include:
06 Rocket, Thomas
07 Mallard, The Ghan
09 The A-Train
13 Indian Pacific, Orient Express, Trans-Siberian
14 Flying Scotsman
15 Hogwarts Express

trained
03 fit **08** schooled **10** discerning **11** experienced

trainee
01 L **02** AT, ET **04** tiro **05** cadet, pupil **06** intern, novice **07** interne, learner, student **08** beginner **10** apprentice **11** probationer

trainer
02 PT **05** coach, tutor **06** mentor

07 handler, teacher **08** educator **10** instructor
See also **footwear**; **horseman, horsewoman**

training
◇ *anagram indicator*
02 PT **03** CAT, CBT **05** drill **07** lessons, nurture, tuition, workout **08** coaching, exercise, learning, pedagogy, practice, teaching, tutoring **09** education, grounding, schooling **10** bringing up, discipline, tirocinium, upbringing, working-out **11** instruction, preparation **14** apprenticeship

• out of training
04 soft

• youth in training
04 page

traipse
03 gad **04** plod, slog, trek **05** trail, tramp, trape **06** slouch, trudge **08** slattern

trait
04 thew **05** quirk, touch, trick **06** stroke **07** feature, quality **08** property **09** attribute **11** peculiarity **12** idiosyncrasy **14** characteristic

traitor
03 dog **05** Judas, kulak **07** nithing **08** betrayer, deceiver, defector, deserter, informer, proditor, quisling, renegade, traditor, treacher, turncoat, two-timer **09** traitress, treachour **11** backstabber, treachetour **12** collaborator, double-dealer **13** double-crosser **14** fifth columnist

traitorous
05 false **06** untrue **08** apostate, disloyal, renegade **09** faithless, seditious **10** perfidious, unfaithful **11** treacherous, treasonable **13** dishonourable, double-dealing **14** double-crossing

trajectory
04 line, path **05** orbit, route, track, trail **06** course, flight **10** flight path

trammel
◇ *anagram indicator*
03 bar, net, tie **04** bond, clog, curb, rein **05** block, catch, chain, check **06** enmesh, entrap, fetter, hamper, hinder, hobble, impede **07** capture, confine, ensnare, inhibit, shackle **08** entangle, handicap, obstacle, restrain, restrict **09** hindrance, restraint **10** impediment **14** stumbling-block

tramp
03 bum **04** hike, hobo, plod, roam, rove, slag, slut, step, tart, trek, walk **05** caird, jakey, march, piker, rogue, stamp, stomp, stump, trail, tread, tromp, wench, whore **06** dosser, hooker, ramble, sloven, toerag, truant, trudge, vagrom, walker, whaler **07** dingbat, floater, floozie, gangrel, swagger, swagman, tinkler, traipse, trample, trollop, vagrant **08** clochard, cursitor, derelict, footslog, scrubber, slattern, straggle, stroller, vagabond

trample

09 landloper, sundowner, toeragger **10** down-and-out, loose woman, prostitute **11** rinthereout, scatterling, Weary Willie **12** hallan-shaker **15** knight of the road

trample

04 foil **05** crush, poach, potch, stamp, tramp, tread, tromp **06** insult, squash, stramp **07** flatten, hobnail **08** override, ride down

trance

04 daze **05** dream, spell **06** stupor, transe **07** ecstasy, rapture, reverie **08** entrance **09** catalepsy **12** somnambulism **15** unconsciousness

tranche

03 cut **04** part **05** block, piece, slice, wedge **06** length **07** portion, section, segment **10** instalment

tranquil

04 calm, cool, easy **05** quiet, still **06** hushed, placid, sedate, serene, silent **07** pacific, relaxed, restful **08** composed, laid-back, peaceful **09** reposeful, unexcited **10** untroubled **11** undisturbed, unflappable **12** even-tempered **13** imperturbable, unimpassioned **14** disimpassioned

tranquillity

03 lee **04** calm, hush, rest **05** peace, quiet **06** repose **07** ataraxy, silence **08** ataraxia, calmness, coolness, quietism, quietude, serenity **09** composure, placidity, quietness, stillness **10** equanimity, sedateness **11** restfulness **12** peacefulness

tranquillize

04 calm, lull **05** quell, quiet, relax **06** opiate, pacify, sedate, serene, soothe **07** compose **09** narcotize

tranquillizer

06 downer, opiate **07** bromide **08** narcotic, quietive, sedative **09** calmative **10** depressant **11** barbiturate **12** sleeping pill
See also **sedative**

transact

02 do **05** enact **06** handle, manage, settle **07** carry on, conduct, execute, perform **08** carry out, conclude, despatch, dispatch **09** discharge, negotiate, prosecute **10** accomplish

transaction

03 job **04** deal, deed **06** action, affair, annals, doings, gamble, matter, record **07** affairs, bargain, minutes, passage, reports **08** business, concerns, debt swap, goings-on, handling, straddle **09** agreement, discharge, enactment, execution **10** enterprise, proceeding, put-through, settlement, swap option **11** arrangement, negotiation, proceedings, undertaking **12** control event, part-exchange, publications

transactions

02 tr **07** affairs, dealing, journal, memoirs

transcend

04 beat **05** excel, outdo **06** exceed **07** eclipse, surpass **08** go beyond, outshine, outstrip, overstep, surmount **09** rise above **11** leave behind

transcendence

09 greatness, sublimity, supremacy **10** ascendancy, excellence, paramouncy **11** paramountcy, pre-eminence, superiority **12** predominance **13** matchlessness, transcendency **15** incomparability

transcendent

07 sublime, supreme **08** numinous, peerless **09** excellent, excelling, ineffable, matchless, spiritual **10** superhuman, surpassing **11** magnificent, superlative **12** incomparable, supernatural, transcending, unparalleled **13** unsurpassable

transcendental

05 vague **08** mystical **09** excelling, spiritual **10** mysterious **12** metaphysical, otherworldly, supereminent, supernatural, transcending **13** preternatural

transcribe

04 copy, note **06** copy up, record, render **07** Braille, copy out, rewrite, write up **08** take down, write out **09** reproduce, translate **13** transliterate

transcript

04 copy, note **05** tenor **06** record, tenour **07** version **09** duplicate **10** manuscript **11** translation **12** reproduction **13** transcription **15** exemplification, transliteration

transcription

07 version **10** writing-out **11** translation **12** reproduction, transumption **15** transliteration

transfer

◇ *anagram indicator*
02 ET **03** EFT, PET, PMT **04** deed, flit, GIFT, hand, move, pass, take, turn, ZIFT **05** carry, grant, ladle, remit, shift **06** assign, change, convey, pounce, remove **07** consign, pipette, removal **08** alienate, give over, hand over, handover, movement, relocate, sign away, sign over, transmit **09** negotiate, transhume, transport, transpose **10** assignment, changeover, conveyance, relocation, transplant **12** displacement, transduction, transference, transmission **13** transposition

transfigure

◇ *anagram indicator*
05 alter, exalt, morph **06** change **07** convert, glorify **08** idealize **09** transform, translate, transmute **11** apotheosize **12** metamorphose

transfix

04 hold, spit, stun **05** rivet, spear, spike, stick **06** empale, impale, pierce, skewer **07** bestick, engross,

petrify **08** paralyse **09** fascinate, hypnotize, mesmerize, spellbind **10** run through

transform

◇ *anagram indicator*
04 turn **05** adapt, alter, morph, renew **06** absorb, change, mutate, reform **07** commute, convert, lithify, rebuild, receive, remodel, resolve **08** disclose **09** sovietize, translate, transmute, transpose **10** trans-shape, transverse **11** reconstruct, transfigure **12** decentralize, metamorphose, transmogrify **13** revolutionize **15** unprotestantize

transformation

◇ *anagram indicator*
03 wig **06** change, reform **07** turning **08** dilation, mutation, petalody, phyllody, reaction, rotation, sepalody **09** reflexion, sea change, variation **10** alteration, conversion, dilatation, metaplasia, metastasis, reflection, revolution **11** reformation, translation **13** metamorphosis, transmutation **15** theriomorphosis, transfiguration

transfuse

05 imbue **06** instil **07** pervade, suffuse **08** permeate, transfer

transgress

03 err, sin **04** defy **05** break, lapse **06** breach, exceed, offend **07** disobey, violate **08** encroach, infringe, overstep, trespass **09** misbehave **10** contravene **11** prevaricate

transgression

03 sin **04** debt, slip **05** crime, error, fault, lapse, scape, wrong **06** breach, escape **07** misdeed, offence, offense **08** iniquity, peccancy, trespass **09** overgoing, violation **10** infraction, peccadillo, wrongdoing **12** disobedience, encroachment, infringement, misbehaviour, misdemeanour, overstepping **13** contravention

transgressor

05 felon **06** debtor, sinner **07** culprit, villain **08** criminal, evil-doer, offender **09** miscreant, wrongdoer **10** delinquent, lawbreaker, malefactor, trespasser

transience

07 brevity **08** caducity, fugacity **09** briefness, shortness **11** evanescence **12** ephemerality, fleetingness, fugitiveness, impermanence **13** deciduousness, temporariness **14** transitoriness

transient

05 brief, fleet, short **06** bubble, flying **07** passing **08** fleeting, volatile **09** ephemeral, fugacious, momentary, short-term, temporary **10** evanescent, short-lived, transitory **11** impermanent **13** summer-seeming

transistor

03 FET

transit

05 route **06** travel **07** haulage, journey, passage, reverse **08** carriage, crossing, movement, shipment, transfer **10** conveyance, journeying, pass across **11** culmination **14** transportation

• **in transit**

05 by air, by sea **06** by rail, by road **07** en route **08** on the way **10** travelling

transition

04 flux, leap, move **05** shift **06** change, switch **07** passage, passing **08** movement, progress **09** evolution, metabasis **10** alteration, changeover, conversion, metastasis, unbecoming **11** composition, development, progression **12** transitional **13** metamorphosis, rite of passage, transmutation **14** transformation

transitional

05 fluid **07** interim, passing **08** changing, twilight **09** temporary, unsettled **11** provisional **12** evolutionary, intermediate **13** developmental

transitory

05 brief, fleet, short **06** flying **07** passing **08** fleeting **09** deciduous, ephemeral, fugacious, momentary, short-term, temporary, transient **10** evanescent, fly-by-night, short-lived **11** impermanent

translate

◇ *anagram indicator*
◇ *foreign word indicator*

03 put **04** move, turn **05** alter, shift **06** change, decode, encode, reduce, render, reword **07** conster, convert, English, explain, improve, traduce **08** construe, decipher, relocate, renovate, simplify, transfer **09** enrapture, interpret, transform, transmute, transport **10** metaphrase, paraphrase, transcribe **12** transmogrify **13** transliterate

translation

◇ *anagram indicator*

03 key **04** crib, move, pony **05** gloss, horse, shift **06** change, motion **07** version **08** transfer **09** rendering, rendition, rewording **10** alteration, conversion, metaphrase, paraphrase, rephrasing, traduction **11** explanation, metaphrasis **12** transumption **13** metamorphosis, transcription, transmutation **14** interpretation, simplification, transformation **15** transliteration

translator

02 tr **03** CLT **07** exegete, glosser, Rhemist **08** dragoman, linguist, polyglot **09** Englisher, exegetist, glossator **10** glossarist, metaphrast, paraphrast **11** interpreter, paraphraser

translucent

05 clear **06** limpid **08** lancelet, pellucid **10** diaphanous, membranous, see-through, translucid

transmigration

07 rebirth **13** reincarnation **14** metempsychosis, Pythagoreanism, transformation

transmission

04 show **06** entail, signal, spread **07** beaming, episode, message, passage, sending **08** carriage, despatch, dispatch, relaying, shipment, transfer **09** broadcast, diffusion, imparting, programme, simulcast, transport **10** convection, conveyance, production, trajection **11** consignment, performance **12** broadcasting, presentation, transference **13** communication, dissemination, transmittance

• **end of transmission**

04 over **10** over and out

transmit

03 fax **04** beam, bear, buzz, pass, pipe, send **05** carry, modem, radio, relay, remit **06** convey, hand on, impart, pass on, report, send on, spread **07** conduct, consign, diffuse, forward, mediate, message, network, radiate, send out, traduce, traject **08** despatch, dispatch, hand down, telecast, televise, transfer **09** broadcast, propagate, satellite, transport **11** communicate, disseminate, interrogate

transmute

◇ *anagram indicator*

05 alter **06** change, remake **07** convert, permute, sublime **08** transmew **09** alchemize, permutate, sublimate, transform, translate, transmove **10** transverse **11** transfigure **12** metamorphose, transmogrify

transparency

05 photo, slide, water **07** clarity, picture **08** openness, overhead **09** clearness, filminess, frankness, gauziness, limpidity, plainness, sheerness **10** candidness, directness, limpidness, patentness, photograph **11** obviousness, pellucidity **12** apparentness, distinctness, explicitness, pellucidness, translucence, translucency **13** translucidity **14** diaphanousness, forthrightness **15** perspicuousness, unambiguousness

transparent

04 open **05** clear, filmy, gauzy, lucid, plain, sheer, white **06** candid, direct, limpid, patent, watery **07** evident, hyaline, hyaloid, obvious, tiffany, visible **08** apparent, distinct, explicit, manifest, pellucid **10** colourless, diaphanous, forthright, noticeable, see-through **11** discernible, perceptible, translucent, unambiguous, undisguised, unequivocal **12** semipellucid, transpicuous, unmistakable **15** straightforward

transparently

07 clearly, plainly **08** patently **09** evidently, obviously **10** distinctly, explicitly, noticeably **11** discernibly, perceptibly **12** unmistakably **13** unambiguously, unequivocally

transpire

05 arise, ensue, occur, prove **06** appear, befall, exhale, happen **07** come out, turn out **09** come about, take place **10** come to pass **11** become known, be disclosed, come to light **14** become apparent

transplant

04 move **05** graft, repot, shift **06** remove, uproot **07** replant **08** displace, plant out, relocate, resettle, transfer **12** cluster graft

transport

◇ *anagram indicator*

02 MT **03** AST, fit, lag, put, ren, rin, run, SST **04** bear, haul, move, rail, rape, rush, ship, take, waft **05** bliss, bring, carry, cycle, exile, fetch, shift, witch **06** convey, deport, frenzy, ravish, remove, thrill **07** delight, ecstasy, elation, freight, haulage, medevac, overjoy, rapture, removal, traject, transit, vehicle **08** carriage, entrance, euphoria, shipment, shipping, transfer **09** captivate, carry away, electrify, enrapture, spellbind, translate **10** conveyance **12** exhilaration **13** seventh heaven, transportance **14** transportation

See also **travel**; **vehicle**

03 bus, cab **04** taxi, tram, tube **05** ferry, metro, train **07** omnibus, railway, trolley **10** stage-coach, trolleybus **11** park-and-ride, underground **12** light railway

transportation

07 airlift, freight, haulage, railage, removal, traffic, transit, waftage **08** carriage, shipment, shipping, transfer **09** fishyback **10** conveyance

transported

◇ *anagram indicator*

04 rapt **05** piped **08** traveled **09** rhapsodic, travelled

transpose

◇ *anagram indicator*

02 tr **04** move, swap, turn **05** alter, shift **06** change, invert, switch **07** convert, reorder **08** exchange, flip-flop, transfer **09** rearrange, transform **10** substitute **11** interchange, metathesize **13** anagrammatize

transverse

05 cross **06** thwart **07** oblique, reverse **08** diagonal **09** crossways, crosswise, transform **10** overthwart **11** transversal

trap

◇ *containment indicator*

03 gin, gob, net, pit, pot **04** drop, dupe,

11 membraneous, transparent **13** membranaceous

fall, grin, hook, lime, lure, mesh, ploy, ruse, take, toil, weel, wile **05** bazoo, catch, creel, decoy, fault, mouth, noose, plant, snare, spell, sting, toils, trick **06** ambush, bunker, corner, danger, device, enmesh, entrap, hazard, tangle **07** beguile, capture, confine, deceive, ensnare, flytrap, gin trap, mantrap, mist-net, pin down, pitfall, putcher, rat-trap, springe **08** artifice, cakehole, catch-pit, dead-fall, fall-trap, inveigle, putcheon, trapdoor, traphole, trickery **09** booby-trap, deception, mouse-trap, snaphance, stratagem **10** catch-basin, dig a pit for, potato trap, snaphaunce, snaphaunch, subterfuge

See also **carriage**

trapped
◇ *insertion indicator*
05 duped, stuck **06** caught, netted, snared **07** tricked **08** ambushed, beguiled, cornered, deceived, ensnared **09** inveigled **10** surrounded **11** in by the week

trapper
06 hunter **08** covering, huntsman, voyageur **12** backwoodsman, frontiersman

trappings
04 gear **05** dress **06** finery, livery, things **07** clothes, panoply, raiment **08** fittings, fixtures, housings **09** equipment, furniture, ornaments, trimmings **10** adornments, fripperies **11** accessories, decorations, furnishings **13** accoutrements, paraphernalia **14** accompaniments

trash
◇ *anagram indicator*
03 mar, pan, rot **04** blah, bosh, bull, bunk, carp, dust, guff, junk, ruin, scum, sink, slam **05** balls, blame, break, check, decry, dreck, dregs, hooey, tripe, waste, wreck **06** attack, drivel, grunge, harass, kitsch, litter, rabble, ravage, refuse, scraps, trudge **07** baloney, censure, condemn, destroy, eyewash, garbage, hogwash, rhubarb, rubbish, run down, shatter, torpedo, wear out **08** badmouth, canaille, demolish, denounce, malarkey, nonsense, riff-raff, trashery, write off **09** criticize, denigrate, devastate, disparage, excoriate, gibberish, moonshine, sweepings, trashtrie, vandalize **10** balderdash, come down on, go to town on, vituperate **11** pick holes in **12** disapprove of, gobbledygook, offscourings, pull to pieces, put the boot in, tear to shreds, undesirables **13** find fault with, play havoc with, tear a strip off **15** do a hatchet job on, pass judgement on

trashy
04 naff **05** cheap **06** crappy, flimsy, kitsch, paltry, shabby, shoddy, tawdry, tinsel **07** kitschy **08** inferior, rubbishy

09 cheap-jack, third-rate, worthless **12** meretricious

trauma
04 hurt, jolt, pain **05** agony, grief, shock, upset, wound **06** damage, injury, lesion, ordeal, strain, stress **07** anguish, torture **08** disorder, distress, upheaval **09** suffering **11** disturbance

traumatic
07 harmful, hurtful, painful **08** shocking, wounding **09** agonizing, injurious, stressful, upsetting **10** disturbing, unpleasant **11** distressing, frightening

traumatize
04 daze, hurt, numb, stun **05** amaze, appal, shock, upset **06** dismay, grieve, offend **07** astound, horrify, outrage, stagger, startle, stupefy **08** distress, paralyse

travail
04 slog, toil **05** grind, sweat, tears **06** effort, labour, strain, stress, throes, travel **07** travois, trouble **08** distress, drudgery, exertion, hardship **09** suffering **10** birth-pangs, childbirth **11** labour pains, tribulation

travel
02 go **03** ren, rin, run **04** meve, move, pass, ride, roam, rove, tour, trip, tube, walk, wend, wing **05** cover, cross, vroom, wagon, wheel **06** ramble, troupe, voyage, waggon, wander **07** advance, conduct, explore, impetus, journey, passage, proceed, touring, tourism, travail, trolley, wayfare **08** go abroad, progress, traverse **09** excursion, make a trip **10** expedition, go overseas, journeying, travelling, wanderings **11** make your way, see the world, sightseeing **13** globetrotting

See also **space**

03 bus, fly, row, ski
04 bike, hike, punt, ride, sail, tour, trek, trip, walk
05 cycle, drive, jaunt, march, motor, pilot, skate, steam, visit
06 aviate, cruise, flight, outing, paddle, ramble, safari, voyage
07 commute, holiday, journey, mission, shuttle
09 excursion, freewheel, hitch-hike, migration, orienteer
10 expedition, pilgrimage
11 exploration

traveller
03 rep **05** agent, Gypsy, hiker, nomad, rider, tramp **06** bagman, spacer, tinker, tourer, viator **07** aviator, bushman, drifter, drummer, migrant, rambler, tourist, tripper, vagrant, voyager **08** aviatrix, commuter, explorer, roadster, salesman, seafarer, spaceman, wanderer, wayfarer **09** itinerant, passenger, peregrine,

sightseer **10** commercial, saleswoman, spacewoman **11** salesperson **12** excursionist, globetrotter, holidaymaker **14** representative **15** knight of the road

travelling
◇ *anagram indicator*
04 road, rode **06** mobile, moving, roving **07** migrant, nomadic, roaming, sailing, touring, vagrant **08** homeless **09** itinerant, itinerary, migrating, migratory, on the move, on the road, unsettled, wandering, wayfaring **11** peripatetic

travel-worn
05 tired, weary **07** seasick, waygone, wayworn **08** footsore **09** jet-lagged **10** saddle-sore **11** travel-weary

traverse
03 lap, ply, ren, rin, run **04** deny, ford, pace, plod, race, ride, roam, span, walk, wear, wind, wing **05** cover, cross, motor, range, stump, trace, track, tramp **06** bridge, denial, oppose, overgo, parade, screen, thwart, voyage, wander **07** barrier, curtain, descend, dispute, examine, measure, oblique, parapet **08** consider, crossing, go across, pass over, progress, walk over **09** adversity, go through, negotiate, partition **10** contradict, crosspiece **11** obstruction, pass through, peregrinate **12** travel across **13** contradiction, travel through

travesty
04 sham **05** farce, spoof **06** parody, send-up, wind-up **07** apology, mockery, take-off **08** disguise **09** black mass, burlesque, tall story **10** caricature, corruption, distortion, perversion

trawl
04 comb, hunt, sift, wade **06** search **07** look for **11** investigate

treacherous
03 icy **05** dirty, false, Punic, risky, snaky **06** guiled, trappy, unsafe, untrue **08** disloyal, perilous, slippery **09** dangerous, deceitful, faithless, hazardous, two-timing **10** perfidious, precarious, traitorous, unfaithful, unreliable **11** duplicitous **12** backstabbing, false-hearted **13** double-hearted, hollow-hearted, untrustworthy **14** double-crossing

treacherously
07 falsely **08** mala fide **10** disloyally **11** deceitfully, faithlessly **12** perfidiously

treachery
07 treason **08** bad faith, betrayal, sabotage, trahison **09** duplicity, falseness, Judas kiss, perfidy, two-timing **10** disloyalty, hollowness, infidelity, Punic faith **11** fides Punica, traitorhood **12** backstabbing **13** deceitfulness, double-dealing, faithlessness **14** double-crossing, unfaithfulness

tread

02 go **04** beat, form, gait, hike, pace, plod, step, trek, walk **05** clamp, clump, crush, dance, march, press, spurn, stamp, trace, track, trade, tramp **06** squash, stramp, stride, trudge, walk on **07** chalaza, flatten, footing, oppress, trample **08** business, copulate, footfall, footmark, footstep **09** footprint, press down **11** cicatricula

• **tread on someone's toes**
03 irk, vex **04** hurt **05** annoy, upset **06** bruise, injure, offend **07** affront **08** infringe **10** discommode, disgruntle **13** inconvenience

treason

06 mutiny **07** perfidy **08** sedition, trahison **09** duplicity, rebellion, treachery **10** disloyalty, subversion **11** lese-majesty, leze-majesté, leze-majesty, perduellion, traitorhood **12** disaffection **14** traitorousness

treasonable

05 false **08** disloyal, mutinous **09** faithless, seditious **10** perfidious, rebellious, subversive, traitorous, unfaithful

treasure

03 gem **04** cash, gems, gold, love **05** adore, cache, guard, hoard, money, prize, value **06** dote on, esteem, jewels, revere, riches, taonga, wealth **07** cherish, darling, fortune, idolize, worship **08** hold dear, preserve **09** valuables **11** masterpiece, pride and joy **13** think highly of **14** crème de la crème

treasurer

06 bursar, fiscal, purser **07** cashier, steward **08** quaestor **10** camerlengo, camerlingo, cash-keeper **11** purse-bearer

treasury

04 bank, fisc, fisk **05** cache, chest, funds, hoard, money, store, vault **06** assets, camera, corpus **07** bursary, capital, coffers **08** finances, revenues **09** exchequer, resources, thesaurus **10** repository, storehouse

treat

◇ *anagram indicator*
02 do **03** buy, fun, rub, tar, tub, use, vat, vet, wax **04** cure, gift, give, heal, tend, view, wine, worm **05** amuse, apply, besee, cover, dress, feast, lay on, nurse, paint, party, prime, put on, serve, smear, stand, study, waste, wheel **06** doctor, handle, manage, outing, parley, pay for, regale, regard, review, thrill **07** banquet, care for, delight, discuss, present, provide, take out **08** attend to, consider, deal with, medicate, pleasure, spread on, surprise **09** amusement, cover with, enjoyment, entertain, excursion, look after, negotiate, poeticize, tartarize **10** indulgence, minister to, pay the bill **11** celebration, foot the bill, negotiation **13** behave towards, entertainment, gratification

treatable

07 curable **08** moderate, operable **09** medicable, reparable, tractable **10** reformable, remediable **11** rectifiable

treatise

05 essay, ethic, paper, study, summa, tract **06** Cybele, system, thesis **07** pandect **08** Almagest, lapidary, pamphlet, prodrome, tractate **09** cosmology, discourse, festilogy, festology, monograph **10** arithmetic, dendrology, exposition, halieutics **11** gnomonology **12** disquisition, dissertation

treatment

◇ *anagram indicator*
03 EST, use **04** care, cure, deal **05** doing, usage **06** action, demean, notice, reason, remedy **07** affront, conduct, dealing, demaine, demayne, demeane, healing, measure, nursing, quarter, regimen, surgery, therapy **08** cosmesis, coverage, dealings, handling **09** behaviour, discursus, going-over **10** asepticism, discussion, management, medicament, medication, observance **12** manipulation, therapeutics **13** antisepticism **14** discountenance

treaty

04 bond, deal, pact **05** peace **06** pledge **07** bargain, compact, concord **08** alliance, assiento, contract, covenant, entreaty, protocol **09** agreement, concordat **10** convention, engagement **11** negotiation **12** pacification

Treaties and agreements include:

03 Edo (Treaty of)
04 Jay's (Treaty), Rome (Treaty of), SALT
05 Baden, Dover (Treaty of), Ghent (Treaty of), Kyoto (accord), Lyons (Treaty of), Paris (Treaties of), Union (Treaty of)
06 Amiens (Treaty of), Berlin (Treaty of), London (Treaties of), Madrid (Treaty of), Passau (Treaty of), Poland (Partitions of), Tilsit (Treaties of), Vienna (Treaties of)
07 Barrier (Treaties), Dresden (Treaty of), Nanjing (Treaty of), Nystadt (Treaty of), Tianjin (Treaty of), Utrecht (Peace of)
08 Brussels (Treaty of), Kanagawa (Treaty of), Lausanne (Treaty of), Pyrenees (Treaty of the), Tientsin (Treaty of)
09 Bucharest (Treaties of), Hay-Herrán (Treaty), Karlowitz (Treaty of), Pressburg (Treaty of), St Germain (Treaty of)
10 Adrianople (Treaty of), Anglo-Iraqi (Treaty), Maastricht (Treaty), Magna Carta, Paris Pacts, San Stefano (Treaty of), Versailles (Treaty of), Warsaw Pact, Washington (Treaty of), Westphalia (Peace of)
11 Fort Stanwix (Treaties of), Locarno Pact, Vereeniging (Peace of), Westminster (Treaty of)
12 Brest-Litovsk (Treaty of), Lateran Pacts
13 North Atlantic (Treaty), Social Chapter, Triple Entente
14 Hague Agreement, Hoare-Laval Pact
15 Entente Cordiale, Munich Agreement

treble

04 high **05** sharp **06** piping, shrill, triple **07** soprano **09** threefold **11** high-pitched

tree

04 bush, limb, spar **05** shrub **06** corner, wooden **07** gallows **08** pedigree

See also **palm**; **pine**; **rubber**

Tree types include:

03 nut
04 palm
05 covin, fruit
06 bonsai, citron, citrus, forest, timber
07 conifer, dwarfed
08 hardwood, softwood
09 broad-leaf, Christmas, deciduous, evergreen
10 ornamental

Trees include:

02 bo, ti
03 ash, asp, bay, bel, box, elm, fig, fir, gum, ita, jak, koa, may, nim, oak, sal, tea, ule, yew
04 acer, akee, arar, atap, bito, coco, cola, dali, dhak, dika, dita, eugh, gean, holm, hule, ilex, jack, kola, lime, lind, mate, mowa, neem, nipa, olea, ombu, palm, pear, pine, plum, poon, rata, rimu, shea, sorb, teak, teil, toon, upas, yang
05 ackee, afara, alder, apple, aspen, assai, balsa, beech, birch, cacao, carob, cedar, china, ebony, elder, fruit, guava, hazel, holly, karri, kauri, larch, lemon, lilac, lotus, mango, maple, morus, olive, papaw, peach, pecan, piñon, pipal, plane, rowan, salix, thorn, tulip, yucca
06 acacia, almond, bamboo, banana, banyan, baobab, bonsai, cashew, cassia, cherry, damson, gingko, jarrah, laurel, linden, papaya, pawpaw, poplar, prunus, quince, rubber, sapele, spruce, walnut, willow
07 apricot, Banksia, blue gum, conifer, cork oak, cypress, dogwood, hickory, quassia, redwood, sequoia, wych elm
08 chestnut, date palm, Dutch elm, ghost gum, hardwood, hawthorn, hornbeam, mahogany, mandarin, mangrove, mulberry, oleaster, softwood, sycamore, tamarisk
09 araucaria, blackwood, Chile pine, crab apple, deciduous, evergreen, jacaranda, kauri-pine, leylandii, melaleuca, paperbark, persimmon, Scots pine, stone pine,

whitebeam, wych-hazel
10 blackthorn, breadfruit, cottonwood, Douglas fir, eucalyptus, ornamental, sandalwood, witch hazel
11 bottle brush, bristlecone, coconut palm, copper beech, false acacia, golden larch, London plane, mountain ash, pussy willow, silver birch, silver maple
12 monkey puzzle, Monterey pine, Wellingtonia
13 angel's trumpet, horse chestnut, Japanese maple, sweet chestnut, weeping willow
14 cedar of Lebanon, Lombardy poplar
15 bristlecone pine

• **abounding in trees**
04 elmy, oaky, piny
• **clump of trees**
03 mot **04** mott **05** bluff, copse, motte, plump **06** spinny **07** spinney
• **embedded tree**
04 snag
• **isolated tree**
04 ombu
• **tree stump**
04 runt
• **tree trunk**
03 log **04** bole, butt, stud **06** ricker

tree-planted walk
04 xyst **06** xystos, xystus

trek
04 drag, hike, plod, roam, rove, slog, trip, walk, yomp **05** march, stage, tramp **06** ramble, safari, trudge **07** journey, migrate, odyssey, traipse **09** migration **10** expedition

trellis
03 net **04** grid, mesh **05** grate **06** grille **07** grating, lattice, network, treille **08** espalier **09** framework **11** latticework **12** reticulation

tremble
◇ *anagram indicator*
04 rock **05** quake, shake **06** dither, dodder, hotter, judder, quaver, quiver, shiver, tremor, wobble, wuther **07** shudder, vibrate, whither **09** vibration **13** tremulousness

trembling
◇ *anagram indicator*
04 yips **06** quaver, shakes **07** quaking, rocking, shaking **09** juddering, quavering, quivering, shivering, tremulous, vibration **10** heart-quake, shuddering **11** oscillation, trepidation

tremendous
04 huge, vast **05** great **06** wicked **07** amazing, corking, howling, immense, massive **08** colossal, dreadful, enormous, gigantic, smashing, terrific, towering **09** wonderful **10** formidable, impressive, incredible, marvellous, prodigious, remarkable, stupendous, thundering **11** exceptional, sensational, spectacular **13** extraordinary **14** out of this world

tremendously
04 very **06** highly, really **07** acutely, awfully, greatly, utterly **08** severely **09** decidedly, extremely, intensely, unusually **10** remarkably, thoroughly, uncommonly **11** exceedingly, excessively, frightfully **12** immoderately, inordinately, terrifically, unreasonably **13** exceptionally **15** extraordinarily

tremor
05 quake, shake, shock **06** dindle, dinnle, quaver, quiver, shiver, thrill, wobble **07** shudder, temblor, tremble **09** agitation, foreshock, marsquake, moonquake, quavering, trembling, vibration **10** earthquake, titubation

tremulous
◇ *anagram indicator*
05 aspen, jumpy, shaky, timid **06** afraid, aspine, scared **07** anxious, excited, fearful, jittery, nervous, quivery, shaking, trembly **08** agitated, timorous, unsteady, wavering **09** quavering, quivering, shivering, trembling, vibrating **10** frightened

trench
03 cut, fur, pit, sap **04** dike, dyke, foss, furr, grip, leat, leet, line, moat, rill **05** boyau, ditch, drain, fosse, gripe, verge **06** border, furrow, gullet, gutter, trough **07** channel, cunette, slidder **08** encroach, entrench, parallel, waterway **09** earthwork **10** excavation **12** entrenchment
See also **ocean**

trenchant
05 acute, blunt, clear, sharp, terse **06** astute, biting **07** acerbic, caustic, cutting, mordant, pungent **08** clear-cut, distinct, emphatic, forceful, incisive, scathing, vigorous **09** effective **10** forthright, no-nonsense, perceptive **11** penetrating, unequivocal **13** perspicacious

trend
03 fad **04** bend, bent, flow, look, mode, rage, tide, turn, wind **05** craze, drift, style, vogue **06** course, downer, latest **07** bearing, current, fashion, leaning **08** downturn, tendency **09** bandwagon, consensus, direction, downswing **10** mainstream, rising tide **11** inclination, radical chic **13** name of the game

trendsetter
05 model **06** leader, new man **07** pioneer **08** new woman **09** innovator, modernist, modern man **11** modern woman, trailblazer **12** avant-gardist **13** avant-gardiste, groundbreaker

trendy
02 in **03** hip, now **04** cool **05** funky, natty **06** groovy, latest, modish, snazzy, with it **07** right-on, stylish, voguish **10** all the rage **11** fashionable **13** up-to-the-minute

trepidation
04 fear **05** alarm, dread, worry

06 dismay, fright, nerves, qualms, tremor, unease **07** anxiety, emotion, jitters, shaking **08** disquiet **09** agitation, cold sweat, quivering, trembling **10** excitement, misgivings, uneasiness **11** butterflies, nervousness, palpitation **12** apprehension, perturbation **13** consternation

trespass
03 sin **05** poach, wrong **06** invade, offend **07** impinge, intrude, offence, violate **08** encroach, infringe, invasion, obdurate, poaching **09** intrusion, violation **10** transgress, wrongdoing **12** encroachment, infringement, misdemeanour **13** contravention, transgression

trespasser
06 sinner **07** burglar, poacher **08** criminal, evil-doer, intruder, offender **10** delinquent, encroacher **12** transgressor

tress
04 curl, hair, lock, tail **05** braid, bunch, plait, swits **06** strand, switch **07** pigtail, ringlet **08** trammels

trial
03 try **04** bane, case, exam, pest, test **05** assay, check, cross, dummy, grief, pilot, probe, study **06** appeal, assess, assize, bother, burden, dry run, hassle, misery, ordeal, sample, screen, trinal, try out, try-out **07** analyse, approof, attempt, contest, examine, hearing, inquiry, lawsuit, retrial, scratch, testing, test run, trouble **08** appraise, audition, distress, dummy run, endeavor, evaluate, hardship, nuisance, practice, tribunal, vexation **09** adventure, adversity, annoyance, endeavour, probation, rehearsal, selection, suffering, threefold **10** affliction, experiment, litigation, temptation **11** approbation, competition, cross to bear, examination, exploratory, investigate, provisional, tribulation **12** cause célèbre, experimental, probationary **13** pain in the neck **14** experiment with **15** thorn in the flesh

triangle
Triangles include:		

05 right
07 Bermuda, eternal, Pascal's, scalene, similar, warning
09 cocked hat, congruent, isosceles, spherical
11 acute-angled, equilateral, right-angled
12 obtuse-angled

triangular
08 trigonal, trigonic **09** trigonous **10** three-sided, trilateral, triquetral **11** triquetrous **13** three-cornered **14** triangle-shaped
• **triangular piece**
04 gair, gare, gore **05** fichu, godet

tribal

05 class, group **06** ethnic, family, native **08** gentilic **09** sectional **10** indigenous

tribe

03 iwi, rod **04** clan, hapu, race, sept **05** blood, breed, caste, class, group, house, ngati, stock **06** branch, family, nation, people **07** dynasty **08** division **11** ethnic group

Tribes of Israel:

03 Dan, Gad
05 Asher, Judah
06 Reuben, Simeon
07 Ephraim, Zebulun
08 Benjamin, Issachar, Manasseh, Naphtali

See also **Aboriginal**; **African**; **American**; **Asian**; **European**

tribulation

03 woe **04** blow, care, pain **05** curse, grief, trial, worry **06** burden, misery, ordeal, sorrow **07** anxiety, reverse, travail, trouble **08** distress, hardship, vexation **09** adversity, heartache, suffering **10** affliction, misfortune **11** unhappiness **12** wretchedness

tribunal

03 bar, EAT **04** rota **05** bench, court, trial **07** hearing **09** Areopagus, committee **11** examination, inquisition **12** confessional **13** kangaroo court

tribune

04 bema

tributary

04 fork **05** bogan, river **06** branch, feeder, stream **08** influent **09** confluent **10** head-stream **12** contributing

tribute

03 due, fee, tax **04** cain, duty, gift, kain, levy, scat, skat, toll **05** gavel, paean, proof, scatt **06** charge, credit, eulogy, homage, honour, praise, tariff **07** payment, pension, present, respect **08** accolade, applause, encomium, evidence, good word, offering, Rome-scot **09** drift-land, gratitude, panegyric, Rome-penny **10** compliment, dedication **11** good opinion, high opinion, Peter's pence, recognition, testimonial **12** commendation, contribution **15** acknowledgement

trice

02 mo **03** sec **04** haul, tick **05** flash, jiffy, shake **06** minute, moment, pulley, second **07** instant **09** twinkling

trichosanthin

01 Q

trick

◇ *anagram indicator*
02 do **03** art, con, fix, fob, fun, gag, kid, rig, tip, toy **04** dupe, fake, feat, flam, fool, gift, gull, hang, have, hoax, jape, joke, mock, pass, pawk, ploy, rook, ruse, scam, sell, sham, trap, trim, turn, vice, wile **05** antic, bluff, bogus, caper, cheat, cozen, dodge, false, flair, fraud, glaik, gleek, knack, plant, prank, quirk, skill, skite, skyte, spell, stall, stunt, watch **06** adroit, antick, begunk, chouse, deceit, delude, device, diddle, double, ersatz, forged, frolic, genius, have on, illude, juggle, lead on, mirage, outwit, palter, rip-off, secret, shavie, take in, talent **07** ability, anticke, antique, beguile, chicane, deceive, defraud, faculty, fantasy, fast one, feigned, frame-up, knowhow, leg-pull, mislead, pliskie, roughie, skylark, slinter, swindle, trinket, wrinkle **08** artifice, capacity, doubling, facility, flimflam, gimcrack, hoodwink, illusion, jimcrack, prestige, skin game, subtlety **09** deception, defective, expedient, gold brick, imitation, manoeuvre, mousetrap, stratagem, technique, underplot **10** apparition, artificial, capability, hocus-pocus, pleasantry, subterfuge, subtleness, under-craft, unreliable **11** conjuration, counter-cast, counterfeit, galliardise, hornswoggle, legerdemain, monkey shine, pull one over **12** starting hole, take for a ride, trick of light **13** double-shuffle, practical joke, sleight of hand **14** pull a fast one on, three-card monte

• number of tricks

03 nap **04** book, slam

• trick out

04 do up, fard, tiff **05** adorn, array **06** attire, bedeck, doll up, tart up **07** dress up, trick up **08** decorate, ornament, spruce up

trickery

04 trap **05** fraud, guile **06** deceit, ropery, slight **07** cantrip, cunning, dodgery, jookery, joukery, sleight **08** artifice, cheating, illusion, jugglery, practice, pretence, wiliness **09** chicanery, deception, duplicity, imposture, stratagem, swindling **10** conveyance, dishonesty, hanky-panky, hocus-pocus, imposition, shenanigan, subterfuge **11** contrivance, legerdemain, shenanigans, skulduggery **12** skullduggery **13** double-dealing, funny business, jiggery-pokery, sleight of hand **14** joukery-pawkery, monkey business **15** smoke and mirrors

trickle

03 ren, rin, run **04** drib, drip, drop, leak, ooze, seep **05** exude **06** filter, gutter **07** dribble, driblet, drizzle, dropple, seepage **08** dribblet, ticklish **09** percolate **10** flow slowly, precarious

trickster

04 hood, rook **05** cheat, fraud, joker, rogue, shark **06** con man, dodger, hoaxer, rascal **07** cozener, diddler, hoodlum, hustler, tricker **08** con woman, deceiver, impostor, swindler **09** artificer, charlatan, con artist, fraudster, pretender, tregetour **10** dissembler, mountebank **11** illy whacker

tricky

◇ *anagram indicator*
03 sly **04** foxy, wily **05** dicey, dodgy, elvan, elven, nasty **06** artful, crafty, elfish, elvish, knotty, pretty, shifty, subtle, thorny **07** awkward, cunning, devious, finicky **08** delicate, scheming, slippery, ticklish **09** deceitful, difficult, sensitive **11** complicated, legerdemain, problematic

tried

06 proved, proven, tested **07** trusted **08** reliable **10** dependable **11** established, trustworthy

trifle

03 bit, fig, toy **04** dash, doit, drop, fool, iota, play, song, spot **05** dally, flirt, sport, straw, touch, trace, wally **06** bauble, dabble, daidle, faddle, fiddle, fisgig, fizgig, frivol, geegaw, gewgaw, little, meddle, niggle, paddle, palter, peddle, piffle, pingle, potter, tiddle, trivia, wanton **07** flamfew, fribble, nothing, old song, quiddle, trinket **08** falderal, fal de rol, flea-bite, folderol, niffnaff, whim-wham **09** bagatelle, mess about, plaything **10** dilly-dally, knick-knack, mess around, triviality **11** fiddlestick, inessential, small amount **12** fiddle-faddle **13** play the wanton

trifling

04 idle **05** empty, minor, petty, potty, seely, silly, small **06** faddle, fallal, futile, paltry, slight **07** fooling, foolish, puerile, shallow, trivial **08** baubling, boy's play, childish, fiddling, frippery, immoment, nonsense, nugatory, piddling, piffling **09** dalliance, desipient, fribbling, fribblish, frivolous, whifflery, worthless **10** negligible **11** superficial, unimportant **12** fiddle-faddle **13** insignificant **14** inconsiderable **15** inconsequential

trigger

04 spur **05** catch, cause, lever, start **06** elicit, prompt, set off, switch **07** produce, provoke **08** activate, generate, initiate, spark off, stimulus, touch off **09** day-length **10** bring about **11** set in action, set in motion

trill

04 lilt, pipe, roll, sing **05** flute, shake, twirl **06** quaver, warble **07** trundle

trim

◇ *head deletion indicator*
◇ *tail deletion indicator*
03 cut, dub, fit, fur, lop, net, way **04** barb, chop, clip, cool, crop, dink, dock, edge, face, form, lace, neat, nett, pare, slim, snip, snod, tidy, tosh, trig **05** adorn, array, braid, cheat, dress, frill, guard, natty, order, prune, roach, ruche, shape, shave, shear, slick, smart, smirk, state, tight, trick **06** adjust, border, dapper, donsie, edging, fettle, fit out, fringe, health, humour, neaten, plight, reduce, smooth, snazzy, spruce, svelte, temper, thrash, tidy up, trimly

07 arrange, balance, compact, curtail, cut down, festoon, fitness, garnish, orderly, slender **08** clean-cut, contract, decorate, decrease, diminish, fittings, ornament, trimming, well-kept **09** condition, cut back on, embellish, scale down, shipshape, underbear **10** decoration **11** clean-limbed, disposition, in good order, presentable, streamlined, well-dressed, well-groomed **12** spick-and-span **13** well-turned-out

trimming
03 end **04** gimp, gymp, trim **05** braid, extra, frill, guard, guimp, robin **06** border, edging, fringe, paring, piping, robing **07** cascade, cutting, falbala, garnish, macramé, macrami, marabou **08** clipping, frou-frou, furbelow, marabout **09** accessory, adornment, balancing, garniture, passement **10** decoration **11** fimbriation **13** accompaniment, embellishment, ornamentation, passementerie

Trinidad and Tobago
02 TT **03** TTO

trinket
04 seal **05** bijou, charm, jewel, trick **06** bauble, doodad, doodah, geegaw, gewgaw, trifle **07** flamfew, trankum **08** delicacy, gimcrack, kickshaw, ornament, whim-wham **09** bagatelle, kickshaws **10** knick-knack **11** whigmaleery **12** whigmaleerie

trio
05 triad **06** triune, troika **07** musette, trilogy, trinity, triplet **08** terzetto, triunity **09** threesome **10** triplicity **11** triumvirate
See also **three; threesome**

trip
◇ *anagram indicator*
03 hop, ren, rin, run **04** buzz, fall, flip, high, hurl, kilt, link, ride, sail, skip, slip, spin, tilt, tour **05** caper, dance, dream, drive, error, flock, foray, gaffe, jaunt, jolly, lapse, slide, spurn, waltz, whirl **06** booboo, bummer, gambol, howler, outing, sortie, spring, tiptoe, tootle, totter, tumble, vision, voyage **07** bloomer, blunder, clanger, fantasy, faux pas, journey, mistake, stagger, stumble **08** freak-out, illusion **09** excursion, false step **10** apparition, expedition, experience, inaccuracy **13** hallucination **15** lose your footing
• **trip up**
04 trap **05** catch, snare, trick **06** ambush, outwit, waylay **07** ensnare **08** catch out, fall over, outsmart, surprise **09** wrongfoot **10** disconcert **15** throw off balance

tripe
03 rot **04** blah, bosh, guff, tosh **05** balls, hooey, trash **06** bunkum, drivel **07** baloney, eyewash, garbage, hogwash, inanity, rhubarb, rubbish, twaddle **08** claptrap, entrails, malarkey,

nonsense, tommyrot **09** bullswool, moonshine, poppycock **10** balderdash

triple
04 trio **05** third, triad **06** treble, triune, troika **07** perfect, trilogy, trinity, triplet **08** three-ply, three-way, triunity **09** threefold, threesome **10** sdrucciola, three times, tripartite, triplicate, triplicity **11** triumvirate

tripod
03 cat, pod **06** trivet **08** triangle **09** brand-iron

tripper
07 grockle, tourist, voyager **09** sightseer, traveller **12** excursionist, holidaymaker

trite
04 dull, worn **05** banal, corny, stale, stock, tired **06** beaten, common **07** cliché'd, routine, worn-out **08** clichéed, cornball, ordinary, overdone, overused, overworn, tritical, truistic, well-worn **09** hackneyed, rinky-dink **10** threadbare, uninspired, unoriginal **11** commonplace, Mickey Mouse, novelettish, predictable, stereotyped, well-trodden **12** run-of-the-mill **13** platitudinous

tritium
01 T **13** heavy hydrogen

triton
03 eft **04** evet, newt

triumph
03 hit, joy, win **04** beat, coup, crow, feat, pomp **05** exult, gloat, glory, paean, revel, trump **06** defeat, insult **07** conquer, elation, mastery, pageant, prevail, prosper, rejoice, succeed, success, swagger, victory **08** conquest, dominate, jubilate, overcome, overcrow, vanquish, walkover **09** celebrate, exultance, exultancy, festivity, happiness, overwhelm, rejoicing, sensation, win the day **10** attainment, exultation, jubilation, observance **11** achievement, celebration, gain mastery **12** masterstroke **13** flying colours **14** accomplishment
• **expression of triumph**
02 ha, ho, io **03** aha, hah, hey, hoa, hoh, Jai, oho, olé **04** ha-ha **05** heigh, there **06** yippee **07** so there

triumphant
05 proud **06** elated, joyful **07** crowing, winning **08** boastful, exultant, gloating, glorious, jubilant **09** cock-a-hoop, rejoicing, triumphal **10** conquering, successful, swaggering, victorious **11** celebratory **12** prize-winning

trivia
03 pap **06** Hecate **07** details, trifles **08** minutiae **12** trivialities **13** irrelevancies **14** technicalities

trivial
04 bald **05** banal, dinky, minor, petty, small, trite **06** flimsy, frothy, little,

measly, paltry **08** everyday, gimcrack, piddling, piffling, snippety, trifling **09** frivolous, quibbling, rinky-dink, small beer, worthless **10** incidental, negligible, peppercorn, vernacular **11** commonplace, meaningless, unimportant **12** cutting no ice, pettifogging **13** insignificant, no great shakes **14** inconsiderable **15** inconsequential, of no consequence

triviality
06 detail, trifle **07** nothing **08** banality, frippery, nonsense, pretence **09** frivolity, pettiness, puerility, smallness **10** nothingism **11** foolishness **12** technicality, unimportance **13** worthlessness **14** insignificance **15** meaninglessness

trivialize
07 devalue, scoff at **08** belittle, minimize, play down **09** underplay **10** depreciate, undervalue **12** Hollywoodize **13** underestimate

troglodyte
04 wren **11** cave-dweller

troll
03 elf **04** drow, harl, jinn, roll, rove, spin, trow **05** dwarf, gnome, pooka **06** allure, goblin, ramble, stroll **07** trundle **08** trolling **09** circulate **10** repetition

trolley
04 corf **05** bogey, bogie, brute, dolly, truck **07** tramcar **09** caddie car **10** caddie cart, traymobile **11** dinnerwagon

trollop
03 pro, pug, tom **04** bawd, dell, drab, moll, punk, road, stew, tart **05** brass, broad, quail, quiff, stale, tramp, trull, wench, whore **06** bulker, callet, geisha, harlot, hooker, mutton, plover **07** cocotte, floozie, hetaera, hostess, hustler, lorette, polecat, rent-boy, venture **08** bona-roba, callgirl, dolly-mop, magdalen, strumpet **09** courtesan, hierodule, loose fish **10** cockatrice, convertite, fancy woman, loose woman, prostitute, rough trade, vizard-mask **11** fallen woman, fille de joie, laced mutton, night-walker, poule de luxe, public woman, working girl **12** fille des rues, painted woman, scarlet woman, street-walker **13** grande cocotte **14** lady of the night, woman of the town

troop
02 go, tp **03** mob **04** army, band, body, crew, gang, herd, kern, pack, team, turm, unit, walk **05** bunch, crowd, flock, group, horde, kerne, march, squad, swarm, turme **06** parade, school, stream, throng, troupe, trudge **07** cavalry, company, consort, convoys, gunners, militia, traipse **08** assemble, brigades, division, fighters, military, platoons, soldiers, squadron **09** commandos, fusiliers, gathering,

multitude, regiments, squadrons
10 assemblage, contingent,
paratroops, servicemen **11** armed
forces, infantrymen **12** paratroopers,
servicewomen

trophy
03 cup, pot **05** award, prize **06** spoils
07 laurels, memento **08** souvenir
10 silverware

Trophies include:
02 TT
05 FA Cup
06 Fed Cup
07 Auld Mug, Gold Cup, Grey Cup,
Uber Cup
08 Davis Cup, Ryder Cup, The Ashes,
World Cup
09 Aresti Cup, Curtis Cup, Thomas
Cup, Walker Cup
10 Masters Cup, Solheim Cup, Stanley
Cup, Winston Cup
11 Admiral's Cup, America's Cup,
Eschborn Cup, Kinnaird Cup,
McCarthy Cup
12 Camanachd Cup, Lugano Trophy
13 Heisman trophy, Leonard Trophy,
Sam Maguire Cup
14 Continental Cup, Jesters' Club Cup
15 Champions Trophy, Lilienthal
Medal, Louis Vuitton Cup, Nascar
Nextel Cup, Scotch Whisky Cup

See also **award**

tropical
03 hot **05** humid **06** steamy, sultry,
torrid **07** boiling, very hot **08** stifling
09 luxuriant **10** boiling hot, figurative,
sweltering

trot
03 jog, ren, rin, run **04** crib, pace
05 crone **06** bustle, canter, scurry
07 dogtrot, heigh-ho, jogtrot, passage,
scamper, scuttle, tripple **08** heich-
how
• **on the trot**
04 busy **06** in a row, in turn **10** back to
back **12** continuously, sequentially,
successively **13** consecutively
15 uninterruptedly
• **trot out**
06 adduce, drag up, recite, relate,
repeat **07** bring up, exhibit **08** bring
out, rehearse **09** reiterate **12** bring
forward

troubadour
04 poet **06** singer **08** jongleur,
mariachi, minstrel, trouvère, trouveur
09 balladeer, cantabank
11 Minnesinger

trouble
◇ *anagram indicator*
03 ado, ail, dog, fix, jam, noy, vex, woe
04 care, fash, fuss, gram, heat, mess,
moil, pain, rile, work **05** annoy, grame,
grief, kaugh, muddy, pains, sturt, trial,
upset, visit, weigh, worry **06** barrat,
bother, burden, corner, cumber,
defect, effort, harass, hassle, hatter,
kiaugh, molest, pickle, put out, sadden,
scrape, shadow, shtook, shtuck, strife,

tsuris, tumult, unease, unrest **07** afflict,
agitate, ailment, anxiety, concern,
disease, disturb, failure, illness,
mismake, perplex, perturb, problem,
schtook, schtuck, thought, torment,
travail, tsouris **08** disorder, disquiet,
distress, exercise, exertion, fighting,
hardship, headache, hot water, irritate,
nuisance, problems, shutdown,
stalling, stopping, struggle, upheaval,
vexation **09** adversity, agitation,
annoyance, attention, breakdown,
commotion, complaint, heartache,
packing-up, suffering, tight spot, weigh
down **10** affliction, conking-out,
cutting-out, difficulty, disability,
discommode, disconcert, irritation,
misfortune, solicitude, uneasiness
11 botheration, disturbance,
malfunction, tribulation
13 inconvenience, make the effort
14 solicitousness, thoughtfulness

troubled
◇ *anagram indicator*
05 tense, upset **06** afraid, on edge,
uneasy **07** anxious, fearful, fretful,
nervous, uptight, worried
08 agonized, bothered, dismayed,
strained **09** concerned, disturbed, ill at
ease, perturbed **10** disquieted,
distracted, distraught, distressed,
frightened **11** overwrought
12 apprehensive **14** hot and bothered

troublemaker
05 mixer **07** inciter, stirrer **08** agitator
09 bovver boy **10** incendiary,
instigator, ringleader **12** rabble-rouser
13 mischief-maker

troublesome
◇ *anagram indicator*
04 hard **05** pesky, rowdy, spiny
06 infest, plaguy, taxing, thorny, tricky,
trying, unruly **07** awkward, brickle,
irksome, plaguey, testing **08** annoying,
exacting, fashious, tiresome
09 demanding, difficult, laborious,
turbulent, vexatious, wearisome,
worrisome **10** bothersome, disturbing,
irritating, perturbing, plaguesome,
rebellious **11** importunate,
mischievous **12** incommodious,
inconvenient **13** insubordinate, unco-
operative

trough
03 gum, hod, tie, tye **04** crib, duct
05 chute, ditch, drain, flame, gully,
hutch, shoot, shute, stock, trunk
06 backet, feeder, furrow, groove,
gutter, hollow, hopper, manger, sluice,
straik, strake, trench, valley **07** channel,
conduit, launder **08** sheep-dip
09 sand table **10** depression
12 seasoning-tub **13** feeding trough
14 watering-trough

trounce
04 beat, best, drub, lick, rout **05** crush,
paste, thump **06** defeat, hammer,
harass, indict, punish, rebuke, thrash,
wallop **07** clobber, shellac
09 overwhelm, slaughter

troupe
03 set **04** band, cast **05** group, troop
06 ballet **07** company

trouper
05 actor **06** player **07** artiste, old hand,
veteran **08** thespian **09** performer
10 theatrical **11** entertainer

trousers
04 bags, daks, keks **05** cords, jeans,
kecks, Levis®, longs, pants, trews
06 Capris, chinos, denims, shorts,
slacks, trouse **07** gauchos, nankins,
trouses **08** bloomers, breeches,
bumsters, flannels, nankeens, overalls,
trossers, trowsers **09** corduroys,
dungarees, moleskins, strossers
10 Capri pants, cargo pants,
drainpipes, Oxford bags, spongebags
12 innominables, reach-me-downs
14 indescribables, inexpressibles
• **part of trousers**
03 fly

trout
04 peal, peel **05** sewen, sewin
06 finnac **07** finnack, finnock, herling,
hirling, rainbow **08** gillaroo, whitling
09 steelhead **10** fingerling,
squeteague

Troy
01 t **05** Ilium

truancy
07 absence, jigging, skiving, wagging
08 shirking **11** absenteeism, French
leave, malingering

truant
03 jig, kip, wag **04** bunk **05** dodge,
hooky, idler, miche, mitch, mooch,
shirk, skive **06** absent, desert, dodger,
hookey, skiver **07** goof off, missing,
runaway, shirker, vagrant **08** absentee,
deserter, malinger, skive off **09** play
hooky **10** malingerer, play the wag,
play truant

truce
03 pax **04** lull, rest, stay **05** break, fains,
let-up, peace **06** barley, fains l
07 respite, treague **08** fainites, interval
09 armistice, ceasefire, cessation
10 moratorium, suspension
12 intermission, pacification

truck
02 PU **03** HGV, ute, van **04** skip, tram
05 bogey, bogie, chore, dolly, float,
lorry, trade, wagon **06** bakkie, barter,
crummy, dumper, pick-up, tipper,
waggon **07** bargain, contact, rubbish,
traffic, trolley, trundle, utility
08 business, commerce, dealings,
exchange **09** honey-cart, persevere,
relations **10** connection, honey-
wagon, juggernaut **11** association,
honey-waggon, intercourse
12 curtain-sider, utility truck
13 communication **14** utility vehicle

truculence
08 defiance, rudeness, violence
09 hostility, pugnacity **11** bellicosity
12 belligerence, disobedience

14 aggressiveness **15** bad-temperedness, quarrelsomeness

truculent
04 rude **05** cross, cruel **06** fierce, savage, sullen **07** defiant, hostile, violent **09** bellicose, combative **10** aggressive, pugnacious **11** bad-tempered, belligerent, contentious, disobedient, ill-tempered, quarrelsome **12** antagonistic, discourteous, obstreperous **13** argumentative, disrespectful

trudge
03 pad **04** haul, hike, plod, slog, toil, trek, vamp, walk **05** clump, march, stump, tramp, trash **06** labour, lumber, stodge, taigle, trapes **07** shuffle, splodge, splotch, traipse, trudger **10** pad the hoof

true
04 fast, firm, flat, just, leal, real, trew, very **05** close, exact, loyal, plumb, right, sooth, truly, truth, valid **06** actual, dinkum, honest, proper, trusty, truthy **07** correct, devoted, dinki-di, exactly, factual, genuine, precise, rightly, sincere, staunch, typical **08** absolute, accurate, constant, faithful, honestly, properly, reliable, rightful, straight, truthful, unerring **09** authentic, corrected, correctly, dedicated, perfectly, precisely, steadfast, veracious, veritable, veritably **10** accurately, dependable, fair dinkum, faithfully, honourable, legitimate, truthfully, undeniable, unerringly **11** conformable, true-hearted, trustworthy, veraciously
• **hold true**
02 go

true-blue
04 true **05** loyal **06** trusty **07** devoted, diehard, staunch **08** constant, faithful, orthodox **09** committed, confirmed, dedicated **10** unwavering **12** card-carrying **13** dyed-in-the-wool **14** uncompromising

truism
05 axiom, truth **06** cliché **07** bromide **09** platitude **11** commonplace

truly
04 fegs, full, real, true, very **05** quite **06** certes, indeed, in fact, really, simply, surely, verily **07** exactly, greatly, in truth, rightly, soothly **08** actually, honestly, of a truth, on my word, properly **09** certainly, correctly, extremely, genuinely, in reality, precisely, sincerely, soothlich, veritable **10** constantly, definitely, on my honour, truthfully, undeniably **11** indubitably, steadfastly, undoubtedly **13** exceptionally, o' my conscience, without a doubt **14** upon conscience

trump
03 cap, top **04** ruff **05** blast, outdo **06** allege **07** deceive, eclipse, surpass, triumph, trumpet, upstage **08** Jew's-harp, outshine **13** knock spots off

• **trump up**
04 fake **06** cook up, create, devise, invent, make up **07** concoct, falsify **08** contrive **09** fabricate

trumped-up
04 fake **05** bogus, faked, false **06** made-up, phoney, untrue **08** cooked-up, invented, spurious **09** concocted, contrived, falsified **10** fabricated

trumpery
05 cheap, nasty, showy **06** flashy, shabby, shoddy, tawdry, trashy **07** mockado, rubbish, useless **08** rubbishy, trifling **09** valueless, worthless **10** pasteboard **12** meretricious

trumpet
03 bay, cry, lur **04** call, horn, lure, parp, roar, toot, tuba **05** blare, blast, bugle, chide, clang, conch, shell, shout, sound, trump **06** bellow, cornet, corona, herald, lituus, sennet, summon, tucket **07** alchemy, alchymy, buccina, clarino, clarion, corolla, salpinx, tantara **08** announce, denounce, proclaim, ram's horn, trombone **09** advertise, broadcast, celebrate, last trump **11** taratantara **12** watering-call

• **blow your own trumpet**
04 brag, crow **05** boast, skite, swank **07** show off, talk big **09** loudmouth **15** blow your own horn

trumps
• **ace of trumps**
03 tib

• **no trumps**
02 NT

truncate
03 cut, lop **04** clip, crop, dock, maim, pare, trim **05** prune **06** reduce **07** curtail, shorten **08** cut short, diminish **10** abbreviate

truncheon
04 club, cosh **05** baton, billy, carve, staff, stick **06** batoon, billie, cudgel **09** shillalah **10** billystick, knobkerrie, nightstick, shillelagh

trundle
04 bowl, chug, hoop, roll, spin **05** trill, troll, truck, twirl **06** castor, cruise, roller **07** trindle **09** freewheel

trunk
03 box, leg, log **04** body, bole, bulk, butt, case, nose, runt, stem, tube **05** chest, crate, frame, shaft, snout, stalk, stick, stock, torso **06** coffer **08** Saratoga, sea chest, suitcase **09** proboscis, telescope **10** pea-shooter **11** portmanteau

truss
03 pad, tie **04** bind, hang, pack, prop, stay, wrap **05** brace, joist, shore, strap, strut **06** bundle, corbel, fasten, lace up, pack up, pinion, secure, tether, tuck up **07** bandage, binding, dorlach, make off, support **08** bundle up,

buttress, muffle up, string up **09** principal

trust
03 EZT,VCT **04** affy, care, duty, give, hope, tick, trow **05** faith **06** assign, assume, bank on, belief, charge, commit, credit, expect, rely on **07** believe, combine, confide, consign, count on, custody, entrust, imagine, presume, suppose, surmise, swear by **08** be sure of, credence, delegate, depend on, fidelity, reliance, turn over **09** assurance, believe in, certainty **10** commitment, confidence, conviction, dependance, dependence, obligation, protection, street cred **11** expectation, safekeeping, trusteeship **12** guardianship **14** put your trust in, responsibility

trustee
02 tr **05** agent **06** keeper **08** assignee, executor, guardian **09** custodian, executrix, fiduciary **10** depositary **13** administrator

trusting
05 naive **06** unwary **08** gullible, innocent, trustful **09** confiding, credulous, ingenuous, unguarded **12** unsuspecting **13** unquestioning

trustworthiness
05 steel **07** honesty, loyalty **08** devotion **09** integrity, stability **10** commitment **11** reliability **12** faithfulness, sensibleness **13** dependability, steadfastness **14** honourableness, responsibility **15** faithworthiness, level-headedness

trustworthy
04 safe, true **05** loyal, sound **06** honest, stable, trusty **07** devoted, ethical, staunch, upright **08** faithful, reliable, sensible **09** authentic, committed, steadfast **10** creditable, dependable, honourable, principled **11** level-headed, responsible **14** good as your word

trusty
04 firm, true **05** loyal, solid **06** honest, stanch, steady, strong **07** staunch, upright **08** faithful, reliable **09** greatcoat **10** dependable, supportive **11** responsible, trustworthy **15** straightforward

truth
04 fact, true **05** axiom, facts, maxim, right, sooth **06** honour, truism, verity **07** candour, honesty, loyalty, realism, reality **08** accuracy, fidelity, validity, veracity **09** actualité, actuality, constancy, exactness, frankness, home truth, integrity, knowledge, precision, principle, rightness, sincerity **10** cold turkey, legitimacy **11** correctness, genuineness, historicity, uprightness **12** authenticity, faithfulness, truthfulness **14** honourableness, the gospel truth

• **in truth**
05 sooth, troth, truly **06** indeed, in fact,

really, surely, troggs **07** insooth, soothly **08** actually, en vérité, forsooth, honestly, in effect **09** assuredly, in reality, soothlich **10** to be honest **11** truth to tell **12** in actual fact **13** if truth be told, in point of fact **15** as a matter of fact

truthful
04 open, true **05** exact, frank, right, sooth, valid **06** candid, honest **07** correct, factual, precise, sincere **08** accurate, faithful, reliable, soothful, straight **09** realistic, soothfast, veracious, veridical, veritable **10** forthright, veridicous **11** trustworthy

truthfully
05 truly **06** openly **08** honestly, reliably **09** correctly, factually, precisely, sincerely **10** accurately, faithfully

truthfulness
06 verity **07** candour, honesty **08** openness, veracity **09** frankness, sincerity **11** uprightness **12** straightness **13** righteousness

try
02 go **03** aim, sap, tax **04** bash, fand, fond, hear, pree, pull, seek, shot, sift, stab, test, tire **05** annoy, assay, crack, drain, essay, fling, judge, prove, taste, tempt, trial, weary, whirl **06** choice, effort, purify, refine, render, sample, strain, stress, strive, try out, weaken **07** afflict, attempt, examine, exhaust, extract, have a go, inspect, stretch, turn out, undergo, venture, wear out **08** appraise, evaluate, irritate, purified **09** appraisal, endeavour, give it a go, have a bash, have a shot, have a stab, undertake **10** evaluation, experience, experiment, have a crack **11** investigate **13** make demands on
• **try out**
04 test **05** taste, try on **06** sample **07** inspect **08** appraise, check out, evaluate **10** have a pop at, take a pop at

trying
04 hard **05** tough, trial **06** severe, taxing **07** arduous, testing **08** annoying, tiresome **09** demanding, difficult, searching, stressful, vexatious, wearisome **10** bothersome, irritating **11** aggravating, distressing, troublesome **12** exasperating
• **trying situation**
03 cow

tub
03 dan, keg, kid, kit, tun, vat **04** back, bath, butt, cask, cowl, kier **05** basin, keeve, kieve, stand **06** barrel, bucket, pulpit **07** bathtub, bran-pie, bran tub, salt-fat, washtub **08** ash-leach, hogshead, lucky dip, salt-foot, swill-tub **09** container

tubby
03 fat **05** buxom, obese, plump, podgy, pudgy, stout **06** chubby, portly, rotund **07** paunchy **08** roly-poly **09** corpulent **10** overweight **15** well-upholstered

tube
03 CRT, vas **04** duct, hose, pipe, vein

05 inlet, shaft, spout, trunk **06** outlet, tubing **07** channel, conduit, snorkel **08** aircraft, cylinder **09** capillary **13** television set, umbilical cord
See also **London**

tuber
03 set **04** coco, eddo **05** cocco **06** jicama, mashua, potato, yautia **08** earth-nut **10** seed potato **11** sweet potato **13** water chestnut

tuberculosis
02 TB **05** lupus **08** phthisis, scrofula **11** consumption **12** pearl disease

tubular
04 pipy **05** piped, tubal, tubar **06** tubate **07** quilled **08** pipelike, tubelike, tubiform, tubulate, tubulous, vasiform

tuck
03 tap **04** beat, chow, cram, ease, eats, fold, food, grub, kilt, nosh, push **05** meals, pleat, scoff, scrab, snack, stuff **06** crease, gather, hamper, insert, pucker, rapier, ruffle, snacks, stroke, thrust **08** eatables **11** comestibles **12** gird yourself
• **tuck away**
04 hide, save **05** hoard, store **06** save up **07** conceal **09** stash away
• **tuck in, tuck into**
◊ *insertion indicator*
03 eat, sup **04** dine **05** eat up, feast, gorge, scoff **06** devour, gobble **08** wolf down **11** eat heartily
• **tuck in, tuck up**
04 kilt **05** truss **06** fold in, wrap up **07** cover up **08** make snug, put to bed **09** fold under **15** make comfortable

Tuesday
02 Tu **03** Tue **04** Tues

tuft
03 dag, top **04** coma, hank, knop, knot, lock, tait, tate, tuzz, wisp **05** beard, brush, bunch, clump, crest, flock, plume, quiff, scopa, swits, truss, tuffe, whisk **06** dallop, dollop, goatee, pencil, pompom, pompon, switch, tassel, toorie, tourie, tuffet **07** cluster, cowlick, daglock, fetlock, flaught, floccus, hassock, pompoon, scopula, topknot, tussock **08** aigrette, corn silk, dislodge, fascicle, imperial, plumelet **09** fascicule, flocculus, scalp lock **10** fasciculus **12** witches' broom

tug
03 lug, pug, rug, tit, tow **04** drag, draw, haul, jerk, pull, rive, tire, toil, yank **05** heave, pluck **06** jigger, strain, strive, wrench **07** saccade, tow boat, tracker

tuition
05 grind **07** lessons **08** coaching, guidance, teaching, training, tutelage **09** education, schooling **11** instruction **12** guardianship

tumble
◊ *anagram indicator*
04 dive, drop, fall, flop, reel, roll, sway, toss, trip **05** heave, lurch, pitch, slide,

touse, touze, towse, towze **06** jumble, plunge, rumple, topple, tousle, touzle, trip up, unseat, welter **07** decline, plummet, stumble **08** collapse, decrease, dishevel, disorder, fall over, nosedive **09** knock down, overthrow, tumble-dry **10** disarrange, somersault, throw about **12** fall headlong
• **tumble to**
03 get **04** suss, twig **05** grasp, savvy **07** realize **08** perceive **09** latch on to **10** comprehend, cotton on to, understand **13** become aware of, get the picture

tumbledown
◊ *anagram indicator*
05 shaky **06** ruined, unsafe **07** crumbly, rickety, ruinous **08** decrepit, unstable, unsteady **09** crumbling, tottering **10** broken-down, ramshackle **11** dilapidated **14** disintegrating

tumbler
03 cup, mug **05** glass **06** beaker, goblet **07** acrobat, gymnast, tumbrel **10** water glass **13** contortionist, drinking-glass **15** jerry-come-tumble

tumid
06 turgid **07** bloated, bulbous, bulging, flowery, fulsome, pompous, stilted, swollen **08** affected, enlarged, inflated, puffed up **09** bombastic, distended, grandiose, high-flown, overblown, tumescent **10** euphuistic **11** pretentious, protuberant **12** magniloquent **13** grandiloquent

tummy
03 gut **05** belly **06** inside, paunch **07** abdomen, insides, stomach **08** pot-belly **11** bread basket, corporation

tumour
03 -oma **04** lump, onco- **06** cancer, growth **08** neoplasm, swelling **09** turgidity **10** malignancy

Tumours include:
05 gumma, myoma, Wilm's **06** epulis, glioma, lipoma, myxoma **07** adenoma, angioma, fibroma, myeloma, sarcoma **08** lymphoma, melanoma, teratoma, xanthoma **09** carcinoma, papilloma, syphiloma **10** meningioma **11** astrocytoma, rodent ulcer **12** glioblastoma, mesothelioma, osteosarcoma **13** neuroblastoma **14** retinoblastoma

tumult
◊ *anagram indicator*
03 din, row **04** coil, riot, rore, rout, stir **05** babel, brawl, chaos, deray, hurly, noise, stoor, stour, surge, whirl **06** affray, bedlam, bustle, fracas, hubbub, mutiny, racket, romage, ruffle, rumpus, stowre, strife, unrest, uproar **07** brattle, clamour, ferment, turmoil **08** disarray, disorder, shouting,

stramash, upheaval, williwaw
09 agitation, commotion, confusion,
hurricane **10** hullabaloo, hurly-burly,
rabblement **11** disturbance,
pandemonium **12** pandaemonium

tumultuous
04 loud, wild **05** noisy, rowdy
06 fierce, hectic, raging, stormy, unruly
07 excited, fervent, riotous, violent
08 agitated, frenzied, restless,
troubled, vehement **09** clamorous,
deafening, disturbed, troublous,
turbulent **10** boisterous, disorderly,
hurly-burly, tumultuary
12 uncontrolled

tumulus
03 how, low **04** howe, mote **05** motte
06 barrow

tune
03 air, set, toy **04** ayre, dump, lilt, note,
port, rant, song, tone, toon **05** adapt,
dance, ditty, loure, motif, pitch, round,
theme, utter **06** adjust, attune, choral,
chorus, jingle, maggot, melody, spring,
strain, temper **07** express, hunt's-up,
melisma, ragtime **08** folk-tune,
regulate, saraband, serenade
09 harmonize, sarabande, siciliano,
signature, theme song, theme tune
10 light-o'-love **11** schottische,
synchronize **13** melodiousness,
signature tune
• **change your tune**
14 change your mind
• **in tune with**
04 true **07** d'accord **12** agreeing with,
in accord with **13** in harmony with
14 in sympathy with **15** in agreement
with
• **out of tune**
04 ajar **05** false **06** at odds, off-key
07 jarring, untuned **08** distuned,
mistuned, out of key, scordato
11 disagreeing

tuneful
04 tuny **06** catchy, mellow **07** melodic,
musical, tunable **08** pleasant,
sonorous, tuneable **09** agreeable,
melodious **10** euphonious,
harmonious **11** mellifluous

tuneless
05 harsh **06** atonal, silent **08** clashing
09 dissonant, unmelodic, unmusical
10 discordant, unpleasant
11 cacophonous, horrisonant,
unmelodious **12** disagreeable

tungsten
01 W

tunic
05 ao dai, kurta **06** blouse, camese,
camise, chiton, kabaya, kameez,
khurta, kirtle, tabard, taberd
07 choroid, tunicle **08** chorioid
09 laticlave **12** chorioid coat

tuning device
03 peg **08** magic eye

Tunisia
02 TN **03** TUN

tunnel
03 dig, sap **04** bore, flue, head, hole,
mine **05** cundy, drift, qanat, shaft
06 burrow, condie, subway, syrinx
07 chimney, gallery, incline, passage
08 excavate, wormhole **09** penetrate,
undermine, underpass **10** passageway

Tunnels include:
03 Aki, Box
05 Keijo, Rokko
06 FATIMA, Fréjus, Fucino, Haruna,
Hoosac, Kanmon, Mersey, Moffat,
Seikan, Thames
07 Arlberg, Cascade, Channel,
Chunnel, Holland, Laerdal,
Øresund, Simplon, Vereina
08 Apennine, Flathead, Hokuriku,
Hyperion, Lierasen, Nakayama,
Posilipo, Tronquoy
09 Dayaoshan, Eupalinus, Furka Base,
Mont Blanc
10 Chesbrough, Dai-shimizu,
Gorigamine, Lotschberg, Qinling I-
II, Rogers Pass, St Gotthard
11 Kilsby Ridge, Mt MacDonald, Shin
shimizu, Tower Subway
12 Detroit River, Moscow subway
13 Great Apennine, Iwate Ichinohe,
Severomuyskiy
14 NEAT St Gotthard, Romeriksporten
15 Monte Santomarco, Orange-Fish
River

tunny
04 tuna **13** horse mackerel

turban
05 mitre, pagri, toque **06** tulban
07 puggery, puggree, turband, turbant,
turbond **08** puggaree, tulipant
09 turribant

turbid
03 dim **04** foul, hazy **05** dense, foggy,
fuzzy, muddy, murky, riley, roily, thick
06 cloudy, drumly, impure, opaque
07 clouded, muddled, unclear
08 confused, feculent **09** turbulent,
unsettled **10** disordered, incoherent

turbulence
◇ *anagram indicator*
05 chaos, storm **06** buller, tumult,
unrest **07** boiling, turmoil **08** disorder,
upheaval **09** agitation, commotion,
confusion, roughness **10** disruption
11 instability, pandemonium

turbulent
◇ *anagram indicator*
04 wild **05** noisy, rough, rowdy
06 choppy, raging, stormy, unruly
07 foaming, furious, riotous, violent
08 agitated, blustery, confused,
factious, mutinous, unstable **09** in
turmoil, unbridled, unsettled
10 boisterous, disordered, disorderly,
outrageous, rebellious, tumultuous
11 combustious, tempestuous
12 obstreperous **13** insubordinate,
undisciplined

turf
03 sod **04** clod, fail, feal, lawn, terf
05 divot, gazon, glebe, grass, green,

patch, scraw, sward, terfe **06** gazoon
07 flaught **09** territory **12** putting
green
• **turf out**
04 fire, oust, sack **05** eject, elbow,
evict, expel **06** banish, remove
07 dismiss, kick out, turn out **08** chuck
out, fling out, throw out **09** discharge
10 dispossess **14** give the elbow to

turgid
07 dilated, flowery, fulsome, pompous,
stilted, swollen, turgent **08** affected,
inflated **09** bombastic, grandiose,
high-flown, overblown **11** extravagant,
pretentious **12** magniloquent,
ostentatious **13** grandiloquent

Turkey
02 TR **03** TUR

Turkmenistan
02 TM **03** TKM

Turks and Caicos Islands
03 TCA

turmoil
◇ *anagram indicator*
03 din, row **04** dust, moil, stir, toil
05 chaos, noise, stoor, stour
06 bedlam, bustle, flurry, hubbub,
pother, pudder, stowre, tumult, uproar
07 ferment, trouble **08** disarray,
disorder, disquiet, upheaval
09 agitation, commotion, confusion
10 turbulence **11** disturbance,
pandemonium, tracasserie
12 pandaemonium **13** Sturm und
Drang **14** the devil and all
• **place of turmoil**
04 hell **11** Pandemonium
12 Pandaemonium

turn
◇ *anagram indicator*
◇ *reversal indicator*
01 U **02** go **03** act, aim, fit, jar, lot, rev,
say, set, uey **04** bash, bend, bent, bias,
bout, cast, form, grow, loop, make,
move, pass, reel, roll, send, shot, slew,
slue, sour, spin, stab, time, veer, wind
05 adapt, alter, apply, crack, curve,
cycle, drift, drive, focus, go bad, go off,
hinge, issue, mould, pivot, point,
round, scare, shape, shift, shock, spell,
spoil, start, stint, swing, trend, trick,
twirl, twist, whirl **06** adjust, appeal,
attend, become, chance, change,
circle, corner, crisis, curdle, depend,
direct, divert, do a uey, favour, fright,
gyrate, invert, manner, modify, mutate,
period, render, resort, return, rotate,
spiral, swerve, swivel, take up
07 benefit, convert, deflect, develop,
deviate, fashion, go round, heading,
illness, leaning, remodel, reverse,
revolve, routine, service, winding
08 aptitude, come to be, courtesy,
exigency, give back, good deed,
gyration, hand over, kindness,
nauseate, occasion, reversal, rotation,
round off, surprise, tendency, transfer
09 chuck a uey, deviation, direction,
faintness, infatuate, performer,
transform, translate, transmute,

variation **10** alteration, appearance, difference, divergence, make rancid, propensity, revolution **11** culmination, inclination, nervousness, opportunity, performance, vicissitude **12** become rancid, have recourse, metamorphose **13** act of kindness **15** go round and round

• **to a turn**
07 exactly **09** correctly, perfectly, precisely **12** to perfection

• **turn against**
07 dislike **08** distrust **12** disapprove of **13** make hostile to **15** become hostile to

• **turn aside**
04 daff **05** avert, parry, swits, twist **06** depart, divert, put off, swerve, switch **07** askance, deflect, deviate, diverge, diverse, fend off, reverse, ward off **08** withdraw **09** sidetrack

• **turn away**
05 avert **06** depart, refuse, reject, return **07** decline, deflect, deviate **08** move away, send away **09** discharge **12** cold shoulder, cold-shoulder

• **turn back**
◊ *reversal indicator*
05 clock, repel **06** go back, return, revert, revolt **07** reflect, retreat **09** drive back, force back, retrovert

• **turn down**
04 bend, mute, veto **05** lower, spurn **06** double, invert, lessen, muffle, rebuff, reduce, refuse, reject, soften **07** decline, quieten **08** decrease **09** knock back, repudiate **11** make quieter

• **turn in**
04 sell, shop **05** dob in, enter, grass, rat on **06** betray, give in, give up, hand in, invert, retire, return, rumble, submit, tell on, tender **07** deliver, go to bed, let down, sack out, sell out, split on, stool on **08** denounce, give back, go back on, hand over, inform on, register, renege on, squeal on **09** hit the hay, surrender, walk out on **10** hit the sack **11** double-cross, turn traitor **12** be disloyal to **13** stab in the back **14** be unfaithful to, break faith with

• **turn of events**
06 affair, result **07** outcome **08** incident **09** happening **10** occurrence, phenomenon

• **turn off**
04 bore, hang, kill, quit, stop **05** leave, repel **06** divert, offend, put off, sicken, unplug **07** deviate, disgust, dismiss, pull off, shut off, turn out **08** alienate, complete, nauseate, shut down **09** branch off, displease, switch off **10** depart from, disconnect, discourage, disenchant **11** turn against

• **turn of phrase**
05 idiom, style **06** saying **07** diction **08** locution, metaphor **10** expression, foreignism **11** phraseology

• **turn on**
04 plug **05** put on, start **06** arouse, attack, excite, fall on, hang on, please, plug in, rest on, ride on, thrill **07** attract,

connect, hinge on, lay into, round on, set upon, start on, start up **08** activate, depend on, switch on **09** start in on, stimulate **14** be contingent on

• **turn out**
02 go **03** try **04** come, fire, make, rout, sack, sort, trie **05** clear, dress, eject, empty, end up, ensue, evict, expel, fadge, issue, prove **06** appear, arrive, attend, banish, become, bounce, clothe, deport, emerge, happen, muster, pan out, result, show up, turn up, unplug **07** develop, dismiss, drum out, fall out, kick out, present, produce, succeed, turf out, turn off **08** assemble, chuck out, churn out, clean out, clear out, throw out **09** be present, come about, discharge, eventuate, fabricate, switch off, transpire **10** disconnect **11** manufacture

• **turn over**
◊ *reversal down indicator*
02 TO **03** rob **04** flip, mill, mull, roll **05** upend, upset, volve **06** assign, invert, pass on, ponder, tumble **07** capsize, consign, deliver, examine, reverse, start up **08** consider, hand over, keel over, meditate, mull over, overturn, roll over, ruminate, transfer **09** reflect on, surrender, think over **10** deliberate, think about, turn turtle **11** contemplate

• **turn up**
◊ *reversal down indicator*
02 go **03** act, dig **04** bash, bend, bias, cock, come, find, loop, plow, root, rout, shew, show, spin, stab, time **05** crack, curve, cycle, dig up, drift, raise, round, scare, shift, shock, spell, stint, trend, twirl, twist, whirl, wroot **06** appear, arrive, attend, cast up, chance, change, circle, corner, expose, fright, grub up, invert, look up, period, plough, reveal, show up, swivel **07** amplify, disgust, disturb, illness, leaning, routine, subsoil, turn out, uncover, unearth **08** disclose, discover, gyration, increase, occasion, reversal, rotation, tendency **09** be present, deviation, direction, faintness, intensify, performer, variation **10** alteration, appearance, difference, divergence, make louder, propensity, revolution, strengthen **11** inclination, materialize, nervousness, opportunity, performance **12** bring to light

turncoat
03 rat **04** fink, scab **07** seceder, traitor **08** apostate, blackleg, defector, deserter, renegade, renegate **10** backslider **11** Vicar of Bray **13** tergiversator

turned
◊ *reversal indicator*
03 off **04** sour **06** soured **08** reversed **09** fashioned **10** upside down

turning
◊ *anagram indicator*
◊ *reversal indicator*
04 bend, fork, turn **05** curve **07** shaping, turn-off, winding

08 junction, reversal, rotation **09** deviation **10** conversion, crossroads **14** transformation

turning-point
04 crux, turn **06** crisis, moment, tropic **08** solstice **09** watershed **10** crossroads **13** moment of truth **14** critical moment, decisive moment

turnip
04 neep **05** navew, swede **07** tumshie **09** breadroot **10** dunderhead

turnout
04 gate, gear, team, togs **05** array, crowd, dress, get-up **06** attire, muster, number, outfit, output, siding, strike, things **07** clobber, clothes, display, striker **08** assembly, audience **09** gathering **10** appearance, assemblage, attendance **12** congregation

turnover
◊ *reversal indicator*
04 flow **05** yield **06** bridie, change, income, output, volume **07** outturn, profits, revenue **08** business, movement **10** production **11** replacement **12** productivity, transference

turpitude
04 evil **07** badness **08** baseness, foulness, iniquity, vileness, villainy **09** depravity **10** corruption, degeneracy, immorality, sinfulness, wickedness **11** corruptness, criminality, viciousness **13** nefariousness **14** flagitiousness

tusk
03 gam **04** tush **05** torsk

tussle
03 vie **04** bout, fray **05** brawl, fight, mêlée, scrap, scrum, set-to, touse, touze, towse, towze **06** battle, dust-up, fracas, tousle, touzle **07** compete, contend, contest, grapple, punch-up, scuffle, tuilyie, tuilzie, wrestle **08** conflict, scramble, struggle **09** scrimmage **10** contention **11** competition

tutelage
03 eye **04** care **05** aegis **06** charge **07** custody, tuition **08** guidance, teaching, wardship **09** education, patronage, schooling, vigilance **10** protection **11** instruction, preparation **12** guardianship

tutor
04 abbé, guru **05** coach, drill, guide, teach, train **06** direct, mentor, school **07** control, dominie, educate, lecture, teacher **08** educator, governor, guardian, instruct, lecturer **09** governess, preceptor, supervise **10** discipline, instructor, répétiteur, supervisor **11** preceptress **12** schoolmaster

tutorial
05 class **06** lesson **07** guiding, seminar, teach-in **08** coaching, didactic,

teaching **09** educative, educatory **13** instructional

Tuvalu
03 TUV

TV *see* **television**

twaddle
03 rot **04** blah, bosh, bunk, guff, tosh **05** balls, hooey, stuff, trash **06** bunkum, drivel, gabble, gossip, hot air, piffle, tattle, waffle **07** baloney, eyewash, fadaise, garbage, hogwash, inanity, rhubarb, rubbish, twattle **08** blathers, blethers, claptrap, malarkey, nonsense, slipslop, tommyrot **09** bullswool, moonshine, poppycock **10** balderdash **12** gobbledygook

tweak
◇ *anagram indicator*
03 fit, nip, tug **04** jerk, pull, suit **05** adapt, pinch, twist **06** adjust, change, modify, tuning, twinge, twitch **07** fitting, shaping, squeeze **08** fine-tune, revision **09** agitation, amendment, arranging **10** adaptation, adjustment, alteration, conversion, fine-tuning, perplexity **11** accommodate, rearranging, remodelling **12** modification **13** accommodation, rearrangement **15** make adjustments

twee
04 cute **05** sweet **06** cutesy, dainty, pretty, quaint **08** affected, precious **11** sentimental

twelve
02 dz **03** doz, XII **05** dozen **06** zodiac

Twelve Days of Christmas *see* **Christmas**

twenty
02 XX

twice
◇ *repetition indicator*
02 bi-, di- **03** bin-, bis **06** doubly

twiddle
◇ *anagram indicator*
04 turn **05** twirl, twist **06** adjust, fiddle, finger, rotate, swivel, wiggle **07** twitter **08** ornament

• **twiddle your thumbs**
08 kill time **13** kick your heels **15** have nothing to do

twig
03 get, see **04** reis, rice, whip, with **05** birch, grasp, shoot, spray, sprig, stick, swits, twist, withe, withy **06** branch, fathom, fettle, rumble, switch, wattle, wicker **07** catch on, fashion, observe, ramulus, realize, sarment **08** cotton on, offshoot, perceive, tumble to **10** comprehend, understand
See also **understand**

twilight
03 dim, ebb **04** dusk, last **05** dying, final, gloom **06** ebbing, sunset **07** decline, dimness, evening, obscure, partial, shadowy **08** cockshut, demi-jour, evenfall, gloaming, glooming,

owl-light **09** crepuscle, darkening, declining, half-light **10** crepuscule, indefinite **11** crepuscular **12** transitional **15** Götterdämmerung

twin
04 dual, join, link, mate, pair, part, yoke **05** clone, gemel, match **06** couple, double, fellow, paired, ringer **07** combine, couplet, deprive, matched, twofold **08** didymous, likeness, matching, parallel, separate **09** corollary, duplicate, identical, lookalike **10** complement, dead ringer, equivalent **11** counterpart, symmetrical **13** corresponding

Twins include:
04 Esau, Gibb (Maurice), Gibb (Robin), Kray (Reggie), Kray (Ronnie)
05 Diana, Jacob, Remus, Viola, Waugh (Mark), Waugh (Steve)
06 Apollo, Bunker (Chang), Bunker (Eng), Castor, Dromio (of Ephesus), Dromio (of Syracuse), Pollux
07 Artemis, Piccard (Auguste), Piccard (Jean-Felix), Romulus, Stanley (Francis), Stanley (Freelon), Weasley (Fred), Weasley (George)
08 Hercules, Iphicles, Louis XIV, Philippe
09 O'Sullivan (Isabel), O'Sullivan (Pat), Sebastian
10 Antipholus (of Ephesus), Antipholus (of Syracuse), Tweedledee, Tweedledum

twine
04 bend, coil, cord, curl, knit, loop, part, wind, wrap, yarn **05** braid, plait, twist, weave **06** spiral, string, tangle, thread **07** deprive, entwine, wreathe, wriggle **08** encircle, separate, surround, whipping **09** intorsion, intortion **10** intertwine

twinge
04 ache, grip, pain, pang, stab **05** cramp, pinch, prick, spasm, throb, throe, twang, tweak **06** stitch, twitch **08** shooting

twinkle
◇ *anagram indicator*
04 wink **05** blink, flash, gleam, glint, light, shine, twink **06** quiver **07** flicker, glimmer, glisten, glitter, shimmer, shining, sparkle, vibrate **09** coruscate, twinkling **11** coruscation, scintillate **13** scintillation

twinkling
◇ *anagram indicator*
02 mo **03** sec **04** jiff, tick, wink **05** flash, jiffy, nitid, shake, trice, twink **06** bright, minute, moment, no time, second **07** instant, shining, winking **08** blinking, flashing, gleaming, polished **09** short time, sparkling **10** flickering, glimmering, glistening, glittering, shimmering **11** coruscating **13** scintillating, scintillation

twirl
◇ *anagram indicator*
04 coil, curl, spin, turn, wind **05** pivot,

trill, twist, wheel, whirl, whorl **06** gyrate, rotate, spiral, swivel **07** revolve, trundle, twiddle, twizzle **08** gyration, rotation **09** pirouette **10** revolution **11** convolution **12** tirlie-wirlie

twirling
◇ *anagram indicator*
05 gyral **07** pivotal **08** gyratory, pivoting, rotating, rotatory, spinning, whirling **09** revolving **10** swivelling **11** pirouetting

twist
◇ *anagram indicator*
03 arc, cue **04** bend, coil, cord, curl, flaw, kink, loop, rick, roll, rove, skew, slew, slue, spin, turn, twig, warp, whim, wind **05** alter, angle, braid, break, curve, freak, plait, quirk, screw, slant, twine, twirl, weave, wrest, wrick, wring **06** change, defect, deform, foible, garble, oddity, rotate, spiral, sprain, squirm, strain, strand, swivel, tangle, thread, wamble, wigwag, wimple, wreath, wrench, writhe, zigzag **07** contort, distort, entwine, falsify, pervert, revolve, swindle, torsion, twizzle, whimple, wreathe, wriggle **08** entangle, misquote, misshape, squiggle, surprise, wresting **09** misreport, turnabout, variation **10** aberration, contortion, distortion, intertwine, perversion **11** convolution, peculiarity **12** idiosyncrasy, imperfection, misrepresent

• **twist someone's arm**
05 bully, force **06** coerce, lean on **07** dragoon **08** bulldoze, persuade **10** intimidate, pressurize **14** put the screws on

twisted
◇ *anagram indicator*
03 odd **04** wavy **05** kinky, thraw **06** thrawn, thrown, warped **07** deviant, sinuous, strange, tortile, winding **08** peculiar, squiggly **09** contorted, perverted, unnatural

twister
04 gale **05** cheat, crook, fraud, rogue, storm **06** con man, phoney, squall **07** cyclone, monsoon, tempest, tornado, typhoon **08** con woman, deceiver, swindler **09** con artist, hurricane, scoundrel, trickster, whirlwind **10** blackguard

twisty
06 zigzag **07** curving, sinuous, winding **08** indirect, tortuous **10** circuitous, meandering, roundabout, serpentine

twit
03 ass, git **04** berk, clot, dope, dork, fool, geek, goop, nerd, nerk, prat **05** chump, clown, dweeb, idiot, ninny, twerp **06** nig-nog, nitwit **07** airhead, halfwit, plonker, saphead, twitter **08** imbecile **09** blockhead, simpleton **10** nincompoop **11** knuckle-head **13** proper Charlie

twitch

◇ *anagram indicator*
03 tic, tig, tit, tug **04** jerk, jump, pull, yips **05** blink, pluck, shake, spasm, start, tweak **06** quiver, shiver, snatch, tremor **07** flutter, the yips, tremble **09** vellicate **10** convulsion

twitchy

04 edgy **05** het up, jerky, jumpy, nervy, shaky, tense **06** on edge, uneasy **07** anxious, fidgety, in a stew, jittery, keyed up, nervous, panicky, restive, uptight, wound up **08** agitated, in a sweat, in a tizzy **12** apprehensive

twitter

03 cry, gab **04** chat, sing, song **05** cheep, chirp, tweet **06** babble, gabble, gossip, jabber, jargon, warble, witter **07** blather, blether, chatter, chirrup, chitter, prattle, twaddle, whistle **08** chirping, tweeting **09** palpitate **10** chirruping

two

02 II **04** pair **05** deuce, twain **06** couple
• **the two**
04 both

two-faced

05 false, lying **07** devious **09** deceitful, insincere **10** Janus-faced, perfidious **11** dissembling, duplicitous, treacherous **12** hypocritical **13** double-dealing, untrustworthy

twofold

04 dual, twin **05** duple **06** bifold, binary, double, duplex **07** twafald, twifold, twyfold **09** duplicate

two-master

04 buss

twosome

03 duo **04** duet, pair **06** couple **09** tête-à-tête

two-up

03 swy **05** swy-up **07** swy game

two-wheeler

04 cart

Tyche

07 Fortuna

tycoon

05 baron, mogul **06** fat cat **07** magnate, supremo **08** big noise **09** big cheese, financier, moneybags **10** capitalist **12** entrepreneur, moneyspinner **13** industrialist

Tyler

03 Wat

Tyneside

02 NE

type

◇ *anagram indicator*
03 ilk, key, set **04** face, font, form, hair, kind, make, mark, norm, sort **05** brand, breed, class, fount, genre, genus, group, model, order, print, stamp, style **06** emblem, letter, number, strain, symbol **07** epitome, example, letters, numbers, pattern, species, symbols, variety **08** category, exemplar, insignia, original, printing, specimen, standard, typeface **09** archetype, character, exemplify, lettering, prefigure, prototype, symbolize, typewrite **10** characters, embodiment, foreshadow **11** description, designation, subdivision **12** anticipation, quintessence **13** foreshadowing **14** classification
• **confused type**
02 pi **03** pie, pye
• **type size**
03 gem **04** body, pica **05** canon **06** minion **07** brevier, English **09** bourgeois, Columbian, nonpareil **10** longprimer **11** emerald type, Great Primer

typeface

Typefaces include:

05 Arial
06 Bell MT, Impact, Lucida, Modern, Tahoma
07 Courier, Curlz MT, Marlett, MS Serif, Verdana
08 Garamond, Jokerman, MS Gothic, MS Mincho, Playbill, Rockwell, Webdings
09 Colonna MT, Wide Latin, Wingdings
10 Arial Black, Courier New, Lucida Sans
11 Baskerville, Book Antiqua, Comic Sans MS, MS Sans Serif, Poor Richard, Trebuchet MS
13 Century Gothic, Lucida Console, Times New Roman
14 Franklin Gothic
15 Bookman Old Style

typhoon

05 storm **06** squall, typhon **07** cyclone, tempest, tornado, twister **09** hurricane, whirlwind

typical

04 trew, true **05** model, stock, typal, typic, usual **06** normal, Podunk **07** average, classic **08** ordinary, orthodox, standard, true-bred **10** archetypal, emblematic, figurative, indicative, stereotype **11** distinctive **12** conventional, illustrative, run-of-the-mill **13** typographical **14** characteristic, quintessential, representative

typically

07 as a rule, usually **08** normally **09** routinely **10** habitually, ordinarily **11** classically, customarily

typify

05 image **06** embody, imbody, shadow **08** indicate **09** epitomize, exemplify, personify, represent, symbolize **10** foreshadow, illustrate **11** encapsulate, foresignify **12** characterize

tyrannical

05 cruel, harsh **06** lordly, severe, strict, unjust **08** absolute, despotic, Neronian, ruthless, satrapal, tyrannic **09** arbitrary, imperious **10** autocratic, despotical, high-handed, oppressive, peremptory, repressive **11** dictatorial, domineering, magisterial, overbearing **12** overpowering, totalitarian, unreasonable **13** authoritarian

tyrannize

04 lord **05** bully, crush **06** coerce **07** dictate, enslave, oppress, repress **08** browbeat, domineer, suppress **09** subjugate, terrorize **10** intimidate, lord it over

tyranny

07 cruelty, liberty **08** severity **09** autocracy, despotism, harshness, injustice **10** absolutism, domination, oppression, strictness **12** dictatorship, ruthlessness **13** imperiousness **14** high-handedness

tyrant

05 bully, pewee **06** despot, peewee **08** autocrat, dictator, martinet **09** oppressor, tyranness **10** absolutist, taskmaster **11** slave-driver **13** authoritarian

See also **despot**

tyro *see* **tiro, tyro**

U

U
07 uniform 10 upper-class

ubiquitous
06 common, global 08 frequent
09 pervasive, universal
10 everywhere, ubiquarian, wall-to-wall 11 ever-present, omnipresent

ubiquity
09 frequency 10 commonness, popularity, prevalence
12 omnipresence, universality
13 pervasiveness

Uganda
03 EAU, UGA

ugliness
04 evil 06 danger, horror, menace
08 disgrace, enormity, vileness
09 deformity, nastiness, plainness
10 homeliness, horridness
11 heinousness, hideousness, monstrosity 12 unloveliness
13 frightfulness, offensiveness, repulsiveness, unsightliness
14 unpleasantness

ugly
◊ anagram indicator
04 evil, foul, loth, vile 05 grave, loath, nasty, plain 06 gorgon, grotty, homely, horrid, oughly, ouglie, unfair
07 hideous, hostile, ogreish
08 alarming, deformed, horrible, ill-faced, ill-faste, ill-faurd, plug-ugly, shocking, sinister, terrible, unlovely
09 dangerous, frightful, grotesque, loathsome, misshapen, monstrous, obnoxious, offensive, repulsive, revolting, ugly as sin, unsightly
10 disgusting, ill-looking, ill-natured, unpleasant 11 disquieting, ill-favoured, threatening 12 disagreeable, evil-favoured, unattractive
13 objectionable 15 unprepossessing

UK see **United Kingdom**

Ukraine
02 UA 03 UKR

ulcer
04 boil, noma, sore 05 issue, rupia
06 aphtha, canker, fester 07 abscess, bedsore, fistula, sycosis 08 open sore
09 impostume 10 plague-sore, ulceration 11 peptic ulcer 13 varicose ulcer 14 decubitus ulcer

ulster
02 NI 04 coat

ulterior
06 covert, hidden, secret 07 private,

remoter, selfish 08 personal
09 concealed, secondary
10 underlying, unrevealed
11 undisclosed, unexpressed

ultimate
◊ tail selection indicator
03 end, ult 04 best, last, peak 05 basic, final, ideal 06 height, summit, utmost
07 closing, epitome, extreme, highest, maximum, perfect, primary, radical, supreme, topmost 08 eventual, furthest, greatest, last word, limiting, remotest, terminal 09 elemental
10 concluding, perfection, the mostest
11 chef d'oeuvre, culmination, fundamental, masterpiece, summum bonum, superlative 12 consummation
14 daddy of them all

ultimately
◊ tail selection indicator
03 ult 06 at last 07 finally 08 after all, in the end 09 basically, primarily
10 eventually 13 fundamentally, sooner or later 15 in the last resort

ultra-
05 extra 09 extremely, unusually
10 especially, remarkably 11 excessively
13 exceptionally 15 extraordinarily

ultraviolet
02 UV

ululate
03 cry, sob 04 hoot, howl, keen, moan, wail, weep 05 mourn 06 holler, lament, scream 07 screech

umbrage
• **take umbrage**
06 be hurt, resent 07 be angry, be upset 08 be miffed, be put out, get huffy 09 be annoyed 10 be insulted, be offended, feel put out 11 take offence
13 be exasperated, take exception
14 take personally

umbrella
05 aegis, cover, 06 agency 08 auspices
09 en tout cas 10 protection

04 gamp, mush
05 dumpy
06 brolly, chatta
07 gingham
08 marquise, mushroom, ombrella, sunshade, umbrello
09 en tout cas
11 bumbershoot

umpire
03 ref, ump 05 judge 06 odd-man

07 arbiter, control, daysman, mediate, oddsman, referee 08 linesman, mediator, moderate, oversman, stickler
09 arbitrate, birlieman, byrlaw-man, moderator 10 adjudicate, arbitrator
11 adjudicator
See also **cricket**

umpteen
06 plenty 08 millions, numerous, very many 09 a good many, countless, thousands 11 innumerable

UN see **United Nations**

unabashed
04 bold 06 brazen 07 blatant
09 abashless, confident, unashamed, undaunted 10 undismayed 11 bold as brass, unconcerned 13 in countenance, unembarrassed

unable
04 weak 05 unfit 06 cannot
08 impotent 09 incapable, powerless
10 inadequate, unequipped
11 incompetent, ineffectual, unqualified

unabridged
04 full 05 uncut, whole 06 entire
08 complete 10 full-length
11 uncondensed, unshortened
12 unexpurgated

unacceptable
04 non-U 05 wrong 07 a bit off
09 obnoxious, offensive, unwelcome
10 unpleasant, unsuitable
11 intolerable, undesirable
12 disagreeable, inadmissible
13 beyond the pale, disappointing, objectionable 14 unsatisfactory

unaccommodating
05 rigid 08 perverse, stubborn
09 obstinate, unbending 10 inflexible, unyielding 11 disobliging
12 intransigent 13 uncomplaisant, unco-operative 14 uncompromising

unaccompanied
04 lone, solo 05 alone, secco
06 lonely, silent, single 09 on your own
10 by yourself, unattended, unescorted 12 single-handed

unaccountable
03 odd 04 free 05 queer 06 immune
07 bizarre, curious, strange, unusual
08 baffling, peculiar, puzzling, singular, uncommon 09 insoluble, unheard-of
10 mysterious 11 astonishing
12 impenetrable, inexplicable, unfathomable 13 extraordinary, not answerable, unexplainable 14 not responsible

unaccountably
09 strangely **10** bafflingly, incredibly, puzzlingly **12** inexplicably, miraculously, mysteriously, mystifyingly **13** unexplainably

unaccustomed
03 new **06** unused, unwont **07** strange, unusual **08** uncommon, unwonted, wontless **09** different, insitate **10** remarkable, surprising, unexpected, unfamiliar **11** unpractised **12** unacquainted **13** extraordinary, inexperienced, unprecedented

unacquainted
06 unused **07** strange, unknown, unusual **08** ignorant **10** unfamiliar, uninformed **12** unaccustomed **13** inexperienced

unadorned
04 bald, bare **05** plain, stark **06** severe, simple **07** undight **08** homespun **10** restrained **11** undecorated, unvarnished **12** unornamented **13** unembellished **15** straightforward

unadulterated
04 neat, pure, real, true **05** sheer, solid, total, utter **06** simple **07** genuine, natural, perfect, sincere, unmixed **08** absolute, complete, flawless, straight, thorough **09** authentic, downright, unalloyed, undiluted **11** unmitigated, unqualified **14** unsophisticate **15** unsophisticated

unaffected
04 real, true **05** naive, plain **06** candid, honest, immune, simple **07** artless, genuine, natural, sincere, unmoved **08** unspoilt **09** guileless, ingenuous, unaltered, unchanged, untouched **10** impervious, unassuming **11** indifferent, unconcerned **13** unpretentious **15** straightforward, unsophisticated

unafraid
05 brave **06** daring **08** fearless, intrepid, unfeared **09** confident, dauntless, undaunted **10** courageous, unshakable **11** unshakeable **13** imperturbable

unalterable
05 final, fixed, rigid **09** immovable, immutable, permanent **10** inflexible, invariable, unchanging, unyielding **11** hard and fast, reverseless **12** unchangeable

unaltered
04 as is **09** invariant

unanimity
05 unity **06** accord, unison **07** concert, concord, harmony **09** agreement, consensus **10** congruence **11** concurrence, consistency **14** like-mindedness

unanimous
05 as one, joint, solid **06** common, united **08** in accord **09** concerted **10** concordant, consistent,

harmonious, like-minded **11** in agreement **12** single-minded

unanimously
05 as one **06** nem con **08** as one man **09** in concert, of one mind, unopposed **10** conjointly **12** with one voice **15** by common consent

unannounced
06 abrupt, chance, sudden **07** amazing, unusual **09** startling **10** accidental, fortuitous, surprising, unexpected, unforeseen **11** astonishing, unlooked-for **13** unanticipated, unpredictable

unanswerable
05 final **08** absolute **10** conclusive, unarguable, undeniable **11** irrefutable **12** indisputable, irrefragable **13** incontestable

unanswered
04 open **05** vexed **07** in doubt **09** undecided, unsettled **10** unrequited, unresolved, up in the air

unappetizing
07 insipid **09** tasteless, unsavoury **10** off-putting, unexciting, uninviting, unpleasant **11** distasteful, unappealing, unpalatable **12** disagreeable, unattractive **13** uninteresting

unapproachable
04 cold, cool **05** aloof **06** remote **07** distant **08** reserved **09** withdrawn **10** forbidding, unfriendly, unsociable **11** standoffish **12** inaccessible, unresponsive **15** uncommunicative

unapt
04 slow **05** inapt, unfit **08** unfitted, unsuited, untimely **10** inapposite, malapropos, unsuitable **12** inapplicable, unseasonable **13** inappropriate

unarmed
04 bare, open, weak **05** inerm, naked **07** exposed **08** helpless **10** unweaponed, vulnerable **11** defenceless, unprotected

unashamed
04 open **06** direct, honest **07** blatant **08** bashless **09** shameless, unabashed **10** impenitent **11** unconcealed, undisguised, unrepentant

unasked
08 unbidden, unsought, unwanted **09** uninvited, voluntary **10** unrequired **11** spontaneous, unannounced, unrequested, unsolicited

unassailable
05 sound **06** proven, secure **08** absolute, positive **09** well-armed **10** conclusive, invincible, inviolable, undeniable **11** impregnable, irrefutable **12** indisputable, inexpugnable, invulnerable **13** incontestable, well-fortified

unassertive
03 shy **04** meek **05** mousy, quiet, timid **06** mousey **07** bashful **08** backward,

retiring, timorous **09** diffident **10** unassuming **12** self-effacing

unassuming
03 shy **04** meek **05** quiet **06** demure, humble, modest, simple **07** natural **08** reticent, retiring **10** restrained **11** unassertive, unobtrusive **12** self-effacing, underbearing **13** unpretentious

unattached
04 free **05** loose **06** single **08** detached **09** available, fancy-free, footloose, on your own, unengaged, unmarried **10** by yourself, with no ties **11** independent, uncommitted **12** unaffiliated

unattended
05 alone **07** ignored **08** forsaken **09** abandoned, forgotten, neglected, unguarded, unwatched **10** unescorted **11** disregarded **12** unsupervised **13** unaccompanied

unattractive
04 ugly **05** plain, warby **06** grungy, homely, skanky **08** ill-faurd, uncomely, unlovely **09** offensive, repellent, unsavoury, unsightly, unwelcome **10** disgusting, off-putting, unexciting, uninviting, unpleasant **11** distasteful, ill-favoured, unappealing, undesirable, unpalatable **12** disagreeable, unappetizing **13** no oil painting, objectionable **15** not much to look at, unprepossessing

unauthorized
07 illegal, illicit **08** unlawful **09** forbidden, irregular **10** prohibited, unapproved, unlicensed, unofficial **11** unchartered, unwarranted **12** illegitimate, unsanctioned

unavailing
04 vain **06** beaten, failed, futile, losing **07** sterile, unlucky, useless **08** abortive, defeated, luckless, nugatory, thwarted **09** fruitless **10** frustrated **11** ineffective, unfortunate **12** unprevailing, unproductive, unprofitable, unsuccessful

unavoidable
04 sure **05** fatal, fated **07** certain **08** destined, required **09** mandatory, necessary **10** compulsory, inevitable, inexorable, obligatory **11** ineluctable, inescapable, predestined

unaware
04 deaf **05** blind **07** witless **08** heedless, ignorant, wareless **09** in the dark, oblivious, unknowing, unmindful, unwitting **10** insentient, uninformed, with no idea **11** incognizant, unconscious **12** unsuspecting **13** unenlightened

unawares
05 aback **07** unwares **08** abruptly, off guard, on the hop, suddenly **09** in the dark, red-handed **10** by surprise, mistakenly, unprepared **11** insidiously, unknowingly, unwittingly

12 accidentally, à l'improviste, unexpectedly, unthinkingly **13** inadvertently, unconsciously **15** unintentionally

unbalanced
◇ *anagram indicator*
03 mad **05** barmy, crazy **06** biased, insane, mental, uneven, unfair, unjust **07** erratic, lunatic, unequal, unsound **08** crackers, demented, deranged, doolally, lopsided, one-sided, partisan, unstable, unsteady **09** disturbed, stir-crazy **10** irrational, prejudiced **11** dysharmonic, inequitable, mentally ill **12** asymmetrical, round the bend **13** round the twist **14** wrong in the head

unbearable
06 too bad **07** too much **08** the limit **10** importable **11** intolerable, unendurable **12** excruciating, insufferable, the last straw, unacceptable **13** insupportable

unbeatable
04 best **07** supreme **09** excellent, matchless, rock-solid **10** invincible **11** indomitable, unstoppable **13** unconquerable, unsurpassable

unbeaten
07 supreme, unbowed, winning **09** unsubdued **10** triumphant, undefeated, victorious **11** unconquered, unsurpassed **12** unvanquished

unbecoming
08 improper, indecent, infra dig, unseemly, unworthy **09** unfitting, unseeming, unsightly **10** indecorous, indelicate, misseeming, unladylike, unsuitable **11** unbefitting **12** ill-beseeming, unattractive **13** inappropriate, ungentlemanly **15** infra dignitatem

unbeknown
• unbeknown to
07 unknown **09** unheard of **10** unrealized **11** unperceived **13** unbeknownst to

unbelief
05 doubt **07** atheism **09** disbelief **10** scepticism **11** agnosticism, incredulity

unbelievable
06 unreal **07** amazing **08** unlikely **10** far-fetched, impossible, improbable, incredible, outlandish, remarkable, staggering **11** astonishing, implausible, incredulous, unthinkable **12** preposterous, unconvincing, unimaginable **13** extraordinary, inconceivable

unbelievably
09 amazingly **10** incredibly **12** outlandishly, unimaginably **13** inconceivably **15** extraordinarily

unbeliever
06 zendik **07** atheist, doubter, infidel, sceptic **08** agnostic **11** disbeliever, nullifidian **14** doubting Thomas

unbelieving
07 dubious, infidel **08** doubtful, doubting **09** miscreant, sceptical **10** suspicious **11** distrustful, incredulous, nullifidian, unconvinced, unpersuaded **12** disbelieving

unbend
04 thaw, undo **05** relax **06** uncoil, uncurl **08** loosen up, unbuckle, unbutton, unfasten, unfreeze **10** straighten

unbending
04 firm **05** aloof, rigid, stern, stiff, tough **06** formal, severe, strict **07** distant **08** Catonian, hardline, relaxing, reserved, resolute, stubborn **10** forbidding, formidable, inflexible, unyielding **12** intransigent **14** uncompromising

unbiased
04 fair, just **06** candid **07** neutral **08** balanced **09** equitable, impartial, objective **10** even-handed, fair-minded, open-minded, uncoloured **11** independent **12** uninfluenced, unprejudiced **13** disinterested, dispassionate

unbidden
04 free **07** unasked, willing **08** unforced, unwanted **09** uninvited, unwelcome, voluntary **10** unprompted **11** spontaneous, unsolicited

unbind
04 free, undo **05** loose, solve, untie **06** loosen, unyoke **07** release, set free, unchain, unloose **08** liberate, unfasten, unfetter, unloosen **09** unshackle

unblemished
04 pure **05** clear, white **07** perfect **08** flawless, spotless, unflawed **09** unspotted, unstained, unsullied, untainted **10** immaculate **11** untarnished **13** unimpeachable **14** irreproachable

unblinking
04 calm, cool **06** steady **07** assured **08** composed, fearless, unafraid **09** impassive **10** unwavering **11** emotionless, unemotional, unfaltering, unflinching, unshrinking **13** imperturbable

unblushing
04 bold **06** amoral, brazen **07** blatant **08** immodest, impudent **09** shameless, unabashed, unashamed **13** unembarrassed **15** conscience-proof

unborn
06 coming, future, to-come **07** awaited, in utero **08** expected, unyeaned **09** embryonic **10** subsequent, succeeding **11** non-existent

unbosom
04 bare, tell **05** admit **06** let out, reveal **07** confess, confide, divulge, lay bare, pour out, tell all, uncover **08** disclose, unburden

unbounded
04 vast **07** endless **08** infinite **09** boundless, limitless, unbridled, unchecked, unlimited **12** immeasurable, unconfinable, uncontrolled, unrestrained, unrestricted

unbreakable
05 solid, tough **06** rugged, strong **07** durable **09** resistant, toughened **10** adamantine **11** infrangible **12** shatterproof **14** indestructible

unbridled
04 wild **07** rampant, riotous **08** unbitted, uncurbed **09** excessive, unchecked **10** immoderate, licentious, profligate, ungoverned **11** intemperate **12** uncontrolled, unrestrained **13** unconstrained

unbroken
04 wild **05** rough, sheer, solid, whole **06** entire, in a row, intact, single **07** endless, non-stop, unbroke, untamed **08** complete, constant, seamless, unbeaten **09** ceaseless, incessant, perpetual, unceasing, undivided, unmatched **10** continuate, continuous, successive, unequalled, unrivalled **11** progressive, unremitting, unsurpassed **13** uninterrupted **14** undomesticated

unburden
04 bare, tell **05** admit **06** let out, reveal **07** cast off, confess, confide, divulge, lay bare, offload, pour out, tell all, uncover **08** disclose **09** discharge

unbutton
04 undo

uncalled-for
07 unasked **08** needless, unsought **09** unwelcome **10** gratuitous, undeserved, unprompted, unprovoked **11** unjustified, unnecessary, unsolicited, unwarranted

uncannily
05 oddly **08** spookily **09** bizarrely, strangely **10** incredibly, remarkably **11** unnaturally **12** mysteriously **14** supernaturally **15** extraordinarily

uncanny
03 odd **05** eerie, queer, weird **06** creepy, spooky, unsafe **07** bizarre, strange **08** eldritch, pokerish **09** fantastic, unearthly, unnatural, wanchancy **10** incredible, mysterious, remarkable, wanchancie **11** exceptional **12** supernatural **13** extraordinary, preternatural, unaccountable

uncared-for
07 run-down, squalid **08** derelict, deserted, forsaken, stranded, untended, untilled, unweeded **09** abandoned, neglected, overgrown **11** dilapidated, disregarded, undervalued, unhusbanded **12** uncultivated, unmaintained **13** unappreciated

uncaring
04 cold 07 callous, unmoved
09 unfeeling 11 indifferent,
unconcerned 12 uninterested
13 inconsiderate, marble-hearted,
unsympathetic 14 marble-breasted

unceasing
07 endless, non-stop, undying
08 constant, unbroken, unending
09 ceaseless, continual, continued,
incessant, perpetual 10 continuous,
persistent, relentless 11 everlasting,
never-ending, unrelenting,
unremitting

unceremonious
04 rude 06 abrupt, casual, direct,
sudden 07 off-hand, relaxed
08 familiar, impolite, informal, laid-
back, sans gêne 09 easy-going
10 unofficial 11 undignified
12 discourteous 13 disrespectful

uncertain
◊ *anagram indicator*
04 iffy, open 05 dicey, dodgy, risky,
shaky, vague 06 chancy, fitful, slippy,
unsure 07 chancey, dubious, erratic,
unclear, unknown, vagrant, various
08 doubtful, hesitant, insecure,
slippery, unsteady, variable, wavering
09 hazardous, irregular, undecided,
unsettled 10 ambivalent, changeable,
inconstant, indefinite, in two minds, of
two minds, precarious, touch-and-go,
unreliable, unresolved, up in the air
11 speculative, unconfirmed,
unconvinced, vacillating
12 equivocating, in the balance,
questionable, undetermined
13 indeterminate, unforeseeable,
unpredictable

uncertainly
05 shyly 06 warily 07 timidly
09 dubiously, haltingly 10 delayingly,
doubtfully, hesitantly, in two minds,
waveringly 11 reluctantly, sceptically,
tentatively, unwillingly 12 indecisively,
irresolutely, stammeringly, stutteringly
13 half-heartedly, vacillatingly

uncertainty
02 if 05 doubt, qualm 06 qualms
07 dilemma 09 ambiguity, confusion,
misgiving, riskiness, vagueness
10 hesitation, insecurity, perplexity,
puzzlement, scepticism, uneasiness
11 ambivalence, contingency
12 bewilderment, irresolution,
peradventure 13 unreliability

unchallengeable
05 final 07 sacless 08 absolute
10 conclusive 11 impregnable,
irrefutable 12 inappellable,
indisputable, irrefragable
13 incontestable

unchangeable
05 final, fixed 07 eternal 08 constant
09 immutable, permanent
10 changeless, invariable, unchanging
11 stereotyped 12 irreversible
14 intransmutable

unchanging
04 same 06 steady 07 abiding, eternal,
lasting 08 constant, enduring
09 permanent, perpetual, phaseless,
steadfast, unvarying 10 changeless,
invariable

uncharitable
04 hard, mean 05 cruel, harsh, stern
06 severe, unkind 07 callous
09 unfeeling 10 unfriendly, ungenerous
11 hard-hearted, insensitive,
unchristian, unforgiving
13 unsympathetic
15 uncompassionate

uncharted
03 new 05 alien 06 virgin 07 foreign,
strange, unknown 09 unplumbed
10 unexplored, unfamiliar, unsurveyed
12 undiscovered

unchaste
04 lewd 05 frail, light, loose 06 fallen,
impure, wanton 07 defiled, immoral,
wappend 08 depraved, immodest
09 dishonest, dissolute 10 licentious
11 light-heeled, promiscuous

unchecked
03 raw 04 wild 06 unruly 07 rampant,
riotous, violent 08 uncurbed, unreined
09 unbridled 10 boisterous,
unhindered 12 uncontrolled,
unrestrained 13 undisciplined

uncivil
04 curt, rude 05 gruff, surly 06 abrupt,
coarse 07 bearish, boorish, brusque,
ill-bred, uncouth 08 churlish, impolite,
unseemly 09 menseless
10 ungracious, unmannerly 11 bad-
mannered, ill-mannered
12 discourteous 13 disrespectful

uncivilized
04 wild 05 rough 06 savage
07 boorish, brutish, heathen, salvage,
uncouth, untamed 08 barbaric,
impolite 09 barbarian, barbarous,
primitive, unrefined 10 antisocial,
heathenish, illiterate, tramontane,
uncultured, uneducated
13 unenlightened 15 unsophisticated

unclassifiable
05 vague 07 elusive 08 doubtful
09 uncertain 10 ill-defined, indefinite,
indistinct 11 indefinable, undefinable
13 indescribable, indeterminate
14 unidentifiable

unclassified
05 basic, known 06 lowest, public
07 general, minimal, minimum
08 official, revealed, ungraded
09 disclosed, published 11 on the
record 12 unrestricted 14 for
publication

uncle
03 eme, oom 10 pawnbroker

Uncles include:

03 Bob, Joe, Pio, Sam, Tom
05 Henry, Lynch (Andrew), Remus,
Silas, Vanya

06 Domkin (George), Fester, Jasper
(John), Julius, Shandy (Toby),
Wilson (Arthur)
07 Flowers (Philip), Forsyte (Old
Jolyon), Trotter (Albert), Quentin
08 Bulgaria, Claudius, McCaslin
(Buck), McCaslin (Buddy)
09 Cobbleigh (Tom), Old Jolyon
10 Richard III
11 Pumblechook
15 Richard the Third

unclean
03 bad 04 evil, foul, lewd 05 dirty,
grimy 06 filthy, grubby, impure, soiled,
wicked 07 corrupt, defiled, profane,
sullied, tainted 08 ordurous, polluted
10 unhygienic 11 adulterated,
unwholesome 12 contaminated

unclear
03 dim 04 hazy, iffy 05 foggy, vague
06 unsure 07 dubious, obscure
08 doubtful 09 ambiguous, equivocal,
non liquet, uncertain, unsettled
10 convoluted, indefinite, indistinct
12 undetermined

unclothed
04 bare, nude 05 naked 06 unclad
08 disrobed, in the raw, starkers,
stripped 09 in the buff, undressed
10 stark-naked 15 in the altogether

uncomfortable
04 cold, hard, mean 05 tense,
unked, unket, unkid 06 on edge,
uneasy 07 anxious, awkward,
cramped, nervous, painful, worried
08 troubled 09 disturbed, ill at ease
10 disquieted, distressed, ill-fitting,
irritating 11 discomfited,
embarrassed 12 disagreeable 13 self-
conscious

uncommitted
04 free 07 neutral 08 floating
09 available, fancy-free, footloose,
undecided 10 non-aligned,
unattached, uninvolved 11 non-
partisan 12 free-floating

uncommon
◊ *anagram indicator*
03 odd 04 rare, seld, very 05 queer
06 scarce 07 bizarre, curious, notable,
special, strange, unusual 08 abnormal,
atypical, peculiar, singular, striking
10 infrequent, remarkable, remarkably,
unfamiliar 11 distinctive, exceptional,
out of the way, outstanding 12 like gold
dust 13 extraordinary 15 thin on the
ground

uncommonly
◊ *anagram indicator*
04 seld, very 06 rarely, seldom
09 extremely, strangely, unusually
10 abnormally, peculiarly, remarkably,
singularly 12 infrequently, occasionally,
particularly 13 exceptionally,
outstandingly

uncommunicative
03 shy 04 curt 05 aloof, brief, close,
quiet 06 silent 08 reserved, reticent,

retiring, taciturn **09** diffident,
secretive, withdrawn **10** buttoned-up,
unsociable **11** tight-lipped
12 unresponsive **13** unforthcoming

uncomplicated
◇ *anagram indicator*
04 easy **05** clear **06** direct, simple
10 uninvolved **11** undemanding
15 straightforward

uncompromising
04 firm **05** rigid, stiff, tough **06** gritty,
strict **07** diehard **08** hardline,
obdurate, stubborn **09** hard-faced,
hardshell, immovable, obstinate, out-
and-out, unbending **10** inexorable,
inflexible, unyielding **12** intransigent
15 unaccommodating

unconcealable
05 clear, plain **07** obvious **08** manifest
09 insistent **13** irrepressible
14 insuppressible, uncontrollable

unconcealed
04 open, pert **05** frank, naked, overt
06 patent, public **07** blatant, evident,
obvious, visible **08** admitted,
apparent, manifest, unveiled
09 unashamed **10** noticeable
11 conspicuous **12** ill-concealed,
undissembled **13** self-confessed
15 undistinguished

unconcern
06 apathy **09** aloofness
10 detachment, negligence,
remoteness **11** callousness, disinterest,
insouciance, nonchalance
12 indifference **13** pococurantism

unconcerned
04 cool **05** aloof, sober **06** casual,
remote **07** callous, distant, relaxed,
unmoved **08** carefree, careless,
composed, detached, not fussy,
uncaring **09** apathetic, impartial, not
fussed, oblivious, unruffled, unworried
10 complacent, insouciant,
nonchalant, uninvolved, untroubled
11 indifferent, pococurante,
unperturbed **12** uninterested
13 disinterested, dispassionate,
unsympathetic

unconditional
04 full, pure **05** total, utter **06** entire
07 plenary **08** absolute, complete,
definite, outright, positive, termless
09 categoric, downright, out-and-out,
unlimited **10** conclusive, unreserved
11 categorical, unequivocal,
unqualified **12** unrestricted,
wholehearted **13** thoroughgoing

unconditionally
05 fully **06** purely **07** totally **08** entirely
10 absolutely, completely **11** simpliciter
12 unreservedly **13** categorically,
unequivocally **14** wholeheartedly

unconfirmed
08 ignorant, unproved, unproven
10 unratified, unverified
14 uncorroborated
15 unauthenticated, unsubstantiated

unconformity
12 irregularity **13** disconformity,
discontinuity

uncongenial
08 unsuited **09** unsavoury
10 discordant, unfriendly, uninviting,
unpleasant **11** displeasing, distasteful,
unappealing **12** antagonistic,
antipathetic, disagreeable,
incompatible, unattractive
13 unsympathetic

unconnected
07 foreign **08** confused, detached,
separate **09** illogical, unrelated
10 disjointed, incoherent, irrational,
irrelevant, unattached **11** independent,
off the point **12** disconnected
13 inappropriate, unco-ordinated
14 beside the point

unconquerable
08 enduring **09** ingrained
10 inveterate, invincible, unbeatable,
unyielding **11** indomitable, insuperable
12 irresistible, overpowering,
undefeatable **13** irrepressible
14 insurmountable

unconscionable
06 amoral, unholy **07** extreme,
ungodly **08** criminal **09** excessive,
unearthly, unethical **10** exorbitant,
immoderate, inordinate, outrageous
11 extravagant **12** preposterous,
unpardonable, unprincipled,
unreasonable, unscrupulous
13 unjustifiable, unwarrantable

unconscious
03 out **04** deaf **05** blind, dazed
06 asleep, innate, latent, put out, reflex,
zonked **07** drugged, fainted, in a coma,
out cold, stunned, unaware, witless
08 comatose, heedless, ignorant,
knee-jerk, lifeless **09** automatic,
collapsed, concussed, impulsive,
oblivious, passed out, repressed,
senseless, unmindful, unwitting
10 accidental, blacked out, insensible,
knocked out, subliminal, suppressed,
unthinking **11** inadvertent,
incognizant, inconscient, inconscious,
instinctive, involuntary
12 subconscious **13** unintentional
14 dead to the world, out for the
count

• **render unconscious**
04 stun **06** lay out, put out **07** garotte,
garrote **08** garrotte, knock out

unconsciously
10 heedlessly, insensibly **11** impulsively,
obliviously, unmindfully, unwittingly
12 accidentally, subliminally,
unthinkingly **13** automatically,
inadvertently, instinctively,
involuntarily **15** unintentionally

unconsciousness
04 coma, doze **05** faint, sleep
06 snooze, torpor, trance **08** blackout,
daydream, narcosis, numbness
12 inconscience, stupefaction
13 insensibility

unconstraint
07 abandon, freedom **08** openness
09 unreserve **10** liberality, relaxation
11 unrestraint **12** laissez-faire

uncontrollable
03 mad **04** wild **06** strong, unruly
07 furious, violent **08** absolute
10 disorderly **11** intractable
12 indisputable, out of control,
ungovernable, unmanageable
13 irrepressible

uncontrolled
◇ *anagram indicator*
04 wild **06** random, randon, unruly
07 rampant, riotous, runaway, violent
08 uncurbed **09** unbridled, unchecked
10 boisterous, unhindered,
unmastered **12** unrestrained
13 undisciplined

unconventional
◇ *anagram indicator*
03 odd **04** rare, zany **05** gipsy, gypsy,
spacy, wacky, weird **06** far-out, freaky,
fringe, spacey, way-out **07** bizarre,
oddball, offbeat, radical, unusual
08 abnormal, bohemian, freakish,
original, uncommon **09** different,
eccentric, irregular, left-field **10** avant-
garde, individual, long-haired,
unorthodox **11** alternative,
uncustomary **12** experimental
13 idiosyncratic

unconvincing
04 lame, weak **05** fishy **06** farfet,
feeble, flimsy **07** dubious, suspect
08 doubtful, unlikely **10** far-fetched,
improbable **11** implausible
12 questionable

uncooked
03 raw **09** au naturel

unco-operative
04 rude **07** awkward, cubbish, stroppy
08 stubborn **09** obstinate, unhelpful
10 unpleasant **12** bloody-minded

unco-ordinated
◇ *anagram indicator*
05 inept **06** clumsy **07** awkward
08 bumbling, bungling, ungainly
09 maladroit **10** disjointed, ungraceful
11 clodhopping

uncork
04 open, undo **05** clear, crack
06 broach, expose, unseal **07** uncover
08 push open **09** break open, burst
open, force open, prise open, slide open

uncouth
◇ *anagram indicator*
04 rude **05** crude, rough **06** clumsy,
coarse, gauche, rugged, rustic, unrude,
vulgar **07** awkward, boorish, loutish,
unknown **08** impolite, improper,
ungainly, unseemly **09** graceless,
rough-hewn, unrefined **10** uncultured,
unfamiliar, ungraceful **11** bad-
mannered, ill-mannered, uncivilized
12 uncultivated **15** unsophisticated

uncover
04 bare, leak, open, peel, rake, show

05 dig up, strip, unlid **06** detect, exhume, expose, reveal, unheal, unhele, unmask, unrake, unveil, unwrap **07** dismask, divulge, lay bare, lay open, unearth **08** disclose, discover, unbonnet, unshroud **09** make known, unsheathe **12** bring to light **13** blow the lid off, lift the lid off, take the lid off

uncritical
05 naive **07** unfussy **08** gullible, trusting **09** accepting, credulous, incurious **11** superficial, unselective **12** undiscerning **13** unquestioning **14** non-judgemental

unctuous
04 glib, oily **05** slick, suave **06** creamy, greasy, smarmy, smooth **07** fawning, gushing, servile **09** insincere, pietistic, plausible **10** obsequious **11** sycophantic **12** ingratiating **13** sanctimonious

uncultivated
03 new **04** wild **05** feral, rough, waste **06** desert, fallow, incult **07** natural, wilding **11** unhusbanded

uncultured
04 hick, rude **05** crude, ocker, rough **06** coarse, incult, rustic **07** boorish, ill-bred, uncouth **09** barbarous, unrefined **10** philistine **11** uncivilized **12** uncultivated **14** unintellectual **15** unsophisticated

undaunted
04 bold **05** brave **07** impavid, unbowed **08** fearless, intrepid, resolute, unafraid **09** dauntless, steadfast, unalarmed **10** courageous, undeterred, undismayed, unflagging **11** indomitable **13** undiscouraged

undecided
04 moot, open **05** vague **06** unsure **07** dubious, in doubt, unknown **08** doubtful, hesitant, wavering **09** debatable, dithering, uncertain, unsettled **10** ambivalent, indecisive, indefinite, in two minds, irresolute, of two minds, unresolved, up in the air **11** uncommitted **12** equivocating, in the balance **13** unestablished

undecorated
05 plain, stark **06** severe, simple **07** austere **08** inornate **09** classical, unadorned **10** functional **12** unornamented **13** unembellished

undefeated
07 supreme, unbowed, winning **08** unbeaten **09** unsubdued **10** triumphant, victorious **11** unconquered, unsurpassed **12** unvanquished

undefended
04 open **05** naked **07** exposed, unarmed **09** pregnable, unguarded **10** vulnerable **11** defenceless, unfortified, unprotected

undefiled
04 pure **05** clean, clear **06** chaste,

intact, virgin **07** sinless **08** flawless, spotless, unsoiled, virginal **09** inviolate, unspotted, unstained, unsullied **10** immaculate, intemerate **11** unblemished

undefined
04 hazy **05** vague **06** woolly **07** inexact, shadowy, tenuous, unclear **08** formless, nebulous **09** imprecise **10** ill-defined, indefinite, indistinct **11** unexplained, unspecified **13** indeterminate

undemonstrative
04 cold, cool **05** aloof, stiff **06** formal, remote **07** distant **08** reserved, reticent **09** impassive, withdrawn **10** phlegmatic, restrained **11** unemotional **12** unresponsive **15** uncommunicative

undeniable
04 sure **05** clear **06** patent, proven **07** certain, evident, obvious **08** definite, manifest, positive **09** excellent, hard facts, undoubted **11** beyond doubt, indubitable, irrefutable **12** indisputable, unmistakable **13** incontestable **14** beyond question, unquestionable **15** unexceptionable

undeniably
09 certainly **10** definitely, positively **11** beyond doubt, indubitably, undoubtedly **12** indisputably, unmistakably **14** beyond question, unquestionably

undependable
06 fickle **07** erratic **08** unstable, variable **09** mercurial, uncertain **10** capricious, changeable, inconstant, unreliable **11** fair-weather, treacherous **12** inconsistent **13** irresponsible, unpredictable, untrustworthy

under
◇ *juxtaposition down indicator*
04 down, less **05** below, lower **06** within **07** beneath **08** downward, junior to, less than, under par **09** lower than **10** inferior to, underneath **11** secondary to, subordinate **13** subordinate to, subservient to

underclothes *see* **underwear**

undercover
03 sly **06** covert, hidden, secret **07** furtive, private **08** hush-hush, stealthy **09** concealed **11** clandestine, underground **12** confidential, intelligence **13** surreptitious

undercurrent
04 aura, hint **05** drift, sense, tinge, trend **07** feeling, flavour **08** movement, overtone, tendency, underset, undertow **09** underflow, undertone **10** atmosphere, suggestion

undercut
04 mine **05** filet **08** excavate, gouge out, scoop out, underbid **09** hollow out, undermine, undersell

10 tenderloin, underprice **11** undercharge **14** charge less than

underdog
04 prey **05** loser **06** victim **07** outcast **08** outsider **09** little man **11** unfortunate, weaker party **12** the exploited

underdone
04 rare **09** half-baked

underestimate
07 dismiss **08** belittle, minimize, misjudge, play down **09** disparage, sell short, underrate **10** look down on, trivialize, undervalue **12** miscalculate

undergarment *see* **underwear**

undergo
04 bear **05** enjoy, stand **06** endure, suffer **07** sustain, weather **08** submit to, tolerate, underlie **09** go through, put up with, withstand **10** experience **11** pass through

underground
04 tube **05** metro **06** buried, covert, hidden, secret, subway, sunken **07** covered, furtive, illegal, radical **08** secretly **09** concealed, hypogeous **10** avant-garde, hypogaeous, subversive, undercover, unofficial, unorthodox **11** alternative, below ground, clandestine **12** experimental, subterranean **13** revolutionary, surreptitious **15** below the surface

Underground and metro transport systems include:
01 T
04 BART, DART
07 the Tube
09 Chicago El, Rome Metro
10 City Circle, Paris Métro
11 Berlin S-Bahn, Berlin U-Bahn, Madrid Metro, Munich S-Bahn, Munich U-Bahn
13 New York Subway
15 Clockwork Orange, Washington Metro

See also **London**

undergrowth
05 brush, scrub **06** briars, bushes, shrubs, spring **07** bracken, thicket **08** brambles **09** brushwood, shrubbery, underwood **10** vegetation **11** ground cover

underhand
03 sly **05** shady **06** crafty, secret, shonky, sneaky **07** crooked, devious, furtive, immoral, oblique **08** improper, scheming, sinister, sneaking, stealthy **09** deceitful, deceptive, dishonest, unethical **10** backstairs, fraudulent **11** clandestine, unobtrusive **12** unscrupulous **13** hole-and-corner, surreptitious

underline
04 mark **06** stress **07** point up **09** emphasize, highlight, italicize **10** accentuate, foreground, underscore **15** draw attention to

underling

05 slave **06** lackey, menial, minion, nobody **07** flunkey, servant **08** hireling, inferior, munchkin, weakling **09** nonentity **11** subordinate

underlying

04 root **05** basal, basic **06** hidden, latent, veiled **07** lurking, primary, subject **08** inherent **09** concealed, essential, intrinsic, subjacent **10** elementary **11** fundamental, subordinate

undermine

03 dig, mar, sap **04** mine **05** erode **06** damage, impair, injure, tunnel, weaken **07** cripple, destroy, handbag, subvert, vitiate **08** excavate, sabotage, undercut, wear away **09** underwork **14** make less secure

undernourished

06 hungry **07** starved **08** anorexic, underfed **09** anorectic **12** malnourished

underprivileged

04 poor **05** needy **06** in need, in want **08** deprived **09** destitute, oppressed **10** in distress **11** impecunious **12** impoverished **13** disadvantaged

underrate

07 dismiss **08** belittle, inferior **09** disparage, downgrade, extenuate, sell short **10** depreciate, look down on, undervalue **13** underestimate

under-secretary

02 US

undersell

03 cut **05** slash **06** reduce **08** mark down, play down, undercut **09** disparage, sell short **10** depreciate, understate **11** undercharge

undershirt

04 vest **06** semmit **07** singlet, surcoat

undersized

03 wee **04** puny, tiny **05** dwarf, pygmy, scrub, small, teeny **06** little, minute, teensy **07** runtish, stunted **08** pint-size **09** atrophied, miniature, pint-sized **11** underweight **14** underdeveloped **15** achondroplastic

understand

03 dig, get, see **04** gaum, gorm, hear, know, read, take, twig **05** catch, click, get it, grasp, imply, learn, savey, savvy, think **06** accept, assume, fathom, follow, gather, make of, rumble, savvey, take in **07** believe, comfort, discern, elusive, feel for, get wise, make out, presume, realize, support, suppose, suss out **08** conceive, conclude, contrive, cotton on, perceive, tumble to **09** apprehend, empathize, enter into, figure out, interpret, latch onto, penetrate, recognize **10** appreciate, comprehend, sympathize **11** commiserate, make sense of **12** feel sorry for, get a handle on, get the hang of, identify with, know the ropes **13** get the message, get the picture, the penny drops

• failure to understand

04 anan, anon

understandable

05 clear, lucid, plain **06** direct **07** natural **08** expected **10** acceptable, accessible, admissible, penetrable, reasonable **11** transparent, unambiguous **12** intelligible, unsurprising **14** comprehensible, self-explaining **15** self-explanatory, straightforward

understanding

03 ken **04** gaum, gorm, head, idea, kind, pact, view, with **05** grasp, sense, trust **06** accord, belief, loving, notion, tender, uptake, wisdom **07** bargain, comfort, command, compact, conceit, empathy, entente, feeling, harmony, insight, lenient, opinion, patient, support **08** sympathy, tolerant **09** agreement, awareness, forgiving, hindsight, intellect, judgement, knowledge, sensitive **10** compassion, discerning, forbearing, impression, perception, supportive, thoughtful **11** arrangement, considerate, consolation, discernment, intelligent, sympathetic **12** appreciation, apprehension, intelligence **13** commiseration, compassionate, comprehension **14** interpretation

understate

07 dismiss **08** belittle, minimize, play down **09** soft-pedal, underplay **11** make light of

understated

04 mild **05** faint **06** low-key, subtle **07** implied **08** indirect **09** toned-down **10** indefinite, indistinct

understatement

07 litotes, meiosis **09** dismissal, restraint **12** minimization, underplaying

understood

05 tacit **07** assumed, implied **08** accepted, familiar, implicit, inferred, presumed, unspoken, unstated **09** unwritten **11** transparent

understudy

05 locum **06** deputy, double, fill-in, relief **07** reserve, stand-in **10** substitute **11** replacement

undersurface

03 pad **04** sole **05** belly **08** intrados, pavilion **09** gastraeum

undertake

03 try **05** agree, begin **06** accept, assume, pledge, tackle, take on **07** attempt, promise, receive **08** commence, contract, covenant, deal with, embark on, perceive, set about, shoulder **09** endeavour, get down to, guarantee, set in hand, underfong **10** enterprise, take in hand **13** put your hand to, set your hand to **14** commit yourself, get to grips with, grasp the nettle, turn your hand to **15** apply yourself to

undertaker

06 editor, surety **07** sponsor **08** compiler, upholder **09** mortician, projector, publisher **10** contractor **12** entrepreneur **15** funeral director

undertaking

03 job, vow **04** call, plan, task, word **06** affair, effort, pledge, scheme **07** attempt, emprise, project, promise, venture, warrant **08** business, campaign, contract, warranty **09** assurance, challenge, endeavour, guarantee, operation **10** commitment, enterprise **12** enterprising

undertone

04 aura, hint **05** tinge, touch, trace **06** murmur **07** feeling, flavour, whisper **09** undernote, undersong **10** atmosphere, intimation, suggestion **11** connotation **12** undercurrent

undervalue

07 disable, dismiss **08** disprize, minimize, misjudge, misprise, misprize **09** disparage, sell short, underrate **10** depreciate, look down on **13** underestimate

underwater

06 sunken **08** demersal, demersed, immersed, undersea, undertow **09** submarine, submerged **10** subaquatic, subaqueous

underwear

06 smalls, undies **08** grundies, lingerie, scanties, skivvies, underset **09** innerwear **10** underlinen **11** underthings **12** underclothes **13** underclothing, undergarments **14** unmentionables

Underwear includes:

03 bra
04 body, coms, jump, slip, vest
05 bania, cimar, combs, cymar, jupon, pants, shift, tanga, teddy, thong, tunic
06 banian, banyan, basque, briefs, corset, garter, girdle, knicks, semmit, skivvy, teddie, trunks
07 chemise, drawers, G-string, hosiery, linings, panties, singlet, spencer, Y-fronts
08 bloomers, camisole, chuddies, frillies, knickers, subucula, thermals
09 brassière, crinoline, jockstrap, long johns, petticoat, stockings, union suit, wyliecoat
10 suspenders, underdress, underpants, undershirt, underskirt
11 boxer shorts, directoires, undershorts
12 body stocking, camiknickers, combinations
13 liberty bodice, suspender-belt
14 French knickers

underweight

04 thin **08** underfed **10** undersized **11** half-starved **14** undernourished

underworld

03 Dis, pit **04** Ades, fire, hell **05** abyss,

below, Hades, Sheol **06** Erebus, the mob, Tophet **07** Abaddon, Acheron, Gehenna, inferno **08** gangland, Tartarus **09** down there, Malebolge, perdition **10** other place, subterrene **11** nether world, underground **12** lower regions **13** bottomless pit, criminal world **14** organized crime **15** abode of the devil, infernal regions

underwrite
04 back, fund, sign **05** write **06** insure **07** approve, confirm, endorse, finance, initial, sponsor, support **08** sanction **09** authorize, guarantee, subscribe, subsidize **11** countersign

undesirable
04 foul **05** nasty **08** disliked, riff-raff, unwanted **09** obnoxious, offensive, repugnant, unwelcome **10** unpleasant, unsuitable **11** distasteful, unwished-for **12** disagreeable, unacceptable **13** objectionable

undeveloped
04 rude **06** latent, neuter **07** dwarfed, stunted **08** immature, inchoate, unformed **09** embryonic, infantile, potential, unfledged **10** developing, primordial, Third World **12** less advanced **14** underdeveloped

undignified
06 clumsy **07** foolish **08** improper, ungainly, unseemly **09** inelegant **10** indecorous, unbecoming, unsuitable **13** inappropriate

undiluted
04 neat, pure **05** heady, sheer, utter **06** strong **07** unmixed **08** straight, unspoilt **09** unalloyed, unblended **11** unmitigated, unqualified **12** concentrated

undisciplined
◇ *anagram indicator*
04 wild **06** unruly, wanton, wilful **07** wayward **08** unsteady **09** untrained **10** unreliable, unschooled **11** disobedient **12** disorganized, obstreperous, uncontrolled, unrestrained, unsystematic **13** unpredictable

undisguised
04 bald, open **05** frank, naked, overt, stark, utter **06** patent **07** blatant, evident, genuine, obvious **08** apparent, explicit, manifest, outright, unmasked, unveiled **09** unadorned **11** transparent, unconcealed **12** undissembled **13** thoroughgoing

undisguisedly
06 openly **07** frankly, overtly **08** outright, patently **09** blatantly, obviously **12** unreservedly **13** transparently

undisputed
04 fact, sure **07** certain **08** accepted, unargued **09** undoubted **10** conclusive, recognized, undeniable **11** indubitable, irrefutable, uncontested

12 acknowledged, indisputable, unchallenged, unquestioned

undistinguished
04 so-so **05** banal, plain **06** common **07** ordinar, plebean **08** everyday, inferior, mediocre, nameless, ordinary, plebeian **10** not much cop, pedestrian **11** indifferent, not up to much **12** run-of-the-mill, unimpressive, unremarkable **13** no great shakes, unexceptional

undisturbed
04 calm, even **05** quiet **06** placid, serene **07** equable **08** composed, tranquil, wakeless **09** collected, quietsome, unruffled, untouched **10** motionless, unaffected, untroubled **11** unconcerned, unperturbed **13** uninterrupted

undivided
03 one **04** full **05** solid, total, whole **06** entire, intact, single, united **07** serious, sincere **08** combined, complete, unbroken **09** dedicated, exclusive, unanimous **10** individual, unreserved **11** individuate, pro indiviso, unqualified **12** concentrated, wholehearted

undo
◇ *anagram indicator*
03 dup, mar **04** free, open, poop, ruin **05** annul, crush, loose, poupe, quash, solve, spoil, untie, unzip, upset, wreck **06** cancel, defeat, loosen, offset, repeal, revoke, seduce, unbend, unclew, unhook, unlace, unlock, unwind, unwork, unwrap **07** destroy, nullify, release, retract, reverse, shatter, subvert, undight, unravel, unshape **08** overturn, separate, set aside, unbuckle, unbutton, unfasten **09** disanoint, undermine **10** invalidate, neutralize, obliterate **11** disentangle

undoing
◇ *anagram indicator*
04 ruin **05** shame **06** defeat **07** opening **08** collapse, disgrace, downfall, reversal, weakness **09** defeature, overthrow, ruination **10** defeasance **11** destruction, unfastening

undomesticated
04 wild **05** feral **06** savage **07** natural, untamed **11** uncivilized **12** ferae naturae

undone
◇ *anagram indicator*
04 left, lost, open **05** loose **06** adrift, opened, ruined, untied **07** ignored, omitted, seduced, unlaced **08** annulled, betrayed, unlocked **09** destroyed, forgotten, neglected, unwrought **10** incomplete, passed over, unbuttoned, unfastened, unfinished **11** outstanding, uncompleted, unfulfilled **14** unaccomplished

• **come undone**
03 run

undoubted
04 sure **06** patent **07** certain, obvious **08** definite **10** undisputed **11** indubitable, irrefutable, uncontested, undesirable **12** acknowledged, indisputable, unchallenged, unquestioned **14** unquestionable

undoubtedly
04 sure **06** surely **07** no doubt **08** of course **09** assuredly, certainly, doubtless **10** definitely, manifestly, no question, undeniably **11** beyond doubt, indubitably **12** unmistakably, without doubt **14** unquestioningly

undreamed-of
07 amazing **08** undreamt **09** unheard-of **10** incredible, miraculous, unexpected, unforeseen, unhoped-for, unimagined **11** astonishing, unsuspected **13** inconceivable

undress
04 peel, shed **05** strip **06** devest, divest, nudity, remove, streak, uncase, unrobe **07** discase, disrobe, peel off, take off **08** disarray, unclothe **09** disattire, nakedness **10** déshabillé, dishabille **11** make unready **13** get your kit off

undressed
04 nude **05** naked **08** disrobed, en cuerpo, in the raw, starkers, stripped, untented **09** in the buff, self-faced, unclothed **10** stark-naked **12** not a stitch on **15** in the altogether

undue
07 extreme **08** improper, needless **09** excessive, obtrusive **10** immoderate, inordinate, undeserved **11** exaggerated, extravagant, superfluous, uncalled-for, unjustified, unnecessary, unwarranted **12** unreasonable **13** inappropriate

undulate
04 roll, wave, wavy **05** heave, surge, swell **06** billow, ripple **07** vibrate **11** rise and fall

undulating
04 wavy **05** waved **06** undate **07** rolling, sinuous **08** flexuose, flexuous, rippling, undulant, undulose, undulous **09** billowing, up-and-down **10** undulatory

unduly
◇ *anagram indicator*
03 too **04** over **08** overmuch **10** wrongfully **11** excessively, obtrusively **12** immoderately, inordinately, unreasonably **13** exaggeratedly, unjustifiably, unnecessarily

undutiful
05 slack **06** remiss **08** careless, disloyal, unfilial **09** negligent **10** defaulting, delinquent, neglectful

undying
07 abiding, eternal, lasting **08** constant, immortal, infinite,

unearth

unending, unfading **09** deathless, perennial, permanent, perpetual, unceasing **10** continuing **11** everlasting, sempiternal **12** imperishable, undiminished **14** indestructible

unearth

04 find **05** dig up **06** detect, dig out, exhume, expose, reveal **07** uncover **08** discover, disinter, excavate **12** bring to light

unearthly

05 eerie, weird **06** absurd, creepy, unholy **07** ghostly, phantom, strange, uncanny, ungodly **08** eldritch **09** appalling, celestial, unheard-of **10** horrendous, outrageous **12** otherworldly, preposterous, supernatural, unreasonable **13** preternatural, spine-chilling **14** unconscionable

unease

05 alarm, doubt, worry **06** qualms **07** anxiety, dis-ease **08** disquiet **09** agitation, misgiving, suspicion **10** discomfort, inquietude, uneasiness **11** nervousness **12** apprehension, perturbation

uneasily

04 hard

uneasiness

05 alarm, doubt, qualm, worry **06** qualms, unease **07** anxiety, dis-ease, malaise, misease, trouble **08** disquiet **09** agitation, dysphoria, misgiving, suspicion **10** discomfort, inquietude, solicitude **11** nervousness **12** apprehension, perturbation **14** distemperature, solicitousness **15** dissatisfaction

uneasy

◇ *anagram indicator*
04 edgy **05** nervy, shaky, tense, upset **06** on edge, queasy, queazy, unsure **07** alarmed, anxious, fidgety, jittery, keyed up, nervous, restive, twitchy, unquiet, worried, wound up **08** agitated, disquiet, insecure, restless, strained, troubled, worrying **09** disturbed, ill at ease, impatient, perturbed, troubling, unnerving, unrestful, unsettled **10** disquieted, disturbing, perturbing, unsettling **11** disquieting **12** apprehensive **13** disconcerting, uncomfortable

uneconomic

10 loss-making **12** uncommercial, unprofitable **15** non-profit-making

unedifying

04 idle

uneducated

06 unread **08** ignorant, untaught **09** benighted, lack-Latin, unlearned **10** illiterate, philistine, uncultured, uninformed, unschooled **12** uncultivated

unemotional

04 cold, cool **05** bland **06** stolid

08 detached, reserved **09** apathetic, bloodless, impassive, objective, unfeeling **10** phlegmatic **11** indifferent, passionless, unexcitable **12** phlegmatical, unresponsive **13** dispassionate **15** undemonstrative

unemphatic

08 downbeat **10** played-down **11** underplayed, understated, unobtrusive **12** soft-pedalled **14** unostentatious

unemployed

04 idle **07** jobless, laid off, unwaged **08** workless **09** on the dole, out of work, redundant **10** unoccupied

unending

07 endless, eternal, undated, undying **08** constant **09** ceaseless, continual, incessant, perpetual, unceasing **10** continuous **11** everlasting, never-ending, unremitting **12** interminable **13** thorough-going, uninterrupted

unendurable

10 shattering, unbearable **11** intolerable **12** insufferable, overwhelming **13** insupportable

unenthusiastic

04 cool, damp **05** blasé, bored **07** neutral, unmoved **08** lukewarm **09** apathetic, Laodicean **10** nonchalant **11** half-hearted, indifferent, unimpressed **12** uninterested, unresponsive

unenviable

09 dangerous, difficult, thankless **10** unpleasant **11** uncongenial, undesirable **12** disagreeable **13** uncomfortable

unequal

06 biased, uneven, unfair, unjust, unlike **07** not up to, varying **08** lopsided, unfitted, unsuited **09** different, disparate, excessive, incapable, irregular, unmatched **10** dissimilar, inadequate, unbalanced **11** incompetent, inequitable, unqualified **12** asymmetrical, not cut out for **14** discriminatory

unequalled

06 unique **07** supreme **08** peerless, unbeaten, unpeered **09** matchless, nonpareil, paramount, unmatched **10** inimitable, pre-eminent, surpassing, unrivalled **11** exceptional, unpatterned, unsurpassed **12** incomparable, transcendent, unparalleled

unequivocal

05 clear, plain **06** direct, square **07** evident, express **08** absolute, definite, distinct, explicit, outright, positive, straight **10** unreserved **11** categorical, unambiguous, unqualified **12** unmistakable **15** straightforward

unequivocally

06 firmly **07** clearly **08** directly **10** definitely, distinctly, explicitly,

positively **12** unmistakably **13** unambiguously **14** unquestionably

unerring

04 dead, sure **05** clean, exact **07** certain, perfect, uncanny **08** accurate, inerrant **09** faultless, unfailing **10** impeccable, infallible

unerringly

04 bang, dead **10** accurately, infallibly **11** unfailingly

unethical

04 evil **05** shady, wrong **06** wicked **07** illegal, illicit, immoral **08** improper **09** dishonest, underhand **12** disreputable, unprincipled, unscrupulous **13** dishonourable **14** unprofessional

uneven

◇ *anagram indicator*
03 odd **05** bumpy, jerky, lumpy, rough, ruggy, stony **06** coarse, craggy, fitful, jagged, patchy, rugged, spotty, unfair **07** crooked, erratic, ruffled, rumpled, streaky, unequal **08** lopsided, one-sided, scratchy, unsteady, variable **09** inequable, irregular, spasmodic **10** accidented, changeable, ill-matched, unbalanced **11** fluctuating, inequitable **12** asymmetrical, inconsistent, intermittent

uneventful

04 dull **05** quiet **06** boring **07** humdrum, routine, tedious **08** everyday, ordinary, unvaried **10** monotonous, unexciting **11** commonplace, unmemorable **12** run-of-the-mill, unremarkable **13** unexceptional, uninteresting

unexampled

05 novel **06** unique **09** unheard-of, unmatched **10** unequalled **11** unpatterned **12** incomparable, unparalleled **13** unprecedented **15** never before seen

unexceptionable

04 mild, safe **05** bland **08** harmless, innocent **09** excellent, innocuous, peaceable **10** undeniable **11** inoffensive **15** unobjectionable

unexceptional

04 so-so **05** usual **06** common, normal **07** average, typical **08** everyday, mediocre, ordinary **10** not much cop **11** indifferent, not up to much, unmemorable **12** run-of-the-mill, unimpressive, unremarkable **13** no great shakes **15** undistinguished

unexcitable

04 calm, cool **06** serene **07** relaxed **08** composed, laid-back **09** contained, easy-going, impassive **10** phlegmatic **11** passionless **13** dispassionate, imperturbable, self-possessed, unimpassioned

unexpected

◇ *anagram indicator*
04 snap **05** shock **06** abrupt, chance, sudden, unware, unwary, wonder

07 amazing, unhoped, unusual, unwarie **08** emergent, unweened **09** inopinate, startling **10** accidental, fortuitous, surprising, unforeseen **11** astonishing, unlooked-for **13** unanticipated, unpredictable

unexpectedly
◇ *anagram indicator*
06 unware **08** abruptly, by chance, suddenly, unawares, unwarely **11** ex improviso **12** accidentally, à l'improviste, fortuitously, out of the blue, phenomenally, refreshingly, surprisingly **13** unpredictably **14** without warning

unexpressive
05 blank **06** vacant **07** deadpan **08** immobile **09** impassive **11** emotionless, inscrutable **12** inexpressive **13** inexpressible **14** expressionless

unfading
04 fast **07** abiding, durable, lasting, undying **08** constant, enduring, fadeless **09** evergreen, unfailing **12** imperishable **13** immarcescible

unfailing
04 sure, true **05** loyal **06** steady **07** certain, staunch, undying **08** constant, faithful, reliable, unerring, unfading **09** steadfast **10** dependable, infallible **12** indefectible, inexhaustive **13** inexhaustible

unfair
◇ *anagram indicator*
04 bent, foul, ugly **05** crook, shady, thick **06** biased, unjust **07** a bit off, bigoted, crooked, partial, slanted **08** one-sided, partisan, weighted, wrongful **09** arbitrary, deceitful, dishonest, unethical, unmerited **10** prejudiced, unbalanced, undeserved **11** inequitable, uncalled-for, unwarranted **12** below the belt, over the score, unprincipled, unreasonable, unscrupulous **14** discriminatory

unfairly
◇ *anagram indicator*
04 foul **07** wrongly **08** biasedly, unjustly **09** illegally, partially **10** improperly, unlawfully **11** dishonestly, inequitably **12** unreasonably

unfairness
04 bias **05** cross **07** bigotry, unright **08** inequity, misusage **09** injustice, prejudice **10** partiality **12** one-sidedness, partisanship **14** discrimination **15** inequitableness

unfaithful
05 false **06** fickle, unleal, untrue **07** godless **08** cheating, disloyal **09** deceitful, dishonest, faithless, insincere, two-timing **10** adulterous, inconstant, perfidious, unreliable **11** duplicitous, treacherous, unbelieving **13** double-dealing, untrustworthy

unfaltering
04 firm **05** fixed **06** steady **08** constant, resolute, tireless, untiring **09** steadfast, unfailing **10** unflagging, unswerving, unwavering, unyielding **11** unflinching **12** pertinacious **13** indefatigable

unfamiliar
◇ *anagram indicator*
03 new **05** alien, novel **07** curious, foreign, strange, uncouth, unknown, unusual **08** selcouth, uncommon, unversed **09** different, uncharted, unskilled **10** unexplored, uninformed **11** unpractised **12** unaccustomed, unacquainted, unconversant **13** inexperienced

unfashionable
03 out **04** lame **05** daggy, dated, dowdy, passé **06** démodé, old hat, square **08** obsolete, outmoded, unmodish **09** out of date, shapeless, unpopular **10** antiquated **12** old-fashioned, out of fashion

unfasten
04 open, undo **05** loose, unbar, unfix, unpin, untie, unzip **06** detach, loosen, unbend, unhasp, unlock, unwrap **07** unclasp, unloose, untruss **08** separate, unbuckle, uncouple, unloosen **10** disconnect

unfathomable
04 deep **06** hidden **07** abysmal **08** abstruse, baffling, esoteric, profound **09** unplumbed, unsounded **10** bottomless, fathomless, mysterious, unknowable **11** inscrutable, unsoundable **12** immeasurable, impenetrable, inexplicable **14** indecipherable

unfavourable
03 bad, ill **04** foul, poor **07** adverse, hostile, ominous, unlucky **08** contrary, critical, inimical, negative, untimely, untoward **09** ill-suited **10** prejudiced, unfriendly **11** in a bad light, inopportune, threatening, unfortunate, unpromising **12** discouraging, inauspicious, unseasonable **15** disadvantageous, uncomplimentary

unfavourably
03 ill **05** badly **06** poorly **09** adversely, in bad part, in ill part, unhappily **10** negatively **13** unfortunately, unpromisingly

unfeeling
04 cold, hard **05** cruel, harsh, stony **06** brutal **07** callous, inhuman **08** hardened, pitiless, uncaring **09** heartless, merciless **10** impassible, iron-headed, iron-witted **11** hard-hearted, insensitive, iron-hearted **13** unsympathetic

unfeigned
04 pure, real **05** frank **07** genuine, natural, sincere **08** unforced **09** heartfelt **10** unaffected **11** spontaneous **12** undissembled, wholehearted

unfettered
04 free **09** chainless, unbridled, unchecked **10** unconfined, unhampered, unhindered, unshackled **11** uninhibited **12** unrestrained, untrammelled **13** unconstrained

unfinished
◇ *tail deletion indicator*
05 crude, rough **06** undone **07** lacking, sketchy, wanting **08** half-done, inchoate **09** deficient, imperfect, incondite **10** incomplete **11** uncompleted, unfulfilled **14** unaccomplished

unfit
◇ *anagram indicator*
04 weak **05** inapt **06** feeble, flabby, impair, unable, unmeet **07** unequal, useless **08** decrepit, disabled, improper, unsuited **09** condemned, incapable, unhealthy, untrained **10** inadequate, ineligible, out of shape, unprepared, unsuitable **11** debilitated, ill-equipped, incompetent, ineffective, unqualified **12** disqualified **13** inappropriate, incapacitated **14** out of condition

unflagging
05 fixed **06** steady **07** staunch **08** constant, tireless, untiring **09** assiduous, unceasing, unfailing **10** persistent, unswerving **11** persevering, undeviating, unfaltering, unremitting **12** never-failing, single-minded **13** indefatigable

unflappable
04 calm, cool **07** equable **08** composed, laid-back **09** collected, easy-going, impassive, supercool, unruffled, unworried **10** phlegmatic **11** level-headed, unexcitable **13** imperturbable, self-possessed

unflattering
05 blunt **06** candid, honest **08** critical **09** outspoken **10** unbecoming **12** unattractive, unfavourable **15** uncomplimentary, unprepossessing

unflinching
04 bold, firm, sure **05** fixed **06** steady **07** staunch **08** constant, resolute, stalwart, unshaken **09** steadfast **10** determined, unblenched, unblinking, unswerving, unwavering **11** unblenching, unfaltering, unshrinking

unflinchingly
04 fast **06** boldly, firmly **08** steadily **09** staunchly **10** resolutely **11** steadfastly **12** unswervingly, unwaveringly **13** unfalteringly, unshrinkingly

unfold
04 grow, open, show, tell, undo **06** deploy, emerge, evolve, extend, relate, result, reveal, spread, unclew, uncoil, unfurl, unroll, untuck, unwrap **07** clarify, develop, display, explain, flatten, narrate, open out, present, uncover, unravel, work out

08 describe, disclose, shake out, undouble **09** come about, elaborate, explicate, interpret, make known, spread out **10** disenvelop, disinvolve, illustrate, straighten, stretch out **13** straighten out

unforeseen
06 casual, sudden **07** amazing, unusual **09** startling **10** surprising, unexpected **11** astonishing, unavoidable, unlooked-for, unpredicted **13** unanticipated, unpredictable

unforgettable
07 notable, special **08** historic, striking **09** important, indelible, memorable, momentous **10** impressive, noteworthy, remarkable **11** distinctive, exceptional, significant **13** extraordinary

unforgivable
08 shameful **10** deplorable, outrageous **11** disgraceful, inexcusable, intolerable **12** contemptible, indefensible, unpardonable **13** reprehensible, unjustifiable

unforgiven
10 unabsolved, unredeemed **11** unrepentant **12** unregenerate

unfortunate
◊ *anagram indicator*
03 ill **04** evil, poor **05** tough **06** doomed **07** adverse, hapless, ruinous, unhappy, unlucky **08** hopeless, ill-fated, ill-timed, luckless, untimely, untoward, wretched **09** ill-omened **10** calamitous, deplorable, disastrous, ill-advised, lamentable, unpleasant, unsuitable **11** evil-starred, injudicious, inopportune, misfortuned, regrettable **12** disaventrous, unfavourable, unsuccessful **13** inappropriate, misadventured **14** disadventurous **15** disadvantageous

unfortunately
◊ *anagram indicator*
04 alas **05** sadly **08** sad to say **09** unhappily, unluckily, worse luck **11** regrettably, sad to relate **13** I am sorry to say

unfounded
04 idle **05** false **08** baseless, spurious, unproven **09** trumped-up **10** bottomless, fabricated, groundless **11** conjectural, unjustified, unsupported **14** uncorroborated **15** unsubstantiated

unfrequented
04 lone **06** lonely, remote, untrod **08** deserted, desolate, isolated, secluded, solitary, untraded, wasteful **09** untrodden, unvisited **11** god-forsaken, sequestered, uninhabited

unfriendly
04 cold, cool, sour **05** aloof, chill, fraim, fremd, surly **06** chilly, fremit,

frosty, frozen, unkind, wintry **07** distant, hostile, wintery **08** inimical, strained, unkindly **10** aggressive, unpleasant, unsociable **11** ill-disposed, quarrelsome, standoffish, uncongenial, unwelcoming **12** antagonistic, disagreeable, inauspicious, inhospitable, inimicitious **13** unneighbourly **14** unapproachable

unfrock
06 demote, depose, ungown **07** degrade, dismiss, suspend

unfruitful
04 arid **06** barren **07** sterile **08** infecund **09** exhausted, fruitless, infertile **10** unprolific **11** infructuous, unrewarding **12** impoverished, unproductive, unprofitable

unfurl
04 grow, open, undo **05** break **06** emerge, evolve, extend, result, spread, uncoil, unfold, unroll, unwrap **07** develop, display, flatten, open out, uncover, unravel, work out **09** come about, spread out **10** straighten, stretch out **13** straighten out

ungainly
◊ *anagram indicator*
05 gawky **06** clumsy, gauche, ungain **07** awkward, loutish, uncouth **08** gangling, unwieldy **09** awkwardly, inelegant, lumbering, maladroit **10** ungraceful **13** unco-ordinated

ungodly
05 world **06** sinful, wicked **07** corrupt, godless, immoral, impious, profane **08** depraved, unsocial **09** unearthly **10** horrendous, iniquitous, outrageous **11** blasphemous, intolerable, irreligious **12** preposterous, unreasonable **14** unconscionable

ungovernable
04 wild **06** unruly **10** disorderly, masterless, rebellious, refractory, ungoverned **12** unmanageable **14** uncontrollable, unrestrainable

ungracious
04 rude **07** boorish, ill-bred, mesquin, offhand, uncivil **08** churlish, impolite, mesquine **09** graceless **10** ungraceful, unhandsome, unmannerly **11** bad-mannered, disgracious **12** discourteous **13** disrespectful

ungrateful
04 rude **07** ingrate, irksome, selfish, uncivil **08** heedless, impolite **09** thankless **10** ungracious, unthankful **11** ill-mannered **12** disagreeable **14** unappreciative

unguarded
04 rash **06** unwary **07** exposed, foolish **08** careless, heedless, off guard **09** foolhardy, impolitic, imprudent, lippening, unweighed **10** incautious, indiscreet, undefended, unscreened, unthinking, vulnerable **11** defenceless, inadvertent, inattentive, thoughtless, unpatrolled, unprotected

12 undiplomatic **13** ill-considered, uncircumspect

ungulate
03 cow **04** deer **05** horse, takin, tapir **06** hoofed **09** Dinoceras **10** Deinoceras, mesohippus, rhinoceros, rhinocerot **11** rhinocerote **12** hippopotamus, Uintatherium **13** Palaeotherium, Titanotherium

unhappily
◊ *anagram indicator*
04 alas **05** sadly **08** sad to say, shrewdly **09** unluckily, worse luck **11** maliciously, regrettably, sad to relate **12** unfavourably **13** unfortunately **14** unsuccessfully

unhappy
◊ *anagram indicator*
03 low, sad **04** blue, down, glum **05** fed up, inapt, upset **06** clumsy, gloomy **07** awkward, hapless, unlucky **08** dejected, downcast, ill-fated, luckless, mournful, tactless **09** depressed, ill-chosen, long-faced, miserable, sorrowful, woebegone **10** despondent, dispirited, ill-advised, ill-starred, melancholy, unsuitable **11** crestfallen, injudicious, mischievous, unfortunate **12** disconsolate, infelicitous **13** inappropriate **14** down in the dumps

unharmed
04 safe **05** sound, whole **06** intact, unhurt **09** undamaged, uninjured, unscathed, untouched

unhealthy
03 ill **04** sick, weak **05** crook, frail, pasty **06** ailing, feeble, infirm, morbid, poorly, sickly, unwell **07** harmful, invalid, noxious, unsound **08** diseased, epinosic **09** dangerous, injurious, unnatural **10** indisposed, insalutary, insanitary, unhygienic, unsanitary **11** debilitated, detrimental, unwholesome **12** insalubrious

unheard-of
03 new **06** unsung **07** obscure, unknown, unusual **08** shocking **09** offensive **10** outrageous, unfamiliar, unheralded **11** exceptional, undreamed-of, unthinkable **12** preposterous, unacceptable, unbelievable, undiscovered, unimaginable **13** extraordinary, inconceivable, unprecedented

unheeded
07 ignored, unnoted **08** unminded, untented **09** disobeyed, forgotten, neglected, unnoticed **10** overlooked, unobserved, unremarked **11** disregarded

unhelpful
04 rude **06** rustic, touchy **07** awkward, boorish, cubbish, loutish, prickly, stroppy **08** stubborn **09** irritable, obstinate **10** unpleasant **11** disobliging, obstructive, troublesome **12** bloody-minded **13** oversensitive, unco-operative **15** unaccommodating

unheralded
06 unsung **08** surprise **09** unnoticed **10** unexpected, unforeseen **11** unannounced **12** unadvertised, unproclaimed, unpublicized, unrecognized

unhesitating
05 ready **06** prompt **07** instant **08** implicit **09** automatic, confident, immediate **10** unwavering **11** spontaneous, unfaltering **12** wholehearted **13** instantaneous, unquestioning

unhinge
05 craze, upset **06** madden **07** confuse, derange, unnerve **08** disorder, distract, drive mad, unsettle **09** unbalance

unhinged
03 mad **04** nuts **05** barmy, crazy, loony, loopy, nutty, potty **06** insane **07** berserk, bonkers, frantic, lunatic **08** confused, demented, deranged **09** delirious, disturbed, unsettled **10** disordered, distraught, irrational, out to lunch, unbalanced **11** not all there **12** round the bend **13** off your rocker, of unsound mind, out of your mind, round the twist **15** non compos mentis

unholy
◊ *anagram indicator*
04 evil **06** sinful, wicked **07** corrupt, godless, immoral, impious, ungodly **08** depraved, dreadful, shocking, terrible **09** unearthly, unnatural **10** horrendous, iniquitous, outrageous **11** blasphemous, irreligious **12** unreasonable **14** unconscionable

unhook
04 free, undo **05** loose, untie **06** loosen **07** release **08** unfasten

unhoped-for
10 incredible, surprising, unexpected, unforeseen **11** undreamed-of, unlooked-for **12** unbelievable, unimaginable **13** unanticipated

unhurried
04 calm, easy, slow **06** sedate **07** relaxed **08** laid-back **09** easy-going, leisurely **10** deliberate

unhurt
02 OK **04** okay, safe **05** sound, whole **06** intact **08** all right, unharmed **09** uninjured, unscathed, untouched **12** whole-skinned

unhygienic
04 foul **05** dirty **06** filthy, impure **07** dirtied, noisome, noxious, unclean **08** feculent, infected, infested, polluted **09** unhealthy **10** insanitary **11** unhealthful, unsanitized **12** contaminated, insalubrious **13** disease-ridden

unidentified
06 secret **07** obscure, strange, unknown, unnamed **08** nameless, unmarked **09** anonymous, incognito **10** mysterious, unfamiliar **12** unclassified, unrecognized

unification
05 union **06** enosis, fusion, merger **07** uniting **08** alliance **09** coalition **10** federation **11** coalescence, combination, integration **12** amalgamation **13** confederation, incorporation

uniform
01 U **03** rig **04** even, flat, garb, like, same, sole, suit **05** alike, dress, equal, habit, level, robes **06** livery, outfit, smooth, stable, steady **07** costume, equable, regalia, regular, similar **08** constant, insignia, of a piece, unbroken **09** identical, unvarying **10** consistent, invariable, monotonous, throughout, unchanging **11** homogeneous, regimentals, undeviating

uniformity
06 tedium **08** drabness, dullness, evenness, flatness, monotony, sameness **09** constancy **10** regularity, similarity, similitude **11** homogeneity **12** homomorphism **13** invariability

unify
03 mix **04** bind, fuse, join, weld **05** blend, merge, unite **07** combine **08** coalesce **09** integrate **10** amalgamate **11** consolidate **12** come together **13** bring together

unifying
06 unific **07** henotic, uniting **11** combinatory, esemplastic, reconciling **13** consolidative

unimaginable
07 amazing **08** unlikely **09** fantastic, unheard-of **10** far-fetched, impossible, incredible, outlandish, staggering **11** astonishing, implausible, undreamed-of, unthinkable **12** mind-boggling, preposterous, unbelievable, unconvincing **13** extraordinary, inconceivable

unimaginative
03 dry **04** dull, tame **05** banal, samey, stale, usual **06** barren, boring **07** mundane, prosaic, routine **08** lifeless, ordinary **09** hackneyed **10** flat-footed, pedestrian, unexciting, uninspired, unoriginal **11** predictable **12** matter-of-fact

unimpaired
05 sound **06** entire, intact **08** integral
• **remain unimpaired**
04 last

unimpeachable
07 perfect **08** reliable, spotless **09** blameless, faultless **10** dependable, immaculate, impeccable **11** unblemished **12** unassailable **14** irreproachable, unquestionable **15** unchallengeable

unimpeded
04 free, open **05** clear **08** all-round **09** unblocked, unchecked

unimportant
04 idle **05** light, minor, petty **06** slight **07** trivial **08** marginal, nugatory, peddling, trifling **09** minuscule, no big deal, secondary, small-time, worthless **10** immaterial, incidental, irrelevant, negligible, peripheral **11** down-the-line, Mickey Mouse **12** inconsequent **13** insignificant, insubstantial, no great shakes **14** inconsiderable **15** inconsequential, of no consequence

unimpressive
04 dull **06** common **07** average **08** mediocre, ordinary **10** unexciting, unimposing **11** commonplace, indifferent **12** unremarkable **13** unexceptional, uninteresting, unspectacular **15** undistinguished

uninhabited
04 lone **05** empty **06** desert, lonely, vacant **08** deserted, desolate, wasteful **09** abandoned, unpeopled, unsettled **10** unoccupied **11** unpopulated

uninhibited
04 free, open **05** frank **06** candid, rave-up **07** natural, relaxed **08** informal **09** abandoned, liberated, outspoken **10** unreserved **11** spontaneous **12** uncontrolled, unrestrained, unrestricted **13** unconstrained **15** unself-conscious

uninspired
04 dull **05** samey, stale, stock, trite **06** boring **07** humdrum, pompier, prosaic **08** ordinary **10** flat-footed, pedestrian, unexciting, unoriginal **11** commonplace, indifferent, uninspiring **13** unexceptional, unimaginative, uninteresting **15** undistinguished

uninspiring
03 dry **04** dull, flat, tame **05** ho-hum, samey, stale, trite **06** boring, dreary, jejune, tiring **07** humdrum, insipid, prosaic, routine, tedious **08** tiresome, unvaried **10** long-winded, monotonous, uneventful, unexciting **11** commonplace, repetitious, stultifying **13** institutional, unimaginative, uninteresting **14** soul-destroying

unintelligent
04 dull, dumb, slow **05** dense, silly, thick **06** obtuse, stupid **07** fatuous, foolish, witless **08** gormless **09** brainless **10** half-witted, unthinking **11** empty-headed, unreasoning

unintelligible
07 complex, garbled, jumbled, muddled, obscure **08** involved, puzzling **09** illegible, scrambled **10** incoherent, mysterious, unreadable **11** complicated, double Dutch **12** impenetrable, inarticulate, unfathomable **14** indecipherable

unintentional
8 careless **09** unplanned, unwilling, unwitting **10** accidental, fortuitous, unintended **11** inadvertent, involuntary, unconscious **2** uncalculated **14** unpremeditated

uninterested
5 blasé, bored **07** distant **08** listless **9** apathetic, impassive, incurious **0** uninvolved **11** indifferent, nococurante, unconcerned **2** unresponsive **14** not giving a damn, not giving a hoot, not giving a toss, unenthusiastic

uninteresting
3 dry **04** drab, dull, flat, tame **5** samey, stale **06** boring, dreary **7** humdrum, prosaic, tedious **8** tiresome **09** incurious, wearisome **0** monotonous, pedestrian, uneventful, unexciting **11** indifferent, uninspiring **12** unimpressive

uninterrupted
6 steady **07** endless, non-stop **8** constant, peaceful, straight, unbroken, unending **09** ceaseless, continual, continued, incessant, sustained, unceasing **10** continuous **1** undisturbed, unremitting

uninvited
7 unasked **08** unbidden, unsought, unwanted **09** unwelcome **1** unsolicited

uninviting
9 offensive, repellent, repulsive, unsavoury **10** forbidding, off-putting, unpleasant **11** distasteful, unappealing, undesirable, unwelcoming **2** disagreeable, unappetizing, unattractive

uninvolved
4 free **06** dégagé **09** fancy-free, footloose, unengaged **10** unattached, unhampered, unhindered **1** independent, uncommitted **12** untrammelled

union
1 U **04** club, yoke **05** blend, close, unity **06** accord, cement, fusion, league, merger **07** harmony, joining, mixture, uniting, wedding, wedlock **8** alliance, juncture, marriage, nuptials, spousage **09** agreement, coalition, espousals, matrimony, synthesis, unanimity **10** consortium, couplement, federation, trade union, Zollverein **11** association, cementation, coadunation, coalescence, combination, concurrence, confederacy, conjugation, conjunction, unification **12** amalgamation **13** confederation, consolidation **14** conglutination

See also **rugby**

2 AU, CU, EU
3 AUT, CDU, CGT, CWU, EIS, EMU, FBU, GMB, ITU, NFU, NUJ, NUM,
NUS, NUT, RFU, RMT
04 BIFU, CCCP, TGWU, UEFA, USSR, ZANU, ZAPU
05 BECTU, T and G
06 Amicus, Soviet, UNISON
07 African
08 European

unionist
01 U **02** UU

unique
03 one **04** lone, only, sole **05** alone **06** one-off, single **07** unusual **08** peerless, singular, solitary **09** matchless, nonpareil, unmatched **10** inimitable, one and only, one of a kind, pre-eminent, sui generis, unequalled, unrivalled **11** idiographic **12** incomparable, unparalleled **13** unprecedented

uniquely
04 only **06** singly, solely **08** by itself, markedly **09** specially **10** inimitably, peculiarly, peerlessly, remarkably, singularly **11** in its own way, matchlessly **12** incomparably **13** distinctively

unison
05 unity **06** accord **07** concert, concord, harmony **09** agreement, unanimity **11** co-operation
● **in unison**
08 in chorus **09** in harmony **10** homophonic **11** in agreement **13** at the same time, in co-operation **14** simultaneously **15** at the same moment

unit
03 ace, one **04** item, part **05** corps, force, piece, squad, whole **06** entity, module, patrol, system **07** brigade, element, portion, section, segment **08** assembly **09** component, task force **10** detachment, individual **11** constituent

See also **measurement**; **military**; **measurement of pressure** *under* **pressure**; **unit of weight** *under* **weight**

unite
03 fay, lap, tie, wad, wed **04** ally, band, fuse, join, knit, knot, link, lock, meng, ming, pool, weld **05** blend, clasp, close, joint, marry, menge, merge, twist, unify **06** cement, cleave, couple, embody, imbody, splice **07** accrete, combine, conjoin, connect, consort **08** coalesce, copulate, federate **09** associate, coadunate, conjugate, co-operate, synoecize **10** amalgamate, close ranks, join forces **11** confederate, consolidate, incorporate **12** concorporate, conglutinate, pull together **15** consubstantiate, make common cause

united
01 U **03** one **04** ment **05** meint, meynt **06** agreed, allied, menged, minged, pooled **07** unified **08** combined, conjoint, in accord **09** concerted, conjoined, corporate, unanimous **10** affiliated, collective, like-minded **11** amalgamated, conjunctive, co-operative, in agreement **12** incorporated **13** concorporated

United Arab Emirates
03 ARE, UAE

United Kingdom
02 UK

See also **prime minister**

03 Ely
04 Bath, York
05 Derby, Leeds, Newry, Ripon, Truro, Wells
06 Armagh, Bangor, Dundee, Durham, Exeter, London, Oxford
07 Belfast, Bristol, Cardiff, Chester, Glasgow, Lincoln, Lisburn, Newport, Norwich, Preston, Salford, Swansea
08 Aberdeen, Bradford, Carlisle, Coventry, Hereford, Kingston, Plymouth, St Albans, St David's, Stirling
09 Cambridge, Edinburgh, Inverness, Lancaster, Leicester, Lichfield, Liverpool, Newcastle, Salisbury, Sheffield, Wakefield, Worcester
10 Birmingham, Canterbury, Chichester, Gloucester, Manchester, Nottingham, Portsmouth, Sunderland, Winchester
11 Londonderry, Southampton, Westminster
12 Brighton
13 Wolverhampton

04 Fens, Tyne
06 Big Ben, Exmoor, Mersey, Severn, Thames
07 Avebury, Glencoe, Needles, Snowdon
08 Balmoral, Bass Rock, Ben Nevis, Dartmoor, Land's End, Loch Ness
09 Cape Wrath, Chilterns, Cotswolds, Helvellyn, London Eye, New Forest, Offa's Dyke, Royal Mile, Snowdonia, Tay Bridge
10 Beachy Head, Cader Idris, Holy Island, Ironbridge, Kew Gardens, Loch Lomond, Lough Earne, Lough Neagh, Stonehenge, The Gherkin, Windermere
11 Arthur's Seat, Canary Wharf, Forth Bridge, Hever Castle, Isle of Wight, John O'Groats, Leeds Castle, Lizard Point, Menai Bridge, Old Man of Hoy, Scafell Pike, York Minster
12 Antonine Wall, Brighton Pier, Castle Howard, Cheddar Gorge, Forest of Dean, Hadrian's Wall, Hampton Court, Humber Bridge, Lake District, Peak District, Seven Sisters, Severn Bridge
13 Arundel Castle, Blue John Caves, Brecon Beacons, Bridge of Sighs, Hatfield House, Liver Building,

Norfolk Broads, Robin Hood's Bay, Royal Pavilion, Tower of London, Warwick Castle, Windsor Castle

14 Blackpool Tower, Blenheim Palace, Giant's Causeway, Holyrood Palace, Inverary Castle, Isle of Anglesey, Sherwood Forest, Stirling Castle, Wells Cathedral

15 Angel of the North, Bodleian Library, Caledonian Canal, Cerne Abbas Giant, Chatsworth House, Edinburgh Castle, Flamborough Head, Grand Union Canal, Post Office Tower, St Michael's Mount

See also **town**

United Nations

United Nations members:

04 Chad, Cuba, Fiji, Iran, Iraq, Laos, Mali, Oman, Peru, Togo

05 Benin, Chile, China, Congo, Egypt, Gabon, Ghana, Haiti, India, Italy, Japan, Kenya, Libya, Malta, Nauru, Nepal, Niger, Palau, Qatar, Samoa, Spain, Sudan, Syria, Tonga, Yemen

06 Angola, Belize, Bhutan, Brazil, Canada, Cyprus, France, Greece, Guinea, Guyana, Israel, Jordan, Kuwait, Latvia, Malawi, Mexico, Monaco, Norway, Panama, Poland, Russia, Rwanda, Sweden, Turkey, Tuvalu, Uganda, Zambia

07 Albania, Algeria, Andorra, Armenia, Austria, Bahrain, Belarus, Belgium, Bolivia, Burundi, Comoros, Croatia, Denmark, Ecuador, Eritrea, Estonia, Finland, Georgia, Germany, Grenada, Hungary, Iceland, Ireland, Jamaica, Lebanon, Lesotho, Liberia, Moldova, Morocco, Myanmar, Namibia, Nigeria, Romania, Senegal, Somalia, St Lucia, Tunisia, Ukraine, Uruguay, Vanuatu, Vietnam

08 Barbados, Botswana, Bulgaria, Cambodia, Cameroon, Colombia, Djibouti, Dominica, Ethiopia, Honduras, Kiribati, Malaysia, Maldives, Mongolia, Pakistan, Paraguay, Portugal, Slovakia, Slovenia, Sri Lanka, Suriname, Tanzania, Thailand, Zimbabwe

09 Argentina, Australia, Cape Verde, Costa Rica, East Timor, Guatemala, Indonesia, Lithuania, Macedonia, Mauritius, Nicaragua, San Marino, Singapore, Swaziland, The Gambia, Venezuela

10 Azerbaijan, Bangladesh, El Salvador, Kazakhstan, Kyrgyzstan, Luxembourg, Madagascar, Mauritania, Mozambique, New Zealand, North Korea, Seychelles, South Korea, Tajikistan, The Bahamas, Uzbekistan

11 Afghanistan, Burkina Faso, Côte d'Ivoire, Philippines, Saudi Arabia, Sierra Leone, South Africa, Switzerland

12 Guinea-Bissau, Turkmenistan

13 Czech Republic, Liechtenstein, United Kingdom

14 Papua New Guinea, Solomon Islands, The Netherlands

15 Marshall Islands, St Kitts and Nevis

16 Brunei Darussalam, Equatorial Guinea

17 Antigua and Barbuda, Dominican Republic, Trinidad and Tobago

18 São Tomé and Príncipe, United Arab Emirates

19 Serbia and Montenegro

20 Bosnia and Herzegovina

21 United States of America

22 Central African Republic

25 St Vincent and the Grenadines

27 Federated States of Micronesia

28 Democratic Republic of the Congo

United States of America

02 US **03** USA

See also **president**

US cities include:

02 LA, NY

03 NYC

05 Boise, Dover, Miami, Salem

06 Albany, Austin, Boston, Dallas, Denver, Helena, Juneau, Pierre, St Paul, Topeka

07 Atlanta, Augusta, Chicago, Concord, Detroit, Houston, Jackson, Lansing, Lincoln, Madison, Memphis, New York, Olympia, Phoenix, Raleigh, Santa Fe, Seattle, Trenton

08 Bismarck, Cheyenne, Columbia, Columbus, Hartford, Honolulu, Las Vegas, Portland, Richmond, San Diego

09 Annapolis, Baltimore, Des Moines, Frankfort, Milwaukee, Nashville

10 Baton Rouge, Carson City, Charleston, Harrisburg, Little Rock, Los Angeles, Montgomery, Montpelier, New Orleans, Pittsburgh, Providence, Sacramento, San Antonio, Washington

11 New York City, Springfield, Tallahassee

12 Indianapolis, Oklahoma City, Philadelphia, Salt Lake City, San Francisco, Washington DC

13 Jefferson City

US landmarks include:

05 Yukon

07 Capitol, Rockies

08 Colorado, Lake Erie, Missouri, Mt Elbert, Mt Vernon, Pentagon, Yosemite

09 Graceland, Hollywood, Hoover Dam, Lake Huron, Milwaukee, Mt Rainier

10 Everglades, Great Lakes, Joshua Tree, Mt McKinley, Mt Rushmore, Mt St Helens, Sears Tower, White House

11 Grand Canyon, Lake Ontario, Liberty Bell, Mississippi, Pearl Harbor, Space Needle, Yellowstone

12 Appalachians, Carnegie Hall, Lake Michigan, Lake Superior, Niagara Falls

13 Great Salt Lake

14 Brooklyn Bridge, Monument Valley, Rocky Mountains

15 Lincoln Memorial, Statue of Liberty

See also **president**; **state**

unity

03 one **05** peace, union **06** accord **07** concert, concord, harmony, oneness **09** agreement, consensus, integrity, unanimity, wholeness **10** solidarity **11** unification **12** amalgamation, togetherness

universal

01 U **03** all **05** total, whole **06** common, cosmic, entire, global, varsal, versal **07** general **08** all-round, catholic, ecumenic **09** unlimited, worldwide **10** ecumenical, ubiquitous **11** omnipresent **12** all-embracing, all-inclusive **13** comprehensive **14** across-the-board

universality

08 entirety, totality, ubiquity **10** commonness, generality, prevalence **11** catholicity **12** completeness, predominance **14** generalization

universally

06 always **09** uniformly **10** everywhere, invariably **12** ubiquitously

universe

03 all **05** world **06** cosmos, nature **07** heavens **08** creation, everyone **09** firmament, macrocosm **14** the sum of things

university

01 U **03** uni **07** academy, college, varsity **08** academia **09** institute **11** polytechnic

Ivy League universities:

04 Yale

05 Brown

07 Cornell, Harvard

08 Columbia

09 Dartmouth, Princeton

12 Pennsylvania

Seven Sisters colleges:

05 Smith

06 Vassar

07 Barnard

08 Bryn Mawr

09 Radcliffe, Wellesley

12 Mount Holyoke

Universities include:

02 OU

03 LSE, MIT, UCL

04 City, Open, UCLA

05 Aston, Keele, UMIST

06 Brunel, Durham, Leiden, Napier, Oxford

07 Caltech, Warwick

08 Ann Arbor, Berkeley, Sorbonne, Stanford

09 Cambridge, St Andrews

10 De Montfort, Heriot-Watt

12 Robert Gordon, Thames Valley
13 Royal Holloway
14 Trinity College
15 California State, Imperial College, Juilliard School

See also **college**

● **at university**
02 up

unjust
05 wrong **06** biased, unfair, wanton
07 partial, unequal **08** one-sided, partisan, wrongful, wrongous
10 iniquitous, prejudiced, undeserved
11 inequitable, unjustified, unrighteous
12 unreasonable

unjustifiable
05 undue **09** excessive
10 immoderate, outrageous
11 inexcusable, uncalled-for, unwarranted **12** indefensible, unacceptable, unforgivable, unpardonable, unreasonable

unkempt
◇ *anagram indicator*
05 messy, ratty, rough, tousy, touzy, towsy, towzy **06** frowsy, frowzy, scungy, shabby, sloppy, untidy
07 rumpled, scraggy, scruffy, squalid, tousled **08** scraggly, slobbish, slovenly, uncombed **09** mal soigné, shambolic, ungroomed **10** disordered, scraggling, unpolished **11** dishevelled

unkind
04 mean **05** cruel, harsh, nasty, snide
06 bitchy, shabby **07** callous, inhuman, vicious **08** inhumane, pitiless, ruthless, spiteful, uncaring, unkindly
09 heartless, malicious, unfeeling
10 malevolent, unfriendly **11** cold-hearted, disobliging, hard-hearted, insensitive, thoughtless
12 uncharitable **13** inconsiderate, unsympathetic

unkindness
05 spite **07** cruelty **08** meanness
09 harshness **10** ill-feeling, inhumanity
11 callousness **13** insensitivity, maliciousness **14** unfriendliness
15 hard-heartedness

unknowable
06 untold **08** infinite **12** incalculable, unfathomable, unimaginable
13 unconditioned, unforeseeable, unpredictable **15** unascertainable

unknowing
06 chance, unwist **07** unaware
08 ignorant **09** unplanned, unwitting
10 accidental, unintended, unthinking
11 inadvertent, involuntary, unconscious **12** unsuspecting
13 unintentional

unknown
01 X, Y, Z **03** ign, new **04** dark **05** alien
06 hidden, occult, secret, unkent, untold **07** foreign, obscure, strange, unnamed **08** nameless, unkenned
09 anonymous, concealed, incognito, uncharted, unheard-of **10** mysterious,

substance x, undivulged, unexplored, unfamiliar, unrevealed **11** undisclosed
12 undiscovered, unidentified

unlawful
06 banned **07** illegal, illicit, vicious
08 criminal, non licet, outlawed, wrongful **09** forbidden **10** prohibited, unlicensed **12** illegitimate, unauthorized, unsanctioned
13 against the law

unleash
04 free **05** let go, loose, untie
07 deliver, release, set free, unloose
08 let loose, untether

unless
03 but **04** less, nisi, save **06** except
07 without

unlettered
08 ignorant, untaught **09** unlearned, untutored **10** illiterate, uneducated, unlessoned, unschooled

unlike
06 unlich **07** difform, diverse, opposed, unequal, various **08** distinct, opposite **09** as against, different, disparate, divergent, unconform, unrelated **10** contrasted, dissimilar, ill-matched **11** as opposed to
12 dissimilar to, incompatible, in contrast to **13** different from, heterogeneous **14** out of character

unlikely
◇ *anagram indicator*
04 last, slim **05** faint, fishy, small
06 farfet, remote, slight, unlike
07 distant, dubious, outside, suspect
08 doubtful **09** fictional **10** far-fetched, improbable, improbably, incredible, suspicious, unexpected, unsuitable
11 implausible, unpromising
12 questionable, unbelievable, unconvincing, unimaginable
13 inconceivable **14** inconsiderable
15 unprepossessing

unlimited
◇ *ends deletion indicator*
04 full, vast **05** great, total **06** untold
07 endless, immense **08** absolute, complete, infinite **09** boundless, countless, extensive, limitless, shoreless, unbounded, unchecked, unimpeded, universal **10** indefinite, unconfined, unhampered
11 confineless, illimitable, unqualified
12 immeasurable, incalculable, uncontrolled, unrestricted
13 inexhaustible, unconditional, unconstrained **15** all-encompassing

unload
04 dump **05** empty, strip **06** remove, unlade, unpack, unship, vacate
07 disload, offload, relieve
08 unburden, uncharge **09** disburden, discharge, unfraught **10** disburthen

unlock
04 free, open, undo **05** unbar
06 unbolt **07** release, unlatch
08 disclose, unfasten

unlooked-for
05 lucky **06** chance **08** surprise
09 fortunate **10** fortuitous, surprising, unexpected, unforeseen, unhoped-for
11 undreamed-of, unpredicted, unthought-of **13** unanticipated

unloved
05 hated **06** dumped **07** spurned
08 detested, disliked, forsaken, loveless, rejected, unwanted
09 neglected, unpopular **10** uncared-for

unluckily
04 alas **05** sadly **08** sad to say
09 unhappily, worse luck **11** regrettably, sad to relate **13** I am sorry to say, unfortunately

unlucky
04 poor **05** black, stiff, tough
06 cursed, donsie, doomed, jinxed, wicked **07** adverse, hapless, infaust, ominous, unhappy **08** ill-fated, luckless, sinister, unchancy, untoward, wretched **09** ill-omened, mischancy, miserable, wanchancy **10** calamitous, disastrous, ill-starred, left-handed, unpleasant, wanchancie **11** star-crossed, unfortunate, unpromising
12 catastrophic, inauspicious, unfavourable, unpropitious, unsuccessful **14** down on your luck
15 disadvantageous

unmanageable
04 wild **05** bulky **06** gallus, unruly, wanton **07** awkward, gallows, ropable, unhandy, unweldy **08** ropeable, unwieldy **09** difficult, wieldless
10 cumbersome, disorderly, refractary, refractory, weeldlesse **11** intractable, troublesome **12** incommodious, inconvenient, obstreperous, recalcitrant, ungovernable
13 impracticable **14** uncontrollable

unmanly
03 wet **04** base, soft, weak **05** cissy, weedy, wussy **06** craven, effete, feeble, yellow **07** wimpish **08** cowardly, womanish **09** weak-kneed
10 effeminate, namby-pamby **11** lily-livered **13** dishonourable **14** chicken-hearted

unmannerly
04 rude **07** boorish, ill-bred, low-bred, uncivil, uncouth **08** impolite
09 graceless, misleared **10** ungracious
11 bad-mannered, ill-mannered
12 badly-behaved, discourteous
13 disrespectful

unmarried
04 free, lone **05** unwed **06** maiden, single **08** celibate, divorced
09 available, on your own, separated
10 unattached **11** partnerless

unmask
04 bare, show **06** detect, expose, reveal, show up, unveil **07** uncloak, uncover, unvisor **08** disclose, discover, unvizard

unmatched
03 odd **04** orra **06** unique **07** supreme **08** peerless **09** matchless, nonpareil, paramount **10** consummate, unequalled, unexampled, unfellowed, unrivalled **11** unparagoned, unsurpassed **12** incomparable, unparalleled **13** beyond compare

unmentionable
05 taboo **08** immodest, indecent, shameful, shocking **09** forbidden **10** abominable, scandalous, unpleasant **11** disgraceful, unspeakable, unutterable **12** embarrassing

unmerciful
04 hard **05** cruel **06** brutal **07** callous **08** pitiless, ruthless, sadistic, uncaring **09** heartless, merciless, spareless, unfeeling, unsparing **10** implacable, relentless **11** remorseless, unrelenting

unmethodical
06 random **07** muddled **08** confused **09** desultory, haphazard, illogical, irregular **10** disorderly **11** unorganized **12** unsystematic **13** unco-ordinated

unmindful
03 lax **04** deaf **05** blind, slack **06** remiss **07** unaware **08** careless, heedless **09** forgetful, negligent, oblivious, unheeding **10** neglectful, regardless **11** inattentive, indifferent, unconscious

unmistakable
04 sure **05** clear, frank, plain **06** patent **07** blatant, certain, decided, evident, glaring, obvious **08** clear-cut, definite, distinct, explicit, manifest, positive, striking, univocal **10** pronounced, undeniable **11** conspicuous, indubitable, unambiguous, unequivocal, well-defined **12** indisputable **14** beyond question, unquestionable

unmistakably
06 surely **07** clearly, plainly **08** proclaim **09** blatantly, certainly, evidently, obviously **10** definitely, distinctly, manifestly, undeniably **11** doubtlessly, indubitably **12** indisputably, without doubt **13** conspicuously, unambiguously, unequivocally **14** unquestionably **15** without question

unmitigated
04 grim, pure, rank **05** harsh, sheer, utter **06** arrant **07** intense, perfect **08** absolute, complete, outright, thorough, unabated, unbroken **09** downright, out-and-out **10** consummate, persistent, relentless, unmodified, unredeemed, unrelieved **11** unqualified, unrelenting, unremitting **12** unalleviated, undiminished **13** thoroughgoing

unmixed
03 net, raw **04** mere, neat, nett, pure **07** sincere **09** unallayed

12 unadulterate, uncompounded **13** unadulterated

unmoved
04 calm, cold, firm **06** steady **07** adamant, dry-eyed **08** resolute, resolved, unshaken **09** impassive, unbending, unchanged, unfeeling, unstirred, untouched **10** determined, inflexible, unaffected, unwavering **11** indifferent, unconcerned, undeviating, unimpressed **12** unresponsive **13** dispassionate

unnamed
04 anon **05** house **09** anonymous

unnatural
◊ *anagram indicator*
03 odd **05** false, queer, stiff **06** farfet, forced, formal, staged, unholy, wooden **07** bizarre, feigned, fustian, heinous, inhuman, pompous, stilted, strange, uncanny, unusual **08** abnormal, absonant, affected, freakish, kindless, laboured, peculiar, strained, uncommon, unkindly **09** anomalous, contrived, insincere, irregular, monstrous, perverted **10** artificial, disnatured, far-fetched, forcedness, monstruous **11** constrained, stiff-necked **12** cataphysical, supernatural **13** against nature, extraordinary, self-conscious, unspontaneous

unnaturally
◊ *anagram indicator*
05 oddly **08** unkindly **09** strangely, unusually **10** abnormally, peculiarly, uncommonly **11** irregularly **15** extraordinarily

unnecessarily
10 needlessly **11** excessively **12** immoderately **13** superfluously

unnecessary
06 wasted **08** needless, unneeded, unwanted **09** excessive, redundant **10** expendable, gratuitous, unrequired **11** dispensable, inessential, superfluous, uncalled-for **12** non-essential, tautological

unnerve
05 alarm, daunt, scare, shake, unman, upset, worry **06** deject, dismay, put out, rattle, weaken **07** fluster, perturb, shake up **08** confound, disquiet, frighten, unsettle **10** demoralize, disconcert, discourage, dishearten, intimidate

unnoticed
06 unseen **07** ignored **08** unheeded **09** neglected **10** overlooked, unobserved, unremarked **11** disregarded **12** undiscovered, unrecognized

unobstructed
04 fair, open **05** plain

unobtrusive
05 quiet **06** humble, low-key, modest **07** subdued **08** retiring **09** underhand **10** restrained, unassuming **11** unassertive **12** self-effacing,

unaggressive, unnoticeable **13** inconspicuous, unpretentious **14** unostentatious

unobtrusively
06 humbly **07** on the QT, quietly **08** modestly **10** on the quiet **15** inconspicuously, surreptitiously, unpretentiously

unoccupied
04 free, idle, room, void **05** empty, waste **06** otiose, vacant **07** jobless **08** deserted, forsaken, inactive, workless **09** at liberty, désoeuvré **10** disengaged, unemployed **11** uninhabited, unpopulated

unofficial
04 curb, kerb **05** black **06** fringe **07** illegal, private **08** informal, personal **10** undeclared, unratified **11** alternative, unconfirmed **12** confidential, off-the-record, unauthorized **15** unauthenticated

unoriginal
05 stale, trite **06** copied **07** cribbed, derived, slavish **09** hackneyed, ready-made **10** derivative, second-hand, uninspired **11** predictable **12** cliché-ridden **13** unimaginative

unorthodox
◊ *anagram indicator*
03 new **04** cult, zany **05** fresh, novel **06** fringe, way-out **07** unusual **08** abnormal, creative **09** eccentric, heterodox, irregular, left-field **10** innovative, off the wall **11** alternative **13** nonconformist **14** unconventional

unpaid
03 due **04** free **05** owing **06** unfeed **07** overdue, payable, pending, pro bono, unwaged **08** honorary **09** remaining, unsettled, voluntary **10** unsalaried **11** outstanding, uncollected **14** pro bono publico, unremunerative

unpalatable
05 nasty **06** bitter **07** insipid **08** inedible **09** offensive, repellent, repugnant, uneatable, unsavoury **10** disgusting, unpleasant **11** distasteful **12** disagreeable, unappetizing, unattractive

unparalleled
04 rare **06** unique **07** supreme **08** peerless **09** matchless, unmatched **10** unequalled, unrivalled **11** exceptional, superlative, unsurpassed **12** incomparable, without equal **13** beyond compare, unprecedented

unpardonable
08 shameful, shocking **10** deplorable, outrageous, scandalous **11** disgraceful, inexcusable **12** indefensible, irremissible, unforgivable **13** reprehensible, unjustifiable **14** unconscionable

unperturbed
04 calm, cool **06** placid, poised,

unpleasant

serene **08** composed, tranquil
09 collected, impassive, unexcited,
unruffled, unworried **10** untroubled
11 undisturbed, unflappable,
unflinching, unflustered **13** self-
possessed

unpleasant
03 bad **04** foul, grim, mean, rude, sour
05 awful, crook, nasty, surly **06** filthy,
mingin', stinky, ungain, unkind
07 drastic, hostile, minging, noisome
08 impolite **09** offensive, repugnant,
repulsive, traumatic **10** aggressive,
disgusting, ill-natured, unfriendly
11 bad-tempered, distasteful,
quarrelsome, troublesome,
undesirable, unpalatable
12 disagreeable, discourteous,
unappetizing, unattractive
13 objectionable

unpleasantness
04 fuss **05** upset **06** bother, furore
07 scandal, trouble **08** bad blood
09 annoyance, esclandre, nastiness
10 bad feeling, ill-feeling
13 embarrassment

unpolished
04 bare, rude **05** crude, rough
06 coarse, vulgar **07** sketchy, uncouth,
unfiled, unkempt **08** agrestic, home-
bred, unpolite, unworked
09 unrefined **10** provincial, uncultured,
unfinished **11** uncivilized, unfashioned
12 uncultivated **13** rough and ready,
wild and woolly **15** unsophisticated

unpopular
05 hated **07** avoided, ignored,
shunned, unloved **08** detested,
disliked, rejected, unwanted
09 neglected, unwelcome
10 friendless **11** undesirable
12 unattractive **13** unfashionable,
unsought-after

unprecedented
03 new **07** unheard, unknown, unusual
08 abnormal, freakish, original,
uncommon **09** unheard-of
10 remarkable, unequalled,
unexampled, unrivalled **11** exceptional
12 unparalleled **13** extraordinary,
revolutionary

unpredictable
◇ *anagram indicator*
06 chance, fickle, random, slippy
07 erratic **08** slippery, unstable,
variable, volatile **09** mercurial
10 capricious, changeable, inconstant,
unexpected, unreliable **12** incalculable
13 unforeseeable

unprejudiced
04 fair, just **08** balanced, detached,
unbiased **09** impartial, objective
10 even-handed, fair-minded, open-
minded, uncoloured **11** enlightened,
non-partisan, unpossessed
12 cosmopolitan **13** dispassionate

unpremeditated
07 offhand **09** extempore, impromptu,
impulsive, unplanned **10** fortuitous,

off-the-cuff, unprepared
11 spontaneous, unmeditated,
unrehearsed **13** unintentional **15** spur-
of-the-moment

unprepared
03 raw **05** ad-lib, crude **07** napping,
unready **09** half-baked, surprised,
unplanned, unwilling **10** flat-footed,
improvised, incomplete, off-the-cuff,
unfinished, unpurvaide, unpurveyed
11 ill-equipped, spontaneous,
unrehearsed **12** unsuspecting **14** on
the wrong foot

unprepossessing
04 ugly **05** plain **06** homely
08 ordinary, unlikely, unlovely
10 forbidding, unexciting, unpleasing
11 indifferent, unappealing
12 unattractive, unremarkable
13 unexceptional, uninteresting
15 undistinguished

unpretentious
05 plain **06** homely, honest, humble,
modest, simple **07** natural **08** discreet,
ordinary **10** penny-plain, unaffected,
unassuming **11** unobtrusive
14 unostentatious **15** straightforward

unprincipled
07 corrupt, crooked, devious, immoral
09 deceitful, dishonest, reprobate,
underhand, unethical **10** profligate
12 uninstructed, unscrupulous
13 discreditable, dishonourable
14 unprofessional

unproductive
03 dry, shy **04** arid, dead, idle, lean,
poor, vain, yeld, yell **05** blank, waste
06 barren, futile, otiose **07** sterile,
useless **09** fruitless, infertile, worthless
10 unfruitful **11** ineffective,
unrewarding **12** unprofitable
13 inefficacious **14** unremunerative

unprofessional
03 lax **06** casual, sloppy **08** improper,
inexpert, unseemly **09** negligent,
unethical, unskilled, untrained
10 amateurish, indecorous
11 incompetent, inefficient
12 inadmissible, unacceptable,
unprincipled, unscrupulous
13 inexperienced

unprofitable
04 lean **08** bootless

unpromising
06 gloomy **07** adverse, ominous
08 doubtful, unlikely **10** depressing
11 dispiriting **12** discouraging,
inauspicious, unfavourable,
unpropitious

unprotected
04 open, soft **05** naked **06** liable
07 exposed, unarmed **08** helpless
09 uncovered, unguarded
10 unattended, undefended,
unshielded, vulnerable **11** defenceless,
unfortified, unsheltered

unprovable
12 unverifiable **14** indemonstrable,

indeterminable, undemonstrable
15 unascertainable

unqualified
05 inapt, round, total, unfit, utter
07 amateur, perfect, plenary
08 absolute, complete, outright,
positive, thorough **09** downright,
incapable, out-and-out, unallayed,
untrained **10** consummate, ineligible,
unlicensed, unprepared, unreserved,
unsuitable **11** categorical, ill-equipped,
incompetent, unequivocal,
unmitigated **12** unrestricted,
wholehearted **13** inexperienced,
unconditional

unquestionable
04 sure **05** clear **06** patent **07** certain,
obvious **08** absolute, definite, flawless,
manifest **09** faultless **10** conclusive,
undeniable **11** indubitable, irrefutable,
self-evident, unequivocal
12 indisputable, unchallenged,
unmistakable **13** incontestable
14 beyond question

unquestionably
06 firmly **07** clearly **08** directly
09 certainly **10** definitely, distinctly,
explicitly, manifestly, positively
11 indubitably, irrefutably
12 unmistakably **13** unambiguously,
unequivocally

unquestioning
08 implicit **11** unqualified
12 questionless, unhesitating,
wholehearted **13** unconditional

unravel
◇ *anagram indicator*
04 fray, free, undo **05** solve **06** evolve,
unknit, unknot, unwind **07** clear up,
explain, resolve, sort out, work out
08 separate, untangle **09** extricate,
figure out, interpret, penetrate, puzzle
out **11** disentangle **13** straighten out

unreadable
07 complex, garbled, jumbled,
muddled, obscure **08** involved,
puzzling **09** illegible, scrambled
10 incoherent, mysterious
11 complicated, double Dutch
12 impenetrable, inarticulate,
unfathomable **14** indecipherable,
unintelligible

unreal
04 fake, faux, mock, sham **05** false,
phony **06** aerial, ersatz, hollow, made-
up, phoney, shadow, untrue
07 amazing, bizarre, phantom, pretend
08 aeriform, fanciful, illusive, illusory,
mythical, nebulous, notional
09 fairytale, fantastic, imaginary,
legendary, moonshiny, phantosme,
storybook, synthetic, visionary,
whimsical **10** artificial, chimerical,
fictitious, immaterial, incredible,
ungrounded **11** Disneyesque, make-
believe, non-existent **12** hypothetical,
unbelievable **13** insubstantial

unrealistic
08 quixotic, romantic, wild-eyed

10 idealistic, impossible, unworkable **11** impractical, theoretical **12** unreasonable **13** impracticable **14** over-optimistic

unreality
09 irreality, phoniness **10** hollowness, phoneyness **11** bizarreness, make-believe **12** fancifulness, illusoriness, nebulousness, non-existence **13** artificiality, imaginariness

unreasonable
03 mad, OTT **05** silly, steep, undue **06** absurd, biased, stupid, unfair, unjust **07** foolish, froward, obscene **08** a bit much, exacting, perverse **09** arbitrary, excessive, expensive, illogical, ludicrous, senseless **10** exorbitant, far-fetched, headstrong, immoderate, iniquitous, irrational, outrageous, over the top, scandalous **11** extravagant, nonsensical, opinionated, uncalled-for, unchristian, unjustified, unrealistic, unwarranted **12** extortionate, inconsistent, preposterous, unacceptable **13** unco-operative, unjustifiable

unreasoning
04 wild **05** brute, crazy, silly **06** absurd, unwise **07** brutish, foolish, invalid, unsound **09** arbitrary, beastlike, illogical, senseless **10** groundless, irrational, ridiculous **11** implausible, nonsensical **12** inconsistent, unreasonable **14** beside yourself

unrecognizable
07 altered, changed **09** disguised, incognito **10** unknowable **12** incognizable **14** unidentifiable

unrecognized
06 unseen **07** ignored **08** unheeded **09** neglected, unnoticed **10** overlooked, unobserved, unremarked **11** disregarded **12** undiscovered

unrefined
03 raw **05** blunt, crude, rough **06** coarse, earthy, rustic, vulgar **07** bestial **09** rough-hewn, untreated **10** uncultured, unfinished, unpolished, unpurified **11** unprocessed **12** uncultivated **15** unsophisticated

unregenerate
06 sinful, wicked **07** natural **08** hardened, obdurate, stubborn **09** abandoned, obstinate, shameless **10** impenitent, persistent, refractory, unreformed **11** intractable, unconverted, unrepentant **12** incorrigible, recalcitrant

unrelated
06 unlike **07** foreign **08** distinct, separate **09** different, disparate **10** dissimilar, extraneous, irrelevant **11** independent, off the point, unconnected **12** inconsequent, relationless, unassociated **14** beside the point

unrelenting
05 cruel, stern **06** steady **07** endless

08 constant, pitiless, ruthless, unabated, unbroken **09** ceaseless, continual, incessant, merciless, perpetual, unceasing, unsparing **10** continuous, implacable, inexorable, relentless, unmerciful **11** remorseless, unforgiving, unremitting **12** intransigent **14** uncompromising

unreliable
◇ *anagram indicator*
04 iffy **05** dodgy, false, trick **06** fickle, shonky **07** unsound **08** doubtful, fallible, in-and-out, mistaken, slippery, unstable **09** deceptive, erroneous, sieve-like, uncertain **10** fly-by-night, inaccurate **11** implausible **12** disreputable, questionable, unconvincing, undependable **13** irresponsible, temperamental, untrustworthy

unremitting
08 constant, tireless, unabated, unbroken **09** assiduous, ceaseless, continual, continued, incessant, intensive, perpetual, unceasing **10** continuous, relentless **11** irremissive, remorseless, unrelenting **13** indefatigable

unrepentant
07 callous **08** hardened, obdurate **09** confirmed, shameless, unabashed, unashamed **10** impenitent **12** incorrigible, unapologetic, unregenerate

unrequited
07 ignored, snubbed, spurned **08** rejected **09** discarded, neglected **10** unanswered **11** not returned **12** unrecognized **14** unacknowledged, unreciprocated

unreserved
04 free, full, open **05** frank, total **06** candid, direct, entire **08** absolute, complete, explicit, outgoing, unbooked **09** extrovert, outspoken, talkative, unlimited **10** forthright **11** uninhibited, unqualified, whole-footed **12** heart-to-heart, unhesitating, unrestrained, unrestricted, wholehearted **13** communicative, demonstrative, unconditional

unreservedly
03 out **05** fully **07** totally, utterly **08** entirely, outright **09** out-and-out **10** absolutely, completely **14** unhesitatingly, wholeheartedly **15** unconditionally

unresisting
04 meek **06** docile **07** passive **08** obedient **09** unsisting **10** submissive

unresolved
04 moot **05** vague, vexed **07** pending **08** doubtful, unsolved **09** undecided, unsettled **10** indefinite, irresolute, unanswered, up in the air **12** undetermined **13** problematical

unresponsive
04 cool **05** aloof **06** frigid **07** unmoved **08** echoless **09** apathetic, withdrawn **10** unaffected **11** indifferent **12** uninterested **13** unsympathetic

unrest
◇ *anagram indicator*
05 worry **06** unease **07** discord, protest, turmoil **08** disorder, disquiet **09** agitation, commotion, rebellion **10** discontent, dissension, uneasiness **11** disturbance **12** disaffection, perturbation, restlessness **15** dissatisfaction

unrestrained
◇ *anagram indicator*
04 free, wild **05** frank, loose **06** hearty, lavish, wanton **07** natural, rampant, unyoked **08** impotent **09** abandoned, libertine, unbounded, unbridled, unchecked **10** boisterous, immoderate, inordinate, unbuttoned, unfettered, unhindered, unlaboured, unreserved **11** extravagant, full-frontal, intemperate, uninhibited, unrepressed **12** uncontrolled **13** irrepressible, unconstrained, wild and woolly

unrestricted
◇ *anagram indicator*
04 free, open **05** clear **06** public **08** absolute, open door **09** chainless, unbounded, unimpeded, unlimited, unopposed **10** free-for-all, unhindered, unreserved **12** discretional, unobstructed **13** discretionary, unconditional

unripe
05 green **07** unready **08** immature **09** unripened **11** out of season, undeveloped

unrivalled
07 supreme **08** peerless **09** matchless, nonpareil, unmatched, untouched **10** inimitable, unequalled **11** superlative, unsurpassed **12** incomparable, unparalleled, without equal **13** beyond compare

unruffled
04 calm, cool, even **05** level **06** serene, smooth **08** composed, peaceful, tranquil **09** collected **10** untroubled **11** undisturbed, unperturbed **13** imperturbable

unruly
◇ *anagram indicator*
04 rag'd, wild **05** ragde, rowdy **06** stormy, wanton, wilful **07** lawless, riotous, rulesse, wayward **08** mutinous, ruleless, torn-down **09** camstairy, camsteary, turbulent **10** camsteerie, disorderly, disruptive, headstrong, rebellious, refractory, refractry **11** disobedient, intractable **12** obstreperous, recalcitrant, ungovernable, unmanageable **13** insubordinate, undisciplined **14** uncontrollable

unsafe
05 dicey, fishy, hairy, risky **06** chancy

unsaid

07 exposed, uncanny, unsound
08 high-risk, insecure, perilous, unstable 09 dangerous, hazardous, uncertain 10 precarious, unreliable, vulnerable 11 defenceless, treacherous

unsaid

08 unspoken, unstated, unvoiced
09 unuttered 10 undeclared
11 unexpressed, unmentioned
12 unpronounced

unsatisfactory

04 lame, poor, ropy, tame, weak
05 empty, lousy, rocky, ropey, wrong
06 faulty 08 inferior, mediocre
09 defective, deficient, imperfect, off-colour 10 inadequate, unsuitable
11 displeasing, frustrating
12 insufficient, unacceptable, unsatisfying 13 disappointing, dissatisfying

unsavoury

05 nasty 06 sordid 07 squalid
09 obnoxious, offensive, on the nose, repellent, repugnant, repulsive, revolting, sickening, tasteless
10 disgusting, nauseating, unpleasant
11 distasteful, undesirable, unpalatable
12 disagreeable, disreputable, unappetizing, unattractive
13 objectionable

unscathed

04 safe 05 sound, whole 06 intact, unhurt 08 unharmed 09 undamaged, uninjured, untouched 13 with whole skin

unscramble

◇ *anagram indicator*
06 decode 08 decipher

unscrupulous

07 corrupt, crooked, immoral
08 improper, ruthless 09 dishonest, shameless, unethical 10 Rottweiler, unscrupled, villainous 12 unprincipled
13 dishonourable 14 unconscionable

unseasonable

08 ill-timed, mistimed, untimely
10 malapropos, out of place, seasonable, unsuitable 11 inopportune
12 intempestive 13 inappropriate

unseasoned

05 green 08 unprimed 09 unmatured, untreated 10 unprepared, untempered

unseat

04 oust 05 throw 06 depose, remove, topple, unship 07 dismiss, unhorse
08 dethrone, dishorse, dismount, displace, unsaddle 09 discharge, overthrow

unseemly

◇ *anagram indicator*
05 undue 06 indign 07 uncivil
08 improper, uncomely, unhonest
09 unrefined 10 ill-looking, indecorous, indelicate, unbecoming, unhandsome, unsuitable
11 unbefitting, undignified
12 disreputable 13 discreditable, inappropriate

unseen

06 hidden, uneyed, veiled 07 cryptic, lurking, obscure 09 concealed, invisible, unnoticed 10 unbeholden, undetected, unobserved
11 unobtrusive 13 inexperienced

unselfish

04 kind 05 noble 07 liberal
08 generous, selfless 10 altruistic, charitable, open-handed, single-eyed
11 magnanimous, self-denying
12 humanitarian 13 disinterested, philanthropic 14 public-spirited, self-forgetting 15 self-sacrificing

unsentimental

05 tough 09 hard-faced, hardnosed, practical, pragmatic, realistic, unfeeling 10 hard-headed, iron-headed, unromantic 11 hard as nails, level-headed, unemotional

unserviceable

02 U/S

unsettle

◇ *anagram indicator*
04 faze 05 feese, feeze, phase, phese, shake, throw, unfix, upset 06 bother, pheese, pheeze, rattle, ruffle
07 agitate, confuse, disturb, fluster, perturb, trouble 09 discomfit, unbalance 10 discompose, disconcert
11 destabilize

unsettled

◇ *anagram indicator*
04 edgy, open 05 fazed, owing, shaky, tense, upset 06 futile, on edge, queasy, queazy, roving, shaken, uneasy, unpaid
07 aimless, anxious, fidgety, lawless, overdue, payable, vagrant 08 agitated, confused, deserted, desolate, doubtful, drifting, goalless, insecure, rambling, restless, troubled, unguided, unnerved, unstable, unsteady, vagabond, variable 09 abandoned, disturbed, flustered, in arrears, pointless, turbulent, uncertain, undecided, unpeopled, wandering
10 changeable, inconstant, irresolute, undirected, unoccupied, unresolved, up in the air 11 disoriented, outstanding, purposeless, to be decided, undiscussed, uninhabited, unmotivated, unpopulated
12 indetermined, in the balance, undetermined 13 directionless, unpredictable 14 in a state of flux

unshakable, unshakeable

04 firm, sure 05 fixed 06 stable
07 staunch 08 constant, resolute
09 immovable, steadfast 10 determined, unswerving, unwavering 11 well-founded 12 unassailable

unsightly

04 ugly 07 hideous 09 repugnant, repulsive, revolting 10 off-putting, unpleasant 11 carbuncular
12 disagreeable, unattractive
15 unprepossessing

unskilful

03 bad 05 inept 06 clumsy, gauche

07 awkward 08 bungling, fumbling, inexpert, unartful, untaught
09 maladroit, unskilled, untrained
10 amateurish, uneducated, unhandsome, untalented
11 incompetent, unpractised, unqualified 13 inexperienced
14 unprofessional

unskilled

04 rude 06 simple, ungain 07 unwitty
08 inexpert 09 unperfect, untrained
10 amateurish 11 incompetent, unpractised, unqualified
13 inexperienced 14 unprofessional

unsociable

04 cold, cool 05 aloof 06 chilly
07 distant, hostile 08 reserved, retiring, solitary, taciturn 09 reclusive, withdrawn 10 insociable, unfriendly
11 introverted, standoffish, uncongenial 12 inhospitable
13 unforthcoming, unneighbourly
15 uncommunicative, uncompanionable

unsoiled *see* unsullied

unsolicited

07 unasked 08 unsought, unwanted
09 sponte sua, uninvited, unwelcome, voluntary 10 gratuitous, unasked-for
11 spontaneous, uncalled-for, unrequested

unsophisticated

03 jay 04 naif 05 basic, crude, naive, plain 06 direct, native, simple
07 artless, genuine, natural, verdant
08 cornball, corn-pone, innocent
09 childlike, guileless, ingenuous, small-town, unrefined, unworldly
10 provincial, unaffected, uninvolved
11 rudimentary, undeveloped
13 inexperienced, unadulterated, uncomplicated, unpretentious
15 straightforward

unsound

◇ *anagram indicator*
03 ill 04 weak 05 false, frail, shaky, wonky 06 ailing, broken, faulty, flawed, hollow, rotten, unsafe, unwell, wobbly 07 damaged, injured, invalid, rickety 08 delicate, deranged, diseased, insecure, unhinged, unstable, unsteady 09 dangerous, defective, erroneous, illogical, unfounded, unhealthy, untenable
10 disordered, fallacious, ill-founded, unbalanced, unreliable
11 unwholesome

unsparing

04 hard 05 harsh, round, stern
06 lavish, severe 07 drastic, liberal, profuse 08 abundant, generous, rigorous, ruthless, slashing
09 bountiful, merciless, plenteous
10 implacable, munificent, open-handed, relentless, ungrudging, unmerciful, unstinting 11 unforgiving
14 uncompromising

unspeakable

05 awful 08 dreadful, horrible,

unspeakably

nameless, shocking, terrible
09 appalling, execrable, frightful, monstrous, nefandous 10 horrendous 11 unthinkable, unutterable 12 unbelievable, unimaginable 13 inconceivable, indescribable, inexpressible, unmentionable

unspeakably

07 awfully 08 terribly 11 appallingly, frightfully, unthinkably, unutterably 12 horrendously, unbelievably, unimaginably 13 inconceivably, indescribably, inexpressibly

unspecified

05 vague 07 obscure, unknown, unnamed 09 uncertain, undecided, undefined 10 indefinite, mysterious 12 undetermined, unidentified

unspectacular

04 dull 06 boring, common 07 average 08 mediocre, ordinary, plodding 10 unexciting 12 unimpressive, unremarkable 13 uninteresting

unspoilt

07 natural, perfect 08 pristine, unharmed 09 preserved, unchanged, undamaged, untouched 10 unaffected, unimpaired 11 unblemished 15 unsophisticated

unspoken

04 mute 05 tacit 06 silent, unsaid 07 assumed, implied 08 implicit, inferred, unstated, wordless 09 unuttered, voiceless 10 undeclared, understood 11 unexpressed

unstable

◇ *anagram indicator*
03 mad 04 nuts, weak 05 barmy, batty, crazy, daffy, dippy, dodgy, loony, loopy, moody, nutty, risky, shaky 06 fitful, infirm, insane, labile, mental, slippy, tickle, unsafe, wankle, wobbly 07 bananas, bonkers, brittle, bruckle, erratic, flighty, meshuga, rickety, unsound 08 crackers, deranged, insecure, instable, ricketty, shifting, slippery, ticklish, unhinged, unstayed, unsteady, variable, volatile, wavering 09 disturbed, mercurial, tottering, unsettled 10 capricious, changeable, inconstant, off balance, off the wall, out to lunch, precarious, unbalanced, unreliable 11 fluctuating, light-minded, off your head, unballasted, vacillating 12 inconsistent, round the bend 13 off your rocker, round the twist, unpredictable, untrustworthy 14 off your trolley, wrong in the head

unsteady

◇ *anagram indicator*
05 dotty, giddy, shaky, totty, warby 06 cranky, groggy, titupy, unsafe, wambly, wavery, wobbly 07 doddery, rickety, tittupy 08 insecure, skittish, unstable, variable, waverous 09 irregular, tottering, versatile 10 flickering, inconstant, precarious, unreliable 11 light-headed, treacherous, unballasted

● **be unsteady**

04 flit 05 waver 06 coggle, wobble 09 vacillate

unstinting

04 full 05 ample, large 06 lavish 07 liberal, profuse 08 abundant, generous, prodigal 09 abounding, bountiful, plentiful, unsparing 10 munificent, ungrudging

unstoppable

07 undying 08 unending 09 unceasing 10 inevitable 11 unavoidable, unrelenting, unremitting 13 without a let-up

unsubstantial

04 airy 07 shadowy 10 cloud-built

unsubstantiated

07 dubious 08 unproved, unproven 09 debatable 10 disputable, unattested, unverified 11 unconfirmed, unsupported 12 questionable 13 unestablished 14 uncorroborated

unsuccessful

04 lost, sour, vain 06 beaten, failed, futile, losing 07 bungled, fumbled, sterile, unlucky, useless 08 abortive, defeated, luckless, thwarted, washed-up 09 fruitless 10 frustrated, miscarried, trade-falne, unavailing 11 ineffective, ineffectual, trade-fallen, unfortunate 12 unproductive, unprofitable

unsuitable

05 amiss, inapt, inept, unapt, unfit 08 improper, unlikely, unseemly, unsorted, unsuited 09 unfitting 10 inapposite, ineligible, malapropos, out of place, unbecoming 11 incongruent, incongruous 12 incompatible, inconvenient, infelicitous, unacceptable 13 inappropriate

unsullied

04 pure 05 clean 06 intact 07 perfect 08 pristine, spotless, unsoiled 09 stainless, undefiled, unspoiled, unspotted, unstained, untainted, untouched 10 immaculate 11 unblackened, unblemished, uncorrupted, untarnished

unsung

07 obscure, unknown 08 unhailed 09 anonymous, forgotten, neglected, unpraised 10 overlooked, unhonoured 11 disregarded, unacclaimed 12 uncelebrated, unrecognized 14 unacknowledged

unsure

05 vague 07 dubious, unknown 08 doubtful, hesitant, insecure, wavering 09 dithering, sceptical, tentative, uncertain, undecided 10 ambivalent, indefinite, in two minds, irresolute, precarious, suspicious 11 uncommitted, unconvinced, unpersuaded 12 equivocating 13 untrustworthy

unsurpassed

07 supreme 08 unbeaten 09 matchless, unmatched 10 surpassing, unequalled, unexcelled, unrivalled 11 exceptional, superlative 12 incomparable, second-to-none, transcendent, unparalleled 13 state-of-the-art

unsurprising

08 expected, forecast, foreseen, hoped-for, promised 09 looked-for, predicted, wished-for 10 forseeable 11 anticipated, predictable

unsuspecting

05 naive 06 simple, unwary 07 unaware 08 gullible, innocent, off guard, trustful, trusting 09 credulous, ingenuous 11 unconscious 12 unsuspicious

unswerving

04 firm, sure, true 05 fixed 06 direct, steady 07 devoted, staunch 08 constant, resolute, untiring 09 dedicated, immovable, steadfast 10 unflagging, unwavering 11 undeviating, unfaltering 12 single-minded

unsympathetic

04 cold, hard 05 cruel, harsh, stony 06 unkind 07 callous, hostile, inhuman, unmoved 08 pitiless, soulless, uncaring 09 hard-faced, heartless, unfeeling, unpitying 11 hard as nails, hard-hearted, ill-disposed, indifferent, insensitive, unconcerned 12 antagonistic, unresponsive

unsystematic

06 random, sloppy, untidy 07 chaotic, jumbled, muddled 08 confused, slapdash 09 haphazard, illogical, irregular, shambolic, unplanned 10 disorderly 11 unorganized 12 disorganized, unmethodical, unstructured 13 unco-ordinated 14 indiscriminate

untamed

04 wild 05 feral 06 fierce, savage 07 haggard, salvage 08 unmanned 09 barbarous 10 unmellowed, untameable 14 undomesticated

untangle

04 undo 05 solve 07 resolve, unravel, work out 09 extricate 11 disentangle 13 straighten out

untarnished

04 pure 05 clean 06 bright, intact 07 glowing, shining 08 polished, pristine, spotless, unsoiled, unspoilt 09 burnished, stainless, unbraided, unspotted, unstained, unsullied 10 immaculate, impeccable 11 unblemished 13 unimpeachable

untenable

05 rocky, shaky 06 flawed 07 unsound 09 illogical, intenable 10 fallacious 11 inexcusable 12 indefensible, unreasonable 13 insupportable, unjustifiable, unsustainable 14 unmaintainable

unthinkable
06 absurd 08 shocking, unlikely
09 illogical, unheard-of 10 impossible,
improbable, incredible, outrageous,
staggering 11 implausible, incogitable
12 preposterous, unbelievable,
unimaginable, unreasonable
13 inconceivable

unthinking
04 rash, rude 06 unkind, vacant
08 careless, heedless, impolite, knee-
jerk, tactless 09 automatic, impulsive,
negligent, Pavlovian 10 incogitant,
indiscreet, mechanical 11 insensitive,
instinctive, involuntary, thoughtless,
unconscious 12 undiplomatic,
unrespective 13 inconsiderate

unthinkingly
06 rashly, rudely 08 stupidly
09 foolishly 10 carelessly, impolitely,
recklessly, tactlessly 11 unfeelingly
12 indiscreetly 13 inattentively,
insensitively, thoughtlessly
15 inconsiderately

untidily
07 dirtily, messily 08 sloppily
09 scruffily 10 disorderly, sluttishly
11 chaotically 12 topsy-turvily
13 shambolically 15 like a dog's
dinner

untidy
◇ anagram indicator
04 foul 05 dirty, messy, ratty, tatty
06 sloppy 07 chaotic, haywire,
jumbled, muddled, raunchy, rumpled,
scruffy, unkempt 08 slipshod, slovenly,
sluttish 09 cluttered, shambolic
10 bedraggled, disorderly, slatternly,
topsy-turvy 11 dishevelled
12 disorganized, unsystematic

untie
04 free, undo 05 loose, solve
06 loosen, unbind, unknit, unknot,
unwrap 07 release, resolve, unhitch,
untruss 08 unfasten

until
02 to 04 till, unto, up to 05 hasta, prior,
while 06 before, up till 07 prior to
08 as late as 11 earlier than, up to the
time

untimely
05 early 07 awkward 08 ill-timed,
immature, timeless 09 importune,
premature 10 malapropos, unsuitable
11 inopportune, prematurely,
unfortunate 12 inauspicious,
inconvenient, infelicitous,
intempestive, unseasonable,
unseasonably 13 inappropriate,
inopportunely

untiring
06 dogged, steady 07 devoted,
staunch 08 constant, resolute, tireless
09 dedicated, incessant, tenacious,
unceasing, unfailing 10 determined,
persistent, unflagging 11 persevering,
unfaltering, unremitting
13 indefatigable

untold
08 infinite 09 boundless, countless,
uncounted 10 unnumbered,
unreckoned 11 innumerable,
measureless, uncountable,
undreamed-of, unutterable
12 immeasurable, incalculable,
unimaginable 13 inconceivable,
indescribable, inexhaustible,
inexpressible

untouched
04 safe 06 intact, unhurt, virgin
08 pristine, unharmed 09 unaltered,
unchanged, undamaged, uninjured,
unscathed, unstirred 10 unaffected,
unimpaired, unrivalled 11 unimpressed

untoward
05 amiss 07 adverse, awkward,
froward, ominous, unlucky
08 annoying, contrary, ill-timed,
improper, unseemly, untimely,
worrying 09 unfitting, vexatious
10 disastrous, indecorous, irritating,
unbecoming, unexpected, unsuitable
11 inopportune, troublesome,
unfortunate 12 inauspicious,
inconvenient, unfavourable,
unpropitious 13 inappropriate

untrained
03 raw 06 unbred 07 amateur
08 inexpert, untaught 09 unskilled
10 uneducated, unschooled
11 incompetent, unpractised,
unqualified 13 inexperienced,
undisciplined 14 unprofessional

untried
03 new 05 novel 08 unproved,
untested 10 innovative, innovatory
11 exploratory 12 experimental
13 unestablished

untroubled
04 calm, cool 06 placid, serene,
steady 08 composed, peaceful,
tranquil 09 impassive, unexcited,
unruffled, unstirred, unworried
11 unconcerned, undisturbed,
unflappable, unflustered, unperturbed
14 inapprehensive

untrue
◇ anagram indicator
05 false, wrong 06 made-up, mythic
07 inexact, untruly 08 disloyal,
mistaken, mythical, two-faced
09 deceitful, deceptive, dishonest,
erroneous, incorrect, legendary,
trumped-up, two-timing
10 fabricated, fallacious, fraudulent,
inaccurate, misleading, perfidious,
unfaithful, unofficial, untruthful
11 inauthentic 12 untruthfully
13 untrustworthy

untrustworthy
05 false 06 fickle, sleeky, slippy,
unsure, untrue 08 disloyal, slippery,
two-faced, untrusty 09 deceitful,
dishonest, faithless 10 capricious, fly-
by-night, unfaithful, unreliable,
untruthful 11 duplicitous, treacherous
12 disreputable 13 dishonourable

untruth
03 fib, lie 04 crap, tale 05 false, lying,
porky, story 06 deceit 07 falsity,
fiction, perjury, whopper
09 falsehood, falseness, invention, tall
story 10 inveracity 11 fabrication,
made-up story 14 unfaithfulness,
untruthfulness

untruthful
05 false, lying 06 untrue 07 crooked
08 invented, two-faced 09 deceitful,
dishonest, erroneous, fictional,
insincere 10 fabricated, fallacious,
mendacious 11 unveracious
12 hypocritical

untutored
06 simple 07 artless 08 ignorant,
inexpert, unversed 09 unlearned,
unrefined, untrained 10 illiterate,
uneducated, unlessoned,
unschooled 11 unpractised
12 uninstructed 13 inexperienced
15 unsophisticated

untwine
06 uncoil, unwind 07 unravel, untwist
10 disentwine

untwist
05 ravel, unlay 06 detort, uncoil,
unwind 07 unravel, untwine

unused
03 new 04 idle 05 blank, clean, extra,
fresh, spare 06 maiden 07 surplus,
unusual 08 left over, pristine,
untapped, unwonted 09 available,
remaining, untouched
10 unemployed, unfamiliar
11 unexploited, unpractised
12 unaccustomed, unacquainted
13 inexperienced

unusual
◇ anagram indicator
03 odd 04 rare, unco 05 freak, kinky,
queer, weird 06 exotic, freaky, unwont
07 bizarre, curious, offbeat, special,
strange 08 abnormal, atypical,
freakish, peculiar, singular, uncommon,
unwonted 09 anomalous, different,
eccentric, irregular 10 phenomenal,
remarkable, surprising, unexpected,
unfamiliar, unorthodox 11 exceptional,
out of the way 12 unacquainted
13 extraordinary, unprecedented
14 unconventional
See also **strange**

unusually
◇ anagram indicator
04 very 05 oddly 08 devilish
09 bizarrely, curiously, extremely
10 especially, peculiarly, remarkably,
singularly 11 exceedingly
12 particularly, prodigiously,
tremendously 13 exceptionally
15 extraordinarily

unutterable
07 extreme 09 egregious, ineffable,
nefandous 11 unspeakable
12 overwhelming, unimaginable
13 indescribable, inexpressible

unvarnished
04 bare, pure **05** frank, naked, plain,
sheer, stark **06** candid, honest, simple
07 sincere **09** unadorned
11 undisguised **13** unembellished
15 straightforward

unveil
04 bare **06** betray, expose, reveal,
unmask **07** divulge, lay bare, lay open,
uncover **08** disclose, discover
09 make known **11** disenshroud
12 bring to light **13** take the lid off

unwanted
05 extra **06** otiose **07** outcast, surplus,
useless **08** rejected, unneeded
09 discarded, redundant, undesired,
uninvited, unwelcome **10** unrequired
11 superfluous, unnecessary,
unsolicited

unwarranted
05 wrong **06** unjust **10** gratuitous,
groundless, undeserved, unprovoked
11 inexcusable, uncalled-for,
unjustified, unnecessary
12 indefensible, unreasonable
13 unjustifiable

unwary
04 rash **05** hasty **08** careless, heedless,
off guard, reckless **09** imprudent,
unguarded **10** incautious, indiscreet,
unthinking **11** thoughtless

unwashed
04 dark, dull, foul, miry **05** black, dirty,
dusty, grimy, manky, messy, mucky,
muddy, slimy, sooty, yucky **06** chatty,
clarty, cloudy, cruddy, filthy, greasy,
grotty, grubby, grungy, scungy, shabby,
soiled **07** clouded, defiled, grufted,
scruffy, squalid, stained, sullied,
unclean **08** polluted, unsoaped
09 tarnished **10** flea-bitten, insanitary,
unhygienic
• the great unwashed
05 plebs **06** the mob **07** the herd
08 riff-raff, the crowd **09** the crowds,
the masses, the rabble **12** the hoi polloi
13 the lower class **14** the proletariat,
the rank and file **15** the common
people, the lower classes, the working
class

unwavering
06 steady, sturdy **07** staunch
08 resolute, unshaken, untiring
09 dedicated, rock-solid, steadfast,
tenacious **10** consistent, determined,
unflagging, unshakable, unswerving
11 down-the-line, undeviating,
unfaltering, unshakeable **12** single-
minded **13** unquestioning

unwelcome
08 excluded, rejected, unwanted,
worrying **09** uninvited, unpopular,
upsetting **10** unpleasant **11** distasteful,
undesirable, unpalatable
12 disagreeable, unacceptable

unwell
03 bad, ill **04** ropy, sick **05** badly, crook,
dicky, queer, ropey, rough, unfit, warby
06 ailing, groggy, poorly, sickly **07** run

down **09** in a bad way, off-colour,
unhealthy **10** indisposed, out of sorts
15 under the weather

unwholesome
03 bad, wan **04** evil, junk, pale
05 pasty **06** morbid, pallid, sickly,
wicked **07** anaemic, harmful, immoral,
noxious, tainted, unsound **08** epinosic
09 degrading, depraving, poisonous,
unhealthy **10** corrupting, insalutary,
insanitary, perverting, unhygienic
12 demoralizing, innutritious,
insalubrious

unwieldy
05 bulky, hefty **06** clumsy
07 awkward, hulking, massive, weighty
08 cumbrous, ungainly **09** ponderous
10 cumbersome **12** incommodious,
inconvenient, unmanageable

unwilling
04 loth, slow **05** loath **06** averse
07 opposed **08** backward, grudging,
hesitant, loathful **09** reluctant,
repugnant, resistant **10** indisposed
11 disinclined **13** unintentional **14** not
having any of, unenthusiastic

unwillingness
08 nolition, slowness **09** hesitancy,
objection **10** reluctance
12 backwardness, loathfulness
13 indisposition **14** disinclination

unwind
◇ *anagram indicator*
03 veg **04** undo **05** chill, relax **06** cool
it, unclew, uncoil, unreel, unroll,
unwrap, veg out **07** slacken, unravel,
unreave, untwist **08** calm down, chill
out, wind down **09** hang loose **10** take
it easy **11** disentangle **13** let yourself go,
put your feet up **14** take things easy
15 let your hair down

unwise
◇ *anagram indicator*
04 rash **05** silly **06** insane, stupid,
unredy **07** foolish, unready **08** reckless
09 foolhardy, ill-judged, impolitic,
imprudent, senseless **10** ill-advised,
indiscreet **11** improvident, inadvisable,
inexpedient, injudicious, thoughtless
12 short-sighted **13** ill-considered,
irresponsible

unwitting
06 chance **07** unaware **09** unknowing,
unplanned, unweeting **10** accidental,
unintended, unthinking **11** inadvertent,
involuntary, unconscious
12 unsuspecting **13** unintentional

unwonted
04 rare **07** strange, unusual
08 atypical, peculiar, singular,
uncommon **09** unheard-of
10 infrequent, unexpected, unfamiliar
11 exceptional, uncustomary
12 unaccustomed **13** extraordinary

unworldly
05 green, naive **08** gullible, innocent
09 ingenuous, spiritual, visionary
10 idealistic **11** impractical

12 metaphysical, otherworldly
13 inexperienced **14** transcendental
15 unsophisticated

unworried
08 composed, downbeat
09 collected, unabashed, unruffled
10 undismayed, untroubled
11 unperturbed

unworthy
04 base **06** indign, shabby **07** ignoble
08 improper, inferior, shameful,
unseemly, wanwordy **09** unfitting,
worthless **10** despicable, ineligible,
unbecoming, undeserved, unsuitable
11 disgraceful, incongruous,
unbefitting, undeserving
12 contemptible, disreputable
13 discreditable, dishonourable,
inappropriate **14** unprofessional

unwritten
04 oral **05** tacit **06** verbal **08** accepted,
implicit, unpenned **09** customary
10 recognized, understood,
unrecorded **11** traditional, word-of-
mouth **12** conventional

unwrought
03 raw **04** live, rude

unyielding
04 firm, grim, hard **05** rigid, solid, stern,
stiff, stout, tough **06** marble
07 adamant, granite, staunch
08 hardline, obdurate, resolute,
stubborn **09** immovable, inelastic,
iron-bound, obstinate, steadfast,
unbending **10** determined,
implacable, inexorable, inflexible,
relentless, rock-ribbed, unwavering
11 intractable, unrelenting
12 intransigent, pertinacious
14 uncompromising

unzip
04 free, open, undo **06** detach, loosen,
unhook, unpack, unwind **07** release
08 separate **10** decompress

up
◇ *reversal down indicator*

up-and-coming
05 eager **07** pushing **09** ambitious,
assertive, go-getting, promising
12 enterprising

up and down
◇ *palindrome indicator*

upbeat
04 rosy **06** bright, cheery **07** bullish,
buoyant, hopeful **08** cheerful, positive
09 promising **10** favourable,
heartening, optimistic **11** encouraging
14 forward-looking

upbraid
04 twit **05** chide, scold, storm
06 berate, rebuke, upbray **07** censure,
reproof, reprove, shake up
08 admonish, reproach **09** castigate,
criticize, go crook at, go crook on,
reprimand **10** exprobrate

upbringing
04 care **07** nurture, raising, rearing,

tending **08** breeding, teaching, training **09** education, parenting **10** bringing-up **11** cultivation, instruction

upcoming

04 near **05** close **06** at hand, coming **07** looming **08** imminent, in the air, on the way **09** impending **11** approaching, forthcoming, in the offing **12** on the horizon **13** about to happen, almost upon you **14** round the corner **15** fast approaching

update

05 amend, renew **06** revamp, revise **07** correct, upgrade **08** renovate **09** modernize

up-front

04 free, open **05** bluff, blunt, early, first, frank, plain **06** candid, direct, honest, sooner **07** advance, earlier, genuine, initial, primary, sincere **08** explicit, straight, truthful **09** downright, in advance, initially, outspoken **10** beforehand, forthright **11** hard-hitting, plain-spoken **12** introductory **15** straightforward

upgrade

05 raise **06** better, uphill, uprate **07** advance, elevate, enhance, improve, promote **09** modernize **10** ameliorate, make better

upheaval

05 chaos, upset **06** romage, uplift, upturn **07** rummage, shake-up, turmoil, upthrow **08** disorder, shake-out **09** confusion, overthrow **10** disruption, earthquake, revolution **11** disturbance

uphill

04 hard **05** tough **06** ascent, taxing, tiring **07** arduous, onerous, upgrade **09** ascending, difficult, gruelling, laborious, punishing, strenuous, wearisome **10** burdensome, exhausting

uphold

04 back, keep **06** defend, hold to **07** confirm, endorse, fortify, justify, promote, stand by, stand to, support, sustain, warrant **08** advocate, champion, maintain **09** vindicate **10** strengthen **11** countenance

upkeep

04 care, keep **06** outlay, repair **07** oncosts, running, support **08** expenses, overheads **10** sustenance **11** expenditure, maintenance, subsistence **12** conservation, preservation, running costs **14** operating costs

uplift

◇ *reversal down indicator*
04 draw, lift **05** boost, edify, elate, exalt, heave, hoist, raise **06** better, lift up, mark-up, refine **07** advance, collect, elevate, improve, inspire, raising, upgrade, upthrow **08** civilize, increase, upheaval **09** cultivate,

elevation, enlighten **10** ameliorate, betterment, enrichment, refinement **11** advancement, cultivation, edification, enhancement, improvement **13** enlightenment

upmarket

04 fine, high **05** prime, prize **06** choice, de luxe, select **07** quality, upscale **08** prestige, superior, top-notch **09** admirable, excellent, exclusive, expensive, first-rate, high-class, reputable, top-flight **10** first-class, respectful, unrivalled **11** exceptional, good-quality, prestigious **13** distinguished, par excellence

upper

03 top **04** high, over **06** higher, senior **07** eminent, exalted, greater, loftier, topmost **08** elevated, superior **09** important, uppermost

• **upper hand**
04 edge, sway **07** control, mastery **08** dominion, eminence, forehand **09** advantage, dominance, supremacy **10** ascendancy, domination **11** superiority

upper-class

01 U **04** posh **05** élite, noble **06** plummy, swanky **07** toffish **08** cutglass, high-born, well-born, well-bred **09** exclusive, high-class, patrician, top-drawer **11** blue-blooded **12** aristocratic

uppermost

03 top **04** main **05** chief, first, major **07** highest, leading, primary, supreme, topmost **08** dominant, foremost, greatest, loftiest **09** paramount, principal **10** pre-eminent **11** predominant

uppity

05 cocky **06** swanky **07** stuck-up **08** affected, arrogant, assuming, snobbish **09** bigheaded, bumptious, conceited **10** hoity-toity **11** impertinent, overweening, toffee-nosed **12** presumptuous, supercilious **13** self-important

upright

04 good, just **05** erect, moral, noble, sheer, steep, white **06** decent, honest, supine, worthy **07** ethical **08** straight, vertical, virtuous **09** elevation, reputable, righteous **10** high-minded, honourable, principled, upstanding **11** respectable, trustworthy, verticality **13** at right angles, incorruptible, perpendicular

• **set upright**
04 cock, rear **05** erect **10** straighten

uprising

◇ *reversal down indicator*
06 mutiny, putsch, revolt, rising **08** intifada **09** coup d'état, overthrow, rebellion **10** insurgence, revolution **12** insurrection

uproar

03 din **04** flaw, hell, riot **05** noise, raird, rammy, reird **06** bedlam, clamor,

dirdam, dirdum, émeute, fracas, furore, hubbub, mayhem, outcry, racket, randan, rumpus, tumult **07** clamour, garboil, ruction, turmoil, whoobub **08** brouhaha, disorder, hubbuboo **09** commotion, confusion, imbroglio **10** hullabaloo, rough music, turbulence **11** pandemonium **12** insurrection, katzenjammer, Pandaemonium **13** collieshangie

uproarious

04 loud, wild **05** noisy, rowdy **07** killing, riotous **08** confused **09** clamorous, deafening, hilarious **10** boisterous, hysterical, rip-roaring, rollicking, rowdy-dowdy **11** rib-tickling **12** unrestrained **13** side-splitting

uproot

04 weed **05** rip up **06** pull up, remove **07** destroy, root out, weed out, wipe out **08** displace, supplant **09** eradicate **11** averruncate

upset

◇ *anagram indicator*
◇ *reversal down indicator*
03 bug, eat, tip **04** coup, cowp, hurt, purl **05** het up, shake, shock, spill, worry **06** bother, chew up, choked, dismay, grieve, gutrot, gutted, jangle, malady, put out, ruffle, sadden, shaken, take on, tip out, topple, upcast **07** agitate, ailment, annoyed, anxious, break up, capsize, confuse, disrupt, disturb, fluster, grieved, illness, jealous, overset, perturb, reverse, shake up, shake-up, trouble, unhappy, unnerve, uptight, worried **08** agitated, bothered, confused, dismayed, disorder, disquiet, distress, in a state, irritate, overturn, renverse, sickness, surprise, troubled, unsteady, upheaval, worked up **09** aggrieved, agitation, complaint, disturbed, flustered, in a bad way, knock over, mess about, overthrow, perturbed, shattered, unsettled **10** discompose, disconcert, disruption, distressed, mess around, traumatize, tumble over **11** coup the cran, destabilize, discomposed, disorganize, disturbance **12** disconcerted, perturbation, play hell with **13** play havoc with **14** discomboberate, discombobulate

upsetting

◇ *anagram indicator*
08 alarming, assuming, worrying **09** conceited, overthrow, startling **10** disturbing, off-putting, perturbing, unsettling **11** distressing, frightening, overturning, presumption **13** disconcerting

upshot

03 aim, end **05** issue, loose, proof **06** finish, pay-off, result, sequel **07** outcome, success **10** conclusion, dénouement **11** consequence, culmination

upside down

◇ *reversal down indicator*
05 upset **06** turned **07** chaotic,

inverse, jumbled, muddled, up-ended
08 confused, inverted, messed up,
upturned **10** disordered, in disarray,
overturned, resupinate, topsy-turvy,
wrong way up **11** wrong side up
13 heels o'er gowdy, heels over head
• **turn upside down**
05 up-end, upset **06** invert, mess up
07 disturb, whemmle, whomble,
whommle, whummle **08** demolish
09 overthrow **10** make untidy, topsy-
turvy **11** disorganize **13** turn inside out

upstage
03 top **04** beat, best **05** dwarf, excel,
outdo **07** eclipse, outrank, surpass
08 outclass, outshine, outstrip,
superior **09** transcend **10** overshadow,
put to shame **11** stand-offish **13** put in
the shade

upstanding
04 firm, good, true **05** erect, moral
06 honest, strong **07** ethical, upright
08 virtuous **10** four-square,
honourable, principled **11** trustworthy
13 incorruptible

upstart
06 nobody **07** parvenu **08** jumped-
up, mushroom **09** arriviste **10** new-
fangled **12** nouveau riche **13** social
climber

upsurge
04 gain, hike, rise **05** boost, surge
06 growth, spread, step-up, upturn
07 advance, build-up **08** addition,
increase **09** expansion, extension,
increment, rocketing **10** escalation
11 development, enlargement,
heightening, mushrooming,
snowballing **12** augmentation,
skyrocketing **13** proliferation
15 intensification

uptight
04 edgy **05** angry, nervy, tense
06 hung-up, on edge, uneasy
07 anxious, prickly **09** irritated **11** strait-
laced **12** conventional

up-to-date
02 in **03** hip, new, now, rad **04** cool,
gear **06** groovy, latest, modern, recent,
trendy, with it **07** à la page, current
08 space-age, swinging **09** in fashion,
prevalent **10** all the rage, present-day
11 fashionable, in the groove
12 contemporary **13** state-of-the-art,
up to the minute
• **bring up-to-date**
09 modernize

upturn
◇ *anagram indicator*
◇ *reversal down indicator*
04 rise **05** boost **07** revival, upsurge,
upswing **08** increase, recovery,
upheaval **10** betterment
11 disturbance, improvement
12 amelioration

upward, upwards
◇ *reversal down indicator*
03 top **06** rising, uphill **07** going up
08 moving up **09** ascending

• **upwards of**
04 over **05** above **08** more than
09 exceeding **10** higher than, in excess
of

uranium
01 U

urban
04 city, town **05** civic **07** built-up,
oppidan **09** inner-city, municipal
12 metropolitan **13** megalopolitan

urbane
05 civil, suave **06** smooth **07** elegant,
refined **08** cultured, debonair,
mannerly, polished, well-bred
09 civilized, courteous **10** cultivated
12 well-mannered **13** sophisticated

urbanity
04 ease **05** charm, grace **06** polish
07 culture, suavity **08** civility,
courtesy, elegance **10** eutrapelia,
refinement, smoothness **11** cultivation,
worldliness **12** mannerliness
14 sophistication

urchin
03 elf, imp, kid **04** brat, waif **05** child,
gamin, rogue **06** rascal **07** mudlark
08 hedgehog, hurcheon, township
09 hunchback **10** ragamuffin
11 guttersnipe

urge
03 beg, hie, nag, yen **04** goad, hist,
itch, need, prod, push, spur, wish
05 chevy, chirp, chivy, drive, egg on,
fancy, force, impel, plead, press
06 advise, appeal, chivvy, compel,
desire, excite, exhort, hasten, incite,
induce, libido, threap, threep
07 beseech, counsel, enforce, entreat,
impetus, implore, impulse, incense,
longing, procure **08** advocate,
persuade, perswade, yearning
09 cacoethes, constrain, eagerness,
encourage, instigate, prompting,
recommend, stimulate **10** compulsion
11 inclination

• **urge on**
02 ca' **03** caa', egg, hie **04** edge, mush,
spur **05** whoop, yoick **06** compel,
giddap, giddup, halloa, halloo, hoicks,
whet on, yoicks **07** giddy-up
09 instigate **11** whet forward

urgency
04 need **05** haste, hurry, press
06 preace, prease, stress **07** gravity,
preasse **08** clamancy, exigency,
instance, instancy, pressure, priority
09 extremity, necessity **10** importance
11 importunity, seriousness
14 imperativeness

urgent
04 dire **05** acute, eager, grave, prior,
vital **07** crucial, earnest, exigent,
instant, serious **08** critical, emergent,
pressing, strident **09** emergency,
essential, immediate, important,
importune, insistent, necessary,
strenuous **10** compelling, imperative,
persistent, persuasive **11** top-priority

urinate
02 go **03** pee, wee, wet **04** leak, whiz
05 slash, stale, urine, whizz **06** pee-
pee, piddle, tiddle, tinkle, wee-wee,
widdle **07** relieve **09** make water,
micturate, pass water, take a leak
11 spend a penny **12** be taken short,
ease yourself **13** be caught short
15 relieve yourself

urn
04 olla **07** kitchen, ossuary, samovar
08 the Ashes **09** ballot box

Uruguay
01 U **03** ROU, Uru, URY

US
◇ *dialect word indicator*

usable
05 valid **07** current, working **08** fit to
use **09** available, practical
10 functional **11** exploitable,
operational, serviceable

usage
03 law, use, way **04** form, mode, rule
05 habit, idiom, style **06** custom,
method, usance **07** control, meaning,
practic, routine, running **08** handling,
parlance, practice **09** etiquette,
formalism, modernism, operation,
procedure, tradition, treatment
10 consuetude, convention,
employment, expression,
management, regulation
11 application, institution, phraseology,
terminology **12** way of writing **13** way
of speaking

use
◇ *anagram indicator*
02 do **03** end, ply, try, ure **04** call, good,
help, milk, need, work **05** abuse, apply,
avail, bleed, cause, enjoy, point, right,
spend, treat, usage, value, waste, wield,
worth **06** custom, demand, draw on,
employ, expend, follow, handle,
misuse, object, profit, resort **07** ability,
benefit, consume, exhaust, exploit,
observe, operate, purpose, service,
utilize **08** accustom, cash in on, deal
with, exercise, impose on, occasion,
practise, put to use, resort to
09 advantage, go through, habituate,
make use of, manoeuvre, necessity,
operation, privilege, regularly
10 employment, get through,
imposition, manipulate, permission,
usefulness **11** application, utilization
12 exploitation, manipulation,
mistreatment **13** bring into play **15** take
advantage of
• **used to**
06 wont to **07** given to, prone to
08 inured to **10** adjusted to, at home
with **11** practised in **12** accustomed to,
familiar with, habituated to, in the
habit of, no stranger to **14** acclimatized
to
• **use up**
◇ *reversal down indicator*
03 sap **04** burn, take **05** drain, spend,
waste **06** absorb, devour, finish,
peruse, work up **07** consume, deplete,

eat into, exhaust, fritter, tire out
08 squander **09** go through

used
◇ *anagram indicator*
04 wont, worn **05** usual **06** expert,
soiled **07** cast-off **08** dog-eared, pre-
owned **09** customary, nearly-new
10 hand-me-down, second-hand
11 experienced

useful
04 able **05** handy, nifty **06** expert
07 helpful, skilful, skilled **08** behovely,
fruitful, valuable **09** competent,
effective, practical, practised,
rewarding **10** all-purpose, beneficial,
convenient, functional, productive,
proficient, profitable, worthwhile
11 experienced, serviceable
12 advantageous **14** general-purpose

usefulness
03 use **04** good, help **05** avail, value,
worth **06** profit **07** benefit, fitness,
service, utility **08** efficacy
09 advantage **10** efficiency
11 convenience **12** practicality
13 functionality **15** serviceableness

useless
◇ *anagram indicator*
03 bad, dud **04** bung, idle, poor, ropy,
vain, void, weak **05** awful, kaput, lousy,
ropey **06** futile, grotty, no good
07 botched **08** bootless, frippery,
hopeless, pathetic, terrible, unusable
09 fruitless, half-assed, incapable,
pointless, to no avail, unhelpful,
worthless **10** broken-down, clapped-
out, effectless, unavailing, unworkable
11 impractical, incompetent,
ineffective, ineffectual, inefficient
12 unproductive, unprofitable
13 inefficacious **14** a load of garbage, a
load of rubbish, good-for-nothing

uselessness
08 futility, idleness **09** inutility
10 ineptitude **12** hopelessness,
incompetence **14** impracticality,
ineffectuality **15** ineffectiveness

usher
04 lead, show **05** guide, macer, pilot,
steer **06** direct, escort **07** chobdar,
conduct, marshal **08** Black Rod,
huissier **09** accompany, assistant,
attendant, introduce, usherette
10 doorkeeper
• **usher in**
06 herald, launch, ring in **07** precede
08 announce, initiate **09** introduce
10 inaugurate **13** pave the way for
14 mark the start of

usual
05 stock **06** common, normal, wonted
07 average, general, ordinar, regular,
routine, typical **08** accepted,
customed, everyday, expected,
familiar, habitual, ordinary, orthodox,
standard **09** customary
10 accustomed, exceptless,
recognized, regulation
11 commonplace, established,

predictable, traditional
12 conventional **13** unexceptional

usually
03 usu **06** mainly, mostly **07** as a rule,
chiefly **08** commonly, normally
09 generally, in the main, on average,
regularly, routinely, typically **10** by and
large, habitually, on the whole,
ordinarily **13** traditionally **14** for the
most part

usurer
05 gripe **07** Shylock **09** loan-shark
10 gombeen-man, note-shaver
11 money-lender **12** extortionist

usurp
04 take **05** annex, seize, steal
06 assume **08** arrogate, supplant, take
over **10** commandeer **11** appropriate

usury
06 excess **07** gombeen **08** interest
09 extortion **12** money-lending

Utah
02 UT

utensil
04 tool **06** device, gadget
09 apparatus, appliance, implement
10 instrument **11** contrivance

Kitchen utensils include:
03 bin, pan, wok
04 etna, fork
05 corer, ladle, mouli, sieve, tongs,
whisk
06 baster, bun tin, grater, juicer, karahi,
mincer, peeler, shears, sifter,
skewer, stoner, tureen, zester
07 blender, cake tin, cleaver, cocotte,
flan tin, grinder, loaf tin, milk pan,
ramekin, skillet, skimmer, spatula,
steamer, terrine
08 blini pan, breadbin, colander, crêpe
pan, cruet set, egg-timer, grill pan,
ham stand, herb mill, mandolin, pie
plate, saucepan, scissors, stockpot,
tea caddy, teaspoon, wine rack
09 bain marie, blowtorch, brochette,
can-opener, casserole, corkscrew,
dough hook, egg slicer, fish slice,
fondue set, frying pan, gravy boat,
mezzaluna, muffin tin, paella pan,
pie funnel, punch bowl, sharpener,
spice rack, tin-opener, toast rack
10 breadboard, breadknife, butter
dish, cook's knife, egg coddler, egg
poacher, fish kettle, jelly mould,
knife block, liquidizer, mixing bowl,
nutcracker, pasta ladle, pasta maker,
pepper mill, quiche dish, rice
cooker, rolling pin, slow cooker,
steak knife, storage jar, table knife,
tea infuser, waffle iron, wine cooler
11 baking sheet, boning knife, butter
knife, cheese board, cheese knife,
cooling rack, garlic press, melon
baller, omelette pan, oyster knife,
pastry board, pastry brush, potato
ricer, roasting pan, sandwich tin,
soufflé dish, tea strainer,
thermometer, wooden spoon
12 bottle opener, butter curler, carving

knife, cheese slicer, deep-fat fryer,
dessert spoon, egg separator, flour
dredger, icing syringe, measuring
jug, nutmeg grater, palette knife,
pastry cutter, potato masher,
pudding basin, pudding mould,
salad spinner, serving spoon,
yoghurt maker
13 butcher's block, chopping-board,
draining spoon, food processor,
ice-cream scoop, kitchen scales,
lemon squeezer, preserving pan
14 measuring spoon, pressure cooker,
straining spoon, vegetable knife
15 grapefruit knife, meat thermometer,
mortar and pestle

utilitarian
05 lowly **06** useful **08** sensible
09 effective, efficient, practical,
pragmatic **10** convenient, functional
11 down-to-earth, serviceable
13 unpretentious

utility
03 use, ute **04** good, help, tool **05** avail,
value, worth **06** profit **07** benefit,
fitness, service **08** efficacy
09 advantage **10** efficiency, usefulness
11 convenience **12** practicality
15 serviceableness

utilize
03 use **05** adapt **06** employ **07** exploit
08 put to use, resort to **09** make use of
13 turn to account **15** take advantage of

utmost
03 end, top **04** best, last, most, peak
05 final **07** extreme, hardest, highest,
maximum, supreme **08** farthest,
furthest, greatest, remotest, ultimate
09 outermost, paramount
11 furthermost

Utopia
04 Eden **05** bliss **06** heaven **07** Elysium
08 paradise **09** Shangri-la **12** Garden
of Eden **13** heaven on earth, seventh
heaven

Utopian
04 airy **05** dream, ideal **07** Elysian,
perfect, wishful **08** fanciful, illusory,
romantic **09** fantastic, imaginary,
visionary **10** chimerical, idealistic,
unworkable **11** impractical

utter
◇ *homophone indicator*
03 say **04** dead, emit, pass, pure, rank,
talk, tell, vend, vent **05** outer, plain,
sheer, sound, speak, stark, state, total,
voice **06** accent, arrant, entire,
goddam, put out, reveal, tongue
07 declaim, declare, deliver, divulge,
express, extreme, goddamn, perfect
08 absolute, announce, complete,
monotone, outright, positive,
proclaim, thorough, vocalize
09 downright, enunciate, goddamned,
out-and-out, pronounce, verbalize
10 articulate, consummate
11 categorical, come out with,
unmitigated, unqualified **12** put into
words **13** thoroughgoing

utterance
03 cry **04** talk, word **05** drawl, mouth, voice **06** remark, speech, tongue **07** comment, inanity, opinion **08** delivery, prophecy **09** outgiving, prolation, speech act, statement **10** expression, outpouring **11** declaration, enunciation **12** announcement, articulation, proclamation **13** pronouncement

utterly
03 dog **04** dead, pure, rank **05** fully, plumb, stark **06** goddam, wholly **07** goddamn, totally **08** entirely **09** downright, goddamned, perfectly, to the wide **10** absolutely, completely, thoroughly **13** categorically

U-turn
03 uey **07** wheelie **08** reversal **09** about-turn, backtrack, volte-face

Uzbekistan
02 UZ **03** UZB

V

V
03 vee **06** victor

vacancy
03 gap, job **04** hole, post, room
05 blank, place **07** inanity, leisure,
opening, vacuity **08** idleness, position
09 blankness, emptiness, situation
10 inactivity **11** opportunity

vacant
04 free, void **05** blank, empty, inane
06 absent, dreamy, unused
07 deadpan, vacuous **08** deserted,
gaumless, gormless, not in use, unfilled
09 abandoned, available
10 unoccupied, unthinking
11 inattentive, uninhabited **12** absent-
minded **14** expressionless

vacate
04 quit **05** annul, leave, waive
06 unload **07** abandon **08** evacuate,
withdraw

vacated
03 red **04** redd

vacation
03 vac **04** hols, long, rest, trip
05 break, leave **06** recess **07** holiday,
leisure, non-term, time off, vacance,
voiding **08** furlough, holidays
12 intermission

vaccinate
03 jab, jag **07** protect, syringe
08 immunize **09** inoculate

vaccination
03 jab **04** dose, shot **09** injection
11 inoculation **12** immunization

vacillate
◇ anagram indicator
04 halt, sway, wave **05** haver, waver
06 didder, dither, teeter, waffle, wobble
07 whiffle **08** hesitate **09** fluctuate,
oscillate, temporize **11** back and fill
12 shilly-shally, tergiversate **14** blow
hot and cold, go back and forth

vacillating
◇ anagram indicator
06 feeble **08** hesitant, waffling,
wavering **09** spineless, uncertain
10 indecisive, irresolute, unresolved,
willy-nilly **11** oscillating **15** shilly-
shallying

vacillation
◇ anagram indicator
06 waffle **08** wavering, wobbling
09 dithering, hesitancy **10** hesitation,
indecision **11** fluctuation, inconstancy
12 irresolution, shilly-shally

13 temporization **14** indecisiveness,
tergiversation **15** shilly-shallying

vacuity
04 void **05** space **06** apathy, hollow,
vacuum **07** inanity **08** idleness
09 blankness, emptiness
11 nothingness, vacuousness
12 listlessness

vacuous
04 idle, void **05** blank, empty, inane
06 stupid, vacant **07** foolish **08** unfilled
09 apathetic **11** empty-headed
14 expressionless

vacuum
03 gap, vac **04** void **05** chasm, space
06 Hoover®, lacuna **07** vacuity
09 emptiness **11** nothingness
• **vacuum flask**
05 dewar **07** Thermos®

vagabond
03 bum **04** hobo **05** caird, nomad,
piker, rogue, rover, scamp, tramp
06 beggar, dosser, rascal, roving
07 dingbat, floater, gadling, gangrel,
migrant, outcast, vagrant **08** clochard,
cursitor, palliard, runabout, runagate,
straggle, wanderer **09** itinerant,
landloper, sundowner, unsettled
10 down-and-out, land-louper
11 rinthereout, scattering, Weary
Willie **12** hallan-shaker **15** knight of the
road

vagary
04 whim **05** fancy, prank, quirk
06 fegary, humour, megrim, whimsy
07 caprice **08** crotchet, rambling
10 digression

vagrancy
08 nomadism **09** wandering
10 itinerancy, travelling
12 homelessness, rootlessness

vagrant
◇ anagram indicator
03 bum **04** hobo **05** caird, derro,
rogue, scamp, tramp **06** beggar,
dosser, rascal, roving, truant, vagrom,
walker **07** drifter, erratic, floater,
gangrel, nomadic, roaming, tinkler
08 cursitor, homeless, rootless,
straggle, stroller, vagabond, wanderer
09 itinerant, landloper, shiftless,
uncertain, unsettled, wandering
10 inconstant, land-louper, travelling
11 rinthereout, scattering **12** gang-
there-out, hallan-shaker, rolling stone
14 circumforanean
15 circumforaneous

vague
◇ anagram indicator
03 dim, lax **04** hazy **05** faint, foggy,
fuzzy, loose, misty, rough, woozy
06 unsure, wander, woolly **07** blurred,
evasive, general, inexact, obscure, of a
sort, of sorts, shadowy, sketchy,
unclear **08** nebulous, yonderly
09 ambiguous, amorphous, imprecise,
uncertain, undefined, unfocused **10** ill-
defined, indefinite, indistinct, out of
focus, unspecific **11** approximate,
generalized **12** undetermined, woolly-
minded **13** indeterminate
14 transcendental

vaguely
◇ anagram indicator
05 dimly **07** faintly **08** slightly, vacantly
09 distantly, inexactly, obscurely
11 imprecisely **14** absent-mindedly

vagueness
07 dimness **08** haziness **09** ambiguity,
faintness, fuzziness, looseness,
obscurity **10** generality, impression,
woolliness **11** imprecision, uncertainty
12 inexactitude

vain
04 idle **05** empty, proud, vogie, waste
06 devoid, futile, hollow, snooty
07 foppish, haughty, stuck-up, useless
08 abortive, affected, arrogant,
nugatory, vaporous, wasteful
09 bigheaded, conceited, coxcombic,
fruitless, pointless, worthless
10 coxcomical, groundless,
peacockish, sleeveless, swaggering,
unavailing **11** coxcombical, egotistical,
empty-headed, pretentious, swell-
headed, thoughtless **12** narcissistic,
ostentatious, unproductive,
unprofitable **13** high and mighty, self-
important, swollen-headed
• **in vain**
04 no go **06** vainly **07** in waste
09 fruitless, to no avail, uselessly **10** for
nothing **11** fruitlessly **13** ineffectually
14 unsuccessfully

vainglorious
04 vain **05** cocky, proud **06** swanky
07 crowing **08** arrogant, boastful,
bragging, puffed up **09** bigheaded,
conceited **10** swaggering **11** egotistical
13 swollen-headed **14** self-flattering

vainly
04 no go **07** for vain, to no end **09** to no
avail, uselessly **10** for nothing
11 fruitlessly **13** ineffectually
14 unsuccessfully

vale *see* **farewell; valley**

valediction
05 adieu, aloha 06 shalom, so long
07 goodbye, send-off 08 farewell
11 leave-taking 14 shalom aleichem

valedictory
04 last 05 final 07 parting 08 farewell
10 apopemptic

valet
03 man 06 Jeeves, lackey 07 lacquey
10 manservant 11 body servant
14 valet de chambre

valetudinarian
04 weak 05 frail 06 feeble, infirm,
sickly, weakly 07 invalid 08 delicate,
neurotic 13 hypochondriac

valiant
04 bold, prow 05 brave 06 heroic,
mighty, plucky, strong 07 gallant,
staunch 08 fearless, intrepid, valorous
09 audacious, dauntless
10 courageous, determined
11 indomitable, lion-hearted,
redoubtable 12 stout-hearted

valiantly
06 boldly 07 bravely 08 pluckily
09 gallantly, staunchly 10 fearlessly,
heroically, intrepidly 11 audaciously,
dauntlessly, indomitably
12 courageously 14 stout-heartedly

valid
04 good, just 05 legal, sound
06 cogent, lawful, proper, strong
07 binding, genuine, logical, weighty
08 bona fide, credible, licensed, official
09 authentic, available, effectual
10 accredited, applicable, approbated,
legitimate, meaningful, reasonable
11 justifiable, substantial, well-founded
12 acknowledged, well-grounded

validate
06 attest, ratify, verify 07 certify,
confirm, endorse 08 accredit, legalize
09 authorize, formalize 10 underwrite
11 corroborate 12 authenticate,
substantiate

validation
11 attestation, endorsement
12 confirmation, ratification
13 accreditation, authorization,
corroboration, formalization
14 authentication

validity
05 force, logic, point, vigor 06 vigour,
weight 07 cogency, grounds
08 legality, strength 09 authority,
soundness, substance 10 lawfulness,
legitimacy 14 justifiability

valley
03 cwm, den, ria 04 comb, dale, dean,
dell, dene, gill, glen, park, vale, wadi,
wady 05 combe, coomb, griff, grike,
gryke, gulch, heuch, heugh, slade,
Tempe, water 06 clough, coombe,
dingle, graben, griffe, hollow, strath,
Tophet, trough 07 Gehenna, wind gap
09 re-entrant

valorous
04 bold 05 brave 06 heroic, plucky
07 doughty, gallant, valiant 08 fearless,
intrepid, stalwart 09 dauntless
10 courageous, mettlesome 11 lion-
hearted 12 stout-hearted

valour
05 value, worth 06 mettle, spirit, virtue
07 bravery, courage, heroism, prowess
08 boldness, valiance, valiancy, war-
proof 09 fortitude, gallantry
11 doughtiness, intrepidity
12 fearlessness 15 lion-heartedness

valuable
04 dear 05 noble 06 costly, golden,
prized, useful, valued, worthy
07 helpful 08 fruitful, precious
09 cherished, deserving, expensive,
important, priceless, treasured
10 beneficial, invaluable, profitable,
worthwhile 12 advantageous,
constructive

valuation
05 price, prise, prize, stent, value
06 extent, survey 08 estimate
09 appraisal, expertise 10 assessment,
evaluation 11 stocktaking
12 appraisement

value
03 use 04 cost, gain, good, prys, rate
05 merit, price, prize, worth
06 admire, assess, esteem, ethics,
morals, profit, survey 07 benefit,
cherish, respect, revere, utility
08 appraise, efficacy, estimate,
evaluate, hold dear, treasure
09 advantage, standards
10 appreciate, excellence, importance,
principles, usefulness 11 put a price on
12 desirability, significance 15 set great
store by
• **of little value**
03 low 05 cheap 06 common
• **something of little value**
04 damn 06 button, trifle
10 boondoggle

valued
04 dear 05 loved 06 priced, prized
07 beloved 08 esteemed
09 cherished, respected, treasured
14 highly regarded

valueless
04 naff, poor 05 cheap 06 futile, paltry,
trashy 07 trivial, useless 08 nugatory,
rubbishy, trifling, unusable
09 pointless, worthless 10 unavailing
11 ineffectual, meaningless,
unimportant 13 insignificant

valve

04 ball, blow, gate, side, tube
05 bleed, choke, clack, diode, heart,
slide
06 escape, mitral, mixing, needle,
poppet, puppet, safety, triode,
ventil
07 exhaust, petcock, seacock, snifter,
tetrode

08 bicuspid, bistable, cylinder,
dynatron , snifting, throttle,
turncock
09 air-intake, butterfly, induction,
injection, magnetron, non-return,
semilunar, thyratron
10 Eustachian, thermionic

vamp
05 Circe, flirt, siren 06 trudge
07 charmer, Delilah, Lorelei, patch up
08 coquette 09 temptress
10 seductress 11 enchantress, femme
fatale

van
02 RV 03 ute 04 wing 05 lorry, truck,
wagon 06 camper, pick-up, waggon
07 caravan, minivan, trailer, utility
08 carriage, vanguard 09 advantage,
Dormobile®, meat wagon, motor
home, Winnebago® 10 baggage-car,
black Maria, freight-car, mobile home,
panel truck 11 patrol-wagon, railroad
car 12 pantechnicon, utility truck
14 utility vehicle

vanadium
01 V

vandal
03 yob 04 lout, thug 05 rough, rowdy,
tough 06 locust, mugger 07 hoodlum,
mobster, ravager, ruffian, wrecker
08 hooligan 09 bovver boy, desolater,
despoiler, ransacker 10 delinquent,
demolisher 11 annihilator

vandalize
◇ *anagram indicator*
04 ruin, sink 05 break, smash, trash,
wreck 06 ravage 07 destroy, shatter,
torpedo 08 demolish, write off
09 devastate

vane
03 fan, web 04 fane, wing 05 blade,
plume 07 dogvane 08 windsail
11 weathercock

vanguard
03 van 04 fore, lead 05 front
09 forefront, front line, spearhead
10 firing line

vanish
04 exit, fade 05 faint, ghost, leave
06 depart, die out, exhale 07 emanate,
evanish, fade out 08 disperse, dissolve,
evanesce, fade away, melt away, peter
out 09 disappear, evaporate, fizzle out
11 go up in smoke 12 end up in smoke
13 dematerialize

vanity
04 airs, pomp 05 folly, pride
07 conceit, egotism, foppery
08 futility, idleness, self-love, vainesse,
vainness 09 arrogance 10 narcissism,
pretension, snootiness, triviality
11 affectation, haughtiness,
ostentation, self-conceit
12 extravagance 13 bigheadedness,
conceitedness, dressing-table

vanquish
04 beat, drub, lick, rout 05 crush,
paste, quell, smash, thump 06 defeat,

hammer, humble, master, subdue, thrash **07** clobber, conquer, repress, trounce **08** confound, overcome **09** overpower, overwhelm, subjugate **10** annihilate **11** triumph over **15** make mincemeat of

Vanuatu
03 VUT

vapid
04 dull, flat, limp, weak **05** banal, bland, stale, trite **06** boring, flashy, jejune, watery **07** insipid, tedious, vacuous **08** lifeless, tiresome **10** colourless, wishy-washy **11** uninspiring

vaporous
04 fumy, vain **05** foggy, misty **06** flimsy, fumous, steamy **07** gaseous **08** fanciful, halitous **10** chimerical **13** insubstantial

vapour
03 fog **04** brag, damp, fume, haze, mist, reek, roke **05** boast, fumes, smoke, steam **06** breath **07** halitus, show off, swagger **09** evaporate **10** exhalation

variable
01 X, Y, Z **03** var **04** Mira **05** Algol **06** factor, fickle, fitful, uneven **07** moonish, mutable, Protean **08** flexible, shifting, unstable, unsteady, wavering **09** fluxional, irregular, parameter **10** changeable, fluxionary, inconstant **11** chameleonic, fluctuating, vacillating **13** pulsating star, temperamental, unpredictable

variance
04 odds **06** strife **07** discord, dispute, dissent **08** conflict, division **09** deviation, dichotomy, variation **10** alteration, difference, dissension, divergence **11** discrepancy **12** disagreement **13** inconsistency
• **at variance**
03 odd **06** at odds, at outs **07** arguing **08** clashing **09** differing, out of step **10** in conflict **11** conflicting, disagreeing, quarrelling **13** at loggerheads **14** in disagreement

variant
◇ *anagram indicator*
03 var **05** rogue **07** derived, deviant, variate, varying, version **08** modified **09** changeful, character, different, divergent, variation **11** alternative, diversified

variation
◇ *anagram indicator*
05 pulse **06** change **07** fluxion, novelty, variant, variety, varying **08** variance **09** departure, deviation, diversity, saltation **10** alteration, alternance, difference, inflection, modulation **11** discrepancy, fluctuation **12** orthogenesis

varied
◇ *anagram indicator*
05 dedal, mixed **06** daedal, motley,

sundry **07** diverse, various **08** assorted **09** different **10** accidented **11** wide-ranging **12** multifarious **13** heterogeneous, miscellaneous

variegated
◇ *anagram indicator*
04 pied **05** jaspe, paned, vairé **06** broken, motley, veined **07** brocked, brockit, clouded, dappled, marbled, mottled, various **08** distinct, speckled, streaked **09** checkered, chequered, dapple-bay, harlequin, proud-pied **10** poikilitic **12** varicoloured **13** multicoloured, parti-coloured, party-coloured

variety
◇ *anagram indicator*
03 var **04** brew, kind, make, sort, type **05** brand, breed, class, color, range **06** change, colour, medley, strain **07** mixture, species **08** category **09** diversity, pot-pourri, variation **10** assortment, collection, difference, miscellany, subspecies **11** versatility **12** multiplicity **13** dissimilarity **14** classification

various
◇ *anagram indicator*
04 many **05** mixed **06** motley, sundry, unlike, varied **07** diverse, several, varying **08** assorted, distinct **09** different, differing, disparate, uncertain **10** changeable, dissimilar, variegated **11** diversified **13** heterogeneous, miscellaneous

varnish
03 lac **04** coat, dope **05** glair, glaze, gloss, japan, resin **06** dammar, dammer, enamel, lacker, mastic, polish, veneer **07** coating, lacquer, mastich, shellac **08** kauri gum, shell-lac **10** lacquering, nail enamel, nail polish **12** French polish, Japan lacquer, vernis martin **13** etching ground

vary
◇ *anagram indicator*
04 hunt **05** alter, clash, range, spice, waver **06** change, depart, differ, modify **07** deviate, diverge, inflect, qualify, variate **08** be at odds, disagree, modulate **09** alternate, diversify, embellish, fluctuate, oscillate, permutate, transform **12** metamorphose

vase
03 jar, jug, urn **04** ewer **05** diota, flask **06** hydria, luster, lustre, vessel **07** amphora, Canopus, pitcher, potiche **09** moon flask **10** Canopic jar, Canopic urn, cornucopia

vassal
03 man **04** serf **05** liege, slave **06** client, thrall **07** bondman, servile, subject, villein **08** bondsman, liegeman, retainer **09** dependant **11** bondservant, subordinate

vassalage
03 fee **04** fief **07** bondage, prowess, serfdom, slavery **08** thraldom

09 servitude **10** dependence, subjection, villeinage **11** subjugation

vast
04 huge **05** great **07** immense, massive **08** colossal, cyclopic, enormous, far-flung, gigantic, infinite, sweeping **09** boundless, cyclopean, cyclopian, extensive, limitless, monstrous, unlimited **10** monumental, tremendous **11** appreciable, never-ending **12** considerable, immeasurable

vastly
06 hugely **07** greatly **09** immensely, massively **10** enormously, infinitely **11** boundlessly, extensively, limitlessly **12** immeasurably **13** without limits

vat
03 fat, tub **04** back, case, keir, kier, tank **05** cuvée, keeve, stand **06** barrel, girnel, tan-pit **07** wine fat **08** pressfat

Vatican City
01 V **03** VAT

vault
◇ *anagram indicator*
04 arch, dome, jump, leap, over, roof, span, tomb, vaut **05** bound, clear, crypt, embow, vaute, vawte **06** cavern, cellar, cupola, heaven, hurdle, spring **07** concave **08** leap-frog **09** cul-de-four, mausoleum, wagon roof **10** depository, repository, strongroom, undercroft, wine-cellar **11** safe-deposit **13** safety-deposit

vaunt
03 gab **04** brag, crow **05** boast, swank **06** flaunt, parade **07** exult in, show off, trumpet **08** vanguard **15** blow your own horn

veer
04 cast, tack, turn, wind **05** sheer, shift, slack, swing, wheel **06** broach, change, pay out, swerve, wester **07** box-haul, deviate, diverge, norther, peel off, souther, whiffle **09** come round

vegetable

Vegetables include:

03 oca, pea, yam
04 bean, cole, eddo, kale, leek, neep, okra, sium, spud, taro, wort
05 chard, choko, cress, gumbo, laver, mooli, onion, swede
06 bhindi, carrot, celery, chives, chocho, daikon, endive, fennel, garlic, lentil, manioc, marrow, pepper, potato, radish, rocket, sorrel, squash, tomato, turnip
07 avocado, bok choy, cabbage, cardoon, cassava, chayote, chicory, lettuce, pak choi, parsnip, pumpkin, salsify, shallot, skirret, spinach, tapioca
08 baby corn, beetroot, borecole, broccoli, capsicum, celeriac, cucumber, eggplant, finochio, kohlrabi, leaf beet, mushroom, red onion, soya bean, zucchini
09 artichoke, asparagus, aubergine,

bean shoot, broad bean, calabrese, courgette, finocchio, mange tout, petit pois, red pepper, Romanesco, sweetcorn

10 bean sprout, butter bean, French bean, lollo rosso, red cabbage, runner bean, swiss chard, watercress

11 cauliflower, Chinese leaf, green pepper, lady's finger, spring onion, sweet potato

12 marrow-squash, savoy cabbage, summer squash, turnip greens, winter squash, yellow pepper

13 ladies' fingers

14 Brussels sprout, Chinese cabbage, globe artichoke

15 vegetable marrow

See also **bean**

vegetarian
05 vegan, vegie **06** veggie **08** ovo-lacto **09** lactarian **11** Pythagorean

vegetate
04 idle **07** moulder **08** go to seed, languish, stagnate **09** do nothing, rusticate **10** degenerate **11** deteriorate

vegetation
04 sudd **05** flora, plant, trees **06** plants **07** flowers, herbage, verdure, vesture **08** greenery, savagery

vehemence
04 fire, heat, zeal **05** force, power, verve **06** ardour, energy, fervor, vigour, warmth **07** fervour, passion, urgency **08** emphasis, fervency, strength, violence **09** animation, intensity **10** enthusiasm **12** forcefulness

vehement
03 hot **04** keen, warm **05** eager **06** ardent, fervid, fierce, heated, strong, urgent **07** earnest, fervent, intense, violent, zealous **08** animated, emphatic, forceful, forcible, powerful, spirited, vigorous **10** passionate, thunderous **11** impassioned **12** enthusiastic

vehicle
05 means, organ **06** agency, medium **07** channel **09** mechanism, transport **10** conveyance, instrument

Vehicles include:
03 bus, cab, car, cat, fly, gig, HGV, tip, ute, van
04 arba, biga, bike, boat, cart, drag, dray, duck, ekka, hack, Jeep®, kago, kart, scow, ship, sled, solo, tank, taxi, tram, trap, tube, wain
05 araba, coach, cycle, lorry, plane, stage, sulky, train, truck, Vespa®, wagon
06 bakkie, camper, hansom, hearse, Humvee®, jalopy, jinker, landau, litter, Maglev, sidecar, sledge, sleigh, surrey, tandem, troika, tuk tuk
07 bicycle, caravan, dog-cart, minibus, minivan, omnibus, phaeton, Pullman, ricksha, scooter, sleeper, tractor, trailer, Transit®, trishaw

08 barouche, brougham, Cape cart, golf cart, monorail, rickshaw, toboggan, tricycle, wagon-lit
09 bobsleigh, buck-wagon, charabanc, motorbike
10 boneshaker, four-in-hand, jinricksha, jinrikisha, juggernaut, motorcycle, post-chaise, Scotch cart, sedan-chair, service car, stagecoach, trolleybus
11 caravanette, jinrickshaw, steam-roller
12 double-decker, pantechnicon
13 fork-lift truck, penny-farthing
15 hackney-carriage

See also **aircraft**; **bicycle**; **car**; **carriage**; **ship**

International Vehicle Registration codes include:
01 A (Austria), B (Belgium), C (Cuba), D (Germany), E (Spain), F (France), G (Gabon), H (Hungary), I (Italy), J (Japan), K (Cambodia), L (Luxembourg), M (Malta), N (Norway), P (Portugal), Q (Qatar), S (Sweden), T (Thailand), V (Vatican City), Z (Zambia)
02 AL (Albania), AM (Armenia), AZ (Azerbaijan), BD (Bangladesh), BF (Burkina Faso), BG (Bulgaria), BH (Belize), BR (Brazil), BS (The Bahamas), BW (Botswana), BY (Belarus), BZ (Belize), CH (Switzerland), CI (Côte d'Ivoire), CL (Sri Lanka), CO (Colombia), CR (Costa Rica), CU (Cuba), CY (Cyprus), CZ (Czech Republic), DK (Denmark), DY (Benin), DZ (Algeria), EC (Ecuador), ES (El Salvador), ET (Egypt), FL (Liechtenstein), FR (Faroe Islands), GB (Great Britain), GE (Georgia), GH (Ghana), GR (Greece), HK (Hong Kong), HR (Croatia), IL (Israel), IR (Iran), IS (Iceland), JA (Jamaica), KS (Kyrgyzstan), KZ (Kazakhzstan), LB (Liberia), LS (Lesotho), LT (Lithuania), LV (Latvia), MA (Morocco), MC (Monaco), MD (Moldova), MK (Macedonia), MS (Mauritius), MW (Malawi), NA (Netherlands Antilles), NL (Netherlands), NZ (New Zealand), PA (Panama), PE (Peru), PK (Pakistan), PL (Poland), PY (Paraguay), QA (Qatar), RA (Argentina), RB (Benin), RC (Taiwan), RG (Guinea), RH (Haiti), RI (Indonesia), RL (Lebanon), RM (Madagascar), RN (Niger), RO (Romania), RP (Philippines), RU (Burundi), SA (Saudi Arabia), SD (Swaziland), SK (Slovakia), SN (Senegal), SO (Somalia), SU (Belarus), SY (Seychelles), TG (Togo), TJ (Tajikistan), TM (Turkmenistan), TN (Tunisia), TR (Turkey), TT (Trinidad and Tobago), UA (Ukraine), UZ (Uzbekistan), VN (Vietnam), WD (Dominica), WG (Grenada), WL (St Lucia), WS

(Samoa), WV (St Vincent and the Grenadines), YV (Venezuela), ZA (South Africa), ZW (Zimbabwe)
03 AFG (Afghanistan), AND (Andorra), ARM (Armenia), AUS (Australia), BDS (Barbados), BIH (Bosnia and Herzegovina), BOL (Bolivia), BRN (Bahrain), BRU (Brunei), BUR (Myanmar), CAM (Cameroon), CDN (Canada), DOM (Dominican Republic), EAK (Kenya), EAT (Tanzania), EAU (Uganda), EAZ (Tanzania), EST (Estonia), ETH (Ethiopia), FIN (Finland), FJI (Fiji), GAB (Gabon), GBA (Alderney), GBG (Guernsey), GBJ (Jersey), GBM (Isle of Man), GBZ (Gibraltar), GCA (Guatemala), GUY (Guyana), HKJ (Jordan), IND (India), IRL (Ireland), IRQ (Iraq), KWT (Kuwait), LAO (Laos), LAR (Libya), MAL (Malaysia), MEX (Mexico), MGL (Mongolia), MOC (Mozambique), NAM (Namibia), NAU (Nauru), NEP (Nepal), NGR (Nigeria), NIC (Nicaragua), PNG (Papua New Guinea), RCA (Central African Republic), RCB (Republic of Congo), RCH (Chile), RGB (Guinea-Bissau), RIM (Mauritania), RMM (Mali), ROK (South Korea), ROU (Uruguay), RSM (San Marino), RUS (Russia), RWA (Rwanda), SCG (Serbia and Montenegro), SGP (Singapore), SLO (Slovenia), SME (Suriname), SUD (Sudan), SVN (Slovenia), SYR (Syria), TCH (Chad), USA (United States of America), WAG (The Gambia), WAL (Sierra Leone), WAN (Nigeria), YAR (Yemen), ZRE (Democratic Republic of the Congo)

veil
04 caul, film, hide, mask, mist, vail, vele **05** blind, burka, burqa, cloak, cover, scarf, scene, shade, veale, velum, volet **06** boorka, canopy, chadar, chador, kiss-me, mantle, purdah, shroud, sudary, weeper, wimple **07** bourkha, chaddar, chaddor, chuddah, chuddar, conceal, cover up, curtain, humeral, modesty, obscure, veiling, whimple, yashmak **08** chrismal, covering, disguise, kalyptra, mantilla, sudarium **09** encurtain **10** camouflage, lambrequin **11** concealment, kiss-me-quick

See also **scarf**

veiled
06 covert, hidden, masked, secret **07** cloaked, covered, obscure **08** indirect, shrouded **09** concealed, disguised **13** surreptitious

vein
03 rib **04** lode, mode, mood, seam, tone, vena **05** costa, nerve, style, tenor, varix **06** cavity, humour, marble, strain, streak, stripe **07** fissure, nervure, stratum **08** stringer **11** blood vessel, disposition, inclination, temperament

05 aorta, iliac, renal, ulnar
06 portal, radial, thread, tibial
07 basilic, carotid, coeliac, femoral, frontal, gastric, hepatic, jugular, organic, precava, saphena, splenic
08 axillary, brachial, coronary, postcava, praecava, superior, temporal, varicose, vena cava
09 popliteal, pulmonary, spermatic
10 innominate, mesenteric, subclavian
11 common iliac
14 anterior tibial
15 brachiocephalic, posterior tibial

veined
05 jaspe **06** venose, venous
07 marbled **08** streaked **10** reticulate, variegated

velocity
01 v **04** pace, rate **05** speed
08 celerity, rapidity **09** fleetness, quickness, swiftness

• **velocity constant**
01 k

velvet
05 gains, panne **06** dévoré, vellet, velour, velure **07** mockado, velours
08 chenille, suedette, winnings
09 three-pile

venal
04 bent **06** venous **07** buyable, corrupt
08 bribable, grafting **09** mercenary
10 simoniacal **11** corruptible

vendetta
04 feud **06** enmity **07** quarrel, rivalry
08 bad blood **09** blood-feud

vendor
06 seller, trader **07** butcher, camelot
08 merchant, salesman, stockist, supplier

veneer
04 mask, show **05** front, gloss, guise, layer **06** façade, fineer, finish
07 coating, display, surface
08 covering, pretence **09** grass-moth
10 appearance, lamination

venerable
03 Ven **04** aged, Bede, wise **06** august
07 revered **08** esteemed, honoured
09 dignified, respected, venerated
10 worshipped

venerate
04 fear **05** adore **06** esteem, honour, revere **07** iconize, respect, worship
09 reverence

veneration
03 awe **05** dulia, honor **06** esteem, honour, latria **07** douleia, respect, worship **08** devotion **09** adoration, aniconism, reverence, sublimity
10 hyperdulia, Mariolatry, Maryolatry
12 symbololatry

Venezuela
02 YV **03** VEN

vengeance
03 utu **04** harm **05** curse, wrack,

wreak **07** revenge **08** mischief, reprisal, requital **09** extremely, vengement **10** avengement
11 exceedingly, retaliation, retribution

• **with a vengeance**
05 fully **07** flat out, greatly **09** furiously, like crazy, to the full, violently
10 forcefully, powerfully, thoroughly, vigorously **11** exceedingly, to the utmost, with a wanion **12** with a witness **13** energetically **14** to a great degree, to a great extent **15** with a wild wanion

vengeful
08 avenging, punitive, spiteful
09 rancorous **10** implacable, revengeful, vindictive **11** retaliatory, retributive

venial
05 minor **06** slight **07** trivial **08** trifling
09 excusable **10** forgivable, negligible, pardonable **11** permissible
13 insignificant

venom
04 hate **05** spite, toxin, virus **06** enmity, malice, poison **07** envenom, ill-will, rancour, swelter **08** acrimony
09 animosity, hostility, poisonous, virulence **11** malevolence

venomous
05 fatal, toxic **06** bitter, deadly, lethal
07 baleful, baneful, noxious, vicious
08 spiteful, viperish, viperous, virulent **09** malicious, malignant, poisonous, rancorous **10** malevolent, vindictive

vent
03 air, gap **04** duct, emit, flue, hole, pipe, sale **05** salse, scent, sniff, snuff, utter, voice, wreak **06** crenel, escape, let out, market, outlet, smoker
07 airhole, chimney, express, opening, orifice, passage, pour out, publish, release **08** aperture, blowhole, breather, emission, spiracle, vomitory
09 discharge, solfatara **10** mud volcano **11** black smoker, let off steam, take it out on **14** counter-opening

ventilate
03 air, fan **04** cool **06** aerate, debate, winnow **07** discuss, express, freshen

ventilation
06 airing **07** cooling **08** aeration
10 freshening

venture
03 put **04** dare, jump, luck, mint, risk, sink **05** assay, fling, foray, stake, throw, wager **06** chance, gamble, hazard, venter, ventre **07** advance, exploit, imperil, presume, pretend, project, suggest **08** be so bold, endanger, make bold **09** adventure, endeavour, operation, promotion, speculate, volunteer **10** enterprise, prostitute, put forward **11** speculation, undertaking
14 take the liberty

venturesome
04 bold **05** brave, risky **06** daring,

plucky **07** doughty **08** fearless, intrepid, spirited **09** audacious, daredevil, dauntless **10** courageous
11 adventurous **12** enterprising

venue *see* **stadium**

venus
04 clam **05** cohog **06** copper, Hesper, quahog, venery, vesper **07** Lucifer, quahaug **08** Hesperus **09** Aphrodite, round clam **11** evening star, morning star

veracious
04 true **05** exact, frank **06** honest
07 factual, genuine **08** accurate, credible, faithful, truthful

veracity
05 truth **07** candour, honesty, probity
08 accuracy **09** frankness, integrity, rectitude **10** exactitude **12** truthfulness

veranda
05 lanai, porch, stoep, stoop **06** piazza
07 decking, gallery, terrace, viranda, virando

verbal
◇ *homophone indicator*
04 oral, said **05** abuse, vocal **06** insult, spoken **07** literal, uttered, voluble
09 invective **10** articulate, linguistic
11 word-of-mouth

verbalize
03 say **04** tell, word **05** speak, state, utter, voice **06** assert, convey, report
07 declare, get over, put over
08 announce, point out **09** enunciate, formulate, pronounce, put across
10 articulate, put in words
11 communicate, give voice to **12** put into words

verbatim
07 closely, exactly **09** literally, precisely
11 to the letter, word for word

verbiage
06 waffle **07** wordage, wording
08 pleonasm **09** prolixity, verbosity
10 repetition **11** periphrasis, perissology **14** circumlocution

verbose
05 gassy, windy, wordy **06** prolix
07 diffuse, voluble, wordish
09 garrulous **10** long-winded, loquacious, pleonastic **12** periphrastic
14 circumlocutory

verbosity
08 verbiage **09** garrulity, loquacity, prolixity, windiness, wordiness
10 logorrhoea, multiloquy **14** long-windedness, loquaciousness

verdant
04 lush **05** fresh, green, leafy, virid
06 virent **11** viridescent

verdict
05 vardy **06** ruling, verdit **07** finding, opinion **08** decision, judgment, recovery, sentence **09** judgement
10 assessment, conclusion
12 adjudication, rough justice

verdure

05 grass **07** foliage, greenth, herbage, leafage **08** greenery, verdancy, viridity **09** freshness, greenness **12** viridescence

verge

03 rim, rod **04** brim, edge, pale, tend **05** brink, limit, merge, point, range, scope, slope, touch, virge **06** border, edging, margin, trench **07** horizon, incline **08** boundary, precinct **09** threshold **11** long paddock **12** jurisdiction

• **verge on**

04 near **08** approach, border on **11** come close to, tend towards

verification

05 audit, proof **08** checking **10** validation **11** attestation **12** ascertaining, confirmation, constatation **13** corroboration **14** authentication, substantiation

verify

05 audit, check, prove **06** attest **07** bear out, confirm, support **08** accredit, validate **09** ascertain **11** corroborate **12** authenticate, substantiate

verisimilitude

07 realism **09** semblance **10** likeliness **11** credibility, resemblance, ring of truth **12** authenticity, plausibility **13** vraisemblance

veritable

04 fair, rank, real, true **05** right, sheer, utter **06** actual **07** genuine, perfect, regular **08** absolute, complete, outright, positive, thorough **09** out-and-out **10** consummate **11** unmitigated

verity

05 sooth, truth **07** reality **08** validity, veracity **09** actuality, soundness **12** authenticity, truthfulness

vermin

Vermin include:

03 rat **04** lice, mice, moth **05** louse, mouse **06** pigeon, weevil **09** cockroach

See also **rodent**

Vermont

02 VT

vermouth

02 It **06** French **07** Cinzano®, Martini®

vernacular

05 idiom, lingo, local **06** common, jargon, native, speech, tongue, vulgar **07** dialect, endemic, popular, trivial **08** informal, language, parlance **09** idioticon **10** colloquial, indigenous **12** vulgar tongue

Veronica

04 Hebe **09** speedwell

versatile

◊ *anagram indicator*
05 handy **07** Protean **08** all-round, flexible, unsteady, variable **09** adaptable, many-sided **10** adjustable, all-purpose, changeable **12** multifaceted, multipurpose

verse

01 v **04** line, rime, sijo, vers **05** haiku, Ionic, meter, metre, rhyme **06** heroic, jingle, poetry, riddle, stanza **07** doggrel, elegiac, iambics, Leonine, pennill, stichos, strophe, versify **08** doggerel, elegiacs, glyconic, singsong, trochaic, versicle **09** amphigory, vers libre **11** acatalectic, septenarius **12** Archilochian, nursery rhyme **13** vers de société, vers d'occasion, versification

versed

02 up **04** deep, read **06** strong, traded, turned **07** learned, perfect, skilled, studied, versant **08** deep-read, familiar, overseen, reversed, scienced, seasoned **09** competent, practised **10** conversant, proficient **11** experienced **13** knowledgeable

versifier

04 poet **06** rhymer, verser **07** poetess, rhymist **09** metrifier, poetaster, poeticule, rhymester **10** verse-maker, verse-smith **11** verse-monger **12** versificator

version

◊ *anagram indicator*
02 EV, NV, RV **04** form, kind, sort, type **05** cover, Itala, model, style **06** design, report, Rev Ver, Targum, update **07** account, edition, reading, turning, variant **08** rough cut **09** microcosm, portrayal, rendering **10** adaptation, paraphrase **11** translation **14** interpretation, King James Bible

versus

01 v **02** vs **06** facing **07** against, playing **08** opposing **09** as against, instead of **10** rather than **11** as opposed to **12** in contrast to **14** in opposition to

vertex

03 top **04** acme, apex, peak **05** crown **06** apogee, height, summit, zenith **08** pinnacle **09** extremity **12** highest point

vertical

05 apeak, apeek, erect, on end, plumb, sheer **07** upright **10** straight up, upstanding **13** perpendicular

vertigo

06 megrim **09** dizziness, giddiness, wooziness **15** light-headedness

verve

03 zip **04** brio, dash, élan, life **05** force, gusto **06** energy, relish, spirit, vigour, whammo **07** fervour, passion, pizzazz, sparkle **08** vitality, vivacity **09** animation **10** enthusiasm, liveliness

very

01 v **02** ae **03** e'er, way **04** ever, fell, mega, mere, pure, real, same, self, très, true, unco **05** assai, awful, dooms, exact, hefty, ideal, jolly, molto, plain, quite, sheer, stiff, truly, utter **06** actual, as hell, damned, deeply, dogged, ever so, highly, mighty, pretty, proper, really, simple **07** acutely, all that, awfully, genuine, good and, gradely, greatly, hell of a, hellova, helluva, majorly, only too, passing, perfect, precise **08** bitching, devilish, graithly, selfsame, spanking, stinking, suitable, terribly, uncommon **09** eminently, extremely, identical, unusually **10** absolutely, abundantly, incredibly, not a little, remarkably, uncommonly **11** exceedingly, excessively **12** particularly, unbelievably

vessel

03 ark, jar, jug, pot, tun, vat **04** boat, bowl, ewer, ship **05** craft, plate **06** barque, holder **07** airship, pitcher, vassail, vessail **09** container **10** receptacle

See also **container**; **ship**

vest

03 bib **04** garb, robe **05** drape, dress, endow, grant, lodge **06** bestow, clothe, confer, invest, semmit, supply **07** descend, devolve, empower, entrust, garment, singlet **08** sanction, vestment **09** authorize, waistcoat **10** undershirt **11** sequestrate

Vesta

06 Hestia

vestibule

04 hall **05** entry, foyer, lobby, porch **06** atrium, exedra **07** exhedra, hallway, narthex, portico, pronaos, tambour **08** anteroom, entrance **09** forecourt **11** oeil-de-boeuf **12** entrance hall

vestige

04 hint, mark, sign **05** print, scrap, shred, token, touch, trace, track, whiff **06** relics **07** glimmer, inkling, remains, remnant, residue **09** footprint, remainder, suspicion **10** impression, indication

vestigial

07 reduced **09** remaining, surviving **10** incomplete **11** rudimentary, undeveloped

vestment

04 vest **09** vestiment

Clerical vestments include:

03 alb **04** cope, cowl, hood **05** amice, cotta, ephod, frock, habit, mitre, scarf, stole **06** mantle, rochet, saccos, sakkos, tippet, wimple **07** biretta, cassock, chimere, humeral, maniple, pallium, soutane, tallith, tunicle **08** chasuble, dalmatic, mozzetta, rational, scapular, skullcap, surplice, yarmulka **09** dog-collar, phelonion

10 Geneva gown, omophorion, phaelonion, sticharion
11 Geneva bands, humeral veil
12 superhumeral
14 clerical collar

vet
04 scan **05** audit, check **06** review, screen, survey **07** examine, inspect **08** appraise, check out **10** scrutinize **11** investigate

vetch
03 ers **04** tare, tine **05** fitch

veteran
03 old, pro **05** adept **06** expert, master **07** old hand, warrior **08** old-timer, seasoned **09** old stager, practised **10** campaigner, pastmaster, proficient **11** experienced, long-serving **13** battle-scarred, old campaigner

veto
03 ban, nix **05** block **06** forbid, negate, reject **07** embargo, rule out **08** disallow, negative, prohibit, turn down **09** blackball, interdict, proscribe **10** thumbs-down **11** prohibition **12** proscription

vex
03 bug, noy **04** fret, haze, hump, rile **05** annoy, grief, spite, upset, worry **06** bother, enrage, excess, grieve, harass, hassle, molest, needle, pester, put out, rankle, wind up **07** afflict, agitate, chagrin, discuss, disturb, hack off, perturb, provoke, tick off, torment, trouble **08** bepester, brass off, distress, irritate **09** aggravate, cheese off **10** exasperate

vexation
03 noy **04** bind, bore, fury, pain **05** anger, pique, upset, worry **06** bother, plague **07** chagrin **08** headache, irritant, nuisance **09** annoyance **11** aggravation, frustration **12** exasperation **14** disappointment
See also **annoyance**

vexatious
05 pesky **06** noyous, plaguy, trying, vexing **07** irksome, nagging, nimious, peevish, plaguey, teasing **08** annoying, fashious, worrying **09** pestilent, provoking, upsetting, worrisome **10** bothersome, burdensome, irritating, tormenting **11** aggravating, infuriating, pestiferous, troublesome **12** exasperating

vexed
04 moot, sore **05** irate, riled, tough, upset **06** knotty, miffed, narked, peeved, put out, tricky **07** annoyed, awkward, debated, hassled, nettled, ruffled, worried **08** agitated, bothered, confused, disputed, harassed, provoked, troubled **09** contested, difficult, disturbed, flustered, in dispute, irritated, perplexed **10** aggravated, displeased, infuriated **11** exasperated

viability
10 expedience **11** feasibility, possibility, workability **12** practicality **13** achievability **14** practicability, reasonableness

viable
05 sound **08** feasible, operable, possible, workable **10** achievable, commercial **11** practicable, sustainable

vibes
04 aura, feel **08** ambience, emotions, feelings **10** atmosphere, vibrations

vibrancy
02 go **04** life, zest **05** oomph **06** energy, spirit, vigour **07** pizzazz, sparkle, stamina **08** strength, vitality, vivacity **09** animation **10** exuberance, get-up-and-go, liveliness

vibrant
05 vivid **06** bright, lively **07** dynamic **08** animated, electric, resonant, spirited, striking, vigorous **09** brilliant, colourful, energetic, sparkling, thrilling, vibrating, vivacious **12** electrifying

vibrate
◇ *anagram indicator*
03 jar **04** dirl, ring, sway **05** quake, shake, swing, thirl **06** dindle, dinnle, hotter, judder, quiver, shimmy, shiver, thrill, tingle **07** flutter, pulsate, resound, shudder, tremble, twinkle **08** brandish, resonate, undulate **09** oscillate, pendulate **11** reverberate

vibration
03 jar **04** dirl **05** pulse, quake, throb **06** dindle, dinnle, hotter, judder, quiver, shimmy, thrill, tremor **07** diadrom, flutter, frisson, shaking **08** fremitus **09** juddering, pulsation, resonance, trembling **10** resounding **11** oscillation, seismic wave **12** seismic shock **13** reverberation, tremulousness

vicar
03 Rev, Vic **06** cleric, curate, deputy, parson, pastor, priest, rector **08** chaplain, minister, preacher, reverend **09** clergyman **10** arch-priest, substitute **11** clergywoman **15** perpetual curate

vicarious
06 acting **08** indirect **09** surrogate **10** empathetic, second-hand **11** substituted

vice
03 sin **04** evil, flaw, grip, tool **05** fault, screw **06** defect, foible **07** blemish, buffoon, failing **08** bad habit, iniquity, weakness **09** depravity, evil-doing **10** bestiality, degeneracy, immorality, profligacy, wickedness, wrongdoing **12** besetting sin, imperfection **13** transgression

vice versa
02 vv **09** inversely **10** conversely, oppositely **12** contrariwise, reciprocally

vicinity
04 area **08** district, environs, locality, nearness **09** precincts, proximity **11** propinquity **12** surroundings **13** neighbourhood

vicious
03 bad **04** foul, mean, vile **05** catty, cruel, nasty **06** bitchy, brutal, faulty, fierce, impure, lethal, morbid, savage, wicked **07** heinous, immoral, violent **08** depraved, impaired, mistaken, spiteful, unlawful, venomous, virulent **09** barbarous, dangerous, ferocious, malicious, malignant **10** malevolent, vindictive **11** bad-tempered

viciously
06 wildly **07** cruelly **08** brutally, fiercely, lethally, savagely **09** violently

viciousness
05 spite, venom **06** malice **07** cruelty, rancour **08** ferocity, savagery **09** brutality, depravity, viciosity, virulence, vitiosity **10** bitchiness, wickedness **11** malevolence **12** spitefulness

vicissitude
04 turn **05** shift, twist **06** change **07** weather **08** mutation **09** deviation, variation **10** alteration, revolution **11** alternation, fluctuation

victim
04 butt, dupe, fool, host, mark, prey **05** patsy **06** martyr, muggee, nebish, quarry, sucker, target **07** fall guy, nebbich, nebbish **08** casualty, fatality, murderee, paranoic, soft mark, sufferer **09** paranoeic, paranoiac, sacrifice, scapegoat **11** sitting duck **13** sitting target
• **fall victim to**
05 catch **07** develop, fall for **08** contract **09** succumb to **10** fall prey to **11** be taken in by **12** be attacked by, be deceived by, be overcome by **14** be stricken with **15** become a target of

victimize
03 con **04** dupe, fool, rook **05** bully, cheat, frame, shaft, sting, trick **06** fleece, pick on, prey on, rip off **07** deceive, defraud, exploit, swindle **08** hoodwink, stitch up **09** bamboozle, persecute **11** have it in for

victor
01 V **05** champ, first **06** top dog, winner **08** bangster, champion **09** conqueror **10** vanquisher **11** pancratiast, prize-winner **13** victor ludorum

Victoria
02 VR **03** Vic **04** Nike

victorious
03 top **05** first **07** winning **08** champion, unbeaten **09** prevalent **10** conquering, successful, triumphant **11** vanquishing **12** prize-winning

victory
01 V **02** VE, VJ **03** Jai, win **04** gree, Nike **07** mastery, success, triumph, winning

08 conquest, squeaker, walk-away, walkover **09** checkmate, landslide **11** subjugation, superiority, triple crown
• **sign of victory**
01 V

victuals
04 chow, eats, food, grub, nosh, tuck **05** bread, scran **06** stores, viands **07** aliment, edibles, rations, vittles **08** eatables, supplies **10** provisions, sustenance **11** comestibles

vie
03 bid **05** fight, rival, stake **06** strive **07** compare, compete, contend, contest, declare **08** corrival, struggle **09** challenge

Vietnam
02 VN **03** VNM

view
02 Vw **03** see **04** espy, idea, look, scan **05** angle, judge, range, scene, sight, study, vista, watch **06** aspect, belief, descry, gaze at, look at, notion, regard, review, sketch, survey, vision **07** account, examine, feeling, glimpse, inspect, observe, opinion, outlook, picture, purpose, thought, witness **08** attitude, consider, eyesight, panorama, perceive, portrait, prospect, scrutiny **09** intention, judgement, landscape, portrayal, sentiment, spectacle **10** appearance, assessment, conviction, estimation, impression, inspection, perception, scrutinize **11** contemplate, examination, expectation, observation, perspective **13** contemplation, range of vision
• **in view of**
07 whereas **11** considering **13** bearing in mind
• **on view**
05 shown **06** on show **07** showing **09** displayed, exhibited, on display, presented **10** made public

viewer
07 goggler, watcher **08** observer, onlooker **09** inspector, spectator

viewpoint
05 angle, slant **06** stance **07** feeling, opinion **08** attitude, position, prospect **10** standpoint **11** observatory, perspective, point of view

vigil
04 wake **05** watch **07** lookout **08** stake-out, watching **10** deathwatch **11** wakefulness **12** pernoctation

vigilance
05 guard, watch **07** caution **09** alertness **11** carefulness, guardedness, observation, wakefulness **12** watch and ward, watchfulness **13** attentiveness **14** circumspection

vigilant
05 alert, awake, aware **07** careful, jealous, wakeful **08** cautious, wakerife,

watchful **09** Argus-eyed, attentive, observant, wide-awake **10** on the watch, unsleeping **11** circumspect, on your guard **12** on the lookout, on the qui vive

vigilante
05 guard, watch **07** lookout **08** sentinel, watchman **10** armed guard **11** watchperson **13** Guardian Angel, security guard

vignette
03 act **04** plan, turn **05** cameo, draft, scene **06** design, sketch **07** diagram, drawing, outline **08** abstract, skeleton **14** representation

vigorous
◇ *anagram indicator*
04 go-go, hard, rank **05** alive, brisk, green, hefty, lusty, round, sound, stout, tough, vital, vivid, young **06** active, bouncy, lively, manful, punchy, raucle, robust, rugged, sprack, strong, vegete **07** dynamic, healthy, intense, lustick, nervous **08** animated, athletic, forceful, forcible, lustique, muscular, powerful, spirited, swanking, youthful **09** energetic, gymnastic, strenuous **11** flourishing, full-blooded, gymnastical

vigorously
◇ *anagram indicator*
04 hard **06** lively **07** briskly, eagerly, lustily **08** heartily, strongly **09** in a big way **10** forcefully, like billy-o, powerfully **11** like billy-oh, strenuously **12** like old boots **13** energetically

vigour
03 pep, vim, zip **04** bant, birr, brio, dash, élan, fire, pith **05** flush, force, gusto, heart, might, moxie, oomph, power, verve **06** energy, health, spirit, stingo **07** pizzazz, potency, stamina **08** activity, dynamism, strength, virility, vitality, vivacity **09** animation, toughness **10** liveliness, robustness **12** forcefulness **13** vivaciousness

vile
◇ *anagram indicator*
03 bad, low **04** base, evil, foul, mean, vild **05** nasty, vilde **06** horrid, impure, paltry, scurvy, sinful, wicked **07** beastly, corrupt, debased, earthly, noxious, scabbed, vicious **08** depraved, horrible, infamous, wretched **09** appalling, degrading, loathsome, miserable, obnoxious, offensive, repugnant, repulsive, revolting, sickening, villanous, worthless **10** degenerate, despicable, detestable, disgusting, iniquitous, nauseating, scandalous, unpleasant, villainous **11** disgraceful, distasteful **12** contemptible, disagreeable

vileness
04 evil **06** infamy **07** outrage **08** baseness, foulness, meanness, ugliness **09** depravity, nastiness, profanity, turpitude **10** corruption, degeneracy, wickedness **11** noxiousness **13** offensiveness

vilification
03 mud **05** abuse **07** calumny **09** aspersion, contumely, criticism, invective **10** defamation, revilement, scurrility **11** denigration, mud-slinging **12** calumniation, vituperation **13** disparagement

vilify
04 slag, slam **05** abuse, decry, knock, slate, smear, snipe **06** berate, debase, defame, malign, revile **07** asperse, rubbish, run down, slag off, slander, traduce **08** badmouth, denounce, vilipend **09** denigrate, disparage **10** calumniate, stigmatize, vituperate

village
03 vil **04** dorp, duar, gram, vill, wick **05** aldea, douar, dowar, kraal, thorp **06** hamlet, kainga, thorpe **07** clachan, endship, kampong, kirkton, outport **08** kirk town, township **09** borghetto, community, rancheria **10** Chautauqua, settlement

villain
04 base **05** baddy, bravo, devil, heavy, knave, rogue **06** baddie, rascal, wretch **07** low-born, villein **08** criminal, escapado, evildoer, scelerat **09** miscreant, reprobate, scelerate, scoundrel, wrongdoer **10** malefactor

Villains include:
04 Case, Cass (Dunstan), Hyde (Mr), Iago
05 Bates (Norman), Doone (Carver), Queeg (Captain), Regan
06 Lecter (Dr Hannibal), Oswald, Silver (Long John)
07 Antonio, Bateman (Patrick), Blofeld (Ernst), Goneril
08 Cornwall (Duke of), Injun Joe
09 Voldemort (Lord)
10 Darth Vader, Goldfinger (Auric), Richard III
12 Aaron the Moor
14 Bonnie and Clyde, Sauron the Great

villainous
03 bad **04** evil, vile **05** cruel **06** gallus, sinful, wicked **07** debased, gallows, heinous, inhuman, roguish, vicious **08** criminal, depraved, fiendish, terrible **09** miscreant, nefarious, notorious **10** degenerate, detestable, iniquitous **11** disgraceful, opprobrious

villainy
03 sin **04** vice **05** crime **07** badness, knavery, roguery **08** atrocity, baseness, disgrace, iniquity **09** depravity, rascality, turpitude **10** wickedness **11** criminality, delinquency

vindicate
04 free **05** clear, right, salve **06** acquit, assert, avenge, uphold, verify **07** absolve, darrain, darrayn, deraign, justify, warrant **08** advocate, champion, darraign, darraine, maintain **09** darraigne, exculpate, exonerate **11** corroborate

vindication
07 apology, defence, defense, support **08** apologia, theodicy **09** assertion **10** apologetic **11** exculpation, exoneration, extenuation **12** compurgation, verification **13** justification **14** substantiation

vindictive
08 punitive, spiteful, vengeful, venomous **09** malicious, rancorous **10** implacable, malevolent, revengeful **11** retributive, unforgiving, vindicative

vine
06 muscat **08** grape ivy, heartpea, muscadel, muscatel **09** ayahuasco, heartseed **10** wonga-wonga **12** winter cherry

vinegar
05 eisel **06** alegar, eisell, energy, vigour **07** souring **08** wood acid **10** acetic acid

vintage
03 cru, era, old **04** best, crop, fine, ripe, time, wine, year **05** epoch, prime **06** choice, gather, mature, origin, period, select **07** classic, harvest, quality, supreme, veteran **08** enduring, superior **09** gathering **11** high-quality

viol
02 gu **03** gju, gue **05** quint, rebec **06** quinte, rebeck

viola
04 alto **05** gamba, pance, pansy **06** paunce, pawnce, violet

violate
◇ anagram indicator
04 rape **05** abuse, break, flout, fract, wreck **06** breach, defile, invade, molest, offend, ravish **07** debauch, defiled, despoil, disobey, disrupt, disturb, infract, outrage, profane, vitiate **08** infringe, stuprate **09** desecrate, dishonour **10** contravene, transgress **13** interfere with

violation
◇ anagram indicator
04 rape **05** abuse, crime **06** breach, mopery **07** offence, outrage **08** invasion, trespass **09** injustice, sacrilege, vitiation **10** defilement, disruption, infraction, spoliation, stupration **11** desecration, profanation **12** infringement, private wrong **13** breach of trust, contravention, transgression

violence
04 fury, rage, rape **05** force, might, power, wrath **06** frenzy, injury, tumult **07** cruelty, outrage, passion **08** ferocity, fighting, foul play, savagery, severity, strength, wildness **09** bloodshed, brutality, intensity, roughness, vehemence **10** aggression, fierceness, turbulence **11** hostilities, profanation **12** forcefulness

violent
◇ anagram indicator
03 het, hot **04** high, rage, rank, rude, wild **05** acute, cruel, fiery, force, great, harsh, heady, hefty, rough, sharp, tough **06** brutal, fierce, savage, severe, stormy, strong, sturdy **07** drastic, extreme, flaming, furious, intense, riotous, rousing, ruffian, vicious **08** dramatic, forceful, forcible, maddened, powerful, slap-bang, towering, vehement **09** ferocious, hot-headed, impetuous, murderous, turbulent **10** aggressive, headstrong, outrageous, passionate, tumultuous **11** destructive, devastating **12** bloodthirsty, excruciating, ungovernable, unrestrained **15** blood-and-thunder

violently
◇ anagram indicator
04 rank, slap **05** amain, tough **06** wildly **07** cruelly, greatly, sharply **08** brutally, fiercely, savagely, severely, slap-bang, strongly **09** extremely, intensely, viciously **10** powerfully **11** ferociously, hot-headedly, impetuously **12** aggressively, dramatically **14** uncontrollably, with a vengeance

violin
02 gu **03** gju, gue, kit **05** Amati, strad **06** catgut, fiddle, leader **07** chikara **10** Stradivari **12** Stradivarius

• violin part
03 nut, rib **04** back, neck, soul **05** belly, f-hole, table **06** bridge, button **07** bass-bar **08** purfling **09** sound post **11** fingerboard

VIP
03 nib, pot **04** lion, star **06** bigwig, top dog **07** big name, big shot, magnate, notable **08** big noise, luminary, somebody **09** big cheese, celebrity, dignitary, personage **11** heavyweight

viper
03 asp **05** adder **08** cerastes, mocassin, moccasin **09** berg-adder, river-jack **10** fer-de-lance **11** rattlesnake

virago
04 fury **05** randy, scold, shrew, vixen **06** amazon, dragon, gorgon, randie, tartar **08** harridan **09** battle-axe, brimstone, termagant, Xanthippe

virgin
03 new **04** girl, maid, pure **05** fresh, Virgo **06** chaste, intact, maiden, modest, vestal **07** Madonna, pucelle **08** celibate, maidenly, spotless, unspoilt, virginal **09** stainless, undefiled, unsullied, untainted, untouched **10** immaculate, unattained **11** unblemished, unexploited

virginal
04 pure **05** fresh, snowy, white **06** chaste, vestal, virgin **08** celibate, maidenly, pristine, spotless **09** stainless, undefiled, untouched **10** immaculate **11** uncorrupted, undisturbed **15** parthenogenetic

Virginia
02 VA

Virgin Islands
02 VI **03** BVI, VGB, VIR

virginity
05 honor **06** cherry, honour, purity, virtue **08** chastity, pucelage **09** innocence **10** chasteness, maidenhead, maidenhood

virile
05 lusty, macho, manly **06** potent, robust, rugged, strong **08** forceful, muscular, vigorous **09** masculine, strapping **10** red-blooded

virility
06 energy, vigour **07** manhood, potency **08** machismo **09** manliness **10** ruggedness **11** masculinity

virtual
07 implied **08** implicit, in effect, virtuous **09** effective, essential, potential, practical **11** prospective **12** in all but name

virtually
06 almost, nearly **08** as good as, in effect **09** in essence **10** more or less **11** effectively, practically **12** in all but name, to all intents

virtue
04 good, plus **05** asset, merit, vertu, worth **06** credit, dharma, honour, valour, vertue **07** benefit, honesty, probity, quality **08** efficacy, goodness, morality, strength **09** advantage, attribute, rectitude, virginity **10** excellence, worthiness **11** saving grace **14** accomplishment, high-mindedness

The seven virtues:
04 hope
05 faith
07 charity, justice
08 prudence
09 fortitude
10 temperance

• by virtue of
07 by way of, owing to **08** by dint of, thanks to **09** because of, by means of **11** on account of **13** with the help of

virtuosity
05 éclat, flair, skill **06** finish, polish **07** bravura, finesse, mastery, panache **08** artistry, wizardry **09** expertise **10** brilliance

virtuoso
06 expert, genius, master **07** maestro, prodigy, skilful **08** dazzling, masterly **09** brilliant, excellent

virtuous
04 good **05** moral **06** chaste, decent, graced, honest, worthy **07** angelic, ethical, upright, virtual **08** innocent **09** blameless, continent, exemplary, righteous **10** honourable, upstanding **11** clean-living, respectable **12** squeaky-clean **13** incorruptible, unimpeachable **14** above suspicion, high-principled, irreproachable **15** beyond suspicion

virulence
05 spite, venom **06** hatred, malice, poison, rancor, spleen **07** rancour, vitriol **08** acrimony, toxicity **09** hostility, malignity **10** antagonism, bitterness, malignancy **11** malevolence, viciousness **14** vindictiveness

virulent
05 fatal, toxic **06** bitter, deadly, lethal, severe **07** extreme, hostile, intense, vicious, waspish **08** spiteful, venomous **09** injurious, malicious, malignant, poisonous, rancorous, vitriolic **10** blistering, malevolent, pernicious, vindictive **11** acrimonious

virus
Viruses include:

03 CDV, DNA, EBV, flu, FLV, HIV, HPV, pox, pro, RNA
04 arbo, cold, ECHO, filo, HTLV, myxo, rota
05 Ebola, flavi, hanta, irido, lenti, parvo, phage, retro, rhino
06 baculo, calici, cowpox, herpes, papova
07 oncorna, picorna, polyoma, variola
08 morbilli, Vaccinia
09 Coxsackie, influenza, papilloma
10 hepatitis A, hepatitis B, hepatitis C, Lassa fever, leaf mosaic
11 Epstein-Barr
13 bacteriophage, parainfluenza
14 human papilloma
15 canine distemper

visa
04 pass, visé **06** carnet, docket, permit **07** licence, warrant **08** passport, sanction **09** green card **10** permission **11** endorsement, safe-conduct **13** authorization, laissez-passer **14** permis de séjour

vis-à-vis
06 facing **08** opposite **09** as regards **10** face-to-face **11** over against **12** in relation to

viscera
04 guts **06** bowels, vitals **07** giblets, innards, insides **08** entrails, gralloch, harigals **09** harigalds **10** intestines

viscous
04 slab **05** gluey, gooey, gummy, stiff, tacky, thick, tough **06** glairy, mucous, sticky, viscid **07** treacly, viscose **08** glareous **09** glaireous, glutinous, resistant **10** gelatinous **12** mucilaginous

Vishnu *see* **incarnation**

visible
04 open **05** clear, overt, plain **06** patent, visual **07** evident, exposed, in sight, obvious, showing **08** apparent, manifest, palpable **10** aspectable, in evidence, noticeable, observable **11** conspicuous, discernible, perceivable, perceptible, unconcealed, undisguised **12** recognizable **15** distinguishable

visibly
06 openly **07** clearly, overtly, plainly **08** patently **09** evidently, obviously **10** manifestly, noticeably **11** perceptibly **13** conspicuously

vision
04 idea, look, view **05** dream, ghost, ideal, image, sight **06** glance, mirage, seeing, wraith **07** aisling, chimera, fantasy, imagine, insight, phantom, picture, spectre **08** daydream, delusion, eyesight, illusion, phantasm **09** foresight, intuition, phantosme **10** apparition, conception, perception, revelation **11** fata Morgana, imagination, mental image **13** hallucination, mental picture **14** far-sightedness **15** optical illusion

visionary
04 aery, seer **05** aerie **06** dreamy, mystic, unreal **07** dreamer, prophet, utopian **08** airdrawn, fanciful, idealist, illusory, quixotic, romantic, theorist **09** fantasist, imaginary, moonshiny, prophetic **10** daydreamer, Don Quixote, far-sighted, idealistic, ideologist, ivory-tower, perceptive **11** impractical, translunary, unpractical, unrealistic **13** impracticable, rainbow-chaser

visit
03 gam, see **04** call, chat, mump, stay, stop, take **05** curse, haunt, pop in, smite **06** call by, call in, call on, come by, drop by, look in, look up, plague, punish, stop by, stop in, take in, wait on **07** afflict, examine, inflict, inspect, sojourn, stop off, trouble **08** call in on, drop in on, frequent, go and see, go over to, stay with, stop in at, stop over, wait upon **09** call round, come round, excursion, first-foot, go round to, house call, stop off at **10** salutation, stop over at **13** spend time with

visitation
05 trial, visit **06** blight, ordeal **08** calamity, disaster, haunting **10** appearance, infliction, inspection, punishment **11** catastrophe, examination **13** manifestation

visitor
05 guest **06** caller **07** company, tourist **08** manuhiri, stranger **09** traveller **12** holidaymaker **13** bird of passage

visor
05 sight **06** mesail, mezail, umbrel, umbril **07** umbrere **08** umbriere

vista
04 view **05** scene **06** avenue, vision **07** outlook **08** enfilade, panorama, prospect **11** perspective

visual
05 optic **06** ocular, visive **07** optical, visible **08** specular **10** observable

visualize
03 see **07** imagine, picture **08** conceive, envisage, envision

vital
03 key **05** alive, basic **06** lively, living,

urgent, zoetic **07** animate, crucial, dynamic, vibrant **08** animated, critical, decisive, forceful, spirited, vigorous **09** energetic, essential, important, necessary, requisite, vivacious **10** imperative, life-giving, quickening **11** fundamental, significant **12** invigorating, life-and-death **13** indispensable

vitality
02 go **03** sap, zap **04** life, zest, zing **05** juice, oomph **06** bounce, energy, fizzen, foison, spirit, vigour **07** fushion, pizzazz, sparkle, stamina, vivency **08** strength, vivacity **09** animation **10** exuberance, get-up-and-go, liveliness **13** vivaciousness

vitally
08 urgently **09** crucially **10** critically, decisively **11** essentially, importantly **13** fundamentally, significantly

vitamin
Vitamins include:

01 A, B, C, D, E, G, H, K, P
06 biotin, citrin, niacin
07 adermin, aneurin, retinol, thiamin
08 carotene, thiamine
09 folic acid, menadione
10 calciferol, pyridoxine, riboflavin, tocopherol
11 menaquinone, pteroic acid
12 ascorbic acid, bioflavonoid, linoleic acid
13 linolenic acid, nicotinic acid, phylloquinone
14 cyanocobalamin, dehydroretinol, ergocalciferol, phytomenadione
15 cholecalciferol, pantothenic acid, vitamin B complex

vitiate
03 mar **04** harm, rape, ruin **05** blend, spoil, sully, taint **06** blight, debase, defile, impair, injure, mucker, weaken **07** blemish, corrupt, debauch, deprave, devalue, nullify, pervert, pollute, violate **09** undermine **10** adulterate, invalidate **11** contaminate

vitriolic
06 biting, bitter **07** abusive, acerbic, caustic, mordant, vicious **08** sardonic, scathing, venomous, virulent **09** malicious, trenchant **11** acrimonious, destructive **12** vituperative

vituperate
03 nag **04** slag, slam **05** abuse, blame, knock, slang, slate **06** berate, rebuke, revile, vilify **07** censure, rubbish, run down, slag off, upbraid **08** denounce, reproach **09** castigate **10** blackguard

vituperation
04 flak **05** abuse, blame, stick **07** censure, obloquy **08** diatribe, knocking, reproach **09** contumely, invective, philippic, reprimand **10** revilement, rubbishing, scurrility

11 castigation, objurgation, slagging-off 12 vilification

vituperative

05 harsh 07 abusive 08 sardonic, scornful 09 insulting, withering 10 belittling, censorious, derogatory, scurrilous 11 fulminatory, opprobrious 12 calumniatory, denunciatory

vivacious

05 jolly, merry, smart 06 bright, bubbly, chirpy, lively 08 animated, cheerful, spirited, sportive 09 ebullient, in spirits, long-lived, sparkling, sprightly 12 effervescent, high-spirited, light-hearted

vivacity

02 go 03 fiz, zap 04 brio, élan, fizz, life, zing 05 oomph 06 energy, spirit, vigour 07 pizzazz, sparkle, spirits 08 activity, dynamism, vitality 09 animation, merriness 10 ebullience, liveliness 13 effervescence

vivid

04 live, rich, vive 05 clear, lurid, sharp 06 bright, lively, strong 07 dynamic, eidetic, glaring, glowing, graphic, intense, vibrant 08 animated, dazzling, distinct, dramatic, lifelike, powerful, spirited, striking, vigorous 09 brilliant, colourful, graphical, memorable, pictorial, realistic 11 picturesque

vividly

06 richly 07 clearly 08 brightly, strongly 09 intensely, memorably, vibrantly 10 distinctly, powerfully 11 brilliantly, graphically 12 dramatically, flamboyantly

vividness

04 glow, life 05 color 06 colour 07 clarity, realism 08 lucidity, radiance, strength 09 intensity, sharpness 10 brightness, brilliancy, refulgence

viz

02 ie, sc 04 scil, sciz 05 to wit 06 namely, that is 08 scilicet 09 videlicet 11 that is to say 12 in other words, specifically

vocabulary

04 cant 05 idiom, lexis, vocab, words 07 lexicon 08 glossary, language, wordbook 09 idioticon, thesaurus 10 dictionary 11 nomenclator 12 Basic English, nomenclature

vocal

◇ *homophone indicator*
04 oral, said, sung 05 blunt, frank, noisy 06 phonal, shrill, spoken, voiced 07 uttered 08 eloquent, strident 09 expressed, outspoken, talkative 10 articulate, expressive, forthright, resounding, vociferous

vocalize

03 air, say 04 sing, tell, vent, word 05 speak, state, utter, voice 06 assert, convey, report 07 declare, express, get over, put over 08 announce, intimate, point out 09 enunciate, formulate, pronounce, put across, ventilate,

verbalize 10 articulate 11 communicate, give voice to 12 put into words

vocally

10 eloquently, stridently 12 articulately, expressively, forthrightly

vocation

03 job 04 line, post, role, work 05 craft, trade 06 career, métier, office 07 calling, mission, pursuit 08 business 10 employment, occupation, profession

vociferous

04 loud 05 blunt, frank, noisy, vocal 08 shouting, strident, vehement 09 clamorous, outspoken 10 forthright, thundering 12 obstreperous

vociferously

06 loudly 07 bluntly, frankly, noisily, vocally 10 stridently, vehemently 11 outspokenly

vogue

03 fad 04 mode, rage 05 craze, style, taste, trend 06 custom 07 fashion, the rage 08 the thing 09 the latest 10 popularity 11 fashionable
• **in vogue**
02 in 06 modish, trendy, with it 07 current, popular, stylish, voguish 09 prevalent 11 fashionable 13 up-to-the-minute

voice

03 air, say, vox 04 alto, bass, cast, pipe, tone, view, vote, will, wish 05 elect, mezzo, mouth, organ, sound, taish, tenor, utter, words 06 airing, assert, convey, medium, report, rumour, singer, speech, taisch, talk of, throat, tongue, treble 07 acclaim, appoint, declare, divulge, express, mention, opinion, soprano, speak of 08 approval, castrato, decision, disclose, falsetto, language, nominate 09 contralto, enunciate, utterance, verbalize 10 articulate, expression, give tongue, inflection, instrument, intonation, mouthpiece, reputation 11 contra-tenor, Heldentenor 12 articulation, counter-tenor, mezzo-soprano

void

03 gap 04 emit, lack, null, vain, want 05 abyss, annul, avoid, belch, blank, chasm, clear, drain, eject, empty, inane, inept, space 06 cancel, cavity, devoid, hollow, lacuna, remove, vacant, vacuum 07 dismiss, drained, emptied, invalid, lacking, nullify, opening, rescind, send out, useless, vacuity 08 abnegate, annulled, defecate, deserted, evacuate, nugatory, send away, unfilled 09 blankness, cancelled, clear away, discharge, emptiness, nullified, worthless 10 invalidate, unoccupied, unutilized 11 ineffectual

volatile

◇ *anagram indicator*
05 giddy, Latin 06 fickle, fitful, lively

07 erratic, flighty 08 fleeting, restless, skittish, unstable, unsteady, variable, volcanic 09 explosive, irregular, mercurial, transient, unsettled, up and down 10 capricious, changeable, inconstant, short-lived 11 light-winged 13 temperamental, unpredictable

volatility

09 shakiness 10 fickleness, fitfulness, insecurity 11 flightiness, fluctuation, inconstancy, instability, uncertainty, variability 12 irresolution, unsteadiness 13 unreliability 14 capriciousness, changeableness, precariousness

volcano

05 salse 08 spitfire 15 burning mountain

Volcanoes include:

03 Apo, Awu, Usu
04 Etna, Fuji, Laki, Taal
05 Hekla, Kenya, Mayon, Pelée, Thera, Thira, Unzen
06 Ararat, Erebus, Hudson, Katmai, Sangay
07 Jurullo, Kilauea, Rainier, Ruapehu, Surtsey, Tambora, Vulcano
08 Cotopaxi, Krakatoa, Mauna Kea, Mauna Loa, Pinatubo, St Helens, Tarawera, Vesuvius
09 Aconcagua, Coseguina, El Chichon, Helgafell, Karisimbi, Lamington, Paricutín, Pichincha, Santorini, Stromboli, Tongariro
10 Bezymianny, Chimborazo, Galunggung, La Soufrire, Lassen Peak, Tungurahua
11 Kilimanjaro, Nyamuragira
12 Citlaltépetl, Ixtaccihuatl, Klyuchevskoy, Popocatèpetl
13 Nevado del Ruiz, Ojos del Salado, Soufrire Hills, Volcán El Misti
14 Cerro Incahuasi
15 Haleakala Crater

vole

08 Arvicola, water dog, water rat 10 water mouse 11 meadow mouse

volition

04 will 06 choice, option 07 purpose 08 choosing, election, free will, velleity 10 preference, resolution 13 determination
• **of your own volition**
06 freely 08 by choice 09 purposely, willingly 11 consciously, voluntarily 12 deliberately 13 intentionally, spontaneously 15 of your own accord

volley

04 hail, tire 05 blast, burst, round, salvo 06 flight, shower 07 barrage, platoon 08 cannonry 09 cannonade, discharge, fusillade 11 bombardment

volte-face

◇ *reversal indicator*
05 U-turn 08 reversal 09 about-face, about-turn, turnabout 13 enantiodromia

voluble

06 chatty, fluent, verbal 07 twining,

verbose 09 garrulous, talkative **10** articulate, changeable, loquacious **11** forthcoming

volume
01 v **03** tom, vol **04** body, book, bulk, code, mass, rise, roll, size, tome **05** codex, noise, sound, space, swell **06** amount, scroll **07** omnibus **08** capacity, decibels, loudness, quantity, solidity **09** aggregate, amplitude **10** dimensions **11** publication

voluminous
03 big **04** full, huge, vast **05** ample, bulky, large, roomy **08** spacious **09** billowing, capacious

voluntarily
06 freely **08** by choice, by my will **09** purposely, willingly **12** deliberately **13** intentionally **15** of your own accord

voluntary
03 vol **04** free **06** unpaid, votive, willed **07** willing **08** designed, free-will, optional, postlude, unforced **09** volunteer **10** deliberate, gratuitous, purposeful, ultroneous, unsalaried, without pay **11** intentional, spontaneous, unsolicited

volunteer
03 vol **05** offer **06** tender **07** advance, proffer, propose, suggest **08** activist, do-gooder, fencible **09** home guard, reformado, voluntary **10** put forward **11** come forward, helping hand, step forward **15** voluntary worker
- **volunteers**
02 TA **03** AVR, CDV, UVF, VAD **04** RNVR

voluptuary
07 playboy **08** hedonist, sybarite **09** bon vivant, bon viveur, debauchee, epicurean, libertine **10** profligate, sensualist **14** pleasure-seeker

voluptuous
05 buxom **06** sultry **07** opulent, sensual, shapely **08** enticing, luscious, sensuous **09** luxurious, seductive **10** curvaceous, effeminate, goloptious, goluptious, hedonistic **11** full-figured **13** self-indulgent

vomit
03 cat **04** barf, boak, bock, boke, honk, puke, sick, spew, spue **05** heave, retch **06** be sick, emetic, sick up **07** bring up, chuck up, chunder, fetch up, throw up, upchuck **08** disgorge, parbreak **10** egurgitate **11** regurgitate

vomiting
04 puke, sick **06** emesis, puking **07** barfing, spewing **08** ejection, parbreak, retching, sickness **10** chundering, sick as a dog **11** hyperemesis **12** anacatharsis,

haematemesis 13 regurgitation **15** morning sickness

voracious
04 avid **06** greedy, hungry **07** swinish **08** edacious, gourmand, ravening, ravenous **09** devouring, rapacious **10** gluttonous, insatiable, omnivorous, prodigious, voraginous

voracity
05 greed **06** hunger **07** avidity, edacity **08** rapacity **12** ravenousness

vortex
04 eddy **05** whirl **09** maelstrom, whirlpool, whirlwind **10** tourbillon **11** tourbillion

votary
06 addict **07** devotee, Paphian, sectary **08** adherent, bacchant, believer, disciple, follower **10** worshipper

vote
01 X **02** no **03** aye, nay, yea, yes **04** poll **05** elect, go for, put in, voice **06** ballot, choose, opt for, return **07** declare, propose, re-elect, suggest, write-in **08** division, election, plump for, suffrage **09** franchise **10** plebiscite, referendum **11** ballot paper, show of hands **12** go to the polls **15** enfranchisement
- **vote in**
04 pick **05** adopt, co-opt, elect, voice **06** choose, opt for, prefer, return, select **07** appoint, vote for **08** decide on, plump for **09** designate, determine
- **vote out**
04 oust **06** demote, remove, topple, unseat **07** boot out, dismiss, turf out **08** dethrone, displace **09** overthrow

voter
02 no **03** nay, yea, yes **04** vote **05** fagot **06** faggot **07** burgher, citizen **08** balloter, colonist, outvoter **10** franchiser, free person, ten-pounder **11** constituent **13** floating voter

vouch
- **vouch for**
04 back **06** affirm, assert, assure, avouch, uphold, verify **07** certify, confirm, endorse, support, swear to, warrant **08** attest to, speak for **09** answer for, guarantee **10** asseverate

voucher
02 LV **04** chit, note **05** paper, token **06** chitty, coupon, ticket **07** warrant **08** document **09** book token, gift token **11** youth credit

vouchsafe
04 cede, give **05** deign, grant, vouch, yield **06** accord, bestow, beteem, confer, impart **07** beteeme **09** guarantee **10** condescend

vow
03 vum **04** avow, hest, hete, oath

05 heast, hecht, hight, swear **06** affirm, behote, bename, devote, heaste, pledge **07** behight, profess, promise, protest **08** dedicate **09** nuncupate, undertake **11** nuncupation **12** give your word

vowel
01 a, e, i, o, u
- **vowel sound**
05 schwa

voyage
04 sail, tour, trip **06** course, cruise, safari, travel **07** journey, odyssey, passage, traffic, travels **08** crossing, put to sea, shipping, traverse **10** enterprise, expedition, navigation **12** rough passage **13** middle passage

Vulcan
10 Hephaestus

vulgar
03 low **04** lewd, loud, naff, rude, vulg **05** bawdy, broad, cheap, crude, dirty, flash, gaudy, rough, showy, tacky, tarty, usual **06** coarse, common, filthy, flashy, garish, glitzy, kitsch, public, ribald, risqué, tawdry **07** boorish, general, ill-bred, obscene, plebean, popular, uncouth, upstart **08** banausic, gorblimy, impolite, improper, indecent, low-lived, ordinary, plebeian **09** customary, gorblimey, hoi polloi, low-minded, off-colour, offensive, pandemian, prevalent, tasteless, unrefined **10** indecorous, indelicate, suggestive, threepenny, uncultured, vernacular **11** commonplace, distasteful, near the bone, picturesque **12** ostentatious **13** cheap and nasty **15** unsophisticated

vulgarian
04 pleb, snob **05** tiger **07** plebean, tigress **08** plebeian

vulgarity
07 crudity **08** ribaldry, rudeness **09** crudeness, gaudiness, indecency **10** coarseness, garishness, tawdriness **11** ostentation

vulnerable
◇ *anagram indicator*
04 open, weak **06** tender **07** exposed **08** helpless, high-risk, in danger, insecure, wide open **09** powerless, pregnable, sensitive, unguarded **11** defenceless, susceptible, unprotected **12** open to attack **15** exposed to danger

vulture
05 gripe, grype, urubu **06** condor **08** aasvogel, zopilote **09** gallinazo, gier-eagle, ossifrage **11** carrion crow, lammergeier, lammergeyer **13** turkey buzzard

W
07 double-u, whiskey **09** double-you

wacky
◇ *anagram indicator*
03 odd **04** daft, wild, zany **05** crazy, goofy, loony, loopy, nutty, silly **06** screwy **07** bonkers, erratic, offbeat **09** eccentric **10** irrational **13** unpredictable

wad
03 bun, pad **04** ball, cake, hunk, lump, mass, plug, roll **05** block, chunk, marry, wodge **06** bundle, dossil, pledge **07** pledget **08** sandwich, security

wadding
06 filler, lining **07** batting, filling, packing, padding **08** stuffing **10** cotton wool **14** quilting-cotton

waddle
04 rock, sway **06** clumsy, daidle, hoddle, toddle, totter, wobble **07** shuffle

wade
02 go **04** ford, roll **05** cross, lurch **06** paddle, splash, wallow, welter **08** flounder, traverse
• **wade in**
05 set to **06** tear in **07** pitch in **08** launch in **10** get stuck in **11** wade through **12** trawl through **13** plough through

wader, wading bird *see* bird

wafer
04 host, seal **05** matza, matzo **06** matzah, matzoh

waffle
04 guff, wave **05** gofer, waver **06** babble, gaufer, gaufre, gopher, hot air, jabber **07** blather, blether, padding, prattle **08** blathers, blethers, nonsense, rabbit on, witter on **09** vacillate, verbosity, wittering, wordiness **10** cotton wool **11** vacillation **12** gobbledygook

waft
04 blow, puff, turn, wave, wing **05** carry, drift, float, glide, scent, whiff **06** beckon, breath, breeze, winnow **07** current, draught **08** transmit **09** transport

wag
◇ *anagram indicator*
03 bob, nod, wit **04** fool, lick, move, rock, stir, sway, walk, wave **05** clown, comic, droll, joker, shake, swing, troll **06** fellow, gagman, jester, quiver, truant, waggle, wiggle, wobble **07** flutter, vibrate **08** banterer, brandish, comedian, humorist **09** oscillate

wage
03 fee, pay, war **04** gage, hire, levy, meed **05** bribe, screw **06** battle, hazard, pledge, pursue, reward, salary **07** carry on, conduct, contend, execute, imprest, payment, pension, returns, stipend **08** earnings, engage in, penny-fee, pittance, practise **09** allowance, emolument, undertake **10** recompense, wage-packet **12** compensation, remuneration

wager
03 bet, lay, wad, wed **04** gage, punt, risk **05** put on, sport, stake **06** chance, gamble, hazard, pledge **07** flutter, lay odds, venture **09** speculate **11** speculation **14** gaming contract

waggish
04 arch **05** droll, funny, merry, witty **06** facete, impish, jocose **07** amusing, comical, jesting, jocular, playful, puckish, risible, roguish **08** humorous, sportive **09** bantering, facetious **10** frolicsome **11** mischievous

waggle
◇ *anagram indicator*
03 wag **04** wave **05** shake **06** bobble, jiggle, wiggle, wobble **07** flutter **09** oscillate **12** niddle-noddle

wagon
03 car, van **04** cart, corf, drag, dray, wain **05** buggy, float, gambo, hutch, lorry, train, truck **06** boxcar, camion, hopper, telega **07** caisson, chariot, cocopan, flatcar, fourgon, gondola, kibitka, tank car, tartana **08** carriage, democrat, schooner **09** low-loader **10** freight-car, luggage-van **15** prairie schooner
• **on the wagon**
02 TT **06** tee-tee **08** teetotal

waif
04 puff, weft **05** stray, wefte **06** orphan, streak, urchin **07** wasting **09** foundling, neglected, wandering **10** ragamuffin

wail
02 io **03** cry, sob **04** howl, keen, moan, weep, yowl **05** groan **06** bemoan, lament, yammer **07** ululate, vagitus, weeping **08** complain **09** complaint, ululation

waistcoat
04 vest **05** gilet **06** bodice, bolero, jerkin **07** surcoat

wait
03 spy **04** bide, halt, hold, rest, stay, tend **05** abide, await, delay, lurch, pause, stand, tarry, watch **06** ambush, attend, escort, expect, hang in, hang on, hold-up, linger, remain, sit out, taihoa **07** stand by **08** hang fire, hesitate, hold back, interval, sentinel, watchman **09** bide tryst, hang about **10** hang around, hesitation **12** bide your time **13** lick your chops
• **wait on**
03 see **04** tend **05** serve **06** attend **07** work for **08** attend to **09** look after **10** minister to, take care of

waiter, waitress
04 host, tray **05** Nippy **06** busboy, butler, carhop, commis, garçon, mousmé, Nippie, salver, server **07** busgirl, hostess, maître d', mousmee, pannier, steward, waitron **08** watchman **09** attendant, sommelier **10** stewardess **12** maître d'hôtel

waive
04 cede **05** avoid, defer, evade, forgo, yield **06** forego, give up, ignore, reject, resign, vacate **07** abandon, forsake, put away **08** postpone, renounce, set aside **09** do without, surrender **10** relinquish **12** dispense with, strain a point

waiver
08 deferral **09** remission, surrender **10** abdication, disclaimer **11** abandonment, resignation **12** postponement, renunciation **14** relinquishment

wake
04 fire, goad, path, prod, rear, rise, stir, warn, wash, whet **05** alert, arise, awake, egg on, get up, rouse, track, trail, train, vigil, waken, watch, waves **06** arouse, awaken, come to, excite, notify, revive, signal, stir up **07** animate, funeral **08** activate, backwash, festival, lichwake, lykewake, serenade **09** aftermath, galvanize, reanimate, stimulate **10** bring round, death-watch **11** make aware of **13** become aware of **15** make conscious of

wakeful
04 wary **05** alert **06** waking **07** heedful, rousing **08** restless, vigilant, wakerife, watchful, waukrife **09** attentive, awakening, insomniac, observant, sleepless **10** unsleeping

wakefulness
05 vigil **08** insomnia **09** vigilance

12 restlessness, watchfulness
13 attentiveness, sleeplessness

waken
04 fire, rise, stir, wake, whet **05** awake, evoke, get up, rouse **06** arouse, awaken, excite, ignite, kindle, stir up, waking **07** animate, enliven, quicken **08** activate **09** galvanize, stimulate

Wales *see* **council**; **town**

walk
03 lag, leg, pad, wag, way **04** beat, foot, gait, hike, hump, lane, lead, limp, mall, move, pace, path, pawn, plod, step, trek, trog, turn, xyst, yomp **05** allée, alley, amble, drive, flock, guide, march, paseo, round, route, steps, stump, track, trail, tramp, tread, usher **06** avenue, behave, depart, escort, foot it, hoof it, pasear, ramble, rounds, sashay, spread, stride, stroll, trapes, trudge, xystos, xystus **07** alameda, berceau, circuit, conduct, gallery, passage, pathway, saunter, terrace, traipse, walkway **08** ambulate, carriage, footpath, frescade, go on foot, pavement, shepherd, sidewalk, traverse, withdraw **09** accompany, boulevard, circulate, disappear, esplanade, promenade **10** ambulatory, pad the hoof, pipe-opener **11** perambulate **13** hunting-ground, pedestrianize **15** stretch your legs
• **walk off with, walk away with**
03 bag, nip **04** lift, nick, whip **05** filch, pinch, steal, swipe **06** nobble, pocket **07** knock up, snaffle **08** knock off, liberate, souvenir **09** duckshove, go off with, relieve of **10** run off with **11** make off with **14** help yourself to
• **walk of life**
04 area, line **05** arena, field, trade **06** career, course, métier, sphere **07** calling, pursuit **08** activity, vocation **10** background, occupation, profession
• **walk out**
05 leave **06** mutiny, revolt, strike **07** protest **08** stop work **09** down tools **10** go on strike
• **walk out on**
04 dump, jilt **06** desert **07** abandon, forsake **08** run out on **15** leave high and dry, leave in the lurch
• **walk over**
05 abuse, cross **06** misuse **07** oppress **08** ill-treat, impose on, traverse **09** profiteer, trample on **10** manipulate **12** take for a ride **13** take liberties **14** play off against, pull a fast one on **15** take advantage of
• **walk unsteadily**
04 halt, stot **06** daddle, hobble, paddle, totter **07** shamble, stumble

walker
03 ped **05** hiker **06** fuller, ganger **07** rambler, vagrant **08** forester **09** ambulator **10** colporteur, pedestrian **11** stick insect

walking-stick
04 cane **05** waddy **06** kebbie, waddie

07 hickory **08** ash-plant **10** blackthorn **11** Malacca-cane **12** Penang-lawyer
See also **stick**

walk-out
06 revolt, strike **07** protest **08** stoppage **09** rebellion

walkover
02 WO **05** cinch **06** doddle **07** easy win, laugher **08** cakewalk, pushover **10** child's play **11** easy victory, piece of cake

walkway
04 lane, path, road **07** passage, pathway **08** footpath, pavement, sidewalk **09** esplanade, promenade

wall
02 wa' **04** mure

Wall types include:
03 dam, sea
04 dike, dyke
05 block, brick, death, fence, hedge, inner, mural, party
06 bailey, cavity, garden, paling, screen, shield
07 barrier, bulwark, curtain, divider, parapet, rampart, sea-wall
08 abutment, bulkhead, buttress, dry-stone, obstacle, palisade, stockade
09 barricade, enclosure, partition, retaining
10 embankment
11 breeze-block, load-bearing, outer bailey
13 fortification, stud partition
14 flying buttress

Walls include:
05 Great
06 Berlin
07 Wailing, Western
08 Antonine, Hadrian's
• **go to the wall**
04 fail, flop, fold **05** slump **06** finish, go bust **07** founder, go under **08** collapse **09** break down **11** come to an end, fall through **12** disintegrate **13** come to nothing
• **wall in**
03 pen **04** cage, hold, ring, wrap **05** bound, fence, frame, hedge, hem in **06** circle, corral, shut in **07** close in, confine, enclose, envelop **08** encircle, surround **09** encompass **10** circummure **12** circumscribe

wallaby
06 quokka, tammar **13** brush kangaroo

wallet
04 case **05** pouch, purse **06** folder, holder **08** bill-fold, notecase, pochette **10** pocketbook

wallop
03 hit, lam **04** bash, beat, beer, belt, blow, bonk, drub, kick, lick, rout, swat, whop **05** clout, crush, paste, pound, punch, smack, swipe, thump, whack **06** batter, buffet, defeat, gallop, hammer, pummel, strike, thrash,

thwack **07** clobber, heavily, noisily, trounce **08** flounder, vanquish
See also **beer**; **blow**

wallow
03 lie **04** bask, blow, loll, roll, wade **05** enjoy, glory, heave, lurch, revel, surge **06** muddle, relish, splash, tumble, well up, welter **07** delight, indulge, slubber **08** flounder **09** luxuriate

walrus
05 morse **06** sea cow **08** seahorse **09** rosmarine

wan
04 dark, pale, took, weak **05** ashen, bleak, faint, lurid, pasty, waxen, weary, white **06** feeble, gained, gloomy, pallid, sickly **07** anaemic, ghastly **08** mournful **09** washed out, whey-faced **10** colourless **11** discoloured

wand
03 rod **04** mace, twig, vare **05** baton, sprig, staff, stick **06** batoon **07** sceptre, thyrsus **08** caduceus **09** goldstick

wander
◊ *anagram indicator*
03 err, gad **04** moon, rave, roam, roll, rove, veer, wend **05** amble, drift, mooch, mouch, prowl, range, ratch, stray, taver, vague, wheel **06** babble, cruise, depart, gibber, maraud, mither, moider, ramble, streel, stroam, stroll, swerve, taiver, wilder **07** deviate, digress, diverge, maunder, meander, moither, pilgrim, saunter, swan off, traipse **08** aberrate, bewilder, divagate, go astray, squander, straggle, stravaig, traverse, turn away **09** bat around, excursion, expatiate, forwander, kick about, moon about **10** kick around, moon around, pilgrimage, ratch about **11** extravagate, lose your way, peregrinate, vagabondize **12** stooge around, talk nonsense **14** walk the streets

wanderer
04 waif **05** Gypsy, nomad, rover, stray **06** nomade, ranger **07** drifter, erratic, pilgrim, rambler, vagrant, voyager **08** prodigal, stroller, vagabond, wayfarer **09** itinerant, straggler, traveller **12** rolling stone

wandering
03 gad **04** roam, rove, waff, waif **05** drift, error **06** errant, erring, flight, roving **07** erratic, journey, meander, nomadic, odyssey, strayed, travels, vagrant **08** aberrant, drifting, errantry, homeless, rambling, rootless, vagabond, voyaging **09** departure, deviation, erroneous, evagation, excursion, itinerant, migratory, strolling, unsettled, walkabout, wayfaring **10** aberration, digression, divergence, journeying, meandering, solivagant, travelling **11** extravagant, noctivagant, peripatetic

13 peregrination, peregrinatory
14 circumforanean
15 circumforaneous

wane
03 dim, ebb **04** drop, fade, fail, fall, sink, welk **05** abate, decay, droop, welke **06** fading, lessen, shrink, vanish, weaken, wither **07** atrophy, decline, dwindle, failure, sinking, subside **08** contract, decrease, diminish, fade away, peter out, taper off **09** abatement, dwindling, lessening, weakening **10** diminution, subsidence **11** contraction, tapering off **12** degeneration
• **on the wane**
06 ebbing, fading **08** dropping, moribund **09** declining, dwindling, lessening, subsiding, weakening, withering **11** obsolescent, on the way out, tapering off **12** degenerating, on the decline **13** deteriorating, on its last legs

wangle
03 fix **04** work **06** fiddle, manage, scheme **07** arrange, falsify, finagle, pull off **08** contrive, engineer **09** manoeuvre **10** manipulate **12** wheel and deal

want
04 lack, like, lust, miss, mole, need, pine, will, wish **05** covet, crave, fancy **06** besoin, dearth, defect, demand, desire, hunger, penury, pining, thirst **07** absence, blemish, call for, craving, hope for, long for, longing, paucity, pine for, poverty, require **08** appetite, coveting, feel like, scarcity, shortage, yearn for, yearning **09** be without, hunger for, indigence, privation, thirst for **10** deficiency, desiderate, feebleness, inadequacy, scantiness **11** destitution, requirement **13** be deficient in, insufficiency

wanting
03 for **04** less, poor **05** needy, short **06** absent, faulty **07** lacking, missing, without **08** amissing, desirous **09** defective, deficient, imperfect **10** inadequate **11** substandard **12** insufficient, unacceptable **13** disappointing **14** not up to scratch, unsatisfactory

wanton
◇ *anagram indicator*
03 gay, rig **04** idle, lewd, nice, rake, rash, roué, slut, tart, wild **05** cadgy, whore **06** frisky, frolic, harlot, impure, jovial, kidgie, lecher, toyish, trifle, unjust, unruly **07** amorous, Don Juan, immoral, riggish, smicker, toysome, trifler, trollop, twigger **08** arrogant, Casanova, immodest, insolent, petulant, prodigal, reckless, skittish, sportive, strumpet **09** abandoned, arbitrary, debauchee, dissipate, dissolute, lecherous, libertine, malicious, merciless, pointless, shameless **10** capricious, cork-heeled, dissipated, gratuitous, groundless,

lascivious, malevolent, prostitute, unprovoked, voluptuary
11 extravagant, promiscuous
12 unmanageable, unrestrained
13 self-indulgent, undisciplined, unjustifiable

war
04 army **05** clash, excel, fight, worse, worst **06** combat, defeat, enmity, stoush, strife, strive **07** contend, contest, ill-will, make war, wage war, warfare **08** campaign, conflict, fighting **09** bloodshed **10** antagonism, contention, take up arms **11** cross swords, hostilities **13** confrontation

War types include:
03 hot
04 cold, germ, holy
05 blitz, civil, jihad, total, trade, world
06 ambush, attack, battle, jungle, nerves, trench
07 assault, limited, nuclear, private
08 chemical, intifada, invasion, skirmish, struggle
09 attrition, guerrilla
10 asymmetric, biological, blitzkrieg, engagement, manoeuvres, resistance
11 bombardment
12 asymmetrical, state of siege
13 armed conflict, counter-attack

Wars include:
03 Cod
04 1812, Boer, Gulf, Iraq, Sikh, Zulu
05 Chaco, Dutch, Great, Maori, Opium, Punic, Roses, World
06 Afghan, Balkan, Barons', Gallic, Indian, Korean, Six-Day, Trojan, Vendée, Winter
07 Bishops', Crimean, Italian, Mexican, Pacific, Persian, Servile, Vietnam
08 Crusades, Football, Iran-Iraq, Peasants', Religion, Ten Years'
09 Black Hawk, Falklands, Yom Kippur
10 Devolution, Jenkins' Ear, Napoleonic, Peninsular, Queen Anne's, Seven Years', Suez Crisis
11 Arab-Israeli, Eighty Years', Indian Civil, King Philip's, Thirty Years'
12 English Civil, Hundred Years', Independence, King William's, Russian Civil, Russo-Finnish, Russo-Turkish, Spanish Civil
13 American Civil, Grand Alliance, Russo-Japanese
14 Boxer Rebellion, Franco-Prussian, Indian Uprising, July Revolution, Triple Alliance
15 Easter Rebellion

See also **battle**
• **war cry**
04 hoop, word **05** havoc, whoop **06** banzai, slogan **07** war song **08** Geronimo **09** alalagmos, battle-cry, watchword **11** rallying-cry
• **war god**
03 Tiu, Tiw, Tyr **04** Mars **08** Quirinus

warble
03 cry **04** call, sing, song **05** carol,

chirl, chirp, trill, yodel **06** quaver, record, relish **07** chirrup, rellish, twitter

ward
04 area, care, fend, room, unit, zone **05** guard, minor, parry, pupil, spike, watch **06** charge **07** cubicle, custody, lookout, protégé, quarter **08** district, division, precinct, protégée **09** apartment, dependant, maternity **10** protection, sanatorium, sanitarium **11** compartment **12** guardianship
• **ward off**
04 fend, wear, weir **05** avert, avoid, block, dodge, evade, parry, repel **06** defend, shield, thwart **07** beat off, deflect, fend off, forfend **08** stave off, turn away **09** drive back, forestall, turn aside **11** averruncate

warden
06 keeper, ranger, regent, warder **07** curator, janitor, steward **08** bearward, guardian, meter man, overseer, sentinel, watchman **09** caretaker, concierge, constable, custodian, meter maid, protector **10** gatekeeper, supervisor **11** housekeeper, lollipop man **12** lollipop lady **13** administrator, lollipop woman **14** superintendent

warder
05 guard, screw **06** jailer, keeper, warden **08** wardress **09** beefeater, custodian **13** prison officer

wardrobe
04 robe **06** attire, closet, locker, outfit **07** almirah, apparel, armoire, cabinet, clothes **08** cupboard, garments **09** garderobe

warehouse
04 hong, shed **05** depot, store **06** bodega, godown, lock-up **07** store up **08** entrepot **09** goods shed, stockroom **10** depository, repository, storehouse **11** freight shed

wares
05 goods, stock, stuff **07** brokery, pedlary, produce **08** ironware, products **11** charcuterie, commodities, merchandise

warfare
03 war **04** arms **05** blows **06** battle, combat, strife **07** contest, discord, feuding **08** campaign, conflict, fighting, struggle **10** contention **11** hostilities **13** confrontation, passage of arms

warily
06 cagily **07** charily **08** gingerly, uneasily, with care **09** carefully, guardedly **10** cautiously, hesitantly, vigilantly, watchfully **12** suspiciously **13** circumspectly, distrustfully **14** apprehensively

wariness
04 care **06** cautel, unease **07** caution **08** caginess, distrust, prudence, wariment **09** alertness, attention,

foresight, hesitancy, suspicion, vigilance **10** discretion **11** carefulness, heedfulness, mindfulness **12** apprehension, watchfulness **14** circumspection

warlike
07 hawkish, hostile, martial **08** cavalier, militant, military **09** bellicose, combative **10** aggressive, battailous, pugnacious, unfriendly **11** belligerent **12** antagonistic, bloodthirsty, militaristic, warmongering

warlock
05 demon, witch **06** wizard **08** conjurer, magician, sorcerer **09** enchanter **11** necromancer

warm
03 het, hot, lew, sun **04** beat, fine, heat, kind, luke, melt, rich, stir, thaw **05** angry, balmy, calid, close, eager, fresh, rouse, sunny, tepid, toast **06** ardent, caring, excite, genial, hearty, heated, heat up, kindly, lively, loving, mellow, please, reheat, tender, toasty **07** affable, amiable, amorous, animate, beating, cheer up, cordial, delight, earnest, enliven, excited, fervent, glowing, intense, liven up, sincere, thermal, zealous **08** cheerful, friendly, interest, lukewarm, make warm, relaxing, vehement, well-to-do **09** harassing, heartfelt, stimulate, strenuous, temperate **10** hospitable, indelicate, passionate **11** comfortable, kind-hearted, sympathetic **12** affectionate, enthusiastic **15** put some life into
• **warm to**
11 begin to like
• **warm up**
04 heat **07** prepare **08** exercise, limber up, loosen up

warm-blooded
04 rash **06** ardent, lively **07** earnest, fervent **08** spirited **09** emotional, excitable, impetuous, vivacious **10** hot-blooded, passionate **11** endothermic, homothermal, homothermic **12** enthusiastic, homothermous, idiothermous

warm-hearted
04 kind **06** ardent, genial, hearty, kindly, loving, tender **07** cordial **08** generous **11** kind-hearted, sympathetic **12** affectionate **13** compassionate, tender-hearted

warmonger
04 hawk **09** aggressor **10** militarist **12** sabre-rattler

warmth
04 care, fire, glow, heat, love, zeal **05** ardor, flame **06** ardour **07** fervour, hotness, passion, unction **08** fervency, kindness, sympathy, warmness **09** affection, eagerness, intensity, sincerity, vehemence **10** compassion, cordiality, enthusiasm, kindliness, tenderness **11** hospitality **12** friendliness

warn
03 vor **04** tell, urge **05** alert, awarn, shore **06** advise, exhort, forbid, inform, notify, rebuke, summon, tip off **07** caution, command, counsel, let know, portend, presage, reprove, warrant **08** admonish, forewarn, instruct **09** factorize, premonish, reprimand **10** give notice **13** sound the alarm **14** put on your guard

warning
04 call, hint, omen, sign, wire **05** alarm, alert **06** advice, augury, caveat, lesson, notice, signal, threat, tip-off **07** caution, counsel, example, ominous, portent, presage, summons **08** monition, monitory **10** admonition, admonitory, cautionary, wake-up call, yellow card **11** information, premonition, premonitory, threatening **12** notification **13** advance notice

See also **signal**
• **expression of warning**
03 nix, now **04** cave, fore, gang, mind **06** timber **07** Achtung, you wait! **08** gardyloo **09** scaldings

warp
◇ *anagram indicator*
04 bend, bent, bias, cast, kink, turn **05** kedge, quirk, throw, twist **06** buckle, defect, deform, spring, swerve **07** contort, corrupt, deviate, distort, entwine, pervert **08** miscarry, misshape **09** deviation **10** contortion, distortion, perversion **11** deformation **12** irregularity

warrant
04 able, back, fiat, keep, warn **05** allow, proof, sepad, swear **06** affirm, assure, avouch, behote, defend, excuse, pardon, permit, pledge, uphaud, uphold **07** approve, behight, call for, caption, certify, consent, declare, defence, deserve, empower, endorse, entitle, justify, licence, license, precept, predict, presage, promise, protect, require, support, voucher **08** defender, detainer, guaranty, mittimus, sanction, security, transire, vouch for, warranty **09** answer for, assurance, authority, authorize, consent to, diligence, execution, guarantee, underclay, vouchsafe **10** commission, permission, underwrite, validation **11** necessitate **12** bench-warrant, death warrant, fugie-warrant, peace-warrant **13** authorization, justification, search warrant **14** lettre de cachet
• **warrant officer**
02 WO **03** CSM, RSM **04** bos'n **05** bosun **09** boatswain

warrantable
05 legal, right **06** lawful, proper **09** allowable, estimable, excusable, necessary **10** defensible, reasonable **11** accountable, justifiable, permissible

warranty
04 bond **06** pledge **08** contract, covenant, evidence **09** assurance, guarantee **11** certificate **13** authorization, justification

warring
◇ *anagram indicator*
05 at war **07** hostile, opposed **08** fighting, opposing **09** combatant, embattled **10** contending **11** belligerent, conflicting **14** at daggers drawn

warrior
05 brave, ghazi **06** Amazon, haiduk, wardog, warman **07** berserk, fighter, heyduck, soldier, warlock, warwolf **08** champion, warhorse **09** berserker, combatant **11** fighting man

warship
03 cog, ram **06** galley **07** cruiser, man-o'-war **08** man-of-war **09** blockship, destroyer, first-rate **10** battleship, turret ship **11** capital ship, dreadnaught, dreadnought, torpedo boat **13** battle-cruiser

wart
03 wen **04** lump **06** anbury, growth **07** verruca **09** keratosis, papilloma **10** angleberry **11** excrescence **12** protuberance

wary
04 cagy, ware **05** alert, aware, cagey, chary, leery, tenty **06** tentie **07** careful, guarded, heedful, prudent, thrifty **08** cautious, vigilant, watchful **09** attentive, wide-awake **10** on the alert, suspicious **11** circumspect, distrustful, on your guard **12** on the lookout **14** circumspective

wash
03 fen, lap, lip, mop, wet **04** bath, beat, coat, dash, flow, hold, lave, lick, roll, sind, slop, soak, synd, wave, wipe **05** bathe, clean, layer, marsh, rinse, scrub, souse, stain, stick, sujee, surge, sweep, swell, swill **06** douche, lotion, shower, sloosh, soogee, soogie, soojey, splash, sponge, stream **07** cleanse, coating, launder, laundry, moisten, shampoo, stand up, washing **08** cleaning, swab down **09** cleansing, freshen up, have a bath, have a wash, hold water **10** be accepted, laundering, pass muster **11** be plausible, carry weight, have a shower **12** bear scrutiny, be believable, be convincing, get cleaned up **15** bear examination
• **wash your hands of**
07 abandon **08** give up on

washed-out
03 wan **04** flat, pale **05** all in, ashen, drawn, faded, spent, weary **06** pallid **07** anaemic, drained, haggard, worn-out **08** blanched, bleached, dog-tired, fatigued, tired-out **09** exhausted, knackered **10** colourless, lacklustre **14** dead on your feet

Washington
02 WA **04** Wash

washout
04 flop, mess **06** fiasco **07** debacle,

failure **08** disaster **11** lead balloon
14 disappointment

wasp

05 vespa **06** hornet **07** gallfly **08** ruby-
tail **09** cuckoo fly, mud dauber, velvet
ant **12** yellow jacket

waspish

05 cross, testy **06** bitchy, crabby,
grumpy, touchy **07** crabbed, grouchy,
peevish, prickly **08** captious, critical,
petulant, snappish, spiteful, virulent
09 crotchety, irascible, irritable **11** bad-
tempered, ill-tempered
12 cantankerous

wastage

04 loss **05** decay **07** atrophy
08 draining, marasmus **10** emaciation,
exhausting **11** dissipation, squandering
12 degeneration **14** frittering away

waste

◇ *anagram indicator*
03 nub **04** bare, blow, crud, gash, kill,
knub, lose, loss, pass, pine, rape, raze,
ruin, sack, slag, vain, wild **05** abuse,
bleak, drain, dregs, dross, empty,
erode, extra, husks, offal, scrap, slops,
spend, spill, spoil, trash **06** barren,
debris, desert, dismal, dreary, expend,
injure, lavish, litter, misuse, ravage,
refuse, shrink, slurry, unused, wither
07 atrophy, consume, despoil, destroy,
exhaust, garbage, neglect, pillage,
rubbish, ruinous, shrivel, splurge,
useless **08** cast away, desolate,
effluent, emaciate, lay waste, left-over,
misspend, rejected, squander,
unwanted **09** depredate, devastate,
dissipate, go through, leftovers,
profusion, recrement, throw away,
worthless **10** desolation, devastated,
dilapidate, get through, impoverish,
unoccupied **11** consumption,
destruction, dissipation, expenditure,
fritter away, offscouring, prodigality,
prodigalize, squandering, superfluous,
uninhabited **12** extravagance,
offscourings, uncultivated,
unproductive, unprofitable,
wastefulness **13** supernumerary
14 misapplication **15** become
emaciated

See also **kill**

wasted

◇ *anagram indicator*
04 high, lost, weak **05** drunk, gaunt,
spent **07** useless, war-worn, worn-out
08 ill-spent, needless, shrunken,
weakened, withered **09** atrophied,
emaciated, exhausted, washed-out
10 shrivelled, squandered, unrequired
11 unexploited, unnecessary **12** down
the drain

wasteful

04 vain **06** lavish **07** ruinous
08 desolate, prodigal, wastfull, wastrife
09 unthrifty, wasterife **10** profitless,
profligate, thriftless **11** extravagant,
improvident, spendthrift, uninhabited
12 uneconomical, unfrequented

wasteland

04 fell, void, wild **05** waste, wilds
06 desert **07** thwaite **08** badlands
09 emptiness **10** barrenness,
wilderness

wasting

05 tabes **07** atrophy **08** marasmic,
marasmus, phthisis, syntexis
09 cirrhosis, consuming, symptosis
10 colliquant, destroying, emaciating,
enfeebling, tabescence **11** colliquable,
consumption, consumptive,
devastating, tabefaction
12 colliquative, contabescent

wastrel

04 waif **05** idler, waste **06** feeble,
loafer, refuse, skiver **07** goof-off,
lounger, shirker **08** layabout
09 lazybones **10** malingerer, ne'er-do-
well, profligate **11** spendthrift **14** good-
for-nothing

watch

03 eye, nit, see, spy **04** espy, heed,
keep, mark, mind, nark, note, scan,
tend, tout, view, wait, wake, ward
05 await, clock, flock, guard, scout,
spial, vigil **06** follow, gape at, gaze at,
look at, look on, look to, notice, peer at,
regard, shadow, survey, ticker
07 inspect, look out, lookout, monitor,
observe, outlook, overeye, protect,
stare at **08** repeater, sentinel, take care,
take heed, tick-tick **09** alertness,
attention, be careful, look after,
timepiece, vigilance **10** inspection,
keep tabs on, stemwinder, take care of,
wristwatch **11** chronometer,
contemplate, keep an eye on,
observation, superintend, supervision
12 pay attention, pernoctation,
surveillance, watchfulness

See also **clock**

• **watch out**
04 mind **06** notice **07** keep nit, look
out **08** cockatoo, stand nit **10** be
vigilant **12** keep a lookout **13** stand
cockatoo

• **watch over**
04 mind, tend, ward **05** guard
06 defend, shield **07** protect, shelter
08 preserve, sentinel, shepherd
09 look after, supervise **10** take care of
11 keep an eye on **14** stand guard over

watchdog

07 monitor **08** guard dog, guardian,
house-dog **09** custodian, inspector,
ombudsman, protector, regulator,
vigilante **10** scrutineer **11** housekeeper

watcher

03 spy **05** Argus **06** viewer **07** lookout,
witness **08** audience, looker-on,
observer, onlooker **09** spectator
10 eyewitness, televiewer

watchful

04 wary **05** alert, chary **07** guarded,
heedful **08** cautious, open-eyed,
vigilant, wakerife, waukrife
09 adviceful, attentive, avizefull,
observant, wide awake **10** suspicious

11 circumspect, on your guard **12** on
the lookout, on the qui vive

watchfulness

07 caution **08** wariness **09** alertness,
attention, dragonism, suspicion,
vigilance **10** observance **11** heedfulness
12 cautiousness **13** attentiveness
14 circumspection, suspiciousness

watchman

04 wait **05** guard **06** waiter **07** Charley,
Charlie, rug gown, wakeman
08 chokidar, night-man **09** caretaker,
chowkidar, custodian **10** speculator
13 security guard

watchword

03 cry **05** maxim, motto **06** byword,
signal, slogan **07** nayword, tag line
08 buzz word, password **09** battle-cry,
catchword, magic word, principle
10 shibboleth **11** catchphrase, rallying-
cry

water

02 aq, ea **03** eau, sea, wet **04** aqua,
hose, lake, rain, soak **05** class, douse,
drink, flood, ocean, river, spray
06 dampen, drench, lustre, saliva,
stream **07** current, moisten, quality,
torrent **08** flooding, irrigate, moisture,
saturate, sprinkle, surround **09** Adam's
wine **10** excellence **12** transparency

See also **lake**; **river**; **sea**

05 Evian®
06 Buxton®, Ty Nant®, Vittel®,
Volvic®
07 Perrier®
08 Aqua Pura®
10 Strathmore®
13 Pennine Spring®, San Pellegrino®
14 Highland Spring®

• **hold water**
04 hold, wash, work **05** stand, stick
06 cohere, hold up **07** stand up
08 convince, ring true **09** make sense
10 be accepted **11** be plausible, carry
weight, pass the test, remain valid
12 bear scrutiny, be believable, be
convincing **15** bear examination

• **water carrier**
06 bhisti **07** bheesty, bhistee
08 Aquarius, bheestie

• **water down**
03 mix **04** thin **06** dilute, soften,
weaken **07** qualify **08** mitigate,
moderate, play down, tone down
09 attenuate, soft-pedal **10** adulterate

watercourse

04 burn, khor, lead, nala, rean, reen,
wadi **05** brook, canal, ditch, drain,
nalla, nulla, rhine, rhyne, river, shott,
whelm **06** arroyo, nallah, nullah, spruit,
stream **07** channel **09** sunk fence
12 water-channel

See also **river**

waterfall

03 lin **04** drop, fall, foss, linn, salt
05 chute, falls, force, rapid, sault,
shoot, shute, spout **06** lasher, rapids

07 cascade, chignon, necktie, torrent
08 cataract, overfall 10 salmon leap

Waterfalls include:

05 Angel, Della, Glass, Pilao, Tysse
06 Boyoma, Iguaçu, Krimml, Ormeli, Ribbon, Tugela
07 Mtarazi, Niagara, Stanley, Thukela
08 Cuquenán, Gavarnie, Gullfoss, Itatinga, Kaieteur, Takkakaw, Victoria, Wallaman, Yosemite
09 Churchill, Dettifoss, Giessbach, Multnomah, Staubbach
10 Cleve-Garth, Sutherland, Wollomombi
11 Reichenbach, Trummelbach
12 Cusiana River, Paulo Alfonso, Silver Strand
13 Mardalsfossen, Tyssetrengane, Upper Yosemite, Vestre Mardola

waterproof, waterproof material
03 mac 04 mack 05 loden 06 anorak, arctic, cagoul, camlet, coated, kagool, kagoul, poncho 07 Barbour®, cagoule, camelot, jaconet, kagoule, oilskin, proofed, slicker, tanking 09 damp-proof, macintosh, sou'wester, tarpaulin 10 impervious, mackintosh, rubberized, tarpauling, trench coat, watertight 11 Barbour® coat, gutta-percha, impermeable 12 antigropelos 13 antigropeloes, Barbour® jacket 14 water-repellent, water-resistant

watertight
04 firm 05 sound 06 sealed, stanch 07 staunch 08 airtight, flawless, hermetic 09 foolproof 10 waterproof 11 impregnable 12 indisputable, unassailable

watery
03 wet 04 damp, thin, weak 05 blear, eager, fluid, moist, runny, soggy, vapid, washy 06 bleary, liquid, serous, sloppy 07 aqueous, diluted, hydrous, insipid, shilpit 08 hydatoid, skinking, squelchy 09 tasteless 10 wishy-washy 11 adulterated, flavourless, transparent, watered-down

wave
◇ *anagram indicator*
03 sea, waw 04 curl, flap, flow, foam, rash, rush, sign, stir, surf, sway, waff, waft, wawe 05 crimp, drift, float, flood, flote, froth, hover, shake, surge, sweep, swell, swing, trend, waver 06 beckon, billow, comber, direct, quiver, ripple, roller, signal, stream, waffle 07 breaker, current, decuman, feather, flutter, gesture, impulse, soliton, tide rip, upsurge, wavelet 08 backwash, brandish, flourish, increase, indicate, movement, outbreak, tendency, undulate, whitecap 09 tidal wave, vacillate 10 crispation, supersonic, undulation, white horse 11 beachcomber, gesticulate, ground swell
• **make waves**
12 cause trouble 13 disturb things, stir up trouble

• **wave aside**
05 spurn 06 reject, shelve 07 dismiss 08 set aside 09 disregard 10 brush aside 15 pour cold water on
• **wave down**
06 summon 08 flag down 12 signal to stop

waver
◇ *anagram indicator*
04 reel, rock, sway, vary, wave 05 haver, shake 06 change, didder, dither, falter, seesaw, teeter, totter, waffle, wobble 07 give way, stagger, tremble 08 hesitate 09 fluctuate, hum and haw, oscillate, vacillate 10 equivocate 11 be undecided 12 shilly-shally

waverer
07 doubter, haverer, wobbler 08 ditherer 14 shilly-shallier

wavering
◇ *anagram indicator*
04 wavy 05 shaky 07 dithery, stagger 08 doubtful, doubting, firmless, havering, hesitant 09 ambiguous, dithering, hesitance, hesitancy 10 hesitation, indecision, in two minds, of two minds 11 vacillatory 12 double-minded 15 shilly-shallying

wavy
04 undé 05 curly, curvy, oundy, undee 06 nebulé, nebuly, repand, ridged, undate, wiggly, zigzag 07 curling, curving, rippled, sinuate, sinuous, undated, winding 08 sinuated, undulate, wavering 09 snow goose 10 flamboyant, undulating, undulatory 11 fluctuating

wax
03 say 04 cere, grow, kiss, pela, rise, seal, talk, tell 05 mount, speak, state, swell, utter, voice, widen 06 become, expand, extend, spread 07 address, broaden, cerumen, declaim, declare, develop, enlarge, express, fill out, magnify, passion 08 converse, increase, paraffin 09 enunciate, get bigger, hold forth, pronounce 10 articulate 11 communicate

waxen
03 wan 04 pale 05 ashen, livid, white 06 pallid 07 anaemic, ghastly, whitish 09 bloodless 10 colourless

waxy
04 soft 05 irate, pasty, waxen 06 pallid 07 cereous 08 incensed 09 ceraceous 11 impressible 14 impressionable

way
◇ *anagram indicator*
01 E, N, S, W 02 Rd, St, Wy 03 far, via 04 gate, lane, mode, path, plan, road, rode, room, tool, very, will, wise, wont 05 habit, lines, means, route, scope, state, style, track, trait, usage, weigh 06 access, avenue, course, custom, esteem, manner, method, nature, really, street, system, temper 07 channel, conduct, fashion, highway, journey, passage, pathway, process, respect, roadway 08 approach,

district, position, practice, progress, strategy 09 behaviour, condition, direction, mannerism, procedure, technique 10 instrument 11 disposition, peculiarity, personality, temperament 12 idiosyncrasy, thoroughfare 14 characteristic, course of action 15 instrumentality
• **all the way**
02 up 04 thro, thru 07 through 08 straight
• **by the way**
02 ob 03 BTW 06 obiter 07 apropos 09 en passant, in passing 11 secondarily 12 incidentally 14 by the same token 15 à propos de bottes, parenthetically
• **either way**
◇ *palindrome indicator*
• **give way**
02 go 03 sag 04 bend, cede, sink 05 break, burst, crack, yield 06 cave in, fall in, give in, relent, shrink, spring, submit, swerve 07 concede, subside, succumb 08 collapse, fall back, withdraw 09 give place, surrender 10 capitulate, give ground 12 disintegrate
• **make your way**
04 wend 06 travel 07 journey
• **on the way**
07 en route 09 in transit
• **quickest way**
07 beeline
• **under way**
05 afoot, begun, going 06 moving 07 started 08 in motion 10 in progress 11 in operation, progressing 12 off the ground
• **way of life**
04 life 05 world 08 position 09 lifestyle, situation 12 modus vivendi
• **ways and means**
04 cash 05 funds, tools 07 capital, methods 08 capacity, reserves 09 procedure, resources 10 capability 11 wherewithal
• **whichever way you look at it**
◇ *palindrome indicator*

wayfarer
05 Gypsy, nomad, rover 06 viator, walker 07 pilgrim, swagger, swagman, trekker, voyager 08 traveler, wanderer 09 itinerant, journeyer, piepowder, traveller 12 globetrotter

wayfaring
06 roving 07 nomadic, walking 08 drifting, rambling, voyaging 09 itinerant, wandering 10 journeying, travelling 11 peripatetic

waylay
03 lay 05 belay, catch, seize 06 accost, ambush, attack, hold up 07 set upon, stick up 08 obstruct, surprise 09 intercept 10 buttonhole 12 lie in wait for

way-out
04 lost, rapt, wild 05 crazy, wacky, weird 06 exotic, far-out, freaky 07 bizarre, off-beat, unusual 09 eccentric, excellent, fantastic, left-field 10 avant-garde, outlandish,

unorthodox **11** exceptional, progressive **12** experimental **14** unconventional

wayward
06 fickle, unruly, wilful **07** peevish **08** contrary, obdurate, perverse, stubborn **09** irregular, obstinate **10** capricious, changeable, headstrong, rebellious, refractory, self-willed **11** disobedient, intractable, loup-the-dyke **12** contumacious, incorrigible, ungovernable, unmanageable **13** insubordinate, unpredictable

waywardness
08 obduracy **09** contumacy, obstinacy **10** perversity, unruliness, wilfulness **12** contrariness, disobedience, perverseness, stubbornness **14** rebelliousness **15** insubordination

weak
01 W **03** dim, low **04** dull, fade, gone, lame, poor, puny, soft, thin **05** cissy, faint, frail, milky, runny, shaky, weedy **06** debile, facile, faulty, feeble, flimsy, infirm, meagre, pallid, sickly, single, slight, unable, watery **07** brickle, diluted, exposed, fragile, insipid, lacking, muffled, stifled, unsound, useless, worn out **08** cowardly, delicate, fatigued, impotent **09** defective, deficient, enervated, exhausted, forceless, imperfect, powerless, spineless, strung out, tasteless, unguarded, unhealthy, untenable **10** effeminate, fizzenless, foisonless, fusionless, inadequate, indecisive, indistinct, irresolute, unstressed, vulnerable **11** adulterated, debilitated, defenceless, fushionless, impressible, ineffectual, unprotected **12** inconclusive, invertebrate, unconvincing **13** imperceptible **14** inconsiderable, valetudinarian

weaken
03 sap **04** fade, fail, flag, kill, pall, thin, tire **05** abate, appal, craze, delay, droop, lower, taint **06** deduct, dilute, ease up, impair, lessen, reduce, soften, temper **07** cripple, disable, dwindle, exhaust, give way, unnerve **08** diminish, enervate, enfeeble, entender, intender, mitigate, moderate, paralyse, soften up **09** extenuate, undermine, water down **10** debilitate, disconcert, effeminate, effeminize **12** incapacitate **13** disinvigorate **14** take the edge off

weakening
06 easing, fading, waning **07** failing **08** dilution, flagging, lowering **09** abatement, dwindling, lessening, reduction **10** enervation, impairment, moderation **11** extenuation, frontolysis, undermining **12** debilitation, diminishment, enfeeblement

weakling
03 wet **04** drip, tonk, weed, wimp, wuss **05** cissy, mouse, wally **06** coward

07 dilling, doormat, milksop **08** softling, underdog **09** underling **10** namby-pamby

weakly
06 feebly, lamely **07** faintly, frailly **08** slightly **09** tenuously **10** helplessly **11** implausibly, powerlessly **12** dispiritedly, indecisively, pathetically **13** ineffectively

weak-minded
04 daft **07** pliable **09** compliant, spineless, weak-kneed **10** irresolute, submissive **11** complaisant, persuadable, persuasible **12** faint-hearted **13** pusillanimous

weakness
04 flaw **05** doubt, fault, folly **06** defect, dotage, foible, liking **07** acrasia, apepsia, blemish, cachexy, failing, frailty, languor, passion **08** azoturia, cachexia, debility, delicacy, fondness, frailtee, penchant, soft spot, trembles **09** frailness, impotence, infirmity, lassitude, weak point **10** deficiency, effeminacy, enervation, feebleness, flimsiness, incapacity, myasthenia, proclivity **11** dubiousness, inclination, paraparesis, shortcoming, tenuousness, uncertainty, unsoundness **12** Achilles' heel, delicateness, doubtfulness, enfeeblement, imperfection, phonasthenia, predilection, unlikelihood, unlikeliness **13** improbability, powerlessness, vulnerability **14** far-fetchedness, implausibility, predisposition **15** ineffectiveness, second childhood

weal
04 mark, scar, wale, welt **05** bends, ridge, wheal, wound **06** streak, stripe **07** welfare **08** cicatrix **09** cicatrice, contusion **12** commonwealth **14** the sum of things

wealth
04 cash, ease, mass, pelf **05** funds, goods, lucre, means, money, store **06** assets, bounty, estate, mammon, plenty, riches **07** capital, finance, fortune, fulness, tallent, warison **08** fullness, opulence, property, richesse, treasure, treasury, warrison **09** abundance, affluence, plenitude, profusion, resources, substance, wellbeing **10** cornucopia, prosperity **11** copiousness, loadsamoney, possessions

wealthy
04 oofy, posh, rich **05** flush, pluty, solid **06** fat-cat, loaded **07** moneyed, opulent, well-off **08** affluent, well-to-do **10** filthy rich, prosperous, well-heeled **11** comfortable, made of money, rolling in it, substantial **12** stinking rich

weapon
03 arm

03 bow, gas, gun, Uzi
04 bomb, Colt®, cosh, dirk, épée, foil, ICBM, Mace®, mine, pike, Scud
05 arrow, billy, bolas, CS gas, H-bomb, knife, lance, Luger®, panga, rifle, sabre, sling, spear, sword, Taser®, vouge
06 airgun, cannon, cudgel, dagger, Exocet®, glaive, jambok, magnum, Mauser, mortar, musket, pistol, rapier, rocket, six-gun, taiaha, tomboc
07 assegai, balista, bayonet, bazooka, bomblet, Bren gun, caltrop, halberd, harpoon, longbow, machete, pole-axe, poniard, sjambok, sten gun, stun gun, tear-gas, torpedo
08 air rifle, atom bomb, ballista, blowpipe, calthrop, catapult, chemical, claymore, crossbow, field gun, howitzer, landmine, nail bomb, nerve gas, nunchaku, oerlikon, partisan, revolver, scimitar, shuriken, stiletto, threshel, time-bomb, tomahawk, tommy gun
09 automatic, battleaxe, boomerang, Mills bomb, smart bomb, truncheon, turret-gun
10 bowie knife, broadsword, flick-knife, gatling gun, machine-gun, mustard gas, napalm bomb, peashooter, shillelagh, six-shooter
11 Agent Orange, blunderbuss, bow and arrow, cluster-bomb, daisy-cutter, depth-charge, hand grenade, kalashnikov, neutron bomb, submunition, water pistol
12 bunker buster, flame-thrower, hydrogen bomb, quarterstaff
13 Cruise missile, knuckleduster, submachine-gun
14 incendiary bomb, rocket-launcher
15 thermobaric bomb, Winchester® rifle

See also **dagger**; **gun**; **knife**; **missile**; **sword**

wear
◊ *insertion indicator*
03 air, don, fly, rub, use **04** bear, edge, fray, have, pack, pass, show, stub **05** carry, dress, erode, grind, guide, mount, put on, spend, sport, waste, weary **06** abrade, accept, affect, assume, attire, become, damage, endure, have on, outfit **07** believe, clothes, conduct, consume, corrode, costume, display, dress in, erosion, exhaust, exhibit, fashion, service, utility **08** abrasion, clothing, friction, garments, tolerate, traverse **09** corrosion **10** durability, employment, usefulness **11** be clothed in, be dressed in, deteriorate, wear and tear **12** become weaker **13** become thinner, deterioration **14** fray at the edges
• **wear down**
05 erode, grind **06** abrade, impair, lessen, reduce **07** attrite, consume, corrode, degrade, rub away

08 diminish, macerate, overcome, soften up 09 grind down, undermine 10 chip away at
- **wear off**
03 ebb 04 fade, fray, wane 05 abate 06 lessen, weaken 07 dwindle, subside 08 decrease, diminish, peter out 09 disappear
- **wear on**
04 go by, go on, pass 06 elapse
- **wear out**
03 sap 04 fray, mush, tire 05 break, drain, erode, trash, use up, waste 06 harass, impair, peruse, strain, stress 07 consume, exhaust, fatigue, frazzle, knacker, knock up, tire out 08 enervate, forspend, overteem 09 forespend 11 deteriorate, wear through

wearily
07 tiredly 08 drowsily, sleepily 10 listlessly 11 unexcitedly 13 lethargically

weariness
05 ennui 07 fatigue, languor 08 lethargy 09 lassitude, tiredness 10 drowsiness, enervation, exhaustion, sleepiness 11 prostration, Weltschmerz 12 listlessness, taedium vitae
- **expression of weariness**
04 hech 07 heigh-ho

wearing
◇ *containment indicator*
02 in 06 taxing, tiring, trying 07 erosive, irksome 08 tiresome 09 consuming, fatiguing, wearisome 10 durability, exhausting, oppressive 12 exasperating

wearisome
04 dull 06 boring, dreary, trying 07 humdrum, irksome, tedious, wearing 08 annoying, tiresome, weariful 09 fatiguing, vexatious 10 bothersome, burdensome, exhausting, monotonous 11 troublesome 12 exasperating

weary
03 bug, fag, irk, sap, tax 04 bore, cloy, fade, fail, jade, puny, tire 05 all in, annoy, bored, drain, ennui, jaded, tired 06 aweary, betoil, burden, bushed, done in, drowsy, harass, pooped, sicken, sleepy, zonked 07 drained, exhaust, fatigue, tedious, tire out, wear out, whacked, worn out 08 awearied, dead beat, dog-tired, dog-weary, enervate, fatigued, forweary, half-dead, irritate, tiresome, toil-worn, trauchle, wiped out 09 exhausted, fagged out, knackered, overweary, pooped out, ramfeezle, think long, unexcited 10 brassed off, browned off, cheesed off, debilitate, exasperate 11 tuckered out 12 bored to tears, sick and tired, uninterested 14 unenthusiastic

wearying
06 taxing, tiring, trying 07 wearing 08 draining 09 fatiguing, wearisome 10 exhausting

weasel
04 mink 05 stoat, taira, tayra 06 grison, marten 07 whitret 08 whittret 09 delundung, wolverene, wolverine 10 whitterick

weather
03 dry, set, sky 04 gain, pass 05 brave, slope, stand 06 endure, expose, harden, resist, season, suffer 07 climate, dryness, outlook, ride out, survive, toughen 08 forecast, humidity, overcome, stick out, surmount, windward 09 rise above, sunniness, windiness, withstand 10 cloudiness, conditions, get through 11 come through, live through, pull through, temperature

Weather phenomena include:

03 fog, ice
04 gale, hail, haze, mist, rain, smog, snow, thaw, wind
05 cloud, frost, sleet, slush, storm
06 breeze, deluge, shower, squall
07 chinook, cyclone, drizzle, drought, mistral, monsoon, rainbow, tempest, thunder, tornado, twister, typhoon
08 black ice, downpour, heatwave, sunshine
09 hoar frost, hurricane, lightning, snowstorm, whirlwind

See also **cloud**; **ice**; **precipitation**; **snow**; **storm**; **wind**

- **under the weather**
03 ill 04 ropy, sick 05 crook, drunk, lousy, queer, ropey, rough, seedy 06 ailing, groggy, grotty, poorly 08 below par, hung over, nauseous 09 off-colour, squeamish 10 indisposed, out of sorts 15 the worse for wear

weave
◇ *anagram indicator*
03 rya, web 04 cane, fuse, knit, lace, spin, wind 05 braid, merge, plait, tweel, twill, twist, unite 06 create, damask, make up, plight, tissue, zigzag 07 compose, entwine, inweave, texture 08 contrive 09 construct, fabricate, interlace, interwork 10 criss-cross, intercross, intertwine, interweave 11 put together

weaver
04 loom

weaver bird
04 taha 06 bishop, ox-bird, quelea 09 grenadier 10 zebra finch 11 Java sparrow

web
03 mat, net 04 knot, mesh, plot, tela, trap, vane, weft 05 skein, snare 06 tangle 07 complex, lattice, netting, network, texture, webbing 08 intrigue, lacework, mesh-work, vexillum 11 fabrication, interlacing, latticework

wed
03 wad 04 ally, fuse, join, link, yoke 05 blend, marry, merge, unify, unite,

wager 06 pledge, splice 07 combine, espouse 08 coalesce, security 09 commingle 10 get hitched, get married, get spliced, interweave, take to wife, tie the knot 13 take the plunge 14 lead to the altar, lead up the aisle

wedded
06 joined, wifely 07 marital, married, nuptial, spousal 08 conjugal 09 connubial, husbandly 11 matrimonial

wedding
05 union 06 bridal, huppah, mating 07 chuppah, nuptial, wedlock 08 espousal, hymeneal, hymenean, marriage, nuptials, spousage 09 espousals, matrimony 11 epithalamic, matrimonial 15 marriage service

See also **anniversary**; **marriage**

wedge
03 fit, gad, gib, jam, key, ram 04 cram, lump, pack, push, trig 05 block, chock, chunk, cleat, crowd, force, lodge, piece, quoin, stuff, wodge 06 cotter, scotch, thrust 07 blaster, feather, squeeze 08 doorstop, triangle 09 space band, whipstock

wedlock
05 union 08 marriage 09 matrimony 13 holy matrimony

Wednesday
03 Wed 04 Weds

wee
03 pee, sma 04 leak, tiny 05 small, teeny, urine, weeny 06 little, midget, minute, teensy 07 urinate 09 itsy-bitsy, miniature, minuscule 10 diminutive, negligible, teeny-weeny 11 Lilliputian, microscopic 13 insignificant

weed
03 hoe 04 tare

Weeds include:

03 ers
04 dock, moss
05 daisy, vetch
06 fat hen, oxalis, spurge, yarrow
07 bracken, ragweed, ribwort
08 bindweed, duckweed, knapweed, self-heal
09 chickweed, coltsfoot, dandelion, ground ivy, groundsel, horsetail, knotgrass, liverwort, pearlwort, snakeweed, speedwell, sun spurge
10 cinquefoil, common reed, couch grass, curled dock, deadnettle, sow thistle, thale cress
11 ground elder, meadow grass, petty spurge, salad burnet, white clover
12 annual nettle, rough hawkbit, sheep's sorrel
13 common burdock, field wood rush, large bindweed, pineapple weed, small bindweed
14 common plantain, shepherd's purse
15 broad-leaved dock, burnet saxifrage, common chickweed, creeping thistle, greater plantain,

lesser celandine, perennial nettle, stemless thistle

See also **cannabis**; **seaweed**; **tobacco**

• **weed out**
05 purge 06 remove 07 isolate, root out 08 get rid of 09 eliminate, eradicate, extirpate

weedkiller
06 diquat 08 atrazine, Paraquat®, simazine 09 herbicide, weedicide 10 glyphosate 11 glufosinate, graminicide 14 sodium chlorate

weedy
03 wet 04 puny, thin, weak 05 frail, lanky, wussy 06 feeble, skinny 07 insipid, scrawny, wimpish 08 gangling 09 weak-kneed 10 undersized

week
01 w 03 ouk 04 oulk

weekly
09 by the week, every week, once a week 10 hebdomadal 11 hebdomadary 12 hebdomadally

weep
03 cry, sob 04 bawl, blub, drip, leak, moan, ooze, pipe, rain, seep, wail 05 droop, exude, greet, mourn, whine 06 beweep, boo-hoo, greete, grieve, lament, snivel 07 blubber, outweep, whimper 09 be in tears, shed tears 11 pipe your eye

weepy
04 oozy 05 teary 06 crying, labile 07 sobbing, tearful, weeping 08 greeting, sob-stuff 09 melodrama 10 blubbering, lachrymose, tear-jerker 11 sentimental

weigh
03 sit, way 04 ride 05 loose, poise, raise, scale, worry 06 burden, ponder 07 afflict, balance, depress, examine, get down, oppress, perpend, trouble 08 bear down, consider, evaluate, mull over, unanchor 09 disanchor, ponderate, reflect on, think over 10 deliberate, meditate on 11 contemplate 13 have a weight of 14 tip the scales at

• **weigh down**
04 load 05 pease, peaze, peise, peize, peyse, poise, worry 06 burden 07 afflict, depress, get down, oppress, trouble 08 bear down, outweigh, overload 09 press down, weigh upon

• **weigh up**
05 scale 06 assess, ponder, size up 07 balance, compare, discuss, examine 08 chew over, consider, evaluate, mull over 09 think over 10 deliberate 11 contemplate

weighing machine
04 tron 05 trone 06 bismar 09 steelyard

weight
01 w 02 wt 03 agw, gvw 04 bias, bulk, duty, gr wt, last, lead, load, mark, mass, nt wt, onus, pith, sway, tare 05 angle,

clout, flesh, force, pease, peaze, peise, peize, peyse, peyse, poise, power, slang, slant, twist, value, wecht, worry 06 burden, impact, moment, scales, slight, strain 07 ballast, gravity, oppress, plummet, tonnage, trouble 08 gravitas, handicap, live load, poundage, pressure, quantity 09 authority, heaviness, influence, prejudice, substance, unbalance, weigh down 10 importance, importancy, ponderance, ponderancy 11 avoirdupois, consequence, encumbrance 12 significance 13 consideration, preponderance 14 impressiveness, responsibility

See also **boxing**

• **unit of weight**
01 g, k, l, t 02 as, cg, ct, dg, gm, gr, hg, kg, lb, mg, oz, st 03 cwt, grt, kat, kin, kip, mna, oke, tod, ton, wey 04 boll, gram, kati, khat, kilo, mina, obol, pood, rotl, seer, tola, unce 05 candy, carat, catty, kandy, katti, liang, maneh, maund, ounce, picul, pikul, pound, stone, tical, todde, tonne 06 candie, carrat, cental, denier, dirhem, fother, gramme, kantar, shekel, talent 07 centner, lispund, scruple 08 decigram, lispound 09 centigram, milligram 10 decigramme 11 centigramme, milligramme

weightless
04 airy 05 light 11 imponderous 13 insubstantial

weighty
05 bulky, grave, great, heavy, hefty, solid, vital 06 severe, solemn, taxing 07 crucial, massive, onerous, pesante, serious 08 critical, exacting, pregnant, worrying 09 demanding, difficult, important, momentous, ponderous 10 burdensome 11 influential, significant, substantial 13 authoritative, consequential

weir
03 pen 04 wear 05 cauld, garth, guard 06 lasher 07 ward off 09 fish-garth

weird
◇ *anagram indicator*
03 odd, rum 04 doom, eery, fate 05 charm, eerie, queer, spell, witch 06 creepy, far-out, spooky, way-out, weyard 07 bizarre, destine, ghostly, strange, uncanny, weyward 08 eldritch, forewarn, freakish, peculiar, witching 09 grotesque, happening, left-field, unearthly, unnatural 10 mysterious 12 supernatural 13 preternatural

weirdly
06 eerily 08 spookily 09 bizarrely, strangely 11 unnaturally 12 mysteriously 14 supernaturally

weirdo
03 dag, nut 04 card, case, cure, geek, kook, loon, wack 05 crank, flake, freak, loony 06 nutter 07 cupcake, dingbat, nutcase, oddball, odd fish 08 crackpot

09 character, eccentric, fruitcake, queer fish 14 fish out of water

welcome
◇ *containment indicator*
04 free, hail, meet 05 greet 06 accept, salute 07 acclaim, embrace, karanga, popular, powhiri, proface, receive 08 glad hand, greeting, haeremai, pleasant, pleasing 09 agreeable, approve of, ben venuto, desirable, gratulate, reception, red carpet 10 acceptable, acceptance, delightful, gratifying, refreshing, salutation, salutary 11 acclamation, appreciated, hospitality 13 be pleased with 15 be satisfied with

welcoming
04 cosy, warm 06 genial, hearty 07 affable, cordial, earnest 08 amicable, cheerful, friendly, homelike, pleasant, relaxing, sociable 09 agreeable, gemütlich, heartfelt, open-armed 10 hospitable 11 comfortable, stimulating, warm-hearted 12 affectionate, invigorating, wholehearted

weld
04 bind, bond, fuse, join, link, pile, seal, seam, wald 05 braze, joint, seize, unite, wield 06 cement, solder 07 connect 09 dyer's-weed 10 mignonette, yellow-weed 11 dyer's rocket 15 dyer's-yellowweed

welfare
04 good, heal, weal 05 hayle, state 06 health, income, profit 07 benefit, comfort, fortune, payment, pension, sick pay, success 08 interest, security 09 advantage, allowance, happiness, soundness, wellbeing 10 commonweal, prosperity 14 social security

well
02 my, OK, so 03 eye, far, fit, jet, lor, sae, spa 04 ably, bien, eddy, fine, flow, font, good, gush, ooze, pool, pour, rise, rush, seep, weel 05 aweel, fitly, flood, fount, fully, good-o, issue, lucky, right, sound, spout, spurt, surge, swell, wally 06 atweel, cavity, deeply, easily, fairly, geyser, good-oh, highly, kindly, proper, robust, source, spring, stream, strong, supply, warmly 07 adeptly, clearly, closely, cockpit, fortune, greatly, happily, healthy, luckily, Mickery, rightly, spouter, trickle 08 all right, brim over, decently, expertly, fountain, genially, pleasing, probably, properly, suitably, thriving, very much, wellhead 09 advisable, agreeable, agreeably, carefully, certainly, correctly, fittingly, fortunate, glowingly, reservoir, skilfully, to a wonder, water hole 10 able-bodied, abundantly, adequately, admiringly, completely, favourably, generously, hospitably, intimately, pleasantly, profoundly, rigorously, splendidly, thoroughly, very likely, wellspring 11 approvingly, comfortable, comfortably,

competently, conceivably, effectively, efficiently, excellently, flourishing, fortunately, intensively **12** considerably, conveniently, in good health, proficiently, prosperously, satisfactory, successfully, sufficiently, watering hole **13** hale and hearty, industriously, quite possibly, substantially, weeping spring **14** satisfactorily, to a great extent **15** comprehensively

● **as well**
03 als, and, tae, too **04** also, both **06** to boot **07** besides **08** moreover **10** in addition **11** furthermore **14** into the bargain

● **as well as**
09 along with, including **12** in addition to, not to mention, over and above, together with **14** to say nothing of

● **well done**
04 euge **05** bravo **06** encore, hurrah **08** congrats, good show **13** à la bonne heure **15** congratulations

well-advised
04 wise **05** sound **06** shrewd **07** politic, prudent **08** sensible **09** judicious, sagacious **10** far-sighted, reasonable **11** circumspect, long-sighted

well-balanced
04 even, sane **05** level, sober, sound **06** sorted, stable **08** balanced, rational, sensible, together **10** harmonious, reasonable **11** level-headed, symmetrical, well-ordered **12** well-adjusted

well-behaved
04 good **06** polite, orderly **08** mannerly, obedient **09** compliant **10** good as gold, respectful **11** considerate, co-operative **12** under control, well-mannered

wellbeing
04 good **06** health, wealth **07** comfort, welfare **09** eudaemony, happiness **10** eudaemonia, good health

well-bred
05 civil **06** polite, urbane **07** gallant, genteel, refined **08** cultured, ladylike, mannerly **09** courteous **10** cultivated, upper-crust **11** blue-blooded, comme il faut, gentlemanly **12** aristocratic, well-mannered **13** well-brought-up

well-built
05 beefy, burly, stout **06** brawny, strong, sturdy **08** muscular **09** strapping

well-deserved
03 due **04** just, meet **07** condign, merited **08** deserved, rightful **09** justified **11** appropriate

well-disposed
06 toward **07** healthy **08** amicable, friendly, towardly **09** agreeable, well-aimed **10** benevolent, favourable, well-minded, well-placed **11** sympathetic **12** well-arranged

well-dressed
04 chic, neat, tidy, trim **05** natty, smart **06** dapper, spruce **07** elegant, stylish **11** fashionable, well-groomed

well-founded
03 fit **05** right, sound, valid **06** proper **08** sensible **09** plausible, warranted **10** acceptable, reasonable **11** justifiable, sustainable

well-groomed
04 neat, tidy, trim **05** smart **06** dapper, soigné, spruce **07** soignée **11** well-dressed **13** well-turned-out

well-heeled
04 oofy, posh, rich **05** flush, solid **06** fat-cat, loaded **07** moneyed, opulent, wealthy, well-off **08** affluent, well-to-do **10** filthy rich, prosperous **11** comfortable, made of money, rolling in it, substantial **12** stinking rich

well-informed
02 up **06** au fait, sussed **07** clued-up **09** au courant

well-known
04 name **05** famed, noted, usual **06** common, famous, notour, of note **07** eminent, notable **08** familiar, renowned **09** notorious **10** celebrated, proverbial **11** illustrious, widely-known

well-mannered
05 civil **06** polite, urbane **07** gallant, genteel, refined **08** cultured, ladylike, mannerly, well-bred **09** bien élevé, courteous **10** cultivated, upper-crust **11** blue-blooded, gentlemanly **12** aristocratic, house-trained **13** well-brought-up

well-nigh
05 welly **06** all but, almost, nearly **09** just about, virtually **11** practically

well-off
04 bein, bien, rich **05** flush, lucky **06** loaded, monied **07** moneyed, wealthy **08** affluent, thriving, well-to-do **09** fortunate **10** filthy rich, forehanded, in the money, prosperous, successful, well-heeled **11** comfortable, made of money, rolling in it **12** stinking rich **15** with money to burn

well-read
07 studied **08** cultured, educated, lettered, literate **12** well-informed **13** knowledgeable

Wells
02 HG

well-spoken
05 clear **06** fluent **08** coherent, eloquent **10** articulate **13** well-expressed

well-thought-of
07 admired, revered **08** esteemed, honoured **09** respected, venerated **10** looked up to **14** highly regarded

well-to-do
04 oofy, posh, rich, warm **05** flush

06 fat-cat, loaded **07** moneyed, wealthy, well-off **08** affluent **10** filthy rich, prosperous **11** comfortable, made of money, rolling in it, substantial **12** stinking rich

well-versed
02 up **06** au fait **07** trained **08** deep-read, familiar **10** acquainted, conversant **11** experienced **13** knowledgeable

well-wisher
03 fan **06** friend **09** supporter **10** well-willer **11** sympathizer

well-worn
04 worn **05** corny, stale, stock, tired, trite **06** frayed, ragged, shabby **07** cliché'd, scruffy, worn-out **08** clichéed, overused, timeworn **09** hackneyed **10** threadbare, unoriginal **11** commonplace, stereotyped **13** battle-scarred

welsh
01 W **02** do **05** cheat **06** diddle **07** defraud, swindle

Welsh first names include:

03 Dai, Huw, Nye, Wyn
04 Aled, Alun, Ceri, Dewi, Enid, Eryl, Evan, Glyn, Gwen, Gwyn, Ifor, Ioan, Owen, Rees, Rhys, Siôn
05 Carys, Cerys, Dilys, Dylan, Elwyn, Emlyn, Emrys, Ffion, Gavin, Haydn, Howel, Hywel, Idris, Ieuan, Lloyd, Madoc, Megan, Nerys, Olwen, Olwin, Olwyn, Rhian, Tudor
06 Dafydd, Delyth, Dilwyn, Eirian, Eirlys, Eluned, Gareth, Gaynor, Gladys, Glenda, Glenys, Glynis, Gwenda, Gwilym, Howell, Mervyn, Morgan, Olwyne
07 Aneirin, Aneurin, Bronwen, Brynmor, Eiluned, Geraint, Gwenyth, Gwillym, Gwyneth, Myfanwy, Myrddin, Peredur, Vaughan
08 Angharad, Llewelyn, Meredith, Morwenna, Rhiannon
09 Gwendolen, Gwenllian

See also **county; town**

welt
03 dry **04** beat, blow, lash, mark, scar, weal **05** ridge, world, wound **06** streak, stripe, wither **08** cicatrix **09** cicatrice, contusion

welter
03 web **04** mess, roll, toss, wade **05** heave, lurch, pitch **06** jumble, muddle, splash, tangle, wallow **07** smother **08** flounder, mish-mash **09** confusion **10** hotchpotch

wend *see* **Slav**
● **wend your way**
02 go **04** hike, move, plod, walk **05** amble **06** travel, trudge, wander **07** meander, proceed **08** progress **11** make your way

west
01 W **03** Mae **08** New World, Occident **10** Occidental

• go west
◊ *reversal indicator*
03 die **06** perish **11** be destroyed **12** be dissipated

western
01 W **06** ponent **07** westlin **10** occidental

Western Sahara
03 ESH

West Virginia
02 WV **03** W Va

wet
03 dip, wat **04** damp, dank, dram, drip, fool, jerk, moil, nerd, rain, soak, soft, sour, wash, weak, weed, weet, wimp, wuss **05** bewet, cissy, douse, flood, humid, idiot, imbue, madid, moist, muggy, rainy, softy, soggy, soppy, spray, steep, swamp, sweat, tipsy, wally, water, weedy **06** beweep, clammy, daggle, dampen, drench, drippy, effete, embrue, feeble, imbrue, liquid, madefy, slippy, sloppy, sluice, soaked, sodden, soused, splash, spongy, watery **07** debauch, draggle, drizzle, embrewe, milksop, moisten, pouring, raining, showery, soaking, sopping, squidgy, tearful, teeming, wetness, wimpish **08** bedabble, bedrench, dampness, drenched, dripping, humidity, irrigate, moisture, pathetic, saturate, slippery, sprinkle, timorous, weakling, wringing **09** drizzling, irriguous, moistness, saturated, spineless **10** clamminess, imbruement, irresolute, namby-pamby, sopping wet **11** ineffective, ineffectual, madefaction, waterlogged **12** condensation
• **wet behind the ears**
03 new, raw **05** green, naive **06** callow **08** gullible, immature, innocent **09** untrained **13** inexperienced
• **wet patch** *see* **sea**

wetness
03 wet **04** damp **05** water **06** liquid **08** dampness, dankness, humidity, moisture **09** sogginess **10** clamminess, rising damp, soddenness **12** condensation

whack
03 box, cut, hit, lot, rap **04** bang, bash, beat, belt, biff, blow, cuff, part, slap, sock **05** clout, quota, share, smack, stint, thump **06** buffet, murder, strike, stroke, thrash, wallop **07** attempt, clobber, portion, rake-off **08** division **09** allowance, parcel out **10** allocation, percentage, proportion **14** slice of the cake

whacking
04 huge, mega, vast **05** giant, gross, jumbo **07** beating, immense, mammoth, massive, socking, Titanic, whaling **08** almighty, colossal, enormous, gigantic, great big, plonking, whopping **09** ginormous, humongous, monstrous, thrashing, walloping **10** astronomic, gargantuan,

large-scale, prodigious, stupendous, tremendous **11** God-almighty **12** considerable

whale
05 Cetus **06** thrash

03 fin, orc, sei
04 blue, grey, orca
05 black, minke, pigmy, piked, pilot, right, sperm, white
06 baleen, beaked, beluga, caa'ing, finner, killer
07 bowhead, dolphin, finback, grampus, Layard's, narwhal, rorqual, toothed
08 humpback, porpoise
09 Greenland, grindhval, razorback, whalebone
10 bottlenose, humpbacked
11 bottle-nosed, false killer
12 river dolphin, strap-toothed
13 common rorqual, Risso's dolphin, sulphur-bottom
15 gangetic dolphin, harbour porpoise

wharf
03 kay, key **04** dock, pier, quay **05** jetty **06** marina, staith **07** staithe **08** dockyard, quayside **12** landing-stage

what
02 eh, my

what's-its-name
05 gismo, thing **06** doings, doodad, doodah, doofus, jigger, thingy **07** doobrey, doobrie, whatnot, whatsit **08** thingamy **09** doohickey, jigamaree, jiggumbob, thingummy, timenoguy **12** thingummybob, thingummyjig **14** what-d'you-call-it **15** whatchamacallit

wheat
04 corn **05** durum, emmer, fitch, rivet, spelt **06** bulgur, sharps **07** bulghur, einkorn **08** amelcorn, semolina, Triticum

wheedle
03 cog **04** blag, coax, draw **05** carny, charm, court **06** cajole, carney, cozy up, cuiter, entice, induce, phrase, whilly **07** beguile, flatter, tweedle, win over **08** butter up, inveigle, persuade, soft-soap, talk into **09** sweet-talk, whillywha **10** whillywhaw

wheel
◊ *reversal indicator*
04 disc, hoop, reel, ring, roam, roll, spin, turn **05** dolly, orbit, pivot, ratch, rhomb, snail, swing, truck, twirl, whirl **06** circle, dollar, gyrate, roller, rotate, sheave, swivel, wander **07** bicycle, go round, refrain, revolve, trindle, trochus, trolley, truckle **08** encircle, gyration, rotation, tricycle **10** revolution

03 big, cog, fly
04 buff, cart, gear, idle, mill, worm

05 bedel, bevel, crown, drive, idler, sakia, wagon, water
06 castor, charka, escape, Ferris, paddle, prayer, sakieh
07 balance, driving, fortune, potter's, ratchet, sakiyeh
08 roulette, spinning, sprocket, spur gear, steering
09 Catherine
13 spinning jenny, throwing table, whirling-table

• at the wheel
07 driving, turning **08** in charge, steering **09** at the helm, directing, heading up, in command, in control **11** responsible **14** behind the wheel

wheeze
03 gag **04** gasp, hiss, idea, joke, pant, plan, ploy, rasp, ruse **05** antic, cough, crack, prank, story, stunt, trick, whiss **06** scheme **07** whaisle, whaizle, whistle, wrinkle **08** anecdote, chestnut, one-liner **11** catchphrase **13** practical joke

whelp
03 cub, pup **05** puppy **07** brachet **08** bratchet

whereabouts
04 site **05** place **08** location, position, vicinity **09** situation

wherewithal
04 cash, dosh, loot **05** brass, bread, dough, funds, gravy, lolly, means, money, ready, smash **06** greens, moolah, stumpy **07** capital, readies, scratch, shekels **08** greenies, supplies **09** megabucks, necessary, resources **11** spondulicks

whet
04 edge, file, hone, stir **05** grind, preen, rouse **06** arouse, awaken, excite, incite, kindle, stroke **07** provoke, quicken, sharpen **08** appetize, increase **09** stimulate, titillate **11** scythe-stone

whiff
04 gust, hint, puff, reek **05** aroma, blast, cigar, jiffy, odour, scent, smell, sniff, stink, touch, trace **06** breath, inhale, stench **07** draught, glimpse, soupçon **09** cigarette, suspicion **10** suggestion

while
02 as **04** span, time, when **05** spell, throw, until **06** period, season **07** stretch, whereas **08** although, interval **09** the whilst **13** in the middle of
• **while away**
03 use **04** pass **05** spend, use up **06** devote, occupy

whim
03 fad, toy **04** flam, idea, kink, swim, urge **05** crank, craze, fancy, flisk, freak, quirk **06** humour, maggot, megrim, notion, vagary, whimsy **07** caprice, conceit, impulse, passion, whimsey **08** crotchet **11** whigmaleery **12** whigmaleerie

whimper

03 cry, sob **04** mewl, moan, pule, weep **05** groan, whine **06** snivel, whinge **07** grizzle, sniffle

whimsical

03 fay, fey, fie, odd **05** dotty, droll, fairy, funny, queer, weird **06** quaint, quirky, whimsy **07** baroque, curious, playful, toysome, unusual **08** fanciful, peculiar **09** crotchety, eccentric, fantastic, impulsive **10** capricious, crotcheted **11** Disneyesque, fantastical, mischievous **13** unpredictable

whimsy

03 odd **04** tick, whim **05** droll, funny, weird **06** fisgig, fizgig, quaint, quirky **07** curious, playful, unusual **08** fanciful, peculiar **09** eccentric, whimsical **10** changeable **13** unpredictable

whine

03 cry, sob **04** beef, carp, moan, pule, wail **05** bleat, gripe, groan **06** grouch, grouse, kvetch, peenge, whinge, yammer **07** grizzle, grumble, wheenge, whimper **08** complain **09** bellyache, complaint

whinge

04 beef, carp, moan **05** greet, gripe, groan, winge **06** grouse, peenge **07** grumble, wheenge **08** complain **09** bellyache, complaint

whip

◇ *anagram indicator*

03 cat, fly, mix, tan, tat, taw **04** beat, belt, cane, crop, dart, dash, firk, flay, flit, flog, goad, hide, jerk, lash, prod, pull, push, rush, spur, stir, tear, urge, whap, whop, yank **05** birch, braid, drive, flash, knout, outdo, quirt, rouse, steal, strap, swish, thong, whack, whang, whisk **06** beat up, breech, defeat, driver, feague, incite, larrup, prompt, punish, snatch, switch, thrash, wallop **07** agitate, chabouk, cowhide, instant, kurbash, overlay, provoke, rawhide, scourge, sjambok **08** ashplant, bullwhip, chastise, coachman, kourbash, overcast, vapulate **09** bullwhack, castigate, coachwhip, flagellum, horsewhip, instigate, longe whip, lunge whip, stock whip **10** black snake, discipline, flagellate, riding-crop **11** hunting-crop, hunting-whip, lunging whip, overcasting **13** cat-o'-nine-tails

• whip up

◇ *anagram indicator*

04 beat **06** arouse, excite, foment, incite, kindle, stir up, work up **07** agitate, inflame, provoke, psych up **09** instigate, stimulate

whippersnapper

03 imp **05** scamp **06** nipper, rascal **07** upstart, whiffet **08** whipster **09** pipsqueak, scallywag **11** hobbledehoy **14** snipper-snapper

whipping

05 knout **06** caning, defeat, hiding, laldie **07** beating, belting, lashing, tanning **08** birching, flogging,

spanking **09** scourging, thrashing, walloping **10** punishment **11** castigation, overcasting **12** flagellation

whirl

◇ *anagram indicator*

04 daze, eddy, reel, roll, spin, tirl, turn **05** pivot, round, swing, swirl, twirl, twist, waltz, wheel **06** bustle, circle, flurry, gyrate, hubbub, jumble, muddle, rotate, series, swivel, tumult, uproar **07** revolve **08** gyration, rotation **09** agitation, commotion, confusion, giddiness, pirouette, turn round **10** hurly-burly, revolution, succession **12** circumgyrate, merry-go-round

• give something a whirl

03 try **06** strive **07** attempt, have a go, venture **09** endeavour, have a bash, have a lash, have a shot, have a stab **10** have a crack **11** give it a burl

whirlpool

04 eddy, gulf, weal, weel, weil, wiel **05** gurge **06** vortex **08** sea purse, swelchie **09** Charybdis, maelstrom

whirlwind

04 eddy, rash **05** babel, chaos, hasty, noise, quick, rapid, swift **06** bedlam, furore, hubbub, speedy, tumult, typhon, uproar, vortex **07** anarchy, clamour, cyclone, tornado, turmoil, typhoon **08** headlong, madhouse **09** commotion, confusion, impetuous, impulsive, lightning, sand-devil **10** hullabaloo, tourbillon **11** pandemonium, tourbillion, white squall

whisk

◇ *anagram indicator*

03 fly, mix, zip **04** beat, belt, bolt, bomb, dart, dash, dive, lash, pelt, race, rush, stir, tear, tuft, whid, whip, wipe **05** brush, flick, hurry, scoot, shoot, speed, sweep, swish, whist **06** beater, chowri, chowry, hasten, switch, twitch **07** panicle **09** egg beater **12** swizzle-stick

whiskey

01 W

whisky

04 dram, half **05** hooch **06** hootch **08** the grain **09** aqua vitae, good stuff, the cratur **10** barley-bree, barley-broo, usquebaugh **11** barley-broth, mountain dew, the Auld Kirk, water of life

03 rye
04 malt
06 poteen, red-eye, Scotch
07 blended, Bourbon, potheen, spunkie
08 peat-reek, sour mash
09 moonshine
10 cornbrandy, corn whisky, single malt, tanglefoot
12 the real McCoy
13 the real Mackay
14 chain lightning, tarantula juice

whisper

03 bur **04** burr, buzz, hark, hint, hiss, sigh **05** round, sough, tinge, trace, whiff **06** breath, gossip, mumble, murmur, mutter, report, rumour, rustle, tittle, whisht **07** breathe, divulge, soupçon, wheesht **08** intimate, low voice, susurrus **09** insinuate, soft voice, suspicion, susurrate, undertone **10** quiet voice, say quietly, suggestion **11** insinuation, pig's whisper **12** speak quietly, stage whisper **14** whittie-whattie

whistle

04 call, ping, pipe, sing, song, sowf **05** cheep, chirp, siren, sowff, sowth, whiss **06** hooter, siffle, throat, warble **07** catcall, summons, tweedle, warbler, wheeple **09** quail-call, quail-pipe

whit

03 bit, jot, rap **04** atom, dash, drop, fico, haet, ha'it, hate, hoot, iota, mite, snap, spot **05** aught, crumb, grain, piece, pinch, point, scrap, shred, speck, straw, trace **06** little **07** modicum, red cent **08** fragment, particle

white

03 wan **04** hoar, leuc-, leuk-, pale, pure **05** ashen, hoary, leuco-, leuko-, light, moral, pasty, waxen **06** albino, bright, honest, pallid **07** albumen, anaemic, niveous, upright **08** innocent, reliable, spotless, virtuous **09** blameless, bloodless, burnished, stainless, undefiled **10** auspicious, colourless, favourable, honourable, immaculate **11** transparent, unblemished, unburnished **12** light-skinned

04 ecru, grey, lily, opal, whey
05 cream, ivory, milky, snowy
06 argent, creamy, pearly, silver
08 magnolia
09 champagne, lily-white, snow-white
11 silver-white

white-collar

06 office **08** clerical, salaried **09** executive, non-manual **12** professional

whiten

03 cam **04** calm, caum, fade, pale, snow **06** blanch, bleach **08** dealbate, etiolate, pipeclay **09** whitewash

whitewash

04 beat, best, drub, -gate, hide, lick **05** crush, paste **06** granny, hammer, thrash **07** clobber, conceal, cover up, cover-up, grannie, trounce **08** suppress **09** calcimine, deception, gloss over, Kalsomine® **10** camouflage **11** concealment, make light of **13** defeat utterly

whittle

03 cut, hew, use **04** fret, pare, trim **05** carve, erode, peach, shape, shave, use up **06** reduce, scrape **07** blanket, consume, eat away **08** diminish, wear away **09** undermine

whole
03 all, fit, lot, sum **04** full, hale, mint, unit, well **05** piece, sound, total, uncut **06** entire, entity, healed, intact, strong, unhurt **07** healthy, perfect **08** complete, ensemble, entirety, fullness, integral, sum total, totality, unbroken, unedited, unharmed **09** aggregate, inviolate, undamaged, undivided, uninjured **10** altogether, completely, everything, in one piece, unabridged **11** full-blooded
• **on the whole**
06 mostly **07** as a rule **08** all in all **09** generally, in general, in the main **10** by and large **13** predominantly **14** for the most part

wholehearted
04 real, true, warm **06** hearty **07** devoted, earnest, genuine, sincere, zealous **08** complete, emphatic **09** committed, dedicated, heartfelt, unfeigned **10** passionate, unreserved, unstinting **11** boots and all, unqualified **12** enthusiastic

wholeheartedly
06 warmly **08** heartily **09** genuinely, sincerely **10** completely **12** emphatically, passionately, unreservedly

wholesale
04 mass **05** broad, great, total **06** en bloc **07** in gross, massive, totally **08** outright, sweeping **09** extensive, massively **11** extensively, far-reaching, wide-ranging **12** all-inclusive **13** comprehensive **14** indiscriminate **15** comprehensively

wholesome
04 good, pure **05** clean, moral, sound, sweet **06** decent, proper **07** bracing, ethical, healthy, helpful, holesom **08** edifying, healsome, holesome, hygienic, physical, remedial, salutary, sanitary, sensible, virtuous **09** healthful, improving, righteous, uplifting **10** beneficial, healthsome, honourable, nourishing, nutritious, propitious, reasonable, refreshing, salubrious **11** respectable **12** invigorating, squeaky-clean

wholly
03 all **04** only **05** clear, fully, quite **06** in toto, purely **07** sheerly, totally, utterly **08** entirely **09** perfectly, tout à fait **10** absolutely, altogether, completely, thoroughly **11** exclusively **14** in every respect **15** comprehensively

whoop
02 ho! **03** cry **04** hoop, hoot, roar, yell **05** cheer, shout **06** holler, hurrah, scream, shriek

whopper
03 fib, lie **05** fable, giant, whale **07** cracker, mammoth, monster, plumper, slapper, stonker, swapper, swinger, swopper, untruth **08** colossus, scrouger **09** falsehood, leviathan, tall story **10** fairy story,

socdolager, sogdolager **11** fabrication, sockdolager, sockdoliger, sockdoliger **12** hippopotamus, slockdolager
See also **lie**

whopping
03 big **04** huge, mega, vast **05** giant, great, jumbo, large **07** immense, mammoth, massive, whaling **08** almighty, enormous, gigantic, great big, plonking, slapping, whacking **09** ginormous, humongous, thrashing, walloping **10** monumental, prodigious, staggering, tremendous **11** God-almighty **13** extraordinary

whore
03 pro, pug, tom **04** bawd, dell, drab, hoor, moll, punk, road, stew, tart **05** brass, broad, quail, quiff, stale, tramp, trull, wench **06** bulker, callet, geisha, harlot, hooker, mutton, plover **07** cocotte, floozie, hetaera, hostess, hustler, lorette, Paphian, pinnace, polecat, rent-boy, trollop, venture **08** bona-roba, callgirl, dolly-mop, magdalen, strumpet **09** courtesan, hierodule, loose fish **10** cockatrice, convertite, fancy woman, loose woman, prostitute, rough trade, vizard-mask **11** fallen woman, fille de joie, laced mutton, night-walker, poule de luxe, public woman, working girl **12** fille des rues, scarlet woman, street-walker **13** grande cocotte **14** lady of the night, woman of the town
See also **prostitute**

whorehouse
03 kip **04** crib, stew **06** bagnio, bordel **07** brothel, Corinth **08** bordello, cathouse, hothouse, red light **10** bawdy-house, flash-house **12** knocking-shop, leaping-house **13** sporting house, vaulting-house **14** house of ill fame **15** disorderly house

whorl
04 coil, loop, turn **05** helix, twirl, twist **06** spiral, volute, vortex **07** calicle, calycle, corolla **08** calycule, gyration, verticil, volution **09** corkscrew **11** convolution

wicked
◇ *anagram indicator*
03 ace, bad, def, fab, ill, rad **04** cool, evil, foul, mean, mega, neat, vile, wick **05** awful, boffo, brill, cruel, felon, nasty, wrong **06** divine, fierce, groovy, guilty, impish, severe, sinful, unholy, unkind, way-out **07** amazing, corrupt, crucial, debased, harmful, heinous, immoral, intense, naughty, radical, roguish, ungodly, unlucky, vicious **08** clinking, depraved, devilish, dreadful, fabulous, heavenly, perverse, rascally, shameful, spiteful, stonking, terrible, terrific **09** abandoned, admirable, atrocious, brilliant, difficult, dissolute, egregious, excellent, fantastic, felonious, high-viced, injurious, miscreant, nefarious, offensive, scelerate, worthless **10** abominable,

evil-minded, facinorous, flagitious, iniquitous, not half bad, scandalous, unpleasant, villainous **11** distressing, facinerious, mischievous, sensational, the business, troublesome, unrighteous **12** black-hearted, second to none, unprincipled **14** out of this world

wickedness
03 ill, sin **04** evil **06** naught **07** impiety, pravity, villany **08** atrocity, enormity, evilness, foulness, iniquity, vileness, villainy **09** amorality, depravity, reprobacy **10** corruption, immorality, sinfulness **11** abomination, corruptness, heinousness **12** devilishness, fiendishness, shamefulness **13** dissoluteness **15** unrighteousness

wickerwork
05 ratan **06** rattan, wattle, wicker **10** basket-work, wattle-work

wide
01 w **04** full, vast, wily **05** ample, baggy, broad, fully, great, loose, roomy **06** astray, astute, remote **07** dilated, distant, general, immense **08** expanded, extended, spacious **09** all the way, capacious, extensive, off course, off target **10** completely, off the mark **11** far-reaching, wide-ranging **12** latitudinous **13** comprehensive **15** to the full extent

wide-awake
04 keen, wary **05** alert, aware, sharp **06** astute, roused **07** heedful, wakened **08** vigilant, watchful **09** conscious, observant, on the ball **10** fully awake, on the alert, on your toes **11** quick-witted **12** on the qui vive

wide-eyed
04 open **05** dazed, frank, fresh, naive **06** amazed, simple **07** angelic, artless, natural, shocked, stunned **08** dewy-eyed, gullible, innocent, open-eyed, startled, trustful, trusting **09** astounded, childlike, credulous, guileless, ingenuous, staggered, surprised, unworldly **10** astonished, bewildered, bowled over, confounded, gobsmacked, taken aback **11** dumbfounded, open-mouthed **12** lost for words, unsuspecting **13** flabbergasted, inexperienced, knocked for six, thunderstruck **15** unsophisticated

widely
07 broadly **09** generally **11** extensively **15** comprehensively

widen
06 dilate, expand, extend, flanch, let out, spread **07** broaden, distend, enlarge, flaunch, stretch **08** increase

wide-open
04 open, wide **06** gaping, spread **07** exposed **09** outspread **10** vulnerable **11** defenceless, susceptible, unfortified, unprotected **12** outstretched

wide-ranging
05 broad **08** sweeping, thorough
09 extensive, important, momentous,
universal **10** widespread **11** far-
reaching, scattershot, significant
13 comprehensive, thoroughgoing

widespread
04 rife **05** broad **06** common, global
07 general, prolate **08** far-flung,
sweeping **09** extensive, pervasive,
prevalent, universal, unlimited,
wholesale **10** wall-to-wall **11** far-
reaching

widow
04 sati **05** widdy **06** relict, suttee
07 bereave, dowager **08** feme sole,
war widow **10** grass widow **11** hempen
widow **12** queen dowager

width
01 w **04** beam, span **05** girth, range,
reach, scope **06** extent **07** breadth,
compass, measure **08** diameter,
latitude, wideness **09** amplitude,
broadness, largeness, thickness
13 extensiveness

wield
03 ply, use **04** gain, have, hold, play,
rule, sway, wave, weld, wild, wind
05 apply, enjoy, exert, shake, sownd,
swing **06** employ, handle, manage
07 command, control, possess, utilize
08 brandish, exercise, flourish,
maintain **10** manipulate

wife
01 w **02** ux **03** rib **04** dame, frau, lady,
mate **05** bride, dutch, femme, queen,
woman **06** missis, missus, spouse,
vahine, wahine **07** consort, hostess,
old lady, partner **08** helpmate,
helpmeet, princess **09** child-wife,
companion, concubine, first lady, other
half **10** better half, her indoors,
stepmother **11** little woman, sister-in-
law **12** kickie-wickie, married woman
13 daughter-in-law **14** the little
woman

wig
03 jiz, tie **04** gizz, jasy, jazy **05** caxon,
Irish, jasey, major, scold, syrup
06 bagwig, bobwig, Brutus, peruke,
tie-wig, toupee, toupet **07** buzz-wig,
periwig, Ramilie, scratch, spencer
08 perruque, postiche, Ramilies,
Ramillie **09** hairpiece, Ramillies **10** full-
bottom, scratch-wig **14** transformation

wiggle
03 wag **04** jerk **05** shake, twist
06 jiggle, squirm, twitch, waggle,
writhe **07** wriggle

wild
◇ *anagram indicator*
03 mad, shy **04** bush, daft, keen, nuts,
rash **05** angry, crazy, feral, livid, messy,
myall, nutty, potty, rough, rowdy, waste,
weald, wield **06** absurd, barren, casual,
chance, choppy, desert, ferine, fierce,
fuming, gallus, raging, random,
rugged, savage, stormy, unruly,
untame, untidy, unwise **07** agitato,

aimless, bananas, berserk, blazing,
bonkers, brutish, enraged, excited,
fervent, foolish, frantic, furious,
gallows, lawless, natural, rampant,
riotous, ropable, salvage, tousled,
uncouth, unkempt, untamed, violent,
wayward **08** agitated, agrestal,
blustery, chimeric, demented,
desolate, fanciful, forsaken, frenzied,
incensed, reckless, romantic, ropeable,
terrific, unbroken, uncombed,
vehement, warragal, warragle,
warragul, warrigal **09** agrestial,
arbitrary, barbarous, enjoyable,
fanatical, fantastic, ferocious,
foolhardy, haphazard, hit-or-miss,
imprudent, impulsive, irregular,
primitive, turbulent, unsettled
10 accidental, boisterous, chimerical,
disordered, disorderly, distracted,
distraught, fortuitous, hopping mad,
incidental, infuriated, irrational,
licentious, outrageous, passionate,
ridiculous **11** approximate, dishevelled,
extravagant, fantastical, impractical,
purposeless, tempestuous, uncivilized,
uninhabited, unpopulated
12 enthusiastic, ferae naturae,
inhospitable, out of control,
preposterous, unconsidered,
uncontrolled, uncultivated,
ungovernable, unmanageable,
unrestrained **13** impracticable,
serendipitous, undisciplined,
uninhabitable **14** beside yourself,
indiscriminate, skimble-skamble,
uncontrollable, undomesticated

• run wild
◇ *anagram indicator*
04 lamp, riot **05** feral **07** rampage

wild animal *see* animal

wilderness
05 waste, wilds **06** desert, jungle
09 wasteland

wild flower *see* flower

wildlife
05 fauna **07** animals

wildly
◇ *anagram indicator*
07 angrily, noisily **08** absurdly, casually
09 aimlessly, defiantly, foolishly,
furiously, riotously **10** recklessly
11 arbitrarily, chaotically, haphazardly
12 anarchically, boisterously,
outrageously, rebelliously, ridiculously
13 extravagantly, fantastically,
irresponsibly **14** preposterously,
uncontrollably, unmethodically,
unrestrainedly

wilds
06 desert **07** outback **09** the sticks,
wasteland **10** the boonies, wilderness
11 remote areas **12** the boondocks
15 the back of beyond

wiles
05 fraud, guile, ploys, ruses **06** deceit,
dodges, tricks **07** cunning, devices
08 cheating, trickery **09** chicanery,
deception **10** artfulness, craftiness,

manoeuvres, stratagems, subterfuge
12 contrivances

wilful
06 dogged, mulish **07** planned,
wayward, willing **08** contrary,
obdurate, perverse, stubborn, willyard,
willyart **09** conscious, obstinate, pig-
headed, voluntary **10** calculated,
deliberate, determined, headstrong,
inflexible, refractory, self-willed,
unyielding **11** intentional, intractable
12 intransigent, premeditated
14 uncompromising

will
02 'll **03** aim, way **04** lust, mind, Self,
want, wish **05** fancy, leave, order
06 astray, choice, choose, compel,
confer, decree, desire, devise, direct,
intend, option, ordain, pass on **07** at a
loss, command, feeling, purpose,
require, resolve **08** attitude, bequeath,
decision, hand down, pass down,
pleasure, transfer, volition **09** dispose
of, intention, testament, willpower
10 bewildered, discretion, preference,
resolution **11** disposition, inclination,
prerogative **13** determination
14 purposefulness

William
02 Wm **04** Bill, Will **05** Billy, Willy

willing
02 on **04** game, glad, keen **05** eager,
happy, prone, ready **06** chosen
07 content, pleased, up for it
08 amenable, biddable, disposed,
inclined, prepared, so-minded
09 agreeable, compliant, volitient,
voluntary **10** consenting, favourable
11 co-operative, intentional
12 enthusiastic, well-disposed

willingly
04 leve, lief, soon **05** lieve **06** freely,
gladly **07** eagerly, happily, readily
08 by choice, in a hurry **09** like a shot
10 cheerfully **11** voluntarily **12** nothing
loath **14** unhesitatingly

willingness
04 will, wish **06** desire, favour
07 consent **08** volition **09** agreement,
readiness **10** compliance, enthusiasm
11 disposition, inclination
12 complaisance **13** agreeableness

will-o'-the-wisp
06 min min **07** fen-fire, spunkie
08 wildfire **09** nightfire **11** fatuous fire,
ignis fatuus **12** Jack-o'-lantern **13** friar's
lantern

willow
04 sale, seal **05** osier, salix, sauch,
saugh, withy **06** sallow

willowy
04 slim, tall **05** lithe **06** limber,
lissom, supple, svelte **07** slender
08 flexible, graceful **09** lithesome,
sylph-like

willpower
04 grit, will **05** drive **07** resolve
10 commitment, doggedness,

resolution **11** persistence, self-command, self-control, self-mastery **13** determination **14** self-discipline, strength of will

willy-nilly
08 by chance, perforce, randomly **10** carelessly **11** arbitrarily, haphazardly, irregularly, necessarily, of necessity **12** compulsorily, nolens volens **14** unmethodically

wilt
03 ebb, sag, wot **04** fade, fail, flag, flop, sink, wane, woot **05** droop, faint, taint **06** lessen, weaken, wither **07** dwindle, shrivel **08** diminish, grow less, languish

wily
03 fly, sly **04** foxy, wide **05** sharp **06** artful, astute, crafty, shifty, shrewd, tricky **07** crooked, cunning, versute **08** cheating, guileful, scheming **09** deceitful, deceptive, designing, underhand **10** intriguing, streetwise

wimp
03 wet **04** clot, drip, fool, jerk, nerd, tonk, weed, wuss **05** clown, softy, wally **07** milksop **10** namby-pamby

wimpish
03 wet **04** soft, weak **05** cissy, weedy, wussy **06** drippy, effete, feeble **08** pathetic, timorous **09** spineless **10** irresolute, namby-pamby **11** ineffective, ineffectual

win
03 get, net, pot **04** earn, gain, mine **05** carry, catch, penny, reach **06** allure, attain, effect, obtain, open up, result, secure **07** achieve, acquire, collect, conquer, mastery, prevail, procure, receive, succeed, success, triumph, victory **08** atchieve, carry off, conquest, overcome, persuade **09** come first, win the day **10** accomplish, strike gold **11** come in first, finish first, squeeze home **12** be victorious, come out on top, turn up trumps, win hands down **13** hit the jackpot, squeak through **14** achieve success

• **win over**
04 sway **05** bribe, charm **06** allure, engage, nobble **07** attract, buy over, convert **08** convince, persuade, win round **09** influence, talk round **10** bring round, conciliate **11** prevail upon

wince
04 jerk, jump, kick, reel **05** cower, quail, start **06** blench, cringe, flinch, recoil, roller, shrink **08** draw back **09** pull a face

wind
◇ *anagram indicator*
02 go **03** air **04** bend, burp, coil, curl, furl, gale, gust, haul, hint, loop, puff, reel, roll, turn, veer, wrap **05** blast, curve, hoist, snake, twine, twist, weave, wield **06** breath, breeze, enfold, ramble, spiral, writhe, zigzag **07** bluster, conceit, current, deviate, draught, meander, turning, wreathe,

wriggle **08** encircle **10** air-current, flatulence, suggestion **12** twist and turn

04 berg, bise, bora, east, föhn, helm **05** Eurus, north, Notus, trade, zonda **06** Auster, Boreas, buster, doctor, El Niño, levant, samiel, simoom, zephyr **07** Aquilon, austral, chinook, cyclone, etesian, gregale, khamsin, meltemi, mistral, monsoon, pampero, sirocco, tornado, twister **08** Argestes, Favonian, Favonius, libeccio, westerly, williwaw **09** harmattan, hurricane, nor'wester, snow eater, southerly **10** Cape doctor, Euroclydon, prevailing, tramontana, wet chinook, willy-willy **11** anticyclone **15** southerly buster

• **get wind of**
07 learn of **08** discover **09** hear about **12** find out about **13** become aware of
• **in the wind**
06 likely **08** expected, probable **10** on the cards **13** about to happen
• **put the wind up**
05 alarm, daunt, panic, scare, spook **06** boggle, rattle **07** agitate, perturb, startle, unnerve **08** frighten **10** discourage **13** sound the alarm
• **wind down**
04 slow, stop **05** chill, relax **06** cool it, ease up, lessen, reduce, unwind **07** decline, dwindle, subside **08** calm down, chill out, diminish, slow down **09** hang loose, lighten up **10** slacken off, take it easy **11** come to an end, quieten down **12** bring to an end **13** let yourself go, put your feet up **14** take things easy **15** let your hair down
• **wind up**
03 end, kid, rib **04** fool, furl, goof, span, stop **05** anger, annoy, close, end up, hoist, tease, trick, uptie **06** excite, finish, settle **07** agitate, tighten **08** conclude, finalize, finish up, irritate **09** close down, liquidate, make fun of, terminate **10** disconcert **12** bring to an end, find yourself **13** bring to a close **15** pull someone's leg

windbag
04 bore **06** gasbag, gossip **07** blether, boaster **08** bigmouth, braggart

winded
06 puffed **07** panting **09** out of puff, puffed out **10** breathless **11** out of breath

windfall
04 find **05** manna **06** caduac **07** bonanza, godsend, jackpot **12** stroke of luck **13** treasure-trove

winding
◇ *anagram indicator*
04 mazy, turn **06** creeky, spiral **07** bending, coiling, crankle, crooked, curving, devious, sinuate, sinuous, turning, twining **08** flexuose, flexuous,

indirect, sinuated, tortuous, twisting **09** meandrian, meandrous **10** circuitous, convoluted, meandering, roundabout, serpentine **11** anfractuous **12** serpentinous **14** crinkle-crankle

window
05 light **07** opening

03 bay, bow **04** pane, rose, sash, shop **05** oriel **06** dormer, French, lancet, louvre, Norman, screen, ticket **07** compass, lucarne, sliding **08** astragal, bull's eye, casement, fanlight, porthole, skylight **09** decorated, mullioned, patio door **10** windscreen **11** oeil-de-boeuf **12** double-glazed, early English, quarterlight, stained glass **13** double-glazing, perpendicular **14** Catherine wheel **15** secondary-glazed

windpipe
05 pipes **06** larynx, throat **07** pharynx, trachea, weasand **08** thrapple, thropple, throttle **11** weasand-pipe

windswept
04 open **05** bleak, blowy, messy, windy **06** barren, untidy **07** exposed, in a mess, ruffled, tousled, unkempt **08** desolate **09** windblown **10** disordered **11** dishevelled, unprotected, unsheltered

windward
04 luff **07** weather
• **beat to windward**
04 turn, work **06** laveer
• **to windward**
02 up **05** aloof **08** a-weather

windy
04 wild **05** blowy, gusty, nervy, timid, wordy **06** afraid, breezy, on edge, prolix, scared, stormy, turgid, uneasy **07** anxious, chicken, nervous, pompous, squally, ventose, verbose **08** blustery, rambling, stressed **09** bombastic, garrulous, windswept **10** frightened, long-winded **11** tempestuous

wine
02 en- **03** eno-, oen-, oin-, vin **04** oeno-, oino-, vino

03 Dão, dry, red, sec **04** Asti, brut, Cava, fino, hock, port, rosé, sack, Sekt, Tent **05** blush, bombo, Douro, Fitou, Gamay, house, Mâcon, Médoc, plonk, Rioja, Soave, straw, sweet, Syrah, table, Tavel, Tokay, tonic, white **06** Alsace, Barolo, Barsac, Beaune, canary, claret, grappa, Graves, Malaga, Malbec, Merlot, mulled, Muscat, Pontac, sherry, Shiraz **07** alicant, Amarone, Auslese, Barbera,

Bunyuls, Chablis, Chianti, Cinsaut, demi-sec, Madeira, Margaux, Marsala, moselle, oloroso, Orvieto, retsina, sangria, vintage, Vouvray

08 Alicante, Bordeaux, Brunello, bucellas, Burgundy, Carignan, Cinsault, Dolcetto, Frascati, Garnacha, Glühwein, Grenache, house red, jerepigo, Kabinett, Malvasia, Marsanne, Montilla, Muscadet, muscatel, Nebbiolo, New World, Palomino, Pauillac, Pinotage, Pornerol, Riesling, Rousanne, ruby port, Sancerre, Sauterne, Sémillon, Spätlese, Spumante, St Julien, Vermouth

09 Bardolino, Carignane, champagne, Colombard, dry sherry, fortified, Frizzante, Hermitage, Lambrusco, Langue d'Oc, Minervois, Pinot Gris, Pinot Noir, Sauternes, sparkling, St-Émilion, Tarragona, tawny port, Trebbiano, Ugni Blanc, white port, Zinfandel

10 Barbaresco, Beaujolais, Chambertin, Chardonnay, Constantia, Grignolino, house white, Manzanilla, Mateus Rosé, Monastrell, Muscadelle, Piesporter, Pinot Blanc, Sangiovese, Verdicchio, vinho verde

11 alcohol-free, amontillado, Chenin Blanc, Niersteiner, Pinot Grigio, Pouilly-Fumé, Rüdesheimer, Steinberger, sweet sherry, Tempranillo, vintage port

12 Blanc de Noirs, Côtes du Rhône, Johannisberg, medium sherry, Pedro Ximénez, Ruby Cabernet, Tinta Barroca, Valpolicella

13 Blanc de Blancs, Cabernet Franc, Château Lafite, Liebfraumilch, Montepulciano, Pouilly-Fuissé

14 Crémant d'Alsace, Crémant de Loire, Lacrima Christi, Sauvignon Blanc

15 Crozes-Hermitage, Gewürztraminer, lachryma Christi

Wine-bottle sizes include:

06 flagon, magnum
08 jeroboam, rehoboam
09 balthazar
10 methuselah, salmanazar
11 Marie-Jeanne
14 nebuchadnezzar

See also **bottle**

• **wine-grower**
05 viner **08** vigneron

wine glass
05 flute, glass **06** goblet **07** balloon
08 schooner **09** straw-stem

wing
02 el **03** ala, arm, fan, fly, set, van
04 flit, move, part, pass, race, sail, side, soar, vane, waft, zoom **05** alula, flank, flock, glide, group, hurry, penny, pinna, right, speed **06** annexe, branch, circle, flight, hasten, pinion, travel **07** adjunct, coterie, faction, section, segment **08** grouping

09 extension, liverwing **10** attachment
11 parascenium

• **wing it**
04 vamp **05** ad-lib **06** busk it **09** play by ear **11** extemporize **15** speak off the cuff

wingless
◇ ends deletion indicator

wink
04 pink **05** blink, eliad, flash, gleam, glint **06** eyliad, illiad, moment, second **07** connive, eyeliad, flicker, flutter, glimmer, glitter, instant, nictate, sparkle, twinkle **08** oeillade
09 nictation, nictitate **10** glimmering
11 nictitation, split second

• **wink at**
06 ignore **07** condone, neglect
08 overlook, pass over **09** disregard
14 take no notice of **15** turn a blind eye to

winkle
04 pupu, worm **05** flush, force, prise
07 draw out, extract **09** extricate

winner
03 ace, dux **05** champ **06** top dog, victor **08** champion, prizeman
09 conqueror, medallist
10 prizewoman, vanquisher
11 prizewinner, title-holder, world-beater **13** Nobel laureate

winning
02 up **05** sweet **06** lovely **07** amiable, winsome **08** alluring, charming, engaging, fetching, pleasing, unbeaten
09 beguiling, endearing **10** attractive, bewitching, conquering, delightful, enchanting, persuasive, successful, triumphant, undefeated, victorious
11 captivating, vanquishing
13 prepossessing

winnings
05 booty, gains, prize **06** prizes, spoils, velvet **07** jackpot, profits, takings
08 proceeds **10** prize money

winnow
03 fan, fly, van **04** comb, cull, flap, part, sift, sort, waft **06** divide, screen, select
07 diffuse, flutter **08** separate
09 ventilate

winsome
05 sweet **06** comely, lovely, pretty
07 amiable **08** alluring, charming, cheerful, engaging, fetching, pleasant, pleasing **09** appealing, beguiling, endearing **10** attractive, bewitching, delectable, delightful, enchanting
11 captivating **13** prepossessing

wintry
03 icy, raw **04** cold, cool **05** bleak, harsh, snowy **06** arctic, biting, chilly, dismal, frosty, frozen, hiemal, stormy
07 brumous, glacial, hostile
08 desolate, freezing, hibernal, piercing **09** cheerless **10** Decemberly, unfriendly **11** Decemberish

wipe
03 dab, dry, mop, rub **04** blow, dust,

jibe, null, scar, swab **05** brand, brush, clean, clear, dicht, dight, erase, purge, scrub, sweep, swipe **06** cancel, forget, reject, remove, sponge, strike
07 cleanse, deterge, expunct, expunge, sarcasm, take off **08** absterge, get rid of, take away **09** eliminate, eradicate
12 handkerchief

• **wipe out**
03 zap **04** kill, null, raze **05** erase, purge, sweep, waste **06** efface, murder, rub out, sponge **07** abolish, blot out, destroy, expunct, expunge
08 blow away, decimate, demolish, massacre **09** eliminate, eradicate, extirpate, liquidate, polish off
10 annihilate, obliterate **11** exterminate

wire
04 bind, coil **05** cable, snare **06** aerial, needle, tip-off **07** connect, protect, support, warning **08** telegram
09 telegraph, telephone **10** pickpocket
11 information **13** finishing line

wire-pulling
04 pull **05** clout **08** intrigue, plotting, scheming **09** influence **10** conspiring
12 manipulation

wiry
04 lean, wavy **05** rough, tough
06 coarse, sinewy, strong **08** muscular

Wisconsin
02 WI **03** Wis

wisdom
05 sense **06** genius, reason, sanity
07 insight **08** learning, prudence, sagacity, sapience **09** erudition, foresight, judgement, knowledge
10 astuteness, experience **11** common sense, discernment, penetration, skilfulness, speculation **12** intelligence
13 comprehension, enlightenment, judiciousness, understanding
14 circumspection

wise
03 way **04** sage, wice **05** aware, godly, pious, sound, weise, weize, witty
06 astute, clever, manner, owlish, shrewd **07** erudite, knowing, learned, politic, prudent, sapient, skilful
08 discreet, educated, informed, rational, sensible **09** judicious, sagacious **10** discerning, far-sighted, perceptive, proficient, reasonable
11 circumspect, common-sense, enlightened, experienced, intelligent, long-sighted, well-advised **12** well-informed **13** knowledgeable, sophisticated, understanding

• **put wise**
04 tell, warn **05** alert **06** clue in, fill in, inform, notify, tip off, wise up **07** apprise
10 intimate to **15** put in the picture
• **wise man**

The Three Wise Men:

06 Caspar
08 Melchior
09 Balthasar

See also **sage**

wiseacre
03 owl **05** Solon **07** wise guy
08 wiseling **09** Gothamite, smart alec
10 clever dick **11** smartypants

wisecrack
03 gag, pun **04** barb, gibe, jest, joke,
quip **05** funny **06** in-joke **08** one-liner
09 witticism

wisely
06 sagely **07** clearly, soundly
08 sensibly, shrewdly **09** advisedly,
knowingly **10** rationally **11** sagaciously
12 perceptively **13** intelligently

wish
03 ask, bid, wis, yen **04** hope, know,
long, lust, need, pine, urge, want,
whim, will, wist **05** covet, crave, fancy,
order, yearn **06** aspire, desire, direct,
hanker, hunger, liking, prefer, thirst
07 believe, bewitch, bidding,
command, craving, longing, request,
require **08** fondness, instruct, yearning
09 hankering, recommend
10 aspiration, preference
11 inclination, instruction, malediction

- **best wishes**
04 best **08** mazeltov, well-wish
09 good-speed

wishy-washy
04 flat, pale, thin, weak **05** bland, vapid
06 feeble, sloppy, watery **07** diluted,
insipid, vanilla **09** tasteless **10** namby-
pamby **11** ineffective, ineffectual,
watered-down **12** milk-and-water

wisp
04 lock, tuft, wase **05** flock, piece,
plume, shred, twist **06** strand, thread

wispy
04 fine, thin **05** faint, frail, light
06 flimsy, slight **07** fragile **08** delicate,
ethereal, gossamer, straggly
10 attenuated **13** insubstantial

wistful
03 sad **06** dreamy, intent, musing
07 earnest, forlorn, longing, pensive,
wishful **08** dreaming, mournful,
yearning **09** regretful **10** meditative,
melancholy, reflective, thoughtful
12 disconsolate **13** contemplative

wistfully
05 sadly **09** forlornly, longingly,
pensively **10** mournfully **11** plaintively
12 thoughtfully

wit
03 wag **04** know, mind, nous, salt
05 comic, joker, sense **06** banter,
brains, esprit, gagman, humour, levity,
reason, wisdom **07** discern, insight,
marbles, sparkle **08** badinage,
comedian, concetto, drollery,
gumption, humorist, merum sal,
repartee, sagacity, satirist **09** Attic salt,
bel esprit, eutrapely, faculties,
funniness, ingenuity, intellect,
invention, judgement, mother wit,
recognize, wittiness **10** astuteness,
cleverness, eutrapelia, jocularity,
liveliness, shrewdness **11** common

sense, imagination, information,
waggishness **12** homme d'esprit,
intelligence **13** facetiousness,
understanding

witch
04 mage, wich, wych **05** crone, magus
08 magician

Witches, witch doctors and wizards include:
03 hag, hex
05 Hecat, lamia, sibyl, weird
06 Hecate, magian, mganga, shaman,
voodoo, wisard, zendik
07 angekok, carline, sangoma,
warlock, wise man
08 angekkok, conjurer, marabout,
night-hag
09 enchanter, galdragon, occultist,
pythoness, sorceress, wise woman,
witch-wife
10 besom-rider, craigfluke, reim-
kennar
11 enchantress, gyre-carline,
medicine man, necromancer,
thaumaturge
12 Weird Sisters
13 thaumaturgist

Witch- and wizard-related terms include:
03 hex
04 mojo, muti, wart
05 charm, coven, goety, magic, spell,
wicca
06 cackle, potion, Sabbat, voodoo,
voudou
07 cantrip, gramary, hag-seed, pricker,
Sabbath, sorcery
08 black art, black cat, cauldron,
diablery, familiar, gramarye,
pishogue, wizardry
09 diablerie, enchanted, occultism,
the occult, witch's hat
10 black magic, broomstick,
divination, necromancy, witchcraft
11 apotropaism, conjuration,
enchantment, incantation,
thaumaturgy, the black art, witch-
finder
12 witching hour
14 Walpurgis night

witchcraft
03 obi **04** obia **05** magic, obeah, spell,
wicca **06** makatu, voodoo **07** myalism,
sorcery **08** wizardry **09** occultism, the
occult **10** black magic, divination,
necromancy **11** conjuration,
enchantment, incantation, the black
art

witch doctor
06 mganga, shaman **07** angekok,
sangoma **08** magician, marabout
11 medicine man **13** medicine woman

witch hunt
08 hounding **09** hue and cry
11 McCarthyism

with
◇ *juxtaposition indicator*
01 w **02** by, in, of **03** cum, mit **04** avec

05 among, using **06** beside, having
08 together **09** including
10 containing, possessing
13 accompanied by **14** in the company
of

withdraw
◇ *deletion indicator*
02 go **04** pull, walk **05** annul, leave,
unsay **06** abjure, call in, cancel, cry off,
depart, detach, go away, opt out, recall,
recant, recede, recoil, remove, repair,
retire, revoke, secede, shrink
07 abolish, back out, call off, deflect,
draw out, drop out, extract, give way,
go aside, inshell, nullify, pull out,
rescind, retract, retreat, scratch,
subduce, subduct, take out
08 disclaim, draw back, evacuate, fall
back, pull away, pull back, separate,
step down, subtract, take away, take
back **09** turn aside **10** declare off,
shrink back **11** contract out,
discontinue **14** absent yourself

withdrawal
03 tap **04** exit **06** exodus, recall, shrink
07 Dunkirk, removal, retiral, retreat
08 backword, delivery, pullback,
recourse **09** breakaway, departure,
disavowal, recession, revulsion,
secession **10** abjuration, disclaimer,
drawing out, evacuation, extraction,
retirement, revocation, subduction,
taking away **11** abstraction, drawing
back, falling back, pulling back,
recantation, repudiation, subtraction
13 disengagement

withdrawn
03 shy **05** aloof, quiet **06** hidden,
remote, silent **07** distant, private,
retired **08** alienate, detached, isolated,
reserved, retiring, secluded, solitary,
taciturn **09** introvert, shrinking
10 unsociable **11** introverted, out-of-
the-way **12** unresponsive
13 unforthcoming
15 uncommunicative

wither
03 die, dry **04** fade, sear, sere, wane,
welk, welt, wilt **05** arefy, blast, decay,
droop, dry up, taint, waste **06** blight,
die off, gizzen, perish, scorch, shrink,
weaken **07** decline, destroy, dwindle,
miff off, mortify, shrivel **08** fade away,
languish **09** disappear, humiliate
12 disintegrate

withering
06 deadly, fading **08** autumnal,
blasting, scathing, scornful, snubbing,
wounding **09** blighting, scorching
10 marcescent, mortifying
11 destructive, devastating, humiliating
12 contemptuous, death-dealing

withhold
◇ *deletion indicator*
04 curb, hide, keep, stop **05** check
06 deduct, detain, refuse, retain
07 conceal, control, decline, forbear,
repress, reserve **08** hold back, keep
back, postpone, restrain, subtract,
suppress **11** keep in check

within
◇ *hidden indicator*
◇ *insertion indicator*
02 in **04** into **05** intra **06** entire, herein, inside **07** indoors, not over **08** inside of, inwardly **09** in reach of **10** enclosed by **12** surrounded by

with it
02 in **03** hep, hip **04** cool **05** funky, natty, ritzy, vogue **06** glitzy, groovy, modern, modish, snazzy, trendy **08** up-to-date **10** all the rage **11** fashionable, progressive **12** contemporary **13** up-to-the-minute

without
◇ *containment indicator*
01 a-, x **02** an-, ex, w/o **03** sen **04** less, sans, sine **06** beyond, except, unless **07** lacking, needing, outside, wanting **08** free from, in need of **09** not having, outwardly **10** deprived of

withstand
04 bear, defy, face **05** brave, fight, stand **06** endure, hinder, oppose, resist, take on, thwart **07** hold off, hold out, last out, survive, weather **08** confront, cope with, tolerate, tough out **09** put up with, stand fast, stand firm, stand up to **10** tough it out **14** hold your ground **15** stand your ground

witless
04 daft, dull, nuts **05** barmy, crazy, inane, loony, loopy, nutty, potty, silly **06** cuckoo, mental, raving, stupid **07** bonkers, foolish, idiotic, moronic, unaware **08** doolally, gaumless, gormless, mindless **09** cretinous, imbecilic, senseless, up the wall **10** half-witted **11** empty-headed, off the rails, unconscious **12** mad as a hatter, off your chump **13** off your rocker, unintelligent **14** wrong in the head

witness
03 see **04** mark, note, show, sign, view **05** prove, see in, teste, watch **06** affirm, attest, depose, evince, expert, look on, notice, obtest, record, verify, viewer **07** bear out, confirm, endorse, observe, support, testify, vouchee, watcher **08** deponent, evidence, looker-on, observer, onlooker, perceive, speak for, validate **09** attestant, authority, bystander, spectator, testifier, testimony **10** eyewitness, man of skill **11** bear witness, compurgator, corroborate, countersign **12** be evidence of, give evidence
• **bear witness**
04 aver, show **05** prove **06** adjure, affirm, assert, attest, evince, record, verify **07** certify, confirm, declare, display, endorse, testify **08** evidence, manifest, vouch for **10** asseverate **11** corroborate, demonstrate

witter
04 chat **06** babble, drivel, gabble, gossip, jabber, patter, rattle **07** blather,

blether, chatter, twaddle, twattle, twitter

witticism
03 hit, pun **04** jibe, joke, quip **06** bon mot **07** epigram, riposte **08** one-liner, repartee **09** impromptu, wisecrack **10** jeu d'esprit, pleasantry **11** play on words
See also **joke**

wittingly
08 by design, wilfully **09** knowingly, on purpose, purposely, studiedly, willingly **10** designedly **11** consciously **12** calculatedly, deliberately **13** intentionally

witty
04 wise **05** comic, droll, funny, light, salty, smart **06** clever, lively **07** amusing, jocular, lambent, waggish **08** discreet, fanciful, humorous, original, pregnant, sensible **09** brilliant, conceited, facetious, ingenious, sarcastic, sparkling, spiritual, spirituel, whimsical **11** coruscating, sharp-witted, spirituelle

wizard
03 ace, hex **04** good, star, whiz **05** adept, great, super, witch **06** expert, genius, master, superb, wisard **07** hotshot, maestro, prodigy, warlock, wise man **08** conjurer, magician, smashing, sorcerer, terrific, virtuoso **09** brilliant, enchanter, enjoyable, fantastic, occultist, wonderful **10** delightful, marvellous, tremendous **11** necromancer, sensational, thaumaturge
See also **witch**

wizened
04 thin, worn **05** lined **07** dried up, gnarled **08** shrunken, withered, wrinkled **10** shrivelled

wobble
◇ *anagram indicator*
04 rock, sway **05** quake, shake, waver **06** coggle, dither, dodder, quaver, quiver, seesaw, teeter, totter, tremor, wabble **07** precess, quaking, shoggle, stagger, tremble, vibrate **08** hesitate **09** fluctuate, oscillate, vacillate, vibration **11** oscillation **12** shilly-shally, unsteadiness, wibble-wobble

wobbly
◇ *anagram indicator*
05 shaky, wonky **06** uneven, unsafe **07** doddery, rickety **08** unstable, unsteady **09** doddering, quavering, teetering, tottering, trembling **10** unbalanced

Wodehouse
02 PG

woe
02 wo **03** sad, wae **04** bale, dool, dule, pain **05** agony, curse, doole, gloom, grief, sorry, tears, trial **06** burden, misery, sorrow, tsuris **07** anguish, sadness, trouble, tsouris **08** calamity, disaster, distress, hardship, wretched

09 adversity, dejection, heartache, suffering **10** affliction, depression, heartbreak, melancholy, misfortune **11** tribulation, unhappiness **12** wretchedness

woebegone
03 sad **04** blue **06** gloomy **07** doleful, forlorn, tearful **08** dejected, downcast, mournful, troubled, wretched **09** long-faced, miserable, sorrowful **10** dispirited, lugubrious **11** crestfallen, downhearted, tear-stained **12** disconsolate **13** grief-stricken **14** down in the mouth

woeful
◇ *anagram indicator*
03 bad, sad **04** mean, poor **05** awful, cruel, lousy, sorry, waefu' **06** feeble, gloomy, paltry, rotten, tragic, waeful **07** doleful, unhappy, waesome **08** dreadful, grieving, grievous, hopeless, mournful, pathetic, pitiable, shocking, terrible, wretched **09** afflicted, appalling, miserable, sorrowful **10** calamitous, deplorable, disastrous, inadequate, lamentable **11** disgraceful, distressing **12** catastrophic, disconsolate, heart-rending **13** disappointing, heartbreaking

woefully
05 sadly **07** awfully, lousily **08** gloomily, pitiably, terribly **09** dolefully, forlornly, miserably, unhappily **10** deplorably, dreadfully, hopelessly, lamentably, mournfully, shockingly, tragically, wretchedly **11** appallingly **12** disastrously, pathetically **13** disgracefully **14** disconsolately

wolf
04 lobo **05** Romeo **06** coyote, lecher **07** Don Juan, Isegrim, seducer **08** Casanova, Isengrim **09** ladies' man, thylacine, womanizer **10** lady-killer **11** philanderer
• **wolf down**
04 bolt, cram, gulp **05** gorge, scoff, stuff **06** devour, gobble **07** put away **08** pack away

woman
01 w **03** bit, chi, gin, hag, hen, her, she, Tib, tit **04** baby, bint, bird, chai, doll, fair, feme, frau, girl, jane, Judy, lady, lass, maid, Mary, minx, mort, peat, puss, sort, tart, wife **05** belle, biddy, broad, chick, cutie, cutty, dolly, femme, fille, filly, flirt, hussy, lover, madam, peach, popsy, quean, randy, wench **06** au pair, blowze, cummer, damsel, female, geisha, gillet, jillet, kimmer, lassie, maiden, moppet, number, ogress, sheila, shiksa, tomboy, tottie, wahine **07** bag lady, fiancée, mystery, nymphet, partner, reverse **08** mistress, princess **09** charwoman, dolly bird, plain Jane **10** bit of stuff, Cinderella, girlfriend, sweetheart **11** beauty queen **12** bachelorette, bobby-dazzler
See also **girl**

- **first woman**
03 Eve 07 Pandora
- **good woman**
01 S 02 St 04 sant 05 Saint

womanhood
05 woman 08 maturity 09 adulthood,
womankind, womenfolk, womenkind
10 muliebrity, womenfolks

womanizer

*Womanizers and libertines
include:*

04 goat, lech, rake, roué, wolf
05 letch, Romeo
06 gay dog, lecher
07 Don Juan, seducer, wastrel
08 Casanova, Lothario, Lovelace,
palliard, rakehell
09 debauchee, ladies' man, libertine,
reprobate, voluptary
10 Corinthian, lady-killer, profligate,
sensualist
11 gay deceiver, philanderer

womanly
04 kind, warm 06 female, tender
07 shapely 08 feminine, ladylike,
motherly, womanish 10 effeminate,
well-formed

women
- **excluding women**
04 stag
- **Women's Institute**
02 WI

See also **woman**

wonder
03 awe 04 gape, marl, muse 05 doubt,
ferly, marle, query, sight, think
06 admire, marvel, ponder, puzzle,
rarity 07 cruller, inquire, miracle,
prodigy, reflect 08 be amazed,
meditate, pleasure, question, surprise
09 amazement, curiosity, nonpareil,
spectacle, speculate 10 admiration,
conjecture, phenomenon, stand in
awe, wonderment 11 ask yourself, be
astounded, be surprised, fascination
12 astonishment, be astonished,
bewilderment 13 be dumbfounded
14 be lost for words

The Seven Wonders of the World:

15 Pyramids of Egypt
16 Colossus of Rhodes
18 Pharos of Alexandria
21 Statue of Zeus at Olympia
23 Hanging Gardens of Babylon
24 Mausoleum of Halicarnassus,
Temple of Artemis at Ephesus

- **expression of wonder**
01 O 02 oh 03 god, wow 04 gosh,
whew 05 wowee 06 heyday, wheugh
07 good-now 08 gracious 09 Jesus
wept 13 stone the crows

wonderful
03 ace, def, fab, old, rad 04 boss, cool,
keen, mean, mega, neat 05 beaut,
boffo, brill, bully, crack, dicty, dilly,
great, hunky, jammy, lummy, socko,
super, triff 06 castor, divine, famous,

far-out, geason, groovy, mighty,
peachy, superb, way-out, wicked,
wizard 07 amazing, awesome, capital,
classic, crucial, elegant, épatant,
magical, mirable, radical, ripping,
stellar, strange, tipping, topping, triffic,
trimmer 08 champion, clinking,
fabulous, glorious, heavenly, jim-
dandy, knockout, smashing, spiffing,
splendid, stonking, stunning, terrific,
top-notch 09 admirable, brilliant,
copacetic, excellent, fantastic,
righteous, startling 10 astounding,
delightful, incredible, marvellous, not
half bad, phenomenal, remarkable,
staggering, stupendous, surprising,
tremendous 11 astonishing,
fantabulous, magnificent, outstanding,
sensational 12 second to none
13 extraordinary 14 out of this world

wonderfully
06 purely 09 amazingly, extremely
10 incredibly 12 phenomenally,
terrifically, tremendously, unbelievably
13 fantastically

wonky
04 awry, weak 05 amiss, askew, shaky,
wrong 06 wobbly 07 crooked,
unsound 08 unsteady 09 skew-whiff

wont
03 use, way 04 fain, rule, used 05 given,
habit 06 custom 07 routine 08 inclined,
practice 10 accustomed, habituated

wonted
04 tame 05 daily, usual 06 common,
normal 07 regular, routine 08 familiar,
frequent, habitual 09 customary
10 accustomed, habituated
12 conventional

woo
03 wow 04 seek 05 chase, court
06 pursue 07 address, attract, look for,
romance 09 cultivate, encourage
10 make love to, pay court to 13 seek
the hand of

wood
03 mad, wud 04 bowl, hyle, shaw, tree
05 copse, cross, grove, hurst, trees,
woods, xylem 06 fierce, forest, planks,
pulpit 07 coppice, furious, spinney,
thicket 08 woodland 10 plantation
See also **forest**; **golf club**; **timber**

Woods include:

03 ash, box, cam, elm, fir, nut, oak, ply,
red, sap, yew
04 bass, cord, cork, deal, ebon, fire,
hard, iron, lana, lime, pine, pink,
pulp, rose, sasa, soft, teak
05 alder, apple, balsa, beech, black,
brush, cedar, drift, ebony, green,
hazel, heart, larch, maple, match,
olive, peach, plane, ramin, satin,
tiger, torch, tulip, utile, white, zebra
06 acacia, bamboo, bitter, brazil,
candle, cherry, cotton, linden,
lumber, obeche, orange, padauk,
pedauk, poplar, rubber, sandal,
sapele, spruce, timber, veneer,
walnut, willow

07 Amboina, bubinga, hickory,
palmyra, quassia
08 amaranth, chestnut, cocobolo,
hornbeam, kindling, mahogany, red
lauan, seasoned, silky oak,
sycamore
09 chipboard, hardboard, jacaranda,
quebracho
10 afrormosia, Douglas fir, paper birch
11 black cherry, lignum vitae, purple
heart, tulip poplar, white walnut,
yellow birch
13 sweet chestnut

- **measurement of wood**
04 cord 05 stere 06 fathom, square
08 standard 09 board-foot, decastere,
decistere 10 hoppus foot 15 hoppus
cubic foot
- **out of the woods**
04 safe 06 secure 10 home and dry, in
the clear 11 out of danger 12 safe and
sound 15 out of difficulty
- **piece of wood**
03 cat, log 04 beam, chip, lath, slat
05 block, board, dwang, plank, split,
staff, wedge 06 batten, billet, fillet,
flitch, loggat, planch, timber, tipcat
07 bunting 08 splinter 09 four-by-two,
scantling, two-by-four

wooded
05 woody 06 sylvan 08 forested,
nemorous, timbered 09 arboreous
11 arboraceous, tree-covered

wooden
04 dull, hard, slow, tree 05 blank,
empty, heavy, rigid, stiff, treen, woody
06 clumsy, leaden, stodgy, stupid,
timber, vacant 07 awkward, deadpan,
stilted, vacuous 08 lifeless, ligneous
09 graceless, impassive, inhibited,
unnatural 10 insensible, spiritless
11 emotionless, unemotional
12 unresponsive 14 expressionless

woodland
04 bush, wood 05 copse, grove, trees,
woods 06 forest, miombo, timber
07 boscage, boskage, coppice,
spinney, thicket 10 plantation

woodpecker
05 Picus 06 yaffle, yucker 07 awlbird,
flicker, piculet, witwall 08 hickwall,
rainbird 10 yaffingale

wood sorrel
03 oca 06 oxalis 08 shamrock

woody
05 bosky 06 sylvan, wooded, wooden,
xyloid 08 forested, ligneous 11 tree-
covered

wool
02 oo 03 ket 04 coat, down, hair,
kemp, noil, yarn 05 flock, llama, noils
06 Angora, botany, fleece, jersey,
pelage, staple, two-ply, vicuña
07 floccus, morling 08 cashmere,
mortling, shatoosh 09 shahtoosh,
strouding 13 linsey-woolsey
- **pull the wool over someone's
eyes**
03 con 04 dupe, fool 05 trick

06 delude, take in **07** deceive **08** hoodwink **09** bamboozle **12** pull a swiftie, put one over on **14** pull a fast one on

wool-gathering
06 dreamy **11** day-dreaming, distraction, inattention **12** absent-minded **13** forgetfulness, preoccupation

woollen fabric *see* fabric

woolly
04 hazy **05** downy, foggy, fuzzy, hairy, sheep, vague, woozy **06** cloudy, fleecy, fluffy, frizzy, jersey, jumper, lanate, lanose, shaggy **07** blurred, muddled, sweater, unclear, woollen **08** cardigan, confused, floccose, nebulous, pullover **10** flocculent, ill-defined, indefinite, indistinct **12** woolly-haired

woozy
05 dazed, dizzy, rocky, tipsy, vague **06** wobbly, woolly **07** bemused, blurred, fuddled **08** confused, unsteady **09** befuddled, nauseated **11** light-headed

word
03 gen, mot, put, say, vow **04** book, chat, dope, hint, info, name, news, oath, sign, talk, term, text, will **05** couch, order, speak, state, write **06** advice, decree, gossip, honour, lyrics, notice, phrase, pledge, remark, report, rumour, saying, script, signal, war cry **07** account, command, comment, explain, express, flatter, go-ahead, hearsay, low-down, mandate, message, palabra, promise, scandal, tidings, vocable, warning, whisper **08** bulletin, dispatch, libretto, password, thumbs-up **09** assertion, assurance, guarantee, statement, tête-à-tête, utterance, watchword **10** communiqué, discussion, expression, green light **11** commandment, declaration, designation, information, instruction, speculation, undertaking **12** consultation, conversation, intelligence **13** communication
See also speech

• have words
03 row **05** argue **06** bicker **07** dispute, quarrel **08** disagree, squabble
• in a word
07 briefly, in brief, in short, to sum up **09** concisely, to be brief **10** succinctly **11** in a nutshell, summarizing **14** to put it briefly
• in other words
02 ie **05** id est **06** that is
• word for word
06 verbal **07** closely, exactly, literal **08** ad verbum, verbatim **09** literally, precisely **10** accurately

wordiness
06 waffle **07** wordage **08** verbiage **09** garrulity, loquacity, prolixity, verbosity **10** logorrhoea **11** diffuseness, perissology,

verboseness **13** garrulousness **14** long-windedness **15** verbal diarrhoea

wording
04 text **05** style, tenor, words **07** diction, wordage **08** language, phrasing, speaking, verbiage **09** subtitles, utterance, verbalism **10** expression **11** phraseology, terminology **13** choice of words

word-perfect
05 exact **06** spot-on **08** accurate, faithful **13** letter-perfect

wordplay
03 pun, wit **04** puns **07** punning **08** repartee **10** witticisms **11** paronomasia

wordy
05 windy **06** phrasy, prolix **07** diffuse, verbose **08** rambling **09** garrulous **10** discursive, long-winded, loquacious

work
◇ *anagram indicator*
02 do, go, op **03** art, dig, fag, fix, hat, job, ply, ren, rin, run, sew, tut, use **04** ache, acts, book, char, deed, duty, edge, farm, form, fuss, guts, line, make, mill, move, opus, plan, play, poem, shop, slog, take, task, tick, till, toil **05** cause, chore, craft, drive, field, graft, guide, knead, model, mould, parts, piece, plant, purge, shape, shift, skill, slave, study, trade, trick **06** action, cajole, career, charge, create, doings, drudge, effect, effort, fiddle, go well, handle, labour, manage, métier, oeuvre, strain, wangle **07** achieve, actions, arrange, calling, control, execute, factory, fashion, ferment, foundry, innards, mission, operate, peg away, perform, process, prosper, pull off, pursuit, squeeze, succeed, travail, trouble, writing **08** business, contrive, creation, drudgery, engineer, exercise, exertion, function, have a job, industry, movement, painting, plug away, treatise, vocation, workings, workshop **09** cultivate, embroider, influence, machinery, manoeuvre, mechanism, penetrate **10** accomplish, assignment, be employed, bring about, commission, embroidery, employment, livelihood, manipulate, occupation, production, profession **11** achievement, be effective, composition, elbow grease, pull strings, undertaking, workmanship **12** be successful, working parts **13** exert yourself, installations **14** accomplishment, be satisfactory, earn your living, line of business, responsibility **15** slog your guts out
• bit of work
01 J **03** erg **05** joule **08** therblig
• day's work
04 darg **05** stent, stint **06** man-day **07** journey
• the works
06 the lot **10** everything **11** the whole lot **15** the whole shebang

• work out
04 dope, plan, toil **05** drill, serve, solve, total, train **06** come to, deduce, devise, evolve, finish, go well, invent, pan out, warm up **07** add up to, arrange, clear up, come out, develop, dope out, exhaust, expiate, keep fit, prosper, resolve, sort out, succeed, turn out **08** amount to, contrive, exercise, organize, practise **09** calculate, construct, elaborate, figure out, formulate, puzzle out **10** understand **11** be effective, put together
• work up
03 tew **04** meng, ming, move, spur, whet **05** menge, reach, rouse, use up **06** arouse, excite, expand, incite, kindle, stir up, subact **07** achieve, agitate, animate, build up, ferment, inflame **08** generate, summon up **09** elaborate, instigate, stimulate

workable
06 doable, viable **08** feasible, possible **09** practical, realistic **11** practicable

workaday
04 dull **06** common **07** average, humdrum, mundane, prosaic, routine, toiling, work-day, working **08** everyday, familiar, ordinary **09** labouring, practical **11** commonplace **12** run-of-the-mill

worker
03 ant, bee **04** hand, peon, temp **06** coater, Indian, key man, legger, toiler **07** artisan, grinder, ouvrier, workman **08** employee, grisette, labourer, mechanic, ouvrière, strapper, stuccoer **09** craftsman, midinette, operative, salaryman, tradesman, workhorse, workwoman **10** mechanical, painstaker, railroader, wage-earner, workaholic, working man **11** breadwinner, craftswoman, proletarian, tradeswoman **12** Gastarbeiter, willing horse, working woman **13** member of staff

workforce
03 men **05** hands, staff **06** labour **07** workers **08** manpower, skeleton **09** employees, personnel, shop floor **10** workpeople **11** labour force **14** human resources

working
◇ *anagram indicator*
02 on **03** pit **04** guts, live, mine **05** going, parts, shaft, waste, works **06** action, active, in a job, in work, manner, method, quarry, system **07** innards, process, routine, running **08** diggings, employed, movement **09** endeavour, labouring, machinery, mechanism, operating, operation, operative **10** in business **11** excavations, functioning, operational **12** up and running, working parts **13** installations **14** in working order

workman, workwoman
04 hand, hobo **05** hunky, navvy **06** beamer, glazer, master, worker

07 artisan **08** apron-man, employee, gunsmith, labourer, mechanic **09** artificer, craftsman, operative, prud'homme, stage hand **10** journeyman, surfaceman **11** craftswoman **12** manual worker, tradesperson

workmanlike
05 adept **06** expert **07** careful, skilful, skilled **08** masterly, thorough **09** competent, efficient **10** proficient **11** painstaking **12** businesslike, professional, satisfactory

workmanship
03 art **04** work **05** craft, skill **06** finish **07** facture, tooling **08** artifice, artistry **09** execution, expertise, handiwork, technique **10** handicraft **11** manufacture **13** craftsmanship

workmate
03 lad **08** co-worker **09** associate, colleague **10** work-fellow, yoke-fellow **12** fellow-worker

workout
05 drill **06** warm-up **08** aerobics, exercise, practice, training **10** gymnastics, isometrics **11** eurhythmics, limbering up **13** callisthenics

workshop
03 lab **04** mill, shop **05** class, forge, plant, works **06** garage, smithy, studio **07** atelier, factory, seminar **08** plumbery, smithery, workroom **09** cooperage, symposium **10** laboratory, study group **11** machine-shop, rigging-loft **15** discussion group

work-shy
04 idle, lazy, lusk, slow **05** inert, slack, tardy **06** laesie, lither, torpid **07** languid, luskish **08** bone-idle, fainéant, inactive, indolent, slothful, sluggish **09** lethargic **10** languorous, slow-moving **14** good-for-nothing

workwoman *see* **workman,** **workwoman**

world
03 age, era, man, orb **04** area, days, life, star, vale **05** class, earth, epoch, field, globe, group, realm, times **06** cosmos, domain, nature, people, period, planet, public, sphere, system **07** kingdom, mankind, reality, section, society **08** creation, division, everyone, humanity, province, universe **09** everybody, existence, humankind, human race, situation, way of life **10** department, experience, population **11** environment **12** heavenly body

World heritage sites include:

03 Bam, Omo, Taï
04 Agra, Bath, Graz, Lima, Manú, Pisa, Riga, San'a, Troy, Tyre
05 Aksum, Awash, Berne, Bosra, Copán, Cuzco, Delos, Galle, Hatra, Kandy, Lyons, Ohrid, Paris, Petra, Quito, Siena, Sucre, Uluru
06 Abomey, Aleppo, Amazon, Assisi, Bassae, Byblos, Cyrene, Darién, Delphi, Durham, Göreme, Kakadu, Naples, Oporto, Orkney, Paphos, Potosí, Puebla, Sangay, Sousse, Thebes, Toledo, Treves, Venice, Verona, Vienna, Warsaw
07 Abu Mena, Avebury, Avignon, Baalbek, Caracas, Djemila, Garamba, Gwynedd, Holy See, Olympia, San Juan, Segovia, St Kilda, Vicenza, Virunga
08 Agra Fort, Alhambra, Altamira, Carthage, Chartres, Damascas, Durmitor, Florence, Ghadamès, Hattusas, Mount Tai, Palenque, Pyramids, Pyrénées, Sabratha, Salvador, Salzburg, Shark Bay, Sigiriya, Stari Ras, Taj Mahal, Timbuktu, Valletta, Würzburg
09 Abu Simbel, Auschwitz, Ayutthaya, Dubrovnik, Edinburgh, Epidaurus, Greenwich, Gros Morne, Huascarán, Jerusalem, Mesa Verde, Nemrut Dag, Parthenon, Serengeti
10 El Escorial, Everglades, Generalife, Hierapolis, Hildesheim, Ironbridge, Monte Albán, Monticello, Persepolis, Pont du Gard, Stonehenge, Versailles
11 Ajanta caves, Danube Delta, Ellora caves, Gorée Island, Hagia Sophia, Leptis Magna, Machu Picchu, Madara Rider, Mohenjo-daro, Quedlinburg, Teotihuacán, Vatican City, Western Wall, Westminster, Yellowstone
12 Altamira Cave, Ancient Kyoto, Fraser Island, Hadrian's Wall, Koguryo Tombs, Mont-St-Michel, Santo Domingo, The Great Wall
13 Fontainebleau, Fontenay Abbey, Great Zimbabwe, Rila Monastery, Tower of London
14 Aldabra Islands, Blenheim Palace, Elephanta caves, Fountains Abbey, Giant's Causeway, Heraion of Samos, Imperial Palace
15 Aachen Cathedral, Amiens Cathedral, Ironbridge Gorge, Kasbah of Algiers, Kathmandu Valley, Nubian monuments, Speyer Cathedral, Statue of Liberty

• on top of the world
05 happy **06** elated, joyful **08** ecstatic, euphoric, exultant, jubilant, thrilled **09** delighted, exuberant, overjoyed, rapturous **10** enraptured, in raptures **11** exhilarated, high as a kite, on cloud nine, over the moon, tickled pink **14** pleased as Punch **15** in seventh heaven

• out of this world
02 ET **03** ace, rad **04** cool, mean, mega, neat **05** brill, great **06** divine, superb, way-out, wicked **07** crucial, radical **08** fabulous, heavenly, smashing, stonking, stunning, terrific **09** excellent, fantastic, wonderful **10** delightful, incredible, marvellous, phenomenal, remarkable

11 sensational **12** second to none, unbelievable **13** indescribable

worldly
06 carnal, greedy, mortal, urbane **07** earthly, knowing, mondain, mundane, outward, profane, secular, selfish, terrene **08** covetous, grasping, material, mondaine, physical, temporal **09** ambitious, corporeal **10** avaricious, streetwise **11** experienced, terrestrial, unspiritual, worldly-wise **12** cosmopolitan **13** materialistic, sophisticated

worldly-wise
06 shrewd, urbane **07** cynical, knowing, worldly **10** cultivated, perceptive, streetwise **11** experienced **12** cosmopolitan **13** sophisticated

worldwide
06 global **07** general, mondial **08** catholic **09** universal **10** ubiquitous **11** transglobal **13** international

worm
04 grub **05** snake **06** dragon, maggot, squirm **07** remorse

Worms include:

03 eel, lug, pin, rag
04 flat, hook, tape
05 arrow, earth, fluke, leech, round
06 peanut, ribbon, thread
07 annelid, bristle
08 sea mouse
10 blood fluke, liver fluke

worn
03 old **04** bare, used **05** all in, drawn, jaded, spent, tatty, tired, trite, weary **06** bushed, done in, frayed, ragged, shabby **07** haggard, thumbed, worn-out **08** careworn, dog-tired, fatigued, strained, tattered **09** exhausted, hackneyed, in tatters, knackered **10** threadbare **13** weather-bitten

• worn out
03 old **04** beat, gone, past, used **05** all in, banal, corny, rough, seedy, stale, stock, tacky, tatty, tired, trite, warby, weary **06** bushed, common, done in, épuisé, failed, frayed, pooped, ragged, shabby, wasted, zonked **07** cliché'd, épuisée, to-worne, traikit, useless, wearied, whacked, worn-out **08** clichéed, dead-beat, decrepit, dog-tired, dog-weary, forfairn, overused, tattered, time-worn, tired out **09** bedridden, disjaskit, exhausted, geriatric, hackneyed, knackered, moth-eaten, pooped out, shattered, washed-out, worm-eaten **10** broken-down, clapped-out, overworked, pedestrian, shagged out, threadbare, uninspired, unoriginal, yawn-making **11** commonplace, ready to drop, stereotyped, tuckered out, wearing thin **12** cliché-ridden, journey-bated, overscutched, run-of-the-mill **13** on its last legs, platitudinous, unimaginative

worried
◊ *anagram indicator*
04 worn **05** het up, tense, upset, wired

worrisome

05 hairy, scary **06** vexing **07** irksome **08** insecure, worrying **09** agonizing, upsetting, vexatious **10** bothersome, disturbing, nail-biting, perturbing **11** disquieting, distressing, frightening, troublesome

worry

◊ *anagram indicator*

03 bug, dog, eat, nag, tew, tiz, vex **04** bite, care, faze, fear, frab, fret, gnaw, pest, stew **05** annoy, choke, deave, deeve, devil, eat up, feese, feeze, go for, harry, phase, phese, sweat, tease, tizzy, touse, touze, towse, towze, trial, upset **06** attack, badger, bother, burden, hang-up, harass, hassle, misery, niggle, pester, pheese, pheeze, pingle, plague, savage, strain, stress, tear at, unease, worrit **07** agitate, agonize, anguish, anxiety, concern, disturb, perturb, problem, tension, torment, trouble **08** disquiet, distress, headache, irritate, nuisance, unsettle, vexation **09** aggravate, agitation, annoyance, be anxious, misgiving **10** be troubled, irritation, perplexity **11** disturbance, fearfulness **12** apprehension, be distressed, perturbation **13** consternation **14** responsibility

• expression of worry

04 uh-oh, yike **05** yikes **06** cripes

worrying

05 hairy, scary **06** trying, uneasy **07** anxious, weighty **08** alarming, niggling **09** agonizing, harassing, upsetting, worrisome **10** disturbing, nail-biting, perturbing, unsettling **11** disquieting, distressing, troublesome

worsen

04 sink, slip **06** weaken **07** decline, go to pot **08** get worse, heighten, increase **09** aggravate, intensify **10** degenerate, exacerbate, go downhill **11** deteriorate **13** go down the tube **14** go down the tubes

worsening

05 decay **07** decline **10** pejoration **12** degeneration, exacerbation **13** deterioration, retrogression

worship

02 Wp **04** laud, love, puja **05** adore, deify, exalt, extol, glory **06** admire, homage, honour, Ibadat, praise, prayer, pray to, regard, revere **07** adulate, dignity, glorify, idolize, opus Dei, prayers, respect **08** adultery, devotion, geolatry, idolatry, naturism, religion, satanism, venerate **09** adoration, adulation, aniconism, devotions, diabolism, laudation, pyrolatry, reverence, snake cult **10** astrolatry, bardolatry, exaltation, eye-service, heliolatry, iconolatry, litholatry, ophiolatry, reputation, veneration **11** angelolatry, be devoted to, deification, idolization, physiolatry, theriolatry **13** anthropolatry, glorification, thaumatolatry

Places of worship include:
03 wat
04 fane, kirk, shul
05 abbey, gompa
06 bethel, chapel, church, mandir, masjid, mosque, pagoda, shrine, temple, vihara
07 chantry, convent, minster
08 gurdwara
09 cathedral, monastery, synagogue
10 tabernacle
12 meeting-house

See also **abbey**; **religious**

worshipful

02 Wp **04** awed, Wpfl **05** pious **06** devout, humble, loving, solemn **07** adoring, devoted, dutiful **08** admiring, obeisant **10** respectful **11** deferential, reverential

worshipper *see* **believer**

worst

03 war **04** beat, best, drub, lick **05** crush, paste, smash, thump **06** damage, defeat, hammer, master, subdue, thrash **07** clobber, conquer, trounce **08** overcome, pessimal, pessimum, vanquish **09** devastate, overpower, overthrow, slaughter, subjugate, whitewash **10** annihilate **13** run rings round **14** get the better of **15** make mincemeat of

worth

02 be **03** use **04** cost, gain, good, help, rate **05** avail, carat, merit, price, value, virtu **06** become, carrat, credit, desert, happen, profit, virtue **07** benefit, deserts, quality, service, utility **08** eminence, meriting, repaying, valuable **09** advantage, deserving, substance **10** assistance, excellence, excellency, importance, justifying, usefulness, warranting, worthiness **11** possessions **12** significance

worthily

04 well **08** laudably, reliably, valuably **09** admirably **10** creditably, honourably **11** commendably

worthless

03 bad, bum, low **04** base, junk, naff, orra, poor, punk, raca, vile, waff **05** blown, cheap, junky, light, sorry, tripy **06** abject, cruddy, crummy, draffy, drossy, futile, naught, no good, ornery, paltry, trashy, tripey **07** corrupt, drunken, ignoble, mauvais, nothing, shotten, trivial, useless **08** beggarly, castaway, draffish, gimcrack, jimcrack, mauvaise, nugatory, rubbishy, sixpenny, trifling, twopenny, unusable, unworthy, wanwordy, wretched **09** brummagem, cheap-jack, no-account, pointless, valueless **10** despicable, unavailing, unprizable **11** ineffectual, littleworth, meaningless, stramineous, unimportant **12** contemptible **13** insignificant **14** good-for-nothing, not worth shucks

• worthless thing

03 mud **04** dirt, grot **05** nyaff **06** fag end **10** catchpenny

worthlessness

07 ambs-ace, ames-ace **08** futility **09** cheapness **11** lack of worth, nothingness, unusability, uselessness **13** pointlessness **15** ineffectualness, meaninglessness

worthwhile

04 good **05** tanti **06** useful, worthy **07** gainful, helpful, of value **08** valuable **09** estimable, rewarding **10** beneficial, productive, profitable **11** justifiable **12** advantageous, constructive

worthy

03 fit, VIP **04** good, name **05** moral, noble **06** big gun, bigwig, decent, honest, honour, top dog **07** big shot, notable, upright **08** big noise, laudable, luminary, reliable, somebody, top brass, valuable, virtuous **09** admirable, big cheese, deserving, dignitary, estimable, excellent, personage, reputable, righteous **10** creditable, excellence, honourable, notability, worthwhile **11** appropriate, commendable, meritorious, respectable, trustworthy **12** praiseworthy

would

01 'd

would-be

04 keen **05** eager **07** budding, hopeful, longing, wannabe, wishful **08** aspiring, striving **09** ambitious, soi-disant **10** optimistic **12** endeavouring, enterprising

wound

◊ *anagram indicator*

03 cut, hit, pip **04** ache, bite, blow, dunt, gash, harm, hurt, pain, scar, sore, stab, tear, vuln, win't **05** bless, graze, grief, saber, sabre, shock, shoot, slash, touch, upset **06** damage, grieve, injure, injury, insult, lesion, offend, pierce, slight, trauma **07** anguish, mortify, scratch, torment **08** distress, lacerate, puncture, sword-cut **09** vulnerate **10** heartbreak, laceration, traumatism, traumatize

wow

03 boy, cor

wrack

◊ *anagram indicator*

05 wreck **07** remnant, seaweed, torment, torture **08** wreckage **09** vengeance **10** punishment **11** destruction, devastation

wraith

05 ghost, shade, spook **06** double, spirit **07** phantom, spectre **08** revenant **10** apparition, astral body **12** doppelgänger

wrangle

03 rag, row **04** herd, spar, spat, tiff **05** argue, clash, fight, scrap, set-to **06** argufy, barney, bicker, cample, cangle, debate, dust-up, hassle, jangle, tussle **07** brabble, brangle, contend, contest, dispute, fall out, punch-up, quarrel, wrestle **08** argument, disagree, ergotize, squabble **09** altercate, argy-bargy, bickering, have it out, have words **10** digladiate **11** altercation, controversy, cross swords **12** disagreement **13** have it out with, slanging match **15** be at loggerheads, have a bone to pick

wrap

◇ *containment indicator*

03 hap, lap, rug, wap **04** bind, cape, fold, hide, mail, pack, robe, roll, snug, wind **05** amice, boost, cloak, cover, scarf, shawl, sheet, stole, throw **06** clothe, cocoon, emboss, encase, enfold, mantle, muffle, parcel, roll up, shroud, swathe, wimple **07** commend, embrace, enclose, envelop, flannel, immerse, involve, obscure, package, snuggle, swaddle, whimple **08** bemuffle, bundle up, enswathe, entangle, gift-wrap, inswathe, parcel up, surround **09** clingfilm, night-rail **11** acclamation

• **wrap up**

03 end, hap **04** mail **05** dry up **06** belt up, bundle, enfold, infold, pack up, parcel, shut up, wind up **07** be quiet, package **08** complete, conclude, gift-wrap, muffle up, parcel up, pipe down, round off **09** finish off, terminate **11** dress warmly, give it a rest **12** put a sock in it **13** bring to a close, shut your mouth **14** hold your tongue **15** wear warm clothes

wrapper

04 case **05** cover, folio, paper **06** casing, jacket, sheath, sleeve **08** covering, envelope, Jiffy bag®, wrapping **09** packaging **10** dust jacket

wrapping

04 case, foil **05** paper **06** carton, swathe **07** tinfoil, wrapper **08** envelope, Jiffy bag® **09** packaging **10** bubble pack, Cellophane® **11** blister card, blister pack, envelopment, silver paper

wrapt *see* **rapt**

wrath

03 ire **04** fury, rage **05** anger, angry **06** ardour, choler, spleen, temper **07** passion **09** annoyance **10** bitterness, irritation, resentment **11** displeasure, indignation **12** exasperation

wrathful

03 mad **05** angry, cross, irate, ratty, spewy, wroth **06** bitter, choked, ireful, raging **07** crooked, enraged, furious, ropable, stroppy, uptight **08** burned up, furibund, hairless, in a paddy, incensed, up in arms **09** in a lather, indignant, raving mad, seeing red, ticked off **10** aggravated, displeased, hopping mad, infuriated **11** disgruntled, fit to be tied **12** on the warpath

wreak

04 harm, vent **05** cause **06** avenge, bestow, create, damage, effect, punish **07** execute, express, inflict, unleash **08** carry out, drive out, exercise **09** vengeance **10** bring about, perpetrate, punishment

wreath

03 lei **04** band, loop, ring **05** crown, torse **06** anadem, circle **07** chaplet, circlet, coronet, festoon, garland **09** snowdrift **10** civic crown

wreathe

04 coil, turn, wind, wrap **05** adorn, crown, twine, twist, wring **06** enfold, enwrap, shroud **07** contort, entwine, envelop, festoon **08** decorate, encircle, surround **10** intertwine, interweave

wreck

◇ *anagram indicator*

03 gum, mar **04** crab, loss, mess, ruin, sink **05** break, gum up, mouse, smash, split, spoil, trash, wrack **06** cast up, debris, pieces, ravage, rubble **07** chicken, destroy, disable, flotsam, handbag, remains, shatter, torpedo, undoing **08** breaking, cast away, demolish, derelict, disaster, neurotic, smashing, stramash, write off, write-off **09** devastate, fragments, ruination, shipwreck **10** basket-case, demolition, disruption, shattering **11** bag of nerves, destruction, devastation **13** play havoc with **14** bundle of nerves

wreckage

◇ *anagram indicator*

04 ruin **05** lagan, ligan, wrack **06** debris, pieces, rubble **07** flotsam, remains **08** detritus **09** fragments

wrench

03 fit, rip, tug **04** ache, blow, jerk, pain, pang, pull, rick, tear, yank **05** force, shock, twist, wrest, wring **06** sorrow, sprain, strain **07** distort, sadness, spanner **08** upheaval **09** uprooting

wrest

03 win **04** pull, rack, take, turn **05** force, screw, seize, thraw, twist, wring **06** sprain, strain, wrench **07** distort, extract, pervert **10** distortion **12** misinterpret

wrestle

03 vie **05** argue, fight **06** battle, combat, debate, strive, tussle, wraxle, writhe **07** bulldog, contend, contest, dispute, grapple, scuffle, wrangle, wriggle **08** struggle

wrestling

◇ *anagram indicator*

> *Wrestling holds and throws include:*

03 hug
04 lock
06 grovet, nelson, souple, suplex
07 bear hug, buttock, hip-lock
08 arm throw, body lock, headlock, scissors
09 ankle lace, body throw
10 Boston crab, full nelson, hammerlock
11 backbreaker, scissor hold
12 cross-buttock, scissors hold, stranglehold
14 grand amplitude

> *Wrestling-related terms include:*

03 hug, mat, pin
04 bout, fall, hold, open, sumo
05 judge
06 action, bridge, souple
07 default, referee
08 arm throw, body lock, chairman, exposing, reversal, takedown
09 ankle lace, body throw, bridge out, freestyle, grapevine, gut wrench, passivity
10 arm control, Greco-Roman
13 central circle, cross-body ride, passivity zone
14 danger position, grand amplitude, protection area
15 double-leg tackle, single leg tackle, technical points

wretch

03 rat **04** worm **05** being, devil, exile, miser, rogue, snake, swine **06** insect, rascal, vassal **07** cullion, outcast, ruffian, scroyle, villain **08** blighter, creature, recreant, vagabond **09** miscreant, miserable, rakeshame, scoundrel **10** peelgarlic, pilgarlick, rascallion **11** rapscallion **14** good-for-nothing

wretched

◇ *anagram indicator*

02 wo **03** bad, low, sad, woe **04** base, mean, poor, vile **05** awful, ratty, seely, sorry, woful **06** abject, bloody, cursed, damned, darned, dashed, effing, gloomy, odious, paltry, rascal, woeful, wretch **07** blasted, doleful, flaming, forlorn, hapless, hateful, piteous, pitiful, unhappy, unlucky **08** annoying, blinking, blooming, dejected, downcast, dratting, dreadful, fiendish, flipping, hopeless, horrible, inferior, infernal, pathetic, pitiable, shameful, shocking, terrible **09** appalling, atrocious, depressed, life-weary, loathsome, miserable, worthless **10** confounded, deplorable, despicable, detestable, distraught, distressed, melancholy, outrageous, unpleasant **11** crestfallen, unfortunate **12** contemptible, disconsolate **13** broken-hearted

wretchedly

05 sadly **07** awfully, lousily

08 gloomily, pitiably, terribly, woefully **09** dolefully, forlornly, miserably, unhappily **10** deplorably, dreadfully, hopelessly, lamentably, mournfully, shockingly, tragically **11** appallingly **12** disastrously, pathetically **13** disgracefully **14** disconsolately

wriggle
04 bend, duck, edge, jerk, shun, turn, wind, worm **05** crawl, dodge, elude, evade, hedge, shirk, sidle, slink, snake, twine, twist **06** escape, eschew, jiggle, squirm, twitch, waggle, wamble, wiggle, writhe, zigzag **07** forbear, wrestle **08** get out of, get round, scriggle, sidestep, squiggle **09** extricate, give a miss, manoeuvre **10** body-swerve, circumvent **11** abstain from, refrain from, run away from **12** keep away from, stay away from, steer clear of

wring
04 coil, hurt, pain, rack, rend, stab, tear **05** exact, force, pinch, screw, thraw, twist, wound, wrest **06** coerce, extort, harrow, injure, mangle, pierce, wrench, writhe **07** distort, extract, squeeze, torture, wreathe **08** distress, lacerate

wrinkle
03 tip **04** fold, idea, line, lirk, plow, ruck, seam **05** frown, ridge, rivel, whelk **06** crease, furrow, gather, notion, plough, pucker, ruckle, ruck up, ruffle, rumple, runkle, trench, wimple **07** crankle, crimple, crinkle, crumple, frounce, frumple, shrivel, whimple **08** unsmooth **09** corrugate **10** suggestion, unevenness **11** corrugation

wrinkled
04 ropy **05** crêpy, ropey **06** crepey, crimpy, ridged, rucked, rugate, rugose, rugous **07** creased, crinkly, furrowy, puckery, ruffled, rumpled, wizened, wrinkly, wrizled **08** crankled, crinkled, crumpled, frounced, furrowed, puckered, rivelled, writhled **09** chamfered **10** corrugated

wrist
06 carpus **11** shackle-bone

writ
04 tolt **05** brief, sci fa **06** capias, decree, elegit, extent, venire **07** dedimus, latitat, precept, process, summons, warrant **08** mandamus, mittimus, noverint, replevin, subpoena **09** nisi prius **10** certiorari, court order, devastavit, distringas, inhibition, injunction, law-burrows, praemunire **11** fieri facias, jury-process, quo warranto, scire facias, supersedeas, supplicavit **12** habeas corpus, quare impedit, venire facias **13** ad inquirendum, audita querela

write
03 pen **04** copy, note **05** carve, chalk, draft, print, trace **06** create, decree, draw up, indite, pencil, record, scrawl,

scribe, scrive **07** compose, dash off, engrave, jot down, put down, screeve, scrieve, set down **08** foretell, inscribe, note down, register, scribble, sling ink, take down **09** character, poeticize, transpose **10** correspond, transcribe, underwrite **11** communicate, make a note of

• **write off**
05 annul, crash, smash, wreck **06** cancel, delete **07** destroy, nullify, smash up, wipe out **08** amortize, cross out, demolish **09** disregard **11** forget about

writer
03 pen **06** author **12** man of letters **14** woman of letters

04 bard, hack, poet **05** clerk **06** author, editor, fabler, penman, pen-pal, rhymer, scribe **07** copyist, diarist **08** annalist, composer, essayist, lyricist, novelist, penwoman, reporter, satirist **09** columnist, dramatist, historian, pen-friend, penpusher, scribbler, sonneteer, web author **10** biographer, chronicler, copywriter, journalist, librettist, playwright **11** contributor, ghost writer, storyteller **12** leader-writer, poet laureate, scriptwriter, stenographer **13** calligraphist, correspondent, court reporter, fiction writer, lexicographer **14** autobiographer **15** technical author, technical writer

See also **author; biography; chef; diary; essay; fable; historian; journalist; lexicographer; literary; playwright; poet; satirist**

• **the writer**
02 me

• **this writer**
01 I

write-up
05 study **06** rating, report, review, survey **08** analysis, critique, scrutiny **09** appraisal, criticism, judgement, recension, summing-up **10** assessment, commentary, evaluation **11** examination

writhe
◇ *anagram indicator*
03 wry **04** coil, curl, jerk, toss, wind **05** thraw, twist, wring **06** squirm, thrash, thresh, wiggle **07** contort, distort, wrestle, wriggle **08** scriggle, struggle **10** intertwine **12** twist and turn

writing
02 MS **03** pen **04** dite, fist, hand, opus, text, work **05** entry, print, prose, words **06** scrawl, script, volume **08** document, scribble **10** manuscript, penmanship **11** calligraphy, composition, handwriting, publication

03 nib, pen **04** Biro®, reed **05** quill **06** crayon, dip pen, pencil, stylus **07** cane pen **08** brailler, CD marker, steel pen **09** ballpoint, eraser pen, ink pencil, marker pen **10** felt-tip pen, lead-pencil, rollerball, typewriter **11** board marker, fountain pen, highlighter **12** cartridge pen, writing brush **13** laundry marker, Roman metal pen, word-processor **14** calligraphy pen, coloured pencil **15** permanent marker

04 blog, book, news, poem, tale **05** diary, drama, essay, lyric, paper, story, study **06** annals, letter, memoir, record, report, review, satire, script, sketch, sonnet, thesis, weblog **07** account, apology, article, epistle, feature, history, journal, parable, profile **08** apologia, critique, treatise, yearbook **09** biography, chronicle, criticism, discourse, editorial, life story, monograph, narrative, statement, technical **10** commentary, literature, propaganda, scientific, travelogue **11** confessions, copywriting, documentary **12** dissertation **13** autobiography, legal document **14** correspondence **15** advertising copy, curriculum vitae, newspaper column

See also **alphabet; scripture**

written
06 penned **07** drawn up, set down **08** recorded **09** pen-and-ink **10** documental, documented **11** documentary, transcribed

wrong
◇ *anagram indicator*
01 X **03** bad, bum, sin **04** awry, back, bent, evil, harm, tort **05** abuse, amiss, badly, crime, crook, error, false, inapt, spoil **06** astray, curved, damage, delict, faulty, guilty, impair, injure, injury, inside, seduce, sinful, unfair, unjust, wicked **07** abusion, abusive, crooked, defraud, illegal, illicit, immoral, in error, inverse, misdeed, off base, off beam, offence, reverse, to blame, twisted, unright, wrongly **08** contrary, criminal, faultily, improper, inequity, iniquity, inverted, mistaken, opposite, trespass, unlawful, unseemly **09** defective, dishonest, dishonour, erroneous, felonious, grievance, imprecise, incorrect, inexactly, injustice, off target, unethical, unfitting **10** fallacious, immorality, improperly, inaccurate,

inapposite, indecorous, iniquitous, malapropos, mistakenly, out of order, sinfulness, unfairness, unsuitable, up the spout, wickedness, wrongdoing **11** blameworthy, erroneously, imprecisely, incongruous, incorrectly, misinformed, unjustified **12** inaccurately, infelicitous, infringement, unlawfulness **13** dishonourable, hardly the time, inappropriate, reprehensible, transgression, wide of the mark **14** hardly the place, unconventional, unsatisfactory

• **go wrong**
04 fail, miss **05** stray **06** go phut, pack up **07** conk out, pervert, seize up **08** backfire, collapse, go astray, walk awry **09** break down, not make it **11** come to grief, come unglued, come unstuck, malfunction, stop working **12** come a cropper, go on the blink, go on the fritz **13** become unstuck, come to nothing **14** be unsuccessful

• **in the wrong**
04 harm, hurt **05** abuse, cheat **06** guilty, ill-use, injure, malign **07** at fault, in error, oppress, to blame **08** ill-treat, maltreat, mistaken, mistreat **09** discredit, dishonour **11** blameworthy **12** misrepresent

wrongdoer
05 felon **06** sinner **07** culprit **08** criminal, evildoer, offender **09** miscreant **10** delinquent, lawbreaker, malefactor, trespasser **12** transgressor

wrongdoing
03 sin **04** evil, miss **05** crime, error, fault **06** felony **07** misdeed, offence **08** iniquity, mischief **09** misfaring **10** immorality, maleficent, maleficial, sinfulness, wickedness **11** delinquency, lawbreaking, maleficence, malfeasance **13** transgression

wrongful
04 evil **05** wrong **06** unfair, unjust, wicked **07** illegal, illicit, immoral **08** criminal, improper, tortious, unlawful **09** dishonest, injurious, unethical **11** blameworthy, unjustified, unwarranted **12** illegitimate **13** dishonourable, reprehensible

wrongfully
03 ill **06** unduly **08** unfairly, unjustly **09** illegally, illicitly, immorally **10** criminally, improperly **11** dishonestly, unethically **13** against the law **14** illegitimately

wrongly
◇ *anagram indicator*
05 amiss, badly **07** athwart, in error **09** by mistake **10** mistakenly **11** erroneously, incorrectly **12** inaccurately

wrought
◇ *anagram indicator*
04 made **06** beaten, formed, ornate, shaped **08** hammered **09** decorated, fashioned **10** decorative, ornamental, ornamented **12** manufactured

• **wrought up**
05 upset **07** anxious, nervous, ruffled, worried **08** agitated, in a tizzy, troubled, unnerved **09** disturbed, flustered, in a lather, unsettled **10** distraught **12** disconcerted

wry
03 dry **05** askew, canny, cross, droll, pawky, thraw, witty **06** bitter, ironic, swerve, thrawn, uneven, warped, writhe **07** contort, crooked, mocking, pervert, twisted **08** deformed, perverse, sardonic, scoffing **09** contorted, distorted, sarcastic **10** distortion, ill-natured

Wyoming
02 WY **03** Wyo

X

X
02 ex **03** chi, ten **04** xray

xenon
02 Xe

xenophobia
06 racism **09** racialism,
xenophoby **13** ethnocentrism
15 ethnocentricity

xenophobic
06 racist **09** parochial, racialist
12 ethnocentric **13** ethnocentrist

Xerox®
04 copy **05** print **06** run off
09 duplicate, facsimile, photocopy,
Photostat®, reproduce

xylophone
07 gamelan, marimba **08** sticcado,
sticcato **09** xylorimba
12 metallophone

Xmas
02 Xm **04** Noel, Yule **05** Nowel
06 Crimbo, Nowell **08** Chrissie,

Nativity, Yuletide **09** Christmas
13 Christmas-tide, Christmas-time

X-ray, xray
01 X **08** skiagram **09** angiogram,
mammogram, pyelogram,
radiogram, sialogram, skiagraph, X-ray
image **10** mammograph, radiograph,
röntgen ray **11** shadowgraph
13 encephalogram
14 encephalograph, X-ray
photograph

Y

Y
03 wye 06 yankee

yacht
02 MY 04 maxi, scow 06 dragon
07 cruiser 08 keelboat 10 knockabout

yack
03 gab, jaw, yap 04 blah, chat, rant
06 babble, confab, gossip, harp on, hot
air, jabber, tattle 07 blather, chatter,
chinwag, prattle, twattle 08 witter on,
yack-yack 11 yackety-yack

yam
06 camote 09 breadroot, Dioscorea
11 sweet potato

yank
◇ *anagram indicator*
03 tug 04 blow, haul, jerk, pull, slap
05 heave 06 snatch, wrench

yankee
01 y

yap
03 cur, gab, jaw 04 bark, fool, yelp
05 mouth, nyaff, scold 06 babble,
jabber, natter, yatter 07 bumpkin,
chatter, prattle 08 witter on

yard
01 y 02 yd 03 Hof, ree 04 mews, quad,
reed 05 court, garth, meuse
06 garden 08 knackery 09 courtyard
10 quadrangle, rick-barton 13 barrack
square, cloister-garth

yardstick
05 gauge, scale 07 measure
08 standard 09 benchmark, criterion,
guideline 10 comparison, touchstone

yarn
03 abb 04 gimp, gymp, line, tale, tram,
wool 05 fable, fibre, guimp, lisle, story,
twist 06 Angora, bouclé, cotton,
crewel, mohair, saxony, strand, thread,
two-ply, zephyr 07 four-ply, genappe,
textile, worsted 08 anecdote, chenille,
wheeling 09 Crimplene®, fibroline,
fingering, organzine, tall story 10 water
twist 11 fabrication

yawn
04 gant, gape 08 oscitate

yawning
04 huge, vast, wide 06 drowsy, gaping
08 wide-open 09 cavernous,
oscitancy 10 oscitation

yaws
04 boba, buba 10 framboesia
12 button scurvy

yea *see* yes

year
01 a, y 02 yr 03 sun 11 twelvemonth
12 calendar year

See also **animal**

• **many years**
03 age, eon, era 04 aeon 05 calpa,
decad, kalpa, yonks 06 decade, lustre,
pentad 07 century, chiliad, lustrum
08 triennia 09 centenary, decennary,
decennium, great year, millenary,
millennia, septennia, triennial,
triennium 10 centennial, millennium,
quadrennia, septennium
11 bimillenary, quadrennium,
quinquennia 12 donkey's years,
quinquennium
• **in the year**
01 a 02 an 04 anno
• **in this year**
02 ha 07 hoc anno
• **year in, year out**
09 endlessly, regularly 10 repeatedly
11 continually 12 monotonously,
persistently, time and again 13 again
and again

yearbook
06 annual

yearling
03 hog 05 stirk

yearly
02 pa 05 per an 06 annual 07 per year
08 annually, per annum 09 every year,
once a year, perennial 11 perennially

yearn
03 yen 04 ache, earn, erne, itch, long,
pant, pine, sigh, want, wish 05 covet,
crave, fancy, green, grein 06 desire,
hanker, hunger, thirst 08 languish
09 think long

yearning
◇ *anagram indicator*
03 yen 04 wish 05 fancy 06 desire,
hanker, hunger, pining, rennet, thirst
07 craving, longing, panting, wistful
09 hankering 11 nympholepsy

yeast
04 barm, bees, cell, yest 06 leaven,
torula 13 Saccharomyces

yell
03 cry 04 bawl, howl, roar, yeld, yelp,
yowl 05 shout, tiger, whoop 06 barren,
bellow, cry out, holler, scream, shriek,
squall, squeal 07 screech, yelloch
08 skelloch 12 unproductive

yellow
04 nesh, soft, weak, yolk 05 faint,
mangy, timid 06 coward, cowish,
craven, flaxen, fulvid, sallow, scared
07 chicken, citrine, fearful, fulvous,
gutless, jittery, luteous, meacock,
nithing, unmanly, wimpish, xanthic
08 clay-bank, cowardly, icterine,
timorous, unheroic, xanthous
09 dastardly, spineless, vitellary,
vitelline, weak-kneed 10 flavescent,
spiritless 11 icteritious, lily-livered,
milk-livered, sensational, sulphureous
12 faint-hearted, weak-spirited, white-
livered, xanthochroic
13 pusillanimous, yellow-bellied
14 chicken-hearted, chicken-livered

yellowhammer
04 yite 08 yeldring, yeldrock, yoldring

yelp
03 bay, cry, yap, yip 04 bark, yawp, yell,
yowl 05 boast, nyaff, quest 06 squeal

Yemen
03 YAR, YEM

yen
01 Y 02 Yn 04 itch, lust, urge 05 thing,
yearn 06 desire, hunger 07 craving,
longing, passion 08 yearning
09 hankering

yeoman
04 exon 07 goodman 09 beefeater

yes
01 I 02 ay, OK 03 aye, yah, yea, yep
04 okay, ou ay, sure, yeah 05 jokol,
quite, right, uh-huh, yokul 06 agreed,
and how, indeed, ja wohl, rather

07 quite so **08** all right, of course, very well **09** certainly **10** absolutely, by all means, definitely **11** affirmative

yes-man
05 toady **06** lackey, minion **07** crawler **09** sycophant, toad-eater **10** bootlicker

yet
03 but, now, too **04** also, even **05** as yet, by now, howbe, so far, still **06** anyway, by then, even so **07** already, besides, further, howbeit, however, thus far **08** hitherto, moreover, until now **09** up till now **10** all the same, for all that, heretofore, in addition, up till then **11** furthermore, just the same, nonetheless **12** nevertheless, up to this time **14** into the bargain **15** notwithstanding
• **as yet**
05 so far **07** thus far, till now, up to now **08** hitherto **13** up to this point

yield
◊ *anagram indicator*
03 bow, net, pan, pay, sag **04** bear, bend, cede, crop, duck, earn, fall, give, haul, meal, vail **05** admit, agree, allow, defer, fetch, forgo, grant, gross, repay **06** accede, accord, afford, cave in, comply, forego, give in, give up, income, output, permit, profit, render, resign, return, reward, submit, supply **07** abandon, bring in, concede, consent, deliver, furnish, give out, give way, harvest, produce, product, provide, revenue, succumb, takings **08** abdicate, earnings, fructify, generate, give over, part with, proceeds, renounce **09** acquiesce, fructuate, give place, surrender **10** bring forth, capitulate, give ground, knock under, relinquish **11** admit defeat, go along with **12** knuckle under **14** resign yourself **15** throw in the towel

yielding
◊ *anagram indicator*
04 easy, give, soft **05** buxom **06** facile, flabby, pliant, quaggy, spongy, supple **07** ductile, elastic, pliable, springy **08** amenable, biddable, flexible, obedient, obliging **09** compliant, complying, resilient, tractable **10** compliance, submissive **11** acquiescent, complaisant, unresisting **13** accommodating

yob, yobbo
03 hob, lob, oaf, oik **04** boor, calf, clod, coof, cuif, dolt, gawk, hick, hoon, jake, lout, slob, swad **05** yahoo, yobbo

06 lubber **07** bumpkin, hallion, lumpkin **08** bull-calf, loblolly **09** barbarian, lager lout, roughneck **10** clodhopper **11** chuckle-head, hobbledehoy

yobbish
04 rude **05** crude, gawky, gruff, rough **06** coarse, oafish, rustic, vulgar **07** boorish, doltish, ill-bred, loutish, uncouth **08** bungling, churlish, ignorant, impolite **09** unrefined **10** uneducated, unmannerly **11** clodhopping, ill-mannered, uncivilized

yobbo *see* **yob, yobbo**

yoke
03 bow, tie **04** bond, join, link, span, team, tool **05** hitch, thing, union, unite **06** burden, couple, halter, inspan, object, square **07** bondage, bracket, connect, enslave, harness, slavery, tyranny **08** coupling **09** servility, servitude **10** oppression **11** enslavement, subjugation

yokel
04 boor, hick, jake, Jock, rube **06** joskin, rustic **07** bucolic, hayseed, peasant **09** hillbilly **10** clodhopper **13** country cousin **14** country bumpkin

you
01 U **02** du, tu **03** Sie **04** thee, vous
• **you and me**
02 us, we

young
03 fry, kid, new **04** baby **05** brood, early, green, issue, jeune, small **06** babies, family, infant, junior, litter, little, recent, youthy **07** ageless, growing, progeny, teenage, youthly **08** childish, children, immature, juvenile, under age, vigorous, youthful **09** beardless, childlike, fledgling, miniature, offspring, unfledged **10** adolescent, fledgeling, little ones **11** undeveloped **13** inexperienced **15** in the first flush
See also **animal**

younger
02 yr **04** less **05** chota **06** junior **10** latter-born

youngster
03 boy, cub, kid, lad, tot **04** brat, girl, gyte, lass, teen, tyke, wean **05** bairn, bimbo, child, smout, sprog, youth **06** nipper, rug rat, shaver **07** hellion, protegé, subteen, tiny tot, toddler, young 'un **08** teenager, young man

10 adolescent, ankle-biter, knave-bairn, young adult, young woman **11** young person

your
02 yr **03** thy
• **yours**
05 thine
• **yours truly**
02 me **06** myself **09** tout à vous

youth
03 boy, kid, lad **04** colt, lout, lowt, page, teen, yoof **05** child, prime, teens **06** Adonis, childe, chylde, gunsel, infant, keelie, kipper, spring **07** boyhood, homeboy, juvenal, May-lord **08** calf-time, girlhood, homegirl, juvenile, springal, teenager, the young, young man **09** childhood, freshness, greenhorn, hot-rodder, lager lout, salad days, springald, stripling, youngster **10** adolescent, immaturity, recentness, young adult **11** adolescence, hobbledehoy, leaping-time, teeny-bopper, young people **12** inexperience, teenage years

youthful
04 spry **05** fresh, young **06** active, boyish, lively, tender, vernal **07** buoyant, girlish **08** blooming, childish, immature, juvenile, vigorous **09** sprightly, youngling, youngthly **13** inexperienced, well-preserved **14** bread-and-butter **15** in the first flush

youthfulness
06 vigour **08** spryness, vivacity **09** freshness **10** juvenility, liveliness **12** juvenileness **13** sprightliness, vivaciousness

yowl
03 bay, cry **04** bawl, howl, wail, yawl, yell, yelp **06** squall **07** screech, ululate **09** caterwaul

ytterbium
02 Yb

yttrium
01 Y

yuck
02 fy **03** yuk **04** itch, yech

yucky
04 foul **05** dirty, gross, itchy, messy, mucky **06** filthy, grotty, grungy, sickly **08** horrible **09** revolting **10** disgusting, unpleasant

Yukon Territory
02 YT

Z

z
03 zed, zee 04 Zulu 06 izzard

Zambia
01 Z 03 RNR, ZMB

zany
◇ anagram indicator
03 odd 04 daft 05 crazy, droll, funny, kooky, toady, wacky 06 absurd 07 amusing, bizarre, comical 08 clownish, merryman 09 eccentric, screwball, simpleton 10 ridiculous

Zanzibar
03 EAZ

zap
03 hit 04 do in, kill 05 erase, force, shoot 06 rub out, strike 07 bump off, correct, destroy, wipe out 08 vitality 09 finish off

zeal
04 fire, zest 05 gusto, study, verve 06 ardour, energy, fervor, spirit, vigour, warmth 07 bigotry, fervour, passion 08 devotion, keenness 09 eagerness, intensity, vehemence, zelotypia 10 commitment, dedication, enthusiasm, fanaticism 11 earnestness 12 propagandism

zealot
05 bigot 07 fanatic, radical, zealant 08 militant, partisan 09 extremist 10 enthusiast 11 eager beaver

zealous
04 keen, warm 05 eager, fiery 06 ardent, fervid, gung-ho, stanch 07 bigoted, burning, devoted, diehard, earnest, fervent, intense, staunch 08 militant, spirited 09 committed, dedicated, fanatical, strenuous 10 passionate 11 impassioned, true-devoted 12 enthusiastic, wholehearted 14 enthusiastical

zealously
06 keenly 07 eagerly 08 ardently 09 earnestly, fervently, instantly, staunchly 11 fanatically 12 passionately

zenith
01 z 03 top 04 acme, apex, peak 06 apogee, climax, height, summit, vertex 07 optimum 08 meridian, pinnacle 09 high point 11 culmination 12 highest point

zero
01 O, z 03 nil, zip 04 blob, duck, love, null 05 nadir, zilch, zippo 06 bottom, cipher, cypher, naught, nought

07 nothing 08 duck's egg, goose-egg 12 absolute zero
• **zero in on**
05 fix on 06 aim for 07 focus on, head for, level at, train on 08 centre on, direct at, home in on, pinpoint 10 converge on 13 concentrate on

zest
04 husk, peel, rind, rine, skin, tang, zeal, zing 05 crust, gusto, shell, spice, taste 06 relish, savour, vigour 07 epicarp, flavour 08 appetite, interest, keenness, piquancy 09 eagerness, enjoyment 10 enthusiasm, exuberance, integument, liveliness 11 joie de vivre

Zeus
07 Jupiter

zigzag
03 yaw 04 tack, wind 05 curve, snake, twist 07 crooked, meander, sinuous, vandyke, winding 08 indented, traverse, twisting 10 meandering, serpentine 14 crinkle-crankle

Zimbabwe
02 ZW 03 ZWE

zinc
02 Zn

zing
02 go 03 pep, zip 04 brio, dash, élan, life, zest 05 oomph, punch, scorn 06 energy, spirit, vigour 07 pizzazz, sparkle 08 vitality 09 animation, criticize 10 enthusiasm, get-up-and-go, liveliness 11 joie de vivre

zip
01 O 02 go 03 fly, pep 04 belt, dash, élan, life, pelt, race, rush, tear, whiz, zero, zest, zing, zoom 05 drive, flash, gusto, hurry, oomph, punch, scoot, shoot, speed, verve, vroom, whisk, whizz 06 energy, spirit, vigour, whoosh 07 nothing, pizzazz, sparkle 08 vitality 10 enthusiasm, get-up-and-go, liveliness 13 slide fastener
See also **United States of America**

zirconium
02 Zr

zither
06 cither 07 cithern, cittern, kantela, kantele 08 autoharp

zodiac
04 year 07 baldric 08 baldrick 09 baudricke

03 Leo, Ram

04 Bull, Crab, Fish, Goat, Lion 05 Aries, Libra, Twins, Virgo 06 Archer, Cancer, Gemini, Pisces, Scales, Taurus, Virgin 07 Balance, Scorpio 08 Aquarius, Scorpion 09 Capricorn 11 Sagittarius, Water-bearer 12 Water-carrier

zone
01 z 04 area, belt, zona 05 tract 06 girdle, region, sector, sphere 07 section, stratum 08 district, province 09 territory

zoo
06 aviary 08 aquarium 09 menagerie 10 animal park, safari park 14 zoological park

zoology

07 ecology, zoonomy, zootaxy 08 cetology, oecology 09 acarology, hippology, mammalogy, ophiology, therology 10 autecology, conchology, embryology, entomology, limacology, malacology, morphology, nematology 11 arachnology, herpetology, ichthyology, insectology, myrmecology, ornithology 12 gnotobiology, parasitology, protozoology, zoopathology 13 helminthology, neuroethology, palaeozoology, zoophysiology 14 archaeozoology 15 lepidopterology

03 Pye (John David) 04 Beer (Sir Gavin Rylands de), Mayr (Ernst Walter), Owen (Savi) 05 Fabre (Jean Henri), Hubel (David Hunter), Krebs (Sir John), Krogh (August), Kühne (Wilhelm) 06 Darwin (Charles), Flower (Sir William Henry), Frisch (Karl von), Kinsey (Alfred), Lorenz (Konrad Zacharias), Morris (Desmond John), Müller (Johannes Peter), Newton (Alfred), Pavlov (Ivan) 07 Agassiz (Louis), Audubon (John James), Dawkins (Richard), Durrell (Gerald), Galvani (Luigi), Hodgkin (Sir Alan Lloyd), Mantell (Gideon Algernon), Medawar (Sir Peter Brian), Wallace (Alfred Russel) 08 Hamilton (William Donald), Linnaeus (Carolus) 09 Aristotle, Schaudinn (Fritz

Richard), **Tinbergen** (Nikolaas)
10 **Kettlewell** (Henry Bernard David)
11 **Sherrington** (Sir Charles Scott)
12 **Wigglesworth** (Sir Vincent Brian),
    Wynne-Edwards (Vero Copner)

zoom
03 fly, zap, zip **04** belt, buzz, dash,
dive, pelt, race, rush, soar, tear, whiz
05 flash, shoot, speed, vroom, whirl
06 hurtle, streak **08** go all out

zulu
01 Z
• **Zulu warriors**
04 impi